S0-BCY-188

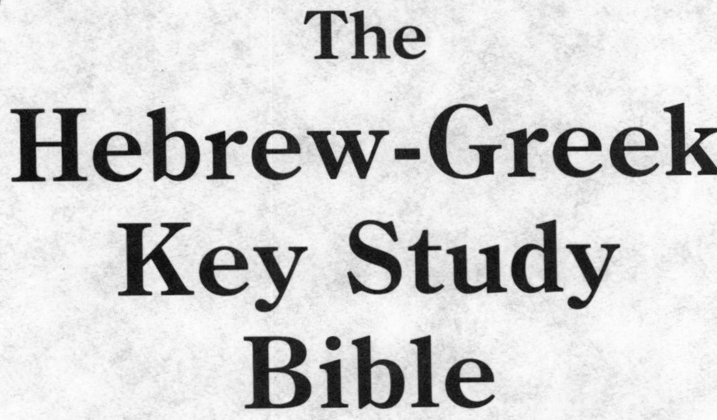

The Hebrew-Greek Key Study Bible

New American Standard

Presented to

---

from

---

occasion

---

date

The Hebrew-Greek Key Study Bible

New American Standard

My Dad - Jon Post

Presented to

David Post

from

Day of Gratitude

occasion

1.3.14 (the year of my wedding)

date

The Hebrew-Greek Key Study Bible

New American Standard

The Hebrew-Greek Key Study Bible

New American Standard

Red Letter Edition

Zodhiates' original and complete system of Bible study

Key words in the text numerically coded to the New American Standard Exhaustive Concordance, Introduction to each book, Exegetical Notes, Center column references, Grammatical helps to the New Testament, Lexical Aids, New American Standard concordance, Strong's dictionaries, and Eight-page color Bible Atlas.

Compiled and edited by
Spiros Zodhiates, Th.D.

AMG PUBLISHERS
CHATTANOOGA, TN 37422, U.S.A.

Black genuine ISBN 0-89957-684-2
Burgundy genuine ISBN 0-89957-683-4
Black bonded ISBN 0-89957-687-7
Burgundy bonded ISBN 0-89957-685-0
Hardbound ISBN 0-89957-690-7

First Printing, June 1990
Hebrew-Greek Key Study Bible
New American Standard

AMG PUBLISHERS

A PERSONAL WORD FROM THE EDITOR

Here is an English Bible which helps you to know what the original Hebrew and Greek words actually mean.

Sometimes words cannot be translated accurately because of the absence of corresponding words in English. For instance, there are three New Testament words in Greek which are translated by the single word "love," and yet each of these Greek words, *agapē, philia,* and *storgē* (only in the compound adjective *astorgoi,* without family affection, in Romans 1:31 and II Timothy 3:3), has a distinctive meaning which gives a different denotation to the verse. Unless you know Hebrew and Greek well, without this Bible it would be very difficult to determine which word is used in the original language.

The lover of God's Word or the expert theologian will treasure this Bible for it contains a whole library of biblical aids under one cover.

It is with an awesome sense of responsibility that my co-workers and I commit this Hebrew-Greek Key Study Bible to you with the prayer that it may enhance your knowledge of God's Word and that the presence of Jesus Christ in your heart may be made more real and satisfying.

SPIROS ZODHIATES

FOREWORD

SCRIPTURAL PROMISE

"The grass withers, the flower fades, but
the word of our God stands forever."
Isaiah 40:8

The New American Standard Bible has been produced with the conviction that the words of Scripture as originally penned in the Hebrew, Aramaic, and Greek were inspired by God. Since they are the eternal Word of God, the Holy Scriptures speak with fresh power to each generation, to give wisdom that leads to salvation, that men may serve Christ to the glory of God.

The Editorial Board had a twofold purpose in making this translation: to adhere as closely as possible to the original languages of the Holy Scriptures, and to make the translation in a fluent and readable style according to current English usage.

THE FOURFOLD AIM OF THE LOCKMAN FOUNDATION

1. These publications shall be true to the original Hebrew, Aramaic, and Greek.

2. They shall be grammatically correct.

3. They shall be understandable to the masses.

4. They shall give the Lord Jesus Christ His proper place, the place which the Word gives Him; therefore, no work will ever be personalized.

PRINCIPLES OF TRANSLATION

MODERN ENGLISH USAGE: The attempt has been made to render the grammar and terminology in contemporary English. When it was felt that the word-for-word literalness was unacceptable to the modern reader, a change was made in the direction of a more current English idiom. In the instances where this has been done, the more literal rendering has been indicated in the notes.

ALTERNATIVE READINGS: In addition to the more literal renderings, notations have been made to include alternate translations, readings of variant manuscripts and explanatory equivalents of the text. Only such notations have been used as have been felt justified in assisting the reader's comprehension of the terms used by the original author.

HEBREW TEXT: In the present translation the latest edition of Rudolf Kittel's Biblia Hebraica has been employed together with the most recent light from lexicography, cognate languages, and the Dead Sea Scrolls.

HEBREW TENSES: Consecution of tenses in Hebrew remains a puzzling factor in translation. The translators have been guided by the requirements of a literal translation, the sequence of tenses, and the immediate and broad contexts.

THE PROPER NAME OF GOD IN THE OLD TESTAMENT: In the Scriptures, the name of God is most significant and understandably so. It is inconceivable to think of spiritual matters without a proper designation for the Supreme Deity. Thus the most common name for the Deity is God, a translation of the original Elohim. One of the titles for God is Lord, a translation of Adonai. There is yet another name which is particularly assigned to God as His special or proper name, that is, the four letters YHWH (Exodus 3:14 and Isaiah 42:8). This name has not been pronounced by the Jews because of reverence for the great sacredness of the divine name. Therefore, it has been consistently translated Lord. The only exception to this translation of YHWH is when it occurs in immediate proximity to the word Lord, that is, Adonai. In that case it is regularly translated God in order to avoid confusion. It is known that for many years YHWH has been transliterated as Yahweh, however no complete certainty attaches to this pronunciation.

GREEK TEXT: Consideration was given to the latest available manuscripts with a view to determining the best Greek text. In most instances the 23rd edition of Eberhard Nestle's Novum Testamentum Graece was followed.

GREEK TENSES: A careful distinction has been made in the treatment of the Greek aorist tense (usually translated as the English past, "He did") and the Greek imperfect tense (rendered either as English past progressive, "He was doing"; or, if inceptive, as "He *began* to do" or "He started to do"; or else if customary past, as "He used to do"). "Began" is italicized if it renders an imperfect tense, in order to distinguish it from the Greek verb for "begin."

On the other hand, not all aorists have been rendered as English pasts ("He did"), for some of them are clearly to be rendered as English perfects ("He has done"), or even as past perfects ("He had done"), judging from the context in which they occur. Such aorists have been rendered as perfects or past perfects in this translation.

As for the distinction between aorist and present imperatives, the translators have usually rendered these imperatives in the customary manner, rather than attempting any such fine distinction as "Begin to do!" (for the aorist imperative), or, "Continually do!" (for the present imperative).

As for sequence of tenses, the translators took care to follow English rules rather than Greek in translating Greek presents, imperfects and aorists. Thus, where English says, "We knew that he was doing," Greek puts it, "We knew that he does"; similarly, "We knew that he had done" is the Greek, "We knew that he did." Likewise, the English, "When he had come, they met him," is represented in Greek by: "When he came, they met him." In all cases a consistent transfer has been made from the Greek tense in the subordinate clause to the appropriate tense in English.

In the rendering of negative questions introduced by the particle **mē** (which always expects the answer, "No") the wording has been altered from a mere, "Will he not do this?" to a more accurate, "He will not do this, will he?"

Editorial Board, THE LOCKMAN FOUNDATION

EXPLANATION OF GENERAL FORMAT

HEBREW-GREEK KEY STUDY BIBLE

INTRODUCTIONS to each book of the Old and New Testaments cover Bible history, archaeology, and customs that are important in understanding the significance of the book in relationship to the whole Bible.

EXPLANATORY NOTES are placed at the lower section of the page and each note identifies the chapter and verse(s) to which it refers at the beginning of the note.

LEXICAL AIDS appear after the book of Revelation. They include:

GRAMMATICAL NOTATION codes, definitions and categories. Multiple superior letters or f, m, and n, preceding a word refer to the grammatical structure of the Greek word and are clarified in this section.

LEXICON TO THE OLD AND NEW TESTAMENTS edited by Spiros Zodhiates, Th.D. Superior numbers following a word are the assigned reference numbers in this lexicon and in the HEBREW AND CHALDEE DICTIONARY of the Old Testament or the GREEK DICTIONARY of the New Testament. These dictionaries are by James Strong, S.T.D., LL.D. It is in these sections that further study material is available. Bold face type is used to identify the number and the word for each entry. Inferior numbers indicate that a word appears only in the dictionary.

A GUIDE TO TRANSLITERATION FROM GREEK TO ENGLISH with modern pronunciation guidelines.

NEW AMERICAN STANDARD BIBLE

NOTES AND CROSS REFERENCES are placed in a column adjoining the text on the page and listed under verse numbers to which they refer. Superior Roman numerals refer to literal renderings, alternate translations or explanations. A single italicized superior letter preceding a word refers to cross references (superior letters not in italic type are grammatical notations). In the center column, cross references in italics are parallel passages.

PARAGRAPHS are designated by bold face numbers or letters.

QUOTATION MARKS are used in the text in accordance with modern English usage.

"THOU," "THEE" AND "THY" are not used in this translation except in the language of prayer when addressing Deity.

PERSONAL PRONOUNS are capitalized when pertaining to Deity.

ITALICS are used in the text to indicate words which are not found in the original Hebrew, Aramaic, or Greek but implied by it. Italics are used in the marginal notes to signify alternate readings for the text.

SMALL CAPS in the New Testament are used in the text to indicate Old Testament quotations or obvious allusions to Old Testament texts. Variations of Old Testament wording are found in New Testament citations depending on whether the New Testament writer translated from a Hebrew text, using existing Greek or Aramaic translations, or paraphrased the material. It should be noted that modern rules for the indication of direct quotation were not used in biblical times thus allowing freedom for omissions or insertions without specific indication of these.

ASTERISKS are used to mark verbs that are historical presents in the Greek which have been translated with an English past tense in order to conform to modern usage. The translators recognized that in some contexts the present tense seems more unexpected and unjustified to the English reader than a past tense would have been. But Greek authors frequently used the present tense for the sake of heightened vividness, thereby transporting their readers in imagination to the actual scene at the time of occurrence. However, the translators felt that it would be wise to change these historical presents to English past tenses.

How to Use the Hebrew

The Gospel According to

JOHN

The Gospel of John stresses the deity of Jesus. It begins with: "In the beginning was the Word, and the Word was with God, and the Word was God," and "the Word became flesh, and dwelt among us" (John 1:1,14). And the Gospel concludes with the author's purpose expressed: "Many other signs therefore Jesus also performed in the presence of the disciples, which are not written in this book; but these have been written that you may believe that Jesus is the Christ, the Son of God; and that believing you may have life in His name" (John 20:30,31). This account of Jesus' life is very different from the Synoptic Gospels (Matthew, Mark, and Luke). It offers the things which Jesus said more than the things which He did. Step by step, this Gospel unfolds its proofs until the reader must reach the inescapable conclusion that Jesus is indeed the Son of God. The literary style is unique: the sentence structure is uncomplicated and easy to understand. Every step in a given narrative is presented as though it is an isolated event or statement, rather than attempting to merge it into an overall framework. The same majestic truths are repeated in intricate parallelisms. It is a book of striking contrasts: light and darkness; truth and falsehood; good and evil; life and death; God and Satan. Only in John's Gospel do we learn that the length of Jesus' public ministry was about 3½ years, by counting the Passover feasts. John is saturated with symbolic representations from ordinary life. Jesus used common things (such as water, bread, light, a vine and its branches, a loving shepherd and his pet sheep) to teach spiritual truths. The Gospel of John was written not so much to retell the historical facts of Jesus' brief stay on earth, but to ask us the question: "What does His coming mean?"

The author merely identifies himself as the disciple "whom Jesus loved" (John 13:23; 20:2). The writer was John the Apostle, one of the "sons of thunder" (Mark 3:17). John was very close to Jesus (Matthew 17:1; Mark 5:37; Luke 8:51). It was young John who leaned against the bosom of Jesus (John 13:23), with whom Jesus entrusted His aged mother (John 19:26,27). John was the first male to believe that Jesus rose from death (John 20:1-10), the first to recognize Him on the shore of Lake Galilee (John 21:1-7).

The Deity of Jesus Christ

1 🔑[a]In the <u>beginning</u>[746] [ipf]was
[b]the <u>Word</u>,[3056] and the Word [ipf]was
[c]with <u>God</u>,[2316] and [d]the Word [ipf]was
[pred]God.
2 [I]He [ipf]was in the <u>beginning</u>[746] with
God.
3 [a]<u>All things</u>[3956] [ao]<u>came into
being</u>[1096] [I]by Him, and apart from Him
nothing [ao]<u>came into being</u>[1096] that has
[pf]<u>come into being</u>.[1096]
4 [a]In Him [ipf]was <u>life</u>,[2222] and the life
[ipf]was [b]the <u>light</u>[5457] of men.
🔑 5 And [a]the light [pin]<u>shines</u>[5316] in the
<u>darkness</u>,[4653] and the darkness did not
[ao] [I]<u>comprehend</u>[2638] it.

The Witness of John

6 There [ao] [I]came a man, [pfpp]sent
from God, whose name was [a]John.
7 [I]He [ao]came [a]for a <u>witness</u>,[3141] that
he might [aosb]<u>bear witness</u>[3140] of the light,
[b]that all might [aosb]believe through him.
8 [Ia]He [ipf]was not the light, but *came*
that he might [aosb]bear witness of the
light.

1 [a]Gen. 1:1; Col. 1:17; 1John 1:1 [b]John 1:14; Rev. 19:13 [c]John 17:5; 1John 1:2 [d]Phil. 2:6
2 [I]Lit., *This one*
3 [I]Or, *through* [a]John 1:10; 1Cor. 8:6; Col. 1:16; Heb. 1:2
4 [a]John 5:26; 11:25; 14:6 [b]John 8:12; 9:5; 12:46
5 [I]Or, *overpower* [a]John 3:19
6 [I]Or, *came into being* [a]Matt. 3:1
7 [I]Lit., *This one* [a]John 1:15, 19, 32; 3:26; 5:33 [b]John 1:12; Acts 19:4; Gal. 3:26
8 [I]Lit., *That one* [a]John 1:20

🔑 **1:1b** See note on I Cor. 12:1-11.
🔑 **1:1c** See note on Phil. 2:6-8.
🔑 **1:5** See notes on Lk. 11:33-36; and general remarks on I John.

INTRODUCTION to each book.

UNDERLINING indicates key words which may be studied further by looking up the attached number in the study helps section.

KEY identifies explanatory notes at bottom of page.

PERSONAL PRONOUNS are capitalized when pertaining to Deity.

A SINGLE ITALICIZED SUPERIOR LETTER preceding a word refers to cross references.

MULTIPLE SUPERIOR LETTERS or f, m and n, preceding a word refer to the grammatical structure of the Greek word and are clarified under the GRAMMATICAL NOTATION section.

ITALICS are used in the text to indicate words which are not found in the original Hebrew, Aramaic, or Greek but implied by it.

Greek Key Study Bible

9 There ipfwas [a]the true light which, coming into the world, pinenlightens[5461] every man.
10 He ipfwas in the world,[2889] and the world was aomade[1096] through Him, and the world did not aoknow[1097] Him.
11 He came to His art-n Iown,[2398, 3588] and those who were His art-mown did not aoreceive[3880] Him.
12 But as many as received Him, to them He aogave the right[1849] to nfbecome[1096] [a]children[5043] of God,[2316] even [b]to those who pptbelieve[4100] in His name,[3686]
13 [a]who were Iborn not of IIblood,[129] nor of the anwill[2307] of the flesh,[4561] nor of the anwill of man,[435] but of God.

9 IOr, *which enlightens every man coming into the world* [a]1John 2:8
10 [a]1Cor. 8:6; Col. 1:16; Heb. 1:2
11 IOr, *own things, possessions, domain*
12 [a]John 11:52; Gal. 3:26 [b]John 1:7; 3:18; 1John 3:23; 5:13
13 IOr, *begotten* IILit., *bloods* [a]John 3:5f.; James 1:18; 1Pet. 1:23; 1John 2:29; 3:9
14 IOr, *tabernacled* IIOr, *unique, only one of His kind* [a]Rev. 19:13

The Word Made Flesh

14 And [a]the Word[3056] ao[b]became[1096] flesh,[4561] and I[c]dwelt among us, and [d]we aobeheld His glory,[1391] glory as of IIthe only begotten[3439] from the anFather, full[4134] of [e]grace[5485] and [f]truth.[225]
15 John pin*[a]bore witness of Him, and cried out, saying, "This was He of whom I said, '[b]He who pptcomes after me pfi Ihas[1096] a higher rank than I, [c]for He ipfexisted before me.' "

[b]Rom. 1:3; Gal. 4:4 Phil. 2:7f.; 1Tim. 3:16; Heb. 2:14; 1John 1:1f.; 4:2; 2John 7 [c]Rev. 21:3 [d]Luke 9:32; John 2:11; 17:22, 24; 2Pet. 1:16f.; 1John 1:1 [e]John 1:17; Rom. 5:21; 6:14 [f]John 8:32; 14:6; 18:37 15 ILit., *is become before me* [a]John 1:7 [b]Matt. 3:11; John 1:27, 30 [c]John 1:30

1:9 See notes on Mt. 13; Heb. 6:1-6.

1:1-18 These are the axiomatic, authoritative statements which John gives concerning the person of Jesus Christ. The rest of the Gospel gives illustrations to confirm these statements found here.

It is the only Gospel which begins with the story of Jesus Christ, not from the time He appeared on earth, but before there was any beginning whatsoever. He had existed as the Logos, the intelligence, which gave birth to everything that is and who also became the expression, the Word, explaining that intelligence which is undiscoverable except through His word and works (Rom. 1:20).

There are two main verbs throughout this passage. There is *ēn*, the imperfect of *eimi* (1510), "to be," which in this context could have been best translated as "had been" for an indefinite time in the past. Thus, an exegetical paraphrase of the first verse would be: "Before there was any beginning, the Word had been, and the Word had been toward the God, and God had been the Word." This verb *ēn* is to be found in every instance in this context where the person of Jesus Christ is referred to in His eternal self-existent state (vv. 1,2,4,8,9,10,15). The other verb to be contrasted with *ēn* is *egeneto,* the aorist of *ginomai* (1096), "to become" something that one was not before. Thus, in v. 14 we find, "And the Word became flesh. . . ." The Lord Jesus at a particular time in the past became that which He was not before, a physical being. Before that He was essentially Spirit (Jn. 4:24). This verb is in the aorist, *egeneto* (vv. 3,6,10,14,17) or in the perfect, *gegone* (vv. 3,15), which means becoming something that one was not before. This refers to some historical time in the past, as the beginning of this new state. It also implies continuing to be that.

In Jn. 1:18 the verse begins with the word "God," *Theon,* without the definite article which refers to God in His general, total, infinite, eternal, as well as special essence as Spirit. John is declaring that no created being has ever seen God in His totality, eternity, infinity, in His special essence as Spirit. This first statement is to be connected with the first verse which speaks of Jesus Christ also in His eternal self-existence as eternal, infinite Spirit. And then to show the very special relationship of the Son to the Father, he calls Him *monogenēs* (3439). The word is unfortunately translated as "the only begotten" thus giving the idea that, in His eternal state, He was generated by the Father. The meaning in this context is as follows: "the unique Son who being (*ōn,* the present participle of *eimi,* 1510), in the bosom of the Father, He Himself brought Him (God) out (*exēgēsato,* 'exegeted' Him at a particular time in the past)." The second part of v. 18 declares that this unique Son or unique God, as some manuscripts have it, who has always been in the bosom of the Father, He is the One who brought Him out to visibility and made Him understood (that is, where our word exegesis comes from). This second declaration of v. 18 agrees with v. 14 which speaks of the incarnation of the Logos. For a complete exegesis of these eighteen verses, see the Editor's book entitled, *Was Christ God?.*

1:12 See notes on Lk. 15; Heb. 6:1-6.

SUBJECT HEADINGS are throughout the text.

ASTERISKS are used to mark verbs that are historical presents in the Greek which have been translated with an English past tense in order to conform to modern usage.

QUOTATION MARKS are used in the text in accordance with modern English usage.

MULTIPLE NUMBERS indicate that an English word or phrase is taken from more than one Greek word.

AN INFERIOR NUMBER indicates the word appears only in Strong's dictionary.

ITALICS IN MARGINAL NOTES are used to signify alternate readings for the text.

SUPERIOR NUMBERS following a word are the assigned reference numbers in the lexical sections where further study material is available.

SUPERIOR ROMAN NUMERALS refer to literal renderings, alternate translations or explanations.

Not Illustrated.

RED LETTER type is used in New Testament to indicate the words of Jesus.

SMALL CAPS in the New Testament are used in the text to indicate Old Testament quotations or obvious allusions to Old Testament texts.

PREFACE TO THE NEW AMERICAN STANDARD BIBLE

In the history of English Bible translations, the King James Version is the most prestigious. This time-honored version of 1611, itself a revision of the Bishops' Bible of 1568, became the basis for the English Revised Version appearing in 1881 (New Testament) and 1885 (Old Testament). The American counterpart of this last work was published in 1901 as the American Standard Version. Recognizing the values of the American Standard Version, the Lockman Foundation felt an urgency to update it by incorporating recent discoveries of Hebrew and Greek textual sources and by rendering it into more current English. Therefore, in 1959 a new translation project was launched, based on the ASV. The result is the New American Standard Bible.

The American Standard Version (1901) has been highly regarded for its scholarship and accuracy. A product of both British and American scholarship, it has frequently been used as a standard for other translations. It is still recognized as a valuable tool for study of the Scriptures. The New American Standard Bible has sought to preserve these and other lasting values of the ASV.

Furthermore, in the preparation of this work numerous other translations have been consulted along with the linguistic tools and literature of biblical scholarship. Decisions about English renderings were made by consensus of a team composed of educators and pastors. Subsequently, review and evaluation by other Hebrew and Greek scholars outside the Editorial Board were sought and carefully considered.

The Editorial Board has continued to function since publication of the complete Bible in 1971. Minor revisions and refinements, recommended over the last several years, are presented in this edition.

PREFACE TO THE HEBREW-GREEK KEY STUDY BIBLE

The Hebrew-Greek Key Study Bible is based on the New American Standard Bible and incorporates the necessary tools to provide for an in-depth appreciation of the English translation of Scripture with or without a knowledge of biblical languages. It includes key Hebrew and Greek words with an explanation of grammatical peculiarities that correspond to the English translation.

This study Bible is the result of many years of study in the original languages by the scholars engaged in the production of this work. Spiros Zodhiates, whose mother tongue is Greek, has brought to it over forty years of study of the Koinē Greek language which was utilized providentially by the Holy Spirit to give mankind the New Testament. Dr. Zodhiates is considered a gifted biblical student by his contemporaries.

Our prayer is that a thorough comprehension of God's Word will bring untold blessings to the reader. We believe, however, that understanding God's Word is not enough. It must be energized by the Holy Spirit in the believer's heart and life so that the written Word may become the living Word to those who have appropriated the Eternal Word, Jesus Christ, in their hearts.

THE EDITORIAL STAFF

ABBREVIATIONS

accus. = accusative
act. = active
adj. = adjective
adv. = adverb
ant. = antonym
aor. = aorist
Aram. = Aramaic
art. = article
cf. = compare
chap. = chapter
Class. = Classical
coll. = collective
comp. = compound
conj. = conjunction
contr. = contrast, contrasted, contraction, contracted
dat. = dative
deriv. = derivative, derivation
DSS = Dead Sea Scrolls
e.g. = for example
emph. = emphatic
f. = singular following
fem. = feminine
ff. = plural following
fut. = future
gen. = genitive
Gr. = Greek translation of O.T. (Septuagint or LXX) or Greek text of N.T.
Heb. = Hebrew text, usually Masoretic
i.e. = that is
imper. = imperative
inf. = infinitive
inten. = intensive
intrans. = intransitive
K.J.V. = King James Version
Lat. = Latin
Lit. = A literal translation
mas. = masculine
mid. = middle
Mod. = Modern
ms. = manuscript
mss. = manuscripts
M.T. = Masoretic text
neg. = negative
neut. = neuter
N.T. = New Testament
obj. = object, objective, objectivity
opp. = opposed, opposition, opposite
Or = An alternate translation justified by the Hebrew, Aramaic, or Greek
O.T. = Old Testament
p. = page
part. = participle
pass. = passively
perf. = perfect
pl. = plural
poss. = possessive
pp. = pages
prep. = preposition
priv. = privative
pron. = pronoun
sing. = singular
sub. = substantive
subj. = subject
syn. = synonym, synonymous
Syr. = Syriac
T.R. = Textus Receptus
trans. = transitive
U.B.S. = United Bible Society
v. = verse
vol. = volume
vv. = verses
Wisd. = Wisdom
[ ] = In text, brackets indicate words probably not in the original writings.
[ ] = In margin, brackets indicate references to a name, place or thing similar to, but not identical with that in the text.

CONTENTS

THE OLD TESTAMENT

THE NEW TESTAMENT

BIBLE STUDY HELPS

THE BOOKS OF THE BIBLE

THE OLD TESTAMENT

Book	Abbrev.	Book	Abbrev.
Genesis	Gen.	Ecclesiastes	Eccl.
Exodus	Ex.	Song of Solomon	Song
Leviticus	Lev.	Isaiah	Is.
Numbers	Num.	Jeremiah	Jer.
Deuteronomy	Deut.	Lamentations	Lam.
Joshua	Josh.	Ezekiel	Ezek.
Judges	Judg.	Daniel	Dan.
Ruth	Ruth	Hosea	Hos.
1 Samuel	1 Sam.	Joel	Joel
2 Samuel	2 Sam.	Amos	Amos
1 Kings	1 Kin.	Obadiah	Obad.
2 Kings	2 Kin.	Jonah	Jon.
1 Chronicles	1 Chr.	Micah	Mic.
2 Chronicles	2 Chr.	Nahum	Nah.
Ezra	Ezra	Habakkuk	Hab.
Nehemiah	Neh.	Zephaniah	Zeph.
Esther	Esth.	Haggai	Hag.
Job	Job	Zechariah	Zech.
Psalms	Ps.	Malachi	Mal.
Proverbs	Prov.		

THE NEW TESTAMENT

Book	Abbrev.	Book	Abbrev.
The Gospel According to:		2 Thessalonians	2 Thess.
Matthew	Matt.	1 Timothy	1 Tim.
Mark	Mark	2 Timothy	2 Tim.
Luke	Luke	Titus	Titus
John	John	Philemon	Philem.
The Acts	Acts	Hebrews	Heb.
Romans	Rom.	James	James
1 Corinthians	1 Cor.	1 Peter	1 Pet.
2 Corinthians	2 Cor.	2 Peter	2 Pet.
Galatians	Gal.	1 John	1 John
Ephesians	Eph.	2 John	2 John
Philippians	Phil.	3 John	3 John
Colossians	Col.	Jude	Jude
1 Thessalonians	1 Thess.	Revelation	Rev.

The

OLD TESTAMENT

GENESIS

The name "Genesis" comes from a Greek word meaning "beginning." This title was taken from the Septuagint, the ancient Greek translation of the Old Testament. The Hebrew title, *Bereshith* ("in beginning," literally, "head"), was derived from the first word of the Hebrew text. The Book of Genesis is an appropriate introduction to the entire Bible. The kernels of all truth are found in Genesis. More than half of all human history is covered in its scant fifty chapters. Genesis answers our gnawing questions about the origins of the universe, of ourselves, of all life forms, of sin and evils in the world. In a more detailed manner Genesis first unfolds the early history of man and then the family records of God's chosen family and related lines of descent, from the dawn of time to the settlement in Egypt.

Although Genesis is, strictly speaking, not a scientific document, only divine inspiration can account for its modern accuracy in a pre-scientific age. Genesis is very clear that all things were created and had a definite beginning point—God. Everything was well designed by a Supreme Intellect and continues on the basis of His purpose, not chance. God controls the cosmos and truly cares about the centerpiece of His creation—mankind. Though the human race departed from God's ordered plan for them and must pay the consequences, God has lovingly provided a way back home to paradise.

Genesis alone fully informs us of the events which predated Moses. Surely Moses wrote it, using some ancient sources under God's direction. Jesus referred to Moses in Lk. 16:31; 24:44; and Jn. 5:46,47.

The Creation

1 [a]In the beginning[7225] [b]God[430]
[c]created[1254] the heavens[8064] and
the earth.[776]
2 And the earth was[1961] [I][a]form-
less[8414] and void, and [b]darkness[2822]
was over the [II]surface of the deep;
and [c]the Spirit[7307] of God [d]was [III]moving
over the [II]surface of the waters.
3 Then [a]God said, "Let there be[1961]
light";[216] and there was light.
4 And God saw[7200] that the light was
[a]good;[2896] and God [b]separated[914] the
light from the darkness.
5 And [a]God called the light day,[3117]
and the darkness[2822] He called[7121]
night.[3915] And [b]there was evening and
there was morning, one day.[3117]
6 Then God said, "Let there be
[I]an [a]expanse[7549] in the midst of the

1 [a]Ps. 102:25; Is. 40:21; John 1:1, 2; Heb. 1:10 [b]Ps. 89:11; 90:2; Acts 17:24; Rom. 1:20; Heb. 11:3 [c]Job 38:4; Is. 42:5; 45:18; Rev. 4:11
2 [I]Or, *a waste and emptiness* [II]Lit., *face of* [III]Or, *hovering* [a]Jer. 4:23 [b]Job 38:9 [c]Ps. 104:30; Is. 40:13, 14 [d]Deut. 32:11; Is. 31:5
3 [a]Ps. 33:6, 9; 2Cor. 4:6 4 [a]Ps. 145:9, 10 [b]Is. 45:7 5 [a]Ps. 74:16 [b]Ps. 65:8 6 [I]Or, *a firmament* [a]Is. 40:22; Jer. 10:12; 2Pet. 3:5

1:1—2:4 A popular topic of discussion is the date of creation. The chronology which one often finds in the marginal columns of many of the older Bibles, notably in the Authorized Version of King James, is *not* a part of the Bible itself by any means! It is the work of Archbishop Ussher, an illustrious prelate of the Irish Church, who lived from A.D. 1580 to 1656. His chronological labors were directed toward affording an idea of the time that elapsed between certain events in recorded history. For this purpose he took the year 1 A.D.—the beginning of the Christian era—as his starting point, and calculated backwards as far as reliable recorded history afforded good working ground. He reckoned as far back as 4004 B.C., and then, finding no more available material in the form of history, either written or inscribed, he had to stop. He did not mean to imply that he had reached the point of creation at all. On the contrary, he had simply gone as far as recorded history enabled him to go.

1:1 God of His own free will and by His absolute power called the whole universe into being, evoking into existence what was previously nonexistent (see Ps. 33:6,9; 102:25; Jer. 10:12; John 1:3; Acts 14:15; 17:24; Rom. 4:17; Heb. 3:4; Rev. 4:11). If we concede the absolute power of God, we must accept His power to create and destroy as stated in the Scriptures. There are many problems which the finite mind cannot completely grasp. We accept those things by faith (Heb. 11:3).

waters, and let it separate[914] the waters
from the waters."
7 And God made[6213] the [I]ex-
panse,[7549] and separated [a]the waters
which were below the [I]expanse from
the waters [b]which were above the
[I]expanse; and it was so.
8 And God called the [I]expanse
heaven.[8064] And there was evening and
there was morning, a second day.
9 Then God said, "[a]Let the waters
below the heavens be gathered into one
place, and let [b]the dry[3004] land appear";[7200] and it was so.
10 And God called the dry land
earth,[776] and the [a]gathering[4723] of the
waters He called seas; and God saw
that it was good.
11 Then God said, "Let the earth
sprout [I][a]vegetation, [II]plants yielding2232
seed,[2233] *and* fruit trees bearing fruit
after [III]their kind, [IV]with seed in them,
on the earth"; and it was so.
12 And the earth brought forth
[I]vegetation, [II]plants yielding seed after
[III]their kind, and trees bearing fruit,
[IV]with seed in them, after [III]their kind;
and God saw that it was good.
13 And there was evening and there
was morning, a third day.
14 Then God said, "Let there be
[I][a]lights[3974] in the [II][b]expanse of the
heavens[8064] to separate[914] the day from
the night, and let them be for [c]signs,[226]
and for [d]seasons,[4150] and for days and
years;
15 and let them be for [I]lights in the
[II]expanse of the heavens to give light
on the earth";[776] and it was so.
16 And God made the two [I]great
lights, the [a]greater [II]light [III]to govern[4475]
the day, and the lesser [II]light [III]to govern
the night; *He made* [b]the stars also.
17 [a]And God placed them in the
[I]expanse of the heavens to give light
on the earth,
18 and [I]to [a]govern the day and the
night, and to separate the light from
the darkness; and God saw that it was
good.
19 And there was evening and there
was morning, a fourth day.
20 Then God said, "Let the waters
[I]teem with swarms of living[2416] creatures, and let birds fly above the earth
[II]in the open [III]expanse of the heavens."
21 And God created [a]the great sea
monsters,[8577] and every living[2416]
creature[5315] that moves, with which the
waters swarmed after their kind, and
every winged bird after its kind; and
God saw that it was good.
22 And God blessed[1288] them, saying, "Be fruitful and multiply, and fill
the waters in the seas, and let birds
multiply on the earth."
23 And there was evening and there
was morning, a fifth day.
24 [a]Then God said, "Let the
earth[776] bring forth living creatures after
[I]their kind: cattle and creeping things
and beasts[2416] of the earth after [I]their
kind"; and it was so.
25 And God made the [a]beasts of the
earth[776] after [I]their kind, and the cattle
after [I]their kind, and everything that
creeps on the ground after its kind; and
God saw that it was good.
🗝 26 Then God[430] said, "Let [a]Us
make[6213] [b]man[120] in Our image,[6754] according to Our likeness;[1823] and let them
[c]rule over the fish[1710] of the sea and
over the birds of the [I]sky[8064] and over
the cattle and over all the earth, and
over every creeping thing that creeps
on the earth."[776]
27 And God created[1254] man [a]in
His own image, in the image of God
He created him; [b]male2145 and female[5347]
He created them.
28 And God blessed them; and God
said to them, "[a]Be fruitful and multiply,

7 [I]Or, *firmament* [a]Job 38:8-11 [b]Ps. 148:4
8 [I]Or, *firmament*
9 [a]Ps. 104:6-9; Jer. 5:22; 2Pet. 3:5 [b]Ps. 24:1, 2; 95:5
10 [a]Ps. 33:7; 95:5; 146:6
11 [I]Or, *grass* [II]Or, *herbs* [III]Lit., *its* [IV]Lit., *in which is its seed* [a]Ps. 65:9-13; 104:14; Heb. 6:7
12 [I]Or, *grass* [II]Or, *herbs* [III]Lit., *its* [IV]Lit., *in which is its seed*
14 [I]Or, *luminaries, light-bearers* [II]Or, *firmament* [a]Ps. 74:16; 136:7 [b]Ps. 19:1; 150:1 [c]Jer. 10:2 [d]Ps. 104:19
15 [I]Or, *luminaries, light-bearers* [II]Or, *firmament*
16 [I]Or, *luminaries, light-bearers* [II]Or, *luminary, light-bearer* [III]Lit., *for the dominion of* [a]Ps. 136:8, 9 [b]Job 38:7; Ps. 8:3; Is. 40:26
17 [I]Or, *firmament* [a]Jer. 33:20, 25
18 [I]Lit., *for the dominion of* [a]Jer. 31:35
20 [I]Or, *swarm* [II]Lit., *on the face of* [III]Or, *firmament*
21 [a]Ps. 104:25-28
24 [I]Lit., *its* [a]Gen. 2:19; 6:20; 7:14; 8:19
25 [I]Lit., *its* [a]Gen. 7:21, 22; Jer. 27:5
26 [I]Lit., *heavens* [a]Gen. 3:22; 11:7 [b]Gen. 5:1; 9:6; 1Cor. 11:7; Eph. 4:24; James 3:9 [c]Ps. 8:6-8
27 [a]Gen. 5:1f.; 1Cor. 11:7; Eph. 4:24; Col. 3:10 [b]Matt. 19:4; Mark 10:6
28 [a]Gen. 9:1, 7; Lev. 26:9; Ps. 127:3, 5

🗝 **1:26,27** Is God singular (Deut. 6:4; 32:39; Isa. 45:5; Jn. 17:3; I Cor. 8:6) or plural (Gen. 3:22; 18:1-3; Isa. 48:16; Jn. 10:34-38)? The Hebrew word for God is *'elohim* (430), a plural noun. In Gen. 1:1 it is used in grammatical agreement with a singular verb *bara'* (1254), "created." When the plural pronouns in "Let us make man in our image after our likeness" are used, does it mean an august *(continued on next page)*

and fill the earth,[776] and subdue it; and
rule[7287] over the fish of the sea and over
the birds of the [I]sky, and over every
living thing[2416] that [II]moves on the
earth."
29 Then God said, "Behold, [a]I have
given you every plant yielding seed that
is on the [I]surface of all the earth, and
every tree [II]which has fruit yielding
seed; it shall be food for you;
30 and [a]to every beast of the earth
and to every bird of the [I]sky and to
every thing that [II]moves on the earth
[III]which has life,[5315] *I have given* every
green plant for food"; and it was so.
31 And God saw all that He had
made,[6213] and behold, it was very
[a]good. And there was evening and there
was morning, the sixth day.

The Creation of Man and Woman

2 Thus the heavens[8064] and the
earth[776] were completed,[3615] and all
[a]their hosts.[6635]
2 And by [a]the seventh day God completed His work[4399] which He had
done;[6213] and [b]He rested[7673] on the seventh day from all His work which He
had done.
3 Then God blessed[1288] the seventh
day and sanctified[6942] it, because in it
He rested from all His work which God
had created[1254] [I]and made.
🗝 4 [Ia]This is the account[8435] of the
heavens and the earth when they were
created, in [b]the day[3117] that the LORD
God made earth and heaven.
5 [a]Now no shrub[7880] of the field[7704]
was yet in the earth,[776] and no plant
of the field had yet sprouted, [b]for the
LORD God had not sent rain upon the
earth; and there was no man to [I]cul-
tivate[5647] the ground.[127]
6 But a [I]mist used to rise from the
earth and water the whole [II]surface of
the ground.
🗝 7 Then the LORD God[430] formed
man[120] of [a]dust[6083] from the ground,[127]
and breathed into his nostrils[639] the
breath[5397] of life;[2416] and [b]man became
a living[2416] [I]being.[5315]

28 [I]Lit., *heavens* [II]Or, *creeps*
29 [I]Lit., *face of* [II]Lit., *in which is the fruit of a tree yielding seed* [a]Ps. 104:14; 136:25
30 [I]Lit., *heavens* [II]Or, *creeps* [III]Lit., *in which is a living soul* [a]Ps. 145:15, 16; 147:9
31 [a]Ps. 104:24, 28; 119:68; 1Tim. 4:4

1 [a]Deut. 4:19; 17:3
2 [a]Ex. 20:8-11; 31:17 [b]Heb. 4:4, 10
3 [I]Lit., *to make*
4 [I]Lit., *These are the generations* [a]Job 38:4-11 [b]Gen. 1:3-31
5 [I]Lit., *work, serve* [a]Gen. 1:11 [b]Ps. 65:9, 10; Jer. 10:12, 13
6 [I]Or, *flow* [II]Lit., *face of*
7 [I]Lit., *soul* [a]Gen. 3:19 [b]1Cor. 15:45

(continued from previous page)
plural of excellence or majesty? Is God speaking to the angels or the earth or nature? Or is this a germinal hint of a distinction in the divine personality? No one can be certain. Until Jesus came, the internal unity of the Godhead was not understood.

God is essentially Spirit (Jn. 4:24). Therefore, man, who is similar to God, possesses an immortal spirit. We resemble God in certain respects (Gen. 1:26) without being equal with Him (Isa. 40:25). Man's likeness to God is what truly distinguishes mankind from the rest of creation. Man is a person with the power to think, feel, and decide. He has the capacity for moral choices and spiritual growth or decline. In the beginning, man loved God and hated unrighteousness. The fall reversed this. Man was still a person with the capacity for good, but his spirit was altered by sin so much that he now generally runs away from God and loves evil more than righteousness (Jn. 3:19,20). After Adam's time, only those who lived uprightly before God were considered to be His offspring (see Mt. 3:7-10; 13:38; Jn. 12:36; Acts 13:10; Col. 3:6). Man is no longer in the perfect state of innocence as at the time of creation. Therefore, he does not have the same spiritual, God-like attributes and qualities of that original state. Jesus, the second Adam (I Cor. 15:45), came to undo Satan's works (I Jn. 3:8), to restore a spiritual likeness to God (II Cor. 3:18).

🗝 **2:4** It is well known that there are actually two accounts of creation in the first two chapters of Genesis, but this need not cause us to conclude that they are incompatible, as some have suggested. The two sections actually complement each other. 1:1—2:4a presents a wide-angle view of all seven days of creation and deals with the creation of man and woman as a single act. Then in 2:4b-24 the author zooms in on the sixth day, giving details which were not possible in an overview like chapter 1. The separate origins of man and woman are brought into sharp focus. Therefore, chapters 1 and 2 are not chronological but 2:4b-24 presents in greater detail some of what 1:11,12,24-31 merely summarizes.

🗝 **2:7** The term "soul" has been used in a variety of senses by different writers in the Bible. The O.T. Hebrew word is *nephesh* (5315) which means "that which breathes." It corresponds to the Greek word

(continued on next page)

🔑 8 And the LORD God planted a
[a]garden toward the east, in Eden; and
there He placed[7760] the man whom He
had formed.[3335]
9 And out of the ground the LORD
God caused to grow [a]every tree that
is pleasing[2530] to the sight and good[2896]
for food; [b]the tree of life[2416] also in the
midst of the garden, and the tree of
the knowledge[1847] of good[2896] and
evil.[7451]
10 Now a [a]river [I]flowed out of Eden
to water the garden; and from there it
divided and became four [II]rivers.
11 The name of the first is Pishon;
it [I]flows around the whole land[776] of
[a]Havilah, where there is gold.
12 And the gold of that land is good;
the bdellium and the onyx stone are
there.
13 And the name of the second river
is Gihon; it [I]flows around the whole land
of Cush.
14 And the name of the third river
is [Ia]Tigris; it [II]flows east of Assyria. And
the fourth river is the [IIIb]Euphrates.
🔑 15 Then the LORD God took the man
and put him into the garden of Eden
to cultivate[5647] it and keep[8104] it.
16 And the LORD God [a]command-
ed[6680] the man, saying, "From any tree
of the garden you may eat freely;
17 but from the tree of the knowledge of good and evil you shall not
[I]eat, for in the day[3117] that you eat from
it [a]you shall surely die."[4191]
🔑 **18** Then the LORD God said, "It is
not good[2896] for the man[120] to be[1961]
alone; [a]I will make him a helper [I]suitable
for him."
🔑 19 And [a]out of the ground the LORD
God formed every beast[2416] of the field
and every bird of the [I]sky,[8064] and
[b]brought *them* to the man[120] to see what
he would call[7121] them; and whatever
the man called a living creature,[5315] that
was its name.
20 And the man gave[7121] names to
all the cattle, and to the birds of the
[I]sky, and to every beast of the field,

8 [a]Gen. 13:10; Is. 51:3; Ezek. 28:13
9 [a]Ezek. 47:12 [b]Gen. 3:22; Rev. 2:7; 22:2, 14
10 [I]Lit., *was going out* [II]Lit., *heads* [a]Ps. 46:4
11 [I]Lit., *surrounds* [a]Gen. 25:18
13 [I]Lit., *is the one surrounding*
14 [I]Heb., *Hiddekel* [II]Lit., *is the one going* [III]Heb., *Perath* [a]Dan. 10:4 [b]Gen. 15:18
16 [a]Gen. 3:2, 3
17 [I]Lit., *eat from it* [a]Deut. 30:15, 19, 20; Rom. 6:23; 1Tim. 5:6; James 1:15
18 [I]Lit., *corresponding to* [a]1Cor. 11:9
19 [I]Lit., *heavens* [a]Gen. 1:24 [b]Gen. 1:26
20 [I]Lit., *heavens*

(continued from previous page)
psuchē (5590) in the N.T., which is usually translated "soul" or "life." See the lexical aid sections for further definition. Here it is used synonymously with spirit. Both spirit and soul refer to the emotional life and also correspond to "heart" in a sense, which is the seat of all thinking, feeling, and purpose. "Soul" and "spirit" are frequently used interchangeably, and it is not easy to define the difference. Hebrew culture tended to view man as being composed of only two parts—soul (spirit) and body. The Greek concept of man was tripartite (see I Thess. 5:23). Broadly defined, the soul usually stood for life, the affections, the will, the consciousness, while the spirit stood for the higher elements by which we comprehend spiritual truths, and the body was, of course, the physical, material body. The author of Hebrews implied that there is a very fine line of distinction between soul and spirit (Heb. 4:12).

🔑 **2:8,9** The tree of knowledge of good and evil was designed as a test of obedience. Our first parents had to choose whether to obey God or break His commandments. When they actually ate the forbidden fruit, the consequences of their actions became self-evident. They found themselves in a different relationship to God and to sin. The tree of life was the antidote against disease and bodily decay. Access to it was based upon a proper relationship with God. The real question which faced Adam, Eve, and us today is: Which path should be chosen? What kind of relationship do we want with God?

🔑 **2:15-17** Man was always meant to work. God intended for him to have something useful to do and to enjoy it. Work only became drudgery after Gen. 3:17-19.

Is it possible for anyone to live a sinless life like Adam before he fell into sin? The circumstances of our lives are so different from those of Adam that they cannot really be compared. We are descendants of a sinful Adam and, therefore, cannot rise above our origins; they affect us. It is theoretically possible to live without sinning, but we know from experience and from Scripture that this never happens (Rom. 3:9-23). No one attains the ideal. Some come nearer to it than others, but in the end everyone needs salvation. That is why Jesus came (Luke 19:10).

🔑 **2:18-20** Man immediately set about to explore and define his domain. God wanted him to come to the conclusion that he was different from all the animals, that bestiality was wrong. He needed a matching sexual partner which corresponded to his own nature.

🔑 **2:19** The Hebrew word for Adam and "man" are the same.

but for [II]Adam there was not found
[a]a helper [III]suitable for him.
🗝 21 So the LORD God caused a
[a]deep sleep to fall upon the man,[120] and
he slept; then He took one of his ribs,
and closed up the flesh[1320] at that place.
22 And the LORD God [I]fashioned into
a woman [a]the rib which He had taken
from the man,[120] and brought her to
the man.
23 And the man[120] said,

"[a]This is now bone[6106] of my
bones,
And flesh[1320] of my flesh;
[I]She shall be called[7121]
[II]Woman,[802]
Because [I]she was taken out of
[III]Man."[376]

24 [a]For this cause a man shall
leave[5800] his father[1] and his mother,[517]
and shall cleave to his wife;[802] and they
shall become one flesh.[1320]
🗝 25 [a]And the man[120] and his wife
were both naked[6174] and were not
ashamed.[954]

The Fall of Man

3 🗝 Now [a]the serpent[5175] was more
crafty[6175] than any beast[2416] of the
field[7704] which the LORD God[430] had
made.[6213] And he said[559] to the woman,[802] "Indeed, has God said, 'You shall
not eat from [I]any tree of the garden'?"
2 And the woman said to the serpent, "'[a]From the fruit of the trees of
the garden we may eat;
3 but from the fruit of the tree which
is in the middle of the garden, God has
said, 'You shall not eat from it or
touch[5060] it, lest you die.' "[4191]
4 [a]And the serpent said to the
woman, "You surely shall not die!
5 "For God knows that in the day
you eat from it your eyes will be opened,
and [a]you will be like God, knowing
good[2896] and evil."[7451]
6 [a]When the woman saw[7200] that the
tree was good[2896] for food, and that it
was a delight to the eyes, and that the
tree was desirable[2530] to make *one*
wise,[7919] she took from its fruit and ate;
and she gave also to her husband[376] with
her, and he ate.
7 Then the eyes of both of them
were opened, and they [a]knew that they
were naked; and they sewed fig leaves
together and made[6213] themselves
[I]loin coverings.
🗝 **8** And they heard[8085] the sound of
[a]the LORD God walking in the garden
in the [I]cool[7307] of the day,[3117] [b]and the

20 [II]Or, *man* [III]Lit., *corresponding to* [a]Gen. 2:18
21 [a]Gen. 15:12
22 [I]Lit., *built* [a]1Cor. 11:8, 9
23 [I]Lit., *This one* [II]Heb., *Ishshah* [III]Heb., *Ish* [a]Gen. 29:14; Eph. 5:28, 29
24 [a]Matt. 19:5; Mark 10:7, 8; 1Cor. 6:16; Eph. 5:31
25 [a]Gen. 3:7, 10, 11

1 [I]Or, *every* [a]2Cor. 11:3; Rev. 12:9; 20:2
2 [a]Gen. 2:16, 17
4 [a]John 8:44; 2Cor. 11:3
5 [a]Is. 14:14; Ezek. 28:2, 12-17
6 [a]Rom. 5:12-19; 1Tim. 2:14; James 1:14, 15; 1John 2:16
7 [I]Or, *girdles* [a]Is. 47:3; Lam. 1:8
8 [I]Lit., *wind, breeze* [a]Gen. 18:33; Lev. 26:12; Deut. 23:14 [b]Job 31:33; Ps. 139:1-12; Hos. 10:8; Amos 9:3; Rev. 6:15-17

🗝 **2:21-24** Monogamy for a lifetime was and is God's original divine plan. The Lord Jesus reemphasized this enduring principle in Matt. 19:3-9.

🗝 **2:25** There was no shame associated with sex before sin entered the world. Only after Adam and Eve sinned did they become self-conscious of their naked bodies (Gen. 3:7,10,21). God intends for intimate, sexual joys only to be fulfilled within the bonds of holy matrimony without shame.

🗝 **3:1-7** This section is historical, not allegorical. There is no valid reason for rejecting the narrative here as being historical or putting any other construction upon the words recorded here than a literal one. Nowhere does the Bible say that the fruit was an apple. This tradition could have come from the Latin *malam* (apple) which is similar to the Latin *malum* (evil). Whatever the fruit may have been, its use was a plain violation of divine prohibition, an unwarranted desire for forbidden knowledge. The gravity of the offense consisted, not in the act itself, but in the fact that Adam and Eve committed it consciously and deliberately against God's explicit and emphatic command. Note that Eve adds the phrase "neither shall ye touch it" to God's words. This is typical of humankind. We find it difficult to leave God's Word alone. We must not add or subtract from His words (Deut. 4:2; Prov. 30:6; Rev. 22:18,19). Satan knew that he could persuade Eve more easily than Adam. Once Eve fell, Satan was confident that she could influence her husband to follow the same course. Satan did not attempt to explain why they would not die; he merely affirmed it! And, he said it so convincingly that Eve believed it. Then the serpent proceeded to impugn God's motives, i.e., God must be trying to keep something away from them. After Eve "bought" these new assumptions, the rest was easy.

🗝 **3:8** Is God omnipresent (Ps. 139:7-10; Jer. 23:23,24; Amos 9:2,3) or not (Gen. 4:16; 11:5; 18:20,21;

(continued on next page)

man[120] and his wife[802] hid themselves
from the presence of the LORD God
among the trees of the garden.
9 Then the LORD God called[7121] to
the man, and said to him, "[a]Where are
you?"
10 And he said, "[a]I heard[8085] the
sound of Thee in the garden, and I was
afraid[3372] because I was naked; so I hid
myself."
11 And He said, "Who told[5046] you
that you were naked? Have you eaten
from the tree of which I commanded[6680]
you not to eat?"
12 [a]And the man[120] said, "The
woman[802] whom Thou gavest *to be* with
me, she gave me from the tree, and I
ate."
13 Then the LORD God said to the
woman, "What is this you have
done?"[6213] And the woman said, "[a]The
serpent deceived me, and I ate."
14 And the LORD God said to the
serpent,
"[a]Because you have done this,
Cursed[779] are you more than all
cattle,
And more than every beast of
the field;
On your belly shall you go,
And [b]dust[6083] shall you eat
All the days[3117] of your life;[2416]
15 And I will put [a]enmity[342]
Between you and the woman,[802]
And between your seed[2233] and
her seed;
[b]He shall [I]bruise you on the
head,[7218]
And you shall bruise him on the
heel."[6119]
16 To the woman He said,
"I will greatly multiply
Your pain[6093] [I]in childbirth,
In pain[6089] you shall [a]bring forth
children;[1121]
Yet your desire[8669] shall be for
your husband,[376]
And [b]he shall rule[4910] over you."
17 Then to Adam[120] He said, "Because you have listened[8085] to the voice
of your wife,[802] and have eaten from
the tree about which I commanded you,
saying, 'You shall not eat from it';
[a]Cursed[779] is the ground[127]
because of you;
[b]In [I]toil you shall eat of it
All the days of your life.
18 "Both thorns and thistles it shall
grow for you;
And you shall eat the [I]plants of
the field;
19 By the sweat of your face[639]
You shall eat bread,
Till you [a]return[7725] to the
ground,
Because [b]from it you were
taken;
For you are dust,[6083]
And to dust you shall return."
🔑 20 Now the man called his wife's
name [I][a]Eve,[2332] because she was the
mother[517] of all *the* living.[2416]
21 And the LORD God made[6213] garments of skin[5785] for Adam and his wife,
and clothed them.
22 Then the LORD God said, "Behold, the man[120] has become like one
of [a]Us, knowing good and evil;[7451] and
now, lest he stretch out his hand,[3027]
and take also from [b]the tree of life, and
eat, and live[2425] forever"—[5769]
23 therefore the LORD God sent him
out from the garden of Eden, to
cultivate[5647] the ground from which he
was taken.
24 So [a]He drove the man out; and

9 [a]Gen. 4:9; 18:9

10 [a]Ex. 20:18, 19; Deut. 5:25

12 [a]Job 31:33; Prov. 28:13

13 [a]2 Cor. 11:3; 1Tim. 2:14

14 [a]Deut. 28:15-20 [b]Is. 65:25; Mic. 7:17

15 [I]Or, *crush* [a]Rev. 12:17 [b]Rom. 16:20

16 [I]Lit., *and your pregnancy, conception* [a]John 16:21; 1Tim. 2:15 [b]1Cor. 14:34

17 [I]Or, *sorrow* [a]Gen. 5:29; Rom. 8:20-22; Heb. 6:8 [b]Job 5:7; 14:1; Eccl. 2:23

18 [I]Lit., *plant*

19 [a]Ps. 90:3; 104:29; Eccl. 12:7 [b]Gen. 2:7

20 [I]I.e., living; or, life [a]2Cor. 11:3; 1Tim. 2:13

22 [a]Gen. 1:26 [b]Gen. 2:9; Rev. 22:14

24 [a]Ezek. 31:11

(continued from previous page)
I Kgs. 19:11,12; Jon. 1:3)? The presence of God from which Adam and Eve fled was the visible and special manifestation to them at that time. This is an anthropomorphic usage, i.e., God is described in human terms so that we can better understand Him. However, God is not a man, and He does not look like him or think like him (Isa. 55:8,9). God is a searching God (Jn. 4:23); He wants us back, like a loving father.

🔑 **3:20** The name, Eve, (in Hebrew *khavvaw,* 2332) means "life." This does not mean that Hebrew was the original language. As thoughts were conveyed from one language to another, proper nouns were adjusted to carry their original meaning.

at the [b]east of the garden of Eden He
stationed the [c]cherubim,[3742] and the
flaming sword[2719] which turned every
direction,[2015] to guard[8104] the way[1870]
to [d]the tree of life.

Cain and Abel

4 🔑 Now the man[120] [I]had relations[3045] with his wife[802] Eve, and
she conceived and gave birth to
[II]Cain,[7014] and she said, "I have gotten[7069] a [III]manchild[376] with *the help of*
the LORD."
2 And again, she gave birth to his
brother[251] Abel.[1893] And [a]Abel was
[b]a keeper of flocks, but Cain was a
tiller[5647] of the ground.[127]
🔑 3 So it came about [I]in the course
of time[3117] that Cain brought an
offering[4503] to the LORD of the fruit of
the ground.
4 And [a]Abel, on his part also brought
of the firstlings of his flock and of their
fat portions. And [b]the LORD had regard
for Abel and for his offering;
5 but [a]for Cain and for his offering
He had no regard. So [b]Cain became very
angry[2734] and his countenance fell.
6 Then the LORD said to Cain, "[a]Why
are you angry? And why has your countenance fallen?[5307]

24 [b]Gen. 2:8 [c]Ex. 25:18-22; Ps. 104:4; Ezek. 10:1-20; Heb. 1:7 [d]Gen. 2:9
1 [I]Lit., *knew* [II]I.e., gotten one [III]Or, *man, the* LORD
2 [a]Luke 11:50, 51 [b]Gen. 46:32; 47:3
3 [I]Lit., *at the end of days*
4 [a]Heb. 11:4 [b]1Sam. 15:22
5 [a]1Sam. 16:7 [b]Is. 3:9; Jude 11
6 [a]Jon. 4:4
7 [I]Or, *surely you will be accepted* [a]Jer. 3:12; Mic. 7:18 [b]Num. 32:23 [c]Job 11:14, 15; Rom. 6:12, 16
8 [I]Lit., *said to* [a]Matt. 23:35; Luke 11:51; 1John 3:12-15; Jude 11
9 [a]Gen. 3:9
10 [a]Num. 35:33; Deut. 21:1-9; Heb. 12:24; Rev. 6:9, 10
11 [a]Gen. 3:14; Deut. 28:15-20; Gal. 3:10
12 [a]Deut. 28:15-24; Joel 1:10-20 [b]Lev. 26:17, 36
14 [a]Gen. 3:24; Jer. 52:3 [b]Deut. 28:64-67

7 "[a]If you do well,[3190] [I]will not *your*
countenance be lifted up?[7613] [b]And if you
do not do well, sin[2403] is crouching at
the door; and its desire[2103] is for you,
[c]but you must master[4910] it."
🔑 8 And Cain [I]told Abel his brother.
And it came about when they were
in the field,[7704] that Cain rose up
against Abel his brother and [a]killed[2026]
him.
9 Then the LORD said to Cain,
"[a]Where is Abel your brother?"[251]
And he said, "I do not know.[3045] Am
I my brother's keeper?"[8104]
10 And He said, "What have you
done?[6213] [a]The voice of your brother's
blood[1818] is crying to Me from the
ground.
11 "And now [a]you are cursed[779]
from the ground,[127] which has opened
its mouth to receive your brother's blood
from your hand.[3027]
12 "[a]When you cultivate[5647] the
ground, it shall no longer yield its
strength to you; [b]you shall be a vagrant
and a wanderer on the earth."[776]
🔑 13 And Cain said to the LORD, "My
punishment[5771] is too great to bear!
14 "Behold, Thou hast [a]driven me
this day[3117] from the face of the ground;
and from Thy face I shall be hidden,
and [b]I shall be a vagrant and a wanderer

🔑 **4:1,2** The Hebrew word *yada'* (3045) indicates the most intimate relationship between a man and a woman, the sexual bond. It could be translated: "And Adam experienced Eve, his wife." It is possible that Cain and Abel were twins, because the text does not repeat the statement that Eve conceived.

🔑 **4:3-7** Is God a respecter of persons (Ex. 2:25; Lev. 26:9; II Kgs. 13:23; Ps. 138:6) or is He completely impartial (Deut. 10:17; II Chr. 19:7; Acts 10:34; Rom. 2:11; Gal. 2:6; Eph. 6:9; I Pet. 1:17)? The first series of texts implies a righteous and benevolent "respect," based upon a proper discrimination as to character. The second series of biblical references denotes a "respect" which is partial, arising out of selfish and unworthy considerations.

Cain's sin began as all other sins begin, with a hostile attitude toward God which leads to disobedience. Cain was not worshipping God in spirit or in truth (Jn. 4:23,24). When Cain saw that Abel was worshipping God properly (Heb. 11:4), he became angry and jealous. He hated his brother and murdered him (1 Jn. 3:12). God is not unjust, and sin does not come upon us accidentally. Sin is pictured here as a predatory animal. However, there is always a sentinel to warn us of its presence. Temptation is not wrong. Jesus was tempted. It is the yielding to temptation which is wrong. If the warning is unheeded, serious danger follows. We are accountable for our actions.

🔑 **4:8** The Greek Septuagint, the Samaritan Pentateuch, and the Ancient Syriac add this phrase: "Let us go out to the field."

🔑 **4:13,14** Cain's cry was one of remorse, not true repentance. He was overwhelmed with a sense of the severity of the sentence, but he was not sorry for his crime. There was no plea for pardon or

(continued on next page)

on the earth, and it will come about[1961]
that [c]whoever finds me will kill[2026]
me."
15 So the LORD said to him, "Therefore whoever kills[2026] Cain, vengeance[5358] will be taken on him [a]seven-
fold." And the LORD [Ib]appointed[7760]
a sign[226] for Cain, lest anyone finding
him should slay[5221] him.
16 Then Cain went out from the
presence [a]of the LORD, and [I]settled in
the land[776] of [II]Nod, east of Eden.
🔑17 And Cain [I]had relations with his
wife and she conceived, and gave birth
to Enoch; and he built a city, and called
the name of the city Enoch, after the
name of his son.[1121]
18 Now to Enoch was born Irad;
and Irad [I]became the father of Mehujael;
and Mehujael [I]became the father of Methushael; and Methushael [I]became the
father of Lamech.
19 And Lamech took to himself
[a]two wives: the name of the one was
Adah, and the name of the other, Zillah.
20 And Adah gave birth to Jabal; he
was the father[1] of those who dwell in
tents[168] and *have* livestock.

14 [c]Num. 35:19
15 [I]Or, *set a mark on* [a]Gen. 4:24 [b]Ezek. 9:4, 6
16 [I]Lit., *dwelt* [II]I.e., wandering [a]2Kin. 24:20; Jer. 23:39; 52:3
17 [I]Lit., *knew*
18 [I]Lit., *begot*
19 [a]Gen. 2:24
23 [I]Or, *kill* [a]Ex. 20:13; Lev. 19:18; Deut. 32:35; Ps. 94:1
24 [a]Gen. 4:15
25 [I]Lit., *knew* [II]Heb., *Sheth* [III]Heb., *shath* [IV]Lit., *seed* [a]Gen. 5:3 [b]Gen. 4:8
26 [I]Or, *by* [a]Luke 3:38 [b]Gen. 12:8; 26:25; 1Kin. 18:24; Ps. 116:17; Joel 2:32; Zeph. 3:9; 1Cor. 1:2

21 And his brother's name was Jubal; he was the father of all those who
play the lyre and pipe.
22 As for Zillah, she also gave birth
to Tubal-cain, the forger of all implements[2794] of bronze and iron; and the
sister of Tubal-cain was Naamah.
🔑23 And Lamech said to his wives,
"Adah and Zillah,
Listen[8085] to my voice,
You wives of Lamech,
Give heed to my speech,[565]
[a]For I [I]have killed[2026] a man[376]
for wounding me;
And a boy for striking me;
24 If Cain is avenged[5358] [a]sevenfold,
Then Lamech seventy-
sevenfold."
25 And [a]Adam [I]had relations with
his wife again; and she gave birth to a
son, and named him [II]Seth,[8352] for, *she
said,* "God[430] [III]has appointed[7896] me another [IV]offspring[2233] in place of Abel;
[b]for Cain killed him."
🔑26 And to Seth, to him also [a]a son
was born; and he called his name Enosh.
Then *men* began [b]to call[7121] [I]upon the
name of the LORD.

(continued from previous page)
expression of sorrow or regret. He was a selfish person who was about to be deprived of all material belongings and driven into the wilderness. Cain was afraid that some of the kinsmen of Abel would find him and kill him in revenge. This was a very real threat to him. Therefore, it logically follows that the population of the world had already multiplied considerably since the expulsion from Eden. No doubt Cain married a relative from among them whose name is not mentioned in the text (Gen. 4:17).

🔑 **4:17** The origin of Cain's wife has perplexed many people. Moses' explanation of the origin of human beings sees Adam as the father of all of us, and this is consistent with the N.T. view of Adam (see Rom. 5:12). Where, then, did Cain get his wife? Genesis does not answer the question directly, but Gen. 5:4 asserts that Adam had other sons *and daughters* besides the three sons whose names appear in the text. Given the longevity of people at that time, Cain could have married one of his own sisters or even a more distant relative.

🔑 **4:23** Other poems and songs in the Bible (besides Psalms and Job) are: Moses and Miriam's song (Ex. 15:1-19,21); war songs (Num. 21:17,18); Moses prophetic song (Deut. 32:1-43); the song of Deborah and Barak (Judg. 5:2-31); Samson's song (Judg. 15:16); Hannah's Magnificat (I Sam. 2:1-10); David's song of the bow (II Sam. 1:19-27); David's song over Abner (II Sam. 3:33,34); David's thanksgiving (I Chr. 16:8-36); Hezekiah's poem (Isa. 38:10-20); Jonah's prayer song (Jon. 2:2-9); Habakkuk's prayer song (Hab. 3:2-19); Mary's song (Lk. 1:46-55); Zechariah's song (Lk. 1:68-79); Simeon's poem (Lk. 2:29-32); and possibly two early Christian songs (Phil. 2:5-11; Eph. 5:14). This particular outburst of Lamech showed a proud and presumptuous self-confidence. This was the boast of a bold, bad man who was elated with the possession of arms which his son Tubal-cain had invented. He felt he could take a human life at will.

🔑 **4:26** Worship, perhaps a mute adoration, already existed (Gen. 4:3,4). This passage may refer to the first institution of regular, solemn, public worship of God. Men were beginning to address God formally in prayer and thanksgiving in the time of Enosh.

Descendants of Adam

5 🗝 This is the book[5612] of the generations[8435] of Adam.[120] In the day[3117] when God[430] created man,[120] He made[6213] him [a]in the likeness[1823] of God.

2 He created them [a]male[2145] and female,[5347] and He [b]blessed[1288] them and named[7121] them [I]Man in the day when they were created.

3 When Adam[120] had lived[2421] one hundred and thirty years, he [I]became the father of *a son* in his own likeness,[6774] according to his image,[6754] and named him Seth.

4 Then the days[3117] of Adam after he became[3205] the father of Seth were eight hundred years, and he had *other* sons[1121] and daughters.

5 So all the days that Adam lived[2425] were nine hundred and thirty years, and he died.[4191]

6 And Seth lived one hundred and five years, and became the father of Enosh.

7 Then Seth lived eight hundred and seven years after he became the father of Enosh, and he had *other* sons and daughters.

8 So all the days of Seth were nine hundred and twelve years, and he died.

9 And Enosh lived ninety years, and became the father of Kenan.

10 Then Enosh lived eight hundred and fifteen years after he became the father of Kenan, and he had *other* sons and daughters.

11 So all the days of Enosh were nine hundred and five years, and he died.

12 And Kenan lived seventy years, and became the father of Mahalalel.

13 Then Kenan lived eight hundred and forty years after he became the father of Mahalalel, and he had *other* sons and daughters.

14 So all the days of Kenan were nine hundred and ten years, and he died.

15 And Mahalalel lived sixty-five years, and became the father of Jared.

16 Then Mahalalel lived eight hundred and thirty years after he became the father of Jared, and he had *other* sons and daughters.

17 So all the days of Mahalalel were eight hundred and ninety-five years, and he died.

18 And Jared lived one hundred and sixty-two years, and became the father of Enoch.

19 Then Jared lived eight hundred years after he became the father of Enoch, and he had *other* sons and daughters.

20 So all the days of Jared were nine hundred and sixty-two years, and he died.

21 And Enoch lived sixty-five years, and became the father of Methuselah.

🗝 22 Then Enoch [a]walked with God[430] three hundred years after he became the father of Methuselah, and he had *other* sons and daughters.

23 So all the days of Enoch were three hundred and sixty-five years.

🗝 24 And [a]Enoch walked with God; and he was not, for God [b]took him.

1 [a]Gen. 1:26, 27; Eph. 4:24; Col. 3:10

2 [I]Lit., *Adam* [a]Matt. 19:4; Mark 10:6 [b]Gen. 1:28

3 [I]Lit., *begot*, and so throughout the ch.

22 [a]Gen. 6:9; 17:1; 24:40; 48:15; Mic. 6:8; Mal. 2:6; 1Thess. 2:12

24 [a]2Kin. 2:11; Jude 14 [b]2Kin. 2:10; Ps. 49:15; 73:24; Heb. 11:5

🗝 **5:1-32** In this chapter Moses gives a ten-person genealogy of pre-flood figures and in chapter 11 a similar one of ten post-flood persons down to Terah, Abraham's father. In both lists, the longevity of these men is far beyond anything in our own day. Yet Moses, who himself lived to be 120 years of age (Deut. 34:7), intended that these figures be taken liteally. This was a time when men were capable of procreating children at 182 years of age (v. 28). Since it is impossible to accurately assess past conditions based upon existing conditions why not accept these statements literally?

🗝 **5:22,24** The original Hebrew adds the definite article before "God" in both instances (vv. 22,24). Perhaps this is an indication that idolatry was emerging, but Enoch lived his in strict compliance to the will of the true God. By so doing, he had recorded of him the testimony that he pleased God (Heb. 11:5). This verse puts forth one of the first hints of the belief of immortality in the O.T. The bodies of both Enoch and Elijah (II Kgs. 2:11) were doubtless transformed as Paul describes in I Cor. 15:51,52. They were given spiritual bodies similar to that of the resurrected Christ (Lk. 24:38-43; Jn. 20:19). Enoch

(continued on next page)

25 And Methuselah lived one hundred and eighty-seven years, and became the father of Lamech.
26 Then Methuselah lived seven hundred and eighty-two years after he became the father of Lamech, and he had *other* sons and daughters.
27 So all the days of Methuselah were nine hundred and sixty-nine years, and he died.
28 And Lamech lived one hundred and eighty-two years, and became the father of a son.
29 Now he called his name Noah, saying, "This one shall [I]give us rest[5162] from our work and from the toil of our hands *arising* from [a]the ground[127] which the LORD has cursed."[779]
30 Then Lamech lived five hundred and ninety-five years after he became the father of Noah, and he had *other* sons and daughters.
31 So all the days of Lamech were seven hundred and seventy-seven years, and he died.
32 And Noah was [a]five hundred years old,[1121] and Noah became the father of Shem, Ham, and Japheth.

The Corruption of Mankind

6 Now it came about, when men[120] began to multiply on the face of the land,[127] and daughters were born to them,
2 that the sons of God[430] saw[7200] that the daughters of men were [I]beautiful;[2896] and they took wives for themselves, whomever they chose.[977]
3 Then the LORD said, "[a]My Spirit[7307] shall not [I]strive with man[120] forever,[5769] [II][b]because he also is flesh;[1320] [III]nevertheless his days[3117] shall be one hundred and twenty years."
🔑4 The [a]Nephilim[5303] were on the earth[776] in those days, and also afterward, when the sons of God came in to the daughters of men, and they bore *children* to them. Those were the mighty men who *were* of old,[5769] men[582] of renown.
5 Then the LORD saw that the wickedness[7451] of man was great on the earth, and that [a]every intent[3336] of the thoughts[4284] of his heart[3820] was only evil[7451] continually.[3117]
🔑6 And [a]the LORD was sorry[5162] that He had made[6213] man on the earth, and He was [b]grieved [I]in His heart.
7 And the LORD said, "[a]I will blot out[4229] man whom I have created[1254] from the face of the land, from man to animals to creeping things and to birds of the [I]sky;[8064] for [b]I am sorry that I have made them."
8 But [a]Noah [b]found favor[2580] in the eyes of the LORD.

29 [I]Lit., *comfort us in* [a]Gen. 3:17-19; 4:11
32 [a]Gen. 7:6
2 [I]Lit., *good*
3 [I]Or, *rule in; some ancient versions read abide in* [II]Or, *in his going astray he is flesh* [III]Or, *therefore* [a]Gal. 5:16, 17; 1Pet. 3:20 [b]Ps. 78:39
4 [a]Num. 13:33
5 [a]Gen. 8:21; Ps. 14:1-3; Prov. 6:18; Matt. 15:19; Rom. 1:28-32
6 [I]Lit., *to* [a]Gen. 6:7; Jer. 18:7-10 [b]Is. 63:10; Eph. 4:30
7 [I]Lit., *heavens* [a]Deut. 28:63; 29:20 [b]Gen. 6:6; Amos 7:3,6
8 [a]Matt. 24:37; Luke 17:26; 1Pet. 3:20 [b]Gen. 19:19; Ex. 33:17; Luke 1:30

(continued from previous page)
is also the speaker of a prophecy (Jude 14, 15). This extract in the N.T. is said to have been a part of an apocryphal book containing various prophecies given by Enoch. However, it is nowhere mentioned that Enoch either wrote down prophetic utterances or had them recorded. It is more likely that Enoch merely spoke these words, and the Lord preserved them through Jude. There is no reason to believe in the authenticity of the apocryphal book of Enoch.

🔑**6:4** *Nephilim* comes from the verb *naphal* (5307) meaning "to fall," in general, but is often associated with violence, hence often translated "overthrow, fall upon." In Num. 13:32,33 it is also noted that they were "men of great stature." Emphasis should be placed upon the fact that they were men of violence who had no respect for other men.

🔑**6:6** This verse has puzzled Bible students for many years. God cannot change (Num. 23:19; I Sam. 15:29; Mal. 3:6; Js. 1:17), nor can He be affected by sorrow or other feelings which are common to humanity, but it was necessary for the inspired biblical writers to use terms which were comprehensible to the minds of human beings. We cannot conceive of God except in human terms. They had brought their punishment upon their own heads by their persistent violation of the laws which He had laid down for the government of the world—a judicial system which was self-operative and from which there could be no escape, except through divine grace, granted in answer to sincere repentance. The wages of sin has always been death (Rom. 6:23). God's foreknowledge (Acts 15:18) in no way contradicts man's free choice. His fixed laws are beneficent to the obedient, but stern and inflexible to the impenitent.

🔑 **9** These are *the records of* the generations[1755] of Noah. Noah was a [a]righteous[6662] man,[376] [Ib]blameless[8549] in his [II]time;[1755] Noah [c]walked with God.[430]

10 And Noah [I]became the father of three sons: Shem, Ham, and Japheth.

11 Now the earth was [a]corrupt[7843] in the sight of God, and the earth was [b]filled with violence.[2555]

12 And God looked on the earth, and behold, it was corrupt; for [a]all flesh[1320] had corrupted[7843] their way[1870] upon the earth.

13 Then God said to Noah, "[a]The end of all flesh has come before Me; for the earth is filled with violence because of them; and behold, I am about to destroy[7843] them with the earth.

14 "Make[6213] for yourself an ark of gopher wood; you shall make the ark with rooms, and shall [I]cover it inside and out with pitch.

🔑 15 "And this is how you shall make it: the length[753] of the ark three hundred [I]cubits, its breadth fifty [I]cubits, and its height thirty [I]cubits.

16 "You shall make a [I]window for the ark, and finish it to a cubit from [II]the top; and set the door of the ark in the side of it; you shall make it with lower, second, and third decks.

17 "And behold, [a]I, even I am bringing the flood of water upon the earth, to destroy[7843] all flesh in which is the breath[7307] of life,[2416] from under heaven;[8064] everything that is on the earth shall perish.[1478]

18 "But I will establish [a]My covenant[1285] with you; and [b]you shall enter the ark—you and your sons and your wife,[802] and your sons' wives with you.

19 "[a]And of every living thing[2416] of all flesh, you shall bring two of every *kind* into the ark, to keep *them* alive[2421] with you; they shall be male[2145] and female.[5347]

20 "[a]Of the birds after their kind, and of the animals after their kind, of every creeping thing of the ground after its kind, two of every *kind* shall come to you to keep *them* alive.

21 "And as for you, take for yourself some of all [a]food which is edible, and gather[622] *it* to yourself; and it shall be for food for you and for them."

22 [a]Thus Noah did; according to all that God had commanded[6680] him, so he did.[6213]

The Flood

7 Then the LORD said to Noah, "Enter the ark, you and all your household;[1004] for you *alone* I have seen[7200] *to be* [a]righteous[6662] before Me in this [I]time.[1755]

2 "You shall take [I]with you of every [a]clean[2889] animal [II]by sevens, a male and his female; and of the animals that are not clean two, a male[376] and his female;[802]

3 also of the birds of the [I]sky,[8064] [II]by sevens, male[2145] and female,[5347] to

9 [I]Lit., *complete, perfect;* or, *having integrity* [II]Lit., *generations* [a]Ps. 37:39; 2Pet. 2:5 [b]Gen. 17:1; Deut. 18:13; Job 1:1 [c]Gen. 5:24

10 [I]Lit., *begot*

11 [a]Deut. 31:29; Judg. 2:19 [b]Ezek. 8:17

12 [a]Ps. 14:1-3

13 [a]Is. 34:1-4; Ezek. 7:2, 3; Amos 8:2; 1Pet. 4:7

14 [I]Or, *pitch*

15 [I]I.e., One cubit equals approx. 18 in.

16 [I]Or, *roof* [II]Lit., *above*

17 [a]2Pet. 2:5

18 [a]Gen. 9:9-16; 17:7 [b]Gen. 7:7

19 [a]Gen. 7:2, 14, 15

20 [a]Gen. 7:3

21 [a]Gen. 1:29, 30

22 [a]Gen. 7:5; Heb. 11:7

1 [I]Lit., *generation* [a]Gen. 6:9

2 [I]Lit., *to* [II]Lit., *seven seven* [a]Lev. 11:1-31; Deut. 14:3-20

3 [I]Lit., *heavens* [II]Lit., *seven seven*

🔑 **6:9** How could Noah be "perfect" when no one is perfect (I Kgs. 8:46; Ps. 14:1-3; Prov. 20:9; Ecc. 7:20; Mk. 10:18; Rom. 3:12,23; I Jn. 1:8)? These passages describe men in their unregenerated state. It is true that no human being (except Jesus) has ever reached the age of accountability without violating God's moral law. Men are not good in the same sense that God is good, only relatively speaking, when comparing good men with bad men. Any good within us derives from God, who is inherently good and loving (Mt. 19:17; I Jn. 3:8). Noah, who lived by faith in a corrupt generation, was a righteous man and much more holy than his contemporaries. He sincerely wanted to do God's will (Heb. 11:7). In a world teeming with wickedness, and amid universal depravity, Noah stood alone, exercising true faith in God. He condemned the sins of men by his virtuous life which was very different from theirs.

🔑 **6:15** The dimensions of the ark present an interesting contrast when set beside those in the flood account on Tablet XI of the longer Epic of Gilgamesh, found at Nineveh in the nineteenth century. There the ark was a perfect cube, 200' by 200' by 200', whereas the one in Genesis follows the proportions of modern ships and would have been far more stable on the high seas. The Gilgamesh account has other crude elements, such as a description of gods descending upon the sacrifice like flies after the ark landed, because the flood had covered up their food source, and they were hungry.

keep [III]offspring[2233] alive on the face of all the earth.[776]

4 "For after [a]seven more days,[3117] I will send rain on the earth [b]forty days and forty nights; and I will blot out[4229] from the face of the land[127] [c]every living thing that I have made."[6213]

5 [a]And Noah did[6213] according to all that the LORD had commanded[6680] him.

6 Now Noah was [a]six hundred years old[1121] when the flood of water [I]came upon the earth.

7 Then [a]Noah and his sons[1121] and his wife[802] and his sons' wives with him entered the ark because of the water of the flood.

8 [a]Of clean animals and animals that are not clean and birds and everything that creeps on the ground,

9 there went into the ark to Noah [I]by twos, male and female, as God[430] had commanded Noah.

10 And it came about after [a]the seven days, that the water of the flood [I]came upon the earth.

11 In the [a]six hundredth year of Noah's life,[2416] in the second month, on the seventeenth day of the month, on the same day all [b]the fountains of the great deep burst open, and the [I]flood-gates of the sky[8064] were opened.

🔑 12 And [a]the rain [I]fell upon the earth for forty days and forty nights.

13 On the very same day[3117] [a]Noah and Shem and Ham and Japheth, the sons of Noah, and Noah's wife and the three wives of his sons with them, entered the ark,

14 they and every beast[2416] after its kind, and all the cattle after [I]their kind, and every creeping thing that creeps on the earth after its kind, and every bird after its kind, [II]all sorts of birds.

15 So they went into the ark to Noah, [a]by twos of all flesh[1320] in which was the breath[7307] of life.

16 And those that entered, male and female of all flesh, entered as God had commanded him; and the LORD closed *it* behind him.

17 Then the flood [I]came upon the earth for [a]forty days; and the water increased and lifted up[5375] the ark, so that it rose above the earth.

18 And the water prevailed and increased greatly upon the earth; and the ark [I]floated on the [II]surface of the water.

19 And the water prevailed more and more upon the earth, so that all the high mountains [I]everywhere under the heavens were covered.

20 The water prevailed fifteen [I]cubits higher, [a]and the mountains were covered.

21 [a]And all flesh that [I]moved on the earth perished,[1478] birds and cattle and beasts and every swarming thing that swarms upon the earth, and all mankind;[120]

22 of all that was on the dry land,[2724] all [a]in whose nostrils[639] was the breath[5397] of the spirit of life,[2416] died.[4191]

23 Thus He blotted out [I]every living thing that was upon the face of the land,[127] from man to animals to creeping things and to birds of the [II]sky, and they were blotted out from the earth; and only [a]Noah was left,[7604] together with those that were with him in the ark.

24 [a]And the water prevailed upon the earth one hundred and fifty days.

3 [III]Lit., *seed*
4 [a]Gen. 7:10 [b]Gen. 7:12, 17 [c]Gen. 6:7, 13
5 [a]Gen. 6:22
6 [I]Lit., *was* [a]Gen. 5:32
7 [a]Gen. 6:18; 7:13; Matt. 24:38f.; Luke 17:27
8 [a]Gen. 6:19, 20; 7:2,3
9 [I]Lit., *two two*
10 [I]Lit., *were* [a]Gen. 7:4
11 [I]Or, *windows of the heavens* [a]Gen. 7:6 [b]Gen. 8:2
12 [I]Lit., *was* [a]Gen. 7:4, 17
13 [a]Gen. 6:18; 7:7
14 [I]Lit., *its* [II]Lit., *every bird, every wing*
15 [a]Gen. 6:19; 7:9
17 [I]Lit., *was* [a]Gen. 7:4
18 [I]Lit., *went* [II]Lit., *face*
19 [I]Lit., *which were under all the heavens*
20 [I]I.e., One cubit equals approx. 18 in. [a]Gen. 8:4
21 [I]Or, *crept* [a]Gen. 6:7, 13, 17; 7:4
22 [a]Gen. 2:7
23 [I]Lit., *all existence* [II]Lit., *heavens* [a]Matt. 24:38, 39; Luke 17:26, 27; Heb. 11:7; 1Pet. 3:20; 2Pet. 2:5
24 [a]Gen. 8:3

🔑 **7:12** The number forty is not merely an arbitrary period or a round number. It was chosen to convey a sense of fullness. Some of its prominent scriptural uses are: Noah opened the window of the ark after another forty days (Gen. 8:6); forty days was the period of the embalming of Joseph (Gen. 50:3); Moses was forty days on the mountain (Ex. 24:18); the spies spent forty days in searching Canaan (Num. 13:25); the Israelites wandered for forty years in the wilderness (Num. 14:33); Moses twice fasted and prayed for forty days (Deut. 9:9,18); the Jews were forbidden to inflict more than forty stripes (Deut. 25:3); Goliath defied Saul's army for forty days (I Sam. 17:16); Elijah, strengthened by food from the angel, fasted for forty days (I Kgs. 19:8); Nineveh was allowed forty days to repent (Jon. 3:4); Ezekiel bore the iniquities of Judah forty days (Ezek. 4:6); the Lord Jesus fasted for forty days (Mt. 4:2); and Christ appeared during a period of forty days teaching the Apostles about the kingdom of God (Acts 1:3).

The Flood Subsides

8 But [a]God[430] remembered[2142] Noah
and all the beasts[2416] and all the cattle that were with him in the ark; and
[b]God caused[6213] a wind[7307] to pass[5674]
over the earth,[776] and the water
subsided.[7918]
2 Also [a]the fountains of the deep
and the [I]floodgates of the sky[8064] were
closed, and [b]the rain from the sky was
restrained;
3 and the water receded steadily
from the earth, and at the end [a]of one
hundred and fifty days the water
decreased.[2637]
4 And in the seventh month, on the
seventeenth day of the month, [a]the ark
rested upon the mountains of Ararat.
5 And the water decreased steadily
until the tenth month; in the tenth
month, on the first day of the month,
the tops[7218] of the mountains became
visible.
6 Then it came about at the end
of forty days, that Noah opened the
[a]window of the ark which he had made;
7 and he sent out a raven, and it
[I]flew here and there until the water was
dried up[3001] [II]from the earth.
8 Then he sent out a dove from him,
to see[7200] if the water was abated[7043]
from the face of the land;[127]
9 but the dove found no resting place
for the sole[3709] of her foot, so she returned to him into the ark; for the water
was on the [I]surface of all the earth. Then
he put out his hand and took her, and
brought her into the ark to himself.
10 So he waited yet another seven
days; and again he sent out the dove
from the ark.
11 And the dove came to him toward
[I]evening; and behold, in her [II]beak was
a freshly picked olive leaf. So Noah knew
that the water was abated from the
earth.
12 Then he waited yet another
seven days, and sent out [a]the dove; but
she did not return to him again.
13 Now it came about in the
[a]six hundred and first year, in the first
month, on the first of the month, the
water was dried up [I]from the earth.
Then Noah removed[5493] the covering
of the ark, and looked,[7200] and behold,
the [II]surface of the ground was dried
up.
14 And in the second month, on the
twenty-seventh day of the month, the
earth was dry.
15 Then God spoke to Noah, saying,
16 "Go out of the ark, you and your
wife[802] and your sons and your sons'
wives with you.
17 "Bring out with you every living
thing of all flesh[1320] that is with you,
birds and animals and every creeping
thing that creeps on the earth, that they
may [Ia]breed abundantly on the earth,
and be fruitful and multiply on the earth."
18 So Noah went out, and his sons
and his wife and his sons' wives with
him.
19 Every beast,[2416] every creeping
thing, and every bird, everything that
moves on the earth, went out [I]by their
families[4940] from the ark.
20 Then Noah built [a]an altar[4196] to
the LORD, and took of every [b]clean[2889]
animal and of every clean bird and
offered[5927] [c]burnt offerings[5930] on the altar.
⊶ 21 And the LORD [a]smelled[7306] the
soothing aroma; and the LORD said [I]to
Himself,[3820] "I will never again [b]curse[7043]
the ground on account of man,[120] for
[c]the [II]intent[3336] of man's heart is evil[7451]
from his youth; [d]and I will never again
[III]destroy[5221] every living thing, as I have
done.[6213]
22 "While the earth remains,[3117]
Seedtime[2233] and harvest,
And cold and heat,

1 [a]Gen. 19:29; Ex. 2:24; 1 Sam. 1:19; Ps. 105:42 [b]Ex. 14:21; 15:10; Job 12:15; Ps. 29:10; Is. 44:27; Nah. 1:4
2 [I]Or, *windows of the heavens* [a]Gen. 7:11 [b]Gen. 7:4, 12
3 [a]Gen. 7:24
4 [a]Gen. 7:20
6 [a]Gen. 6:16
7 [I]Lit., *went out, going and returning* [II]Lit., *from upon*
9 [I]Lit., *face*
11 [I]Lit., *the time of evening* [II]Lit., *mouth*
12 [a]Jer. 48:28
13 [I]Lit., *from upon* [II]Lit., *face* [a]Gen. 7:6
17 [I]Or, *swarm* [a]Gen. 1:22, 28
19 [I]Or, *according to their kind*
20 [a]Gen. 12:7, 8; 13:18; 22:9 [b]Gen. 7:2; Lev. 11:1-47 [c]Gen. 22:2; Ex. 10:25
21 [I]Lit., *to His heart* [II]Or, *inclination* [III]Lit., *smite* [a]Ex. 29:18, 25 [b]Gen. 3:17; 6:7, 13, 17; Is. 54:9 [c]Gen. 6:5; Ps. 51:5; Jer. 17:9; Rom. 1:21; 3:23; Eph. 2:1-3 [d]Gen. 9:11, 15

⊶ **8:21,22** Tucked away in this promise is a stipulation that is easy to miss. Day, night, and the seasons will continue "while the earth remains." The earth was not intended by God to be eternal. Its final destruction is described in poetic imagery in Ps. 102:26, which is quoted in Heb. 1:11,12. The most graphic account of the end of the world, indeed of the entire physical universe, is found in II Pet. 3:10.

And [a]summer and winter,
And [b]day and night
Shall not cease."

Covenant of the Rainbow

9 And God[430] blessed[1288] Noah and
his sons[1121] and said to them, "[a]Be
fruitful and multiply, and fill the earth.[776]
2 "And the fear[4172] of you and the
terror of you shall be on every beast[2416]
of the earth[127] and on every bird of the
[I]sky;[8064] with everything that creeps on
the ground,[127] and all the fish[1709] of the
sea, into your hand they are given.
3 "Every moving thing that is
alive[2416] shall be food for you; I give
all to you, [a]as *I gave* the green plant.
4 "Only you shall not eat flesh[1320]
with its life,[5315] *that is,* [a]its blood.[1818]
5 "And surely I will require [I][a]your
lifeblood;[5315,1818] [II][b]from every beast I
will require it. And [II]from *every* man,[120]
[II]from every man's brother[251] I will require the life of man.
6 "[a]Whoever sheds[8210] man's
blood,
By man his blood shall be shed,
For [b]in the image[6754] of God[430]
He made man.
7 "And as for you, [a]be fruitful and
multiply;
[I]Populate the earth abundantly
and multiply in it."
8 Then God spoke to Noah and to
his sons with him, saying,
9 "Now behold, [a]I Myself do establish My covenant[1285] with you, and with
your [I]descendants[2233] after you;
10 and with every living[2416] creature[5315] that is with you, the birds, the
cattle, and every beast[2416] of the earth
with you; of all that comes out of the
ark, even every beast of the earth.
11 "And I establish My covenant
with you; and all flesh shall [a]never again
be cut off[3772] by the water of the flood,
[b]neither shall there again be a flood to
destroy[7843] the earth."
12 And God said, "This is [a]the
sign[226] of the covenant which I am making between Me and you and every living
creature that is with you, for [I]all successive[5769] generations;[1755]
13 I set My [a]bow in the cloud,[6051]
and it shall be for a sign of a covenant
between Me and the earth.
14 "And it shall come about, when
I bring a cloud over the earth, that the
bow shall be seen in the cloud,
15 and [a]I will remember[2142] My covenant, which is between Me and you
and every living creature of all flesh;
and [b]never again shall the water become
a flood to destroy all flesh.
16 "When the bow is in the cloud,
then I will look upon[7200] it, to remember[2142] the [a]everlasting[5769] covenant between God and every living creature of
all flesh that is on the earth."
17 And God said to Noah, "This is
the sign of the covenant which I have
established between Me and all flesh
that is on the earth."

22 [a]Ps. 74:17 [b]Jer. 33:20, 25
1 [a]Gen. 1:28; 9:7
2 [I]Lit., *heavens*
3 [a]Gen. 1:29
4 [a]Lev. 7:26f.; 17:10-16; 19:26; Deut. 12:16, 23; 15:23; 1Sam. 14:34; Acts 15:20, 29
5 [I]Lit., *your blood of your lives* [II]Lit., *from the hand of* [a]Ex. 20:13; 21:12 [b]Ex. 21:28, 29
6 [a]Ex. 21:12-14; Lev. 24:17; Num. 35:33; Matt. 26:52 [b]Gen. 1:26, 27
7 [I]Lit., *Swarm in the earth* [a]Gen. 9:1
9 [I]Lit., *seed* [a]Gen. 6:18
11 [a]Gen. 8:21 [b]Is. 54:9
12 [I]Or, *everlasting generations* [a]Gen. 9:13, 17; 17:11
13 [a]Ezek. 1:28
15 [a]Lev. 26:42, 45; Deut. 7:9; Ezek. 16:60 [b]Gen. 9:11
16 [a]Gen. 17:13, 19; 2Sam. 23:5

9:3 There is no contradiction between this passage and Deut. 14:3-21. The former refers to men who did not live under the Law of Moses. The latter command was addressed to Jews. Perhaps strict food laws were given to the Jewish people to make them distinct from other nations whose food was often closely associated with idolatry (I Cor. 10:28). Therefore, Israel would be less susceptible to falling into temptation.

9:8-17 Throughout history God has dealt with man through covenants or agreements. Later the Jews regarded this covenant between God and Noah as the basis of the relationship between God and all mankind, but the covenants with Abraham and with Moses at Mount Sinai were seen as forming the basis of God's special relationship with Israel. Some believe that the stipulations laid on the Gentiles in Acts 15:20,29 find some of their source here in the covenant between God and Noah. In spite of the fact that the distinction between clean and unclean animals existed (Gen. 7:2), God allowed the eating of any plant or animal. The only restriction was the eating of animal blood, for that is where the life of the animal resided (Gen. 9:4). Later Israel was forbidden to eat not only blood but also the flesh of certain animals. The Lord removed the clean-unclean distinction from food altogether (Mk. 7:15; Acts 10:15).

🔑 **18** Now the sons of Noah who came out of the ark were Shem and Ham and Japheth; and [a]Ham was the father of Canaan.

19 These three *were* the sons of Noah; and [a]from these the whole earth was [I]populated.[5310]

20 Then Noah began [I]farming and planted a vineyard.

21 And he drank of the wine and [a]became drunk, and uncovered himself inside his tent.

22 And Ham, the father of Canaan, [a]saw[7200] the nakedness[6172] of his father, and told[5046] his two brothers outside.

23 But Shem and Japheth took a garment and laid it upon both their shoulders and walked backward and covered[3680] the nakedness of their father; and their faces were [I]turned away, so that they did not see[7200] their father's nakedness.

24 When Noah awoke from his wine, he knew what his youngest son had done to him.

25 So he said,

"[a]Cursed[779] be Canaan;
[I][b]A servant of servants[5650]
He shall be to his brothers."

26 He also said,

"[a]Blessed[1288] be the LORD,
The God of Shem;
And let Canaan be [I]his servant.

27 "[a]May God enlarge Japheth,
And let him dwell in the tents of Shem;
And let Canaan be [I]his servant."

28 And Noah lived[2421] three hundred and fifty years after the flood.

29 So all the days[3117] of Noah were nine hundred and fifty years, and he died.[4191]

Descendants of Noah

10 Now these are *the records of* the generations[8435] of Shem, Ham, and Japheth, the sons[1121] of Noah; and sons were born to them after the flood.

2 [a]The sons of Japheth *were* [b]Gomer and Magog and [c]Madai and [d]Javan and Tubal and [e]Meshech and Tiras.

3 And the sons of Gomer *were* [a]Ashkenaz and [I]Riphath and [b]Togarmah.

4 And the sons of Javan *were* Elishah and [a]Tarshish, Kittim and [I]Dodanim.

5 From these the coastlands of the nations[1471] [I]were separated into their lands,[776] every one[376] according to his language, according to their families,[4940] into their nations.

6 [a]And the sons of Ham *were* Cush and Mizraim and Put and Canaan.

7 And the sons of Cush *were* [a]Seba and Havilah and Sabtah and [b]Raamah and Sabteca; and the sons of Raamah *were* [c]Sheba and [d]Dedan.

8 Now Cush [I]became the father of Nimrod; he [II]became a mighty one on the earth.[776]

9 He was a mighty hunter before the LORD; therefore it is said, "Like Nimrod a mighty hunter before the LORD."

10 And the beginning[7225] of his kingdom[4467] was [I][a]Babel and Erech and Accad and Calneh, in the land of [b]Shinar.

11 From that land he went forth [a]into Assyria, and built Nineveh and Rehoboth-Ir and Calah,

12 and Resen between Nineveh and Calah; that is the great city.

13 And Mizraim [I]became the father of [a]Ludim and Anamim and Lehabim and Naphtuhim

14 and [a]Pathrusim and Casluhim

18 [a]Gen. 9:25-27; 10:6
19 [I]Lit., *scattered* [a]Gen. 9:1, 7; 10:32; 1Chr. 1:4
20 [I]Lit., to be a *farmer*
21 [a]Prov. 20:1
22 [a]Hab. 2:15
23 [I]Lit., *backward*
25 [I]I.e., The lowest of servants [a]Deut. 27:16 [b]Josh. 9:23
26 [I]Or, *their* [a]Gen. 14:20; 24:27
27 [I]Or, *their* [a]Gen. 10:2-5; Is. 66:19
2 [a]1Chr. 1:5-7 [b]Ezek. 38:2, 6 [c]2Kin. 17:6 [d]Is. 66:19 [e]Ezek. 38:2
3 [I]I.e., In 1Chr. 1:6, *Diphath* [a]Jer. 51:27 [b]Ezek. 27:14
4 [I]I.e., In 1Chr. 1:7, *Rodanim* [a]Ezek. 27:12, 25
5 [I]Or, *separated themselves*
6 [a]1Chr. 1:8-10
7 [a]Is. 43:3 [b]Ezek. 27:22 [c]Ezek. 27:15, 20
8 [I]Lit., *begot* [II]Lit., *began to be*
10 [I]Or, *Babylon* [a]Gen. 11:9 [b]Gen. 11:2; 14:1
11 [a]Mic. 5:6
13 [I]Lit., *begot* [a]Jer. 46:9
14 [a]1Chr. 1:12

🔑 **9:18-25** Was Noah unfair in this instance? First, it cannot be proven that Canaan was cursed for the misconduct of Ham, Canaan's father. It is true that the Bible does teach individual responsibility (Deut. 24:16; Ezek. 18:4,20; Rom. 2:5,6). The Bible also clearly teaches that the consequences of the sins of ancestors do affect later generations (Ex. 20:5; Josh. 7:24-26). In this case, Noah had inspired prophetic foresight about the sins of Ham's future descendants, the Canaanites. Since Ham showed such gross disrespect for his father, Noah, that attitude would soon be passed on, or had already been transmitted, to Canaan. It is even possible that Canaan also witnessed the naked condition of Noah. Could he have done some unspeakable thing which is not mentioned in the text?

(from which came the Philistines) and Caphtorim.

15 And Canaan [I]became the father of [a]Sidon, his first-born, and [b]Heth

16 and [a]the Jebusite and the Amorite and the Girgashite

17 and the Hivite and the Arkite and the Sinite

18 and the Arvadite and the Zemarite and the Hamathite; and afterward the families of the Canaanite were spread abroad.

19 And [a]the territory of the Canaanite [I]extended from Sidon as you go toward Gerar, as far as Gaza; as you go toward [b]Sodom and Gomorrah and Admah and Zeboiim, as far as Lasha.

20 These are the sons of Ham, according to their families, according to their languages, by their lands,[776] by their nations.

21 And also to Shem, the father of all the children[1121] of Eber, *and* the [I]older brother of Japheth, children were born.

22 [a]The sons of Shem *were* [b]Elam and Asshur and [c]Arpachshad and [d]Lud and Aram.

23 And the sons of Aram *were* [a]Uz and Hul and Gether and Mash.

24 And Arpachshad [I]became the father of [a]Shelah; and Shelah [I]became the father of Eber.

25 And [a]two sons were born to Eber; the name of the one *was* [I]Peleg, for in his days[3117] the earth[776] was divided;[6385] and his brother's name *was* Joktan.

26 And Joktan [I]became the father of Almodad and Sheleph and Hazarmaveth and Jerah

27 and Hadoram and Uzal and Diklah

28 and [I]Obal and Abimael and Sheba

29 and Ophir and Havilah and Jobab; all these were the sons of Joktan.

30 Now their [I]settlement[4186] [II]extended from Mesha as you go toward Sephar, the hill country of the east.

31 These are the sons of Shem, according to their families, according to their languages, by their lands, according to their nations.

32 These are the families of the sons of Noah, according to their genealogies,[8435] by their nations; and [a]out of these the nations were separated on the earth after the flood.

Universal Language, Babel, Confusion

11 Now the whole earth[776] [I]used the same language[8193] and [II]the same words.[1697]

2 And it came about as they journeyed east, that they found a plain in the land[776] [a]of Shinar and [I]settled there.

3 And they said to one[376] another,[7453] "Come, let us make bricks and burn[8316] *them* thoroughly."[8316] And they used brick for stone, and they used [a]tar for mortar.

4 And they said, "Come, let us build for ourselves a city, and a tower whose top[7218] [a]*will reach* into heaven,[8064] and let us make[6213] for ourselves [b]a name; lest we [c]be scattered abroad over the face of the whole earth."

5 [a]And the LORD came down to see[7200] the city and the tower which the sons[1121] of men[120] had built.

6 And the LORD said, "Behold, they are one people,[5971] and they all have [I][a]the same language. And this is what they began to do,[6213] and now nothing

15 [I]Lit., *begot* [a]1Chr. 1:13; Jer. 47:4 [b]Gen. 23:3
16 [a]Gen. 15:19-21
19 [I]Lit., *was* [a]Num. 34:2-12 [b]Gen. 14:2, 3
21 [I]Or, *the brother of Japheth the elder*
22 [a]1Chr. 1:17 [b]Gen. 14:1, 9 [c]Gen. 11:10 [d]Is. 66:19
23 [a]Job 1:1; Jer. 25:20
24 [I]Lit., *begot* [a]Gen. 11:12; Luke 3:35
25 [I]I.e., division [a]1Chr. 1:19
26 [I]Lit., *begot*
28 [I]I.e., In 1Chr. 1:22, *Ebal*
30 [I]Lit., *dwelling* [II]Lit., *was*
32 [a]Gen. 9:19
1 [I]Lit., *was one lip* [II]Or, *few or one* set of *words*
2 [I]Lit., *dwelt* [a]Gen. 10:10; 14:1; Dan. 1:2
3 [a]Gen. 14:10
4 [a]Deut. 1:28; 9:1; Ps. 107:26 [b]Gen. 6:4; 2Sam. 8:13 [c]Deut. 4:27
5 [a]Gen. 18:21; Ex. 3:8; 19:11, 18, 20
6 [I]Lit., *one lip* [a]Gen. 11:1

10:15,17 The Hivites formed one of the seven nations of Canaan descended from Canaan (Gen. 10:17; Deut. 7:1). They lived near Lebanon. The Shechemites and Gibeonites were affiliated with them (Gen. 34:2; Josh. 9:3-7; Judg. 3:3). Their land was promised to Israel and they were commanded to destroy them (Deut. 7:2,24). In the reign of Solomon, a remnant of the Hivites was made tributary to Israel (I Kgs. 9:20,21).

11:1-9 A considerable amount of time had elapsed between the great flood of Noah and the building of the Tower of Babel. Josephus, the Jewish historian, says that "a multitude" followed Nimrod's advice to build the tower. This was a flagrant example of corporate pride. Adam and Eve wanted to be God; these men wanted to make a name for themselves, banding together in defiance against God.

which they purpose to do will be [II]impossible for them.

7 "Come, [a]let Us go down and there [b]confuse[1101] their [I]language, that they may not understand[8085] one another's [I]speech."[8193]

8 So the LORD [a]scattered them abroad from there over the face of the whole earth; and they stopped building the city.

9 Therefore its name was called[7121] [Ia]Babel,[894] because there the LORD confused[1101] the [II]language of the whole earth; and from there the LORD scattered them abroad over the face of the whole earth.

Descendants of Shem

🗝 **10** [a]These are *the records of* the generations[8435] of Shem. Shem was one hundred years old,[1121] and [I]became the father of Arpachshad two years after the flood;

11 and Shem lived[2421] five hundred years after he became the father of Arpachshad, and he had *other* sons[1121] and daughters.

12 And Arpachshad lived[2425] thirty-five years, and became the father of Shelah;

13 and Arpachshad lived[2425] four hundred and three years after he became the father of Shelah, and he had *other* sons and daughters.

14 And Shelah lived thirty years, and became the father of Eber;

15 and Shelah lived four hundred and three years after he became the father of Eber, and he had *other* sons and daughters.

16 And Eber lived thirty-four years, and became the father of Peleg;

17 and Eber lived four hundred and thirty years after he became the father of Peleg, and he had *other* sons and daughters.

18 And Peleg lived thirty years, and became the father of Reu;

19 and Peleg lived two hundred and nine years after he became the father of Reu, and he had *other* sons and daughters.

20 And Reu lived thirty-two years, and became the father of Serug;

21 and Reu lived two hundred and seven years after he became the father of Serug, and he had *other* sons and daughters.

22 And Serug lived thirty years, and became the father of Nahor;

23 and Serug lived two hundred years after he became the father of Nahor, and he had *other* sons and daughters.

24 And Nahor lived twenty-nine years, and became the father of [a]Terah;

25 and Nahor lived one hundred and nineteen years after he became the father of Terah, and he had *other* sons and daughters.

26 And Terah lived seventy years, and became [a]the father of Abram, Nahor and Haran.

27 Now these are *the records of* the generations[8435] of Terah. Terah became the father of Abram, Nahor and Haran; and [a]Haran became the father of [b]Lot.

28 And Haran died[4191] [I]in the presence of his father Terah in the land[776] of his birth, in [a]Ur of the Chaldeans.

29 And Abram and [a]Nahor took wives for themselves. The name of Abram's wife[802] was [b]Sarai; and the name of Nahor's wife was [c]Milcah, the daughter of Haran, the father of Milcah [I]and Iscah.

30 And [a]Sarai was barren;[6135] she had no child.

31 And Terah took Abram his son, and Lot the son of Haran, his grandson, and Sarai his daughter-in-law, his son Abram's wife; and they went out [I]together from [a]Ur of the Chaldeans in order to enter the land of Canaan; and they went as far as Haran, and [II]settled there.

32 And the days of Terah were two

6 [II]Lit., *withheld from*

7 [I]Lit., *lip* [a]Gen. 1:26 [b]Gen. 42:23; Ex. 4:11; Deut. 28:49; Is. 33:19; Jer. 5:15

8 [a]Gen. 11:4; Ps. 92:9; Luke 1:51

9 [I]Or, *Babylon;* cf. Heb., *balal,* confuse [II]Lit., *lip* [a]Gen. 10:10

10 [I]Lit., *begot,* and so throughout the ch. [a]Gen. 10:22-25

24 [a]Josh. 24:2

26 [a]Josh. 24:2

27 [a]Gen. 11:31; 12:4 [b]Gen. 13:10; 14:12; 19:1, 29

28 [I]Or, *during the lifetime of* [a]Gen. 11:31

29 [I]Lit., *and the father of* [a]Gen. 24:10 [b]Gen. 17:15; 20:12 [c]Gen. 22:20, 23; 24:15

30 [a]Gen. 16:1

31 [I]Lit., *with them* [II]Lit., *dwelt* [a]Gen. 15:7; Neh. 9:7; Acts 7:4

🗝 **11:10-27** See note on Gen. 5:1-32.

hundred and five years; and Terah died
in Haran.

Abram Journeys to Egypt

12 🗝 Now [a]the LORD said to
Abram,
"[I]Go forth from your country,[776]
And from your relatives
And from your father's
house,[1004]
To the land[776] which I will
show[7200] you;
2 And [a]I will make[6213] you a great
nation,[1471]
And [b]I will bless[1288] you,
And make your name great;
And so [I][c]you shall be a
blessing;[1293]
3 And [a]I will bless those who bless
you,
And the one who [I]curses[7043] you
I will [II]curse.[779]
[b]And in you all the families[4940]
of the earth[127] shall be
blessed."[1288]
4 So Abram went forth as the LORD
had spoken[1696] to him; and [a]Lot went
with him. Now Abram was seventy-five
years old[1121] when he departed from
Haran.
🗝 5 And Abram took Sarai his wife and
Lot his nephew,[1121,251] and all their
[a]possessions which they had accumulated, and [b]the [I]persons[5315] which they
had acquired[6213] in Haran, and they
[II]set out for the land of Canaan; [c]thus
they came to the land of Canaan.
6 And Abram passed[5674] through the
land as far as the site of [a]Shechem, to
the [I]oak of Moreh. Now the Canaanite
was then[227] in the land.
7 And the LORD [a]appeared[7200] to
Abram and said, "[b]To your [I]descend-
ants[2233] I will give this land." So he built
[c]an altar[4196] there to the LORD who had
appeared to him.
8 Then he proceeded from there to
the mountain on the east of Bethel, and
pitched his tent,[168] with [a]Bethel on the
west and Ai on the east; and there he
built an altar to the LORD and [b]called[7121]
upon the name of the LORD.
9 And Abram journeyed on, continuing toward [a]the [I]Negev.
10 Now there was [a]a famine in the
land; so Abram went down to Egypt
to sojourn[1481] there, for the famine was
[b]severe in the land.
🗝 11 And it came about when he
[I]came near to Egypt, that he said to
Sarai his wife,[802] "See now,[4994] I know
that you are a [II][a]beautiful woman;[802]
12 [a]and it will come about when the
Egyptians see[7200] you, that they will
say,[559] 'This is his wife'; and they will
kill[2026] me, but they will let you live.[2421]
13 "Please[4994] say that you are

1 [I]Lit., *Go for yourself* [a]Gen. 15:7; Acts 7:3; Heb. 11:8
2 [I]Lit., *be a blessing* [a]Gen. 17:4-6; 18:18; 46:3; Deut. 26:5 [b]Gen. 22:17 [c]Zech. 8:13
3 [I]Or, *reviles* [II]Or, *bind under a curse* [a]Gen. 24:35; 27:29; Num. 24:9 [b]Gen. 22:18; 26:4; 28:14; Acts 3:25; Gal. 3:8
4 [a]Gen. 11:27, 31
5 [I]Lit., *souls* [II]Lit., *went forth to go to* [a]Gen. 13:6 [b]Gen. 14:14; Lev. 22:11 [c]Gen. 11:31; Heb. 11:8
6 [I]Or, *terebinth* [a]Gen. 35:4; Deut. 11:30
7 [I]Lit., *seed* [a]Gen. 17:1; 18:1 [b]Gen. 13:15; 15:18; Deut. 34:4; Ps. 105: 9-12; Acts 7:5; Gal. 3:16 [c]Gen. 13:4, 18; 22:9
8 [a]Josh. 8:9, 12 [b]Gen. 4:26; 21:33
9 [I]I.e., South country [a]Gen. 13:1, 3; 20:1; 24:62
10 [a]Gen. 26:1 [b]Gen. 43:1
11 [I]Lit., *drew near to enter* [II]Lit., *woman of beautiful appearance* [a]Gen. 26:7; 29:17
12 [a]Gen. 20:11

🗝 **12:1-3** This promise to Abraham and his seed was not for their sake only. It was intended ultimately to bring redemption to the whole world. Through a covenant with God which was stipulated later (Gen. 15:18-21), Abraham's family became a divine protectorate which harbored the hope of its fulfillment. The promise was repeated four more times to the Patriarchs: two times to Abraham (Gen. 17:6-8; 22:16-18), once to Isaac (Gen. 26:3,4), and once to Jacob (Gen. 28:13,14). Each time the promise was repeated, it came at a critical point in the family's history and the circumstances should be carefully observed. Important references to the promise are made in the N.T. in Acts 3:25; Rom. 4:13; Gal. 3:8,29; and Eph. 2:12. In Galatians it is called a preliminary preaching of the Gospel. Both Galatians and Ephesians underline its importance to the Gentiles. Ephesians clearly states that those who were "far off" and "strangers to the covenant of the promise" have been brought near by the blood of Christ.

🗝 **12:5** Did Abraham know his destination or not (Heb. 11:8)? The name of the country was not revealed to him at first. Gen. 11:31 merely shows that Abraham's destination was known to the writer at a later date. Even if the name "Canaan" had been mentioned to Abraham at the very outset, it could still be true that he went forth "not knowing where he was going." It was several hundred miles to the west, and he knew little or nothing about that region.

🗝 **12:11-20** How does this section relate to Gen. 20:2-18? There were two American Presidents named

(continued on next page)

[a]my sister[269] so that it may go well[3190]
with me because of you, and that
[I][b]I may live[2421] on account of you."
14 And it came about when Abram
came into Egypt, the Egyptians [I]saw[7200]
that the woman was very beautiful.
15 And Pharaoh's officials[8269] saw
her and praised[1984] her to Pharaoh; and
[a]the woman was taken into Pharaoh's
house.[1004]
16 Therefore [a]he treated Abram
well[3190] for her sake; and [I][b]gave him
sheep and oxen and donkeys and male
and female servants[5650] and female donkeys and camels.
17 But the LORD [a]struck[5060] Pharaoh
and his house with great plagues[5061] because of Sarai, Abram's wife.
18 Then Pharaoh called[7121] Abram
and said, "[a]What is this you have
done[6213] to me? Why did you not tell[5046]
me that she was your wife?
19 "Why did you say, 'She is my
sister,' so that I took her for my wife?
Now then, [I]here is your wife, take her
and go."
20 And Pharaoh commanded[6680] *his*
men[582] concerning him; and they
[I]escorted him away, with his wife and
all that belonged to him.

Abram and Lot

13 So Abram went up from Egypt
to [a]the [I]Negev, he and his wife[802]
and all that belonged to him; and Lot
with him.
2 Now Abram was [a]very rich[3513] in
livestock, in silver and in gold.
3 And he went [I]on his journeys from
the [II]Negev as far as Bethel, to the place
where his tent[168] had been at the beginning, [a]between Bethel and Ai,
4 to the place of the [a]altar,[4196] which
he had made[6213] there formerly; and
there Abram called[7121] on the name of
the LORD.
5 Now [a]Lot, who went with Abram,
also had flocks and herds and tents.
6 And [a]the land[776] could not [I]sus-
tain[5375] them [II]while dwelling together;
[b]for their possessions were so great that
they were not able to remain together.
7 [a]And there was strife[7379] between
the herdsmen of Abram's livestock and
the herdsmen of Lot's livestock. Now
[b]the Canaanite and the Perizzite were
dwelling then in the land.
8 [a]Then Abram said to Lot, "Please
let there be[1961] no strife between you
and me, nor between my herdsmen and
your herdsmen, for we are brothers.[251]
9 "Is not the whole land before you?
Please separate from me: if *to* the left,
then I will go to the right; or if *to* the
right, then I will go to the left."
10 And Lot lifted up his eyes and
saw[7200] all the [I][a]valley of the Jordan, that
it was well watered everywhere—*this
was* before the LORD [b]destroyed[7843]
Sodom and Gomorrah—like [c]the garden
of the LORD, [d]like the land of Egypt as
you go to [e]Zoar.
11 So Lot chose[977] for himself all
the [I]valley of the Jordan; and Lot journeyed eastward. Thus they separated
from each[376] other.
12 Abram [I]settled in the land of Canaan, while Lot [I]settled in [a]the cities
of the [II]valley, and moved his tents as
far as Sodom.
13 Now [a]the men[582] of Sodom were
wicked[7451] [I]exceedingly and [b]sinners[2400]
against the LORD.
14 And the LORD said to Abram,
after Lot had separated from him, "[a]Now
lift up[5375] your eyes and look[7200] from
the place where you are, [b]northward
and southward and eastward and westward;

13 [I]Lit., *my soul* [a]Gen. 20:2, 5, 12; 26:7 [b]Jer. 38:17, 20
14 [I]Lit., *saw the woman that she was*
15 [a]Gen. 20:2
16 [I]Lit., *he had* [a]Gen. 20:14 [b]Gen. 13:2
17 [a]Gen. 20:18; 1Chr. 16:21; Ps. 105:14
18 [a]Gen. 20:9, 10; 26:10
19 [I]Or, *behold*
20 [I]Lit., *sent*

1 [I]I.e., South country [a]Gen. 12:9
2 [a]Gen. 24:35
3 [I]Lit., *by his stages* [II]I.e., South country [a]Gen. 12:8
4 [a]Gen. 12:7, 8
5 [a]Gen. 12:5
6 [I]Lit., *bear* [II]Lit., *to dwell* [a]Gen. 36:7 [b]Gen. 12:5, 16; 13:2
7 [a]Gen. 26:20 [b]Gen. 12:6; 15:20, 21
8 [a]Prov. 15:18; 20:3
10 [I]Lit., *circle* [a]Gen. 19:17-29; Deut. 34:3 [b]Gen. 19:24 [c]Gen. 2:8, 10 [d]Gen. 47:6 [e]Gen. 14:2, 8; 19:22; Deut. 34:3
11 [I]Lit., *circle*
12 [I]Lit., *dwelt* [II]Lit., *circle* [a]Gen. 14:2; 19:24, 25, 29
13 [I]Lit., *wicked and sinners exceedingly* [a]Gen. 18:20; Ezek. 16:49 [b]Gen. 39:9; Num. 32:23; 2Pet. 2:7, 8
14 [a]Deut. 3:27; 34:1-4; Is. 49:18 [b]Gen. 28:14

(continued from previous page)
Roosevelt who lived within a few years of one another. Similar events are not necessarily identical. The cases of Pharaoh and Abimelech were distinctly different but similar circumstances. In the first instance, Pharaoh was quite taken with the beautiful sixty-five-year-old, middle-aged princess. Abimelech merely wanted a political alliance with a rich, nomadic chieftain. The text does not say that this ninety-year-old woman was beautiful to Abimelech. The case of Isaac in Gen. 26:6-11 is only similar in the use of Abimelech, a mere title of the kings of Gerar.

15 [a]for all the land which you see, [b]I will give it to you and to your [I]descendants[2233] forever.[5769]

16 "And I will make[7760] your [I]descendants [a]as the dust[6083] of the earth;[776] so that if anyone[376] can number the dust of the earth, then your [I]descendants can also be numbered.

17 "Arise, [a]walk about the land through its length and breadth; for [b]I will give it to you."

18 Then Abram moved his tent and came and dwelt by the [Ia]oaks of Mamre, which are in Hebron, and there he built [b]an altar to the LORD.

War of the Kings

14 And it came about in the days of Amraphel king[4428] of [a]Shinar, Arioch king of Ellasar, Chedorlaomer king of [b]Elam, and Tidal king of [I]Goiim,[1471]

2 *that* they made war with Bera king of Sodom, and with Birsha king of Gomorrah, Shinab king of [a]Admah, and Shemeber king of [b]Zeboiim, and the king of Bela (that is, [c]Zoar).

3 All these [I]came as allies to [a]the valley[6010] of Siddim (that is, [b]the Salt Sea).

4 Twelve years they had served[5647] Chedorlaomer, but the thirteenth year they rebelled.[4775]

5 And in the fourteenth year Chedorlaomer and the kings that were with him, came and [I]defeated[5221] the [a]Rephaim[7497] in [b]Ashteroth-karnaim and the Zuzim in Ham and the Emim in [IIc]Shaveh-kiriathaim,

6 and the [a]Horites in their Mount Seir, as far as [b]El-paran, which is by the wilderness.

7 Then they turned back and came to En-mishpat (that is, [a]Kadesh), and [I]conquered all the country[7704] of the Amalekites, and also the Amorites, who lived in [b]Hazazon-tamar.

8 And the king of Sodom and the king of Gomorrah and the king of Admah and the king of Zeboiim and the king of Bela (that is, Zoar) came out; and they arrayed for battle against them in [a]the valley of Siddim,

9 against Chedorlaomer king of Elam and Tidal king of [I]Goiim and Amraphel king of Shinar and Arioch king of Ellasar—four kings against five.

10 Now the valley of Siddim was full of tar pits; and [a]the kings of Sodom and Gomorrah fled, and they fell[5307] [I]into them. But those who survived[7604] fled to the [b]hill country.

11 Then they took all the goods of Sodom and Gomorrah and all their food supply,[400] and departed.

12 And they also took Lot, [a]Abram's nephew, and his possessions and departed, [b]for he was living in Sodom.

13 Then [I]a fugitive came and told[5046] Abram the [a]Hebrew.[5680] Now he was [II]living by the [IIIb]oaks of Mamre the Amorite, brother of Eshcol and brother of Aner, and these were [IVc]allies[1167] with Abram.

14 And when Abram heard that [a]his [I]relative had been taken captive,[7617] he [II]led out his trained men, [b]born in

15 [I]Lit., *seed* [a]Gen. 12:7 [b]Gen. 13:17; 15:7; 17:8; 2Chr. 20:7; Acts 7:5
16 [I]Lit., *seed* [a]Gen. 16:10; 28:14; Num. 23:10
17 [a]Num. 13:17-24 [b]Gen. 13:15
18 [I]Or, *terebinths* [a]Gen. 14:13 [b]Gen. 8:20; 12:7, 8

1 [I]Or, *nations* [a]Gen. 10:10; 11:2 [b]Gen. 10:22; Is. 11:11; Dan. 8:2
2 [a]Gen. 10:19 [b]Deut. 29:23 [c]Gen. 13:10; 19:22
3 [I]Lit., *joined together* [a]Gen. 14:8, 10 [b]Num. 34:12; Deut. 3:17; Josh. 3:16
5 [I]Lit., *smote* [II]Or, *the plain of Kiriathaim* [a]Deut. 3:11, 13 [b]Deut. 1:4; Josh. 9:10 [c]Num. 32:37
6 [a]Gen. 36:20; Deut. 2:12, 22 [b]Gen. 21:21; Num. 10:12
7 [I]Lit., *smote* [a]Num. 13:26 [b]2Chr. 20:2
8 [a]Gen. 14:3
9 [I]Or, *nations*
10 [I]Lit., *there* [a]Gen. 14:17, 21, 22 [b]Gen. 19:17
12 [a]Gen. 11:27 [b]Gen. 13:12
13 [I]Lit., *the* [II]Lit., *abiding* [III]Or, *terebinths* [IV]Lit., *possessors of the covenant* [a]Gen. 40:15; Ex. 3:18 [b]Gen. 13:18;
14:24 [c]Gen. 21:27, 32
14 [I]Lit., *brother* [II]Or, *mustered* [a]Gen. 14:12 [b]Gen. 12:5; 15:3; 17:27; Eccl. 2:7

13:15 Here and in Gen. 15:18 God's gift was not given to Abraham personally (Acts 7:5), but to him as the founder and representative of the nation. The land was given to him "in trust."

14:2 Sodom was a small but populous country. Josephus says that it was rich and flourishing, with five kings controlling its affairs and with a certain degree of ancient civilization. They were idolaters, but they had an opportunity through the presence of Lot and his household to learn about the true God, but they spurned Him (II Pet. 2:7,8). Their wickedness and sexual sin was so persistent that God decided to destroy them completely (Gen. 19:12,13).

14:13 Abram (Abraham) was the first to be called a Hebrew (from the root *'abar* (5674), to cross over). Presumably, it was used in the sense of an immigrant. The name is seldom used of the Israelites in the O.T., except when the speaker is a foreigner, or when the Israelites speak of themselves to one of another nation.

his house,[1004] three hundred and eighteen, and went in pursuit as far as
[c]Dan.
15 And [a]he divided [I]his forces
against them by night, he and his servants,[5650] and [II]defeated them, and pursued them as far as Hobah, which is
[III]north of [b]Damascus.
16 And he [a]brought back all the
goods, and also brought back [b]his
[I]relative Lot with his possessions, and
also the women, and the people.[5971]

God's Promise to Abram

17 Then after his return from the
[I]defeat[5221] of Chedorlaomer and the
kings who were with him, [a]the king of
Sodom went out to meet him at the
valley of Shaveh (that is, [b]the King's
Valley).
18 And [a]Melchizedek[4442] king of Salem brought out [b]bread and wine; now
he was a [c]priest[3548] of [I]God[410] Most
High.[5945]
19 And he blessed[1288] him and said,
"Blessed[1288] be Abram of
[I]God Most High,
[II][a]Possessor of heaven[8064] and
earth;[776]
20 And blessed be [I]God Most High,
Who has delivered your enemies
into your hand."[3027]
[a]And he gave him a tenth[4643] of
all.
21 And the king of Sodom said to
Abram, "Give the [I]people[5315] to me and
take the goods for yourself."
22 And Abram said to the king of
Sodom, "I have [I]sworn to the LORD

14 [c]Deut. 34:1; Judg. 18:29; 1Kin. 15:20
15 [I]Lit., *himself* [II]Lit., *smote* [III]Lit., *on the left* [a]Judg. 7:16 [b]Gen. 15:2
16 [I]Lit., *brother* [a]1Sam. 30:8, 18, 19 [b]Gen. 14:12, 14
17 [I]Lit., *smiting* [a]Gen. 14:10 [b]2Sam. 18:18
18 [I]Heb., *El Elyon* [a]Heb. 7:1-10 [b]Ps. 104:15 [c]Ps. 110:4; Heb. 5:6, 10
19 [I]Heb., *El Elyon* [III]Or, *Creator* [a]Gen. 14:22
20 [I]Heb., *El Elyon* [a]Heb. 7:4
21 [I]Lit., *soul*
22 [I]Lit., *lifted up my hand* [II]Heb., *El Elyon* [III]Or, *Creator* [a]Gen. 14:19 [b]Ps. 24:1
23 [a]2Kin. 5:16
24 [I]Lit., *Not to me except* [a]Gen. 14:13

1 [I]Or, *Your very great reward* [a]Gen. 15:4; 46:2; 1Sam. 15:10 [b]Gen. 21:17; 26:24; Is. 41:10 [c]Deut. 33:29 [d]Num. 18:20; Ps. 58:11
2 [I]Heb., *YHWH*, usually rendered LORD [II]Lit., *go* [III]Lit., *son of acquisition*
3 [I]Lit., *Behold* [II]Lit., *seed* [III]Lit., *and behold, a son of* [a]Gen. 14:14
4 [I]Lit., *inward parts* [a]Gal. 4:28
5 [I]Lit., *seed*

[II][a]God Most High, [III][b]possessor of
heaven and earth,
23 that [a]I will not take a thread or
a sandal[8288] thong or anything that is
yours, lest you should say, 'I have made
Abram rich.'
24 "I will take nothing except what
the young men[5288] have eaten, and the
share of the men who went with me,
[a]Aner, Eshcol, and Mamre; let them
take their share."

Abram Promised a Son

15 After these things [a]the
word[1697] of the LORD came[1961]
to Abram in a vision,[4236] saying,
"[a]Do not fear,[3372] Abram,
I am [b]a shield to you;
[I]Your [c]reward shall be very
great."
2 And Abram said, "O Lord[136]
[I]GOD, what wilt Thou give me, since I
[II]am childless, and the [III]heir[1121] of my
house[1004] is Eliezer of Damascus?"
3 And Abram said, "[I]Since Thou
hast given no [II]offspring[2233] to me,
[III]one [a]born[1121] in my house is my heir."
4 Then behold, the word of the
LORD came to him, saying, "This man
will not be your heir; [a]but one who shall
come forth from your own [I]body,[4578] he
shall be your heir."
5 And He took him outside and said,
"Now look toward the heavens,[8064] and
[a]count the stars, if you are able to
count[5608] them." And He said to him,
"[b]So shall your [I]descendants be."

[a]Gen. 22:17; 26:4; Deut. 1:10 [b]Ex. 32:13; Rom. 4:18; Heb. 11:12

14:18-20 Abram (Abraham) gave Melchizedek the tithe, because, as priest to God Most High, Melchizedek represented God. This brief encounter was the foundation of a Messianic prophecy (Ps. 110:4; Heb. 5:10; 6:20; 7:1-28).

15:1-6 This is one of the classic passages in the entire Bible. It underlines the argument of the Apostle Paul in Romans 4 that justification is by faith. Abraham accepted the divine promise of a son and expected it to be fulfilled even when it was physically impossible. One should note that his faith was accounted to him for righteousness before he personally was circumcised as a sign of his covenant with God and more than 400 years before the law was given to his descendants. Therefore, neither circumcision nor the law had a part in Abraham's righteousness. His trusting faith was accounted as equivalent to righteousness and an acceptable substitute before God for right conduct. God continues to seek men who will trust Him completely through obedience to His Son Jesus, and He will accept that kind of faith as a substitute for perfect righteousness.

6 [a]Then he believed[539] in the LORD; and He reckoned[2803] it to him as righteousness.[6666]

7 And He said to him, "I am the LORD who brought you out of [a]Ur of the Chaldeans, to [b]give you this land[776] to [I]possess it."[3423]

8 And he said, "O Lord [I]GOD, [a]how may I know that I shall [II]possess it?"

9 So He said to him, "[I]Bring Me a three year old heifer, and a three year old female goat, and a three year old ram, and a turtledove, and a young pigeon."

10 Then he [I]brought all these to Him and [a]cut them [II]in two, and laid each[376] half opposite the other; but he [b]did not cut the birds.

11 And the birds of prey came down upon the carcasses,[6297] and Abram drove them away.

12 Now when the sun was going down, [a]a deep sleep fell upon Abram; and behold, [I]terror[367] *and* great darkness[2825] fell upon him.

13 And *God* said to Abram, "Know for certain that [a]your [I]descendants will be strangers[1616] in a land that is not theirs, [II]where [b]they will be enslaved[5647] and oppressed [c]four hundred years.

14 "But I will also judge the nation[1471] whom they will serve;[5647] and afterward they will come out [a]with [I]many possessions.

15 "And as for you, [a]you shall go to your fathers[1] in peace;[7965] you shall be buried[6912] at a good[2896] old age.[7872]

16 "Then in [a]the fourth generation[1755] they shall return here, for [b]the iniquity[5771] of the Amorite is not yet complete."[8003]

17 And it came about when the sun had set, that it was very dark, and behold, *there appeared* a smoking oven and a flaming torch which [a]passed[5674] between these pieces.[1506]

18 On that day[3117] the LORD made[3772] a covenant[1285] with Abram, saying,

"[a]To your [I]descendants I have
given this land,
From [b]the river of Egypt as far
as the great river, the river
Euphrates:

19 [a]the Kenite and the Kenizzite and the Kadmonite

20 and the Hittite and the Perizzite and the Rephaim[7497]

21 and the Amorite and the Canaanite and the Girgashite and the Jebusite."

Sarai and Hagar

16 Now [a]Sarai, Abram's wife[802] had borne him no *children,* and she had [b]an Egyptian maid whose name was Hagar.

2 So Sarai said to Abram, "Now behold, the LORD has prevented me from

---

6 [a]Rom. 4:3, 20-22; Gal. 3:6; James 2:23
7 [I]Or, *inherit* [a]Gen. 11:31 [b]Gen. 13:15, 17
8 [I]Heb., *YHWH,* usually rendered *LORD* [II]Or, *inherit* [a]Judg. 6:36-40; Luke 1:18
9 [I]Lit., *Take*
10 [I]Lit., *took* [II]Lit., *in the midst* [a]Gen. 15:17 [b]Lev. 1:17
12 [I]Or, *a terror of great darkness* [a]Gen. 2:21; 28:11; Job 33:15
13 [I]Lit., *seed* [II]Lit., *and shall serve them; and they shall afflict them* [a]Acts 7:6, 17 [b]Ex. 1:11; Deut. 5:15 [c]Ex. 12:40; Gal. 3:17
14 [I]Lit., *great* [a]Ex. 12:32-38
15 [a]Gen. 25:8; 47:30
16 [a]Gen. 15:13 [b]Lev. 18:24-28
17 [a]Jer. 34:18, 19
18 [I]Lit., *seed* [a]Gen. 17:8; Josh. 21:43; Acts 7:5 [b]Ex. 23:31; Num. 34:1-15; Deut. 1:7,8
19 [a]Ex. 3:17; 23:28; Josh. 24:11; Neh. 9:8
1 [a]Gen. 11:30 [b]Gen. 12:16

15:13-16 God gave Abraham a preview of events in his family's history before they actually possessed the land which He had promised them. They would first be temporary residents in a strange land for 400 years and become slaves. Their bondage in Egypt was certainly a part of God's overall plan. 400 years is a round figure. There is no conflict with the 430 years mentioned in Ex. 12:40,41. The four generations of their sojourn should be understood as four lifetimes. 100 years would have been a conservative estimate for one lifetime in patriarchal times. The events surrounding Israel's departure from Egypt would be a judgment upon that nation. The interval of their sojourn in Egypt would be given to the Amorites, who possessed Canaan at that time. Israel's campaign against them was a matter of God's judgment.

15:16 The Amorites were one of the seven nations of Canaan and were governed by many independent kings (Josh. 5:1; 9:10). Originally they inhabited a mountain district in the South (Num. 13:29), but later they acquired an extensive tract of land from Moab, east of Jordan (Num. 21:26). They had many strong cities (Num. 32:17,33). They were profane, wicked, and idolatrous (Josh. 24:15). They interfered with Israel at times (Num. 21:24), again were peaceful, but were finally brought into bondage by Solomon (I Kgs. 9:20,21).

15:18 God's promise concerning this land both here and in Gen. 17:8 was conditional (Deut. 31:16,17; Josh. 23:16). The literal descendants of Abraham eventually proved to be unworthy, and, therefore, the land was taken away from them. However, a future restoration to the land is promised (Amos 9:11-15).

bearing *children.* [a]Please go in to my
maid; perhaps I shall [I]obtain children
through her." And Abram listened[8085]
to the voice of Sarai.
3 And after Abram had [I]lived [a]ten
years in the land[776] of Canaan, Abram's
wife Sarai took Hagar the Egyptian, her
maid, and gave her to her husband[376]
Abram as his wife.
4 And he went in to Hagar, and she
conceived; and when she saw[7200] that
she had conceived, her mistress[1404] was
despised in her sight.
5 And Sarai said to Abram, "[a]May
the wrong[2555] done me be upon you. I
gave my maid into your [I]arms; but when
she saw that she had conceived, I was
despised in her [II]sight. [b]May the LORD
judge between [III]you and me."
6 But Abram said to Sarai, "Behold,
your maid is in your [I]power;[3027] do to
her what is good in your [II]sight."[5869,2896]
So Sarai treated her harshly, and [a]she
fled from her presence.
7 Now [a]the angel of the LORD found
her by a spring of water in the wilderness, by the spring on the way to
[b]Shur.
8 And he said, "Hagar, Sarai's maid,
[a]where have you come from and where
are you going?" And she said, "I am
fleeing from the presence of my mistress
Sarai."
9 Then the angel of the LORD said
to her, "Return to your mistress, and
submit yourself [I]to her authority."
10 Moreover, the [a]angel of the LORD
said to her, "[b]I will greatly multiply your
[I]descendants[2233] so that [II]they shall be
too many to count."[5608]
11 The angel of the LORD said to
her further,
"Behold, you are with child,
And you shall bear a son;[1121]
And you shall call[7121] his name
[I]Ishmael,
Because [a]the LORD [II]has given
heed[8085] to your affliction.
12 "And he will be a [a]wild donkey
of a man,[120]
His hand[3027] *will be* against
everyone,
And everyone's hand *will be*
against him;
And he will [I]live [II][b]to the east
of all his brothers."
13 Then she called[7121] the name of
the LORD who spoke[1696] to her, "[I]Thou
art [II]a God[410] who sees";[7210] for she said,
"[a]Have I even [III]remained[7200] alive here
after seeing[7210] Him?"
14 Therefore the well was called
[I]Beer-lahai-roi;883 behold, it is between
[a]Kadesh and Bered.
🔑 **15** So Hagar bore Abram a son; and
Abram called the name of his son, whom
Hagar bore, Ishmael.3458
16 And Abram was [a]eighty-six years
old[1121] when Hagar bore Ishmael to
[I]him.

Abraham and the Covenant of Circumcision

17 Now when Abram was ninety-
nine years old, [a]the LORD appeared[7200] to Abram and said to him,
"I am [I]God[410] [a]Almighty;[7706]
Walk before Me, and be
[II][b]blameless.[8549]
2 "And I will [I]establish My
[a]covenant[1285] between Me
and you,
And I will [b]multiply you
exceedingly."
3 And Abram [a]fell on his face, and
God[430] talked with him, saying,

2 [I]Lit., *be built from her* [a]Gen. 30:3, 4, 9, 10
3 [I]Lit., *dwelt* [a]Gen. 12:4
5 [I]Lit., *bosom* [II]Lit., *eyes* [III]Lit., *me and you* [a]Jer. 51:35 [b]Gen. 31:53; Ex. 5:21
6 [I]Lit., *hand* [II]Lit., *eyes* [a]Gen. 16:9
7 [a]Gen. 21:17, 18; 22:11, 15; 31:11 [b]Gen. 20:1; 25:18
8 [a]Gen. 3:9; 1Kin. 19:9, 13
9 [I]Lit., *under her hands*
10 [I]Lit., *seed* [II]Or, *it shall not be counted for multitude* [a]Gen. 22:15-18 [b]Gen. 17:20
11 [I]I.e., God hears [II]Lit., *has heard* [a]Ex. 2:23, 24; 3:7, 9
12 [I]Lit., *dwell* [II]Lit., *before the face of;* or, *in defiance of* [a]Job 24:5; 39:5-8 [b]Gen. 25:18
13 [I]Or, *Thou, God, dost see me* [II]Heb., *Elroi* [III]Lit., *seen here after the one who saw me* [a]Gen. 32:30; Ps. 139:1-12
14 [I]I.e., the well of the living one who sees me [a]Gen. 14:7
16 [I]Lit., *Abram* [a]Gen. 12:4; 16:3

1 [I]Heb., *El Shaddai* [II]Lit., *complete, perfect;* or, *having integrity* [a]Gen. 12:7; 18:1 [b]Gen. 28:3; 35:11 [c]Gen. 6:9; Deut. 18:13
2 [I]Lit., *give* [a]Gen. 15:18 [b]Gen. 13:16; 15:5
3 [a]Gen. 17:17; 18:2

🔑 **16:15,16** The Ishmaelites were the descendants of Ishmael and were divided into twelve tribes (Gen. 25:16). They were also called Hagarites, Hagarenes, and Arabians (I Chr. 5:10; Ps. 83:6; Isa. 13:20). They were governed by kings, were rich in cattle, and lived in tents (Jer. 25:24; Isa. 13:20; I Chr. 5:21). Though they were merchants of the East and traveled around in large caravans (Gen. 37:25; Job 6:19), they were frequently lawless and would waylay and plunder travelers (Jer. 3:2). After harassing Israel, they were overcome by Gideon (Judg. 8:10-21). It would seem that later they became more peacefully inclined, since they sent presents to King Solomon and King Jehoshaphat (I Kgs. 10:15; II Chr. 17:11), however, some tribes fought against King Uzziah (II Chr. 26:7).

4 "As for Me, behold, My covenant
is with you,
And you shall be the father[1] of
a [a]multitude of nations.[1471]
🔑5 "No longer shall your name be
called[7121] [I]Abram,[87]
But [a]your name shall be
[II]Abraham;[85]
For [b]I will make you the father
of a multitude of nations.

6 "And I will make you exceedingly fruitful, and I will make nations of you, and [a]kings[4428] shall come forth from you.

7 "And I will establish My covenant between Me and you and your [I]descendants[2233] after you throughout their generations[1755] for an [a]everlasting[5769] covenant, [b]to be God to you and [c]to your [I]descendants after you.

8 "And [a]I will give to you and to your [I]descendants after you, the land[776] of your sojournings,[4033] all the land of Canaan, for an everlasting possession;[272] and [b]I will be their God."[430]

9 God said further to Abraham, "Now as for you, [a]you shall keep[8104] My covenant, you and your [I]descendants after you throughout their generations.

10 "[a]This is My covenant, which you shall keep, between Me and you and your [I]descendants after you: every male[2145] among you shall be circumcised.

11 "And [a]you shall be circumcised[5243] in the flesh[1320] of your foreskin;[6190] and it shall be the sign[226] of the covenant between Me and you.

12 "And every male among you who is [a]eight days[3117] old[1121] shall be circumcised[4135] throughout your generations, a *servant* who is born in the house[1004] or who is bought with money from any foreigner,[5236] who is not of your [I]descendants.

13 "A *servant* who is born in your house or [a]who is bought with your money shall surely be circumcised; thus shall My covenant be in your flesh for an everlasting covenant.

14 "But an uncircumcised[6189] male who is not circumcised in the flesh of his foreskin, that person[5315] shall be [a]cut off[3772] from his people;[5971] he has broken[6565] My covenant."

15 Then God said to Abraham, "As for Sarai[8297] your wife, you shall not call[7121] her name Sarai, but [I]Sarah[8283] *shall be* her name.

16 "And I will bless[1288] her, and indeed I will give you [a]a son[1121] by her. Then I will bless her, and she shall be *a mother of* nations; [b]kings of peoples shall [I]come from her."

17 Then Abraham [a]fell on his face and laughed,[6711] and said in his heart,[3820] "Will a child be born to a man one hundred years old? And [b]will Sarah, who is ninety years old, bear *a child?*"

18 And Abraham said to God, "Oh that Ishmael might live[2421] before Thee!"

🔑19 But God said, "No, but Sarah your wife shall bear you [a]a son, and you shall call[7121] his name [I]Isaac;[3327] and [b]I will establish My covenant with him for an everlasting covenant for his [II]descendants after him.

20 "And as for Ishmael, I have heard[8085] you; behold, I will bless him, and [a]will make him fruitful, and will multiply him exceedingly. [b]He shall [I]become the father of twelve princes,[5387] and I will make him a [c]great nation.[1471]

21 "But My covenant I will establish with [a]Isaac, whom [b]Sarah will bear to you at this season[4150] next year."

22 And when He finished talking with him, [a]God went up from Abraham.

23 Then Abraham took Ishmael his son, and all *the servants* who were [a]born in his house and all who were bought with his money, every male[2145] among the men[582] of Abraham's house-

4 [a]Gen. 35:11; 48:19
5 [I]I.e., exalted father [II]I.e., father of a multitude [a]Neh. 9:7 [b]Rom. 4:17
6 [a]Gen. 17:16; 35:11
7 [I]Lit., *seed* [a]Gen. 17:13, 19; Ps. 105:9, 10; Luke 1:55 [b]Gen. 26:24; Lev. 11:45; 26:12, 45; Heb. 11:16 [c]Gen. 28:13; Gal. 3:16
8 [I]Lit., *seed* [a]Gen. 12:7; 13:15, 17; Acts 7:5 [b]Ex. 6:7; 29:45; Lev. 26:12; Deut. 29:13; Rev. 21:7
9 [I]Lit., *seed* [a]Ex. 19:5
10 [I]Lit., *seed* [a]John 7:22; Acts 7:8; Rom. 4:11
11 [a]Ex. 12:48; Deut. 10:16; Acts 7:8; Rom. 4:11
12 [I]Lit., *seed* [a]Lev. 12:3
13 [a]Ex. 12:44
14 [a]Ex. 4:24-26
15 [I]I.e., princess
16 [I]Lit., *be* [a]Gen. 18:10 [b]Gen. 17:6; 36:31
17 [a]Gen. 17:3; 18:12; 21:6 [b]Gen. 21:7
19 [I]I.e., he laughs [II]Lit., *seed* [a]Gen. 17:16; 18:10; 21:2 [b]Gen. 26:2-5
20 [I]Lit., *beget twelve princes* [a]Gen. 16:10 [b]Gen. 25:12-16 [c]Gen. 21:18
21 [a]Gen. 17:19; 18:10, 14 [b]Gen. 21:2
22 [a]Gen. 18:33; 35:13
23 [a]Gen. 14:14

🔑 **17:5,6** In Hebrew the name Abram means "exalted father" (87) and the name Abraham means "father of a multitude" (85).

🔑 **17:19** In Hebrew the name Isaac means "laughter" (3327). Both Abraham and Sarah laughed when they thought of the apparent impossibility of this birth (Gen. 17:17; 21:6).

hold, and circumcised[4135] the flesh of
their foreskin in the very same day,
[b]as God had said to him.
24 Now Abraham was ninety-nine
years old when [a]he was circumcised in
the flesh of his foreskin.
25 And [a]Ishmael his son was thirteen years old when he was circumcised
in the flesh of his foreskin.
26 In the very same day Abraham
was circumcised, and Ishmael his son.
27 And all the men of his household,
who were [a]born in the house or bought
with money from a foreigner, were circumcised with him.

Birth of Isaac Promised

18 ⊶ Now [a]the LORD appeared[7200]
to him by the [I][b]oaks of Mamre,
while he was sitting at the tent[168] door
in the heat of the day.[3117]
2 And when he lifted[5375] up his eyes
and looked,[7200] behold, three [a]men[582]
were standing[5324] opposite him; and
when he saw[7200] *them,* he ran from the
tent door to meet them, and bowed[7812]
himself to the earth,[776]
3 and said, "[I]My lord,[136] if now I
have found favor[2580] in [II]your sight,
please do not [III]pass[5674] [II]your servant[5650] by.[5674]
4 "Please[4994] let a little water be
brought and [a]wash your feet, and
[I]rest yourselves under the tree;
5 and I will [I][a]bring a piece of bread,
that you may [II]refresh yourselves;[3820]
after that you may go on, since you have
[III]visited[5674] your servant." And they
said,[1696] "So do, as you have said."
6 So Abraham hurried into the tent
to Sarah, and said, "[I]Quickly, prepare
three [II]measures of fine flour, knead *it,*
and make[6213] bread cakes."
7 Abraham also ran to the herd, and
took a tender and [I]choice[2896] calf, and
gave *it* to the servant; and he hurried
to prepare[6213] it.
8 And he took curds and milk and
the calf which he had prepared,[6213] and
placed *it* before them; and he was standing by them under the tree [I]as they ate.
9 Then they said to him, "Where
is Sarah your wife?" And he said, "Behold, in the tent."
10 And he said, "[a]I will surely
return[7725] to you [I]at this time[6256] next
year; and behold, Sarah your wife shall
have a son."[1121] And Sarah was listening[8085] at the tent door, which was behind him.
11 Now [a]Abraham and Sarah were
old,[2205] advanced in age;[3117] Sarah was
[b]past [I]childbearing.[734,802]
⊶ 12 And Sarah laughed[6711] [I]to herself, saying, "[a]After I have become old,
shall I have pleasure, my [b]lord[113] being
old[2204] also?"
13 And the LORD said to Abraham,
"Why did Sarah laugh,[6711] saying, 'Shall
I indeed[552] [I]bear *a child,* when I am *so*
old?'
14 "[a]Is anything[1697] too [I]difficult[6381]
for the LORD? At the [b]appointed time[4150]
I will return to you, [II]at this time next
year, and Sarah shall have a son."
15 Sarah denied *it* however, saying,
"I did not laugh";[6711] for she was
afraid.[3372] And He said, "No, but you
did laugh."[6711]
16 Then [a]the men rose up from
there, and looked down toward Sodom;
and Abraham was walking with them
to send them off.

23 [b]Gen. 17:9-11
24 [a]Rom. 4:11
25 [a]Gen. 16:16
27 [a]Gen. 14:14
1 [I]Or, *terebinths* [a]Gen. 12:7; 17:1 [b]Gen. 13:18; 14:13
2 [a]Gen. 18:16, 22; 32:24; Josh. 5:13; Judg. 13:6-11; Heb. 13:2
3 [I]Or, *O Lord* [II]Or, *Thy* [III]Lit., *pass away from your servant*
4 [I]Lit., *support* [a]Gen. 19:2; 24:32; 43:24
5 [I]Lit., *take* [II]Lit., *sustain your heart* [III]Lit., *come to* [a]Judg. 6:18, 19; 13:15, 16
6 [I]Lit., *Hasten three measures* [II]Heb., *seah;* i.e., one seah equals approx. eleven qts.
7 [I]Lit., *good*
8 [I]Lit., *and*
10 [I]Lit., *when the time revives* [a]Gen. 21:2; Rom. 9:9
11 [I]Lit., *the manner of women* [a]Gen. 17:17; Rom. 4:19 [b]Heb. 11:11
12 [I]Lit., *within* [a]Gen. 17:17; Luke 1:18 [b]1Pet. 3:6
13 [I]Lit., *surely bear*
14 [I]Or, *wonderful* [II]Lit., *when the time revives* [a]Jer. 32:17, 27; Zech. 8:6; Matt. 19:26; Luke 1:37; Rom. 4:21 [b]Gen. 17:21; 18:10
16 [a]Gen. 18:2, 22; 19:1

⊶ **18:1-33** Did Abraham see God? What about Jn. 1:18, "No man hath seen God at any time."? This theophany (appearance of God to man) in the O.T. is believed to have been Christ, in a physical pre-existent form. The N.T. teaches that Christ existed co-eternally with God the Father (Jn. 1:1; 8:56-58; 17:5; Col. 1:15-17), and it is not inconceivable that He would at times take the appearance of humanity when He chose to do so. Jesus Christ is the personal manifestation of God to man (Jn. 14:9).

⊶ **18:12** There are several different kinds of laughter in the Bible: (1) the laughter of incredulity (Gen. 18:12); (2) the laughter of joyful wonder (Gen. 17:17); (3) the laughter of defiance (Job 5:22); (4) the laughter of approbation (Job 29:24); (5) hollow laughter with undertones of sorrow (Prov. 14:13); (6) the laughter of scorn (Ps. 2:4); (7) the laughter of rapturous delight (Ps. 126:2).

17 And [a]the LORD said, "Shall I hide[3680] from Abraham [b]what I am about to do,

18 since Abraham will surely become a great and [I]mighty nation,[1471] and in him [a]all the nations of the earth[776] will be blessed?[1288]

19 "For I have [Ia]chosen him, in order that he may [b]command his children[1121] and his household[1004] after him to [c]keep[8104] the way[1870] of the LORD by doing[6213] righteousness[6666] and justice;[4941] in order that the LORD may bring upon Abraham [d]what He has spoken[1696] about him."

20 And the LORD said, "[a]The outcry of Sodom and Gomorrah is indeed great, and their sin[2403] is exceedingly grave.[3513]

21 "I will [a]go down now, and see if they have done entirely according to its outcry, which has come to Me; and if not, I will know."

22 Then [a]the men turned away from there and went toward Sodom, while Abraham was still standing before [b]the LORD.

23 And Abraham came near and said, "[a]Wilt Thou indeed sweep away[5595] the righteous[6662] with the wicked?[7563]

24 "Suppose[194] there are fifty righteous within the city; wilt Thou indeed sweep *it* away and not [I]spare the place for the sake of the fifty righteous who are in it?

🔑25 "Far be it from Thee to do[6213] [I]such a thing,[1697] to slay the righteous with the wicked, so that the righteous and the wicked are *treated* alike. Far be it from Thee! Shall not [a]the Judge of all the earth[776] [II]deal justly?"[4941]

26 So the LORD said, "[a]If I find in Sodom fifty righteous within the city, then I will [I]spare[5375] the whole place on their account."

27 And Abraham answered and said, "Now behold, I have [I]ventured to speak to the Lord, although I am *but* [a]dust[6083] and ashes.

28 "Suppose the fifty righteous are lacking five, wilt Thou destroy[7843] the whole city because of five?" And He said, "I will not destroy *it* if I find forty-five there."

29 And he spoke to Him yet again and said, "Suppose forty are found there?" And He said, "I will not do *it* on account of the forty."

30 Then he said, "Oh[4994] may the Lord not be angry[2734], and I shall speak; suppose thirty are found there?" And He said, "I will not do *it* if I find thirty there."

31 And he said, "Now behold, I have [I]ventured to speak to the Lord; suppose twenty are found there?" And He said, "I will not destroy *it* on account of the twenty."

32 Then he said, "[a]Oh may the Lord not be angry, and I shall speak only this once; suppose ten are found there?" And He said, "I will not destroy *it* on account of the ten."

33 And as soon as He had finished speaking to Abraham [a]the LORD departed; and Abraham returned to his place.

The Doom of Sodom

19 Now the [a]two angels came to Sodom in the evening as Lot was sitting in the gate of Sodom. When [b]Lot saw *them,* he rose to meet them and [I]bowed[7812] down *with his* face[639] to the ground.[776]

2 And he said, "Now behold, my lords,[113] please turn aside into your servant's[5650] house,[1004] and spend the night, and wash your feet; then you may rise early and go on your way."[1870] They said however, "No, but we shall spend the night in the square."

17 [a]Gen. 18:22, 26, 33; Amos 3:7 [b]Gen. 18:21; 19:24

18 [I]Or, *populous* [a]Gen. 12:3; 22:18; Acts 3:25; Gal. 3:8

19 [I]Lit., *known* [a]Neh. 9:7; Amos 3:2 [b]Deut. 6:6, 7 [c]Gen. 17:9 [d]Gen. 12:2, 3

20 [a]Gen. 19:13; Ezek. 16:49, 50

21 [a]Gen. 11:5; Ex. 3:8; Ps. 14:2

22 [a]Gen. 18:16; 19:1 [b]Gen. 18:1, 17

23 [a]Ex. 23:7; Num. 16:22; 2Sam. 24:17; Ps. 11:4-7

24 [I]Or, *forgive*

25 [I]Lit., *after this manner* [II]Lit., *do justice* [a]Deut. 1:16, 17; 32:4; Job 8:3, 20; Ps. 58:11; 94:2; Is. 3:10, 11; Rom. 3:5, 6

26 [I]Or, *forgive* [a]Jer. 5:1

27 [I]Lit., *undertaken* [a]Gen. 3:19; Job 30:19; 42:6

31 [I]Lit., *undertaken*

32 [a]Judg. 6:39

33 [a]Gen. 17:22; 35:13

1 [I]Lit., *bowed himself* [a]Gen. 18:2, 22 [b]Gen. 18:2-5

🔑 **18:25** God is a good, moral Governor of the universe (Deut. 32:4; Ps. 92:15; Ezek. 18:25; Rom. 3:3,4). If God were not benign to us (Mt. 5:45), there would be no food or joy (Acts 14:14-17). However, sometimes God arbitrarily chooses key people to suit His eternal purpose (Rom. 9:11-13). He has the unquestionable right to bestow His favors as He sees fit.

3 Yet he urged them strongly, so
they turned aside to him and entered
his house;[1004] [a]and he prepared a
feast[4960] for them, and baked unleavened
bread,[4682] and they ate.
4 Before they lay down, [a]the men[582]
of the city, the men of Sodom, surrounded the house, both young and
old,[2205] all the people[5971] [I]from every
quarter;
5 and they called[7121] to Lot and said
to him, "[a]Where are the men who came
to you tonight? Bring them out to us
that we may [I]have relations with
them."
6 But Lot went out to them at the
doorway, and shut the door behind
him,
7 and said, "Please, my brothers,[251]
do not act wickedly.[7489]
8 "Now behold, [a]I have two daughters who have not [I]had relations[3045] with
man;[376] please let me bring them out
to you, and do[6213] to them [II]whatever
you like;[2896] only do nothing to these
men, inasmuch as they have come under
the [III]shelter of my roof."
9 But they said, "Stand aside." Furthermore, they said, "This one came
in [I]as an alien,[1481] and already [a]he is
acting like a judge; now we will treat
you worse[7489] than them." So they
pressed hard against [II]Lot and came near
to break[7665] the door.
10 But [a]the men reached out their
[I]hands[3027] and brought Lot into the
house [II]with them, and shut the door.
11 And [a]they [I]struck[5221] the men
who were at the doorway of the house
with blindness, both small and great,
so that they wearied *themselves trying*
to find the doorway.
12 Then the men said to Lot,
"Whom else have you here? A son-in-
law, and your sons,[1121] and your daughters, and whomever you have in the
city, bring *them* out of the place;
13 for we are about to destroy[7843]
this place, because [a]their outcry has
become so great before the LORD
that [b]the LORD has sent us to destroy
it."

14 And Lot went out and spoke to
his sons-in-law, who [I]were to marry his
daughters, and said, "Up, [a]get out of
this place, for the LORD will destroy the
city." [b]But he appeared to his sons-in-
law [II]to be jesting.6711
15 And when morning dawned, the
angels urged Lot, saying, "Up, take your
wife and your two daughters, who are
here, lest you be swept away[5595] in the
[I]punishment[5771] of the city."
16 But he hesitated. So the men
[a]seized[2388] his hand and the hand of his
wife and the [I]hands of his two daughters,
for [b]the compassion[2551] of the LORD *was*
upon him; and they brought him out,
and put him outside the city.
17 And it came about when they had
brought them outside, that [I]one said,
"[a]Escape[4422] for your life![5315] [b]Do not
look behind you, and do not stay
[II]anywhere in the [c]valley; escape to
[d]the [III]mountains, lest you be swept
away."
18 But Lot said to them, "Oh no,
my lords![113]
19 "Now behold, your servant has
found favor[2580] in your sight, and you
have magnified your lovingkindness,[2617]
which you have shown[6213] me by
saving[2421] my life; but I cannot escape
to the [I]mountains, lest the disaster[7451]
overtake me and I die;[4191]
20 now behold, this town is near
enough to flee to, and it is small. Please,
let me escape there (is it not small?)
[I]that my life[5315] may be saved."[2421]
21 And he said to him, "Behold, I
grant[5375] you this [I]request[1697] also, not
to overthrow[2015] the town of which you
have spoken.
22 "Hurry, escape there, for I cannot do anything[1697] until you arrive
there." Therefore the name of the town
was called[7121] [Ia]Zoar.
23 The sun had risen over the
earth[776] when Lot came to Zoar.
24 Then the LORD [a]rained on Sodom
and Gomorrah brimstone1614 and fire
from the LORD out of heaven,[8064]
25 and [a]He overthrew those cities,
and all the [I]valley, and all the inhabitants

3 [a]Gen. 18:6-8

4 [I]Or, *without exception;* lit., *from every end* [a]Gen. 13:13; 18:20

5 [I]I.e., have intercourse [a]Lev. 18:22; Judg. 19:22

8 [I]I.e., had intercourse [II]Lit., *as is good in your sight* [III]Lit., *shadow* [a]Judg. 19:24

9 [I]Lit., *to sojourn* [II]Lit., *the man, against Lot* [a]Ex. 2:14

10 [I]Lit., *hand* [II]Lit., *to* [a]Gen. 19:1

11 [I]Lit., *smote* [a]Deut. 28:28, 29; 2Kin. 6:18; Acts 13:11

13 [a]Gen. 18:20 [b]Lev. 26:30-33; Deut. 4:26; 28:45; 1Chr. 21:15

14 [I]Or, *had married;* lit., *were taking* [II]Lit., *like one who was jesting* [a]Num. 16:21, 45; Rev. 18:4 [b]Jer. 43:1, 2

15 [I]Or, *iniquity*

16 [I]Lit., *hand* [a]Deut. 5:15; 6:21; 7:8; 2Pet. 2:7 [b]Ex. 34:7; Ps. 32:10; 33:18, 19

17 [I]Lit., *he* [II]Lit., *in all the circle* [III]Lit., *mountain* [a]Jer. 48:6 [b]Gen. 19:26 [c]Gen. 13:10 [d]Gen. 14:10

19 [I]Lit., *mountain*

20 [I]Lit., *and my soul will live*

21 [I]Lit., *thing*

22 [I]I.e., small [a]Gen. 13:10; 14:2

24 [a]Deut. 29:23; Ps. 11:6; Is. 13:19; Ezek. 16:49, 50; Luke 17:29; Jude 7

25 [I]Lit., *circle* [a]Deut. 29:23; Ps. 107:34; Is. 13:19; Lam. 4:6; 2Pet. 2:6

of the cities, and what grew on the
ground.[127]
🔑 26 But his wife, from behind him,
[a]looked *back;* and she became a pillar
of salt.

27 Now Abraham arose early in the
morning *and went* to [a]the place where
he had stood before the LORD;
28 and he looked down toward
Sodom and Gomorrah, and toward all
the land[776] of the [I]valley, and he saw,
and behold, [a]the smoke of the land[776]
ascended like the smoke of a [II]furnace.
29 Thus it came about, when God[430]
destroyed the cities of the [I]valley, that
[a]God remembered[2142] Abraham, and
[b]sent Lot out of the midst of the overthrow, when He overthrew the cities
in which Lot lived.

Lot Is Debased

30 And Lot went up from Zoar, and
[Ia]stayed in the [II]mountains, and his two
daughters with him; for he was afraid[3372]
to [III]stay in Zoar; and he [I]stayed in a
cave, he and his two daughters.
31 Then the first-born said to the
younger, "Our father is old,[2204] and
there is not a man[376] [I]on earth to

26 [a]Gen. 19:17; Luke 17:32
27 [a]Gen. 18:22
28 [I]Lit., *circle* [II]Lit., *kiln* [a]Rev. 9:2; 18:9
29 [I]Lit., *circle* [a]Deut. 7:8; 9:5, 27 [b]2Pet. 2:7
30 [I]Lit., *dwelt* [II]Lit., *mountain* [III]Lit., *dwell* [a]Gen. 19:17, 19
31 [I]Or, *in the land* [a]Gen. 16:2, 4; 38:8; Deut. 25:5
32 [I]Lit., *seed from our father* [a]Luke 21:34
34 [I]Lit., *seed from our father*
37 [a]Deut. 2:9

[a]come in to us after the manner[1870] of
the earth.
32 "Come, [a]let us make our father
drink wine, and let us lie with him, that
we may preserve[2421] [I]our family[2233]
through our father."
33 So they made their father drink
wine that night, and the first-born went
in and lay with her father; and he did
not know[3045] when she lay down or when
she arose.
34 And it came about on the morrow, that the first-born said to the younger, "Behold, I lay last night with my
father; let us make him drink wine tonight also; then you go in and lie with
him, that we may preserve [I]our family
through our father."
35 So they made their father drink
wine that night also, and the younger
arose and lay with him; and he did not
know when she lay down or when she
arose.
36 Thus both the daughters of Lot
were with child by their father.
🔑 37 And the first-born bore a son,
and called his name [a]Moab;[4124] he is the
father of the Moabites to this day.[3117]
🔑 38 And as for the younger, she also
bore a son, and called his name

🔑 **19:26** The salt of the Dead Sea accumulated around her body and permeated it. In Antiquities 1,11,4, Josephus wrote that this pillar still remained in his day and that he had seen it. It was a peculiar formation of crumbling, crystalline rock associated by tradition with the event in Gen. 19. Clement of Rome, Irenaeus, and Benjamin of Tudela also wrote of the strange formation as visible in their day, but later writers stated that it had ceased to exist.

🔑 **19:37** The Moabites were the descendants of Lot and were neighbors of the Amorites on the opposite side of the Arnon River (Num. 21:13). They were governed by kings and they possessed many great cities (Num. 21:28-30; 23:7; Isa. 15:1). They were prosperous, arrogant, and idolatrous. They were mighty men of war (Isa. 16:6). The Amorites deprived them of a large part of their territory (Num. 21:26). The Moabites refused to let Israel pass through their country and were so greatly impressed and alarmed by the multitude of the Israelite army that, along with Midian, they sent Balaam to curse it (Num. 22-24). Subsequently, Israel was enticed into idolatry and even intermarried with them. They were always hostile to Israel until King Saul subdued them (I Sam. 14:47), and they were later tributary to David and succeeding Jewish kings (II Sam. 8:2,12; II Kgs. 3:4), but finally joined Babylon against Judah (II Kgs. 24:2). On several occasions, God pronounced judgments against Moab (Isa. 15:1-16:14; Jer. 48:1-47; Amos 2:1-3).

🔑 **19:38** The Ammonites were the children of Lot (Deut. 2:19). They were a cruel, covetous, proud, vindictive, and idolatrous nation (see Judg. 10:6; Amos 1:13; Zeph. 2:10; Ezek. 25:3,6). Their chief city was Rabbah (II Sam. 12:26,27), where they were governed by hereditary kings (Jer. 27:3). They had various encounters with Israel. With the Philistines they oppressed Israel for eighteen years (Judg. 10:7-9). King Saul succeeded against them (I Sam. 11:11). David and Joab also overcame them (II Sam. 10:7-14), but Solomon intermarried with them and introduced their idols into Israel (I Kgs. 11:1-5).

Ben-ammi;[1151] he is the father of the
[I]sons of [a]Ammon to this day.

Abraham's Treachery

20 Now Abraham journeyed from
[a]there toward the land of [b]the
[I]Negev,[776] and [II]settled between Kadesh
and Shur; then he sojourned[1481] in
[c]Gerar.
2 And Abraham said of Sarah his
wife,[802] "[a]She is my sister."[269] So
[b]Abimelech king of Gerar sent and took
Sarah.
3 [a]But God[430] came to Abimelech
in a dream of the night, and said to him,
"Behold, [b]you are a dead man because
of the woman[802] whom you have taken,
for she is [I]married."[1166]
4 Now Abimelech had not come near
her; and he said, "Lord,[136] [a]wilt Thou
slay[2026] a nation,[1471] even *though* [I]blame-
less?[6662]
5 "Did he not himself say[559] to me,
'She is my sister'? And she [a]herself said,
'He is my brother.'[251] In [b]the integrity[8537] of my heart[3824] and the innocence[5356] of my [I]hands[3709] I have
done[6213] this."
6 Then God said to him in the
dream, "Yes, I know[3045] that in the integrity of your heart you have done this,
and I also [I][a]kept you from sinning[2398]
against Me; therefore I did not let you
touch[5060] her.
7 "Now therefore, restore[7725] the
man's[376] wife, for [a]he is a prophet,[5030]
and he will pray[6419] for you, and you
will live.[2421] But if you do not restore
her, know that you shall surely die,[4191]
you and all who are yours."
8 So Abimelech arose early in the
morning and called[7121] all his servants[5650]
and told all these things in their
hearing;[241] and the men[582] were greatly
frightened.[3372]
9 [a]Then Abimelech called Abraham
and said to him, "What have you done
to us? And [I]how have I sinned[2398] against
you, that you have brought on me and
on my kingdom[4467] [b]a great sin?[2401] You
have done to me [II]things that ought not
to be done."
10 And Abimelech said to Abraham,
"What have you [I]encountered,[7200] that
you have done this thing?"
11 And Abraham said, "Because I
thought,[559] surely there is no [a]fear[3374]
of God[430] in this place; and [b]they will
kill[2026] me because of my wife.
🔑 12 "Besides, she actually is my sister, the daughter of my father, but not
the daughter of my mother, and she
became my wife;
13 and it came about, when [a]God
caused me to wander from my father's
house,[1004] that I said to her, 'This is
[I]the kindness[2617] which you will show
to me: [II]everywhere we go, [b]say of me,
"He is my brother." ' "
14 [a]Abimelech then took sheep and
oxen and male and female servants,[5650]
and gave them to Abraham, and restored
his wife Sarah to him.
15 And Abimelech said, "[a]Behold,
my land[776] is before you; [I]settle wherever [II]you please."[2896]
16 And to Sarah he said, "Behold,
I have given your [a]brother a thousand
pieces of silver; behold, it is [I]your vindication before all who are with you, and
before all men you are cleared."
17 And [a]Abraham prayed to God;[430]
and God healed Abimelech and his wife
and his maids, so that they bore *children.*
18 [a]For the LORD had closed fast
all the wombs of the household of Abimelech because of Sarah, Abraham's wife.

Isaac Is Born

21 [a]Then the LORD took note[6485] of
Sarah as He had said, and the

38 [I]Heb., *Bene-Ammon* [a]Deut. 2:19

1 [I]I.e., South country [II]Lit., *dwelt* [a]Gen. 18:1 [b]Gen. 12:9 [c]Gen. 26:1, 6

2 [a]Gen. 12:11-13; 20:12; 26:7 [b]Gen. 12:15

3 [I]Lit., *married to a husband* [a]Gen. 12:17, 18 [b]Gen. 20:7

4 [I]Lit., *righteous* [a]Gen. 18:23-25

5 [I]Lit., *palms* [a]Gen. 20:13 [b]1Kin. 9:4; Ps. 7:8; 26:6

6 [I]Lit., *restrained* [a]1Sam. 25:26, 34

7 [a]1Sam. 7:5; 2Kin. 5:11; Job 42:8

9 [I]Lit., *what* [II]Lit., *deeds* [a]Gen. 12:18 [b]Gen. 39:9

10 [I]Lit., *seen*

11 [a]Neh. 5:15; Prov. 16:6 [b]Gen. 12:12; 26:7

13 [I]Lit., *your* [II]Lit., *at every place where* [a]Gen. 12:1-9 [b]Gen. 12:13; 20:5

14 [a]Gen. 12:16

15 [I]Lit., *dwell* [II]Lit., *it is good in your sight* [a]Gen. 13:9; 34:10; 47:6

16 [I]Lit., *for you a covering of the eyes* [a]Gen. 20:5

17 [a]Num. 12:13; 21:7; James 5:16

18 [a]Gen. 12:17

1 [a]Gen. 17:16, 21; 18:10, 14; Gal. 4:23

🔑 **20:12** Abraham speaks of Sarah as his half-sister, the daughter of the same father, but not the same mother. The common Jewish tradition referred to by Josephus (Antiquities 1,6,6) and also by Jerome is that Sarah was identical with Iscah (See Gen. 11:29), daughter of Haran and sister of Lot, who is called Abraham's "brother" (Gen. 13:8).

LORD did[6213] for Sarah as He had [I]promised.[1696]

2 [a]So Sarah conceived and bore a son to Abraham in his old age,[2208] at [b]the appointed time[4150] of which God[430] had spoken to him.

3 And Abraham called the name of his son who was born to him, whom Sarah bore to him, [a]Isaac.

4 Then Abraham circumcised[4135] his son[1121] Isaac when he was [a]eight days[3117] old,[1121] as God had commanded[6680] him.

5 Now Abraham was [a]one hundred years old when his son Isaac[3327] was born to him.

6 And Sarah said, "God has made[6213] [a]laughter[6711] for me; everyone who hears[8085] will laugh[6711] [I]with me."

7 And she said,[559] "[a]Who would have said to Abraham that Sarah would nurse children?[1121] Yet I have borne him a son[1121] in his old age."

8 And the child grew and was weaned, and Abraham made a great feast[4960] on the day that Isaac was weaned.

Sarah Turns against Hagar

9 Now Sarah saw [a]the son of Hagar the Egyptian, whom she had borne to Abraham, [I][b]mocking.[6711]

10 Therefore she said to Abraham, "[a]Drive out this maid and her son, for the son of this maid shall not be an heir with my son [I]Isaac."

11 [a]And the matter[1697] [I]distressed[7489] Abraham greatly because of his son.

12 But God said to Abraham, "[I]Do not be distressed because of the lad and your maid; whatever Sarah tells you, listen[8085] to her, for [a]through Isaac [II]your descendants[2233] shall be named.[7121]

13 "And of [a]the son of the maid I will make a nation[1471] also, because he is your [I]descendant."

14 So Abraham rose early in the morning, and took bread and a [I]skin of water, and gave *them* to Hagar, putting *them* on her shoulder, and *gave her* the boy, and sent her away. And she departed, and wandered about in the wilderness of Beersheba.

15 And the water in the skin was used up, and she [I]left the boy under one of the bushes.[7880]

16 Then she went and sat down opposite him, about a bowshot away, for she said, "Do not let me [I]see[7200] the boy die."[4194] And she sat opposite him, and [a]lifted up[5375] her voice and wept.

17 And God [a]heard[8085] the lad crying; and the angel of God called[7121] to Hagar from heaven,[8064] and said to her, "What is the matter with you, Hagar? [b]Do not fear,[3372] for God has heard the voice of the lad where he is.

18 "Arise, lift up[5375] the lad, and hold[2388] him by [I]the hand; [a]for I will make[7760] a great nation of him."

19 Then God [a]opened her eyes and she saw [b]a well of water; and she went and filled the [I]skin with water, and gave the lad a drink.

20 And [a]God was with the lad, and he grew; and he [I]lived in the wilderness, and became an archer.

21 And [a]he [I]lived in the wilderness of Paran; and his mother[517] took a wife for him from the land[776] of Egypt.

Covenant with Abimelech

22 Now it came about at that time,[6256] that [a]Abimelech and Phicol, the commander[8269] of his army,[6635] spoke to Abraham, saying, "[b]God is with you in all that you do;[6213]

23 now therefore, [a]swear[7650] to me here by God that you will not deal falsely[8266] with me, or with my offspring, or with my posterity; but according to the kindness[2617] that I have shown to you, you shall show to me, and to the land in which you have sojourned."[1481]

24 And Abraham said, "I swear[7650] it."

25 But Abraham [I]complained[3198] to Abimelech because of the well of water which the servants[5650] of Abimelech [a]had seized.

1 [I]Lit., *spoken*

2 [a]Acts 7:8; Gal. 4:22; Heb. 11:11 [b]Gen. 17:21; 18:10, 14

3 [a]Gen. 17:19, 21

4 [a]Gen. 17:12; Acts 7:8

5 [a]Gen. 17:17

6 [I]Lit., *for* [a]Gen. 18:13; Ps. 126:2; Is. 54:1

7 [a]Gen. 18:11, 13

9 [I]Or, *playing* [a]Gen. 16:1, 4, 15 [b]Gal. 4:29

10 [I]Lit., *with Isaac* [a]Gal. 4:30

11 [I]Lit., *was very grievous in Abraham's sight* [a]Gen. 17:18

12 [I]Lit., *Do not let it be grievous in your sight* [II]Lit., *your seed will be called* [a]Rom. 9:7; Heb. 11:18

13 [I]Lit., *seed* [a]Gen. 16:10; 21:18; 25:12-18

14 [I]I.e., a skin used as a bottle

15 [I]Lit., *cast*

16 [I]Lit., *look upon the death of the child* [a]Jer. 6:26; Amos 8:10

17 [a]Ex. 3:7; Deut. 26:7; Ps. 6:8 [b]Gen. 26:24

18 [I]Lit., *your* [a]Gen. 16:10; 21:13; 25:12-16

19 [I]V. 14, note 1 [a]Num. 22:31; 2Kin. 6:17 [b]Gen. 16:7, 14

20 [I]Lit., *dwelt* [a]Gen. 28:15; 39:2, 3, 21

21 [I]Lit., *dwelt* [a]Gen. 25:18

22 [a]Gen. 20:2, 14; 26:26 [b]Gen. 26:28; Is. 8:10

23 [a]Josh. 2:12; 1Sam. 24:21

25 [I]Lit., *reproved* [a]Gen. 26:15, 18, 20-22

26 And Abimelech said, "I do not know[3045] who has done this thing; neither did you tell[5046] me, nor did I hear of it [1]until today."[3117]

27 And Abraham took sheep and oxen, and gave them to Abimelech; and [a]the two of them made[3772] a covenant.[1285]

28 Then Abraham set seven ewe[3535] lambs of the flock by themselves.

29 And Abimelech said to Abraham, "What do these seven ewe lambs mean, which you have set[5324] by themselves?"

30 And he said, "You shall take these seven ewe lambs from my hand in order that it may be a [a]witness[5713] to me, that I dug this well."[875]

31 Therefore he called[7121] that place [a]Beersheba;[884] because there the two of them took an oath.[7650]

32 So they made a covenant at Beersheba; and Abimelech and Phicol, the commander of his army, arose and returned to the land of the Philistines.

33 And *Abraham* planted a tamarisk[815] tree at Beersheba, and there [a]he called[7121] on the name of the LORD, the [b]Everlasting[5769] God.[410]

34 And Abraham sojourned[1481] [a]in the land of the Philistines for many days.

26 [1]Lit., *except*
27 [a]Gen. 26:31
30 [a]Gen. 31:48
31 [a]Gen. 21:14; 26:33
33 [a]Gen. 12:8 [b]Ex. 15:18; Deut. 32:40; Ps. 90:2; 93:2; Is. 40:28; Jer. 10:10; Hab. 1:12; Heb. 13:8
34 [a]Gen. 22:19
1 [a]Deut. 8:2, 16; Heb. 11:17; James 1:12-14 [b]Gen. 22:11
2 [a]Gen. 22:12, 16; John 3:16; 1John 4:9 [b]2Chr. 3:1 [c]Gen. 8:20
6 [a]John 19:17

The Offering of Isaac

22 🗝 Now it came about after these things, that [a]God[430] tested[5254] Abraham, and said to him, "[b]Abraham!" And he said, "Here I am."

2 And He said, "Take now [a]your son,[1121] your only[3173] son, whom you love,[157] Isaac, and go to the land[776] of [b]Moriah; and offer[5927] him there as a [c]burnt offering[5930] on one of the mountains of which I will tell you."

3 So Abraham rose early in the morning and saddled his donkey, and took two of his young men with him and Isaac his son; and he split wood for the burnt offering, and arose and went to the place of which God had told[559] him.

4 On the third day[3117] Abraham raised his eyes and saw[7200] the place from a distance.

5 And Abraham said to his young men, "Stay here with the donkey, and I and the lad will go yonder; and we will worship[7812] and return to you."

6 And Abraham took the wood of the burnt offering and [a]laid[7760] it on Isaac his son, and he took in his hand the fire and the knife. So the two of them walked on together.

🗝 **22:1-19** The story of Abraham and Isaac will always be an important one. It is similar to the love that God has in sacrificing His only Son for us (Jn. 3:16). Abraham did not have to give up his precious son, but he was fully prepared to plunge the knife into Isaac, when suddenly God's angel intervened. According to Rom. 4:20, Abraham's faith in God's promise to give the infant Isaac to him in old age never wavered. When God tested (not tempted) Abraham here with taking away that very child, Abraham believed that God planned to raise Isaac from death (Heb. 11:17-19) after Abraham killed Isaac. He showed his wonderful, absolute obedience to God. If God is all-knowing, how could He say, "For now I know that you fear God" (Gen. 22:12)? The problem of foreknowledge is an extremely difficult one, and discussion about it is usually fruitless. In this case, God speaks of the test of Abraham's faith as a valid experiment. It demonstrated again the soundness of Abraham and how well-made his character was. God found him to be firm in faith and perfect in obedience. Abraham was not imitating idolatrous neighbors. On the contrary, he did not choose this type of sacrifice at all; God issued the command. This incident showed that God did not want human sacrifices; that would be reserved for the sinless Lamb of God (Jn. 1:29).

There is no contradiction between Gen. 22:1 and Js. 1:13. The Hebrew word here is *nissah* (5254) which means to "put to the test." It should not be translated as "tempt." See Hebrew lexical section (5254) for a more detailed explanation. Compare David's testing of Saul's armor (I Sam. 17:39) and the Queen of Sheba's testing of Solomon's wisdom (I Kgs. 10:1). The Geneva Bible has: "God did prove Abraham." God may with good motives allow us to be tested, but He will never place inducements before us to lead us into temptation above what we can bear (I Cor. 10:13). His ultimate objective is what is good for us.

7 And Isaac spoke to Abraham his father and said, "My father!" And he said, "Here I am, my son." And he said, "Behold, the fire and the wood, but where is the [a]lamb for the burnt offering?"

8 And Abraham said, "God will [I]provide[7200] for Himself the lamb for the burnt offering, my son." So the two of them walked on together.

9 Then they came to [a]the place of which God had told him; and Abraham built [b]the altar[4196] there, and arranged the wood, and bound his son Isaac, and [c]laid him on the altar on top of the wood.

10 And Abraham stretched out his hand, and took the knife to slay[7819] his son.

11 But [a]the angel of the LORD called[7121] to him from heaven,[8064] and said, "Abraham, Abraham!" And he said, "Here I am."

12 And he said, "Do not stretch out your hand against the lad, and do nothing to him; for now [a]I know[3045] that you [I]fear[3373] God, since you have not withheld [b]your son, your only son, from Me."

13 Then Abraham raised his eyes and looked,[7200] and behold, behind *him* a ram caught in the thicket by his horns; and Abraham went and took the ram, and offered him up for a burnt offering in the place of his son.

14 And Abraham called the name of that place [I]The LORD Will Provide,3070 as it is said to this day,[3117] "In the mount of the LORD [a]it will [II]be provided."[7200]

15 Then the angel of the LORD called[7121] to Abraham a second time from heaven,

16 and said, "[a]By Myself I have sworn,[7650] declares the LORD, because you have done[6213] this thing,[1697] and have not withheld your son, your only son,

17 indeed I will greatly bless[1288] you, and I will greatly [a]multiply your [I]seed[2233] as the stars of the heavens,[8064] and as [b]the sand which is on the seashore;[8193] and [c]your [I]seed shall possess the gate of [II]their enemies.

18 "And [a]in your [I]seed all the nations[1471] of the earth[776] shall [II]be blessed, because you have [b]obeyed[8085] My voice."

19 [a]So Abraham returned to his young men, and they arose and went together to Beersheba; and Abraham lived at Beersheba.

20 Now it came about after these things, that it was told[5046] Abraham, saying, "Behold, [a]Milcah [I]also has borne children[1121] to your brother Nahor:

21 Uz his first-born and Buz his brother and Kemuel the father of Aram

22 and Chesed and Hazo and Pildash and Jidlaph and Bethuel."

23 And Bethuel [I]became the father of [a]Rebekah: these eight Milcah bore to Nahor, Abraham's brother.

24 And his concubine, whose name was Reumah, [I]also bore Tebah and Gaham and Tahash and Maacah.

Death and Burial of Sarah

23 Now [I]Sarah lived one hundred and twenty-seven years; *these were* the years of the life of Sarah.

🗝 2 And Sarah died[4191] in [a]Kiriath-arba (that is, Hebron) in the land[776] of Canaan; and Abraham [I]went in to mourn for Sarah and to weep for her.

3 Then Abraham rose from before his dead, and spoke to the [a]sons[1121] of Heth, saying,

4 "I am [a]a stranger[1616] and a sojourner[8453] among you; [b]give me [I]a [c]burial[6913] site among you, that I may bury[6912] my dead out of my sight."

7 [a]Ex. 29:38-42; John 1:29, 36; Rev. 13:8
8 [I]Lit., *see*
9 [a]Gen. 22:2 [b]Gen. 12:7, 8; 13:18 [c]Heb. 11:17-19; James 2:21
11 [a]Gen. 16:7-11; 21:17, 18
12 [I]Or, *reverence; lit., are a fearer of God* [a]James 2:21, 22 [b]Gen. 22:2, 16
14 [I]Heb., *YHWH-jireh* [II]Lit., *be seen* [a]Gen. 22:8
16 [a]Ps. 105:9; Luke 1:73; Heb. 6:13, 14
17 [I]Or, *descendants* [II]Lit., *his* [a]Gen. 15:5; 26:4; Jer. 33:22; Heb. 11:12 [b]Gen. 32:12 [c]Gen. 24:60
18 [I]Or, *descendants* [II]Or, *bless themselves* [a]Gen. 12:3; 18:18; Acts 3:25; Gal. 3:8, 16 [b]Gen. 18:19; 22:3, 10; 26:5
19 [a]Gen. 22:5
20 [I]Lit., *she also* [a]Gen. 11:29
23 [I]Lit., *begot* [a]Gen. 24:15
24 [I]Lit., *she also*

1 [I]Lit., *the life of Sarah was*
2 [I]Or, *proceeded* [a]Josh. 14:15; 15:13; 21:11
3 [a]Gen. 10:15; 15:20
4 [I]Lit., *possession of a grave* [a]Gen. 17:8; Lev. 25:23; 1Chr. 29:15; Ps. 39:12; 105:12; 119:19; Heb. 11:9, 13 [b]Acts 7:16 [c]Gen. 49:30

🗝 **23:2,3,19** The Hittites were descendants of Canaan's son, Heth. One of the seven Canaanitish nations, they dwelt in Hebron and were governed by kings (Deut. 7:1; I Kgs. 10:29). Their land was promised to Israel and the Israelites were commanded to destroy them, but Israel did not destroy them entirely (Deut. 7:1,2,24; Judg. 3:5). Among their prominent leaders were Ephron, Ahimelech, and Uriah (Gen. 49:30; I Sam. 26:6; II Sam. 11:6,21). Esau, Solomon, and many other Israelites intermarried with the Hittites. They were warlike people and made many conquests.

5 And the sons[1121] of Heth answered Abraham, saying to him,

6 "Hear us, my lord,[113] you are a [I][a]mighty prince[5387] among us; bury your dead in the choicest of our graves;[6913] none of us will refuse you his grave[6913] for burying your dead."

7 So Abraham rose and bowed[7812] to the people[5971] of the land, the sons of Heth.

8 And he spoke with them, saying, "If it is your [I]wish[5315] *for me* to bury my dead out of my sight, hear me, and approach [a]Ephron the son of Zohar for me,

9 that he may give me the cave of Machpelah which he owns, which is at the end of his field;[7704] for the full price let him give it to me in [I]your presence for [II]a burial site."

10 Now Ephron was sitting among the sons of Heth; and Ephron the Hittite answered Abraham in the hearing[241] of the sons of Heth; *even* [a]of all who went in at the gate of his city, saying,

11 "No, my lord, hear me; [a]I give you the field, and I give you the cave that is in it. In the presence of the sons of my people I give it to you; bury your dead."

12 And Abraham bowed before the people of the land.

13 And he spoke to Ephron in the hearing of the people of the land, saying, "If you will only please listen[8085] to me; I will give the price of the field, accept *it* from me, that I may bury my dead there."

14 Then Ephron answered Abraham, saying to him,

15 "My lord, listen[8085] to me; a piece of land worth four hundred [a]shekels of silver, what is that between me and you? So bury your dead."

16 And Abraham listened[8085] to Ephron; and Abraham [a]weighed out for Ephron the silver which he had named[1696] in the [I]hearing of the sons of Heth, four hundred shekels of silver, [II]commercial standard.

17 So [a]Ephron's field, which was in Machpelah, which faced Mamre, the field and cave which was in it, and all the trees which were in the field, that were [I]within all the confines of its border, [II]were deeded over

18 to Abraham for a possession [a]in the presence of the sons of Heth, before all who went in at the gate of his city.

19 And after this, Abraham buried[6912] Sarah his wife in the cave of the field at Machpelah facing Mamre (that is, Hebron) in the land of Canaan.

20 So the field, and the cave that is in it, [I]were [a]deeded over to Abraham for [II]a burial site by the sons of Heth.

A Bride for Isaac

24 Now [a]Abraham was old,[2204] advanced in age;[3117] and the LORD had [b]blessed[1288] Abraham in every way.

2 And Abraham said to his servant,[5650] the oldest[2205] of his household,[1004] who had [a]charge[4910] of all that he owned, "[b]Please place[7760] your hand under my thigh,[3409]

3 and I will make you swear[7650] by the LORD, [a]the God[430] of heaven[8064] and the God of earth,[776] that you [b]shall not take a wife[802] for my son from the daughters of [c]the Canaanites, among whom I live,

4 but you shall go to [a]my country[776] and to my relatives, and take a wife for my son Isaac."

5 And the servant said to him, "Suppose the woman[802] will not be willing to follow me to this land;[776] should I take your son back to the land from where you came?"

6 Then Abraham said to him, "[a]Beware[8104] lest you take my son back there!

7 "[a]The LORD, the God of heaven, who took me from my father's house and from the land of my birth, and who spoke to me, and who swore[7650] to me, saying, '[b]To your [I]descendants[2233] I will give this land,' He will send [c]His angel before you, and you will take a wife for my son from there.

8 "But if the woman is not willing

---

6 [I]Lit., *prince of God* [a]Gen. 14:14; 20:7

8 [I]Lit., *soul* [a]Gen. 25:9

9 [I]Lit., *the midst of you* [II]Lit., *possession of a burial place*

10 [a]Gen. 23:18; 34:20, 24; Ruth 4:1, 11

11 [a]2Sam. 24:21-24

15 [a]Ex. 30:13; Ezek. 45:12

16 [I]Lit., *ears* [II]Lit., *current according to the merchant* [a]2Sam. 14:26; Jer. 32:9, 10; Zech. 11:12

17 [I]Lit., *in all its border around* [II]Or, *were ratified* [a]Gen. 25:9; 49:29, 30; 50:13

18 [a]Gen. 23:10

20 [I]Or, *were ratified* [II]Lit., *possession of a burial place* [a]Jer. 32:10-14

1 [a]Gen. 18:11 [b]Gen. 12:2; 13:2; 24:35; Gal. 3:9

2 [a]Gen. 39:4-6 [b]Gen. 24:9; 47:29

3 [a]Gen. 14:19, 22 [b]Deut. 7:3; 2Cor. 6:14-17 [c]Gen. 10:15-19; 26:34, 35; 28:1, 8

4 [a]Gen. 12:1; Heb. 11:15

6 [a]Gen. 24:8

7 [I]Lit., *seed* [a]Gen. 24:3 [b]Gen. 12:7; 13:15; 15:18; Ex. 32:13 [c]Gen. 16:7; 21:17; 22:11; Ex. 23:20, 23

to follow you, then you will [a]be free[5352] from this my oath;[7621] [b]only do not take my son back there."

9 So the servant [a]placed his hand under the thigh of Abraham his master,[113] and swore to him concerning this matter.[1697]

10 Then the servant took ten camels from the camels of his master, and set out with a variety of [a]good things[2898] of his master's in his hand; and he arose, and went to [I]Mesopotamia, to [b]the city of Nahor.

11 And he made the camels kneel down outside the city by [a]the well of water at evening time, [b]the time[6256] when women go out to draw water.

12 And he said, "[a]O LORD, the God of my master Abraham, please [I][b]grant me success today,[3117] and show[6213] lovingkindness[2617] to my master Abraham.

13 "Behold, [a]I am standing[5324] by the [I]spring, and the daughters of the men[582] of the city are coming out to draw water;

14 now may it be that the girl to whom I say, 'Please let down your jar so that I may drink,' and [I]who answers, 'Drink, and I will water your camels also';—*may* she *be the one* whom Thou hast appointed for Thy servant Isaac; and by this I shall know that Thou hast shown[6213] lovingkindness to my master."

Rebekah Is Chosen

15 And it came about [a]before he had finished speaking, that behold, [b]Rebekah who was born to Bethuel the son of [c]Milcah, the wife of Abraham's brother Nahor, came out with her jar on her shoulder.

16 And the girl was [a]very beautiful,[2896] a virgin,[1330] and no man[376] had [I]had relations[3045] with her; and she went down to the spring and filled her jar, and came up.

17 Then the servant ran to meet her, and said, "[a]Please let me drink a little water from your jar."

18 And [a]she said, "Drink, my lord";[113] and she quickly lowered her jar to her hand, and gave him a drink.

19 Now when she had finished giving him a drink, [a]she said, "I will draw also for your camels until they have finished drinking."

20 So she quickly emptied her jar into the trough, and ran back to the well to draw, and she drew for all his camels.

21 [a]Meanwhile, the man was gazing at her [I]in silence, to know whether the LORD had made his journey[1870] successful or not.

22 Then it came about, when the camels had finished drinking, that the man took a [a]gold ring weighing a half-shekel and two bracelets for her [I]wrists weighing ten shekels in gold,

23 and said, "Whose daughter are you? Please tell[5046] me, is there room for us to lodge in your father's house?"

24 And she said to him, "[a]I am the daughter of Bethuel, the son of Milcah, whom she bore to Nahor."

25 Again she said to him, "We have plenty of both straw and feed,[4554] and room to lodge in."

26 Then the man [a]bowed low and worshiped[7812] the LORD.

27 And he said, "[a]Blessed[1288] be the LORD, the God of my master Abraham, who has not forsaken[5800] [b]His lovingkindness[2617] and His truth[571] toward my master; as for me, [c]the LORD has guided[5148] me in the way to the house of my master's brothers."

28 Then [a]the girl ran and told[5046] her mother's household about these things.[1697]

29 Now Rebekah had a brother[251] whose name was [a]Laban; and Laban ran outside to the man at the spring.

30 And it came about that when he saw the ring, and the bracelets on his sister's [I]wrists, and when he heard the words[1697] of Rebekah his sister,[269] saying, "[II]This is what the man said[1696] to me," he went to the man; and behold, he was standing by the camels at the spring.

8 [a]Josh. 2:17-20 [b]Gen. 24:6

9 [a]Gen. 24:2

10 [I]Heb., *Aram-naharaim, Aram of the two rivers* [a]Gen. 24:22, 53 [b]Gen. 11:31, 32

11 [a]Gen. 24:42 [b]Ex. 2:16; 1Sam. 9:11

12 [I]Lit., *cause to occur for me* [a]Gen. 24:27, 42, 48; 26:24; Ex. 3:6, 15 [b]Gen. 27:20

13 [I]Lit., *fountain of water* [a]Gen. 24:43

14 [I]Lit., *she will say*

15 [a]Gen. 24:45 [b]Gen. 22:20, 23 [c]Gen. 11:29

16 [I]Lit., *known* [a]Gen. 12:11; 26:7; 29:17

17 [a]John 4:7

18 [a]Gen. 24:14, 46

19 [a]Gen. 24:14

21 [I]Lit., *keeping silent* [a]Gen. 24:12-14, 27, 52

22 [I]Lit., *hands* [a]Gen. 24:47; Ex. 32:2, 3

24 [a]Gen. 24:15

26 [a]Gen. 24:48, 52; Ex. 4:31

27 [a]Gen. 24:12, 42, 48; Ex. 18:10; Ruth 4:14; 1Sam. 25:32; 2Sam. 18:28; Luke 1:68 [b]Gen. 32:10; Ps. 98:3 [c]Gen. 24:21, 48

28 [a]Gen. 29:12

29 [a]Gen. 29:5, 13

30 [I]Lit., *hands* [II]Lit., *Thus the man*

31 And he said, "[a]Come in, [b]blessed of the LORD! Why do you stand outside since [c]I have prepared the house, and a place for the camels?"

32 So the man entered the house. Then [I][a]Laban unloaded the camels, and he gave straw and feed to the camels, and water to wash his feet and the feet of the men who were with him.

33 But when *food* was set[7760] before him to eat, he said, "I will not eat until I have told[1696] my business."[1697] And he said, "Speak on."

34 So he said, "I am [a]Abraham's servant.

35 "And the LORD has greatly [a]blessed my master, so that he has become [I]rich; and He has given him [b]flocks and herds, and silver and gold, and servants[5650] and maids, and camels and donkeys.

36 "Now [a]Sarah my master's wife bore a son to my master [I]in her old[2209] age; and [b]he has given him all that he has.

37 "[a]And my master made me swear, saying, 'You shall not take a wife for my son from the daughters of the Canaanites, in whose land I [I]live;

38 but you shall go to my father's house, and to my relatives,[4940] and take a wife for my son.'

39 "[a]And I said to my master, 'Suppose the woman does not follow me.'

40 "And he said to me, '[a]The LORD, before whom I have [b]walked, will send [c]His angel with you to make your journey successful, and you will take a wife for my son from my relatives, and from my father's house;

41 [a]then you will be free[5355] from my oath,[423] when you come to my relatives; and if they do not give her to you, you will be free from my oath.'

42 "So [a]I came today to the spring, and said, 'O LORD, the God of my master Abraham, if now Thou wilt make my journey on which I go [b]successful;

43 behold, [a]I am standing by the [I]spring, and may it be that the maiden[5959] who comes out to draw, and to whom I say, "[b]Please let me drink a little water from your jar";

44 and she will say to me, "You drink, and I will draw for your camels also"; let her be the woman whom the LORD has appointed for my master's son.'

45 "Before I had finished [a]speaking in my heart,[3820] behold, [b]Rebekah came out with her jar on her shoulder, and went down to the spring and drew; and [c]I said to her, 'Please let me drink.'

46 "And she quickly lowered her jar from her *shoulder,* and said, '[a]Drink, and I will water your camels also'; so I drank, and she watered the camels also.

47 "[a]Then I asked[7592] her, and said, 'Whose daughter are you?' And she said, 'The daughter of Bethuel, Nahor's son, whom Milcah bore to him'; and I put the [b]ring on her nose,[639] and the bracelets on her [I]wrists.

48 "And I [a]bowed low and worshiped the LORD, and blessed[1288] the LORD, the God of my master Abraham, [b]who had guided[5148] me in the right[571] way[1870] to take the daughter of my master's [I]kinsman for his son.

49 "So now if you are going to [I][a]deal[6213] kindly[2617] and truly[571] with my master, tell me; and if not, let me know, that I may turn to the right hand or the left."

50 Then Laban and Bethuel answered and said, "[a]The matter[1697] comes from the LORD; [b]*so* we cannot speak to you bad[7451] or good.[2896]

51 "Behold, Rebekah is before you, take *her* and go, and let her be the wife of your master's son, as the LORD has spoken."[1696]

52 And it came about when Abraham's servant heard their words,[1697] that he [a]bowed himself to the ground[776] [I]before the LORD.

53 And the servant brought out [a]articles of silver and articles of gold, and garments, and gave them to Rebekah; he also gave precious things to her brother and to her mother.

54 Then he and the men who were with him ate and drank and spent the

31 [a]Gen. 29:13 [b]Gen. 26:29; Ruth 3:10; Ps. 115:15 [c]Gen. 18:3-5; 19:2, 3
32 [I]Lit., *he* [a]Gen. 43:24; Judg. 19:21
34 [a]Gen. 24:2
35 [I]Lit., *great* [a]Gen. 24:1 [b]Gen. 13:2
36 [I]Lit., *after she was old* [a]Gen. 21:1-7 [b]Gen. 25:5
37 [I]Lit., *dwell* [a]Gen. 24:2-4
39 [a]Gen. 24:5
40 [a]Gen. 24:7 [b]Gen. 5:22, 24; 17:1 [c]Ex. 23:20
41 [a]Gen. 24:8
42 [a]Gen. 24:11, 12 [b]Neh. 1:11
43 [I]Lit., *fountain of water* [a]Gen. 24:13 [b]Gen. 24:14
45 [a]1Sam. 1:13 [b]Gen. 24:15 [c]Gen. 24:17
46 [a]Gen. 24:18, 19
47 [I]Lit., *hands* [a]Gen. 24:23, 24 [b]Ezek. 16:11, 12
48 [I]Lit., *brother* [a]Gen. 24:26, 52 [b]Gen. 24:27; Ps. 32:8; 48:14; Is. 48:17
49 [I]Lit., *show lovingkindness and truth* [a]Gen. 47:29; Josh. 2:14
50 [a]Ps. 118:23; Mark 12:11 [b]Gen. 31:24, 29
52 [I]Lit., *to* [a]Gen. 24:26, 48
53 [a]Gen. 24:10, 22; Ex. 3:22; 11:2; 12:35

night. When they arose in the morning, he said, "[a]Send me away to my master."

55 But her brother and her mother said, "[a]Let the girl stay with us *a few* days, say ten; afterward she may go."

56 And he said to them, "Do not delay me, since [a]the LORD has prospered my way. Send me away that I may go to my master."

57 And they said, "We will call[7121] the girl and [I]consult[7592] her wishes."

58 Then they called Rebekah and said to her, "Will you go with this man?" And she said, "I will go."

59 Thus they sent away their sister Rebekah and [a]her nurse with Abraham's servant and his men.

60 And they blessed[1288] Rebekah and said to her,

"May you, our sister,[269]
[a]Become thousands[505] of ten
thousands,
And may [b]your [I]descendants
possess
The gate of those who hate[8130]
them."

Isaac Marries Rebekah

61 Then Rebekah arose with her maids, and they mounted the camels and followed the man. So the servant took Rebekah and departed.

62 Now Isaac had come from going to [a]Beer-lahai-roi; for he [I]was living in [b]the [II]Negev.[776]

63 And Isaac went out [a]to [I]meditate in the field[7704] toward evening;[6256] and [b]he lifted up his eyes and looked,[7200] and behold, camels were coming.

64 And Rebekah lifted up her eyes, and when she saw Isaac she dismounted[5307] from the camel.

65 And she said to the servant, "Who is that man walking in the field to meet us?" And the servant said, "He is my master." Then she took her [I]veil and covered[3680] herself.

66 And the servant told[5608] Isaac all the things[1697] that he had done.

67 Then Isaac brought her into his mother[517] Sarah's tent,[168] and [a]he took Rebekah, and she became his wife; and [b]he loved[157] her; thus Isaac was comforted after [c]his mother's death.

Abraham's Death

25 Now Abraham took another wife,[802] [I]whose name was Keturah.

2 And [a]she bore to him Zimran and Jokshan and Medan and Midian and Ishbak and Shuah.

3 And Jokshan [I]became the father of Sheba and Dedan. And the sons of Dedan were Asshurim and Letushim and Leummim.

4 And the sons of Midian *were* Ephah and Epher and Hanoch and Abida and Eldaah. All these *were* the sons of Keturah.

5 [a]Now Abraham gave all that he had to Isaac;

6 but to the sons of [I]his concubines, Abraham gave gifts while he was still living,[2416] and [a]sent them away from his son Isaac eastward, to the land[776] of the east.

7 And these are [I]all the years of Abraham's life that he lived,[2425] [a]one hundred and seventy-five years.

8 And Abraham breathed his last[1478] and died[4191] [a]in a [I]ripe[2896] old age,[7872] an old man[2205] and satisfied *with life;* and he was [b]gathered to his people.[5971]

9 Then his sons Isaac and Ishmael buried[6912] him in [a]the cave of Machpelah, in the field of Ephron the son of Zohar the Hittite, facing Mamre,

10 [a]the field[7704] which Abraham purchased from the sons of Heth; there

54 [a]Gen. 24:56, 59; 30:25
55 [a]Judg. 19:4
56 [a]Gen. 24:40
57 [I]Lit., *ask her mouth*
59 [a]Gen. 35:8
60 [I]Lit., *seed* [a]Gen. 17:16 [b]Gen. 22:17
62 [I]Lit., *was dwelling* [II]I.e., South country [a]Gen. 16:14; 25:11 [b]Gen. 20:1
63 [I]Or, *stroll;* meaning uncertain [a]Josh. 1:8; Ps. 1:2; 77:12; 119:15, 27, 48; 143:5; 145:5 [b]Gen. 18:2
65 [I]Or, *shawl*
67 [a]Gen. 25:20 [b]Gen. 29:18 [c]Gen. 23:1, 2
1 [I]Lit., *and her name*
2 [a]1Chr. 1:32, 33
3 [I]Lit., *begot*
5 [a]Gen. 24:35, 36
6 [I]Lit., *concubines which belonged to Abraham* [a]Gen. 21:14
7 [I]Lit., *the days of* [a]Gen. 12:4
8 [I]Lit., *good* [a]Gen. 15:15; 47:8, 9 [b]Gen. 25:17; 35:29; 49:29, 33
9 [a]Gen. 23:17, 18; 49:29, 30; 50:13
10 [a]Gen. 23:3-16

25:1,2 How can this be reconciled with Gen. 17:17 and Heb. 11:12? "Now" in Gen. 25:1 may resume the narrative after a digression, carrying us back into the lifetime of Sarah. Therefore, Keturah's children were born to Abraham before the disability of old age overtook him. It is also possible that the miraculous quickening of his virile powers, by which he was enabled to become the father of Isaac, was continued for some years later.

Abraham was buried[6912] with Sarah his
wife.
11 And it came about after the
death[4194] of Abraham, that [a]God[430]
blessed[1288] his son Isaac; and Isaac
[I]lived by [b]Beer-lahai-roi.

Descendants of Ishmael

12 Now these are *the records of* the
generations[8435] of [a]Ishmael, Abraham's
son, whom Hagar the Egyptian, Sarah's
maid, bore to Abraham;
13 and these are the names of
[a]the sons of Ishmael, by their names,
[I]in the order of their birth: Nebaioth,
the first-born of Ishmael, and Kedar and
Adbeel and Mibsam
14 and Mishma and Dumah and
Massa,
15 Hadad and Tema, Jetur, Naphish
and Kedemah.
16 These are the sons of Ishmael
and these are their names, by their villages, and by their camps; [a]twelve
princes[5387] according to their [I]tribes.[523]
17 And these are the years of the
life of Ishmael, [a]one hundred and thirty-
seven years; and he breathed his last
and died,[4191] and was [b]gathered to his
people.
18 And they [I]settled from [a]Havilah
to [b]Shur which is [II]east of Egypt [III]as
one goes toward Assyria; [c]he [IV]set-
tled[5307] in defiance of all his [V]relatives.

Isaac's Sons

19 Now these are *the records of*
[a]the generations[8435] of Isaac, Abraham's
son:[1121] Abraham [I]became the father of
Isaac;
20 and Isaac was forty years old[1121]
when he took [a]Rebekah, the [b]daughter
of Bethuel the [I]Aramean of Paddan-
aram, the [c]sister[229] of Laban the
[I]Aramean, to be his wife.
21 And Isaac prayed[6279] to the LORD
on behalf of his wife, because she was
barren;[6135] and [a]the LORD [I]answered him
and Rebekah his wife [b]conceived.
22 But the children[1121] struggled together within her; and she said, "If it
is so, why then am I *this way?*" So she
went to [a]inquire of the LORD.
23 And the LORD said to her,
"[a]Two nations[1471] are in your
womb;[990]
[b]And two peoples[3816] shall be
separated from your
body;[4578]
And one people shall be stronger
than the other;
And [c]the older shall serve[5647] the
younger."
24 When her days[3117] to be delivered were fulfilled, behold, there were
twins in her womb.
25 Now the first[7223] came forth
red,[132] [a]all over like a hairy[8181] garment;
and they named him Esau.[6215]
26 And afterward his brother[251]
came forth with [a]his hand[3027] holding on
to Esau's heel,[6119] so [b]his name was
called [I]Jacob;[3290] and Isaac was [c]sixty
years old when she gave birth to them.
🔑 **27** When the boys grew up, Esau
became a skillful hunter, a man[376] of
the field;[7704] but Jacob was a [I]peaceful[8535]
man, [II][a]living in tents.[168]
28 Now Isaac loved[157] Esau, because [I]he had [a]a taste for game; [b]but
Rebekah loved[157] Jacob.
🔑 29 And when Jacob had cooked[2102]

11 [I]Lit., *dwelt* [a]Gen. 12:2, 3; 22:17; 26:3 [b]Gen. 16:14; 24:62
12 [a]Gen. 16:15
13 [I]Lit., *in regard to their generations* [a]1Chr. 1:29-31
16 [I]Or, *peoples* [a]Gen. 17:20
17 [a]Gen. 16:16 [b]Gen. 25:8; 49:33
18 [I]Lit., *dwelt* [II]Lit., *before* [III]Lit., *as you go* [IV]Lit., *fell over against* [V]Lit., *brothers* [a]1Sam. 15:7 [b]Gen. 20:1 [c]Gen. 16:12
19 [I]Lit., *begot* [a]Matt. 1:2
20 [I]I.e., Syrian [a]Gen. 24:15, 29, 67 [b]Gen. 22:23 [c]Gen. 24:29
21 [I]Lit., *was entreated of him* [a]1Sam. 1:17; 1Chr. 5:20; 2Chr. 33:13; Ezra 8:23; Ps. 127:3 [b]Rom. 9:10
22 [a]1Sam. 9:9; 10:22
23 [a]Gen. 17:4-6, 16; Num. 20:14; Deut. 2:4, 8 [b]Gen. 27:29 [c]Gen. 27:40; Mal. 1:2, 3; Rom. 9:12
25 [a]Gen. 27:11
26 [I]I.e., one who takes by the heel or supplants [a]Hos. 12:3 [b]Gen. 27:36 [c]Gen. 25:20
27 [I]Lit., *complete* [II]Lit., *dwelling* [a]Heb. 11:9
28 [I]Lit., *game was in his mouth* [a]Gen. 27:19 [b]Gen. 27:6-10

🔑 **25:27** Rebekah is one of several women in the Bible who was not able to have children except by God's intervention (Sarah, Rachel, Samson's mother, Hannah, and Elizabeth). The strife between her twin sons Jacob and Esau began even before their birth and continued not only throughout their lives but even between their descendants. Much of the suffering of the Israelites (Jacob) came at the hands of the Edomites (Esau) and is noted throughout the O.T. (Num. 20:20,21; II Sam. 8:13,14; Ps. 137:7; Joel 3:19).

🔑 **25:29-34** There is often confusion about the difference between the birthright and the blessing in the narrative about Jacob and Esau. The birthright is related to the order of birth of sons. According to Deut. 21:17, the right of the firstborn was to be a double portion of his father's inheritance, and the

(continued on next page)

[a]stew,[5138] Esau came in from the field and he was [I]famished;

30 and Esau said to Jacob, "Please let me have a swallow of [I]that red[122] stuff there, for I am [II]famished." Therefore his name was called[7121] [III]Edom.

31 But Jacob said, "[I]First[3117] sell me your [a]birthright."[1062]

32 And Esau said, "Behold, I am about to die; so of what *use* then is the birthright to me?"

33 And Jacob said, "[I]First swear[7650] to me"; so he swore to him, and [a]sold his birthright to Jacob.

34 Then Jacob gave Esau bread and lentil stew; and he ate and drank, and rose and went on his way. Thus Esau despised his birthright.

Isaac Settles in Gerar

26 Now there was [a]a famine in the land,[776] besides the previous famine that had occurred in the days[3117] of Abraham. So Isaac went to Gerar, to [b]Abimelech king of the Philistines.

2 And the LORD [a]appeared[7200] to him and said, "Do not go down to Egypt; [I][b]stay in the land of which I shall tell you.

3 "Sojourn[1481] in this land[776] and [a]I will be with you and [b]bless[1288] you, for [c]to you and to your [I]descendants[2233] I will give all these lands,[776] and I will establish [d]the oath[7621] which I swore[7650] to your father[1] Abraham.

4 "And [a]I will multiply your [I]descendants as the stars of heaven,[8064] and will give your [I]descendants all these lands; and [b]by your [I]descendants all the nations[1471] of the earth[776] [II]shall be blessed;

5 because Abraham [I][a]obeyed[8085] Me and kept[8104] My charge,[4931] My commandments,[4687] My statutes[2708] and My laws."[8451]

6 So Isaac [I]lived in Gerar.

7 When the men[582] of the place asked about his wife, he said, "[a]She is my sister,"[269] for he was [b]afraid[3372] to say, "my wife," *thinking,* "[I]the men of the place might kill[2026] me on account of Rebekah, for she is [c]beautiful."[2896]

8 And it came about, when he had been there a long time,[3117] that Abimelech king of the Philistines looked out through a window, and saw,[7200] and behold, Isaac was caressing[6711] his wife Rebekah.

9 Then Abimelech called Isaac and said, "Behold, certainly she is your wife! How then did you say,[559] 'She is my sister'?" And Isaac said to him, "Because I said, 'Lest I die[4191] on account of her.' "

10 And [a]Abimelech said, "What is this you have done[6213] to us? One of the people[5971] might easily have lain with your wife, and you would have brought guilt[817] upon us."

11 So Abimelech charged[6680] all the people, saying, "He who [a]touches[5060] this man[376] or his wife shall surely be put to death."

12 Now Isaac sowed in that land,[776] and [I]reaped in the same year a hundredfold. And [a]the LORD blessed[1288] him,

13 and the man [a]became rich, and continued to grow [I]richer until he became very [I]wealthy;

14 for [a]he had possessions of flocks [I]and herds and a great household,[5657] so that the Philistines envied[7065] him.

15 Now [a]all the wells which his father's servants[5650] had dug in the days of Abraham his father, the Philistines stopped up [I]by filling them with earth.[6083]

16 Then Abimelech said to Isaac, "Go away from us, for you are [I][a]too powerful for us."

29 [I]Lit., *weary* [a]2Kin. 4:38
30 [I]Lit., *the red, this red* [II]Lit., *weary* [III]I.e., red
31 [I]Lit., *Today* [a]Deut. 21:16, 17; 1Chr. 5:1, 2
33 [I]Lit., *Today* [a]Heb. 12:16

1 [a]Gen. 12:10 [b]Gen. 20:1, 2
2 [I]Lit., *dwell* [a]Gen. 12:7; 17:1; 18:1 [b]Gen. 12:1
3 [I]Lit., *seed* [a]Gen. 26:24; 28:15; 31:3 [b]Gen. 12:2 [c]Gen. 12:7; 13:15; 15:18 [d]Gen. 22:16-18; Ps. 105:9
4 [I]Lit., *seed* [II]Or, *bless themselves* [a]Gen. 15:5; 22:17; Ex. 32:13 [b]Gen. 22:18; Gal. 3:8
5 [I]Lit., *hearkened to My voice* [a]Gen. 22:16
6 [I]Lit., *dwelt*
7 [I]Lit., *lest . . . place* [a]Gen. 12:13; 20:2, 12 [b]Prov. 29:25 [c]Gen. 12:11; 24:16; 29:17
10 [a]Gen. 20:9
11 [a]Ps. 105:15
12 [I]Lit., *found* [a]Gen. 24:1; 26:3; Job 42:12; Prov. 10:22
13 [I]Lit., *great* [a]Prov. 10:22
14 [I]Lit., *and possessions of herds* [a]Gen. 24:35; 25:5
15 [I]Lit., *and filled them* [a]Gen. 21:25, 30
16 [I]Lit., *much mightier than we* [a]Ex. 1:9

(continued from previous page)
father could not alter it. In this case Esau gave in to Jacob's extortion and sold the birthright to his brother. None of this had anything to do with Esau's blessing, as Esau, himself, recognized (Gen. 27:36), because a father could bless his son in any way he saw fit. Therefore, when Jacob deceived his father and got Esau's blessing, he stole something from his brother to which he had no right.

17 And Isaac departed from there
and camped in the valley of Gerar, and
[I]settled there.

Quarrel over the Wells

18 Then Isaac dug again the wells
of water which [I]had been dug in the
days of his father Abraham, for the Philistines had stopped them up after the
death[4194] of Abraham; and he [II]gave[7121]
them the same names which his father
had [III]given them.
19 But when Isaac's servants dug
in the valley and found there a well of
[I]flowing[2416] water,
20 the herdsmen of Gerar [a]quar-
reled[7378] with the herdsmen of Isaac,
saying, "The water is ours!" So he
named the well [I]Esek,[6230] because they
contended[6229] with him.
21 Then they dug another well, and
they quarreled[7378] over it too, so he
named it [I]Sitnah.[7856]
22 And he moved away from there
and dug another well, and they did not
quarrel over it; so he named it [I]Reho-
both,[7344] for he said, "[II][a]At last the LORD
has made [III]room[7337] for us, and we shall
be [b]fruitful in the land."
23 Then he went up from there to
[a]Beersheba.
24 And the LORD [a]appeared to him
the same night and said,
"[a]I am the God[430] of your father
Abraham;
[b]Do not fear,[3372] for I am with
you.
I [c]will bless[1288] you, and multiply
your [I]descendants,
For the sake of My servant
Abraham."
25 So he built an [a]altar[4196] there,
and called upon the name of the LORD,
and pitched his tent[168] there; and there
Isaac's servants dug a well.

Covenant with Abimelech

26 Then [a]Abimelech came to him
from Gerar [I]with his adviser Ahuzzath,
and Phicol the commander[8269] of his
army.[6635]
27 And Isaac said to them, "[a]Why
have you come to me, since you hate[8130]
me, and have sent me away from you?"
28 And they said, "We see[7200]
plainly [a]that the LORD has been with you;
so we said, 'Let there now be an oath[423]
between us, *even* between [I]you and us,
and let us make[3772] a covenant[1285] with
you,
29 that you will do us no harm,[7451]
just as we have not touched[5060] you
[I]and have done to you nothing but
good,[2896] and have sent you away in
peace.[7965] You are now the [a]blessed[1288]
of the LORD.' "
30 Then [a]he made them a feast,[4960]
and they ate and drank.
31 And in the morning they arose
early[7925] and [I][a]exchanged oaths;[7650] then
Isaac sent them away and they departed
from him in peace.
32 Now it came about on the same
day,[3117] that Isaac's servants came in
and told[5046] him about the well[875] which
they had dug, and said to him, "We have
found water."
33 So he called it Shibah;[7656] therefore the name of the city is [a]Beer-
sheba[884] to this day.
34 And when Esau was forty years
old [a]he [I]married Judith the daughter of
Beeri the Hittite, and Basemath the
daughter of Elon the Hittite;
35 and [a]they [I]brought grief to Isaac
and Rebekah.

Jacob's Deception

27 🗝 Now it came about,[1961] when
Isaac was old,[2204] and [a]his eyes
were too dim to see,[7200] that he called

17 [I]Lit., *dwelt*
18 [I]Lit., *they had dug* [II]Lit., *called their names as the names* [III]Lit., *called*
19 [I]Lit., *living*
20 [I]I.e., contention [a]Gen. 21:25
21 [I]I.e., enmity
22 [I]I.e., broad places [II]Lit., *Truly now* [III]Or, *broad* [a]Ps. 4:1; Is. 54:2, 3 [b]Gen. 17:6; Ex. 1:7
23 [a]Gen. 22:19
24 [I]Lit., *seed* [a]Gen. 26:2 [b]Gen. 17:7, 8; 24:12; Ex. 3:6; Acts 7:32 [c]Gen. 15:1 [d]Gen. 22:17; 26:3, 4
25 [a]Gen. 12:7, 8; 13:4, 18; Ps. 116:17
26 [I]Lit., *and his confidential friend* [a]Gen. 21:22
27 [a]Judg. 11:7
28 [I]Lit., *us and you* [a]Gen. 21:22, 23
29 [I]Lit., *and just as we* [a]Gen. 24:31; Ps. 115:15
30 [a]Gen. 19:3
31 [I]Lit., *swore one to another* [a]Gen. 21:31
33 [a]Gen. 21:31
34 [I]Lit., *took as wife* [a]Gen. 28:8; 36:2
35 [I]Lit., *were a bitterness of spirit to* [a]Gen. 27:46
1 [a]Gen. 48:10; 1Sam. 3:2

🗝 **27:1-40** Esau had sold his birthright to Jacob, now Jacob was seeking by deception, with his mother's help, to have it officially recognized by his father, Isaac. God had recognized Jacob before the boys were born (Gen. 25:23), but one should not come to the conclusion that God condones lying and fraud *(continued on next page)*

his [b]older son[1121] Esau and said to him, "My son." And he said to him, "Here I am."

2 [a]And [I]Isaac said, "Behold now, I am old *and* I do not know the day[3117] of my death.[4194]

3 "Now then, please take[5375] your gear, your quiver and your bow, and go out to the field and [a]hunt game for me;

4 and prepare[6213] a savory dish for me such as I love,[157] and bring it to me that I may eat, so that [a]my soul[5315] may bless[1288] you before I die."[4191]

5 And Rebekah was listening while Isaac spoke to his son Esau. So when Esau went to the field[7704] to hunt for game to bring *home,*

6 [a]Rebekah said[559] to her son Jacob, "Behold, I heard[8085] your father speak to your brother[251] Esau, saying,

7 'Bring me *some* game and prepare a savory dish for me, that I may eat, and bless you in the presence of the LORD before my death.'

8 "Now therefore, my son, [a]listen[8085] to [I]me [II]as I command[6680] you.

9 "Go now to the flock and [I]bring me two choice [II]kids from there, that I may prepare them *as* a savory dish for your father, such as he loves.

10 "Then you shall bring *it* to your father, that he may eat, so that he may bless you before his death."

11 And Jacob [I]answered his mother[517] Rebekah, "Behold, Esau my brother is a [a]hairy[8163] man[376] and I am a smooth man.

12 "[a]Perhaps my father will feel me, then I shall be as a [I]deceiver in his sight; and I shall bring upon myself a curse[7045] and not a blessing."[1293]

13 But his mother said to him, "Your curse be on me, my son; only [a]obey my voice, and go, get *them* for me."

14 So he went and got *them,* and brought *them* to his mother; and his mother made savory food such as his father loved.

15 Then Rebekah took the [I]best [a]garments of Esau her elder son, which were with her in the house,[1004] and put them on Jacob her younger son.

16 And she put the skins[5785] of the [I]kids on his hands and on the smooth part of his neck.

17 She also gave the savory food and the bread, which she had made,[6213] [I]to her son Jacob.

18 Then he came to his father and said, "My father." And he said, "Here I am. Who are you, my son?"

19 And Jacob said to his father, "I am Esau your first-born; I have done as you told[1696] me. [a]Get up, please, sit and eat of my game, that [I][b]you may bless me."

20 And Isaac said to his son, "How is it that you have *it* so quickly, my son?" And he said, "[a]Because the LORD your God[430] caused *it* to happen to me."

21 Then Isaac said to Jacob, "Please come close, that [a]I may feel you, my son, whether you are really my son Esau or not."

22 So Jacob came close to Isaac his father, and he felt him and said, "The voice is the voice of Jacob, but the hands are the hands of Esau."

23 And he did not recognize[5234] him, because his hands[3027] were [a]hairy like his brother Esau's hands; so he blessed[1288] him.

1 [b]Gen. 25:25, 33, 34
2 [I]Lit., *he* [a]Gen. 47:29
3 [a]Gen. 25:28
4 [a]Gen. 27:19, 25, 31; 48:9, 15, 16; Deut. 33:1; Heb. 11:20
6 [a]Gen. 25:28
8 [I]Lit., *my voice* [II]Lit., *according to what* [a]Gen. 27:13, 43
9 [I]Lit., *take* [II]Lit., *kids of goats*
11 [I]Lit., *said to* [a]Gen. 25:25
12 [I]Lit., *mocker* [a]Gen. 27:21, 22
13 [a]Gen. 27:8
15 [I]Lit., *desirable;* or, *choice* [a]Gen. 27:27
16 [I]Lit., *kids of the goats*
17 [I]Lit., *into the hand of*
19 [I]Lit., *your soul* [a]Gen. 27:31 [b]Gen. 27:4
20 [a]Gen. 24:12
21 [a]Gen. 27:12
23 [a]Gen. 27:16

(continued from previous page)

to accomplish His will. In this act, Jacob realized the true meaning of his name, "the one who supplants." God did not approve of Jacob's conduct. In fact, it was most unjustifiable, but the Bible does not attempt to conceal the faults of good men. The text simply relates how Jacob's wrongdoing led to his banishment from home and final separation from his mother, with whom he was very close. Genesis tells how he himself suffered retribution from the trickery of Laban, his uncle. Jacob felt much anguish when he heard that his brother, Esau, was approaching with 400 men. Finally, Jacob fell a pathetic victim to the deceit of his own sons about the alleged death of his favorite son, Joseph. The whole story of his life shows that he was continually learning by hard experience about the evils of his early vices of duplicity and hard bargaining, but Jacob apparently repented of his deceptions. God confirmed the blessing upon him (Gen. 28:12-15) and later changed his name to Israel (Gen. 32:28).

24 And he said, "Are you really my
son Esau?" And he said, "I am."
25 So he said, "Bring *it* to me, and
I will eat of my son's game, that
[Ia]I may bless you." And he brought *it*
to him, and he ate; he also brought him
wine and he drank.
26 Then his father Isaac said to him,
"Please come close and kiss me, my
son."
27 So he came close and kissed him;
and when he smelled[7306] the smell of
his garments, he [a]blessed[1288] him and
said,

"See, [a]the smell of my son
Is like the smell of a field
[b]which the LORD has blessed;
28 Now may [a]God give you of the
dew of heaven,[8064]
And of the [b]fatness of the
earth,[776]
And an abundance of grain and
new wine;
29 [a]May peoples[5971] serve[5647] you,
And nations[3816] bow down to
you;
[b]Be master of your brothers,
[c]And may your mother's sons
bow down[7812] to you.
[d]Cursed[779] be those who
curse[779] you,
And blessed[1288] be those who
bless you."

The Stolen Blessing

30 Now it came about, as soon as
Isaac had finished blessing[1288] Jacob, and
Jacob had hardly gone out from the presence of Isaac his father, that Esau his
brother came in from his hunting.
31 Then he also made savory food,
and brought it to his father; and he said
to his father, "[a]Let my father arise, and
eat of his son's game, that [Ib]you may
bless me."
32 And Isaac his father said to him,
"[a]Who are you?" And he said, "I am
your son, [b]your first-born, Esau."
33 Then Isaac [I]trembled[2729] violently,[1419] and said, "[a]Who was he then
that hunted game and brought *it* to me,
so that I ate of all *of it* before you came,
and blessed him? [b]Yes, and he shall be
blessed."
34 When Esau heard the words[1697]
of his father, [a]he cried out with an exceedingly great and bitter[4751] cry, and
said to his father, "Bless[1288] me, *even*
me also, O my father!"
35 And he said, "[a]Your brother
came deceitfully,[4820] and has taken away
your blessing."[1293]
36 Then he said, "[I]Is he not rightly
named[7121] [a]Jacob, for he has supplanted
me these two times? He took away my
birthright,[1062] and behold, now he has
taken away my blessing." And he said,
"Have you not reserved a blessing for
me?"
37 But Isaac answered and said to
Esau, "Behold, I have made[7760] him
[a]your master, and all his [I]relatives I have
given to him [II]as servants;[5650] and with
grain and new wine I have sustained
him. Now as for you then, what can I
do, my son?"
38 And Esau said to his father, "Do
you have only one blessing, my father?
Bless me, *even* me also, O my father."
So Esau lifted his voice and [a]wept.
39 Then [a]Isaac his father answered
and said to him,

"Behold, [Ia]away from the
[II]fertility of the earth shall be
your dwelling,[4186]
And [I]away from the dew of
heaven from above.
40 "And by your sword you shall live,
And your brother [a]you shall
serve;
But it shall come about
[b]when you become
restless,[7300]

25 [I]Lit., *my soul* [a]Gen. 27:4
27 [a]Heb. 11:20 [b]Song 4:11 [c]Ps. 65:10
28 [a]Gen. 27:39; Deut. 33:13, 28; Prov. 3:20; Zech. 8:12 [b]Num. 18:12
29 [a]Gen. 25:23; Is. 45:14; 49:7, 23; 60:12, 14 [b]Gen. 9:26, 27; 27:37 [c]Gen. 37:7, 10 [d]Gen. 12:3; Num. 24:9
31 [I]Lit., *your soul* [a]Gen. 27:19 [b]Gen. 27:4
32 [a]Gen. 27:18 [b]Gen. 25:33, 34
33 [I]Lit., *trembled with a very great trembling* [a]Gen. 27:35 [b]Gen. 25:23; 28:3, 4; Num. 23:20
34 [a]Heb. 12:17
35 [a]Gen. 27:19
36 [I]Or, *Was he then named Jacob that he has* [a]Gen. 25:26, 32-34
37 [I]Lit., *brothers* [II]Lit., *for* [a]Gen. 27:28, 29
38 [a]Heb. 12:17
39 [I]Or, *of* [II]Lit., *fatness* [a]Heb. 11:20 [b]Gen. 27:28; Deut. 33:13, 28
40 [a]Gen. 25:23; 27:29 [b]2Kin. 8:20-22

27:39,40 The Edomites were the descendants of Esau. They inhabited a rich, fertile country which was especially given to them (Deut. 2:5). Their country was traversed by roads, though it was mountainous and rocky (Num. 20:17; Jer. 49:16). They were ruled by dukes and later by kings (Gen. 36:15-43). In

(continued on next page)

That you shall [I]break his yoke
from your neck.”

41 So Esau [a]bore a grudge against[7852] Jacob because of the blessing with which his father had blessed him; and Esau said [I]to himself,[3820] “[b]The days of mourning for my father are near; then I will kill[2026] my brother[251] Jacob.”

42 Now when the words of her elder son Esau were reported[5046] to Rebekah, she sent and called her younger son Jacob, and said to him, “Behold your brother Esau is consoling[5162] himself concerning you, *by planning* to kill[2026] you.

43 “Now therefore, my son, [a]obey my voice, and arise, [I]flee to [b]Haran, to my brother [c]Laban!

44 “And stay with him [a]a few days,[3117] until your brother's fury[2534] [I]subsides,

45 until your brother's anger[639] [I]against you subsides,[7725] and he forgets [a]what you did to him. Then I shall send and get you from there. Why should I be bereaved of you both in one day?”[3117]

46 And Rebekah said to Isaac, “I am tired[6973] of [I]living[2416] because of [a]the daughters of Heth; [b]if Jacob takes a wife from the daughters of Heth, like these, from the daughters of the land,[776] what good will my life be to me?”

Jacob Is Sent Away

28 So Isaac called Jacob and [a]blessed[1288] him and charged[6680] him, and said to him, “[b]You shall not take a wife[802] from the daughters of Canaan.

2 “Arise, go to Paddan-aram, to the house[1004] of [a]Bethuel your mother's father; and from there take to yourself a wife from the daughters of Laban your mother's brother.

3 “And may [I][a]God[410] Almighty[7706] [b]bless you and [c]make you fruitful and [d]multiply you, that you may become a [e]company[6951] of peoples.[5971]

4 “May He also give you the [a]blessing[1293] of Abraham, to you and to your [I]descendants[2233] with you; that you may [b]possess the land[776] of your [c]sojournings,[4033] which God[430] gave to Abraham.”

5 Then [a]Isaac sent Jacob away, and he went to Paddan-aram to Laban, son of Bethuel the Aramean, the brother of Rebekah, the mother[517] of Jacob and Esau.

6 Now Esau saw[7200] that Isaac had blessed[1288] Jacob and sent him away to Paddan-aram, to take to himself a wife from there, *and that* when he blessed[1288] him he charged him, saying, “[a]You shall not take a wife from the daughters of Canaan,”

7 and that Jacob had obeyed[8085] his father and his mother and had gone to Paddan-aram.

8 So Esau saw that [a]the daughters of Canaan displeased[7451] [I]his father[1] Isaac;

9 and Esau went to Ishmael, and [I]married, [a]besides the wives that he had, Mahalath the daughter of Ishmael, Abraham's son, the sister of Nebaioth.

Jacob's Dream

🔑 **10** Then Jacob departed from [a]Beersheba and went toward [b]Haran.

40 [I]Lit., *tear off*

41 [I]Lit., *in his heart* [a]Gen. 32:3-11; 37:4, 8 [b]Gen. 50:2-4, 10

43 [I]Lit., *flee for yourself* [a]Gen. 27:8, 13 [b]Gen. 11:31 [c]Gen. 24:29

44 [I]Lit., *turns away* [a]Gen. 31:41

45 [I]Lit., *turns away from you* [a]Gen. 27:12, 19, 35

46 [I]Lit., *my life* [a]Gen. 26:34, 35; 28:8 [b]Gen. 24:3

1 [a]Gen. 27:33 [b]Gen. 24:3, 4

2 [a]Gen. 25:20

3 [I]Heb., *El Shaddai* [a]Gen. 17:1; 35:11; 48:3 [b]Gen. 22:17 [c]Gen. 17:6, 20 [d]Gen. 17:2; 26:4, 24 [e]Gen. 35:11; 48:4

4 [I]Lit., *seed* [a]Gen. 12:2; 22:17 [b]Gen. 15:7, 8; 17:8 [c]1Chr. 29:15; Ps. 39:12

5 [a]Gen. 27:43

6 [a]Gen. 28:1

8 [I]Lit., *in the eyes of his* [a]Gen. 24:3; 26:34, 35; 27:46

9 [I]Lit., *took for his wife* [a]Gen. 26:34; 36:2

10 [a]Gen. 26:23 [b]Gen. 12:4, 5; 27:43

(continued from previous page)
character they are said to have been shrewd, proud, and self-confident, strong, cruel, and idolatrous (Jer. 27:3; 49:7,16,19; Ezek. 25:12; II Chr. 25:14,20). They inhabited the cities of Avith, Pau, Bozrah, Teman, and others. Though they were implacable enemies of Israel, it was forbidden to hate them (Deut. 23:7). They could be received into the congregation in the third generation (Deut. 23:8). King Saul made war against them and David conquered them (I Sam. 14:47; II Sam. 8:14). They took refuge in Egypt and returned after David's death (I Kgs. 11:17-22) when they joined with Israel's enemies only to again be overthrown (II Chr. 20:22,23) but finally aided Babylon against Judah (Ps. 137:7; Obad. 11).

🔑 **28:10-19** Jacob's spiritual nature began to change slightly at Bethel. Here he realized that God

(continued on next page)

11 And he [I]came to [II]a [a]certain place
and spent the night there, because the
sun had set; and he took one of the
stones of the place and put[7760] it
[III]under his head, and lay down in that
place.
12 And [a]he had a dream, and behold,
a ladder was set on[5324] the earth[776] with
its top[7218] reaching[5060] to heaven;[8064]
and behold, [b]the angels of God were
ascending[5927] and descending on it.
13 And behold, [a]the LORD stood[5324]
[I]above it and said, "I am the LORD,
[b]the God of your father Abraham and
the God of Isaac; the land on which you
lie, I will give it [c]to you and to [d]your
[II]descendants.
14 "Your [I]descendants shall also be
like [a]the dust[6083] of the earth,[776] and
you shall [II]spread out [b]to the west and
to the east and to the north and to the
south; and [c]in you and in your [I]descend-
ants shall all the families[4940] of the earth
be blessed.[1288]
15 "And behold, [a]I am with you, and
[b]will keep[8104] you wherever you go, and
[c]will bring you back[7725] to this land;[127]
for [d]I will not leave[5800] you until I have
done what I have [I]promised you."
16 Then Jacob [a]awoke from his
sleep and said, "[b]Surely the LORD is in
this place, and I did not know[3045] it."
17 And he was afraid[3372] and said,
"[a]How awesome[3372] is this place! This
is none other than the house[1004] of
God,[430] and this is the gate of heaven."
18 So Jacob rose early in the morning, and took [a]the stone that he had
put[7760] [I]under his head and set it up as
a pillar,[4676] and poured oil[8081] on its top.
19 And he called the name of that
place [I][a]Bethel;[1008] however, [II]previously
the name of the city had been [b]Luz.
20 Then Jacob [a]made[5087] a vow,[5088]
saying, "[b]If God will be with me and
will keep me on this journey[1870] that I
[I]take, and will give me [II][c]food to eat
and garments to wear,
21 and [a]I return to my father's house
in [I]safety,[7965] [b]then the LORD will be my
God.
22 "And this stone, which I have
set up[7760] as a pillar, [a]will be God's
house; and [b]of all that Thou dost give
me I will surely give a tenth to Thee."

Jacob Meets Rachel

29 Then Jacob [I]went on his journey,
and came to the land[776] of
[a]the sons[1121] of the east.
2 And he looked, and [I]saw [a]a well
in the field, and behold, three flocks of
sheep were lying there beside it, for
from that well they watered the flocks.
Now the stone on the mouth[6310] of the
well was large.
3 When all the flocks were gathered
there, they would then roll[1556] the stone
from the mouth of the well, and water
the sheep, and put the stone back in
its place on the mouth of the well.
4 And Jacob said to them, "My
brothers, where are you from?" And
they said, "We are from [a]Haran."
5 And he said to them, "Do you
know[3045] Laban the [a]son[1121] of Nahor?"
And they said, "We know *him*."
6 And he said to them, "Is it well[7965]
with him?" And they said, "It is well,
and behold, [a]Rachel his daughter is coming with the sheep."
7 And he said, "Behold, it is still
high day;[3117] it is not time[6256] for the
livestock to be gathered. Water the
sheep, and go, pasture them."

11 [I]Lit., *lighted on* [II]Lit., *the place* [III]Lit., *at his head-place* [a]Gen. 28:19
12 [a]Gen. 41:1; Num. 12:6 [b]John 1:51
13 [I]Or, *beside him* [II]Lit., *seed* [a]Gen. 35:1; Amos 7:7 [b]Gen. 26:3, 24 [c]Gen. 13:15, 17; 26:3 [d]Gen. 12:7; 15:18
14 [I]Lit., *seed* [II]Lit., *break through* [a]Gen. 13:16; 22:17 [b]Gen. 13:14, 15 [c]Gen. 12:3; 18:18; 22:18; 26:4
15 [I]Lit., *spoken to* [a]Gen. 26:3, 24; 31:3 [b]Num. 6:24; Ps. 121:5, 7, 8 [c]Gen. 48:21; Deut. 30:3 [d]Num. 23:19; Deut. 7:9; 31:6, 8
16 [a]1Kin. 3:15; Jer. 31:26 [b]Ex. 3:4-6; Josh. 5:13-15; Ps. 139:7-12
17 [a]Ps. 68:35
18 [I]Lit., *at his head-place* [a]Gen. 28:11; 35:14
19 [I]I.e., the house of God [II]Lit., *at the first* [a]Judg. 1:23 [b]Gen. 35:6; 48:3
20 [I]Lit., *go* [II]Lit., *bread* [a]Gen. 31:13; Judg. 11:30; 2Sam. 15:8 [b]Gen. 28:15 [c]1Tim. 6:8
21 [I]Lit., *peace* [a]Judg. 11:31 [b]Deut. 26:17
22 [a]Gen. 35:7 [b]Lev. 27:30; Deut. 14:22

1 [I]Lit., *lifted up his feet* [a]Judg. 6:3, 33
2 [I]Lit., *behold* [a]Gen. 24:10, 11; Ex. 2:15, 16
4 [a]Gen. 28:10
5 [b]Gen. 24:24, 29 **6** [a]Ex. 2:16

(continued from previous page)
was in more than one place. He treated his vision at Bethel as a business deal. If God would help him, and give him bread to eat, and bring him back safely, then he would allow God to be his God and he would give God a tenth of everything. At the Jabbok River (Gen. 32:22-32) the crisis was much more far-reaching. There Jacob realized his danger and his need of a blessing. He no longer bargained with God. He saw that his own strength was futile and he humbly sought help from God. From that night on he was a different man.

28:19 Beth means "house of" and El is a short form for "God," worshipped as the Almighty.

8 But they said, "We cannot, until all the flocks are gathered, and they roll the stone from the mouth of the well; then we water the sheep."

9 While he was still speaking with them, Rachel came with her father's sheep, for she was a shepherdess.

10 And it came about, when Jacob saw[7200] Rachel the daughter of Laban his mother's brother, and the sheep of Laban his mother's brother, that Jacob went up, and rolled the stone from the mouth of the well, and watered the flock of Laban his mother's brother.

11 Then Jacob [a]kissed Rachel, and lifted his voice and wept.

12 And Jacob told[5046] Rachel that he was a [I][a]relative of her father and that he was Rebekah's son, and [b]she ran and told her father.

13 So it came about, when [a]Laban heard the news[8088] of Jacob his sister's son, that he ran to meet him, and [b]embraced him and kissed him, and brought him to his house.[1004] Then he related[5608] to Laban all these things.

14 And Laban said to him, "Surely you are [a]my bone[6106] and my flesh."[1320] And he stayed with him a month.

15 Then Laban said to Jacob, "Because you are my [I]relative,[251] should you therefore serve[5647] me for nothing?2600 Tell[5046] me, what shall [a]your wages be?"

16 Now Laban had two daughters; the name of the older was Leah, and the name of the younger was Rachel.

17 And Leah's eyes were weak, but Rachel was [a]beautiful of form and [I]face.

18 Now Jacob [a]loved151 Rachel, so he said, "[b]I will serve[5647] you seven years for your younger daughter Rachel."

19 And Laban said, "It is better[2896] that I give her to you than that I should give her to another man;[376] stay with me."

20 So Jacob served seven years for Rachel and they seemed to him but a few days[3117] [a]because of his love[160] for her.

Laban's Treachery

21 Then Jacob said to Laban, "Give *me* my wife, for my [I]time is completed, that I may [a]go in to her."

22 And Laban gathered all the men[582] of the place, and made a feast.[4960]

23 Now it came about in the evening that he took his daughter Leah, and brought her to him; and *Jacob* went in to her.

24 Laban also gave his maid Zilpah to his daughter Leah as a maid.

25 So it came about in the morning that, behold, it was Leah! And he said to Laban, "[a]What is this you have done[6213] to me? Was it not for Rachel that I served with you? Why then have you [b]deceived me?"

26 But Laban said, "It is not [I]the practice in our place, to [II]marry off the younger before the first-born.

27 "Complete the week of this one, and we will give you the other also for the service[5656] which [a]you shall serve with me for another seven years."

28 And Jacob did so and completed her week, and he gave him his daughter Rachel as his wife.

29 Laban also gave his maid Bilhah to his daughter Rachel as her maid.

30 So *Jacob* went in to Rachel also, and indeed [a]he loved Rachel more than Leah, and he served with [I]Laban for [b]another seven years.

31 Now the LORD saw[7200] that Leah was [I]unloved,[8130] and He opened her womb, but Rachel was barren.6135

32 And Leah conceived and bore a son[1121] and named him [I]Reuben,7205 for she said, "Because the LORD has [II][a]seen[7200] my affliction; surely now my husband[376] will love me."

33 Then she conceived again and bore a son and said, "[a]Because the LORD has [I]heard[8085] that I am [II]unloved, He has therefore given me this *son* also." So she named him Simeon.8095

34 And she conceived again and bore a son and said, "Now this time my husband will become [I]attached3867 to me, because I have borne him three

11 [a]Gen. 33:4
12 [I]Lit., *brother* [a]Gen. 28:5 [b]Gen. 24:28
13 [a]Gen. 24:29-31 [b]Gen. 33:4
14 [a]Gen. 2:23; Judg. 9:2; 2Sam. 5:1; 19:12, 13
15 [I]Lit., *brother* [a]Gen. 31:41
17 [I]Lit., *beautiful of appearance* [a]Gen. 12:11, 14; 26:7
18 [a]Gen. 24:67 [b]Hos. 12:12
20 [a]Song 8:7
21 [I]Lit., *days are* [a]Judg. 15:1
25 [a]Gen. 12:18; 20:9; 26:10 [b]1Sam. 28:12
26 [I]Lit., *done thus in* [II]Lit., *give*
27 [a]Gen. 31:41
30 [I]Lit., *him* [a]Gen. 29:17, 18 [b]Gen. 31:41
31 [I]Lit., *hated*
32 [I]I.e., see, a son [II]Lit., *looked upon* [a]Gen. 16:11; 31:42; Ex. 3:7; 4:31; Deut. 26:7; Ps. 25:18
33 [I]Heb., *shama*, related to Simeon [II]Lit., *hated* [a]Deut. 21:15
34 [I]Heb., *lavah*, related to Levi

sons." Therefore he was named [a]Levi.[3878]

35 And she conceived again and bore a son and said, "This time I will [I]praise[3034] the LORD." Therefore she named him [IIa]Judah.[3063] Then she stopped bearing.

The Sons of Jacob

30 Now when Rachel saw that [a]she bore Jacob no children,[1121] [I]she became jealous[7065] of her sister;[269] and she said to Jacob, "[b]Give me children, or else I die."

2 Then Jacob's anger[639] burned[2734] against Rachel, and he said, "Am I in the place of God, who has [a]withheld from you the fruit of the womb?"[990]

3 And she said, "[a]Here is my maid Bilhah, go in to her, that she may [b]bear on my knees, that [Ic]through her I too may have children."

4 So [a]she gave him her maid Bilhah as a wife, and Jacob went in to her.

5 And Bilhah conceived and bore Jacob a son.[1121]

6 Then Rachel said, "God[430] has [Ia]vindicated[1777] me, and has indeed heard[8085] my voice and has given me a son." Therefore she named[7121] him [II]Dan.[1835]

7 And Rachel's maid Bilhah conceived again and bore Jacob a second son.

8 So Rachel said, "With [I]mighty[430] wrestlings[5319] I have [II]wrestled[6617] with my sister, *and* I have indeed prevailed." And she named him Naphtali.[5321]

9 When Leah saw that she had stopped bearing, she took her maid Zilpah and gave her to Jacob as a wife.

10 And Leah's maid Zilpah bore Jacob a son.

11 Then Leah said, "[I]How fortunate!"[1409] So she named him [II]Gad.[1410]

12 And Leah's maid Zilpah bore Jacob a second son.

13 Then Leah said, "[I]Happy[837] am I! For women [a]will call me happy."[833] So she named him [II]Asher.[836]

14 Now in the days[3117] of wheat harvest Reuben went and found [a]mandrakes[1736] in the field,[7704] and brought them to his mother Leah. Then Rachel said to Leah, "Please give me some of your son's mandrakes."

15 But she said to her, "Is it a small matter for you to take my husband?[376] And would you take my son's mandrakes also?" So Rachel said, "Therefore he may lie with you tonight in return for your son's mandrakes."

16 When Jacob came in from the field in the evening, then Leah went out to meet him and said, "You must come in to me, for I have surely hired you with my son's mandrakes." So he lay with her that night.

17 And God gave heed[8085] to Leah, and she conceived and bore Jacob a fifth son.

18 Then Leah said, "God has given me my [I]wages,[7939] because I gave my maid to my husband." So she named him Issachar.[3485]

19 And Leah conceived again and bore a sixth son to Jacob.

20 Then Leah said, "God has endowed me with a good gift;[2065] now my husband [I]will dwell[2082] with me, because I have borne him six sons." So she named him Zebulun.[2074]

21 And afterward she bore a daughter and named her Dinah.

22 Then [a]God remembered[2142] Rachel, and God gave heed to her and [b]opened her womb.

23 So she conceived and bore a son and said, "God has [a]taken away[622] my reproach."[2781]

24 And she named him Joseph,[3130] saying, "[a]May the LORD [I]give[3254] me another son."

Jacob Prospers

25 Now it came about when Rachel had borne Joseph, that Jacob said to Laban, "[a]Send me away, that I may go to my own place and to my own country.[776]

26 "Give *me* my wives and my children [a]for whom I have served[5647] you,

---

34 [a]Gen. 49:5

35 [I]Heb., *Jadah,* related to Judah [II]Heb., *Jehudah* [a]Gen. 49:8; Matt. 1:2

1 [I]Lit., *Rachel* [a]Gen. 29:31 [b]1Sam. 1:5, 6

2 [a]Gen. 20:18; 29:31

3 [I]Lit., *from her I too may be built* [a]Gen. 16:2 [b]Gen. 50:23; Job 3:12 [c]Gen. 16:2

4 [a]Gen. 16:3, 4

6 [I]Lit., *judged* [II]I.e., He judged [a]Ps. 35:24; 43:1; Lam. 3:59

8 [I]Lit., *wrestlings of God* [II]Heb., *niphtal,* related to Naphtali

11 [I]Lit., *With fortune!* Some versions read *Fortune has come* [II]I.e., Fortune

13 [I]Lit., *With my happiness!* [II]I.e., happy [a]Luke 1:48

14 [a]Song 7:13

18 [I]Heb., *sachar,* related to Issachar

20 [I]Heb., *zabal,* related to Zebulun. Some translate *will honor*

22 [a]1Sam. 1:19, 20 [b]Gen. 29:31

23 [a]Is. 4:1; Luke 1:25

24 [I]Lit., *add to me;* Heb., *Joseph* [a]Gen. 35:17

25 [a]Gen. 24:54, 56

26 [a]Gen. 29:18, 20,27; Hos. 12:12

and let me depart; for you yourself know my service[5656] which I have [I]rendered[5647] you."

27 But Laban said to him, "If now [I]it pleases[2580] you, *stay with me;* I have divined[5172] [a]that the LORD has blessed[1288] me on your account."

28 And he [I]continued, "[a]Name me your wages, and I will give it."

29 But he said to him, "[a]You yourself know how I have served you and how your cattle have [I]fared with me.

30 "For you had little before [I]I came, and it has [II]increased to a multitude; and the LORD has blessed you [III]wherever I turned. But now, when shall I provide[6213] for my own household[1004] also?"

31 So he said, "What shall I give you?" And Jacob said, "You shall not give me anything.[1697] If you will do[6213] this *one* thing for me, I will again pasture *and* keep[8104] your flock:

32 let me pass through[5674] your entire flock today,[3117] removing from there every [a]speckled and spotted sheep, and every black [I]one among the lambs, and the spotted and speckled among the goats; and *such* shall be my wages.

33 "So my [I]honesty[6666] will answer for me later,[3117] when you come concerning my [II]wages. Every one that is not speckled and spotted among the goats and black among the lambs, *if found* with me, will be considered stolen."

34 And Laban said, "[I]Good, let it be according to your word."[1697]

35 So he removed on that day the striped[6124] and spotted male goats and all the speckled and spotted female goats, every one with white in it, and all the black ones among the sheep, and gave them into the [I]care[3027] of his sons.

36 And he put *a distance of* three days'[3117] journey[1870] between himself and Jacob, and Jacob fed the rest[3498] of Laban's flocks.

37 Then Jacob [I]took fresh rods of poplar and almond and plane trees, and peeled[6478] white stripes in them, exposing the white which *was* [II]in the rods.

38 And he set the rods which he had peeled in front of the flocks in the gutters,[7298] *even* in the watering troughs, where the flocks came to drink; and they [I]mated when they came to drink.

39 So the flocks [I]mated by the rods, and the flocks brought forth striped, speckled, and spotted.

40 And Jacob separated the lambs, and [I]made the flocks face toward the striped and all the black in the flock of Laban; and he put his own herds apart, and did not put them with Laban's flock.

41 Moreover, it came about whenever the [I]stronger of the flock [II]were mating, that Jacob would place[7760] the rods in the sight of the flock in the gutters, so that they might [III]mate by the rods;

42 but when the flock was feeble, he did not put *them* in; so the feebler were Laban's and the [I]stronger Jacob's.

43 So [a]the man[376] [I]became exceedingly prosperous, and had large flocks and female and male servants[5650] and camels and donkeys.

Jacob Leaves Secretly for Canaan

31 Now [I]Jacob heard the words of Laban's sons, saying, "Jacob has taken away all that was our father's,[1] and from what belonged to our father he has made[6213] all this [II]wealth."[3519]

2 And Jacob saw[7200] the [I]attitude of Laban, and behold, it was not *friendly* toward him as formerly.

3 Then the LORD said to Jacob, "[a]Return[7725] to the land[776] of your fathers[1] and to your relatives, and [b]I will be with you."

4 So Jacob sent and called Rachel and Leah to his flock in the field,

5 and said to them, "[a]I see your father's [I]attitude, that it is not *friendly* toward me as formerly, but [b]the God[430] of my father has been with me.

6 "And [a]you know that I have served[5647] your father with all my strength.

26 [I]Lit., *served*
27 [I]Lit., *I have found favor in your eyes* [a]Gen. 26:24; 39:3, 5; Is. 61:9
28 [I]Lit., *said* [a]Gen. 29:15; 31:7, 41
29 [I]Lit., *been* [a]Gen. 31:6
30 [I]Lit., *me* [II]Lit., *broken forth* [III]Lit., *at my foot*
32 [I]Lit., *sheep* [a]Gen. 31:8
33 [I]Lit., *righteousness* [II]Lit., *wages which are before you*
34 [I]Lit., *Behold, would that it might be*
35 [I]Lit., *hand*
37 [I]Lit., *took to himself* [II]Lit., *on*
38 [I]Or, *conceived*
39 [I]Or, *conceived*
40 [I]Lit., *set the faces*
41 [I]Lit., *bound ones;* i.e., firm and compact [II]Or, *conceived* [III]Or, *conceive*
42 [I]Lit., *bound ones;* i.e., firm and compact
43 [I]Lit., *broke forth* [a]Gen. 12:16; 13:2; 24:35; 26:13, 14; 30:30
1 [I]Lit., *he* [II]Lit., *glory*
2 [I]Lit., *face*
3 [a]Gen. 32:9 [b]Gen. 28:15
5 [I]Lit., *face* [a]Gen. 31:2 [b]Gen. 21:22; 28:13, 15; 31:29, 42, 53; Is. 41:10; Heb. 13:5
6 [a]Gen. 30:29

7 "Yet your father has [a]cheated me and [b]changed my wages ten times; however, [c]God did not allow him to hurt[7489] me.

8 "If [a]he spoke thus, 'The speckled shall be your wages,' then all the flock brought forth speckled; and if he spoke thus, 'The striped[6124] shall be your wages,' then all the flock brought forth striped.

9 "Thus God has [a]taken away your father's livestock and given *them* to me.

10 "And it came about at the time[6256] when the flock were [I]mating that I lifted up my eyes and saw[7200] in a dream, and behold, the male goats which were [II]mating[5927] *were* striped, speckled, and mottled.

11 "Then [a]the angel of God said to me in the dream, 'Jacob,' and I said, 'Here I am.'

12 "And he said, 'Lift up,[5375] now, your eyes and see *that* all the male goats which are [I]mating are striped, speckled, and mottled; for [a]I have seen[7200] all that Laban has been doing to you.

13 'I am [a]the God[410] *of* Bethel, where you [b]anointed[4886] a pillar,[4676] where you made a vow to Me; now arise, [I]leave this land, and [c]return to the land of your birth.' "

14 And Rachel and Leah answered and said to him, "Do we still have any portion or inheritance[5159] in our father's house?[1004]

15 "Are we not reckoned[2803] by him as foreigners?[5237] For [a]he has sold us, and has also [I]entirely consumed [II]our purchase price.

16 "Surely all the wealth which God has taken away from our father belongs to us and our children;[1121] now then, do[6213] whatever God has said to you."

17 Then Jacob arose and put his children[1121] and his wives upon camels;

18 and he drove away all his livestock and all his property which he had gathered, his acquired livestock which he had gathered in Paddan-aram, [a]to go to the land of Canaan to his father Isaac.

19 When Laban had gone to shear his flock, then Rachel stole the [Ia]household idols[8655] that were her father's.

20 And Jacob [I]deceived[3820] Laban the Aramean, by not telling[5046] him that he was fleeing.

21 So he fled with all that he had; and he arose and crossed[5674] the *Euphrates* River, and set his face toward the hill country of [a]Gilead.

Laban Pursues Jacob

22 When it was told[5046] Laban on the third day[3117] that Jacob had fled,

23 then he took his [I]kinsmen with him, and pursued him *a distance of* seven days' journey; and he overtook him in the hill country of Gilead.

24 And [a]God came to Laban the Aramean in a [b]dream of the night, and said to him, "[Ic]Be careful that you do not speak to Jacob either good[2896] or bad."

25 And Laban caught up with Jacob. Now Jacob had pitched his tent[168] in the hill country, and Laban with his [I]kinsmen camped in the hill country of Gilead.

26 Then Laban said to Jacob, "What have you done[6213] [I]by deceiving[3824] me and carrying away my daughters like captives[7617] of the sword?

27 "Why did you flee secretly and [I]deceive me, and did not tell me, so that I might have sent you away with joy and with songs,[7892] with [a]timbrel[8596] and with [b]lyre;

28 and did not allow me [a]to kiss my sons[1121] and my daughters? Now you have done foolishly.

29 "It is in [I]my power[410] to do[6213] you harm,[7451] but [a]the God[430] of your father[1] spoke to me last night, saying, '[IIb]Be careful not to speak either good or bad[7451] to Jacob.'

30 "And now you have indeed gone away because you longed greatly for your father's house; *but* why did you steal [a]my gods?"[430]

31 Then Jacob answered and said to Laban, "Because I was afraid,[3372] for I said, 'Lest[6435] you would take your daughters from me by force.'

32 "[a]The one with whom you find

7 [a]Gen. 29:25 [b]Gen. 31:41 [c]Gen. 15:1; 31:29

8 [a]Gen. 30:32

9 [a]Gen. 31:1, 16

10 [I]Or, *conceiving* [II]Lit., *leaping upon the flock*

11 [a]Gen. 16:7-11; 22:11, 15; 31:13; 48:16

12 [I]Lit., *leaping upon the flock* [a]Ex. 3:7

13 [I]Lit., *go out from* [a]Gen. 28:13, 19 [b]Gen. 28:18, 20 [c]Gen. 28:15; 32:9

15 [I]I.e., enjoyed the benefit of [II]Lit., *our money* [a]Gen. 29:20, 23, 27

18 [a]Gen. 35:27

19 [I]Heb., *teraphim* [a]Gen. 31:30, 34; 35:2; Judg. 17:5; 1Sam. 19:13; Hos. 3:4

20 [I]Lit., *stole the heart of*

21 [a]Gen. 37:25

23 [I]Lit., *brothers*

24 [I]Lit., *Take heed to yourself* [a]Gen. 20:3; 31:29 [b]Gen. 20:3, 6; 31:11 [c]Gen. 24:50; 31:7, 29

25 [I]Lit., *brothers*

26 [I]Lit., *and you have stolen my heart*

27 [I]Lit., *steal me* [a]Ex. 15:20 [b]Gen. 4:21

28 [a]Gen. 31:55

29 [I]Lit., *the power of my hand* [II]Lit., *Take heed to yourself* [a]Gen. 31:5, 24, 42, 53 [b]Gen. 31:24

30 [a]Gen. 31:19; Josh. 24:2; Judg. 18:24

32 [a]Gen. 44:9

your gods shall not live; in the presence of our [I]kinsmen [II]point[5234] out what is yours [III]among my belongings and take *it* for yourself." For Jacob did not know[3045] that Rachel had stolen them.

33 So Laban went into Jacob's tent, and into Leah's tent, and into the tent of the two maids, but he did not find *them.* Then he went out of Leah's tent and entered Rachel's tent.

34 Now Rachel had taken the [I]household idols and put them in the camel's saddle, and she sat on them. And Laban felt through all the tent, but did not find *them.*

35 And she said to her father, "Let not my lord[113] be angry[2734] that I cannot [a]rise before you, for the manner[1870] of women is upon me." So he searched, but did not find the [Ib]household idols.

36 Then Jacob became angry[2734] and contended[7378] with Laban; and Jacob answered and said to Laban, "What is my transgression?[6588] What is my sin,[2403] that you have hotly pursued me?

37 "Though you have felt through all my goods, what have you found of all your household[1004] goods? Set[7760] *it* here before my [I]kinsmen and your [I]kinsmen, that they may decide[3198] between us two.

38 "These twenty years I *have been* with you; your ewes[7353] and your female goats have not miscarried, nor have I eaten the rams of your flocks.

39 "That which was torn *of beasts* I did not bring to you; I bore the loss[2398] of it myself. You required it of my hand *whether* stolen by day or stolen by night.

40 "*Thus* I was: by day the [I]heat consumed me, and the frost by night, and my sleep fled from my eyes.

41 "These twenty years I have been in your house; [a]I served you fourteen years for your two daughters, and six years for your flock, and you [b]changed my wages ten times.

42 "If [a]the God of my father, the God of Abraham, and the fear[6343] of Isaac, had not been for me, surely now you would have sent me away empty-handed. [b]God has seen my affliction and the toil of my hands,[3709] so He [c]rendered judgment last night."

The Covenant of Mizpah

43 Then Laban answered and said to Jacob, "The daughters are my daughters, and the children[1121] are my children, and [a]the flocks are my flocks, and all that you see is mine. But what can I do[6213] this day[3117] to these my daughters or to their children whom they have borne?

44 "So now come, let us [a]make[3772] a covenant,[1285] [I]you and I, and [b]let it be a witness[5707] between [II]you and me."

45 Then Jacob took [a]a stone and set it up *as* a pillar.

46 And Jacob said to his [I]kinsmen, "Gather[3950] stones." So they took stones and made[6213] a heap,[1530] and they ate there by the heap.

47 Now Laban [a]called it [I]Jegar-sahadutha,[3026] but Jacob called[7121] it [II]Galeed.[1567]

48 And Laban said, "[a]This heap is a witness between [I]you and me this day." Therefore it was named Galeed;

49 and [Ia]Mizpah, for he said, "May the LORD watch between [II]you and me when we are [III]absent[5641] one[376] from the other.[7453]

50 "If you mistreat my daughters, or if you take wives besides my daughters, *although* no man[376] is with us, see, [a]God is witness between [I]you and me."

51 And Laban said to Jacob, "Behold this heap and behold the pillar which I have set between [I]you and me.

52 "This heap is a witness,[5707] and the pillar is a witness, that I will not pass by this heap to you for harm, and you will not pass by this heap and this pillar to me, for harm.[7451]

53 "[a]The God of Abraham and the God of Nahor, the God of their father, [b]judge between us." So Jacob swore[7650] by [c]the fear[6343] of his father Isaac.

54 Then Jacob [a]offered a sacrifice[2077] on the mountain, and called[7121] his [I]kinsmen to [II]the meal; and they ate

32 [I]Lit., *brothers* [II]Lit., *recognize* [III]Lit., *with me*

34 [I]Heb., *teraphim*

35 [I]Heb., *teraphim* [a]Lev. 19:32 [b]Gen. 31:19

37 [I]Lit., *brothers*

40 [I]Or, *drought*

41 [a]Gen. 29:27, 30 [b]Gen. 31:7

42 [a]Gen. 31:5, 29, 53 [b]Gen. 29:32; Ex. 3:7 [c]Gen. 31:24, 29

43 [a]Gen. 31:1

44 [I]Lit., *I and you* [II]Lit., *me and you* [a]Gen. 21:27, 32; 26:28 [b]Josh. 24:27

45 [a]Gen. 28:18; Josh. 24:26, 27

46 [I]Lit., *brothers*

47 [I]I.e., the heap of witness, in Aram. [II]I.e., the heap of witness, in Heb. [a]Josh. 22:34

48 [I]Lit., *me and you* [a]Josh. 24:27

49 [I]Lit., *the Mizpah;* i.e., the watchtower [II]Lit., *me and you* [III]Lit., *hidden* [a]Judg. 11:29; 1Sam. 7:5, 6

50 [I]Lit., *me and you* [a]Jer. 29:23; 42:5

51 [I]Lit., *me and you*

53 [a]Gen. 28:13 [b]Gen. 16:5 [c]Gen. 31:42

54 [I]Lit., *brothers* [a]Ex. 18:12 [II]Lit., *eat bread*

[III]the meal and spent the night on the
mountain.
55 [I]And early in the morning Laban
arose, and [a]kissed his sons[1121] and his
daughters and blessed[1288] them. Then
Laban departed and returned to his
place.

Jacob's Fear of Esau

32 Now as Jacob went on his way,
[a]the angels of God[430] met him.
2 And Jacob said when he saw them,
"This is God's [I]camp."[4264] So he named
that place [II][a]Mahanaim.[4266]
3 Then Jacob [a]sent messengers before him to his brother[251] Esau in the
land of [b]Seir, the [I]country[7704] of [c]Edom.
4 He also commanded[6680] them say-
ing, "Thus you shall say to my lord[113]
Esau: 'Thus says your servant[5650] Jacob,
"I have sojourned[1481] with Laban, and
[a]stayed until now;
5 and [a]I have oxen and donkeys *and*
flocks and male and female servants;[5650]
and I have sent to tell[5046] my lord, [b]that
I may find favor[2580] in your sight." ' "
6 And the messengers returned to
Jacob, saying, "We came to your brother
Esau, and furthermore [a]he is coming
to meet you, and four hundred men[376]
are with him."
7 Then Jacob was [a]greatly afraid[3372]
and distressed; and he divided the
people[5971] who were with him, and the
flocks and the herds and the camels,
into two companies;[4264]
8 for he said, "If Esau comes to the
one company[4264] and [I]attacks[5221] it, then
the company which is left[7604] will
escape."[6413]
9 And Jacob said, "O [a]God of my
father[1] Abraham and God of my father
Isaac, O LORD, who didst say to me,
'[b]Return[7725] to your country[776] and to
your relatives, and I will [I]prosper[3190]
you,'
10 [I]I am unworthy [a]of all the
lovingkindness[2617] and of all the [II]faith-
fulness[571] which Thou hast shown[6213]
to Thy servant; for with my staff *only*
I crossed[5674] this Jordan, and now I have
become two companies.
11 "[a]Deliver[5337] me, I pray, [b]from
the hand[3027] of my brother, from the
hand of Esau; for I fear[3373] him, lest
he come and [I]attack me, the [c]mothers
with the children.[1121]
12 "For Thou didst say, '[a]I will
surely[3190] [I]prosper[3190] you, and
[b]make[7760] your [II]descendants[2233] as the
sand of the sea, which cannot be
numbered[5608] for multitude.' "
13 So he spent the night there.
Then he [I]selected from what [II]he had
with him a [a]present[4503] for his brother
Esau:
14 two hundred female goats and
twenty male goats, two hundred
ewes[7353] and twenty rams,
15 thirty milking camels and their
colts,[1121] forty cows[6510] and ten bulls,
twenty female donkeys and ten male
donkeys.
16 And he delivered *them* into the
hand of his servants, every drove by
itself, and said to his servants, "Pass
on before me, and put a space[7305] between droves."
17 And he commanded the [I]one in
front,[7223] saying, "When my brother
Esau meets you and asks[7592] you, saying, 'To whom do you belong, and where
are you going, and to whom do these
animals in front of you belong?'
18 then you shall say, '*These* belong
to your servant Jacob; it is a present
sent to my lord Esau. And behold, he
also is behind us.' "
19 Then he commanded also the
second and the third, and all those who
followed the droves, saying, "After this
manner you shall speak to Esau when
you find him;
20 and you shall say, 'Behold, your
servant Jacob also is behind us.' " For
he said, "I will appease[6440] him with the
present that goes before me. Then afterward I will see[7200] his face; perhaps[194]
he will accept[5375] me."
21 So the present passed on[5674] before him, while he himself spent that
night in the camp.

54 [III]Lit., *bread*
55 [I]Ch. 32:1 in Heb. [a]Gen. 31:28, 43
1 [a]2Kin. 6:16, 17; Ps. 34:7
2 [I]Or, *company* [II]I.e., Two Camps, or, Two Companies [a]Josh. 21:38; 2Sam. 2:8
3 [I]Lit., *field* [a]Gen. 27:41, 42; 32:7, 11 [b]Gen. 14:6; 33:14 [c]Gen. 25:30; 36:8, 9
4 [a]Gen. 31:41
5 [a]Gen. 30:43 [b]Gen. 33:8
6 [a]Gen. 33:1
7 [a]Gen. 32:11
8 [I]Lit., *smites*
9 [I]Lit., *do good with you* [a]Gen. 28:13; 31:42 [b]Gen. 28:15; 31:3, 13
10 [I]Lit., *I am less than all* [II]Or, *truth* [a]Gen. 24:27
11 [I]Lit., *smite* [a]Ps. 59:1, 2 [b]Gen. 27:41, 42; 33:4 [c]Hos. 10:14
12 [I]Lit., *do good with* [II]Lit., *seed* [a]Gen. 28:14 [b]Gen. 22:17
13 [I]Lit., *took* [II]Lit., *had come to his hand* [a]Gen. 43:11
17 [I]Lit., *first*

22 Now he arose that same night and took his two wives and his two maids and his eleven children, and crossed[5674] the ford of the [a]Jabbok.

23 And he took them and sent them across the stream. And he sent across whatever he had.

Jacob Wrestles

24 Then Jacob was left[3498] alone, and a man[376] [a]wrestled with him until daybreak.

25 And when he saw that he had not prevailed against him, he touched[5060] the socket[3709] of his thigh;[3409] so the socket of Jacob's thigh was dislocated while he wrestled with him.

26 Then he said, "Let me go, for the dawn is breaking."[5927] But he said, "[a]I will not let you go unless you bless[1288] me."

27 So he said to him, "What is your name?" And he said, "Jacob."

🗝 28 And [a]he said, "Your name shall no longer be Jacob,3290 but [I]Israel;3478 for you have striven with God and with men[582] and have prevailed."

29 Then [a]Jacob asked him and said, "Please tell[5046] me your name." But he said, "Why is it that you ask my name?" And he blessed[1288] him there.

🗝 30 So Jacob named the place [I]Peniel,6439 for *he said,* "[a]I have seen[7200] God[430] face to face,6440 yet my [II]life[5315] has been preserved."[5337]

31 Now the sun rose upon him just as he crossed[5674] over [a]Penuel, and he was limping on his thigh.

32 Therefore, to this day[3117] the sons[1121] of Israel do not eat the sinew of the hip which is on the socket of the thigh, because he touched the socket of Jacob's thigh in the sinew of the hip.

Jacob Meets Esau

33 Then Jacob lifted his eyes and looked,[7200] and behold, [a]Esau was coming, and four hundred men[376] with him. So he divided the children [I]among Leah and Rachel and the two maids.

2 And he put the maids and their children [I]in front, and Leah and her children [II]next, and Rachel and Joseph [II]last.[314]

3 But he himself passed on[5674] ahead of them and [a]bowed[7812] down to the ground[776] seven times, until he came near to his brother.[251]

4 Then Esau ran to meet him and embraced him, and [a]fell on his neck and kissed him, and they wept.

5 And he lifted his eyes and saw[7200] the women and the children, and said, "[I]Who are these with you?" So he said, "[a]The children whom God[430] has graciously given[2603] your servant."[5650]

6 Then the maids came near [I]with their children, and they bowed down.

7 And Leah likewise came near with her children, and they bowed down; and afterward Joseph came near with Rachel, and they bowed down.

8 And he said, "What do you mean by [a]all this company[4264] which I have met?" And he said, "[b]To find favor[2580] in the sight of my lord."[113]

9 But Esau said, "[a]I have plenty, my brother; let what you have be your own."

10 And Jacob said, "No, please, if now I have found favor in your sight, then take my present[4503] from my hand, [I]for I see your face as one sees the face of God, and you have received me favorably.[7521]

11 "Please take my [I][a]gift[1293] which has been brought to you, [b]because God has dealt graciously with me, and because I have [II]plenty." Thus he urged him and he took *it.*

12 Then [I]Esau said, "Let us take our journey and go, and I will go before you."

13 But he said to him, "My lord

22 [a]Deut. 3:16; Josh. 12:2
24 [a]Hos. 12:3, 4
26 [a]Hos. 12:4
28 [I]I.e., he who strives with God; or, God strives [a]Gen. 35:10; 1Kin. 18:31
29 [a]Judg. 13:17, 18
30 [I]I.e., the face of God [II]Lit., *soul* [a]Gen. 16:13; Ex. 24:10, 11; 33:20; Num. 12:8; Judg. 6:22; 13:22
31 [a]Judg. 8:8
1 [I]Or, *to* [a]Gen. 32:6
2 [I]Lit., *first* [II]Lit., *behind*
3 [a]Gen. 42:6; 43:26
4 [a]Gen. 45:14, 15
5 [I]Or, *What relation are these to you?* [a]Gen. 48:9; Ps. 127:3; Is. 8:18
6 [I]Lit., *they and*
8 [a]Gen. 32:13-16 [b]Gen. 32:5
9 [a]Gen. 27:39, 40
10 [I]Lit., *for therefore I have seen your face like seeing God's face*
11 [I]Lit., *blessing* [II]Lit., *all* [a]1Sam. 25:27 [b]Gen. 30:43
12 [I]Lit., *he*

🗝 **32:28** The Hebrew name Israel means "striver with God."
🗝 **32:30** The name Peniel in Hebrew means "face of God."

knows that the children are frail and that
the flocks and herds which are nursing
are [I]a care to me. And if they are driven
hard one day,[3117] all the flocks will die.
14 "Please let my lord pass on[5674]
before his servant; and I will proceed
at my leisure, according to the pace of
the cattle[4399] that are before me and
according to the pace of the children,
until I come to my lord at [a]Seir."
15 And Esau said, "Please let me
leave with you some of the people[5971]
who are with me." But he said, "[I]What
need is there? [a]Let me find favor in the
sight of my lord."
16 So Esau returned that day on his
way to Seir.
17 And Jacob journeyed to [Ia]Suc-
coth; and built for himself a house,[1004]
and made[6213] booths[5521] for his livestock,
therefore the place is named[7121] Succoth.

Jacob Settles in Shechem

18 Now Jacob came safely to the
city of [a]Shechem, which is in the land[776]
of Canaan, when he came from [b]Paddan-
aram, and camped before the city.
19 And [a]he bought the piece of
land[7704] where he had pitched his tent[168]
from the hand of the sons[1121] of Hamor,
Shechem's father, for one hundred
[I]pieces of money.
20 Then he erected[5324] there an al-
tar,[4196] and called it [I]El-Elohe-Israel.[415]

The Treachery of Jacob's Sons

34 Now [a]Dinah the daughter of
Leah, whom she had borne to
Jacob, went out to [I]visit[7200] the daughters of the land.[776]
2 And when Shechem the son of Hamor [a]the Hivite, the prince[5387] of the
land,[776] saw her, he took her and lay
with her [I]by force.
3 And [I]he was deeply attracted to
Dinah the daughter of Jacob, and he
loved[157] the girl and [II]spoke tenderly[3820]
to her.
4 So Shechem [a]spoke to his father
Hamor, saying, "Get me this young girl
for a wife."
5 Now Jacob heard that he had
defiled[2930] Dinah his daughter; but his
sons were with his livestock in the
field,[7704] so Jacob kept silent until they
came in.
6 Then Hamor the father of Shechem went out to Jacob to speak with
him.
7 Now the sons[1121] of Jacob came
in from the field when they heard *it;*
and the men[582] were grieved, and they
were very angry[2734] because he had
done[6213] a [Ia]disgraceful thing in Israel
[II]by lying with Jacob's daughter, for such
a thing ought not to be done.
8 But Hamor spoke with them, saying, "The soul of my son Shechem
longs[2836] for your daughter; please give
her to him [I]in marriage.
9 "And intermarry with us; give
your daughters to us, and take our
daughters for yourselves.
10 "Thus you shall [I]live with us, and
[a]the land shall be *open* before you;
[I]live and [b]trade in it, and [c]acquire property in it."
11 Shechem also said to her father
and to her brothers, "If I find favor[2580]
in your sight, then I will give whatever
you say to me.
12 "Ask me ever so much bridal[4119]
payment and gift, and I will give according as you say to me; but give me the
girl [I]in marriage."
13 But Jacob's sons answered Shechem and his father Hamor, with deceit,[4820] and spoke to them, because he
had defiled Dinah their sister.[269]
14 And they said to them, "We can-
not do[6213] this thing,[1697] to give our sister to [a]one[376] who is uncircumcised,[6190]
for that would be a disgrace[2781] to us.
15 "Only on this *condition* will we
consent to you: if you will become like
us, in that every male[2145] of you be circumcised,
16 then we will give our daughters
to you, and we will take your daughters
for ourselves, and we will [I]live with you
and become one people.[5971]

13 [I]Lit., *upon me*
14 [a]Gen. 32:3
15 [I]Lit., *Why this?* [a]Ruth 2:13
17 [I]I.e., booths [a]Josh. 13:27; Judg. 8:5, 14; Ps. 60:6
18 [a]Gen. 12:6; Josh. 24:1; Judg. 9:1 [b]Gen. 25:20; 28:2
19 [I]Heb., *qesitah* [a]Josh. 24:32; John 4:5
20 [I]I.e., God, the God of Israel
1 [I]Lit., *see* [a]Gen. 30:21
2 [I]Lit., *and humbled her* [a]Gen. 34:30
3 [I]Lit., *his soul clung* [II]Lit., *spoke to the heart of the girl*
4 [a]Judg. 14:2
7 [I]Lit., *senseless* [II]Lit., *to lie* [a]Deut. 22:20-30; Judg. 20:6; 2Sam. 13:12
8 [I]Lit., *for a wife*
10 [I]Lit., *dwell* [a]Gen. 13:9; 20:15 [b]Gen. 42:34 [c]Gen. 47:27
12 [I]Lit., *for a wife*
14 [a]Gen. 17:14
16 [I]Lit., *dwell*

17 "But if you will not listen[8085] to us to be circumcised, then we will take our daughter and go."

18 Now their words[1697] seemed [I]reasonable[3190] to Hamor and Shechem, Hamor's son.

19 And the young man did not delay to do the thing, because he was delighted[2654] with Jacob's daughter. Now he was more respected[3513] than all the household[1004] of his father.

20 So Hamor and his son Shechem came to the [a]gate of their city, and spoke to the men of their city, saying,

21 "These men are [I]friendly with us; therefore let them [II]live in the land and trade in it, for behold, the land is [III]large enough for them. Let us take their daughters [IV]in marriage, and give our daughters to them.

22 "Only on this *condition* will the men consent to us to [I]live with us, to become one people: that every male among us be circumcised[4135] as they are circumcised.

23 "Will not their livestock and their property and all their animals be ours? Only let us consent to them, and they will [I]live with us."

24 And [a]all who went out of the gate of his city listened to Hamor and to his son Shechem, and every male was circumcised, all who went out of the gate of his city.

25 Now it came about on the third day, when they were in pain, that two of Jacob's sons, [a]Simeon and Levi, Dinah's brothers,[251] each took his sword and came upon the city unawares, and killed[2026] every male.

26 And they killed[2026] Hamor and his son Shechem with the edge[6310] of the sword, and took Dinah from Shechem's house, and went forth.

27 Jacob's sons came upon the slain[2491] and looted the city, because they had defiled their sister.

28 They took their flocks and their herds and their donkeys, and that which was in the city and that which was in the field;

29 and they captured[7617] and looted all their wealth[2428] and all their little ones[2945] and their wives, even all that *was* in the houses.

30 Then Jacob said to Simeon and Levi, "You have [a]brought trouble on me, by [b]making me odious[887] among the inhabitants of the land, among [c]the Canaanites and the Perizzites; and [I][d]my men being few in number, they will gather together against me and [II]attack[5221] me and I shall be destroyed,[8045] I and my household."[1004]

31 But they said, "Should he [I]treat our sister as a harlot?"[2181]

Jacob Moves to Bethel

35 Then God[430] said to Jacob, "Arise, go up to [a]Bethel, and [I]live there; and make[6213] an altar[4196] there to [b]God,[410] who appeared to you [c]when you fled [II]from your brother[251] Esau."

2 So Jacob said to his [a]household[1004] and to all who were with him, "Put away[5493] [b]the foreign[5236] gods[430] which are among you, and [c]purify yourselves, and change your garments;

3 and let us arise and go up to Bethel; and I will make[6213] [a]an altar there to God, [b]who answered me in the day[3117] of my distress, and [c]has been with me [I]wherever I have gone."

4 So they gave to Jacob all the foreign gods which [I]they had, and the rings which were in their ears; and Jacob hid them under the [II]oak which was near Shechem.

5 As they journeyed, there was [I][a]a great terror upon the cities which were around them, and they did not pursue the sons of Jacob.

6 So Jacob came to [a]Luz (that is, Bethel), which is in the land[776] of Canaan, he and all the people[5971] who were with him.

7 And [a]he built an altar there, and called the place [I]El-bethel,[416] because there God[430] had revealed Himself to him, when he fled [II]from his brother.

8 Now [a]Deborah, Rebekah's nurse, died,[4191] and she was buried below

18 [I]Lit., *good*

20 [a]Ruth 4:1; 2Sam. 15:2

21 [I]Lit., *peaceful* [II]Lit., *dwell* [III]Lit., *wide of hands before them* [IV]Lit., *to us for wives*

22 [I]Lit., *dwell*

23 [I]Lit., *dwell*

24 [a]Gen. 23:10

25 [a]Gen. 49:5-7

30 [I]Lit., *I, few in number* [II]Lit., *smite* [a]Josh. 7:25 [b]Ex. 5:21; 1Sam. 13:4; 2Sam. 10:6 [c]Gen. 13:7; 34:2 [d]Gen. 46:26, 27; Deut. 4:27; 1Chr. 16:19; Ps. 105:12

31 [I]Or, *make*

1 [I]Lit., *dwell* [II]Lit., *from the face of* [a]Gen. 28:19 [b]Gen. 28:13 [c]Gen. 27:43

2 [a]Gen. 18:19; Josh. 24:15 [b]Gen. 31:19, 30, 34 [c]Ex. 19:10, 14

3 [I]Lit., *in the way which* [a]Gen. 28:20-22 [b]Ps. 107:6 [c]Gen. 28:15; 31:3, 42

4 [I]Lit., *were in their hand* [II]Or, *terebinth*

5 [I]Or, *a terror of God* [a]Ex. 15:16; 23:27; Deut. 2:25

6 [a]Gen. 28:19; 48:3

7 [I]I.e., the God of Bethel [II]Lit., *from the face of* [a]Gen. 35:3

8 [a]Gen. 24:59

Bethel under the oak; it was named [I]Allon-bacuth.

Jacob Is Named Israel

9 Then God appeared[7200] to Jacob again when he came from Paddan-aram, and He [a]blessed[1288] him.

10 And [a]God said to him,
"Your name is Jacob;
[I]You shall no longer be called[7121] Jacob,
But Israel shall be your name."
Thus He called [II]him Israel.

11 God also said to him,
"I am [Ia]God[410] Almighty;[7706]
[b]Be fruitful and multiply;
A nation[1471] and a [c]company[6951] of nations shall [II]come from you,
And [d]kings[4428] shall [II]come forth from [III]you.

12 "And [a]the land which I gave to Abraham and Isaac,
I will give it to you,
And I will give the land to your [I]descendants[2233] after you."

13 Then [a]God went up from him in the place where He had spoken[1696] with him.

14 And Jacob set up[5324] [a]a pillar[4676] in the place where He had spoken with him, a pillar of stone, and he poured[5258] out a [I]libation[5262] on it; he also poured oil[8081] on it.

15 So Jacob named the place where God had spoken[1696] with him, [Ia]Bethel.

16 Then they journeyed from Bethel; and when there was still some distance[776] to go to [a]Ephrath, Rachel began to give birth[3205] and she [I]suffered severe labor.

17 And it came about when she was in severe labor that the midwife said to her, "Do not fear,[3372] for now [a]you have *another* son."[1121]

18 And it came about as her soul was departing (for she died[4191]), that she named[7121] him [I]Ben-oni;[1126] but his father[1] called him [II]Benjamin.[1144]

19 So [a]Rachel died[4191] and was buried[6912] on the way to [b]Ephrath (that is, Bethlehem).

20 And Jacob set up a pillar over her grave; that is the [a]pillar of Rachel's grave[6900] to this day.[3117]

21 Then Israel journeyed on and pitched his tent[168] beyond the [Ia]tower of [II]Eder.

22 And it came about while Israel was dwelling in that land, that [a]Reuben went and lay with Bilhah his father's concubine; and Israel heard *of it.*

The Sons of Israel

Now there were twelve sons[1121] of Jacob—

🔑 23 [a]the sons of Leah: Reuben, Jacob's first-born, then Simeon and Levi and Judah and Issachar and Zebulun;

24 [a]the sons of Rachel: Joseph and Benjamin;

25 and [a]the sons of Bilhah, Rachel's maid: Dan and Naphtali;

26 and [a]the sons of Zilpah, Leah's maid: Gad and Asher. These are the sons of Jacob who were born to him in Paddan-aram.

27 And Jacob came to his father Isaac at [a]Mamre of [b]Kiriath-arba (that is, Hebron), where Abraham and Isaac had sojourned.[1481]

28 Now the days[3117] of Isaac were [a]one hundred and eighty years.

29 And Isaac breathed his last[1478] and died,[4191] and was [a]gathered to his people, an [b]old[2205] man [I]of ripe age;[3117] and [c]his sons Esau and Jacob buried[6912] him.

8 [I]I.e., oak of weeping
9 [a]Gen. 32:29
10 [I]Lit., *Your name* [II]Lit., *his name* [a]Gen. 17:5; 32:28
11 [I]Heb., *El Shaddai* [II]Or, *come into being* [III]Lit., *your loins* [a]Gen. 17:1; 28:3; Ex. 6:3 [b]Gen. 9:1, 7 [c]Gen. 48:4 [d]Gen. 17:6, 16; 36:31
12 [I]Lit., *seed* [a]Gen. 12:7; 13:15; 26:3, 4; 28:13; Ex. 32:13
13 [a]Gen. 17:22; 18:33
14 [I]Or, *drink offering* [a]Gen. 28:18, 19; 31:45
15 [I]I.e., the house of God [a]Gen. 28:19
16 [I]Lit., *had difficulty in her giving birth* [a]Gen. 35:19; 48:7; Ruth 4:11; Mic. 5:2
17 [a]Gen. 30:24
18 [I]I.e., the son of my sorrow [II]I.e., the son of the right hand
19 [a]Gen. 48:7 [b]Ruth 1:2; 4:11; Mic. 5:2
20 [a]1Sam. 10:2
21 [I]Heb., *Migdal-eder* [II]Or, *flock* [a]Mic. 4:8
22 [a]Gen. 49:4; 1Chr. 5:1
23 [a]Gen. 29:31-35; 30:18-20; 46:8; Ex. 1:1-4
24 [a]Gen. 30:22-24; 35:18
25 [a]Gen. 30:5-8
26 [a]Gen. 30:10-13
27 [a]Gen. 13:18; 18:1; 23:19 [b]Josh. 14:15
28 [a]Gen. 25:26
29 [I]Lit., *and satisfied with days* [a]Gen. 25:8; 49:33 [b]Gen. 15:15 [c]Gen. 25:9

🔑 **35:23-26** This brief listing of Jacob's twelve sons and their mothers follows a longer account of the circumstances of their births. Although later there would be twelve tribes of Israel, Jacob's sons and the heads of the tribes are not the same in every case. Ten of the sons, excluding Levi and Joseph, had tribes named for them. Levi headed up a special thirteenth tribe of priests and their assistants. Jacob's favorite son was Joseph. So, he was afforded the honor of having two tribes come from him through his sons, Ephraim and Manasseh.

Esau Moves

36 Now these are *the records of* the generations[8435] of [a]Esau (that is, Edom).

2 Esau [a]took his wives from the daughters of Canaan: Adah the daughter of Elon the Hittite, and [b]Oholibamah the daughter of Anah and the [c]granddaughter of Zibeon the Hivite;

3 also Basemath, Ishmael's daughter, the sister of Nebaioth.

4 And Adah bore [a]Eliphaz to Esau, and Basemath bore Reuel,

5 and Oholibamah bore Jeush and Jalam and Korah. These are the sons[1121] of Esau who were born to him in the land of Canaan.

6 [a]Then Esau took his wives and his sons and his daughters and all [I]his household,[5315] and his livestock and all his cattle and all his goods which he had acquired in the land[776] of Canaan, and went to *another* land[776] away from his brother[251] Jacob.

7 [a]For their property had become too great for them to [I]live together, and the [b]land where they [c]sojourned[4033] could not sustain[5375] them because of their livestock.

8 So Esau lived in the hill country of [a]Seir; Esau is [b]Edom.

9 These then are *the records of* the generations of Esau the father[1] of [I]the Edomites in the hill country of Seir.

Descendants of Esau

10 These are the names of Esau's sons: Eliphaz the son of Esau's wife Adah, Reuel the son of Esau's wife Basemath.

11 And the sons of Eliphaz were Teman, Omar, [I]Zepho and Gatam and Kenaz.

12 And Timna was a concubine of Esau's son Eliphaz and she bore [a]Amalek to Eliphaz. These are the sons of Esau's wife Adah.

13 And these are the sons of Reuel: Nahath and Zerah, Shammah and Mizzah. These were the sons of Esau's wife Basemath.

14 And these were the sons of Esau's wife Oholibamah, the daughter of Anah and the [I]granddaughter of Zibeon: [II]she bore to Esau, Jeush and Jalam and Korah.

15 These are the chiefs[441] of the sons of Esau. The sons of Eliphaz, the first-born of Esau, are chief Teman, chief Omar, chief Zepho, chief Kenaz,

16 chief Korah, chief Gatam, chief Amalek. These are the chiefs [I]descended from Eliphaz in the land of Edom; these are the sons of Adah.

17 And these are the sons of Reuel, Esau's son: chief Nahath, chief Zerah, chief Shammah, chief Mizzah. These are the chiefs [I]descended from Reuel in the land of Edom; these are the sons of Esau's wife Basemath.

18 And these are the sons of Esau's wife Oholibamah: chief Jeush, chief Jalam, chief Korah. These are the chiefs [I]descended from Esau's wife Oholibamah, the daughter of Anah.

19 These are the sons of Esau (that is, Edom), and these are their chiefs.

20 These are the sons of Seir [a]the Horite, the inhabitants of the land: Lotan and Shobal and Zibeon and Anah,

21 and Dishon and Ezer and Dishan. These are the chiefs [I]descended from the Horites, the sons[1121] of Seir in the land of Edom.

22 And the sons of Lotan were Hori and [I]Hemam; and Lotan's sister was Timna.

23 And these are the sons of Shobal: [I]Alvan and Manahath and Ebal, [II]Shepho and Onam.

24 And these are the sons of Zibeon: Aiah and Anah—he is the Anah who found the hot springs in the wilderness when he was pasturing the donkeys of his father Zibeon.

25 And these are the children of Anah: Dishon, and Oholibamah, the daughter of Anah.

26 And these are the sons of [I][a]Dishon: [II]Hemdan and Eshban and Ithran and Cheran.

27 These are the sons of Ezer: Bilhan and Zaavan and [I]Akan.

---

1 [a]Gen. 25:30
2 [a]Gen. 28:9 [b]Gen. 36:25 [c]Gen. 36:24
4 [a]1Chr. 1:35
6 [I]Lit., *the souls of his house* [a]Gen. 12:5
7 [I]Lit., *dwell* [a]Gen. 13:6 [b]Gen. 17:8; Heb. 11:9 [c]1Chr. 29:15; Ps. 39:12
8 [a]Gen. 32:3 [b]Gen. 36:1, 19
9 [I]Lit., *Edom*
11 [I]In 1Chr. 1:36, *Zephi*
12 [a]Ex. 17:8-16; Num. 24:20; Deut. 25:17-19; 1Sam. 15:2, 3
14 [I]Gr., *son* [II]Lit., *and she*
16 [I]Lit., *of Eliphaz*
17 [I]Lit., *of Reuel*
18 [I]Lit., *of Oholibamah, Esau's wife*
20 [a]Gen. 14:6; Deut. 2:12, 22; 1Chr. 1:38-42
21 [I]Lit., *of the Horites*
22 [I]In 1Chr. 1:39, *Homam*
23 [I]In 1Chr. 1:40, *Alian* [II]In 1Chr. 1:40, *Shephi*
26 [I]Heb., *Dishan* [II]In 1Chr. 1:41, *Hamran* [a]1Chr. 1:41
27 [I]In 1Chr. 1:42, *Jaakan*

28 These are the sons of Dishan:
Uz and Aran.
29 These are the chiefs [I]descended
from the Horites: chief Lotan, chief Shobal, chief Zibeon, chief Anah,
30 chief Dishon, chief Ezer, chief
Dishan. These are the chiefs [I]descended
from the Horites, according to their *various* chiefs in the land of Seir.
31 Now these are the kings who
reigned[4427] in the land of Edom before
any [a]king reigned over the sons of Israel.
32 [I][a]Bela the son of Beor reigned
in Edom, and the name of his city was
Dinhabah.
33 Then Bela died,[4191] and Jobab the
son of Zerah of Bozrah became king in
his place.
34 Then Jobab died, and Husham
of the land of the Temanites became
king in his place.
35 Then Husham died, and Hadad
the son of Bedad, who [I]defeated[5221]
Midian in the field of Moab, became king
in his place; and the name of his city
was Avith.
36 Then Hadad died, and Samlah of
Masrekah became king in his place.
37 Then Samlah died, and Shaul of
Rehoboth on the *Euphrates* River became king in his place.
38 Then Shaul died, and Baal-hanan
the son of Achbor became king in his
place.
39 Then Baal-hanan the son of Achbor died, and [I]Hadar became king in his
place; and the name of his city was
[II]Pau; and his wife's name was Mehetabel, the daughter of Matred, daughter
of Mezahab.
40 Now these are the names of the
chiefs [I]descended from Esau, according
to their families[4940] *and* their localities,
by their names: chief Timna, chief
[II]Alvah, chief Jetheth,
41 chief Oholibamah, chief Elah,
chief Pinon,
42 chief Kenaz, chief Teman, chief
Mibzar,
⚿ 43 chief Magdiel, chief Iram. These
are the chiefs of Edom (that is, Esau,
the father of [I]the Edomites), according
to their habitations[4186] in the land of their
possession.[272]

Joseph's Dream

37 ⚿ Now Jacob lived in [a]the
land[776] [I]where his father[1] had sojourned,[4033] in the land of Canaan.
2 These are *the records of* the
generations[8435] of Jacob.
Joseph, when [a]seventeen years of
age,[1121] was pasturing the flock with his
brothers while he was *still* a youth, along
with [b]the sons[1121] of Bilhah and the sons
of Zilpah, his father's wives. And Joseph
brought back a [c]bad[7451] report about
them to their father.
3 Now Israel loved[157] Joseph more
than all his sons,[1121] because he was
[a]the son[1121] of his old age;[2208] and he
made[6213] him a [I][b]varicolored tunic.
4 And his brothers[251] saw[7200] that
their father loved him more than all his
brothers; and *so* they [a]hated[8130] him and

29 [I]Lit., *of the Horites*
30 [I]Lit., *of the Horites*
31 [a]Gen. 17:6, 16; 35:11; 1Chr. 1:43
32 [I]Lit., *And Bela* [a]1Chr. 1:43
35 [I]Or, *smote*
39 [I]In 1Chr. 1:50, *Hadad* [II]In 1Chr. 1:50, *Pai*
40 [I]Lit., *of Esau* [II]In 1Chr. 1:51, *Aliah*
43 [I]Heb., *Edom*
1 [I]Lit., *of his father's sojournings* [a]Gen. 17:8; 28:4
2 [a]Gen. 41:46 [b]Gen. 35:25, 26 [c]1Sam. 2:22-24
3 [I]Or, *full-length robe* [a]Gen. 44:20 [b]Gen. 37:23, 32
4 [a]Gen. 27:41; 1Sam. 17:28

⚿ **36:43** There are many believed to have been successors of the original inhabitants of Idumea and of the Horites. Esau has been called "the father of the Edomites" here. With Esau's immense family he retired to Mount Seir, from which they gradually dispossessed the existing population and held it for many generations. During the course of the Maccabean wars, the children of Esau lost their independent existence and merged with the house of Israel.

⚿ **37:1-11** Joseph was special from conception. He was God's answer to the prayers of his barren mother, Rachel. The princely robe given to him by his father was a source of jealousy among his brothers. The dreams that he had at this time were another source of envy for his brothers, but they were also a sign of God's special blessing to him. Later the ability to understand the dreams of others in Egypt (the butler, the baker, and Pharaoh) were further signs of God's use of him to accomplish His ends. Through much adversity in his life Joseph never complained. Later he became a fountainhead of blessing to his brothers as well as to all people in the region by providing food in time of famine. Joseph was the most important instrument whom God used to help his family to become a mighty nation which would depend upon God as Joseph did throughout his lifetime.

could not speak to him [I]on friendly terms.[7965]

5 Then Joseph [I][a]had a dream, and when he told[5046] it to his brothers, they hated him even more.

6 And he said to them, "Please listen to this dream which I have [I]had;

7 for behold, we were binding sheaves in the field,[7704] and lo, my sheaf rose up and also stood erect;[5324] and behold, your sheaves gathered around and [a]bowed down[7812] to my sheaf."

8 Then his brothers said to him, "[a]Are you actually going to reign[4427] over us? Or are you really going to rule[4910] over us?" So they hated him even more for his dreams and for his words.

9 Now he [I]had still another dream, and related it to his brothers, and said,[5608] "Lo, I have [I]had still another dream; and behold, the sun and the moon and eleven stars were bowing down to me."

10 And he related *it* to his father and to his brothers; and his father rebuked[1605] him and said to him, "What is this dream that you have [I]had? Shall I and your mother and [a]your brothers actually come to bow ourselves down[7812] before you to the ground?"[776]

11 And [a]his brothers[251] were jealous[7065] of him, but his father [b]kept[8104] the saying[1697] *in mind.*

12 Then his brothers went to pasture their father's flock in Shechem.

13 And Israel said to Joseph, "Are not your brothers pasturing *the flock* in [a]Shechem? Come, and I will send you to them." And he said to him, "[I]I will go."

14 Then he said to him, "Go now and see about the welfare[7965] of your brothers and the welfare of the flock; and bring word[1697] back to me." So he sent him from the valley[6010] of [a]Hebron, and he came to Shechem.

15 And a man[376] found him, and behold, he was wandering in the field; and the man asked him, [I]"What are you looking for?"

16 And he said, "I am looking for my brothers; please tell[5046] me where they are pasturing *the flock.*"

17 Then the man said, "They have moved from here; for I heard *them* say, 'Let us go to [a]Dothan.'" So Joseph went after his brothers and found them at Dothan.

The Plot against Joseph

18 [I]When they saw[7200] him from a distance and before he came close to them, they [a]plotted against him to put him to death.

19 And they said to one[376] another,[251] "[I]Here comes this dreamer![1167]

20 "Now then, come and let us kill[2026] him and throw him into one of the pits;[953] and [a]we will say, 'A wild[7451] beast[2416] devoured him.' Then let us see[7200] what will become of his dreams!"

21 But [a]Reuben heard *this* and rescued him out of their hands[3027] and said, "Let us not [I]take his life."[5221]

22 Reuben further said to them, "Shed[8210] no blood.[1818] Throw him into this pit that is in the wilderness, but do not lay hands on him"—that he might rescue him out of their hands, to restore him to his father.

23 So it came about, when Joseph [I]reached his brothers, that they stripped Joseph of his [II]tunic, the varicolored tunic that was on him;

24 and they took him and threw him into the pit. Now the pit was empty, without any water in it.

🗝 **25** Then they sat down to eat [I]a meal. And as they raised their eyes and looked,[7200] behold, a caravan of [a]Ishmaelites was coming from Gilead, with their camels bearing[5375] [II][b]aromatic gum and [III][c]balm and [IV]myrrh,[3910] [V]on their way to bring *them* down to Egypt.

4 [I]Lit., *in peace*
5 [I]Lit., *dreamed* [a]Gen. 28:12; 31:10, 11, 24
6 [I]Lit., *dreamed*
7 [a]Gen. 42:6, 9; 43:26; 44:14
8 [a]Gen. 49:26; Deut. 33:16
9 [I]Lit., *dreamed*
10 [I]Lit., *dreamed* [a]Gen. 27:29
11 [a]Acts 7:9 [b]Dan. 7:28; Luke 2:19, 51
13 [I]Lit., *Behold me.* [a]Gen. 33:18-20
14 [a]Gen. 13:18; 23:2, 19; 35:27; Josh. 14:14, 15; Judg. 1:10
15 [I]Lit., *saying, "What. . .?"*
17 [a]2Kin. 6:13
18 [I]Or, *And* [a]Ps. 31:13; 37:12, 32; Mark 14:1; John 11:53; Acts 23:12
19 [I]Lit., *Behold, this master of dreams comes*
20 [a]Gen. 37:32, 33
21 [I]Lit., *smite his soul* [a]Gen. 42:22
23 [I]Lit., *came to* [II]Or, *full-length robe*
25 [I]Lit., *bread* [II]Or, *ladanum spice* [III]Or, *mastic* [IV]Or, *resinous bark* [V]Lit., *going* [a]Gen. 16:11, 12; 37:28; 39:1 [b]Gen. 43:11 [c]Jer. 8:22; 46:11

🗝 **37:25,28,36** The Midianites and the Ishmaelites were often confused because of their common descent from Abraham and the similarity of their customs and mode of life. It is possible that the Ishmaelites may have been the owners of the caravan, which was mostly made of Midianites.

26 And Judah said to his brothers,
"What profit is it for us to kill our
brother[251] and [a]cover up[3680] his blood?
27 "[a]Come and let us sell him to
the Ishmaelites and not lay our hands
on him; for he is our brother, our *own*
flesh."[1320] And his brothers listened *to*
him.
🔑28 Then some [a]Midianite traders
passed by,[5674] so they pulled *him* up
and lifted[5927] Joseph out of the pit, and
[b]sold [I]him to the Ishmaelites for twenty
shekels of silver. Thus [c]they brought Joseph into Egypt.
29 Now Reuben returned to the pit,
and behold, Joseph was not in the pit;
so he [a]tore his garments.
30 And he returned to his brothers
and said, "[a]The boy is not *there;* as for
me, where am I to go?"
31 So [a]they took Joseph's tunic, and
slaughtered[7819] a male goat,[8163] and
dipped[2881] the tunic in the blood;[1818]
32 and they sent the varicolored
tunic and brought it to their father and
said, "We found this; please [I]examine[5234]
it to *see* whether it is your son's tunic
or not."
33 Then he [I]examined it and said,
"It is my son's tunic. [a]A wild beast has
devoured him; [b]Joseph has surely been
torn to pieces!"
34 So Jacob [a]tore his clothes, and
put sackcloth on his loins, and mourned
for his son many days.
35 Then all his sons[1121] and all his
daughters arose to comfort[5162] him, but
he refused[3985] to be comforted. And he
said, "Surely I will [a]go down to Sheol[7585]
in mourning for my son." So his father
wept for him.
🔑36 Meanwhile, the [I]Midianites [a]sold
him in Egypt to Potiphar, Pharaoh's
officer,[5631] the captain[8269] of the bodyguard.

Judah and Tamar

38 And it came about at that
time,[6256] that Judah [I]departed
from his brothers, and [II]visited a
certain[376] [a]Adullamite, whose name was
Hirah.
2 And Judah saw there a daughter
of a certain[376] Canaanite whose name
was [a]Shua; and he took her and went
in to her.
3 So she conceived and bore a
son[1121] and he named him [a]Er.
4 Then she conceived again and
bore a son and named him [a]Onan.
5 And she bore still another son and
named him [a]Shelah; and it was at Chezib
[I]that she bore him.
6 Now Judah took a wife for Er his
first-born, and her name *was* Tamar.
7 But [a]Er, Judah's first-born, was
evil[7451] in the sight of the LORD, so the
LORD took his life.
🔑8 Then Judah said to Onan, "[a]Go
in to your brother's[251] wife, and perform
your duty as a brother-in-law to her,
and raise up [I]offspring[2233] for your
brother."
9 And Onan knew that the [Ia]offspring
would not be his; so it came about that
when he went in to his brother's wife,
he [II]wasted[7843] his seed on the
ground,[776] in order not to give [I]offspring
to his brother.
10 But what he did[6213] was displeasing[3415] in the sight of the LORD;
so He [a]took his life also.
11 Then Judah said to his daughter-
in-law Tamar, "[a]Remain a widow in your
father's house until my son Shelah grows
up"; for he [I]thought, "[II]*I am afraid* that
he too may die[4191] like his brothers."
So Tamar went and lived in her father's
house.
12 Now [I]after a considerable
time[3117] Shua's daughter, the wife of Judah, died; and when [II]the time of mourning was ended, Judah went up to his
sheepshearers at [a]Timnah, he and his
friend[7453] Hirah the Adullamite.
13 And it was told[5046] to Tamar,
"[I]Behold, your father-in-law is going up
to [a]Timnah to shear his sheep."
14 So she [I]removed her widow's

26 [a]Gen. 37:20
27 [a]Gen. 42:21
28 [I]Lit., *Joseph* [a]Gen. 37:25; Judg. 6:1-3; 8:22, 24 [b]Gen. 45:4, 5; Ps. 105:17; Acts 7:9 [c]Gen. 39:1
29 [a]Gen. 37:34; 44:13
30 [a]Gen. 42:13, 36
31 [a]Gen. 37:3, 23
32 [I]Or, *recognize*
33 [I]Or, *recognized* [a]Gen. 37:20 [b]Gen. 44:28
34 [a]Gen. 37:29
35 [a]Gen. 25:8; 35:29; 42:38; 44:29, 31
36 [I]Lit., *Medanites* [a]Gen. 39:1

1 [I]Lit., *went down* [II]Lit., *turned aside to* [a]Josh. 15:35; 1Sam. 22:1
2 [a]1Chr. 2:3
3 [a]Gen. 46:12; Num. 26:19
4 [a]Gen. 46:12
5 [I]Lit., *when* [a]Num. 26:20
7 [a]Gen. 46:12; Num. 26:19; 1Chr. 2:3
8 [I]Lit., *seed* [a]Deut. 25:5, 6; Matt. 22:24
9 [I]Lit., *seed* [II]Lit., *spilled on the ground* [a]Deut. 25:6
10 [a]Gen. 46:12; Num. 26:19
11 [I]Lit., *said* [II]Lit., *Lest he also die* [a]Ruth 1:12, 13
12 [I]Lit., *the days became many and* [II]Lit., *Judah was comforted, he* [a]Josh. 15:10, 57
13 [I]Lit., *saying, Behold* [a]Josh. 15:10, 57; Judg. 14:1
14 [I]Lit., *removed from herself*

🔑 **38:8** See note on Ruth 4:1-12.

garments and [a]covered[3680] *herself* with a [II]veil, and wrapped herself, and sat in the gateway of [III]Enaim, which is on the road to Timnah; for she saw that Shelah had grown up, and [b]she had not been given to him as a wife.[802]

15 When Judah saw[7200] her, he thought[2803] she *was* a harlot,[2181] for she had covered her face.

16 So he turned aside to her by the road, and said, "[I]Here now, let me come in to you"; for he did not know[3045] that she was his daughter-in-law. And she said, "What will you give me, that you may come in to me?"

17 He said, therefore, "I will send you a [I]kid from the flock." She said, moreover, "Will you give a pledge until you send *it?*"

18 And he said, "What pledge shall I give you?" And she said, "[a]Your seal and your cord, and your staff[4294] that is in your hand." So he gave *them* to her, and went in to her, and she conceived by him.

19 Then she arose and departed, and [I]removed her [II]veil and put on her widow's garments.

20 When Judah sent the [I]kid by his friend the Adullamite, to receive the pledge from the woman's[802] hand, he did not find her.

21 And he asked[7592] the men[582] of her place, saying, "Where is the temple prostitute[6948] who was by the road at Enaim?" But they said, "There has been no temple prostitute here."

22 So he returned to Judah, and said, "I did not find her; and furthermore, the men of the place said, 'There has been no temple prostitute here.' "

23 Then Judah said, "Let her [I]keep them, lest we become a laughingstock. [II]After all, I sent this kid, but you did not find her."

24 Now it was about three months later that Judah was informed, "[I]Your daughter-in-law Tamar has played the harlot,[2181] and behold, she is also with child by harlotry."[2183] Then Judah said, "Bring her out and [a]let her be burned!"

25 It was while she was being brought out that she sent to her father-in-law, saying, "I am with child by the man[376] to whom these things belong." And she said, "[a]Please examine[5234] and see, whose signet ring and cords and staff are these?"

26 And Judah recognized[5234] *them,* and said, "[a]She is more righteous[6663] than I, inasmuch as [b]I did not give her to my son Shelah." And he did not [I]have relations with her again.

27 And it came about at the time[6256] she was giving birth, that behold, there were [a]twins in her womb.[990]

28 Moreover, it took place while she was giving birth,[3205] one put out a hand, and the midwife took and tied a scarlet *thread* on his hand,[3027] saying, "This one came out first."[7223]

29 But it came about as he drew back his hand, that behold, his brother came out. Then she said, "What a breach[6556] you have made for yourself!" So he was named [Ia]Perez.[6557]

30 And afterward his brother came out who had the scarlet *thread* on his hand; and he was named [Ia]Zerah.

Joseph's Success in Egypt

39 Now Joseph had been taken down to Egypt; and Potiphar, an Egyptian officer[5631] of Pharaoh, the captain[8269] of the bodyguard, bought him [I]from the [a]Ishmaelites, who had taken him down there.

2 And [a]the LORD was with Joseph, so he became a [I]successful man.[376] And he was in the house[1004] of his master,[113] the Egyptian.

3 Now his master [a]saw[7200] that the LORD was with him and *how* the LORD [b]caused all that he did[6213] to prosper in his hand.

4 So Joseph [a]found favor[2580] in his sight, and [I]became his personal servant;[8334] and he made him overseer[6485] over his house,[1004] and [b]all that he owned he put in his [II]charge.

5 And it came about that from the time[227] he made him overseer in his house, and over all that he owned, the

---

14 [II]Or, *shawl* [III]In Josh. 15:34, *Enam* [a]Gen. 24:65 [b]Gen. 38:11, 26

16 [I]Or, *Come, now*

17 [I]Lit., *kid of goats*

18 [a]Gen. 38:25; 41:42

19 [I]Lit., *removed from herself* [II]Or, *shawl*

20 [I]Lit., *kid of goats by the hand of*

23 [I]Lit., *take for herself* [II]Lit., *Behold*

24 [I]Lit., *saying, Your* [a]Lev. 21:9

25 [a]Gen. 37:32

26 [I]Lit., *know her yet again* [a]1Sam. 24:17 [b]Gen. 38:14

27 [a]Gen. 25:24-26

29 [I]I.e., a breach [a]Gen. 46:12; Ruth 4:12

30 [I]I.e., a dawning or brightness [a]1Chr. 2:4

1 [I]Lit., *from the hand of* [a]Gen. 37:25, 28, 36; Ps. 105:17

2 [I]Or, *prosperous* [a]Gen. 39:3, 21, 23; Acts 7:9

3 [a]Gen. 21:22; 26:28 [b]Ps. 1:3

4 [I]Or, *ministered to him* [II]Lit., *hand* [a]Gen. 18:3; 19:19 [b]Gen. 24:2; 39:8, 22

LORD [a]blessed[1288] the Egyptian's house on account of Joseph; thus [b]the LORD's blessing[1293] was upon all that he owned, in the house and in the field.

6 So he left[5800] everything he owned in Joseph's [I]charge;[3027] and with him *there* he did not [II]concern[3045] himself with anything except the [III]food which he [IV]ate. Now Joseph was [a]handsome in form and appearance.

7 And it came about after these events [a]that his master's wife[802] [I]looked with desire at Joseph, and she said, "[b]Lie with me."

8 But [a]he refused[3985] and said to his master's wife, "Behold, with me *here,* my master [I]does not concern[3045] himself with anything in the house, and he has put all that he owns in my [II]charge.

9 "[I][a]There is no one greater in this house than I, and he has withheld nothing from me except you, because you are his wife. How then could I do[6213] this great evil,[7451] and [b]sin[2398] against God?"[430]

10 And it came about as she spoke to Joseph day after day,[3117] that he did not listen[8085] to her to lie beside her, *or* be with her.

11 Now it happened [I]one day[3117] that he went into the house to do his work,[4399] and none of the men[582] of the household was there inside.

12 And she caught him by his garment, saying, "Lie with me!" And he left his garment in her hand and fled, and went outside.

13 [I]When she saw[7200] that he had left[5800] his garment in her hand, and had fled outside,

14 she called[7121] to the men of her household, and said to them, "See,[7200] he has brought in a [I]Hebrew[5680] to us to make sport of us; he came in to me to lie with me, and I [II]screamed.

15 "And it came about when he heard that I raised my voice and [I]screamed, that he left his garment beside me and fled, and went outside."

16 So she [I]left his garment beside her until his master[113] came home.

17 Then she [a]spoke to him [I]with these words, "[II]The Hebrew slave,[5650] whom you brought to us, came in to me to make sport of me;

18 and it happened as I raised my voice and [I]screamed, that he left his garment beside me and fled outside."

Joseph Imprisoned

19 Now it came about when his master heard the words of his wife, which she spoke to him, saying, "[I]This is what your slave did to me," that [a]his anger[693] burned.[2734]

20 So Joseph's master took him and [a]put him into the jail, the place where the king's prisoners were confined; and he was there in the jail.

21 But [a]the LORD was with Joseph and extended kindness[2617] to him, and [b]gave him favor[2580] in the sight of the chief[8269] jailer.

22 And the chief jailer [a]committed to Joseph's [I]charge all the prisoners who were in the jail; so that whatever was done there, he was [II]responsible *for it.*

23 [a]The chief jailer did not supervise anything under [I]Joseph's charge because [b]the LORD was with him; and whatever he did, [c]the LORD made to prosper.

Joseph Interprets a Dream

40 Then it came about after these things [a]the cupbearer and the baker for the king of Egypt offended[2398] their lord,[113] the king of Egypt.

2 And Pharaoh was [a]furious with his two officials,[5631] the chief[8269] cupbearer and the chief baker.

3 So he put them in confinement in the house of the [a]captain[8269] of the bodyguard, in the jail, the *same* place where Joseph was imprisoned.

4 And the captain of the bodyguard put Joseph in charge[6485] of them, and he [I]took care[8334] of them; and they were in confinement for [II]some time.[3117]

5 Then the cupbearer and the baker for the king of Egypt, who were confined in jail, both had a dream the same night, each man[376] with his *own* dream *and*

5 [a]Gen. 30:27 [b]Deut. 28:3, 4, 11

6 [I]Lit., *hand* [II]Lit., *know* [III]Lit., *bread* [IV]Or, *used to eat* [a]Gen. 29:17; 1Sam. 16:12

7 [I]Lit., *lifted up her eyes at* [a]Prov. 7:15-20 [b]2Sam. 13:11

8 [I]Lit., *does not know what is in the house* [II]Lit., *hand* [a]Prov. 6:23, 24

9 [I]Or, *He is not greater* [a]Gen. 41:40 [b]Gen. 20:6; 42:18; 2Sam. 12:13; Ps. 51:4

11 [I]Lit., *about this day*

13 [I]Lit., *And it came about when*

14 [I]Lit., *Hebrew man* [II]Lit., *called with a great voice.*

15 [I]Lit., *called out*

16 [I]Lit., *let. . .lie beside*

17 [I]Lit., *according to* [II]Lit., *saying, "The* [a]Ex. 23:1; Prov. 26:28

18 [I]Lit., *called out*

19 [I]Lit., *According to these things your slave* [a]Prov. 6:34

20 [a]Gen. 40:3; Ps. 105:18

21 [a]Gen. 39:2; Ps. 105:19; Acts 7:9 [b]Ex. 3:21; 11:3; 12:36

22 [I]Lit., *hand* [II]Lit., *the doer* [a]Gen. 39:4; 40:3, 4

23 [I]Lit., *his hand* [a]Gen. 39:3, 8 [b]Gen. 39:2, 3 [c]Gen. 39:3

1 [a]Gen. 40:11, 13; Neh. 1:11

2 [a]Prov. 16:14

3 [a]Gen. 39:1, 20

4 [I]Lit., *ministered to* [II]Lit., *days*

each dream with its *own* interpretation.

6 [I]When Joseph came to them in the morning and observed[7200] them, [II]behold, they were dejected.[2196]

7 And he asked Pharaoh's officials who were with him in confinement in his master's house, "[I][a]Why are your faces so sad[7451] today?"[3117]

8 Then they said to him, "[a]We have [I]had a dream and there is no one to interpret it." Then Joseph said to them, "[b]Do not interpretations belong to God?[430] Tell[5608] *it* to me, please."

9 So the chief cupbearer told his dream to Joseph, and said to him, "In my dream, [I]behold, *there was* a vine in front of me;

10 and on the vine *were* three branches. And as it was budding, its blossoms came out, *and* its clusters produced ripe grapes.

11 "Now Pharaoh's cup was in my hand;[3027] so I took the grapes and squeezed them into Pharaoh's cup, and I put the cup into Pharaoh's [I]hand."

12 Then Joseph said to him, "This is the [a]interpretation of it: the three branches are three days;[3117]

13 within three more days Pharaoh will [I]lift up[5375] your head and restore you to your [II]office; and you will put Pharaoh's cup into his hand according to your former custom when you were his cupbearer.

14 "Only [I]keep me in mind[2142] when it goes well[3190] with you, and please [a]do[6213] me a kindness[2617] [II]by mentioning[2142] me to Pharaoh, and get me out of this house.

15 "For [a]I was in fact kidnapped from the land[776] of the Hebrews, and even here I have done nothing that they should have put[7760] me into the [I]dungeon."[953]

16 When the chief baker saw[7200] that he had interpreted favorably,[2896] he said to Joseph, "I also *saw* in my dream, and behold, *there were* three baskets of white bread on my head;

17 and in the top[5945] basket *there were* some of all [I]sorts of baked food for Pharaoh, and the birds were eating them out of the basket on my head."

18 Then Joseph answered and said, "This is its interpretation: the three baskets are three days;

19 within three more days Pharaoh will lift up your head from you and will hang you on a tree; and the birds will eat your flesh[1320] off you."

20 Thus it came about on the third day, *which was* [a]Pharaoh's birthday, that he made a feast[4960] for all his servants; [b]and he lifted up the head of the chief cupbearer and the head of the chief baker among his servants.

21 And he restored the chief cupbearer to his [I]office, and [a]he put the cup into Pharaoh's [II]hand;

22 but [a]he hanged the chief baker, just as Joseph had interpreted to them.

23 Yet the chief cupbearer did not remember Joseph, but [a]forgot him.

Pharaoh's Dream

41 Now it happened at the end of two full[3117] years that Pharaoh had a dream, and behold, he was standing by the Nile.

2 And lo, from the Nile there came up seven cows,[6510] sleek and [I]fat;[1277] and they grazed in the [a]marsh grass.

3 Then behold, seven other cows came up after them from the Nile, ugly[7451][4758] and [I]gaunt,[1851][1320] and they stood by the *other* cows on the bank[8193] of the Nile.

4 And the ugly and [I]gaunt cows ate up the seven sleek and fat cows. Then Pharaoh awoke.

5 And he fell asleep and dreamed a second time; and behold, seven ears of grain came up on a single stalk, plump and good.[2896]

6 Then behold, seven ears, thin and scorched by the east wind, sprouted up after them.

7 And the thin ears swallowed up the seven plump and full ears. Then Pharaoh awoke, and behold, *it was* a dream.

8 Now it came about in the morning that [a]his spirit[7307] was troubled, so he

6 [I]Or, *And* [II]Lit., *and behold*

7 [I]Lit., *saying, Why* [a]Neh. 2:2

8 [I]Lit., *dreamed* [a]Gen. 41:15 [b]Gen. 41:16; Dan. 2:27, 28

9 [I]Lit., *and behold*

11 [I]Lit., *palm*

12 [a]Dan. 2:36; 4:18, 19

13 [I]Or possibly, *forgive you* [II]Lit., *place*

14 [I]Lit., *remember me with yourself* [II]Lit., *and mention* [a]Josh. 2:12; 1Sam. 20:14; 1Kin. 2:7

15 [I]Or, *pit* [a]Gen. 37:26-28

17 [I]Lit., *food for Pharaoh made by a baker*

20 [a]Matt. 14:6 [b]2Kin. 25:27; Jer. 52:31

21 [I]Lit., *wine-pouring* [II]Lit., *palm* [a]Gen. 40:13

22 [a]Gen. 40:19; Esth. 7:10

23 [a]Job 19:14; Ps. 31:12; Eccl. 9:15

2 [I]Lit., *fat of flesh* [a]Job 8:11; Is. 19:6, 7

3 [I]Lit., *lean of flesh*

4 [I]Lit., *lean of flesh*

8 [a]Dan. 2:1, 3

sent and called[7121] for all the [I][b]magicians[2748] of Egypt, and all its [c]wise men.[2450] And Pharaoh told[5608] them his [II]dreams, but [d]there was no one who could interpret them to Pharaoh.

9 Then the chief[8269] cupbearer spoke to Pharaoh, saying, "I would make mention[2142] today[3117] of [a]my *own* [I]offenses.[2399]

10 "Pharaoh was [a]furious[7107] with his servants,[5650] and [b]he put me in confinement in the house of the captain[8269] of the bodyguard, *both* me and the chief baker.

11 "And [a]we had a dream [I]on the same night, [II]he and I; each[376] of us dreamed according to the interpretation of his *own* dream.

12 "Now a Hebrew[5680] youth *was* with us there, a [a]servant of the captain of the bodyguard, and we related *them* to him, and [b]he interpreted our dreams for us. To each one he interpreted according to his *own* dream.

13 "And it came about that just [a]as he interpreted for us, so it happened; he restored me in my [I]office, but he hanged him."

Joseph Interprets

14 Then Pharaoh sent and [a]called for Joseph, and they [b]hurriedly brought him out of the dungeon;[953] and when he had shaved himself and changed his clothes, he came to Pharaoh.

15 And Pharaoh said to Joseph, "I have had a dream, [a]but no one can interpret it; and [b]I have heard [I]it said about you, that [II]when you hear[8085] a dream you can interpret it."

16 Joseph then answered Pharaoh, saying, "[I][a]It is not in me; [b]God[430] will [II]give Pharaoh a favorable[7965] answer."

17 So Pharaoh spoke to Joseph, "In my dream, behold, I was standing on the bank[8193] of the Nile;

18 and behold, seven cows, [I]fat and sleek came up out of the Nile; and they grazed in the marsh grass.

19 "And lo, seven other cows came up after them, poor and very ugly and [I]gaunt, such as I had never seen for [II]ugliness[7455] in all the land[776] of Egypt;

20 and the lean and [I]ugly cows ate up the first seven fat cows.

21 "Yet when they had [I]devoured them, it could not be [II]detected that they had [I]devoured them; [III]for they were just as ugly as [IV]before. Then I awoke.

22 "I saw[7200] also in my dream, and behold, seven ears, full and good, came up on a single stalk;

23 and lo, seven ears, withered, thin, *and* scorched by the east wind, sprouted up after them;

24 and the thin ears swallowed the seven good ears. Then [a]I told it to the [I]magicians, but there was no one who could explain[5046] it to me."

25 Now Joseph said to Pharaoh, "Pharaoh's [I]dreams are one *and the same;* [a]God has told[5046] to Pharaoh what He is about to do.[6213]

26 "The seven good[2896] cows are seven years; and the seven good ears are seven years; the [I]dreams are one *and the same.*

27 "And the seven lean and ugly cows that came up after them are seven years, and the seven thin ears scorched by the east wind [a]shall be seven years of famine.

28 "[I]It is as[1697] I have spoken to Pharaoh: [a]God has shown[7200] to Pharaoh what He is about to do.

29 "Behold, [a]seven years of great abundance are coming in all the land of Egypt;

30 and after them [a]seven years of famine will [I]come, and all the abundance will be forgotten in the land of Egypt; and the famine will [II]ravage the land.

31 "So the abundance will be unknown in the land because of that subsequent famine; for it *will be* very severe.

32 "Now as for the repeating of the dream to Pharaoh twice, *it means* that [a]the matter is determined by God, and God will quickly bring it about.[6213]

33 "And now let Pharaoh look[7200] for a man[376] [a]discerning[995] and wise,[2450] and set him over the land of Egypt.

34 "Let Pharaoh take action[6213] to

8 [I]Or, *soothsayer priests* [II]Lit., *dream* [b]Ex. 7:11, 22; Dan. 1:20; 2:2 [c]Matt. 2:1 [d]Dan. 2:27; 4:7
9 [I]Or, *sins* [a]Gen. 40:14, 23
10 [a]Gen. 40:2, 3 [b]Gen. 39:20
11 [I]Lit., *one night* [II]Lit., *I and he* [a]Gen. 40:5
12 [a]Gen. 37:36 [b]Gen. 40:12
13 [I]Lit., *place* [a]Gen. 40:21, 22
14 [a]Ps. 105:20 [b]Dan. 2:25
15 [I]Lit., *about you, saying* [II]Lit., *you hear a dream to interpret it* [a]Gen. 41:8 [b]Dan. 5:16
16 [I]Lit., *Apart from me* [II]Lit., *answer the peace of Pharaoh* [a]Dan. 2:30; Zech. 4:6; Acts 3:12; 2Cor. 3:5 [b]Gen. 40:8; 41:25, 28, 32; Deut. 29:29; Dan. 2:22, 28, 47
18 [I]Lit., *fat of flesh*
19 [I]Lit., *lean of flesh* [II]Lit., *badness*
20 [I]Lit., *bad*
21 [I]Lit., *entered their inward parts* [II]Or, *known* [III]Lit., *and* [IV]Lit., *in the beginning*
24 [I]Or, *soothsayer priests* [a]Is. 8:19; Dan. 4:7
25 [I]Lit., *dream is* [a]Gen. 41:28, 32; Dan. 2:28, 29, 45
26 [I]Lit., *dream is*
27 [a]2Kin. 8:1
28 [I]Lit., *That is the thing which I spoke* [a]Gen. 41:25, 32
29 [a]Gen. 41:47
30 [I]Lit., *arise* [II]Lit., *destroy* [a]Gen. 41:54, 56; 47:13; Ps. 105:16
32 [a]Gen. 41:25, 28
33 [a]Gen. 41:39

appoint[6485] overseers[6496] [I]in charge of the land, and let him exact a fifth *of the produce* of the land of Egypt in the seven years of abundance.

35 "Then let them [a]gather[6908] all the food of these good years that are coming, and store[8104] up the grain for food in the cities under Pharaoh's authority, and let them guard *it*.

36 "And let the food become as a reserve[6487] for the land for the seven years of famine which will occur in the land of Egypt, so that the land may not perish[3772] during the famine."

37 Now the [I]proposal seemed good[3190] [II]to Pharaoh and [II]to all his servants.

Joseph Is Made a Ruler of Egypt

38 Then Pharaoh said to his servants, "Can we find a man like this, [a]in whom is a divine spirit?"[7307]

39 So Pharaoh said to Joseph, "Since God has informed you of all this, there is no one so [a]discerning and wise as you are.

40 "[a]You shall be[1961] over my house,[1004] and according to your [I]command[6310] all my people[5971] shall [II]do homage; only in the throne[3678] I will be greater than you."

41 And Pharaoh said to Joseph, "See I have set you [a]over all the land of Egypt."

🗝 42 Then Pharaoh [a]took off his signet ring from his hand, and put it on Joseph's hand, and clothed him in garments[899] of fine linen, and [b]put the gold necklace around his neck.

43 And he had him ride in [I]his second chariot; and they proclaimed[7121] before him, "[II]Bow the knee!" And he set him over all the land of Egypt.

44 Moreover, Pharaoh said to Joseph, "*Though* I am Pharaoh, yet [a]without [I]your permission no one shall raise his hand or foot in all the land of Egypt."

45 Then Pharaoh named Joseph [I]Zaphenath-paneah; and he gave him Asenath, the daughter of Potiphera priest[3548] of [II][a]On, as his wife. And Joseph went forth over the land of Egypt.

46 Now Joseph was [a]thirty years old[1121] when he [I]stood before Pharaoh, king[4428] of Egypt. And Joseph went out from the presence of Pharaoh, and went through all the land of Egypt.

47 And during the seven years of plenty the land brought forth [I]abundantly.

48 So he gathered all the food of *these* seven years which occurred in the land of Egypt, and placed the food in the cities; he placed in every city the food from its own surrounding fields.

49 Thus Joseph stored up grain [I]in great abundance like the sand of the sea, until he stopped [II]measuring[5608] *it,* for it was [III]beyond measure.

The Sons of Joseph

50 Now before the year of famine came, [a]two sons[1121] were born to Joseph, whom Asenath, the daughter of Potiphera priest of [I]On, bore to him.

51 And Joseph named the first-born [I]Manasseh,[4519] "For," *he said,* "God has made me forget[5382] all my trouble[5999] and all my father's household."

52 And he named[7121] the second [I]Ephraim,[669] "For," *he said,* "[a]God has made me fruitful[6509] in the land of my affliction."

53 When the seven years of plenty

34 [I]Lit., *over*
35 [a]Gen. 41:48
37 [I]Lit., *word* [II]Lit., *in the sight of*
38 [a]Job 32:8; Dan. 4:8, 9, 18; 5:11, 14
39 [a]Gen. 41:33
40 [I]Lit., *mouth* [II]Lit., *kiss* [a]Ps. 105:21; Acts 7:10
41 [a]Gen. 42:6; Ps. 105:21; Dan. 6:3; Acts 7:10
42 [a]Esth. 3:10; 8:2 [b]Dan. 5:7, 16, 29
43 [I]Lit., *the second. . .which was his* [II]Heb., *Abreck: Attention* or *Make way*
44 [I]Lit., *you no one* [a]Ps. 105:22
45 [I]Probably Egyptian for "God speaks; he lives" [II]Or, *Heliopolis* [a]Jer. 43:13; Ezek. 30:17
46 [I]Or, *entered the service of* [a]Gen. 37:2
47 [I]Lit., *by handfuls*
49 [I]Lit., *very much* [II]Lit., *numbering* [III]Or, *without number*
50 [I]Or, *Heliopolis* [a]Gen. 48:5
51 [I]I.e., making to forget
52 [I]I.e., fruitfulness [a]Gen. 17:6; 28:3; 49:22

🗝 **41:42-44** Joseph had reached the very summit of political power in one of the mightiest nations in the world. Besides the personal ring and fine clothing which Pharaoh gave him, he also placed him in his second chariot for a public procession. Kings often went out to battle with two chariots. One for the battle and the other to return home in case of disaster. The fact that Joseph rode in the second chariot would seem to indicate that he was second in command. In Gen. 42:6 he is also called the governor over the land. Therefore, he was in charge of the practical matters of administration in everyday life in Egypt.

which had been in the land of Egypt
came to an end,
54 and [a]the seven years of famine
began to come, just as Joseph had said,
then there was famine in all the lands;[776]
but in all the land of Egypt there was
bread.
55 So when all the land of Egypt
was famished, the people cried out to
Pharaoh for bread; and Pharaoh said to
all the Egyptians, "Go to Joseph;
[a]whatever he says to you, you shall do."
56 When the famine was *spread* over
all the face of the earth,[776] then Joseph
opened all [I]the storehouses, and sold
to the Egyptians; and the famine was
severe[2388] in the land of Egypt.
57 And *the people of* all the earth[776]
came to Egypt to buy grain from Joseph,
because [a]the famine was severe[2388] in
all the earth.[776]

Joseph's Brothers Sent to Egypt

42 Now [a]Jacob saw[7200] that there
was grain[7668] in Egypt, and Jacob
said to his sons,[1121] "Why are you
staring at one another?"[7200]
2 And he said, "Behold, [a]I have
heard[8085] that there is grain in Egypt;
go down there and buy *some* for us
[I]from that place, [b]so that we may live[2421]
and not die."[4191]
3 Then ten brothers[251] of Joseph
went down to buy grain from Egypt.
4 But Jacob did not send Joseph's
brother[251] [a]Benjamin with his brothers,
for he said,[559] "[I][b]I am afraid[194] that harm
may befall him."
5 So the sons of Israel came to buy
grain among those who were coming,
[a]for the famine was in the land[776] of Canaan *also.*
6 Now [a]Joseph was the ruler[7989]
over the land; he was the one who sold
to all the people[5971] of the land. And
Joseph's brothers came and [b]bowed
down[7812] to him with *their* faces[639] to
the ground.
7 When Joseph saw[7200] his brothers
he recognized[5234] them, but he disguised
himself[5234] to them and [a]spoke to them
harshly.[7186] And he said to them,
"Where have you come from?" And they
said, "From the land of Canaan, to buy
food."
🔑 **8** But Joseph had recognized[5234] his
brothers, although [a]they did not recognize him.
9 And Joseph [a]remembered[2142] the
dreams which he [I]had about them, and
said to them, "You are spies; you have
come to look[7200] at the [II]undefended
parts[6172] of our land."
10 Then they said to him, "No,
[a]my lord,[113] but your servants[5650] have
come to buy food.
11 "We are all sons of one man;[376]
we are [a]honest[3651] men, your servants
are not spies."
12 Yet he said to them, "No, but
you have come to look at the [I]unde-
fended parts of our land!"
13 But they said, "Your servants are
twelve brothers[251] *in all,* the sons[1121]
of one man in the land of Canaan; and
behold, the youngest is with [a]our father[1]
today,[3117] and [b]one is no more."
14 And Joseph said to them, "It is
as I said [I]to you, you are spies;
15 by this you will be tested:[974]
[a]by the life[2416] of Pharaoh, you shall not
go from this place unless your youngest
brother comes here!
16 "Send one of you that he may
get your brother, while you remain confined, that your words[1697] may be
tested, whether there is [a]truth[571] in you.
But if not, by the life of Pharaoh, surely
you are spies."
17 So he put them all together in
[a]prison for three days.
18 Now Joseph said to them on the

54 [a]Gen. 41:30; Ps. 105:16; Acts 7:11
55 [a]John 2:5
56 [I]Lit., *that which was in them*
57 [a]Gen. 12:10
1 [a]Acts 7:12
2 [I]Lit., *from there* [a]Acts 7:12 [b]Gen. 43:8; Ps. 33:18, 19
4 [I]Lit., *Lest harm* [a]Gen. 35:24 [b]Gen. 42:38
5 [a]Gen. 12:10; 26:1; 41:57; Acts 7:11
6 [a]Gen. 41:41, 55 [b]Gen. 37:7-10; 41:43; Is. 60:14
7 [a]Gen. 42:30
8 [a]Gen. 37:2; 41:46
9 [I]Lit., *had dreamed* [II]Lit., *nakedness of the land* [a]Gen. 37:6-9
10 [a]Gen. 37:8
11 [a]Gen. 42:16, 19, 31, 34
12 [I]Lit., *naked-ness of the land*
13 [a]Gen. 43:7 [b]Gen. 37:30; 42:32; 44:20
14 [I]Lit., *to you, saying*
15 [a]1Sam. 17:55
16 [a]Gen. 42:11
17 [a]Gen. 40:4, 7

🔑 **42:8** Why did Joseph's brother's not recognize him? About 20 years had passed. Joseph was only a teenager when they sold him as a slave. They never expected to see him again. As an Egyptian, he would have been clean-shaven and well-dressed. And, since he spoke through an interpreter, they would never have dreamed that it could be Joseph.

third day, "Do[6213] this and live,[2421] for [a]I fear[3373] God:[430]

19 if you are honest men, let one of your brothers be confined in [I]your prison; but as for *the rest of* you, go, carry grain for the famine of your households,

20 and [a]bring your youngest brother to me, so your words may be verified,[539] and you will not die." And they did[6213] so.

21 Then they said to one[376] another,[250] "[a]Truly we are guilty[816] concerning our brother,[251] because we saw[7200] the distress[6869] of his soul[5315] when he pleaded[2603] with us, yet we would not listen; therefore this distress has come upon us."

22 And Reuben answered them, saying, "[a]Did I not tell[559] [I]you, 'Do not sin[2398] against the boy'; and you would not listen? [II][b]Now comes the reckoning for his blood."[1818]

23 They did not know,[3045] however, that Joseph understood,[8085] for there was an interpreter[3887] between them.

24 And he turned away from them and [a]wept. But when he returned to them and spoke to them, he [b]took Simeon from them and bound him before their eyes.

25 [a]Then Joseph gave orders[6680] to fill their bags with grain and to restore every man's[376] money in his sack, and to give them provisions for the journey.[1870] And thus it was done for them.

26 So they loaded[5375] their donkeys with their grain, and departed from there.

27 And as one *of them* opened his sack to give his donkey fodder[4554] at the lodging place, he saw[7200] his [a]money; and behold, it was in the mouth[6310] of his sack.

28 Then he said to his brothers, "My money has been returned,[7725] and behold, it is even in my sack." And their hearts[3820] [I]sank, and they *turned* [II]trembling[2729] to one another, saying, "[a]What is this that God has done[6213] to us?"

Simeon Is Held Hostage

29 When they came to their father Jacob in the land of Canaan, they told[5046] him all that had happened to them, saying,

30 "The man, the lord of the land,[776] [a]spoke harshly with us, and took us for spies of the country.[776]

31 "But we said to him, 'We are [a]honest men; we are not spies.

32 'We are twelve brothers, sons of our father; one is no more, and the youngest is with our father today in the land of Canaan.'

33 "And the man, the lord of the land, said to us, '[a]By this I shall know that you are honest men: leave one of your brothers with me and take *grain for* the famine of your households, and go.

34 'But bring your youngest brother to me that I may know that you are not spies, but [I]honest men. I will give your brother to you, and you may [a]trade[5503] in the land.' "

35 Now it came about as they were emptying their sacks, that behold, [a]every man's bundle of money *was* in his sack; and when they and their father saw their bundles of money, they were dismayed.[3372]

36 And their father Jacob said to them, "You have [a]bereaved me of my children: Joseph is no more, and Simeon is no more, and you would take Benjamin; all these things are against me."

37 Then Reuben spoke to his father, saying, "You may put my two sons to death if I do not bring him *back* to you; put him in my [I]care,[3027] and I will return him to you."

38 But [I]Jacob said, "My son shall not go down with you; for his [a]brother is dead,[4191] and he alone is left.[7604] [b]If harm should befall him on the journey [II]you are taking, then you will [c]bring my gray hair[7872] down to Sheol[7585] in sorrow."

The Return to Egypt

43

Now[a] the famine was severe in the land.[776]

---

18 [a]Gen. 39:9; Lev. 25:43; Neh. 5:15

19 [I]Lit., *the house of your prison*

20 [a]Gen. 42:34; 43:5; 44:23

21 [a]Gen. 37:26-28; 45:3; Hos. 5:15

22 [I]Lit., *you saying* [II]Lit., *And behold, his blood also is required* [a]Gen. 37:21, 22 [b]Gen. 9:5, 6; 1Kin. 2:32; 2Chr. 24:22; Ps. 9:12

24 [a]Gen. 43:30; 45:14, 15 [b]Gen. 43:14, 23

25 [a]Gen. 44:1; Rom. 12:17, 20, 21; 1Pet. 3:9

27 [a]Gen. 43:21, 22

28 [I]Lit., *went out* [II]Lit., *trembled* [a]Gen. 43:23

30 [a]Gen. 42:7

31 [a]Gen. 42:11

33 [a]Gen. 42:19, 20

34 [I]Lit., *you are honest* [a]Gen. 34:10

35 [a]Gen. 43:12, 15, 21

36 [a]Gen. 43:14

37 [I]Lit., *hand*

38 [I]Lit., *he* [II]Lit., *on which you are going* [a]Gen. 37:33, 34; 42:13; 44:27, 28 [b]Gen. 42:4 [c]Gen. 37:35; 44:29, 31

1 [a]Gen. 12:10; 26:1; 41:56, 57

2 So it came about when they had finished eating the grain[7668] which they had brought from Egypt, that their father said to them, "Go back, buy us a little food."

3 Judah spoke to him, however, saying, "[a]The man[376] solemnly warned[5749] [I]us, 'You shall not see my face unless your brother[251] is with you.'

4 "If you send our brother with us, we will go down and buy you food.

5 "But if you do not send *him,* we will not go down; for the man said[559] to us, 'You shall not see my face unless your brother is with you.' "

6 Then Israel said, "Why did you treat me so badly[7489] [I]by telling[5046] the man whether you still had *another* brother?"

7 But they said, "The man questioned[7592] particularly about us and our relatives, saying, '[a]Is your father[1] still alive?[2416] Have you *another* brother?' So we [I]answered[5046] his questions. Could we possibly know that he would say, 'Bring your brother down'?"

8 And Judah said to his father Israel, "Send the lad with me, and we will arise and go, [a]that we may live and not die,[4191] we as well as you and our little ones.[2945]

9 "[a]I myself will be surety for him; [I]you may hold me responsible[3027] for him. If I do not bring him *back* to you and set him before you, then [II]let me bear the blame[2398] before you forever.[3117, 3605]

10 "For if we had not delayed, surely by now we could have returned twice."

11 Then their father Israel said to them, "If *it must be* so, then do[6213] this: take some of the best products of the land in your [I]bags, and carry down to the man [a]as a present,[4503] a little [II][b]balm and a little honey, [III]aromatic gum and [IV]myrrh,[3910] pistachio nuts and almonds.

12 "And take double *the* money in your hand, and take back in your hand [a]the money that was returned in the mouth of your sacks; perhaps[194] it was a mistake.

13 "Take your brother also, and arise, return to the man;

14 and may [I][a]God[410] Almighty[7706] [b]grant you compassion[7356] in the sight of the man, that he may release to you [c]your other brother and Benjamin. And as for me, [d]if I am bereaved of my children, I am bereaved."

15 So the men[582] took [a]this present, and they took double *the* money in their hand, and Benjamin; then they arose and went down to Egypt and stood before Joseph.

Joseph Sees Benjamin

16 When Joseph saw[7200] Benjamin with them, he said to his [a]house[1004] steward, "Bring the men into the house,[1004] and slay[2873] *an animal* and make ready; for the men are to dine with me at noon."

17 So the man[376] did[6213] as Joseph said,[559] and [I]brought the men to Joseph's house.[1004]

18 Now the men were afraid,[3372] because they were brought to Joseph's house; and they said, "*It is* because of the money that was returned in our sacks the first time that we are being brought in, that he may [I]seek occasion[1556] against us and fall upon us, and take us for slaves[5650] with our donkeys."

19 So they came near to Joseph's house steward,[376] and spoke to him at the entrance of the house,

20 and said, "Oh, my lord,[113] we indeed came down the first time to buy food,

21 and it came about when we came to the lodging place, that we opened our sacks, and behold, [a]each man's money was in the mouth of his sack, our money in [I]full. So [b]we have brought it back in our hand.

22 "We have also brought down other money in our hand to buy food; we do not know[3045] who put[7760] our money in our sacks."

23 And he said, "[I]Be at ease,[7965] do not be afraid.[3372] [a]Your God[430] and

---

3 [I]Lit., *us, saying* [a]Gen. 43:5; 44:23

6 [I]Lit., *to tell*

7 [I]Lit., *told him according to these words* [a]Gen. 42:13; 43:27

8 [a]Gen. 42:2

9 [I]Lit., *from my hand you may require him* [II]Lit., *I shall have sinned before you all the days* [a]Gen. 42:37; 44:32; Philem. 18, 19

11 [I]Or, *vessels* [II]Or, *mastic* [III]Or, *ladanum spice* [IV]Or, *resinous bark* [a]Gen. 32:20; 43:25, 26 [b]Gen. 37:25; Jer. 8:22; Ezek. 27:17

12 [a]Gen. 42:25, 35; 43:21, 22

14 [I]Heb., *El Shaddai* [a]Gen. 17:1; 28:3; 35:11 [b]Ps. 106:46 [c]Gen. 42:24 [d]Gen. 42:36

15 [a]Gen. 43:11

16 [a]Gen. 44:1

17 [I]Lit., *the man brought*

18 [I]Lit., *roll himself upon us*

21 [I]Lit., *its weight* [a]Gen. 42:27, 35 [b]Gen. 43:12, 15

23 [a]Gen. 42:28 [I]Lit., *Peace be to you*

the God of your father[1] has given you treasure in your sacks; [II]I had your money." Then [b]he brought Simeon out to them.

24 Then the man brought the men into Joseph's house and [a]gave them water, and they [b]washed[7364] their feet; and he gave their donkeys fodder.[4554]

25 So they prepared [a]the present [I]for Joseph's coming at noon; for they had heard that they were to eat [II]a meal there.

26 When Joseph came home, they brought into the house to him the present which was in their hand and [a]bowed[7812] to the ground[776] before him.

27 Then he asked[7592] them about their welfare,[7965] and said, "[a]Is your old[2205] father well,[7965] of whom you spoke?[559] Is he still alive?"

28 And they said, "Your servant[5650] our father is well; he is still alive." [a]And they bowed down [I]in homage.[7812]

29 As he lifted his eyes and saw his brother[251] Benjamin, his mother's son, he said, "Is this [a]your youngest brother, of whom you spoke to me?" And he said, "[b]May God be gracious[2603] to you, my son."

30 And Joseph hurried *out* for [I][a]he was deeply stirred[3648,7356] over his brother, and he sought *a place* to weep; and he entered his chamber and [b]wept there.

31 Then he washed his face, and came out; and he [a]controlled himself and said, "[I]Serve the meal."

32 So they served him by himself, and them by themselves, and the Egyptians, who ate with him, by themselves; because the Egyptians could not eat bread with the Hebrews, for that is [I][a]loathsome[8441] to the Egyptians.

33 Now they [I]were seated before him, [a]the first-born according to his birthright[1062] and the youngest according to his youth, and the men looked at one another[7453] in astonishment.

34 And he took portions[4864] to them from [I]his own table; [a]but Benjamin's portion was five times as much as any of theirs. So they feasted and drank freely with him.

The Brothers Are Brought Back

44 Then he commanded[6680] his house steward, saying, "Fill the men's[582] sacks with food, as much as they can carry,[5375] and put each man's[376] money in the mouth of his sack.

2 "And put[7760] my cup, the silver cup, in the mouth of the sack of the youngest, and his money for the grain."[7668] And he did[6213] [I]as Joseph had told *him*.

3 [I]As soon as it was light, the men were sent away, they with their donkeys.

4 They had *just* gone out of [a]the city, *and* were not far off, when Joseph said to his house steward, "Up, follow the men; and when you overtake them, say to them, 'Why have you repaid evil[7451] for good?[2896]

5 'Is not this the one from which my lord[113] drinks, and which he indeed uses for [a]divination?[5172] You have done wrong[7489] in doing this.' "[6213]

6 So he overtook them and spoke these words to them.

7 And they said to him, "Why does my lord speak such words as these? Far be it from your servants[5650] to do such a thing.

8 "Behold, [a]the money which we found in the mouth of our sacks we have brought back to you from the land[776] of Canaan. How then could we steal silver or gold from your lord's house?

9 "[a]With whomever of your servants it is found, let him die,[4191] and we also will be my lord's [b]slaves."[5650]

10 So he said, "Now let it also be according to your words; he with whom it is found shall be my slave, and *the rest of* you shall be innocent."[5355]

11 Then they hurried, each man lowered his sack to the ground,[776] and each man opened his sack.

12 And he searched, beginning with

23 [II]Lit., *your money had come to me* [b]Gen. 42:24

24 [a]Gen. 18:4; 19:2; 24:32 [b]Luke 7:44; John 13:5; 1Tim. 5:10

25 [I]Lit., *until* [II]Lit., *bread* [a]Gen. 43:11, 15

26 [a]Gen. 37:7, 10

27 [a]Gen. 43:7; 45:3

28 [I]Lit., *and prostrated themselves* [a]Gen. 37:7, 10

29 [a]Gen. 42:13 [b]Num. 6:25; Ps. 67:1

30 [I]Lit., *his compassion grew warm* [a]1Kin. 3:26 [b]Gen. 42:24; 45:2, 14, 15; 46:29

31 [I]Lit., *Set on bread.* [a]Gen. 45:1

32 [I]Lit., *an abomination* [a]Gen. 46:34; Ex. 8:26

33 [I]Lit., *sat* [a]Gen. 42:7

34 [I]Lit., *his face* [a]Gen. 35:24; 45:22

1 [a]Gen. 42:25

2 [I]Or, *according to the word*

3 [I]Lit., *The morning was light*

4 [a]Gen. 44:13

5 [a]Gen. 30:27; 44:15; Lev. 19:26; Deut. 18:10-14

8 [a]Gen. 43:21

9 [a]Gen. 31:32 [b]Gen. 44:16

the oldest and ending with the youngest, and [a]the cup was found in Benjamin's sack.

13 Then they [a]tore their clothes, and when each man loaded his donkey, they returned to [b]the city.

14 When Judah and his brothers came to Joseph's house, he was still there, and [a]they fell[5307] to the ground before him.

🔑 15 And Joseph said to them, "What is this deed that you have done?[6213] Do you not know[3045] that such a man as I can indeed practice [a]divination?"[5172]

16 So Judah said, "What can we say to my lord? What can we speak? And how can we justify[6663] ourselves? God[430] has found out the iniquity[5771] of your servants; behold, we are my lord's [a]slaves, both we and the one in whose [I]possession the cup has been found."

17 But he said, "Far be it from me to do this. The man in whose [I]possession the cup has been found, he shall be my slave; but as for you, go up in peace[7965] to your father."[1]

18 Then Judah approached him, and said, "Oh my lord, may your servant please speak a word[1697] in my lord's ears,[241] and [I][a]do not be angry[639] with your servant; for [b]you are equal to Pharaoh.

19 "[a]My lord asked[7592] his servants, saying, 'Have you a father or a brother?'[251]

20 "And we said to my lord, 'We have an old[2205] father and [a]a little child of *his* old age.[2208] Now [b]his brother is dead,[4191] so he alone is left[3498] of his mother,[517] and his father loves[157] him.'

21 "Then you said to your servants, '[a]Bring him down to me, that I may set my eyes on him.'

22 "But we said to my lord, 'The lad cannot leave[5800] his father, for if he should leave his father, [I]his father would die.'

23 "You said to your servants, however, '[a]Unless your youngest brother comes down with you, you shall not see[7200] my face again.'

24 "Thus it came about when we went up to your servant my father, we told[5046] him the words of my lord.

25 "And [a]our father said, 'Go back, buy us a little food.'

26 "But we said, 'We cannot go down. If our youngest brother is with us, then we will go down; for we cannot see the man's face unless our youngest brother is with us.'

27 "And your servant my father said to us, 'You know[3045] that [a]my wife bore me two sons;

28 and the one went out from me, and [a]I said, "Surely he is torn in pieces," and I have not seen him since.

29 'And if you take this one also from [I]me, and harm befalls him, you will [a]bring my gray hair[7872] down to Sheol[7585] in [II]sorrow.'[7451]

30 "Now, therefore, when I come to your servant my father, and the lad is not with us, since [I][a]his life is bound up in the lad's life,[5315]

31 it will come about when he sees that the lad is not *with us*, that he will die. Thus your servants will [a]bring the gray hair of your servant our father down to Sheol in sorrow.

32 "For your servant [a]became surety[6148] for the lad to my father, saying, 'If I do not bring him *back* to you, then [I]let me bear the blame[2398] before my father forever.'[3117][3605]

33 "Now, therefore, please let your servant remain instead of the lad a slave to my lord, and let the lad go up with his brothers.

34 "For how shall I go up to my father if the lad is not with me, lest I see[7200] the evil[7451] that would [I]overtake my father?"

Joseph Deals Kindly with His Brothers

45 Then Joseph could not control himself before all those who

12 [a]Gen. 44:2
13 [a]Gen. 37:29, 34; Num. 14:6; 2Sam. 1:11 [b]Gen. 44:4
14 [a]Gen. 37:7, 10
15 [a]Gen. 44:5
16 [I]Lit., *hand* [a]Gen. 44:9
17 [I]Lit., *hand*
18 [I]Lit., *let not your anger burn against* [a]Gen. 18:30, 32; Ex. 32:22 [b]Gen. 37:7, 8; 41:40-44
19 [a]Gen. 43:7
20 [a]Gen. 37:3; 43:8; 44:30 [b]Gen. 37:33; 42:13, 38
21 [a]Gen. 42:15, 20
22 [I]Lit., *he would*
23 [a]Gen. 43:3, 5
25 [a]Gen. 43:2
27 [a]Gen. 46:19
28 [a]Gen. 37:31-35
29 [I]Lit., *my face* [II]Lit., *evil* [a]Gen. 42:38; 44:31
30 [I]Lit., *his soul is bound with his soul* [a]1Sam. 18:1
31 [a]Gen. 44:29
32 [I]Lit., *and I shall have sinned for all the days before my father* [a]Gen. 43:9
34 [I]Lit., *find*

🔑 **44:15** There was a common practice in Egypt similar to "crystal gazing." Joseph's gift of telling the future was no doubt associated with that, but Joseph's trust was in God, not in a silver cup.

stood[5324] by him, and he cried,[7121] "Have everyone[376][3605] go out from me." So there [I]was no man with him [a]when Joseph made himself known to his brothers.[251]

2 And [a]he [I]wept so loudly that the Egyptians heard *it,* and the household[1004] of Pharaoh heard *of it.*

3 Then Joseph said to his brothers, "[a]I am Joseph! [b]Is my father[1] still alive?"[2416] But his brothers could not answer him, for [c]they were dismayed[926] at his presence.

4 Then Joseph said to his brothers, "Please come [I]closer to me." And they came [I]closer. And he said, "I am your brother[251] Joseph, whom you [a]sold into Egypt.

5 "And now do not be grieved[6087] or angry[2734] [I]with yourselves, because [a]you sold me here; for [b]God[430] sent me before you to preserve life.[4241]

6 "For the famine *has been* in the land[776] [a]these two years, and there are still five years in which there will be neither plowing nor harvesting.

7 "And [a]God sent me before you to preserve[7760] for you a remnant[7611] in the earth,[776] and to keep you alive[2421] by a great [I]deliverance.[6413]

8 "Now, therefore, it was not you who sent me here, but God; and He has made[7760] me a [a]father to Pharaoh and lord[113] of all his household and ruler[4910] over all the land of Egypt.

9 "Hurry and go up to my father, and [a]say to him, 'Thus says your son[1121] Joseph, "God has made[7760] me lord of all Egypt; come down to me, do not delay.

10 "And you shall [I]live in the land of [a]Goshen, and you shall be near me, you and your children and your children's children and your flocks and your herds and all that you have.

11 "There I will also [a]provide for you, for there are still five years of famine *to come,* lest you and your household[1004] and all that you have be impoverished." '

12 "And behold, your eyes see,[7200] and the eyes of my brother Benjamin *see,* that it is my mouth[6310] which is speaking to you.

13 "Now you must tell[5046] my father of all my splendor[3519] in Egypt, and all that you have seen; and you must hurry and [a]bring my father down here."

14 Then he fell on his brother Benjamin's neck and [a]wept; and Benjamin wept on his neck.

15 And he kissed all his brothers and wept on them, and afterward his brothers talked[1696] with him.

16 Now when [a]the [I]news was heard[8085] in Pharaoh's house [II]that Joseph's brothers had come, it [III]pleased[3190] Pharaoh and his servants.[5650]

17 Then Pharaoh said to Joseph, "Say to your brothers, 'Do[6213] this: load your beasts and [I]go to the land of Canaan,

18 and take your father and your households and come to me, and [a]I will give you the [I]best[2898] of the land of Egypt and you shall eat the fat of the land.'

19 "Now you are ordered,[6680] 'Do this: [I]take [a]wagons from the land of Egypt for your little ones[2945] and for your wives, and bring[5375] your father and come.

20 'And do not [I]concern yourselves with your goods, for the [II]best of all the land of Egypt is yours.' "

21 Then the sons of Israel did[6213] so; and Joseph gave them [a]wagons according to the [I]command[6310] of Pharaoh, and gave them provisions for the journey.

22 To [I]each[376] of them he gave [a]changes of garments, but to Benjamin he gave three hundred *pieces of* silver and [b]five changes of garments.

23 And to his father he sent [I]as follows: ten donkeys loaded[5375] with the [II]best things[2898] of Egypt, and ten female donkeys loaded with grain and bread and sustenance for his father [III]on the journey.

24 So he sent his brothers away, and [I]as they departed, he said to them, "Do not [II]quarrel on the journey."

1 [I]Lit., *stood* [a]Acts 7:13

2 [I]Lit., *gave forth his voice in weeping* [a]Gen. 45:14, 15; 46:29

3 [a]Acts 7:13 [b]Gen. 43:27 [c]Gen. 37:20-28; 42:21, 22

4 [I]Lit., *near* [a]Gen. 37:28

5 [I]Lit., *in your eyes* [a]Gen. 37:28 [b]Gen. 45:7, 8; 50:20; Ps. 105:17

6 [a]Gen. 37:2; 41:46, 53

7 [I]Lit., *escaped company* [a]Gen. 45:5

8 [a]Judg. 17:10

9 [a]Acts 7:14

10 [I]Lit., *dwell* [a]Gen. 46:28, 34; 47:1

11 [a]Gen. 47:12

13 [a]Acts 7:14

14 [a]Gen. 45:2

16 [I]Lit., *voice* [II]Lit., *saying, "Joseph's brothers have come."* [III]Lit., *was good in the eyes of* [a]Acts 7:13

17 [I]Lit., *come, go*

18 [I]Lit., *good* [a]Gen. 27:28

19 [I]Lit., *take for yourselves* [a]Gen. 45:21, 27; 46:5; Num. 7:3-8

20 [I]Lit., *let your eye look with regret upon your vessels* [II]Lit., *good*

21 [I]Lit., *mouth* [a]Gen. 45:19

22 [I]Lit., *all of them he gave each man* [a]2Kin. 5:5 [b]Gen. 43:34

23 [I]Lit., *like this* [II]Lit., *good* [III]Lit., *for*

24 [I]Lit., *they departed; and he said* [II]Lit., *be agitated*

25 Then they went up from Egypt,
and came to the land of Canaan to their
father Jacob.
26 And they told[5046] him, saying,
"Joseph is still alive, and indeed he is
ruler[4910] over all the land of Egypt." But
[I]he was stunned, for [a]he did not believe[539] them.
27 When they told him all the
words[1697] of Joseph that he had
spoken[1696] to them, and when he saw[7200]
the [a]wagons that Joseph had sent to
carry him, the spirit[7307] of their father
Jacob revived.[2421]
28 Then Israel said, "It is enough;
my son Joseph is still alive. I will go
and see him before I die."[4191]

Jacob Moves to Egypt

46 So Israel set out with all that
he had, and came to [a]Beersheba,
and offered sacrifices[2077] to the [b]God[430]
of his father[1] Isaac.
2 And [a]God spoke to Israel [I]in
visions[4759] of the night and said, "[b]Jacob,
Jacob." And he said, "Here I am."
3 And He said, "[a]I am God,[410] the
God of your father; do not be afraid[3372]
to go down to Egypt, for I will [b]make[7760]
you a great nation[1471] there.
4 "[a]I will go down with you to Egypt,
and [b]I will also surely bring you up again;
and [c]Joseph will [I]close[3027] your eyes."
5 Then Jacob arose from Beer-
sheba; and the sons[1121] of Israel carried
their father Jacob and their little ones[2945]
and their wives, in the [a]wagons which
Pharaoh had sent to carry[5375] him.
6 And they took their livestock and
their property, which they had acquired
in the land[776] of Canaan, and [a]came to
Egypt, Jacob and all his [I]descendants[2233]
with him:
7 his sons and his grandsons with
him, his daughters and his granddaugh-
ters, and all his [I]descendants he brought
with him to Egypt.

Those Who Came to Egypt

8 Now these are the [a]names of the
sons[1121] of Israel, Jacob and his sons,[1121]
who went to Egypt: Reuben, Jacob's
first-born.
9 And the sons of Reuben: Hanoch
and Pallu and Hezron and Carmi.
10 And the [a]sons of Simeon:
[I]Jemuel and Jamin and Ohad and [II]Jachin
and [III]Zohar and Shaul the son of a Canaanite woman.
11 And the sons of Levi: [I]Gershon,
Kohath, and Merari.
12 And the sons of Judah: Er and
Onan and Shelah and Perez and Zerah
(but Er and Onan died[4191] in the land
of Canaan). And the [a]sons of Perez were
Hezron and Hamul.
13 And the sons of Issachar: Tola
and [I]Puvvah and [II]Iob and Shimron.
14 And the sons of Zebulun: Sered
and Elon and Jahleel.
15 These are the sons[1121] of Leah,
whom she bore to Jacob in Paddan-aram,
with his daughter Dinah; [I]all his sons[5315]
and his daughters *numbered* thirty-
three.
16 And the [a]sons of Gad: [I]Ziphion
and Haggi, Shuni and [II]Ezbon, Eri and
[III]Arodi and Areli.
17 And the [a]sons of Asher: Imnah
and Ishvah and Ishvi and Beriah and their
sister Serah. And the [b]sons of Beriah:
Heber and Malchiel.
18 These are the sons of Zilpah,
whom Laban gave to his daughter Leah;
and she bore to Jacob these sixteen persons.
19 The sons of Jacob's wife Rachel:
Joseph and Benjamin.
20 [a]Now to Joseph in the land of
Egypt were born Manasseh and
Ephraim, whom Asenath, the daughter
of Potiphera, priest[3548] of On, bore to
him.
21 And the [a]sons of Benjamin: Bela
and Becher and Ashbel, Gera and Naaman, [I]Ehi and Rosh, [II]Muppim and
[III]Huppim and Ard.
22 These are the sons of Rachel,
who were born to Jacob; *there were* fourteen persons in all.
23 And the sons of Dan: [I]Hushim.
24 And the sons of Naphtali:
[I]Jahzeel and Guni and Jezer and [II]Shillem.

26 [I]Lit., *his heart grew numb* [a]Gen. 37:31-35
27 [a]Gen. 45:19
1 [a]Gen. 21:31; 28:10 [b]Gen. 26:24; 28:13; 31:42
2 [I]Lit., *in the visions* [a]Gen. 15:1; Num. 12:6; Job 33:14, 15 [b]Gen. 22:11; 31:11
3 [a]Gen. 17:1; 28:13 [b]Gen. 12:2; Ex. 1:9; Deut. 26:5
4 [I]Lit., *put his hand on* [a]Gen. 28:15; 48:21 [b]Gen. 50:24; Ex. 3:8 [c]Gen. 50:1
5 [a]Gen. 45:21
6 [I]Lit., *seed* [a]Deut. 26:5; Josh. 24:4; Ps. 105:23; Is. 52:4; Acts 7:15
7 [I]Lit., *seed*
8 [a]Ex. 1:1-4; Num. 26:4, 5; 1Chr. 2:1ff.
10 [I]In Num. 26:12 and 1Chr. 4:24, *Nemuel* [II]In 1Chr. 4:24, *Jarib* [III]In Num. 26:13 and 1Chr. 4:24, *Zerah* [a]Ex. 6:15
11 [I]In 1Chr. 6:16, *Gershom*
12 [a]1Chr. 2:5
13 [I]In Num. 26:23, *Puvah;* in 1Chr. 7:1, *Puah* [II]In Num. 26:24 and 1Chr. 7:1, *Jashub*
15 [I]Lit., *all the souls of*
16 [I]In Num. 26:15, *Zephon* [II]In Num. 26:16, *Ozni* [III]In Num. 26:17, *Arod* [a]Num. 26:15-18
17 [a]1Chr. 7:30 [b]1Chr. 7:31
20 [a]Gen. 41:50-52
21 [I]In Num. 26:38, *Ahiram* [II]In Num. 26:39, *Shephupham;* in 1Chr. 7:12, *Shuppim* [III]In Num. 26:39, *Hupham* [a]1Chr. 7:6
23 [I]In Num. 26:42, *Shuham*
24 [I]In 1Chr. 7:13, *Jahziel* [II]In 1Chr. 7:13, *Shallum*

25 These are the [a]sons of Bilhah, whom [b]Laban gave to his daughter Rachel, and she bore these to Jacob; *there were* seven persons in all.

26 [a]All the persons belonging to Jacob, who came to Egypt, [I]his direct descendants, not including[3409] the wives of Jacob's sons, *were* sixty-six persons in all,

🗝 27 and the sons of Joseph, who were born to him in Egypt were [I]two; [a]all the persons of the house[1004] of Jacob, who came to Egypt, *were* seventy.

28 Now he sent Judah before him to Joseph, to point out[3384] *the way* before him to [a]Goshen; and they came into the land of Goshen.

29 And Joseph [I]prepared his chariot and went up to Goshen to meet his father Israel; as soon as he appeared[7200] [II]before him, he fell on his neck and [a]wept on his neck a long time.

30 Then Israel said to Joseph, "Now let me die,[4191] since I have seen your face, that you are still alive."

31 And Joseph said to his brothers[251] and to his father's household, "[a]I will go up and tell[5046] Pharaoh, and will say to him, 'My brothers and my father's household, who *were* in the land of Canaan, have come to me;

32 and the men[582] are shepherds, for they have been [I]keepers of livestock; and they have brought their flocks and their herds and all that they have.'

33 "And it shall come about when Pharaoh calls[7121] you and says, '[a]What is your occupation?'

🗝 34 that you shall say, 'Your servants[5650] have been [Ia]keepers of livestock from our youth even until now, both we and our fathers,' that you may [II]live in the land of [b]Goshen; for every shepherd is [IIIc]loathsome[8441] to the Egyptians."

Jacob's Family Settles in Goshen

47 Then [a]Joseph went in and told[5046] Pharaoh, and said, "My father[1] and my brothers[251] and their flocks and their herds and all that they have, have come out of the land[776] of Canaan; and behold, they are in the land of [b]Goshen."

2 And he took five men[582] from among his brothers, and [a]presented them to Pharaoh.

3 Then Pharaoh said to his brothers, "[a]What is your occupation?" So they said to Pharaoh, "Your servants[5650] are [b]shepherds, both we and our fathers."

4 And they said to Pharaoh, "[a]We have come to sojourn[1481] in the land, for there is no pasture for your servants' flocks, for [b]the famine is severe in the land of Canaan. Now, therefore, please let your servants [Ic]live in the land of Goshen."

5 Then Pharaoh said to [I]Joseph, "Your father and your brothers have come to you.

6 "The land of Egypt is [I]at your

25 [a]Gen. 30:5, 7 [b]Gen. 29:29
26 [I]Lit., *who came out of his loins* [a]Ex. 1:5
27 [I]Lit., *two souls* [a]Ex. 1:5; Deut. 10:22; Acts 7:14
28 [a]Gen. 45:10
29 [I]Lit., *tied, harnessed* [II]Lit., *to* [a]Gen. 45:14, 15
31 [a]Gen. 47:1
32 [I]Lit., *men*
33 [a]Gen. 47:2, 3
34 [I]Lit., *men* [II]Lit., *dwell* [III]Lit., *an abomination* [a]Gen. 13:7, 8; 26:20; 37:2 [b]Gen. 45:10, 18; 47:6, 11 [c]Gen. 43:32; Ex. 8:26
1 [a]Gen. 46:31 [b]Gen. 45:10; 46:28
2 [a]Acts 7:13
3 [a]Gen. 46:33 [b]Gen. 46:34
4 [I]Lit., *dwell* [a]Gen. 15:13; Deut. 26:5; Ps. 105:23 [b]Gen. 43:1; Acts 7:11 [c]Gen. 46:34
5 [I]Lit., *Joseph, saying*
6 [I]Lit., *before you*

🗝 **46:27** Jacob's children, grandchildren, and great-grandchildren amounted to sixty-six (Gen. 46:8-26). Adding Jacob himself, and Joseph with his two sons, we have seventy. If we add to the sixty-six the nine wives of Jacob's sons (Judah's wives and Simeon's wives were dead; Joseph could not be said to call himself, his own wife, or his two sons into Egypt; and Jacob is specified separately by Stephen in Acts 7:14), we have seventy-five persons, as in Acts.

🗝 **46:34** There was a historical reason for the hatred of the shepherds. The Hyksos (or, Shepherd Kings), hundreds of years before Joseph's time, had invaded and conquered Lower Egypt and ruled the Delta, and were still in power at the time of Joseph. They came from the East and were probably Arabians, and are represented as having been a cruel and arrogant race who subjected the Egyptians to great hardships. They were finally driven out of the country by a coalition of forces under several kings. The Hebrews were probably called Shepherds because of the simplicity of their life, which was largely pastoral. Manetho, the Egyptian historian, said that they were the builders of Jerusalem, but his reference is probably to the Canaanites rather than to the Jews. Some writers suggest that they were the progenitors of the Bedouins, and that the Amalekites, Midianites, and other hostile nations who opposed the Israelites after the Exodus were also descended from the same stock of the expelled Shepherds. It is not improbable that the Philistines may also have been a branch of the same Shepherd family.

disposal; [II]settle your father and your
brothers in [a]the best of the land, let[7760]
them [III]live in the land of Goshen; and
if you know any [b]capable[2428] men among
them, then [IV]put them in charge[8269] of
my livestock."
7 Then Joseph brought his father Jacob and [I]presented him to Pharaoh; and
Jacob [a]blessed[1288] Pharaoh.
8 And Pharaoh said to Jacob, "How
many [I]years[3117] have you lived?"
9 So Jacob said to Pharaoh, "The
[Ia]years[3117] of my sojourning[4033] are one
hundred and [II]thirty; few and [III]un-
pleasant[7451] have been the [I]years of my
life, nor have they [IV]attained [b]the
[I]years [V]that my fathers lived during the
days of their sojourning."
10 And Jacob [a]blessed Pharaoh, and
went out from [I]his presence.
11 So Joseph [I]settled his father and
his brothers, and gave them a
possession[272] in the land of Egypt, in
[a]the best of the land, in the land of
[b]Rameses, as Pharaoh had ordered.[6680]
12 And Joseph [a]provided his father
and his brothers and all his father's
household[1004] with [I]food, according to
their little ones.[2945]
13 Now there was no [I]food in all
the land, because the famine was very
severe, so that [a]the land of Egypt and
the land of Canaan languished because
of the famine.
14 And [a]Joseph gathered[3950] all the
money that was found in the land of
Egypt and in the land of Canaan for the
grain[7668] which they bought, and Joseph
brought the money into Pharaoh's
house.[1004]
15 And when the money was all
spent[8552] in the land of Egypt and in
the land of Canaan, all the Egyptians
came to Joseph [I]and said, "Give us
[II]food, for [a]why should we die[4191] in your
presence? For *our* money [III]is gone."
16 Then Joseph said, "Give up your
livestock, and I will give you *food* for
your livestock, since *your* money
[I]is gone."
17 So they brought their livestock
to Joseph, and Joseph gave them
[I]food in exchange for the horses and
the [II]flocks and the herds and the donkeys; and he [III]fed them with [I]food in
exchange for all their livestock [IV]that
year.
18 And when that year was end-
ed,[8552] they came to him the [I]next year
and said to him, "We will not hide from
my lord[113] that our money is all
spent,[8552] and the [II]cattle are my lord's.
There is nothing left [III]for my lord except
our bodies[1472] and our lands.[127]
19 "Why should we die before your
eyes, both we and our land? Buy us
and our land for [I]food, and we and our
land will be slaves to Pharaoh. So give
us seed,[2233] that we may live[2421] and
not die, and that the land may not be
desolate."[3456]

Result of the Famine

20 So Joseph bought all the land of
Egypt for Pharaoh, for [I]every[376] Egyptian sold his field, because the famine
was severe[2388] upon them. Thus the land
became Pharaoh's.
21 And as for the people,[5971] he
removed[5674] them to the cities from one
end of Egypt's border to the other.
22 Only the land of the priests[3548]
he did not buy, for the priests had an
allotment[2706] from Pharaoh, and they
[I]lived off the allotment which Pharaoh
gave them. Therefore, they did not sell
their land.
23 Then Joseph said to the people,
"Behold, I have today[3117] bought you
and your land for Pharaoh; now, *here*
is seed for you, and you may sow the
land.
24 "And [I]at the harvest you shall
give a [a]fifth to Pharaoh, and [II]four-fifths
shall be your own for seed of the field
and for your food and for those of your
households and as food for your little
ones."
25 So they said, "You have saved
our lives![2421] Let us find favor[2580] in the
sight of my lord, and we will be Pharaoh's slaves."
26 And Joseph made[7760] it a

6 [II]Lit., *cause them to dwell* [III]Lit., *dwell* [IV]Lit., *appoint them rulers* [a]Gen. 45:10, 18; 47:11 [b]Ex. 18:21, 25; 1Kin. 11:28; Prov. 22:29

7 [I]Lit., *set him before* [a]Gen. 47:10; 2Sam. 14:22; 1Kin. 8:66

8 [I]Lit., *are the days of the years of your life*

9 [I]Lit., *days of the years* [II]Lit., *thirty years* [III]Lit., *evil* [IV]Lit., *reached* [V]Lit., *of the life of my fathers* [a]Heb. 11:9, 13 [b]Gen. 25:7; 35:28

10 [I]Lit., *Pharaoh's* [a]Gen. 47:7

11 [I]Lit., *caused to dwell* [a]Gen. 47:6, 27 [b]Ex. 1:11; 12:37

12 [I]Or, *bread* [a]Gen. 45:11

13 [I]Or, *bread* [a]Gen. 41:30; Acts 7:11

14 [a]Gen. 41:56

15 [I]Lit., *saying* [II]Or, *bread* [III]Lit., *ceases* [a]Gen. 47:19

16 [I]Lit., *ceases*

17 [I]Or, *bread* [II]Lit., *livestock of the flocks and livestock of the herds* [III]Lit., *led them as a shepherd* [IV]Lit., *in that year*

18 [I]Lit., *second* [II]Lit., *livestock of the cattle* [III]Lit., *in the presence of*

19 [I]Or, *bread*

20 [I]Lit., *Egypt, every man*

22 [I]Lit., *ate their allotment*

24 [I]Lit., *it shall come about that you shall* [II]Lit., *four parts* [a]Gen. 41:34

statute[2706] concerning the land of
Egypt *valid* to this day, that Pharaoh
should have the fifth; [a]only the land
of the priests [I]did not become Pharaoh's.
27 Now Israel [I]lived in the land of
Egypt, in [II]Goshen, and they [a]acquired
property in it and [b]were fruitful and became very numerous.
28 And Jacob lived[2421] in the land
of Egypt [a]seventeen years; so the
[I]length[3117] of Jacob's life was one hundred and forty-seven years.
29 When [Ia]the time[3117] for Israel to
die drew near, he called his son[1121] Joseph and said to him, "Please, if I have
found favor in your sight, [b]place[7760] now
your hand under my thigh[3409] and
[c]deal[6213] with me in kindness[2617] and
[II]faithfulness.[571] Please do not bury[6912]
me in Egypt,
30 but when I [a]lie down with my
fathers, you shall carry[5375] me out of
Egypt and bury[6912] me in [b]their burial
place."[6913] And he said,[559] "I will do[6213]
as you have said."
🔑 31 And he said, "[a]Swear[7650] to me."
So he swore to him. Then [b]Israel
bowed[7812] *in worship* at the head[7218] of
the bed.

Israel's Last Days

48 Now it came about after these
things[1697] that [I]Joseph was told,
"Behold, your father[1] is sick." So he
took his two sons [a]Manasseh and
Ephraim with him.
2 When [I]it was told[5046] to Jacob,
"Behold, your son Joseph has come
to you," Israel [II]collected his
strength[2388] and sat [III]up in the bed.
3 Then Jacob said to Joseph,
"[Ia]God[410] Almighty[7706] appeared to me
at [b]Luz in the land of Canaan and
blessed[1288] me,
4 and He said to me, 'Behold, I will
make you fruitful and numerous, and I
will make you a company[6951] of peoples,[5971] and will give this land[776] to your
[I]descendants[2233] after you for [a]an everlasting[5769] possession.'[272]
🔑 5 "And now your two sons, who
were born to you in the land of Egypt
before I came to you in Egypt, are mine;
[a]Ephraim and Manasseh shall be mine,
as [b]Reuben and Simeon are.
6 "But your offspring that [I]have
been born after them shall be yours;
they shall be called[7121] by the [II]names
of their brothers[251] in their inheritance.[5159]
7 "Now as for me, when I came from
[a]Paddan, [b]Rachel died,[4191] [I]to my sorrow, in the land[776] of Canaan on the
journey, when there was still some distance to go to Ephrath; and I buried[6912]
her there on the way[1870] to Ephrath (that
is, Bethlehem)."
8 When Israel [a]saw[7200] Joseph's
sons,[1121] he said, "Who are these?"
9 And Joseph said to his father,
"[a]They are my sons, whom God[430]
has given me here." So he said, "Bring
them to me, please, that [b]I may bless
them."
10 Now [a]the eyes of Israel were *so*
dim[3513] from age[2207] *that* he could not

26 [I]Lit., *alone did* [a]Gen. 47:22
27 [I]Lit., *dwelt* [II]Lit., *in the land of Goshen* [a]Gen. 47:11 [b]Gen. 17:6; 26:4; 35:11; Ex. 1:7; Deut. 26:5; Acts 7:17
28 [I]Lit., *days of Jacob, the years of his life* [a]Gen. 47:9
29 [I]Lit., *the days of Israel to die drew near* [II]Lit., *truth* [a]Deut. 31:14; 1Kin. 2:1 [b]Gen. 24:2 [c]Gen. 24:49
30 [a]Gen. 15:15; Deut. 31:16 [b]Gen. 23:17-20; 25:9, 10; 35:29; 49:29-32; 50:5, 13; Acts 7:15, 16
31 [a]Gen. 21:23, 24; 24:3; 31:53; 50:25 [b]1Kin. 1:47

1 [I]Lit., *one said to Joseph* [a]Gen. 41:51, 52; Josh. 14:4
2 [I]Lit., *one told Jacob and said* [II]Lit., *strengthened himself* [III]Lit., *upon the bed*
3 [I]Heb., *El Shaddai* [a]Gen. 28:13f.; 35:9-12 [b]Gen. 28:19; 35:6
4 [I]Lit., *seed* [a]Gen. 17:8
5 [a]Gen. 41:50-52; 46:20; 48:1; Josh. 14:4 [b]1Chr. 5:1, 2
6 [I]Lit., *you have begotten* [II]Lit., *name*
7 [I]Lit., *upon me* [a]Gen. 33:18 [b]Gen. 35:19, 20
8 [a]Gen. 48:10
9 [a]Gen. 33:5 [b]Gen. 27:4
10 [a]Gen. 27:1

🔑 **47:31** Did Jacob support himself on the head of the bed, or did he support himself by his staff (Heb. 11:21)? Genesis represents Jacob as not yet sick (just old) and Hebrews speaks of Jacob as "dying." Therefore, it is quite possible that the two passages may not be referring to the same incident. Our present Hebrew vocalization (*mittah*) is translated as "bed," while the Greek Septuagint and the Epistle to the Hebrews follows a different vocalization (*matteh*), which is translated as "staff." All Hebrew vowels were inserted into the Hebrew consonantal text late. Therefore, we cannot be sure what the correct reading is.

🔑 **48:5** Jacob formally adopted his two grandsons Ephraim and Manasseh as his own sons. Through them Joseph received a double portion of his father's inheritance. In the future development of Israel, God claimed the tribe of Levi as His own, therefore, they had no portion of the inheritance of Israel. With the double portion of the sons of Joseph there still remained twelve tribes who would share in the inheritance which God promised to Israel.

see.7200 Then [I]Joseph brought them close to him, and he [b]kissed them and embraced them.

11 And Israel said to Joseph, "I never [I]expected6419 to see your face, and behold, God has let me see7200 your [II]children as well."

12 Then Joseph [I]took them from his knees, and [a]bowed7812 with his face639 to the ground.776

13 And Joseph took them both, Ephraim with his right hand toward Israel's left, and Manasseh with his left hand toward Israel's right, and brought them close to him.

14 But Israel stretched out his right hand3225 and laid it on the head of Ephraim, who was the younger, and his left hand on Manasseh's head, [I]crossing7919 his hands, [II]although [a]Manasseh was the first-born.

15 And he blessed1288 Joseph, and said,

"[a]The God before whom my
fathers Abraham and Isaac
walked,
[b]The God who has been my
shepherd [I]all my life to this
day,3117

16 [a]The angel who has
redeemed1350 me from all
evil,7451
[b]Bless the lads;
And may my name [I]live on in
them,
And the [II]names of my fathers
Abraham and Isaac;
And [c]may they grow1711 into a
multitude in the midst of the
earth."

17 When Joseph saw7200 that his father [a]laid his right hand on Ephraim's head, it displeased3415 him; and he grasped his father's hand to remove it from Ephraim's head to Manasseh's head.

18 And Joseph said to his father, "Not so, my father, for this one is the first-born. Place7760 your right hand on his head."

19 But his father refused3985 and said, "I know,3045 my son, I know; he also shall become a people and he also shall be great. However, his younger brother shall be greater than he, and [a]his [I]descendants shall become a [II]multitude of nations."1471

20 And [a]he blessed1288 them that day, saying,

"By you Israel shall pronounce
blessing, saying,
'May God make you like Ephraim
and Manasseh!'"

Thus he put Ephraim before Manasseh.

21 Then Israel said to Joseph, "Behold, I am about to die, but [a]God will be with you, and [b]bring you back7725 to the land776 of your fathers.

22 "And I give you one [I]portion more than your brothers, [a]which I took from the hand of the Amorite with my sword and my bow."

Israel's Prophecy Concerning His Sons

49 Then Jacob summoned7121 his sons1121 and said, "Assemble yourselves that I may tell5046 you what shall befall you [a]in the [I]days3117 to come.319

2 "Gather together and hear,8085
O sons of Jacob;
And [a]listen8085 to Israel your
father.1

3 "Reuben, you are my first-born;
My might and [a]the beginning7225
of my strength,
[I]Preeminent3499 in dignity and
[I]preeminent in power.

4 "[I]Uncontrolled as water, you shall
not have preeminence,
[a]Because you went up to your
father's bed;
Then you defiled2490 *it*—he went
up to my couch.

5 "[a]Simeon and Levi are brothers;
Their swords are implements of
violence.2555

6 "[a]Let my soul5315 not enter into
their council;5475
Let not my glory3519 be united
with their assembly;6951
Because in their anger639 they
slew2026 [I]men,376

---

10 [I]Lit., *the* [b]Gen. 27:27

11 [I]Lit., *meditated, judged* [II]Lit., *seed*

12 [I]Lit., *made them come out* [a]Gen. 42:6

14 [I]Or, *consciously directing* [II]Lit., *when* [a]Gen. 41:51, 52

15 [I]Lit., *from the continuance of me* [a]Gen. 17:1 [b]Gen. 49:24

16 [I]Lit., *be called* [II]Lit., *name* [a]Gen. 22:11, 15-18; 28:13-15; 31:11 [b]Heb. 11:21 [c]Gen. 28:14; 46:3

17 [a]Gen. 48:14

19 [I]Lit., *seed* [II]Lit., *fulness* [a]Gen. 28:14; 46:3

20 [a]Heb. 11:21

21 [a]Gen. 26:3 [b]Gen. 28:15; 46:4; 50:24

22 [I]Or, *ridge;* lit., *shoulder;* Heb., *Shechem* [a]Josh. 24:32; John 4:5

1 [I]Lit., *end of the days* [a]Num. 24:14

2 [a]Ps. 34:11

3 [I]Lit., *preeminence* [a]Deut. 21:17; Ps. 78:51; 105:36

4 [I]Or, *Boiling over;* lit., *recklessness* [a]Gen. 35:22; Deut. 27:20; 1Chr. 5:1

5 [a]Gen. 34:25-30

6 [I]Lit., *a man* [a]Ps. 64:2

And in their self-will[7522] they
lamed [II]oxen.
7 "Cursed[779] be their anger, for it
is fierce;
And their wrath,[5678] for it is
cruel.
[a]I will [I]disperse them in Jacob,
And scatter them in Israel.
8 "Judah, your brothers shall praise
you;
Your hand shall be on the neck
of your enemies;
[a]Your father's sons[1121] shall
bow[7812] down to you.
9 "Judah is a [a]lion's whelp;[1482]
From the prey, my son, you
have gone up.
[b]He [I]couches,[3766] he lies down
as a lion,
And as a [II]lion, who [III]dares rouse
him up?
⊶ 10 "[a]The scepter[7626] shall not depart
from Judah,
Nor the ruler's[2710] staff from
between his feet,
[I]Until Shiloh[7886] comes,
And [b]to him *shall be* the
obedience of the peoples.[5971]
11 "[I][a]He ties *his* foal to the vine,
And his donkey's colt[1121] to the
choice vine;
[b]He washes[3526] his garments in
wine,
And his robes in the blood[1818]
of grapes.
12 "His eyes are [I]dull from wine,
And his teeth [II]white from milk.
13 "[a]Zebulun shall dwell at the seashore;
And he *shall be* [I]a haven for
ships,
And his flank *shall be* toward
Sidon.
14 "Issachar is [I]a strong donkey,
[a]Lying down between the
[II]sheepfolds.

15 "When he saw[7200] that a resting
place was good[2896]
And that the land[776] was
pleasant,
He bowed his shoulder to bear
burdens,
And became a slave[5647] at forced
labor.
16 "[a]Dan shall [b]judge his people,
As one of the tribes[7626] of Israel.
17 "Dan shall be a serpent[5175] in the
way,
A horned snake[8207] in the
path,[734]
That bites the horse's heels,[6119]
So that his rider falls backward.
18 "[a]For Thy salvation[3444] I wait,[6960]
O LORD.
19 "[a]As for Gad, [I]raiders[1416] shall
raid him,
But he shall raid *at* their
[II]heels.[6119]
20 "[I][a]As for [b]Asher, his [II]food shall
be [III]rich,
And he shall yield royal dainties.
21 "[a]Naphtali is a doe[355] let loose,
He gives beautiful words.[561]
22 "[a]Joseph is a fruitful [I]bough,[1121]
A fruitful [I]bough by a spring;
Its [II]branches run over a wall.
23 "The archers[1167] bitterly[4843]
attacked him,
And shot *at him* and harassed[7852]
him;
24 But his [a]bow remained [I]firm,
And [II][b]his arms were agile,
From the hands[3027] of the
[c]Mighty One of Jacob
(From there is [d]the Shepherd,
[e]the Stone of Israel),
25 From [a]the God[410] of your father
who helps you,
And [I][b]by the [II]Almighty[7706] who
blesses[1288] you

6 [II]Lit., *an ox*
7 [I]Lit., *divide* [a]Josh. 19:1, 9; 21:1-42
8 [a]Gen. 27:29; 1Chr. 5:2
9 [I]Lit., *bows down* [II]Or, *lioness* [III]Lit., *shall* [a]Ezek. 19:5-7; Mic. 5:8 [b]Num. 24:9
10 [I]Or, *Until he comes to Shiloh*; or, *Until he comes to whom it belongs* [a]Num. 24:17; Ps. 60:7; 108:8 [b]Ps. 2:6-9; 72:8-11; Is. 42:1, 4; 49:6
11 [I]Lit., *Binding of* [a]Deut. 8:7, 8; 2Kin. 18:32 [b]Is. 63:2
12 [I]Or, *darker than* [II]Or, *whiter than*
13 [I]Lit., *for a shore of ships* [a]Deut. 33:18, 19
14 [I]Lit., *a donkey of bone* [II]Or, *saddlebags* [a]Judg. 5:16; Ps. 68:13
16 [a]Deut. 33:22; Judg. 18:26, 27 [b]Gen. 30:6
18 [a]Ex. 15:2; Ps. 25:5; 40:1-3; 119:166, 174; Is. 25:9; Mic. 7:7
19 [I]Lit., *a raiding band* [II]Lit., *heel* [a]Deut. 33:20
20 [I]Lit., *From* [II]Or, *bread* [III]Lit., *fat* [a]Deut. 33:24, 25 [b]Gen. 30:13
21 [a]Deut. 33:23
22 [I]Lit., *son* [II]Lit., *daughters* [a]Deut. 33:13-17
24 [I]I.e., in an unyielding position [II]Lit., *the arms of his hands* [a]Job 29:20 [b]Ps. 18:34; 73:23; Is. 41:10 [c]Ps. 132:2, 5; Is. 1:24; 49:26 [d]Ps. 23:1; 80:1 [e]Ps. 118:22; Is. 28:16; 1Pet. 2:6-8
25 [I]Or, *with* [II]Heb., *Shaddai* [a]Gen. 28:13; 32:9 [b]Gen. 28:3; 48:3

⊶ **49:10** This verse probably means that Judah would maintain its identity as a people with an established government until the coming of Shiloh (or Christ?). In fact, Judah alone, of all the tribes of Israel, remained a distinct organized political unity until the Messiah came. However, it lost that position a short time later with the destruction of Jerusalem in A.D. 70. This passage is not quoted in the N.T. with reference to Messianic prophecy.

With [c]blessings[1293] of heaven[8064]
above,
Blessings of the deep that lies
beneath,
Blessings of the breasts and of
the womb.
26 "The blessings of your father
Have surpassed the blessings of
my ancestors
Up to the [I]utmost bound of
[a]the everlasting[5769] hills;
May they be on the head of
Joseph,
And on the crown of the head
of the one distinguished[5139]
among his brothers.
27 "Benjamin is a [I]ravenous[2963] wolf;
In the morning he devours the
prey,
And in the evening he divides
the spoil."
28 All these are the twelve tribes
of Israel, and this is what their father
said[1696] to them [I]when he blessed[1288]
them. He blessed them, every one[376]
[II]with the blessing appropriate to him.
29 Then he charged[6680] them and
said to them, "I am about to be [a]gathered
to my people; [b]bury me with my fathers
in the cave that is in [c]the field[7704] of
Ephron the Hittite,
30 in the [a]cave that is in the field
of Machpelah, which is before Mamre,
in the land of Canaan, which Abraham
bought along with the field from Ephron
the Hittite for a [I]burial site.[6913]
31 "There they buried[6912] [a]Abraham
and his wife [b]Sarah, there they buried
[c]Isaac and his wife Rebekah, and there
I buried Leah—
32 the field and the cave that is in
it, purchased from the sons of Heth."
33 When Jacob finished charging[6680]
his sons, he drew his feet into the bed
and [a]breathed his last,[1478] and was
[b]gathered to his people.

The Death of Israel

50 Then Joseph fell on his father's[1]
face, and wept over him and
kissed him.
2 And Joseph commanded[6680] his
servants[5650] the physicians to embalm
his father. So the physicians [a]embalmed
Israel.
3 Now forty days[3117] were [I]required
for [II]it, for [III]such is the period required
for embalming. And the Egyptians
[a]wept for him seventy days.
4 And when the days of [I]mourning
for him were past,[5674] Joseph spoke to
the household[1004] of Pharaoh, saying,
"If now I have found favor[2580] in your
sight, please speak [II]to Pharaoh, saying,
5 '[a]My father made me swear,[7650]
saying, "Behold, I am about to die; in
my grave[6913] [b]which I dug for myself
in the land[776] of Canaan, there you shall
bury[6912] me." Now therefore, please let
me go up and bury my father; then I
will return.' "[7725]
6 And Pharaoh said, "Go up and
bury your father, as he made you
swear."
7 So Joseph went up to bury his father, and with him went up all the servants of Pharaoh, the elders[2205] of his
household and all the elders of the land
of Egypt,
8 and all the household of Joseph
and his brothers[251] and his father's
household; they left[5800] only their little
ones[2945] and their flocks and their herds
in the land of Goshen.
9 There also went up with him both
chariots and horsemen; and it was a very
great company.[4264]
10 When they came to the [I]thresh-
ing floor of Atad, which is beyond the
Jordan, they [a]lamented there with a very
great and [II]sorrowful lamentation; and
he [III]observed[6213] seven days mourning
for his father.
11 Now when the inhabitants of the
land, the Canaanites, saw[7200] the mourning at [I]the threshing floor of Atad, they
said, "This is a [II]grievous [III]mourning[60]
for the Egyptians." Therefore it was
named[7121] [IV]Abel-mizraim,[67] which is beyond the Jordan.

Burial at Machpelah

12 And thus his sons[1121] did[6213] for
him as he had charged[6680] them;

25 [c]Gen. 27:28
26 [I]Lit., *limit;* or, *desire* [a]Deut. 33:15, 16
27 [I]Lit., *a wolf that tears*
28 [I]Lit., *and* [II]Lit., *according to his blessing*
29 [a]Gen. 25:8 [b]Gen. 47:30 [c]Gen. 23:16-20; 50:13
30 [I]Lit., *possession of a burial place* [a]Gen. 23:3-20
31 [a]Gen. 25:9 [b]Gen. 23:19 [c]Gen. 35:29
33 [a]Gen. 25:8; Acts 7:15 [b]Gen. 49:29
2 [a]Gen. 50:26; 2Chr. 16:14; Matt. 26:12; Mark 16:1; John 19:39, 40
3 [I]Lit., *fulfilled* [II]Or, *him* [III]Lit., *so are fulfilled the days of embalming* [a]Gen. 50:10; Num. 20:29; Deut. 34:8
4 [I]Lit., *weeping* [II]Lit., *In the ears of*
5 [a]Gen. 47:29-31 [b]2Chr. 16:14; Is. 22:16; Matt. 27:60
10 [I]Heb., *Goren ha-Atad* [II]Lit., *heavy* [III]Lit., *made a mourning for seven days* [a]Acts 8:2
11 [I]Heb., *Goren ha-Atad* [II]Lit., *heavy* [III]Heb., *ebel* [IV]I.e., the meadow (or mourning) of Egypt

13 for his sons carried[5375] him to the land of Canaan, and buried him in [a]the cave of the field[7704] of Machpelah before Mamre, which Abraham had bought along with the field for a [I]burial site[6913] from Ephron the Hittite.

14 And after he had buried his father, Joseph returned[7725] to Egypt, he and his brothers, and all who had gone up with him to bury his father.

15 When Joseph's brothers saw that their father was dead,[4191] they said, "[a]What if[3863] Joseph should bear a grudge against[7852] us and pay us back in full for all the wrong[7451] which we did[1580] to him!"

16 So they [I]sent *a message*[6680] to Joseph, saying, "Your father charged before he died,[4194] saying,

17 'Thus you shall say to Joseph, "Please forgive,[5375] I beg you,[577] the transgression[6588] of your brothers[251] and their sin,[2403] for they did you wrong." ' And now, please forgive the transgression of the servants of the God[430] of your father." And Joseph wept when they spoke to him.

18 Then his brothers also came and [a]fell down before him and said, "Behold, we are your servants."

19 But Joseph said to them, "Do not be afraid,[3372] for am I in God's place?

20 "And as for you, [a]you meant[2803] evil against me, *but* God meant it for good[2896] in order to bring about[6213] [I]this present result, to preserve[2421] many people[5971] alive.[2421]

21 "So therefore, do not be afraid; [a]I will provide for you and your little ones." So he comforted[5162] them and spoke [I]kindly[3820] to them.

Death of Joseph

22 Now Joseph stayed in Egypt, he and his father's household,[1004] and Joseph lived[2421] one hundred and ten years.

23 And Joseph saw the third generation of Ephraim's sons;[1121] also the sons of Machir, the son of Manasseh, were [a]born on Joseph's knees.

24 And Joseph said to his brothers, "[a]I am about to die, but God will surely [I]take care of[6485] you, and bring you up from this land to the land which He [II]promised on oath[7650] to [b]Abraham, to [c]Isaac and to [d]Jacob."

25 Then Joseph made the sons of Israel swear,[7650] saying, "God will surely [I]take care of you, and [a]you shall carry my bones[6106] up from here."

26 So Joseph died[4191] at the age of one hundred and ten years; and [I]he was [a]embalmed and placed in a coffin[727] in Egypt.

---

13 [I]Lit., *possession of a burial place* [a]Gen. 23:16-20; Acts 7:16

15 [a]Gen. 37:28; 42:21, 22

16 [I]Lit., *commanded*

18 [a]Gen. 37:8-10; 41:43

20 [I]Lit., *as it is this day* [a]Gen. 37:26, 27; 45:5, 7

21 [I]Lit., *to their heart* [a]Gen. 45:11; 47:12

23 [a]Gen. 30:3

24 [I]Or, *visit* [II]Lit., *swore* [a]Gen. 48:21; Ex. 3:16, 17; Heb. 11:22 [b]Gen. 13:15, 17; 15:7, 8, 18 [c]Gen. 26:3 [d]Gen. 28:13; 35:12

25 [I]Or, *visit* [a]Gen. 47:29, 30; Ex. 13:19; Josh. 24:32; Heb. 11:22

26 [I]Lit., *they embalmed him* [a]Gen. 50:2

EXODUS

Exodus is a Greek word which is composed of two parts, *ek,* "out," and *hodos,* "road." The Book of Exodus describes the departure of the nation of Israel from their bondage in the land of Egypt. Centuries before the Patriarch, Jacob, had brought his extended family to Egypt to avoid starvation (see Gen. 46:1-27). Because of a shift in political power, the descendants of Joseph and his brothers fell into slavery, but they became quite numerous. The emphasis in Genesis upon one family has given way to a focus upon the nation of Israel in the Book of Exodus. They are slowly shaped into a people who are in a covenant relationship with Jehovah God.

The main theme of Exodus is redemption. All people may have hope, no matter how desperate the situation. God will send a deliverer to display His awesome power, and deliverance will come through blood. Moses is clearly a type of Jesus Christ. God keeps His promises.

There can be little doubt that Moses wrote the Book of Exodus. He penned it from first-hand experience with God and with the people of Israel. There are two distinct portions: (1) the historical section (chapters 1—19); (2) the regulations (chapters 20—40).

Israel Multiplies in Egypt

1 Now these are the [a]names of the
sons[1121] of Israel who came to Egypt
with Jacob; they came each one[376]
[I]with his household:[1004]
2 Reuben, Simeon, Levi and Judah;
3 Issachar, Zebulun and Benjamin;
4 Dan and Naphtali, Gad and Asher.
5 And all the [I]persons[5315] who came
from the loins[3409] of Jacob were [a]seventy
[II]in number, but Joseph was *already* in
Egypt.
🔑6 And [a]Joseph died, and all his
brothers[251] and all that generation.[1755]
7 But the sons of Israel [a]were fruitful and [I]increased greatly, and multiplied, and became exceedingly [II]mighty,
so that the land[776] was filled with them.
🔑8 Now a new [a]king[4428] arose over
Egypt, who did not know[3045] Joseph.
9 And [a]he said[559] to his people,[5971]
"Behold, the people of the sons of Israel
are [I]more and mightier than we.
10 "Come, let us [a]deal wisely with
them, lest they multiply and [I]in the event
of war, they also join themselves to
those who hate us,[8130] and fight against
us, and [II]depart[5927] from the land."
11 So they appointed [a]taskmas-
ters[8269] over them to afflict them with
[I][b]hard labor. And they built for Pharaoh
[c]storage cities, Pithom and [d]Raamses.
12 But the more they afflicted them,
[a]the more they multiplied and the more
they [I]spread out, so that they were in
dread[6973] of the sons of Israel.
13 And the Egyptians compelled the
sons of Israel [a]to labor rigorously;

1 [I]Lit., *and* [a]Gen. 46:8-27 **5** [I]Lit., *souls* [II]Lit., *as to souls* [a]Gen. 46:26, 27; Deut. 10:22 **6** [a]Gen. 50:26 **7** [I]Lit., *swarmed* [II]Or, *numerous* [a]Gen. 12:2; 28:3; 35:11; 46:3; 47:27; 48:4; Deut. 26:5; Ps. 105:24; Acts 7:17 **8** [a]Acts 7:18, 19 **9** [I]Or, *too many and too mighty for us* [a]Ps. 105:24, 25 **10** [I]Lit., *it came about when war befalls that* [II]Lit., *go up from* [a]Acts 7:19 **11** [I]Lit., *their burdens* [a]Gen. 15:13; Ex. 3:7; 5:6 [b]Ex. 1:14; 2:11; 5:4-9; 6:6f. [c]1Kin. 9:19; 2Chr. 8:4 [d]Gen. 47:11 **12** [I]Lit., *broke forth* [a]Ex. 1:7 **13** [a]Gen. 15:13; Deut. 4:20

🔑 **1:6** The word "generation" is used in a variety of ways in the Scriptures. In some cases it refers to a period of time without set limits (Ps. 102:24) while at other times it is used as a simple reference to the past (Isa. 51:8) or the future (Ps. 100:5). It is also used to designate men with particular characteristics or of a certain class. Here it refers to all of a particular class living at a designated time.

🔑 **1:8** Joseph went to Egypt during a period when a foreign Semitic people, known as the Hyksos, had taken over and ruled Egypt. The fact that Joseph was Semitic and from the same general area probably made it easier for the Pharaoh to elevate him to such a high post than if the Pharaoh had been a native Egyptian. When the Hyksos were finally expelled, not only would the Egyptians have regarded foreign Semitic people who had settled in Egypt under the preceding administration as a military threat (see Ex. 1:9,10), but their continued presence would have been a constant reminder of their former foreign overlords. Hence, all the ingredients were present for the enslavement of Israel, although they had nothing to do with the earlier subjugation of the Egyptians by the Hyksos.

14 and they made [a]their lives[2416] bitter with hard labor[5656] in mortar and
bricks and at all *kinds* of labor[5656]
in the field,[7704] all their labors[5647]
which they rigorously [I]imposed[5647] on
them.
15 Then the king of Egypt spoke[559]
to the Hebrew midwives, one of whom
[I]was named Shiphrah, and the other
[I]was named Puah;
16 and he said, "When you are helping the Hebrew women to give birth
and see[7200] *them* upon the birthstool,
[a]if it is a son, then you shall put him to
death; but if it is a daughter, then she
shall live."[2425]
🔑17 But the midwives [Ia]feared[3372]
God,[430] and [b]did[6213] not do as the king
of Egypt had [II]commanded[1696] them, but
let[2421] the boys live.[2421]
18 So the king of Egypt called[7121]
for the midwives, and said to them,
"Why have you done this thing,[1697] and
let the boys live?"
19 And the midwives said to Pharaoh, "Because the Hebrew women are
not as the Egyptian women; for they
are vigorous,[2422] and they give birth[2962]
before the midwife [I]can get to
them."
20 So [a]God was good to the midwives, and [b]the people multiplied, and
became very [I]mighty.
21 And it came about because the
midwives [Ia]feared[3372] God, that He
[IIb]established[6213] [III]households[1004] for
them.
22 Then Pharaoh commanded[6680] all
his people, saying,[559] "[a]Every son who
is born [I]you are to cast into [b]the Nile,
and every daughter you are to keep
alive."

14 [I]Lit., *worked through them* [a]Ex. 2:23; 6:9; Num. 20:15; Acts 7:19

15 [I]Lit., *the name was*

16 [a]Acts 7:19

17 [I]Or, *revered* [II]Lit., *spoken to* [a]Ex. 1:21; Prov. 16:6 [b]Acts 4:18-20; 5:29

19 [I]Lit., *comes to*

20 [I]Or, *numerous* [a]Prov. 11:18; Eccl. 8:12; Heb. 6:10 [b]Ex. 1:12; Is. 3:10

21 [I]Or, *revered* [II]Lit., *made* [III]Or, *families* [a]Ex. 1:17 [b]1Sam. 2:35; 2Sam. 7:11, 27; 1Kin. 2:24; 11:38

22 [I]Some versions insert *to the Hebrews* [a]Acts 7:19 [b]Gen. 41:1

1 [I]Lit., *took* [a]Ex. 6:16, 18, 20

2 [I]Lit., *him that* [II]Lit., *good* [a]Acts 7:20; Heb. 11:23

3 [I]I.e., papyrus reeds [II]Or, *chest* [a]Is. 18:2 [b]Is. 19:6

4 [I]Lit., *know* [II]Lit., *be done* [a]Ex. 15:20; Num. 26:59

5 [I]Or, *chest* [a]Ex. 7:15; 8:20

6 [I]Heb., *saw it, the child* [II]Or, *lad*

7 [I]Lit., *a woman giving suck*

The Birth of Moses

2 Now a man[376] from [a]the house[1004]
of Levi went and [I]married a daughter of Levi.
2 And the woman[802] conceived and
bore a son;[1121] and when she saw[7200]
[I]that he was [IIa]beautiful,[2896] she hid him
for three months.
3 But when she could hide him no
longer, she got him a [Ia]wicker [II]basket
and covered it over with tar and pitch.
Then she put the child into it, and set
it among the [b]reeds[5488] by the bank[8193]
of the Nile.
4 And [a]his sister[269] stood at a distance to [I]find out[3045] what would
[II]happen[6213] to him.
5 Then the daughter of Pharaoh
came down [a]to bathe at the Nile, with
her maidens walking alongside[3027] the
Nile; and she saw the [I]basket among
the reeds and sent her maid, and she
brought it *to her*.
6 When she opened *it*, she [I]saw the
child, and behold, *the* [II]boy was crying.
And she had pity on him and said,[559]
"This is one of the Hebrews' children."
7 Then his sister said to Pharaoh's
daughter, "Shall I go and call[7121]
[I]a nurse for you from the Hebrew
women, that she may nurse the child
for you?"
8 And Pharaoh's daughter said to
her, "Go *ahead*." So the girl[5959] went
and called the child's mother.[517]
9 Then Pharaoh's daughter said to
her, "Take this child away and nurse
him for me and I shall give *you* your
wages." So the woman took the child
and nursed him.
🔑10 And the child grew, and she

🔑 **1:17-20** God has instituted civil government for the good of the people (Rom. 13:1-5). Throughout the Scriptures He instructs His people to be in submission and obedient to those powers (Ecc. 8:2; I Pet. 2:13,14). But those powers are not granted the right to compel men to do things which are contrary to God's law (Dan. 3:16,18; Acts 4:19; 5:29). The question arises here as to whether the Hebrew midwives were lying and refusing obedience to the king. If they did, it was done to avoid committing murder. Of the two evils, they chose the lesser. However, there is no proof that they were guilty of falsehood. It seems that Pharaoh accepted their explanation of the case, which rested upon a well-known physiological fact. God gave His approval to their action.

🔑 **2:10** The name Moses (in Hebrew *mosheh*) is from the verb *mashah* (4871) meaning "to draw

(continued on next page)

brought him to Pharaoh's daughter, and [a]he became her son. And she named[7121] him [I]Moses, and said, "Because I [II]drew him out of the water."

11 Now it came about in those days,[3117] [a]when Moses had grown up, that he went out to his brethren[251] and looked on their [I][b]hard labors; and [c]he saw an Egyptian beating[5221] a Hebrew, one of his brethren.

12 So he [I]looked this way and that, and when he saw there was no one *around,* he [a]struck down[5221] the Egyptian and hid him in the sand.

13 And he went out [a]the next day, and behold, two Hebrews[582] were [I]fighting with each other; and he said to the [II]offender,[7563] "Why are you striking[5221] your companion?"[7453]

14 But he said, "[a]Who made[7760] you a [I]prince[8269] or a judge[8199] over us? Are you [II]intending[559] to kill[2026] me, as you killed the Egyptian?" Then Moses was afraid,[3372] and said, "Surely the matter[1697] has become known."

Moses Escapes to Midian

🗝 15 When Pharaoh heard[8085] of this matter, he tried to kill[2026] Moses. But [a]Moses fled from the presence of Pharaoh and [I]settled in the land of Midian; and he sat down [b]by a well.

🗝 **16** Now [a]the priest[3548] of Midian had seven daughters; and [b]they came to draw water, and filled the troughs to water their father's flock.

17 Then the shepherds came and drove them away, but [a]Moses stood up and helped them, and watered their flock.

18 When they came to [a]Reuel their father, he said, "Why have you come *back* so soon today?"[3117]

19 So they said, "An Egyptian delivered us from the hand[3027] of the shepherds; and what is more, he even drew the water for us and watered the flock."

20 And he said to his daughters, "Where is he then? Why is it that you have left[5800] the man behind? Invite[7121] him [I]to have something to eat."

21 [a]And Moses was willing[2974] to dwell with the man, and he gave his daughter [b]Zipporah to Moses.

🗝 22 Then she gave birth to [a]a son,[1121] and he named him [I]Gershom, for he said, "I have been [b]a [II]sojourner[1616] in a foreign[5237] land."[776]

23 Now it came about in *the course of* those many days[3117] that the king[4428] of Egypt died. And the sons of Israel [a]sighed because of the bondage,[5656] and they cried out; and [b]their cry for help because of *their* bondage rose up[5927] to God.[430]

24 So [a]God heard[8085] their groaning; and God remembered [b]His covenant[1285] with Abraham, Isaac, and Jacob.

25 And [a]God saw the sons of Israel, and God [I]took notice[3045] *of them.*

10 [I]Heb., *Mosheh,* from *mashah* [II]Heb., *mashah* [a]Acts 7:21
11 [I]Lit., *burdens* [a]Acts 7:23; Heb. 11:24-26 [b]Ex. 1:11; 5:4, 5; 6:6, 7 [c]Acts 7:24
12 [I]Lit., *turned* [a]Acts 7:24, 25
13 [I]Or, *quarreling* [II]Or, *the guilty one* [a]Acts 7:26-28
14 [I]Lit., *man, a prince* [II]Lit., *saying in your heart* [a]Gen. 19:9; Acts 7:27, 28
15 [I]Lit., *dwelt* [a]Acts 7:29; Heb. 11:27 [b]Gen. 24:11; 29:2
16 [a]Ex. 3:1; 18:12 [b]Gen. 24:11, 13, 19; 29:9, 10; 1Sam. 9:11
17 [a]Gen. 29:3, 10
18 [a]Ex. 3:1; Num. 10:29
20 [I]Lit., *that he may eat bread*
21 [a]Acts 7:29 [b]Ex. 4:25; 18:2
22 [I]Heb., *ger sham, a stranger there* [II]Heb., *ger* [a]Ex. 4:20; 18:3, 4 [b]Gen. 23:4; Lev. 25:23; Acts 7:29; Heb. 11:13, 14
23 [a]Ex. 6:5, 9 [b]Ex. 3:7, 9; Deut. 26:7; James 5:4
24 [a]Ex. 6:5; Acts 7:34 [b]Gen. 15:13f.; 22:16-18; 26:2-5; 28:13-15; Ps. 105:8, 42
25 [I]Lit., *knew* them [a]Ex. 3:7; 4:31; Acts 7:34

(continued from previous page)
out." Some have objected that an Egyptian princess would not have given a Hebrew name to her foster child. However, a comparison of Hebrew and Egyptian names reveals that there was an Egyptian name virtually identical in sound and meaning to *Mosheh,* as in the case with a number of personal names in modern Western languages. It may be that the princess gave him an Egyptian name and the sacred writer chose its Hebrew counterpart. The text in the Hebrew Bible could also be construed to mean that it was Moses' mother who named him.

🗝 **2:15** The Midianites were descendants of Abraham by another wife, Keturah, whom he married after Sarah died (Gen. 25:1,2).

🗝 **2:16** In Num. 12:1 Moses wife is said to be an Ethiopian. Since Ethiopia was settled by descendants of Cush whose names are certainly interchangeable. It has been argued from Hab. 3:7 that "Cushite" and "Midian" are interchangeable names also, and therefore Zipporah was the Ethiopian wife. Another possible solution is that, at the point of Num. 12:1, Zipporah had died and Moses married an Ethiopian woman just as Abraham had married Keturah after the death of Sarah.

🗝 **2:22** In Hebrew this name suggests a foreigner who was banished into exile. Moses' second son, Eliezer ("God is a Helper"), is mentioned in Ex. 18:4.

The Burning Bush

3 Now Moses was pasturing the flock of [a]Jethro his father-in-law, the priest[3548] of Midian; and he led the flock to the [I]west side of the wilderness, and came to [b]Horeb, the [c]mountain of God.[430]

2 And [a]the angel of the LORD appeared[7200] to him in a blazing fire from the midst of [I]a [b]bush; and he looked,[7200] and behold, the bush was burning with fire, yet the bush was not consumed.

3 So Moses said, "[I][a]I must turn aside now, and see this [II]marvelous sight, why the bush is not burned up."

4 When the LORD saw that he turned aside[5493] to look,[7200] [a]God called[7121] to him from the midst of the bush, and said, "Moses, Moses!" And he said, "Here I am."

5 Then He said, "Do not come near here;[7126] [a]remove your sandals from your feet, for the place on which you are standing is holy[6944] ground."[127]

6 He said also, "[a]I am the God[430] of your father,[1] the God of Abraham, the God of Isaac, and the God of Jacob." [b]Then Moses hid his face, for he was [c]afraid[3372] to look at God.

7 And the LORD said, "I have surely [a]seen[7200] the affliction of My people[5971] who are in Egypt, and have given heed[8085] to their cry because of their taskmasters, for I am aware[3045] of their sufferings.

8 "So I have come down [a]to deliver them from the [I]power[3027] of the Egyptians, and to bring them up[5927] from that land[776] to a [b]good[2896] and spacious land, to a land flowing with milk and honey, to the place of [c]the Canaanite and the Hittite and the Amorite and the Perizzite and the Hivite and the Jebusite.

9 "And now, behold, [a]the cry of the sons[1121] of Israel has come to Me; furthermore, I have seen the oppression with which the Egyptians are oppressing them.

The Mission of Moses

10 "Therefore, come now, and I will send you to Pharaoh, [a]so that you may bring My people, the sons of Israel, out of Egypt."

11 But Moses said to God, "[a]Who am I, that I should go to Pharaoh, and that I should bring the sons of Israel out of Egypt?"

12 And He said, "Certainly [a]I will be with you, and this shall be the sign[226] to you that it is I who have sent you: [b]when you have brought the people out of Egypt, [c]you shall [I]worship God at this mountain."

13 Then Moses said to God,[430] "Behold, I am going to the sons of Israel, and I shall say to them, 'The God of your fathers has sent me to you.' Now they may say to me, 'What is His name?' What shall I say to them?"

14 And God said to Moses, "[I][a]I AM WHO [I]I AM";[1961] and He said, "Thus you shall say to the sons of Israel, '[I]I AM has sent me to you.' "

15 And God, furthermore, said to Moses, "Thus you shall say to the sons of Israel, '[a]The LORD, the God of your fathers, the God of Abraham, the God of Isaac, and the God of Jacob, has sent me to you.' This is My name forever,[5769] and this is My [b]memorial-name[2146] [I]to all generations.[1755]

16 "Go and [a]gather[622] the elders[2205] of Israel together, and say to them, '[b]The LORD, the God of your fathers,[1]

1 [I]Or, *rear part* [a]Ex. 2:18; 4:18; 18:12; Num. 10:29 [b]Ex. 3:12; 17:6; 33:6; 1Kin. 19:8 [c]Ex. 4:27; 18:5; 24:13
2 [I]Lit., *the* [a]Gen. 16:7-11; 21:17; 22:11, 15; Ex. 3:4-11, 16; Judg. 13:13-21; Acts 7:30 [b]Deut. 33:16; Mark 12:26; Luke 20:37; Acts 7:30
3 [I]Lit., *Let me turn* [II]Lit., *great* [a]Acts 7:31
4 [a]Ex. 4:5
5 [a]Josh. 5:15; Acts 7:33
6 [a]Gen. 28:13; Ex. 3:16; 4:5; Matt. 22:32; Mark 12:26; Luke 20:37 [b]Acts 7:32 [c]Judg. 13:22; Rev. 1:17
7 [a]Ex. 2:25; Neh. 9:9; Ps. 106:44; Is. 63:9; Acts 7:34
8 [I]Lit., *hand* [a]Gen. 15:13-16; 46:4; 50:24, 25; Ex. 6:6-8; 12:51 [b]Ex. 3:17; 13:5; Num. 13:27; Deut. 1:25; 8:7-9; Jer. 11:5; Ezek. 20:6 [c]Gen. 15:19-21; Josh. 24:11
9 [a]Ex. 2:23
10 [a]Gen. 15:13, 14; Ex. 12:40, 41; Mic. 6:4; Acts 7:6, 7
11 [a]Ex. 4:10; 6:12; 1Sam. 18:18
12 [I]Or, *serve* [a]Gen. 31:3; Ex. 4:12, 15; 33:14-16; Deut. 31:23; Josh. 1:5; Is. 43:2 [b]Ex. 19:1 [c]Ex. 19:2, 3; Acts 7:7
14 [I]Related to the name of God, *YHWH,* rendered *LORD,* which is derived from the verb *HAYAH,* to *be* [a]Ex. 6:3; John 8:24, 28, 58; Heb. 13:8; Rev. 1:8; 4:8
15 [I]Lit., *to generation of generation* [a]Ex. 3:6, 13 [b]Ps. 30:4; 97:12; 102:12; 135:13; Hos. 12:5
16 [a]Ex. 4:29 [b]Gen. 28:13; 48:15; Ex. 3:2, 6; 4:5

3:14 The phrase "I AM" in Hebrew is closely related to God's personal name (Ex. 6:3; Jehovah or Yahweh or YHWH) which occurs more than 6,000 times in the O.T. Though the meaning is not completely clear to biblical scholars, it seems to suggest the timelessness of God, the very foundation of all existence. Perhaps there is a hint of this in Rev. 1:4, "from Him who is, and who was, and who is to come." Jesus probably alluded to this in Jn. 8:58, "Before Abraham was born, I AM." Christ is the same yesterday, and today, *yes* and forever (Heb. 13:8).

the God of Abraham, Isaac and Jacob,
has appeared to me, saying, "[I][c]I am indeed concerned[6485] about you and what
has been done to you in Egypt.
17 "So [a]I said, I will bring you up
out of the affliction of Egypt to the land
of [b]the Canaanite and the Hittite and
the Amorite and the Perizzite and the
Hivite and the Jebusite, to a land
[c]flowing with milk and honey." '
18 "And [a]they will [I]pay heed[8085] to
what you say; and [b]you with the elders
of Israel will come to the king[4428] of
Egypt, and you will say to him, 'The
LORD, the God of the Hebrews, has met
with us. So now, please, let us go a
[c]three days'[3117] journey[1870] into the wilderness, that we may sacrifice[2076] to
the LORD our God.'
19 "But I know[3045] that the king of
Egypt [a]will not permit you to go,
[b]except [I]under compulsion.[2389]
20 "So I will stretch out [a]My hand,
and strike Egypt with all My
[b]miracles[6381] which I shall do[6213] in the
midst of it; and [c]after that he will let
you go.
21 "And I will grant this people
[a]favor[2580] in the sight of the Egyptians;
and it shall be that when you go, you
will not go empty-handed.
22 "But every woman[802] [a]shall
ask[7592] of her neighbor[7934] and the
woman who lives[1481] in her house,[1004]
articles of silver and articles of gold,
and clothing; and you will put them on
your sons and daughters. Thus you will
[b]plunder[5337] the Egyptians."

Moses Given Powers

4 Then Moses answered and said,
"What if they will not believe[539] me,
or [a]listen[8085] [I]to what I say? For they
may say, '[b]The LORD has not appeared
to you.' "
2 And the LORD said to him, "What
is that in your hand?"[3027] And he said,
"[a]A staff."[4294]
3 Then He said, "Throw it on the
ground."[776] So he threw it on the
ground, and [a]it became a serpent;[5175]
and Moses fled from it.
4 But the LORD said to Moses,
"Stretch out your hand[3709] and grasp *it*
by its tail"—so he stretched out his hand
and caught it, and it became a staff in
his [I]hand—
5 "that [a]they may believe that [b]the
LORD, the God[430] of their fathers,[1] the
God of Abraham, the God of Isaac, and
the God of Jacob, has appeared to you."
6 And the LORD furthermore said
to him, "Now put your hand into your
bosom." So he put his hand into his
bosom, and when he took it out, behold,
his hand was [a]leprous like snow.
7 Then He said, "Put[7725] your hand
into your bosom again." So he put his
hand into his bosom again; and when
he took it out of his bosom, behold,
[a]it was restored[7725] like *the rest of* his
flesh.[1320]
8 "And it shall come about that if
they will not believe you or [I]heed the
[II]witness of the first[7223] sign,[226] they may
believe the [II]witness of the last sign.
9 "But it shall be that if they will
not believe even these two signs or heed
what you say, then you shall take some
water from the Nile and pour[8210] it on
the dry[3004] ground; and the water which
you take from the Nile [a]will become
blood[1818] on the dry ground."
10 Then Moses said to the LORD,
"Please, Lord,[136] [a]I have never been
[I]eloquent,[1697] neither [II]recently nor in
time past, nor since Thou hast spoken
to Thy servant;[5650] for I am [III]slow of
speech[6310] and [III]slow of tongue."
11 And the LORD said to him, "Who
has made[7760] man's[120] mouth?[6310] Or
[a]who makes *him* dumb or deaf, or seeing
or blind? Is it not I, the LORD?
12 "Now then go, and [a]I, even I,
will be with your mouth, and [b]teach you
what you are to say."[1696]
13 But he said, "Please, Lord, now
[I]send *the message* by whomever Thou
wilt."

16 [I]Lit., *Visiting I have visited* [c]Ex. 4:31; Ps. 33:18f.
17 [a]Gen. 15:13-21; 46:4; 50:24, 25 [b]Josh. 24:11 [c]Ex. 3:8
18 [I]Lit., *hear your voice* [a]Ex. 4:31 [b]Ex. 5:1 [c]Ex. 5:3; 8:27
19 [I]Lit., *by a strong hand* [a]Ex. 5:2 [b]Ex. 6:1
20 [a]Ex. 6:1; 7:4, 5; 9:15; 13:3, 9, 14 [b]Ex. 7:3; 15:11; Deut. 6:22; Neh. 9:10; Ps. 105:27; 135:9; Jer. 32:20; Acts 7:36 [c]Ex. 11:1; 12:31-33
21 [a]Ex. 11:3; 12:36; 1Kin. 8:50; Ps. 105:37f.; 106:46; Prov. 16:7
22 [a]Gen. 15:14; Ex. 11:2; 12:35 [b]Ezek. 39:10

1 [I]Lit., *to my voice* [a]Ex. 3:18; 6:30 [b]Ex. 3:15, 16
2 [a]Ex. 4:17, 20
3 [a]Ex. 7:10-12
4 [I]Lit., *palm*
5 [a]Ex. 4:31; 19:9 [b]Gen. 28:13; 48:15; Ex. 3:6, 15
6 [a]Num. 12:10; 2Kin. 5:27
7 [a]Num. 12:13-15; Deut. 32:39; 2Kin. 5:14; Matt. 8:3; Luke 17:12-14
8 [I]Lit., *listen to* [II]Lit., *voice*
9 [a]Ex. 7:19, 20
10 [I]Lit., *a man of words* [II]Lit., *yesterday* [III]Lit., *heavy* [a]Ex. 3:11; 4:1; 6:12; Jer. 1:6
11 [a]Ps. 94:9; 146:8; Matt. 11:5; Luke 1:20, 64
12 [a]Ex. 4:15, 16; Deut. 18:18; Is. 50:4; Jer. 1:9 [b]Matt. 10:19, 20; Mark 13:11; Luke 12:11, 12; 21:14, 15
13 [I]Lit., *send by the hand which Thou sendest*

4:10 See note on Jer. 1:5.

Aaron to Be Moses' Mouthpiece

14 Then the anger[639] of the LORD burned[2734] against Moses, and He said, "Is there not your brother[251] Aaron the Levite? I know[3045] that [I]he speaks fluently.[1696] And moreover, behold, [a]he is coming out to meet you; when he sees[7200] you, he will be glad in his heart.[3820]

15 "And you are to speak[1696] to him and [a]put[7760] the words[1697] in his mouth; and I, even I, will be with your mouth and his mouth, and I will teach you what you are to do.[6213]

16 "Moreover, [a]he shall speak[1696] for you to the people;[5971] and it shall come about that he shall be as a mouth for you, and you shall be as God to him.

17 "And you shall take in your hand [a]this staff, [b]with which you shall perform the signs."

18 Then Moses departed and returned[7725] to [I]Jethro [a]his father-in-law, and said to him, "Please, let me go, that I may return to my brethren[251] who are in Egypt, and see[7200] if they are still alive."[2416] And Jethro said to Moses, "Go in peace."[7965]

19 Now the LORD said to Moses in Midian, "Go [I]back[7725] to Egypt, for [a]all the men[582] who were seeking your life[5315] are dead."[4191]

20 So Moses took his wife[802] and his [a]sons[1121] and mounted them on a donkey, and he returned to the land[776] of Egypt. Moses also took the [b]staff of God[430] in his hand.

21 And the LORD said to Moses, "When you go [I]back to Egypt see[7200] that you perform before Pharaoh all [a]the wonders[4159] which I have put in your [II]power; but [b]I will harden[2388] his heart so that he will not let the people go.

22 "Then you shall say to Pharaoh, 'Thus says[559] the LORD, "[a]Israel is My son, My first-born.

23 "So I said to you, "[a]Let My son go, that he may serve Me'; but you have refused to let him go. Behold, [b]I will kill[2026] your son, your first-born." ' "

24 Now it came about at the lodging place on the way[1870] that the LORD met him and [a]sought to put him to death.

25 Then Zipporah took [a]a flint and cut off[3772] her son's foreskin[6190] and [I]threw[5060] *it* at Moses' feet, and she said, "You are indeed a bridegroom of blood[1818] to me."

26 So He let him alone.[7503] At that time she said, "*You are* a bridegroom of blood"—[I]because of the circumcision.[4139]

27 [a]Now the LORD said to Aaron, "Go to meet Moses in the wilderness." So he went and met him at the [b]mountain of God, and he kissed him.

28 And [a]Moses told[5046] Aaron all the words of the LORD with which He had sent him, and [b]all the signs that He had commanded[6680] him *to do.*

29 Then Moses and Aaron went and [a]assembled[622] all the elders[2205] of the sons[1121] of Israel;

30 and [a]Aaron spoke[1696] all the words which the LORD had spoken to Moses. He then performed the [b]signs in the sight of the people.

31 So [a]the people believed;[539] and when they heard[8085] that the LORD [I][b]was concerned[6485] about the sons of Israel and that He had seen[7200] their affliction, then [c]they bowed low and worshiped.[7812]

Israel's Labor Increased

5 And afterward Moses and Aaron came and said to Pharaoh, "[a]Thus says[559] the LORD, the God[430] of Israel, '[b]Let My people[5971] go that they may celebrate a feast to Me in the wilderness.' "

2 But Pharaoh said, "[a]Who is the LORD that I should obey[8085] His voice to let Israel go? I do not know[3045] the LORD, and besides, [b]I will not let Israel go."

3 Then they said, "[a]The God of the Hebrews has met with us. Please, let us go a three days' journey into the wilderness that we may sacrifice[2076] to the LORD our God, lest He fall upon us with pestilence[1698] or with the sword."

14 [I]Lit., *speaking he speaks* [a]Ex. 4:27
15 [a]Ex. 4:12, 30; 7:1f.; Num. 23:5, 12, 16; Deut. 18:18; Is. 51:16; 59:21; Jer. 1:9
16 [a]Ex. 7:1, 2
17 [a]Ex. 4:2, 20; 17:9 [b]Ex. 7:9-20; 14:16
18 [I]Heb., *Jether* [a]Ex. 2:21; 3:1
19 [I]Lit., *return* [a]Ex. 2:15, 23
20 [a]Ex. 18:3, 4; Acts 7:29 [b]Ex. 4:17; 17:9; Num. 20:8, 9, 11
21 [I]Lit., *to return* [II]Lit., *hand* [a]Ex. 3:20; 11:9, 10 [b]Ex. 7:3, 13; 9:12, 35; 10:1, 20, 27; 14:4, 8; Deut. 2:30; Josh. 11:20; 1Sam. 6:6; Is. 63:17; John 12:40; Rom. 9:18
22 [a]Is. 63:16; 64:8; Jer. 31:9; Hos. 11:1; Rom. 9:4
23 [a]Ex. 5:1; 6:11; 7:16 [b]Ex. 11:5; 12:29; Ps. 105:36; 135:8; 136:10
24 [a]Num. 22:22
25 [I]Lit., *made it touch at his feet* [a]Gen. 17:14; Josh. 5:2, 3
26 [I]Lit., *with reference to*
27 [a]Ex. 4:14 [b]Ex. 3:1; 18:5; 24:13
28 [a]Ex. 4:15f. [b]Ex. 4:8f.
29 [a]Ex. 3:16
30 [a]Ex. 4:15, 16 [b]Ex. 4:1-9
31 [I]Lit., *had visited* [a]Ex. 3:18; 4:8f.; 19:9 [b]Gen. 50:24; Ex. 3:16 [c]Gen. 24:26; Ex. 12:27; 1Chr. 29:20

1 [a]Ex. 3:18 [b]Ex. 4:23; 6:11; 7:16
2 [a]2Kin. 18:35; 2Chr. 32:14; Job 21:15 [b]Ex. 3:19
3 [a]Ex. 3:18

4 But the king[4428] of Egypt said to them, "Moses and Aaron, why do you [I]draw the people away from their [II]work? Get *back* to your [III][a]labors!"

5 Again Pharaoh said, "Look, [a]the people of the land are now many, and you would have them cease[7673] from their labors!"

6 So the same day[3117] Pharaoh commanded[6689] [a]the taskmasters over the people and their [b]foremen,[7860] saying,

7 "You are no longer to give the people straw to make brick as previously; let them go and gather straw for themselves.

8 "But the quota of bricks which they were making previously, you shall impose on them; you are not to reduce any of it. Because they are [a]lazy,[7503] therefore they cry out, '[I]Let us go and sacrifice to our God.'

9 "Let the labor[5656] be heavier on the men,[582] and let them work[6213] at it that they may pay no attention to false[8267] words."

10 So [a]the taskmasters of the people and their foremen went out and spoke to the people, saying, "Thus says Pharaoh, 'I am not going to give you *any* straw.

11 'You go *and* get straw for yourselves wherever you can find *it;* but none of your labor will be reduced.' "

12 So the people scattered through all the land of Egypt to gather stubble for straw.

13 And the taskmasters pressed them, saying,[559] "Complete[3615] your [I]work quota, [II]*your* daily[3117] amount,[1697] just as when [III]you had straw."

14 Moreover, [a]the foremen of the sons[1121] of Israel, whom Pharaoh's taskmasters had set[7760] over them, [b]were beaten[5221] [I]and were asked,[559] "Why have you not completed[3615] your required amount[2706] either yesterday or today[3117] in making brick as previously?"

15 Then the foremen of the sons of Israel came and cried out to Pharaoh, saying, "Why do you deal[6213] this way with your servants?[5650]

16 "There is no straw given to your servants, yet they keep saying to us, 'Make bricks!' And behold, your servants are being beaten; but it is the fault[2398] of your *own* people."

17 But he said, "You are [a]lazy, *very* lazy; therefore you say, 'Let us go *and* sacrifice to the LORD.'

18 "So go now *and* work; for you shall be given no straw, yet you must deliver the quota of bricks."

19 And the foremen of the sons of Israel saw[7200] that they were in trouble[7451] [I]because they were told, "You must not reduce [II]*your* daily amount of bricks."

20 When they left Pharaoh's presence, they met Moses and Aaron as they were [I]waiting for them.

21 And [a]they said to them, "[b]May the LORD look upon you and judge[8199] *you,* for you have [c]made [I]us odious in Pharaoh's sight and in the sight of his servants, to put a sword[2719] in their hand[3027] to kill[2026] us."

22 Then Moses returned[7725] to the LORD and said, "[a]O Lord,[136] why hast Thou brought harm to this people? Why didst Thou ever send me?

23 "Ever since I came to Pharaoh to speak[1696] in Thy name, he has done harm to this people; [a]and Thou hast not delivered Thy people at all."

God Promises Action

6 Then the LORD said to Moses, "Now you shall see[7200] what I will do[6213] to Pharaoh; for [I][a]under compulsion[2389] he shall let them go, and [I]under compulsion[3027] he shall drive them out of his land."

2 God[430] spoke[1696] further to Moses and said to him, "I am [a]the LORD;

🔑 3 and I appeared[7200] to Abraham,

---

4 [I]Lit., *loose* [II]Lit., *works* [III]Lit., *burdens* [a]Ex. 1:11; 2:11; 6:5-7

5 [a]Ex. 1:7, 9

6 [a]Ex. 1:11; 3:7; 5:10, 13, 14 [b]Ex. 5:10, 14, 15, 19

8 [I]Lit., *saying, 'Let* [a]Ex. 5:17

10 [a]Ex. 1:11; 3:7; 5:6

13 [I]Lit., *works* [II]Lit., *the matter of a day in its day* [III]Lit., *there was*

14 [I]Lit., *saying* [a]Ex. 5:6 [b]Is. 10:24

17 [a]Ex. 5:8

19 [I]Lit., *saying* [II]Lit., *from your bricks the matter of a day in its day*

20 [I]Lit., *standing to meet*

21 [I]Lit., *our savor to stink* [a]Ex. 14:11; 15:24; 16:2 [b]Gen. 16:5; 31:53 [c]Gen. 34:30; 1Sam. 13:4; 27:12; 2Sam. 10:6; 1Chr. 19:6

22 [a]Num. 11:11; Jer. 4:10

23 [a]Ex. 3:8

1 [I]Lit., *by a strong hand* [a]Ex. 3:19, 20; 7:4, 5; 11:1; 12:31, 33, 39; 13:3

2 [a]Ex. 3:14, 15

🔑 **6:3** In light of such passages as Gen. 12:8 and 14:22, in which LORD is equivalent to JEHOVAH, this name was evidently known among the Patriarchs. Some scholars have suggested that Moses,

(continued on next page)

Isaac, and Jacob, as [Ia]God[410] Almighty,[7706] but *by* [b]My name, [II]LORD, I
did not make Myself known to them.
4 "And I also established [a]My
covenant[1285] with them, to give them
the land[776] of Canaan, the [I]land in which
they sojourned.[1481]
5 "And furthermore I have
[a]heard[8085] the groaning of the sons[1121]
of Israel, because the Egyptians are
holding them in bondage; and I have
remembered My covenant.
6 "Say, therefore, to the sons of
Israel, '[a]I am the LORD, and [b]I will bring
you out from under the burdens of the
Egyptians, and I will deliver you from
their bondage.[5656] I will also [c]redeem[1350]
you with [d]an outstretched arm and with
great judgments.[8201]
7 'Then I will take you [Ia]for My people,[5971] and [b]I will be [II]your God; and
[c]you shall know[3045] that I am the LORD
your God, who brought you out from
under the burdens of the Egyptians.
8 'And I will bring you to the land
which [a]I [I]swore[3027] to give to Abraham,
Isaac, and Jacob, and [b]I will give it to
you *for* a possession;[4181] [c]I am the
LORD.' "
9 So Moses spoke thus to the sons
of Israel, but they did not listen[8085] to
Moses on [a]account of *their* [I]despondency
and cruel bondage.
10 Now the LORD spoke to Moses,
saying,
11 "[a]Go, [I]tell[1696] Pharaoh king[4428] of
Egypt [II]to let the sons of Israel go out
of his land."
12 But Moses spoke before the
LORD, saying, "Behold, the sons of Israel have not listened to me; [a]how then
will Pharaoh listen[8085] to me, for I am
[Ib]unskilled[6189] in speech?"[8193]
13 Then the LORD spoke to Moses
and to Aaron, and gave them a charge[6680]
to the sons of Israel and to Pharaoh
king of Egypt, to bring the sons of Israel
out of the land of Egypt.

The Heads of Israel

14 These are the heads[7218] of their
fathers'[1] households.[1004] [a]The sons[1121]
of Reuben, Israel's first-born: Hanoch
and Pallu, Hezron and Carmi; these are
the families[4940] of Reuben.
15 And the [a]sons of Simeon: Jemuel
and Jamin and Ohad and Jachin and Zohar
and Shaul the son of a Canaanite woman;
these are the families of Simeon.
16 And these are the names of
[a]the sons of Levi according to their
generations:[8435] Gershon and Kohath
and Merari; and the [I]length of Levi's
life[2416] was one hundred and thirty-
seven years.
17 [a]The sons of Gershon: [I]Libni and
Shimei, according to their families.
18 And [a]the sons of Kohath: Amram
and Izhar and Hebron and Uzziel; and
the [I]length of Kohath's life was one hundred and thirty-three years.
19 And [a]the sons of Merari: Mahli
and Mushi. These are the families of
the Levites according to their generations.

3 [I]Heb., *El Shaddai* [II]Heb., *YHWH*, usually rendered LORD [a]Gen. 17:1; 35:11; 48:3 [b]Ps. 68:4; 83:18; Is. 52:6; Jer. 16:21; Ezek. 37:6,13
4 [I]Lit., *land of their sojournings in which* [a]Gen. 12:7; 15:18; 17:4, 7; 26:3, 4; 28:4, 13
5 [a]Ex. 2:24
6 [a]Ex. 13:3, 14; 20:2; Deut. 6:12 [b]Ex. 3:17; 7:4; 12:51; 16:6; 18:1; Deut. 26:8; Ps. 136:11 [c]Ex. 15:13; Deut. 7:8; 1Chr. 17:21; Neh. 1:10 [d]Deut. 4:34; 5:15; 26:8; Ps. 136:11f.
7 [I]Lit., *to Me for a people* [II]Lit., *to you for a God* [a]Ex. 19:5; Deut. 4:20; 7:6; 2Sam. 7:24 [b]Gen. 17:7f.; Ex. 29:45f.; Lev. 11:45; 26:12, 13, 45; Deut. 29:13 [c]Ex. 16:12; Is. 41:20; 49:23, 26; 60:16
8 [I]Lit., *lifted up My hand* [a]Gen. 15:18; 26:3; Num. 14:30; Neh. 9:15; Ezek. 20:5, 6 [b]Josh. 24:13; Ps. 136:21, 22 [c]Ex. 6:6
9 [I]Lit., *shortness of spirit* [a]Ex. 2:23
11 [I]Lit., *speak to* [II]Lit., *that he let* [a]Ex. 4:22, 23
12 [I]Lit., *uncircumcised of lips* [a]Ex. 4:1, 10; 6:30 [b]Jer. 1:6

14 [a]Gen. 46:9; Num. 26:5-11; 1Chr. 5:3
15 [a]Gen. 46:10; 1Chr. 4:24 **16** [I]Lit., *years* [a]Gen. 46:11; Num. 3:17; 26:57f.; 1Chr. 6:1, 16-19 **17** [I]In 1Chr. 23:7, *Ladan* [a]Num. 3:18-20; 1Chr. 6:17-19
18 [I]Lit., *years* [a]Num. 3:19; 1Chr. 6:2, 18 **19** [a]Num. 3:20; 1Chr. 6:19; 23:21

(continued from previous page)
because of his personal knowledge of the Lord at this time, inserted the name in the passages in Genesis when he wrote it at a later time. However, the key to this problem probably lies in a proper understanding of the Hebrew word *yadah* "known." The meaning of this word is "to know by instruction or observation." Israel was about to witness, through the events of their exodus from Egypt, a demonstration of His power in a more graphic way than had their forefathers. It was by this name, the LORD, that His powerful works of salvation would be done. Israel would know by its experience the full meaning of the name. Though they knew He was called the LORD, the Patriarchs had not seen such a demonstration of power and, therefore, had not known all the implications of that name. Note also Ex. 3:13-15 where I AM is from the same Hebrew root as YHWH.

🔑20 And [a]Amram [I]married his father's
sister Jochebed, and she bore him Aaron
and Moses; and the [II]length of Amram's
life was one hundred and thirty-seven
years.
21 And [a]the sons of Izhar: Korah
and Nepheg and Zichri.
22 [a]And the sons of Uzziel: Mishael
and [I]Elzaphan and Sithri.
23 And Aaron [I]married Elisheba, the
daughter of [a]Amminadab, the sister of
[b]Nahshon, and she bore him [c]Nadab and
Abihu, Eleazar and Ithamar.
24 And the [a]sons of Korah: Assir
and Elkanah and [I]Abiasaph; these are
the families of the Korahites.
25 And Aaron's son [a]Eleazar
[I]married one of the daughters of Putiel,
and she bore him [b]Phinehas. These are
the heads of the fathers' *households* of
the Levites according to their families.
26 It was *the same* Aaron and Moses
to whom the LORD said, "[a]Bring out the
sons of Israel from the land of Egypt
according to their [b]hosts."[6635]
27 They were the ones [a]who spoke
to Pharaoh king of Egypt [I]about bringing
out the sons of Israel from Egypt; it
was *the same* Moses and Aaron.
28 Now it came about on the day[3117]
when the LORD spoke to Moses in the
land of Egypt,
29 that the LORD spoke to Moses,
saying, "[a]I am the LORD; [b]speak to Pharaoh king of Egypt all that I speak[1696]
to you."
30 But Moses said before the LORD,
"Behold, I am [I][a]unskilled in speech; how
then will Pharaoh listen[8085] to me?"

"I Will Stretch Out My Hand"

7 Then the LORD said to Moses,
"[a]See,[7200] I make you *as* God[430] to
Pharaoh, and your brother Aaron shall
be your prophet.[5030]
2 "You shall speak[1696] all that I
command[6680] you, and your brother
[a]Aaron shall speak to Pharaoh that he
let the sons[1121] of Israel go out of his
land.[776]
🔑3 "But [a]I will harden Pharaoh's
heart[3820] that I may [b]multiply My signs[226]
and My wonders[4159] in the land of Egypt.
4 "When [a]Pharaoh will not listen[8085]
to you, then I will lay My hand[3027] on
Egypt, and [b]bring out My hosts,[6635] My
people[5971] the sons of Israel, from the
land of Egypt by [c]great judgments.[8201]
5 "And [a]the Egyptians shall
know[3045] that I am the LORD, when I
[b]stretch out My hand on Egypt and bring
out the sons of Israel from their midst."
6 So Moses and Aaron did *it;* [a]as
the LORD commanded[6680] them, thus
they did.[6213]
7 And Moses was [a]eighty years
old[1121] and Aaron [I]eighty-three, when
they spoke to Pharaoh.

Aaron's Rod Becomes a Serpent

8 Now the LORD spoke to Moses
and Aaron, saying,
9 "When Pharaoh speaks to you,
saying, '[I][a]Work a miracle,'[4159] then you
shall say to Aaron, '[b]Take your staff[4294]
and throw *it* down before Pharaoh, *that*
it may become a serpent.' "[8577]
10 So Moses and Aaron came to
Pharaoh, and thus they did just as the
LORD had commanded; and Aaron threw
his staff down before Pharaoh and
[I]his servants,[5650] and it [a]became a serpent.
11 Then Pharaoh also [a]called[7121] for

20 [I]Lit., *took to him to wife* [II]Lit., *years* [a]Ex. 2:1, 2; Num. 26:59
21 [a]Num. 16:1; 1Chr. 6:37, 38
22 [I]In Num. 3:30, *Elizaphan* [a]Lev. 10:4; Num. 3:30
23 [I]Lit., *took to him to wife* [a]Ruth 4:19, 20; 1Chr. 2:10 [b]Num. 1:7; 2:3 [c]Lev. 10:1; Num. 3:2; 26:60; 1Chr. 6:3; 24:1
24 [I]In 1Chr. 6:23 and 9:19, *Ebiasaph* [a]Num. 26:11; 1Chr. 6:22, 23, 37
25 [I]Lit., *took to him to wife* [a]Josh. 24:33 [b]Num. 25:7-13; Josh. 24:33; Ps. 106:30
26 [a]Ex. 3:10; 6:13 [b]Ex. 7:4; 12:17, 51
27 [I]Lit., *to bring out* [a]Ex. 5:1
29 [a]Ex. 6:2, 6, 8 [b]Ex. 6:11; 7:2
30 [I]Lit., *uncircumcised of lips* [a]Ex. 4:10; 6:12; Jer. 1:6

1 [a]Ex. 4:16
2 [a]Ex. 4:15
3 [a]Ex. 4:21 [b]Ex. 11:9; Acts 7:36
4 [a]Ex. 3:19, 20; 7:13, 16, 22; 8:15, 19; 9:12; 11:9 [b]Ex. 12:51; 13:3, 9 [c]Ex. 6:6
5 [a]Ex. 7:17; 8:19, 22; 10:7; 14:4, 18, 25 [b]Ex. 3:20
6 [a]Gen. 6:22; 7:5; Ex. 7:2
7 [I]Lit., *83 years old* [a]Deut. 29:5; 31:2; 34:7; Acts 7:23, 30
9 [I]Lit., *Show a wonder for yourselves* [a]Is. 7:11; John 2:18; 6:30 [b]Ex. 4:2, 17
10 [I]Lit., *before his* [a]Ex. 4:3; 7:9
11 [a]Dan. 2:2; 4:6; 5:7

🔑**6:20** A variant reading in the Greek Septuagint, the Syriac, and the Latin Vulgate indicates that Jochebed was Amram's paternal cousin.

🔑**7:3** Those who have long persisted in the ways of evil reach a point at which they are unable to distinguish right from wrong or good from evil. They grow hardened and morally incorrigible. Without doubt this was the state of Pharaoh. Being a man accustomed to the abuse of power, he steeled himself against all sense of justice and mercy. In Rom. 1:24 God is said to have given up immoral men

(continued on next page)

the wise men[2450] and *the* sorcerers,[3784] and they also, the [Ib]magicians[2748] of Egypt, did [II]the same with [c]their secret arts.[3858]

12 For each one threw down his staff and they turned into serpents. But Aaron's staff swallowed up their staffs.

13 Yet [a]Pharaoh's heart was [I]hardened,[2388] and he did not listen[8085] to them, as the LORD had said.[1696]

Water Is Turned to Blood

14 Then the LORD said to Moses, "Pharaoh's heart is [I]stubborn; he refuses[3985] to let the people go.

15 "Go to Pharaoh in the morning [I]as [a]he is going out to the water, and station[5324] yourself to meet him on the bank[8193] of the Nile; and you shall take in your hand [b]the staff that was turned[2015] into a serpent.[5175]

16 "[a]And you will say to him, 'The LORD, the God[430] of the Hebrews, sent me to you, saying, "[b]Let My people go, that they may serve Me in the wilderness. But behold, you have not listened[8085] until now."

17 'Thus says[559] the LORD, "[a]By this you shall know[3045] that I am the LORD: behold, I will strike [I]the water that is in the Nile with the staff that is in my hand, and [b]it shall be turned[2015] to blood.[1818]

18 "And [a]the fish[1710] that are in the Nile will die, and the Nile will [I]become foul;[887] and the Egyptians will [IIb]find difficulty in drinking water from the Nile." ' "

19 Then the LORD said to Moses, "Say to Aaron, 'Take your staff and [a]stretch out your hand over the waters of Egypt, over their rivers, over their [I]streams, and over their pools,[4723] and over all their reservoirs of water, that they may become blood; and there shall be blood throughout all the land of Egypt, both in *vessels of* wood and in *vessels of* stone.' "

20 So Moses and Aaron did even as the LORD had commanded. And he lifted up [Ia]the staff and struck[5221] the water that *was* in the Nile, in the sight of Pharaoh and in the sight of his servants, and [b]all the water that *was* in the Nile was turned[2015] to blood.

21 And the fish that *were* in the Nile died,[4191] and the Nile [I]became foul, so that the Egyptians could not drink water from the Nile. And the blood was through all the land of Egypt.

22 [a]But the [I]magicians of Egypt did [II]the same with their secret arts;[3909] and Pharaoh's heart was [III]hardened, and he did not listen to them, as the LORD had said.

23 Then Pharaoh turned and went into his house[1004] [I]with no concern[3820] even for this.

24 So all the Egyptians dug around the Nile for water to drink, for they could not drink of the water of the Nile.

25 And seven days [I]passed after the LORD had struck[5221] the Nile.

Frogs over the Land

8 [I]Then the LORD said[559] to Moses, "Go to Pharaoh and say to him, 'Thus says the LORD, "[a]Let My people go, that they may serve Me.

2 "But if you refuse[3985] to let *them* go, behold, I will smite your whole territory with frogs.

3 "And the Nile will [a]swarm with frogs, which will come up[5927] and go into your house[1004] and into your bedroom and on your bed, and into the houses of your servants[5650] and on your people,[5971] and into your ovens and into your kneading bowls.

4 "So the frogs will come up on you

11 [I]Or, *soothsayer priests* [II]Lit., *thus* [b]Gen. 41:8; Ex. 7:22; Dan. 2:2; 2Tim. 3:8 [c]Ex. 7:22; 8:7, 18; 2Tim. 3:9; Rev. 13:13, 14
13 [I]Lit., *strong* [a]Ex. 4:21; 7:3, 22; 8:15, 19, 32; 9:7, 12, 34, 35; 10:1, 20, 27
14 [I]Or, *hard;* lit., *heavy*
15 [I]Lit., *behold* [a]Ex. 2:5; 8:20 [b]Ex. 4:2, 3; 7:10
16 [a]Ex. 3:13, 18; 4:22; 5:1 [b]Ex. 4:23; 5:1, 3
17 [I]Lit., *upon the waters* [a]Ex. 5:2; 7:5; 10:2; Ps. 9:16; Ezek. 25:17 [b]Ex. 4:9; 7:20; Rev. 11:6; 16:4, 6
18 [I]I.e., have a bad smell [II]Or, *be weary of* [a]Ex. 7:21 [b]Ex. 7:24
19 [I]Or, *canals* [a]Ex. 8:5, 6, 16; 9:22; 10:12, 21; 14:21, 26
20 [I]Lit., *with the staff* [a]Ex. 17:5 [b]Ps. 78:44; 105:29
21 [I]I.e., had a bad smell
22 [I]Or, *soothsayer priests* [II]Lit., *thus* [III]Lit., *strong* [a]Ex. 7:11; 8:7
23 [I]Lit., *and he did not set his heart even to this*
25 [I]Lit., *were fulfilled*
1 [I]Ch. 7:26 in Heb. [a]Ex. 3:18; 4:23; 5:1, 3
3 [a]Ps. 105:30

(continued from previous page)
to the path they were determined to follow. In the same way God allowed Pharaoh to follow the course he was determined to follow. God did not force him to act in an evil way nor did He by divine decree determine that Pharaoh would not repent if he so chose.

and your people and all your servants." ' "
5 [I]Then the LORD said to Moses,
"Say to Aaron, '[a]Stretch out your
hand[3027] with your staff[4294] over the
rivers, over the [II]streams and over the
pools, and make frogs come up on the
land[776] of Egypt.' "
6 So Aaron stretched out his hand
over the waters of Egypt, and the
[I][a]frogs came up and covered[3680] the land
of Egypt.
7 [a]And the [I]magicians[2748] did[6213]
[II]the same with their secret arts,[3909]
[III]making frogs come up on the land of
Egypt.
8 Then Pharaoh [a]called[7121] for Moses and Aaron and said, "[b]Entreat[6279]
the LORD that He remove the frogs from
me and from my people; and [c]I will let
the people go, that they may sacrifice[2076]
to the LORD."
9 And Moses said to Pharaoh, "[I]The
honor is yours to tell me: when shall I
entreat for you and your servants and
your people, that the frogs be
[II]destroyed[3772] from you and your
houses, *that* they may be left[7604] only
in the Nile?"
10 Then he said, "Tomorrow." So
he said, "*May it be* according to your
word,[1697] that you may know[3045] that
there is [a]no one like the LORD our
God.[430]
11 "And the [a]frogs will depart[5493]
from you and your houses and your servants and your people; they will be left
only in the Nile."
12 Then Moses and Aaron went out
from Pharaoh, and [a]Moses cried to the
LORD concerning the frogs which He had
[I]inflicted upon Pharaoh.
13 And the LORD did according to
the word of Moses, and the frogs died
out of the houses, the courts, and the
fields.
14 So they piled them in heaps, and
the land[776] [I]became foul.
15 But when Pharaoh saw[7200] that
there was relief,[7309] he [I]hardened his
heart[3820] and [a]did not listen[8085] to them,
as the LORD had said.[1696]

The Plague of Insects

16 Then the LORD said to Moses,
"Say to Aaron, 'Stretch out your staff
and strike[5221] the dust[6083] of the earth,
that it may become [I]gnats through all
the land of Egypt.' "
17 And they did so; and Aaron
stretched out his hand with his staff,
and struck[5221] the dust of the earth,
and there were [I]gnats on man[120] and
beast. All the dust of the earth became [I][a]gnats through all the land of
Egypt.
18 And the [I]magicians tried with
their secret arts to bring forth [II]gnats,
but [a]they could not; so there were
[II]gnats on man and beast.
19 Then the [I]magicians said to Pharaoh, "[a]This is the finger of God." But
Pharaoh's heart was [II]hardened, and he
did not listen to them, as the LORD had
said.
20 Now the LORD said to Moses,
"[a]Rise early in the morning and present
yourself before Pharaoh, [I]as [b]he comes
out to the water, and say to him, 'Thus
says the LORD, "[c]Let My people go,
that they may serve Me.
21 "For if you will not let My people
go, behold, I will send swarms of insects
on you and on your servants and on
your people and into your houses; and
the houses of the Egyptians shall be
full of swarms of insects, and also the
ground[127] on which they *dwell*.
22 "[a]But on that day[3117] I will set
apart the land[776] of Goshen, where My
people are [I]living, so that no swarms
of insects will be there, in order that
you may know that [II][b]I, the LORD, am
in the midst of the land.[776]
23 "And I will [I]put a division[6304] between My people and your people. Tomorrow this sign[226] shall occur." ' "
24 Then the LORD did so. And there
came [I]great swarms of insects into the
house of Pharaoh and the houses of his
servants and the land was [a]laid waste[7843]
because of the swarms of insects in all
the land of Egypt.
25 And Pharaoh [a]called for Moses

5 [I]Ch. 8:1 in Heb. [II]Or, *canals* [a]Ex. 7:19
6 [I]Lit., *frog* [a]Ps. 78:45; 105:30
7 [I]Or, *soothsayer priests* [II]Lit., *thus* [III]Lit., *and made* [a]Ex. 7:11, 22
8 [a]Ex. 8:25; 9:27; 10:16 [b]Ex. 8:28; 9:28; 10:17; Num. 21:7; 1Kin. 13:6 [c]Ex. 8:15, 29, 32
9 [I]Lit., *Glory over me* [II]Lit., *cut off*
10 [a]Ex. 9:14; Deut. 4:35, 39; 33:26; 2Sam. 7:22; 1Chr. 17:20; Ps. 86:8; Is. 46:9; Jer. 10:6, 7
11 [a]Ex. 8:13
12 [I]Lit., *placed* [a]Ex. 8:30; 9:33; 10:18
14 [I]I.e., had a bad smell
15 [I]Lit., *made heavy* [a]Ex. 7:4
16 [I]Or, *lice*
17 [I]Or, *lice* [a]Ps. 105:31
18 [I]Or, *soothsayer priests* [II]Or, *lice* [a]Ex. 7:11, 12; 8:7; 9:11
19 [I]Or, *soothsayer priests* [II]Lit., *strong* [a]Ex. 7:5; 10:7; Ps. 8:3; Luke 11:20
20 [I]Lit., *behold* [a]Ex. 7:15; 9:13 [b]Ex. 2:5; 7:15 [c]Ex. 3:18; 4:23; 5:1, 3; 8:1
22 [I]Lit., *standing* [II]Or, *I am the LORD in the midst of the earth* [a]Ex. 9:4, 6, 24; 10:23; 11:7 [b]Ex. 9:29; 19:5; 20:11
23 [I]Lit., *set a ransom*
24 [I]Lit., *heavy* [a]Ps. 78:45; 105:31
25 [a]Ex. 8:8; 9:27; 10:16

and Aaron and said, "[b]Go, sacrifice to your God within the land."[776]

26 But Moses said,[559] "It is not right to do so, for we shall sacrifice[2076] to the LORD our God [I]what is [a]an abomination[8841] to the Egyptians. If we sacrifice [I]what is an abomination to the Egyptians before their eyes, will they not then stone us?

27 "We must go a [a]three days' journey into the wilderness and sacrifice[2076] to the LORD our God as He [I]commands[559] us."

28 And Pharaoh said, "[a]I will let you go, that you may sacrifice to the LORD your God in the wilderness; only you shall not go very far away. [b]Make supplication for me."

29 Then Moses said, "Behold, I am going out from you, and I shall make supplication[6279] to the LORD that the swarms of insects may depart from Pharaoh, from his servants, and from his people tomorrow; only do not let Pharaoh [a]deal deceitfully again in not letting the people go to sacrifice to the LORD."

30 So [a]Moses went out from Pharaoh and made supplication to the LORD.

31 And the LORD did [I]as Moses asked, and removed the swarms of insects from Pharaoh, from his servants and from his people; not one remained.

32 But Pharaoh [I]hardened his heart this time also, and [a]he did not let the people go.

Egyptian Cattle Die

9 Then the LORD said to Moses, "Go to Pharaoh and speak[1696] to him, 'Thus says[559] the LORD, the God[430] of the Hebrews, "[a]Let My people[5971] go, that they may serve Me.

2 "For [a]if you refuse to let *them* go, and [I]continue to hold[2388] them,

3 behold, [a]the hand[3027] of the LORD [I]will come[1961] *with* a very severe pestilence[1698] on your livestock which are in the field,[7704] on the horses, on the donkeys, on the camels, on the herds, and on the flocks.

25 [b]Ex. 9:28; 10:8, 24; 12:31
26 [I]Lit., *the abomination of Egypt* [a]Gen. 43:32; 46:34; Deut. 7:25f.
27 [I]Lit., *says to us* [a]Ex. 3:18; 5:3
28 [a]Ex. 8:8, 15, 29, 32 [b]Ex. 8:8; 9:28; 1Kin. 13:6
29 [a]Ex. 8:8, 15
30 [a]Ex. 8:12
31 [I]Lit., *according to the word of Moses*
32 [I]Lit., *made heavy* [a]Ex. 4:21; 8:8, 15

1 [a]Ex. 4:23; 8:1
2 [I]Lit., *still hold* [a]Ex. 8:2
3 [I]Lit., *will be* [a]Ex. 7:4; 1Sam. 5:6; Ps. 39:10; Acts 13:11
4 [a]Ex. 8:22 [b]Ex. 9:6
6 [a]Ex. 9:19, 20, 25; Ps. 78:48 [b]Ex. 9:4
7 [I]Lit., *heavy* [a]Ex. 7:14; 8:32
9 [a]Deut. 28:27; Rev. 16:2
11 [I]Or, *soothsayer priests* [II]Lit., *and on all* [a]Ex. 8:18
12 [I]Lit., *made strong* [a]Ex. 4:21; 10:1, 20; 14:8; Josh. 11:20; John 12:40
13 [a]Ex. 8:20 [b]Ex. 4:23
14 [I]Lit., *to your heart* [a]Ex. 8:10; Deut. 3:24; 2Sam. 7:22; 1Chr. 17:20; Ps. 86:8; Is. 45:5-8; 46:9; Jer. 10:6, 7

4 "[a]But the LORD will make a distinction between the livestock of Israel and the livestock of Egypt, so that [b]nothing will die of all that belongs to the sons[1121] of Israel." ' "

5 And the LORD set a definite time,[4150] saying, "Tomorrow the LORD will do[6213] this thing[1697] in the land."

6 So the LORD did this thing on the morrow, and [a]all the livestock of Egypt died;[4191] [b]but of the livestock of the sons of Israel, not one died.

7 And Pharaoh sent, and behold, there was not even one of the livestock of Israel dead. But [a]the heart[3820] of Pharaoh was [I]hardened, and he did not let the people go.

The Plague of Boils

8 Then the LORD said to Moses and Aaron, "Take for yourselves handfuls of soot from a kiln, and let Moses throw[2236] it toward the sky[8064] in the sight of Pharaoh.

9 "And it will become fine dust[80] over all the land of Egypt, and will become [a]boils breaking out with sores[76] on man[120] and beast through all the land of Egypt."

10 So they took soot from a kiln, and stood before Pharaoh; and Moses threw it toward the sky, and it became boils breaking out with sores on man and beast.

11 [a]And the [I]magicians[2748] could not stand before Moses because of the boils, for the boils were on the magicians [II]as well as on all the Egyptians.

12 And [a]the LORD [I]hardened[2388] Pharaoh's heart, and he did not listen to them, just as the LORD had spoken[1696] to Moses.

13 Then the LORD said to Moses, "[a]Rise up early in the morning and stand before Pharaoh and say to him, 'Thus says the LORD, the God of the Hebrews, "[b]Let My people go, that they may serve Me.

14 "For this time I will send all My plagues [I]on you and your servants[5658] and your people, so that [a]you may

know[3945] that there is no one like Me
in all the earth.[776]
15 "For *if by* now I had put forth
My hand and struck[5221] you and your
people with pestilence,[1698] you would
then have been cut off from the earth.
16 "But, indeed, [a]for this cause I
have allowed you to [I]remain, in order
to show[7200] you My power, and in order
to proclaim[5608] My name through all the
earth.
17 "Still you exalt[5549] yourself
against My people [I]by not letting them
go.

The Plague of Hail

18 "Behold, about this time[6256] tomorrow, [a]I will [I]send a very heavy hail,
such as has not been *seen* in Egypt
from the day it was founded[3245] [II]until
now.
19 "Now therefore send, bring
[a]your livestock and whatever you have
in the field to safety. [b]Every man and
beast that is found in the field and is
not brought[622] home,[1004] when the hail
comes down on them, will die.[4191]" ' "
20 [a]The one among the servants of
Pharaoh who [I]feared the word[1697] of the
LORD made his servants and his livestock
flee into the houses;[1004]
21 but he who [I]paid no regard[3820]
to the word of the LORD [II]left[5800] his
servants and his livestock in the field.
22 Now the LORD said to Moses,
"Stretch out your hand toward the sky,
that [I][a]hail may fall on all the land[776] of
Egypt, on man and on beast and on every
plant of the field, throughout the land
of Egypt."
23 And Moses stretched out his
staff[4294] toward the sky, and the LORD
[I]sent [II]thunder and [a]hail, and fire ran
down to the earth.[776] And the LORD
rained hail on the land of Egypt.
24 So there was hail, and fire
[I]flashing continually in the midst of the
hail, very severe, such as had not been
in all the land of Egypt since it became
a nation.[1471]
25 And [a]the hail struck all that was
in the field through all the land of Egypt,
both man and beast; the hail also struck
every plant of the field and shattered[7665]
every tree of the field.
26 [a]Only in the land[776] of Goshen,
where the sons of Israel *were,* there
was no hail.
27 Then Pharaoh [I][a]sent[7121] for Moses and Aaron, and said to them, "[b]I
have sinned[2398] this time; the LORD is
the righteous[6662] one, and I and my people are the wicked[7563] ones.
28 "[a]Make supplication[6279] to the
LORD, for there has been enough of
God's [I]thunder and hail; and [b]I will let
you go, and you shall stay no longer."
29 And Moses said to him, "As soon
as I go out of the city, I will [a]spread
out my [I]hands[3709] to the LORD; the
[II]thunder will cease, and there will be
hail no longer, that you may know that
[b]the earth[776] is the LORD'S.
30 "[a]But as for you and your servants, I know[3045] that [b]you do not yet
[I]fear[3372] [II]the LORD God."
31 (Now the flax and the [a]barley
were [I]ruined,[5221] for the barley was in
the ear and the flax was in bud.
🔑 32 But the wheat and the spelt were
not [I]ruined, for they *ripen* late.)
33 [a]So Moses went out of the city
from Pharaoh, and spread out his
[I]hands[3709] to the LORD; and the [II]thunder
and the hail ceased, and rain [III]no longer
poured on the earth.
34 But when Pharaoh saw[7200] that
the rain and the hail and the [I]thunder
had ceased, he sinned[2398] again and
[II]hardened his heart, he and his servants.
35 And Pharaoh's heart was [I]hard-
ened,[2388] and he did not let the sons
of Israel go, just as the [a]LORD had spoken
through[3027] Moses.

16 [I]Lit., *stand* [a]Prov. 16:4; Rom. 9:17
17 [I]Lit., *so as not to let*
18 [I]Lit., *cause to rain* [II]Lit., *and until now* [a]Ex. 9:23, 24
19 [a]Ex. 9:6 [b]Ex. 9:25
20 [I]Or, *revered* [a]Prov. 13:13
21 [I]Lit., *did not set his heart to* [II]Lit., *then left*
22 [I]Lit., *there may be hail* [a]Rev. 16:21
23 [I]Lit., *gave* [II]Lit., *sounds* [a]Gen. 19:24; Josh. 10:11; Ps. 18:13; 78:47; 105:32; Is. 30:30; Ezek. 38:22; Rev. 8:7
24 [I]Lit., *taking hold of itself*
25 [a]Ex. 9:19; Ps. 78:47, 48; 105:32, 33
26 [a]Ex. 8:22; 9:4, 6; 11:7
27 [I]Lit., *sent and called* [a]Ex. 8:8 [b]Ex. 10:16, 17; 2Chr. 12:6; Ps. 129:4; 145:17; Lam. 1:18
28 [I]Lit., *sounds* [a]Ex. 8:8, 28; 10:17 [b]Ex. 8:25; 10:8, 24
29 [I]Lit., *palms* [II]Lit., *sounds* [a]1Kin. 8:22, 38; Ps. 143:6; Is. 1:15 [b]Ex. 8:22; 19:5; 20:11; Ps. 24:1; 1Cor. 10:26
30 [I]Or, *reverence* [II]Lit., *before the LORD* [a]Ex. 8:29 [b]Is. 26:10
31 [I]Lit., *smitten* [a]Ruth 1:22; 2:23
32 [I]Lit., *smitten*
33 [I]Lit., *palms* [II]Lit., *sounds* [III]Lit., *was not poured* [a]Ex. 8:12; 9:29
34 [I]Lit., *sounds* [II]Lit., *made heavy*
35 [I]Lit., *strong* [a]Ex. 4:21

🔑 **9:32** Rye or spelt was a wild wheat which was more edible than barley, but it was not as good as wheat. It matured later than barley and was difficult to separate from its chaff. Egypt used it for basic bread.

The Plague of Locusts

10 Then the LORD said to Moses, "Go to Pharaoh, for [a]I have [I]hardened his heart and the heart[3820] of his servants,[5650] that I may [II]perform these signs[226] of Mine [III]among them,

2 and [a]that you may tell in the [I]hearing[241] of your son,[1121] and of your grandson, how I made a mockery of the Egyptians, and how I [II]performed[7760] My signs among them; [b]that you may know[3045] that I am the LORD."

3 And Moses and Aaron went to Pharaoh and said to him, "Thus says[559] the LORD, the God[430] of the Hebrews, 'How long will you refuse[3985] to [a]humble yourself before Me? [b]Let My people[5971] go, that they may serve Me.

4 'For if you refuse[3985] to let My people go, behold, tomorrow I will bring locusts into your territory.

5 'And they shall cover[3680] the surface of the land,[776] so that no one shall be able to see[7200] the land. [a]They shall also eat the rest[3499] of what has escaped—[6413] what is left[7604] to you from the hail—and they shall eat every tree which sprouts[7604] for you out of the field.[7704]

6 'Then [a]your houses[1004] shall be filled, and the houses of all your servants and the houses of all the Egyptians, *something* which neither your fathers[1] nor your grandfathers have seen,[7200] from the day[3117] that they [I]came upon the earth[127] until this day.'" And he turned and went out from Pharaoh.

7 And [a]Pharaoh's servants said to him, "How long will this man be [b]a snare[4170] to us? Let the men[582] go, that they may serve the LORD their God. Do you not [I]realize[3045] that Egypt is destroyed?"[6]

8 So Moses and Aaron [a]were brought back to Pharaoh, and he said to them, "[b]Go, serve the LORD your God! [I]Who are the ones that are going?"

9 And Moses said, "[a]We shall go with our young and our old;[2205] with our sons and our daughters, [b]with our flocks and our herds we will go, for we [I]must hold a feast[2282] to the LORD."

10 Then he said to them, "Thus may the LORD be with you, [I]if ever I let you and your little ones[2945] go! Take heed,[7200] for evil[7451] is [II]in your mind.

11 "Not so! Go now, the men[1397] *among you,* and serve the LORD, for [I]that is what you desire." So [a]they were driven out from Pharaoh's presence.

12 Then the LORD said to Moses, "[a]Stretch out your hand[3027] over the land[776] of Egypt for the locusts, that they may come up on the land of Egypt, and [b]eat every plant of the land, *even* all that the hail has left."

13 So Moses stretched out his staff[4294] over the land of Egypt, and the LORD directed an east wind[7307] on the land all that day and all that night;[3915] and when it was morning, the east wind [I]brought the [a]locusts.

14 And [a]the locusts came up over all the land of Egypt and settled in all the territory of Egypt; *they were* very [I]numerous. There had never been so *many* [II]locusts, nor would there be so *many* [III]again.

15 For they covered[3680] the surface of the whole land, so that the land was darkened; and they [a]ate every plant of the land and all the fruit of the trees that the hail had left.[3498] Thus nothing green was left[3498] on tree or plant of the field through all the land of Egypt.

16 Then Pharaoh hurriedly [a]called[7121] for Moses and Aaron, and he said, "[b]I have sinned[2398] against the LORD your God and against you.

17 "Now therefore, please forgive my sin[2403] only this once, and [a]make supplication[6279] to the LORD your God, that He would only remove this death[4194] from me."

18 And [a]he went out from Pharaoh and made supplication to the LORD.

19 So the LORD shifted[2015] *the wind* to a very strong[2389] west wind which took up the locusts and drove them into the [I]Red Sea; not one locust was left in all the territory of Egypt.

20 But [a]the LORD [I]hardened[2388] Pha-

---

1 [I]Lit., *made heavy* [II]Lit., *put* [III]Lit., *in his midst* [a]Ex. 4:21; 7:13; Josh. 11:20; John 12:40; Rom. 9:18

2 [I]Lit., *ears* [II]Lit., *put* [a]Ex. 12:26, 27; 13:8, 14, 15; Deut. 4:9; Ps. 44:1; 78:5; Joel 1:3 [b]Ex. 7:5, 17

3 [a]1Kin. 21:29; 2Chr. 34:27; James 4:10; 1Pet. 5:6 [b]Ex. 4:23

5 [a]Joel 1:4; 2:25

6 [I]Lit., *were* [a]Ex. 8:3, 21

7 [I]Lit., *know* [a]Ex. 7:5; 8:19; 12:33 [b]Ex. 23:33; Josh. 23:13; 1Sam. 18:21; Eccl. 7:26

8 [I]Lit., *Who and who are* [a]Ex. 8:8 [b]Ex. 8:25

9 [I]Lit., *have a feast* [a]Ex. 12:37, 38 [b]Ex. 10:26

10 [I]Lit., *when I* [II]Lit., *before your face*

11 [I]Lit., *you desire it* [a]Ex. 10:28

12 [a]Ex. 7:19 [b]Ex. 10:5, 15

13 [I]Lit., *carried* [a]Ps. 78:46; 105:34

14 [I]Lit., *heavy* [II]Lit., *locusts like them before them* [III]Lit., *after them* [a]Deut. 28:38; Ps. 78:46; 105:34; Joel 1:4, 7; 2:1-11; Rev. 9:3

15 [a]Ex. 10:5; Ps. 105:34f.

16 [a]Ex. 8:8 [b]Ex. 9:27

17 [a]Ex. 8:8, 28; 9:28; 1Kin. 13:6

18 [a]Ex. 8:30

19 [I]Lit., *Sea of Reeds*

20 [I]Lit., *made strong* [a]Ex. 4:21; 11:10

raoh's heart, and he did not let the sons of Israel go.

Darkness over the Land

21 Then the LORD said to Moses, "[a]Stretch out your hand toward the sky,[8064] that there may be darkness[2822] over the land of Egypt, even a darkness [b]which may be felt."

22 So Moses stretched out his hand toward the sky, and there was [a]thick[653] darkness in all the land of Egypt for three days.

23 They did not see one another,[251] nor did anyone rise from his place for three days, [a]but all the sons of Israel had light in their dwellings.[4186]

24 Then Pharaoh [a]called[7121] to Moses, and said, "Go, serve the LORD; only let your flocks and your herds be detained. Even [b]your little ones may go with you."

25 But Moses said, "You must also [I]let us[3027] have sacrifices[2077] and burnt offerings,[5930] that we may [II]sacrifice[6213] *them* to the LORD our God.

26 "[a]Therefore, our livestock, too, will go with us; not a hoof will be left behind, for we shall take some of them to serve the LORD our God. And until we arrive there, we ourselves do not know with what we shall serve the LORD."

27 But [a]the LORD [I]hardened[2388] Pharaoh's heart, and he was not willing to let them go.

28 Then Pharaoh said to him, "[a]Get away from me! [I]Beware,[8104] do not see my face again, for in the day[3117] you see my face you shall die!"

29 And Moses said, "You are right;[1696] [a]I shall never see your face again!"

The Last Plague

11 Now the LORD said to Moses, "One more plague[5061] I will bring on Pharaoh and on Egypt; [a]after that he will let you go from here. When he lets you go, he will surely drive you out from here completely.

2 "Speak[1696] now in the [I]hearing of the people[5971] that [a]each man ask[7592] from his neighbor[7453] and each woman[802] from her neighbor[7468] for articles of silver and articles of gold."

3 [a]And the LORD gave the people favor[2580] in the sight of the Egyptians. [b]Furthermore, the man[376] Moses *himself* was [I]greatly esteemed in the land[776] of Egypt, *both* in the sight of Pharaoh's servants[5650] and in the sight of the people.

4 And Moses said, "Thus says[559] the LORD, 'About [a]midnight I am going out into the midst of Egypt,

5 and [a]all the first-born in the land of Egypt shall die,[4191] from the first-born of the Pharaoh who sits on his throne,[3678] even to the first-born of the slave girl who is behind the millstones; all the first-born of the cattle as well.

6 'Moreover, there shall be [a]a great cry in all the land of Egypt, such as there has not been *before* and such as shall never be again.

7 '[a]But against any of the sons[1121] of Israel a dog shall not *even* [I]bark, whether against man[376] or beast, that you may [II]understand[3045] how the LORD makes a distinction between Egypt and Israel.'

8 "And [a]all these your servants will come down to me and bow[7812] themselves [I]before me, saying, 'Go out, you and all the people who [II]follow you,' and after that I will go out." [b]And he went out from Pharaoh in hot anger.[639]

9 Then the LORD said to Moses, "[a]Pharaoh will not listen[8085] to you, so [b]that My wonders[4159] will be multiplied in the land of Egypt."

10 And [a]Moses and Aaron performed[6213] all these wonders before Pharaoh; yet [b]the LORD [I]hardened[2388] Pharaoh's heart, and he did not let the sons of Israel go out of his land.

---

21 [a]Ex. 9:22 [b]Deut. 28:29
22 [a]Ps. 105:28; Rev. 16:10
23 [a]Ex. 8:22
24 [a]Ex. 8:8, 25 [b]Ex. 10:10
25 [I]Lit., *give into our hand* [II]Lit., *make*
26 [a]Ex. 10:9
27 [I]Lit., *made strong* [a]Ex. 4:21; 10:20; 14:4, 8
28 [I]Lit., *Take heed to yourself* [a]Ex. 10:11
29 [a]Ex. 11:8; Heb. 11:27
1 [a]Ex. 12:31, 33, 39
2 [I]Lit., *ears* [a]Ex. 3:22; 12:35, 36
3 [I]Lit., *very great* [a]Ex. 3:21; 12:36; Ps. 106:46 [b]Deut. 34:10-12
4 [a]Ex. 12:29
5 [a]Ex. 12:12, 29; Ps. 78:51; 105:36; 135:8; 136:10
6 [a]Ex. 12:30
7 [I]Lit., *sharpen his tongue* [II]Lit., *know* [a]Ex. 8:22; Josh. 10:21
8 [I]Lit., *to* [II]Lit., *are at your feet* [a]Ex. 12:31-33 [b]Heb. 11:27
9 [a]Ex. 7:4 [b]Ex. 7:3
10 [I]Lit., *made strong* [a]Ex. 4:21 [b]Ex. 7:3; 9:12; 10:20, 27; Josh. 11:20; Is. 63:17; John 12:40

The Passover Lamb

12 Now the LORD said to Moses and Aaron in the land[776] of [I]Egypt,

🗝 2 "[a]This month shall be the beginning[7218] of months for you; it is to be the first[7223] month of the year to you.

3 "Speak[1696] to all the congregation[5712] of Israel, saying, 'On the tenth of this month they are each one to take a [I]lamb for themselves, according to their fathers'[1] households,[1004] a [I]lamb for [II]each household.

4 'Now if the household[1004] is too small for a [I]lamb, then he and his neighbor[7934] nearest to his house are to take one according to the [II]number of persons[5315] *in them;* according to [III]what each man should eat, you are to [IV]divide the lamb.

5 'Your [I]lamb shall be [a]an unblemished[8549] male[2145] a year old;[1121] you may take it from the sheep or from the goats.

6 'And [I]you shall keep[4931] it until the [a]fourteenth day of the same month, then the whole assembly[6951] of the congregation of Israel is to kill[7819] it [II][b]at twilight.

7 '[a]Moreover, they shall take some of the blood[1818] and put it on the two doorposts and on the lintel [I]of the houses[1004] in which they eat it.

8 'And they shall eat the flesh[1320] [a]that *same* night,[3915] [b]roasted with fire, and they shall eat it with [c]unleavened bread [I][d]and bitter herbs.

9 'Do not eat any of it raw or boiled[1310] at all with water, but rather [a]roasted with fire, *both* its head and its legs along with [b]its entrails.[7130]

10 '[a]And you shall not leave any of it over[3498] until morning, but whatever is left of it until morning, you shall burn with fire.

11 'Now you shall eat it in this manner: *with* your loins girded, your sandals on your feet, and your staff in your hand;[3027] and you shall eat it in haste—it is [a]the LORD'S Passover.[6453]

12 'For [a]I will go[5674] through the land of Egypt on that night, and will strike down all the first-born in the land of Egypt, both man and beast; and [b]against all the gods[430] of Egypt I will execute[6213] judgments—[8201] [c]I am the LORD.

13 'And [a]the blood shall be a sign[226] for you on the houses where you [I]live; and when I see[7200] the blood I will pass over[6452] you, and no plague[5063] will befall you [II]to destroy[4889] *you* when I strike[5221] the land of Egypt.

Feast of Unleavened Bread

14 'Now [a]this day[3117] will be [b]a memorial[2146] to you, and you shall celebrate it *as* a feast[2282] to the LORD; throughout your generations[1755] you are to celebrate it *as* [I][c]a permanent[5769] ordinance.[2708]

15 '[a]Seven days you shall eat unleavened bread,[2557] but on the first day you shall [I]remove[7673] leaven from your houses; for whoever eats anything leavened from the first day until the seventh day, [b]that [II]person shall be cut off[3772] from Israel.

16 'And [a]on the first day you shall have a holy[6944] assembly,[4744] and *another* holy assembly on the seventh day; no work[4399] at all shall be done[6213] on them, except what must be eaten [I]by every person,[5315] that alone may be [II]prepared by you.

17 'You shall also observe[8104] [a]the *Feast of* Unleavened Bread, for on this [b]very day I brought your hosts[6635]

1 [I]Lit., *Egypt, saying*
2 [a]Ex. 13:4; 23:15; 34:18; Deut. 16:1
3 [I]Or, *kid* [II]Lit., *the*
4 [I]Or, *kid* [II]Or, *amount* [III]Lit., *each man's eating* [IV]Lit., *compute for*
5 [I]Or, *kid* [a]Lev. 22:18-21; 23:12; Heb. 9:14; 1Pet. 1:19
6 [I]Lit., *it shall be to you for a guarding* [II]Lit., *between the two evenings* [a]Ex. 12:14, 17; Lev. 23:5; Num. 9:1-3, 11; 28:16 [b]Ex. 16:12; Deut. 16:4, 6
7 [I]Lit., *upon* [a]Ex. 12:22
8 [I]Lit., *in addition to* [a]Ex. 34:25; Num. 9:12 [b]Deut. 16:7 [c]Deut. 16:3, 4; 1Cor. 5:8 [d]Num. 9:11
9 [a]Ex. 12:8 [b]Ex. 29:13, 17, 22
10 [a]Ex. 16:19; 23:18; 34:25
11 [a]Ex. 12:13, 21, 27, 43
12 [a]Ex. 11:4, 5 [b]Num. 33:4; Ps. 82:1 [c]Ex. 6:2
13 [I]Lit., *are* [II]Lit., *for destruction* [a]Heb. 11:28
14 [I]Or, *an eternal* [a]Ex. 12:6; Lev. 23:4, 5; 2Kin. 23:21 [b]Ex. 13:9 [c]Ex. 12:17, 24; 13:10
15 [I]Lit., *cause to cease* [II]Lit., *soul* [a]Ex. 13:6, 7; 23:15; 34:18; Lev. 23:6; Num. 28:17; Deut. 16:3, 8 [b]Gen. 17:14; Ex. 12:19; Num. 9:13

16 [I]Lit., *pertaining to* [II]Lit., *done* [a]Lev. 23:7, 8; Num. 28:18, 25 **17** [a]Deut. 16:3-8 [b]Ex. 12:41

🗝 **12:2** The Jewish calendar, based on lunar months rather than solar months as our present calendar, had its beginning at this time. The first month was called Abib (Ex. 13:4) until the exile. Afterward it was called Nisan (see Neh. 2:1; Esth. 3:7). On modern calendars it corresponds to the latter part of March and the first part of April.

out of the land of Egypt; therefore you
shall observe this day throughout your
generations as [c]a [I]permanent ordinance.
18 "[a]In the first *month,* on the fourteenth day of the month at evening, you
shall eat unleavened bread, until the
twenty-first day of the month at evening.
19 "[a]Seven days there shall be no
leaven found in your houses; for whoever eats what is leavened, that [Ib]person
shall be cut off from the congregation
of Israel, whether *he is* an alien[1616] or
a native of the land.
20 'You shall not eat anything leavened; in all your dwellings[4186] you shall
eat unleavened bread.' "
21 Then [a]Moses called[7121] for all the
elders[2205] of Israel, and said to them,
"[I]Go and [b]take for yourselves [II]lambs
according to your families,[4940] and
slay[7819] [c]the Passover *lamb.*
22 "[a]And you shall take a bunch of
hyssop[231] and dip[2881] it in the blood which
is in the basin,[5592] and [I]apply[5060] some
of the blood that is in the basin to the
lintel[4947] and the two doorposts; and
none of you shall go outside the door
of his house until morning.

A Memorial of Redemption

23 "For [a]the LORD will pass
through[5674] to smite[5062] the Egyptians;
and when He sees the blood on the lintel
and on the two doorposts, the LORD
will pass over the door and will [b]not
allow the [c]destroyer[7843] to come in to
your houses to smite *you.*
24 "And [a]you shall observe this
event[1697] as an ordinance[2706] for you and
your children[1121] forever.
25 "And it will come about when you
enter the land which the LORD will give
you, as He has [I]promised,[1696] that you
shall observe[8104] this [II]rite.[5656]
26 "[a]And it will come about when
your children[1121] will say to you, '[I]What
does this rite mean to you?'
27 that you shall say, 'It is a Passover sacrifice[2077] to [a]the LORD [I]who
passed over the houses of the sons of
Israel in Egypt when He smote the
Egyptians, but [II]spared our homes.' "
[b]And the people[5971] bowed low and
worshiped.[7812]
28 Then the sons of Israel went and
did[6213] *so;* just as the LORD had
commanded[6680] Moses and Aaron, so
they did.
29 Now it came about at [a]midnight
that [b]the LORD struck all [c]the first-born
in the land of Egypt, from the first-born
of Pharaoh who sat on his throne[3678]
to the first-born of the captive[7628] who
was in the dungeon,[953] and all the first-
born of [d]cattle.
30 And Pharaoh arose in the
night,[3915] he and all his servants[5650] and
all the Egyptians; and there was
[a]a great cry in Egypt, for there was
no home where there was not someone
dead.
31 Then [a]he called for Moses and
Aaron at night and said, "Rise up,
[b]get out from among my people, both
you and the sons of Israel; and go,
[I]worship the LORD, as you have said.
32 "Take [a]both your flocks and your
herds, as you have said,[1696] and go, and
bless[1288] me also."

Exodus of Israel

33 And [a]the Egyptians urged[2388] the
people, to send them out of the land
in haste, for they said, "We shall all
be dead."
34 So the people took[5375] [a]their
dough before it was leavened,[2556] *with*
their kneading bowls bound up in the
clothes on their shoulders.
35 [a]Now the sons of Israel had done
according to the word[1697] of Moses, for

17 [I]Or, *eternal* [c]Ex. 12:14; 13:3, 10
18 [a]Ex. 12:2; Lev. 23:5-8; Num. 28:16-25
19 [I]Lit., *soul* [a]Ex. 12:15; 23:15; 34:18 [b]Num. 9:13
21 [I]Lit., *Draw out* [II]Lit., *sheep* [a]Num. 9:4; Heb. 11:28 [b]Ex. 12:3 [c]Ex. 12:11
22 [I]Lit., *cause to touch* [a]Ex. 12:7
23 [a]Ex. 11:4; 12:12, 13 [b]Rev. 7:3; 9:4 [c]1Cor. 10:10; Heb. 11:28
24 [a]Ex. 12:14, 17; 13:5, 10
25 [I]Lit., *spoken* [II]Lit., *service*
26 [I]Lit., *What is this service to you?* [a]Ex. 10:2; 13:8, 14, 15; Deut. 32:7; Josh. 4:6; Ps. 78:6
27 [I]Lit., *because He* [II]Lit., *delivered* [a]Ex. 12:11 [b]Ex. 4:31
29 [a]Ex. 11:4, 5 [b]Num. 8:17; 33:4; Ps. 135:8; 136:10 [c]Ex. 4:23; Ps. 78:51; 105:36 [d]Ex. 9:6
30 [a]Ex. 11:6
31 [I]Or, *serve* [a]Ex. 8:8 [b]Ex. 8:25
32 [a]Ex. 10:9, 26
33 [a]Ex. 10:7; 11:1; 12:39; Ps. 105:38
34 [a]Ex. 12:39
35 [a]Ex. 3:21, 22; 11:2, 3; Ps. 105:37

12:22 Hyssop is a small, fragrant plant of the mint family. It is very bushy in texture and serves well as a brush.

12:35 The Revised Version correctly translates "They asked of the Egyptians . . ." It was not regarded

(continued on next page)

they had requested[7592] from the Egyptians articles of silver and articles of gold, and clothing;

36 and the LORD had given the people favor[2580] in the sight of the Egyptians, so that they let them have[7592] their request. Thus they [a]plundered the Egyptians.

37 Now the [a]sons[2945] of Israel journeyed from [b]Rameses to Succoth, about [c]six hundred thousand men[1397] on foot, aside from children.

38 And a [a]mixed[6154] multitude also went up[5927] with them, [I]along with flocks and herds, a [b]very large number of livestock.

39 And they baked the dough which they had brought out of Egypt into cakes of unleavened bread. For it had not become leavened, since they were [a]driven out of Egypt and could not delay, nor had they [I]prepared[6313] any provisions[6720] for themselves.

🔑40 Now the time [I]that the sons[4186] of Israel lived in Egypt was [a]four hundred and thirty years.

41 And it came about at the end of four hundred and thirty years, [I]to [a]the very day, that [b]all the hosts[6635] of the LORD went out from the land of Egypt.

Ordinance of the Passover

42 [a]It is a night [I]to be observed for the LORD for having brought them out from the land of Egypt; this night is for the LORD, [I]to be observed [II]by all the sons of Israel throughout their generations.

43 And the LORD said to Moses and Aaron, "This is the ordinance[2708] of [a]the Passover: no [Ib]foreigner[5236] is to eat of it;

44 but every man's [a]slave purchased with money, after you have circumcised him, then he may eat of it.

45 "[a]A sojourner[8453] or a hired servant shall not eat of it.

🔑46 "It is to be eaten in a single house; you are not to bring forth any of the flesh outside of the house, [a]nor are you to break[7665] any bone[6106] of it.

47 "[a]All the congregation of Israel are to [I]celebrate[6213] this.

48 "But [a]if a [I]stranger sojourns[1481] with you, and [II]celebrates[6213] the Passover to the LORD, let all his males be circumcised,[4135] and then let him come near[7126] to [III]celebrate it; and he shall be like a native of the land. But no uncircumcised[6189] person may eat of it.

49 "[Ia]The same law[8451] shall [II]apply to the native as to the [III]stranger who sojourns among you."

50 Then all the sons of Israel did *so;* they did just as the LORD had commanded Moses and Aaron.

🔑51 And it came about on that same day that [a]the LORD brought the sons

36 [a]Ex. 3:22
37 [a]Num. 33:3, 5 [b]Gen. 47:11 [c]Ex. 38:26; Num. 1:46; 2:32; 11:21; 26:51
38 [I]Lit., *and* [a]Num. 11:4 [b]Ex. 17:3; Num. 20:19; 32:1; Deut. 3:19
39 [I]Lit., *made* [a]Ex. 6:1; 11:1; 12:31-33
40 [I]Or, *of the sons of Israel who dwelt* [a]Gen. 15:13, 16; Acts 7:6; Gal. 3:17
41 [I]Lit., *that it happened on this very day* [a]Ex. 12:17 [b]Ex. 3:8, 10; 6:6
42 [I]Or, *of vigil* [II]Lit., *to the sons* [a]Ex. 13:10; 34:18; Deut. 16:1
43 [I]Lit., *son of a stranger* [a]Ex. 12:11; Num. 9:14 [b]Ex. 12:48
44 [a]Gen. 17:12, 13; Lev. 22:11
45 [a]Lev. 22:10
46 [a]Num. 9:12; Ps. 34:20; John 19:33, 36
47 [I]Lit., *do* [a]Ex. 12:6; Num. 9:13, 14
48 [I]Lit., *sojourner* [II]Lit., *does* [III]Lit., *do* [a]Num. 9:14
49 [I]Lit., *One law* [II]Lit., *be* [III]Lit., *sojourner* [a]Lev. 24:22; Num. 15:15, 16, 29
51 [a]Ex. 12:41

(continued from previous page)
as a loan. It was customary at the parting of friends or leaving of a servant to give a gift. The Israelites had long been servants of the Egyptians. Probably in the state of panic which followed these events the Egyptians were willing to give them anything if they would leave and do so quickly.

🔑 **12:40** The Samaritan Pentateuch and the Septuagint add after "Egypt" the words "and in the land of Canaan."

🔑 **12:46** The Passover was at the very center of the religion of Israel, as it is with Jews to this day. For Christians it also forms part of the important background for Jesus' death on the cross. In this verse and in Num. 9:12, the breaking of the lamb's bones is forbidden, and in Jn. 19:36 the fact that Jesus' legs were not broken on the cross is regarded by John as a fulfillment of this very verse. In a passage reminiscent of Ex. 12, Paul refers to Jesus as the Christians' Passover Lamb (I Cor. 5:7). The identification of Jesus as the Lamb of God, however, may go back as much to Isa. 53 as it does to Ex. 12. Furthermore, in the Book of Hebrews Jesus' death is regarded as the equivalent of the Day of Atonement sacrifice, a different O.T. offering (Heb. 9:12, 28). This conforms to the picture that we often get of Jesus in the N.T. In Him *all* of the hopes of the O.T. are fulfilled.

🔑 **12:51** Since the sons of Israel had kept their family records for centuries, they could move quickly by families, clans, and tribes.

of Israel out of the land of Egypt [I][b]by their hosts.

Consecration of the First-born

13 Then the LORD spoke[1696] to Moses, saying,

2 "[a]Sanctify[6942] to Me every first-born, the first [I]offspring of every womb among the sons[1121] of Israel, both of man[120] and beast; it belongs to Me."

3 And Moses said to the people,[5971] "[a]Remember this day[3117] in which you went out from Egypt, from the house[1004] of [I]slavery;[5650] for [b]by [II]a powerful[2392] hand[3027] the LORD brought you out from this place. [c]And nothing leavened[2557] shall be eaten.

🗝 4 "On this day in the [a]month of Abib, you are about to go forth.

5 "And it shall be when the LORD [a]brings you to the land[776] of the Canaanite, the Hittite, the Amorite, the Hivite and the Jebusite, which [b]He swore[7650] to your fathers[1] to give you, a land flowing with milk and honey, [c]that you shall [I]observe[5647] this rite[5656] in this month.

6 "For [a]seven days you shall eat unleavened bread, and on the seventh day there shall be a feast[2282] to the LORD.

7 "Unleavened bread shall be eaten throughout the seven days; and [a]nothing leavened shall be seen[7200] [I]among you, nor shall any leaven be seen [I]among you in all your borders.

8 "[a]And you shall tell[5046] your son[1121] on that day, saying, 'It is because of what the LORD did[6213] for me when I came out of Egypt.'

9 "And [a]it shall [I]serve as a sign[226] to you on your hand, and as a reminder[2146] [II]on your forehead, that the law[8451] of the LORD may be in your mouth;[6310] for with [b]a powerful[2389] hand the LORD brought you out of Egypt.

10 "Therefore, you shall [a]keep[8104] this ordinance[2708] at its appointed time[4150] from [I]year to year.[3117]

11 "Now it shall come about when [a]the LORD brings you to the land of the Canaanite, as [b]He swore to you and to your fathers, and gives it to you,

12 that [a]you shall [I]devote[5674] to the LORD the first [II]offspring of every womb, and [III]the first offspring of every beast that you own; the males[2145] belong to the LORD.

13 "But [a]every first [I]offspring of a donkey you shall redeem[6299] with a lamb, but if you do not redeem *it,* then you shall break its neck; and [b]every first-born of man among your sons you shall redeem.

14 "[a]And it shall be when your son asks[7592] you in time to come, saying, 'What is this?' then you shall say to him, '[b]With a [I]powerful[2392] hand the LORD brought us out of Egypt, from the house of [II]slavery.

15 'And it came about, when Pharaoh was stubborn about letting us go, that the [a]LORD killed[2026] every first-born in the land of Egypt, both the first-born of man and the first-born of beast. Therefore, I sacrifice[2076] to the LORD the males, the first [I]offspring of every womb, but every first-born of my sons I redeem.'

16 "So [a]it shall [I]serve as a sign[226] on your hand, and as [II]phylacteries[2903] [III]on your forehead, for with a [IV]powerful hand the LORD brought us out of Egypt."

God Leads the People

17 Now it came about when Pharaoh had let the people go, that God[430] did not lead[5148] them by the way[1870] of the land of the Philistines, even though it was near; for God said, "[a]Lest the people change their minds when they see[7200] war, and they return[7725] to Egypt."

51 [I]Lit., *according to* [b]Ex. 6:26
2 [I]Lit., *opening* [a]Ex. 13:12, 13, 15; 22:29; Lev. 27:26; Num. 3:13; 8:16f.; 18:15; Deut. 15:19; Luke 2:23
3 [I]Lit., *slaves* [II]Lit., *strength of hand* [a]Ex. 12:42; Deut. 16:3 [b]Ex. 3:20; 6:1 [c]Ex. 12:19
4 [a]Ex. 12:2; 23:15; 34:18; Deut. 16:1
5 [I]Lit., *serve this service* [a]Ex. 3:8, 17; Josh. 24:11 [b]Ex. 6:8 [c]Ex. 12:25
6 [a]Ex. 12:15-20
7 [I]Lit., *to* [a]Ex. 12:19
8 [a]Ex. 10:2; 12:26f.; 13:14; Ps. 44:1
9 [I]Lit., *be for* [II]Lit., *between your eyes* [a]Ex. 12:14; 13:16; Num. 15:39; Deut. 6:8; 11:18 [b]Ex. 13:3
10 [I]Lit., *days to days* [a]Ex. 12:24, 25; 13:5
11 [a]Ex. 13:5 [b]Gen. 15:18; 17:8; 28:15; Ps. 105:42-45
12 [I]Lit., *cause to pass over* [II]Lit., *opening* [III]Lit., *every issue the offspring of a beast* [a]Ex. 13:1, 2; 22:29; 34:19; Lev. 27:26; Num. 18:15; Ezek. 44:30; Luke 2:23
13 [I]Lit., *opening* [a]Ex. 34:20; Num. 18:15 [b]Num. 3:46
14 [I]Lit., *strength of hand* [II]Lit., *slaves* [a]Ex. 10:2; 12:26, 27; 13:8; Deut. 6:20; Josh. 4:6, 21 [b]Ex. 13:3, 9
15 [I]Lit., *opening* [a]Ex. 12:29
16 [I]Lit., *be for* [II]Or, *frontlet-bands* [III]Lit., *between your eyes* [IV]Lit., *strength of hand* [a]Ex. 13:9; Deut. 6:8
17 [a]Ex. 14:11, 12; Num. 14:1-4; Deut. 17:16

🗝 **13:4** Abib is the first month of the Hebrew year. Since they used the lunar calendar, the exact date cannot remain static in our solar calendar.

18 Hence God led the people around by the way of the wilderness to the [I]Red Sea; and the sons of Israel went up[5927] [a]in martial array from the land of Egypt.

19 And Moses took [a]the bones[6106] of Joseph with him, for he had made the sons of Israel solemnly swear,[7650] saying, "God shall surely [I]take care of[6485] you; and you shall carry[5927] my bones from here with you."

20 Then they set out from [a]Succoth and camped in Etham on the edge of the wilderness.

21 And [a]the LORD was going before them in a pillar of cloud[6051] by day to lead them on the way, and in a pillar of fire by night[3915] to give them light, that they might [I]travel by day and by night.

22 [I]He [a]did not take away the pillar of cloud by day, nor the pillar of fire by night, from before the people.

Pharaoh in Pursuit

14 Now the LORD spoke[1696] to Moses, saying,

2 "Tell[1696] the sons[1121] of Israel to turn[7725] back and camp before [a]Pi-hahiroth, between [b]Migdol and the sea; you shall camp in front of Baal-zephon, opposite it, by the sea.

3 "For Pharaoh will say[559] of the sons of Israel, 'They are wandering aimlessly[943] in the land;[776] the wilderness has shut them in.'

4 "Thus [a]I will [I]harden[2388] Pharaoh's heart,[3820] and [b]he will chase after them; and I will be honored through Pharaoh and all his army,[2428] and [c]the Egyptians will know[3045] that I am the LORD." And they did[6213] so.

5 When the king[4428] of Egypt was told[5046] that the people[5971] had fled, [I]Pharaoh and his servants[5650] had a change[2015] of heart[3820] toward the people, and they said, "What is this we have done,[6213] that we have let Israel go from serving us?"

6 So he made his chariot ready and took his people with him;

7 and he took six hundred select chariots, and all the *other* chariots of Egypt with officers[7991] over all of them.

8 And [a]the LORD [I]hardened[2388] the heart of Pharaoh, king of Egypt, and he chased after the sons of Israel as the sons of Israel were going out [II][b]boldly.[3027]

9 Then [a]the Egyptians chased after them *with* all the horses *and* chariots of Pharaoh, his horsemen and his army,[2428] and they overtook them camping by the sea, [b]beside Pi-hahiroth, in front of Baal-zephon.

10 And as Pharaoh drew near, the sons of Israel [I]looked,[5375] and behold, the Egyptians were marching after them, and they became very frightened;[3372] [a]so the sons of Israel cried out to the LORD.

11 Then [a]they said to Moses, "Is it because there were no graves[6913] in Egypt that you have taken us away to die in the wilderness? Why have you dealt with us in this way, [I]bringing us out of Egypt?

12 "[a]Is this not the word[1697] that we spoke[1696] to you in Egypt, saying, '[I]Leave us alone that we may serve the Egyptians'? For it would have been better[2896] for us to serve the Egyptians than to die in the wilderness."

The Sea Is Divided

13 But Moses said to the people, "[a]Do not fear![3372] [I]Stand by and see[7200] [b]the salvation[3444] of the LORD which He will accomplish[6213] for you today;[3117] for the Egyptians whom you have seen[7200] today, you will never see[7200] them again forever.[5769]

14 "[a]The LORD will fight for you while [b]you keep silent."

15 Then the LORD said to Moses, "Why are you crying out to Me? Tell the sons of Israel to go forward.

16 "And as for you, lift up [a]your staff[4294] and stretch out your hand over the sea and divide it, and the sons of Israel shall [I]go through the midst of the sea on dry[3004] land.

---

18 [I]Lit., *Sea of Reeds* [a]Josh. 1:14; 4:12, 13
19 [I]Lit., *visit* [a]Gen. 50:24, 25; Josh. 24:32; Acts 7:15, 16
20 [a]Ex. 12:37; Num. 33:6
21 [I]Lit., *go* [a]Ex. 14:19, 24; 33:9, 10; Num. 9:15; 14:14; Deut. 1:33; Neh. 9:12; Ps. 78:14; 99:7; 105:39; Is. 4:5; 1Cor. 10:1
22 [I]Or, *The pillar of cloud by day and the pillar of fire by night did not depart* [a]Neh. 9:19

2 [a]Num. 33:7 [b]Jer. 44:1
4 [I]Lit., *make strong* [a]Ex. 4:21; 7:3; 14:17 [b]Ex. 14:23 [c]Ex. 7:5; 14:25
5 [I]Lit., *the heart of Pharaoh. . . was changed*
8 [I]Lit., *made strong* [II]Lit., *with a high hand* [a]Ex. 14:4 [b]Num. 33:3; Acts 13:17
9 [a]Ex. 15:9; Josh. 24:6 [b]Ex. 14:2
10 [I]Lit., *lifted up their eyes* [a]Josh. 24:7; Neh. 9:9; Ps. 34:17; 107:6
11 [I]Lit., *so as to bring* [a]Ex. 5:21; 15:24; 16:2; Ps. 106:7, 8
12 [I]Lit., *Cease from us* [a]Ex. 6:9
13 [I]Or, *Take your stand* [a]Gen. 15:1; 46:3; Ex. 20:20; 2Chr. 20:15, 17; Is. 41:10, 13, 14 [b]Ex. 14:30; 15:2
14 [a]Ex. 14:25; 15:3; Deut. 1:30; 3:22; Josh. 23:3; 2Chr. 20:29; Neh. 4:20 [b]Is. 30:15
16 [I]Lit., *enter the* [a]Ex. 4:17, 20; 7:19; 14:21, 26; 17:5, 6, 9; Num. 20:8, 9, 11; Is. 10:26

17 "And as for Me, behold, [a]I will [I]harden[2388] the hearts[3820] of the Egyptians so that they will go in after them; and I will be honored through Pharaoh and all his army, through his chariots and his horsemen.

18 "[a]Then the Egyptians will know that I am the LORD, when I am honored through Pharaoh, through his chariots and his horsemen."

19 And [a]the angel of God,[430] who had been going before the camp[4264] of Israel, moved and went behind them; and the pillar of cloud[6051] moved from before them and stood behind them.

20 So it came between the camp of Egypt and the camp of Israel; and there was the cloud [I]along with the darkness,[2822] yet it gave light at night. Thus the one did not come near[7126] the other all night.[3915]

21 [a]Then Moses stretched out his hand over the sea; and the LORD [I]swept the sea *back* by a strong east wind[7307] all night, and turned the sea into [b]dry land,[2724] so [c]the waters were divided.

22 [a]And the sons of Israel [I]went through the midst of the sea on the dry land, and [b]the waters *were like* a wall to them on their right hand and on their left.

23 Then [a]the Egyptians took up the pursuit, and all Pharaoh's horses, his chariots and his horsemen went in after them into the midst of the sea.

24 And it came about at the morning watch, that [a]the LORD looked down on the [I]army of the Egyptians [II]through the pillar of fire and cloud and brought the [I]army of the Egyptians into confusion.

17 [I]Lit., *make strong* [a]Ex. 14:4, 8
18 [a]Ex. 14:25
19 [a]Ex. 13:21, 22
20 [I]Lit., *and the darkness*
21 [I]Lit., *caused to go* [a]Ex. 7:19; 14:16 [b]Ps. 66:6; 106:9; 136:13, 14 [c]Ex. 15:8; Josh. 3:16; 4:23; Neh. 9:11; Ps. 74:13; 78:13; 114:3, 5; Is. 63:12, 13
22 [I]Lit., *entered the* [a]Ex. 15:19; Josh. 3:17; 4:22; Neh. 9:11; Ps. 66:6; 78:13; Heb. 11:29 [b]Ex. 14:29; 15:8
23 [a]Ex. 14:4, 17
24 [I]Lit., *camp* [II]Or, *in* [a]Ex. 13:21
25 [I]Or, *removed* [II]Lit., *me* [a]Ex. 14:4, 14, 18
26 [a]Ex. 14:16
27 [I]Lit., *to meet it* [II]Lit., *shook off* [a]Josh. 4:18 [b]Ex. 15:1, 7; Deut. 11:4; Neh. 9:11; Ps. 78:53; Heb. 11:29
28 [I]Lit., *in respect to* [a]Ps. 78:53; 106:11
29 [a]Ex. 14:22; Ps. 66:6; Is. 11:15
30 [a]Ex. 14:13; Ps. 106:8, 10; Is. 63:8, 11 [b]Ps. 58:10; 59:10
31 [I]Lit., *hand* [II]Lit., *done* [III]Or, *revered* [a]Ex. 4:31; 19:9; Ps. 106:12; John 2:11; 11:45

1 [I]Lit., *and said, saying* [a]Ps. 106:12; Rev. 15:3

25 And He [I]caused their chariot wheels[212] to swerve, and He made them drive with difficulty; so the Egyptians said, "Let [II]us flee from Israel, [a]for the LORD is fighting for them against the Egyptians."

26 Then the LORD said to Moses, "[a]Stretch out your hand over the sea so that the waters may come back[7725] over the Egyptians, over their chariots and their horsemen."

27 So Moses stretched out his hand over the sea, and [a]the sea returned[7725] to its normal state at daybreak, while the Egyptians were fleeing [I]right into it; then the LORD [II][b]overthrew the Egyptians in the midst of the sea.

28 And the waters returned and covered[3680] the chariots and the horsemen, [I]even Pharaoh's entire army that had gone into the sea after them; [a]not even one of them remained.

29 But the sons of Israel walked on [a]dry land through the midst of the sea, and the waters *were like* a wall to them on their right hand and on their left.

🗝 30 [a]Thus the LORD saved Israel that day[3117] from the hand of the Egyptians, and Israel [b]saw[7200] the Egyptians dead on the seashore.[8193]

31 And when Israel saw the great [I]power[3027] which the LORD had [II]used against the Egyptians, the people [III]feared[3372] the LORD, and [a]they believed[539] in the LORD and in His servant Moses.

The Song of Moses and Israel

15 [a]Then Moses and the sons[1121] of Israel sang[7891] this song[7892] to the LORD, [I]and said,

🗝 **14:30,31** As Moses commanded Israel in verse thirteen to "stand by and see the salvation of the Lord," the confirmation is made that on that day the Lord had *saved* them, that they *saw* His great work and they *believed*. The Lord had led them into a position in which they were not able to save themselves. They could only depend upon Him for that salvation. This is a central theme throughout the O.T.: God saved Israel. The story of that salvation went before them. As they moved in to possess Canaan, forty years later, their adversaries remembered the demonstration of the power of their God in their flight from Egypt (Josh. 2:10). Throughout their history the descendants of these Israelites remembered the events of that day (II Kgs. 17:7; II Chr. 6:4,5). In times of apostasy, the Lord called upon Israel to remember that work of salvation (Jer. 11:3,4; Hos. 12:13). This is a powerful, graphic type of the salvation which he worked for all men through Jesus Christ.

"[II][b]I will sing to the LORD, for He
[III]is highly exalted;[1342]
[c]The horse and its rider He has
hurled into the sea.
2 "[I][a]The LORD is my strength and
song,
And He has become my salvation;[3444]
[b]This is my God,[410] and I will
praise Him;
[c]My father's[1] God,[430] and I will
[d]extol Him.
3 "[a]The LORD is a warrior;[376]
[I][b]The LORD is His name.
4 "[a]Pharaoh's chariots and his
army[2428] He has cast[3384] into
the sea;
And the choicest of his
officers[7991] are [I]drowned in
the [II]Red Sea.
5 "The deeps cover[3680] them;
[a]They went down into the depths
like a stone.
6 "[a]Thy right hand, O LORD, is
majestic[142] in power,
[b]Thy right hand, O LORD,
shatters the enemy.
7 "And in the greatness of Thine
[I]excellence Thou [a]dost
overthrow those who rise up
against Thee;
[b]Thou dost send forth Thy
burning anger, *and* it
[c]consumes them as chaff.
8 "[a]And at the blast[7307] of Thy
nostrils[639] the waters were
piled up,[6192]
[b]The flowing waters stood up[5324]
like a heap;
The deeps were congealed in the
heart[3820] of the sea.
9 "[a]The enemy said,[559] 'I will pursue, I will overtake, I will
[b]divide the spoil;
My [I]desire[5315] shall be
[II]gratified against them;
I will draw out my sword, my
hand[3027] shall [III]destroy[3423]
them.'
10 "[a]Thou didst blow with Thy
wind,[7307] the sea covered[3680]
them;
[b]They sank like lead in the
[I]mighty[117] waters.
11 "[a]Who is like Thee among the
gods,[410] O LORD?
Who is like Thee, [b]majestic in
holiness,[6944]
[c]Awesome[3372] in praises,[8416]
[d]working[6213] wonders?[6382]
12 "[a]Thou didst stretch out Thy right
hand,
The earth[776] swallowed them.
13 "In Thy lovingkindness[2617] Thou
hast [a]led[5148] the people[5971]
whom Thou hast
[b]redeemed;[1350]
In Thy strength Thou hast
guided *them* [c]to Thy holy[6944]
habitation.
14 "[a]The peoples have heard,[8085]
they tremble;[7264]
Anguish has gripped the
inhabitants of Philistia.
15 "Then the [a]chiefs[441] of Edom
were dismayed;[926]
[b]The leaders of Moab,
trembling[7461] grips them;
[c]All the inhabitants of Canaan
have melted away.
16 "[a]Terror[367] and dread[6343] fall[5307]
upon them;
[b]By the greatness of Thine arm
they are motionless as stone;
Until Thy people pass over,[5674]
O LORD,
Until the people pass over whom
Thou [c]hast purchased.
17 "[a]Thou wilt bring them and
[b]plant them in [c]the mountain
of Thine inheritance,[5159]
[d]The place, O LORD, which Thou
hast made for Thy dwelling,
[e]The sanctuary,[4720] O LORD,[136]
which Thy hands have
established.
18 "[a]The LORD shall reign[4427]
forever[5769] and ever."[5703]
19 [a]For the horses of Pharaoh with
his chariots and his horsemen went into

1 [II]Or, *Let me sing* [III]Or, *triumphed gloriously* [b]Is. 12:5; 42:10-12 [c]Jer. 51:21
2 [I]Heb., *YAH* [a]Ps. 18:1, 2; Is. 12:2; Hab. 3:18f. [b]Ps. 48:14 [c]Ex. 3:6, 15, 16 [d]2Sam. 22:47; Ps. 99:5; Is. 25:1
3 [I]Heb., *YHWH*, usually rendered *LORD* [a]Ex. 14:14; Rev. 19:11 [b]Ex. 3:15; 6:2, 3, 7, 8; Ps. 24:8; 83:18
4 [I]Lit., *sunk* [II]Lit., *Sea of Reeds* [a]Ex. 14:6, 7, 17, 28
5 [a]Ex. 15:10; Neh. 9:11
6 [a]Ex. 3:20; 6:1 [b]Ps. 118:15, 16
7 [I]Or, *exaltation* [a]Ex. 14:27 [b]Ps. 78:49, 50 [c]Deut. 4:24; Is. 5:24; Heb. 12:29
8 [a]Ex. 14:22, 29; Job 4:9 [b]Ps. 78:13
9 [I]Lit., *soul* [II]Lit., *be filled with them* [III]Or, *dispossess, bring to ruin* [a]Ex. 14:5, 8, 9 [b]Judg. 5:30; Is. 53:12; Luke 11:22
10 [I]Or, *majestic* [a]Ex. 14:27, 28 [b]Ex. 15:5
11 [a]Ex. 8:10; 9:14; Deut. 3:24; 2Sam. 7:22; 1Kin. 8:23; Ps. 71:19; 86:8; Mic. 7:18 [b]Is. 6:3; Rev. 4:8 [c]Ps. 22:23 [d]Ps. 72:18; 136:4
12 [a]Ex. 15:6
13 [a]Neh. 9:12; Ps. 77:20 [b]Ex. 15:16; Ps. 77:15 [c]Ex. 15:17; Ps. 78:54
14 [a]Deut. 2:25; Hab. 3:7
15 [a]Gen. 36:15, 40 [b]Num. 22:3, 4 [c]Josh. 2:9, 11, 24; 5:1
16 [a]Ex. 23:27; Deut. 2:25; Josh. 2:9 [b]Ex. 15:5, 6 [c]Ex. 15:13; Ps. 74:2; Is. 43:1; Jer. 31:11; Titus 2:14; 2Pet. 2:1
17 [a]Ex. 23:20; 32:34 [b]Ps. 44:2; 80:8, 15 [c]Ps. 2:6; 78:54, 68 [d]Ps. 68:16; 76:2; 132:13, 14 [e]Ps. 78:69
18 [a]Ps. 10:16; 29:10; Is. 57:15 **19** [a]Ex. 14:23, 28

the sea, and the LORD brought back[7725] the waters of the sea on them; but the sons of Israel walked on [b]dry land through the midst of the sea.

20 And [a]Miriam the prophetess, Aaron's sister,[269] took the [b]timbrel[8596] in her hand, and all the women went out after her with timbrels and with [Ic]dancing.

21 And Miriam answered them,
"[a]Sing to the LORD, for He
[I]is highly exalted;
The horse and his rider He has
hurled into the sea."

The LORD Provides Water

22 [a]Then Moses [I]led Israel from the [II]Red Sea, and they went out into [b]the wilderness of [c]Shur; and they went three days in the wilderness and found no water.

23 And when they came to [a]Marah, they could not drink the waters [I]of Marah, for they were [II]bitter; therefore it was named [III]Marah.

24 So the people [a]grumbled at Moses, saying, "What shall we drink?"

25 Then he [a]cried out to the LORD, and the LORD showed[3384] him [b]a tree; and he threw *it* into the waters, and the waters became[7760] sweet. There He [c]made for them a statute[2706] and regulation,[4941] and there He [d]tested[5254] them.

26 And He said, "[a]If you will give earnest heed[8085] to the voice of the LORD your God, and do[6213] what is right in His sight, and give ear[238] [b]to His commandments,[4687] and keep[8104] all His statutes, [c]I will put none of the diseases[4245] on you which I have put on the Egyptians; for I, [d]the LORD, am your healer."

27 Then they came to [a]Elim where there *were* twelve springs of water and seventy date palms, and they camped there beside the waters.

The LORD Provides Manna

16 Then they set out from Elim, and all the congregation[5712] of the sons[1121] of Israel came to the wilderness of [a]Sin, which is between Elim and Sinai, on [b]the fifteenth day of the second month after their departure from the land[776] of Egypt.

2 And the whole congregation of the sons of Israel [a]grumbled against Moses and Aaron in the wilderness.

3 And the sons of Israel said to them, "[a]Would that we had died by the LORD's hand[3027] in the land of Egypt, [b]when we sat by the pots of [I]meat,[1320] when we ate bread to the full; for you have brought us out into this wilderness to kill this whole assembly[6951] with hunger."

4 Then the LORD said to Moses, "Behold, [a]I will rain bread from heaven[8064] for you; and the people[5971] shall go out and gather[3950] a day's portion[1697] every day,[3117] that I may [b]test[5254] them, whether or not they will walk in My [I]instruction.[8451]

5 "And it will come about [a]on the sixth day, when they prepare what they bring in, it will be twice as much as they gather daily."

6 So Moses and Aaron said to all the sons of Israel, "At evening [Ia]you will know[3045] that the LORD has brought you out of the land of Egypt;

7 and in the morning [I]you will see[7200] [a]the glory[3519] of the LORD, for [b]He hears[8085] your grumblings against the

19 [b]Ex. 14:22, 29
20 [I]Lit., *dances* [a]Ex. 2:4; Num. 26:59; 1Chr. 6:3; Mic. 6:4 [b]Judg. 11:34; 1Sam. 18:6; 1Chr. 15:16; Ps. 68:25; 81:2; 149:3; Jer. 31:4 [c]Judg. 11:34; 21:21; 1Sam. 18:6; Ps. 30:11; 150:4
21 [I]Or, *has triumphed gloriously* [a]Ex. 15:1
22 [I]Lit., *caused Israel to journey* [II]Lit., *Sea of Reeds* [a]Ps. 77:20; 78:52, 53 [b]Num. 33:8 [c]Gen. 16:7; 20:1; 25:18
23 [I]Lit., *from* [II]Heb., *Marim* [III]I.e., bitterness [a]Num. 33:8; Ruth 1:20
24 [a]Ex. 14:11; 16:2; Ps. 106:13
25 [a]Ex. 14:10 [b]Ezek. 47:7, 8 [c]Josh. 24:25 [d]Ex. 16:4; Deut. 8:2, 16; Judg. 2:22; 3:1, 4; Ps. 66:10
26 [a]Ex. 19:5, 6; Deut. 7:12 [b]Ex. 20:2-17 [c]Deut. 7:15; 28:58, 60 [d]Ex. 23:25; Deut. 32:39; Ps. 41:3, 4; 103:3; 147:3
27 [a]Num. 33:9

1 [a]Num. 33:10, 11; Ezek. 30:15 [b]Ex. 12:6, 51; 19:1
2 [a]Ex. 14:11; 15:24; Ps. 106:25; 1Cor. 10:10
3 [I]Or, *flesh* [a]Ex. 17:3; Num. 14:2, 3; 20:3; Lam. 4:9 [b]Num. 11:4, 5
4 [I]Or, *law* [a]Neh. 9:15; Ps. 78:23-25; 105:40; John 6:31; 1Cor. 10:3 [b]Ex. 15:25; Deut. 8:2, 16
5 [a]Ex. 16:22
6 [I]Lit., *and you* [a]Ex. 6:7
7 [I]Lit., *and you* [a]Ex. 16:10, 12; Is. 35:2; 40:5; John 11:4, 40 [b]Num. 14:27; 17:5

15:23-25 The Lord did not take Israel to Canaan by the most direct route. They needed not only to observe the mighty works of His power but also to depend upon Him in a practical way for the very necessities of life. Ultimately they needed to understand that all would be accomplished not by their own ability but by God's own power. At Marah they needed water, but that which was available was not fit for drinking until God acted. This was clearly a statement by Him that the same power which defeated the Egyptian army and brought them safely out would provide the water necessary for life.

LORD; and [c]what are we, that you grumble against us?"

The LORD Provides Meat

8 And Moses said, *"This will happen* when the LORD gives you [I]meat to eat in the evening, and bread to the full in the morning; for the LORD hears your grumblings which you grumble against Him. And what are we? Your grumblings are [a]not against us but against the LORD."

9 Then Moses said to Aaron, "Say to all the congregation of the sons of Israel, '[a]Come near[7126] before the LORD, for He has heard your grumblings.' "

10 And it came about as Aaron spoke to the whole congregation of the sons of Israel, that they [I]looked toward the wilderness, and behold, [a]the glory of the LORD appeared in the cloud.[6051]

11 And the LORD spoke[1696] to Moses, saying,

12 "[a]I have heard the grumblings of the sons of Israel; speak[1696] to them, saying, '[I]At twilight you shall eat [II]meat,[1320] and in the morning you shall be filled with bread; and [b]you shall know that I am the LORD your God.' "[430]

🔑 13 So it came about at evening that [a]the quails came up and covered[3680] the camp,[4264] and in the morning [b]there was a layer of dew around the camp.[4264]

14 [a]When the layer of dew [I]evaporated, behold, on the [II]surface of the wilderness [b]there was a fine flake-like thing, fine as the frost[3713] on the ground.[776]

15 When the sons of Israel saw[7200] *it,* they said to one[376] another, "[I]What is[4479] it?" For they did not know[3045] what it was. And Moses said to them, "[a]It is the bread which the LORD has given you to eat.

16 "This is [I]what[1697] the LORD has commanded,[6680] 'Gather of it every man[376] [II]as much as he should eat; you shall take [III][a]an omer[6016] apiece according to the number of persons[5315] each of you has in his tent.' "[168]

17 And the sons of Israel did[6213] so, and *some* gathered much and *some* little.

18 When they measured[4058] it with an omer, [a]he who had gathered much had no excess, and he who had gathered little had no lack; every man gathered [I]as much as he should eat.

19 And Moses said to them, "Let[3498] no man leave[3498] any of it until morning."

20 But they did not listen[8085] to Moses, and some left[3498] part of it until morning, and it bred worms and became foul; and Moses was angry[7107] with them.

21 And they gathered it morning by morning, every man [I]as much as he should eat; but when the sun grew hot, it would melt.

The Sabbath Observed

22 [a]Now it came about on the sixth day they gathered twice as much bread, two omers[6016] for each one. When all the [b]leaders[5387] of the congregation came and told[5046] Moses,

23 then he said[1696] to them, "This is what the LORD [I]meant: [a]Tomorrow is a sabbath observance,[7677] a holy[6944]

7 [c]Num. 16:11
8 [I]Or, *flesh* [a]1Sam. 8:7; Luke 10:16; Rom. 13:2; 1Thess. 4:8
9 [a]Num. 16:16
10 [I]Lit., *turned* [a]Ex. 13:21; 16:7; Num. 16:19; 1Kin. 8:10f.
12 [I]Lit., *Between the two evenings* [II]Or, *flesh* [a]Ex. 16:8; Num. 14:27 [b]Ex. 6:7; 16:7; 1Kin. 20:28; Joel 3:17
13 [a]Num. 11:31; Ps. 78:27-29; 105:40 [b]Num. 11:9
14 [I]Lit., *had gone up* [II]Lit., *face of* [a]Num. 11:7-9 [b]Ex. 16:31; Neh. 9:15; Ps. 78:24; 105:40
15 [I]Heb., *Man hu,* cf. v. 31 [a]Ex. 16:4; Neh. 9:15; Ps. 78:24; John 6:31; 1Cor. 10:3
16 [I]Lit., *the thing which* [II]Lit., *according to his eating* [III]Lit., *an omer for a head* [a]Ex. 16:32, 36
18 [I]Lit., *according to his eating* [a]2Cor. 8:15
19 [a]Ex. 12:10; 16:23; 23:18
21 [I]Lit., *according to his eating*
22 [a]Ex. 16:5 [b]Ex. 34:31
23 [I]Lit., *spoke* [a]Gen. 2:3; Ex. 20:8-11; 23:12; 31:15; 35:2; Lev. 23:3; Neh. 9:13, 14

🔑 **16:13-15** This is yet another step in the faith-building experience of Israel. They were about to learn that the Lord would give them not only the water that they drank, but the very food they would eat daily. Quail were common. They regularly migrated across the Red Sea into the Sinai peninsula. The Lord's work could be seen in the time of day that they arrived as well as in the abundance and regularity with which they came. There are also several phenomena in that area similar to the manna, substances that are excreted from certain trees or bushes and other substances deposited on the trees by insects which dry and form a crust-like layer but melt with the sun's heat. The manna, on the other hand, was "bread from heaven" (verse 4). It came six days each week and was absent on the Sabbath. At the end of each day the remainder of the morning's gathering would be destroyed by worms. Israel would have to depend upon God *every day!* Jesus presents manna as an antitype of Himself who is the "true bread out of heaven," (Jn. 6:32-35).

sabbath[7676] to the LORD. Bake what you
will bake and boil what you will boil,
and [b]all that is left over [II]put aside to
be kept[4931] until morning."
24 So they [I]put it aside until morning, as Moses had ordered, and [a]it did
not become foul, nor was there any
worm in it.
25 And Moses said, "Eat it today,
for today is a sabbath to the LORD; today
you will not find it in the field.[7704]
26 "[a]Six days you shall gather it,
but on the seventh day, *the* sabbath,
there will be [I]none."
27 And it came about on the seventh
day that some of the people went out
to gather, but they found none.
28 Then the LORD said to Moses,
"[a]How long do you refuse[3985] to keep[8104]
My commandments[4687] and My [I]instruc-
tions?
29 "See,[7200] [I]the LORD has given you
the sabbath; therefore He gives you
bread for two days on the sixth day.
Remain every man in his place; let no
man go out of his place on the seventh
day."
30 So the people rested[7673] on the
seventh day.
31 And the house[1004] of [a]Israel
named[7121] it [I]manna, and it was like
[b]coriander seed,[2233] white; and its
taste[2940] was like wafers with honey.
32 Then Moses said, "This is
[I]what the LORD has commanded,[6680] 'Let
an omerful of it be kept throughout your
generations,[1755] that they may see the
bread that I fed you in the wilderness,
when I brought you out of the land of
Egypt.' "
33 And Moses said to Aaron, "[a]Take
a jar and put an omerful of manna in
it, and place it before the LORD, to be
kept throughout your generations."

23 [II]Lit., *lay up for you* [b]Ex. 16:19
24 [I]Lit., *laid it up* [a]Ex. 16:20
26 [I]Lit., *none on it* [a]Ex. 20:9, 10
28 [I]Or, *laws* [a]2Kin. 17:14; Ps. 78:10; 106:13
29 [I]Lit., *for the* LORD
31 [I]Heb., *man,* cf. v. 15 [a]Num. 11:7-9; Deut. 8:3, 16 [b]Ex. 16:14
32 [I]Lit., *the thing which*
33 [a]Heb. 9:4; Rev. 2:17
34 [a]Ex. 25:16, 21; 27:21; 40:20; Num. 17:10
35 [a]Deut. 8:2f.; Josh. 5:12; Neh. 9:20, 21
36 [I]I.e., Approx. one bu. [a]Ex. 16:16

1 [I]Lit., *their journeyings* [II]Lit., *mouth* [a]Ex. 16:1; Num. 33:12 [b]Ex. 19:2; Num. 33:14
2 [a]Ex. 14:11; Num. 20:2, 3, 13 [b]Ex. 16:8 [c]Deut. 6:16; Ps. 78:18, 41; Matt. 4:7; 1Cor. 10:9
3 [I]Lit., *the people* [II]Lit., *me* [III]Lit., *my* [a]Ex. 16:2, 3 [b]Ex. 12:38
4 [a]Num. 14:10; 1Sam. 30:6
5 [a]Ex. 3:16, 18 [b]Ex. 7:20
6 [a]Ex. 3:1 [b]Num. 20:10, 11; Deut. 8:15; Neh. 9:15; Ps. 78:15; 105:41; 114:8; 1Cor. 10:4

34 As the LORD commanded Moses,
so Aaron placed it before [a]the Testimony,[5715] to be kept.
35 [a]And the sons of Israel ate the
manna forty years, until they came to
an inhabited land; they ate the manna
until they came to the border of the
land of Canaan.
36 (Now [a]an omer is a tenth of an
[I]ephah.)

Water in the Rock

17 Then all the congregation[5712] of
the sons[1121] of Israel journeyed
by [I]stages from the wilderness of
[a]Sin, according to the [II]command[6310] of
the LORD, and camped at [b]Rephidim,
and there was no water for the
people[5971] to drink.
2 Therefore the people [a]quar-
reled[7378] with Moses and said, "Give
us water that we may drink." And Moses
said to them, "[b]Why do you quarrel with
me? [c]Why do you test[5254] the LORD?"
3 But the people thirsted there for
water; and [I]they [a]grumbled against Moses and said, "Why, now, have you
brought us up[5927] from Egypt, to kill
[II]us and [III]our children and [III][b]our livestock with thirst?"
4 So Moses cried out to the LORD,
saying, "What shall I do[6213] to this people? A [a]little more and they will stone
me."
5 Then the LORD said to Moses,
"Pass[5674] before the people and take
with you some of [a]the elders[2205] of Israel; and take in your hand[3027] your
staff[4294] with which [b]you struck[5221] the
Nile, and go.
🔑 6 "Behold, I will stand before you
there on the rock at [a]Horeb; and
[b]you shall strike the rock, and water

🔑 **17:6** Allegory is one of the several methods that N.T. writers used to interpret the O.T. Only Gal. 4:21-31 is identified as an allegory, but there are others, including one in 1 Cor. 10:4, where Paul allegorized the accounts of God giving Israel manna and water from a rock during their time in the wilderness. Ex. 17:6 (see also Num. 20:8-11; Ps. 78:15,16) is one of the passages to which Paul was probably referring. An allegorical interpretation does not necessarily deny the literal meaning of a passage, but it merely asserts that there is another, deeper meaning which God intended. In 1 Cor. 10:4 Paul

(continued on next page)

will come out of it, that the people may drink." And Moses did so in the sight of the elders of Israel.

7 And he named[7121] the place [Ia]Massah[4531] and [IIb]Meribah because of the quarrel[7379] of the sons of Israel, and because they [c]tested the LORD, saying, "Is the LORD among us, or not?"

Amalek Fought

🔑 **8** Then [a]Amalek came and fought against Israel at [b]Rephidim.

9 So Moses said to [a]Joshua, "Choose men[582] for us, and go out, fight against Amalek. Tomorrow I will station[5324] myself on the top[7218] of the hill with [b]the staff of God[430] in my hand."

10 And Joshua did as Moses [I]told[559] him, [II]and fought against Amalek; and Moses, Aaron, and [a]Hur went up[5927] to the top of the hill.

11 So it came about when Moses held his hand up, that Israel prevailed, and when he let his hand [I]down, Amalek prevailed.

12 But Moses' hands were heavy. Then they took a stone and put it under him, and he sat on it; and Aaron and Hur [a]supported his hands, one on one side and one on the other. Thus his hands were steady[530] until the sun set.

13 So Joshua [I]overwhelmed Amalek and his people with the edge[6310] of the sword.

14 Then the LORD said to Moses, "[a]Write this in [I]a book[5612] as a memorial,[2146] and [II]recite it to Joshua, [III]that [b]I will utterly blot out[4229] the memory[2143] of Amalek from under heaven."[8064]

15 And Moses built an [a]altar,[4196] and named it [b]The LORD is My Banner;

16 and he said, "[Ia]The LORD has sworn; the LORD will have war against Amalek from generation[1755] to generation."

7 [I]I.e., test [II]I.e., quarrel [a]Deut. 6:16; 9:22; Ps. 95:8 [b]Num. 20:13, 24; 27:14; Ps. 81:7 [c]Num. 14:22; Deut. 33:8
8 [a]Gen. 36:12; Num. 24:20; Deut. 25:17-19; 1Sam. 15:2 [b]Ex. 17:1
9 [a]Ex. 24:13 [b]Ex. 4:20
10 [I]Lit., *said to* [II]Lit., *to fight* [a]Ex. 24:14; 31:2
11 [I]Lit., *rest*
12 [a]Is. 35:3
13 [I]Lit., *weakened*
14 [I]Lit., *the book* [II]Lit., *place it in the ears of* [III]Or, *for* [a]Ex. 24:4; 34:27; Num. 33:2 [b]Deut. 25:19; 1Sam. 15:3
15 [a]Ex. 24:4 [b]Gen. 22:14; Judg. 6:24
16 [I]Or, *Because a hand is against the throne of the* LORD; lit., *Because a hand upon the throne of* YAH [a]Gen. 22:16

1 [a]Ex. 2:16, 18; 3:1
2 [a]Ex. 2:21; 4:25
3 [I]Lit., *the name of the one was* [II]Heb., *ger* [a]Ex. 2:22; 4:20; Acts 7:29 [b]Ex. 2:22
4 [I]Lit., *the name of the other was* [II]Heb., *El-ezer;* i.e., my God is help [a]1Chr. 23:15, 17 [b]Gen. 49:25
5 [I]Lit., *unto* [a]Ex. 3:1, 12; 4:27; 24:13
6 [I]Lit., *said*
7 [a]Gen. 43:26, 28 [b]Gen. 29:13; Ex. 4:27 [c]Gen. 43:27; 2Sam. 11:7
8 [a]Ex. 4:23; 7:4, 5 [b]Num. 20:14; Neh. 9:32 [c]Ex. 15:6, 16
9 [I]Lit., *in that He had delivered* [II]Lit., *him* [a]Is. 63:7-14
10 [a]Gen. 14:20; 2Sam. 18:28; 1Kin. 8:56; Ps. 68:19, 20

Jethro, Moses' Father-in-law

18 Now [a]Jethro, the priest[3548] of Midian, Moses' father-in-law, heard of all that God[430] had done[6213] for Moses and for Israel His people,[5971] how the LORD had brought Israel out of Egypt.

2 And Jethro, Moses' father-in-law, took Moses' wife[802] [a]Zipporah, after he had sent her away,

3 and her [a]two sons,[1121] of whom [I]one was named Gershom, for he said, "I have been [b]a [II]sojourner[1616] in a foreign[5237] land."[776]

4 And [I]the other was named [IIa]Eliezer, for *he said,* "[b]The God of my father[1] was my help, and delivered[5337] me from the sword[2719] of Pharaoh."

5 Then Jethro, Moses' father-in-law, came with his sons and his wife to Moses [I]in the wilderness where he was camped, at [a]the mount of God.

6 And he [I]sent word to Moses, "I, your father-in-law Jethro, am coming to you with your wife and her two sons with her."

7 Then Moses went out to meet his father-in-law, and [a]he bowed down[7812] and [b]kissed him; and they [c]asked[7592] each[376] other[7453] of their welfare,[7965] and went into the tent.[168]

8 And Moses told his father-in-law all that the LORD had done to Pharaoh and to the Egyptians [a]for Israel's sake, all the [b]hardship that had befallen them on the journey, and *how* [c]the LORD had delivered them.

9 And Jethro rejoiced over all [a]the goodness[2896] which the LORD had done to Israel, [I]in delivering [II]them from the hand[3027] of the Egyptians.

10 So Jethro said, "[a]Blessed[1288] be

(continued from previous page)
maintained that, in a preexistent state, Christ was that rock which provided Israel with water in the wilderness. Paul's purpose was to show the close connection between the Corinthian Christians and their spiritual forefathers, so that they would learn from Israel's poor example.

🔑 **17:8-13** See note on Num. 27:18-23.

the LORD who delivered you from the hand of the Egyptians and from the hand of Pharaoh, *and* who delivered the people from under the hand of the Egyptians.

11 "Now I know[3045] that [a]the LORD is greater than all the gods;[430] [I]indeed, [b]it was proven when they dealt proudly against [II]the people."

12 [a]Then Jethro, Moses' father-in-law, took a burnt offering[5930] and sacrifices[2077] for God, and Aaron came with all the elders[2205] of Israel to eat [I]a meal with Moses' father-in-law before God.

13 And it came about the next day that Moses sat to judge[8199] the people, and the people stood about Moses from the morning until the evening.

14 Now when Moses' father-in-law saw[7200] all that he was doing for the people, he said, "What is this thing that you are doing for the people? Why do you alone sit *as judge* and all the people stand[5324] about you from morning until evening?"

15 And Moses said to his father-in-law, "Because the people come to me [a]to inquire of God.

16 "When they have a [Ia]dispute,[1697] it comes to me, and I judge between a man and his neighbor,[7453] and make known the statutes[2706] of God and His laws."[8451]

Jethro Counsels Moses

17 And Moses' father-in-law said to him, "The thing that you are doing is not good.[2896]

18 "[a]You will surely wear out, both yourself and [I]these people who are with you, for the [II]task is too heavy for you; [b]you cannot do[6213] it alone.

19 "Now listen[8085] to [I]me: I shall give you counsel,[3289] and God be with you. [II]You be the people's representative before God, and you [a]bring the [III]disputes[1697] to God,

20 [a]then teach[2094] them the statutes[2706] and the laws, and make known to them [b]the way in which they are to walk, and the work they are to do.[6213]

21 "Furthermore, you shall [I]select[2372] out of all the people [a]able[2428] men[582] [b]who fear[3373] God, men of truth,[571] those who [c]hate dishonest gain;[1215] and you shall place[7760] *these* over them, *as* leaders[8269] of thousands, [II]of hundreds, [II]of fifties and [II]of tens.

22 "And let them judge the people at all times;[6256] and let it be [a]that every major [I]dispute they will bring to you, but every minor [I]dispute they themselves will judge. So it will be easier[7043] for you, and [b]they will bear *the burden* with you.

23 "If you do this thing and God *so* commands[6680] you, then you will be able to [I]endure, and all [II]these people also will go to [III]their place in peace."

24 So Moses listened[8085] [I]to his father-in-law, and did all that he had said.

25 And Moses chose [a]able men out of all Israel, and made them heads[7218] over the people, leaders of thousands, [I]of hundreds, [I]of fifties and [I]of tens.

26 And they judged the people at all times; [a]the difficult [I]dispute[1697] they would bring to Moses, but every minor [I]dispute[1697] they themselves would judge.

27 Then Moses [Ia]bade his father-in-law farewell, and he went his way into his own land.

Moses on Sinai

19 🔑 [a]In the third month after the sons[1121] of Israel had gone out of the land[776] of Egypt, [I]on that very day[3117] they came into the wilderness of [b]Sinai.

2 When they set out from

11 [I]Lit., *indeed, in the thing in which they* [II]Lit., *them* [a]Ex. 12:12; 15:11; 2Chr. 2:5; Ps. 95:3; 97:9; 135:5 [b]Luke 1:51
12 [I]Lit., *bread* [a]Gen. 31:54; Ex. 24:5
15 [a]Num. 9:6, 8; 27:5; Deut. 17:8-13
16 [I]Lit., *matter* [a]Ex. 24:14
18 [I]Lit., *this* [II]Lit., *matter* [a]Num. 11:14, 17; Deut. 1:12 [b]Deut. 1:9
19 [I]Lit., *my voice* [II]Lit., *You be for the people in front of God* [III]Lit., *matters* [a]Num. 27:5
20 [a]Deut. 1:18; 4:1, 5; 5:1 [b]Ps. 143:8
21 [I]Lit., *see* [II]Lit., *leaders of* [a]Ex. 18:25; Deut. 1:13, 15; 2Chr. 19:5-10; Ps. 15:1-5; Acts 6:3 [b]Gen. 42:18; 2Sam. 23:3 [c]Deut. 16:19
22 [I]Lit., *matter* [a]Deut. 1:17, 18 [b]Num. 11:17
23 [I]Lit., *stand* [II]Lit., *this* [III]Lit., *his*
24 [I]Lit., *to the voice of*
25 [I]Lit., *leaders of* [a]Ex. 18:21; Deut. 1:15
26 [I]Lit., *matter* [a]Ex. 18:22
27 [I]Lit., *sent off his father-in-law* [a]Num. 10:29, 30
1 [I]Lit., *on this day* [a]Ex. 12:6, 51; 16:1 [b]Deut. 1:6; 4:10, 15; 5:2
2 [a]Ex. 17:1; Num. 33:15

🔑 **19:1** Israel had now arrived at Mount Sinai, where they remained for almost a year (compare Ex. 19:1 with Num. 10:11). Some of the high points and low points of their history occurred here. At Sinai *(continued on next page)*

[a]Rephidim, they came to the wilderness
of Sinai, and camped in the wilderness;
and there Israel camped in front of
[b]the mountain.
3 And Moses went up[5927] to God,[430]
and [a]the LORD called[7121] to him from
the mountain, saying, "Thus you shall
say to the house[1004] of Jacob and tell[5046]
the sons of Israel:
4 '[a]You yourselves have seen[7200]
what I did[6213] to the Egyptians, and *how*
I bore[5375] you on [b]eagles' wings, and
brought you to Myself.
🗝 5 'Now then, [a]if you will indeed
obey[8085] My voice and [b]keep[8104] My covenant,[1285] then you shall be [c]My [I]own
possession[5459] among all the peoples,[5971] for [d]all the earth[776] is Mine;
6 and you shall be to Me [a]a kingdom[4467] of priests[3548] and [b]a holy[6918]
nation.'[1471] These are the words[1697] that
you shall speak[1696] to the sons of Israel."
7 [a]So Moses came and called the
elders[2205] of the people, and set before
them all these words which the LORD
had commanded[6680] him.
8 [a]And all the people answered together and said, "All that the LORD has
spoken[1696] we will do!"[6213] And Moses
brought back[7725] the words of the people
to the LORD.
9 And the LORD said to Moses, "Behold, I shall come to you in [a]a thick
cloud,[6051] in order that the [b]people may
hear when I speak with you, and may
also believe[539] in you forever."[5769] Then
Moses told the words of the people to
the LORD.
10 The LORD also said to Moses,
"Go to the people and [a]consecrate[6942]

2 [b]Ex. 3:1, 12; 18:5
3 [a]Ex. 3:4
4 [a]Deut. 29:2 [b]Deut. 32:11; Rev. 12:14
5 [I]Or, *special treasure* [a]Ex. 15:26; Deut. 5:2f. [b]Ps. 78:10 [c]Deut. 4:20; 7:6; 14:2; 26:18; Ps. 135:4; Titus 2:14; 1Pet. 2:9 [d]Ex. 9:29; Deut. 10:14; Job 41:11; Ps. 50:12; 1Cor. 10:26
6 [a]1Pet. 2:5, 9; Rev. 1:6; 5:10 [b]Deut. 7:6; 14:21; 26:19; Is. 62:12
7 [a]Ex. 4:29, 30
8 [a]Ex. 4:31; 24:3, 7; Deut. 5:27; 26:17
9 [a]Ex. 19:16; 24:15, 16; Deut. 4:11; Ps. 99:7 [b]Deut. 4:12, 36
10 [a]Lev. 11:44, 45 [b]Gen. 35:2; Lev. 15:5; Num. 8:7, 21; 19:19; Rev. 22:14
11 [a]Ex. 19:16
12 [I]Lit., *Take heed to yourselves* [a]Heb. 12:20
13 [I]I.e., with arrows [a]Heb. 12:20 [b]Ex. 19:17
16 [I]Lit., *sounds* [a]Heb. 12:18, 19, 21
17 [I]Lit., *lower part*
18 [a]Deut. 4:11; Ps. 104:32; 144:5

them today[3117] and tomorrow, and let
them [b]wash[3526] their garments;
11 and let them be ready[3559] for the
third day, for on [a]the third day the LORD
will come down on Mount Sinai in the
sight of all the people.
12 "And you shall set bounds for
the people all around, saying, '[I]Be-
ware[8104] that you do not go up on the
mountain or touch[5060] the border of it;
[a]whoever touches the mountain shall
surely be put to death.
13 'No hand[3027] shall touch him, but
[a]he shall surely be stoned or [I]shot[3384]
through; whether beast or man,[376] he
shall not live.'[2421] When the ram's horn
sounds a long blast, they shall come up
to [b]the mountain."
14 So Moses went down from the
mountain to the people and consecrated[6942] the people, and they washed
their garments.
15 And he said to the people, "Be
ready for the third day; do not go[5066]
near a woman."
16 [a]So it came about on the third
day, when it was morning, that there
were [I]thunder and lightning flashes and
a thick cloud upon the mountain and a
very loud[2389] trumpet sound, so that all
the people who *were* in the camp[4264]
trembled.[2729]
17 And Moses brought the people
out of the camp to meet God, and they
stood at the [I]foot[8482] of the mountain.

The LORD Visits Sinai

18 [a]Now Mount Sinai *was* all in
smoke[6225] because the LORD descended

(continued from previous page)
they rebelled against God and made an idol of gold, but also at this holy mountain they received and ratified the Ten Commandments and most of the Law of Moses. Ex. 19—24, Leviticus, and Num. 1:1—10:10 all relate to Mount Sinai. Israel's nearly forty years of wandering in the wilderness are narrated in the rest of Numbers. Deuteronomy is a second giving of the law by Moses at the end of the forty years, as the nation prepared to enter Canaan under Joshua.

🗝 **19:5,6** God here makes a conditional promise to Israel that if they would obey Him and keep His covenant, He would regard and treat them in a special way. The people chose, instead, to make a golden calf and forsake the God who had rescued them from Egyptian slavery. This and persistent infidelity throughout most of her history greatly limited the extent to which Israel could realize these promises. In the case at hand, the application is made to Christians in I Pet. 2:9,10, with elements from both Ex. 19:5,6 and Isa. 43:20,21 being fulfilled.

upon it [b]in fire; and its smoke ascended
like [c]the smoke of a furnace, and
[d]the whole mountain [I]quaked[2729] violently.
19 When the sound of the trumpet
grew louder[2390] and louder, Moses
spoke and [a]God answered him with
[I]thunder.
20 [a]And the LORD came down on
Mount Sinai, to the top[7218] of the mountain; and the LORD called Moses to the
top of the mountain, and Moses went
up.
21 Then the LORD spoke to Moses,
"Go down, [I]warn the people, lest
[a]they break through to the LORD to
gaze,[7200] and many of them [II]perish.[5307]
22 "And also let the [a]priests[3548] who
come near[5066] to the LORD consecrate[6942] themselves, lest the LORD
break out against them."
23 And Moses said to the LORD,
"The people cannot come up to Mount
Sinai, for Thou didst [I]warn us, saying,
'[a]Set bounds about the mountain and
consecrate it.' "
24 Then the LORD said to him, "[I]Go
down and come up *again,* [a]you and Aaron
with you; but do not let the [b]priests
and the people break through to come
up to the LORD, lest He break forth upon
them."
25 So Moses went down to the people and told them.

The Ten Commandments

20 🔑 Then God[430] spoke[1696] all
these words,[1697] saying,
2 "[a]I am the LORD your God,
[b]who brought you out of the land[776] of
Egypt, out of the house[1004] of [I]slav-
ery.[5650]
3 "[a]You shall have no other [b]gods[430]
[I]before Me.
🔑 4 "[a]You shall not make[6213] for yourself [I]an idol,[6459] or any likeness[8544] of
what is in heaven[8064] above or on the
earth[776] beneath or in the water under
the earth.
🔑 5 "[a]You shall not worship[7812] them
or serve them; for I, the LORD your
God,[410] am a [b]jealous[7067] God, [c]visit-
ing[6485] the iniquity[5771] of the fathers[1] on
the children,[1121] on the third and the
fourth generations of those who hate
Me,
6 but showing[6213] lovingkindness[2617]
to [a]thousands, to those who love[157] Me
and keep[8104] My commandments.[4687]
7 "[a]You shall not take[5375] the name
of the LORD your God in vain,[7723] for
the LORD will not [I]leave him unpunished
who takes His name in vain.
8 "Remember [a]the sabbath[7676]
day,[3117] to keep it holy.[6942]
9 "[a]Six days[3117] you shall labor and
do[6213] all your work,[4399]
10 but the seventh day is a sabbath
of the LORD your God; *in it* [a]you shall
not do any work, you or your son[1121]
or your daughter, your male or your
female servant[5650] or your cattle or your
sojourner[1616] who [I]stays with you.
11 "[a]For in six days the LORD made
the heavens and the earth, the sea and

18 [I]Or, *trembled* [b]Ex. 3:2; 24:17; Deut. 5:4; 2Chr. 7:1-3; Heb. 12:18 [c]Gen. 15:17; 19:28 [d]Judg. 5:5; Ps. 68:7, 8; Jer. 4:24
19 [I]Or, *a voice;* lit., *a sound* [a]Ps. 81:7
20 [a]Neh. 9:13
21 [I]Lit., *testify to* [II]Lit., *fall* [a]Ex. 3:5; 1Sam. 6:19
22 [a]Ex. 19:24; 24:5; Lev. 10:3; 21:6-8
23 [I]Lit., *testify to* [a]Ex. 19:12
24 [I]Lit., *Go, descend* [a]Ex. 24:1, 9, 12 [b]Ex. 19:22

2 [I]Lit., *slaves* [a]Lev. 26:1; Deut. 5:6; Ps. 81:10 [b]Ex. 13:3; 15:13, 16; Deut. 7:8
3 [I]Or, *besides Me* [a]Deut. 6:14; 2Kin. 17:35; Jer. 25:6; 35:15 [b]Ex. 15:11; 20:23
4 [I]Or, *a graven image* [a]Lev. 19:4; 26:1; Deut. 4:15-19; 27:15
5 [a]Ex. 23:24; Josh. 23:7; 2Kin. 17:35 [b]Ex. 34:14; Deut. 4:24; Josh. 24:19; Nah. 1:2 [c]Ex. 34:6, 7; Num. 14:18, 33; Deut. 5:9, 10; 1Kin. 21:29; Jer. 32:18
6 [a]Deut. 7:9
7 [I]Or, *hold him guiltless* [a]Lev. 19:12; Deut. 6:13; 10:20
8 [a]Ex. 23:12; 31:13-16; Lev. 26:2; Deut. 5:12
9 [a]Ex. 34:21; 35:2, 3; Lev. 23:3; Deut. 5:13; Luke 13:14
10 [I]Lit., *is in your gates* [a]Neh. 13:16-19
11 [a]Gen. 2:2, 3; Ex. 31:17

🔑 **20:1-17** With these Ten Commandments the covenant with Israel begins. The ancient rabbis isolated 613 separate commandments in the entire Law of Moses, but these ten are the principles upon which the rest are based. By themselves they are called "the words of the covenant" (Ex. 34:28). The first four commandments deal with reverence for God directly, while the latter six refer to man's relationship with his fellow man. In the N.T. Jesus reduced the commandments of the O.T. to two, and they correspond to these two categories in the Ten Commandments (Mt. 22:35-40). The first is total love for God, as expressed in Deut. 6:5. The second is a rather obscure statement in Lev. 19:18: "You shall love your neighbor as yourself." Therefore, Jesus took what started out as 613 commandments and was summed up in ten in the Law of Moses and reduced them to two. All of God's commandments in the O.T. as to how His people should live may be abbreviated simply to have love for God and for man.

🔑 **20:4** See note on Num. 21:4-9.

🔑 **20:5** See note on Ezek. 18:1-4.

all that is in them, and rested on the seventh day; therefore the LORD blessed[1288] the sabbath day and made it holy.[6942]

12 "[a]Honor your father[1] and your mother,[517] that your [b]days may be prolonged[748] in the land[127] which the LORD your God gives you.

13 "[a]You shall not murder.[7523]

14 "[a]You shall not commit adultery.[5003]

15 "[a]You shall not steal.

16 "[a]You shall not bear false[8269] witness against your [b]neighbor.[7453]

17 "[a]You shall not covet[2530] your neighbor's house;[1004] [b]you shall not covet[2530] your neighbor's wife[802] or his male servant or his female servant or his ox or his donkey or anything that belongs to your neighbor."

18 [a]And all the people[5971] perceived[7200] the [I]thunder and the lightning flashes and the sound of the trumpet and the mountain smoking; and when the people saw[7200] *it,* they trembled and stood at a distance.

19 [a]Then they said to Moses, "Speak[1696] [I]to us yourself and we will listen;[8085] but let not God speak[1696] [I]to us, lest we die."

20 And Moses said to the people, "[a]Do not be afraid;[3372] for God[430] has come in order [b]to test[5254] you, and in order that [c]the fear of Him may [I]remain with you, so that you may not sin."[2398]

21 So the people stood at a distance, while Moses approached[5066] [a]the thick cloud[6205] where God *was.*

22 Then the LORD said to Moses, "Thus you shall say to the sons of Israel, 'You yourselves have seen[7200] that [a]I have spoken[1696] [I]to you from heaven.

23 '[a]You shall not make *other gods*[430] besides Me; [b]gods of silver or gods of gold, you shall not make for yourselves.

24 'You shall make [a]an altar[4196] of earth[127] for Me, and you shall sacrifice[2076] on it your [b]burnt offerings[5930] and your [c]peace offerings,[8002] [d]your sheep and your oxen; in every place [e]where I cause My name to be remembered, I will come to you and bless you.

25 'And if you make an altar of stone for Me, [a]you shall not build it of cut[1496] stones, for if you wield[5130] your tool[2719] on it, you will profane it.

26 'And you shall not go up by steps to My altar, that [a]your nakedness[6172] may not be exposed[1540] on it.'

Ordinances for the People

21 "Now these are the [a]ordinances[4941] which you are to set before them.

2 "If you buy [a]a Hebrew slave,[5650] he shall serve for six years; but on the seventh he shall go out as a free man without payment.

3 "If he comes [I]alone, he shall go out [I]alone; if he is the husband[1167] of a wife, then his wife shall go out with him.

4 "If his master[113] gives him a wife, and she bears him sons[1121] or daughters, the wife and her children shall belong to her master, and he shall go out [I]alone.

5 "But [a]if the slave plainly says,[559] 'I love[157] my master, my wife and my children;[1121] I will not go out as a free man,'

6 then his master shall bring[5066] him to [I]God,[430] then he shall bring him to the door or the doorpost. And his master shall pierce his ear with an awl;[4836] and he shall serve[5647] him permanently.[5769]

7 "[a]And if a man[376] sells his daughter as a female slave, she is not to [I]go free [b]as the male slaves [I]do.

8 "If she is [I]displeasing[7451] in the eyes of her master [II]who designated[3259] her for himself, then he shall let her be redeemed.[6299] He does not have authority[4910] to sell her to a foreign[5237] people[5971] because of his [III]unfairness[898] to her.

9 "And if he designates her for his

12 [a]Lev. 19:3; Deut. 27:16; Matt. 15:4; 19:19; Mark 7:10; 10:19; Luke 18:20; Eph. 6:2 [b]Deut. 5:16, 33; 6:2; 11:8,9; Jer. 35:7
13 [a]Gen. 9:6; Ex. 21:12; Lev. 24:17; Matt. 5:21; 19:18; Mark 10:19; Luke 18:20; Rom. 13:9; James 2:11
14 [a]Lev. 20:10; Deut. 5:18; Matt. 5:27; 19:18; Rom. 13:9
15 [a]Ex. 21:16; Lev. 19:11, 13; Matt. 19:18; Rom. 13:9
16 [a]Ex. 23:1, 7; Deut. 5:20; Matt. 19:18 [b]Lev. 19:18
17 [a]Deut. 5:21; Rom. 7:7; 13:9; Eph. 5:3, 5 [b]Prov. 6:29; Matt. 5:28
18 [I]Lit., *sounds* [a]Ex. 19:16, 18; Heb. 12:18, 19
19 [I]Lit., *with* [a]Deut. 5:5, 23-27; Gal. 3:19; Heb. 12:19
20 [I]Lit., *be before* [a]Ex. 14:13; Is. 41:10, 13 [b]Ex. 15:25; Deut. 13:3 [c]Deut. 4:10; 6:24; Prov. 3:7; 16:6; Is. 8:13
21 [a]Ex. 19:16; Deut. 5:22
22 [I]Lit., *with* [a]Deut. 4:36; 5:24, 26; Neh. 9:13
23 [a]Ex. 20:3 [b]Ex. 32:1, 2, 4; Deut. 29:17
24 [a]Ex. 20:25; 27:1-8 [b]Ex. 10:25; 18:12 [c]Ex. 24:5; Lev. 1:2 [d]Deut. 12:5; 16:6, 11; 26:2; 2Chr. 6:6 [e]Deut. 12:5; 26:2
25 [a]Deut. 27:5, 6; Josh. 8:31
26 [a]Ex. 28:42, 43

1 [a]Ex. 24:3, 4; Deut. 4:14; 6:1
2 [a]Lev. 25:39-43; Deut. 15:12-18; Jer. 34:14
3 [I]Lit., *by himself*
4 [I]Lit., *by himself*

5 [a]Deut. 15:16, 17 **6** [I]Or, *the judges who acted in God's name* **7** [I]Lit., *go out* [a]Neh. 5:5 [b]Ex. 21:2, 3
8 [I]Lit., *bad* [II]Another reading is *so that he did not designate her* [III]Lit., *dealing treacherously*

son, he shall deal[6213] with her according
to the custom of[4941] daughters.
10 "If he takes to himself another
woman, he may not reduce her [I]food,[7607]
her clothing, or [a]her conjugal rights.
11 "And if he will not do these three
things for her, then she shall go out
for nothing, without *payment of* money.

Personal Injuries

12 "[a]He who strikes[5221] a man so
that he dies[4191] shall surely be put to
death.
13 "[a]But [I]if he did not lie in wait[6658]
for him, but [b]God[430] let *him* fall into
his hand,[3027] then I will appoint[7760] you
a place to which he may flee.
14 "[a]If, however, a man acts presumptuously toward his neighbor,[7453] so
as to kill[2026] him craftily,[6195] you are to
take him *even* from My altar,[4196] that
he may die.
15 "And he who strikes his father[1]
or his mother[517] shall surely be put to
death.
16 "[a]And he who [I]kidnaps a man,
whether he sells him or he is found in
his [II]possession, shall surely be put to
death.
17 "[a]And he who curses[7043] his father or his mother shall surely be put
to death.
18 "And if men[582] have a quarrel[7378]
and one strikes the other with a stone
or with *his* fist, and he does not die
but [I]remains in bed;
19 if he gets up and walks around
outside on his staff, then he who struck
him shall[5352] go unpunished; he shall only
pay for his [I]loss of time, and [II]shall
take care of him until he is completely
healed.
20 "And if a man strikes his male
or female slave with a rod[7626] and he
dies [I]at his hand, he shall [II]be punished.[5358]
21 "If, however, he [I]survives a day
or two,[3117] no vengeance shall be taken;
[a]for he is his [II]property.
22 "And *if* men struggle with each
other and strike[5062] a woman with child
so that [I]she has a miscarriage, yet there
is no *further* injury,[611] he shall surely
be fined as the woman's husband[1167]
[II]may demand of him; and he shall
[a]pay [III]as the judges[6414] *decide.*
23 "But if there is *any further* injury,
[a]then you shall appoint *as a penalty*
life[5315] for life,
24 [a]eye for eye, tooth for tooth,
hand for hand, foot for foot,
25 burn for burn, wound for wound,
[I]bruise for bruise.
26 "And if a man strikes the eye
of his male or female slave, and
destroys[7843] it, he shall let him go free
on account of his eye.
27 "And if he [I]knocks[5307] out a tooth
of his male or female slave, he shall
let him go free on account of his tooth.
28 "And if an ox gores a man[376]
or a woman [I]to death, [a]the ox shall surely
be stoned and its flesh[1320] shall not be
eaten; but the owner[1167] of the ox shall
go unpunished.[5355]
29 "If, however, an ox was previously in the habit of[5056] goring, and its
owner has been warned, yet he does
not confine[8104] it, and it kills a man or
a woman, the ox shall be stoned and
its owner also shall be put to death.
30 "If a ransom[3724] is [I]demanded of
him, then he shall give for the redemption[6306] of his life whatever is
[I]demanded of him.
31 "Whether it gores a son or
[I]a daughter, it shall be done to him according to [II]the same rule.
32 "If the ox gores a male or female
slave, [I]the owner shall give his *or her*
master [a]thirty shekels of silver, and the
ox shall be stoned.
33 "And if a man opens a pit,[953]
or [I]digs a pit and does not cover[3680] it
over, and an ox or a donkey falls into
it,
34 the owner of the pit shall make
restitution; he shall [I]give money to its
owner, and the dead *animal* shall become his.
35 "And if one man's ox hurts another's so that it dies, then they shall
sell the live[2416] ox and divide its price

10 [I]Lit., *flesh* [a]1Cor. 7:3, 5
12 [a]Gen. 9:6; Lev. 24:17; Num. 35:30; Matt. 26:52
13 [I]Lit., *he who* [a]Num. 35:10-34; Deut. 19:1-13; Josh. 20:1-9 [b]1Sam. 24:4, 10, 18
14 [a]Deut. 19:11, 12; 1Kin. 2:28-34
16 [I]Lit., *steals* [II]Lit., *hand* [a]Deut. 24:7
17 [a]Lev. 20:9; Prov. 20:20; Matt. 15:4; Mark 7:10
18 [I]Lit., *lies*
19 [I]Lit., *his sitting* [II]Lit., *healing, he shall cause to be healed*
20 [I]Lit., *under* [II]Lit., *suffer vengeance*
21 [I]Lit., *stands* [II]Lit., *money* [a]Lev. 25:44-46
22 [I]Or, *an untimely birth occurs;* lit., *her children come out* [II]Lit., *lays on him* [III]Lit., *by arbitration* [a]Ex. 21:30; Deut. 22:18, 19
23 [a]Lev. 24:19; Deut. 19:21
24 [a]Lev. 24:20; Deut. 19:21; Matt. 5:38
25 [I]Lit., *welt*
27 [I]Lit., *causes to fall*
28 [I]Lit., *so that he dies* [a]Gen. 9:5; Ex. 21:32
30 [I]Lit., *laid on him*
31 [I]Lit., *gores a daughter* [II]Lit., *this judgment*
32 [I]Lit., *he* [a]Zech. 11:12; Matt. 26:15; 27:3, 9
33 [I]Lit., *if a man digs*
34 [I]Lit., *give back*

equally; and also they shall divide the
dead *ox*.
36 "Or *if* it is known that the ox
was previously in the habit of goring,
yet its owner has not confined it, he
shall surely pay[7999] ox for ox, and the
dead *animal* shall become his.

Property Rights

22 "If a man[376] steals an ox or a
sheep, and slaughters[2873] it or
sells it, he shall pay five oxen for the
ox and [a]four sheep for the sheep.
2 "[I]If the [a]thief is [II]caught while
breaking in, and is struck[5221] so that
he dies,[4191] there will be no bloodguiltiness[1818] on his account.
3 "*But* if the sun has risen on him,
there will be bloodguiltiness on his account. He shall surely[7999] make restitution; if he owns nothing, then he shall
be [a]sold for his theft.
4 "If what he stole is actually found
alive[2416] in his [I]possession,[3027] whether
an ox or a donkey or a sheep, [a]he shall
pay double.
5 "If a man lets a field or vineyard
be grazed *bare* and lets his animal loose
so that it grazes in another man's
field,[7704] he shall make restitution from
the best of his own field and the best
of his own vineyard.
6 "If a fire breaks out and spreads
to thorn bushes, so that stacked grain
or the standing grain or the field *itself*
is consumed, he who started the fire
shall surely make restitution.[7999]
7 "[a]If a man gives his neighbor[7453]
money or goods to keep[8104] *for him*,
and it is stolen from the man's house,[1004]
if the thief is [I]caught, he shall pay double.
8 "If the thief is not [I]caught, then
the owner[1167] of the house shall [II]appear
before [III][a]the judges,[430] *to* determine
whether he [IV]laid his hands on his neighbor's property.[4399]
9 "For every [I]breach[1697] of trust,[6588]
whether it is for ox, for donkey, for
sheep, for clothing, *or* for any lost thing
about which one says,[559] 'This is it,' the
[II]case[1697] of both parties shall come before [III][a]the judges; he whom [III]the judges
condemn[7561] shall pay double to his
neighbor.
10 "If a man gives his neighbor a
donkey, an ox, a sheep, or any animal
to keep *for him*, and it dies or is hurt[7665]
or is driven away[7617] while no one is
looking,[7200]
11 an [a]oath[7621] before the LORD shall
be made by the two of them, [I]that he
has not [II]laid hands on his neighbor's
property; and its owner[1167] shall accept
it, and he shall not make restitution.[7999]
12 "But if it is actually stolen from
him, he shall make restitution to its
owner.
13 "If it is all torn to pieces, let him
bring it as evidence; he shall not make
restitution for what has been torn to
pieces.
14 "And if a man [I]borrows[7592] *anything* from his neighbor, and it is injured
or dies while its owner is not with it,
he shall make full restitution.
15 "If its owner is with it, he shall
not make restitution; if it is hired, it
came for its hire.

Sundry Laws

16 "[a]And if a man seduces[6601] a
virgin[1330] who is not engaged,[781] and lies
with her, he must pay a dowry for her
to be his wife.
17 "If her father[1] absolutely refuses
to give her to him, he shall [I]pay money
equal to the [a]dowry[4119] for virgins.[1330]
18 "You shall not allow[2421] a
[a]sorceress[3784] to live.[2421]
19 "[a]Whoever lies with an animal
shall surely be put to death.
20 "[a]He who sacrifices[2076] to [I]any
god, other than to the LORD alone, shall
be [II]utterly destroyed.[2763]
21 "And [a]you shall not wrong[3238] a
stranger[1616] or oppress him, for you
were strangers in the land of Egypt.
22 "[a]You shall not afflict any widow
or orphan.
23 "If you afflict him at all, *and*
[a]if he does cry out to Me, [b]I will surely
hear[8085] his cry;

1 [I]Ch. 21:37 in Heb. [a]2Sam. 12:6; Luke 19:8
2 [I]Ch. 22:1 in Heb. [II]Lit., *found* [a]Matt. 6:19; 24:43; 1Pet. 4:15
3 [a]Matt. 18:25
4 [I]Lit., *hand* [a]Ex. 22:7
7 [I]Lit., *found* [a]Lev. 6:1-7
8 [I]Lit., *found* [II]Lit., *approach to* [III]Or, *God* [IV]Lit., *stretched his hand* [a]Ex. 22:9; Deut. 17:8, 9; 19:17
9 [I]Or, *matter of transgression* [II]Lit., *matter* [III]Or, *God* [a]Ex. 22:8, 28; Deut. 25:1
11 [I]Lit., *whether* [II]Lit., *stretched his hand* [a]Heb. 6:16
14 [I]Lit., *asks*
16 [a]Deut. 22:28, 29
17 [I]Lit., *weigh out silver* [a]Gen. 34:12; 1Sam. 18:25
18 [a]Lev. 19:31; 20:6, 27; Deut. 18:10, 11; 1Sam. 28:3; Jer. 27:9, 10
19 [a]Lev. 18:23; 20:15, 16; Deut. 27:21
20 [I]Lit., *the gods* [II]Lit., *put under the ban* [a]Ex. 32:8; 34:15; Lev. 17:7; Num. 25:2; Deut. 17:2, 3, 5; 1Kin. 18:40; 2Kin. 10:25
21 [a]Ex. 23:9; Lev. 19:33, 34; 25:35; Deut. 1:16; 10:19; 27:19; Zech. 7:10
22 [a]Deut. 24:17, 18; Prov. 23:10, 11; Jer. 7:6, 7
23 [a]Deut. 15:9; Job 35:9; Luke 18:7 [b]Deut. 10:18; Job 34:28; Ps. 10:14, 17, 18; 18:6; 68:5; James 5:4

24 and My anger[639] will be kindled,[2734] and I will kill[2026] you with the sword; [a]and your wives shall become widows and your children[1121] fatherless.

25 “[a]If you lend money to My people,[5971] to the poor [I]among you, you are not to [II]act as a creditor to him; you shall not [III]charge him [b]interest.

26 “If you ever take your neighbor’s cloak [a]as a pledge, you are to return[7725] it to him before the sun sets,

27 for that is his only covering; it is his cloak for his [I]body.[5785] What else shall he sleep in? And it shall come about that [a]when he cries out to Me, I will hear[8085] *him,* for [b]I am gracious.[2587]

28 “You shall not [Ia]curse[7043] God,[430] [b]nor curse[779] a ruler[5387] of your people.

29 “[a]You shall not delay *the offering from* [I]your harvest and your vintage. [b]The first-born of your sons[1121] you shall give to Me.

30 “[a]You shall do[6213] the same with your oxen *and* with your sheep. It shall be with its mother[517] seven days; [b]on the eighth day you shall give it to Me.

31 “[a]And you shall be holy[6944] men[582] to Me, therefore [b]you shall not eat *any* flesh[1320] torn to pieces in the field; you shall throw it to the dogs.

Sundry Laws

23 “[a]You shall not bear[5375] a false[7723] report;[8088] do not join your hand[3027] with a wicked[7563] man to be a [b]malicious[2555] witness.

2 “You shall not follow [I]a multitude in doing evil,[7451] nor shall you [II]testify[1696] in a dispute[7379] so as to turn aside after [I]a multitude in order to [a]pervert *justice;*

3 [a]nor shall you [I]be partial to a poor man in his dispute.

4 “[a]If you meet your enemy’s ox or his donkey wandering away,[8582] you shall surely return[7725] it to him.

5 “[a]If you see the donkey of one who hates you lying *helpless* under its load,[4853] you shall refrain from leaving it to him, you shall surely release *it* with him.

6 “[a]You shall not pervert the justice[4941] *due* to your needy *brother* in his dispute.

7 “[a]Keep far from a false[8267] charge,[1697] and [b]do not kill[2026] the innocent[5355] or the righteous,[6662] for [c]I will not acquit[6663] the guilty.

8 “[a]And you shall not take a bribe, for a bribe blinds the clear-sighted and [I]subverts the cause[1697] of the just.

9 “[a]And you shall not oppress a [I]stranger,[1616] since you yourselves know[3045] the [II]feelings[5315] of a [I]stranger, for you *also* were [I]strangers in the land of Egypt.

The Sabbath and Land

10 “[a]And you shall sow your land[776] for six years and gather[622] in its yield,

🗝 11 but *on* the seventh year you shall let it [I]rest and lie fallow, so that the needy of your people[5971] may eat; and whatever they leave[3499] the beast[2416] of the field[7704] may eat. You are to do[6213] the same with your vineyard *and* your olive grove.

12 “[a]Six days you are to do[6213] your work, but on the seventh day you shall cease[7673] *from labor* in order that your ox and your donkey may rest, and the son of your female slave, as well as [I]your stranger, may refresh themselves.

13 “Now [a]concerning everything which I have said to you, be on your guard;[8104] and [b]do not mention the name of other gods,[430] nor let *them* be heard[8085] [I]from your mouth.[6310]

24 [a]Ps. 109:2, 9
25 [I]Lit., *with* [II]Lit., *be* [III]Lit., *lay upon* [a]Lev. 25:35-37; Deut. 15:7-11 [b]Deut. 23:19, 20; Neh. 5:7; Ps. 15:5; Ezek. 18:8
26 [a]Deut. 24:6, 10-13; Job 24:3; Prov. 20:16; Amos 2:8
27 [I]Lit., *skin* [a]Ex. 22:23 [b]Ex. 34:6
28 [I]Or, *revile* [a]Lev. 24:15, 16 [b]Eccl. 10:20; Acts 23:5
29 [I]Lit., *your fulness and your tears* [a]Ex. 23:16, 19; Deut. 26:2-11; Prov. 3:9 [b]Ex. 13:2, 12
30 [a]Lev. 22:27; Deut. 15:19; [b]Gen. 17:12; Lev. 12:3
31 [a]Ex. 19:6; Lev. 11:44; 19:2 [b]Lev. 7:24; 17:15; Ezek. 4:14

1 [a]Ex. 20:16; Lev. 19:11f.; Deut. 5:20; Ps. 101:5; Prov. 10:18 [b]Deut. 19:16-21; Ps. 35:11; Prov. 19:5; Acts 6:11
2 [I]Lit., *many men* [II]Or, *answer* [a]Deut. 16:19; 24:17
3 [I]Lit., *honor* [a]Ex. 23:6; Lev. 19:15; Deut. 1:17; 16:19
4 [a]Deut. 22:1-4
5 [a]Deut. 22:4
6 [a]Ex. 23:2, 3; Lev. 19:15
7 [a]Ex. 20:16; Ps. 119:29; Eph. 4:25 [b]Ex. 20:13; Deut. 27:25 [c]Ex. 34:7; Deut. 25:1; Rom. 1:18
8 [I]Or, *distorts the words* [a]Deut. 10:17; 16:19; Prov. 15:27; 17:8, 23; Is. 5:22, 23
9 [I]Or, *sojourner(s)* [II]Lit., *soul* [a]Ex. 22:21; Lev. 19:33f.; Deut. 24:17f.; 27:19
10 [a]Lev. 25:1-7
11 [I]Lit., *drop*
12 [I]Lit., *the sojourner* [a]Ex. 20:8-11; 31:15; 34:21; 35:2, 3; Lev. 23:3; Deut. 5:13f.
13 [I]Lit., *on* [a]Deut. 4:9, 23; 1Tim. 4:16 [b]Josh. 23:7; Ps. 16:4; Hos. 2:17

🗝 **23:11** This was a sabbath rest for the land. A fuller form of this law of the sabbatical year is found in Lev. 25:1-7. Though it followed sound agricultural principles, restoring fertility to the soil, this was not the purpose stated for its observance. The volunteer growth of the grain and fruit would be a much needed resource for the poor and even provide food for the wild beasts.

Three National Feasts

🔑 **14** "[a]Three times a year you shall celebrate a feast to Me.

15 "You shall observe[8104] [a]the Feast[2282] of Unleavened Bread; for seven days you are to eat unleavened bread, as I commanded[6680] you, at the appointed time[4150] in the [b]month Abib, for in it you came out of Egypt. And [I][c]none shall appear[7200] before Me empty-handed.

16 "Also *you shall observe* [a]the Feast of the Harvest *of* the first fruits of your labors *from* what you sow in the field; also the Feast of the Ingathering at the end of the year [b]when you gather[622] in *the fruit of* your labors from the field.

17 "[a]Three times a year all your males shall appear before the Lord[113] [I]GOD.

18 "[a]You shall not offer[2076] the blood[1818] of My sacrifice[2077] with leavened bread;[2557] [b]nor is the fat of My [I]feast to remain overnight until morning.

19 "You shall bring [a]the choice first[7225] fruits of your soil[127] into the house[1004] of the LORD your God.[430] [b]You are not to boil a kid in the milk of its mother.[517]

Conquest of the Land

20 "Behold, I am going to send [a]an angel before you to guard[8104] you along the way,[1870] and [b]to bring you into the place which I have prepared.

21 "Be on your guard[8104] before him and obey[8085] his voice; [a]do not be rebellious toward him, for he will not pardon[5375] your transgression,[6588] since [b]My name is in him.

22 "But if you will truly obey[8085] his voice and do[6213] all that I say, then [a]I will be an enemy to your enemies and an adversary to your adversaries.

🔑 23 "[a]For My angel will go before you and bring you in to *the land of* the Amorites, the Hittites, the Perizzites, the Canaanites, the Hivites and the Jebusites; and I will completely destroy them.

24 "[a]You shall not worship[7812] their gods, nor serve them, nor do according to their deeds; [b]but you shall utterly overthrow them, and break[7665] their [c]*sacred* pillars[4676] in pieces.

25 "[a]But you shall serve[5647] the LORD your God, [I]and He will bless[1288] your bread and your water; and [b]I will remove sickness from your midst.

26 "There shall be no one miscarrying or [a]barren[6135] in your land; [b]I will fulfill the number of your days.[3117]

27 "I will [a]send My terror[367] ahead of you, and [b]throw into confusion[2000] all the people among whom you come, and I will [c]make all your enemies turn *their* backs to you.

28 "And I will send [a]hornets ahead of you, that they may [b]drive out the Hivites, the Canaanites, and the Hittites before you.

29 "[a]I will not drive them out before you in a single year, that the land may not become desolate,[8077] and the beasts of the field become too numerous for you.

30 "I will drive them out before you [a]little by little, until you become fruitful and take possession[5157] of the land.

14 [a]Ex. 23:17; 34:22-24; Deut. 16:16
15 [I]Lit., *they not* [a]Ex. 12:14-20; Lev. 23:6-8; Num. 28:16-25 [b]Ex. 12:2; 13:4 [c]Ex. 22:29; 34:20
16 [a]Ex. 34:22; Lev. 23:10; Num. 28:26 [b]Lev. 23:39
17 [I]Heb., *YHWH*, usually rendered LORD [a]Ex. 23:14; 34:23; Deut. 16:16
18 [I]Or, *festival* [a]Ex. 34:25; Lev. 2:11 [b]Ex. 12:10; Lev. 7:15; Deut. 16:4
19 [a]Ex. 22:29; 34:26; Deut. 26:2, 10; Neh. 10:35; Prov. 3:9 [b]Deut. 14:21
20 [a]Ex. 3:2; 14:19; 23:23; 32:34; 33:2 [b]Ex. 15:16, 17
21 [a]Deut. 9:7; Ps. 78:40, 56 [b]Ex. 3:14; 6:3; 34:5-7
22 [a]Gen. 12:3; Num. 24:9; Deut. 30:7
23 [a]Ex. 23:20; Josh. 24:8, 11
24 [a]Ex. 20:5; 23:13, 33; Deut. 12:30f. [b]Num. 33:52; Deut. 7:5; 12:3; 2Kin. 18:4 [c]Ex. 34:13; Lev. 26:1; 2Kin. 3:2
25 [I]Or, *that He may bless* [a]Lev. 26:3-13; Deut. 6:13; 10:12; 28:1-14; Josh. 22:5; 1Sam. 12:20; Matt. 4:10 [b]Ex. 15:26; Deut. 7:15
26 [a]Deut. 7:14 [b]Deut. 4:40; Job 5:26
27 [a]Gen. 35:5; Ex. 15:16; Deut. 2:25; Josh. 2:9 [b]Deut. 7:23 [c]Ps. 18:40; 21:12
28 [a]Deut. 7:20; Josh. 24:12 [b]Ex. 33:2; 34:11
29 [a]Deut. 7:22 **30** [a]Deut. 7:22

🔑 **23:14-17** These three appearances before the Lord were the three annual feasts of the Jews (see Lev. 23:16,17,33-36). They are listed as the Feast of Unleavened Bread which was closely associated with the Passover (see Ex. 12:1-11, 14-20; Lev. 23:4-8; Deut. 16:1-8), the Feast of Harvest or Firstfruits, later called the Feast of Weeks and in N.T. times known as Pentecost (see Lev. 23:9-14; Deut. 16:9-12), and the Feast of Ingathering, later called the Feast of Tabernacles (see Lev. 23:33-36, 39-43; Deut. 16:13-15). At the time of each of these feats all males were to make a pilgrimage to the sanctuary, which was at this time the tabernacle and later the temple after its construction.

🔑 **23:23** Note how "I" and "My Angel" are used interchangeably. The same is true in the incident of the burning bush (Ex. 3:2-5) and the commissioning of Gideon (Judg. 6:12,14,16). There is strong evidence that the Son of God is the Angel of Jehovah.

31 "[a]And I will fix your boundary from the [I]Red Sea to the sea of the Philistines, and from the wilderness to the River *Euphrates;* [b]for I will deliver the inhabitants of the land into your hand, and you will [c]drive them out before you.

32 "[a]You shall [I]make[3772] no covenant[1285] with them [b]or with their gods.

33 "[a]They shall not live in your land, lest they make you sin[2398] against Me; for *if* you serve their gods, [b]it will surely be a snare[4170] to you."

People Affirm Their Covenant with God

24 Then He said to Moses, "[a]Come up to the LORD, you and Aaron, [b]Nadab and Abihu and [c]seventy of the elders[2205] of Israel, and you shall worship[7812] at a distance.

2 "Moses alone, however, shall come near to the LORD, but they shall not come near,[5066] nor shall the people[5971] come up[5927] with him."

3 Then Moses came and recounted to the people all the words[1697] of the LORD and all the [I]ordinances;[4941] and all the people answered with one voice, and said,[1696] "[a]All the words which the LORD has spoken we will do!"[6213]

4 And [a]Moses wrote down all the words of the LORD. Then he arose early in the morning, and built an [b]altar[4196] [I]at the foot of the mountain with twelve pillars[4676] for the twelve tribes[7626] of Israel.

5 And he sent young men of the sons[1121] of Israel, [a]and they offered[5927] burnt offerings[5930] and sacrificed[2076] young bulls as peace[8002] offerings[2077] to the LORD.

6 And [a]Moses took half of the blood[1818] and put *it* in basins,[101] and the *other* half of the blood he sprinkled[2236] on the altar.

7 Then he took [a]the book[5612] of the covenant[1285] and read[7121] *it* in the hearing[241] of the people; and they said, "[b]All that the LORD has spoken we will do, and we will be obedient!"[8085]

8 So [a]Moses took the blood and sprinkled *it* on the people, and said, "Behold [b]the blood of the covenant,[1285] which the LORD has [I]made[3772] with you [II]in accordance with all these words."

9 Then Moses went up [I]with Aaron, [a]Nadab and Abihu, and seventy of the elders of Israel,

10 and [a]they saw[7200] the God[430] of Israel; and under His feet [I][b]there appeared to be a pavement of sapphire, [II]as clear[2892] as the sky[8064] itself.

11 Yet He did not stretch out His hand[3027] against the nobles[678] of the sons of Israel; and [a]they beheld[2372] God, and they ate and drank.

12 Now the LORD said to Moses, "Come up to Me on the mountain and [I]remain there, and [a]I will give you the stone tablets [II]with the law[8451] and the commandment[4687] which I have written for their instruction."[3384]

13 So Moses arose [I]with [a]Joshua his [II]servant,[8334] and Moses went up to [b]the mountain of God.

14 But to the elders he said, "[a]Wait here for us until we return to you. And behold, [b]Aaron and Hur are with you; whoever [I]has a legal matter,[1697] let him approach them."

15 Then Moses went up to the mountain, and [a]the cloud[6051] covered[3680] the mountain.

16 And [a]the glory[3519] of the LORD [I]rested[7931] on Mount Sinai, and the cloud covered it for six days; and on the seventh day He [b]called[7121] to Moses from the midst of the cloud.

17 [a]And to the eyes of the sons of Israel the appearance of the glory of the LORD was like a [b]consuming fire on the mountain top.[7218]

18 And Moses entered the midst of the cloud [I]as he went up to the mountain; and Moses was on the mountain [a]forty days and forty nights.

31 [I]Lit., *Sea of Reeds* [a]Gen. 15:18; Deut. 1:7, 8; 11:24 [b]Deut. 2:36; Josh. 21:44 [c]Josh. 24:12, 18
32 [I]Lit., *cut* [a]Ex. 34:12; Deut. 7:2 [b]Ex. 23:13, 24
33 [a]Deut. 7:1-5, 16 [b]Ex. 34:12; Deut. 12:30; Josh. 23:13; Judg. 2:3; Ps. 106:36

1 [a]Ex. 19:24 [b]Ex. 6:23; 28:1; Lev. 10:1, 2 [c]Num. 11:16
3 [I]Or, *judgments* [a]Ex. 19:8; 24:7; Deut. 5:27
4 [I]Lit., *under* [a]Ex. 17:14; 34:27; Deut. 31:9 [b]Ex. 17:15
5 [a]Ex. 18:12
6 [a]Heb. 9:18
7 [a]Ex. 24:4; Heb. 9:19 [b]Ex. 24:3
8 [I]Lit., *cut* [II]Lit., *on all* [a]Heb. 9:19, 20 [b]Zech. 9:11; Matt. 26:28; Mark 14:24; Luke 22:20; 1Cor. 11:25; Heb. 13:20
9 [I]Lit., *and* [a]Ex. 24:1
10 [I]Lit., *like a pavement* [II]Lit., *and as* [a]Ex. 24:11; Num. 12:8; Is. 6:5; John 1:18; 6:46 [b]Ezek. 1:26; 10:1; Rev. 4:3
11 [a]Gen. 16:13; 32:30; Ex. 24:10
12 [I]Lit., *be* [II]Lit., *and* [a]Ex. 31:18; 32:15; Deut. 5:22
13 [I]Lit., *and* [II]Or, *minister* [a]Ex. 17:9-14; 33:11 [b]Ex. 3:1
14 [I]Lit., *is a master of matters* [a]Gen. 22:5 [b]Ex. 17:10, 12
15 [a]Ex. 19:9
16 [I]Lit., *dwelt* [a]Ex. 16:10; Num. 14:10 [b]Ps. 99:7
17 [a]Ex. 3:2; Ezek. 1:28 [b]Deut. 4:24; 9:3; Heb. 12:29
18 [I]Lit., *and* [a]Ex. 34:28; Deut. 9:9; 10:10

24:13 See note on Num. 27:18-23.

Offerings for the Sanctuary

25 Then the LORD spoke[1696] to Moses, saying,

2 “[a]Tell[1696] the sons[1121] of Israel to [I]raise a [II]contribution[8641] for Me; [b]from every man whose heart[3820] moves him[5068] you shall [I]raise My [II]contribution.

3 “And this is the [I]contribution which you are to [II]raise from them: gold, silver and bronze,

4 [I][a]blue, purple and scarlet *material,* fine linen, goat *hair,*

5 rams' skins[5785] dyed red, porpoise skins, acacia wood,

6 [a]oil[8081] for lighting,[3974] [b]spices for the anointing[4888] oil and for the fragrant incense,[7004]

🔑 7 onyx stones and setting stones, for the [a]ephod and for the [I][b]breastpiece.

🔑 8 “And let them [a]construct[6213] a sanctuary[4720] for Me, [b]that I may dwell[7931] among them.

9 “[a]According to all that I am going to show[7200] you, *as* the pattern of the tabernacle[4908] and the pattern[8403] of all its furniture, just so you shall construct[6213] *it.*

Ark of the Covenant

10 “[a]And they shall construct an ark[727] of acacia wood two and a half [I]cubits [II]long,[753] and one and a half cubits [III]wide, and one and a half cubits [IV]high.

11 “And you shall [a]overlay it with pure[2889] gold, inside[1004] and out you shall overlay it, and you shall make a gold molding [I]around it.

12 “And you shall cast four gold rings for it, and [I]fasten them on its four feet, and two rings shall be on one side of it and two rings on the other side of it.

13 “And you shall make poles of acacia wood and overlay them with gold.

14 “And you shall put the poles into the rings on the sides of the ark, to carry[5375] the ark with them.

15 “The [a]poles shall [I]remain in the rings of the ark; they shall not be removed from it.

16 “And you shall [a]put into the ark the testimony[5715] which I shall give you.

17 “And you shall [a]make a [I]mercy seat[3727] of pure gold, two and a half [II]cubits [III]long and one and a half cubits [IV]wide.

18 “And you shall make two cherubim[3742] of gold, make them of hammered work [I]at the two ends of the mercy seat.

19 “And make one cherub[3742] [I]at one end and one cherub [I]at the other end; you shall make the cherubim *of one piece* with the mercy seat at its two ends.

20 “And [a]the cherubim shall have *their* wings spread upward, covering the mercy seat with their wings and [I]facing one another; the faces of the cherubim are to be *turned* toward the mercy seat.

21 “And [a]you shall put the mercy

2 [I]Lit., *take* [II]Or, *heave offering* [a]Ex. 35:4-9 [b]Ex. 35:21; 1Chr. 29:3, 5, 9; Ezra 2:68; 2Cor. 8:11, 12; 9:7
3 [I]Or, *heave offering* [II]Lit., *take*
4 [I]Or, *violet* [a]Ex. 28:5, 6, 8
6 [a]Ex. 27:20 [b]Ex. 30:23f.
7 [I]Or, *pouch* [a]Ex. 28:4, 6-14 [b]Ex. 28:4, 15-30
8 [a]Ex. 36:1-5 [b]Ex. 29:45, 46; Num. 5:3; Deut. 12:11; 1Kin. 6:13; 2Cor. 6:16; Rev. 21:3
9 [a]Ex. 25:40; 26:30; Acts 7:44; Heb. 8:2, 5
10 [I]I.e., One cubit equals approx. 18 in. [II]Lit., *its length* [III]Lit., *its width* [IV]Lit., *its height* [a]Ex. 37:1-9; Deut. 10:3; Heb. 9:4
11 [I]Lit., *on it round about* [a]Heb. 9:4
12 [I]Or, *put*
15 [I]Lit., *be* [a]1Kin. 8:8
16 [a]Ex. 40:20; Deut. 10:2; 31:26; 1Kin. 8:9; Heb. 9:4
17 [I]Lit., *propitiatory,* and so through v. 22 [II]I.e., One cubit equals approx. 18 in. [III]Lit., *its length* [IV]Lit., *its width* [a]Ex. 37:6
18 [I]Lit., *from*
19 [I]Lit., *from*
20 [I]Lit., *their faces to* [a]1Kin. 8:7; 1Chr. 28:18; Heb. 9:5
21 [a]Ex. 26:34; 40:20

🔑 **25:7** The word “ephod” (646) is a Hebrew name for the sacred upper garment of the priest, of plain linen for the regular priest. It was multi-colored and embroidered especially for the high priest. The breastplate, which was worn by the high priest alone, went on top of the ephod or upper garment. It was square and twelve precious stones, one for each tribe, were inset. It reached from the waist to the shoulders and was connected at the shoulders by a gem. The robe was sleeveless under the ephod and came down to the ankles.

🔑 **25:8,9** The Lord commanded Moses to build a sanctuary. It was to be a tabernacle or moveable tent which would be suitable for Israel's nomadic life. The Levites would have responsibility for it (Num. 18:2-4). It was to be a dwelling place for the Lord among His people (Ex. 25:8) and a depository for the tables of the law or testimony, hence it was called “the tabernacle of testimony” (Ex. 38:21). Also known as “the tent of meeting” (Ex. 40:34), because the Lord met His people there, its general designation was “the house of the Lord” (Ex. 34:26). It was to be filled with “the glory of the Lord” (Ex. 40:36-38) and by His presence there He would personally lead the children of Israel on their journey.

seat [I]on top of the ark, and [b]in the ark
you shall put the testimony which I shall
give to you.
22 "And [a]there I will meet with you;
and from above the mercy seat, from
[b]between the two cherubim which are
upon the ark of the testimony, I will
speak[1696] to you about all that I will give
you in commandment[6680] for the sons
of Israel.

The Table of Showbread

23 "[a]And you shall make a table of
acacia wood, two cubits [I]long and one
cubit [II]wide and one and a half cubits
[III]high.
24 "And you shall overlay it with
pure gold and make a gold [a]border
around it.
25 "And you shall make for it a rim
of a handbreadth around *it;* and you shall
make a gold border for the rim around
it.
26 "And you shall make four gold
rings for it and put rings on the four
corners which are on its four feet.
27 "The rings shall be close to the
rim as holders for the poles to carry
the table.
28 "And you shall make the poles
of acacia wood and overlay them with
gold, so that with them the table may
be carried.
29 "And you shall make its [Ia]dishes
and its pans[3709] and its jars and its
[II]bowls, with which to pour libations;
you shall make them of pure gold.
30 "And you shall set [a]the bread of
the [I]Presence on the table before Me
[II]at all times.[8548]

The Golden Lampstand

31 "[a]Then you shall make a lampstand of pure gold. The lampstand *and*
its base and its shaft[3409] are to be made
of hammered work; its cups, its [I]bulbs
and its flowers shall be *of one piece* with
it.
32 "And [a]six branches shall go out
from its sides; three branches of the
lampstand from its one side, and three
branches of the lampstand from its
[I]other side.
33 "[a]Three cups *shall be* shaped like
almond *blossoms* in the one branch, a
[I]bulb and a flower, and three cups shaped
like almond *blossoms* in the [II]other
branch, a [I]bulb and a flower—so for six
branches going out from the lampstand;
34 and [a]in the lampstand four cups
shaped like almond *blossoms,* its [I]bulbs
and its flowers.
35 "[a]And a [I]bulb shall be under the
first pair of branches *coming* out of it,
and a [I]bulb under the *second* pair of
branches *coming* out of it, and a [I]bulb
under the *third* pair of branches *coming*
out of it, for the six branches coming
out of the lampstand.
36 "[a]Their [I]bulbs and their branches
shall be of one piece with it; all of it shall
be one piece of hammered work of pure
gold.
37 "Then you shall make its
lamps[5216] seven *in number;* and [a]they
shall [I]mount its lamps so as to shed light
on the space in front of it.
38 "And its snuffers and [I]their trays
shall be of pure gold.
39 "It shall be made from a talent
of pure gold, with all these utensils.
40 "And [a]see[7200] that you make *them*
[b]after the pattern for them, which was
shown[7200] to you on the mountain.

Curtains of Linen

26 "[a]Moreover you shall make[6213]
the tabernacle[4908] with ten curtains of fine twisted linen and [I]blue and
purple and scarlet *material;* you shall
make them with cherubim,[3742] the work
of a skillful[2803] workman.
2 "The length of each curtain shall
be twenty-eight [I]cubits, and the width
of each curtain four [I]cubits; all the curtains shall have [II]the same measurements.
3 "Five curtains shall be [I]joined to
one another; and *the other* five curtains
shall be [I]joined to one[802] another.[269]
4 "And you shall make[6213] loops of

21 [I]Lit., *above, upon* [b]Ex. 25:16
22 [a]Ex. 29:42, 43; 30:6, 36; Lev. 16:2; Num. 17:4 [b]Num. 7:89; 1Sam. 4:4; 2Sam. 6:2; 2Kin. 19:15; Ps. 80:1; Is. 37:16
23 [I]Lit., *its length* [II]Lit., *its width* [III]Lit., *its height* [a]Ex. 37:10-16
24 [a]Ex. 25:11
29 [I]Or, *platters* [II]Lit., *libation bowls* [a]Ex. 37:16; Num. 4:7
30 [I]Lit., *Face* [II]Or, *continually* [a]Ex. 39:36; 40:23; Lev. 24:5-9
31 [I]Or, *calyx* [a]Ex. 37:17-24; 1Kin. 7:49; Zech. 4:2
32 [I]Lit., *second* [a]Ex. 37:18
33 [I]Or, *calyx* [II]Lit., *one branch* [a]Ex. 37:19
34 [I]Or, *calyxes* [a]Ex. 37:20
35 [I]Or, *calyx* [a]Ex. 37:21
36 [I]Or, *calyxes* [a]Ex. 37:22
37 [I]Lit., *raise up* [a]Num. 8:2
38 [I]Lit., *its snuff dishes*
40 [a]Heb. 8:5 [b]Ex. 25:9; 26:30; Num. 8:4; Acts 7:44
1 [I]Or, *violet* [a]Ex. 36:8-19
2 [I]I.e., One cubit equals approx. 18 in. [II]Lit., *one measure*
3 [I]Or, *coupled*

[I]blue on the edge[8193] of the [II]outermost curtain in the *first* set, and likewise you shall make *them* on the edge of the curtain that is outermost in the second [III]set.

5 "You shall make fifty loops in the one curtain, and you shall make fifty loops on the [I]edge of the curtain that is in the second [II]set; the loops shall be opposite each other.

6 "And you shall make fifty clasps[7165] of gold, and [I]join the curtains to one another[802] with the clasps, that the [II]tabernacle may be a unit.

Curtains of Goats' Hair

7 "Then [a]you shall make curtains of goats' *hair* for a tent[168] over the tabernacle; you shall make eleven curtains in all.

8 "The length of each curtain *shall be* thirty [I]cubits, and the width of each curtain four cubits; the eleven curtains shall have [II]the same measurements.

9 "And you shall [I]join five curtains by themselves, and the *other* six curtains by themselves, and you shall double over the sixth curtain [II]at the front of the tent.[168]

10 "And you shall make fifty loops on the edge of the [I]curtain that is outermost in the *first* [II]set, and fifty loops on the edge of the curtain *that is outermost in* the second [II]set.

11 "And you shall make fifty clasps of [I]bronze, and you shall put the clasps into the loops and [II]join the tent[168] together, that it may be [III]a unit.

12 "And the [I]overlapping part that is left over in the curtains of the tent, the half curtain that is left over, shall lap over the back of the tabernacle.

13 "And the cubit on one side and the cubit on the other, of what is left over in the length of the curtains of the tent, shall lap over the sides of the tabernacle on one side and on the other, to cover[3680] it.

14 "And [a]you shall make a covering for the tent of rams' skins [I]dyed red, and a covering of porpoise skins above.

Boards and Sockets

15 "Then you shall make [a]the boards for the tabernacle of acacia wood, standing upright.

16 "Ten cubits *shall be* the length of [I]each board, and one and a half cubits the width of each board.

17 "There *shall be* two tenons[3027] for each board, [I]fitted to one another; thus you shall do for all the boards of the tabernacle.

18 "And you shall make the boards for the tabernacle: twenty boards [I]for the south side.

19 "And you shall make forty [Ia]sockets of silver under the twenty boards, two [I]sockets under one board for its two tenons and two [I]sockets under another board for its two tenons;

20 and for the second side of the tabernacle, on the north side, twenty boards,

21 and their forty [I]sockets of silver; two [I]sockets under one board and two [I]sockets under another board.

22 "And for the [I]rear of the tabernacle, to the west, you shall make six boards.

23 "And you shall make two boards for the corners of the tabernacle at the [I]rear.

24 "And they shall be double[8382] beneath, and together they shall be complete [I]to its top[7218] [II]to the first ring; thus it shall be with both of them: they shall form the two corners.

25 "And there shall be eight boards with their [I]sockets of silver, sixteen [I]sockets; two [I]sockets under one board and two [I]sockets under another board.

26 "Then you shall make [a]bars of acacia wood, five for the boards of one side of the tabernacle,

27 and five bars for the boards of the [I]other side of the tabernacle, and five bars for the boards of the side of the tabernacle for the [II]rear *side* to the west.

28 "And the middle bar in the [I]center of the boards shall pass through from end to end.

4 [I]Or, *violet* [II]Lit., *one curtain from the end in the coupling* [III]Lit., *coupling*
5 [I]Lit., *end* [II]Lit., *coupling*
6 [I]Or, *couple* [II]Or, *dwelling place,* and so throughout the ch.
7 [a]Ex. 36:14
8 [I]I.e., One cubit equals approx. 18 in. [II]Lit., *one measure*
9 [I]Or, *couple* [II]Lit., *toward the front of the face of the tent*
10 [I]Lit., *one curtain* [II]Lit., *coupling*
11 [I]Or, *copper* [II]Or, *couple* [III]Lit., *one*
12 [I]Lit., *excess*
14 [I]Or, *tanned* [a]Ex. 36:19
15 [a]Ex. 36:20-34
16 [I]Lit., *the*
17 [I]Lit., *bound*
18 [I]Lit., *toward the side of the Negev to the south*
19 [I]Or, *bases* [a]Ex. 38:27
21 [I]Or, *bases*
22 [I]Lit., *extreme parts*
23 [I]Lit., *extreme parts*
24 [I]Or, *at its head* [II]Or, *with reference to*
25 [I]Or, *bases*
26 [a]Ex. 36:31
27 [I]Lit., *second* [II]Lit., *extreme parts*
28 [I]Lit., *midst*

29 "And you shall overlay the boards with gold and make their rings of gold *as* holders for the bars; and you shall overlay the bars with gold.

30 "Then you shall erect the tabernacle [a]according to its plan[4941] which you have been shown[7200] in the mountain.

The Veil and Screen

🔑 **31** "And you shall make [a]a veil of [I]blue and purple and scarlet *material* and fine twisted linen; it shall be made with cherubim, the work of a skillful workman.

32 "And you shall [I]hang it on four pillars of acacia overlaid with gold, their hooks *also being of* gold, on four [II]sockets of silver.

33 "And you shall [I]hang up the veil under the clasps, and shall bring in [a]the ark[727] of the testimony[5715] there within the veil; and the veil shall [II]serve for you as a partition [b]between the holy[6944] place and the holy of holies.

34 "And [a]you shall put the mercy seat[3727] on the ark of the testimony in the holy of holies.

35 "And [a]you shall set the table outside the veil, and the [b]lampstand opposite the table on the side of the tabernacle toward the south; and you shall put the table on the north side.

36 "And [a]you shall make a screen for the doorway of the tent of [I]blue and purple and scarlet *material* and fine twisted linen, the work of a [II]weaver.

37 "And [a]you shall make five pillars of acacia for the screen, and overlay them with gold, their hooks *also being of* gold; and you shall cast five [I]sockets of [II]bronze for them.

30 [a]Ex. 25:9, 40; Acts 7:44; Heb. 8:5

31 [I]Or, *violet* [a]Ex. 36:35, 36; 2Chr. 3:14; Matt. 27:51; Heb. 9:3

32 [I]Lit., *put* [II]Or, *bases*

33 [I]Lit., *put* [II]Lit., *separate for you between* [a]Ex. 25:16; 40:21 [b]Heb. 9:2f.

34 [a]Ex. 25:21; 40:20; Lev. 16:2

35 [a]Ex. 40:22 [b]Ex. 40:24

36 [I]Or, *violet* [II]Lit., *variegator;* i.e., a weaver in colors [a]Ex. 36:37

37 [I]Or, *bases* [II]Or, *copper* [a]Ex. 36:38

1 [I]I.e., One cubit equals approx. 18 in. [a]Ex. 38:1-7

2 [I]Or, *copper,* and so for *bronze* throughout the ch. [a]Ps. 118:27

4 [I]Lit., *on*

7 [a]Num. 4:15

8 [a]Ex. 25:40; 26:30; Acts 7:44; Heb. 8:5

9 [I]Or, *dwelling place* [II]Lit., *For the side of the Negev to the south* [a]Ex. 38:9-20

10 [I]Or, *bases*

The Bronze Altar

27 "And you shall make[6213] [a]the altar[4196] of acacia wood, five [I]cubits long[753] and five cubits wide; the altar shall be square, and its height shall be three cubits.

2 "And you shall make [a]its horns on its four corners; its horns shall be of one piece with it, and you shall overlay it with [I]bronze.

3 "And you shall make[6213] its pails for removing its ashes, and its shovels and its basins[4219] and its forks and its firepans; you shall make all its utensils of bronze.

4 "And you shall make for it a grating of network of bronze, and on the net you shall make four bronze rings [I]at its four corners.

5 "And you shall put it beneath, under the ledge of the altar, that the net may reach halfway up the altar.

6 "And you shall make poles for the altar, poles of acacia wood, and overlay them with bronze.

7 "And its poles shall be inserted into the rings, so that the poles shall be on the two sides of the altar [a]when it is carried.[5375]

8 "You shall make it hollow with planks; [a]as it was shown[7200] to you in the mountain, so they shall make *it.*

Court of the Tabernacle

9 "And you shall make [a]the court of the [I]tabernacle.[4908] [II]On the south side *there shall be* hangings for the court of fine twisted linen one hundred cubits long for one side;

10 and its pillars *shall be* twenty, with their twenty [I]sockets of bronze;

🔑 **26:31-35** The veil, literally "a separation," was hung between the Holy of Holies and the Holy Place. Its function was to separate all men, even the priests, from the presence of God. Only one man, the high priest, went beyond that veil and he was permitted to do so only once a year, on the Day of Atonement (Lev. 16:1-19). His purpose was to take the blood of the bull and the goat for his sins and the sins of the people. The meaning was clear—man was separated from God by reason of his sin and could approach Him only through blood which was presented by a priest. When Jesus died on the cross the veil hanging in the temple was torn in two (Mt. 27:51). Jesus went beyond that veil (Heb. 9:12,24) as high priest (Heb. 9:11; 7:23-28) taking His own blood (Heb. 9:12), and making full atonement (Heb. 10:10,12).

the hooks of the pillars and their [II]bands[2838] *shall be* of silver.

11 "And likewise for the north side in length *there shall be* hangings one hundred *cubits* long, and its twenty pillars with their twenty [I]sockets of bronze; the hooks of the pillars and their bands *shall be* of silver.

12 "And *for* the width of the court on the west side *shall be* hangings of fifty cubits *with* their ten pillars and their ten [I]sockets.

13 "And the width of the court on the [I]east side *shall be* fifty cubits.

14 "The hangings for the *one* [I]side *of the gate shall be* fifteen cubits *with* their three pillars and their three [II]sockets.

15 "And for the [I]other [II]side *shall be* hangings of fifteen cubits *with* their three pillars and their three [III]sockets.

16 "And for the gate of the court there *shall be* a screen of twenty cubits, of [I]blue and purple and scarlet *material* and fine twisted linen, the work of a [II]weaver, *with* their four pillars and their four [III]sockets.

17 "All the pillars around the court shall be furnished[2836] with silver bands *with* their hooks of silver and their [I]sockets of bronze.

18 "The length of the court *shall be* one hundred cubits, and the width fifty throughout, and the height five cubits of fine twisted linen, and their [I]sockets of bronze.

19 "All the utensils of the tabernacle *used* in all its service,[5656] and all its pegs, and all the pegs of the court, *shall be* of bronze.

20 "And you shall charge[6680] the sons[1121] of Israel, that they bring you [a]clear[2134] oil[8081] of beaten olives for the [I]light,[3974] to make a lamp[5216] [II]burn[5927] continually.[8548]

21 "In the [a]tent[168] of meeting,[4150] outside [b]the veil which is before the testimony,[5715] [c]Aaron and his sons[1121] shall keep it in order from evening to morning before the LORD; *it shall be* a perpetual[5769] [d]statute[2708] throughout their generations[1755] [I]for the sons of Israel.

Garments of the Priests

28 🗝 "Then [a]bring near to yourself Aaron your brother, and his sons[1121] with him, from among the sons[1121] of Israel, to minister as priest to Me—Aaron, [b]Nadab and Abihu, Eleazar and Ithamar, Aaron's sons.

2 "And you shall make[6213] [a]holy[6944] garments for Aaron your brother, for glory[3519] and for beauty.[8597]

3 "And you shall speak[1696] to all the [I][a]skillful[2450] persons [b]whom I have endowed with [II]the spirit[7307] of wisdom,[2451] that they make Aaron's garments to consecrate[6942] him, that he may minister as priest to Me.

4 "And these are the garments which they shall make:[6213] a [I][a]breastpiece and an ephod and a robe and a tunic of checkered work, a turban[4701] and a sash,[73] and they shall make holy garments for Aaron your brother and his sons, that he may minister as priest to Me.

5 "And they shall take [a]the gold and the [I]blue and the purple and the scarlet *material* and the fine linen.

6 "They shall also make [a]the ephod of gold, of [I]blue and purple *and* scarlet *material* and fine twisted linen, the work of the skillful workman.

7 "It shall have two shoulder pieces joined to its two ends, that it may be joined.

8 "And the skillfully woven band,[2805] which is on it, shall be like its workmanship, [I]of the same material: of gold, of [II]blue and purple and scarlet *material* and fine twisted linen.

9 "And you shall take two onyx stones and engrave on them the names of the sons of Israel,

10 six of their names on the one stone, and the names of the remaining[3498] six on the [I]other stone, according to their birth.[8435]

10 [II]Or, *fillets, rings*
11 [I]Or, *bases*
12 [I]Or, *bases*
13 [I]Lit., *east side eastward*
14 [I]Lit., *shoulder* [II]Or, *bases*
15 [I]Lit., *second* [II]Lit., *shoulder* [III]Or, *bases*
16 [I]Or, *violet* [II]Lit., *variegator;* i.e., a weaver in colors [III]Or, *bases*
17 [I]Or, *bases*
18 [I]Or, *bases*
20 [I]Or, *luminary* [II]Lit., *ascend* [a]Ex. 35:8, 28; Lev. 24:1-4
21 [I]Lit., *from* [a]Ex. 25:22; 29:42; 30:36 [b]Ex. 26:31, 33 [c]Ex. 30:8; 1Sam. 3:3; 2Chr. 13:11 [d]Ex. 28:43; 29:9; Lev. 3:17; 16:34; Num. 18:23; 19:21; 1Sam. 30:25

1 [a]Num. 18:7; Ps. 99:6; Heb. 5:1, 4 [b]Ex. 24:1, 9
2 [a]Ex. 29:5, 29; 31:10; 39:1-31; Lev. 8:7-9, 30
3 [I]Lit., *wise of heart* [II]I.e., artistic skill [a]Ex. 31:6; 35:25, 31-35; 36:1 [b]Ex. 31:3; Is. 11:2; 1Cor. 12:7-11; Eph. 1:17
4 [I]Or, *pouch* [a]Ex. 28:15-43
5 [I]Or, *violet* [a]Ex. 25:3
6 [I]Or, *violet* [a]Ex. 39:2-7; Lev. 8:7
8 [I]Lit., *from it* [II]Or, *violet*
10 [I]Lit., *second*

🗝 **28:1-5** See note on Ex. 32:25-29.

11 "[I]As a jeweler engraves a signet, you shall engrave the two stones according to the names of the sons of Israel; you shall [II]set them in filigree *settings*[4865] of gold.

12 "And you shall put the two stones on the shoulder pieces of the ephod, *as* stones of memorial[2146] for the sons of Israel, and Aaron shall [a]bear[5375] their names before the LORD on his two shoulders [b]for a memorial.

13 "[a]And you shall make filigree *settings* of gold,

14 and two chains of pure[2889] gold; you shall make them of twisted cordage[5688] work, and you shall put the corded chains on the filigree *settings.*

15 "And [a]you shall make a [I]breastpiece of judgment,[4941] the work of a skillful workman; like the work of the ephod you shall make it: of gold, of [II]blue and purple and scarlet *material* and fine twisted linen you shall make it.

16 "It shall be square *and* folded double, a span [I]in length and a span [I]in width.

17 "And you shall [I]mount on it four rows of stones; the first row *shall be* a row of ruby, topaz and emerald;

18 and the second row a turquoise, a sapphire and a diamond;

19 and the third row a jacinth, an agate and an amethyst;

20 and the fourth row a beryl and an onyx and a jasper; they shall be [I]set in gold filigree.

21 "And the stones shall be according to the names of the sons of Israel: twelve, according to their names; they shall be *like* the engravings of a seal, each [a]according to his name for the twelve tribes.[7626]

22 "And you shall make on the [I]breastpiece chains of twisted cordage work in pure gold.

23 "And you shall make on the breastpiece two rings of gold, and shall put the two rings on the two ends of the breastpiece.

24 "And you shall put the two cords of gold on the two rings at the ends of the breastpiece.

25 "And you shall put the *other* two ends of the two cords on the two filigree *settings,* and put them on the shoulder pieces of the ephod, at the front of it.

26 "And you shall make two rings of gold and shall place them on the two ends of the breastpiece, on the edge[8193] of it, which is toward the inner side[1004] of the ephod.[8193]

27 "And you shall make two rings of gold and put them on the bottom of the two shoulder pieces of the ephod, on the front of it close to the place where it is joined, above the skillfully woven band of the ephod.

28 "And they shall bind the breastpiece by its rings to the rings of the ephod with a [I]blue cord, that it may be on the skillfully woven band of the ephod, and that the breastpiece may not come loose from the ephod.

29 "And Aaron shall carry the names of the sons of Israel in the breastpiece of judgment over his heart when he enters the holy place, for a memorial before the LORD continually.[8548]

⊶ 30 "And [a]you shall put in the breastpiece of judgment the [I][b]Urim[217] and the

11 [I]Lit., *A work of a lapidary, engravings of a seal* [II]Lit., *make them to be surrounded*

12 [a]Ex. 28:29; 39:6f. [b]Ex. 39:7; Lev. 24:7; Num. 31:54; Josh. 4:7; 1Cor. 11:24f.

13 [a]Ex. 39:16-18

15 [I]Or, *pouch* [II]Or, *violet* [a]Ex. 39:8-21

16 [I]Lit., *its*

17 [I]Lit., *fill in a setting of stones, four rows of stones*

20 [I]Lit., *interwoven with gold in their settings*

21 [a]Rev. 7:4-8; 21:12

22 [I]Or, *pouch,* and so through v. 30

28 [I]Or, *violet*

30 [I]I.e., lights and perfections [a]Lev. 8:8 [b]Num. 27:21; Deut. 33:8; Ezra 2:63; Neh. 7:65

⊶ **28:30** This is the first Old Testament mention of these sacred objects called the Urim and Thummim. They were used by the priests to receive divine messages and were kept in the high priest's breastplate. The mention of the ephod in connection with simple oracles (I Sam. 23:6,9-12) suggests that at times these objects may have been associated with the priest's ephod. No one knows what the Urim and Thummim looked like or how they worked, but one plausible theory is that they were two flat objects with one side meaning Urim and the other Thummim. When they were thrown down and both Urim sides came up, God's answer was no. The opposite would be the case with two Thummim, but if one each came up, then God was not giving an answer. This would help explain King Saul's inability to get an answer from God on two different occasions (I Sam. 14:36,37; 28:6). The Urim and Thummim are not mentioned in the Old Testament between the early monarchy and post-exilic times, which may not be a coincidence, since this was the period of the prophets, when God revealed Himself much more fully than in the simple answers to questions posed by priests.

Thummim,[8537] and they shall be over Aaron's heart when he goes in before the LORD; and Aaron shall carry the judgment of the sons of Israel over his heart before the LORD continually.

31 "[a]And you shall make the robe of the ephod all[3632] of [I]blue.

32 "And there shall be an opening[6310] [I]at its top[7218] in the middle of it; around its opening there shall be a binding[8193] of woven work, as *it were* the opening of a coat of mail,[8473] that it may not be torn.

33 "And you shall make on its hem pomegranates of blue and purple and scarlet *material,* all around on its hem, and bells of gold between them all around:

34 a golden bell and a pomegranate, a golden bell and a pomegranate, all around on the hem of the robe.

35 "And it shall be on Aaron [I]when he ministers;[8334] and [II]its tinkling may be heard[8085] when he enters and [III]leaves the holy place before the LORD, that he may not die.

36 "You shall also make [a]a plate of pure gold and shall engrave on it, like the engravings of a seal, '[b]Holy[6944] to the LORD.'

37 "And you shall [I]fasten it on a [II]blue cord, and it shall be on the turban; it shall be at the front of the turban.

38 "And it shall be on Aaron's forehead, and Aaron shall [I][a]take away the iniquity[5771] of the holy things[6944] which the sons of Israel consecrate,[6942] with regard to all their holy gifts; and it shall always[8548] be on his forehead, that [b]they may be accepted[7522] before the LORD.

39 "And you shall weave [a]the tunic of checkered work of fine linen, and shall make a turban of fine linen, and you shall make a sash,[73] the work of a [I]weaver.

40 "And for Aaron's sons you shall make [a]tunics; you shall also make sashes[73] for them, and you shall make [I][b]caps for them, for glory and for beauty.

41 "And you shall put them on Aaron your brother and on his sons with him; and you shall [a]anoint[4886] them and [I]ordain[4390] them and consecrate[6942] them, that they may serve Me as priests.

42 "And you shall make for them [a]linen breeches to cover[3680] *their* bare flesh;[6172] they shall [I]reach from the loins even to the thighs.[3409]

43 "And they shall be on Aaron and on his sons when they enter the tent[168] of meeting,[4150] or [a]when they approach[5066] the altar[4196] to minister in the holy place, so that they do not incur[5375] [I]guilt and die.[4191] [b]It *shall be* a statute[2708] forever to him and to his [II]descendants[2233] after him.

Consecration of the Priests

29 "[a]Now this is [I]what[1697] you shall do[6213] to them to consecrate[6942] them to minister as priests to Me: take one young bull and two rams without blemish,[8549]

2 and [a]unleavened bread and unleavened cakes mixed with oil,[8081] and unleavened wafers [I]spread with oil; you shall make them of fine wheat[2406] flour.

3 "And you shall put them in one basket, and present them in the basket along with the bull and the two rams.

4 "Then [a]you shall bring[7126] Aaron and his sons to the doorway of the tent[168] of meeting,[4150] and wash[7364] them with water.

5 "And you shall take the garments, and put on Aaron the [a]tunic and [b]the robe of the ephod and [c]the ephod and [d]the [I]breastpiece, and gird him with the skillfully [e]woven band[2805] of the ephod;

6 and you shall set the [a]turban on his head,[7218] and put [b]the holy[6944] crown[5145] on the turban.[4701]

7 "Then you shall take [a]the anointing[4888] oil, and pour it on his head and anoint[4886] him.

8 "And you shall bring his sons and put [a]tunics on them.

9 "And you shall gird them with [a]sashes,[73] Aaron and his sons, and bind [I]caps on them, and they shall have [b]the priesthood[3550] by a perpetual[5769] statute.[2708] So you shall [II][c]ordain[3027] Aaron and his sons.

---

31 [I]Or, *violet* [a]Ex. 39:22-26
32 [I]Or, *for his head*
35 [I]Lit., *for ministering* [II]Lit., *its sound* [III]Lit., *comes out from*
36 [a]Ex. 39:30, 31; Lev. 8:9 [b]Zech. 14:20
37 [I]Lit., *place* [II]Or, *violet*
38 [I]Or, *bear* [a]Lev. 10:17; 22:16; Num. 18:1 [b]Lev. 1:4; 22:27; 23:11; Is. 56:7
39 [I]Lit., *variegator;* i.e., a weaver in colors [a]Ex. 39:27-29
40 [I]Lit., *headgear* [a]Ex. 28:4; 39:27, 41 [b]Ex. 29:9; 39:28; Lev. 8:13; Ezek. 44:18
41 [I]Lit., *fill their hand* [a]Ex. 29:7, 9; 30:30; 40:15; Lev. 8:1-36; 10:7
42 [I]Lit., *be* [a]Ex. 39:28; Lev. 6:10; 16:4; Ezek. 44:18
43 [I]Or, *iniquity* [II]Lit., *seed* [a]Ex. 20:26 [b]Ex. 27:21

1 [I]Lit., *the thing which* [a]Lev. 8:1-34
2 [I]Or, *anointed* [a]Lev. 2:4; 6:19-23
4 [a]Ex. 40:12; Lev. 8:6
5 [I]Or, *pouch* [a]Ex. 28:39; Lev. 8:7 [b]Ex. 28:31 [c]Ex. 28:6 [d]Ex. 28:15 [e]Ex. 28:8
6 [a]Ex. 28:4, 39 [b]Ex. 28:36, 37; Lev. 8:9
7 [a]Ex. 30:25; Lev. 8:12; 21:10; Num. 35:25; Ps. 133:2
8 [a]Ex. 28:39, 40; Lev. 8:13
9 [I]Lit., *headgear* [II]Lit., *fill the hand of* [a]Ex. 28:40 [b]Ex. 40:15; Num. 3:10; 18:7; 25:13; Deut. 18:5 [c]Ex. 28:41; Lev. 8:1-36

The Sacrifices

10 "Then you shall bring[7126] the bull before the tent of meeting, and Aaron and his sons shall [a]lay their hands[3027] on the head of the bull.

11 "And you shall slaughter[7819] the bull before the LORD at the doorway of the tent of meeting.

12 "And you shall [a]take some of the blood[1818] of the bull and put *it* on [b]the horns of the altar[4196] with your finger; and you shall pour[8210] out all the blood at the base[3247] of the altar.

13 "And you shall [a]take all the fat that covers[3680] the entrails[7130] and the [I]lobe of the liver, and the two kidneys and the fat that is on them, and offer them up in smoke[6999] on the altar.

14 "But [a]the flesh[1320] of the bull and its hide[5785] and its refuse, you shall burn with fire outside the camp;[4264] it is a sin offering.[2403]

15 "[a]You shall also take the one ram, and Aaron and his sons shall lay their hands on the head of the ram;

16 and you shall slaughter the ram and shall take its blood and sprinkle[2236] it around on the altar.

17 "Then you shall cut the ram into its pieces, and wash its entrails and its legs, and put *them* [I]with its pieces and [II]its head.

18 "And you shall offer up in smoke the whole ram on the altar; it is a burnt offering[5930] to the LORD: [a]it is a soothing aroma, an offering by fire[801] to the LORD.

19 "Then [a]you shall take the [I]other ram, and Aaron and his sons shall lay their hands on the head of the ram.

20 "And you shall slaughter the ram, and take some of its blood and put *it* on the lobe of Aaron's right ear and on the lobes of his sons' right ears and on the thumbs of their right hands and on the big toes of their right feet, and sprinkle the *rest of the* blood around on the altar.

21 "Then you shall take some of the blood that is on the altar and some of the [a]anointing oil, and sprinkle *it* on Aaron and on his garments, and on his sons and on his sons' garments with him; so he and his garments shall be consecrated,[6942] as well as his sons and his sons' garments with him.

22 "You shall also take the fat from the ram and the fat tail, and the fat that covers the entrails and the [I]lobe of the liver, and the two kidneys and the fat that is on them and the right thigh (for it is a ram of [II]ordination),

23 and one cake of bread and [a]one cake of bread *mixed with* oil and one wafer from the basket of unleavened bread which is *set* before the LORD;

24 and you shall put [I]all these [II]in the [III]hands[3709] of Aaron and [II]in the [III]hands of his sons, and shall wave[5130] them as a wave offering[8573] before the LORD.

25 "And [a]you shall take them from their hands, and offer them up in smoke on the altar on the burnt offering for a soothing aroma before the LORD; it is an offering by fire to the LORD.

26 "Then you shall take [a]the breast of Aaron's ram of [I]ordination, and wave it as a wave offering before the LORD; and it shall be your portion.

27 "And you shall consecrate[6942] the breast of the wave offering and the thigh of the heave offering[8641] which was waved and which was [I]offered[7311] from the ram of [II]ordination, from the one which was for Aaron and from the one which was for his sons.

28 "And it shall be for Aaron and his sons[1121] as *their* portion[2706] forever[5769] from the sons[1121] of Israel, for it is a heave offering; and it shall be a heave offering from the sons of Israel from the sacrifices[2077] of their peace offerings,[8002] *even* their heave offering to the LORD.

29 "And [a]the holy garments of Aaron shall be for his sons after him, [I]that in them they may be anointed[4888] and ordained.

30 "For seven days the one of his sons who is priest[3548] in his stead shall put them on when he enters the tent of meeting to minister[8334] in the holy place.

10 [a]Lev. 1:4; 8:14

12 [a]Lev. 8:15 [b]Ex. 27:2; 30:2

13 [I]Or, *appendage on* [a]Lev. 3:3, 4

14 [a]Lev. 4:11, 12, 21; Heb. 13:11

15 [a]Lev. 8:18

17 [I]Lit., *on* [II]Lit., *on its*

18 [a]Gen. 8:21; Ex. 29:25

19 [I]Lit., *second* [a]Lev. 8:22f.

21 [a]Ex. 30:25, 31; Lev. 8:30

22 [I]Or, *appendage on* [II]Lit., *filling*

23 [a]Lev. 8:26

24 [I]Lit., *the whole* [II]Lit., *on* [III]Lit., *palms*

25 [a]Lev. 8:28

26 [I]Lit., *filling* [a]Lev. 7:31, 34; 8:29

27 [I]Lit., *heaved;* or, *lifted up* [II]Lit., *filling*

29 [I]Lit., *for anointing in them and filling their hand in them* [a]Num. 20:26, 28

Food of the Priests

31 “And you shall take the ram of [I]ordination and [a]boil its flesh in a holy[6918] place.

32 “And Aaron and his sons shall eat the flesh of the ram, and the bread that is in the basket, at the doorway of the tent of meeting.

33 “Thus [a]they shall eat [I]those things by which atonement was made[3722] [II]at their ordination *and* consecration;[6942] but a [IIIb]layman[2114] shall not eat *them,* because they are holy.

34 “And [a]if any of the flesh of [I]ordination or any of the bread remains[3498] until morning, then you shall burn[8313] the remainder[3498] with fire; it shall not be eaten, because it is holy.

35 “And thus you shall do[6213] to Aaron and to his sons, according to all that I have commanded[6680] you; you shall [I]ordain them through [a]seven days.

36 “And [a]each day[3117] you shall offer a bull as a sin offering for atonement,[3725] and you shall [I]purify[2398] the altar when you make atonement[3722] [II]for it; and [b]you shall anoint it to consecrate it.

37 “For seven days you shall make atonement [I]for the altar and consecrate it; then [a]the altar shall be most holy,[6942] *and* whatever touches[5060] the altar shall be holy.

38 “Now [a]this is what you shall offer on the altar: two one[1121] year old lambs each day, continuously.[8548]

39 “The [a]one lamb you shall offer in the morning, and the [I]other lamb you shall offer at [II]twilight;

40 and there *shall be* one-tenth *of an ephah* of fine flour mixed with one-fourth of a hin of beaten oil, and one-fourth of a hin of wine for a libation[5262] with one lamb.

41 “And the [I]other lamb you shall offer at [II]twilight, and shall offer with it [III]the same grain offering[4503] as the morning and [IV]the same libation, for a soothing aroma, an offering by fire to the LORD.

42 “It shall be a continual burnt offering throughout your generations[1755] at the doorway of the tent of meeting before the LORD, [a]where I will meet with you, to speak to you there.

43 “And I will meet there with the sons of Israel, and it shall be consecrated[6942] by My glory.[3519]

44 “And I will consecrate the tent of meeting and the altar; I will also consecrate Aaron and his sons to minister as priests to Me.

45 “And [a]I will dwell among the sons of Israel and will be their God.[430]

46 “And they shall know[3045] that [a]I am the LORD their God who brought them out of the land[776] of Egypt, that I might dwell[7931] among them; I am the LORD their God.

The Altar of Incense

30 “Moreover, you shall make[6213] [a]an altar[4196] as a place for burning incense;[7004] you shall make[6213] it of acacia wood.

2 “Its length *shall be* a [I]cubit, and its width a cubit, it shall be square, and its height *shall be* two cubits; its horns *shall be* [II]of one piece with it.

3 “And you shall overlay it with pure[2889] gold, its top and its [I]sides all around, and its horns; and you shall make a gold molding all around for it.

4 “And you shall make two gold rings for it under its molding; you shall make *them* on its two side walls—on [I]opposite sides—and [II]they shall be holders for poles with which to carry[5375] it.

5 “And you shall make the poles of acacia wood and overlay them with gold.

6 “And you shall put [I]this altar in front of the veil that is [II]near the ark[727] of the testimony,[5715] in front of the [IIIa]mercy seat[3727] that is over *the ark of* the testimony, where I will meet with you.

7 “And Aaron shall burn[6999] fragrant incense on it; he shall burn it every morning when he trims the lamps.[5216]

8 “And when Aaron [I]trims[5927] the lamps at [II]twilight, he shall burn incense. *There shall be* perpetual[8548] incense

31 [I]Lit., *filling* [a]Lev. 8:31

33 [I]Lit., *them* [II]Lit., *to fill their hand to sanctify them* [III]Lit., *stranger* [a]Lev. 10:14 [b]Lev. 22:10, 13

34 [I]Lit., *filling* [a]Ex. 12:10; 23:18; 34:25; Lev. 8:32

35 [I]Lit., *fill their hand* [a]Lev. 8:33

36 [I]Or, *offer a sin offering on the altar* [II]Lit., *upon* [a]Heb. 10:11 [b]Ex. 40:10

37 [I]Lit., *upon* [a]Ex. 30:28f.

38 [a]Num. 28:3-31; 29:6-38

39 [I]Lit., *second* [II]Lit., *between the two evenings* [a]Ezek. 46:13-15

41 [I]Lit., *second* [II]Lit., *between the two evenings* [III]Lit., *according to the grain offering of the morning* [IV]Lit., *according to its*

42 [a]Ex. 25:22; Num. 17:4

45 [a]Ex. 25:8; Lev. 26:12; Num. 5:3; Deut. 12:11; Zech. 2:10; 2Cor. 6:16; Rev. 21:3

46 [a]Ex. 20:2

1 [a]Ex. 37:25-29

2 [I]I.e., One cubit equals approx. 18 in. [II]Lit., *from itself*

3 [I]Lit., *walls*

4 [I]Lit., *its two* [II]Lit., *it*

6 [I]Lit., *it* [II]Lit., *upon* or *over* [III]Lit., *propitiatory* [a]Ex. 25:21f.

8 [I]Lit., *causes to ascend* [II]Lit., *between the two evenings*

before the LORD throughout your generations.[1755]
9 "You shall not offer[5927] any
strange[2114] incense on [I]this altar, or
burnt offering[5930] or meal offering;[4503]
and you shall not pour out a libation[5262]
on it.
10 "And Aaron shall [a]make atonement[3722] on its horns once a year; he
shall make atonement on it with the
blood[1818] of the sin offering[2403] of atonement[3725] once a year throughout your
generations. It is most holy[6944] to the
LORD."
11 The LORD also spoke[1696] to Moses, saying,
12 "When you take [a]a [I]census[7218]
of the sons[1121] of Israel [II]to number
them, then each one[376] of them shall
give [b]a ransom[3724] for [III]himself[5315] to
the LORD, when you [IV]number[6485] them,
that there may be no plague[5063] among
them when you [IV]number them.
13 "This is what everyone who
[I]is numbered[5674] shall give: half a shekel
according to the shekel of the sanctuary
([a]the shekel is twenty gerahs),[1626] half
a shekel as a [II]contribution[8641] to the
LORD.
14 "Everyone who [I]is numbered,
from twenty years old[1121] and over, shall
give the [II]contribution to the LORD.
15 "The rich shall not pay more, and
the poor shall not pay less than the half
shekel, when you give the [I]contribution
to the LORD to make atonement for
[II]yourselves.
16 "And you shall take the atonement[3725] money from the sons of Israel, and shall give it for the service[5656]
of the tent[168] of meeting,[4150] that it may
be a memorial[2146] for the sons of Israel
before the LORD, to make atonement
for [I]yourselves."
17 And the LORD spoke to Moses,
saying,
18 "You shall also make [a]a laver[3595]
of [I]bronze, with its base of bronze, for
washing; and you shall [b]put it between
the tent of meeting and the altar, and
you shall put water in it.
19 "And Aaron and his sons[1121] shall
[a]wash[7364] their hands[3027] and their feet
from it;
20 when they enter the tent of
meeting, they shall wash with water,
that they may not die; or when they
approach[5066] the altar to minister,[8334] by
offering up in smoke a fire *sacrifice* to
the LORD.
21 "So they shall wash their hands
and their feet, that they may not die;
and [a]it shall be a perpetual[5769] statute[2706]
for them, for [I]Aaron and his [II]descend-
ants[2233] throughout their generations."

The Anointing Oil

22 Moreover, the LORD spoke to
Moses, saying,
23 "Take also for yourself the
finest[7218] of spices: of flowing myrrh[4753]
five hundred *shekels,* and of fragrant cinnamon half as much, two hundred and
fifty, and of fragrant cane[7070] two hundred and fifty,
24 and of cassia[6916] five hundred,
according to the shekel of the sanctuary,
and of olive oil[8081] a hin.
25 "And you shall make [I]of these a
holy anointing[4888] oil, a perfume mixture,
the work of a perfumer;[7543] it shall be
[a]a holy anointing[4888] oil.
26 "And with it [a]you shall anoint[4886]
the tent of meeting and the ark of the
testimony,
27 and the table and all its utensils,
and the lampstand and its utensils, and
the altar of incense,
28 and the altar of burnt offering and
all its utensils, and the laver and its
stand.
29 "You shall also consecrate[6942]
them, that they may be most holy; whatever touches[5060] them shall be holy.
30 "[a]And you shall anoint[4886] Aaron
and his sons, and consecrate[6942] them,
that they may minister as priests to Me.
31 "And you shall speak to the sons
of Israel, saying, 'This shall be a holy
anointing oil to Me throughout your generations.
32 'It shall not be poured on
[I]anyone's[120] body,[1320] nor shall you make

9 [I]Lit., *it*
10 [a]Lev. 16:18
12 [I]Lit., *sum* [II]Lit., *for their being mustered* [III]Lit., *his soul* [IV]Lit., *muster* [a]Ex. 38:25, 26; Num. 1:2; 26:2 [b]Num. 31:50
13 [I]Lit., *passes over to those who are mustered* [II]Lit., *heave offering* [a]Lev. 27:25; Num. 3:47; Ezek. 45:12
14 [I]V. 13, note 1 [II]Lit., *heave offering of the LORD*
15 [I]Lit., *heave offering of the LORD* [II]Lit., *your souls*
16 [I]Lit., *your souls*
18 [I]Or, *copper* [a]Ex. 38:8 [b]Ex. 40:30
19 [a]Ex. 40:31f.; Is. 52:11
21 [I]Lit., *him* [II]Lit., *seed* [a]Ex. 28:43
25 [I]Lit., *it* [a]Ex. 37:29; 40:9; Lev. 8:10
26 [a]Ex. 40:9; Lev. 8:10; Num. 7:1
30 [a]Ex. 29:7; Lev. 8:12
32 [I]Lit., *the flesh of man*

any like it, in [II]the same proportions; [a]it is holy, *and* it shall be holy to you.

33 "[a]Whoever shall mix *any* like it, or whoever puts any of it on a [I]layman,[2114] [II][b]shall be cut off[3772] from his people.' "[5971]

The Incense

34 Then the LORD said to Moses, "Take for yourself spices, stacte[5198] and onycha and galbanum,[2464] spices with pure[2134] frankincense;[3828] there shall be an equal part of each.

35 "And with it you shall make incense, a perfume,[7004] the work of a perfumer, salted, pure, *and* holy.

36 "And you shall beat[7833] some of it very fine, and put part of it before the testimony in the tent of meeting, [a]where I shall meet with you; it shall be most holy to you.

37 "And the incense which you shall make, [a]you shall not make in [I]the same proportions for yourselves; it shall be holy to you for the LORD.

38 "[a]Whoever shall make *any* like it, to [I]use as perfume,[7306] [II]shall be cut off from his people."

The Skilled Craftsmen

31 [a]Now the LORD spoke[1696] to Moses, saying,

2 "See,[7200] I have called by name Bezalel, the [a]son of Uri, the son of Hur, of the tribe[4294] of Judah.

3 "And I have [a]filled him with the Spirit[7307] of God[430] in wisdom,[2451] in understanding,[8394] in knowledge,[1847] and in all *kinds of* [I]craftsmanship,[4399]

4 to [I]make[2803] artistic designs[4284] for work[6213] in gold, in silver, and in [II]bronze,

5 and in the cutting of stones [I]for settings, and in the carving of wood, that he may work in all *kinds of* [II]craftsmanship.

6 "And behold, I Myself have [I]appointed with him [a]Oholiab, the son of Ahisamach, of the tribe of Dan; and in the hearts[3820] of all who are [II]skillful[2450] I have put [III]skill, that they may make[6213] all that I have commanded[6680] you:

7 [a]the tent[168] of meeting,[4150] and [b]the ark[727] of testimony,[5715] and [c]the [I]mercy seat[3727] upon it, and all the furniture of the tent,

8 [a]the table also and its [I]utensils, and the [b]pure *gold* lampstand with all its [I]utensils, and [c]the altar[4196] of incense,[7004]

9 [a]the altar of burnt offering also with all its [I]utensils, and [b]the laver[3595] and its stand,

10 the [I][a]woven garments as well, and the holy[6944] garments for Aaron the priest,[3548] and the garments of his sons, *with which* to [II]carry on their priesthood;

11 [a]the anointing[4888] oil[8081] also, and the [b]fragrant incense for the holy place, they are to make[6213] *them* according to all that I have commanded you."

The Sign of the Sabbath

12 And the LORD spoke to Moses, saying,

13 "But as for you, speak[1696] to the sons[1121] of Israel, saying, '[a]You shall surely observe[8104] My sabbaths;[7676] for *this* is [b]a sign[226] between Me and you throughout your generations,[1755] that you may know[3045] that I am the LORD who sanctifies[6942] you.

14 'Therefore you are to observe the sabbath, for it is holy to you. [a]Everyone who profanes[2490] it shall surely be put to death; for whoever does any work on it, that person[5315] shall be cut off[3772] from among his people.[5971]

15 '[a]For six days work may be done,[6213] but on the seventh day there is a [b]sabbath of complete rest,[7677] holy to the LORD; [c]whoever does any work on the sabbath day shall surely be put to death.

16 'So the sons of Israel shall observe the sabbath, to [I]celebrate[6213] the sabbath throughout their generations as a perpetual[5769] covenant.'[1285]

17 "[a]It is a sign between Me and the sons of Israel forever;[5769] [b]for in six days the LORD made[6213] heaven[8064] and earth,[776] but on the seventh day

---

[II]Lit., *its proportion* [a]Ex. 30:25, 37

33 [I]Lit., *stranger* [II]Lit., *even he shall* [a]Ex. 30:38 [b]Gen. 17:14; Ex. 12:15; Lev. 7:20f.

36 [a]Ex. 29:42

37 [I]Lit., *its proportion* [a]Ex. 30:32

38 [I]Lit., *smell of it* [II]Lit., *even he shall* [a]Ex. 30:33

1 [a]Ex. 35:30-36:1

2 [a]1Chr. 2:20

3 [I]Or, *workmanship* [a]Ex. 35:31; 1Kin. 7:14; 1Cor. 12:4-8

4 [I]Lit., *devise devices* [II]Or, *copper*

5 [I]Lit., *to fill in (for a setting)* [II]Or, *workmanship*

6 [I]Lit., *given* [II]Lit., *wise of heart* [III]Lit., *wisdom* [a]Ex. 35:34

7 [I]Lit., *propitiatory* [a]Ex. 36:8-38 [b]Ex. 37:1-5 [c]Ex. 37:6-9

8 [I]Or, *vessels* [a]Ex. 37:10-16 [b]Ex. 37:17-24; Lev. 24:4 [c]Ex. 37:25-29

9 [I]Or, *vessels* [a]Ex. 38:1-7 [b]Ex. 38:8

10 [I]Or, *service garments* [II]Lit., *minister as priests* [a]Ex. 39:1

11 [a]Ex. 30:23-32 [b]Ex. 30:34-38

13 [a]Ex. 20:8 [b]Ex. 31:17; Ezek. 20:12, 20

14 [a]Ex. 31:15; 35:2; Num. 15:32, 35; John 7:23

15 [a]Ex. 20:9-11; 23:12; 34:21; 35:2; Lev. 23:3; Deut. 5:12-14 [b]Gen. 2:2f.; Ex. 16:23; 20:8; 35:2, 3 [c]Ex. 31:14

16 [I]Lit., *do*

17 [a]Ex. 31:13; Ezek. 20:12 [b]Gen. 1:31; 2:2, 3; Ex. 20:11

He ceased[7673] *from labor,* and was refreshed."
18 And when He had finished[3615]
speaking[1696] with him upon Mount Sinai,
He gave Moses [a]the two tablets of the
testimony, tablets of stone, [b]written by
the finger of God.

The Golden Calf

32 Now when the people[5971] saw[7200]
that Moses [a]delayed to come
down from the mountain, the people
assembled[6950] about Aaron, and said to
him, "Come, [b]make us [1]a god[430] who
will go before us; as for [c]this Moses,
the man[376] who brought us up[5927] from
the land[776] of Egypt, we do not know[3045]
what has become of him."
2 And Aaron said to them, "[a]Tear
off the gold rings which are in the ears
of your wives, your sons, and your
daughters, and bring *them* to me."
3 Then all the people tore off the
gold rings which were in their ears, and
brought *them* to Aaron.
4 And he took *this* from their
hand,[3027] and fashioned it with a
graving[2747] tool, and made it into a
[a]molten[4541] calf; and they said, "[1]This
is your god, O Israel, who brought you
up from the land of Egypt."
5 Now when Aaron saw *this,* he built
an altar[4196] before it; and Aaron made
a proclamation[7121] and said, "Tomorrow
shall be a feast[2282] to the LORD."
6 So the next day they rose early
and [a]offered[5927] burnt offerings,[5930] and
brought[5066] peace offerings;[8002] and [b]the
people sat down to eat and to drink,
and rose up [c]to play.
7 Then the LORD spoke[1696] to Moses, "Go [1]down at once, for your people,
whom [a]you brought up from the land
of Egypt, have [b]corrupted[7843] *themselves.*
8 "They have quickly turned
aside[5493] from the way[1870] which I
commanded[6680] them. [a]They have
made[6213] for themselves a molten calf,
and have worshiped[7812] it, and [b]have
sacrificed[2076] to it, and said, '[1][c]This is
your god, O Israel, who brought you
up from the land of Egypt!' "
9 [a]And the LORD said to Moses, "I
have seen[7200] this people, and behold,
they are [1][b]an obstinate people.
10 "Now then [a]let Me alone, that
My anger[639] may burn[2734] against them,
and that I may destroy[3615] them; and
[b]I will make[6213] of you a great nation."[1471]

Moses' Entreaty

11 Then [a]Moses entreated the LORD
his God,[430] and said, "O LORD, why doth
Thine anger burn against Thy people
whom Thou hast brought out from the
land of Egypt with great power and with
a mighty[2389] hand?
12 "Why should [a]the Egyptians
speak, saying, 'With evil *intent*[7451] He
brought them out to kill[2026] them in the
mountains and to destroy[3615] them from
the face of the earth'?[127] Turn[7725] from
Thy burning anger and change[5162] Thy
mind about *doing* harm[7451] to Thy people.
13 "Remember Abraham, Isaac,
and Israel, Thy servants[5650] to whom
Thou didst [a]swear[7650] by Thyself, and
didst say to them, 'I will [b]multiply your
[1]descendants[2233] as the stars of the heavens,[8064] and [c]all this land of which I have
spoken[559] I will give to your [1]descend-
ants, and they shall inherit[5157] *it*
forever.' "[5769]
14 [a]So the LORD changed His mind
about the harm which He said[1696] He
would do to His people.
15 [a]Then Moses turned and went
down from the mountain with the two
tablets of the testimony[5715] in his hand,
[b]tablets which were written on both
[1]sides; they were written on one *side*
and the other.
16 And the tablets were God's
work, and the writing was God's writing
engraved on the tablets.
🔑 17 Now when Joshua heard[8085] the

18 [a]Ex. 24:12; 34:29; Deut. 4:13; 5:22; 9:10f. [b]Ex. 32:15, 16; 34:1, 28; Deut. 9:10
1 [1]Or, *gods* [a]Ex. 24:18; Deut. 9:11, 12 [b]Acts 7:40 [c]Ex. 14:11
2 [a]Ex. 35:22
4 [1]Or, *These are your gods* [a]Deut. 9:16; Neh. 9:18; Ps. 106:19; Acts 7:41
6 [a]Acts 7:41 [b]1Cor. 10:7 [c]Ex. 32:17-19; Num. 25:2
7 [1]Lit., *go down* [a]Ex. 32:4, 11; Deut. 9:12 [b]Gen. 6:11f.
8 [1]Or, *These are your gods* [a]Ex. 20:3, 4, 23 [b]Ex. 22:20; 34:15; Deut. 32:17 [c]1Kin. 12:28
9 [1]Or, *a stiff-necked* [a]Num. 14:11-20 [b]Ex. 33:3, 5; 34:9; Is. 48:4; Acts 7:51
10 [a]Deut. 9:14 [b]Num. 14:12
11 [a]Deut. 9:18, 26
12 [a]Num. 14:13-19; Deut. 9:28; Josh. 7:9
13 [1]Lit., *seed* [a]Gen. 22:16-18; Heb. 6:13 [b]Gen. 15:5; 26:4 [c]Gen. 12:7; 13:15; 15:18; 17:8; 35:12; Ex. 13:5, 11; 33:1
14 [a]Ps. 106:45
15 [1]Lit., *their sides* [a]Deut. 9:15 [b]Ex. 31:18

🔑 **32:17** See note on Num. 27:18-23.

sound of the people [I]as they shouted, he said to Moses, "There is a sound of war in the camp."[4264]

18 But he said,

"It is not the sound of the cry
of triumph,
Nor is it the sound of the cry
of defeat;
But the sound of singing I
hear."[8085]

Moses' Anger

19 And it came about, as soon as [I]Moses came near[7126] the camp, that [a]he saw the calf and *the* dancing; and Moses' anger[639] burned, and [b]he threw the tablets from his hands and shattered[7665] them [II]at the foot of the mountain.

20 [a]And he took the calf which they had made and burned *it* with fire, and ground it to powder, and scattered[2219] it over the surface of the water, and made the sons[1121] of Israel drink *it.*

21 Then Moses said to Aaron, "What did this people do to you, that you have brought *such* great sin[2401] upon them?"

22 And Aaron said, "Do not let the anger of my lord[113] burn; you know[3045] the people yourself, [a]that they are [I]prone to evil.

23 "For [a]they said to me, 'Make [I]a god for us who will go before us; for this Moses, the man who brought us up from the land of Egypt, we do not know what has become of him.'

24 "And I said to them, 'Whoever has any gold, let them tear it off.' So they gave *it* to me, and [a]I threw[7993] it into the fire, and out came[3335] this calf."

🔑 **25** Now when Moses saw that the people were [I]out of control—for Aaron had [a]let them [II]get out of control[6544] to be a derision among [III]their enemies—

🔑 26 then Moses stood in the gate of the camp, and said, "Whoever is for the LORD, *come* to me!" And all the sons[1121] of Levi gathered[622] together to him.

27 And he said to them, "Thus says[559] the LORD, the God of Israel, 'Every man *of you* put his sword upon his thigh,[3409] and go back[5674] and forth[7725] from gate to gate in the camp, and kill[2026] every man his brother,[251] and every man his friend, and every man his [I]neighbor.' "[7453]

28 So [a]the sons of Levi did[6213] [I]as Moses instructed,[1697] and about three thousand men of the people[376] fell[5307] that day.[3117]

29 Then Moses said, "Dedicate[3027] yourselves today[3117] to the LORD—for every man has been against his son and against his brother—in order that He may bestow a blessing[1293] upon you today."

30 And it came about on the next day that Moses said to the people, "[a]You yourselves have [I]committed[2398] a great

17 [I]Lit., *in its shouting*
19 [I]Lit., *he* [II]Lit., *beneath* [a]Ex. 32:6; Deut. 9:16 [b]Deut. 9:17
20 [a]Deut. 9:21
22 [I]Lit., *in evil* [a]Deut. 9:24
23 [I]Or, *gods* [a]Ex. 32:1-4
24 [a]Ex. 32:4
25 [I]Lit., *let loose* [II]Lit., *go loose* [III]Lit., *those who rise against them* [a]1Kin. 12:28-30; 14:16
27 [I]Or, *kin*
28 [I]Lit., *according to Moses' word* [a]Num. 25:7-13; Deut. 33:9
29 [I]Lit., *Fill your hand*
30 [I]Lit., *sinned* [a]1Sam. 12:20, 23

🔑 **32:25-29** In this passage, where we see Moses' righteous indignation toward Israel's apostasy in making the golden calf, we learn how the Levites won the privilege of serving in the tabernacle. Apparently some people were still rebellious, so the Levites responded to Moses' question of who was on the Lord's side by going throughout the camp executing the rebels. For their loyalty to God, they became His special ministers. The distinction between the Levites in general and the priests in particular must, however, be carefully made. The priests were a special class within the tribe of Levi whose ministry included the more sacred functions from which other members of the tribe were barred. Even though, in a general sense, God wanted all Israel to be "a kingdom of priests" (Ex. 19:6), a special priesthood already existed (Ex. 19:22,24). Only Aaron and his sons could be priests (Ex. 28:1; Num. 3:10), but that was not made an hereditary appointment until Phinehas' act of zealous loyalty to God shortly before Israel entered Canaan (Num. 25:6-13).

🔑 **32:26,27** Though the Law expressly forbade murder (Ex. 20:13; Deut. 5:17) God was bringing *His* judgment upon these men. Israel had lapsed into gross idolatry, breaking their covenant with God, and committing treason against their King, the Lord Himself. God in His infinite wisdom judged them worthy of capital punishment.

sin;[2401] and now I am going up[5927] to the LORD, perhaps[194] I can [b]make atonement[3722] for your sin."[2403]

31 Then Moses returned[7725] to the LORD, and said, "Alas, this people has [I]committed a great sin, and they have made [II]a [a]god of gold for themselves.

32 "But now, if Thou wilt, forgive[5375] their sin—and if not, please blot me out from Thy [a]book[5612] which Thou hast written!"

33 And the LORD said to Moses, "Whoever has sinned against Me, [a]I will blot him out[4229] of My book.

34 "But go now, lead[5148] the people [a]where I told[1696] you. Behold, [b]My angel shall go before you; nevertheless [c]in the day when I [I]punish,[6485] [d]I will [II]punish them for their sin."

35 [a]Then the LORD smote[5062] the people, because of [b]what they did with the calf which Aaron had made.

The Journey Resumed

33 Then the LORD spoke[1696] to Moses, "Depart, go up from here, you and the people[5971] whom you have brought up[5927] from the land[776] of Egypt, to the land of which [a]I swore[7650] to Abraham, [b]Isaac, and [c]Jacob, saying, '[d]To your [I]descendants[2233] I will give it.'

2 "And I will send [a]an angel before you and [b]I will drive out the Canaanite, the Amorite, the Hittite, the Perizzite, the Hivite and the Jebusite.

3 "*Go up* to a land [a]flowing with milk and honey; for I will not go up[5927] in your midst, because you are [I][b]an obstinate people, lest [c]I destroy[3615] you on the way."

4 When the people heard[8085] this [I]sad[7451] word,[1697] [a]they went into mourning, and none of them put on his ornaments.

5 For the LORD had said to Moses, "Say to the sons[1121] of Israel, 'You are [I][a]an obstinate people; should I go up in your midst for one moment, I would destroy[3615] you. Now therefore, put off your ornaments from you, that I may know[3045] what I will do[6213] with you.' "

6 So the sons of Israel stripped[5337] themselves of their ornaments from Mount Horeb *onward.*

7 Now Moses used to take [a]the tent and pitch it outside the camp,[4264] a good distance from the camp, and he called[7121] it the tent[168] of meeting.[4150] And it came about, that [b]everyone who sought the LORD would go out to the tent of meeting which was outside the camp.

8 And it came about, whenever Moses went out to the tent, that all the people would arise and stand,[5324] each[376] at the entrance of his tent, and gaze after Moses until he entered the tent.

9 And it came about, whenever Moses entered the tent, [a]the pillar of cloud[6051] would descend and stand at the entrance of the tent; [b]and [I]the LORD would speak[1696] with Moses.

10 When all the people saw[7200] the pillar of cloud standing at the entrance of the tent, all the people would arise and worship,[7812] each at the entrance of his tent.[168]

🔑 11 Thus [a]the LORD used to speak[1696] to Moses face to face, just as a man speaks[1696] to his friend.[7453] When [I]Moses returned[7725] to the camp, [b]his servant[8334] Joshua, the son of Nun, a young man, would not depart from the tent.

Moses Intercedes

12 Then Moses said to the LORD, "See,[7200] Thou dost say to me, '[a]Bring up this people!' But Thou Thyself hast not let me know [b]whom Thou wilt send with me. [c]Moreover, Thou hast said, 'I have known[3045] you by name, and you have also found favor[2580] in My sight.'

13 "Now therefore, I pray Thee, if I have found favor in Thy sight, [a]let me know[3045] Thy ways,[1870] that I may know Thee, so that I may find favor in Thy sight. [b]Consider[7200] too, that this nation[1471] is Thy people."

30 [b]Num. 25:13

31 [I]Lit., *sinned* [II]Or, *gods* [a]Ex. 20:23

32 [a]Ps. 69:28; Is. 4:3; Dan. 12:1; Mal. 3:16, 17; Phil. 4:3; Rev. 3:5; 21:27

33 [a]Ex. 17:14; Deut. 29:20; Ps. 9:5; Rev. 3:5

34 [I]Lit., *visit* [II]Lit., *visit their sin upon them* [a]Ex. 3:17 [b]Ex. 23:20 [c]Deut. 32:35; Rom. 2:5, 6 [d]Ps. 99:8

35 [a]Ex. 32:28 [b]Ex. 32:4, 24

1 [I]Lit., *seed* [a]Ex. 32:13 [b]Gen. 26:1-3 [c]Gen. 28:10 [d]Gen. 12:7

2 [a]Ex. 32:34 [b]Ex. 23:27-31; Josh. 24:11

3 [I]Lit., *a stiff-necked* [a]Ex. 3:8, 17 [b]Ex. 32:9; 33:5 [c]Ex. 32:10

4 [I]Lit., *evil* [a]Num. 14:1, 39

5 [I]Lit., *a stiff-necked* [a]Ex. 33:3

7 [a]Ex. 18:7, 12-16 [b]Ex. 29:42f.

9 [I]Lit., *He* [a]Ex. 13:21 [b]Ps. 99:7

11 [I]Lit., *he* [a]Num. 12:8; Deut. 34:10 [b]Ex. 24:13

12 [a]Ex. 3:10; 32:34 [b]Ex. 33:2 [c]Ex. 33:17

13 [a]Ps. 25:4; 27:11; 51:13; 86:11; 119:33 [b]Ex. 3:7, 10; 5:1; 32:12, 14; Deut. 9:26, 29

🔑 **33:11** See note on Num. 27:18-23.

14 And He said, "[a]My presence shall go *with you,* and [b]I will give you rest."

15 Then he said to Him, "[a]If Thy presence does not go *with us,* do not lead us up from here.

16 "For how then can it be known[3045] that I have found favor in Thy sight, I and Thy people? Is it not by Thy going with us, so that [a]we, I and Thy people, may be distinguished from all the *other* people who are upon the [I]earth?"[127]

17 And the LORD said to Moses, "I will also do this thing[1697] of which you have spoken; [a]for you have found favor in My sight, and I have known you by name."

18 [a]Then [I]Moses said, "I pray[4994] Thee, show[7200] me Thy glory!"[3519]

19 And He said, "[a]I Myself will make all My goodness[2896] pass[5674] before you, and will proclaim[7121] the name of the LORD before you; and [b]I will be gracious[2603] to whom I will be gracious, and will show compassion[7355] on whom I will show compassion."

20 But He said, "You cannot see[7200] My face, [a]for no man[120] can see[7200] Me and live!"[2425]

21 Then the LORD said, "Behold, there is a place [I]by Me, and [a]you shall stand *there* on the rock;

22 and it will come about, while My glory is passing by,[5674] that I will put[7760] you in the cleft of the rock and [a]cover you with My hand[3709] until I have passed by.

23 "Then I will take My hand away and you shall see My back, but [a]My face shall not be seen."[7200]

The Two Tablets Replaced

34 Now the LORD said to Moses, "Cut out[6458] for yourself [a]two stone tablets like the former ones,[7223] and [b]I will write on the tablets the words[1697] that were on the former tablets which you shattered.[7665]

2 "So be ready[3559] by morning, and come up in the morning to [a]Mount Sinai, and [I]present[5324] yourself there to Me on the top[7218] of the mountain.

3 "And [a]no man is to come up with you, nor let any man be seen[7200] [I]anywhere on the mountain; even the flocks and the herds may not graze in front of that mountain."

4 So he cut out[6458] [a]two stone tablets like the former ones, and Moses rose up early in the morning and went up[5927] to Mount Sinai, as the LORD had commanded[6680] him, and he took two stone tablets in his hand.[3027]

5 And [a]the LORD descended in the cloud[6051] and stood there with him as [I]he called[7121] upon the name of the LORD.

6 Then the LORD passed by[5674] in front of him and proclaimed, "The LORD, the LORD God,[410] [a]compassionate and gracious,[2587] slow to anger,[639] and abounding[7227] in lovingkindness[2617] and [I]truth;[571]

7 who [a]keeps[5341] lovingkindness[2617] for thousands, who forgives iniquity,[5771] transgression[6588] and sin;[2403] yet He [b]will by no means leave *the guilty* unpunished, [c]visiting[6485] the iniquity of fathers[1] on the children[1121] and on the grandchildren to the third and fourth generations."

8 And Moses made haste [I][a]to bow low toward the earth[776] and worship.[7812]

9 And he said, "[a]If now I have found favor[2580] in Thy sight, O Lord,[136] I pray, let the Lord[136] go along in our midst, even though [I][b]the people[5971] are so obstinate; and do Thou [c]pardon[5545] our iniquity and our sin,[2403] and [d]take us as Thine own [II]possession."[5157]

The Covenant Renewed

10 Then [I]God said, "Behold, [a]I am going to make[3772] a covenant.[1285] Before all your people [b]I will perform[6213] miracles[6381] which have not been [II]produced in all the earth, nor among any of the nations;[1471] and all the people [III]among whom you live will see[7200] the working of the LORD, for it is a fearful[3372] thing that I am going to perform with you.

---

14 [a]Deut. 4:37; Is. 63:9 [b]Deut. 12:10; 25:19; Josh. 21:44; 22:4
15 [a]Ps. 80:3, 7, 19
16 [I]Lit., *ground* [a]Lev. 20:24, 26
17 [a]Ex. 33:12
18 [I]Lit., *he* [a]Ex. 33:20-23
19 [a]Ex. 34:6, 7 [b]Rom. 9:15
20 [a]Is. 6:5; 1Tim. 6:16
21 [I]Lit., *with* [a]Ps. 18:2, 46; 27:5; 61:2; 62:7
22 [a]Ps. 91:1, 4; Is. 49:2; 51:16
23 [a]Ex. 33:20; John 1:18

1 [a]Ex. 24:12; 31:18; 32:16, 19 [b]Deut. 10:2, 4
2 [I]Or, *place yourself before* [a]Ex. 19:11, 18, 20
3 [I]Lit., *on all* [a]Ex. 19:12, 13
4 [a]Ex. 34:1
5 [I]Or, *he called out with the name of the LORD* [a]Ex. 19:9; 33:9
6 [I]Or, *faithfulness* [a]Num. 14:18; Deut. 4:31; Neh. 9:17; Ps. 86:15; 103:8; 108:4; 145:8; Joel 2:13; Rom. 2:4
7 [a]Ex. 20:5, 6; Deut. 5:10; 7:9; Ps. 103:3; 130:3, 4; 1John 1:9 [b]Ex. 23:7; Deut. 7:10; Job 10:14; Nah. 1:3 [c]Deut. 5:9
8 [I]Lit., *and bowed . . . worshiped* [a]Ex. 4:31
9 [I]Lit., *it is a people stiff-necked* [II]Or, *inheritance* [a]Ex. 33:13 [b]Ex. 32:9 [c]Ex. 34:7 [d]Deut. 4:20; 9:26, 29; 32:9; Ps. 33:12
10 [I]Lit., *He* [II]Lit., *created* [III]Lit., *in whose midst you are* [a]Ex. 34:27, 28; Deut. 5:2 [b]Deut. 4:32; Ps. 72:18; 136:4

11 "[I]Be sure to observe[8141] what I am commanding[6680] you this day:[3117] behold, [a]I am going to drive out the Amorite before you, and the Canaanite, the Hittite, the Perizzite, the Hivite and the Jebusite.

12 "[a]Watch[8104] yourself that you make[3772] no covenant with the inhabitants of the land[776] into which you are going, lest it become a snare[4170] in your midst.

13 "[a]But *rather,* you are to tear down[5422] their altars[4196] and smash[7665] their *sacred* pillars[4676] and cut down[3772] their [I][b]Asherim[842]

14 —for [a]you shall not worship any other god, for the LORD, whose name is Jealous,[7067] is a jealous God—[410]

15 lest you make a covenant with the inhabitants of the land and they play the harlot[2181] with their gods,[430] and [a]sacrifice[2076] to their gods, and someone [b]invite you [I]to eat of his sacrifice;[2077]

🔑 16 and [a]you take some of his daughters for your sons, and his daughters play the harlot with their gods, and cause your sons *also* to play the harlot with their gods.

17 "[a]You shall make for yourself no molten gods.

18 "You shall observe[8104] [a]the Feast[2282] of Unleavened Bread. For [b]seven days you are to eat unleavened bread, [I]as I commanded you, at the appointed time[4150] in the [c]month of Abib, for in the month of Abib you came out of Egypt.

19 "[a]The first offspring from every womb[7358] belongs to Me, and all your male livestock, the first offspring from [I]cattle and sheep.

20 "[a]And you shall redeem[6299] with a lamb the [I]first offspring from a donkey; and if you do not redeem *it,* then you shall break its neck. You shall redeem [b]all the first-born of your sons. And [II][c]none shall appear[7200] before Me empty-handed.

21 "You shall work [a]six days, but on the seventh day you shall rest;[7673] *even* during plowing time and harvest you shall rest.

22 "And you shall celebrate [a]the Feast of Weeks, *that is,* the first fruits of the wheat harvest, and the Feast of Ingathering at the turn of the year.

🔑 23 "[a]Three times a year all your males are to appear before the Lord[113] [I]GOD, the God[430] of Israel.

24 "For I will [I][a]drive out nations[1471] before you and enlarge your borders, and no man shall covet[2530] your land when you go up three times a year to appear before the LORD your God.

25 "[a]You shall not [I]offer the blood[1818] of My sacrifice with leavened[2557] bread, [b]nor is the sacrifice of the Feast of the Passover[6453] to [II]be left over until morning.

26 "You shall bring [a]the very first[7225] of the first fruits of your soil[127] into the house[1004] of the LORD your God. You shall not boil a kid in its mother's milk."

27 Then the LORD said to Moses, "[a]Write [I]down these words, for in accordance with these words I have made[3772] [b]a covenant with you and with Israel."

28 So he was there with the LORD [a]forty days and forty nights; he did not eat bread or drink water. And [b]he wrote on the tablets the words of the covenant, [c]the Ten [I]Commandments.[1697]

Moses' Face Shines

29 And it came about when Moses was coming down from Mount Sinai (and the [a]two tablets of the testimony[5715] *were* in Moses' hand as he was coming down from the mountain), that Moses did not know[3045] that [b]the skin[5785] of his face shone because of his speaking[1696] with Him.

30 So when Aaron and all the sons of Israel saw[7200] Moses, behold, the skin of his face shone, and [a]they were afraid[3372] to come near[5066] him.

31 Then Moses called[7121] to them,

11 [I]Lit., *Observe for yourself* [a]Ex. 33:2
12 [a]Ex. 23:32, 33
13 [I]I.e., wooden symbols of a female deity [a]Ex. 23:24; Deut. 12:3 [b]Deut. 16:21; Judg. 6:25, 26; 2Kin. 18:4; 2Chr. 34:3f.
14 [a]Ex. 20:3, 5; Deut. 4:24
15 [I]Lit., *and you eat* [a]Ex. 22:20; 32:8 [b]Num. 25:1, 2; Deut. 32:37, 38
16 [a]Deut. 7:3; Josh. 23:12, 13; 1Kin. 11:1-4
17 [a]Ex. 20:4, 23; Lev. 19:4; Deut. 5:8
18 [I]Or, *which* [a]Ex. 12:17; Lev. 23:6; Num. 28:16f. [b]Ex. 12:15, 16 [c]Ex. 12:2; 13:4
19 [I]Or, *oxen* [a]Ex. 13:2; 22:29f.
20 [I]Lit., *first opening of* [II]Lit., *they shall not* [a]Ex. 13:13 [b]Ex. 13:15; Num. 3:45 [c]Ex. 22:29; 23:15; Deut. 16:16
21 [a]Ex. 20:9f.; 23:12; 31:15; 35:2; Lev. 23:3; Deut. 5:13f.
22 [a]Ex. 23:16; Num. 28:26
23 [I]Heb., *YHWH,* usually rendered *LORD* [a]Ex. 23:14-17
24 [I]Or, *dispossess* [a]Ex. 33:2; Ps. 78:55
25 [I]Lit., *slaughter* [II]Lit., *remain overnight* [a]Ex. 23:18 [b]Ex. 12:10
26 [a]Ex. 23:19; Deut. 26:2
27 [I]Lit., *for yourself* [a]Ex. 17:14; 24:4 [b]Ex. 34:10
28 [I]Lit., *Words* [a]Ex. 24:18 [b]Ex. 31:18; 34:1 [c]Deut. 4:13; 10:4
29 [a]Ex. 32:15 [b]Matt. 17:2; 2Cor. 3:7
30 [a]2Cor. 3:7

🔑 **34:16** Since Israel was married to Jehovah, idolatry was tantamount to adultery.
🔑 **34:23** See note at Ex. 23:14-17.

and Aaron and all the rulers[5387] in the congregation[5712] returned to him; and Moses spoke[1696] to them.

32 And afterward all the sons of Israel came near,[5066] and he commanded[6680] them *to do* everything that the LORD had spoken[1696] [I]to him on Mount Sinai.

33 When Moses had finished[3615] speaking[1696] with them, [a]he put a veil over his face.

34 But whenever Moses went in before the LORD to speak with Him, [a]he would take off the veil until he came out; and whenever he came out and spoke to the sons of Israel what he had been commanded,

35 [a]the sons of Israel would see the face of Moses, that the skin of Moses' face shone. So Moses would replace[7725] the veil over his face until he went in to speak with Him.

The Sabbath Emphasized

35 Then Moses assembled[6950] all the congregation[5712] of the sons[1121] of Israel, and said to them, "[a]These are the things[1697] that the LORD has commanded[6680] *you* to [I]do.

2 "[a]For six days[3117] work[4399] may be done,[6213] but on the seventh day[3117] you shall have a holy *day,*[6944] [b]a sabbath[7676] of complete rest[7677] to the LORD; [c]whoever does any work on it shall be put to death.

3 "[a]You shall not kindle a fire in any of your dwellings[4186] on the sabbath day."

4 And Moses spoke to all the congregation of the sons of Israel, saying, "This is the thing[1697] which the LORD has commanded, saying,

5 '[a]Take from among you a [I]contribution[8641] to the LORD; whoever is of a willing[5081] heart,[3820] let him bring it as the LORD's [I]contribution: gold, silver, and [II]bronze,

6 and [I]blue, purple and scarlet *material,* fine linen, goats' *hair,*

7 and rams' skins [I]dyed red, and porpoise skins, and acacia wood,

8 and oil[8081] for lighting,[3974] and spices for the anointing[4888] oil, and for the fragrant incense,[7004]

9 and onyx stones and setting stones, for the ephod and for the [I]breastpiece.

Tabernacle Workmen

10 'And [a]let every skillful[2450] man among you come, and make[6213] all that the LORD has commanded:

11 the [I][a]tabernacle,[4908] its tent[168] and its covering, its hooks[7165] and its boards, its bars, its pillars, and its [II]sockets;

12 the [a]ark[727] and its poles, the [I]mercy seat,[3727] and the curtain of the screen;

13 the [a]table and its poles, and all its [I]utensils, and the bread of the [II]Presence;

14 the [a]lampstand also for the light and its utensils and its lamps[5216] and the oil for the light;

15 and the [a]altar[4196] of incense and its poles, and the [b]anointing oil and the [c]fragrant incense, and the screen for the doorway at the [I]entrance of the tabernacle;

16 [a]the altar of burnt offering[5930] with its [I]bronze grating, its poles, and all its [II]utensils, the [III]basin[3595] and its stand;

17 [a]the hangings of the court, its pillars and its [I]sockets, and the screen for the gate of the court;

18 the pegs of the tabernacle and the pegs of the court and their cords;

19 the [I][a]woven garments, for ministering[8334] in the holy[6944] place, the holy garments for Aaron the priest,[3548] and the garments of his sons, to minister as priests.' "

Gifts Received

20 Then all the congregation of the sons of Israel departed from Moses' presence.

21 And [a]everyone[376] whose heart [I]stirred him and everyone whose

---

32 [I]Lit., *with*
33 [a]2Cor. 3:13
34 [a]2Cor. 3:16
35 [a]2Cor. 3:13
1 [I]Lit., *do them.* [a]Ex. 34:32
2 [a]Ex. 20:9, 10; 23:12; 31:15; 34:21; Lev. 23:3; Deut. 5:13f. [b]Ex. 16:23 [c]Num. 15:32-36
3 [a]Ex. 12:16; 16:23
5 [I]Or, *heave offering* [II]Or, *copper* [a]Ex. 25:1-9
6 [I]Or, *violet*
7 [I]Or, *tanned*
9 [I]Or, *pouch*
10 [a]Ex. 31:6
11 [I]Lit., *dwelling place* [II]Or, *bases* [a]Ex. 26:1-30
12 [I]Lit., *propitiatory* [a]Ex. 25:10-22
13 [I]Or, *vessels* [II]Lit., *Face* [a]Ex. 25:23-30
14 [a]Ex. 25:31ff.
15 [I]Or, *doorway* [a]Ex. 30:1-6 [b]Ex. 30:25 [c]Ex. 30:34-38
16 [I]Or, *copper* [II]Or, *vessels* [III]Or, *laver* [a]Ex. 27:1-8
17 [I]Or, *bases* [a]Ex. 27:9-18
19 [I]Or, *service garments* [a]Ex. 31:10; 39:1
21 [I]Lit., *lifted up* [a]Ex. 25:2; 35:5, 22, 26, 29; 36:2

spirit[7307] [II]moved[5068] him came *and*
brought the LORD's [III]contribution for
the work of the tent[168] of meeting[4150]
and for all its service[5656] and for the
holy garments.
22 Then all [I]whose hearts moved
them, both men[582] and women, came
and brought brooches and [II]earrings and
signet rings and bracelets,[3558] all articles
of gold; so *did* every man[376] who
[III]presented an offering[5130] of gold to the
LORD.
23 And every man, [I]who had in his
possession [II]blue and purple and scarlet
material and fine linen and goats' *hair*
and rams' skins [III]dyed red and porpoise
skins, brought them.
24 Everyone who could make a
[I]contribution of silver and [II]bronze
brought the LORD's [I]contribution; and
every man, [III]who had in his possession
acacia wood for any work of the service,
brought it.
25 And all the [I]skilled women spun
with their hands,[3027] and brought what
they had spun, *in* [II]blue and purple *and*
scarlet *material* and *in* fine linen.
26 And all the women whose heart
[I]stirred with a skill[2451] spun the goats'
hair.
27 And the rulers[5387] brought the
onyx stones and the stones for setting
for the ephod and for the [I]breastpiece;
28 and [a]the spice and the oil for the
light and for the anointing oil and for
the fragrant incense.
29 The [I]Israelites, all the men and
women, whose heart [II]moved[6213] them
to bring *material* for all the work, which
the LORD had commanded through Moses to be done, brought a [a]freewill
offering[5071] to the LORD.
30 [a]Then Moses said to the sons
of Israel, "See,[7200] the LORD has called
by name Bezalel the son of Uri, the
son of Hur, of the tribe[4294] of Judah.
31 "And He has filled him with the
Spirit of God,[430] in wisdom, in understanding[8394] and in knowledge[1847] and in
all [I]craftsmanship;
32 [I]to make designs for working[4284]
in gold and in silver and in [II]bronze,
33 and in the cutting of stones for
settings, and in the carving of wood,
so as to perform in every inventive[4284]
work.
34 "He also has put in his heart to
teach,[3384] both he and [a]Oholiab, the son
of Ahisamach, of the tribe of Dan.
35 "[a]He has filled them with [I]skill
to perform every work of an engraver
and of a designer[2803] and of an embroiderer, in [II]blue and in purple *and* in scarlet *material,* and in fine linen, and of a
weaver, as performers of every work
and makers[2803] of designs.

The Tabernacle Underwritten

36 "Now Bezalel and Oholiab, and
every [I]skillful[3820] person in whom
the LORD has put [II]skill[2451] and
understanding[8394] to know[3045] how to
perform[6213] all the work[4399] [III]in the
construction[5656] of the sanctuary, shall
perform in accordance with all that the
LORD has commanded."[6688]
2 Then Moses called Bezalel and
Oholiab and every [I]skillful person in
[II]whom the LORD had put [III]skill, [a]every-
one whose heart stirred him, to come
to the work to perform it.
3 And they received from Moses all
the [I]contributions[8641] which the sons[1121]
of Israel had brought [II]to perform the
work [III]in the construction of the sanctuary.[6944] And they still *continued* bringing to him freewill offerings[5071] every
morning.
4 And all the [I]skillful men who were
performing[6213] all the work of the sanctuary came, each from [II]the work which
[III]he was performing,
5 and they said to [I]Moses, "[a]The
people[5971] are bringing much more than
enough for the [II]construction work which
the LORD commanded *us* to [III]perform."
6 So Moses issued a command,[6680]
and a [I]proclamation was circulated[5674]
throughout the camp, saying, "Let neither man nor woman any longer
perform[6213] work for the [II]contributions
of the sanctuary." Thus the people were
restrained from bringing *any more.*

21 [II]Or, *made him willing* [III]Or, *heave offering*
22 [I]Or, *who were willing-hearted* [II]Or, *nose rings* [III]Lit., *waved a wave offering*
23 [I]Lit., *with whom was found* [II]Or, *violet* [III]Or, *tanned*
24 [I]Or, *heave offering* [II]Or, *copper* [III]Lit., *with whom was found*
25 [I]Lit., *women wise of heart* [II]Or, *violet*
26 [I]Lit., *lifted them up in wisdom*
27 [I]Or, *pouch*
28 [a]Ex. 30:23ff.
29 [I]Lit., *sons of Israel* [II]Lit., *made them willing* [a]Ex. 35:21; 1Chr. 29:9
30 [a]Ex. 31:1-6
31 [I]Or, *work*
32 [I]Lit., *devise devices* [II]Or, *copper*
34 [a]Ex. 31:6
35 [I]Lit., *wisdom of heart* [II]Or, *violet* [a]Ex. 31:3, 6; 35:31; 1Kin. 7:14

1 [I]Lit., *man wise of heart* [II]Lit., *wisdom* [III]Or, *connected with the service of;* lit., *of the service of*
2 [I]Lit., *man wise of heart* [II]Lit., *whose heart* [III]Lit., *wisdom* [a]Ex. 35:21, 26
3 [I]Lit., *lifted offering* [II]Lit., *to perform it for the work* [III]Lit., *of the service of*
4 [I]Lit., *wise* [II]Lit., *his* [III]Lit., *they were*
5 [I]Lit., *Moses, saying,* [II]Lit., *service for the work* [III]Lit., *perform it* [a]2Chr. 24:14; 31:6-10
6 [I]Lit., *voice* [II]Lit., *heave offering*

7 [a]For the [I]material they had was sufficient and more than enough for all the work, to perform it.

Construction Proceeds

8 [a]And all the [I]skillful men among those who were performing the work made the [II]tabernacle[4908] with ten curtains; of fine twisted linen and [III]blue and purple and scarlet *material,* with cherubim,[3742] the work of a skillful workman,[4399] [IV]Bezalel made them.

9 The length of each curtain was twenty-eight [I]cubits, and the width of each curtain four [I]cubits; all the curtains had [II]the same measurements.

10 And he [I]joined five curtains to one another, and *the other* five curtains he [I]joined to one another.

11 And he made loops of [I]blue on the edge[8193] of the [II]outermost curtain in the first [III]set; he did likewise on the edge of the curtain that was [II]outermost in the second [III]set.

12 He made [a]fifty loops in the one curtain and he made fifty loops on the [I]edge of the curtain that was in the second [II]set; the loops were opposite each other.

13 And he made [a]fifty clasps[7165] of gold, and [I]joined the curtains to one another with the clasps, so the tabernacle was [II]a unit.

14 Then [a]he made curtains of goats' *hair* for a tent[168] over the tabernacle; he made eleven curtains [I]in all.

15 The length of each curtain was thirty cubits, and four cubits the width of each curtain; the eleven curtains had [I]the same measurements.

16 And he [I]joined five curtains by themselves, and *the other* six curtains by themselves.

17 Moreover, he made fifty loops on the edge of the curtain that was outermost in the *first* [I]set, and he made fifty loops on the edge of the curtain *that was outermost in* the second [I]set.

18 And he made fifty clasps of [I]bronze to [II]join the tent together, that it might be [III]a unit.

19 And he made a covering for the tent of rams' skins [I]dyed red, and a covering of porpoise skins above.

20 [a]Then he made the boards for the tabernacle of acacia wood, standing upright.

21 Ten cubits was the length of [I]each board, and one and a half cubits the width of each board.

22 There were two tenons[3027] for each board, [I]fitted to one another; thus he did for all the boards of the tabernacle.

23 And he made the boards for the tabernacle: twenty boards [I]for the south side;

24 and he made forty [I]sockets of silver under the twenty boards; two [I]sockets under one board for its two tenons and two [I]sockets under another board for its two tenons.

25 Then for the second side of the tabernacle, on the north side, he made twenty boards,

26 and their forty [I]sockets of silver; two [I]sockets under one board and two [I]sockets under another board.

27 And for the [I]rear of the tabernacle, to the west, he made six boards.

28 And he made two boards for the corners of the [I]tabernacle at the [II]rear.

29 And they were double beneath, and together they were complete to its [I]top[7218] [II]to the first ring; thus he did with both of them for the two corners.

30 And there were eight boards with their [I]sockets of silver, sixteen [I]sockets, [II]two under every board.

31 Then he made [a]bars of acacia wood, five for the boards of one side of the tabernacle,

32 and five bars for the boards of the [I]other side of the tabernacle, and five bars for the boards of the tabernacle for the [II]rear *side* to the west.

33 And he made the middle bar to pass through in the [I]center of the boards from end to end.

34 And he overlaid the boards with gold and made their rings of gold *as* holders for the bars, and overlaid the bars with gold.

7 [I]Lit., *work* [a]1Kin. 8:64
8 [I]Lit., *wise of heart* [II]Lit., *dwelling place* [III]Or, *violet* [IV]Lit., *he* [a]Ex. 26:1-14
9 [I]I.e., One cubit equals approx. 18 in. [II]Lit., *one measure*
10 [I]Or, *coupled*
11 [I]Or, *violet* [II]Lit., *one curtain from the end in the coupling* [III]Lit., *coupling*
12 [I]Lit., *end* [II]Lit., *coupling* [a]Ex. 26:5
13 [I]Or, *coupled* [II]Lit., *one* [a]Ex. 26:6
14 [I]Lit., *in number* [a]Ex. 26:7-14
15 [I]Lit., *one measure*
16 [I]Or, *coupled*
17 [I]Lit., *coupling*
18 [I]Or, *copper* [II]Or, *couple* [III]Lit., *one*
19 [I]Or, *tanned*
20 [a]Ex. 26:15-29
21 [I]Lit., *the*
22 [I]Lit., *bound*
23 [I]Lit., *to the side of the Negev, to the south*
24 [I]Or, *bases*
26 [I]Or, *bases*
27 [I]Lit., *extreme parts*
28 [I]Lit., *dwelling place* [II]Lit., *extreme parts*
29 [I]Or, *head* [II]Or, *with reference to*
30 [I]Or, *bases* [II]Lit., *two sockets*
31 [a]Ex. 26:26-29
32 [I]Or, *second* [II]Lit., *extreme parts*
33 [I]Lit., *midst*

35 [a]Moreover, he made the veil of
[I]blue and purple and scarlet *material,*
and fine twisted linen; he made it with
cherubim, the work of a skillful workman.
36 And he made four pillars of acacia
for it, and overlaid them with gold, with
their hooks of gold; and he cast four
[I]sockets of silver for them.
37 And he made a [a]screen for the
doorway of the tent,[168] of [I]blue and purple and scarlet *material,* and fine twisted
linen, the work of a [II]weaver;
38 and *he made* its [a]five pillars with
their hooks, and he overlaid their
tops[7218] and their [I]bands[2838] with gold;
but their five [II]sockets were of [III]bronze.

Construction Continues

37 [a]Now Bezalel made[6213] the ark[727]
of acacia wood; its length was
two and a half [I]cubits, and its width one
and a half cubits, and its height one and
a half cubits;
2 and he overlaid it with pure[2889]
gold inside and out, and made a gold
molding for it all around.
3 And he cast four rings of gold for
it on its four feet; even two rings on
one side of it, and two rings on the
[I]other side of it.
4 And he made poles of acacia wood
and overlaid them with gold.
5 And he put the poles into the rings
on the sides of the ark, to carry[5375]
[I]it.
6 And he made a [I]mercy seat[3727]
of pure gold, two and a half cubits
[II]long, and one and a half cubits [III]wide.
7 And he made[6213] two cherubim[3742]
of gold; he made them of hammered
work, [I]at the two ends of the mercy
seat;
8 one cherub[3742] [I]at the one end,
and one cherub [I]at the other end; he
made the cherubim *of one piece* with the
mercy seat [I]at the two ends.
9 And the cherubim had *their* wings
spread upward, covering the [I]mercy
seat with their wings, with their faces
toward each other; the faces of the
cherubim were toward the mercy seat.
10 [a]Then he made the table of acacia wood, two [I]cubits [II]long and a cubit
[III]wide and one and a half cubits [IV]high.
11 And he overlaid it with pure gold,
and made a gold molding for it all around.
12 And he made a rim for it of a
handbreadth all around, and made a gold
molding for its rim all around.
13 And he cast four gold rings for
it and put the rings on the four corners
that were on its four feet.
14 Close by the rim were the rings,
the holders for the poles to carry the
table.
15 And he made the poles of acacia
wood and overlaid them with gold, to
carry the table.
16 And he made the utensils which
were on the table, its [I]dishes and its
pans[3709] and its [II]bowls and its jars, with
which to pour out libations, of pure gold.
17 [a]Then he made the lampstand
of pure gold. He made the lampstand
of hammered work, its base and its
shaft;[3409] its cups, its [I]bulbs and its flowers were *of one piece* with it.
18 And there were six branches going out of its sides; three branches of
the lampstand from the one side of it,
and three branches of the lampstand
from the [I]other side of it;
19 three cups shaped like almond
blossoms, a [I]bulb and a flower in one
branch, and three cups shaped like almond *blossoms,* a [I]bulb and a flower in
the other branch—so for the six
branches going out of the lampstand.
20 And in the lampstand *there were*
four cups shaped like almond *blossoms,*
its [I]bulbs and its flowers;
21 and a [I]bulb was under the *first*
pair of branches *coming* out of it, and
a [I]bulb under the *second* pair of branches
coming out of it, and a [I]bulb under the
third pair of branches *coming* out of it,
for the six branches coming out of the
lampstand.
22 Their [I]bulbs and their branches
were *of one piece* with it; the whole of
it *was* a single hammered work of pure
gold.

35 [I]Or, *violet* [a]Ex. 26:31-37
36 [I]Or, *bases*
37 [I]Or, *violet* [II]Lit., *variegator;* i.e., a weaver in colors [a]Ex. 26:36
38 [I]Or, *fillets, rings* [II]Or, *bases* [III]Or, *copper* [a]Ex. 26:37
1 [I]I.e., One cubit equals approx. 18 in. [a]Ex. 25:10-20
3 [I]Lit., *second*
5 [I]Lit., *the ark*
6 [I]Lit., *propitiatory* [II]Lit., *its length* [III]Lit., *its width*
7 [I]Lit., *from*
8 [I]Lit., *from*
9 [I]Lit., *propitiatory*
10 [I]I.e., One cubit equals approx. 18 in. [II]Lit., *its length* [III]Lit., *its width* [IV]Lit., *its height* [a]Ex. 25:23-29
16 [I]Or, *platters* [II]Lit., *libation bowls*
17 [I]Or, *calyxes* [a]Ex. 25:31-39
18 [I]Lit., *second*
19 [I]Or, *calyx*
20 [I]Or, *calyxes*
21 [I]Or, *calyx*
22 [I]Or, *calyxes*

23 And he made its seven lamps[5216] with its snuffers and its [I]trays of pure gold.

24 He made it and all its utensils from a talent of pure gold.

25 [a]Then he made the altar[4196] of incense[7004] of acacia wood: a cubit [I]long and a cubit [II]wide, square, and two cubits [III]high; its horns were *of one piece* with it.

26 And he overlaid it with pure gold, its top and its [I]sides all around, and its horns; and he made a gold molding for it all around.

27 And he made two golden rings for it under its molding, on its two sides—on opposite sides—as holders for poles with which to carry it.

28 And he made the poles of acacia wood and overlaid them with gold.

29 [a]And he made the holy[6944] anointing[4888] oil[8081] and the pure, fragrant incense of spices, the work of a perfumer.[7543]

The Tabernacle Completed

38 [a]Then he made[6213] the altar[4196] of burnt offering[5930] of acacia wood, five [I]cubits [II]long, and five cubits [III]wide, square, and three cubits [IV]high.

2 And he made its horns on its four corners, its horns [I]being *of one piece* with it, and he overlaid it with [II]bronze.

3 And he made[6213] all the utensils of the altar, the pails and the shovels and the basins,[4219] the flesh hooks and the firepans; he made all its utensils of bronze.

4 And he made for the altar a grating of bronze network beneath, under its ledge, reaching halfway up.

5 And he cast four rings on the four ends of the bronze grating *as* holders for the poles.

6 And he made the poles of acacia wood and overlaid them with bronze.

7 And he inserted the poles into the rings on the sides of the altar, with which to carry[5375] it. He made it hollow with planks.

8 [a]Moreover, he made the laver[3595] of bronze with its base of bronze, [I]from the mirrors[4759] of the serving[6633] women who served at the doorway of the tent[168] of meeting.[4150]

9 [a]Then he made the court: [I]for the south side the hangings of the court were of fine twisted linen, one hundred cubits;

10 their twenty pillars, and their twenty [I]sockets, *made* of bronze; the hooks of the pillars and their [II]bands[2838] *were* of silver.

11 And for the north side *there were* one hundred cubits; their twenty pillars and their twenty [I]sockets *were* of bronze, the hooks of the pillars and their [II]bands *were* of silver.

12 And for the west side *there were* hangings of fifty cubits *with* their ten pillars and their ten [I]sockets; the hooks of the pillars and their [II]bands *were* of silver.

13 And for the [I]east side fifty cubits.

14 The hangings for the *one* [I]side *of the gate were* fifteen cubits, *with* their three pillars and their three [II]sockets,

15 and so for the [I]other [II]side. [III]On both sides of the gate of the court *were* hangings of fifteen cubits, *with* their three pillars and their three [IV]sockets.

16 All the hangings of the court all around *were* of fine twisted linen.

17 And the [I]sockets for the pillars *were* of [II]bronze, the hooks of the pillars and their [III]bands, of silver; and the overlaying of their tops,[7218] of silver, and all the pillars of the court were furnished with silver [III]bands.[2836]

18 And the screen of the gate of the court was the work of the [I]weaver, of [II]blue and purple and scarlet *material*, and fine twisted linen. And the length was twenty cubits and the [III]height was five cubits, corresponding to the hangings of the court.

19 And their four pillars and their four [I]sockets *were* of bronze; their hooks *were* of silver, and the overlaying of their tops and their [II]bands *were* of silver.

20 And all the pegs of the [I]tabernacle[4908] and of the court all around *were* of bronze.

---

23 [I]Lit., *snuff dishes*

25 [I]Lit., *its length* [II]Lit., *its width* [III]Lit., *its height* [a]Ex. 30:1-5

26 [I]Lit., *walls*

29 [a]Ex. 30:23-25, 34, 35

1 [I]I.e., One cubit equals approx. 18 in. [II]Lit., *its length* [III]Lit., *its width* [IV]Lit., *its height* [a]Ex. 27:1-8

2 [I]Lit., *were* [II]Or, *copper*, and so for *bronze* throughout the ch.

8 [I]Lit., *with* [a]Ex. 30:18

9 [I]Lit., *to the side of the Negev, to the south* [a]Ex. 27:9-19

10 [I]Or, *bases* [II]Or, *fillets, rings*

11 [I]Or, *bases* [II]Or, *fillets, rings*

12 [I]Or, *bases* [II]Or, *fillets, rings*

13 [I]Lit., *east side, eastward*

14 [I]Lit., *shoulder* [II]Or, *bases*

15 [I]Lit., *second* [II]Lit., *shoulder* [III]Lit., *On this side and on that side* [IV]Or, *bases*

17 [I]Or, *bases* [II]Or, *copper* [III]Or, *fillets, rings*

18 [I]Lit., *variegator;* i.e., a weaver in colors [II]Or, *violet* [III]Lit., *height in width*

19 [I]Or, *bases* [II]Or, *fillets, rings*

20 [I]Lit., *dwelling place*

The Cost of the Tabernacle

21 [I]This is the number[6485] of *the*
things for the [II]tabernacle, the [II]taberna-
cle of the testimony,[5715] as they were
[III]numbered[6485] according to the [IV]com-
mand[6310] of Moses, for the service[5656]
of the Levites, by the hand[3027] of Ithamar, the son of Aaron the priest.[3548]
22 Now [a]Bezalel, the son of Uri the
son of Hur, of the tribe[4294] of Judah,
made all that the LORD had commanded[6680] Moses.
23 And with him was [a]Oholiab, the
son of Ahisamach, of the tribe of Dan,
an engraver and a skillful workman and
a [I]weaver in [II]blue and in purple and in
scarlet *material,* and fine linen.
24 All the gold that was used[6213]
for the work, in all the work of the sanctuary,[6944] even the gold of the wave offering, was 29 talents and 730 shekels,
according to [a]the shekel of the sanctuary.
25 [a]And the silver of those of the
congregation[5712] who were [I]num-
bered[6485] was 100 talents and 1,775
shekels, according to the shekel of the
sanctuary;[6944]
26 [a]a beka a head (*that is,* half a
shekel according to the shekel of the
sanctuary), for each one who passed[5674]
over to those who were [I]numbered,
from twenty years old[1121] and upward,
for [b]603,550 men.
27 And the hundred talents of silver
were for casting the [I]sockets of the sanctuary and the [I]sockets of the veil; one
hundred [I]sockets for the hundred talents, a talent for a [I]socket.
28 And of the 1,775 *shekels,* he
made hooks for the pillars and overlaid
their tops and made [I]bands for them.
29 And the bronze of the wave offering was 70 talents, and 2,400 shekels.
30 And with it he made the [I]sockets
to the doorway of the tent of meeting,
and the bronze altar and its bronze grating, and all the utensils of the altar,
31 and the [I]sockets of the court all
around and the [I]sockets of the gate of
the court, and all the pegs of the
[II]tabernacle and all the pegs of the court
all around.

The Priestly Garments

39 Moreover, from the [I][a]blue and
purple and scarlet *material,* they
made[6213] finely [b]woven garments for
ministering[8334] in the holy[6944] place,
[II]as well as the holy garments which
were for Aaron, just as the LORD had
commanded[6680] Moses.
2 [a]And he made the ephod of gold,
and of [I]blue and purple and scarlet *ma-*
terial, and fine twisted linen.
3 Then they hammered out gold
sheets and cut *them* into threads
[I]to be woven[6213] in *with* the [II]blue and
the purple and the scarlet *material,* and
the fine linen, the work of a skillful workman.
4 They made attaching shoulder
pieces for [I]the ephod; it was attached
at its two *upper* ends.
5 And the skillfully woven band[2805]
which was on it was like its workmanship, [I]of the same material: of gold *and*
of [II]blue and purple and scarlet *material,*
and fine twisted linen, just as the LORD
had commanded Moses.
6 And [a]they made the onyx stones,
set in gold filigree *settings;*[4865] they were
engraved *like* the engravings of a signet,
according to the names of the sons[1121]
of Israel.
7 And [a]he placed them on the shoulder pieces of the ephod, *as* memorial[2146]
stones for the sons of Israel, just as
the LORD had commanded Moses.
8 [a]And he made the breastpiece, the
work of a skillful workman, like the
workmanship of the ephod: of gold *and*
of [I]blue and purple and scarlet *material*
and fine twisted linen.
9 It was square; they made the
breastpiece folded double, a span
[I]long and a span [II]wide when folded double.
10 And they [I]mounted four rows of
stones on it. The first row *was* a row
of ruby, topaz, and emerald;

21 [I]Lit., *These are the appointed things of the tabernacle* [II]Lit., *dwelling place* [III]Lit., *appointed* [IV]Lit., *mouth*

22 [a]Ex. 31:2

23 [I]Lit., *variegator;* i.e., a weaver in colors [II]Or, *violet* [a]Ex. 31:6

24 [a]Ex. 30:13; Lev. 27:25; Num. 3:47; 18:16

25 [I]Lit., *mustered* [a]Ex. 30:11-16

26 [I]Lit., *mustered* [a]Ex. 30:13, 15 [b]Ex. 12:37; Num. 1:46; 26:51

27 [I]Or, *bases*

28 [I]Or, *fillets, rings*

30 [I]Or, *bases*

31 [I]Or, *bases* [II]Lit., *dwelling place*

1 [I]Or, *violet* [II]Lit., *and they made* [a]Ex. 35:23 [b]Ex. 31:10; 35:19

2 [I]Or, *violet* [a]Ex. 28:6-12

3 [I]Lit., *to work* [II]Or, *violet*

4 [I]Lit., *it*

5 [I]Lit., *from it* [II]Or, *violet*

6 [a]Ex. 28:9-11

7 [a]Ex. 28:12

8 [I]Or, *violet* [a]Ex. 28:15-28

9 [I]Lit., *its length* [II]Lit., *its width*

10 [I]Lit., *filled*

11 and the second row, a turquoise, a sapphire and a diamond;

12 and the third row, a jacinth, an agate, and an amethyst;

13 and the fourth row, a beryl, an onyx, and a jasper. They were set in gold filigree *settings* when they were [I]mounted.

14 And the stones were corresponding to the names of the sons of Israel; they were twelve, corresponding to their names, *engraved with* the engravings of a signet, each with its name for the twelve tribes.[7626]

15 And they made on the breastpiece chains like cords, of twisted[5688] cordage work in pure[2889] gold.

16 And they made two gold filigree *settings* and two gold rings, and put the two rings on the two ends of the breastpiece.

17 Then they put the two gold cords in the two rings at the ends of the breastpiece.

18 And they put the *other* two ends of the two cords on the two filigree *settings,* and put them on the shoulder pieces of the ephod at the front of it.

19 And they made two gold rings and placed *them* on the two ends of the breastpiece, on its inner[1004] edge[8193] which was next to the ephod.

20 Furthermore, they made two gold rings and placed them on the bottom of the two shoulder pieces of the ephod, on the front of it, close to the place where it joined, above the woven band of the ephod.

21 And they bound the breastpiece by its rings to the rings of the ephod with a [I]blue cord, that it might be on the woven band of the ephod, and that the breastpiece might not come loose from the ephod, just as the LORD had commanded Moses.

22 [a]Then he made the robe of the ephod of woven work, all[3632] of [I]blue;

23 [a]and the opening[6310] of the robe was *at the top* in the center, as the opening of a coat of mail,[8473] with a binding[8193] all around its opening, that it might not be torn.

24 And they made pomegranates of [I]blue and purple and scarlet *material and* twisted *linen* on the hem of the robe.

25 They also made bells of pure gold, and put the bells between the pomegranates all around on the hem of the [I]robe,

26 [I]alternating a bell and a pomegranate all around on the hem of the robe, for the service,[8334] just as the LORD had commanded Moses.

27 [a]And they made the tunics of finely woven linen for Aaron and his sons,

28 and the turban[4701] of fine linen, and the decorated [I]caps of fine linen, and the linen breeches of fine twisted linen,

29 and the sash[73] of fine twisted linen, and [I]blue and purple and scarlet *material,* the work of the [II]weaver, just as the LORD had commanded Moses.

30 [a]And they made the plate of the holy crown[5145] of pure gold, and [I]inscribed it like the engravings of a signet, "Holy[6944] to the LORD."

31 And they [I]fastened a [II]blue cord to it, to [I]fasten it on the turban above, just as the LORD had commanded Moses.

32 Thus all the work[5656] of the [I]tabernacle[4908] of the tent[168] of meeting[4150] was completed;[3615] and the sons of Israel did according to all that the LORD had commanded Moses; so they did.

33 And they brought the tabernacle to Moses, the tent and all its [I]furnishings: its clasps,[7165] its boards, its bars, and its pillars and its [II]sockets;

34 and the covering of rams' skins [I]dyed red, and the covering of porpoise skins, and the screening veil;

35 the ark[727] of the testimony[5715] and its poles and the [I]mercy seat;[3727]

36 the table, all its utensils, and the bread of the [I]Presence;

37 the pure *gold* lampstand, [I]with its arrangement of lamps[5216] and all its utensils, and the oil[8081] for the light;[3974]

38 and the gold altar,[4196] and the anointing[4888] oil and the fragrant

13 [I]Lit., *filled*

21 [I]Or, *violet*

22 [I]Or, *violet* [a]Ex. 28:31, 34

23 [a]Ex. 28:32

24 [I]Or, *violet*

25 [I]Lit., *robe, between the pomegranates*

26 [I]Lit., *a bell and a pomegranate, a bell. . .*

27 [a]Ex. 28:39, 40, 42

28 [I]Lit., *headgear*

29 [I]Or, *violet* [II]Lit., *variegator;* i.e., a weaver in colors

30 [I]Lit., *wrote on it a writing* [a]Ex. 28:36, 37

31 [I]Lit., *put* [II]Or, *violet*

32 [I]Lit., *dwelling place*

33 [I]Or, *utensils* [II]Or, *bases*

34 [I]Or, *tanned*

35 [I]Lit., *propitiatory*

36 [I]Lit., *Face*

37 [I]Lit., *its lamps, the lamps set in order*

incense,[7004] and the veil for the doorway
of the tent;[168]
39 the [I]bronze altar and its [I]bronze
grating, its poles and all its utensils, the
laver[3595] and its stand;
40 the hangings for the court, its
pillars and its [I]sockets, and the screen
for the gate of the court, its cords and
its pegs and all the [II]equipment for the
service[5656] of the tabernacle, for the tent
of meeting;
41 the woven garments for ministering in the holy place and the holy
garments for Aaron the priest[3548] and
the garments of his sons, to minister
as priests.
42 So the sons of Israel did all the
work according to all that the LORD had
commanded Moses.
43 And Moses [I]examined[7200] all the
work[4399] and behold, they had done it;
just as the LORD had commanded, this
they had done. So Moses [a]blessed[1288]
them.

The Tabernacle Erected

40 Then the LORD spoke[1696] to Moses, saying,
2 "[a]On the first day of the first
month you shall set up the [I]taberna-
cle[4908] of the tent[168] of meeting.[4150]
3 "And [a]you shall place the ark[727]
of the testimony[5715] there, and you shall
screen the ark with the veil.
4 "And you shall [a]bring in the table
and [I][b]arrange what belongs on it; and
you shall [c]bring in the lampstand and
[II]mount its lamps.[5216]
5 "Moreover, you shall [a]set the gold
altar[4196] of incense[7004] before the ark
of the testimony, and set up the veil
for the doorway to the tabernacle.
6 "And you shall set the altar of
burnt offering[5930] in front of the doorway
of the tabernacle of the tent of meeting.
7 "And you shall [a]set the laver[3595]
between the tent of meeting and the
altar, and put water [I]in it.
8 "And you shall set up the court
all around and [I]hang up the veil for the
gateway of the court.
9 "Then you shall take the anoint-
ing[4888] oil[8081] and [a]anoint[4886] the tabernacle and all that is in it, and shall consecrate[6942] it and all its [I]furnishings; and
it shall be holy.[6944]
10 "And you shall anoint the altar
of burnt offering and all its utensils, and
consecrate[6942] the altar; and [a]the altar
shall be most holy.
11 "And you shall anoint the laver
and its stand, and consecrate it.
12 "Then you shall [a]bring[7126] Aaron
and his sons[1121] to the doorway of the
tent[168] of meeting and wash[7364] them
with water.
13 "And [a]you shall put the holy garments on Aaron and anoint him and consecrate him, that he may minister as a
priest to Me.
14 "And you shall bring his sons and
put tunics on them;
15 and you shall anoint them even
as you have anointed their father,[1] that
they may minister as priests[3550] to Me;
and their anointing shall [I]qualify them
for a [a]perpetual[5769] priesthood throughout their generations."[1755]
16 Thus Moses did;[6213] according
to all that the LORD had commanded[6680]
him, so he did.
17 Now it came about [a]in the first
month [I]of the second year, on the first
day of the month, that the [II]tabernacle
was erected.
18 And Moses erected the tabernacle and [I]laid its [II]sockets, and set up
its boards, and [I]inserted its bars and
erected its pillars.
19 And he spread the tent over the
tabernacle and put the covering of the
tent [I]on top of it, just as the LORD had
commanded Moses.
20 Then he took [a]the testimony and
put *it* into the ark, and [I]attached the
poles to the ark, and put the [II]mercy
seat[3727] [III]on top of the ark.
21 And he brought the ark into the
tabernacle, and [a]set up a veil for
the screen, and screened off the ark
of the testimony, just as the LORD had
commanded Moses.
22 Then he [a]put the table in the tent

---

39 [I]Or, *copper*
40 [I]Or, *bases* [II]Or, *utensils*
43 [I]Lit., *saw* [a]Lev. 9:22, 23; Num. 6:23-26
2 [I]Lit., *dwelling place* [a]Ex. 19:1; 40:17; Num. 1:1
3 [a]Ex. 26:33; 40:21; Num. 4:5
4 [I]Lit., *arrange its arrangement* [II]Or, *light* [a]Ex. 26:35; 40:22 [b]Ex. 25:30; 40:23 [c]Ex. 40:24f.
5 [a]Ex. 40:26
7 [I]Lit., *there* [a]Ex. 30:18; 40:30
8 [I]Lit., *put the screen*
9 [I]Or, *utensils* [a]Ex. 30:26; Lev. 8:10
10 [a]Ex. 29:37
12 [a]Lev. 8:1-6
13 [a]Ex. 28:41; Lev. 8:13
15 [I]Lit., *be for them* [a]Ex. 29:9; Num. 25:13
17 [I]Lit., *in* [II]Lit., *dwelling place* [a]Ex. 40:2
18 [I]Lit., *put* [II]Or, *bases*
19 [I]Lit., *over it above*
20 [I]Lit., *set* [II]Lit., *propitiatory* [III]Lit., *over the ark above* [a]Ex. 25:16; Deut. 10:5; 1Kin. 8:9; 2Chr. 5:10; Heb. 9:4
21 [a]Ex. 26:33
22 [a]Ex. 26:35

of meeting, on the north side[3409] of the tabernacle, outside the veil.

23 And he set the arrangement of [a]bread in order on it before the LORD, just as the LORD had commanded Moses.

24 Then he placed the lampstand in the tent of meeting, opposite the table, on the south side of the tabernacle.

25 And he [a]lighted[5927] the lamps before the LORD, just as the LORD had commanded Moses.

26 Then he [a]placed the gold altar in the tent of meeting in front of the veil;

27 and he [a]burned[6999] fragrant incense on it, just as the LORD had commanded Moses.

28 Then he set up the [I]veil for the doorway of the tabernacle.

29 And he [a]set the altar of burnt offering *before* the doorway of the tabernacle of the tent of meeting, and [b]offered[5927] on it the burnt offering and the meal offering,[4503] just as the LORD had commanded Moses.

30 And he placed the laver between the tent of meeting and the altar, and put water in it for washing.

31 [a]And from it Moses and Aaron and his sons washed their hands[3027] and their feet.

32 When they entered the tent of meeting, and when they approached[7126] the altar, they washed, just as the LORD had commanded Moses.

33 And he [a]erected the court all around the [I]tabernacle and the altar, and [II]hung up the veil for the gateway of the court. Thus Moses finished[3615] the work.[4399]

The Glory of the LORD

34 [a]Then the cloud[6051] covered[3680] the tent of meeting, and the [b]glory[3519] of the LORD filled the tabernacle.

35 And Moses [a]was not able to enter the tent of meeting because the cloud had settled on it, and the glory of the LORD filled the tabernacle.

36 And throughout all their journeys [a]whenever the cloud was taken up from over the tabernacle, the sons[1121] of Israel would set out;

37 but [a]if the cloud was not taken up, then they did not set out until the day when it was taken up.

38 For throughout all their journeys, [a]the cloud of the LORD was on the tabernacle by day, and there was fire in it by night,[3915] in the sight of all the house[1004] of Israel.

23 [a]Ex. 25:30; Lev. 24:5, 6
25 [a]Ex. 25:37; 40:4
26 [a]Ex. 30:6; 40:5
27 [a]Ex. 30:7
28 [I]Or, *screen*
29 [a]Ex. 40:6 [b]Ex. 29:38-42
31 [a]Ex. 30:19, 20
33 [I]Or, *dwelling place* [II]Lit., *put the screen* [a]Ex. 27:9-18; 40:8
34 [a]Num. 9:15-23 [b]1Kin. 8:11; Ezek. 43:4f.; Rev. 15:8
35 [a]1Kin. 8:11; 2Chr. 5:13, 14
36 [a]Num. 9:17; Neh. 9:19
37 [a]Num. 9:19-22
38 [a]Ex. 13:21; Num. 9:12, 15; Ps. 78:14; Is. 4:5

40:34 Israel had built the sanctuary according to the plans which the Lord had given them. Now "the glory of the Lord filled the tabernacle," indicating that He approved of their work. This glory was seen by Israel in the form of a cloud. This was the same cloud, evidently, by which the Lord Himself went before the people when they came out of Egypt. At night it took the form of a pillar of fire (Ex. 13:21,22). In this form He led them throughout their journey (v. 38). When Solomon had completed the temple (II Chr. 5:13,14) the Lord once again showed His approval when the house of the Lord was filled with the glory of the Lord in the form of a cloud. During the time of Zedekiah that glory departed (Ezek. 11:22,23) never to return. When the second temple was built God promised that the "latter glory of this house shall be greater than the former . . . and in this place I shall give peace" (Hag. 2:9). This was fulfilled in Jesus Christ who referred to His body as the temple (Jn. 2:19-21) and manifested the glory of God seen by men (Jn. 1:14). His Church is His body upon the earth today (Eph. 1:22,23). It is a holy temple unto the Lord in which Christians are built together for a dwelling place of God (Eph. 2:21,22).

LEVITICUS

The Book of Moses is called by the title of "Leviticus," because it records the duties of the Levites. This book describes the role of sacrifice in God's plan. Though mankind has sinned, God will accept a substitute for the death of the sinner. It is a portent of things to come in the New Testament, where Jesus, "the Lamb of God," takes away the sin of the world (Jn. 1:29).

Leviticus contains material which delineates civil, sanitary, ceremonial, moral, and religious laws from God. The main purpose of this book is to show that God is holy and that man is sinful. However, if man will recognize this fact and obey, he is permitted to approach God. Each type of offering was commanded to teach God's way to this new nation.

The Law of Burnt Offerings

1 Then [a]the LORD called[7121] to Moses and spoke to him from the tent[168] of meeting,[4150] saying,[559]

2 "Speak[1696] to the sons[1121] of Israel and say[559] to them, 'When any man[120] of you brings an [1a]offering[7133] to the LORD, you shall bring your [1]offering of animals from [b]the herd or the flock.

3 'If his offering is a [a]burnt offering[5930] from the herd, he shall offer it, a male[2145] [b]without defect;[8549] he shall offer it [c]at the doorway of the tent of meeting, that he may be accepted before the LORD.

4 '[a]And he shall lay his hand[3027] on the head[7218] of the burnt offering,[5930] that it may be accepted[7521] for him to make [b]atonement[3722] on his behalf.

5 'And [a]he shall slay[7819] the [1]young bull before the LORD; and Aaron's sons,[1121] the priests,[3548] shall offer[7126] up [b]the blood[1818] and [c]sprinkle[2236] the blood around on the altar[4196] that is at the doorway of the tent of meeting.

6 '[a]He shall then skin[6584] the burnt offering and cut it into its pieces.

7 '[a]And the sons of Aaron the priest shall put fire on the altar and arrange wood on the fire.

8 'Then Aaron's sons, the priests, shall arrange the pieces, the head, and the [a]suet over the wood which is on the fire that is on the altar.

9 'Its [a]entrails, however, and its legs he shall wash[7364] with water. And [b]the priest shall offer up in smoke[6999] all of it on the altar for a burnt offering, an offering by fire[801] of [c]a soothing aroma to the LORD.

10 'But if his offering is from the flock, of the sheep or of the goats, for a burnt offering, he shall offer it a [a]male without defect.

11 'And [a]he shall slay it on the side[3409] of the altar northward before the LORD, and Aaron's sons, the priests, shall sprinkle its blood around on the altar.

12 'He shall then cut it into its pieces with its head and its [a]suet, and the priest shall arrange them on the wood which is on the fire that is on the altar.

13 'The entrails, however, and the legs he shall wash with water. And [a]the priest shall offer all of it, and offer it up in smoke on the altar; it is a burnt offering, an offering by fire of a soothing aroma to the LORD.

14 'But if his offering to the LORD is a burnt offering of birds, then he shall bring his offering from the [a]turtledoves or from young pigeons.

1 [a]Ex. 19:3; 25:22; Num. 7:89
2 [1]Heb., *qorban* [a]Mark 7:11 [b]Lev. 22:18f.
3 [a]Lev. 6:8-13 [b]Ex. 12:5; Lev. 22:20-24; Deut. 15:21; 17:1 [c]Lev. 17:8, 9; Deut. 12:5, 6, 11
4 [a]Ex. 29:10, 15, 19; Lev. 3:2, 8 [b]Ex. 29:33; Lev. 4:20, 26, 31; 2Chr. 29:23, 24
5 [1]Or, *one of the herd;* lit., *son of the herd* [a]Ex. 29:11, 16, 20 [b]Lev. 17:11 [c]Lev. 1:11; 3:2, 8, 13; Heb. 12:24; 1Pet. 1:2
6 [a]Lev. 7:8
7 [a]Lev. 6:8-13
8 [a]Lev. 1:12; 3:3, 4; 8:20
9 [a]Ex. 12:9 [b]Num. 15:8-10; 28:11-14 [c]Gen. 8:21; Ex. 29:18, 25; Lev. 1:13; Num. 15:3; Eph. 5:2
10 [a]Ex. 12:5; Lev. 1:3; Ezek. 43:22; 1Pet. 1:19
11 [a]Ex. 24:6; Lev. 1:5; 8:19; 9:12
12 [a]Lev. 3:3, 4
13 [a]Num. 15:4-7; 28:11-14
14 [a]Gen. 15:9; Lev. 5:7, 11; 12:8; Luke 2:24

1:1 The fact that Jehovah called Moses is mentioned fifty-six times in the twenty-seven chapters of Leviticus. In the Book of Exodus, God spoke from Mount Sinai, but in the Book of Leviticus He speaks from the Holy of Holies in the tabernacle from above the mercy seat of the ark of the covenant.

1:14-17 This was a poor man's offering. Compare the offering brought by Mary and Joseph to the temple soon after Jesus was born (Lk. 2:24).

15 'And the priest shall bring it to
the altar and wring off its head, and offer
it up in smoke on the altar; and its blood
is to be drained out [a]on the side of the
altar.
16 'He shall also take away[5493] its
crop with its feathers, and cast it beside
the altar eastward, to the place of the
[I][a]ashes.
17 'Then he shall tear it by its wings,
but [a]shall not sever *it*.[914] And the priest
shall offer it up in smoke on the altar
on the wood which is on the fire;
[b]it is a burnt offering, an offering by fire
of a soothing aroma to the LORD.

The Law of Grain Offerings

2 'Now when anyone[5315] presents a
[a]grain[4503] offering[7133] as an offering
to the LORD, his offering shall be of fine
flour, and he shall pour oil[8081] on it and
put frankincense[3828] on it.
2 'He shall then bring it to Aaron's
sons,[1121] the priests;[3548] and shall take
from it [a]his handful of its fine flour and
of its oil with all of its frankincense. And
the priest shall offer *it* up in smoke[6999]
as its [b]memorial portion on the altar,[4196]
an offering by fire of a soothing aroma
to the LORD.
3 'And [a]the remainder[3498] of the
grain offering[4503] belongs to [b]Aaron and
his sons: a thing most holy,[6944] of the
offerings to the LORD by fire.[801]
4 'Now when you bring an offering[7133] of a grain offering baked in an
oven, *it shall be* [a]unleavened cakes of
fine flour mixed[1101] with oil, or unleavened wafers [I]spread[4886] with oil.
5 'And if your offering is a grain offering *made* [a]on the griddle, *it shall be*
of fine flour, unleavened, mixed with
oil;
6 you shall break it into bits, and
pour oil on it; it is a grain offering.
7 'Now if your offering is a grain
offering *made* [a]in a [I]pan, it shall be made
of fine flour with oil.
8 'When you bring[5066] in the grain
offering which is made of these things
to the LORD, it shall be presented[7126]
to the priest and he shall bring it to
the altar.
9 'The priest then shall take up from
the grain offering [a]its memorial portion,
and shall offer *it* up in smoke on the
altar *as* an offering by fire of a soothing
aroma to the LORD.
10 'And [a]the remainder[3498] of the
grain offering belongs to Aaron and his
sons: a thing most holy, of the offerings
to the LORD by fire.
11 '[a]No grain offering, which you
bring to the LORD, shall be made with
leaven,[2557] for you shall not offer [I]up
in smoke any leaven or any honey as
an [b]offering by fire to the LORD.
12 '[a]As an offering of first fruits,[7225]
you shall bring them to the LORD, but
they shall not ascend[5927] for a soothing
aroma on the altar.
13 'Every grain offering of yours,
moreover, you shall season with salt,
so that [a]the salt of the covenant[1285] of
your God[430] shall not be lacking[7673] from
your grain offering; with all your offerings you shall offer salt.
14 'Also if you bring a grain offering
of early ripened things to the LORD, you
shall bring [a]fresh heads of grain roasted
in the fire, grits of new growth, for the
grain offering of your early ripened
things.
15 'You shall then put oil on it and
lay[7760] incense on it; it is a grain offering.
16 'And the priest shall offer up in
smoke [a]its memorial portion, part of its
grits and its oil with all its incense as
an offering by fire to the LORD.

The Law of Peace Offerings

3 'Now if his offering[7133] is a [a]sacri-
fice[2077] of peace offerings,[8002] if he
is going to offer out of the herd, whether
male[2145] or female,[5347] he shall offer it
[b]without defect[8549] before the LORD.
2 '[a]And he shall lay his hand[3027] on
the head of his offering[7133] and [b]slay[7819]
it at the doorway of the tent[168] of
meeting,[4150] and Aaron's sons,[1121]
the priests,[3548] shall sprinkle[2236] the
blood[1818] around on the altar.[4196]

---

15 [a]Lev. 5:9
16 [I]Or, *fat ashes* [a]Lev. 6:10
17 [a]Gen. 15:10; Lev. 5:8 [b]Lev. 9:13

1 [a]Lev. 6:14-18; Num. 15:4
2 [a]Lev. 5:12; 6:15 [b]Lev. 2:9, 16; 5:12; 24:7; Acts 10:4
3 [a]Lev. 2:10; 6:16 [b]Lev. 10:12, 13
4 [I]Lit., *anointed* [a]Ex. 29:2
5 [a]Lev. 6:21; 7:9
7 [I]Lit., *lidded cooking pan* [a]Lev. 7:9
9 [a]Lev. 2:2, 16; 5:12
10 [a]Lev. 2:3; 6:16
11 [I]Lit., *up from it* [a]Ex. 23:18; 34:25; Lev. 6:16, 17 [b]Ex. 29:25; Lev. 1:13
12 [a]Ex. 34:22; Lev. 7:13; 23:10, 17, 18
13 [a]Num. 18:19; 2Chr. 13:5; Ezek. 43:24
14 [a]Lev. 23:14
16 [a]Lev. 2:2

1 [a]Lev. 7:11-34; 17:5 [b]Lev. 1:3; 22:20-24
2 [a]Lev. 1:4 [b]Ex. 29:11, 16, 20

3 'And from the sacrifice of the peace offerings, he shall present[7126] an offering by fire to the LORD, the fat that covers[3680] the entrails and all the fat that is on the entrails,

4 and the two kidneys with the fat that is on them, which is on the loins, and the [I]lobe of the liver, which he shall remove[5493] with the kidneys.

5 'Then [a]Aaron's sons shall offer *it* up in smoke[6999] on the altar [b]on the burnt offering,[5930] which is on the wood that is on the fire; [c]it is an offering by fire[801] of a soothing aroma to the LORD.

6 'But if his offering for a sacrifice of peace offerings to the LORD is from the flock, he shall offer it, male or female, [a]without defect.

7 'If he is going to offer [a]a lamb for his offering, then he shall offer it [b]before the LORD,

8 and [a]he shall lay his hand on the head of his offering, and [b]slay it before the tent of meeting; and Aaron's sons shall [c]sprinkle its blood around on the altar.

9 'And from the [a]sacrifice of peace offerings he shall bring as an offering by fire to the LORD, its fat, [I]the entire fat tail which he shall remove close to the backbone, and the fat that covers the entrails and all the fat that is on the entrails,

10 and the two kidneys with the fat that is on them, which is on the loins, and the [I]lobe of the liver, which he shall remove [a]with the kidneys.

11 'Then the priest shall offer *it* up in smoke [a]on the altar, *as* [b]food, an offering by fire to the LORD.

12 'Moreover, if his offering is [a]a goat, then he shall offer it before the LORD,

13 and he shall lay his hand on its head and slay it before the tent of meeting; and the sons of Aaron shall sprinkle its blood around on the altar.

14 'And from it he shall present his offering as an offering by fire to the LORD, the fat that covers the entrails and all the fat that is on the entrails,

15 and the two kidneys with the fat that is on them, which is on the loins, and the [I]lobe of the liver, which he shall remove [a]with the kidneys.

16 'And the priest shall offer them up in smoke on the altar *as* food, an offering by fire for a soothing aroma; [a]all fat is the LORD's.

17 'It is a [a]perpetual[5769] statute[2708] throughout your generations[1755] in all your dwellings:[4186] you shall not eat any fat [b]or any blood.'"

The Law of Sin Offerings

4 Then the LORD spoke to Moses, saying,[559]

2 "Speak[1696] to the sons[1121] of Israel, saying, 'If a person[5315] sins [a]unintentionally[7684] in any of the [I]things which the LORD has [b]commanded[4687] not to be done, and commits any of them,

3 [a]if the anointed[4899] priest[3548] sins so as to bring guilt[819] on the people,[5971] then let him offer[7126] to the LORD a [I]bull without defect[8549] as a sin offering[2403] for the sin[2403] he has [II]committed.[2398]

4 'And he shall bring the bull to the doorway of the tent[168] of meeting[4150] before the LORD, and [a]he shall lay his hand[3027] on the head of the bull, and slay[7819] the bull before the LORD.

5 'Then the [a]anointed priest is to take some of the blood[1818] of the bull and bring it to the tent of meeting,

6 and the priest shall dip[2881] his finger in the blood, and sprinkle some of the blood seven times before the LORD, in front of [a]the veil of the sanctuary.[6944]

7 'The priest shall also put some of the blood on the horns of [a]the altar[4196] of fragrant incense[7004] which is before the LORD in the tent of meeting; and all the blood of the bull he shall pour[8210] out at the base[3247] of the altar of burnt offering[5930] which is at the doorway of the tent of meeting.

8 '[a]And he shall remove from it all the fat of the bull of the sin offering: the fat that covers[3680] the entrails, and all the fat which is on the entrails,

---

4 IOr, *appendage on*

5 aLev. 7:28-34 bEx. 29:38-42; Num. 28:3-10 cNum. 15:8-10; 28:12-14

6 aLev. 3:1; 22:20-24

7 aNum. 15:4, 5; 28:4-8 bLev. 17:8, 9; 1Kin. 8:62

8 aLev. 1:4 bLev. 3:2 cLev. 1:5

9 ILit., *the fat tail, entire* aLev. 17:5; Num. 7:88; 1Sam. 10:8; 2Sam. 6:17; 1Kin. 3:15; 8:63, 64; 1Chr. 16:1

10 IOr, *appendage on* aLev. 3:4, 15

11 aLev. 3:5 bLev. 3:16; 21:6, 8, 17, 22

12 aNum. 15:6-11

15 IOr, *appendage on* aLev. 3:4; 7:4

16 aLev. 7:23-25

17 aLev. 6:18, 22; 7:34, 36; 10:9, 15; 16:29; 17:7; 23:14, 21; 24:3 bLev. 7:26; 17:10-16

2 ILit., *commands of the LORD which are not to be done* aLev. 4:22, 27; 5:15-18; 22:14 bLev. 4:13

3 IOr, *bull of the herd* IILit., *sinned* aLev. 4:14, 23, 28

4 aLev. 1:4; 4:15; Num. 8:12

5 aLev. 4:3, 17

6 aEx. 40:21, 26

7 aLev. 4:18, 25, 30, 34; 8:15; 9:9; 16:18

8 aLev. 3:3, 4

9 and the two kidneys with the fat
that is on them, which is on the loins,
and the [I]lobe of the liver, which he shall
remove[5493] [a]with the kidneys
10 (just as it is removed from the
ox of the sacrifice[2077] of peace offerings),[8002] and the priest is to offer[6999]
them up in smoke on the altar of burnt
offering.
11 'But [a]the hide[5785] of the bull and
all its flesh[1320] with its head and its legs
and its entrails and its refuse,
12 [I]that is, all *the rest of* the bull,
he is to bring out to [a]a clean[2889] place
outside the camp[4264] where the [II]ashes
are poured out, and burn[8313] it on wood
with fire; where the [II]ashes are poured
out it shall be burned.
13 "[a]Now if the whole congregation[5712] of Israel commits error,[7686]
and the matter [I]escapes the notice of
the assembly,[6951] and they commit any
of the [II]things which the LORD has
commanded not to be done, and they
become guilty;[816]
14 [a]when the sin [I]which they have
[II]committed becomes known, then the
assembly[6951] shall offer [b]a [III]bull of the
herd for a sin offering, and bring it before
the tent of meeting.
15 'Then [a]the elders[2205] of the congregation shall lay their hands on the
head of the bull before the LORD, and
the bull shall be slain [b]before the LORD.
16 'Then the anointed priest is to
bring some of the blood of the bull to
the tent of meeting;
17 and [a]the priest shall dip his finger
in the blood, and sprinkle *it* seven times
before the LORD, in front of the veil.
18 'And he shall put some of the
blood on the horns of [a]the altar which
is before the LORD [I]in the tent of meeting; and all the blood he shall pour out
at the base of the altar of burnt offering
which is at the doorway of the tent of
meeting.
19 "[a]And he shall remove all its fat
from it and offer it up in smoke on the
altar.
20 'He shall also do with the bull
just as he did with [a]the bull of the sin
offering; thus he shall do with it. So
[b]the priest shall make atonement[3722] for
them, and they shall be forgiven.[5545]
21 'Then he is to bring out the bull
to *a place* outside the camp, and burn
it as he burned the first bull; it is
[a]the sin offering for the assembly.
22 'When [a]a leader[5387] [b]sins and unintentionally does any one of all the
[I]things which the LORD God[430] has commanded not to be done, and he becomes
guilty,
23 [I][a]if his sin [II]which he has committed is made known[3045] to him, he shall
bring for his offering[7133] a [III][b]goat, [c]a
male[2145] without defect.
24 'And he shall lay his hand on the
head of the male goat, and slay it in
the place where [I]they slay the burnt
offering before the LORD; it is a sin offering.
25 'Then the priest is to take some
of the blood of the sin offering with his
finger, and put it on [a]the horns of the
altar of burnt offering; and *the rest of*
its blood he shall pour out at the base
of the altar of burnt offering.
🔑 26 "[a]And all its fat he shall offer up
in smoke on the altar as *in the case of*
the fat of the sacrifice of peace offerings.
Thus [b]the priest shall make atonement
for him in regard to his sin, and he shall
be forgiven.
27 'Now if [I]anyone of [II]the com-

9 [I]Or, *appendage on* [a]Lev. 3:4
11 [a]Lev. 9:11; Num. 19:5
12 [I]Lit., *and* [II]Or, *fat ashes are* [a]Lev. 4:21; 6:10, 11; 16:27
13 [I]Lit., *is hidden from the eyes of* [II]Lit., *commands of the LORD which are not to be done* [a]Num. 15:24-26
14 [I]Lit., *concerning which* [II]Lit., *sinned* [III]Lit., *son of the herd* [a]Lev. 4:3 [b]Lev. 4:3, 23, 28
15 [a]Lev. 8:14, 18, 22; Num. 8:10, 12 [b]Lev. 1:3
17 [a]Lev. 4:6
18 [I]Lit., *which is in* [a]Lev. 4:7, 25, 30, 34
19 [a]Lev. 4:8
20 [a]Lev. 4:8, 21 [b]Num. 15:25, 28
21 [a]Lev. 4:13f.; 16:15-17; Num. 15:24-26
22 [I]Lit., *commands of the LORD which are not to be done* [a]Num. 31:13; 32:2 [b]Lev. 4:2, 27
23 [I]Lit., *or* [II]Lit., *in which he has sinned* [III]Lit., *buck of the goats* [a]Lev. 4:3 [b]Lev. 4:3, 14, 28 [c]Lev. 4:28
24 [I]Lit., *one slays*
25 [a]Lev. 4:7, 18, 30, 34
26 [a]Lev. 4:19 [b]Lev. 4:20, 31; 5:10, 13, 16, 18; 6:7
27 [I]Lit., *one soul* [II]Lit., *the people of the land*

🔑 **4:26** One of the enduring problems in Christian biblical scholarship is whether or not complete atonement for sins was possible under the O.T. sacrificial system. Several O.T. passages, including this one, give no indication that atonement and forgiveness were anything but complete. The writer of Hebrews acknowledged the connection between blood sacrifice and forgiveness in the Law (Heb. 9:22), but he went on to deny that animal sacrifices could ever take away sins (Heb. 10:4,11). Apparently he regarded O.T. forgiveness as either incomplete or in anticipation of Jesus' final solution for sin, because he asserted that the effects of Jesus' sacrifice went back to those under the first covenant, as well as forward (Heb. 9:15).

mon[776] people sins [a]unintentionally in doing any of the [III]things which the LORD has commanded not to be done, and becomes guilty,

28 [I][a]if his sin, which he has [II]committed is made known to him, then he shall bring for his offering a [III][b]goat, a [c]female[5347] without defect, for his sin which he has [II]committed.

29 'And [a]he shall lay his hand on the head of the sin offering, and [b]slay the sin offering at the place of the burnt offering.

30 'And the priest shall take some of its blood with his finger and put it on the horns of [a]the altar of burnt offering; and [b]all *the rest of* its blood he shall pour out at the base of the altar.

31 '[a]Then he shall remove all its fat, just as the fat was removed[5493] from the sacrifice of peace offerings; and the priest shall offer it up in smoke on the altar for [b]a soothing aroma to the LORD. Thus the priest shall make atonement for him, [I]and he shall be forgiven.

32 'But if he brings [a]a lamb as his offering for a sin offering, he shall bring it, a female without defect.

33 'And [a]he shall lay his hand on the head of the sin offering, and slay it for a sin offering [b]in the place where [I]they slay the burnt offering.

34 'And the priest is to take some of the blood of the sin offering with his finger and put it on the horns of [a]the altar of burnt offering; and [b]all *the rest of* its blood he shall pour out at the base of the altar.

35 'Then he shall remove [a]all its fat, just as the fat of the lamb is removed from the sacrifice of the peace offerings, and the priest shall offer them up in smoke on the altar, on the offerings by fire[801] to the LORD. Thus [b]the priest shall make atonement for him in regard to his sin which he has [I]committed, and he shall be forgiven.

The Law of Guilt Offerings

5 'Now if a person sins, after he hears[8085] a [I]public [a]adjuration[423] *to testify*, when he is a witness, whether he has seen[7200] or *otherwise* known,[3045] if he does not tell[5046] *it*, then he will bear[5375] his [II]guilt.[5771]

2 'Or if a person touches[5060] [a]any unclean[2931] thing,[1697] whether a carcass of an unclean beast,[2416] or the carcass[5038] of unclean cattle, or a carcass of unclean swarming things, though it is hidden from him, and he is unclean, then he will be guilty.[816]

3 'Or if he touches human uncleanness,[2932] of whatever *sort* his uncleanness *may* be with which he becomes unclean,[2930] and it is hidden from him, and then he comes to know *it*, he will be guilty.

4 'Or if a person [a]swears thoughtlessly with his lips[8193] to do evil[7489] or to do good, in whatever matter a man may speak thoughtlessly with an oath,[7621] and it is hidden from him, and then he comes to know *it*, he will be guilty in one of these.

5 'So it shall be when he becomes guilty in one of these, that he shall [a]confess[3034] that in which he has sinned.[2398]

6 'He shall also bring his guilt offering[817] to the LORD for his sin which he has [I]committed, [a]a female[5347] from the flock, a lamb or a [II]goat as a sin offering.[2403] So the priest[3548] shall make atonement[3722] on his behalf for his sin.

7 'But if [I]he cannot afford[5060] a lamb, then he shall bring to the LORD his guilt[817] offering for that in which he has sinned,[2398] two turtledoves or two young[1121] pigeons, [a]one for a sin offering and the other for a burnt offering.[5930]

8 'And he shall bring them to the priest, who shall offer[7126] first that which is for the sin offering and shall nip its head at the front of its neck, but he [a]shall not sever *it*.

9 'He shall also sprinkle some of the blood[1818] of the sin offering [a]on the side of the altar,[4196] while the rest[7604] of the blood shall be drained out [b]at the base[3247] of the altar: it is a sin offering.

10 'The second he shall then prepare as a burnt offering [a]according to

27 [III]Lit., *commands of the* LORD *which are not to be done* [a]Lev. 4:2; Num. 15:27

28 [I]Lit., *or* [II]Lit., *sinned* [III]Or, *female goat* [a]Lev. 4:3 [b]Lev. 4:3, 14, 23, 32 [c]Lev. 4:23

29 [a]Lev. 1:4; 4:4, 24 [b]Lev. 1:5, 11

30 [a]Lev. 4:7, 18, 25, 34 [b]Lev. 4:7

31 [I]Or, *so that he may be* [a]Lev. 4:8 [b]Gen. 8:21; Ex. 29:18; Lev. 1:9, 13; 2:2, 9, 12

32 [a]Lev. 4:28

33 [I]Lit., *one slays* [a]Lev. 1:4, 5 [b]Lev. 4:29

34 [a]Lev. 4:7, 18, 25, 30 [b]Lev. 4:7

35 [I]Lit., *sinned* [a]Lev. 4:26, 31 [b]Lev. 4:20

1 [I]Lit., *voice of an oath* [II]Or, *iniquity* [a]Prov. 29:24; Jer. 23:10

2 [a]Lev. 11:8, 11, 24-40; Num. 19:11-16; Deut. 14:8

4 [a]Num. 30:6, 8; Ps. 106:33

5 [a]Lev. 16:21; 26:40; Num. 5:7; Prov. 28:13

6 [I]Lit., *sinned* [II]Lit., *female goat* [a]Lev. 4:28, 32

7 [I]Lit., *his hand does not reach enough for* [a]Lev. 12:6, 8; 14:22, 30, 31

8 [a]Lev. 1:17

9 [a]Lev. 1:15 [b]Lev. 4:7, 18

10 [a]Lev. 1:14-17

the ordinance.[4941] [b]So the priest shall make atonement on his behalf for his sin which he has [I]committed, and it shall be forgiven[5545] him.

11 'But [a]if his [I]means are insufficient for two turtledoves or two young pigeons, then for his offering[7133] for that which he has sinned, he shall bring the tenth of an [II]ephah of fine flour for a sin offering; [b]he shall not put oil[8081] on it or place incense[3828] on it, for it is a sin offering.

12 'And he shall bring it to the priest, and the priest shall take his handful of it as its memorial portion and offer *it* up in smoke[6999] on the altar, [I]with the offerings of the LORD by fire: it is a sin offering.

13 'So the priest shall make atonement for him concerning his sin which he has [I]committed from [a]one of these, and it shall be forgiven him; then [b]*the rest* shall become the priest's, like the grain offering.' "[4503]

14 Then the LORD spoke to Moses, saying,[559]

15 "[a]If a person acts unfaithfully[4604] and sins [b]unintentionally[7684] against the LORD's holy things,[6944] then he shall bring his [c]guilt offering to the LORD: [d]a ram without defect[8549] from the flock, according to your valuation in silver by shekels, in *terms of* the [e]shekel of the sanctuary,[6944] for a guilt offering.

16 "[a]And he shall make restitution for that which he has sinned[2398] against the holy thing, and shall add to it a fifth part of it, and give it to the priest. [b]The priest shall then make atonement for him with the ram of the guilt offering, and it shall be forgiven him.

17 "Now if a person sins and does[6213] any of the things [I]which the LORD has commanded[4687] not to be done, [a]though he was unaware,[3045] still he is guilty, and shall bear his punishment.

18 "He is then to bring to the priest [a]a ram without defect from the flock, according to your valuation, for a guilt offering. So the priest shall make atonement for him concerning his error in which he sinned[7683] [b]unintentionally and did not know *it*, and it shall be forgiven him.

19 "It is a guilt offering; he was certainly guilty[816] before the LORD."

Guilt Offering

6 Then the LORD spoke to Moses, saying,[559]

2 "[a]When a person[5315] sins and acts[4603] unfaithfully against the LORD, and deceives his companion in regard to a deposit[6487] or a security entrusted[6487] *to him*, or through robbery, or *if* he has extorted from his companion,

3 or [a]has found what was lost[9] and lied about it and sworn[7650] falsely,[8267] so that he sins in regard to any one of the things a man[120] may do;

4 then it shall be, when he sins and becomes guilty,[816] that he shall [a]restore[7725] what he took by robbery, or what he got by extortion, or the deposit which was [I]entrusted to him, or the lost thing which he found,

5 or anything about which he swore falsely; [a]he shall make restitution for it [I]in full, and add to it one-fifth more. [b]He shall give it to the one to whom it belongs on the day[3117] *he presents* his guilt offering.[819]

6 "Then he shall bring to the priest[3548] his guilt offering[817] to the LORD, [a]a ram without defect[8549] from the flock, according to your valuation, for a guilt offering,

7 and [a]the priest shall make atonement for him before the LORD; and he shall be forgiven for any one of the things which he may have done to incur guilt."

The Priest's Part in the Offerings

8 [I]Then the LORD spoke to Moses, saying,

9 "Command[6680] Aaron and his sons,[1121] saying,[559] 'This is [a]the law[8541] for the burnt offering:[5930] the burnt offering itself *shall remain* on the hearth on the altar[4196] all night[3915] until the

10 [I]Lit., *sinned* [b]Lev. 4:20, 26; 5:13, 16

11 [I]Lit., *hand does not reach* [II]I.e., Approx. one bu. [a]Lev. 14:21-32; 27:8 [b]Lev. 2:1, 2

12 [I]Lit., *upon*

13 [I]Lit., *sinned* [a]Lev. 5:4, 5 [b]Lev. 2:3

15 [a]Num. 5:5-8 [b]Lev. 4:2; 22:14 [c]Lev. 7:1-10 [d]Lev. 6:6 [e]Ex. 30:13

16 [a]Lev. 6:5; 22:14; Num. 5:7, 8 [b]Lev. 7:2-7

17 [I]Lit., *the commands of the LORD which are* [a]Lev. 4:2; 5:19

18 [a]Lev. 5:15 [b]Lev. 5:17

1 [I]Ch. 5:20 in Heb.

2 [a]Ex. 22:7-15

3 [a]Ex. 23:4; Deut. 22:1-4

4 [I]Or, *deposited with* [a]Lev. 24:18, 21

5 [I]Lit., *in its sum* [a]Lev. 5:16 [b]Num. 5:8

6 [a]Lev. 5:15

7 [a]Lev. 7:2-5

8 [I]Ch. 6:1 in Heb.

9 [a]Ex. 29:38-42; Num. 28:3-10

morning, and [b]the fire on the altar is
to be kept burning on it.
10 'And the priest is to put[7760] on
[a]his linen robe, and he shall put on undergarments next to his flesh;[1320] and he
shall take up the [I]ashes *to* which the
fire [II]reduces the burnt offering on the
altar, and place them beside the altar.
11 'Then he shall take off his garments and put on other garments, and
carry the [I]ashes outside the camp[4264]
to a clean place.
12 'And the fire on the altar shall
be kept burning on it. It shall not go
out, but the priest shall burn[6999] wood
on it every morning; and he shall lay
out the burnt offering on it, and offer
up in smoke the fat portions of the peace
offerings[8002] [a]on it.
13 'Fire shall be kept burning continually[8548] on the altar; it is not to go
out.
14 'Now this is the law of the grain
offering:[4503] the sons of Aaron shall
present[7126] it before the LORD in front
of the altar.
15 '[a]Then one *of them* shall lift up
from it a handful of the fine flour of the
grain offering, [I]with its oil[8081] and all the
incense[3828] that is on the grain offering,
and he shall offer *it* up in smoke on the
altar, a soothing aroma, as its memorial
offering to the LORD.
16 '[a]And what is left[3498] of it Aaron
and his sons are to eat. It shall be eaten
as unleavened cakes in a holy[6918] place;
they are to eat it in the court of the
tent[168] of meeting.[4150]
17 '[a]It shall not be baked with
leaven.[2557] I have given it as their share
from My offerings by fire;[801] [b]it is most
holy[6944], like the sin offering[2403] and
[c]the guilt offering.
18 '[a]Every male[2145] among the
sons[1121] of Aaron may eat it; it is a
permanent[5769] ordinance[2706] throughout
your generations,[1755] from the offerings by fire to the LORD. [b]Whoever
touches[5060] them shall become consecrated.' "[6942]
19 Then the LORD spoke to Moses,
saying,
20 "This is the offering[7133] which
Aaron and his sons are to present to
the LORD on the day when he is anointed;
the tenth of an [a]ephah of fine flour as
[b]a [I]regular[8548] grain offering, half of it
in the morning and half of it in the evening.
21 "It shall be prepared with oil on
a [a]griddle. When it is *well* stirred, you
shall bring it. You shall present the grain
offering in baked pieces as a soothing
aroma to the LORD.
22 "And the anointed[4899] priest who
will be in his place [I]among his sons shall
[II]offer it. By a permanent ordinance it
shall be entirely[3632] offered up in smoke
to the LORD.
23 "So every grain offering of the
priest shall be burned entirely. It shall
not be eaten."
24 Then the LORD spoke to Moses,
saying,
25 "Speak[1696] to Aaron and to his
sons, saying, 'This is the law of the sin
offering: [a]in the place where the burnt
offering is slain the sin offering shall be
slain before the LORD; it is most holy.
26 '[a]The priest who offers it for sin
shall eat it. It shall be eaten in a holy
place, in the court of the tent of meeting.
27 '[a]Anyone who touches its flesh
shall become consecrated; and when any
of its blood[1818] [I]splashes[5137] on a garment, in a holy place you shall wash[3526]
what was splashed on.
28 'Also [a]the earthenware[2789] vessel
in which it was boiled[1310] shall be
broken;[7665] and if it was boiled in a
bronze vessel, then it shall be scoured
and rinsed in water.
29 '[a]Every male among the priests
may eat of it; [b]it is most holy.
30 'But no sin offering [a]of which any
of the blood is brought into the tent of
meeting to make atonement[3722] [b]in the
holy place shall be eaten; [c]it shall be
burned[8313] with fire.

The Priest's Part in the Offerings

7 'Now this is the law[8451] of the
[a]guilt offering;[817] it is most holy.[6944]

9 [b]Lev. 6:12, 13
10 [I]Or, *fat ashes* [II]Lit., *consumes* [a]Ex. 28:39, 42; 39:27, 28
11 [I]Or, *fat ashes*
12 [a]Lev. 3:5
15 [I]Lit., *and some of* [a]Lev. 2:2, 9
16 [a]Lev. 2:3; 10:12-14; Ezek. 44:29
17 [a]Lev. 2:11 [b]Ex. 40:10; Lev. 6:25, 26, 29, 30; Num. 18:9 [c]Lev. 7:7; 10:16-18
18 [a]Lev. 6:29; 7:6; Num. 18:10; 1Cor. 9:13 [b]Lev. 6:27
20 [I]Lit., *grain offering continually* [a]Lev. 5:11 [b]Num. 4:16
21 [a]Lev. 2:5
22 [I]Lit., *from among* [II]Lit., *do*
25 [a]Lev. 1:11
26 [a]Lev. 6:29
27 [I]Lit., *one sprinkles* [a]Lev. 7:19
28 [a]Lev. 11:33; 15:12
29 [a]Lev. 6:18 [b]Lev. 6:17, 25
30 [a]Lev. 4:1-21 [b]Lev. 4:7, 18 [c]Lev. 4:11, 12, 21
1 [a]Lev. 5:14-6:7

2 'In [a]the place where they slay[7819] the burnt offering[5930] they are to slay the guilt offering, and he shall sprinkle its blood[1818] around on the altar.[4196]

3 'Then he shall offer from it all its fat: the [a]fat tail and the fat that covers[3680] the entrails,

4 and the two kidneys with the fat that is on them, which is on the loins, and the lobe on the liver he shall remove[5493] [a]with the kidneys.

5 'And the priest[3548] shall offer them up in smoke[6999] on the altar as an offering by fire[801] to the LORD; it is a guilt offering.

6 "[a]Every male[2145] among the priests may eat of it. It shall be eaten in a holy[6918] place; it is most holy.

7 'The guilt offering[2403] is like the [a]sin offering, there is one law for them; the [b]priest who makes atonement with it [I]shall have it.

8 'Also the priest who presents any man's[272] burnt offering, [I]that priest shall have for himself the skin[5785] of the burnt offering which he has presented.[7126]

9 'Likewise, every grain offering[4503] that is baked in the oven, and everything prepared in a [I]pan or on a [a]griddle, [II]shall belong to the priest who presents it.

10 'And every grain offering mixed[1101] with oil,[8081] or dry,[2720] shall [I]belong to all the sons[1121] of Aaron, [II]to all[376] alike.[251]

11 'Now this is the law of the [a]sacrifice[2077] of peace offerings[8002] which shall be presented to the LORD.

12 'If he offers it by way of [a]thanksgiving,[8426] then along with the sacrifice of thanksgiving he shall offer [b]unleavened cakes mixed with oil, and unleavened wafers [I]spread[4886] with oil, and cakes *of well* stirred fine flour mixed with oil.

13 'With the sacrifice of his peace offerings for thanksgiving, he shall present his offering[7133] with cakes of [a]leavened[2557] bread.

14 'And of [I]this he shall present one of every offering[7133] as a [II]contribution[8641] to the LORD; [a]it shall [III]belong to the priest who sprinkles the blood of the peace offerings.

15 '[a]Now *as for* the flesh[1320] of the sacrifice of his thanksgiving peace offerings, it shall be eaten on the day[3117] of his offering; he shall not leave any of it over until morning.

16 'But if the sacrifice of his offering is a [a]votive[5088] or a freewill offering,[5071] it shall be eaten on the day that he offers[7126] his sacrifice; and on the [I]next day what is left[3498] of it may be eaten;

17 [a]but what is left over from the flesh of the sacrifice on the third day shall be burned with fire.

18 'So if any of the flesh of the sacrifice of his peace offerings should *ever* be eaten on the third day, he who offers it shall not be accepted,[7521] *and* it shall not be reckoned[2803] to his *benefit.* It shall be an [a]offensive thing,[6292] and the person[5315] who eats of it shall bear[5375] his *own* iniquity.[5771]

19 'Also the flesh that touches[5060] anything unclean[2931] shall not be eaten; it shall be burned with fire. [I]As for *other* flesh, anyone who is clean[2889] may eat *such* flesh.

20 '[a]But the person who eats the flesh of the sacrifice of peace offerings which belong to the LORD, [I]in his uncleanness,[2932] that person [b]shall be cut off[3772] from his people.[5971]

21 '[a]And when anyone touches anything unclean, whether human[120] uncleanness, or an unclean animal, or any unclean [I]detestable thing, and eats of the flesh of the sacrifice of peace offerings which belong to the LORD, that person shall be cut off from his people.' "

22 Then the LORD spoke to Moses, saying,[559]

23 "Speak[1696] to the sons[1121] of Israel, saying, 'You shall not eat [a]any fat *from* an ox, a sheep, or a goat.

24 'Also the fat of *an animal* which dies,[5038] and the fat of an animal [a]torn *by beasts,* may be put to any other use,[4399] but you must certainly not eat it.

25 'For whoever eats the fat of the

2 [a]Lev. 1:11
3 [a]Lev. 3:9
4 [a]Lev. 3:4
6 [a]Lev. 6:18, 29; Num. 18:9
7 [I]Lit., *it shall be for him* [a]Lev. 6:25, 26, 30 [b]1Cor. 9:13; 10:18
8 [I]Lit., *for the priest, it shall be for him*
9 [I]Lit., *lidded cooking pan* [II]Lit., *for the priest, it shall be for him* [a]Lev. 2:5
10 [I]Lit., *be* [II]Lit., *a man as his brother*
11 [a]Lev. 3:1
12 [I]Or, *anointed* [a]Lev. 7:15 [b]Lev. 2:4; Num. 6:15
13 [a]Lev. 2:12; 23:17, 18; Amos 4:5
14 [I]Lit., *it* [II]Or, *heave offering* [III]Lit., *be for* [a]Num. 18:8, 11, 19
15 [a]Lev. 22:29, 30
16 [I]Lit., *morrow and what* [a]Lev. 19:5-8
17 [a]Ex. 12:10
18 [a]Lev. 19:7; Prov. 15:8
19 [I]Lit., *And the flesh*
20 [I]Lit., *and his uncleanness is on him* [a]Lev. 22:3-7; Num. 19:13 [b]Lev. 7:25
21 [I]Some mss. read *swarming thing* [a]Lev. 5:2, 3
23 [a]Lev. 3:17
24 [a]Ex. 22:31; Lev. 17:15; 22:8

animal from which [I]an offering by fire is offered to the LORD, even the person who eats shall be cut off from his people.

26 "[a]And you are not to eat any blood, either of bird or animal, in any of your dwellings.[4186]

27 'Any person who eats any blood, even that person shall be cut off from his people.' "

28 Then the LORD spoke to Moses, saying,

29 "Speak to the sons of Israel, saying, 'He who offers [a]the sacrifice of his peace offerings to the LORD shall bring his offering to the LORD from the sacrifice of his peace offerings.

30 'His own hands[3027] are to bring offerings by fire to the LORD. He shall bring the fat with the breast, that the [a]breast may be [I]presented as a wave offering before the LORD.

31 'And the priest shall offer up the fat in smoke on the altar; but [a]the breast shall belong to Aaron and his sons.

32 'And you shall give [a]the right thigh to the priest as a [I]contribution from the sacrifices of your peace offerings.

33 'The one among the sons of Aaron who offers the blood of the peace offerings and the fat, the right thigh shall be his as *his* portion.

34 'For I have taken [a]the breast of the wave offering and the thigh of the [I]contribution from the sons of Israel from the sacrifices of their peace offerings, and have given them to Aaron the priest and to his sons as *their* due[2706] forever[5769] from the sons of Israel.

35 'This is [I]that which is consecrated[4886] to Aaron and [I]that [a]which is consecrated to his sons from the offerings by fire to the LORD, in that day when he presented[3547] them to serve as priests[3547] to the LORD.

36 '[I]These the LORD had commanded[6680] to be given them from the sons of Israel in the day that He [a]anointed[4886] them. It is *their* due[2708] forever throughout their generations.' "[1755]

37 This is the law of the burnt offering, the grain offering and the sin offering and the guilt offering and [a]the ordination offering and the sacrifice of peace offerings,

38 [a]which the LORD commanded Moses at Mount Sinai in the day that He commanded the sons of Israel to [I]present their offerings[7133] to the LORD in the wilderness of Sinai.

25 [I]Lit., *he offers an offering by fire*

26 [a]Gen. 9:4; Lev. 17:10-16; 19:26; Deut. 12:23; 1Sam. 14:33; Acts 15:20

29 [a]Lev. 3:1

30 [I]Lit., *waved* [a]Ex. 29:26, 27; Lev. 8:29; Num. 6:20

31 [a]Num. 18:11; Deut. 18:3

32 [I]Or, *heave offering* [a]Ex. 29:27; Lev. 7:34; 9:21; Num. 6:20

34 [I]Or, *heave offering* [a]Ex. 29:27; Lev. 10:14, 15; Num. 18:18

35 [I]Lit., *the anointed portion of* [a]Num. 18:8

36 [I]Lit., *which* [a]Ex. 40:13-15; Lev. 8:12, 30

37 [a]Ex. 29:22-34; Lev. 8:22, 23

38 [I]Or, *offer* [a]Lev. 1:1; 26:46; 27:34; Deut. 4:5

2 [a]Ex. 28:1 [b]Lev. 6:10 [c]Ex. 30:25

6 [a]Ex. 29:4-6 [b]Ex. 30:19, 20; Ps. 26:6; 1Cor. 6:11; Eph. 5:26

7 [I]Lit., *and with it* [a]Ex. 28:4

8 [I]Lit., *pouch* [II]I.e., the lights and perfections [a]Ex. 28:30; Num. 27:21; Deut. 33:8; 1Sam. 28:6; Ezra 2:63; Neh. 7:65

9 [a]Ex. 28:36

10 [I]Or, *dwelling place* [a]Ex. 30:26-29; Lev. 8:2

The Consecration of Aaron and His Sons

8 Then the LORD spoke to Moses, saying,

2 "[a]Take Aaron and his sons[1121] with him, and the [b]garments and [c]the anointing[4886] oil[8081] and the bull of the sin offering,[2403] and the two rams and the basket of unleavened bread;

3 and assemble all the congregation[5712] at the doorway of the tent[168] of meeting."[4150]

4 So Moses did[6213] just as the LORD commanded[6680] him. When the congregation[5712] was assembled[6950] at the doorway of the tent of meeting,

5 Moses said to the congregation, "This is the thing[1697] which the LORD has commanded to do."[6213]

6 Then [a]Moses had Aaron and his sons come near, and [b]washed[7364] them with water.

7 And he [a]put the tunic on him and girded him with the sash,[73] and clothed him with the robe, and put the ephod on him; and he girded him with the artistic band[2805] of the ephod, [I]with which he tied *it* to him.

🔑 8 He then placed the [I]breastpiece on him, and in the [I]breastpiece he put[7760] [IIa]the Urim[217] and the Thummim.[8537]

9 He also placed the turban[4701] on his head, and on the turban, at its front, he placed [a]the golden plate, the holy[6944] crown,[5145] just as the LORD had commanded Moses.

10 Moses then took [a]the anointing oil and anointed[4886] the [I]tabernacle[4908]

🔑 **8:8** On the Urim and Thummim see note on Ex. 28:30.

and all that was in it, and consecrated[6942]
them.
11 And he sprinkled some of it on
the altar[4196] seven times and anointed
the altar and all its utensils, and the
basin and its stand,[3595] to [a]consecrate
them.
12 Then he poured some of the
[a]anointing oil on Aaron's head and
anointed him, to consecrate him.
13 [a]Next Moses had Aaron's sons
come near and clothed them with tunics,
and girded them with sashes,[73] and
bound [I]caps on them, just as the LORD
had commanded Moses.
14 Then he brought[5066] [a]the bull of
the sin offering, and Aaron and his sons
laid their hands[3027] on the head of the
bull of the sin offering.
15 Next [I]Moses slaughtered *it* and
took the blood[1818] and with his finger
[a]put *some of it* around on the horns of
the altar, and purified the altar. Then
he poured out *the rest of* the blood at
the base[3247] of the altar and consecrated
it, to make atonement[3722] for it.
16 He also [a]took all the fat that was
on the entrails and the [I]lobe of the liver,
and the two kidneys and their fat; and
Moses offered it up in smoke[6999] on the
altar.
17 [a]But the bull and its hide[5785] and
its flesh[1320] and its refuse, he burned[8313]
in the fire outside the camp,[4264] just as
the LORD had commanded Moses.
18 Then he presented [a]the ram of
the burnt offering,[5930] and Aaron and
his sons laid their hands on the head
of the ram.
19 And [I]Moses slaughtered *it* and
sprinkled the blood around on the altar.
20 When he had cut the ram into
its pieces, Moses [a]offered up the head
and the pieces and the suet in smoke.
21 After he had washed[7364] the entrails and the legs with water, Moses
[a]offered up the whole ram in smoke on
the altar. It was a burnt offering for a
soothing aroma; it was an offering by
fire[801] to the LORD, just as the LORD
had commanded Moses.
22 Then he presented the second
ram, [a]the ram of [I]ordination; and Aaron
and his sons laid their hands on the head
of the ram.
23 And [I]Moses slaughtered *it* and
took some of its blood and [a]put it on
the lobe of Aaron's right ear,[241] and on
the thumb of his right hand, and on the
big toe of his right foot.
24 He also had Aaron's sons come
near; and Moses put some of the blood
on the lobe of their right ear, and on
the thumb of their right hand, and on
the big toe of their right foot. Moses
then [a]sprinkled *the rest of* the blood
around on the altar.
25 And he took the fat, and the fat
tail, and all the fat that was on the entrails, and the [I]lobe of the liver and the
two kidneys and their fat and the right
thigh.
26 And [a]from the basket of unleavened bread that was before the LORD,
he took one unleavened cake and one
cake of bread *mixed with* oil and one
wafer, and placed *them* on the portions
of fat and on the right thigh.
27 He then [a]put all *these* on the
hands[3709] of Aaron and on the hands of
his sons, and presented them as a wave
offering before the LORD.
28 Then Moses [a]took them from
their hands and offered them up in smoke
on the altar with the burnt offering. They
were an ordination offering for [b]a soothing aroma; it was an offering by fire to
the LORD.
29 Moses also took [a]the breast and
presented it for a wave offering before
the LORD; it was [b]Moses' portion of the
ram of ordination, just as the LORD had
commanded Moses.
30 So Moses [a]took some of the
anointing oil and some of the blood which
was on the altar, and sprinkled it on
Aaron, on his garments, on his sons,
and on the garments of his sons with
him; and he consecrated Aaron, his garments, and his sons, and the garments
of his sons with him.
31 Then Moses said to Aaron and
to his sons, "[a]Boil the flesh at the doorway of the tent of meeting, and eat it

11 [a]Ex. 29:36, 37; 30:29
12 [a]Ex. 29:7; 30:30; Lev. 21:10, 12; Ps. 133:2
13 [I]Lit., *headgear* [a]Ex. 29:8, 9
14 [a]Ex. 29:10; Lev. 4:4; Ps. 66:15; Ezek. 43:19
15 [I]Lit., *he slaughtered it and Moses took* [a]Ex. 29:12; Lev. 4:7; Ezek. 43:20
16 [I]Or, *appendage on* [a]Ex. 29:13
17 [a]Ex. 29:14; Lev. 4:11, 12
18 [a]Ex. 29:15; Lev. 8:2
19 [I]Lit., *he slaughtered it and Moses sprinkled*
20 [a]Lev. 1:8
21 [a]Ex. 29:18
22 [I]Lit., *filling,* and so throughout the ch. [a]Ex. 29:31; Lev. 8:2
23 [I]Lit., *he slaughtered it and Moses took* [a]Ex. 29:20, 21
24 [a]Heb. 9:18-22
25 [I]Or, *appendage on*
26 [a]Ex. 29:23
27 [a]Ex. 29:24
28 [a]Ex. 29:25 [b]Gen. 8:21
29 [a]Lev. 7:31-34 [b]Ex. 29:26; Ps. 99:6
30 [a]Ex. 29:21
31 [a]Ex. 29:31

there together with the bread which is in the basket of the ordination offering, just as I commanded, [b]saying,[559] 'Aaron and his sons shall eat it.'

32 "And [a]the remainder[3498] of the flesh and of the bread you shall burn in the fire.

33 "[a]And you shall not go outside the doorway of the tent of meeting for seven days, until the day that the period of your ordination is fulfilled; for he will [I]ordain you through seven days.

34 "The LORD has commanded to do as has been done this day, to make atonement[3722] on your behalf.

35 "At the doorway of the tent of meeting, moreover, you shall remain day[3119] and night[3915] for seven days, and [a]keep[8104] the charge[4931] of the LORD, that you may not die,[4191] for so I have been commanded."

36 Thus Aaron and his sons did all the things which the LORD had commanded through Moses.

Aaron Offers Sacrifices

9 Now it came about [a]on the eighth day that Moses called[7121] Aaron and his sons[1121] and the elders[2205] of Israel;

2 and he said to Aaron, "[a]Take for yourself a calf, a bull, for a sin offering[2403] and a ram for a burnt offering,[5930] *both* without defect,[8549] and offer[7126] *them* before the LORD.

3 "Then to the sons[1121] of Israel you shall speak, saying, 'Take a male goat for a sin offering, and a calf and a lamb, both one year old,[1121] without defect, for a burnt offering,

4 and an ox and a ram for peace offerings,[8002] to sacrifice before the LORD, and a grain offering[4503] mixed[1101] with oil;[8081] for today[3117] [a]the LORD shall appear[7200] to you.'"

5 So they took what Moses had commanded[6680] to the front of the tent[168] of meeting,[4150] and the whole congregation[5712] came near[7126] and stood before the LORD.

6 And Moses said, "This is the thing[1697] which the LORD has commanded you to do,[6213] that [a]the glory[3519] of the LORD may appear to you."

7 Moses then said to Aaron, "Come near[7126] to the altar[4196] and [Ia]offer[6213] your sin offering[7133] and your burnt offering, that you may make atonement for yourself and for the people;[5971] then make the offering [II]for the people, that you may make atonement for them, just as the LORD has commanded."

8 [a]So Aaron came near to the altar and slaughtered the calf of the sin offering which was for himself.

9 [a]And Aaron's sons presented the blood[1818] to him; and he dipped[2881] his finger in the blood, and [b]put *some* on the horns of the altar, and poured out *the rest of* the blood at the base[3247] of the altar.

10 The fat and the kidneys and the [I]lobe of the liver of the sin offering, he then offered up in smoke[6999] on the altar just as the LORD had commanded Moses.

11 [a]The flesh[1320] and the skin,[5785] however, he burned[8313] with fire outside the camp.[4264]

12 Then he slaughtered the burnt offering; and Aaron's sons handed the blood to him and he sprinkled it around on the altar.

13 And they handed the burnt offering to him in [I]pieces with the head, and he offered *them* up in smoke on the altar.

14 He also washed[7364] the entrails and the legs, and offered *them* up in smoke with the burnt offering on the altar.

15 Then he presented the people's offering,[7133] and took the [a]goat of the sin offering which was for the people, and slaughtered it and offered it for sin, like the first.

16 He also presented the burnt offering, and [I]offered[6213] it according to [a]the ordinance.

17 Next he presented [a]the grain offering, and filled his [I]hand[3709] with some of it and offered *it* up in smoke on the altar, [b]besides the burnt offering of the morning.

18 Then [a]he slaughtered the ox and the ram, the sacrifice[2077] of peace

31 [b]Ex. 29:32
32 [a]Ex. 29:34
33 [I]Lit., *fill your hands* [a]Ex. 29:35
35 [a]Num. 3:7; 9:19; Deut. 11:1; 1Kin. 2:3; Ezek. 48:11
1 [a]Ezek. 43:27
2 [a]Ezek. 29:1; Lev. 4:3
4 [a]Ex. 29:43
6 [a]Ex. 24:16; Lev. 9:23
7 [I]Lit., *make* [II]Lit., *of* [a]Heb. 5:3; 7:27
8 [a]Lev. 4:1-12
9 [a]Lev. 9:12, 18 [b]Lev. 4:7
10 [I]Or, *appendage on*
11 [a]Lev. 4:11, 12; 8:17
13 [I]Lit., *its pieces*
15 [a]Lev. 4:27-31
16 [I]Lit., *made* [a]Lev. 1:1-13
17 [I]Lit., *palm* [a]Lev. 2:1-3 [b]Lev. 3:5
18 [a]Lev. 3:1-11

offerings which was for the people; and
Aaron's sons handed the blood to him
and he sprinkled it around on the altar.
19 As for the portions of fat from
the ox and from the ram, the fat tail,
and the *fat* [a]covering, and the kidneys
and the [I]lobe of the liver,
20 they now placed the portions of
fat on the breasts; and he offered
[I]them up in smoke on the altar.
21 But [a]the breasts and the right
thigh Aaron [I]presented as a wave offering before the LORD, just as Moses had
commanded.
22 Then Aaron lifted[5375] up his
hands[3027] toward the people and
[a]blessed[1288] them, and he stepped down
after making the sin offering[6213] and the
burnt offering and the peace offerings.
23 And Moses and Aaron went into
the tent of meeting. When they came
out and blessed the people, [a]the glory
of the LORD appeared to all the people.
24 [a]Then fire came out from before
the LORD and consumed the burnt offering and the portions of fat on the altar;
and when all the people saw[7200] *it*, they
shouted and fell[5307] on their faces.

The Sin of Nadab and Abihu

10 Now [a]Nadab and Abihu, the
sons[1121] of Aaron, took their[272]
respective [b]firepans, and after putting
fire in them, placed[7760] incense[7004] on
it and offered strange[2114] fire before the
LORD, which He had not commanded[6680]
them.
2 [a]And fire came out from the presence of the LORD and consumed them,
and they died[4191] before the LORD.
3 Then Moses said to Aaron, "It
is what the LORD spoke,[1696] saying,
'By those who [a]come near Me I
[Ib]will be treated as holy,[6942]
And before all the people[5971] I
will [c]be honored.' "[3513]
So Aaron, therefore, kept silent.
4 Moses called also to [a]Mishael and
Elzaphan, the sons of Aaron's uncle Uzziel, and said to them, "Come forward,[7126] carry your [I]relatives[251] away
from the front of the sanctuary[6944] to
the outside of the camp."[4264]
5 So they came forward and
carried[5375] them still in their [a]tunics to
the outside of the camp, as Moses had
said.[1696]
6 Then Moses said to Aaron and
to his sons Eleazar and Ithamar, "[a]Do
not [I]uncover[6544] your heads[7218] nor
tear[6533] your clothes, so that you may
not die, and that He may not [b]be-
come wrathful against all the congregation.[5712] But your [II]kinsmen, the whole
house[1004] of Israel, shall bewail[1058] the
burning which the LORD has [III]brought
about.[8313]
7 "You shall not even go out from
the doorway of the tent[168] of meeting,[4150] lest you die; for [a]the LORD's
anointing[4886] oil[8081] is upon you." So they
did[6213] according to the word[1697] of Moses.
8 The LORD then spoke to Aaron,
saying,[559]
9 "[a]Do not drink wine or strong
drink, neither you nor your sons with
you, when you come into the tent of
meeting, so that you may not die—it
is a perpetual[5769] statute[2708] throughout
your generations—[1755]
10 and [a]so as to make a distinction between the holy and the profane,
and between the unclean[2931] and the
clean,[2889]
11 and [a]so as to teach[3384] the sons
of Israel all the statutes[2706] which the
LORD has spoken to them through
Moses."

19 [I]Or, *appendage on* [a]Lev. 3:9
20 [I]Lit., *the portions of fat*
21 [I]Lit., *waved* [a]Ex. 29:26, 27; Lev. 7:30-34
22 [a]Num. 6:22-26; Deut. 21:5; Luke 24:50
23 [a]Lev. 9:6; Num. 16:19
24 [a]1Kin. 18:38, 39; 2Chr. 7:1

1 [a]Ex. 24:1, 9; Num. 3:2; 26:61 [b]Lev. 16:12
2 [a]Num. 3:4; 16:35; 26:61
3 [I]Or, *will show Myself holy* [a]Ex. 19:22; Lev. 21:6 [b]Ex. 30:30; Ezek. 38:16 [c]Ex. 14:4, 17; Is. 49:3; Ezek. 28:22
4 [I]Lit., *brothers* [a]Ex. 6:22
5 [a]Ex. 29:5; Lev. 8:13
6 [I]Lit., *unbind* [II]Lit., *brothers* [III]Lit., *burned* [a]Lev. 21:1-5, 10-12 [b]Num. 1:53; 16:22, 46; 18:5; Josh. 7:1; 22:18, 20; 2Sam. 24:1
7 [a]Ex. 28:41; Lev. 21:12
9 [a]Prov. 20:1; 31:5; Is. 28:7; Ezek. 44:21; Hos. 4:11; Luke 1:15; Eph. 5:18; 1Tim. 3:3; Titus 1:7
10 [a]Lev. 11:47; 20:25; Ezek. 22:26
11 [a]Deut. 17:10, 11; 33:10

10:1-3 This is one of several examples in the Bible where sin was punished quickly and directly by God. Exactly why God intervened in each case is not clear, but the stated reason here is the preservation of His holiness. Apparently such immediate correction was necessary here at the beginning of Israel's life under the covenant to impress upon the people how serious obedience was to God. A similar instance happened in the early church when Ananias and Sapphira died immediately after lying to God, and it had a beneficial sobering effect upon all who heard about it (Acts 5:1-11).

12 Then Moses spoke[1696] to Aaron, and to his surviving[3498] sons, [a]Eleazar and Ithamar, "[b]Take the grain offering[4503] that is left[3498] over from the LORD's offerings by fire[801] and eat it unleavened beside the altar,[4196] for it is most holy.

13 "You shall eat it, moreover, in a holy[6918] place, because it is your due[2706] and your sons' due out of the LORD's offerings by fire; for thus I have been commanded.

14 "[a]The breast of the wave offering, however, and the thigh[8641] of the offering you may eat in a clean place, you and your sons and your daughters with you; for they have been given as your due and your sons' due out of the sacrifices[2077] of the peace offerings[8002] of the sons of Israel.

15 "[a]The thigh offered by lifting up and the breast offered by waving, they shall bring along with the offerings by fire of the portions of fat, to present as a wave offering before the LORD; so it shall be a thing perpetually due you and your sons with you, just as the LORD has commanded."

16 But Moses searched carefully for the [a]goat of the sin offering,[2403] and behold, it had been burned up! So he was angry with Aaron's surviving sons Eleazar and Ithamar, saying,

17 "Why [a]did you not eat the sin offering at the holy place? For it is most holy, and [I]He gave it to you to bear[5375] away [b]the guilt[5771] of the congregation,[5712] to make atonement[3722] for them before the LORD.

18 "Behold, [a]since its blood[1818] had not been brought inside, into the sanctuary, you should certainly have [b]eaten it in the sanctuary, just as I commanded."

19 But Aaron spoke[1696] to Moses, "Behold, this very day[3117] they [a]presented[7126] their sin offering and their burnt offering[5930] before the LORD. When things like these happened to me, if I had eaten a sin offering today, would it have been good[3190] in the sight of the LORD?"

12 [a]Ex. 6:23; Num. 3:2 [b]Lev. 6:14-18
14 [a]Lev. 7:30-34; Num. 18:11
15 [a]Lev. 7:34
16 [a]Lev. 9:3, 15
17 [I]Or, *was given* [a]Lev. 6:24-30 [b]Ex. 28:38; Lev. 22:16; Num. 18:1
18 [a]Lev. 6:30 [b]Lev. 6:26
19 [a]Lev. 9:8, 12
2 [a]Deut. 14:3-21
4 [a]Acts 10:14
6 [I]Or, *hare*
9 [a]Deut. 14:9
10 [a]Deut. 14:10
11 [I]Lit., *detestable things*
12 [I]Lit., *detestable things*
13 [I]Lit., *a detestable thing* [II]Or, *vulture* [III]Or, *black vulture* [a]Deut. 14:12-19

20 And when Moses heard *that,* it seemed good in his sight.

Laws about Animals for Food

11 The LORD spoke again to Moses and to Aaron, saying to them,

2 "Speak[1696] to the sons[1121] of Israel, saying,[559] '[a]These are the creatures[2416] which you may eat from all the animals that are on the earth.[776]

3 'Whatever divides a hoof, thus making split hoofs, *and* chews[5927] the cud, among the animals, that you may eat.

4 'Nevertheless, [a]you are not to eat of these, among those which chew the cud, or among those which divide the hoof: the camel, for though it chews cud, it does not divide the hoof, it is unclean[2931] to you.

5 'Likewise, the rock badger, for though it chews cud, it does not divide the hoof, it is unclean to you;

6 the [I]rabbit also, for though it chews cud, it does not divide the hoof, it is unclean to you;

7 and the pig, for though it divides the hoof, thus making a split hoof, it does not chew cud, it is unclean to you.

8 'You shall not eat of their flesh[1320] nor touch[5060] their carcasses;[5038] they are unclean to you.

9 '[a]These you may eat, whatever is in the water: all that have fins and scales, those in the water, in the seas or in the rivers, you may eat.

10 '[a]But whatever is in the seas and in the rivers, that do not have fins and scales among all the teeming life of the water, and among all the living creatures[5315] that are in the water, they are detestable things to you,

11 and they shall be [I]abhorrent to you; you may not eat of their flesh, and their carcasses you shall detest.

12 'Whatever in the water does not have fins and scales is [I]abhorrent to you.

Avoid the Unclean

13 'These, moreover, [a]you shall detest among the birds; they are

[I]abhorrent, not to be eaten: the [II]eagle
and the vulture and the [III]buzzard,
14 and the kite and the falcon in its
kind,
15 every raven in its kind,
16 and the ostrich and the owl and
the sea gull and the hawk in its kind,
17 and the little owl and the cormorant and the [I]great owl,
18 and the white owl and the
[I]pelican and the carrion vulture,
19 and the stork, the heron in its
kinds, and the hoopoe, and the bat.
20 'All the [I]winged insects that walk
on *all* fours are detestable to you.
21 'Yet these you may eat among
all the [I]winged insects which walk on
all fours: those which have above their
feet jointed legs with which to jump on
the earth.
22 'These of them you may eat: the
locust in its kinds, and the devastating
locust in its kinds, and the cricket in
its kinds, and the grasshopper in its
kinds.
23 'But all other [I]winged insects
which are four-footed are detestable to
you.
24 'By these, moreover, you will
be made unclean:[2930] whoever touches
their carcasses becomes unclean until
evening,
25 and [a]whoever picks up any of
their carcasses shall wash[3526] his clothes
and be unclean[2930] until evening.
26 'Concerning all the animals which
divide the hoof, but do not make a split
hoof, or which do not chew cud, they
are unclean to you: whoever touches
them becomes unclean.
27 'Also whatever walks on its
paws,[3709] among all the creatures that
walk on *all* fours, are unclean to you;
whoever touches their carcasses becomes unclean until evening,
28 and the one who picks up their
carcasses shall wash his clothes and be
unclean until evening; they are unclean
to you.
29 'Now these are to you the unclean among the swarming things which
swarm on the earth: the mole, and the
mouse, and the [I]great lizard in its kinds,
30 and the gecko, and the [I]crocodile,
and the lizard, and the [II]sand reptile,
and the chameleon.
31 'These are to you the unclean
among all the swarming things; whoever
touches them when they are dead[4194]
becomes unclean until evening.
32 'Also anything on which one of
them may fall[5307] when they are dead,
becomes unclean, including any wooden
article, or clothing, or a skin,[5785] or a
sack—any article [I]of which use[4399] is
made—[a]it shall be put in the water and
be unclean until evening, then it becomes clean.[2891]
33 'As for any [a]earthenware[2789] vessel into which one of them may fall, whatever is in it becomes unclean and you
shall break[7665] [I]the vessel.
34 'Any of the [I]food which may be
eaten, on which water comes, shall become unclean; and any [I]liquid which may
be drunk in every vessel shall become
unclean.
35 'Everything, moreover, on which
part of their carcass may fall becomes
unclean; an oven or a [I]stove shall be
smashed;[5422] they are unclean and shall
continue as unclean to you.
36 'Nevertheless a spring or a
cistern[953] [I]collecting[4723] water shall be
clean,[2889] though the one who touches
their carcass shall be unclean.
37 'And if a part of their carcass falls
on any seed[2233] for sowing which is to
be sown, it is clean.
38 'Though if water is put on the
seed, and a part of their carcass falls
on it, it is unclean to you.
39 'Also if one of the animals
dies[4191] which you have for food, the
one who touches its carcass becomes
unclean until evening.
40 '[a]He too, who eats some of its
carcass shall wash his clothes and be
unclean until evening; and the one who
picks up its carcass shall wash his clothes
and be unclean until evening.
41 '[a]Now every swarming thing that
swarms on the earth is detestable, not
to be eaten.

17 [I]Specifically, *great horned owl*
18 [I]Or, *owl or jackdaw*
20 [I]Lit., *swarming things with wings*
21 [I]V. 20, note 1
23 [I]V. 20, note 1
25 [a]Lev. 11:40
29 [I]Or, *thorn-tailed lizard*
30 [I]Or, *lizard* [II]Species as yet undefined
32 [I]Lit., *with which work is done* [a]Lev. 15:12
33 [I]Lit., *it* [a]Lev. 6:28; 15:12
34 [I]I.e., if touched by a carcass; cf. vv. 29-32
35 [I]Lit., *hearth for supporting (two) pots*
36 [I]Lit., *of a gathering of*
40 [a]Lev. 17:15; 22:8; Deut. 14:21; Ezek. 44:31
41 [a]Lev. 11:29

42 'Whatever crawls on its belly,
and whatever walks on *all* fours, whatever has many feet, in respect to every
swarming thing that swarms on the
earth, you shall not eat them, for they
are detestable.
43 "[a]Do not render [I]yourselves detestable through any of the swarming
things that swarm; and you shall not
make yourselves unclean with them so
that you become unclean.[2933]
🔑 44 'For [a]I am the LORD your God.[430]
Consecrate yourselves therefore, and
[b]be holy; for I am holy.[6918] And you shall
not make yourselves unclean with any
of the swarming things that swarm on
the earth.
45 '[a]For I am the LORD, who brought
you up from the land of Egypt, to be
your God; thus [b]you shall be holy for I
am holy.' "
46 This is the law[8451] regarding the
animal, and the bird, and every living[2416]
thing that moves in the waters, and
everything that swarms on the earth,
47 [a]to make a distinction between
the unclean and the clean, and between
the edible creature and the creature
which is not to be eaten.

Laws of Motherhood

12 Then the LORD spoke to Moses,
saying,
2 "Speak[1696] to the sons of Israel,
saying,[559] 'When a woman[802] [I]gives birth
and bears a male *child*,[2145] then she shall
be unclean[2930] for seven days, [a]as in
the days of [II]her menstruation she shall
be unclean.[2930]
3 'And on [a]the eighth day the
flesh[1320] of his foreskin[6190] shall be
circumcised.[4135]

43 [I]Lit., *your souls* [a]Lev. 20:25

44 [a]Ex. 6:7; 16:12; 23:25; Is. 43:3; 51:15 [b]Lev. 19:2; 1Pet. 1:16

45 [a]Ex. 6:7; 20:2; Lev. 22:33; 25:38; 26:45 [b]Lev. 19:2; 1Pet. 1:16

47 [a]Lev. 10:10; Ezek. 22:26; 44:23

2 [I]Lit., *produces seed* [II]Lit., *the impurity of her sickness* [a]Lev. 15:19; 18:19

3 [a]Gen. 17:12; Luke 1:59; 2:21

5 [I]Lit., *impurity*

6 [a]Luke 2:22 [b]Lev. 5:7

7 [I]Lit., *fountain*

8 [I]Lit., *her hand does not find a sufficiency of a lamb* [a]Luke 2:22-24 [b]Lev. 5:7 [c]Lev. 4:26

2 [I]Lit., *flesh* [II]Lit., *a mark, stroke*, and so throughout the ch. [a]Deut. 24:8

4 'Then she shall remain in the
blood[1818] of *her* purification[2892] for thirty-
three days; she shall not touch[5060] any
consecrated thing,[6944] nor enter the
sanctuary,[4720] until the days of her purification are completed.
5 'But if she bears a female *child*,[5347]
then she shall be unclean for two weeks,
as in her [I]menstruation; and she shall
remain in the blood of *her* purification
for sixty-six days.
6 'And [a]when the days of her purification are completed, for a son[1121] or
for a daughter, she shall bring to the
priest[3548] at the doorway of the tent[168]
of meeting,[4150] a one[1121] year old lamb
for a burnt offering,[5930] and a young[1121]
pigeon or a turtledove [b]for a sin offering.[2403]
7 'Then he shall offer[7126] it before
the LORD and make atonement[3722] for
her; and she shall be cleansed[2891] from
the [I]flow of her blood. This is the law[8451]
for her who bears *a child, whether* a
male[2145] or a female.[5347]
8 'But if [I]she cannot afford a lamb,
then she shall take [a]two turtledoves or
two young pigeons, [b]the one for a burnt
offering and the other for a sin offering;
and the [c]priest shall make atonement
for her, and she shall be clean.' "

The Test for Leprosy

13 Then the LORD spoke to Moses
and to Aaron, saying,[559]
2 "When a man[120] has on the skin[5785]
of his [I]body[1320] a swelling or a scab or
a bright spot, and it becomes [II]an infection of leprosy[5061] on the skin of his
[I]body, [a]then he shall be brought to Aaron
the priest,[3548] or to one of his sons[1121]
the priests.

🔑 **11:44,45** The holiness of the Lord is a major concern in the O.T., but this passage is of particular interest, because it connected this characteristic of God with His people's need to imitate it. In the N.T., Peter quoted from these verses, or the same statement in Lev. 19:2 or 20:26, to encourage his readers to lead pure lives (I Pet. 1:16). The Greek word translated "holy" in I Peter is the same one used several times in the N.T. to refer to Christians as "saints." The basic idea in the word is the otherness or apartness of the person to whom it refers. In the case of Israel, and later imitated in the N.T., based on His holiness, God's people were to live different lives, because they had been set apart from the world and dedicated to God.

3 "And the priest shall look[7200] at the mark on the skin of the [I]body, and if the hair in the infection has turned[2015] white and the infection appears to be deeper than the skin of his [I]body, it is an infection of leprosy; when the priest has looked at him, he shall pronounce him unclean.

4 "But if the bright spot is white on the skin of his [I]body, and [II]it does not appear to be deeper than the skin, and the hair on it has not turned white, then the priest shall [III]isolate *him who has* the infection for seven days.

5 "And the priest shall look at him on the seventh day, and if in his eyes the infection [I]has not changed, *and* the infection has not spread on the skin, then the priest shall [II]isolate him for seven more days.

6 "And the priest shall look at him again on the seventh day; and if the infection has faded, and the mark has not spread on the skin, then the priest shall pronounce him clean;[2891] it is *only* a scab. And he shall [a]wash[3526] his clothes and be clean.

7 "But if the scab spreads farther on the skin, after he has shown himself to the priest for his cleansing,[2893] he shall appear again to the priest.

8 "And the priest shall look, and if the scab has spread on the skin, then the priest shall pronounce him unclean; it is leprosy.

9 "When the infection of leprosy is on a man, then he shall be brought to the priest.

10 "The priest shall then look, and if there is a [a]white swelling in the skin, and it has turned the hair white, and there is quick[4241] raw[2416] flesh in the swelling,

11 it is [I]a chronic leprosy on the skin of his [II]body, and the priest shall pronounce him unclean;[2931] he shall not [III]isolate him, for he is unclean.

12 "And if the leprosy breaks out farther on the skin, and the leprosy covers[3680] all the skin of *him who has* the infection from his head[7218] even to his feet, [I]as far as the priest can see,

13 then the priest shall look, and behold, *if* the leprosy has covered all his [I]body, he shall pronounce clean[2889] *him who has* the infection; it has all turned white *and* he is clean.

14 "But whenever raw flesh appears[7200] on him, he shall be unclean.[2930]

15 "And the priest shall look at the raw flesh, and he shall pronounce him unclean; the raw flesh is unclean, it is leprosy.

16 "Or if the raw flesh turns again[7725] and is changed[2015] to white, then he shall [a]come to the priest,

17 and the priest shall look at him, and behold, *if* the infection has turned to white, then the priest shall pronounce clean *him who has* the infection; he is clean.

18 "And when the [I]body has a boil on its skin, and it is healed,

19 and in the place of the boil there is a white swelling or a reddish-white,[122] bright spot, then it shall be shown to the priest;

20 and the priest shall look, and behold, *if* [I]it appears to be lower than the skin, and the hair on it has turned white, then the priest shall pronounce him unclean; it is the infection of leprosy, it has broken out in the boil.

21 "But if the priest looks at it, and behold, there are no white hairs in it and it is not lower than the skin and is faded, then the priest shall [I]isolate him for seven days;

22 and if it spreads farther on the skin, then the priest shall pronounce him unclean; it is an infection.

23 "But if the bright spot remains in its place, and does not spread, it is *only* the scar of the boil; and the priest shall pronounce him clean.

24 "Or if the [I]body sustains in its skin a burn by fire, and the raw *flesh* of the burn becomes a bright spot, reddish-white, or white,

25 then the priest shall look at it. And if the hair in the bright spot has [a]turned[2015] white, and it appears to be deeper than the skin, it is leprosy; it has broken out in the burn. Therefore,

3 [I]Lit., *flesh*
4 [I]Lit., *flesh* [II]Lit., *the appearance of it is not deeper* [III]Lit., *shut up*
5 [I]Lit., *has stood* [II]Lit., *shut up*
6 [a]Lev. 11:25; 14:8
10 [a]Num. 12:10; 2Kin. 5:27; 2Chr. 26:19, 20
11 [I]Lit., *an old* [II]Lit., *flesh* [III]Lit., *shut up*
12 [I]Lit., *with regard to the whole sight of the priest's eyes*
13 [I]Lit., *flesh*
16 [a]Luke 5:12-14
18 [I]Lit., *flesh*
20 [I]Lit., *the appearance of it is lower*
21 [I]Lit., *shut up*
24 [I]Lit., *flesh*
25 [a]Ex. 4:6; Num. 12:10; 2Kin. 5:27

the priest shall pronounce him unclean; it is an infection of leprosy.

26 "But if the priest looks at it, and indeed, there is no white hair in the bright spot, and it is no [I]deeper than the skin, but is dim, then the priest shall [II]isolate him for seven days;

27 and the priest shall look at him on the seventh day. If it spreads farther in the skin, then the priest shall pronounce him unclean; it is an infection of leprosy.

28 "But if the bright spot remains in its place, and has not spread in the skin, but is dim, it is the swelling from the burn; and the priest shall pronounce him clean, for it is *only* the scar of the burn.

29 "Now if a man[376] or woman[802] has an infection on the head or on the beard,[2206]

30 then the priest shall look at the infection, and if it appears to be deeper than the skin, and there is thin yellowish hair in it, then the priest shall pronounce him unclean; it is a scale,[5424] it is leprosy of the head or of the beard.

31 "But if the priest looks at the infection of the scale, and indeed, it appears to be no deeper than the skin, and there is no black hair in it, then the priest shall [I]isolate *the person* with the scaly infection for seven days.

32 "And on the seventh day the priest shall look at the infection, and if the scale has not spread, and no yellowish hair has [I]grown in it, and the appearance of the scale is no deeper than the skin,

33 then he shall shave himself, but he shall not shave the scale; and the priest shall [I]isolate *the person* with the scale seven more days.

34 "Then on the seventh day the priest shall look at the scale, and if the scale has not spread in the skin, and it appears to be no deeper than the skin, the priest shall pronounce him clean; and he shall wash his clothes and be clean.

35 "But if the scale spreads farther in the skin after his cleansing,

36 then the priest shall look at him, and if the scale has spread in the skin, the priest need not seek for the yellowish hair; he is unclean.

37 "If in his sight the scale has remained, however, and black hair has grown in it, the scale has healed, he is clean; and the priest shall pronounce him clean.

38 "And when a man or a woman has bright spots on the skin of the [I]body, *even* white bright spots,

39 then the priest shall look, and if the bright spots on the skin of their [I]bodies are a faint white, it is [II]eczema that has broken out on the skin; he is clean.

40 "Now if a [I]man loses the hair of his head, he is [a]bald; he is clean.

41 "And if his head becomes bald at the [I]front and sides, he is bald on the forehead; he is clean.

42 "But if on the bald head or the bald forehead, there occurs a reddish-white infection, it is leprosy breaking out on his bald head or on his bald forehead.

43 "Then [a]the priest shall look at him; and if the swelling of the infection is reddish-white on his bald head or on his bald forehead, like the appearance of leprosy in the skin of the [I]body,

44 he is a leprous man, he is unclean. The priest shall surely pronounce him unclean; his infection is on his head.

45 "As for the leper who has the infection, his clothes shall be torn, and [a]the hair of his head shall be [I]uncovered, and he shall [b]cover his mustache and cry,[7121] '[c]Unclean! Unclean!'

46 "He shall remain unclean all the days during which he has the infection; he is unclean. He shall live alone; his dwelling[4186] shall be [a]outside the camp.[4264]

47 "When a garment has a [I]mark of leprosy in it, whether it is a wool garment or a linen garment,

48 whether in [I]warp[8359] or woof,[6154] of linen or of wool, whether in leather or in any article made[4399] of leather,

26 [I]Lit., *lower* [II]Lit., *shut up*

31 [I]Lit., *shut up*

32 [I]Lit., *been*

33 [I]Lit., *shut up*

38 [I]Lit., *flesh*

39 [I]Lit., *flesh* [II]Lit., *tetter*

40 [I]Lit., *man's head becomes bald* [a]2Kin. 2:23; Is. 15:2; Amos 8:10

41 [I]Lit., *border of his face*

43 [I]Lit., *flesh* [a]Lev. 10:10; Ezek. 22:26

45 [I]Or, *disheveled* [a]Lev. 10:6 [b]Ezek. 24:17, 22; Mic. 3:7 [c]Lam. 4:15

46 [a]Num. 5:1-4; 12:14

47 [I]Lit., *infection, and so throughout the ch.*

48 [I]Or, *weaving or texture*

49 if the mark is greenish or reddish
in the garment or in the leather, or in
the [I]warp or in the woof, or in any article
of leather, it is a leprous mark and shall
be shown to the priest.
50 "Then [a]the priest shall look at
the mark, and shall [I]quarantine the article with the mark for seven days.
51 "He shall then look at the mark
on the seventh day; if the mark has
spread in the garment, whether in the
warp or in the woof, or in the leather,
whatever the purpose for which the
leather is used, the mark is a [I]leprous
malignancy, it is unclean.
52 "So he shall burn[8313] the garment, whether the warp or the woof,
in wool or in linen, or any article of
leather in which the mark occurs, for
it is a [I]leprous malignancy; it shall be
burned in the fire.
53 "But if the priest shall look, and
indeed, the mark has not spread in the
garment, either in the warp or in the
woof, or in any article of leather,
54 then the priest shall order[6680]
them to wash the thing in which the
mark occurs, and he shall [I]quarantine
it for seven more days.
55 "After the article with the mark
has been washed, the priest shall again
look, and if the mark has not changed[2015]
its appearance, even though the mark
has not spread, it is unclean; you shall
burn it in the fire, whether an eating
away has produced bareness on the top
or on the front of it.
56 "Then if the priest shall look,
and if the mark has faded after it has
been washed, then he shall tear[7167] it
out of the garment or out of the leather,
whether from the warp or from the
woof;
57 and if it appears[7200] again in the
garment, whether in the warp or in the
woof, or in any article of leather, it is
an outbreak; the article with the mark
shall be burned in the fire.
58 "And the garment, whether the
warp or the woof, or any article of
leather from which the mark has
departed[5493] when you washed[3526] it, it

49 [I]Or, *weaving or texture*

50 [I]Lit., *shut up* [a]Ezek. 44:23

51 [I]Lit., *malignant leprosy*

52 [I]Lit., *malignant leprosy*

54 [I]Lit., *shut up*

2 [a]Matt. 8:4; Mark 1:44; Luke 5:14; 17:14

3 [I]Lit., *mark, stroke,* and so throughout the ch. [a]Lev. 13:46

4 [I]Lit., *scarlet color and* [a]Lev. 14:6, 49, 51, 52; Num. 19:6

5 [I]Lit., *living*

6 [I]Lit., *scarlet color and* [II]Lit., *living* [a]Lev. 14:4 [b]Ps. 51:7

7 [a]Ezek. 36:25

8 [a]Lev. 11:25; 13:6; Num. 8:7 [b]Lev. 14:9, 20 [c]Num. 5:2, 3; 12:14, 15; 2Chr. 26:21

9 [I]Lit., *flesh* [a]Lev. 14:8, 20

shall then be washed a second time and
shall be clean."
59 This is the law[8451] for the mark
of leprosy in a garment of wool or linen,
whether in the warp or in the woof, or
in any article of leather, for pronouncing
it clean or unclean.

Law of Cleansing a Leper

14 Then the LORD spoke to Moses,
saying,[559]
2 "This shall be the law[8451] of the
leper in the day of his cleansing.[2893]
[a]Now he shall be brought to the
priest,[3548]
3 and the priest shall go [a]out to the
outside of the camp.[4264] Thus the priest
shall look,[7200] and if the [I]infection[5061] of
leprosy has been healed in the leper,
4 then the priest shall give
orders[6680] to take two live[2416] clean[2889]
birds and [a]cedar wood and a [I]scarlet
string and hyssop[231] for the one who
is to be cleansed.[289]
5 "The priest shall also give orders
to slay[7819] the one bird in an earthenware[2789] vessel over [I]running water.
6 "*As for* the live[2416] bird, he shall
take it, together with [a]the cedar wood
and the [I]scarlet string and the [b]hyssop,
and shall dip[2881] them and the live bird
in the blood[1818] of the bird that was slain
over the [II]running water.
7 "[a]He shall then sprinkle seven
times the one who is to be cleansed
from the leprosy, and shall pronounce
him clean, and shall let the live bird go
free over the open field.
8 "[a]The one to be cleansed shall
then wash[3526] his clothes and shave off
all his hair, and bathe[7364] in water and
[b]be clean.[2891] Now afterward, he may
enter the camp, but he [c]shall stay outside
his tent[168] for seven days.
9 "And it will be on the seventh day
that he shall shave off all his hair: he
shall shave his head[7218] and his beard[2206]
and his eyebrows, even all his hair. He
shall then wash his clothes and bathe
his [I]body[1320] in water and [a]be clean.
10 "Now on the eighth day he is

to take two male lambs without defect,[8549] and a yearling ewe3535 lamb without defect, and three-tenths *of an* [I]*ephah* of fine flour mixed with oil[8081] for a grain offering,[4503] and one [IIa]log of oil;

11 and the priest who pronounces him clean shall present the man[376] to be cleansed[2891] and the [I]aforesaid before the LORD at the doorway of the tent of meeting.[4150]

12 "Then the priest shall take the one male lamb and bring[7126] it for a [a]guilt offering,[817] with the [Ib]log of oil, and present them as a [c]wave offering before the LORD.

13 "Next he shall slaughter the male lamb in [a]the place where they slaughter the sin offering[2403] and the burnt offering,[5930] at the place of the sanctuary—[6944]for the guilt offering, [b]like the sin offering, belongs to the priest; it is most holy.

14 "The priest shall then take some of the blood of the [a]guilt offering, and the priest shall put *it* on [b]the lobe of the right ear[241] of the one to be cleansed, and on the thumb of his right hand, and on the big toe of his right foot.

15 "The priest shall also take some of the [Ia]log of oil, and pour *it* into his left palm;[3709]

16 the priest shall then dip his right-hand finger into the oil that is in his left palm, and with his finger sprinkle some of the oil seven times before the LORD.

17 "And of the remaining[3499] oil which is in his palm, the priest shall put some on the right ear lobe of the one to be cleansed, and on the thumb of his right hand, and on the big toe of his right foot, on the blood of the guilt offering;

18 while the rest[3498] of the oil that is in the priest's palm, he shall put on the head of the one to be cleansed. So the priest shall make [a]atonement[3722] on his behalf before the LORD.

19 "The priest shall next offer[6213] the [a]sin offering and make atonement for the one to be cleansed from his uncleanness.[2932] Then afterward, he shall slaughter the burnt offering.

20 "And the priest shall offer[5927] up the burnt offering and the grain offering on the altar.[4196] Thus the priest shall make atonement for him, and [a]he shall be clean.

21 "[a]But if he is poor, and his [I]means are insufficient, then he is to take one male lamb for a [b]guilt offering as a wave offering to make atonement[3722] for him, and one-tenth *of an* [II]*ephah* of fine flour mixed[1101] with oil for a grain offering, and a [IIIc]log of oil,

22 and two turtledoves or two young[1121] pigeons which [I]are within his means, [a]the one shall be a [b]sin offering and the other a burnt offering.

23 "[a]Then the eighth day he shall bring them for his cleansing to the priest, at the doorway of the tent of meeting, before the LORD.

24 "And the priest shall take the lamb of the guilt offering, and [a]the [I]log of oil, and the priest shall offer them for a wave offering before the LORD.

25 "Next he shall slaughter the lamb of the guilt offering; and the priest is to take some of the blood of the guilt offering and put *it* on [a]the lobe of the right ear of the one to be cleansed and on the thumb of his right hand, and on the big toe of his right foot.

26 "The priest shall also pour some of the oil into his left palm;

27 and with his right-hand finger the priest shall sprinkle some of the oil that is in his left palm seven times before the LORD.

28 "The priest shall then put some of the oil that is in his palm on the lobe of the right ear of the one to be cleansed, and on the thumb of his right hand, and on the big toe of his right foot, on the place of the blood of the guilt offering.

29 "Moreover, the rest[3498] of the oil that is in the priest's palm he shall put on the head of the one to be cleansed, to make atonement on his behalf before the LORD.

30 "He shall then offer one of the

10 [I]I.e., Approx. one bu. [II]I.e., Approx. one pt. [a]Lev. 14:12, 15, 21, 24

11 [I]Lit., *them*

12 [I]I.e., Approx. one pt. [a]Lev. 5:6, 18; 6:6; 14:19 [b]Lev. 14:10 [c]Ex. 29:22-24, 26

13 [a]Ex. 29:11; Lev. 1:11; 4:24 [b]Lev. 6:24-30; 7:7

14 [a]Lev. 14:19 [b]Ex. 29:20; Lev. 8:23, 24

15 [I]I.e., Approx. one pt. [a]Lev. 14:10

18 [a]Lev. 4:26; Num. 15:28; Heb. 2:17

19 [a]Lev. 14:12

20 [a]Lev. 14:8, 9

21 [I]Lit., *hand is not reaching* [II]I.e., Approx. one bu. [III]I.e., Approx. one pt. [a]Lev. 5:11; 12:8; 27:8 [b]Lev. 14:22 [c]Lev. 14:10

22 [I]Lit., *his hand reaches* [a]Lev. 5:7 [b]Lev. 14:21, 24, 25

23 [a]Lev. 14:10, 11

24 [I]I.e., Approx. one pt. [a]Lev. 14:10

25 [a]Lev. 14:14

turtledoves or young pigeons, [I]which are within his means.

31 "*He shall offer* what [I]he can afford, [a]the one for a sin offering, and the other for a burnt offering, together with the grain offering. So the priest shall make atonement before the LORD on behalf of the one to be cleansed.

32 "This is the law *for him* in whom there is an infection of leprosy, whose [I]means are limited for his cleansing."

Cleansing a Leprous House

33 The LORD further spoke to Moses and to Aaron, saying,

34 "[a]When you enter the land[776] of Canaan, which I give you for a possession,[272] and I put a mark of leprosy on a house[1004] in the land of your possession,

35 then the one who owns the house shall come and tell[5046] the priest, saying, '*Something* like [a]a mark *of leprosy* has become visible to me in the house.'

36 "The priest shall then order that they empty the house before the priest goes in to look at the mark, so that everything in the house need not become unclean;[2930] and afterward the priest shall go in to look at the house.

37 "So he shall look at the mark, and if the mark on the walls of the house has greenish or reddish[122] depressions, and appears deeper than the [I]surface;

38 then the priest shall come out of the house, to the [I]doorway, and [II]quarantine the house for seven days.

39 "And the priest shall return[7725] on the seventh day and [I]make an inspection. If the mark has indeed spread in the walls of the house,

40 then the priest shall order them to tear out the stones with the mark in them and throw them away [I]at an unclean[2931] place outside the city.

41 "And he shall have the house scraped all around [I]inside, and they shall dump[8210] the plaster[6083] that they scrape off at an unclean place outside the city.

42 "Then they shall take other stones and replace *those* stones; and he shall take other plaster[6083] and replaster the house.

43 "If, however, the mark breaks out again in the house, after he has torn out the stones and scraped the house, and after it has been replastered,

44 then the priest shall come in and [I]make an inspection. If he sees that the mark has indeed spread in the house, it is [a]a malignant mark in the house; it is unclean.

45 "He shall therefore tear down[5422] the house, its stones, and its timbers, and all the plaster of the house, and he shall take *them* outside the city to an [a]unclean place.

46 "Moreover, whoever goes into the house during the time that he has [I]quarantined it, becomes [a]unclean until evening.

47 "Likewise, whoever lies down in the house shall wash[3526] his clothes, and whoever eats in the house shall wash his clothes.

48 "If, on the other hand, the priest comes in and [I]makes an inspection, and the mark has not indeed spread in the house after the house has been replastered, then the priest shall pronounce the house clean because the mark has [II]not reappeared.

49 "To cleanse the house then, he shall take [a]two birds and cedar wood and a [I]scarlet string and hyssop,

50 and he shall slaughter the one bird in an earthenware vessel over [I]running water.

51 "Then he shall take the cedar wood and the [a]hyssop and the [I]scarlet string, with the live bird, and dip them in the blood of the slain bird, as well as in the [II]running water, and sprinkle the house seven times.

52 "He shall thus cleanse the house with the blood of the bird and with the [I]running water, along with the live bird and with the cedar wood and with the hyssop and with the [II]scarlet string.

53 "However, he shall let the live bird go free outside the city into the open field. So he shall make atonement for the house, and it shall be clean."

30 [I]Lit., *from those which his hand can reach*
31 [I]Lit., *his hand can reach* [a]Lev. 5:7
32 [I]Lit., *hand does not reach*
34 [a]Gen. 17:8; Num. 32:22; Deut. 7:1; 32:49
35 [a]Ps. 91:10
37 [I]Lit., *wall*
38 [I]Lit., *doorway of the house* [II]Lit., *shut up*
39 [I]Lit., *look*
40 [I]Lit., *to*
41 [I]Lit., *from the house around*
44 [I]Lit., *look* [a]Lev. 13:51
45 [a]Lev. 14:41
46 [I]Lit., *shut up* [a]Num. 19:7, 10, 21, 22
48 [I]Lit., *looks* [II]Lit., *healed*
49 [I]Lit., *scarlet color* [a]Lev. 14:4
50 [I]Lit., *living*
51 [I]Lit., *scarlet color* [II]Lit., *living* [a]1Kin. 4:33; Ps. 51:7
52 [I]Lit., *living* [II]Lit., *scarlet color*

54 This is the law for any mark of
leprosy—even for a [a]scale,
55 and for the [a]leprous garment or
house,
56 and [a]for a swelling, and for a scab,
and for a bright spot—
57 to teach[3384] [I]when they are unclean, and [II]when they are clean. This
is the law of leprosy.

Cleansing Unhealthiness

15 The LORD also spoke to Moses
and to Aaron, saying,
2 "Speak[1696] to the sons[1121] of Israel, and say[559] to them, '[a]When any
man[376] has a discharge from his
[I]body,[1320] [II]his discharge is unclean.[2931]
3 'This, moreover, shall be his
uncleanness[2932] in his discharge: it is
his uncleanness whether his body allows
its discharge to flow, or whether his
body obstructs its discharge.
4 'Every bed on which the person
with the discharge lies becomes unclean,[2930] and everything on which he
sits becomes unclean.
5 'Anyone, moreover, who touches[5060] his bed shall wash[3526] his
clothes and bathe[7364] in water and be
unclean[2930] until evening;
6 and whoever sits on the thing on
which the man with the discharge has
been sitting, shall wash his clothes and
bathe in water and be unclean until evening.
7 'Also whoever touches the
[I]person with the discharge shall wash
his clothes and bathe in water and be
unclean until evening.
8 'Or if the man with the discharge
spits on one who is clean,[2889] he too
shall wash[3526] his clothes and bathe in
water and be unclean until evening.
9 'And every saddle on which the
person with the discharge rides becomes unclean.
10 'Whoever then touches any of the
things which were under him shall be
unclean until evening, and he who carries them shall wash his clothes and
bathe in water and be unclean until evening.
11 'Likewise, whomever the one
with the discharge touches without having rinsed[7857] his hands[3027] in water shall
wash his clothes and bathe in water and
be unclean until evening.
12 'However, an [a]earthenware[2789]
vessel which the person with the discharge touches shall be broken,[7665] and
every wooden vessel shall be rinsed in
water.
13 'Now when the man with the discharge becomes cleansed[2891] from his
discharge, then he [a]shall count[5608] off
for himself seven days for his
cleansing;[2893] he shall then wash his
clothes and bathe his body in [I]running[2416]
water and shall become clean.
14 'Then on the eighth day he shall
take for himself [a]two turtledoves or two
young pigeons, and come before the
LORD to the doorway of the tent of meeting, and give them to the priest;[3548]
15 and the priest shall offer[6213]
them, [a]one for a sin offering, and the
other for a burnt offering.[5930] So
[b]the priest shall make atonement[3722] on
his behalf before the LORD because of
his discharge.
16 '[a]Now if a [I]man has a seminal[2233]
emission,[7902] he shall bathe all his body
in water and be unclean until evening.
17 'As for any garment or any
leather[5785] on which there is seminal
emission, it shall be washed with
water and be unclean until evening.
18 'If a man lies with a woman[802]
so that there is a seminal emission, they
shall both bathe in water and be [a]unclean
until evening.
19 '[a]When a woman has a discharge, *if* her discharge in her body is
blood,[1818] she shall continue in her menstrual impurity for seven days; and
whoever touches her shall be unclean
until evening.
20 'Everything also on which she
lies during her menstrual impurity shall
be unclean, and everything on which she
sits shall be unclean.
21 'And anyone who touches her

54 [a]Lev. 13:30
55 [a]Lev. 13:47-52
56 [a]Lev. 13:2
57 [I]Lit., *in the day of uncleanness* [II]Lit., *in the day of cleanness*
2 [I]Lit., *flesh,* and so throughout the ch. [II]Or, *by his discharge, he is unclean* [a]Lev. 22:4; Num. 5:2; 2Sam. 3:29
7 [I]Lit., *flesh*
12 [a]Lev. 6:28; 11:33
13 [I]Lit., *living* [a]Lev. 8:33; 14:8
14 [a]Lev. 14:22, 23
15 [a]Lev. 5:7; 14:31 [b]Lev. 14:19, 31
16 [I]Lit., *man's . . . goes out from him* [a]Lev. 22:4; Deut. 23:10, 11
18 [a]1Sam. 21:4
19 [a]Lev. 12:2

bed shall wash his clothes and bathe in water and be unclean until evening.

22 'And whoever touches any thing on which she sits shall wash his clothes and bathe in water and be unclean until evening.

23 'Whether it be on the bed or on the thing on which she is sitting, when he touches it, he shall be unclean until evening.

24 "[a]And if a man actually lies with her, so that her menstrual impurity is on him, he shall be unclean seven days, and every bed on which he lies shall be unclean.

25 '[a]Now if a woman has a discharge of her blood many days, not at the period[6256] of her menstrual impurity, or if she has a discharge beyond [I]that period, all the days of her impure discharge she shall continue as though [II]in her menstrual impurity; she is unclean.

26 'Any bed on which she lies all the days of her discharge shall be to her like [I]her bed at menstruation; and every thing on which she sits shall be unclean, like [II]her uncleanness at that time.

27 'Likewise, whoever touches them shall be unclean and shall wash[3526] his clothes and bathe in water and be unclean until evening.

28 'When she becomes clean[2891] from her discharge, she shall count off for herself seven days; and afterward she shall be clean.

29 'Then on the eighth day she shall take for herself two turtledoves or two young pigeons, and bring them in to the priest, to the doorway of the tent of meeting.

30 'And the priest shall offer the [a]one for a sin offering and the other for a burnt offering. So the priest shall make atonement on her behalf before the LORD because of her impure discharge.'

31 "Thus you shall keep the sons of Israel separated[5144] from their uncleanness, lest they die[4191] in their uncleanness by their [a]defiling My [I]tabernacle[4908] that is among them."

32 This is the law[8451] for the one with a discharge, and for the man [I]who has a seminal emission so that he is unclean[2930] by it,

33 and for the woman who is ill because of menstrual impurity, and for the one who has a discharge, whether a male[2145] or a female,[5347] or a man who lies with an unclean woman.

Law of Atonement

16 Now the LORD spoke to Moses after [a]the death[4194] of the two sons[1121] of Aaron, when they had approached[7126] the presence of the LORD and died.[4191]

🗝 2 And the LORD said to Moses, "Tell[1696] your brother[251] Aaron that he shall not enter [a]at any time[6256] into the holy[6944] place inside[1004] the veil, before the [I]mercy seat[3727] which is on the ark,[727] lest he die; for [b]I will appear[7200] in the cloud[6051] over the [I]mercy seat.

3 "Aaron shall enter the holy place with this: with a [I]bull for a [a]sin offering[2403] and a ram for a burnt offering.[5930]

4 "He shall put on the [a]holy linen tunic, and the linen undergarments shall be next to his [I]body,[1320] and he shall be girded with the linen sash,[73] and attired with the linen turban[4701] (these are holy garments). Then he shall [b]bathe[7364] his [I]body in water and put them on.

5 "And he shall take from the congregation[5712] of the sons[1121] of Israel [a]two male goats for a sin offering and one ram for a burnt offering.

6 "Then [a]Aaron shall offer[7126] the bull for the sin offering which is for himself, that he may make atonement[3722] for himself and for his household.[1004]

7 "And he shall take the two goats and present them before the LORD at the doorway of the tent of meeting.[4150]

8 "And Aaron shall cast lots for the

24 [a]Lev. 18:19; 20:18

25 [I]Lit., *her menstrual impurity* [II]Lit., *in the days of* [a]Matt. 9:20; Mark 5:25; Luke 8:43

26 [I]Lit., *the bed of her menstrual impurity* [II]Lit., *the uncleanness of her menstrual impurity*

30 [a]Lev. 5:7

31 [I]Or, *dwelling place* [a]Lev. 20:3; Num. 19:13, 20; Ezek. 5:11; 36:17

32 [I]Lit., *whose seminal emission goes out from him*

1 [a]Lev. 10:1, 2

2 [I]Lit., *propitiatory* [a]Ex. 30:10; Heb. 6:19; 9:7, 25 [b]Ex. 25:21, 22; 40:34; 1Kin. 8:10-12

3 [I]Or, *bull of the herd* [a]Lev. 4:1-12; 16:6; Heb. 9:7

4 [I]Lit., *flesh* [a]Ex. 28:39, 42 [b]Ex. 30:20; Lev. 16:24; Heb. 10:22

5 [a]Lev. 4:13-21; 2Chr. 29:21; Ezek. 45:22

6 [a]Heb. 5:3

🗝 **16:2,14** See note on Ex. 26:25-31.

two goats, one lot for the LORD and the other lot for the [I]scapegoat.5799

9 "Then Aaron shall offer the goat on which the lot for the LORD fell,[5927] and make[6213] it a sin offering.

10 "But the goat on which the lot for the [I]scapegoat fell, shall be presented alive[2416] before the LORD, to make [a]atonement[3722] upon it, to send it into the wilderness as the [I]scapegoat.

11 "Then Aaron shall offer the bull of the sin offering [a]which is for himself, and make atonement for himself and [b]for his household, and he shall slaughter[7819] the bull of the sin offering which is for himself.

12 "And he shall take a [a]firepan full of coals of fire from upon the altar[4196] before the LORD, and [I]two handfuls of finely ground [b]sweet incense,[7004] and bring *it* inside the veil.

13 "And he shall put the incense on the fire before the LORD, that the cloud of incense may cover[3680] the [Ia]mercy seat that is on *the ark of* the testimony,[5715] [b]lest he die.

14 "Moreover, [a]he shall take some of the blood[1818] of the bull and sprinkle *it* [b]with his finger on the [I]mercy seat on the east *side*; also in front of the [I]mercy seat he shall sprinkle some of the blood with his finger seven times.

15 "Then he shall slaughter the goat of the sin offering [a]which is for the people,[5971] and bring its blood inside the veil, and do with its blood as he did with the blood of the bull, and sprinkle it on the [I]mercy seat and in front of the [I]mercy seat.

16 "And [a]he shall make atonement for the holy place, because of the impurities[2932] of the sons of Israel, and because of their transgressions,[6588] in regard to all their sins; and thus he shall do for the tent[168] of meeting which abides with them in the midst of their impurities.

17 "When he goes in to make atonement in the holy place, no one[120] shall be in the tent of meeting[6951] until he comes out, that he may make atonement for himself and for his household and for all the assembly of Israel.

18 "Then he shall go out to the altar that is before the LORD and make atonement for it, and shall take some of the blood of the bull and of the blood of the goat, and [a]put it on the horns of the altar on all sides.

19 "And [a]with his finger he shall sprinkle some of the blood on it seven times, and cleanse it, and from the impurities of the sons of Israel consecrate[6942] it.

20 "When he finishes[3615] atoning for the holy place, and the tent of meeting and the altar, he shall offer the live[2416] goat.

21 "Then Aaron shall lay both of his hands[3027] on the head[7218] of the live goat, and [a]confess[3034] over it all the iniquities[5771] of the sons of Israel, and all their transgressions [I]in regard to all their sins; and he shall lay them on the head of the goat and send *it* away into the wilderness by the hand of a man[376] who *stands* in readiness.

22 "And the goat shall bear[5375] on itself all their iniquities to a solitary land;[776] and he shall release the goat in the wilderness.

23 "Then Aaron shall come into the tent of meeting, and take off [a]the linen garments which he put on when he went into the holy place, and shall leave them there.

24 "And [a]he shall bathe his [I]body with water in a holy[6918] place and put on [b]his clothes, and come forth and offer his burnt offering and the burnt offering of the people, and make atonement for himself and for the people.

25 "Then he shall offer up in smoke[6999] the fat of the sin offering on the altar.

26 "And the one who released the goat as the [I]scapegoat [a]shall wash[3526] his clothes and bathe his [II]body with water; then afterward he shall come into the camp.

27 "But the bull of the sin offering and the goat of the sin offering, [a]whose blood was brought in to make atonement

8 [I]Lit., *goat of removal,* or else a name: *Azazel*

10 [I]Lit., *goat of removal,* or else a name: *Azazel* [a]Is. 53:4-10; Rom. 3:25; 1John 2:2

11 [a]Heb. 7:27; 9:7 [b]Lev. 16:33

12 [I]Lit., *the filling of the hollow of his hands* [a]Lev. 10:1; Num. 16:18 [b]Ex. 30:34-38

13 [I]Lit., *propitiatory* [a]Ex. 25:21 [b]Ex. 28:43; Lev. 22:9; Num. 4:15, 20

14 [I]Lit., *propitiatory* [a]Heb. 9:25 [b]Lev. 4:6, 17

15 [I]Lit., *propitiatory* [a]Heb. 7:27; 9:7, 12

16 [a]Ex. 29:36, 37; 30:10; Heb. 2:17

18 [a]Lev. 4:25; Ezek. 43:20, 22

19 [a]Lev. 16:14; Ezek. 43:20

21 [I]Lit., *in addition to* [a]Lev. 5:5

23 [a]Lev. 16:4; Ezek. 42:14; 44:19

24 [I]Lit., *flesh* [a]Lev. 16:4 [b]Ex. 28:40, 41

26 [I]Lit., *goat of removal,* or else a name: *Azazel* [II]Lit., *flesh* [a]Lev. 11:25, 40

27 [a]Lev. 6:30; Heb. 13:11

in the holy place, shall be taken outside
the camp,[4264] and they shall burn[8313]
their hides,[5785] their flesh, and their
refuse in the fire.
28 "Then the [a]one who burns them
shall wash his clothes and bathe his body
with water, then afterward he shall come
into the camp.

An Annual Atonement

🔑**29** "And *this* shall be a permanent[5769] statute[2708] for you: [a]in the seventh month, on the tenth day of the
month, you shall humble your souls,[5315]
and not [b]do any work,[4399] whether the
native, or the alien[1616] who sojourns[1481]
among you;
30 for it is on this day[3117] that
[I]atonement shall be made for you to
[a]cleanse you; you shall be clean from
all your sins[2403] before the LORD.
31 "It is to be a sabbath[7676] of solemn rest[7677] for you, that you may
[a]humble your souls; it is a permanent
statute.
32 "So the priest[3548] who is anointed
and [I]ordained to serve as priest[3547] in
his father's[1] place shall make atonement:
he shall thus put on [a]the linen garments,
the holy garments,
33 and make atonement for the holy
sanctuary;[4720] and he shall make atonement for the tent of meeting and for
the altar. He shall also make atonement
for [a]the priests and for all the people
of the assembly.
34 "Now you shall have this as a
[a]permanent statute, to [b]make atonement
for the sons of Israel for all their sins
once every year." And just as the LORD
had commanded[6680] Moses, *so* he did.

Blood for Atonement

17 Then the LORD spoke to Moses,
saying,
2 "Speak[1696] to Aaron and to his
sons,[1121] and to all the sons[1121] of Israel,
and say[559] to them, 'This is what[1697]
the LORD has commanded,[6680] saying,
🔑3 "Any man[272] from the house[1004]
of Israel who slaughters an ox, or a lamb,
or a goat in the camp, or who
slaughters[7819] it outside the camp,[4264]
4 and [a]has not brought it to the doorway of the tent[4908] of meeting[4150] to
present[7126] *it* as an offering[7133] to the
LORD before the [I]tabernacle[168] of the
LORD, bloodguiltiness[1818] is to be
reckoned[2803] to that man. He has
shed[8210] blood and that man shall be cut
off[3772] from among his people.[5971]
5 "[I]The reason is so that the sons
of Israel may bring their sacrifices[2077]
which they were sacrificing[2076] in the
open field, that they may bring them
in to the LORD, at the doorway of the
tent of meeting to the priest,[3548] and
sacrifice them as sacrifices of peace
offerings[8002] to the LORD.
6 "And the priest shall sprinkle[2236]
the blood on the altar[4196] of the LORD
at the doorway of the tent of meeting,
and [a]offer up the fat in smoke[6999] as a
soothing aroma to the LORD.
7 "And [a]they shall no longer sacrifice
their sacrifices to the [I]goat demons[8163]
with which they play the harlot.[2181] This
shall be a permanent[5769] statute[2708] to
them throughout their genera-
tions."'[1755]
8 "Then you shall say to them, 'Any
man from the house of Israel, or from
the aliens[1616] who sojourn[1481] among
them, who offers[5927] a burnt offering[5930]
or sacrifice,
9 and [a]does not bring it to the doorway of the tent of meeting to [I]offer[6213]
it to the LORD, that man also shall be
cut off from his people.
10 "[a]And any man from the house
of Israel, or from the aliens who sojourn

28 [a]Num. 19:8
29 [a]Lev. 23:27; Num. 29:7 [b]Ex. 31:14, 15
30 [I]Lit., *he shall make atonement* [a]Ps. 51:2; Jer. 33:8; Eph. 5:26
31 [a]Lev. 23:32; Ezra 8:21; Is. 58:3, 5; Dan. 10:12
32 [I]Lit., *whose hand is filled* [a]Lev. 16:4
33 [a]Lev. 16:11
34 [a]Lev. 23:31 [b]Heb. 9:7
4 [I]Lit., *dwelling place* [a]Deut. 12:5-21
5 [I]Lit., *In order that*
6 [a]Num. 18:17
7 [I]Or, *goat-idols* [a]Ex. 22:20; 32:8; 34:15; Deut. 32:17; 2Chr. 11:15; Ps. 106:37f.; 1Cor. 10:20
9 [I]Lit., *do* [a]Ex. 20:24; Lev. 17:4
10 [a]Gen. 9:4; Lev. 3:17; 7:26, 27; Deut. 12:16, 23-25; 1Sam. 14:33

🔑 **16:29** Here the Day of Atonement is said to be on the tenth day of the seventh month, whereas Lev. 23:32 specifies the ninth day of the month. The wording of the latter passage here is the key. It says that the rest is to begin on the ninth day of the month *at evening.* According to the ancient Hebrew calendar, the tenth day began on the evening of the ninth day.

🔑 **17:3,4** See note on Deut. 12:15,16.

among them, who eats any blood,
[b]I will set My face against that person[5315]
who eats blood, and will cut him off from
among his people.
11 'For [a]the [I]life[5315] of the flesh[1320]
is in the blood, and I have given it to
you on the altar to make atonement[3722]
for your souls; for [b]it is the blood by
reason of the [I]life that makes atonement.'
12 "Therefore I said to the sons of
Israel, 'No person among you may eat
blood, nor may any alien who sojourns
among you eat blood.'
13 "So when any man from the sons
of Israel, or from the aliens who sojourn
among them, [I]in hunting catches[6679] a
beast[2416] or a bird which may be eaten,
[a]he shall pour out its blood and cover[3680]
it with earth.[6083]
14 "[a]For *as for the* [I]life of all flesh,
its blood is *identified* with its [I]life. Therefore I said to the sons of Israel, 'You
are not to eat the blood of any flesh,
for the [I]life of all flesh is its blood; whoever eats it shall be cut off.'
15 "[a]And when any person eats *an
animal* which dies,[5038] or is torn *by
beasts*, whether he is a native or an alien,
he shall wash[3526] his clothes and
bathe[7364] in water, and remain unclean[2930] until evening; then he will become clean.[2891]
16 "But if he does not wash[3526] *them*
or bathe his body, then [a]he shall bear[5375]
his [I]guilt."[5771]

Laws on Immoral Relations

18 Then the LORD spoke to Moses,
saying,
2 "Speak[1696] to the sons[1121] of Israel
and say[559] to them, '[a]I am the LORD
your God.[430]
3 'You shall not do [I]what is [a]done
in the land[776] of Egypt where you lived,
nor are you to do[6213] [I]what is [b]done in
the land of Canaan where I am bringing
you; you shall not walk in their statutes.[2708]
4 'You are to perform My judg-
ments[4941] and keep[8104] My statutes, [I]to
live in accord with them; [a]I am the LORD
your God.
5 'So you shall keep[8104] My statutes[2708] and My judgments, [a]by which
a man[120] may live[2425] if he does them;
I am the LORD.
6 'None of you shall approach[7126]
any blood relative[7607] [I]of his[1320] to
uncover[1540] nakedness;[6172] I am the
LORD.
7 '[a]You shall not uncover the nakedness of your father,[1] that is, the nakedness of your mother.[517] She is your
mother; you are not to uncover her
nakedness.
8 '[a]You shall not uncover the nakedness of your father's wife;[802] it is your
father's nakedness.
9 '[a]The nakedness of your sister,[269]
either your father's daughter or your
mother's daughter, whether born at
home[1004] or born outside, their nakedness you shall not uncover.
10 'The nakedness of your son's
daughter or your daughter's[1121] daughter, their nakedness you shall not uncover; for [I]their nakedness is yours.
11 'The nakedness of your father's
wife's daughter, [I]born[4138] to your father,
she is your sister, you shall not uncover
her nakedness.
12 '[a]You shall not uncover the
nakedness of your father's sister; she
is your father's blood relative.
13 'You shall not uncover the nakedness of your mother's sister, for she
is your mother's blood relative.
14 '[a]You shall not uncover the
nakedness of your father's brother;[251]
you shall not approach his wife, she is
your aunt.
15 '[a]You shall not uncover the
nakedness of your daughter-in-law; she
is your son's wife, you shall not uncover
her nakedness.
16 '[a]You shall not uncover the
nakedness of your brother's wife; it is
your brother's nakedness.
17 '[a]You shall not uncover the
nakedness of a woman[802] and of her
daughter, nor shall you take her son's
daughter or her daughter's daughter,

10 [b]Lev. 20:3, 6; Jer. 44:11
11 [I]Lit., *soul* [a]Gen. 9:4; Lev. 17:14 [b]Heb. 9:22
13 [I]Lit., *who in hunting* [a]Deut. 12:16
14 [I]Lit., *soul* [a]Gen. 9:4; Lev. 17:11
15 [a]Ex. 22:31; Lev. 7:24; 22:8; Deut. 14:21
16 [I]Or, *iniquity* [a]Num. 19:20
2 [a]Ex. 6:7; Lev. 11:44; Ezek. 20:5
3 [I]Lit., *according to the deed of* [a]Ezek. 20:7, 8 [b]Lev. 18:24-30; 20:23
4 [I]Lit., *to walk in them* [a]Lev. 18:2
5 [a]Neh. 9:29; Ezek. 18:9; 20:11; Luke 10:28; Rom. 10:5; Gal. 3:12
6 [I]Lit., *of his flesh*
7 [a]Lev. 20:11; Deut. 27:20; Ezek. 22:10
8 [a]Lev. 20:11; Deut. 22:30; 27:20; 1Cor. 5:1
9 [a]Lev. 18:11; 20:17; Deut. 27:22
10 [I]Lit., *they are your nakedness*
11 [I]Lit., *begotten of*
12 [a]Lev. 20:19
14 [a]Lev. 20:20
15 [a]Lev. 20:12
16 [a]Lev. 20:21
17 [a]Lev. 20:14

to uncover her nakedness; they are blood relatives. It is [I]lewdness.[2154]

18 'And you shall not [I]marry a woman in addition to [II]her sister [III]as a rival[6887] while she is alive,[2416] to uncover her nakedness.

19 '[a]Also you shall not approach a woman to uncover her nakedness during her [b]menstrual[5079] impurity.[2932]

20 '[a]And you shall not have intercourse[7903] with your neighbor's wife, to be defiled[2930] with her.

21 'Neither shall you give any of your offspring[2233] [a]to [I]offer[5674] them to Molech, nor shall you [b]profane[2490] the name of your God; I am the LORD.

22 '[a]You shall not lie with a male[2145] as [I]one lies with a female; it is an abomination.[8441]

23 '[a]Also you shall not have intercourse with any animal to be defiled with it, nor shall any woman stand before an animal to [I]mate with it; it is a perversion.

24 'Do not defile yourselves by any of these things; for by all these [a]the nations[1471] which I am casting out before you have become defiled.

25 'For the land has become defiled,[2930] [a]therefore I have visited[6485] its [I]punishment[5771] upon it, so the land [b]has spewed out its inhabitants.

26 'But as for you, you are to keep My statutes and My judgments, and shall not do any of these abominations, *neither* the native, nor the alien[1616] who sojourns[1481] among you

27 (for the men[582] of the land who have been before you have done[6213] all these abominations, and the land has become defiled);

28 so that the land may not spew you out, should you defile it, as it has spewed out the nation which has been before you.

29 'For whoever does any of these abominations, [I]those persons[5315] who do *so* shall be cut off[3772] from among their people.[5971]

30 'Thus you are to keep [a]My charge,[4931] that you do not practice[6213] any of the abominable customs which have been practiced before you, so as not to defile yourselves with them; [b]I am the LORD your God.' "

Idolatry Forbidden

19 Then the LORD spoke to Moses, saying,

2 "Speak[1696] to all the congregation[5712] of the sons[1121] of Israel and say[559] to them, '[a]You shall be holy,[6918] for I the LORD your God[430] am holy.

3 'Every one[376] of you [a]shall reverence[3372] his mother[517] and his father,[1] and you shall keep [b]My sabbaths;[7676] [c]I am the LORD your God.

4 'Do not turn to [a]idols[457] or make[6213] for yourselves molten[4541] [b]gods; I am the LORD your God.

5 'Now when you offer[2076] a sacrifice[2077] of peace offerings[8002] to the LORD, you shall offer it so that you may be accepted.

6 'It shall be eaten the same day you offer *it,* and the next day; but what remains[3498] until the third day shall be burned[8313] with fire.

7 'So if it is eaten at all on the third day, it is an offense;[6292] it will not be accepted.[7521]

8 'And everyone who eats it will bear[5375] his iniquity,[5771] for he has profaned the holy thing[6944] of the LORD;

17 [I]Or, *wickedness*

18 [I]Lit., *take a wife* [II]Or, *another* [III]Lit., *to be*

19 [a]Lev. 15:24; 20:18 [b]Lev. 12:2

20 [a]Lev. 20:10; Prov. 6:29; Matt. 5:27, 28; 1Cor. 6:9; Heb. 13:4

21 [I]Lit., *cause to pass over* [a]Lev. 20:2-5; Deut. 12:31 [b]Lev. 19:12; 20:3; 21:6; Ezek. 36:20; Mal. 1:12

22 [I]Lit., *those who lie* [a]Lev. 20:13; Deut. 23:18 mg.; Rom. 1:27

23 [I]Or, *lie* [a]Ex. 22:19; Lev. 20:15, 16; Deut. 27:21

24 [a]Lev. 18:3; Deut. 18:12

25 [I]Lit., *iniquity* [a]Lev. 20:23; Deut. 9:5; 18:12 [b]Lev. 18:28; 20:22

29 [I]Or, *and the*

30 [a]Lev. 22:9; Deut. 11:1 [b]Lev. 18:2

2 [a]Ex. 19:6; Lev. 11:44; 20:7, 26; Eph. 1:4; 1Pet. 1:16

3 [a]Ex. 20:12; 31:13; Deut. 5:16 [b]Ex. 20:8 [c]Lev. 11:44

4 [a]Lev. 26:1; Ps. 96:5; 115:4-7 [b]Ex. 20:23; 34:17

18:21 One of the darker sides of the religion of some of Israel's neighbors when they settled Canaan was human sacrifice. This passage and others (Lev. 20:2; Deut. 18:10) show God's total opposition to such a practice. Still, even kings of Judah sacrificed their sons to Molech, the Ammonite national deity (II Kgs. 16:3; 21:6), and the people of Judah at one point even built a special high place to use to sacrifice their sons and daughters (Jer. 7:31). All of this was done in worship to foreign gods, which made the sin doubly evil. The Lord's attitude is clear. In the only instance of possible human sacrifice where God was involved, Abraham's attempted offering of Isaac, God intervened and stopped the sacrifice.

19:2 See note on Lev. 11:44,45.

and that person[5315] shall be cut off[3772]
from his people.[5971]

Sundry Laws

🗝 **9** "[a]Now when you reap the harvest
of your land,[776] you shall not reap[3615]
to the very corners of your field,[7704]
neither shall you gather the gleanings
of your harvest.
10 'Nor shall you glean your vineyard, nor shall you gather the fallen fruit
of your vineyard; you shall leave[5800]
them for the needy and for the
stranger.[1616] I am the LORD your God.
11 "[a]You shall not steal, nor deal
falsely, [b]nor lie to one another.
12 "[a]And you shall not swear falsely[8267] by My name, so as to [b]profane
the name of your God; I am the LORD.
13 "[a]You shall not oppress your
neighbor,[7453] nor rob *him*. [b]The wages
of a hired man are not to remain with
you all night until morning.
14 'You shall not curse[7043] a deaf
man, nor [a]place a stumbling block[4383]
before the blind, but you shall revere[3372]
your God; I am the LORD.
15 "[a]You shall do no injustice[5766] in
judgment;[4941] you shall not be partial
to the poor nor defer[1921] to the great,
but you are to judge[8199] your neighbor
fairly.[6664]
16 'You shall not go about as [a]a
slanderer among your people, and you
are not to [I]act against the [IIb]life[1818] of
your neighbor; I am the LORD.
17 'You [a]shall not hate[8130] your
[I]fellow countryman[251] in your heart;[3824]
you [b]may surely reprove[3198] your neighbor, but shall not incur[5375] sin because
of him.
🗝 18 "[a]You shall not take vengeance,[5358] [b]nor bear any grudge against
the sons of your people, but [c]you shall
love[157] your neighbor as yourself; I am
the LORD.
19 'You are to keep My statutes.[2708] You shall not breed together[7250] two kinds of your cattle;
[a]you shall not sow your field with two
kinds of seed, nor wear a garment upon
you of two kinds of material mixed together.
20 "[a]Now if a man lies carnally[7902]
with a woman[802] who is a slave
acquired[2778] for *another* man,[272] but who
has in no way been redeemed,[6299] nor
given her freedom, there shall be
punishment;[1244] they shall not, *however,*
be put to death,[4191] because she was
not free.
21 'And he shall bring his guilt
offering[817] to the LORD to the doorway
of the tent of meeting,[4150] [a]a ram for a
guilt offering.
22 'The priest[3548] shall also make
atonement[3722] for him with the ram of
the guilt offering before the LORD for
his sin[2403] which he has committed,[2398]
and the sin which he has committed shall
be forgiven[5545] him.
23 'And when you enter the land
and plant all kinds of trees for food, then
you shall count their fruit as [I]forbid-
den.[6189] Three years it shall be [I]forbid-
den to you; *it* shall not be eaten.
24 'But in the fourth year all its fruit
shall be holy, an offering of praise to
the LORD.
25 'And in the fifth year you are to
eat of its fruit, that its yield may increase
for you; I am the LORD your God.
26 'You shall not eat *anything*
[a]with the blood, nor practice [b]divina-
tion[5172] or soothsaying.
27 "[a]You shall not round[5362] off the
side-growth of your heads, nor harm[7843]
the edges of your beard.[2206]
28 'You shall not make any cuts in

9 [a]Lev. 23:22; Deut. 24:20-22
11 [a]Ex. 20:15, 16 [b]Jer. 9:3-5; Eph. 4:25
12 [a]Ex. 20:7; Deut. 5:11; Matt. 5:33 [b]Lev. 18:21
13 [a]Ex. 22:7-15, 21-27 [b]Deut. 24:15; James 5:4
14 [a]Deut. 27:18
15 [a]Ex. 23:3, 6; Deut. 1:17; 10:17; 16:19
16 [I]Lit., *stand* [II]Lit., *blood* [a]Ps. 15:3; Jer. 6:28; 9:4; Ezek. 22:9 [b]Ex. 23:7; Deut. 27:25
17 [I]Lit., *brother* [a]1John 2:9, 11; 3:15 [b]Matt. 18:15; Luke 17:3
18 [a]Deut. 32:35; Rom. 12:19; Heb. 10:30 [b]Ps. 103:9 [c]Matt. 19:19; Mark 12:31; Luke 10:27; Rom. 13:9; Gal. 5:14; James 2:8
19 [a]Deut. 22:9, 11
20 [a]Deut. 22:23-27
21 [a]Lev. 6:1-7
23 [I]Lit., *uncircumcised*
26 [a]Gen. 9:4; Lev. 7:26f.; 17:10; Deut. 12:16, 23 [b]Deut. 18:10; 2Kin. 17:17
27 [a]Lev. 21:5; Deut. 14:1

🗝 **19:9,10** The Law of Moses contains a large number of humanitarian laws to protect poor people and foreigners. These verses and Lev. 23:22, which fall into this category of legislation, put restrictions on how closely crops could be harvested, so the poor would have something to glean. That the law was being followed during the period of the Judges is evident from the fact that Ruth gleaned the field of Boaz, her future husband (Ruth 2:2-7).

🗝 **19:18** See note on Ex. 20:1-17.

your [I]body[1320] for the [II]dead,[5315] nor
make any tattoo marks on yourselves:
I am the LORD.
29 '[a]Do not [I]profane[2490] your daughter by making her a harlot, so that the
land may not fall to harlotry,[2181] and the
land become full of lewdness.[2154]
30 'You shall [a]keep My sabbaths and
[b]revere My sanctuary;[4720] I am the
LORD.
31 'Do not turn to [I][a]mediums[178] or
spiritists;[3049] do not seek them out to
be defiled[2930] by them. I am the LORD
your God.
32 '[a]You shall rise up before the
grayheaded,[7872] and honor the [I]aged,[2205]
and you shall revere your God; I am
the LORD.
🔑 33 '[a]When a stranger resides[1481]
with you in your land, you shall not do
him wrong.[3238]
34 'The stranger who resides[1481]
with you shall be to you as the native
among you, and [a]you shall love him as
yourself; for you were aliens in the land
of Egypt: I am the LORD your God.
35 '[a]You shall do no wrong in judgment, in measurement of weight, or capacity.
36 'You shall have [a]just[6664] balances,
just weights, a just [I]ephah, and a just
[II]hin: I am the LORD your God, who
brought you out from the land of Egypt.
37 'You shall thus observe[8104] all My
statutes, and all My ordinances, and
do[6213] them: I am the LORD.' "

On Human Sacrifice and Immoralities

20 Then the LORD spoke to Moses,
saying,
🔑 2 "You shall also say to the sons[1121]
of Israel, 'Any man[376] from the sons of
Israel or from the aliens[1616] sojourning[1481] in Israel, [a]who gives any of his
[I]offspring[2233] to Molech, shall surely
be put to death;[4191] [b]the people[5971]
of the land[776] shall stone him with
stones.
3 'I will also set My face against that
man[376] and will cut him[3772] off from
among his people, because he has given
some of his [I]offspring to Molech,
[a]so as to defile My sanctuary[4720] and
[b]to profane[2490] My holy[6944] name.
4 'If the people of the land, however,
[I]should ever disregard that man when
he gives any of his [II]offspring to Molech,
so as not to put him to death,[4191]
5 then I Myself will set My face
against that man and against his
family;[4940] and I will cut off from among
their people both him and all those who
play the harlot[2181] after him, by playing
the harlot[2181] after Molech.
6 'As for the person[5315] who turns
to [I][a]mediums and to spiritists,[178] to play
the harlot[2181] after them, I will also set
My face against that person and will cut
him off from among his people.
7 'You shall consecrate yourselves
therefore and [a]be holy, for I am the LORD
your God.[430]
8 'And [a]you shall keep[8104] My
statutes[2708] and practice[6213] them; I am
the LORD who sanctifies[6942] you.
9 '[a]If *there is* anyone who curses[7043]
his father[1] or his mother,[517] he shall
surely be put to death; he has cursed
his father or his mother, his bloodguiltiness[1818] is upon him.
10 '[a]If *there is* a man who commits
adultery with another man's wife,[802] one
who commits adultery[5003] with his
friend's[7453] wife, the adulterer[5003] and

28 [I]Lit., *flesh* [II]Lit., *soul*
29 [I]Or, *degrade* [a]Lev. 21:9; Deut. 22:21; 23:17, 18
30 [a]Lev. 19:3 [b]Lev. 26:2
31 [I]Or, *ghosts or spirits* [a]Lev. 20:6, 27; Deut. 18:11; 1Sam. 28:3; Is. 8:19
32 [I]Lit., *face of the aged* [a]Prov. 23:22; Lam. 5:12; 1Tim. 5:1
33 [a]Ex. 22:21; Deut. 24:17, 18
34 [a]Lev. 19:18
35 [a]Deut. 25:13-16; Ezek. 45:10
36 [I]I.e., Approx. one bu. [II]I.e., Approx. one gal. [a]Deut. 25:13-15; Prov. 20:10

2 [I]Lit., *seed* [a]Lev. 18:21 [b]Lev. 20:27; 24:14-23; Num. 15:35, 36; Deut. 21:21
3 [I]Lit., *seed* [a]Lev. 15:31 [b]Lev. 18:21
4 [I]Lit., *hiding they hide their eyes from* [II]Lit., *seed*
6 [I]Or, *ghosts and spirits* [a]Lev. 19:31
7 [a]Eph. 1:4; 1Pet. 1:16
8 [a]Ex. 31:13
9 [a]Ex. 21:17; Deut. 27:16
10 [a]Ex. 20:14; Lev. 18:20; Deut. 5:18

🔑 **19:33,34** This general ethical principle should not be read as eliminating all distinctions between Israelites and foreigners living among them. In certain contexts, especially the lending of money, the two groups were to be treated differently. The usual reason to lend to a fellow countryman was to help a poor man get back on his feet, so that no interest could be exacted (Lev. 25:35-37). The case was different for foreigners, who could be charged interest (Deut. 23:20) and whose debts were not cancelled on the sabbatical year (Deut. 15:1-3). Nevertheless, Lev. 19:33,34 expresses the overriding ethical concern, and it is based theologically on the fact that they themselves had been foreigners in Egypt.

🔑 **20:2** See note on Lev. 18:21.

the adulteress[5003] shall surely be put to death.

11 "[a]If *there is* a man who lies with his father's wife, he has uncovered[1540] his father's nakedness;[6172] both of them shall surely be put to death, their bloodguiltiness is upon them.

12 "[a]If *there is* a man who lies with his daughter-in-law, both of them shall surely be put to death; they have committed [I]incest, their bloodguiltiness is upon them.

13 "[a]If *there is* a man who lies with a male[2145] as those who lie with a woman,[802] both of them have committed a detestable act;[8441] they shall surely be put to death. Their bloodguiltiness is upon them.

14 "[a]If *there is* a man who [I]marries a woman and her mother, it is immorality;[2154] both he and they shall be burned[8313] with fire, that there may be no immorality in your midst.

15 "[a]If *there is* a man who lies with an animal, he shall surely be put to death; you shall also kill[2026] the animal.

16 'If *there is* a woman who approaches any animal to [I]mate with it, you shall kill[2026] the woman and the animal; they shall surely be put to death. Their bloodguiltiness is upon them.

17 "[a]If *there is* a man who takes his sister,[269] his father's daughter or his mother's daughter, so that he sees[7200] her nakedness and she sees his nakedness, it is a disgrace;[2617] and they shall be cut off[3772] in the sight of the sons of their people. He has uncovered his sister's nakedness; he bears[5375] his guilt.[5771]

18 "[a]If *there is* a man who lies with a [I]menstruous woman and uncovers her nakedness, he has laid bare her flow, and she has [II]exposed the flow of her blood; thus both of them shall be cut off from among their people.

19 "[a]You shall also not uncover the nakedness of your mother's sister or of your father's sister, for such a one has made naked his [I]blood relative;[7607] they shall bear their guilt.

20 "[a]If *there is* a man who lies with his uncle's wife he has uncovered his uncle's nakedness; they shall bear their sin. They shall die[4191] childless.

21 "[a]If *there is* a man who takes his brother's[251] wife, it is [I]abhorrent; he has uncovered his brother's nakedness. They shall be childless.

22 'You are therefore to keep all My statutes and all My ordinances and do them, so that the land to which I am bringing you to [I]live will not [a]spew you out.

23 'Moreover, you shall not [I]follow [a]the customs[2708] of the nation[1471] which I shall drive out before you, for they did all these things, and [b]therefore I have abhorred[6973] them.

24 'Hence I have said to you, "[a]You are to possess[3423] their land,[127] and I Myself will give it to you to possess[3423] it, a land flowing with milk and honey." I am the LORD your God, who has [b]separated[914] you from the peoples.

25 '[a]You are therefore to make a distinction between the clean[2889] animal and the unclean,[2931] and between the unclean bird and the clean; and you shall not make [I]yourselves detestable by animal or by bird or by anything [II]that creeps on the ground, which I have separated for you as unclean.

🔑 26 'Thus you are to be holy to Me, for I the LORD am holy; and I [a]have set you apart[914] from the peoples to be Mine.

27 'Now a man or a woman [a]who is a medium or a [I]spiritist shall surely be put to death. They shall be stoned with stones, their bloodguiltiness is upon them.' "

Regulations Concerning Priests

21 Then the LORD said to Moses, "Speak to the priests,[3548] the sons[1121] of Aaron, and say[559] to them,

11 [a]Lev. 18:7, 8; Deut. 27:20
12 [I]Lit., *confusion;* i.e., a violation of divine order [a]Lev. 18:15
13 [a]Lev. 18:22
14 [I]Lit., *takes* [a]Lev. 18:17; Deut. 27:23
15 [a]Lev. 18:23; Deut. 27:21
16 [I]Lit., *lie*
17 [a]Lev. 18:9; Deut. 27:22
18 [I]Lit., *sick* [II]Or, *uncovered* [a]Lev. 15:24; 18:19
19 [I]Lit., *flesh* [a]Lev. 18:12, 13
20 [a]Lev. 18:14
21 [I]Or, *an impure deed* [a]Lev. 18:16
22 [I]Lit., *dwell in it* [a]Lev. 18:28
23 [I]Lit., *walk in the statutes* [a]Lev. 18:3 [b]Lev. 18:25
24 [a]Ex. 13:5; 33:1-3 [b]Ex. 33:16; Lev. 20:26
25 [I]Lit., *your souls* [II]Lit., *with which the ground creeps* [a]Lev. 10:10; 11:1-47; Deut. 14:3-21
26 [a]Lev. 20:24
27 [I]Lit., *spiritist among them* [a]Lev. 19:31

🔑 **20:26** See note on Lev. 11:44,45.

"[a]No one shall defile himself for a dead person[5315] among his people,[5971]

2 [a]except for his relatives[7607] who are nearest to him, his mother[517] and his father[1] and his son and his daughter and his brother,[251]

3 also for his virgin[1330] sister,[269] who is near to him [I]because she has had no husband;[376] for her he may defile himself.

4 'He shall not defile himself as a [I]relative by marriage[1167] among his people, and so profane himself.

5 '[a]They shall not make any baldness on their heads, [b]nor shave off the edges of their beards,[2206] [c]nor make any cuts in their flesh.[1320]

6 'They shall be holy[6918] to their God[430] and [a]not profane[2490] the name of their God, for they present the offerings by fire[801] [I]to the LORD, [b]the bread of their God; so they shall be holy.[6944]

7 '[a]They shall not take a woman[802] who is profaned[2491] by harlotry,[2181] nor shall they take a woman[802] divorced from her husband; for he is holy to his God.

8 'You shall consecrate[6942] him, therefore, for he offers [a]the bread of your God; he shall be holy to you; for I the LORD, who sanctifies you, am holy.

9 '[a]Also the daughter of any[376] priest, if she profanes herself by harlotry,[2181] she profanes her father; she shall be burned[8313] with fire.

10 'And the priest who is the highest among his brothers, on whose head the anointing[4886] oil[8081] has been poured, and [I]who has been consecrated to wear the garments, [a]shall not [II]uncover[6544] his head, nor tear his clothes;

11 [a]nor shall he approach any dead[4191] person,[5315] nor defile himself *even* for his father or his mother;

12 [a]nor shall he go out of the sanctuary,[4720] nor profane the sanctuary of his God; for [b]the consecration[5145] of the anointing oil of his God is on him: I am the LORD.

13 'And he shall take a wife in her virginity.[1331]

14 '[a]A widow, or a divorced[1644] woman, or one who is profaned by harlotry,[2181] these he may not take; but rather he is to [I]marry a virgin of his own people;

15 that he may not profane his [I]offspring[2233] among his people: for I am the LORD who sanctifies him.' "

16 Then the LORD spoke to Moses, saying,

17 "Speak[1696] to Aaron, saying,[559] 'No man[376] of your [I]offspring throughout their generations[1755] who has a defect[3971] shall approach to offer[7126] the [a]bread of his God.

18 '[a]For no one who has a defect shall approach: a blind man, or a lame man, or he who has a [I][b]disfigured *face*,[2763] or any deformed *limb*,

19 or a man who has a broken foot[7667] or broken hand,

20 or a hunchback or a dwarf, or *one who has* a [I]defect[8400] in his eye or eczema[1618] or scabs or [a]crushed testicles.

21 'No man among the [I]descendants of Aaron the priest, who has a defect, is to come near[5066] to offer the LORD's offerings by fire; *since* he has a defect, he shall not come near to offer [a]the bread of his God.

22 'He may eat [a]the bread of his God, *both* of the most holy[6944] and of the holy,[6944]

23 only he shall not go in to the veil or come near the altar[4196] because he has a defect, that he may not profane My sanctuaries. For I am the LORD who sanctifies them.' "

24 So Moses spoke[1696] to Aaron and to his sons and to all the sons of Israel.

Sundry Rules for Priests

22 Then the LORD spoke to Moses, saying,[559]

2 "Tell[1696] Aaron and his sons[1121] to be careful with the holy *gifts* of the sons of Israel, which they dedicate to Me, so as not to profane[2490] My holy name; I am the LORD.

3 "Say to them, '[a]If any man[376] among all your [I]descendants[2233] throughout your generations[1755]

---

1 [a]Lev. 19:28; Ezek. 44:25
2 [a]Lev. 21:11
3 [I]Or, *whom no man has had*
4 [I]Lit., *husband among*
5 [a]Deut. 14:1; Ezek. 44:20 [b]Lev. 19:27 [c]Deut. 14:1
6 [I]Lit., *of* [a]Lev. 18:21 [b]Lev. 3:11
7 [a]Lev. 21:13, 14
8 [a]Lev. 21:6
9 [a]Gen. 38:24; Lev. 19:29
10 [I]Lit., *whose hand has been filled* [II]Lit., *unbind* [a]Lev. 10:6
11 [a]Lev. 19:28; Num. 19:14
12 [a]Lev. 10:7 [b]Ex. 29:6, 7
14 [I]Lit., *take as wife* [a]Lev. 21:7; Ezek. 44:22
15 [I]Lit., *seed*
17 [I]Lit., *seed* [a]Lev. 21:6
18 [I]Lit., *slit* [a]Lev. 22:19-25
20 [I]Lit., *obscurity* [a]Deut. 23:1; Is. 56:3-5
21 [I]Lit., *seed* [a]Lev. 21:6
22 [a]1Cor. 9:13
3 [I]Lit., *seed* [a]Lev. 7:20, 21; Num. 19:13

approaches[7126] the holy *gifts* which the
sons of Israel dedicate to the LORD,
while he has an uncleanness,[2932] that
person[5315] shall be cut off[3772] from before
Me. I am the LORD.
4 '[a]No man,[376] of the [I]descendants
of Aaron, who is a leper or who has a
discharge, may eat of the holy *gifts* until
he is clean. [b]And if one touches[5060] anything made unclean[2931] by a corpse[5315]
or if [c]a man has a seminal emission,
5 or [a]if a man touches any teeming
things, by which he is made unclean,[2930]
or any man[120] by whom he is made unclean, whatever his uncleanness;
6 a [I]person who touches any such
shall be unclean[2930] until evening, and
shall not eat of the holy *gifts*, unless
he has bathed[7364] his [II]body[1320] in water.
7 'But when the sun sets, he shall
be clean,[2891] and afterward he shall eat
of the holy *gifts*, for [a]it is his [I]food.
8 'He shall not eat [a]*an animal* which
dies[5038] or is torn *by beasts*, becoming
unclean[2930] by it; I am the LORD.
9 'They shall therefore keep[8104]
[a]My charge,[4931] so that [b]they may not
bear[5375] sin because of it, and die[4191]
thereby because they profane it; I am
the LORD who sanctifies them.
10 '[a]No [I]layman,[2114] however, is to
eat the holy *gift*; a sojourner[8453] with
the priest[3548] or a hired man shall not
eat of the holy *gift*.
11 '[a]But if a priest buys a [I]slave as
his property with his money, [II]that one
may eat of it, and those who are born
in his house[1004] may eat of his [III]food.
12 'And if a priest's daughter is married to a [I]layman, she shall not eat of
the [II]offering[8641] of the *gifts*.
13 'But if a priest's daughter becomes a widow or divorced,[1644] and has
no child and returns[7725] to her father's[1]
house as in her youth, she shall eat of
her father's [I]food; [a]but no [II]layman shall
eat of it.
14 '[a]But if a man eats a holy *gift*
unintentionally,[7684] then he shall add to
it a fifth of it and shall give the holy
gift to the priest.
15 'And [a]they shall not profane the
holy *gifts* of the sons of Israel which
they offer to the LORD,
16 and *so* cause them [a]to bear
[I]punishment[5771] for guilt[819] by eating
their holy *gifts*; for I am the LORD who
sanctifies them.' "

Flawless Animals for Sacrifice

17 Then the LORD spoke to Moses,
saying,
18 "Speak to Aaron and to his sons
and to all the sons of Israel, and say[559]
to them, '[a]Any man of the house of Israel
or of the aliens[1616] in Israel who presents
his offering,[7133] whether it is any of their
[I]votive[5088] or any of their freewill offerings,[5071] which they present to the LORD
for a burnt offering—[5930]
19 [a]for you to be accepted—*it must
be* a male[2145] without defect[8549] from the
cattle, the sheep, or the goats.
20 '[a]Whatever has a defect,[3971] you
shall not offer, for it will not be accepted[7522] for you.
21 'And when a man offers a sacrifice[2077] of peace offerings[8002] to the
LORD [a]to [I]fulfill[6381] a special vow, or for
a freewill offering, of the herd or of the
flock, it must be perfect to be accepted;[7522] there shall be no defect in
it.
22 'Those *that are* blind or frac-
tured[7665] or maimed or having a running
sore or eczema[1618] or scabs, you shall
not offer to the LORD, nor make of
them an offering by fire[801] on the altar[4196] to the LORD.
23 'In respect to an ox or a lamb
which has an [I]overgrown or stunted
member, you may present it for a freewill
offering, but for a vow it shall not be
accepted.[7521]
24 'Also [a]anything *with its testicles*
bruised or crushed[3807] or torn or cut,[3772]
you shall not offer to the LORD, or
[I]sacrifice in your land,[776]
25 nor shall you accept any such
from the hand[3027] of a foreigner[5236] for
offering [a]as the [I]food of your God;[430]
for their corruption is in them, they have

4 [I]Lit., *seed* [a]Lev. 14:1-32 [b]Lev. 11:24-28, 39, 40 [c]Lev. 15:16, 17

5 [a]Lev. 11:23-28

6 [I]Lit., *soul* [II]Lit., *flesh*

7 [I]Lit., *bread* [a]Num. 18:11

8 [a]Lev. 7:24; 11:39, 40; 17:15

9 [a]Lev. 18:30 [b]Ex. 28:43; Lev. 22:16; Num. 18:22

10 [I]Lit., *stranger* [a]Ex. 29:33; Lev. 22:13; Num. 3:10

11 [I]Lit., *soul* [II]Lit., *he may* [III]Lit., *bread* [a]Gen. 17:13; Ex. 12:44

12 [I]Lit., *stranger* [II]Lit., *heave offering*

13 [I]Lit., *bread* [II]Lit., *stranger* [a]Lev. 22:10

14 [a]Lev. 5:15, 16

15 [a]Num. 18:32

16 [I]Or, *iniquity requiring a guilt offering* [a]Lev. 10:17; 22:9

18 [I]Lit., *vows* [a]Num. 15:14

19 [a]Lev. 21:18-21; Deut. 15:21

20 [a]Deut. 15:21; 17:1; Mal. 1:8, 14; Heb. 9:14; 1Pet. 1:19

21 [I]Or, *make a special votive offering* [a]Num. 15:3, 8

23 [I]Or, *a deformed*

24 [I]Lit., *do* [a]Lev. 21:20

25 [I]Lit., *bread* [a]Lev. 21:22

a defect, they shall not be accepted[7521] for you.' "

26 Then the LORD spoke to Moses, saying,

27 "When an ox or a sheep or a goat is born, it shall [I]remain [a]seven days [II]with its mother,[517] and from the eighth day on it shall be accepted[7521] as a sacrifice of an offering[7133] by fire to the LORD.

28 "[a]But, *whether* it is an ox or a sheep,[7716] you shall not kill[7819] *both* it and its young[1121] in one day.

29 "And when you sacrifice[2076] [a]a sacrifice of thanksgiving[8426] to the LORD, you shall sacrifice it so that you may be accepted.

30 "It shall be eaten on the same day, you shall leave none of it until morning: I am the LORD.

31 "[a]So you shall keep My commandments,[4687] and do[6213] them: I am the LORD.

32 "And you shall not profane My holy name, but I will be sanctified[6942] among the sons of Israel: I am the LORD who sanctifies[6942] you,

33 [a]who brought you out from the land of Egypt, to be your God: I am the LORD."

Laws of Religious Festivals

23 The LORD spoke again to Moses, saying,

2 "Speak[1696] to the sons[1121] of Israel, and say[559] to them, '[a]The LORD's appointed times[4150] which you shall [b]proclaim[7121] as holy[6944] convocations—[4744] My appointed times are these:

3 '[a]For six days work[4399] may be done; but on the seventh day there is a sabbath[7676] of complete rest,[7677] a holy convocation.[4744] You shall not do[6213] any work; it is a sabbath to the LORD in all your dwellings.[4186]

4 'These are the [a]appointed times of the LORD, holy convocations which you shall proclaim at the times appointed for them.

5 '[a]In the first month, on the fourteenth day of the month [I]at twilight is the LORD's Passover.[6453]

6 'Then on the fifteenth day of the same month there is the [a]Feast[2282] of Unleavened Bread to the LORD; for seven days you shall eat unleavened bread.

7 'On the first day you shall have a holy convocation; you shall [a]not do any laborious[5656] work.

8 'But for seven days you shall present[7126] an offering by fire[801] to the LORD. On the seventh day is a holy convocation; you shall not do any laborious work.' "

9 Then the LORD spoke to Moses, saying,[559]

10 "Speak to the sons of Israel, and say to them, 'When you enter the land[776] which I am going to give to you and [a]reap its harvest, then you shall bring in the sheaf of the first fruits[7225] of your harvest to the priest.[3548]

11 'And he shall wave the sheaf before the LORD for you to be accepted;[7522] on the day after the sabbath the priest shall wave it.

12 'Now on the day when you wave the sheaf, you shall offer[6213] a male lamb one[1121] year old without defect[8546] for a burnt offering[5930] to the LORD.

13 'Its [a]grain offering[4503] shall then be two-tenths *of an ephah* of fine flour mixed[1101] with oil,[8081] an offering by fire to the LORD *for* a soothing aroma, with its libation,[5262] a fourth of a [I]hin of wine.

14 'Until this same day, until you have brought in the offering[7133] of your God,[430] [a]you shall eat neither bread nor roasted grain nor new growth. It is to be a perpetual[5769] statute[2708] throughout your generations[1755] in all your dwelling places.

15 '[a]You shall also count[5608] for yourselves from the day after the sabbath, from the day when you brought in the sheaf of the wave offering; there shall be seven complete[8549] sabbaths.

16 'You shall count[5608] fifty days to the day after the seventh sabbath; then you shall present a [a]new grain offering to the LORD.

27 [I]Lit., *be* [II]Lit., *under* [a]Ex. 22:30
28 [a]Deut. 22:6, 7
29 [a]Lev. 7:12
31 [a]Lev. 19:37; Num. 15:40; Deut. 4:40
33 [a]Lev. 11:45
2 [a]Lev. 23:4, 37, 44; Num. 29:39 [b]Lev. 23:21
3 [a]Ex. 20:9, 10; 23:12; 31:13-17; 35:2, 3; Lev. 19:3; Deut. 5:13, 14
4 [a]Ex. 23:14; Lev. 23:2
5 [I]Lit., *between the two evenings* [a]Ex. 12:18, 19; Num. 28:16-25; Deut. 16:1; Josh. 5:10
6 [a]Ex. 12:14-20; 23:15; 34:18; Deut. 16:3-8
7 [a]Lev. 23:8, 21, 25, 35, 36
10 [a]Ex. 23:19; 34:26
13 [I]I.e., Approx. one gal. [a]Lev. 6:20
14 [a]Ex. 34:26; Num. 15:20, 21
15 [a]Num. 28:26-31; Deut. 16:9-12
16 [a]Num. 28:26

17 'You shall bring in from your dwelling places[4186] two *loaves* of bread for a wave offering, made of two-tenths *of an* [I]*ephah*; they shall be of a fine flour, baked [a]with leaven[2557] as first fruits to the LORD.

18 'Along with the bread, you shall present seven one year old male lambs without defect, and a bull of the herd, and two rams; they are to be a burnt offering to the LORD, with their grain offering and their libations, an offering by fire of a soothing aroma to the LORD.

19 'You shall also offer[6213] [a]one male goat for a sin offering[2398] and two male lambs one year old for a sacrifice[2077] of peace offerings.[8002]

20 'The priest shall then wave them with the bread of the first fruits for a wave offering with two lambs before the LORD; they are to be holy to the LORD for the priest.

21 'On this same day you shall [a]make a proclamation as well; you are to have a holy convocation. You shall do no laborious [b]work. It is to be a perpetual statute in all your dwelling places throughout your generations.

🔑 22 "[a]When you reap the harvest of your land, moreover, you shall not reap[3615] to the very corners of your field,[7704] nor gather the gleaning of your harvest; you are to leave[5800] them for the needy and the alien.[1616] I am the LORD your God.' "

23 Again the LORD spoke to Moses, saying,

24 "Speak to the sons of Israel, saying, '[a]In the seventh month on the first of the month, you shall have a [I]rest,[7677] a [b]reminder[2146] by blowing *of trumpets*, a holy convocation.

25 'You shall [a]not do any laborious work, but you shall present an offering by fire to the LORD.' "

The Day of Atonement

26 And the LORD spoke to Moses, saying,

27 "On exactly [a]the tenth day of this seventh month is [b]the day of atonement;[3725] it shall be a holy convocation for you, and you shall humble your souls[5315] and present an offering by fire to the LORD.

28 "Neither shall you do any work on this same day, for it is a [a]day of atonement, [b]to make atonement[3722] on your behalf before the LORD your God.

29 "If there is any [I]person who will not humble himself on this same day, [a]he shall be cut off[3772] from his people.[5971]

30 "As for any person who does any work on this same day, that person I will destroy from among his people.

31 "You shall do no work at all. It is to be a perpetual statute throughout your generations in all your dwelling places.

🔑 32 "It is to be a sabbath of complete rest to you, and you shall humble your souls; on the ninth of the month at evening, from evening until evening you shall keep[7673] your sabbath."

33 Again the LORD spoke to Moses, saying,

34 "Speak to the sons of Israel, saying, 'On [a]the fifteenth of this seventh month is the [b]Feast of Booths[5521] for seven days to the LORD.

35 'On the first day is a holy convocation; you shall do [a]no laborious work of any kind.

36 '[a]For seven days you shall present an offering by fire to the LORD. On [b]the eighth day you shall have a holy convocation and present an offering by fire to the LORD; it is an assembly.[6116] You shall do no laborious work.

37 'These are [a]the appointed times of the LORD which you shall proclaim as holy convocations, to present offerings by fire to the LORD—burnt offerings and grain offerings, sacrifices and libations, [b]*each* day's matter[1697] on its own day—

38 besides *those of* the sabbaths of

17 [I]I.e., Approx. one bu. [a]Lev. 2:12; 7:13
19 [a]Lev. 4:23; Num. 28:30
21 [a]Lev. 23:2, 4 [b]Lev. 23:7
22 [a]Lev. 19:9, 10; Deut. 24:19; Ruth 2:15f.
24 [I]Lit., *sabbath rest* [a]Num. 29:1 [b]Num. 10:9, 10
25 [a]Lev. 23:21
27 [a]Lev. 16:29; 25:9; Num. 29:7 [b]Ex. 30:10; Lev. 16:30; 23:28; Num. 29:7-11
28 [a]Lev. 23:27 [b]Lev. 16:34
29 [I]Lit., *soul* [a]Gen. 17:14; Lev. 13:46; Num. 5:2
34 [a]Num. 29:12 [b]Lev. 23:42, 43; Deut. 16:13, 16; Ezra 3:4; Neh. 8:14; Zech. 14:16; John 7:2
35 [a]Lev. 23:25
36 [a]Num. 29:12-34 [b]Num. 29:35-38
37 [a]Lev. 23:2 [b]Num. 28:1-29:38

🔑 **23:22** See note on Lev. 19:9-10.
🔑 **23:32** See note on Lev. 16:29.

the LORD, and besides your gifts, and besides all your [I]votive[5088] and freewill offerings,[5071] which you give to the LORD.

39 'On exactly the fifteenth day of the seventh month, [a]when you have gathered in the crops of the land, you shall celebrate the feast of the LORD for seven days, with a [I]rest on the first day and a [I]rest on the eighth day.

40 'Now on the first day you shall take for yourselves the [I]foliage of beautiful[1926] trees, palm branches and boughs of leafy trees and willows of the brook; and you shall rejoice before the LORD your God for seven days.

41 'You shall thus celebrate it *as* a feast to the LORD for seven days in the year. It *shall be* a perpetual statute throughout your generations; you shall celebrate it in the seventh month.

42 'You shall [I]live [a]in booths for seven days; all the native-born in Israel shall [I]live in booths,[5521]

43 so that [a]your generations may know[3045] that I had the sons of Israel live in booths when I brought them out from the land of Egypt. I am the LORD your God.' "

44 So Moses declared[1696] to the sons of Israel [a]the appointed times of the LORD.

The Lamp and the Bread of the Sanctuary

24 Then the LORD spoke to Moses, saying,

2 "Command the sons[1121] of Israel that they bring to you [a]clear[2134] oil[8081] from beaten olives for the [I]light,[3974] to make[5927] a lamp[5216] [II]burn[5927] continually.[8548]

3 "Outside the veil of testimony[5715] in the tent[168] of meeting,[4150] Aaron shall keep it in order from evening to morning before the LORD continually; *it shall be* a perpetual statute[2708] throughout your generations.[1755]

4 "He shall keep the lamps in order on the [a]pure[2889] *gold* lampstand before the LORD continually.

38 [I]Lit., *vows, and besides all your*
39 [I]Lit., *sabbath rest* [a]Ex. 23:16
40 [I]Lit., *products, fruit*
42 [I]Lit., *dwell* [a]Lev. 23:34
43 [a]Deut. 31:13; Ps. 78:5f.
44 [a]Lev. 23:37
2 [I]Or, *luminary* [II]Lit., *ascend* [a]Ex. 27:20, 21
4 [a]Ex. 25:31; 31:8; 37:17
5 [a]Ex. 25:30; 39:36; 40:23
6 [a]Ex. 25:24; 1Kin. 7:48
7 [a]Lev. 2:2, 9, 16
8 [I]Lit., *from* [a]Matt. 12:5 [b]Ex. 25:30; Num. 4:7; 2Chr. 2:4
9 [a]Matt. 12:4; Mark 2:26; Luke 6:4
11 [a]Ex. 3:15; 22:28; Job 2:5, 9; Is. 8:21
12 [I]Or, *prison* [II]Lit., *to declare distinctly to them according to the mouth of the* LORD [a]Ex. 18:15; Num. 15:34
14 [a]Deut. 13:9; 17:7 [b]Lev. 20:2, 27; Deut. 21:21
15 [a]Ex. 22:28
16 [a]1Kin. 21:10; Matt. 12:31; Mark 3:28f.

5 "[a]Then you shall take fine flour and bake twelve cakes with it; two-tenths *of an ephah* shall be *in* each cake.

6 "And you shall set[7760] them *in* two rows, six *to* a row,[4635] on the [a]pure *gold* table before the LORD.

7 "And you shall put pure frankincense[3828] on each row, that it may be [a]a memorial portion for the bread, *even* an offering by fire[801] to the LORD.

8 "[a]Every sabbath[7676] day he shall set it in order before the LORD [b]continually; it is an everlasting[5769] covenant[1285] [I]for the sons of Israel.

9 "[a]And it shall be for Aaron and his sons, and they shall eat it in a holy[6918] place; for it is most holy[6944] to him from the LORD'S offerings by fire, *his* portion[2706] forever."[5769]

10 Now the son of an Israelite woman,[802] whose father was an Egyptian, went out among the sons of Israel; and the Israelite woman's son and a man[272] of Israel struggled with each other in the camp.[4264]

11 And the son of the Israelite woman blasphemed[5344] the [a]Name and cursed.[7043] So they brought him to Moses. (Now his mother's name was Shelomith, the daughter of Dibri, of the tribe[4294] of Dan.)

12 And they put him in [I]custody [II]so that [a]the command[6310] of the LORD might be made clear to them.

13 Then the LORD spoke to Moses, saying,

14 "Bring the one who has cursed outside the camp, and let all who heard[8085] him [a]lay their hands[3027] on his head;[7218] then [b]let all the congregation[5712] stone him.

15 "And you shall speak to the sons of Israel, saying,[559] '[a]If anyone[376] curses[7043] his God,[430] then he shall bear[5375] his sin.

16 'Moreover, the one who [a]blasphemes[5344] the name of the LORD shall surely be put to death; all the congregation shall certainly stone him. The alien[1616] as well as the native, when he blasphemes[5344] the Name, shall be put to death.[4191]

"An Eye for an Eye"

17 'And if a man takes the life[5221] of any human being,[120] he shall surely be put to death.
18 'And the one who takes the life of an animal shall make it good, life for life.
19 'And if a man injures[3971] his neighbor, just as he has done,[6213] so it shall be done to him:
20 fracture[7667] for fracture, eye for eye, tooth for tooth; just as he has injured a man, so it shall be inflicted on him.
21 'Thus the one who kills an animal shall make it good, but the one who kills a man shall be put to death.
22 'There shall be one standard[4941] for you; it shall be for the stranger as well as the native, for I am the LORD your God.' "
23 Then Moses spoke to the sons of Israel, and they brought the one who had cursed outside the camp and stoned him with stones. Thus the sons of Israel did, just as the LORD had commanded[6680] Moses.

The Sabbatic Year and Year of Jubilee

25 The LORD then spoke to Moses at Mount Sinai, saying,
2 "Speak to the sons[1121] of Israel, and say[559] to them, 'When you come into the land[776] which I shall give you, then the land shall have[7673] a sabbath[7676] to the LORD.
3 'Six years you shall sow your field,[7704] and six years you shall prune your vineyard and gather[622] in its crop,
4 but during the seventh year the land shall have a sabbath rest,[7677] a sabbath to the LORD; you shall not sow your field nor prune your vineyard.
5 'Your harvest's aftergrowth[5599] you shall not reap, and your grapes of untrimmed vines[5139] you shall not gather; the land shall have a sabbatical year.
6 'And all of you shall have the sabbath *products* of the land for food; yourself, and your male and female slaves,[5650] and your hired man and your foreign[8453] resident, those who live as aliens[1481] with you.
7 'Even your cattle and the animals[2416] that are in your land shall have all its crops to eat.
8 'You are also to count[5608] off seven sabbaths of years for yourself, seven times seven years, so that you have the time of the seven sabbaths of years, *namely,* forty-nine years.
9 'You shall then sound[5674] a ram's horn abroad on the tenth day of the

17 Lit., *smites* Gen. 9:6; Ex. 21:12; Num. 35:30, 31; Deut. 27:24
18 Lit., *smites* Lev. 24:21
19 Lit., *gives a blemish*
20 Lit., *given a blemish* Lit., *given* Ex. 21:23; Deut. 19:21 Matt. 5:38
21 Lit., *smites* Lev. 24:17
22 Lit., *judgment* Ex. 12:49; Num. 9:14; 15:15, 16, 29
1 Or, *on*
3 Ex. 23:10, 11
4 Lev. 25:20
5 Lit., *growth from spilled kernels*
6 Lev. 25:20, 21
9 Lev. 23:27

25:1-55 This chapter contains one of the most sophisticated pieces of social legislation to emerge from the ancient world. Much of its intent was to eliminate poverty, as is explicitly stated in the parallel in Deut. 15:4,5. No evidence exists that the system was ever fully implemented, but had it been, Israel's history would have been far different, and the prophets would have had far less to denounce. The provisions of this chapter prevent overworking the land, call for regular land redistribution and forbid perpetual servitude. Years are divided into groups of seven, with the seventh as a sabbatical year (year of rest). No farming was to be done on that year (Lev 25:3-5), debts were to be cancelled (Deut. 15:2), and indentured servants were to go free (Deut. 15:12). This cycle was to repeat itself seven times, for a total of forty-nine years. The next year was to be a special one called Jubilee (Lev. 25:8,9). What was true during a sabbatical year applied to this year also, but in addition all real estate, except that within walled cities, automatically reverted to the family to which it had originally been assigned (Lev. 25:13). This is not just social legislation; theological considerations played and even greater part. Servants were to be released, because all Israelites already belonged to God as His servants, since He had rescued them from Egypt (Lev. 25:55). The land was to be redeemed regularly, because it actually belonged to God, not Israel (Lev. 25:23,24). That some Israelites, even centuries later, regarded the keeping of ancestral real estate in the family as a sacred duty can be seen in Naboth's reason for his refusal to sell King Ahab his vineyard (I Kgs. 21:3). For an example of the influence of this legislation during the period of the Judges, see the note on Ruth 4:1-12.

seventh month; on the day of atonement[3725] you shall sound a horn all through your land.

10 'You shall thus consecrate[6942] the fiftieth year and [a]proclaim[7121] [I]a release through the land to all its inhabitants. It shall be a jubilee[3104] for you, [II]and [b]each[376] of you shall return to his own property,[272] [II]and each of you shall return to his family.[4940]

11 'You shall have the fiftieth year as a jubilee; you shall not sow, nor reap its aftergrowth, nor gather in *from* its untrimmed vines.

12 'For it is a jubilee; it shall be holy[6944] to you. You shall eat its crops out of the field.

13 '[a]On this year of jubilee each of you shall return to his own property.

14 'If you make a sale, moreover, to your friend, or buy from your friend's hand, [a]you shall not wrong[3238] one another.[251]

15 'Corresponding to the number of years after the jubilee, you shall buy from your [I]friend; he is to sell to you according to the number of years of crops.

16 '[a]In proportion to the [I]extent of the years you shall increase its price, and in proportion to the fewness of the years, you shall diminish its price; for *it is* a number of crops he is selling to you.

17 'So [a]you shall not wrong one another, but you shall [I]fear[3372] your God;[430] for I am the LORD your God.

18 'You shall thus observe[6213] My statutes,[2708] and keep My judgments,[4941] so as to carry them out, that [a]you may live securely[983] on the land.

19 'Then the land will yield its produce, so that you can eat your fill and live securely on it.

20 'But if you say, "[a]What are we going to eat on the seventh year [I]if we do not sow or gather in our crops?"

21 then [a]I will so order[6680] My blessing[1293] for you in the sixth year that it will bring forth the crop for three years.

22 'When you are sowing the eighth year, you can still eat [a]old things from the crop, eating *the old* until the ninth year when its crop comes in.

The Law of Redemption

23 'The land, moreover, shall not be sold permanently,[6783] for [a]the land is Mine; for [b]you are *but* aliens[1616] and sojourners with Me.

24 'Thus for every [I]piece of your property, you are to provide for the redemption[1353] of the land.

25 '[a]If a [I]fellow countryman[251] of yours becomes so poor he has to sell[1350] part of his property, then his nearest kinsman is to come and buy back what his [I]relative has sold.

26 'Or in case a man has no kinsman, but so [I]recovers his means as to find sufficient for its redemption,

27 [a]then he shall calculate[2803] the years since its sale and refund[7725] the balance[5736] to the man to whom he sold it, and so return to his property.

28 'But if [I]he has not found sufficient means to get it back for himself, then what he has sold shall remain in the hands of its purchaser until the year of jubilee; but at the jubilee it shall [II]revert, that [a]he may return to his property.

29 'Likewise, if a man sells a dwelling[4186] house[1004] in a walled city, then his redemption right remains valid until a full[8552] year from its sale; his right of redemption lasts a full year.

30 'But if it is not bought back for him within the space of a full[8549] year, then the house that is in the walled city passes permanently to its purchaser throughout his generations;[1755] it does not [I]revert in the jubilee.

31 'The houses of the villages, however, which have no surrounding wall shall be considered[2803] [I]as open fields;[776] they have redemption rights and [II]revert in the jubilee.

32 'As for [a]cities of the Levites, the Levites have a permanent[5769] right of redemption for the houses of the cities which are their possession.

33 'What, therefore, [I]belongs to the

10 [I]Or, *liberty* [II]Or, *when* [a]Jer. 34:8, 15, 17 [b]Lev. 25:13, 28, 54

13 [a]Lev. 25:10; 27:24

14 [a]Lev. 25:17

15 [I]Lit., *friend's hands*

16 [I]Lit., *multitude* [a]Lev. 25:27, 51, 52

17 [I]Or, *reverence* [a]Lev. 25:14; Prov. 14:31; 22:22; Jer. 7:5, 6; 1Thess. 4:6

18 [a]Lev. 26:5; Deut. 12:10; Jer. 23:6

20 [I]Or, *behold* [a]Lev. 25:4

21 [a]Deut. 28:8

22 [a]Lev. 26:10

23 [a]Ex. 19:5 [b]Gen. 23:4; 1Chr. 29:15; Ps. 39:12; Heb. 11:13; 1Pet. 2:11

24 [I]Lit., *land*

25 [I]Lit., *brother* [a]Ruth 2:20; 4:4, 6

26 [I]Lit., *his hand reaches*

27 [a]Lev. 25:16

28 [I]Lit., *his hand has not found sufficient to* [II]Lit., *go out* [a]Lev. 25:10, 13

30 [I]Lit., *go out*

31 [I]Lit., *according to* [II]Lit., *go out*

32 [a]Num. 35:1-8; Josh. 21:2

33 [I]Lit., *is from*

Levites may be redeemed and a house
sale [II]in the city of this possession
[III]reverts in the jubilee, for the houses
of the cities of the Levites are their
possession among the sons of Israel.
34 "[a]But pasture fields of their cities
shall not be sold, for that is their perpetual[5769] possession.

Of Poor Countrymen

35 "[a]Now in case a [I]countryman of
yours becomes poor and his [II]means with
regard to you falter, then you are to
sustain[2388] him, like a stranger or a sojourner, that he may live with you.
36 "[a]Do not take [I]usurious interest
from him, but revere your God, that
your [II]countryman may live with you.
37 'You shall not give him your silver
at interest, nor your food[400] for gain.
38 "[a]I am the LORD your God, who
brought you out of the land of Egypt
to give you the land of Canaan *and*
[b]to be your God.
39 "[a]And if a [I]countryman of yours
becomes so poor with regard to you
that he sells himself to you, you shall
not subject[5647] him to a slave's service.
40 'He shall be with you as a hired
man, as [a]if he were a sojourner with
you, until the year of jubilee.
41 'He shall then go out from you,
he and his sons with him, and shall go
back to his family, that he may return
to the property of his forefathers.[1]
42 'For they are My servants whom
I brought out from the land of Egypt;
they are not to be sold *in* a slave
sale.
43 "[a]You shall not rule[7287] over him
with severity, but are to revere your
God.
44 'As for your male and female
slaves whom you may have—you may
acquire male and female slaves[5650] from
the pagan nations[1471] that are around
you.
45 'Then, too, *it is* out of the sons
of the sojourners[8453] who live as aliens
among you that you may gain acquisition,
and out of their families who are with
you, whom they will have [I]produced in
your land; they also may become your
possession.
46 'You may even bequeath them
to your sons after you, to receive[3423]
as a possession; you can use them as
permanent[5769] slaves.[5647] [a]But in respect to your [I]countrymen, the sons of
Israel, you shall not rule with severity
over one another.

Of Redeeming a Poor Man

47 'Now if the [I]means of a stranger
or of a sojourner with you becomes sufficient, and a [II]countryman of yours becomes so poor with regard to him as
to sell himself to a stranger who is
sojourning[1616] with you, or to the descendants of a stranger's family,
48 then he shall have redemption
right after he has been sold. One of
his brothers may redeem him,
49 or his uncle, or his uncle's son,
may redeem him, or one of his blood
relatives[7607] from his family may redeem
him; or [I][a]if he prospers, he may redeem
himself.
50 'He then with his purchaser shall
calculate[2803] from the year when he sold
himself to him up to the year of jubilee;
and the price of his sale shall correspond
to the number of years. *It is* like the
days of a hired man *that* he shall be
with him.
51 'If there are still many years,
[a]he shall refund[7725] part of his purchase
price in proportion to them for his own
redemption;[1353]
52 and if few years remain until the
year of jubilee, he shall so calculate with
him. In proportion to his years he is
to refund *the amount for* his redemption.
53 'Like a man hired year by year
he shall be with him; [a]he shall not rule
over him with severity in your sight.
54 'Even if he is not redeemed by
[I]these *means*, [a]he shall still go out in

33 [II]Lit., *and* [III]Lit., *goes out*
34 [a]Num. 35:2-5
35 [I]Lit., *brother* [II]Lit., *hand* [a]Deut. 15:7-11; 24:14, 15
36 [I]Lit., *interest and usury* [II]Lit., *brother* [a]Ex. 22:25; Deut. 23:19, 20
38 [a]Lev. 11:45 [b]Gen. 17:7
39 [I]Lit., *brother* [a]Ex. 21:2-6; Deut. 15:12-18; 1Kin. 9:22
40 [a]Ex. 21:2
43 [a]Ex. 1:13, 14; Lev. 25:46, 53; Ezek. 34:4; Col. 4:1
45 [I]Lit., *begotten*
46 [I]Lit., *brothers* [a]Lev. 25:43
47 [I]Lit., *hand reaches* [II]Lit., *brother*
49 [I]Lit., *if his hand has reached and* [a]Lev. 25:26, 27
51 [a]Lev. 25:16
53 [a]Lev. 25:43
54 [I]Or, *these years* [a]Lev. 25:10, 13, 28

25:35-38 See note on Lev. 19:33,34.

the year of jubilee, he and his sons with
him.
55 'For the sons of Israel are My
servants; they are My servants whom
I brought out from the land of Egypt.
I am the LORD your God.

Blessings of Obedience

26 'You shall not make[6213] for yourselves [I][a]idols,[6459] nor shall you
set up for yourselves [b]an image[4676] or
[c]a *sacred* pillar, nor shall you place a
[d]figured stone in your land[776] to bow
down[7812] [II]to it; for I am the LORD your
God.[430]
2 '[a]You shall keep My sabbaths[7676]
and reverence[3372] My sanctuary;[4720] I
am the LORD.
3 '[a]If you walk in My statutes[2708]
and keep My commandments[4687] so as
to carry them out,
4 then [a]I shall give you rains in their
season,[6256] so that the land will yield
its produce and the trees of the field
will bear their fruit.
5 '[a]Indeed, your threshing will last
for you until grape gathering, and grape
gathering will last until sowing time.[2233]
You will thus eat your [I]food to the full
and [b]live securely[983] in your land.
6 '[a]I shall also grant peace[7965] in the
land, so that [b]you may lie down with
no one making *you* tremble. [c]I shall also
eliminate[7673] harmful[7451] beasts[2416] from
the land, and [d]no sword[2719] will pass[5674]
through your land.
7 'But you will chase your enemies,
and they will fall[5307] before you by the
sword;
8 [a]five of you will chase a hundred,
and a hundred of you will chase ten thousand, and your enemies will fall before
you by the sword.
🔑9 'So I will turn toward you and
[a]make you fruitful and multiply you, and
I will [b]confirm My covenant[1285] with
you.
10 '[a]And you will eat the old supply
and clear out the old because of the
new.
11 '[a]Moreover, I will make My
[I]dwelling[4908] among you, and My soul[5315]
will not [II]reject you.
12 '[a]I will also walk among you and
be your God, and you shall be My
people.[5971]
13 '[a]I am the LORD your God, who
brought you out of the land of Egypt
so that *you* should not be their slaves,
and [b]I broke the bars of your yoke and
made you walk erect.

Penalties of Disobedience

14 '[a]But if you do not obey Me and
do not carry out all these commandments,
15 if, instead, you [a]reject[3988] My
statutes, and if your soul abhors My
ordinances[4941] so as not to carry out[6213]
all My commandments, *and* so
[b]break[6565] My covenant,
16 I, in turn, will do this to you: I
will appoint[6485] over you a [a]sudden terror,[928] consumption and fever that shall
waste away[3615] the eyes and cause the
[b]soul to pine away; also, [c]you shall sow
your seed uselessly, for your enemies
shall eat it up.
17 'And I will set My face against
you so that you shall be struck down
before your enemies; and [a]those who
hate[8130] you shall rule[7287] over you, and
[b]you shall flee when no one is pursuing
you.
18 'If also after these things, you
do not obey Me, then I will punish[3256]
you [a]seven times more for your
sins.[2403]
19 'And I will also [a]break[7665] down
your pride of power; I will also make
your sky[8064] like iron and your earth
like bronze.
20 'And [a]your strength shall be
spent[8552] uselessly, for your land shall
not yield its produce and the trees of
the land shall not yield their fruit.

1 [I]Or, *graven images* [II]Lit., *over* [a]Lev. 19:4; Deut. 5:8 [b]Ex. 20:4; Deut. 16:21f. [c]Ex. 23:24 [d]Num. 33:52
2 [a]Lev. 19:30
3 [a]Deut. 7:12-26; 11:13; 28:1-14
4 [a]Deut. 11:14
5 [I]Lit., *bread* [a]Deut. 11:15; Joel 2:19, 26; Amos 9:13 [b]Lev. 25:18, 19; Ezek. 34:25
6 [a]Ps. 29:11; 85:8; 147:14 [b]Zeph. 3:13 [c]Lev. 26:22 [d]Lev. 26:25
8 [a]Deut. 32:30
9 [a]Gen. 17:6; 22:17; 48:4 [b]Gen. 17:7
10 [a]Lev. 25:22
11 [I]Or, *tabernacle* [II]Lit., *abhor* [a]Ex. 25:8; 29:45, 46; Ezek. 37:26
12 [a]Gen. 3:8; Deut. 23:14; 2Cor. 6:16
13 [a]Ex. 20:2 [b]Ezek. 34:27
14 [a]Deut. 28:15-68; Josh. 23:15
15 [a]Lev. 26:11; 2Kin. 17:15 [b]Lev. 26:9
16 [a]Deut. 28:22; Ps. 78:33 [b]1Sam. 2:33; Ezek. 24:23; 33:10 [c]Judg. 6:3-6; Job 31:8
17 [a]Ps. 106:41 [b]Lev. 26:36, 37; Ps. 53:5; Prov. 28:1
18 [a]Lev. 26:21, 24, 28
19 [a]Is. 28:1-3; Ezek. 24:21
20 [a]Ps. 127:1; Is. 17:10, 11; 49:4; Jer. 12:13

🔑 **26:9** This was a confirmation of the same promise that God had made to Abraham in Gen. 12:1-3; 13:16; 15:5; 17:5,6; 18:18; 22:17,18.

21 'If then, you [I][a]act with hostility against Me and are unwilling to obey[8085] Me, I will increase the plague on you [b]seven times according to your sins.

22 'And [a]I will let loose among you the beasts of the field, which shall bereave you of your children and destroy[3772] your cattle and reduce your number so that [b]your roads[1870] lie deserted.

23 '[a]And if by these things you are not turned[3256] to Me, but act with hostility against Me,

24 then I will [a]act with hostility against you; and I, even I, will strike you [b]seven times for your sins.

25 'I will also bring upon you a sword which will execute[5358] [a]vengeance[5359] for the covenant; and when you gather together into your cities, I will send [b]pestilence[1698] among you, so that you shall be delivered into enemy hands.[3027]

26 '[a]When I break your staff[4294] of bread, ten women will bake your bread in one oven, and they will bring back[7725] your bread [I]in rationed amounts, so that you will [b]eat and not be satisfied.

27 'Yet if in spite of this, you do not obey Me, but act with hostility against Me,

28 then [a]I will act with wrathful[2534] hostility against you; and I, even I, will punish[3256] you seven times for your sins.

29 'Further, [a]you shall eat the flesh[1320] of your sons[1121] and the flesh of your daughters you shall eat.

30 'I then [a]will destroy[8045] your high places,[1116] and cut down[3772] your [b]incense altars,[2553] and heap your [I]remains[6297] on the [I]remains of your idols;[1544] for My soul shall abhor[1602] you.

31 'I will [I]lay [a]waste[2723] your cities as well, and will make your [b]sanctuaries desolate; and I will not [c]smell[7306] your soothing aromas.

32 'And I will make [a]the land desolate [b]so that your enemies who settle in it shall be appalled over it.

33 'You, however, I [a]will scatter among the nations[1471] and will draw out a sword after you, as your land becomes desolate[8077] and your cities become waste.

34 '[a]Then the land will [I]enjoy[7521] its sabbaths all the days[3117] of the desolation, while you are in your enemies' land; then the land will rest and [I]enjoy its sabbaths.

35 'All the days of *its* desolation it will observe the rest[7673] which it did not observe on your sabbaths, while you were living on it.

36 'As for those of you who may be left,[7604] I will also bring [a]weakness into their hearts[3824] in the lands of their enemies. And the sound of a driven leaf will chase them and even when no one is pursuing, they will flee [I]as though from the sword, and they will fall.

37 '[a]They will therefore stumble over each[376] other as if *running* from the sword, although no one is pursuing; and you will have *no strength* [I]to stand up before your enemies.

38 'But [a]you will perish[6] among the nations, and your enemies' land will consume you.

39 '[a]So those of you who may be left will rot[4743] away because of their iniquity[5771] in the lands of your enemies; and also because of the iniquities of their forefathers[1] they will rot away with them.

40 '[a]If they confess[3034] their iniquity and the iniquity of their forefathers, in their unfaithfulness[4603] which they committed[4603] against Me, and also in their acting with hostility against Me—

41 I also was acting with hostility against them, to bring them into the land of their enemies—[a]or if their uncircumcised[6189] heart becomes humbled so that [b]they then make amends[7521] for their iniquity,

42 then I will remember[2142] [a]My covenant with Jacob, and I will remember also [b]My covenant with Isaac, and [c]My covenant with Abraham as well, and I will remember the land.

43 '[a]For the land shall be abandoned[5800] by them, and shall make up for its sabbaths while it is made desolate without them. They, meanwhile, shall

---

21 [I]Lit., *walk,* and so throughout the ch. [a]Lev. 26:23, 27, 40 [b]Lev. 26:18
22 [a]2Kin. 17:25 [b]Judg. 5:6
23 [a]Lev. 26:21; Jer. 5:3
24 [a]Lev. 26:28, 41 [b]Lev. 26:21
25 [a]Jer. 50:28; 51:11 [b]Num. 14:12
26 [I]Lit., *by weight* [a]Is. 3:1; Ezek. 4:16, 17; 5:16 [b]Mic. 6:14
28 [a]Lev. 26:24, 41; Is. 59:18
29 [a]2Kin. 6:29
30 [I]Lit., *corpses* [a]2Kin. 23:20; Ezek. 6:3, 6; Amos 7:9 [b]2Chr. 34:4, 7; Is. 27:9
31 [I]Lit., *give desolation to* [a]Neh. 2:3; Jer. 44:2, 6, 22 [b]Is. 63:18; Lam. 2:7 [c]Amos 5:21
32 [a]Jer. 9:11; 12:11; 25:11; 33:10 [b]Jer. 18:16; 19:8
33 [a]Deut. 4:27; 28:64; Ps. 44:11; 106:27; Jer. 31:10; Ezek. 12:15; 20:23; Zech. 7:14
34 [I]Lit., *satisfy* [a]Lev. 26:43; 2Chr. 36:21
36 [I]Lit., *the flight of the sword* [a]Is. 30:17; Lam. 1:3, 6; 4:19; Ezek. 21:7
37 [I]Lit., *you will stand* [a]Jer. 6:21; Nah. 3:3
38 [a]Deut. 4:26
39 [a]Ezek. 4:17; 33:10
40 [a]Jer. 3:12-15; 14:20; Hos. 5:15
41 [a]Jer. 4:4; 9:25, 26; Ezek. 44:7, 9; Acts 7:51 [b]Ezek. 20:43
42 [a]Gen. 28:13-15; 35:11, 12 [b]Gen. 26:2-5 [c]Gen. 22:15-18
43 [a]Lev. 26:34

be making amends for their iniquity,
[I]because they rejected[3988] My ordinances and their [b]soul abhorred My statutes.
44 'Yet in spite of this, when they
are in the land of their enemies, I will
not reject them, nor will I so [a]abhor
them as [b]to destroy[3615] them, [c]breaking
My covenant with them; for I am the
LORD their God.
45 'But I will remember for them
the [a]covenant with their ancestors,[7223]
whom I brought out of the land of Egypt
in the sight of the nations, that [b]I might
be their God. I am the LORD.' "
46 [a]These are the statutes[2706] and
ordinances and laws[8451] which the LORD
established between Himself and the
sons[1121] of Israel [I]through Moses at
Mount Sinai.

Rules Concerning Valuations

27 Again, the LORD spoke to Moses, saying,
2 "Speak to the sons[1121] of Israel,
and say[559] to them, '[a]When a man[376]
makes a difficult[6381] vow,[5088] he *shall*
be valued according to your valuation
of persons[5315] belonging to the LORD.
3 'If your valuation is of the male[2145]
from twenty years even to sixty years
old,[1121] then your valuation shall be fifty
shekels of silver, after [a]the shekel of
the sanctuary.[6944]
4 'Or if it is a female,[5347] then your
valuation shall be thirty shekels.
5 'And if it be from five years even
to twenty years old then your valuation
for the male shall be twenty shekels,
and for the female ten shekels.
6 'But if *they are* from a month even
up to five years old, then your valuation
shall be [a]five shekels of silver for the
male, and for the female your valuation
shall be three shekels of silver.
7 'And if *they are* from sixty years
old and upward, if it is a male, then
your valuation shall be fifteen shekels,
and for the female ten shekels.
8 'But if he is poorer than your valuation, then he shall be placed before the
priest,[3548] and the priest shall value him;
[a]according to [I]the means[3027] of the one
who vowed,[5087] the priest shall value
him.
9 'Now if it is an animal of the kind
which [I]men can present as an offering[7133]
to the LORD, any such that one gives
to the LORD shall be holy.[6944]
10 '[a]He shall not replace[2498] it or exchange it, a good[2896] for a bad,[7451] or a
bad for a good; or if he does exchange[8545]
animal for animal, then both it and its
substitute shall become holy.
11 'If, however, it is any unclean[2931]
animal of the kind which [I]men do not
present as an offering to the LORD, then
he shall place the animal before the
priest.
12 'And the priest shall value it
[I]as either good or bad; as you, the priest,
value it, so it shall be.
13 'But if he should ever *wish to*
redeem it, then he shall add one-fifth
of it to your valuation.
14 'Now if a man consecrates his
house[1004] as holy to the LORD, then the
priest shall value it [I]as either good or
bad; as the priest values it, so it shall
stand.
15 'Yet if the one who consecrates
it should *wish to* redeem his house, then
he shall add one-fifth of your valuation
price to it, so that it may be his.
16 'Again, if a man consecrates to
the LORD part of the fields[7704] of his
own property,[272] then your valuation
shall be [I]proportionate to the seed[2233]
needed for it: a homer[2563] of barley seed
at fifty shekels of silver.
17 'If he consecrates his field as of
the year of jubilee,[3104] according to your
valuation it shall stand.
18 'If he consecrates his field after
the jubilee, however, then the priest
shall calculate[2803] the price for [I]him
[II]proportionate to the years that are
left[3498] until the year of jubilee; and it
shall be deducted[1639] from your valuation.
19 'And if the one who consecrates
it should ever wish to redeem the field,
then he shall add one-fifth of your valua-

43 [I]Lit., *because and by the cause* [b]Lev. 26:11
44 [a]Lev. 26:11 [b]Deut. 4:31; Jer. 30:11 [c]Jer. 33:20-26
45 [a]Ex. 6:6-8 [b]Gen. 17:7
46 [I]Lit., *by the hand of* [a]Lev. 7:38; 27:34; Deut. 4:5; 29:1
2 [a]Num. 6:2; Deut. 23:21-23
3 [a]Ex. 30:13; Lev. 27:25; Num. 3:47; 18:16
6 [a]Num. 18:16
8 [I]Lit., *what the hand reaches* [a]Lev. 5:11; 14:21-24
9 [I]Lit., *they*
10 [a]Lev. 27:33
11 [I]Lit., *they*
12 [I]Lit., *between*
14 [I]Lit., *between good*
16 [I]Lit., *according to its seed*
18 [I]Or, *it* [II]Lit., *according to the years*

tion price to it, so that it may pass to
him.
20 'Yet if he will not redeem the
field, [I]but has sold the field to another
man, it may no longer be redeemed;
21 and when it [I]reverts in the jubilee, the field shall be holy to the LORD,
like a field [II]set apart;[2764] [a]it shall be
for the priest as his [III]property.
22 'Or if he consecrates to the LORD
a field which he has bought, which is
not a part of the field of his own
[I]property,
23 then the priest shall calculate for
[I]him the amount of your valuation up
to the year of jubilee; and he shall on
that day give your valuation as holy to
the LORD.
24 'In the year of jubilee the field
shall return[7725] to the one from whom
he bought it, to whom the possession
of the land[776] belongs.
25 'Every valuation of yours, moreover, shall be after [a]the shekel of the
sanctuary. The shekel shall be twenty
gerahs.[1626]
26 [a]'However, a first-born among
animals, which as a first-born belongs
to the LORD, no man may consecrate
it; whether ox or sheep, it is the LORD'S.
27 'But if *it is* among the unclean
animals, then he shall [I]redeem[6299] it according to your valuation, and add to it
one-fifth of it; and if it is not redeemed,
then it shall be sold according to your
valuation.
28 'Nevertheless, [a]anything which
a man[120] [I]sets apart[2763] to the LORD out
of all that he has, of man or animal or
of the fields of his own property, shall
not be sold or redeemed. Anything
[II]devoted to destruction is most holy to
the LORD.
29 'No [I]one who may have been
[II]set apart[2763] among men shall be ransomed; he shall surely be put to
death.[4191]
30 'Thus [a]all the tithe[4643] of the
land, of the seed of the land or of the
fruit of the tree, is the LORD'S; it is
holy to the LORD.
31 'If, therefore, a man wishes to
redeem part of his tithe, he shall add
to it one-fifth of it.
32 'And for every tenth part of herd
or flock, whatever [a]passes under the
rod,[7626] the tenth one shall be holy to
the LORD.
33 [a]'He is not to be concerned
whether *it is* good or bad, nor shall he
exchange it; or if he does exchange it,
then both it and its substitute shall
become holy. It shall not be redeemed.' "
34 [a]These are the commandments[4687] which the LORD commanded[6680] Moses for the sons of Israel at
Mount Sinai.

20 [I]Or, *if he*

21 [I]Lit., *goes out* [II]Or, *devoted, banned* [III]Lit., *possession* [a]Num. 18:14; Ezek. 44:29

22 [I]Lit., *possession*

23 [I]Or, *it*

25 [a]Ex. 30:13; Lev. 27:3; Num. 3:47; 18:16

26 [a]Ex. 13:2

27 [I]Or, *ransom*

28 [I]Lit., *anything devoted;* or, *banned* [II]Or, *puts under the ban* [a]Num. 18:14; Josh. 6:17-19

29 [I]Lit., *one devoted;* or, *banned* [II]Or, *put under the ban*

30 [a]Gen. 28:22; 2Chr. 31:5; Neh. 13:12

32 [a]Jer. 33:13; Ezek. 20:37

33 [a]Lev. 27:10

34 [a]Lev. 26:46; Deut. 4:5

NUMBERS

Numbers, believed to be the fourth book of Moses, was so named because the sons of Israel were numbered in chapter 1 and chapter 26. As in former books, Moses is the principal figure. The central theme of the Book of Numbers is service. The nation of Israel had become, at least temporarily, nomadic. God was weeding out the dead wood during a period of about forty years. Those who did not truly believe in God's promise were not permitted to enter into the land of Canaan, but their children were being prepared for battle. The younger generation was full of faith and courage. This book describes how they wandered in the wilderness for thirty-eight years, while the older generation died off and a new nation, trained to obey God, was ready for an assault upon the land which "flowed with milk and honey." There are many lessons for us to learn from them today. We must never complain against God or doubt Him. God could get them out of Egypt, but it was difficult to get Egypt out of them!

The Census of Israel's Warriors

1 Then the LORD spoke[1696] to Moses in the wilderness of Sinai, in
the tent[168] of meeting,[4150] on [a]the first
of the second month, in the second year
after they had come out of the land of
Egypt, saying,
2 "[a]Take[5375] a [l]census[7218] of all the
congregation[5712] of the sons[1121] of Israel,
by their families,[4940] by their fathers'[1]
households,[1004] according to the number
of names, every male, head by head[1538]
3 from [a]twenty years old[1121] and upward, whoever *is able to* go out to
war[6635] in Israel, you and Aaron shall
[l]number[6485] them by their armies.[6635]
4 "With you, moreover, there shall
be a man[376] of each tribe,[4294] [a]each
one[376] head[7218] of his father's household.
5 "These then are the names of the
men[582] who shall stand with you:
[a]of Reuben, Elizur the son[1121] of Shedeur;
6 of Simeon, Shelumiel the son of
Zurishaddai;
7 of Judah, [a]Nahshon the son of Amminadab;
8 of Issachar, Nethanel the son of
Zuar;
9 of Zebulun, Eliab the son of Helon;
10 of the sons of Joseph: of Ephra-

1 [a]Ex. 40:2, 17

2 [l]Lit., *sum* [a]Ex. 12:37; 38:25, 26; Num. 26:2

3 [l]Lit., *muster*, and so throughout the ch. [a]Ex. 30:14; 38:26

4 [a]Ex. 18:21, 25; Num. 1:16; Deut. 1:15

5 [a]Gen. 29:32; Ex. 1:2; Deut. 33:6; Rev. 7:5

7 [a]Ruth 4:20; 1Chr. 2:10; Luke 3:32

1:1 The Lord began to speak on this occasion one month after the construction of the tabernacle had been completed (Ex. 40:17) and one year and fifteen days after the original Passover when Israel began its journey from Egypt (Ex. 12:6; Num. 33:3).

1:2 The Book of Numbers, as its names suggests, records the taking of two censuses of Israel. The procedure for the twelve tribes was different than for the tribe of Levi. The former count was a military census, since it numbered only the males of the military age of twenty years old and older. The first census was taken just before Israel left Mount Sinai, because their intention was to conquer Canaan immediately. Unfortunately, the people sinned at Kadesh-barnea, so they had to spend a total of forty years in the wilderness, until all the men who rebelled had died. Approximately thirty-seven years after the first census, a second one was taken following the same procedure (Num. 26:1-51), and the figures were to be used in determining the size of the territory allotted to each tribe (Num. 26:52-56). When the figures from the two censuses are compared, some interesting facts emerge. The first numbering found 603,550 fighting men in the twelve tribes (Num. 1:46), a remarkable number in light of the fact that a few centuries before at most, only about seventy members of Jacob's family had migrated to Egypt. The totals for the second census were 601,730 (Num. 26:51), which reflects almost no change in thirty-seven years. The composition of the two groups was, however, totally different. Only two men, Joshua and Caleb, who had not rebelled at Kadesh-barnea, were counted in both censuses. Had the 24,000 who were killed just before the second census because of their sin at Baal-peor (Num. 25:9) still been alive, the adult male population would have shown a modest increase. For the censuses of the tribe of Levi, see the note on Num. 3:39.

im, Elishama the son of Ammihud; of Manasseh, Gamaliel the son of Pedahzur;

11 of Benjamin, Abidan the son of Gideoni;

12 of Dan, Ahiezer the son of Ammishaddai;

13 of Asher, Pagiel the son of Ochran;

14 of Gad, Eliasaph the son of [a]Deuel;

15 of Naphtali, Ahira the son of Enan.

16 "These are they who were [a]called[7121] of the congregation, the leaders[5387] of their fathers' tribes;[4294] they were the [b]heads[7218] of [1]divisions[505] of Israel."

17 So Moses and Aaron took these men who had been designated[5344] by name,

18 and they assembled all the congregation together on the [a]first of the second month. Then they registered by [b]ancestry in their families, by their fathers' households, according to the number of names, from twenty years old and upward, head by head,

19 just as [a]the LORD had commanded[6680] Moses. So he numbered[6485] them in the wilderness of Sinai.

20 [a]Now the sons of Reuben, Israel's first-born, their genealogical registration[8435] by their families, by their fathers' households, according to the number of names, head by head, every male from twenty years old and upward, whoever *was able to* go out to war,

21 their numbered men, of the tribe of Reuben, *were* 46,500.

22 [a]Of the sons of Simeon, their genealogical registration by their families, by their fathers' households, their numbered men, according to the number of names, head by head, every male from twenty years old and upward, [b]whoever *was able to* go out to war,

23 their numbered men, of the tribe of Simeon, *were* 59,300.

24 [a]Of the sons of Gad, their genealogical registration by their families, by their fathers' households, according to the number of names, from twenty years old and upward, whoever *was able to* go out to war,

25 their numbered men, of the tribe of Gad, *were* 45,650.

26 [a]Of the sons of Judah, their genealogical registration by their families, by their fathers' households, according to the number of names, from twenty years old and upward, whoever *was able to* go out to war,

27 their numbered men, of the tribe of Judah, *were* 74,600.

28 [a]Of the sons of Issachar, their genealogical registration by their families, by their fathers' households, according to the number of names, from twenty years old and upward, whoever *was able to* go out to war,

29 their numbered men, of the tribe of Issachar, *were* 54,400.

30 [a]Of the sons of Zebulun, their genealogical registration by their families, by their fathers' households, according to the number of names, from twenty years old and upward, whoever *was able to* go out to war,

31 their numbered men, of the tribe of Zebulun, *were* 57,400.

32 [a]Of the sons of Joseph, *namely,* of the sons of Ephraim, their genealogical registration by their families, by their fathers' households, according to the number of names, from twenty years old and upward, whoever *was able to* go out to war,

33 their numbered men, of the tribe of Ephraim, *were* 40,500.

34 [a]Of the sons of Manasseh, their genealogical registration by their families, by their fathers' households, according to the number of names, from twenty years old and upward, whoever *was able to* go out to war,

35 their numbered men, of the tribe of Manasseh, *were* 32,200.

36 [a]Of the sons of Benjamin, their genealogical registration by their families, by their fathers' households, according to the number of names, from twenty years old and upward, whoever *was able to* go out to war,

14 [a]Num. 2:14
16 [1]Lit., *thousands;* or, *clans* [a]Ex. 18:21; Num. 7:2; 16:2; 26:9 [b]Ex. 18:25
18 [a]Num. 1:1 [b]Ezra 2:59; Heb. 7:3
19 [a]2Sam. 24:1
20 [a]Num. 26:5-7
22 [a]Num. 26:12-14 [b]Ps. 144:1
24 [a]Gen. 30:11; Num. 26:15-18; Josh. 4:12; Jer. 49:1
26 [a]Gen. 29:35; Num. 26:19-22; 2Sam. 24:9; Ps. 78:68; Matt. 1:2
28 [a]Num. 26:23-25
30 [a]Num. 26:26, 27
32 [a]Num. 26:35-37; Deut. 33:13-17; Jer. 7:15; Obad. 19
34 [a]Num. 26:28-34
36 [a]Gen. 49:27; Num. 26:38-41; 2Chr. 17:17; Rev. 7:8

37 their numbered men, of the tribe of Benjamin, *were* 35,400.

38 [a]Of the sons of Dan, their genealogical registration by their families, by their fathers' households, according to the number of names, from twenty years old and upward, whoever *was able to* go out to war,

39 their numbered men, of the tribe of Dan, *were* 62,700.

40 [a]Of the sons of Asher, their genealogical registration by their families, by their fathers' households, according to the number of names, from twenty years old and upward, whoever *was able to* go out to war,

41 their numbered men, of the tribe of Asher, *were* 41,500.

42 [a]Of the sons of Naphtali, their genealogical registration by their families, by their fathers' households, according to the number of names, from twenty years old and upward, whoever *was able to* go out to war,

43 their numbered men, of the tribe of Naphtali, *were* 53,400.

44 These are the ones who were numbered, whom Moses and Aaron numbered, with the leaders of Israel, twelve men,[376] each[376] of whom was of his father's household.

45 So all the numbered men of the sons of Israel by their fathers' households, from twenty years old and upward, whoever *was able to* go out to war in Israel,

46 even all the numbered men were [a]603,550.

Levites Exempted

47 [a]The Levites, however, were not numbered among them by their fathers' tribe.

48 For the LORD had spoken[1696] to Moses, saying,

49 "Only the tribe of Levi [a]you shall not number, nor shall you take their [I]census among the sons of Israel.

50 "But you shall [a]appoint[6485] the Levites over the [I]tabernacle[4908] of the testimony,[5715] and over all its furnishings and over all that belongs to it. They shall carry[5375] the tabernacle and all its furnishings, and they shall take care[8334] of it; they shall also camp around the [I]tabernacle.

51 "[a]So when the tabernacle is to set out, the Levites shall take it down; and when the tabernacle encamps, the Levites shall set it up. But [b]the [I]layman[2114] who comes near shall be put to death.[4191]

52 "[a]And the sons of Israel shall camp, each man by his own camp,[4264] and each man by his own standard, according to their armies.[6635]

53 "[a]But the Levites shall camp around the tabernacle of the testimony, that there may be [b]no wrath[7110] on the congregation of the sons of Israel. [c]So the Levites shall keep[8104] charge[4931] of the tabernacle of the testimony."

54 Thus the sons of Israel did;[6213] according to all which the LORD had commanded Moses, so they did.

Arrangement of the Camps

2 Now the LORD spoke[1696] to Moses and to Aaron, saying,

2 "[a]The sons[1121] of Israel shall camp, each[376] by his own standard, with the [I]banners[226] of their fathers'[1] households;[1004] they shall camp around the tent[168] of meeting[4150] [II]at a distance.

3 "Now those who camp on the east side toward the sunrise *shall be* of the standard of the camp[4264] of Judah, by their armies,[6635] and the leader[5387] of the sons of Judah: [a]Nahshon the son of Amminadab,

4 and his army, even their [I]numbered[6485] men, 74,600.

5 "And those who camp next to him *shall be* the tribe[4294] of Issachar, and the leader of the sons of Issachar: [a]Nethanel the son of Zuar,

6 and his army, even their numbered men, 54,400.

7 "Then *comes* the tribe of Zebulun, and the leader of the sons of Zebulun: [a]Eliab the son of Helon,

38 [a]Gen. 30:6; 46:23; Num. 2:25; 26:42, 43

40 [a]Num. 26:44-47

42 [a]Num. 26:48-50

46 [a]Ex. 12:37; 38:26; Num. 2:32; 26:51

47 [a]Num. 2:33; 3:14-39; 4:49; 26:57-64

49 [I]Lit., *sum* [a]Num. 26:62

50 [I]Lit., *dwelling place*, and so throughout the ch. [a]Ex. 38:21; Num. 3:6-8, 25-37; 4:15, 25-27, 31, 32

51 [I]Lit., *stranger* [a]Num. 4:1-33 [b]Num. 3:10, 38; 4:15, 19, 20

52 [a]Num. 2:2, 34

53 [a]Num. 3:23, 29, 35, 38 [b]Lev. 10:6; Num. 16:46; 18:5 [c]Num. 8:24; 18:2-4; 1Chr. 23:32

2 [I]Lit., *signs* [II]Or, *facing it* [a]Num. 1:52; 24:2

3 [a]Num. 1:7; 10:14; Ruth 4:20; 1Chr. 2:10; Luke 3:32, 33

4 [I]Lit., *mustered*, and so throughout the ch.

5 [a]Num. 1:8; 7:18, 23

7 [a]Num. 1:9

8 and his army, even his numbered men, 57,400.

9 "The total of the numbered men of the camp of Judah: 186,400, by their armies. [a]They shall set out first.[7223]

10 "On the south side *shall be* the standard of the camp of Reuben by their armies, and the leader of the sons of Reuben: [a]Elizur the son of Shedeur,

11 and his army, even their numbered men, 46,500.

12 "And those who camp next to him *shall be* the tribe of Simeon, and the leader of the sons of Simeon: [a]Shelumiel the son of Zurishaddai,

13 and his army, even their numbered men, 59,300.

14 "Then *comes* the tribe of Gad, and the leader of the sons[1121] of Gad: [a]Eliasaph the son of [I]Deuel,

15 and his army, even their numbered men, 45,650.

16 "The total of the numbered men of the camp of Reuben: 151,450 by their armies. And [a]they shall set out second.

17 "[a]Then the tent of meeting shall set out *with* the camp of the Levites in the midst of the camps; just as they camp, so they shall set out, every man in his place, by their standards.

18 "On the west side *shall be* the standard of the camp of [a]Ephraim by their armies, and the leader of the sons of Ephraim *shall be* [b]Elishama the son of Ammihud,

19 and his army, even their numbered men, 40,500.

20 "And next to him *shall be* the tribe of Manasseh, and the leader of the sons of Manasseh: [a]Gamaliel the son of Pedahzur,

21 and his army, even their numbered men, 32,200.

22 "Then *comes* the tribe of [a]Benjamin, and the leader of the sons of Benjamin: [b]Abidan the son of Gideoni,

23 and his army, even their numbered men, 35,400.

24 "The total of the numbered men of the camp of Ephraim: 108,100, by their armies. And [a]they shall set out third.

25 "On the north side *shall be* the standard of the camp of Dan by their armies, and the leader of the sons of Dan: [a]Ahiezer the son of Ammishaddai,

26 and his army, even their numbered men, 62,700.

27 "And those who camp next to him *shall be* the tribe of Asher, and the leader of the sons of Asher: [a]Pagiel the son of Ochran,

28 and his army, even their numbered men, 41,500.

29 "Then *comes* the tribe of [a]Naphtali, and the leader of the sons of Naphtali: [b]Ahira the son of Enan,

30 and his army,[6635] even their numbered men, 53,400.

31 "The total of the numbered men of the camp of Dan, *was* 157,600. [a]They shall set out last[314] by their standards."

32 These are the numbered men of the sons of Israel by their fathers'[1] households; the total of the numbered men of the camps[4264] by their armies,[6635] [a]603,550.

33 [a]The Levites, however, were not numbered among the sons of Israel, just as the LORD had commanded[6680] Moses.

34 Thus the sons of Israel did;[6213] according to all that the LORD commanded Moses, so they camped by their standards, and so they set out, every one[376] by his family,[4940] according to his father's household.

Levites to Be Priesthood

3 [a]Now these are *the records of* the generations[8435] of Aaron and Moses at the time[3117] when the LORD spoke[1696] with Moses on Mount Sinai.

2 [a]These then are the names of the sons[1121] of Aaron: Nadab the first-born, and Abihu, Eleazar and Ithamar.

3 These are the names of the sons of Aaron, the [a]anointed priests,[3548] whom he [I]ordained[4886] to serve[8334] as priests.[3547]

4 [a]But Nadab and Abihu died before the LORD when they offered[7126]

9 [a]Num. 10:14
10 [a]Num. 1:5
12 [a]Num. 1:6
14 [I]Many mss. read *Reuel* [a]Num. 1:14; 7:42
16 [a]Num. 10:18
17 [a]Num. 1:53
18 [a]Gen. 48:14-20; Jer. 31:9, 18-20 [b]Num. 1:10
20 [a]Num. 1:10
22 [a]Ps. 68:27 [b]Num. 1:11
24 [a]Num. 10:22
25 [a]Num. 1:12
27 [a]Num. 1:13
29 [a]Gen. 30:8 [b]Num. 1:15
31 [a]Num. 10:25
32 [a]Ex. 38:26; Num. 1:46
33 [a]Num. 1:47; 26:57-62
1 [a]Ex. 6:20-27
2 [a]Ex. 6:23; Num. 26:60
3 [I]Lit., *filled their hand* [a]Ex. 28:41
4 [a]Lev. 10:1, 2; Num. 26:61

strange[2114] fire before the LORD in the
wilderness of Sinai; and they had no
children.[1121] So Eleazar and Ithamar
served as priests [I]in the lifetime of their
father[1] Aaron.
5 Then the LORD spoke to Moses,
saying,
6 "[a]Bring[7126] the tribe[4294] of Levi
near and set them before Aaron the
priest,[3548] that they may serve him.
7 "And they shall perform[8104] the
duties[4931] for [I]him and for the whole
congregation[5712] before the tent[168] of
meeting,[4150] to do[5647] the [a]service[5656]
of the tabernacle.[4908]
8 "They shall also keep all the furnishings of the tent of meeting, along
with the duties of the sons of Israel,
to do the service of the tabernacle.
9 "You shall thus [a]give the Levites
to Aaron and to his sons; they are wholly
given to him from among the sons of
Israel.
10 "So you shall appoint[6485] Aaron
and his sons that [a]they may keep[8104]
their priesthood,[3550] but [b]the [I]layman[2114]
who comes near shall be put to
death."[4191]
11 Again the LORD spoke to Moses,
saying,
12 "Now, behold, I [a]have taken the
Levites from among the sons of Israel
instead of every [b]first-born, the first issue of the womb[7358] among the sons
of Israel. So the Levites shall be Mine.
13 "For [a]all the first-born are Mine;
on the day that I struck down[5221] all
the first-born in the land of Egypt, I
sanctified to Myself all the first-born in
Israel, from man[120] to beast. They shall
be Mine; I am the LORD."
14 Then the LORD spoke to Moses
[a]in the wilderness of Sinai, saying,
15 "[I][a]Number the sons of Levi by
their fathers'[1] households,[1004] by their
families;[4940] every male from a month
old[1121] and upward you shall number."
16 So Moses numbered[6485] them according to the [I]word of the LORD, just
as he had been commanded.[6680]
17 [a]These then are the sons of Levi
by their names: Gershon and Kohath
and Merari.
18 And these are the names of the
[a]sons of Gershon by their families: Libni
and Shimei;
19 and the sons of Kohath by their
families: Amram and Izhar, Hebron and
Uzziel;
20 and the sons of Merari by their
families: Mahli and Mushi. These are
the families of the Levites according to
their fathers' households.
21 Of Gershon *was* the family[4940]
of the Libnites and the family of the
Shimeites; these *were* the families of the
Gershonites.
22 Their numbered men, in the
numbering of every male[2145] from a
month old and upward, *even* their numbered men *were* 7,500.
23 The families of the Gershonites
were to camp behind the [I]tabernacle
westward,
24 and the leader of the fathers'
households of the Gershonites *was* Eliasaph the son[1121] of Lael.

Duties of the Priests

25 Now [a]the duties of the sons of
Gershon in the tent of meeting *involved*
the tabernacle and [b]the tent,[168] its covering, and [c]the screen for the doorway
of the tent of meeting,
26 and [a]the hangings of the court,

4 [I]Lit., *before the face*
6 [a]Num. 8:6-22; 18:1-7; Deut. 10:8
7 [I]Lit., *him and the duties of the whole congregation* [a]Num. 1:50
9 [a]Num. 18:6
10 [I]Lit., *stranger* [a]Ex. 29:9 [b]Num. 1:51
12 [a]Num. 3:45; 8:14 [b]Ex. 13:2
13 [a]Ex. 13:2; Lev. 27:26; Neh. 10:36
14 [a]Ex. 19:1
15 [I]Lit., *muster*, and so throughout the ch. [a]Num. 1:47
16 [I]Lit., *mouth*
17 [a]Ex. 6:16-22
18 [a]Ex. 6:17
23 [I]Lit., *dwelling place*, and so throughout the ch.
25 [a]Num. 4:24-26 [b]Ex. 26:1, 7, 14 [c]Ex. 26:36
26 [a]Ex. 27:9, 12, 14, 15

3:10 See note on Ex. 32:25-29.

3:12,13 In the time of the Patriarchs the firstborn son had a position of special honor and responsibility in the family structure. God proclaimed Israel to be His firstborn (Ex. 4:22). With the death of the Egyptians' firstborn sons, those of Israel who had been saved took on new importance for the covenant people (Ex. 11:4,5; 12:21-29). The firstborn among them were set apart for the Lord and it was necessary to make a sacrifice for their redemption (Ex. 22:29). In this passage another change was about to take place. All the male members of the tribe of Levi, from one month old and above, were substituted for the firstborn males of the rest of the tribes of Israel (see verses 41,45). The Levites were to be consecrated for the Lord's service.

and [b]the screen for the doorway of the court, which is around the tabernacle and the altar,[4196] and its cords, according to all the service [I]concerning them.

27 And of Kohath *was* the family of the Amramites and the family of the Izharites and the family of the Hebronites and the family of the Uzzielites; these were the families of the Kohathites.

28 In the numbering of every male from a month old and upward, *there were* 8,600, performing[8104] the duties of the sanctuary.[6944]

29 The families of the sons of Kohath were to camp on the southward side[3409] of the tabernacle,

30 and the leader of the fathers' households of the Kohathite families was [I]Elizaphan the son of Uzziel.

31 Now [a]their duties *involved* [b]the ark,[727] [c]the table, [d]the lampstand, [e]the altars,[4196] and the utensils of the sanctuary with which they minister, and the screen, and all the service [I]concerning them;

32 and Eleazar the son of Aaron the priest *was* the chief of the leaders of Levi, *and had* the oversight[6486] of those who perform the duties of the sanctuary.

33 Of Merari *was* the family of the Mahlites and the family of the Mushites; these *were* the families of Merari.

34 Their numbered men in the numbering of every male from a month old and upward, *were* 6,200.

35 And the leader of the fathers' households of the families of Merari *was* Zuriel the son of Abihail. They *were* to [a]camp on the northward side of the tabernacle.

36 Now the appointed[6486] duties of the sons of Merari *involved* the frames of the tabernacle, its bars, its pillars, its sockets, all its equipment, and the service concerning them,

37 and the pillars around the court with their sockets and their pegs and their cords.

38 Now those who were to [a]camp before the tabernacle eastward, before the tent of meeting toward the sunrise, are Moses and Aaron and his sons, performing the duties of the sanctuary[4720] for the obligation of the sons of Israel; but [b]the [I]layman coming near was to be put to death.

39 All the numbered men of the Levites, whom Moses and Aaron numbered at the [I]command[6310] of the LORD by their families, every male from a month old and upward, *were* [a]22,000.

First-born Redeemed

40 Then the LORD said[559] to Moses, "[a]Number[6485] every first-born male of the sons of Israel from a month old and upward, and [I]make a list[5375] of their names.

41 "And you [a]shall take the Levites for Me, I am the LORD, instead of all the first-born among the sons of Israel, and the cattle of the Levites instead of all the first-born among the cattle of the sons of Israel."

42 So Moses numbered all the first-born among the sons of Israel, just as the LORD had commanded him;

43 and all the first-born males by the number of names from a month old and upward, for their numbered men were [a]22,273.

44 Then the LORD spoke to Moses, saying,

45 "[a]Take the Levites instead of all the first-born among the sons of Israel and the cattle of the Levites. And the Levites shall be Mine; I am the LORD.

26 [I]Lit., *of it* [b]Ex. 27:16
30 [I]In Ex. 6:22, *Elzaphan*
31 [I]Lit., *of it* [a]Num. 4:15 [b]Ex. 25:10-22 [c]Ex. 25:23-28 [d]Ex. 25:31-40 [e]Ex. 27:1, 2; 30:1-5
35 [a]Num. 1:53; 2:25
38 [I]Lit., *stranger* [a]Num. 1:53; 2:3 [b]Num. 1:51
39 [I]Lit., *word* [a]Num. 3:43; 4:48; 26:62
40 [I]Lit., *take the number* [a]Num. 3:15
41 [a]Num. 3:12, 45
43 [a]Num. 3:39
45 [a]Num. 3:12

3:39 The numbering of the tribe of Levi followed a different procedure than the rest of Israel, and the figures were kept separate, since Levi was not to be given a separate tribal territory. All males as old as one month were counted, and the total for the census before Israel left Mount Sinai was 22,000. Using the same method, 23,000 were recorded at the second census, about thirty-seven years later (Num. 26:26).

🗝 46 "[a]And for the ransom[6302] of the 273 of the first-born of the sons of Israel who are in excess beyond the Levites,

47 you shall take [a]five shekels apiece, per head;[1538] you shall take *them* in [b]terms of the shekel of the sanctuary ([c]the shekel is twenty [I]gerahs),[1626]

48 and give the money, the ransom of those who are in excess among them, to Aaron and to his sons."

49 So Moses took the ransom[6306] money from those who were in excess, beyond those ransomed[6306] by the Levites;

50 from the first-born of the sons of Israel he took the money in terms of the shekel of the sanctuary, 1,365.

51 Then Moses gave the ransom money to Aaron and to his sons, at the [I]command of the LORD, just as the LORD had commanded Moses.

Duties of the Kohathites

4 Then the LORD spoke[1696] to Moses and to Aaron, saying,

2 "Take[5375] [I]a census[7218] of the [II]descendants[1121] of Kohath from among the sons of Levi, by their families,[4940] by their fathers'[1] households,[1004]

3 from [a]thirty years[1121] and upward, even to fifty years old, all who enter the service[6635] to do[6213] the work in the tent[168] of meeting.[4150]

4 "This is the work[5656] of the [I]descendants of Kohath in the tent of meeting, *concerning* the most holy things.[6944]

5 "When the camp[4264] sets out, Aaron and his sons shall go in and they shall take down [a]the veil of the screen and cover[3680] the [b]ark[727] of the testimony[5715] with it;

6 and they shall lay a [a]covering of porpoise skin on it, and shall spread over *it* a cloth of pure[3632] [I]blue, and shall insert[7760] its poles.

7 "Over the table of the bread of the Presence they shall also spread a cloth of [I]blue and put on it the dishes and the pans[3709] and the sacrificial bowls and the jars for the libation, and [a]the continual[8548] bread shall be on it.

8 "And they shall spread over them a cloth of scarlet *material,* and cover the same with a covering of porpoise skin, and they shall insert its poles.

9 "Then they shall take a [I]blue cloth and cover the [a]lampstand for the light,[3974] [b]along with its lamps[5216] and its snuffers, and its [II]trays and all its oil[8081] vessels, by which they serve[8334] it;

10 and they shall put it and all its utensils in a covering of porpoise skin, and shall put it on the carrying bars.

11 "And over the golden altar[4196] they shall spread a [I]blue cloth and cover it with a covering of porpoise skin, and shall insert its poles;

12 and they shall take all the utensils of service,[8335] with which they serve in the sanctuary,[6944] and put them in a [I]blue cloth and cover them with a covering of porpoise skin, and put them on the carrying bars.

13 "Then they shall take away the [I]ashes from the [a]altar, and spread a purple cloth over it.

14 "They shall also put on it all its utensils by which they serve in connection with it: the firepans, the forks and shovels and the basins, all the utensils of the altar; and they shall spread a cover of porpoise skin over it and insert its poles.

46 [a]Ex. 13:13, 15; Num. 18:15, 16
47 [I]I.e., A gerah equals approx. one-fortieth oz. [a]Lev. 27:6; Num. 18:16 [b]Ex. 30:13 [c]Lev. 27:25; Ezek. 45:12
51 [I]Lit., *mouth*
2 [I]Lit., *the sum* [II]Lit., *sons*
3 [a]Num. 4:23, 30, 35; 8:24; 1Chr. 23:3, 24, 27; Ezra 3:8
4 [I]Lit., *sons*
5 [a]Ex. 40:5; Lev. 16:2; 2Chr. 3:14; Matt. 27:51; Heb. 9:3 [b]Ex. 25:10-16
6 [I]Or, *violet* [a]Num. 4:25
7 [I]Or, *violet* [a]Ex. 25:30; Lev. 24:5-9
9 [I]Or, *violet* [II]Lit., *snuff dishes* [a]Ex. 25:31 [b]Ex. 25:37, 38
11 [I]Or, *violet*
12 [I]Or, *violet*
13 [I]Or, *fat ashes;* i.e., soaked with fat [a]Ex. 27:1-8

🗝 **3:46-51** The firstborn of Israel were numbered at 22,273 and the Levites at 22,000 (verse 39), a difference of 273. In the substitution of the Levites for the firstborn these 273 extra among the firstborn were to be redeemed by a contribution of five shekels of silver apiece which were to be given to Aaron and his sons, the priestly family. The shekel of the sanctuary was a weight measurement of silver which had been established for the contributions for the maintenance of the tabernacle (Ex. 30:13-16). The shekel of silver was to weigh 20 gerahs. A gerah has been estimated at slightly less than six-tenths of a gram. Therefore, the shekel would have weighed approximately eleven and one-half grams or four-tenths of an ounce.

15 "And when Aaron and his sons have finished[3615] covering[3680] the holy *objects* and all the furnishings of the sanctuary, when the camp is to set out, after that the sons of Kohath shall come to carry[5375] *them,* so that they may not touch[5060] the holy *objects*[6944] [a]and die.[4191] These are the [I]things in the tent of meeting which the sons of Kohath are to carry.[4853]

16 "And the responsibility[6486] of Eleazar the son[1121] of Aaron the priest[3548] is [a]the oil for the light and the [b]fragrant incense[7004] and [c]the continual[8548] grain offering[4503] and [d]the anointing[4888] oil—the responsibility[6486] of all the [I]tabernacle[4908] and of all that is in it, with the sanctuary and its furnishings."

17 Then the LORD spoke to Moses and to Aaron, saying,

18 "Do not let the tribe[7626] of the families of the Kohathites be cut[3772] off from among the Levites.

19 "But do this to them that they may live[2421] and [a]not die when they approach the most holy *objects:* Aaron and his sons shall go in and assign[7760] each[376] of them to his work and to his load;

20 but [a]they shall not go in to see the holy *objects* even for a moment, lest they die."

Duties of the Gershonites

21 Then the LORD spoke to Moses, saying,

22 "Take [I]a census of the sons of Gershon [II]also, by their fathers' households,[1004] by their families;

23 from [a]thirty years and upward to fifty years old, you shall [I]number[6485] them; all who enter to perform[6633] the service to do[5647] the work in the tent of meeting.

24 "This is the service of the families of the Gershonites, in serving[5647] and in carrying:[4853]

25 they shall carry [a]the curtains of the tabernacle and the tent of meeting *with* its covering and [b]the covering of porpoise skin that is on top of it, and the screen for the doorway of the tent of meeting,

26 and [a]the hangings of the court, and the screen for the doorway of the gate of the court which is around the tabernacle and the altar, and their cords and all the equipment for their service; and all that is to be done,[6213] [I]they shall perform.

27 "All the service[6310] of the sons of the Gershonites, in all their loads and in all their work, shall be *performed* at the [I]command of Aaron and his sons; and you shall assign[6485] to them as a duty[4931] all their loads.

28 "This is the service of the families of the sons of the Gershonites in the tent of meeting, and their duties *shall be* [I]under the direction[3027] of Ithamar the son of Aaron the priest.

Duties of the Merarites

29 "*As for* the sons of Merari, you shall number them by their families, by their fathers' households;

30 from [a]thirty years and upward even to fifty years old, you shall number them, everyone who enters the service to do the work of the tent of meeting.

31 "Now this is the duty of their loads, for all their service in the tent of meeting: the boards of the tabernacle and its bars and its pillars and its [I]sockets,

32 and the pillars around the court and their [I]sockets and their pegs and their cords, with all their equipment and with all their service; and you shall assign *each man* by name the items [II]he is to carry.

33 "This is the service of the families of the sons of Merari, according to all their service in the tent of meeting, [I]under the direction of Ithamar the son of Aaron the priest."

34 So Moses and Aaron and the leaders of the congregation[5712] numbered[6485] the sons of the Kohathites by their families, and by their fathers' households,

---

15 [I]Lit., *burden . . . of the sons* [a]Num. 1:51; 4:19, 20; 2Sam. 6:6, 7

16 [I]Lit., *dwelling place,* and so throughout the ch. [a]Lev. 24:1-3 [b]Ex. 30:34-38 [c]Lev. 6:20 [d]Ex. 30:22-33

19 [a]Num. 4:15

20 [a]Ex. 19:21; 1Sam. 6:19

22 [I]Lit., *the sum* [II]Lit., *also them*

23 [I]Lit., *muster,* and so throughout the ch. [a]Num. 4:3; 1Chr. 23:3, 24, 27

25 [a]Ex. 40:19 [b]Ex. 26:14; Num. 4:6

26 [I]Lit., *so they shall serve* [a]Ex. 38:9

27 [I]Lit., *mouth*

28 [I]Lit., *in the hand*

30 [a]Num. 4:3; 8:24-26

31 [I]Or, *bases*

32 [I]Or, *bases* [II]Lit., *of the duty of their loads.*

33 [I]Lit., *in the hand*

35 from [a]thirty years and upward even to fifty years old, everyone who entered the service for work in the tent of meeting.

36 And their numbered men by their families were 2,750.

37 These are the numbered men of the Kohathite families, everyone who was serving in the tent of meeting, whom Moses and Aaron numbered according to the [I]commandment[6310] of the LORD [II]through Moses.

38 And the numbered men of the sons of Gershon by their families, and by their fathers' households,

39 from thirty years and upward even to fifty years old, everyone who entered the service for work in the tent of meeting.

40 And their numbered men by their families, by their fathers' households, were 2,630.

41 These are the numbered men of the families of the sons of Gershon, everyone who was serving in the tent of meeting, whom Moses and Aaron numbered according to the [I]commandment of the LORD.

42 And the numbered men of the families of the sons of Merari by their families, by their fathers' households,

43 from [a]thirty years and upward even to fifty years old, everyone who entered the service for work in the tent of meeting.

44 And their numbered men by their families were 3,200.

45 These are the numbered men of the families of the sons of Merari, whom Moses and Aaron numbered according to the [I]commandment of the LORD [II]through Moses.

46 All the numbered men of the Levites, whom Moses and Aaron and the leaders of Israel numbered, by their families and by their fathers' households,

47 from thirty years and upward even to fifty years old, everyone who could enter to do the work of service[5656] and the work of carrying in the tent of meeting.

48 And their numbered men were [a]8,580.

49 According to the [I]commandment of the LORD [II]through Moses, they [a]were numbered, everyone[376] by his serving or carrying; thus these were his numbered men, just as the LORD had commanded[6680] Moses.

On Defilement

5 [a]Then the LORD spoke[1696] to Moses, saying,

2 "Command[6680] the sons[1121] of Israel that they [a]send away from the camp[4264] every leper and everyone having a [b]discharge and everyone who is [c]unclean[2931] because of a *dead* person.

3 "You shall send away both male and female;[5347] you shall send them outside the camp so that they will not defile[2930] their camp[4264] where I dwell[7931] [a]in their midst."

4 And the sons of Israel did[6213] so and sent them outside the camp; just as the LORD had spoken to Moses, thus the sons of Israel did.

5 Then the LORD spoke to Moses, saying,

6 "Speak[1696] to the sons of Israel, '[a]When a man[376] or woman[802] commits[6213] any of the sins[2403] of mankind,[120] acting[6213] unfaithfully[4604] against the LORD, and that person[5315] is guilty,[816]

7 then [I]he shall [a]confess[3034] [II]his sins which [III]he has committed,[6213] and he [b]shall make restitution[7725] in full[7218] for his wrong, and add to it one-fifth of it, and give *it* to him whom he has wronged.[816]

8 'But if the man has no [I]relative[1350] to whom restitution may be made for the wrong, the restitution[7725] which is made for the wrong *must go* to the LORD for the priest,[3548] besides the ram of atonement,[3725] by which atonement is made for him.

35 [a]1Chr. 23:24
37 [I]Lit., *mouth* [II]Lit., *by the hand of*
41 [I]Lit., *mouth*
43 [a]Num. 8:24-26
45 [I]Lit., *mouth* [II]Lit., *by the hand of*
48 [a]Num. 3:39
49 [I]Lit., *mouth* [II]Lit., *by the hand of* [a]Num. 1:47
2 [a]Lev. 13:8, 46; Num. 12:10, 14, 15 [b]Lev. 15:2 [c]Lev. 21:1; Num. 9:6-10; 19:11
3 [a]Lev. 26:12; Num. 35:34
6 [a]Lev. 5:14-6:7
7 [I]Lit., *they* [II]Lit., *their* [III]Lit., *they have* [a]Lev. 5:5; 26:40, 41; Josh. 7:19 [b]Lev. 6:4, 5
8 [I]Lit., *redeemer*

5:1-4 This appears to be an addition to some of the laws already set forth in the Book of Leviticus.

9 “[a]Also every [I]contribution[8641] pertaining to all the holy *gifts*[6944] of the sons
of Israel, which they offer[7126] to the
priest, shall be his.
10 ‘So every man’s holy *gifts*[6944]
shall be his; whatever any man gives
to the priest, it [a]becomes his.’ ”

The Adultery Test

11 Then the LORD spoke to Moses,
saying,
12 “Speak to the sons of Israel, and
say[559] to them, ‘If any man’s wife[802]
[a]goes astray and is unfaithful to him,
13 and a man has [a]intercourse[2233]
with her and it is hidden from the eyes
of her husband[376] and she is [I]undetected,
although she has defiled[2930] herself, and
there is no witness against her and she
has not been caught in the act,
14 [I]if a spirit[7307] of [a]jealousy[7068]
comes over him and he is jealous of
his wife when she has defiled herself,
or if a spirit of jealousy comes over him
and he is jealous of his wife when she
has not defiled herself,
15 the man shall then bring his wife
to the priest, and shall bring *as* [I]an
offering[7133] for her one-tenth of an
[II]ephah of barley meal; he shall not pour
oil[8081] on it, nor put frankincense[3828] on
it, for it is a grain offering[4503] of jealousy,
a grain offering of memorial, [a]a reminder[2142] of iniquity.[5771]
16 ‘Then the priest shall bring her
near and have her stand before the
LORD,
17 and the priest shall take holy[6918]
water in an earthenware[2789] vessel; and
[I]he shall take some of the dust[6083] that
is on the floor of the tabernacle[4908] and
put *it* into the water.
18 ‘The priest shall then have the
woman stand before the LORD and let
the hair of the woman’s[802] head[7218] go
loose,[6544] and place the grain offering
of memorial [I]in her hands,[3709] which is
the grain offering of jealousy, and in the
hand[3027] of the priest is to be the water
of bitterness[4751] that brings a curse.[779]
19 ‘And the priest shall have her
take an oath and shall say to the woman,
“If no man has lain with you and if you
have not [a]gone astray into uncleanness,[2932] *being* under *the authority of*
your husband, be [I]immune[5352] to this
water of bitterness that brings a curse;
20 if you, however, have [a]gone
astray, *being* under *the authority of* your
husband, and if you have defiled yourself
and a man other than your husband has
had intercourse with you”
21 (then the priest shall have the
woman [a]swear with the oath[7621] of the
curse,[423] and the priest shall say to
the woman), “the LORD make you a
curse[423] and an oath among your people[5971] by the LORD’S making your
thigh[3409] [I]waste away[5307] and your abdomen[990] swell;
22 and this water that brings a curse
shall go into your [I]stomach,[4578] and make
your abdomen swell and your thigh
[II]waste away.” And the woman [a]shall
say, “Amen. Amen.”[543]
23 ‘The priest shall then write these
curses[423] on a scroll,[5612] and he shall
[I]wash[4229] them off into the water of bitterness.
24 ‘Then he shall make the woman
drink the water of bitterness that brings
a curse, so that the water which brings
a curse will go into her [I]and *cause* bitterness.
25 ‘And the priest shall take the
grain offering of jealousy from the woman’s hand, and he shall wave[5130] the grain
offering before the LORD and bring it
to the altar;[4196]
26 and [a]the priest shall take a handful of the grain offering as its memorial

9 [I]Lit., *heave offering* [a]Lev. 7:32, 34; 10:14, 15
10 [a]Lev. 10:13
12 [a]Num. 5:19-21, 29
13 [I]Lit., *concealed* [a]Lev. 18:20; 20:10
14 [I]Lit., *and* [a]Prov. 6:34; Song 8:6
15 [I]Lit., *her* [II]I.e., Approx. one bu. [a]1Kin. 17:18; Ezek. 29:16
17 [I]Lit., *the priest*
18 [I]Lit., *on her palms*
19 [I]Lit., *free from* [a]Num. 5:12
20 [a]Num. 5:12
21 [I]Lit., *fall* [a]Josh. 6:26; 1Sam. 14:24; Neh. 10:29
22 [I]Or, *inward parts* [II]Lit., *fall* [a]Deut. 27:15
23 [I]Lit., *wipe*
24 [I]Lit., *to*
26 [a]Lev. 2:2, 9

5:11-31 When the sexual infidelity of a married woman was suspected, God’s personal judgment was to be sought in the matter. It was a violation not only of the marriage vows but also of God’s covenant. The punishment for such unfaithfulness was death (Lev. 20:10). Sometimes called the “law of jealousy,” this passage contains the prescribed ritual by which the priest was to seek God’s judgment to determine whether she was guilty or blameless.

offering and offer *it* up in smoke[6999] on
the altar, and afterward he shall make
the woman drink the water.
27 'When he has made her drink the
water, then it shall come about, if she
has defiled herself and has been unfaithful to her husband, that the water which
brings a curse shall go into her [I]and *cause*
bitterness, and her abdomen will swell
and her thigh will [II]waste away, and the
woman will become [a]a curse among[7130]
her people.
28 'But if the woman has not defiled
herself and is clean,[2893] she will then
be free and conceive [I]children.[2233]
29 'This is the law[8451] of jealousy:[7068] when a wife, *being* under *the*
authority of her husband, [a]goes astray
and defiles herself,
30 or when a spirit of jealousy comes
over a man and he is jealous of his wife,
he shall then make the woman stand
before the LORD, and the priest shall
apply all this law to her.
31 'Moreover, the man shall be
free[5352] from [I]guilt, but that woman shall
[a]bear[5375] her [I]guilt.' "

Law of the Nazirites

6 Again the LORD spoke[1696] to Moses,
saying,
2 "Speak[1696] to the sons[1121] of Israel, and say[559] to them, 'When a man[376]
or woman[802] makes a [I]special vow,[5087]
the vow[5088] of [a]a [II]Nazirite,[5139] to [III]dedi-
cate himself[5144] to the LORD,
3 he shall [a]abstain from wine and
strong drink; he shall drink no vinegar,
whether made from wine or strong
drink, neither shall he drink any grape
juice, nor eat fresh or dried[3002] grapes.
4 'All the days[3117] of his [I]separa-
tion[5145] he shall not eat anything that
is produced by the grape vine, from *the*
seeds even to *the* skin.
5 'All the days of his vow of separation [a]no razor shall pass over his
head.[7218] He shall be holy until the days
are fulfilled for which he separated[5144]
himself to the LORD; he shall let the
locks of hair on his head grow long.
6 '[a]All the days of his separation to
the LORD he shall not go near to a dead
person.[5315]
7 'He [a]shall not make himself
unclean[2930] for his father[1] or for his
mother,[517] for his brother[251] or for his
sister,[269] when they die,[4194] because his
separation[5145] to God[430] is on his head.
8 'All the days of his separation he
is holy to the LORD.
9 'But if a man dies very suddenly
beside him and he defiles[2930] his dedicated head *of hair,* then [a]he shall shave
his head on the day[3117] when he becomes
clean;[2893] [b]he shall shave it on the seventh day.
10 'Then on the eighth day he shall
bring [a]two turtledoves or two young[1121]
pigeons to the priest,[3548] to the doorway
of the tent[168] of meeting.[4150]
11 'And the priest shall offer[6213]
[a]one for a sin[2403] offering and *the* other
for a burnt offering,[5930] and make atonement[3722] for him [I]concerning his sin[2398]
because of the *dead* person. And that
same day he shall consecrate[6942] his
head,
12 and shall dedicate[5144] to the LORD
his days [I]as a [II]Nazirite, and shall bring
a male lamb a year old[1121] for a guilt
offering;[817] but the former[7223] days shall
be void because his separation was defiled.
13 'Now this is the law[8451] of the

27 [I]Lit., *to* [II]Lit., *fall* [a]Jer. 29:18; 42:18; 44:12
28 [I]Lit., *seed*
29 [a]Num. 5:12
31 [I]Or, *iniquity* [a]Lev. 20:17
2 [I]Or, *difficult* [II]I.e., one separated [III]Or, *live as a Nazirite* [a]Judg. 13:5; 16:17; Amos 2:11, 12
3 [a]Luke 1:15
4 [I]Or, *living as a Nazirite,* and so through v. 21
5 [a]1Sam. 1:11
6 [a]Lev. 21:1-3; Num. 19:11-22
7 [a]Num. 9:6
9 [a]Lev. 14:8, 9 [b]Num. 6:18
10 [a]Lev. 5:7; 14:22
11 [I]Lit., *because of that which he sinned* [a]Lev. 5:7
12 [I]Or, *of dedication* [II]I.e., one separated

6:2-21 The word Nazarite, not to be confused with Nazarene, means "separated," and in this context of the covenant meant specifically "one who was separated unto the Lord." It was probably similar to a vow which existed among the Hebrews prior to Mount Sinai but which is here brought under the regulation of the law. By the terms of the vow, a man or woman could voluntarily separate himself unto the Lord for a specific period of time, even for life. He did not, however, become a hermit, separating himself from society. Samson (Judg. 13:5) and Samuel (I Sam. 1:11,28) are two notable Nazarites in the Bible. It is also thought that John the Baptist may have been a Nazarite (Lk. 1:15) and that perhaps this is the vow associated with Paul (Acts 21:23-26).

Nazirite [a]when the days of his separation are fulfilled, he shall bring [I]the offering to the doorway of the tent of meeting.

14 'And he shall present[7126] his offering[7133] to the LORD: one male lamb a year old without defect[8549] for a burnt offering and one [a]ewe-lamb[3535] a year old without defect for a sin offering and one ram without defect for a peace offering,

15 and a basket of [a]unleavened[4682] cakes of fine flour mixed[1101] with oil[8081] and unleavened wafers spread[4886] with oil, along with [b]their grain offering and their libations.[5262]

16 'Then the priest shall present[7126] *them* before the LORD and shall offer his sin offering and his burnt offering.

17 'He shall also offer the ram for a sacrifice[2077] of peace offerings to the LORD, together with the basket of unleavened cakes; the priest shall likewise offer its grain offering and its libation.

18 '[a]The Nazirite shall then shave his dedicated head *of hair* at the doorway of the tent of meeting, and take the dedicated hair of his head and put *it* on the fire which is under the sacrifice of peace offerings.

19 '[a]And the priest shall take the ram's shoulder *when it has been* boiled,[1311] and one unleavened cake out of the basket, and one unleavened wafer, and shall put *them* on the [I]hands[3709] of the Nazirite after he has shaved his [II]dedicated *hair*.

20 'Then the priest shall wave[5130] them for a wave offering[8573] before the LORD. It is holy[6944] for the priest, together with the breast offered by waving[8573] and the thigh offered by lifting up;[8641] and [a]afterward the Nazirite may drink wine.'

21 "This is the law of the Nazirite who vows his offering to the LORD according to his separation, in addition to what *else* [I]he can[3027] afford; according to his vow which he takes, so he shall do[6213] according to the law of his separation."

13 [I]Lit., *it* [a]Acts 21:26
14 [a]Lev. 14:10; Num. 15:27
15 [a]Ex. 29:2; Lev. 2:4 [b]Num. 15:1-7
18 [a]Num. 6:9; Acts 21:23, 24
19 [I]Lit., *palms* [II]Or, *separated* [a]Lev. 7:28-34
20 [a]Eccl. 9:7
21 [I]Lit., *his hand can reach*
23 [a]1Chr. 23:13
24 [a]Deut. 28:3-6; Ps. 28:9 [b]1Sam. 2:9; Ps. 17:8
25 [a]Ps. 80:3, 7, 19 [b]Ps. 86:16
26 [a]Ps. 4:6; 44:3 [b]Ps. 29:11; 37:37
27 [I]Lit., *put* [a]2Sam. 7:23; 2Chr. 7:14
1 [a]Ex. 40:17 [b]Ex. 40:9-11; Num. 7:10, 84, 88
2 [I]Lit., *stood* [II]Lit., *mustered* [a]Num. 1:5-16 [b]2Chr. 35:8
3 [a]Is. 66:20
5 [I]Lit., *for serving*

Aaron's Benediction

22 Then the LORD spoke to Moses, saying,

23 "Speak to Aaron and to his sons,[1121] saying, 'Thus [a]you shall bless[1288] the sons of Israel. You shall say to them:

24 The LORD [a]bless you, and
[b]keep[8104] you;
25 The LORD [a]make His face shine
on you,
And [b]be gracious[2603] to you;
26 The LORD [a]lift up His
countenance on you,
And [b]give[7760] you peace.'[7965]

27 "So they shall [I][a]invoke My name on the sons of Israel, and I then will bless them."

Offerings of the Leaders

7 Now it came about on [a]the day[3117] that Moses had finished setting up the tabernacle,[4908] he [b]anointed[4886] it and consecrated[6942] it with all its furnishings and the altar[4106] and all its utensils; he anointed them and consecrated them also.

2 Then [a]the leaders[5387] of Israel, the heads[7218] of their fathers'[1] households,[1004] [b]made an offering[7126] (they were the leaders of the tribes;[4294] they were the ones who [I]were over the [II]numbered[6485] men).

3 When they brought[7126] their offering before the LORD, six [a]covered carts and twelve oxen, a cart for *every* two of the leaders and an ox for each[376] one, then they presented them before the tabernacle.

4 Then the LORD spoke[559] to Moses, saying,

5 "Accept *these things* from them, that they may be [I]used[5647] in the service[5656] of the tent[168] of meeting,[4150] and you shall give them to the Levites, *to* each man[376] according to his service."

6 So Moses took the carts and the oxen, and gave them to the Levites.

7 Two carts and four oxen he gave

to the sons[1121] of Gershon, according
to [a]their service,
8 and four carts and eight oxen he
gave to the sons of Merari, according
to [a]their service, under the [I]direction[3027]
of Ithamar the son[1121] of Aaron the
priest.[3548]
9 But he did not give *any* to the
sons of Kohath because theirs *was*
[a]the service of the holy *objects*,[6944] which
they carried[5375] on the shoulder.
10 And the leaders offered the
dedication[2598] *offering* [I]for the altar
[II]when [a]it was anointed, so the leaders
offered their offering before the altar.
🗝 11 Then the LORD said[559] to Moses,
"Let them present[7126] their offering, one
leader[5387] each day, for the dedication
of the altar."
12 Now the one who presented his
offering on the first[7223] day *was* Nahshon
the son of Amminadab, of the tribe[4294]
of Judah;
13 and his offering[4503] *was* one silver
[I][a]dish whose weight *was* one hundred
and thirty *shekels*, one silver bowl of
seventy shekels, [b]according to [II]the
shekel of the sanctuary, both of them
full of fine flour mixed[1101] with oil[8081]
for a grain offering;
14 one gold pan of ten *shekels*, full
of incense;[7004]
15 one [I]bull, one ram, one male lamb
one[1121] year old, for a burnt offering;[5930]
16 [a]one male[8163] goat for a sin[2403]
offering;
17 and for the sacrifice[2077] of peace
offerings,[8002] two oxen, five rams, five
male goats, five male lambs one year
old. This *was* the offering[7133] of [a]Nah-
shon the son of Amminadab.
18 On the second day Nethanel the
son of Zuar, leader of Issachar, presented *an offering;*
19 he presented as his offering one
silver dish whose weight *was* one hundred and thirty *shekels*, one silver bowl
of seventy shekels, according to the

7 [a]Num. 4:24-26
8 [I]Lit., *hand* [a]Num. 4:31, 32
9 [a]Num. 4:5-15
10 [I]Lit., *of* [II]Lit., *in the day that* [a]Num. 7:1; 2Chr. 7:9
13 [I]Or, *platter*, and so through v. 85 [II]I.e., Approx. one-half oz., and so through v. 86 [a]Ex. 25:29; 37:16 [b]Num. 3:47
15 [I]Or, *bull of the herd*, and so through v. 81
16 [a]Lev. 4:23
17 [a]Luke 3:32, 33
23 [a]Lev. 7:11-13
27 [a]Is. 53:7; John 1:29; 1Pet. 1:19
33 [a]Heb. 9:28

shekel of the sanctuary, both of them
full of fine flour mixed with oil for a grain
offering;
20 one gold pan of ten *shekels*, full
of incense;
21 one bull, one ram, one male lamb
one year old, for a burnt offering;
22 one male goat for a sin offering;
23 and for the sacrifice of [a]peace
offerings, two oxen, five rams, five male
goats, five male lambs one year old.
This *was* the offering of Nethanel the
son of Zuar.
24 On the third day *it was* Eliab
the son of Helon, leader of the sons[1121]
of Zebulun;
25 his offering *was* one silver dish
whose weight *was* one hundred and
thirty *shekels*, one silver bowl of seventy
shekels, according to the shekel of the
sanctuary, both of them full of fine flour
mixed with oil for a grain offering;
26 one gold pan of ten *shekels*, full
of incense;
27 one young bull, one ram, one
[a]male lamb one year old, for a burnt
offering;
28 one male goat for a sin offering;
29 and for the sacrifice of peace offerings, two oxen, five rams, five male
goats, five male lambs one year old.
This *was* the offering of Eliab the son
of Helon.
30 On the fourth day *it was* Elizur
the son of Shedeur, leader of the sons
of Reuben;
31 his offering *was* one silver dish
whose weight *was* one hundred and
thirty *shekels*, one silver bowl of seventy
shekels, according to the shekel of the
sanctuary, both of them full of fine flour
mixed with oil for a grain offering;
32 one gold pan of ten *shekels*, full
of incense;
33 one bull, one ram, one [a]male lamb
one year old, for a burnt offering;
34 one male goat for a sin offering;
35 and for the sacrifice of peace

🗝 **7:11** The court was limited in space. The sheer numbers would not allow the receiving, the slaughtering, and the preparation of 252 animals in one day in the court, not counting the 36 whole animals and the fat parts of 216 animals on the altar.

offerings, two oxen, five rams, five male goats, five male lambs one year old. This *was* the offering of Elizur the son of Shedeur.

36 On the fifth day *it was* Shelumiel the son of Zurishaddai, leader of the children of Simeon;

37 his offering *was* one silver dish whose weight *was* one hundred and thirty *shekels,* one silver bowl of seventy shekels, according to the shekel of the sanctuary, both of them full of fine flour mixed with oil for a grain offering;

38 one gold pan of ten *shekels,* full of incense;

39 one bull, one ram, one male lamb one year old, for a burnt offering;

40 one male goat for a sin offering;

41 and for the sacrifice of peace offerings, two oxen, five rams, five male goats, five male lambs one year old. This *was* the offering of Shelumiel the son of Zurishaddai.

42 On the sixth day *it was* [a]Eliasaph the son of Deuel, leader of the sons of Gad;

43 his offering *was* one silver dish whose weight *was* one hundred and thirty *shekels,* one silver bowl of seventy shekels, according to the shekel of the sanctuary, both of them full of [a]fine flour mixed with oil for a grain offering;

44 one gold pan of ten *shekels,* full of incense;

45 [a]one bull, one ram, one male lamb one year old, for a burnt offering;

46 one male goat for a sin offering;

47 and for the sacrifice of peace offerings, two oxen, five rams, five male goats, five male lambs one year old. This *was* the offering of Eliasaph the son of Deuel.

48 On the seventh day *it was* [a]Elishama the son of Ammihud, leader of the sons of Ephraim;

49 his offering *was* one silver dish whose weight *was* one hundred and thirty *shekels,* one silver bowl of seventy shekels, according to the shekel of the sanctuary, both of them full of fine flour mixed with oil for a grain offering;

50 one gold pan of ten *shekels,* full of [a]incense;

51 [a]one bull, one ram, one male lamb one year old, for a burnt offering;

52 one male goat for a sin offering;

53 and for the sacrifice of peace offerings, two oxen, five rams, five male goats, five male lambs one year old. This *was* the offering of Elishama the son of Ammihud.

54 On the eighth day *it was* [a]Gamaliel the son of Pedahzur, leader of the sons of Manasseh;

55 his offering *was* one silver dish whose weight *was* one hundred and thirty *shekels,* one silver bowl of seventy shekels, according to the shekel of the sanctuary, both of them full of fine flour mixed with oil for a grain offering;

56 one gold pan of ten *shekels,* full of [a]incense;

57 one bull, one ram, one [a]male lamb one year old, for a burnt offering;

58 one male goat for a sin offering;

59 and for the [a]sacrifice of peace offerings, two oxen, five rams, five male goats, five male lambs one year old. This *was* the offering of Gamaliel the son of Pedahzur.

60 On the ninth day *it was* [a]Abidan the son of Gideoni, leader of the sons of Benjamin;

61 his offering *was* one silver dish whose weight *was* one hundred and thirty *shekels,* one silver bowl of seventy shekels, according to the shekel of the sanctuary, both of them full of fine flour mixed with oil for a grain offering;

62 one gold pan of ten *shekels,* full of [a]incense;

63 one bull, one ram, one male lamb one year old, for a burnt offering;

64 one male goat for a [a]sin offering;

65 and for the sacrifice of [a]peace offerings, two oxen, five rams, five male goats, five male lambs one year old. This *was* the offering of Abidan the son of Gideoni.

66 On the tenth day *it was* [a]Ahiezer the son of Ammishaddai, leader of the sons of Dan;

67 his offering *was* one silver dish

42 [a]Num. 1:14; 10:20
43 [a]Lev. 2:5; 14:10
45 [a]Ps. 50:8-14; Is. 1:11
48 [a]Num. 1:10; 2:18; 1Chr. 7:26
50 [a]Deut. 33:10; Ezek. 8:11; Luke 1:10
51 [a]Mic. 6:6-8
54 [a]Num. 2:20
56 [a]Ex. 30:7
57 [a]Ex. 12:5; Acts 8:32; Rev. 5:6
59 [a]Lev. 3:1-17
60 [a]Num. 1:11; 2:22
62 [a]Rev. 5:8; 8:3, 4
64 [a]2Cor. 5:21
65 [a]Col. 1:20
66 [a]Num. 1:12; 2:25

whose weight *was* one hundred and thirty *shekels,* one silver bowl of seventy shekels, according to the [a]shekel of the sanctuary, both of them full of fine flour mixed with oil for a grain offering;

68 one gold pan of ten *shekels,* full of [a]incense;

69 one bull, one ram, one male lamb one year old, for a burnt offering;

70 one male goat for a sin offering;

71 and for the sacrifice of peace offerings, two oxen, five rams, five male goats, five male lambs one year old. This *was* the offering of Ahiezer the son of Ammishaddai.

72 On the eleventh day *it was* [a]Pagiel the son of Ochran, leader of the sons of Asher;

73 his offering *was* one silver dish whose weight *was* one hundred and thirty *shekels,* one silver bowl of seventy shekels, according to the shekel of the sanctuary, both of them full of fine flour mixed with oil for a grain offering;

74 one gold pan of ten *shekels,* full of [a]incense;

75 one bull, one ram, one male lamb one year old, for a burnt offering;

76 one male goat for a sin offering;

77 and for the sacrifice of peace offerings, two oxen, five rams, five male goats, five male lambs one year old. This *was* the offering of Pagiel the son of Ochran.

78 On the twelfth day *it was* [a]Ahira the son of Enan, leader of the sons of Naphtali;

79 his offering *was* one [a]silver dish whose weight *was* one hundred and thirty *shekels,* one silver bowl of seventy shekels, according to the shekel of the sanctuary, both of them full of fine flour mixed with oil for a grain offering;

80 one gold pan of ten *shekels,* full of incense;

81 one bull, one ram, one male lamb one year old, for a burnt offering;

82 one male goat for a sin offering;

83 and for the sacrifice of peace offerings, two oxen, five rams, five male goats, five male lambs one year old.

67 [a]Ex. 30:13; Lev. 27:25

68 [a]Ps. 141:2

72 [a]Num. 1:13; 2:27

74 [a]Mal. 1:11

78 [a]Num. 1:15; 2:29

79 [a]Ezra 1:9, 10; Dan. 5:2

84 [I]Lit., *of* [II]Lit., *in the day that* [a]Num. 7:10 [b]Num. 7:1

86 [a]Ex. 30:13

88 [a]Num. 7:1, 10

89 [I]Lit., *propitiatory* [a]Ex. 40:34, 35 [b]Ex. 25:21, 22 [c]Ps. 80:1; 99:1

2 [I]Lit., *raise up* [a]Ex. 25:37; Lev. 24:2, 4

3 [I]Lit., *raised up*

4 [a]Ex. 25:31-40 [b]Ex. 25:9, 31-40; 26:30; 37:17-24

This *was* the offering of Ahira the son of Enan.

84 This *was* [a]the dedication[2598] *offering* [I]for the altar from the leaders of Israel [II]when [b]it was anointed: twelve silver dishes, twelve silver bowls, twelve gold pans,[3709]

85 each silver dish *weighing* one hundred and thirty *shekels* and each bowl seventy; all the silver of the utensils *was* 2,400 *shekels,* according to the shekel of the sanctuary;

86 the twelve gold pans, full of incense, *weighing* ten *shekels* apiece, according to the [a]shekel of the sanctuary, all the gold of the pans 120 *shekels;*

87 all the oxen for the burnt offering twelve bulls, *all* the rams twelve, the male lambs one year old with their grain offering twelve, and the male[8169] goats for a sin offering twelve;

88 and all the oxen for the sacrifice of peace offerings 24 bulls, *all* the rams 60, the male goats 60, the male lambs one year old 60. [a]This *was* the dedication *offering* for the altar after it was anointed.

89 Now when [a]Moses went into the tent of meeting to speak[1696] with Him, he heard[8085] the voice speaking[1696] to him from above [b]the [I]mercy seat that was on the ark[727] of the testimony,[5715] from [c]between the two cherubim,[3742] so He spoke to him.

The Seven Lamps

8 Then the LORD spoke[1696] to Moses, saying,

2 "Speak[1696] to Aaron and say[559] to him, 'When you [I]mount[5927] the lamps,[5216] the seven lamps will [a]give light[216] in the front of the lampstand.' "

3 Aaron therefore did[6213] so; he [I]mounted its lamps at the front of the lampstand, just as the LORD had commanded[6680] Moses.

4 [a]Now this was the workmanship of the lampstand, hammered work of gold; from its base to its flowers, it was hammered work; [b]according to the pat-

tern which the LORD had showed[7200] Moses, so he made the lampstand.

Cleansing the Levites

5 Again the LORD spoke to Moses, saying,

6 "Take the Levites from among the sons[1121] of Israel and [a]cleanse[2891] them.

7 "And thus you shall do[6213] to them, for their [I]cleansing: *sprinkle*[5137] [II]purifying [a]water on them, and let them [III][b]use a razor over their whole [IV]body,[1320] and [c]wash[3526] their clothes, and they shall be clean.[2891]

8 "Then let them take a [I]bull[6499,1121,1241] with [a]its grain offering,[4503] fine flour mixed[1101] with oil;[8081] and a second [I]bull you shall take for a sin[2403] offering.

9 "So [a]you shall present[7126] the Levites before the tent[168] of meeting.[4150] [b]You shall also assemble the whole congregation[712] of the sons of Israel,

10 and present the Levites before the LORD; and the sons of Israel [a]shall lay their hands[3027] on the Levites.

11 "Aaron then shall [I]present the Levites before the LORD as a [a]wave offering from the sons of Israel, that they may [II]qualify to perform the service[5656] of the LORD.

12 "Now [a]the Levites shall lay their hands on the heads[7218] of the bulls; then offer[6213] the one for a sin offering and the other for a burnt offering[5930] to the LORD, to make atonement[3722] for the Levites.

13 "And you shall have the Levites stand before Aaron and before his sons[1121] so as to present them as a wave offering to the LORD.

14 "Thus you shall separate[914] the Levites from among the sons of Israel, and [a]the Levites shall be Mine.

15 "Then after that the Levites may go in to serve[5647] the tent of meeting. But you shall cleanse them and [a]present them as a wave offering;

16 for they are [a]wholly given to Me from among the sons of Israel. I have taken them for Myself [b]instead of every first issue of the womb, the first-born of all the sons of Israel.

17 "For [a]every first-born among the sons of Israel is Mine, among the men[120] and among the animals; on the day[3117] that I struck down[5221] all the first-born in the land of Egypt I sanctified[6942] them for Myself.

18 "But I have taken the Levites instead of every first-born among the sons of Israel.

19 "And [a]I have given the Levites as [I]a gift to Aaron and to his sons from among the sons of Israel, to perform the service of the sons of Israel at the tent of meeting, and to make atonement on behalf of the sons of Israel, that there may be no [b]plague[5063] among the sons of Israel by [II]their coming near[5066] to the sanctuary."[6944]

20 Thus did Moses and Aaron and all the congregation[5712] of the sons of Israel to the Levites; according to all that the LORD had commanded Moses concerning the Levites, so the sons of Israel did to them.

21 [a]The Levites, too, purified[2398] themselves from sin and washed[3526] their clothes; and Aaron presented[5130] them as a wave offering before the LORD. Aaron also made atonement for them to cleanse them.

22 Then after that the Levites went in to perform their service in the tent of meeting before Aaron and before his sons; just as the LORD had commanded Moses concerning the Levites, so they did to them.

Retirement

23 Now the LORD spoke to Moses, saying,

24 "This is what *applies* to the Levites: from [a]twenty-five years old[1121] and upward [I]they shall enter to perform[6633] service in the work of the tent of meeting.

25 "But at the age of fifty years they shall [I]retire from service in the work and not work[5647] any more.

6 [a]Is. 52:11

7 [I]Lit., *this their cleansing* [II]Lit., *water of sin* [III]Lit., *cause to pass* [IV]Lit., *flesh* [a]Num. 19:9, 13, 20 [b]Lev. 14:8, 9 [c]Num. 8:21

8 [I]Or, *bull of the herd* [a]Lev. 2:1; Num. 15:8-10

9 [a]Ex. 29:4; 40:12 [b]Lev. 8:3

10 [a]Lev. 1:4

11 [I]Lit., *wave*, and so throughout the ch. [II]Lit., *be able* [a]Lev. 7:30, 34

12 [a]Ex. 29:10

14 [a]Num. 3:12; 16:9

15 [a]Ex. 29:24

16 [a]Num. 3:9 [b]Ex. 13:2; Num. 3:12, 45

17 [a]Ex. 13:2, 12, 13, 15; Luke 2:23

19 [I]Lit., *given ones* [II]Lit., *the sons of Israel's* [a]Num. 3:9 [b]Num. 1:53; 16:46

21 [a]Num. 8:7

24 [I]Lit., *he* [a]Num. 4:3; 1Chr. 23:3, 24, 27

25 [I]Lit., *return*

26 "They may, however, [I]assist[8334] their brothers[251] in the tent of meeting, [a]to keep[8104] an obligation;[4931] but they *themselves* shall do no work. Thus you shall deal with the Levites concerning their obligations."

The Passover

9 Thus the LORD spoke[1696] to Moses in the wilderness of Sinai, in [a]the first[7223] month of the second year after they had come out of the land of Egypt, saying,

2 "Now, let the sons[1121] of Israel observe[6213] the Passover[6453] at [a]its appointed time.[4150]

3 "On the fourteenth day[3117] of this month, [I]at twilight, you shall observe it at its appointed time; you shall observe it according to all its statutes and according to all its ordinances."[4941]

4 So Moses [I]told the sons of Israel to observe the Passover.

5 And [a]they observed[6213] the Passover in the first *month,* on the fourteenth day of the month, at twilight, in the wilderness of Sinai; [b]according to all that the LORD had commanded[6680] Moses, so the sons of Israel did.[6213]

🔑 6 But there were *some* men[582] who were [a]unclean[2931] because of *the* [I]dead person,[5315] so that they could not observe Passover on that day; so [b]they came before Moses and Aaron on that day.

7 And those men said[559] to him, "*Though* we are unclean because of *the* [I]dead person, why are we restrained from presenting[7126] the offering[7133] of the LORD at its appointed time among the sons of Israel?"

8 Moses therefore said to them, "[Ia]Wait, and I will listen to[8085] what the LORD will command[6680] concerning you."

9 Then the LORD spoke to Moses, saying,

🔑 10 "Speak[1696] to the sons of Israel, saying, 'If any one of you or of your generations becomes unclean[2931] because of a *dead* [I]person, or is on a distant journey, he may, however, observe the Passover to the LORD.

11 'In the second month on the [a]fourteenth day at twilight, they shall observe it; they [b]shall eat it with unleavened bread[4682] and bitter herbs.

🔑 12 'They [a]shall leave[7604] none of it until morning, [b]nor break[7665] a bone[6106] of it; according to all the statute[2708] of the Passover they shall observe it.

13 '[a]But the man who is clean[2889] and is not on a journey, and yet [I]neglects to observe the Passover, that [II]person[5315] shall then be cut off[3772] from his people,[5971] for he did not present[7126] the offering of the LORD at its appointed time. That man [b]shall bear[5375] his sin.[2399]

14 '[a]And if an alien[1616] sojourns[1481] among you and [I]observes the Passover to the LORD, according to the statute[2708] of the Passover and according to its ordinance,[4941] so he shall do; you shall have [b]one statute, both for the alien and for the native of the land.' "

The Cloud on the Tabernacle

15 Now on [a]the day that the tabernacle[4908] was erected [b]the cloud[6051] covered[3680] the tabernacle, the [c]tent[168] of the testimony,[5715] and [d]in the evening it was like the appearance of fire over the tabernacle, until morning.

16 So it was continuously;[8548] [a]the cloud would cover it *by day,* and the appearance of fire by night.[3915]

17 [a]And whenever the cloud was lifted[5927] from over the tent,[168] afterward the sons of Israel would then set out; and in the place where the cloud settled down,[7931] there the sons of Israel would camp.

18 At the [I]command[6310] of the LORD

26 [I]Lit., *serve* [a]Num. 1:53
1 [a]Ex. 40:2, 17; Num. 1:1
2 [a]Ex. 12:6; Lev. 23:5; Deut. 16:1, 2
3 [I]Lit., *between the two evenings,* and so throughout the ch.
4 [I]Lit., *spoke to*
5 [a]Josh. 5:10 [b]Ex. 12:1-13
6 [I]Lit., *soul of man* [a]Num. 5:2; 19:11-22 [b]Ex. 18:15; Num. 27:2
7 [I]Lit., *soul of man*
8 [I]Lit., *Stand* [a]Ex. 18:15; Ps. 85:8
10 [I]Lit., *soul*
11 [a]2Chr. 30:2, 15 [b]Ex. 12:8
12 [a]Ex. 12:10 [b]Ex. 12:46; John 19:36
13 [I]Or, *ceases* [II]Lit., *soul* [a]Gen. 17:14; Ex. 12:15, 47 [b]Num. 5:31
14 [I]Or, *would observe* [a]Ex. 12:48 [b]Ex. 12:49; Lev. 24:22; Num. 15:15, 16, 29
15 [a]Ex. 40:2, 17 [b]Ex. 40:34 [c]Num. 17:7 [d]Ex. 13:21, 22
16 [a]Ex. 40:34; Neh. 9:12
17 [a]Ex. 40:36-38; Num. 10:11, 12
18 [I]Lit., *mouth*

🔑 **9:6** An unclean person could not participate in a sacrificial meal (Lev. 7:20,21; cf. I Cor. 11:28,29).
🔑 **9:10,11** If for some reason a man could not observe the Passover, or be present at the sanctuary at the prescribed time, provisions were made for him to keep it one month later.
🔑 **9:12** See note on Ex. 12:46.

the sons of Israel would set out, and at the [I]command of the LORD they would camp; [a]as long as the cloud settled over the tabernacle, they remained camped.

19 Even when the cloud lingered over the tabernacle for many days,[3117] [I]the sons of Israel would keep[8104] the LORD's charge[4931] and not set out.

20 If [I]sometimes the cloud remained a few days over the tabernacle, [a]according to the [II]command of the LORD they remained camped. Then according to the [II]command of the LORD they set out.

21 If [I]sometimes the cloud [II]remained from evening until morning, when the cloud was lifted in the morning, they would move out; or *if it remained* in the daytime[3119] and at night, whenever the cloud was lifted, they would set out.

22 Whether it was two days or a month or a year that the cloud lingered over the tabernacle, staying[7931] above it, the sons of Israel remained camped and did not set out; but [a]when it was lifted, they did set out.

23 [a]At the [I]command of the LORD they camped, and at the [I]command of the LORD they set out; they kept the LORD's charge, according to the [I]command of the LORD through[3027] Moses.

The Silver Trumpets

10 The LORD spoke[1696] further to Moses, saying,

2 "Make[6213] yourself two trumpets of silver, of hammered work you shall make them; and you shall use them for [a]summoning[4744] the congregation[712] and for having the camps[4264] set out.

3 "And [a]when both are blown,[8628] all the congregation shall gather[3259] themselves to you at the doorway of the tent[168] of meeting.[4150]

4 "Yet if *only* one is blown, then the [a]leaders,[5387] the heads[7218] of the [I]divisions[505] of Israel, shall assemble[3259] before you.

5 "But when you blow an alarm, the camps that are pitched [a]on the east side shall set out.

6 "And when you blow an alarm the second time, the camps that are pitched on [a]the south side shall set out; an alarm is to be blown for them to set out.

7 "When convening[6950] the assembly,[6951] however, you shall blow without [a]sounding an alarm.[7321]

8 "[a]The priestly[3548] sons[1121] of Aaron, moreover, shall blow the trumpets; and [I]this shall be for you a perpetual[5769] statute[2708] throughout your generations.[1755]

9 "And when you go to war in your land against the adversary who [a]attacks you, then you shall sound an alarm[7321] with the trumpets, that you may be [b]remembered[2142] before the LORD your God,[430] and be saved from your enemies.

10 "Also in the day[3117] of your gladness and in your appointed[4150] [I]feasts, and on the first *days*[7218] of your months, [a]you shall blow the trumpets over your burnt offerings,[5930] and over the sacrifices[2077] of your peace offerings;[8002] and they shall be as a reminder of you before your God. I am the LORD your God."

The Tribes Leave Sinai

11 Now it came about in [a]the second year, in the second month, on the twentieth of the month, that the cloud[6051] was lifted from over the [I]tabernacle[4908] of the testimony;[5715]

12 and the sons[1121] of Israel set out on [a]their journeys from the wilderness of Sinai. Then the cloud settled down[7931] in the [b]wilderness of Paran.

13 [a]So they moved out for the first[7223] time according to the [I]commandment[6310] of the LORD through[3027] Moses.

14 And the standard of the camp[4264] of the sons of Judah, according to their armies,[6635] [a]set out first, with Nahshon

18 [a]1Cor. 10:1
19 [I]Lit., *and the*
20 [I]Lit., *it was that* [II]Lit., *mouth* [a]Ps. 48:14; Prov. 3:5, 6
21 [I]Lit., *it was that* [II]Lit., *was*
22 [a]Ex. 40:36, 37
23 [I]Lit., *mouth* [a]Ps. 73:24; 107:7; Is. 63:14
2 [a]Is. 1:13
3 [a]Jer. 4:5; Joel 2:15
4 [I]Lit., *thousands;* or, *clans* [a]Ex. 18:21; Num. 1:16; 7:2
5 [a]Num. 10:14
6 [a]Num. 10:18
7 [a]Joel 2:1
8 [I]Lit., *it* [a]Num. 31:6; Josh. 6:4; 2Chr. 13:12
9 [a]Judg. 2:18; 1Sam. 10:18; Ps. 106:42 [b]Gen. 8:1; Ps. 106:4
10 [I]Or, *times* [a]Ps. 81:3-5
11 [I]Lit., *dwelling place,* and so throughout the ch. [a]Ex. 40:17
12 [a]Ex. 40:36 [b]Gen. 21:21; Num. 12:16
13 [I]Lit., *mouth* [a]Deut. 1:6
14 [a]Num. 2:3-9

10:10 On "the first days of your months," see Num. 28:11-15.

the son[1121] of Amminadab, over its
army,[6635]
15 and Nethanel the son of Zuar,
over the tribal[4294] army of the sons of
Issachar;
16 and Eliab the son of Helon over
the tribal army of the sons of Zebulun.
17 [a]Then the tabernacle was taken
down; and the sons of Gershon and the
sons of Merari, who were carrying[5375]
the tabernacle, set out.
18 Next [a]the standard of the camp
of Reuben, according to their armies,
set out with Elizur the son of Shedeur,
over its army,
19 and Shelumiel the son of Zurishaddai over the tribal army of the sons
of Simeon,
20 and Eliasaph the son of Deuel
was over the tribal army of the sons
of Gad.
21 [a]Then the Kohathites set out,
carrying the holy *objects;*[4720] and [b]the
tabernacle was set up before their arrival.
22 [a]Next the standard of the camp
of the sons of Ephraim, according to
their armies, was set out, with Elishama
the son of Ammihud over its army,
23 and Gamaliel the son of Pedahzur
over the tribal army of the sons of Manasseh;
24 and Abidan the son of Gideoni
over the tribal army of the sons of Benjamin.
25 [a]Then the standard of the camp
of the sons of Dan, according to their
armies,[6635] *which formed* the [b]rear
guard[622] for all the camps, set out, with
Ahiezer the son of Ammishaddai over
its army,
26 and Pagiel the son of Ochran over
the tribal army of the sons of Asher;
27 and Ahira the son of Enan over
the tribal army of the sons of Naphtali.
28 [I]This was the order of march of
the sons of Israel by their armies as
they set out.
29 Then Moses said[559] to [a]Hobab
the son of [b]Reuel the Midianite, Moses'
father-in-law, "We are setting out to the
place of which the LORD said, '[c]I will
give it to you'; [d]come with us and we
will do you good,[2895] for the LORD
[e]has [I]promised[1696] good[2896] concerning
Israel."
30 But he said to him, "[a]I will not
come, but rather will go to my *own* land
and relatives."
31 Then he said, "Please[4994] do not
leave[5800] us, inasmuch as you know[3045]
where we should camp in the wilderness, and you [a]will be as eyes for us.
🔑 32 "So it will be, if you go with us,
it will come about that [Ia]whatever
good[2896] the LORD [II]does for us, [b]we
will [III]do for you."
33 [a]Thus they set out from the
mount of the LORD three days'[3117] journey,[1870] with [b]the ark[727] of the covenant[1285] of the LORD journeying in front
of them for the [I]three days, to seek
out [c]a resting place for them.
34 [a]And the cloud of the LORD was
over them by day,[3119] when they set
out from the camp.
35 Then it came about when the
ark set out that Moses said,
"[a]Rise up, O LORD!
And let Thine enemies be
scattered,
And let those [b]who hate[8130] Thee
flee [I]before Thee."
36 And when it came to rest, he
said,
"[a]Return[7725] Thou, O LORD,
To the myriad [b]thousands of
Israel."

The People Complain

11 🔑 Now the people[5971] became
like [a]those who complain of

17 [a]Num. 4:21-32
18 [a]Num. 2:10-16
21 [a]Num. 4:4-20 [b]Num. 10:17
22 [a]Num. 2:18-24
25 [a]Num. 2:25-31 [b]Josh. 6:9, 13
28 [I]Lit., *These are the settings out of the sons*
29 [I]Lit., *spoken* [a]Judg. 4:11 [b]Ex. 2:18; 3:1; 18:12 [c]Gen. 12:7; Ex. 6:4-8 [d]Ps. 95:1-7; 100:1-5 [e]Deut. 4:40; 30:5
30 [a]Judg. 1:16; Matt. 21:28, 29
31 [a]Job 29:15
32 [I]Lit., *that good which* [II]Lit., *does good* [III]Lit., *do good* [a]Ps. 22:27-31; 67:5-7 [b]Lev. 19:34; Deut. 10:18
33 [I]Lit., *three days' journey* [a]Num. 10:12 [b]Deut. 1:33 [c]Is. 11:10
34 [a]Num. 9:15-23
35 [I]Or, *from Thy presence* [a]Ps. 68:1, 2; Is. 17:12-14 [b]Deut. 7:10; 32:41
36 [a]Is. 63:17 [b]Deut. 1:10
1 [a]Num. 14:2; 16:11; 17:5

🔑 **10:32** Since Hobab's descendants are mentioned later as living in Canaan (Judg. 1:16; I Sam. 15:6), he must have complied with Moses' request, although his decision was not recorded.

🔑 **11:1-5** The source of discontent and complaint is described as the "rabble," which is rendered in other versions as "mixed multitude" and "foreigners." Since they were not Hebrews, they had no personal

(continued on next page)

adversity [b]in the hearing of the LORD;
and when the LORD heard[8085] *it,* His anger[639] was kindled,[2734] and the fire of
the LORD burned among them and consumed *some* of the outskirts of the
camp.[4264]
2 [a]The people therefore cried out
to Moses, and Moses prayed[6419] to the
LORD, and the fire [I]died out.
3 So the name of that place was
called[7121] [I][a]Taberah, because the fire of
the LORD burned among them.
4 And the [a]rabble who were
among[7130] them [I]had greedy desires; and
also the sons[1121] of Israel wept again
and said, "[b]Who will give us [II]meat[1320]
to eat?
5 "[a]We remember[2142] the fish[1710]
which we used to eat free in Egypt,
the cucumbers and the melons and the
leeks[2682] and the onions and the garlic,
6 but now [a]our [I]appetite[5315] is
gone.[3001] There is nothing at all [II]to look
at except this manna."[4478]
7 [a]Now the manna was like coriander seed,[2233] and its appearance like that
of [b]bdellium.
8 The people would go about and
gather[3950] *it* and grind *it* [I]between two
millstones or beat *it* in the mortar, and
boil *it* in the pot and make[6213] cakes
with it; and its taste[2940] was as the taste
of [II]cakes baked with oil.[8081]
9 [a]And when the dew fell on the
camp at night,[3915] the manna would fall
[I]with it.

The Complaint of Moses

10 Now Moses heard the people
weeping throughout their families,[4940]
each man[376] at the doorway of his
tent;[168] and the anger of the LORD was
kindled greatly, and [I]Moses was displeased.
11 [a]So Moses said to the LORD,
"Why hast Thou [I]been so hard[7489] on
Thy servant?[5650] And why have I not
found favor[2580] in Thy sight, that Thou
hast laid the burden[4853] of all this people
on me?
12 "Was it I who conceived all this
people? Was it I who brought them
forth,[3205] that Thou shouldest say[559] to
me, 'Carry[5375] them in your bosom as
a [I][a]nurse carries a nursing[539] infant, to
the land[127] which [b]Thou didst swear[7650]
to their fathers'?[1]
13 "Where am I to get meat to give
to [a]all this people? For they weep before
me, saying, 'Give us meat that we may
eat!'
14 "[a]I alone am not able to carry[5375]
all this people, because it is too [I]burden-
some for me.
15 "[a]So if Thou art going to deal[6213]
thus with me, please[4994] kill me at once,
if I have found favor in Thy sight, and
do not let me see my wretchedness."[7451]

Seventy Elders to Assist

16 The LORD therefore said to Mo-
ses, "Gather[622] for Me [a]seventy men[376]
from the elders[2205] of Israel, [b]whom you
know[3045] to be the elders of the people
and their officers and bring them to the
tent[168] of meeting,[4150] and let them take
their stand there with you.
17 "[a]Then I will come down and
speak[1696] with you there, and I will take
of [b]the Spirit[7307] who is upon you, and
will put *Him* upon them; and they shall
bear the burden of the people with you,
so that you shall not bear *it* all alone.
18 "And say to the people, '[a]Con-
secrate[6942] yourselves for tomorrow,
and you shall eat meat; for you have
wept [b]in the ears[241] of the LORD, saying, "Oh that someone would give us
meat to eat! For we were well-off[2895]

1 [b]Num. 11:18; 14:28
2 [I]Lit., *sank down* [a]Num. 12:11, 13; 21:7
3 [I]I.e., burning [a]Deut. 9:22
4 [I]Lit., *desired a desire* [II]Lit., *flesh,* and so throughout the ch. [a]Ex. 12:38; 1Cor. 10:6 [b]Ps. 78:20
5 [a]Ex. 16:3
6 [I]Lit., *soul is dried up* [II]Lit., *for our eyes* [a]Num. 21:5
7 [a]Ex. 16:31 [b]Gen. 2:12
8 [I]Lit., *with* [II]Lit., *juice of oil*
9 [I]Lit., *on* [a]Ex. 16:13, 14
10 [I]Lit., it was *evil in Moses' sight*
11 [I]Lit., *dealt ill with* [a]Ex. 5:22; Deut. 1:12
12 [I]Or, *foster-father* [a]2 Kin. 10:1, 5; Is. 49:23 [b]Gen. 24:7; Ex. 13:5, 11; 33:1
13 [a]Num. 11:21, 22; John 6:5-9
14 [I]Lit., *heavy* [a]Ex. 18:18; Deut. 1:12
15 [a]Ex. 32:32
16 [a]Ex. 24:1, 9 [b]Ex. 18:25
17 [a]Num. 11:25 [b]1Sam. 10:6; Joel 2:28
18 [a]Ex. 19:10, 22 [b]Num. 11:1

(continued from previous page)
attachment either to the promise or to God. They had come out of Egypt with Israel (Ex. 12:38). They were tired of the manna and, forgetting all of the reasons for fleeing from Egypt, they remembered only the fish, onions, and garlic which was formerly available to them. They soon infected Israel with their deep dissatisfaction. They are also referred to as "sojourners" in various prescriptions of the Law (Lev. 25:35,40,47). They were evidently held in low esteem by the Israelites although Israel allowed themselves to be influenced by their grumbling.

in Egypt." Therefore the LORD will give
you meat and you shall eat.
19 'You shall eat, not one day,[3117]
nor two days, nor five days, nor ten
days, nor twenty days,
🔑 20 [I]but a whole[3117] month, until it
comes out of your nostrils[639] and becomes loathsome to you; because
[a]you have rejected[3988] the LORD who
is among you and have wept before Him,
saying, "Why did we ever leave
Egypt?" ' "
21 But Moses said, "The people,
among whom I am, are 600,000 on foot;
yet Thou hast said, 'I will give them
meat in order that they may eat for a
whole month.'
22 "Should flocks and herds be
slaughtered[7819] for them, to be sufficient
for them? Or should all the fish[1709] of
the sea be gathered[622] together for
them, to be sufficient for them?"
23 And the LORD said to Moses, "Is
[a]the LORD's [I]power[3027] limited? Now you
shall see whether [b]My word[1697] will
[II]come true for you or not."
24 So Moses went out and [a]told the
people the words[1697] of the LORD. Also,
he gathered seventy men of the elders
of the people, and stationed them around
the tent.
25 [a]Then the LORD came down in
the cloud[6051] and spoke[1696] to him; and
He took of the Spirit who was upon him
and placed *Him* upon the seventy elders.
And it came about that when the Spirit
rested upon them, they prophesied.[5012]
But they did not do *it* again.
26 But two men[582] had remained
in the camp; the name of one was Eldad
and the name of the [I]other Medad. And
[a]the Spirit rested upon them (now they
were among those who had been registered, but had not gone out to the tent),
and they prophesied in the camp.
27 So a young man ran and told[5046]
Moses and said, "Eldad and Medad are
prophesying[5012] in the camp."
28 Then [a]Joshua the son[1121] of Nun,
the attendant[8334] of Moses from his
youth, answered and said, "[b]Moses, my
lord,[113] restrain them."
29 But Moses said to him, "Are you
jealous[7065] for my sake? [a]Would that all
the LORD's people were prophets,[5030]
that the LORD would put His Spirit upon
them!"
30 Then Moses [I]returned to the
camp, *both* he and the elders of Israel.

The Quail and the Plague

31 [a]Now there went forth a wind[7307]
from the LORD, and it brought quail from
the sea, and let *them* fall beside the
camp, about a day's journey[1870] on this
side and a day's journey on the other
side, all around the camp, and [I]about
two [II]cubits *deep* on the surface of the
ground.[776]
32 And the people [I]spent all day and
all night and all the next day, and
gathered the quail (he who gathered
least gathered ten [II][a]homers)[2563] and
they spread *them* out for themselves
all around the camp.
33 [a]While the meat was still between their teeth, before[2962] it was
chewed,[3772] the anger[639] of the LORD
was kindled against the people, and the
LORD struck[5221] the people with a very
severe plague.[4347]
34 So the name of that place was
called [I][a]Kibroth-hattaavah, because
there they buried[6912] the people who
had been greedy.[183]
35 From Kibroth-hattaavah [a]the
people set out for Hazeroth, and they
[I]remained at Hazeroth.

The Murmuring of Miriam and Aaron

12 Then Miriam and Aaron
spoke[1696] against Moses because
of the Cushite woman[802] whom he had
married (for he had married a [a]Cushite
woman);

20 [I]Lit., *until* [a]Josh. 24:27; 1Sam. 10:19
23 [I]Lit., *hand short* [II]Lit., *befall you* [a]Is. 50:2; 59:1 [b]Ezek. 12:25; 24:14
24 [a]Num. 11:16
25 [a]Num. 11:17; 12:5
26 [I]Lit., *second* [a]Num. 24:2; 1Sam. 10:6; 2Chr. 15:1; Neh. 9:30
28 [a]Ex. 33:11; Josh. 1:1 [b]Mark 9:38-40
29 [a]1Cor. 14:5
30 [I]Lit., *removed himself*
31 [I]Or, from *about two cubits above* [II]I.e., One cubit equals approx. 18 in. [a]Ex. 16:13; Ps. 78:26-28; 105:40
32 [I]Lit., *rose* [II]I.e., One homer equals approx. 11 bu. [a]Ezek. 45:11
33 [a]Ps. 78:29-31; 106:15
34 [I]I.e., the graves of greediness [a]Deut. 9:22
35 [I]Lit., *were* [a]Num. 33:17
1 [a]Ex. 2:21

🔑 **11:20** God notices the actions, words, and thoughts of each individual (Prov. 5:21; Mt. 12:36,37; Heb. 4:13).

2 [a]and they said,[559] "Has the LORD
indeed spoken[1696] only through Moses?
Has He not spoken through us as well?"
And the LORD heard[8085] it.
🔑3 (Now the man[376] Moses was
[a]very humble, more than any man[120] who
was on the face of the earth.)[127]
4 And suddenly the LORD said to
Moses and Aaron and to Miriam, "You
three come out to the tent[168] of meeting." So the three of them came out.
5 [a]Then the LORD came down in a
pillar of cloud[6051] and stood at the doorway of the tent, and He called[7121]
[1]Aaron and Miriam. When they had both
come forward,
6 He said,
"Hear[8085] now My words:[1697]
If there is a prophet[5030] among
you,
I, the LORD, shall make Myself
known[3045] to him in a [a]vision.
I shall speak[1696] with him in a
[b]dream.
🔑7 "Not so, with [a]My servant[5650]
Moses,
[b]He is faithful[539] in all My
household;[1004]
8 [a]With him I speak mouth[6310] to
mouth,
Even openly, and not in dark
sayings,[2420]
And he beholds [b]the form[8544] of
the LORD.
Why then were you not afraid[3372]
To speak against My servant,
against Moses?"
9 So the anger[639] of the LORD

2 [a]Num. 16:3
3 [a]Matt. 11:29
5 [1]Or, *"Aaron and Miriam!"* [a]Ex. 19:9; 34:5
6 [a]Gen. 46:2; 1Sam. 3:15 [b]Gen. 31:11; 1Kin. 3:5, 15
7 [a]Josh. 1:1 [b]Heb. 3:2, 5
8 [a]Deut. 34:10; Hos. 12:13 [b]Ex. 20:4; 24:10, 11; Deut. 5:8; Ps. 17:15
9 [a]Gen. 17:22; 18:33
10 [a]Deut. 24:9 [b]Ex. 4:6; 2Kin. 5:27
11 [a]2Sam. 19:19; 24:10
13 [a]Ps. 30:2; 41:4; Is. 30:26; Jer. 17:14
14 [a]Deut. 25:9; Job 17:6; 30:10; Is. 50:6 [b]Num. 5:1-4
15 [a]Deut. 24:9
1 [a]Deut. 1:22, 23
2 [a]Deut. 1:22; 9:23

burned[2734] against them and [a]He departed.
🔑10 But when the cloud had withdrawn[5493] from over the tent, behold,
[a]Miriam *was* leprous, as [b]*white as* snow.
As Aaron turned toward Miriam, behold,
she *was* leprous.
11 Then Aaron said to Moses, "Oh,
my lord,[113] I beg[4994] you, [a]do not account
this sin[2403] to us, in which we have acted
foolishly and in which we have
sinned.[2398]
12 "Oh, do not let her be like one
dead,[4191] whose flesh[1320] is half eaten
away when he comes from his
mother's[517] womb!"
13 And Moses cried out to the
LORD, saying, "O God,[410] [a]heal her, I
pray!"
14 But the LORD said to Moses, "If
her father[1] had but [a]spit in her face,
would she not bear her shame for seven
days?[3117] Let her be shut up for seven
days [b]outside the camp,[4264] and afterward she may be received again."
15 So [a]Miriam was shut up outside
the camp for seven days, and the
people[5971] did not move on until Miriam
was received again.
16 Afterward, however, the people
moved out from Hazeroth and camped
in the wilderness of Paran.

Spies View the Land

13 Then [a]the LORD spoke[1696] to Moses saying,
2 "[a]Send out for yourself men[582] so

🔑 **12:3** Some scholars have thought it necessary to consider this verse a later insertion in the text, possibly by Joshua, as it did not seem proper for Moses (the author) to glorify himself. However, the purpose of the statement was not to glorify Moses but to explain why he took no steps to justify himself when Miriam and Aaron questioned his authority as God's spokesman. If written by Moses, it was done under the Spirit's direction and with the same objectivity that allowed him to record his own faults and sins.

🔑 **12:7** Moses was more than the leader or prophet of Israel. The writer of Hebrews sets him forth as a type of Christ (Heb. 3:2-6). He was chosen by God to be a deliverer (Ex. 3:1-10). He was designated as a prophet (Deut. 18:15). As a servant in God's house, he was deemed faithful and trustworthy even though he was not the Son (Heb. 3:5,6). And he was a mediator between the Lord and Israel (Ex. 17:1-7; 32:30-35) as Christ is for His church (I Jn. 2:1,2).

🔑 **12:10** Miriam had apparently initiated this instruction (v. 1). Aaron was again showing his lack of spiritual backbone, just as he did in the incident of the golden calf (Ex. 32:1-6; 21-24). God wants strong male leadership. See note on I Cor. 14:33-40.

that they may spy out the land[776] of
Canaan, which I am going to give to
the sons[1121] of Israel; you shall send a
man[376] from each of their fathers'
tribes,[4294] every one a leader[5387] among
them."
3 So Moses sent them from the wilderness of Paran at the [I]command[6310]
of the LORD, all of them men who were
heads[7218] of the sons of Israel.
4 These then *were* their names:
from the tribe of Reuben, Shammua the
son[1121] of Zaccur;
5 from the tribe of Simeon, Shaphat
the son of Hori;
6 from the tribe of Judah, [a]Caleb the
son of Jephunneh;
7 from the tribe of Issachar, Igal the
son of Joseph;
8 from the tribe of Ephraim,
[a]Hoshea the son of Nun;
9 from the tribe of Benjamin, Palti
the son of Raphu;
10 from the tribe of Zebulun, Gaddiel the son of Sodi;
11 from the tribe of Joseph, from
the tribe of Manasseh, Gaddi the son
of Susi;
12 from the tribe of Dan, Ammiel
the son of Gemalli;
13 from the tribe of Asher, Sethur
the son of Michael;
14 from the tribe of Naphtali, Nahbi
the son of Vophsi;
15 from the tribe of Gad, Geuel the
son of Machi.
16 These are the names of the men
whom Moses sent to spy out the land;
but Moses called[7121] [a]Hoshea the son
of Nun, Joshua.
17 When Moses sent them to spy
out the land of Canaan, he said[559] to
them, "Go up [I]there into [a]the [II]Negev;
then go up[5927] into the hill country.
18 "And see what the land is like,
and whether the people[5971] who live in
it are strong[2389] *or* weak, whether they
are few or many.
19 "And how is the land in which
they live, is it good[2896] or bad?[7451] And
how are the cities in which they live,
are *they* [I]like *open* camps[4264] or with fortifications?
20 "And [a]how is the land, is it fat
or lean? Are there trees in it or not?
[I]Make an [b]effort[2388] then to get some
of the fruit of the land." Now the time
was the time[3117] of the first ripe grapes.
21 So they went up[5927] and spied
out the land from [a]the wilderness of Zin
as far as Rehob, [I][b]at Lebo-hamath.
22 When they had gone up into
[a]the Negev, [I]they came to Hebron
where [b]Ahiman, Sheshai and Talmai, the
[II]descendants of [c]Anak were. (Now Hebron was built seven years before
[d]Zoan in Egypt.)
23 Then they came to the [I]valley
of [II][a]Eshcol and from there cut down[3772]
a branch with a single cluster of grapes;
and they carried[5375] it on a pole between
two *men,* with some of the pomegranates and the figs.
24 That place was called the valley
of [I]Eshcol, because of the cluster which
the sons of Israel cut down from there.

3 [I]Lit., *mouth*

6 [a]Num. 14:6, 30; Josh. 14:6

8 [a]Num. 13:16; Deut. 32:44

16 [a]Num. 13:8; Deut. 32:44

17 [I]Lit., *here* [II]I.e., South country, and so throughout the ch. [a]Gen. 12:9; 13:1, 3

19 [I]Lit., *in*

20 [I]Lit., *Use your strength* [a]Deut. 1:24, 25 [b]Deut. 31:6, 23

21 [I]Or, *to the entrance of Hamath* [a]Num. 20:1; 27:14; 33:36 [b]Josh. 13:5

22 [I]Lit., Most mss. read *one came* [II]Lit., *children* [a]Num. 13:17 [b]Josh. 15:14 [c]Num. 13:28, 33 [d]Ps. 78:12, 43

23 [I]Or, *wadi* [II]I.e., cluster [a]Gen. 14:13; Num. 13:24; 32:9; Deut. 1:24

24 [I]I.e., cluster

13:16 See note on Num. 27:18-23.

13:17 The term "Negev" could be rendered here "south country." It was a well-defined territory forming the southernmost and least fertile part of Canaan and was subsequently a part of Judah's inheritance. It extended northward from Kadesh to within a few miles of Hebron and from the Dead Sea westward to the Mediterranean. "The hill country" was the country of southern and central Canaan, mostly within the borders of the inheritance of Judah and Ephraim. It began a few miles south of Hebron and extended northward to the plain of Jezreel and eventually northwest to the sea just above Mount Carmel.

13:22 Zoan was also called Avaris or Tanis in Greek. It was an important city in the delta region of Egypt built about 1700 B.C. Founded by the Hyksos kings as their northern capital, it was probably also used by Raamses for that purpose (Ex. 1:11). The reference to Zoan establishes that Hebron had been founded very early. It was near this city that the Hebrew Patriarchs had been buried (Gen. 23:19; 49:31; 50:13).

The Spies' Reports

25 When they returned[7725] from
spying out the land, at the end of forty
days,[3117]
🔑 26 they proceeded to come to Moses and Aaron and to all the congregation[5712] of the sons of Israel [I]in
the wilderness of Paran, at [a]Kadesh;
and they brought back word[1697] to them
and to all the congregation and
showed[7200] them the fruit of the land.
27 Thus they told[5608] him, and said,
"We went in to the land where you sent
us; and [a]it certainly does flow with milk
and honey, and [b]this is its fruit.
🔑 28 "Nevertheless, [a]the people who
live in the land are strong, and the cities
are fortified *and* very large; and moreover, we saw[7200] [b]the [I]descendants of
Anak there.
29 "Amalek is living in the land of
[a]the Negev and the Hittites and the Jebusites and [b]the Amorites are living in the
hill country, and [c]the Canaanites are living by the sea and by the side of the
Jordan."
🔑 **30** Then Caleb quieted the people
[I]before Moses, and said, "We should
by all means go up and take possession[3423] of it, for we shall surely[2895]
overcome it."
31 But the men who had gone up
with him said, "[a]We are not able to go
up against the people, for they are too
strong[2389] for us."
🔑 32 So they gave out to the sons of
Israel [a]a bad report of the land which
they had spied out, saying, "The land
through which we have gone, in spying
it out, is [b]a land that devours its [I]in-
habitants; and [c]all the people whom we
saw in it are men of *great* size.
33 "There also we saw the

26 [I]Lit., *to* [a]Num. 20:1, 14; 32:8
27 [a]Ex. 3:8, 17; 13:5 [b]Deut. 1:25
28 [I]Lit., *born ones* [a]Deut. 1:28; 9:1, 2 [b]Num. 13:33
29 [a]Num. 13:17; 14:25, 45 [b]Josh. 10:6 [c]Num. 14:43, 45
30 [I]Lit., *toward*
31 [a]Deut. 1:28; 9:1-3
32 [I]Or, *settlers* [a]Num. 14:36, 37; Ps. 106:24 [b]Ezek. 36:13, 14 [c]Amos 2:9

🔑 **13:26** Kadesh, otherwise known as Kadesh-barnea, was an oasis in the wilderness just south of Canaan. It figured prominently in Israel's history during the wilderness wanderings, but Israel's experience there was almost entirely negative. The spies were sent out from Kadesh, but upon their return, the people rebelled (Num. 14:1-10). The author of Psalm 95 expanded on the consequences of this rebellion, making the point that this prevented Israel from entering God's rest (vv. 7b-11). The writer of Hebrews based a major section of his exhortation to faithfulness upon this incident, as it was interpreted in Ps. 95 (Heb. 3:7–4:11). His point was that, although Israel had been promised a rest, God revoked the promise because of their sin. The promise was still standing, so God's people now could claim a sabbath rest (a reference to heaven), if they did not "fall through following the same example of disobedience" as Israel did (Heb. 4:9,11). Israel's reluctance to conquer Canaan soon turned into rash action, and they were soundly repulsed when they initiated an unauthorized attack from Kadesh (Num. 14:40-45). Decades later, near the end of the forty years in the wilderness, Miriam, the sister of Moses and Aaron, died and was buried at Kadesh (Num. 20:1). Finally, while they were still at Kadesh, Moses and Aaron sinned in the way that they provided water for the people, and were punished by not being allowed to lead the nation into Canaan (Num. 20:10-12). Within a short time Aaron died on Mount Hor (Num. 20:23-29), and later, after he had turned over the reigns of leadership to Joshua, Moses died on Mount Nebo (Deut. 34:1-5).

🔑 **13:28** "Cities are fortified and very large." Modern archeologists have found that indeed there were numerous large walled fortresses throughout Palestine even at that early date. Some of them were as large as ten acres. These made invasion by foreign armies extremely difficult.

🔑 **13:30** Caleb and Joshua were the spies who brought back the minority report that, with the Lord's help, Canaan could easily be taken (Num. 14:6-9). For their faithfulness, God said that they alone would survive the wilderness experience and enter Canaan (Num. 14:30). When the second census was taken as preparations were being made to move into Canaan (see the note on Num. 1:2), only Caleb and Joshua were alive from the original group (Num. 26:64,65). After the major campaigns of the conquest were completed, and Joshua was parceling out land in Canaan, Caleb was the first to be given his land, in keeping with God's promise forty-five years earlier (Num. 14:24; Josh. 14:6-15). He was allotted Hebron, near the Cave of Machpelah, where the Patriarchs had been buried.

🔑 **13:32,33** The Israelite spies reported two great obstacles to their invasion of Canaan: (1) men of great size; (2) Nephilim. Reference is made to them in Gen. 6:4 (see note). The Nephilim were men of violence. The sons of Anak were among the Nephilim and in Deut. 2:10,11 they are also referred to as giants (in Hebrew *rapha* not *nephilim*).

[a]Nephilim[5303] (the sons[1121] of Anak are
part of the Nephilim); and [b]we became
like grasshoppers in our own sight, and
so we were in their sight."

The People Rebel

14 🔑Then all the congregation[5712] [I]lifted up their voices
and cried, and the people[5971] wept [II]that
night.[3915]
2 And all the sons[1121] of Israel
[a]grumbled against Moses and Aaron; and
the whole congregation said[559] to them,
"[b]Would that we had died in the land[776]
of Egypt! Or would that we had died
in this wilderness!
3 "And why is the LORD bringing
us into this land, [a]to fall by the sword?[2719]
[b]Our wives[802] and our little ones[2945] will
become plunder; would it not be bet-
ter[2896] for us to return[7725] to Egypt?"
4 So they said to one[376] another,
"[a]Let us appoint a leader and return to
Egypt."
5 [a]Then Moses and Aaron fell[5307]
on their faces in the presence of all the
assembly[6951] of the congregation of the
sons of Israel.
🔑6 And Joshua the son[1121] of Nun and
Caleb the son of Jephunneh, of those
who had spied out the land, tore their
clothes;
7 and they spoke[559] to all the congregation[5712] of the sons of Israel, saying,
"[a]The land which we passed[5674] through
to spy out is an exceedingly good[2896]
land.
8 "[a]If the LORD is pleased[2654] with
us, then He will bring us into this land,
and give it to us—[b]a land which flows
with milk and honey.
9 "Only [a]do not rebel[4775] against the
LORD; and do not [b]fear[3372] the people
of the land, for they shall be our
[I]prey. Their [II]protection has been
removed[5493] from them, and the LORD
is with us; do not fear them."
10 [a]But all the congregation said to
stone them with stones. Then [b]the
glory[3519] of the LORD appeared[7200] in the
tent[168] of meeting[4150] to all the sons of
Israel.

Moses Pleads for the People

11 [a]And the LORD said to Moses,
"How long will this people spurn[5006]
Me? And how long will [b]they not believe[539] in Me, despite all the signs[226]
which I have performed[6213] in their
midst?[7130]
12 "I will smite[5221] them with [I][a]pesti-
lence[1698] and dispossess them, and I
[b]will make[6213] you into a nation[1471]
greater and mightier than they."
13 [a]But Moses said to the LORD,
"Then the Egyptians will hear[8085] of it,
for by Thy strength Thou didst bring
up[5927] this people from their midst,
14 and they will tell[559] *it* to the inhabitants of this land. They have
heard[8085] that Thou, O LORD, art in the
midst of this people, for [a]Thou, O
LORD, art seen[7200] eye to eye, while Thy
cloud[6051] stands over them; and Thou
dost go before them in a pillar of cloud
by day[3119] and in a pillar of fire by night.
15 "Now if Thou dost slay[4191] this
people as one man,[376] [a]then the
nations[3816] who have heard of Thy
fame[8088] will [I]say,[559]
16 'Because the LORD [a]could not
bring this people into the land which
He promised them by oath,[7650] therefore
He slaughtered[7819] them in the wilderness.'
17 "But now, I pray,[4994] let the
power of the Lord[136] be great, just as
Thou hast [I]declared,[1696]
18 '[a]The LORD is slow to anger and
abundant in lovingkindness,[2617] forgiving[5375] iniquity[5771] and transgression;[6588]
but [b]He will by no means clear *the*
guilty, [c]visiting the iniquity of the
fathers[1] on the children[1121] [I]to the third
and the fourth *generations.*'
19 "[a]Pardon,[5545] I pray, the iniquity

33 [a]Gen. 6:4 [b]Deut. 1:28; 9:2; Josh. 11:21
1 [I]Lit., *lifted and gave their voice* [II]Lit., *in that*
2 [a]Num. 11:1 [b]Num. 11:5; 16:13; 20:3, 4; 21:5
3 [a]Ex. 5:21; 16:3 [b]Num. 14:31; Deut. 1:39
4 [a]Neh. 9:17
5 [a]Num. 16:4
7 [a]Num. 13:27; Deut. 1:25
8 [a]Deut. 10:15 [b]Ex. 3:8; Num. 13:27
9 [I]Lit., *food* [II]Lit., *shadow* [a]Deut. 1:26; 9:23, 24 [b]Deut. 1:21, 29
10 [a]Ex. 17:4 [b]Ex. 16:10; Lev. 9:23
11 [a]Ex. 32:9-13 [b]Ps. 106:24
12 [I]Lit., *the pestilence* [a]Lev. 26:25; Deut. 28:21 [b]Ex. 32:10
13 [a]Ex. 32:11-14; Ps. 106:23
14 [a]Ex. 13:21; Deut. 5:4
15 [I]Lit., *speak, saying* [a]Ex. 32:12
16 [a]Josh. 7:7
17 [I]Lit., *spoken, saying*
18 [I]Lit., *on* [a]Ex. 20:6; 34:6, 7; Deut. 5:10; 7:9; Ps. 103:8; 145:8; Jon. 4:2 [b]Ex. 20:5; Deut. 5:9; 7:10 [c]Ex. 34:7
19 [a]Ex. 32:32; 34:9

🔑 **14:1-10** See note on Num. 13:26.
🔑 **14:6-9** See note on Num. 13:30.

of this people according to the greatness
of Thy lovingkindness, just as Thou also
hast forgiven[5375] this people, from Egypt
even until now."

The LORD Pardons and Rebukes

20 So the LORD said, "[a]I have
pardoned[5545] *them* according to your
word;[1697]
21 but indeed, [a]as I live,[2416] [I][b]all the
earth[776] will be filled with the glory of
the LORD.
22 "Surely [a]all the men[582] who have
seen My glory and My signs,[226] which
I performed[6213] in Egypt and in the wilderness, yet [b]have put Me to the test[5254]
these ten times and have not listened[8085]
to My voice,
23 [a]shall by no means see the land
which I swore to their fathers, nor shall
any of those who spurned[5006] Me see it.
24 "But My servant[5650] Caleb, [a]be-
cause he has had a different spirit[7307]
and has followed Me fully, [I][b]I will bring
into the land [II]which he entered, and
his [III]descendants[2233] shall take possession[3423] of it.
25 "[a]Now the Amalekites and the
Canaanites live in the valleys; turn tomorrow and set out to the wilderness
by the way[1870] of the [I]Red Sea."
26 And the LORD spoke[1696] to Moses and Aaron, saying,
27 "How long *shall I bear* with this
evil[7451] congregation who are [a]grumbling
against Me? I have heard the complaints
of the sons of Israel, which they are
[I]making against Me.
28 "Say[559] to them, '[a]As I live,' says
the LORD, 'just as [b]you have spoken in
My hearing,[241] so I will surely do[6213]
to you;
29 [a]your corpses[6297] shall fall in this
wilderness, even all [b]your [I]numbered[6485]
men, according to your complete number from twenty years old[1121] and upward, who have grumbled against Me.
30 'Surely you shall not come into
the land in which I [I]swore to settle[7931]
you, [a]except Caleb the son of Jephunneh
and Joshua the son of Nun.
31 '[a]Your children,[2945] however,
whom you said would become a prey—
I will bring them in, and they shall
know[3045] the land which you have rejected.[3988]
32 '[a]But as for you, your corpses
shall fall in this wilderness.
33 'And your sons shall be shepherds for [a]forty years in the wilderness,
and they shall [I]suffer *for* your [II]unfaithful-
ness,[2184] until your corpses [III]lie[8552] in
the wilderness.
34 'According to the [a]number of
days[3117] which you spied out the land,
forty days, for every day you shall bear
your [I]guilt[5771] a year, *even* forty years,
and you shall know My opposition.
35 '[a]I, the LORD, have spoken,[1696]
surely this I will do to all this evil congregation who are gathered[3259] together
against Me. In this wilderness they shall
be destroyed, and there they shall
die.' "[4191]
36 [a]As for the men whom Moses
sent to spy out the land and who returned[7725] and made all the congregation grumble against him by bringing out
a bad report concerning the land,
37 even [a]those men who brought
out the very bad report of the land died
by a [b]plague before the LORD.
38 But Joshua the son of Nun and
Caleb the son of Jephunneh remained
alive[2421] out of those men who went to
spy out the land.

20 [a]Mic. 7:18-20
21 [I]Lit., *and all* [a]Num. 14:28; Deut. 32:40; Is. 49:18 [b]Is. 6:3; Hab. 2:14
22 [a]1 Cor. 10:5 [b]Ex. 5:21; 14:11; 15:24; 16:2; 17:2, 3; 32:1; Num. 11:1, 4; 12:1; 14:2
23 [a]Num. 26:65; 32:11; Heb. 3:18
24 [I]Lit., *him I* [II]Lit., *where* [III]Lit., *seed* [a]Num. 14:6-9 [b]Num. 26:65; 32:12; Deut. 1:36; Josh. 14:6-15
25 [I]Lit., *Sea of Reeds* [a]Num. 13:29
27 [I]Lit., *complaining* [a]Num. 11:1
28 [a]Num. 14:21 [b]Num. 14:2; Deut. 2:14, 15; Heb. 3:17
29 [I]Lit., *mustered* [a]Heb. 3:17 [b]Num. 1:45, 46
30 [I]Lit., *raised My hand* [a]Num. 14:24
31 [a]Num. 14:3
32 [a]Num. 26:64, 65; 32:13; 1Cor. 10:5
33 [I]Lit., *bear* [II]Lit., *fornications* [III]Lit., *are finished* [a]Deut. 2:7; 8:2, 4; 29:5
34 [I]Or, *iniquities* [a]Num. 13:25
35 [a]Num. 23:19
36 [a]Num. 13:4-16, 32
37 [a]1Cor. 10:10; Heb. 3:17, 18 [b]Num. 16:49

14:22 The number ten is not to be taken literally here. It is symbolic of completeness. The Lord had had enough. The promised judgment of Ex. 32:34 must be executed. God will punish sin (Job 4:8; Gal. 6:7).
14:24 See note on Num. 13:30.
14:25 This was a hard lesson, but their unbelief had cost them the blessing which God had promised to them.
14:30 See note n Num. 13:30.

Israel Repulsed

39 And when Moses spoke [a]these words[1697] to all the sons of Israel, [b]the people mourned greatly.

🔑40 In the morning, however, they rose up early and went up to the [I]ridge[7218] of the hill country, saying, "[a]Here we are; [II]we have indeed sinned,[2398] but we will go up[5927] to the place which the LORD has promised."[559]

41 But Moses said, "[a]Why then are you transgressing[5674] the [I]commandment[6310] of the LORD, when it will not succeed?

42 "[a]Do not go up, lest you be struck down[5062] before your enemies, for the LORD is not among you.

43 "For the Amalekites and the Canaanites will be there in front of you, and you will fall by the sword, inasmuch as you have turned back from following the LORD. And the LORD will not be with you."

🔑44 But they went up heedlessly to the [I]ridge of the hill country; neither [a]the ark[727] of the covenant[1285] of the LORD nor Moses left the camp.[4264]

45 Then the Amalekites and the Canaanites who lived in that hill country came down, and struck[5221] them and beat them down[3807] as far as [a]Hormah.

Laws for Canaan

15 Now the LORD spoke[1696] to Moses, saying,

2 "[a]Speak[1696] to the sons[1121] of Israel, and say[559] to them, 'When you enter the land [I]where you are to live,[4186] which I am giving you,

3 then make[6213] [a]an offering by fire to the LORD, a burnt offering[5930] or a sacrifice[2077] to [I][b]fulfill[6381] a special vow,[5088] or as a freewill offering[5071] or in your [c]appointed times,[4150] to make a [d]soothing aroma to the LORD, from the herd or from the flock.

4 "[a]And the one who presents his offering[7133] shall present[7126] to the LORD a grain offering[4503] of one-tenth *of an ephah* of fine flour mixed[1101] with one-fourth of a [I]hin of oil,[8081]

5 and you shall prepare wine for the libation,[5262] one-fourth of a hin, with the burnt offering or for the sacrifice, for [a]each lamb.

6 'Or for a ram you shall prepare as a grain offering two-tenths *of an ephah* of fine flour mixed with one-third of a hin of oil;

7 and for the libation you shall offer one-third of a hin of wine as a soothing aroma to the LORD.

8 'And when you prepare [a]a bull as a burnt offering or a sacrifice, to [I]fulfill a special vow, or for peace offerings[8002] to the LORD,

9 then you shall offer with the bull a grain offering of three-tenths *of an ephah* of fine flour mixed with one-half a hin of oil;

10 and you shall offer as the libation one-half a hin of wine as an offering by fire, as a soothing aroma to the LORD.

11 'Thus it shall be done[6213] for each ox, or for each ram, or for each of the male lambs, or of the goats.

12 'According to the number that you prepare, so you shall do[6213] for everyone according to their number.

13 'All who are native shall do these things in this manner, in presenting an offering by fire, as a soothing aroma to the LORD.

Law of the Sojourner

14 'And if an alien[1616] sojourns[1481] with you, or one who may be among you throughout your generations,[1755] and he *wishes to* make[6213] an offering by fire, as a soothing aroma to the LORD, just as you do, so he shall do.

15 '*As for* the assembly,[6951] there shall be [a]one statute[2708] for you and for the alien who sojourns[1481] *with you,* a perpetual[5769] statute throughout your

39 [a]Num. 14:28-35 [b]Ex. 33:4

40 [I]Or, *top of the mountain* [II]Or, *and we will go up. . . for we have sinned* [a]Deut. 1:41-44

41 [I]Lit., *mouth* [a]2Chr. 24:20

42 [a]Deut. 1:42

44 [I]Or, *top of the mountain* [a]Num. 31:6

45 [a]Num. 21:3

2 [I]Lit., *of your dwellings* [a]Lev. 23:10

3 [I]Or, *make a special votive offering* [a]Lev. 1:2, 3 [b]Lev. 22:21 [c]Lev. 23:1-44 [d]Gen. 8:21; 2Cor. 2:15, 16; Phil. 4:18

4 [I]I.e., Approx. one gal., and so through v. 10 [a]Num. 28:1-29:40

5 [a]Lev. 1:10; 3:6; Num. 15:11

8 [I]Or, *make a special votive offering* [a]Lev. 1:3; 3:1

15 [a]Num. 9:14; 15:29

🔑**14:40-45** See note on Num. 13:26.

🔑**14:44** They were adding the sin of presumptuous self-confidence to their sin of unbelief (vv. 1-4).

generations; as you are, so shall the alien be before the LORD.

16 'There is to be [a]one law[8451] and one ordinance[4941] for you and for the alien who sojourns with you.' "

17 Then the LORD spoke to Moses, saying,

18 "Speak to the sons of Israel, and say to them, 'When you enter the land where I bring you,

19 then it shall be, that when you eat of the [I][a]food of the land, you shall lift up [II]an offering[8641] to the LORD.

20 '[a]Of the first[7225] of your [I]dough you shall lift up a cake as an [II]offering; as [b]the [II]offering of the threshing floor, so you shall lift[7311] it up.

21 'From the first of your [I]dough you shall give to the LORD an [II]offering throughout your generations.

22 'But when you [a]unwittingly fail[7686] and do not observe all these commandments, which the LORD has spoken[1696] to Moses,

23 *even* all that the LORD has commanded[6680] you [I]through[3027] Moses, from the day[3117] when the LORD gave commandment and onward throughout your generations,

24 then it shall be, if it is done [a]unintentionally,[7684] [I]without the knowledge of the congregation,[5712] that all the congregation shall offer one bull[6499,1121,1241] for a burnt offering, as a soothing aroma to the LORD, [b]with its grain offering, and its libation, according to the ordinance, and one male[8163] goat for a sin offering.

25 'Then [a]the priest[3548] shall make atonement[3722] for all the congregation of the sons of Israel, and they shall be forgiven;[5545] for it was an error, and they have brought their offering, an offering by fire[801] to the LORD, and their sin offering before the LORD, for their error.

26 'So all the congregation of the sons of Israel will be forgiven, with the alien who sojourns among them, for *it happened* to all the people[5971] through [a]error.

27 'Also if one person[5315] sins[2398] [a]unintentionally, then he shall offer a one year old female goat for a sin[2403] offering.

28 'And [a]the priest shall make atonement before the LORD for the person who goes astray[7683] when he sins[2398] unintentionally,[7684] making atonement for him [I]that he may be forgiven.

29 'You shall have one law for him who does *anything*[6213] unintentionally, for him who is native among the sons of Israel and for the alien who sojourns among them.

30 'But the person who does[6213] *anything* [a]defiantly, whether he is native or an alien, that one is blaspheming the LORD; and that person shall be cut off[3772] from among[7130] his people.

31 'Because he has [a]despised the word[1697] of the LORD and has broken[6565] His commandment,[4687] that person shall be completely cut off; [b]his [I]guilt[5771] *shall be* on him.' "

Sabbath-breaking Punished

32 Now while the sons of Israel were in the wilderness, they found a man[376] [a]gathering wood on the sabbath[7676] day.

33 And those who found him gathering wood brought[7126] him to Moses and Aaron, and to all the congregation;

34 and they put him in [I]custody [a]because it had not been [II]declared what should be done to him.

35 Then the LORD said[559] to Moses, "The man shall surely be put to death;[4191] [a]all the congregation shall stone him with stones outside the camp."[4264]

36 So all the congregation brought him outside the camp, and stoned him [I]to death with stones, just as the LORD had commanded Moses.

⊶ **37** The LORD also spoke[559] to Moses, saying,

16 [a]Lev. 24:22
19 [I]Lit., *bread* [II]Or, *a heave offering* [a]Josh. 5:11, 12
20 [I]Or, *coarse meal* [II]Or, *heave offering* [a]Ex. 34:26; Lev. 23:14 [b]Deut. 14:22, 23; 16:13
21 [I]Or, *coarse meal* [II]Or, *offering lifted up*
22 [a]Lev. 4:2
23 [I]Lit., *by the hand of*
24 [I]Lit., *from the eyes of the congregation* [a]Lev. 4:2, 22, 27; 5:15, 18 [b]Num. 15:8-10
25 [a]Lev. 4:20; Heb. 2:17
26 [a]Num. 15:24
27 [a]Lev. 4:27-31; Luke 12:48
28 [I]Or, *and he shall* [a]Lev. 4:35
30 [a]Num. 14:40-44; Deut. 1:43; 17:12, 13
31 [I]Or, *iniquity* [a]2Sam. 12:9; Prov. 13:13 [b]Ezek. 18:20
32 [a]Ex. 31:14, 15; 35:2, 3
34 [I]Or, *prison* [II]Lit., *declared distinctly* [a]Num. 9:8
35 [a]Lev. 20:2, 27; 24:14-23; Deut. 21:21
36 [I]Lit., *with stones and he died*

⊶ **15:37-40** These blue fringes placed upon the borders of their garments were to be a daily reminder

(continued on next page)

38 "Speak to the sons of Israel, and tell[559] them that they shall make[6213] for themselves [a]tassels on the corners of their garments throughout their generations, and that they shall put on the tassel of each corner a cord of blue.

39 "And it shall be a tassel for you [I]to look at and [a]remember[2142] all the commandments of the LORD, so as to do them and not [II]follow after your own heart[3824] and your own eyes, after which you played the harlot,[2181]

40 in order that you may remember to do all My commandments, and [a]be holy[6918] to your God.

41 "I am the LORD your God[430] who brought you out from the land[776] of Egypt to be your God; I am the LORD your God."

Korah's Rebellion

16 Now [a]Korah the son[1121] of Izhar, the son of Kohath, the son of Levi, with [b]Dathan and Abiram, the sons[1121] of Eliab, and On the son of Peleth, sons of Reuben, took *action,*

2 and they rose up before Moses, [I]together with some[582] of the sons[1121] of Israel, two hundred and fifty leaders[5387] of the congregation,[712] [II][a]chosen in the assembly,[4150] men[582] of renown.

3 And they assembled[6950] together [a]against Moses and Aaron, and said[559] to them, "[I][b]You have gone far enough, for all the congregation[5712] are holy,[6918] every one of them, and [c]the LORD is in their midst; so why do you exalt yourselves above the assembly[6951] of the LORD?"

4 When Moses heard[8085] *this,* [a]he fell[5307] on his face;

5 and he spoke[1696] to Korah and all his company,[5712] saying, "Tomorrow morning the LORD will show[3045] who is His, and [a]who is holy, and will bring *him* near[7126] to Himself; even [b]the one whom He will choose,[977] He will bring near to Himself.

6 "Do[6213] this: take censers for yourselves, Korah and all [I]your company,

7 and put fire in them, and lay incense[7004] upon them in the presence of the LORD tomorrow; and the man[376] whom the LORD chooses[977] *shall be* the one who is holy. [I][a]You have gone far enough, you sons of Levi!"

8 Then Moses said to Korah, "Hear[8085] now, you sons of Levi,

9 [a]is it [I]not enough for you that the God[430] of Israel has separated[914] you from the *rest of* the congregation of Israel, [b]to bring[7126] you near to Himself, to do[5647] the service[5656] of the tabernacle[4908] of the LORD, and to stand before the congregation to minister[8334] to them;

10 and that He has brought[7126] you near, *Korah,* and all your brothers,[251] sons of Levi, with you? And are you [a]seeking for the priesthood[3550] also?

11 "Therefore you and all your company are gathered[3259] together [a]against the LORD; but as for Aaron, [I]who is he that [b]you grumble against him?"

12 Then Moses sent [I]a summons[7121] to Dathan and Abiram, the sons of Eliab; but they said, "We will not come up.[5927]

13 "Is it [I]not enough that you have brought[5927] us up out of a [a]land[776] flowing with milk and honey [b]to have us die in the wilderness, but you would also lord[8323] it over us?

14 "Indeed, you have not brought us [a]into a land flowing with milk and honey, nor have you given us an inheritance[5159] of [b]fields[7704] and vineyards. Would you [I][c]put out the eyes of [II]these men? We will not come up!"

15 Then Moses became very angry[2734] and said to the LORD, "[a]Do not regard their offering![4503] [b]I have not

38 [a]Deut. 22:12; Matt. 23:5

39 [I]Lit., *and you shall look at it* [II]Lit., *seek* [a]Deut. 4:23; 6:12; 8:11, 14, 19

40 [a]Lev. 11:44, 45

1 [a]Ex. 6:21; Jude 11 [b]Num. 26:9; Deut. 11:6

2 [I]Lit., *and men from* [II]Lit., *called ones of* [a]Num. 1:16; 26:9

3 [I]Lit., *It is much for you* [a]Num. 12:2; Ps. 106:16 [b]Num. 16:7 [c]Num. 5:3

4 [a]Num. 14:5

5 [a]Lev. 10:3; Ps. 65:4 [b]Num. 17:5, 8

6 [I]Lit., *his*

7 [I]Lit., *It is much for you* [a]Num. 16:3

9 [I]Or, *too little for you* [a]Is. 7:13 [b]Num. 3:6, 9; Deut. 10:8

10 [a]Num. 3:10; 18:1-7

11 [I]Lit., *what* [a]Ex. 16:7 [b]1Cor. 10:10

12 [I]Lit., *to call*

13 [I]Lit., *a little thing* [a]Ex. 16:3; Num. 11:4-6 [b]Num. 14:2, 3

14 [I]Lit., *bore out* [II]Lit., *those* [a]Num. 13:27; 14:8 [b]Ex. 22:5; 23:10, 11; Num. 20:5 [c]Judg. 16:21; 1Sam. 11:2

15 [a]Gen. 4:4, 5 [b]1Sam. 12:3

(continued from previous page)

to Israel of the Lord's commandments and of the fact that they were a holy or separated people to God. Jesus accused some Jewish leaders of making their fringes extremely long in order to make a show of their religion, without being committed to the Lord's commandments (Mt. 23:5).

taken[5375] a single donkey from them,
nor have I done harm[7489] to any of
them."
16 And Moses said to Korah, "You
and all your company be present before
the LORD tomorrow, both you and they
along with Aaron.
17 "And each of you take his firepan
and put incense on [I]it, and each of you
bring his censer before the LORD, two
hundred and fifty firepans; also you and
Aaron *shall* each[376] *bring* his firepan."
18 So they each took his *own* censer
and put fire on [I]it, and laid[7760] incense
on [I]it; and they stood at the doorway
of the tent[168] of meeting, with Moses
and Aaron.
19 Thus Korah assembled all the
congregation against them at the doorway of the tent of meeting. And [a]the
glory[3519] of the LORD appeared[7200] to
all the congregation.
20 Then the LORD spoke to Moses
and Aaron, saying,
21 "[a]Separate[914] yourselves from
among this congregation, [b]that I may
consume[3615] them instantly."
22 But they fell on their faces, and
said, "O God,[410] [a]Thou God of the
spirits[7307] of all flesh,[1320] [b]when one man
sins,[2398] wilt Thou be angry[7107] with the
entire congregation?"
23 Then the LORD spoke to Moses,
saying,
24 "Speak[1696] to the congregation,
saying, '[a]Get back from around the
dwellings of Korah, Dathan and Abiram.'"
25 Then Moses arose and went to
Dathan and Abiram, with the elders[2205]
of Israel following him,
26 and he spoke to the congregation, saying, "[a]Depart[5493] now from the
tents[168] of these wicked[7563] men, and
touch[5060] nothing that belongs to them,
[b]lest you be swept away[5595] in all their
sin."
27 So they got back from around
the dwellings of Korah, Dathan and Abiram; and Dathan and Abiram came out
and stood[5324] at the doorway of their
tents, along with their wives[802] and
[a]their sons and their little ones.[2945]
28 And Moses said, "By this you
shall know[3045] that [a]the LORD has sent
me to do all these deeds; for this is
not [I]my doing.
29 "If these men[120] die[4191] [I]the
death[4194] of all men, or [II]if they suffer[6485]
the [a]fate[6486] of all men, *then* the LORD
has not sent me.
30 "But [a]if the LORD [I]brings about
an entirely new thing and the ground[127]
opens its mouth[6310] and swallows[1104]
them up with all that is theirs, and they
[b]descend alive[2416] into [II]Sheol,[7585] then
you will understand that these men have
spurned[5006] the LORD."
31 Then it came about as he
finished[3615] speaking[1696] all these
words,[1697] that the ground[127] that was
under them split open;
🔑 32 and [a]the earth[776] opened its
mouth and swallowed them up, and their
households,[1004] and [b]all the men who
belonged to Korah, with *their* possessions.
33 So they and all that belonged to
them went down alive[2416] to [I]Sheol; and
the earth closed over them, and they
perished[6] from the midst of the assembly.
34 And all Israel who *were* around
them fled at their [I]outcry, for they said,
"[II]The earth may swallow us up!"
35 [a]Fire also came forth from the
LORD and consumed the [b]two hundred
and fifty men[376] who were offering[7126]
the incense.
36 [I]Then the LORD spoke to Moses,
saying,
37 "Say[559] to Eleazar, the son of
Aaron the priest,[3548] that he shall take
up the censers out of the midst of the
[I]blaze,[8316] for they are holy;[6942] and you
scatter the [II]burning coals abroad.

17 [I]Lit., *them*
18 [I]Lit., *them*
19 [a]Num. 14:10; 16:42; 20:6
21 [a]Num. 16:45 [b]Ex. 32:10, 12
22 [a]Num. 27:16 [b]Gen. 18:23-32; Lev. 4:3
24 [a]Num. 16:45
26 [a]Is. 52:11 [b]Gen. 19:15, 17
27 [a]Num. 26:11
28 [I]Lit., *from my heart* [a]Ex. 3:12-15; 4:12, 15
29 [I]Lit., *like the death* [II]Lit., *the visitation of all men be visited upon them* [a]Eccl. 3:19
30 [I]Lit., *creates a new creation* [II]I.e., the nether world [a]Job 31:2, 3 [b]Ps. 55:15
32 [a]Num. 26:10; Deut. 11:6; Ps. 106:17 [b]Num. 26:11
33 [I]I.e., the nether world
34 [I]Or, *voice* [II]Lit., *Lest the earth*
35 [a]Num. 11:1-3; 26:10 [b]Num. 16:2
36 [I]Ch. 17:1 in Heb.
37 [I]Or, *place of burning* [II]Lit., *the fire*

🔑 **16:32** Not all of Korah's sons perished. Some of his descendants are mentioned in Num. 26:58; I Chr. 9:19; and in Psalms 84, 85, 87, 88.

38 "As for the censers of these [I]men[2400] who have sinned at the cost of their lives,[5315] let them be made into hammered[7555] sheets[6341] for a plating of the altar,[4196] since they did present them before the LORD and they are holy; and [a]they shall be for a sign[226] to the sons of Israel."

39 So Eleazar the priest took the bronze censers which the men who were burned[8313] had offered; and they hammered them out as a plating[6341] for the altar,

40 as a [I]reminder to the sons of Israel that [a]no [II]layman[2114] who is not of the [III]descendants[2233] of Aaron should come near [b]to burn incense before the LORD; that he might not become like Korah and his company—just as the LORD had spoken[1696] to him [IV]through[3027] Moses.

Murmuring and Plague

41 But on the next day all the congregation of the sons of Israel [a]grumbled against Moses and Aaron, saying, "You are the ones who have caused the death of the LORD's people."[5971]

42 It came about, however, when the congregation had assembled against Moses and Aaron, that they turned toward the tent of meeting, and behold, the cloud[6051] covered[1642] it and [a]the glory of the LORD appeared.

43 Then Moses and Aaron came to the front of the tent of meeting,

44 and the LORD spoke to Moses, saying,

45 "[I][a]Get away from among this congregation, that I may consume them instantly." Then they fell on their faces.

46 And Moses said to Aaron, "Take your censer and put in it fire from the altar, and lay incense *on it;* then bring it quickly to the congregation and [a]make atonement[3722] for them, for [b]wrath[7110] has gone forth from the LORD, the plague[5063] has begun!"

38 [I]Lit., *sinners against their lives* [a]Ezek. 14:8; 2Pet. 2:6

40 [I]Or, *memorial* [II]Lit., *stranger* [III]Lit., *seed* [IV]Lit., *by the hand of* [a]Num. 1:51 [b]Ex. 30:7-10

41 [a]Num. 16:3

42 [a]Num. 16:19

45 [I]Or, *Arise* [a]Num. 16:21, 24

46 [a]Num. 25:13; Is. 6:6, 7 [b]Num. 18:5; Deut. 9:22

47 [a]Num. 25:6-8, 13

49 [a]Num. 25:9 [b]Num. 16:32, 35

1 [I]Ch. 17:16 in Heb.

4 [a]Ex. 25:16, 21, 22; Num. 17:7

5 [a]Num. 16:5

7 [a]Num. 1:50, 53; 9:15

47 Then Aaron took *it* as Moses had spoken,[1696] and ran into the midst of the assembly, for behold, the plague had begun among the people. [a]So he put *on* the incense and made atonement for the people.

48 And he took his stand between the dead[4191] and the living,[2416] so that the plague was checked.

49 [a]But those who died by the plague were 14,700, besides those who [b]died on account[1697] of Korah.

50 [I]Then Aaron returned[7725] to Moses at the doorway of the tent of meeting, for the plague had been checked.

Aaron's Rod Buds

17 [I]Then the LORD spoke[1696] to Moses, saying,

2 "Speak[1696] to the sons[1121] of Israel, and get from them a rod[4294] for each father's[1] household:[1004] twelve rods,[4294] from all their leaders[5387] according to their fathers' households. You shall write each name on his rod,

3 and write Aaron's name on the rod of Levi; for there is one rod for the head[7218] *of each* of their fathers' households.

4 "You shall then deposit them in the tent[168] of meeting[4150] in front of [a]the testimony,[5715] where I meet[3259] with you.

5 "And it will come about that the rod of [a]the man whom I choose[977] will sprout. Thus I shall lessen from upon Myself the grumblings of the sons of Israel, who are grumbling against you."

6 Moses therefore spoke to the sons of Israel, and all their leaders gave him a rod apiece, for each[376] leader[5387] according to their fathers'[1] households,[1004] twelve rods, with the rod of Aaron among their rods.

7 So Moses deposited the rods before the LORD in [a]the tent of the testimony.[5715]

🔑 8 Now it came about on the next

🔑 **17:8** God used Aaron's rod as an answer to Israel who complained against Moses and Aaron after

(continued on next page)

day that Moses went into the tent of
the testimony; and behold, [a]the rod of
Aaron for the house of Levi had sprouted
and put forth buds and produced blossoms, and it bore[1580] ripe almonds.
9 Moses then brought out all the
rods from the presence of the LORD
to all the sons of Israel; and they
looked,[7200] and each man[376] took his rod.
10 But the LORD said[559] to Moses,
"Put back the rod of Aaron [a]before the
testimony [I]to be kept[4931] as a sign[226]
against the [IIb]rebels,[4805] that you may
put an end to their grumblings against
Me, so that they should not die."[4191]
11 Thus Moses did;[6213] just as the
LORD had commanded[6680] him, so he
did.
12 Then the sons of Israel spoke[559]
to Moses, saying, "[a]Behold, we perish,[1478] we are dying, we are all dying!
13 "[a]Everyone who comes near,
who comes near to the tabernacle[4908]
of the LORD, must die. Are we to
perish[1478] completely?"

Duties of Levites

18 So the LORD said[559] to Aaron,
"You and your sons[1121] and your
father's[1] household[1004] with you shall
[a]bear[5375] the guilt[5771] [I]in connection with
the sanctuary;[4720] and you and your sons
with you shall bear the guilt [II]in connection with your priesthood.[3550]
2 "But bring with you also your
brothers,[251] the tribe[4294] of Levi, the
tribe[7626] of your father,[1] that they may
be [a]joined with you and serve[8334] you,
while you and your sons with you are
before the tent[168] of the testimony.[5715]
3 "And they shall thus attend[8104] to
your obligation[4931] and the obligation of
all the tent, but [a]they shall not come
near to the furnishings of the sanctuary[6944] and [b]the altar,[4196] lest both they
and you die.
4 "And they shall be joined with you
and attend to the obligations of the tent
of meeting,[4250] for all the service[5656] of
the tent; but an [I]outsider[2114] may not
come near you.
5 "So you shall attend to the
[a]obligations of the sanctuary and the obligations of the altar, [b]that there may no
longer be wrath[7110] on the sons[1121] of
Israel.
6 "And behold, I Myself [a]have taken
your [I]fellow Levites from among the
sons of Israel; they are [b]a gift to you,
[II]dedicated to the LORD, to perform[5647]
the service for the tent of meeting.
7 "But you and your sons with you
shall [a]attend to your priesthood[3550] for
everything[3605,1697] concerning the altar
and inside[1004] the veil, and you are to
perform service.[5647] I am giving you the
priesthood as [b]a [I]bestowed service, but
[c]the [II]outsider who comes near shall be
put to death."[4191]

The Priests' Portion

8 Then the LORD spoke[1696] to
Aaron, "Now behold, I Myself have
given you charge of My [Ia]offerings,[8641]
even all the holy gifts[6944] of the sons
of Israel, I have given them to you as
a portion,[4888] and to your sons as a
perpetual[5769] allotment.[2706]
9 "This shall be yours from the most
holy *gifts*,[6944] *reserved* from the fire; every offering[7133] of theirs, even [a]every
grain offering and every [b]sin[2403] offering
and every guilt offering,[817] which they
shall render[7725] to Me, shall be most
holy[6944] for you and for your sons.
10 "As the most holy *gifts* you shall
eat it; every male shall eat it. It shall
be holy to you.

8 [a]Ezek. 17:24; Heb. 9:4
10 [I]Lit., *for preserving* [II]Lit., *sons of rebellion* [a]Num. 17:4 [b]Deut. 9:7, 24
12 [a]Is. 6:5
13 [a]Num. 1:51
1 [I]Lit., *of the sanctuary* [II]Lit., *of your priesthood* [a]Ex. 28:38; Lev. 10:17; 22:16
2 [a]Num. 3:5-10
3 [a]Num. 4:15-20 [b]Num. 1:51; 18:7
4 [I]Lit., *a stranger*
5 [a]Ex. 27:21; Lev. 24:3 [b]Num. 16:46
6 [I]Lit., *brethren the* [II]Lit., *given* [a]Num. 3:12, 45 [b]Num. 3:9
7 [I]Lit., *service of gift* [II]Lit., *stranger* [a]Ex. 29:9 [b]Num. 18:20; Deut. 18:2; Matt. 10:8; 1Pet. 5:2, 3 [c]Num. 1:51
8 [I]Lit., *heave offerings*, and so throughout the ch. [a]Lev. 6:16, 18; 7:28-34
9 [a]Lev. 2:1-16 [b]Lev. 6:30

(continued from previous page)
many unfaithful people had been killed during the rebellion of Korah. Though it had long been severed from the parent tree (probably an almond tree), God caused it to produce fruit as a sign of His approval. The rod itself was to be placed in front of the ark of the covenant as a sign to those who would rebel and complain against God and His spokesmen. Apparently it was later placed within the ark (Heb. 9:4).
18:5 This had happened twice before (Lev. 10:2 and Num. 16:35).

11 "This also is yours, [a]the
offering[8641] of their gift, even all the
wave[8573] offerings of the sons of Israel;
I have [b]given them to you and to your
sons and daughters with you, as a perpetual allotment.[2706] Everyone of your
household who is clean[2889] may eat it.
12 "[a]All the [I]best of the fresh oil[8081]
and all the [I]best of the fresh wine and
of the grain, the first fruits[7225] of those
which they give to the LORD, I give them
to you.
13 "[a]The first ripe fruits of all that
is in their land,[776] which they bring to
the LORD, shall be yours; everyone of
your household who is clean may eat it.
14 "[a]Every devoted thing[2764] in Israel shall be yours.
15 "[I][a]Every first issue of the
womb7358 of all flesh,[1320] whether man[120]
or animal, which they offer to the LORD,
shall be yours; nevertheless the first-
born of man[120] you shall surely redeem,
and the first-born of unclean[2931] animals
you shall redeem.[6299]
16 "And as to their redemption[6299]
price, from a month old[1121] you shall
redeem them, by your valuation, five
[I]shekels in silver, according to the
[I]shekel of the sanctuary, which is twenty
gerahs.1626
17 "But [a]the first-born of an ox or
the first-born of a sheep or the first-
born of a goat, you shall not redeem;
they are holy. [b]You shall sprinkle[2236]
their blood[1818] on the altar and shall offer
up their fat in smoke[6999] *as* an offering
by fire, for a soothing aroma to the
LORD.
18 "And their [I]meat shall be yours;
it shall be yours like the [a]breast of a
wave offering and like the right thigh.
19 "[a]All the offerings of the holy
gifts, which the sons of Israel offer to
the LORD, I have given to you and your
sons and your daughters with you, as
a perpetual allotment. It is [b]an everlasting covenant[1285] of salt before the LORD
to you and your [I]descendants[2233] with
you."
20 Then the LORD said[559] to Aaron,
"[a]You shall have no inheritance[5157] in
their land, nor own any portion among
them; [b]I am your portion and your
inheritance[5159] among the sons of Israel.
21 "And to the sons of Levi, behold,
I have given all the [a]tithe[4643] in Israel
for an inheritance, in return for their
service which they perform, the service
of the tent of meeting.
22 "And [a]the sons of Israel shall not
come near the tent of meeting again,
lest they bear sin[2399] and die.
23 "Only the Levites shall perform
the service of the tent of meeting, and
they shall [a]bear their iniquity; it shall
be a perpetual statute[2708] throughout
your generations,[1755] and among the
sons of Israel [b]they shall have no inheritance.
24 "For the tithe[4643] of the sons of
Israel, which they offer as an offering[8641]
to the LORD, I have given to the Levites
for an inheritance;[5159] therefore I have
said concerning them, '[a]They shall have
no inheritance among the sons of Israel.' "
25 Then the LORD spoke to Moses,
saying,
26 "Moreover, you shall speak[1696]
to the Levites and say[559] to them, 'When
you take from the sons of Israel [a]the
tithe which I have given you from them
for your inheritance, then you shall present an offering from it to the LORD, a
[b]tithe of the tithe.[4643]
27 'And your offering shall be
reckoned[2803] to you as the grain from
the threshing floor or the full produce
from the wine vat.
28 'So you shall also present an offering to the LORD from your tithes,
which you receive from the sons of Israel; and from it you shall give the LORD's
offering to Aaron the priest.[3548]
29 'Out of all your gifts you shall
present every offering due to the LORD,
from all the [I]best of them, [II]the sacred
part[4720] from them.'
30 "And you shall say to them,
'When you have [I]offered7311 from it the
best of it, then *the rest* shall be
reckoned[2803] to the Levites as the prod-

---

11 [a]Num. 18:1; Deut. 18:3 [b]Lev. 22:1-16
12 [I]Lit., *fat* [a]Deut. 18:4; 32:14; Ps. 81:16; 147:14
13 [a]Ex. 22:29; 23:19; 34:26
14 [a]Lev. 27:1-33
15 [I]Lit., *Everything that opens* [a]Ex. 13:13, 15; Num. 3:46
16 [I]I.e., A shekel equals approx. one-half oz.
17 [a]Deut. 15:19 [b]Lev. 3:2
18 [I]Lit., *flesh* [a]Lev. 7:31
19 [I]Lit., *seed* [a]Num. 18:11 [b]2Chr. 13:5
20 [a]Deut. 10:9; 12:12; 14:27, 29 [b]Deut. 18:2; Josh. 13:33; Ezek. 44:28
21 [a]Lev. 27:30-33; Deut. 14:22-29
22 [a]Num. 1:51
23 [a]Num. 18:1 [b]Num. 18:20
24 [a]Deut. 10:9
26 [a]Num. 18:21 [b]Neh. 10:38
29 [I]Lit., *fat* [II]Lit., *its*
30 [I]Lit., *lifted*

uct of the threshing floor, and as the
product of the wine vat.
31 'And you may eat it anywhere,
you and your households,[1004] for it is
your compensation in return for your
service in the tent of meeting.
32 'And you shall bear no sin by reason of it, when you have [I]offered the
[II]best of it. But you shall not [a]profane[2490]
the sacred gifts of the sons of Israel,
lest you die.' "

Ordinance of the Red Heifer

19 Then the LORD spoke[1696] to Moses and Aaron, saying,
2 "This is the statute[2708] of the
law[8451] which the LORD has command-
ed,[6680] saying, 'Speak[1696] to the sons[1121]
of Israel that they bring you an
[a]unblemished[8549] red[122] heifer in which
is no defect,[3971] *and* [b]on which a yoke
has never [I]been placed.
3 'And you shall give it to [a]Eleazar
the priest,[3548] and it shall [b]be brought
outside the camp[4264] and be
slaughtered[7819] in his presence.
4 'Next Eleazar the priest shall take
some of its blood[1818] with his finger,
and [a]sprinkle[5137] some of its blood toward the front of the tent[168] of meeting[4150] seven times.
5 'Then the heifer shall be
burned[8316] in his sight; [a]its hide[5785] and
its flesh[1320] and its blood, with its refuse,
shall be burned.
6 'And the priest shall take [a]cedar
wood and hyssop[231] and scarlet *material,*
and cast it into the midst of the [I]burn-
ing[8316] heifer.
7 'The priest [a]shall then wash[3526] his
clothes and bathe[7364] his [I]body in water,
and afterward come into the camp, but
the priest shall be unclean[2930] until evening.
8 'The one who burns[8313] it shall also
wash his clothes in water and bathe his
[I]body in water, and shall be unclean until
evening.
9 'Now a man[376] who is clean[2889]
shall gather[622] up the ashes of the heifer
and deposit them outside the camp in
a clean place, and [I]the congregation[5712]
of the sons of Israel shall keep it as
[a]water to remove impurity; it is [II]purifi-
cation from sin.[2403]
10 'And the one who gathers[622] the
ashes of the heifer [a]shall wash his clothes
and be unclean until evening; and it shall
be a perpetual[5769] statute[2708] to the sons
of Israel and to the alien[1616] who
sojourns[1481] among them.
11 '[a]The one who touches[5060] the
corpse[4191,5315] of any [I]person[120] shall be
unclean for seven days.[3117]
12 'That one shall [a]purify[2398] himself
from uncleanness with [I]the water on the
third day[3117] and on the seventh day,
and then he shall be clean;[2891] but if
he does not purify himself on the third
day and on the seventh day, he shall
not be clean.
13 '[a]Anyone who touches a corpse,
the [I]body of a man who has died, and
does not purify himself, [b]defiles[2930] the
[II]tabernacle[4908] of the LORD; and that
person[5315] shall be cut off[3772] from Israel.
Because the water for impurity was not
[III][c]sprinkled[2236] on him, he shall be
unclean;[2931] his uncleanness[2932] is still
on him.
14 'This is the law when a man
dies[4191] in a tent:[168] everyone who
comes into the tent and everyone who
is in the tent shall be unclean for seven
days.
15 'And every open vessel, which
has no covering [I]tied down on it, shall
be unclean.
16 '[a]Also, anyone who in the open
field touches one who has been slain[2491]
with a sword[2719] or who has died *naturally,* or a human bone[6106] or a grave,[6913]
shall be unclean for seven days.
17 'Then for the unclean *person* they
shall take some of the [I]ashes[6083] of the
[II]burnt[8316] [III][a]purification from sin and
[IV]flowing[2416] water shall be [V]added to
them in a vessel.
18 'And a clean[2889] person shall take
hyssop and dip[2881] *it* in the water, and
sprinkle *it* on the tent and on all the
furnishings and on the persons[5315] who

32 [I]Lit., *lifted* [II]Lit., *fat* [a]Lev. 22:15, 16

2 [I]Lit., *come up* [a]Lev. 22:20-25 [b]Deut. 21:3

3 [a]Num. 3:4 [b]Lev. 4:11, 12, 21; Num. 19:9

4 [a]Lev. 4:6, 17; 16:14

5 [a]Ex. 29:14; Lev. 4:11, 12

6 [I]Lit., *burning of the heifer* [a]Lev. 14:4

7 [I]Lit., *flesh* [a]Lev. 16:26, 28; 22:6

8 [I]Lit., *flesh*

9 [I]Lit., *it shall be to the congregation. . . Israel, for a guarding as water of impurity* [II]Or, *a sin offering* [a]Num. 8:7; 31:23

10 [a]Num. 19:7

11 [I]Lit., *soul of man* [a]Lev. 21:1, 11; Num. 5:2; 6:6; Acts 21:26, 27

12 [I]Lit., *it* [a]Num. 19:19; 31:19

13 [I]Lit., *soul* [II]Lit., *dwelling place* [III]Or, *thrown* [a]Lev. 7:21; 22:3-7 [b]Lev. 15:31; 20:3; Num. 19:20 [c]Num. 19:19

15 [I]Lit., *cord*

16 [a]Num. 31:19

17 [I]Lit., *dust* [II]Lit., *burning of the* [III]Or, *sin offering* [IV]Lit., *living* [V]Lit., *put* [a]Num. 19:9

were there, and on the one who
touched[5060] the bone or the one slain
or the one dying *naturally* or the grave.
19 'Then the clean *person* [a]shall
sprinkle on the unclean on the third day
and on the seventh day; and on the seventh day he shall purify him from uncleanness, and he shall wash his clothes
and bathe *himself* in water and shall be
clean by evening.
20 'But the man who is unclean and
does not purify himself from uncleanness, that person shall be cut off from
the midst of the assembly,[6951] because
he has [a]defiled[2930] the sanctuary[4720] of
the LORD; the water for impurity has
not been sprinkled on him, he is unclean.
21 'So it shall be a perpetual[5769] statute for them. And he [a]who sprinkles[5137]
the water for impurity shall wash his
clothes, and he who touches the water
for impurity shall be unclean until evening.
22 '[a]Furthermore, anything that the
unclean *person* touches shall be unclean;
and the person who touches *it* shall be
unclean until evening.' "

Death of Miriam

20 Then the sons[1121] of Israel,
the whole congregation,[5712]
came to the [a]wilderness of Zin in the
first[7223] month; and the people[5971]
stayed at Kadesh. Now Miriam died
there and was buried[6912] there.
2 [a]And there was no water for the
congregation; [b]and they assembled[6950]
themselves against Moses and Aaron.
3 [a]The people thus contended[7378]
with Moses and spoke,[559] saying, "[b]If
only we had perished[1478] [c]when our
brothers[251] perished before the LORD!

19 [a]Ezek. 36:25; Heb. 10:22
20 [a]Num. 19:13
21 [a]Num. 19:7
22 [a]Lev. 5:2, 3; 7:21; 22:5, 6
1 [a]Num. 13:21; 27:14; 33:36
2 [a]Ex. 17:1 [b]Num. 16:19, 42
3 [a]Ex. 17:2 [b]Num. 14:2, 3 [c]Num. 16:31-35
4 [I]Lit., *there* [a]Ex. 17:3
5 [I]Lit., *seed* [a]Num. 16:14
6 [a]Num. 14:5
8 [a]Ex. 4:17, 20; 17:5, 6
9 [a]Num. 17:10
10 [a]Ps. 106:33
11 [a]Ps. 78:16; Is. 48:21; 1Cor. 10:4
12 [a]Num. 20:24; 27:14; Deut. 1:37; 3:26, 27

4 "[a]Why then have you brought the
LORD'S assembly[6951] into this wilderness, for us and our beasts to die[4191]
[I]here?
5 "And why have you made us come
up[5927] from Egypt, to bring us in to this
wretched[7451] place? [a]It is not a place
of [I]grain[2233] or figs or vines or pomegranates, nor is there water to drink."
6 Then Moses and Aaron came in
from the presence of the assembly[6951]
to the doorway of the tent[168] of meeting,[4150] and [a]fell[5307] on their faces. Then
the glory[3519] of the LORD appeared[7200]
to them;
7 and the LORD spoke[1696] to Moses,
saying,

The Water of Meribah

8 "Take [a]the rod;[4294] and you and
your brother[251] Aaron assemble the
congregation[712]
and speak[1696] to the rock before their
eyes, that it may yield its water. You
shall thus bring forth water for them
out of the rock and let the congregation
and their beasts drink."
9 So Moses took the rod [a]from before the LORD, just as He had commanded[6680] him;
10 and Moses and Aaron gathered
the assembly before the rock. And he
said[559] to them, "[a]Listen[8085] now, you
rebels;[4784] shall we bring forth water
for you out of this rock?"
11 Then Moses lifted up his hand[3027]
and struck[5221] the rock twice with his
rod; and [a]water came forth abundantly,
and the congregation and their beasts
drank.
12 But the LORD said to Moses
and Aaron, "[a]Because you have not

20:1 See note on Num. 13:26.
20:8-11 See note on Ex. 17:6.
20:10-12 See note on Num. 13:26.
20:12 Moses was excluded from the number of those entering Canaan. This was God's judgment on him for his attitude and action when providing water from the rock for Israel. At Horeb (Ex. 17:6) God had commanded Moses to strike the rock, but on this occasion only to speak to it (v. 8). In v. 11 he displayed a presumptuous attitude in striking the rock and apparently assumed for himself and Aaron the power to perform such a miracle and excluded the Lord. Here his sin is indicated as unbelief and in *(continued on next page)*

believed[539] Me, to treat Me as holy[6942] in the sight of the sons of Israel, therefore you shall not bring this assembly into the land which I have given them."

13 Those *were* the waters of [I][a]Meribah, [II]because the sons of Israel contended[7378] with the LORD, and He proved Himself holy[6942] among them.

14 From Kadesh Moses then sent messengers[4397] to [a]the king[4428] of Edom: "Thus your brother Israel has said, 'You [b]know[3045] all the hardship that has befallen us;

15 that our fathers[1] went down to Egypt, and we stayed in Egypt a long time, and the Egyptians treated us and our fathers badly.[7489]

16 'But [a]when we cried out to the LORD, He heard[8085] our voice and sent [b]an angel[4397] and brought us out from Egypt; now behold, we are at Kadesh, a town on the edge of your territory.

🔑 17 'Please[4994] [a]let us pass through your land.[776] We shall not pass through[5674] field[7704] or through vineyard; we shall not even drink water from a well. We shall go along the king's[4428] highway,[1870] not turning to the right or left, until we pass[5674] through your territory.'"

18 [a]Edom, however, said to him, "You shall not pass through [I]us, lest I come out with the sword[2719] against you."

19 Again, the sons of Israel said to him, "We shall go up by the highway, and if I and [a]my livestock do drink any of your water, [b]then I will [I]pay its price. Let me only pass through on my feet, [II]nothing[1697] *else*."

13 [I]I.e., contention [II]Or, *where* [a]Ex. 17:7; Ps. 95:8
14 [a]Gen. 36:31-39; Deut. 2:4 [b]Josh. 2:9, 10; 9:9, 10, 24
16 [a]Ex. 2:23; 3:7 [b]Ex. 14:19
17 [a]Num. 21:22
18 [I]Lit., *me* [a]Num. 24:18
19 [I]Lit., *give* [II]Or, *no great thing* [a]Ex. 12:38 [b]Deut. 2:6, 28
20 [I]Lit., *people* [a]Judg. 11:17
21 [a]Judg. 11:17 [b]Deut. 2:8
22 [a]Num. 20:1, 14
23 [a]Num. 33:37
24 [I]Lit., *mouth* [a]Gen. 25:8 [b]Num. 20:5, 10
25 [a]Num. 3:4
26 [a]Num. 20:24
28 [a]Ex. 29:29 [b]Num. 33:38; Deut. 10:6; 32:50

20 But he said, "[a]You shall not pass through." And Edom came out against him with a heavy [I]force, and with a strong[2389] hand.

21 [a]Thus Edom refused[3985] to allow Israel to pass[5674] through his territory; [b]so Israel turned away from him.

22 Now when they set out from [a]Kadesh, the sons of Israel, the whole congregation, came to Mount Hor.

🔑 23 Then the LORD spoke to Moses and Aaron at [a]Mount Hor by the border of the land of Edom, saying,

The Death of Aaron

24 "Aaron shall be [a]gathered[622] to his people; for he shall not enter the land which I have given to the sons of Israel, because [b]you rebelled[4784] against My [I]command at the waters of Meribah.

25 "Take Aaron and his son[1121] [a]Eleazar, and bring them up to Mount Hor;

26 and strip Aaron of his garments and put them on his son Eleazar. So Aaron will be [a]gathered *to his people*, and will die there."

27 So Moses did[6213] just as the LORD had commanded, and they went up[5927] to Mount Hor in the sight of all the congregation.

28 And after Moses had stripped Aaron of his garments and [a]put them on his son Eleazar, [b]Aaron died there on the mountain top.[7218] Then Moses and Eleazar came down from the mountain.

29 And when all the congregation saw[7200] that Aaron had died,[1478] all the

---

(continued from previous page)
Num. 27:14 as rebellion while in Deut. 32:51 it is breaking faith with God and not holding Him in reverence before the people. Israel was also blamed for his sin (Deut. 1:37; Ps. 106:32). Certainly Moses and Aaron did not doubt God's power, but, perhaps fearing a revolt of the proportions and nature of the one in chapter 14, they were asserting themselves before the people.

🔑 **20:17** "King's highway." This was the direct road from the Gulf of Aqabah to Syria on the east side of the Dead Sea and Jordan valley. Its entire length has been a rich mine of archeological information for modern scholars. Ruins found there indicate that it was in use as early as the twenty-third century B.C. During Solomon's reign it was part of the commercial trade route from Ezion-geber to Judah and Syria. Recovered Roman milestones indicate that Trajan had used part of it in his road system in the second century A.D. Today a modern highway covers a part of that route.

🔑 **20:23-39** See note on Num. 13:26.

house[1004] of Israel wept for Aaron thirty
[a]days.[3117]

Arad Conquered

21 When the Canaanite, the king[4428]
of [a]Arad, who lived in the
[I]Negev, heard[8085] that Israel was coming
by the way[1870] of [II]Atharim, then he
fought against Israel, and took some of
them captive.[7628]
2 So [a]Israel made a vow[5088] to the
LORD, and said,[559] "If Thou wilt indeed
deliver this people[5971] into my hand,[3027]
then I will [I]utterly destroy[2763] their cities."
3 And the LORD heard[8085] the voice
of Israel, and delivered up the Canaanites; then they [I]utterly destroyed[2763]
them and their cities. Thus the name
of the place was called[7121] [II][a]Hormah.
🔑4 Then they set out from Mount
Hor by the way of the [I]Red Sea, to
[a]go around the land of Edom; and the
[II]people[5315,7971] became impatient[7114] because of the journey.
5 And the people spoke[1696] against
God[430] and Moses, "[a]Why have you
brought[5927] us up out of Egypt to die[4191]
in the wilderness? For there is no
[I]food and no water, and [II][b]we loathe[6973]
this miserable food."

The Bronze Serpent

6 [a]And the LORD sent fiery[8314] serpents[5175] among the people and [b]they
bit the people, so that [c]many people
of Israel died.

29 [a]Gen. 1:5; 50:3, 10; Deut. 34:8

1 [I]I.e., South country [II]Or, *the spies* [a]Num. 33:40; Josh. 12:14; Judg. 1:16

2 [I]Lit., *devote to destruction* [a]Gen. 28:20; Judg. 11:30

3 [I]Lit., *devoted to destruction* [II]I.e., a devoted thing; or, Destruction [a]Num. 14:45

4 [I]Lit., *Sea of Reeds* [II]Lit., *soul of the people was short* [a]Deut. 2:8

5 [I]Lit., *bread* [II]Lit., *our soul loathes* [a]Num. 14:2, 3 [b]Num. 11:6

6 [a]Deut. 8:15 [b]Jer. 8:17 [c]1Cor. 10:9

7 [a]Num. 11:2; Ps. 78:34; Is. 26:16; Hos. 5:15 [b]Ex. 8:8; 1Sam. 12:19; Acts 8:24

8 [I]Lit., *Make for yourself* [a]Is. 14:29; 30:6; John 3:14

9 [a]2Kin. 18:4; John 3:14, 15

10 [a]Num. 33:43, 44

11 [I]Lit., *sunrise*

12 [I]I.e., a dry ravine except during rainy season [a]Num. 33:45

13 [a]Num. 22:36; Judg. 11:18

15 [a]Num. 21:28; Deut. 2:9, 18, 29

7 [a]So the people came to Moses and
said, "We have sinned,[2398] because we
have spoken[1696] against the LORD and
you; [b]intercede[6419] with the LORD, that
He may remove the serpents from us."
And Moses interceded[6419] for the people.
8 Then the LORD said to Moses,
"[I]Make[6213] a [a]fiery *serpent,* and set[7760]
it on a standard; and it shall come about,
that everyone who is bitten, when he
looks[7200] at it, he shall live."[2425]
9 And Moses made[6213] a [a]bronze
serpent[5175] and set it on the standard;
and it came about, that if a serpent bit
any man,[376] when he looked to the
bronze serpent, he lived.[2425]
10 [a]Now the sons[1121] of Israel
moved out and camped in Oboth.
11 And they journeyed from Oboth,
and camped at Iyeabarim, in the wilderness which is opposite Moab, to the
[I]east.
12 [a]From there they set out and
camped in [I]Wadi Zered.
13 From there they journeyed and
camped on the other side of the Arnon, which is in the wilderness that
comes out of the border of the Amorites, [a]for the Arnon is the border
of Moab, between Moab and the Amorites.
14 Therefore it is said in the
Book[5612] of the Wars of the LORD,
"Waheb in Suphah,
And the wadis of the Arnon,
15 And the slope of the wadis
That extends to the site
of [a]Ar,

🔑 **21:4-9** From a Christian perspective, this is one of the most important incidents in the Pentateuch, but it had a far-reaching influence upon Israel herself. In commanding a bronze serpent to be made, God made an exception to the second of the Ten Commandments, which forbade the making of an image of any creature found on the earth (Ex. 20:4). The reason for this law is graphically illustrated by the fact that hundreds of years later this bronze serpent was being worshiped as a religious object (II Kgs. 18:4). In the N.T., Paul made a brief historical reference to the fact that God had sent serpents to punish Israel (I Cor. 10:9), but the principal allusion to the incident comes from the lips of Jesus Himself. In His conversation with Nicodemus, Jesus likened His being lifted up on the cross to Moses' lifting up of the serpent in the wilderness (Jn. 3:14). Much of the significance of this lies in the fact that this reference to Moses and the bronze serpent brought about the most famous statement in the N.T., Jn. 3:16, the golden text of the Bible. At least one of the church fathers carried the imagery even further than Jesus did. Since it would be necessary to have a crossbeam in order to support a snake, he saw in the pole itself an allegorical reference to the cross.

And leans[8172] to the border of
Moab."
16 [a]And from there *they continued*
to [I]Beer, that is the well where the LORD
said to Moses, "Assemble[622] the people,
that I may give them water."
17 [a]Then Israel sang[7891] this
song:[7892]

"Spring[5927] up, O well! Sing
to it!
18 "The well, which the leaders[8269]
sank,
Which the nobles[5081] of the
people dug,
With the scepter[2710] *and* with
their staffs."

And from the wilderness *they continued*
to Mattanah,
19 and from Mattanah to Nahaliel,
and from Nahaliel to Bamoth,
20 and from Bamoth to the valley
that is in the land[7704] of Moab, at the
top[7718] of Pisgah which overlooks the
[I]wasteland.

Two Victories

21 [a]Then Israel sent messengers[4397] to Sihon, king of the Amorites,
saying,
22 "[a]Let me pass through[5674] your
land. We will not turn off into field[7704]
or vineyard; we will not drink water from
wells. We will go by the king's[4428] highway until we have passed through your
border."
23 [a]But Sihon would not permit Israel to pass through his border. So Sihon
gathered all his people and went out
against Israel in the wilderness, and
came to [b]Jahaz and fought against Israel.
24 Then [a]Israel [I]struck[5221] him with
the edge[6310] of the sword,[2719] and took
possession[3423] of his land from the Arnon
to the Jabbok, as far as the sons of Ammon; for the [b]border of the sons of Ammon *was* [II]Jazer.
25 And Israel took all these cities
and [a]Israel lived in all the cities of the
Amorites, in Heshbon, and in all her
[I]villages.

16 [I]I.e., a well [a]Num. 33:46-49

17 [a]Ex. 15:1; Ps. 105:2

20 [I]Or, *Jeshimon*

21 [a]Deut. 2:26-37; Judg. 11:19

22 [a]Num. 20:16, 17

23 [a]Num. 20:21 [b]Deut. 2:32

24 [I]Lit., *smote*, so with Gr. and Lat. [II]M.T. reads *strong* [a]Amos 2:9 [b]Deut. 2:37

25 [I]Lit., *daughters* [a]Amos 2:10

28 [I]Lit., *lords of the* [II]Or, *Bamoth* [a]Jer. 48:45 [b]Num. 21:15 [c]Num. 22:41; Is. 15:2; 16:12

29 [a]Jer. 48:46 [b]Judg. 11:24; 1Kin. 11:33; 2Kin. 23:13 [c]Is. 15:5 [d]Is. 16:2

30 [a]Num. 32:3, 34; Jer. 48:18, 22

32 [a]Num. 32:1, 3, 35; Jer. 48:32

33 [I]Lit., *he and* [a]Deut. 3:1-7 [b]Josh. 13:12

34 [a]Deut. 3:2

35 [I]Lit., *smote* [a]Deut. 3:3, 4

26 For Heshbon was the city of Sihon, king of the Amorites, who had
fought against the former king of Moab
and had taken all his land out of his hand,
as far as the Arnon.
27 Therefore those who use proverbs say,[559]

"Come to Heshbon! Let it be
built!
So let the city of Sihon be
established.[3559]
28 "[a]For a fire went forth from
Heshbon,
A flame from the town of Sihon;
It devoured [b]Ar of Moab,
The [I][c]dominant [II]heights[1116] of
the Arnon.
29 "[a]Woe to you, O Moab!
You are ruined, O people of
[b]Chemosh!
[c]He has given his sons[1121] as
fugitives,
[d]And his daughters into
captivity,[7628]
To an Amorite king, Sihon.
30 "But we have cast them
down,[3384]
Heshbon is ruined[6] as far as
[a]Dibon,
Then we have laid waste[8074]
even to Nophah,
Which *reaches* to Medeba."

31 Thus Israel lived in the land of
the Amorites.
32 And Moses sent to spy out
[a]Jazer, and they captured its villages and
dispossessed the Amorites who *were*
there.
33 [a]Then they turned and went
up[5927] by the way of Bashan, and Og
the king of Bashan went out [I]with all
his people, for battle at [b]Edrei.
34 But the LORD said to Moses,
"[a]Do not fear[3372] him, for I have given
him into your hand, and all his people
and his land; and you shall do[6213] to him
as you did to Sihon, king of the Amorites,
who lived at Heshbon."
35 So [a]they [I]killed him and his sons
and all his people, until there was no
remnant left[7604] him; and they possessed
his land.

Balak Sends for Balaam

22 [a]Then the sons[1121] of Israel journeyed, and camped in the plains[6160] of Moab beyond the Jordan *opposite* Jericho.

2 Now [a]Balak the son[1121] of Zippor saw[7200] all that Israel had done[6213] to the Amorites.

3 [a]So Moab was in great fear[1481] because of the people,[5971] for they were numerous; and Moab was in dread[6973] of the sons of Israel.

4 And Moab said[559] to the elders[2205] of [a]Midian, "Now this [I]horde[6951] will lick up all that is around us, as the ox licks up the grass of the field."[7704] And Balak the son of Zippor was king[4428] of Moab at that time.[6256]

🗝 5 So he sent messengers[4397] to [a]Balaam the son of Beor, at [b]Pethor, which is near the [I]River, *in* the land of the sons of his people, to call[7121] him, saying, "Behold, a people came out of Egypt; behold, they cover[3680] the surface of the land,[776] and they are living opposite me.

6 "[a]Now, therefore, please[4994] come, [b]curse[779] this people for me since they are too [I]mighty for me; perhaps[194] I may be able to [II]defeat[5221] them and drive them out of the land. For I know[3045] that he whom you bless is blessed,[1288] and he whom you curse[779] is cursed."[779]

7 So the elders of Moab and the elders of Midian departed with the *fees for* [a]divination[7081] in their hand;[3027] and they came to Balaam and [I]repeated[1696] Balak's words[1697] to him.

8 And he said to them, "Spend the night[3915] here, and I will bring word[1697] back to you as the LORD may speak[1696] to me." And the leaders[8269] of Moab stayed with Balaam.

9 Then [a]God[430] came to Balaam and said, "Who are these men[582] with you?"

10 And Balaam said to God, "Balak the son of Zippor, king of Moab, has sent *word* to me,

11 'Behold, there is a people who came out of Egypt and they cover[3680] the surface of the land; now come, curse[6895] them for me; perhaps I may be able to fight against them, and drive them out.' "

12 And God said to Balaam, "Do not go with them; [a]you shall not curse the people; for they [b]are blessed."

13 So Balaam arose in the morning and said to Balak's leaders, "Go back to your land, for the LORD has refused[3985] to let me go with you."

14 And the leaders of Moab arose and went to Balak, and said, "Balaam refused to come with us."

15 Then Balak again sent leaders, more numerous and more distinguished[3513] than [I]the former.

16 And they came to Balaam and said to him, "Thus says Balak the son of Zippor, 'Let nothing, I beg you, hinder you from coming to me;

17 for I will indeed honor[3513] you richly, and I will do[6213] whatever you say[1697] to me. [a]Please come then, curse this people for me.' "

1 [a]Num. 33:48, 49

2 [a]Judg. 11:25

3 [a]Ex. 15:15

4 [I]Lit., *assembly* [a]Num. 25:15-18; 31:1-3

5 [I]I.e., Euphrates [a]Josh. 24:9; 2Pet. 2:15f.; Jude 11 [b]Deut. 23:4

6 [I]Or, *numerous* [II]Lit., *smite* [a]Num. 22:17; 23:7, 8 [b]Num. 22:12; 24:9

7 [I]Lit., *spoke* [a]Num. 23:23; 24:1; Josh. 13:22

9 [a]Gen. 20:3

12 [a]Num. 23:8; 24:9 [b]Gen. 12:2; 22:17

15 [I]Lit., *these*

17 [a]Num. 22:6

🗝 **22:5—24:25** Balaam was from the town of Pethor on the Euphrates river in Mesopotamia, some distance from Moab where king Balak begged him to come and place a curse upon Israel for fear that the Israelites would annihilate his people along with the Midianites. Though a diviner, Balaam recognized the Lord as real, but perhaps as only one of a number of gods. At first Balaam obeyed God's refusal to let him come but later, in light of the abundance of gifts offered by Moab and Midian, decided to come. He continually refused to curse Israel because of his fear of the Lord, but instead pronounced blessings upon them. However, in the end he gave evil counsel to Balak, pointing out how he could lead them into sexual immorality and idolatry, thus bringing about their downfall. In chapter 25 Israel was instructed to take revenge on Midian. When this judgment was later carried out in chapter 31 Balaam, for his part in the plot against Israel, suffered a most dishonorable death as a warning to future generations. In fact, two N.T. writers inform us that Balaam was an example of one who would do wrong for personal gain (II Pet. 2:15; Jude 11). John said that Balaam was an example of one who taught others how to sin (Rev. 2:14).

18 And Balaam answered and said to the servants[5650] of Balak, "[a]Though Balak were to give me his house[1004] full of silver and gold, I could not do anything, either small or great, contrary[5674] to the [I]command of the LORD my God.

19 "And now please, you also stay here tonight, and I will find out[3045] what else the LORD will speak[1696] to me."

20 And God came to Balaam at night and said to him, "If the men have come to call you, rise up *and* go with them; but [a]only the word which I speak to you shall you do."

21 [a]So Balaam arose in the morning, and saddled[2280] his donkey, and went with the leaders of Moab.

The Angel and Balaam

22 But God was angry[639] because he was going, [a]and the angel[4397] of the LORD took his stand in the way[1870] as an adversary[7854] against him. Now he was riding on his donkey and his two servants were with him.

23 When the donkey saw the angel of the LORD standing[5324] in the way with his drawn sword[2719] in his hand, the donkey turned off from the way and went into the field; but Balaam struck[5221] the donkey to turn her back into the way.

24 Then the angel of the LORD stood in a narrow path of the vineyards, *with* a wall on this side and a wall on that side.

25 When the donkey saw the angel of the LORD, she pressed herself to the wall and pressed Balaam's foot against the wall, so he struck her again.

26 And the angel of the LORD went further, and stood in a narrow place where there was no way to turn to the right hand or the left.

27 When the donkey saw the angel of the LORD, she lay down under Balaam; so [a]Balaam was angry and struck the donkey with his stick.

28 And [a]the LORD opened the mouth[6310] of the donkey, and she said to Balaam, "What have I done to you, that you have struck[5221] me these three times?"

29 Then Balaam said to the donkey, "Because you have made a mockery of me! If there had been a sword in my hand, [a]I would have killed[2026] you by now."

30 And the donkey said[559] to Balaam, "Am I not your donkey on which you have ridden all your life to this day?[3117] Have I ever been accustomed[5532] to do so to you?" And he said, "No."

31 Then the LORD opened the eyes of Balaam, and he saw [a]the angel of the LORD standing in the way with his drawn sword in his hand; and he bowed [I]all the way to the ground.[7812,639,6911]

32 And the angel of the LORD said to him, "Why have you struck your donkey these three times? Behold, I have come out as an adversary,[7854] because your way was [Ia]contrary to me.

33 "But the donkey saw me and turned aside from me these three times. If she had not turned aside from me, I would surely have killed[2026] you just now, and let her live."

34 And Balaam said to the angel of the LORD, "[a]I have sinned,[2398] for I did not know[3045] that you were standing[5324] in the way against me. Now then, if it is displeasing to you, I will turn back."

35 But the angel of the LORD said to Balaam, "Go with the men, but [a]you shall speak only the word which I shall [I]tell you." So Balaam went along with the leaders of Balak.

36 When Balak heard[8085] that Balaam was coming, he went out to meet him at the city of Moab, which is on the Arnon border, [I]at the extreme end of the border.

37 Then Balak said to Balaam, "Did I not urgently send to you to call you? Why did you not come to me? Am I really[552] unable to honor you?"

38 So Balaam said to Balak, "Behold, I have come now to you! [a]Am I able to speak anything at all? The word that God puts[7760] in my mouth, that I shall speak."

18 [I]Lit., *mouth* [a]Num. 22:38; 24:13; 1Kin. 22:14; 2Chr. 18:13

20 [a]Num. 22:35; 23:5, 12, 16, 26; 24:13

21 [a]2Pet. 2:15

22 [a]Ex. 23:20

27 [a]James 1:19

28 [a]2Pet. 2:16

29 [a]Prov. 12:10; Matt. 15:19

31 [I]Lit., *and prostrated himself to his face* [a]Josh. 5:13-15

32 [I]Lit., *reckless* [a]2Pet. 2:15

34 [a]Num. 14:40

35 [I]Or, *speak to* [a]Num. 22:20

36 [I]Lit., *which is at*

38 [a]Num. 22:18

39 And Balaam went with Balak, and
they came to Kiriath-huzoth.
40 And Balak sacrificed[2076] oxen and
sheep, and sent *some* to Balaam and
the leaders who were with him.
41 Then it came about in the morning that Balak took Balaam, and
brought[5927] him up to [I][a]the high places[1116]
of Baal; and he saw from there [II]a
[b]portion of the people.

The Prophecies of Balaam

23 Then Balaam said[559] to Balak,
"Build seven altars[4196] for me
here, and prepare[3559] seven bulls and
seven rams for me here."
2 And Balak did[6213] just as Balaam
had spoken,[1696] and Balak and Balaam
offered[5927] up a bull and a ram on each
altar.[4196]
3 Then Balaam said to Balak, "Stand
beside your burnt offering,[5930] and I will
go; perhaps[194] the LORD will come to
meet me, and whatever He shows me
I will tell[5046] you." So he went to a bare
hill.[8205]
4 Now God[430] met Balaam, and he
said to Him, "I have set up the seven
altars, and I have offered up a bull and
a ram on each altar."
5 Then the LORD [a]put a word[1697]
in Balaam's mouth[6310] and said, "Return[7725] to Balak, and you shall speak[1696]
thus."
6 So he returned[7725] to him, and behold, he was standing[5324] beside his
burnt offering,[5930] he and all the leaders[8269] of Moab.
7 And he took up his [I]discourse and
said,

"From [a]Aram Balak has
brought[5148] me,
Moab's king[4428] from the
mountains of the East,
'[b]Come curse[779] Jacob for me,
And come, denounce[2194] Israel!'

8 "[a]How shall I curse, whom God[410]
has not cursed?[6895]
And how can I denounce, whom
the LORD has not
denounced?[2194]

9 "As I see him from the top[7218]
of the rocks,
And I look at him from the hills;
[a]Behold, a people[5971] *who* dwells
apart,
And shall not be reckoned[2803]
among the nations.[1471]
10 "[a]Who can count the dust[6083] of
Jacob,
Or number the fourth part of
Israel?
[b]Let [I]me die[4191] the death[4194] of
the upright,
[c]And let my end[319] be like
his!"

11 Then Balak said to Balaam,
"What have you done[6213] to me?
[a]I took you to curse[6895] my enemies,
but behold, you have actually blessed[1288]
them!"
12 And he answered and said,
"Must I not be careful to speak [a]what
the LORD puts in my mouth?"
13 Then Balak said to him,
"Please[4994] come with me to another
place from where you may see them,
although you will only see the extreme
end of them, and will not see all of them;
and curse them for me from there."
14 So he took him to the field[7704]
of Zophim, to the top of Pisgah, and
built seven altars and offered a bull and
a ram on *each* altar.
15 And he said to Balak, "Stand here
beside your burnt offering, while I myself meet *the LORD* yonder."
16 Then the LORD met Balaam and
[a]put a word in his mouth and said,
"Return[7725] to Balak, and thus you shall
speak."[1696]
17 And he came to him, and behold,
he was standing beside his burnt offering, and the leaders of Moab with him.
And Balak said to him, "What has the
LORD spoken?"
18 Then he took up[5375] his [I]dis-
course and said,

"Arise, O Balak, and hear;[8085]
Give ear to me, O son[1121] of
Zippor!
19 "[a]God is not a man,[376] that He
should lie,[3576]

41 [I]Or, *Bamoth-baal* [II]Lit., *the end of the camp* [a]Num. 21:28 [b]Num. 23:13

5 [a]Num. 22:20; Deut. 18:18; Jer. 1:9

7 [I]Lit., *parable* [a]Num. 22:5; Deut. 23:4 [b]Num. 22:6

8 [a]Num. 22:12

9 [a]Deut. 32:8; 33:28

10 [I]Lit., *my soul* [a]Gen. 13:16; 28:14 [b]Is. 57:1 [c]Ps. 37:37

11 [a]Neh. 13:2

12 [a]Num. 22:20

16 [a]Num. 22:20

18 [I]Lit., *parable*

19 [a]1Sam. 15:29

Nor a son of man,[120] that He
should repent;[5162]
[b]Has He said, and will He not
do[6213] it?
Or has He spoken, and will He
not make it good?
20 "Behold, I have received *a*
command to bless;[1288]
[a]When He has blessed, then
[b]I cannot revoke[7725] it.
21 "[a]He has not observed
[I]misfortune[205] in Jacob;
[b]Nor has He seen[7200] trouble[5999]
in Israel;
[c]The LORD his God is with him,
[d]And the shout of a king is among
them.
22 "[a]God brings them out of Egypt,
He is for them like the
[b]horns of the wild ox.
23 "[a]For there is no omen[5172] against
Jacob,
Nor is there any divination[7081]
against Israel;
At the proper time it shall be
said to Jacob
And to Israel, what God has
done.
24 "[a]Behold, a people rises like a
lioness,
And as a lion it lifts itself;
It shall not lie down until it
devours the prey,
And drinks the blood[1818] of the
slain."[2491]

25 Then Balak said to Balaam, "Do
not curse them at all nor bless them
at all!"
26 But Balaam answered and said
to Balak, "Did I not tell you, '[I][a]Whatever
the LORD speaks, that I must do'?"
27 Then Balak said to Balaam,
"Please come, I will take you to another
place; perhaps it will be [I]agreeable[3477]
with God that you curse them for me
from there."
28 So Balak took Balaam to the top
of Peor which overlooks the [I]wasteland.
29 And Balaam said to Balak, "Build
seven altars for me here and prepare
seven bulls and seven rams for me
here."
30 And Balak did just as Balaam had
said, and offered up a bull and a ram
on *each* altar.

The Prophecy from Peor

24 When Balaam saw[7200] that it
[I]pleased[2895] the LORD to bless[1288]
Israel, he did not go as at other times
to [II]seek [a]omens[5172] but he set his face
toward the [b]wilderness.
2 And Balaam lifted up his eyes and
saw Israel [I]camping[7931] tribe by tribe;[7626]
and [a]the Spirit[7307] of God[430] came upon
him.
3 And he took up his [I]discourse and
said,[559]
"[a]The oracle of Balaam the son[1121]
of Beor,
And the oracle of the man whose
eye is opened;
4 The oracle of him who
[a]hears[8085] the [I]words[561] of
God,[410]
Who sees[2372] the [b]vision[4236] of
[II]the Almighty,[7706]
Falling down, yet having his eyes
uncovered,[1540]
5 How fair[2896] are your tents,[168]
O Jacob,
Your dwellings,[4908] O Israel!
6 "Like [I]valleys that stretch out,
Like gardens beside the river,
Like [a]aloes[174] planted by the
LORD,
Like [b]cedars beside the waters.
7 "Water shall flow from his
buckets,
And his seed[2233] *shall be* by many
waters,
And his king[4428] shall be higher
than [a]Agag,
[b]And his kingdom[4438] shall be
exalted.[5375]

19 [b]Is. 40:8; 55:11
20 [a]Gen. 12:2; 22:17; Num. 22:12 [b]Is. 43:13
21 [I]Or, *iniquity* [a]Num. 14:18, 19, 34; Ps. 32:2, 5 [b]Deut. 9:24; 32:5; Jer. 50:20 [c]Ex. 3:12; Deut. 31:23 [d]Deut. 33:5; Ps. 89:15-18
22 [a]Num. 24:8 [b]Deut. 33:17
23 [a]Num. 22:7; 24:1; Josh. 13:22
24 [a]Gen. 49:9; Nah. 2:11, 12
26 [I]Lit., *saying, Whatever* [a]Num. 22:18
27 [I]Lit., *right in the sight of God*
28 [I]Or, *Jeshimon*
1 [I]Lit., *was good in the eyes of* [II]Lit., *encounter* [a]Num. 22:7; 23:23 [b]Num. 23:28
2 [I]Lit., *dwelling* [a]Num. 11:26; 1Sam. 19:20; Rev. 1:10
3 [I]Lit., *parable,* and so throughout the ch. [a]Num. 24:15, 16
4 [I]Lit., *sayings* [II]Heb., *Shaddai* [a]Num. 22:20 [b]Gen. 15:1; Num. 12:6
6 [I]Or possibly, *palm trees* [a]Ps. 45:8 [b]Ps. 1:3
7 [a]Num. 24:20; 1Sam. 15:8 [b]Ps. 145:11-13

24:7 Agag was a general title given to the Amalekite kings, just as Pharaoh was the general title for a king in Egypt. Since the Amalekites were the very first to oppose Israel after they left Egypt (Ex. 17:8), they represent the non-Jewish kingdoms in opposition to God's kingdom.

8 "[a]God brings him out of Egypt,
He is for him like the horns of the wild ox.
[b]He shall devour the nations[1471] *who are* his adversaries,
And shall crush their bones[6106] in pieces,
And shatter[4272] *them* with his [c]arrows.
9 "[a]He [I]couches,[3766] he lies down as a lion,
And as a [II]lion, who [III]dares rouse him?
[b]Blessed[1288] is everyone who blesses[1288] you,
And cursed[779] is everyone who curses[779] you."
10 Then Balak's anger[639] burned[2734]
against Balaam, and he struck[5606] his
[I]hands[3709] together; and Balak said to
Balaam, "I called[7121] you to curse[6895]
my enemies, but behold, you have
persisted in blessing them these three
times!
11 "Therefore, [I]flee to your place
now. I said[559] I would honor[3515] you
greatly, but behold, the LORD has held
you back from honor."[3519]
12 And Balaam said[1696] to Balak,
"[a]Did I not tell your messengers[4397]
whom you had sent to me, saying,
13 'Though Balak were to give me
his house[1004] full of silver and gold, I
could not do anything contrary[5674] to the
[I]command[6310] of the LORD, either
good[2896] or bad,[7451] [a]of my own
[II]accord.[3820] [b]What the LORD speaks,[1696]
that I will speak'?[1696]
14 "And now behold, [a]I am going
to my people;[5971] come, *and* I will
advise[3289] you what this people will do
to your people in the [I]days[3117] to
come."[319]
15 And he took up his discourse and
said,
"[a]The oracle of Balaam the son of Beor,
And the oracle of the man whose eye is opened,
16 The oracle of him who hears the [I]words of God,
And knows[3045] the knowledge[1847] of the [II]Most High,[5945]
Who sees the vision of [III]the Almighty,
Falling down, yet having his eyes uncovered.
17 "I see him, but not now;
I behold him, but not near;
A star shall come forth from Jacob,
[a]And a scepter[7626] shall rise from Israel,
[b]And shall crush[4272] through the [I]forehead of Moab,
And [II]tear down all the sons[1121] of [III]Sheth.
18 "[a]And Edom shall be a possession,[3424]
[b]Seir, its enemies, also shall be a possession,
While Israel performs valiantly.[2428]
19 "One from Jacob shall have dominion,[7287]
And shall destroy[6] the remnant[8300] from the city."
20 And he looked[7200] at Amalek and
took up his discourse and said,
"Amalek was the first[7225] of the nations,
[a]But his end[5703] *shall be* [I]destruction."[8]
21 And he looked at the [a]Kenite,
and took up his discourse and said,
"Your dwelling place is enduring,
And your nest is set[7760] in the cliff.
22 "Nevertheless Kain shall be consumed;
How long shall [a]Asshur [I]keep you captive?"[7617]
23 And he took up his discourse and
said,
"Alas, who can live[2421] except God has ordained[6213] it?
24 "But ships *shall come* from the coast of [a]Kittim,
And they shall afflict Asshur and shall afflict [b]Eber;
[c]So they also *shall come* to destruction."
25 Then Balaam arose and departed

---

8 [a]Num. 23:22 [b]Num. 23:24; Ps. 2:9 [c]Ps. 45:5
9 [I]Lit., *bows down* [II]Or, *lioness* [III]Lit., *shall* [a]Gen. 49:9; Num. 23:24 [b]Gen. 12:3; 27:29
10 [I]Lit., *palms*
11 [I]Lit., *flee for yourself*
12 [a]Num. 22:18
13 [I]Lit., *mouth* [II]Lit., *heart* [a]Num. 16:28 [b]Num. 22:20
14 [I]Lit., *end of the days* [a]Num. 31:8, 16; Josh. 13:22
15 [a]Num. 24:3, 4
16 [I]Lit., *sayings* [II]Heb., *Elyon* [III]Heb., *Shaddai*
17 [I]Lit., *corners* [II]Another reading is *the crown of the head of* [III]I.e., tumult [a]Gen. 49:10 [b]Num. 21:29; Is. 15:1-16:14
18 [a]Gen. 27:29; Amos 9:11, 12 [b]Gen. 32:3
20 [I]Lit., *to destroying* [a]Num. 24:24
21 [a]Gen. 15:19
22 [I]Lit., *take* [a]Gen. 10:21, 22
24 [a]Gen. 10:4; Ezek. 27:6 [b]Gen. 10:21 [c]Num. 24:20

and returned[7725] to [a]his place, and Balak
also went his way.[1870]

The Sin of Peor

25 While Israel remained at
[a]Shittim, the people[5971] began
[b]to play the harlot[2181] with the daughters
of Moab.
2 For [a]they invited[7121] the people
to the sacrifices[2077] of their gods,[430] and
the people ate and bowed[7812] down to
their gods.
3 So [a]Israel joined themselves to
[I]Baal of Peor, and the LORD was angry[639]
against Israel.
4 And the LORD said[559] to Moses,
"Take all the leaders[7218] of the people
and execute them [I]in broad daylight before the LORD, [a]so that the fierce anger
of the LORD may turn away from Israel."
5 So Moses said to the judges[8199]
of Israel, "Each[376] of you [a]slay[2026] his
men[582] who have joined themselves to
[I]Baal of Peor."
🔑**6** Then behold, one of the sons[1121]
of Israel came and brought[7126] to his
[I]relatives[251] a [a]Midianite woman, in the
sight of Moses and in the sight of all
the congregation of the sons of Israel,
[b]while they were weeping at the doorway of the tent[168] of meeting.[4150]
7 [a]When Phinehas the son[1121] of
Eleazar, the son of Aaron the priest,[3548]
saw[7200] it, he arose from the midst of
the congregation,[5712] and took a spear
in his hand;[3027]
8 and he went after the man[376] of
Israel into the [I]tent,[6898] and pierced both
of them through, the man of Israel and
the woman,[802] through the [II]body.
[a]So the plague on the sons of Israel was
checked.
9 [a]And those who died by the plague
were 24,000.

The Zeal of Phinehas

10 Then the LORD spoke[1696] to Moses, saying,
11 "[a]Phinehas the son of Eleazar,
the son of Aaron the priest, has turned
away My wrath[2534] from the sons of Israel, in that he was jealous[7065] with My
jealousy[7068] among them, so that I did
not destroy[3615] the sons of Israel [b]in
My jealousy.[7068]
12 "Therefore say,[559] '[a]Behold, I
give him My [b]covenant[1285] of peace;[7965]
13 and it shall be for him and his
[I]descendants[2233] after him, a covenant
of a [a]perpetual[5769] priesthood,[3550] because he was jealous for his God,[430] and
[b]made atonement[3722] for the sons of Israel.'"
14 Now the name of the [I]slain man
of Israel who was [I]slain[5221] with the Midianite woman, was Zimri the son of
Salu, a leader[5387] of a father's household[1004] among the Simeonites.
15 And the name of the Midianite
woman who was [I]slain was [a]Cozbi the
daughter of [b]Zur, [II]who was head[7218] of
the people[523] of a father's household in
Midian.
16 Then the LORD spoke to Moses,
saying,
17 "[a]Be hostile[6887] to the Midianites
and strike[5221] them;
18 for they have been hostile to you
with their tricks, with which they have
deceived you in the affair[1697] of Peor,
and in the affair of Cozbi, the daughter
of the leader of Midian, their sister[269]
who was slain on the day[3117] of the
plague because of Peor."

Census of a New Generation

26 🔑[I]Then it came about after the
[a]plague, [II]that the LORD spoke[559]
to Moses and to Eleazar the son[1121] of
Aaron the priest,[3548] saying,
2 "[a]Take[5375] a [I]census[7218] of all the
congregation[5712] of the sons[1121] of Israel
from twenty years old[1121] and upward,
by their fathers'[1] households,[1004] whoever is able to go out to war[6635] in Israel."

25 [a]Num. 24:14

1 [a]Num. 33:49; Josh. 2:1 [b]Num. 31:16; 1Cor. 10:8; Rev. 2:14

2 [a]Ex. 34:15; Deut. 32:38

3 [I]Or, *Baal-peor* [a]Ps. 106:28, 29; Hos. 9:10

4 [I]Lit., *in front of the sun* [a]Deut. 13:17

5 [I]Or, *Baal-peor* [a]Ex. 32:27

6 [I]Lit., *brothers* [a]Num. 22:4 [b]Joel 2:17

7 [a]Ps. 106:30

8 [I]Or, *inner rooms* [II]Or, *belly* [a]Num. 16:46-48

9 [a]Num. 14:37; 16:48-50; 31:16

11 [a]Ps. 106:30 [b]Ex. 20:5

12 [a]Ps. 106:30, 31 [b]Is. 54:10; Ezek. 34:25; 37:26

13 [I]Lit., *seed* [a]Ex. 29:9 [b]Num. 16:46

14 [I]Lit., *smitten*

15 [I]Lit., *smitten* [II]Lit., *he* [a]Num. 25:18 [b]Num. 31:8

17 [a]Num. 25:1; 22:4; 31:1-3

1 [I]Ch. 25:19 in Heb. [II]Ch. 26:1 in Heb. [a]Num. 25:9

2 [I]Lit., *sum* [a]Ex. 30:11-16; 38:25, 26; Num. 1:2

🔑**25:6-13** See note on Ex. 32:25-29.
🔑**26:1-51** See note on Num. 1:2.

3 So Moses and Eleazar the priest spoke[1696] with them [a]in the plains[6160] of Moab by the Jordan at Jericho, saying,

4 "*Take a census of the people* from twenty years old and upward, as the LORD has commanded[6680] Moses."

Now the sons of Israel who came out of the land of Egypt *were:*

5 Reuben, Israel's first-born, the sons of Reuben: *of* Hanoch, the family[4940] of the Hanochites; of Pallu, the family of the Palluites;

6 of Hezron, the family[4940] of the Hezronites; of Carmi, the family of the Carmites.

7 These are the families[4940] of the Reubenites, and those who were numbered[6485] of them were [a]43,730.

8 And the son[1121] of Pallu: Eliab.

9 And the sons of Eliab: Nemuel and Dathan and Abiram. These are the Dathan and Abiram who were [a]called[7121] by the congregation, who contended against Moses and against Aaron in the company[5712] of Korah, when they contended against the LORD,

10 and [a]the earth[776] opened its mouth[6310] and swallowed them up along with Korah, when that company died,[4194] [b]when the fire devoured 250 men,[376] so that they became a [I]warning.

11 [a]The sons of Korah, however, did not die.

12 The sons of Simeon according to their families: of [I]Nemuel, the family of the Nemuelites; of Jamin, the family of the Jaminites; of [II]Jachin, the family of the Jachinites;

13 of [I]Zerah, the family of the Zerahites; of Shaul, the family of the Shaulites.

14 These are the families of the Simeonites, [a]22,200.

15 The sons of Gad according to their families: of [I]Zephon, the family of the Zephonites; of Haggi, the family of the Haggites; of Shuni, the family of the Shunites;

16 of [I]Ozni, the family of the Oznites; of Eri, the family of the Erites;

17 of [I]Arod, the family of the Arodites; of Areli, the family of the Arelites.

18 These are the families of the sons of Gad according to those who were numbered of them, [a]40,500.

19 The [a]sons of Judah *were* Er and Onan, but Er and Onan died in the land of Canaan.

20 And the [a]sons of Judah according to their families were: of Shelah, the family of the Shelanites; of Perez, the family of the Perezites; of Zerah, the family of the Zerahites.

21 And the sons of Perez were: of Hezron, the family of the Hezronites; of Hamul, the family of the Hamulites.

22 These are the families of Judah according to those who were numbered of them, [a]76,500.

23 The [a]sons of Issachar according to their families: *of* Tola, the family of the Tolaites; of [I]Puvah, the family of the Punites;

24 of [I]Jashub, the family of the Jashubites; of Shimron, the family of the Shimronites.

25 These are the families of Issachar according to those who were numbered of them, [a]64,300.

26 The [a]sons of Zebulun according to their families: of Sered, the family of the Seredites; of Elon, the family of the Elonites; of Jahleel, the family of the Jahleelites.

27 These are the families of the Zebulunites according to those who were numbered of them, [a]60,500.

28 The [a]sons of Joseph according to their families: Manasseh and Ephraim.

29 The sons of Manasseh: of Machir, the family of the Machirites; and [a]Machir [I]became the father of Gilead: of Gilead, the family of the Gileadites.

30 These are the sons of Gilead: *of* [I]Iezer, the family of the [a]Iezerites; of Helek, the family of the Helekites;

31 and *of* Asriel, the family of the Asrielites; and *of* Shechem, the family of the Shechemites;

32 and *of* Shemida, the family of the Shemidaites; and *of* Hepher, the family of the Hepherites.

33 Now Zelophehad the son of

---

3 [a]Num. 22:1; 33:48; 35:1
7 [a]Num. 1:21
9 [a]Num. 1:16; 16:2
10 [I]Lit., *sign* [a]Num. 16:32 [b]Num. 16:35, 38
11 [a]Num. 16:27, 33; Deut. 24:16
12 [I]In Gen. 46:10 and Ex. 6:15, *Jemuel* [II]In 1Chr. 4:24, *Jarib*
13 [I]In Gen. 46:10, *Zohar*
14 [a]Num. 1:23
15 [I]In Gen. 46:16, *Ziphion*
16 [I]In Gen. 46:16, *Ezbon*
17 [I]In Gen. 46:16, *Arodi*
18 [a]Num. 1:25
19 [a]Gen. 38:2; 46:12
20 [a]Gen. 49:8; 1Chr. 2:3; Rev. 7:5
22 [a]Num. 1:27
23 [I]In Gen. 46:13, *Puvvah;* in 1Chr. 7:1, *Puah* [a]Gen. 46:13; 1Chr. 7:1
24 [I]In Gen. 46:13, *Iob*
25 [a]Num. 1:29
26 [a]Gen. 46:14
27 [a]Num. 1:31
28 [a]Gen. 46:20; Deut. 33:16f.
29 [I]Lit., *begot* [a]Josh. 17:1; 1Chr. 7:14f.
30 [I]In Josh. 17:2, *Abiezer* [a]Judg. 6:11, 24, 34

Hepher had no sons, but only daughters; and [a]the names of the daughters of Zelophehad were Mahlah, Noah, Hoglah, Milcah and Tirzah.

34 These are the families of Manasseh; and those who were numbered of them were [a]52,700.

35 These are the sons of Ephraim according to their families: of Shuthelah, the family of the Shuthelahites; of [I]Becher, the family of the Becherites; of Tahan, the family of the Tahanites.

36 And these are the sons of Shuthelah: of Eran, the family of the Eranites.

37 These are the families of the sons[1121] of Ephraim according to those who were numbered of them, [a]32,500. These are the sons of Joseph according to their families.

38 The sons of Benjamin according to their families: of Bela, the family of the Belaites; of Ashbel, the family of the Ashbelites; of [I]Ahiram, the family of the Ahiramites;

39 of [I]Shephupham, the family of the Shuphamites; of [II]Hupham, the family of the Huphamites.

40 And the sons of Bela were [I]Ard and Naaman: *of Ard,* the family of the Ardites; of Naaman, the family of the Naamites.

41 These are the sons of Benjamin according to their families; and those who were numbered of them were [a]45,600.

42 These are the sons of Dan according to their families: of [I]Shuham, the family of the Shuhamites. These are the families of Dan according to their families.

43 All the families of the Shuhamites, according to those who were numbered of them, were [a]64,400.

44 The [a]sons of Asher according to their families: of Imnah, the family of the Imnites; of Ishvi, the family of the Ishvites; of Beriah, the family of the Beriites.

45 Of the sons of Beriah: of Heber, the family of the Heberites; of Malchiel, the family of the Malchielites.

46 And the name of the daughter of Asher *was* Serah.

47 These are the families of the sons of Asher according to those who were numbered of them, [a]53,400.

48 The [a]sons of Naphtali according to their families: of Jahzeel, the family of the Jahzeelites; of Guni, the family of the Gunites;

49 of Jezer, the family of the Jezerites; of [a]Shillem, the family of the Shillemites.

50 These are the families of Naphtali according to their families; and those who were numbered of them were [a]45,400.

51 These are those who were numbered of the sons of Israel, [a]601,730.

🔑 **52** Then the LORD spoke to Moses, saying,

53 "[I]Among these the land shall be divided for an inheritance[5159] according to the number of names.

54 "[a]To the larger *group* you shall increase their inheritance, and to the smaller *group* you shall diminish their inheritance; each shall be given their inheritance according to those who were numbered of them.

55 "But the land shall be [a]divided by lot. They shall [I]receive their inheritance[5157] according to the names of the tribes[4294] of their fathers.[1]

56 "According to the selection by lot, their inheritance shall be divided between the larger and the smaller *groups.*"

57 And [a]these are those who were numbered of the Levites according to their families: of Gershon, the family of the Gershonites; of Kohath, the family of the Kohathites; of Merari, the family of the Merarites.

58 These are the families of Levi: the family of the Libnites, the family of the Hebronites, the family of the Mahlites, the family of the Mushites, the

33 [a]Num. 27:1
34 [a]Num. 1:35
35 [I]In 1Chr. 7:20, *Bered*
37 [a]Num. 1:33
38 [I]In Gen. 46:21, *Ehi;* in 1Chr. 8:1, *Aharah*
39 [I]In Gen. 46:21, *Muppim;* in 1Chr. 7:12, *Shuppim* [II]In Gen. 46:21, *Muppim* and *Huppim*
40 [I]In 1Chr. 8:3, *Addar*
41 [a]Num. 1:37
42 [I]In Gen. 46:23, *Hushim*
43 [a]Num. 1:39
44 [a]Gen. 46:17; 1Chr. 7:30
47 [a]Num. 1:41
48 [a]Gen. 46:24; 1Chr. 7:13
49 [a]1Chr. 7:13
50 [a]Num. 1:43
51 [a]Ex. 12:37; 38:26; Num. 1:46; 11:21
53 [I]Lit., *To*
54 [a]Num. 33:54
55 [I]Lit., *inherit according to* [a]Num. 33:54; 34:13
57 [a]Gen. 46:11; Ex. 6:16; 1Chr. 6:1, 16

🔑 **26:52-56** See note on Num. 1:2.

family of the Korahites. [a]And Kohath
[I]became the father of Amram.
59 And the name of Amram's wife[802]
[a]was Jochebed, the daughter of Levi,
who was born to Levi in Egypt; and
she bore to Amram: Aaron and Moses
and their sister[269] Miriam.
60 [a]And to Aaron were born Nadab
and Abihu, Eleazar and Ithamar.
61 [a]But Nadab and Abihu died when
they offered[7126] strange[2114] fire before
the LORD.
62 And those who were numbered
of them were [a]23,000, every male[2145]
from a month old and upward, for
[b]they were not numbered among the
sons of Israel [c]since no inheritance was
given to them among the sons of Israel.
63 These are those who were numbered by Moses and Eleazar the priest,
who numbered the sons of Israel in the
plains of Moab by the Jordan at Jericho.
64 [a]But among these there was not
a man[376] of those who were numbered
by Moses and Aaron the priest, who
numbered the sons of Israel in the wilderness of Sinai.
65 For the LORD had said[559] [I]of
them, "[a]They shall surely die[4191] in the
wilderness." And not a man was left[3498]
of them, [b]except Caleb the son of Jephunneh, and Joshua the son of Nun.

A Law of Inheritance

27 Then [a]the daughters of Zelophehad, the son[1121] of Hepher, the
son of Gilead, the son of Machir, the
son of Manasseh, of the families[4940] of
Manasseh the son of Joseph, came near;
and these are [b]the names of his daughters: Mahlah, Noah and Hoglah and Milcah and Tirzah.
2 And they stood before Moses and
before Eleazar the priest[3548] and before
the leaders[5387] and all the congregation,[5712] at the doorway of the tent[168]
of meeting,[4150] saying,
3 "Our father[1] [a]died in the wilderness, yet he was not among the
company[5712] of those who gathered[3259]
themselves together against the LORD
in the company of Korah; but he died
in his own sin,[2399] and [b]he had no
sons.[1121]
4 "Why should the name of our father be withdrawn from among his
family[4940] because he had no son? Give
us a possession[272] among our father's
brothers."[251]
5 [a]And Moses brought[7126] their case
before the LORD.
6 Then the LORD spoke[559] to Moses, saying,
7 "[a]The daughters of Zelophehad
are right in *their* statements.[1696] You
shall surely give them a hereditary[5159]
possession among their father's[1]
brothers, and you shall transfer the inheritance of their father to them.
8 "Further, you shall speak to the
sons[1121] of Israel, saying, 'If a man[376]
dies[4191] and has no son, then you shall
transfer his inheritance to his daughter.
9 'And if he has no daughter, then
you shall give his inheritance to his
brothers.
10 'And if he has no brothers, then
you shall give his inheritance to his father's brothers.
11 'And if his father has no brothers,
then you shall give his inheritance to
his nearest relative[7607] in his own family,
and he shall possess[3423] it; and it shall
be a [a]statutory[2708] ordinance[4941] to the
sons of Israel, just as the LORD commanded[6680] Moses.'"
12 [a]Then the LORD said[559] to Moses, "Go up to this [b]mountain of Abarim,
and see the land which I have given to
the sons of Israel.
13 "And when you have seen[7200] it,
you too [a]shall be gathered[622] to your
people,[5971] [b]as Aaron your brother[251]
[I]was;
14 for in the wilderness of Zin, during the strife of the congregation,
[a]you rebelled[4784] against My [I]com-

58 [I]Lit., *begot* [a]Ex. 6:20
59 [a]Ex. 2:1, 2; 6:20
60 [a]Num. 3:2
61 [a]Lev. 10:1, 2; Num. 3:4
62 [a]Num. 3:39 [b]Num. 1:47 [c]Num. 18:23, 24
64 [a]Num. 14:29-35; Deut. 2:14-16; Heb. 3:17
65 [I]Or, *to* [a]Num. 14:26-35; Ps. 90:3-10; 1Cor. 10:5 [b]Deut. 1:36; Josh. 14:6-10
1 [a]Num. 26:33; 36:1 [b]Num. 26:33
3 [a]Num. 26:64, 65 [b]Num. 26:33
5 [a]Num. 9:8; 27:21
7 [a]Num. 36:2; Josh. 17:4
11 [a]Num. 35:29
12 [a]Deut. 3:23-27; 32:48-52 [b]Num. 33:47, 48
13 [I]Lit., *was gathered* [a]Num. 31:2 [b]Num. 20:24, 28; Deut. 10:6
14 [I]Lit., *mouth* [a]Num. 20:12; Deut. 32:51; Ps. 106:32

26:62 See note on Num. 3:39.
26:64,65 See note on Num. 13:30.

mand[6310] [II]to treat Me as holy[6942] before their eyes at the water." (These are the waters of Meribah of Kadesh in the wilderness of Zin.)

Joshua to Succeed Moses

15 Then Moses spoke[1696] to the LORD, saying,

16 "[a]May the LORD, the God[430] of the spirits[7307] of all flesh,[1320] appoint a man over the congregation,

17 who [a]will go out [I]and come in before them, and who will lead them out and [II]bring them in, that the congregation of the LORD may not be [b]like sheep which have no shepherd."

🗝 18 So the LORD said to Moses, "[I]Take Joshua the son of Nun, a man [a]in whom is the Spirit,[7307] and [b]lay your hand[3027] on him;

19 and have him stand before Eleazar the priest and before all the congregation; and [a]commission[6680] him in their sight.

20 "And you shall put some of your [I]authority[1935] on him, in order that all the congregation of the sons of Israel may obey[8085] *him.*

21 "Moreover, he shall stand before Eleazar the priest, who shall inquire[7592] for him [a]by the judgment of the Urim before the LORD. At his [I]command they shall go out and at his [I]command they shall come in, *both* he and the sons of Israel with him, even all the congregation."

22 And Moses did[6213] just as the LORD commanded him; and he took Joshua and set him before Eleazar the priest, and before all the congregation.

23 Then he laid his hands[3027] on him and [a]commissioned him, just as the LORD had spoken[1696] [I]through Moses.

Laws for Offerings

28 Then the LORD spoke[1696] to Moses, saying,

2 "Command[6680] the sons[1121] of Israel and say[559] to them, 'You shall [I]be careful[8104] to present[7126] My offering, My [a]food for My offerings[7133] by fire, of a soothing aroma to Me, at their appointed time.'[4150]

3 "[a]And you shall say to them, 'This is the offering by fire which you shall offer to the LORD; two male lambs one[1121] year old without defect[8549] *as* a continual[8548] burnt offering[5930] every day.[3117]

4 'You shall offer the one lamb in the morning, and the other lamb you shall offer [I]at twilight;

5 also [a]a tenth of an ephah of fine flour for a [b]grain offering,[4503] mixed[1101] with a fourth of a hin of beaten oil.[8081]

6 'It is a continual burnt offering which was ordained in Mount Sinai as a soothing aroma, an offering by fire[801] to the LORD.

7 'Then the libation[5262] with it *shall be* a fourth of a hin for each lamb, [a]in the holy[6944] place you shall pour[5258] out a libation of strong drink to the LORD.

8 'And the other lamb you shall offer [I]at twilight; as the grain offering of the morning and as its libation, you shall offer it, an offering by fire, a soothing aroma to the LORD.

9 'Then on the sabbath[7676] day two male lambs one year old without defect,

14 [II]Lit., *for My sanctity*
16 [a]Num. 16:22
17 [I]Lit., *before them and who will* [II]Lit., *who will bring* [a]Deut. 31:2; 2Chr. 1:10 [b]1Kin. 22:17; Ezek. 34:5; Matt. 9:36; Mark 6:34
18 [I]Lit., *Take for yourself* [a]Num. 11:25-29; Deut. 34:9 [b]Num. 27:23
19 [a]Deut. 3:28; 31:3, 7, 8, 23
20 [I]Lit., *majesty*
21 [I]Lit., *mouth* [a]Ex. 28:30; 1Sam. 28:6
23 [I]Lit., *by the hand of* [a]Deut. 31:23
2 [I]Lit., *watch* [a]Lev. 3:11
3 [a]Ex. 29:38-42
4 [I]Lit., *between the two evenings*
5 [a]Ex. 16:36; Num. 15:4 [b]Lev. 2:1
7 [a]Ex. 29:42
8 [I]Lit., *between the two evenings*

🗝 **27:18-23** With his death approaching, Moses asked God to choose a successor to lead Israel in his place. God selected Joshua, a man who had been Moses' close associate and servant as far back as when Israel was still at Mount Sinai (Ex. 24:13; 32:17; 33:11). Even before their arrival at Sinai, Moses had appointed Joshua to be the leader of the army against Amalek (Ex. 17:8-13). His public commissioning here in Num. 27 involved more than the role of military leader, but it was in this area that he was to make his greatest mark. Joshua is mentioned by name twice in the N.T. (Acts 7:45; Heb. 4:8), which the K.J.V. unfortunately translated as "Jesus." The basis of the confusion is the fact that "Jesus" is the Greek equivalent of the Hebrew word "Joshua." This correspondence in names was not missed by the church fathers, some of whom saw the O.T. Joshua as a type of Jesus Christ. One of them even found special significance in the fact that Moses renamed Joshua (Num. 13:8,16), believing that this enabled certain of his actions to be interpreted as those of Jesus Himself.

and two-tenths *of an* [I]*ephah* of fine flour mixed with oil as a grain offering, and its libation:

10 '*This is* the burnt offering of every sabbath in addition to the [a]continual burnt offering and its libation.

🗝 **11** 'Then [a]at the beginning[7218] of each of your months you shall present[7126] a burnt offering to the LORD; two [I]bulls and one ram, seven male lambs one year old without defect,

12 [a]and three-tenths *of an* [I]*ephah* of fine flour for a grain offering, mixed with oil, for each bull; and two-tenths of fine flour for a grain offering, mixed with oil, for the one ram;

13 and a tenth *of an* [I]*ephah* of fine flour mixed with oil for a grain offering for each lamb, for a burnt offering of a soothing aroma, an offering by fire to the LORD.

14 'And their libations shall be half a hin of wine for a bull and a third of a hin for the ram and a fourth of a hin for a lamb; this is the burnt offering of each month throughout the months of the year.

15 'And one male[8163] goat for a sin[2403] offering to the LORD; it shall be offered[6213] with its libation in addition to the [a]continual burnt offering.

16 '[a]Then on the fourteenth day of the first[7223] month shall be the LORD's Passover.[6453]

17 'And [a]on the fifteenth day of this month *shall be* a [b]feast, unleavened bread[4682] *shall be* eaten for seven days.[3117]

18 'On the [a]first day *shall be* a holy convocation;[4744] you shall do[6213] no laborious[5656] work.

19 'And you shall present an offering by fire, a burnt offering to the LORD: two [I]bulls and one ram and seven male lambs one year old, [a]having them without defect.[8549]

20 'And for their grain offering, you shall offer fine flour mixed with oil: three-tenths *of an* [I]*ephah* for a bull and two-tenths for the ram.

21 'A tenth *of an* [I]*ephah* you shall offer for [II]each of the seven lambs,

22 and one male goat for a [a]sin offering, to make atonement[3722] for you.

23 'You shall present these besides [a]the burnt offering of the morning, which is for a continual burnt offering.

24 'After this manner you shall present daily,[3117] for seven days, [a]the food of the offering by fire, of a soothing aroma to the LORD; it shall be presented with its libation in addition to the [b]continual burnt offering.

25 'And on the seventh day you shall have a holy convocation; [a]you shall do no laborious work.

26 'Also on [a]the day of the first fruits, when you present[7126] a new grain offering to the LORD in your *Feast of* Weeks, you shall have a holy convocation; [b]you shall do no laborious work.

27 'And you shall offer a burnt offering for a soothing aroma to the LORD, two young bulls, one ram, seven male lambs one year old,

28 and their grain offering, fine flour mixed with oil, three-tenths *of an* [I]*ephah* for each bull, two-tenths for the one ram,

29 a tenth for [I]each of the seven lambs,

30 one male goat to make atonement for you.

31 '[a]Besides the continual burnt offering and its grain offering, you shall present *them* with their libations. They shall be [I]without defect.

9 [I]I.e., Approx. one bu.
10 [a]Num. 28:3
11 [I]Lit., *bulls of the herd* [a]Num. 10:10; Ezek. 46:6, 7
12 [I]I.e., Approx. one bu. [a]Num. 15:4-12
13 [I]I.e., Approx. one bu.
15 [a]Num. 28:3
16 [a]Ex. 12:1-20; Lev. 23:5-8; Deut. 16:1-8
17 [a]Lev. 23:6 [b]Ex. 23:15; 34:18; Deut. 16:3-8
18 [a]Lev. 23:7
19 [I]Or, *bulls of the herd* [a]Deut. 15:21
20 [I]I.e., Approx. one bu.
21 [I]I.e., Approx. one bu. [II]Lit., *each lamb*
22 [a]Lev. 16:18; Rom. 8:3; Gal. 4:4f.
23 [a]Num. 28:3
24 [a]Lev. 3:11 [b]Num. 28:3
25 [a]Num. 28:18
26 [a]Ex. 23:16; 34:22; Lev. 23:15-21; Deut. 16:9-12 [b]Num. 28:18
28 [I]I.e., Approx. one bu.
29 [I]Lit., *each lamb*
31 [I]Lit., *without defect to you* [a]Num. 28:3

🗝 **28:11-15** The reference here is to the observance of the new moon (I Chr. 23:31; Ezra 3:5). Though it was characterized by the blowing of trumpets it is not to be confused with the feast of trumpets (Num. 29:1-6), which was celebrated at the beginning of the seventh month, while this observation was held on the first day of every month. Special sacrifices were offered. It was a time of inquiring of God's messengers and worshiping at God's house, as well as a time for fellowship (I Sam. 20:5,18; II Kgs. 4:23). The observance was one of great solemnity; all business and work was to cease. When Israel began to approach it with insincerity as a mere ritual, God condemned its observance (Isa. 1:13,14).

Offerings of the Seventh Month

29 "[a]Now in the seventh month, on the first day[3117] of the month, you shall also have a holy[6944] convocation;[4744] [b]you shall do[6213] no laborious[5656] work. It will be to you a day for blowing trumpets.

2 'And you shall offer a burnt offering[5930] as a soothing aroma to the LORD: one [I]bull, one ram, *and* seven male lambs one[1121] year old without defect;[8549]

3 also their grain offering,[4503] fine flour mixed[1101] with oil,[8081] three-tenths *of an* [I]*ephah* for the bull, two-tenths for the ram,

4 and one-tenth for [I]each of the seven lambs.

5 'And *offer* one male[8163] goat for a sin[2403] offering, to make atonement[3722] for you,

6 [a]besides the burnt offering of the new moon, and its grain offering, and the [b]continual[8548] burnt offering and its grain offering, and their libations,[5262] according to their ordinance,[4941] for a soothing aroma, an offering by fire[801] to the LORD.

7 'Then on [a]the tenth day of this seventh month you shall have a holy convocation, and you shall humble yourselves;[5315] you shall not do any work.

8 'And you shall present[7126] a burnt offering to the LORD *as* a soothing aroma: one bull, one ram, seven male lambs one year old, [a]having them without defect;

9 and their grain offering, fine flour mixed with oil, three-tenths *of an* [I]*ephah* for the bull, two-tenths for the one ram,

10 a tenth for each of the seven lambs;

11 one male goat for a sin offering, besides [a]the sin offering of atonement and [b]the continual[4744] burnt offering and its grain offering, and their libations.

12 'Then on [a]the fifteenth day of the seventh month you shall have a holy convocation; you [b]shall do no laborious work, and you shall observe a feast to the LORD for seven days.[3117]

13 'And you shall present a burnt offering, an offering by fire as a soothing aroma to the LORD: thirteen bulls, two rams, fourteen male lambs one year old, which are without defect,

14 and their grain offering, fine flour mixed with oil, three-tenths *of an* [I]*ephah* for [II]each of the thirteen bulls, two-tenths for [III]each of the two rams,

15 and a tenth for each of the fourteen lambs;

16 and one male goat for a sin offering, [a]besides the continual burnt offering, its grain offering and its libation.

17 'Then on [a]the second day: twelve bulls, two rams, fourteen male lambs one year old without defect;[8549]

18 and their grain offering and their libations for the bulls, for the rams and for the lambs, by their number [a]according to the ordinance;

19 and one male goat for a sin offering, [a]besides the continual burnt offering and its grain offering, and their libations.

20 'Then on the third day: eleven bulls, two rams, fourteen male lambs one year old without defect;

21 and their grain offering and their libations for the bulls, for the rams and for the lambs, by their number according to the ordinance;

22 and one male goat for a sin offering, besides the continual burnt offering and its grain offering and its libation.

23 'Then on the fourth day: ten bulls, two rams, fourteen male lambs one year old without defect;

24 their grain offering and their libations for the bulls, for the rams and for the lambs, by their number according to the ordinance;

25 and one male goat for a sin offering, besides the continual burnt offering, its grain offering and its libation.

26 'Then on the fifth day: nine bulls, two rams, fourteen male lambs one year old [a]without defect;

27 and their grain offering and their libations for the bulls, for the rams and

---

1 [a]Ex. 23:16; 34:22; Lev. 23:23-25 [b]Num. 28:26
2 [I]Or, *bull of a herd,* and so throughout the ch.
3 [I]I.e., Approx. one bu.
4 [I]Lit., *each lamb,* and so throughout the ch.
6 [a]Num. 28:27 [b]Num. 28:3
7 [a]Lev. 16:29-34; 23:26-32
8 [a]Lev. 22:20; Deut. 15:21; 17:1
9 [I]I.e., Approx. one bu.
11 [a]Lev. 16:3, 5 [b]Num. 28:3
12 [a]Lev. 23:33-35; Deut. 16:13-15 [b]Num. 29:1
14 [I]I.e., Approx. one bu. [II]Lit., *each bull* [III]Lit., *each ram*
16 [a]Num. 28:3
17 [a]Lev. 23:36
18 [a]Lev. 2:1-16
19 [a]Num. 28:8
26 [a]Heb. 7:26

for the lambs, by their number according to the ordinance;

28 and one male goat for a sin offering, besides the continual burnt offering and its grain offering and its libation.

29 'Then on the sixth day: eight bulls, two rams, fourteen male lambs one year old without defect;

30 and their grain offering and their libations for the bulls, for the rams and for the lambs, by their number according to the ordinance;

31 and one male goat for a sin offering, besides the continual burnt offering, its grain offering and its libations.

32 'Then on the seventh day: seven bulls, two rams, fourteen male lambs one year old without defect;

33 and their grain offering and their libations for the bulls, for the rams and for the lambs, by their number according to the ordinance;

34 and one male goat for a sin offering, besides the continual burnt offering, its grain offering and its libation.

35 '[a]On the eighth day you shall have a solemn assembly;[6116] you shall do no laborious work.

36 'But you shall present a burnt offering, an offering by fire, as a soothing aroma to the LORD: one bull, one ram, seven male lambs one year old without defect;

37 their grain offering and their libations for the bull, for the ram and for the lambs, by their number according to the ordinance;

38 and one male goat for a sin offering, besides the continual burnt offering and its grain offering and its libation.

39 'You shall present these to the LORD at your [a]appointed times,[4150] besides your [I]votive offerings[5088] and your freewill offerings,[5071] for your burnt offerings and for your grain offerings[4503] and for your libations and for your peace offerings.' "[8002]

40 [I]And Moses spoke to the sons[1121] of Israel in accordance with all that the LORD had commanded[6680] Moses.

35 [a]Lev. 23:36

39 [I]Lit., *vows* [a]Lev. 23:2

40 [I]Ch. 30:1 in Heb.

1 [a]Num. 1:4, 16; 7:2

2 [a]Deut. 23:21-23; Matt. 5:33

4 [I]Lit., *is silent to her*, and so throughout the ch.

6 [I]Lit., *be to a husband* [II]Lit., *her vows are on her*

8 [I]Lit., *is on her*

The Law of Vows

30 Then Moses spoke[1696] to [a]the heads[7218] of the tribes[4294] of the sons[1121] of Israel, saying, "This is the word[1697] which the LORD has commanded.[6680]

2 "[a]If a man[376] makes[5087] a vow[5088] to the LORD, or takes[7650] an oath[7621] to bind himself[5315] with a binding obligation, he shall not violate[2490] his word;[1697] he shall do[6213] according to all that proceeds out of his mouth.[6310]

3 "Also if a woman[802] makes a vow to the LORD, and binds herself by an obligation in her father's[1] house[1004] in her youth,

4 and her father[1] hears[8085] her vow and her obligation by which she has bound herself, and her father [I]says nothing to her, then all her vows[5088] shall stand, and every obligation by which she has bound herself shall stand.

5 "But if her father should forbid her on the day[3117] he hears[8085] *of it,* none of her vows or her obligations by which she has bound herself shall stand; and the LORD will forgive[5545] her because her father had forbidden her.

6 "However, if she should [I]marry[1961,376] while [II]under her vows or the rash statement of her lips[8193] by which she has bound herself,

7 and her husband hears[8085] of it and says nothing to her on the day he hears *it,* then her vows shall stand and her obligations by which she has bound herself shall stand.

8 "But if on the day her husband hears *of it,* he forbids her, then he shall annul her vow which [I]she is under and the rash statement of her lips by which she has bound herself; and the LORD will forgive her.

9 "But the vow of a widow or of a divorced[1644] woman, everything by which she has bound herself,[5315] shall stand against her.

10 "However, if she vowed in her husband's house, or bound herself by an obligation with an oath,

11 and her husband heard *it,* but said

nothing to her *and* did not forbid her, then all her vows shall stand, and every obligation by which she bound herself shall stand.

12 "But if her husband indeed annuls[6565] them on the day he hears *them,* then whatever proceeds out of her lips concerning her vows or concerning the obligation of herself, shall not stand; her husband has annulled them, and the LORD will forgive her.

13 "Every vow and every binding oath to humble herself, her husband may confirm it or her husband may annul it.

14 "But if her husband indeed says nothing to her from day to day, then he confirms[6965] all her vows or all her obligations which are on her; he has confirmed them, because he said nothing to her on the day he heard them.

15 "But if he indeed annuls them after he has heard them, then he shall bear[5375] her guilt."[5771]

16 These are the statutes[2706] which the LORD commanded Moses, *as* between a man and his wife,[802] *and as* between a father and his daughter, *while she is* in her youth in her father's house.

The Slaughter of Midian

31 Then the LORD spoke[1696] to Moses, saying,

2 "[a]Take full vengeance for the sons[1121] of Israel on the Midianites; afterward you will be [b]gathered[622] to your people."[5971]

3 And Moses spoke to the people, saying, "Arm men from among you for the war,[6635] that they may [I]go against Midian, to execute [a]the LORD's vengeance on Midian.

4 "A thousand from each tribe[4294] of all the tribes[4294] of Israel you shall send to the war."

5 So there were [I]furnished from the thousands[505] of Israel, a thousand from each tribe, twelve thousand armed for war.

6 And Moses sent them, a thousand from each tribe, to the war, and Phinehas the son[1121] of Eleazar the priest,[3548] to the war with them, [a]and the holy[6944] vessels and [b]the trumpets for the alarm in his hand.[3027]

7 So they made war[6633] against Midian, just as the LORD had commanded[6680] Moses, and [a]they killed[2026] every male.[2145]

8 And they killed the kings of Midian along with the *rest of* their slain:[2491] [a]Evi and Rekem and [b]Zur and Hur and Reba, the five kings[4428] of Midian; they also killed [c]Balaam the son of Beor with the sword.[2719]

9 And the sons of Israel captured[7617] the women[802] of Midian and their little ones;[2945] and all their cattle and all their flocks and all their goods, they plundered.[7617]

10 Then they burned[8313] all their cities where they lived and all their camps with fire.

11 And [a]they took all the spoil and all the prey, both of man[120] and of beast.

12 And they brought the captives[7628] and the prey and the spoil to Moses, and to Eleazar the priest and to the congregation[5712] of the sons of Israel, to the camp[4264] at the plains[6160] of Moab, which are by the Jordan opposite Jericho.

13 And Moses and Eleazar the priest and all the leaders[5387] of the congregation went out to meet them outside the camp.

14 And Moses was angry[7107] with the officers[6485] of the army,[2428] the captains of thousands and the captains of hundreds, who had come from service in the war.

15 And Moses said[559] to them, "Have you [I]spared [a]all the women?

16 "[a]Behold, these [I]caused the sons of Israel, through the [II]counsel[1697] of [b]Balaam, to [III]trespass[4604] against the LORD in the matter[1697] of Peor, so the plague was among the congregation of the LORD.

17 "[a]Now therefore, kill every male among the little ones, and kill every

2 [a]Num. 25:1, 16, 17 [b]Num. 20:24, 26; 27:13
3 [I]Lit., *be* [a]Lev. 26:25
5 [I]Lit., *delivered*
6 [a]Num. 14:44 [b]Num. 10:8, 9
7 [a]Deut. 20:13; Judg. 21:11; 1Kin. 11:15, 16
8 [a]Josh. 13:21 [b]Num. 25:15 [c]Num. 31:16; Josh. 13:22
11 [a]Deut. 20:14
15 [I]Lit., *let. . .live* [a]Deut. 20:14
16 [I]Lit., *were to* [II]Lit., *word* [III]Possibly, *defect from the Lord* [a]Num. 25:1-9 [b]Num. 31:8
17 [a]Deut. 7:2; 20:16-18

woman[802] who has known[3045] man [I]intimately.

18 "But all the [I]girls[2945] who have not known man [II]intimately, [III]spare for yourselves.

19 "[a]And you, camp outside the camp seven days; whoever has killed[2026] any person,[5315] and whoever has touched[5060] any slain, purify[2398] yourselves, you and your captives, on the third day[3117] and on the seventh day.

20 "And you shall purify for yourselves every garment and every article of [I]leather and all the work of goats' *hair,* and all articles of wood."

21 Then Eleazar the priest said to the men[582] of war who had gone to battle, "This is the statute[2708] of the law which the LORD has commanded Moses:

22 only the gold and the silver, the bronze, the iron, the tin and the lead,

23 everything[3605,1697] that can stand the fire, you shall pass through the fire, and it shall be clean,[2891] but it shall be purified[2398] with [a]water for impurity. But whatever cannot stand the fire you shall pass through the water.

24 "And you shall wash[3526] your clothes on the seventh day and be clean, and afterward you may enter the camp."

Division of the Booty

25 Then the LORD spoke[559] to Moses, saying,

26 "You and Eleazar the priest and the heads[7218] of the fathers'[1] *households* of the congregation, take[5375] a count[7218] of the booty [I]that was captured, both of man[120] and of animal;

27 and [a]divide the booty between the warriors who went out to battle[6635] and all the congregation.

28 "[a]And levy a tax for the LORD from the men of war who went out to battle, one[5315] [I]in five hundred of the persons[120] and of the cattle and of the donkeys and of the sheep;

29 take it from their half and give it to Eleazar the priest, as an [I]offering[8641] to the LORD.

30 "And from the sons of Israel's half, you shall take one drawn out of every fifty of the persons, of the cattle, of the donkeys and of the sheep, from all the animals, and give them to the Levites who [a]keep[8104] charge[4931] of the tabernacle[4908] of the LORD."

31 And Moses and Eleazar the priest did[6213] just as the LORD had commanded Moses.

32 Now the booty[4455] that remained[3499] from the spoil which the [I]men of war had plundered was 675,000 sheep,

33 and 72,000 cattle,

34 and 61,000 donkeys,

35 and of human beings, of the women who had not known man [I]intimately, all the persons were 32,000.

36 And the half, the portion of those who went out to war, was *as follows:* the number of sheep was 337,500,

37 and the LORD's levy of the sheep was 675,

38 and the cattle were 36,000, from which the LORD's levy was 72.

39 And the donkeys were 30,500, from which the LORD's levy was 61.

40 And the human beings were 16,000, from whom the LORD's levy was 32 persons.

41 And Moses gave the levy *which was* the LORD's offering to Eleazar the priest, just [a]as the LORD had commanded Moses.

42 As for the sons of Israel's half, which Moses [I]separated from the men who had gone to war—

43 now the congregation's half was 337,500 sheep,

44 and 36,000 cattle,

45 and 30,500 donkeys,

46 and the human beings were 16,000—

47 and from the sons of Israel's half, Moses took one drawn out of every fifty, both of man[120] and of animals, and gave them to the Levites, who kept[8104] charge of the tabernacle of the LORD, just as the LORD had commanded Moses.

48 Then the officers who were over the thousands of the army,[6635] the cap-

---

17 [I]Lit., *by lying with a man*

18 [I]Lit., *female children* [II]Lit., *by lying with a man* [III]Lit., *keep alive*

19 [a]Num. 19:11-22

20 [I]Or, *skin*

23 [a]Num. 19:9, 17

26 [I]Lit., *of captives*

27 [a]Josh. 22:8

28 [I]Lit., *soul from* [a]Num. 18:21-30

29 [I]Lit., *heave offering,* and so throughout the ch.

30 [a]Num. 3:7, 8, 25, 26, 31, 36, 37; 18:3, 4

32 [I]Lit., *people*

35 [I]Lit., *by lying with a man*

41 [a]Num. 5:9, 10; 18:19

42 [I]Or, *divided*

tains of thousands and the captains of hundreds, approached[5066] Moses;

49 and they said to Moses, "Your servants[5650] have taken a census of men of war who are in our charge, and no man[376] of us is missing.[6485]

50 "So we have brought[7126] as an offering[7133] to the LORD what each man found, articles of gold, armlets and bracelets, signet rings, earrings and necklaces,3558 [a]to make atonement[3722] for ourselves[5315] before the LORD."

51 And Moses and Eleazar the priest took the gold from them, all kinds of wrought articles.

52 And all the gold of the offering which they offered up to the LORD, from the captains of thousands and the captains of hundreds, was 16,750 shekels.

53 [a]The men of war had taken booty, every man for himself.

54 So Moses and Eleazar the priest took the gold from the captains[8269] of thousands and of hundreds, and brought it to the tent[168] of meeting[4150] as [a]a memorial for the sons of Israel before the LORD.

Reuben and Gad Settle in Gilead

32 Now the sons[1121] of Reuben and the sons of Gad had an [a]exceedingly large number of livestock. So when they saw[7200] the land of [b]Jazer and the land of Gilead, that [I]it was indeed a place suitable for livestock,

2 the sons of Gad and the sons of Reuben came and spoke[559] to Moses and to Eleazar the priest[3548] and to the leaders[5387] of the congregation,[5712] saying,

3 "[a]Ataroth, Dibon, Jazer, Nimrah, Heshbon, Elealeh, Sebam, Nebo and Beon,

4 the land[776] [a]which the LORD [I]conquered[5221] before the congregation of Israel, is a land for livestock; and your servants[5650] have livestock."

5 And they said,[559] "If we have found favor[2580] in your sight, let this land be given to your servants as a possession;[272] do not take us across the Jordan."

6 But Moses said to the sons of Gad and to the sons of Reuben, "Shall your brothers[251] go to war while you yourselves sit here?

7 "[a]Now why are you [I]discouraging5106 the sons of Israel from crossing over[5674] into the land which the LORD has given them?

8 "[I]This is what your fathers[1] did[6213] when I sent them from [a]Kadesh-barnea to see the land.

9 "For when they went up[5927] to [a]the [I]valley of Eshcol and saw the land, they [II]discouraged the sons of Israel so that they did not go into the land which the LORD had given them.

10 "So [a]the LORD'S anger[639] burned[2734] in that day,[3117] and He swore,[7650] saying,

11 '[a]None of the men[582] who came up[5927] from Egypt, from twenty years old[1121] and upward, shall see the land which I swore to Abraham, to Isaac and to Jacob; for they did not follow Me fully,

12 except Caleb the son[1121] of Jephunneh the Kenizzite and Joshua the son of Nun, [a]for they have followed the LORD fully.'

13 "[a]So the LORD'S anger burned against Israel, and He made them wander in the wilderness forty years, until the entire generation[1755] of those who had done[6213] evil[7451] in the sight of the LORD was destroyed.[8552]

14 "Now behold, you have risen up in your fathers'[1] place, a brood of sinful[2400] men, to add still more to the burning [a]anger of the LORD against Israel.

15 "For if you [a]turn away[7725] from following Him, He will once more abandon them in the wilderness; and you will destroy[7843] all these people."[5971]

16 Then they came near[5066] to him and said, "We will build here sheepfolds for our livestock and cities for our little ones;[2945]

17 [a]but we ourselves will be armed ready *to go* before the sons of Israel,

50 [a]Ex. 30:12-16
53 [a]Num. 31:32; Deut. 20:14
54 [a]Ex. 30:16
1 [I]Lit., *behold, the place, a place for* [a]Ex. 12:38 [b]Num. 21:32
3 [a]Num. 32:34-38
4 [I]Lit., *smote* [a]Num. 21:34
7 [I]Lit., *restraining the hearts of* [a]Num. 13:27-14:4
8 [I]Lit., *Thus your fathers* [a]Num. 13:3, 26; Deut. 1:19-25
9 [I]Or, *wadi* [II]Lit., *restrained the hearts of* [a]Num. 13:24; Deut. 1:24
10 [a]Num. 14:11f.; Deut. 1:34
11 [a]Num. 14:28-30
12 [a]Deut. 1:36; Josh. 14:8f.
13 [a]Num. 14:33-35
14 [a]Deut. 1:34f.
15 [a]Deut. 30:17, 18; 2Chr. 7:19, 20
17 [a]Josh. 4:12, 13

until we have brought them to their place, while our little ones live in the fortified cities because of the inhabitants of the land.

18 "[a]We will not return[7725] to our homes[1004] until every one[376] of the sons of Israel has possessed his inheritance.[5159]

19 "For we will not have an inheritance[5157] with them on the other side of the Jordan and beyond, because our inheritance has fallen to us [a]on this side of the Jordan toward the east."

20 [a]So Moses said to them, "If you will do[6213] [I]this,[1697] if you will arm yourselves before the LORD for the war,

21 and all of you armed men cross over the Jordan before the LORD until He has driven His enemies out from before Him,

22 [a]and the land is subdued before the LORD, then afterward you shall return and be free of obligation[5355] toward the LORD and toward Israel, and this land shall be yours for a possession before the LORD.

23 "But if you will not do so, behold, you have sinned[2398] against the LORD, and be sure[3045] [a]your sin[2403] will find you out.

24 "Build yourselves cities for your little ones, and sheepfolds for your sheep; and [a]do [I]what you have promised."[6310]

25 And the sons of Gad and the sons of Reuben spoke to Moses, saying, "Your servants will do just as my lord[113] commands.[6680]

26 "[a]Our little ones, our wives,[802] our livestock and all our cattle shall [I]remain there in the cities of Gilead;

27 while your servants, everyone who is armed for war,[6635] will [a]cross over in the presence of the LORD to battle, just as my lord says."

28 So Moses gave command[6680] concerning them to Eleazar the priest, and to Joshua the son of Nun, and to the heads[7218] of the fathers' *households* of the tribes[4294] of the sons of Israel.

29 And Moses said to them, "If the sons of Gad and the sons of Reuben, everyone who is armed for battle, will cross with you over the Jordan in the presence of the LORD, and the land will be subdued before you, then you shall give them the land of Gilead for a possession;

30 but if they will not cross over with you armed, they shall have possessions among you in the land of Canaan."

31 And the sons of Gad and the sons of Reuben answered, saying, "As the LORD has said[1696] to your servants, so we will do.

32 "We ourselves will cross over armed in the presence of the LORD into the land of Canaan, and the possession of our inheritance *shall remain* with us across the Jordan."

33 [a]So Moses gave to them, to the sons of Gad and to the sons of Reuben and to the half-tribe[7626] of Joseph's son Manasseh, the kingdom[4467] of Sihon, king of the Amorites and the kingdom of Og, the king[4428] of Bashan, the land with its cities with *their* [I]territories, the cities of the surrounding land.

34 And the sons of Gad built Dibon and Ataroth and [a]Aroer,

35 and Atroth-shophan and Jazer and Jogbehah,

36 and [a]Beth-nimrah and Beth-haran as fortified cities, and sheepfolds for sheep.

37 And the sons of Reuben built Heshbon and Elealeh and Kiriathaim,

38 and [a]Nebo and Baal-meon—*their* names being changed—and Sibmah, and they gave *other* names to the cities which they built.

39 And the sons of [a]Machir the son of Manasseh went to Gilead and took it, and dispossessed[3423] the Amorites who were in it.

40 So Moses gave [a]Gilead to Machir the son of Manasseh, and he lived in it.

41 And Jair the son of Manasseh went and took its [I]towns, and called[7121] them [II][a]Havvoth-jair.

42 And Nobah went and took Kenath and its villages, and called it Nobah after [a]his own name.

18 [a]Josh. 22:1-4
19 [a]Josh. 12:1; 13:8
20 [I]Lit., *this thing* [a]Deut. 3:18
22 [a]Deut. 3:20
23 [a]Gen. 4:7; 44:16; Is. 59:12
24 [I]Lit., *that which has come out of your mouth* [a]Num. 30:2
26 [I]Lit., *be* [a]Josh. 1:14
27 [a]Josh. 4:12
33 [I]Lit., *borders* [a]Deut. 3:8-17; Josh. 12:1-6
34 [a]Deut. 2:36
36 [a]Num. 32:3
38 [a]Is. 46:1
39 [a]Gen. 50:23
40 [a]Deut. 3:12, 13, 15; Josh. 17:1
41 [I]Lit., *tent villages* [II]I.e., the towns of Jair [a]Deut. 3:14; Judg. 10:4
42 [a]2Sam. 18:18; Ps. 49:11

Review of the Journey from Egypt to Jordan

33 These are the journeys of the
sons[1121] of Israel, by which they
came out from the land of Egypt by their
armies,[6635] under [a]the [I]leadership[3027] of
Moses and Aaron.
2 And Moses recorded their starting
places according to their journeys by
the [I]command[6310] of the LORD, and these
are their journeys according to their
starting places.
3 [a]And they journeyed from Rameses in the first[7223] month, on the fifteenth day[3117] of the first month; on the
[I]next day after the Passover[6453] the sons
of Israel [b]started out [II]boldly in the sight
of all the Egyptians,
4 while the Egyptians were burying[6912] all their first-born whom the
LORD had struck down[5221] among them.
The LORD had also executed[6213] judgments[8201] [a]on their gods.[430]
5 Then [a]the sons of Israel journeyed
from Rameses, and camped in Succoth.
6 [a]And they journeyed from Succoth, and camped in Etham, which is
on the edge of the wilderness.
7 [a]And they journeyed from Etham,
and turned back[7725] to Pi-hahiroth, which
faces Baal-zephon; and they camped before Migdol.
8 [a]And they journeyed [I]from before
Hahiroth, and passed[5674] through the
midst of the sea into the wilderness;
and [b]they went three days'[3117] journey
in the wilderness of Etham, and camped
at Marah.
9 [a]And they journeyed from Marah,
and came to Elim; and in Elim there
were twelve springs of water and seventy palm trees; and they camped there.
10 And they journeyed from Elim,
and camped by the [I]Red Sea.
11 And they journeyed from the
[I]Red Sea, and camped in [a]the wilderness
of Sin.
12 And they journeyed from the wilderness of Sin, and camped at Dophkah.
13 And they journeyed from Dophkah, and camped at Alush.

1 [I]Lit., *hand* [a]Ps. 77:20; 105:26; Mic. 6:4
2 [I]Lit., *mouth*
3 [I]Lit., *morrow* [II]Lit., *with a high hand* [a]Ex. 12:37 [b]Ex. 14:8
4 [a]Ex. 12:12
5 [a]Ex. 12:37
6 [a]Ex. 13:20
7 [a]Ex. 14:1, 2
8 [I]Many mss. read *from Pi-hahiroth* [a]Ex. 14:22 [b]Ex. 15:22, 23
9 [a]Ex. 15:27
10 [I]Lit., *Sea of Reeds*
11 [I]Lit., *Sea of Reeds* [a]Ex. 16:1
14 [a]Ex. 17:1
15 [a]Ex. 19:1
16 [a]Num. 11:34
17 [a]Num. 11:35
20 [a]Deut. 1:1
30 [a]Deut. 10:6
32 [a]Gen. 36:27; Deut. 10:6; 1Chr. 1:42
33 [a]Deut. 10:7
35 [a]Deut. 2:8
36 [a]Num. 20:1

14 And they journeyed from Alush,
and camped [a]at Rephidim; now it was
there that the people[5971] had no water
to drink.
15 And they journeyed from Rephidim, and camped in [a]the wilderness of
Sinai.
16 And they journeyed from the wilderness of Sinai, and camped at [a]Kib-
roth-hattaavah.
17 And they journeyed from Kibroth-hattaavah, and camped at [a]Haze-
roth.
18 And they journeyed from Hazeroth, and camped at Rithmah.
19 And they journeyed from Rithmah, and camped at Rimmon-perez.
20 And they journeyed from Rimmon-perez, and camped at [a]Libnah.
21 And they journeyed from Libnah,
and camped at Rissah.
22 And they journeyed from Rissah,
and camped in Kehelathah.
23 And they journeyed from Kehelathah, and camped at Mount Shepher.
24 And they journeyed from Mount
Shepher, and camped at Haradah.
25 And they journeyed from Haradah, and camped at Makheloth.
26 And they journeyed from Makheloth, and camped at Tahath.
27 And they journeyed from Tahath,
and camped at Terah.
28 And they journeyed from Terah,
and camped at Mithkah.
29 And they journeyed from Mithkah, and camped at Hashmonah.
30 And they journeyed from Hashmonah, and camped at [a]Moseroth.
31 And they journeyed from Moseroth, and camped at Bene-jaakan.
32 And they journeyed from [a]Bene-
jaakan, and camped at Hor-haggidgad.
33 And they journeyed from Hor-
haggidgad, and camped at [a]Jotbathah.
34 And they journeyed from Jotbathah, and camped at Abronah.
35 And they journeyed from Abronah, and camped at [a]Ezion-geber.
36 And they journeyed from Ezion-
geber, and camped in the wilderness of
[a]Zin, that is, Kadesh.

37 And they journeyed from Kadesh, and camped at [a]Mount Hor, [b]at the edge of the land of Edom.

38 [a]Then Aaron the priest[3548] went up[5927] to Mount Hor at the [I]command of the LORD, and died there, in the fortieth year after the sons of Israel had come from the land of Egypt on the first *day* in the fifth month.

39 And Aaron was one hundred twenty-three years old[1121] when he died[4194] on Mount Hor.

40 Now the Canaanite, the king[4428] of [a]Arad [I]who lived in the [II]Negev in the land of Canaan, heard[8085] of the coming of the sons of Israel.

41 Then they journeyed from Mount Hor, and camped at Zalmonah.

42 And they journeyed from Zalmonah, and camped at Punon.

43 And they journeyed from Punon, and camped at [a]Oboth.

44 And they journeyed from Oboth, and camped at Iye-abarim, at the border of Moab.

45 And they journeyed from Iyim, and camped at Dibon-gad.

46 And they journeyed from Dibon-gad, and camped at Almon-diblathaim.

47 And they journeyed from Almon-diblathaim, and camped in the mountains of [a]Abarim, before Nebo.

48 And they journeyed from the mountains of Abarim, and [a]camped in the plains[6160] of Moab by the Jordan *opposite* Jericho.

49 And they camped by the Jordan, from Beth-jeshimoth as far as [a]Abel-shittim in the plains of Moab.

Law of Possessing the Land

50 Then the LORD spoke[1696] to Moses in the plains of Moab by the Jordan *opposite* Jericho, saying,

51 "Speak[1696] to the sons of Israel and say[559] to them, '[a]When you cross over the Jordan into the land of Canaan,

52 then you shall drive out[3423] all the inhabitants of the land from before you, and [a]destroy[6] all their figured stones,[4906] and destroy all their molten images and demolish[8045] all their high places;[1116]

53 [a]and you shall take possession[3423] of the land and live in it, for I have given the land to you to possess[3423] it.

54 '[a]And you shall inherit[5157] the land by lot according to your families;[4940] to the larger you shall give more inheritance,[5157] and to the smaller you shall give less inheritance. Wherever the lot falls to anyone, that shall be his. You shall inherit[5157] according to the tribes[4294] of your fathers.[1]

55 'But if you do not drive out the inhabitants of the land from before you, then it shall come about that those whom you let remain of them *will become* [a]as pricks in your eyes and as thorns in your sides, and they shall trouble you in the land in which you live.

56 'And it shall come about that as I plan to do to them, so I will do to you.' "

Instruction for Apportioning Canaan

34 Then the LORD spoke[1696] to Moses, saying,

2 "Command[6680] the sons[1121] of Israel and say[559] to them, 'When you enter [a]the land of Canaan, this is the land that shall fall to you as an inheritance,[5159] *even the* land of Canaan according to its borders.

3 '[a]Your southern [I]sector shall [II]extend from the wilderness of Zin along the side of Edom, and your southern border shall [II]extend from the end of the Salt Sea [b]eastward.

4 'Then your border shall turn *direction* from the south to the ascent of Akrabbim, and [I]continue to Zin, and its [II]termination shall be to the south of [a]Kadesh-barnea; and it shall [III]reach Hazaraddar, and [I]continue to Azmon.

5 'And the border shall turn *direction* from Azmon to the brook of Egypt, and its termination shall be at [a]the sea.

6 'As for the western border, you shall have the Great Sea, that is, *its*

37 [a]Num. 20:22 [b]Num. 20:16
38 [I]Lit., *mouth* [a]Num. 20:28; Deut. 10:6
40 [I]Lit., *and he* [II]I.e., South country [a]Num. 21:1
43 [a]Num. 21:10, 11
47 [a]Num. 27:12
48 [a]Num. 22:1
49 [a]Num. 25:1
51 [a]Josh. 3:17
52 [a]Ex. 23:24; Lev. 26:1; Deut. 7:5; 12:3, 30; Ps. 106:34-36
53 [a]Deut. 11:31; 17:14; Josh. 21:43
54 [a]Num. 26:53-56
55 [a]Josh. 23:13
2 [a]Gen. 17:8; Ps. 78:54, 55; 105:11
3 [I]Lit., *side* [II]Lit., *be* [a]Josh. 15:1-3 [b]Josh. 15:5
4 [I]Lit., *pass along* [II]Lit., *goings out*, and so throughout the ch. [III]Lit., *go forth to* [a]Num. 32:8
5 [a]Josh. 15:4

[I]coastline; this shall be your west border.
7 "[a]And this shall be your north border: you shall draw your *border* line from
the Great Sea to Mount Hor.
8 'You shall draw a line from Mount
Hor to [a]the [I]Lebo-hamath, and the termination of the border shall be at Zedad;
9 and the border shall proceed to
Ziphron, and its termination shall be at
Hazar-enan. This shall be your north
border.
10 'For your eastern border you
shall also draw a line from Hazar-enan
to Shepham,
11 and the border shall go down
from Shepham to [a]Riblah on the east
side of Ain; and the border shall go down
and reach to the [I]slope on the east side
of the Sea of [b]Chinnereth.
12 'And the border shall go down
to the Jordan and its termination shall
be at the Salt Sea. This shall be your
land according to its borders all
around.'"
13 So Moses commanded[6680] the
sons of Israel, saying, "[a]This is the land
that you are to apportion[5157] by lot
among you as a possession, which the
LORD has commanded to give to the nine
and a half tribes.[4294]
14 "[a]For the tribe of the sons of
Reuben have received *theirs* according
to their fathers'[1] households,[1004] and the
tribe of the sons of Gad according to
their fathers' households, and the half-
tribe of Manasseh have received their
possession.
15 "The two and a half tribes have
received their possession across the Jordan opposite Jericho, eastward toward
the sunrising."
16 Then the LORD spoke to Moses,
saying,
17 "[a]These are the names of the
men[582] who shall apportion[5157] the land
to you for inheritance: Eleazar the
priest[3548] and Joshua the son[1121] of Nun.
18 "And you shall take one
leader[5387] of every tribe to apportion
the land for inheritance.[5157]
19 "And these are the names of the

6 [I]Lit., *border*

7 [a]Ezek. 47:15-17

8 [I]Or, *entrance of Hamath* [a]Josh. 13:5

11 [I]Lit., *shoulder* [a]2Kin. 23:33 [b]Deut. 3:17; Josh. 13:27

13 [a]Gen. 15:18; Num. 26:52-56; Deut. 11:24; Josh. 14:1-5

14 [a]Num. 32:33

17 [a]Josh. 14:1, 2

19 [a]Gen. 29:35; Deut. 33:7; Ps. 60:7 [b]Num. 13:6, 30; 26:65; Deut. 1:36

20 [a]Gen. 29:33; 49:5; Ezek. 48:24

21 [a]Gen. 49:27; Deut. 33:12; Ps. 68:27

1 [a]Lev. 25:32-34

4 [I]Lit., *and outward*

men: of the tribe of [a]Judah, [b]Caleb the
son of Jephunneh.
20 "And of the tribe of the sons of
[a]Simeon, Samuel the son of Ammihud.
21 "Of the tribe of [a]Benjamin, Elidad
the son of Chislon.
22 "And of the tribe of the sons of
Dan a leader, Bukki the son of Jogli.
23 "Of the sons of Joseph: of the
tribe of the sons of Manasseh a leader,
Hanniel the son of Ephod.
24 "And of the tribe of the sons of
Ephraim a leader, Kemuel the son of
Shiphtan.
25 "And of the tribe of the sons of
Zebulun a leader, Elizaphan the son of
Parnach.
26 "And of the tribe of the sons of
Issachar a leader, Paltiel the son of
Azzan.
27 "And of the tribe of the sons of
Asher a leader, Ahihud the son of Shelomi.
28 "And of the tribe of the sons of
Naphtali a leader, Pedahel the son of
Ammihud."
29 These are those whom the LORD
commanded to apportion the inheritance
to the sons of Israel in the land of Canaan.

Cities for the Levites

35 [a]Now the LORD spoke[1696] to Moses in the plains[6160] of Moab by
the Jordan opposite Jericho, saying,
2 "Command[6680] the sons[1121] of Israel that they give to the Levites from
the inheritance[5159] of their possession,[272] cities to live in; and you shall
give to the Levites pasture lands around
the cities.
3 "And the cities shall be theirs to
live in; and their pasture lands shall be
for their cattle and for their herds and
for all their beasts.[2416]
4 "And the pasture lands of the cities which you shall give to the Levites
shall extend from the wall of the city
[I]outward a thousand cubits around.
5 "You shall also measure outside
the city on the east side two thousand

cubits, and on the south side two thousand cubits, and on the west side two thousand cubits, and on the north side two thousand cubits, with the city in the center. This shall become theirs as pasture lands for the cities.

Cities of Refuge

6 "And the cities which you shall give to the Levites *shall be* the [a]six cities of refuge, which you shall give for the manslayer[7523] to flee to; and in addition to them you shall give forty-two cities.

7 "All the cities which you shall give to the Levites *shall be* [a]forty-eight cities, [I]together with their pasture lands.

8 "[a]As for the cities which you shall give from the possession of the sons of Israel, you shall take more from the larger and you shall take less from the smaller; each[376] shall give some of his cities to the Levites in proportion to his possession which he inherits."

9 Then the LORD spoke to Moses, saying,

10 "[a]Speak[1696] to the sons of Israel and say[559] to them, 'When you cross[5674] the Jordan into the land of Canaan,

11 [a]then you shall select for yourselves cities to be your [b]cities of refuge, that the manslayer[7523] who has [I]killed[5221] any person[5315] [c]unintentionally[7684] may flee there.

12 'And [a]the cities shall be to you as a refuge from the avenger,[1350] so that the manslayer may not die[4191] until he stands before the congregation[5712] for [I]trial.[4941]

13 'And the cities which you are to give shall be your six cities of refuge.

14 'You [a]shall give three cities across the Jordan and three cities [I]in the land of Canaan; they are to be cities of refuge.

15 'These six cities shall be for refuge for the sons of Israel, and for the alien[1616] and for the sojourner[8453] among them; that anyone who [I]kills a person [a]unintentionally may flee there.

16 "[a]But if he struck[5221] him down with an iron object, so that he died,

6 [a]Josh. 20:7-9

7 [I]Lit., *them* [a]Josh. 21:41

8 [a]Lev. 25:32-34; Num. 26:54; 33:54; Josh. 21:1-42

10 [a]Josh. 20:1-9

11 [I]Lit., *smote* [a]Deut. 19:1-13 [b]Josh. 20:2f. [c]Ex. 21:13; Lev. 4:2f., 22f.; Num. 35:22-25

12 [I]Lit., *judgment* [a]Deut. 19:4-6; Josh. 20:2, 3

14 [I]Lit., *you shall give in* [a]Deut. 4:41

15 [I]Lit., *smites* [a]Num. 35:11

16 [a]Ex. 21:12, 14; Lev. 24:17

17 [a]Num. 35:31

20 [a]Gen. 4:8; 2Sam. 3:27; 20:10 [b]Ex. 21:14; Deut. 19:11

22 [a]Num. 35:11

23 [I]Lit., *by which he may die*

24 [a]Josh. 20:6

he is a murderer; the murderer shall surely be put to death.[4191]

17 'And if he struck him down with a stone in the hand, by which he may die, and *as a result* he died, he is a murderer; the murderer [a]shall surely be put to death.

18 'Or if he struck him with a wooden object in the hand,[3027] by which he may die, and *as a result* he died, he is a murderer; the murderer shall surely be put to death.

19 'The blood[1818] avenger[1350] himself shall put[4191] the murderer to death;[4191] he shall put him to death when he meets him.

20 'And [a]if he pushed him of hatred, or threw something at him [b]lying in wait and *as a result* he died,

21 or if he struck him down with his hand in enmity,[342] and *as a result* he died, the one who struck[5221] him shall surely be put to death,[4191] he is a murderer; the blood avenger shall put the murderer to death when he meets him.

22 "[a]But if he pushed him suddenly without enmity, or threw something at him without lying in wait,

23 or with any [I]deadly object of stone, and without seeing[7200] it dropped[5307] on him so that he died, while he was not his enemy nor seeking his injury,[7451]

24 then [a]the congregation shall judge[8199] between the slayer and the blood avenger according to these ordinances.

25 'And the congregation shall deliver[5337] the manslayer from the hand of the blood avenger, and the congregation shall restore[7725] him to his city of refuge to which he fled; and he shall live in it until the death[4194] of the high priest[3548] who was anointed[4886] with the holy[6944] oil.[8081]

26 'But if the manslayer shall at any time go beyond the border of his city of refuge to which he may flee,

27 and the blood avenger finds him outside the border of his city of refuge, and the blood avenger kills[7523] the man-

slayer, he shall not be guilty[816] of blood

28 because he should have remained in his city of refuge until the death of the high priest. But after the death of the high priest the manslayer shall return[7725] to the land of his possession.

29 'And these things shall be for a [a]statutory[2708] ordinance to you throughout your generations[1755] in all your dwellings.[4186]

30 '[a]If anyone kills a person, the murderer shall be put to death at the [I]evidence[6310] of witnesses, but [b]no person shall be put to death on the testimony of one witness.

31 'Moreover, you shall not take ransom[3724] for the life[5315] of a murderer who is guilty[7563] of death, but he shall surely be put to death.[4191]

32 'And you shall not take ransom for him who has fled to his city of refuge, that he may return[7725] to live in the land [I]before the death of the priest.

33 '[a]So you shall not pollute[2610] the land in which you are; for blood pollutes[2610] the land and no expiation[3722] can be made for the land for the blood that is shed[8210] on it, except [b]by the blood of him who shed it.

34 'And you shall not [a]defile[2930] the land in which you live, in the midst of which [b]I dwell;[7931] for I the LORD am dwelling in the midst of the sons of Israel.' "

Inheritance by Marriage

36 [a]And the heads[7218] of the fathers'[1] *households* of the family[4940] of the sons[1121] of Gilead, the son[1121] of Machir, the son[1121] of Manasseh, of the families of the sons of Joseph, came near[5066] and spoke[1696] before Moses and before the leaders,[5387] the heads of the fathers' *households* of the sons of Israel,

2 and they said,[559] "The LORD[113] commanded[6680] my lord to give the land by lot to the sons of Israel as an inheritance,[5159] and my lord [a]was commanded by the LORD to give the inheritance of Zelophehad our brother[251] to his daughters.

3 "But if they [I]marry one of the sons of the *other* tribes[7626] of the sons of Israel, their inheritance will be withdrawn from the inheritance of our fathers and will be added to the inheritance of the tribe to which they belong; thus it will be withdrawn from our allotted inheritance.

4 "And when the [a]jubilee of the sons of Israel [I]comes, then their inheritance will be added to the inheritance of the tribe to which they belong; so their inheritance will be withdrawn from the inheritance of the tribe of our fathers."

5 Then Moses commanded the sons of Israel according to the [I]word of the LORD, saying, "The tribe of the sons of Joseph are right in *their* statements.[1696]

6 "[a]This is [I]what[1697] the LORD has commanded[6680] concerning the daughters of Zelophehad, saying, 'Let them marry [II]whom they wish;[2896] only they must marry within the family[4940] of the tribe of their father.'[1]

7 "Thus [a]no inheritance of the sons of Israel shall [I]be transferred from tribe to tribe, for the sons of Israel shall each[376] [II]hold to the inheritance of the tribe of his fathers.

8 "[a]And every daughter who comes into possession[3423] of an inheritance of any tribe of the sons of Israel, shall be wife[802] to one of the family of the tribe of her father, so that the sons of Israel each[376] may possess the inheritance of his fathers.

9 "Thus no inheritance shall [I]be transferred from one tribe to another tribe, for the tribes[4294] of the sons of Israel shall each [II]hold to his own inheritance."

10 Just as the LORD had commanded Moses, so the daughters of Zelophehad did:[6213]

11 [a]Mahlah, Tirzah, Hoglah, Milcah and Noah, the daughters of Zelophehad married their uncles' sons.

---

29 [a]Num. 27:11
30 [I]Lit., *mouth* [a]Num. 35:16 [b]Deut. 17:6; 19:15; Matt. 18:16; John 7:51; 8:17, 18
32 [I]Or, *until*
33 [a]Deut. 21:7, 8; Ps. 106:38 [b]Gen. 9:6
34 [a]Lev. 18:24, 25 [b]Num. 5:3
1 [a]Num. 27:1
2 [a]Num. 27:5-7
3 [I]Lit., *become wives to,* in this ch.
4 [I]Lit., *shall be* [a]Lev. 25:10
5 [I]Lit., *mouth*
6 [I]Lit., *the thing which* [II]Lit., *to the good one in their eyes* [a]Num. 27:7
7 [I]Lit., *turn about* [II]Lit., *cleave* [a]1 Kin. 21:3
8 [a]1 Chr. 23:22
9 [I]Lit., *turn about* [II]Lit., *cleave*
11 [a]Num. 26:33

12 They married *those* from the families of the sons of Manasseh the son of Joseph, and their inheritance [I]remained with the tribe of the family of their father.

13 [a]These are the commandments and the ordinances3613 which the LORD commanded to the sons of Israel through3027 Moses in the plains6160 of Moab by the Jordan *opposite* Jericho.

12 [I]Lit., *was*

13 [a]Lev. 26:46; 27:34; Num. 22:1

DEUTERONOMY

The name "Deuteronomy" is a Greek word and is an inexact rendering of Deut. 17:18 in the Septuagint, the Greek translation of the Old Testament. It should have been translated: "this is the repetition of the Law." This book is not a "second Law," but only a partial restatement and expansion of former laws in the writings of Moses. The Jews called the book "the five-fifths of the Law," since it is the last of the five books of Moses. Deuteronomy resumes where the Book of Numbers leaves off. Israel is now in the Plains of Moab, poised for invasion. The laws of Moses were rehearsed and expounded for this new generation as they were about to take possession of the land which was promised to them by God. Deuteronomy contains the last words of Moses in the final week of his life. Since God would not allow him to cross the Jordan River with them, under the direct inspiration of God Moses reemphasized God's Law in view of the new conditions which they would soon face. Moses warned them against disobeying God and he encouraged them to follow the true path.

Israel's History after the Exodus

1 These are the words[1697] which
Moses spoke[1696] to all Israel
[a]across the Jordan in the wilderness,
in the [b]Arabah[6160] opposite [I]Suph, between Paran and Tophel and Laban and
Hazeroth and Dizahab.
2 It is eleven days'[3117] *journey* from
[a]Horeb by the way[1870] of Mount [b]Seir
to [c]Kadesh-barnea.
3 And it came about in the [a]fortieth
year, on the first day of the eleventh
month, that Moses spoke to the
children[1121] of Israel, [b]according to all
that the LORD had commanded him *to*
give to them,
4 after he had [Ia]defeated[5221] Sihon
the king[4428] of the Amorites, who lived
in Heshbon, and [b]Og the king of Bashan,
who lived in [c]Ashtaroth [II]and Edrei.
5 Across the Jordan in the land of
Moab, Moses undertook to expound this
law,[8451] saying,
6 "The LORD our God[430] [a]spoke to
us at Horeb, saying, 'You have [I]stayed
long enough at this mountain.
7 'Turn and set your journey, and
go to [a]the hill country of the Amorites,
and to all their neighbors in the Arabah,
in the hill country and in the lowland[8219]
and in [b]the [I]Negev and by the seacoast,
the land of the Canaanites, and Lebanon,
as far as the great river, the river Euphrates.
8 'See, I have placed the land before
you; go in and possess the land which
the LORD [a]swore[7650] to give to your fathers, to Abraham, to Isaac, and to Jacob, to them and their [I]descendants[2233]
after them.'
9 "And I spoke[559] to you at that
time,[6256] saying, '[a]I am not able to
bear[5357] *the burden* of you alone.
10 'The LORD your God has [a]multi-
plied you, and behold, you are this day[3117]
as the stars of heaven[8064] for multitude.
11 'May the LORD, the God of your
fathers, increase you a thousand-fold
more than you are, and bless[1288] you,
[a]just as He has [I]promised[1696] you!
12 'How can I alone bear the load[2960]
and burden[4853] of you and your strife?[7379]
13 '[Ia]Choose wise[2450] and discerning[995] and experienced[3045] men from

1 [I]Perhaps Red Sea [a]Deut. 4:46 [b]Deut. 2:8
2 [a]Ex. 3:1; 17:6 [b]Gen. 32:3 [c]Num. 13:26; 32:8; Deut. 9:23
3 [a]Num. 33:38 [b]Deut. 4:1,2
4 [I]Lit., *smitten* [II]So with ancient versions; M.T. omits *and* [a]Num. 21:21-26; Deut. 2:26-35; Josh. 13:10; Neh. 9:22 [b]Num. 21:33-35; Josh. 13:12 [c]Josh. 12:4
6 [I]Lit., *dwelt* [a]Num. 10:11-13
7 [I]I.e., South country [a]Gen. 15:18; Deut. 11:24; Josh. 10:40 [b]Gen. 12:9
8 [I]Lit., *seed* [a]Gen. 12:7; 26:3; 28:13; Ex. 33:1; Num. 14:23; 32:11; Heb. 6:13, 14
9 [a]Ex. 18:18, 24; Num. 11:14
10 [a]Gen. 15:5; 22:17; Ex. 32:13; Deut. 7:7; 10:22; 26:5; 28:62
11 [I]Lit., *spoken to* [a]Deut. 1:8, 10
13 [I]Lit., *Give for yourselves* [a]Ex. 18:21

1:1 The phrase "across the Jordan" should be translated as "beyond Jordan" as it is in Deut. 3:20,25. This was the common term used for the district east of Jordan. With the Greek infiltration at a later date it came to be called Perea. "The wilderness" is a reference to the desert of Arabia and "Arabah" refers to the tract of sterile land which stretches along the lower Jordan to the Dead Sea and continues to the Gulf of Aqabah. The word "Suph" is a transliteration from the original Hebrew text. The reference is uncertain but probably indicates the Gulf of Aqabah which is an extension of the Red Sea.

your tribes,[7626] and I will appoint[7760]
them as your heads.'[7218]
14 "And you answered me and
said,[559] 'The thing[1697] which you have
said[1696] to do is good.'[2896]
15 "So I took the heads[7218] of your
tribes, wise and experienced men, and
[I]appointed them heads[7218] over you,
leaders[8269] of thousands,[505] and [II]of hundreds, [II]of fifties and [II]of tens, and
officers[7860] for your tribes.
🗝 **16** "Then I charged[6680] your
judges[8199] at that time, saying, 'Hear[8085]
the cases between your [I]fellow countrymen,[251] and [a]judge[8199] righteously[6664]
between a man[376] and his [II]fellow countryman,[251] or the alien[1616] who is with
him.
17 "[a]You shall not show partiality in
judgment;[4941] you shall hear the small
and the great alike. You shall [b]not
fear[1481] [I]man, for the judgment is God's.
And [c]the case[1697] that is too hard for
you, you shall bring[7126] to me, and I
will hear it.'
18 "[a]And I commanded[6680] you at
that time all the things[1697] that you
should do.
19 "Then we set out from [a]Horeb,
and went through all that [b]great and
terrible[3372] wilderness which you
saw,[7200] on the way to the [c]hill country
of the Amorites, just as the LORD our
God had commanded us; and we came
to [d]Kadesh-barnea.
20 "And I said to you, 'You have
come to the hill country of the Amorites
which the LORD our God is about to
give us.
21 'See, the LORD your God has
placed the land before you; go up,[5927]
take possession, as the LORD, the God
of your fathers, has spoken[1696] to you.
[a]Do not fear[3372] or be dismayed.'[2865]
22 "[a]Then all of you approached me
and said, 'Let us send men before us,
that they may search out the land for
us, and bring back to us word[1697] of
the way by which we should go up, and
the cities which we shall enter.'
23 "And the thing[1697] pleased[3190] me
and I took twelve of your men, one man
for each tribe.[7626]
24 "And [a]they turned and went
up[5927] into the hill country, and came
to the valley of Eshcol, and spied it out.
25 "Then they took *some* of the fruit
of the land in their hands[3027] and brought
it down to us; and they brought us back
a report and said, 'It is a good land which
the LORD our God is about to give us.'
26 "[a]Yet you were not willing[14] to
go up, but [b]rebelled[4784] against the [I]com-
mand[6310] of the LORD your God;
27 and [a]you grumbled in your
tents[168] and said, 'Because the LORD
hates us, He has brought us out of the
land of Egypt to deliver us into the
hand[3027] of the Amorites to destroy[8045]
us.
28 'Where can we go up? Our brethren have made our hearts[3824] melt, saying, "The people[5971] are bigger and taller
than we; the cities are large and fortified
to heaven. And besides, we saw[7200]
[a]the sons[1121] of the Anakim there." '
29 "Then I said to you, 'Do not be
shocked,[6206] nor fear them.
30 'The LORD your God who goes
before you will [a]Himself fight on your
behalf, [I]just as He did[6213] for you in
Egypt before your eyes,
31 and in the wilderness where you
saw how [a]the LORD your God carried[5375]
you, just as a man carries his son,[1121]
in all the way which you have walked,
until you came to this place.'
32 "But [I][a]for all this, you did not
trust[539] the LORD your God,
33 [a]who goes before you on *your*
way, [b]to seek out a place for you to
encamp, in fire by night and cloud[6051]
by day,[3119] to show[7200] you the way in
which you should go.

15 [I]Lit., *gave* [II]Lit., *leaders of*
16 [I]Lit., *brothers* [II]Lit., *brother* [a]Deut. 16:18; John 7:24
17 [I]Lit., *because of man* [a]Deut. 10:17; 16:19; 24:17; 2Chr. 19:5, 6; Prov. 24:23-26; Acts 10:34; James 2:1, 9 [b]Prov. 29:25 [c]Ex. 18:22, 26
18 [a]Ex. 18:20
19 [a]Deut. 1:2 [b]Deut. 2:7; 8:15; 32:10; Jer. 2:6 [c]Deut. 1:7 [d]Deut. 1:2
21 [a]Josh. 1:6, 9
22 [a]Num. 13:1-3
24 [a]Num. 13:21-25
26 [I]Lit., *mouth* [a]Num. 14:1-4 [b]Deut. 9:23
27 [a]Deut. 9:28; Ps. 106:25
28 [a]Num. 13:28,33; Deut. 9:2
30 [I]Lit., *according to all that* [a]Ex. 14:14; Deut. 3:22; 20:4; Neh. 4:20
31 [a]Deut. 32:10-12; Is. 46:3, 4; 63:9; Hos. 11:3; Acts 13:18
32 [I]Lit., *in this matter* [a]Num. 14:11; Ps. 106:24; Heb. 3:19; 4:2; Jude 5
33 [a]Ex. 13:21; Num. 9:15-23; Neh. 9:12; Ps. 78:14 [b]Num. 10:33

🗝 **1:16** The Hebrew word here (*ger*) is translated as "sojourner," "stranger," "immigrant," or "alien." They were non-Israelite residents who, for the most part, enjoyed equal rights under the Law of Moses with their Hebrew neighbors. If they were poor, they were provided for along with the Levites, the orphans, and the widows, but they were required to be circumcised and conform to the Law of Moses.

34 "Then the LORD heard[8085] the
sound of your words, and He was
angry[7107] and [a]took an oath, saying,
35 '[a]Not one[376] of these men, this
evil[7451] generation,[1755] shall see the good
land which I swore to give your fathers,
36 except Caleb the son of Jephunneh; he shall see it, and [a]to him and to
his sons I will give the land on which
he has set foot, because he has followed
the LORD fully.'
🗝 37 "[a]The LORD was angry[599] with
me also on your account, saying, '[b]Not
even you shall enter there.
38 'Joshua the son of Nun, who
stands before you, [a]he shall enter there;
encourage[2388] him, for [b]he shall cause
Israel to inherit it.
39 'Moreover, [a]your little ones[2945]
who you said would become a prey, and
your sons, who this day have [b]no
knowledge[3045] of good or evil, shall enter
there, and I will give it to them, and
they shall possess it.
40 'But as for you, [a]turn around and
set out for the wilderness by the way
to the [I]Red Sea.'
41 "[a]Then you answered and said
to me, 'We have sinned[2398] against the
LORD; we will indeed go up and fight,
just as the LORD our God commanded
us.' And every man of you girded on
his weapons of war, and regarded it as
easy to go up into the hill country.
42 "[a]And the LORD said to me,
'Say[559] to them, "Do not go up, nor
fight, for I am not among[7130] you; lest
you be [I]defeated[5062] before your enemies." '
43 "So I spoke to you, but you would
not listen. Instead [a]you rebelled against
the [I]command of the LORD, and acted
presumptuously and went up into the
hill country.
44 "[a]And the Amorites who [I]lived
in that hill country came out against you,
and chased you [b]as bees do, and
crushed[3807] you from Seir to Hormah.
45 "Then you returned[7725] and wept
before the LORD; but the [a]LORD did not
listen[8085] to your voice, nor give ear[238]
to you.
46 "So you remained in [a]Kadesh
many days,[3117] [I]the days that you spent
there.

Wanderings in the Wilderness

2 "Then we turned and set out for
the wilderness by the way[1870] to
the [I]Red Sea, as the LORD spoke[1696]
to me, and circled [a]Mount Seir for many
days.[3117]
2 "And the LORD spoke[559] to me,
saying,
3 'You have circled this mountain
long enough. *Now* turn north,
4 [a]and command[6680] the people,[5971]
saying, "You will pass through[5674] the
[b]territory of your brothers[251] the
sons[1121] of Esau who live in Seir; and
[c]they will be afraid of you. So be very
careful;
5 do not [I]provoke them, for I will
not give you any of their land, even *as*
little as a [II]footstep [a]because I have given
Mount Seir to Esau as a possession.[3425]
6 "You shall buy food from them
with money so that you may eat, and
you shall also purchase water from them
with money so that you may drink.
7 "For the LORD your God[430] has
blessed[1288] you in all [I]that you[3027] have
done; He has known your [II]wanderings
through this [a]great wilderness. These
[b]forty years the LORD your God has
been with you; you have not lacked a
thing." '
8 "So we passed[5674] beyond our
brothers the sons of Esau, who live in
Seir, away from the [a]Arabah[6160] road,
away from Elath and [b]from Ezion-geber.
And we turned and passed through by
the way of the wilderness of Moab.
9 "Then the LORD said[559] to me, 'Do
not harass Moab, nor provoke them to
war, for I will not give you any of
[I]their land as a possession, because I
have given [a]Ar to [b]the sons of Lot as
a possession.

34 [a]Num. 14:28-30; Heb. 3:18
35 [a]Ps. 95:11; 106:26; Ezek. 20:15; 1Cor. 10:5; Heb. 3:14-19
36 [a]Num. 14:24; Josh. 14:9
37 [a]Num. 20:12; Deut. 3:26; 4:21 [b]Num. 27:13, 18
38 [a]Num. 14:30 [b]Num. 34:17; Deut. 3:28; 31:7; Josh. 11:23
39 [a]Num. 14:3, 31 [b]Is. 7:15, 16
40 [I]Lit., *Sea of Reeds* [a]Num. 14:25
41 [a]Num. 14:40
42 [I]Lit., *smitten* [a]Num. 14:41-43
43 [I]Lit., *mouth* [a]Num. 14:40
44 [I]Lit., *dwelt* [a]Num. 14:45 [b]Ps. 118:12
45 [a]Job 27:8, 9; Ps. 66:18; John 9:31
46 [I]Lit., *as the days* [a]Num. 20:1, 22; Deut. 2:7, 14; Judg. 11:17

1 [I]Lit., *Sea of Reeds* [a]Num. 21:4 [b]Deut. 1:2
4 [a]Num. 20:14-21 [b]Gen. 36:8 [c]Ex. 15:15, 16
5 [I]Or, *engage in strife with* [II]Lit., *treading of a sole of a foot* [a]Gen. 36:8; Josh. 24:4
7 [I]Lit., *the work of your hand* [II]Lit., *goings* [a]Deut. 1:19 [b]Num. 14:33, 34; 32:13; Deut. 2:14
8 [a]Deut. 1:1 [b]Num. 33:35; 1Kin. 9:26
9 [I]Lit., *his* [a]Num. 21:15, 28; Deut. 2:18, 29 [b]Gen. 19:36, 37

🗝 **1:37** See note on Num. 20:12.

🔑 10 (The [a]Emim lived there formerly, a people as great, numerous, and tall as the Anakim.

11 Like the Anakim, they are also regarded[2803] as [a]Rephaim,[7497] but the Moabites call[7121] them Emim.

12 [a]The Horites formerly lived in Seir, but the sons of Esau dispossessed them and destroyed[8045] them from before them and settled in their place, [b]just as Israel did[6213] to the land of [I]their possession which the LORD gave to them.)

13 'Now arise and cross over the [I]brook Zered yourselves.' So we crossed over[5674] the [I]brook Zered.

14 "Now the [I]time[3117] that it took for us to come from Kadesh-barnea, until we crossed over[5674] the [II]brook Zered, was [a]thirty-eight years; until [b]all the generation[1755] of the men of war perished[8552] from within[7130] the camp,[4264] as [c]the LORD had sworn[7650] to them.

15 "[a]Moreover the hand of the LORD was against them, to destroy[2000] them from within the camp, until they all perished.

16 "So it came about when [a]all the men of war had finally perished[4191] from among[7130] the people,

17 that the LORD spoke to me, saying,

18 'You shall cross over [a]Ar, the border of Moab, today.[3117]

19 'And when you come opposite[7126] the [a]sons of Ammon, do not harass them nor provoke them, for I will not give you any of the land of the sons of Ammon as a possession, because I have given it to [b]the sons of Lot as a possession.'

20 (It is also regarded as the land of the [a]Rephaim, *for* Rephaim formerly lived in it, but the Ammonites call them Zamzummin,

21 a people as great, numerous, and tall as the Anakim, but the LORD destroyed them before them. And they dispossessed them and settled in their place,

🔑 22 just as He did for the sons of Esau, who [a]live in Seir, when He destroyed [b]the Horites from before them; and they dispossessed them, and settled in their place even to this day.

🔑 23 And the [a]Avvim, who lived in villages as far as Gaza, the [I][b]Caphtorim who came from [II][c]Caphtor, destroyed them and lived in their place.)

24 'Arise, set out, and pass through the [I][a]valley of Arnon. Look![7200] I have given Sihon the Amorite, king[4428] of Heshbon, and his land into your hand; begin to take possession and contend with him in battle.

25 'This day I will begin to put [a]the dread[6343] and fear[3374] of you [I]upon the peoples[5971] [II]everywhere under the heavens,[8064] who, when they hear[8085] the report[8088] of you, [b]shall tremble and be in anguish[2342] because of you.'

26 "[a]So I sent messengers[4397] from the wilderness of Kedemoth to Sihon king of Heshbon with words[1697] of peace,[7965] saying,

27 'Let me pass through your land, I will [I]travel only on the highway; I will not turn aside to the right or to the left.

28 'You will sell me food for money so that I may eat, and give me water for money so that I may drink, [a]only let me pass through on [I]foot,

29 just as the sons of Esau who live

10 [a]Gen. 14:5
11 [a]Gen. 14:5; Deut. 2:20
12 [I]Lit., *his* [a]Gen. 36:20; Deut. 2:22 [b]Num. 21:25, 35
13 [I]Or, *wadi*
14 [I]Lit., *days in which we went* [II]Or, *wadi* [a]Deut. 2:7 [b]Num. 14:29-35; 26:64, 65; Ps. 106:26; 1Cor. 10:5 [c]Deut. 1:34, 35
15 [a]Jude 5
16 [a]Deut. 2:14
18 [a]Deut. 2:9
19 [a]Gen. 19:38 [b]Deut. 2:9
20 [a]Deut. 2:11
22 [a]Gen. 36:8; Deut. 2:5 [b]Deut. 2:12
23 [I]I.e., Philistines [II]I.e., Crete [a]Josh. 13:3 [b]Gen. 10:14; 1Chr. 1:12 [c]Jer. 47:4; Amos 9:7
24 [I]Or, *wadi* [a]Num. 21:13, 14; Judg. 11:18
25 [I]Lit., *in front of* [II]Lit., *under all the heavens* [a]Ex. 23:27; Deut. 11:25; Josh. 2:9 [b]Ex. 15:14-16
26 [a]Num. 21:21-32; Deut. 1:4; Judg. 11:19-21
27 [I]Lit., *go by the way*
28 [I]Lit., *my feet* [a]Num. 20:19

🔑 **2:10,11** See note on Num. 13:32,33.

🔑 **2:22** "To this day" is a phrase which is found often throughout the Pentateuch and historical books of the O.T. It meant up to the time when that particular book was written. (See Gen. 22:14; 32:32; 35:20; Deut. 3:14; 34:6; Josh. 4:9; 7:26; Judg. 1:21; 10:4; I Sam. 6:18; II Sam. 4:3; I Kgs. 9:13; II Kgs. 8:22).

🔑 **2:23** "Villages" could also mean "enclosures." The Avvim are called Avvites in Josh. 13:3. They are the scattered remnant of a people conquered by the Caphtorim (Gen. 10:14). The word means "ruins," and seems to be a statement about their fallen state.

in Seir and the Moabites who live in
[a]Ar did for me, until I cross over the
Jordan into the land which the LORD our
God is giving to us.'
30 "But [a]Sihon king of Heshbon was
not willing[14] for us to pass [I]through his
land; for the [b]LORD your God hardened
his spirit[7307] and made his heart[3824] obstinate, in order to deliver him into your
hand, as *he is* today.
31 "And the LORD said to me, 'See,
I have begun to deliver Sihon and his
land [I]over to you. Begin to [II]occupy,
that you may possess[3423] his land.'
32 "Then Sihon [I]with all his people
came out to meet us in battle at Jahaz.
33 "And [a]the LORD our God delivered him [I]over to us; and we [II][b]de-
feated[5221] him with his sons[1121] and all
his people.
34 "So we captured all his cities at
that time,[6256] and [I][a]utterly destroyed[2763]
[II]the men, women[802] and children[2945] of
every city. We left[7604] no survivor.[8300]
35 "We took [a]only the animals as
our booty and the spoil of the cities which
we had captured.
36 "From [a]Aroer which is on the
edge[8193] of the [I]valley of Arnon and *from*
the city which is in the [I]valley, even to
Gilead, there was no city that was too
high for us; the LORD our God delivered
all [II]over to us.
37 "[a]Only you did not go near to
the land of the sons of Ammon, all along
the [I]river [b]Jabbok and the cities of the
hill country, and wherever the LORD our
God had commanded us.

Conquests Recounted

3 "[a]Then we turned and went up[5927]
the road[1870] to Bashan, and Og,
king[4428] of Bashan, [I]with all his people[5971]
came out to meet us in battle at Edrei.
2 "But the LORD said[559] to me, 'Do
not fear[3372] him, for I have delivered
him and all his people and his land into
your hand;[3027] and you shall do to him
just as you did[6213] to Sihon king of the
Amorites, who lived at Heshbon.'
3 "So the LORD our God[430] delivered
Og also, king of Bashan, with all his
people into our hand,[3027] and we
smote[5221] [I]them until no survivor[7604] was
[II]left.[8300]
4 "And we captured all his cities at
that time;[6256] there was not a city which
we did not take from them: sixty cities,
all the region[2256] of [a]Argob, the kingdom[4467] of Og in Bashan.
5 "All these were cities fortified with
high walls, gates and bars, besides a
great many [I]unwalled towns.
6 "And we [I]utterly destroyed them,
as we did[6213] to [a]Sihon king of Heshbon, [II][b]utterly destroying[2763] [III]the men,
women[802] and children[2945] of every city.
7 "[a]But all the animals and the spoil
of the cities we took as our booty.
8 "[a]Thus we took the land at that
time from the hand of the two kings[4428]
of the Amorites who were beyond the
Jordan, from the [I]valley of Arnon to
Mount Hermon
9 (Sidonians [a]call[7121] Hermon [b]Siri-
on, and the Amorites call it [c]Senir):
10 all the cities of the tableland and
all Gilead and [a]all Bashan, as far as Salecah and Edrei, cities of the kingdom
of Og in Bashan.
11 (For only Og king of Bashan was
left[7604] of the remnant[3499] of the [a]Repha-
im.[7497] Behold, his [I]bedstead was an iron
[I]bedstead; it is in [b]Rabbah of the sons[1121]
of Ammon. Its length was nine cubits
and its width four cubits [II]by ordinary
cubit.)
12 "So we took possession[3423] of
this land at that time. From [a]Aroer,
which is by the [I]valley of Arnon, and
half the hill country of [b]Gilead and its
cities, I gave to the Reubenites and to
the Gadites.
13 "And the rest of Gilead, and all
Bashan, the kingdom of Og, I gave to
the half-tribe[7626] of Manasseh, all the
region of Argob (concerning all Bashan,
it is called[7121] the land of Rephaim.
14 [a]Jair the son[1121] of Manasseh
took all the region[2256] of Argob as far
as the border of the Geshurites and the
Maacathites, and called [I]it, *that is*,

29 [a]Deut. 2:9
30 [I]Lit., *by him* [a]Num. 21:23 [b]Ex. 4:21; Josh. 11:20
31 [I]Lit., *before you* [II]Lit., *possess*
32 [I]Lit., *he and*
33 [I]Lit., *before us* [II]Lit., *smote* [a]Ex. 23:31; Deut. 7:2 [b]Deut. 29:7
34 [I]Or, *put under the ban* [II]Lit., *every city of man. . .* [a]Deut. 3:6; 7:2
35 [a]Deut. 3:7
36 [I]Or, *wadi* [II]Lit., *before us* [a]Deut. 3:12; 4:48; Josh. 12:2; 13:9
37 [I]Or, *wadi* [a]Deut. 2:19 [b]Gen. 32:22; Num. 21:24; Deut. 3:16

1 [I]Lit., *he and* [a]Num. 21:33-35
3 [I]Lit., *him* [II]Lit., *left to him*
4 [a]Deut. 3:13, 14; 1Kin. 4:13
5 [I]Or, *rural*
6 [I]Or, *put them under the ban* [II]Or, *putting under the ban* [III]Lit., *every city of men. . .* [a]Deut. 1:4 [b]Deut. 2:34
7 [a]Deut. 2:35
8 [I]Or, *wadi* [a]Num. 32:33; Josh. 12:1-7; 13:8-12
9 [a]Deut. 4:48; Josh. 11:17; Ps. 42:6; 133:3 [b]Ps. 29:6 [c]1Chr. 5:23
10 [a]Josh. 13:11
11 [I]Or, *couch* [II]Lit., *by a man's forearm* [a]Gen. 14:5; Deut. 2:11, 20 [b]2Sam. 11:1; 12:26; Jer. 49:2
12 [I]Or, *wadi* [a]Deut. 2:36 [b]Num. 32:32-38; Josh. 13:8-13
14 [I]Lit., *them* [a]Num. 32:41; 1Chr. 2:22

Bashan, after his own name, [II]Havvoth-
jair, *as it is* to this day.)[3117]
15 "[a]And to Machir I gave Gilead.
16 "And to the Reubenites and to
the Gadites, I gave from Gilead even
as far as the [I]valley of Arnon, the middle
of the [I]valley [II]as a border and as far
as the [I]river [a]Jabbok, the border of the
sons of Ammon;
17 the Arabah[6160] also, with the Jordan [I]as *a* border, from [II][a]Chinnereth
[b]even as far as the sea of the Arabah,
[c]the Salt Sea, [III]at the foot of the slopes
of Pisgah on the east.
18 "Then I commanded[6680] you at
that time, saying, '[a]The LORD your God
has given you this land to possess it;
[b]all you valiant men shall cross over
armed before your brothers,[251] the sons
of Israel.
19 '[a]But your wives[802] and your little
ones[2945] and your livestock (I know[3045]
that you have [b]much livestock), shall
remain in your cities which I have given
you,
20 [a]until the LORD gives rest to your
fellow countrymen as to you, and they
also possess the land which the LORD
your God will give them beyond the Jordan. [b]Then you may return[7725] every
man to his possession,[3425] which I have
given you.'
21 "And I commanded Joshua at that
time, saying, 'Your eyes have seen[7200]
all that the LORD your God has done[6213]
to these two kings; so the LORD shall
do to all the kingdoms[4467] into which
you are about to cross.[5674]
22 'Do not fear them, for the LORD
your God [a]is the one fighting for you.'
23 "I also pleaded[2603] with the LORD
at that time, saying,
24 'O Lord[136] [I]GOD, Thou hast begun to show[7200] Thy servant[5650] [a]Thy
greatness and Thy strong[2389] hand; for
what [b]god[410] is there in heaven[8064] or
on earth[776] who can do such works and
mighty acts as Thine?
25 'Let me, I pray,[4994] cross
over[5674] and see the [a]fair[2896] land that
is beyond the Jordan, [I]that good[2896] hill
country and Lebanon.'
26 "But [a]the LORD was angry[5674]
with me on your account, and would
not listen[8085] to me; and the LORD said
to me, '[I]Enough! Speak[1696] to Me no
more of this matter.[1697]
27 'Go up to the top[7218] of [a]Pisgah
and lift up[5375] your eyes to the west
and north and south and east, and see[7200]
it with your eyes, [b]for you shall not cross
over this Jordan.
28 '[a]But charge[6680] Joshua and
encourage[2388] him and strengthen him;
[b]for he shall go across [I]at the head of
this people, and he shall give them as
an inheritance[5157] the land which you
will see.'
29 "So we remained in the valley
opposite [a]Beth-peor.

Israel Urged to Obey God's Law

4 "And now, O Israel, listen[8085] to
the statutes[2706] and the judgments[4941] which [a]I am teaching[3925] you
to perform, in order that [b]you may
live[2421] and go in and take possession
of the land which the LORD, the God[430]
of your fathers, is giving you.
2 "[a]You shall not add to the word[1697]
which [b]I am commanding[6680] you, nor
take away from it, that you may keep[8104]
the commandments of the LORD your
God which I command you.
3 "[a]Your eyes have seen[7200] what
the LORD has done[6213] in the case of
Baal-peor, for all the men[376] who followed Baal-peor, the LORD your God
has destroyed[8045] [I]them from among[7130]
you.
4 "But you who held fast to the LORD
your God are alive[2416] today,[3117] every
one of you.
5 "See,[7200] I have taught[3925] you
statutes and judgments [a]just as the LORD
my God commanded[6680] me, that you
should do thus in the land where you
are entering to possess it.
6 "So keep and do *them,* [a]for that
is your wisdom[2451] and your understanding[998] in the sight of the peoples[4171]
who will hear[8085] all these statutes
and say,[559] 'Surely this great

14 [II]I.e., the towns of Jair
15 [a]Num. 32:39, 40
16 [I]Or, *wadi* [II]Lit., *and* [a]Num. 21:24; Deut. 2:37
17 [I]Lit., *and* [II]I.e., the Sea of Galilee [III]Lit., *under* [a]Num. 34:11; Josh. 13:27 [b]Josh. 12:3 [c]Gen. 14:3; Josh. 3:16
18 [a]Josh. 1:13 [b]Num. 32:20; Josh. 4:12,13
19 [a]Josh. 1:14 [b]Ex. 12:38
20 [a]Josh. 1:15 [b]Josh. 22:4
22 [a]Ex. 14:14; Deut. 1:30; 20:4; Neh. 4:20
24 [I]Heb., *YHWH,* usually rendered *LORD* [a]Deut. 11:2 [b]Ex. 8:10; 15:11; 2Sam. 7:22; Ps. 71:19; 86:8
25 [I]Lit., *this* [a]Deut. 4:22
26 [I]Lit., *Enough for you* [a]Deut. 1:37
27 [a]Num. 23:14; 27:12 [b]Deut. 1:37
28 [I]Lit., *before this people* [a]Num. 27:18; Deut. 31:3, 7, 8, 23 [b]Deut. 1:38
29 [a]Num. 25:1-3; Deut. 4:46; 34:6

1 [a]Deut. 1:3 [b]Lev. 18:5; Deut. 5:33; 8:1; 16:20; 30:16, 19; Ezek. 20:11; Rom. 10:5
2 [a]Deut. 12:32; Prov. 30:6; Rev. 22:18 [b]Deut. 4:5, 14, 40
3 [I]Lit., *him* [a]Num. 25:1-9
5 [a]Lev. 26:46; 27:34
6 [a]Deut. 30:19, 20; 32:46, 47; Job 28:28; Ps. 19:7; 111:10; Prov. 1:7; 2Tim. 3:15

nation is a wise[2450] and understanding[995] people.'[5971]
7 "For [a]what great nation is there
that has a god [b]so near to it as is the
LORD our God [c]whenever we call[7121] on
Him?
8 "Or what great nation is there that
has [a]statutes and judgments as righteous
as this whole law[8451] which I am setting
before you today?
9 "Only [a]give heed to yourself and
keep your soul[5315] diligently, lest you
forget the things[1697] which your eyes
have seen, and lest they depart[5493] from
your heart[3824] [b]all the days[3117] of your
life;[2416] but [c]make them known[3045] to
your sons[1121] and your grandsons.
10 "*Remember* the day you stood before the LORD your God at Horeb, when
the LORD said[559] to me, 'Assemble the
people to Me, that I may let them hear
My words[1697] [a]so they may learn[3925] to
[1]fear[3372] Me all the days they live[2416]
on the earth,[127] and that they may
[b]teach their children.'[1121]
11 "And you came near and stood
at the foot of the mountain, [a]and the
mountain burned with fire to the *very*
heart[3820] of the heavens:[8064] darkness,[2822] cloud[6051] and thick gloom.[6205]
12 "Then the LORD spoke[1696] to you
from the midst of the fire; you heard[8085]
the sound of words, but you saw[7200]
no form—[8544] only a voice.
13 "So He declared[5046] to you His
covenant[1285] which He commanded you
to perform,[6213] *that is,* [a]the Ten [1]Com-
mandments; and [b]He wrote them on two
tablets of stone.
🔑 14 "And the LORD commanded me
at that time[6256] to teach you statutes
and judgments, that you might perform
them in the land where you are going
over[5647] to possess it.
15 "So [a]watch yourselves carefully,
since you did not see any [b]form on the
day the LORD spoke to you at Horeb
from the midst of the fire,
16 lest you [a]act corruptly[7843] and
[b]make[6213] a graven image[6459] for yourselves in the form of any figure,[5566] the
likeness[8403] of male[2145] or female,[5347]
17 the likeness of any animal that
is on the earth,[776] the likeness of
[a]any winged bird that flies in the sky,[8064]
18 the likeness of anything that
creeps on the ground,[127] the likeness
of any fish[1710] that is in the water below
the earth.
19 "And *beware,* lest you lift up your
eyes to heaven and see the sun and
the moon and the stars, [a]all the host[6635]
of heaven, [b]and be drawn away and
worship[7812] them and serve[5647] them,
those which the LORD your God has allotted to all the peoples under the whole
heaven.
20 "But the LORD has taken you and
brought you out of [a]the iron furnace,
from Egypt, to [b]be a people for His own
possession,[5159] as today.
21 "[a]Now the LORD was angry[599]
with me on your account, and swore[7650]
that I should not cross the Jordan, and
that I should not enter the good land
which the LORD your God is giving you
as an inheritance.
22 "For [a]I shall die[4191] in this land,
I shall not cross the Jordan, but you
shall cross and take possession of this
[b]good land.
23 "So watch yourselves, [a]lest you
forget the covenant of the LORD your
God, which He made with you, and
[b]make for yourselves a graven image
in the form[8544] of anything *against* which
the LORD your God has commanded[6680]
you.
24 "For the LORD your God is a
[a]consuming fire, a [b]jealous God.[410]

7 [a]Deut. 4:32-34; 2Sam. 7:23 [b]Ps. 34:17, 18; 145:18; 148:14; Is. 55:6 [c]Ps. 34:18; 85:9
8 [a]Ps. 89:14; 97:2; 119:144, 160, 172
9 [a]Deut. 4:23; 6:12; 8:11, 14, 19; Prov. 4:23; 23:19 [b]Deut. 6:2; 12:1; 16:3 [c]Gen. 18:19; Deut. 4:10; 6:7, 20-25; 11:19; 32:46; Ps. 78:5, 6; Prov. 22:6; Eph. 6:4
10 [1]Or, *reverence* [a]Deut. 14:23; 17:19; 31:12, 13 [b]Deut. 4:9
11 [a]Ex. 19:18; Heb. 12:18, 19
13 [1]Lit., *Words* [a]Ex. 34:28; Deut. 10:4 [b]Ex. 31:18; 34:1, 28
15 [a]Josh. 23:11 [b]Is. 40:18
16 [a]Deut. 4:25; 9:12; 31:29 [b]Ex. 20:4; Lev. 26:1; Deut. 5:8, 9; 27:15; Rom. 1:23
17 [a]Rom. 1:23
19 [a]Gen. 2:1; Deut. 17:3; 2Kin. 17:16; 21:3 [b]Deut. 13:5, 10; Job 31:26-28
20 [a]1Kin. 8:51; Jer. 11:4 [b]Ex. 19:5; Deut. 7:6; 14:2; 26:18; Titus 2:14; 1Pet. 2:9
21 [a]Num. 20:12; Deut. 1:37
22 [a]Num. 27:13, 14 [b]Deut. 3:25
23 [a]Deut. 4:9 [b]Deut. 4:16
24 [a]Ex. 24:17; Deut. 9:3; Is. 30:27; 33:14; Heb. 12:29 [b]Deut. 5:9; 6:15

🔑 **4:14** This was the covenant made at Mount Horeb, based on the Ten Commandments, which God spoke directly to the people. But, when the people became fearful and could bear no more, the Lord commanded Moses to send them to their tents, while Moses remained to receive the rest of the Law (Ex. 31:18; Heb. 12:19,20), which the people were to obey when they settled in their new home in Canaan. These laws were delivered in the plain of Moab as Moses' third discourse in Deuteronomy (12-26).

25 "When you [I]become the father of children and children's children and have remained long in the land, and [a]act corruptly, and [b]make an [II]idol in the form of anything, and [c]do that which is evil[7451] in the sight of the LORD your God *so as* to provoke Him to anger,[3707]

26 I [a]call heaven and earth to witness[5749] against you today, that you shall [b]surely perish[6] quickly from the land where you are going over the Jordan to possess it. You shall not [I]live[748] long on it, but shall be utterly destroyed.

27 "And the LORD will [a]scatter you among the peoples, and you shall be left[7604] few in number among the nations,[1471] where the LORD shall drive you.

28 "And [a]there you will serve gods,[430] the work of man's[120] hands,[3027] [b]wood and stone, [c]which neither see nor hear nor eat nor smell.[7306]

29 "[a]But from there you will seek the LORD your God, and you will find *Him* if you search for Him [b]with all your heart and all your soul.

30 "When you [a]are in distress and all these things have come upon you, [b]in the latter days, [c]you will return[7725] to the LORD your God and listen[8085] to His voice.

31 "For the LORD your God is a [a]compassionate God; [b]He will not fail[7503] you nor [c]destroy[7843] you nor [d]forget the covenant with your fathers which He swore to them.

32 "Indeed, [a]ask[7592] now concerning the former days which were before you, since the [b]day that God created[1254] [I]man[120] on the earth, and *inquire* [c]from one end of the heavens to the other. [d]Has *anything* been done like this great thing,[1697] or has *anything* been heard like it?

33 "[a]Has *any* people heard the voice of God speaking[1696] from the midst of the fire, as you have heard *it*, and survived?

34 "[a]Or has a god tried[5254] to go to take for himself a nation from within[7130] *another* nation [b]by trials,[4531] by signs[226] and wonders[4159] and by war and [c]by a mighty[2389] hand[3027] and by an outstretched arm and by great terrors,[4172] [I]as the LORD your God did for you in Egypt before your eyes?

35 "To you it was shown[7200] that you might know[3045] that the LORD, He is God; [a]there is no other besides Him.

36 "[a]Out of the heavens He let you hear His voice [b]to discipline[3256] you; and on earth He let you see His great fire, and you heard[8085] His words from the midst of the fire.

37 "[I][a]Because He loved your fathers,[1] therefore He chose[977] [II]their descendants[2233] after them. And He [III][b]personally brought you from Egypt by His great power,

38 driving out[3423] from before you nations[1471] greater and mightier than you, to bring you in *and* [a]to give you their land for an inheritance, as it is today.

39 "Know therefore today, and take it to your heart, that [a]the LORD, He is God in heaven above and on the earth below; there is no other.

40 "[a]So you shall keep His statutes and His commandments which I am [I]giving you today, that [b]it may go well[3190] with you and with your children after you, and [c]that you may [II]live long on the land which the LORD your God is giving you for all time."

41 [a]Then Moses set apart[914] three cities across the Jordan to the [I]east,

42 that a manslayer[7523] might flee there, who unintentionally[1097,1847] slew his neighbor without having enmity[8130] toward him in time past; and by fleeing to one of these cities he might live:

43 [a]Bezer in the wilderness on the plateau[776] for the Reubenites, and Ramoth in Gilead for the Gadites, and Golan in Bashan for the Manassites.

44 Now this is the law which Moses set[7760] before the sons of Israel;

25 [I]Lit., *beget* [II]Or, *a graven image* [a]Deut. 4:16 [b]Deut. 4:23 [c]2Kin. 17:17
26 [I]Lit., *prolong your days* [a]Deut. 30:19; 31:28; 32:1; Is. 1:2; Mic. 6:2 [b]Deut. 7:4; 8:19, 20
27 [a]Lev. 26:33; Deut. 28:64; 29:28; Neh. 1:8
28 [a]Deut. 28:36, 64; Jer. 16:13 [b]Deut. 29:17 [c]Ps. 115:4-8; 135:15-18; Is. 44:12-20
29 [a]Deut. 30:1-3, 10; 2Chr. 15:4; Is. 55:6; Jer. 29:13 [b]Deut. 6:5; 10:12
30 [a]Ps. 18:6; 59:16; 107:6, 13 [b]Deut. 31:29; Jer. 23:20; Hos. 3:5; Heb. 1:2 [c]Jer. 4:1, 2
31 [a]Ex. 34:6; 2Chr. 30:9; Neh. 9:31; Ps. 103:8; 111:4; 116:5; Jon. 4:2 [b]Deut. 31:6, 8; Josh. 1:5; 1Chr. 28:20; Heb. 13:5 [c]Jer. 30:11 [d]Lev. 26:45
32 [I]Or, *Adam* [a]Deut. 32:7; Job 8:8 [b]Gen. 1:27; Is. 45:12 [c]Deut. 28:64; Matt. 24:31 [d]Deut. 4:7; 2Sam. 7:23
33 [a]Ex. 20:22; Deut. 5:24, 26
34 [I]Lit., *according to all that* [a]Ex. 14:30; Deut. 33:29 [b]Deut. 7:19 [c]Deut. 5:15; 6:21; Ps. 136:12
35 [a]Ex. 8:10; 9:14; Deut. 4:39; 32:12, 39; 1Sam. 2:2; Is. 43:10-12; 44:6-8; 45:5-7; Mark 12:32
36 [a]Ex. 19:9, 19; 20:18, 22; Deut. 4:33; Neh. 9:13; Heb. 12:25 [b]Deut. 8:5
37 [I]Lit., *And instead, because* [II]Lit., *his seed* [III]Lit., *with His presence* [a]Deut. 7:7, 8; 10:15; 33:3 [b]Ex. 33:14; Is. 63:9
38 [a]Num. 32:4; 34:14, 15
39 [a]Deut. 4:35; Josh. 2:11
40 [I]Lit., *commanding* [II]Lit., *prolong your days* [a]Lev. 22:31; Deut. 4:2; Ps. 105:45 [b]Deut. 4:1; 5:16, 29, 33; 6:3, 18; 12:25, 28; 22:7 [c]Ex. 23:26; Deut. 32:47
41 [I]Lit., *sunrise* [a]Num. 35:6; Deut. 19:2-13; Josh. 20:7-9
43 [a]Josh. 20:8

45 these are the testimonies[5713] and the statutes and the ordinances which Moses spoke to the sons of Israel, when they came out from Egypt,

46 across the Jordan, in the valley [a]opposite Beth-peor, in the land of [b]Sihon king[4428] of the Amorites who lived at Heshbon, whom Moses and the sons of Israel [I]defeated[5221] when they came out from Egypt.

47 And they took possession[3423] of his land and the land of [a]Og king of Bashan, the two kings[4428] of the Amorites, *who were* across the Jordan to the [I]east,

48 from [a]Aroer, which is on the edge[8143] of the [I]valley of Arnon, even as far as [b]Mount Sion (that is, Hermon),

49 with all the Arabah[6160] across the Jordan to the east, even as far as the sea of the Arabah, [I]at the foot of the slopes of Pisgah.

The Ten Commandments Repeated

5 Then Moses summoned[7121] all Israel, and said[559] to them, "Hear,[8085] O Israel, the statutes[2706] and the ordinances[4941] which I am speaking[1696] today[3117] in your [I]hearing,[241] that you may learn[3925] them and observe[8104] [II]them carefully.

2 "The LORD our God[430] made[3772] [a]a covenant[1285] with us at Horeb.

3 "[a]The LORD did not make this covenant with our fathers,[1] but with us, *with* all those of [I]us alive[2416] here today.

4 "The LORD spoke[1696] to you [a]face to face at the mountain [b]from the midst of the fire,

5 *while* [a]I was standing between the LORD and you at that time,[6256] to declare[5046] to you the word[1697] of the LORD; [b]for you were afraid because of the fire and did not go up the mountain. [I]He said,

6 "[a]I am the LORD your God, who brought you out of the land of Egypt, out of the house[1004] of [I]slavery.[5650]

7 "[a]You shall have no other gods[430] [I]before Me.

8 "[a]You shall not make for yourself [I]an idol,[6459] *or* any likeness[8544] *of* what is in heaven[8064] above [II]or on the earth[776] beneath [II]or in the water under the earth.

9 'You shall not worship[7812] them or serve[5647] them; for I, the LORD your God, am a jealous God,[410] [a]visiting the iniquity[5771] of the fathers on the children,[1121] and on the third and the fourth *generations* of those who hate[8130] Me,

10 but [a]showing lovingkindness[2617] to thousands,[505] to those who love[157] Me and keep My commandments.

11 "[a]You shall not take[5375] the name of the LORD your God in vain,[7723] for the LORD will not [I]leave him unpunished[5352] who takes His name in vain.

12 "[a]Observe the sabbath[7676] day to keep it holy,[6942] as the LORD your God commanded[6680] you.

13 'Six days[3117] you shall labor[5647] and do all your work,

14 but [a]the seventh day is a sabbath of the LORD your God; *in it* you shall not do any work, you or your son[1121] or your daughter or your male servant[5650] or your female servant or your ox or your donkey or any of your cattle or your sojourner[1616] who [I]stays with you, so that your male servant and your female servant may rest as well as you.

15 "[a]And you shall remember[2142] that you were a slave[5650] in the land of Egypt, and the LORD your God brought you out of there by a mighty[2389] hand and by an outstretched arm; therefore the LORD your God commanded you to observe[6213] the sabbath day.

16 "[a]Honor your father[1] and your mother, as the LORD your God has commanded you, [b]that your days may be prolonged,[748] and that it may go well[3190] with you on the land[127] which the LORD your God gives you.

17 "[a]You shall not murder.

46 [I]Lit., *smote* [a]Deut. 3:29 [b]Num. 21:21-25
47 [I]Lit., *sunrise* [a]Deut. 1:4; 3:3, 4
48 [I]Or, *wadi* [a]Deut. 2:36; 3:12 [b]Deut. 3:9; Ps. 133:3
49 [I]Lit., *under*

1 [I]Lit., *ears* [II]Lit., *to do them*
2 [a]Ex. 19:5; Mal. 4:4
3 [I]Lit., *us ourselves* [a]Jer. 31:32; Heb. 8:9
4 [a]Num. 14:14; Deut. 34:10 [b]Deut. 4:33
5 [I]Lit., *saying* [a]Gal. 3:19 [b]Ex. 19:16, 21-24; 20:18; Heb. 12:18-21
6 [I]Lit., *slaves* [a]Ex. 20:2-17; Lev. 26:1; Deut. 6:4; Ps. 81:10
7 [I]Or, *besides* [a]Ex. 20:3
8 [I]Or, *a graven image* [II]Lit., *or what is* [a]Ex. 20:4-6; Lev. 26:1; Deut. 4:15-18; 27:15; Ps. 97:7
9 [a]Ex. 34:7; Num. 14:18; Deut. 7:10
10 [a]Num. 14:18; Deut. 7:9; Jer. 32:18
11 [I]Or, *hold him guiltless* [a]Ex. 20:7; Lev. 19:12; Deut. 6:13; 10:20; Matt. 5:33
12 [a]Ex. 16:23-30; 20:8-11; 31:13f.; Mark 2:27f.
14 [I]Lit., *is in your gates* [a]Gen. 2:2; Heb. 4:4
15 [a]Ex. 20:11
16 [a]Ex. 20:12; Lev. 19:3; Deut. 27:16; Matt. 15:4; 19:19; Mark 7:10; 10:19; Luke 18:20; Eph. 6:2, 3; Col. 3:20 [b]Deut. 4:40
17 [a]Gen. 9:6; Ex. 20:13; Lev. 24:17; Matt. 5:21f.; 19:18; Mark 10:19; Rom. 13:9; James 2:11

5:9 See note on Ezek. 18:1-4.

18 [a]"You shall not commit adultery.[5003]

19 [a]"You shall not steal.

20 [a]"You shall not bear false[7723] witness against your neighbor.

21 [a]"You shall not covet your neighbor's wife,[802] and you shall not desire[183] your neighbor's house, his field[7704] or his male servant or his female servant, his ox or his donkey or anything that belongs to your neighbor.'

Moses Interceded

22 "These words[1697] the LORD spoke[1696] to all your assembly[6951] at the mountain from the midst of the fire, *of* the cloud[6680] and *of* the thick gloom,[6205] with a great voice, and He added no more. And [a]He wrote them on two tablets of stone and gave them to me.

23 "And it came about, when you heard[8085] the voice from the midst of the darkness,[2822] while the mountain was burning with fire, that you came near to me, all the heads[7218] of your tribes[7626] and your elders.[2205]

24 "And you said, 'Behold, the LORD our God has shown[7200] us His glory[3519] and His greatness, and we have heard His voice from the midst of the fire; we have seen[7200] today that God speaks[1696] with man, yet he lives.[2425]

25 [a]'Now then why should we die?[4191] For this great fire will consume us; if we hear the voice of the LORD our God any longer, then we shall die.

26 'For [a]who is there of all flesh,[1320] who has heard the voice of the living[2416] God speaking[1696] from the midst of the fire, as we *have*, and lived?[2421]

27 '[I]Go near[7126] and hear all that the LORD our God says;[559] then speak to us all that the LORD our God will speak to you, and we will hear and do *it*.'

28 "And the LORD heard the voice of your words when you spoke to me, [a]and the LORD said to me, 'I have heard the voice of the words of this people[5971] which they have spoken[1696] to you. They have done well in all that they have spoken.

29 [a]'Oh that they had such a heart[3824] in them, that they would fear[3372] Me, and [b]keep all My commandments always, that [c]it may be well with them and with their sons forever![5769]

30 'Go, say to them, "Return to your tents."[168]

31 [a]'But as for you, stand here by Me, that I may speak to you all the commandments and the statutes and the judgments which you shall teach[3925] them, that they may observe *them* in the land[776] which I give them to possess.'

32 "So you shall observe[8104] to do just as the LORD your God has commanded you; [a]you shall not turn aside to the right or to the left.

33 "[a]You shall walk in all the way[1870] which the LORD your God has commanded you, [b]that you may live,[2421] and that it may be well[2895] with you, and that you may prolong[748] *your* days in the land which you shall possess.

Obey God and Prosper

6 "Now this is the commandment, the statutes[2706] and the judgments[4941] which the LORD your God[430] has commanded[6680] *me* to teach[3925] you, that you might do *them* in the land where you are going over to possess it,

2 so that you and your son[1121] and your grandson might [a]fear[3372] the LORD your God, to keep[8104] all His statutes[2708] and His commandments, which I command[6680] you, [b]all the days[3117] of your life,[2416] and that your days may be prolonged.[748]

3 "O Israel, you should listen[8085] and [I]be careful[8104] to do *it*, that [a]it may be well[3190] with you and that you may multiply greatly, just as the LORD, the God of your fathers,[1] has promised[1696] you, *in* [b]a land flowing with milk and honey.

18 [a]Ex. 20:14; Lev. 20:10; Matt. 5:27f.; 19:18; Mark 10:19; Luke 18:20; Rom. 13:9; James 2:11
19 [a]Ex. 20:15; Lev. 19:11
20 [a]Ex. 20:16; 23:1; Matt. 19:18
21 [a]Ex. 20:17; Rom. 7:7; 13:9
22 [a]Ex. 24:12; 31:18; Deut. 4:13
25 [a]Ex. 20:18, 19; Deut. 18:16
26 [a]Deut. 4:33
27 [I]Lit., *Go yourself*
28 [a]Deut. 18:17
29 [a]Ps. 81:13; Is. 48:18 [b]Deut. 11:1 [c]Deut. 5:16, 33
31 [a]Ex. 24:12
32 [a]Deut. 17:20; 28:14; Josh. 1:7; 23:6; Prov. 4:27
33 [a]Deut. 10:12; Jer. 7:23; Luke 1:6 [b]Deut. 4:1, 40; 12:25, 28; 22:7; Eph. 6:3
2 [a]Ex. 20:20; Deut. 10:12; Ps. 111:10; 128:1; Eccl. 12:13 [b]Deut. 4:9
3 [I]Lit., *keep* [a]Deut. 5:33 [b]Ex. 3:8, 17

🔑 **4** "[a]Hear, O Israel! The LORD is our
God, the [b]LORD is one!
5 "And [a]you shall love[157] the LORD
your God [b]with all your heart[3824] and
with all your soul[5315] and with all your
might.
6 "And [a]these words,[1697] which I am
commanding you today,[3117] shall be on
your heart;
7 and [a]you shall teach them diligently[8150] to your sons[1121] and shall
talk[1696] of them when you sit in your
house[1004] and when you walk by the
way[1870] and when you lie down and when
you rise up.
8 "[a]And you shall bind them as a
sign[226] on your hand[3027] and they shall
be as [I]frontals[2903] [II]on your forehead.
9 "[a]And you shall write them on the
doorposts of your house and on your
gates.
10 "Then it shall come about when
the LORD your God brings you into the
land which He swore[7650] to your fathers,
Abraham, Isaac and Jacob, to give you,
[a]great and splendid[2896] cities which you
did not build,
11 and houses full of all good things
which you did not fill, and hewn
cisterns[953] which you did not dig, vineyards and olive trees which you did not
plant, and [a]you shall eat and be satisfied,
12 then watch[8104] yourself, lest
[a]you forget the LORD who brought you
from the land of Egypt, out of the house
of [I]slavery.[5650]

4 [a]Matt. 22:37; Mark 12:29, 30; Luke 10:27 [b]Deut. 4:35, 39; John 10:30; 1Cor. 8:4; Eph. 4:6
5 [a]Matt. 22:37; Mark 12:30; Luke 10:27 [b]Deut. 4:29; 10:12
6 [a]Deut. 11:18
7 [a]Deut. 4:9; 11:19; Eph. 6:4
8 [I]Or, *frontlet bands* [II]Lit., *between your eyes* [a]Ex. 12:14; 13:9, 16; Deut. 11:18; Prov. 3:3; 6:21; 7:3
9 [a]Deut. 11:20
10 [a]Deut. 9:1; 19:1; Josh. 24:13; Ps. 105:44
11 [a]Deut. 8:10; 11:15; 14:29
12 [I]Lit., *slaves* [a]Deut. 4:9
13 [I]Or, *reverence* [II]Or, *serve* [a]Deut. 13:4; Matt. 4:10; Luke 4:8 [b]Deut. 5:11; 10:20; Ps. 63:11; Matt. 5:33
14 [a]Jer. 25:6
15 [I]Lit., *destroy* [a]Deut. 4:24; 5:9
16 [a]Matt. 4:7; Luke 4:12 [b]Ex. 17:7
17 [a]Deut. 11:22; Ps. 119:4
18 [a]Deut. 4:40
20 [a]Ex. 13:8, 14

🔑 13 "[a]You shall [I]fear *only* the LORD
your God; and you shall [II]worship[5647]
Him, and [b]swear[7650] by His name.
14 "[a]You shall not follow other
gods,[430] any of the gods of the peoples[5971] who surround you,
15 for the LORD your God in the
midst[7130] of you is a [a]jealous God;[410]
otherwise the anger of the LORD your
God will be kindled[2734] against you, and
He will [I]wipe[8045] you off the face of the
earth.
🔑 **16** "[a]You shall not put the LORD
your God to the test,[5254] [b]as you
tested[5254] *Him* at Massah.
17 "[a]You should diligently keep[8104]
the commandments of the LORD your
God, and His testimonies[5713] and His
statutes which He has commanded
you.
18 "And you shall do what is right
and good[2896] in the sight of the LORD,
that [a]it may be well with you and that
you may go in and possess the good
land which the LORD swore to *give* your
fathers,
19 by driving out all your enemies
from before you, as the LORD has
spoken.[1696]
20 "[a]When your son asks[7592] you
in time to come, saying, 'What *do* the
testimonies and the statutes and the
judgments *mean* which the LORD our
God commanded you?'
21 then you shall say[559] to your son,
'We were slaves[5650] to Pharaoh in

🔑 **6:4-9** To the Jews, this is the most important text in Deuteronomy, and this agrees with Jesus' own assessment, because He called v. 5 "the great and foremost commandment" (Mt. 22:36-38; see note on Ex. 20:1-17). The Jews refer to these verses as the Shema, since that is the first word in the text, meaning to listen in the sense of obeying. It is the central tenet of monotheism. Moses was here trying to teach Israel where her priorities lay and how to guarantee that she would never forget them. Unfortunately, before Israel and Judah went into exile, the people did forget and national tragedy resulted. Hosea put his finger on part of the problem when he attributed it to their lack of knowledge (Hos. 4:6). Had Israel taught the Shema to her children and displayed it as Moses prescribed, her history would certainly have been much different. Recently, in one of the Dead Sea caves, a phylactery has been discovered which contained these six verses.

🔑 **6:13** Jesus quoted part of this verse and Deut. 10:20 in response to one of Satan's temptations in the wilderness (Mt. 4:10; Lk. 4:8). In fact, this early part of Deuteronomy, which was spoken by Moses while Israel was still in the period of her wilderness wanderings, formed the basis of all three of Jesus' responses to Satan. "You shall not put the Lord your God to the test" (Mt. 4:7; Lk. 4:12) comes from Deut. 6:16, and "Man shall not live on bread alone" (Mt. 4:4; Lk. 4:4) is a quotation of Deut. 8:3.

🔑 **6:16** See note on Deut. 6:13.

Egypt; and the LORD brought us from Egypt with a mighty[2389] hand.

22 'Moreover, the LORD showed great and distressing[7451] signs[226] and wonders[4159] before our eyes against Egypt, Pharaoh and all his household;[1004]

23 and He brought us out from there in order to bring us in, to give us the land which He had sworn to our fathers.'

24 "So the LORD commanded us to observe all these statutes, [a]to fear the LORD our God for our good always and [b]for our survival,[2421] as *it is* today.

25 "And [a]it will be righteousness[6666] for us if we [I]are careful to observe all this commandment before the LORD our God, just as He commanded us.

Warnings

7 "[a]When the LORD your God[430] shall bring you into the land where you are entering to possess it, and shall clear away many nations[1471] before you, the Hittites and the Girgashites and the Amorites and the Canaanites and the Perizzites and the Hivites and the Jebusites, [b]seven nations greater and stronger than you,

2 and when the LORD your God shall deliver them before you, and you shall [I]defeat[5221] them, [a]then you shall [II]utterly destroy[2763] them. [b]You shall make no covenant[1285] with them [c]and show no favor to them.

3 "Furthermore, [a]you shall not intermarry with them; you shall not give your [I]daughters to [II]their sons,[1121] nor shall you take [III]their daughters for your [IV]sons.

4 "For [I]they will turn your [II]sons away from [III]following Me to serve[5647] other gods;[430] then the anger of the LORD will be kindled[2734] against you, and [a]He will quickly destroy[8045] you.

5 "But thus you shall do[6213] to them: [a]you shall tear down[5422] their altars, and smash[7665] their *sacred* pillars, and hew down their [I]Asherim,[842] and burn[8313] their graven images[6456] with fire.

🔑 6 "For you are [a]a holy[6918] people[5971] to the LORD your God; the LORD your God has chosen[977] you to be [b]a people for His [I]own possession[5459] out of all the peoples who are on the face of the [II]earth.

7 "[a]The LORD did not set His love[2836] on you nor choose[977] you because you were more in number than any of the peoples, for you were the fewest of all peoples,

8 but because the LORD loved[160] you and kept[8104] the [a]oath[7621] which He swore[7650] to your forefathers,[1] [b]the LORD brought you out by a mighty[2389] hand,[3027] and redeemed[6299] you from the house[1004] of [I]slavery,[5650] from the hand of Pharaoh king[4428] of Egypt.

9 "Know[3045] therefore that the LORD your God, [a]He is God, [b]the faithful[539] God,[410] [c]who keeps[8104] [I]His covenant and [I]His lovingkindness[2617] to a thousandth generation[1755] with those who [d]love[157] Him and keep His commandments;

10 but [a]repays those who hate[8130] Him to [I]their faces, to destroy[6] [II]them; He will not delay[309] [III]with him who hates[8130] Him, He will repay[7999] him to his face.

11 "Therefore, you shall keep the commandment and the statutes[2706] and the judgments[4941] which I am commanding[6680] you today,[3117] to do them.

Promises of God

12 "[a]Then it shall come about, because you listen[8085] to these judgments and keep and do them, that the LORD your God will keep with you [I]His covenant and [I]His lovingkindness which He swore[7650] to your forefathers.

13 "And He will [a]love you and bless[1288] you and [b]multiply you; He will

24 [a]Deut. 10:12; Jer. 32:39 [b]Ps. 41:2; Luke 10:28
25 [I]Lit., *keep* [a]Deut. 24:13; Rom. 10:3
1 [a]Deut. 20:16-18 [b]Acts 13:19
2 [I]Lit., *smite* [II]Lit., *surely devote to the ban* [a]Num. 31:17; Josh. 11:11 [b]Ex. 23:32 [c]Deut. 7:16; 13:8
3 [I]Lit., *daughter* [II]Lit., *his son* [III]Lit., *his daughter* [IV]Lit., *son* [a]Ex. 34:15, 16; Josh. 23:12; Ezra 9:2
4 [I]Lit., *he* [II]Lit., *son* [III]Lit., *after* [a]Deut. 4:26
5 [I]I.e., wooden symbols of a female deity [a]Ex. 23:24; 34:13; Deut. 12:3
6 [I]Or, *special treasure* [II]Lit., *ground* [a]Ex. 19:6; Deut. 14:2, 21; Ps. 50:5; Jer. 2:3 [b]Ex. 19:5; Deut. 4:20; 14:2; 26:18; Ps. 135:4; Titus 2:14; 1Pet. 2:9
7 [a]Deut. 4:37
8 [I]Lit., *slaves* [a]Ex. 32:13 [b]Ex. 13:3
9 [I]Lit., *the* [a]Deut. 4:35, 39 [b]Is. 49:7; 1Cor. 1:9; 1Thess. 5:24; 2Tim. 2:13 [c]Ex. 20:6; Dan. 9:4 [d]Deut. 5:10
10 [I]Lit., *his face* [II]Lit., *him* [III]Lit., *to* [a]Is. 59:18; Nah. 1:2
12 [I]Lit., *the* [a]Lev. 26:3-13; Deut. 28:1-14
13 [a]Ps. 146:8; Prov. 15:9; John 14:21 [b]Lev. 26:9; Deut. 13:17; 30:5

🔑 **7:6** In Hebrew the word translated as "holy" means "separate" or "set apart." Israel had to be unique among the nations because she belonged to God in a special way. The moral implications of this isolationism becomes clearer in later passages.

also bless the fruit of your womb[990] and the fruit of your ground,[127] your grain and your new wine and your oil,[3323] the increase of your herd[504] and the young of your flock, [I]in the land which He swore to your forefathers to give you.

14 "You shall be blessed[1288] above all peoples; there shall be no male or female [a]barren[6135] among you or among your cattle.

15 "And [a]the LORD will remove from you all sickness; and He will not put on you any of the harmful[7451] diseases[4064] of Egypt which you have known,[3045] but He will lay them on all who hate you.

16 "And you shall consume all the peoples whom the LORD your God will deliver to you; [a]your eye shall not pity them, neither shall you serve their gods, for that *would be* [b]a snare[4170] to you.

17 "If you should say[559] in your heart,[3824] 'These nations are greater than I; how can I [a]dispossess[3423] them?'

18 you shall not be afraid of them; you shall well [a]remember[2142] what the LORD your God did[6213] to Pharaoh and to all Egypt:

19 [a]the great trials[4531] which your eyes saw[7200] and the signs[226] and the wonders[4159] and the mighty hand and the outstretched arm by which the LORD your God brought you out. So shall the LORD your God do to all the peoples of whom you are afraid.[3373]

20 "Moreover, the LORD your God will send [a]the hornet against them, until those who are left[7604] and hide themselves from you perish.[6]

21 "You shall not dread[6206] [I]them, for [a]the LORD your God is in your midst,[7130] [b]a great and awesome[3372] God.

22 "[a]And the LORD your God will clear away these nations before you little by little; you will not be able to put an end to them[3615] quickly, lest the [I]wild[7704] beasts[2416] grow too numerous for you.

23 "[a]But the LORD your God shall deliver them before you, and will [I]throw[2000] them into great confusion[4103] until they are destroyed.[8045]

24 "[a]And He will deliver their kings[4428] into your hand so that you shall make their name perish from under heaven;[8064] [b]no man will be able to stand before you until you have destroyed them.

25 "The graven images of their gods you are to [a]burn with fire; you shall [b]not covet the silver or the gold that is on them, nor take it for yourselves, lest you be [c]snared[3369] by it, for it is an [d]abomination[8441] to the LORD your God.

26 "And you shall not bring an abomination into your house, and like it come under the [a]ban;[2764] you shall utterly detest[8262] it and you shall utterly abhor[8581] it, for it is something banned.

God's Gracious Dealings

8 "All the commandments that I am commanding[6680] you today[3117] you shall be careful[8104] to do, that you [a]may live[2421] and multiply, and go in and possess the land[776] which the LORD swore[7650] *to give* to your forefathers.[1]

2 "[a]And you shall remember[2142] all the way[1870] which the LORD your God[430] has [b]led you in the wilderness these forty years, that He might humble you, [c]testing[5254] you, to know[3045] what was in your heart,[3824] whether you would keep[8104] His commandments or not.

3 "And He humbled you and let you be hungry, and fed you with manna[4478] which you did not know,[3045] nor did your fathers know, that He might make you [I]understand that [a]man[120] does not live by bread alone, but man[120] lives by everything that proceeds out of the mouth[6310] of the LORD.

4 "[a]Your clothing did not wear out on you, nor did your foot swell these forty years.

5 "[a]Thus you are to know[3045] in your heart that the LORD your God was

13 [I]Lit., *on the ground*
14 [a]Ex. 23:26
15 [a]Ex. 15:26
16 [a]Deut. 7:2 [b]Ex. 23:33; Judg. 8:27; Ps. 106:36
17 [a]Num. 33:53
18 [a]Ps. 105:5
19 [a]Deut. 4:34
20 [a]Ex. 23:28; Josh. 24:12
21 [I]Lit., *from before them* [a]Ex. 29:45; Josh. 3:10 [b]Deut. 10:17; Neh. 1:5; 9:32
22 [I]Lit., *beasts of the field* [a]Ex. 23:29, 30
23 [I]Lit., *confuse them with* [a]Ex. 23:27; Josh. 10:10
24 [a]Josh. 6:2; 10:23-25 [b]Deut. 11:25; Josh. 1:5; 10:8; 23:9
25 [a]Ex. 32:20; Deut. 12:3; 1Chr. 14:12 [b]Ex. 20:17 [c]Deut. 7:16; Judg. 8:27 [d]Deut. 17:1
26 [a]Lev. 27:28f.
1 [a]Deut. 4:1
2 [a]Deut. 8:16 [b]Ps. 136:16; Amos 2:10 [c]Ex. 15:25; 20:20; 2Chr. 32:31
3 [I]Lit., *know* [a]Matt. 4:4; Luke 4:4
4 [a]Deut. 29:5; Neh. 9:21
5 [a]Deut. 4:36; 2Sam. 7:14; Prov. 3:12; Heb. 12:6; Rev. 3:19

8:3 See note on Deut. 6:13.

disciplining you just as a man[376] disciplines his son.[1121]

6 "Therefore, you shall keep the commandments of the LORD your God, to walk in His ways[1870] and to [I]fear[3372] Him.

7 "For [a]the LORD your God is bringing you into a good[2896] land, a land of brooks of water, of fountains and springs, flowing forth in valleys and hills;

8 a land of wheat and barley, of vines and fig trees and pomegranates, a land of olive oil[8081] and honey;

9 a land where you shall eat food without scarcity, in which you shall not lack anything; a land whose stones are iron, and out of whose hills you can dig copper.

10 "When [a]you have eaten and are satisfied, you shall bless[1288] the LORD your God for the good land which He has given you.

11 "[I]Beware[8104] lest you [a]forget the LORD your God by not keeping[8104] His commandments and His ordinances[4941] and His statutes[2708] which I am commanding you today;

12 lest, [a]when you have eaten and are satisfied, and have built good[2896] houses[1004] and lived *in them,*

13 and when your herds and your flocks multiply, and your silver and gold multiply, and all that you have multiplies,

14 then your heart becomes [I]proud, and you [a]forget the LORD your God who brought you out from the land of Egypt, out of the house[1004] of [II]slavery.[5650]

15 "He led you through [a]the great and terrible[3372] wilderness, *with its* [b]fiery[8314] serpents[5175] and scorpions and thirsty ground where there was no water; He [c]brought water for you out of the rock of flint.

16 "In the wilderness He fed you manna [a]which your fathers did not know,[3045] that He might humble you and that He might [b]test you, to do good[3190] for you [I]in the end.

17 "Otherwise, [a]you may say[559] in your heart, 'My power and the strength of my hand[3027] made[6213] me this wealth.'[2428]

18 "But you shall remember the LORD your God, for [a]it is He who is giving you power to make wealth, that He may confirm His covenant[1285] which He swore to your fathers, as *it is* this day.

19 "And it shall come about if you ever forget the LORD your God, and go after other gods[430] and serve[5647] them and worship[7812] them, [a]I testify[5749] against you today that you shall surely perish.[6]

20 "Like the nations[1471] that the LORD makes to perish before you, so [a]you shall perish; because you would not listen[8085] to the voice of the LORD your God.

Israel Provoked God

9 "Hear,[8085] O Israel! You are crossing over the Jordan today[3117] to go in to dispossess [a]nations[1471] greater and mightier than you, great cities [I][b]fortified to heaven,[8064]

2 a people[5971] great and tall, the sons[1121] of the Anakim, whom you know[3045] and of whom you have heard *it said,*[8085] '[a]Who can stand before the sons of Anak?'

3 "Know therefore today that [a]it is the LORD your God[430] who is crossing over before you as [b]a consuming fire. He will destroy[8045] them and He will subdue them before you, so that [c]you may drive them out and destroy[6]

6 [I]Or, *reverence*
7 [a]Deut. 11:9-12; Jer. 2:7
10 [a]Deut. 6:11
11 [I]Lit., *Take heed to yourself* [a]Deut. 4:9
12 [a]Prov. 30:9; Hos. 13:6
14 [I]Lit., *lifted up* [II]Lit., *slaves* [a]Deut. 8:11; Ps. 106:21
15 [a]Deut. 1:19; Jer. 2:6 [b]Num. 21:6 [c]Ex. 17:6; Num. 20:11; Deut. 32:13; Ps. 78:15; 114:8
16 [I]Lit., *at your end* [a]Ex. 16:15 [b]Deut. 8:2
17 [a]Deut. 9:4
18 [a]Prov. 10:22; Hos. 2:8
19 [a]Deut. 4:26; 30:18
20 [a]Ezek. 5:5-17
1 [I]Lit., *and fortified* [a]Deut. 4:38; 7:1; 11:23 [b]Deut. 1:28
2 [a]Num. 13:22, 28, 33; Josh. 11:21, 22
3 [a]Deut. 31:3; Josh. 3:11 [b]Deut. 4:24; Heb. 12:29 [c]Ex. 23:31; Deut. 7:24

9:1-29 As Moses set before Israel the tremendous task of driving the Canaanites out of the land which God had promised them, he called upon them to remember their rebellion in the wilderness and all of its ramifications for the task at hand. Essentially he was making the same statement that the Apostle Paul made to Christians centuries later in Eph. 2:8,9 "For by grace you have been saved through faith; and that not of yourselves, it is the gift of God; not as a result of works, that no one should boast."

9:2 See note on Num. 13:32,33.

them quickly, just as the LORD has
spoken[1696] to you.
4 "[a]Do not say[559] in your heart[3824]
when the LORD your God has driven
them out before [I]you, 'Because of my
righteousness[6666] the LORD has brought
me in to possess this land,' but *it is*
[b]because of the wickedness[7564] of these
nations *that* the LORD is dispossessing
them before you.
5 "It is [a]not for your righteousness
or for the uprightness[3476] of your heart
that you are going to possess their land,
but *it is* because of the wickedness of
these nations *that* the LORD your God
is driving them out before you, in order
to confirm [b]the [I]oath[1697] which the LORD
swore[7650] to your fathers,[1] to Abraham,
Isaac and Jacob.
6 "Know, then, *it is* not because of
your righteousness *that* the LORD your
God is giving you this good[2896] land to
possess, for you are [a]a [I]stubborn people.
7 "Remember,[2142] do not forget
how you provoked the LORD your God
to wrath[7107] in the wilderness; [a]from the
day that you left the land of Egypt until
you arrived at this place, you have been
rebellious against the LORD.
8 "Even [a]at Horeb you provoked the
LORD to wrath, and the LORD was so
angry[599] with you that He would have
destroyed[8045] you.
9 "When I went up[5927] to the mountain to receive the tablets of stone, the
tablets of the covenant[1285] which the
LORD had made with you, then I remained on the mountain forty days[3117]
and nights;[3915] [a]I neither ate bread nor
drank water.
10 "And the LORD gave me the two
tablets of stone [a]written by the finger
of God; and on them *were* all the
words[1697] which the LORD had spoken[1696] with you at the mountain from
the midst of the fire on the day of the
assembly.[6951]
11 "And it came about [a]at the end
of forty days and nights that the LORD
gave me the two tablets of stone, the
tablets of the covenant.
12 "[a]Then the LORD said[559] to me,
'Arise, go down from here quickly, for
your people whom you brought out of
Egypt have acted corruptly.[7843] They
have [b]quickly turned aside from the
way[1870] which I commanded[6680] them;
they have made[6213] a molten image for
themselves.'
13 "The [a]LORD spoke[559] further to
me, saying, 'I have seen[7200] this people,
and indeed, it is a [I][b]stubborn people.
14 "[a]Let Me alone,[7503] that I may
destroy them and [b]blot out[4229] their
name from under heaven; and I will
make[6213] of you a nation[1471] mightier and
greater than they.'
15 "[a]So I turned and came down
from the mountain while the mountain
was burning with fire, and the two tablets of the covenant were in my two
hands.[3027]
16 "And I saw[7200] that you had indeed sinned[2398] against the LORD your
God. You had made for yourselves a
molten calf; you had turned aside[5493]
quickly from the way which the LORD
had commanded you.
17 "And I took hold of the two tablets and threw them from my hands,
and smashed[7665] them before your eyes.
18 "[a]And I fell down[5307] before the
LORD, [b]as at the first,[7223] forty days and
nights; [c]I neither ate bread nor drank
water, [d]because of all your sin which
you had committed in doing[6213] what was
evil[7451] in the sight of the LORD to provoke Him to anger.[3707]
19 "For [a]I was afraid[3025] of the anger
and hot displeasure[2534] with which the
LORD was wrathful[7107] against you in order to destroy you, [b]but the LORD
listened[8085] to me that time also.
20 "And the LORD was angry[599]
enough with Aaron to destroy him; so
I also prayed[6419] for Aaron at the same
time.[6256]
21 "[a]And I took your [I]sinful[2403]
thing, the calf which you had made, and
burned[8313] it with fire and crushed[3807]
it, grinding it very small until it was as
fine as dust;[6083] and I threw its dust
into the brook that came down from the
mountain.

4 [I]Lit., *you saying* [a]Deut. 8:17; 9:7, 24; 31:27 [b]Lev. 18:3, 24-30; Deut. 12:31; 18:9-14

5 [I]Lit., *word* [a]Titus 3:5 [b]Gen. 12:7; 13:15; 15:7; 17:8; 26:4; 28:13

6 [I]Or, *stiff-necked* [a]Deut. 9:13; 10:16; 31:27

7 [a]Ex. 14:10f.; Num. 14:22

8 [a]Ex. 32:7-10; Ps. 106:19

9 [a]Ex. 24:18; 34:28; Deut. 8:3; 9:18

10 [a]Deut. 4:13

11 [a]Deut. 9:9

12 [a]Ex. 32:7, 8 [b]Judg. 2:17

13 [I]Or, *stiff-necked* [a]Ex. 32:9 [b]Deut. 10:16; 31:27; 2Kin. 17:14

14 [a]Ex. 32:10 [b]Ps. 9:5; 109:13

15 [a]Ex. 32:15-19

18 [a]Ex. 34:28 [b]Deut. 10:10 [c]Deut. 9:9 [d]Ex. 34:9

19 [a]Ex. 32:10f.; Heb. 12:21 [b]Ex. 34:10; Deut. 10:10

21 [I]Lit., *sin* [a]Ex. 32:20

22 "Again at [a]Taberah and at
[b]Massah and at [c]Kibroth-hattaavah you
provoked the LORD to wrath.
23 "And when the LORD sent you
from [a]Kadesh-barnea, saying, '[b]Go
up[5927] and possess the land which I have
given you,' then you rebelled[4784] against
the [I]command[6310] of the LORD your God;
[c]you neither believed[539] Him nor listened
to His voice.
24 "[a]You have been rebellious
against the LORD from the day I knew[3045]
you.
25 "[a]So I fell down before the LORD
the forty days and nights, which I
[I]did because the LORD had said He would
destroy you.
26 "[a]And I prayed to the LORD, and
said, 'O Lord[136] GOD, do not destroy[7843]
Thy people, even Thine inheritance,[5159]
whom Thou hast redeemed[6299] through
Thy greatness, whom Thou hast
brought out of Egypt with a mighty
hand.[3027]
27 'Remember Thy servants,[5650]
Abraham, Isaac, and Jacob; do not look
at the stubbornness of this people or
at their wickedness[7562] or their sin.
28 'Otherwise the land from which
Thou didst bring us may say, "[a]Because
the LORD was not able to bring them
into the land which He had [I]promised[1696]
them and because He hated them He
has brought them out to slay[4191] them
in the wilderness."
29 'Yet they are Thy people, even
[a]Thine inheritance, whom Thou hast
brought out by Thy [b]great power and
Thine outstretched arm.'

The Tablets Rewritten

10 🔑 "At that time the LORD said[559]
to me, '[a]Cut out[6458] for yourself
two tablets of stone like the former[7223]
ones, and come up[5927] to Me on the
mountain, and [b]make an ark[727] of wood
for yourself.
2 'And [a]I will write on the tablets
the words[1697] that were on the former
tablets which you shattered,[7665] and
[b]you shall put them in the ark.'[727]
3 "So [a]I made[6213] an ark[727] of acacia
wood and [b]cut out[6458] two tablets of
stone like the former ones, and went
up[5927] on the mountain with the two tablets in my hand.[3027]
4 "And He wrote on the tablets, like
the former writing, [a]the Ten [I]Command-
ments [b]which the LORD had spoken[1696]
to you on the mountain from the midst
of the fire [c]on the day[3117] of the assembly;[6951] and the LORD gave them to me.
5 "Then I turned and [a]came down
from the mountain, and [b]put the tablets
in the ark[727] which I had made; [c]and
there they are, as the LORD commanded[6680] me."
6 (Now the sons[1121] of Israel set
out from [I]Beeroth [a]Bene-jaakan to
Moserah. [b]There Aaron died[4191] and
there he was buried[6912] and Eleazar his
son[1121] ministered as priest[3547] in his
place.
7 [a]From there they set out to Gudgodah; and from Gudgodah to Jotbathah,
a land of brooks of water.
8 [a]At that time the LORD set apart[914]
the tribe[7626] of Levi to carry[5375] the
ark[727] of the covenant[1285] of the LORD,
to stand before the LORD [b]to serve[8334]
Him and to bless[1288] in His name until
this day.
9 [a]Therefore, Levi does not have
a portion or inheritance[5159] with his
brothers;[251] the LORD is his inheritance,
just as the LORD your God[430] spoke[1696]
to him.)
10 "[a]I, moreover, stayed on the
mountain forty days[3117] and forty

---

22 [a]Num. 11:3 [b]Ex. 17:7 [c]Num. 11:34
23 [I]Lit., *mouth* [a]Deut. 1:2 [b]Deut. 1:21 [c]Deut. 1:26; Ps. 106:24
24 [a]Deut. 9:7; 31:27
25 [I]Lit., *fell down* [a]Deut. 9:18
26 [a]Ex. 32:11-13; 1Sam. 7:9; Jer. 15:1
28 [I]Lit., *spoken to* [a]Ex. 32:12; Num. 14:16
29 [a]Deut. 4:20; 1Kin. 8:51; Neh. 1:10; Ps. 106:40 [b]Deut. 4:34
1 [a]Ex. 34:1 [b]Ex. 25:10
2 [a]Deut. 4:13 [b]Ex. 25:16
3 [a]Ex. 25:5; 37:1-9 [b]Ex. 34:4
4 [I]Lit., *Words* [a]Ex. 34:28; Deut. 4:13 [b]Ex. 20:1 [c]Deut. 9:10; 18:16
5 [a]Ex. 34:29 [b]Ex. 40:20 [c]1Kin. 8:9
6 [I]Or, *the wells of the sons of Jaakan* [a]Num. 33:30, 31 [b]Num. 20:25-28; 33:38
7 [a]Num. 33:33, 34
8 [a]Num. 3:6; 18:1-7; Deut. 31:9 [b]Deut. 17:12; 18:5; 21:5
9 [a]Num. 18:20, 24; Deut. 18:1, 2; Ezek. 44:28
10 [a]Ex. 34:28; Deut. 9:18

🔑 **10:1-5** God once again wrote His commandments on new plates, a symbolic act of how He would rewrite His law in the human heart through Christ whose body was broken for sinners. God gives man his second chance through Christ. The ark was a symbol of Christ in whom the commandments of God could be kept (Col. 2:9). The words God wrote on the second tablets were the same as on the first set pointing to the immutability of God. His laws are eternal. In and through Christ, God restores to Himself what He originally meant man to be, the inn-keeper of His covenant.

nights[3915] like the first time,[3117] and the
LORD listened[8085] to me that time also;
the LORD was not willing[14] to destroy[7843]
you.
11 "Then the LORD said to me,
'Arise, proceed on your journey ahead
of the people,[5971] that they may go in
and possess the land which I swore[7650]
to their fathers[1] to give them.'
12 "[a]And now, Israel, what does
the LORD your God require from you,
but to [I]fear[3372] the LORD your God, to
walk in all His ways[1870] and [b]love[157] Him,
and to serve[5647] the LORD your God with
[c]all your heart[3824] and with all your
soul,[5315]
13 *and* to keep[8104] the LORD's commandments and His statutes which I
am commanding[6680] you today for your
good?[2896]
14 "Behold, [a]to the LORD your God
belong heaven[8064] and the [I]highest
heavens,[8064] [b]the earth[776] and all that
is in it.
15 "[a]Yet on your fathers did the
LORD set His affection[2836] to love them,
and He chose[977] their [I]descendants[2233]
after them, *even* you above all peoples,
as *it is* this day.
🔑 16 "[a]Circumcise[4135] then [I]your
heart, and [b]stiffen your neck no more.
17 "[a]For the LORD your God is the
God of gods[430] and the [b]Lord[113] of lords,
the great, the mighty, and the
awesome[3372] God[410] [c]who does not show
partiality,[5375] nor [d]take a bribe.
18 "He executes justice[4941] for
[a]the orphan and the widow, and shows
His love[157] for the alien[1616] by giving
him food and clothing.
19 "[a]So show your love for the alien,
for you were aliens[1616] in the land of
Egypt.
🔑 20 "You shall fear the LORD your
God; you shall serve Him and [a]cling to
Him, and [b]you shall swear[7650] by His
name.
21 "He is [a]your praise[8416] and He
is your God, who has done[6213] these
great and awesome things[3372] for you
which your eyes have seen.[7200]
22 "[a]Your fathers went down to
Egypt seventy persons[5315] *in all,*
[b]and now the LORD your God has
made[7760] you as numerous as the stars
of heaven.

Rewards of Obedience

11 "You shall therefore [a]love[157] the
LORD your God,[430] and always
[b]keep[8104] His charge,[4931] His statutes,
His ordinances,[4941] and His commandments.
2 "And know[3045] this day[3117] [a]that
I *am* not *speaking* with your sons[1121]
who have not known[3045] and who have
not seen[7200] the [I]discipline of the
LORD your God—His greatness, His
mighty[2389] hand,[3027] and His outstretched arm,
3 and [a]His signs[226] and His works
which He did[6213] in the midst of Egypt
to Pharaoh the king[4428] of Egypt and
to all his land;
4 and what He did to Egypt's
army,[2428] to its horses and its chariots,
[a]when He made the water of the
[I]Red Sea to [II]engulf them while they
were pursuing you, and the LORD
[III]completely destroyed[6] them;
5 and what He did to you in the wilderness until you came to this place;
6 and [a]what He did to Dathan and
Abiram, the sons[1121] of Eliab, the son[1121]
of Reuben, when the earth[776] opened
its mouth[6310] and swallowed them, their
households,[1004] their tents,[168] and

12 [I]Or, *reverence* [a]Mic. 6:8 [b]Deut. 6:5; Matt. 22:37; 1Tim. 1:5 [c]Deut. 4:29
14 [I]Lit., *heaven of heavens* [a]1 Kin. 8:27; Neh. 9:6; Ps. 68:33; 115:16 [b]Ps. 24:1
15 [I]Lit., *seed* [a]Deut. 4:37
16 [I]Lit., *the foreskin of your heart* [a]Lev. 26:41; Jer. 4:4 [b]Deut. 9:6
17 [a]Josh. 22:22; Ps. 136:2; Dan. 2:47; 1Tim. 6:15; Rev. 19:16 [b]Rev. 17:14 [c]Deut. 1:17; Acts 10:34; Rom. 2:11; Gal. 2:6; Eph. 6:9 [d]Deut. 16:19
18 [a]Ex. 22:22-24; Ps. 68:5; 146:9
19 [a]Lev. 19:34; Ezek. 47:22, 23
20 [a]Deut. 11:22; 13:4 [b]Deut. 5:11; 6:13; Ps. 63:11
21 [a]Ps. 109:1; 148:14; Jer. 17:14
22 [a]Gen. 46:27 [b]Gen. 15:5; 22:17; Deut. 1:10

1 [a]Deut. 6:5; 10:12 [b]Lev. 18:30; 22:9
2 [I]Or, *instruction* [a]Deut. 4:34
3 [a]Ex. 7:8-21
4 [I]Lit., *Sea of Reeds* [II]Lit., *flow over their faces* [III]Lit., *to this day* [a]Ex. 14:28; Deut. 1:40; 2:1
6 [a]Num. 16:1-35; Ps. 106:16-18

🔑 **10:16** Abraham and all his male descendants after thim were required by God to be circumcised as a sign of the covenant which He made with them (Gen. 17:9-14). They themselves had renewed that covenant and been circumcised. Moses stated in this verse that there were spiritual implications to that circumcision. They had to purge themselves of the obstinance and perverseness which had plagued them throughout their journey and caused God to punish them. Their physical circumcision was not valid if it was not accompanied by the proper attitute toward God.

🔑 **10:20** See note on Deut. 6:13.

[b]every living thing that [I]followed them,
among[7130] all Israel—
7 but your own eyes have seen all
the great work of the LORD which He
did.
8 "You shall therefore keep every
commandment which I am command-
ing[6680] you today, [a]so that you may be
strong[2388] and go in and possess the
land into which you are about to cross
to possess it;
9 [a]so that you may prolong[748] *your*
days[3117] on the land[127] which the LORD
swore[7650] to your fathers[1] to give to
them and to their [I]descendants,[2233]
[b]a land[776] flowing with milk and honey.
10 "For the land, into which you are
entering to possess it, is not like the
land of Egypt from which you came,
where you used to sow your seed and
water it with your [I]foot like a vegetable
garden.
11 "But [a]the land into which you are
about to cross to possess it, a land of
hills and valleys, drinks water from the
rain of heaven,[8064]
12 a land for which the LORD your
God cares; [a]the eyes of the LORD your
God are always on it, from the [I]begin-
ning[7225] even to the end[319] of the year.
13 "And it shall come about,
[a]if you listen obediently[8085] to my commandments which I am commanding you
today, [b]to love the LORD your God and
to serve[5647] Him [c]with all your heart[3824]
and all your soul,[5315]
14 that [Ia]He will give the rain for
your land in its season,[6256] the [IIb]early
and [III]late rain, that you may gather[622]
in your grain and your new wine and
your oil.[3323]
15 "And [Ia]He will give grass in your
fields[7704] for your cattle, and [b]you shall
eat and be satisfied.
16 "[Ia]Beware, lest your hearts be
deceived and you turn away and serve
other gods[430] and worship[7812] them.
17 "Or [a]the anger[639] of the LORD
will be kindled[2734] against you, and He
will [b]shut up the heavens [c]so that there
will be no rain and the ground will not
yield its fruit; and [d]you will perish[6]
quickly from the good[2896] land which the
LORD is giving you.
18 "[a]You shall therefore [I]im-
press[7760] these words[1697] of mine on
your heart and on your soul; and you
shall bind them as a sign[226] on your hand,
and they shall be as [II]frontals[2903] [III]on
your forehead.
19 "[a]And you shall teach[3925] them
to your sons, talking[1696] of them when
you sit in your house[1004] and when you
walk along the road[1870] and when you
lie down and when you rise up.
20 "[a]And you shall write them on
the doorposts of your house and on your
gates,
21 so that [a]your days and the days
of your sons may be multiplied on the
land which the LORD swore to your fathers to give them, as [Ib]long as the heavens *remain* above the earth.
22 "For if you are [a]careful to
keep[8104] all this commandment which I
am commanding you, to do it, [b]to love
the LORD your God, to walk in all His
ways[1870] and [c]hold fast to Him;
23 then the LORD will [a]drive out[3423]
all these nations[1471] from before you,
and you will [b]dispossess nations greater
and mightier than you.
24 "[a]Every place on which the
sole[3709] of your foot shall tread shall be
yours; [b]your border shall be from the
wilderness to Lebanon, *and* from the
river, the river Euphrates, as far as
[I]the western sea.
25 "[a]There shall no man[376] be able
to stand before you; the LORD your God
shall lay the dread[4172] of you and the
fear[6343] of you on all the land on which
you set foot, as He has spoken[1696] to
you.
26 "[a]See,[7200] I am setting before
you today a blessing[1293] and a curse:[7045]
27 the [a]blessing, if you listen[8085] to
the commandments of the LORD your
God, which I am commanding you today;
28 and the [a]curse, if you do not listen
to the commandments of the LORD your
God, but turn aside from the way which
I am commanding you today, [I]by follow-

6 [I]Lit., *was at their feet* [b]Num. 26:10, 11
8 [a]Deut. 31:6, 7, 23; Josh. 1:6, 7
9 [I]Lit., *seed* [a]Deut. 4:40; 5:16, 33; 6:2; Prov. 10:27 [b]Ex. 3:8
10 [I]I.e., probably a treadmill
11 [a]Deut. 8:7
12 [I]Lit., *beginning of the year* [a]1Kin. 9:3
13 [a]Lev. 26:3; Deut. 7:12 [b]Deut. 11:1 [c]Deut. 4:29
14 [I]So some ancient versions; M.T. reads *I* [II]I.e., autumn [III]I.e., spring [a]Lev. 26:4; Deut. 28:12 [b]Joel 2:23; James 5:7
15 [I]So some ancient versions; M.T. reads *I* [a]Ps. 104:14 [b]Deut. 6:11
16 [I]Lit., *Watch yourselves* [a]Job 31:27
17 [a]Deut. 6:15; 9:19 [b]1Kin. 8:35; 2Chr. 6:26; 7:13 [c]Deut. 28:24 [d]Deut. 4:26
18 [I]Lit., *put* [II]Lit., *frontlet bands* [III]Lit., *between your eyes* [a]Ex. 13:9, 16; Deut. 6:8
19 [a]Deut. 4:9, 10; 6:7; Prov. 22:6
20 [a]Deut. 6:9
21 [I]Lit., *the days of the heavens* [a]Prov. 3:2; 4:10; 9:11 [b]Ps. 72:5
22 [a]Deut. 6:17 [b]Deut. 11:1 [c]Deut. 10:20
23 [a]Deut. 4:38 [b]Deut. 9:1
24 [I]I.e., the Mediterranean [a]Josh. 1:3; 14:9 [b]Gen. 15:18; Ex. 23:31; Deut. 1:7, 8
25 [a]Ex. 23:27; Deut. 7:24
26 [a]Deut. 30:1, 19
27 [a]Deut. 28:1-14
28 [I]Lit., *to follow* [a]Deut. 28:15-68

ing other gods which you have not known.

29 "And it shall come about, when the LORD your God brings you into the land where you are entering to possess it, [a]that you shall place the blessing on Mount Gerizim and the curse on Mount Ebal.

30 "Are they not across the Jordan, west of the way toward the sunset, in the land of the Canaanites who live in the Arabah,[6160] opposite [a]Gilgal, beside [b]the [I]oaks of Moreh?

31 "For you are about to cross the Jordan to go in to possess the land which the LORD your God is giving you, and [a]you shall possess it and live in it,

32 and you shall be careful[8104] to do all the statutes[2706] and the judgments which I am setting before you today.

Laws of the Sanctuary

12 "These are the statutes[2706] and the judgments[4941] which you shall carefully observe[8104] in the land which the LORD, the God[430] of your fathers,[1] has given you to possess [I][a]as long as[3117] you live[2416] on the [II]earth.[127]

2 "You shall utterly destroy[6] all the places where the nations[1471] whom you shall dispossess serve[5647] their gods,[430] on the [a]high mountains and on the hills and under every green tree.

3 "And [a]you shall tear down[5422] their altars and smash[7665] their *sacred* pillars and burn[8313] their [I]Asherim[842] with fire, and you shall cut[1438] down the engraved images[6456] of their gods, and you shall [b]obliterate their name from that place.

4 "You shall not act like this toward the LORD your God.

🔑 5 "[a]But you shall seek *the LORD* at the place which the LORD your God shall choose[977] from all your tribes,[7626] to establish His name there for His dwelling, and there you shall come.

6 "And there you shall bring your burnt offerings,[5930] your sacrifices,[2077] [a]your tithes,[4643] the [I]contribution[8641] of your hand,[3027] your votive offerings,[5088] your freewill offerings,[5071] and the first-born of your herd and of your flock.

7 "There also you and your households[1004] shall eat before the LORD your God, and [a]rejoice in all [I]your undertakings in which the LORD your God has blessed[1228] you.

8 "You shall not do at all what we are doing here today,[3117] every man[376] *doing* whatever is right in his own eyes;

9 for you have not as yet come to [a]the resting place and the [b]inheritance[5159] which the LORD your God is giving you.

10 "When you cross[5647] the Jordan and live in the land which the LORD your God is giving you to inherit,[5157] and [a]He gives you rest from all your enemies around *you* so that you live in security,

11 [a]then it shall come about that the place in which the LORD your God shall choose for His name to dwell,[7931] there you shall bring all that I command[6680] you: your burnt offerings and your sacrifices, your tithes and the [I]contribution[8641] of your hand, and all your choice votive offerings which you will vow[5087] to the LORD.

12 "And you shall [a]rejoice before the LORD your God, you and your sons[1121] and daughters, your male[5650] and female servants,[5650] and the [b]Levite who is within your gates, since [c]he has no portion or inheritance with you.

13 "[a]Be careful that you do not offer your burnt offerings in every *cultic* place you see,

14 but in the place which the LORD chooses in one of your tribes, there you shall offer your burnt offerings, and there you shall do all that I command you.

🔑 15 "[a]However, you may

29 [a]Deut. 27:12; Josh. 8:33
30 [I]Lit., *terebinths* [a]Josh. 4:19 [b]Gen. 12:6
31 [a]Deut. 17:14; Josh. 21:43
1 [I]Lit., *all the days* [II]Lit., *ground* [a]Deut. 4:9, 10; 1Kin. 8:40
2 [a]2Kin. 16:4; 17:10, 11
3 [I]I.e., wooden symbols of a female deity [a]Num. 33:52; Deut. 7:5; Judg. 2:2 [b]Ex. 23:13; Ps. 16:4; Zech. 13:2
5 [a]Ex. 20:24; Deut. 12:11, 13; 2Chr. 7:12; Ps. 78:68
6 [I]Or, *heave offering* [a]Deut. 14:22
7 [I]Lit., *the putting forth of your hand* [a]Lev. 23:40; Deut. 12:12, 18; 14:26; 28:47; Eccl. 3:12, 13; 5:18-20
9 [a]Deut. 3:20; 25:19; Ps. 95:11 [b]Deut. 4:21
10 [a]Josh. 11:23
11 [I]Or, *heave offering* [a]Deut. 12:5; 15:20; 16:2; 17:8; 18:6
12 [a]Deut. 12:7 [b]Deut. 12:18, 19; 26:11-13 [c]Deut. 10:9; 14:29
13 [a]Deut. 12:5, 11
15 [a]Deut. 12:20-23

🔑 **12:5** "The place which the LORD your God shall choose" is the phrase which was regularly used in Deuteronomy for the legitimate sanctuary to which Israel must go to worship God.

🔑 **12:15,16** This law modified an earlier one in Lev. 17:3,4, which stated that the slaughtered animal

(continued on next page)

slaughter[2076] and eat meat[1320] within any
of your gates, [I]whatever you[5315] desire,
according to the blessing[1293] of the LORD
your God which He has given you; the
unclean[2931] and the clean[2889] may eat
of it, as of [b]the gazelle[6643] and the deer.
16 "[a]Only you shall not eat the
blood; [b]you are to pour[8210] it out on the
ground[776] like water.
17 "[a]You are not allowed to eat
within your gates the tithe[4643] of your
grain, or new wine, or oil,[3233] or the
first-born of your herd or flock, or any
of your votive offerings which you
vow,[5087] or your freewill offerings, or
the [I]contribution of your hand.
18 "But [a]you shall eat them before
the LORD your God in [b]the place which
the LORD your God will choose, you and
your son[1121] and daughter, and your
male[5650] and female servants,[5650] and the
[c]Levite who is within your gates; and
you shall [d]rejoice before the LORD your
God in all [I]your undertakings.[3027]
19 "[a]Be careful that you do not
forsake[5800] the Levite [I]as long[3117] as you
live in your land.
20 "When the LORD your God extends your border [a]as He has promised[1696] you, and you say,[559] 'I will eat
meat,' because [I]you desire to eat meat,
then you may eat meat, [II]whatever you
desire.
21 "If the place which the LORD your
God chooses[977] to put His name is too
far from you, then you may slaughter
of your herd and flock which the LORD
has given you, as I have commanded[6680]
you; and you may eat within your gates
[I]whatever you desire.
22 "Just as a gazelle or a deer is
eaten, so you shall eat it; the unclean
and the clean alike may eat of it.
23 "Only be sure[2388] [a]not to eat the
blood, for the blood is the [I]life,[5315] and
you shall not eat the [I]life with the flesh.
24 "You shall not eat it; you shall
pour it out on the ground like water.
25 "You shall not eat it, in order
that [a]it may be well[3190] with you and
your sons[1121] after you, for [b]you will
be doing what is right in the sight of
the LORD.
26 "[a]Only your holy things[6944] which
you may have and your votive offerings,
you shall take and go to the place which
the LORD chooses.
27 "And [a]you shall offer[6213] your
burnt offerings, the flesh and the blood,
on the altar of the LORD your God; and
the blood of your sacrifices shall be
poured out[8210] on the altar[4196] of the
LORD your God, and [b]you shall eat the
flesh.
28 "Be careful to listen[8085] to all
these words[1697] which I command you,
in order that [a]it may be well with you
and your sons after you forever, for you
will be doing[6213] what is good[2896] and
right in the sight of the LORD your God.
29 "When [a]the LORD your God cuts
off[3772] before you the nations which you
are going in to dispossess, and you dispossess[3423] them and dwell in their land,
30 beware that you are not
ensnared[3369] [I]to follow them, after they
are destroyed[8045] before you, and that
you do not inquire after their gods, saying, 'How do these nations serve[5647]
their gods, that I also may do likewise?'
31 "[a]You shall not behave thus toward the LORD your God, for every
abominable act which the LORD hates[8130]
they have done[6213] for their gods; for
[b]they even burn[8313] their sons and
daughters in the fire to their gods.
32 "[I][a]Whatever[1697] I command you,
you shall be careful to do; [b]you shall
not add to nor take away from it.

Shun Idolatry

13 "[I][a]If a prophet[5030] or a dreamer of dreams arises among[7130]
you and gives you a sign[226] or a wonder,

15 [I]Lit., *in every desire of your soul* [b]Deut. 12:22; 14:5; 15:22
16 [a]Gen. 9:4; Lev. 7:26; 17:10-12; 1Sam. 14:33f.; Acts 15:20, 29 [b]Deut. 15:23
17 [I]Lit., *heave offering* [a]Deut. 12:26
18 [I]Lit., *the putting forth of your hand* [a]Deut. 14:23 [b]Deut. 12:5 [c]Deut. 12:12 [d]Deut. 12:7; Eccl. 3:12f.; 5:18-20
19 [I]Lit., *all your days upon your land* [a]Deut. 14:27
20 [I]Lit., *your soul desires* [II]Lit., *in every desire of your soul* [a]Gen. 15:18; Deut. 11:24; 19:8
21 [I]Lit., *in every desire of your soul*
23 [I]Lit., *soul* [a]Gen. 9:4; Lev. 17:10-14; Deut. 12:16
25 [a]Deut. 4:40; Is. 3:10 [b]Ex. 15:26; 1Kin. 11:38
26 [a]Num. 5:9f.; 18:19; Deut. 12:17
27 [a]Lev. 1:9, 13 [b]Lev. 3:1-17
28 [a]Deut. 4:40; Eccl. 8:12
29 [a]Josh. 23:4
30 [I]Lit., *after them*
31 [a]Deut. 9:5 [b]Lev. 18:21; Deut. 18:10; Ps. 106:37; Jer. 32:35
32 [I]Lit., *Everything that* [a]Deut. 4:2; Josh. 1:7 [b]Prov. 30:6; Rev. 22:18

1 [I]Ch. 13:2 in Heb. [a]Matt. 24:24; Mark 13:22; 2Thess. 2:9

(continued from previous page)
must be presented at the central sanctuary. The situation had now changed from a nation camped around the tabernacle to one preparing to disperse into the towns of Canaan.

13:1-5 See note on Deut. 18:20-22.

2 and the sign or the wonder comes true, concerning which he spoke[1696] to you, saying, '[a]Let us go after other gods[430] (whom you have not known)[3045] and let us serve[5647] them,'

3 you shall not listen[8085] to the words[1697] of that prophet or that dreamer of dreams; for the LORD your God[430] is [a]testing[5254] you to find out[3045] if [b]you love[157] the LORD your God with all your heart[3824] and with all your soul.[5315]

4 "[a]You shall follow the LORD your God and fear[3372] Him; and you shall keep[8104] His commandments, listen[8085] to His voice, serve Him, and [b]cling to Him.

5 "But that prophet or that dreamer of dreams shall be [a]put to death,[4191] because he has [I]counseled[1696] [II]rebellion against[5627] the LORD your God who brought you from the land of Egypt and redeemed[6299] you from the house[1004] of [III]slavery,[5650] [b]to seduce you from the way[1870] in which the LORD your God commanded[6680] you to walk. [c]So you shall purge the evil[7451] from among you.

6 "[a]If your brother,[251] your mother's son,[1121] or your son or daughter, or the wife[802] [I]you cherish, or your friend[7453] who is as your own soul, entice[5496] you secretly, saying, '[b]Let us go and serve other gods' (whom neither you nor your fathers[1] have known,

7 of the gods of the peoples[5971] who are around you, near you or far from you, from one end of the earth[776] to the other end),

8 [a]you shall not yield[14] to him or listen[8085] to him; [b]and your eye shall not pity him, nor shall you spare or conceal[3680] him.

9 "[a]But you shall surely kill him; [b]your hand[3027] shall be first[7223] against him to put him to death, and afterwards the hand of all the people.

10 "So you shall stone him [I]to death[4191] because he has sought [a]to seduce you from the LORD your God who brought you out from the land of Egypt, out of the house of [II]slavery.

2 [a]Deut. 13:6, 13

3 [a]Ex. 20:20; Deut. 8:2, 16; 1Cor. 11:19 [b]Deut. 6:5

4 [a]2Kin. 23:3; 2Chr. 34:31; 2John 6 [b]Deut. 10:20

5 [I]Lit., *spoken* [II]Lit., *turning aside* [III]Lit., *slaves* [a]Deut. 13:9, 15; 17:5; 1Kin. 18:40 [b]Deut. 4:19; 13:10 [c]1Cor. 5:13

6 [I]Lit., *of your bosom* [a]Deut. 17:2-7; 29:18 [b]Deut. 13:2

8 [a]Prov. 1:10 [b]Deut. 7:2

9 [a]Deut. 13:5 [b]Lev. 24:14; Deut. 17:7

10 [I]Lit., *with stones so that he dies* [II]Lit., *slaves* [a]Deut. 13:5

11 [a]Deut. 19:20

13 [a]Deut. 13:2

15 [I]Or, *putting it under the ban* [a]Deut. 13:5

16 [I]Lit., *mound* [a]Deut. 7:25, 26 [b]Josh. 8:28; Is. 17:1; 25:2; Jer. 49:2

17 [a]Ex. 32:12; Num. 25:4 [b]Deut. 30:3 [c]Deut. 7:13 [d]Gen. 22:17; 26:4, 24; 28:14

18 [I]Or, *for* [II]Lit., *to keep* [III]Lit., *to do*

1 [I]Lit., *make a baldness between your eyes* [a]Rom. 8:16; 9:8, 26; Gal. 3:26; 1John 3:1 [b]Lev. 19:28; 21:5; Jer. 16:6; 41:5

2 [I]Or, *special treasure* [a]Lev. 20:26; Deut. 7:6; Rom. 12:1 [b]Ex. 19:5; Deut. 4:20; 26:18; Titus 2:14; 1Pet. 2:9

11 "Then [a]all Israel will hear[8085] and be afraid, and will never again do such a wicked[7451] thing among[7130] you.

12 "If you hear in one of your cities, which the LORD your God is giving you to live in, *anyone* saying *that*

13 some worthless men[582] have gone out from among[7130] you and have seduced the inhabitants of their city, saying, '[a]Let us go and serve other gods' (whom you have not known),

14 then you shall investigate and search out and inquire[7592] thoroughly.[3190] And if it is true[571] *and* the matter[1697] established that this abomination has been done[6213] among[7130] you,

15 [a]you shall surely strike[5221] the inhabitants of that city with the edge[6310] of the sword,[2719] [I]utterly destroying[2763] it and all that is in it and its cattle with the edge of the sword.

16 "[a]Then you shall gather[6908] all its booty into the middle of its open square and burn[8313] the city and all its booty[3632] with fire as a whole burnt offering to the LORD your God; and it shall be a [I][b]ruin forever.[5769] It shall never be rebuilt.

17 "And nothing[3972] from that which is put under the ban[2764] shall cling to your hand, in order that the LORD may turn from [a]His burning anger and [b]show mercy to you, and have compassion[7355] on you and [c]make you increase, just [d]as He has sworn[7650] to your fathers,

18 [I]if you will listen to the voice of the LORD your God, [II]keeping all His commandments which I am commanding[6680] you today,[3117] [III]and doing what is right in the sight of the LORD your God.

Clean and Unclean Animals

14 "You are [a]the sons[1121] of the LORD your God;[430] [b]you shall not cut[1413] yourselves nor [I]shave[7760] your forehead for the sake of the dead.[4191]

2 "For you are [a]a holy[6918] people[5971] to the LORD your God; and the LORD has chosen[977] you to be a [b]people for His [I]own possession[5459] out of all the

peoples[5971] who are on the face of the
earth.[127]
3 "[a]You shall not eat any detestable
thing.[8441]
4 "[a]These are the animals which you
may eat: the ox, the sheep, the goat,
5 [I]the deer, the gazelle,[6643] the roe-
buck, the wild goat, the ibex, the antelope[1788] and the mountain sheep.
6 "And any animal that divides the
hoof and has the hoof split in [I]two *and*
[II]chews[5927] the cud, among the animals,
that you may eat.
7 "Nevertheless, you are not to eat
of these among those which [I]chew[5927]
the cud, or among those that divide the
hoof in [II]two: the camel and the [III]rabbit
and the rock-badger, for though they
[I]chew the cud, they do not divide the
hoof; they are unclean[2931] for you.
8 "And the pig, because it divides
the hoof but *does* not *chew* the cud, it
is unclean for you. You shall not eat
any of their flesh[1320] nor touch[5060] their
carcasses.[5038]
9 "These you may eat of all that
are in water: anything that has fins and
scales you may eat,
10 but anything that does not have
fins and scales you shall not eat; it is
unclean for you.
11 "You may eat any clean[2889] bird.
12 "But [a]these are the ones which
you shall not eat: the [I]eagle and the
vulture and the [II]buzzard,
13 and the red kite,[7201] the falcon,
and the kite in their kinds,
14 and every raven in its kind,
15 and the ostrich, the owl, the sea
gull, and the hawk in their kinds,
16 the little owl, the [I]great owl, the
white owl,
17 the pelican, the carrion vulture,
the cormorant,
18 the stork, and the heron in their
kinds, and the hoopoe and the bat.
19 "And all the [I]teeming life with
wings are unclean to you; they shall not
be eaten.

3 [a]Ezek. 4:14

4 [a]Lev. 11:2-45; Acts 10:14

5 [I]Exact identification of these animals is uncertain

6 [I]Lit., *two hoofs* [II]Lit., *brings up*

7 [I]Lit., *brings up* [II]Lit., *a cleaving* [III]Or, *hare*

12 [I]Or, *vulture* [II]Or, *black vulture* [a]Lev. 11:13

16 [I]Or, *great horned owl*

19 [I]I.e., flying insects

21 [I]Lit., *gates* [a]Lev. 17:15; 22:8; Ezek. 4:14; 44:31 [b]Deut. 14:2 [c]Ex. 23:19; 34:26

22 [I]Lit., *your seed* [a]Lev. 27:30; Deut. 12:6, 17; Neh. 10:37

23 [a]Deut. 12:5 [b]Deut. 4:10; Ps. 2:11; 111:10; 147:11; Is. 8:13; Jer. 32:38-40

24 [I]Lit., *way* [II]Lit., *carry it* [a]Deut. 12:5, 21

25 [I]Lit., *give in money*

26 [I]Lit., *soul* [II]Lit., *asks of you* [a]Deut. 12:7

27 [I]Lit., *gates* [a]Deut. 12:12 [b]Num. 18:20; Deut. 10:9; 18:12

28 [I]Lit., *gates* [a]Deut. 26:12

29 [I]Or, *fatherless* [II]Lit., *gates* [a]Deut. 10:9 [b]Deut. 16:11, 14; 24:19-21; 26:12; Ps. 94:6; Is. 1:17 [c]Deut. 6:11

20 "You may eat any clean bird.
🗝 21 "[a]You shall not eat anything
which dies *of itself*. You may give it to
the alien[1616] who is in your [I]town, so
that he may eat it, or you may sell it
to a foreigner,[5237] for you are [b]a holy
people to the LORD your God. [c]You shall
not boil a kid in its mother's[517] milk.
22 "You [a]shall surely tithe all the
produce from [I]what you sow,[2233] which
comes out of the field[7704] every year.
23 "And you shall eat in the presence of the LORD your God, [a]at the place
where He chooses[977] to establish His
name, the tithe[4643] of your grain, your
new wine, your oil,[3323] and the first-born
of your herd and your flock, in order
that you may [b]learn[3925] to fear[3372] the
LORD your God always.
24 "And if the [I]distance[1870] is so
great for you that you are not able to
[II]bring[5375] *the tithe,* since the place where
the LORD your God chooses [a]to set[7760]
His name is too far away from you when
the LORD your God blesses[1288] you,
25 then you shall [I]exchange *it* for
money, and bind the money in your
hand[3027] and go to the place which the
LORD your God chooses.
26 "And you may spend the money
for whatever your [I]heart[5315] desires, for
oxen, or sheep, or wine, or strong drink,
or whatever your [I]heart [II]desires; and
[a]there you shall eat in the presence of
the LORD your God and rejoice, you and
your household.[1004]
27 "Also you shall not neglect[5800]
[a]the Levite who is in your [I]town,
[b]for he has no portion or inheritance[5159]
among you.
28 "[a]At the end of every third year
you shall bring out all the tithe of your
produce in that year, and shall deposit
it in your [I]town.
29 "And the Levite, [a]because he has
no portion or inheritance among you,
and [b]the alien, the [I]orphan and the widow
who are in your [II]town, shall come and
[c]eat and be satisfied, in order that

🗝 **14:21** Boiling a young goat in its own mother's milk would be a heartless deed. The milk of its mother was intended to keep the kid alive, not contribute to its death.

[d]the LORD your God may bless[1288] you in all the work of your hand which you do.[6213]

The Sabbatic Year

15 🗝 "[a]At the end of *every* seven years you shall [I]grant[6213] a remission *of debts*.[8059]

2 "And this is the manner of remission: every creditor shall release what he has loaned to his neighbor; he shall not exact it of his neighbor and his brother,[251] because the LORD's remission has been proclaimed.[7121]

3 "[a]From a foreigner[5237] you may exact *it,* but your hand[3027] shall release whatever of yours is with your brother.

4 "However, there shall be no poor among[7130] you, since [a]the LORD will surely bless[1288] you in the land which the LORD your God[430] is giving you as an inheritance[5159] to possess,

5 if only you listen obediently[8085] to the voice of the LORD your God, to observe[8104] carefully all this commandment which I am commanding[6680] you today.[3117]

6 "[a]For the LORD your God shall bless[1288] you as He has promised[1696] you, and you will lend to many nations,[1471] but you will not borrow; and you will rule[4910] over many nations, but they will not rule over you.

7 "If there is [a]a poor man with you, one of your brothers,[251] in any of your [I]towns in your land which the LORD your God is giving you, [b]you shall not harden your heart,[3824] nor close your hand from your poor brother;

8 but [a]you shall freely open your hand to him, and shall generously lend him sufficient for his need *in* whatever he lacks.

9 "Beware,[8104] lest there is a base[1100] [I]thought[1697] in your heart, saying, '[a]The seventh year, the year of remission, is near,'[7126] and [b]your eye is hostile[7489] toward your poor brother, and you give him nothing;[3808] then he [c]may cry to the LORD against you, and it will be a sin[2403] in you.

10 "You shall generously give to him, and your heart shall not be grieved when you give to him, because [a]for this thing[1697] the LORD your God will bless you in all your work and in all [I]your undertakings.

11 "[a]For the poor will never cease *to be* [I]in the land; therefore I command you, saying, 'You shall freely open your hand to your brother, to your needy and poor in your land.'

12 "[a]If your [I]kinsman, a Hebrew man or woman, is sold to you, then he shall serve[5647] you six years, but in the seventh year you shall set him [II]free.

13 "And when you set him [I]free, you shall not send him away empty-handed.

14 "You shall furnish him liberally from your flock and from your threshing floor and from your wine vat; you shall give to him as the LORD your God has blessed[1288] you.

15 "And you shall remember[2142] that you were a slave[5650] in the land of Egypt, and the LORD your God redeemed[6299] you; therefore I command you [I]this today.

16 "And it shall come about [a]if he says[559] to you, 'I will not go out from you,' because he loves[157] you and your household,[1004] since he fares well[2895] with you;

17 then you shall take an awl[4836] and pierce it through his ear[241] into the door, and he shall be your servant[5650] forever.[5769] And also you shall do likewise to your maidservant.

18 "It shall not seem hard to you when you set him [I]free, for he has given you six years *with* [II]double the service of a hired man; so the LORD your God will bless you in whatever you do.[6213]

19 "[a]You shall consecrate[6942] to the LORD your God all the first-born males[2145] that are born of your herd and

29 [d]Deut. 15:10; Mal. 3:10

1 [I]Lit., *make a release* [a]Deut. 31:10

3 [a]Deut. 23:20

4 [a]Deut. 28:8

6 [a]Deut. 28:12, 13

7 [I]Lit., *gates* [a]Lev. 25:35; Deut. 15:11 [b]1John 3:17

8 [a]Matt. 5:42; Luke 6:34; Gal. 2:10

9 [I]Lit., *word* [a]Deut. 15:1 [b]Matt. 20:15 [c]Ex. 22:23; Deut. 24:15; Job 34:28; Ps. 12:5; James 5:4

10 [I]Lit., *the putting forth of your hand* [a]Deut. 14:29; Ps. 41:1; Prov. 22:9

11 [I]Lit., *in the midst of* [a]Matt. 26:11; Mark 14:7; John 12:8

12 [I]Lit., *brother* [II]Lit., *free from you* [a]Ex. 21:2-6; Lev. 25:39-43; Jer. 34:14

13 [I]Lit., *free from you*

15 [I]Lit., *this thing*

16 [a]Ex. 21:5, 6

18 [I]Lit., *free from you* [II]Lit., *double the amount*

19 [a]Ex. 13:2, 12

🗝 **15:1-3** See note on Lev. 19:33,34.

🗝 **15:1-18** See note on Lev. 25:1-55.

of your flock; you shall not work with the first-born of your herd, nor shear the first-born of your flock.

20 "[a]You and your household[1004] shall eat it every year before the LORD your God in the place which the LORD chooses.[977]

21 "[a]But if it has any [I]defect,[3971] *such as* lameness or blindness, *or* any serious [I]defect, you shall not sacrifice[2076] it to the LORD your God.

22 "You shall eat it within your gates; [a]the unclean[2931] and the clean[2889] alike *may eat it,* as [b]a gazelle[6643] or a deer.

23 "Only [a]you shall not eat its blood; you are to pour[8210] it out on the ground[776] like water.

The Feasts of Passover, of Weeks, and of Booths

16 "Observe[8104] [a]the month of Abib and [I][b]celebrate[6213] the Passover[6453] to the LORD your God,[430] for in the month of Abib the LORD your God brought you out of Egypt by night.[3915]

2 "And you shall sacrifice[2076] the Passover to the LORD your God from the flock and the herd, in the place where the LORD chooses[977] to establish His name.

3 "[a]You shall not eat leavened bread[2557] with it; seven days[3117] you shall eat with it unleavened bread,[4682] the bread of affliction (for you came out of the land of Egypt in haste), in order that you may remember[2142] [b]all the days[3117] of your life[2416] the day when you came out of the land of Egypt.

4 "For seven days no leaven shall be seen[7200] with you in all your territory, and [a]none of the flesh[1320] which you sacrifice[2076] on the evening of the first[7223] day shall remain overnight until morning.

5 "You are not allowed to sacrifice the Passover in any of your [I]towns which the LORD your God is giving you;

6 but [a]at the place where the LORD your God chooses to establish His name, you shall sacrifice the Passover in the evening at sunset, at the time[4150] that you came out of Egypt.

7 "And you shall [a]cook and eat *it* in the place which the LORD your God chooses. And in the morning you are to return to your tents.[168]

8 "Six days you shall eat unleavened bread, and [a]on the seventh day there shall be [b]a solemn assembly[6116] to the LORD your God; you shall do no work *on it.*

9 "[a]You shall count[5608] seven weeks for yourself; you shall begin to count seven weeks from the time you begin to put the sickle to the standing grain.

10 "Then you shall [I]celebrate the Feast of Weeks to the LORD your God with a tribute of a freewill offering[5071] of your hand,[3027] which you shall give just as the LORD your God blesses[1288] you;

11 and you shall [a]rejoice before the LORD your God, you and your son[1121] and your daughter and your male and female servants[5650] and [b]the Levite who is in your [I]town, and [c]the stranger[1616] and the [II]orphan and the widow who are in your midst,[7130] in the place where the LORD your God chooses[977] to establish His name.

12 "And [a]you shall remember that you were a slave[5650] in Egypt, and you shall be careful to observe these statutes.[2706]

13 "[a]You shall [I]celebrate the Feast of Booths[5521] seven days after you have gathered[622] in from your threshing floor and your wine vat;

14 and you shall [a]rejoice in your feast, you and your son and your daughter and your male and female servants and the Levite and the stranger and the [I]orphan and the widow who are in your [II]towns.

15 "Seven days you shall celebrate a feast to the LORD your God in the place which the LORD chooses, because

20 [a]Lev. 7:15-18; Deut. 12:5; 14:23
21 [I]Lit., *blemish* [a]Lev. 22:19-25; Deut. 17:1
22 [a]Deut. 12:15, 16, 22
23 [a]Gen. 9:4; Lev. 7:26; 17:10; 19:26; Deut. 12:16, 23
1 [I]Lit., *perform* [a]Ex. 12:2 [b]Num. 28:16
3 [a]Ex. 12:8, 15, 19, 39; 13:3; 34:18 [b]Deut. 4:9
4 [a]Ex. 12:8, 10; 34:25
5 [I]Lit., *gates*
6 [a]Deut. 12:5
7 [a]Ex. 12:8; 2Chr. 35:13
8 [a]Num. 28:25 [b]Ex. 12:16; 13:6; Lev. 23:8, 36
9 [a]Ex. 23:16; 34:22; Lev. 23:15; Num. 28:26
10 [I]Lit., *perform*
11 [I]Lit., *gates* [II]Or, *fatherless* [a]Deut. 12:7 [b]Deut. 12:12 [c]Deut. 14:29
12 [a]Deut. 15:15
13 [I]Lit., *perform* [a]Lev. 23:34-43
14 [I]Or, *fatherless* [II]Lit., *gates* [a]Deut. 16:11

16:1-12 See note on Ex. 23:14-17.

the LORD your God will bless[1288] you in all your produce and in all the work of your hands,[3027] so that you shall be altogether joyful.

16 "[a]Three times in a year all your males shall appear[7200] before the LORD your God in the place which He chooses, at the Feast of Unleavened Bread and at the Feast of Weeks and at the Feast of Booths, and [b]they shall not appear before the LORD empty-handed.

17 "Every man[376] [I]shall give as he is able,[3027] according to the blessing[1288] of the LORD your God which He has given you.

18 "You shall appoint for yourself judges[8199] and officers[7860] in all your [I]towns which the LORD your God is giving you, according to your tribes,[7626] and they shall judge[8199] the people[5971] with righteous[6664] judgment.[4941]

19 "[a]You shall not distort justice; [b]you shall not [I]be partial, and [c]you shall not take a bribe, for a bribe blinds the eyes of the wise[2450] and perverts the words[1697] of the righteous.

20 "Justice, *and only* justice,[6664] you shall pursue, that [a]you may live[2421] and possess[3423] the land which the LORD your God is giving you.

21 "[a]You shall not plant for yourself an [I]Asherah[842] of any kind of tree beside the altar[4196] of the LORD your God, which you shall make[6213] for yourself.

22 "[a]Neither shall you set up for yourself a *sacred* pillar which the LORD your God hates.[8130]

Administration of Justice

17 "[a]You shall not sacrifice[2076] to the LORD your God[430] an ox or a sheep which has a blemish[3971] or any [I]defect,[7451] for that is a detestable thing to the LORD your God.

2 "[a]If there is found in your midst,[7130] in any of your [I]towns, which the LORD your God is giving you, a man[376] or a woman[802] who does[6213] what is evil[7451] in the sight of the LORD your God, by transgressing[5674] His covenant,[1285]

3 and has gone and [a]served[5674] other gods[430] and worshiped[7812] them, [b]or the sun or the moon or any of the heavenly[8064] host,[6635] [c]which I have not commanded,[6680]

4 and if it is told[5046] you and you have heard[8085] of it, then you shall inquire thoroughly.[3190] And behold, if it is true and the thing[1697] certain that this detestable thing has been done in Israel,

5 then you shall bring out that man or that woman who has done this evil[7451] deed, to your gates, *that is,* the man or the woman, and [a]you shall stone them to [I]death.[4191]

6 "[a]On the [I]evidence[6310] of two witnesses or three witnesses, he who is to die shall be put to death;[4191] he shall not be put to death on the [I]evidence of one witness.

7 "[a]The hand[3027] of the witnesses shall be first[7223] against him to put him to death, and afterward the hand of all the people.[5971] [b]So you shall purge the evil from your midst.[7130]

8 "[a]If any case[1697] is too difficult[6381] for you to decide,[4941] between [I]one kind of homicide or another, between [II]one kind of lawsuit[1779] or another, and between [III]one kind of assault[5061] or another, being cases of dispute[7379] in your [IV]courts, then you shall arise and go up to [b]the place which the LORD your God chooses.[977]

9 "So you shall come to [a]the Levitical priest[3548] or the judge[8199] who is *in office* in those days,[3117] and you shall inquire *of them,* and they will declare[5046] to you the verdict[1697] in the case.

10 "And you shall do according to the [I]terms of the verdict which they declare to you from that place which the LORD chooses; and you shall be careful to observe according to all that they teach[3384] you.

11 "[a]According to the [I]terms[6310] of the law[8451] which they teach[3384] you, and according to the verdict which they tell[559] you, you shall do; you shall not turn aside from the word which they declare to you, to the right or the left.

12 "And the man who acts

16 [a]Ex. 23:14-17; 34:23, 24 [b]Ex. 34:20

17 [I]Lit., *according to the gift of his hand,*

18 [I]Lit., *gates*

19 [I]Lit., *regard persons* [a]Ex. 23:2; Lev. 19:15; Deut. 1:17; 10:17 [b]Prov. 24:23 [c]Ex. 23:8; Prov. 17:23; Eccl. 7:7

20 [a]Deut. 4:1

21 [I]I.e., wooden symbol of a female deity [a]Deut. 7:5; 2Kin. 17:16; 21:3; 2Chr. 33:3

22 [a]Lev. 26:1

1 [I]Lit., *evil thing* [a]Deut. 15:21

2 [I]Lit., *gates* [a]Deut. 13:6-11

3 [a]Ex. 22:20 [b]Job 31:26-28 [c]Jer. 7:22

5 [I]Lit., *death with stones* [a]Lev. 24:14; Josh. 7:25

6 [I]Lit., *mouth* [a]Num. 35:30; Deut. 19:15; Matt. 18:16; John 8:17; 2Cor. 13:1; 1Tim. 5:19; Heb. 10:28

7 [a]Lev. 24:14; Deut. 13:9 [b]1Cor. 5:13

8 [I]Lit., *blood to blood* [II]Lit., *judgment to judgment* [III]Lit., *stroke to stroke* [IV]Lit., *gates* [a]2Chr. 19:10; Hag. 2:11 [b]Deut. 12:5; Ps. 122:5

9 [a]Deut. 19:17

10 [I]Lit., *mouth*

11 [I]Lit., *mouth* [a]Deut. 25:1

[a]presumptuously[2087] by not listening[8085]
to the priest who stands there to
serve[8334] the LORD your God, nor to
the judge, that man shall die; thus you
shall purge the evil from Israel.
13 "Then all the people will hear[8085]
and be afraid,[3372] and will not act [a]pre-
sumptuously again.
🔑 **14** "When you enter the land which
the LORD your God gives you, and you
[a]possess it and live in it, and you say,[559]
"[b]I will set a king[4428] over me like all
the nations[1471] who are around me,'
15 you shall surely set a king over
you whom the LORD your God chooses,
one [a]from among[7130] your [I]country-
men[251] you shall set as king over yourselves; you may not put a foreigner over
yourselves who is not your [I]country-
man.[251]
16 "[a]Moreover, he shall not multiply
horses for himself, nor shall he [b]cause
the people to return[7725] to Egypt to multiply horses, since [c]the LORD has said[559]
to you, 'You shall never again return
that way.'[1870]
17 "[a]Neither shall he multiply
wives[802] for himself, [I]lest his heart[3824]
turn away; nor shall he greatly increase
silver and gold for himself.
18 "Now it shall come about when
he sits on the throne[3678] of his kingdom,[4467] he shall write for himself a copy
of this law on a scroll[5612] [I][a]in the presence
of the Levitical priests.
19 "And it shall be with him, and
he shall read[7121] it [a]all the days of his
life,[2416] that he may learn[3925] to fear the
LORD his God, [I]by carefully observing[8104]
all the words[1697] of this law and these
statutes,[2706]
20 that his heart may not be lifted
up above his [I]countrymen [a]and that he
may not turn aside from the commandment,[4687] to the right or the left; in order
that he and his sons[1121] may continue
long[748] in his kingdom in the midst of
Israel.

Portion of the Levites

18 "[a]The Levitical priests,[3548] the
whole tribe[7626] of Levi, shall have
no portion or inheritance[5159] with Israel;
they shall eat the LORD's offerings by
fire and His [I]portion.
2 "[a]And they shall have no inheritance among[7130] their [I]countrymen;[251]
the LORD is their inheritance, as He
[II]promised[1696] them.
3 "[a]Now this shall be the priests'[3548]
due[4941] from the people,[5971] from those
who offer[2076] a sacrifice,[2077] either an
ox or a sheep, of which they shall give
to the priest the shoulder and the two
cheeks and the stomach.[6896]
4 "You shall give him the [a]first fruits
of your grain, your new wine, and your
oil,[3323] and the first[7225] shearing of your
sheep.
5 "[a]For the LORD your God has
chosen[977] him and his sons[1121] from all
your tribes,[7626] to [b]stand [I]and serve[8334]
in the name of the LORD forever.
6 "Now if a Levite comes from any
of your [I]towns throughout Israel where
he [a]resides,[1481] and comes [II]whenever
he desires[183] to the place which the LORD
chooses,[977]
7 then he shall serve in the name
of the LORD his God, like all his fellow
Levites who stand there before the
LORD.
8 "[a]They shall eat [I]equal portions,
except *what they receive* from the sale
of their fathers' *estates.*

12 [a]Num. 15:30; Deut. 1:43; 17:13; 18:20; Hos. 4:4
13 [a]Deut. 17:12
14 [a]Deut. 11:31; Josh. 21:43 [b]1Sam. 8:5, 19, 20; 10:19
15 [I]Lit., *brother(s)* [a]Jer. 30:21
16 [a]1Kin. 4:26; 10:26-29; Ps. 20:7 [b]Is. 31:1; Ezek. 17:15 [c]Ex. 13:17, 18; Hos. 11:5
17 [I]Lit., *nor* [a]2Sam. 5:13; 12:11; 1Kin. 11:3,4
18 [I]Lit., *from before* [a]Deut. 31:24-26
19 [I]Lit., *to keep to do them* [a]Deut. 4:9, 10; Josh. 1:8
20 [I]Lit., *brothers* [a]Deut. 5:32; 1Kin. 15:5

1 [I]Or, *inheritance* [a]Deut. 10:9; 1Cor. 9:13
2 [I]Lit., *brothers* [II]Lit., *spoke to* [a]Num. 18:20
3 [a]Lev. 7:32-34; Num. 18:11, 12
4 [a]Num. 18:12
5 [I]Lit., *to* [a]Ex. 29:9 [b]Deut. 10:8
6 [I]Lit., *gates* [II]Lit., *with all the desire of his soul* [a]Num. 35:2; 3
8 [I]Lit., *portion like portion* [a]Lev. 27:30-33; Num. 18:21-24; 2Chr. 31:4; Neh. 12:44

🔑 **17:14-20** Moses predicted that eventually Israel would beg for a king. Even though their reasons would not be approved by God, He had already incorporated it into His plan. He would establish His throne with the house of David in preparation for the coming reign of His Son, Jesus. In the East in ancient times the horse was not used for agricultural purposes or for travel. Usually it was used only for war. It seemed that this prohibition was placed upon future kings of Israel so that they should not be like the rulers of other nations and place their trust in elaborate and costly preparations for war (see Hos. 1:7). Both David and Solomon later acquired for themselves horses, wives, silver, and gold in spite of this prohibition.

Spiritism Forbidden

9 "When you enter the land which
the LORD your God gives you, you shall
not learn[3925] to [1][a]imitate the detestable
things of those nations.[1471]
10 "There shall not be found among
you anyone [a]who makes his son[1121] or
his daughter pass through[5674] the fire,
one who uses divination,[7081] one [b]who
practices witchcraft, or one who interprets omens,[5172] or a sorcerer,[3784]
11 or one who casts a spell,[2267]
[a]or a medium,[7592] or a spiritist, or one
who calls[3049] up the dead.[4191]
12 "For whoever does these things
is detestable to the LORD; and [a]because
of these detestable things the LORD your
God will drive them out before you.
13 "[a]You shall be [1]blameless[8549] before the LORD your God.
14 "For those nations, which you
shall dispossess, listen[8085] to those who
[a]practice witchcraft and to diviners,[7080]
but as for you, the LORD your God has
not allowed you *to do* so.
15 "[a]The LORD your God[430] will
raise up for you a prophet[5030] like me
from among you, from your [1]country-
men, you shall listen[8085] to him.
16 "This is [a]according to all that you
asked of the LORD your God in Horeb
on the day[3117] of the assembly,[6951]
saying, 'Let me not hear[8085] again the
voice of the LORD my God, let me
not see this great fire anymore, lest I
die.'
17 "[a]And the LORD said[559] to me,
'They have [1]spoken[1696] well.[3190]
18 'I will raise up a prophet from
among their [1]countrymen like you, and
[a]I will put My words[1697] in his mouth,[6310]
and [b]he shall speak[1696] to them all that
I command[6680] him.
19 "[a]And it shall come about that
whoever[376] will not listen to My words
which he shall speak in My name, I Myself will require *it* of him.
20 'But the prophet who shall speak
a word[1697] [a]presumptuously in My name
which I have not commanded[6680] him
to speak, or [b]which he shall speak in

9 [1]Lit., *do according to* [a]Deut. 9:5
10 [a]Deut. 12:31 [b]Ex. 22:18; Lev. 19:26, 31; 20:6; Jer. 27:9, 10; Mal. 3:5
11 [a]Lev. 19:31
12 [a]Lev. 18:24
13 [1]Lit., *complete, perfect;* or, *having integrity* [a]Gen. 6:9; 17:1; Matt. 5:48
14 [a]2Kin. 21:6
15 [1]Lit., *brothers* [a]Matt. 21:11; Luke 2:25-34; 7:16; 24:19; John 1:21, 25; 4:19; Acts 3:22; 7:37
16 [a]Ex. 20:18, 19; Deut. 5:23-27
17 [1]Lit., *done well what they have spoken* [a]Deut. 5:28
18 [1]Lit., *brothers* [a]Is. 51:16; John 17:8 [b]John 4:25; 8:28; 12:49, 50
19 [a]Acts 3:23; Heb. 12:25
20 [a]Deut. 13:5; 17:12 [b]Deut. 13:1, 2; Jer. 14:14; Zech. 13:3

18:10 See note on Lev. 18:21.

18:15-19 The identity of this unnamed prophet is not revealed anywhere in the O.T. By Jesus' day, the Jews had developed a clear-cut expectation of a yet future figure who would fulfill Moses' words here. Priests and Levites from Jerusalem asked John the Baptist if he were the prophet, and he responded in the negative (Jn. 1:21). On more than one occasion during Jesus' ministry, people concluded that He was this figure (Jn. 6:14; 7:40). In point of fact, he *was* the Prophet, as Peter asserted in his temple sermon (Acts. 3:22,23). Although Jesus was also the Messiah, the two figures should not be confused (see Jn. 1:20,21). The Messiah was to be a royal figure who would reign, but the Prophet was to be a teacher.

18:20-22 The existence of prophets during the period of the monarchy raised a number of problems, one of which was how to distinguish between the true and false ones. Turbulent times, when the people especially wanted to hear words of hope and security, saw the greatest outbreak of prophets for hire and seers with optimistic lies. Shortly after Judah started going into Babylonian exile, but before the fall of Jerusalem, Jeremiah and Ezekiel had to contend with a rash of these charlatans, upon whom they issued stern denunciations (Jer. 23:9-32; Ezek. 13:1-23). The penalty for being a false prophet was death (Deut. 13:5; 18:20; see Jer. 28:16), but there had to be a way to prove the charge. In this passage in Deut. 18, Moses gave a simple test. If the prophet's message did not come true as predicted, he was a false prophet (see also I Kgs. 22:28). In this conflict with the false prophet, Hananiah, Jeremiah expressed the test positively, so that if the prophecy came true, all would know that Hananiah was a true prophet (Jer. 28:9). This was only a general rule which applied to the case at hand, because it was possible for a false prophet to utter a true message, either as a lucky guess or as a test from the Lord (Deut. 13:1-3). The content of his message had to be consistent with the basic elements of Israel's faith. So, if a prophet said that Israel should serve another god, he was obviously false (Deut. 13:1-3). In the N.T. both Paul and John taught that the content of the message already received was the standard by which to measure any new message, even if it came from Paul himself or an angel (Gal. 1:8) or a spirit masquerading as God's Spirit (I Jn. 4:1-3). One final general test, which would not always apply, was that an easy message in hard times is often unreliable (Jer. 23:16,17,29; 28:8,9; Ezek. 13:10-16).

the name of other gods,[430] [I]that prophet shall die.'

21 "And [I]you may say[559] in your heart,[3824] 'How shall we know[3045] the word which the LORD has not spoken?'

22 "[a]When a prophet speaks in the name of the LORD, if the thing[1697] does not come about or come true, that is the thing which the LORD has not spoken. The prophet has spoken it [b]presumptuously;[2087] you shall not be afraid[1481] of him.

Cities of Refuge

19 "[a]When the LORD your God[430] cuts off[3772] the nations,[1471] whose land the LORD your God gives you, and you dispossess[3423] them and settle in their cities and in their houses,[1004]

2 [a]you shall set aside[914] three cities for yourself in the midst of your land, which the LORD your God gives you to [I]possess.

3 "You shall prepare the [I]roads[1870] for yourself, and divide into three parts the territory of your land, which the LORD your God will give you as a possession,[5157] [II]so that any manslayer[7523] may flee there.

4 "[a]Now this is the case of the manslayer who may flee there and live: when he [I]kills[5221] his friend [II]unintentionally,[1847] [III]not hating[8130] him previously—

5 as when *a man* goes into the forest with his friend to cut 2404 wood, and his hand[3027] [I]swings the axe to cut down[3772] the tree, and the iron *head* slips off the [II]handle 6086 and [III]strikes his friend so that he dies—[4191] he may flee to one of these cities and live;

6 lest the avenger[1350] of blood pursue the manslayer [I]in the heat of his anger, and overtake him, because the way is long, and [II]take his life,[5221] though he was not deserving of death,[4194] since he had not hated him previously.

7 "Therefore, I command[6680] you, saying, 'You shall set aside three cities for yourself.'

8 "And if the LORD your God [a]enlarges your territory, just as He has sworn[7650] to your fathers,[1] and gives you all the land which He [I]promised[1696] to give your fathers—

9 if you [I]carefully observe[8104] all this commandment, which I command you today,[3117] [a]to love[157] the LORD your God, and to walk in His ways[1870] always—[b]then you shall add three more cities for yourself, besides these three.

10 "So innocent[5355] blood will not be shed[8210] in the midst of your land which the LORD your God gives you as an inheritance, and [a]bloodguiltiness be on you.

11 "But [a]if there is a man who hates[8130] his neighbor and lies in wait for him and rises up against him and strikes[5221] [I]him so that he dies,[4191] and he flees to one of these cities,

12 then the elders[2205] of his city shall send and take him from there and deliver him into the hand of the avenger of blood, that he may die.

13 "[I][a]You shall not pity him, but [b]you shall purge the blood of the innocent from Israel, that it may go well[2895] with you.

Laws of Landmark and Testimony

14 "[a]You shall not move your neighbor's boundary mark, which the ancestors[7223] have set, in your inheritance which you shall inherit in the land that the LORD your God gives you to [I]possess.

15 "[a]A single witness shall not rise up against a man on account of any iniquity 5571 or any sin[2403] [I]which he has committed;[2398] on the [II]evidence[6310] of two or three witnesses a matter[1697] shall be confirmed.

16 "[a]If a malicious[2555] witness rises up against a man to [I]accuse him of [II]wrongdoing,[5627]

17 then both the men who have the dispute[7379] shall stand [a]before the LORD, before the priests[3548] and the judges[8199] who will be *in office* in those days.[3117]

18 "And the judges [a]shall investigate 1875 thoroughly;[3190] and if the wit-

---

20 [I]Lit., *and that*
21 [I]Lit., *if you say*
22 [a]Jer. 28:9 [b]Deut. 18:20

1 [a]Deut. 6:10, 11
2 [I]Lit., *possess it* [a]Deut. 4:41; Josh. 20:2
3 [I]Lit., *road* [II]Lit., *and it shall be for every manslayer to flee there*
4 [I]Lit., *smites* [II]Lit., *without knowledge* [III]Lit., *and he was not hating him previously* [a]Num. 35:9-34
5 [I]Lit., *is thrust with* [II]Lit., *wood* [III]Lit., *finds*
6 [I]Lit., *while his heart is hot* [II]Lit., *smite him in the soul*
8 [I]Lit., *spoke* [a]Gen. 15:18
9 [I]Lit., *keep. . . to do it* [a]Deut. 6:5 [b]Josh. 20:7
10 [a]Num. 35:33; Deut. 21:1-9
11 [I]Lit., *him in the soul* [a]Ex. 21:12; Num. 35:16; 1John 3:15
13 [I]Lit., *Your eye* [a]Deut. 7:2 [b]1Kin. 2:31
14 [I]Lit., *possess it* [a]Deut. 27:17; Job 24:2; Prov. 22:28; Hos. 5:10
15 [I]Lit., *in any sin, which he sins* [II]Lit., *mouth of two witnesses, or by the mouth of three* [a]Num. 35:30; Deut. 17:6; Matt. 18:16; John 8:17; 2Cor. 13:1; 1Tim. 5:19; Heb. 10:28
16 [I]Lit., *testify against* [II]Lit., *turning aside* [a]Ex. 23:1; Ps. 27:12
17 [a]Deut. 17:9
18 [a]Deut. 25:1

ness is a false[8267] witness *and* he has [I]accused his brother[251] falsely,[8267]

19 then [a]you shall do to him just as he had intended[2161] to do[6213] to his brother. Thus you shall purge the evil[7451] from among you.

20 "And [a]the rest will hear[8085] and be afraid,[3372] and will never again do[6213] such an evil thing among you.

21 "Thus [Ia]you shall not show pity: [b]life for life,[5315] [c]eye for eye, tooth for tooth, hand for hand, foot for foot.

Laws of Warfare

20 "When you go out to battle against your enemies and see [a]horses and chariots *and* people[5971] more numerous than you, [b]do not be afraid[3372] of them; for the LORD your God,[430] who brought[5927] you up from the land of Egypt, is with you.

2 "Now it shall come about that when you are approaching the battle, the priest shall come near and speak[1696] to the people.

3 "And he shall say[559] to them, 'Hear,[8085] O Israel, you are approaching[7126] the battle against your enemies today.[3117] Do not be fainthearted. [a]Do not be afraid,[3372] or panic,[6206] or tremble before them,

4 for the LORD your God [a]is the one who goes with you, to fight for you against your enemies, to save[3467] you.'

5 "The officers[7860] also shall speak to the people, saying, 'Who is the man that has built a new house[1004] and has not [a]dedicated[2596] it? Let him depart and return[7725] to his house, lest he die[4191] in the battle and another man[376] dedicate[2596] it.

6 'And who is the man that has planted a vineyard and has not [I]begun to use[2490] its fruit? Let him depart and return to his house, lest he die in the battle and another man [I]begin to use its fruit.

7 "[a]And who is the man that is engaged[781] to a woman[802] and has not [I]married her? Let him depart and return to his house, lest he die in the battle and another man [II]marry her.'

8 "Then the officers shall speak further to the people, and they shall say, '[a]Who is the man that is afraid[3373] and fainthearted? Let him depart and return to his house, so that [I]he might not make his brothers' hearts melt like his heart.'[3824]

9 "And it shall come about that when the officers have finished[3615] speaking[1696] to the people, they shall appoint commanders[8269] of armies[6635] at the head of the people.

10 "When you approach[7126] a city to fight against it, you shall [I]offer it terms[7121] of peace.

11 "And it shall come about, if it [I]agrees to make peace with you and opens to you, then it shall be that all the people who are found in it shall become your [a]forced labor and shall serve[5647] you.

12 "However, if it does not make peace with you, but makes war against you, then you shall besiege it.

13 "When the LORD your God gives it into your hand,[3027] [a]you shall strike[5221] all the [I]men in it with the edge[6310] of the sword.

14 "Only the women[802] and the children[2945] and [a]the animals and all that is in the city, all its spoil, you shall take as booty for yourself; and you shall [I]use the spoil of your enemies which the LORD your God has given you.

15 "Thus you shall do to all the cities that are very far from you, which are not of the cities of these nations[1471] [I]nearby.

🔑 16 "[a]Only in the cities of these

18 [I]Lit., *testified against*
19 [a]Prov. 19:5
20 [a]Deut. 17:13; 21:21
21 [I]Lit., *your eye* [a]Deut. 19:13 [b]Ex. 21:23; Lev. 24:20 [c]Matt. 5:38
1 [a]Deut. 3:22; 7:18; 31:6, 8; Ps. 20:7; Is. 31:1 [b]2Chr. 32:7, 8; Ps. 23:4; Is. 41:10
3 [a]Deut. 20:1; Josh. 23:10
4 [a]Deut. 1:30; 3:22; Josh. 23:10
5 [a]Neh. 12:27
6 [I]Lit., *treat(ed) it as common*
7 [I]Lit., *taken* [II]Lit., *take* [a]Deut. 24:5
8 [I]So with Gr. and other ancient versions [a]Judg. 7:3
10 [I]Lit., *call to it for peace*
11 [I]Lit., *answers peace* [a]1Kin. 9:21
13 [I]Lit., *males* [a]Num. 31:7
14 [I]Lit., *eat* [a]Josh. 8:2
15 [I]Lit., *here*
16 [a]Ex. 23:31-33; Num. 21:2, 3; Deut. 7:1-5; Josh. 11:14

🔑 **20:16-18** This was not the judgment of Israel being expressed but the judgment of God based upon His omniscience and justice. He had given them more than 500 years to repent and they had rejected His mercy (Gen. 15:16). There were two reasons given for the unexcelled severity of this verdict: (1) Their overwhelming wickedness. They burned their children in honor of their gods. They practiced

(continued on next page)

peoples that the LORD your God is giving you as an inheritance,[5159] you shall not leave alive[2421] anything that breathes.

17 "But you shall [I]utterly destroy[2763] them, the Hittite and the Amorite, the Canaanite and the Perizzite, the Hivite and the Jebusite, as the LORD your God has commanded[6680] you,

18 in order that they may not teach[3925] you to do [a]according to all their detestable things which they have done for their gods, so that you would [b]sin[2398] against the LORD your God.

19 "When you besiege a city a long time,[3117] to make war against it in order to capture it, you shall not destroy[7843] its trees by swinging an axe against them; for you may eat from them, and you shall not cut[3772] them down. [I]For is the tree of the field[7704] a man,[120] that it should [II]be besieged by you?

20 "Only the trees which you know[3045] [I]are not fruit trees you shall destroy and cut down, that you may construct siegeworks against the city that is making[6213] war with you until it falls.

Expiation of a Crime

21 "If a slain person is found lying[5307] in the open country[7704] in the land[127] which the LORD your God[430] gives you to [I]possess, *and* it is not known[3045] who has struck[2491] him,

2 then your elders[2205] and your judges[8199] shall go out and measure *the distance* to the cities which are around the slain one.

3 "And it shall be that the city which is nearest to the slain man,[376] that is, the elders of that city, shall take a heifer of the herd, which has not been worked[5647] and which has not pulled in a yoke;

4 and the elders of that city shall bring the heifer down to a valley with running water, which has not been plowed[5647] or sown, and shall break the heifer's neck there in the valley.

5 "Then [a]the priests,[3548] the sons[1121] of Levi, shall come near,[5066] for the LORD your God has chosen[977] them to serve[8334] Him and to bless[1288] in the name of the LORD; and every dispute[7379] and every [I]assault [II]shall be settled by them.

6 "And all the elders of that city [I]which is nearest to the slain man shall [a]wash[7364] their hands[3027] over the heifer whose neck was broken in the valley;

7 and they shall answer and say,[559] 'Our hands have not shed[8210] this blood, nor did our eyes see[7200] *it*.

8 '[I]Forgive[3722] Thy people[5971] Israel whom Thou hast redeemed,[6299] O LORD, and do not place the guilt of [a]innocent[5355] blood in the midst of Thy people Israel.' And the bloodguiltiness shall be [II]forgiven[3722] them.

9 "[a]So you shall remove the guilt of innocent blood from your midst, when you do what is right in the eyes of the LORD.

Domestic Relations

10 "When you go out to battle against your enemies, and [a]the LORD your God delivers them into your hands, and you take them away captive,[7617]

11 and see among the captives[7633] a beautiful woman,[802] and have a desire[2836] for her and would take her as a wife[802] for yourself,

12 then you shall bring her home to your house,[1004] and she shall [a]shave her head[7218] and [I]trim her nails.

13 "She shall also [I]remove the clothes of her captivity[7633] and shall

17 [I]Or, *put them under the ban*

18 [a]Ex. 34:12-16; Deut. 7:4; 9:5; 12:30, 31 [b]Ex. 23:33; 2Kin. 21:3-15; Ps. 106:34-41

19 [I]Read as interrogative with ancient versions [II]Lit., *come before you in the siege*

20 [I]Lit., *they are not trees for food*

1 [I]Lit., *possess it*

5 [I]Lit., *stroke* [II]Lit., *shall be according to their mouth* [a]Deut. 17:9-11; 19:17; 1Chr. 23:13

6 [I]Lit., *who are* [a]Matt. 27:24

8 [I]Lit., *Cover over, atone for* [II]Lit., *covered over, atoned for* [a]Num. 35:33, 34; Jon. 1:14

9 [a]Deut. 19:13

10 [a]Josh. 21:44

12 [I]Lit., *do* [a]Lev. 14:8, 9; Num. 6:9

13 [I]Lit., *remove from her*

(continued from previous page)

sodomy, bestiality and other vices just as repulsive. Because they were so depraved, the land is represented as vomiting out her inhabitants (See Lev. 18;21-25). (2) Their contaminating example. For the same reason covenants and marriages were strictly prohibited between the people of Israel and these seven tribes (Deut. 7:1-4). The disastrous consequences of Israel's association with the Moabites is a convincing example of the wisdom of such a prohibition (Num. 25:1-3). It was completely impossible to live near people so totally given to idolatry without being defilled by them.

remain in your house, and [a]mourn[1058]
her father[1] and mother a full[3117] month;
and after that you may go in to her and
be her husband[1167] and she shall be
your wife.
14 "And it shall be, if you are not
pleased[2654] with her, then you shall let
her go [I]wherever she wishes; but you
shall certainly not sell her for money,
you shall not [II]mistreat her, because you
have [a]humbled her.
15 "If a man has two wives,[802] the
one loved[157] and [a]the other[259] [I]un-
loved,[8130] and *both* the loved and the
[I]unloved[8130] have borne him sons,[1121]
if the first-born son[1121] belongs to the
[I]unloved,[8146]
16 then it shall be in the day he
[I]wills what he has to his sons, he cannot
make the son of the loved the first-born
before the son of the [II]unloved, who is
the first-born.
17 "But he shall acknowledge[5234]
the first-born, the son of the [I]unloved,
by giving him a double portion of all that
[II]he has, for he is the [a]beginning[7225] of
his strength; [b]to him belongs the
right[4941] of the first-born.
18 "If any man has a stubborn[5637]
and rebellious son who will [a]not obey[8085]
his father or his mother, and when they
chastise him, he will not even listen[8085]
to them,
19 then his father and mother shall
seize him, and bring him out to the elders
of his city [I]at the gateway of his home
town.
20 "And they shall say to the elders
of his city, 'This son of ours is stubborn
and rebellious, he will not obey us, he
is a glutton and a drunkard.'
21 "[a]Then all the men of his city
shall stone him to death;[4191] so [b]you shall
remove the evil[7451] from your midst,
and [c]all Israel shall hear[8085] *of it* and
fear.[3372]
22 "And if a man has committed[1961]
a sin [a]worthy of death,[4194] and he is
put to death,[4191] and you hang him on
a tree,
23 [a]his corpse shall not hang all
night[3915] on the tree, but you shall surely
bury[6912] him on the same day[3117] (for
[b]he who is hanged is [I]accursed[7045] of
God), so that you [c]do not defile your
land which the LORD your God gives
you as an inheritance.[5159]

Sundry Laws

22 "[a]You shall not see your [I]country-
man's[251] ox or his sheep straying
away, and [II]pay no attention to them;
you shall certainly bring them back to
your countryman.[251]
2 "And if your countryman is not
near you, or if you do not know[3045] him,
then you shall bring[622] it home to your
house,[1004] and it shall remain with you
until your countryman looks for it; then
you shall restore[7725] it to him.
3 "And thus you shall do with his
donkey, and you shall do the same with
his garment, and you shall do likewise
with anything lost[9] by your countryman,
which he has lost and you have found.
You are not allowed to [I]neglect *them.*
4 "You shall not see your countryman's donkey or his ox fallen down on
the way,[1870] and [I]pay no attention to
them; you shall certainly help him to
raise *them* up.
5 "A woman[802] shall not wear man's
clothing, nor shall a man[1397] put on a
woman's[802] clothing; for whoever does
these things is an abomination to the
LORD your God.[430]
6 "If you happen to come upon a
bird's nest along the way, in any tree
or on the ground,[776] with young ones
or eggs, and the mother[517] sitting on
the young or on the eggs, [a]you shall
not take the mother with the young;[1121]
7 you shall certainly let the mother
go, but the young you may take for yourself, [a]in order that it may be well[3190]
with you, and that you may prolong[748]
your days.[3117]
8 "When you build[1129] a new house,
you shall make[6213] a parapet for your
roof, that you may not bring bloodguilt
on your house if anyone falls from it.
9 "[a]You shall not sow your vineyard
with two kinds of seed,[2233] lest [I]all the

---

13 [a]Ps. 45:10

14 [I]Lit., *according to her soul* [II]Or, *enslave* [a]Gen. 34:2

15 [I]Lit., *hated* [a]Gen. 29:33

16 [I]Lit., *makes to inherit* [II]Lit., *hated*

17 [I]Lit., *hated* [II]Lit., *is found with him* [a]Gen. 49:3 [b]Gen. 25:31

18 [a]Ex. 20:12; Lev. 19:3; Prov. 1:8; Eph. 6:1-3

19 [I]Lit., *and to the gate of his place*

21 [a]Lev. 20:2, 27; 24:14-23; Num. 15:25, 36 [b]Deut. 19:19 [c]Deut. 13:11

22 [a]Deut. 22:26; Matt. 26:66; Mark 14:64; Acts 23:29

23 [I]Lit., *the curse of God* [a]Josh. 8:29; 10:26, 27; John 19:31 [b]Gal. 3:13 [c]Lev. 18:25; Num. 35:34

1 [I]Lit., *brother*, and so through v. 4 [II]Lit., *hide yourself from them* [a]Ex. 23:4, 5; Prov. 27:10; Zech. 7:9

3 [I]Lit., *hide yourself*

4 [I]Lit., *hide yourself from them.*

6 [a]Lev. 22:28

7 [a]Deut. 4:40

9 [I]Lit., *the fulness* [a]Lev. 19:19

produce of the seed which you have sown, and the increase of the vineyard become defiled.[6942]

10 "[a]You shall not plow with an ox and a donkey together.

11 "[a]You shall not wear a material mixed of wool and linen together.

12 "[a]You shall make yourself tassels on the four corners of your garment with which you cover yourself.

Laws on Morality

13 "[a]If any man[376] takes a wife[802] and goes in to her and *then* [I]turns against[8130] her,

14 and charges[7760] her with shameful deeds and [I]publicly defames[7451] her, and says,[559] 'I took this woman, *but* when I came near her, I did not find her a virgin,'[1331]

15 then the girl's[5291] father[1] and her mother shall take and bring out the *evidence* of the girl's virginity[1331] to the elders[2205] of the city at the gate.

16 "And the girl's father shall say to the elders, 'I gave my daughter to this man for a wife, but he [I]turned against[8130] her;

17 and behold, he has charged her with shameful deeds, saying, "I did not find your daughter a virgin." But [I]this is the *evidence* of my daughter's virginity.' And they shall spread the garment before the elders of the city.

18 "So [a]the elders of that city shall take the man and chastise[3256] him,

19 and they shall fine[6064] him a hundred *shekels* of silver and give it to the girl's father, because he [I]publicly defamed a virgin[1330] of Israel. And she shall remain his wife; he cannot [II]divorce her all his days.

20 "But if this [I][a]charge[1697] is true, that the girl was not found a virgin,

21 then they shall bring out the girl to the doorway of her father's[1] house, and the men of her city shall stone her [I]to death[4191] because she has [a]committed[6213] an act of folly in Israel, by playing the harlot[2181] in her father's house; thus [b]you shall purge the evil from among you.

22 "[a]If a man is found lying with a married[1166] woman, then both of them shall die, the man who lay with the woman, and the woman; thus you shall purge the evil from Israel.

23 "[a]If there is a girl who is a virgin engaged[781] to a man,[376] and *another* man finds her in the city and lies with her,

24 then you shall bring them both out to the gate of that city and you shall stone them [I]to death; the girl, because she did not cry out in the city, and the man, because he has violated his neighbor's wife. Thus you shall purge the evil from among you.

25 "But if in the field[7704] the man finds the girl who is engaged, and the man forces her and lies with her, then only the man who lies with her shall die.

26 "But you shall do nothing[1697] to the girl; there is no sin[2399] in the girl worthy of death,[4194] for just as a man rises against his neighbor and murders[7523] him, so is this case.[1697]

27 "When he found her in the field, the engaged girl cried out, but there was no one to save her.

28 "[a]If a man finds a girl who is a virgin, who is not engaged, and seizes her and lies with her and they are discovered,

29 then the man who lay with her shall give to the girl's father fifty *shekels* of silver, and she shall become his wife because he has violated her; he cannot divorce her all his days.

30 "[I][a]A man shall not take his father's wife so that he shall not uncover[1540] his father's skirt.

Persons Excluded from the Assembly

23

"[a]No one who is [I]emasculated, or has his male organ cut off,[3772] shall enter the assembly[6951] of the LORD.

---

10 [a]2Cor. 6:14-16
11 [a]Lev. 19:19
12 [a]Num. 15:37-41; Matt. 23:5
13 [I]Lit., *hates her* [a]Gen. 29:21; Deut. 24:1; Judg. 15:1
14 [I]Lit., *causes an evil name to go out against her*
16 [I]Lit., *hated her*
17 [I]Lit., *these are*
18 [a]Ex. 18:21; Deut. 1:9-18
19 [I]Lit., *caused an evil name to go out against a virgin* [II]Lit., *send her away*
20 [I]Lit., *matter* [a]Deut. 17:4
21 [I]Lit., *with stones so that she dies* [a]Gen. 34:7; Lev. 19:29; 21:9; Deut. 23:17, 18; Judg. 20:5-10; 2Sam. 13:12, 13 [b]Deut. 13:5; 17:7; 19:19
22 [a]Lev. 20:10; Ezek. 16:38; Matt. 5:27, 28; John 8:5; 1Cor. 6:9; Heb. 13:4
23 [a]Lev. 19:20-22; Matt. 1:18, 19
24 [I]Lit., *with stones so that they die*
28 [a]Ex. 22:16
30 [I]Ch. 23:1 in Heb. [a]Lev. 18:8; 20:11; Deut. 27:20; 1Cor. 5:1
1 [I]Lit., *wounded by crushing of testicles* [a]Lev. 21:20; 22:24

2 "No one of illegitimate birth shall enter the assembly of the LORD; none of his *descendants,* even to the tenth generation,[1755] shall enter the assembly of the LORD.

3 "[a]No Ammonite or Moabite shall enter the assembly of the LORD; none of their *descendants,* even to the tenth generation, shall ever[5769] enter the assembly of the LORD,

4 [a]because they did not meet you with [I]food and water on the way[1870] when you came out of Egypt, and because they hired against you [b]Balaam the son[1121] of Beor from Pethor of [II]Mesopotamia, to curse[7043] you.

5 "Nevertheless, the LORD your God[430] was not willing[14] to listen[8085] to Balaam, but the LORD your God [a]turned[2015] the curse[7045] into a blessing[1288] for you because the LORD your God [b]loves[157] you.

6 "[a]You shall never seek their peace[7965] or their prosperity[2896] all your days.[3117]

7 "You shall not detest[8581] an Edomite, for [a]he is your brother;[251] you shall not detest an Egyptian, [b]because you were an alien[1616] in his land.[776]

8 "The sons[1121] of the third generation who are born[3205] to them may enter the assembly of the LORD.

9 "When you go out as [I]an army[4264] against your enemies, then you shall keep[8104] yourself from every evil[4751] thing.[1697]

10 "[a]If there is among you any man[376] who is unclean[2889] because of a nocturnal[3915] emission, then he must go outside the camp;[4264] he may not [I]reenter the camp.

11 "But it shall be when evening approaches, he shall bathe[7364] himself with water, and at sundown he may [I]reenter the camp.

12 "You shall also have a place outside the camp and go out there,

13 and you shall have a [I]spade[3489] among your tools, and it shall be when you sit down outside, you shall dig with it and shall turn[7725] [II]to cover[3680] up your excrement.

14 "Since [a]the LORD your God walks in the midst[7130] of your camp to deliver[5337] you and to [I]defeat your enemies before you, therefore your camp must be [b]holy;[6918] and He must not see [II]anything indecent[6172] among you [III]lest He turn away[7725] from you.

15 "[a]You shall not hand over to his master[113] a slave[5650] who has [I]escaped[5337] from his master to you.

16 "He shall live with you in your midst, in the place which he shall choose[977] in one of your [I]towns where it pleases[2896] him; [a]you shall not mistreat[3238] him.

17 "[a]None of the daughters of Israel shall be a cult prostitute,[6948] [b]nor shall any of the sons[1121] of Israel be a cult prostitute.[6945]

🔑 18 "You shall not bring the hire of a harlot[2181] or the wages of a [Ia]dog into the house[1004] of the LORD your God for any votive[5088] offering, for both of these are an abomination to the LORD your God.

🔑 19 "[a]You shall not charge interest to your [I]countrymen: interest on money, food,[400] *or* anything that may be loaned at interest.

20 "[a]You may charge interest to a foreigner, but to your [I]countryman you shall not charge interest, so that [b]the LORD your God may bless[1288] you in all [II]that you undertake[3027] in the land which you are about to enter to [III]possess.

21 "[a]When you make a vow to the LORD your God, you shall not delay[309] to pay it, for it would be sin[2399] in you, [I]and the LORD your God will surely require it of you.

22 "However, if you refrain from vowing, it would not be sin in you.

23 "You shall be careful to perform[6213] what goes out from your lips,[8193] just as you have voluntarily[5071]

3 [a]Neh. 13:1, 2
4 [I]Lit., *bread* [II]Heb., *Aram-naharaim* [a]Neh. 13:2 [b]Num. 22:5; 23:7; Josh. 24:9; 2Pet. 2:15; Jude 11
5 [a]Prov. 26:2 [b]Deut. 4:37
6 [a]Ezra 9:12
7 [a]Gen. 25:24-26; Obad. 10, 12 [b]Ex. 22:21; 23:9; Lev. 19:34; Deut. 10:19
9 [I]Or, *a camp*
10 [I]Lit., *come to the midst of* [a]Lev. 15:16
11 [I]Lit., *come to the midst of*
13 [I]Lit., *peg* [II]Lit., *and*
14 [I]Lit., *give* [II]Lit., *nakedness of anything* [III]Lit., *and* [a]Lev. 26:12 [b]Ex. 3:5
15 [I]Lit., *delivered himself* [a]1Sam. 30:15
16 [I]Lit., *gates* [a]Ex. 22:21; Prov. 22:22
17 [a]Lev. 19:29; Deut. 22:21 [b]Gen. 19:5; 2Kin. 23:7
18 [I]I.e., male prostitute, sodomite [a]Lev. 18:22; 20:13
19 [I]Lit., *brothers* [a]Ex. 22:25; Lev. 25:35-37; Neh. 5:2-7; Ps. 15:5
20 [I]Lit., *brother* [II]Lit., *the putting forth of your hand* [III]Lit., *possess it* [a]Deut. 28:12 [b]Deut. 15:10
21 [I]Lit., *for* [a]Num. 30:1, 2; Job 22:27; Ps. 61:8; Eccl. 5:4, 5; Matt. 5:33

🔑 **23:18** "Dog" here means a male prostitute.
🔑 **23:19,20** See note on Lev. 19:33,34.

vowed to the LORD your God, what you have [I]promised.[1696]

24 "When you enter your neighbor's vineyard, then you may eat grapes [I]until you are fully satisfied,[5315] but you shall not put any in your [II]basket.

25 "[a]When you enter your neighbor's standing grain, then you may pluck the heads with your hand, but you shall not wield[5130] a sickle in your neighbor's standing grain.

Law of Divorce

24 "When a man[376] takes a wife[802] and marries[1166] her, and it happens [I]that she finds no favor[2580] in his eyes because he has found some [a]indecency in her, and [b]he writes her a certificate[5612] of divorce[3748] and puts *it* in her hand[3027] and sends her out from his house,[1004]

2 and she leaves his house and goes and becomes another man's *wife,*

3 and if the latter husband[376] [I]turns against[8130] her and writes her a certificate of divorce and puts *it* in her hand and sends her out of his house, or if the latter husband dies[4191] who took her to be his wife,

4 *then* her [a]former husband[1167] who sent her away is not allowed to take her again to be his wife, since she has been defiled; for that is an abomination before the LORD, and you shall not bring sin[2398] on the land which the LORD your God[430] gives you as an inheritance.[5159]

5 "[a]When a man takes a new wife, he shall not go out with the army,[6635] nor be charged with any duty;[1697] he shall be free[5355] at home[1004] one year and shall [b]give happiness to his wife whom he has taken.

Sundry Laws

6 "No one shall take a handmill[3747] or an upper millstone in pledge, for he would be taking a life[5315] in pledge.[2254]

7 "[a]If a man is [I]caught kidnapping any of his [II]countrymen[251] of the sons[1121] of Israel, and he deals with him violently, or sells him, then that thief shall die; so you shall purge the evil[7451] from among you.

8 "[a]Be careful against [I]an infection[5061] of leprosy, that you diligently observe and do according to all that the Levitical priests shall teach[3384] you; as I have commanded[6680] them, so you shall be careful to do.

9 "Remember[2142] what the LORD your God did[6213] [a]to Miriam on the way[1870] as you came out of Egypt.

10 "[a]When you make your neighbor[7453] a loan of any sort, you shall not enter his house to take his pledge.

11 "You shall remain outside, and the man to whom you make the loan shall bring the pledge out to you.

12 "And if he is a poor man, you shall not sleep with his pledge.

13 "[a]When the sun goes down you shall surely return[7725] the pledge to him, that he may sleep in his cloak and bless[1288] you; and [b]it will be righteousness[6666] for you before the LORD your God.

14 "[a]You shall not oppress a hired servant *who is* poor and needy, whether *he is* one of your [I]countrymen or one of your aliens[1616] who is in your land in your [II]towns.

15 "[a]You shall give him his wages on his day[3117] [I]before the sun sets, for he is poor and sets his [II]heart[5315] on it; so that [b]he may not cry against you to the LORD and it become sin[2399] in you.

⊶ 16 "[a]Fathers[1] shall not be put to death[4191] [I]for *their* sons, nor shall sons be put to death [I]for *their* fathers; everyone shall be put to death for his own sin.

17 "[a]You shall not pervert the justice[4941] [I]due an alien[1616] *or* [II]an orphan,

23 [I]Lit., *spoken with your mouth*

24 [I]Lit., *according to your satisfaction of your soul* [II]Or, *vessel*

25 [a]Matt. 12:1; Mark 2:23; Luke 6:1

1 [I]Lit., *if* [a]Num. 5:12, 28; Deut. 22:13-21 [b]Matt. 5:31; 19:7-9; Mark 10:4, 5

3 [I]Lit., *hates her*

4 [a]Jer. 3:1

5 [a]Deut. 20:7 [b]Prov. 5:18

7 [I]Lit., *found stealing* [II]Lit., *brothers* [a]Ex. 21:16

8 [I]Lit., *a mark or stroke* [a]Lev. 13:1-14, 57

9 [a]Num. 12:10

10 [a]Ex. 22:26, 27

13 [a]Ex. 22:26 [b]Deut. 6:25; Ps. 106:31; Dan. 4:27

14 [I]Lit., *brothers* [II]Lit., *gates* [a]Lev. 19:13; 25:35-43; Deut. 15:7-18; Prov. 14:31; Amos 4:1; 1Tim. 5:18

15 [I]Lit., *that the sun shall not go down on it* [II]Lit., *soul* [a]Lev. 19:13; Jer. 22:13; James 5:4 [b]Ex. 22:23; Deut. 15:9; Job 35:9; James 5:4

16 [I]Or, *with* [a]2Kin. 14:6; 2Chr. 25:4; Jer. 31:29, 30; Ezek. 18:20

17 [I]Lit., *of* [II]Or, *the fatherless* [a]Ex. 23:9; Lev. 19:33; Deut. 1:17; 10:17; 16:19; 27:19

⊶ **24:16** In earlier times the moral unit was the family; many children died for the crimes of their fathers. However, in Israel the responsibility of the individual was also taught (Jer. 31:29,30; Ezek. 18:1-4). See the note on Ezek. 18:1-4.

nor [b]take a widow's garment in pledge.
18 "But you shall remember that
you were a slave[5650] in Egypt, and that
the LORD your God redeemed[6299] you
from there; therefore I am commanding[6680] you to do this thing.[1697]
19 "[a]When you reap your harvest
in your field[7704] and have forgotten a
sheaf in the field, you shall not go back
to get it; it shall be [b]for the alien, for
the [I]orphan, and for the widow, in order
that the LORD your God [c]may bless you
in all the work of your hands.[3027]
20 "[a]When you beat your olive tree,
you shall not go over the boughs[6286]
[I]again; it shall be [b]for the alien, for the
[II]orphan, and for the widow.
21 "When you gather the grapes of
your vineyard, you shall not [I]go over
it again; it shall be for the alien, for
the [II]orphan, and for the widow.
22 "And you shall remember that
you were a slave in the land of Egypt;
therefore I am commanding you to do
this thing.

Sundry Laws

25 "[a]If there is a dispute[7379] between men and they go to
[I]court,[4941] and [II]the judges decide their
case,[8199] [b]and they justify[6663] the righteous and condemn[7561] the wicked,[7563]
2 then it shall be if the wicked man
[I][a]deserves to be beaten,[5221] the judge
shall then make him lie down[5307] and
be beaten in his presence with the number of stripes according to his [II]guilt.[7564]
3 "[a]He may beat[5221] him forty times
but no more, lest he beat[5221] him with
many more stripes[4347] than these, and
your brother[251] be [b]degraded[7043] in your
eyes.
4 "[a]You shall not muzzle the ox
while he is threshing.
5 "When brothers[251] live together
and one of them dies[4191] and has no
son,[1121] the wife[802] of the deceased[4191]
shall not be *married* outside *the family*
to a strange man.[2114] [a]Her husband's
brother shall go in to her and take her
to himself as wife and perform the duty
of a husband's brother to her.
6 "And it shall be that the first-born
whom she bears shall [I]assume the name
of his dead brother, that [a]his name may
not be blotted out[4229] from Israel.
7 "[a]But if the man[376] does not desire[2654] to take his brother's wife, then
his brother's wife shall go up[5927] to the
gate to the elders[2205] and say,[559] 'My
husband's brother refuses[3985] to establish a name for his brother in Israel;
he is not willing to perform the duty of
a husband's brother to me.'
8 "Then the elders of his city shall
summon[7121] him and speak[1696] to him.
And *if* he persists and says, 'I do not
desire to take her,'
9 [a]then his brother's[251] wife shall
come to him in the sight of the elders,
and pull his sandal off his foot and
[b]spit in his face; and she shall [I]declare,
'Thus it is done[6213] to the man who does
not build up his brother's house.'[1004]
10 "And in Israel his name shall be
called,[7121] 'The house of him whose sandal is removed.'
11 "If *two* men, a man and his
[I]countryman, are struggling together,
and the wife of one comes near[7126] to
deliver[5337] her husband[376] from the
hand[3027] of the one who is striking him,
and puts out her hand and seizes[2388]
his genitals,
12 then you shall cut off her
[I]hand;[3709] [II][a]you shall not show pity.
13 "[a]You shall not have in your
bag [I]differing weights, a large and a
small.
14 "You shall not have in your house
[I]differing measures, a large and a small.
15 "You shall have a full[8003] and
just[6664] weight; you shall have a full and
just [I]measure, [a]that your days[3117] may
be prolonged in the [II]land[127] which the
LORD your God[430] gives you.
16 "For [a]everyone who does these
things, everyone who acts unjustly[5766]

17 [b]Ex. 22:22

19 [I]Or, *fatherless* [a]Lev. 19:9, 10; 23:22 [b]Deut. 14:29 [c]Prov. 19:17

20 [I]Lit., *after yourself* [II]Or, *fatherless* [a]Lev. 19:10 [b]Deut. 24:19

21 [I]Lit., *glean it after yourself* [II]Or, *fatherless*

1 [I]Lit., *the judgment* [II]Lit., *they judge them* [a]Deut. 17:8-13; 19:17 [b]Deut. 1:16, 17

2 [I]Lit., *is a son of beating* [II]Or, *wickedness* [a]Prov. 19:29; Luke 12:48

3 [a]2Cor. 11:24 [b]Job 18:3

4 [a]Prov. 12:10; 1Cor. 9:9; 1Tim. 5:18

5 [a]Matt. 22:24; Mark 12:19; Luke 20:28

6 [I]Lit., *stand on* [a]Ruth 4:5, 10

7 [a]Ruth 4:5, 6

9 [I]Lit., *answer and say* [a]Ruth 4:7, 8 [b]Num. 12:14

11 [I]Lit., *brother*

12 [I]Lit., *palm* [II]Lit., *your eye* [a]Deut. 7:2; 19:13

13 [I]Lit., *a stone and a stone* [a]Lev. 19:35-37; Prov. 11:1; 20:23; Ezek. 45:10; Mic. 6:11

14 [I]Lit., *an ephah and an ephah*

15 [I]Lit., *ephah* [II]Lit., *ground* [a]Ex. 20:12

16 [a]Prov. 11:1

25:5-10 For a discussion of an example of this practice, see note on Ruth 4:1-12.

is an abomination to the LORD your God.

17 "[a]Remember[2142] what Amalek did[6213] to you along the way[1870] when you came out from Egypt,

18 how he met you along the way and attacked[5221] among you all the stragglers[2179] at your rear when you were faint and weary; and he [a]did not [I]fear[3373] God.

19 "Therefore it shall come about when the LORD your God has given you [a]rest from all your surrounding enemies, in the land[127] which the LORD your God gives you as an inheritance[5159] to [I]possess, you shall blot out[4229] the memory[2143] of Amalek from under heaven;[8064] you must not forget.

Offering First Fruits

26 "Then it shall be, when you enter the land which the LORD your God[430] gives you as an inheritance,[5159] and you possess it and live in it,

2 that you shall take some of [a]the first[7225] of all the produce of the ground[127] which you shall bring in from your land that the LORD your God gives you, and you shall put *it* in a basket and [b]go to the place where the LORD your God chooses[977] to establish[7931] His name.

3 "And you shall go to the priest who is in office at that time,[3117] and say[559] to him, 'I declare[5046] this day[3117] to the LORD [I]my God that I have entered the land[776] which the LORD swore[7650] to our fathers[1] to give us.'

4 "Then the priest shall take the basket from your hand[3027] and set it down before the altar[4196] of the LORD your God.

5 "And you shall answer and say before the LORD your God, '[a]My father[1] was a [I]wandering[6] Aramean, and he went down to Egypt and [II]sojourned[1481] there, [b]few in number; but there he became a [c]great, mighty and populous nation.[1471]

6 'And the [a]Egyptians treated us harshly[7489] and afflicted us, and imposed hard[7186] labor on us.

7 'Then [a]we cried to the LORD, the God of our fathers, and the LORD heard[8085] our voice and saw[7200] our affliction and our toil[5999] and our oppression;

8 [a]and the LORD brought us out of Egypt with a mighty[2389] hand and an outstretched arm and with great terror[4172] and with signs[226] and wonders;[4159]

9 and He has brought us to this place, and has given us this land, [a]a land flowing with milk and honey.

10 'And now behold, I have brought the first[7225] of the produce[6529] of the ground[127] [a]which Thou, O LORD hast given me.' And you shall set it down before the LORD your God, and worship[7812] before the LORD your God;

11 and you and [a]the Levite and the alien[1616] who is among you shall [b]rejoice in all the good[2896] which the LORD your God has given you and your household.[1004]

12 "[a]When you have finished[3615] [I]paying[6237] all the tithe[4643] of your increase in the third year, the year of tithing, then you shall give it to the Levite, to the stranger, to the [II]orphan and to the widow, that they may eat in your [III]towns, and be satisfied.

13 "And you shall say before the LORD your God, 'I have removed the sacred *portion*[6944] from *my* house, and also have given it to the Levite and the alien, the [I]orphan and the widow, according to all Thy commandments which Thou hast commanded[6680] me; [a]I have not transgressed[5674] or forgotten any of Thy commandments.

14 'I have not eaten of it [I]while mourning, nor have I removed any of it while I was unclean,[2931] nor offered any of it to the dead.[4191] I have listened[8085] to the voice of the LORD my God; I have done[6213] according to all that Thou hast commanded me.

15 '[a]Look down from Thy holy[6944] habitation, from heaven,[8064] and bless[1288] Thy people[5971] Israel, and the ground[776] which Thou hast given us, [b]a land flowing with milk and honey, as Thou didst swear to our fathers.'

---

17 [a]Ex. 17:8-16

18 [I]Or, *reverence* [a]Ps. 36:1; Rom. 3:18

19 [I]Lit., *possess it* [a]Deut. 12:9

2 [a]Ex. 22:29; 23:16, 19; Num. 18:13; Prov. 3:9 [b]Deut. 12:5

3 [I]So with Gr.; Heb., *your*

5 [I]Or, *perishing* [II]Or, *lived as an alien* [a]Gen. 43:1-14 [b]Gen. 46:27 [c]Deut. 1:10; 10:22

6 [a]Ex. 1:8-11

7 [a]Ex. 2:23-25; 3:9

8 [a]Deut. 4:34; 34:11, 12

9 [a]Ex. 3:8, 17

10 [a]Deut. 8:18; Prov. 10:22

11 [a]Deut. 12:12 [b]Deut. 12:7; 16:11; Eccl. 3:12, 13; 5:18-20

12 [I]Lit., *tithing* [II]Or, *fatherless* [III]Lit., *gates* [a]Lev. 27:30; Num. 18:24; Deut. 14:28, 29; Heb. 7:5, 9, 10

13 [I]Or, *fatherless* [a]Ps. 119:141, 153, 176

14 [I]Lit., *while in my*

15 [a]Ps. 80:14; Is. 63:15; Zech. 2:13 [b]Deut. 26:9

16 "This day the LORD your God
commands you to do these statutes[2706]
and ordinances.[4941] You shall therefore
be careful[8104] to do them [a]with all your
heart[3824] and with all your soul.[5315]
17 "[a]You have today declared[559] the
LORD to be your God, and [I]that you
would walk in His ways[1870] and keep
His statutes, His commandments and
His ordinances, and listen[8085] to His
voice.
18 "And the LORD has today declared you to be [a]His people, a treasured
possession,[5459] as He promised[1696] you,
and [I]that you should keep all His commandments;
19 and [I]that He shall [a]set you
high[5945] above all nations[1471] which He
has made,[6213] for praise,[8416] fame, and
honor;[8597] and that you shall be [b]a consecrated people to the LORD your God,
as He has spoken."[1696]

The Curses of Mount Ebal

27 Then Moses and the elders[2205]
of Israel charged[6680] the peo-
ple,[5971] saying, "Keep[8104] all the commandments which I command[6680] you
today.
2 "[a]So it shall be on the day when
you shall cross the Jordan to the land
which the LORD your God[430] gives you,
that you shall set up for yourself large
stones, and coat them with lime
3 and write on them all the words[1697]
of this law,[8451] when you cross[5674] over,
in order that you may enter the land
which the LORD your God gives you,
[a]a land flowing with milk and honey, as
the LORD, the God of your fathers,[1]
[I]promised[1696] you.
4 "So it shall be when you cross[5674]
the Jordan, you shall set up [a]on Mount
Ebal, these stones, [I]as I am commanding
you today, and you shall coat them with
lime.
5 "Moreover, you shall build there
an altar[4196] to the LORD your God, an
altar of stones; you [a]shall not [I]wield[5130]
an iron *tool* on them.
6 "You shall build the altar[4196] of the
LORD your God of [I]uncut[8003] stones; and
you shall offer on it burnt offerings[5930]
to the LORD your God;
7 and you shall sacrifice peace
offerings[8002] and eat there, and you shall
[a]rejoice before the LORD your God.
8 "And you shall write on the
[I]stones all the words of this law very
distinctly."
9 Then Moses and the Levitical
priests[3548] spoke[1696] to all Israel, saying,
"Be silent and listen,[8085] O Israel! This
day you have become[1961] a people for
the LORD your God.
10 "You shall therefore [I]obey[8085] the
LORD your God, and do His commandments and His statutes[2706] which I command you today."
11 Moses also charged[6680] the people on that day, saying,
12 "When you cross[5674] the Jordan,
these shall stand on [a]Mount Gerizim to
bless[1288] the people: [b]Simeon, Levi, Judah, Issachar, Joseph, and Benjamin.
13 "And for the curse,[7045] these
shall stand on Mount Ebal: Reuben,
Gad, Asher, Zebulun, Dan, and Naphtali.
14 "The Levites shall then answer
and say[559] to all the men[376] of Israel
with a loud voice,
15 'Cursed[779] is the man[376] who
makes [I][a]an idol or a molten image, an
abomination to the LORD, the work of
the hands[3027] of the craftsman, and
sets[7760] *it* up in secret.' And [b]all the
people shall answer and say, 'Amen.'[543]
16 '[a]Cursed is he who dishonors his
father[1] or mother.' And all the people
shall say, 'Amen.'
17 '[a]Cursed is he who moves his
neighbor's boundary mark.' And all the
people shall say, 'Amen.'
18 '[a]Cursed is he who misleads[7686]
a blind *person* on the road.'[1870] And all
the people shall say, 'Amen.'
19 '[a]Cursed is he who distorts the
justice[4941] due an alien,[1616] [I]orphan, and
widow.' And all the people shall say,
'Amen.'
20 '[a]Cursed is he who lies with his
father's[1] wife,[802] because he has

16 [a]Deut. 4:29
17 [I]Lit., *to walk in* [a]Ps. 48:14
18 [I]Lit., *to keep all* [a]Ex. 6:7; 19:5; Deut. 4:20; 7:6; 14:2; 28:9; 29:13; Titus 2:14; 1Pet. 2:9
19 [I]Lit., *to set you* [a]Deut. 4:7, 8; 28:1, 13 [b]Ex. 19:6; Deut. 7:6; Is. 62:12; Jer. 2:3; 1Pet. 2:9
2 [a]Josh. 8:30-32
3 [I]Lit., *spoke to* [a]Deut. 26:9
4 [I]Lit., *which* [a]Deut. 11:29; Josh. 8:30
5 [I]Lit., *lift up* [a]Ex. 20:25; Josh. 8:31
6 [I]Lit., *whole*
7 [a]Deut. 26:11
8 [I]I.e., stones coated with lime, cf. v. 4
10 [I]Lit., *listen to the voice of*
12 [a]Deut. 11:29 [b]Josh. 8:33-35
15 [I]Or, *a graven image* [a]Ex. 20:4, 23; 34:17; Lev. 19:4; 26:1; Deut. 4:16, 23; 5:8; Is. 44:9 [b]1Cor. 14:16
16 [a]Ex. 20:12; 21:17; Lev. 19:3; 20:9; Deut. 5:16; Ezek. 22:7
17 [a]Deut. 19:14; Prov. 22:28
18 [a]Lev. 19:14
19 [I]Or, *fatherless* [a]Ex. 22:21; 23:9; Lev. 19:33; Deut. 10:18; 24:17
20 [a]Lev. 18:8; 20:11; Deut. 22:30; 1Cor. 5:1

uncovered his father's skirt.' And all the people shall say, 'Amen.'

21 "[a]Cursed is he who lies with any animal.' And all the people shall say, 'Amen.'

22 "[a]Cursed is he who lies with his sister,[269] the daughter of his father or of his mother.' And all the people shall say, 'Amen.'

23 "[a]Cursed is he who lies with his mother-in-law.' And all the people shall say, 'Amen.'

24 "[a]Cursed is he who strikes his neighbor in secret.' And all the people shall say, 'Amen.'

25 "[a]Cursed is he who accepts a bribe to strike[5221] down an innocent[5355] person.'[5315] And all the people shall say, 'Amen.'

26 "[a]Cursed is he who does not confirm the words of this law[8451] by doing them.' And all the people shall say, 'Amen.'

Blessings at Gerizim

28 "[a]Now it shall be, if you will diligently [I]obey[8085] the LORD your God,[430] being careful to do all His commandments which I command[6680] you today,[3117] the LORD your God [b]will set you high[5945] above all the nations[1471] of the earth.[776]

2 "And all these blessings[1293] shall come upon you and [a]overtake you, if you will [I]obey the LORD your God.

3 "Blessed[1288] *shall* you *be* in the city, and blessed *shall* you *be* [a]in the [I]country.[7704]

4 "Blessed *shall be* the [I]offspring of your [II]body[990] and the [I]produce of your ground[127] and the [I]offspring of your beasts, the increase of your herd[504] and the young of your flock.

5 "Blessed *shall be* your basket and your kneading bowl.

6 "Blessed *shall* you *be* [a]when you come in, and blessed *shall* you *be* when you go out.

7 "The LORD will cause your enemies who rise up against you to be [I]defeated[5062] before you; they shall come out against you one way[1879] and shall flee before you seven ways.[1870]

8 "The LORD will command the blessing[1293] upon you in your barns and in [a]all that you put your hand[3027] to, and He will bless[1288] you in the land[127] which the LORD your God gives you.

9 "[a]The LORD will establish you as a holy[6918] people[5971] to Himself, as He swore[7650] to you, if you will keep[8104] the commandments of the LORD your God, and walk in His ways.

10 "So all the peoples of the earth shall see that [Ia]you are called[7121] by the name of the LORD; and they shall be afraid of you.

11 "[a]And the LORD will make you abound in prosperity, in the [I]offspring of your [II]body and in the [I]offspring of your beast and in the [I]produce of your ground, in the land which the LORD swore[7650] to your fathers[1] to give you.

12 "The LORD will open for you His good[2896] storehouse, the heavens,[8064] to give rain to your land[776] in its season[6256] and to bless all the work of your hand; and [a]you shall lend to many nations, but you shall not borrow.

13 "[a]And the LORD shall make you the head[7218] and not the tail, and you only shall be above, and you shall not be underneath, if you will listen to the commandments of the LORD your God, which I charge you today, to [I]observe *them* carefully,

14 and [a]do not turn aside from any of the words[1697] which I command you today, to the right or to the left, to go after other gods[430] to serve[5667] them.

Consequences of Disobedience

15 "[a]But it shall come about, if you will not [I]obey the LORD your God, to observe to do all His commandments and His statutes[2708] with which I charge you today, that all these curses[7045] shall come upon you and overtake you.

16 "[a]Cursed[779] *shall* you *be* in the city, and cursed *shall* you *be* in the [I]country.

---

21 [a]Ex. 22:19; Lev. 18:23; 20:15

22 [a]Lev. 18:9; 20:17

23 [a]Lev. 20:14

24 [a]Ex. 21:12; Lev. 24:17; Num. 35:30, 31

25 [a]Ex. 23:7; Deut. 10:17; Ps. 15:5; Ezek. 22:12

26 [a]Ps. 119:21; Jer. 11:3; Gal. 3:10

1 [I]Lit., *listen to the voice of* [a]Ex. 15:26; 23:22-27; Lev. 26:3-13; Deut. 7:12-26; 11:13 [b]Deut. 28:13; 26:19; 1Chr. 14:2

2 [I]Lit., *listen to the voice of* [a]Zech. 1:6

3 [I]Or, *field* [a]Gen. 39:5

4 [I]Lit., *fruit* [II]Lit., *womb*

6 [a]Ps. 121:8

7 [I]Lit., *smitten*

8 [a]Deut. 15:10

9 [a]Ex. 19:5

10 [I]Lit., *the name of the LORD is called upon you* [a]2Chr. 7:14

11 [I]Lit., *fruit* [II]Or, *womb* [a]Deut. 28:4; Prov. 10:22

12 [a]Deut. 23:20

13 [I]Lit., *keep and do* [a]Deut. 28:1, 44

14 [a]Deut. 5:32; Josh. 1:7

15 [I]Lit., *listen to the voice of* [a]Lev. 26:14-43; Josh. 23:15; Dan. 9:11

16 [I]Or, *field* [a]Deut. 28:3

17 "[a]Cursed *shall be* your basket and your kneading bowl.

18 "[a]Cursed *shall be* the [I]offspring of your [II]body and the [I]produce of your ground, the increase of your herd and the young of your flock.

19 "[a]Cursed *shall* you *be* when you come in, and cursed *shall* you *be* when you go out.

🔑 **20** "[a]The LORD will send upon you curses,[3994] confusion,[4103] and [b]rebuke, in all [I]you undertake to do, until you are destroyed[8045] and until [c]you perish[6] quickly, on account of the evil[7455] of your deeds, because you have forsaken[5800] Me.

21 "[a]The LORD will make the pestilence[1698] cling to you until He has consumed[3615] you from the land, where you are entering to possess it.

22 "[a]The LORD will smite[5221] you with consumption and with fever and with inflammation and with fiery heat and with [I]the sword[2719] and [b]with blight and with mildew, and they shall pursue you until [c]you perish.

23 "And [I]the heaven which is over your head shall be bronze, and the earth which is under you, iron.

24 "[a]The LORD will make the rain of your land powder[80] and dust;[6083] from heaven it shall come down on you until you are destroyed.

25 "[a]The LORD will cause you to be [I]defeated before your enemies; you shall go out one way against them, but you shall flee seven ways before them, and you shall [b]be *an example of* terror to all the kingdoms[4467] of the earth.

26 "[a]And your carcasses[5038] shall be food to all birds of the sky and to the beasts of the earth, and there shall be no one to frighten *them* away.

27 "[a]The LORD will smite you with the boils[7822] of Egypt and with [b]tumors[6076] and with the scab and with the itch, from which you cannot be healed.

28 "The LORD will smite you with madness and with blindness and with bewilderment of heart;[3824]

29 and you shall [Ia]grope at noon, as the blind man gropes in darkness,[653] and you shall not prosper in your ways; but you shall only be oppressed and robbed continually, with none to save you.

30 "[a]You shall betroth[781] a wife,[802] but another man shall violate her; [b]you shall build a house,[1004] but you shall not live in it; you shall plant a vineyard, but you shall not [I]use its fruit.

31 "Your ox shall be slaughtered[2873] before your eyes, but you shall not eat of it; your donkey shall be torn away from you, and shall not be restored[7725] to you; your sheep shall be given to your enemies, and you shall have none to save you.

32 "[a]Your sons[1121] and your daughters shall be given to another people, while your eyes shall look on and yearn[3615] for them continually; but there shall be nothing [I]you can do.

33 "[a]A people[5971] whom you do not know[3045] shall eat up the produce of your ground and all your labors, and you shall never be anything but oppressed and crushed continually.

34 "And you shall be driven mad by the sight of [I]what you see.

35 "[a]The LORD will strike you on the knees and legs with sore[7451] boils, from which you cannot be healed, from the sole[3709] of your foot to the crown of your head.

36 "[a]The LORD will bring you and your king,[4428] whom you shall set over you, to a nation[1471] which neither you nor your fathers have known,[3045] and there you shall serve other gods, [b]wood and stone.

37 "And [a]you shall become[1961] a horror, a proverb, and a taunt among all the people[5971] where the LORD will drive you.

38 "[a]You shall bring out much seed[2233] to the field but you shall

17 [a]Deut. 28:5
18 [I]Lit., *fruit* [II]Or, *womb* [a]Deut. 28:4
19 [a]Deut. 28:6
20 [I]Lit., *the putting forth of your hand which you do* [a]Deut. 28:8; Mal. 2:2 [b]Ps. 80:16; Is. 51:20; 66:15 [c]Deut. 4:26
21 [a]Lev. 26:25; Num. 14:12; Jer. 24:10; Amos 4:10
22 [I]Another reading is *drought* [a]Lev. 26:16 [b]Amos 4:9 [c]Deut. 4:26
23 [I]Lit., *your*
24 [a]Deut. 11:17; 28:12
25 [I]Lit., *smitten* [a]Deut. 28:7; Is. 30:17 [b]2 Chr. 29:8; Jer. 15:4; 24:9; Ezek. 23:46
26 [a]Jer. 7:33; 16:4; 19:7; 34:20
27 [a]Ex. 9:9; Deut. 7:15; 28:60, 61 [b]1Sam. 5:6
29 [I]Lit., *be groping* [a]Ex. 10:21
30 [I]Lit., *begin it* [a]Job 31:10; Jer. 8:10 [b]Amos 5:11
32 [I]Lit., *in the power of your hand* [a]Deut. 28:41
33 [a]Jer. 5:15, 17
34 [I]Lit., *your eyes which you*
35 [a]Deut. 28:27
36 [a]2Kin. 17:4, 6; 24:12, 14; 25:7, 11; 2Chr. 36:1-21; Jer. 39:1-9 [b]Deut. 4:28; Jer. 16:13
37 [a]1Kin. 9:7, 8; Jer. 19:8; 24:9; 25:9; 29:18
38 [a]Is. 5:10; Mic. 6:15; Hag. 1:6

🔑 **28:20** The words of Moses are blending with the words of God (see also 11:14,15; 17:3; 29:5,6). The prophets often spoke for God in the first person.

gather[622] in little, for [b]the locust shall
consume it.
39 "[a]You shall plant and cultivate[5647]
vineyards, but you shall neither drink
of the wine nor gather *the grapes,* for
the worm shall devour them.
40 "[a]You shall have olive trees
throughout your territory but you shall
not anoint[5480] yourself with the oil,[8081]
for your olives shall drop off.
41 "[a]You shall [I]have sons and daughters but they shall not be yours, for
they shall go into captivity.[7628]
42 "[a]The cricket shall possess[3423] all
your trees and the produce of your
ground.
43 "[a]The alien[1616] who is among[7130]
you shall rise above you higher and
higher, but you shall go down lower and
lower.
44 "[a]He shall lend to you, but you
shall not lend to him; [b]he shall be the
head, and you shall be the tail.
45 "So all these curses shall come
on you and pursue you and overtake
you [a]until you are destroyed, because
you would not [I]obey[8085] the LORD your
God by keeping His commandments and
His statutes which He commanded[6680]
you.
46 "And they shall become [a]a sign[226]
and a wonder on you and your [I]descend-
ants forever.[5769]
47 "[a]Because you did not serve[5647]
the LORD your God with joy and a
glad[2898] heart, for the abundance of all
things;
48 therefore you shall serve your
enemies whom the LORD shall send
against you, [a]in hunger, in thirst, in
nakedness, and in the lack of all things;
and He [b]will put an iron yoke on your
neck until He has destroyed you.
49 "[a]The LORD will bring[5375] a nation against you from afar, from the end
of the earth, [b]as the eagle swoops down,
a nation whose language you shall not
understand,[8085]
50 a nation of fierce countenance
who shall [a]have no respect[5375] for the
old,[2205] nor show favor[2603] to the young.
51 "Moreover, it shall eat the
[I]offspring of your herd and the produce
of your ground until you are destroyed,[6]
who also leaves[7604] you no grain, new
wine, or oil,[3323] nor the increase of your
herd or the young of your flock until
they have caused you to perish.
52 "[a]And it shall besiege you in all
your [I]towns until your high and fortified
walls in which you trusted[982] come down
throughout your land, and it shall besiege you in all your [I]towns throughout
your land which the LORD your God has
given you.
53 "[a]Then you shall eat the [I]off-
spring of your own body, the flesh[1320]
of your sons and of your daughters
whom the LORD your God has given you,
during the siege and the distress by
which your enemy shall [II]oppress you.
54 "The man who is [I]refined and
very delicate among you [II]shall be
hostile[7489] toward his brother[251] and toward the wife [III]he cherishes and toward
the rest[3499] of his children who remain,[3498]
55 so that he will not give *even* one
of them any of the flesh of his children
which he shall eat, since he has nothing
else left,[7604] during the siege and the
distress by which your enemy shall
[I]oppress you in all your [II]towns.
56 "[a]The [I]refined and delicate
woman among you, who would not
venture[5254] to set the sole of her foot
on the ground[776] for delicateness and
[II]refinement, [III]shall be hostile toward
the husband[376] [IV]she cherishes and toward her son[1121] and daughter,
57 and toward her afterbirth which
issues from between her [I]legs and toward her children whom she bears; for
[a]she shall eat them secretly for lack of
anything *else,* during the siege and the
distress by which your enemy shall
[II]oppress you in your [III]towns.
58 "If you are not careful to observe
all the words of this law[8451] which are
written in this book,[5612] to [I][a]fear[3372] this
honored[3513] and awesome[3372] [b]name,
[II]the LORD your God,
59 then the LORD will bring
extraordinary[6381] plagues on you and

38 [b]Ex. 10:4; Joel 1:4
39 [a]Is. 5:10; 17:10, 11
40 [a]Jer. 11:16; Mic. 6:15
41 [I]Lit., *beget* [a]Deut. 28:32
42 [a]Deut. 28:38
43 [a]Deut. 28:13
44 [a]Deut. 28:12 [b]Deut. 28:13
45 [I]Lit., *listen to the voice of* [a]Deut. 4:25, 26
46 [I]Lit., *seed* [a]Num. 26:10; Is. 8:18; Ezek. 5:15; 14:8
47 [a]Deut. 12:7; Neh. 9:35-37
48 [a]Lam. 4:4-6 [b]Jer. 28:13, 14
49 [a]Is. 5:26-30; 7:18-20; Jer. 5:15; 6:22, 23 [b]Jer. 48:40; 49:22; Lam. 4:19; Hos. 8:1
50 [a]Is. 47:6
51 [I]Lit., *fruit*
52 [I]Lit., *gates* [a]Jer. 10:17, 18; Zeph. 1:15, 16
53 [I]Lit., *fruit* [II]Or, *distress* [a]Lev. 26:29; 2Kin. 6:28, 29; Jer. 19:9; Lam. 2:20; 4:10
54 [I]Lit., *tender* [II]Lit., *his eye shall be evil toward* [III]Lit., *of his bosom*
55 [I]Or, *distress* [II]Lit., *gates*
56 [I]Lit., *tender* [II]Lit., *tenderness* [III]Lit., *her eye shall be evil toward* [IV]Lit., *of her bosom* [a]Lam. 4:10
57 [I]Lit., *feet* [II]Or, *distress* [III]Lit., *gates* [a]2Kin. 6:28, 29; Lam. 4:10
58 [I]Or, *reverence* [II]Heb., *YHWH* [a]Ps. 99:3; Mal. 1:14 [b]Is. 42:8

[I]your descendants, even [II]severe and
lasting[539] plagues, and miserable and
chronic sicknesses.
60 "[a]And He will bring back on you
all the diseases[4064] of Egypt of which
you were afraid, and they shall cling to
you.
61 "Also every sickness and every
plague[4347] which, not written in the book
of this law, the LORD will bring on you
[a]until you are destroyed.
62 "Then you shall be left few in
number, [a]whereas you were as the stars
of heaven for multitude, because you
did not [I]obey[8085] the LORD your God.
63 "And it shall come about that as
the LORD [a]delighted over you to prosper[3191]
you, and multiply you, so the
LORD will [b]delight over you to make you
perish and destroy[6] you; and you shall
be [c]torn from the land where you are
entering to possess it.
64 "Moreover, the LORD will [a]scatter
you among all peoples, from one end
of the earth to the other end of the
earth; and there you shall [b]serve other
gods, wood and stone, which you or
your fathers have not known.
65 "And [a]among those nations you
shall find no rest, and there shall be
no resting place for the sole of your
foot; but there [b]the LORD will give you
a trembling[7626] heart, failing of eyes, and
despair of soul.[5315]
66 "So your life[2416] shall [I]hang in
doubt before you; and you shall be in
dread[6342] night[3915] and day,[3119] and shall
have no assurance[539] of your life.
67 "[a]In the morning you shall say,[559]
'Would that it were evening!' And at
evening you shall say, 'Would that it
were morning!' because of the dread[6343]
of your heart which you dread, and for
the sight of your eyes which you shall
see.
68 "And the LORD will bring you
back to Egypt in ships, by the way about
which I spoke[559] to you, 'You will never
see it again!' And there you shall offer

59 [I]Lit., *plague on your seed* [II]Lit., *great*
60 [a]Deut. 28:27
61 [a]Deut. 4:25, 26
62 [I]Lit., *listen to the voice of* [a]Deut. 1:10; Neh. 9:23
63 [a]Jer. 32:41 [b]Prov. 1:26 [c]Jer. 12:14; 45:4
64 [a]Lev. 26:33; Deut. 4:27; Neh. 1:8 [b]Deut. 4:28; 29:26; 32:17
65 [a]Lam. 1:3 [b]Lev. 26:36
66 [I]Lit., *be hung for you in front*
67 [a]Job 7:4
1 [I]Ch. 28:69 in Heb. [a]Lev. 26:46; 27:34 [b]Deut. 5:2, 3
2 [I]Ch. 29:1 in Heb.
3 [a]Deut. 4:34; 7:19
4 [a]Is. 6:9, 10; Ezek. 12:2; Matt. 13:14; Acts 28:26, 27; Rom. 11:8
5 [a]Deut. 8:4
6 [a]Deut. 8:3
7 [I]Lit., *came to* [II]Lit., *smote* [a]Num. 21:21-24, 33, 35; Deut. 2:26-3:17
8 [a]Num. 32:32, 33; Deut. 3:12, 13
9 [a]Deut. 4:6; 1Kin. 2:3 [b]Josh. 1:7

yourselves for sale to your enemies as
male and female slaves,[5650] but there
will be no buyer."

The Covenant in Moab

29 [I][a]These are the words[1697] of the
covenant[1285] which the LORD
commanded[6680] Moses to make with the
sons[1121] of Israel in the land[776] of Moab,
besides the [b]covenant which He had
made[3772] with them at Horeb.
2 [I]And Moses summoned[7121] all Israel
and said[559] to them, "You have
seen[7200] all that the LORD did before
your eyes in the land of Egypt to Pharaoh
and all his servants and all his land;
3 [a]the great trials[4531] which your
eyes have seen, those great signs[226]
and wonders.
4 "Yet to this day[3117] [a]the LORD has
not given you a heart[3820] to know,[3045]
nor eyes to see, nor ears[241] to hear.[8085]
5 "And I have led you forty years
in the wilderness; [a]your clothes have
not worn out on you, and your sandal
has not worn out on your foot.
6 "[a]You have not eaten bread, nor
have you drunk wine or strong drink,
in order that you might know[3045] that I
am the LORD your God.[430]
7 "[a]When you [I]reached this place,
Sihon the king[4428] of Heshbon and Og
the king of Bashan came out to meet
us for battle, but we [II]defeated[5221] them;
8 and we took their land and
[a]gave it as an inheritance[5159] to the Reubenites,
the Gadites, and the half-tribe[7626]
of the Manassites.
9 "[a]So keep[8104] the words of this
covenant to do them, [b]that you may
prosper in all that you do.
10 "You stand[5324] today, all of
you, before the LORD your God: your
chiefs,[7218] your tribes,[7626] your elders[2205]
and your officers,[7860] *even* all
the men[376] of Israel,
11 your little ones,[2945] your
wives,[802] and the alien[1616] who is within

28:68 See note on Jer. 18:7-10.
29:11 See note on Num. 11:1-5.

your camps,[4264] from [a]the one who chops[2404] your wood to the one who draws your water,

12 that you may enter[5674] into the covenant with the LORD your God, and into His oath which the LORD your God is making[3772] with you today,

13 in order that He may establish you today as His people[5971] and that [a]He may be your God, just as He spoke[1696] to you and as He swore[7650] to your fathers,[1] to Abraham, Isaac, and Jacob.

14 "Now not with you alone am I [a]making this covenant and this oath,

15 [a]but both with those who stand here with us today in the presence of the LORD our God and with those who are not with us here today

16 (for you know how we lived in the land of Egypt, and how we came through the midst of the nations[1471] through which you passed.[5674]

17 "Moreover, you have seen their abominations and their idols[1544] *of* [a]wood, stone, silver, and gold, which *they had* with them);

18 [a]lest there shall be among you a man[376] or woman,[802] or family[7940] or tribe, whose heart turns away today from the LORD our God, to go and serve[5647] the gods[430] of those nations; lest there shall be among you [b]a root bearing poisonous fruit[7219] and wormwood.[3939]

19 "And it shall be when he hears[8085] the words of this curse,[423] that he will [I]boast,[1288] saying, 'I have peace[7965] though I walk in the stubbornness[8307] of my heart in order [II]to destroy the watered[7302] *land* with the dry.'

20 "The LORD shall never be willing to forgive him, but rather the anger of the LORD and [a]His jealousy[7068] will [I][b]burn[6225] against that man, and every curse[423] which is written in this book[5612] will [II]rest on him, and the LORD will [c]blot out[4229] his name from under heaven.[8064]

21 "Then the LORD will single him out[914] for [I]adversity[7451] from all the tribes of Israel, according to all the curses of the covenant [a]which are written in this book of the law.[8451]

22 "Now the generation[1755] to come, your sons who rise up after you and [a]the foreigner who comes from a distant land, when they see the plagues of the land and the diseases with which the LORD has [I]afflicted it, will say,[559]

23 'All its land is [a]brimstone[1614] and salt, [b]a burning[8316] waste, [I]unsown and unproductive, and no grass grows in it, like the overthrow of [c]Sodom and Gomorrah, Admah and Zeboiim, which the LORD overthrew[2015] in His anger and in His wrath.'[2534]

24 "And all the nations shall say, '[a]Why has the LORD done[6213] thus to this land? Why this great [I]outburst of anger?'

25 "Then *men* shall say, '[a]Because they forsook[5800] the covenant of the LORD, the God of their fathers, which He made with them when He brought them out of the land of Egypt.

26 'And they went and served[5647] other gods and worshiped[7812] them, gods whom they have not known[3045] and whom He had not [I]allotted to them.

27 'Therefore, the anger of the LORD burned[2734] against that land, [a]to bring upon it every curse[7045] which is written in this book;

28 and [a]the LORD uprooted them from their land[127] in anger and in fury and in great wrath,[7110] and cast them into another land, as *it is* this day.'

29 "[a]The secret things belong to the LORD our God, but [b]the things revealed[1540] belong to us and to our sons forever,[5769] that we may observe all the words of this law.

Restoration Promised

30 "So it shall be when all of these things[1697] have come upon you, [a]the blessing[1293] and the curse[7045] which I have set before you, and you [I]call *them* to mind[3824] [b]in all nations[1471] where the LORD your God[430] has banished you,

2 and you [a]return[7725] to the LORD your God and [I]obey[8085] Him [b]with all

11 [a]Josh. 9:21, 23, 27
13 [a]Gen. 17:7; Ex. 6:7
14 [a]Jer. 31:31; Heb. 8:7, 8
15 [a]Acts 2:39
17 [a]Ex. 20:23; Deut. 4:28; 28:36
18 [a]Deut. 13:6 [b]Deut. 32:32; Heb. 12:15
19 [I]Lit., *bless himself in his heart* [II]I.e., to destroy everything
20 [I]Lit., *smoke* [II]Lit., *lie down* [a]Ps. 79:5; Ezek. 23:25 [b]Ps. 74:1; 80:4 [c]Ex. 32:33; Deut. 9:14; 2 Kin. 14:27
21 [I]Lit., *evil* [a]Deut. 30:10
22 [I]Lit., *made it sick* [a]Jer. 19:8; 49:17; 50:13
23 [I]Lit., *it is not sown and does not cause to sprout* [a]Gen. 19:24; Is. 34:9; Jer. 17:6; Zeph. 2:9 [b]Is. 1:7; 64:11 [c]Jude 7
24 [I]Lit., *heat* [a]1Kin. 9:8; Jer. 22:8
25 [a]2Kin. 17:9-23; 2Chr. 36:13-21
26 [I]Lit., *portioned*
27 [a]Dan. 9:11
28 [a]2Chr. 7:20; Ps. 52:5; Prov. 2:22; Ezek. 19:12, 13
29 [a]Acts 1:7 [b]John 5:39; Acts 17:11; 2Tim. 3:16

1 [I]Lit., *cause them to return to your heart* [a]Deut. 11:26; 30:15, 19 [b]Lev. 26:40-45; Deut. 28:64; 29:28; 1Kin. 8:47
2 [I]Lit., *listen to His voice* [a]Deut. 4:29, 30; Neh. 1:9 [b]Deut. 4:29

your heart[3824] and soul[5315] according to
all that I command[6680] you today,[3117] you
and your sons,[1121]
3 then the LORD your God will
[a]restore [I]you from captivity,[7622] and
have compassion[7355] on you, and [b]will
gather[6908] you again from all the peoples[5971] where the LORD your God has
[c]scattered you.
4 "If your outcasts are at the ends
of the [I]earth,[8064] [a]from there the LORD
your God will gather you, and from there
He will [II]bring you back.
5 "And [a]the LORD your God will
bring you into the land which your
fathers[1] possessed,[3423] and you shall
possess it; and He will prosper[3190] you
and [b]multiply you more than your fathers.
6 "Moreover [a]the LORD your God
will circumcise[4135] your heart and the
heart of your [I]descendants,[2233] [b]to
love[157] the LORD your God with all your
heart and with all your soul, in order
that you may live.[2416]
7 "[a]And the LORD your God will
[I]inflict all these curses[423] on your enemies and on those who hate[8130] you,
who persecuted you.
8 "And you shall again [I]obey the
LORD, and observe all His commandments which I command you today.
9 "[a]Then the LORD your God will
[I]prosper you abundantly in all the work
of your hand,[3027] in the [II]offspring of
your [III]body[990] and in the [II]offspring of
your cattle and in the [II]produce of your
ground,[127] for [b]the LORD will again rejoice over you for good,[2896] just as He
rejoiced over your fathers;
10 [I]if you [II]obey[8085] the LORD your
God to keep[8104] His commandments and
His statutes which [a]are written in this
book[5612] of the law,[8451] [I]if you turn to
the LORD your God [b]with all your heart
and soul.
11 "For this commandment[4687]
which I command you today is not too
difficult for you, nor is it [I]out of reach.[6381]
12 "It is not in heaven, [I]that you
should say,[559] '[a]Who will go up[5927] to
heaven for us to get it for us and make
us hear[8085] it, that we may observe it?'
13 "Nor is it beyond the sea, [I]that
you should say, 'Who will cross[5647] the
sea for us to get it for us and make us
hear it, that we may observe it?'
14 "But the word[1697] is very near
you, in your mouth[6310] and in your heart,
that you may observe it.

Choose Life

15 "See, [a]I have set before you today life[2416] and [I]prosperity, and death[4191]
and [II]adversity;[7451]
16 in that I command you today
[a]to love the LORD your God, to walk
in His ways[1870] and to keep His commandments and His statutes and His
judgments, that you [b]may live[2421] and
multiply, and that the LORD your God
may bless[1288] you in the land where you
are entering to possess it.
17 "But if your heart turns away
and you will not obey, but are drawn
away and worship[7812] other gods[430] and
serve[5647] them,
18 I declare[5046] to you today[3117] that
[a]you shall surely perish.[6] You shall not
prolong[748] *your* days in the land where
you are crossing[5674] the Jordan to enter
[I]and possess it.
19 "[a]I call heaven and earth[776] to
witness against you today, that I have
set before you life and death, [b]the blessing and the curse.[7045] So choose[977] life
in order that you may live, you and your
[I]descendants,
20 [a]by loving the LORD your God,
by obeying His voice, and [b]by holding
fast to Him; [c]for [I]this is your life and
the length of your days, [II]that you may
live in [d]the land which the LORD
swore[7650] to your fathers, to Abraham,
Isaac, and Jacob, to give them."

Moses' Last Counsel

31 So Moses went and spoke[1696]
these words[1697] to all Israel.
2 And he said[559] to them, "I am
[a]a hundred and twenty years old[1121]
today;[3117] [b]I am no longer able to come

3 [I]Lit., *your captivity* [a]Gen. 28:15; 48:21; Ps. 126:1, 4; Jer. 29:14 [b]Ps. 147:2; Jer. 32:37; Ezek. 34:13 [c]Deut. 4:27
4 [I]Lit., *sky* [II]Lit., *take you* [a]Neh. 1:9; Is. 43:6; 48:20; 62:11
5 [a]Jer. 29:14; 30:3 [b]Deut. 7:13; 13:17
6 [I]Lit., *seed* [a]Deut. 10:16 [b]Deut. 6:5
7 [I]Lit., *put* [a]Deut. 7:15
8 [I]Lit., *listen to the voice of*
9 [I]Lit., *make you have excess for good* [II]Lit., *fruit* [III]Lit., *womb* [a]Jer. 31:27, 28 [b]Jer. 32:41
10 [I]Or, *for you will* [II]Lit., *listen to the voice of* [a]Deut. 29:21 [b]Deut. 4:29
11 [I]Lit., *far off*
12 [I]Lit., *to say* [a]Rom. 10:6-8
13 [I]Lit., *to say*
15 [I]Lit., *good* [II]Lit., *evil* [a]Deut. 11:26
16 [a]Deut. 6:5 [b]Deut. 4:1; 30:19
18 [I]Lit., *to* [a]Deut. 4:26; 8:19
19 [I]Lit., *seed* [a]Deut. 4:26 [b]Deut. 30:1
20 [I]Lit., *that* [II]Lit., *to dwell* [a]Deut. 6:5 [b]Deut. 10:20 [c]Deut. 4:1; 32:47; Acts 17:25, 28 [d]Gen. 12:7; 17:1-8
2 [a]Deut. 34:7 [b]Num. 27:17; 1Kin. 3:7

and go, and the LORD has said to me, '[c]You shall not cross[5647] this Jordan.'

3 "[a]It is the LORD your God[430] who will cross ahead of you; He will destroy[8045] these nations[1471] before you, and you shall dispossess them. [b]Joshua is the one who will cross ahead of you, just as the LORD has spoken.[1696]

4 "And the LORD will do to them just as He did[6213] to Sihon and Og, the kings[4428] of the Amorites, and to their land,[776] when He destroyed[8045] them.

5 "And [a]the LORD will deliver them up before you, and you shall do to them according to all the commandments which I have commanded[6680] you.

6 "[a]Be strong[2388] and courageous,[2896] [b]do not be afraid[3372] or tremble[6206] at them, for [c]the LORD your God is the one who goes with you. [d]He will not fail[7503] you or forsake[5800] you."

7 Then Moses called[7121] to Joshua and said to him in the sight of all Israel, "[a]Be strong and courageous, for you shall go with this people[5971] into the land which the LORD has sworn[7650] to their fathers[1] to give them, and you shall give it to them as an inheritance.[5157]

8 "And [a]the LORD is the one who goes ahead of you; He will be with you. [b]He will not fail you or forsake you. Do not fear, or be dismayed."[2865]

9 So Moses wrote this law[8451] and gave it to the priests,[3548] the sons[1121] of Levi [a]who carried[5375] the ark[727] of the covenant[1285] of the LORD, and to all the elders[2205] of Israel.

10 Then Moses commanded them, saying, "At the end of *every* seven years, at the time[4150] of [a]the year of remission[8059] of debts, at the [b]Feast of Booths,[5521]

11 when all Israel comes [a]to appear[7200] before the LORD your God at [b]the place which He will choose,[977] [c]you shall read[7121] this law in front of all Israel in their hearing.[241]

12 "Assemble the people, the men[582] and the women[802] and children[2945] and [I]the alien[1616] who is in your [II]town, in order that they may hear[8085] and [a]learn[3925] and fear the LORD your God, and be careful to observe all the words of this law.

13 "And their children,[1121] who have not known,[3045] will hear and learn to fear the LORD your God, as long as[3117] you live[2416] on the land[127] [I]which you are about to cross the Jordan to [II]possess."

Israel Will Fall Away

14 Then the LORD said to Moses, "Behold, [Ia]the time[3117] for you to die[4191] is near;[7126] call[7121] Joshua, and present yourselves at the tent[168] of meeting,[4150] that I may commission[6680] him." [b]So Moses and Joshua went and presented themselves at the tent of meeting.

15 [a]And the LORD appeared[7200] in the tent in a pillar of cloud,[6051] and the pillar of cloud stood at the doorway of the tent.

16 And the LORD said to Moses, "Behold, [a]you are about to lie down with your fathers; and [b]this people will arise and play the harlot[2181] with the strange gods[430] of the land, into the midst of which they are going, and [c]will forsake Me and break[6565] My covenant which I have made with them.

17 "[a]Then My anger will be kindled[2734] against them in that day, and [b]I will forsake them and [c]hide My face from them, and they shall be consumed, and many evils and troubles shall come upon them; so that they will say[559] in that day, '[d]Is it not because our God is not among us that these evils have come upon us?'

18 "But I will surely hide My face in that day because of all the evil which they will do,[6213] for they will turn to other gods.

19 "Now therefore, [a]write this song[7892] for yourselves, and teach[3925] it to the sons of Israel; put it [I]on their lips,[6310] in order that this song may be a witness for Me against the sons of Israel.

20 "[a]For when I bring them into the land flowing with milk and honey, which

---

2 [c]Deut. 1:37; 3:27
3 [a]Deut. 9:3 [b]Num. 27:18
5 [a]Deut. 7:2
6 [a]Josh. 10:25; 1Chr. 22:13 [b]Deut. 1:29; 7:18; 20:1 [c]Deut. 20:4 [d]Josh. 1:5; Heb. 13:5
7 [a]Deut. 1:38; 3:28
8 [a]Ex. 13:21; 33:14 [b]Deut. 31:6; Josh. 1:5; Heb. 13:5
9 [a]Num. 4:5, 6, 15; Deut. 10:8; 31:25, 26; Josh. 3:3
10 [a]Deut. 15:1, 2 [b]Lev. 23:34; Deut. 16:13
11 [a]Deut. 16:16 [b]Deut. 12:5 [c]Josh. 8:34; 2Kin. 23:2
12 [I]Lit., *your alien* [II]Lit., *gates* [a]Deut. 4:10
13 [I]Lit., *where* [II]Lit., *possess it*
14 [I]Lit., *your days to die are* [a]Num. 27:12, 13; Deut. 4:22; 32:50 [b]Ex. 33:9-11
15 [a]Ex. 33:9
16 [a]Gen. 15:15 [b]Ex. 34:15; Deut. 4:25-28; Judg. 2:11, 12, 17 [c]Judg. 10:6; 1Kin. 18:18; 19:10; Jer. 2:13
17 [a]Judg. 2:14; 6:13 [b]2Chr. 15:2; 24:20 [c]Ps. 104:29; Is. 8:17 [d]Num. 14:42
19 [I]Lit., *in their mouths* [a]Deut. 31:22
20 [a]Deut. 6:10-12; 8:10, 19; 11:16, 17

I swore[7650] to their fathers, and they
have eaten and are satisfied and [b]become
[I]prosperous,[1878] then they will turn to
other gods and serve[5647] them, and
spurn[5006] Me and break My covenant.
21 "Then it shall come about,
[a]when many evils and troubles have
come upon them, that this song will testify before them as a witness (for it shall
not be forgotten from the [I]lips of their
descendants);[2233] for [b]I know[3045] their
intent[3336] which they are [II]developing today, before I have brought them into
the land which I swore."
22 [a]So Moses wrote this song the
same day, and taught[3925] it to the sons
of Israel.

Joshua Is Commissioned

23 [a]Then He commissioned Joshua
the son[1121] of Nun, and said, "[b]Be strong
and courageous, for you shall bring the
sons of Israel into the land which I swore
to them, and [c]I will be with you."
24 And it came about, when Moses
finished[3615] writing the words of this law
in a book[5612] until they were complete,[8552]
25 that Moses commanded the Le-
vites [a]who carried the ark[727] of the covenant of the LORD, saying,
26 "Take this book of the law and
place it beside the ark[727] of the covenant of the LORD your God, that it
may [I]remain there as a witness against
you.
27 "For I know [a]your rebellion and
[b]your [I]stubbornness;[7186] behold, while
I am still alive[2416] with you today, you
have been rebellious against the LORD;
how much more, then, after my
death?[4194]
28 "Assemble to me all the elders
of your tribes[7626] and your officers,[7860]
that I may speak[1696] these words in their
hearing[241] and [a]call the heavens[8064] and
the earth[776] to witness against them.
29 "For I know that after my death
you will [a]act corruptly[7843] and turn[5493]
from the way[1870] which I have commanded you; and evil[7451] will befall you

20 [I]Lit., *fat* [b]Deut. 32:15-17

21 [I]Lit., *mouth of its seed* [II]Lit., *making* [a]Lev. 26:41; Deut. 4:30 [b]1Chr. 28:9; John 2:24, 25

22 [a]Deut. 31:19

23 [a]Num. 27:23; Deut. 31:7 [b]Josh. 1:6 [c]Ex. 3:12

25 [a]Deut. 31:9

26 [I]Lit., *be*

27 [I]Lit., *stiff neck* [a]Deut. 9:7, 24 [b]Ex. 32:9; Deut. 9:6, 13

28 [a]Deut. 4:26; 30:19; 32:1

29 [a]Judg. 2:19

1 [a]Deut. 4:26; Ps. 50:4; Is. 1:2; Jer. 6:19

2 [a]Is. 55:10, 11 [b]Ps. 72:6

3 [a]Ex. 33:19; 34:5, 6 [b]Deut. 3:24; 5:24

4 [I]Or, *judgment* [a]Deut. 32:15, 18, 30; 2Sam. 22:31 [b]Gen. 18:25; Dan. 4:37 [c]Deut. 7:9

5 [I]Lit., *It has* [a]Deut. 4:25; 31:29 [b]Matt. 17:17

6 [a]Ps. 116:12 [b]Deut. 32:28 [c]Deut. 1:31; Ps. 74:2; Is. 63:16 [d]Deut. 32:15

7 [a]Ex. 12:26; Ps. 78:5-8

in the latter days, for you will do that
which is evil in the sight of the LORD,
provoking Him to anger[3707] with the
work of your hands."[3027]
30 Then Moses spoke in the hearing of all the assembly of Israel the words
of this song, until they were complete:[8552]

The Song of Moses

32 "[a]Give ear,[238] O heavens,[8064] and
let me speak;[1696]
And let the earth[776] hear[8085] the
words[561] of my mouth.[6310]
2 "[a]Let my teaching[3948] drop[6201] as
the rain,
My speech[565] distill[5140] as the
dew,
[b]As the droplets on the fresh
grass
And as the showers on the herb.
3 "[a]For I proclaim the name of the
LORD;
[b]Ascribe greatness to our
God![430]
4 "[a]The Rock! His work is
perfect,[8549]
[b]For all His ways[1870] are
[I]just;[4941]
[c]A God[410] of faithfulness[530] and
without injustice,[5766]
Righteous[6662] and upright is He.
5 "[I][a]They have acted corruptly[7843]
toward Him,
They are not His children,[1121]
because of their defect;[3971]
[b]*But are* a perverse and crooked
generation.[1755]
6 "Do you thus [a]repay[1580] the LORD,
[b]O foolish and unwise
people?[5971]
[c]Is not He your Father[1] who has
bought you?
[d]He has made[6213] you and
established[3559] you.
7 "Remember[2142] the days[3117] of
old,[5769]
Consider[995] the years of all
generations.[1755]
[a]Ask[7592] your father, and he will
inform[5046] you,

Your elders,[2205] and they will
tell[559] you.
8 "[a]When the Most High[5945] gave
the nations[1471] their
inheritance,[5157]
When He separated the sons[1121]
of [I]man,
He set the boundaries of the
peoples
[b]According to the number of the
sons of Israel.
9 "[a]For the LORD's portion is His
people;
Jacob is the allotment[2256] of His
inheritance.[5159]
10 "[a]He found him in a desert land,
And in the howling waste[8414] of
a wilderness;
He encircled him, He cared[995]
for him,
He guarded[5341] him as
[b]the pupil of His eye.
11 "[a]Like an eagle that stirs up its
nest,
That hovers over its young,
[b]He spread His wings and caught
them,
He carried them on His pinions.
12 "[a]The LORD alone guided[5148] him,
[b]And there was no foreign[5246]
god with him.
13 "[a]He made him ride on the high
places of the earth,
And he ate the produce of the
field;
[b]And He made him suck honey
from the rock,
And [c]oil[8081] from the flinty rock,
14 Curds of cows,[1241] and milk of
the flock,
With fat of lambs,[3733]
And rams, the breed of Bashan,
and goats,
[a]With the finest of the wheat—
And of the [b]blood of grapes you
drank wine.
15 "[a]But [I]Jeshurun grew fat and
kicked—
You are grown fat, thick, and
sleek—
[b]Then he forsook[5203] God
[c]who made him,

8 [I]Or, *Adam* [a]Acts 17:26 [b]Num. 23:9; Deut. 33:28

9 [a]1Sam. 10:1; 1Kin. 8:51, 53; Jer. 10:16

10 [a]Deut. 1:19 [b]Ps. 17:8; Prov. 7:2; Zech. 2:8

11 [a]Ex. 19:4; Deut. 33:12 [b]Ps. 18:10-18

12 [a]Deut. 4:35, 39 [b]Deut. 32:39; Is. 43:12

13 [a]Is. 58:14 [b]Deut. 8:8; Ps. 81:16 [c]Job 29:6

14 [a]Ps. 81:16; 147:14 [b]Gen. 49:11

15 [I]I.e., Israel [a]Deut. 31:20 [b]Judg. 10:6 [c]Deut. 32:6 [d]Deut. 32:4; Ps. 89:26

16 [a]Ps. 78:58 [b]Ps. 106:29

17 [a]Lev. 17:7; 1Cor. 10:20 [b]Deut. 28:64 [c]Judg. 5:8

18 [a]Deut. 32:4 [b]Ps. 106:21

19 [a]Lev. 26:30; Ps. 106:40 [b]Jer. 44:21-23

20 [a]Deut. 31:29 [b]Deut. 32:5 [c]Deut. 9:23

21 [I]Lit., *vanities* [a]Deut. 32:16; 1Cor. 10:22 [b]Deut. 32:17; 1Kin. 16:13, 26 [c]Rom. 10:19

22 [I]I.e., the nether world [a]Num. 16:33-35; Ps. 18:7, 8; Lam. 4:11 [b]Lev. 26:20

23 [a]Deut. 29:21 [b]Ps. 18:14; 45:5

24 [I]Lit., *burning heat* [a]Deut. 28:22, 48

And scorned [d]the Rock of his
salvation.[3444]
16 "[a]They made Him jealous[7065] with
strange[2114] *gods;*
[b]With abominations they
provoked Him to anger.[3707]
17 "[a]They sacrificed[2076] to
demons[7700] who were not
God,
[b]To gods[430] whom they have not
known,[3045]
[c]New *gods* who came lately,
Whom your fathers[1] did not
dread.[8175]
18 "You neglected [a]the Rock who
begot you,
[b]And forgot the God who gave
you birth.[2342]
19 "[a]And the LORD saw[7200] *this,* and
spurned[5006] *them*
[b]Because of the provocation of
His sons and daughters.
20 "Then He said,[559] 'I will hide My
face from them,
[a]I will see what their end[319] *shall
be;*
[b]For they are a perverse[8419]
generation,
[c]Sons in whom is no faithfulness.
21 '[a]They have made Me jealous
with *what* is not God;
They have provoked Me to
anger[3707] with their [Ib]idols.
[c]So I will make[5130] them jealous
with *those who* are not a
people;
I will provoke them to anger with
a foolish nation,[1471]
22 [a]For a fire is kindled in My anger,
And burns to the lowest part of
[I]Sheol,
[b]And consumes the earth with
its yield,
And sets on fire the
foundations[4146] of the
mountains.
23 '[a]I will heap[5595] misfortunes[7451]
on them;
[b]I will use[3615] My arrows on
them.
24 '[a]*They shall be* wasted by famine,
and consumed by [I]plague

[b]And bitter destruction;[6986]
[c]And the teeth of beasts I will
send upon them,
[d]With the venom[2534] of crawling
things[2119] of the dust.[6083]
25 '[a]Outside the sword[2719] shall
bereave,
And inside terror—[367]
[b]Both young man[367] and
virgin,[1330]
The nursling with the man of
gray hair.[7872]
26 'I would have said, "[a]I will cut
them to pieces,
[b]I will remove[7673] the
memory[2143] of them from
men,"[582]
27 Had I not feared the
provocation[3708] by the
enemy,
Lest their adversaries should
misjudge,
Lest they should say,[559] "[a]Our
hand[3027] is [I]triumphant,
And the LORD has not done[6213]
all this." '
28 "[a]For they are a nation
[I]lacking in counsel,[6098]
And there is no
understanding[8394] in them.
29 "[a]Would that they were wise,[2449]
that they understood this,
[b]That they would discern their
[I]future![319]
30 "[a]How could one chase a
thousand,
And two put ten thousand to
flight,
Unless their [b]Rock had sold
them,
And the LORD had given them
up?
31 "Indeed their rock is not like our
Rock,
[a]Even our enemies [I]themselves
judge[6414] this.
32 "For their vine is from the vine
of Sodom,
And from the fields of
Gomorrah;
Their grapes are grapes of
[a]poison,[7219]

24 [b]Ps. 91:6 [c]Lev. 26:22 [d]Amos 5:18, 19
25 [a]Lam. 1:20; Ezek. 7:15 [b]2Chr. 36:17; Lam. 2:21
26 [a]Deut. 4:27; 28:64 [b]Deut. 9:14
27 [I]Lit., *high* [a]Num. 15:30
28 [I]Lit., *perishing* [a]Deut. 32:6
29 [I]Or, *latter end* [a]Deut. 5:29 [b]Deut. 31:29
30 [a]Lev. 26:7, 8 [b]Deut. 32:4; Ps. 44:12
31 [I]Lit., *are judges* [a]Ex. 14:25
32 [a]Deut. 29:18
33 [I]Lit., *dragons* [II]Lit., *cruel*
34 [a]Job 14:17; Jer. 44:21
35 [a]Ps. 94:1; Rom. 12:19; Heb. 10:30 [b]Jer. 23:12 [c]Ezek. 7:5-10
36 [I]Lit., *hand* [a]Ps. 135:14; Heb. 10:30 [b]Lev. 26:43-45; Deut. 30:1-3
37 [a]Judg. 10:14; Jer. 2:28
38 [a]Num. 25:1, 2 [b]Jer. 11:12
39 [a]Is. 41:4; 43:10 [b]Deut. 32:12; Is. 45:5 [c]1Sam. 2:6; Ps. 68:20 [d]Ps. 51:8 [e]Ps. 50:22
40 [a]Ezek. 20:5, 6; 21:4, 5
41 [I]Or, *lightning* [a]Is. 34:6-8 [b]Jer. 50:28-32

Their clusters, bitter.
33 "Their wine is the venom of
[I]serpents,[8577]
And the [II]deadly poison of
cobras.[6620]
34 "[a]Is it not laid up in store with
Me,
Sealed up in My treasuries?
35 '[a]Vengeance[5359] is Mine, and
retribution,
[b]In due[4941] time[6256] their foot will
slip;
[c]For the day[3117] of their
calamity[343] is near,
And the impending things are
hastening upon them.'
36 "[a]For the LORD will vindicate[1777]
His people,
[b]And will have compassion[5162] on
His servants;[5650]
When He sees[7200] that *their*
[I]strength[3027] is gone,
And there is none *remaining,*
bond or free.[5800]
37 "And He will say, '[a]Where are
their gods,
The rock in which they sought
refuge?[2620]
38 '[a]Who ate the fat of their
sacrifices,[2077]
And drank the wine of their
libation?[5257]
[b]Let them rise up and help
you,
Let them be your hiding place!
39 '[a]See now that I, I am He,
[b]And there is no god besides Me;
[c]It is I who put to death and give
life.
[d]I have wounded, and it is I who
heal;
[e]And there is no one who can
deliver[5337] from My hand.
40 'Indeed, [a]I lift up[5375] My hand to
heaven,[8064]
And say, as I live[2416] forever,[5769]
41 [a]If I sharpen[8150] My [I]flashing
sword,
And My hand takes hold on
justice,
[b]I will render[7725] vengeance on
My adversaries,

And I will repay[7999] those who hate[8130] Me.
42 "[a]I will make My arrows drunk with blood,
[b]And My sword shall devour flesh,[1320]
With the blood of the slain[2491] and the captives,[7633]
From the long-haired[7218] [I]leaders[6546] of the enemy.'
43 "[a]Rejoice, O nations, *with* His people;
[b]For He will avenge the blood of His servants,
[c]And will render vengeance on His adversaries,
[d]And will atone[3722] for His land[127] *and* His people."
44 Then Moses came and spoke[1696]
all the words[1697] of this song in the
hearing[241] of the people, he, with
[Ia]Joshua the son[1121] of Nun.
45 When Moses had finished[3615]
speaking[1696] all these words to all Israel,
46 he said to them, "[a]Take[7760] to
your heart all the words with which I
am warning[5749] you today, which you
shall command[6680] [b]your sons to observe
[I]carefully, *even* all the words of this
law.[8451]
47 "For it is not an idle word[1697]
for you; indeed [a]it is your life.[2416] And
[b]by this word you shall prolong[748] your
days in the land, [I]which you are about
to cross[5674] the Jordan to [II]possess."
48 And [a]the LORD spoke to Moses
that very same day, saying,
49 "[a]Go up to this mountain of the
Abarim, Mount Nebo, which is in the
land[776] of Moab [I]opposite Jericho, and
look[7200] at the land[776] of Canaan, which
I am giving to the sons of Israel for a
possession.[272]
50 "Then die[4191] on the mountain
where you ascend, and be [a]gathered to
your people, as Aaron your brother[251]
died[4191] on Mount Hor and was gathered[622] to his people,
🔑 51 [a]because you broke faith[4603] with
Me in the midst of the sons of Israel
at the waters of Meribah-kadesh, in the
[b]wilderness of Zin, because you did not
treat Me as holy[6942] in the midst of the
sons of Israel.
52 "[a]For you shall see the land at
a distance, but [b]you shall not go there,
into the land which I am giving the sons
of Israel."

The Blessing of Moses

33 Now this is the blessing[1293] with
which Moses [a]the man of God[430]
blessed[1288] the sons[1121] of Israel before
his death.[4194]
2 And he said,[559]
"[a]The LORD came from Sinai,
[b]And [I]dawned on them from Seir;
[c]He shone forth from Mount Paran,
And He came from [d]the [II]midst of ten thousand holy ones;
[e]At His right hand there was [III]flashing lightning[1881] for them.
3 "[a]Indeed, He loves[2245] [I]the people;[5971]
[b]All [II]Thy holy ones[6918] are in Thy hand,[3027]
[c]And they [III]followed in Thy steps;
Everyone receives[5375] of Thy words.[1703]
4 "[a]Moses charged[6680] us with a law,[8451]
[b]A possession for the assembly[6952] of Jacob.
5 "[a]And He was king[4428] in Jeshurun,
When the heads[7218] of the people were gathered,
The tribes[7626] of Israel together.[622]
6 "[a]May Reuben live[2421] and not die,[4191]
Nor his men be few."
7 [a]And this regarding Judah; so he
said,

42 [I]Lit., *head* [a]Deut. 32:23 [b]Jer. 12:12; 46:10, 14
43 [a]Rom. 15:10 [b]2Kin. 9:7; Rev. 6:10; 19:2 [c]Is. 1:24, 25 [d]Ps. 65:3; 79:9; 85:1
44 [I]Lit., *Hoshea* [a]Num. 13:8, 16
46 [I]Lit., *to do* [a]Ezek. 40:4; 44:5 [b]Deut. 4:9
47 [I]Lit., *where* [II]Lit., *possess it* [a]Deut. 8:3; 30:20 [b]Deut. 4:40; 33:25
48 [a]Num. 27:12
49 [I]Lit., *which is opposite* [a]Num. 27:12-14; Deut. 3:27
50 [a]Gen. 25:8
51 [a]Num. 20:12 [b]Num. 27:14
52 [a]Deut. 34:1-3 [b]Deut. 1:37; 3:27
1 [a]Josh. 14:6
2 [I]Lit., *rose to* [II]Lit., *myriads of holiness* [III]Or, *a fiery law* [a]Ex. 19:18, 20; Ps. 68:8, 17 [b]Judg. 5:4 [c]Num. 10:12; Hab. 3:3 [d]Dan. 7:10; Acts 7:53 [e]Ex. 23:20-22
3 [I]Lit., *peoples* [II]Lit., *His* [III]Or, *lie down at Thy feet* [a]Deut. 4:37; Mal. 1:2 [b]Deut. 7:6; 14:2 [c]Deut. 6:1-9; Luke 10:39
4 [a]Deut. 4:2; John 7:19 [b]Ps. 119:111
5 [a]Num. 23:21
6 [a]Gen. 49:3, 4
7 [a]Gen. 49:8-12

🔑 **32:51** See note on Num. 20:12.

"Hear,[8085] O LORD, the voice of
Judah,
And bring him to his people.
With his hands[3027] he contended
for [I]them;
And mayest Thou be a help
against his adversaries."
8 And of Levi he said,
"*Let* Thy [a]Thummim and Thy
Urim *belong* to [I]Thy
[b]godly[2623] man
[c]Whom Thou didst prove at
Massah,[5254]
With whom Thou didst
contend[7378] at the waters of
Meribah;
9 [a]Who said of his father[1] and his
mother,
'I did not consider[7200] them';
And he did not acknowledge[5234]
his brothers,[251]
Nor did he regard[3045] his own
sons,
For [b]they observed[8104] Thy
word,[565]
And kept[5341] Thy covenant.[1285]
10 "[a]They shall teach Thine
ordinances[4941] to Jacob,
And Thy law to Israel.
[b]They shall put incense[7004]
[I]before Thee,
And [c]whole burnt offerings[3632]
on Thine altar.[4196]
11 "O LORD, bless[1288] his substance,
And accept[7521] the work of his
hands;
Shatter the loins of those who
rise up against him,
And those who hate[8130] him, so
that they may not rise *again*."
12 Of Benjamin he said,
"[a]May the beloved[3039] of the LORD
dwell[7931] in security by
Him,
[b]Who shields him all the day,
[c]And he dwells between His
shoulders."
13 And of Joseph he said,
"[a]Blessed of the LORD *be* his
land,[776]
With the choice things of
heaven,[8064] with the dew,
And from the deep lying
beneath,
14 And with the choice yield of the
sun,
And with the choice produce of
the months.
15 "And with the [I]best[7218] things of
[a]the ancient[6924] mountains,
And with the choice things of
the everlasting[5769] hills,
16 And with the choice things
of the earth[776] and its fulness,
And the favor[7522] [a]of Him who
dwelt[7931] in the bush.
Let it come to the head[7218] of
Joseph,
And to the crown of the head
of the one distinguished
among his brothers.
17 "As the first-born of his ox,
majesty[1926] is his,
And his horns are the horns of
[a]the wild ox;
With them he shall [b]push the
peoples,
All [I]at once, *to* the ends of the
earth.
And those are the ten thousands
of Ephraim,
And those are the thousands[505]
of Manasseh."
18 [a]And of Zebulun he said,
"Rejoice, Zebulun, in your going
forth,
And, Issachar, in your tents.[168]
19 "[a]They shall call[7121] peoples *to* the
mountain;
There they shall offer
[b]righteous[6664] sacrifices;[2077]
For they shall [I]draw out [c]the
abundance of the seas,
And the hidden treasures of the
sand."
20 [a]And of Gad he said,
"Blessed is the one who enlarges
Gad;
He lies down[7931] [b]as a [I]lion,
And tears the arm, also the
crown of the head.
21 "[a]Then he [I]provided[7200] the
first[7225] *part* for himself,

7 [I]Lit., *him*

8 [I]Lit., *him* [a]Ex. 28:30; Lev. 8:8 [b]Ps. 106:16 [c]Ex. 17:7; Num. 20:13, 24; Deut. 6:16

9 [a]Ex. 32:27-29 [b]Mal. 2:5

10 [I]Lit., *in Thy nostrils* [a]Lev. 10:11; Deut. 31:9-13 [b]Lev. 16:12, 13 [c]Ps. 51:19

12 [a]Deut. 4:37f.; 12:10 [b]Deut. 32:11 [c]Ex. 28:12

13 [a]Gen. 27:27, 28; 49:22-26

15 [I]Or, *chief* [a]Hab. 3:6

16 [a]Ex. 2:2-6; 3:2, 4

17 [I]Or, *together* [a]Num. 23:22 [b]1Kin. 22:11; Ps. 44:5

18 [a]Gen. 49:13-15

19 [I]Lit., *suck* [a]Ex. 15:17; Ps. 2:6; Is. 2:3 [b]Ps. 4:5; 51:19 [c]Is. 60:5

20 [I]Or, *lioness* [a]Gen. 49:19 [b]Gen. 49:9

21 [I]Lit., *saw* [a]Num. 32:1-5

[b]For there the ruler's[2710] portion
was [II]reserved;
[c]And he came *with* the leaders
of the people;
[d]He executed[6213] the justice[6666]
of the LORD,
And His ordinances with Israel."
22 [a]And of Dan he said,
"Dan is [b]a lion's whelp,[1482]
That leaps forth from Bashan."
23 And of Naphtali he said,
"[a]O Naphtali, satisfied with
favor,[7522]
And full of the blessing of the
LORD,
Take possession of the sea and
the south."
24 [a]And of Asher he said,
"More blessed than sons is
Asher;
May he be favored[7522] by his
brothers,
[b]And may he dip[2881] his foot in
oil.
25 "[a]Your locks shall be iron and
bronze,
[b]And according to your days,[3117]
so shall your leisurely walk
be.
26 "[a]There is none like the God[410]
of [I]Jeshurun,
[b]Who rides the heavens
[II]to your help,
And through the skies[7834] in His
majesty.
27 "[a]The eternal[6924] God is a
[I]dwelling place,
[b]And underneath are the
everlasting[5769] arms;
[c]And He drove out the enemy
from before you,
[d]And said,[559] 'Destroy!'[8045]
28 "[a]So Israel dwells in security,
[b]The fountain of Jacob secluded,

21 [II]Or, *covered up* [b]Num. 34:14 [c]Josh. 4:12 [d]Josh. 22:1-3
22 [a]Gen. 49:16 [b]Ezek. 19:2,3
23 [a]Gen. 49:21
24 [a]Gen. 49:20 [b]Job 29:6
25 [a]Ps. 147:13 [b]Deut. 4:40; 32:47
26 [I]I.e., Israel [II]Lit., *in* [a]Ex. 15:11; Deut. 4:35; Ps. 86:8; Jer. 10:6 [b]Deut. 10:14; Ps. 68:33, 34; 104:3; Hab. 3:8
27 [I]Or, *refuge* [a]Ps. 90:1, 2 [b]Gen. 49:24 [c]Ex. 34:11; Josh. 24:18 [d]Deut. 7:2
28 [a]Deut. 33:12; Jer. 23:6 [b]Num. 23:9; Deut. 32:8 [c]Gen. 27:28, 37 [d]Deut. 33:13
29 [a]Ps. 1:1; 32:1, 2 [b]Deut. 4:32; 2Sam. 7:23 [c]Gen. 15:1; Ps. 33:20; 115:9-11 [d]Ps. 68:34 [e]Ps. 66:3 [f]Num. 33:52

1 [a]Deut. 32:49 [b]Deut. 32:52
2 [I]I.e., Mediterranean Sea [a]Deut. 11:24
3 [I]I.e., South country [a]Judg. 1:16; 3:13; 2Chr. 28:15
4 [I]Lit., *seed* [a]Gen. 12:7; 26:3; 28:13
5 [I]Lit., *mouth* [a]Num. 12:7; Josh. 1:1, 2 [b]Deut. 32:50
6 [a]Deut. 3:29; 4:46 [b]Jude 9
7 [a]Deut. 31:2

[c]In a land of grain and new wine;
[d]His heavens[8064] also drop[6201]
down dew.
29 "[a]Blessed[835] are you, O Israel;
[b]Who is like you, a people saved
by the LORD,
[c]Who is the shield of your help,
[d]And the sword[2719] of your
majesty!
[e]So your enemies shall cringe
before you,
[f]And you shall tread upon their
high places."[1116]

The Death of Moses

34 [a]Now Moses went up[5927] from
the plains[6160] of Moab to Mount
Nebo, to the top[7218] of Pisgah, which
is opposite Jericho. And the LORD
[b]showed him all the land,[776] Gilead as
far as Dan,
2 and all Naphtali and the land of
Ephraim and Manasseh, and all the land
of Judah as far as the [Ia]western sea,
3 and the [I]Negev and the plain in
the valley of Jericho, [a]the city of palm
trees, as far as Zoar.
4 Then the LORD said[559] to him,
"This is the land which [a]I swore[7650] to
Abraham, Isaac, and Jacob, saying, 'I
will give it to your [I]descendants';[2233] I
have let you see *it* with your eyes, but
you shall not go over[5674] there."
🗝 5 So Moses [a]the servant[5650] of the
LORD [b]died[4191] there in the land of Moab,
according to the [I]word of the LORD.
6 And He buried[6912] him in the valley
in the land of Moab, [a]opposite Beth-
peor; but [b]no man[376] knows his burial
place[6900] to this day.
7 Although Moses was [a]one hundred and twenty years old[1121] when he

🗝 **34:5-8** By secretly burying Moses Himself, God avoided any possibility of Israel later making a shrine out of Moses' burial place. This also thwarted the devil, because he later had a dispute with Michael, the archangel, concerning the body of Moses (Jude 9). Moses died when he was 120 years old, and his life falls neatly into three periods of forty years each. The first forty years were spent in Egypt as a member of Pharaoh's household (Acts 7:21-23). Next, he lived a private family life in the land of Midian (Acts 7:29,30). Finally, he lived forty years from God's call at the burning bush until his death.

died,[4194] [b]his eye was not dim, nor his
vigor abated.[5127]
8 So the sons[1121] of Israel wept for
Moses in the plains of Moab thirty
days;[3117] then the days of weeping *and*
mourning for Moses came to an end.[8552]
9 Now Joshua the son[1121] of Nun
was [a]filled with the spirit[7307] of wisdom,[2451] for Moses had laid his hands[3027]
on him; and the sons of Israel listened[8085]
to him and did[6213] as the LORD had
commanded[6680] Moses.

10 Since then [a]no prophet[5030] has
risen in Israel like Moses, whom [b]the
LORD knew[3045] face to face,
11 for all the signs[226] and wonders[4159] which the LORD sent him to
perform in the land of Egypt against
Pharaoh, all his servants,[5650] and all his
land,
12 and for all the mighty [1]power[3027]
and for all the great terror[4172] which
Moses performed in the sight of all Israel.

7 [b]Gen. 27:1; 48:10

9 [a]Num. 27:18, 23; Is. 11:2

10 [a]Deut. 18:15, 18 [b]Ex. 33:11; Num. 12:8; Deut. 5:4

12 [1]Lit., *hand*

The Book of

JOSHUA

The Book of Joshua describes the conquest of the land of Canaan under the leadership of Joshua, the successor of Moses. Joshua had been an excellent understudy of Moses throughout the forty years of wandering in the wilderness. He was with Moses at Mount Sinai (Ex. 24:13) when Moses received the Ten Commandments. Joshua was one of the twelve spies (Num. 13:8,16). Of the older generation, only he and Caleb were permitted to cross the Jordan River. Joshua was indeed a great man of tremendous faith, courage, and leadership ability, who believed that God could do what He promised. The Greek form of his name is "Jesus" (Heb. 4:8, in the K.J.V.). The deliverance which was begun in the Book of Exodus was completed in the Book of Joshua. Israel had to cross two bodies of water enroute to their final destination: (1) the Red Sea; (2) the Jordan River. Many never made it past the second one because of their unbelief and disobedience. Joshua was victorious in destroying the Canaanites because of a new breed of Israelite, those who took God at His word. The main purpose of the Book of Joshua was to show how God kept His original promise to Abraham and how the wicked were expelled. The children of those who had been redeemed out of Egypt by the blood of the Passover were now claiming the blessing of that redemption.

God's Charge to Joshua

1 ⊶ Now it came about after the
death[4194] of Moses the servant[5650]
of the LORD that the LORD spoke[559] to
Joshua the son[1121] of Nun, Moses'
[I]servant,[8334] saying,
2 "Moses [a]My servant is dead;[4191]
now therefore arise, [b]cross this Jordan,
you and all this people,[5971] to the land[776]
which I am giving to them, to the
sons[1121] of Israel.
3 "[a]Every place on which the
sole[3709] of your foot treads, I have given
it to you, just as I spoke[1696] to Moses.
4 "[a]From the wilderness and this
Lebanon, even as far as the great river,
the river Euphrates, all the land of the
Hittites, and as far as the Great Sea
toward the setting of the sun, will be
your territory.
5 "[a]No man[376] will *be able to* stand
before you all the days[3117] of your
life.[2416] Just as I have been with Moses,
I will be with you; [b]I will not fail[7503]
you or forsake[5800] you.
6 "[a]Be strong[2388] and courageous,
for you shall give this people possession[5157] of the land which I swore[7650]
to their fathers[1] to give them.

1 [I]Or, *minister*
2 [a]Num. 12:7; Deut. 34:5 [b]Josh. 1:11
3 [a]Deut. 11:24
4 [a]Gen. 15:18; Num. 34:3
5 [a]Deut. 7:24 [b]Deut. 31:6, 7; Heb. 13:5
6 [a]Deut. 31:6, 7, 23

⊶ **1:1** Joshua is introduced as "Moses' servant." There is no success without a successor. In Num. 13:16 his name was changed from Hoshea to Joshua, which is the equivalent of Jesus (see Introduction). Moses, representing the Law, was already dead, and now Joshua was ordered by God and permitted to do what Moses could not do—to lead Israel into the promised land. It could be construed that Joshua was "Moses' servant" in the sense that Christ was "made under the Law" (Gal. 4:4). He had performed faithfully under Moses; now it was he, not Moses, who would be the means of accomplishing the blessings which God had promised under the Law. God had spoken to Moses "mouth to mouth" (Num. 12:8). When Joshua had been selected as Moses' successor, he was instructed to ask counsel through Eleazar the priest "by the judgment of the Urim" (Num. 27:18-23). This was evidently a means to be used for determining the proper course when there was some doubt or in extremely difficult cases. Here, however, Joshua, as the appointed leader who knew the plan of the Lord well, needed to be incited to prompt action, and the people needed to be encouraged by the renewal of divine command. It is reasonable to assume that on such an important occasion, prior to entry into the promised land, God was speaking "mouth to mouth," or intimately, as He had with Moses.

🔑 7 "Only be strong and very courageous; [I][a]be careful to do[6213] according to all the law[8451] which Moses My servant commanded[6680] you; do not turn from it to the right or to the left, so that you may [II]have success wherever you go.

8 "[a]This book[5612] of the law shall not depart from your mouth,[6310] but you shall meditate[1897] on it day[3119] and night,[3915] so that you may [I]be careful to do according to all that is written in it; [b]for then you will make your way[1870] prosperous, and then you will [II]have success.

9 "Have I not commanded you? [a]Be strong and courageous! [b]Do not tremble[6206] or be dismayed,[2865] for the LORD your God[430] is with you wherever you go."

Joshua Assumes Command

10 Then Joshua commanded the officers[7860] of the people, saying,

11 "Pass through[5674] the midst of the camp[4264] and command[6680] the people, saying, 'Prepare[3559] provisions[6720] for yourselves, for within [a]three days you are to cross this Jordan, to go in to possess[3423] the land which the LORD your God is giving you, to possess it.' "

12 [a]And to the Reubenites and to the Gadites and to the half-tribe[7626] of Manasseh, Joshua [I]said,

🔑 13 "Remember the word[1697] which Moses the servant of the LORD commanded you, saying, '[a]The LORD your God gives you rest, and will give you this land.'

14 "Your wives,[802] your little ones,[2945] and your cattle shall remain in the land which Moses gave you beyond the Jordan, but you shall cross before your brothers[251] in battle array, all your valiant[2428] warriors, and shall help them,

15 until the LORD gives your brothers rest, as *He gives* you, and they also possess[3423] the land which the LORD your God is giving them. [a]Then you shall return[7725] to [I]your own land, and possess[3425] [II]that which Moses [b]the servant of the LORD gave you beyond the Jordan toward the sunrise."

16 And they answered Joshua, saying, "All that you have commanded[6680] us we will do, and wherever you send us we will go.

17 "Just as we obeyed[8085] Moses in all things, so we will obey[8085] you; only [a]may the LORD your God be with you, as He was with Moses.

18 "Anyone[376] who rebels against your [I]command[6310] and does not obey your words[1697] in all that you command him, shall be put to death;[4191] only be strong and courageous."

Rahab Shelters Spies

2 🔑 Then Joshua the son[1121] of Nun sent two men as spies secretly from [a]Shittim, saying, "Go, view the land,[776] especially Jericho." So they went and came into the house[1004] of [b]a harlot[2181]

7 [I]Lit., *observe* [II]Or, *act wisely* [a]Deut. 5:32

8 [I]Lit., *observe* [II]Or, *act wisely* [a]Deut. 31:24; Josh. 8:34 [b]Deut. 29:9; Ps. 1:1-3

9 [a]Josh. 1:7 [b]Deut. 31:8

11 [a]Josh. 3:2

12 [I]Lit., *said, saying* [a]Num. 32:20-22

13 [a]Deut. 3:18-20

15 [I]Lit., *the land of your possession* [II]Lit., *it* [a]Josh. 22:4 [b]Josh. 1:1

17 [a]Josh. 1:5, 9

18 [I]Lit., *mouth*

1 [a]Num. 25:1; Josh. 3:1 [b]Heb. 11:31; James 2:25

🔑 **1:7** Jehovah had promised this land to the Israelites, but now they needed to show courage in the face of hardship and war. More than ever before, they had to obey God's law.

🔑 **1:13** See Num. 32:20-27.

🔑 **2:1** Attempts have been made to see in this passage "the house of a woman" or "house of an innkeeper," instead of "the house of a harlot." The same Hebrew term, *zanah* (2181), is commonly used for one who is given to committing adultery (Lev. 21:7; Jer. 5:7). As in Luke 7:37, "a woman . . . who was a sinner" under the law, Rahab remains as an example of a woman who, because of her faith, was not only pardoned but was raised to a position of honor. Rahab was admitted among the people of God. She married into a respected family of one of the chief tribes, and found a prominent place in God's history of salvation as the great-great grandmother of David (see Ruth 4:21,22) in the lineage leading to Christ (Mt. 1:5). Thus, she received some of the temporal blessings of the covenant in great abundance. She is commended in the New Testament for her faith (Heb. 11:31; Js. 2:25). The spies would naturally go to a house such as hers in Jericho, because they could do so without attracting much attention. They had probably met her outside the city, because of her profession, and determined where she lived beforehand.

whose name was Rahab, and [I]lodged
there.
2 And it was told the king of Jericho,
saying, "Behold, men from the sons[1121]
of Israel have come here tonight to
search out the land."[776]
3 And the king of Jericho sent *word*
to Rahab, saying, "Bring out the men
who have come to you, who have entered your house, for they have come
to search out all the land."
4 But the [a]woman[802] had taken the
two men and hidden them, and she
said,[559] "Yes, the men came to me, but
I did not know[3045] where they were
from.
5 "And it came about when *it was*
time to shut the gate, at dark,[2822] that
the men went out; I do not know[3045]
where the men went. Pursue them
quickly, for you will overtake them."
6 But [a]she had brought[5927] them up
to the roof and hidden them in the stalks
of flax which she had laid in order on
the roof.
7 So the men pursued them on the
road[1870] to the Jordan to the fords; and
as soon as those who were pursuing
them had gone out, they shut the gate.
8 Now before they lay down,
[I]she came up[5927] to them on the roof,
9 and said to the men, "[a]I know[3045]
that the LORD has given you the land,
and that the [b]terror[367] of you has
fallen[5307] on us, and that all the inhabitants of the land have [I]melted away before you.
10 "[a]For we have heard[8085] how the
LORD dried up[3001] the water of the
[I]Red Sea before you when you came
out of Egypt, and [b]what you did[6213] to
the two kings[4428] of the Amorites who
were beyond the Jordan, to Sihon and
Og, whom you [II]utterly destroyed.[2763]

1 [I]Lit., *lay down*
4 [a]2Sam. 17:19
6 [a]James 2:25
8 [I]Lit., *then she*
9 [I]Or, *become demoralized* [a]Num. 20:24; Josh. 9:24 [b]Ex. 23:27; Deut. 2:25; Josh. 9:9, 10
10 [I]Lit., *Sea of Reeds* [II]Or, *put under the ban* [a]Ex. 14:21; Num. 23:22; 24:8 [b]Num. 21:21-35
11 [I]Lit., *spirit arose* [a]Josh. 5:1; 7:5; Ps. 22:14; Is. 13:7; 19:1 [b]Deut. 4:39
12 [I]Or, *faithfulness* [a]Josh. 2:18, 19
13 [I]Lit., *let live* [II]Lit., *souls*
14 [I]Lit., *soul* [II]Lit., *instead of you to die* [III]Or, *truly* [a]Gen. 24:49
16 [a]James 2:25
17 [I]Lit., *of yours* [a]Gen. 24:8
18 [I]Lit., *behold* [a]Josh. 2:12

11 "And when we heard *it*, [a]our
hearts[3824] melted and no [I]courage remained in any man[376] any longer because
of you; for the [b]LORD your God,[430] He
is God in heaven[8064] above and on
earth[776] beneath.
12 "Now therefore, please[4994]
swear[7650] to me by the LORD, since I
have dealt[6213] kindly[2617] with you, that
you also will deal[6213] kindly with my
father's[1] household, and give me a
[a]pledge[226] of [I]truth,[571]
13 and [I]spare[2421] my father[1] and my
mother[517] and my brothers[251] and my
sisters,[269] with all who belong to them,
and deliver[5337] our [II]lives[5315] from
death."[4194]
14 So the men said[559] to her, "Our
[I]life[5315] [II]for yours if you do not tell[5046]
this business[1697] of ours; and it shall
come about when the LORD gives us
the land that we will [a]deal kindly[2617] and
[III]faithfully[571] with you."

The Promise to Rahab

15 Then she let them down by a
rope[2256] through the window, for her
house was on the city wall, so that she
was living on the wall.
16 And she said to them, "[a]Go to
the hill country, lest the pursuers happen upon you, and hide yourselves there
for three days,[3117] until the pursuers
return.[7725] Then afterward you may go
on your way."
17 And the men said to her, "[a]We
shall be free[5355] from this oath[7621] [I]to
you which you have made us swear,
18 [I]unless, when we come into the
land, you tie this cord of scarlet thread
in the window through which you let
us down, and [a]gather[622] to yourself into
the house[1004] your father and your

2:18 The bright scarlet "line" or cord would have caught the eye at once and distinguished the house of Rahab from all others. Because scarlet was so closely associated with Levitical rituals, especially with those connected with the putting away of sin and its consequences (see Lev. 14:4,6,51; Num. 19:6), the church fathers from Clement of Rome onward saw in this thread a symbolic connection with the blood of the Passover (Ex. 12:7,13), a symbol of salvation by the blood of Christ, a salvation common to both Christ's messengers and those whom they visit. Certainly to Rahab and her house it was a means of salvation.

mother and your brothers and all your
father's household.[1004]
19 "And it shall come about that anyone who goes out of the doors of your
house into the street, his blood[1818] *shall*
be on his own head,[7218] and we *shall*
be free;[5355] but anyone who is with you
in the house, [a]his blood *shall be* on our
head, if a hand[3027] is *laid* on him.
20 "But if you tell this business of
ours, then we shall be free[5355] from the
oath which you have made us swear."
21 And she said, "According to your
words,[1697] so be it." So she sent them
away, and they departed; and she tied
the scarlet cord in the window.
22 And they departed and came to
the hill country, and remained there for
three days until the pursuers returned.
Now the pursuers had sought *them*
[I]all along the road, but had not found
them.
23 Then the two men returned and
came down from the hill country and
crossed over[5674] and came to Joshua the
son of Nun, and they related[5608] to him
all that had happened to them.
24 And they said to Joshua, "Surely
the LORD has given all the land into our
hands,[3027] and [a]all the inhabitants of the
land, moreover, have [I]melted away before us."

Israel Crosses the Jordan

3 Then Joshua rose early in the morning; and he and all the sons[1121] of
Israel set out from [a]Shittim and came
to the Jordan, and they lodged there
before they crossed.[5674]
2 And it came about [a]at the end of
three days[3117] that the officers[7860] went
through the midst of the camp;[4264]
3 and they commanded[6680] the people,[5971] saying, "When you see the
[a]ark[727] of the covenant[1285] of the LORD
your God[430] with the Levitical priests[3548]
carrying[5375] it, then you shall set out
from your place and go after it.
4 "However, there shall be between
you and it a distance of about 2,000
[I]cubits by measure. Do not come near
it, that you may know[3045] the way[1870]
by which you shall go, for you have not
passed this way before."
5 Then Joshua said[559] to the people,
"[a]Consecrate[6942] yourselves, for tomorrow the LORD will do[6213] wonders[6381]
among[7130] you."
6 And Joshua spoke[559] to the
priests, saying, "Take[5375] up the ark[727]
of the covenant and cross over ahead
of the people." So they took up[5375] the
ark of the covenant and went ahead of
the people.
7 Now the LORD said to Joshua,
"This day[3117] I will begin to [a]exalt you
in the sight of all Israel, that they may
know that just as I have been with Moses, I will be with you.
8 "You shall, moreover, com-
mand[6680] the priests who are carrying
the ark[727] of the covenant, saying,
'When you come to the edge of the waters of the Jordan, you shall stand *still*
in the Jordan.'"
9 Then Joshua said to the sons of
Israel, "Come here, and hear[7181] the
words[1697] of the LORD your God."
10 And Joshua said, "By this you
shall know that [a]the living[2416] God[410] is
among[7130] you, and that He will assuredly [b]dispossess[3423] from before you
the Canaanite, the Hittite, the Hivite,
the Perizzite, the Girgashite, the Amorite, and the Jebusite.
11 "Behold, the ark[727] of the covenant of [a]the Lord[113] of all the earth[776]
is crossing over[5674] ahead of you into
the Jordan.
12 "Now then, [a]take for yourselves
twelve men from the tribes[7626] of Israel,
one man[376] for each tribe.[7626]
13 "And it shall come about when
the soles[3709] of the feet of the priests
who carry the ark[727] of the LORD, the
Lord of all the earth, shall rest in the
waters of the Jordan, the waters of
the Jordan shall be cut off,[3772] *and* the
waters which are [I]flowing down from
above [II]shall [a]stand in one heap."
14 So it came about when the people set out from their tents[168] to cross
the Jordan with the priests carrying

19 [a]Matt. 27:25
22 [I]Lit., *through all the road*
24 [I]Or, *become demoralized* [a]Josh. 2:9
1 [a]Josh. 2:1
2 [a]Josh. 1:11
3 [a]Deut. 31:9
4 [I]I.e., One cubit equals approx. 18 in.
5 [a]Ex. 19:10, 11; Josh. 7:13
7 [a]Josh. 4:14
10 [a]Deut. 5:26; 1Thess. 1:9 [b]Ex. 33:2; Deut. 7:1
11 [a]Job 41:11; Ps. 24:1; Zech. 6:5
12 [a]Josh. 4:2
13 [I]Lit., *going* [II]Lit., *and they shall* [a]Ex. 15:8

[a]the ark[727] of the covenant before the
people,
15 and when those who carried[5375]
the ark[727] came into the Jordan, and the
feet of the priests carrying the ark were
dipped[2881] in the edge of the water (for
the [a]Jordan overflows all its banks all
the days[3117] of harvest),
16 [a]that the waters which were
[I]flowing down from above stood *and*
rose up in [b]one heap, a great distance
away at Adam, the city that is beside
Zarethan; and those which were [I]flowing
down toward the sea of the [c]Arabah,[6160]
the Salt Sea, were completely cut off.[8552]
So the people crossed opposite Jericho.
17 And the priests who carried the
ark[727] of the covenant of the LORD stood
firm[3559] [a]on dry ground[2724] in the middle
of the Jordan while all Israel crossed
on dry ground, until all the nation[1471]
had finished[8552] crossing the Jordan.

Memorial Stones from Jordan

4 Now it came about when all the
nation had finished crossing[5674]
the [a]Jordan, that the LORD spoke[559] to
Joshua, saying,
2 "[a]Take for yourselves twelve men
from the people,[5971] one man[376] from
each tribe,[7626]
3 and command[6680] them, saying,
'Take[5375] up for yourselves twelve
stones from here out of the middle of
the Jordan, from the place where the
priests'[3548] feet are standing firm,[3559]
and carry them over with you, and lay
them down in [a]the lodging place where
you will lodge tonight.' "[3915]
4 So Joshua called[7121] the twelve
men whom he had appointed from the
sons[1121] of Israel, one man from each
tribe;[7626]
5 and Joshua said[559] to them,
"[I]Cross again to the ark[727] of the LORD
your God[430] into the middle of the Jordan, and each of you take up a stone
on his shoulder, according to the number
of the tribes of the sons of Israel.
6 "[I]Let this be a sign[226] among[7130]
you, so that [a]when your children ask[7592]
[II]later, saying, 'What do these stones
mean to you?'
7 then you shall say[559] to them, 'Because the [a]waters of the Jordan were
cut off[3772] before the ark[727] of the
covenant[1285] of the LORD; when it
crossed the Jordan, the waters of the
Jordan were cut off.' So these stones
shall become a [b]memorial to the sons
of Israel forever."[5769]
8 And thus the sons of Israel did,[6213]
as Joshua commanded,[6680] and took[5375]
up twelve stones from the middle of
the Jordan, just as the LORD spoke[1696]
to Joshua, according to the number of
the tribes of the sons of Israel; and they
carried[5674] them over with them to

14 [a]Ps. 132:8; Acts 7:44f.
15 [a]1Chr. 12:15; Jer. 12:5; 49:19
16 [I]Lit., *going* [a]Ps. 66:6; 74:15; 114:3, 5 [b]Josh. 3:13 [c]Deut. 1:1
17 [a]Ex. 14:21, 22, 29
1 [a]Deut. 27:2; Josh. 3:17
2 [a]Josh. 3:12
3 [a]Josh. 4:20
5 [I]Lit., *Cross before the ark*
6 [I]Lit., *That this may be* [II]Lit., *tomorrow* [a]Ex. 12:26; 13:14; Josh. 4:21
7 [a]Josh. 3:13 [b]Ex. 12:14; Num. 16:40

3:15-17 The Lord did not act until their feet stepped down to the water! He was severely testing the faith of the priests here. The phrase "Jordan overflows all its banks" should rather be translated "is full up to all his banks," i.e., brimful. These verses illustrate how suddenly and how completely the Lord showed His power in Israel's behalf to bring them into the promised land. The Jordan flows at the bottom of a deep valley. Descent is made to the water on both sides by two, and occasionally three, terraces. Ordinarily the water flows only in the lower part of this course and is usually less than 100 feet wide. The bank is overgrown with a veritable jungle of tamarisks and willows. In the spring the rising waters reach well up into the trees and undergrowth. Occasionally the rising water fills the ravine to the brim. Such was the case when Joshua brought the people to the crossing. Under these conditions the river cannot be forded at all and crossing can be made only by swimming. At best this is a hazardous task. Though it was no doubt the means used by the two spies, it was completely out of the question for the large multitude that followed Joshua. The fact that this great number of people passed over the Jordan at that season was a clear demonstration that God's power was continuing to work for them. There were absolutely no human means available to produce such an effect. Just as God had sent a strong east wind to clear a wide path in the Red Sea for Israel (Ex. 14:21,22), so He could cause a great upheaval or a tremendous landslide to dam the waters of the Jordan. He can use physical things to accomplish His divine purpose.

[a]the lodging place, and put them down there.

🔑 9 Then Joshua set up twelve [a]stones in the middle of the Jordan at the place where the feet of the priests[3548] who carried[5375] the ark[727] of the covenant were standing, and they are there to this day.[3117]

🔑 10 For the priests who carried the ark[727] were standing in the middle of the Jordan until everything[1697] was completed[8552] that the LORD had commanded Joshua to speak[1696] to the people, according to all that Moses had commanded Joshua. And the people hurried and crossed;

11 and it came about when all the people had finished crossing, that the ark[727] of the LORD and the priests crossed before the people.

12 [a]And the sons of Reuben and the sons of Gad and the half-tribe of Manasseh crossed over in battle array before the sons of Israel, just as Moses had spoken to them;

13 about 40,000, equipped for war,[6635] crossed for battle before the LORD to the desert plains[6160] of Jericho.

14 [a]On that day the LORD exalted Joshua in the sight of all Israel; so that they [I]revered[3372] him, just as they had [I]revered Moses all the days[3117] of his life.[2416]

15 Now the LORD said to [I]Joshua,

16 "Command the priests who carry [a]the ark[727] of the testimony[5715] that they come up[5927] from the Jordan."

17 So Joshua commanded the priests, saying, "Come up from the Jordan."

18 And it came about when the priests who carried the ark[727] of the covenant of the LORD had come up from the middle of the Jordan, and the soles[3709] of the priests' feet were [I]lifted up to the dry[2724] ground,[776] that the waters of the Jordan returned[7725] to their place, and went over all its banks as before.

🔑 **19** Now the people came up[5927] from the Jordan on the [a]tenth of the first[7223] month and camped at Gilgal on the eastern edge of Jericho.

20 [a]And [I]those twelve stones which they had taken from the Jordan, Joshua set up [b]at Gilgal.

21 And he said to the sons of [I]Israel, "When your children ask[7592] their fathers in time to come, saying, 'What are these stones?'

22 then you shall inform[3045] your children, saying, 'Israel crossed[5674] this Jordan on [a]dry[3004] ground.'

23 "For the LORD your God dried[3001] up the waters of the Jordan before you until you had crossed, just as the LORD your God had done to the [I]Red Sea, [a]which He dried up before us until we had crossed;[5674]

24 that [a]all the peoples of the earth[776] may know that the [b]hand[3027] of the LORD is mighty,[2389] so that you may [I][c]fear[3372] the LORD your God [II]forever."

Israel Is Circumcised

5 Now it came about when all the kings[4428] of the Amorites who *were* beyond the Jordan to the west, and

8 [a]Josh. 4:20
9 [a]Gen. 28:18; Josh. 24:26f.; 1Sam. 7:12
12 [a]Num. 32:17
14 [I]Or, *feared* [a]Josh. 3:7
15 [I]Lit., *Joshua, saying*
16 [a]Ex. 25:16
18 [I]Lit., *drawn out*
19 [a]Deut. 1:3
20 [I]Lit., *these* [a]Josh. 4:8 [b]Josh. 4:3, 8
21 [I]Lit., *Israel, saying,*
22 [a]Josh. 3:17
23 [I]Lit., *Sea of Reeds* [a]Ex. 14:21
24 [I]Or, *reverence* [II]Lit., *all the days* [a]1Kin. 8:42; 2Kin. 19:19; Ps. 106:8 [b]Ex. 15:16; 1Chr. 29:12; Ps. 89:13 [c]Ex. 14:31; Ps. 76:7f.; Jer. 10:7

🔑 **4:9** When the Book of Joshua was written, the two pillars of stones were still standing. There were twelve stones in Gilgal and twelve stones in the Jordan River. During the ten months when the Jordan was not overflowing its banks, the twelve stones were plainly visible to succeeding generations.

🔑 **4:10** See Deut. 31:7,8.

🔑 **4:19** After crossing the Jordan, Israel camped at Gilgal for a while before the conquest of Canaan began. Several things happened at Gilgal which signified that the wilderness wanderings were over and Israel was embarking on a new phase of her national history. First, Joshua had the people set up twelve stones as a monument to the miraculous drying up of the Jordan for their crossing (Josh. 4:19-24). Next, the young males were circumcised with flint knives, thereby reinstituting a practice which had not been kept for forty years (5:2-9). With that accomplished (see Ex. 12:48), they could then observe the Passover (5:10). Finally, and probably most indicative of the end of their wanderings, on the day after the Passover, the manna stopped, and they ate from the produce of Canaan (5:11,12).

all the kings of the [a]Canaanites who
were by the sea, [b]heard[8085] how the
LORD had dried up the waters of the
Jordan before the sons[1121] of Israel
until [I]they had crossed,[5674] that their
hearts[3824] melted, and there was no
spirit[7307] in them any longer, because
of the sons of Israel.
2 At that time the LORD said[559] to
Joshua, "Make[6213] for yourself [a]flint
knives[2719] and circumcise[4135] again the
sons of Israel the second time."
3 So Joshua made himself flint
knives and circumcised[4135] the sons of
Israel at [I]Gibeath-haaraloth.[6190]
4 And this is the reason[1697] why
Joshua circumcised them: [a]all the people
who came out of Egypt who were
males,[2145] all the men of war, died[4191]
in the wilderness along the way,[1870] after
they came out of Egypt.
5 For all the people who came out
were circumcised, but all the people who
were born in the wilderness along the
way as they came out of Egypt had not
been circumcised.
6 For the sons of Israel walked
[a]forty years in the wilderness, until all
the nation,[1471] *that is,* the men of war
who came out of Egypt, [I]perished[8552]
because they did not listen[8085] to the
voice of the LORD, [b]to whom the LORD
had sworn[7650] that He would not let
them see[7200] the land[776] which the LORD
had sworn to their fathers[1] to give us,
a land flowing with milk and honey.
7 And their children whom He raised
up in their place, Joshua [I]circumcised;
for they were uncircumcised,[6189] because they had not circumcised them
along the way.
8 Now it came about when they had
finished circumcising[4135] all the nation,
that they remained in their places in the
camp[4264] until they were [I]healed.[2421]
9 Then the LORD said to Joshua,
"Today[3117] I have rolled[1556] away
[a]the reproach[2781] of Egypt from you."
So the name of that place is called[7121]
[I]Gilgal to this day.
10 While the sons of Israel camped
at Gilgal, [a]they observed[6213] the Passover[6453] on the evening of the [b]four-
teenth day of the month on the desert
plains[6160] of Jericho.
11 And on the [I]day after the Passover, on [II]that very day, they ate some
of the produce of the land, unleavened[4682] cakes and parched *grain.*
12 And [a]the manna[4478] ceased[7673] on
the [I]day after they had eaten some of
the produce of the land, so that the sons
of Israel no longer had manna, but they
ate some of the yield of the land of Canaan during that year.
⊶ **13** Now it came about when Joshua
was by Jericho, that he lifted up[5375]
his eyes and looked,[7200] and behold, [a]a
man[376] was standing opposite him with
his sword[7219] drawn in his hand,[3027] and
Joshua went to him and said to him,
"Are you for us or for our adversaries?"
14 And he said, "No, rather I indeed
come now *as* captain[8269] of the host[6635]
of the LORD." And Joshua [a]fell[5307] on
his face to the earth,[776] and bowed
down,[7812] and said to him, "What has
my lord[113] to say[1696] to his servant?"[5650]
15 And the captain of the LORD's
host said to Joshua, "[a]Remove your sandals from your feet, for the place where
you are standing is holy."[6944] And Joshua
did so.

The Conquest of Jericho

6 ⊶ Now Jericho was tightly shut because of the sons[1121] of Israel; no
one went out and no one came in.
2 And the LORD said[559] to Joshua,

1 [I]Other mss. read *we* [a]Num. 13:29 [b]Josh. 2:10, 11
2 [a]Ex. 4:25
3 [I]I.e., the hill of the foreskins
4 [a]Deut. 2:14
6 [I]Lit., *were finished* [a]Deut. 2:7, 14 [b]Num. 14:29-35; 26:63-65
7 [I]Lit., *circumcised them*
8 [I]Lit., *revived*
9 [I]I.e., rolling [a]Zeph. 2:8
10 [a]Ex. 12:18 [b]Josh. 4:19
11 [I]Lit., *morrow* [II]Lit., *this*
12 [I]Lit., *morrow* [a]Ex. 16:35
13 [a]Gen. 18:1, 2; 32:24, 30; Num. 22:31
14 [a]Gen. 17:3
15 [a]Ex. 3:5

⊶ **5:13-15** This place was made holy in the presence of the Divine Messenger. The Angel is the Lord Himself (cf. Ex. 3:2-6; Judg. 6:12,16).
⊶ **6:1-7** This was not a mere military confrontation with a people who were entrenched in a formidable stronghold. The implications are more spiritual than political. God was bringing judgment upon those who had long refused Him and was working on behalf of that people with whom He had just renewed

(continued on next page)

"See, I have given Jericho into your
hand,[3027] with [a]its king *and* the
valiant[2428] warriors.
3 "And you shall march around the
city, all the men of war circling[5362] the
city once. You shall do[6213] so for six
days.[3117]
4 "Also seven priests shall carry
seven [a]trumpets of rams' horns before
the ark;[727] then on the seventh day[3117]
you shall march around the city seven
times, and the priests[3548] shall blow[8628]
the trumpets.
5 "And it shall be that when they
make a long blast with the ram's horn,
and when you hear[7181] the sound of the
trumpet, all the people[5971] shall shout[7321]
with a great shout; and the wall of the
city will fall down [I]flat, and the people
will go up every man[376] [II]straight ahead."
6 So Joshua the son[1121] of Nun
called[7121] the priests and said to them,
"Take[5375] up the ark[727] of the covenant,[1285] and let seven priests carry
seven trumpets of rams' horns before
the ark of the LORD."
7 Then [I]he said to the people, "Go
forward, and march around the city, and
let the armed men go on before the
ark of the LORD."
8 And it was *so,* that when Joshua
had spoken[559] to the people, the seven
priests carrying[5375] the seven trumpets
of rams' horns before the LORD went[5674]
forward and blew[8628] the trumpets; and
the ark[727] of the covenant of the LORD
followed them.
9 And the armed men went before
the priests who blew the trumpets, and
[a]the rear guard[622] came after the ark,[727]
while they continued to blow[8628] the
trumpets.
10 But Joshua commanded[6680] the
people, saying, "You shall not shout nor
let your voice be heard, nor let a
word[1697] proceed out of your mouth,[6310]
until the day I tell[559] you, 'Shout!' Then
you shall shout!"
11 So he had the ark[727] of the LORD
[I]taken around the city, circling *it* once;
then they came into the camp[4264] and
spent the night in the camp.
12 Now Joshua rose early in the
morning, and the priests took up[5375] the
ark[727] of the LORD.
13 And [a]the seven priests carrying
the seven trumpets of rams' horns before the ark[727] of the LORD went on continually, and blew the trumpets; and the
armed men went before them, and
[b]the rear guard came after the ark of
the LORD, while they continued to blow
the trumpets.
14 Thus the second day they
marched around the city once and
returned[7725] to the camp; they did[6213]
so for six days.
15 Then it came about on the seventh day that they rose early at the
dawning of the day and marched around
the city in the same manner[4941] seven
times; only on that day they marched
around the city seven times.
16 And it came about at the seventh time, when the priests blew the
trumpets, Joshua said to the people,
"[a]Shout! For the LORD has given you
the city.

2 [a]Deut. 7:24
4 [a]Lev. 25:9
5 [I]Lit., *in its place* [II]Lit., *before himself*
7 [I]Or, *they*
9 [a]Josh. 6:13; Is. 52:12
11 [I]Lit., *to go around*
13 [a]Josh. 6:4 [b]Josh. 6:9
16 [a]2Chr. 13:14f.

(continued from previous page)
His covenant. The fall of Jericho cogently taught the Canaanites that Israel's successes were not mere human victories of man against man but victories of the God of Israel over their gods. This feat, following closely upon the crossing of the Jordan by miraculous means, impressed upon the people that the same God who had led their fathers out of Egypt and through the Red Sea was with Joshua just as surely as He had been with Moses. This statement of the Lord regarding the means by which Jericho would fall is a condensed form of the actual fact (see vv. 8-10,16,17,20). The trumpets employed were not the silver ones used for assembling the people as well as for signals in military campaigns (Num. 10:2), but the trumpets to be used for introducing the Jubilee (Lev. 25:9,10). Though there was much enthusiasm early in this century for archeological finds at Jericho claiming to demonstrate the historical validity of this event, later studies have ascertained that all remains at the site of Jericho are from a time prior to the fall described here. This in no way, however, detracts from the credibility of this passage.

17 "And the city shall be [a]under the
ban,[2764] it and all that is in it belongs
to the LORD; only Rahab the harlot[2181]
[I]and all who are with her in the house[1004]
shall live,[2421] because she hid the
messengers[4397] whom we sent.
18 "But as for you, only keep[8104]
yourselves from the things under the
ban, lest you [I]covet *them* and [a]take some
of the things under the ban,[2763] so you
would make[7760] the camp of Israel
accursed[2763] and bring trouble on it.
19 "[a]But all the silver and gold and
articles of bronze and iron are holy to
the LORD; they shall go into the treasury
of the LORD."
20 So the people shouted,[7321] and
[I]*priests* blew the trumpets; and it came
about, when the people heard[8085] the
sound of the trumpet, that the people
shouted with a great shout and the
[a]wall fell down[5307] [II]flat, so that the people went[5927] up into the city, every man
straight [III]ahead, and they took the city.
21 [a]And they [I]utterly destroyed[2763]
everything in the city, both man and
woman,[802] young and old, and ox and
sheep and donkey, with the edge[6310] of
the sword.[2719]
22 And Joshua said to the two men
who had spied out the land,[776] "[a]Go into
the harlot's[2181] house and bring the
woman and all she has out of there, as
you have sworn[7650] to her."
23 So the young men who were
spies went in and [a]brought out Rahab
and her father[1] and her mother[517] and
her brothers[251] and all she had; they
also brought out all her relatives,[4940] and
placed them outside the camp of Israel.
24 [a]And they burned[8313] the city
with fire, and all that was in it. Only
the silver and gold and articles of bronze
and iron, they put into the treasury of
the [I]house of the LORD.
25 However, [a]Rahab the harlot and
her father's[1] household[1004] and all she
had, Joshua [I]spared; and she has lived
in the midst of Israel to this day, for
[b]she hid the messengers whom Joshua
sent to spy out Jericho.
26 Then Joshua made them take an
oath[7650] at that time, saying, "[a]Cursed[779]
before the LORD is the man who rises
up and builds this city Jericho; with *the
loss of* his first-born he shall lay its foundation,[3245] and with *the loss of* his youngest son he shall set up[5324] its gates."
27 So [a]the LORD was with Joshua,
and his [b]fame was in all the land.

Israel Is Defeated at Ai

7 [a]But the sons[1121] of Israel acted
unfaithfully[4604] in regard to the things

17 [I]Lit., *she and all* [a]Lev. 27:28; Deut. 20:17
18 [I]Lit., *devote* [a]Josh. 7:1
19 [a]Num. 31:11, 12, 21-23
20 [I]Or, *they* [II]Lit., *in its place* [III]Lit., *before himself* [a]Heb. 11:30
21 [I]Or, *put under the ban* [a]Deut. 20:16
22 [a]Josh. 2:12-19
23 [a]Heb. 11:31
24 [I]I.e., tabernacle [a]Deut. 20:16-18
25 [I]Lit., *let live* [a]Heb. 11:31 [b]Josh. 2:6
26 [a]1Kin. 16:34
27 [a]Gen. 39:2; Judg. 1:19 [b]Josh. 9:1, 3
1 [a]Josh. 6:17-19

6:17 The order from the Lord regarding the plunder of Jericho was to treat it as the firstfruits of Canaan. It was not applied elsewhere (Deut. 20:10-18). Whatever they took was "reserved" exclusively for God, because the firstfruits belonged to Him (Ex. 23:19).

6:21 This severe measure was taken to prevent alien elements of Canaanite culture and worship from infecting Israel. This was justified on the basis of their total incorrigibility before God (see Rom. 1:18-32).

6:26 See I Kgs. 16:34 for the sad fulfillment of this curse. It was a local custom to dedicate the gates and walls of a new city by burying children inside the foundations.

7:1 The sin of Achan stood as a lesson to all Israel of the consequences to one who breaks faith with God. The nation as a collective whole was in a covenant relationship with God and was dealt with by Him not merely as a group of people living together under a common law for their own protection and to accomplish their own goals. Instead, He treated them as an organic whole. Understanding this concept is essential to understanding Paul in Rom. 5:12-21. Achan had defiled not only himself but all of Israel. They were no longer acceptable to God because they, in the person of Achan, had broken the covenant. Therefore, God would no longer work for them in driving out the Canaanites. Only after Achan (and his family, because of their involvement with him in the deed) had been dealt with did God release Israel from their guilt in the matter. Achan's sin was not simply one of stealing goods or even of covetousness. He had clearly defiled God by disobeying His command (vv. 1,11). Achan's punishment (Josh. 22:20) was a warning to all that they should never allow their greed to cause them to forget God's will.

under the ban,[2764] for Achan, the son[1121] of Carmi, the son of Zabdi, the son of Zerah, from the tribe[4294] of Judah, took some of the things under the ban, therefore the anger[639] of the LORD burned[2734] against the sons of Israel.

🔑**2** Now Joshua sent men from Jericho to Ai, which is near [a]Beth-aven, east of Bethel, and said[559] to them, "[I]Go up[5927] and spy out the land."[776] So the men went up[5927] and spied out Ai.

3 And they returned[7725] to Joshua and said[559] to him, "Do not let all the people[5971] go up; *only* about two or three thousand men need go up [I]to Ai; do not make all the people toil up there, for they are few."

4 So about three thousand men from the people went up there, but [a]they fled [I]from the men of Ai.

5 And the men of Ai struck[5221] down about thirty-six of their men, and pursued them [I]from the gate as far as Shebarim, and struck them down on the descent, so the [a]hearts[3824] of the people melted and became as water.

6 Then Joshua [a]tore his clothes and fell[5307] to the earth[776] on his face before the ark[727] of the LORD until the evening,[6153] *both* he and the elders[2205] of Israel; and [b]they put dust[6083] on their heads.[7218]

7 And Joshua said, "Alas, O Lord[136] [I]GOD, why didst Thou ever bring this people over the Jordan, *only* to deliver us into the hand[3027] of the Amorites, to destroy[6] us? If only we had been willing[2974] [II]to dwell beyond the Jordan!

8 "O Lord, what can I say[559] since Israel has turned[2015] *their* [I]back before their enemies?

9 "[a]For the Canaanites and all the inhabitants of the land[776] will hear[7181] of it, and they will surround us and cut off[3772] our name from the earth. And what wilt Thou do[6213] for Thy great name?"

10 So the LORD said to Joshua, "Rise up! Why is it that you have fallen[5307] on your face?

11 "Israel has sinned,[2398] and [a]they have also transgressed[5674] My covenant[1285] which I commanded[6680] them. And they have even taken some of the things under the ban[2764] and have both stolen and deceived. Moreover, they have also put *them* among[7130] their own things.

12 "Therefore the [a]sons of Israel cannot stand before their enemies; they turn *their* [I]backs before their enemies, for they have become accursed.[2764] I will not be with you anymore unless you destroy[8045] the things under the ban from your midst.[7130]

13 "Rise up! [a]Consecrate[6942] the people and say, 'Consecrate yourselves for tomorrow, for thus the LORD, the God[430] of Israel, has said,[559] "[b]There are things under the ban[2764] in your midst,[7130] O Israel. You cannot stand before your enemies until you have removed the things under the ban from your midst."[7130]

14 'In the morning then you shall come near[7126] by your tribes.[7626] And it shall be that the tribe[7626] which [a]the LORD takes *by lot* shall come near by families,[4940] and the family[4940] which the LORD takes shall come near by households,[1004] and the household[1004] which the LORD takes shall come near man by man.[1397]

15 'And [a]it shall be that the one who is taken with the things under the ban[2764] shall be burned[8313] with fire, he and all that belongs to him, because he has transgressed the covenant of the LORD, and because he [b]has committed[6213] a disgraceful thing in Israel.' "

The Sin of Achan

16 So Joshua arose early in the morning and brought Israel near by [I]tribes, and the tribe of Judah was taken.

2 [I]Lit., *saying, Go* [a]Josh. 18:12; 1Sam. 13:5; 14:23

3 [I]Lit., *and smite*

4 [I]Lit., *before* [a]Lev. 26:17; Deut. 28:25

5 [I]Or, *before* [a]Lev. 26:36; Josh. 2:11; Ezek. 21:7; Nah. 2:10

6 [a]Job 2:12 [b]Job 42:6; Lam. 2:10; Rev. 18:19

7 [I]Heb., *YHWH, usually rendered* LORD [II]Lit., *and had dwelt*

8 [I]Lit., *neck*

9 [a]Ex. 32:12; Deut. 9:28

11 [a]Josh. 6:18, 19

12 [I]Lit., *necks* [a]Num. 14:39, 45; Judg. 2:14

13 [a]Josh. 3:5 [b]Josh. 6:18

14 [a]Prov. 16:33

15 [a]1Sam. 14:38f. [b]Gen. 34:7; Judg. 20:6

16 [I]Lit., *its tribes*

🔑**7:2-5** This unsuccessful first battle at Ai illustrates the partnership between God and Israel during the conquest of Canaan. Joshua and his men did the fighting, but God guaranteed the victory. What should have been an easy victory turned into a painful defeat, because God was not with them.

17 And he brought the family of Judah near, and he took the family of the Zerahites; and he brought the family of the Zerahites near man by man, and Zabdi was taken.

18 And he brought his household near man by man; and [a]Achan, son of Carmi, son of Zabdi, son of Zerah, from the tribe of Judah, was taken.

19 Then Joshua said to Achan, "My son, I implore[4994] you, [a]give[7760] glory[3519] to the LORD, the God of Israel, and give praise[8426] to Him; and tell[5046] me now what you have done.[6213] Do not hide it from me."

20 So Achan answered Joshua and said, "Truly,[546] I have sinned against the LORD, the God of Israel, and [I]this is what I did:

21 when I saw[7200] among the spoil a beautiful[2896] mantle from Shinar and two hundred shekels of silver and a bar of gold fifty shekels in weight, then I [a]coveted[2530] them and took them; and behold, they are concealed in the earth inside my tent[168] with the silver underneath it."

22 So Joshua sent messengers,[4397] and they ran to the tent; and behold, it was concealed in his tent with the silver underneath it.

23 And they took them from inside the tent and brought them to Joshua and to all the sons of Israel, and they poured them out before the LORD.

24 Then Joshua and all Israel with him, took Achan the son of Zerah, the silver, the mantle, the bar of gold, his sons,[1121] his daughters, his [I]oxen, his donkeys, his sheep, his tent and all that belonged to him; and they brought[5927] them up to [a]the valley of [II]Achor.

🔑 25 And Joshua said, "Why have you [a]troubled us? The LORD will trouble you this day."[3117] And all Israel stoned [I]them with stones; and they burned[8313] them with fire [II]after they had stoned them with stones.

26 And they raised over him a great heap of stones that stands to this day, and the LORD turned from the fierceness of His anger.[639] Therefore the name of that place has been called[7121] [a]the valley of [I]Achor to this day.

The Conquest of Ai

8 Now the LORD said[559] to Joshua, "[a]Do not fear[3372] or be dismayed.[2865] Take all the people[5971] of war with you and arise, go up[5927] to Ai; see, [b]I have given into your hand[3027] the king of Ai, his people, his city, and his land.[776]

2 "And you shall do[6213] to Ai and its king just as you did[6213] to Jericho and its king; you shall [a]take only its spoil and its cattle as plunder for yourselves. [I]Set[7760] an ambush for the city behind it."

3 So Joshua rose with all the people of war to go up to Ai; and Joshua chose[977] 30,000 men, valiant[2428] warriors, and sent them out at night.[3915]

4 And he commanded[6680] them, saying, "See,[7200] you are [a]going to ambush the city from behind [I]it. Do not go very far from the city, but all of you be ready.[3559]

5 "Then I and all the people who are with me will approach[7126] the city. And it will come about when they come out to meet us as at the first,[7223] that [a]we will flee before them.

6 "And they will come out after us until we have drawn them away from the city, for they will say,[559] '*They* are fleeing before us as at the first.' So we will flee before them.

7 "And you shall rise from *your* ambush and take possession of the city, for the LORD your God[430] will deliver it into your hand.

8 "Then it will be when you have seized the city, that you shall set the city on fire. You shall do *it* [a]according to the word[1697] of the LORD. See, I have commanded you."

9 So Joshua sent them away, and

18 [a]Num. 32:23; Acts 5:1-10
19 [a]1Sam. 6:5; 2Chr. 30:22; Jer. 13:16; John 9:24
20 [I]Lit., *thus and thus I did*
21 [a]Eph. 5:5; 1Tim. 6:10
24 [I]Or, *cattle* [II]I.e., trouble [a]Josh. 15:7
25 [I]Lit., *him* [II]Lit., *and they stoned* [a]Josh. 6:18
26 [I]I.e., trouble [a]Is. 65:10; Hos. 2:15

1 [a]Josh. 1:9; 10:8 [b]Josh. 6:2
2 [I]Lit., *Set for yourself* [a]Deut. 20:14; Josh. 8:27
4 [I]Lit., *the city* [a]Judg. 20:29
5 [a]Judg. 20:32
8 [a]Deut. 20:16-18; Josh. 8:2

🔑 **7:25** Since Deut. 24:16 prohibited the execution of children for the sins of their fathers, it follows logically that Achan's children must have condoned what he did.

they went to the place of ambush and remained between Bethel and Ai, on the west side of Ai; but Joshua spent that night among the people.

10 Now Joshua [a]rose early in the morning and mustered[6485] the people, and he went up[5927] with the elders[2205] of Israel before the people to Ai.

11 Then all the people of war who *were* with him went up and drew near and arrived in front of the city, and camped on the north side of Ai. Now *there was* a valley between him and Ai.

12 And he took about 5,000 men and set[7760] them in ambush between [a]Bethel and Ai, on the west side of the [I]city.

13 So they stationed the people, all the army[4264] that was on the north side of the city, and its rear guard on the west side of the city, and Joshua spent that night in the midst of the valley.

14 And it came about when the king of Ai saw[7200] *it,* that the men of the city hurried and rose up early and went out to meet Israel in battle, he and all his people at the appointed[4150] place before the desert plain.[6160] But he did not know[3045] that *there was* an ambush against him behind the city.

15 And Joshua and all Israel pretended to be beaten[5060] before them, and fled [a]by the way[1870] of the wilderness.

16 And all the people who were in the city were called together[2199] to pursue them, and they pursued Joshua, and [a]were drawn away from the city.

17 So not a man[376] was left[7604] in Ai or Bethel who had not gone out after Israel, and they left[5800] the city [I]unguarded and pursued Israel.

18 Then the LORD said to Joshua, "[a]Stretch out the javelin that is in your hand toward Ai, for I will give it into your hand." So Joshua stretched out the javelin that was in his hand toward the city.

19 And the *men in* ambush rose quickly from their place, and when he had stretched out his hand, they ran and entered the city and captured it; and they quickly set the city on fire.

20 When the men[582] of Ai turned [I]back and looked, behold, the smoke of the city ascended[5927] to the sky,[8064] and they had no place[3027] to flee this way or that, for the people who had been fleeing to the wilderness turned[2015] against the pursuers.

21 When Joshua and all Israel saw that the *men in* ambush had captured the city and that the smoke of the city ascended, they turned back[7725] and [I]slew[5221] the men of Ai.

22 And [I]the others came out from the city to encounter them, so that they were *trapped* in the midst of Israel, [II]some on this side and some on that side; and they [III]slew[5221] them until [a]no one was left [IV]of those who survived[8300] or escaped.

23 But they took alive[2416] the king of Ai and brought[7126] him to Joshua.

24 Now it came about when Israel had finished[3615] killing all the inhabitants of Ai in the field[7704] in the wilderness where they pursued them, and all of them were fallen[5307] by the edge[6310] of the sword[2719] until they were destroyed,[8552] then all Israel returned[7725] to Ai and struck it with the edge of the sword.

25 [a]And all who fell[5307] that day,[3117] both men[376] and women,[802] were 12,000—all the [I]people of Ai.

26 For Joshua [a]did not withdraw his hand with which he stretched out the javelin until he had [I]utterly destroyed[2763] all the inhabitants of Ai.

27 [a]Israel took only the cattle and the spoil of that city as plunder for themselves, according to the word[1697] of the LORD which He had commanded Joshua.

28 So Joshua burned[8313] Ai and made[7760] it [a]a heap forever,[5769] a desolation[8077] until this day.

29 [a]And he hanged the king of Ai on a tree until evening;[6153] and at sunset Joshua gave command and they took his body[5038] down from the tree, and threw it at the entrance of the city gate, and

10 [a]Gen. 22:3
12 [I]I.e., Ai [a]Gen. 12:8; 28:19; Judg. 1:22
15 [a]Josh. 15:61; 16:1; 18:12
16 [a]Judg. 20:31
17 [I]Lit., *open*
18 [a]Ex. 14:16; 17:9-13; Josh. 8:26
20 [I]Lit., *behind them*
21 [I]Lit., *smote*
22 [I]Lit., *these came* [II]Lit., *these. . .those* [III]Lit., *smote* [IV]Lit., *for it* [a]Josh. 8:8
25 [I]Lit., *men* [a]Deut. 20:16-18
26 [I]Or, *put under the ban* [a]Ex. 17:11, 12
27 [a]Josh. 8:2
28 [a]Deut. 13:16
29 [a]Deut. 21:22, 23

raised over it a great heap of stones *that stands* to this day.

30 Then Joshua built an altar[4196] to the LORD, the God of Israel, in [a]Mount Ebal,

31 just as Moses the servant[5650] of the LORD had commanded the sons[1121] of Israel, as it is written in the book[5612] of the law[8451] of Moses, [a]an altar[4196] of uncut[8003] stones, on which no man had wielded[5130] an iron *tool;* and they offered[5927] burnt offerings[5930] on it to the LORD, and sacrificed[2076] peace offerings.[8002]

32 And he [a]wrote there on the stones a copy of the law of Moses, which [I]he had written, in the presence of the sons of Israel.

33 [a]And all Israel with their elders and officers[7860] and their judges[8199] were standing on both sides of the ark[727] before the Levitical priests[3548] who carried[5375] the ark of the covenant[1285] of the LORD, the stranger[1616] as well as the native. Half of them *stood* in front of [b]Mount Gerizim and half of them in front of Mount Ebal, just as Moses the servant of the LORD had given command at first[7223] to bless[1288] the people of Israel.

34 Then afterward he read[7121] all the words[1697] of the law, the blessing[1293] and the curse,[7045] according to all that is written in [a]the book of the law.

35 There was not a word of all that Moses had commanded which Joshua did not read before all the assembly[6951] of Israel [a]with the women and the little ones[2945] and the strangers[1616] who were [I]living among[7130] them.

Guile of the Gibeonites

9 Now it came about when [a]all the kings[4428] who were beyond the Jordan, in the hill country and in the lowland and on all the [b]coast of the Great Sea toward Lebanon, [c]the Hittite and the Amorite, the Canaanite, the Perizzite, the Hivite and the Jebusite, heard[8085] of it,

2 that they gathered[6908] themselves together with [I][a]one accord[6310] to fight with Joshua and with Israel.

3 When the inhabitants of [a]Gibeon heard what Joshua had done[6213] to Jericho and to Ai,

4 they also acted[6213] craftily[6195] and [I]set out as envoys,[6735] and took worn-out sacks on their donkeys, and wineskins, worn-out and torn and [II]mended,

5 and worn-out and patched[2921] sandals on their feet, and worn-out clothes on themselves; and all the bread of their provision was dry[3001] *and* had become crumbled.

6 And they went to Joshua to the [a]camp[4264] at Gilgal, and said[559] to him and to the men[376] of Israel, "We have come from a far country;[776] now therefore, make a covenant[1285] with us."

7 And the men of Israel said to the [a]Hivites, "Perhaps[194] you are living [I]within[7130] our land; [b]how then shall we make a covenant with you?"

8 But they said to Joshua, "[a]We are your servants."[5650] Then Joshua said to them, "Who are you, and where do you come from?"

9 And they said to him, "Your servants have come from [a]a very far country because of the [I]fame of the LORD your God;[430] for [b]we have heard the report of Him and all that He did in Egypt,

10 and all that He did to the two kings of the Amorites who were beyond the Jordan, to Sihon king of Heshbon and to Og king of Bashan who was at Ashtaroth.

11 "So our elders[2205] and all the inhabitants of our country spoke[559] to us, saying, 'Take provisions[6720] in your hand for the journey,[1870] and go to meet them and say[559] to them, "[a]We are your servants; now then, make a covenant with us."'

12 "This our bread *was* warm *when* we took it for our provisions out of our houses[1004] on the day[3117] that we left to come to you; but now behold, it is dry and has become crumbled.

13 "And these wineskins which we filled were new, and behold, they are torn; and these our clothes and our san-

30 [a]Deut. 27:2-8

31 [a]Ex. 20:25

32 [I]I.e., Moses [a]Deut. 27:2, 3, 8

33 [a]Deut. 27:11-14 [b]Deut. 11:29

34 [a]Josh. 1:8

35 [I]Lit., *walking* [a]Ex. 12:38; Deut. 31:12; Zech. 8:23

1 [a]Num. 13:29; Josh. 3:10 [b]Num. 34:6 [c]Ex. 3:17; 23:23

2 [I]Lit., *one mouth* [a]Ps. 83:3, 5

3 [a]Josh. 9:17, 22; 10:2; 21:17

4 [I]Lit., *went and traveled as envoys* [II]Lit., *tied up*

6 [a]Josh. 5:10

7 [I]Lit., *among us* [a]Josh. 9:1; 11:19 [b]Ex. 23:32; Deut. 7:2

8 [a]Deut. 20:11; 2Kin. 10:5

9 [I]Or, *name* [a]Josh. 9:16, 17 [b]Josh. 2:9; 9:24

11 [a]Josh. 9:8

dals are worn out because of the very
long journey."
14 So the men[582] *of Israel* took some
of their provisions, and [a]did not ask[7592]
for the [I]counsel of the LORD.
15 [a]And Joshua made peace[7965] with
them and made[6213] a covenant with
them, to let them live;[2421] and the leaders[5387] of the congregation[5712] swore[7650]
an oath to them.
16 And it came about at the end
of three days[3117] after they had made
a covenant[3772] with them, that they
heard that they were neighbors and
that they were living [I]within[7130] their
land.
17 Then the sons[1121] of Israel set
out and came to their cities on the third
day. Now their cities *were* [a]Gibeon and
Chephirah and Beeroth and Kiriath-
jearim.
18 And the sons of Israel did not
strike[5221] them because the leaders of
the congregation had sworn[7650] to them
by the LORD the God of Israel. And the
whole congregation grumbled against
the leaders.
19 But all the leaders said to the
whole congregation, "We have sworn
to them by the LORD, the God of Israel,
and now we cannot touch[5060] them.
20 "This we will do[6213] to them,
even let them live, lest wrath[7110] be upon
us for the oath[7621] which we swore to
them."
21 And the leaders said to them,
"Let them live." So they became [a]hew-
ers[2404] of wood and drawers of water
for the whole congregation, just as the
leaders had spoken[1696] to them.
22 Then Joshua called[7121] for them
and spoke[1696] to them, saying, "Why
have you deceived us, saying, 'We are
very far from you,' [a]when you are living
[I]within[7130] our land?
23 "Now therefore, you are
[a]cursed,[779] and [I]you shall never
cease[3772] being slaves,[5650] both hewers
of wood and drawers of water for the
house[1004] of my God."
24 So they answered Joshua and
said, "[a]Because it was certainly told[5046]
your servants that the LORD your God
had commanded[6680] His servant[5650] Moses to give you all the land,[776] and to
destroy[8045] all the inhabitants of the land
before you; therefore we feared[3372]
greatly for our lives[5315] because of you,
and have done this thing.[1697]
25 "And now behold, [a]we are in your
hands;[3027] do as it seems good[2896] and
right in your sight to do to us."
26 Thus he did to them, and delivered[5337] them from the hands of the
sons of Israel, and they did not kill[2026]
them.
27 But Joshua made them that day
hewers of wood and drawers of water
for the congregation and for the altar[4196]
of the LORD, to this day, [a]in the place
which He would choose.[977]

Five Kings Attack Gibeon

10 Now it came about when Adoni-zedek king of Jerusalem
heard[8085] that Joshua had captured Ai,
and had [I]utterly destroyed[2763] it (just
[a]as he had done[6213] to Jericho and its
king, so he had done to Ai and its king),
and that the inhabitants of Gibeon had
[b]made peace with Israel and were
[II]within[7130] their land,
2 that [I]he [a]feared[3372] greatly, because Gibeon *was* a great city, like one
of the royal[4467] cities, and because it
was greater than Ai, and all its men[582]
were mighty.
3 Therefore Adoni-zedek king of Jerusalem sent *word* [a]to Hoham king of
Hebron and to Piram king of Jarmuth
and to Japhia king of Lachish and to Debir
king of Eglon, saying,
4 "Come up[5927] to me and help me,
and let us [I]attack Gibeon, for it has

14 [I]Lit., *mouth* [a]Num. 27:21
15 [a]Ex. 23:32
16 [I]Lit., *among them*
17 [a]Josh. 18:25
21 [a]Deut. 29:11
22 [I]Lit., *among us* [a]Josh. 9:16
23 [I]Lit., *a servant shall not be cut off from you* [a]Gen. 9:25
24 [a]Josh. 9:9
25 [a]Gen. 16:6
27 [a]Deut. 12:5
1 [I]Or, *put under the ban* [II]Lit., *among them* [a]Josh. 8:21f. [b]Josh. 9:15
2 [I]Lit., *they* [a]Ex. 15:14-16
3 [a]Josh. 10:23
4 [I]Lit., *smite*

9:27 The Lord indicated to Israel where they were to erect altars for worshiping Him. The Gibeonites helped to rebulid the walls of Jerusalem after the exile (Neh. 7:25). Solomon received a message from God in a dream at Gibeon (I Kgs. 3:5-15).

[a]made peace with Joshua and with the sons[1121] of Israel."

5 So the five kings[4428] of [a]the Amorites, the king of Jerusalem, the king of Hebron, the king of Jarmuth, the king of Lachish, *and* the king of Eglon, gathered[622] together and went up,[5927] they with all their armies,[4264] and camped by Gibeon and fought against it.

6 Then the men of Gibeon sent *word* to Joshua to the camp[4264] at Gilgal, saying, "Do not [I]abandon[7503] your servants;[5650] come up to us quickly and save[3467] us and help us, for all the kings of the Amorites that live in the hill country have assembled[6908] against us."

7 So Joshua went up from Gilgal, he and [a]all the people[5971] of war with him and all the valiant[2428] warriors.

8 And the LORD said[559] to Joshua, "[a]Do not fear[3372] them, for I have given them into your hands; not [I]one[376] of them shall stand before you."

9 So Joshua came upon them suddenly [I]by marching all night[3915] from Gilgal.

10 [a]And the LORD confounded them before Israel, and He [I]slew[5221] them with a great slaughter[4347] at Gibeon, and pursued them by the way[1870] of the ascent of Beth-horon, and struck[5221] them as far as Azekah and Makkedah.

11 And it came about as they fled from before Israel, *while* they were at the descent of Beth-horon, that [a]the LORD threw large stones from heaven[8064] on them as far as Azekah, and they died; *there were* more who died[4191] [I]from the hailstones than those whom the sons of Israel killed[2026] with the sword.[2789]

12 Then Joshua spoke[1696] to the LORD in the day[3117] when the LORD delivered up the Amorites before the sons of Israel, and he said in the sight of Israel,

"O [a]sun, stand still at Gibeon,
And O moon in the valley of Aijalon."

13 [a]So the sun stood still, and the moon stopped,
Until the nation[1471] avenged[5358] themselves of their enemies.

Is it not written in [b]the book[5612] of Jashar?[3477] And [c]the sun stopped in the middle of the sky, and did not hasten to go *down* for about a whole[8549] day.

14 And there was no day like that before it or after it, when the LORD listened[8085] to the voice of a man; for [a]the LORD fought for Israel.

15 Then Joshua and all Israel with him returned[7725] to the camp to Gilgal.

Victory at Makkedah

16 Now these [a]five kings had fled and hidden themselves in the cave at Makkedah.

17 And it was told[5046] Joshua, saying, "The five kings have been found hidden in the cave at Makkedah."

18 And Joshua said, "Roll[1556] large stones against the mouth[6310] of the cave, and assign men by it to guard[8104] them,

19 but do not stay *there* yourselves; pursue your enemies and [I]attack them in the rear.[2179] Do not allow them to enter their cities, for the LORD your God[430] has delivered them into your hand."

20 And it came about when Joshua and the sons of Israel had finished[3615] [I]slaying[5221] them with a very great slaughter, [a]until they were destroyed,[8552] and the survivors[8300] *who* remained of them [II]had entered the fortified cities,

21 that all the people returned to the camp to Joshua at Makkedah in peace.[7965] No one [I]uttered a word against any of the sons of Israel.

22 Then Joshua said, "Open the

4 [a]Josh. 9:15
5 [a]Num. 13:29
6 [I]Lit., *slacken your hands from*
7 [a]Josh. 8:1
8 [I]Lit., *a man* [a]Josh. 1:5, 9
9 [I]Lit., *he went up*
10 [I]Lit., *struck* [a]Deut. 7:23
11 [I]Lit., *with* [a]Ps. 18:12f.; Is. 28:2
12 [a]Hab. 3:11
13 [a]Hab. 3:11 [b]2Sam. 1:18 [c]Is. 38:8
14 [a]Ex. 14:14; Deut. 1:30; Josh. 10:42
16 [a]Josh. 10:5
19 [I]Lit., *smite their tail*
20 [I]Lit., *striking* [II]Lit., *and had* [a]Deut. 20:16
21 [I]Lit., *sharpened his tongue*

10:12-14 At Joshua's request, God caused the sun to stand still for several hours so that Israel could achieve a greater victory. This is one of two times in the O.T. when God interrupted the celestial clock as a favor or a sign to a man. The other occasion was the turning back of the sundial ten points for the benefit of Hezekiah (Isa. 38:7,8).

mouth of the cave and bring these five kings out to me from the cave."

23 And they did[6213] so, and [a]brought these five kings out to him from the cave: the king of Jerusalem, the king of Hebron, the king of Jarmuth, the king of Lachish, *and* the king of Eglon.

24 And it came about when they brought these kings out to Joshua, that Joshua called[7121] for all the men[376] of Israel, and said to the chiefs[8269] of the men of war who had gone with him, "Come near,[7126] [a]put your feet on the necks of these kings." So they came near and put their feet on their necks.

25 Joshua then said to them, "[a]Do not fear or be dismayed![2865] Be strong[2388] and courageous, for thus the LORD will do[6213] to all your enemies with whom you fight."

26 So afterward Joshua struck them and put them to death,[4191] and he [a]hanged them on five trees; and they hung on the trees until evening.

27 And it came about at [I]sunset that Joshua commanded,[6680] and [a]they took them down from the trees and threw them into the cave where they had hidden themselves, and put[7760] large stones over the mouth of the cave, to this very day.

28 Now Joshua captured Makkedah on that day, and struck it and its king with the edge[6310] of the sword; [a]he [I]utterly destroyed [II]it and every [III]person[5315] who was in it. He left no survivor.[8300] Thus he did to the king of Makkedah [b]just as he had done to the king of Jericho.

Joshua's Conquest of SouthernPalestine

29 Then Joshua and all Israel with him passed[5674] on from Makkedah to [a]Libnah, and fought against Libnah.

30 And the LORD gave it also with its king into the hands of Israel, and he struck it and every person who *was* in it with the edge of the sword. He left no survivor in it. Thus he did to its king just as he had done to the king of Jericho.

31 And Joshua and all Israel with him passed on from Libnah to Lachish, and they camped by it and fought against it.

32 And the LORD gave Lachish into the hands of Israel; and he captured it on the second day, and struck it and every person who *was* in it with the edge of the sword, according to all that he had done to Libnah.

🗝 **33** Then Horam king of [a]Gezer came up[5927] to help Lachish, and Joshua [I]defeated him and his people until he had left[7604] him no survivor.[8300]

34 And Joshua and all Israel with him passed on from Lachish to Eglon, and they camped by it and fought against it.

35 And they captured it on that day and struck it with the edge of the sword; and he [I]utterly destroyed that day every person who *was* in it, according to all that he had done to Lachish.

36 Then Joshua and all Israel with him went up from Eglon to [a]Hebron, and they fought against it.

37 And they captured it and struck it and its king and all its cities and all the persons who *were* in it with the edge of the sword. He left no survivor, according to all that he had done to Eglon. And he [I]utterly destroyed it and every person who *was* in it.

38 Then Joshua and all Israel with him returned to [a]Debir, and they fought against it.

39 And he captured it and its king and all its cities, and they struck them with the edge of the sword, and [I]utterly destroyed every person *who was* in it. He left no survivor. Just as he had done to Hebron, so he did to Debir and its king, as he had also done to Libnah and its king.

40 Thus Joshua struck all the land,[776] [a]the hill country and the [I]Negev

23 [a]Deut. 7:24
24 [a]Mal. 4:3
25 [a]Josh. 10:8
26 [a]Josh. 8:29
27 [I]Lit., *the time of the going of the sun* [a]Deut. 21:22, 23
28 [I]Or, *put under the ban* [II]Some mss. read *them* [III]Lit., *soul,* and so throughout the ch. [a]Deut. 20:16 [b]Josh. 6:21
29 [a]Josh. 15:42; 21:13
33 [I]Lit., *smote* [a]Josh. 16:3, 10; Judg. 1:29; 1Kin. 9:16f.
35 [I]Or, *put under the ban*
36 [a]Num. 13:22; Judg. 1:10, 20; 2Sam. 5:1, 3, 5, 13; 2Chr. 11:10
37 [I]Or, *put it under the ban*
38 [a]Josh. 15:15; Judg. 1:11; 1Chr. 6:58
39 [I]Or, *put it under the ban*
40 [I]I.e., South country [a]Deut. 1:7

🗝 **10:33** Because Gezer remained as a Canaanite stronghold long after Joshua's time (Josh. 16:10; Judg. 1:29), Joshua probably never did vanquish it.

and the lowland[8219] and the slopes and
[b]all their kings. He left no survivor, but
[c]he [II]utterly destroyed all who breathed,
just as the LORD, the God of Israel, had
commanded.
41 And Joshua struck them from Kadesh-barnea even as far as Gaza, and
all the country of [a]Goshen even as far
as Gibeon.
42 And Joshua captured all these
kings and their lands[776] at one time, because [a]the LORD, the God of Israel,
fought for Israel.
43 So Joshua and all Israel with him
returned to the camp at Gilgal.

Northern Palestine Taken

11 Then it came about, when Jabin
king of [a]Hazor heard[8085] *of it,* that
he sent to Jobab king of Madon and to
the king of Shimron and to the king of
Achshaph,
2 and to the kings[4428] who were of
the north in the hill country, and in the
[a]Arabah—[6160] south of [I]Chinneroth and
in the lowland and on the [II]heights of
Dor on the west—
3 to the Canaanite on the east and
on the west, and the Amorite and the
Hittite and the Perizzite and the Jebusite
in the hill country, and [a]the Hivite
[I]at the foot of [b]Hermon in the land[776]
of [c]Mizpeh.
4 And they came out, they and all
their armies[4264] with them, [a]*as* many
people[5971] *as* the sand that is on the
seashore,[8193] with very many horses and
chariots.
5 So all of these kings having agreed
to meet, came and encamped together
at the waters of Merom, to fight against
Israel.
🔑 **6** Then the LORD said[559] to Joshua,
"[a]Do not be afraid[3372] because of them,
for tomorrow at this time I will deliver all of them slain[2491] before Israel;
you shall [b]hamstring[6131] their horses
and burn[8313] their chariots with fire."
7 So Joshua and all the people of
war with him came upon them suddenly by the waters of Merom, and
attacked[5307] them.
8 And the LORD delivered them into
the hand[3027] of Israel, so that they
[I]defeated[5221] them, and pursued them
as far as Great Sidon and [a]Misrephoth-
maim and the valley of [b]Mizpeh to the
east; and they struck them until no
survivor[8300] was left[7604] to them.
9 And Joshua did[6213] to them as the
LORD had told him; he [a]hamstrung[6131]
their horses, and burned[8313] their chariots with fire.
10 Then Joshua turned back at that
time, and captured [a]Hazor and struck
its king with the sword; for Hazor formerly was the head[7218] of all these
kingdoms.[4467]
11 [a]And they struck every per-
son[5315] who was in it with the edge[6310]
of the sword, [I]utterly destroying[2763]
them; there was no one left[3498] who
breathed. And he burned Hazor with
fire.
12 And Joshua captured all the cities
of these kings, and all their kings, and
he struck them with the edge of the
sword, *and* utterly destroyed[2763] them;
just [a]as Moses the servant[5650] of the
LORD had commanded.[6680]
13 However, Israel did not burn[8313]
any cities that stood on their mounds,
except Hazor alone, *which* Joshua
burned.
14 [a]And all the spoil of these cities
and the cattle, the sons[1121] of Israel took
as their plunder; but they struck every
man with the edge of the sword, until
they had destroyed[8045] them. They left
no one who breathed.
15 Just as the LORD had commanded
Moses his servant, so Moses commanded[6680] Joshua, and so Joshua did;
he left nothing[1697] undone[5403] of all
that the LORD had commanded Moses.
16 Thus Joshua took all that land:

40 [II]Or, *put it under the ban* [b]Deut. 7:24 [c]Deut. 20:16
41 [a]Josh. 11:16; 15:51
42 [a]Josh. 10:14
1 [a]Josh. 11:10
2 [I]I.e., Sea of Galilee [II]Or, *Naphoth-dor* [a]Josh. 12:3; 13:27
3 [I]Lit., *under* [a]Deut. 7:1; Judg. 3:3, 5; 1Kin. 9:20 [b]Josh. 11:17; 13:5, 11 [c]Josh. 15:38; 18:26
4 [a]Judg. 7:12
6 [a]Josh. 10:8 [b]2Sam. 8:4
8 [I]Lit., *smote* [a]Josh. 13:6 [b]Josh. 11:3
9 [a]Josh. 11:6
10 [a]Josh. 11:1
11 [I]Or, *putting them under the ban,* and so throughout the ch. [a]Deut. 20:16
12 [a]Num. 33:50-52; Deut. 7:2; 20:16f.
14 [a]Num. 31:11, 12

🔑 **11:6** Cutting the tendons of the legs rendered the horses unfit for military service. Israel was forbidden to develop a cavalry (Deut. 17:16) because God wanted them to depend upon Him, not the strength of horses (Isa. 31:1,3).

[a]the hill country and all the [I]Negev, all that land of Goshen, the lowland, [b]the Arabah,[6160] the hill country of Israel and its lowland

17 from [a]Mount Halak, that rises toward Seir, even as far as Baal-gad in the valley of Lebanon [I]at the foot of Mount Hermon. And he captured [b]all their kings and struck them down and put them to death.[4191]

18 Joshua waged[6213] war a long time[3117] with all these kings.

19 There was not a city which made peace with the sons of Israel except [a]the Hivites living in Gibeon; they took them all in battle.

20 [a]For it was of the LORD to [I]harden their hearts,[3820] to meet Israel in battle in order that he might [b]utterly destroy[2763] them, that they might [II]receive no mercy,[8467] but that he might destroy[8045] them, just as the LORD had commanded Moses.

🔑 **21** Then Joshua came at that time and cut off[3772] [a]the Anakim from the hill country, from Hebron, from Debir, from Anab and from all the hill country of Judah and from all the hill country of Israel. Joshua utterly destroyed them with their cities.

22 There were no Anakim left in the land of the sons of Israel; only in Gaza, in [a]Gath, and in [b]Ashdod some remained.[7604]

🔑 23 So Joshua took the whole land, according to all that the LORD had spoken[1696] to Moses, and [a]Joshua gave it for an inheritance[5159] to Israel according to their divisions by their tribes.[7626] [b]Thus the land had rest[8252] from war.

16 [I]I.e., South country [a]Josh. 10:40, 41 [b]Josh. 11:2

17 [I]Lit., *under* [a]Josh. 12:7 [b]Deut. 7:24

19 [a]Josh. 9:3, 7

20 [I]Lit., *make strong* [II]Lit., *have* [a]Ex. 14:17 [b]Deut. 7:16

21 [a]Num. 13:33; Deut. 9:2

22 [a]1Sam. 17:4; 1Kin. 2:39; 1Chr. 8:13 [b]Josh. 15:46f.; 1Sam. 5:1; Is. 20:1

23 [a]Deut. 1:38 [b]Deut. 12:9, 10; 25:19; Heb. 4:8

1 [I]Lit., *smote* [a]Num. 32:33; Deut. 3:8-17

2 [a]Deut. 2:36

3 [I]I.e., Galilee [II]Lit., *the way of* [III]Lit., *under* [a]Josh. 11:2 [b]Josh. 13:20

4 [a]Deut. 3:11 [b]Deut. 1:4

5 [a]Deut. 3:10; Josh. 13:11; 1Chr. 5:11 [b]Deut. 3:14; 1Sam. 27:8

6 [I]Lit., *smote* [a]Num. 32:33; Deut. 3:12

7 [I]Lit., *smote*

Kings Defeated by Israel

12 🔑 Now these are the [a]kings[4428] of the land[776] whom the sons[1121] of Israel [I]defeated,[5221] and whose land they possessed[3423] beyond the Jordan toward the sunrise, from the valley of the Arnon as far as Mount Hermon, and all the Arabah[6160] to the east:

2 Sihon king of the Amorites, who lived in Heshbon, *and* ruled[4910] [a]from Aroer, which is on the edge[8193] of the valley of the Arnon, both the middle of the valley and half of Gilead, even as far as the brook Jabbok, the border of the sons of Ammon;

3 and the [a]Arabah as far as the Sea of [I]Chinneroth toward the east, and as far as the sea of the Arabah, *even* the Salt Sea, eastward [II]toward[1870] [b]Beth-jeshimoth, and on the south, [III]at the foot of the slopes of Pisgah;

4 and the territory of Og king of Bashan, one of [a]the remnant[3499] of Rephaim,[7497] who lived at [b]Ashtaroth and at Edrei,

5 and ruled[4910] over Mount Hermon and [a]Salecah and all Bashan, as far as [b]the border of the Geshurites and the Maacathites, and half of Gilead, *as far as* the border of Sihon king of Heshbon.

6 Moses the servant[5650] of the LORD and the sons of Israel [I]defeated[5221] them; and [a]Moses the servant of the LORD gave it to the Reubenites and the Gadites, and the half-tribe[7626] of Manasseh as a possession.[3425]

7 Now these are the kings of the land[776] whom Joshua and the sons of Israel [I]defeated beyond the Jordan

---

🔑 **11:21** The Anakim were the giants who were so feared by the twelve spies (Num. 13:33). The Anakim recaptured Hebron and Debir later, but Caleb finally conquered them (Josh. 15:14).

🔑 **11:23** Although conflict ended on a larger scale, local resistance did continue for a long time. However, in general, Joshua had accomplished what the Lord commanded. Israel was now dominant in Canaan, but it remained for each tribe to exterminate the last pockets of pagan culture (Ex. 23:28-33).

🔑 **12:1** The extent of the conquest under Joshua's leadership was vast, but his advanced age prevented him from completing the task (Josh. 13:1-6). During the six to seven-year military campaign (see Josh. 14:7-10), the borders of Israel were expanded from Kadesh-barnea in the south (Josh. 10:41) to the foothills of Mount Hermon in the north (Josh. 11:17). Joshua's task now was to distribute the land among the tribes and leave the further conquest to God (Josh. 13:6,7). Chapters 13—21 are concerned with that distribution.

toward the west, from Baal-gad in the valley of Lebanon even as far as [a]Mount Halak, which rises toward Seir; and Joshua gave it to the <u>tribes</u>[7626] of Israel as a possession according to their divisions,

8 in [a]the hill country, in the lowland, in the <u>Arabah</u>,[6160] on the slopes, and in the wilderness, and in the [I]Negev; the Hittite, the Amorite and the Canaanite, the Perizzite, the Hivite and the Jebusite:

9 the [a]king of Jericho, one; the [b]king of Ai, which is beside Bethel, one;

10 the [a]king of Jerusalem, one; the king of Hebron, one;

11 the king of Jarmuth, one; the king of Lachish, one;

12 the king of Eglon, one; the king of Gezer, one;

13 the king of Debir, one; the king of Geder, one;

14 the king of Hormah, one; the king of [a]Arad, one;

15 the king of Libnah, one; the king of Adullam, one;

16 the king of Makkedah, one; the king of Bethel, one;

17 the king of Tappuah, one; the [a]king of Hepher, one;

18 the king of [a]Aphek, one; the king of Lasharon, one;

19 the king of Madon, one; the king of Hazor, one;

20 the king of Shimron-meron, one; the king of Achshaph, one;

21 the king of Taanach, one; the king of Megiddo, one;

22 the king of [a]Kedesh, one; the king of Jokneam in Carmel, one;

🗝 23 the king of Dor in the [I]heights of Dor, one; the king of [a]<u>Goiim</u>[1471] in Gilgal, one;

24 the king of Tirzah, one: [a]in all, thirty-one kings.

Canaan Divided Among the Tribes

13 🗝 Now [a]Joshua was <u>old</u>[2204] *and* advanced in years when the LORD <u>said</u>[559] to him, "You are old *and* advanced in years, and very much of the <u>land</u>[776] <u>remains</u>[7604] to be <u>possessed</u>.[3423]

2 "This is the land that remains: all the regions *of* the Philistines and all *those of* the [a]Geshurites;

🗝 3 from the Shihor which is [I]east of Egypt, even as far as the border of Ekron to the north (it is <u>counted</u>[2803] as Canaanite); the [a]five <u>lords</u>[5633] of the Philistines: the Gazite, the Ashdodite, the Ashkelonite, the Gittite, the Ekronite; and the Avvite

4 [I]to the south, all the land of the Canaanite, and Mearah that belongs to the Sidonians, as far as [a]Aphek, to the border of the [b]Amorite;

5 and the land of the [a]Gebalite, and all of Lebanon, toward the [I]east, [b]from Baal-gad below Mount Hermon as far as [II]Lebo-hamath.

6 "All the inhabitants of the hill country from Lebanon as far as [a]Misrephoth-maim, all the Sidonians, I will [I]<u>drive</u> them <u>out</u>[3423] from before the <u>sons</u>[1121] of Israel; [b]only allot it to Israel for an inheritance as I have <u>commanded</u>[6680] you.

🗝 7 "Now therefore, apportion this land for an inheritance to the nine <u>tribes</u>,[7626] and the half-<u>tribe</u>[7626] of Manasseh."

8 With [I]the other half-tribe, the Reubenites and the Gadites received their inheritance which Moses gave them [a]beyond the Jordan to the east, just as Moses the <u>servant</u>[5650] of the LORD gave to them;

9 from Aroer, which is on the edge of the valley of the Arnon, with the city

7 [a]Josh. 11:17
8 [I]I.e., South country [a]Josh. 11:16
9 [a]Josh. 6:2 [b]Josh. 8:29
10 [a]Josh. 10:23
14 [a]Num. 21:1
17 [a]1Kin. 4:10
18 [a]Josh. 13:4; 2Kin. 13:17
22 [a]Josh. 19:37; 20:7; 21:32
23 [I]Or, *Naphath-dor* [a]Gen. 14:1
24 [a]Deut. 7:24
1 [a]Josh. 14:10
2 [a]Josh. 13:11; 1Sam. 27:8
3 [I]Lit., *on the face of* [a]1Sam. 6:4, 16
4 [I]Or, *from the Teman* [a]Josh. 12:18; 19:30; 1Sam. 4:1; 1Kin. 20:26, 30 [b]Ezek. 16:3; Amos 2:10
5 [I]Lit., *sunrise* [II]Or, *the entrance of Hamath* [a]1Kin. 5:18 [b]Josh. 12:7
6 [I]Or, *dispossess* [a]Josh. 11:8 [b]Num. 33:54
8 [I]Lit., *it, the* [a]Josh. 12:1-6

🗝 **12:23** This is not the same Gilgal which is mentioned as being near Jericho or the one which was near Bethel. This Gilgal was probably located about 42 miles north of Jerusalem, just south of Carmel.
🗝 **13:1-7** See note on Josh. 12:1.
🗝 **13:3** See note on Deut. 2:23.
🗝 **13:7** Although the conquest of Canaan was still incomplete, Joshua knew that an early distribution of the land would give the sons of Israel a taste of success and would spur them on to greater victories.

which is in the middle of the valley, and all the plain of Medeba, as far as Dibon;

10 and all the cities of Sihon king of the Amorites, who reigned[4427] in Heshbon, as far as the border of the sons of Ammon;

11 and [a]Gilead, and the [I]territory of the Geshurites and Maacathites, and all Mount Hermon, and all Bashan as far as Salecah;

12 all the kingdom1312 of [a]Og in Bashan, who reigned in Ashtaroth and in Edrei (he alone was left[7604] of the remnant[3499] of the Rephaim[7497]); for Moses [b]struck[5221] them and dispossessed[3423] them.

13 But the sons of Israel did not dispossess[3423] the Geshurites or the Maacathites; for Geshur and Maacath live among7136 Israel until this day.[3117]

🗝 14 [a]Only to the tribe of Levi he did not give an inheritance; the offerings[2077] by fire to the LORD, the God[430] of Israel, are [I]their inheritance, as He spoke[1696] to him.

15 So Moses gave *an inheritance* to the tribe[4294] of the sons of Reuben according to their families.[4940]

16 And their [I]territory was [a]from Aroer, which is on the edge of the valley of the Arnon, with the city which is in the middle of the valley and all the plain by Medeba;

17 Heshbon, and all its cities which are on the plain: Dibon and Bamoth-baal and Beth-baal-meon,

18 and [a]Jahaz and Kedemoth and Mephaath,

19 and [a]Kiriathaim and Sibmah and Zereth-shahar on the hill of the valley,

20 and Beth-peor and the slopes of Pisgah and Beth-jeshimoth,

21 even all the cities of the plain and all the kingdom of Sihon king of the Amorites who reigned in Heshbon, whom Moses struck[5221] with the chiefs[5387] of Midian, [a]Evi and Rekem and Zur and Hur and Reba, the princes[5257] of Sihon, who lived in the land.[776]

🗝 22 The sons of Israel also killed[2026] [a]Balaam the son[1121] of Beor, the diviner,[7080] with the sword[2719] among *the rest of* their slain.[2491]

23 And the border of the sons of Reuben was the [I]Jordan. This was the inheritance of the sons of Reuben according to their families, the cities and their villages.

24 Moses also gave *an inheritance* to the tribe of Gad, to the sons of Gad, according to their families.

25 And their territory was [a]Jazer, and all the cities of Gilead, and half the land of the sons of Ammon, as far as Aroer which is before Rabbah;

26 and from Heshbon as far as Ramath-mizpeh and Betonim, and from Mahanaim as far as the border of [I]Debir;

27 and in the valley, Beth-haram and Beth-nimrah and Succoth and Zaphon, the rest[3499] of the kingdom of Sihon king of Heshbon, with the Jordan [I]as a border, as far as the *lower* end of the Sea of [IIa]Chinnereth beyond the Jordan to the east.

28 This is the inheritance of the sons of Gad according to their families, the cities and their villages.

29 Moses also gave *an inheritance* to the half-tribe of Manasseh; and it was for the half-tribe of the sons of Manasseh according to their families.

30 And their territory was from Mahanaim, all Bashan, all the kingdom of Og king of Bashan, and all [a]the [I]towns of Jair, which are in Bashan, sixty cities;

31 also half of Gilead, with [a]Ashtaroth and Edrei, the cities of the kingdom of Og in Bashan, *were* for the sons of Machir the son of Manasseh, for half of the sons of Machir according to their families.

32 These are *the territories* which Moses apportioned for an inheritance[5157]

11 [I]Or, *border* [a]Gen. 37:25; Num. 32:29; Josh. 13:25; 17:5f.
12 [a]Deut. 3:11 [b]Num. 21:24
14 [I]Lit., *his* [a]Deut. 18:1, 2
16 [I]Or, *border* [a]Josh. 13:9
18 [a]Num. 21:23; Judg. 11:20; Is. 15:4; Jer. 48:34
19 [a]Num. 32:37; Jer. 48:1, 23; Ezek. 25:9
21 [a]Num. 31:8
22 [a]Num. 31:8
23 [I]Lit., *Jordan and border*
25 [a]Num. 21:32; Josh. 21:39; 2Sam. 24:5; 1Chr. 6:81; 26:31; Is. 16:8f.; Jer. 48:32
26 [I]Or, *Lidebir*
27 [I]Lit., *and border* [II]I.e., Galilee [a]Num. 34:11; Deut. 3:17
30 [I]Lit., *tent villages* [a]Num. 32:41
31 [a]Josh. 9:10; 12:4; 13:12; Judg. 10:6; 1Sam. 7:3f.; 12:10; 1Chr. 6:71

🗝 **13:14** See Num. 18:20.
🗝 **13:22** See Num. 31:8.

in the plains[6160] of Moab, beyond the
Jordan at Jericho to the east.
33 But [a]to the tribe of Levi, Moses
did not give an inheritance; the LORD,
the God of Israel, is their inheritance,
as He had [l]promised to them.

Caleb's Request

14 Now these are *the territories*
which the sons[1121] of Israel inherited in the land[776] of Canaan, which
[a]Eleazar the priest, and Joshua the
son[1121] of Nun, and the heads[7218] of the
[l]households of the tribes[4294] of the sons
of Israel apportioned to them for an
inheritance,[5157]
2 by the [a]lot of their inheritance,[5159]
as the LORD commanded[6680] [l]through[3027]
Moses, for the nine tribes and the half-
tribe.[4294]
3 For [a]Moses had given the inheritance of the two tribes and the half-tribe
beyond the Jordan; but [b]he did not give
an inheritance to the Levites among
them.
4 For the sons of Joseph were two
tribes, [a]Manasseh and Ephraim, and
they did not give a portion to the Levites
in the land, except cities to live in, with
their pasture lands for their livestock
and for their property.
5 Thus the sons of Israel did[6213] just
[a]as the LORD had commanded Moses,
and they divided the land.
🔑6 Then the sons of Judah drew near
to Joshua in Gilgal, and [a]Caleb the son
of Jephunneh the Kenizzite said[559] to
him, "You know[3045] the word[1697] which
the LORD spoke[1696] to Moses the man[376]
of God[430] concerning [l]you and me in Kadesh-barnea.
7 "I was forty years old[1121] when
[a]Moses the servant[5650] of the LORD sent
me from Kadesh-barnea to spy out the
land, and I brought word[1697] back to him
as *it was* in my heart.[3824]
8 "Nevertheless my brethren[251]
who went up[5927] with me made the
heart[3820] of the people[5971] [l]melt with
fear; but [a]I followed the LORD my God
fully.
🔑9 "So Moses swore[7650] on that
day,[3117] saying, 'Surely [a]the land on
which your foot has trodden shall be
an inheritance to you and to your children forever,[5769] because you have followed the LORD my God fully.'
10 "And now behold, the LORD has
let me live, just as He spoke, these
forty-five years, from the time that the
LORD spoke[1696] this word to Moses,
when Israel walked in the wilderness;
and now behold, I am eighty-five years
old today.
11 "[a]I am still as strong[2389] today
as I was in the day Moses sent me; as
my strength was then, so my strength
is now, for war and for [b]going out and
coming in.
12 "Now then, give me this hill
country about which the LORD spoke
on that day, for you heard[8085] on that
day that [a]Anakim *were* there, with great
fortified cities; perhaps the LORD will
be with me, and I shall [l]drive them out
as the LORD has spoken."
13 So Joshua [a]blessed[1288] him, and
[b]gave Hebron to Caleb the son of Jephunneh for an inheritance.
14 Therefore, Hebron became the
inheritance of Caleb the son of Jephunneh the Kenizzite until this day, because
he followed the LORD God of Israel
fully.
15 Now the name of Hebron was
formerly [l]Kiriath-arba; *for Arba* was the
greatest man[120] among the Anakim.
[a]Then the land had rest[8252] from war.

33 [l]Lit., *spoken to* [a]Deut. 18:1f.; Josh. 13:14
1 [l]Lit., *fathers'* [a]Num. 34:16-29
2 [l]Lit., *by the hand of* [a]Num. 26:55; 33:54; 34:13
3 [a]Num. 32:33 [b]Josh. 13:14
4 [a]Gen. 41:51f.; 46:20; 48:1, 5; Num. 26:28; 2Chr. 30:1
5 [a]Num. 35:1f.; Josh. 21:2
6 [l]Lit., *me and concerning you* [a]Num. 13:6, 30; 14:6, 24, 30
7 [a]Num. 13:1-31
8 [l]Lit., *become demoralized* [a]Num. 14:24; Deut. 1:36
9 [a]Deut. 1:36
11 [a]Deut. 34:7 [b]Deut. 31:2
12 [l]Or, *dispossess* [a]Num. 13:33
13 [a]Josh. 22:6 [b]Judg. 1:20; 1Chr. 6:55f.
15 [l]I.e., the city of Arba [a]Josh. 11:23

🔑 **14:6** Kenaz was an Edomite tribe. Caleb was associated with Judah (Num. 3:6; 34:19) because the Kenizzite and Judahite strains were blended by marriage. Compare I Chr. 2:4,5,18,19; 4:13-15.

🔑 **14:6-15** See note on Num. 13:30.

🔑 **14:9** When Caleb was on his spy mission, he visited the Anakim (Deut. 1:28). Moses promised him the same region which he had visited for a possession (Deut. 1:36).

Territory of Judah

15 Now [a]the lot for the tribe[4294] of the sons[1121] of Judah according to their families[4940] [I]reached the [b]border of Edom, southward to the [c]wilderness of Zin at the extreme south.

2 And their south border was from the lower end of the Salt Sea, from the bay that turns to the south.

3 Then it proceeded southward to the ascent of Akrabbim and continued[5674] to Zin, then went up by the south of Kadesh-barnea and continued to Hezron, and went up[5927] to Addar and turned about to Karka.

4 And it [a]continued to Azmon and proceeded to the [Ib]brook of Egypt; and the [II]border ended at the sea. This shall be your south border.

5 And the [a]east border *was* the Salt Sea, as far as the [I]mouth of the Jordan. And the [b]border of the north side was from the bay of the sea at the [I]mouth of the Jordan.

6 Then the border went up to Beth-hoglah, and continued on the north of Beth-arabah, and the border went up to the stone of Bohan the son[1121] of Reuben.

🔑 7 And the border went up to Debir from [a]the valley of Achor, and turned northward toward Gilgal which is opposite the ascent of Adummim, which is on the south of the valley; and the border continued to the waters of En-shemesh, and [I]it ended at En-rogel.

🔑 8 Then the border went up the valley of Ben-hinnom to the slope of the [a]Jebusite on the south (that is, Jerusalem); and the border went up to the top[7218] of the mountain which is before the valley of Hinnom to the west, which is at the end of the valley of Rephaim[7497] toward the north.

9 And from the top of the mountain the border curved to the spring of the waters of Nephtoah and proceeded to the cities of Mount Ephron, then the border curved to [a]Baalah (that is, [b]Kiriath-jearim).

10 And the border turned about from Baalah westward to Mount Seir, and continued to the slope of Mount Jearim on the north (that is, Chesalon), and went down to Beth-shemesh and continued through [a]Timnah.

11 And the border proceeded to the side of Ekron northward. Then the border curved to Shikkeron and continued to Mount Baalah and proceeded to Jabneel, and the [I]border ended at the sea.

12 And the west border *was* [a]at the Great Sea, even *its* [I]coastline. This is the border around the sons of Judah according to their families.

13 Now [a]he gave to Caleb the son of Jephunneh a portion [b]among the sons of Judah, according to the [I]command[6310] of the LORD to Joshua, *namely,* [II]Kiriath-arba, *Arba being* the father[1] of Anak (that is, Hebron).

14 And [a]Caleb [I]drove out from there the three [b]sons[1121] of Anak: Sheshai and Ahiman and Talmai, the children of Anak.

15 Then [a]he went up from there against the inhabitants of Debir; now the name of Debir formerly was Kiriath-sepher.

16 And Caleb said,[559] "The one who [I]attacks Kiriath-sepher and captures it, [II]I will give him Achsah my daughter as a wife."[802]

17 And [a]Othniel the son of Kenaz, the brother[251] of Caleb, captured it; so he gave him Achsah his daughter as a wife.

18 [a]And it came about that when she came *to him,* she persuaded him to ask[7592] her father for a field.[7704] So she alighted from the donkey, and

1 [I]Lit., *was to* [a]Num. 34:3, 4 [b]Num. 20:16 [c]Deut. 32:51
4 [I]Or, *wadi* [II]Lit., *goings out of the border were* [a]Num. 34:5 [b]Gen. 15:18; 1Kin. 8:65
5 [I]Lit., *end* [a]Num. 34:3, 10-12 [b]Josh. 18:15-19
7 [I]Lit., *the goings out of it were* [a]Josh. 7:24
8 [a]Josh. 15:63
9 [a]1Chr. 13:6 [b]Judg. 18:12
10 [a]Gen. 38:13; Judg. 14:1
11 [I]Lit., *goings out. . .were*
12 [I]Lit., *border* [a]Num. 34:6
13 [I]Lit., *mouth* [II]I.e., the city of Arba [a]Josh. 14:13-15 [b]Num. 13:6
14 [I]Or, *dispossessed* [a]Josh. 11:21, 22 [b]Num. 13:33; Deut. 9:2
15 [a]Josh. 10:38
16 [I]Lit., *smites* [II]Lit., *and I*
17 [a]Judg. 1:13; 3:9
18 [a]Judg. 1:14

🔑 **15:7** This was not the Gilgal which was Israel's first campsite (Josh. 4:19). It is the Geliloth of Josh. 18:17.

🔑 **15:8** Later the Valley of Hinnom was the site for human sacrifices in the worship of Moloch (II Kgs. 23:10; II Chr. 28:3; 33:6; Jer. 7:31). The Hebrew, "Ge-Hinnom," became the Greek word, "Gehenna," which was the word for "hell" (Mt. 5:29,30). See notes in the N.T. lexical aids section on this Greek word.

Caleb said to her, "What do you want?"
19 Then she said,[559] "Give me a blessing;[1293] since you have given me the land of the [I]Negev,[776] give me also springs of water." So he gave her the upper springs and the lower[8482] springs.
20 This is the inheritance of the tribe of the sons of Judah according to their families.
21 Now the cities at the extremity of the tribe of the sons of Judah toward the border of Edom in the south were Kabzeel and [a]Eder and Jagur,
22 and Kinah and Dimonah and Adadah,
23 and Kedesh and Hazor and Ithnan,
24 Ziph and Telem and Bealoth,
25 and Hazor-hadattah and Kerioth-hezron (that is, Hazor),
26 Amam and Shema and Moladah,
27 and Hazar-gaddah and Heshmon and Beth-pelet,
28 and Hazar-shual and [a]Beersheba and Biziothiah,
29 Baalah and Iim and Ezem,
30 and Eltolad and Chesil and Hormah,
31 and [a]Ziklag and Madmannah and Sansannah,
32 and Lebaoth and Shilhim and Ain and Rimmon; in all, twenty-nine cities with their villages.
33 In the lowland: [a]Eshtaol and Zorah and Ashnah,
34 and Zanoah and En-gannim, Tappuah and Enam,
35 Jarmuth and [a]Adullam, Socoh and Azekah,
36 and Shaaraim and Adithaim and Gederah and Gederothaim; fourteen cities with their villages.
37 Zenan and Hadashah and Migdalgad,
38 and Dilean and Mizpeh and Joktheel,
39 [a]Lachish and Bozkath and Eglon,
40 and Cabbon and Lahmas and Chitlish,

19 [I]I.e., South country
21 [a]Gen. 35:21
28 [a]Gen. 21:31
31 [a]1 Sam. 27:6; 30:1
33 [a]Judg. 13:25; 16:31
35 [a]1Sam. 22:1
39 [a]Josh. 10:3; 2Kin. 14:19
46 [I]Lit., *hand*
47 [I]Or, *wadi* [II]Lit., *border* [a]Josh. 15:4
63 [a]Judg. 1:21; 2Sam. 5:6; 1Chr. 11:4

41 and Gederoth, Beth-dagon and Naamah and Makkedah; sixteen cities with their villages.
42 Libnah and Ether and Ashan,
43 and Iphtah and Ashnah and Nezib,
44 and Keilah and Achzib and Mareshah; nine cities with their villages.
45 Ekron, with its towns and its villages;
46 from Ekron even to the sea, all that were by the [I]side of Ashdod, with their villages.
47 Ashdod, its towns and its villages; Gaza, its towns and its villages; as far as [a]the [I]brook of Egypt and the Great Sea, even *its* [II]coastline.
48 And in the hill country: Shamir and Jattir and Socoh,
49 and Dannah and Kiriath-sannah (that is, Debir),
50 and Anab and Eshtemoh and Anim,
51 and Goshen and Holon and Giloh; eleven cities with their villages.
52 Arab and Dumah and Eshan,
53 and Janum and Beth-tappuah and Aphekah,
54 and Humtah and Kiriath-arba (that is, Hebron), and Zior; nine cities with their villages.
55 Maon, Carmel and Ziph and Juttah,
56 and Jezreel and Jokdeam and Zanoah,
57 Kain, Gibeah and Timnah; ten cities with their villages.
58 Halhul, Beth-zur and Gedor,
59 and Maarath and Beth-anoth and Eltekon; six cities with their villages.
60 Kiriath-baal (that is, Kiriath-jearim), and Rabbah; two cities with their villages.
61 In the wilderness: Beth-arabah, Middin and Secacah,
62 and Nibshan and the City of Salt and Engedi; six cities with their villages.
🗝 **63** Now as for the [a]Jebusites, the inhabitants of Jerusalem, the sons of Ju-

🗝 **15:63** Although Jerusalem was located in the territory of Benjamin (Josh. 18:28), Judah conquered

(continued on next page)

dah could not [I]drive them out; so the
Jebusites live with the sons of Judah at
Jerusalem until this day.[3117]

Territory of Ephraim

16 Then the lot for the sons[1121] of
Joseph went from the Jordan at
Jericho to the waters of Jericho on the
east into [a]the wilderness, going up from
Jericho through the hill country to
Bethel.
2 And it went from Bethel to Luz,
and [a]continued[5674] to the border of the
Archites at Ataroth.
3 And it went down westward to
the territory of the Japhletites, as far
as the territory of lower8481 [a]Beth-horon
even to [b]Gezer, and [I]it ended at the
sea.
4 And the [a]sons of Joseph, Manasseh and Ephraim, received their inheritance.[5157]
5 Now *this* was the territory of the
sons of Ephraim according to their
families:[4940] the border of their inheritance[5159] eastward was [a]Ataroth-addar,
as far as upper[5945] Beth-horon.
6 Then the border went westward
at [a]Michmethath on the north, and the
border turned about eastward to Taanath-shiloh, and continued *beyond*[5674] it
to the east of Janoah.
7 And it went down from Janoah to
Ataroth and to [a]Naarah, then reached[6293]
Jericho and came out at the Jordan.
8 From [a]Tappuah the border continued westward to the [I]brook of Kanah,
and [II]it ended at the sea. This is the
inheritance of the tribe[4294] of the sons
of Ephraim according to their families,
9 *together* with the cities which were

63 [I]Or, *dispossess them*

1 [a]Josh. 8:15; 18:12

2 [a]Josh. 18:13

3 [I]Lit., *the goings out of it were* [a]Josh. 18:13; 1Kin. 9:17 [b]Josh. 10:33

4 [a]Josh. 17:14

5 [a]Josh. 18:13

6 [a]Josh. 17:7

7 [a]1Chr. 7:28

8 [I]Or, *wadi* [II]Lit., *the goings out of it were* [a]Josh. 17:8

10 [I]Or, *dispossess* [a]Judg. 1:29; 1Kin. 9:16 [b]Josh. 17:12, 13

1 [I]Lit., *and there was to him* [a]Gen. 41:51; 46:20; 48:17f.

3 [a]Num. 26:33; 27:1-7

4 [a]Num. 27:5-7

set apart for the sons of Ephraim in
the midst of the inheritance of the sons
of Manasseh, all the cities with their
villages.
10 [a]But they did not [I]drive out the
Canaanites who lived in Gezer, so
[b]the Canaanites live in the midst[7130] of
Ephraim to this day,[3117] and they became forced laborers.[5647]

Territory of Manasseh

17 Now *this* was the lot for the
tribe[4294] of [a]Manasseh, for he
was the first-born of Joseph. To Machir
the first-born of Manasseh, the father[1]
of Gilead, [I]was allotted Gilead and
Bashan, because he was a man[376] of
war.
2 So *the lot* was *made* for the rest[3498]
of the sons[1121] of Manasseh according
to their families:[4940] for the sons of
Abiezer and for the sons of Helek and
for the sons of Asriel and for the sons
of Shechem and for the sons of Hepher
and for the sons of Shemida; these *were*
the male2145 *descendants* of Manasseh
the son[1121] of Joseph according to their
families.
3 However, [a]Zelophehad, the son
of Hepher, the son of Gilead, the son
of Machir, the son of Manasseh, had
no sons,[1121] only daughters; and these
are the names of his daughters: Mahlah and Noah, Hoglah, Milcah and Tirzah.
4 And they came near before Eleazar the priest and before Joshua the son
of Nun and before the leaders,[5387] saying, "The LORD commanded[6680] Moses
to give us an inheritance among our
brothers."[251] So [a]according to the

(continued from previous page)
it and burned it after the death of Joshua (Judg. 1:8). However, the Jebusites must have rebuilt it, because the Benjamites were unable to drive them out (Judg. 1:21). Not until the time of David was the site of Jerusalem finally conquered (II Sam. 5:6-10).

16:2 The name of Bethel was formerly Luz (Gen. 28:19; Josh. 18:13; Judg. 1:23).

16:10 Gezer was conquered by the king of Egypt, who gave it to Solomon as a dowry (I Kgs. 9:16).

17:3 Approximately 350 years had elapsed between the lifetimes of Manasseh and the daughters of Zelophehad.

[I]command[6310] of the LORD he gave them an inheritance among their father's brothers.

5 Thus there fell[5307] ten portions[2256] to Manasseh, besides the land[776] of Gilead and Bashan, which is beyond the Jordan,

6 because the daughters of Manasseh received an inheritance[5157] among his sons. And the [a]land of Gilead belonged to the rest of the sons of Manasseh.

7 And the border of Manasseh [I]ran from Asher to Michmethath which was east of Shechem; then the border went [II]southward to the inhabitants of En-tappuah.

8 The land of Tappuah belonged to Manasseh, but [a]Tappuah on the border of Manasseh *belonged* to the sons of Ephraim.

9 And the [a]border went down to the [I]brook of Kanah, southward of the [I]brook (these cities *belonged* to Ephraim among the cities of Manasseh), and the border of Manasseh *was* on the north side of the [I]brook, and [II]it ended at the sea.

10 The south side *belonged* to Ephraim and the north side to Manasseh, and the sea was [I]their border; and they reached to Asher on the north and to Issachar on the east.

11 And in Issachar and in Asher, [a]Manasseh had Beth-shean and its towns and Ibleam and its towns, and the inhabitants of Dor and its towns, and the inhabitants of En-dor and its towns, and the inhabitants of Taanach and its towns, and the inhabitants of Megiddo and its towns, the third is [b]Napheth.

12 [a]But the sons of Manasseh could not take possession[3423] of these cities, because the Canaanites persisted in living in that land.

13 And it came about when the sons of Israel became strong,[2388] [a]they put the Canaanites to forced labor, but they did not [I]drive them out completely.

14 Then the [a]sons of Joseph spoke[1696] to Joshua, saying, "Why have you given me only one lot and one portion for an inheritance,[5154] since I am a numerous people[5971] whom the LORD has thus far blessed?"[1288]

15 And Joshua said[559] to them, "If you are a numerous people, go [I]up to the forest[3293] and [II]clear a place for yourself there in the land of the Perizzites and of the Rephaim,[7497] since the hill country of Ephraim is too narrow for you."

16 And the sons of Joseph said,[559] "The hill country is not enough for us, and all the Canaanites who live in the valley land have [a]chariots of iron, both those who are in Beth-shean and its towns, and those who are in the valley of Jezreel."

17 And Joshua spoke[559] to the house[1004] of Joseph, to Ephraim and Manasseh, saying, "You are a numerous people and have great power; you shall not have one lot *only,*

18 but the hill country shall be yours. For though it is a forest, you shall [I]clear it, and to its [II]farthest borders it shall be yours; for you shall [III]drive out the Canaanites, even though they have [a]chariots of iron *and* though they are strong."[2389]

Rest of the Land Divided

18 ⚷ Then the whole congregation[5712] of the sons[1121] of Israel assembled[6950] themselves at [a]Shiloh, and set[7931] up the tent[168] of meeting[4150] there; and the land[776] was subdued before them.

2 And there remained[3498] among the sons of Israel seven tribes[7626] who had not divided their inheritance.[5159]

4 [I]Lit., *mouth*
6 [a]Josh. 13:30, 31
7 [I]Lit., *was* [II]Lit., *to the right hand*
8 [a]Josh. 16:8
9 [I]Or, *wadi* [II]Lit., *goings out of it were* [a]Josh. 16:8f.
10 [I]Lit., *its*
11 [a]1Chr. 7:29 [b]Josh. 11:2; 12:23
12 [a]Judg. 1:27
13 [I]Or, *dispossess* [a]Josh. 16:10
14 [a]Num. 13:7
15 [I]Lit., *up for yourself* [II]Lit., *cut down*
16 [a]Josh. 17:18; Judg. 1:19; 4:3, 13
18 [I]Lit., *cut it down* [II]Lit., *goings out* [III]Or, *dispossess* [a]Josh. 17:16
1 [a]Judg. 21:19; Jer. 7:12; 26:6, 9

⚷ **18:1** The tabernacle (tent) had been standing at Gilgal. Shiloh was a strategic site in the hill country which could be defended better, and it was more centrally located for all the tribes. Israel was a large religious congregation, not just a nation. This holy tent was of natural importance to them because it was where they met with God (Ex. 29:42-46).

3 So Joshua said[559] to the sons of
Israel, "[a]How long will you put off[7503]
entering to take possession[3423] of the
land which the LORD, the God[430] of your
fathers,[1] has given you?
4 "Provide for yourselves three
men[582] from [I]each tribe[7626] that I may
send them, and that they may arise and
walk through the land and write a description of it according to their inheritance; then they shall [II]return to me.
5 "And they shall divide it into seven
portions; [a]Judah shall stay in its territory on the south, and the house[1004] of Joseph shall stay in their territory on the
north.
6 "And you shall describe the land
in seven divisions, and bring *the descrip-*
tion here to me. [a]And I will cast[3384] lots
for you here before the LORD our God.
🔑 7 "For [a]the Levites have no portion
among[7130] you, because the priesthood[3550] of the LORD is [I]their inheritance.
Gad and Reuben aad the half-tribe
of Manasseh also have received their
inheritance eastward beyond the Jordan, which Moses the servant[5650] of the
LORD gave them."
8 Then the men arose and went,
and Joshua commanded[6680] those who
went to describe the land, saying, "Go
and walk through the land and describe
it, and return[7725] to me; then I will cast
lots for you here before the LORD in
[a]Shiloh."
9 So the men went and passed[5674]
through the land, and described it by
cities in seven divisions in a book;[5612]
and they came to Joshua to the camp[4264]
at Shiloh.
10 And [a]Joshua cast lots for them
in Shiloh before the LORD, and there
Joshua divided the land to the sons of
Israel according to their divisions.

The Territory of Benjamin

11 Now the lot of the tribe[4294] of
the sons of Benjamin came up[5927] ac-

3 [a]Judg. 18:9
4 [I]Lit., *the* [II]Lit., *come*
5 [a]Josh. 15:1
6 [a]Josh. 14:2
7 [I]Lit., *his* [a]Num. 18:7, 20; Josh. 13:33
8 [a]Josh. 18:1
10 [a]Num. 34:16-29; Josh. 19:51
11 [I]Lit., *went out*
12 [I]Lit., *the goings out of it were* [a]Josh. 16:1
13 [a]Gen. 28:19; Judg. 1:23 [b]Josh. 16:3
14 [I]Lit., *the goings out of it were*
15 [a]Josh. 15:5-9
16 [a]2Kin. 23:10
17 [a]Josh. 15:6
19 [I]Lit., *goings out of the border were*

cording to their families,[4940] and the territory of their lot [I]lay between the sons
of Judah and the sons of Joseph.
12 And [a]their border on the north
side was from the Jordan, then the border went up[5927] to the side of Jericho
on the north, and went up through the
hill country westward; and [I]it ended at
the wilderness of Beth-aven.
13 And from there the border continued[5674] to [a]Luz, to the side of Luz
(that is, Bethel) southward; and the border went down to Ataroth-addar, near
the hill which *lies* on the south of
[b]lower[8481] Beth-horon.
14 And the border extended *from*
there, and turned round on the west side
southward, from the hill which *lies* before Beth-horon southward; and [I]it
ended at Kiriath-baal (that is, Kiriath-
jearim), a city of the sons of Judah. This
was the west side.
15 Then the [a]south side *was* from
the edge of Kiriath-jearim, and the border went westward and went to the
fountain of the waters of Nephtoah.
16 And the border went down to
the edge of the hill which is in the
[a]valley of Ben[1121]-hinnom, which is in
the valley of Rephaim[7497] northward; and
it went down to the valley of Hinnom,
to the slope of the Jebusite southward,
and went down to En-rogel.
17 And it extended northward and
went to En-shemesh and went to Geliloth, which is opposite the ascent of
Adummim, and it went down to the
[a]stone of Bohan the son of Reuben.
18 And it continued[5674] to the side
in front of the Arabah northward, and
went down to the Arabah.
19 And the border continued to the
side of Beth-hoglah northward; and the
[I]border ended at the north bay of the
Salt Sea, at the south end of the Jordan.
This *was* the south border.
20 Moreover, the Jordan was its
border on the east side. This *was* the
inheritance of the sons of Benjamin,

🔑 **18:7** The Levites were scattered throughout the Israelites in order to minister to them.

according to their families *and* according to its borders all around.

21 Now the cities of the tribe of the sons of Benjamin according to their families were Jericho and Beth-hoglah and Emek-keziz,

22 and Beth-arabah and Zemaraim and Bethel,

23 and Avvim and Parah and Ophrah,

24 and Chephar-ammoni and Ophni and [a]Geba; twelve cities with their villages.

25 Gibeon and Ramah and Beeroth,

26 and Mizpeh and Chephirah and Mozah,

27 and Rekem and Irpeel and Taralah,

28 and [a]Zelah, Haeleph and the Jebusite (that is, Jerusalem), Gibeah, Kiriath; fourteen cities with their villages. This is the inheritance of the [b]sons of Benjamin according to their families.

Territory of Simeon

19 Then the second lot [I]fell to Simeon, to the tribe of the sons[1121] of Simeon according to their families,[4940] and their inheritance was in the midst of the inheritance of the sons of Judah.

2 So they had as their inheritance Beersheba or [I]Sheba and Moladah,

3 and Hazar-shual and Balah and Ezem,

4 and Eltolad and Bethul and Hormah,

5 and Ziklag and Beth-marcaboth and Hazar-susah,

6 and Beth-lebaoth and Sharuhen, thirteen cities with their villages;

7 Ain, Rimmon and Ether and Ashan, four cities with their villages;

8 and all the villages which *were* around these cities as far as Baalath-beer, Ramah of the [I]Negev. This *was* the inheritance of the tribe of the sons of Simeon according to their families.

9 The inheritance[5159] of the sons of Simeon *was taken* from the portion of the sons of Judah, for the share of the sons of Judah was too large for them; so the sons of Simeon received *an* inheritance[5157] in the midst of [I]Judah's inheritance.

Territory of Zebulun

10 Now the third lot came up[5927] for the sons of Zebulun according to their families. And the territory of their inheritance was as far as Sarid.

11 Then their border went up[5927] to the west and to Maralah, it then [I]touched[6293] Dabbesheth, and reached to the [II]brook that is before Jokneam.

12 Then it turned from Sarid to the east toward the sunrise as far as the border of Chisloth-tabor, and it proceeded to Daberath and [I]up to Japhia.

13 And from there it continued[5674] eastward toward the sunrise to Gath-hepher, to Eth-kazin, and it proceeded to Rimmon [I]which stretches to Neah.

14 And the border circled around it on the north to Hannathon, and [I]it ended at the valley of Iphtahel.

15 *Included* also *were* Kattah and Nahalal and Shimron and Idalah and Bethlehem; twelve cities with their villages.

16 This *was* the inheritance of the sons of Zebulun according to their families, these cities with their villages.

Territory of Issachar

17 The fourth lot [I]fell to Issachar, to the sons of Issachar according to their families.

24 [a]Ezra 2:26; Is. 10:29

28 [a]2Sam. 21:14 [b]Num. 26:38

1 [I]Lit., *came out*

2 [I]In Josh. 15:26, *Shema*

8 [I]I.e., South country

9 [I]Lit., *their*

11 [I]Or, *reached to* [II]Or, *wadi*

12 [I]Lit., *went up*

13 [I]Or, *and is marked off*

14 [I]Lit., *the goings out of it were*

17 [I]Lit., *came out*

19:1-9 Simeon's allotment was in the extreme south in the territory which was already given to Judah, because Judah was not large enough to fill all of her land. This had consequences for later times. During the period of the divided monarchy, although Simeon was politically a part of the ten tribes of Israel, her proximity to Judah led to her eventual assimilation into Judah.

18 And their territory was to Jezreel
and *included* Chesulloth and [a]Shunem,
19 and Hapharaim and Shion and Anaharath,
20 and Rabbith and Kishion and
Ebez,
21 and Remeth and En-gannim and
En-haddah and Beth-pazzez.
22 And the border reached[6293] to
[a]Tabor and Shahazumah and Beth-shemesh, and [I]their border ended at the
Jordan; sixteen cities with their villages.
23 This *was* the inheritance of the
tribe of the sons of Issachar according
to their families, the cities with their
villages.

Territory of Asher

24 Now the fifth lot [I]fell to the tribe
of the sons of Asher according to their
families.
25 And their territory was Helkath
and Hali and Beten and Achshaph,
26 and Allammelech and Amad and
Mishal; and it reached to Carmel on the
west and to Shihor-libnath.
27 And it turned[7725] toward the
[I]east to Beth-dagon, and reached to
Zebulun, and to the valley of Iphtahel
northward to Beth-emek and Neiel; then
it proceeded on [II]north to [a]Cabul,
28 and Ebron and Rehob and Hammon and Kanah, as far as Great [a]Si-
don.
29 And the border[2256] turned to Ramah, and to the fortified city of Tyre;
then the border turned to Hosah, and
[I]it ended at the sea by the region of
[a]Achzib.
30 *Included* also *were* Ummah, and
Aphek and Rehob; twenty-two cities
with their villages.
31 This *was* the inheritance of the
tribe of the sons of Asher according to
their families, these cities with their villages.

18 [a]1Sam. 28:4; 2Kin. 4:8

22 [I]Lit., *the goings out of their border were* [a]Judg. 4:6; Ps. 89:12

24 [I]Lit., *came out*

27 [I]Lit., *sunrise* [II]Lit., *from the left hand* [a]1Kin. 9:13

28 [a]Gen. 10:19; Judg. 1:31; Acts 27:3

29 [I]Lit., *the goings out of it were* [a]Judg. 1:31

32 [I]Lit., *came out*

33 [I]Lit., *the goings out of it were*

34 [I]Or, *reached to* [II]Lit., *sunrise*

35 [a]Gen. 10:18; 1Kin. 8:65 [b]Deut. 3:17

40 [I]Lit., *came out*

46 [I]Heb., *Japho*

Territory of Naphtali

32 The sixth lot [I]fell to the sons
of Naphtali; to the sons of Naphtali according to their families.
33 And their border was from Heleph, from the oak in Zaanannim and
Adami-nekeb and Jabneel, as far as Lakkum; and [I]it ended at the Jordan.
34 Then the border turned westward to Aznoth-tabor, and proceeded
from there to Hukkok; and it reached
to Zebulun on the south and [I]touched
Asher on the west, and to Judah at the
Jordan toward the [II]east.
35 And the fortified cities *were* Ziddim, Zer and [a]Hammath, Rakkath and
[b]Chinnereth,
36 and Adamah and Ramah and Hazor,
37 and Kedesh and Edrei and En-
hazor,
38 and Yiron and Migdal-el, Horem
and Beth-anath and Beth-shemesh;
nineteen cities with their villages.
39 This *was* the inheritance of the
tribe of the sons of Naphtali according
to their families, the cities with their
villages.

Territory of Dan

🗝 **40** The seventh lot [I]fell to the tribe
of the sons of Dan according to their
families.
41 And the territory of their inheritance was Zorah and Eshtaol and Ir-
shemesh,
42 and Shaalabbin and Aijalon and
Ithlah,
43 and Elon and Timnah and Ekron,
44 and Eltekeh and Gibbethon and
Baalath,
45 and Jehud and Bene-berak and
Gath-rimmon,
46 and Me-jarkon and Rakkon, with
the territory over against [I]Joppa.

🗝 **19:40-48** Dan's inheritance was on the coastal plain south of the territory given to Ephraim, but she was unable to possess it. Therefore, the tribe took the city of Leshem, above the Sea of Galilee in the extreme north and settled it and the surrounding territory (Judg. 18:27-29). The tribe renamed the city "Dan," and it became a popular designation of the northern extremity of Israel ("from Dan to Beersheba").

47 And the territory of the [a]sons of Dan proceeded [I]beyond them; for the sons of Dan went up and fought with Leshem and captured it. Then they struck[5221] it with the edge[6310] of the sword[2719] and possessed[3423] it and [II]settled in it; and they called[7121] [III][b]Leshem Dan after the name of Dan their father.[1]

48 This *was* the inheritance of the tribe of the sons of Dan according to their families, these cities with their villages.

🔑 **49** When they finished[3615] apportioning the land[776] for inheritance by its borders, the sons of Israel gave an inheritance in their midst to Joshua the son[1121] of Nun.

50 In accordance with the [I]command of the LORD they gave him the city for which he asked,[7592] [a]Timnath-serah in the hill country of Ephraim. So he built the city and [II]settled in it.

51 [a]These are the inheritances which Eleazar the priest and Joshua the son of Nun and the heads[7218] of the [I]households[1] of the tribes[4294] of the sons of Israel distributed by lot in Shiloh before the LORD, at the doorway of the tent[168] of meeting. So they finished dividing the land.[776]

Six Cities of Refuge

20 Then the LORD spoke[1696] to Joshua, saying,

🔑 2 "Speak[1696] to the sons[1121] of Israel, saying, '[I]Designate [a]the cities of refuge, of which I spoke to you [II]through[3027] Moses,

3 that the manslayer[7523] who [I]kills[5221] any person[5315] unintentionally,[7684] without premeditation,[1087,1847] may flee there, and they shall become your refuge from the avenger[1350] of blood.[1818]

4 'And he shall flee to one of these cities, and shall stand at the entrance of the [a]gate of the city and state[1696] his case[1697] in the hearing[241] of the elders[2205] of that city; and they shall [I]take him into the city to them and give him a place, so that he may dwell among them.

5 'Now [a]if the avenger of blood pursues him, then they shall not deliver the manslayer into his hand, because he struck[5221] his neighbor without premeditation and did not hate[8130] him beforehand.

6 'And he shall dwell in that city [a]until he stands before the congregation[5712] for judgment,[4941] until the death[4194] of the one who is high priest in those days.[3117] Then the manslayer shall [I]return[7725] to his own city and to his own house,[1004] to the city from which he fled.' "

7 So they [I]set apart [a]Kedesh in [II]Galilee in the hill country of Naphtali and Shechem in the hill country of Ephraim, and Kiriath-arba (that is,

47 [I]Lit., *from* [II]Lit., *dwelt* [III]I.e., Laish [a]Judg. 18:1 [b]Judg. 18:29
50 [I]Lit., *mouth* [II]Lit., *dwelt* [a]Num. 13:8; Josh. 24:30
51 [I]Lit., *fathers* [a]Josh. 18:10
2 [I]Lit., *Set for yourselves* [II]Lit., *by the hand of* [a]Num. 35:6-34; Deut. 4:41-43; 19:2ff.
3 [I]Lit., *smites*
4 [I]Lit., *gather* [a]Ruth 4:1; Job 5:4; Jer. 38:7
5 [a]Num. 35:12
6 [I]Lit., *return and come* [a]Num. 35:12
7 [I]Lit., *sanctified* [II]Heb., *Galil* [a]Josh. 21:32; 1Chr. 6:76

🔑 **19:49,50** When the twelve spies returned from Canaan, while Israel was camped at Kadesh, Joshua and Caleb stood alone as the only two among them who remained faithful to the Lord (Num. 14:6-9). For Caleb's faithfulness he was awarded a special portion in the Promised Land. However, nothing is said of a special allotment being reserved for Joshua. The name of the city given to Joshua was Timnath-serah meaning "the portion remains." The name was probably given to it at this time because Joshua's was the last portion given in the whole distribution of the land among the tribes and individuals. It is also called Timnath-heres, which means "portion of the sun," in Judg. 2:9 by a transposition of two letters at the end of the Hebrew word. The ancient rabbis explained that this latter name was given because a representation of the sun had been fixed to Joshua's tomb in memory of the command given by him that the sun should stand still (Josh. 10:12-14). It is more probable that it is an accidental transposition of the letters which has been retained in the text.

🔑 **20:2** See Num. 35:9-34; Deut. 19:1-3. This is how justice was assured in the case of accidental homicide (without malice). Also, the community was protected from a wanton murderer. This procedure replaced the custom in which the manslayer fled to the Lord's altar (Ex. 21:12-14; I Kgs. 1:50-53; 2:28-34). The most primitive method of dealing with such criminals was an unrelenting cycle of revenge (cf. Gen. 4:14,15).

Hebron) in [b]the hill country of Judah.
8 And beyond the Jordan east of Jericho, they [I]designated Bezer in the wilderness on the plain from the tribe of
Reuben, and Ramoth in Gilead from the
tribe of Gad, and Golan in Bashan from
the tribe of Manasseh.
9 [a]These were the appointed cities
for all the sons of Israel and for the
stranger[1616] who sojourns[1481] among
them, that whoever [I]kills any person
unintentionally may flee there, and not
die by the hand of the avenger of blood
until he stands before the congregation.

Forty-eight Cities of the Levites

21 Then the heads[7218] of [I]house-
holds[1] of [a]the Levites approached[5066] Eleazar the priest and
Joshua the son[1121] of Nun and the heads
of [I]households of the tribes of the
sons[1121] of Israel.
🔑 2 And they spoke[1696] to them at Shiloh in the land[776] of Canaan, saying,
"[a]The LORD commanded[6680] [I]through[3027]
Moses to give us cities to live in, with
their pasture lands for our cattle."
3 So the sons of Israel gave the Levites from their inheritance[5159] these cities with their pasture lands, according
to the [I]command[6310] of the LORD.
4 Then the lot came out for the
families[4940] of the Kohathites. And the
sons of Aaron the priest, who were of
the Levites, [I]received thirteen cities by
lot from the tribe of Judah and from the
tribe of the Simeonites and from the
tribe of Benjamin.
5 And the rest[3498] of the sons of
Kohath [I]received ten cities by lot from
the families of the tribe of Ephraim and
from the tribe of Dan and from the half-
tribe of Manasseh.
6 And the sons of Gershon [I]received
thirteen cities by lot from the families
of the tribe of Issachar and from the
tribe of Asher and from the tribe of
Naphtali and from the half-tribe of Manasseh in Bashan.
7 The sons of Merari according to
their families [I]received twelve cities
from the tribe of Reuben and from the
tribe of Gad and from the tribe of Zebulun.
8 Now the [a]sons of Israel gave by
lot to the Levites these cities with their
pasture lands, as the LORD had commanded [I]through Moses.
9 And they gave these cities which
are *here* mentioned by name from the
tribe of the sons of Judah and from the
tribe of the sons of Simeon;
10 and they were for the sons of
Aaron, one of the families of the Kohathites, of the sons of Levi, for the lot
was theirs first.[7223]
11 Thus [a]they gave them Kiriath-
arba, *Arba being* the [b]father[1] of Anak
(that is, Hebron), in the hill country of
Judah, with its surrounding pasture
lands.
12 But the fields[7704] of the city and
its villages, they gave to Caleb the son
of Jephunneh as his possession.[272]
13 So [a]to the sons of Aaron the
priest they gave [b]Hebron, the city of
refuge for the manslayer,[7523] with its
pasture lands, and [c]Libnah with its pasture lands,
14 and [a]Jattir with its pasture lands
and [b]Eshtemoa with its pasture lands,
15 and [I]Holon with its pasture lands
and [a]Debir with its pasture lands,
16 and [I]Ain with its pasture lands
and [a]Juttah with its pasture lands *and*
[b]Beth-shemesh with its pasture lands;
nine cities from these two tribes.[7626]
17 And from the tribe of Benjamin,
[a]Gibeon with its pasture lands, [b]Geba
with its pasture lands,
🔑 18 Anathoth with its pasture lands
and [I]Almon with its pasture lands; four
cities.

7 [b]Josh. 21:11; Luke 1:39
8 [I]Lit., *set*
9 [I]Lit., *smites* [a]Num. 35:13ff.
1 [I]Lit., *fathers* [a]Num. 35:1-8
2 [I]Lit., *by the hand of* [a]Num. 35:2
3 [I]Lit., *mouth*
4 [I]Lit., *had*
5 [I]Lit., *had*
6 [I]Lit., *had*
7 [I]Lit., *had*
8 [I]Lit., *by the hand of* [a]Gen. 49:5ff.
11 [a]1Chr. 6:55 [b]Josh. 14:15; 15:13
13 [a]1Chr. 6:57 [b]Josh. 15:54 [c]Josh. 15:42
14 [a]Josh. 15:48 [b]Josh. 15:50
15 [I]In 1Chr. 6:58, *Hilen* [a]Josh. 15:49
16 [I]In 1Chr. 6:59, *Ashan* [a]Josh. 15:55 [b]Josh. 15:10
17 [a]Josh. 18:25 [b]Josh. 18:24
18 [I]In 1Chr. 6:60, *Allemeth*

🔑 **21:2** The Levites were not the only ones to occupy these cities; they lived in quarters which met their needs.
🔑 **21:18** See note on Jer. 1:1.

19 All the cities of the sons of Aaron, the <u>priests</u>,[3548] were thirteen cities with their pasture lands.

20 Then the cities from the tribe of Ephraim were allotted to the [a]families of the sons of Kohath, the Levites, *even to* the <u>rest</u>[3498] of the sons of Kohath.

21 And they gave them [a]Shechem, the city of refuge for the manslayer, with its pasture lands, in the hill country of Ephraim, and Gezer with its pasture lands,

22 and Kibzaim with its pasture lands and Beth-horon with its pasture lands; four cities.

23 And from the tribe of Dan, Elteke with its pasture lands, Gibbethon with its pasture lands,

24 Aijalon with its pasture lands, Gath-rimmon with its pasture lands; four cities.

25 And from the half-tribe of Manasseh, *they allotted* Taanach with its pasture lands and Gath-rimmon with its pasture lands; two cities.

26 All the cities with their pasture lands for the families of the rest of the sons of Kohath were ten.

27 And [a]to the sons of Gershon, one of the families of the Levites, from the half-tribe of Manasseh, *they gave* Golan in Bashan, the city of refuge for the manslayer, with its pasture lands, and Be-eshterah with its pasture lands; two cities.

28 And from the tribe of Issachar, *they gave* Kishion with its pasture lands, Daberath with its pasture lands,

29 Jarmuth with its pasture lands, En-gannim with its pasture lands; four cities.

30 And from the tribe of Asher, *they gave* Mishal with its pasture lands, Abdon with its pasture lands,

31 Helkath with its pasture lands and Rehob with its pasture lands; four cities.

32 And from the tribe of Naphtali, *they gave* [a]Kedesh in Galilee, the city of refuge for the manslayer, with its pasture lands and Hammoth-dor with its pasture lands and Kartan with its pasture lands; three cities.

33 All the cities of the Gershonites according to their families were thirteen cities with their pasture lands.

34 And to the families of [a]the sons of Merari, the rest of the Levites, *they gave* from the tribe of Zebulun, Jokneam with its pasture lands and Kartah with its pasture lands.

35 Dimnah with its pasture lands, Nahalal with its pasture lands; four cities.

36 And from the tribe of Reuben, *they gave* [a]Bezer with its pasture lands and Jahaz with its pasture lands,

37 Kedemoth with its pasture lands and Mephaath with its pasture lands; four cities.

38 And from the tribe of Gad, *they gave* [a]Ramoth in Gilead, the city of refuge for the manslayer, with its pasture lands and [b]Mahanaim with its pasture lands,

39 Heshbon with its pasture lands, Jazer with its pasture lands; four cities in all.

40 All *these were* the cities of the sons of Merari according to their families, the rest of the families of the Levites; and their lot was twelve cities.

41 [a]All the cities of the Levites in the midst of the possession of the sons of Israel were forty-eight cities with their pasture lands.

42 These cities each had its surrounding pasture lands; thus *it was* with all these cities.

43 [a]So the LORD gave Israel all the land which He had <u>sworn</u>[7650] to give to their fathers, and [b]they <u>possessed</u>[3423] it and lived in it.

44 And the LORD [a]gave them rest on every side, according to all that He had sworn to their fathers, and [b]no <u>one</u>[376] of all their enemies stood before them; [c]the LORD gave all their enemies into their hand.

45 [a]Not [I]one of the <u>good</u>[2896] <u>promises</u>[1697] which the LORD had [II]<u>made</u>[1696] to the <u>house</u>[1004] of Israel <u>failed</u>;[5307] all came to pass.

20 [a]1Chr. 6:66

21 [a]Josh. 20:7

27 [a]1Chr. 6:71

32 [a]Josh. 20:7

34 [a]1Chr. 6:

36 [a]Deut. 4:43; Josh. 20:8

38 [a]Deut. 4:43; 1Kin. 4:13 [b]Gen. 32:2; 2Sam. 2:8

41 [a]Num. 35:7

43 [a]Deut. 34:4 [b]Num. 33:53; Deut. 11:31; 17:14

44 [a]Josh. 1:13; 23:1 [b]Deut. 7:24 [c]Ex. 23:31

45 [I]Lit., *a word from every good word* [II]Lit., *spoken* [a]Josh. 23:14; 1Kin. 8:56

Tribes beyond Jordan Return

22 [a]Then Joshua summoned[7121] the Reubenites and the Gadites and the half-tribe[4294] of Manasseh,

2 and said to them, "You have kept[8104] all that Moses the servant[5650] of the LORD commanded[6680] you, [a]and have listened[8085] to my voice in all that I commanded you.

3 "You have not forsaken[5800] your brothers[251] these many days[3117] to this day, but have kept the charge[4931] of the commandment[6310] of the LORD your God.[430]

4 "And now [a]the LORD your God has given rest to your brothers, as He spoke[1696] to them; therefore turn now and go to your tents,[168] to the land[776] of your possession,[272] which Moses the servant of the LORD gave you beyond the Jordan.

5 "Only be very careful to observe[6213] the commandment and the law[8451] which Moses the servant of the LORD commanded[6680] you, to [a]love[157] the LORD your God and walk in all His ways[1870] and keep[8104] His commandments and hold fast to Him and serve[5647] Him [b]with all your heart[3824] and with all your soul."[5315]

6 So Joshua [a]blessed[1288] them and sent them away, and they went to their tents.

7 Now [a]to the one half-tribe[7626] of Manasseh Moses had given *a possession* in Bashan, but [b]to the other half Joshua gave *a possession* among their brothers westward beyond the Jordan. So when Joshua sent them away to their tents, he blessed them,

8 and said[559] to [I]them, "Return[7725] to your tents with great riches and with very much livestock, with silver, gold, bronze, iron, and with very many clothes; [a]divide the spoil of your enemies with your brothers."

9 And the sons[1121] of Reuben and the sons of Gad and the half-tribe of Manasseh returned[7725] *home* and departed from the sons of Israel at Shiloh which is in the land[776] of Canaan, to go to the [a]land of Gilead, to the land of their possession which they had possessed,[3423] according to the [I]command of the LORD [II]through[3027] Moses.

The Offensive Altar

10 And when they came to the region of the Jordan which is in the land of Canaan, the sons of Reuben and the sons of Gad and the half-tribe of Manasseh built an altar[4196] there by the Jordan, a large altar in appearance.

11 And the sons of Israel heard[8085] *it* [I]said,[559] "Behold, the sons of Reuben and the sons of Gad and the half-tribe of Manasseh have [a]built an altar[4196] at the [II]frontier of the land of Canaan, in the region of the Jordan, on the side *belonging to* the sons of Israel."

12 And when the sons of Israel heard *of it,* the whole congregation[5712] of the sons of Israel gathered[6950] themselves at [a]Shiloh, to go up[5927] against them in war.[6635]

13 Then the sons of Israel sent to the sons of Reuben and to the sons of Gad and to the half-tribe of Manasseh, into the land of Gilead, [a]Phinehas the son[1121] of Eleazar the priest,

14 and with him ten chiefs,[5387] one chief[5387] for each father's household[1004] from each of the tribes[4294] of Israel; and [a]each one[376] of them *was* the head[7218] of his father's[1] household among the [I]thousands[505] of Israel.

15 And they came to the sons of Reuben and to the sons of Gad and to the half-tribe of Manasseh, to the land of Gilead, and they spoke[1696] with them saying,

⊶ 16 "Thus says[559] the whole congregation of the LORD, 'What is this unfaithful act[4604] which you have committed against the God of Israel, turning away[7725] from following the LORD this

1 [a]Num. 32:20-22
2 [a]Josh. 1:12-18
4 [a]Num. 32:18; Deut. 3:20
5 [a]Deut. 5:10 [b]Deut. 4:29
6 [a]Gen. 47:7; Josh. 14:13; 2Sam. 6:18; Luke 24:50
7 [a]Num. 32:33 [b]Josh. 17:1-13
8 [I]Lit., *them, saying, "Return* [a]Num. 31:27; 1Sam. 30:16
9 [I]Lit., *mouth* [II]Lit., *by the hand of* [a]Num. 32:1, 26, 29
11 [I]Lit., *saying* [II]Lit., *front* [a]Deut. 12:5; Josh. 22:19
12 [a]Josh. 18:1
13 [a]Num. 25:7, 11; 31:6
14 [I]Or, *families* [a]Num. 1:4

⊶ **22:16** This should have been called a monument, not an altar. To build a second "altar" would have been a violation of Deut. 12:1-14. However, this was not for the purpose of offering sacrifices.

day, by [a]building yourselves an altar,[4196] to rebel[4775] against the LORD this day?

17 'Is not [a]the iniquity[5771] of Peor [I]enough for us, from which we have not cleansed[2891] ourselves to this day, although a plague[5063] came on the congregation of the LORD,

18 that you must turn away this day from following the LORD? And it will come about if you rebel against the LORD today,[3117] that [a]He will be angry with the whole congregation of Israel tomorrow.

19 'If, however, the land of your possession is unclean,[2931] then [I]cross into the land of the possession of the LORD, where the LORD's tabernacle[4908] [II]stands,[7931] and take possession among us. Only do not rebel against the LORD, or rebel against us by [a]building an altar[4196] for yourselves, besides the altar of the LORD our God.

20 'Did not [a]Achan the son of Zerah act unfaithfully in the things under the ban,[2764] and wrath[7110] fall[1961] on all the congregation of Israel? And that man[376] did not perish[1478] alone in his iniquity.' "

21 Then the sons of Reuben and the sons of Gad and the half-tribe of Manasseh answered, and spoke[1696] to the heads[7218] of the [I]families of Israel.

22 "The [a]Mighty One, God,[410] the LORD, the Mighty One, God, the LORD! [b]He knows, and may Israel itself know.[3045] If *it was* in rebellion,[4777] or if in an unfaithful act[4604] against the LORD do not Thou save[3467] us this day!

23 "If we have built us an altar[4196] to turn away from following the LORD, or if to [a]offer a burnt offering[5930] or grain offering[4503] on it, or if to offer[6213] sacrifices of peace offerings[8002] on it, may the LORD Himself require it.

24 "But truly we have done[6213] this out of concern,[1674] [I]for a reason,[1697] saying, 'In time to come your sons may say[559] to our [II]sons, "What have you to do with the LORD, the God of Israel?

25 "For the LORD has made the Jordan a border between us and you, *you* sons of Reuben and sons of Gad; you have no portion in the LORD." So your sons may make our sons stop[7673] fearing[3372] the LORD.'

26 "Therefore we said,[559] 'Let us [I]build an altar,[4196] not for burnt offering or for sacrifice;[2077]

27 rather it shall be [a]a witness between us and you and between our generations[1755] after us, that we are to [b]perform[5647] the service[5656] of the LORD before Him with our burnt offerings, and with our sacrifices[2077] and with our peace offerings, that your sons may not say to our sons in time to come, "You have no portion in the LORD." '

28 "Therefore we said, 'It shall also come about if they say *this* to us or to our generations in time to come, then we shall say, "See[7200] the copy of the altar[4196] of the LORD which our fathers made,[6213] not for burnt offering or for sacrifice; rather it is a witness between us and you." '

29 "Far be it from us that we should rebel against the LORD and turn away from following the LORD this day, by [a]building an altar[4196] for burnt offering, for grain offering[4503] or for sacrifice, besides the altar of the LORD our God which is before His [I]tabernacle."

30 So when Phinehas the priest and the leaders of the congregation, even the heads of the [I]families of Israel who *were* with him, heard the words[1697] which the sons of Reuben and the sons of Gad and the sons of Manasseh spoke, it pleased them.

31 And Phinehas the son of Eleazar the priest said to the sons of Reuben and to the sons of Gad and to the sons of Manasseh, "Today we know that the [a]LORD is in our midst, because you have not committed this unfaithful act against the LORD; now you have delivered[5337] the sons of Israel from the hand of the LORD."

32 Then Phinehas the son of Eleazar the priest and the leaders returned from the sons of Reuben and from the sons of Gad, from the land of Gilead, to the land of Canaan, to the sons of Israel, and brought back word[1697] to them.

16 [a]Josh. 22:11
17 [I]Lit., *little for us* [a]Num. 25:1-9
18 [a]Num. 16:22
19 [I]Lit., *cross for yourselves* [II]Lit., *abides* [a]Josh. 22:11
20 [a]Josh. 7:1-26
21 [I]Lit., *thousands*
22 [a]Deut. 10:17 [b]1Kin. 8:39; Job 10:7; Ps. 44:21
23 [a]Deut. 12:11
24 [I]Lit., *from* [II]Lit., *sons, saying*
26 [I]Lit., *prepare to build for ourselves*
27 [a]Gen. 31:48; Josh. 24:27 [b]Deut. 12:6, 11, 26f.
29 [I]Lit., *dwelling place* [a]Deut. 12:13f.
30 [I]Lit., *thousands*
31 [a]Ex. 25:8; Lev. 26:11f.; 2Chr. 15:2

33 And the word pleased the sons of Israel, and the sons of Israel [a]blessed God; and they did not speak of[559] going up against them in war,[6635] to destroy[7843] the land in which the sons of Reuben and the sons of Gad were living.

34 And the sons of Reuben and the sons of Gad [a]called the altar[4196] *Witness;* "For," *they said,* "it is a witness between us that the LORD is God."

Joshua's Farewell Address

23 Now it came about after many days,[3117] when the LORD had given [a]rest to Israel from all their enemies [I]on every side, and Joshua was old,[2204] advanced in years,

2 that [a]Joshua called[7121] for all Israel, for their elders[2205] and their heads[7218] and their judges[8199] and their officers,[7860] and said[559] to them, "I am old, advanced in years.

3 "And you have seen[7200] all that the LORD your God[430] has done[6213] to all these nations[1471] because of you, for [a]the LORD your God is He who has been fighting for you.

4 "See,[7200] [a]I have apportioned to you these nations which remain as an inheritance[5159] for your tribes,[7626] with all the nations which I have cut off,[3772] from the Jordan even to the Great Sea toward the setting of the sun.

5 "And the LORD your God, He shall thrust them out from before you and [I][a]drive them from before you; and [b]you shall possess[3423] their land,[776] just as the LORD your God [II]promised[1696] you.

6 "[a]Be very firm,[2388] then, to keep[8104] and do[6213] all that is written in the book[5612] of the law[8451] of Moses, so that you may not turn aside from it to the right hand or to the left,

7 in order that you may not [I]associate with these nations, these which remain among you, or [a]mention the name of their gods,[430] or [b]make[1697] *anyone* swear[7650] *by them,* or [c]serve[5647] them, or bow down to them.

8 "But you are to cling to the LORD your God, as you have done to this day.[3117]

9 "[a]For the LORD has [I]driven out great and strong nations from before you; and as for you, [b]no man[376] has stood before you to this day.

10 "[a]One of your men puts to flight a thousand, for the LORD your God is [b]He who fights for you, just as He [I]promised you.

11 "So take diligent heed to yourselves to love[157] the LORD your God.

🗝 12 "For if you ever go back and [a]cling to the rest[3499] of these nations, these which remain among you, and [b]intermarry with them, so that you [I]associate with them and they with you,

13 know[3045] with certainty that the LORD your God will not continue to [I]drive these nations out from before you; but they shall be a [a]snare[6341] and a trap[4170] to you, and a whip[7850] on your sides and thorns in your eyes, until you perish[6] from off this good[2896] land[127] which the LORD your God has given you.

14 "Now behold, today [a]I am going the way[1870] of all the earth,[776] and you know in all your hearts[3824] and in all your souls[5315] that [b]not one word[1697] of all the good words[1697] which the LORD your God spoke[1696] concerning you has failed;[5307] all have [I]been fulfilled for you, not [II]one of them has failed.

15 "And it shall come about that just as all the good words which the LORD your God spoke to you have come upon you, so [a]the LORD will bring upon you all the threats,[7451] until He has destroyed[8045] you from off this good land which the LORD your God has given you.

16 "[a]When you transgress[5674] the covenant[1285] of the LORD your God,

33 [a]1Chr. 29:20; Dan. 2:19; Luke 2:28
34 [a]Gen. 31:47-49
1 [I]Lit., *from round about* [a]Josh. 21:44
2 [a]Josh. 24:1
3 [a]Deut. 1:30
4 [a]Ex. 23:30
5 [I]Or, *dispossess* [II]Lit., *spoke to* [a]Ex. 23:20 [b]Num. 33:53
6 [a]Deut. 5:32; Josh. 1:7
7 [I]Lit., *go among* [a]Ex. 23:13; Ps. 16:4 [b]Deut. 6:13; 10:20 [c]Ex. 20:5
9 [I]Or, *dispossessed* [a]Ex. 23:23, 30 [b]Deut. 7:24
10 [I]Lit., *spoke to* [a]Lev. 26:8; Deut. 28:7; 32:20 [b]Deut. 3:22; Josh. 23:3
12 [I]Lit., *go among* [a]Ex. 34:15, 16; Ps. 106:34, 35 [b]Deut. 7:3, 4; Ezra 9:2; Neh. 13:25
13 [I]Or, *dispossess* [a]Ex. 23:33; 34:12; Deut. 7:16
14 [I]Lit., *come* [II]Lit., *one word* [a]1Kin. 2:2 [b]Josh. 21:45
15 [a]Lev. 26:14-33; Deut. 28:15
16 [a]Deut. 4:25, 26

🗝 **23:12-16** In the last two chapters of the book, Joshua addressed Israel twice. One of the features of this first speech is a stern warning abut the consequences of apostasy. Although God intended to drive out the remaining Canaanites (Josh. 13:2-6), He would not do it if Israel was unfaithful to Him. The Book of Judges tells the tragic story of that infidelity and the disastrous results for Israel.

which He commanded[6680] you, and go
and serve[5647] other gods, and bow
down[7812] to them, then the anger[639] of
the LORD will burn[2734] against you, and
you shall perish quickly from off the good
land which He has given you."

Joshua Reviews Israel's History

24 Then [a]Joshua gathered[622]
all the tribes[7626] of Israel to Shechem, and called[7121] for the elders[2205]
of Israel and for their heads[7218] and their
judges[8199] and their officers;[7860] and they
presented themselves before God.[430]
2 And Joshua said[559] to all the people,[5971] "Thus says[559] the LORD, the God
of Israel, 'From ancient times your
fathers[1] lived beyond the [I]River, *namely,*
[a]Terah, the father of Abraham and the
father[1] of Nahor, and they served[5647]
other gods.[430]
3 'Then [a]I took your father Abraham
from beyond the [I]River, and led him
through all the land[776] of Canaan, and
[b]multiplied his [II]descendants[2233] and
gave him [c]Isaac.
4 'And to Isaac I gave [a]Jacob and
Esau, and [b]to Esau I gave Mount Seir,
to possess[3423] it; but [c]Jacob and his
sons[1121] went down to Egypt.
5 'Then [a]I sent Moses and Aaron,
and I plagued Egypt [I]by what I did[6213]
in its midst;[7130] and afterward I brought
you out.
6 'And I brought your fathers out
of Egypt, and [a]you came to the sea;
and Egypt pursued your fathers with
chariots and horsemen to the [I]Red Sea.
7 'But when they cried out to the
LORD, He put darkness between you
and the Egyptians, and brought the sea
upon them and covered[3680] them; and
your own eyes saw[7200] what I did[6213]
in Egypt. And [a]you lived in the wilderness for a long time.[3117]
8 'Then [a]I brought you into the land
of the Amorites who lived beyond the
Jordan, and they fought with you; and
I gave them into your hand,[3027] and you
took possession of their land when I
destroyed[8045] them before you.
9 'Then [a]Balak the son[1121] of Zippor,
king of Moab, arose and fought against
Israel, and he sent and summoned
Balaam the son of Beor to curse[7043]
you.
10 'But I [a]was not willing[14] to
listen[8085] to Balaam. So he had to
bless[1288] you, and I delivered[5337] you
from his hand.
11 'And [a]you crossed[5674] the Jordan
and came to Jericho; and the citizens[1167]
of Jericho fought against you, *and*
[b]the Amorite and the Perizzite and the
Canaanite and the Hittite and the Girgashite, the Hivite and the Jebusite.
Thus [c]I gave them into your hand.
12 'Then I [a]sent the hornet before
you and it [I]drove out the two kings[4428]
of the Amorites from before you, *but*
[b]not by your sword[2719] or your bow.
13 'And [a]I gave you a land on which
you had not labored, and cities which
you had not built, and you have lived
in them; you are eating of vineyards
and olive groves which you did not
plant.'

"We Will Serve the Lord"

14 "Now, therefore, [I][a]fear[3372] the
LORD and serve[5647] Him in sincerity[8549]
and [II]truth;[571] and put away[5493] the gods
which your fathers served beyond the
[III]River and in Egypt, and serve the
LORD.
15 "And if it is disagreeable[7489] in

1 [a]Josh. 23:2
2 [I]I.e., Euphrates [a]Gen. 11:27-32
3 [I]I.e., Euphrates [II]Lit., *seed* [a]Gen. 12:1; 24:7 [b]Gen. 15:5 [c]Gen. 21:3
4 [a]Gen. 25:25, 26 [b]Gen. 36:8; Deut. 2:5 [c]Gen. 46:6, 7
5 [I]Lit., *according to* [a]Ex. 4:14-17
6 [I]Lit., *Sea of Reeds* [a]Ex. 14:2-31
7 [a]Deut. 1:46; 2:14
8 [a]Num. 21:21-32
9 [a]Num. 22:2-6
10 [a]Deut. 23:5
11 [a]Josh. 3:14-17 [b]Ex. 23:23, 28; Deut. 7:1 [c]Ex. 23:31
12 [I]Lit., *drove them out* [a]Ex. 23:28; Deut. 7:20 [b]Ps. 44:3
13 [a]Deut. 6:10, 11
14 [I]Or, *reverence* [II]Or, *faithfulness* [III]I.e., Euphrates [a]Deut. 10:12; 18:13; 1Sam. 12:24

24:1 Schechem was a historic site. Here the Lord first promised the land of Canaan to Abram (Gen. 12:6,7). Here Jacob destroyed the idols which had been brought from Mesopotamia (Gen. 35:2-5). And here the Law of Moses was officially enacted (Josh. 8:30-35).

24:2 Actually, Terah had three sons (Gen. 11:27), but only Abraham and Nahor were mentioned because they were direct ancestors of Israel. Nahor was the grandfather of Rebekah (Gen. 22:20-23) and the great-grandfather of Rachel and Leah (Gen. 29:10,16).

24:15,16 This invitation of Joshua is similar to that extended by Moses to Israel on the other side

(continued on next page)

your sight to serve the LORD, choose[977]
for yourselves today[3117] whom you will
serve: whether the gods which your fathers served which were beyond the
River, or [a]the gods of the Amorites in
whose land you are living; but as for
me and my house,[1004] we will serve the
LORD."
16 And the people answered and
said, "Far be it from us that we should
forsake[5800] the LORD to serve other
gods;
17 for the LORD our God is He who
brought us and our fathers up out of
the land of Egypt, from the house of
[I]bondage,[5650] and who did these great
signs[226] in our sight and preserved[8104]
us through all the way[1870] in which we
went and among all the peoples
through[7130] whose midst we passed.[5674]
18 "And the LORD drove out from
before us all the peoples, even the
Amorites who lived in the land. We
also will serve the LORD, for He is our
God."
19 Then Joshua said to the people,
"You will not be able to serve the LORD,
[a]for He is a holy[6918] God. He is [b]a jealous
God;[410] [c]He will not forgive[5375] your
transgression[6588] or your sins.
20 "[a]If you forsake the LORD and
serve foreign[5236] gods, then He will
turn[7725] and do you harm[7489] and
consume[3615] you after He has done
good[3190] to you."
21 And the people said to Joshua,
"No, but we will serve the LORD."
22 And Joshua said to the people,
"You are witnesses against yourselves
that [a]you have chosen[977] for yourselves
the LORD, to serve Him." And they said,
"We are witnesses."
23 "Now therefore, put away the
foreign gods which are in your midst,[7130]
and [a]incline your hearts[3824] to the LORD,
the God of Israel."
24 [a]And the people said to Joshua,
"We will serve the LORD our God and
we will [I]obey[8085] His voice."
25 [a]So Joshua made[3772] a covenant[1285] with the people that day, and
made[7760] for them a statute[2706] and an
ordinance[4941] in Shechem.
26 And Joshua [a]wrote these
words[1697] in the book[5612] of the law[8451]
of God; and he took a large stone and
set it up there under the oak that was
by the sanctuary[4720] of the LORD.
27 And Joshua said to all the people,
"Behold, [a]this stone shall be for a
witness[5713] against us, for it has
heard[8085] all the words[561] of the LORD
which He spoke[1696] [I]to us; thus it shall
be for a witness against you, lest you
deny your God."
28 Then Joshua dismissed the people, each to his inheritance.[5159]

Joshua's Death and Burial

29 And it came about after these
things[1697] that Joshua the son of Nun,
the servant[5650] of the LORD, died,[4191]
being one hundred and ten years old.[1121]
30 And they buried[6912] him in the
territory of his inheritance in [a]Timnath-
serah, which is in the hill country of
Ephraim, on the north of Mount Gaash.

15 [a]Judg. 6:10
17 [I]Lit., *bondmen*
19 [a]Lev. 19:2; 20:7, 26 [b]Ex. 20:5; 34:14 [c]Ex. 23:21
20 [a]Deut. 4:25, 26
22 [a]Ps. 119:173
23 [a]1Kin. 8:57, 58; Ps. 119:36; 141:4
24 [I]Lit., *listen to* [a]Ex. 19:8; 24:3, 7; Deut. 5:27
25 [a]Ex. 24:8
26 [a]Deut. 31:24
27 [I]Lit., *with* [a]Josh. 22:27, 34
30 [a]Josh. 19:50

(continued from previous page)
of the Jordan (Deut. 30:15-20). He recognized that one can only serve God in sincerity and truth if he has freely and willingly pledged in his heart to do so. He summarizes the options that are open to Israel: (1) They could return to serve the gods of their ancestors. "Beyond the River" is better translated "on the other side of the river," i.e., the Euphrates (the same is true in vv. 2,14). "The gods which your fathers served" is a reference to Terah, Abraham's father (see v. 2). These were probably the "images" or teraphim which their ancestor Laban called "his gods" (Gen. 31:19,30,34). Perhaps there were some secret adherents to these gods among the people (see vv. 14,23). (2) They could serve the gods of the Amorites. Amorites was a term, though referring to a specific people, which was also used in a generic sense for all people living in Canaan, hence the reference is probably to the Baalim and Ashteroth in Judg. 10:6. (3) They could follow the example of him and his family, i.e., to serve the Lord. This stands as one of the great affirmations of faith in all the Bible.

🔑31 And [a]Israel served the LORD
all the days[3117] of Joshua and all the
days of the elders who [I]survived Joshua, and had known[3045] all the deeds
of the LORD which He had done for Israel.
🔑**32** Now [a]they buried the bones[6106]
of Joseph, which the sons of Israel
brought up from Egypt, at Shechem,
in the piece of ground [b]which Jacob had
bought from the sons[1121] of Hamor the
father of Shechem for one hundred
[I]pieces of money; and they became the
inheritance of Joseph's sons.
33 And Eleazar the son of Aaron
died; and they buried him [I]at Gibeah
of [a]Phinehas his son, which was given
him in the hill country of Ephraim.

31 [I]Lit., *prolonged days after* [a]Judg. 2:6f.

32 [I]Heb., *qesitah* [a]Gen. 50:24, 25; Ex. 13:19 [b]Gen. 33:19; John 4:5; Acts 7:15f.

33 [I]Or, *on the hill* [a]Josh. 22:13

🔑**24:31** Moses had trained Joshua to be his successor, but Joshua and the elders were too busy conquering the Canaanites to train their own successors, to thoroughly ground new leaders in the faith of Israel. As a result, the next generation succumbed to Canaanite idolatry. God's people are always just one generation away from apostasy. Therefore, we must train our young people to walk in the fear of the Lord today before they become the leaders of tomorrow.

🔑**24:32** Compare Gen. 50:24,25; Ex. 13:19.

The Book of

JUDGES

The term “judges” is not a good translation of the Hebrew word. God raised up these heroes (and a heroine) to deliver a given local tribe of Israel from apostasy and then govern them. The people of Israel had become a very disorganized, loose confederacy after their conquest of the land of Canaan under Joshua. Therefore, without leadership, they repeatedly fell into idolatry, foreign political domination, intermarriage with pagans, and other major sins. They were in a general state of spiritual confusion. A key verse says, “Every man did that which was right in his own eyes” (Judges 17:6). The Book of Judges is fragmentary and it is not chronological. Many scholars believe that some of the events were concurrent. The nation of Israel was in disarray; they needed help from God. The Book of Judges portrays some of the blackest pages in the history of the sons of Israel. In effect it was their Dark Ages. There were regular cycles of falling away, salvation, restoration, and falling away again. Over and over they forgot who the true God was. Each tribe of Israel was mostly isolated from the other tribes. They had lost their sense of national unity under God. They adopted Baal worship, the local religion, abandoning the spiritual purity which the Lord required. They were surrounded by hostile nations who wanted the land which the Israelites had taken, the land which God had promised to them as an inheritance. They were an easy prey for enemy invasion. About 350 years are covered by the Book of Judges. One can decipher seven apostasies, seven bondages, and seven deliverances. The book begins with compromise and ends with anarchy. The author is unknown.

Jerusalem Is Captured

1 🔑Now it came about after the
death of Joshua that the sons[1121] of
Israel [a]inquired[7592] of the LORD, saying,
“Who shall go up[5927] first for us [b]against
the Canaanites, to fight against them?”
2 And the LORD said,[559] “[a]Judah shall
go up; behold, I have given the land[776]
into his hand.”[3027]
3 Then Judah said to Simeon his
brother, “Come up[5927] with me into
[I]the territory allotted me, that we may
fight against the Canaanites; and
[II]I in turn will go with you into [III]the
territory allotted you.” So Simeon went
with him.
4 And Judah went up,[5927] and
[a]the LORD gave the Canaanites and the
Perizzites into their hands; and they
[I]defeated[5221] ten thousand men[376] at Bezek.
5 And they found Adoni-bezek in
Bezek and fought against him and they
[I]defeated the Canaanites and the Perizzites.
6 But Adoni-bezek fled; and they
pursued him and caught him and cut off
his [I]thumbs and big toes.
7 And Adoni-bezek said, “Seventy
kings[4428] with their thumbs and their big
toes cut off used to gather[3950] up *scraps*
under my table; [a]as I have done,[6213] so
God[430] has repaid[7999] me.” So they
brought him to Jerusalem and he died
there.
🔑8 Then the sons of Judah fought
against [a]Jerusalem and captured it and

1 [a]Num.27:21 [b]Judg.1:27; 2:21-23; 3:1-6
2 [a]Gen. 49:8
3 [I]Lit., *my lot* [II]Lit., *I, even I* [III]Lit., *your lot*
4 [I]Lit., *smote them* [a]Ps. 44:2; 78:55
5 [I]Lit., *smote*
6 [I]Lit., *thumbs of his hands and his feet*
7 [a]Lev. 24:19
8 [a]Josh. 15:63; Judg. 1:21

🔑 **1:1** The phrase “inquired of the LORD” is found only in the Books of Judges and Samuel. The civil ruler of Israel had the right to ask the high priest to consult the Urim and the Thummim for him (Num. 27:21). This was the means which was set up by God for the judges, and later the kings, to have the Lord’s judgment on any particular matter available before making a decision. There is some question about the chronology of events here since the record of Joshua’s death is given later in 2:8.

🔑 **1:8** The early history of Jerusalem is not certain, because the city was known by several different names during its history, and it is difficult to determine which name applied at what time. The city is

(continued on next page)

struck[5221] it with the edge[6310] of the sword[2719] and set the city on fire.

9 And afterward the sons of Judah went down to fight against the Canaanites living in the hill country and in the [I]Negev and in the lowland.

10 [a]So Judah went against the Canaanites who lived in Hebron (now the name of Hebron formerly *was* Kiriath-arba); and they struck Sheshai and Ahiman and Talmai.

Capture of Other Cities

11 Then [a]from there he went against the inhabitants of Debir (now the name of Debir formerly *was* Kiriath-sepher).

12 And Caleb said, "The one who attacks Kiriath-sepher and captures it, I will even give him my daughter Achsah for a wife."[802]

13 And [a]Othniel the son[1121] of Kenaz, Caleb's younger brother, captured it; so he gave him his daughter Achsah for a wife.

14 Then [a]it came about when she came *to him,* that she persuaded him to ask[7592] her father[1] for a field.[7704] Then she alighted from [I]her donkey, and Caleb said to her, "What [II]do you want?"

15 And she said to him, "Give me a blessing,[1293] since you have given me the land of the [I]Negev, give me also springs of water." So Caleb gave her the upper springs and the lower[8482] springs.

16 And the [I]descendants of [a]the Kenite, Moses' father-in-law, went up from the [b]city of palms with the sons of Judah, to the wilderness of Judah which is in the south of [c]Arad; and they went and lived with the people.

17 Then Judah went with Simeon his brother, and they struck the Canaanites living in Zephath, and utterly destroyed[2763] it. So the name of the city was called[7121] [a]Hormah.

18 And Judah took [a]Gaza with its territory and Ashkelon with its territory and Ekron with its territory.

19 Now the LORD was with Judah, and they took possession of the hill country; but they could not [I]drive out the inhabitants of the valley because they had [a]iron chariots.

20 Then they gave Hebron to Caleb, [a]as Moses had [I]promised;[1696] and he drove out[3423] from there [b]the three sons[1121] of Anak.

21 [a]But the sons of Benjamin did not drive out the [b]Jebusites who lived in Jerusalem; so the Jebusites have lived with the sons of Benjamin in Jerusalem to this day.[3117]

22 Likewise the house[1004] of Joseph went up against Bethel, and the LORD was with them.

23 And the house of Joseph spied out Bethel ([a]now the name of the city was formerly Luz).

24 And the spies[8104] saw[7200] a man[376] coming out of the city, and they said to him, "Please[4994] show[7200] us the entrance to the city and [a]we will treat[6213] you kindly."[2617]

25 So he showed[7200] them the entrance to the city, and they struck[5221] the city with the edge of the sword, [a]but they let the man and all his family[4940] go free.

26 And the man went into the land of the Hittites and built a city and named it Luz [I]which is its name to this day.

Places Not Conquered

27 [a]But Manasseh did not take possession of Beth-shean and its villages, or Taanach and its villages, or the inhab-

9 [I]I.e., South country
10 [a]Josh. 15:13-19
11 [a]Josh. 15:15
13 [a]Judg. 3:9
14 [I]Lit., *the* [II]Lit., *for yourself* [a]Josh. 15:18
15 [I]I.e., South country
16 [I]Lit., *sons* [a]Num. 10:29-32; Judg. 4:11 [b]Deut. 34:3; Judg. 3:13 [c]Num. 21:1
17 [a]Num. 21:3
18 [a]Josh. 11:22
19 [I]Or, *dispossess* [a]Josh. 17:16; Judg. 4:3, 13
20 [I]Lit., *spoken* [a]Josh. 14:9 [b]Josh. 15:14; Judg. 1:10
21 [a]Josh. 15:63; Judg. 1:8 [b]1Chr. 11:4
23 [a]Gen. 28:19
24 [a]Josh. 2:12
25 [a]Josh. 6:25
26 [I]Lit., *it*
27 [a]Josh. 17:12

(continued from previous page)

called Salem in Ps. 76:2. Therefore, if the Salem of Gen. 14:18 applies to the same site, Melchizedek was one of its early kings. It did not become the capital of Israel until David drove out the Jebusites from the fortified southern hill known as Mount Zion (II Sam. 5:6-8; I Chr. 11:4-7). Apparently, during the period of the judges, the name "Jerusalem" could refer to a larger area than Mount Zion, because members of the tribe of Benjamin and the Jebusites may have coexisted in the city (Judg. 1:21).

itants of Dor and its villages, or the inhabitants of Ibleam and its villages, or the inhabitants of Megiddo and its villages; so [b]the Canaanites persisted in living in that land.

28 And it came about when Israel became strong,[2388] that they put the Canaanites to forced labor, but they did not drive them out completely.

29 [a]Neither did Ephraim drive out the Canaanites who were living in Gezer; so the Canaanites lived in Gezer among[7130] them.

30 Zebulun did not drive out the inhabitants of Kitron, or the inhabitants of Nahalol; so the Canaanites lived among them and became subject to forced labor.

31 Asher did not drive out the inhabitants of Acco, or the inhabitants of Sidon, or of Ahlab, or of Achzib, or of Helbah, or of Aphik, or of Rehob.

32 So the Asherites lived among the Canaanites, the inhabitants of the land; for they did not drive them out.

33 Naphtali did not drive out the inhabitants of Beth-shemesh, or the inhabitants of Beth-anath, but lived among the Canaanites, the inhabitants of the land; and the inhabitants of Beth-shemesh and Beth-anath became forced labor for them.

34 Then the Amorites [I]forced the sons of Dan into the hill country, for they did not allow them to come down to the valley;

35 yet the Amorites persisted in [I]living in Mount Heres, in Aijalon and in Shaalbim; but when the [II]power of the house of Joseph [III]grew strong,[3513] they became forced labor.

36 And the border of the Amorites ran from the [a]ascent of Akrabbim, from Sela and upward.

Israel Rebuked

2 Now [a]the angel[4397] of the LORD came up[5927] from Gilgal to [b]Bochim. And he said,[559] "[c]I brought you up[5927] out of Egypt and led you into the land which I have sworn[7650] to your fathers;[1] and I said, '[d]I will never break[6565] My covenant[1285] with you,

2 and as for you, [a]you shall make no covenant[1285] with the inhabitants of this land; [b]you shall tear down[5422] their altars.'[4196] But you have not [I]obeyed[8085] Me; what is this you have done?[6213]

3 "Therefore I also said, '[a]I will not drive them out before you; but they shall [I]become [b]*as thorns* in your sides, and their gods[430] shall be a snare[4170] to you.' "

4 And it came about when the angel of the LORD spoke[1696] these words[1697] to all the sons[1121] of Israel, that the people lifted up[5375] their voices and wept.

5 So they named[7121] that place [I]Bochim; and there they sacrificed[2076] to the LORD.

Joshua Dies

6 [a]When Joshua had dismissed the people, the sons of Israel went each[376] to his inheritance[5159] to possess[3423] the land.

7 And the people served[5647] the LORD all the days of Joshua, and all the days of the elders[2205] who [I]survived Joshua, who had seen[7200] all the great work of the LORD which He had done for Israel.

8 Then Joshua the son[1121] of Nun, the servant[5650] of the LORD, died at the age[1121] of one hundred and ten.

🔑 9 And they buried[6912] him in the territory of [a]his inheritance in Timnath-heres, in the hill country of Ephraim, north of Mount Gaash.

10 And all that generation[1755] also were gathered[622] to their fathers; and there arose another generation after them who [a]did not know[3045] the LORD, nor yet the work which He had done[6213] for Israel.

27 [b]Judg. 1:1
29 [a]Josh. 16:10
34 [I]Lit., *pressed*
35 [I]Lit., *dwelling* [II]Lit., *hand* [III]Lit., *was heavy*
36 [a]Josh. 15:3
1 [a]Judg. 6:11; 13:2-21 [b]Judg. 2:5 [c]Ex. 20:2 [d]Gen. 17:7, 8; Lev. 26:42, 44; Deut. 7:9
2 [I]Lit., *listened to My voice* [a]Ex. 23:32; Deut. 7:2-5 [b]Ex. 34:12, 13
3 [I]Some ancient mss. read *be adversaries, and* [a]Josh. 23:13 [b]Num. 33:55
5 [I]I.e., weepers
6 [a]Josh. 24:28-31
7 [I]Lit., *prolonged days after*
9 [a]Josh. 19:49f.
10 [a]Ex. 5:2; 1Sam. 2:12

🔑 **2:9** See note on Josh. 19:49,50.

Israel Serves Baals

11 Then the sons of Israel did
[a]evil[7451] in the sight of the LORD, and
[I]served the [b]Baals,
12 and [a]they forsook[5800] the LORD,
the God[430] of their fathers, who had
brought them out of the land of Egypt,
and followed other gods from *among* the
gods of the peoples who were around
them, and bowed[7812] themselves down
to them; thus they provoked the LORD
to anger.[3707]
🔑 13 So they forsook the LORD and
[a]served Baal and the Ashtaroth.
14 [a]And the anger[639] of the LORD
burned[2734] against Israel, and He gave
them into the hands[3027] of plunderers[8154]
who plundered them; and [b]He sold them
into the hands of their enemies around
them, so that they could no longer stand
before their enemies.
15 Wherever they went, the
hand[3027] of the LORD was against them
for evil, as the LORD had spoken[1696]
and [a]as the LORD had sworn[7650] to
them, so that they were severely distressed.
🔑 16 [a]Then the LORD raised up
judges[8199] [I]who delivered[3467] them from
the hands of those who plundered[8154]
them.
17 And yet they did not listen[8085]
to their judges, for they played the
harlot[2181] after other gods and bowed
themselves down to them. They turned
aside quickly from the way[1870] [a]in which
their fathers had walked in obeying the
commandments of the LORD; they did
not do as *their fathers.*
18 And when the LORD raised up
judges for them, [a]the LORD was with
the judge[8199] and delivered them from
the hand of their enemies all the days
of the judge; for the LORD was [b]moved
to pity[5162] by their groaning because of
those who oppressed and afflicted[1766]
them.
19 But it came about when the judge
died,[4191] that they would turn back[7725]

11 [I]Or, *worshiped* [a]Judg. 3:7, 12; 4:1; 6:1 [b]Judg. 6:25; 8:33; 10:6
12 [a]Deut. 31:16
13 [a]Judg. 10:6
14 [a]Deut. 31:17; Ps. 106:40-42 [b]Deut. 28:25; 32:30
15 [a]Lev. 26:14-39; Deut. 28:15-68
16 [I]Lit., *and they* [a]Ps. 106:43-45
17 [a]Judg. 2:7
18 [a]Josh. 1:5 [b]Deut. 32:36; Ps. 106:44

🔑 **2:13** The Canaanite deities mentioned in this verse seduced Israel for hundreds of years until she finally went into her two exiles. Thanks to a major archaeological find in Syria, the Ras Shamra (also known as Ugaritic) tablets have greatly enhanced our knowledge of Canaanite religion. The Book of Judges mentions at least four deities of a fairly extensive pantheon: Baal (2:13), Dagon (16:23), Asherah (3:7) and Ashtar (2:13). In the Baal Epic, found at Ugarit, Baal was the principal figure, although his father, El, was the highest of the Canaanite gods. The exploits of Baal and his sister and consort, Anath, were reenacted every year in the Canaanite agricultural calendar. In the epic, Baal was killed by monsters generated by Asherah, his mother and mortal enemy. Anath buried Baal, and when Mot, his brother and enemy, boasted about his power over Baal as god of death, Anath's anger turned into rage, and she cut him to pieces, burned him, ground the remains, and sowed them in a field. This action brought Baal back to life, and the tablets end with an intense struggle between Baal and Mot. Canaanite agriculture was so inextricably tied to religion that even the processes of sowing and reaping had complete religious overtones. Archaeologists have pointed out that even though, as a nomadic people, Israel was culturally inferior to the established urban Canaanites, the latter were in a period of decline and reflected by far the most degrading and corrupt culture in the whole area. God's judgment upon the Canaanites was such that there was nothing to redeem. Therefore, peaceful coexistence was not possible, and the Canaanite society had to be totally destroyed. The results of the seductive influence of Canaanite religion upon Israel for the next several hundred years proved God's judgment to be correct.

🔑 **2:16** This is the first mentioned of the term "judges" from which this book derived its name. Following Joshua's death, a period of decline began in Israel because of their unfaithfulness. There were recurring times of submission to the remaining people in the land and then of being delivered from them. In this unstable time before the appearance of the prophets God gave them leaders called "judges" to work their deliverance. There were thirteen judges in all, of which eleven are mentioned in this book. Eli and Samuel come at the end of this period and are treated in the Book of First Samuel. The term "judge" implied that their leadership extended not only to legal cases but also to government and the military as well. They did not have the stature of Moses and Joshua before them nor the prestige of the kings who followed. None of them had the total support of all twelve tribes. It was a time of confusion and turmoil.

and act more corruptly[7843] than their fathers, in following other gods to
serve[5647] them and bow down to them;
they did not abandon their practices or
their stubborn[7186] ways.
20 [a]So the anger of the LORD burned
against Israel, and He said, "Because
this nation[1471] has transgressed[5674] My
covenant which I commanded[6680] their
fathers, and has not listened[8085] to My
voice,
21 [a]I also will no longer drive out
before them any of the nations[1471] which
Joshua left[5800] when he died,
22 in order to [a]test[5254] Israel by
them, whether they will keep[8104] the
way of the LORD to walk in it as their
fathers [I]did, or not."
23 So the LORD allowed those nations to remain, not driving them out
quickly; and He did not give them into
the hand of Joshua.

Idolatry Leads to Servitude

3 [a]Now these are the nations[1471]
which the LORD left, to test[5254] Israel by them (*that is,* all who had not
[I]experienced[3045] any of the wars of Canaan;
2 only in order that the generations[1755] of the sons[1121] of Israel
might [I]be taught[3925] war, [II]those who
had not [III]experienced[3045] it formerly).
3 *These nations are:* the five
lords[5633] of the Philistines and all the
Canaanites and the Sidonians and
[a]the Hivites who lived in Mount Lebanon, from Mount Baal-hermon as far
as [I]Lebo-hamath.
4 And they were for [I][a]testing Israel,
to find out if they would [II]obey[8085] the
commandments of the LORD, which He
had commanded[6680] their fathers[1]
[III]through[3027] Moses.
5 And [a]the sons of Israel lived
among[7130] the Canaanites, the Hittites,
the Amorites, the Perizzites, the Hivites, and the Jebusites;
6 and [a]they took their daughters for
themselves as wives,[802] and gave their
own daughters to their sons,[1121] and
served[5647] their gods.[430]
7 And the sons of Israel did [a]what
was evil[7451] in the sight of the LORD,
and [b]forgot the LORD their God,[430] and
[c]served the Baals and the [I]Asheroth.[842]
8 Then the anger[639] of the LORD was
kindled[2734] against Israel, so that He sold
them into the hands of Cushan-rishathaim king[4428] of [I]Mesopotamia; and the
sons of Israel served Cushan-rishathaim
eight years.

The First Judge Delivers Israel

9 And when the sons of Israel
cried[2199] to the LORD, the LORD raised
up a deliverer[3467] for the sons of Israel
to deliver[3467] them, [a]Othniel the son[1121]
of Kenaz, Caleb's younger brother.[251]
10 And [a]the Spirit[7307] of the LORD
came upon him, and he judged[8199] Israel.
When he went out to war, the LORD
gave Cushan-rishathaim king of [I]Meso-
potamia into his hand, so that [II]he prevailed over Cushan-rishathaim.
11 Then the land[776] had rest[8252]
forty years. And Othniel the son of
Kenaz died.
12 Now the sons of Israel again
[a]did evil in the sight of the LORD. So
[b]the LORD strengthened[2388] Eglon the
king of Moab against Israel, because
they had done[6213] evil in the sight of
the LORD.
13 And he gathered[622] to himself the
sons of Ammon and Amalek; and he
went and [I]defeated[5221] Israel, and they
possessed[3423] [a]the city of the palm trees.
14 And the sons of Israel served
Eglon the king of Moab eighteen years.

Ehud Delivers from Moab

15 But when the sons of Israel
[a]cried to the LORD, the LORD raised up
a deliverer for them, Ehud the son of

20 [a]Judg. 2:14
21 [a]Josh. 23:4, 5, 13
22 [I]Lit., *kept* [a]Deut. 8:2; 13:3
1 [I]Lit., *known* [a]Judg. 1:1; 2:21, 22
2 [I]Lit., *know, to teach them* [II]Lit., *only* [III]Lit., *known*
3 [I]Or, *the entrance of Hamath* [a]Josh. 9:7; 11:19
4 [I]Lit., *testing by them* [II]Lit., *hear* [III]Lit., *by the hand of* [a]Deut. 8:2
5 [a]Ps. 106:35
6 [a]Ex. 34:15, 16; Deut. 7:3, 4; Josh. 23:12
7 [I]I.e., wooden symbol of a female deity [a]Judg. 2:11 [b]Deut. 4:9 [c]Judg. 2:13
8 [I]Heb., *Aram-naharaim*
9 [a]Judg. 1:13
10 [I]Heb., *Aram* [II]Lit., *his hand was strong* [a]Num. 11:25-29; 24:2
12 [a]Judg. 2:11 [b]Judg. 2:14
13 [I]Lit., *smote* [a]Deut. 34:3; Judg. 1:16
15 [a]Ps. 78:34

3:7 The word transliterated "Asheroth" refers to the shrines of the Canaanites goddess, Asherah. See note on Judg. 2:13.

Gera, the Benjamite, a left-handed man.[376] And the sons of Israel sent tribute[4503] by [I]him to Eglon the king of Moab.

16 And Ehud made[6213] himself a sword which had two edges, a cubit in length;[753] and he bound it on his right thigh[3409] under his cloak.

17 And he presented[7126] the tribute to Eglon king of Moab. Now Eglon was a very fat man.

18 And it came about when he had finished[3615] presenting the tribute, that he sent away the people[5971] who had carried[5375] the tribute.

19 But he himself turned back[7725] from the idols[6456] which were at Gilgal, and said,[559] "I have a secret message for you, O king." And he said, "Keep[8104] silence." And all who attended him left him.

20 And Ehud came to him while he was sitting alone in his cool roof chamber. And Ehud said, "I have a message from God for you." And he arose from his seat.[3678]

21 And Ehud stretched out his left hand, took the sword from his right thigh and thrust it into his belly.[990]

22 The handle also went in after the blade, and the fat closed over the blade, for he did not draw the sword out of his belly; and the refuse came out.

23 Then Ehud went out into the vestibule and shut the doors of the roof chamber behind him, and locked *them*.

24 When he had gone out, his servants[5650] came and looked,[7200] and behold, the doors of the roof chamber were locked; and they said, "[a]He is only [I]relieving himself in the cool room."

25 And they waited[2342] until they [I]became anxious;[954] but behold, he did not open the doors of the roof chamber. Therefore they took the key and opened them, and behold, their master[113] had fallen[5307] to the [II]floor[776] dead.[4191]

26 Now Ehud escaped[4422] while they were delaying, and he passed by[5674] the idols and escaped to Seirah.

27 And it came about when he had arrived, that [a]he blew[8628] the trumpet in the hill country of Ephraim; and the sons of Israel went down with him from the hill country, and he *was* in front of them.

28 And he said to them, "Pursue *them*, for the LORD has given your enemies the Moabites into your hands." So they went down after him and seized [a]the fords of the Jordan opposite Moab, and did not allow anyone to cross.

29 And they struck down[5221] at that time[6256] about ten thousand Moabites, all robust and valiant[2428] men;[376] and no one escaped.

30 So Moab was subdued that day[3117] under the hand of Israel. And the land was undisturbed for eighty years.

Shamgar Delivers from Philistines

31 And after him came [a]Shamgar the son of Anath, who struck down six hundred Philistines with an oxgoad;[4451] and he also saved Israel.

Deborah and Barak Deliver from Canaanites

4 Then [a]the sons[1121] of Israel again did evil[7451] in the sight of the LORD, after Ehud died.[4191]

🗝 2 And the LORD sold them into the hand[3027] of [a]Jabin king[4428] of Canaan, who reigned in Hazor; and the commander[8269] of his army[6635] was Sisera, who lived in [b]Harosheth-hagoyim.[1471]

3 And the sons of Israel cried to the LORD; for he had nine hundred [a]iron chariots, and he oppressed the sons of Israel severely for twenty years.

15 [I]Lit., *his hand*
24 [I]Lit., *covering his feet* [a]1Sam. 24:3
25 [I]Lit., *were ashamed* [II]Lit., *earth*
27 [a]Judg. 6:34; 1Sam. 13:3
28 [a]Judg. 7:24; 12:5
31 [a]Judg. 5:6
1 [a]Judg. 2:19
2 [a]Josh. 11:1, 10 [b]Judg. 4:13, 16
3 [a]Judg. 1:19

🗝 **4:2** Jabin was probably a title for the king of the Canaanites (Josh. 11:1; Judg. 4:23,24), just as Pharaoh was a title for the kings of Egypt.

4 Now Deborah, a [I]prophetess,[5031]
the wife[802] of Lappidoth, was judging[8199]
Israel at that time.[6256]
5 And she used to [I]sit under the
[a]palm tree of Deborah between Ramah
and Bethel in the hill country of Ephraim;
and the sons of Israel came up[5927] to
her for judgment.[4941]
6 Now she sent and summoned[7121]
[a]Barak the son[1121] of Abinoam from Ke-
desh-naphtali, and said[559] to him, "[I]Be-
hold, the LORD, the God[430] of Israel,
has commanded,[6680] 'Go and march to
Mount Tabor, and take with you ten
thousand men[376] from the sons of Naphtali and from the sons of Zebulun.
7 'And I will draw out to you Sisera,
the commander of Jabin's army,[6635] with
his chariots and his [I]many *troops* to the
river Kishon; and [a]I will give him into
your hand.' "
8 Then Barak said to her, "If you
will go with me, then I will go; but if
you will not go with me, I will not go."
9 And she said, "I will surely go with
you; nevertheless, the honor[8597] shall
not be yours on the journey that you
are about to take, [a]for the LORD will
sell Sisera into the hands of a woman."[802]
Then Deborah arose and went with Barak to Kedesh.
10 And Barak called [a]Zebulun and
Naphtali together to Kedesh, and ten
thousand men went up[5927] [I][b]with him;
Deborah also went up with him.
11 Now Heber [a]the Kenite had separated himself from the Kenites, from
the sons of Hobab the father-in-law of
Moses, and had pitched his tent[168] as
far away as the [I]oak in [b]Zaanannim,
which is near Kedesh.
12 Then they told[5046] Sisera that
Barak the son of Abinoam had gone[5927]
up to Mount Tabor.
13 And Sisera called together[2199] all
his chariots, [a]nine hundred iron chariots,
and all the people[5971] who *were* with him,
from [b]Harosheth-hagoyim to the river
Kishon.
14 And Deborah said to Barak,
"Arise! For this is the day[3117] in which
the LORD has given Sisera into your
hands; [I]behold, [a]the LORD has gone out
before you." So Barak went down from
Mount Tabor with ten thousand men
following him.
15 [a]And the LORD [I]routed[2000] Sisera
and all *his* chariots and all *his* army,[4264]
with the edge[6310] of the sword[2719] before
Barak; and Sisera alighted from *his* chariot and fled away on foot.
16 But Barak pursued the chariots
and the army as far as Harosheth-
hagoyim, and all the army of Sisera
fell[5307] by the edge of the sword; [a]not
even one was left.[7604]
17 Now Sisera fled away on foot
to the tent of Jael the wife of Heber
the Kenite, for *there was* peace[7965] between Jabin the king of Hazor and the
house[1004] of Heber the Kenite.
18 And Jael went out to meet Sisera,
and said to him, "Turn aside, my master,[113] turn aside to me! Do not be
afraid."[3372] And he turned aside[5493] to
her into the tent, and she covered[3680]
him with a [I]rug.[8063]
19 [a]And he said to her, "Please[4994]
give me a little water to drink, for I
am thirsty." So she opened a [I]bottle of
milk and gave him a drink; then she
covered him.
20 And he said to her, "Stand in
the doorway of the tent, and it shall
be if anyone[376] comes and inquires[7592]
of you, and says,[559] 'Is there anyone
here?' that you shall say, 'No.' "
21 But Jael, Heber's wife, [a]took a
tent peg and [I]seized a hammer in her
hand, and went secretly to him and

4 [I]Lit., *woman prophetess*
5 [I]Or, *live* [a]Gen. 35:8
6 [I]Or, *Has not . . . commanded . . .?* [a]Heb. 11:32
7 [I]Lit., *multitude* [a]Ps. 83:9
9 [a]Judg. 4:21
10 [I]Lit., *at his feet* [a]Judg. 5:18 [b]Judg. 4:14; 5:15
11 [I]Or, *terebinth* [a]Judg. 1:16 [b]Josh. 19:33
13 [a]Judg. 4:3 [b]Judg. 4:2
14 [I]Or, *has not the LORD gone . . .?* [a]Deut. 9:3; 2Sam. 5:24; Ps. 68:7
15 [I]Lit., *confused* [a]Deut. 7:23; Josh. 10:10
16 [a]Ex. 14:28; Ps. 83:9
18 [I]Or, *blanket*
19 [I]I.e., skin container [a]Judg. 5:24-27
21 [I]Lit., *placed* [a]Judg. 5:26

4:4 Deborah means "bee." She was also called "a prophetess." In vv. 6,9,14 are examples of her prophetic powers. Though no other judge is expressly called a prophet, they all seem to have had direct communications from God either through special knowledge or power.

4:6,8 Barak's hesitancy to lead armies apart from Deborah's presence resulted in the diminution of his glory (v. 9). Nevertheless, he is listed among the heroes of faith (Heb. 11:32). His faith consisted of his obedience to God's commands issued through Deborah (vv. 6,10,14).

drove the peg into his temple, and it went through into the ground;[776] for he was sound asleep and exhausted. So he died.

22 And behold, as Barak pursued Sisera, Jael came out to meet him and said to him, "Come, and I will show[7200] you the man whom you are seeking." And he entered [I]with her, and behold Sisera was lying dead with the tent peg in his temple.

23 So [a]God subdued on that day Jabin the king of Canaan before the sons of Israel.

24 And the hand of the sons of Israel pressed heavier and heavier upon Jabin the king of Canaan, until they had [I]destroyed[3772] Jabin the king of Canaan.

The Song of Deborah and Barak

5 [a]Then Deborah and Barak the son of Abinoam sang[7891] on that day,[3117] saying,

2 "[a]That [I]the leaders led in Israel,
That [b]the people volunteered,[5068]
Bless[5971] the LORD!
3 "Hear,[8085] O kings;[4428] give ear,[238] O rulers![7336]
[a]I—to the LORD, I will sing,[7891]
I will sing praise[2167] to the LORD, the God[430] of Israel.
4 "[a]LORD, when Thou didst go out from Seir,
When Thou didst march from the field[7704] of Edom,
[b]The earth[776] quaked,[7493] the heavens[8064] also dripped,
Even the clouds dripped water.
5 "[a]The mountains [I]quaked at the presence of the LORD,
[b]This Sinai, at the presence of the LORD, the God of Israel.
6 "In the days of [a]Shamgar the son of Anath,
In the days of [b]Jael, the highways[734] [I]were deserted,
And travelers [II]went by [III]roundabout ways.
7 "The peasantry ceased, they ceased in Israel,
Until I, Deborah, arose,
Until I arose, a mother[517] in Israel.
8 "[a]New gods[430] were chosen;[977]
Then war *was* in the gates.
Not a shield or a spear was seen[7200]
Among forty thousand in Israel.
9 "My heart[3820] *goes out* to [a]the commanders[2710] of Israel,
The volunteers[5068] among the people;
Bless[1288] the LORD!
10 "[a]You who ride on [I]white donkeys,
You who sit on *rich* carpets,
And you who travel on the road—[1870] [II]sing[7878]
11 "At the sound of those who divide *flocks* among [a]the watering places,
There they shall recount [b]the righteous deeds[6666] of the LORD,
The righteous deeds for His [I]peasantry in Israel.
Then the people of the LORD went down [c]to the gates.
12 "[a]Awake, awake, Deborah;
Awake, awake, [I]sing a song![7892]
Arise, Barak, and [b]take away[7617] your captives,[7628] O son of Abinoam.
13 "Then survivors[8300] came down[7287] to the nobles;[117]
The people of the LORD came down to me as warriors.
14 "From Ephraim those whose root is [a]in Amalek *came down,*
Following you, Benjamin, with your peoples;
From Machir commanders came down,
And from Zebulun those who wield[5608] the staff of [I]office.
15 "And the [I]princes[8269] of Issachar *were* with Deborah;
As *was* Issachar, so *was* Barak;
Into the valley they rushed [a]at his [II]heels;

22 [I]Lit., *to*
23 [a]Neh. 9:24; Ps. 18:47
24 [I]Lit., *cut off*
1 [a]Ex. 15:1
2 [I]Or, *locks hung loose in* [a]Judg. 5:9 [b]Ps. 110:3
3 [a]Ps. 27:6
4 [a]Deut. 33:2; Ps. 68:7 [b]Ps. 68:8, 9
5 [I]Lit., *flowed* [a]Ex. 19:18 [b]Ps. 68:8
6 [I]Lit., *had ceased* [II]Lit., *walked* [III]Lit., *twisted* [a]Judg. 3:31 [b]Judg. 4:17
8 [a]Deut. 32:17
9 [a]Judg. 5:2
10 [I]Or, *tawny* [II]Or, *declare it* [a]Judg. 10:4; 12:14
11 [I]Or, *rural dwellers* [a]Gen. 24:11; 29:2, 3 [b]1Sam. 12:7; Mic. 6:5 [c]Judg. 5:8
12 [I]Or, *utter* [a]Ps. 57:8 [b]Ps. 68:18; Eph. 4:8
14 [I]Lit., *the scribe* [a]Judg. 12:15
15 [I]So with ancient versions; Heb., *My princes* [II]Lit., *feet* [a]Judg. 4:10

Among the divisions[6391] of
Reuben
There were great resolves[2711] of
heart.
16 "Why did you sit[3427] among
[a]the [I]sheepfolds,
To hear the piping[8292] for the
flocks?
Among the divisions of Reuben
There were great searchings of
heart.
17 "[a]Gilead [I]remained[7931] across the
Jordan;
And why did Dan stay in ships?
Asher sat at the seashore,
And [I]remained by its landings.
18 "[a]Zebulun *was* a people who
despised their lives *even* to
death,[4191]
And Naphtali also, on the high
places of the field.
19"[a]The kings came *and* fought;
Then fought the kings of Canaan
[b]At Taanach near the waters of
Megiddo;
[c]They took no plunder in silver.
20 "[a]The stars fought from
heaven,[8064]
From their courses they fought
against Sisera.
21 "The torrent of Kishon swept
them away,
The ancient torrent, the torrent
Kishon.
[a]O my soul,[5315] march on with
strength.
22 "[a]Then the horses' hoofs beat[1986]
From the dashing, the dashing
of his [I]valiant[47] steeds.
23 'Curse[779] Meroz,' said[559] the
angel[4397] of the LORD,
'Utterly curse[779] its inhabitants;
[a]Because they did not come to
the help of the LORD,
To the help of the LORD against
the warriors.'
24"[a]Most blessed[1288] of women[802]
is Jael,
The wife[802] of Heber the Kenite;
Most blessed is she of women
in the tent.[168]

25 "He asked[7592] for water *and* she
gave him milk;
In a magnificent[117] bowl she
brought[7126] him curds.
26 "She reached out her hand[3027] for
the tent peg,
And her right hand for the
workmen's hammer.
Then she struck[1986] Sisera, she
smashed[4277] his head;[7218]
And she shattered and
pierced[4272] his temple.
27 "Between her feet he bowed,[3766]
he fell, he lay;
Between her feet he bowed, he
fell;[5307]
Where he bowed, there he
fell[5307] [I]dead.[7703]
28"Out of the window she looked
and lamented,
The mother of Sisera through
the [I]lattice,[822]
'Why does his chariot delay in
coming?
Why do the [II]hoofbeats of his
chariots tarry?'
29 "Her wise[2450] princesses[8282]
would answer[559] her,
Indeed she repeats[7725] her
words to herself,
30 '[a]Are they not finding, are they
not dividing the spoil?
A maiden, two maidens for
every warrior;[1397]
To Sisera a spoil of dyed work,
A spoil of dyed work
embroidered,
Dyed work of double
embroidery on the [I]neck of
the spoiler?'
31 "[a]Thus let all Thine enemies
perish,[6] O LORD;
[b]But let those who love[157] Him
be like the rising of the sun
in its might."
And the land[766] was undisturbed[8252] for
forty years.

Israel Oppressed by Midian

6 Then the sons[1121] of Israel [a]did what
was evil[7451] in the sight of the LORD;

16 [I]Or, *saddlebags* [a]Num. 32:1, 2, 24, 36
17 [I]Or, *dwelt* [a]Josh. 22:9
18 [a]Judg. 4:6, 10
19 [a]Josh. 11:1-5; Judg. 4:13 [b]Judg. 1:27 [c]Judg. 5:30
20 [a]Josh. 10:12-14
21 [a]Ex. 15:2; Ps. 44:5
22 [I]Lit., *mighty ones* [a]Job 39:19-25
23 [a]Judg. 5:13
24 [a]Judg. 4:19-21
27 [I]Lit., *devastated*
28 [I]Or, *window* [II]Lit., *steps*
30 [I]Lit., *necks of the spoil* [a]Ex. 15:9
31 [a]Ps. 68:2; 92:9 [b]Ps. 19:4-6; 89:36, 37
1 [a]Judg. 2:11

and the LORD gave them into the hands[3027] of [b]Midian seven years.

2 And the [I]power of Midian prevailed against Israel. Because of Midian the sons of Israel made[6213] for themselves [a]the dens which were in the mountains and the caves and the strongholds.

3 For it was when Israel had sown, that the Midianites would come up[5927] with the Amalekites and the sons of the east and [I]go against them.

4 So they would camp against them and [a]destroy[7843] the produce of the earth[776] [I]as far as Gaza, and [b]leave no sustenance[4241] in Israel as well as no sheep, ox, or donkey.

5 For they would come up with their livestock and their tents,[168] they would come in [a]like locusts for number, both they and their camels were innumerable; and they came into the land[776] to devastate[7843] it.

6 So Israel was brought [a]very low because of Midian, and the sons of Israel cried[2199] to the LORD.

7 Now it came about when the sons of Israel cried to the LORD on account of Midian,

8 that the LORD sent a prophet[5030] to the sons of Israel, and [a]he said[559] to them, "Thus says[559] the LORD, the God[430] of Israel, 'It was I who brought[5927] you up from Egypt, and brought you out from the house[1004] of [I]slavery.[5650]

9 'And I delivered[5337] you from the hands of the Egyptians and from the hands of all your oppressors, and dispossessed them before you and gave you their land,

10 and I said to you, "I am the LORD your God; you [a]shall not fear[3372] the gods[430] of the Amorites in whose land you live. But you have not [I]obeyed[8085] Me." ' "

Gideon Is Visited

11 Then [a]the angel[4397] of the LORD came and sat under the [I]oak that was in Ophrah, which belonged to Joash the [b]Abiezrite as his son[1121] [c]Gideon was beating out wheat in the wine press in order to save *it* from the Midianites.

12 And the angel of the LORD appeared[7200] to him and said to him, "The LORD is with you, O valiant[2428] warrior."

13 Then Gideon said to him, "O my lord,[113] if the LORD is with us, why then has all this happened to us? And where are all His miracles[6381] which our fathers[1] told[5046] us about, saying, 'Did not the LORD bring us up from Egypt?' But [a]now the LORD has abandoned[5203] us and given us into the hand[3709] of Midian."

14 And the LORD [I]looked at him and said, "[a]Go in this your strength and deliver[3467] Israel from the hand of Midian. Have I not sent you?"

15 [a]And he said to Him, "O Lord, [I]how shall I deliver Israel? Behold, my family is the least in [b]Manasseh, and I am the youngest in my father's[1] house."

16 [a]But the LORD said to him, "Surely I will be with you, and you shall [I]defeat[5221] Midian as one man."[376]

17 So [I]Gideon said to Him, "If now I have found favor[2580] in Thy sight, then show[6213] me [a]a sign[226] that it is Thou who speakest[1696] with me.

18 "Please[4994] do not depart from here, until I come *back* to Thee, and bring out my offering[4503] and lay it before Thee." And He said, "I will remain until you return."[7725]

19 Then Gideon went in and [a]prepared a kid and unleavened[4682] bread from an [I]ephah of flour; he put the meat[1320] in a basket [II]and the broth in a pot, and brought *them* out to him under the [III]oak, and presented[5066] *them*.

20 And the angel of God said to him, "Take the meat and the unleavened bread and lay them on this rock, and pour[8210] out the broth." And he did so.

21 Then the angel of the LORD put out the end of the staff that was in his hand and touched[5060] the meat and the unleavened bread; and [a]fire sprang up[5927] from the rock and consumed the meat and the unleavened bread. Then

1 [b]Num. 22:4; 25:15-18; 31:1-3
2 [I]Lit., *hand* [a]1Sam. 13:6; Heb. 11:38
3 [I]Lit., *go up*
4 [I]Lit., *until your coming to* [a]Lev. 26:16 [b]Deut. 28:31
5 [a]Judg. 7:12; 8:10
6 [a]Deut. 28:43
8 [I]Lit., *slaves* [a]Judg. 2:1, 2
10 [I]Lit., *listened to My voice* [a]2Kin. 17:35; Jer. 10:2
11 [I]Or, *terebinth* [a]Judg. 2:1; 6:14; 13:3 [b]Josh. 17:2; Judg. 6:15 [c]Heb. 11:32
13 [a]Judg. 6:1; Ps. 44:9
14 [I]Or, *turned toward* [a]Heb. 11:32-34
15 [I]Lit., *with what* [a]Ex. 3:11 [b]Judg. 6:11
16 [I]Lit., *smite* [a]Ex. 3:12; Josh. 1:5
17 [I]Lit., *he* [a]Judg. 6:37; Is. 38:7, 8
19 [I]I.e., Approx. one bu. [II]Lit., *and he put* [III]Or, *terebinth* [a]Gen. 18:6-8
21 [a]Lev. 9:24

the angel of the LORD [I]vanished from his sight.

22 [a]When Gideon saw[7200] that he was the angel of the LORD,[136] [I]he said, "Alas, O Lord [II]GOD! For now I have seen[7200] the angel of the LORD face to face."

23 And the LORD said to him, "Peace[7965] to you, do not fear; you shall not die."[4191]

24 Then Gideon built an altar there to the LORD and named[7121] it [I]The LORD is Peace. To this day[3117] it is still [a]in Ophrah of the Abiezrites.

25 Now the same night[3915] it came about that the LORD said to him, "Take your father's bull [I]and a second bull seven years old, and pull down[2040] the altar of Baal which belongs to your father,[1] and cut down[3772] the [IIa]Asherah[842] that is beside it;

26 and build an altar to the LORD your God on the top[7218] of this stronghold in an orderly manner, and take a second bull and offer a burnt offering[5930] with the wood of the Asherah which you shall cut down."

27 Then Gideon took ten men[582] of his servants[5650] and did[6213] as the LORD had spoken[1696] to him; and it came about, because he was too afraid[3372] of his father's household[1004] and the men of the city to do[6213] it by day,[3119] that he did it by night.

The Altar of Baal Destroyed

28 When the men of the city arose early in the morning, behold, the altar of Baal was torn down,[5422] and the Asherah which was beside it was cut down, and the second bull was offered[5927] on the altar which had been built.

29 And they said to one[376] another,[7453] "Who did[6213] this thing?"[1697] And when they searched about and inquired, they said, "Gideon the son of Joash did this thing."

30 Then the men of the city said to Joash, "Bring out your son, that he may die, for he has torn down the altar of Baal, and indeed, he has cut down the Asherah which was beside it."

31 But Joash said to all who stood against him, "Will you contend[7378] for Baal, or will you deliver him? Whoever will [I]plead for him shall be put to death[4191] by morning. If he is a god, let him contend for himself, because someone has torn down his altar."

32 Therefore on that day he named him [a]Jerubbaal, that is to say, "Let Baal contend against him," because he had torn down[5422] his altar.

33 Then all the Midianites and the Amalekites and the sons of the east assembled[622] themselves; and they crossed over[5674] and camped in [a]the valley of Jezreel.

34 So [a]the Spirit[7307] of the LORD [I]came upon Gideon; and he [b]blew[8628] a trumpet, and the Abiezrites were called together[2199] to follow him.

35 And he sent messengers[4397] throughout Manasseh, and they also were called together to follow him; and he sent messengers to Asher, [a]Zebulun, and Naphtali, and [b]they came up to meet them.

Sign of the Fleece

🗝 **36** Then Gideon said to God, "[a]If Thou wilt deliver Israel [I]through me, as Thou hast spoken,

37 behold, I will put a fleece of wool on the threshing floor. If there is dew on the fleece only, and it is dry on all

21 [I]Or, *departed*

22 [I]Lit., *Gideon* [II]Heb., *YHWH,* usually rendered LORD [a]Gen. 32:30; Ex. 33:20; Judg. 13:21, 22

24 [I]Heb., *Yahweh-shalom* [a]Judg. 8:32

25 [I]Or, *even* [II]I.e., wooden symbol of a female deity, also vv. 26, 28, 30 [a]Ex. 34:13

31 [I]Or, *contend*

32 [a]Judg. 7:1

33 [a]Josh. 17:16

34 [I]Lit., *clothed* [a]Judg. 3:10 [b]Judg. 3:27

35 [a]Judg. 4:6, 10; 5:18 [b]Judg. 7:3

36 [I]Lit., *by my hand* [a]Judg. 6:14, 16, 17

🗝 **6:36,37** Gideon wanted full assurance that he really had a promise from God. The caution he used here in no way implies that he doubted God's faithfulness or ability to fulfil His promise. He was simply seeking divine confirmation that he indeed was being guided by God's will. That there is no trace of doubt in his character is further confirmed in the N.T. when Gideon is set forth as a worthy example of faith (Heb. 11:32). The threshing floor was usually outside in the open air where it would normally collect moisture during the night from the dew. The second sign in v. 40 was even more convincing than this because it was the nature of the fleece to attract and retain moisture.

the ground, then I will know[3045] that
Thou wilt deliver Israel [I]through me,
as Thou hast spoken."
38 And it was so. When he arose
early the next morning and squeezed
the fleece, he drained the dew from the
fleece, a bowl full of water.
39 Then Gideon said to God, "[a]Do
not let Thine anger[639] burn[2734] against
me that I may speak[1696] once more;
please let me make a test[5254] once more
with the fleece, let it now be dry only
on the fleece, and let there be dew on
all the ground."[776]
40 And God did so that night; for
it was dry only on the fleece, and dew
was on all the ground.

Gideon's 300 Chosen Men

7 Then [a]Jerubbaal (that is, Gideon)
and all the people[5971] who were with
him, rose early and camped beside
[I]the spring of Harod; and the camp[4264]
of Midian was on the north side of
[II]them by the hill of [b]Moreh in the valley.
2 And the LORD said[559] to Gideon,
"The people who are with you are too
many for Me to give Midian into their
hands,[3027] [a]lest Israel [I]become boastful,[6286] saying, 'My own [II]power[3027] has
delivered me.'
3 "Now therefore [I]come,[4994] proclaim[7121] in the hearing[241] of the people, saying, '[a]Whoever is afraid[3373] and
trembling,[2730] let him return[7725] and depart from Mount Gilead.'" So 22,000
people returned,[7725] but 10,000 remained.[7604]
4 [a]Then the LORD said to Gideon,
"The people are still too many; bring
them down to the water and I will test[6884]
them for you there. Therefore it shall
be that he of whom I say[559] to you,
'This one shall go with you,' he shall
go with you; but everyone of whom I
say to you, 'This one shall not go with
you,' he shall not go."
5 So he brought the people down
to the water. And the LORD said to Gideon, "You shall separate everyone who
laps the water with his tongue, as a
dog laps, as well as everyone who
kneels[3766] to drink."
6 Now the number of those who
lapped, putting their hand to their
mouth,[6310] was 300 men; but all the
rest[3499] of the people kneeled[3766] to
drink water.
7 And the LORD said to Gideon, "I
will deliver[3467] you [a]with the 300 men
who lapped and will give the Midianites
into your hands; so let all the *other* people go, each man[376] to his [I]home."
8 So [I]the 300 men took the people's
provisions[6720] and their trumpets into
their hands. And [II]Gideon sent all the
other men of Israel, each to his tent,[168]
but retained the 300 men; and the camp
of Midian was below him in the valley.
9 Now the same night[3915] it came
about that the LORD said to him, "Arise,
go down against the camp, [a]for I have
given it into your hands.
10 "But if you are afraid[3373] to go
down, go with Purah your servant down
to the camp,
11 and you will hear[8085] what they
say;[1696] and [a]afterward your hands will
be strengthened[2388] that you may go
down against the camp." So he went
with Purah his servant down to the
[I]outposts of the army that was in the
camp.
12 Now the Midianites and the Amalekites and all the sons[1121] of the east
were lying in the valley [a]as numerous
as locusts; and their camels were without number, [b]as numerous as the sand
on the seashore.[8193,3220]
13 When Gideon came, behold, a
man was relating[5608] a dream to his
friend.[7453] And he said, "Behold, I
[I]had a dream; [II]a loaf of barley bread
was tumbling[2015] into the camp of
Midian, and it came to the tent and

37 [I]Lit., *by my hand*
39 [a]Gen. 18:32
1 [I]Or, *En-Harod* [II]Lit., *him* [a]Judg. 6:32 [b]Gen. 12:6; Deut. 11:30
2 [I]Lit., *glorify itself against me* [II]Lit., *hand* [a]Deut. 8:17, 18
3 [I]Or, *please* [a]Deut. 20:8
4 [a]1Sam. 14:6
7 [I]Lit., *place* [a]1Sam. 14:6
8 [I]Lit., *they* [II]Lit., *he*
9 [a]Josh. 2:24; 10:8; 11:6
11 [I]Lit., *extremity of the battle array* [a]Judg. 7:15; 1Sam. 14:9, 10
12 [a]Judg. 6:5; 8:10 [b]Josh. 11:4
13 [I]Lit., *dreamed* [II]Lit., *and behold, a loaf*

7:5 Those who cupped the water in their hands could scan the area for enemies while they drank. They were more alert than the majority of the soldiers.

struck[5221] it so that it fell,[5307] and turned
it [III]upside down so that the tent lay
flat."
14 And his friend answered and said,
"This is nothing less than the sword[2719]
of Gideon the son[1121] of Joash, a man
of Israel; God[430] has given Midian and
all the camp [a]into his hand."
15 And it came about when Gideon
heard[8085] the account of the dream and
its interpretation,[7667] that he bowed in
worship.[7812] He returned to the camp
of Israel and said, "Arise, for the LORD
has given the camp of Midian into your
hands."
16 And he divided the 300 men into
three [I]companies,[7218] and he put trumpets and empty pitchers into the hands
of all of them, with torches inside the
pitchers.
17 And he said to them, "Look at
me, and do[6213] likewise. And behold,
when I come to the outskirts of the
camp,[4264] [I]do as I do.
18 "When I and all who are with
me blow the trumpet, then you also
blow[8628] the trumpets all around the
camp, and say, 'For the LORD and for
Gideon.' "

Confusion of the Enemy

19 So Gideon and the hundred men
who were with him came to the outskirts
of the camp at the beginning[7218] of the
middle watch, when they had just posted
the watch;[8104] and they blew[8628] the
trumpets and smashed the pitchers that
were in their hands.
20 When the three [I]companies blew
the trumpets and broke[7665] the pitchers, they held[2388] the torches in their
left hands and the trumpets in their
right hands for blowing, and cried,[7121]
"A sword for the LORD and for Gideon!"
21 And each stood in his place
around the camp; and [a]all the [I]army ran,
crying out[7321] as they fled.
22 And when they blew 300 trumpets, the [a]LORD set[7760] the sword of

13 [III]Lit., *upwards*
14 [a]Josh. 2:9
16 [I]Lit., *heads*
17 [I]Lit., *it shall come about that just as I do, so you shall do.*
20 [I]Lit., *heads*
21 [I]Or, *camp* [a]2Kin. 7:7
22 [I]Or, *camp* [a]1Sam. 14:20 [b]1Kin. 4:12; 19:16
23 [a]Judg. 6:35
24 [I]Lit., *to meet* [a]Judg. 3:28
25 [a]Ps. 83:11; Is. 10:26 [b]Judg. 8:4
1 [a]Judg. 12:1
3 [I]Lit., *spirit* [II]Lit., *this thing*
4 [a]Judg. 7:25
5 [a]Gen. 33:17

one against another even throughout the
whole [I]army; and the [I]army fled as far
as Beth-shittah toward Zererah, as far
as the edge[8193] of [b]Abel-meholah, by
Tabbath.
23 And the men of Israel were
summoned from [a]Naphtali and Asher
and all Manasseh, and they pursued
Midian.
24 And Gideon sent messen-
gers[4397] throughout all the hill country
of Ephraim, saying, "Come down
[I]against Midian and [a]take the waters
before them, as far as Beth-barah
and the Jordan." So all the men of
Ephraim were summoned, and they took
the waters as far as Beth-barah and the
Jordan.
25 And they captured the two
leaders[8269] of Midian, [a]Oreb and Zeeb,
and they killed[2026] Oreb at the rock of
Oreb, and they killed Zeeb at the wine
press of Zeeb, while they pursued
Midian; and they brought the heads[7218]
of Oreb and Zeeb to Gideon [b]from
across the Jordan.

Zeba and Zalmunna Routed

8 Then the men[376] of Ephraim said[559]
to him, "[a]What is this thing you have
done to us, not calling[7121] us when you
went to fight against Midian?" And they
contended with him vigorously.[2394]
2 But he said to them, "What have
I done[6213] now in comparison with you?
Is not the gleaning *of the grapes* of
Ephraim better[2896] than the vintage of
Abiezer?
3 "God[430] has given the leaders[8269]
of Midian, Oreb and Zeeb into your
hands;[3027] and what was I able to do[6213]
in comparison with you?" Then their
[I]anger toward him subsided[7503] when he
said[1696] [II]that.
4 Then Gideon and the 300 men
who were with him came [a]to the Jordan
and crossed[5674] over, weary yet pursuing.
5 And he said to the men[582] of
[a]Succoth, "Please[4994] give loaves of

bread to the people[5971] who are following me, for they are weary, and I am pursuing Zebah and Zalmunna, the kings[4428] of Midian."

6 And the leaders of Succoth said, "[I][a]Are the hands[3709] of Zebah and Zalmunna already in your hands,[3027] that we should give bread to your army?"[6635]

7 And Gideon said, "[I]All right, [a]when the LORD has given Zebah and Zalmunna into my hand, then I will [II]thrash your [III]bodies[1320] with the thorns of the wilderness and with briers."

8 And he went up[5927] from there to [I][a]Penuel, and spoke[1696] similarly to them; and the men of Penuel answered him just as the men of Succoth had answered.

9 So he spoke[559] also to the men of Penuel, saying, "When I return[7725] safely,[7965] [a]I will tear down[5422] this tower."

10 Now Zebah and Zalmunna were in Karkor, and their [I]armies[4264] with them, about 15,000 men, all who were left[3498] of the entire [II]army of the sons[1121] of the east; [a]for the fallen[5307] were 120,000 [III]swordsmen.[376,8025,2719]

11 And Gideon went up by the way[1870] of those who lived[7931] in tents[168] on the east of Nobah and Jogbehah, and [I]attacked[5221] the camp,[4264] when the camp was [II]unsuspecting.

12 When Zebah and Zalmunna fled, he pursued them and captured the two kings of Midian, Zebah and Zalmunna, and routed[2729] the whole [I]army.

13 Then Gideon the son[1121] of Joash returned[7725] from the battle [I]by the ascent of Heres.

14 And he captured a youth [I]from Succoth and questioned[7592] him. Then *the youth* wrote down for him the princes of Succoth and its elders,[2205] seventy-seven men.

15 And he came to the men of Succoth and said, "Behold Zebah and Zalmunna, concerning whom you taunted[2778] me, saying, '[I][a]Are the hands of Zebah and Zalmunna already in your hand, that we should give bread to your men who are weary?' "

16 And he took the elders of the city, and thorns of the wilderness and briers, and he [I]disciplined[3045] the men of Succoth with them.

17 [a]And he tore down[5422] the tower of Penuel and killed[2026] the men of the city.

18 Then he said to Zebah and Zalmunna, "What kind of men *were* they whom you killed at Tabor?" And they said,[559] "They were like you, each one [I]resembling the son of a king."[4428]

19 And he said, "They *were* my brothers,[251] the sons[1121] of my mother.[517] *As* the LORD lives,[2416] if only you had let them live, I would not kill[2026] you."

20 So he said to Jether his first-born, "Rise, kill them." But the youth did not draw his sword, for he was afraid,[3372] because he was still a youth.

21 Then Zebah and Zalmunna said, "Rise up yourself, and fall on us; for as the man,[376] so is his strength." [a]So Gideon arose and killed Zebah and Zalmunna, and [b]took the crescent ornaments which were on their camels' necks.

22 Then the men of Israel said to Gideon, "Rule[4910] over us, both you and your son, also your son's son, for you have delivered[3467] us from the hand of Midian."

23 But Gideon said to them, "I will not rule over you, nor shall my son rule over you; [a]the LORD shall rule over you."

24 Yet Gideon said to them, "I would [I]request[7596] of you, that each of you give me [II]an earring from his spoil." (For they had gold earrings, because they were [a]Ishmaelites.)

25 And they said, "We will surely give *them*." So they spread out a garment, and every one of them threw an earring there from his spoil.

26 And the weight of the gold earrings that he requested[7592] was 1,700 *shekels* of gold, besides the crescent ornaments and the pendants and the purple robes which *were* on the kings of Midian,

---

6 [I]Lit., *Is the palm* [a]Judg. 8:15

7 [I]Lit., *For thus* [II]Or, *trample* [III]Lit., *flesh* [a]Judg. 7:15

8 [I]In Gen. 32:30, *Peniel* [a]Gen. 32:31

9 [a]Judg. 8:17

10 [I]Or, *camps* [II]Or, *camp* [III]Lit., *men who drew sword* [a]Judg. 6:5; 7:12; Is. 9:4

11 [I]Lit., *smote* [II]Or, *secure*

12 [I]Or, *camp*

13 [I]Or, *from*

14 [I]Lit., *of the men of*

15 [I]Lit., *Is the palm* [a]Judg. 8:6

16 [I]Lit., *made the men . . . to know*

17 [a]Judg. 8:9

18 [I]Lit., *like the form of the sons*

21 [a]Ps. 83:11 [b]Judg. 8:26

23 [a]1Sam. 8:7; 10:19; 12:12; Ps. 10:16

24 [I]Lit., *request a request* [II]Or, *a nose ring* [a]Gen. 25:13-16

and besides the neck bands that *were*
on their camels' necks.
🗝 27 And Gideon made[6213] it into
[a]an ephod, and placed it in his city,
Ophrah, and all Israel played the
harlot[2181] with it there, so that it became a snare[4170] to Gideon and his
household.[1004]

Forty Years of Peace

28 So Midian was subdued before
the sons of Israel, and they did not lift
up[5375] their heads[7218] anymore. And the
land[776] was undisturbed[8252] for forty
years in the days of Gideon.
29 Then [a]Jerubbaal the son of Joash
went and lived in his own house.
30 Now Gideon had [a]seventy sons
who [I]were his direct descendants,[3318]
for he had many wives.[802]
31 And his concubine who was in
Shechem also bore him a son, and he
[I]named him Abimelech.
32 And Gideon the son of Joash died
at a ripe[2896] old age[7872] and was
buried[6912] in the tomb[6913] of his father[1]
Joash, in Ophrah of the Abiezrites.
🗝 **33** Then it came about, as soon as
Gideon was dead,[4191] [a]that the sons of
Israel again[7725] played the harlot[2181] with
the Baals, and made[7760] [b]Baal-berith
their god.
34 Thus the sons of Israel [a]did not
remember[2142] the LORD their God, who
had delivered[5337] them from the hands
of all their enemies on every side;
35 [a]nor did they show[6213] kindness[2617] to the household of Jerubbaal (*that is,* Gideon), in accord with
all the good[2896] that he had done to Israel.

27 [a]Ex. 28:6-35; Judg. 17:5; 18:14-20
29 [a]Judg. 7:1
30 [I]Lit., *came from his loins* [a]Judg. 9:2, 5
31 [I]Lit., *appointed his name*
33 [a]Judg. 2:11, 12 [b]Judg. 9:4, 27, 46
34 [a]Deut. 4:9; Judg. 3:7
35 [a]Judg. 9:16-18
1 [I]Lit., *brothers* [a]Judg. 8:31, 35
2 [a]Judg. 8:30; 9:5, 18 [b]Gen. 29:14
3 [I]Lit., *brothers* [II]Lit., *their hearts inclined after* [III]Lit., *brother* [a]Gen. 29:15
4 [a]Judg. 8:33
5 [a]2Kin. 11:1, 2; [b]Judg. 8:30; 9:2, 18
6 [I]Or, *the house of Millo* [II]Or, *terebinth*
7 [a]Deut. 11:29, 30

Abimelech's Conspiracy

9 And [a]Abimelech the son[1121] of Jerubbaal went to Shechem to his
mother's[517] [I]relatives,[251] and spoke to
them and to the whole clan[4940] of the
household[1004] of his mother's father,[1]
saying,
2 "Speak,[1696] now, in the hearing[241]
of all the leaders[1167] of Shechem, 'Which
is better[2896] for you, that [a]seventy
men,[376] all the sons[1121] of Jerubbaal,
rule[4910] over you, or that one man rule
over you?' Also, remember[2142] that I
am [b]your bone[6106] and your flesh."[1320]
3 And his mother's [I]relatives
spoke[1696] all these words[1697] on his behalf in the hearing of all the leaders of
Shechem; and [II]they were inclined to
follow Abimelech, for they said,[559] "He
is [a]our [III]relative."[251]
4 And they gave him seventy *pieces*
of silver from the house of [a]Baal-berith
with which Abimelech hired worthless
and reckless fellows,[582] and they followed him.
5 Then he went to his father's[1]
house at Ophrah, and [a]killed[2026] his
brothers the sons of Jerubbaal, [b]seventy
men, on one stone. But Jotham the
youngest son of Jerubbaal was left,[3498]
for he hid himself.
6 And all the men of Shechem and
all [I]Beth-millo assembled[622] together,
and they went and made Abimelech
king,[4428] by the [II]oak of the pillar[5324]
which was in Shechem.
🗝 **7** Now when they told[5046] Jotham,
he went and stood on the top[7218] of
[a]Mount Gerizim, and lifted[5375] his voice
and called[7121] out. Thus he said to them,
"Listen[8085] to me, O men of Shechem,
that God[430] may listen to you.

🗝 **8:27** The "ephod" mentioned here (see also Judg. 17:5) seems to be different from the priestly garment of the same name (Ex. 28:5-12). An ephod of gold could hardly be worn as a garment. It was apparently used for purposes of divination. The human tendency is to worship objects instead of God.

🗝 **8:33** A strange contrast is made here between Baal-berith, which means "Baal (the lord) of the covenant," and Yahweh, the Lord, with whom Israel had made their covenant. They were in fact exchanging one Lord for another! This apostasy was centered in Shechem. No doubt Gideon had opened the way for this apostasy by making the ephod.

🗝 **9:7-15** This is one of the few parables in the O.T.

8 "Once the trees went forth to anoint[4886] a king over them, and they said to the olive tree, 'Reign[4427] over us!'

9 "But the olive tree said to them, 'Shall I leave my fatness with [I]which God and men[376] are honored,[3513] and go to wave over the trees?'

10 "Then the trees said to the fig tree, 'You come, reign over us!'

11 "But the fig tree said to them, 'Shall I leave my sweetness and my good[2896] [I]fruit, and go to wave over the trees?'

12 "Then the trees said to the vine, 'You come, reign over us!'

13 "But the vine said to them, 'Shall I leave my new wine, which cheers God and men, and go to wave over the trees?'

14 "Finally all the trees said to the bramble, 'You come, reign over us!'

15 "And the bramble said to the trees, 'If in [I]truth[571] you are anointing me as king over you, come and take refuge[2620] in my shade; but if not, may fire come out from the bramble and consume the cedars of Lebanon.'

16 "Now therefore, if you have dealt[6213] in [I]truth[571] and integrity[8549] in making Abimelech king,[4427] and if you have dealt[6213] well[2895] with [a]Jerubbaal and his house, and [II]have dealt with him [III]as he deserved—

17 for my father fought for you and [I]risked[7993] his life[5315] and delivered you from the hand[3027] of Midian;

18 but you have risen against my father's house today[3117] and have killed[2026] [a]his sons, seventy men, on one stone, and have made Abimelech, [b]the son of his maidservant, king over the men of Shechem, because he is your [I]relative—

19 if then you have dealt in [I]truth and integrity with Jerubbaal and his house this day, rejoice in Abimelech, and let him also rejoice in you.

20 "But if not, let fire come out from Abimelech and consume the men of Shechem and [I]Beth-millo; and let fire come out from the men of Shechem and from [I]Beth-millo, and consume Abimelech."

21 Then Jotham escaped and fled, and went to Beer and remained there because of Abimelech his brother.

Shechem and Abimelech Fall

22 Now Abimelech ruled over[7786] Israel three years.

23 [a]Then God sent an evil[7451] spirit[7307] between Abimelech and the men of Shechem; and the men of Shechem [b]dealt treacherously[898] with Abimelech,

24 [a]in order that the violence[2555] [I]done to the seventy sons of Jerubbaal might come, and [b]their blood might be laid[7760] on Abimelech their brother, who killed them, and on the men of Shechem, who strengthened his hands to kill his brothers.

25 And the men of Shechem set [I]men in ambush against him on the tops of the mountains, and they robbed all who might pass by them along the road;[1870] and it was told to Abimelech.

26 Now Gaal the son of Ebed came with his [I]relatives, and crossed over[5674] into Shechem; and the men of Shechem put their trust in him.

27 And they went out into the field[7704] and gathered *the grapes of* their vineyards and trod *them,* and held[6213] a [I]festival; and they went into the house of [a]their god, and ate and drank and cursed[7043] Abimelech.

28 Then Gaal the son of Ebed said, "Who is Abimelech, and who is Shechem, that we should serve[5647] him? Is he not the son of Jerubbaal, and *is* Zebul *not* his [I]lieutenant? Serve the men[582] of [a]Hamor the father of Shechem; but why should we serve him?

29 "[I][a]Would, therefore, that this people[5971] were under my authority! Then I would remove Abimelech." And he said to Abimelech, "Increase your army,[6635] and come out."

30 And when Zebul the ruler[8269] of the city heard[8085] the words of Gaal the son of Ebed, his anger[639] burned.[2734]

31 And he sent messengers[4397] to Abimelech [I]deceitfully,[8649] saying,

9 [I]Lit., *which by me*

11 [I]Or, *produce*

15 [I]Or, *sincerity*

16 [I]Or, *sincerity* [II]Lit., *if you have* [III]Lit., *according to the dealing of his hands* [a]Judg. 8:35

17 [I]Lit., *cast his soul in front*

18 [I]Lit., *brother* [a]Judg. 8:30; 9:2, 5 [b]Judg. 8:31

19 [I]Or, *sincerity*

20 [I]Or, *the house of Millo*

23 [a]1Sam. 16:14; Is. 19:2, 14 [b]Is. 33:1

24 [I]Lit., *of the seventy* [a]Deut. 27:25; Judg. 9:56, 57 [b]Num. 35:33

25 [I]Lit., *liers-in-wait for*

26 [I]Lit., *brothers*

27 [I]Lit., *rejoicing* [a]Judg. 8:33; 9:46

28 [I]Lit., *overseer* [a]Gen. 34:2

29 [I]Lit., *And who will give this people into my hand* [a]2Sam. 15:4

31 [I]Or, *in Tormah*

"Behold, Gaal the son of Ebed and his [II]relatives have come to Shechem; and behold, they are [III]stirring up the city against you.

32 "Now therefore, arise by night,[3915] you and the people who are with you, and lie in wait in the field.[7704]

33 "And it shall come about in the morning, as soon as the sun is up, that you shall rise early and rush upon the city; and behold, when he and the people who are with him come out against you, you shall [a]do[6213] to them [I]whatever you can."

34 So Abimelech and all the people who *were* with him arose by night and lay in wait against Shechem in four [I]companies.[7218]

35 Now Gaal the son of Ebed went out and stood in the entrance of the city gate; and Abimelech and the people who *were* with him arose from the ambush.

36 And when Gaal saw[7200] the people, he said to Zebul, "[I]Look, people are coming down from the tops of the mountains." But Zebul said to him, "You are seeing the shadow of the mountains as *if they were* men."

37 And Gaal spoke again and said, "Behold, people are coming down from [a]the [I]highest part of the land,[776] and one [II]company[7218] comes by the way of [III]the diviners' [IV]oak."[6049]

38 Then Zebul said to him, "Where is your [I]boasting[6310] now with which you said,[559] 'Who is Abimelech that we should serve him?' Is this not the people whom you despised?[3988] Go out now and fight with them!"

39 So Gaal went out before the leaders of Shechem and fought with Abimelech.

40 And Abimelech chased him, and he fled before him; and many fell[5307] wounded[2491] up to the entrance of the gate.

41 Then Abimelech remained at Arumah, but Zebul drove out Gaal and his [I]relatives so that they could not remain in Shechem.

42 Now it came about the next day, that the people went out to the field, and it was told to Abimelech.

43 So he took [I]his people and divided them into three [II]companies, and lay in wait in the field; when he looked[7200] and [III]saw the people coming out from the city, he arose against them and [IV]slew[5221] them.

44 Then Abimelech and the [I]company who was with him dashed forward and stood in the entrance of the city gate; the other two [II]companies then dashed against all who *were* in the field and [III]slew[5221] them.

45 And Abimelech fought against the city all that day, and he captured the city and killed the people who *were* in it; then he [a]razed[5422] the city and sowed it with salt.

46 When all the leaders of the tower of Shechem heard of *it,* they entered the inner chamber of the [I]temple of [a]El-berith.[410]

47 And it was told Abimelech that all the leaders of the tower of Shechem were gathered together.[6908]

48 So Abimelech went up to Mount [a]Zalmon, he and all the people who *were* with him; and Abimelech took [I]an axe in his hand and cut down[3772] a branch from the trees, and lifted[5375] it and laid *it* on his shoulder. Then he said to the people who *were* with him, "What you have seen[7200] me do, hurry *and* do [II]likewise."

49 And all the people also cut down each one his branch and followed Abimelech, and put *them* on the inner chamber and set the inner chamber on fire over those *inside,* so that all the men[376] of the tower of Shechem also died, about a thousand men and women.[802]

50 Then Abimelech went to Thebez, and he camped against Thebez and captured it.

51 But there was a strong tower in the center of the city, and all the men and women with all the leaders of the city fled there and shut themselves in; and they went up on the roof of the tower.

52 So Abimelech came to the tower

31 [II]Lit., *brothers* [III]Lit., *besieging*

33 [I]Lit., *as your hand can find* [a]1Sam. 10:7

34 [I]Lit., *heads*

36 [I]Lit., *Behold*

37 [I]Or, *center* [II]Lit., *head* [III]Heb., *Elom-meonenim* [IV]Or, *terebinth* [a]Ezek. 38:12

38 [I]Lit., *mouth*

41 [I]Lit., *brothers*

43 [I]Lit., *the* [II]Lit., *heads* [III]Lit., *behold* [IV]Lit., *smote*

44 [I]Singular with Gr.; Heb. plural, *heads* [II]Lit., *heads* [III]Lit., *smote*

45 [a]2Kin. 3:25

46 [I]Lit., *house* [a]Judg. 8:33

48 [I]Lit., *the axes* [II]Lit., *like me* [a]Ps. 68:14

and fought against it, and approached the entrance of the tower to burn[8313] it with fire.

53 But [a]a certain woman[802] threw an upper millstone on Abimelech's head,[7218] crushing his skull.

54 Then [a]he called[7121] quickly to the young man, his armor bearer, and said to him, "Draw your sword[2719] and kill[4191] me, lest it be said[559] of me, 'A woman slew him.'" So [I]the young man pierced him through, and he died.

55 And when the men of Israel saw that Abimelech was dead,[4191] each departed to his [I]home.

56 Thus [a]God repaid[7725] the wickedness[7451] of Abimelech, which he had done to his father, in killing his seventy brothers.

57 Also God returned[7725] all the wickedness of the men of Shechem on their heads,[7218] and the curse[7045] of Jotham the son of Jerubbaal came [I]upon them.

Oppression of Philistines and Ammonites

10 Now after Abimelech died, Tola the son[1121] of Puah, the son of Dodo, a man[376] of Issachar, [a]arose to save[3467] Israel; and he lived in Shamir in the hill country of Ephraim.

2 And he judged[8199] Israel twenty-three years. Then he died and was buried[6912] in Shamir.

3 And after him, Jair the Gileadite arose, and judged Israel twenty-two years.

4 And he had thirty sons[1121] who rode on thirty donkeys, and they had thirty cities [I]in the land[776] of Gilead [a]that are called[7121] [II]Havvoth-jair to this day.[3117]

5 And Jair died and was buried in Kamon.

6 Then the sons[1121] of Israel again did[6213] evil[7451] in the sight of the LORD, [a]served[5647] the Baals and the Ashtaroth, the gods[430] of Aram, the gods of Sidon, the gods of Moab, [b]the gods of the sons of Ammon, and the gods of the Philistines; thus [c]they forsook[5800] the LORD and did not serve Him.

7 And the anger of the LORD burned[2734] against Israel, and He [a]sold them into the hands[3027] of the Philistines, and into the hands of the sons of Ammon.

8 And they [I]afflicted[7492] and crushed the sons of Israel [II]that year; for eighteen years they *afflicted* all the sons of Israel who were beyond the Jordan [III]in Gilead in the land of the Amorites.

9 And the sons of Ammon crossed[5674] the Jordan to fight also against Judah, Benjamin, and the house[1004] of Ephraim, so that Israel was greatly distressed.

10 Then the [a]sons of Israel cried[2199] out to the LORD, saying, "We have sinned[2398] against Thee, for indeed, we have forsaken[5800] our God[430] and served the Baals."

11 And the LORD said[559] to the sons of Israel, "*Did I* not *deliver you* [a]from the Egyptians, [b]the Amorites, [c]the sons of Ammon, and the Philistines?

12 "Also when the Sidonians, the Amalekites and the Maonites [a]oppressed you, you cried out to Me, and I delivered[3467] you from their hands.[3027]

13 "Yet [a]you have forsaken Me and served other gods; therefore I will deliver you no more.

14 "[a]Go and cry[2199] out to the gods which you have chosen;[977] let them deliver you in the time[6256] of your distress."

15 And the sons of Israel said to the LORD, "We have sinned, [a]do[6213] to us whatever seems good[2896] to Thee; only please[4994] deliver[5337] us this day."

16 [a]So they put away[5493] the foreign[5236] gods from among them, and served the LORD; and [I][b]He could bear the misery[5999] of Israel no longer.

17 Then the sons of Ammon were summoned, and they camped in Gilead. And the sons of Israel gathered[622] together, and camped in [a]Mizpah.

53 [a]2Sam. 11:21
54 [I]Lit., *his* [a]1Sam. 31:4
55 [I]Lit., *place*
56 [a]Gen. 9:5, 6; Ps. 94:23
57 [I]Lit., *to*
1 [a]Judg. 2:16
4 [I]Lit., *which are in* [II]I.e., the towns of Jair [a]Num. 32:41
6 [a]Judg. 2:13 [b]Judg. 11:24 [c]Deut. 31:16, 17; 32:15
7 [a]1Sam. 12:9
8 [I]Lit., *shattered* [II]Lit., *in that* [III]Lit., *which is in*
10 [a]1Sam. 12:10
11 [a]Judg. 2:12 [b]Num. 21:21-25 [c]Judg. 3:13
12 [a]Ps. 106:42
13 [a]Jer. 2:13
14 [a]Deut. 32:37
15 [a]1Sam. 3:18
16 [I]Lit., *His soul was short with the misery* [a]Josh. 24:23 [b]Deut. 32:36
17 [a]Judg. 11:29

18 And the people,[5271] the
leaders[8269] of Gilead, said to one[376]
another,[7453] "Who is the man who will
begin to fight against the sons of Ammon? He shall become head[7218] over all
the inhabitants of Gilead."

Jephthah the Ninth Judge

11 Now [a]Jephthah the Gileadite was
a [I]valiant[2428] warrior, but he was
the son[1121] of a harlot.[2181] And Gilead
[II]was the father of Jephthah.
2 And Gilead's wife[802] bore him
sons;[1121] and when his wife's[802] sons
grew up, they drove Jephthah out and
said[559] to him, "You shall not have an
inheritance[5157] in our father's[1] house,[1004]
for you are the son of another
woman."[802]
3 So Jephthah fled from his broth-
ers[251] and lived in the land[776] of [a]Tob;
and worthless fellows gathered[3850]
themselves [I]about Jephthah, and they
went out with him.
4 And it came about after a while[3117]
that [a]the sons[1121] of Ammon fought
against Israel.
5 And it happened when the sons
of Ammon fought against Israel that the
elders[2205] of Gilead went to get Jephthah
from the land of Tob;
6 and they said to Jephthah, "Come
and be our chief that we may fight against
the sons of Ammon."
7 Then Jephthah said to the elders
of Gilead, "[a]Did you not hate[8130] me and
drive me from my father's house? So
why have you come to me now when
you are in trouble?"
8 And the elders of Gilead said to
Jephthah, "For this reason we have now
returned[7725] to you, that you may go
with us and fight with the sons of Ammon
and [a]become head[7218] over all the inhabitants of Gilead."
9 So Jephthah said to the elders of
Gilead, "If you take me back to fight
against the sons of Ammon and the LORD
gives them up [I]to me, will I become
your head?"
10 And the elders of Gilead said to
Jephthah, "[a]The LORD is [I]witness[8085] between us; surely we will do[6213] [II]as you
have said."[1697]
11 Then Jephthah went with the elders of Gilead, and the people[5271]
made[7760] him head and chief over them;
and Jephthah spoke all his words before
the LORD at [a]Mizpah.
12 Now Jephthah sent messengers[4397] to the king[4428] of the sons of
Ammon, saying, "What is between
you and me, that you have come to me
to fight against my land?"
13 And the king of the sons of Ammon said[559] to the messengers of Jephthah, "Because Israel [a]took away my
land when they came up[5927] from Egypt,
from the Arnon as far as the [b]Jabbok
and the Jordan; therefore, return[7725]
them peaceably now."
14 But Jephthah sent messengers
again to the king of the sons of Ammon,
15 and they said to him, "Thus
says[559] Jephthah, 'Israel did not take
away the land of Moab, nor the land of
the sons of Ammon.
16 'For when they came up from
Egypt, and Israel [a]went through the wilderness to the [I]Red Sea and [b]came to
Kadesh,
17 then Israel [a]sent messengers to
the king of Edom, saying, "Please[4994]
let us pass through[5674] your land," but
the king of Edom would not listen.[8085]
[b]And they also sent to the king of Moab,
but he would not consent.[14] So Israel
remained at Kadesh.
18 'Then they went through the wilderness and [a]around the land of Edom
and the land of Moab, and came to the
east side of the land of Moab, and they
camped beyond the Arnon; but they
[b]did not enter the territory of Moab,
for the Arnon *was* the border of Moab.

1 [I]Or, *mighty man of valor* [II]Lit., *begat* [a]Heb. 11:32
3 [I]Lit., *to* [a]2Sam. 10:6, 8
4 [a]Judg. 10:9, 17
7 [a]Gen. 26:27
8 [a]Judg. 10:18
9 [I]Lit., *before*
10 [I]Lit., *hearer* [II]Lit., *according to your word* [a]Gen. 31:50; Jer. 29:23; 42:5; Mic. 1:2
11 [a]Judg. 10:17; 11:29; 20:1; 1Sam. 10:17
13 [a]Num. 21:24 [b]Gen. 32:22
16 [I]Lit., *Sea of Reeds* [a]Num. 14:25; Deut. 1:40 [b]Num. 20:1, 4-21
17 [a]Num. 20:14-21 [b]Josh. 24:9
18 [a]Num. 21:4; Deut. 2:8 [b]Deut. 2:9, 18, 19

10:18 It is not accurate to think that the judges succeeded one another. Eli ruled for forty years, Jair for twenty-two years, Jephthah for six years, Izban for seven years, Elon for ten years, Abdon for eight years, and Samson for twenty years, but many of these periods overlapped.

19 'And Israel sent [a]messengers to Sihon king of the Amorites, the king of Heshbon, and Israel said to him, "Please let us pass through your land to our place."

20 'But Sihon did not trust Israel to pass through his territory; so Sihon gathered[622] all his people and camped in Jahaz, and fought with Israel.

21 'And the LORD, the God[430] of Israel, gave Sihon and all his people into the hand[3027] of Israel, and they [1a]defeated[5221] them; so Israel possessed[3423] all the land of the Amorites, the inhabitants of that country.[776]

22 '[a]So they possessed all the territory of the Amorites, from the Arnon as far as the Jabbok, and from the wilderness as far as the Jordan.

23 'Since now the LORD, the God of Israel, drove out[3423] the Amorites from before His people Israel, are you then to possess[3423] it?

24 'Do you not possess what [a]Chemosh your god gives you to possess? So whatever the LORD our God has driven out before us, we will possess it.

25 'And now are you any better[2896] than [a]Balak the son of Zippor, king of Moab? Did he ever strive[7378] with Israel, or did he ever fight against them?

26 '[a]While Israel lived in Heshbon and its villages, and in Aroer and its villages, and in all the cities that are on the banks of the Arnon, three hundred years, why did you not recover[5337] them within that time?[6256]

27 'I therefore have not sinned[2398] against you, but you are doing[6213] me wrong[7451] by making war against me; [a]may the LORD, the Judge,[8199] judge today[3117] between the sons of Israel and the sons of Ammon.' "

28 But the king of the sons of Ammon [1]disregarded[3808,8085] the message which Jephthah sent him.

Jephthah's Tragic Vow

29 Now [a]the Spirit[7307] of the LORD came upon Jephthah, so that he passed through[5674] Gilead and Manasseh; then he passed through Mizpah of Gilead, and from Mizpah of Gilead he went on to the sons of Ammon.

30 And Jephthah made a vow[5088] to the LORD and said, "If Thou wilt indeed give the sons of Ammon into my hand,[3027]

31 then it shall be that whatever comes out of the doors of my house to meet me when I return[7725] in peace[7965] from the sons of Ammon, it shall be the LORD'S, and I will offer it up as a burnt offering."[5930]

32 So Jephthah crossed over to the sons of Ammon to fight against them; and the LORD gave them into his hand.

33 And he struck them with a very great slaughter[4347] from Aroer [1]to the entrance of [a]Minnith, twenty cities, and as far as Abel-keramim. So the sons of Ammon were subdued before the sons of Israel.

34 When Jephthah came to his house at [a]Mizpah, behold, his daughter was coming out to meet him [b]with tambourines[8596] and with dancing. Now she was his one *and* only child;[3173] besides her he had neither son nor daughter.

35 And it came about when he saw[7200] her, that he tore his clothes and said, "Alas, my daughter! You have brought me very low, and you are among those who trouble me; for I have [1]given my word[6310] to the LORD, and [a]I cannot take *it* back."

36 So she said to him, "My father,[1]

19 [a]Num. 21:21-32; Deut. 2:26-36
21 [1]Lit., *smote* [a]Num. 21:24; Deut. 2:32-34
22 [a]Deut. 2:36, 37
24 [a]Num. 21:29; 1Kin. 11:7
25 [a]Num. 22:2; Josh. 24:9; Mic. 6:5
26 [a]Num. 21:25, 26; Deut. 2:36
27 [a]Gen. 16:5; 18:25; 31:53; 1Sam. 24:12, 15
28 [1]Lit., *did not listen to the words*
29 [a]Judg. 3:10
33 [1]Lit., *even until you are coming to* [a]Ezek. 27:17
34 [a]Judg. 10:17; 11:11 [b]Ex. 15:20; 1Sam. 18:6; Jer. 31:4
35 [1]Lit., *opened my mouth* [a]Num. 30:2; Eccl. 5:4, 5

11:29-33 Jephthah was sanctioned by God to be a judge of Israel. This declaration is the distinctive mark which stamps this as divine history. Verse 31 indicates clearly that Jephthah intended, if victorious, to offer a human sacrifice to the Lord. This is probably a throwback to his origins in Syria (Gilead, see Judg. 11:1-3). That God's Spirit was upon him does not imply that God had given him spiritual knowledge and wisdom or that God condoned such sacrifices. It implies only that He had given to Jephthah a special measure of valor and might to conquer the Ammonites.

you have [I]given your word to the LORD; [a]do to me [II]as you have said, since the LORD has avenged[5360] you of your enemies, the sons of Ammon."

37 And she said to her father, "Let this thing[1697] be done[6213] for me; let me alone[7503] two months, that I may [I]go to the mountains and weep[1058] because of [a]my virginity,[1331] I and my companions."

38 Then he said, "Go." So he sent her away for two months; and she left with her companions, and wept[1058] on the mountains because of her virginity.

39 And it came about at the end of two months that she returned[7725] to her father, who did[6213] to her according to the vow which he had made; and she [I]had no relations[3045] with a man.[376] Thus it became a custom[2706] in Israel,

40 that the daughters of Israel went yearly[3117] to [I]commemorate the daughter of Jephthah the Gileadite four days in the year.

Jephthah and His Successors

12 Then the men[376] of Ephraim were summoned, and they crossed [I]to Zaphon and [a]said[559] to Jephthah, "Why did you cross over to fight against the sons[1121] of Ammon without calling[7121] us to go with you? We will burn[8313] your house[1004] down on you."

2 And Jephthah said to them, "I and my people[5971] were at great strife[7379] with the sons of Ammon; when I called you, you did not deliver[3467] me from their hand.[3027]

3 "And when I saw[7200] that you would not deliver *me,* I [I][a]took my life[5315] in my hands[3709] and crossed over[5674] against the sons of Ammon, and the LORD gave them into my hand.[3027] Why then have you come up[5927] to me this day,[3117] to fight against me?"

4 Then Jephthah gathered[6908] all the men[582] of Gilead and fought Ephraim; and the men of Gilead [I]defeated[5221] Ephraim, because they said, "You are fugitives of Ephraim, O Gileadites, in the midst of Ephraim *and* in the midst of Manasseh."

5 And the Gileadites [a]captured the fords of the Jordan opposite Ephraim. And it happened when *any of* the fugitives of Ephraim said, "Let me cross over,"[5674] the men of Gilead would say to him, "Are you an Ephraimite?" If he said, "No,"

🔑 6 then they would say to him, "Say[559] now, 'Shibboleth.' " But he said, "Sibboleth," for he could not [I]pronounce it correctly. Then they seized him and slew[7819] him at the fords of the Jordan. Thus there fell[5307] at that time[6256] 42,000 of Ephraim.

7 And Jephthah judged[8199] Israel six years. Then Jephthah the Gileadite died and was buried[6912] in *one of* the cities of Gilead.

8 Now Ibzan of Bethlehem judged Israel after him.

9 And he had thirty sons,[1121] and thirty daughters *whom* he [I]gave in marriage outside *the family,* and he brought in thirty daughters from outside for his sons. And he judged Israel seven years.

10 Then Ibzan died and was buried in Bethlehem.

11 Now Elon the Zebulunite judged Israel after him; and he judged Israel ten years.

12 Then Elon the Zebulunite died and was buried at Aijalon in the land[776] of Zebulun.

13 Now Abdon the son[1121] of Hillel the Pirathonite judged Israel after him.

14 And he had forty sons and thirty grandsons who rode on seventy donkeys; and he judged Israel eight years.

15 Then Abdon the son of Hillel the Pirathonite died and was buried at

36 [I]Lit., *opened your mouth* [II]Lit., *according to what has proceeded from your mouth* [a]Num. 30:2

37 [I]Lit., *go and go down on* [a]Gen. 30:23; Luke 1:25

39 [I]Lit., *knew no man*

40 [I]Lit., *recount;* ancient versions, *lament*

1 [I]Or, *northward* [a]Judg. 8:1

3 [I]Lit., *put my soul in my palm* [a]1Sam. 19:5; 28:21; Job 13:14

4 [I]Lit., *smote*

5 [a]Judg. 3:28

6 [I]Lit., *speak so*

9 [I]Lit., *sent outside*

🔑 **12:6** This was a linguistic test given in order to tell whether or not a man was an Ephraimite. The word "shibboleth" meant "a stream in flood time." However, an Ephraimite, because of the nature of his dialect, said "sibboleth," substituting the "s" sound for the "sh" sound. Even though he denied being an Ephraimite his tongue would betray him, bringing certain death.

Pirathon in the land[776] of Ephraim, in the hill country of the Amalekites.

Philistines Oppress Again

13 Now the sons[1121] of Israel [a]again did[6213] evil[7451] in the sight of the LORD, so that the LORD gave them into the hands[3027] of the Philistines forty years.

2 And there was a certain man[376] of [a]Zorah, of the family[4940] of the Danites, whose name was Manoah; and his wife[802] was barren[6135] and had borne no *children.*

3 [a]Then the angel[4397] of the LORD appeared[7200] to the woman,[802] and said[559] to her, "Behold now, you are barren and have borne no *children,* but you shall conceive and give birth to a son.[1121]

4 "Now therefore, be careful[8104] [a]not to drink wine or strong drink, nor eat any unclean[2931] thing.

5 "[a]For behold, you shall conceive and give birth to a son, and no razor shall come upon his head,[7218] for the boy shall be a [b]Nazirite[5139] to God[430] from the womb;[990] and he shall begin to deliver Israel from the hands of the Philistines."

6 Then the woman came and told[5046] her husband,[376] saying, "[a]A man of God came to me and his appearance was like the appearance of the angel of God, very awesome.[3372] And I did not ask[7592] him where he *came* from, nor did he tell me his name.

7 "But he said to me, 'Behold, you shall conceive and give birth to a son, and now you shall not drink wine or strong drink nor eat any unclean[2932] thing, for the boy shall be a Nazirite to God from the womb to the day[3117] of his death.' "[4191]

8 Then Manoah entreated[6279] the LORD and said, "O Lord, please let [a]the man of God whom Thou hast sent come to us again that he may teach[3384] us what to do[6213] for the boy who is to be born."

9 And God listened[8085] to the voice of Manoah; and [a]the angel of God came again to the woman as she was sitting in the field,[7704] but Manoah her husband was not with her.

10 So the woman ran quickly and told[5046] her [I]husband, "Behold, [a]the man who [II]came the *other* day has appeared to me."

11 Then Manoah arose and followed his wife, and when he came to the man he said to him, "Are you [a]the man who spoke[1696] to the woman?" And he said, "I am."

12 And Manoah said, "Now when your words[1697] come *to pass,* what shall be the boy's mode of life[4941] and his vocation?"

13 So [a]the angel of the LORD said to Manoah, "[b]Let the woman pay attention [I]to all that I said.

14 "She should not eat anything that comes from the [a]vine nor drink wine or strong drink, nor eat any unclean thing; let her observe[8104] all that I commanded."[6680]

15 Then Manoah said to [a]the angel of the LORD, "Please let us detain you so that we may prepare[6213] a kid for you."

16 And the angel of the LORD said to Manoah, "Though you detain me, [a]I will not eat your [I]food, but if you prepare a burnt offering,[5930] *then* offer[6213] it to the LORD." For Manoah did not know[3045] that he was the angel of the LORD.

17 And Manoah said to the angel of the LORD, "[a]What is your name, so

1 [a]Judg. 2:11
2 [a]Josh. 19:41
3 [a]Judg. 6:11, 14; 13:6, 8, 10, 11; Luke 1:11-13
4 [a]Num. 6:2, 3; Luke 1:15
5 [a]Luke 1:15 [b]Num. 6:2-5
6 [a]Judg. 6:11; 13:8, 10, 11
8 [a]Judg. 13:3, 7
9 [a]Judg. 13:8
10 [I]Lit., *husband, and said to him* [II]Lit., *came to me* [a]Judg. 13:9
11 [a]Judg. 13:8
13 [I]Lit., *from* [a]Judg. 13:11 [b]Judg. 13:4
14 [a]Num. 6:4
15 [a]Judg. 13:3
16 [I]Lit., *bread* [a]Judg. 6:20
17 [a]Gen. 32:29

13:1 The Philistines were originally from Caphtor on the island of Crete. They are sometimes referred to historically as "the sea people." When their invasion of Egypt failed, they settled along the coast of Canaan in the thirteenth century B.C. From there they began filtering into the foothills of Dan and Judah. Their defeat by Samson was not final. They continued to plague Israel even in the time of David (II Sam. 5:17-25).

13:5 See note on Nazirite in Num. 6:2-21.

that when your words[1697] come *to pass,*
we may honor[3513] you?"
18 But the angel of the LORD said
to him, "Why do you ask my name, seeing it is [Ia]wonderful?"[6383]
19 So [a]Manoah took the kid with
the grain offering[4503] and offered[5922] it
on the rock to the LORD, and He performed wonders while Manoah and his
wife looked[7200] on.
20 For it came about when the flame
went up[5927] from the altar toward
heaven,[8064] that the angel of the LORD
ascended in the flame of the altar. When
Manoah and his wife saw *this,* they
[a]fell[5307] on their faces to the ground.[776]
21 Now the angel of the LORD
appeared[7200] no more to Manoah or his
wife. [a]Then Manoah knew that he was
the angel of the LORD.
22 So Manoah said to his wife, "[a]We
shall surely die,[4191] for we have seen[7200]
God."
23 But his wife said to him, "If the
LORD had desired[2654] to kill us, He would
not have accepted a burnt offering and
a grain offering from our hands,[3027] nor
would He have [a]shown us all these
things, nor would He have let us hear[8085]
things like this at this time."[6256]
24 Then the woman gave birth to
a son and named[7121] him Samson; and
the [a]child grew up and the LORD
blessed[1288] him.

18 [I]I.e., incomprehensible [a]Is. 9:6
19 [a]Judg. 6:20, 21
20 [a]Lev. 9:24; 1Chr. 21:16; Ezek. 1:28; Matt. 17:6
21 [a]Judg. 13:16
22 [a]Gen. 32:30; Deut. 5:26; Judg. 6:22
23 [a]Ps. 25:14
24 [a]1Sam. 3:19; Luke 1:80
25 [I]I.e., the camp of Dan [a]Judg. 3:10 [b]Judg. 18:11, 12
2 [I]Lit., *up* [II]Lit., *mother, saying,*
3 [I]Lit., *brothers* [II]Lit., *my* [III]Lit., *is right in my eyes* [a]Gen. 24:3, 4 [b]Ex. 34:16; Deut. 7:3
4 [a]Josh. 11:20

25 And [a]the Spirit[7307] of the LORD
began to stir him in [Ib]Mahaneh-
dan,[4264,1835] between Zorah and Eshtaol.

Samson's Marriage

14 Then Samson went down to Timnah and saw[7200] a woman[802] in
Timnah, *one* of the daughters of the Philistines.
2 So he came [I]back[5927] and told[5046]
his father[1] and [II]mother,[517] "I saw[7200]
a woman in Timnah, *one* of the daughters
of the Philistines; now therefore, get
her for me as a wife."[802]
3 Then his father and his mother
said to him, "Is there no woman among
the daughters of your [Ia]relatives,[251] or
among all [II]our people,[5971] that you go
to [b]take a wife from the uncircumcised[6189] Philistines?" But Samson
said to his father, "Get her for me, for
she [III]looks good[3477] to me."
4 However, his father and mother
did not know[3045] that [a]it was of the LORD,
for He was seeking an occasion against
the Philistines. Now at that time[6256] the
Philistines were ruling[7287] over Israel.
5 Then Samson went down to Timnah with his father and mother, and came
as far as the vineyards of Timnah; and
behold, a young lion *came* roaring toward
him.

13:18,19 The Messianic prophecy of Isa. 9:6 uses a cognate Hebrew word, *peli* (6382) meaning wonderful. This suggests that this Angel was Jesus!

13:22 It was a common belief that if a man ever saw God or His Angel, then he would soon die (cf. Judg. 6:22ff.; Ex. 33:20; Deut. 5:26).

13:24 Samson was born into the tribe of Dan on the border of the Philistine territory. He was selected by God even before his birth to be a deliverer of Israel against the Philistine oppression (v. 5). To accomplish this feat God gave him superhuman strength. Even with these blessings, he gave in to his own physical desires. His life was ultimately ruined because of his insistence upon having whatever he wanted. In captivity he was blinded by his Philistine captors. At the end of his life he repented and literally gave his life to vindicate God before the pagans, for which he is mentioned in the N.T. as a man of faith (Heb. 11:32). He was the last of the judges mentioned in this book.

14:3,4 Mixed marriages were forbidden (Deut. 7:3). Samson's parents were right to oppose his marriage to a heathen woman from the people who constantly oppressed Israel. We should not understand here that God had forced Samson into this marriage. Samson had made the decision. Though it was not right, God found a way to accomplish His will in spite of the lack of wisdom of one of His servants. It proved to be the crucial link in the liberation of Israel (Judg. 15:1-8). The N.T. teaches that Christians should not be "bound together with unbelievers" (II Cor. 6:14) and they should marry "only in the Lord" (I Chr. 7:39).

6 And [a]the Spirit[7307] of the LORD [I]came upon him mightily, so that [b]he tore him as one tears a kid though he had nothing in his hand;[3027] but he did not tell his father or mother what he had done.[6213]

7 So he went down and talked[1696] to the woman; and she [I]looked good[3477] to Samson.

8 When he returned[7725] later[3117] to take her, he turned aside[5493] to look at the carcass[4658] of the lion; and behold, a swarm of bees and honey were in the body[1472] of the lion.

9 So he scraped [I]the honey into his [II]hands[3709] and went on, eating as he went. When he came to his father and mother, he gave *some* to them and they ate *it;* but he did not tell them that he had scraped the honey out of the body of the lion.

10 Then his father went down to the woman; and Samson made a feast[4960] there, for the young men customarily did this.

11 And it came about when they saw him that they brought thirty companions to be with him.

Samson's Riddle

12 Then Samson said to them, "Let me now [a]propound a riddle[2420] to you; if you will indeed tell[5046] it to me within the seven days of the feast, and find it out, then I will give you thirty linen wraps and thirty [b]changes of clothes.

13 "But if you are unable to tell me, then you shall give me thirty linen wraps and thirty changes of clothes." And they said to him, "Propound your riddle, that we may hear[8085] it."

14 So he said to them,

"Out of the eater came something
to eat,
And out of the strong came
something sweet."

But they could not tell[5046] the riddle in three days.

15 Then it came about on the [I]fourth day[3117] that they said to Samson's wife, "[a]Entice[6601] your husband,[376] that he may tell us the riddle, [b]lest we burn[8313] you and your father's[1] house[1004] with fire. Have you invited[7121] us to impoverish us? Is this not *so?*"

16 And Samson's wife wept before him and said, "[a]You only hate[8130] me, and you do not love me; you have propounded a riddle to the sons[1121] of my people, and have not told *it* to me." And he said to her, "Behold, I have not told *it* to my father or mother; so should I tell[5046] you?"

17 However she wept before him seven days while their feast lasted. And it came about on the seventh day that he told her because she pressed him so hard. She then told the riddle to the sons of her people.

18 So the men[582] of the city said to him on the seventh day before the sun went down,

"What is sweeter than honey?
And what is stronger than a
lion?"

And he said to them,

"If you had not plowed with my
heifer,
You would not have found out
my riddle."

19 Then [a]the Spirit of the LORD [I]came upon him mightily, and he went down to Ashkelon and killed[5221] thirty of them[376] and took their spoil, and gave the changes *of clothes* to those who told the riddle. And his anger burned,[2734] and he went up[5927] to his father's house.

20 But Samson's wife was [a]*given* to his companion who had been his [I]friend.

Samson Burns Philistine Crops

15 But after a while, in the time[3117] of wheat harvest, it came about that Samson visited[6485] his wife[802] [a]with a young goat, and said,[559] "I will go in to my wife in *her* room." But her father[1] did not let him enter.

2 And her father said, "I really thought[559] that you hated[8130] her intensely; so I [a]gave her to your companion. Is not her younger sister[269] [I]more

6 [I]Lit., *rushed upon* [a]Judg. 3:10 [b]1Sam. 17:34-36
7 [I]Lit., *was right in Samson's eyes*
9 [I]Lit., *it* [II]Lit., *palms*
12 [a]Ezek. 17:2 [b]Gen. 45:22; 2Kin. 5:22
15 [I]So with some ancient versions; Heb., *seventh* [a]Judg. 16:5 [b]Judg. 15:6
16 [a]Judg. 16:15
19 [I]Lit., *rushed upon* [a]Judg. 3:10; 13:25
20 [I]Or, *best man* [a]Judg. 15:2
1 [a]Gen. 38:17
2 [I]Lit., *better* [a]judg. 14:20

beautiful[2896] than she? Please[4994] let her be yours [II]instead."

3 Samson then said to them, "This time I shall be blameless[5352] in regard to the Philistines when I do[6213] them harm."[7451]

4 And Samson went and caught three hundred foxes, and took torches, and turned *the foxes* tail to tail, and put one torch in the middle between two tails.

5 When he had set fire to the torches, he released [I]the foxes into the standing grain of the Philistines, thus burning up both the shocks and the standing grain, along with the vineyards *and* groves.

6 Then the Philistines said, "Who did[6213] this?" And they said,[559] "Samson, the son-in-law of the Timnite, because [I]he took his wife and gave her to his companion." So the Philistines came up[5927] and [a]burned[8313] her and her father with fire.

7 And Samson said to them, "Since you act like this, I will surely take revenge[5358] on you, but after that I will quit."

8 And he struck[5221] them [I]ruthlessly with a great slaughter;[4347] and he went down and lived in the cleft of the rock of Etam.

9 Then the Philistines went up[5927] and camped in Judah, and spread[5203] out in Lehi.

10 And the men[376] of Judah said, "Why have you come up[5927] against us?" And they said, "We have come up to bind Samson in order to do to him as he did to us."

11 Then 3,000 men of Judah went down to the cleft of the rock of Etam and said to Samson, "Do you not know[3045] [a]that the Philistines are rulers[4910] over us? What then is this that you have done to us?" And he said to them, "As they did[6213] to me, so I have done to them."

12 And they said to him, "We have come down to bind you so that we may give you into the hands of the Philistines." And Samson said to them, "Swear[7650] to me that you will not [I]kill me."

13 So they said[559] to [I]him, "No, but we will bind you fast and give you into their hands; yet surely we will not kill you." Then they bound him with two new ropes and brought[5927] him up from the rock.

🗝 **14** When he came to Lehi, the Philistines shouted[7321] as they met him. And [a]the Spirit[7307] of the LORD [I]came upon him mightily so that the ropes that were on his arms were as flax that is burned with fire, and his bonds [II]dropped from his hands.[3027]

15 And he found a fresh jawbone of a donkey, so he [I]reached out and took it and [II]killed[5221] [a]a thousand men with it.

16 Then Samson said,

"With the jawbone of a donkey,
[I]Heaps upon heaps,
With the jawbone of a donkey
I have [II]killed[5221] a thousand
men."

17 And it came about when he had finished[3615] speaking,[1696] that he threw the jawbone from his hand; and he named[7121] that place [I]Ramath-lehi.

18 Then he became very thirsty, and he [a]called to the LORD and said, "Thou hast given this great deliverance[8668] by the hand of Thy servant,[5650] and now [I]shall I die[4191] of thirst [II]and fall into the hands of the uncircumcised?"[6189]

2 [II]Lit., *instead of her*
5 [I]Lit., *them*
6 [I]I.e., the Timnite [a]Judg. 14:15
8 [I]Lit., *leg on thigh*
11 [a]Lev. 26:25; Deut. 28:43f.; Judg. 13:1; 14:4; Ps. 106:40-42
12 [I]Lit., *fall upon me yourselves*
13 [I]Lit., *him, saying*
14 [I]Lit., *rushed upon* [II]Lit., *were melted* [a]Judg. 14:19; 1Sam. 11:6
15 [I]Lit., *stretched out his hand* [II]Lit., *smote* [a]Lev. 26:8; Josh. 23:10
16 [I]Lit., *Heap, two heaps;* Heb. is same root as donkey [II]Lit., *smitten*
17 [I]I.e., the high place of the jawbone
18 [I]Or, *I shall . . . uncircumcised* [II]Or, *or* [a]Judg. 16:28

🗝 **15:14,15** The great statement of these verses is that the true source of Samson's great strength was not in his long hair or in abstaining from strong drink. It was to be found in his dedication to God and the personal relationship that he maintained with Him. His admission to Delilah in Judg. 16:17 should be interpreted then as a denial of that trust and a breaking of his covenant vow, for which the Lord left him (Judg. 16:20). His strength returned one more time, allowing him to decimate the Philistines, but only after he had admitted that the Lord was the Source of that strength (Judg. 16:28), which was apparently a statement of repentance.

19 But God[430] split the hollow place that is in Lehi so that water came out of it. When he drank, [a]his [I]strength returned and he revived. Therefore, he named it [II]En-hakkore, which is in Lehi to this day.[3117]

20 So [a]he judged[8199] Israel twenty years in [b]the days of the Philistines.

Samson's Weakness

16 Now Samson went to [a]Gaza and saw[7200] a harlot[2181] there, and went in to her.

2 *When it was told* to the Gazites, saying, "Samson has come here," they [a]surrounded *the place* and lay in wait for him all night[3915] at the gate of the city. And they kept silent all night, saying, "*Let us wait* until the morning light, then we will kill him."

3 Now Samson lay until midnight, and at midnight he arose and took hold of the doors of the city gate and the two posts and pulled them up along with the bars; then he put them on his shoulders and carried them up to the top[7218] of the mountain which is opposite Hebron.

4 After this it came about that he loved[157] a woman[802] in the valley of Sorek, whose name was Delilah.

5 And the [a]lords[5633] of the Philistines came up[5927] to her, and said[559] to her, "[b]Entice him, and see where his great strength *lies* and [I]how we may overpower him that we may bind him to afflict him. Then we will each[376] give you eleven hundred *pieces* of silver."

6 So Delilah said to Samson, "Please[4994] tell[5046] me where your great strength is and [I]how you may be bound to afflict you."

7 And Samson said to her, "If they bind me with seven fresh cords that have not been dried, then I shall become weak and be like any *other* man."[120]

8 Then the lords of the Philistines brought[5927] up to her seven fresh cords that had not been dried, and she bound him with them.

9 Now she had *men* lying in wait in an inner room. And she said to him, "The Philistines are upon you, Samson!" But he snapped the cords as a string of tow snaps when it [I]touches[7306] fire. So his strength was not discovered.[3045]

10 Then Delilah said to Samson, "Behold, you have deceived me and told me lies; now please tell me, [I]how you may be bound."

11 And he said to her, "If they bind me tightly with new ropes [I]which have not been used, then I shall become weak and be like any *other* man."

12 So Delilah took new ropes and bound him with them and said to him, "The Philistines are upon you, Samson!" For the *men* were lying in wait in the inner room. But he snapped [I]the ropes from his arms like a thread.

⊶**13** Then Delilah said to Samson, "Up to now you have deceived me and told me lies; tell me [I]how you may be bound." And he said to her, "If you weave the seven locks of my [II]hair[7218] with the web [III][and fasten it with a pin, then I shall become weak and be like any other man."

14 So while he slept, Delilah took the seven locks of his [I]hair and wove them into the web]. And she fastened[8628] *it* with the pin, and said to him, "The Philistines are upon you, Samson!" But he awoke from his sleep and pulled out the pin of the loom and the web.

Delilah Extracts His Secret

15 Then she said to him, "[a]How can you say,[559] 'I love[157] you,' when your heart[3820] is not with me? You have deceived me these three times and have not told[5046] me where your great strength is."

19 [I]Lit., *spirit* [II]I.e., the spring of him who called [a]Is. 40:29

20 [a]Judg. 16:31; Heb. 11:32 [b]Judg. 13:1

1 [a]Josh. 15:47

2 [a]1Sam. 23:26; Ps. 118:10-12

5 [I]Lit., *by what* [a]Josh. 13:3 [b]Judg. 14:15

6 [I]Lit., *by what*

9 [I]Lit., *smells*

10 [I]Lit., *by what*

11 [I]Lit., *with which work has not been done*

12 [I]Lit., *them*

13 [I]Lit., *by what* [II]Lit., *head* [III]The passage in brackets is found in Gr. but not in any Heb. mss.

14 [I]Lit., *head*

15 [a]Judg. 14:16

⊶**16:13** The web was undoubtedly the cloth which Delilah was weaving in a loom. The pin was the object with which the braided locks were fastened to the web. She probably wove his hair into the cloth.

16 And it came about when she pressed him daily with her words[1697] and urged him, that his soul[5315] was [I]annoyed[7114] to death.

🔑 17 So he told her all *that was* in his heart and said to her, "A razor has never come on my head, for I have been a [a]Nazirite[5139] to God[430] from my mother's[517] womb.[990] If I am shaved, then my strength will leave me and I shall become weak and be like any *other* man."

18 When Delilah saw that he had told her all *that was* in his heart, she sent and called[7121] the lords of the Philistines, saying, "Come up once more, for he has told[5046] me all *that is* in his heart." Then the lords of the Philistines came up to her, and brought the money in their hands.[3027]

19 And she made him sleep on her knees, and called for a man[376] and had him shave off the seven locks of his [I]hair. Then she began to afflict him, and his strength left him.

20 And she said, "The Philistines are upon you, Samson!" And he awoke from his sleep and said, "I will go out as at other times and shake myself free." But he did not know[3045] that [a]the LORD had departed[5493] from him.

21 Then the Philistines seized him and gouged out his eyes; and they brought him down to Gaza and bound him with bronze chains, and he was a grinder in the prison.

22 However, the hair of his head began to grow again after it was shaved off.

🔑 **23** Now the lords of the Philistines assembled[6908] to offer[2076] a great sacrifice[2077] to [a]Dagon their god, and to rejoice, for they said,

"Our god has given Samson our
enemy into our hands."

24 When the people[5971] saw him, [a]they praised[1984] their god, for they said,

"Our god has given our enemy
into our hands,[3027]
Even the destroyer of our
country,[776]
Who has slain[2491] many of us."

25 It so happened when [I]they were in high[2896] spirits,[3820] that they said, "Call[7121] for Samson, that he may amuse us." So they called for Samson from the prison, and he [II]entertained them. And they made him stand between the pillars.

26 Then Samson said to the boy who was holding his hand, "Let me feel the pillars on which the house rests,[3559] that I may lean[8172] against them."

27 Now the house was full of men[582] and women,[802] and all the lords of the Philistines were there. And about 3,000 men[376] and women were on the roof looking on while Samson was amusing *them*.

Samson Is Avenged

28 [a]Then Samson called to the LORD and said, "O Lord[136] [I]GOD, please remember[2142] me and please strengthen[2388] me just this time, O God, that I may at once [b]be avenged[5358] of the Philistines for my two eyes."

29 And Samson grasped the two middle pillars on which the house rested,[3559] and braced himself against them, the one with his right hand and the other with his left.

30 And Samson said, "Let me die[4191] with the Philistines!" And he bent with [I]all his might so that the house fell[5307] on the lords and all the people who were in it. So the dead[4191] whom he killed at his death were more than those whom he killed in his life.[2416]

31 Then his brothers[251] and all his father's[1] household came down, took[5375] him, brought him up, and buried[6912] him between Zorah and Eshtaol in the

16 [I]Lit., *impatient to the point of*
17 [a]Num. 6:2, 5; Judg. 13:5
19 [I]Lit., *head*
20 [a]Num. 14:42, 43; Josh. 7:12; 1Sam. 16:14
23 [a]1Sam. 5:2
24 [a]1Sam. 31:9; 1Chr. 10:9; Ps. 97:7
25 [I]Lit., *their heart was pleasant* [II]Lit., *made sport before them*
28 [I]Heb., *YHWH,* usually rendered LORD [a]Judg. 15:18 [b]Jer. 15:15
30 [I]Lit., *strength*

🔑 **16:17** See note on Judg. 15:14,15.
🔑 **16:23** The Philistines were a sea people. Therefore, it is not surprising that one of their gods was Dagon, the fish god. See note on Judg. 2:13.

tomb[6913] of Manoah his father. [a]Thus
he had judged[8199] Israel twenty years.

Micah's Idolatry

17 Now there was a man[376] of the
hill country of Ephraim whose
name was Micah.
2 And he said[559] to his mother,[517]
"The eleven hundred *pieces* of silver
which were taken from you, about which
you uttered[559] a curse[422] [I]in my hearing,[241] behold, the silver is with me; I
took it." And his mother said,
"Blessed[1288] be my son[1121] by the
LORD."
3 He then returned[7725] the eleven
hundred *pieces* of silver to his mother,
and his mother said, "I wholly dedicate[6942] the silver from my hand[3027] to
the LORD for my son [a]to make[6213] a
graven image[6459] and a molten image;
now therefore, I will return[7725] [I]them
to you."
4 So when he returned the silver
to his mother, his mother took two hundred *pieces* of silver and gave them to
the silversmith[6884] who made[6213]
[I]them into a graven image and a molten
image, and [II]they were in the house[1004]
of Micah.
5 And the man Micah had a [Ia]shrine
and he made an [b]ephod and [IIc]household
idols[8655] and [III]consecrated one of his
sons,[1121] [d]that he might become his
priest.
6 In those days [a]there was no
king[4428] in Israel; [b]every man did[6213]
what was right in his own eyes.
7 Now there was a young man from
[a]Bethlehem in Judah, of the family[4940]
of Judah, who was a Levite; and he was
[I]staying[1481] there.
8 Then the man departed from the
city, from Bethlehem in Judah, to
[I]stay[1481] wherever he might find *a place;*
and as he made his journey, he came
to the [a]hill country of Ephraim to the
house of Micah.
9 And Micah said to him, "Where
do you come from?" And he said to him,
"I am a Levite from Bethlehem in Judah,

31 [a]Judg. 15:20

2 [I]Lit., *and also spoke it in my ears*

3 [I]Lit., *it* [a]Ex. 20:4, 23; 34:17

4 [I]Lit., *it* [II]Lit., *it was*

5 [I]Lit., *house of gods* [II]Heb., *teraphim* [III]Lit., *filled the hand of* [a]Judg. 18:24 [b]Judg. 8:27; 18:14 [c]Gen. 31:19 [d]Num. 3:10

6 [a]Judg. 18:1; 19:1 [b]Deut. 12:8; Judg. 21:25

7 [I]Or, *sojourning* [a]Judg. 19:1; Ruth 1:1, 2; Mic. 5:2; Matt. 2:1

8 [I]Or, *sojourn* [a]Josh. 24:33

9 [I]Or, *sojourn*

10 [a]Judg. 18:19

12 [I]Lit., *filled the hand of* [II]Lit., *was* [a]Num. 16:10; 18:1-7

1 [I]Lit., *it* [II]Lit., *fallen* [a]Judg. 17:6; 19:1 [b]Josh. 19:40-48

2 [I]Lit., *men, sons of valor* [a]Judg. 13:25 [b]Judg. 17:1

4 [a]Judg. 17:12

and I am going to [I]stay wherever I may
find *a place.*"
10 Micah then said to him, "Dwell
with me and be [a]a father[1] and a priest
to me, and I will give you ten *pieces* of
silver a year, a suit of clothes, and your
maintenance."[4241] So the Levite went
in.
11 And the Levite agreed[2974] to live
with the man; and the young man became to him like one of his sons.
12 So Micah [I]consecrated the Levite, and the young man [a]became his
priest and [II]lived in the house of Micah.
13 Then Micah said, "Now I
know[3045] that the LORD will prosper[3190]
me, seeing I have a Levite as priest."

Danites Seek Territory

18 [a]In those days there was no
king[4428] of Israel; and [b]in those
days the tribe[7626] of the Danites was
seeking an inheritance for themselves
to live in, for until that day[3117] [I]an
inheritance[5159] had not [II]been allotted[5307]
to them as a possession among the
tribes[7626] of Israel.
2 So the sons[1121] of Dan sent from
their family[4940] five men[582] out of their
whole number, [I]valiant[2428] men from
[a]Zorah and Eshtaol, to spy out the land[776]
and to search it; and they said[559] to
them, "Go, search the land." And they
came to [b]the hill country of Ephraim,
to the house[1004] of Micah, and lodged
there.
3 When they were near the house
of Micah, they recognized[5234] the voice
of the young man, the Levite; and they
turned aside[5493] there, and said to him,
"Who brought you here? And what are
you doing[6213] in this *place?* And what
do you have here?"
4 And he said to them, "Thus and
so has Micah done to me, and he has
hired me, and [a]I have become his
priest."
5 And they said to him, "Inquire[7592]
of God,[430] please,[4994] that we may
know[3045] whether our way[1870] on which
we are going will be prosperous."

6 And the priest said to them, "Go in peace;[7965] your way in which you are going [I]has the LORD's approval."

7 Then the five men departed and came to [a]Laish and saw[7200] the people[5971] who were in it[7130] living in security, after the manner[4941] of the Sidonians, quiet[8252] and secure;[982] for there was no [I]ruler humiliating *them* for anything[1697] in the land, and they were far from the Sidonians and had no dealings[1697] with anyone.[120]

8 When they came back to their brothers[251] at Zorah and Eshtaol, their brothers said to them, "What *do* you *report?*"

9 And they said, "Arise, and let us go up[5927] against them; for we have seen[7200] the land, and behold, it is very good.[2896] And will you [I]sit still? Do not delay to go, to enter, to possess[3423] the land.

10 "When you enter, you shall come to a secure people with a spacious land; for God has given it into your hand,[3027] [a]a place where there is no lack of anything that is on the earth."[776]

11 Then from the family of the Danites, from Zorah and from Eshtaol, six hundred men[376] armed with weapons of war set out.

12 And they went up[5927] and camped at Kiriath-jearim in Judah. Therefore they called[7121] that place [I][a]Mahaneh-dan to this day; behold, it is [II]west of Kiriath-jearim.

13 And they passed[5674] from there to the hill country of Ephraim and came to the house of Micah.

Danites Take Micah's Idols

14 Then the five men who went to spy out the country[776] of Laish answered and said to their kinsmen, "Do[6213] you know that there are in these houses[1004] [a]an ephod and [I]household idols[8655] and a graven image[6459] and a molten image? Now therefore, consider[3045] what you should do."

15 And they turned aside there and came to the house of the young man, the Levite, to the house of Micah, and asked[7592] him of his welfare.[7965]

16 And the six hundred men armed with their weapons of war, who were of the sons of Dan, stood[5324] by the entrance of the gate.

17 Now the five men who went to spy out the land went up *and* entered there, *and* took [a]the graven image and the ephod and [I]household idols and the molten image, while the priest stood by the entrance of the gate with the six hundred men armed with weapons of war.

18 And when these went into Micah's house and took the graven image,[6459] the ephod and [I]household idols and the molten image, the priest said to them, "What are you doing?"

19 And they said to him, "Be silent, [a]put[7760] your hand[3027] over your mouth[6310] and come with us, and be to us [b]a father[1] and a priest. Is it better[2896] for you to be a priest to the house of one man,[376] or to be priest to a tribe and a family in Israel?"

20 And the priest's[3548] heart[3820] was glad,[3190] and he took the ephod and [I]household idols and the graven image, and went among[7130] the people.

21 Then they turned and departed, and put the little ones[2945] and the livestock and the valuables in front of them.

22 When they had gone some distance from the house of Micah, the men who *were* in the houses near Micah's house assembled[2199] and overtook the sons of Dan.

23 And they cried[7121] to the sons of Dan, who turned [I]around and said to Micah, "What is *the matter* with you, that you have assembled together?"

24 And he said, "You have taken away my gods[430] which I made,[6213] and the priest, and have gone away, and what do I have besides? So how can you say to me, 'What is *the matter* with you?' "

25 And the sons of Dan said to him, "Do not let your voice be heard[8085]

---

6 [I]Lit., *is before the LORD*

7 [I]Lit., *possessor of restraint* [a]Josh.19:47; Judg. 18:29

9 [I]Lit., *be*

10 [a]Deut. 8:9

12 [I]I.e., the camp of Dan [II]Lit., *behind* [a]Judg. 13:25

14 [I]Heb., *teraphim* [a]Judg. 17:5

17 [I]Heb., *teraphim* [a]Gen. 31:19, 30; Is. 41:29; Mic. 5:13

18 [I]Heb., *teraphim*

19 [a]Job 21:5; 29:9; 40:4 [b]Judg. 17:10

20 [I]Heb., *teraphim*

23 [I]Lit., *their faces*

among us, lest [I]fierce[4751] men fall upon you and you [II]lose[622] your life,[5315] with the lives of your household."[1004]

26 So the sons of Dan went on their way; and when Micah saw that they were too strong[2389] for him, he turned and went back to his house.

27 Then they took what Micah had made and the priest who had belonged to him, and came to [a]Laish, to a people quiet and secure, and struck[5221] them with the edge[6310] of the sword;[2719] and they burned[8313] the city with fire.

28 And there was no one to deliver *them,* because it was far from Sidon and they had no dealings with anyone, and it was in the valley which is near [a]Beth-rehob. And they rebuilt the city and lived in it.

29 And [a]they called the name of the city Dan, after the name of Dan their father who was born in Israel; however, the name of the city formerly[7223] was Laish.

30 And the sons of Dan set up for themselves [a]the graven image; and Jonathan, the son[1121] of [b]Gershom, the son of [I]Manasseh, [c]he and his sons[1121] were priests[3548] to the tribe of the Danites until the day of the captivity[1546] of the land.

31 So they set[7760] up for themselves Micah's graven image which he had made, all the time that the [a]house of God was at Shiloh.

A Levite's Concubine Degraded

19 Now it came about in those days, when [a]there was no king[4428] in Israel, that there was a certain[376] Levite [I]staying in the remote part of the hill country of Ephraim, who took a concubine for himself from Bethlehem in Judah.

2 But his concubine played the harlot[2181] against him, and she went away from him to her father's[1] house[1004] in Bethlehem in Judah, and was there for a period[3117] of four months.

3 Then her husband[376] arose and went after her to [a]speak[1696] [I]tenderly[3820] to her in order to bring her back, [II]taking with him his servant and a pair of donkeys. So she brought him into her father's house, and when the girl's father[1] saw[7200] him, he was glad to meet him.

4 And his father-in-law, the girl's father, detained him; and he remained with him three days. So they ate and drank and lodged there.

5 Now it came about on the fourth day[3117] that they got up early in the morning, and he [I]prepared to go; and the girl's father said[559] to his son-in-law, "[a]Sustain [II]yourself with a piece of bread, and afterward you may go."

6 So both of them sat down and ate and drank together; and the girl's father said to the man,[376] "Please[4994] be willing[2974] to spend the night,[3915] and [a]let your heart be merry."[3190]

7 Then the man arose to go, but his father-in-law urged him so that he spent the night there again.

8 And on the fifth day he arose to go early in the morning, and the girl's father said, "Please sustain [I]yourself, and wait until [II]afternoon"; so both of them ate.

9 When the man arose to go along with his concubine and servant, his father-in-law, the girl's father, said to him, "Behold now, the day has drawn[7503] [I]to a close; please spend the night. Lo, the day is [II]coming to an end; spend the night here that your heart may be merry. Then tomorrow you may arise early for your journey so that you may go [III]home."

10 But the man was not willing[14] to spend the night, so he arose and departed and came to *a place* opposite [a]Jebus (that is, Jerusalem). And there were with him a pair of saddled[2280] donkeys; his concubine also was with him.

11 When they *were* near Jebus, the day was almost gone; and [a]the servant said to his master,[113] "Please come, and let us turn aside into this city of the Jebusites and spend the night in it."

---

25 [I]Lit., *bitter of soul* [II]Lit., *gather*

27 [a]Josh. 19:47; Judg. 18:7

28 [a]2Sam. 10:6

29 [a]Josh. 19:47

30 [I]Some ancient versions read *Moses* [a]Judg. 17:3, 5 [b]Ex. 2:22; 18:3 [c]Judg. 17:3, 5

31 [a]Josh. 18:1

1 [I]Or, *sojourning* [a]Judg. 18:1

3 [I]Lit., *to her heart* [II]Lit., *and* [a]Gen. 34:3; 50:21

5 [I]Lit., *arose* [II]Lit., *your heart* [a]Gen. 18:5; Judg. 19:8

6 [a]Judg. 16:25; 19:9, 22; Ruth 3:7; 1Kin. 21:7; Esth. 1:10

8 [I]Lit., *your heart* [II]Lit., *the day declines*

9 [I]Lit., *toward evening* [II]Lit., *declining* [III]Lit., *to your tent*

10 [a]1Chr. 11:4, 5

11 [a]Judg. 19:19

12 However, his master said to him,
"We will not turn aside[5493] into the city
of foreigners who are not of the sons[1121]
of Israel; but we will go on as far as
Gibeah."
13 And he said to his servant,
"Come and let us approach one of these
places; and we will spend the night in
Gibeah or Ramah."
14 So they passed[5674] along and
went their way, and the sun set on
them near Gibeah which belongs to
Benjamin.
15 And they turned aside[5493] there
in order to enter *and* lodge in Gibeah.
When [I]they entered, [I]they sat down in
the open square of the city, for no one
took them into *his* house to spend the
night.
16 Then behold, an old man[2205] was
coming out of the field[7704] from his work
at evening. Now the man was from
[a]the hill country of Ephraim, and he was
[I]staying[1481] in Gibeah, but the men[582]
of the place [b]were Benjamites.
17 And he lifted up[5375] his eyes and
saw the traveler[732] in the open square
of the city; and the old man said, "Where
are you going, and where do you come
from?"
18 And he said to him, "We are
passing[5674] from Bethlehem in Judah to
the remote part of the hill country of
Ephraim, *for* I am from there, and I
went to Bethlehem in Judah. But I am
now going to [I]my house, and no man
will take me into his house.
19 "Yet there is both straw and
fodder[4554] for our donkeys, and also
bread and wine for me, [I]your maidservant, and [a]the young man who is with
your servants;[5650] there is no lack of
anything."[1697]
20 And the old man said, "[a]Peace[7965]
to you. Only let me *take care of* all your
needs; however, do not spend the night
in the open square."
21 [a]So he took him into his house
and gave the donkeys fodder,[1101] and
they washed[7364] their feet and ate and
drank.
22 While they were [I]making merry,
behold, [a]the men of the city, certain[582]
[II][b]worthless[1108] fellows,[1121] surrounded
the house, pounding the door; and they
spoke[559] to the owner[1167] of the house,
the old man, saying, "Bring out the man
who came into your house that we may
have [III]relations[3045] with him."
23 Then the man, the owner of the
house, went out to them and said to
them, "No, my fellows,[251] please do[6213]
not act so wickedly; since this man has
come into my house, [a]do not commit
this act of folly.
24 "[a]Here is my virgin daughter and
his concubine. Please let me bring them
out that you may ravish them and do
to them [I]whatever you wish. But do
not commit such an act of folly[5039] against
this man."
25 But the men would not listen[8085]
to him, so the man seized[2388] his concubine and brought *her* out to them. And
they raped[3045] her and abused[5953] her
all night until morning, then let her go
at the approach[5927] of dawn.
26 [I]As the day began to dawn, the
woman[802] came and fell down[5307] at the
doorway of the man's house where her
master[113] was, until *full* daylight.[216]
27 When her master arose in the
morning and opened the doors of the
house and went out to go on his way,
then behold, his concubine was lying[5307]
at the doorway of the house, with her
hands[3027] on the threshold.
28 And he said to her, "Get up and
let us go," [a]but there was no answer.
Then he placed her on the donkey;
and the man arose and went to his
[I]home.
29 When he entered his house, he
took a knife and laid hold of his concubine
and [a]cut her in twelve pieces, limb by
limb,[6106] and sent her throughout the
territory of Israel.
30 And it came about that all who
saw *it* said, "Nothing like this has *ever*
happened[1961] or been seen[7200] from the
day when the sons of Israel came up
from the land[776] of Egypt to this day.
Consider[7760] it, [a]take counsel and speak
up!"

15 [I]So with Gr.; M.T., *he*

16 [I]Or, *sojourning* [a]Judg. 19:1 [b]Judg. 19:14

18 [I]Heb., *the house of the Lord,* cf. v. 29

19 [I]I.e., my concubine [a]Judg. 19:11

20 [a]Gen. 43:23; Judg. 6:23

21 [a]Gen. 24:32, 33

22 [I]Lit., *making their hearts merry* [II]Lit., *sons of Belial* [III]Lit., *intercourse* [a]Gen. 19:4, 5; Ezek. 16:46-48 [b]Deut. 13:13; 1Sam. 2:12; 1Kin. 21:10; 2Cor. 6:15

23 [a]Gen. 34:7; Deut. 22:21; Judg. 20:6; 2Sam. 13:12

24 [I]Lit., *the good in your eyes* [a]Gen. 19:8

26 [I]Lit., *At the turning of the morning*

28 [I]Lit., *place* [a]Judg. 20:5

29 [a]1Sam. 11:7

30 [a]Judg. 20:7; Prov. 13:10

Resolve to Punish the Guilty

20 Then all the sons[1121] of Israel from Dan to Beersheba, including the land[776] of Gilead, came out, and the congregation[5712] assembled[6950] as one man[376] to the LORD at [a]Mizpah.

2 And the [I]chiefs of all the people,[5971] *even* of all the tribes[7626] of Israel, took their stand in the assembly[6951] of the people of God,[430] 400,000 foot [II]soldiers [a]who drew the sword.[2719]

3 (Now the sons of Benjamin heard[8085] that the sons of Israel had gone up[5927] to Mizpah.) And the sons of Israel said,[559] "Tell[1696] *us,* how did this wickedness[7451] take place?"

4 So the Levite, the husband[376] of the woman[802] who was murdered,[7523] answered and said, "I came with my concubine to spend the night at Gibeah which belongs to Benjamin.

5 "But the [a]men[1167] of Gibeah rose up against me and surrounded the house[1004] at night[3915] because of me. They intended to kill[2026] me; instead, they [b]ravished my concubine so that she died.[4191]

6 "And I [a]took hold of my concubine and cut her in pieces and sent her throughout the land[7704] of Israel's inheritance;[5159] for [b]they have committed[6213] a lewd[2154] and disgraceful act in Israel.

7 "Behold, all you sons of Israel, [a]give your advice[1697] and counsel[6098] here."

8 Then all the people arose as one man, saying, "Not one of us will go to his tent,[168] nor will any of us return to his house.

9 "But now this is the thing[1697] which we will do[6213] to Gibeah; *we will go up* against it by lot.

10 "And we will take 10 men[582] out of 100 throughout the tribes of Israel, and 100 out of 1,000, and 1,000 out of 10,000 to [I]supply food[6720] for the people, that when they come to [II]Gibeah of Benjamin, they may [III]punish *them* for all the disgraceful acts that they have committed[6213] in Israel."

11 Thus all the men[376] of Israel were gathered[622] against the city, united as one man.

12 Then the tribes of Israel sent men through the entire [I]tribe[7626] of Benjamin, saying, "What is this wickedness that has taken place[1961] among you?

13 "Now then, deliver up the men, the [Ia]worthless fellows in Gibeah, that we may put them to death[4191] and [b]remove *this* wickedness[7451] from Israel." But the sons of Benjamin would[14] not listen[8085] to the voice of their brothers,[251] the sons of Israel.

14 And the sons of Benjamin gathered from the cities to Gibeah, to go out to battle against the sons of Israel.

15 And from the cities on that day the [a]sons of Benjamin were [I]numbered,[6485] 26,000 men who draw the sword, besides the inhabitants of Gibeah who were [I]numbered, 700 choice men.

16 Out of all these people 700 [a]choice men were left-handed; each one could sling a stone at a hair and not miss.[2398]

17 Then the men of Israel besides Benjamin were [I]numbered, 400,000 men who draw the sword; all these were men of war.

Civil War, Benjamin Defeated

18 Now the sons of Israel arose, went up[5927] to Bethel, and [a]inquired[7592] of God, and said, "Who shall go up[5927] first for us to battle against the sons of Benjamin?" Then the LORD said, "Judah *shall go up* first."

19 So the sons of Israel arose in the morning and camped against Gibeah.

20 And the men of Israel went out to battle against Benjamin, and the men

1 [a]1Sam. 7:5

2 [I]Lit., *corner-stones* [II]Lit., *men* [a]Judg. 8:10

5 [a]Judg. 19:22 [b]Judg. 19:25f.

6 [a]Judg. 19:29 [b]Gen. 34:7; Josh. 7:15

7 [a]Judg. 19:30

10 [I]Lit., *take* [II]Heb., *Geba* [III]Lit., *do*

12 [I]Lit., *tribes*

13 [I]Lit., *sons of Belial* [a]2Cor. 6:15 [b]Deut. 13:5; 17:12; 1Cor. 5:13

15 [I]Or, *mustered* [a]Num. 1:36, 37; 2:23; 26:41

16 [a]Judg. 3:15; 1Chr. 12:2

17 [I]Or, *mustered*

18 [a]Num. 27:21; Judg. 20:23, 27

20:1 The phrase "from Dan to Beersheba" does not imply that Dan's settlement of its portion, recorded in chapter 18, had already been completed. It only shows that in the writer's time "from Dan to Beersheba" had become a proverbial expression for all Israel.

of Israel arrayed for battle against them
at Gibeah.
21 Then the sons of Benjamin came
out of Gibeah and [Ia]felled[7843] to the
ground[776] on that day[3117] 22,000 men
of Israel.
22 But the people, the men of Israel,
encouraged[2388] themselves and arrayed
for battle again in the place where they
had arrayed themselves the first[7223] day.
🔑 23 [a]And the sons of Israel went up
and wept before the LORD until evening,
and [b]inquired of the LORD, saying, "Shall
we again draw near[5066] for battle against
the sons of my brother[251] Benjamin?"
And the LORD said, "Go up against
him."
24 Then the sons of Israel [I]came
against the sons of Benjamin the second
day.
25 And Benjamin went out [I]against
them from Gibeah the second day and
[II]felled to the ground again 18,000 men
of the sons of Israel; all these drew the
sword.
26 Then [a]all the sons of Israel and
all the people went up and came to
Bethel and wept; thus they remained
there before the LORD and fasted that
day until evening. And they offered[5927]
burnt offerings[5930] and peace offerings[8002] before the LORD.
27 And the sons of Israel [a]in-
quired[7592] of the LORD (for the ark of
the covenant[1285] of God *was* there in
those days,
28 and Phinehas the son of Eleazar,
Aaron's son,[1121] stood before it to *minister* in those days), saying, "Shall I yet
again go out to battle against the sons
of my brother Benjamin, or shall I
cease?" And the LORD said, "Go up,
[a]for tomorrow I will deliver them into
your hand."[3027]
29 [a]So Israel set[7760] men in ambush
around Gibeah.
30 And the sons of Israel went up
against the sons of Benjamin on the third
day and arrayed themselves against
Gibeah, as at other times.
31 [a]And the sons of Benjamin went
out [I]against the people and were drawn
away from the city, and they began to
strike[5221] [II]and kill[2491] some of the people, as at other times, on the highways,
one of which goes up to Bethel and the
other to Gibeah, *and* in the field,[7704]
about thirty men of Israel.
32 And the sons of Benjamin said,
"They are struck down[5062] before us,
as at the first." But the sons of Israel
said, "Let us flee that we may draw
them away from the city to the highways."
33 Then all the men of Israel arose
from their place and arrayed themselves
at Baal-tamar; [a]and the men of Israel
in ambush broke out of their place, even
out of Maareh-geba.
34 When ten thousand choice men
from all Israel came against Gibeah, the
battle became [I]fierce;[3513] [a]but [II]Benjamin
did not know[3045] that [III]disaster was
[IV]close to them.
35 And the LORD struck[5062] Benjamin before Israel, so that the sons of
Israel destroyed 25,100 men of Benjamin that day, all [I]who draw the sword.
36 So the sons of Benjamin saw[7200]
that they were [I]defeated. [a]When the
men of Israel gave [II]ground to Benjamin
because they relied[982] on the men in
ambush whom they had set against
Gibeah,
37 [a]the men in ambush hurried and
rushed against Gibeah; the men in ambush also deployed and struck[5221] all the
city with the edge of the sword.
38 Now the appointed sign[226] between the men of Israel and the men
in ambush was [a]that they should make
a great cloud of smoke rise[5927] from the
city.
39 Then the men of Israel turned
in the battle, and Benjamin began to
strike [I]and kill about thirty men of Israel,

21 [I]Lit., *destroyed* [a]Judg. 20:25
23 [a]Josh. 7:6, 7 [b]Judg. 20:18
24 [I]Lit., *approached*
25 [I]Lit., *to meet* [II]Lit., *destroyed*
26 [a]Judg. 20:23; 21:2
27 [a]Judg. 20:18
28 [a]Judg. 7:9
29 [a]Josh. 8:4
31 [I]Lit., *to meet* [II]Lit., *slain ones* [a]Josh. 8:16
33 [a]Josh. 8:19
34 [I]Lit., *heavy* [II]Lit., *they* [III]Lit., *evil* [IV]Lit., *touching* [a]Josh. 8:14; Job 21:13
35 [I]Lit., *these*
36 [I]Lit., *smitten* [II]Lit., *place* [a]Josh. 8:15
37 [a]Josh. 8:19
38 [a]Josh. 8:20
39 [I]Lit., *slain ones*

🔑 **20:23** Apparently the Israelites trusted in their army and the righteousness of their cause, and they did not include God in their planning. All Israel needed a strong disciplinary lesson, and God used their enemies to teach it to them.

[a]for they said, "Surely they are [II]de-
feated before us, as in the first battle."
40 But when the cloud began to rise
from the city in a column of smoke, Benjamin looked [a]behind them; and behold,
the whole city was going up *in smoke*
to heaven.
41 Then the men of Israel
turned,[2015] and the men of Benjamin
were terrified;[926] for they saw that
[I][a]disaster was [II]close to them.
42 Therefore, they turned their
backs before the men of Israel [a]toward
the direction[1870] of the wilderness, but
the battle overtook them while those
who came out of the cities destroyed
them in the midst of them.
43 [a]They surrounded Benjamin,
pursued them without rest *and* trod
them down opposite Gibeah toward the
[I]east.
44 Thus 18,000 men of Benjamin
fell;[5307] all these were valiant[2428] warriors.
45 [I]The rest turned and fled toward
the wilderness to the rock of [a]Rimmon,
but they [II]caught 5,000 of them on the
highways and overtook them [III]at Gidom
and [IV]killed[5221] 2,000 of them.
46 So all of Benjamin who fell that
day were 25,000 men who draw the
sword; all these were valiant warriors.
47 But 600 men turned and fled toward the wilderness to the rock of Rimmon, and they remained at the rock of
Rimmon four months.
48 The men of Israel then turned
back[7725] against the sons of Benjamin
and struck them with the edge of the
sword, both the entire city with the cattle and all that they found; they also
set on fire all the cities which they found.

Mourning Lost Tribe

21 Now the men[376] of Israel
[a]had sworn[7650] in Mizpah, saying,
"None of us shall give his daughter to
Benjamin [I]in marriage."[802]
2 [a]So the people[5971] came to
Bethel[1004] and sat there before God[430]
until evening, and lifted up[5375] their
voices and wept [I]bitterly.
3 And they said,[559] "Why, O LORD,
God of Israel, has this come about in
Israel, so that one tribe[7626] should be
missing[6485] today[3117] in Israel?"
4 And it came about the next day
that the people arose early and built
[a]an altar there, and offered[5927] burnt
offerings[5930] and peace offerings.
5 Then the sons[1121] of Israel said,
"Who is there among all the tribes[7626]
of Israel who did not come up in the
assembly[6951] to the LORD?" For [I]they
had taken a great oath[7621] concerning
him [a]who did not come up to the LORD
at Mizpah, saying, "He shall surely be
put to death."[4191]
6 And the sons of Israel were
sorry[5162] for their brother[251] Benjamin
and said, "One tribe is cut off from Israel
today.
7 "What shall we do[6213] for wives[802]
for those who are left,[3498] since we have
[a]sworn by the LORD not to give them
any of our daughters in marriage?"

Provision for Their Survival

8 And they said, "What one is there
of the tribes[7626] of Israel who did not
come up to the LORD at Mizpah?" And
behold, no one had come to the camp[4264]
from Jabesh-gilead to the assembly.[6951]
9 For when the people were
[I]numbered,[6485] behold, not one of the
inhabitants of Jabesh-gilead was there.
10 And the congregation[5712] sent
12,000 of the valiant warriors there, and
commanded[6680] them, saying, "Go and
[a]strike[5221] the inhabitants of Jabesh-
gilead with the edge[6310] of the
sword,[2719] with the women[802] and the
little ones.[2945]
11 "And this is the thing[1697] that you
shall do: you [a]shall utterly destroy[2763]
every man[2145] and every woman[802] who
has [II]lain with a man."
12 And they found among the inhabitants of Jabesh-gilead 400 young
virgins[1330] who had not known[3045] a
man[376] by lying with [I]him; and they

39 [II]Lit., *smitten* [a]Judg. 20:32
40 [a]Josh. 8:20
41 [I]Lit., *evil* [II]Lit., *touching* [a]Prov. 5:22; 11:5, 6; 29:6
42 [a]Josh. 8:15, 24
43 [I]Lit., *sunrise* [a]Hos. 9:9; 10:9
45 [I]So with Gr.; Heb., *And they* [II]Lit., *gleaned* [III]Lit., *as far as* [IV]Lit., *smote* [a]Judg. 21:13
1 [I]Lit., *for a wife* [a]Judg. 21:7, 18
2 [I]Lit., *with great weeping* [a]Judg. 20:26
4 [a]Deut. 12:5; 2Sam. 24:25
5 [I]Lit., *there was a great oath* [a]Judg. 5:23
7 [a]Judg. 21:1
9 [I]Or, *mustered*
10 [a]Num. 31:17; Judg. 5:23; 1Sam. 11:7
11 [I]Lit., *known lying with* [a]Num. 31:17
12 [I]Lit., *a male*

brought them to the camp at Shiloh, which is in the land[776] of Canaan.

13 Then the whole congregation sent *word* and spoke[1696] to the sons of Benjamin who were [a]at the rock of Rimmon, and [b]proclaimed[7121] peace to them.

14 And Benjamin returned at that time,[6256] and they gave them the women whom they had kept alive from the women of Jabesh-gilead; yet they [I]were not enough for them.

15 And the people were sorry for Benjamin because the LORD had made[6213] a breach in the tribes of Israel.

🔑 **16** Then the elders[2205] of the congregation said, "What shall we do for wives for those who are left, since the women are destroyed[8045] out of Benjamin?"

17 And they said, "*There must be* an inheritance[3425] for the survivors of Benjamin, that a tribe may not be blotted out[4229] from Israel.

18 "But we cannot give them wives of our daughters." For the sons of Israel [a]had sworn, saying, "Cursed[779] is he who gives a wife to Benjamin."

19 So they said, "Behold, there is a feast[2282] of the LORD from year to year[3117] in [a]Shiloh, which is on the north side of Bethel, on the east side of the highway that goes up from Bethel to Shechem, and on the south side of Lebonah."

20 And they commanded the sons of Benjamin, saying, "Go and lie in wait in the vineyards,

21 and watch; and behold, if the daughters of Shiloh come out to [Ia]take part in the dances, then you shall come out of the vineyards and each of you shall catch his wife from the daughters of Shiloh, and go to the land[776] of Benjamin.

22 "And it shall come about, when their fathers[1] or their brothers[251] come to complain[7378] to us, that we shall say[559] to them, 'Give them to us voluntarily,[2603] because we did not take for each man *of Benjamin* [I]a wife in battle, [IIa]nor did you give *them* to them, *else* you would now be guilty.' "[816]

23 And the sons of Benjamin did[6213] so, and took[5375] wives according to their number from those who danced, whom they carried away. And they went and returned[7725] to their inheritance,[5159] and [a]rebuilt the cities and lived in them.

24 And the sons of Israel departed from there at that time,[6256] every man to his tribe and family,[4940] and each one of them went out from there to his inheritance.

25 [a]In those days there was no king[4428] in Israel; everyone did what was right in his own eyes.

13 [a]Judg. 20:47 [b]Deut. 20:10
14 [I]Lit., *did not find it so*
18 [a]Judg. 21:1
19 [a]Josh. 18:1; Judg. 18:31; 1Sam. 1:3
21 [I]Lit., *dance* [a]Ex. 15:20; Judg. 11:34
22 [I]Lit., *his* [II]Lit., *because* [a]Judg. 21:1, 18
23 [a]Judg. 20:48
25 [a]Judg. 17:6; 18:1; 19:1

🔑 **21:16-24** The festival spoken of in v. 19 is probably the Passover or one of the three great Jewish feasts (Ex. 23:14-17). In these unsettled times the men went up to Shiloh only once a year instead of three times (I Sam. 1:3). Only the males kept the feasts, therefore the virgins of Shiloh would naturally be the only maidens present. The public festival would be a likely occasion for their festive dances. It is possible that this was simply a local festival which was peculiar to Shiloh, like the yearly sacrifice of David's family at Bethlehem (I Sam. 20:29). The men of Israel had made a hasty oath in the heat of anger (v. 1). Later, when they saw the plight of Benjamin, that without wives the tribe would soon cease to exit, they felt compassion for them. However, the terms of their oath stood. Though they would not give their daughters as wives to the Benjamites, they instructed them in detail how to go up to Shiloh and carry off the girls at the festival. In their mind they would not be guilty of breaking the oath, and the Benjamites would have wives and be preserved as a tribe even though the women were gained by violent means.

The Book of

RUTH

The Book of Ruth is a love story. It took place during the turbulent period of the Judges. The inspired author is unknown. Ruth, the main character, was a heathen girl from Moab who married one of the sons of Elimelech and Naomi. However, Elimelech and both of his sons died in Moab. Ruth decided to return to Bethlehem with Naomi, and eventually came to believe that Jehovah was the only true God. Boaz was a close relative to Elimelech. According to God's Law in Lev. 25:25-28 and Deut. 25:5-10, Boaz had the right to be a kinsman-redeemer and marry Ruth to perpetuate the family of Elimelech. Through the providence of God, Boaz, who was the son of Rahab, a former prostitute in pagan Jericho (Jos. 2:1; Mt. 1:5), did marry Ruth, a young woman who had no opportunity to know the God of Israel in childhood. This marriage produced a son named Obed who fathered Jesse, and Jesse was the father of King David. Therefore, the great-grandparents of the royal Messianic line had roots *outside* Israel. How fitting it is that Jesus, the Son of David, descended from such a family!

Naomi Widowed

1 🔑 Now it came about in the days[3117] [a]when the judges [I]governed, that there was [b]a famine in the land.[776] And a certain man [c]of Bethlehem in Judah went to sojourn[1481] in the land[7704] of Moab [II]with his wife[802] and his two sons.[1121]

2 And the name of the man *was* Elimelech, and the name of his wife, Naomi; and the names of his two sons *were* Mahlon and Chilion, Ephrathites of Bethlehem in Judah. Now they [a]entered the land of Moab and remained there.

3 Then Elimelech, Naomi's husband, died; and she was left[7604] with her two sons.

4 And they took[5375] for themselves Moabite women *as* wives; the name of the one was Orpah and the name of the other Ruth. And they lived there about ten years.

5 Then [I]both Mahlon and Chilion also died; and the woman[802] was bereft of her two children and her husband.

6 Then she arose with her daughters-in-law that she might return from the land of Moab, for she had heard[8085] in the land of Moab that the LORD had [a]visited[6485] His people[5971] in [b]giving them food.

7 So she departed from the place where she was, and her two daughters-in-law with her; and they went on the way[1870] to return[7725] to the land[776] of Judah.

8 And Naomi said to her two daughters-in-law, "Go, return[7725] each[802] of you to her mother's[517] house.[1004] [a]May the LORD deal[6213] kindly[2617] with you as you have dealt[6213] with the dead and with me.

9 "May the LORD grant that you may find rest, each in the house of her husband." Then she kissed them, and they lifted up[5375] their voices and wept.

10 And they said to her, "*No,* but we will surely return[7725] with you to your people."

11 But Naomi said, "Return,[7725] my daughters. Why should you go with me? Have I yet sons in my womb,[4578] that [a]they may be your husbands?[582]

12 "Return, my daughters! Go, for I am too old[2204] to have a husband. If I said[559] I have hope, if I should even have a husband tonight and also bear sons,

13 would you therefore wait until

1 [I]Or, *judged* [II]Lit., *he, and* [a]Judg. 2:16-18 [b]Gen. 12:10; 26:1; 2Kin. 8:1 [c]Judg. 17:8; Mic. 5:2

2 [a]Judg. 3:30

5 [I]Lit., *both of them*

6 [a]Ex. 4:31; Jer. 29:10; Zeph. 2:7 [b]Ps. 132:15; Matt. 6:11

8 [a]2Tim. 1:16

11 [a]Gen. 38:11; Deut. 25:5

🔑 **1:1** These events occurred about 1100 B.C. during the period of the judges.

they were grown? Would you therefore
refrain from marrying? No, my daughters; for it is [I]harder for me than for
you, for [a]the hand[3027] of the LORD has
gone forth against me."

Ruth's Loyalty

14 And they lifted up their voices
and wept again; and Orpah kissed her
mother-in-law, but Ruth clung to her.
15 Then she said, "Behold, your
sister-in-law has gone back[7725] to her
people and her [a]gods;[430] return[7725] after
your sister-in-law."
16 But Ruth said, "Do not urge[6293]
me to leave[5800] you *or* turn back from
following you; for where you go, I will
go, and where you lodge, I will lodge.
Your people[5971] *shall be* my people, and
your God,[430] my God.
17 "Where you die, I will die, and
there I will be buried.[6912] Thus may
[a]the LORD do[6213] to me, and worse, if
anything but death[4194] parts you and
me."
18 When [a]she saw[7200] that she was
determined to go with her, she [I]said
no more to her.
19 So they both went until they
came to Bethlehem. And it came about
when they had come to Bethlehem, that
[a]all the city was stirred[1949] because of
them, and [I]the women said, "Is this
Naomi?"
20 And she said to them, "Do not
call me [I]Naomi; call me [II]Mara,[4755] for
[III][a]the Almighty[7706] has dealt very bitterly with me.
21 "I went out full, but [a]the LORD
has brought me back[7725] empty. Why
do you call me Naomi, since the LORD
has witnessed against me and [I]the Almighty has afflicted[7489] me?"
22 So Naomi returned,[7725] and with
her Ruth the Moabitess, her daughter-
in-law, who returned from the land of
Moab. And they came to Bethlehem at
[a]the beginning of barley harvest.

Ruth Gleans in Boaz' Field

2 🔑 Now Naomi had [I]a kinsman[1350]
of her husband, a [II]man of great
wealth,[2428] of the family of [a]Elimelech,
whose name was Boaz.
🔑 2 And Ruth the Moabitess said to
Naomi, "Please let me go to the field[7704]
and [a]glean[3950] among the ears of grain
after one in whose sight I may find
favor."[2580] And she said to her, "Go,
my daughter."
3 So she departed and went and
gleaned in the field after the reapers;
and [I]she happened to come to the portion
of the field belonging to Boaz, who was
of the family of Elimelech.
4 Now behold, Boaz came from
Bethlehem and said to the reapers,
"[a]May the LORD be with you." And they
said to him, "May the LORD bless[1288]
you."
5 Then Boaz said to his servant who
was [I]in charge of[5324,5921] the reapers,
"Whose young woman is this?"
6 And the servant [I]in charge of
the reapers answered and said, "She
is the young Moabite woman who

13 [I]Lit., *more bitter* [a]Judg. 2:15; Job 19:21; Ps. 32:4
15 [a]Josh. 24:15; Judg. 11:24
17 [a]1Sam. 3:17; 2Kin. 6:31
18 [I]Lit., *ceased to speak* [a]Acts 21:14
19 [I]Lit., *they* [a]Matt. 21:10
20 [I]I.e., pleasant [II]I.e., bitter [III]Heb., *Shaddai* [a]Ex. 6:3; Job 6:4
21 [I]Heb., *Shaddai* [a]Job 1:21
22 [a]Ex. 9:31; Lev. 23:10, 11

1 [I]Or, *an acquaintance* [II]Or, *mighty, valiant man* [a]Ruth 1:2
2 [a]Lev. 19:9, 10; 23:22; Deut. 24:19; Ruth 2:7
3 [I]Lit., *her chance chanced upon*
4 [a]Judg. 6:12; Ps. 129:8; Luke 1:28; 2Thess. 3:16
5 [I]Lit., *appointed over*
6 [I]Lit., *who was appointed over*

🔑 **2:1** Boaz was the son of Salmon (Ruth 4:21), the husband of Rahab the harlot (Mt. 1:5), who had helped the spies prepare for the battle against Jericho (Josh. 2:1-21). Boaz' marriage to Ruth, a native of Moab (Ruth 1:4), resulted in the royal bloodline of David, and hence of Jesus, the Messiah, having two Gentile women in it. Ruth and Boaz were David's great grandparents (Ruth 4:21,22; Mt. 1:5,6). See note on Josh 2:1.

🔑 **2:2** The field of Boaz, which tour guides to this day point out on the outskirts of Bethlehem, is important in the Bible on several counts. Not only did Ruth and Boaz meet here, but, as part of his family's ancestral lands, this is where David the shepherd boy would have tended his father's sheep. Much later, Joseph (Mary's husband), as a direct descendant of David, was drawn back to his family lands in Bethlehem during the census under Emperor Augustus, and thus, Jesus was born in the City of David. Even then, shepherds in the vicinity were tending their flocks, just as David had done centuries earlier.

2:2-7 See note on Lev. 19:9-10.

returned[7725] with Naomi from the land[7704] of Moab.

7 "And she said, 'Please let me glean and gather[622] after the reapers among the sheaves.' Thus she came and has remained from the morning until now; she has been sitting in the house[1004] for a little while."

8 Then Boaz said to Ruth, "[I]Listen[8085] carefully, my daughter. Do not go to glean[3950] in another field; furthermore, do not go[5674] on from this one, but stay here with my maids.

9 "Let your eyes be on the field which they reap, and go after them. Indeed, I have commanded[6680] the servants not to touch you. When you are thirsty, go to the [I]water jars and drink from what the servants draw."

10 Then she [a]fell on her face, bowing[7812] to the ground[776] and said to him, "Why have I found favor in your sight that you should take notice[5234] of me, since I am a foreigner?"[5237]

11 And Boaz answered and said to her, "All that you have done[6213] for your mother-in-law after the death[4194] of your husband has been fully reported to me, and how you left[5800] your father[1] and your mother[517] and the land[776] of your birth, and came to a people[5971] that you did not previously know.[3045]

12 "[a]May the LORD reward your work, and your wages be full[8003] from the LORD, the God of Israel, [b]under whose wings you have come to seek refuge."[2620]

13 Then she said, "I have found favor[2580] in your sight, my lord,[113] for you have comforted[5162] me and indeed have spoken[1696] [I]kindly[3820] to your maidservant, though I am not like one of your maidservants."

14 And at mealtime[6256,400] Boaz said to her, "[I]Come[5066] here, that you may eat of the bread and dip[2881] your piece of bread in the vinegar." So she sat beside the reapers; and he [II]served her roasted grain, and she ate and was satisfied [a]and had some left.

15 When she rose to glean, Boaz commanded[6680] his servants, saying, "Let her glean[3950] even among the sheaves, and do not insult her.

16 "And also you shall purposely pull out for her *some grain* from the bundles and leave[5800] *it* that she may glean, and do not rebuke[1605] her."

17 So she gleaned in the field until evening. Then she beat out what she had gleaned, and it was about an ephah of barley.

18 And she took *it* up[5375] and went into the city, and her mother-in-law saw[7200] what she had gleaned. She also took *it* out and [a]gave [I]Naomi what she had left after [II]she was satisfied.

19 Her mother-in-law then said to her, "Where did you glean today[3117] and where did you work?[6213] May he who [a]took notice of you be blessed."[1288] So she told her mother-in-law with whom she had worked and said, "The name of the man with whom I worked today is Boaz."

20 And Naomi said to her daughter-in-law, "[a]May he be blessed of the LORD who has not withdrawn his kindness[2617] to the living[2416] and to the dead." Again Naomi said to her, "The man is [I]our relative, he is one of our [II]closest relatives."[1350]

21 Then Ruth the Moabitess said, "[I]Furthermore, he said[559] to me, 'You should stay close to my servants until they have finished[3615] all my harvest.' "

22 And Naomi said to Ruth her daughter-in-law, "It is good,[2896] my daughter, that you go out with his maids, lest *others* fall upon you in another field."

23 So she stayed close by the maids of Boaz in order to glean until [a]the end[3615] of the barley harvest and the wheat harvest. And she lived with her mother-in-law.

Boaz Will Redeem Ruth

3 Then Naomi her mother-in-law said to her, "My daughter, shall I not seek [I]security for you, that it may be well[3190] with you?

2 "And now is not Boaz [a]our

8 [I]Lit., *Have you not heard*
9 [I]Lit., *vessels*
10 [a]1Sam. 25:23
12 [a]1Sam. 24:19 [b]Ruth1:16; Ps. 17:8; 36:7; 57:1; 61:4; 63:7; 91:4
13 [I]Lit., *to the heart of your*
14 [I]Lit., *Draw near* [II]Lit., *held out to* [a]Ruth 2:18
18 [I]Lit., *her* [II]Lit., *her satiety* [a]Ruth 2:14
19 [a]Ps. 41:1
20 [I]Lit., *near to us* [II]Lit., *redeemers* [a]2Sam. 2:5
21 [I]Lit., *Also that*
23 [a]Deut. 16:9
1 [I]Lit., *rest*
2 [a]Deut. 25:5-10

[I]kinsman, with whose maids you were? Behold, he winnows[2219] barley at the threshing floor tonight.

3 "Wash[7364] yourself therefore, and anoint[5480] yourself and put on your *best* clothes, and go down to the threshing floor; *but* do not make yourself known[3045] to the man until he has finished[3615] eating and drinking.

4 "And it shall be when he lies down, that you shall [I]notice[3045] the place where he lies, and you shall go and uncover[1540] his feet and lie down; then he will tell you what you shall do."[6213]

5 And she said to her, "[a]All that you say I will do."

6 So she went down to the threshing floor and did according to all that her mother-in-law had commanded[6680] her.

7 When Boaz had eaten and drunk and [a]his heart was merry,[3190] he went to lie down at the end of the heap of grain; and she came secretly, and uncovered his feet and lay down.

8 And it happened in the middle of the night that the man was startled[2729] and [I]bent forward; and behold, a woman[802] was lying at his feet.

9 And he said, "Who are you?" And she answered, "I am Ruth your maid. So spread your covering over your maid, for you are a [I]close relative."[1350]

10 Then he said, "[a]May you be blessed[1288] of the LORD, my daughter. You have shown[3190] your last kindness[2617] to be better than the first[7223] by not going after young men, whether poor or rich.

11 "And now, my daughter, do not fear. I will do[6213] for you whatever you [I]ask, for all my people[5971] in the [II]city know[3045] that you are [a]a woman of excellence.[2428]

12 "And now it is true[551] I am a [I]close relative; however, there is a [I]relative closer than I.

13 "Remain this night, and when morning comes, [a]if he will [I]redeem you, good;[2896] let him redeem you. But if he does not wish[2654] to [I]redeem[1350] you, then I will redeem[1350] you, [b]as the LORD lives.[2416] Lie down until morning."

14 So she lay at his feet until morning and rose before one could recognize[5234] another;[7453] and he said, "[a]Let it not be known[3045] that the woman came to the threshing floor."

15 Again he said, "Give me the cloak that is on you and hold it." So she held it, and he measured six *measures* of barley and laid *it* on her. Then [I]she went into the city.

16 And when she came to her mother-in-law, she said, "[I]How did it go, my daughter?" And she told her all that the man had done[6213] for her.

17 And she said, "These six *measures* of barley he gave to me, for he said,[559] 'Do not go to your mother-in-law empty-handed.' "

18 Then she said, "Wait, my daughter, until you know[3045] how the matter[1697] [I]turns out; for the man will not rest[8252] until he has [II]settled[3615] it today."[3117]

The Marriage of Ruth

4 ⚷ Now Boaz went up[5927] to the gate and sat down there, and behold, [a]the [I]close relative[1350] of whom Boaz spoke[1696] was passing by, so he said, "Turn aside, [II]friend, sit down here." And he turned aside and sat down.

2 And he took ten men[582] of the [a]elders[2205] of the city and said, "Sit down here." So they sat down.

2 [I]Or, *acquaintance*
4 [I]Lit., *know*
5 [a]Eph. 6:1; Col. 3:20
7 [a]Judg. 19:6, 9; 2Sam. 13:28; 1Kin. 21:7; Esth. 1:10
8 [I]Lit., *twisted himself*
9 [I]Or, *redeemer*
10 [a]Ruth 2:20
11 [I]Lit., *say* [II]Lit., *gate* [a]Prov. 12:4; 31:10
12 [I]Or, *redeemer*
13 [I]Or, *act as close relative to* [a]Deut. 25:5; Matt. 22:24 [b]Judg. 8:19; Jer. 4:2; 12:16
14 [a]Rom. 14:16; 2Cor. 8:21
15 [I]So with many mss.; M.T., *he*
16 [I]Lit., *Who are you?*
18 [I]Lit., *falls* [II]Lit., *finished the matter*
1 [I]Or, *redeemer* [II]Lit., *a certain one* [a]Ruth 3:12
2 [a]1Kin. 21:8; Prov. 31:23

⚷ **4:1-12** Here we see two separate laws in the Pentateuch coming into play. First, Boaz was willing to perform the duty of next of kin to redeem a piece of land, so it could stay in the family (see Lev. 25:25), but there was a person who was a closer relative. This case, however, was further complicated by the need to contract a levirate marriage. Therefore, the other relative deferred to Boaz, who willingly married Ruth. The legal basis for this practice is found in Deut. 25:5-10, including the shaming of a man who would not perform his duty. This obligation dates back to the Patriarchs (Gen. 38:8), and the legal ramifications of such cases were still being discussed in Jesus' day (Mt. 22:23-28).

3 Then he said to the [I]closest relative, "Naomi, who has come back[7725] from the land[7704] of Moab, has to sell the piece of land[7704] [a]which belonged to our brother[251] Elimelech.

4 "So I thought[559] to [I]inform[1540] you, saying, '[a]Buy *it* before those who are sitting *here,* and before the elders of my people.[5971] If you will redeem[1350] *it,* redeem *it;* but if [II]not, tell me that I may know;[3045] for [b]there is no one but you to redeem *it,* and I am after you.' " And he said, "I will redeem *it.*"

5 Then Boaz said, "On the day[3117] you buy the field[7704] from the hand[3027] of Naomi, you must also acquire Ruth the Moabitess, the widow[802] of the deceased, in order [a]to raise up the name of the deceased on his inheritance."[5159]

6 And [a]the [I]closest relative said, "I cannot redeem *it* for myself, lest I [II]jeopardize[7843] my own inheritance. Redeem *it* for yourself; you *may have* my right of redemption,[1353] for I cannot redeem *it.*"

7 Now this was [a]*the custom* in former times in Israel concerning the redemption[1353] and the exchange *of land* to confirm any matter:[1697] a man removed his sandal and gave it to another; and this was the *manner of* attestation[8584] in Israel.

8 So the [I]closest relative said to Boaz, "Buy *it* for yourself." And he removed his sandal.

9 Then Boaz said to the elders and all the people,[5971] "You are witnesses today[3117] that I have bought from the hand of Naomi all that belonged to Elimelech and all that belonged to Chilion and Mahlon.

10 "Moreover, I have acquired Ruth the Moabitess, the widow of Mahlon, to be my wife in order to raise up the name of the deceased on his inheritance, so [a]that the name of the deceased may not be cut off[3772] from his brothers[251] or from the [I]court of his *birth* place; you are witnesses today."

11 And all the people who were in the [I]court, and the elders, said, "*We are* witnesses. May the LORD make the woman[802] who is coming into your home[1004] [a]like Rachel and Leah, both of whom built the house of Israel; and may you achieve[6213] [II]wealth[2428] in Ephrathah and [III]become famous in Bethlehem.

12 "Moreover, may your house be like the house of [a]Perez whom Tamar bore to Judah, through the [I]offspring[2233] which the LORD shall give you by this young woman."

13 So Boaz took Ruth, and she became his wife,[802] and he went in to her. And [a]the LORD [I]enabled her to conceive, and she gave birth to a son.[1121]

14 Then the [a]women said to Naomi, "Blessed[1288] is the LORD who has not left[7673] you without a [I]redeemer today, and may his name [II]become famous in Israel.

15 "May he also be to you a restorer[7725] of life[5315] and a sustainer of your old age;[7872] for your daughter-in-law, who loves[157] you [I][a]and is better[2896] to you than seven sons, has given birth to him."

The Line of David Began Here

16 Then Naomi took the child [I]and laid him in her lap, and became his nurse.[539]

17 And the neighbor[7934] women gave him a name, saying, "A son has been born to Naomi!" So they named him Obed. He is the father[1] of Jesse, the father of David.

18 Now these are the generations[8435] of Perez: [a]to Perez [I]was born Hezron,

19 and to Hezron was born Ram, and to Ram, Amminadab,

20 and to Amminadab was born Nahshon, and to Nahshon, Salmon,

🗝 21 and to Salmon was born Boaz, and to Boaz, Obed,

22 and to Obed was born Jesse, and to Jesse, David.

3 [I]Lit., *redeemer* [a]Lev. 25:25

4 [I]Lit., *uncover your ear* [II]Lit., *no one will redeem* [a]Jer. 32:7f. [b]Lev. 25:25

5 [a]Gen. 38:8; Deut. 25:5f.; Matt. 22:24

6 [I]Lit., *redeemer* [II]Lit., *ruin* [a]Lev. 25:25

7 [a]Deut. 25:8-10

8 [I]Lit., *redeemer*

10 [I]Lit., *gate* [a]Deut. 25:6

11 [I]Lit., *gate* [II]Or, *power* [III]Lit., *call the name in* [a]Gen. 29:25-30

12 [I]Lit., *seed* [a]Gen. 38:29; 46:12; Ruth 4:18

13 [I]Lit., *gave her conception* [a]Gen. 29:31; 33:5

14 [I]Or, *closest relative* [II]Lit., *be called in* [a]Luke 1:58

15 [I]Lit., *who* [a]Ruth 1:16, 17; 2:11, 12

16 [I]I.e., as her own

18 [I]Lit., *begot,* and so through v. 22 [a]Matt. 1:3-6

🗝 **4:21,22** See note on Ruth 2:1.

The First Book of

SAMUEL

Originally, in the Hebrew Bible, the first and second books of Samuel were just one book. Also, I Kings and II Kings formed one continuous story which followed chronologically. I Samuel opens with a touching story about total dedication toward God. Samuel, which means "asked of God," was a young boy who was given to God by his mother, Hannah, for God's service under the direction of Eli, the old priest, judge, and leader of God's people. Samuel was destined to become one of the greatest leaders—a judge, a prophet, and a priest—in the Old Testament. He even established schools of prophets for guiding Israel. God communicated directly to the prophets and they, in turn, spoke to the people. Although God was the real King of Israel, the people clamored for a physical king to lead them. God allowed Samuel to assist in the transition to a unified kingdom. Samuel anointed Saul with oil to be the first king of Israel. Though Saul was tall, brave, and handsome, he proved to be a very disappointing spiritual leader. He forsook God's directives and ignored the counsel of Samuel. Saul sank lower and lower spiritually. Finally, God chose an unknown to be the new king of Israel. His name was David. Though David certainly had his shortcomings, God used him mightily to teach many important spiritual lessons. Jesus Christ was called the "Son of David" (Matt. 20:30). The main purpose of the book of I Samuel was to show the folly of wanting a human king instead of God, and that God's purpose would be accomplished in spite of man. Samuel and David were obedient to God and were consequently blessed. Saul was disobedient to God and was eventually destroyed.

Elkanah and His Wives

1 Now there was a certain man from
[a]Ramathaim-zophim from the [b]hill
country of Ephraim, and his name was
[c]Elkanah the son[1121] of Jeroham, the
son of Elihu, the son of Tohu, the son
of Zuph, an Ephraimite.
2 And he had [a]two wives:[802] the
name of one was [b]Hannah and the name
of the other Peninnah; and Peninnah had
children, but Hannah had no children.
3 Now this man would go up from
his city [a]yearly[3117] [b]to worship[7812] and
to sacrifice[2076] to the LORD of hosts in
[c]Shiloh. And the two sons[1121] of Eli,
Hophni and Phinehas were priests[3548]
to the LORD there.
4 And when the day came that Elkanah sacrificed,[2076] he [a]would give portions to Peninnah his wife[802] and to all
her sons and her daughters;
5 but to Hannah he would give a
double portion, for he loved[157] Hannah,
[a]but the LORD had closed her womb.
6 Her rival, however, [a]would provoke[3707] her bitterly[3708] to irritate her,
because the LORD had closed her womb.
7 And it happened[6213] year after
year, as often as she went up to the
house of the LORD, she would provoke
her, so she wept and would not eat.
8 Then Elkanah her husband said
to her, "Hannah, why do you weep and
why do you not eat and why is your
heart sad? [a]Am I not better[2896] to you
than ten sons?"
9 Then Hannah rose after eating and
drinking in Shiloh. Now Eli the priest[3548]
was sitting on the seat[3678] by the doorpost of [a]the temple of the LORD.
10 And she, [I]greatly distressed,[4751]
prayed[6419] to the LORD and wept bitterly.
11 And she [a]made a vow[5087] and
said, "O LORD of hosts, if Thou wilt

1 [a]1Sam. 1:19 [b]Josh. 17:17, 18; 24:33 [c]1Chr. 6:22-28, 33-38
2 [a]Deut. 21:15-17 [b]Luke 2:36
3 [a]Ex. 34:23; 1Sam. 1:21; Luke 2:41 [b]Ex. 23:14; Deut. 12:5-7; 16:16 [c]Josh. 18:1
4 [a]Deut. 12:17, 18
5 [a]Gen. 16:1; 30:1
6 [a]Job 24:21
8 [a]Ruth 4:15
9 [a]1Sam. 3:3
10 [I]Lit., *bitter of soul*
11 [a]Num. 30:6-11

1:11 The outward sign which Hannah mentioned in connection with the vow that she made for her son was associated with the vow of the Nazarite (See note on Num. 6:2-21). Apparently he, as Samson before him (see Judg. 13:4,5), was to be a Nazarite for life. The difference was that Samson was a

(continued on next page)

indeed [b]look on the affliction of Thy maidservant and remember me, and not forget Thy maidservant, but wilt give Thy
maidservant a [I]son,[2233] then I will give
him to the LORD all the days[3117] of his
life,[2416] and [c]a razor shall never come
on his head."
12 Now it came about, as she
[I]continued praying[6419] before the LORD,
that Eli was watching her mouth.
13 As for Hannah, [a]she was speaking[1696] in her heart, only her lips[8193]
were moving, but her voice was not
heard. So Eli thought she was drunk.
14 Then Eli said to her, "[a]How long
will you make yourself drunk? Put away
your wine from you."
15 But Hannah answered and said,
"No, my lord,[113] I am a woman[802] [I]op-
pressed[7186] in spirit;[7307] I have drunk neither wine nor strong drink, but I [a]have
poured[8210] out my soul before the LORD.
16 "Do not [I]consider your maidservant as a worthless woman;[1100] for I
have spoken[1696] until now out of my
great concern[7878] and [II]provocation."[3708]
17 Then Eli answered and said,
"[a]Go in peace;[7965] and may the God[430]
of Israel [b]grant your petition[7596] that you
have asked[7592] of Him."
18 And she said, "[a]Let your maidservant find favor[2580] in your sight." So
the woman went her way[1870] and ate,
and [b]her face was no longer *sad.*

Samuel Is Born to Hannah

19 Then they arose early in the
morning and worshiped[7812] before the
LORD, and returned again to their house
in [a]Ramah. And Elkanah [I]had relations
with Hannah[3045] his wife, and [b]the LORD
remembered her.
20 And it came about [I]in due time,
after Hannah had conceived, that she
gave birth to a son; and she named[7121]
him Samuel, *saying,* "[a]Because I have
asked him of the LORD."

21 Then the man Elkanah [a]went up
with all his household to offer[2076] to the
LORD the yearly sacrifice[2077] and *pay* his
vow.
22 But Hannah did not go up, for
she said to her husband, "*I will not go
up* until the child is weaned; then I will
[a]bring him, that he may appear[7200] before
the LORD and [b]stay there forever."
23 And [a]Elkanah her husband said
to her, "Do[6213] what seems best[2896]
[I]to you. Remain until you have weaned
him; only [b]may the LORD confirm His
word."[1697] So the woman remained and
nursed her son until she weaned him.
24 Now when she had weaned him,
[a]she took him up with her, with a three-
year-old bull and one ephah of flour and
a jug of wine, and brought him to
[b]the house of the LORD in Shiloh, although the child was young.
25 Then [a]they slaughtered[2819] the
bull, and [b]brought the boy to Eli.
26 And she said, "Oh, my lord!
[a]As your soul lives,[2416] my lord, I am
the woman who stood[5324] here beside
you, praying to the LORD.
27 "[a]For this boy I prayed,[6419] and
the LORD has given me my petition which
I asked of Him.
28 "[a]So I have also [I]dedicated[7592]
him to the LORD; as long as he lives
he is [I]dedicated to the LORD." And
[b]he worshiped the LORD there.

Hannah's Song of Thanksgiving

2 Then Hannah [a]prayed[6419] and said,
"My heart exults in the LORD;
[b]My [I]horn is exalted in the LORD,
My mouth [II]speaks boldly against
my enemies,
Because [c]I rejoice in Thy
salvation.
2 "[a]There is no one holy like the
LORD,
Indeed, [b]there is no one besides
Thee,

11 [I]Lit., *seed of men* [b]Gen. 29:32 [c]Num. 6:5; Judg. 13:5
12 [I]Lit., *multiplied*
13 [a]Gen. 24:42-45
14 [a]Acts 2:4, 13
15 [I]Lit., *severe* [a]Job 30:16; Ps. 42:4; 62:8; Lam. 2:19
16 [I]Lit., *give* [II]Lit., *my provocation*
17 [a]Judg. 18:6; 1Sam. 25:35; 2Kin. 5:19; Mark 5:34; Luke 7:50 [b]Ps. 20:3-5
18 [a]Gen. 33:15; Ruth 2:13 [b]Rom. 15:13
19 [I]Lit., *knew* [a]1Sam. 1:1; 2:11 [b]Gen. 21:1; 30:22
20 [I]Lit., *at the circuit of the days* [a]Gen. 41:51, 52; Ex. 2:10, 22; Matt. 1:21
21 [a]Deut. 12:11; 1Sam. 1:3
22 [a]Luke 2:22 [b]1Sam. 1:11,28
23 [I]Lit., *in your eyes* [a]Num. 30:7, 10, 11 [b]1Sam. 1:17
24 [a]Num. 15:9, 10; Deut. 12:5, 6 [b]Josh. 18:1; 1Sam. 4:3, 4
25 [a]Lev. 1:5 [b]Luke 2:22
26 [a]2Kin. 2:2, 4,6; 4:30
27 [a]1Sam. 1:11-13; Ps. 6:9; 66:19, 20
28 [I]Lit., *lent* [a]1Sam. 1:11, 22 [b]Gen. 24:26, 52

1 [I]I.e., strength [II]Lit., *is enlarged* [a]1Sam. 2:1-10; Luke 1:46-55 [b]Deut. 33:17; Job 16:15; Ps. 75:10; 89:17, 24; 92:10; 112:9 [c]Ps. 9:14; 13:5; 35:9; Is. 12:2, 3
2 [a]Ex. 15:11; Lev. 19:2; Ps. 86:8 [b]2Sam. 22:32

(continued from previous page)
Nazarite by God's instruction and Samuel's mother made the vow for her son. Because of her obvious attitude toward God and her faith in Him, Hannah's supplication is an example of prayer to be carefully studied.

[c]Nor is there any rock like our
God.[430]
3 "[I]Boast no more so very proudly,
[a]Do not let arrogance come out
of your mouth;
[b]For the LORD is a God of
knowledge,[1844]
[c]And with Him actions are
weighed.
4 "[a]The bows of the mighty are
shattered,
[b]But the feeble[3782] gird on
strength.[2428]
5 "Those who were full hire
themselves out for bread,
But those who were hungry
cease *to hunger.*
[a]Even the barren[6135] gives birth
to seven,
But [b]she who has many
children[1121] languishes.
6 "[a]The LORD kills[4191] and makes
alive;
[b]He brings down to [I]Sheol[7585]
and raises up.
7 "[a]The LORD makes poor and rich;
[b]He brings low, He also exalts.
8 "[a]He raises the poor from the
dust,
[b]He lifts the needy from the ash
heap[6083]
[c]To make them sit with
nobles,[5081]
And inherit[5157] a seat of honor;
[d]For the pillars of the earth[776]
are the LORD'S,
And He set the world[8398] on
them.
9 "[a]He keeps[8104] the feet of His
godly ones,[2623]
[b]But the wicked[6563] ones are
silenced in darkness;[2822]
[c]For not by might shall a man
prevail.
10 "[a]Those who contend[7378] with the
LORD will be shattered;[2865]
[b]Against them He will thunder
in the heavens,
[c]The LORD will judge[1777] the
ends of the earth;

2 [c]Deut. 32:30, 31
3 [I]Lit., *Talk much* [a]Prov. 8:13 [b]1Sam. 16:7; 1Kin. 8:39 [c]Prov. 16:2; 24:12
4 [a]Ps. 37:15; 46:9 [b]Ps. 18:39; Heb. 11:32-34
5 [a]Ruth 4:15; Ps. 113:9 [b]Jer. 15:9
6 [I]I.e., the nether world [a]Deut. 32:39; 2Kin. 5:7; Rev. 1:18 [b]Is. 26:19
7 [a]Deut. 8:17, 18 [b]Job 5:11; Ps. 75:7; James 4:10
8 [a]Job 42:10-12; Ps. 75:7; 113:7 [b]2Sam. 7:8; Dan. 2:48; James 2:5 [c]Job 36:7; Ps. 113:8 [d]Job 38:4-6; Ps. 75:3; 104:5
9 [a]Ps. 91:11, 12; 121:3; Prov. 3:26; 1Pet. 1:5 [b]Matt. 8:12 [c]Ps. 33:16, 17
10 [I]I.e., strength [a]Ex. 15:6; Ps. 2:9 [b]1Sam. 7:10; 2Sam. 22:14; Ps. 18:13, 14 [c]Ps. 96:13; 98:9; Matt. 25:31, 32 [d]Ps. 21:1, 7 [e]Ps. 89:24
11 [a]1Sam. 1:1, 19 [b]1Sam. 1:28; 2:18; 3:1
12 [I]Lit., *sons of Belial* [a]Jer. 2:8; 9:3, 6; 2Cor. 6:15
13 [a]Lev. 7:29-34
15 [a]Lev. 3:3-5, 16
16 [I]Lit., *offer up in smoke* [II]Lit., *like the day* [III]Lit., *your soul*
17 [a]Mal. 2:7-9
18 [I]Lit., *girded with* [a]1Sam. 2:11; 3:1 [b]1Sam. 2:28; 22:18; 2Sam. 6:14; 1Chr. 15:27
19 [a]Ex. 28:31

[d]And He will give strength to
His king,[4428]
[e]And will exalt the [I]horn of His
anointed."[4899]
11 Then Elkanah went to his home
at [a]Ramah. [b]But the boy ministered to
the LORD before Eli the priest.[3548]

The Sin of Eli's Sons

12 Now the sons[1121] of Eli were
[Ia]worthless men;[1100] they did not
know[3045] the LORD
13 [a]and the custom[4941] of the
priests[3548] with the people.[5971] When
any man was offering[2076] a sacrifice,[2077]
the priest's servant would come while
the meat[1320] was boiling, with a three-
pronged fork in his hand.
14 Then he would thrust it into the
pan, or kettle, or caldron, or pot; all
that the fork brought up[5927] the priest
would take for himself. Thus they did[6213]
in Shiloh to all the Israelites who came
there.
15 Also, before [a]they burned[6999] the
fat, the priest's servant would come and
say to the man who was sacrificing,[2076]
"Give the priest meat for roasting, as
he will not take boiled[1310] meat from
you, only raw."
16 And if the man said to him, "They
must surely [I]burn[6999] the fat [II]first,[3117]
and then take as much as [III]you[5315] desire," then he would say,[559] "No, but
you shall give *it to me* now; and if not,
I will take it by force."
17 Thus the sin[2403] of the young men
was very great before the LORD, for
the men [a]despised[5006] the offering[4503]
of the LORD.

Samuel before the Lord as a Boy

18 Now [a]Samuel was ministering
before the LORD, *as* a boy [Ib]wearing a
linen ephod.
19 And his mother would make him
a little [a]robe and bring it to him from

2:10 On "His anointed" see note on I Sam. 16:13.

year to year when she would come up with her husband to offer[2076] [b]the yearly[3117] sacrifice.

20 Then Eli would [a]bless[1288] Elkanah and his wife[802] and say, "May the LORD give[7760] you [I]children[2233] from this woman[802] in place of [II]the one she [b]dedicated[7592] to the LORD." And they went to their own [III]home.

21 And [a]the LORD visited[6485] Hannah; and she conceived and gave birth to three sons and two daughters. And [b]the boy Samuel grew before the LORD.

Eli Rebukes His Sons

22 Now Eli was very old;[2204] and he heard [a]all that his sons were doing to all Israel, and how they lay with [b]the women[802] who served[6633] at the doorway of the tent of meeting.[4150]

23 And he said to them, "Why do[6213] you do such things, the evil[7451] things that I hear from all these people?

24 "No, my sons; for the report is not good[2896] [a]which I hear [I]the LORD's people circulating.

25 "If one man sins[2398] against another, [a]God[430] will mediate for him; but [b]if a man sins against the LORD, who can intercede for him?" But they would not listen to the voice of their father,[1] for the [c]LORD desired[2654] to put them to death.[4191]

26 Now the boy [a]Samuel [I]was growing in stature and in favor[2896] both with the LORD and with men.

27 Then [a]a man of God came to Eli and said to him, "Thus says the LORD, '[b]Did I *not* indeed reveal[1540] Myself to the house of your father when they were in Egypt *in bondage* to Pharaoh's house?

28 'And [a]did I *not* choose[977] them from all the tribes of Israel to be My priests, to go up to My altar,[4196] to burn incense,[7004] to carry an ephod before Me; and did I *not* [b]give to the house of your father all the fire *offerings* of the sons of Israel?

29 'Why do you [a]kick at My sacrifice and at My offering [b]which I have commanded[6680] *in My* [c]dwelling, and [d]honor your sons above Me, by making yourselves fat with the [I]choicest[7225] of every offering of My people Israel?'

30 "Therefore the LORD God of Israel declares,[5001] '[a]I did indeed say that your house and the house of your father should walk before Me forever'; but now the LORD declares, 'Far be it from Me—for [b]those who honor Me I will honor, and those [c]who despise Me will be lightly esteemed.

🔑 31 'Behold, [a]the days[3117] are coming when I will break your [I]strength and the [I]strength of your father's[1] house so that there will not be an old man in your house.

32 'And you will see [a]the distress of *My* dwelling, in *spite of* all that [I]I do good for Israel; and an [b]old man will not be in your house forever.

33 'Yet I will not cut[3772] off every man of yours from My altar [I]that your eyes may fail[3615] *from weeping* and your soul grieve, and all the increase of your house will die[4191] [II]in the prime of life.

34 'And this will be [a]the sign[226] to you which shall come concerning your two sons, Hophni and Phinehas: [b]on the same day[3117] both of them shall die.

35 'But [a]I will raise up for Myself a faithful[539] priest who will do according to what is in My heart and in My soul; and [b]I will build him an enduring[539] house, and he will walk before [c]My anointed always.

36 'And it shall come about that everyone who is left[3498] in your house shall come and bow down[7812] to him for a [I]piece of silver or a loaf of bread, and say, "Please[4994] [II]assign me to one of the priest's offices so that I may eat a piece of bread." ' "

19 [b]1Sam. 1:3,21
20 [I]Lit., *seed* [II]Lit., *the one asked for which was lent* [III]Lit., *place* [a]Luke 2:34 [b]1Sam. 1:11, 27,28
21 [a]Gen. 21:1 [b]Judg. 13:24; 1Sam. 2:26; 3:19-21; Luke 1:80; 2:40
22 [a]1Sam. 2:13-17 [b]Ex. 38:8
24 [I]Or, *making the LORD's people transgress* [a]1Kin. 15:26
25 [a]Deut. 1:17 [b]Num. 15:30; 1Sam. 3:14; Heb. 10:26, 27 [c]Josh. 11:20
26 [I]Lit., *was going on both great and good* [a]1Sam. 2:21; Luke 2:52
27 [a]Deut. 33:1; Judg. 13:6 [b]Ex. 4:14-16; 12:1, 43
28 [a]Ex. 28:1-4; 30:7, 8; Lev. 8:7, 8 [b]Lev. 7:35, 36
29 [I]Or, *first* [a]1Sam. 2:13-17 [b]Deut. 12:5-9 [c]Ps. 26:8 [d]Matt. 10:37
30 [a]Ex. 29:9; Num. 25:13 [b]Ps. 50:23 [c]Mal. 2:9
31 [I]Or, *arm* [a]1Sam. 4:11-18; 22:17-20
32 [I]Lit., *He does* [a]1Kin. 2:26, 27 [b]Zech. 8:4
33 [I]Lit., *to waste away your eyes and to grieve your soul* [II]Lit., *as men*
34 [a]1Sam. 10:7-9; 1Kin. 13:3 [b]1Sam. 4:11, 17
35 [a]1Sam. 3:1; 7:9; 9:12, 13 [b]1Sam. 8:3-5; 25:28; 2Sam. 7:11, 27; 1Kin. 11:38 [c]1Sam. 10:9, 10; 12:3; 16:13
36 [I]Or, *payment* [II]Lit., *attach*

🔑 **2:31-36** See note on I Kgs. 2:26,27.

The Prophetic Call to Samuel

3 Now [a]the boy Samuel was ministering to the LORD before Eli. And [b]word[1697] from the LORD was rare in those days,[3117] [I]visions[2377] were infrequent.

2 And it happened at that time as Eli was lying down in his place (now [a]his eyesight had begun to grow dim *and* he could not see well),

3 and [a]the lamp[5216] of God[430] had not yet[2962] gone out, and Samuel was lying down in the temple of the LORD where the ark[727] of God *was,*

4 that the LORD called[7121] Samuel; and he said,[559] "[a]Here I am."

5 Then he ran to Eli and said, "Here I am, for you called[7121] me." But he said, "I did not call, lie down again." So he went and lay down.

6 And the LORD called yet again, "Samuel!" So Samuel arose and went to Eli, and said, "Here I am, for you called[7121] me." But he [I]answered, "I did not call, my son,[1121] lie down again."

7 [a]Now Samuel did not yet know[3045] the LORD, nor had the word of the LORD yet been revealed to him.

8 So the LORD called Samuel again for the third time. And he arose and went to Eli, and said, "Here I am, for you called me." Then Eli discerned[995] that the LORD was calling the boy.

9 And Eli said to Samuel, "Go lie down, and it shall be if He calls you, that you shall say, 'Speak,[1696] LORD, for Thy servant[5650] is listening.' " So Samuel went and lay down in his place.

10 Then the LORD came and stood and called as at other times, "Samuel! Samuel!" And Samuel said, "Speak, for Thy servant is listening."

11 And the LORD said to Samuel, "Behold, [a]I am about to do[6213] a thing in Israel at which both ears[241] of everyone who hears it will tingle.

12 "In that day[3117] [a]I will carry out against Eli all that I have spoken[1696] concerning his house, from beginning to end.[3615]

🔑 13 "For [a]I have told him that I am about to judge[8199] his house forever for [b]the iniquity[5771] which he knew, because [c]his sons[1121] brought a curse[7043] on themselves and [d]he did not rebuke them.

14 "And therefore I have sworn to the house of Eli that [a]the iniquity of Eli's house shall not be atoned[3722] for by sacrifice[2077] or offering[4503] forever."

15 So Samuel lay down until morning. Then he [a]opened the doors of the house of the LORD. But Samuel was afraid[3372] to tell[5046] [b]the vision to Eli.

16 Then Eli called Samuel and said, "Samuel, my son." And he said, "Here I am."

17 And he said,[1696] "What is the word that He spoke to you? Please[4994] do not hide it from me. [a]May God do so to you, and more also, if you hide anything from me of all the words that He spoke to you."

18 So Samuel told him everything[1697] and hid nothing from him. And he said, "[a]It is the LORD; let Him do what seems good[2896] to Him."

19 Thus [a]Samuel grew and [b]the LORD was with him and [c]let none of his words[1697] [I]fail.

20 And all Israel [a]from Dan even to Beersheba knew[3045] that Samuel was confirmed[539] as a prophet[5030] of the LORD.

21 And [a]the LORD appeared[7200] again at Shiloh, [b]because the LORD revealed Himself to Samuel at Shiloh by the word of the LORD.

Philistines Take the Ark in Victory

4 Thus the word[1697] of Samuel came to all Israel. Now Israel went out to meet the Philistines in battle and camped beside [a]Ebenezer while the Philistines camped in [b]Aphek.

2 And the Philistines drew up in battle array to meet Israel. When the battle

1 ILit., *no vision spread abroad* a1Sam. 2:11, 18 bPs. 74:9; Ezek. 7:26; Amos 8:11, 12
2 aGen. 27:1; 48:10; 1Sam. 4:15
3 aEx. 25:31-37; Lev. 24:2, 3
4 aIs. 6:8
6 ILit., *said*
7 aActs 19:2; 1Cor. 13:11
11 a2Kin. 21:12; Jer. 19:3
12 a1Sam. 2:27-36
13 a1Sam. 2:29-31 b1Sam. 2:22 c1Sam. 2:12, 17, 22 dDeut. 17:12; 21:18
14 aLev. 15:31; Is. 22:14
15 a1Chr. 15:23 b1Sam. 3:10
17 a2Sam. 3:35
18 aEx. 34:5-7; Lev. 10:3; Job 2:10; Is. 39:8
19 ILit., *fall to the ground* a1Sam. 2:21 bGen. 21:22; 28:15; 39:2 c1Sam. 9:6
20 aJudg. 20:1
21 aGen. 12:7 b1Sam. 3:10
1 a1Sam. 7:12 bJosh. 12:18; 1Sam. 29:1

🔑 **3:13** No doubt Eli had spoken to his sons about their bad behavior before, but he failed to discipline them. We must love our children while being firm with them (Eph. 6:4; Heb. 12:5-8).

spread,[5203] Israel was [I]defeated before the Philistines who killed[5221] about four thousand men on the battlefield.[7704]

🔑 3 When the people[5971] came into the camp,[4264] the elders[2205] of Israel said, "[a]Why has the LORD defeated us today before the Philistines? [b]Let us take to ourselves from Shiloh the ark[727] of the covenant[1285] of the LORD, that [I]it may come among[7130] us and deliver[3467] us from the power of our enemies."

4 So the people sent to Shiloh, and from there they carried[5375] the ark of the covenant of the LORD of hosts [a]who sits *above* the cherubim;[3742] and the two sons[1121] of Eli, Hophni and Phinehas, *were* there with the ark of the covenant of God.[430]

5 And it happened as the ark of the covenant of the LORD came into the camp, that [a]all Israel shouted[7321] with a great shout, so that the earth[776] resounded.

6 And when the Philistines heard the noise of the shout, they said, "What *does* the noise of this great shout in the camp of the Hebrews *mean?*" Then they understood[3045] that the ark of the LORD had come into the camp.

7 And the Philistines were afraid,[3372] for they said, "God has come into the camp." And they said, "[a]Woe to us! For nothing like this has happened before.

8 "Woe to us! Who shall deliver[5337] us from the hand of these mighty gods?[430] These are the gods who smote[5221] the Egyptians with all *kinds of* plagues[4347] in the wilderness.

9 "[a]Take courage[2388] and be[1961] men, O Philistines, lest you become slaves to the Hebrews, [b]as they have been slaves to you; therefore, be men and fight."

10 So the Philistines fought and [a]Israel was [I]defeated, and [b]every man fled to his tent, and the slaughter was very great; for there fell[5307] of Israel thirty thousand foot soldiers.

11 And the ark of God was taken; and [a]the two sons of Eli, Hophni and Phinehas, died.[4191]

12 Now a man of Benjamin ran from the battle line and came to Shiloh the same day[3117] with [a]his clothes torn and [I]dust[127] on his head.

13 When he came, behold, [a]Eli was sitting on *his* seat[3678] [I]by the road eagerly watching, because his heart was trembling for the ark of God. So the man came to tell *it* in the city, and all the city cried[2199] out.

14 When Eli heard the noise of the outcry, he said, "What *does* the noise of this commotion *mean?*" Then the man came hurriedly and told Eli.

15 Now Eli was ninety-eight years old,[1121] and [a]his eyes were set so that he could not see.

16 And the man said to Eli, "I am the one who came from the battle line. Indeed, I escaped from the battle line today." And he said, "[a]How did things go, my son?"[1121]

17 Then the one who brought the news answered and said, "Israel has fled before the Philistines and there has also been a great slaughter among the people, and your two sons also, Hophni and Phinehas, are dead,[4191] and the ark of God has been taken."

18 And it came about when he mentioned the ark of God that [I][a]Eli fell off the seat backward beside[3027] the gate, and his neck was broken[7665] and he died,[4191] for [II]he was old[2204] and heavy. Thus he judged[8199] Israel forty years.

19 Now his daughter-in-law, Phinehas' wife,[802] was pregnant and about to give birth; and when she heard the news that the ark of God was taken and that her father-in-law and her husband had died, she kneeled down[3766] and gave birth,[3205] for her pains came upon her.

20 And about the time of her death[4191] the women who stood[5324] by her said[1696] to her, "[a]Do not be

2 [I]Lit., *smitten*
3 [I]Or, *he* [a]Josh. 7:7, 8 [b]Num. 10:35; Josh. 6:6
4 [a]Ex. 25:22; 2Sam. 6:2; Ps. 80:1
5 [a]Josh. 6:5, 20
7 [a]Ex. 15:14
9 [a]1Cor. 16:13 [b]Judg. 13:1; 1Sam. 14:21
10 [I]Lit., *smitten* [a]Deut. 28:15, 25; 1Sam. 4:2 [b]2Sam. 18:17; 19:8; 2Kin. 14:12; 2Chr. 25:22
11 [a]1Sam. 2:34; Ps. 78:56-64
12 [I]Lit., *ground* [a]Josh. 7:6; 2Sam. 1:2; 15:32; Neh. 9:1; Job 2:12
13 [I]Gr. version reads *beside the gate watching the road* [a]1Sam. 1:9; 4:18
15 [a]1Sam. 3:2; 1Kin. 14:4
16 [a]2Sam. 1:4
18 [I]Lit., *he* [II]Lit., *the man* [a]1Sam. 4:13
20 [a]Gen. 35:16-19

🔑 **4:3** They tried to force God to do things their way. See Isa. 55:8,9.

afraid,[3372] for you have given birth to a
son." But she did not answer or pay
attention.
21 And she called[7121] the boy [I]Icha-
bod, saying, "[a]The glory has departed[1540] from Israel," because [b]the ark
of God was taken and because of her
father-in-law and her husband.
22 And she said, "The glory has departed from Israel, for the ark of God
was taken."

Capture of the Ark Provokes God

5 Now the Philistines took the ark[727]
of God[430] and [a]brought it from Ebenezer to [b]Ashdod.
2 Then the Philistines took the ark
of God and brought it to [a]the house of
Dagon, and set it by Dagon.
3 When the Ashdodites arose early
the next morning, behold, [a]Dagon had
fallen[5307] on his face to the ground[776]
before the ark of the LORD. So they
took Dagon and [b]set him in his place
again.
4 But when they arose early the
next morning, behold, [a]Dagon had fallen
on his face to the ground[776] before the
ark of the LORD. And the head of Dagon and both the palms[3709] of his hands
were cut off[3772] on the threshold;
[I]only the trunk of Dagon was left[7604] to
him.
5 Therefore neither the priests[3548]
of Dagon nor all who enter Dagon's
house [a]tread on the threshold of Dagon
in Ashdod to this day.[3117]
6 Now [a]the hand of the LORD was
heavy on the Ashdodites, and [b]He
ravaged[8074] them and smote[5221] them
with [c]tumors,6076 both Ashdod and its
territories.
7 When the men of Ashdod saw[7200]
that it was so, they said, "The ark of
the God of Israel must not remain with
us, for His hand is severe on us and
on Dagon our god."
8 So they sent and [a]gathered[622] all
the lords[5633] of the Philistines to them
and said, "What shall we do[6213] with the
ark of the God of Israel?" And they
said,[559] "Let the ark of the God of Israel
be brought around to Gath." And they
brought the ark of the God of Israel
around.
9 And it came about that after they
had brought it around, [a]the hand of the
LORD was against the city with very
great confusion;[4103] and He smote the
men of the city, both young and old,
so that [b]tumors broke out on them.
10 So they sent the ark of God to
Ekron. And it happened as the ark of
God came to Ekron that the Ekronites
cried[2199] out, saying, "They have
brought the ark of the God of Israel
around to [I]us, to kill[4191] [I]us and [II]our
people."[5971]
11 They [a]sent therefore and
gathered all the lords of the Philistines
and said, "Send away the ark of the
God of Israel, and let it return to its
own place, that it may not kill [I]us and
[II]our people." For there was a deadly
confusion throughout the city; [b]the hand
of God was very heavy there.
12 And the men who did not die[4191]
were smitten[5221] with tumors and [a]the
cry of the city went up to heaven.

The Ark Returned to Israel

6 Now the ark[727] of the LORD had been
in the [I]country[7704] of the Philistines
seven months.
2 And [a]the Philistines called[7121] for
the priests[3548] and the diviners,[7080] saying, "What shall we do[6213] with the ark
of the LORD? Tell us [I]how we shall send
it to its place."
3 And they said, "If you send away
the ark of the God[430] of Israel, [a]do not
send it empty; but you shall surely
[b]return to Him a guilt offering. Then
you shall be healed and it shall be
known[3045] to you why His hand is not
removed from you."

21 [I]I.e., No glory [a]Ps. 26:8; Jer. 2:11 [b]1Sam. 4:11

1 [a]1Sam. 4:1; 7:12 [b]Josh. 13:3

2 [a]Judg. 16:23-30; 1Chr. 10:8-10

3 [a]Is. 19:1; 46:1, 2 [b]Is. 46:7

4 [I]So with ancient versions; Heb., *only Dagon* [a]Ezek. 6:4, 6; Mic. 1:7

5 [a]Zeph. 1:9

6 [a]Ex. 9:3; 1Sam. 5:7, 11; Ps. 32:4; 145:20; 147:6; Acts 13:11 [b]1Sam. 6:5 [c]Deut. 28:27; Ps. 78:66

8 [a]1Sam. 5:11; 29:6-11

9 [a]Deut. 2:15; 1Sam. 5:11; 7:13; 12:15 [b]1Sam. 5:6

10 [I]Lit., *me* [II]Lit., *my*

11 [I]Lit., *me* [II]Lit., *my* [a]1Sam. 5:8 [b]1Sam. 5:6, 9

12 [a]Ex. 12:30; Is. 15:3

1 [I]Lit., *field*

2 [I]Or, *with what* [a]Gen. 41:8; Ex. 7:11; Is. 2:6

3 [a]Ex. 23:15; Deut. 16:16 [b]Lev. 5:15, 16

5:2 On Dagon see note on Judg. 2:13.

4 Then they said, "What shall be the guilt offering which we shall return to Him?" And they said,[559] "Five golden [a]tumors[6076] and five golden mice [b]*according to* the number of the lords[5633] of the Philistines, for one plague was on all of [I]you and on your lords.

5 "So you shall make likenesses[6754] of your tumors and likenesses of your mice that ravage the land,[776] and [a]you shall give glory to the God of Israel; perhaps[194] [b]He will ease[7043] His hand from you, [c]your gods,[430] and your land.

6 "Why then do you harden your hearts [a]as the Egyptians and Pharaoh hardened their hearts? When He had severely dealt with them, [b]did they not allow [I]the people to go, and they departed?

🗝 7 "Now therefore take and [a]prepare a new cart and two milch cows[6510] on which there [b]has never been a yoke; and hitch the cows to the cart and take their calves[1121] home, away from them.

8 "And take the ark of the LORD and place it on the cart; and put [a]the articles of gold which you return to Him as [b]a guilt offering in a box by its side. Then send it away that it may go.

9 "And watch, if it goes up by the way[1870] of its own territory to [a]Beth-shemesh, then He has done[6213] us this great evil.[7451] But if not, then [b]we shall know[3045] that it was not His hand that struck[5060] us; it happened to us by chance."

10 Then the men did[6213] so, and took two milch cows and hitched them to the cart, and shut up their calves at home.

11 And they put[7760] the ark of the LORD on the cart, and the box with the golden mice and the likenesses of their tumors.[2914]

12 And the cows took the straight[3474] way in the [I]direction of [a]Beth-shemesh; they went along [b]the highway, lowing[1600] as they went, and did not turn aside to the right or to the left. And the lords of the Philistines followed them to the border of Beth-shemesh.

13 Now *the people of* Beth-shemesh were reaping their wheat harvest in the valley, and they raised their eyes and saw[7200] the ark and were glad to see *it.*

14 And the cart came into the field[7704] of Joshua the Beth-shemite and stood there where there *was* a large stone; and they split the wood of the cart and [a]offered[5927] the cows as a burnt offering to the LORD.

15 And [a]the Levites took down the ark of the LORD and the box that was with it, in which were the articles of gold, and put them on the large stone; and the men of Beth-shemesh offered burnt offerings and sacrificed[2076] sacrifices that day[3117] to the LORD.

16 And when the [a]five lords of the Philistines saw[7200] it, they returned to Ekron that day.

17 And [a]these are the golden tumors which the Philistines returned for a guilt offering to the LORD: one for Ashdod, one for Gaza, one for Ashkelon, one for Gath, one for Ekron;

18 and the golden mice, *according* to the number of all the cities of the Philistines belonging to the five lords, [a]both of fortified cities and of country villages. [b]The large [I]stone on which they set the ark of the LORD *is a witness* to this day in the field of Joshua the Beth-shemite.

19 And [a]He struck down[5221] some of the men of Beth-shemesh because they had looked[7200] into the ark of the LORD. He struck down of all the people,[5971] 50,070 men, and the people mourned because the LORD had struck[5221] the people with a great slaughter.[4347]

20 And the men of Beth-shemesh said, "[a]Who is able to stand before the

4 [I]Lit., *them* [a]1Sam. 5:6, 9, 12; 6:17 [b]Josh. 13:3; Judg. 3:3; 1Sam. 6:17, 18

5 [a]Josh. 7:19; 1Chr. 16:28, 29; Is. 42:12; Jer. 13:16; John 9:24; Rev. 14:7 [b]1Sam. 5:6, 11 [c]1Sam. 5:3, 4, 7

6 [I]Lit., *them* [a]Ex. 7:13; 8:15, 32; 9:34; 14:17 [b]Ex. 12:31

7 [a]2Sam. 6:3 [b]Num. 19:2; Deut. 21:3, 4

8 [a]1Sam. 6:4, 5 [b]1Sam. 6:3

9 [a]Josh. 15:10; 21:16 [b]1Sam. 6:3

12 [I]Lit., *way* [a]1Sam. 6:9 [b]Num. 20:19

14 [a]2Sam. 24:22; 1Kin. 19:21

15 [a]Josh. 3:3

16 [a]Josh. 13:3; Judg. 3:3

17 [a]1Sam. 6:4

18 [I]So some mss. and versions; Heb., *Abel* [a]Deut. 3:5 [b]1Sam. 6:14, 15

19 [a]Ex. 19:21; Num. 4:5, 15, 20; 2Sam. 6:7

20 [a]Lev. 11:44, 45; 2Sam. 6:9; Mal. 3:2; Rev. 6:17

🗝 **6:7** Normally, it would be difficult to drive even the best-trained cows straight on a road, especially when their calves have just been taken away from them. The behavior of the cows indicated that God was overruling their natural instincts.

LORD, this holy God? And to whom shall
He go up from us?"
21 So they sent messengers to the
inhabitants of [a]Kiriath-jearim, saying,
"The Philistines have brought back the
ark of the LORD; come down and take
it up to you."

Deliverance from the Philistines

7 And the men of Kiriath-jearim came
and took the ark[727] of the LORD and
[a]brought it into the house of Abinadab
on the hill, and consecrated[6942] Eleazar
his son[1121] to keep[8104] the ark of the
LORD.
2 And it came about from the day[3117]
that the ark remained at Kiriath-jearim
that the time was long, for it was twenty
years; and all the house of Israel lamented after the LORD.
3 Then Samuel spoke[559] to all the
house of Israel, saying, "[a]If you return
to the LORD with all your heart, [b]remove
the foreign[5236] gods[430] and the [c]Ashta-
roth from among you and [d]direct[3559] your
hearts to the LORD and [e]serve[5647] Him
alone; and He will deliver[5337] you from
the hand of the Philistines."
4 So the sons[1121] of Israel removed
the Baals and the Ashtaroth and served
the LORD alone.
5 Then Samuel said, "Gather[6908] all
Israel to [a]Mizpah, and [b]I will pray[6419]
to the LORD for you."
6 And they gathered[6908] to Mizpah,
and drew water and [a]poured[8210] it out
before the LORD, and [b]fasted on that
day,[3117] and said there, "[c]We have
sinned[2398] against the LORD." And Samuel judged[8199] the sons of Israel at
Mizpah.
7 Now when the Philistines heard
that the sons of Israel had gathered to
Mizpah, the lords[5633] of the Philistines
went up against Israel. And when the
sons of Israel heard it, [a]they were afraid
of the Philistines.
8 Then the sons of Israel said to
Samuel, "[a]Do not cease to cry[2199] to
the LORD our God[430] for us, that He
may save[3467] us from the hand of the
Philistines."
9 And Samuel took [a]a suckling lamb
and offered[5927] it for a whole[3632] burnt
offering to the LORD; and Samuel
cried[2199] to the LORD for Israel and
[b]the LORD answered him.
10 Now Samuel was offering up[5927]
the burnt offering, and the Philistines
drew near[5066] to battle against Israel.
But [a]the LORD thundered with a great
[I]thunder on that day against the Philistines and [b]confused them, so that they
were [II]routed[5062] before Israel.
11 And the men of Israel went out
of Mizpah and pursued the Philistines,
and struck[5221] them down as far as below
Beth-car.
12 Then Samuel [a]took a stone and
set[7760] it between Mizpah and Shen, and
named[7121] it [I]Ebenezer, saying, "Thus
far the LORD has helped us."
13 [a]So the Philistines were subdued
and [b]they did not come anymore within
the border of Israel. And the hand of
the LORD was against the Philistines all
the days[3117] of Samuel.
14 And the cities which the Philistines had taken from Israel were restored to Israel, from Ekron even to
Gath; and Israel delivered their territory
from the hand of the Philistines. So there
was peace[7965] between Israel and [a]the
Amorites.

Samuel's Ministry

15 Now Samuel [a]judged Israel all
the days of his life.[2416]
16 And he used to go annually on
circuit to [a]Bethel and [b]Gilgal and [c]Miz-
pah, and he judged Israel in all these
places.
17 Then his return *was* to [a]Ramah,
for his house *was* there, and there he
judged Israel; and he [b]built there an
altar[4196] to the LORD.

21 [a]Josh. 9:17; 15:9, 60; 1Chr. 13:5, 6
1 [a]2Sam. 6:3, 4
3 [a]1Kin. 8:48; Is. 55:7; Hos. 6:1; Joel 2:12-14 [b]Gen. 35:2; Josh. 24:14, 23; Judg. 10:16 [c]Judg. 2:13; 1Sam. 31:10 [d]Deut. 13:4; 2Chr. 19:3 [e]Deut. 6:13; 10:20; 13:4; Josh. 24:14; Matt. 4:10; Luke 4:8
5 [a]Judg. 10:17; 20:1 [b]1Sam. 8:6; 12:17-19
6 [a]1Sam. 1:15; Ps. 62:8; Lam. 2:19 [b]Lev. 16:29; Neh. 9:1 [c]Judg. 10:10; 1Kin. 8:47; Ps. 106:6
7 [a]1Sam. 13:6; 17:11
8 [a]1Sam. 12:19-24; Is. 37:4
9 [a]Lev. 22:27 [b]Ps. 99:6; Jer. 15:1
10 [I]Lit., *voice* [II]Lit., *smitten* [a]1Sam. 2:10; 2Sam. 22:14, 15; Ps. 29:3, 4 [b]Josh. 10:10; Ps. 18:14
12 [I]I.e., The stone of help [a]Gen. 35:14; Josh. 4:9; 24:26
13 [a]Judg. 13:1-15 [b]1Sam. 13:5
14 [a]Num. 13:29; Josh. 10:5-10
15 [a]1Sam. 7:6
16 [a]Gen. 28:19; 35:6 [b]Josh. 5:9, 10 [c]1Sam. 7:5
17 [a]1Sam. 1:1, 19; 2:11 [b]Judg. 21:4

7:4 Concerning the Baals and Ashtaroth see note on Judg. 2:13.

Israel Demands a King

8 And it came about when Samuel
was old[2204] that [a]he appointed his
sons[1121] judges[8199] over Israel.
2 Now the name of his first-born
was Joel, and the name of his second,
Abijah; *they* were judging in [a]Beer-
sheba.
3 His sons, however, did not walk
in his ways,[1870] but turned aside after
dishonest gain1215 and [a]took bribes and
perverted justice.[4941]
4 Then all the elders[2205] of Israel
gathered[6908] together and came to Samuel at [a]Ramah;
5 and they said to him, "Behold, you
have grown old, and your sons do not
walk in your ways. Now [a]appoint a
king[4428] for us to judge[8199] us like all
the nations."[1471]
6 But the thing was [Ia]displeasing[7489]
in the sight of Samuel when they said,
"Give us a king to judge us." And
[b]Samuel prayed[6419] to the LORD.
7 And the LORD said to Samuel,
"Listen to the voice of the people[5971]
in regard to all that they say to you,
for [a]they have not rejected you, but they
have rejected Me from being king over
them.
8 "Like all the deeds which they
have done[6213] since the day[3117] that I
brought[5927] them up from Egypt even
to this day—in that they have
forsaken[5800] Me and served other
gods—[430] so they are doing[6213] to you
also.
9 "Now then, listen to their voice;
[a]however, you shall solemnly [I]warn[5749]
them and tell[5046] them of [b]the [II]pro-
cedure of the king who will reign over
them."

Warning concerning a King

10 So Samuel spoke all the
words[1697] of the LORD to [a]the people
who had asked[7592] of him a king.
11 And he said, "[a]This will be the
[I]procedure of the king who will reign
over you: [b]he will take your sons and
place[7760] *them* for himself in his chariots
and among his horsemen and [c]they will
run before his chariots.
12 "And [a]he will appoint for himself
commanders[8269] of thousands and of fifties, and *some* to [I]do his plowing and
to reap his harvest and to make his
weapons of war and equipment for his
chariots.
13 "He will also take your daughters
for perfumers7543 and cooks and bakers.
14 "And [a]he will take the best[2896]
of your fields[7704] and your vineyards and
your olive groves, and give *them* to his
servants.
15 "And he will take a tenth of your
seed[2233] and of your vineyards, and give
to his officers[5631] and to his servants.
16 "He will also take your male servants and your female servants and your
best[2896] young men and your donkeys,
and [I]use *them* for his work.[4399]
17 "He will take a tenth of your
flocks, and you yourselves will become
his servants.
18 "Then [a]you will cry[2199] out in that
day because of your king whom you have
chosen[977] for yourselves, but [b]the LORD
will not answer you in that day."
19 Nevertheless, the people [a]re-
fused to listen to the voice of Samuel,
and they said, "No, but there shall be
a king over us,
20 [a]that we also may be like all the
nations, that our king may judge us and

1 [a]Deut. 16:18, 19
2 [a]Gen. 22:19; 1Kin. 19:3; Amos 5:5
3 [a]Ex. 23:6, 8; Deut. 16:19
4 [a]1Sam. 7:17
5 [a]Deut. 17:14, 15
6 [I]Or, *evil* [a]1Sam. 12:17 [b]1Sam. 15:11
7 [a]Ex. 16:8; 1Sam. 10:19
9 [I]Lit., *testify to* [II]Lit., *custom* [a]Ezek. 3:18 [b]1Sam. 8:11-18; 10:25
10 [a]1Sam. 8:4
11 [I]Lit., *custom* [a]Deut. 17:14-20; 1Sam. 10:25 [b]1Sam. 14:52 [c]2Sam. 15:1
12 [I]Lit., *plow his plowing* [a]Num. 31:14; 1Sam. 22:7
14 [a]1Kin. 21:7; Ezek. 46:18
16 [I]Lit., *make*
18 [a]Is. 8:21 [b]Prov. 1:25-28; Is. 1:15; Mic. 3:4
19 [a]Is. 66:4; Jer. 44:16
20 [a]1Sam. 8:5

8:3 Like Eli, Samuel neglected his sons. Perhaps, like many servants of God, he was away from home too much and too busy trying to help others. He failed to notice the trouble signs.

8:5-7 In Deut. 17:14,15 there is a prophetic statement that upon entering the land they would request a king. This is not a divine sanction of that request but a simple recognition of what their attitude would be. God implied from the beginning that He would be their king (Ex. 19:5,6; Deut. 4:39,40). The later Jewish explanation of their sin was that it was not in asking for a king but the way in which they asked for one. They wanted a king "like all the nations." In any case, their request was a rejection of God and a sign of distrust in Him.

go out before us and fight our battles."
21 Now after Samuel had heard all
the words of the people, [a]he repeated
them in the LORD's hearing.[241]
22 And the LORD said to Samuel,
"[a]Listen to their voice, and [1]appoint them
a king." So Samuel said to the men of
Israel, "Go every man to his city."

Saul's Search

9 Now there was a man of Benjamin
whose name was [a]Kish the son of
Abiel, the son of Zeror, the son[1121] of
Becorath, the son of Aphiah, the son
of a Benjamite, a mighty man of
[1]valor.[2428]
2 And he had a son whose name
was Saul, a [a]choice and handsome
man,[2896] and there was not a more handsome person[376] than he among the
sons[1121] of Israel; [b]from his shoulders
and up he was taller than any of the
people.[5971]
3 Now the donkeys of Kish, Saul's
father,[1] were lost.[6] So Kish said to his
son Saul, "Take now with you one of
the servants, and arise, go search for
the donkeys."
4 And he passed[5674] through
[a]the hill country of Ephraim and passed
through the land[776] of [b]Shalishah, but
they did not find *them*. Then they passed
through the land of [c]Shaalim, but *they*
were not *there*. Then he passed through
the land of the Benjamites, but they did
not find *them*.
5 When they came to the land of
[a]Zuph, Saul said to his servant who was
with him, "Come, and let us return,
[b]lest my father cease *to be concerned*
about the donkeys and become anxious
for us."
6 And he said to him, "Behold now,
there is [a]a man of God[430] in this city,
and the man is held in honor; [b]all that
he says[1696] surely comes true. Now let
us go there, [c]perhaps[194] he can tell[5046]
us about our journey[1870] on which we
have set out."
7 Then Saul said to his servant, "But
behold, if we go, what shall we bring
the man? For the bread is gone from
our sack and there is [a]no present to
bring to the man of God. What do we
have?"
8 And the servant answered Saul
again and said, "Behold, I have in my
hand a fourth of a shekel of silver; I
will give *it* to the man of God and he
will [a]tell us our way."
9 (Formerly in Israel, when a man
went to inquire of God, he used to
say,[559] "Come, and let us go to the
seer";[7200] for *he who is called* a
prophet[5030] now was formerly called[7121]
[a]a seer.)
10 Then Saul said to his servant,
"Well said; come, let us go." So they
went to the city where the man of God
was.
11 As they went up the slope to
the city, [a]they found young women going
out to draw water, and said to them,
"Is the seer here?"
12 And they answered them and
said, "He is; [1]see, *he is* ahead of you.
Hurry now, for he has come into the
city today, for [a]the people have a
sacrifice[2077] on [b]the high place today.
13 "As soon as you enter the city
you will find him before he goes up to
the high place to eat, for the people
will not eat until he comes, because
[a]he must bless[1288] the sacrifice; afterward those who are invited[7121] will eat.
Now therefore, go up for you will find
him at once."
14 So they went up to the city. As
they came into the city, behold, Samuel
was coming out toward them to go up
to the high place.

God's Choice for King

15 Now a day[3117] before Saul's coming, [a]the LORD had [1]revealed *this* to Samuel saying,
16 "About this time tomorrow I will
send you a man from the land of Benjamin, and [a]you shall anoint[4886] him to be
prince[5057] over My people Israel; and
he shall deliver[3467] My people from the
hand of the Philistines. For [b]I have

21 [a]Judg. 11:11
22 [1]Lit., *cause a king to reign for them* [a]1Sam. 8:7
1 [1]Or, *wealth or influence* [a]1Sam. 14:51; 1Chr. 8:33; 9:36-39
2 [a]1Sam. 10:24 [b]1Sam. 10:23
4 [a]Josh. 24:33 [b]2Kin. 4:42 [c]Josh. 19:42
5 [a]1Sam. 1:1 [b]1Sam. 10:2
6 [a]Deut. 33:1; 1Kin. 13:1; 2Kin. 5:8 [b]1Sam. 3:19 [c]Gen. 24:42
7 [a]1Kin. 14:3; 2Kin. 5:15; 8:8, 9; Ezek. 13:19
8 [a]1Sam. 9:6
9 [a]2Sam. 24:11; 2Kin. 17:13; 1Chr. 9:22; 26:28; 29:29; Is. 30:10; Amos 7:12
11 [a]Gen. 24:11, 15; 29:8, 9; Ex. 2:16
12 [1]Or, *behold* [a]Gen. 31:54; Num. 28:11-15; 1Kin. 3:2 [b]1Sam. 7:17; 10:5
13 [a]Luke 9:16; John 6:11
15 [1]Lit., *uncovered the ear* [a]1Sam. 15:1; Acts 13:21
16 [a]1Sam. 10:1 [b]Ex. 3:7, 9

regarded[7200] My people, because their cry has come to Me.”

17 When Samuel saw[7200] Saul, the LORD [I]said to him, “[a]Behold, the man of whom I spoke to you! This one shall rule over My people.”

18 Then Saul approached[5066] Samuel in the gate, and said, “Please[4994] tell me where the seer's house is.”

19 And Samuel answered Saul and said, “I am the seer. Go up before me to the high place, for you shall eat with me today; and in the morning I will let you go, and will tell you all that is on your mind.

20 “And [a]as for your donkeys which were lost three days[3117] ago, do not set[7760] your mind on them, for they have been found. And [b]for whom is all that is desirable in Israel? Is it not for you and for all your father's[1] household?”

🔑 21 And Saul answered and said, “[a]Am I not a Benjamite, of [b]the smallest of the tribes of Israel, and my family[4940] the least of all the families[4940] of the [I]tribe of Benjamin? Why then do you speak[1696] to me in this way?”

22 Then Samuel took Saul and his servant and brought them into the hall, and gave them a place at the head of those who were invited, who were about thirty men.[376]

23 And Samuel said to the cook, “[I]Bring the portion that I gave you, concerning which I said to you, ‘Set it [II]aside.’ ”

24 Then the cook [a]took up the leg with what was on it and set *it* before Saul. And *Samuel* said, “Here is what has been reserved![7604] Set *it* before you *and* eat, because it has been kept[8104] for you until the appointed time, [I]since I said I have invited[7121] the people.” So Saul ate with Samuel that day.

25 When they came down from the high place into the city, *Samuel* spoke with Saul [a]on the roof.[I]

26 And they arose early; and it came about at daybreak[5927] that Samuel called to Saul on the roof, saying, “Get up, that I may send you away.” So Saul arose, and both he and Samuel went out into the street.

27 As they were going down to the edge of the city, Samuel said to Saul, “Say[559] to the servant that he might go ahead[5674] of us and pass on, but you remain standing now,[3117] that I may proclaim the word[1697] of God to you.”

Saul among Prophets

10

Then [a]Samuel took the flask of oil,[8081] poured it on his head, [b]kissed[5401] him and said, “Has not [c]the LORD anointed[4886] you a ruler[5057] over [d]His inheritance?[5159]

2 “When you go from me today, then you will find two men close to [a]Rachel's tomb[6900] in the territory of Benjamin at Zelzah; and they will say to you, ‘[b]The donkeys which you went to look for have been found. Now behold, your father[1] has [I]ceased[5203] to be concerned[1697] about the donkeys and is anxious[1672] for you, saying, “What shall I do about my son?” ’[1121]

3 “Then you will go on further from there, and you will come as far as the [I][a]oak of Tabor, and there three men going up [b]to God[430] at Bethel will meet you, one carrying three kids, another carrying three loaves of bread, and another carrying a jug of wine;

4 and they will greet[7965] you and give you two *loaves* of bread, which you will accept from their hand.

5 “Afterward you will come to [I][a]the hill of God where the Philistine garrison is; and it shall be as soon as you have come there to the city, that you will meet [b]a group[2256] of prophets[5030] coming down from the high place with harp, tambourine,[8596] flute, and a lyre before them, and [c]they will be prophesying.[5012]

6 “Then [a]the Spirit[7307] of the LORD will come upon you mightily, and

17 [I]Lit., *answered* [a]1Sam. 16:12

20 [a]1Sam. 9:3 [b]1Sam. 8:5; 12:13

21 [I]So some ancient versions; Heb., *tribes* [a]1Sam. 15:17 [b]Judg. 20:46-48

23 [I]Lit., *Give* [II]Lit., *with you*

24 [I]Lit., *saying* [a]Ex. 29:22, 27; Lev. 7:32, 33; Num. 18:18

25 [I]Gr. adds *and they spread a bed for Saul on the roof and he slept.* [a]Deut. 22:8; Luke 5:19; Acts 10:9

1 [a]Ex. 30:23-33; 1Sam. 16:13; 2Kin. 9:3, 6 [b]Ps. 2:12 [c]1Sam. 16:13; 26:9; 2Sam. 1:14 [d]Deut. 32:9; Ps. 78:71

2 [I]Lit., *abandoned the matter of* [a]Gen. 35:16-20; 48:7 [b]1Sam. 9:3-5

3 [I]Or, *terebinth* [a]Gen. 35:8 [b]Gen. 28:19; 35:1, 3, 7

5 [I]Or, *Gibeath-haelohim* [a]1Sam. 13:2, 3 [b]1Sam. 19:20; 2Kin. 2:3, 5, 15 [c]2Kin. 3:15; 1Chr. 25:1-6; 1Cor. 14:1

6 [a]Num. 11:25, 29; Judg. 14:6

🔑 **9:21** The tribe of Benjamin had been reduced to only 600 men (Judg. 20:47).

[b]you shall prophesy with them and be
changed into another man.
7 "And it shall be when these
signs[226] come to you, [a]do for yourself
what [I]the occasion requires;[5647] for
[b]God is with you.
8 "And [a]you shall go down before
me to Gilgal; and behold, I will come
down to you to offer burnt offerings and
[b]sacrifice[2076] peace offerings. [c]You shall
wait seven days[3117] until I come to you
and show[3045] you what you should do."
9 Then it happened when he turned
his back to leave Samuel, God [a]changed
[I]his heart; and all those signs came about
on that day.[3117]
10 [a]When they came to [I]the hill
there, behold, a group of prophets met
him; and the Spirit of God came upon
him mightily, so that he prophesied[5012]
among them.
11 And it came about, when all who
knew[3045] him previously saw[7200] that he
prophesied now with the prophets, that
the people[5971] said to one[376] another,[7453]
"What has happened to the son of Kish?
[a]Is Saul also among the prophets?"
12 And a man there answered and
said, "Now, who is their father?" Therefore it became a proverb: "[a]Is Saul also
among the prophets?"
13 When he had finished[3615] prophesying, he came to the high place.
14 Now [a]Saul's uncle said to him
and his servant, "Where did you go?"
And he said, "[b]To look for the donkeys.
When we saw that they could not be
found, we went to Samuel."
15 And Saul's uncle said, "Please[4994]
tell me what Samuel said to you."
16 So Saul said to his uncle, "[a]He
told us plainly[5046] that the donkeys had
been found." But he did not tell him

6 [b]1Sam. 10:10; 19:23, 24

7 [I]Lit., *your hand finds* [a]Eccl. 9:10 [b]Josh. 1:5; Judg. 6:12; Heb. 13:5

8 [a]1Sam. 11:14; 13:8 [b]1Sam. 11:15 [c]1Sam. 13:8

9 [I]Lit., *for him another heart* [a]1Sam. 10:6

10 [I]Or, *Gibeath* [a]1Sam. 10:5, 6; 19:20

11 [a]1Sam. 19:24; Amos 7:14, 15; Matt. 13:54-57; John 7:15

12 [a]1Sam. 19:23, 24

14 [a]1Sam. 14:50 [b]1Sam. 9:3-6

16 [a]1Sam. 9:20

17 [a]Judg. 20:1; 1Sam. 7:5

18 [I]Lit., *hand* [a]Judg. 6:8, 9

19 [I]So with several mss. and versions; M.T., *said to Him* [a]1Sam. 8:6, 7; 12:12 [b]Josh. 7:14-18; 24:1; Prov. 16:33

22 [a]1Sam. 23:2, 4

23 [a]1Sam. 9:2

24 [a]Deut. 17:15; 2Sam. 21:6

about the matter of the kingdom which
Samuel had mentioned.[559]

Saul Publicly Chosen King

17 Thereafter Samuel called the
[a]people together to the LORD at Mizpah;
18 and he said to the sons[1121] of
Israel, "[a]Thus says[559] the LORD, the God
of Israel, 'I brought[5927] Israel up from
Egypt, and I delivered[5337] you from the
hand of the Egyptians, and from the
[I]power of all the kingdoms[4467] that were
oppressing you.'
19 "But you [a]today rejected your
God, who delivers[3467] you from all your
calamities[7451] and your distresses; yet
you have [I]said, 'No, but set[7760] a king[4428]
over us!' Now therefore, [b]present yourselves before the LORD by your tribes
and by your clans."
20 Thus Samuel brought all the
tribes of Israel near, and the tribe of
Benjamin was taken by lot.
21 Then he brought the tribe of Benjamin near by its families,[4940] and the
Matrite family[4940] was taken. And Saul
the son of Kish was taken; but when
they looked for him, he could not be
found.
22 Therefore [a]they inquired[7592] further of the LORD, "Has the man come
here yet?" So the LORD said,[559] "Behold,
he is hiding himself by the baggage."
23 So they ran and took him from
there, and when he stood among the
people, [a]he was taller than any of the
people from his shoulders upward.
24 And Samuel said to all the people,
"Do you see him [a]whom the LORD has
chosen?[977] Surely there is no one like
him among all the people." So all the

10:10 See note on II Kgs. 2:3,5.

10:20-24 Though the people chose Saul by lot (v. 21), the Lord himself made the ultimate choice (v. 24). When selections or decisions were made by lot, the Jews understood this to be a means by which they were being led by God, which course the disciples followed in choosing Matthias (Acts 1:26). That Saul was a Benjamite has been problematic for some since Judah had been designated as the royal tribe (Gen. 49:10). Saul laid the foundation for the greater kingdom of David, who was finally able to take possession of the whole territory which was promised to Abraham (Gen. 15:18) and bring a unity to Israel that had been lacking up to this time.

people shouted[7321] and said, "[I][b]*Long live*[2421] the king!"

25 Then Samuel told the people [a]the ordinances of the kingdom, and wrote *them* in the book[5612] and [b]placed *it* before the LORD. And Samuel sent all the people away, each one to his house.

26 And Saul also went [a]to his house at Gibeah; and the valiant *men* whose hearts God had touched went with him.

27 But certain [I][a]worthless men[1100] said, "How can this one deliver us?" And they despised him and [b]did not bring him any present.[4503] But he kept silent.

Saul Defeats the Ammonites

11 Now [a]Nahash the Ammonite came up and [I]besieged [b]Jabesh-gilead; and all the men of Jabesh said to Nahash, "Make [c]a covenant[1285] with us and we will serve[5647] you."

2 But Nahash the Ammonite said[559] to them, "I will make *it* with you on this condition, [a]that I will gouge out the right eye of every one of you, thus I will make[7760] it [b]a reproach on all Israel."

3 And [a]the elders[2205] of Jabesh said to him, "Let us alone for seven days,[3117] that we may send messengers throughout the territory of Israel. Then, if there is no one to deliver us, we will come out to you."

4 Then the messengers came [a]to Gibeah of Saul and spoke these words in the hearing[241] of the people,[5971] and all the people [b]lifted up their voices and wept.

5 Now behold, Saul was coming from the field[7704] [a]behind the oxen; and [I]he said, "What is *the matter* with the people that they weep?" So they related to him the words of the men of Jabesh.

6 Then [a]the Spirit[7307] of God[430] came upon Saul mightily when he heard these words, and [I]he became very angry.[639]

7 And he took a yoke of oxen and [a]cut[5408] them in pieces, and sent *them* throughout the territory of Israel by the hand of messengers, saying, "[b]Whoever does not come out after Saul and after Samuel, so shall it be done[6213] to his oxen." Then the dread of the LORD fell[5307] on the people, and they came out [c]as one man.

8 And he [I]numbered them in [a]Bezek; and the [b]sons[1121] of Israel were 300,000, and the men of Judah 30,000.

9 And they said to the messengers who had come, "Thus you shall say to the men of Jabesh-gilead, 'Tomorrow, by the time the sun is hot, you shall have deliverance.' " So the messengers went and told[5046] the men of Jabesh; and they were glad.

10 Then the men of Jabesh said, "[a]Tomorrow we will come out to you, and you may do[6213] to us whatever seems good[2896] [I]to you."

11 And it happened the next morning that Saul put the people [a]in three companies;[7128] and they came into the midst of the camp at the morning watch, and struck down[5221] the Ammonites until the heat of the day.[3117] And it came about that those who survived were scattered, so that no two of them were left[7604] together.

12 Then the people said to Samuel, "[a]Who is he that said, 'Shall Saul reign over us?' [I][b]Bring the men, that we may put them to death."[4191]

13 But Saul said, "[a]Not a man shall be put to death this day, for today [b]the LORD has accomplished deliverance in Israel."

14 Then Samuel said to the people, "Come and let us go to [a]Gilgal and [b]renew the kingdom there."

15 So all the people went to Gilgal, and there they made Saul king[4427] [a]before the LORD in Gilgal. There they also [b]offered[2076] sacrifices of peace offerings before the LORD; and there Saul and all the men of Israel rejoiced greatly.

Samuel Addresses Israel

12 Then Samuel said to all Israel, "Behold, [a]I have listened to your voice in all that you said to me, and I [b]have [I]appointed a king[4428] over you.

---

24 [I]Lit., *May the king live* [b]1Kin. 1:25, 34, 39

25 [a]Deut. 17:14-20; 1Sam. 8:11-18 [b]Deut. 31:26

26 [a]1Sam. 11:4; 15:34

27 [I]Lit., *sons of Belial,* cf. 2Cor. 6:15 [a]Deut. 13:13; 1Sam. 25:17 [b]1Kin. 10:25; 2Chr. 17:5

1 [I]Lit., *camped against* [a]1Sam. 12:12 [b]Judg. 21:8; 1Sam. 31:11 [c]Gen. 26:28; 1Kin. 20:34; Job 41:4; Ezek. 17:13

2 [a]Num. 16:14 [b]1Sam. 17:26; Ps. 44:13

3 [a]1Sam. 8:4

4 [a]1Sam. 10:26; 15:34 [b]Gen. 27:38; Judg. 2:4; 20:23, 26; 21:2; 1Sam. 30:4

5 [I]Lit., *Saul* [a]1Kin. 19:19

6 [I]Lit., *his anger burned exceedingly* [a]Judg. 3:10; 6:34; 11:29; 13:25; 14:6; 1Sam. 10:10; 16:13

7 [a]Judg. 19:29 [b]Judg. 21:5, 8 [c]Judg. 20:1

8 [I]Lit., *mustered* [a]Judg. 1:5 [b]Judg. 20:2

10 [I]Lit., *in your sight* [a]1Sam. 11:3

11 [a]Judg. 7:16, 20

12 [I]Lit., *Give* [a]1Sam. 10:27 [b]Luke 19:27

13 [a]1Sam. 10:27; 2Sam. 19:22 [b]Ex. 14:13, 30; 1Sam. 19:5

14 [a]1Sam. 7:16; 10:8 [b]1Sam. 10:25

15 [a]1Sam. 10:17 [b]1Sam. 10:8

1 [I]Lit., *made* [a]1Sam. 8:7, 9, 22 [b]1Sam. 10:24; 11:14, 15

2 "And now, [a]here is the king walking before you, but [b]I am old[2204] and gray, and behold [c]my sons[1121] are with you. And [d]I have walked before you from my youth even to this day.[3117]

3 "Here I am; bear witness against me before the LORD and [a]His anointed.[4899] [b]Whose ox have I taken, or whose donkey have I taken, or whom have I defrauded? Whom have I oppressed, or [c]from whose hand have I taken a bribe to blind my eyes with it? I will restore *it* to you."

4 And they said, "You have not defrauded us, or oppressed us, or taken anything from any man's hand."

5 And he said to them, "The LORD is witness against you, and His anointed is witness this day that [a]you have found nothing [b]in my hand." And they said,[559] "*He is* witness."

6 Then Samuel said to the people,[5971] "It is the LORD who [1a]appointed Moses and Aaron and who brought[5927] your fathers[1] up from the land[776] of Egypt.

7 "So now, take your stand, [a]that I may plead with you before the LORD concerning all the righteous acts of the LORD which He did[6213] for you and your fathers.

8 "[a]When Jacob went into Egypt and [b]your fathers cried[2199] out to the LORD, then [c]the LORD sent Moses and Aaron [1d]who brought your fathers out of Egypt and settled them in this place.

9 "But [a]they forgot the LORD their God,[430] so [b]He sold them into the hand of Sisera, captain[8269] of the army of Hazor, and [c]into the hand of the Philistines and [d]into the hand of the king of Moab, and they fought against them.

10 "And [a]they cried out to the LORD and said, 'We have sinned[2398] because we have forsaken[5800] the LORD and have served [b]the Baals and the Ashtaroth; but [c]now deliver[5337] us from the hands of our enemies, and we will serve Thee.'

11 "Then the LORD sent [a]Jerubbaal and [1b]Bedan and [c]Jephthah and [d]Samuel, and delivered[5337] you from the hands of your enemies all around, so that you lived in security.

The King Confirmed

12 "When you saw[7200] [a]that Nahash the king of the sons[1121] of Ammon came against you, you said to me, '[b]No, but a king shall reign over us,' [c]although the LORD your God *was* your king.

13 "Now therefore, [a]here is the king whom you have chosen,[977] [b]whom you have asked for,[7592] and behold, the LORD has set a king over you.

14 "[a]If you will fear[3372] the LORD and serve Him, and listen to His voice and not rebel against the [1]command[6310] of the LORD, then both you and also the king who reigns over you will follow the LORD your God.

15 "And [a]if you will not listen to the voice of the LORD, but rebel against the [1]command of the LORD, then [b]the hand of the LORD will be against you, [c]*as it was* against your fathers.

16 "Even now, [a]take your stand and see this great thing which the LORD will do[6213] before your eyes.

17 "[a]Is it not the wheat harvest today? [b]I will call[7121] to the LORD, that He may send [1]thunder and rain. Then you will know[3045] and see that [c]your wickedness[7451] is great which you have done[6213] in the sight of the LORD by asking[7592] for yourselves a king."

18 So Samuel called[7121] to the LORD, and the LORD sent [1]thunder and rain that day; and [a]all the people greatly feared[3372] the LORD and Samuel.

19 Then all the people said to Samuel, "[a]Pray for your servants to the LORD your God, so that we may not die,[4191] for we have added to all our sins [b]*this* evil[7451] by asking[7592] for ourselves a king."

20 And Samuel said to the people, "Do not fear. You have committed all this evil, yet [a]do not turn aside from following the LORD, but serve the LORD with all your heart.

21 "And you must not turn aside, for *then you would go* after [a]futile[8414]

2 [a]1Sam. 8:20 [b]1Sam. 8:1, 5 [c]1Sam. 8:3, 5 [d]1Sam. 3:10, 19; 20
3 [a]1Sam. 10:1; 24:6; 2Sam. 1:14 [b]Ex. 20:17; Num. 16:15; Acts 20:33 [c]Ex. 23:8; Deut. 16:19
5 [a]Acts 23:9; 24:20 [b]Ex. 22:4
6 [1]Lit., *made* [a]Ex. 6:26; Mic. 6:4
7 [a]Ezek. 20:35; Mic. 6:1-5
8 [1]Lit., *and they brought* [a]Gen. 46:5, 6 [b]Ex. 2:23-25 [c]Ex. 3:10; 4:14-16 [d]1Sam. 10:18
9 [a]Deut. 32:18; Judg. 3:7 [b]Judg. 4:2 [c]Judg. 3:31; 10:7; 13:1 [d]Judg. 3:12-30
10 [a]Judg. 10:10 [b]Judg. 2:13; 3:7 [c]Judg. 10:15, 16
11 [1]Gr. and Syr. read *Barak* [a]Judg. 6:31, 32; 7:1 [b]Judg. 4:6; 11:1 [c]Judg. 11:29 [d]1Sam. 3:20
12 [a]1Sam. 11:1, 2 [b]1Sam. 8:6, 19 [c]Judg. 8:23; 1Sam. 8:7
13 [a]1Sam. 10:24 [b]1Sam. 8:5; 12:17, 19; Hos. 13:11
14 [1]Lit., *mouth* [a]Josh. 24:14
15 [1]Lit., *mouth* [a]Lev. 26:14, 15; Josh. 24:20; Is. 1:20 [b]1Sam. 5:9 [c]1Sam. 12:9
16 [a]Ex. 14:13, 31
17 [1]Lit., *sounds* [a]Prov. 26:1 [b]1Sam. 7:9, 10; James 5:16ff. [c]1Sam. 8:7
18 [1]Lit., *sounds* [a]Ex. 14:31
19 [a]Ex. 9:28; 1Sam. 12:23; Jer. 15:1; 1John 5:16 [b]1Sam. 12:17, 20
20 [a]Deut. 11:16
21 [a]Deut. 11:16; Is. 41:29; Hab. 2:18

things which can not profit or deliver, because they are futile.

22 "For [a]the LORD will not abandon[5203] His people [b]on account of His great name, because the LORD [c]has been pleased[2974] to make you a people for Himself.

23 "Moreover, as for me, [a]far be it from me that I should sin[2398] against the LORD by ceasing to pray for you; but [b]I will instruct you in the good[2896] and right way.[1870]

24 "[a]Only [I]fear the LORD and serve Him in truth with all your heart; for consider[7200] [b]what great things He has done for you.

25 "[a]But if you still do wickedly, [b]both you and your king [c]shall be swept away."[5995]

War with the Philistines

13 Saul was *forty* years old when he began to reign, and he reigned *thirty*-two years over Israel.

2 Now Saul chose[977] for himself 3,000 men of Israel, of which 2,000 were with Saul in [a]Michmash and in the hill country of Bethel, while 1,000 were with Jonathan at [b]Gibeah of Benjamin. But he sent away the rest of the people,[5971] each to his tent.

3 And Jonathan smote[5221] [a]the garrison of the Philistines that was in [b]Geba, and the Philistines heard of *it.* Then Saul [c]blew[8628] the trumpet throughout the land,[776] saying, "Let the Hebrews hear."

4 And all Israel heard [I]the news that Saul had smitten[5221] the garrison of the Philistines, and also that Israel [a]had become odious to the Philistines. The people were then summoned [II]to Saul at Gilgal.

5 Now the Philistines assembled[622] to fight with Israel, 30,000 chariots and 6,000 horsemen, and [a]people like the sand which is on the seashore[8193] in abundance; and they came up and camped in Michmash, east of [b]Beth-aven.

6 When the men of Israel saw[7200] that they were in a strait[6887] (for the people were hard-pressed), then [a]the people hid themselves in caves, in thickets, in cliffs, in cellars, and in pits.[953]

7 Also *some of* the Hebrews crossed the Jordan into the land of [a]Gad and Gilead. But as for Saul, he *was* still in Gilgal, and all the people followed him trembling.

8 Now [a]he waited seven days,[3117] according to the appointed time set by Samuel, but Samuel did not come to Gilgal; and the people were scattering from him.

9 So Saul said, "Bring[5066] to me the burnt offering and the peace offerings." And [a]he offered[5927] the burnt offering.

10 And it came about as soon as he finished[3615] offering[5927] the burnt offering, that behold, Samuel came; and [a]Saul went out to meet him *and* to [I]greet[1288] him.

Saul Assumes Priestly Office

11 But Samuel said, "What have you done?"[6213] And Saul said, "Because I saw that the people were scattering from me, and that you did not come within the appointed[4150] days, and that [a]the Philistines were assembling at Michmash,

12 therefore I said, 'Now the Philistines will come down against me at Gilgal, and I have not asked the favor of the LORD.' So I forced myself and offered the burnt offering."

🔑 13 And Samuel said to Saul, "[a]You have acted foolishly; [b]you have not

22 [a]Deut. 31:6; 1Kin. 6:13 [b]Ex. 32:12; Num. 14:13; Josh. 7:9; Ps. 106:8; Jer. 14:21 [c]Deut. 7:6-11; 1Pet. 2:9

23 [a]Rom. 1:9; 1Cor. 9:16; Col. 1:9; 1Thess. 3:10; 2Tim. 1:3 [b]1Kin. 8:36; Ps. 34:11; Prov. 4:11

24 [I]Or, *reverence* [a]Eccl. 12:13 [b]Deut. 10:21; Is. 5:12

25 [a]Is. 1:20; 3:11 [b]Josh. 24:20 [c]1Sam. 31:1-5; Hos. 10:3

2 [a]1Sam. 13:5; 14:31 [b]1Sam. 10:26

3 [a]1Sam. 10:5 [b]1Sam. 13:16; 14:5 [c]Judg. 3:27; 6:34

4 [I]Lit., *saying* [II]Lit., *after* [a]Gen. 34:30; Ex.5:21; 2Sam. 10:6

5 [a]Josh. 11:4 [b]Josh. 18:12; 1Sam. 14:23

6 [a]Judg. 6:2

7 [a]Num. 32:33

8 [a]1Sam. 10:8

9 [a]Deut. 12:5-14; 2Sam. 24:25; 1Kin. 3:4

10 [I]Lit., *bless* [a]1Sam. 15:13

11 [a]1Sam. 13:2, 5, 16, 23

13 [a]2Chr. 16:9 [b]1Sam. 15:11, 22, 28

🔑 **13:13,14** Saul showed himself to be a man without regard for God's will. Samuel had told Saul that he should wait for him in Gilgal for seven days. Saul, seeing that Samuel had not arrived, took the priestly responsibility upon himself, which apparently he had no right to do, and offered the burnt sacrifice. This is all summed up by Samuel as disobedience to the commandment of the Lord. Though Samuel *(continued on next page)*

kept[8104] the commandment[4687] of the
LORD your God,[430] which He commanded[6680] you, for now the LORD
would have established[3559] your kingdom[4467] [I]over Israel [c]forever.
14 "But [a]now your kingdom shall not
endure. [b]The LORD has sought out for
Himself a man after His own heart, and
the LORD has appointed him as ruler[5057]
over His people, because you have not
kept what the LORD commanded you."
15 Then Samuel arose and went up
from Gilgal to [a]Gibeah of Benjamin. And
Saul [I]numbered the people who were
present with him, [b]about six hundred
men.
16 Now Saul and his son[1121] Jonathan and the people who were present
with them were staying in [a]Geba of Benjamin while the Philistines camped at
Michmash.
17 And [a]the [I]raiders[7843] came from
the camp[4264] of the Philistines in three
[II]companies:[7218] one [III]company[7218]
turned [IV]toward[1870] [b]Ophrah, to the land
of Shual,
18 and another [I]company turned
[II]toward [a]Beth-horon, and another [I]com-
pany turned [II]toward the border which
overlooks the valley of [b]Zeboim toward the wilderness.
19 Now [a]no blacksmith could be
found in all the land of Israel, for the
Philistines said, "Lest the Hebrews
make [I][b]swords[2719] or spears."
20 So all Israel went down to the
Philistines, each to sharpen his plowshare, his mattock,[4281] his axe, and his
hoe.[855]
21 And the charge was [I]two-thirds
of a shekel for the plowshares, the mat-
tocks, the forks, and the axes, and to
fix the hoes.
22 So it came about on the day[3117]
of battle that [a]neither sword[2719] nor
spear was found in the hands of any of
the people who *were* with Saul and Jonathan, but they were found with Saul and
his son Jonathan.
23 And [a]the garrison of the Philistines went out to [b]the pass of Michmash.

Jonathan's Victory

14 Now the day[3117] came that Jonathan, the son[1121] of Saul, said
to the young man who was carrying[5375]
his armor, "Come and let us cross over
to the Philistines' garrison that is on
yonder side." But he did not tell his
father.[1]
2 And Saul was staying in the outskirts of [a]Gibeah under the pomegranate
tree which is in [b]Migron. And the
people[5971] who *were* with him *were*
[c]about six hundred men,
3 and Ahijah, the [a]son of Ahitub,
[b]Ichabod's brother,[251] the son of Phinehas, the son of Eli, the priest[3548] of
the LORD at [c]Shiloh, [d]was [I]wearing an
ephod. And the people did not know[3045]
that Jonathan had gone.
4 And [a]between the passes by which
Jonathan sought to cross over to the
Philistines' garrison, there was a sharp
crag on the one side, and a sharp crag
on the other side, and the name of the
one was Bozez, and the name of the
other Seneh.
5 The one crag rose on the north
opposite Michmash, and the other on
the south opposite Geba.
6 Then Jonathan said to the young
man who was carrying his armor, "Come
and let us cross over to the garrison
of [a]these uncircumcised;[6189] perhaps the
LORD will work[6213] for us, for [b]the LORD
is not restrained to save by many or
by few."
7 And his armor bearer said to him,
"Do[6213] all that is in your heart; turn
yourself, *and* here I am with you according to your [I]desire."
8 Then Jonathan said, "[a]Behold, we

13 [I]Lit., *to* [c]1Sam. 1:22
14 [a]1Sam. 15:28 [b]Acts 7:46; 13:22
15 [I]Lit., *mustered* [a]1Sam. 13:2 [b]1Sam. 13:2, 6, 7; 14:2
16 [a]1Sam. 13:2,3
17 [I]Lit., *destroyers* [II]Lit., *heads* [III]Lit., *head* [IV]Lit., *toward the direction of* [a]1Sam. 14:15 [b]Josh. 18:23
18 [I]Lit., *head* [II]Lit., *the direction of* [a]Josh. 16:3; 18:13, 14 [b]Neh. 11:34
19 [I]Lit., *sword or spear* [a]Judg. 5:8; 2Kin. 24:14; Jer. 24:1; 29:2 [b]Judg. 5:8
21 [I]Heb., *pim*
22 [a]Judg. 5:8
23 [a]1Sam. 14:1; 2Sam. 23:14 [b]1Sam. 14:4, 5; Is. 10:28
2 [a]1Sam. 13:15, 16 [b]Is. 10:28 [c]1Sam. 13:15
3 [I]Lit., *carrying* [a]1Sam. 22:9-12, 20 [b]1Sam. 4:21 [c]1Sam. 1:3 [d]1Sam. 2:28
4 [a]1Sam. 13:23
6 [a]1Sam. 17:26, 36; Jer. 9:25, 26 [b]Judg. 7:4, 7; 1Sam. 17:46, 47; Ps. 115:3; 135:6; Zech. 4:6; Matt. 19:26
7 [I]Lit., *heart*
8 [a]Judg. 7:9-14

(continued from previous page)
affirmed that, because of Saul's disobedience, the kingdom would pass from him to another, Saul did not repent. He continued to disobey according to his own whims. Later Samuel stated that it is better to obey than to sacrifice (I Sam. 15:22).

will cross over[5674] to the men and reveal[1540] ourselves to them.

9 "If they [I]say to us, 'Wait until we come[5060] to you'; then we will stand in our place and not go up to them.

10 "But if they [I]say, 'Come up to us,' then we will go up, for the LORD has given them into our hands; and [a]this shall be the sign[226] to us."

11 And when both of them revealed themselves to the garrison of the Philistines, the Philistines said, "Behold, [a]Hebrews are coming out of the holes where they have hidden themselves."

12 So the men of the garrison [I]hailed Jonathan and his armor bearer and said, "Come up to us and [a]we will tell you something." And Jonathan said to his armor bearer, "Come up after me, for [b]the LORD has given them into the hands of Israel."

13 Then Jonathan climbed up on his hands and feet, with his armor bearer behind him; and they fell[5307] before Jonathan, and his armor bearer put some to death[4191] after him.

14 And that first slaughter[4347] which Jonathan and his armor bearer made was about twenty men within about half a furrow in an acre of land.

15 And there was a trembling in the camp, in the field,[7704] and among all the people. Even the garrison and [a]the raiders[7843] trembled, and [b]the earth[776] quaked so [c]that it became a [I]great trembling.

16 Now Saul's watchmen in Gibeah of Benjamin looked,[7200] and behold, the multitude melted away; and they went here and *there.*

17 And Saul said to the people who *were* with him, "[I]Number[6485] now and see who has gone from us." And when they had [I]numbered, behold, Jonathan and his armor bearer were not *there.*

18 Then Saul said to Ahijah, "[a]Bring the ark[727] of God[430] here." For the ark of God was at that time with the sons[1121] of Israel.

19 And it happened [a]while Saul talked to the priest, that the commotion in the camp of the Philistines continued and increased; so Saul said to the priest, "Withdraw[622] your hand."

20 Then Saul and all the people who *were* with him rallied[2199] and came to the battle; and behold, [a]every man's sword[2719] was against his fellow,[7453] *and there was* very great confusion.[4103]

21 Now the Hebrews *who* were with the Philistines previously, who went up with them all around in the camp,[4264] even [a]they also *turned* to be with the Israelites who *were* with Saul and Jonathan.

22 When all the [a]men of Israel who had hidden themselves in the hill country of Ephraim heard that the Philistines had fled, even they also pursued them closely in the battle.

23 So [a]the LORD delivered[3467] Israel that day, and the battle [I]spread[5674] beyond [b]Beth-aven.

Saul's Foolish Order

24 Now the men of Israel were hard-pressed on that day, for Saul had [a]put the people under oath,[422] saying, "Cursed[779] be the man who eats food [I]before evening, and until I have avenged myself on my enemies." So none of the people tasted food.

25 And all *the people of* the land[776] entered the forest, and there was honey on the ground.[7704]

26 When the people entered the for-

9 [I]Lit., *say thus*

10 [I]Lit., *say thus* [a]Gen. 24:14; Judg. 6:36

11 [a]1Sam. 13:6; 14:22

12 [I]Lit., *answered* [a]1Sam. 17:43, 44 [b]2Sam. 5:24

15 [I]Lit., *trembling of God* [a]1Sam. 13:17, 18 [b]1Sam. 7:10 [c]Gen. 35:5; 2Kin. 7:6

17 [I]Lit., *muster(ed)*

18 [a]1Sam. 23:9; 30:7

19 [a]Num. 27:21

20 [a]Judg. 7:22; 2Chr. 20:23

21 [a]1Sam. 29:4

22 [a]1Sam. 13:6

23 [I]Lit., *passed over* [a]Ex. 14:30; 1Sam. 10:19; 14:23; 1Chr. 11:14; 2Chr. 32:22; Ps. 44:7 [b]1Sam. 13:5

24 [I]Lit., *until* [a]Josh. 6:26

14:18 Saul desired to know God's will by seeking the ark of God. In the Septuagint (the Greek translation of the O.T.) the word "ephod" is used instead of the word "ark." The ephod was in Saul's camp at Gibeah (I Sam. 14:3). The ark, however, was at Kiriath Jearim (also called Baale-judah) where it remained for twenty years until David brought it to Jerusalem (II Sam. 6:1-17). The ephod with the Urim and Thummim was used for such purposes (23:9; 30:7; 2:18,28).

14:19 Withdrawing the hand is more appropriate in regard to the ephod (see note on 14:18, also II Sam. 6:6,7).

est, behold, [a]*there was* a flow of honey; but no man put his hand to his mouth, for the people feared[3372] the oath.[7621]

27 But Jonathan had not heard when his father put the people under oath[7650]; therefore, [a]he put out the end of the staff that *was* in his hand and dipped[2881] it in the honeycomb, and put his hand to his mouth, and [b]his eyes brightened.

28 Then one of the people answered and said, "Your father strictly put the people under oath, saying, 'Cursed be the man who eats food today.'" And the people were weary.

29 Then Jonathan said, "[a]My father has troubled the land. See now, how my eyes have brightened because I tasted a little of this honey.

30 "How much more, if only the people had eaten freely today of the spoil of their enemies which they found! For now the slaughter among the Philistines has not been great."

31 And they struck[5221] among the Philistines that day from [a]Michmash to [b]Aijalon. And the people were very weary.

32 And [a]the people [I]rushed greedily upon the spoil, and took sheep and oxen and calves, and slew[7819] *them* on the ground;[776] and the people ate *them* [b]with the blood.[1818]

33 Then they told Saul, saying, "Behold, the people are [a]sinning[2398] against the LORD by eating with the blood." And he said, "You have acted treacherously; roll a great stone to me today."

34 And Saul said, "Disperse yourselves among the people and say to them, 'Each one of you bring me his ox or his sheep, and slaughter[7819] *it* here and eat; and do not sin against the LORD by eating with the blood.'" So all the people that night[3915] brought[5066] each one his ox [I]with him, and slaughtered *it* there.

35 And [a]Saul built an altar[4196] to the LORD; it was the first altar that he built to the LORD.

🔑 **36** Then Saul said, "Let us go down after the Philistines by night and take spoil among them until the morning light,[216] and let us not leave[7604] a man of them." And they said, "Do whatever seems good[2896] [I]to you." So [a]the priest said, "Let us draw near to God here."

37 And Saul [a]inquired[7592] of God, "Shall I go down after the Philistines? Wilt Thou give them into the hand of Israel?" But [b]He did not answer him on that day.

38 And Saul said, "[a]Draw near[5066] here, all you [I]chiefs of the people, and investigate[3045] and see how this sin[2403] has happened today.

39 "For [a]as the LORD lives,[2416] who delivers[3467] Israel, though it is in Jonathan my son, he shall surely die."[4191] But not one of all the people answered him.

40 Then he said to all Israel, "You shall be on one side and I and Jonathan my son will be on the other side." And the people said to Saul, "Do what seems good [I]to you."

41 Therefore, Saul said to the LORD, the God of Israel, "[a]Give a perfect *lot.*" And Jonathan and Saul were taken, but the people escaped.

42 And Saul said, "Cast[5307] *lots* between me and Jonathan my son." And Jonathan was taken.

43 Then Saul said to Jonathan, "[a]Tell me what you have done."[6213] So Jonathan told him and said, "[b]I indeed tasted a little honey with the end of the staff that was in my hand. Here I am, I must die!"

44 And Saul said,[559] "[a]May God do [I]this *to me* and more also, for [b]you shall surely die, Jonathan."

45 But the people said to Saul, "Must Jonathan die, who has [I]brought about this great deliverance[3444] in Israel? Far from it! As the LORD lives, [a]there shall not one hair of his head fall to the ground, for [b]he has worked with God

26 [a]Matt. 3:4

27 [a]1Sam. 14:43 [b]1Sam. 30:12

29 [a]Josh. 7:25; 1Kin. 18:18

31 [a]1Sam. 14:5 [b]Josh. 10:12

32 [I]Lit., *did with regard to the spoil* [a]1Sam. 15:19 [b]Gen. 9:4; Lev. 3:17; 17:10-14; 19:26; Deut. 12:16, 23; Acts 15:20

33 [a]Lev. 7:26, 27; 19:26; Deut. 12:16, 23-25; 15:23

34 [I]Lit., *in his hand*

35 [a]1Sam. 7:12, 17; 2Sam. 24:25; James 4:8

36 [I]Lit., *in your eyes* [a]1Sam. 14:3, 18, 19

37 [a]1Sam. 10:22 [b]1Sam. 28:6

38 [I]Lit., *corners* [a]Josh. 7:11,12; 1Sam. 10:19, 20

39 [a]1Sam. 14:24, 44; 2Sam. 12:5

40 [I]Lit., *in your eyes*

41 [a]Acts 1:24

43 [a]Josh. 7:19 [b]1Sam. 14:27

44 [I]Lit., *thus* [a]Ruth 1:17; 1Sam. 25:22 [b]1Sam. 14:39

45 [I]Lit., *worked* [a]2Sam. 14:11; 1Kin. 1:52; Luke 21:18; Acts 27:34 [b]2Cor. 6:1

🔑 **14:36,37** See note on Ex. 28:30.

this day." So the people [II]rescued Jonathan and he did not die.[4191]

46 Then Saul went up from [I]pursuing the Philistines, and the Philistines went to their own place.

Constant Warfare

47 Now when Saul had taken the kingdom over Israel, he fought against all his enemies on every side, against Moab, [a]the sons of Ammon, Edom, [b]the kings[4428] of Zobah, and [c]the Philistines; and wherever he turned, he [I]inflicted punishment.[7561]

48 And he acted valiantly and [Ia]defeated the Amalekites, and delivered[5337] Israel from the hands of [II]those who plundered[8154] them.

49 Now [a]the sons[1121] of Saul were Jonathan and Ishvi and Malchi-shua; and the names of his two daughters *were these:* the name of the first-born [b]Merab and the name of the younger [c]Michal.

50 And the name of Saul's wife[802] was Ahinoam the daughter of Ahimaaz. And [a]the name of the captain[8269] of his army was Abner the son of Ner, Saul's uncle.

51 [a]And Kish *was* the father of Saul, and Ner the father of Abner *was* the son of Abiel.

52 Now the war against the Philistines was severe[2389] all the days[3117] of Saul; and when Saul saw[7200] any mighty man or any valiant man, he [Ia]attached him to [II]his staff.

Saul's Disobedience

15 Then Samuel said to Saul, "[a]The LORD sent me to anoint[4886] you as king[4428] over His people,[5971] over Israel; now therefore, listen to the [I]words[1697] of the LORD.

2 "Thus says[559] the LORD of hosts, 'I will [I]punish Amalek [a]*for* what he did[6213] to Israel, how he set[7760] himself against him on the way[1870] while he was coming up from Egypt.

3 'Now go and strike[5221] Amalek and [a]utterly destroy all that he has, and do not spare him; but [b]put to death[4191] both man and woman,[802] child and infant, ox and sheep, camel and donkey.'"

4 Then Saul summoned[8085] the people and [I]numbered them in [a]Telaim, 200,000 foot soldiers and 10,000 men of Judah.

5 And Saul came to the city of Amalek, and set an ambush in the valley.

6 And Saul said to [a]the Kenites, "Go, depart,[5493] go down from among the Amalekites, lest I destroy you with them; for [b]you showed[6213] kindness[2617] to all the sons[1121] of Israel when they came up from Egypt." So the Kenites departed from among the Amalekites.

7 So [a]Saul [I]defeated[5221] the Amalekites, from [b]Havilah as you go to [c]Shur, which is [II]east of Egypt.

8 And he captured [a]Agag the king of the Amalekites alive,[2416] and [b]utterly destroyed[2763] all the people with the edge[6310] of the sword.[2719]

9 But Saul and the people [a]spared Agag and the best of the sheep, the oxen, the fatlings, the lambs,[3733] and all that was good,[2896] and were not willing[14] to destroy them utterly; but everything despised[5240] and worthless, that they utterly destroyed.

Samuel Rebukes Saul

10 Then the word[1697] of the LORD came to Samuel, saying,

11 "[a]I regret that I have made Saul king, for [b]he has turned back from [I]following Me, and has not carried out My commands."[1697] And Samuel was distressed and [c]cried[2199] out to the LORD all night.[3915]

12 And Samuel rose early in the

45 [II]Lit., *ransomed*
46 [I]Lit., *after*
47 [I]Or, *condemned* [a]1Sam. 11:1-13 [b]2Sam. 8:3-10 [c]1Sam. 14:52
48 [I]Lit., *smote* [II]Lit., *its plunderers* [a]1Sam. 15:3, 7
49 [a]1Sam. 31:2; 1Chr. 8:33; 10:2 [b]1Sam. 18:17-19 [c]1Sam. 18:20, 27; 19:12; 2Sam. 6:20-23
50 [a]2Sam. 2:8
51 [a]1Sam. 9:1, 21
52 [I]Lit., *gathered* [II]Lit., *himself* [a]1Sam. 8:11
1 [I]Lit., *sound of the words* [a]1Sam. 9:16; 10:1
2 [I]Or, *visit* [a]Ex. 17:8-16; Num. 24:20; Deut. 25:17-19
3 [a]Num. 24:20; Deut. 20:16-18; Josh. 6:17-21 [b]1Sam. 22:19
4 [I]Lit., *mustered* [a]Josh. 15:24
6 [a]Num. 24:21; Judg. 1:16; 4:11 [b]Ex. 18:9, 10; Num. 10:29-32
7 [I]Lit., *smote* [II]Lit., *before* [a]1Sam. 14:48 [b]Gen. 25:18 [c]Gen. 16:7; Ex. 15:22; 1Sam. 27:8
8 [a]Num. 24:7; 1Sam. 15:20; Esth. 3:1 [b]1Sam. 27:8, 9; 30:1; 2Sam. 8:12
9 [a]1Sam. 15:3, 15, 19
11 [I]Lit., *after* [a]Gen. 6:6, 7; Ex. 32:14; 1Sam. 15:35; 2Sam. 24:16 [b]Josh. 22:16; 1Sam. 13:13; 1Kin. 9:6, 7 [c]Ex. 32:11-13; Luke 6:12

15:12 Carmel, which means "garden," does not refer to the famous mountain in the western part of Galilee but to a town in Judah which lay about seven miles south of Hebron. It was directly on Saul's way as he returned from battle against the Amalekites.

morning to meet Saul; and it was told Samuel, saying, "Saul came to [a]Carmel, and behold, he set[5324] up a monument for himself, then turned and proceeded[5674] on [I]down to [b]Gilgal."

13 And Samuel came to Saul, and Saul said to him, "[a]Blessed[1288] are you of the LORD! I have carried out the command[1697] of the LORD."

14 But Samuel said, "[a]What then is this [I]bleating[6963] of the sheep in my ears,[241] and the [I]lowing[6963] of the oxen which I hear?"

15 And Saul said, "They have brought them from the Amalekites, for [a]the people spared the best of the sheep and oxen, to sacrifice[2076] to the LORD your God;[430] but the rest we have utterly destroyed."

16 Then Samuel said[1696] to Saul, "Wait, and let me tell you what the LORD said to me last night." And he said to him, "Speak!"[1696]

17 And Samuel said, "Is it not true, [a]though you were little in your own eyes, you were *made* the head of the tribes of Israel? And the LORD anointed[4886] you king over Israel,

18 and the LORD sent you on a [I]mission,[1870] and said, "[a]Go and utterly destroy the sinners,[2400] the Amalekites, and fight against them until they are exterminated.'[3615]

19 "Why then did[6213] you not obey the voice of the LORD, [a]but rushed upon the spoil and did what was evil[7451] in the sight of the LORD?"

20 Then Saul said to Samuel, "[a]I did obey[8085] the voice of the LORD, and went on the [I]mission on which the LORD sent me, and have brought back Agag the king of Amalek, and have utterly destroyed the Amalekites.

21 "But [a]the people took *some* of the spoil, sheep and oxen, the choicest[7225] of the things devoted to destruction, to sacrifice to the LORD your God at Gilgal."

22 And Samuel said,

"[a]Has the LORD as much
delight[2656] in burnt offerings
and sacrifices
As in obeying the voice of the
LORD?
Behold, [b]to obey is better[2896]
than sacrifice,[2077]
And to heed than the fat of rams.

23 "For rebellion is as the sin[2403] of
[a]divination,
And insubordination is as
[b]iniquity[205] and idolatry.[8655]
Because you have rejected the
word of the LORD,
[c]He has also rejected you from
being king."

24 Then Saul said to Samuel, "[a]I have sinned;[2398] [b]I have indeed transgressed the [I]command[6310] of the LORD and your words, because I feared[3372] the people and listened to their voice.

25 "Now therefore, [a]please[4994] pardon[5374] my sin and return with me, that I may worship[7812] the LORD."

26 But Samuel said to Saul, "I will not return with you; for [a]you have rejected the word of the LORD, and the LORD has rejected you from being king over Israel."

27 And as Samuel turned to go, [a]*Saul* seized the edge of his robe,[4598] and it tore.

28 So Samuel said to him, "[a]The LORD has torn the kingdom[4468] of Israel from you today,[3117] and has given it to your neighbor[7453] who is better than you.

29 "And also the [I][a]Glory[5331] of Israel [b]will not lie[8266] or change His mind; for He is not a man that He should change His mind."

30 Then he said, "I have sinned; [a]*but* please honor me now before the elders[2205] of my people and before Israel, and go back with me, [b]that I may worship the LORD your God."

31 So Samuel went back following Saul, and Saul worshiped[7812] the LORD.

32 Then Samuel said, "Bring me Agag, the king of the Amalekites." And Agag came to him [I]cheerfully. And Agag said, "Surely the bitterness[4751] of death[4194] is past."

33 But Samuel said, "[a]As your sword has made women[802] childless, so

---

12 [I]Lit., *and went down* [a]Josh. 15:55; 1Sam. 25:2 [b]1Sam. 13:12, 15

13 [a]Gen. 14:19; Judg. 17:2; Ruth 3:10; 2Sam. 2:5

14 [I]Lit., *sound* [a]Ex. 32:21-24

15 [a]Gen. 3:12, 13; Ex. 32:22, 23; 1Sam. 15:9, 21

17 [a]1Sam. 9:21; 10:22

18 [I]Lit., *way* [a]1Sam. 15:3

19 [a]1Sam. 14:32

20 [I]Lit., *way* [a]1Sam. 15:13

21 [a]Ex. 32:22, 23; 1Sam. 15:15

22 [a]Ps. 40:6-8; 51:16, 17; Is. 1:11-15; Mic. 6:6-8; Heb. 10:6-9 [b]Jer. 7:22, 23; Hos. 6:6; Matt. 12:7; Mark 12:33

23 [a]Deut. 18:10 [b]Gen. 31:19, 34 [c]1Sam. 13:14

24 [I]Lit., *mouth* [a]Num. 22:34; 2Sam. 12:13; Ps. 51:4 [b]Prov. 29:25; Is. 51:12, 13

25 [a]Ex. 10:17

26 [a]1Sam. 13:14; 16:1

27 [a]1Kin. 11:30, 31

28 [a]1Sam. 28:17, 18; 1Kin. 11:31

29 [I]Or, *Eminence* [a]1Chr. 29:11 [b]Num. 23:19; Ezek. 24:14; Titus 1:2

30 [a]John 5:44; 12:43 [b]Is. 29:13

32 [I]Or, *in bonds*

33 [a]Gen. 9:6; Judg. 1:7; Matt. 7:2

shall your mother be childless among women." And Samuel hewed[8158] Agag to pieces before the LORD at Gilgal.

34 Then Samuel went to [a]Ramah, but Saul went up to his house at [b]Gibeah of Saul.

35 And [a]Samuel did not see Saul again until the day of his death; for Samuel [b]grieved over Saul. And the LORD regretted that He had made Saul king[4427] over Israel.

Samuel Goes to Bethlehem

16 Now the LORD said to Samuel, "[a]How long will you grieve over Saul, since [b]I have rejected him from being king over Israel? [c]Fill your horn with oil,[8081] and go; I will send you to [d]Jesse the Bethlehemite, for I have [e]selected[7200] a king[4428] for Myself among his sons."[1121]

2 But Samuel said, "How can I go? When Saul hears *of it,* he will kill[2026] me." And the LORD said, "[a]Take a heifer with you, and say,[559] 'I have come to sacrifice[2076] to the LORD.'

3 "And you shall invite[7121] Jesse to the sacrifice[2077], and [a]I will show[3045] you what you shall do;[6213] and [b]you shall anoint[4886] for Me the one whom I [1]designate to you."

4 So Samuel did[6213] what the LORD said,[1696] and came to [a]Bethlehem. And the elders[2205] of the city came trembling to meet him and said, "[b]Do you come in peace?"[7965]

5 And he said, "In peace; I have come to sacrifice to the LORD. [a]Consecrate[6942] yourselves and come with me to the sacrifice." He also consecrated[6942] Jesse and his sons, and invited[7121] them to the sacrifice.

34 [a]1Sam. 7:17 [b]1Sam. 11:4
35 [a]1Sam. 19:24 [b]1Sam. 16:1
1 [a]1Sam. 15:35 [b]1Sam. 13:13, 14; 15:23 [c]1Sam. 9:16; 10:1; 2Kin. 9:1 [d]Ruth 4:17-22 [e]Ps. 78:70, 71; Acts 13:22
2 [a]1Sam. 20:29
3 [1]Lit., *say to you* [a]Ex. 4:15; Acts 9:6 [b]Deut. 17:14,15; 1Sam. 9:16
4 [a]Gen. 48:7; Luke 2:4 [b]1Kin. 2:13; 2Kin. 9:22; 1Chr. 12:17, 18
5 [a]Gen. 35:2; Ex. 19:10
6 [a]1Sam. 17:13
7 [1]So with Gr.; Heb., He does *not see what man sees* [a]1Sam. 2:3; 1Kin. 8:39; 1Chr. 28:9; Luke 16:15
8 [a]1Sam. 17:13
9 [1]In 2Sam. 13:3, *Shimeah;* in 1Chr. 2:13, *Shimea* [a]1Sam. 17:13
11 [1]Lit., *take* [a]1Sam. 17:12; 2Sam. 13:3
12 [a]Gen. 39:6; Ex. 2:2; Acts 7:20 [b]1Sam. 9:17
13 [a]1Sam. 10:1 [b]Num. 27:18; 1Sam. 10:6, 9, 10

6 Then it came about when they entered, that he looked[7200] at [a]Eliab and thought, "Surely the LORD's anointed[4899] is before Him."

7 But the LORD said to Samuel, "Do not look at his appearance or at the height of his stature, because I have rejected him; for [1]God *sees* not as man sees, for man looks[7200] at the outward appearance, [a]but the LORD looks at the heart."

8 Then Jesse called [a]Abinadab, and made him pass before Samuel. And he said, "Neither has the LORD chosen[977] this one."

9 Next Jesse made [1a]Shammah pass by. And he said, "Neither has the LORD chosen this one."

10 Thus Jesse made seven of his sons pass before Samuel. But Samuel said to Jesse, "The LORD has not chosen these."

11 And Samuel said to Jesse, "Are these all the children?" And he said, "[a]There remains yet the youngest, and behold, he is tending the sheep." Then Samuel said to Jesse, "Send and [1]bring him; for we will not sit down until he comes here."

David Anointed

12 So he sent and brought him in. Now he was ruddy, with [a]beautiful eyes and a handsome[2896] appearance. And the LORD said, "[b]Arise, anoint him; for this is he."

🗝 13 Then Samuel took the horn of oil and [a]anointed[4886] him in the midst of his brothers;[251] and [b]the Spirit[7307] of the LORD came mightily upon David from that day[3117] forward. And Samuel arose and went to Ramah.

🗝 **16:13** This picture of the selection of David, the former shepherd boy, to be king over Israel is important to our understanding of the coming of Jesus. In N.T. times, it was recognized by Jews that the Christ would come from the seed of David (Jn. 7:42). Jesus was designated as the Christ which means "anointed," as David was here the anointed one of God (see I Sam. 2:10). A title repeatedly applied to Jesus was "the Son of David." A comparison could also be made in the fact that Jesus came as a Shepherd (Jn. 10:11), just as David had been a shepherd. Just as David ascended to the throne of Israel, Jesus left His work of shepherding on earth to ascend to the throne in heaven (Acts 2:30-34), which is seen as an extension of the throne of David.

14 [a]Now the Spirit of the LORD departed from Saul, and [b]an evil[7451] spirit from the LORD terrorized him.
15 Saul's servants then said to him, "Behold now, an evil spirit from God[430] is terrorizing you.
16 "Let our lord[113] now command your servants who are before you. Let them seek a man who is a skillful player on the harp; and it shall come about when the evil spirit from God is on you, that [a]he shall play *the harp* with his hand, and you will be well."[2895]
17 So Saul said to his servants, "Provide[7200] for me now a man who can play well,[3190] and bring *him* to me."
🗝 18 Then one of the young men answered and said, "Behold, I have seen[7200] a son[1121] of Jesse the Bethlehemite who is a skillful musician, [a]a mighty man of valor, a warrior, one prudent[995] in speech, and a handsome[8389] man;[376] and [b]the LORD is with him."
19 So Saul sent messengers to Jesse, and said, "Send me your son David who is with the flock."
20 And Jesse [a]took a donkey *loaded with* bread and a jug of wine and a young goat, and sent *them* to Saul by David his son.
21 Then David came to Saul and [I][a]attended him, and [II]Saul loved[157] him greatly; and he became his armor bearer.
22 And Saul sent to Jesse, saying, "Let David now stand before me; for he has found favor[2580] in my sight."
23 So it came about whenever [a]the *evil* spirit from God came to Saul, David would take the harp and play *it* with his hand; and Saul would be refreshed and be well, and the evil spirit would depart from him.

Goliath's Challenge

17 Now [a]the Philistines gathered[622] their armies for battle; and they were gathered at Socoh which belongs to Judah, and they camped between [b]Socoh and [c]Azekah, in [d]Ephes-dammim.
2 And Saul and the men of Israel were gathered, and camped in [a]the valley of Elah, and drew up in battle array to encounter the Philistines.
3 And the Philistines stood on the mountain on one side while Israel stood on the mountain on the other side, with the valley between them.
4 Then a champion came out from the armies[4264] of the Philistines named [a]Goliath, from [b]Gath, whose height was six [I]cubits and a span.
5 And *he had* a bronze helmet on his head, and he was clothed with scale-armor [I]which weighed five thousand shekels of bronze.
6 *He* also *had* bronze [I]greaves[4697] on his legs and a [a]bronze javelin *slung* between his shoulders.
7 And [a]the shaft of his spear was like a weaver's beam, and the head of his spear *weighed* six hundred shekels of iron; [b]his shield-carrier[5375] also walked before him.
8 And he stood and shouted[7121] to the ranks of Israel, and said to them, "Why do you come out to draw up in

14 [a]Judg. 16:20; 1Sam. 11:6; 18:12; 28:15 [b]Judg. 9:23; 1Sam. 16:15, 16; 18:10; 19:9; 1Kin. 22:19-22
16 [a]1Sam. 18:10; 19:9; 2Kin. 3:15
18 [a]1Sam. 17:32-36 [b]1Sam. 3:19
20 [a]1Sam. 10:4, 27; Prov. 18:16
21 [I]Lit., *stood before him* [II]Lit., *he* [a]Gen. 41:46; Prov. 22:29
23 [a]1Sam. 16:14-16
1 [a]1Sam. 13:5 [b]Josh. 15:35; 2Chr. 28:18 [c]Josh. 10:10 [d]1Chr. 11:13
2 [a]1Sam. 21:9
4 [I]I.e., One cubit equals approx. 18 in. [a]2Sam. 21:19 [b]Josh. 11:22
5 [I]Lit., *and the weight of the armor was*
6 [I]Or, *shin guards* [a]1Sam. 17:45
7 [a]2Sam. 21:19; 1Chr. 11:23 [b]1Sam. 17:41

🗝 **16:18** If David is here recognized as a mighty and valiant man, why did Saul play down this fact shortly after (I Sam. 17:33)? Note that here the statement is made by a servant of Saul when the king was searching for a minstrel to play the lyre for his entertainment. The servant may have intentionally overstated David's prowess to impress Saul. Though well developed physically for his age and fearless, he was still just a youth. Probably several years had passed when David offered to go out against Goliath, but he was still just a boy compared to the men in the king's army, and certainly in comparison to Goliath. No statement is made that Saul recognized who David was, even though he had served as the king's minstrel. Indeed, in I Sam. 17:55, Saul asked, after the victory over Goliath, who this young man was. Possibly these few years had completely changed David's appearance, so that Saul did not recognize him as the youth who had played music for him. It is also possible that Saul might have simply pretended not to know him.

battle array? Am I not the Philistine and you [a]servants[5650] of Saul? Choose a man for yourselves and let him come down to me.

9 "[a]If he is able to fight with me and [I]kill me, then we will become your servants; but if I prevail against him and [I]kill him, then you shall become our servants and serve us."

10 Again the Philistine said, "[a]I defy the ranks of Israel this day;[3117] give me a man that we may fight together."

11 When Saul and all Israel heard these words[1697] of the Philistine, they were dismayed[2865] and greatly afraid.[3372]

12 Now David was [a]the son[1121] of [I]the [b]Ephrathite of Bethlehem in Judah, whose name was Jesse, and [c]he had eight sons. And [II]Jesse was old[2204] in the days[3117] of Saul, advanced *in years* among men.

13 And the three older sons of Jesse had [I]gone after Saul to the battle. And [a]the names of his three sons who went to the battle were Eliab the first-born, and the second to him Abinadab, and the third Shammah.

14 And [a]David was the youngest. Now the three oldest followed Saul,

15 [a]but David went back and forth from Saul [b]to tend his father's[1] flock at Bethlehem.

16 And the Philistine came [I]forward[5066] morning and evening for forty days, and took his stand.

17 Then Jesse said to David his son, "[a]Take now for your brothers[251] an ephah of this roasted grain and these ten loaves, and run to the camp to your brothers.

18 "[a]Bring also these ten cuts of cheese to the commander[8269] of *their* thousand, [b]and look into the welfare[7965] of your brothers, and bring back [I]news[6161] of them.

19 "For Saul and they and all the men of Israel are in the valley of Elah, fighting with the Philistines."

David Accepts the Challenge

20 So David arose early in the morning and left[5203] the flock with a keeper[8104] and took *the supplies* and went as Jesse had commanded[6680] him. And he came to the [a]circle of the camp while the army was going out in battle array shouting[7321] the war cry.

21 And Israel and the Philistines drew up in battle array, army against army.

22 Then David left his [a]baggage in the [I]care of the baggage keeper, and ran to the battle line and entered in order to greet[7965] his brothers.

23 As he was talking with them, behold, the champion, the Philistine from Gath named Goliath, was coming up from the army of the Philistines, and he spoke[1696] [a]these same words; and David heard *them.*

24 When all the men of Israel saw[7200] the man, they fled from him and were greatly afraid.

25 And the men of Israel said, "Have you seen[7200] this man who is coming up? Surely he is coming up to defy Israel. And it will be that the king[4428] will enrich the man who kills[5221] him with great riches and [a]will give him his daughter and make his father's house [I]free in Israel."

26 Then David spoke[559] to the men who were standing by him, saying, "What will be done[6213] for the man who kills this Philistine, and takes away [a]the reproach from Israel? For who is this [b]uncircumcised[6189] Philistine, that he should [c]taunt the armies of [d]the living[2416] God?"[430]

27 And the people[5971] [I]answered[559] him in accord with this word, saying, "[a]Thus it will be done for the man who kills him."

28 Now Eliab his oldest brother[251] heard when he spoke[1696] to the men; and [a]Eliab's anger[639] burned[2734] against David and he said, "Why have you come

8 [a]1Sam. 8:17
9 [I]Lit., *smite* [a]2Sam. 2:12-16
10 [a]1Sam. 17:26, 36, 45; 2Sam. 21:21
12 [I]Lit., *this* [II]Lit., *the man* [a]Ruth 4:22; 1Sam. 16:18 [b]Gen. 35:19 [c]1Sam. 16:10, 11; 1Chr. 2:13-15
13 [I]Lit., *gone; they went* [a]1Sam. 16:6, 8, 9
14 [a]1Sam. 16:11
15 [a]1Sam. 16:21-23 [b]1Sam. 16:11, 19
16 [I]Lit., *near*
17 [a]1Sam. 25:18
18 [I]Lit., *their pledge* [a]1Sam. 16:20 [b]Gen. 37:13,14
20 [a]1Sam. 26:5,7
22 [I]Lit., *hand* [a]Judg. 18:21; Is. 10:28
23 [a]1Sam. 17:8-10
25 [I]I.e., free from taxes and public service [a]Josh. 15:16
26 [a]1Sam. 11:2 [b]1Sam. 14:6; 17:36; Jer. 9:25, 26 [c]1Sam. 17:10 [d]Deut. 5:26; 2Kin. 19:4; Jer. 10:10
27 [I]Lit., *said to* [a]1Sam. 17:25
28 [a]Gen. 37:4, 8-36; Prov. 18:19; Matt. 10:36

17:11 Everyone knew, including Saul, that there was only one man large enough to go against Goliath—Saul!

down? And with whom have you left
those few sheep in the wilderness? I
know[3045] your insolence[2087] and the
wickedness[7455] of your heart; for you
have come down in order to see the
battle."
29 But David said, "What have I
done now? Was it not just a
[I]question?"[1697]
30 Then he turned [I]away from him
to another and [a]said[559] the same thing;
and the people answered the same thing
as [II]before.[7223]

David Kills Goliath

31 When the words which David
spoke[1696] were heard, they told *them*
[I]to Saul, and he sent for him.
32 And David said to Saul, "[a]Let no
man's heart fail on account of him;
[b]your servant[5650] will go and fight with
this Philistine."
🔑 33 Then Saul said to David, "[a]You
are not able to go against this Philistine
to fight with him; for you are *but* a youth
while he has been a warrior from his
youth."
34 But David said to Saul, "Your
servant was tending his father's sheep.
When a lion or a bear came and took a
lamb from the flock,
35 I went out after him and
[I]attacked[5221] him, and [a]rescued[5337] *it*
from his mouth; and when he rose up
against me, I seized[2388] *him* by his
beard[2206] and [I]struck him and killed[4191]
him.
36 "Your servant has [I]killed[5221] both
the lion and the bear; and this uncircumcised Philistine will be like one of them,
since he has taunted[2778] the armies of
the living God."
37 And David said, "[a]The LORD who
delivered me from the paw of the lion
and from the paw of the bear, He will
deliver[5337] me from the hand of this Philistine." And Saul said to David, "[b]Go,
and may the LORD be with you."
38 Then Saul clothed David with his
garments and put a bronze helmet on
his head, and he clothed him with armor.
39 And David girded his sword[2719]
over his armor and tried to walk,[2974]
for he had not tested[5254] *them.* So David
said to Saul, "I cannot go with these,
for I have not tested *them.*" And David
took them [I]off.
40 And he took his stick in his hand
and chose[977] for himself five smooth
stones from the brook, and put them
in the shepherd's bag which he had, even
in *his* pouch,[3219] and [a]his sling was in
his hand; and he approached the Philistine.
41 Then the Philistine came on and
approached David, with the shield-
bearer[5375] in front of him.
42 When the Philistine looked and
saw David, [a]he disdained him; for he
was *but* a youth, and [b]ruddy, with a handsome appearance.
43 And the Philistine said to David,
"[a]Am I a dog, that you come to me with
sticks?" And [b]the Philistine cursed[7043]
David by his gods.[430]
44 The Philistine also said to David,
"Come to me, and I will give your
flesh[1320] [a]to the birds of the sky[8064] and
the beasts of the field."[7704]
45 Then David said to the Philistine,
"You come to me with a sword, a spear,
and a javelin, [a]but I come to you in the
name of the LORD of hosts, the God of
the armies of Israel, whom you have
taunted.
46 "This day the LORD will deliver
you up into my hands, and I will strike[5221]
you down and remove your head from
you. And I will give the [a]dead bodies[6297]
of the army of the Philistines this day
to the birds of the sky and the wild
beasts[2416] of the earth,[776] [b]that all the
earth may know that there is a God in
Israel,
47 and that all this assembly[6951] may
know that [a]the LORD does not deliver[3467]
by sword or by spear; [b]for the battle
is the LORD's and He will give you into
our hands."

29 [I]Lit., *word*
30 [I]Lit., *from beside him* [II]Lit., *the former word* [a]1Sam. 17:26, 27
31 [I]Lit., *before*
32 [a]Deut. 20:1-4 [b]1Sam. 16:18
33 [a]Num. 13:31
35 [I]Lit., *smote* [a]Amos 3:12
36 [I]Lit., *smitten*
37 [a]2Cor. 1:10; 2Tim. 4:17, 18 [b]1Sam. 20:13; 1Chr. 22:11, 16
39 [I]Lit., *off from himself*
40 [a]Judg. 20:16
42 [a]Ps. 123:4; Prov. 16:18 [b]1Sam. 16:12
43 [a]1Sam. 24:14; 2Sam. 3:8; 2Kin. 8:13 [b]1Kin. 20:10
44 [a]1Sam. 17:46
45 [a]2Sam. 22:35; 2Chr. 32:8; Ps. 124:8; Heb. 11:32-34
46 [a]Deut. 28:26 [b]Josh. 4:24; 1Kin. 8:43; 18:36; 2Kin. 19:19; Is. 37:20
47 [a]1Sam. 14:6; 2Chr. 14:11; 20:15; Ps. 44:6; Hos. 1:7; Zech. 4:6 [b]2Chr. 20:15

🔑 **17:33** See note on I Sam. 16:18.

48 Then it happened when the Philistine rose and came and drew near to
meet David, that [a]David ran quickly toward the battle line to meet the Philistine.
49 And David put his hand into his
bag and took from it a stone and slung[7044]
it, and struck the Philistine on his forehead. And the stone sank into his forehead, so that he fell[5307] on his face to
the ground.
50 Thus David prevailed[2388] over
the Philistine with a sling and a stone,
and he struck the Philistine and killed[4191]
him; but there was no sword in David's
hand.
51 Then David ran and stood over
the Philistine and [a]took his sword and
drew it out of its sheath and killed him,
and cut[3772] off his head with it. [b]When
the Philistines saw that their champion
was dead,[4191] they fled.
52 And the men of Israel and Judah
arose and shouted and pursued the Philistines [I]as far as the valley, and to the
gates of [a]Ekron. And the slain[2491] Philistines [II]lay along the way[1870] to [b]Shaa-
raim, even to Gath and Ekron.
53 And the sons[1121] of Israel returned from chasing the Philistines and
plundered[8154] their camps.
54 Then David took the Philistine's
head and brought it to Jerusalem, but
he put his weapons in his tent.
🔑 **55** Now when Saul saw David going
out against the Philistine, he said to Abner the commander of the army, "Abner, whose son is [a]this young man?"
And Abner said, "By your life,[2416] O
king, I do not know."
56 And the king said, "You
inquire[7592] whose son the youth[5958] is."
57 So when David returned from
killing[5221] the Philistine, Abner took him
and [a]brought him before Saul with the
Philistine's head in his hand.
58 And Saul said to him, "Whose
son are you, young man?" And David
answered, "[a]*I am* the son of your servant Jesse the Bethlehemite."

Jonathan and David

18 Now it came about when he had
finished[3615] speaking[1696] to Saul,
that [a]the soul[5315] of Jonathan was knit
to the soul of David, and [b]Jonathan
loved[157] him as himself.
2 And Saul took him that day[3117] and
[a]did not let him return to his father's[1]
house.
3 Then [a]Jonathan made a cov-
enant[1285] with David because he loved[160]
him as himself.
4 And [a]Jonathan stripped himself of
the robe that was on him and gave it
to David, with his armor, including his
sword[2719] and his bow and his belt.[2290]
5 So David went out wherever Saul
sent him, *and* [I]prospered; and Saul set
him over the men of war. And it was
pleasing[3190] in the sight of all the
people[5971] and also in the sight of Saul's
servants.[5650]
6 And it happened as they were
coming, when David returned from
killing[5221] the Philistine, that [a]the
women[802] came out of all the cities of
Israel, singing[7891] and dancing, to meet
King[4428] Saul, with tambourines,[8596]
with joy and with [I]musical instruments.
7 And the women [a]sang as they
[I]played, and said,

"[b]Saul has slain[5221] his thousands,
[c]And David his ten thousands."

8 Then Saul became very angry,[2734]
for this saying[1697] [I]displeased[7489] him;
and he said, "They have ascribed to David ten thousands, but to me they have
ascribed thousands. Now [a]what more
can he have but the kingdom?"
9 And Saul looked at David with suspicion from that day on.

Saul Turns against David

10 Now it came about on the next
day that [a]an evil[7451] spirit[7307] from God[430]
came mightily upon Saul, and [b]he
raved[5012] in the midst of the house, while
David was playing *the harp* with his hand,

48 [a]Ps. 27:3
51 [a]1Sam. 21:9; 2Sam. 23:21 [b]Heb. 11:34
52 [I]Lit., *until your coming to* [II]Lit., *fell* [a]Josh. 15:11 [b]Josh. 15:36
55 [a]1Sam. 16:12, 21, 22
57 [a]1Sam. 17:54
58 [a]1Sam. 17:12
1 [a]Gen. 44:30 [b]Deut. 13:6; 1Sam. 20:17; 2Sam. 1:26
2 [a]1Sam. 17:15
3 [a]1Sam. 20:8-17
4 [a]Gen. 41:42; 1Sam. 17:38; Esth. 6:8
5 [I]Or, *acted wisely*
6 [I]I.e., triangles; or, three-stringed instruments [a]Ex. 15:20, 21; Judg. 11:34; Ps. 68:25; 149:3
7 [I]Or, *danced* [a]Ex. 15:21; 1Sam. 21:11; 29:5 [b]1Sam. 21:11 [c]2Sam. 18:3
8 [I]Lit., *was evil in his eyes* [a]1Sam. 15:28
10 [a]1Sam. 16:14 [b]1Sam. 19:23, 24

🔑 **17:55** See note on I Sam. 16:18.

[Ic]as usual; and [IId]a spear *was* in Saul's hand.

11 And [a]Saul hurled the spear for he thought, "I will [I]pin[5221] David to the wall." But David [II]escaped from his presence twice.

12 Now [a]Saul was afraid[3372] of David, [b]for the LORD was with him but [c]had departed from Saul.

13 Therefore Saul removed him from [I]his presence, and appointed him as his commander[8269] of a thousand; and [a]he went out and came in before the people.

14 And David was [I]prospering in all his ways[1870] for [a]the LORD *was* with him.

15 When Saul saw[7200] that he was [I]prospering greatly, he dreaded[1481] him.

16 But [a]all Israel and Judah loved David, and he went out and came in before them.

17 Then Saul said to David, "[a]Here is my older daughter Merab; I will give her to you as a wife,[802] only be a valiant man for me and fight [b]the LORD's battles." For Saul thought, "My hand shall not be against him, but [c]let the hand of the Philistines be against him."

18 But David said to Saul, "[a]Who am I, and what is my life[2416] *or* my father's family[4940] in Israel, that I should be the king's son-in-law?"

19 So it came about at the time when Merab, Saul's daughter, should have been given to David, that she was given to [a]Adriel [b]the Meholathite for a wife.

David Marries Saul's Daughter

20 Now [a]Michal, Saul's daughter, loved David. When they told Saul, the thing was agreeable [I]to him.

21 And Saul thought, "I will give her to him that she may become a snare[4170] to him, and [a]that the hand of the Philistines may be against him." Therefore Saul said to David, "[b]For a second time you may be my son-in-law today."

22 Then Saul commanded[6680] his servants, "Speak[1696] to David secretly, saying,[559] 'Behold, the king delights in you, and all his servants love you; now therefore, become the king's[4428] son-in-law.' "

23 So Saul's servants spoke[1696] these words[1697] [I]to David. But David said, "Is it trivial in your sight to become the king's son-in-law, [a]since I am a poor man and lightly esteemed?"

24 And the servants of Saul reported to him [I]according to these words *which* David spoke.

25 Saul then said, "Thus you shall say to David, 'The king does not desire[2656] any [a]dowry[4119] except a hundred foreskins[6190] of the Philistines, [b]to take vengeance on the king's enemies.' " Now [c]Saul planned to make David fall by the hand of the Philistines.

26 When his servants told David these words, [I]it pleased David to become the king's son-in-law. [IIa]Before the days[3117] had expired

27 David rose up and went, [a]he and his men, and struck down[5221] two hundred men among the Philistines. Then [b]David brought their foreskins, and they gave them in full number to the king, that he might become the king's son-in-law. So Saul gave him Michal his daughter for a wife.

28 When Saul saw and knew[3045] that the LORD was with David, and *that* Michal, Saul's daughter, loved him,

29 then Saul was even more afraid of David. Thus Saul was David's enemy continually.

30 Then the commanders[8269] of the Philistines [a]went out *to battle*, and it happened as often as they went out, that David [b]behaved himself more wisely than all the servants of Saul. So his name was highly esteemed.

David Protected from Saul

19 Now Saul told[1696] Jonathan his son[1121] and all his servants[5650] [a]to put David to death.[4191] But [b]Jonathan, Saul's son, greatly delighted[2654] in David.

2 So Jonathan told David saying, "Saul my father[1] is seeking to put you to death. Now therefore, please[4994] be

---

10 [I]Lit., *day by day* [II]Lit., *the* [c]1Sam. 16:23 [d]1Sam. 19:9

11 [I]Lit., *strike David and the wall* [II]Lit., *turned about* [a]1Sam. 19:10; 20:33

12 [a]1Sam. 18:15, 29 [b]1Sam. 16:13, 18 [c]1Sam. 16:14; 28:15

13 [I]Lit., *with him* [a]Num. 27:17; 1Sam. 18:16; 2Sam. 5:2

14 [I]Or, *acting wisely* [a]Gen. 39:2, 3, 23; Josh. 6:27; 1Sam. 16:18

15 [I]Or, *acting very wisely*

16 [a]1Sam. 18:5

17 [a]1Sam. 17:25 [b]Num. 21:14; 1Sam. 17:36, 47; 25:28 [c]1Sam. 18:21, 25

18 [a]1Sam. 9:21; 18:23; 2Sam. 7:18

19 [a]2Sam. 21:8 [b]Judg. 7:22; 1Kin. 19:16

20 [I]Lit., *in his sight* [a]1Sam. 18:28

21 [a]1Sam. 18:17 [b]1Sam. 18:26

23 [I]Lit., *in the ears of* [a]Gen. 29:20; 34:12

24 [I]Lit., *by saying according*

25 [a]Gen. 34:12; Ex. 22:17 [b]1Sam. 14:24 [c]1Sam. 18:17

26 [I]Lit., *it was agreeable in the sight of* [II]Lit., *And the days had not expired* [a]1Sam. 18:21

27 [a]1Sam. 18:17 [b]2Sam. 3:14

30 [a]2Sam. 11:1 [b]1Sam. 18:5

1 [a]1Sam. 18:8, 9 [b]1Sam. 18:1-3

on guard in the morning, and stay in a
secret place and hide yourself.
3 "And I will go out and stand beside
my father in the field[7704] where you are,
and I will speak[1696] with my father about
you; [a]if I [I]find out anything, then I shall
tell you."
4 Then Jonathan [a]spoke well[2896] of
David to Saul his father, and said to
him, "[b]Do not let the king[4428] sin against
his servant[5650] David, since he has not
sinned[2398] against you, and since his
deeds *have been* very [I]beneficial to you.
5 "For [a]he took his life[5315] in his hand
and struck[5221] the Philistine, and
[b]the LORD brought about a great deliverance[8668] for all Israel; you saw[7200]
it and rejoiced. [c]Why then will you sin
against innocent[5355] blood,[1818] by putting
David to death[4191] without a cause?"
6 And Saul listened to the voice of
Jonathan, and Saul vowed,[7650] "As the
LORD lives,[2416] he shall not be put to
death."[4191]
7 Then Jonathan called[7121] David,
and Jonathan told[5046] him all these
words. And Jonathan brought David to
Saul, and he was in his presence as
[a]formerly.
8 When there was war again, David
went out and fought with the Philistines,
and [I]defeated them with great slaughter,
so that they fled before him.
9 Now there was [a]an evil[7451]
spirit[7307] from the LORD on Saul as he
was sitting in his house [b]with his spear
in his hand, [c]and David was playing *the
harp* with *his* hand.
10 [a]And Saul tried to [I]pin[5221] David
to the wall with the spear, but he slipped
away out of Saul's presence, so that
he [II]stuck[5221] the spear into the wall.
And David fled and escaped[4422] that
night.[3915]
11 Then [a]Saul sent messengers to
David's house to watch[8104] him, in order
to put him to death in the morning. But
Michal, David's wife,[802] told him, saying,
"If you do not save[4422] your life tonight,
tomorrow you will be put to death."
12 [a]So Michal let David down
through a window, and he went out and
fled and escaped.
13 And Michal took [a]the [I]household
idol[8655] and laid[7760] *it* on the bed, and
put a quilt of goats' *hair* at its head,[4763]
and covered[3680] *it* with clothes.
14 When Saul sent messengers to
take David, she said, "[a]He is sick."
15 Then Saul sent messengers to
see David, saying, "Bring him up to
me on [I]his bed, that I may put him
to death."
16 When the messengers entered,
behold, the [I]household idol *was* on the
bed with the quilt of goats' *hair* at its
head.
17 So Saul said to Michal, "Why
have you deceived me like this and let
my enemy go, so that he has escaped?"
And Michal said[559] to Saul, "He said to
me, 'Let me go! [a]Why should I put you
to death?' "
18 Now David fled and escaped and
came [a]to Samuel at Ramah, and told him
all that Saul had done[6213] to him. And
he and Samuel went and stayed in
[b]Naioth.
19 And it was told Saul, saying, "Behold, David is at Naioth in Ramah."
🔑 20 Then [a]Saul sent messengers to
take David, but when they saw[7200]
[b]the company of the prophets[5030]
prophesying, with Samuel standing *and
presiding*[5324] over them, the Spirit of
God[430] came upon the messengers of
Saul; and [c]they also prophesied.[5012]
21 And when it was told Saul, he
sent other messengers, and they also
prophesied. So Saul sent messengers
again the third time, and they also prophesied.
22 Then he himself went to Ramah,
and came as far as the large well[953] that
is in Secu; and he asked[7592] and said,
"Where are Samuel and David?" And
someone said, "Behold, they are at
Naioth in Ramah."

3 [I]Lit., *see* [a]1Sam. 20:9, 13
4 [I]Lit., *good* [a]1Sam. 20:32; Prov. 31:8, 9 [b]Gen. 42:22; Prov. 17:13; Jer. 18:20
5 [a]Judg. 9:17; 1Sam. 17:49, 50; 28:21; Ps. 119:109 [b]1Sam. 11:13; 1Chr. 11:14 [c]Deut. 19:10-13; 1Sam. 20:32; Ps. 94:21; Matt. 27:4
7 [a]1Sam. 16:21; 18:2, 10, 13
8 [I]Lit., *smote*
9 [a]1Sam. 16:14; 18:10, 11 [b]1Sam. 18:10 [c]1Sam. 16:16
10 [I]Lit., *strike David and the wall* [II]Lit., *struck* [a]1Sam. 18:11; 20:33; Prov. 1:16
11 [a]Judg. 16:2; Ps. 59:title
12 [a]Josh. 2:15; Acts 9:25; 2Cor. 11:33
13 [I]Heb., *teraphim* [a]Gen. 31:19; Judg. 18:14, 17
14 [a]Josh. 2:5
15 [I]Lit., *the*
16 [I]Heb., *teraphim*
17 [a]2Sam. 2:22
18 [a]1Sam. 7:17 [b]1Sam. 19:22, 23
20 [a]1Sam. 19:11, 14; John 7:32 [b]1Sam. 10:5, 6, 10 [c]Num. 11:25; Joel 2:28

🔑 **19:20** For "company of the prophets" see note on II Kgs. 2:3,5.

23 And he [I]proceeded there to Naioth in Ramah; and [a]the Spirit of God came upon him also, so that he went along prophesying continually until he came to Naioth in Ramah.

24 And he also stripped off his clothes, and he too prophesied before Samuel and [I]lay down [IIa]naked[6174] all that day[3117] and all that night. Therefore they say,[559] "[b]Is Saul also among the prophets?"

David and Jonathan Covenant

20 Then David fled from Naioth in Ramah, and came and [a]said [I]to Jonathan, "What have I done?[6213] What is my iniquity?[5771] And what is my sin before your father,[1] that he is seeking my life?"[5315]

2 And he said to him, "Far from it, you shall not die.[4191] Behold, my father does[6213] nothing[1697] either great or small [I]without disclosing[1540] it to me. So why should my father hide this thing from me? It is not so!"

3 Yet David [a]vowed[7650] again, [I]saying, "Your father knows well[3045] that I have found favor[2580] in your sight, and he has said,[559] 'Do not let Jonathan know[3045] this, lest he be grieved.' But truly [b]as the LORD lives[2416] and as your soul[5315] lives, there is [II]hardly a step between me and death."[4194]

4 Then Jonathan said to David, "Whatever [I]you say, I will do for you."

5 So David said to Jonathan, "Behold, tomorrow is [a]the new moon, and I ought [b]to sit down to eat with the king.[4428] But let me go, [c]that I may hide myself in the field[7704] until the third evening.[3117]

6 "If your father misses me at all, then say,[559] 'David earnestly asked[7592] *leave* of me to run to [a]Bethlehem his city, because it is [b]the yearly[3117] sacrifice[2077] there for the whole family.'[4940]

7 "If he [I]says, 'It is good,' your servant[5650] *shall be* safe;[7965] but if he is very angry,[2734] [a]know[3045] that he has decided[3615] on evil.[7451]

8 "Therefore deal kindly[2617] with your servant, for [a]you have brought your servant into a covenant[1285] of the LORD with you. But [b]if there is iniquity in me, put me to death[4191] yourself; for why then should you bring me to your father?"

9 And Jonathan said, "Far be it from you! For if I should indeed learn[3045] that evil has been decided by my father to come upon you, then would I not tell you about it?"

10 Then David said to Jonathan, "Who will tell me [I]if your father answers you harshly?"

11 And Jonathan said to David, "Come, and let us go out into the field." So both of them went out to the field.

12 Then Jonathan said to David, "The LORD, the God of Israel, *be witness*! When I have sounded out my father about this time tomorrow, *or* the third day, behold, if there is good[2896] *feeling* toward David, shall I not then send to you and [I]make it known to you?

13 "If it please my father *to do* you harm, [a]may the LORD do[6213] so to Jonathan and more also, if I do not [I]make it known to you and send you away, that you may go in safety. And [b]may the LORD be with you as He has been with my father.

14 "And if I am still alive,[2416] will you not show[6213] me the lovingkindness[2617] of the LORD, that I may not die?

15 "And [a]you shall not cut[3772] off your lovingkindness from my house forever, not even when the LORD cuts off every one[376] of the enemies of David from the face of the earth."[127]

16 So Jonathan made a *covenant* with the house of David, *saying*, "[a]May the LORD require *it* at the hands of David's enemies."

17 And Jonathan made David vow[7650] again because of his love[160] for him, because [a]he loved[157] him as he loved his own life.

18 Then Jonathan said to him, "[a]Tomorrow is the new moon, and you

---

23 [I]Lit., *went* [a]1Sam. 10:10

24 [I]Lit., *fell* [II]I.e., without outward garments [a]2Sam. 6:20; Is. 20:2; Mic. 1:8 [b]1Sam. 10:10-12

1 [I]Lit., *before* [a]1Sam. 24:9

2 [I]Lit., *and he does not uncover my ear*

3 [I]Lit., *and said* [II]Lit., *about* [a]Deut. 6:13 [b]1Sam. 25:26; 2Kin. 2:6

4 [I]Lit., *your soul says*

5 [a]Num. 10:10; 28:11-15; Amos 8:5 [b]1Sam. 20:24, 27 [c]1Sam. 19:2

6 [a]1Sam. 17:58 [b]Deut. 12:5; 1Sam. 9:12

7 [I]Lit., *says thus* [a]1Sam. 25:17

8 [a]1Sam. 18:3; 23:18 [b]2Sam. 14:32

10 [I]Lit., *or what*

12 [I]Lit., *uncover your ear*

13 [I]Lit., *uncover your ear* [a]Ruth 1:17; 1Sam. 3:17 [b]Josh. 1:5; 1Sam. 17:37; 18:12; 1Chr. 22:11, 16

15 [a]2Sam. 9:1, 3

16 [a]Deut. 23:21; 1Sam. 25:22

17 [a]1Sam. 18:1

18 [a]1Sam. 20:5, 25

will be missed because your seat[4186] will be empty.[6485]

19 "When you have stayed for three days,[3117] you shall go down quickly and come to the place where you hid yourself on that eventful day, and you shall remain by the stone Ezel.

20 "And I will shoot[3384] three arrows to the side, as though I shot at a target.

21 "And behold, I will send the lad, *saying,* 'Go, find the arrows.' If I specifically say to the lad, 'Behold, the arrows are on this side of you, get them,' then come; for there is safety for you and [I]no harm, as the LORD lives.

22 "But if I [I]say to the youth, '[a]Behold, the arrows are beyond you,' go, for the LORD has sent you away.

23 "[a]As for the [I]agreement of which you and I have spoken,[1696] behold, [b]the LORD is between you and me forever."

24 So David hid in the field; and when the new moon came, the king sat down to eat food.

25 And the king sat on his seat as usual, the seat by the wall; then Jonathan rose up and Abner sat down by Saul's side, but [a]David's place was empty.

26 Nevertheless Saul did not speak[1696] anything that day, for he thought, "It is an accident, [a]he is not clean,[2889] surely *he is* not clean."

27 And it came about the next day, the second *day* of the new moon, that David's place was empty; so Saul said to Jonathan his son,[1121] "Why has the son of Jesse not come to the meal, either yesterday or today?"

28 Jonathan then answered Saul, "[a]David earnestly asked leave of me *to go* to Bethlehem,

29 for he said, 'Please[4994] [I]let me go, since our family has a sacrifice in the city, and my brother[251] has commanded[6680] me to attend. And now, if I have found favor[2580] in your sight, please let me get away that I may see my brothers.'[251] For this reason he has not come to the king's[4428] table."

Saul Is Angry with Jonathan

30 Then Saul's anger[639] burned[2734] against Jonathan and he said to him, "You son of a perverse,[5753] rebellious woman! Do I not know that you are choosing[977] the son of Jesse to your own shame and to the shame of your mother's nakedness?[6172]

31 "For [I]as long as the son of Jesse lives[2425] on the earth,[127] neither you nor your kingdom[4438] will be established.[3559] Therefore now, send and bring him to me, for [a]he [II]must surely die."

32 But Jonathan answered Saul his father and said to him, "[a]Why should he be put to death? What has he done?"

33 Then [a]Saul hurled his spear at him to strike[5221] him down; [b]so Jonathan knew that his father had decided to put David to death.

34 Then Jonathan arose from the table in fierce[2750] anger, and did not eat food on the second day of the new moon, for he was grieved over David because his father had dishonored him.

35 Now it came about in the morning that Jonathan went out into the field for the appointment[4150] with David, and a little lad *was* with him.

36 And he said to his lad, "[a]Run, find now the arrows which I am about to shoot." As the lad was running, he shot [I]an arrow past him.

37 When the lad reached the place of the arrow which Jonathan had shot, Jonathan called[7121] after the lad, and said, "[a]Is not the arrow beyond you?"

38 And Jonathan called after the lad, "Hurry, be quick, do not stay!" And Jonathan's lad picked up[3950] the arrow and came to his master.

39 But the lad was not aware of anything; only Jonathan and David knew about the matter.

40 Then Jonathan gave his weapons[3627] to his lad and said to him, "Go, bring *them* to the city."

41 When the lad was gone, David rose from the south side and fell[5307] on his face[639] to the ground,[776] and [a]bowed[7812] three times. And they

21 [I]Lit., *there is nothing*
22 [I]Lit., *say thus* [a]1Sam. 20:37
23 [I]Lit., *word* [a]1Sam. 20:14, 15 [b]Gen. 31:49, 53; 1Sam. 20:42
25 [a]1Sam. 20:18
26 [a]Lev. 7:20, 21; 15:5; 1Sam. 16:5
28 [a]1Sam. 20:6
29 [I]Lit., *send me away*
31 [I]Lit., *all the days which* [II]Lit., *is a son of death* [a]2Sam. 12:5
32 [a]Gen. 31:36; 1Sam. 19:5; Prov. 31:9; Matt. 27:23
33 [a]1Sam. 18:11; 19:10 [b]1Sam. 20:7
36 [I]Lit., *the* [a]1Sam. 20:20, 21
37 [a]1Sam. 20:22
41 [a]Gen. 42:6

kissed[5401] each other and wept together,[7453] but [b]David more.

42 And Jonathan said to David, "[a]Go in safety, inasmuch as we have sworn to each other in the name of the LORD, saying, '[b]The LORD will be between me and you, and between my [I]descendants[2233] and your [I]descendants forever.'" [II]Then he rose and departed, while Jonathan went into the city.

David Takes Consecrated Bread

21 🗝 Then David came to [a]Nob to Ahimelech the priest;[3548] and Ahimelech [b]came trembling[2729] to meet David, and said to him, "Why are you alone and no one with you?"

2 And David said to Ahimelech the priest, "The king[4428] has commissioned[6620] me with a matter,[1697] and has said to me, '[a]Let no one know[3045] anything about the matter on which I am sending you and with which I have commissioned you; and I have directed[3045] the young men to a certain place.'

3 "Now therefore, what [I]do you have on hand? Give [II]me five loaves of bread, or whatever can be found."

4 And the priest answered David and said, "There is no ordinary[2455] bread [I]on hand, but there is [a]consecrated bread; if only the young men have [b]kept[8104] themselves from women."[802]

5 And David answered the priest and said to him, "[a]Surely women have been kept from us as previously when I set out and the [b]vessels of the young men were holy, though it was an ordinary journey; how much more then today[3117] will [I]their vessels *be holy*?"

6 So [a]the priest gave him consecrated *bread*; for there was no bread there but the [b]bread of the Presence which was removed from before the LORD, in order to put hot bread *in its place* when it was taken away.

7 Now one of the servants of Saul was there that day, detained before the LORD; and his name was [a]Doeg the Edomite, the [b]chief[47] of Saul's shepherds.

8 And David said to Ahimelech, "Now is there not a spear or a sword [I]on hand? For I brought neither my sword[2719] nor my weapons [II]with me, because the king's[4428] matter was urgent."

9 Then the priest said, "[a]The sword of Goliath the Philistine, whom you [I]killed[5221] [b]in the valley of Elah, behold, it is wrapped in a cloth behind the ephod; if you would take it for yourself, take *it*. For there is no other except it here." And David said, "There is none like it; give it to me."

10 Then David arose and fled that day from Saul, and went to [a]Achish king of Gath.

11 But the [a]servants of Achish said to him, "Is this not David the king of the land?[776] [b]Did they not sing of this one[376] as they danced, saying,

'Saul has slain his thousands,
And David his ten thousands'?"

12 And David [a]took[7760] these words[1697] [I]to heart, and greatly feared[3372] Achish king of Gath.

13 So he [a]disguised his sanity[2940] before them, and acted insanely in their hands, and scribbled on the doors of the gate, and let his saliva run down into his beard.[2206]

14 Then Achish said to his servants, "Behold, you see the man behaving as a madman. Why do you bring him to me?

15 "Do I lack madmen, that you have brought this one to act the madman in my presence? Shall this one come into my house?"

41 [b]1Sam. 18:3
42 [I]Lit., *seed* [II]Ch. 21:1 in Heb. [a]1Sam. 20:22 [b]1Sam. 20:15, 16, 23
1 [a]1Sam. 22:19; Neh. 11:32; Is. 10:32 [b]1Sam. 16:4
2 [a]Ps. 141:3
3 [I]Lit., *is under your hand?* [II]Lit., *in my hand*
4 [I]Lit., *under my hand* [a]Ex. 25:30; Lev. 24:5-9; Matt. 12:4 [b]Ex. 19:15
5 [I]Lit., *it be holy in the vessel* [a]Ex. 19:14, 15 [b]1Thess. 4:4
6 [a]Matt. 12:3, 4; Luke 6:3, 4 [b]Lev. 24:5-9
7 [a]1Sam. 14:47; 22:9; Ps. 52: title [b]1Chr. 27:29, 31
8 [I]Lit., *under your hand* [II]Lit., *in my hand*
9 [I]Lit., *smote* [a]1Sam. 17:51, 54 [b]1Sam. 17:2
10 [a]Ps. 34:title
11 [a]Ps. 56:title [b]1Sam. 18:7; 29:5
12 [I]Lit., *in his* [a]Luke 2:19
13 [a]Ps. 34:title

🗝 **21:1-6** David's deception of the priest cannot be condoned. His eating of the showbread was a violation of the law (See Lev. 24:5-9). Christ did not expressly approve of David's action (Mt. 12:3,4; Mk. 2:25,26; Lk. 6:3,4). When He was assailed by the Jews about the strict observance of the Law, He referred to the incident as an illustration. He reminded them that the king whom they held in such high regard had patently broken the law. Apparently they did not point out this fact in their teaching.

The Priests Slain at Nob

22 So David departed from there and [a]escaped[4422] to [b]the cave of Adullam; and when his brothers[251] and all his father's[1] household heard *of it*, they went down there to him.

2 And everyone[376] who was in distress,[4751] and everyone who [I]was in debt, and everyone who was [II]discontented,[4751] gathered[6908] to him; and he became captain[8269] over them. Now there were [a]about four hundred men with him.

3 And David went from there to Mizpah of Moab; and he said to the king[4428] of Moab, "Please[4994] let my father[1] and my mother come *and stay* with you until I know[3045] what God[430] will do[6213] for me."

4 Then he left[5148] them with the king of Moab; and they stayed with him all the time[3117] that David was in the stronghold.

5 And [a]the prophet[5030] Gad said to David, "Do not stay in the stronghold; depart, and go into the land[776] of Judah." So David departed and went into the forest of Hereth.

6 Then Saul heard that David and the men who were with him had been discovered.[3045] Now [a]Saul was sitting in Gibeah, under the tamarisk tree on the height with his spear in his hand, and all his servants were standing[5324] around him.

7 And Saul said to his servants who stood[5324] around him, "Hear now, O Benjamites! Will the son[1121] of Jesse also give to all of you fields[7704] and vineyards? [a]Will he make you all commanders[8269] of thousands and commanders of hundreds?

8 "For all of you have conspired against me so that there is no one who [I]discloses[241] to me [a]when my son makes *a covenant* with the son of Jesse, and there is none of you [b]who is sorry for me or [I]discloses to me that my son has stirred up my servant[5650] against me to lie in ambush, as *it is* this day."[3117]

9 Then [a]Doeg the Edomite, who was [I]standing[5324] by the servants of Saul, answered and said, "[b]I saw[7200] the son of Jesse coming to Nob, to [c]Ahimelech the son of Ahitub.

10 "And [a]he inquired[7592] of the LORD for him, [b]gave him provisions,[6720] and [c]gave him the sword[2719] of Goliath the Philistine."

11 Then the king sent someone to summon[7121] Ahimelech the priest,[3548] the son of Ahitub, and all his father's household, the priests[3548] who were in Nob; and all of them came to the king.

12 And Saul said, "Listen now, son of Ahitub." And he [I]answered,[559] "Here I am, my lord."[113]

13 Saul then said to him, "Why have you and the son of Jesse conspired against me, in that you have given him bread and a sword and have inquired of God for him, that he should rise up against me [a]by lying in ambush as *it is* this day?"

14 [a]Then Ahimelech answered the king and said, "And who among all your servants is as faithful[539] as David, even the king's[4428] son-in-law, who [I]is captain over your guard, and is honored in your house?

15 "Did I *just* begin [a]to inquire[7592] of God for him today? Far be it from me! [b]Do not let the king impute[7760] anything to his servant *or* to any of the household of my father, for your servant knows[3045] nothing [I]at all of this whole affair."

16 But the king said, "You shall surely die,[4191] Ahimelech, you and all your father's household!"

17 And [a]the king said to the [I]guards who were attending him, "Turn around and put the priests of the LORD to death,[4191] because their hand also is with David and because they knew that he was fleeing and did not [II]reveal[1540] it to me." But the [b]servants of the king were not willing[14] to put forth their hands to [III]attack the priests of the LORD.

18 Then the king said to Doeg, "You turn around and [I]attack[4191] the priests." And Doeg the Edomite turned around and [II]attacked the priests, and [a]he killed

1 [a]Ps. 57:title [b]Josh. 12:15; 15:35; 2Sam. 23:13; Ps. 142:title

2 [I]Lit., *had a creditor* [II]Lit., *bitter of soul* [a]1Sam. 23:13; 25:13

5 [a]2Sam. 24:11; 1Chr. 21:9; 29:29; 2Chr. 29:25

6 [a]Judg. 4:5; 1Sam. 14:2

7 [a]1Sam. 8:12; 1Chr. 12:16-18

8 [I]Lit., *uncovers my ear* [a]1Sam. 18:3; 20:16 [b]1Sam. 23:21

9 [I]Or, *set over* [a]Ps. 52:title [b]1Sam. 21:1 [c]1Sam. 14:3; 21:1

10 [a]Num. 27:21; 1Sam. 10:22 [b]1Sam. 21:6 [c]1Sam. 21:9

12 [I]Lit., *said*

13 [a]1Sam. 22:8

14 [I]So with Gr.; Heb., *turns aside to* [a]1Sam. 19:4, 5; 20:32

15 [I]Lit., *small or great* [a]2Sam. 5:19, 23 [b]2Sam. 19:18, 19

17 [I]Lit., *runners* [II]Lit., *uncover my ear* [III]Lit., *fall upon* [a]2Kin. 10:25 [b]Ex. 1:17

18 [I]Lit., *smite* [II]Lit., *smote* [a]1Sam. 2:31

that day eighty-five men[376] [b]who wore the linen ephod.

19 And [a]he struck[5221] Nob the city of the priests with the edge[6310] of the sword, both men and women,[802] children and infants; also oxen, donkeys, and sheep, *he struck* with the edge of the sword.

20 But [a]one son[1121] of Ahimelech the son of Ahitub, named Abiathar, [b]escaped and fled after David.

21 And Abiathar told[5046] David that Saul had killed[2026] the priests of the LORD.

22 Then David said to Abiathar, "I knew on that day, when [a]Doeg the Edomite was there, that he would surely tell Saul. I have brought about *the death* of every person[5315] in your father's household.

23 "Stay with me, do not be afraid,[3372] for [a]he who seeks my life seeks your life;[5315] for you are [I]safe[4931] with me."

David Delivers Keilah

23 Then they told David, saying, "Behold, the Philistines are fighting against [a]Keilah, and are plundering the threshing floors."

2 So David [a]inquired[7592] of the LORD, saying, "Shall I go and [I]attack[5221] these Philistines?" And the LORD said to David, "Go and [I]attack the Philistines, and deliver Keilah."

3 But David's men said to him, "Behold, we are afraid[3373] here in Judah. How much more then if we go to Keilah against the ranks of the Philistines?"

4 Then David inquired of the LORD once more. And the LORD answered him and said, "Arise, go down to Keilah, for [a]I will give the Philistines into your hand."

5 So David and his men went to Keilah and fought with the Philistines; and he led away their livestock and struck[5221] them with a great slaughter.[5221] Thus David delivered[3467] the inhabitants of Keilah.

⊶ **6** Now it came about, when Abiathar the son[1121] of Ahimelech [a]fled to David at Keilah, *that* he came down *with* an ephod in his hand.

7 When it was told Saul that David had come to Keilah, Saul said, "God[430] has [I]delivered him into my hand, for he shut himself in by entering a city with double gates and bars."

8 So Saul summoned[8085] all the people[5971] for war, to go down to Keilah to besiege David and his men.

9 Now David knew[3045] that Saul was plotting evil against him; so he said to [a]Abiathar the priest,[3548] "[b]Bring[5066] the ephod here."

10 Then David said, "O LORD God of Israel, Thy servant[5650] has heard for certain that Saul is seeking to come to Keilah to destroy[7843] the city on my account.

11 "Will the men of Keilah surrender me into his hand? Will Saul come down just as Thy servant has heard? O LORD God of Israel, I pray,[4994] tell Thy servant." And the LORD said, "He will come down."

12 Then David said, "Will the men of Keilah surrender me and my men into the hand of Saul?" And the LORD said, "[a]They will surrender you."

13 Then David and his men, [a]about six hundred, arose and departed from Keilah, and they went [b]wherever they could go. When it was told Saul that David had escaped[4422] from Keilah, he [I]gave up the pursuit.

14 And David stayed in the wilderness in the strongholds, and remained in the hill country in the wilderness of [a]Ziph. And Saul sought him every day,[3117] but [b]God did not deliver him into his hand.

Saul Pursues David

15 Now David [I]became aware[7200] that Saul had come out to seek his life[5315]

18 [b]1Sam. 2:18
19 [a]1Sam. 15:3
20 [a]1Sam. 23:6, 9; 30:7; 1Kin. 2:26, 27 [b]1Sam. 23:6
22 [a]1Sam. 21:7
23 [I]Lit., *a charge* [a]1Kin. 2:26
1 [a]Josh. 15:44; Neh. 3:17, 18
2 [I]Lit., *smite* [a]1Sam. 23:4, 6, 9-12; 2Sam. 5:19, 23
4 [a]Josh. 8:7; Judg. 7:7
6 [a]1Sam. 22:20
7 [I]Lit., *alienated*
9 [a]1Sam. 22:20 [b]1Sam. 23:6; 30:7
12 [a]Judg. 15:10-13; 1Sam. 23:20
13 [I]Lit., *ceased going out* [a]1Sam. 22:2; 25:13 [b]2Sam. 15:20
14 [a]Josh. 15:55; 2Chr. 11:8 [b]Ps. 32:7
15 [I]Lit., *saw*

⊶ **23:6** See note on Ex. 28:30.

while David was in the wilderness of Ziph at Horesh.

16 And Jonathan, Saul's son, arose and went to David at Horesh, and [I][a]encouraged[2388] him in God.

17 Thus he said to him, "[a]Do not be afraid,[3372] because the hand of Saul my father[1] shall not find you, and you will be king[4427] over Israel and I will be next to you; and [b]Saul my father knows that also."

18 So [a]the two of them made a covenant[1285] before the LORD; and David stayed at Horesh while Jonathan went to his house.

19 Then [a]Ziphites came up to Saul at Gibeah, saying, "Is David not hiding with us in the strongholds at Horesh, on [b]the hill of Hachilah, which is on the [I]south of [II]Jeshimon?

20 "Now then, O king,[4428] come down according to all the desire[183] of your soul[5315] to [I]do so; and [a]our part *shall be* to surrender him into the king's[4428] hand."

21 And Saul said, "May you be blessed[1288] of the LORD; [a]for you have had compassion on me.

22 "Go now, make more sure,[3559] and investigate[3045] and see his place where his [I]haunt is, *and* who has seen[7200] him there; for I am told that he is very cunning.

23 "So look, and learn[3045] about all the hiding places where he hides himself, and return to me with certainty,[3559] and I will go with you; and it shall come about if he is in the land[776] that I will search him out among all the thousands of Judah."

24 Then they arose and went to Ziph before Saul. Now David and his men were in the wilderness of [a]Maon, in the Arabah[6160] to the [I]south of [II]Jeshimon.

25 When Saul and his men went to seek *him,* they told David, and he came down to the rock and stayed in the wilderness of Maon. And when Saul heard *it,* he pursued David in the wilderness of Maon.

26 And Saul went on one side of the mountain, and David and his men on the other side of the mountain; and David was hurrying to get away from Saul, for Saul and his men [a]were surrounding David and his men to seize them.

27 But a messenger came to Saul, saying, "Hurry and come, for the Philistines have made a raid on the land."

28 So Saul returned from pursuing David, and went to meet the Philistines; therefore they called[7121] that place [I]the Rock of Escape.

29 [I]And David went up from there and stayed in the strongholds of [a]Engedi.

David Spares Saul's Life

24 Now it came about [a]when Saul returned from pursuing the Philistines, [b]he was told, saying, "Behold, David is in the wilderness of Engedi."

2 Then [a]Saul took three thousand chosen men from all Israel, and went to seek David and his men in front of the Rocks of the Wild Goats.

3 And he came to the sheepfolds[1448] on the way,[1870] where there *was* a cave; and Saul [a]went in to [I]relieve himself. Now [b]David and his men were sitting in the inner recesses of the cave.

4 And the men of David said[559] to him, "Behold, [a]*this is* the day[3117] of which the LORD said to you, 'Behold; [b]I am about to give your enemy into your hand, and you shall do[6213] to him as it seems good[3190] [I]to you.' " Then David arose and cut[3772] off the edge of Saul's robe secretly.[3909]

5 And it came about afterward that [a]David's [I]conscience bothered[5221] him because he had cut off the edge of Saul's *robe.*

6 So he said to his men, "[a]Far be it from me because of the LORD that I should do this thing to my lord, the LORD'S anointed,[4899] to stretch out my

16 [I]Lit., *strengthened his hand* [a]1Sam. 30:6; Neh. 2:18

17 [a]Ps. 27:1, 3; 118:6; Is. 54:17; Heb. 13:6 [b]1Sam. 20:31; 24:20

18 [a]1Sam. 18:3; 20:12-17, 42; 2Sam. 9:1; 21:7

19 [I]Lit., *right side* [II]Or, *the desert* [a]1Sam. 26:1; Ps. 54:title [b]1Sam. 26:3

20 [I]Lit., *come down* [a]1Sam. 23:12

21 [a]1Sam. 22:8

22 [I]Lit., *foot*

24 [I]Lit., *right side* [II]Or, *the desert* [a]Josh. 15:55; 1Sam. 25:2

26 [a]Ps. 17:9

28 [I]Heb., *Selahammahlekoth*

29 [I]Ch. 24:1 in Heb. [a]Josh. 15:62; 2Chr. 20:2

1 [a]1Sam. 23:28, 29 [b]1Sam. 23:19

2 [a]1Sam. 26:2

3 [I]Lit., *cover his feet* [a]Judg. 3:24 [b]Ps. 57:title; 142:title

4 [I]Lit., *in your sight* [a]1Sam. 23:17; 25:28-30 [b]1Sam. 26:8, 11

5 [I]Lit., *heart struck* [a]2Sam. 24:10

6 [a]1Sam. 26:11

hand against him, since he is the LORD's anointed."

7 And David [I]persuaded his men[582] with *these* words[1697] and did not allow them to rise up against Saul. And Saul arose, [II]left the cave, and went on *his* way.

8 Now afterward David arose and went out of the cave and called[7121] after Saul, saying, "My lord[113] the king!"[4428] And when Saul looked behind him, [a]David bowed with his face[639] to the ground[776] and prostrated[7812] himself.

9 And David said to Saul, "Why do you listen to the words of men, saying, 'Behold, David seeks [I]to harm you'?

10 "[a]Behold, this day your eyes have seen[7200] that the LORD had given you today into my hand in the cave, and [b]some said to kill[2026] you, but *my eye* had pity on you; and I said, 'I will not stretch out my hand against my lord, for he is the LORD's anointed.'

11 "Now, [a]my father,[1] see! Indeed, see the edge of your robe in my hand! For in that I cut off the edge of your robe and did not kill[2026] you, know[3045] and perceive that there is no evil[7451] or [I]rebellion in my hands, and I have not sinned[2398] against you, though you [b]are lying in wait for my life[5315] to take it.

12 "[a]May the LORD judge[8199] between [I]you and me, and may the LORD avenge[5358] me on you; but my hand shall not be against you.

13 "As the proverb of the ancients says,[559] '[a]Out of the wicked[7563] comes forth wickedness';[7562] but my hand shall not be against you.

14 "After whom has the king of Israel come out? Whom are you pursuing? [a]A dead[4191] dog, [b]a single flea?

15 "[a]The LORD therefore be judge and decide between [I]you and me; and may He see and [b]plead[7378] my cause,[7379] and [II]deliver[8199] me from your hand."

16 Now it came about when David had finished[3615] speaking[1696] these words to Saul, that Saul said, "[a]Is this your voice, my son[1121] David?" Then Saul lifted up his voice and wept.

17 [a]And he said to David, "You are more righteous than I; for [b]you have dealt well[2896] with me, while I have dealt wickedly with you.

18 "And you have declared[5046] today that you have done[6213] good to me, that [a]the LORD delivered me into your hand and *yet* you did not kill[2026] me.

19 "For if a man [a]finds his enemy, will he let him go away [I]safely? May the LORD therefore reward you with good in return for what you have done[6213] to me this day.

20 "And now, behold, [a]I know that you shall surely be king,[4427] and that [b]the kingdom[4467] of Israel shall be established in your hand.

21 "So now [a]swear[7650] to me by the LORD that you will not cut off my [I]descendants[2233] after me, and that you will not destroy[8045] my name from my father's[1] household."

22 And David swore[7650] to Saul. And Saul went to his home, but David and his men went up to [a]the stronghold.

Samuel's Death

25 [a]Then Samuel died;[4191] and all Israel gathered[6908] together and [b]mourned for him, and [c]buried[6912] him at his house in Ramah. And David arose and went down to the [d]wilderness of Paran.

Nabal and Abigail

2 Now *there was* a man in [a]Maon whose business was in [b]Carmel; and the man was very [I]rich, and he had three thousand sheep and a thousand goats. And it came about while [c]he was shearing his sheep in Carmel

3 (now the man's name was Nabal, and his [a]wife's[802] name was Abigail. And the woman[802] was [I]intelligent[7922] and beautiful in appearance, but the man was harsh[7186] and evil in *his* dealings, and he was [b]a Calebite),

4 that David heard in the wilderness

---

7 [I]Lit., *tore apart* [II]Lit., *from*

8 [a]1Sam. 25:23, 24; 1Kin. 1:31

9 [I]Lit., *your hurt*

10 [a]Ps. 7:3, 4 [b]1Sam. 24:4

11 [I]Lit., *transgression* [a]2Kin. 5:13 [b]1Sam. 23:14, 23; 26:20

12 [I]Lit., *me and you* [a]Gen. 16:5; 31:53; Judg. 11:27; 1Sam. 26:10, 23

13 [a]Matt. 7:16-20

14 [a]2Sam. 9:8 [b]1Sam. 26:20

15 [I]Lit., *me and you* [II]Lit., *vindicate* [a]1Sam. 24:12 [b]Ps. 35:1; 43:1; 119:154; Mic. 7:9

16 [a]1Sam. 26:17

17 [a]1Sam. 26:21 [b]Matt. 5:44

18 [a]1Sam. 26:23

19 [I]Lit., *on a good road* [a]1Sam. 23:17

20 [a]1Sam. 23:17 [b]1Sam. 13:14

21 [I]Lit., *seed* [a]Gen. 21:23; 1Sam. 20:14-17; 2Sam. 21:6-8

22 [a]1Sam. 23:29

1 [a]1Sam. 28:3 [b]Num. 20:29; Deut. 34:8 [c]2Kin. 21:18; 2Chr. 33:20 [d]Gen. 21:21; Num. 10:12; 13:3

2 [I]Lit., *great* [a]1Sam. 23:24 [b]Josh. 15:55 [c]Gen. 38:13; 2Sam. 13:23

3 [I]Lit., *of good understanding* [a]Prov. 31:10 [b]Josh. 15:13; 1Sam. 30:14

that Nabal was shearing his sheep.

5 So David sent ten young men, and David said[559] to the young men, "Go up to Carmel, [I]visit Nabal and greet[7965] him in my name;

6 and thus you shall say, '[I]Have a long life,[2416] [a]peace[7965] be to you, and peace be to your house, and peace be to all that you have.

7 'And now I have heard [a]that you have shearers; now your shepherds have been with us and we have not insulted them, [b]nor have they missed anything all the days[3117] they were in Carmel.

8 'Ask[7592] your young men and they will tell[5046] you. Therefore let *my* young men find favor[2580] in your eyes, for we have come on [a]a [I]festive day.[3117] Please[4994] give whatever you find at hand to your servants and to your son[1121] David.'"

9 When David's young men came, they spoke[1696] to Nabal according to all these words[1697] in David's name; then they waited.

10 But Nabal answered David's servants, and said, "[a]Who is David? And who is the son of Jesse? There are many servants today[3117] who are each breaking away from his master.

11 "Shall I then [a]take my bread and my water and my meat[2878] that I have slaughtered[2873] for my shearers, and give it to men [I]whose origin I do not know?"[3045]

12 So David's young men retraced their way[1870] and went back; and they came and told him according to all these words.[1697]

13 And David said to his men, "Each *of you* gird on his sword."[2719] So each man girded on his sword. And David also girded on his sword, and about [a]four hundred men went up behind David while two hundred [b]stayed with the baggage.

14 But one of the young men told Abigail, Nabal's wife, saying, "Behold, David sent messengers from the wilderness to [I][a]greet[1288] our master, and he scorned them.

15 "Yet the men were very good to us, and we were not [a]insulted, nor did we miss anything [I]as long as we went about with them, while we were in the fields.[7704]

16 "[a]They were a wall to us both by night[3915] and by day,[3119] all the time we were with them tending the sheep.

17 "Now therefore, know and [I]consider[7200] what you should do,[6213] for evil is plotted[3615] against our master and against all his household; and he is such a [II]worthless[1100] man that no one can speak[1696] to him."

Abigail Intercedes

18 Then Abigail hurried and [a]took two hundred *loaves* of bread and two jugs of wine and five sheep already prepared[6213] and five measures of roasted grain and a hundred clusters of raisins and two hundred cakes of figs, and loaded[7760] *them* on donkeys.

19 And she said to her young men, "[a]Go on before me; behold, I am coming after you." But she did not tell her husband Nabal.

20 And it came about as she was riding on her donkey and coming down by the hidden part[5643] of the mountain, that behold, David and his men were coming down toward her; so she met them.

21 Now David had said, "Surely in vain[8267] I have guarded[8104] all that this *man* has in the wilderness, so that nothing was missed of all that belonged to him; and he has [a]returned me evil for good.

22 "[a]May God[430] do so to the enemies of David, and more also, [b]if by morning I leave[7604] *as much as* one [I]male of any who belong to him."

23 When Abigail saw[7200] David, she hurried and dismounted from her donkey, and fell[5307] on her face before David, [a]and bowed[7812] herself to the ground.[776]

24 And she fell at his feet and said,

---

5 [I]Lit., *go into*

6 [I]Lit., *To life* [a]1Chr. 12:18; Ps. 122:7; Luke 10:5

7 [a]2Sam. 13:23, 24 [b]1Sam. 25:15, 21

8 [I]Lit., *good* [a]Neh. 8:10-12; Esth. 9:19, 22

10 [a]Judg. 9:28

11 [I]Lit., *from where they are* [a]Judg. 8:6, 15

13 [a]1Sam. 23:13 [b]1Sam. 30:24

14 [I]Lit., *bless* [a]1Sam. 13:10; 15:13

15 [I]Lit., *all the days* [a]1Sam. 25:7, 21

16 [a]Ex. 14:22; Job 1:10

17 [I]Lit., *see* [II]Lit., *son of Belial*

18 [a]2Sam. 16:1; 1Chr. 12:40

19 [a]Gen. 32:16, 20

21 [a]Ps. 109:5; Prov. 17:13

22 [I]Lit., *who urinates against the wall* [a]1Sam. 3:17; 20:13 [b]1Kin. 14:10

23 [a]1Sam. 20:41

"On me [I]alone, my lord,[113] be the blame.[5771] And please let your maidservant speak [II]to you, and listen to the words of your maidservant.

25 "Please do not let my lord [I]pay attention to this [II]worthless man, Nabal, for as his name is, so is he. [III]Nabal is his name and folly is with him; but I your maidservant did not see the young men of my lord whom you sent.

26 "Now therefore, my lord, as the LORD lives, and as your soul[5315] lives, since the LORD has restrained[4513] you from [I]shedding blood,[1818] and [a]from [II]avenging[3467] yourself by your own hand, now then [b]let your enemies, and those who seek evil against my lord, be as Nabal.

27 "And now let [a]this [I]gift[1293] which your maidservant has brought to my lord be given to the young men who [II]accompany my lord.

28 "Please forgive[5375] [a]the transgression of your maidservant; for [b]the LORD will certainly make for my lord an enduring house, because my lord is [c]fighting the battles of the LORD, and [d]evil shall not be found in you all your days.

29 "And should anyone rise up to pursue you and to seek your [I]life,[5315] then the [I]life of my lord shall be bound in the bundle of the living[2416] with the LORD your God; but the [I]lives of your enemies [a]He will sling out [II]as from the hollow of a sling.

30 "And it shall come about when the LORD shall do[6213] for my lord according to all the good that He has spoken[1696] concerning you, and [a]shall appoint[6680] you ruler over Israel,

31 that this will not [I]cause grief or a troubled[4383] heart to my lord, both by having shed[8210] blood without cause and by my lord having [II]avenged himself. [a]When the LORD shall deal[6213] well[3190] with my lord, then remember your maidservant."

32 Then David said to Abigail,

24 [I]Lit., *even me* [II]Lit., *in your ears*

25 [I]Lit., *set his heart to* [II]Lit., *man of Belial* [III]I.e., Fool

26 [I]Lit., *coming in with blood* [II]Lit., *saving* [a]Heb. 10:30 [b]2Sam. 18:32

27 [I]Lit., *blessing* [II]Lit., *walk at the feet of* [a]Gen. 33:11; 1Sam. 30:26

28 [a]1Sam. 25:24 [b]1Sam. 22:14; 2Sam. 7:11, 16 [c]1Sam. 18:17 [d]1Sam. 24:11; Ps. 7:3

29 [I]Lit., *soul* [II]Lit., *in the midst* [a]Jer. 10:18

30 [a]1Sam. 13:14

31 [I]Lit., *become staggering to you or a stumbling of the heart* [II]Lit., *saved* [a]Gen. 40:14; 1Sam. 25:30

32 [a]Ex. 18:10; 1Kin. 1:48; Ps. 41:13; 72:18; 106:48; Luke 1:68

33 [I]Lit., *coming in with blood* [II]Lit., *saving* [a]1Sam. 25:26

34 [I]Lit., *who urinates against the wall* [a]1Sam. 25:26

35 [I]Lit., *your voice* [II]Lit., *lifted up your face* [a]1Sam. 20:42; 2Kin. 5:19 [b]Gen. 19:21

36 [I]Lit., *small or large* [a]2Sam. 13:28 [b]Prov. 20:1; Is. 5:11; Hos. 4:11 [c]1Sam. 25:19

38 [a]1Sam. 26:10; 2Sam. 6:7; Ps. 104:29

39 [I]Lit., *and spoke* [a]1Sam. 24:15; Prov. 22:23 [b]1Sam. 25:26, 34 [c]Song 8:8

41 [a]1Sam. 25:23

"[a]Blessed[1288] be the LORD God of Israel, who sent you this day to meet me,

33 and blessed be your discernment,[2940] and blessed be you, [a]who have kept me this day from [I]bloodshed, and from [II]avenging myself by my own hand.

34 "Nevertheless, as the LORD God of Israel lives, [a]who has restrained me from harming you, unless you had come quickly to meet me, surely there would not have been left[3498] to Nabal until the morning light *as much as* one [I]male."

35 So David received from her hand what she had brought him, and he said to her, "[a]Go up to your house in peace. See, I have listened to [I]you and [II][b]granted[5375] your request."

36 Then Abigail came to Nabal, and behold, he was holding [a]a feast in his house, like the feast[4960] of a king.[4428] And Nabal's heart was merry within him, [b]for he was very drunk; so [c]she did not tell him anything[1697] [I]at all until the morning light.

37 But it came about in the morning, when the wine had gone out of Nabal, that his wife told him these things, and his heart died within[7130] him so that he became *as* a stone.

38 And about ten days later, it happened that [a]the LORD struck[5062] Nabal, and he died.

David Marries Abigail

39 When David heard that Nabal was dead,[4191] he said, "Blessed be the LORD, who has [a]pleaded[7378] the cause[7379] of my reproach from the hand of Nabal, and [b]has kept back His servant[5650] from evil. The LORD has also returned the evildoing[7451] of Nabal on his own head." Then David sent [I][c]a proposal to Abigail, to take her as his wife.

40 When the servants of David came to Abigail at Carmel, they spoke to her, saying, "David has sent us to you, to take you as his wife."

41 And she arose [a]and bowed with

25:25 The name Nabal in Hebrew means "fool" or "foolish."

her face[639] to the ground[776] and said, "Behold, your maidservant is a maid [b]to wash[7364] the feet of my lord's servants."

42 Then [a]Abigail quickly arose, and rode on a donkey, with her five maidens who [I]attended her; and she followed the messengers of David, and became his wife.

43 David had also taken Ahinoam of [a]Jezreel, and [b]they both became his wives.[802]

🗝 **44** Now Saul had given [a]Michal his daughter, David's wife, to Palti the son of Laish, who was from [b]Gallim.

David Again Spares Saul

26 Then the Ziphites came to Saul at Gibeah, saying, "[a]Is not David hiding on the hill of Hachilah, *which is* before [I]Jeshimon?"

2 So Saul arose and went down to the wilderness of Ziph, having with him [a]three thousand chosen men of Israel, to search for David in the wilderness of Ziph.

3 And Saul camped in the hill of Hachilah, which is before [I]Jeshimon, [a]beside the road,[1870] and David was staying in the wilderness. When [b]he saw[7200] that Saul came after him into the wilderness,

4 David sent out spies, and he knew[3045] that Saul was definitely coming.

5 David then arose and came to the place where Saul had camped. And David saw[7200] the place where Saul lay, and [a]Abner the son[1121] of Ner, the commander[8269] of his army; and Saul was lying in the circle of the camp, and the people[5971] were camped around him.

6 Then David answered and said[559] to Ahimelech [a]the Hittite and to [b]Abishai the son of Zeruiah, Joab's brother,[251] saying, "Who [c]will go down with me to Saul in the camp?"[4264] And Abishai said, "I will go down with you."

7 So David and Abishai came to the people by night,[3915] and behold, Saul lay sleeping inside the circle of the camp, with his spear stuck in the ground[776] at his head;[4763] and Abner and the people were lying around him.

8 Then Abishai said to David, "Today[3117] God[430] has delivered your enemy into your hand; now therefore, please[4994] let me strike[5221] him with the spear [I]to the ground[776] with one stroke, and I will not [II]strike him the second time."

9 But David said to Abishai, "Do not destroy[7843] him, for [a]who can stretch out his hand against the LORD's anointed and be without guilt?"[5352]

10 David also said, "As the LORD lives,[2416] [a]surely the LORD will strike[5062] him, or [b]his day will come that he dies,[4191] or [c]he will go down into battle and perish.[5595]

11 "[a]The LORD forbid that I should stretch out my hand against the LORD's anointed; but now please take the spear that is at his head and the jug[6835] of water, and let us go."

12 So David took the spear and the jug of water from *beside* Saul's head, and they went away, but no one saw or knew[3045] *it,* nor did any awake, for they were all asleep, because [a]a sound sleep from the LORD had fallen[5307] on them.

13 Then David crossed over to the other side, and stood on top of the mountain at a distance *with* a large area between them.

14 And David called[7121] to the people and to Abner the son of Ner, saying, "Will you not answer, Abner?" Then Abner answered and said, "Who are you who calls[7121] to the king?"[4428]

15 So David said to Abner, "Are you not a man? And who is like you in Israel? Why then have you not guarded[8104] your

41 [b]Mark 1:7
42 [I]Lit., *walked at her feet* [a]Gen. 24:61-67
43 [a]Josh. 15:56 [b]1Sam. 27:3; 30:5
44 [a]1Sam. 18:27; 2Sam. 3:14 [b]Is. 10:30
1 [I]Or, *the desert* [a]1Sam. 23:19; Ps. 54:title
2 [a]1Sam. 13:2; 24:2
3 [I]Or, *the desert* [a]1Sam. 24:3 [b]1Sam. 23:15
5 [a]1Sam. 14:50, 51; 17:55
6 [a]Gen. 23:3; 26:34; Josh. 3:10; 1Kin. 10:29; 2Kin. 7:6 [b]1Chr. 2:16 [c]Judg. 7:10, 11
8 [I]Lit., *even into* [II]Lit., *repeat with respect to him*
9 [a]1Sam. 24:6, 7; 2Sam. 1:14, 16
10 [a]Deut. 32:35; 1Sam. 25:26, 38; Rom. 12:19; Heb. 10:30 [b]Gen. 47:29; Deut. 31:14; Ps. 37:13 [c]1Sam. 31:6
11 [a]1Sam. 24:6, 12; Rom. 12:17, 19; 1Pet. 3:9
12 [a]Gen. 2:21; 15:12; Is. 29:10

🗝 **25:44** Saul's second daughter, Michal, had been given to David for his slaying of Goliath. However, Saul, while pursuing David, decided to give her to another man. Later David demanded her back (II Sam. 3:14), but she no longer loved him (II Sam. 6:16). She died childless (II Sam. 6:23).

lord[113] the king? For one of the people came to destroy the king your lord.

16 "This thing that you have done[6213] is not good.[2896] As the LORD lives, *all* of you [I][a]must surely die,[4194] because you did not guard your lord, the LORD's anointed.[4899] And now, see where the king's[4428] spear is, and the jug of water that was at his head."

17 Then Saul recognized[5234] David's voice and said, "[a]Is this your voice, my son David?" And David said, "It is my voice, my lord the king."

18 He also said, "[a]Why then is my lord pursuing his servant?[5650] For what have I done? Or what evil[7451] is in my hand?

19 "Now therefore, please let my lord the king listen to the words[1697] of his servant. If [a]the LORD has stirred you up against me, [b]let Him [I]accept[7306] an offering;[4503] but [c]if it is [II]men, cursed[779] are they before the LORD, for [d]they have driven me out today that I should have no attachment with the inheritance[5159] of the LORD, saying, 'Go, serve other gods.'[430]

20 "Now then, do not let my blood[1818] fall to the ground away from the presence of the LORD; for the king of Israel has come out to search for [a]a single flea, just as one hunts a partridge in the mountains."

21 Then Saul said, "[a]I have sinned.[2398] Return, my son David, for I will not harm you again because my life[5315] was precious in your sight this day. Behold, I have played the fool and have committed a serious error."[7683]

22 And David answered and said, "Behold the spear of the king! Now let one of the young men come over and take it.

23 "And [a]the LORD will repay each man *for* his righteousness and his faithfulness;[530] for the LORD delivered you into *my* hand today, but [b]I refused to stretch out my hand against the LORD's anointed.

24 "Now behold, as your life[5315] was [a]highly valued in my sight this day, so may my life be highly valued in the sight of the LORD, and may He [b]deliver[5337] me from all distress."

25 Then Saul said to David, "[a]Blessed[1288] are you, my son David; you will both accomplish[6213] much and surely prevail." So [b]David went on his way, and Saul returned to his place.

David Flees to the Philistines

27 Then David said[559] [I]to himself, "Now I will perish[5595] one day[3117] by the hand of Saul. [a]There is nothing better[2896] for me than [II]to escape[4422] into the land[776] of the Philistines. Saul then will despair[2976] of searching for me anymore in all the territory of Israel, and I will escape from his hand."

2 So David arose and crossed[5674] over, he and [a]the six hundred men who were with him, to [b]Achish the son[1121] of Maoch, king[4428] of Gath.

3 And David lived with Achish at Gath, he and his men, [a]each with his household, *even* David with [b]his two wives,[802] Ahinoam the Jezreelitess, and Abigail the Carmelitess, Nabal's [I]widow.[802]

4 Now it was told Saul that David had fled to Gath, so he no longer searched for him.

5 Then David said to Achish, "If now I have found favor[2580] in your sight, let them give me a place in one of the cities in the country,[7704] that I may live there; for why should your servant[5650] live in the royal city with you?"

6 So Achish gave him Ziklag that day; therefore [a]Ziklag has belonged to the kings[4428] of Judah to this day.

7 And the number of days that David lived in the country of the Philistines was [a]a year and four months.

8 Now David and his men went up and raided [a]the Geshurites and the Girzites and [b]the Amalekites; for they were

16 [I]Lit., *are surely sons of death* [a]1Sam. 20:31
17 [a]1Sam. 24:16
18 [a]1Sam. 24:9, 11-14
19 [I]Lit., *smell* [II]Lit., *sons of men* [a]2Sam. 16:11 [b]Gen. 8:21 [c]1Sam. 24:9 [d]Josh. 22:25-27
20 [a]1Sam. 24:14
21 [a]Ex. 9:27; 1Sam. 15:24, 30; 24:17
23 [a]1Sam. 24:19; Ps. 7:8; 18:20; 62:12 [b]1Sam. 24:12
24 [a]1Sam. 18:30 [b]Ps. 54:7
25 [a]1Sam. 24:19 [b]1Sam. 24:22
1 [I]Lit., *in his heart* [II]Lit., *that I should surely escape* [a]1Sam. 26:19
2 [a]1Sam. 25:13 [b]1Sam. 21:10; 1Kin. 2:39
3 [I]Lit., *wife* [a]1Sam. 30:3; 2Sam. 2:3 [b]1Sam. 25:42, 43
6 [a]Josh. 15:31; 19:5; Neh. 11:28
7 [a]1Sam. 29:3
8 [a]Josh. 13:2, 13 [b]Ex. 17:8; 1Sam. 15:7, 8

26:21 Saul meant every word at that moment, but David wisely did not place himself in Saul's power. Saul was too changeable.

the inhabitants of the land from ancient[5769] times, as you come to [c]Shur even as far as the land of Egypt.

9 And David [I]attacked[5221] the land and did not leave a man or a woman[802] alive, and he [a]took away the sheep, the cattle, the donkeys, the camels, and the clothing. Then he returned and came to Achish.

10 Now Achish said, "Where have you [a]made a raid today?" And David said, "Against the [I]Negev of Judah and against the [I]Negev of [b]the Jerahmeelites and against the [I]Negev of [c]the Kenites."

11 And David did not leave[2421] a man or a woman alive, to bring to Gath, saying, "Lest they should tell about us, saying, 'So has David done[6213] and so *has been* his practice all the time[3117] he has lived in the country of the Philistines.' "

12 So Achish believed[539] David, saying, "He has surely made himself odious[887] among his people[5971] Israel; therefore he will become my servant forever."

Saul and the Spirit Medium

28 Now it came about in those days[3117] that [a]the Philistines gathered[6908] their armed camps for war,[6635] to fight against Israel. And Achish said[559] to David, "Know[3045] assuredly that you will go out with me in the camp, you and your men."

2 And David said to Achish, "Very well, you shall know what your servant[5650] can do."[6213] So Achish said to David, "Very well, I will make you [I]my bodyguard[8104] [a]for life."

3 Now [a]Samuel was dead,[4191] and all Israel had lamented him and buried[6912] him [b]in Ramah his own city. And Saul had removed from the land[776] those who [c]were mediums and spiritists.[3049]

4 So the Philistines gathered together and came and camped [a]in Shunem; and Saul gathered all Israel together and they camped in [b]Gilboa.

5 When Saul saw[7200] the camp of the Philistines, he was afraid[3372] and his heart trembled greatly.

🔑 6 [a]When Saul inquired[7592] of the LORD, [b]the LORD did not answer him, either by [c]dreams or by [d]Urim[217] or by prophets.[5030]

7 Then Saul said to his servants, "Seek for me a woman[802] who is a medium, that I may go to her and inquire of her." And his servants said to him, "Behold, [a]there is a woman who is a medium at [b]En-dor."

8 Then Saul [a]disguised himself by putting on other clothes, and went, he and two men with him, and they came to the woman by night;[3915] and he said, "[b]Conjure up[7080] for me, please,[4994] and [c]bring up for me whom I shall [I]name to you."

9 But the woman said to him, "Behold, you know[3045] [a]what Saul has done,[6213] how he has cut[3772] off those who are mediums and spiritists from the land. Why are you then laying a snare[5367] for my life[5315] to bring about my death?"[4191]

10 And Saul vowed[7650] to her by the LORD, saying, "As the LORD lives,[2416] there shall no punishment[5771] come upon you for this thing."

11 Then the woman said, "Whom shall I bring up for you?" And he said, "Bring up Samuel for me."

12 When the woman saw Samuel, she cried[2199] out with a loud voice; and the woman spoke[559] to Saul, saying, "Why have you deceived me? For you are Saul."

13 And the king[4428] said to her, "Do not be afraid; but what do you see?"[7200] And the woman said to Saul, "I see a [I]divine being[430] coming up[5927] out of the earth."[776]

14 And he said to her, "What is his form?" And she said, "An old[2205] man is coming up, and [a]he is wrapped with a robe."[4598] And Saul knew[3045] that it was Samuel, and [b]he bowed with his

8 [c]Ex. 15:22
9 [I]Lit., *smote* [a]1Sam. 15:3; Job 1:3
10 [I]I.e., South country [a]1Sam. 23:27 [b]1Sam. 30:29; 1Chr. 2:9, 25 [c]Judg. 1:16; 4:11
1 [a]1Sam. 29:1
2 [I]Lit., *keeper of my head* [a]1Sam. 1:22, 28
3 [a]1Sam. 25:1 [b]1Sam. 7:17 [c]Lev. 19:31; 20:27; Deut. 18:10; 1Sam. 15:23
4 [a]Josh. 19:18; 1Sam. 28:4; 1Kin. 1:3; 2Kin. 4:8 [b]1Sam. 31:1
6 [a]1Chr. 10:13, 14 [b]1Sam. 14:37; Prov. 1:24-31 [c]Num. 12:6; Joel 2:28 [d]Ex. 28:30; Num. 27:21
7 [a]Acts 16:16 [b]Josh. 17:11; Ps. 83:10
8 [I]Lit., *say* [a]2Chr. 18:29; 35:22 [b]1Chr. 10:13; Is. 8:19 [c]Deut. 18:10, 11
9 [a]1Sam. 28:3
13 [I]Or, *god*
14 [a]1Sam. 15:27 [b]1Sam. 24:8

🔑 **28:6** See note on Ex. 28:30.

face[639] to the ground[776] and did homage.[7812]

15 Then Samuel said to Saul, "Why have you disturbed me by bringing me up?" And Saul answered, "I am greatly distressed; for the Philistines are waging war against me, and [a]God[430] has departed from me and [b]answers me no more, either through prophets or by dreams; therefore I have called[7121] you, that you may make known[3045] to me what I should do."

16 And Samuel said, "Why then do you ask[7592] me, since the LORD has departed from you and has become[1960] your adversary?

17 "And the LORD has done [I]accordingly [a]as He spoke[1696] through me; for the LORD has torn the kingdom out of your hand and given it to your neighbor,[7453] to David.

18 "As [a]you did not [I]obey[8085] the LORD and did not execute[6213] His fierce wrath[639] on Amalek, so the LORD has done this thing to you this day.[3117]

19 "Moreover the LORD will also give over Israel along with you into the hands of the Philistines, therefore tomorrow [a]you and your sons[1121] will be with me. Indeed the LORD will give over the army of Israel into the hands of the Philistines!"

20 Then Saul immediately fell[5307] full length[4116] upon the ground and was very afraid because of the words[1697] of Samuel; also there was no strength in him, for he had eaten no [I]food all day and all night.

21 And the woman came to Saul and saw that he was terrified, and said to him, "Behold, your maidservant has [I]obeyed[8085] you, and [a]I have [II]taken my life in my hand, and have listened to your words which you spoke[1696] to me.

22 "So now also, please listen to the voice of your maidservant, and let me set a piece of bread before you that *you may* eat and have strength when you go on *your* way."[1870]

23 But he refused and said, "[a]I will not eat." [b]However, his servants together with the woman urged him, and he listened to [I]them. So he arose from the ground and sat on [c]the bed.

24 And the woman had a [a]fattened calf in the house, and she quickly slaughtered[2076] it; and she [b]took flour, kneaded it, and baked unleavened[4682] bread from it.

25 And she brought[5066] *it* before Saul and his servants, and they ate. Then they arose and went away that night.

The Philistines Mistrust David

29 Now [a]the Philistines gathered[6908] together all their armies to [b]Aphek, while the Israelites were camping by the spring which is in [c]Jezreel.

2 And the lords[5633] of the Philistines were proceeding[5674] on by hundreds and by thousands, and [a]David and his men were proceeding on in the rear[314] with Achish.

3 Then the commanders[8269] of the Philistines said,[559] "What *are* these Hebrews *doing here*?" And Achish said to the commanders of the Philistines, "Is this not David, the servant[5650] of Saul the king[4428] of Israel, [a]who has been with me these days,[3117] or *rather* these years, and [b]I have found no fault in him from the day he [I]deserted[5307] *to me* to this day?"[3117]

4 But the commanders of the Philistines were angry[7107] with him, and the commanders of the Philistines said to him, "Make the man[376] go back, that he may return [a]to his place where you have assigned him, and do not let him go down to battle with us, [b]lest in the battle he become an adversary[7854] to us. For with what could this *man* make himself acceptable to his lord? *Would it* not *be* with the heads of [I]these men?

5 "Is this not David, [a]of whom they sing in the dances, saying,

'Saul has slain[5221] his thousands,
And David his ten thousands'?"

6 Then Achish called[7121] David and said to him, "*As* the LORD lives,[2416] you *have been* upright,[3477] and [a]your going out and your coming in with me in the

---

15 [a]1Sam. 16:14; 18:12 [b]1Sam. 28:6

17 [I]Lit., *for himself* [a]1Sam. 15:28

18 [I]Lit., *listen to the voice of* [a]1Sam. 15:20, 26; 1Kin. 20:42

19 [a]1Sam. 31:2; Job 3:17-19

20 [I]Lit., *bread*

21 [I]Lit., *listened to your voice* [II]Lit., *put* [a]Judg. 12:3; 1Sam. 19:5; Job 13:14

23 [I]Lit., *their voices* [a]1Kin. 21:4 [b]2Kin. 5:13 [c]Esth. 1:6; Ezek. 23:41

24 [a]Gen. 18:7; Luke 15:23, 27, 30 [b]Gen. 18:6

1 [a]1Sam. 28:1 [b]Josh. 12:18; 19:30; 1Sam. 4:1; 1Kin. 20:30 [c]1Kin. 21:1; 2Kin. 9:30

2 [a]1Sam. 28:1,2

3 [I]Lit., *fell* [a]1Sam. 27:7 [b]1Sam. 27:1-6; 1Chr. 12:19, 20; Dan. 6:5

4 [I]Lit., *those* [a]1Sam. 27:6 [b]1Sam. 14:21

5 [a]1Sam. 18:7; 21:11

6 [a]2Sam. 3:25; 2Kin. 19:27; Is. 37:28

army are pleasing[2896] in my sight;
[b]for I have not found evil[7451] in you from
the day of your coming to me to this
day. Nevertheless, you are not
pleasing[2896] in the sight of the lords.
7 "Now therefore return, and go in
peace, that you may not displease the
lords of the Philistines."
8 And David said to Achish, "[a]But
what have I done?[6213] And what have
you found in your servant from the day
when I came before you to this day,
that I may not go and fight against the
enemies of my lord[113] the king?"
9 But Achish answered and said to
David, "I know[3045] that you are pleasing
in my sight, [a]like an angel[4397] of God;[430]
nevertheless [b]the commanders of the
Philistines have said, 'He must not go
up with us to the battle.'
10 "Now then arise early in the
morning [a]with the servants of your lord
who have come with you, and as soon
as you have arisen early in the morning
and have light,[216] depart."
11 So David arose early, he and his
men, to depart in the morning, to return
to the land[776] of the Philistines. And the
Philistines went up to Jezreel.

David's Victory over the Amalekites

30 Then it happened when David
and his men came to [a]Ziklag on
the third day,[3117] that [b]the Amalekites
had made a raid on the [I]Negev and on
[c]Ziklag, and had [II]overthrown[5221] Ziklag
and burned[8313] it with fire;
2 and they took captive[7617] the
women[802] *and all* who were in it, both
small and great, [I][a]without killing[4191] anyone, and carried *them* off and went their
way.[1870]
3 And when David and his men came
to the city, behold, it was burned with
fire, and their wives and their sons[1121]
and their daughters had been taken captive.
4 Then David and the people[5971]
who were with him [a]lifted their voices
and wept until there was no strength
in them to weep.
5 Now [a]David's two wives had been
taken captive, Ahinoam the Jezreelitess
and Abigail the [I]widow[802] of Nabal the
Carmelite.
6 Moreover David was greatly distressed because [a]the people spoke[559]
of stoning him, for all the people were
[I]embittered, each one because of his
sons and his daughters. But [b]David
strengthened[2388] himself in the LORD his
God.[430]
7 Then [a]David said[559] to [b]Abiathar
the priest,[3548] the son[1121] of Ahimelech,
"Please[4994] bring[5066] me the ephod." So
Abiathar brought[5066] the ephod to David.
8 And [a]David inquired[7592] of the
LORD, saying, "[b]Shall I pursue this band?
Shall I overtake them?" And He said[559]
to him, "Pursue, for you shall surely
overtake them, [c]and you shall surely rescue *all*."
9 So David went, [a]he and the six
hundred men who were with him, and
came to the brook Besor, *where* those
left[3498] behind remained.
10 But David pursued, he and four
hundred men, for [a]two hundred who
were too exhausted to cross the brook
Besor, remained *behind*.
11 Now they found an Egyptian in
the field[7704] and brought him to David,
and gave him bread and he ate, and they
provided him water to drink.
12 And they gave him a piece of
fig cake and two clusters of raisins, and
he ate; [a]then his spirit[7307] [I]revived. For
he had not eaten bread or drunk water
for three days[3117] and three nights.[3915]
13 And David said to him, "To whom
do you belong? And where are you
from?" And he said, "I am a young man
of Egypt, a servant[5650] of an Amalekite;
and my master left[5800] me behind when
I fell sick three days ago.
14 "We made a raid on [a]the [I]Negev
of the Cherethites, and on that which
belongs to Judah, and on [b]the [I]Negev
of Caleb, and [c]we burned Ziklag with
fire."
15 Then David said to him, "Will

6 [b]1Sam. 27:8-12; 29:3
8 [a]1Sam. 27:10-12
9 [a]2Sam. 14:17, 20; 19:27 [b]1Sam. 29:4
10 [a]1Chr. 12:19, 22

1 [I]I.e., South country [II]Lit., *smote* [a]1Sam. 29:4, 11 [b]1Sam. 15:7; 27:8-10 [c]1Sam. 27:6, 8
2 [I]Lit., *they did not kill* [a]1Sam. 27:11
4 [a]Num. 14:1
5 [I]Lit., *wife* [a]1Sam. 25:42, 43; 2Sam. 2:2
6 [I]Lit., *bitter in soul* [a]Ex. 17:4; John 8:59 [b]1Sam. 23:16; Ps. 18:2; 27:14; 31:24; 71:4, 5; Rom. 4:20
7 [a]1Sam. 23:6, 9 [b]1Sam. 22:20-23
8 [a]1Sam. 23:2, 4; Ps. 50:15; 91:15 [b]Ex. 15:9 [c]1Sam. 30:18
9 [a]1Sam. 27:2
10 [a]1Sam. 30:9, 21
12 [I]Lit., *returned to him* [a]Judg. 15:19
14 [I]I.e., South country [a]1Sam. 30:1, 16; 2Sam. 8:18; 1Kin. 1:38, 44; Ezek. 25:16; Zeph. 2:5 [b]Josh. 14:13; 15:13; 21:12 [c]1Sam. 30:1

you bring me down to this band?"[1466]
And he said, "Swear[7650] to me by God
that you will not kill[4191] me or deliver
me into the hands of my master, and I
will bring you down to this band."
16 And when he had brought him
down, behold, they were [I]spread[5203]
over all the land,[776] [a]eating and drinking
and [II]dancing because of [b]all the great
spoil that they had taken from the land[776]
of the Philistines and from the land of
Judah.
17 And David [I]slaughtered[5221] them
[a]from the twilight [II]until the evening of
[III]the next day; and not a man of them
escaped,[4422] except four hundred young
men who rode on [b]camels and fled.
18 So David [a]recovered all that the
Amalekites had taken, and [I]rescued his
two wives.
19 But nothing of theirs was missing, whether small or great, sons or
daughters, spoil or anything that they
had taken for themselves; [a]David
brought *it* all back.
20 So David had [I]captured all the
sheep and the cattle *which the people*
drove ahead of [II]the *other* livestock, and
they said, "[a]This is David's spoil."

The Spoils Are Divided

21 When [a]David came to the two
hundred men who were too exhausted
to follow David, who had also been left
at the brook Besor, and they went out
to meet David and to meet the people who were with him, then David approached[5066] the people and
greeted[7965] them.
22 Then all the wicked[7451] and
worthless[1100] men among those who
went with David answered and said,
"Because they did not go with [I]us, we
will not give them any of the spoil that
we have recovered, except to every
man his wife and his children,[1121] that
they may lead *them* away and depart."
23 Then David said, "You must not
do[6213] so, my brothers,[251] with what the
LORD has given us, who has kept us
and delivered into our hand the band
that came against us.
24 "And who will listen to you in
this matter? For [a]as his share is who
goes down to the battle, so shall his
share be who stays by the baggage; they
shall share alike."
25 And so it has been from that day
forward, that he made it a statute[2706]
and an ordinance[4941] for Israel to this
day.
26 Now when David came to Ziklag,
he sent *some* of the spoil to the elders[2205]
of Judah, to his friends,[7453] saying, "Behold, [a]a [I]gift[1293] for you from the spoil
of [b]the enemies of the LORD:
27 to those who were in [a]Bethel,
and to those who were in [b]Ramoth of
the [I]Negev, and to those who were in
[c]Jattir,
28 and to those who were in
[a]Aroer, and to those who were in Siphmoth, and to those who were in [b]Esh-
temoa,
29 and to those who were in Racal,
and to those who were in the cities of
[a]the Jerahmeelites, and to those who
were in the cities of [b]the Kenites,
30 and to those who were in
[a]Hormah, and to those who were in
[b]Bor-ashan, and to those who were
in Athach,
31 and to those who were in
[a]Hebron, and to all the places where
David himself and his men were
accustomed[1980] to [b]go."

Saul and His Sons Slain

31 🔑 [a]Now the Philistines were
fighting against Israel, and the
men of Israel fled from before the Philistines and fell[5307] slain[2491] [b]on Mount Gilboa.
2 And the Philistines overtook Saul
and his sons;[1121] and the Philistines
[I]killed[5221] [a]Jonathan and Abinadab and
Malchi-shua the sons of Saul.
3 And [a]the battle went heavily[3513]

16 [I]Lit., *left* [II]Lit., *keeping a pilgrim-feast* [a]Luke 12:19; 17:27f. [b]1Sam. 30:14
17 [I]Lit., *smote* [II]Lit., *even until* [III]Lit., *their* [a]1Sam. 11:11 [b]Judg. 7:12; 1Sam. 15:3
18 [I]Lit., *David rescued* [a]Gen. 14:16
19 [a]1Sam. 30:8
20 [I]Lit., *taken* [II]Lit., *those livestock* [a]1Sam. 30:26-31
21 [a]1Sam. 30:10
22 [I]Lit., *me*
24 [a]Num. 31:27; Josh. 22:8
26 [I]Lit., *blessing* [a]1Sam. 25:27 [b]1Sam. 18:17; 25:28
27 [I]I.e., South country [a]Gen. 12:8; Josh. 7:2; 8:9; 16:1 [b]Josh. 19:8 [c]Josh. 15:48; 21:14
28 [a]Josh. 13:16; 1Chr. 11:44 [b]Josh. 15:50
29 [a]1Sam. 27:10 [b]Judg. 1:16; 1Sam. 15:6
30 [a]Num. 14:45; 21:3; Josh. 12:14; 15:30; 19:4; Judg. 1:17 [b]Josh. 15:42; 19:7
31 [a]Num. 13:22; Josh. 14:13-15; 21:11-13; 2Sam. 2:1 [b]1Sam. 23:22
1 [a]1Chr. 10:1-12 [b]1Sam. 28:4
2 [I]Lit., *smote* [a]1Chr. 8:33f.
3 [a]2Sam. 1:6

🔑 **31:1-13** See I Chr. 10:1-12.

against Saul, and the archers[3384]
[I]hit him; and he was badly wounded[2342]
by the archers.
4 [a]Then Saul said[559] to his armor
bearer, "Draw your sword[2719] and
pierce me through with it, lest [b]these
uncircumcised[6189] come and pierce me
through and make sport of me." But
his armor bearer would[14] not, for he
was greatly afraid. [c]So Saul took his
sword and fell on it.
5 And when his armor bearer
saw[7200] that Saul was dead,[4191] he also
fell on his sword and died[4191] with him.
6 Thus Saul died with his three sons,
his armor bearer, and all his men on
that day[3117] together.
7 And when the men of Israel who
were on the other side of the valley,
with those who were beyond the Jordan,
saw that the men of Israel had fled and
that Saul and his sons were dead, they
abandoned[5800] the cities and fled; then
the Philistines came and lived in them.
8 And it came about on the [I]next
day when the Philistines came to strip
the slain, that they found Saul and his
three sons fallen on Mount[5307] Gilboa.
9 And they cut[3772] off his head, and
stripped off his weapons, and sent *them*
[I]throughout the land[776] of the Philistines,
[a]to carry the good news[1319] [b]to the house
of their idols[6091] and to the people.[5971]
10 And they put his weapons in the
[I]temple of [a]Ashtaroth, and [b]they
fastened[8628] his body[1472] to the wall of
[c]Beth-shan.
11 Now when [a]the inhabitants of Jabesh-gilead heard [I]what the Philistines
had done[6213] to Saul,
12 [a]all the valiant men rose and
walked all night,[3915] and took the body
of Saul and the bodies[1472] of his sons
from the wall of Beth-shan, and they
came to Jabesh, and [b]burned[8313] them
there.
13 And they took their bones[6106] and
[a]buried[6912] them under [b]the tamarisk
tree at Jabesh, and [c]fasted seven
days.[3117]

3 [I]Lit., *found*

4 [a]Judg. 9:54; 1Chr. 10:4 [b]Judg. 14:3; 1Sam. 14:6; 17:26, 36 [c]2Sam. 1:6, 10

8 [I]Lit., *morrow*

9 [I]Lit., *into . . . around* [a]2Sam. 1:20 [b]Judg. 16:23, 24

10 [I]Lit., *house* [a]Judg. 2:13; 1Sam. 7:3 [b]1Sam. 31:12; 2Sam. 21:12 [c]Josh. 17:11

11 [I]Lit., *about him what* [a]1Sam. 11:1-13

12 [a]2Sam. 2:4-7 [b]2Chr. 16:14

13 [a]2Sam. 21:12-14 [b]1Sam. 22:6 [c]2Sam. 1:12

The Second Book of

SAMUEL

The Second Book of Samuel narrates the career of David in considerable detail. He was probably the strongest king that Israel ever had. He had great ability as an administrator, a soldier, and a musician. However, his greatest quality was spirituality. He was truly close to the God of Israel. When David was a young man, the Lord sought him because he was "a man after His own heart" (I Sam. 13:14). He engendered outstanding loyalty in his followers. He was an exceptional spiritual leader. Under inspiration David wrote the famed Twenty-third Psalm as well as other psalms in which he praised God. He had so many things going for him when he slipped and fell. He lusted after Bathsheba, committed adultery with her, and had her husband abandoned in battle to be killed. God sent Nathan the prophet to expose David's sin. Shortly after this time David truly repented. That contrition is recorded in Psalm 51. II Samuel focuses upon the restoration of order following the chaos of Saul's reign. David emerges as the king of all the people, and Zion (Jerusalem) is the seat of power. God made a special covenant with David in II Samuel 7:8-17 to establish a continuous, royal lineage which would end with Jesus Christ who would sit upon the throne of David. God's original promise to Abraham of blessing the whole world is further explained by this new prophecy; all nations would be blessed through a particular descendant of David, Jesus Christ. The closing years of David were more peaceful than his earlier years, but he was forced to live with the memories of a turbulent life.

David Learns of Saul's Death

1 🔑Now it came about after [a]the
death[4194] of Saul, when David had
returned from [b]the slaughter of the
Amalekites, that David remained two
days in Ziklag.
2 And it happened on the third
day,[3117] that behold, [a]a man came out
of the camp from Saul, [b]with his clothes
torn and [I]dust[127] on his head. And it
came about when he came to David that
[c]he fell[5307] to the ground[776] and prostrated himself.[7812]
3 Then David said to him, "From
where do you come?" And he said to
him, "I have escaped[4422] from the camp
of Israel."
4 And David said to him, "[a]How did
things go? Please tell me." And he
said,[559] "The people have fled from the
battle, and also many of the people have
fallen[5307] and are dead;[4191] and Saul and
Jonathan his son are dead also."
5 So David said to the young man
who told him, "How do you know[3045]
that Saul and his son Jonathan are dead?"
6 And the young man who told him
said, "By chance I happened to be on
[a]Mount Gilboa, and behold, [b]Saul was
leaning[8172] on his spear. And behold,
the chariots and the horsemen pursued
him closely.
7 "And when he looked behind him,
he saw me and called[7121] to me. And I
said, 'Here I am.'
8 "And he said to me, 'Who are you?'
And I [I]answered him, '[a]I am an Amalekite.'
9 "Then he said to me, 'Please stand
beside me and kill me; for agony[7661] has
seized me because my [I]life[5315] still lingers in me.'
10 "So I stood beside him [a]and killed
him, because I knew that he could not
live[2421] after he had fallen. And [b]I took
the crown[5145] which *was* on his head
and the bracelet which *was* on his arm,

1 [a]1Sam. 31:6 [b]1Sam. 30:1, 17, 26
2 [I]Lit., *ground* [a]2Sam. 4:10 [b]1Sam. 4:12 [c]1Sam. 25:23
4 [a]1Sam. 4:16
6 [a]1Sam. 28:4; 31:1-6; 1Chr. 10:4-10 [b]1Sam. 31:2-4
8 [I]Lit., *said to* [a]1Sam. 15:3; 30:1, 13, 17
9 [I]Lit., *whole life is still in me*
10 [a]Judg. 9:54 [b]2Kin. 11:12

🔑 **1:1-10** The story of the Amalekite is different from the record of I Sam. 31:3-5. Apparently, this man discovered Saul's body and looted it. Some time later he told his own version to David, hoping that he would be rewarded for this "good news." See II Sam. 4:10.

and I have brought them here to my
lord."[113]

11 Then [a]David took hold of his
clothes and tore them, and *so* also *did*
all the men who *were* with him.
12 And they mourned and wept and
[a]fasted until evening for Saul and his
son Jonathan and for the people of the
LORD and the house of Israel, because
they had fallen by the sword.
13 And David said to the young man
who told him, "Where are you from?"
And he [I]answered, "[a]I am the son of
an alien, an Amalekite."
14 Then David said to him, "How
is it you were not afraid[3372] [a]to stretch
out your hand to destroy[7843] the LORD's
anointed?"[4899]
15 And David called one of the
young men and said, "Go, [I]cut him
down." [a]So he struck him and he
died.[4191]
16 And David said to him, "[a]Your
blood[1818] is on your head, for [b]your
mouth has testified against you, saying,
'I have killed the LORD's anointed.'"

David's Dirge for Saul and Jonathan

17 Then David [a]chanted with this
lament over Saul and Jonathan his son,
🔑 18 and he told *them* to teach the
sons[1121] of Judah *the song of* the bow;
behold, it is written in [a]the book[5612] of
Jashar.[3477]
19 "[I]Your beauty,[6643] O Israel, is
slain on your high places!
[a]How have the mighty fallen!
20 "[a]Tell *it* not in Gath,
Proclaim it not in the streets of
Ashkelon;
Lest [b]the daughters of the
Philistines rejoice,
Lest the daughters of [c]the
uncircumcised[6189] exult.

11 [a]Gen. 37:29, 34; Josh. 7:6; 2Chr. 34:27; Ezra 9:3
12 [a]2Sam. 3:35
13 [I]Lit., *said* [a]2Sam. 1:8
14 [a]1Sam. 24:6; 26:9, 11, 16
15 [I]Lit., *fall upon him* [a]2Sam. 4:10, 12
16 [a]1Sam. 26:9; 2Sam. 3:28, 29; 1Kin. 2:32 [b]2Sam. 1:10; Luke 19:22
17 [a]2Chr. 35:25
18 [a]Josh. 10:13
19 [I]Lit., *The* [a]2Sam. 1:25, 27
20 [a]1Sam. 31:8-13; Mic. 1:10 [b]Ex. 15:20, 21; 1Sam. 18:6 [c]1Sam. 14:6
21 [a]1Sam. 31:1 [b]Ezek. 31:15 [c]Is. 21:5
22 [a]Deut. 32:42; Is. 34:6 [b]1Sam. 18:4
23 [a]Jer. 4:13 [b]Judg. 14:18
25 [a]2Sam. 1:19, 27
26 [a]1Sam. 18:1-4
27 [a]2Sam. 1:19, 25 [b]Is. 13:5
1 [a]1Sam. 23:2, 4, 9-12

21 "[a]O mountains of Gilboa,
[b]Let not dew or rain be on
you, nor fields[7704] of
offerings;[8641]
For there the shield of the
mighty was defiled,
The shield of Saul, not
[c]anointed with oil.[8081]
22 "[a]From the blood of the slain,
from the fat of the mighty,
[b]The bow of Jonathan did not
turn back,
And the sword of Saul did not
return empty.
23 "Saul and Jonathan, beloved and
pleasant in their life,
And in their death they were not
parted;
[a]They were swifter than eagles,
[b]They were stronger than lions.
24 "O daughters of Israel, weep over
Saul,
Who clothed you luxuriously in
scarlet,
Who put ornaments of gold on
your apparel.
25 "[a]How have the mighty fallen in
the midst of the battle!
Jonathan is slain on your high
places.
🔑 26 "I am distressed for you, my
brother[251] Jonathan;
You have been very pleasant to
me.
[a]Your love[160] to me was more
wonderful[6381]
Than the love of women.[802]
27 "[a]How have the mighty fallen,
And [b]the weapons of war
perished!"

David Made King over Judah

2 Then it came about afterwards that
[a]David inquired[7592] of the LORD, saying, "Shall I go up to one of the cities

🔑 **1:18** The book of Jasher is also mentioned in Josh. 10:13. It is apparently a historical book of military poetry, a collection of songs about heros. It grew larger as the years went by, but it is now lost. Jasher is probably a name used for Israel. We find it in Deut. 32:15 under the form Jeshurun which means "the righteous or upright one." The book printed under this name in modern times is spurious.
🔑 **1:26** David truly loved Jonathan because Jonathan was noble, unselfish, and loyal. Even though Jonathan was the heir apparent, he was willing to take second place for the sake of David, his friend.

of Judah?" And the LORD said to him,
"Go up." So David said, "Where shall
I go up?" And He said, "[b]To Hebron."
2 So David went up there, and
[a]his two wives[802] also, Ahinoam the
Jezreelitess and Abigail the [I]widow[802]
of Nabal the Carmelite.
3 And [a]David brought up his men
who *were* with him, each with his household; and they lived in the cities of Hebron.
4 Then the men of Judah came and
there [a]anointed[4886] David king[4428] over
the house of Judah.
And they told David, saying, "It was
[b]the men of Jabesh-gilead who buried[6912]
Saul."
5 And David sent messengers to the
men of Jabesh-gilead, and said to them,
"[a]May you be blessed[1288] of the LORD
because you have [I]shown this kindness[2617] to Saul your lord, and have
buried him.
6 "And now [a]may the LORD [I]show
lovingkindness and truth to you; and I
also will [I]show this goodness to you,
because you have done[6213] this thing.
7 "Now therefore, let your hands
be strong, and be [I]valiant; for Saul your
lord is dead,[4191] and also the house of
Judah has anointed me king[4428] over
them."

Ish-bosheth Made King over Israel

8 But [a]Abner the son of Ner,
commander[8269] of Saul's army, had taken
[I]Ish-bosheth the son of Saul, and brought
him over to [b]Mahanaim.
9 And he made him king[4427] over
[a]Gilead, over the [b]Ashurites, over [c]Jez-
reel, over Ephraim, and over Benjamin,
even over all Israel.
10 Ish-bosheth, Saul's son, was
forty years old[1121] when he became king
over Israel, and he was king for two
years. The house of Judah, however,
followed David.
11 And [a]the [I]time that David was
king in Hebron over the house of Judah
was seven years and six months.

Civil War

12 Now Abner the son of Ner, went
out from Mahanaim to [a]Gibeon with the
servants of Ish-bosheth the son of Saul.
13 And [a]Joab the son of Zeruiah and
the servants of David went out and met
[I]them by the pool of Gibeon; and they
sat down, [II]one on the one side of the
pool and [II]the other on the other side
of the pool.
14 Then Abner said to Joab, "Now
let the young men arise and [I][a]hold a
contest before us." And Joab said, "Let
them arise."
15 So they arose and went over by
count, twelve for Benjamin and Ish-
bosheth the son of Saul, and twelve of
the servants of David.
16 And each one[376] of them
seized[2388] his [I]opponent[7453] by the head,
and *thrust* his sword in his [II]opponent's
side; so they fell[5307] down together.

1 [b]Josh. 14:13; 1Sam. 30:31
2 [I]Lit., *wife* [a]1Sam. 25:42, 43
3 [a]1Sam. 30:9; 1Chr. 12:1
4 [a]1Sam. 16:13; 2Sam. 5:3, 5 [b]1Sam. 31:11-13
5 [I]Lit., *done* [a]1Sam. 23:21; Ps. 115:15
6 [I]Lit., *do* [a]Ex. 34:6; 2Tim. 1:16
7 [I]Lit., *sons of valor*
8 [I]I.e., man of shame; cf. 1Chr. 8:33, *Eshbaal* [a]1Sam. 14:50 [b]Gen. 32:2; 2Sam. 17:24
9 [a]Josh. 22:9 [b]Judg. 1:32 [c]1Sam. 29:1
11 [I]Lit., *number of days* [a]2Sam. 5:5
12 [a]Josh. 10:12; 18:25
13 [I]Lit., *them together* [II]Lit., *these* [a]2Sam. 8:16; 1Chr. 2:16; 11:6
14 [I]Lit., *make sport* [a]2Sam. 2:16, 17
16 [I]Lit., *fellow* [II]Lit., *fellow's*

2:9 Abner was himself a close relative of Saul (I Sam. 14:50). Abner wanted as much control as possible after the death of Saul and Jonathan.

2:11 Up to this time David had been accepted as king only by his own tribe, Judah (v. 10). Hebron was his capital while he reigned over them for seven and one-half years. Ishbosheth, the son of Saul, was his rival for two years, reigning over all the other tribes of Israel (vv. 8-10). He depended upon Abner, who had been Saul's commander-in-chief. It was only after Abner's death, though he had already defected to David's side, that Israel's confidence in him began to diminish. After the death of Ishbosheth David was crowned king over all Israel and reigned for thirty-three years (II Sam. 5:1-5). He was king for a total of forty years.

2:13 Joab was the half-nephew of David. Zeruiah was David's half-sister (I Chr. 2:16), probably through the marriage of his mother to Nahash (II Sam. 17:25). This was before David's mother married Jesse, David's father.

2:14 This is similar to the offer made by Goliath (I Sam. 17:8,9). A single contest between champions would avoid much bloodshed.

Therefore that place was called[7121] [III]Helkath-hazzurim, which is in Gibeon.

17 And that day[3117] the battle was very severe, and [a]Abner and the men of Israel were beaten[5062] before the servants of David.

18 Now [a]the three sons of Zeruiah were there, Joab and Abishai and Asahel; and Asahel *was* [b]*as* [I]swift-footed as one of the gazelles which is in the field.

19 And Asahel pursued Abner and did not [I]turn to the right or to the left from following Abner.

20 Then Abner looked behind him and said, "Is that you, Asahel?" And he answered,[559] "It is I."

21 So Abner said to him, "[I]Turn to your right or to your left, and take hold of one of the young men for yourself, and take for yourself his spoil." But Asahel was not willing[14] to turn aside from following him.

22 And Abner repeated again to Asahel, "Turn [I]aside from following me. Why should I strike you to the ground?[776] [a]How then could I lift up my face to your brother[251] Joab?"

23 However, he refused to turn aside; therefore Abner struck him in the belly with the butt end of the spear, so that the spear came out at his back. And he fell there and died[4191] on the spot. And it came about that all who came to the place where [a]Asahel had fallen and died, stood still.

24 But Joab and Abishai pursued Abner, and when the sun was going down, they came to the hill of Ammah, which is in front of Giah by the way[1870] of the wilderness of Gibeon.

25 And the sons[1121] of Benjamin gathered together behind Abner and became one band, and they stood on the top of a certain hill.

26 Then Abner called to Joab and said, "Shall the sword devour forever? Do you not know[3045] that it will be bitter[4751] in the end? How long will you [I]refrain from telling[559] the people to turn back from following their brothers?"[251]

27 And Joab said, "As God[430] lives,[2416] if you had not spoken, surely then the people would have gone away in the morning, each from following his brother."

28 So Joab blew[8628] the trumpet; and all the people halted and pursued Israel no longer, [a]nor did they continue to fight anymore.

29 Abner and his men then went through the Arabah all that night; so they crossed the Jordan, walked all morning, and came to [a]Mahanaim.

30 Then Joab returned from following Abner; when he had gathered all the people together, [I]nineteen of David's servants besides Asahel were missing.

31 But the servants of David had struck down many of Benjamin and Abner's men, *so that* three hundred and sixty men died.

32 And they took up Asahel and buried him [a]in his father's[1] tomb[6913] which was in Bethlehem. Then Joab and his men went all night until the day [I]dawned at Hebron.

The House of David Strengthened

3 Now [a]there was a long[752] war between the house of Saul and the house of David; and David grew steadily stronger, but the house of Saul grew weaker continually.

🔑 **2** [a]Sons were born to David at Hebron: his first-born was Amnon, by [b]Ahinoam the Jezreelitess;

3 and his second, Chileab, by Abigail the [I]widow[802] of Nabal the Carmelite; and the third, Absalom the son of [a]Maacah, the daughter of Talmai, king[4428] of [b]Geshur;

4 and the fourth, [a]Adonijah the son of Haggith; and the fifth, Shephatiah the son of Abital;

5 and the sixth, Ithream, by David's wife Eglah. These were born to David at Hebron.

III I.e., the field of sword-edges

17 [a]2Sam. 3:1

18 [I]Lit., *light in his feet* [a]1Chr. 2:16 [b]1Chr. 12:8; Hab. 3:19

19 [I]Lit., *turn to go to*

21 [I]Lit., *Turn for yourself*

22 [I]Lit., *aside for yourself* [a]2Sam. 3:27

23 [a]2Sam. 20:12

26 [I]Lit., *not tell the people*

28 [a]2Sam. 3:1

29 [a]2Sam. 2:8

30 [I]Lit., *nineteen men*

32 [I]Lit., *lighted on them* [a]Gen. 47:29, 30; Judg. 8:32

1 [a]1Kin. 14:30; Ps. 46:9

2 [a]1Chr. 3:1-3 [b]1Sam. 25:42, 43

3 [I]Lit., *wife* [a]1Sam. 27:8; 1Chr. 3:2 [b]2Sam. 14:32; 15:8

4 [a]1Kin. 1:5

🔑 **3:2-5** See I Chr. 3:1-4.

Abner Joins David

6 And it came about while there was war between the house of Saul and the house of David that [a]Abner was making himself strong in the house of Saul.

🔑 7 Now Saul had a concubine whose name was [a]Rizpah, the daughter of Aiah; and [I]Ish-bosheth said to Abner, "Why have you gone in to my father's[1] concubine?"

8 Then Abner was very angry[2734] over the words[1697] of Ish-bosheth and said, "[a]Am I a dog's head that belongs to Judah? Today[3117] I show kindness[2617] to the house of Saul your father,[1] to his brothers[251] and to his friends, and have not delivered you into the hands of David; and yet today you charge[6485] me with a guilt concerning the woman.[802]

9 "[a]May God[430] do so to Abner, and more also, if [b]as the LORD has sworn to David, I do not accomplish this for him,

10 [a]to transfer the kingdom[4467] from the house of Saul, and to establish the throne of David over Israel and over Judah, [b]from Dan even to Beersheba."

11 And he could no longer answer[7725] Abner a word,[1697] because he was afraid[3372] of him.

12 Then Abner sent messengers to David in his place, saying, "Whose is the land?[776] Make your covenant[1285] with me, and behold, my hand shall be with you to bring all Israel over to you."

13 And he said, "Good! I will make a covenant with you, but I demand one thing of you, [I]namely, [a]you shall not see my face unless you [b]first bring Michal, Saul's daughter, when you come to see [II]me."

14 So David sent messengers to Ish-bosheth, Saul's son, saying, "Give me my wife Michal, to whom I was betrothed[781] [a]for a hundred foreskins[6190] of the Philistines."

15 And Ish-bosheth sent and took her from *her* husband, from [I]Paltiel the son of Laish.

16 But her husband went with her, weeping as he went, and followed her as far as [a]Bahurim. Then Abner said to him, "Go, return." So he returned.

17 Now Abner had [I]consultation with [a]the elders[2205] of Israel, saying, "In times past you were seeking for David to be king over you.

18 "Now then, do *it*! For the LORD has spoken of David, saying, '[a]By the hand of My servant David [I]I will save My people Israel from the hand of the Philistines and from the hand of all their enemies.' "

19 And Abner also spoke in the hearing[241] of Benjamin; and in addition Abner went to speak in the hearing of David in Hebron all that seemed good[2896] to Israel and to [a]the whole house of Benjamin.

20 Then Abner and twenty men with him came to David at Hebron. And David made a feast for Abner and the men who were with him.

21 And Abner said to David, "Let me arise and go, and [a]gather[5908] all Israel to my lord[113] the king that they may make a covenant with you, and that [b]you may be king over all that your soul desires." So David sent Abner away, and he went in peace.

22 And behold, [a]the servants of David and Joab came from a raid and brought much spoil with them; but Abner was not with David in Hebron, for he had sent him away, and he had gone in peace.

6 [a]2Sam. 2:8, 9
7 [I]So some ancient mss. and versions; M.T., *he* [a]2Sam. 21:8-11
8 [a]1Sam. 24:14; 2Sam. 9:8
9 [a]1Kin. 19:2 [b]1Sam. 15:28
10 [a]1Sam. 15:28 [b]1Sam. 3:20
13 [I]Lit., *saying* [II]Lit., *my face* [a]Gen. 43:3 [b]1Sam. 18:20; 19:11
14 [a]1Sam. 18:25, 27
15 [I]In 1Sam. 25:44, *Palti*
16 [a]2Sam. 16:5; 19:16
17 [I]Lit., *a word* [a]1Sam. 8:4
18 [I]So many ancient mss. and versions; M.T., *he* [a]1Sam. 9:16; 15:28
19 [a]1Sam. 10:20, 21; 1Chr. 12:29
21 [a]2Sam. 3:10, 12 [b]1Kin. 11:37
22 [a]1Sam. 27:8

🔑 **3:7** A concubine was much more than a mistress. In a sense, she was a secondary "wife" (Ex. 21:8-10; Deut. 21:11-13). She was considered to be a member of the household, she took her position by an official ceremony of appointment, and she had the rights of a married woman. Unlike a true wife, concubines were usually acquired by purchase or were captives taken in war. She could be "divorced" summarily and then released, but never as a slave (Gen. 16:2,3; 21:10; Ex. 21:7,8; Deut. 21:10-14; Mal. 2:14-16). Abner was a powerful, ambitious man. He knew that possessing one of the court women was tantamount to royal power.

23 When Joab and all the army that was with him arrived, they told Joab, saying, "Abner the son of Ner came to the king, and he has sent him away, and he has gone in peace."

24 Then Joab came to the king and said, "What have you done?[6213] Behold, Abner came to you; why then have you sent him away and he is already gone?

25 "You know[3045] Abner the son of Ner, that he came to deceive you and to learn[3045] of [a]your going out and coming in, and to find out all that you are doing."

Joab Murders Abner

26 When Joab came out from David, he sent messengers after Abner, and they brought him back from the well[953] of Sirah; but David did not know[3045] *it.*

27 So when Abner returned to Hebron, Joab took him aside into the middle of the gate to speak with him privately, and there [a]he struck him in the belly so that he died[4191] on account of the blood[1818] of Asahel his brother.[251]

28 And afterward when David heard it, he said, "I and my kingdom[4467] are innocent[5355] before the LORD forever of the blood of Abner the son of Ner.

29 "[a]May it [I]fall on the head of Joab and on all his father's house; and may there not fail from the house of Joab [b]one who has a discharge, or who is a leper, or who takes hold[2388] of a distaff, or who falls[5307] by the sword, or who lacks bread."

30 So Joab and Abishai his brother killed Abner [a]because he had put their brother Asahel to death in the battle at Gibeon.

David Mourns Abner

31 Then David said to Joab and to all the people who were with him, "[a]Tear[7167] your clothes and gird on sackcloth and lament before Abner." And King David walked behind the bier.

32 Thus they buried[6912] Abner in Hebron; and the king lifted up his voice and wept at [a]the grave[6913] of Abner, and all the people wept.

33 And [a]the king chanted a *lament* for Abner and said,

"Should Abner die as a fool
dies?[4194]

34 "Your hands were not bound, nor
your feet put in fetters;
As one falls before the
[I]wicked, you have fallen."[5307]

And all the people wept again over him.

35 Then all the people came [a]to [I]persuade David to eat bread while it was still day; but David vowed, saying, "[b]May God do so to me, and more also, if I taste bread or anything else [c]before the sun goes down."

36 Now all the people took note *of it,* and it [I]pleased them, just as everything the king did[6213] [II]pleased all the people.

37 So all the people and all Israel understood[3045] that day that it had not been *the will* of the king to put Abner the son of Ner to death.

38 Then the king said to his servants, "Do you not know that a prince and a great man has fallen[5307] this day in Israel?

39 "And I am [a]weak today, though anointed[4886] king; and these men [b]the sons of Zeruiah are too difficult for me. [c]May the LORD repay the evil[7451]doer[6213] according to his evil."[7451]

Ish-bosheth Murdered

4 Now when [I]Ish-bosheth, Saul's son, heard that [a]Abner had died[4191] in Hebron, [II][b]he lost courage,[7503] and all Israel was disturbed.

2 And Saul's son *had* two men who were commanders[8269] of bands:[1416] the name of the one was Baanah and the name of the other Rechab, sons of Rimmon the Beerothite, of the sons[1121] of Benjamin (for [a]Beeroth is also considered [b]*part* of Benjamin,

3 and the Beerothites fled to [a]Gittaim, and have been aliens there until this day).[3117]

4 Now [a]Jonathan, Saul's son, had

25 [a]Deut. 28:6; 1Sam. 29:6; Is. 37:28
27 [a]2Sam. 2:23; 20:9, 10; 1Kin. 2:5
29 [I]Lit., *whirl* [a]Deut. 21:6-9; 1Kin. 2:31-33 [b]Lev. 13:46
30 [a]2Sam. 2:23
31 [a]Gen. 37:34; Judg. 11:35
32 [a]Job 31:28, 29; Prov. 24:17
33 [a]2Sam. 1:17; 2Chr. 35:25
34 [I]Lit., *sons of wickedness*
35 [I]Lit., *cause* [a]2Sam. 12:17 [b]1Sam. 3:17 [c]2Sam. 1:12
36 [I]Lit., *was good in their eyes* [II]Lit., *was good in the eyes of all*
39 [a]1Chr. 29:1; 2Chr. 13:7 [b]2Sam. 19:5-7 [c]1Kin. 2:32-34
1 [I]So some ancient mss.; M.T., *he* [II]Lit., *his hands dropped* [a]2Sam. 3:27 [b]Ezra 4:4
2 [a]Josh. 9:17 [b]Josh. 18:25
3 [a]Neh. 11:33
4 [a]2Sam. 9:3, 6

a son crippled in his feet. He was five
years old[1121] when the [b]report of Saul
and Jonathan came from Jezreel, and
his nurse took him up and fled. And it
happened that in her hurry to flee, he
fell[5307] and became lame. And his name
was [Ic]Mephibosheth.
5 So the sons of Rimmon the Beerothite, Rechab and Baanah, departed
and came to the house of [a]Ish-bosheth
in the heat of the day while he was taking
his midday rest.
6 [I]And they came to the middle of
the house as [II]if to get wheat, and
[a]they struck him in the belly; and Rechab
and Baanah his brother[251] escaped.[4422]
7 Now when they came into the
house, as he was lying on his bed in
his bedroom, they struck him and killed
him and beheaded him. And they took
his head and [Ia]traveled by way of the
Arabah all night.
8 Then they brought the head of Ish-
bosheth to David at Hebron, and said
to the king,[4428] "Behold, the head of
Ish-bosheth, [a]the son of Saul, your enemy, who sought your life;[5315] thus the
LORD has given my lord[113] the king vengeance this day on Saul and his [I]descend-
ants."
9 And David answered Rechab and
Baanah his brother, sons of Rimmon the
Beerothite, and said to them, "As the
LORD lives,[2416] [a]who has redeemed my
life from all distress,
10 [a]when one told me, saying, 'Behold, Saul is dead,' and [I]thought he was
bringing good news, I seized him and
killed him in Ziklag, which was the reward I gave him for *his* news.
11 "How much more, when
wicked[7563] men have killed a righteous
man in his own house on his bed, shall
I not now [a]require his blood[1818] from
your hand, and [I]destroy you from the
earth?"[776]
12 Then [a]David commanded[6680] the
young men, and they killed them and
cut off their hands and feet, and hung
them up beside the pool in Hebron. But
they took the head of Ish-bosheth
[b]and buried[6912] it in the grave[6913] of Abner in Hebron.

David King over All Israel

5 [a]Then all the tribes of Israel
came to David at Hebron and
[I]said, "Behold, we are [b]your bone[6106]
and your flesh.[1320]
2 "Previously, when Saul was
king[4428] over us, [a]you were the one who
led Israel out and in. And the LORD said
to you, '[b]You will shepherd My people
Israel, and you will be [c]a ruler[5057] over
Israel.' "
3 So all the elders[2205] of Israel came
to the king at Hebron, and King David
[a]made a covenant[1285] with them before
the LORD at Hebron; then [b]they
anointed[4886] David king over Israel.
4 David was [a]thirty years old[1121]
when he became king, *and* [b]he reigned
forty years.
5 At Hebron [a]he reigned over Judah
seven years and six months, and in Jerusalem he reigned thirty-three years over
all Israel and Judah.
6 [a]Now the king and his men went
to [b]Jerusalem against the Jebusites, the

4 [I]I.e., *Merib-baal* [b]1Sam. 31:1-4 [c]1Chr. 8:34; 9:40
5 [a]2Sam. 2:8
6 [I]Lit., *And here* [II]Lit., *takers of wheat* [a]2Sam. 2:23
7 [I]Lit., *went* [a]2Sam. 2:29
8 [I]Lit., *seed* [a]1Sam. 24:4; 25:29
9 [a]Gen. 48:16; 1Kin. 1:29; Ps. 31:7
10 [I]Lit., *he was as a bearer of good news in his own eyes* [a]2Sam. 1:2, 4, 15
11 [I]Lit., *burn* [a]Gen. 9:5; Ps. 9:12
12 [a]2Sam. 1:15 [b]2Sam. 3:32

1 [I]Lit., *said, saying* [a]1Chr. 11:1-3 [b]2Sam. 19:13
2 [a]1Sam. 18:5, 13, 16 [b]Gen. 49:24; 2Sam. 7:7 [c]1Sam. 25:30
3 [a]2Sam. 3:21 [b]1Sam. 16:13; 2Sam. 2:4
4 [a]Gen. 41:46; Num. 4:3; Luke 3:23 [b]1Kin. 2:11; 1Chr. 26:31
5 [a]2Sam. 2:11; 1Chr. 3:4; 29:27
6 [a]1Chr. 11:4-9 [b]Josh. 15:63; 18:28; Judg. 1:21

5:1-5 See parallel passage in I Chr. 11:1-3. See note on II Sam. 2:11.

5:6 The fortress of Zion was almost impenetrable in the mountains of Judah. Therefore, it was an important, strategic military site which was centrally located between Israel in the north and Judah in the south.

5:6-10 David's first task, after being crowned king over all Israel, was to conquer the city of Jerusalem. Salem (Gen. 14:18) was possibly an early reference to Jerusalem. If so, it was ruled by Melchizedek who was also a priest of the Most High God. When Israel returned from Egypt, Salem was in the hands of an indigenous band of Amorites called Jebusites. They called the city Jebus. The tribe of Judah had attacked the city early in the conquest of Canaan (Judg. 1:8) but was able to capture only the part outside the city walls. The tribe of Benjamin inhabited that part of the city and lived in apparent

(continued on next page)

inhabitants of the land,[776] and they said to [I]David, "You shall not come in here, but the blind and lame shall turn you away"; [II]thinking, "David cannot enter here."

7 Nevertheless, David captured the stronghold of Zion, that is [a]the city of David.

🔑8 And David said on that day,[3117] "Whoever would strike the Jebusites, let him reach the lame and the blind, who are hated by David's soul, through the water tunnel."[6794] Therefore they say, "The blind or the lame shall not come into the house."

9 So David lived in the stronghold, and called[7121] it [a]the city of David. And David built all around from the [Ib]Millo and inward.[1004]

10 And [a]David became greater and greater, for the LORD God[430] of hosts was with him.

🔑**11** [a]Then Hiram king of Tyre sent messengers to David with cedar trees and carpenters and stonemasons; and [b]they built a house for David.

12 And David realized that the LORD had established[3559] him as king over Israel, and that He had exalted his kingdom[4467] for the sake of His people Israel.

🔑**13** Meanwhile [a]David took more concubines and wives[802] from Jerusalem, after he came from Hebron; and more sons and daughters were born to David.

14 Now [a]these are the names of those who were born to him in Jerusalem: Shammua, Shobab, Nathan, Solomon,

15 Ibhar, Elishua, Nepheg, Japhia,

16 Elishama, Eliada and Eliphelet.

War with the Philistines

🔑**17** When the Philistines heard that they had anointed David king over Israel, [a]all the Philistines went up to seek out David; and when David heard *of it,* he went down to the [b]stronghold.

18 Now the Philistines came and spread themselves out in [a]the valley of Rephaim.

19 Then [a]David inquired[7592] of the LORD, saying, "Shall I go up against the Philistines? Wilt Thou give them into my hand?" And [b]the LORD said to David, "Go up, for I will certainly give the Philistines into your hand."

20 So David came to [a]Baal-perazim, and [I]defeated them there; and he said, "The LORD has broken through my enemies before me like the breakthrough of waters." Therefore he named that place [II]Baal-perazim.

21 And they abandoned[5800] their idols[6091] there, so [a]David and his men carried them away.[5375]

22 Now [a]the Philistines came up once again and spread themselves out in the valley of Rephaim.

23 And when [a]David inquired of the LORD, He said, "You shall not go *directly* up; circle around behind them and come at them in front of the [I]balsam trees.

24 "And it shall be, when [a]you hear the sound of marching in the tops of the [I]balsam trees, then you shall act promptly, for then [b]the LORD will have gone out before you to strike the army of the Philistines."

25 Then David did[6213] so, just as the LORD had commanded[6680] him, and struck down the Philistines from [Ia]Geba [II]as far as [b]Gezer.

6 [I]Lit., *David, saying* [II]Lit., *saying*
7 [a]2Sam. 6:12, 16; 1Kin. 2:10; 9:24
9 [I]I.e., citadel [a]2Sam. 5:7 [b]1Kin. 9:15, 24
10 [a]2Sam. 3:1
11 [a]1Kin. 5:1, 10, 18; 1Chr. 14:1 [b]Ps. 30:title
13 [a]Deut. 17:17; 1Chr. 3:9
14 [a]1Chr. 3:5-8
17 [a]1Sam. 29:1 [b]2Sam. 23:14; 1Chr. 11:16
18 [a]Gen. 14:5; Josh. 15:8; 17:15; 18:16
19 [a]1Sam. 23:2 [b]2Sam. 2:1
20 [I]Lit., *David smote* [II]I.e., the master of breakthrough [a]1Chr. 14:11; Is. 28:21
21 [a]1Chr. 14:12
22 [a]2Sam. 5:18
23 [I]Or, *baka-shrubs* [a]2Sam. 5:19
24 [I]Or, *baka-shrubs* [a]2Kin. 7:6 [b]Judg. 4:14
25 [I]In 1Chr. 14:16, *Gibeon* [II]Lit., *until you are coming to* [a]Is. 28:21 [b]Josh. 12:12; 21:21

(continued from previous page)
peace with the Jebusites who controlled the fortress (Judg. 1:21). After his victory there, David began to rebuild and expand the city. It became the seat of his kingdom. The "Millo," which means "the filling," was apparently a part of the defense system of the walled city of the Jebusites. Solomon rebuilt it during his reign (I Kgs. 11:27). See the parallel passage in I Chr. 11:4-9.

🔑**5:8** This was a concealed passageway which was cut down through the rock under the city.

🔑**5:11,12** See I Chr. 14:1,2.

🔑**5:13-16** See I Chr. 3:5-9; 14:3-7.

🔑**5:17-25** See I Chr. 14:8-17.

Peril in Moving the Ark

6 🗝 [a]Now David again gathered all the chosen men of Israel, thirty thousand.

🗝 2 And David arose and went with all the people who were with him to [I][a]Baale-judah, to bring up from there the ark[727] of God[430] which is called[7121] by the [b]Name, the very name of the LORD of hosts who [c]is [II]enthroned *above* the cherubim.[3742]

3 And they [I]placed the ark of God on [a]a new cart that they might bring[5375] it from the house of Abinadab which was on the hill; and Uzzah and Ahio, the sons of Abinadab, were leading the new cart.

4 So [a]they brought it with the ark of God from the house of Abinadab, which was on the hill; and Ahio was walking ahead of the ark.

5 Meanwhile, David and all the house of Israel [a]were celebrating before the LORD [b]with all kinds of *instruments made of* [I]fir wood, and with lyres, harps, tambourines,[8596] castanets and cymbals.

6 But when they came to the [a]threshing floor of Nacon, Uzzah [b]reached out toward the ark of God and took hold of it, for the oxen nearly upset *it*.

🗝 7 And the anger[639] of the LORD burned[2734] against Uzzah, and [a]God struck him down there for [I]his irreverence;[7944] and he died[4191] there by the ark of God.

8 And David became angry[2734] because [I]of the LORD's outburst against Uzzah, and that place is called [II]Perez-uzzah to this day.[3117]

9 So [a]David was afraid[3372] of the LORD that day; and he said, "How can the ark of the LORD come to me?"

10 And David was unwilling[3808,14] to move the ark of the LORD into the city of David with him; but David took it aside to the house of [a]Obed-edom the Gittite.

11 Thus the ark of the LORD remained in the house of Obed-edom the Gittite three months, and the LORD [a]blessed[1288] Obed-edom and all his household.

The Ark Is Brought to Jerusalem

🗝 **12** Now it was told King[4428] David, saying, "The LORD has blessed the house of Obed-edom and all that belongs to him, on account of the ark of God." [a]And David went and brought[5927] up the ark of God from the house of Obed-edom into [b]the city of David with gladness.

13 And so it was, that when the [a]bearers[5375] of the ark of the LORD had gone six paces, he sacrificed an [b]ox and a fatling.

14 And [a]David was dancing before the LORD with all *his* might, and David was [I][b]wearing a linen ephod.

15 So David and all the house of Israel were bringing up the ark of the LORD with shouting and the sound of the trumpet.

16 Then it happened *as* the ark of the LORD came into the city of David that [a]Michal the daughter of Saul looked out of the window and saw King David leaping and dancing before the LORD; and she despised him in her heart.

1 [a]1Chr. 13:5-14
2 [I]I.e., Kiriath-jearim [II]Lit., *sitting* [a]Josh. 15:9, 10; 1Sam. 7:1 [b]Lev. 24:16 [c]Ex. 25:22
3 [I]Lit., *caused to ride* [a]Num. 7:4-9; 1Sam. 6:7
4 [a]1Sam. 7:1; 1Chr. 13:7
5 [I]Or, *cypress* [a]1Sam. 18:6, 7 [b]1Chr. 13:8
6 [a]1Chr. 13:9 [b]Num. 4:15, 19, 20
7 [I]Lit., *the* [a]1Sam. 6:19
8 [I]Lit., *the LORD broke through a breakthrough* [II]I.e., the breakthrough of Uzzah
9 [a]Ps. 119:120; Luke 5:8
10 [a]1Chr. 26:4-8
11 [a]Gen. 30:27; 39:5
12 [a]1Chr. 15:25-16:3 [b]1Kin. 8:1
13 [a]Num. 4:15; Josh. 3:3; 1Chr. 15:2, 15 [b]1Kin. 8:5
14 [I]Lit., *girded with* [a]Ex. 15:20, 21; Judg. 11:34 [b]Ex. 19:6; 1Sam. 2:18, 28
16 [a]2Sam. 3:14

🗝 **6:1-11** See I Chr. 13:5-14.

🗝 **6:2** Baale of Judah was also known as Baalah and Kiriath-jearim (I Chr. 13:6). The Ark of the Covenant had stayed in the house of Abinadab for almost a century (cf. I Sam. 14:18) after its capture by the Philistines and its subsequent return (I Sam. 7:1).

🗝 **6:7** God's severity toward Uzzah served notice forever that He must be revered and obeyed. There were two violations: (1) The ark never should have been mounted upon a cart. Num. 4:15 specifically stated that it must be carried by hand. (2) The ark was supposed to be carried upon staves and should never have been touched even by the priests, those who were authorized to carry it (Num. 4:15). However, nowhere does the text indicate that Uzzah's personal, eternal salvation was involved; his intentions were good. It is not for us to judge his eternal destiny (Mt. 7:1).

🗝 **6:12-23** See I Chr. 15:1—16:6.

17 So they brought in the ark of the LORD and set it [a]in its place inside the tent which David had pitched for it; and [b]David offered[5927] burnt offerings and peace offerings before the LORD.

18 And when David had finished[3615] offering[5927] the burnt offering and the peace offering, [a]he blessed the people in the name of the LORD of hosts.

19 Further, he distributed to all the people, to all the multitude of Israel, both to men and women,[802] a cake of bread and one of dates and one of raisins to each one.[376] Then all the people departed each to his house.

20 But when David returned to bless[1288] his household, Michal the daughter of Saul came out to meet David and said, "How the king of Israel distinguished himself today! [a]He uncovered[1540] himself today in the eyes of his servants' maids as one of the [b]foolish ones shamelessly uncovers himself!"

21 So David said to Michal, "[a]*It was* before the LORD, who chose[977] me above your father[1] and above all his house, to appoint[6680] me ruler over the people of the LORD, over Israel; therefore I will celebrate before the LORD.

22 "And I will be more lightly esteemed[7043] than this and will be humble in my own eyes, but with the maids of whom you have spoken, with them I will be distinguished."

23 And Michal the daughter of Saul had no child to the day of her death.[4194]

David Plans to Build a Temple

7 🔑 [a]Now it came about when the king[4428] lived in his house, and the LORD had given him rest on every side from all his enemies,

2 that the king said to [a]Nathan the prophet, "See now, I dwell in [b]a house of cedar, but the ark[727] of God[430] [c]dwells within tent curtains."

3 And Nathan said to the king, "[a]Go, do[6213] all that is in your mind, for the LORD is with you."

🔑 4 But it came about in the same night that the word[1697] of the LORD came to Nathan, saying,

5 "Go and say to My servant David, 'Thus says the LORD, "[a]Are you the one who should build Me a house to dwell in?

6 "For [a]I have not dwelt in a house since the day I brought[5927] up the sons[1121] of Israel from Egypt, even to this day;[3117] but I have been moving about [b]in a tent, even in a [1]tabernacle.

7 "[a]Wherever I have gone with all the sons of Israel, did I speak a word with one of the tribes of Israel, [b]which I commanded[6680] to shepherd My people Israel, saying, 'Why have you not built Me a house of cedar?' " '

God's Covenant with David

8 "Now therefore, thus you shall say to My servant David, 'Thus says the LORD of hosts, "[a]I took you from the pasture,[5116] from following the sheep, [b]that you should be ruler over My people Israel.

9 "And [a]I have been with you wherever you have gone and [b]have cut[3772] off all your enemies from before you; and I will make you a great name, like the names of the great men who are on the earth.[776]

10 "I will also appoint[7760] a place for My people Israel and [a]will plant them, that they may live[7931] in their own place and not be disturbed again, [b]nor will the

---

17 [a]1Chr. 15:1; 2Chr. 1:4 [b]1Kin. 8:62-65
18 [a]1Kin. 8:14, 15
20 [a]2Sam. 6:14, 16; Eccl. 7:17 [b]Judg. 9:4
21 [a]1Sam. 13:14; 15:28
1 [a]1Chr. 17:1-27
2 [a]2Sam. 7:17; 12:1; 1Kin. 1:22; 1Chr. 29:29; 2Chr. 9:29 [b]2Sam. 5:11 [c]Ex. 26:1
3 [a]1Kin. 8:17, 18; 1Chr. 22:7
5 [a]1Kin. 5:3, 4; 8:19
6 [1]Lit., *dwelling place* [a]Josh. 18:1; 1Kin. 8:16 [b]Ex. 40:18, 34
7 [a]Lev. 26:11, 12 [b]2Sam. 5:2
8 [a]1Sam. 16:11, 12; Ps. 78:70, 71 [b]2Sam. 6:21
9 [a]1Sam. 5:10 [b]Ps. 18:37-42
10 [a]Ex. 15:17; Is. 5:2, 7 [b]Ps. 89:22, 23; Is. 60:18

🔑 **7:1-29** See I Chr. 17:1-27.

🔑 **7:4-16** Shortly after David transferred his residence to Jerusalem he had the ark of the Lord brought up also (II Sam. 6:12-19). Shortly afterward, he proposed that it was not right for him to dwell in a house of cedar while the Lord dwells in a tent (v. 2). The Lord answered through the prophet Nathan that His house would be built by David's son (v. 13). The reason given was that David had been a man who shed blood (I Kgs. 5:3; I Chr. 22:8; 28:3). He had been a man of war, not peace. Nevertheless,

(continued on next page)

[I]wicked[5766] afflict them any more as formerly,

11 even [a]from the day that I commanded judges[8199] to be over My people Israel; and [b]I will give you rest from all your enemies. The LORD also declares to you that [c]the LORD will make a house for you.

12 "[a]When your days are complete and you [b]lie down with your fathers,[1] [c]I will raise up your [I]descendant after you, who will come forth from [II]you, and I will establish his kingdom.[4467]

13 "[a]He shall build a house for My name, and [b]I will establish the throne of his kingdom forever.

🔑 14 "[a]I will be a father[1] to him and he will be a son to Me; [b]when he commits iniquity,[5753] I will correct[3198] him with the rod of men and the strokes of the sons[1121] of men,

15 but My lovingkindness shall not depart[5493] from him, [a]as I took *it* away from Saul, whom I removed from before you.

16 "And [a]your house and your kingdom shall endure[539] before [I]Me forever; your throne shall be established[3559] forever." ' "

17 In accordance with all these words[1697] and all this vision,[2384] so Nathan spoke to David.

David's Prayer

18 Then David the king went in and sat before the LORD, and he said, "[a]Who am I, O Lord[136] [I]GOD, and what is my house, that Thou hast brought me this far?

19 "And yet this was insignificant in Thine eyes, O Lord GOD, [a]for Thou hast spoken also of the house of Thy servant concerning the distant future. And [b]this is the [I]custom of man, O Lord GOD.

20 "And again what more can David say to Thee? For [a]Thou knowest[3045] Thy servant, O Lord GOD!

21 "[a]For the sake of Thy word, and according to Thine own heart, Thou hast done[6213] all this greatness to let Thy servant know.[3045]

22 "For this reason [a]Thou art great, O Lord GOD; for [b]there is none like Thee, and there is no God besides Thee, [c]according to all that we have heard with our ears.[241]

23 "And [a]what one nation on the earth is like Thy people Israel, whom God went to redeem for Himself as a people and to make a name for Himself, and [b]to do a great thing for Thee and awesome things for Thy land,[776] before [c]Thy people whom [d]Thou hast redeemed for Thyself from Egypt, *from* nations and their gods?

🔑 24 "For [a]Thou hast established[3559] for Thyself Thy people Israel as Thine own people forever, and [b]Thou, O LORD, hast become[1961] their God.

25 "Now therefore, O LORD God, the word that Thou hast spoken concerning Thy servant and his house, confirm *it* forever, and do as Thou hast spoken,

26 [a]that Thy name may be magnified forever, by saying, 'The LORD of hosts is God over Israel'; and may the house of Thy servant David be established before Thee.

10 [I]Lit., *sons of wickedness*
11 [a]Judg. 2:14-16; 1Sam. 12:9-11 [b]2Sam. 7:1 [c]1Sam. 25:28; 2Sam. 7:27
12 [I]Lit., *seed* [II]Lit., *your bowels* [a]1Kin. 2:1 [b]Deut. 31:16; Acts 13:36 [c]1Kin. 8:20; Ps. 132:11
13 [a]1Kin. 6:12; 8:19 [b]Is. 9:7; 49:8
14 [a]Ps. 89:26, 27; 2Cor. 6:18; Heb. 1:5 [b]1Kin. 11:34; Ps. 89:30-33
15 [a]1Sam. 15:23; 16:14
16 [I]So with Gr. and some ancient mss.; M.T., *you* [a]2Sam. 7:13; Ps. 89:36, 37
18 [I]Heb., *YHWH*, usually rendered *LORD*, and so throughout the ch. [a]Ex. 3:11; 1Sam. 18:18
19 [I]Or, *law* [a]2Sam. 7:11-16; 1Chr. 17:17 [b]Is. 55:8, 9
20 [a]1Sam. 16:7; John 21:17
21 [a]1Chr. 17:19; Eph. 4:32
22 [a]Deut. 3:24; Ps. 48:1; 86:10 [b]Ex. 15:11; 1Sam. 2:2 [c]Ex. 10:2; Ps. 44:1
23 [a]Deut. 4:32-38 [b]Deut. 10:21 [c]Deut. 15:15 [d]Deut. 9:26
24 [a]Deut. 32:6 [b]Gen. 17:7, 8; Ex. 6:7
26 [a]Ps. 72:18, 19; Matt. 6:9

(continued from previous page)
God intended to bless David. In fact, the promise that He made to him was an extension of the promise to Abraham (Gen. 17:6). God would make him a prince over his people giving him royal authority (v. 8). The Lord would make for him a great name, thus establishing his dynasty (v. 9). He would give him a kingdom to reign over, including both land and people (v. 10). His house and kingdom would last forever (v. 16). This is certainly a reference to the continuance of the Kingdom of God through Christ, who was to be *the* descendant of the house of David (Lk. 1:31-33; Acts 2:25-35).

🔑 **7:14** Eventually this referred to Jesus Christ, the promised Descendant of David (Lk. 1:32,33), who occupies the eternal throne as God's Son (Heb. 1:5). See Ps. 2:7; Acts 13:33; Heb. 5:5.

🔑 **7:24** These words contain the central promise of both the O.T. and N.T. (Gen. 17:7; Ex. 6:7; Rev. 21:3).

27 "For Thou, O LORD of hosts, the God of Israel, hast [I]made a revelation to Thy servant, saying, '[a]I will build you a house'; therefore Thy servant has found [II]courage to pray this prayer to Thee.

28 "And now, O Lord GOD, Thou art God, and [a]Thy words are truth, and Thou hast [I]promised this good thing to Thy servant.

29 "Now therefore, may it please Thee to bless[1288] the house of Thy servant, that it may continue forever before Thee. For Thou, O Lord GOD, hast spoken; and [a]with Thy blessing[1293] may the house of Thy servant be blessed[1288] forever."

David's Triumphs

8 [a]Now after this it came about that David [I]defeated the Philistines and subdued them; and David took [II]control of the chief city from the hand of the Philistines.

2 And [a]he [I]defeated [b]Moab, and measured them with the line,[2256] making them lie down on the ground;[776] and he measured two lines[2256] to put to death[4191] and one full line to keep alive. And [c]the Moabites became servants to David, [d]bringing[5375] tribute.[4503]

3 Then David [I]defeated [a]Hadadezer, the son of Rehob king[4428] of Zobah, as [b]he went to restore his [II]rule at the [III]River.

4 And David captured from him 1,700 horsemen and 20,000 foot soldiers; and David [a]hamstrung[6131] the chariot horses, but reserved *enough* of them for 100 chariots.

5 And when [a]the Arameans of Damascus came to help[5826] Hadadezer, king of Zobah, David [I]killed 22,000 Arameans.

6 Then David put garrisons among the Arameans of Damascus, and [a]the Arameans became servants to David, bringing tribute. And [b]the LORD helped David wherever he went.

7 And David took the shields of gold which were [I]carried by the servants of Hadadezer, and brought them to Jerusalem.

8 And from [I]Betah and from [a]Berothai, cities of Hadadezer, King David took a very large amount of bronze.

9 Now when Toi king of [a]Hamath heard that David had [I]defeated all the army of Hadadezer,

10 Toi sent [I]Joram his son to King David to [II]greet him and bless[1288] him, because he had fought against Hadadezer and [III]defeated him; for Hadadezer [IV]had been at war with Toi. And [V]*Joram* brought with him articles of silver, of gold and of bronze.

11 King David also [a]dedicated[6942] these to the LORD, with the silver and gold that he had dedicated from all the nations which he had subdued:

12 from [I]Aram and [a]Moab and [b]the sons[1121] of Ammon and [c]the Philistines and [d]Amalek, and from the spoil of Hadadezer, son of Rehob, king of Zobah.

13 So [a]David made a name *for himself* when he returned from [I]killing[5221] 18,000 [II]Arameans in [b]the Valley of Salt.

14 And he put garrisons in Edom. In all Edom he put garrisons, and [a]all the Edomites became servants to David. And [b]the LORD helped David wherever he went.

15 So David reigned over all Israel; and David [I]administered[6213] justice[4941]

27 [I]Lit., *uncovered the ear of* [II]Lit., *his heart* [a]2Sam. 7:13
28 [I]Or, *spoken* [a]Ex. 34:6; John 17:17
29 [a]Num. 6:24-26
1 [I]Lit., *smote* [II]Lit., *the bridle of the mother city* [a]1Chr. 18
2 [I]Lit., *smote* [a]Num. 24:17 [b]1Sam. 22:3, 4 [c]2Sam. 8:6; 1Kin. 4:21 [d]2Kin. 3:4; 17:3
3 [I]Lit., *smote* [II]Lit., *hand* [III]I.e., Euphrates [a]1Sam. 14:47; 2Sam. 10:16, 19 [b]2Sam. 10:15-19
4 [a]Josh. 11:6, 9
5 [I]Lit., *smote* [a]1Kin. 11:23-25
6 [a]2Sam. 8:2 [b]2Sam. 3:18
7 [I]Lit., *on*
8 [I]In 1Chr. 18:8, *Tibhath* [a]Ezek. 47:16
9 [I]Lit., *smitten* [a]1Kin. 8:65; 2Chr. 8:4
10 [I]In 1Chr. 18:10, *Hadoram* [II]Lit., *ask him of his welfare* [III]Lit., *smitten* [IV]Lit., *was a man of wars* [V]Lit., *there were in his hand*
11 [a]1Kin. 7:51
12 [I]Some mss. read *Edom* [a]2Sam. 8:2 [b]2Sam. 10:14 [c]2Sam. 5:17-25 [d]1Sam. 27:8; 30:17-20
13 [I]Lit., *smiting* [II]Some mss. read *Edom* [a]2Sam. 7:9 [b]2Kin. 14:7
14 [a]Gen. 27:37-40; Num. 24:17, 18 [b]2Sam. 8:6
15 [I]Lit., *was doing*

7:27 "House" does not refer to a building, but a dynasty (a lineage).

8:1-14 See I Chr. 18:1-13.

8:13 I Chr. 8:12 records this same event. In Hebrew, there is only one letter difference between "Edom" and "Syria." However, the Syrians did sometimes ally themselves with Israel's enemies (II Sam. 8:5). As II Chr. 25:11 identifies the Edomites as inhabitants of the "valley of salt," it is more likely that the Edomites were the enemies here rather than the Syrians who lived a distance to the north of Israel.

8:15-18 See II Sam. 20:23-26; I Chr. 18:14-17.

and righteousness[6666] for all his people.

16 And [a]Joab the son of Zeruiah *was* over the army, and [b]Jehoshaphat the son of Ahilud *was* [c]recorder.

17 And [a]Zadok the son of Ahitub and Ahimelech the son of Abiathar *were* [b]priests, and Seraiah *was* [c]secretary.

18 And [a]Benaiah the son of Jehoiada [I]was over the [b]Cherethites and the Pelethites; and David's sons were [II][c]chief ministers.

David's Kindness to Mephibosheth

9 Then David said, "Is there yet [I]anyone left[3498] of the house of Saul, [a]that I may show him kindness[2617] for Jonathan's sake?"

2 Now there was a servant of the house of Saul whose name was Ziba, and they called[7121] him to David; and the king[4428] said to him, "Are you [a]Ziba?" And he said, "*I am* your servant."

3 And the king said, "Is there not yet anyone of the house of Saul to whom I may show the [a]kindness of God?"[430] And Ziba said to the king, "[b]There is still a son of Jonathan who is crippled in both feet."

4 So the king said to him, "Where is he?" And Ziba said to the king, "Behold, he is [a]in the house of Machir the son of Ammiel in Lo-debar."

5 Then King David sent and brought him from the house of Machir the son of Ammiel, from Lo-debar.

6 And [a]Mephibosheth, the son of Jonathan the son of Saul, came to David and [b]fell[5307] on his face and prostrated himself. And David said,[559] "Mephibosheth." And he said, "Here is your servant!"

7 And David said to him, "Do not fear,[3372] for [a]I will surely show kindness to you for the sake of your father[1] Jonathan, and [b]will restore to you all the [I]land of your [II]grandfather[1] Saul; and [c]you shall [III]eat at my table regularly."[8548]

8 Again he prostrated[7812] himself and said, "What is your servant, that you should regard [a]a dead[4191] dog like me?"

9 Then the king called Saul's servant Ziba, and said to him, "[a]All that belonged to Saul and to all his house I have given to your master's [I]grandson.

10 "And you and your sons and your servants shall cultivate the land[127] for him, and you shall bring in *the produce* so that your master's grandson may have food; nevertheless [a]Mephibosheth your master's grandson [b]shall [I]eat at my table regularly."[8548] Now Ziba had fifteen sons and twenty servants.

11 Then Ziba said to the king, "According [a]to all that my lord[113] the king commands[6680] his servant so your servant will do."[6213] So Mephibosheth ate at [I]David's table as one of the king's[4428] sons.

12 And Mephibosheth had a young son whose name was Mica. And all who lived in the house of Ziba were servants to Mephibosheth.

13 So Mephibosheth lived in Jerusalem, for [a]he ate at the king's table regularly. Now [b]he was lame in both feet.

Ammon and Aram Defeated

10 [key] [a]Now it happened afterwards that [b]the king[4428] of the Ammonites died,[4191] and Hanun his son became king in his place.

2 Then David said, "I will show kindness[2617] to Hanun the son of [a]Nahash, just as his father[1] showed kindness to me." So David sent [I]some of his servants to console[5162] him concerning his father. But when David's servants came to the land[776] of the Ammonites,

3 the princes of the Ammonites said to Hanun their lord,[113] "[I]Do you think that David is honoring your father because he has sent consolers[5162] to you? [a]Has David not sent his servants to you

16 [a]1Chr. 11:6 [b]1Kin. 4:3 [c]2Kin. 18:18, 37

17 [a]1Chr. 6:4-8 [b]1Chr. 16:39, 40 [c]2Kin. 18:18

18 [I]Lit., *and the Cherethites* [II]Lit., *priests* [a]1Kin. 4:4 [b]1Sam. 30:14; 2Sam. 15:18; 20:7, 23; 1Kin. 1:38, 44 [c]1Chr. 18:17

1 [I]Lit., *he who is* [a]1Sam. 20:14-17, 42

2 [a]2Sam. 16:1-4; 19:17, 29

3 [a]1Sam. 20:14 [b]2Sam. 4:4

4 [a]2Sam. 17:27-29

6 [a]2Sam. 16:4; 19:24-30 [b]1Sam. 25:23

7 [I]Lit., *field* [II]Lit., *father* [III]Lit., *eat bread* [a]2Sam. 9:1, 3 [b]2Sam. 12:8 [c]2Sam. 19:28; 1Kin. 2:7; 2Kin. 25:29

8 [a]2Sam. 16:9; 24:14

9 [I]Lit., *son* [a]2Sam. 16:4; 19:29

10 [I]Lit., *eat bread* [a]2Sam. 9:7, 11, 13 [b]2Sam. 19:28; 1Kin. 2:7

11 [I]Lit., *my* [a]2Sam. 16:1-4; 19:24-30

13 [a]2Sam. 9:7, 11 [b]2Sam. 9:3

1 [a]1Chr. 19:1-19 [b]1Sam. 11:1

2 [I]Lit., *by the hand of* [a]1Sam. 11:1

3 [I]Lit., *In your eyes is David honoring* [a]Gen. 42:9, 16

[key] **10:1-19** See I Chr. 19:1-19.

in order to search the city, to spy it
out and overthrow[2015] it?"
4 So Hanun took David's servants
and [a]shaved off half of their beards,[2206]
and [b]cut off[3772] their garments in the
middle as far as their hips, and sent
them away.
5 When they told *it* to David, he
sent to meet them, for the men were
greatly humiliated. And the king said,
"[I]Stay at Jericho until your beards grow,
and *then* return."
6 Now when the sons of Ammon
saw that [a]they had become odious to
David, the sons of Ammon sent and
[b]hired the Arameans of [c]Beth-rehob and
the [d]Arameans of Zobah, 20,000 foot
soldiers, and the king of [e]Maacah with
1,000 men, and the men of Tob with
12,000 men.
7 When David heard *of it,* he sent
Joab and all the army, the mighty men.
8 And the sons of Ammon came out
and drew up in battle array [a]at the entrance of the [I]city, while the Arameans
of Zobah and of Rehob and the men of
[b]Tob and Maacah *were* by themselves
in the field.[7704]
9 Now when Joab saw that [I]the battle was set against him in front and in
the rear, he selected[977] from all the
choice[977] men of Israel, and arrayed
them against the Arameans.
10 But the remainder of the people
he placed in the hand of Abishai his
brother,[251] and he arrayed *them* against
the sons of Ammon.
11 And he said, "If the Arameans
are too strong for me, then you shall
help me, but if the sons of Ammon are
too strong for you, then I will come to
help you.
12 "[a]Be strong,[2388] and let us show
ourselves courageous[2388] for the sake
of our people and for the cities of our
God;[430] and [b]may the LORD do[6213] what
is good in His sight."
13 So Joab and the people who were
with him drew near to the battle against
the Arameans, and [a]they fled before him.
🔑 14 When the sons of Ammon saw
that the Arameans fled, they *also* fled
before Abishai and entered the city.
[a]Then Joab returned from *fighting*
against the sons of Ammon and came
to Jerusalem.
15 When the Arameans saw that
they had been [I]defeated by Israel, they
gathered[622] themselves together.
16 [a]And Hadadezer sent and
brought out the Arameans who were
beyond the [I]River, and they came to
Helam; and [b]Shobach the commander[8269] of the army of Hadadezer
[II]led them.
17 Now when it was told David, he
gathered all Israel together and crossed
the Jordan, and came to Helam. And
the Arameans arrayed themselves to
meet David and fought against him.
18 But the Arameans fled before Israel, and David killed [a]700 charioteers
of the Arameans and 40,000 horsemen
and struck down Shobach the commander of their army, and he died there.
19 When all the kings,[4428] servants
of Hadadezer, saw that they were
[I]defeated by Israel, [a]they made peace
with Israel and served them. So the Arameans feared[3372] to help the sons of Ammon anymore.

Bathsheba, David's Great Sin

11 [a]Then it happened [I][b]in the spring,
at the time when kings go out
to battle, that David sent Joab and his
servants with him and all Israel, and
they destroyed[7843] the sons[1121] of Ammon and [c]besieged Rabbah. But David
stayed at Jerusalem.
2 Now when evening[6153] came David arose from his bed and walked
around on [a]the roof of the king's[4428]
house, and from the roof he saw a
woman[802] bathing;[7364] and the woman
was very beautiful[2896] in appearance.
3 So David sent and inquired about

4 [a]Is. 15:2; Jer. 41:5 [b]Is. 20:4
5 [I]Lit., *Return to*
6 [a]Gen. 34:30; 1Sam. 27:12 [b]2Sam. 8:3, 5; 2Kin. 7:6 [c]Judg. 18:28 [d]2Sam. 8:3 [e]Deut. 3:14
8 [I]Lit., *gate* [a]1Chr. 19:9 [b]Judg. 11:3, 5
9 [I]Lit., *the faces of the battle were against*
12 [a]Deut. 31:6; Josh. 1:6; 1Cor. 16:13 [b]1Sam. 3:18
13 [a]1Kin. 20:13-21
14 [a]2Sam. 11:1
15 [I]Lit., *smitten before*
16 [I]I.e., Euphrates [II]Lit., *before* [a]2Sam. 8:3-8 [b]1Chr. 19:16
18 [a]1Chr. 19:18
19 [I]Lit., *smitten before* [a]2Sam. 8:6
1 [I]Lit., *at the return of the year* [a]1Chr. 20:1 [b]2Sam. 10:14; 1Kin. 20:22, 26 [c]2Sam. 12:26-29; Jer. 49:2, 3; Amos 1:14
2 [a]Deut. 22:8; 1Sam. 9:25; Matt. 24:17; Acts 10:9

🔑 **10:14** It was too late in the year to undertake a full-scale siege. After the rain season was over, Joab commenced the next spring (II Sam. 11:1).

the woman. And one said, "Is this not
[a]Bathsheba, the daughter of Eliam, the
wife[802] of [b]Uriah the Hittite?"
🗝 4 And David sent messengers and
took her, and when she came to him,
[a]he lay with her; [b]and when she had
purified herself from her uncleanness,[2932] she returned to her house.
5 And the woman conceived; and
she sent and told David, and said, "[a]I
am pregnant."
6 Then David sent to Joab, *saying,*
"Send me Uriah the Hittite." So Joab
sent Uriah to David.
7 When Uriah came to him, [a]David
asked[7592] concerning the welfare of Joab
and [I]the people and the state of the
war.
8 Then David said to Uriah, "Go
down to your house, and [a]wash[7364] your
feet." And Uriah went out of the
king's[4428] house, and a present from the
king [I]was sent out after him.
9 But Uriah slept [a]at the door of
the king's house with all the servants
of his lord,[113] and did not go down to
his house.
10 Now when they told David, saying, "Uriah did not go down to his
house," David said to Uriah, "Have you
not come from a journey?[1870] Why did
you not go down to your house?"
11 And Uriah said to David, "[a]The
ark[727] and Israel and Judah are staying
in [I]temporary shelters, and my lord Joab
and [b]the servants of my lord are camping
in the open field.[7704] Shall I then go to
my house to eat and to drink and to
lie with my wife? By your life and the
life[2416] of your soul, I will not do[6213] this
thing."
12 Then David said to Uriah, "[a]Stay
here today[3117] also, and tomorrow I will
let you go." So Uriah remained in Jerusalem that day and the [I]next.
13 Now David called[7121] him, and
he ate and drank before him, and he
[a]made him drunk; and in the evening
he went out to lie on his bed [b]with his
lord's servants, but he did not go down
to his house.
14 Now it came about in the morning that David [a]wrote a letter[5612] to Joab,
and sent *it* by the hand of Uriah.
15 And [a]he had written in the letter,
saying, "[I]Place Uriah in the front line
of the [II]fiercest battle and withdraw from
him, [b]so that he may be struck down
and die."[4191]
16 So it was as Joab kept watch[8104]
on the city, that he put Uriah at the
place where he knew[3045] there *were* valiant men.
17 And the men of the city went
out and fought against Joab, and some
of the people among David's servants
fell;[5307] and [a]Uriah the Hittite also
died.[4191]
18 Then Joab sent and reported to
David all the events of the war.
19 And he charged[6680] the messenger, saying, "When you have finished[3615]
telling all the events of the war to the
king,
20 and if it happens that the king's
wrath[5927] rises and he says to you, 'Why
did you go so near to the city to fight?
Did you not know that they would shoot
from the wall?
21 'Who [a]struck down Abimelech
the son of Jerubbesheth? Did not a
woman throw an upper millstone on him
from the wall so that he died at Thebez?
Why did you go so near the wall?'—
then you shall say, 'Your servant Uriah
the Hittite is dead[4191] also.' "
22 So the messenger departed and
came and reported to David all that Joab
had sent him *to tell.*
23 And the messenger said to David, "The men prevailed against us and
came out against us in the field,[7704] but
we [I]pressed them as far as the entrance
of the gate.
24 "Moreover, the archers shot at
your servants from the wall; so some
of the king's servants are dead, and your
servant Uriah the Hittite is also dead."

3 [a]1Chr. 3:5 [b]2Sam. 23:39
4 [a]Ps. 51:title; James 1:14, 15 [b]Lev. 12:2-5; 15:18-28; 18:19
5 [a]Lev. 20:10; Deut. 22:22
7 [I]Lit., *welfare of* [a]Gen. 37:14; 1Sam. 17:22
8 [I]Lit., *went out* [a]Gen. 43:24; Luke 7:44
9 [a]1Kin. 14:27, 28
11 [I]Or, *booths* [a]2Sam. 7:2, 6 [b]2Sam. 20:6
12 [I]Lit., *morrow* [a]Job 20:12-14
13 [a]Prov. 20:1; 23:29-35 [b]2Sam. 11:9
14 [a]1Kin. 21:8-10
15 [I]Lit., *Give* [II]Lit., *strong* [a]Eccl. 8:11; Jer. 17:9 [b]2Sam. 12:9
17 [a]2Sam. 11:21
21 [a]Judg. 9:50-54
23 [I]Lit., *were upon*

🗝 **11:4** "Uncleanness" refers to menstruation (Lev. 15:19). Polygamy was strictly forbidden in Deut. 17:17.

25 Then David said to the messenger, "Thus you shall say to Joab, 'Do
not let this thing [I]displease you, for the
sword devours one as well as another;
make your battle against the city
stronger and overthrow it'; and *so*
encourage[2388] him."
26 Now when the wife of Uriah
heard that Uriah her husband was dead,
[a]she mourned for her husband.
27 When the *time of* mourning was
over, David sent and [I]brought[622] her to
his house and [a]she became his wife; then
she bore him a son. But [b]the thing that
David had done[6213] was evil[7489] in the
sight of the LORD.

Nathan Rebukes David

12 Then the LORD sent [a]Nathan
to David. And [b]he came to him,
and [I]said,
"There were two men in one city,
the one rich and the other
poor.
2 "The rich man had a great many
flocks and herds.
3 "But the poor man had nothing
except [a]one little ewe[3535]
lamb
Which he bought and nourished;
And it grew up together with
him and his children.[1121]
It would eat of his [I]bread and
drink of his cup and lie in his
bosom,
And was like a daughter to him.
4 "Now a traveler came to the rich
man,
And he [I]was unwilling to take
from his own flock or his own
herd,
To prepare[6213] for the
wayfarer[732] who had come to
him;
Rather he took the poor man's
ewe lamb and prepared[6213] it
for the man who had come
to him."
5 Then David's anger[639] burned[2734]
greatly against the man, and he said to
Nathan, "As the LORD lives,[2416] surely
the man who has done[6213] this [Ia]deserves
to die.[4194]
6 "And he must make restitution for
the lamb [a]fourfold, because he did[6213]
this thing and had no compassion."
7 Nathan then said to David, "[a]You
are the man! Thus says the LORD God[430]
of Israel, '[b]It is I who anointed[4886] you
king[4428] over Israel and it is I who
delivered[5337] you from the hand of
Saul.
8 'I also gave you [a]your master's
house and your master's wives[802] into
your [I]care, and I gave you the house
of Israel and Judah; and if *that had been*
too little, I would have added to you
many more things like these!
9 'Why [a]have you despised the
word[1697] of the LORD by doing[6213] evil[7451]
in His sight? [b]You have struck down[5221]
Uriah the Hittite with the sword,
[c]have taken his wife[802] to be your wife,
and have killed him with the sword of
the sons of Ammon.
10 'Now therefore, [a]the sword shall
never depart[5493] from your house, because you have despised Me and have

25 [I]Lit., *be evil in your sight*
26 [a]Gen. 50:10; Deut. 34:8; 1Sam. 31:13
27 [I]Lit., *gathered* [a]2Sam. 12:9 [b]Ps. 51:4,5
1 [I]Lit., *said to him* [a]2Sam. 7:2, 4, 17 [b]Ps. 51:title
3 [I]Lit., *morsel* [a]2Sam. 11:3
4 [I]Lit., *spared*
5 [I]Lit., *is a son of death* [a]1Sam. 26:16
6 [a]Ex. 22:1; Luke 19:8
7 [a]1Kin. 20:42 [b]1Sam. 16:13
8 [I]Lit., *bosom* [a]2Sam. 9:7
9 [a]1Sam. 15:23, 26 [b]2Sam. 11:14-17 [c]2Sam. 11:27
10 [a]2Sam. 13:28; 18:14; 1Kin. 2:25

12:1-14 This passage records the consequences of one of the blackest hours in David's life. He had been guilty of both adultery and murder. He had actually disobeyed four of the Ten Commandments of the Law: thou shalt not kill, thou shalt not commit adultry, thou shalt not steal and thou shalt not covet thy neighbor's wife. Nathan's parable has long been a focal point of moral teaching in the Bible. Though David's repentance was immediate and sincere, there would be necessary repercussions in David's life: (1) The sword would never depart from his house (v. 10). Observe that David was a man of war, and life was very difficult for the rest of his days. (2) Evil would come upon him out of his own house and his wives would be taken from him and shamed publicly (vv. 11,12). This was apparently fulfilled in II Sam. 16:22. (3) The child would die (v. 14). This was immediately fulfilled in II Sam. 12:15-19. This is an important event because it openly shows the presence of sin, even in the life of a man of God, and how that man responded with deep humility and repentance, even when its consequences plagued him throughout his life. (See Ps. 51.)

taken the wife of Uriah the Hittite to
be your wife.'
11 "Thus says the LORD, 'Behold,
I will raise up evil against you from your
own household; [a]I will even take your
wives before your eyes, and give *them*
to your companion, and he shall lie with
your wives in [I]broad daylight.
12 'Indeed [a]you did[6213] it secretly,
but [b]I will do this thing before all Israel,
and [I]under the sun.'"
🔑 13 Then David said to Nathan, "[a]I
have sinned against the LORD." And Nathan said to David, "The LORD also has
[Ib]taken away your sin; you shall not
die.[4191]
14 "However, because by this deed
you have [a]given occasion to the enemies
of the LORD to blaspheme,[5006] the
child[1121] also that is born to you shall
surely die."
15 So Nathan went to his house.

Loss of a Child

Then the LORD struck the child that
Uriah's [I]widow bore to David, so that
he was *very* sick.
16 David therefore inquired of God
for the child; and David [a]fasted and went
and [b]lay all night on the ground.[776]
17 And [a]the elders[2205] of his household stood beside him in order to raise
him up from the ground, but he was
unwilling and would[14] not eat food with
them.
18 Then it happened on the seventh
day[3117] that the child died.[4191] And the
servants of David were afraid[3372] to tell
him that the child was dead,[4191] for they
said, "Behold, while the child was *still*
alive,[2416] we spoke to him and he did
not listen to our voice. How then can
we tell him that the child is dead, since
he might do *himself* harm!"[7451]
19 But when David saw that his servants were whispering[3907] together, David perceived that the child was dead;
so David said to his servants, "Is the
child dead?" And they said, "He is dead."
20 So David arose from the ground,
[a]washed,[7364] anointed[5480] *himself,* and
changed his clothes; and he came into
the house of the LORD and [b]wor-
shiped.[7812] Then he came to his own
house, and when he requested, they
set food before him and he ate.
21 Then his servants said to him,
"What is this thing that you have done?
[I]While the child was alive, you fasted
and wept; but when the child died, you
arose and ate food."
22 And he said, "While the child was
still alive, [a]I fasted and wept; for I said,
'[b]Who knows, the LORD may be
gracious[2603] to me, that the child may
live.'[2416]
23 "But now he has died; why
should I fast? Can I bring him back again?
[a]I shall go to him, but [b]he will not return
to me."

Solomon Born

🔑 24 Then David comforted[5162] his
wife Bathsheba, and went in to her and
lay with her; and she gave birth to a
son, and [Ia]he named[7121] him Solomon.
Now the LORD loved[157] him
25 and sent *word* through Nathan
the prophet, and he named him [I]Jedidiah
for the LORD's sake.

War Again

🔑 26 [a]Now Joab fought against
[b]Rabbah of the sons of Ammon, and captured the royal city.
27 And Joab sent messengers to David and said, "I have fought against

11 [I]Lit., *the sight of this sun* [a]Deut. 28:30; 2Sam. 16:21, 22
12 [I]Lit., *before* [a]2Sam. 11:4-15 [b]2Sam. 16:22
13 [I]Lit., *caused your sin to pass away* [a]1Sam. 15:24, 30; 2Sam. 24:10; Luke 18:13 [b]Lev. 20:10; 24:17; Prov. 28:13; Mic. 7:18
14 [a]Is. 52:5; Rom. 2:24
15 [I]Lit., *wife*
16 [a]Neh. 1:4 [b]2Sam. 13:31
17 [a]Gen. 24:2
20 [a]Ruth 3:3; Matt. 6:17 [b]Ps. 95:6-8; 103:1, 8-17; Prov. 3:7
21 [I]Lit., *On account of*
22 [a]Is. 38:1-3 [b]Jon. 3:9
23 [a]Gen. 37:35 [b]Job 7:8-10
24 [I]Some mss. read *she* [a]1Chr. 22:9; Matt. 1:6
25 [I]I.e., beloved of the Lord
26 [a]1Chr. 20:1-3 [b]Deut. 3:11

🔑 **12:13** See David's Psalm 51 and Psalm 32 where he showed true contrition and expressed deep feelings of guilt before God pardoned him.

🔑 **12:24** Solomon was the fourth son of David and Bathsheba (I Chr. 3:5). Perhaps, after three years and two sons, Solomon was born.

🔑 **12:26-31** See I Chr. 20:1-3.

Rabbah, I have even captured the city
of waters.
28 "Now therefore, gather[622] the
rest of the people together and camp
against the city and capture it, lest
I capture the city myself and it be named
after me."
29 So David gathered[622] all the people and went to Rabbah, fought against
it, and captured it.
30 Then [a]he took the crown of
[I]their king[4428] from his head; and its
weight *was* a talent of gold, and *in it*
[II]*was* a precious stone; and it was *placed*
on David's head. And he brought out
the spoil of the city in great amounts.
31 He also brought out the people
who were in it, and [a]set *them* under
saws, sharp iron instruments,[2757] and
iron axes, and made them pass through
the brickkiln. And thus he did to all the
cities of the sons of Ammon. Then David
and all the people returned *to* Jerusalem.

Amnon and Tamar

13 Now it was after this that
[a]Absalom the son of David had
a beautiful sister whose name was
[b]Tamar, and [c]Amnon the son of David
loved[157] her.
2 And Amnon was so frustrated[3334]
because of his sister Tamar that he made
himself ill, for she was a virgin,[1330] and
it seemed [I]hard to Amnon to do[6213] anything to her.
3 But Amnon had a friend[7453] whose
name was Jonadab, the son of [I][a]Shimeah,
David's brother;[251] and Jonadab was a
very shrewd man.
4 And he said to him, "O son of
the king,[4428] why are you so depressed
morning after morning? Will you not tell
me?" Then Amnon said to him, "I am
in love[157] with Tamar, the sister of my
brother Absalom."
5 Jonadab then said to him, "Lie
down on your bed and pretend to be
ill; when your father[1] comes to see you,
say to him, 'Please let my sister Tamar
come and give me *some* food to eat,
and let her prepare[6213] the food in my
sight, that I may see *it* and eat from
her hand.' "
6 So Amnon lay down and pretended
to be ill; when the king[4428] came to see
him, Amnon said to the king, "Please
let my sister Tamar come and [a]make
me a couple of cakes in my sight, that
I may eat from her hand."
7 Then David sent to the house for
Tamar, saying, "Go now to your brother
Amnon's house, and prepare food for
him."
8 So Tamar went to her brother Amnon's house, and he was lying down.
And she took dough, kneaded *it,* made
cakes in his sight, and baked the cakes.
9 And she took the pan and [I]dished
them out before him, but he refused to
eat. And Amnon said, "[a]Have everyone
go out from me." So everyone went
out from him.
10 Then Amnon said to Tamar,
"Bring the food into the [I]bedroom, that
I may eat from your hand." So Tamar
took the cakes which she had made and
brought them into the bedroom to her
brother Amnon.
11 When she brought[5066] *them* to
him to eat, he [a]took hold of her and
said to her, "Come, lie with me, my
sister."
12 But she answered[559] him, "No,
my brother, do not violate me, for
[a]such a thing is not done[6213] in Israel;
do not do this [b]disgraceful thing!
13 "As for me, where could I
[I]get rid of my reproach? And as for you,
you will be like one of the [II]fools in Israel.
Now therefore, please speak to the king,
for [a]he will not withhold me from you."
14 However, he would[14] not listen
to [I]her; since he was stronger than she,
he [a]violated her and lay with her.
15 Then Amnon hated her with a
very great hatred; for the hatred with
which he hated her was greater than

30 [I]Or, *Malcam;* c.f. Zeph. 1:5 [II]Or, *were precious stones* [a]1Chr. 20:2
31 [a]1Chr. 20:3; Heb. 11:37
1 [a]2Sam. 3:2, 3; 1Chr. 3:2 [b]1Chr. 3:9 [c]2Sam. 3:2
2 [I]Lit., *hard in Amnon's eyes*
3 [I]In 1Sam. 16:9, *Shammah;* in 1Chr. 2:13, *Shimea* [a]1Sam. 16:9
6 [a]Gen. 18:6
9 [I]Lit., *poured* [a]Gen. 45:1
10 [I]Or, *inner room*
11 [a]Gen. 39:12
12 [a]Lev. 20:17 [b]Judg. 19:23; 20:6
13 [I]Lit., *cause to go* [II]Or, *disgraceful ones* [a]Gen. 20:12
14 [I]Lit., *her voice* [a]Lev. 18:9; Deut. 22:25; 27:22; 2Sam. 12:11

13:15 This passage proves that there can be desire without love. Once Amnon's lust was satisfied, a feeling of revulsion set in.

the love with which he had loved her. And Amnon said to her, "Get up, go away!"

16 But she said to him, "No, because this wrong[7451] in sending me away is greater than the other that you have done[6213] to me!" Yet he would not listen to her.

17 Then he called[7121] his young man who attended him and said, "Now throw this woman out of my *presence*, and lock the door behind her."

18 Now she had on [a]a [I]long-sleeved garment; for in this manner the virgin[1330] daughters of the king dressed themselves in robes. Then his attendant took her out and locked the door behind her.

19 And [a]Tamar put [I]ashes on her head, and [b]tore her [II]long-sleeved garment which *was* on her; and [c]she put[7760] her hand on her head and went away, crying aloud as she went.

20 Then Absalom her brother said to her, "Has Amnon your brother been with you? But now keep silent, my sister, he is your brother; do not take this matter to heart." So Tamar remained and was desolate[8076] in her brother Absalom's house.

21 Now when King David heard of all these matters, he was very angry.[2734]

22 But Absalom did not speak to Amnon [a]either good[2896] or bad;[7451] for [b]Absalom hated Amnon because he had violated his sister Tamar.

23 Now it came about after two full[3117] years that Absalom [a]had sheepshearers in Baal-hazor, which is near Ephraim, and Absalom invited[7121] all the king's sons.

Absalom Avenges Tamar

24 And Absalom came to the king and said, "Behold now, your servant has sheepshearers; please[4994] let the king and his servants go with your servant."

25 But the king said to Absalom, "No, my son, we should not all go, lest we be burdensome[3513] to you." Although he [I]urged him, he would not go, but blessed[1288] him.

26 Then [a]Absalom said, "If not, please let my brother Amnon go with us." And the king said to him, "Why should he go with you?"

27 But when Absalom [I]urged him, he let Amnon and all the king's sons go with him.

🗝 **28** And Absalom commanded[6680] his servants, saying, "See now, [a]when Amnon's heart is merry with wine, and when I say to you, 'Strike Amnon,' then put him to death.[4191] Do not fear;[3372] have not I myself commanded you? Be courageous[2388] and be [I]valiant."

29 And the servants of Absalom did[6213] to Amnon just as Absalom had commanded. Then all the king's sons arose and each mounted [a]his mule and fled.

30 Now it was while they were on the way[1870] that the report came to David, saying, "Absalom has struck down all the king's sons, and not one of them is left."[3498]

31 Then the king arose, [a]tore his clothes and [b]lay on the ground;[776] and all his servants were standing by with clothes torn.

32 And [a]Jonadab, the son of Shimeah, David's brother, [I]responded, "Do not let my lord[113] [II]suppose they have put to death all the young men, the king's sons, for Amnon alone is dead;[4191] because by the [III]intent[6310] of Absalom this has been determined[7760] since the day that he violated his sister Tamar.

33 "Now therefore, do not let my lord the king [a]take the report to [I]heart, namely, 'all the king's sons are dead,' for only Amnon is dead."

34 Now [a]Absalom had fled. And [b]the young man who was the watchman raised his eyes and looked,[7200] and

18 [I]Lit., *a varicolored tunic* [a]Gen. 37:3, 23
19 [I]Or, *dust* [II]Lit., *varicolored tunic* [a]1Sam. 4:12; Esth. 4:1 [b]Gen. 37:29; 2Sam. 1:11 [c]Jer. 2:37
22 [a]Gen. 31:24 [b]Lev. 19:17; 1John 2:9, 11; 3:10, 12, 15
23 [a]1Sam. 25:7
25 [I]Lit., *broke through*
26 [a]2Sam. 3:27; 11:13-15
27 [I]Lit., *broke through*
28 [I]Lit., *sons of valor* [a]Judg. 19:6, 9, 22; 1Sam. 25:36-38
29 [a]2Sam. 18:9; 1Kin. 1:33, 38
31 [a]2Sam. 1:11 [b]2Sam. 12:16
32 [I]Lit., *answered and said* [II]Lit., *say* [III]Lit., *mouth* [a]2Sam. 13:3-5
33 [I]Lit., *his heart* [a]2Sam. 19:19
34 [a]2Sam. 13:37, 38 [b]2Sam. 18:24

🗝 **13:28** Just as David had ruined another man's home, now his home was being destroyed. First there was incest, then a murder ensued.

behold, many people were coming from
the road behind him by the side of the
mountain.
35 And Jonadab said to the king,
"Behold, the king's sons have come;
according to your servant's word, so it
happened."
36 And it came about as soon as
he had finished[3615] speaking, that behold, the king's sons came and lifted
their voices and wept; and also the king
and all his servants wept [I]very bitterly.
37 Now [a]Absalom fled and went to
[b]Talmai the son of Ammihud, the king
of [c]Geshur. And *David* mourned for his
son every day.
38 [a]So Absalom had fled and gone
to Geshur, and was there three years.
39 And *the heart of* King David
longed[3615] to go out to Absalom; for
[a]he was comforted[5162] concerning Amnon, since he was dead.

The Woman of Tekoa

14 Now Joab the son of Zeruiah perceived that [a]the king's[4428] heart
was inclined toward Absalom.
2 So Joab sent to [a]Tekoa and
[I]brought a wise[2450] woman[802] from there
and said to her, "Please pretend to be
a mourner, and put on mourning garments now, and do not [b]anoint[5480] yourself with oil,[8081] but be like a woman
who has been mourning for the dead[4191]
many days;
3 then go to the king[4428] and speak
to him in this manner." So Joab put
[a]the words[1697] in her mouth.
4 Now when the woman of Tekoa
[I]spoke to the king, she fell[5307] on her
face[639] to the ground[776] and [a]pros-
trated[7812] herself and said, "[b]Help, O
king."
5 And the king said to her, "What
is your trouble?" And she [I]answered,[559]
"Truly I am a widow, for my husband
is dead.
6 "And your maidservant had two
sons, but the two of them struggled together in the field,[7704] and there was
no [I]one to separate them, so one struck
the other and killed him.
7 "Now behold, [a]the whole family[4940] has risen against your maidservant, and they say, 'Hand over the one
who struck his brother,[251] that we may
put him to death[4191] for the life[5315] of
his brother whom he killed, [b]and
destroy[8045] the heir also.' Thus they will
extinguish my coal which is left,[7604] so
as to [I]leave[7604] my husband neither name
nor remnant on the face of the earth."[127]
8 Then the king said to the woman,
"Go to your house, and I will give
orders[6680] concerning you."
🔑 9 And the woman of Tekoa said to
the king, "O my lord,[113] the king,
[a]the iniquity[5771] is on me and my father's[1]
house, but [b]the king and his throne are
guiltless."[5355]
10 So the king said, "Whoever
speaks to you, bring him to me, and
he will not touch you anymore."
11 Then she said, "Please let the
king remember the LORD your God,[430]
[a]*so that* the avenger of blood[1818] may
not continue to destroy,[7843] lest they
destroy my son." And he said, "[b]As the
LORD lives,[2416] not one hair of your son
shall fall to the ground."[776]
12 Then the woman said, "Please
let your maidservant speak a word[1697]
to my lord the king." And he said,
"Speak."
13 And the woman said, "[a]Why then
have you planned such a thing against
the people of God? For in speaking this
word the king is as one who is guilty,[818]
in that the king does not bring back
[b]his banished one.
14 "For [a]we shall surely die[4191] and
are [b]like water spilled on the ground

36 [I]Lit., *with a very great weeping*
37 [a]2Sam. 13:34 [b]2Sam. 3:3 [c]2Sam. 14:23, 32
38 [a]2Sam. 13:34
39 [a]2Sam. 12:19-23
1 [a]2Sam. 13:39
2 [I]Lit., *took* [a]2Sam. 23:26; 2Chr. 11:6; Amos 1:1 [b]2Sam. 12:20
3 [a]2Sam. 14:19
4 [I]Many mss. and ancient versions read *came* [a]1Sam. 25:23 [b]2Kin. 6:26-28
5 [I]Lit., *said*
6 [I]Lit., *deliverer between*
7 [I]Lit., *set* [a]Num. 35:19; Deut. 19:12, 13 [b]Matt. 21:38
9 [a]Gen. 43:9; 1Sam. 25:24 [b]1Kin. 2:33
11 [a]Num. 35:19, 21; Deut. 19:4-10 [b]1Sam. 14:45; 1Kin. 1:52; Matt. 10:30
13 [a]2Sam. 12:7; 1Kin. 20:40-42 [b]2Sam. 13:37, 38
14 [a]Job 30:23; 34:15; Heb. 9:27 [b]Ps. 58:7

🔑 **14:9** This woman from Tekoa was very shrewd. She knew that a pardon from David for an unpremeditated crime would not be enough to urge the king to forgive Absalom. Therefore, she induced David to grant a pardon against a much more serious guilt and to confirm it with an oath. So, David had no valid excuse for not accepting Absalom in a similar way.

which cannot be gathered[622] up again. Yet God does not take away life, but plans[2803] [I]ways so that [c]the banished one may not be cast out from him.

15 "Now [I]the reason I have come to speak this word to my lord the king is because the people have made me afraid;[3372] so your maidservant said, 'Let me now speak to the king, perhaps the king will perform the [II]request of his maidservant.

16 'For the king will hear [I]and deliver[5337] his maidservant from the [II]hand of the man who would destroy [III]both me and my son from [a]the inheritance[5159] of God.'

🗝 17 "Then your maidservant said, 'Please let the word of my lord the king be [I]comforting, for as [a]the angel[4397] of God, so is my lord the king to discern[8085] good[2896] and evil.[7451] And may the LORD your God be with you.' "

18 Then the king answered and said to the woman, "Please do not hide anything from me that I am about to ask[7592] you." And the woman said, "Let my lord the king please speak."

19 So the king said, "Is the hand of Joab with you in all this?" And the woman answered and said, "As your soul lives, my lord the king, no one can turn to the right or to the left from anything that my lord the king has spoken. Indeed, it was [a]your servant Joab who commanded me, and it was he who put all these words in the mouth of your maidservant;

20 in order to change the appearance of things your servant Joab has done[6213] this thing. But my lord is wise, [a]like the wisdom[2451] of the angel of God, to know[3045] all that is in the earth."

Absalom Is Recalled

21 Then the king said to Joab, "Behold now, [a]I will surely do this thing; go therefore, bring back the young man Absalom."

22 And Joab fell on his face to the ground, prostrated[7812] himself and blessed the king; then Joab said, "Today[3117] your servant knows that I have found favor[2580] in your sight, O my lord, the king, in that the king has performed[6213] the [I]request of his servant."

23 So Joab arose and went to [a]Geshur, and brought Absalom to Jerusalem.

24 However the king said, "Let him turn to [a]his own house, and let him not see my face." So Absalom turned to his own house and did not see the king's face.

25 Now in all Israel was no one as handsome as Absalom, so highly praised; [a]from the sole of his foot to the crown of his head there was no defect[3971] in him.

26 And when he [a]cut the hair of his head (and it was at the end of every year that he cut *it,* for it was heavy on him so he cut it), he weighed the hair of his head at 200 shekels by the king's weight.

27 And [a]to Absalom there were born three sons, and one daughter whose name was [b]Tamar; she was a woman of beautiful appearance.

28 Now Absalom lived two full[3117] years in Jerusalem, [a]and did not see the king's face.

29 Then Absalom sent for Joab, to send him to the king, but he would[14] not come to him. So he sent again a second time, but he would not come.

30 Therefore he said to his servants, "See, [a]Joab's [I]field is next to mine, and he has barley there; go and set it on fire." So Absalom's servants set the [I]field on fire.

31 Then Joab arose, came to Absalom at his house and said to him, "Why have your servants set my [I]field on fire?"

14 [I]Lit., *devices* [c]Num. 35:15, 25,28
15 [I]Lit., *that* [II]Lit., *word*
16 [I]Lit., *to* [II]Lit., *palm* [III]Lit., *together* [a]Deut. 32:9; 1Sam. 26:19
17 [I]Lit., *for rest* [a]1Sam. 29:9; 2Sam. 14:20; 19:27
19 [a]2Sam. 14:3
20 [a]2Sam. 14:17; 19:27
21 [a]2Sam. 14:11
22 [I]Lit., *word*
23 [a]Deut. 3:14; 2Sam. 13:37, 38
24 [a]2Sam. 13:20
25 [a]Deut. 28:35; Job 2:7; Is. 1:6
26 [a]Ezek. 44:20
27 [a]2Sam. 18:18 [b]2Sam. 13:1
28 [a]2Sam. 14:24
30 [I]Lit., *portion* [a]Judg. 15:3-5
31 [I]Lit., *portion*

🗝 **14:17** The Angel of God is more than an ordinary angel. This was the infallible Guide of Israel, distinct from God the Father, yet possessing the attributes of deity and to be identified with the preincarnate Christ (Gen. 16:7-13; Ex. 3:2-5).

32 And Absalom [I]answered Joab,
"Behold, I sent for you, saying, 'Come
here, that I may send you to the king,
to say, "Why have I come from Geshur?
It would be better for me still to be
there." ' Now therefore, let me see the
king's face; [a]and if there is iniquity in
me, let him put me to death."
33 So when Joab came to the king
and told him, he called[7121] for Absalom.
Thus he came to the king and prostrated
himself on his face to the ground before
the king, and [a]the king kissed[5401] Absalom.

Absalom's Conspiracy

15 Now it came about after this
that [a]Absalom provided for himself a chariot and horses, and fifty men
as runners before him.
2 And Absalom used to rise early
and [a]stand beside the way[1870] to the
gate; and it happened that when any
man had a suit[7379] to come to the king[4428]
for judgment,[4941] Absalom would call[7121]
to him and say, "From what city are
you?" And he would say, "Your servant
is from one of the tribes of Israel."
3 Then Absalom would say to him,
"See, [a]your [I]claims are good[2896] and
right, but no man listens to you on the
part of the king."
4 Moreover, Absalom would say,
"[a]Oh that one would appoint me judge[8199]
in the land,[776] then every man who has
any suit or cause[4941] could come to me,
and I would give him justice."[6663]
5 And it happened that when a man
came near to prostrate[7812] himself before him, he would put out his hand and
take hold of him and [a]kiss[5401] him.
6 And in this manner Absalom
dealt[6213] with all Israel who came to the
king for judgment; [a]so Absalom stole
away the hearts of the men of Israel.
7 Now it came about at the end of
[I]forty years that Absalom said to the
king, "Please let me go and pay my vow
which I have vowed[5087] to the LORD,
in [a]Hebron.
8 "For your servant [a]vowed a vow
while I was living at Geshur in Aram,
saying, '[b]If the LORD shall indeed bring
me back to Jerusalem, then I will serve
the LORD.' "
9 And the king said to him, "Go in
peace." So he arose and went to Hebron.
10 But Absalom sent spies throughout all the tribes of Israel, saying, "As
soon as you hear the sound of the trumpet, then you shall say, '[a]Absalom is
king in Hebron.' "
11 Then two hundred men went
with Absalom from Jerusalem, [a]who
were invited and [b]went [I]innocently, and
they did not know[3045] anything.
12 And Absalom sent for [a]Ahitho-
phel the Gilonite, David's counselor,[3289]
from his city [b]Giloh, while he was
offering[2076] the sacrifices. And the conspiracy was strong, for [c]the people increased continually with Absalom.

David Flees Jerusalem

13 Then a messenger came to David, saying, "[a]The hearts of the men
of Israel are [I]with Absalom."
14 And David said to all his servants
who were with him at Jerusalem, "[a]Arise
and let us flee, for *otherwise* none of
us shall escape[6413] from Absalom. Go
in haste, lest he overtake us quickly
and bring down calamity[7451] on us and
strike the city with the edge[6310] of the
sword."
15 Then the king's[4428] servants said
to the king, "Behold, your servants *are*

32 [I]Lit., *said to* [a]1Sam. 20:8; Prov. 28:13
33 [a]Gen. 33:4; Luke 15:20
1 [a]1Kin. 1:5
2 [a]Ruth 4:1; 2Sam. 19:8
3 [I]Lit., *words* [a]Prov. 12:2
4 [a]Judg. 9:29
5 [a]2Sam. 14:33; 20:9
6 [a]Rom. 16:18
7 [I]Some ancient versions render *four* [a]2Sam. 3:2, 3
8 [a]2Sam. 13:37, 38 [b]Gen. 28:20, 21
10 [a]1Kin. 1:34; 2Kin. 9:13
11 [I]Lit., *in their integrity* [a]1Sam. 9:13 [b]1Sam. 22:15
12 [a]2Sam. 15:31 [b]Josh. 15:51 [c]Ps. 3:1
13 [I]Lit., *after* [a]Judg. 9:3; 2Sam. 15:6
14 [a]2Sam. 12:11; Ps. 3:title

15:1 These were signs that Absalom was assuming royal power (I Sam. 8:11). David was showing weakness by allowing this to happen.

15:2 Judicial cases were decided at the city gate (Deut. 21:19; 22:15).

15:12 I Chr. 27:33 shows that Ahithophel had been a member of David's cabinet. Perhaps Ahithophel turned against David because he was Bathsheba's grandfather (compare II Sam. 11:3 and II Sam. 23:34).

ready to do whatever my lord[113] the king
chooses."[977]
16 So the king went out and all his
household [I]with him. But [a]the king
left[5800] ten concubines[802] to keep[8104] the
house.
17 And the king went out and all
the people [I]with him, and they stopped
at the last house.
🔑18 Now all his servants passed on
beside him, [a]all the Cherethites, all the
Pelethites, and all the Gittites, [b]six hundred men who had come [I]with him from
Gath, passed on before the king.
19 Then the king said to [a]Ittai the
Gittite, "Why will you also go with us?
Return and remain with the king, for
you are a foreigner and also an exile;[1540]
return to your own place.
20 "You came *only* yesterday, and
shall I today[3117] make you wander with
us, while [a]I go where I will? Return and
take back your brothers;[251] [b]mercy and
[I]truth be with you."
21 But Ittai answered the king[4428]
and said, "As the LORD lives,[2416] and
as my lord the king lives, surely
[a]wherever my lord the king may be,
whether for death[4194] or for life,[2416]
there also your servant will be."
22 Therefore David said to Ittai,
"Go and pass over." So Ittai the Gittite
passed over with all his men and all the
little ones who *were* with him.
23 While all the country[776] was
weeping with a loud voice, all the people
passed over. The king also passed over
[a]the brook Kidron, and all the people
passed over toward [b]the way of the wilderness.
24 Now behold, [a]Zadok also *came,*
and all the Levites with him [b]carrying[5375]
the ark[727] of the covenant[1285] of God.[430]
And they set down the ark of God, and
[c]Abiathar came up until all the people
had finished[8552] passing from the city.

16 [I]Lit., *at his feet* [a]2Sam. 16:21, 22
17 [I]Lit., *at his feet*
18 [I]Lit., *at his feet* [a]2Sam. 8:18 [b]1Sam. 23:13; 25:13; 30:1, 9
19 [a]2Sam. 18:2
20 [I]Or, *faithfulness* [a]1Sam. 23:13 [b]2Sam. 2:6
21 [a]Ruth 1:16, 17; Prov. 17:17
23 [a]1Kin. 15:13; 2Chr. 29:16 [b]2Sam. 15:28; 16:2
24 [a]2Sam. 8:17; 20:25 [b]Num. 4:15; 1Sam. 4:4, 5 [c]1Sam. 22:20
25 [a]Ps. 43:3 [b]Ex. 15:13; Jer. 25:30
26 [I]Lit., *in His sight* [a]2Sam. 11:27; 1Chr. 21:7 [b]1Sam. 3:18
27 [a]1Sam. 9:6-9 [b]2Sam. 17:17
28 [a]Josh. 5:10; 2Sam. 17:16
30 [a]Esth. 6:12; Ezek. 24:17, 23 [b]Is. 20:2-4
31 [a]2Sam. 15:12 [b]2Sam. 16:23; 17:14, 23
32 [I]Or, *tunic* [II]Lit., *ground* [a]Josh. 16:2
33 [a]2Sam. 19:35
34 [a]2Sam. 16:19

25 And the king said to Zadok, "Return the ark of God to the city. If I
find favor[2580] in the sight of the LORD,
then [a]He will bring me back again, and
show me both it and [b]His habitation.
26 "But if He should say thus, '[a]I
have no delight[2654] in you,' behold, here
I am, [b]let Him do[6213] to me as seems
good [I]to Him."
27 The king said also to Zadok the
priest, "Are you *not* [a]a seer? Return
to the city in peace and your [b]two sons
with you, your son Ahimaaz and Jonathan the son of Abiathar.
28 "See, I am going to wait [a]at the
fords of the wilderness until word[1697]
comes from you to inform me."
29 Therefore Zadok and Abiathar
returned the ark of God to Jerusalem
and remained there.
🔑**30** And David went up the ascent
of the *Mount of* Olives, and wept as
he went, and [a]his head was covered and
he walked [b]barefoot. Then all the people
who were with him each covered his
head and went up weeping as they went.
31 Now someone told David, say-
ing, "[a]Ahithophel is among the conspirators with Absalom." And David said,
"O LORD, I pray, [b]make the counsel[6098]
of Ahithophel foolishness."
32 It happened as David was coming
to the summit, where God was worshiped,[7812] that behold, Hushai the
[a]Archite met him with his [I]coat torn,
and [II]dust[127] on his head.
33 And David said to him, "If you
pass over with me, then you will be
[a]a burden[4853] to me.
34 "But if you return to the city,
and [a]say to Absalom, 'I will be your servant, O king; as I have been your
father's[1] servant in time past, so I will
now be your servant,' then you can
thwart[6565] the counsel of Ahithophel for
me.

🔑 **15:18** Originally, the 600 men had composed David's band of rebels and fled with him to the Philistine city of Gath to escape from King Saul (I Sam. 27:2) and then they continued with him in Ziklag, Hebron, and Jerusalem (I Sam. 30:1; II Sam. 2:3; 5:6). Now, some thirty years later, this honored unit of faithful veterans were still together.

🔑 **15:30** These were signs of mourning (Esth. 6:12; Ezek. 24:17).

35 "And are not Zadok and Abiathar the priests with you there? So it shall be that [a]whatever you hear from the king's house, you shall report to Zadok and Abiathar the priests.

36 "Behold [a]their two sons are with them there, Ahimaaz, Zadok's son and Jonathan, Abiathar's son; and [b]by them you shall send me everything that you hear."

37 So Hushai, [a]David's friend, came into the city, and [b]Absalom came into Jerusalem.

Ziba, a False Servant

16 Now when David had passed [a]a little beyond the summit, behold, [b]Ziba the servant of Mephibosheth met him [c]with a couple of saddled donkeys, and on them *were* two hundred loaves of bread, a hundred clusters of raisins, a hundred summer fruits, and a jug of wine.

2 And the king said to Ziba, "Why do you have these?" And Ziba said, "[a]The donkeys are for the king's[4428] household to ride, and the bread and summer fruit for the young men to eat, and the wine, [b]for whoever is faint in the wilderness to drink."

3 Then the king said, "And where is [a]your master's son?" And [b]Ziba said to the king, "Behold, he is staying in Jerusalem, for he said, 'Today[3117] the house of Israel will restore the kingdom[4468] of my father[1] to me.' "

⊶ 4 So the king said to Ziba, "Behold, all that belongs to Mephibosheth is yours." And Ziba said, "I prostrate[7812] myself; let me find favor[2580] in your sight, O my lord,[113] the king!"

David Is Cursed

5 When King David came to [a]Bahurim, behold, there came out from there a man of the family[4940] of the house of Saul [b]whose name was Shimei, the son of Gera; he came out [c]cursing[7043] continually as he came.

6 And he threw stones at David and at all the servants of King David; and all the people and all the mighty men were at his right hand and at his left.

7 And thus Shimei said when he cursed, "Get out, get out, [a]you man of bloodshed,[1818] and worthless[1100] fellow!

⊶ 8 "[a]The LORD has returned upon you all [b]the bloodshed[1818] of the house of Saul, in whose place you have reigned; and the LORD has given the kingdom into the hand of your son Absalom. And behold, you are *taken* in your own evil, for you are a man of bloodshed!"

9 Then [a]Abishai the son of Zeruiah said to the king, "Why should [b]this dead[4191] dog [c]curse[7043] my lord the king? Let me go over now, and [1]cut off his head."

10 But the king said, "[a]What have I to do with you, O sons of Zeruiah? [b]If he curses, and if the LORD has told him, 'Curse David,' [c]then who shall say, 'Why have you done[6213] so?' "

11 Then David said to Abishai and to all his servants, "Behold, [a]my son who came out from [1]me seeks my life;[5315] how much more now this Benjamite? Let him alone and let him curse, [b]for the LORD has told[559] him.

12 "Perhaps the LORD will look on my affliction and [1a]return good[2896] to me instead of his cursing[7045] this day."

13 So David and his men went on the way;[1870] and Shimei went along on the hillside parallel with him and as he went he cursed, and cast stones and threw[6080] dust[6083] at him.

⊶ 14 And the king and all the people who were with him arrived weary and he refreshed himself there.

35 [a]2Sam. 17:15, 16
36 [a]2Sam. 15:27 [b]2Sam. 17:17
37 [a]2Sam. 16:16; 1Chr. 27:33 [b]2Sam. 16:15
1 [a]2Sam. 15:32 [b]2Sam. 9:2-13 [c]1Sam. 25:18
2 [a]Judg. 10:4 [b]2Sam. 17:29
3 [a]2Sam. 9:9, 10 [b]2Sam. 19:26, 27
5 [a]2Sam. 3:16; 17:18 [b]2Sam. 19:16-23; 1Kin. 2:8, 9, 44 [c]Ex. 22:28; 1Sam. 17:43
7 [a]2Sam. 12:9
8 [a]2Sam. 21:1-9 [b]2Sam. 1:16; 3:28, 29; 4:11, 12
9 [1]Lit., *take off* [a]1Sam. 26:8; 2Sam. 19:21; Luke 9:54 [b]2Sam. 9:8 [c]Ex. 22:28
10 [a]2Sam. 3:39; 19:22 [b]John 18:11 [c]Rom. 9:20
11 [1]Lit., *my body* [a]2Sam. 12:11 [b]Gen. 45:5; 1Sam. 26:19
12 [1]Lit., *the LORD will return* [a]Deut. 23:5; Rom. 8:28

⊶ **16:4** This decision was too hasty. According to II Sam. 19:24-28, Ziba was lying; Mephibosheth's loyalty to David never wavered.

⊶ **16:8** Here he was referring to the seven descendants of Saul whom David permitted to be killed by the Gibeonites at the time of the famine (II Sam. 21:1-9).

⊶ **16:14** He arrived at the fords of the Jordan River (II Sam. 15:28). David is believed to have written Psalm 3 and Psalm 63 while fleeing through the wilderness of Judah.

Absalom Enters Jerusalem

15 [a]Then Absalom and all the people, the men of Israel, entered Jerusalem, and Ahithophel with him.
16 Now it came about when [a]Hushai
the Archite, David's friend, came to Absalom, that [b]Hushai said to Absalom,
"[c]*Long* live the king! *Long* live the king!"
17 And Absalom said to Hushai, "Is
this your [I]loyalty[2617] to your friend?[7453]
[a]Why did you not go with your friend?"
18 Then Hushai said to Absalom,
"No! For whom the LORD, this people,
and all the men of Israel have chosen,[977]
his will I be, and with him I will remain.
19 "And besides, [a]whom should I
serve? *Should I* not *serve* in the presence
of his son? As I have served in your
father's[1] presence, so I will be in your
presence."
20 Then Absalom said to Ahithophel, "Give your advice.[6098] What shall
we do?"[6213]
21 And Ahithophel said to Absalom,
"[a]Go in to your father's concubines,
whom he has left to keep[8104] the house;
then all Israel will hear that you have
made yourself odious[887] to your father.
The hands of all who are with you will
also be strengthened."
🔑22 So they pitched a tent for Absalom on the roof, [a]and Absalom went in
to his father's concubines [b]in the sight
of all Israel.
23 And [a]the advice[3289] of Ahithophel, which he [I]gave in those days, *was*
as if one inquired[7592] of the word[1697] of
God; [b]so was all the advice of Ahithophel *regarded* by both David and Absalom.

Hushai's Counsel

17 Furthermore, Ahithophel said
to Absalom, "Please let me
choose[977] 12,000 men that I may arise
and pursue David tonight.
2 "And [a]I will come upon him while
he is weary and [I]exhausted and will
terrify[2729] him so that all the people who
are with him will flee. Then [b]I will strike
down the king[4428] alone,
3 and I will bring back all the people
to you. [I]The return of everyone depends
on the man you seek; *then* all the people
shall be at [a]peace."
4 So the [I]plan pleased Absalom and
all the elders[2205] of Israel.
5 Then Absalom said, "Now call[7121]
[a]Hushai the Archite also, and let us hear
what [I]he has to say."
6 When Hushai had come to Absalom, Absalom said to [I]him, "Ahithophel
has spoken [II]thus. Shall we [III]carry
out[6213] his plan? If not, you speak."
7 So Hushai said to Absalom, "[a]This
time the advice[6098] that Ahithophel has
[I]given is not good."[2896]
8 Moreover, Hushai said, "You
know[3045] your father[1] and his men, that
they are mighty men and they are
[I]fierce,[4751] [a]like a bear robbed of her
cubs in the field.[7704] And your father is
an [II]expert in warfare, and will not spend
the night with the people.
9 "Behold, he has now hidden himself in one of the [I]caves or in another
place; and it will be [II]when he falls[5307]
on them at the first attack, that whoever
hears *it* will say, 'There has been a
slaughter among the people who follow
Absalom.'
10 "And even the one who is valiant,
whose heart is like the heart of a lion,
[a]will completely [I]lose heart; for all Israel
knows that your father is a mighty man
and those who are with him are valiant
men.
11 "But I counsel[3289] that all Israel
be surely gathered[622] to you, [a]from Dan
even to Beersheba, [b]as the sand that
is by the sea in abundance, and that
[I]you personally go into battle.
12 "So we shall come to him in one
of the places where he can be found,
and we will [I]fall on him [a]as the dew
falls[5307] on the ground;[127] and of him

15 [a]2Sam. 15:12, 37

16 [a]2Sam. 15:37 [b]2Sam. 15:34 [c]1Sam. 10:24; 2Kin. 11:12

17 [I]Or, *kindness* [a]2Sam. 19:25

19 [a]2Sam. 15:34

21 [a]2Sam. 15:16; 20:3

22 [a]2Sam. 15:16; 20:3 [b]2Sam. 12:11, 12

23 [I]Lit., *advised* [a]2Sam. 17:14, 23 [b]2Sam. 15:12

2 [I]Lit., *slack of hands* [a]2Sam. 16:14 [b]1Kin. 22:31

3 [I]Lit., *Like the return of the whole is the man whom you seek* [a]Jer. 6:14

4 [I]Lit., *word was pleasing in the sight of*

5 [I]Lit., *is in his mouth—even he* [a]2Sam. 15:32-34

6 [I]Lit., *him, saying* [II]Lit., *according to this word* [III]Lit., *do his word*

7 [I]Lit., *advised* [a]2Sam. 16:21

8 [I]Lit., *bitter of soul* [II]Lit., *man of war* [a]Hos. 13:8

9 [I]Lit., *pits* [II]Lit., *according to a falling among them*

10 [I]Lit., *melt* [a]Josh. 2:9-11

11 [I]Lit., *your face go* [a]1Sam. 3:20 [b]Gen. 22:17; 1Sam. 13:5

12 [I]Lit., *settle down* [a]Ps. 110:3; Mic. 5:7

🔑 **16:22** See note on II Sam. 12:1-14. It was what Nathan predicted. Besides the fact that this was forbidden by God, it made reconciliation with David impossible and forced the people to take sides.

and of all the men who are with him, not even one will be left.[3498]

13 "And if he withdraws into a city, then all Israel shall bring[5375] ropes to that city, and we will [a]drag it into the [I]valley until not even a small stone is found there."

14 Then Absalom and all the men of Israel said, "The counsel of Hushai the Archite is better[2896] than the counsel of Ahithophel." For [a]the LORD had ordained[6680] to thwart[6565] the good counsel of Ahithophel, in order that the LORD might bring calamity[7451] on Absalom.

Hushai's Warning Saves David

15 Then [a]Hushai said to Zadok and to Abiathar the priests, "[I]This is what Ahithophel counseled Absalom and the elders of Israel, and [I]this is what I have counseled.[3289]

16 "Now therefore, send quickly and tell David, saying, '[a]Do not spend the night at the fords of the wilderness, but by all means cross over, lest the king and all the people who are with him be [I]destroyed.' "

17 [a]Now Jonathan and Ahimaaz were staying at [b]En-rogel, and a maidservant would go and tell them, and they would go and tell King David, for they could not be seen entering the city.

18 But a lad did see them, and told Absalom; so the two of them departed quickly and came to the house of a man [a]in Bahurim, who had a well in his courtyard, and they went down [I]into it.

19 And [a]the woman[802] [I]took a covering and spread it over the well's mouth and scattered grain on it, so that nothing was known.[3045]

20 Then Absalom's servants came to the woman at the house and said, "Where are Ahimaaz and Jonathan?" And [a]the woman said to them, "They have crossed the brook of water." And when they searched and could not find *them,* they returned to Jerusalem.

21 And it came about after they had departed that they came up out of the well and went and told King David; and they said to David, "[a]Arise and cross over the water quickly for thus Ahithophel has counseled against you."

22 Then David and all the people who *were* with him arose and crossed the Jordan; and by [I]dawn[216] not even one remained who had not crossed the Jordan.

23 Now when Ahithophel saw that his counsel was not [I]followed, he [II]saddled *his* donkey and arose and went to his home, to [a]his city, and [III][b]set his house in order, and [c]strangled himself; thus he died[4191] and was buried[6912] in the grave[6913] of his father.

24 Then David came to [a]Mahanaim. And Absalom crossed the Jordan, he and all the men of Israel with him.

25 And Absalom set [a]Amasa over the army in place of Joab. Now Amasa was the son of a man whose name was [I]Ithra the Israelite, who went in to Abigail the daughter of [b]Nahash, sister of Zeruiah, Joab's mother.

26 And Israel and Absalom camped in the land[776] of Gilead.

27 Now when David had come to Mahanaim, Shobi [a]the son of Nahash from [b]Rabbah of the sons[1121] of Ammon, [c]Machir the son of Ammiel from Lodebar, and [d]Barzillai the Gileadite from Rogelim,

28 brought[5066] [a]beds, basins,[5592] pottery,[3335] wheat, barley, flour, parched *grain,* beans, lentils, parched *seeds,*

⊶ 29 honey, curds, sheep, and cheese of the herd,[1241] for David and for the people who *were* with him, [a]to eat; for they said, "The people are hungry and weary and thirsty in the wilderness."

Absalom Slain

18 Then David [I]numbered the people who were with him and [a]set over them commanders[8269] of thousands and commanders of hundreds.

---

13 [I]Or, *wadi* [a]Mic. 1:6
14 [a]2Sam. 15:31, 34; Ps. 9:15, 16
15 [I]Lit., *Thus and thus* [a]2Sam. 15:35, 36
16 [I]Lit., *swallowed up* [a]2Sam. 15:28
17 [a]2Sam. 15:27, 36 [b]Josh. 15:7; 18:16
18 [I]Lit., *there* [a]2Sam. 3:16; 16:5
19 [I]Lit., *took and spread the covering* [a]Josh. 2:4-6
20 [a]Lev. 19:11; Josh. 2:3-5; 1Sam. 19:12-17
21 [a]2Sam. 17:15, 16
22 [I]Lit., *the light of the morning*
23 [I]Lit., *done* [II]Lit., *bound* [III]Lit., *gave charge to* [a]2Sam. 15:12 [b]2Kin. 20:1 [c]Matt. 27:5
24 [a]Gen. 32:2, 10; 2Sam. 2:8
25 [I]In 1Chr. 2:17, *Jether the Ishmaelite* [a]2Sam. 19:13; 20:9-12; 1Kin. 2:5, 32 [b]1Chr. 2:16
27 [a]1Sam. 11:1; 2Sam. 10:1, 2 [b]2Sam. 12:26, 29 [c]2 Sam.9:4 [d]2Sam. 19:31-39; 1Kin. 2:7
28 [a]Prov. 11:25; Matt. 5:7
29 [a]2Sam. 16:2, 14; Prov. 21:26; Eccl. 11:1; Rom. 12:13

1 [I]Lit., *mustered* [a]Ex. 18:25; Num. 31:14; 1Sam. 22:7

⊶ **17:29** David may have written Psalms 61 and 62 about this time.

2 And David sent the people out,
[a]one third under the [I]command of Joab,
one third under the [I]command of Abishai
the son of Zeruiah, Joab's brother,[251]
and one third under the [I]command of
[b]Ittai the Gittite. And the king[4428] said
to the people, "I myself will surely go
out with you also."
3 But the people said,[559] "[a]You
should not go out; for if we indeed flee,
they will not care about us, even if half
of us die,[4191] they will not care about
us. But [I]you are worth ten thousand
of us; therefore now it is better[2896] that
you *be ready* to help[5826] us from the city."
4 Then the king said to them,
"Whatever seems best to you I will
do."[6213] So [a]the king stood beside the
gate, and all the people went out by
hundreds and thousands.
5 And the king charged[6680] Joab and
Abishai and Ittai, saying, "*Deal* gently
for my sake with the young man Absalom." And [a]all the people heard when
the king charged[6680] all the commanders
concerning Absalom.
6 Then the people went out into the
field[7704] against Israel, and the battle
took place in [a]the forest of Ephraim.
7 And the people of Israel were
[I]defeated there before the servants of
David, and the slaughter there that
day[3117] was great, 20,000 men.
8 For the battle there was spread
over the whole countryside,[776] and the
forest devoured more people that day
than the sword devoured.
9 Now Absalom happened to meet
the servants of David. For Absalom was
riding on *his* mule, and the mule went
under the thick branches of a great oak.
And [a]his head caught[2388] fast in the oak,
so he was [I]left hanging between heaven
and earth,[776] while the mule that was
under him kept going.
10 When a certain man saw *it,* he
told Joab and said, "Behold, I saw Absalom hanging in an oak."
11 Then Joab said to the man who
had told him, "Now behold, you saw
him! Why then did you not strike him
there to the ground?[776] And I would have
given you ten *pieces* of silver and a
belt."[2290]
12 And the man said to Joab, "Even
if I should receive a thousand *pieces of*
silver in my hand, I would not put out
my hand against the king's[4428] son; for
[a]in our hearing the king charged[6680] you
and Abishai and Ittai, saying, '[I]Pro-
tect[8104] for me the young man Absalom!'
13 "Otherwise, if I had dealt
treacherously[8267] against his life[5315] (and
[a]there is nothing hidden from the king),
then you yourself would have stood
aloof."
14 Then Joab said, "I will not
[I]waste time here with you." [a]So he took
three spears in his hand and thrust them
through the heart of Absalom while he
was yet alive[2416] in the [II]midst of the
oak.
15 And ten young men who carried[5375] Joab's armor gathered around
and struck Absalom and killed him.
16 Then [a]Joab blew[8628] the trumpet, and the people returned from pursuing Israel, for Joab restrained the people.
17 And they took Absalom and cast
him into [I]a deep pit in the forest and
[a]erected[5324] over him a very great heap
of stones. And [b]all Israel fled, each[376]
to his tent.
18 Now Absalom in his lifetime[2416]
had taken and [a]set up for himself a pillar
which is in [b]the King's Valley, for he
said, "[c]I have no son [I]to preserve my
name." So he named[7121] the pillar after
his own name, and it is called Absalom's
monument to this day.

David Is Grief-stricken

19 Then [a]Ahimaaz the son of Zadok
said, "Please let me run and bring the
king news [b]that the LORD has [I]freed[8199]
him from the hand of his enemies."
20 But Joab said to him, "You are
not the man to carry news this day,
but you shall carry news another day;
however, you shall carry no news today
because the king's son is dead."[4191]
21 Then Joab said to the Cushite,

2 [I]Lit., *hand* [a]Judg. 7:16; 1Sam. 11:11 [b]2Sam. 15:19-22
3 [I]So with some ancient versions; M.T., *for now there are ten thousand like us* [a]2Sam. 21:17
4 [a]2Sam. 18:24
5 [a]2Sam. 18:12
6 [a]Josh. 17:15, 18; 2Sam. 17:26
7 [I]Lit., *smitten*
9 [I]Lit., *placed* [a]2Sam. 14:26
12 [I]So with some mss. and the ancient versions; M.T., *Take care whoever you are of* [a]2Sam. 18:5
13 [a]2Sam. 14:19, 20
14 [I]Lit., *tarry thus* [II]Lit., *heart* [a]2Sam. 14:30
16 [a]2Sam. 2:28; 20:22
17 [I]Lit., *the great* [a]Deut. 21:20, 21; Josh. 7:26; 8:29 [b]2Sam. 19:8; 20:1, 22
18 [I]Lit., *for the sake of remembering* [a]1Sam. 15:12 [b]Gen. 14:17 [c]2Sam. 14:27
19 [I]Lit., *vindicated* [a]2Sam. 15:36 [b]2Sam. 18:31

"Go, tell the king what you have seen." So the Cushite bowed[7812] to Joab and ran.

22 Now Ahimaaz the son of Zadok said once more to Joab, "But whatever happens, please let me also run after the Cushite." And Joab said, "Why would you run, my son, since [a]you will have no reward for going?"

23 "But whatever happens," *he said,* "I will run." So he said to him, "Run." Then Ahimaaz ran by way[1870] of the plain and passed up[5674] the Cushite.

24 Now [a]David was sitting between the two gates; and [b]the watchman went up to the roof of the gate by the wall, and raised his eyes and looked,[7200] and behold, a man running by himself.

25 And the watchman called[7121] and told the king. And the king said, "If he is by himself there is good news in his mouth." And he came nearer and nearer.

26 Then the watchman saw another man running; and the watchman called to the gatekeeper[7778] and said, "Behold, *another* man running by himself." And the king said, "This one also is bringing good news."

27 And the watchman said, "I [I]think the running of the first one[7223] [a]is like the running of Ahimaaz the son of Zadok." And the king said, "[b]This is a good man and comes with good[2896] news."

28 And Ahimaaz called and said to the king, "[I]All is well."[7965] And [a]he prostrated himself before the king with his face[639] to the ground. And he said, "[b]Blessed[1288] is the LORD your God,[430] who has delivered up the men who lifted their hands against my lord[113] the king."

29 And the king said, "[a]Is it well with the young man Absalom?" And Ahimaaz answered, "When Joab sent the king's servant, and your servant, I saw a great tumult, but [b]I did not know[3045] what *it was.*"

30 Then the king said, "Turn aside and stand here." So he turned aside and stood still.

31 And behold, the Cushite arrived, and the Cushite said, "Let my lord the king receive good news, for [a]the LORD has [I]freed you this day from the hand of all those who rose up against you."

32 Then the king said to the Cushite, "[a]Is it well with the young man Absalom?" And the Cushite answered, "[b]Let the enemies of my lord the king, and all who rise up against you for evil, be as that young man!"

33 [I]And the king was deeply moved and went up to the chamber over the gate and wept. And thus he said as he walked, "[a]O my son Absalom, my son, my son Absalom! [b]Would I had died[4191] instead of you, O Absalom, my son, my son!"

Joab Reproves David's Lament

19 Then it was told Joab, "Behold, [a]the king[4428] is weeping and mourns for Absalom."

2 And the [I]victory[8668] that day[3117] was turned to mourning for all the people, for the people heard *it* said that day, "The king is grieved for his son."

3 So the people went by stealth into the city that day, as people who are humiliated steal away when they flee in battle.

4 And the king [a]covered his face and [I]cried[2199] out with a loud voice, "[b]O my son Absalom, O Absalom, my son, my son!"

5 Then Joab came into the house to the king and said, "Today you have covered with shame the faces of all your servants, who today have saved your life[5315] and the lives[5315] of your sons and daughters, the lives of your wives,[802] and the lives of your concubines,

6 by loving[157] those who hate you,[8030] and by hating those who love you.[157] For you have shown today that [I]princes and servants are nothing to you; for I know this day that if Absalom were alive[2416] and all of us were dead[4191] today, then [II]you would be pleased.

7 "Now therefore arise, go out and speak [I]kindly[3820] to your servants, for

22 [a]2Sam. 18:29

24 [a]2Sam. 19:8 [b]2Sam. 13:34; 2Kin. 9:17

27 [I]Lit., *see* [a]2Kin. 9:20 [b]1Kin. 1:42

28 [I]Lit., *Peace.* [a]1Sam. 25:23; 2Sam. 14:4 [b]1Sam. 17:46

29 [a]2Sam. 20:9; 2Kin. 4:26 [b]2Sam. 18:22

31 [I]Lit., *vindicated* [a]Judg. 5:31; 2Sam. 18:19

32 [a]2Sam. 18:29 [b]1Sam. 25:26

33 [I]Ch. 19:1 in Heb. [a]2Sam. 19:4 [b]Ex. 32:32; Rom. 9:3

1 [a]2Sam. 18:5, 14

2 [I]Lit., *salvation*

4 [I]Lit., *the king cried* [a]2Sam. 15:30 [b]2Sam. 18:33

6 [I]Or, *commanders* [II]Lit., *it would be right in your eyes*

7 [I]Lit., *to the heart*

I swear by the LORD, if you do not go
out, surely [a]not a man[376] will pass the
night with you, and this will be worse[7489]
for you than all the evil[7451] that has come
upon you from your youth until now."

David Restored as King

8 So the king arose and sat in the
gate. When they told all the people, saying, "Behold, the king is [a]sitting in the
gate," then all the people came before
the king.
Now [a]Israel had fled, each to his tent.
9 And all the people were quarreling
throughout all the tribes of Israel, saying, "[a]The king delivered us from the
[I]hand of our enemies and [b]saved[4422] us
from the [I]hand of the Philistines, but
now [c]he has fled out of the land[776] from
Absalom.
10 "However, Absalom, whom we
anointed[4886] over us, has died[4191] in battle. Now then, why are you silent about
bringing the king back?"
11 Then King David sent to
[a]Zadok and Abiathar the priests, saying,
"Speak to the elders[2205] of Judah, saying,
'Why are you the last to bring the king
back to his house, since the word of
all Israel has come to the king, *even* to
his house?
12 'You are my brothers;[251] [a]you are
my bone[6106] and my flesh.[1320] Why then
should you be the last to bring back
the king?'
13 "And say to [a]Amasa, 'Are you
not my bone[6106] and my flesh? [b]May
God[430] do[6213] so to me, and more also,
if you will not be [c]commander[8269] of the
army before me continually [d]in place of
Joab.'"
14 Thus he turned the hearts of all
the men of Judah [a]as one man, so that
they sent *word* to the king, *saying*, "Return, you and all your servants."
15 The king then returned and came
as far as the Jordan. And Judah came
to [a]Gilgal in order to go to meet the
king, to bring[5674] the king across the
Jordan.
16 Then [a]Shimei the son of Gera,
the Benjamite who was from Bahurim,
hurried and came down with the men
of Judah to meet King David.
17 And there were a thousand men
of Benjamin with him, with [a]Ziba the
servant of the house of Saul, and his
fifteen sons and his twenty servants with
him; and they rushed to the Jordan before the king.
18 Then they kept crossing the ford
to bring over the king's[4428] household,
and to do what was good[2896] in his sight.
And Shimei the son of Gera fell[5307] down
before the king as he was about to cross
the Jordan.
19 So he said to the king, "[a]Let not
my lord[113] consider[2803] me guilty,[5771] nor
remember what your servant did wrong
on the day when my lord the king came
out from Jerusalem, so that the king
should [I]take *it* to heart.
20 "For your servant knows[3045] that
I have sinned; therefore behold, I have
come today, [a]the first[7223] of all the house
of Joseph to go down to meet my lord
the king."
21 But Abishai the son of Zeruiah
answered and said, "[a]Should not Shimei
be put to death[4191] for this, [b]because
he cursed[7043] the LORD's anointed?"[4899]
22 David then said, "[a]What have I
to do with you, O sons of Zeruiah, that
you should this day be an adversary[7853]
to me? [b]Should any man be put to death
in Israel today? For do I not know[3045]
that I am king over Israel today?"
🔑 23 And the king said to Shimei,
"[a]You shall not die."[4191] Thus the king
swore to him.
🔑 **24** Then [a]Mephibosheth the [I]son of
Saul came down to meet the king; and
[b]he had neither [II]cared for[6213] his feet,
nor [II]trimmed his mustache,[8222] nor
[c]washed[3526] his clothes, from the day
the king departed until the day he came
home in peace.

7 [a]Prov. 14:28
8 [a]2Sam. 15:2; 18:24 [b]2Sam. 18:17
9 [I]Lit., *palm* [a]2Sam. 8:1-14 [b]2Sam. 5:20; 8:1 [c]2Sam. 15:14
11 [a]2Sam. 15:29
12 [a]2Sam. 5:1
13 [a]2Sam. 17:25 [b]1Kin. 19:2 [c]2Sam. 8:16 [d]2Sam. 3:27-39; 19:5-7
14 [a]Judg. 20:1
15 [a]Josh. 5:9; 1Sam. 11:14, 15
16 [a]2Sam. 16:5-13; 1Kin. 2:8
17 [a]2Sam. 16:1-4; 19:26, 27
19 [I]Lit., *set* [a]1Sam. 22:15; 2Sam. 16:6-8
20 [a]2Sam. 16:5
21 [a]2Sam. 16:7, 8 [b]Ex. 22:28
22 [a]2Sam. 3:39; 16:9, 10 [b]1Sam. 11:13
23 [a]1Kin. 2:8
24 [I]I.e., grandson [II]Lit., *done* [a]2Sam. 9:6-10 [b]2Sam. 12:20 [c]Ex. 19:10

🔑 **19:23** Compare I Kgs. 2:8,9. David had not really forgiven Shimei; it was only expedient for Shimei.
🔑 **19:24** These were signs of mourning (Ezek. 24:17).

25 And it was when he came from Jerusalem to meet the king, that the king said to him, "[a]Why did you not go with me, Mephibosheth?"

26 So he answered,[559] "O my lord, the king, my servant deceived me; for your servant said, 'I will saddle a donkey for myself that I may ride on it and go with the king,' [a]because your servant is lame.

27 "Moreover, [a]he has slandered your servant to my lord the king; but my lord the king is [b]like the angel[4397] of God, therefore do what is good in your sight.

28 "For [a]all my father's[1] household was nothing but dead[4194] men before my lord the king; [b]yet you set your servant among those who ate at your own table. What right do I have yet that I should [I]complain[2199] anymore to the king?"

29 So the king said to him, "Why do you still speak of your affairs? I have [I]decided, 'You and Ziba shall divide the land.'"

30 And Mephibosheth said to the king, "Let him even take it all, since my lord the king has come safely to his own house."

31 Now [a]Barzillai the Gileadite had come down from Rogelim; and he went on to the Jordan with the king to [I]escort him over the Jordan.

32 Now Barzillai was very old, being eighty years old;[1121] and he had [Ia]sustained the king while he stayed at Mahanaim, for he was a very great man.

33 And the king said to Barzillai, "You cross over with me and I will [I]sustain you in Jerusalem with me."

34 But Barzillai said to the king, "[a]How long [I]have I yet to live,[2416] that I should go up with the king to Jerusalem?

35 "I am [I]now [a]eighty years old. Can I distinguish[3045] between good and bad? Or can your servant taste what I eat or what I drink? Or can I hear anymore [b]the voice of singing men and women? [c]Why then should your servant be an added burden[4853] to my lord the king?

36 "Your servant would merely cross over the Jordan with the king. Why should the king compensate me *with* this reward?

37 "Please let your servant return, that I may die in my own city near the grave[6913] of my father[1] and my mother. However, here is your servant [a]Chimham, let him cross over with my lord the king, and do for him what is good in your sight."

38 And the king answered, "Chimham shall cross over with me, and I will do for him what is good in your sight; and whatever you [I]require of me, I will do for you."

39 All the people crossed over the Jordan and the king crossed too. The king then [a]kissed[5401] Barzillai and blessed[1288] him, and he returned to his place.

40 Now the king went on to Gilgal, and Chimham went on with him; and all the people of Judah and also [a]half the people of Israel [I]accompanied the king.

41 And behold, all the men of Israel came to the king and said to the king, "[a]Why had our brothers [b]the men of Judah stolen you away, and brought the king and his household and all David's men with him over the Jordan?"

42 Then all the men of Judah answered the men of Israel, "Because [a]the king is a close relative to [I]us. Why then [II]are you angry[2734] about this matter? Have we eaten at all at the king's *expense*, or has [III]anything been taken for us?"

43 But the men of Israel answered the men of Judah and said, "[Ia]We have ten parts in the king, therefore [I]we also have more *claim* on David than you. Why then did you treat us with contempt?[7043] Was it not [I]our advice[1697] first to bring back [I]our king?" Yet the words of the men of Judah were harsher than the words[1697] of the men of Israel.

Sheba's Revolt

20 Now [a]a worthless[1100] fellow happened to be there whose name

25 [a]2Sam. 16:17
26 [a]2Sam. 9:3
27 [a]2Sam. 16:3, 4 [b]2Sam. 14:17, 20
28 [I]Lit., *cry out* [a]2Sam. 21:6-9 [b]2Sam. 9:7, 10, 13
29 [I]Lit., *said*
31 [I]Lit., *send* [a]2Sam. 17:27-29; 1Kin. 2:7
32 [I]Or, *provided food for* [a]2Sam. 17:27-29
33 [I]Or, *provide food for*
34 [I]Lit., *are the days of the years of my life* [a]Gen. 47:8
35 [I]Lit., *today* [a]Ps. 90:10 [b]Eccl. 2:8; Is. 5:11, 12 [c]2Sam. 15:33
37 [a]2Sam. 19:40; 1Kin. 2:7; Jer. 41:17
38 [I]Lit., *choose*
39 [a]Gen. 31:55; Ruth 1:14; 2Sam. 14:33
40 [I]Lit., *crossed over with* [a]2Sam. 19:9, 10
41 [a]Judg. 8:1; 12:1 [b]2Sam. 19:11, 12
42 [I]Lit., *me* [II]Lit., *is it hot to you* [III]Or, *a gift* [a]2Sam. 19:12
43 [I]Singular in Heb. [a]2Sam. 5:1; 1Kin. 11:30, 31
1 [a]2Sam. 16:7

was Sheba, the son of [b]Bichri, a Benjamite; and he blew[8628] the trumpet and
said,
"[c]We have no portion in David,
Nor do we have inheritance[5159]
in [d]the son of Jesse;
[e]Every man to his tents, O
Israel!"
2 So all the men of Israel [I]withdrew
from following David, *and* followed
Sheba the son of Bichri; but the men
of Judah [II]remained steadfast to their
king,[4428] from the Jordan even to Jerusalem.
3 Then David came to his house at
Jerusalem, and [a]the king took the ten
women,[802] the concubines whom he had
left to keep[8104] the house, and placed
them under guard[4931] and provided them
with sustenance, but did not go in to
them. So they were shut up until the
day[3117] of their death,[4191] living[2424] as
widows.
4 Then the king said to [a]Amasa,
"Call out the men of Judah for me within
three days, and be present here yourself."
5 So Amasa went to call out *the men
of* Judah, but he [a]delayed longer than
the set time which he had appointed[3259]
him.
6 And David said to [a]Abishai, "Now
Sheba the son of Bichri will do us more
harm than Absalom; [b]take your lord's
servants and pursue him, lest he find
for himself fortified cities and escape
from our sight."
7 So Joab's men went out after him,
[a]along with the Cherethites and the
Pelethites and all the mighty men; and
they went out from Jerusalem to pursue
Sheba the son of Bichri.
8 When they were at the large stone
which is in [a]Gibeon, Amasa came
[I]to meet them. Now Joab was [II]dressed
in his military attire, and over it was a
belt[2290] with a sword in its sheath fastened at his waist; and as he went forward, it fell[5307] out.
9 And Joab said to Amasa, "Is it well
with you, my brother?"[251] And [a]Joab
took Amasa by the beard[2206] with his
right hand to kiss[5401] him.

Amasa Murdered

10 But Amasa was not on guard
against the sword which was in Joab's
hand so [a]he struck him in the belly with
it and poured out his inward parts[4578]
on the ground,[776] and did not *strike* him
again; and he died.[4191] Then Joab and
Abishai his brother pursued Sheba the
son of Bichri.
11 Now there stood by him one[376]
of Joab's young men, and said, "Whoever favors[2654] Joab and whoever is for
David, [a]*let him* follow Joab."
12 But Amasa lay wallowing[1556] in
his blood in the middle of the highway.
And when the man saw that all the people stood still, he [I]removed Amasa from
the highway into the field[7704] and threw
a garment over him when he saw that
everyone who came by him stood still.

Revolt Put Down

13 As soon as he was removed from
the highway, all the men passed on after
Joab to pursue Sheba the son of Bichri.
14 Now he went through all the
tribes of Israel to Abel even to Beth-
maacah and all the Berites; and they
were gathered together and also went
after him.
15 And they came and besieged
him in [a]Abel Beth-maacah, and [b]they
[I]cast[8210] up a mound against the city,
and it stood by the rampart; and all the
people who were with Joab were wreak-
ing destruction in order to topple the
wall.
🗝 16 Then [a]a wise[2450] woman[802]

1 [b]Gen. 46:21 [c]2Sam. 19:43; 1Kin. 12:16 [d]1Sam. 22:7-9 [e]1Sam. 13:2; 2Sam. 18:17; 2Chr. 10:16
2 [I]Lit., *went up* [II]Lit., *clung to*
3 [a]2Sam. 15:16; 16:21, 22
4 [a]2Sam. 17:25; 19:13
5 [a]1Sam. 13:8
6 [a]2Sam. 21:17 [b]2Sam. 11:11; 1Kin. 1:33
7 [a]2Sam. 8:18; 1Kin. 1:38
8 [I]Lit., *before* [II]Lit., *girded with military garment as clothing* [a]2Sam. 2:13; 3:30
9 [a]Matt. 26:49
10 [a]2Sam. 2:23; 3:27; 1Kin. 2:5
11 [a]2Sam. 20:13
12 [I]Lit., *caused to turn*
15 [I]Lit., *poured out* [a]1Kin. 15:20; 2Kin. 15:29 [b]2Kin. 19:32; Ezek. 4:2
16 [a]2Sam. 14:2

🗝 **20:16** The "wise woman" was a member of a special group in Israel. Jer. 18:18 explains that God guided His people through the counsel of the wise men, through the Law of the priests, through the word of the prophets.

called[7121] from the city, "Hear, hear! Please tell Joab, 'Come here that I may speak with you.'"

17 So he approached her, and the woman said, "Are you Joab?" And he answered,[559] "I am." Then she said to him, "Listen to the words[1697] of your maidservant." And he answered, "I am listening."

18 Then she spoke, saying, "Formerly they used to say, 'They will surely ask[7592] *advice* at Abel,' and thus they ended[8552] *the dispute.*

19 "I am of those who are peaceable *and* faithful[539] in Israel. [a]You are seeking to destroy[4191] a city, even a mother in Israel. Why would you swallow up [b]the inheritance of the LORD?"

20 And Joab answered and said, "Far be it, far be it from me that I should swallow up or destroy![7843]

21 "Such is not the case. But a man from [a]the hill country of Ephraim, [b]Sheba the son of Bichri by name, has lifted up his hand against King David. Only hand him over, and I will depart from the city." And the woman said to Joab, "Behold, his head will be thrown to you over the wall."

22 Then the woman [a]wisely[2451] came to all the people. And they cut[3772] off the head of Sheba the son of Bichri and threw it to Joab. So [b]he blew the trumpet, and they were dispersed from the city, each to his tent. Joab also returned to the king at Jerusalem.

🔑 **23** [a]Now Joab was over the whole army of Israel, and Benaiah the son of Jehoiada was over the Cherethites and the Pelethites;

24 and Adoram was over the forced labor, and [a]Jehoshaphat the son of Ahilud was the recorder;

25 and Sheva was scribe, and Zadok and [a]Abiathar were priests;

26 and Ira the Jairite was also a priest to David.

Gibeonite Revenge

21 Now there was [a]a famine in the days of David for three years, year after year; and [b]David sought the presence of the LORD. And the LORD said,[559] "It is for Saul and his bloody[1818] house, because he put the Gibeonites to death."

2 So the king[4428] called[7121] the Gibeonites and spoke to them (now the Gibeonites were not of the sons of Israel but of the remnant of the Amorites, and [a]the sons[1121] of Israel [I]made a covenant with them, but Saul had sought to [II]kill them in his zeal[7065] for the sons of Israel and Judah).

3 Thus David said to the Gibeonites, "What should I do[6213] for you? And how can I make atonement[3722] that you may bless[1288] [a]the inheritance[5159] of the LORD?"

4 Then the Gibeonites said to him, "[a]We have no *concern* of silver or gold with Saul or his house, nor is it for us to put any man to death[4191] in Israel." And he said, "I will do for you whatever you say."

5 So they said to the king, "[a]The man who consumed[3615] us, and who planned [I]to exterminate us from remaining within any border of Israel,

6 let seven men from his sons be given to us, and we will [I]hang them [a]before the LORD in Gibeah of Saul, [b]the chosen of the LORD." And the king said, "I will give *them.*"

7 But the king spared [a]Mephibosheth, the son of Jonathan the son of Saul, [b]because of the oath[7621] of the LORD which was between them, between David and Saul's son Jonathan.

8 So the king took the two sons of [a]Rizpah the daughter of Aiah, Armoni and Mephibosheth whom she had born to Saul, and the five sons of [I][b]Merab the daughter of Saul, whom she had born to Adriel the son of Barzillai the [c]Meholathite.

---

19 [a]Deut. 20:10 [b]1Sam. 26:19; 2Sam. 14:16; 21:3
21 [a]Josh. 24:33 [b]2Sam. 20:2
22 [a]2Sam. 20:16; Eccl. 9:13-16 [b]2Sam. 20:1
23 [a]2Sam. 8:16-18; 1Kin. 4:3-6
24 [a]1Kin. 4:3
25 [a]1Kin. 4:4

1 [a]Gen. 12:10; 26:1; 42:5 [b]Num. 27:21
2 [I]Lit., *had sworn to* [II]Lit., *smite* [a]Josh. 9:3, 15-20
3 [a]1Sam. 26:19; 2Sam. 20:19
4 [a]Num. 35:31, 32
5 [I]Lit., *against us that we should be exterminated* [a]2Sam. 21:1
6 [I]Lit., *expose them* [a]Num. 25:4 [b]1Sam. 10:24
7 [a]2Sam. 4:4; 9:10 [b]1Sam. 18:3; 20:12-17; 23:18; 2Sam. 9:1-7
8 [I]So Gr. and Heb. mss. [a]2Sam. 3:7 [b]1Sam. 18:19 [c]1Kin. 19:16

🔑 **20:23-26** See II Sam. 8:15-18; I Chr. 18:14-17.

9 Then he gave them into the hands
of the Gibeonites, and they [I]hanged
them in the mountain before the LORD,
so that the seven of them fell[5307] together; and they were put to death[4191]
in the first[7223] days of harvest at [a]the
beginning of barley harvest.
10 [a]And Rizpah the daughter of Aiah
took sackcloth and spread it for herself
on the rock, from the beginning of harvest until [I]it rained on them from the
sky; and [b]she [II]allowed neither the birds
of the sky[8064] to rest on them by day[3119]
nor the beasts[2416] of the field[7704] by
night.
11 When it was told David what
Rizpah the daughter of Aiah, the concubine of Saul, had done,[6213]
12 then David went and took
[a]the bones[6106] of Saul and the bones[6106]
of Jonathan his son from the men of
Jabesh-gilead, who had stolen them from
the open square of [b]Bethshan, [c]where
the Philistines had hanged them on the
day [d]the Philistines struck down Saul
in Gilboa.
13 And he brought[5927] up the bones
of Saul and the bones of Jonathan his
son from there, and they gathered[622]
the bones of those who had been
[I]hanged.
14 And they buried[6912] the bones
of Saul and Jonathan his son in the
country[776] of Benjamin in [a]Zela, in the
grave[6913] of Kish his father;[1] thus they
did all that the king commanded,[6680] and
after that [b]God[430] was moved by entreaty[6279] for the land.[776]
15 Now when [a]the Philistines were
at war again with Israel, David went
down and his servants with him; and
as they fought against the Philistines,
David became weary.
16 Then Ishbi-benob, who was
[a]among the descendants of the [I]giant,[7497]
the weight of whose spear was three
hundred *shekels* of bronze in weight,
[II]was girded with a new *sword,* and he
[III]intended to kill David.
17 But [a]Abishai the son of Zeruiah
helped[5826] him, and struck the Philistine
and killed[4191] him. Then the men of David swore to him, saying, "[b]You shall
not go out again with us to battle, that
you may not extinguish [c]the lamp[5216]
of Israel."
18 [a]Now it came about after this
that there was war again with the Philistines at Gob; then [b]Sibbecai the Hushathite struck down Saph, who was
among the descendants of the [I]giant.
19 And there was war with the Philistines again at Gob, and Elhanan the
son of Jaare-oregim the Bethlehemite
[I]killed [II]Goliath the Gittite, [a]the shaft of
whose spear was like a weaver's beam.
20 And there was war at Gath again,
where there was a man of *great* stature
who had six fingers on each hand and
six toes on each foot, twenty-four in
number; and he also had been born
[a]to the [I]giant.
21 And when he defied[2778] Israel,
Jonathan the son of Shimei, David's
brother, struck him down.
22 [a]These four were born to the
[I]giant in Gath, and they fell by the hand
of David and by the hand of his servants.

David's Psalm of Deliverance

22 [a]And David spoke [b]the
words[1697] of this song to the
LORD in the day[3117] that the LORD
delivered[5337] him from the [I]hand of all
his enemies and from the [I]hand of Saul.

9 [I]Lit., *exposed them* [a]Ex. 9:31, 32
10 [I]Lit., *water was poured* [II]Lit., *gave* [a]Deut. 21:23 [b]1Sam. 17:44, 46
12 [a]1Sam. 31:11-13 [b]Josh. 17:11 [c]1Sam. 31:10 [d]1Sam. 31:3, 4
13 [I]Lit., *exposed*
14 [a]Josh. 18:28 [b]Josh. 7:26; 2Sam. 24:25
15 [a]2Sam. 5:17-25
16 [I]Heb., *Raphah* [II]Lit., *and he was* [III]Lit., *said* [a]Num. 13:22, 28; Josh.15:14; 2Sam. 21:18-22
17 [a]2Sam. 20:6-10 [b]2Sam. 18:3 [c]2Sam. 22:29; 1Kin. 11:36
18 [I]Heb., *Raphah* [a]1Chr. 20:4-8 [b]1Chr. 11:29; 27:11
19 [I]Lit., *smote* [II]In 1Chr. 20:5, *Lahmi, the brother of Goliath* [a]1Sam. 17:7
20 [I]Heb., *Raphah* [a]2Sam. 21:16, 18
22 [I]Heb., *Raphah* [a]1Chr. 20:8
1 [I]Lit., *palm* [a]Ps. 18:2-50 [b]Ex. 15:1; Deut. 31:30

21:20-22 See I Chr. 20:6-8.

22:1-51 This and the next chapter (see also Ps. 18:1-50) fit into David's life-story revealing his true character. Suggested outline: Jehovah, the source of David's strength (2-4); all deliverances are ascribed directly to God (5-19); such deliverances depend on the right conduct of God's people (20-25); God is to man what man is to God (26-28); David's personal testimony to the truth of the things sung (29-46); the doxology (47-51). Lessons: God's absolute sovereignty; His omnipotent power to deliver; the necessity of obedience to His law; obedience is rewarded by His action. This song was probably composed soon after David's victories over his enemies (8:1-14) and prior to his sin with Bathsheba (11:21-25; cf. I Kgs. 15:5).

2 And he said,
"[a]The LORD is my [I]rock and my fortress and my deliverer;
3 [Ia]My God,[430] my rock, in whom I take refuge;
My [b]shield and [c]the horn of my salvation, my stronghold and [d]my refuge;
My savior, Thou dost save me from violence.[2555]
4 "I call[7121] upon the LORD,
[a]who is worthy to be praised;
And I am saved from my enemies.
5 "For [a]the waves of death[4194] encompassed me;
[b]The torrents of [I]destruction [II]overwhelmed[1204] me;
6 [a]The cords of [I]Sheol surrounded me;
The snares of death confronted me.
7 "[a]In my distress I called[7121] upon the LORD,
Yes, I [I]cried[7121] to my God;
And from His temple He heard my voice,
And my cry for help *came* into His ears.[241]
8 "Then [a]the earth[776] shook and quaked,
[b]The foundations[4146] of heaven were trembling
And were shaken, because He was angry.[2734]
9 "Smoke went up [I]out of His nostrils,
[a]And fire from His mouth devoured;
[b]Coals were kindled by it.
10 "He bowed the heavens also, and came down
With [a]thick darkness[6205] under His feet.
11 "[a]And He rode on a cherub[3742] and flew;
And He [I]appeared on [b]the wings of the wind.[7307]
12 "[a]And He made darkness[2822] [I]canopies around Him,
A mass of waters, thick clouds of the sky.

2 [I]Lit., *crag* [a]1Sam. 23:25; 24:2; Ps. 31:3; 71:3
3 [I]Lit., *God of my rock* [a]Deut. 32:4, 37; 1Sam. 2:2 [b]Gen. 15:1; Deut. 33:29 [c]Luke 1:69 [d]Ps. 9:9
4 [a]Ps. 48:1; 96:4
5 [I]Heb., *Belial* [II]Or, *terrified* [a]Ps. 93:4; Jon. 2:3 [b]Ps. 69:14, 15
6 [I]I.e., the nether world [a]Ps. 116:3
7 [I]Or, *called* [a]Ps. 116:4; 120:1
8 [a]Judg. 5:4; Ps. 97:4 [b]Job 26:11
9 [I]Or, *in His wrath* [a]Ps. 97:3; Heb. 12:29 [b]2Sam. 22:13
10 [a]Ex. 19:16; 1Kin. 8:12; Ps. 97:2; Nah. 1:3
11 [I]Many mss. read *sped* [a]2Sam. 6:2 [b]Ps. 104:3
12 [I]Or, *pavilions* [a]Job 36:29
13 [a]2Sam. 22:9
14 [a]Job 37:2-5; Ps. 29:3
15 [I]Lit., *confused* [a]Deut. 32:23; Josh. 10:10; 1Sam. 7:10
16 [I]Or, *uncovered* [a]Ex. 15:8; Nah. 1:4
17 [a]Ps. 144:7 [b]Ex. 2:10
19 [a]Ps. 23:4
20 [a]Ps. 31:8; 118:5 [b]2Sam. 15:26
21 [a]1Sam. 26:23; 1Kin. 8:32 [b]Ps. 24:4
22 [a]Gen. 18:19; Ps. 128:1; Prov. 8:32
23 [I]Lit., *it* [a]Deut. 6:6-9; Ps. 119:30, 102
24 [I]Lit., *complete;* or, *having integrity* [a]Gen. 6:9; 7:1; Eph. 1:4; Col. 1:21, 22
25 [a]2Sam. 22:21

13 "From the brightness before Him
[a]Coals of fire were kindled.
14 "[a]The LORD thundered from heaven,
And the Most High uttered His voice.
15 "[a]And He sent out arrows, and scattered them,
Lightning, and [I]routed[2000] them.
16 "Then the channels of the sea appeared,[7200]
The foundations of the world[8398] were [I]laid bare,
By the rebuke of the LORD,
[a]At the blast of the breath[7307] of His nostrils.
17 "[a]He sent from on high, He took me;
[b]He drew me out of many waters.
18 "He delivered me from my strong enemy,
From those who hated me, for they were too strong for me.
19 "They confronted me in the day of my calamity,[343]
[a]But the LORD was my support.
20 "[a]He also brought me forth into a broad place;
He rescued[2502] me, [b]because He delighted[2654] in me.
21 "[a]The LORD has rewarded me according to my righteousness;
[b]According to the cleanness[1252] of my hands He has recompensed me.
22 "[a]For I have kept[8104] the ways[1870] of the LORD,
And have not acted wickedly[7561] against my God.
23 "[a]For all His ordinances[4941] *were* before me;
And *as for* His statutes, I did not depart[5493] from [I]them.
24 "[a]I was also [I]blameless[8549] toward Him,
And I kept[3045] myself from my iniquity.[5771]
25 "[a]Therefore the LORD has recompensed me according to my righteousness,

According to my cleanness
before His eyes.
26 "[a]With the [I]kind Thou dost show
Thyself [I]kind,
With the [II]blameless[8549] Thou
dost show Thyself
[II]blameless;
27 [a]With the pure Thou dost show
Thyself pure,
[b]And with the perverted[6141]
Thou dost show Thyself
[I]astute.
28 "[a]And Thou dost save an afflicted
people;
[b]But Thine eyes are on the
haughty *whom* Thou dost
abase.
29 "[a]For Thou art my lamp,[5216] O
LORD;
And the LORD illumines my
darkness.
30 "[a]For by Thee I can [I]run upon a
troop;
By my God I can leap over a
wall.
31 "[a]As for God,[410] His way[1870] is
[I]blameless;
[b]The word[565] of the LORD is
tested;
[c]He is a shield[4043] to all who take
refuge in Him.
32 "[a]For who is God, besides the
LORD?
[b]And who is a rock, besides our
God?
33 "[a]God is my strong fortress;
And He [I]sets the [II]blameless in
[III]His way.
34 "[a]He makes [I]my feet like hinds'[355]
feet,
[b]And sets me on my high
places.
35 "[a]He trains my hands for battle,
[b]So that my arms can bend a
bow of bronze.
36 "Thou hast also given me
[a]the shield of Thy salvation,
And Thy [I]help makes me
great.
37 "[a]Thou dost enlarge my steps
under me,
And my [I]feet have not slipped.

26 [I]Or, *loyal* [II]Lit., *complete;* or, *having integrity* [a]Matt. 5:7
27 [I]Lit., *twisted* [a]Matt. 5:8; 1John 3:3 [b]Lev. 26:23, 24; Rom. 1:28
28 [a]Ex. 3:7, 8; Ps. 72:12, 13 [b]Is. 2:11, 12, 17; 5:15
29 [a]2Sam. 21:17; 1Kin. 11:36; Ps. 27:1
30 [I]Or, *crush a troop* [a]2Sam. 5:6-8
31 [I]Lit., *complete;* or, *having integrity* [a]Deut. 32:4; Matt. 5:48 [b]Ps. 12:6; 119:140; Prov. 30:5 [c]2Sam. 22:3; Ps. 84:9
32 [a]1Sam. 2:2 [b]2Sam. 22:2
33 [I]Or, *sets free* [II]Lit., *complete;* or, *having integrity* [III]Another reading is *my* [a]2Sam. 22:2; Ps. 31:3,4
34 [I]Another reading is *His* [a]2Sam. 2:18; Hab. 3:19 [b]Deut. 32:13
35 [a]Ps. 144:1 [b]Job 20:24
36 [I]Lit., *answering* [a]Eph. 6:16, 17
37 [I]Lit., *ankles* [a]2Sam. 22:20; Prov. 4:12
38 [a]Ex. 15:9
39 [a]Mal. 4:3
40 [I]Lit., *caused to bow down* [a]Ps. 44:5
41 [I]Or, *silenced* [a]Ex. 23:27; Josh. 10:24
42 [a]Is. 17:7, 8 [b]1Sam. 28:6; Is. 1:15
43 [a]2Kin. 13:7 [b]Is. 10:6; Mic. 7:10
44 [a]2Sam. 3:1; 19:9, 14 [b]2Sam. 8:1-14 [c]Is. 55:5
45 [a]Ps. 66:3; 81:15
46 [I]Lit., *languish* [II]Lit., *gird themselves* [III]Lit., *fastnesses* [a]1Sam. 14:11; Mic. 7:17
47 [I]Lit., *the God of the rock* [a]2Sam. 22:3; Ps. 89:26
48 [a]1Sam. 24:12; 25:39; 2Sam. 4:8; Ps. 94:1 [b]Ps. 144:2

38 "I pursued my enemies and
[a]destroyed them,
And I did not turn back until they
were consumed.[3615]
39 "And I have devoured them and
shattered[4272] them, so that
they did not rise;
And [a]they fell[5307] under my feet.
40 "For Thou hast girded me with
strength for battle;
Thou hast [I]subdued under me
[a]those who rose up against
me.
41 "Thou hast also [a]made my
enemies turn *their* backs to
me,
And I [I]destroyed[6789] those who
hated me.
42 "[a]They looked, but there was
none to save;
[b]*Even* to the LORD, but He did
not answer them.
43 "[a]Then I pulverized[7833] them as
the dust[6083] of the earth,
[b]I crushed *and* stamped
them as the mire of the
streets.
44 "[a]Thou hast also delivered me
from the contentions of my
people;
[b]Thou hast kept me as head of
the nations;
[c]A people whom I have not
known serve me.
45 "[a]Foreigners pretend obedience
to me;
As soon as they hear, they
obey[8085] me.
46 "Foreigners [I]lose heart,
[a]And [II]come trembling out of
their [III]fortresses.
47 "The LORD lives,[2416] and
blessed[1288] be my rock;
And exalted be [I][a]God, the rock
of my salvation,
48 [a]The God who executes
vengeance[5360] for me,
[b]And brings down peoples under
me,
49 Who also brings me out from
my enemies;
Thou dost even lift me above

[a]those who rise up against
me;
[b]Thou dost rescue me from the
violent[2555] man.
50 "[a]Therefore I will give thanks to
Thee, O LORD, among the
nations,
And I will sing praises to Thy
name.
51 "[a]*He* is a tower of [I]deliverance
to His king,[4428]
And [b]shows lovingkindness to
His anointed,[4899]
[c]To David and his [II]descendants
forever."[5769]

David's Last Song

23 Now these are the last
words[1697] of David.
David the son of Jesse declares,
[a]And the man who was raised
on high declares,
[b]The anointed[4899] of the God[430]
of Jacob,
And the sweet psalmist of Israel,
2 "[a]The Spirit of the LORD spoke
by me,
And His word[4405] was on my
tongue.
3 "The God of Israel said,
[a]The Rock of Israel spoke to me,
'[b]He who rules over men
righteously,[6662]
[c]Who rules in the fear of God,
4 [a]Is as the light[216] of the morning
when the sun rises,
A morning without clouds,
When the tender grass *springs*
out of the earth,[776]
Through sunshine after rain.'
5 "Truly is not my house so with
God?[410]
For [a]He has made an
everlasting[5769]
covenant[1285] with me,
Ordered in all things, and
secured;
For all my salvation and all *my*
desire,[2656]
Will He not indeed make *it*
grow?
6 "[a]But the worthless,[1100] every
one of them will be thrust
away like thorns,
Because they cannot be taken
in hand;
7 But the man who touches them
Must be [I]armed with iron and
the shaft of a spear,
And [a]they will be completely
burned[8313] with fire in *their*
[II]place."

His Mighty Men

8 [a]These are the names of the
mighty men whom David had: Josheb-
basshebeth a Tahchemonite, chief[7218] of
the [I]captains,[7791] he was *called* Adino
the Eznite, because of eight hundred
slain *by him* at one time;
9 and after him was Eleazar the son
of [a]Dodo the [b]Ahohite, one of the three
mighty men with David when they
[I]defied[2778] the Philistines who were
gathered[622] there to battle and the men
of Israel had [II]withdrawn.
10 [a]He arose and struck the Philistines until his hand was weary and
[I]clung to the sword, and [b]the LORD
brought about a great [II]victory[8668] that
day;[3117] and the people returned after
him only to strip *the slain*.
11 Now after him was Shammah the
son of Agee a [a]Hararite. And the Philistines were gathered [I]into a troop, where
there was a plot of ground[7704] full of
lentils, and the people fled from the Philistines.
12 But he took his stand in the midst
of the plot, defended it and struck the

49 [a]Ps. 44:5 [b]Ps. 140:1, 4, 11
50 [a]Rom. 15:9
51 [I]I.e., victories; lit., *salvation* [II]Lit., *seed* [a]Ps. 144:10 [b]Ps. 89:24 [c]2Sam. 7:12-16
1 [a]2Sam. 7:8, 9; Ps. 78:70, 71 [b]1Sam. 16:12, 13; Ps. 89:20
2 [a]Matt. 22:43; 2Pet. 1:21
3 [a]2Sam. 22:2, 3, 32 [b]Ps. 72:1-3; Is. 11:1-5 [c]2Chr. 19:7, 9
4 [a]Judg. 5:31; Ps. 72:6
5 [a]2Sam. 7:12-16; Ps. 89:29; Is. 55:3
6 [a]Matt. 13:41
7 [I]Lit., *filled* [II]Lit., *sitting* [a]Matt. 3:10; 13:30; Heb. 6:8
8 [I]Or, *three* [a]1Chr. 11:11-47
9 [I]Lit., *re-proached* [II]Lit., *gone up* [a]1Chr. 27:4 [b]1Chr. 8:4
10 [I]Lit., *his hand clung* [II]Lit., *salvation* [a]1Chr. 11:13 [b]1Sam. 11:13; 19:5
11 [I]Possibly, at Lehi [a]2Sam. 23:33

23:1-7 This son was much more than a simple farewell. It was like the final blessing of Jacob in Gen. 49. it was an inspired prophecy of the Messiah to come and of the Mediator's new covenant of salvation. This song was patterned along the same lines as that of Balaam's (Num. 24:15-24).
23:5 Compare Isa. 11:1; Jer. 23:5; Zech. 3:8.
23:8-38 See I Chr. 11:10-47.

Philistines; and [a]the LORD brought about a great [I]victory.

13 Then three of the thirty chief men went down and came to David in the harvest time to the [a]cave of Adullam, while the troop of the Philistines was camping in [b]the valley of Rephaim.

14 And David was then [a]in the stronghold, while the garrison of the Philistines was then in Bethlehem.

15 [a]And David had a craving[183] and said, "Oh that someone would give me water to drink from the well[953] of Bethlehem which is by the gate!"

16 [a]So the three mighty men broke through the camp of the Philistines, and drew water from the well of Bethlehem which was by the gate, and took *it* and brought *it* to David. Nevertheless he would[14] not drink it, but [b]poured it out to the LORD;

17 and he said, "Be it far from me, O LORD, that I should do[6213] this. [a]*Shall I drink* the blood[1818] of the men who went in *jeopardy* of their lives?"[5315] Therefore he would not drink it. These things the three mighty men did.[6213]

18 And [a]Abishai, the brother[251] of Joab, the son of Zeruiah, was [b]chief of the [I]thirty. And he swung his spear against three hundred [II]and killed *them,* and had a name as well as the three.

19 He was most honored of the thirty, therefore he became their commander;[8269] however, he did not attain to the three.

20 Then [a]Benaiah the son of Jehoiada, the son of a valiant man of [b]Kabzeel, who had done[6213] mighty deeds, [I]killed the [II]two *sons of* Ariel of Moab. He also went down and killed a lion in the middle of a pit on a snowy day.

21 And he [I]killed an Egyptian, [II]an impressive man. Now the Egyptian *had* a spear in his hand, but he went down to him with a club and snatched the spear from the Egyptian's hand, and killed him with his own spear.

22 These *things* [a]Benaiah the son of Jehoiada did, and had a name as well as the three mighty men.

23 He was honored among the thirty, but he did not attain to the three. And David appointed him over his guard.[4928]

24 [a]Asahel the brother of Joab was among the thirty; Elhanan the son of Dodo of Bethlehem,

25 [a]Shammah the [b]Harodite, Elika the Harodite,

26 Helez the Paltite, Ira the son of Ikkesh the [a]Tekoite,

27 Abiezer the [a]Anathothite, Mebunnai the Hushathite,

28 Zalmon the Ahohite, Maharai the [a]Netophathite,

29 [a]Heleb the son of Baanah the Netophathite, Ittai the son of Ribai of [b]Gibeah of the sons[1121] of Benjamin,

30 Benaiah a [a]Pirathonite, Hiddai of the brooks of [b]Gaash,

31 Abi-albon the Arbathite, Azmaveth the [a]Barhumite,

32 Eliahba the [a]Shaalbonite, the sons of Jashen, Jonathan,

33 [a]Shammah the Hararite, Ahiam the son of Sharar the Ararite,

34 Eliphelet the son of Ahasbai, the son of [a]the Maacathite, [b]Eliam the son of [c]Ahithophel the Gilonite,

35 [a]Hezro the [b]Carmelite, Paarai the Arbite,

36 Igal the son of Nathan of [a]Zobah, Bani the Gadite,

37 Zelek the Ammonite, Naharai the [a]Beerothite, armor bearers of Joab the son of Zeruiah,

38 Ira the [a]Ithrite, Gareb the Ithrite,

39 [a]Uriah the Hittite; thirty-seven in all.

12 [I]Lit., *salvation* [a]2Sam. 23:10
13 [a]1Sam. 22:1 [b]2Sam. 5:18
14 [a]1Sam. 22:4,5
15 [a]1Chr. 11:17
16 [a]1Chr. 11:18 [b]Gen.35:14
17 [a]Lev. 17:10
18 [I]So two Heb. mss. and Syriac; M.T., *three* [II]Lit., *slain ones* [a]2Sam. 10:10, 14; 18:2 [b]1Chr. 11:20, 21
20 [I]Lit., *smote* [II]Or, *two lion-like heroes* [a]2Sam. 8:18; 20:23 [b]Josh. 15:21
21 [I]Lit., *smote* [II]Lit., *a man of appearance*
22 [a]2Sam. 23:20
24 [a]2Sam. 2:18; 1Chr. 27:7
25 [a]1Chr. 11:27 [b]Judg. 7:1
26 [a]2Sam. 14:2
27 [a]Josh. 21:18
28 [a]2Kin. 25:23
29 [a]1Chr. 11:30 [b]Josh. 18:28
30 [a]Judg. 12:13, 15 [b]Josh. 24:30
31 [a]2Sam. 3:16
32 [a]Josh. 19:42
33 [a]2Sam. 23:11
34 [a]2Sam. 10:6, 8; 20:14 [b]2Sam. 11:3 [c]2Sam. 15:12
35 [a]1Chr. 11:37 [b]Josh. 15:55
36 [a]2Sam. 8:3
37 [a]2Sam. 4:2
38 [a]1Chr. 2:53
39 [a]2Sam. 11:3,6

The Census Taken

24 🔑 [a]Now [b]again the anger[639] of the LORD burned[2734] against Israel, and it incited David against them

1 [a]1Chr. 21:1 [b]2Sam. 21:1, 2

🔑 **24:1-14** It appears that God had told David to take a census of Israel and Judah, but David did it in an improper manner, i.e., to determine his own strength rather than to trust in the Lord. Instead of

(continued on next page)

to say, "[c]Go, number Israel and Judah."
2 And the king[4428] said to Joab the
commander[8269] of the army who was
with him, "Go about now through all
the tribes of Israel, [a]from Dan to
Beersheba, and [I]register the people,
that I may know[3045] the number of the
people."
3 But Joab said to the king, "[a]Now
may the LORD your God[430] add to the
people a hundred times as many as they
are, while the eyes of my lord[113] the
king *still* see; but why does my lord
the king delight[2654] in this thing?"
4 Nevertheless, the king's[4428]
word[1697] prevailed against Joab and
against the commanders[8269] of the army.
So Joab and the commanders of the army
went out from the presence of the king,
to [I]register the people of Israel.
5 And they crossed the Jordan and
camped in [a]Aroer, on the right side of
the city that is in the middle of the valley
of Gad, and toward [b]Jazer.
6 Then they came to Gilead and
to [I]the land[776] of Tahtim-hodshi, and
they came to Dan-jaan and around to
[a]Sidon,
7 and came to the [a]fortress of Tyre
and to all the cities of the [b]Hivites and
of the Canaanites, and they went out
to the south of Judah, *to* [c]Beersheba.
8 So when they had gone about
through the whole land, they came to
Jerusalem at the end of nine months
and twenty days.
9 And Joab gave [a]the number of the
[I]registration of the people to the king;
and there were in Israel [b]eight hundred
thousand valiant men who drew the
sword, and the men of Judah were five
hundred thousand men.
10 Now [a]David's heart [I]troubled
him after he had numbered the people.
So David said to the LORD, "[b]I have
sinned greatly in what I have done.[6213]
But now, O LORD, please [II]take away
the iniquity[5771] of Thy servant, for
[c]I have acted very foolishly."
11 When David arose in the morning, the word of the LORD came to
[a]the prophet Gad, David's [b]seer, saying,
12 "Go and speak to David, 'Thus
the LORD says, "I am offering you three
things; choose[977] for yourself one of
them, which I may do[6213] to you." ' "
13 So Gad came to David and told
him, and said to him, "Shall [a]seven years
of famine come to you in your land?
Or will you flee three months before
your foes while they pursue you? Or
shall there be three days'[3117] pestilence
in your land? Now consider and see what
answer[1697] I shall return to Him who
sent me."
14 Then David said to Gad, "I am
in great distress.[6887] Let us now fall into
the hand of the LORD [a]for His mercies
are great, but do not let me fall into
the hand of man."

Pestilence Sent

15 So [a]the LORD [I]sent a pestilence
upon Israel from the morning until the
appointed[4150] time; and seventy thousand men of the people [b]from Dan to
Beersheba died.[4191]
16 [a]When the angel stretched out
his hand toward Jerusalem to destroy[7843]
it, [b]the LORD relented from the calamity,[7451] and said to the angel who
destroyed[7843] the people, "It is enough!
Now relax your hand!" And the angel
of the LORD was by the threshing floor
of Araunah the Jebusite.
17 Then David spoke to the LORD
when he saw the angel[4397] who was

1 [c]1Chr. 27:23, 24
2 [I]Lit., *muster* [a]Judg. 20:1; 2Sam. 3:10
3 [a]Deut. 1:11
4 [I]Lit., *muster*
5 [a]Deut. 2:36; Josh. 13:9, 16 [b]Num. 21:32; 32:35
6 [I]Or, *Kadesh in the land of the Hittite* [a]Josh. 19:28; Judg. 1:31
7 [a]Josh. 19:29 [b]Josh. 11:3; Judg. 3:3 [c]Gen. 21:22-33
9 [I]Lit., *muster* [a]Num. 1:44-46 [b]1Chr. 21:5
10 [I]Lit., *smote* [II]Lit., *cause to pass away* [a]1Sam. 24:5 [b]2Sam. 12:13 [c]1Sam. 13:13; 2Chr. 16:9
11 [a]1Sam. 22:5; 1Chr. 29:29 [b]1Sam. 9:9
13 [a]1Chr. 21:12; Ezek. 14:21
14 [a]Ps.51:1; 130:4, 7
15 [I]Lit., *gave* [a]1Chr. 21:14; 27:24 [b]2Sam. 24:2
16 [a]Ex. 12:23; 2Kin. 19:35; Acts 12:23 [b]Ex. 32:14; 1Sam. 15:11

(continued from previous page)
depending on God's promise for protection, he desired tangible military strength. He recognized his sin and the Lord gave him his choice of three different punishments: (1) three years of famine in the land, (2) three months of flight before his enemies, or (3) three days of pestilence in the land. His unfaltering trust in the Lord is seen in his choice (v. 14), a statement that the man of God should consider carefully. Even when God is punishing us, we know He has our best interests in mind, and we can trust Him.

24:1-25 See I Chr. 21:1-27.

striking down the people, and said, "Behold, [a]it is I who have sinned, and it is
I who have done[6213] wrong; but [b]these
sheep, what have they done? Please let
Thy hand be against me and against my
father's[1] house."

David Builds an Altar

18 So Gad came to David that
day[3117] and said to him, "[a]Go up, erect
an altar[4196] to the LORD on the threshing
floor of [I]Araunah the Jebusite."
19 And David went up according to
the word of Gad, just as the LORD had
commanded.[6680]
20 And Araunah looked down and
saw the king and his servants crossing
over toward him; and Araunah went out
and bowed his face[639] to the ground[776]
before the king.
21 Then Araunah said, "Why has my
lord the king come to his servant?" And
David said, "To buy the threshing floor
from you, in order to build an altar to
the LORD, [a]that the plague may be held
back from the people."
22 And Araunah said to David, "Let
my lord the king take and offer up what
is good[2896] in his sight. Look,[7200]
[a]the oxen for the burnt offering, the
threshing sledges and the yokes of the
oxen for the wood.
23 "Everything, O king, Araunah
gives to the king." And Araunah said
to the king, "May the LORD your God
[a]accept[7521] you."
24 However, the king said to Araunah, "No, but I will surely buy *it* from
you for a price, for [a]I will not offer burnt
offerings to the LORD my God [I]which
cost me nothing." So [b]David bought the
threshing floor and the oxen for fifty
shekels of silver.
25 And David built there an altar
to the LORD, and offered[5927] burnt offerings and peace offerings. [a]Thus the LORD
was moved by entreaty[6279] for the land,
and the plague was held back from Israel.

17 [a]2Sam. 24:10 [b]2Sam. 7:8; Ps. 74:1

18 [I]In 2Chr. 3:1, *Ornan* [a]1Chr. 21:18

21 [a]Num. 16:44-50

22 [a]1Sam. 6:14; 1Kin. 19:21

23 [a]Ezek. 20:40, 41

24 [I]Lit., *gratuitously* [a]Mal. 1:13, 14 [b]1Chr. 21:24, 25

25 [a]2Sam. 21:14

The First Book of the
KINGS

As with I Samuel and II Samuel, the First and Second Books of Kings were originally one book in the Hebrew text. I Kings and II Kings tell of David's death, the golden age of Solomon's reign, how the nation divided into two kingdoms, and their eventual captivity by heathen powers. Solomon, David's son, began his rule with great wealth, glory, and power, but it ended in disgrace. He did not seem to have the same spiritual toughness of his father. Solomon compromised some of the most sacred spiritual principles in order to achieve his political ends. In other words, the end justified the means. He taxed the people so much that the stage was set for rebellion. Also, he began to depend on military might instead of the true God. The spiritual condition of Israel was of paramount importance to the writer amidst political changes. The author registers a spiritual judgment concerning each king: Those kings who tried to maintain the traditional worship of the God of Israel were good, and those who abandoned the true God were evil. The apostate northern kingdom (Israel) which had been established by Jeroboam finally went too far and was destroyed, but the smaller, southern kingdom (Judah) proved to be more penitent. The ancestry of Jesus Christ was traced through the tribe of Judah. The main messages of the Book of I Kings are: (1) Human governments are faulty even at their best, but this is especially true when God is not included in the scheme of things. (2) God's rule continues despite the foibles of man. The will and purpose of God will indeed prevail. He still spoke through His prophets even when some did not want to listen. God showed His power through the forces of nature and he incited foreign hostile armies to accomplish His purpose. God is always in control.

David in Old Age

1 Now King David was old, advanced in age; and they covered[3680] him with clothes, but he could not keep warm.

2 So his servants said to him, "Let them seek a young virgin for my lord the king, and let her [I]attend the king and become his nurse; and let her lie in your bosom, that my lord the king may keep warm."

3 So they searched for a beautiful girl[5291] throughout all the territory of Israel, and found Abishag the [a]Shunammite, and brought her to the king.

4 And the girl was very beautiful; and she became the king's nurse and served him, but the king did not [I]cohabit with her.

2 [I]Lit., *stand before*

3 [a]Josh. 19:18; 1Sam. 28:4

4 [I]Lit., *know her*

5 [a]2Sam. 3:4 [b]2Sam. 15:1

6 [I]Lit., *pained him* [II]Lit., *she gave him birth* [a]2Sam. 3:3, 4

7 [I]Lit., *his words were* [a]1Chr. 11:6 [b]1Sam. 22:20, 23; 2Sam. 20:25 [c]1Kin. 2:22

8 [a]2Sam. 20:25; 1Chr. 16:39 [b]2Sam. 8:18 [c]2Sam. 12:1 [d]1Kin. 4:18 [e]2Sam. 23:8-39

🔑 5 Now [a]Adonijah the son of Haggith exalted himself, saying, "I will be king." So [b]he prepared for himself chariots and horsemen with fifty men to run before him.

6 And his father[1] had never [I]crossed[6087] him at any time by asking, "Why have you done[6213] so?" And he was also a very handsome[2896] man; and [II][a]he was born after Absalom.

7 And [I]he had conferred with [a]Joab the son of Zeruiah and with [b]Abiathar the priest; and following [c]Adonijah they helped him.

8 But [a]Zadok the priest, [b]Benaiah the son of Jehoiada, [c]Nathan the prophet, [d]Shimei, Rei, and [e]the mighty men who belonged to David, were not with Adonijah.

9 And Adonijah sacrificed sheep and

🔑 **1:5** According to the custom of the time, the birthright belonged to the oldest son in a family. In the case of royal families that would include also accession to the throne. Though he was David's fourth son, Adonijah was apparently the oldest living son, and thus it was assumed that he would be the next king. David had not informed him that this custom was not to be followed. He was necessarily presumptuous in seeking the throne (I Kgs. 2:15).

oxen and fatlings by the [I]stone of Zoheleth, which is beside [a]En-rogel; and he invited[7121] all his brothers,[251] the king's sons, and all the men of Judah, the king's servants.

10 But he did not invite Nathan the prophet, Benaiah, the mighty men, and [a]Solomon his brother.[251]

Nathan and Bathsheba

11 Then Nathan spoke to [a]Bathsheba the mother of Solomon, saying, "Have you not heard that Adonijah the son of Haggith has become king, and David our lord does not know *it?*

12 "So now come, please let me [a]give you counsel[6098] and save your life and the life of your son Solomon.

13 "Go [I]at once to King David and say to him, 'Have you not, my lord, O king, sworn to your maidservant, saying, "[a]Surely Solomon your son shall be king after me, and he shall sit on my throne"? Why then has Adonijah become king?'

14 "Behold, while you are still there speaking with the king, I will come in after you and confirm your words."

15 So Bathsheba went in to the king in the bedroom. Now [a]the king was very old, and Abishag the Shunammite was ministering to the king.

16 Then Bathsheba bowed and prostrated[7812] herself [I]before the king. And the king said, "What [II]do you wish?"

17 And she said to him, "My lord, you swore to your maidservant by the LORD your God,[430] *saying,* '[a]Surely your son Solomon shall be king after me and he shall sit on my throne.'

18 "And now, behold, Adonijah is king; and now, my lord the king, you do not know *it.*

19 "And [a]he has sacrificed oxen and fatlings and sheep in abundance, and has invited all the sons of the king and Abiathar the priest and Joab the commander[8269] of the army; but he has not invited Solomon your servant.

20 "And as for you now, my lord the king, the eyes of all Israel are on you, to tell them who shall sit on the throne of my lord the king after him.

21 "Otherwise it will come about, [a]as soon as my lord the king sleeps with his fathers,[1] that I and my son Solomon will be considered [I]offenders."

22 And behold, while she was still speaking with the king, Nathan the prophet came in.

23 And they told the king, saying, "Here is Nathan the prophet." And when he came in before the king, he prostrated[7812] himself [I]before the king with his face[639] to the ground.[776]

24 Then Nathan said, "My lord the king, have you said, 'Adonijah shall be king after me, and he shall sit on my throne'?

25 "[a]For he has gone down today[3117] and has sacrificed oxen and fatlings and sheep in abundance, and has invited all the king's sons and the commanders[8269] of the army and Abiathar the priest, and behold, they are eating and drinking before him; and they say, '[b]*Long* live King Adonijah!'

26 "[a]But me, *even* me your servant, and Zadok the priest and Benaiah the son of Jehoiada and your servant Solomon, he has not invited.

27 "Has this thing been done by my lord the king, and you have not shown to your [I]servants who should sit on the throne of my lord the king after him?"

28 Then King David answered and said, "Call[7121] Bathsheba to me." And she came into the king's presence and stood before the king.

29 And the king vowed and said, "[a]As the LORD lives, who has redeemed my life from all distress,

30 surely as [a]I vowed to you by the LORD the God of Israel, saying, 'Your son Solomon shall be king after me, and he shall sit on my throne in my place'; I will indeed do[6213] so this day."

31 Then Bathsheba bowed with her face to the ground,[776] and prostrated herself [I]before the king and said, "[a]May my lord King David live forever."

32 Then King David said, "Call to me [a]Zadok the priest, Nathan the

9 [I]Or, *Gliding* or *Serpent Stone* [a]Josh. 15:7; 18:16; 2Sam. 17:17
10 [a]2Sam. 12:24
11 [a]2Sam. 12:24
12 [a]Prov. 15:22
13 [I]Lit., *and enter* [a]1Kin. 1:30; 1Chr. 22:9-13
15 [a]1Kin. 1:1
16 [I]Lit., *to* [II]Lit., *to you*
17 [a]1Kin. 1:13
19 [a]1Kin. 1:9
21 [I]Lit., *sinners* [a]Deut. 31:16; 2Sam. 7:12; 1Kin. 2:10
23 [I]Lit., *to*
25 [a]1Kin. 1:9 [b]1Sam. 10:24
26 [a]1Kin. 1:8, 10
27 [I]Some mss. read *servant*
29 [a]2Sam. 4:9
30 [a]1Kin. 1:13, 17
31 [I]Lit., *to* [a]Dan. 2:4; 3:9
32 [a]1Kin. 1:8

prophet, and Benaiah the son of Jehoiada." And they came into the king's presence.

33 And the king said to them, "Take with you [a]the servants of your lord, and have my son Solomon ride on my own mule, and bring him down to [b]Gihon.

34 "And let Zadok the priest and Nathan the prophet [a]anoint[4886] him there as king over Israel, and [b]blow[8628] the trumpet and say, '[c]*Long* live King Solomon!'

35 "Then you shall come up after him, and he shall come and sit on my throne and be king in my place; for I have appointed[6680] him to be ruler over Israel and Judah."

36 And Benaiah the son of Jehoiada answered the king and said, "Amen![543] Thus may the LORD, the God of my lord the king, say.

37 "[a]As the LORD has been with my lord the king, so may He be with Solomon, and [b]make his throne greater than the throne of my lord King David!"

Solomon Anointed King

38 So [a]Zadok the priest, Nathan the prophet, Benaiah the son of Jehoiada, [b]the Cherethites,[3746] and the Pelethites went down and had Solomon ride on King David's mule, and brought him to [c]Gihon.

39 Zadok the priest then [a]took the horn of oil from the tent and [b]anointed[4886] Solomon. Then they [c]blew[8628] the trumpet, and all the people said, "[d]*Long* live King Solomon!"

40 And all the people went up after him, and the people [I]were playing on flutes and rejoicing with great joy, so that the earth [II]shook at their noise.

41 Now Adonijah and all the guests[7121] who were with him heard *it,* as they finished[3615] eating. When Joab heard the sound of the trumpet, he said, "Why [I]is the city making such an uproar?"

42 While he was still speaking, behold, [a]Jonathan the son of Abiathar the priest came. Then Adonijah said, "Come in, for [b]you are a valiant man and bring good[2896] news."

43 But Jonathan answered and said to Adonijah, "No! Our lord King David has made Solomon king.

44 "The king has also sent with him Zadok the priest, Nathan the prophet, Benaiah the son of Jehoiada, the Cherethites, and the Pelethites; and they have made him ride on the king's mule.

45 "And Zadok the priest and Nathan the prophet have anointed him king in Gihon, and they have come up from there rejoicing, [a]so that the city is in an uproar. This is the noise which you have heard.

46 "Besides, [a]Solomon has even taken his seat on the throne of the kingdom.

47 "And moreover, the king's servants came to bless[1288] our lord King David, saying, 'May [a]your God make the name of Solomon better[3190] than your name and his throne greater than your throne!' And [b]the king bowed himself on the bed.

48 "The king has also said thus, 'Blessed[1288] be the LORD, the God of Israel, who [a]has granted one to sit on my throne today while my own eyes see *it.*'"

49 Then all the guests of Adonijah were terrified;[2729] and they arose and each went on his way.

50 And Adonijah was afraid[3372] of Solomon, and he arose, went and [a]took hold[2388] of the horns of the altar.[4196]

51 Now it was told Solomon, saying, "Behold, Adonijah is afraid of King Solomon, for behold, he has taken hold of the horns of the altar, saying, 'Let King Solomon swear to me today that he will not put his servant to death with the sword.'"

52 And Solomon said, "If he will be a worthy man, [a]not one of his hairs will fall to the ground; but if wickedness is found in him, he will die."[4191]

53 So King Solomon sent, and they brought him down from the altar. And he came and prostrated himself [I]before

33 [a]2Sam. 20:6, 7 [b]2Chr. 32:30; 33:14
34 [a]1Sam. 10:1; 16:3, 12; 2Sam. 5:3; 1Kin. 19:16; 2Kin. 9:3 [b]2Sam. 15:10 [c]1Kin. 1:25
37 [a]Josh. 1:5, 17; 1Sam. 20:13 [b]1Kin. 1:47
38 [a]1Kin. 1:8 [b]2Sam. 8:18 [c]1Kin. 1:33
39 [a]Ex. 30:23-32; Ps. 89:20 [b]1Chr. 29:22 [c]1Kin. 1:34 [d]1Sam. 10:24
40 [I]Lit., *fluting* [II]Lit., *was split*
41 [I]Lit., *is the sound of the city an uproar*
42 [a]2Sam. 15:27, 36; 17:17 [b]2Sam. 18:27
45 [a]1Kin. 1:40
46 [a]1Chr. 29:23
47 [a]1Kin. 1:37 [b]Gen. 47:31
48 [a]2Sam. 7:12; 1Kin. 3:6
50 [a]Ex. 27:2; 30:10; 1Kin. 2:28
52 [a]1Sam. 14:45; 2Sam. 14:11; Acts 27:34
53 [I]Lit., *to*

King Solomon, and Solomon said to him,
"Go to your house."

David's Charge to Solomon

2 As David's [I][a]time[3117] to die[4191] drew
near, he charged[6680] Solomon his
son, saying,
2 "[a]I am going the way of all the
earth.[776] [b]Be strong, therefore, and
[I]show yourself a man.
3 "And keep the charge[4931] of the
LORD your God,[430] to walk in His ways,
to keep His statutes, His commandments,[4687] His ordinances,[4941] and His
testimonies, [a]according to what is written in the law of Moses, that [b]you may
succeed in all that you do and wherever
you turn,
4 so that [a]the LORD may carry out
His promise which He spoke concerning
me, saying, '[b]If your sons[1121] are careful
of their way, [c]to walk before Me in
[I]truth with all their heart and with all
their soul, [II][d]you shall not lack a man
on the throne of Israel.'
5 "Now you also know what Joab
the [a]son of Zeruiah did[6213] to me, what
he did to the two commanders[8269] of
the armies of Israel, to [b]Abner the son
of Ner, and to [c]Amasa the son of Jether,
whom he killed; he also [I]shed the blood
of war in peace. And he put the blood[1818]
of war on his belt[2290] [II]about his waist,
and on his sandals [III]on his feet.
6 "[a]So act[6213] according to your wisdom, and do not let his gray hair[7872]
go down to [I]Sheol[7585] in peace.
7 "But [a]show kindness to the sons
of Barzillai the Gileadite, and [b]let them
be among those who eat at your table;
[c]for they [I]assisted me when I fled from
Absalom your brother.[251]
8 "And behold, [a]there is with you
Shimei the son of Gera the Benjamite,
of Bahurim; now it was he who
cursed[7043] me with a [I]violent curse[7045]
on the day[3117] I went to Mahanaim. But
when [b]he came down to me at the Jordan, I swore to him by the LORD, saying,
'I will not put you to death[4191] with the
sword.'
9 "Now therefore, do not let him
go unpunished,[5352] [a]for you are a wise
man; and you will know what you ought
to do to him, and you will bring his gray
hair down to [I]Sheol with blood."

Death of David

🔑 **10** Then [a]David slept with his fathers[1] and was buried[6912] in [b]the city
of David.
11 And [a]the days that David reigned
over Israel *were* forty years: [b]seven
years he reigned in Hebron, and thirty-
three years he reigned in Jerusalem.
12 And [a]Solomon sat on the throne
of David his father,[1] and his kingdom
was firmly established.[3559]
13 Now Adonijah the son of Haggith
came to Bathsheba the mother of Solomon. And she said, "[a]Do you come
peacefully?" And he said, "Peacefully."
14 Then he said, "I have something
to say to you." And she said, "Speak."
🔑 15 So he said, "You know that
[a]the kingdom was mine and [b]that all Israel [I]expected me to be king; [c]however,
the kingdom has turned about and
become[1961] my brother's,[251] [d]for it was
his from the LORD.
16 "And now I am making[7592] one
request of you; do not [I]refuse me." And
she said to him, "Speak."
17 Then he said, "Please speak to
Solomon the king, for he will not
[I]refuse you, that he may give me
[a]Abishag the Shunammite as a wife."
18 And Bathsheba said, "Very well;
I will speak to the king for you."

Adonijah Executed

19 So Bathsheba went to King Solomon to speak to him for Adonijah. And

1 [I]Lit., *days* [a]Gen. 47:29; Deut. 31:14

2 [I]Lit., *become a man* [a]Josh. 23:14 [b]Deut. 31:7, 23; Josh. 1:6, 7

3 [a]Deut. 17:18-20 [b]1Chr. 22:12, 13

4 [I]Or, *faithfulness* [II]Lit., *there shall not be cast off to you a man from before Me* [a]2Sam. 7:25 [b]Ps. 132:12 [c]2Kin. 20:3 [d]2Sam. 7:12, 13; 1Kin. 8:25; 9:5

5 [I]Lit., *made* [II]Lit., *that was about* [III]Lit., *that were on* [a]2Sam. 2:13, 18 [b]2Sam. 3:27; 1Kin. 2:32 [c]2Sam. 20:10

6 [I]I.e., the nether world [a]1Kin. 2:9

7 [I]Lit., *came near to* [a]2Sam. 19:31-38 [b]2Sam. 9:7, 10 [c]2Sam. 17:27-29

8 [I]Or, *grievous* [a]2Sam. 16:5-8 [b]2Sam. 19:18-23

9 [I]I.e., the nether world [a]1Kin. 2:6

10 [a]Acts 2:29; 13:36 [b]2Sam. 5:7; 1Kin. 3:1

11 [a]2Sam. 5:4, 5; 1Chr. 3:4; 29:26, 27 [b]2Sam. 5:5

12 [a]1Chr. 29:23; 2Chr. 1:1

13 [a]1Sam. 16:4

15 [I]Lit., *set their faces on me* [a]2Sam. 3:3, 4; 1Kin. 2:22 [b]1Kin. 1:5-25 [c]1Kin. 1:38-50 [d]1Chr. 22:9, 10; 28:5-7

16 [I]Lit., *turn away my face*

17 [I]Lit., *turn away your face* [a]1Kin. 1:3, 4

🔑 **2:10-12** See I Chr. 29:26-30.
🔑 **2:15** See note on I Kgs. 1:5.

the king arose to meet her, bowed[7812] before her, and sat on his throne; then he [a]had a throne set for the king's mother, and [b]she sat on his right.

20 Then she said, "I am making one small request of you; [a]do not [I]refuse me." And the king said to her, "Ask, my mother, for I will not [II]refuse you."

21 So she said, "[a]Let Abishag the Shunammite be given to Adonijah your brother as a wife."

🗝 22 And King Solomon answered and said to his mother, "And why are you asking Abishag the Shunammite for Adonijah? [a]Ask for him also the kingdom—[b]for he is my older brother—even for him, for [c]Abiathar the priest, and for Joab the son of Zeruiah!"

23 Then King Solomon swore by the LORD, saying, "May God do so to me and more also, if Adonijah has [a]not spoken this word against his own [I]life.

24 "Now therefore, as the LORD lives, who has established me and set me on the throne of David my father, and [a]who has made me a house as He promised, surely Adonijah will be put to death today."

25 So King Solomon [a]sent Benaiah the son of Jehoiada; and he fell upon him so that he died.[4191]

🗝 **26** Then to Abiathar the priest the king said, "[a]Go to Anathoth to your own field,[7704] [b]for you [I]deserve to die;[4194] but I will not put you to death[4191] at this time, because [c]you carried the ark[727] of the Lord [II]GOD before my father David, and because [d]you were afflicted in everything with which my father was afflicted."

27 So Solomon dismissed Abiathar from being priest to the LORD, in order to fulfill [a]the word of the LORD, which He had spoken concerning the house of Eli in Shiloh.

Joab Executed

28 Now the news came to Joab, [a]for Joab had followed Adonijah, [b]although he had not followed Absalom. And Joab fled to the tent of the LORD and [c]took hold of the horns of the altar.[4196]

29 And it was told King Solomon that Joab had fled to the tent of the LORD, and behold, he is beside the altar. Then Solomon [a]sent Benaiah the son of Jehoiada, saying, "[b]Go, fall upon him."

30 So Benaiah came to the tent of the LORD, and said to him, "Thus the king has said, 'Come out.' " But he said, "No, for I will die here." And Benaiah brought the king word again, saying, "Thus spoke Joab, and thus he answered me."

31 And the king said to him, "[a]Do as he has spoken and fall upon him and bury[6912] him, [b]that you may remove from me and from my father's house the blood which Joab shed without cause.

32 "And [a]the LORD will return his blood on his own head, [b]because he fell upon two men more righteous and better[2896] than he and killed them with the sword, while my father David did not know *it:* [c]Abner the son of Ner, commander[8269] of the army of Israel, and [d]Amasa the son of Jether, commander of the army of Judah.

33 "[a]So shall their blood return on the head of Joab and on the head of his [I]descendants forever; but to David and his [I]descendants and his house and his throne, may there be peace from the LORD forever."

34 Then [a]Benaiah the son of Jehoi-

19 [a]1Kin. 15:13 [b]Ps. 45:9
20 [I]Lit., *turn away my face* [II]Lit., *turn away your face* [a]1Kin. 2:16
21 [a]1Kin. 1:3, 4
22 [a]2Sam. 12:8 [b]1Kin. 1:6; 2:15; 1Chr. 3:2, 5 [c]1Kin. 1:7
23 [I]Lit., *soul* [a]Ruth 1:17
24 [a]2Sam. 7:11, 13; 1Chr. 22:10
25 [a]2Sam. 8:18
26 [I]Lit., *are a man of death* [II]Heb., *YHWH*, usually rendered *LORD* [a]Josh. 21:18; Jer. 1:1 [b]1Sam. 26:16 [c]1Sam. 23:6; 2Sam. 15:24-29 [d]1Sam. 22:20-23; 23:8, 9
27 [a]1Sam. 2:27-36
28 [a]1Kin. 1:7 [b]2Sam. 17:25; 18:2 [c]1Kin. 1:50
29 [a]1Kin. 2:25 [b]Ex. 21:14
31 [a]Ex. 21:14 [b]Num. 35:33; Deut. 19:13; 21:8, 9
32 [a]Gen. 9:6; Judg. 9:24, 57; Ps. 7:16 [b]2Chr. 21:13, 14 [c]2Sam. 3:27 [d]2Sam. 20:9, 10
33 [I]Lit., *seed* [a]2Sam. 3:29
34 [a]1Kin. 2:25

🗝 **2:22** Because of the relationship of Abishag to David, she could now only be married to a king.

🗝 **2:26,27** For his support of Adonijah in usurping the throne, Solomon banished Abiathar to his home in Anathoth and removed him from being priest. This fulfilled the prophesy of I Sam. 2:31-36 that the priesthood would depart from the family of Eli of which Abiathar was a descendant. When Zadok was appointed priest (v. 35) the priesthood was returned to its ancient lineage since Zadok was a descendant of Eleazar the son of Aaron (I Chr. 6:1-8). With regard to Anathoth, it is of interest to note that Jeremiah the prophet descended from the priests of that place (Jer. 1:1). See the note on Jer. 1:1.

ada went up and fell upon him and put
him to death, and he was buried at his
own house [b]in the wilderness.
🔑 35 And [a]the king appointed Benaiah
the son of Jehoiada over the army in
his place, and the king appointed
[b]Zadok the priest [c]in the place of Abiathar.

Shimei Executed

36 Now the king sent and called[7121]
for [a]Shimei and said to him, "Build for
yourself a house in Jerusalem and live
there, and do not go out from there to
any place.
37 "For it will happen on the day
you go out and [a]cross over the [I]brook
Kidron, you will know for certain that
you shall surely die; [b]your blood shall
be on your own head."
38 Shimei then said to the king,
"The word is good.[2896] As my lord
the king has said, so your servant will
do." So Shimei lived in Jerusalem many
days.
39 But it came about at the end of
three years, that two of the servants
of Shimei ran away [a]to Achish son of
Maacah, king of Gath. And they told
Shimei, saying, "Behold, your servants
are in Gath."
40 Then Shimei arose and saddled
his donkey, and went to Gath to Achish
to look for his servants. And Shimei
went and brought his servants from
Gath.
41 And it was told Solomon that
Shimei had gone from Jerusalem to
Gath, and had returned.
42 So the king sent and called for
Shimei and said to him, "Did I not make
you swear by the LORD and solemnly
warn you, saying, 'You will know for
certain that on the day you depart and
go anywhere, you shall surely die'? And
you said to me, 'The word which I have
heard is good.'
43 "Why then have you not kept the
oath of the LORD, and the command[4687]
which I [I]have laid on you?"
44 The king also said to Shimei,
"[a]You know all the evil which [I]you acknowledge in your heart, which you
did[6213] to my father David; therefore
[b]the LORD shall return your evil on your
own head.
45 "But King Solomon shall be
blessed,[1288] and [a]the throne of David
shall be established before the LORD forever."
46 [a]So the king commanded[6680] Benaiah the son of Jehoiada, and he went
out and fell upon him so that he died.
[b]Thus the kingdom was established in
the hands of Solomon.

Solomon's Rule Consolidated

3 Then [a]Solomon [I]formed a marriage
alliance[2859] with Pharaoh king of
Egypt, and took Pharaoh's daughter
[b]and brought her to the city of David,
[c]until he had finished[3615] building his own
house and the house of the LORD and
[d]the wall around Jerusalem.
2 [a]The people were still sacrificing
on the high places, because there was
no house built for the name of the LORD
until those days.[3117]
🔑 **3** Now [a]Solomon loved the LORD,
[b]walking in the statutes of his father[1]
David, except he sacrificed and burned
incense[6999] on the high places.
4 [a]And the king went to [b]Gibeon to
sacrifice there, [c]for that was the great
high place; Solomon offered a thousand
burnt offerings on that altar.[4196]
5 [a]In Gibeon the LORD appeared[7200]
to Solomon [b]in a dream at night; and
God[430] said, "[c]Ask[7592] what *you wish* me
to give you."

Solomon's Prayer

6 Then Solomon said, "[a]Thou hast
shown great lovingkindness to Thy

34 [b]Josh. 15:61; Matt. 3:1
35 [a]1Kin. 4:4 [b]1Chr. 6:53; 24:3; 29:22 [c]1Kin. 2:27
36 [a]2Sam. 16:5; 1Kin. 2:8
37 [I]Or, *wadi* [a]2Sam. 15:23; 2Kin. 23:6; John 18:1 [b]Josh. 2:19; 2Sam. 1:16; Ezek. 18:13
39 [a]1Sam. 27:2
43 [I]Lit., *commanded*
44 [I]Lit., *your heart acknowledges* [a]2Sam. 16:5-13 [b]1Sam. 25:39; 2Kin. 11:1, 12-16; Ps. 7:16
45 [a]2Sam. 7:13; Prov. 25:5
46 [a]1Kin. 2:25, 34 [b]1Kin. 2:12; 2Chr. 1:1
1 [I]Lit., *made himself a son-in-law of Pharaoh* [a]1Kin. 7:8; 9:16, 24; 2Chr. 8:11 [b]1Kin. 9:24 [c]1Kin. 7:1; 9:10 [d]1Kin. 9:15
2 [a]Lev. 17:3-5; Deut. 12:2, 13, 14; 1Kin. 22:43
3 [a]Deut. 6:5; 10:12, 13; 11:13; 30:16; Ps. 31:23; 145:20; 1Cor. 8:3 [b]1Kin. 2:3; 9:4; 11:4, 6, 38
4 [a]2Chr. 1:3 [b]Josh. 18:21-25 [c]1Chr. 16:39; 21:29
5 [a]1Kin. 9:2; 11:9 [b]Num. 12:6; Matt. 1:20; 2:13 [c]John 15:7
6 [a]2Sam. 7:8-17; 2Chr. 1:8

🔑 **2:35** See note on I Kgs. 2:26,27.
🔑 **3:3-15** See II Chr. 1:1-13.

servant David my father, [b]according as he walked before Thee in [I]truth and righteousness and uprightness of heart toward Thee; and [c]Thou hast [II]reserved for him this great lovingkindness, that Thou hast given him a son to sit on his throne, as *it is* this day.[3117]

7 "And now, O LORD my God, [a]Thou hast made Thy servant king in place of my father David, yet [b]I am but a little child; [c]I do not know how to go out or come in.

8 "And [a]Thy servant is in the midst of Thy people which Thou hast chosen,[977] [b]a great people who cannot be numbered or counted for multitude.

9 "So [a]give Thy servant [I]an understanding heart to judge[8199] Thy people [b]to discern[995] between good[2896] and evil.[7451] For who is able to judge this [II]great people of Thine?"

God's Answer

10 And [I]it was pleasing in the sight of the Lord that Solomon had asked[7592] this thing.

11 And God said to him, "Because you have asked this thing and have [a]not asked for yourself [I]long life, nor have asked riches for yourself, nor have you asked for the life of your enemies, but have asked for yourself [II]discernment[8085] to understand justice,[4941]

12 behold, [a]I have done[6213] according to your words. Behold, [b]I have given you a wise and discerning heart, so that there has been no one like you before you, nor shall one like you arise after you.

13 "[a]And I have also given you what you have not asked, both [b]riches and honor, so that there will not be any among the kings like you all your days.

14 "And [a]if you walk in My ways, keeping My statutes and commandments,[4687] as your father David walked, then I will [b]prolong your days."

15 Then [a]Solomon awoke, and behold, it was a dream. And he came to Jerusalem and stood before the ark[727] of the covenant[1285] of the Lord, and offered burnt offerings and made peace offerings, and [b]made a feast for all his servants.

Solomon Wisely Judges

16 Then two women who were harlots came to the king and stood before him.

17 And the one woman said, "Oh, my lord, [I]this woman and I live in the same house; and I gave birth to a child while she *was* in the house.

18 "And it happened on the third day after I gave birth, that this woman also gave birth to a child, and we were together. There was no stranger with us in the house, only the two of us in the house.

19 "And this woman's son[1121] died[4191] in the night, because she lay on it.

20 "So she arose in the middle of the night and took my son from beside me while your maidservant slept, and laid him in her bosom, and laid her dead[4191] son in my bosom.

21 "And when I rose in the morning to nurse my son, behold, he was dead; but when I looked at him carefully in the morning, behold, he was not my son, whom I had borne."

22 Then the other woman said, "No! For the living one is my son, and the dead one is your son." But [I]the first woman said, "No! For the dead one is your son, and the living one is my son." Thus they spoke before the king.

23 Then the king said, "[I]The one says, 'This is my son who is living, and your son is the dead one'; and [I]the other says, 'No! For your son is the dead one, and my son is the living one.' "

24 And the king said, "Get me a sword." So they brought a sword before the king.

25 And the king said, "Divide[1504] the living child in two, and give half to the one and half to the other."

26 Then the woman whose child *was* the living one spoke to the king, for [Ia]she was deeply stirred over her son

6 [I]Or, *faithfulness* [II]Lit., *kept* [b]1Kin. 9:4 [c]1Kin. 1:48
7 [a]1Chr. 22:9-13 [b]1Chr. 29:1; Jer. 1:6, 7 [c]Num. 27:17
8 [a]Ex. 19:6; Deut. 7:6 [b]Gen. 15:5; 22:17
9 [I]Lit., *a hearing* [II]Lit., *heavy* [a]2Chr. 1:10; Ps. 72:1, 2; Prov. 2:3-9; James 1:5 [b]2Sam. 14:17; Heb. 5:14
10 [I]Lit., *the thing*
11 [I]Lit., *many days* [II]Lit., *hearing* [a]James 4:3
12 [a]1John 5:14, 15 [b]1Kin. 4:29-31; 5:12; 10:23, 24; Eccl. 1:16
13 [a]1Kin. 4:21-24; 10:23, 27; Matt. 6:33; Eph. 3:20 [b]Prov. 3:16
14 [a]1Kin. 3:6 [b]Ps. 91:16; Prov. 3:2
15 [a]Gen. 41:7 [b]1Kin. 8:65
17 [I]Lit., *I and this woman*
22 [I]Lit., *this one was saying*
23 [I]Lit., *this one*
26 [I]Lit., *her compassion grew warm* [a]Gen. 43:30; Is. 49:15; Jer. 31:20; Hos. 11:8

and said, "Oh, my lord, give her the living child, and by no means kill him." But the other said, "He shall be neither mine nor yours; divide *him!*"

27 Then the king answered and said, "Give [I]the first woman the living child, and by no means kill him. She is his mother."

28 When all Israel heard of the judgment which the king had [I]handed down,[8199] they feared[3372] the king; for [a]they saw that the wisdom of God was in him to [II]administer[6213] justice.

Solomon's Officials

4 Now King Solomon was king over all Israel.

2 And these were his officials: Azariah the son of Zadok *was* [a]the priest;

3 Elihoreph and Ahijah, the sons of Shisha *were* secretaries; [a]Jehoshaphat the son of Ahilud *was* the recorder;

4 and [a]Benaiah the son of Jehoiada *was* over the army; and Zadok and [b]Abiathar *were* priests;

5 and Azariah the son of Nathan *was* over [a]the deputies; and Zabud the son of Nathan, a priest, *was* the king's friend;

6 and Ahishar was over the household; and Adoniram the son of Abda *was* over the men subject to forced labor.

7 And Solomon had twelve deputies over all Israel, who [I]provided for the king and his household; each man had to [II]provide for a month in the year.

8 And these are their names: Ben-hur, in the [a]hill country of Ephraim;

9 Ben-deker in Makaz and [a]Shaalbim and [b]Beth-shemesh and Elonbeth-hanan;

10 Ben-hesed, in Arubboth ([a]Socoh *was* his and all the land of [b]Hepher);

11 Ben-abinadab, *in* all [I]the [a]height of Dor (Taphath the daughter of Solomon was his wife);

12 Baana the son of Ahilud, *in* [a]Taanach and Megiddo, and all [b]Beth-shean which is beside [c]Zarethan below Jezreel, from Beth-shean to [d]Abel-meholah as far as the other side of [e]Jokmeam;

13 Ben-geber, in [a]Ramoth-gilead ([b]the towns of Jair, the son of Manasseh, which are in Gilead were his: [c]the region of Argob, which is in Bashan, sixty great cities with walls and bronze bars *were* his);

14 Ahinadab the son of Iddo, *in* [a]Mahanaim;

15 [a]Ahimaaz, in Naphtali (he also married Basemath the daughter of Solomon);

16 Baana the son of [a]Hushai, in Asher and [I]Bealoth;

17 Jehoshaphat the son of Paruah, in Issachar;

18 [a]Shimei the son of Ela, in Benjamin;

19 Geber the son of Uri, in the land[776] of Gilead, [a]the country of Sihon king of the Amorites and of Og king of Bashan; and *he was* the only deputy who *was* in the land.

Solomon's Power, Wealth and Wisdom

20 [a]Judah and Israel *were* as numerous as the sand that is on the [I]seashore in abundance; *they* were eating and drinking and rejoicing.

21 [Ia]Now Solomon ruled over all the kingdoms [b]from the [II]River *to* the land of the Philistines and to the border of Egypt; [c]*they* brought[5066] tribute and served Solomon all the days[3117] of his life.

22 And Solomon's [I]provision for one day was thirty [II]kors of fine flour and sixty [II]kors of meal,

23 ten fat oxen, twenty [I]pasture-fed oxen, a hundred sheep besides deer, gazelles, roebucks,[6643] and fattened fowl.

24 For he had dominion[7287] over everything [I]west of the [II]River, from Tiphsah even to [a]Gaza, [b]over all the kings [I]west of the [II]River; and [c]he had peace on all sides around about him.

25 [a]So Judah and Israel lived in safety, every man under his vine and his fig tree, [b]from Dan even to Beersheba, all the days of Solomon.

27 [I]Lit., *her the living child*
28 [I]Lit., *judged* [II]Lit., *do* [a]1Kin. 3:9, 11, 12; Dan. 1:17; Col. 2:2, 3
2 [a]1Chr. 6:10
3 [a]2Sam. 8:16
4 [a]1Kin. 2:35 [b]1Kin. 2:27
5 [a]1Kin. 4:7
7 [I]Lit., *nourished* [II]Lit., *nourish*
8 [a]Josh. 24:33
9 [a]Judg. 1:35 [b]Josh. 21:16
10 [a]Josh. 15:35 [b]Josh. 12:17
11 [I]Or, *Naphoth-dor* [a]Josh. 11:1, 2
12 [a]Judg. 5:19 [b]Josh. 17:11 [c]Josh. 3:16 [d]1Kin. 19:16 [e]1Chr. 6:68
13 [a]1Kin. 22:3-15 [b]Num. 32:41 [c]Deut. 3:4
14 [a]Josh. 13:26
15 [a]2Sam. 15:27
16 [I]Or, *in Aloth* [a]2Sam. 15:32
18 [a]1Kin. 1:8
19 [a]Deut. 3:8-10
20 [I]Lit., *sea* [a]Gen. 22:17; 32:12; 1Kin. 3:8
21 [I]Ch. 5:1 in Heb. [II]I.e., Euphrates [a]2Chr. 9:26 [b]Gen. 15:18; Josh. 1:4 [c]2Sam. 8:2, 6
22 [I]Lit., *bread* [II]I.e., 1 kor equals approx. 10 bu.
23 [I]Lit., *oxen of the pasture*
24 [I]Lit., *beyond* [II]I.e., Euphrates [a]Judg. 1:18 [b]Ps. 72:11 [c]1Chr. 22:9
25 [a]Jer. 23:6; Mic. 4:4; Zech. 3:10 [b]1Sam. 3:20

26 [a]And Solomon had [I]40,000 stalls of horses for his chariots, and 12,000 horsemen.

27 And those deputies [I]provided for King Solomon and all who came to King Solomon's table, each in his month; they left nothing lacking.

28 They also brought barley and straw for the horses and [a]swift steeds to the place where it should be, each according to his charge.

29 Now [a]God[430] gave Solomon wisdom and very great discernment and breadth of [I]mind, [b]like the sand that is on the seashore.

30 And Solomon's wisdom surpassed the wisdom of all [a]the sons[1121] of the east and [b]all the wisdom of Egypt.

🗝 31 For [a]he was wiser than all men, than [b]Ethan the Ezrahite, Heman, [c]Calcol and [I]Darda, the sons of Mahol; and his [II]fame was *known* in all the surrounding nations.

32 [a]He also spoke 3,000 proverbs, and his songs were 1,005.

33 And he spoke of trees, from the cedar that is in Lebanon even to the hyssop[231] that grows on the wall; he spoke also of animals and birds and creeping things and fish.[1709]

34 And [I]men [a]came from all peoples to hear the wisdom of Solomon, from all the kings of the earth[776] who had heard of his wisdom.

Alliance with King Hiram

5 🗝 Now Hiram king of Tyre sent his servants to Solomon, when he heard that they had anointed[4886] him king in place of his father,[1] for [a]Hiram had [II]always been a friend of David.

2 Then [a]Solomon sent *word* to Hiram, saying,

🗝 3 "You know that [a]David my father was unable to build a house for the name of the LORD his God[430] because of the wars which surrounded him, until the LORD put them under the soles of his feet.

4 "But now [a]the LORD my God has given me rest on every side; there is neither adversary nor [I]misfortune.[7451]

5 "And behold, [a]I [I]intend to build a house for the name of the LORD my God, as the LORD spoke to David my father, saying, 'Your son, whom I will set on your throne in your place, he will build the house for My name.'

6 "Now therefore, command[6680] that they cut[3772] for me [a]cedars from Lebanon, and my servants will be with your servants; and I will give you wages for your servants according to all that you say,[559] for you know that there is no one among us who knows how to cut timber like the Sidonians."

7 And it came about when Hiram heard the words of Solomon, that he rejoiced greatly and said, "Blessed[1288] be the LORD today,[3117] who has given to David a wise son over this great people."

8 So Hiram sent *word* to Solomon, saying, "I have heard[8085] *the message* which you have sent me; I will do[6213] [I]what you desire[2656] concerning the cedar and cypress timber.

9 "My servants will bring *them* down from Lebanon to the sea; and I will make them into rafts *to go* by sea [a]to the place where you [I]direct me, and I will have them broken up there, and you shall carry *them* away. Then [b]you shall accomplish[6213] my desire by giving food to my household."

10 So [I]Hiram [II]gave Solomon [III]as much as he desired of the cedar and cypress timber.

11 [a]Solomon then gave Hiram 20,000 [I]kors of wheat as food for his household, and twenty [I]kors of beaten oil; thus Solomon would give Hiram year by year.

26 [I]One ms. reads *4000*, cf. 2Chr. 9:25 [a]1Kin. 10:26; 2Chr. 1:14
27 [I]Or, *nourished*
28 [a]Esth. 8:10, 14; Mic. 1:13
29 [I]Lit., *heart* [a]1Kin. 3:12 [b]1Kin. 4:20
30 [a]Gen. 29:1; Judg. 6:33 [b]Is. 19:11; Acts 7:22
31 [I]In 1Chr. 2:6, *Dara* [II]Lit., *name* [a]1Kin. 3:12 [b]1Chr. 15:19; Ps. 89:title [c]1Chr. 2:6
32 [a]Prov. 1:1; 10:1; 25:1; Eccl. 12:9; Song 1:1
34 [I]Lit., *they* [a]1Kin. 10:1; 2Chr. 9:23
1 [I]Ch. 5:15 in Heb. [II]Lit., *all the day* [a]2Chr. 2:3 [b]2Sam. 5:11; 1Chr. 14:1
2 [a]2Chr. 2:3
3 [a]2Sam. 7:5; 1Chr. 28:2, 3
4 [I]Lit., *evil occurrence* [a]1Kin. 4:24; 1Chr. 22:9
5 [I]Lit., *say* [a]2Sam. 7:12, 13; 1Chr. 17:12; 22:10; 28:6; 2Chr. 2:4
6 [a]2Chr. 2:8
8 [I]Lit., *all your pleasure*
9 [I]Lit., *send* [a]2Chr. 2:16 [b]Ezra 3:7; Ezek. 27:17
10 [I]Heb., *Hirom* [II]Lit., *was giving* [III]Lit., *all his desire*
11 [I]I.e., 1 kor equals approx. 10 bu. [a]2Chr. 2:10

🗝 **4:31** Psalm 88 was written by Heman, and Psalm 89 was composed by Ethan. They were among five famous brothers in the tribe of Judah (I Chr. 2:6).
🗝 **5:1-18** See II Chr. 2:1-18.
🗝 **5:3** See note on II Sam. 7:4-16.

12 And [a]the LORD gave wisdom to Solomon, just as He [I]promised him; and there was peace between Hiram and Solomon, and the two of them made a covenant.

Conscription of Laborers

13 Now [a]King Solomon [I]levied forced laborers from all Israel; and the forced laborers [II]numbered 30,000 men.

14 And he sent them to Lebanon, 10,000 a month in relays; they were in Lebanon a month *and* two months at home. And [a]Adoniram *was* over the forced laborers.

15 Now [a]Solomon had 70,000 [I]transporters,[5375] and 80,000 hewers[2672] *of stone* in the mountains,

16 [a]besides Solomon's 3,300 chief deputies who *were* over the [I]project *and* who ruled over the people who were doing the work.

17 Then [a]the king commanded,[6680] and they quarried great stones, costly stones, to lay the foundation[3245] of the house with cut[1496] stones.

18 So Solomon's builders[1129] and [I]Hiram's builders and [a]the Gebalites[1382] [II]cut[6458] them, and prepared the timbers and the stones to build the house.

The Building of the Temple

6 🗝 [a]Now it came about in the four hundred and eightieth year after the sons[1121] of Israel came out of the land of Egypt, in the fourth year of Solomon's reign over Israel, in the month of Ziv which is the second month, that he [I]began to build the house of the LORD.

🗝 2 As for the house which King Solomon built for the LORD, its length *was* sixty [I]cubits and its width twenty *cubits* and its height thirty cubits.

3 And the porch in front of the nave of the house *was* twenty cubits [I]in length, [II]corresponding to the width of the house, *and* its [III]depth along the front of the house *was* ten cubits.

4 Also for the house [a]he made windows with *artistic* frames.

5 And [a]against the wall of the house he built stories encompassing the walls of the house around both the nave and the [b]inner sanctuary; thus he made [c]side chambers all around.

6 The lowest[8481] story *was* five cubits wide, and the middle *was* six cubits wide, and the third *was* seven cubits wide; for on the outside he [I]made offsets *in the wall* of the house all around in order that *the beams* should not [II]be inserted in the walls of the house.

7 And [a]the house, while it was being built, was built of stone [I]prepared at the quarry, and there was neither hammer nor axe nor any iron tool heard in the house while it was being built.

8 The doorway for the [I]lowest side chamber *was* on the right side of the house; and they would go up by winding stairs to the middle *story,* and from the middle to the third.

9 So [a]he built the house and finished[3615] it; and he covered the house with beams and [I]planks of cedar.

10 He also built the stories against the whole house, each five [I]cubits high; and they [II]were fastened to the house with timbers of cedar.

11 Now the word of the LORD came to Solomon saying,

12 "*Concerning* this house which you are building, [a]if you will walk in My statutes and execute My ordinances[4941] and keep all My commandments[4687] by

12 [I]Lit., *spoke to* [a]1Kin. 3:12
13 [I]Lit., *raised up* [II]Lit., *was* [a]1Kin. 4:6; 9:15
14 [a]1Kin. 4:6; 12:18
15 [I]Or, *burden bearers* [a]1Kin. 9:20-22; 2Chr. 2:17, 18
16 [I]Lit., *work* [a]1Kin. 9:23
17 [a]1Kin. 6:7; 1Chr. 22:2
18 [I]Heb., *Hirom's* [II]Or, *chiseled* [a]Josh. 13:5; Ezek. 27:9

1 [I]Lit., *built* [a]2Chr. 3:1, 2
2 [I]I.e., One cubit equals approx. 18 in.
3 [I]Lit., *in its length* [II]Lit., *on the face of* [III]Lit., *width*
4 [a]Ezek. 40:16; 41:16
5 [a]Ezek. 41:6 [b]1Kin. 6:16, 19, 20 [c]Ezek. 41:5
6 [I]Lit., *gave* [II]Lit., *take hold*
7 [I]Lit., *finished* [a]Ex. 20:25; Deut. 27:5, 6
8 [I]So with Gr. and versions; M.T., *middle*
9 [I]Lit., *rows* [a]1Kin. 6:14, 38
10 [I]I.e., One cubit equals approx. 18 in. [II]Lit., *took hold*
12 [a]2Sam. 7:5-16; 1Kin. 9:4

🗝 **6:1-38** See II Chr. 3:1-14.

🗝 **6:2** Calculations based on Ex. 26 indicate that the tabernacle proper had been thirty cubits long and ten cubits wide. The permanent structure of the temple maintained the same proportions except that the length and breadth were doubled in size. Depending upon the length of the cubit currently in use then, it ranged in size from 90 to 100 feet long by 30 to 35 feet wide. In any case, it was not a large structure. This was the sanctuary proper. A number of more imposing and magnificent structures surrounded it.

walking in them, then I will carry out My word with you which I spoke to David your father.[1]

13 "And [a]I will dwell[7931] among the sons of Israel, and [b]will not forsake[5800] My people Israel."

14 [a]So Solomon built the house and finished it.

15 Then he [a]built the walls of the house on the inside with boards of cedar; from the floor of the house to the [I]ceiling he overlaid *the walls* on the inside with wood, and he overlaid the floor of the house with boards of cypress.

16 [a]And he built twenty cubits on the rear part of the house with boards of cedar from the floor to the [I]ceiling; he built *them* for it on the inside as an inner sanctuary, *even* as [b]the most holy place.

17 And the house, that is, the nave in front of *the inner sanctuary,* was forty [I]cubits *long.*

18 And there was cedar on the house within, carved *in the shape* of [a]gourds and open flowers; all was cedar, there was no stone seen.

19 Then he prepared an inner sanctuary within the house in order to place there the ark[727] of the covenant[1285] of the LORD.

20 And [I]the inner sanctuary *was* twenty cubits in length, twenty cubits in width, and twenty cubits in height, and he overlaid it with pure gold. He also overlaid the altar[4196] with cedar.

21 So Solomon overlaid the inside of the house with pure gold. And he drew chains of gold across the front of the inner sanctuary; and he overlaid it with gold.

22 And he overlaid the whole house with gold, until all the house was finished.[8552] Also [a]the whole altar which was by the inner sanctuary he overlaid with gold.

23 [a]Also in the inner sanctuary he made two cherubim[3742] of olive wood, each ten cubits high.

24 And five cubits *was* the one wing of the cherub[3742] and five cubits the other wing of the cherub; from the end of one wing to the end of the other wing *were* ten cubits.

25 And the other cherub *was* ten cubits; both the cherubim were of the same measure and the same form.

26 The height of the one cherub *was* ten cubits, and so *was* the other cherub.

27 And he placed the cherubim in the midst of the inner house, and [a]the wings of the cherubim were spread out, so that the wing of the one was touching the *one* wall, and the wing of the other cherub was touching the other wall. So their wings were touching each other in the center of the house.

28 He also overlaid the cherubim with gold.

29 Then he carved all the walls of the house round about with carved engravings of cherubim, palm trees, and open flowers, inner and outer *sanctuaries.*

30 And he overlaid the floor of the house with gold, inner and outer *sanctuaries.*

31 And for the entrance of the inner sanctuary he made doors of olive wood, the lintel[352] *and* five-sided doorposts.

32 So *he made* two doors of olive wood, and he carved on them carvings of cherubim, palm trees, and open flowers, and overlaid them with gold; and he spread the gold on the cherubim and on the palm trees.

33 So also he made for the entrance of the nave four-sided doorposts of olive wood

34 and [a]two doors of cypress wood; the two leaves of the one door turned on pivots, and the two [I]leaves of the other door turned on pivots.

35 And he carved *on it* cherubim, palm trees, and open flowers; and he overlaid *them* with gold evenly applied[3474] on the engraved work.

36 And [a]he built the inner court with three rows of cut[1496] stone and a row of cedar beams.

37 [a]In the fourth year the foundation[3245] of the house of the LORD was laid, in the month of Ziv.

38 And in the eleventh year, in the

13 [a]Ex. 25:8; 29:45; Lev. 26:11 [b]Deut. 31:6; Josh. 1:5; Heb. 13:5
14 [a]1Kin. 6:9, 38
15 [I]Lit., *walls of ceiling* [a]1Kin. 7:7
16 [I]Lit., *walls* [a]2Chr. 3:8 [b]Ex. 26:33, 34; Lev. 16:2; 1Kin. 8:6; Heb. 9:3
17 [I]I.e., One cubit equals approx. 18 in.
18 [a]1Kin. 7:24
20 [I]Lit., *before*
22 [a]Ex. 30:1, 3, 6
23 [a]Ex. 37:7-9; 2Chr. 3:10-12
27 [a]Ex. 25:20; 37:9; 1Kin. 8:7
34 [I]So with Gr.; M.T., *curtains* [a]Ezek. 41:23-25
36 [a]1Kin. 7:12; Jer. 36:10
37 [a]1Kin. 6:1

month of Bul, which is the eighth month, the house was finished throughout all its parts and according to all its plans.[4941] So he was seven years in building it.

Solomon's Palace

7 Now [a]Solomon was building his own house thirteen years, and he finished[3615] all his house.

2 And [a]he built the house of the forest of Lebanon; its length was 100 [I]cubits and its width 50 cubits and its height 30 cubits, on four rows of cedar pillars with cedar beams on the pillars.

3 And it was paneled with cedar above the side chambers which were on the 45 pillars, 15 in each row.

4 And *there were artistic window* frames in three rows, and window was opposite window in three ranks.

5 And all the doorways and doorposts *had* squared *artistic* frames, and window was opposite window in three ranks.

6 Then he made [a]the hall of pillars; its length was 50 cubits and its width 30 cubits, and a porch *was* in front of them and pillars and a [b]threshold in front of them.

7 And he made the hall of the [a]throne where he was to judge,[8199] the hall of judgment,[4941] and [b]it was paneled with cedar from floor to floor.

8 And his house where he was to live, the other court inward from the hall, was of the same workmanship. [a]He also made a house like this hall for Pharaoh's daughter, [b]whom Solomon had married.

9 All these were of costly stones, of stone cut[1496] according to measure, sawed with saws, inside and outside; even from the foundation to the coping, and so on the outside to the great court.

10 And the foundation[3245] was of costly stones, *even* large stones, stones of ten cubits and stones of eight cubits.

11 And above were costly stones, stone cut according to measure, and cedar.

12 So [a]the great court all around *had* three rows of cut stone and a row of cedar beams even as the inner court of the house of the LORD, and [b]the porch of the house.

Hiram's Work in the Temple

🔑**13** Now [a]King Solomon sent and brought Hiram from Tyre.

14 [a]He was a widow's son from the tribe of Naphtali, and his father[1] was a man of Tyre, a worker in bronze; and [b]he was filled with wisdom and understanding and skill[1847] for doing any work in bronze. So he came to King Solomon and [c]performed all his work.

15 And he fashioned [a]the two pillars of bronze; [b]eighteen cubits was the height of one pillar, and a line of twelve cubits [I]measured the circumference of both.

16 He also made two capitals of molten bronze to set on the tops of the pillars; the height of the one capital was five [I]cubits and the height of the other capital was five cubits.

17 *There were* nets of network and twisted threads of chainwork for the capitals which were on the top of the pillars; seven for the one capital and seven for the other capital.

18 So he made the pillars, and two rows around on the one network to cover[3680] the capitals which were on the top of the pomegranates; and so he did[6213] for the other capital.

19 And the capitals which *were* on the top of the pillars in the porch were of lily design, four cubits.

20 And *there were* capitals on the two pillars, even above *and* close to the [I]rounded projection[990] which was beside the network; and [a]the pomegranates *numbered* two hundred in rows around [II]both capitals.

21 [a]Thus he set up the pillars at the

1 [a]1Kin. 3:1; 9:10; 2Chr. 8:1
2 [I]I.e., One cubit equals approx. 18 in. [a]1Kin. 10:17, 21; 2Chr. 9:16
6 [a]1Kin. 7:12 [b]Ezek. 41:25, 26
7 [a]Ps. 122:5; Prov. 20:8 [b]1Kin. 6:15, 16
8 [a]1Kin. 9:24; 2Chr. 8:11 [b]1Kin. 3:1
12 [a]1Kin. 6:36 [b]1Kin. 7:6
13 [a]2Chr. 2:13, 14; 4:11
14 [a]2Chr. 2:14 [b]Ex. 28:3; 31:3-5; 35:31; 36:1 [c]2Chr. 4:11-16
15 [I]Lit., *went around the other pillar* [a]2Kin. 25:17; 2Chr. 3:15; 4:12; Jer. 52:21 [b]1Kin. 7:41
16 [I]I.e., One cubit equals approx. 18 in.
20 [I]Lit., *belly* [II]Lit., *on the other capital* [a]1Kin. 7:42; 2Chr. 3:16; 4:13; Jer. 52:23
21 [a]2Chr. 3:17

🔑**7:13** This man's mother was a Hebrew. He is not the same man as King Hiram.
🔑**7:13-22** See II Chr. 2:13-14; 3:15-17.

[b]porch of the nave; and he set up the
right pillar and named[7121] it [I]Jachin, and
he set up the left pillar and named it
[II]Boaz.
22 And on the top of the pillars was
lily design. So the work of the pillars
was finished.[8552]
🔑 **23** [a]Now he made the sea of
[b]cast *metal* ten cubits from brim[8193] to
brim, circular in form, and its height
was five cubits, and [I]thirty cubits in circumference.
24 And under its brim [a]gourds went
around encircling[5362] it ten to a cubit,
[b]completely surrounding the sea; the
gourds were in two rows, cast [I]with
the rest.
25 [a]It stood on twelve oxen, three
facing north, three facing west, three
facing south, and three facing east; and
the sea *was set* on top of them, and all
their rear parts *turned* inward.[1004]
26 And it was a handbreadth thick,
and its brim was made like the brim of
a cup, *as* a lily blossom; it could hold
two thousand baths.
27 Then [a]he made the ten stands
of bronze; the length of each stand was
four cubits and its width four cubits and
its height three cubits.
28 And this was the design of the
stands: they had borders, even borders
between the [I]frames,
29 and on the borders which were
between the [I]frames *were* lions, oxen
and cherubim;[3742] and on the [I]frames
there *was* a pedestal above, and beneath
the lions and oxen *were* wreaths of hanging work.
30 Now each stand had four bronze
wheels with bronze axles, and its four
feet had supports; beneath the basin[3595]
were cast supports with wreaths at each
side.
31 And its opening inside the crown
at the top *was* a cubit, and its opening
was round like the design of a pedestal,
a cubit and a half; and also on its opening
there were engravings,[4734] and their borders were square, not round.

32 And the four wheels *were* underneath the borders, and the axles of the
wheels *were* on the stand. And the height
of a wheel *was* a cubit and a half.
33 And the workmanship of the
wheels *was* like the workmanship of a
chariot wheel. Their axles, their
rims,[1354] their spokes, and their hubs
were all cast.
34 Now *there were* four supports at
the four corners of each stand; its supports *were* part of the stand itself.
35 And on the top of the stand *there*
was a circular form half a [I]cubit high,
and on the top of the stand its [II]stays
and its borders *were* part of it.
36 And he engraved[6605] on the
plates of its stays and on its borders,
cherubim, lions and palm trees, according to the clear space on each, with
wreaths *all* around.
37 [a]He made the ten stands[4350] like
this: all of them had one casting, one
measure and one form.
38 [a]And he made ten basins[3595] of
bronze, one basin held forty baths; each
basin *was* four cubits, *and* on each of
the ten stands *was* one basin.
39 Then he set the stands, five on
the right side of the house and five on
the left side of the house; and he set
the sea *of cast metal* on the right side
of the house eastward toward the south.
40 Now Hiram made the basins[3595]
and the shovels and the bowls.[4219] So
Hiram finished[3615] doing[6213] all the work
which he performed for King Solomon
in the house of the LORD:
41 the two pillars and the *two* bowls
of the capitals which *were* on the top
of the [a]two pillars, and the two networks
to cover the two bowls of the capitals
which *were* on the top of the pillars;
42 and the [a]four hundred pomegranates for the two networks, two rows
of pomegranates for each network to
cover the two bowls of the capitals which
were on the tops of the pillars;
43 and the ten stands with the ten
basins on the stands;

21 [I]I.e., he shall establish [II]I.e., in it is strength [b]1Kin. 6:3
23 [I]Lit., *a line of 30 cubits went around it* [a]2Chr. 4:2 [b]2Kin. 16:17; 25:13
24 [I]Lit., *in its casting* [a]1Kin. 6:18 [b]2Chr. 4:3
25 [a]2Chr. 4:4, 5; Jer. 52:20
27 [a]1Kin. 7:38; 2Kin. 25:13; 2Chr. 4:14
28 [I]Or, *crossbars*
29 [I]Or, *crossbars*
35 [I]I.e., One cubit equals approx. 18 in. [II]Lit., *hands*
37 [a]2Chr. 4:14
38 [a]Ex. 30:18; 2Chr. 4:6
41 [a]1Kin. 7:17, 18
42 [a]1Kin. 7:20

🔑 **7:23-51** See II Chr. 4:1—5:1.

44 and [a]the one sea and the twelve oxen under the sea;

45 and [a]the pails and the shovels and the bowls; even all these utensils which Hiram made for King Solomon *in* the house of the LORD *were* of polished bronze.

46 [a]In the plain of the Jordan the king cast them, in the clay ground[127] between [b]Succoth and [c]Zarethan.

47 And Solomon left all the utensils *unweighed,* because *they were* too many; [a]the weight of the bronze could not be ascertained.

48 And Solomon made all the furniture which *was in* the house of the LORD: [a]the golden altar[4196] and the golden table on which *was* the [b]bread of the Presence;

49 and the lampstands, five on the right side and five on the left, in front of the inner sanctuary, of pure gold; and [a]the flowers and the lamps and the tongs, of gold;

50 and the cups and the snuffers and the bowls and the spoons and the [a]firepans, of pure gold; and the hinges both for the doors of the inner house, the most holy place, *and* for the doors of the house, *that is,* of the nave, of gold.

51 [a]Thus all the work that King Solomon performed *in* the house of the LORD was finished.[7999] And [b]Solomon brought in the things dedicated[6944] by his father David, the silver and the gold and the utensils, *and* he put them in the treasuries of the house of the LORD.

The Ark Brought into the Temple

8 🗝 [a]Then Solomon assembled[6950] the elders[2205] of Israel and all [b]the heads of the tribes, the leaders[5387] of the fathers'[1] *households* of the sons[1121] of Israel, to King Solomon in Jerusalem, [c]to bring up the ark[727] of the covenant[1285] of the LORD from [d]the city of David, which is Zion.

2 And all the men of Israel assembled themselves to King Solomon at [a]the feast,[2282] in the month Ethanim, which is the seventh month.

3 Then all the elders of Israel came, and [a]the priests took up the ark.

4 And they brought[5927] up the ark of the LORD and [a]the tent of meeting[4150] and all the holy utensils, which were in the tent, and the priests and the Levites brought them up.

5 And King Solomon and all the congregation[5712] of Israel, who were assembled[3259] to him, [a]were with him before the ark, sacrificing [l]so many sheep and oxen they could not be counted or numbered.

6 Then [a]the priests brought the ark of the covenant of the LORD [b]to its place, into the inner sanctuary of the house, to the most holy place, [c]under the wings of the cherubim.[3742]

7 For the cherubim spread *their* wings over the place of the ark, and the cherubim made a covering over the ark and its poles from above.

8 But [a]the poles were so long that the ends of the poles could be seen from the holy place before the inner sanctuary, but they could not be seen outside; they are there to this day.[3117]

9 [a]There was nothing in the ark except the two tablets of stone which Moses put there at Horeb, where [b]the LORD made a covenant with the sons of Israel, when they came out of the land of Egypt.

10 And it came about when the priests came from the holy place, that [a]the cloud[6051] filled the house of the LORD,

11 so that the priests could not stand to minister because of the cloud, for the glory of the LORD filled the house of the LORD.

Solomon Addresses the People

🗝 **12** [a]Then Solomon said,
"The LORD has said that

44 [a]1Kin. 7:23, 25
45 [a]Ex. 27:3; 2Chr. 4:16
46 [a]2Chr. 4:17 [b]Gen. 33:17; Josh. 13:27 [c]Josh. 3:16
47 [a]1Chr. 22:3, 14
48 [a]Ex. 30:1-3; 37:10-29; 2Chr. 4:8 [b]Ex. 25:30
49 [a]Ex. 25:31-38
50 [a]Ex. 27:3; 2Kin. 25:15
51 [a]2Chr. 5:1 [b]2Sam. 8:11; 1Chr. 18:11; 2Chr. 5:1
1 [a]2Chr. 5:2-10 [b]Num. 1:4; 7:2 [c]2Sam. 6:12-17; 1Chr. 15:25-29 [d]2Sam. 5:7
2 [a]Lev. 23:34; 1Kin. 8:65; 2Chr. 7:8-10
3 [a]Num. 7:9; Deut. 31:9; Josh. 3:3, 6
4 [a]1Kin. 3:4; 2Chr. 1:3
5 [l]Lit., *sheep and oxen . . . numbered for multitude* [a]2Sam. 6:13; 2Chr. 1:6
6 [a]1Kin. 8:3 [b]1Kin. 6:19 [c]1Kin. 6:27
8 [a]Ex. 25:13-15; 37:4, 5
9 [a]Ex. 25:16, 21; Deut. 10:2-5; Heb. 9:4 [b]Ex. 24:7, 8; 40:20; Deut. 4:13
10 [a]Ex. 40:34, 35; 2Chr. 7:1, 2
12 [a]2Chr. 6:1

🗝 **8:1-11** See II Chr. 5:2-14.
🗝 **8:12-66** See II Chr. 6:1—7:10.

[b]He would dwell[7931] in the
thick cloud.[6205]

13 "[a]I have surely built Thee a lofty
house,
[b]A place for Thy dwelling
forever."

14 Then the king [I]faced about and [a]blessed[1288] all the assembly[6951] of Israel, while all the assembly of Israel was standing.

15 And he said, "[a]Blessed be the LORD, the God[430] of Israel, [b]who spoke with His mouth to my father[1] David and has fulfilled *it* with His hand, saying,

16 '[a]Since the day that I brought My people Israel from Egypt, I did not choose[977] a city out of all the tribes of Israel *in which* to build a house that [b]My name might be there, but [c]I chose David to be over My people Israel.'

17 "[a]Now it was [I]in the heart of my father David to build a house for the name of the LORD, the God of Israel.

18 "But the LORD said to my father David, 'Because it was [I]in your heart to build a house for My name, you did well that it was [I]in your heart.

19 '[a]Nevertheless you shall not build the house, but your son who [I]shall be born to you, he shall build the house for My name.'

20 "Now the LORD has fulfilled His word which He spoke; for [a]I have risen in place of my father David and sit on the throne of Israel, as the LORD [I]promised, and have built the house for the name of the LORD, the God of Israel.

21 "And there I have set a place for the ark, [a]in which is the covenant of the LORD, which He made with our fathers when He brought them from the land of Egypt."

The Prayer of Dedication

22 Then [a]Solomon stood before the altar[4196] of the LORD in the presence of all the assembly of Israel and [b]spread out his hands toward heaven.

23 And he said, "O LORD, the God of Israel, [a]there is no God like Thee in heaven above or on earth[776] beneath, [b]who art keeping covenant and *showing* lovingkindness to Thy servants who walk before Thee with all their heart,

24 who hast kept with Thy servant, my father David, that which Thou hast [I]promised him; indeed, Thou hast spoken with Thy mouth and hast fulfilled it with Thy hand as it is this day.

25 "Now therefore, O LORD, the God of Israel, keep with Thy servant David my father that which Thou hast [I]promised him, saying, '[II][a]You shall not lack a man to sit on the throne of Israel, if only your sons take heed to their way to walk before Me as you have walked.'

26 "Now therefore, O God of Israel, let Thy word, I pray Thee, be confirmed [a]which Thou hast spoken to Thy servant, my father David.

27 "But will God indeed[552] dwell on the earth? Behold, [a]heaven and the [I]highest heaven cannot contain Thee, how much less this house which I have built!

28 "Yet have regard to the [a]prayer of Thy servant and to his supplication, O LORD my God, to listen to the cry and to the prayer which Thy servant prays before Thee today;

29 [a]that Thine eyes may be open toward this house night and day, toward [b]the place of which Thou hast said, 'My name shall be there,' to listen to the prayer which Thy servant shall pray toward this place.

30 "And [a]listen to the supplication of Thy servant and of Thy people Israel, [b]when they pray toward this place; hear Thou in heaven Thy dwelling place; hear and [c]forgive.[5545]

31 "[a]If a man sins against his neighbor and is made to take an oath, and

12 [b]Lev. 16:2; Ps. 18:11; 97:2
13 [a]2Sam. 7:13 [b]Ex. 15:17; Ps. 132:14
14 [I]Lit., *turned his face about* [a]2Sam. 6:18; 1Kin. 8:55
15 [a]1Chr. 29:10, 20; Neh. 9:5; Luke 1:68 [b]2Sam. 7:12, 13; 1Chr. 22:10
16 [a]2Sam. 7:4, 5; 1Chr. 17:3-10; 2Chr. 6:5 [b]Deut. 12:5, 11 [c]1Sam. 16:1; 2Sam. 7:8
17 [I]Lit., *with* [a]2Sam. 7:2, 3; 1Chr. 17:1, 2
18 [I]Lit., *with*
19 [I]Lit., *is to come forth from your loins* [a]2Sam. 7:5, 12, 13; 1Kin. 5:3, 5; 1Chr. 17:11, 12; 22:8-10
20 [I]Lit., *spoke* [a]1Chr. 28:5, 6
21 [a]Deut. 31:26; 1Kin. 8:9
22 [a]1Kin. 8:54; 2Chr. 6:12 [b]Ex. 9:33; Ezra 9:5
23 [a]1Sam. 2:2; 2Sam. 7:22 [b]Deut. 7:9; Neh. 1:5; 9:32; Dan. 9:4
24 [I]Lit., *spoken to*
25 [I]Lit., *spoken to* [II]Lit., *There shall not be cut off to you a man from before Me.* [a]1Kin. 2:4
26 [a]2Sam. 7:25
27 [I]Lit., *heaven of heavens* [a]2Chr. 2:6; Ps. 139:7-16; Is. 66:1; Jer. 23:24; Acts 7:49
28 [a]Phil. 4:6
29 [a]2Chr. 7:15; Neh. 1:6 [b]Deut. 12:11
30 [a]Neh. 1:6 [b]Dan. 6:10 [c]Ex. 34:6, 7; Ps. 85:2; Dan. 9:9; 1John 1:9
31 [a]Ex. 22:8-11

8:27 See note on Isa. 66:1,2. God is Spirit (Jn. 4:24). Therefore, he cannot be limited to time-space dimensions. Today Christians are themselves God's temple and the Spirit of God dwells in them (I Cor. 3:16,17; 6:19,20).

he comes *and* takes an oath before Thine altar in this house,

32 then hear Thou in heaven and act[6213] and judge[8199] Thy servants, [a]condemning[7561] the wicked by bringing his way on his own head and justifying[6663] the righteous by giving him according to his righteousness.

33 "[a]When Thy people Israel are [I]defeated before an enemy, because they have sinned against Thee, [b]if they turn to Thee again and confess[3034] Thy name and pray and make supplication to Thee in this house,

34 then hear Thou in heaven, and forgive the sin of Thy people Israel, and bring them back to the land which Thou didst give to their fathers.

35 "[a]When the heavens are shut up and there is no rain, because they have sinned against Thee, and they pray toward this place and confess Thy name and turn from their sin when Thou dost afflict them,

36 then hear Thou in heaven and forgive the sin of Thy servants and of Thy people Israel, [a]indeed, teach them the good[2896] way in which they should walk. And [b]send rain on Thy land, which Thou hast given Thy people for an inheritance.[5159]

37 "[a]If there is famine in the land, if there is pestilence, if there is blight *or* mildew, locust *or* grasshopper, if their enemy besieges them in the land of their [I]cities, whatever plague, whatever sickness there is,

38 whatever prayer or supplication is made by any man *or* by all Thy people Israel, [I]each knowing the [II]affliction of his own heart, and spreading his [III]hands toward this house;

39 then hear Thou in heaven Thy dwelling place, and forgive and act and render to each according to all his ways, [a]whose heart Thou knowest, for [b]Thou alone dost know the hearts of all the sons of men,

40 that they may [I]fear[3372] Thee all the days[3117] that they live [II]in the land which Thou hast given to our fathers.

41 "Also concerning the foreigner who is not of Thy people Israel, when he comes from a far country[776] for Thy name's sake

42 (for they will hear of Thy great name [a]and Thy mighty hand, and of Thine outstretched arm); when he comes and prays toward this house,

43 hear Thou in heaven Thy dwelling place, and do[6213] according to all for which the foreigner calls[7121] to Thee, in order [a]that all the peoples of the earth may know Thy name, to [I]fear Thee, as *do* Thy people Israel, and that they may know that [II]this house which I have built is called[7121] by Thy name.

44 "When Thy people go out to battle against [I]their enemy, by whatever way Thou shalt send them, and [a]they pray to the LORD [II]toward the city which Thou hast chosen[977] and the house which I have built for Thy name,

45 then hear in heaven their prayer and their supplication, and maintain their [I]cause.

46 "When they sin against Thee (for [a]there is no man who does not sin) and Thou art angry[599] with them and dost deliver them to an enemy, so that [I]they take them away captive[7617] [b]to the land of the enemy, far off or near;

47 [a]if they [I]take thought[7725] in the land where they have been taken captive, and repent and make supplication to Thee in the land of those who have taken them captive, saying, '[b]We have sinned and have committed iniquity, we have acted wickedly';

48 [a]if they return to Thee with all their heart and with all their soul in the land of their enemies who have taken them captive,[7617] and [b]pray to Thee toward their land which Thou hast given to their fathers, the city which Thou hast chosen, and the house which I have built for Thy name;

49 then hear their prayer and their supplication in heaven Thy dwelling place, and maintain their [I]cause,[4941]

50 and forgive Thy people who have sinned against Thee and all their transgressions which they have transgressed

32 [a]Deut. 25:1
33 [I]Lit., *smitten* [a]Lev. 26:17, 25; Deut. 28:25, 48 [b]Lev. 26:40-42
35 [a]Lev. 26:19; Deut. 11:16, 17; 2Sam. 24:10-13
36 [a]1Sam. 12:23; Ps. 5:8; 25:4, 5; 27:11; 86:11; 119:133; Jer. 6:16 [b]1Kin. 18:1, 41-45; Jer. 14:22
37 [I]Lit., *gates* [a]Lev. 26:16, 25, 26; Deut. 28:21-23, 38-42
38 [I]Lit., *who shall know each* [II]Lit., *plague* [III]Lit., *palms*
39 [a]1Sam. 2:3; 16:7 [b]1Chr. 28:9; Ps. 11:4; Jer. 17:10; John 2:24, 25; Acts 1:24
40 [I]Or, *revere* [II]Lit., *on the face of the land*
42 [a]Ex. 13:3; Deut. 3:24
43 [I]Or, *reverence* [II]Lit., *Thy name is called upon this house which I have built* [a]Josh. 4:23, 24; 1Sam. 17:46; Ps. 67:2
44 [I]Lit., *his* [II]Lit., *in the way of* [a]2Chr. 14:11
45 [I]Lit., *right* or *justice*
46 [I]Lit., *their captors take them captive* [a]Ps. 130:3, 4; 143:2; Prov. 20:9; Eccl. 7:20; Rom. 3:23; 1John 1:8-10 [b]Lev. 26:34-39; 2Kin. 17:6, 18; 25:21
47 [I]Lit., *return to their heart* [a]Lev. 26:40-42; Neh. 9:2 [b]Ezra 9:6, 7; Neh. 1:6; Ps. 106:6; Dan. 9:5
48 [a]Deut. 4:29; 1Sam. 7:3, 4; Neh. 1:9 [b]Dan. 6:10; Jon. 2:4
49 [I]Lit., *judgment*

against Thee, and [a]make them *objects of* compassion[7356] before those who have taken them captive, that they may have compassion on them

51 ([a]for they are Thy people and Thine inheritance which Thou hast brought forth from Egypt, [b]from the midst of the iron furnace),

52 [a]that Thine eyes may be open to the supplication of Thy servant and to the supplication of Thy people Israel, to listen to them whenever they call[7121] to Thee.

53 "For Thou hast separated them from all the peoples of the earth as Thine inheritance, [a]as Thou didst speak through Moses Thy servant, when Thou didst bring our fathers forth from Egypt, O Lord [I]GOD."

Solomon's Benediction

54 [a]And it came about that when Solomon had finished[3615] praying this entire prayer and supplication to the LORD, [b]he arose from before the altar of the LORD, from kneeling on his knees with his [I]hands spread toward heaven.

55 And he stood and [a]blessed all the assembly of Israel with a loud voice, saying,

56 "Blessed be the LORD, who has given rest to His people Israel, [a]according to all that He [I]promised; [b]not one word has [II]failed[5307] of all His good [III]promise, which He [I]promised through Moses His servant.

57 "May the LORD our God be with us, as He was with our fathers; [a]may He not leave us or forsake[5203] us,

58 that [a]He may incline our hearts to Himself, to walk in all His ways and to keep His commandments[4687] and His statutes and His ordinances,[4941] which He commanded[6680] our fathers.

59 "And may these words of mine, with which I have made supplication before the LORD, be near to the LORD our God day[3119] and night, that He may maintain the [I]cause of His servant and the [I]cause of His people Israel, [II]as each day requires,

🔑 60 so [a]that all the peoples of the earth may know that [b]the LORD is God; there is no one else.

61 "[a]Let your heart therefore be [I]wholly devoted to the LORD our God, to walk in His statutes and to keep His commandments, as at this day."

Dedicatory Sacrifices

62 [a]Now the king and all Israel with him [b]offered sacrifice before the LORD.

63 And Solomon offered for the sacrifice of peace offerings, which he offered to the LORD, 22,000 oxen and 120,000 sheep. [a]So the king and all the sons of Israel dedicated[2596] the house of the LORD.

64 On the same day the king consecrated[6942] the middle of the court that *was* before the house of the LORD, because there he [I]offered the burnt offering and the grain offering and the fat of the peace offerings; for [a]the bronze altar that *was* before the LORD *was* too small to hold the burnt offering and the grain offering and the fat of the peace offerings.

65 So [a]Solomon observed the feast at that time, and all Israel with him, a great assembly [b]from the entrance of Hamath [c]to the brook of Egypt, before the LORD our God, for seven days and seven *more* days, *even* fourteen days.

66 On the eighth day he sent the people away and they blessed the king. Then they went to their tents joyful and glad[2896] of heart for all the goodness that the LORD had [I]shown[6213] to David His servant and to Israel His people.

God's Promise and Warning

9 🔑 [a]Now it came about when Solomon had finished[3615] building the

50 [a]2Chr. 30:9; Ps. 106:46; Acts 7:10
51 [a]Ex. 32:11, 12; Deut. 9:26-29 [b]Deut. 4:20; Jer. 11:4
52 [a]1Kin. 8:29
53 [I]Heb., *YHWH*, usually rendered *LORD* [a]Ex. 19:5, 6; Deut. 9:26-29
54 [I]Lit., *palms* [a]2Chr. 7:1 [b]2Chr. 6:13
55 [a]Num. 6:23-26; 2 Sam. 6:18; 1Kin. 8:14
56 [I]Lit., *spoke* [II]Lit., *fallen* [III]Lit., *word* [a]Deut. 12:10 [b]Josh. 21:45; 23:14, 15
57 [a]Deut. 31:6, 17; Josh. 1:5; 1Sam. 12:22; Rom. 8:31; Heb. 13:5
58 [a]Ps. 119:36; Jer. 31:33
59 [I]Lit., *judgment* [II]Lit., *the thing of a day in its day*
60 [a]Josh. 4:24; 1Sam. 17:46; 1Kin. 8:43; 2 Kin. 19:19 [b]Deut. 4:35; 1Kin. 18:39; Jer. 10:10-12
61 [I]Lit., *complete with* [a]Deut. 18:13; 1Kin. 11:4; 2Kin. 20:3
62 [a]2Chr. 7:4-10 [b]2Sam. 6:17-19; Ezra 6:16, 17
63 [a]Ezra 6:15-18; Neh. 12:27
64 [I]Lit., *made* [a]2Chr. 4:1
65 [a]Lev. 23:34-42; 1Kin. 8:2 [b]Num. 34:8; Josh. 13:5; Judg. 3:3; 2Kin. 14:25 [c]Gen. 15:18; Ex. 23:31; Num. 34:5; Josh. 13:3
66 [I]Lit., *done*
1 [a]2Chr. 7:11

🔑 **8:60** Compare Deut. 4:39.
🔑 **9:1-9** See II Chr. 7:11-22.

house of the LORD, and [b]the king's
house, and [c]all [I]that Solomon desired[2839]
to do,[6213]
2 that [a]the LORD appeared[7200] to
Solomon a second time, as He had appeared to him at Gibeon.
3 And the LORD said to him, "[a]I have
heard your prayer and your supplication,
which you have made before Me; I have
consecrated this house which you have
built [b]by putting My name there forever,
and [c]My eyes and My heart will be there
perpetually.
4 "And as for you, [a]if you will walk
before Me as your father[1] David walked,
in integrity[8537] of heart and uprightness,
doing according to all that I have
commanded[6680] you *and* will keep My
statutes and My ordinances,[4941]
5 then [a]I will establish the throne
of your kingdom over Israel forever,
just as I [I]promised to your father David,
saying, '[II]You shall not lack a man on
the throne of Israel.'
6 "[a]But if you or your sons[1121] shall
indeed turn away from following Me,
and shall not keep My commandments[4687] and My statutes which
I have set before you and shall go
and serve other gods[430] and worship
them,
7 [a]then I will cut off[3772] Israel from
the land which I have given them, and
[b]the house which I have consecrated
for My name, I will [I]cast out of My sight.
So [c]Israel will become a proverb and a
byword among all peoples.
8 "And this house will become
[I][a]a heap of ruins; everyone who passes
by will be astonished[8074] and hiss and
say, '[b]Why has the LORD done thus to
this land and to this house?'
9 "And they will say,[559] '[a]Because
they forsook[5800] the LORD their God,[430]
who brought their fathers[1] out of the
land of Egypt, and adopted other gods
and worshiped them and served them,
therefore the LORD has brought all this
adversity[7451] on them.' "

Cities Given to Hiram

🔑 **10** [a]And it came about [b]at the end
of twenty years in which Solomon had
built the two houses, the house of the
LORD and the king's house
11 (Hiram king of Tyre had
supplied[5375] Solomon with cedar and cypress timber and gold according to all
his desire),[2656] then King Solomon gave
Hiram twenty cities in the land of Galilee.
12 So Hiram came out from Tyre
to see the cities which Solomon had
given him, and they [I]did not please him.
13 And he said, "What are these
cities which you have given me, my
brother?"[251] So [I]they were called[7121] the
land of [II][a]Cabul to this day.[3119]
14 [a]And Hiram sent to the king 120
talents of gold.
15 Now this is the account of the
forced labor which King Solomon
[a]levied to build the house of the LORD,
his own house, the [I][b]Millo, the wall of
Jerusalem, [c]Hazor, [d]Megiddo, and
[e]Gezer.
16 *For* Pharaoh king of Egypt had
gone up and captured Gezer, and
burned[8313] it with fire, and killed the
[a]Canaanites who lived in the city, and
had [b]given it *as* a dowry to his daughter,
Solomon's wife.
17 So Solomon rebuilt Gezer and the
lower[8481] [a]Beth-horon
18 and [a]Baalath and Tamar in the
wilderness, in the land *of Judah,*
19 and all the storage cities which
Solomon had, even [a]the cities for
[I]his chariots and the cities for [I][b]his horsemen, and [II][c]all that it pleased[2836] Solomon
to build in Jerusalem, in Lebanon, and
in all the land [III]under his rule.[4475]
20 *As for* all the people who were
left of the Amorites, the Hittites,
the Perizzites, the Hivites and the Jebusites, who were not of the sons of Israel,
21 [a]their descendants who were left

1 [I]Lit., *Solomon's desire which he was pleased to do* [b]1Kin. 7:1, 2 [c]2Chr. 8:6
2 [a]1Kin. 3:5; 11:9; 2Chr. 1:7
3 [a]2Kin. 20:5; Ps. 10:17; 34:17 [b]1Kin. 8:29 [c]Deut. 11:12; 2Chr. 6:40
4 [a]1Kin. 3:6, 14; 11:4, 6, 8; 2Kin. 20:3; Ps. 128:1
5 [I]Lit., *spoke* [II]Lit., *There shall not be cut off to you a man* [a]2Sam. 7:12,16; 1Kin. 2:4; 6:12; 1Chr. 22:10
6 [a]2Sam. 7:14-16; 1Chr. 28:9; Ps. 89:30ff.
7 [I]Lit., *send* [a]Lev. 18:24-29; Deut. 4:26; 2Kin. 17:23 [b]Jer. 7:4-14 [c]Deut. 28:37; Ps. 44:14; Jer. 24:9
8 [I]Heb., *high* [a]2Kin. 25:9; 2Chr. 36:19 [b]Deut. 29:24-26; 2Chr. 7:21; Jer. 22:8,9,28
9 [a]Deut. 29:25-28; Jer. 2:10-13
10 [a]2Chr. 8:1 [b]1Kin. 6:37, 38; 7:1; 9:1
12 [I]Lit., *were not right in his sight*
13 [I]Lit., *he called them* [II]I.e., as good as nothing [a]Josh. 19:27
14 [a]1Kin. 9:11
15 [I]I.e., citadel [a]1Kin. 5:13 [b]2Sam. 5:9; 1Kin. 9:24 [c]Josh. 11:1; 19:36 [d]Josh. 17:11 [e]Judg. 1:29
16 [a]Josh. 16:10 [b]1Kin. 3:1; 7:8
17 [a]Josh. 10:10; 16:3; 21:22; 2Chr. 8:5
18 [a]Josh. 19:44
19 [I]Lit., *the* [II]Lit., *the desire of Solomon which he desired to build in Jerusalem* [III]Lit., *of* [a]1Kin. 10:26; 2Chr. 1:14 [b]1Kin. 4:26 [c]1Kin. 9:1
21 [a]Judg. 1:21-29; 3:1

🔑 **9:10-28** See II Chr. 8:1-18.

after them in the land [b]whom the sons
of Israel were unable to destroy[2763] utterly, [c]from them Solomon levied
[d]forced laborers,[5647] even to this day.
22 But Solomon [a]did not make
slaves[5650] of the sons of Israel; for they
were men of war, his servants, his
princes, his captains,[7991] his chariot
commanders, and his horsemen.
23 These *were* the [I][a]chief officers
who were over Solomon's work, five
hundred and fifty, [b]who ruled over the
people doing the work.
24 As soon as [a]Pharaoh's daughter
came up from the city of David to her
house which *Solomon* had built for her,
[b]then he built the Millo.
25 Now [a]three times in a year Solomon offered burnt offerings[5930] and
peace offerings on the altar[4196] which
he built to the LORD, burning incense[6999]
with them *on the altar* which *was* before
the LORD. So he finished[7999] the house.
26 King Solomon also built a
[a]fleet of ships in [b]Ezion-geber, which
is near Eloth on the shore of the
[I]Red Sea, in the land of Edom.
27 [a]And Hiram sent his servants
with the fleet, sailors who knew the sea,
along with the servants of Solomon.
28 And they went to [a]Ophir, and
took four hundred and twenty talents
of gold from there, and brought *it* to
King Solomon.

The Queen of Sheba

10 Now when the [a]queen of
[b]Sheba heard about the fame[8088]
of Solomon concerning the name of the
LORD, she came [c]to test him with difficult
questions.
2 So she came to Jerusalem with a
very large retinue, with camels [a]carry-
ing[5375] spices and very much gold and
precious stones. When she came to Solomon, she spoke with him about all that
was in her heart.
3 And Solomon [I]answered all her
questions; nothing was hidden from the
king which he did not [II]explain to her.
4 When the queen of Sheba perceived all the wisdom of Solomon, the
house that he had built,
5 the food of his table, the seating
of his servants, the attendance of his
waiters and their attire, his cupbearers,
and [I]his stairway by which he went up
to the house of the LORD, there was
no more spirit in her.
6 Then she said to the king, "It was
a true report which I heard in my own
land about your words[1697] and your wisdom.
7 "Nevertheless I did not believe[539]
the [I]reports, until I came and my eyes
had seen it. And behold, the half was
not told me. You exceed *in* wisdom and
prosperity the report which I heard.
8 "How [a]blessed are your men, how
blessed are these your servants who
stand before you continually[8548] *and* hear
your wisdom.
9 "[a]Blessed[1288] be the LORD your
God[430] who delighted[2654] in you to set
you on the throne of Israel; [b]because
the LORD loved Israel forever, therefore
He made you king, [c]to do[6213] justice[4941]
and righteousness."[6666]
10 And [a]she gave the king a hundred
and twenty talents of gold, and a very
great *amount* of spices and precious
stones. Never again did such abundance
of spices come in as that which the queen
of Sheba gave King Solomon.
11 [a]And also the ships of Hiram,
which brought gold from Ophir,
brought[5375] in from Ophir a very great
number of almug[484] trees and precious
stones.
12 And [a]the king made of the almug
trees supports for the house of the LORD

21 [b]Josh. 15:63; 17:12, 13 [c]Judg. 1:28, 35 [d]Gen. 9:25, 26; Ezra 2:55,58
22 [a]Lev. 25:39
23 [I]Or, *officers of the deputies* [a]2Chr. 8:10 [b]1Kin. 5:16
24 [a]1Kin. 3:1; 7:8 [b]2Sam. 5:9; 1Kin. 9:15; 11:27; 2Chr. 32:5
25 [a]Ex. 23:14-17; Deut. 16:16
26 [I]Lit., *Sea of Reeds* [a]1Kin. 22:48 [b]Num. 33:35; Deut. 2:8; 1Kin. 22:48
27 [a]1Kin. 5:6, 9; 10:11
28 [a]1Chr. 29:4; 2Chr. 8:18
1 [a]2Chr. 9:1; Matt. 12:42; Luke 11:31 [b]Gen. 10:7, 28; Ps. 72:10, 15 [c]Judg. 14:12-14; Ps. 49:4
2 [a]1Kin. 10:10
3 [I]Lit., *told her all her words* [II]Lit., *tell her*
5 [I]Or, *his burnt offering which he offered*
7 [I]Lit., *words*
8 [a]Prov. 8:34
9 [a]1Kin. 5:7 [b]1Chr. 17:22; 2Chr. 2:11 [c]2Sam. 8:15; 23:3; Ps. 72:2
10 [a]1Kin. 10:2
11 [a]1Kin. 9:27, 28; Job 22:24
12 [a]2Chr. 9:11

10:1,2 Sheba is a reference to Saba, the land of the Sabeans in southwestern Arabia. It is roughly equivalent to the eastern part of the modern state of Yemen. It controlled the trade route by which precious spices, metals, and other commodities were transported from southern Arabia to Palestine and beyond.

10:1-13 See II Chr. 9:1-12.

and for the king's house, also lyres and harps for the singers; such almug trees have not come in *again,* nor have they been seen to this day.[3117]

13 And King Solomon gave to the queen of Sheba all her desire[2656] which she requested,[7592] besides what he gave her according to [I]his royal bounty.[3027] Then she turned and went to her own land[776] [II]together with her servants.

Wealth, Splendor and Wisdom

🔑 **14** [a]Now the weight of gold which came in to Solomon in one year *was* 666 talents of gold,

15 besides *that* from the traders and the [I]wares[4536] of the merchants and all the kings of the [a]Arabs and the governors[6346] of the country.

16 And [a]King Solomon made 200 large shields of beaten[7820] gold, [I]using 600 *shekels of* gold on each large shield.

17 And *he made* [a]300 shields of beaten gold, [I]using three minas of gold on each shield, and [b]the king put them in the house of the forest of Lebanon.

18 Moreover, the king made a great throne of [a]ivory and overlaid it with refined gold.

19 There *were* six steps to the throne and a round top to the throne at its rear, and [I]arms [II]on each side of the seat, and two lions standing beside the [I]arms.

20 And twelve lions were standing there on the six steps on the one side and on the other; nothing like *it* was made for any other kingdom.

21 And all King Solomon's drinking vessels *were* of gold, and all the vessels of the house of the forest of Lebanon *were* of pure gold. None was of silver; it was not considered [I]valuable[2803] in the days[3117] of Solomon.

🔑 22 For [a]the king had at sea the ships of Tarshish with the ships of Hiram; once every three years the ships of Tarshish came bringing[5375] gold and silver, ivory and apes and peacocks.

23 [a]So King Solomon became greater than all the kings of the earth[776] in riches and in wisdom.

24 And all the earth was seeking the presence of Solomon, [a]to hear his wisdom which God had put in his heart.

25 And [a]they brought every man his gift, articles of silver and gold, garments, weapons,[5402] spices, horses, and mules, so much year by year.

🔑 **26** [a]Now Solomon gathered chariots and horsemen; and he had 1,400 chariots and 12,000 horsemen, and he [I]stationed them in the [b]chariot cities and with the king in Jerusalem.

27 [a]And the king made silver *as common* as stones in Jerusalem, and he made cedars as plentiful as sycamore trees that are in the [I]lowland.[8219]

28 [a]Also Solomon's import of horses was from Egypt and Kue, and the king's merchants procured *them* from Kue for a price.

29 And a chariot [I]was imported from Egypt for 600 *shekels* of silver, and a horse for 150; and [II]by the same means they exported them [a]to all the kings of the Hittites and to the kings of the Arameans.

Solomon Turns from God

11 Now [a]King Solomon loved many foreign women along with the daughter of Pharaoh: Moabite, Ammonite, Edomite, Sidonian, and Hittite women,

13 [I]Lit., *the hand of King Solomon* [II]Lit., *she and*
14 [a]2Chr. 9:13-28
15 [I]Or, *traffic* [a]2Chr. 9:14
16 [I]Lit., *he brought up* [a]1Kin. 14:26-28; 2Chr. 12:9,10
17 [I]Lit., *he brought up* [a]1Kin. 14:26 [b]1Kin. 7:2
18 [a]1Kin. 10:22; 2Chr. 9:17; Ps. 45:8
19 [I]Lit., *hands* [II]Lit., *on this side and on this at the place of the seat*
21 [I]Lit., *anything*
22 [a]1Kin. 9:26-28; 22:48; 2Chr. 20:36
23 [a]1Kin. 3:12, 13; 4:30
24 [a]1Kin. 3:9, 12, 28
25 [a]Ps. 68:29
26 [I]So with ancient versions; Heb., *led* [a]1Kin. 4:26; 2Chr. 1:14-17; 9:25 [b]1Kin. 9:19
27 [I]Heb., *Shephelah* [a]Deut. 17:17; 2Chr. 1:15
28 [a]Deut. 17:16; 2Chr. 1:16; 9:28
29 [I]Lit., *came up and went out from* [II]Lit., *in like manner by their hand* [a]2Kin. 7:6, 7
1 [a]Deut. 17:17; Neh. 13:23-27

🔑 **10:14-25** See II Chr. 9:13-24.

🔑 **10:22** "The ships of Tarshish" are usually identified with Tartessos in southern Spain. However, some scholars now suggest that this word was formed on the Hebrew root which means "to refine." If so, these ships were in some way connected with refineries and mines of which archaeologists have found remains near Ezion-geber on the Red Sea. At any rate, this was a reference to a type of ship, not to its destination.

🔑 **10:26-29** See II Chr. 1:14-17; 9:25-28.

2 from the nations concerning which the LORD had said to the sons[1121] of Israel, "[a]You shall not [l]associate with them, neither shall they [l]associate with you, *for* they will surely turn your heart away after their gods."[430] Solomon held fast to these in love.

3 [a]And he had seven hundred wives, princesses, and three hundred concubines, and his wives turned his heart away.

4 For it came about when Solomon was old, his wives turned his heart away after other gods; and [a]his heart was not [l]wholly devoted to the LORD his God,[430] as the heart of David his father[1] *had been.*

5 For Solomon went after [a]Ashtoreth the goddess[430] of the Sidonians and after [1b]Milcom the detestable idol[8251] of the Ammonites.

6 And Solomon did[6213] what was evil[7451] in the sight of the LORD, and did not follow the LORD fully, as David his father *had done.*

7 Then Solomon built a high place for [a]Chemosh the detestable idol of Moab, on the mountain which is [l]east of Jerusalem, and for [b]Molech the detestable idol of the sons of Ammon.

8 Thus also he did for all his foreign wives, who burned incense[6999] and sacrificed to their gods.

9 Now [a]the LORD was angry[599] with Solomon [b]because his heart was turned away from the LORD, the God of Israel, [c]who had appeared[7200] to him twice,

10 and [a]had commanded[6680] him concerning this thing, that he should not go after other gods; but he did not observe what the LORD had commanded.

11 So the LORD said to Solomon, "Because [l]you have done this, and you have not kept My covenant[1285] and My statutes, which I have commanded you, [a]I will surely tear[7167] the kingdom from you, and will give it to your servant.

12 "Nevertheless I will not do[6213] it in your days[3117] for the sake of your father[1] David, *but* I will tear it out of the hand of your son.

13 "However, [a]I will not tear away all the kingdom, *but* [b]I will give one tribe to your son for the sake of My servant David and [c]for the sake of Jerusalem which I have chosen."[977]

God Raises Adversaries

14 Then the LORD raised up an adversary to Solomon, Hadad the Edomite; he was of the [l]royal line in Edom.

15 For it came about, [a]when David was in Edom, and Joab the commander[8269] of the army had gone up to bury[6912] the slain, and had [b]struck down every male in Edom

16 (for Joab and all Israel stayed there six months, until he had cut off[3772] every male in Edom),

17 that Hadad fled [l]to Egypt, he and certain[582] Edomites of his father's servants with him, while Hadad *was* a young boy.

18 And they arose from Midian and came to [a]Paran; and they took men with them from Paran and came to Egypt, to Pharaoh king of Egypt, who gave him a house and assigned[559] him food[3899] and gave him land.

19 Now Hadad found great favor[2580] [l]before Pharaoh, so that he gave him in marriage the sister of his own wife, the sister of Tahpenes the queen.

20 And the sister of Tahpenes bore his son Genubath, whom Tahpenes weaned in Pharaoh's house; and Genubath was in Pharaoh's house among the sons of Pharaoh.

21 But [a]when Hadad heard in Egypt that David slept with his fathers,[1] and that Joab the commander of the army was dead,[4191] Hadad said to Pharaoh, "Send me away, that I may go to my own country."[776]

22 Then Pharaoh said to him, "But what have you lacked with me, that behold, you are seeking to go to your own country?" And he answered,[559] "Nothing; nevertheless you must surely [l]let me go."

23 [a]God also raised up *another* adversary to him, Rezon the son of Eliada,

2 [l]Lit., *go among* [a]Ex. 23:31-33; 34:12-16; Deut. 7:3
3 [a]2Sam. 5:13-16
4 [l]Lit., *complete with* [a]1Kin. 9:4
5 [l]In Jer. 49:1, 3, *Malcam* [a]Judg. 2:13; 10:6; 1Sam. 7:3, 4 [b]1Kin. 11:7
7 [l]Lit., *before* [a]Num. 21:29; Judg. 11:24; 2Kin. 23:13 [b]Lev. 20:2-5; 2Kin. 23:10; Acts 7:43
9 [a]Ps. 90:7 [b]1Kin. 11:2, 4 [c]1Kin. 3:5; 9:2
10 [a]1Kin. 6:12; 9:6, 7
11 [l]Lit., *this is with you* [a]1Sam. 2:30; 1Kin. 11:29-31; 12:15, 16, 20; 2Kin. 17:15, 21
13 [a]2Sam. 7:15; 1Chr. 17:13; Ps. 89:33 [b]1Kin. 11:32, 36; 12:20 [c]1Kin. 8:29
14 [l]Lit., *king's seed*
15 [a]2Sam. 8:14; 1Chr. 18:12, 13 [b]Deut. 20:13
17 [l]Lit., *to go into*
18 [a]Num. 10:12; Deut. 1:1
19 [l]Lit., *in the sight of*
21 [a]1Kin. 2:10
22 [l]Lit., *send me away*
23 [a]1Kin. 11:14

who had fled from his lord [b]Hadadezer king of Zobah.

24 And he gathered[6908] men to himself and became leader of a marauding band,[1416] [a]after David slew them of *Zobah;* and they went to Damascus and stayed [I]there, and reigned in Damascus.

25 So he was an adversary to Israel all the days of Solomon, along with the evil that Hadad *did;* and he abhorred[6973] Israel and reigned over Aram.

26 Then [a]Jeroboam the son of Nebat, an Ephraimite of Zeredah, Solomon's servant, whose mother's name was Zeruah, a widow, [b]also [I]rebelled against the king.

27 Now this was the reason[1697] why he [I]rebelled against the king: [a]Solomon built the [II]Millo, *and* closed up the breach of the city of his father David.

28 Now the man Jeroboam was a valiant warrior, and when [a]Solomon saw that the young man was [I]industrious,[4399] he appointed him over all the [II]forced labor of the house of Joseph.

29 And it came about at that time, when Jeroboam went out of Jerusalem, that [a]the prophet Ahijah the Shilonite found him on the road. Now [I]Ahijah had clothed[3680] himself with a new cloak; and both of them were alone in the field.[7704]

30 Then [a]Ahijah took hold of the new cloak which was on him, and tore it into twelve pieces.

⚿ 31 And he said to Jeroboam, "Take for yourself ten pieces; for thus says the LORD, the God of Israel, 'Behold, [a]I will tear the kingdom out of the hand of Solomon and give you ten tribes

32 ([a]but he will have one tribe, for the sake of My servant David and for the sake of Jerusalem, [b]the city which I have chosen from all the tribes of Israel),

33 because they have forsaken[5800] Me, and [a]have worshiped Ashtoreth the goddess of the Sidonians, [b]Chemosh the god of Moab, and Milcom the god of the sons of Ammon; and they have not walked in My ways, doing what is right in My sight and *observing* My statutes and My ordinances,[4941] as his father David *did.*

34 'Nevertheless I will not take the whole kingdom out of his hand, but I will make him [I]ruler all the days of his life, for the sake of My servant David whom I chose,[977] who observed My commandments[4687] and My statutes;

35 but [a]I will take the kingdom from his son's hand and give it to you, *even* ten tribes.

36 'But [a]to his son I will give one tribe, [b]that My servant David may have a lamp always before Me in Jerusalem, [c]the city where I have chosen for Myself to put My name.

37 'And I will take you, and you shall reign over whatever [I]you desire, and you shall be king over Israel.

38 'Then it will be, that if you listen to all that I command[6680] you and walk in My ways, and do what is right in My sight by observing My statutes and My commandments, as My servant David did, then [a]I will be with you and [b]build you an enduring house as I built for David, and I will give Israel to you.

39 'Thus I will afflict the [I]descendants of David for this, but not always.' "

40 Solomon sought therefore to put Jeroboam to death; but Jeroboam arose and fled to Egypt to [a]Shishak king of Egypt, and he was in Egypt until the death[4194] of Solomon.

23 [b]2Sam. 8:3; 10:16
24 [I]Lit., *in it* [a]2Sam. 10:8, 18
26 [I]Lit., *lifted up a hand* [a]1Kin. 11:11, 28; 12:2, 20; 2Chr. 13:6 [b]2Sam. 20:21
27 [I]Lit., *lifted up a hand* [II]I.e., citadel [a]1Kin. 9:15, 24
28 [I]Lit., *a doer of work* [II]Lit., *burden* [a]Prov. 22:29
29 [I]Lit., *he* [a]1Kin. 12:15; 14:2; 2Chr. 9:29
30 [a]1Sam. 15:27, 28
31 [a]1Kin. 11:11, 12
32 [a]1Kin. 11:13; 12:21 [b]1Kin. 11:13; 14:21
33 [a]1Sam. 7:3; 1Kin. 11:5-8 [b]Num. 21:29; Jer. 48:7, 13
34 [I]Or, *prince*
35 [a]1Kin. 11:12; 12:16, 17
36 [a]1Kin. 11:13 [b]1Kin. 15:4; 2Kin. 8:19; Ps. 132:17 [c]1Kin. 11:13
37 [I]Lit., *your soul desires*
38 [a]Deut. 31:8; Josh. 1:5 [b]2Sam. 7:11, 27
39 [I]Lit., *seed*
40 [a]1Kin. 14:25; 2Chr. 12:2-9

⚿ **11:31-35** Rehoboam reigned over only one tribe, the tribe of Judah, while Jeroboam became the king over ten tribes (I Kgs. 12:16.17). A question has been raised about the twelfth tribe. Levi was not counted because it had no land possessions (Num. 18:20-24). The tribe of Joseph was divided into two parts, Ephraim and Manasseh, which were usually spoken of as two distinct tribes. Apparently in this division Joseph was counted as only one tribe making Jeroboam's ten. Although Rehoboam at first retained only the tribe of Judah, later most of the tribe of Benjamin joined his kingdom. Still later, the tribes of Simeon and Dan also became part of the kingdom of Judah.

The Death of Solomon

🗝 **41** [a]Now the rest of the acts[1697] of
Solomon and whatever he did, and his
wisdom, are they not written in the
book[5612] of the acts of Solomon?
42 Thus [a]the time that Solomon
reigned in Jerusalem over all Israel was
forty years.
43 And Solomon [a]slept with his fathers and was buried[6912] in the city of
his father David, and his son [b]Rehoboam
reigned in his place.

King Rehoboam Acts Foolishly

12 🗝 [a]Then Rehoboam went to
Shechem, for all Israel had come
to [b]Shechem to make him king.
2 Now it came about [a]when Jeroboam the son of Nebat heard *of it,* that
[I]he was living in Egypt (for he was yet
in Egypt, where he had fled from the
presence of King Solomon).
3 Then they sent and called[7121] him,
and Jeroboam and all the assembly[6951]
of Israel came and spoke to Rehoboam,
saying,
4 "[a]Your father[1] made our yoke
hard;[7186] now therefore lighten the hard
service of your father and his heavy yoke
which he put on us, and we will serve
you."
5 Then he said to them, "[a]Depart
[I]for three days,[3117] then return to me."
So the people departed.
6 And King Rehoboam [a]con-
sulted[3298] with the elders who had
[I]served his father Solomon while he was
still alive, saying, "How do you counsel
me to answer[7725,1697] this people?"
7 Then they spoke to him, saying,
"[a]If you will be a servant to this people
today,[3117] will serve them, [I]grant them
their petition, and speak good[2896] words
to them, then they will be your servants
forever."
8 But he forsook[5800] the counsel[6098]
of the elders which they had given him,
and consulted with the young men who
grew up with him [I]and served him.
9 So he said to them, "What
counsel[3289] do you give that we may
answer this people who have spoken
to me, saying, 'Lighten the yoke which
your father put on us'?"
10 And the young men who grew
up with him spoke to him, saying, "Thus
you shall say to this people who spoke
to you, saying, 'Your father made our
yoke heavy, now you make it lighter
for us!' But you shall speak to them,
'My little finger is thicker than my
father's[1] loins!
11 'Whereas my father loaded you
with a heavy yoke, I will add to your
yoke; my father disciplined[3256] you with
whips, but I will discipline[3256] you with
scorpions.'"
12 Then Jeroboam and all the people came to Rehoboam on the third day
as the king had [I]directed,[1696] saying,
"[a]Return to me on the third day."
13 And the king answered the people harshly, for he forsook the advice
of the elders which they had [I]given
him,
14 and he spoke to them according
to the advice of the young men, saying,
"[a]My father made your yoke heavy, but
I will add to your yoke; my father disciplined you with whips, but I will discipline you with scorpions."
15 So the king did not listen to the
people; [a]for it was a turn *of events* from
the LORD, [b]that He might establish His
word, which the LORD spoke through
Ahijah the Shilonite to Jeroboam the son
of Nebat.

The Kingdom Divided Jeroboam Rules Israel

16 When all Israel *saw* that the king
did not listen to them, the people answered the king, saying,

"What portion do we have in
David?

---

41 [a]2Chr. 9:29
42 [a]2Chr. 9:30
43 [a]1Kin. 2:10; 2Chr. 9:31 [b]1Kin. 14:21; Matt. 1:7
1 [a]2Chr. 10:1 [b]Judg. 9:6
2 [I]Lit., *Jeroboam* [a]1Kin. 11:26, 40
4 [a]1Sam. 8:11-18; 1Kin. 4:7, 21-25; 9:15
5 [I]Lit., *yet three* [a]1Kin. 12:12
6 [I]Lit., *stood before* [a]1Kin. 4:1-6; Job 12:12; 32:7
7 [I]Lit., *answer them* [a]2Chr. 10:7; Prov. 15:1
8 [I]Lit., *who stood before*
12 [I]Lit., *spoken* [a]1Kin. 12:5
13 [I]Lit., *advised*
14 [a]Ex. 1:13, 14; 5:5-9, 16-18
15 [a]Deut. 2:30; Judg. 14:4; 1Kin. 12:24; 2Chr. 10:15 [b]1Kin. 11:11, 31

🗝 **11:41-43** See II Chr. 9:29-31.
🗝 **12:1-24** See II Chr. 10:1—11:4.

We have no inheritance[5159] in the
son of Jesse;
[a]To your tents, O Israel!
Now look after your own house,
David!"
So Israel departed to their tents.
17 But [a]as for the sons[1121] of Israel
who lived in the cities of Judah, Rehoboam reigned over them.
18 Then King Rehoboam sent
[a]Adoram, who was over the forced labor, and all Israel stoned him [I]to
death.[4191] And King Rehoboam made
haste to mount his chariot to flee to
Jerusalem.
19 [a]So Israel has been in rebellion
against the house of David to this day.
20 And it came about when all Israel
heard that Jeroboam had returned, that
they sent and called him to the
assembly[5712] and made him king over
all Israel. [a]None but the tribe of Judah
followed the house of David.
21 [a]Now when Rehoboam had come
to Jerusalem, he assembled[6950] all the
house of Judah and the tribe of Benjamin,
180,000 chosen men who were warriors, to fight against the house of Israel
to restore the kingdom to Rehoboam
the son of Solomon.
22 But the word of God[430] came to
[a]Shemaiah the man of God, saying,
23 "Speak to Rehoboam the son of
Solomon, king of Judah, and to all the
house of Judah and Benjamin and to the
[a]rest of the people, saying,
24 'Thus says the LORD, "You must
not go up and fight against your
[I]relatives[251] the sons of Israel; return
every man to his house, [a]for this thing
has come from Me." '" So they listened
to the word of the LORD, and returned
and went *their way* according to the word
of the LORD.

Jeroboam's Idolatry

25 Then [a]Jeroboam built Shechem
in the hill country of Ephraim, and lived
[I]there. And he went out from there and
built [b]Penuel.
26 And Jeroboam said in his heart,
"Now the kingdom will return to the
house of David.
27 "[a]If this people go up to offer[6213]
sacrifices in the house of the LORD at
Jerusalem, then the heart of this people
will return to their lord, *even* to Rehoboam king of Judah; and they will kill
me and return to Rehoboam king of Judah."
🔑 28 So the king [I]consulted, and
[a]made two golden [b]calves, and he said
to them, "It is too much for you to go
up to Jerusalem; [c]behold your gods,[430]
O Israel, that brought[5927] you up from
the land of Egypt."
29 And he set [a]one in [b]Bethel, and
the other he put in [c]Dan.
30 Now [a]this thing became a sin,
for the people went *to worship* before
the one as far as Dan.
31 And [a]he made houses on high
places, and [b]made priests from among
[I]all the people who were not of the sons
of Levi.
32 And Jeroboam [I]instituted a
feast[2282] in the eighth month on the fifteenth day of the month, [a]like the feast
which is in Judah, and he [II]went up to
the altar;[4196] thus he did[6213] in Bethel,
sacrificing to the calves which he had
made. And he stationed in Bethel
[b]the priests of the high places which
he had made.
33 Then he [I]went up to the altar
which he had made in Bethel on the
fifteenth day in the eighth month, even
in the month which he had [II][a]devised
[III]in his own heart; and he [II]instituted a
feast for the sons of Israel, and [I]went
up to the altar [b]to burn [IV]incense.[6999]

Jeroboam Warned, Stricken

13 Now behold, there came [a]a man
of God[430] from Judah to Bethel

16 [a]2Sam. 20:1
17 [a]1Kin. 11:13, 36
18 [I]Lit., *with stones that he died* [a]2Sam. 20:24; 1Kin. 4:6; 5:14
19 [a]2Kin. 17:21
20 [a]1Kin. 11:13, 32, 36
21 [a]2Chr. 11:1
22 [a]2Chr. 11:2; 12:5-7
23 [a]1Kin. 12:17
24 [I]Lit., *brothers* [a]1Kin. 12:15
25 [I]Lit., *in it* [a]Gen. 12:6; Judg. 9:45-49 [b]Gen. 32:30, 31; Judg. 8:8, 17
27 [a]Deut. 12:5-7, 14
28 [I]Lit., *took counsel* [a]2Kin. 10:29; 17:16; Hos. 8:4-7 [b]Hos. 10:5 [c]Ex. 32:4, 8
29 [a]Hos. 10:5 [b]Gen. 28:19 [c]Judg. 18:26-31
30 [a]1Kin. 13:34; 2Kin. 17:21
31 [I]Or, *extremities of* [a]1Kin. 13:32 [b]1Kin. 13:33; 2Kin. 17:32; 2Chr. 11:15; 13:9
32 [I]Lit., *made* [II]Or, *offered upon* [a]Lev. 23:33, 34; Num. 29:12; 1Kin. 8:2, 5 [b]Amos 7:10-13
33 [I]Or, *offered upon* [II]Lit., *made* [III]Lit., *from* [IV]Or, *sacrifices* [a]Num. 15:39 [b]1Kin. 13:1
1 [a]1Kin. 12:22; 2Kin. 23:17

🔑 **12:28** These were the very words used near Mount Sinai. When Moses did not return immediately, the people began to worship the golden calf (Ex. 32:4).

by the word of the LORD, while Jeroboam was standing by the altar[4196] [b]to burn incense.[6999]

2 And [a]he cried[7121] against the altar by the word of the LORD, and said, "O altar, altar, thus says the LORD, 'Behold, a son[1121] shall be born to the house of David, [b]Josiah by name; and on you he shall sacrifice the priests of the high places who burn incense on you, and human bones[6106] shall be burned[8313] on you.' "

3 Then he gave a [I]sign the same day,[3117] saying, "[a]This is the [I]sign which the LORD has spoken, 'Behold, the altar shall be split apart and the [II]ashes which are on it shall be poured out.' "

4 Now it came about when the king heard the saying of the man of God, which he cried against the altar in Bethel, that Jeroboam stretched out his hand from the altar, saying, "Seize him." But his hand which he stretched out against him dried[3001] up, so that he could not draw it back to himself.

5 The altar also was split apart and the [I]ashes were poured out from the altar, according to the [II]sign which the man of God had given by the word of the LORD.

6 And the king answered and said to the man of God, "Please [I][a]entreat the LORD your God, and pray for me, that my hand may be restored to me." So [b]the man of God [II]entreated the LORD, and the king's hand was restored to him, and it became as it was before.[7223]

7 Then the king said to the man of God, "Come home with me and refresh yourself, and [a]I will give you a reward."

8 But the man of God said to the king, "[a]If you were to give me half your house I would not go with you, nor would I eat bread or drink water in this place.

9 "For so [I]it was commanded[6680] me by the word of the LORD, saying, 'You shall eat no bread, nor drink water, nor return by the way which you came.' "

10 So he went another way, and did not return by the way which he came to Bethel.

The Disobedient Prophet

11 Now [a]an old prophet was living in Bethel; and his [I]sons came and told him all the deeds which the man of God had done[6213] that day in Bethel; the words which he had spoken to the king, these also they related to their father.[1]

12 And their father said to them, "[I]Which way did he go?" Now his sons [II]had seen the way which the man of God who came from Judah had gone.

13 Then he said to his sons, "Saddle the donkey for me." So they saddled the donkey for him and he rode away on it.

14 So he went after the man of God and found him sitting under [I]an oak; and he said to him, "Are you the man of God who came from Judah?" And he said, "I am."

15 Then he said to him, "Come home with me and eat bread."

16 And he said, "[a]I cannot return with you, nor go with you, nor will I eat bread or drink water with you in this place.

17 "For a command *came* to me [a]by the word of the LORD, 'You shall eat no bread, nor drink water there; do not return by going the way which you came.' "

18 And he said to him, "[a]I also am a prophet like you, and [b]an angel[4397] spoke to me by the word of the LORD, saying, 'Bring him back with you to your house, that he may eat bread and drink water.' " *But* [c]he lied to him.

19 So he went back with him, and ate bread in his house and drank water.

20 Now it came about, as they were sitting down at the table, that the word of the LORD came to the prophet who had brought him back;

21 and he cried to the man of God who came from Judah, saying, "Thus says the LORD, 'Because you have [I]disobeyed[4784] the [II]command of the LORD, and have not observed the commandment[4687] which the LORD your God commanded[6680] you,

22 but have returned and eaten

---

1 [b]1Kin. 12:33
2 [a]1Kin. 13:32 [b]2Kin. 23:15, 16
3 [I]Lit., *wonder* [II]Lit., *ashes of fat* [a]Ex. 4:1-5; Judg. 6:17; Is. 38:7; John 2:18; 1Cor. 1:22
5 [I]Lit., *ashes of fat* [II]Lit., *wonder*
6 [I]Lit., *soften the face of* [II]Lit., *softened the face of* [a]Ex. 8:8, 28; 9:28; 10:17; Acts 8:24; James 5:16 [b]Luke 6:27, 28
7 [a]1Sam. 9:7, 8; 2Kin. 5:15
8 [a]Num. 22:18; 24:13; 1Kin. 13:16, 17
9 [I]Lit., *he commanded me*
11 [I]Lit., *son* [a]1Kin. 13:25; 2Kin. 23:18
12 [I]Lit., *Where is the way he went* [II]Some ancient versions read *showed him*
14 [I]Or, *a terebinth*
16 [a]1Kin. 13:8, 9
17 [a]1Kin. 20:35
18 [a]Matt. 7:15; 1John 4:1 [b]Gal. 1:8 [c]Prov. 12:19, 22; 19:5; Jer. 29:31, 32; Ezek. 13:8, 9; 1Tim. 4:1, 2
21 [I]Lit., *rebelled against* [II]Lit., *mouth*

bread and drunk water in the place of
which He said to you, "Eat no bread
and drink no water"; your body[5038] shall
not come to the grave[6913] of your
fathers.'"[1]
23 And it came about after he had
eaten bread and after he had drunk, that
he saddled the donkey for him, for the
prophet whom he had brought back.
24 Now when he had gone, [a]a lion
met him on the way and killed him, and
his body was thrown on the road, with
the donkey standing beside it; the lion
also was standing beside the body.
25 And behold, men passed by and
saw the body thrown on the road, and
the lion standing beside the body; so
they came and told *it* in the city where
[a]the old prophet lived.
26 Now when the prophet who
brought him back from the way heard
it, he said, "It is the man of God, who
[I]disobeyed[4784] the [II]command of the
LORD; therefore the LORD has given him
to the lion, which has torn him and killed
him, according to the word of the LORD
which He spoke to him."
27 Then he spoke to his sons, saying, "Saddle the donkey for me." And
they saddled *it.*
28 And he went and found his body
thrown on the road with the donkey and
the lion standing beside the body; the
lion had not eaten the body nor torn
the donkey.
29 So the prophet took up the body
of the man of God and laid it on the
donkey, and brought it back and he came
to the city of the old prophet to mourn
and to bury[6912] him.
30 And he laid his body in his own
grave,[6913] and they mourned over him,
saying, "[a]Alas, my brother!"[251]
31 And it came about after he had
buried[6912] him, that he spoke to his sons,
saying, "When I die,[4191] bury me in the
grave in which the man of God is buried;
[a]lay my bones beside his bones.
32 "[a]For the thing shall surely come
to pass which he cried by the word of
the LORD against the altar in Bethel and
[b]against all the houses of the high places

24 [a]1Kin. 20:36

25 [a]1Kin. 13:11

26 [I]Lit., *rebelled against* [II]Lit., *mouth*

30 [a]Jer. 22:18

31 [a]Ruth 1:17; 2Kin. 23:17, 18

32 [a]1Kin. 13:2 [b]Lev. 26:30; 1Kin. 12:31 [c]1Kin. 16:24; John 4:5; Acts 8:14

33 [I]Or, *extremities of* [a]1Kin. 12:31, 32 [b]Judg. 17:5

34 [I]Lit., *by this thing he became* [a]1Kin. 12:30; 2Kin. 17:21 [b]1Kin. 14:10; 15:29, 30

2 [a]1Sam. 28:8; 2Sam. 14:2; 2Chr. 18:29 [b]Josh. 18:1 [c]1Kin. 11:29-31

3 [a]1Sam. 9:7, 8; 1Kin. 13:7; 2Kin. 4:42

4 [I]Lit., *set* [a]1Kin. 14:2 [b]1Kin. 11:29 [c]1Sam. 3:2; 4:15

5 [I]Lit., *seek a word from* [a]2Sam. 14:2

7 [a]2Sam. 12:7; 1Kin. 11:28-31; 16:2

8 [a]1Kin. 11:31

which are in the cities of [c]Samaria."
33 After this event Jeroboam did
not return from his evil[7451] way, but
[a]again he made priests of the high places
from among [I]all the people; [b]any who
would, he ordained, to be priests of the
high places.
34 [a]And [I]this event became sin to
the house of Jeroboam, [b]even to blot
it out and destroy[8045] *it* from off the
face of the earth.[127]

Ahijah Prophesies against the King

14 At that time Abijah the son of
Jeroboam became sick.
2 And Jeroboam said to his wife,
"Arise now, and [a]disguise yourself so
that they may not know that you are
the wife of Jeroboam, and go to [b]Shiloh;
behold, Ahijah the prophet is there, who
[c]spoke concerning me *that I would be*
king over this people.
3 "[a]And take ten loaves with you,
some cakes[5350] and a jar[1228] of honey,
and go to him. He will tell you what
will happen[1961] to the boy."
4 And Jeroboam's wife did[6213] so,
and arose and went to [a]Shiloh, and came
to the house of [b]Ahijah. Now Ahijah
could not see, [c]for his eyes were
[I]dim because of his age.
5 Now the LORD had said to Ahijah,
"Behold, the wife of Jeroboam is coming
to [I]inquire of you concerning her son,
for he is sick. You shall say thus and
thus to her, for it will be when she arrives that [a]she will pretend[5234] to be
another woman."
6 And it came about when Ahijah
heard the sound of her feet coming in
the doorway, that he said, "Come in,
wife of Jeroboam, why do you
pretend[5234] to be another woman? For
I am sent to you *with* a harsh *message.*
7 "Go, say to Jeroboam, 'Thus says
the LORD God[430] of Israel, "[a]Because I
exalted you from among the people and
made you leader over My people Israel,
8 and [a]tore the kingdom away from
the house of David and gave it to you—

[b]yet you have not been like My servant David, who kept My commandments[4687] and who followed Me with all his heart, [c]to do[6213] only that which was right in My sight;

9 you also have done[6213] more evil[7489] than all who were before you, and [a]have gone and made for yourself other gods[430] and [b]molten images to provoke Me to anger,[3707] and have [c]cast Me behind your back—

10 therefore behold, I am bringing calamity[7451] on the house of Jeroboam, and [a]will cut off[3772] from Jeroboam [I]every male person, [b]both bond and free in Israel, and I [c]will make a clean sweep of the house of Jeroboam, as one sweeps away dung until it is all gone.

11 "'[a]Anyone belonging to Jeroboam who dies[4191] in the city the dogs will eat. And he who dies in the field[7704] the birds of the heavens[8064] will eat; for the LORD has spoken *it*.'"

12 "Now you arise, go to your house. [a]When your feet enter the city the child will die.[4191]

13 "And all Israel shall mourn for him and bury[6912] him, for [I]he alone of Jeroboam's *family* shall come to the grave,[6913] because in him [a]something good[2896] was found toward the LORD God of Israel in the house of Jeroboam.

14 "Moreover, [a]the LORD will raise up for Himself a king over Israel who shall cut off the house of Jeroboam this day[3117] [I]and from now on.

15 "For the LORD will strike Israel, as a reed is shaken in the water; and [a]He will uproot Israel from [b]this good land which He gave to their fathers,[1] and [c]will scatter them beyond the *Euphrates* River, [d]because they have made their [I]Asherim,[842] provoking the LORD to anger.

16 "And He will give up Israel [a]on account of the sins of Jeroboam, which he [I]committed and with which he made Israel to sin."

17 Then Jeroboam's wife arose and departed and came to [a]Tirzah. [b]As she was entering the threshold of the house, the child died.[4191]

18 [a]And all Israel buried[6912] him and mourned for him, according to the word of the LORD which He spoke through His servant Ahijah the prophet.

19 Now the rest of the acts[1697] of Jeroboam, [a]how he made war and how he reigned, behold, they are written in the Book[5612] of the Chronicles of the Kings of Israel.

20 And the time[3117] that Jeroboam reigned *was* twenty-two years; and he slept with his fathers, and Nadab his son reigned in his place.

Rehoboam Misleads Judah

🗝 **21** [a]Now Rehoboam the son of Solomon reigned in Judah. Rehoboam was forty-one years old when he became king, and he reigned seventeen years in Jerusalem, [b]the city which the LORD had chosen[977] from all the tribes of Israel to put His name there. And his mother's name was Naamah the Ammonitess.

22 [a]And Judah did evil in the sight of the LORD, and they [b]provoked Him to jealousy more than all that their fathers had done, with [I]the sins which they [II]committed.[2398]

23 For they also built for themselves [a]high places and *sacred* [b]pillars[4676] and [I][c]Asherim on every high hill and [d]beneath every luxuriant tree.

24 And there were also [a]male cult prostitutes[6945] in the land. They did according to all the abominations[8441] of the nations which the LORD dispossessed[3423] before the sons[1121] of Israel.

25 [a]Now it came about in the fifth year of King Rehoboam, that Shishak the king of Egypt came up against Jerusalem.

26 And he took away the treasures of the house of the LORD and the treasures of the king's house, and [a]he took

8 [b]1Kin. 11:33, 38 [c]1Kin. 15:5
9 [a]1Kin. 12:28; 2Chr. 11:15 [b]Ex. 34:17 [c]Neh. 9:26; Ps. 50:17; Ezek. 23:35
10 [I]Lit., *him who urinates against the wall* [a]1Kin. 21:21; 2Kin. 9:8 [b]Deut. 32:36; 2Kin. 14:26 [c]1Kin. 15:29
11 [a]1Kin. 16:4; 21:24
12 [a]1Kin. 14:17
13 [I]Lit., *the one* [a]2Chr. 19:3
14 [I]Lit., *and what even now?* [a]1Kin. 15:27-29
15 [I]I.e., wooden symbols of a female deity [a]Deut. 29:28; 2Kin. 17:6; Ps. 52:5 [b]Josh. 23:15, 16 [c]2Kin. 15:29 [d]Ex. 34:13, 14; Deut. 12:3,4
16 [I]Lit., *sinned* [a]1Kin. 12:30; 13:34; 15:30, 34; 16:2
17 [a]1Kin. 15:21, 33; 16:6-9, 15, 23; Song 6:4 [b]1Kin. 14:12
18 [a]1Kin. 14:13
19 [a]1Kin. 14:30; 2Chr. 13:2-20
21 [a]2Chr. 12:13 [b]1Kin. 11:32, 36
22 [I]Lit., *their* [II]Lit., *sinned* [a]2Chr. 12:1, 14 [b]Deut. 32:21; Ps. 78:58; 1Cor. 10:22
23 [I]I.e., wooden symbols of a female deity [a]Deut. 12:2; Ezek. 16:24 [b]Deut. 16:22 [c]1Kin. 14:15 [d]2Kin. 17:10; Is. 57:5; Jer. 2:20
24 [a]Gen. 19:5; Deut. 23:17; 1Kin. 15:12; 22:46; 2Kin. 23:7
25 [a]1Kin. 11:40; 2Chr. 12:2, 9
26 [a]1Kin. 15:18; 2Chr. 12:9

🗝 **14:21-31** See II Chr. 12:1-16.

everything, [Ib]even taking all the shields
of gold which Solomon had made.
27 So King Rehoboam made shields
of bronze in their place, and [a]com-
mitted[6485] them to the [I]care of the commanders of the [II]guard who guarded the
doorway of the king's house.
28 Then it happened as often as the
king entered the house of the LORD,
that the [I]guards would carry[5375] them
and would bring them back into the
[I]guards' room.
29 [a]Now the rest of the acts of Rehoboam and all that he did, are they
not written in the Book of the Chronicles
of the Kings of Judah?
30 [a]And there was war between Rehoboam and Jeroboam continually.
31 And Rehoboam slept with his fathers, and was buried with his fathers
in the city of David; and [a]his mother's
name was Naamah the Ammonitess.
And Abijam his son became king in his
place.

Abijam Reigns over Judah

15 🔑 [a]Now in the eighteenth year
of King Jeroboam, the son of Nebat, Abijam became king over Judah.
🔑 2 He reigned three years in Jerusalem; and his mother's name was
[Ia]Maacah the daughter of [IIb]Abishalom.
3 And he walked in all the sins of
his father[1] which he had committed[6213]
before him; and [a]his heart was not
[I]wholly devoted to the LORD his God,[430]
like the heart of his father David.
4 But for David's sake the LORD his
God gave him a [a]lamp in Jerusalem, to
raise up his son after him and to establish
Jerusalem;
5 [a]because David did[6213] what was
right in the sight of the LORD, and had
not turned aside from anything that He
commanded[6680] him all the days[3117] of
his life, [b]except in the case of Uriah
the Hittite.
6 [a]And there was war between Rehoboam and Jeroboam all the days of
his life.
7 Now [a]the rest of the acts[1697] of
Abijam and all that he did, are they not
written in the Book[5612] of the Chronicles
of the Kings of Judah? [b]And there was
war between Abijam and Jeroboam.

Asa Succeeds Abijam

8 [a]And Abijam slept with his fathers[1]
and they buried[6912] him in the city of
David; and Asa his son became king in
his place.
🔑 **9** So in the twentieth year of Jeroboam the king of Israel, Asa began to
reign as king of Judah.
10 And he reigned forty-one years
in Jerusalem; and [a]his mother's name
was Maacah the daughter of Abishalom.
11 And [a]Asa did[6213] what was right
in the sight of the LORD, like David his
father.
12 [a]He also put away the male cult
prostitutes[6945] from the land, and
[b]removed all the idols[1544] which his fathers had made.
13 [a]And [I]he also removed Maacah
his mother from *being* queen mother,
because she had made a horrid image[4656]
[II]as an Asherah;[842] and Asa cut down[3772]
her horrid image and [b]burned[8313] *it* at
the brook Kidron.
14 [a]But the high places were not
taken away; nevertheless [b]the heart of
Asa was [I]wholly devoted to the LORD
all his days.
15 And [a]he brought into the house
of the LORD the dedicated[6944] things of

26 [I]Lit., *and he took away* [b]1Kin. 10:17; 2Chr. 9:15, 16
27 [I]Lit., *hand* [II]Lit., *runner* [a]1Sam. 8:11; 22:17
28 [I]Lit., *runners*
29 [a]2Chr. 12:15, 16
30 [a]1Kin. 12:21; 15:6
31 [a]1Kin. 14:21

1 [a]2Chr. 13:1
2 [I]In 2Chr. 13:2, *Micaiah, the daughter of Uriel* [II]In 2Chr. 11:20, *Absalom* [a]2Chr. 13:2 [b]2Chr. 11:21
3 [I]Lit., *complete with* [a]1Kin. 11:4; Ps. 119:80
4 [a]2Sam. 21:17; 1Kin. 11:36; 2Chr. 21:7
5 [a]1Kin. 9:4; 14:8; Luke 1:6 [b]2Sam. 11:3f., 15-17; 12:9, 10
6 [a]1Kin. 14:30; 2Chr. 12:15-13:20
7 [a]2Chr. 13:2, 21, 22 [b]2Chr. 13:3-20
8 [a]2Chr. 14:1
10 [a]1Kin. 15:2
11 [a]2Chr. 14:2
12 [a]Deut. 23:17; 1Kin. 14:24; 22:46 [b]1Kin. 11:7, 8; 14:23; 2Chr. 14:2-5
13 [I]Lit., *also Maacah his mother and he removed her* [II]Or, *for Asherah* [a]2Chr. 15:16-18 [b]Ex. 32:20
14 [I]Lit., *complete with* [a]1Kin. 22:43; 2Kin. 12:3 [b]1Kin. 8:61; 15:3
15 [a]1Kin. 7:51

🔑 **15:1-8** See II Chr. 13:1-22.
🔑 **15:2-10** In v. 10 Maacah was called Asa's mother when in fact she was his grandmother. Her name was mentioned probably to show Asa's claim to the throne. Rehoboam intended that of all his children, only those born to him by Maacah, would be in line of succession to the throne (II Chr. 11:21,22). She is spoken of loosely as Asa's mother, just as David is called his father (v. 11) though he was really his great-great-grandfather.
🔑 **15:9-15** See II Chr. 14:1-5; 15:16-19.

his father and his own dedicated things:
silver and gold and utensils.
🔑 **16** [a]Now there was war between
Asa and Baasha king of Israel all their
days.
17 [a]And Baasha king of Israel went
up against Judah and [1b]fortified Ramah
[c]in order to prevent *anyone* from going out or coming in to Asa king of
Judah.
18 Then [a]Asa took all the silver and
the gold which were left in the treasuries
of the house of the LORD and the treasuries of the king's house, and delivered
them into the hand of his servants. And
[b]King Asa sent them to Ben-hadad the
son of Tabrimmon, the son of Hezion,
king of Aram, who lived in [c]Damascus,
saying,
19 "*Let there be* a [a]treaty between
[1]you and me, *as* between my father and
your father. Behold, I have sent you a
present of silver and gold; go, break[6565]
your treaty with Baasha king of Israel
so that he will withdraw from me."
20 So Ben-hadad listened to King
Asa and sent the commanders[8269] of his
armies against the cities of Israel, and
[1]conquered [a]Ijon, [b]Dan, [c]Abel-beth-maa-
cah and all [d]Chinneroth, besides all the
land of Naphtali.
21 And it came about when Baasha
heard *of it* that [a]he ceased [1]fortifying
Ramah, and remained in [b]Tirzah.
22 Then King Asa made a proclamation to all Judah—none was
exempt[5355]—and they carried away the
stones of Ramah and its timber with
which Baasha had built. And King Asa
built with them [a]Geba of Benjamin and
Mizpah.

Jehoshaphat Succeeds Asa

23 [a]Now the rest of all the acts of
Asa and all his might and all that he
did and the cities which he built, are
they not written in the Book of the
Chronicles of the Kings of Judah? But
in the time of his old age he was
diseased[2470] in his feet.
24 And Asa slept with his fathers
and was buried with his fathers in the
city of David his father; and [a]Jehoshaphat
his son reigned in his place.

Nadab, then Baasha, Rules over Israel

25 Now [a]Nadab the son of Jeroboam
became king over Israel in the second
year of Asa king of Judah, and he reigned
over Israel two years.
26 And he did evil[7451] in the sight
of the LORD, and [a]walked in the way
of his father and [b]in his sin which he
made Israel sin.
27 Then [a]Baasha the son of Ahijah
of the house of Issachar conspired
against him, and Baasha struck him
down at [b]Gibbethon, which belonged to
the Philistines, while Nadab and all Israel
were laying siege to Gibbethon.
28 So Baasha killed him in the third
year of Asa king of Judah, and reigned
in his place.
29 And it came about, as soon as
he was king, he struck down all the
household of Jeroboam. He did not leave
to Jeroboam [1]any persons alive,[5397] until
he had destroyed[8045] them, [a]according
to the word of the LORD, which He spoke
by His servant Ahijah the Shilonite,
30 *and* because of the sins of Jeroboam which he sinned, and [a]which he
made Israel sin, because of his provocation with which he provoked the LORD
God of Israel to anger.[3707]
31 [a]Now the rest of the acts of Nadab and all that he did, are they not
written in the Book of the Chronicles
of the Kings of Israel?

War with Judah

32 [a]And there was war between Asa
and Baasha king of Israel all their days.
33 In the third year of Asa king of

16 [a]1Kin. 15:32
17 [1]Lit., *built* [a]2Chr. 16:1-6 [b]Josh. 18:25; 1Kin. 15:21, 22 [c]1Kin. 12:26-29
18 [a]1Kin. 14:26; 15:15 [b]2Kin. 12:17, 18; 2Chr. 16:2 [c]Gen. 14:15; 1Kin. 11:23, 24
19 [1]Lit., *me and you* [a]2Chr. 16:7
20 [1]Lit., *smote* [a]2Kin. 15:29 [b]Judg. 18:29; 1Kin. 12:29 [c]2Sam. 20:15; 2Kin. 15:29 [d]Josh. 11:2; 12:3
21 [1]Lit., *building* [a]1Kin. 15:17 [b]1Kin. 14:17; 16:15-18
22 [a]Josh. 18:24; 21:17
23 [a]2Chr. 16:11-14
24 [a]1Kin. 22:41-44; 2Chr. 17:1; Matt. 1:8
25 [a]1Kin. 14:20
26 [a]1Kin. 12:28-33; 13:33, 34 [b]1Kin. 14:16; 15:30, 34
27 [a]1Kin. 14:14 [b]Josh. 19:44; 21:23; 1Kin. 16:15
29 [1]Lit., *any breath* [a]1Kin. 14:9-16
30 [a]1Kin. 15:26
31 [a]1Kin. 14:19
32 [a]1Kin. 15:16

🔑 **15:16-24** See II Chr. 16:1-14.

Judah, Baasha the son of Ahijah became king over all Israel at Tirzah, *and reigned* twenty-four years.

34 And he did evil in the sight of the LORD, and [a]walked in the way of Jeroboam and in his sin which he made Israel sin.

Prophecy against Baasha

16 Now the word of the LORD came to [a]Jehu the son of [b]Hanani against Baasha, saying,

2 "Inasmuch as I [a]exalted you from the dust[6083] and made you leader over My people Israel, and [b]you have walked in the way of Jeroboam and have made My people Israel sin, provoking Me to anger[3707] with their sins,

3 behold, [a]I will consume [b]Baasha and his house, and [c]I will make your house like the house of Jeroboam the son of Nebat.

4 "[a]Anyone of Baasha who dies[4191] in the city the dogs shall eat, and anyone of his who dies in the field[7704] the birds of the heavens[8064] will eat."

5 [a]Now the rest of the acts[1697] of Baasha and what he did[6213] and his might, are they not written in the Book[5612] of the Chronicles of the Kings of Israel?

The Israelite Kings

6 And Baasha slept with his fathers[1] and was buried[6912] in [a]Tirzah, and Elah his son became king in his place.

7 Moreover, the word of the LORD through [a]the prophet Jehu the son of Hanani also came against Baasha and his household, both because of all the evil[7451] which he did in the sight of the LORD, provoking Him to anger with [b]the work of his hands, in being like the house of Jeroboam, and because [c]he struck [I]it.

8 In the twenty-sixth year of Asa king of Judah, Elah the son of Baasha became king over Israel at Tirzah, *and reigned* two years.

9 And his servant [a]Zimri, commander[8269] of half his chariots, conspired against him. Now he *was* at Tirzah drinking himself drunk in the house of Arza, [b]who *was* over the household at Tirzah.

10 Then Zimri went in and struck him and put him to death, in the twenty-seventh year of Asa king of Judah, and became king in his place.

11 And it came about, when he became king, as soon as he sat on his throne, that [a]he [I]killed all the household of Baasha; he did not leave [II]a single male, neither of his [III]relatives nor of his friends.[7453]

12 Thus Zimri destroyed[8045] all the household of Baasha, [a]according to the word of the LORD, which He spoke against Baasha through [b]Jehu the prophet,

13 for all the sins of Baasha and the sins of Elah his son, which they sinned and which they made Israel sin, [a]provoking the LORD God[430] of Israel to anger with their [I]idols.

14 [a]Now the rest of the acts of Elah and all that he did, are they not written in the Book of the Chronicles of the Kings of Israel?

15 In the twenty-seventh year of Asa king of Judah, Zimri reigned seven days[3117] at Tirzah. Now the people were camped against [a]Gibbethon, which belonged to the Philistines.

16 And the people who were camped heard [I]it said, "Zimri has conspired and has also struck down the king." Therefore all Israel made Omri, the commander of the army, king over Israel that day[3117] in the camp.

17 Then Omri and all Israel with him went up from Gibbethon, and they besieged Tirzah.

18 And it came about, when Zimri saw that the city was taken, that he went into the citadel of the king's house and burned[8313] the king's house over him with fire, and [a]died,[4191]

19 because of his sins which he sinned, doing[6213] evil in the sight of the LORD, [a]walking in the way of Jeroboam,

---

34 [a]1Kin. 15:26

1 [a]1Kin. 16:7; 2Chr. 19:2; 20:34 [b]2Chr. 16:7-10

2 [a]1Sam. 2:8; 1Kin. 14:7 [b]1Kin. 15:34

3 [a]1Kin. 14:10; 21:21 [b]1Kin. 16:11 [c]1Kin. 15:29

4 [a]1Kin. 14:11; 21:24

5 [a]1Kin. 14:19; 15:31

6 [a]1Kin. 14:17; 15:21

7 [I]Or, *him* [a]1Kin. 16:1 [b]Ps. 115:4; Is. 2:8 [c]1Kin. 14:14; 15:27, 29

9 [a]2Kin. 9:30-33 [b]Gen. 24:2; 39:4; 1Kin. 18:3

11 [I]Lit., *smote* [II]Lit., *him who urinates against the wall* [III]Lit., *redeemers* [a]1Kin. 15:29; 16:3

12 [a]1Kin. 16:3 [b]2Chr. 19:2; 20:34

13 [I]Lit., *vanities* [a]Deut. 32:21; 1Kin. 15:30

14 [a]1Kin. 16:5

15 [a]1Kin. 15:27

16 [I]Lit., *saying*

18 [a]1Sam. 31:4, 5; 2Sam. 17:23

19 [a]1Kin. 12:28; 14:16; 15:26

and in his sin which he did, making Israel sin.

20 [a]Now the rest of the acts of Zimri and his conspiracy which he [I]carried out, are they not written in the Book of the Chronicles of the Kings of Israel?

21 Then the people of Israel were divided into two parts: half of the people followed Tibni the son of Ginath, to make him king; the *other* half followed Omri.

22 But the people who followed Omri prevailed over the people who followed Tibni the son of Ginath. And Tibni died and Omri became king.

23 In the thirty-first year of Asa king of Judah, Omri became king over Israel, *and reigned* twelve years; he reigned six years at [a]Tirzah.

24 And he bought the hill [I]Samaria from Shemer for two talents of silver; and he built on the hill, and named[7121] the city which he built [Ia]Samaria, after the name of Shemer, the owner of the hill.

25 And [a]Omri did evil in the sight of the LORD, and [b]acted more wickedly than all who *were* before him.

26 For he [a]walked in all the way of Jeroboam the son of Nebat and in his sins which he made Israel sin, provoking the LORD God of Israel with their [I]idols.

27 Now the rest of the acts of Omri which he did and his might which he [I]showed, are they not written in the Book of the Chronicles of the Kings of Israel?

28 So Omri slept with his fathers, and was buried in Samaria; and Ahab his son became king in his place.

29 Now Ahab the son of Omri became king over Israel in the thirty-eighth year of Asa king of Judah, and Ahab the son of Omri reigned over Israel in Samaria twenty-two years.

30 And Ahab the son of Omri did evil in the sight of the LORD [a]more than all who were before him.

31 And it came about, as though it had been a trivial thing for him to walk in the sins of Jeroboam the son of Nebat, that [a]he married Jezebel the daughter of Ethbaal king of the [b]Sidonians, and went to serve Baal and worshiped him.

32 So he erected an altar[4196] for Baal in [a]the house of Baal, which he built in Samaria.

33 And Ahab also made [a]the [I]Asherah.[842] Thus [b]Ahab did more to provoke the LORD God of Israel than all the kings of Israel who were before him.

34 [a]In his days Hiel the Bethelite built Jericho; he laid its foundations[3245] with the *loss of* Abiram his first-born, and set up its gates with the *loss of* his youngest son Segub, according to the word of the LORD, which He spoke by Joshua the son of Nun.

Elijah Predicts Drought

17 Now Elijah the Tishbite, who was of [Ia]the settlers[8453] of Gilead, said to Ahab, "[b]As the LORD, the God[430] of Israel lives, before whom I stand, surely [c]there shall be neither dew nor rain these years, except by my word."

20 [I]Lit., *conspired* [a]1Kin. 16:5, 14, 27
23 [a]1Kin. 15:21
24 [I]Heb., *Shomeron* [a]1Kin. 16:28, 29, 32
25 [a]Mic. 6:16 [b]1Kin. 14:9; 16:30-33
26 [I]Lit., *vanities* [a]1Kin. 16:19
27 [I]Lit., *did*
30 [a]1Kin. 14:9; 16:25
31 [a]Deut. 7:1-5 [b]Judg. 18:7; 1Kin. 11:1-5; 2Kin. 10:18; 17:16
32 [a]2Kin. 10:21, 26, 27
33 [I]I.e., wooden symbol of a female deity [a]2Kin. 13:6 [b]1Kin. 14:9; 16:29, 30; 21:25
34 [a]Josh. 6:26
1 [I]Or, *Tishbe in Gilead* [a]Judg. 12:4 [b]1Kin. 18:10; 22:14; 2Kin. 3:14; 5:20 [c]1Kin. 18:1; Luke 4:25; James 5:17

16:34 See Josh. 6:26.

17:1 Elijah must have been quite active before the events of this chapter. Ahab called him "the troubler of Israel" (I Kgs. 18:17) and they had looked everywhere for him (I Kgs. 18:10). The reputation which he had already acquired seemed to have had an effect upon Ahab, especially to cause him to take the prophecy of the drought seriously here. He was the man whom God raised up at this critical time, when the worship of Baal threatened the very existence of worshiping the Lord in Israel. Elijah was perhaps associated with the schools of the prophets at Bethel, Jericho, and Gilgal (II Kgs. 2:3-5). He was to the prophets what Moses had been to the Law. His stature is seen in the fact that the forerunner of Christ was to come with his spirit and power (Lk. 1:17) and he and Moses, as representatives of the Law and the Prophets stood with Jesus on the Mount of Transfiguration (Mt. 17:3; Lk. 9:30).

2 And the word of the LORD came to him, saying,

3 "Go away from here and turn eastward, and hide yourself by the brook Cherith, which is [I]east of the Jordan.

4 "And it shall be that you shall drink of the brook, and [a]I have commanded[6680] the ravens to provide for you there."

5 So he went and did[6213] according to the word of the LORD, for he went and lived by the brook Cherith, which is [I]east of the Jordan.

6 And the ravens brought him bread and meat[1320] in the morning and bread and meat in the evening, and he would drink from the brook.

7 And it happened after a while, that the brook dried[3001] up, because there was no rain in the land.

8 Then the word of the LORD came to him, saying,

9 "Arise, go to [a]Zarephath, which belongs to Sidon, and stay there; behold, [b]I have commanded a widow there to provide for you."

10 So he arose and went to Zarephath, and when he came to the gate of the city, behold, a widow was there gathering sticks; and [a]he called[7121] to her and said, "Please get me a little water in a [I]jar, that I may drink."

11 And as she was going to get *it,* he called to her and said, "Please bring me a piece of bread in your hand."

12 But she said, "[a]As the LORD your God lives, [b]I have no [I]bread, only a handful of flour in the [II]bowl and a little oil in the jar;[6835] and behold, I am gathering [III]a few sticks that I may go in and prepare[6213] for me and my son, that we may eat it and [c]die."[4191]

13 Then Elijah said to her, "Do not fear;[3372] go, do[6213] as you have said, but make me a little bread cake from [I]it first,[7223] and bring *it* out to me, and afterward you may make *one* for yourself and for your son.

14 "For thus says the LORD God of Israel, 'The [I]bowl of flour shall not be exhausted, nor shall the jar of oil [II]be empty, until the day[3117] that the LORD sends rain on the face of the earth.' "[127]

15 So she went and did according to the word of Elijah, and she and he and her household ate for *many* days.[3117]

16 The [I]bowl of flour was not exhausted nor did the jar of oil [II]become empty, according to the word of the LORD which He spoke through Elijah.

Elijah Raises Widow's Son

17 Now it came about after these things, that the son of the woman, the mistress of the house, became sick; and his sickness was so severe, that there was no breath[5397] left in him.

18 So she said to Elijah, "[a]What do I have to do with you, O [b]man of God? [I]You have come to me to bring my iniquity to remembrance, and to put my son to death!"

19 And he said to her, "Give me your son." Then he took him from her bosom and carried him up to the upper room where he was living, and laid him on his own bed.

20 And he called[7121] to the LORD and said, "O LORD my God, hast Thou also brought calamity[7489] to the widow with whom I am [I]staying, by causing her son to die?"

21 [a]Then he stretched himself upon the child three times, and called to the LORD, and said, "O LORD my God, I pray Thee, let this child's life return [I]to him."

22 And the LORD heard the voice of Elijah, [a]and the life of the child returned [I]to him and he revived.

23 And Elijah took the child, and brought him down from the upper room into the house and gave him to his mother; and Elijah said, "See, your son is alive."

24 Then the woman said to Elijah, "[a]Now I know that you are a man of God, and that the word of the LORD in your mouth is truth."

3 [I]Lit., *before*

4 [a]1Kin. 17:9

5 [I]Lit., *before*

9 [a]Obad. 20; Luke 4:26 [b]1Kin. 17:4

10 [I]Or, *vessel* [a]Gen. 24:17; John 4:7

12 [I]Lit., *cake* [II]Lit., *pitcher* [III]Lit., *two* [a]1Kin. 17:1 [b]2Kin. 4:2-7 [c]Gen. 21:15, 16

13 [I]Lit., *there*

14 [I]Lit., *pitcher* [II]Lit., *lack*

16 [I]Lit., *pitcher* [II]Lit., *lack*

18 [I]Or, *Have you come . . . death?* [a]2Sam. 16:10; 2Kin. 3:13; Luke 4:34; John 2:4 [b]1Kin. 12:22

20 [I]Lit., *sojourning*

21 [I]Lit., *upon his inward part* [a]2Kin. 4:34, 35; Acts 20:10

22 [I]Lit., *upon his inward part* [a]Luke 7:14; Heb. 11:35

24 [a]John 2:11; 3:2; 16:30

Obadiah Meets Elijah

18 ⊶ Now it came about [a]*after* many days,[3117] that the word of the LORD came to Elijah in the third year, saying, "Go, show yourself to Ahab, and [b]I will send rain on the face of the earth."[127]

2 So Elijah went to show himself to Ahab. Now the famine *was* severe in Samaria.

⊶ 3 And Ahab called[7121] Obadiah [a]who *was* over the household. (Now Obadiah [1b]feared[3373] the LORD greatly;

4 for it came about, [a]when Jezebel [1]destroyed[3772] the prophets of the LORD, that Obadiah took a hundred prophets and hid them by fifties in a cave, and [b]provided them with bread and water.)

5 Then Ahab said to Obadiah, "Go through the land to all the springs of water and to all the valleys; perhaps[194] we will find grass and keep the horses and mules alive, and not [1]have to kill some of the cattle."

6 So they divided the land between them to [1]survey it; Ahab went one way by himself and Obadiah went another way by himself.

7 Now as Obadiah was on the way, behold, Elijah [1]met him, [a]and he recognized him and fell[5307] on his face and said, "Is this you, Elijah my master?"

8 And he said[559] to him, "It is I. Go, say to your master, 'Behold, Elijah *is here.*' "

9 And he said, "What [1]sin have I committed, that you are giving your servant into the hand of Ahab, to put me to death?

10 "[a]As the LORD your God[430] lives, there is no nation or kingdom where my master has not sent to search for you; and when they said, 'He is not *here,*' he made the kingdom or nation swear that they could not find you.

11 "And now you are saying, 'Go, say to your master, "Behold, Elijah *is here.*" '

12 "And it will come about when I leave you [a]that the Spirit of the LORD will carry[5375] you where I do not know; so when I come and tell Ahab and he cannot find you, he will kill me, although *I* your servant have [1]feared[3372] the LORD from my youth.

13 "[a]Has it not been told to my master what I did[6213] when Jezebel killed the prophets of the LORD, that I hid [1]a hundred prophets of the LORD by fifties in a cave, and provided them with bread and water?

14 "And now you are saying, 'Go, say to your master, "Behold, Elijah *is here*" '; he will then kill me."

15 And Elijah said, "[a]As the LORD of hosts lives, before whom I stand, I will surely show myself to him today."[3117]

16 So Obadiah went to meet Ahab, and told him; and Ahab went to meet Elijah.

17 And it came about, when Ahab saw Elijah that [a]Ahab said to him, "Is this you, you troubler of Israel?"

18 And he said, "I have not troubled Israel, but you and your father's[1] house *have,* because [a]you have forsaken[5800] the commandments[4687] of the LORD, and [b]you have followed the Baals.

19 "Now then send *and* gather[6908] to me all Israel at [a]Mount Carmel, [b]*together* with 450 prophets of Baal and 400 prophets of [c]the Asherah,[842] who eat at Jezebel's table."

God or Baal on Mount Carmel

20 So Ahab sent *a message* among all the sons[1121] of Israel, and brought[6908] the prophets together at Mount Carmel.

21 And Elijah came near to all the people and said, "[a]How long *will* you [1]hesitate between two opinions? [b]If the LORD is God, follow Him; but if Baal, follow him." But the people did not answer him a word.

22 Then Elijah said to the people,

1 [a]1Kin. 17:1; Luke 4:25; James 5:17 [b]Deut. 28:12
3 [1]Or, *revered* [a]1Kin. 16:9 [b]Neh. 7:2; Job 28:28
4 [1]Lit., *cut off* [a]1Kin. 18:13 [b]Matt. 10:40-42
5 [1]Lit., *cut off*
6 [1]Lit., *pass through*
7 [1]Lit., *to meet* [a]2Kin. 1:6-8
9 [1]Lit., *have I sinned*
10 [a]1Kin. 17:1
12 [1]Or, *revered* [a]2Kin. 2:16; Ezek. 3:12, 14; Acts 8:39
13 [1]Lit., *a hundred men of the prophets* [a]1Kin. 18:4
15 [a]1Kin. 17:1
17 [a]Josh. 7:25; 1Kin. 21:20
18 [a]1Kin. 9:9; 2Chr. 15:2 [b]1Kin. 16:31; 21:25, 26
19 [a]Josh. 19:26; 2Kin. 2:25 [b]1Kin. 18:22 [c]1Kin. 16:33
21 [1]Lit., *limp on the two divided opinions* [a]2Kin. 17:41; Matt. 6:24 [b]Josh. 24:15

⊶ **18:1** When Elijah prayed, it rained (Js. 5:17,18).
⊶ **18:3** Obadiah was one of the 7,000 faithful men of whom Elijah was unaware (I Kgs. 19:18).

"I [a]alone am left a prophet of the LORD, but Baal's prophets are [b]450 men.

23 "Now let them give us two oxen; and let them choose[977] one ox for themselves and cut it up, and place it on the wood, but put no fire *under it*; and I will prepare[6213] the other ox, and lay it on the wood, and I will not put a fire *under it*.

24 "Then you call[7121] on the name of your god,[430] and I will call on the name of the LORD, and [a]the God who answers by fire, He is God." And all the people answered and said, "[I]That is a good idea."

25 So Elijah said to the prophets of Baal, "Choose one ox for yourselves and prepare it first[7223] for you are many, and call on the name of your god, but put no fire *under it*."

26 Then they took the ox which [I]was given them and they prepared[6213] it and called on the name of Baal from morning until noon saying, "O Baal, answer us." But there was [a]no voice and no one answered. And they [II]leaped about the altar[4196] which [III]they made.

27 And it came about at noon, that Elijah mocked them and said, "Call out with a loud voice, for he is a god; either he is occupied or gone aside, or is on a journey,[1870] or perhaps he is asleep and needs to be awakened."

28 So they cried[7121] with a loud voice and [a]cut[1413] themselves according to their custom with swords and lances until the blood[1818] gushed out on them.

29 And it came about when midday was past, that they [I]raved [a]until the time of the offering of the *evening* sacrifice; but there was no voice, no one answered, and no [II]one paid attention.

30 Then Elijah said to all the people, "Come near to me." So all the people came near to him. And [a]he repaired the altar of the LORD which had been torn down.

31 And Elijah took twelve stones according to the number of the tribes of the sons of Jacob, to whom the word of the LORD had come, saying, "[a]Israel shall be your name."

22 [a]1Kin. 19:10, 14 [b]1Kin. 18:19

24 [I]Lit., *The matter is good* [a]1Kin. 18:38

26 [I]Lit., *he gave* [II]Lit., *limped;* i.e., a type of ceremonial dance [III]So some mss. and the ancient versions; M.T., *he* [a]Ps. 115:4, 5; Jer. 10:5

28 [a]Lev. 19:28; Deut. 14:1

29 [I]Lit., *prophesied* [II]Lit., *attentiveness* [a]Ex. 29:39, 41

30 [a]1Kin. 19:10, 14; 2Chr. 33:16

31 [a]Gen. 32:28; 35:10; 2Kin. 17:34

32 [I]Heb., *seahs;* i.e., one seah equals approx. 11 qts. [a]Col. 3:17

33 [a]Gen. 22:9; Lev. 1:7, 8

36 [a]1Kin. 18:29 [b]Gen. 28:13; Ex. 3:6; 4:5; Matt. 22:32 [c]1Kin. 8:43 [d]Num. 16:28-32

38 [a]Gen. 15:17; Lev. 9:24; 10:1, 2; Judg. 6:21; 2Kin. 1:12; 1Chr. 21:26; 2Chr. 7:1; Job 1:16

39 [a]1Kin. 18:21, 24

40 [a]Judg. 4:7; 5:21 [b]Deut. 13:5; 18:20; 2Kin. 10:24, 25

42 [a]1Kin. 18:19, 20 [b]James 5:18

32 So with the stones he built an altar in [a]the name of the LORD, and he made a trench around the altar, large enough to hold two [I]measures of seed.

33 [a]Then he arranged the wood and cut the ox in pieces and laid *it* on the wood. And he said, "Fill four pitchers with water and pour *it* on the burnt offering and on the wood."

34 And he said, "Do it a second time," and they did it a second time. And he said, "Do it a third time," and they did it a third time.

35 And the water flowed around the altar, and he also filled the trench with water.

Elijah's Prayer

36 Then it came about [a]at the time of the offering of the *evening* sacrifice, that Elijah the prophet came near and said, "[b]O LORD, the God of Abraham, Isaac and Israel, today let it be known that [c]Thou art God in Israel, and that I am Thy servant, and [d]that I have done[6213] all these things at Thy word.

37 "Answer me, O LORD, answer me, that this people may know that Thou, O LORD, art God, and *that* Thou hast turned their heart back again."

38 Then the [a]fire of the LORD fell, and consumed the burnt offering and the wood and the stones and the dust,[6083] and licked up the water that was in the trench.

39 And when all the people saw it, they fell on their faces; and they said, "[a]The LORD, He is God; the LORD, He is God."

40 Then Elijah said to them, "Seize the prophets of Baal; do not let one of them escape."[4422] So they seized them; and Elijah brought them down to [a]the brook Kishon, [b]and slew them there.

41 Now Elijah said to Ahab, "Go up, eat and drink; for there is the sound of the roar of a *heavy* shower."

42 So Ahab went up to eat and drink. But Elijah went up to the top of [a]Carmel; and he [b]crouched down on the earth,[776]

and put his face between his knees.

43 And he said to his servant, "Go up now, look toward the sea." So he went up and looked and said, "There is nothing." And he said, "Go back" seven times.

44 And it came about at the seventh *time,* that he said, "Behold, [a]a cloud as small as a man's hand is coming up from the sea." And he said, "Go up, say to Ahab, '[I]Prepare *your chariot* and go down, so that the *heavy* shower does not stop you.' "

45 So it came about in a little while, that the sky grew black[6937] with clouds and wind, and there was a heavy shower. And Ahab rode and went to [a]Jezreel.

46 Then [a]the hand of the LORD was on Elijah, and [b]he girded up his loins and [I]outran Ahab [II]to Jezreel.

Elijah Flees from Jezebel

19 Now Ahab told Jezebel all that Elijah had done,[6213] and [I][a]how he had killed all the prophets with the sword.

2 Then Jezebel sent a messenger to Elijah, saying, "[a]So may the gods[430] do[6213] to me and even more, if I do not make your [I]life as the [I]life of one of them by tomorrow about this time."

3 And he [I]was afraid and arose and ran for his [II]life and came to [a]Beersheba, which belongs to Judah, and left his servant there.

4 But he himself went a day's journey[1870] into the wilderness, and came and sat down under a [I]juniper tree; and [a]he requested for himself that he might die,[4191] and said, "It is enough; now, O LORD, take my [II]life, for I am not better[2896] than my fathers."[1]

5 And he lay down and slept under a [I]juniper tree; and behold, there was [a]an angel[4397] touching him, and he said to him, "Arise, eat."

6 Then he looked and behold, there was at his head a bread cake *baked on* hot stones, and a jar[6835] of water. So he ate and drank and lay down again.

7 And the angel of the LORD came again a second time and touched him and said, "Arise, eat, because the journey is too great for you."

8 So he arose and ate and drank, and went in the strength of that food [a]forty days[3117] and forty nights to [b]Horeb, the mountain of God.[430]

Elijah at Horeb

9 Then he came there to a cave, and lodged there; and behold, [a]the word of the LORD *came* to him, and He said to him, "What are you doing here, Elijah?"

10 And he said, "[a]I have been very zealous[7065] for the LORD, the God of hosts; for the sons[1121] of Israel have forsaken[5800] Thy covenant,[1285] [b]torn down Thine altars[4196] and killed Thy prophets with the sword. And [c]I alone am left; and they seek my life, to take it away."

11 So He said, "[a]Go forth, and stand on the mountain before the LORD." And behold, the LORD was passing by! And [b]a great and strong wind was rending the mountains and breaking[7665] in pieces the rocks before the LORD; *but* the LORD *was* not in the wind. And after the wind an earthquake,[7494] *but* the LORD *was* not in the earthquake.

12 And after the earthquake a fire, *but* the LORD *was* not in the fire; and after the fire [a]a sound of a gentle blowing.

13 And it came about when Elijah heard *it,* that [a]he wrapped his face in his mantle,[155] and went out and stood in the entrance of the cave. And behold, [b]a voice *came* to him and said, "What are you doing here, Elijah?"

14 Then he said, "[a]I have been very zealous for the LORD, the God of hosts; for the sons of Israel have forsaken Thy

44 [I]Lit., *Tie, harness* [a]Luke 12:54

45 [a]Josh. 17:16; Judg. 6:33

46 [I]Lit., *ran before* [II]Lit., *until you are coming to* [a]2Kin. 3:15; Is. 8:11; Ezek. 3:14 [b]2Kin. 4:29; Jer. 1:17; 1Pet. 1:13

1 [I]Lit., *all about how* [a]1Kin. 18:40

2 [I]Lit., *soul* [a]Ruth 1:17; 1Kin. 20:10; 2Kin. 6:31

3 [I]Reading of many mss.; Heb. text may read *saw* [II]Lit., *soul* [a]Gen. 21:31

4 [I]Or, *broom-tree* [II]Lit., *soul* [a]Num. 11:15; Jer. 20:14-18; Jon. 4:3, 8

5 [I]Or, *broom-tree* [a]Gen. 28:12

8 [a]Ex. 24:18; 34:28; Deut. 9:9-11, 18; Matt. 4:2 [b]Ex. 3:1; 4:27

9 [a]Ex. 33:21, 22

10 [a]Ex. 20:5; 34:14 [b]Rom. 11:3, 4 [c]1Kin. 18:22

11 [a]Ex. 19:20; 24:12, 18 [b]Ezek. 1:4

12 [a]Job 4:16; Zech. 4:6

13 [a]Ex. 3:6 [b]1Kin. 19:9

14 [a]1Kin. 19:10

18:43 This is an example of persistent prayer (See Lk. 11:5-10; 18:1-8).

covenant, torn down Thine altars and
killed Thy prophets with the sword. And
I alone am left; and they seek my life,
to take it away."
15 And the LORD said to him, "Go,
return on your way to the wilderness
of Damascus, and when you have arrived, [a]you shall anoint[4886] Hazael king
over Aram;
16 and [a]Jehu the son of Nimshi you
shall anoint king over Israel; and
[b]Elisha the son of Shaphat of Abel-meholah you shall anoint as prophet in your
place.
17 "And it shall come about, the
[a]one who escapes[4422] from the sword
of Hazael, Jehu [b]shall put to death, and
the one who escapes from the sword
of Jehu, Elisha shall put to death.
🔑 18 "[a]Yet I will leave 7,000 in Israel,
all the knees that have not bowed[3766]
to Baal and every mouth that has not
[b]kissed him."
19 So he departed from there and
found Elisha the son of Shaphat, while
he was plowing with twelve pairs *of oxen*
before him, and he with the twelfth.
And Elijah passed over to him and threw
[a]his mantle on him.
20 And he left the oxen and ran after
Elijah and said, "Please [a]let me kiss my
father[1] and my mother, then I will follow
you." And he said to him, "Go back
again, for what have I done to you?"
21 So he returned from following
him, and took the pair of oxen and sacrificed them and [a]boiled their flesh[1320] with
the implements of the oxen, and gave
it to the people and they ate. Then he
arose and followed Elijah and ministered
to him.

War with Aram

20 Now [a]Ben-hadad king of Aram
gathered[6908] all his army,
[b]and there *were* thirty-two kings with
him, and horses and chariots. And he
went up and [c]besieged Samaria, and
fought against it.
2 Then he sent messengers to the
city to Ahab king of Israel, and said to
him, "Thus says Ben-hadad,
3 'Your silver and your gold are
mine; your most beautiful[2896] wives and
children[1121] are also mine.' "
4 And the king of Israel answered
and said, "It is according to your word,
my lord, O king; I am yours, and all
that I have."
5 Then the messengers returned
and said, "Thus says [I]Ben-hadad,
'Surely, I sent to you saying, "You shall
give me your silver and your gold and
your wives and your children,"
6 but about this time tomorrow I
will send my servants to you, and they
will search your house and the houses
of your servants; and it shall come about,
[I]whatever is desirable in your eyes,
they will [II]take in their hand and carry
away.' "
7 Then the king of Israel called[7121]
all the elders[2205] of the land and said,
"Please observe and [a]see how this man
is looking for trouble; for he sent to
me for my wives and my children and
my silver and my gold, and I did not
refuse him."
8 And all the elders and all the people said to him, "Do not listen or
consent."[14]
9 So he said to the messengers of
Ben-hadad, "Tell my lord the king, 'All
that you sent for to your servant at the
first[7223] I will do,[6213] but this thing I cannot do.' " And the messengers departed
and brought him word again.
10 And Ben-hadad sent to him and
said, "May [a]the gods[430] do so to me
and more also, if the dust[6083] of Samaria
shall suffice for handfuls for all the people
who [I]follow me."
11 Then the king of Israel answered
and said, "Tell *him*, '[a]Let not him who
girds on *his armor* boast[1984] like him
who takes *it* off.' "

15 [a]2Kin. 8:8-15
16 [a]2Kin. 9:1-10 [b]1Kin. 19:19-21; 2Kin. 2:9, 15
17 [a]2Kin. 8:12; 13:3, 22 [b]2Kin. 9:14-10:25
18 [a]Rom. 11:4 [b]Hos. 13:2
19 [a]1Sam. 28:14; 2Kin. 2:8, 13, 14
20 [a]Matt. 8:21, 22; Luke 9:61, 62; Acts 20:37
21 [a]2Sam. 24:22
1 [a]1Kin. 15:18, 20; 2Kin. 6:24 [b]1Kin. 22:31 [c]1Kin. 16:24; 2Kin. 6:24
5 [I]Lit., *Ben-hadad, saying*
6 [I]Lit., *all the desire of your eyes* [II]Lit., *put*
7 [a]2Kin. 5:7
10 [I]Lit., *are at my feet* [a]1Kin. 19:2; 2Kin. 6:31
11 [a]Prov. 27:1

🔑 **19:18** The Apostle Paul referred to this in Rom. 11:4. If we try to trust in statistics rather than God, then we are not living by faith. Things are not always what they seem to be (Jn. 7:24; Mt. 8:11,12).

12 And it came about when *Ben-hadad* heard this message, as [a]he was drinking [I]with the kings in the [II]temporary shelters, that he said to his servants, "Station *yourselves*." So they stationed *themselves* against the city.

Ahab Victorious

13 Now behold, a prophet approached Ahab king of Israel and said, "Thus says the LORD, 'Have you seen all this great multitude? Behold, [a]I will deliver them into your hand today,[3117] and [b]you shall know that I am the LORD.' "

14 And Ahab said, "By whom?" So he said, "Thus says the LORD, 'By the young men of the rulers of the provinces.' " Then he said, "Who shall [I]begin the battle?" And he [II]answered,[559] "You."

15 Then he mustered the young men of the rulers of the provinces, and there were 232; and after them he mustered all the people, *even* all the sons of Israel, 7,000.

16 And they went out at noon, while [a]Ben-hadad was drinking himself drunk in the [I]temporary shelters [II]with the thirty-two kings who helped him.

17 And the young men of the rulers of the provinces went out first; and Ben-hadad sent out and they told him, saying, "Men have come out from Samaria."

18 [a]Then he said, "If they have come out for peace, take them alive;[2416] or if they have come out for war, take them alive."

19 So these went out from the city, the young men of the rulers of the provinces, and the army[2428] which followed them.

20 And they [I]killed each his man; and the Arameans fled, and Israel pursued them, and Ben-hadad king of Aram escaped[4422] on a horse with horsemen.

21 And the king of Israel went out and [I]struck the horses and chariots, and [I]killed the Arameans with a great slaughter.

22 Then [a]the prophet came near to the king of Israel, and said to him, "Go, strengthen yourself and observe and see what you have to do; for [b]at the turn of the year the king of Aram will come up against you."

23 Now the servants of the king of Aram said to him, "[a]Their gods are gods of the mountains, therefore they were stronger than we; but rather let us fight against them in the plain, *and* surely we shall be stronger than they.

24 "And do this thing: remove the kings, each from his place, and put captains[6346] in their place,

25 and [I]muster an army like the army that you have lost, horse for horse, and chariot for chariot. Then we will fight against them in the plain, and surely we shall be stronger than they." And he listened to their voice and did[6213] so.

Another Aramean War

26 So it came about [a]at the turn of the year, that Ben-hadad mustered the Arameans and went up to [b]Aphek to fight against Israel.

27 And the sons of Israel were mustered and were provisioned and went to meet them; and the sons of Israel camped before them like two little flocks of goats, [a]but the Arameans filled the country.[776]

28 Then [a]a man of God[430] came near and spoke to the king of Israel and said, "Thus says the LORD, 'Because the Arameans have said, "[b]The LORD is a god of *the* mountains, but He is not a god of *the* valleys"; therefore [c]I will give all this great multitude into your hand, and you shall know that I am the LORD.' "

29 So they camped one over against the other seven days.[3117] And it came about that on the seventh day, the battle was joined, and the sons of Israel [I]killed *of* the Arameans 100,000 foot soldiers in one day.

30 But the rest fled to [a]Aphek into the city, and the wall fell[5307] on 27,000 men who were left. And Ben-hadad fled and came into the city [b]into an inner chamber.

12 [I]Lit., *he and* [II]Or, *booths* [a]1Kin. 16:9; Prov. 31:4, 5

13 [a]1Kin. 20:28 [b]1Kin. 18:36

14 [I]Lit., *bind* [II]Lit., *said*

16 [I]Or, *booths* [II]Lit., *he and the 32 kings* [a]1Kin. 16:9; 20:12; Prov. 20:1

18 [a]2Kin. 14:8-12

20 [I]Lit., *smote*

21 [I]Lit., *smote*

22 [a]1Kin. 20:13 [b]2Sam. 11:1; 1Kin. 20:26

23 [a]1Kin. 14:23; Jer. 16:19-21; Rom. 1:21-23

25 [I]Lit., *number*

26 [a]1Kin. 20:22 [b]2Kin. 13:17

27 [a]Judg. 6:3-5; 1Sam. 13:5-8

28 [a]1Kin. 17:18 [b]1Kin. 20:23 [c]1Kin. 20:13

29 [I]Lit., *smote*

30 [a]1Kin. 20:26 [b]1Kin. 22:25; 2Chr. 18:24

31 And [a]his servants said to him,
"Behold now, we have heard that the
kings of the house of Israel are merciful
kings, please let us [b]put sackcloth on
our loins and ropes on our heads, and
go out to the king of Israel; perhaps[194]
he will save your [I]life."
32 So [a]they girded sackcloth on their
loins and *put* ropes on their heads, and
came to the king of Israel and said,
"[b]Your servant Ben-hadad says, 'Please
let me live.'" And he said, "Is he still
alive? He is my brother."[251]
33 Now the men [I]took this as an
omen, and quickly [II]catching his word
said, "Your brother Ben-hadad." Then
he said, "Go, bring him." Then Ben-
hadad came out to him, and he [III]took
him up into the chariot.
34 And *Ben-hadad* said to him,
"[a]The cities which my father[1] took from
your father I will restore, and you shall
make streets for yourself in Damascus,
as my father made in Samaria." *Ahab
said,* "And I will let you go with this
covenant."[1285] So he made a covenant
with him and let him go.
35 Now a certain man of [a]the sons
of the prophets said to [I]another [b]by the
word of the LORD, "Please strike me."
But the man refused to strike him.
36 Then he said to him, "Because
you have not listened to the voice of
the LORD, behold, as soon as you have
departed from me, [a]a lion will [I]kill you."
And as soon as he had departed from
him a lion found him, and [II]killed
him.
37 Then he found another man and
said, "Please [I]strike me." And the man
[II]struck[5221] him, [III]wounding him.
38 So the prophet departed and
waited for the king by the way, and
[a]disguised himself with a bandage over
his eyes.
39 And as the king passed by, he
cried to the king and said, "Your servant
went out into the midst of the battle;
and behold, a man turned aside and
brought a man to me and said, 'Guard
this man; if for any reason he is missing,
[a]then your life shall be for his life, or
else you shall pay a talent of silver.'
40 "And while your servant was
busy[6213] here and there, he was gone."
And the king of Israel said to him, "So
shall your judgment[4941] be; you yourself
have decided *it*."
41 Then he hastily took the bandage
away from his eyes, and the king of
Israel recognized[5234] him that he was
of the prophets.
42 And he said to him, "Thus says
the LORD, 'Because you have let go out
of *your* hand the man whom I had devoted to destruction, therefore [a]your
[I]life shall go for his [I]life, and your people
for his people.'"
43 So [a]the king of Israel went to
his house sullen and vexed,[2198] and came
to Samaria.

Ahab Covets Naboth's Vineyard

21 Now it came about after these
things, that Naboth the Jezreel-
ite had a vineyard which *was* in [a]Jezreel
beside the palace of Ahab king of Samaria.
2 And Ahab spoke to Naboth, saying, "[a]Give me your vineyard, that I may
have it for a vegetable garden because
it is close beside my house, and I will
give you a better[2896] vineyard than it
in its place; if [I]you like, I will give you
the price of [II]it in money."
3 But Naboth said to Ahab, "The
LORD forbid me [a]that I should give you
the inheritance[5159] of my fathers."[1]
4 [a]So Ahab came into his house sullen and vexed[2198] because of the word
which Naboth the Jezreelite had spoken
to him; for he said, "I will not give you
the inheritance of my fathers." And he
lay down on his bed and turned away
his face and ate no [I]food.
5 But Jezebel his wife came to him
and said to him, "How is it that your
spirit is so sullen that you are not eating
[I]food?"

31 [I]Lit., *soul* [a]1Kin. 20:23-26 [b]Gen. 37:34; 2Sam. 3:31
32 [a]1Kin. 20:31 [b]1Kin. 20:3-6
33 [I]Lit., *divined* [II]Lit., *caught from him* [III]Lit., *caused him to come up*
34 [a]1Kin. 15:20
35 [I]Lit., *his neighbor* [a]2Kin. 2:3-7 [b]1Kin. 13:17,18
36 [I]Lit., *smite* [II]Lit., *smote* [a]1Kin. 13:24
37 [I]Lit., *smite* [II]Lit., *smote* [III]Lit., *striking and wounding*
38 [a]1Kin. 14:2
39 [a]2Kin. 10:24
42 [I]Lit., *soul* [a]1Kin. 20:39
43 [a]1Kin. 21:4
1 [a]Judg. 6:33; 1Kin. 18:45, 46
2 [I]Lit., *it is good in your eyes* [II]Lit., *this* [a]1Sam. 8:14
3 [a]Lev. 25:23; Num. 36:7; Ezek. 46:18
4 [I]Lit., *bread* [a]1Kin. 20:43
5 [I]Lit., *bread*

21:3 See note on Lev. 25:1-55.

6 So he said to her, "Because I
spoke to Naboth the Jezreelite, and said
to him, 'Give me your vineyard for
money; or else, if it pleases you, I will
give you a vineyard in its place.' But
he said,[559] 'I will not give you my vineyard.' "
7 And Jezebel his wife said to him,
"[a]Do you now [I]reign over Israel? Arise,
eat bread, and let your heart be joyful;
I will give you the vineyard of Naboth
the Jezreelite."
8 [a]So she wrote letters in Ahab's
name and sealed them with his seal,
and sent letters to [b]the elders[2205] and
to the nobles who were living with Naboth in his city.
9 Now she wrote in the letters, saying, "Proclaim a fast, and seat Naboth
at the head of the people;
10 and seat two [a]worthless[1100] men
before him, and let them testify against
him, saying, '[b]You cursed[1288] God[430] and
the king.' Then take him out and
[c]stone him [I]to death."[4191]

Jezebel's Plot

11 So the men of his city, the elders
and the nobles who lived in his city,
did[6213] as Jezebel had sent *word* to them,
just as it was written in the letters which
she had sent them.
12 They [a]proclaimed a fast and
seated Naboth at the head of the people.
13 Then the two worthless men
came in and sat before him; and the
worthless men testified against him,
even against Naboth, before the people,
saying, "Naboth cursed God and the
king." [a]So they took him outside the
city and stoned him [I]to death[4191] with
stones.
14 Then they sent *word* to Jezebel,
saying, "Naboth has been stoned, and
is dead."[4191]
15 And it came about when Jezebel
heard that Naboth had been stoned and
was dead, that Jezebel said to Ahab,
"Arise, take possession of the vineyard
of Naboth, the Jezreelite, which he refused to give you for money; for Naboth
is not alive,[2416] but dead."
16 And it came about when Ahab
heard that Naboth was dead, that Ahab
arose to go down to the vineyard of
Naboth the Jezreelite, to take possession of it.
17 Then the word of the LORD came
to Elijah the Tishbite, saying,
18 "Arise, go down to meet Ahab
king of Israel, [a]who is in Samaria; behold,
he is in the vineyard of Naboth where
he has gone down to take possession
of it.
19 "And you shall speak to him, saying, 'Thus says the LORD, "[a]Have you
murdered, and also taken possession?" '
And you shall speak to him, saying,
'Thus says the LORD, "[b]In the place
where the dogs licked up the blood[1818]
of Naboth the dogs shall lick up your
blood, even yours." ' "
20 And Ahab said to Elijah, "[a]Have
you found me, O my enemy?" And he
[I]answered, "I have found *you,* [b]because
you have sold yourself to do evil[7451] in
the sight of the LORD.
21 "Behold, I will bring evil upon
you, and [a]will utterly sweep you away,
and will cut off[3772] from Ahab every
male, both bond and free in Israel;
22 and [a]I will make your house
[b]like the house of Jeroboam the son of
Nebat, and like the house of Baasha the
son of Ahijah, because of the provocation
with which you have provoked *Me* to
anger,[3707] and *because* you [c]have made
Israel sin.
23 "And of Jezebel also has the LORD
spoken, saying, '[a]The dogs shall eat Jezebel in the [I]district of Jezreel.'
24 "[a]The one belonging to Ahab,
who dies[4191] in the city, the dogs shall
eat, and the one who dies in the field[7704]
the birds of heaven[8064] shall eat."
25 [a]Surely there was no one like
Ahab who sold himself to do evil in the
sight of the LORD, [I]because Jezebel his
wife incited him.
26 And [a]he acted very abomi-
nably[8581] in following idols,[1544] [b]accord-
ing to all that the Amorites had

7 [I]Lit., *exercise kingship* [a]1Sam. 8:14
8 [a]Esth. 3:12; 8:8, 10 [b]1Kin. 20:7
10 [I]Lit., *so that he dies* [a]1Sam. 2:12; 2Sam. 20:1 [b]Ex. 22:28; Lev. 24:15, 16; Acts 6:11 [c]Lev. 24:14
12 [a]Is. 58:4
13 [I]Lit., *with stones so that he died* [a]2Kin. 9:26; 2Chr. 24:21; Acts 7:58, 59; Heb. 11:37
18 [a]1Kin. 16:29
19 [a]2Sam. 12:9 [b]1Kin. 22:38; 2Kin. 9:26
20 [I]Lit., *said* [a]1Kin. 18:17 [b]1Kin. 21:25; 2Kin. 17:17; Rom. 7:14
21 [a]1Kin. 14:10; 2Kin. 9:8
22 [a]1Kin. 15:29 [b]1Kin. 16:3, 11 [c]1Kin. 12:30; 13:34; 14:16
23 [I]Lit., *portion; some mss. read rampart* [a]2Kin. 9:10, 30-37
24 [a]1Kin. 14:11; 16:4
25 [I]Or, *whom Jezebel his wife incited* [a]1Kin. 16:30-33; 21:20
26 [a]1Kin. 15:12; 2Kin. 17:12 [b]Gen. 15:16; Lev. 18:25-30; 2Kin. 21:11

done,[6213] whom the LORD cast[3423] out before the sons of Israel.

27 And it came about when Ahab heard these words, that [a]he tore his clothes and put [I]on sackcloth and fasted, and he lay in sackcloth and went about [II]despondently.

28 Then the word of the LORD came to Elijah the Tishbite, saying,

29 "Do you see how Ahab has humbled himself before Me? Because he has humbled himself before Me, I will not bring the evil in his days,[3117] *but* I will bring the evil upon his house [a]in his son's days."

Ahab's Third Campaign against Aram

22 And [I]three years passed without war between Aram and Israel.

2 [a]And it came about in the third year, that [b]Jehoshaphat the king of Judah came down to the king of Israel.

3 Now the king of Israel said to his servants, "Do you know that [a]Ramoth-gilead belongs to us, and we [I]are still doing nothing to take it out of the hand of the king of Aram?"

4 And he said to Jehoshaphat, "Will you go with me to battle at Ramoth-gilead?" And Jehoshaphat said to the king of Israel, "[a]I am as you are, my people as your people, my horses as your horses."

5 Moreover, Jehoshaphat said to the king of Israel, "Please inquire [I]first for the word of the LORD."

6 Then [a]the king of Israel gathered[6908] the prophets together, about four hundred men, and said to them, "Shall I go against Ramoth-gilead to battle or shall I refrain?" And they said, "Go up, for the Lord will give *it* into the hand of the king."

7 But [a]Jehoshaphat said, "Is there not yet a prophet of the LORD here, that we may inquire of him?"

8 And the king of Israel said to Jehoshaphat, "There is yet one man by whom we may inquire of the LORD, but I hate him, because he does not prophesy good[2896] concerning me, but evil.[7451] *He is* Micaiah son of Imlah." But Jehoshaphat said, "Let not the king say so."

9 Then the king of Israel called[7121] an officer and said, "[I]Bring quickly Micaiah son of Imlah."

10 Now the king of Israel and Jehoshaphat king of Judah were sitting each[376] on his throne, arrayed in *their* robes, at the threshing floor at the entrance of the gate of Samaria; and [a]all the prophets were prophesying before them.

11 Then Zedekiah the son of Chenaanah made [a]horns of iron for himself and said, "Thus says the LORD, '[b]With these you shall gore the Arameans until they are consumed.' "[3615]

12 And all the prophets were prophesying thus, saying, "Go up to Ramoth-gilead and prosper, for the LORD will give *it* into the hand of the king."

Micaiah Predicts Defeat

13 Then the messenger who went to summon[7121] Micaiah spoke to him saying, "Behold now, the words of the prophets are uniformly favorable to the king. Please let your word be like the word of one of them, and speak favorably."

14 But Micaiah said, "[a]As the LORD lives, what [b]the LORD says to me, that I will speak."

15 When he came to the king, the king said to him, "Micaiah, shall we go to Ramoth-gilead to battle, or shall we refrain?" And he [I]answered[559] him, "[a]Go up and succeed, and the LORD will give *it* into the hand of the king."

16 Then the king said to him, "How many times must I adjure[7650] you to

27 [I]Lit., *sackcloth on his flesh* [II]Or, *softly* [a]Gen. 37:34; 2Sam. 3:31; 2Kin. 6:30
29 [a]2Kin. 9:25-37
1 [I]Lit., *they sat for three years*
2 [a]2Chr. 18:2 [b]1Kin. 15:24
3 [I]Lit., *are silent so as not* [a]Deut. 4:43; Josh. 21:38; 1Kin. 4:13
4 [a]2Kin. 3:7
5 [I]Lit., *as the day*
6 [a]1Kin. 18:19
7 [a]2Kin. 3:11
9 [I]Lit., *Hasten Micaiah*
10 [a]1Kin. 22:6
11 [a]Zech. 1:18-21 [b]Deut. 33:17
14 [a]1Kin. 18:10, 15 [b]Num. 22:18; 24:13
15 [I]Lit., *said to* [a]1Kin. 22:12

22:1-28 See II Chr. 18:2-27.

speak to me nothing but the truth in the name of the LORD?"

17 So he said,

"I saw all Israel
Scattered on the mountains,
[a]Like sheep which have no
shepherd.
And the LORD said, 'These have
no master.
Let each of them return to his
house in peace.'"

18 Then the king of Israel said to Jehoshaphat, "[a]Did I not tell you that he would not prophesy good concerning me, but evil?"

19 And [I]Micaiah said, "Therefore, hear the word of the LORD. [a]I saw the LORD sitting on His throne, and [b]all the host of heaven standing by Him on His right and on His left.

20 "And the LORD said, 'Who will entice Ahab to go up and fall at Ramoth-gilead?' And one said this while another said that.

21 "Then a spirit came forward and stood before the LORD and said, 'I will entice him.'

22 "And the LORD said to him, 'How?' And he said, 'I will go out and [a]be a deceiving spirit in the mouth of all his prophets.' Then He said, 'You are to entice *him* and also prevail. Go and do[6213] so.'

23 "Now therefore, behold, [a]the LORD has put a deceiving spirit in the mouth of all these your prophets; and the LORD has proclaimed disaster against you."

24 Then [a]Zedekiah the son of Chenaanah came near and struck Micaiah on the cheek and said, "[b]How did the Spirit of the LORD pass from me to speak to you?"

25 And Micaiah said, "Behold, you shall see on that day when you [a]enter an inner room to hide yourself."

26 Then the king of Israel said, "Take Micaiah and return him to Amon the governor of the city and to Joash the king's son;

27 and say, 'Thus says the king, "[a]Put this man in prison, and feed him [I]sparingly with bread and water until I return safely."'"

🔑 28 And Micaiah said, "[a]If you indeed return safely the LORD has not spoken by me." And he said, "[b]Listen, all you people."

Defeat and Death of Ahab

🔑 **29** So [a]the king of Israel and Jehoshaphat king of Judah went up against Ramoth-gilead.

30 And the king of Israel said to Jehoshaphat, "[a]I will disguise myself and go into the battle, but you put on your robes." So the king of Israel disguised himself and went into the battle.

31 Now [a]the king of Aram had commanded[6680] the thirty-two captains[8269] of his chariots, saying, "Do not fight with small or great, but with the king of Israel alone."

32 So it came about, when the captains of the chariots saw Jehoshaphat, that they said, "Surely it is the king of Israel," and they turned aside to fight against him, and Jehoshaphat cried out.

33 Then it happened, when the captains of the chariots saw that it was not the king of Israel, that they turned back from pursuing him.

34 Now a certain man drew his bow at random[8537] and struck the king of Israel [I]in a joint of the armor. So he said to the driver of his chariot, "Turn [II]around, and take me out of the [III]fight; [a]for I am severely wounded."

35 And the battle [I]raged[5927] that day, and the king was propped up in his chariot in front of the Arameans, and died[4191] at evening, and the blood[1818] from the wound ran into the bottom of the chariot.

36 [a]Then a cry passed throughout

17 [a]Num. 27:17; 1Kin. 22:34-36; 2Chr. 18:16; Matt. 9:36; Mark 6:34
18 [a]1Kin. 22:8
19 [I]Lit., *he* [a]Is. 6:1; Ezek. 1:26-28; Dan. 7:9, 10 [b]Job 1:6; 2:1; Ps. 103:20, 21; Dan. 7:10; Matt. 18:10; Heb. 1:7, 14
22 [a]Judg. 9:23; 1Sam. 16:14; 18:10; 19:9; Ezek. 14:9; 2Thess. 2:11
23 [a]Ezek. 14:9
24 [a]1Kin. 22:11; Matt. 5:39; Acts 23:2, 3 [b]2Chr. 18:23
25 [a]1Kin. 20:30
27 [I]Lit., *with bread of affliction and water of affliction* [a]2Chr. 16:10; 18:25-27
28 [a]Deut. 18:22 [b]Mic. 1:2
29 [a]1Kin. 22:3, 4
30 [a]2Chr. 35:22
31 [a]1Kin. 20:1, 16, 24; 2Chr. 18:30
34 [I]Lit., *between the scale-armor and the breastplate* [II]Lit., *your hand* [III]Lit., *camp* [a]2Chr. 35:23
35 [I]Lit., *went up*
36 [a]2Kin. 14:12

🔑 **22:28** See note on Deut. 18:20-22.
🔑 **22:29-40** See II Chr. 18:28-34.

the army close to sunset, saying, "Every
man to his city and every man to his
[I]country."[776]
37 So the king died and was brought
to Samaria, and they buried[6912] the king
in Samaria.
38 And they washed the chariot by
the pool of Samaria, and the dogs licked
up his blood (now the harlots bathed
themselves *there*), [a]according to the
word of the LORD which He spoke.
39 Now the rest of the acts[1697] of
Ahab and all that he did[6213] and [a]the
ivory house which he built and all the
cities which he built, are they not written
in the Book[5612] of the Chronicles of the
Kings of Israel?
40 So Ahab slept with his fathers,[1]
and Ahaziah his son became king in his
place.

The New Rulers

🔑**41** [a]Now Jehoshaphat the son of Asa
became king over Judah in the fourth
year of Ahab king of Israel.
42 Jehoshaphat was thirty-five
years old when he became king, and
he reigned twenty-five years in Jerusalem. And his mother's name was Azubah
the daughter of Shilhi.
43 [a]And he walked in all the way
of Asa his father;[1] he did not turn aside
from it, doing[6213] right in the sight of
the LORD. [b]However, the high places
were not taken away; the people still
sacrificed and burnt incense[6999] on the
high places.

🔑44 [a]Jehoshaphat also made peace
with the king of Israel.
45 Now the rest of the acts of Jehoshaphat, and his might which he
showed and how he warred, are they
not written [a]in the Book of the Chronicles of the Kings of Judah?
46 And the remnant of [a]the sod-
omites[6045] who remained in the days[3117]
of his father Asa, he [I]expelled from the
land.
47 Now [a]there was no king in Edom;
a deputy[5324] was king.
48 Jehoshaphat made [a]ships of
Tarshish to go to [b]Ophir for gold, but
[c]they did not go for the ships were
broken[7665] at [d]Ezion-geber.
49 Then Ahaziah the son of Ahab
said to Jehoshaphat, "Let my servants
go with your servants in the ships." But
Jehoshaphat was not willing.
50 [a]And Jehoshaphat slept with his
fathers and was buried with his fathers
in the city of his father David, and Jehoram his son became king in his place.
51 Ahaziah the son of Ahab [a]became
king over Israel in Samaria in the seventeenth year of Jehoshaphat king of Judah,
and he reigned two years over Israel.
52 And he did evil in the sight of
the LORD and [a]walked in the way of his
father and in the way of his mother and
in the way of Jeroboam the son of Nebat,
who caused Israel to sin.
53 [a]So he served Baal and worshiped him and provoked the LORD
God[430] of Israel to anger[3707] according
to all that his father had done.[6213]

36 [I]Lit., *land*
38 [a]1Kin. 21:19
39 [a]Amos 3:15
41 [a]2Chr. 20:31
43 [a]2Chr. 17:3 [b]1Kin. 15:14; 2Kin. 12:3
44 [a]1Kin. 22:2; 2Kin. 8:16, 18; 2Chr. 19:2
45 [a]2Chr. 20:34
46 [I]Lit., *consumed* [a]Gen. 19:5; Deut. 23:17; 1Kin. 14:24; 15:12; Jude 7
47 [a]2Sam. 8:14; 2Kin. 3:9
48 [a]1Kin. 10:22; 2Chr. 20:36 [b]1Kin. 9:28 [c]2Chr. 20:37 [d]1Kin. 9:26
50 [a]2Chr. 21:1
51 [a]1Kin. 22:40
52 [a]1Kin. 15:26; 21:25
53 [a]Judg. 2:11; 1Kin. 16:30-32

🔑**22:41-50** See II Chr. 20:31—21:1.
🔑**22:44** He did so by contracting a marriage between his son and Athaliah, the wicked daughter of Ahab and Jezebel.

The Second Book of the
KINGS

The First and Second Books of Kings are called the Third and Fourth Books of Kingdoms in the Septuagint, the ancient Greek translation of the Old Testament. I Samuel, II Samuel, and I Kings provide the necessary backdrop of historical events which preceded II Kings. The book picks up where I Kings left off, the end of Ahaziah's reign. In painful detail the Book of II Kings narrates the tragic events of the divided kingdom until Israel's fall in 722 B.C. and Judah's captivity in 586 B.C. The start of I Kings is full of hope and promise and the end of II Kings describes a nation in ruins. The people have forsaken their God, the same God who had led them out of Egypt with such awesome power! About 400 years are covered by the two books, which were originally one book in the Hebrew Bible. The author is not known, but many speculate that it could have been the prophet Jeremiah. In addition to the important lessons of I Kings, the Book of Second Kings teaches that once a nation abandons its heritage it loses the ability to discern the difference between right and wrong. The very makeup of the national and individual conscience is affected. Superficial reforms and mere lip service accomplish little. The Lord demands true repentance. The final result of continued sin is always total collapse. However, God's love is so persistent that He will never give up on His people.

Ahaziah's Messengers Meet Elijah

1 Now [a]Moab rebelled against Israel
after the death[4194] of Ahab.
🔑2 And Ahaziah fell through the
lattice[7639] in his upper chamber which
was in Samaria, and became ill. So he
sent messengers and said to them, "Go,
[a]inquire of Baal-zebub, the god[430] of Ekron, [b]whether I shall recover from this
sickness."[2483]
3 But the angel[4397] of the LORD said
to [a]Elijah the Tishbite, "Arise, go up
to meet the messengers of the king[4428]
of Samaria and say to them, 'Is it because
there is no God in Israel *that* you are
going to inquire of [b]Baal-zebub, the god
of Ekron?'
4 "Now therefore thus says the
LORD, '[I][a]You shall not come down from
the bed where you have gone up, but
you shall surely die.' "[4191] Then Elijah
departed.
5 When the messengers returned
to him he said to them, "[I]Why have you
returned?"
6 And they said to him, "A man came
up to meet us and said to us, 'Go, return
to the king who sent you and say to
him, "Thus says the LORD, 'Is it because
there is no God in Israel *that* you are
sending [a]to inquire of Baal-zebub, the
god of Ekron? Therefore [I]you shall not
come down from the bed where you
have gone up, but shall surely die.' " ' "
7 And he said to them, "What kind
of man was he who came up to meet
you and spoke these words[1697] to you?"
🔑8 And they [I]answered[559] him, "[a]*He*
was a hairy man with a leather girdle[232]
[II]bound about his loins." And he said,
"It is Elijah the Tishbite."
9 Then *the king* [a]sent to him a
captain[8269] of fifty with his fifty. And he
went up to him, and behold, he was
sitting on the top of the hill. And he

1 [a]2Sam. 8:2; 2Kin. 3:5
2 [a]2Kin. 1:3, 6, 16; Matt. 10:25; Mark 3:22 [b]2Kin. 8:7-10
3 [a]1Kin. 17:1; 21:17 [b]2Kin. 1:2
4 [I]Lit., *The bed where you went up, you shall not come down from it* [a]2Kin. 1:6, 16
5 [I]Lit., *What is this that you have returned?*
6 [I]V. 4, note 1 [a]2Kin. 1:2
8 [I]Lit., *said* [II]Or, *girt* [a]Zech. 13:4; Matt. 3:4; Mark 1:6
9 [a]2Kin. 6:13, 14

🔑**1:2** In Hebrew Baal-zebub means "lord of flies." How could such a god bring good health? In later times Satan, the prince of demons, was dubbed by the name "Beelzebub" (Mt. 10:25; 12:24). Better Greek texts have "Beelzebul."

🔑**1:8** The description of John the Baptist in the Gospels (Mt. 3:4; Mk. 1:6) is strikingly reminiscent of that of Elijah here. The connection between the two figures is explicitly made in the N.T., based in part on Mal. 4:5-6. See the note on that passage.

said to him, "O man of God, the king says, 'Come down.' "

10 And Elijah answered and said to the captain of fifty, "If I am a man of God, [a]let fire come down from heaven and consume you and your fifty." [b]Then fire came down from heaven and consumed him and his fifty.

11 So he again sent to him another captain of fifty with his fifty. And he answered and said to him, "O man of God, thus says the king, 'Come down quickly.' "

12 And Elijah answered and said to them, "If I am a man of God, let fire come down from heaven and consume you and your fifty." Then the fire of God came down from heaven and consumed him and his fifty.

13 So he [a]again sent the captain of a third fifty with his fifty. When the third captain of fifty went up, he came and bowed down on his knees before Elijah, and begged[2603] him and said to him, "O man of God, please[4994] let my life[5315] and the lives of these fifty servants of yours be precious in your sight.

14 "Behold fire came down from heaven, and consumed the first[7223] two captains[8269] of fifty with their fifties; but now let my [I]life be precious in your sight."

15 And [a]the angel of the LORD said to Elijah, "Go down with him; [b]do not be afraid[3372] of him." So he arose and went down with him to the king.

16 Then he said to him, "Thus says the LORD, 'Because you have sent messengers [a]to inquire of Baal-zebub, the god of Ekron—is it because there is no God in Israel to inquire of His word?—[1697] therefore [I]you shall not come down from the bed where you have gone up, but shall surely die.' "

10 [a]1Kin. 18:36-38; Luke 9:54 [b]Job 1:16
13 [a]Is. 1:5; Jer. 5:3
14 [I]Lit., *soul*
15 [a]2Kin. 1:3 [b]Is. 51:12; Jer. 1:17; Ezek. 2:6
16 [I]V. 4, note 1 [a]2Kin. 1:3
17 [a]2Kin. 3:1; 8:16
1 [I]Or, *windstorm* [a]Gen. 5:24; Heb. 11:5 [b]1Kin. 19:16-21 [c]Josh. 4:19
2 [a]Ruth 1:15 [b]1Kin. 12:28, 29 [c]1Sam. 1:26; 2Kin. 2:4, 6
3 [I]Lit., *your head* [a]2Kin. 4:1, 38; 5:22
4 [a]2Kin. 2:2 [b]Josh. 6:26 [c]2Kin. 2:2
5 [I]Lit., *your head* [II]Lit., *said* [a]2Kin. 2:3 [b]2Kin. 2:3

Jehoram Reigns over Israel

17 So Ahaziah died[4191] according to the word of the LORD which Elijah had spoken. And because he had no son, Jehoram became king in his place [a]in the second year of Jehoram the son of Jehoshaphat, king of Judah.

18 Now the rest of the acts[1697] of Ahaziah which he did,[6213] are they not written in the Book[5612] of the Chronicles of the Kings[4428] of Israel?

Elijah Taken to Heaven

2 And it came about when the LORD was about to [a]take up Elijah by a [I]whirlwind to heaven, that Elijah went with [b]Elisha from [c]Gilgal.

2 And Elijah said to Elisha, "[a]Stay here please,[4994] for the LORD has sent me as far as [b]Bethel." But Elisha said, "[c]As the LORD lives[2416] and as you yourself live, I will not leave[5800] you." So they went down to Bethel.

🗝 3 Then [a]the sons of the prophets[5030] who *were at* Bethel came out to Elisha and said to him, "Do you know[3045] that the LORD will take away your master from over [I]you today?"[3117] And he said, "Yes, I know;[3045] be still."

4 And Elijah said to him, "Elisha, please [a]stay here, for the LORD has sent me to [b]Jericho." But he said, "[c]As the LORD lives, and as you yourself live, I will not leave you." So they came to Jericho.

🗝 5 And [a]the sons of the prophets who *were* at Jericho approached Elisha and said to him, "[b]Do you know that the LORD will take away your master from over [I]you today?" And he [II]answered,[559] "Yes, I know; be still."

🗝 **2:3,5** "The sons of the prophets" is probably a reference to "the school of the prophets." In ancient Israel there were schools taught by the prophets, and the pupils were called "sons of prophets." The earliest mention of the schools are those established by Samuel at Gibeah (I Sam. 10:10) and Naioth (I Sam. 19:20), where they are called a "company of prophets." The prophets whom Obadiah hid from Jezebel (I Kgs. 18:4) were probably pupils in such a school. The reference to a school at Gilgal (II Kgs. 4:38-44) would seem to indicate a kind of college where there was a common table. In II Kgs. 6:1-4 there is an account of the building of such a school. The schools here were at Bethel and Jericho.

6 Then Elijah said to him, "Please [a]stay here, for the LORD has sent me to [b]the Jordan." And he said, "As the LORD lives, and as you yourself live, I will not leave you." So the two of them went on.

7 Now [a]fifty men of the sons of the prophets went and stood opposite *them* at a distance, while the two of them stood by the Jordan.

8 And Elijah [a]took his mantle[155] and folded it together and [b]struck the waters, and they were divided here and there, so that the two of them crossed over on dry[2724] ground.

9 Now it came about when they had crossed over, that Elijah said to Elisha, "Ask[7592] what I shall do[6213] for you before I am taken from you." And Elisha said, "Please, let a [a]double portion of your spirit be upon me."

10 And he said, "You have asked[7592] a hard thing. *Nevertheless,* if you [a]see me when I am taken from you, it shall be so for you; but if not, it shall not be *so.*"

11 Then it came about as they were going along and talking, that behold, *there appeared* [a]a chariot of fire and horses of fire which separated the two of them. And Elijah went up by a [I]whirlwind to heaven.

12 And Elisha saw *it* and cried out, "[a]My father,[1] my father, the [I]chariots of Israel and its horsemen!" And he saw him no more. Then [b]he took hold of his own clothes and tore them in two pieces.

13 He also took up the mantle[155] of Elijah that fell[5307] from him, and returned and stood by the bank[8193] of the Jordan.

14 And he took the mantle[155] of Elijah that fell from him, and struck the waters and said, "Where is the LORD, the God[430] of Elijah?" And when he also had [a]struck the waters, they were divided here and there; and Elisha crossed over.

Elisha Succeeds Elijah

15 Now when [a]the sons of the prophets who *were* at Jericho opposite *him* saw him, they said, "The spirit of Elijah rests on Elisha." And they came to meet him and bowed[7812] themselves to the ground[776] before him.

16 And they said to him, "Behold now, there are with your servants fifty strong men, please let them go and search for your master; [I]perhaps[194] [a]the Spirit of the LORD has taken him up and cast him on some mountain or into some valley." And he said, "You shall not send."

17 But when [a]they urged him until he was ashamed,[954] he said, "Send." They sent therefore fifty men; and they searched three days,[3117] but did not find him.

18 And they returned to him while he was staying at Jericho; and he said to them, "Did I not say to you, 'Do not go'?"

19 Then the men of the city said to Elisha, "Behold now, the situation[4186] of this city is pleasant,[2896] as my lord[113] sees; but the water is bad,[7451] and the land [I]is unfruitful."[7921]

20 And he said, "Bring me a new jar,[6746] and put salt [I]in it." So they brought *it* to him.

21 And he went out to the spring of water, and [a]threw salt [I]in it and said, "Thus says the LORD, 'I have [II]purified these waters; there shall not be from there death[4194] or [III]unfruitfulness any longer.'"

22 So the waters have been [I]purified to this day, according to the word of Elisha which he spoke.

23 Then he went up from there to Bethel; and as he was going up by the way,[1870] young lads came out from the city and [a]mocked him and said to him, "Go up, you baldhead; go up, you baldhead!"

🗝 24 When he looked[7200] behind him

---

6 [a]2Kin. 2:2 [b]Josh. 3:8, 15-17
7 [a]2Kin. 2:15, 16
8 [a]1Kin. 19:13, 19 [b]Ex. 14:21, 22; 2Kin. 2:14
9 [a]Num. 11:17-25; Deut. 21:17
10 [a]Acts 1:10
11 [I]Or, *windstorm* [a]2Kin. 6:17
12 [I]Lit., *chariot* [a]2Kin. 13:14 [b]Gen. 37:34; Job 1:20
14 [a]2Kin. 2:8
15 [a]2Kin. 2:7
16 [I]Lit., *lest* [a]1Kin. 18:12; Acts 8:39
17 [a]2Kin. 8:11
19 [I]Lit., *causes barrenness*
20 [I]Lit., *there*
21 [I]Lit., *there* [II]Lit., *healed* [III]Lit., *barrenness* [a]Ex. 15:25,26; 2Kin. 4:41; 6:6
22 [I]Lit., *healed*
23 [a]2Chr. 36:16; Ps. 31:17, 18

🗝 **2:24** These boys were mocking God when they mocked the ascension of Elijah. "God is not mocked" (Gal. 6:7). Their lives would not have been constructive. See the exegetical note on Mk. 3:28,29.

and saw them, he [a]cursed[7043] them in
the name of the LORD. Then two female
bears came out of the woods and tore
up forty-two lads of [1]their number.
25 And he went from there to
[a]Mount Carmel, and from there he returned to Samaria.

Jehoram Meets Moab Rebellion

3 Now Jehoram the son of Ahab became king over Israel at Samaria
[a]in the eighteenth year of Jehoshaphat
king[4428] of Judah, and reigned twelve
years.
2 And he did evil[7451] in the sight of
the LORD, though not like his father[1]
and his mother; for [a]he put away the
sacred pillar of Baal [b]which his father
had made.
3 Nevertheless, [a]he clung to the
sins of Jeroboam the son of Nebat,
[b]which he made Israel sin; he did not
depart[5493] from them.
4 Now Mesha king of Moab was a
sheep breeder, and [a]used to pay the
king of Israel 100,000 lambs[3733] and the
wool of 100,000 rams.
5 But it came about, [a]when Ahab
died,[4194] the king of Moab rebelled
against the king of Israel.
6 And King Jehoram went out of Samaria [1]at that time and mustered all Israel.
7 Then he went and sent *word* to
Jehoshaphat the king of Judah, saying,
"The king of Moab has rebelled against
me. Will you go with me to fight against
Moab?" And he said, "I will go up;
[a]I am as you are, my people[5971] as your
people, my horses as your horses."
8 And he said, "Which way shall we
go up?" And he [1]answered,[559] "The
way[1870] of the wilderness of Edom."
9 So [a]the king of Israel went with
[b]the king of Judah and [c]the king of Edom;
and they made a circuit of seven days'[3117]
journey,[1870] and there was no water for
the army or for the cattle that followed
them.
10 Then the king of Israel said,
"Alas! For the LORD has called[7121] these
three kings[4428] to give them into the
hand of Moab."
11 But Jehoshaphat said, "[a]Is there
not a prophet[5030] of the LORD here, that
we may inquire of the LORD by him?"
And one of the king of Israel's servants
answered and said, "[b]Elisha the son of
Shaphat is here, [c]who used to pour water
on the hands of Elijah."
12 And Jehoshaphat said, "The
word[1697] of the LORD is with him." So
the king of Israel and Jehoshaphat and
the king of Edom went down to him.
13 Now Elisha said to the king of
Israel, "What do I have to do with you?
[a]Go to the prophets[5030] of your father
and to the prophets of your mother."
And the king of Israel said to him, "No,
for the LORD has called these three kings
together to give them into the hand of
Moab."
14 And Elisha said, "[a]As the LORD
of hosts lives,[2416] before whom I stand,
were it not that I regard the presence
of Jehoshaphat the king of Judah, I would
not look at you nor see you.
15 "But now [a]bring me a minstrel."
And it came about, when the minstrel
played, that [b]the hand of the LORD came
upon him.
16 And he said, "Thus says the
LORD, 'Make this valley full of trenches.'
17 "For thus says the LORD, 'You
shall not see wind[7307] nor shall you see
rain; yet that valley [a]shall be filled with
water, so that you shall drink, both you
and your cattle and your beasts.
18 'And this is but a [a]slight thing
in the sight of the LORD; He shall also
give the Moabites into your hand.
19 '[a]Then you shall strike every fortified city and every choice city, and
fell[5307] every good[2896] tree and stop all
springs of water, and mar every good
piece of land with stones.'"
20 And it happened in the morning
[a]about the time of offering the sacrifice,
that behold, water came by the way of
Edom, and the country[776] was filled with
water.
21 Now all the Moabites heard that
the kings had come up to fight against

24 [1]Lit., *them* [a]Neh. 13:25-27
25 [a]1Kin. 18:19, 20; 2Kin. 4:25
1 [a]2Kin. 1:17
2 [a]Ex. 23:24; 2Kin. 10:18, 26-28 [b]1Kin. 16:31, 32
3 [a]1Kin. 12:28-32 [b]1Kin. 14:9, 16
4 [a]2Sam. 8:2; Is. 16:1, 2
5 [a]2Kin. 1:1
6 [1]Lit., *in that day*
7 [a]1Kin. 22:4
8 [1]Lit., *said*
9 [a]2Kin. 3:1 [b]2Kin. 3:7 [c]1Kin. 22:47
11 [a]1Kin. 22:7 [b]2Kin. 2:25 [c]1Kin. 19:21; John 13:4, 5, 13, 14
13 [a]1Kin. 18:19; 22:6-11, 22-25
14 [a]1Kin. 17:1; 2Kin. 5:16
15 [a]1Sam. 16:23; 1Chr. 25:1 [b]1Kin. 18:46; Ezek. 1:3
17 [a]Ps. 107:35
18 [a]Jer. 32:17, 27; Mark 10:27; Luke 1:37
19 [a]2Kin. 3:25
20 [a]Ex. 29:39, 40

them. And all who were able to [I]put on armor and older were summoned, and stood on the border.

22 And they rose early in the morning, and the sun shone on the water, and the Moabites saw the water opposite *them* as red as blood.[1818]

23 Then they said, "This is blood; the kings have surely fought together, and they have slain one another.[7453] Now therefore, Moab, to the spoil!"

24 But when they came to the camp[4262] of Israel, the Israelites arose and struck the Moabites, so that they fled before them; and they went forward [I]into the land, [II]slaughtering[5221] the Moabites.

25 [a]Thus they destroyed the cities; and each one threw a stone on every piece of good land and filled it. So they stopped all the springs of water and felled all the good trees, until in [b]Kir-hareseth *only* they left[7604] its stones; however, the slingers went about *it* and struck it.

26 When the king of Moab saw that the battle was too fierce for him, he took with him 700 men who drew swords, to break through to the king of Edom; but they could not.

27 Then he took his oldest son who was to reign in his place, and [a]offered him as a burnt offering on the wall. And there came great wrath[7112] against Israel, and they departed from him and returned to their own land.

The Widow's Oil

4 Now a certain woman[802] of the wives[802] of [a]the sons of the prophets[5030] cried out to [I]Elisha, "Your servant my husband is dead,[4191] and you know[3045] that your servant feared[3373] the LORD; and [b]the creditor has come to take my two children to be his slaves."[5650]

2 And Elisha said to her, "What shall I do[6213] for you? Tell me, what do you have in the house?" And she said, "Your maidservant has nothing in the house except [a]a jar of oil."

3 Then he said, "Go, borrow vessels at large for yourself from all your neighbors,[7934] *even* empty vessels; do not get a few.

4 "And you shall go in and shut the door behind you and your sons, and pour out into all these vessels; and you shall set aside what is full."

5 So she went from him and shut the door behind her and her sons; they were bringing[5066] *the vessels* to her and she poured.

6 And it came about when [a]the vessels were full, that she said to her son, "Bring[5066] me another vessel." And he said to her, "There is not one vessel more." And the oil stopped.

7 Then she came and told [a]the man of God.[430] And he said, "Go, sell the oil and pay your debt,[2421] and you *and* your sons[1121] can live on the rest."

The Shunammite Woman

8 Now there came a day[3117] when Elisha passed[5674] over to [a]Shunem, where there was a [I]prominent woman, and she persuaded[2388] him to eat [II]food. And so it was, as often as he passed by, he turned in there to eat [II]food.

9 And she said to her husband, "Behold now, I perceive that this is a holy [a]man of God passing[5674] by us continually.

10 "Please,[4994] let us [a]make a little walled upper chamber and let us set a bed for him there, and a table and a chair and a lampstand; and it shall be, when he comes to us, *that* he can turn in there."

11 [I]One day he came there and turned in to the upper chamber and [II]rested.

12 Then he said to [a]Gehazi his servant, "Call[7121] this Shunammite." And when he had called[7121] her, she stood before him.

13 And he said to him, "Say now to her, 'Behold, you have been [I]careful[2729] for us with all this [II]care;[2731] what can I do[6213] for you? Would you

---

21 [I]Lit., *gird themselves with a belt*
24 [I]Lit., *into it* [II]Lit., *smiting*
25 [a]2Kin. 3:19 [b]Is. 16:7; Jer. 48:31, 36
27 [a]Amos 2:1; Mic. 6:7
1 [I]Lit., *Elisha, saying* [a]2Kin. 2:3 [b]Lev. 25:39-41, 48; 1Sam. 22:2; Neh. 5:2-5
2 [a]1Kin. 17:12
6 [a]Matt. 14:20
7 [a]1Kin. 12:22
8 [I]Lit., *great* [II]Lit., *bread* [a]Josh. 19:18
9 [a]2Kin. 4:7
10 [a]Matt. 10:41, 42; 25:40; Rom. 12:13
11 [I]Lit., *Now a day came that* [II]Lit., *lay there*
12 [a]2Kin. 4:29-31; 5:20-27; 8:4, 5
13 [I]Lit., *fearful* [II]Lit., *fear*

be spoken for to the king[4428] or to the
captain[8269] of the army?' " And she
[III]answered,[559] "I live among my own
people."[5971]
🗝 14 So he said, "What then is to be
done for her?" And Gehazi [I]answered,
"Truly she has no son[1121] and her husband is old."
15 And he said, "Call her." When
he had called her, she stood in the doorway.
16 Then he said, "[a]At this season
[I]next year you shall embrace a son."
And she said, "No, my lord,[113] O man
of God, [b]do not lie[3576] to your maidservant."
17 And the woman conceived and
bore a son at that season [I]the next year,
as Elisha had said to her.

The Shunammite's Son

18 When the child was grown, the
day came that he went out to his father[1]
to the reapers.
19 And he said to his father, "My
head, my head." And he said to his servant, "Carry[5375] him to his mother."
20 When he had taken him and
brought him to his mother, he sat on
her [I]lap until noon, and *then* died.[4191]
21 And she went up and [a]laid him
on the bed of [b]the man of God, and
shut *the door* behind him, and went out.
22 Then she called to her husband
and said, "Please send me one of the
servants and one of the donkeys, that
I may run to the man of God and return."
23 And he said, "Why will you go
to him today? It is neither [a]new moon
nor sabbath." And she said, "*It will be*
well."[7965]
24 Then she saddled a donkey and
said to her servant, "Drive and go forward; do not slow down[6113] [I]the pace
for me unless I tell[559] you."
25 So she went and came to the
man of God to [a]Mount Carmel. And it
came about when the man of God saw
her at a distance, that he said to Gehazi
his servant, "Behold, [I]yonder is the Shunammite.
26 "Please run now to meet her and
say to her, 'Is it well with you? Is it
well with your husband? Is it well with
the child?' " And she [I]answered, "It is
well."
27 When she came to the man of
God [a]to the hill, she caught[2388] hold of
his feet. And Gehazi came near[5066] to
push her away; but the man of God said,
"Let her alone,[7503] for her soul is
[I]troubled[4843] within her; and the LORD
has hidden it from me and has not told
me."
28 Then she said, "Did I ask[7592] for
a son from my lord? Did I not say, '[a]Do
not deceive[7952] me'?"
29 Then he said to Gehazi, "[a]Gird
up your loins and [b]take my staff in your
hand, and go your way; if you meet any
man, do not [c]salute him, and if anyone
salutes you, do not answer him; and
[d]lay[7760] my staff on the lad's face."
30 And the mother of the lad said,
"[a]As the LORD lives[2416] and as you yourself live, I will not leave[5800] you." And
he arose and followed her.
31 Then Gehazi passed on before
them and laid[7760] the staff on the lad's
face, but there was neither sound nor
[I]response. So he returned to meet him
and told [II]him, "The lad [a]has not awakened."
32 When Elisha came into the
house, behold the lad was dead and laid
on his bed.
33 So he entered and [a]shut the door
behind them both,[8147] and prayed[6419] to
the LORD.
34 And [a]he went up and lay on the
child, and put his mouth on his mouth
and his eyes on his eyes and his hands
on his hands, and he stretched himself
on him; and the flesh[1320] of the child
became warm.
35 Then he returned and walked in
the house once back and forth, and went

13 [III]Lit., *said*
14 [I]Lit., *said*
16 [I]Lit., *when the time revives* [a]Gen. 18:14 [b]2Kin. 4:28
17 [I]Lit., *when the time revived*
20 [I]Lit., *knees*
21 [a]2Kin. 4:32 [b]2Kin. 4:7
23 [a]Num. 10:10; 28:11; 1Chr. 23:31
24 [I]Lit., *riding*
25 [I]Lit., *this Shunammite* [a]2Kin. 2:25
26 [I]Lit., *said*
27 [I]Lit., *bitter* [a]2Kin. 4:25
28 [a]2Kin. 4:16
29 [a]1Kin. 18:46; 2Kin. 9:1 [b]Ex. 4:17; 2Kin. 2:14 [c]Luke 10:4 [d]Ex. 7:19, 20; 14:16
30 [a]2Kin. 2:2, 4
31 [I]Lit., *attentiveness* [II]Lit., *him, saying* [a]John 11:11
33 [a]2Kin. 4:4; Matt. 6:6; Luke 8:51
34 [a]1Kin. 17:21-23

🗝 **4:14** She was not present when Elisha and Gehazi conversed further.

up and [a]stretched himself on him; and the lad sneezed seven times and the lad opened his eyes.

36 And he called Gehazi and said, "Call this Shunammite." So he called her. And when she came in to him, he said, "Take up your son."

37 Then she went in and fell[5307] at his feet and bowed[7812] herself to the ground,[776] and [a]she took up her son and went out.

The Poisonous Stew

38 When Elisha returned to [a]Gilgal, *there was* [b]a famine in the land. [I]As [c]the sons of the prophets [d]were sitting before him, he said to his servant, "[e]Put on the large pot and boil stew[5138] for the sons of the prophets."

39 Then one went out into the field[7704] to gather[3950] herbs, and found a wild vine and gathered[3950] from it his lap full of wild gourds, and came and sliced them into the pot of stew, for they did not know[3045] *what they were.*

40 So they poured *it* out for the men to eat. And it came about as they were eating of the stew, that they cried out and said, "O man of God, there is [a]death[4194] in the pot." And they were unable to eat.

41 But he said, "Now bring meal." [a]And he threw it into the pot, and he said, "Pour *it* out for the people that they may eat." Then there was no harm in the pot.

42 Now a man came from Baal-shalishah, and brought the man of God bread of the first fruits, twenty loaves of barley and fresh ears of grain in his sack. And he said, "[a]Give *them* to the people that they may eat."

43 And his attendant[8334] said, "What, [a]shall I set this before a hundred men?" But he said, "Give *them* to the people that they may eat, for thus says the LORD, 'They shall eat and have *some* left[3498] over.'"

44 So he set *it* before them, and they ate and [a]had *some* left[3498] over, according to the word[1697] of the LORD.

Naaman Is Healed

5 Now [a]Naaman, captain[8269] of the army of the king[4428] of Aram, was a great man [I]with his master, and highly respected, because by him the LORD had given victory[8668] to Aram. The man was also a valiant[2428] warrior, *but he was* a leper.

2 Now the Arameans had gone out [a]in bands, and had taken captive a little girl from the land of Israel; and she [I]waited on Naaman's wife.[802]

3 And she said to her mistress, "I wish that my master[113] were [I]with the prophet[5030] who is in Samaria! Then he would cure him of his leprosy."

4 And [I]Naaman went in and told his master, saying, "Thus and thus spoke the girl who is from the land of Israel."

5 Then the king of Aram said, "Go [I]now, and I will send a letter[5612] to the king of Israel." And he departed and [a]took with him ten talents of silver and six thousand *shekels* of gold and ten [b]changes of clothes.

6 And he brought the letter to the king of Israel, saying, "And now as this letter comes to you, behold, I have sent Naaman my servant to you, that you may cure him of his leprosy."

7 And it came about when the king of Israel read the letter, that [a]he tore his clothes and said, "[b]Am I God, to kill[4191] and to make alive, that this man is sending *word* to me to cure a man of his leprosy? But [c]consider[3045] now, and see how he is seeking [I]a quarrel against me."

8 And it happened when Elisha [a]the man of God heard that the king of Israel had torn his clothes, that he sent *word* to the king, saying, "Why have you torn your clothes? Now let him come to me, and he shall know[3045] that there is a prophet in Israel."

9 So Naaman came with his horses

35 [a]1Kin. 17:21
37 [a]Heb. 11:35
38 [I]Lit., *And* [a]2Kin. 2:1 [b]2Kin. 8:1 [c]2Kin. 2:3 [d]Luke 10:39; Acts 22:3 [e]Ezek. 11:3, 7, 11; 24:3
40 [a]Ex. 10:17
41 [a]Ex. 15:25; 2Kin. 2:21
42 [a]Matt. 14:16-21; 15:32-38
43 [a]Luke 9:13; John 6:9
44 [a]Matt. 14:20; 15:37; John 6:13

1 [I]Lit., *before* [a]Luke 4:27
2 [I]Lit., *was before* [a]2Kin. 6:23; 13:20
3 [I]Lit., *before*
4 [I]Lit., *he*
5 [I]Lit., *enter* [a]1Sam. 9:7; 2Kin. 4:42 [b]Judg. 14:12; 2Kin. 5:22, 23
7 [I]Lit., *an occasion* [a]Gen. 37:29 [b]Gen. 30:2; 1Sam. 2:6 [c]1Kin. 20:7; Luke 11:54
8 [a]1Kin. 12:22

4:38-44 See note on II Kgs. 2:3,5.

and his chariots, and stood at the doorway of the house of Elisha.
10 And Elisha sent a messenger to
him, saying, "[a]Go and wash[7364] in the
Jordan seven times, and your flesh[1320]
shall be restored to you and *you shall*
be clean."[2891]
11 But Naaman was furious[7107] and
went away and said, "Behold, I [I]thought,
'He will surely come out to me, and
stand and call[7121] on the name of the
LORD his God, and wave his hand over
the place, and cure the leper.'
12 "Are not [I]Abanah and Pharpar,
the rivers of Damascus, better[2896] than
all the waters of Israel? Could I not wash
in them and be clean?" So he turned
and [a]went away in a rage.
13 [a]Then his servants came near[5066]
and spoke to him and said, "[b]My father,[1]
had the prophet told you *to do some* great
thing, would you not have done[6213] *it?*
How much more *then,* when he says
to you, 'Wash, and be clean'?"
14 So he went down and dipped[2881]
himself seven times in the Jordan, according to the word of the man of God;
and [a]his flesh was restored like the flesh
of a little child, and [b]he was clean.

Gehazi's Greed

15 When he returned to the man
of God [I]with all his company,[4264] and
came and stood before him, he said,
"Behold now, [a]I know that there is no
God in all the earth,[776] but in Israel;
so please [b]take a [II]present[1293] from your
servant now."
16 But he said, "[a]As the LORD
lives,[2416] before whom I stand, [b]I will
take nothing." And he urged him to take
it, but he refused.
17 And Naaman said, "If not, please
let your servant at least be given two
mules' load[4853] of [a]earth;[127] for your servant will no more offer burnt offering
nor will he sacrifice to other gods,[430]
but to the LORD.
18 "In this matter may the LORD
pardon[5545] your servant: when my master goes into the house of Rimmon to
worship[7812] there, and [a]he leans[8172] on
my hand and I bow myself in the house
of Rimmon, when I bow myself in the
house of Rimmon, the LORD pardon your
servant in this matter."
19 And he said to him, "[a]Go in
peace."[7965] So he departed from him
some distance.
20 But [a]Gehazi, the servant of Elisha the man of God, [I]thought, "Behold,
my master has spared this Naaman the
Aramean, [II]by not receiving from his
hands what he brought. [b]As the LORD
lives, I will run after him and take something from him."
21 So Gehazi pursued Naaman.
When Naaman saw one running after
him, he came[5307] down from the chariot
to meet him and said, "Is all well?"[7965]
22 And he said, "[a]All is well. My
master has sent me, saying, 'Behold,
just now two young men of the sons
of the prophets[5030] have come to me
from [b]the hill country of Ephraim. Please
give them a talent of silver and [c]two
changes of clothes.'"
23 And Naaman said, "[a]Be
pleased[2974] to take two talents." And
he urged him, and bound two talents
of silver in two bags with two changes
of clothes, and gave them to two of his
servants; and they carried[5375] *them* before him.
24 When he came to the [I]hill, he
took them from their hand and [a]de-
posited them in the house, and he sent
the men away, and they departed.
25 But he went in and stood before
his master. And Elisha said to him,
"Where have you been, Gehazi?" And
he said, "[a]Your servant went nowhere."
26 Then he said to him, "Did not
my heart go *with you,* when the man
turned from his chariot to meet you?
[a]Is it a time to receive money and to
receive clothes and olive groves and
vineyards and sheep and oxen and male
and female servants?
27 "Therefore, the leprosy of Naaman shall cleave to you and to your
[I]descendants forever." So he went out

10 [a]John 9:7
11 [I]Lit., *said*
12 [I]Another reading is *Amanah* [a]Prov. 14:17; 16:32; 19:11
13 [a]1Sam. 28:23 [b]2Kin. 2:12; 6:21; 8:9
14 [a]2Kin. 5:10; Job 33:25 [b]Luke 4:27; 5:13
15 [I]Lit., *he and* [II]Lit., *blessing* [a]Josh. 2:11; 1Sam. 17:46, 47; 2Kin. 5:8 [b]1Sam. 25:27
16 [a]2Kin. 3:14 [b]Gen. 14:22, 23; 2Kin. 5:20, 26
17 [a]Ex. 20:24
18 [a]2Kin. 7:2, 17
19 [a]Ex. 4:18; 1Sam. 1:17; Mark 5:34
20 [I]Lit., *said* [II]Lit., *from* [a]2Kin. 4:12, 31, 36 [b]Ex. 20:7; 2Kin. 6:31
22 [a]2Kin. 4:26 [b]Josh. 24:33 [c]2Kin. 5:5
23 [a]2Kin. 6:3
24 [I]Lit., *Ophel* [a]Josh. 7:1, 11, 12, 21; 1Kin. 21:16
25 [a]2Kin. 5:22
26 [a]2Kin. 5:16
27 [I]Lit., *seed*

from his presence [a]a leper *as white* as snow.

The Axe Head Recovered

6 Now [a]the sons of the prophets said to Elisha, "Behold now, the place before you where we are living is too limited6862 for us.
2 "Please let us go to the Jordan, and each of us take from there a beam, and let us make a place there for ourselves where we may live." So he said,559 "Go."
3 Then one said, "Please be willing2974 to go with your servants." And he [I]answered, "I shall go."
4 So he went with them; and when they came to the Jordan, they cut down trees.
5 But as one was felling a beam, [I]the axe head fell into the water; and he cried out and said, "Alas, my master! For it was borrowed."
6 Then the man of God430 said, "Where did it fall?" And when he showed him the place, [a]he cut off a stick, and threw *it* in there, and made the iron float.
7 And he said, "Take it up for yourself." So he put out his hand and took it.

The Arameans Plot to Capture Elisha

8 Now the king4428 of Aram was warring against Israel; and he [I]counseled3289 with his servants saying, "In such and such a place shall be my camp."
9 And [a]the man of God sent *word* to the king of Israel saying, "Beware8104 that you do not pass this place, for the Arameans are coming down there."
10 And the king of Israel sent to the place about which the man of God had told him; thus he warned2094 him, so that he guarded himself there, [I]more than once or twice.
11 Now the heart of the king of Aram was enraged over this thing; and he called7121 his servants and said to them, "Will you tell me which of us is for the king of Israel?"
12 And one of his servants said, "No, my lord,113 O king; but Elisha, the prophet who is in Israel, tells the king of Israel the words1697 that you speak in your bedroom."
13 So he said, "Go and see where he is, that I may send and take him." And it was told him, saying, "Behold, he is in [a]Dothan."
14 And he sent horses and chariots and a great army there, and they came by night3915 and surrounded5362 the city.
15 Now when the attendant of the man of God had risen early and gone out, behold, an army with horses and chariots was circling the city. And his servant said to him, "Alas, my master! [I]What shall we do?"6213
16 So he [I]answered, "[a]Do not fear,3372 for [b]those who are with us are more than those who are with them."
17 Then Elisha prayed6419 and said, "[a]O LORD, I pray, open his eyes that he may see." And the LORD opened the servant's eyes, and he saw; and behold, the mountain was full of [b]horses and chariots of fire all around Elisha.
18 And when they came down to him, Elisha prayed to the LORD and said, "Strike this [I]people1471 with blindness, I pray." So He [a]struck them with blindness according to the word1697 of Elisha.
19 Then Elisha said to them, "This is not the way,1870 nor is this the city; follow me and I will bring you to the man whom you seek." And he brought them to Samaria.
20 And it came about when they had come into Samaria, that Elisha said, "O [a]LORD, open the eyes of these *men,* that they may see." So the LORD opened

27 [a]Ex. 4:6; Num. 12:10
1 [a]2Kin. 2:3
3 [I]Lit., *said*
5 [I]Lit., *as for the iron, it fell*
6 [a]Ex. 15:25; 2Kin. 2:21; 4:41
8 [I]Lit., *took counsel*
9 [a]2Kin. 4:1, 7; 6:12
10 [I]Lit., *not once or twice*
13 [a]Gen. 37:17
15 [I]Lit., *How*
16 [I]Lit., *said* [a]Ex. 14:13 [b]2Chr. 32:7, 8; Rom. 8:31
17 [a]2Kin. 6:20 [b]2Kin. 2:11; Ps. 68:17; Zech. 6:1-7
18 [I]Lit., *nation* [a]Gen. 19:11
20 [a]2Kin. 6:17

6:1-4 See note on II Kgs. 2:3,5.
6:17 Elisha did not pray for the heavenly hosts to come; they were already there. The servant was not aware of them. Jesus referred to them in Mt. 18:10.

their eyes, and they saw; and behold, they were in the midst of Samaria.

21 Then the king of Israel when he saw them, said to Elisha, "[a]My father,[1] shall I [I]kill them? Shall I [I]kill them?"

22 And he [I]answered, "You shall not [II]kill *them.* Would you [II][a]kill those you have taken captive with your sword and with your bow? [b]Set bread and water before them, that they may eat and drink and go to their master."

23 So he prepared a great feast for them; and when they had eaten and drunk he sent them away, and they went to their master. And [a]the marauding bands[1416] of Arameans did not come again into the land of Israel.

The Siege of Samaria—Cannibalism

24 Now it came about after this, that [a]Ben-hadad king of Aram gathered[6908] all his army and went up and besieged Samaria.

25 And there was a great [a]famine in Samaria; and behold, they besieged it, until a donkey's head was sold for eighty *shekels* of silver, and a fourth of a [I]kab[6894] of dove's dung for five *shekels* of silver.

26 And as the king of Israel was passing[5674] by on the wall a woman[802] cried out to him, saying, "Help, my lord, O king!"

27 And he said, "[I]If the LORD does not help you, from where shall I help you? From the threshing floor, or from the wine press?"

28 And the king said to her, "[a]What [I]is the matter with you?" And she [II]answered, "This woman said to me, 'Give your son that we may eat him today,[3117] and we will eat my son tomorrow.'

29 "[a]So we boiled my son and ate him; and I said to her on the next day, 'Give your son, that we may eat him'; but she has hidden her son."

30 And it came about when the king heard the words of the woman, that [a]he tore his clothes—now he was passing[5674] by on the wall—and the people[5971] looked,[7200] and behold, he had sackcloth [I]beneath[1004] on his [II]body.[1320]

31 Then he said, "May [a]God do so to me and more also, if the head of Elisha the son of Shaphat [I]remains on him today."

32 Now Elisha was sitting in his house, and [a]the elders[2205] were sitting with him. And *the king* sent a man from his presence; but before[2962] the messenger came to him, he said to the elders, "Do you [b]see how this son of a murderer has sent to take away my head? Look, when the messenger comes, shut the door and [I]hold the door shut against him. Is not the sound of his master's feet behind him?"

33 And while he was still talking with them, behold, the messenger came down to him, and he said, "[a]Behold, this evil[7451] is from the LORD; why should I wait[3176] for the LORD any longer?"

Elisha Promises Food

7 Then Elisha said, "Listen to the word[1697] of the LORD; thus says the LORD, '[a]Tomorrow about this time a [I]measure of fine flour shall be *sold* for a shekel, and two measures of barley for a shekel, in the gate of Samaria.'"

2 And [a]the royal officer[7991] on whose hand the king[4428] was leaning[8172] answered the man of God[430] and said, "Behold, [b]if the LORD should make windows in heaven, could this thing be?" Then he said, "Behold you shall see it with your own eyes, but you shall not eat [I]of it."

Four Lepers Relate Arameans' Flight

3 Now there were four [a]leprous men at the entrance of the gate; and they said to one another,[7453] "Why do we sit here until we die?[4191]

4 "If we say, 'We will enter the city,' then the famine is in the city and we shall die there; and if we sit here, we die also. Now therefore come, and let

---

21 [I]Lit., *smite* [a]2Kin. 2:12; 5:13; 8:9

22 [I]Lit., *said* [II]Lit., *smite* [a]Deut. 20:11-16; 2Chr. 28:8-15 [b]Rom. 12:20

23 [a]2Kin. 5:2; 24:2

24 [a]1Kin. 20:1

25 [I]I.e., one kab equals approx. 2 qts. [a]Lev. 26:26

27 [I]Lit., *No, let the LORD help you*

28 [I]Lit., *to you* [II]Lit., *said* [a]Judg. 18:23

29 [a]Lev. 26:27-29; Deut. 28:52, 53, 57; Lam. 4:10

30 [I]Lit., *within* [II]Lit., *flesh* [a]1Kin. 21:27

31 [I]Lit., *stands* [a]Ruth 1:17; 1Kin. 19:2

32 [I]Lit., *press him with the door* [a]Ezek. 8:1; 14:1; 20:1 [b]1Kin. 18:4, 13, 14; 21:10, 13

33 [a]Is. 8:21

1 [I]Heb., *seah* [a]2Kin. 7:18

2 [I]Lit., *from there* [a]2Kin. 5:18; 7:17, 19 [b]Gen. 7:11; Mal. 3:10

3 [a]Lev. 13:45, 46; Num. 5:2-4; 12:10-14

us [I]go over to [a]the camp of the Arameans. If they spare us, we shall live;[2421]
and if they kill[4191] us, we shall but die."
5 And they arose at twilight to go
to the camp[7121] of the Arameans; when
they came to the outskirts of the camp
of the Arameans, behold, there was no
one there.
6 For [a]the Lord[136] had caused the
army of the Arameans to hear a sound
of chariots and a sound of horses, *even*
the sound of a great army, so that they
said to one another, "Behold, the king
of Israel has hired against us [b]the kings
of the Hittites and [c]the kings[4428] of the
Egyptians, to come upon us."
7 Therefore they [a]arose and fled in
the twilight, and left[5800] their tents and
their horses and their donkeys, even
the camp just as it was, and fled for
their life.[5315]
8 When these lepers came to the
outskirts of the camp, they entered one
tent and ate and drank, and [a]carried[5375]
from there silver and gold and clothes,
and went and hid *them*; and they returned and entered another tent and carried from there *also,* and went and hid
them.
9 Then they said to one another,
"We are not doing[6213] right. This day[3117]
is a day of good[2896] news, but we are
keeping silent; if we wait until morning
light,[216] punishment will [I]overtake us.
Now therefore come, let us go and tell
the king's[4428] household."
10 So they came and called[7121] to
the gatekeepers[7778] of the city, and they
told them, saying, "We came to the
camp of the Arameans, and behold,
there was no one there, nor the voice
of man, only the horses tied and the
donkeys tied, and the tents just as they
were."
11 And the gatekeepers[7778] called,
and told *it* within the king's household.
12 Then the king arose in the
night[3915] and said to his servants, "I will
now tell you what the Arameans have
done[6213] to us. They know[3045] that
[a]we are hungry; therefore they have
gone from the camp [b]to hide themselves
in the field,[7704] saying, 'When they come
out of the city, we shall capture them
alive[2416] and get into the city.'"
13 And one of his servants answered and said, "Please, let some *men*
take five of the horses which remain,
which are left[7604] [I]in the city. Behold,
they *will be in any case* like all the multitude of Israel who are left in it; behold,
they *will be in any case* like all the multitude of Israel who have already perished,[8552] so let us send and see."
14 They took therefore two chariots
with horses, and the king sent after the
army of the Arameans, saying, "Go and
see."

The Promise Fulfilled

15 And they went after them to the
Jordan, and behold, all the way[1870] was
full of clothes and equipment, which the
Arameans had thrown away in their
haste. Then the messengers returned
and told the king.
16 So the people[5971] went out and
plundered the camp of the Arameans.
Then a [I]measure of fine flour *was sold*
for a shekel and two [I]measures of barley
for a shekel, [a]according to the word of
the LORD.
17 Now the king appointed [a]the
royal officer on whose hand he leaned
[I]to have charge of the gate; but the people trampled on him at the gate, and
he died[4191] just as the man of God had
said, [b]who spoke when the king came
down to him.
18 And it came about just as the
man of God had spoken to the king,
saying, "[a]Two [I]measures of barley for
a shekel and a [I]measure of fine flour
for a shekel, shall be *sold* tomorrow
about this time at the gate of Samaria."
19 Then the royal officer answered
the man of God and said, "Now behold,
[a]if the LORD should make windows in
heaven, could such a thing be?" And
he said, "Behold, you shall see it with
your own eyes, but you shall not eat
[I]of it."
20 And so it happened[1961] to him,

4 [I]Lit., *fall* [a]2Kin. 6:24
6 [a]2Sam. 5:24 [b]1Kin. 10:29 [c]2Chr. 12:2, 3; Is. 31:1; 36:9
7 [a]Ps. 48:4-6; Prov. 28:1
8 [a]Josh. 7:21
9 [I]Lit., *find*
12 [a]2Kin. 6:25-29 [b]Josh. 8:4-12
13 [I]Lit., *in it*
16 [I]Heb., *seah;* i.e., one seah equals approx. 11 qts. [a]2Kin. 7:1
17 [I]Lit., *over the gate* [a]2Kin. 7:2 [b]2Kin. 6:32
18 [I]Heb., *seah;* i.e., one seah equals approx. 11 qts. [a]2Kin. 7:1
19 [I]Lit., *from there* [a]2Kin. 7:2

for the people trampled on him at the gate, and he died.

Jehoram Restores the Shunammite's Land

8 Now [a]Elisha spoke to the woman[802] whose son he had restored to life, saying, "Arise and go [I]with your household, and sojourn wherever you can sojourn; for the [b]LORD has called[7121] for a famine, and [c]it shall even come on the land for seven years."

2 So the woman arose and did[6213] according to the word of the man of God,[430] and she went with her household and sojourned in the land of the Philistines seven years.

3 And it came about at the end of seven years, that the woman returned from the land of the Philistines; and she went out to [I]appeal to the king[4428] for her house and for her field.

4 Now the king was talking with [a]Gehazi, the servant of the man of God, saying, "Please relate to me all the great things that Elisha has done."[6213]

5 And it came about, as he was relating to the king [a]how he had restored to life the one who was dead,[4191] that behold, the woman whose son he had restored to life, [I]appealed to the king for her house and for her field. And Gehazi said, "My lord,[113] O king, this is the woman and this is her son, whom Elisha restored to life."

6 When the king asked[7592] the woman, she related *it* to him. So the king appointed for her a certain officer, saying, "Restore all that was hers and all the produce of the field[7704] from the day[3117] that she left[5800] the land even until now."

Elisha Predicts Evil from Hazael

7 Then Elisha came to [a]Damascus. Now [b]Ben-hadad king of Aram was sick, and it was told him, saying, "[c]The man of God has come here."

8 And the king said to [a]Hazael, "[b]Take a gift in your hand and go to meet the man of God, and [c]inquire of the LORD by him, saying, 'Will I recover from this sickness?'"[2483]

9 So Hazael went to meet him and took a gift in his hand, even every kind of good[2898] thing of Damascus, forty camels' loads;[4853] and he came and stood before him and said, "[a]Your son Ben-hadad king of Aram has sent me to you, saying, 'Will I recover from this sickness?'"

🔑 10 Then Elisha said to him, "[a]Go, say to him, 'You shall surely recover,' but the [b]LORD has shown me that he will certainly die."[4191]

11 And he [I]fixed his gaze steadily *on him* [a]until he was ashamed,[954] and [b]the man of God wept.

12 And Hazael said, "Why does my lord weep?" Then he [I]answered,[559] "Because [a]I know[3045] the evil[7451] that you will do[6213] to the sons[1121] of Israel: their strongholds you will set on fire, and their young men you will kill with the sword, and their little ones you [b]will dash in pieces, and their women with child you will rip up."

13 Then Hazael said, "But what is your servant, [a]*who is but* a dog, that he should do this great thing?" And Elisha [I]answered, "[b]The LORD has shown me that you will be king over Aram."

14 So he departed from Elisha and returned to his master, who said to him, "What did Elisha say to you?" And he [I]answered, "He told me that [a]you would surely recover."

15 And it came about on the morrow, that he took the cover and dipped[2881] it in water and spread it on his face, [a]so that he died.[4191] And Hazael became king in his place.

1 [I]Lit., *you and your* [a]2Kin. 4:18, 31-35; [b]Ps. 105:16; Hag. 1:11 [c]Gen. 41:27, 54

3 [I]Lit., *cry out*

4 [a]2Kin. 4:12; 5:20-27

5 [I]Lit., *cried out* [a]2Kin. 4:35

7 [a]1Kin. 11:24 [b]2Kin. 6:24 [c]2Kin. 5:20

8 [a]1Kin. 19:15, 17 [b]1Kin. 14:3 [c]2Kin. 1:2

9 [a]2Kin. 5:13

10 [a]2Kin. 8:14 [b]2Kin. 8:15

11 [I]Lit., *made his face stand fast and he set* [a]2Kin. 2:17 [b]Luke 19:41

12 [I]Lit., *said* [a]2Kin. 10:32, 33; 12:17; 13:3, 7 [b]2Kin. 15:16; Nah. 3:10

13 [I]Lit., *said* [a]1Sam. 17:43; 2Sam. 9:8 [b]1Kin. 19:15

14 [I]Lit., *said* [a]2Kin. 8:10

15 [a]2Kin. 8:10

🔑 **8:10** This is not to be taken literally. It was spoken in sarcasm. Compare Micaiah's sarcasm in I Kgs. 22:15.

Another Jehoram Reigns in Judah

🔑 **16** Now in the fifth year of [a]Joram the son of Ahab king of Israel, Jehoshaphat being then the king of Judah, Jehoram the son of Jehoshaphat king of Judah became king.

17 He was [a]thirty-two years old when he became king, and he reigned eight years in Jerusalem.

18 And he walked in the way[1870] of the kings[4428] of Israel, just as the house of Ahab had done, for [a]the daughter of Ahab became his wife;[802] and he did evil in the sight of the LORD.

19 However, the LORD was not willing[14] to destroy[7843] Judah, for the sake of David His servant, [a]since He had [I]promised him to give a [II]lamp[5216] to him through his sons always.

20 In his days[3117] [a]Edom revolted from under the hand of Judah, and made a king over themselves.

21 Then Joram crossed over to Zair, and all his chariots with him. And it came about that he arose by night[3915] and struck the Edomites who had surrounded him and the captains[8269] of the chariots; [a]but *his* [I]army[5971] fled to their tents.

22 [a]So Edom revolted [I]against Judah to this day. Then [b]Libnah revolted at the same time.

23 And the rest of the acts[1697] of Joram and all that he did, are they not written in the Book[5612] of the Chronicles of the Kings of Judah?

Ahaziah Succeeds Jehoram in Judah

24 So Joram slept with his fathers,[1] and [a]was buried[6912] with his fathers in the city of David; and [b]Ahaziah his son became king in his place.

🔑 **25** [a]In the twelfth year of Joram the son of Ahab king of Israel, Ahaziah the son of Jehoram king of Judah began to reign.

26 [a]Ahaziah *was* twenty-two years old when he became king, and he reigned one year in Jerusalem. And his mother's name *was* Athaliah the granddaughter of Omri king of Israel.

27 And [a]he walked in the way of the house of Ahab, and did[6213] evil in the sight of the LORD, like the house of Ahab *had done,* because he was a son-in-law of the house of Ahab.

28 Then he went with Joram the son of Ahab to war against [a]Hazael king of Aram at [b]Ramoth-gilead, and the Arameans [I]wounded[5221] Joram.

29 So [a]King[4428] Joram returned to be healed in Jezreel of the wounds[4347] which the Arameans had [I]inflicted[5221] on him at [b]Ramah, when he fought against Hazael king of Aram. Then [c]Ahaziah the son of Jehoram king of Judah went down to see Joram the son of Ahab in Jezreel because he was sick.

Jehu Reigns over Israel

9 Now Elisha the prophet called[7121] one of [a]the sons[1121] of the prophets, and said to him, "[b]Gird up your loins, and [c]take this flask of oil in your hand, and go to [d]Ramoth-gilead.

2 "When you arrive there, [I]search out [a]Jehu the son of Jehoshaphat the son of Nimshi, and go in and [II][b]bid him arise from among his brothers,[251] and bring him to an inner room.

3 "Then take the flask of oil and pour it on his head and say, 'Thus says the LORD, "[a]I have anointed[4885] you king[4428] over Israel."' Then open the door and flee and do not wait."

4 So [a]the young man, the servant of the prophet, went to Ramoth-gilead.

5 When he came, behold, the captains[8269] of the army were sitting, and he said, "I have a word for you, O captain."[8269] And Jehu said, "[I]For which *one* of us?" And he said, "For you, O captain."

6 And he arose and went into the

16 [a]2Kin. 1:17; 3:1
17 [a]2Chr. 21:5-10
18 [a]2Kin. 8:27
19 [I]Lit., *said* [II]I.e., descendant on the throne [a]2Sam. 7:12-15; 1Kin. 11:36
20 [a]1Kin. 22:47; 2Kin. 3:9, 26, 27; 8:22
21 [I]Lit., *the people* [a]2Sam. 18:17; 19:8
22 [I]Lit., *from under the hand of* [a]Gen. 27:40 [b]Josh. 21:13; 2Kin. 19:8
24 [a]2Chr. 21:20 [b]2Chr. 21:1, 7
25 [a]2Chr. 22:1-6
26 [a]2Chr. 22:2
27 [a]2Chr. 22:3
28 [I]Lit., *smote* [a]2Kin. 8:15 [b]1Kin. 22:3, 29
29 [I]Lit., *struck* [a]2Kin. 9:15 [b]2Kin. 8:28; 2Chr. 22:5, 6 [c]2Kin. 9:16
1 [a]2Kin. 2:3 [b]2Kin. 4:29 [c]1Sam. 10:1; 16:1; 1Kin. 1:39 [d]2Kin. 8:28, 29
2 [I]Lit., *and look there for* [II]Lit., *cause him to* [a]1Kin. 19:16, 17; 2Kin. 9:14, 20 [b]2Kin. 9:5, 11
3 [a]2Chr. 22:7
4 [a]2Kin. 9:1
5 [I]Lit., *To whom of us all?*

🔑 **8:16-24** See II Chr. 21:1-20.
🔑 **8:25-29** See II Chr. 22:1-6.

house, and he poured the oil on his head
and said to him, "Thus says the LORD,
the <u>God</u>[430] of Israel, '[a]I have anointed
you king over the <u>people</u>[5971] of the LORD,
even over Israel.
7 'And you shall strike the house
of Ahab your master, [a]that I may
<u>avenge</u>[5358] [b]the blood of My servants
the prophets, and the <u>blood</u>[1818] of all
the servants of the LORD, [c]at the hand
of Jezebel.
8 'For the whole house of Ahab shall
<u>perish</u>,[6] and [a]I will <u>cut off</u>[3772] from Ahab
[b]every male person [c]both bond and free
in Israel.
9 'And [a]I will make the house of
Ahab like the house of Jeroboam the
son of Nebat, and [b]like the house of
Baasha the son of Ahijah.
10 'And [a]the dogs shall eat Jezebel
in the territory of Jezreel, and none shall
<u>bury</u>[6912] *her.*' " Then he opened the door
and fled.
11 Now Jehu came out to the servants of his <u>master</u>,[113] and one said to
him, "[a]Is all <u>well</u>?[7965] Why did this
[b]mad fellow come to you?" And he said
to them, "You <u>know</u>[3045] *very well* the
man and his <u>talk</u>."[7879]
12 And they said, "It is a <u>lie</u>,[8267]
tell us now." And he said, "Thus and
thus he said to me, 'Thus says the LORD,
"I have anointed you king over Israel." ' "
13 Then [a]they hurried and each man
took his garment and placed it under
him on the bare steps, and [b]<u>blew</u>[8628]
the trumpet, saying, "Jehu is <u>king</u>!"[4427]

Jehoram (Joram) Is Assassinated

14 So Jehu the son of Jehoshaphat
the son of Nimshi conspired against
Joram. [a]Now Joram [I]with all Israel was
[II]<u>defending</u>[8104] Ramoth-gilead against
Hazael king of Aram,
15 but [a]King [I]Joram had returned
to Jezreel to be healed of the <u>wounds</u>[4347]
which the Arameans had [II]<u>inflicted</u>[5221]
on him when he fought with Hazael king
of Aram. So Jehu said, "If this is your
mind, *then* let no one escape *or* [III]leave
the city to go tell *it* in Jezreel."
16 Then Jehu rode in a chariot and
went to Jezreel, for Joram was lying
there. [a]And Ahaziah king of Judah had
come down to see Joram.
17 Now the watchman was standing
on the tower in Jezreel and he saw the
[I]company of Jehu as he came, and said,
"I see a [I]company." And Joram said,
"Take a horseman and send him to meet
them and let him say, 'Is it <u>peace</u>?' "[7965]
18 So a horseman went to meet him
and said, "Thus says the king, 'Is it
peace?' " And Jehu said, "[a]What have
you to do with peace? Turn behind me."
And the watchman [I]reported, "The messenger came to them, but he did not
return."
19 Then he sent out a second horseman, who came to them and said, "Thus
says the king, 'Is it peace?' " And Jehu
[I]<u>answered</u>,[559] "What have you to do with
peace? Turn behind me."
20 And the watchman [I]reported,
"He came even to them, and he did
not return; and [a]the driving is like the
driving of [b]Jehu the son of Nimshi, for
he drives furiously."
21 Then [I]Joram said, "[II]Get ready."
And they made his chariot ready.
[a]And [I]Joram king of Israel and Ahaziah
king of Judah went out, <u>each</u>[376] in his
chariot, and they went out to meet Jehu
and found him in the [III][b]property of Naboth the Jezreelite.
22 And it came about, when [I]Joram
saw Jehu, that he said, "Is it peace,
Jehu?" And he [II]answered, "What peace,
[a]so long as the <u>harlotries</u>[2183] of your
mother Jezebel and her <u>witchcrafts</u>[3785]
are so many?"
23 So [I]Joram [II]reined about and fled
and said to Ahaziah, "[a]*There is* treachery, O Ahaziah!"
24 And [a]Jehu [I]drew his bow with
his full strength and [II]shot [III]Joram between his arms; and the arrow went
[IV]through his heart, and he sank in his
chariot.
25 Then *Jehu* said to Bidkar his officer, "Take *him* up and [a]cast him into

6 [a]1Sam. 2:7, 8; 1Kin. 19:16; 2Kin. 9:3; 2Chr. 22:7
7 [a]Deut. 32:35, 43 [b]1Kin. 18:4; 21:15, 21, 25 [c]2Kin. 9:32-37
8 [a]1Kin. 21:21; 2Kin. 10:17 [b]1Sam. 25:22 [c]Deut. 32:36; 2Kin. 14:26
9 [a]1Kin. 14:10, 11; 15:29 [b]1Kin. 16:3-5, 11, 12
10 [a]1Kin. 21:23; 2Kin. 9:35, 36
11 [a]2Kin. 9:17, 19, 22 [b]Jer. 29:26; Hos. 9:7; Mark 3:21
13 [a]Matt. 21:7, 8; Mark 11:7, 8 [b]2Sam. 15:10; 1Kin. 1:34, 39
14 [I]Lit., *he and* [II]Lit., *keeping* [a]1Kin. 22:3; 2Kin. 8:28
15 [I]Heb., *Jehoram* [II]Lit., *struck* [III]Lit., *go out from* [a]2Kin. 8:29
16 [a]2Kin. 8:29
17 [I]Lit., *multitude*
18 [I]Lit., *told, saying* [a]2Kin. 9:19, 22
19 [I]Lit., *said*
20 [I]Lit., *told, saying* [a]2Sam. 18:27 [b]1Kin. 19:17
21 [I]Heb., *Jehoram* [II]Lit., *Yoke the chariot* [III]Lit., *portion* [a]2Chr. 22:7 [b]1Kin. 21:1-7, 15-19; 2Kin. 9:26
22 [I]Heb., *Jehoram* [II]Lit., *said* [a]1Kin. 16:30-33; 18:19; 2Chr. 21:13
23 [I]Heb., *Jehoram* [II]Lit., *turned his hands* [a]2Kin. 11:14
24 [I]Lit., *filled his hand with the bow* [II]Lit., *smote* [III]Heb., *Jehoram* [IV]Lit., *out at* [a]1Kin. 22:34
25 [a]1Kin. 21:1

the [I]property of the field[7704] of Naboth the Jezreelite, for I remember when [II]you and I were riding together after Ahab his father,[1] that the [b]LORD laid this [c]oracle[4853] against him:

26 'Surely [a]I have seen yesterday the blood of Naboth and the blood of his sons,' says the LORD, 'and [b]I will repay you in this [I]property,' says the LORD. Now then, take and cast him into the [I]property, according to the word[1697] of the LORD."

Jehu Assassinates Ahaziah

27 [a]When Ahaziah the king of Judah saw *this,* he fled by the way[1870] of the garden house. And Jehu pursued him and said, "[I]Shoot him too, in the chariot." *So they shot him* at the ascent of Gur, which is at [b]Ibleam. But he fled to Megiddo and died[4191] there.

28 [a]Then his servants carried him in a chariot to Jerusalem, and buried[6912] him in his grave[6900] with his fathers[1] in the city of David.

29 Now in [a]the eleventh year of Joram, the son of Ahab, Ahaziah became king over Judah.

30 When Jehu came to Jezreel, Jezebel heard *of it,* and [a]she painted her eyes and adorned her head, and looked out the window.

31 And as Jehu entered the gate, she said, "[a]Is it [I]well, Zimri, [II]your master's murderer?"

32 Then he lifted up his face to the window and said, "Who is on my side? Who?" And two or three officials[5631] looked down at him.

Jezebel Is Slain

33 And he said, "Throw her down." So they threw her down, and some of her blood was sprinkled on the wall and on the horses, and he trampled her under foot.

34 When he came in, he ate and drank; and he said, "See now to [a]this cursed[779] woman and bury her, for [b]she is a king's[4428] daughter."

35 And they went to bury her, but they found no more of her than the skull and the feet and the palms[3709] of her hands.

36 Therefore they returned and told him. And he said, "This is the word of the LORD, which He spoke by His servant Elijah the Tishbite, saying, '[a]In the [I]property of Jezreel the dogs shall eat the flesh[1320] of Jezebel;

37 and [a]the corpse[5038] of Jezebel shall be as dung on the face of the field in the [I]property of Jezreel, so they cannot say, "This is Jezebel." ' "

Judgment upon Ahab's House

10 Now Ahab had seventy sons in [a]Samaria. And Jehu wrote letters[5612] and sent *them* to Samaria, to the rulers of Jezreel, the elders,[2205] and to the guardians of *the children* of Ahab, saying,

2 "And now, [a]when this letter[5612] comes to you, since your master's sons are with you, [I]as well as the chariots and horses and a fortified city and the weapons,[5402]

3 select the best[2896] and [I]fittest[3477] of your master's sons, and set *him* on his father's[1] throne, and fight for your master's house."

4 But they feared[3372] greatly and said, "Behold, [a]the two kings[4428] did not stand before him; how then can we stand?"

5 And the one who *was* over the household, and he who *was* over the city, the elders, and the guardians of *the children,* sent *word* to Jehu, saying, "[a]We are your servants, all that you say[559] to us we will do,[6213] we will not make any man king;[4427] do what is good[2896] in your sight."

🔑6 Then he wrote a letter to them a second time saying, "If you are on

25 [I]Lit., *portion* [II]Lit., *I and you* [b]1Kin. 21:19, 24-29 [c]Is. 13:1
26 [I]Lit., *portion* [a]1Kin. 21:13, 19 [b]2Kin. 9:21, 25
27 [I]Lit., *smite* [a]2Chr. 22:7, 9 [b]Josh. 17:11; Judg. 1:27
28 [a]2Kin. 23:30
29 [a]2Kin. 8:25
30 [a]Jer. 4:30; Ezek. 23:40
31 [I]Lit., *peace* [II]Lit., *his* [a]1Kin. 16:9-20; 2Kin. 9:18-22
34 [a]1Kin. 21:25 [b]1Kin. 16:31
36 [I]Lit., *portion* [a]1Kin. 21:23
37 [I]Lit., *portion* [a]Jer. 8:1-3
1 [a]1Kin. 16:24-29
2 [I]Lit., *and with you the* [a]2Kin. 5:6
3 [I]Lit., *most upright*
4 [a]2Kin. 9:24, 27
5 [a]Josh. 9:8, 11; 1Kin. 20:4, 32; 2Kin. 18:14

🔑 **10:6** All Israel must know that the dynasty of Omri was ended.

my side, and you will listen to my voice,
take the heads of the men, your master's
sons, and come to me at Jezreel tomorrow about this time." Now the king's[4428]
sons, seventy persons,[376] *were* with the
great men of the city, *who* were rearing
them.
7 And it came about when the letter
came to them, that they took the king's
sons, and [a]slaughtered *them,* seventy
persons, and put their heads in baskets,
and sent *them* to him at Jezreel.
8 When the messenger came and
told him, saying, "They have brought
the heads of the king's sons," he said,
"Put[7760] them in two heaps at the entrance of the gate until morning."
9 Now it came about in the morning,
that he went out and stood, and said
to all the people,[5971] "You are [I]innocent;
behold, [a]I conspired against my master
and killed him, but [b]who [II]killed all these?
10 "Know[3045] then that [a]there shall
fall to the earth[776] nothing of the word[1697]
of the LORD, which the LORD spoke concerning the house of Ahab, for the LORD
has done[6213] [b]what He spoke [I]through
His servant Elijah."
11 So Jehu [I]killed all who remained
of the house of Ahab in [a]Jezreel, and
all his great men and his acquaintances[3045] and his priests, until he left[7604]
him without a survivor.
12 Then he arose and departed, and
went to Samaria. On the way[1870] while
he was at [I]Beth-eked of the shepherds,
13 [a]Jehu [I]met the [II]relatives[251] of
Ahaziah king[4428] of Judah and said, "Who
are you?" And they [III]answered,[559] "We
are the [II]relatives of Ahaziah; and we
have come down [IV]to greet the sons of
the king and the sons of the queen
mother."
14 And he said, "Take them
alive."[2416] So they took them alive, and
killed them at the pit of Beth-eked, forty-
two men; and he left none of them.
15 Now when he had departed from
there, he [I]met [a]Jehonadab the son of
[b]Rechab *coming* to meet him; and he
[II]greeted him and said to him, "Is your
heart right, as my heart is with your
heart?" And Jehonadab [III]answered, "It
is." *Jehu said,* "If it is, [c]give *me* your
hand." And he gave him his hand, and
he took him up to him into the chariot.
16 And he said, "Come with me and
[a]see my zeal[7068] for the LORD." So
[I]he made him ride in his chariot.
17 And when he came to Samaria,
[a]he [I]killed all who remained to Ahab in
Samaria, until he had destroyed[8045] him,
[b]according to the word of the LORD,
which He spoke to Elijah.

Jehu Destroys Baal Worshipers

18 Then Jehu gathered[6908] all the
people and said to them, "[a]Ahab served
Baal a little; Jehu will serve him much.
19 "And now, [a]summon[7121] all the
prophets of Baal, all his worshipers and
all his priests; let no one be missing,[6485]
for I have a great sacrifice for Baal;
whoever is missing shall not live."[2421]
But Jehu did[6213] it in [I]cunning, in order
that he might destroy[6] the worshipers[5647] of Baal.
20 And Jehu said, "[a]Sanctify a solemn assembly[6116] for Baal." And
[b]they proclaimed *it.*
21 Then Jehu sent [I]throughout Israel and all the worshipers of Baal came,
so that there was not a man left who
did not come. And when they went
into [a]the house of Baal, the house of
Baal was filled from one end to the
other.
22 And he said to the one who *was*
[I]in charge of the wardrobe,[4458] "Bring
out garments[3830] for all the worshipers
of Baal." So he brought out garments[4403]
for them.
23 And Jehu went into the house
of Baal with Jehonadab the son of Rechab; and he said to the worshipers of
Baal, "Search and see that there may
be here with you none of the servants
of the LORD, but only the worshipers
of Baal."
24 Then they went in to offer sacrifices and burnt offerings. Now Jehu had
stationed[7760] for himself eighty men outside, and he had said, "[a]The one who

7 [a]Judg. 9:5; 2Kin. 11:1

9 [I]Lit., *just* [II]Lit., *smote* [a]2Kin. 9:14-24 [b]2Kin. 10:6

10 [I]Lit., *by the hand of* [a]2Kin. 9:7-10 [b]1Kin. 21:19-29

11 [I]Lit., *smote* [a]Hos. 1:4

12 [I]I.e., house of binding

13 [I]Lit., *found* [II]Lit., *brothers* [III]Lit., *said* [IV]Lit., *about the welfare of* [a]2Kin. 8:24, 29; 2Chr. 21:17; 22:8

15 [I]Lit., *found* [II]Lit., *blessed* [III]Lit., *said* [a]Jer. 35:6-19 [b]1Chr. 2:55 [c]Ezra 10:19; Ezek. 17:18

16 [I]Lit., *they* [a]1Kin. 19:10

17 [I]Lit., *smote* [a]2Kin. 9:8 [b]2Kin. 10:10

18 [a]1Kin. 16:31, 32

19 [I]Lit., *insidiousness* [a]1Kin. 18:19; 22:6

20 [a]Joel 1:14 [b]Ex. 32:4-6

21 [I]Lit., *in all* [a]1Kin. 16:32; 2Kin. 11:18

22 [I]Lit., *over the*

24 [a]1Kin. 20:30-42

permits any of the men whom I bring
into your hands to escape,[4422] [I]shall give
up his life[5315] in exchange."
25 Then it came about, as soon as
he had finished[3615] offering the burnt offering, that Jehu said to the [Ia]guard and
to the royal officers,[7991] "[b]Go in,
[II]kill them; let none come out." And
they [III]killed them with the edge[6310] of
the sword; and the [I]guard and the royal
officers threw *them* out, and went
to the [IV]inner room of the house of
Baal.
26 And they brought out the *sacred*
[a]pillars[4676] of the house of Baal, and
burned[8313] them.
27 They also broke down the *sacred*
pillar of Baal and broke down the house
of Baal, and [a]made it a latrine[4280] to this
day.[3117]
28 Thus Jehu eradicated Baal out
of Israel.
29 However, [a]*as for* the sins of
Jeroboam the son of Nebat, which he
made Israel sin, from these Jehu did
not depart,[5493] *even* the [b]golden
calves that *were* at Bethel and that
were at Dan.
30 And the LORD said to Jehu, "Because you have done[6213] well[2895] in
executing[6213] what is right in My eyes,
and have done to the house of Ahab
according to all that *was* in My heart,
[a]your sons of the fourth generation shall
sit on the throne of Israel."
31 But Jehu [Ia]was not careful to walk
in the law[8451] of the LORD, the God[430]
of Israel, with all his heart; [b]he did not
depart from the sins of Jeroboam, which
he made Israel sin.
32 In those days[3117] the [a]LORD began to cut off *portions* [I]from Israel; and
[b]Hazael [II]defeated them throughout the
territory of Israel:
33 from the Jordan eastward, all the
land of Gilead, the Gadites and the Reubenites and the Manassites, from
[a]Aroer, which is by the valley of the
Arnon, even [b]Gilead and Bashan.

Jehoahaz Succeeds Jehu

34 Now the rest of the acts[1697] of
Jehu and all that he did and all his might,
are they not written in the Book[5612] of
the Chronicles of the Kings of Israel?
35 And Jehu slept with his fathers,[1]
and they buried[6912] him in Samaria. And
Jehoahaz his son became king in his
place.
36 Now the [I]time which Jehu
reigned over Israel in Samaria *was*
twenty-eight years.

Athaliah Queen of Judah

11 [a]When Athaliah the mother
of Ahaziah saw that her son was
dead,[4191] she rose and destroyed[6] all
the royal [I]offspring.
2 But Jehosheba, the daughter of
King[4428] Joram, sister of Ahaziah,
[a]took Joash the son of Ahaziah and stole
him from among the king's[4428] sons who
were being put to death, and placed him
and his nurse in the bedroom. So they
hid him from Athaliah, and he was not
put to death.
3 So he was hidden with her in the
house of the LORD six years, while Athaliah was reigning over the land.
4 [a]Now in the seventh year Jehoiada
sent and brought the captains of hundreds of [b]the Carites and of the [I]guard,
and brought them to him in the house
of the LORD. Then he made a
covenant[1285] with them and put them
under oath in the house of the LORD,
and showed them the king's son.
5 And he commanded[6680] them, saying, "This is the thing that you shall
do:[6213] [a]one third of you, who come in
on the sabbath and keep[8140] watch[4931]
over the king's house
6 (one third also *shall be* at the gate
Sur, and one third at the gate behind
the [I]guards), [II]shall keep[8104] watch over
the house for defense.
7 "And two parts[3027] of you, *even*

24 [I]Lit., *his soul for his soul*
25 [I]Lit., *runners* [II]Lit., *smite* [III]Lit., *smote* [IV]Lit., *city* [a]1Sam. 22:17 [b]1Kin. 18:40
26 [a]1Kin. 14:23; 2Kin. 3:2
27 [a]Ezra 6:11; Dan. 2:5; 3:29
29 [a]1Kin. 12:28-30; 13:33, 34 [b]1Kin. 12:29
30 [a]2Kin. 15:12
31 [I]Lit., *did not watch* [a]Prov. 4:23 [b]2Kin. 10:29
32 [I]Lit., *in* [II]Lit., *smote* [a]2Kin. 13:25; 14:25 [b]1Kin. 19:17; 2Kin. 8:12; 13:22
33 [a]Deut. 2:36 [b]Amos 1:3-5
36 [I]Lit., *days*
1 [I]Lit., *seed* [a]2Chr. 22:10-12
2 [a]2Kin. 11:21; 12:1
4 [I]Lit., *runners* [a]2Chr. 23:1-21 [b]2Sam. 20:23; 2Kin. 11:19
5 [a]1Chr. 9:25
6 [I]Lit., *runners* [II]Lit., *and shall*

11:1-16 See II Chr. 22:10—23:15.

all who go out on the sabbath, shall also keep watch over the house of the LORD for the king.

8 "Then you shall surround[5362] the king, each with his weapons in his hand; and whoever comes within the ranks shall be put to death. And [a]be with the king when he goes out and when he comes in."

9 So the captains of hundreds [a]did[6213] according to all that Jehoiada the priest commanded. And each one of them took his men who were to come in on the sabbath, with those who were to go out on the sabbath, and came to Jehoiada the priest.

10 And [a]the priest gave to the captains of hundreds the spears and shields that had been King David's, which *were* in the house of the LORD.

11 And the [I]guards stood each with his weapons in his hand, from the right [II]side of the house to the left [II]side of the house, by the altar[4196] and by the house, around the king.

12 Then he brought the king's son out and [a]put the crown[5145] on him, and *gave him* [b]the testimony; and they made him king[4427] and anointed[4886] him, and they clapped[5221] their hands and said, "[c]*Long* live the king!"

13 [a]When Athaliah heard the noise of the guard *and of* the people,[5971] she came to the people in the house of the LORD.

14 And she looked[7200] and behold, the king was standing [a]by the pillar, according to the custom, with the captains and the [I]trumpeters beside the king; and [b]all the people of the land rejoiced and blew[8628] trumpets. Then Athaliah [c]tore her clothes and cried, "[d]Treason! Treason!"

15 And Jehoiada the priest commanded the captains of hundreds who were appointed over the army, and said to them, "Bring her out [I]between the ranks, and whoever follows her put to death[4191] with the sword." For the priest said, "Let her not be put to death in the house of the LORD."

16 So they [I]seized[7760,3027] her, and when she arrived at the horses' entrance[1870,3996] of the king's house, she was [a]put to death there.

🔑 **17** Then [a]Jehoiada made a covenant between the LORD and the king and the people, that they should be the LORD'S people, also [b]between the king and the people.

18 And all the people of the land went to [a]the house of Baal, and tore it down; [b]his altars[4196] and his images[6754] they broke[7665] in pieces thoroughly, and [c]killed Mattan the priest of Baal before the altars. And the priest appointed[7760] [I]officers over the house of the LORD.

19 And he took the captains of hundreds and the [a]Carites and the [I]guards and all the people of the land; and they brought the king down from the house of the LORD, and came by the way of [b]the gate of the [I]guards to the king's house. And he sat on the throne of the kings.[4428]

20 So [a]all the people of the land rejoiced and the city was quiet.[8252] For they had put Athaliah to death with the sword at the king's house.

21 [I][a]Jehoash was seven years old when he became king.

Joash (Jehoash) Reigns over Judah

12 🔑 In the seventh year of Jehu, [a]Jehoash became king, and he reigned forty years in Jerusalem; and his mother's name was Zibiah of Beersheba.

2 And Jehoash did[6213] right in the sight of the LORD all his days[3117] in which Jehoiada the priest instructed him.

3 Only [a]the high places were not taken away; the people[5971] still sacrificed and burned incense[6999] on the high places.

8 [a]Num. 27:16, 17
9 [a]2Chr. 23:8
10 [a]2Sam. 8:7; 1Chr. 18:7
11 [I]Lit., *runners* [II]Lit., *shoulder*
12 [a]2Sam. 1:10 [b]Ex. 25:16; 31:18 [c]1Sam. 10:24
13 [a]2Chr. 23:12
14 [I]Lit., *trumpets* [a]2Kin. 23:3; 2Chr. 34:31 [b]1Kin. 1:39, 40 [c]Gen. 37:29; 44:13 [d]2Kin. 9:23
15 [I]Lit., *from within*
16 [I]Lit., *placed hands to her* [a]Gen. 9:6; Lev. 24:17
17 [a]Josh. 24:25; 2Chr. 15:12-14; 34:31 [b]1Sam. 10:25; 2Sam. 5:3
18 [I]Lit., *offices* [a]2Kin. 10:26, 27 [b]Deut. 12:2, 3 [c]1Kin. 18:40
19 [I]Lit., *runners* [a]2Kin. 11:4 [b]2Kin. 11:6
20 [a]Prov. 11:10
21 [I]Ch. 12:1 in Heb. [a]2Chr. 24:1-14
1 [a]2Chr. 24:1
3 [a]2Kin. 14:4; 15:35

🔑 **11:17-21** See II Chr. 23:16-21.
🔑 **12:1-21** See II Chr. 24:1-16.

The Temple to Be Repaired

4 Then Jehoash said to the priests, "All the money of the sacred things [a]which is brought into the house of the LORD, in current[5674] money, *both* [b]the money of each man's assessment *and* all the money [I]which any man's heart prompts him to bring into the house of the LORD,

5 let the priests take it for themselves, each from his acquaintance;[4378] and they shall repair the [I]damages of the house wherever any damage may be found.

6 But it came about that in the twenty-third year of King[4428] Jehoash [a]the priests had not repaired the damages of the house.

🔑7 Then King Jehoash called[7121] for Jehoiada the priest, and for the *other* priests and said to them, "Why do you not repair the damages of the house? Now therefore take no *more* money from your acquaintances,[4378] but pay it for the damages of the house."

8 So the priests agreed that they should take no *more* money from the people, nor repair the damages of the house.

9 But [a]Jehoiada the priest took a chest[727] and bored[5344] a hole in its lid, and put it beside the altar,[4196] on the right side as one comes into the house of the LORD; and the priests who guarded[8104] the threshold put in it all the money which was brought into the house of the LORD.

10 And when they saw that there was much money in the chest, [a]the king's[4428] scribe and the high priest came up and tied *it* in bags and counted the money which was found in the house of the LORD.

11 And they gave the money which was weighed out into the hands of those who did the work,[4399] who had the oversight of the house of the LORD; and they [I]paid it out to the carpenters and the builders,[1129] who worked on the house of the LORD;

12 and [a]to the masons and the stonecutters,[2672] and for buying timber and hewn[4274] stone to repair the damages to the house of the LORD, and for all that was [I]laid out for the house to repair it.

13 But [a]there were not made for the house of the LORD [b]silver cups, snuffers, bowls,[4219] trumpets, any vessels of gold, or vessels of silver from the money which was brought into the house of the LORD;

14 for they gave that to those who did the work, and with it they repaired the house of the LORD.

15 Moreover, [a]they did not require an accounting from the men into whose hand they gave the money to pay to those who did the work, for they dealt[6213] faithfully.[530]

16 The [a]money from the guilt offerings and [b]the money from the sin offerings, was not brought into the house of the LORD; [c]it was for the priests.

17 Then [a]Hazael king of Aram went up and fought against Gath and captured it, and [b]Hazael set his face to go up to Jerusalem.

18 And [a]Jehoash king of Judah took all the sacred things that Jehoshaphat and Jehoram and Ahaziah, his fathers,[1] kings[4428] of Judah, had dedicated,[6942] and [b]his own sacred things and all the gold that was found among the treasuries of the house of the LORD and of the king's house, and sent *them* to Hazael king of Aram. Then he went away from Jerusalem.

Joash (Jehoash) Succeeded by Amaziah in Judah

19 Now the rest of the acts[1697] of Joash and all that he did, are they not

4 [I]Lit., *which it comes into. . .to bring* [a]2Kin. 22:4 [b]Ex. 30:13-16; 35:5, 22, 29; 1Chr. 29:3-9
5 [I]Lit., *breaches,* and so through v. 12
6 [a]2Chr. 24:5
9 [a]Mark 12:41; Luke 21:1
10 [a]2Sam. 8:17; 2Kin. 19:2; 22:3, 4, 12
11 [I]Lit., *brought*
12 [I]Lit., *went out* [a]2Kin. 22:5, 6
13 [a]2Chr. 24:14 [b]1Kin. 7:48, 50
15 [a]2Kin. 22:7; 1Cor. 4:2; 2Cor. 8:20
16 [a]Lev. 5:15-18 [b]Lev. 4:24, 29 [c]Lev. 7:7; Num. 18:19
17 [a]1Kin. 19:17; 2Kin. 8:12; 10:32, 33 [b]2Chr. 24:23,24
18 [a]1Kin. 14:26; 15:18; 2Kin. 16:8; 18:15, 16 [b]2Kin. 12:4

🔑 **12:7** We can infer that donations which were made for repairs had to be used for their own living expenses. The true priests were suffering because so many were worshiping idols.

written in the Book[5612] of the Chronicles of the Kings of Judah?

20 [a]And his servants arose and made a conspiracy, and [b]struck down Joash at [c]the house of Millo *as he was* going down to Silla.

21 For Jozacar the son of Shimeath, and Jehozabad the son of [a]Shomer, his servants, struck *him,* and he died;[4191] and they buried[6912] him with his fathers in the city of David, and [b]Amaziah his son became king in his place.

Kings of Israel: Jehoahaz and Jehoash

13 In the twenty-third year of Joash the son of Ahaziah, king[4428] of Judah, Jehoahaz the son of Jehu became king over Israel at Samaria, *and he reigned* seventeen years.

2 And he did evil[7451] in the sight of the LORD, and followed the sins of Jeroboam the son of Nebat, [a]with which he made Israel sin; he did not turn[5493] from them.

3 [a]So the anger[639] of the LORD was kindled[2734] against Israel, and He gave them continually into the hand of [b]Hazael king of Aram, and into the hand of [c]Ben-hadad the son of Hazael.

4 Then [a]Jehoahaz entreated the favor of the LORD, and the LORD listened to him; for [b]He saw the oppression of Israel, how the king of Aram oppressed them.

5 And the LORD gave Israel a [I][a]deliverer, so that they [II]escaped from under the hand of the Arameans; and the sons[1121] of Israel lived in their tents as formerly.

6 Nevertheless they did not turn away from the sins of the house of Jeroboam, [a]with which he made Israel sin, but walked in [I]them; and [b]the Asherah[842] also remained standing in Samaria.

7 For he left[7604] to Jehoahaz of the [I]army[5971] not more than fifty horsemen and ten chariots and 10,000 footmen, for the king of Aram had destroyed[6] them and [a]made them like the dust[6083] at threshing.

8 Now the rest of the acts[1697] of Jehoahaz, and all that he did and his might, are they not written in the Book[5612] of the Chronicles of the Kings[4428] of Israel?

9 And Jehoahaz slept with his fathers,[1] and they buried[6912] him in Samaria; and Joash his son became king in his place.

10 In the thirty-seventh year of Joash king of Judah, Jehoash the son of Jehoahaz, became king over Israel in Samaria, *and reigned* sixteen years.

11 And he did evil in the sight of the LORD; he did not turn away from all the sins of Jeroboam the son of Nebat, with which he made Israel sin, but he walked in [I]them.

12 [a]Now the rest of the acts of Joash and all that he did[6213] and his might with which he fought against Amaziah king of Judah, are they not written in the Book of the Chronicles of the Kings of Israel?

13 So Joash slept with his fathers, and Jeroboam sat on his throne; and Joash was buried in Samaria with the kings of Israel.

Death of Elisha

14 When Elisha [I]became sick with the illness of which he was to die,[4191] Joash the king of Israel came down to him and wept over [II]him and said, "[a]My father,[1] my father, the chariots of Israel and its horsemen!"

15 And Elisha said to him, "Take a bow and arrows." So he [I]took a bow and arrows.

16 Then he said to the king of Israel, "Put your hand on the bow." And he put his hand *on it,* then Elisha laid his hands on the king's[4428] hands.

17 And he said, "Open the window toward the east," and he opened *it.* Then Elisha said, "Shoot!" And he shot. And he said, "The LORD's arrow of victory,[8668] even the arrow of victory over Aram; for you shall [I]defeat the Arameans at [a]Aphek until you have [II]destroyed[3615] *them.*"

20 [a]2Chr. 24:25-27 [b]2Kin. 14:5 [c]Judg. 9:6; 2Sam. 5:9; 1Kin. 11:27
21 [a]2Chr. 24:26 [b]2Kin. 14:1
2 [a]1Kin. 12:26-33
3 [a]Judg. 2:14 [b]2Kin. 12:17 [c]2Kin. 13:24, 25
4 [a]Num. 21:7-9 [b]Ex. 3:7, 9; 2Kin. 14:26
5 [I]Or, *savior* [II]Lit., *went out* [a]2Kin. 13:25; 14:25, 27; Neh. 9:27
6 [I]Lit., *it* [a]2Kin. 13:2 [b]1Kin. 16:33
7 [I]Lit., *people* [a]Amos 1:3
11 [I]Lit., *it*
12 [a]2Kin. 13:14-19; 14:8-15
14 [I]Lit., *was sick with his sickness* [II]Lit., *his face* [a]2Kin. 2:12
15 [I]Lit., *took to himself*
17 [I]Lit., *smite* [II]Lit., *made an end of* [a]1Kin. 20:26

18 Then he said, "Take the arrows," and he took them. And he said to the king of Israel, "Strike the ground,"[776] and he struck *it* three times and [I]stopped.

19 So [a]the man of God[430] was angry[7107] with him and said, "You should have struck five or six times, then you would have struck Aram until you would have [I]destroyed *it*. But now you shall strike Aram [b]*only* three times."

20 And Elisha died, and they buried him. Now [a]the bands[1416] of the Moabites would invade the land in the spring of the year.

21 And as they were burying[6912] a man, behold, they saw a marauding band;[1416] and they cast the man into the grave[6913] of Elisha. And when the man [I]touched the bones[6106] of Elisha he [a]revived and stood up on his feet.

22 Now [a]Hazael king of Aram had oppressed Israel all the days of Jehoahaz.

23 But the [a]LORD was gracious[2603] to them and [b]had compassion on them and turned to them because of [c]His covenant[1285] with Abraham, Isaac, and Jacob, and would[14] not destroy[6] them or cast them from His presence until now.

24 When Hazael king of Aram died, Ben-hadad his son became king in his place.

25 Then [a]Jehoash the son of Jehoahaz took again from the hand of Ben-hadad the son of Hazael the cities which he had taken in war from the hand of Jehoahaz his father. [b]Three times Joash [I]defeated[5221] him and recovered the cities of Israel.

Amaziah Reigns over Judah

14 🔑 [a]In the second year of Joash son of Joahaz king[4428] of Israel, [b]Amaziah the son of Joash king of Judah became king.

2 He was twenty-five years old when he became king, and he reigned twenty-nine years in Jerusalem. And his mother's name was Jehoaddin of Jerusalem.

3 And he did[6213] right in the sight of the LORD, yet not like David his father;[1] he did according to all that Joash his father had done.

4 Only [a]the high places were not taken away; [b]the people[5971] still sacrificed and burned incense[6999] on the high places.

5 Now it came about, as soon as the kingdom[4467] was firmly[2388] in his hand, that he [Ia]killed his servants who had slain the king his father.

🔑 6 But the sons[1121] of the [I]slayers he did not put to death, according to what is written in the book[5612] of the law[8451] of Moses, as the LORD commanded,[6680] saying, "[a]The fathers[1] shall not be put to death[4191] for the sons, nor the sons be put to death for the fathers; but [b]each shall be put to death for his own sin."

7 He [I]killed *of* Edom in [a]the Valley of Salt 10,000 and took [b]Sela by war, and named[7121] it [c]Joktheel to this day.[3117]

8 [a]Then Amaziah sent messengers to Jehoash, the son of Jehoahaz son of Jehu, king of Israel, saying, "[b]Come, let us face each other."

9 And Jehoash king of Israel sent to Amaziah king of Judah, saying, "[a]The thorn bush which was in Lebanon sent to the cedar which was in Lebanon, saying, 'Give your daughter to my son in marriage.' But there passed[5674] by a wild beast[2416] that was in Lebanon, and trampled the thorn bush.

10 "[a]You have indeed [I]defeated Edom, and [b]your heart has [II]become proud. Enjoy your glory[3513] and stay at home; for why should you provoke trouble so that you, even you, should fall, and Judah with you?"

11 But Amaziah would not listen.

18 [I]Lit., *stood*
19 [I]Lit., *made an end of* [a]2Kin. 5:20 [b]2Kin. 13:25
20 [a]2Kin. 3:7; 24:2
21 [I]Lit., *went and touched* [a]Matt. 27:52
22 [a]2Kin. 8:12, 13
23 [a]2Kin. 14:27 [b]1Kin. 8:28 [c]Gen. 13:16, 17; 17:2-5
25 [I]Lit., *smote* [a]2Kin. 10:32, 33; 14:25 [b]2Kin. 13:18, 19
1 [a]2Chr. 25:1 [b]2Kin. 13:10
4 [a]2Kin. 12:3 [b]2Kin. 16:4
5 [I]Lit., *smote* [a]2Kin. 12:20
6 [I]Lit., *smiters* [a]Deut. 24:16 [b]Jer. 31:30; Ezek. 18:4, 20
7 [I]Lit., *smote* [a]2Sam. 8:13; 1Chr. 18:12; 2Chr. 25:11 [b]Is. 16:1 [c]Josh. 15:38
8 [a]2Chr. 25:17-24 [b]2Sam. 2:14-17
9 [a]Judg. 9:8-15
10 [I]Lit., *smitten* [II]Lit., *lifted you up* [a]2Kin. 14:7 [b]Deut. 8:14; 2Chr. 26:16

🔑 **14:1-16** See II Chr. 25:1-24.
🔑 **14:6** Compare Deut. 24:16; Jer. 31:30; Ezek. 18:4,20.

So Jehoash king of Israel went up; and
he and Amaziah king of Judah <u>faced</u>**[7200]**
each other at [a]Beth-shemesh, which belongs to Judah.
12 And Judah was defeated [I]by Israel, and [a]they fled each to his tent.
13 Then Jehoash king of Israel captured Amaziah king of Judah, the son
of Jehoash the son of Ahaziah, at Beth-
shemesh, and came to Jerusalem and
tore down the wall of Jerusalem from
[a]the Gate of Ephraim to [b]the Corner
Gate, 400 [I]cubits.
14 And [a]he took all the gold and silver and all the utensils which were found
in the house of the LORD, and in
the treasuries of the <u>king's</u>**[4428]** house,
the hostages also, and returned to Samaria.

Jeroboam II Succeeds Jehoash in Israel

15 [a]Now the rest of the <u>acts</u>**[1697]** of
Jehoash which he did, and his might and
how he fought with Amaziah king of Judah, are they not written in the Book
of the Chronicles of the <u>Kings</u>**[4428]** of Israel?
16 So Jehoash slept with his fathers
and was <u>buried</u>**[6912]** in Samaria with the
kings of Israel; and Jeroboam his son
became king in his place.

Azariah (Uzziah) Succeeds Amaziah in Judah

17 [a]And Amaziah the son of Joash
king of Judah <u>lived</u>**[2421]** fifteen years after
the <u>death</u>**[4194]** of Jehoash son of Jehoahaz
king of Israel.
18 Now the rest of the acts of Amaziah, are they not written in the Book
of the Chronicles of the Kings of Judah?
19 And they conspired against him
in Jerusalem, and he fled to [a]Lachish;
but they sent after him to Lachish and
killed him there.
20 Then they <u>brought</u>**[5375]** him on
horses and he was buried at Jerusalem
with his fathers in the city of David.
21 And all the people of Judah took
[I]Azariah, who *was* sixteen years old,
and made him <u>king</u>**[4427]** in the place of
his father Amaziah.
22 [a]He built Elath and restored it
to Judah, after the king slept with his
fathers.
23 In the fifteenth year of Amaziah
the son of Joash king of Judah, Jeroboam
the son of Joash king of Israel became
king in Samaria, *and reigned* forty-one
years.
24 And he did <u>evil</u>**[7451]** in the sight
of the LORD; he <u>did</u> not <u>depart</u>**[5493]** from
all the sins of Jeroboam the son of Nebat,
which he made Israel sin.
25 [a]He restored the border of Israel
from [b]the entrance of Hamath as far as
[c]the Sea of the <u>Arabah</u>,**[6160]** according
to the <u>word</u>**[1697]** of the LORD, the <u>God</u>**[430]**
of Israel, which He spoke [I]through His
servant [d]Jonah the son of Amittai, the
prophet, who was of [e]Gath-hepher.
26 For the [a]LORD saw the affliction
of Israel, *which was* very <u>bitter</u>;**[4784]** for
[b]there was neither bond nor <u>free</u>,**[5800]**
nor was there any helper for Israel.
27 And the [a]LORD did not say that
He would <u>blot</u>**[4229]** out the name of Israel
from under heaven, but He saved them
by the hand of Jeroboam the son of
Joash.

Zechariah Reigns over Israel

28 Now the rest of the acts of Jeroboam and all that he did and his might,
how he fought and how he recovered
for Israel, [a]Damascus and [b]Hamath,
which had belonged to Judah, are they
not written in the Book of the Chronicles
of the Kings of Israel?
29 And Jeroboam slept with his fathers, even with the kings of Israel, and
Zechariah his son became king in his
place.

11 [a]Josh. 19:38
12 [I]Lit., *before* [a]2Sam. 18:17
13 [I]I.e., One cubit equals approx. 18 in. [a]Neh. 8:16; 12:39 [b]2Chr. 25:23
14 [a]1Kin. 14:26; 2Kin. 12:18
15 [a]2Kin. 13:12, 13
17 [a]2Chr. 25:25-28
19 [a]Josh. 10:31; 2Kin. 18:14, 17
21 [I]In 2Chr. 26:1, *Uzziah*
22 [a]1Kin. 9:26; 2Kin. 16:6; 2Chr. 8:17
25 [I]Lit., *by* [a]2Kin. 10:32; 13:25 [b]1Kin. 8:65 [c]Deut. 3:17 [d]Jon. 1:1; Matt. 12:39, 40 [e]Josh. 19:13
26 [a]2Kin. 13:4 [b]Deut. 32:36
27 [a]2Kin. 13:23
28 [a]1Kin. 11:24 [b]2Chr. 8:3

14:17-22 See II Chr. 25:25-28.

Series of Kings: Azariah (Uzziah) over Judah

15 [a]In the twenty-seventh year
of Jeroboam king[4428] of Israel,
Azariah son of Amaziah king of Judah
became king.
2 He was [a]sixteen years old when
he became king, and he reigned fifty-
two years in Jerusalem; and his mother's
name was [1]Jecoliah of Jerusalem.
3 And he did[6213] right in the sight
of the LORD, according to all that his
father[1] Amaziah had done.[6213]
4 Only [a]the high places were not
taken away; the people[5971] still sacrificed
and burned incense[6999] on the high
places.
5 [a]And the LORD struck the king,
so that he was a leper to the day[3117]
of his death.[4194] And he [b]lived in a separate house, [1]while Jotham the king's[4428]
son was over the household, judging[8199]
the people of the land.
6 Now the rest of the acts[1697] of
Azariah and all that he did, are they
not written in the Book[5612] of the Chronicles of the Kings of Judah?
7 And Azariah slept with his fathers,[1] and they buried[6912] him with his
fathers in the city of David, and Jotham
his son became king in his place.

Zechariah over Israel

8 [a]In the thirty-eighth year of Azariah king of Judah, Zechariah the son
of Jeroboam became king over Israel
in Samaria *for* six months.
9 And he did evil[7451] in the sight of
the LORD, as his fathers had done; he
did not depart[5493] from the sins of Jeroboam the son of Nebat, which he made
Israel sin.
10 Then Shallum the son of Jabesh
conspired against him and [a]struck him
before the people and [1]killed him, and
reigned in his place.
11 Now the rest of the acts of Zechariah, behold they are written in the Book
of the Chronicles of the Kings of Israel.
12 This is [a]the word[1697] of the LORD
which He spoke to Jehu, saying, "Your
sons to the fourth generation shall sit
on the throne of Israel." And so it was.
13 Shallum son of Jabesh became
king in the [a]thirty-ninth year of Uzziah
king of Judah, and he reigned one[3117]
month in [b]Samaria.
14 Then Menahem son of Gadi went
up from [a]Tirzah and came to Samaria,
and struck Shallum son of Jabesh in Samaria, and killed him and became king
in his place.
15 Now the rest of the acts of Shallum and his conspiracy which he made,
behold they are written in the Book of
the Chronicles of the Kings of Israel.
16 Then Menahem struck Tiphsah
and all who were in it and its borders
from Tirzah, because they did not open
to him, therefore he struck *it;* and he
ripped up [a]all its women who were with
child.

Menahem over Israel

17 In the [a]thirty-ninth year of Azariah king of Judah, Menahem son of Gadi
became king over Israel *and reigned* ten
years in Samaria.
18 And he did evil in the sight of
the LORD; he did not depart all his
days[3117] from the sins of Jeroboam the
son of Nebat, which he made Israel sin.
19 [a]Pul, king of Assyria, came
against the land, and Menahem gave Pul
a thousand talents of silver so that
his hand might be with him to
[b]strengthen[2388] the kingdom[4467] [1]under
his rule.
20 Then Menahem exacted the
money from Israel, even from all the
mighty men of wealth,[2428] from each man
fifty shekels of silver to pay the king
of Assyria. So the king of Assyria

1 [a]2Kin. 14:17
2 [1]In 2Chr. 26:3, *Jechiliah* [a]2Chr. 26:3, 4
4 [a]2Kin. 12:3
5 [1]Lit., *and* [a]2Chr. 26:21-23 [b]Lev. 13:46; Num. 12:14
8 [a]2Kin. 15:1
10 [1]Lit., *smote* [a]Amos 7:9
12 [a]2Kin. 10:30
13 [a]2Kin. 15:1, 8 [b]1Kin. 16:24
14 [a]1Kin. 14:17
16 [a]2Kin. 8:12; Hos. 13:16
17 [a]2Kin. 15:1, 8, 13
19 [1]Lit., *in his hand* [a]1Chr. 5:25, 26 [b]2Kin. 14:5

15:1 Azariah is usually called Uzziah. Jeroboam II must have hindered his free rule over Judah for a dozen years, because Amaziah, his father, survived Joash of Israel by fifteen years (II Kgs. 14:17).
15:1-7 See II Chr. 26:1-23.

returned and did not remain there in
the land.
21 Now the rest of the <u>acts</u>[1697] of
Menahem and all that he did, are they
not written in the Book of the Chronicles
of the Kings of Israel?
22 And Menahem slept with his fathers, and Pekahiah his son became king
in his place.

Pekahiah over Israel

23 In [a]the fiftieth year of Azariah
king of Judah, Pekahiah son of Menahem
became king over Israel in Samaria, *and*
reigned two years.
24 And he did evil in the sight of
the LORD; he did not depart from the
sins of Jeroboam son of Nebat, which
he made Israel sin.
25 Then Pekah son of Remaliah, his
<u>officer</u>,[7791] conspired against him and
struck him in Samaria, in [a]the <u>castle</u>[759]
of the king's house with Argob and
Arieh; and with him were fifty men of
the Gileadites, and he <u>killed</u>[4191] him and
became king in his place.
26 Now the rest of the acts of Pekahiah and all that he did, behold they are
written in the Book of the Chronicles
of the Kings of Israel.

Pekah over Israel

27 In [a]the fifty-second year of Azariah king of Judah, [b]Pekah son of Remaliah became king over Israel in Samaria,
and reigned twenty years.
28 And he did evil in the sight of
the LORD; he did not depart from the
sins of Jeroboam son of Nebat, which
he made Israel sin.
🔑 **29** In the days of Pekah king of Israel, [I][a]Tiglath-pileser king of Assyria
came and [II]captured Ijon and Abel-beth-
maacah and Janoah and Kedesh and Hazor and Gilead and Galilee, all the land
of Naphtali; and [b]he carried them
<u>captive</u>[1540] to Assyria.
30 And Hoshea the son of Elah made
a conspiracy against Pekah the son of
Remaliah, and struck him and put him
to death and became king in his place,
in the twentieth year of Jotham the son
of Uzziah.
31 Now the rest of the acts of Pekah
and all that he did, behold, they are written in the Book of the Chronicles of
the Kings of Israel.

Jotham over Judah

🔑 **32** In the second year of Pekah the
son of Remaliah king of Israel, Jotham
the son of [I]Uzziah king of Judah became
king.
33 [a]He was twenty-five years old
when he became king, and he reigned
sixteen years in Jerusalem; and his
mother's name *was* Jerusha the daughter
of Zadok.
34 And [a]he did what was right in
the sight of the LORD; he did according
to all that his father Uzziah had done.
35 Only [a]the high places were not
taken away; the people still sacrificed
and <u>burned incense</u>[6999] on the high
places. [b]He built the upper gate of the
house of the LORD.
36 Now the rest of the acts of Jotham and all that he did, are they not
written in the Book of the Chronicles
of the Kings of Judah?
37 In those days [a]the LORD began
to send Rezin king of Aram and Pekah
the son of Remaliah against Judah.
38 And Jotham slept with his fathers, and he was buried with his fathers
in the city of David his father; and Ahaz
his son became king in his place.

Ahaz Reigns over Judah

16 🔑 In the seventeenth year of
Pekah the son of Remaliah,

23 [a]2Kin. 15:1, 8, 13, 17
25 [a]1Kin. 16:18
27 [a]2Kin. 15:23 [b]2Chr. 28:6; Is. 7:1
29 [I]In 1Chr. 5:6, 26, *Tilgath-pilneser* [II]Lit., *took* [a]2Kin. 15:19 [b]2Kin. 17:6
32 [I]I.e., Azariah
33 [a]2Chr. 27:1
34 [a]2Kin. 15:3, 4; 2Chr. 26:4, 5
35 [a]2Kin. 12:3 [b]2Chr. 23:20; 27:3
37 [a]2Kin. 16:5; Is. 7:1

🔑 **15:29,30** See notes on Hos. 8:8,9 and Isa. 7:14.
🔑 **15:32-38** See II Chr. 27:1-9.
🔑 **16:1-20** See II Chr. 28:1-27.

[a]Ahaz the son of Jotham, king[4428] of Judah, became king.
2 [a]Ahaz *was* twenty years old when
he became king, and he reigned sixteen
years in Jerusalem; and he did[6213] not
do what was right in the sight of the
LORD his God,[430] as his father[1] David
had done.
3 But he walked in the way[1870] of
the kings[4428] of Israel, [a]and even made
his son pass through the fire, [b]according
to the abominations[8441] of the nations
whom the LORD had [I]driven[2423] out from
before the sons[1121] of Israel.
4 And he [a]sacrificed and burned
incense[6999] on the high places and on
the hills and under every green tree.
5 Then [a]Rezin king of Aram and
Pekah son of Remaliah, king of Israel,
came up to Jerusalem to *wage* war; and
they besieged Ahaz, [b]but could not
[I]overcome him.
6 At that time Rezin king of Aram
recovered [a]Elath for Aram, and cleared
the Judeans out of [I]Elath entirely; and
the [II]Arameans came to Elath, and have
lived there to this day.[3117]

Ahaz Seeks Help of Aram

7 [a]So Ahaz sent messengers to
[b]Tiglath-pileser king of Assyria, saying,
"I am your servant and your son; come
up and deliver me from the [I]hand of
the king of Aram, and from the [I]hand
of the king of Israel, who are rising up
against me."
8 And [a]Ahaz took the silver and gold
that was found in the house of the LORD
and in the treasuries of the king's[4428]
house, and sent a present to the king
of Assyria.
9 [a]So the king of Assyria listened
to him; and the king of Assyria went
up against Damascus and [b]captured it,
and carried *the people of* it away into
exile[1540] to [c]Kir, and put Rezin to death.

Damascus Falls

10 Now King Ahaz went to Damas-
cus to meet [a]Tiglath-pileser king of Assyria, and saw the altar[4196] which *was*
at Damascus; and King Ahaz sent to
[b]Urijah the priest the [I]pattern[1823] of the
altar and its model,[8403] according to all
its workmanship.
11 So Urijah the priest built an altar;
according to all that King Ahaz had sent
from Damascus, thus Urijah the priest
made *it,* [I]before the coming of King Ahaz
from Damascus.
12 And when the king came from
Damascus, the king saw the altar; then
[a]the king approached[7126] the altar and
[I]went up to it,
13 and [I]burned his burnt offering and
his meal offering, and poured[5258] his libation and sprinkled the blood[1818] of his
peace offerings on the altar.
14 And [a]the bronze altar, which *was*
before the LORD, [I]he brought[7126] from
the front of the house, from between
[b]*his* altar and the house of the LORD,
and he put it on the north side of *his*
altar.
15 Then King Ahaz [I]commanded[6680]
Urijah the priest, saying, "Upon the
great altar [II]burn[6999] [a]the morning burnt
offering and the evening meal offering
and the king's burnt offering and his meal
offering, with the burnt offering of all
the people[5971] of the land and their meal
offering and their libations; and sprinkle
on it all the blood of the burnt offering
and all the blood of the sacrifice. But
[b]the bronze altar shall be for me to inquire *by.*"

1 [a]2Chr. 28:1
2 [a]2Chr. 28:1-4
3 [I]Or, *dispossessed* [a]Lev. 18:21; 2Kin. 17:17; 21:6 [b]Deut. 12:31; 2Kin. 21:2, 11
4 [a]Deut. 12:2; 2Kin. 14:4
5 [I]Lit., *fight* [a]2Kin. 15:37; Is. 7:1 [b]2Chr. 28:5, 6
6 [I]Heb., *Eloth* [II]So with some ancient versions; Heb., *Edomites* [a]2Kin. 14:22; 2Chr. 26:2
7 [I]Lit., *palm* [a]2Chr. 28:16 [b]2Kin. 15:29
8 [a]2Kin. 12:17, 18; 18:15
9 [a]2Chr. 28:21 [b]Amos 1:3-5 [c]Is. 22:6; Amos 9:7
10 [I]Lit., *likeness* [a]2Kin. 15:29 [b]Is. 8:2
11 [I]Lit., *until*
12 [I]Or, *offered on it* [a]2Chr. 26:16, 19
13 [I]Lit., *offered in smoke*
14 [I]Lit., *he also* [a]Ex. 27:1, 2; 40:6, 29; 2Chr. 4:1 [b]2Kin. 16:11
15 [I]Lit., *commanded him, Urijah* [II]Lit., *offer in smoke* [a]Ex. 29:39-41 [b]2Kin. 16:14

16:3 See note on Lev. 18:21.
16:5-9 See note on Isa. 7:14.
16:6 In our modern order of the O.T. Scriptures the word "Judeans" appears here for the first time. The name is derived from the patriarch Judah and was originally applied to all members of the tribe bearing his name. It also came to be used for all subjects of the kingdom of Judah in contrast to the kingdom made up of the ten tribes who seceded. These ten tribes retained the name "Israelites." After the captivity, the name seems to have been applied indiscriminately to the whole race.

16 So Urijah the priest did according to all that King Ahaz commanded.

17 Then King Ahaz [a]cut off the borders of the stands, and removed the laver[3595] from them; he also [b]took down the sea from the bronze oxen which were under it, and put it on a pavement of stone.

18 And the covered way[4329] for the sabbath which they had built in the house, and the outer entry of the king, he removed from the house of the LORD because of the king of Assyria.

Hezekiah Reigns over Judah

19 Now the rest of the acts[1697] of Ahaz which he did, are they not written [a]in the Book[5612] of the Chronicles of the Kings of Judah?

20 So [a]Ahaz slept with his fathers,[1] and [b]was buried[6912] with his fathers in the city of David; and his son Hezekiah reigned in his place.

Hoshea Reigns over Israel

17 In the twelfth year of Ahaz king[4428] of Judah, [a]Hoshea the son of Elah became king over Israel in Samaria, *and reigned* nine years.

2 And he did[6213] evil[7451] in the sight of the LORD, only not as the kings[4428] of Israel who were before him.

3 [a]Shalmaneser king of Assyria came up [b]against him, and Hoshea became his servant and paid him tribute.

4 But the king of Assyria found conspiracy in Hoshea, who had sent messengers to So king of Egypt and had offered[5927] no tribute to the king of Assyria, as *he had done* year by year; so the king of Assyria shut him up and bound him in prison.

5 Then the king of Assyria invaded the whole land and went up to [a]Samaria and besieged it three years.

Israel Captive

⊶ 6 In the ninth year of Hoshea, [a]the king of Assyria captured Samaria and [b]carried Israel away into exile to Assyria, and [c]settled them in Halah and Habor, *on* the river of [d]Gozan, and [e]in the cities of the Medes.

Why Israel Fell

7 Now [a]*this* came about, because the sons[1121] of Israel had sinned against the LORD their God,[430] [b]who had brought them up from the land of Egypt from under the hand of Pharaoh, king of Egypt, [c]and they had [I]feared[3372] other gods[430]

8 and [a]walked in the [I]customs of the nations whom the LORD had driven out before the sons of Israel, and *in the customs* [b]of the kings of Israel which they had [II]introduced.

9 And the sons of Israel [I]did things secretly which were not right, against the LORD their God. Moreover, they built for themselves high places in all their towns, from [a]watchtower[5341] to fortified city.

10 And [a]they set for themselves *sacred* pillars[4676] and [I][b]Asherim[842] on every high hill and under every green tree,

11 and there they burned incense[6999] on all the high places as the nations *did* which the LORD had carried away to exile before them; and they did evil[7451] things provoking the LORD.

12 And they served idols,[1544] [a]concerning which the LORD had said to them, "You shall not do[6213] this thing."

13 Yet the [a]LORD warned Israel and Judah, [b]through all His prophets *and*

---

17 [a]1Kin. 7:27, 28, 38 [b]1Kin. 7:23, 25
19 [a]2Chr. 28:26
20 [a]Is. 14:28 [b]2Chr. 28:27
1 [a]2Kin. 15:30
3 [a]Hos. 10:14 [b]2Kin. 18:9-12
5 [a]Hos. 13:16
6 [a]Hos. 13:16 [b]Deut. 28:64; 29:27, 28 [c]2Kin. 18:11; 1Chr. 5:26 [d]Is. 37:12 [e]Is. 13:17; 21:2
7 [I]Lit., *revered,* and so throughout the ch. [a]Josh. 23:16 [b]Ex. 14:15-30 [c]Judg. 6:10
8 [I]Lit., *statutes* [II]Lit., *made* [a]Lev. 18:3; Deut. 18:9 [b]2Kin. 16:3; 17:19
9 [I]Or, *uttered words which* [a]2Kin. 18:8
10 [I]I.e., wooden symbols of a female deity [a]Ex. 34:12-14 [b]1Kin. 14:23; Mic. 5:14
12 [a]Ex. 20:4
13 [a]Neh. 9:29, 30 [b]2Kin. 17:23

⊶ **17:6-18** The Northern Kingdom of Israel fell in 721 or 722 B.C. Shalmaneser began the attack but died before it was completed, so Israel fell to Sargon II who took them captive. There follows a list of all the ways that they were unfaithful to the Lord. Hosea prophesied that the northern tribes would not return to the land as long as God was dealing with them for breaking His covenant (Hos. 9:3). Yet they were promised restoration to the land after God had finished punishing them (Zech. 10:6,10). See Ezek. 48:1-7,25-28 for future allotments of land by God to the tribes of the Northern Kingdom.

[c]every seer, saying, "[d]Turn from your evil ways[1870] and keep[8104] My commandments,[4687] My statutes according to all the law[8451] which I commanded[4687] your fathers,[1] and which I sent to you through My servants the prophets."

14 However, they did not listen, but [a]stiffened their neck [I]like their fathers, who did not believe[539] in the LORD their God.

15 And [a]they rejected His statutes and [b]His covenant[1285] which He made with their fathers, and His warnings with which He warned them. And [c]they followed vanity and [d]became vain, and *went* after the nations which surrounded them, concerning which the [e]LORD had commanded[6680] them not to do like them.

16 And they forsook[5800] all the commandments of the LORD their God and made for themselves molten images, *even* [a]two calves, and [b]made an [I]Asherah[842] and [c]worshiped[7812] all the host of heaven and [d]served Baal.

17 Then [a]they made their sons and their daughters pass through the fire, and [b]practiced[7080] divination[7081] and enchantments,[5172] and [c]sold themselves to do evil in the sight of the LORD, provoking Him.

18 So the LORD was very angry[559] with Israel, and [a]removed them from His [I]sight; [b]none was left[7604] except the tribe of Judah.

19 Also [a]Judah did not keep[8104] the commandments of the LORD their God, but [b]walked in the [I]customs [II]which Israel had [III]introduced.

20 And the LORD rejected all the [I]descendants of Israel and afflicted them and [a]gave them into the hand of plunderers, until He had cast them [II]out of His sight.

21 When [a]He had torn Israel from the house of David, [b]they made Jeroboam the son of Nebat king.[4427] Then [c]Jeroboam drove Israel away from following the LORD, and made them [I]commit a great sin.

22 And the sons of Israel walked in all the sins of Jeroboam which he did; they did not depart[5493] from them,

23 [a]until the LORD removed Israel from His sight, [b]as He spoke through all His servants the prophets. [c]So Israel was carried away into exile from their own land[127] to Assyria until this day.[3117]

Cities of Israel Filled with Strangers

24 [a]And the king of Assyria brought *men* from Babylon and from Cuthah and from [I][b]Avva and from [c]Hamath and Sephar-vaim, and settled *them* in the cities of Samaria in place of the sons of Israel. So they possessed[3423] Samaria and lived in its cities.

25 And it came about at the beginning of their living there, that they [a]did not fear the LORD; therefore the LORD sent lions among them which killed some of them.

26 So they spoke to the king of Assyria, saying, "The nations[1471] whom you have carried away into exile in the cities of Samaria do not know[3045] the custom of the god of the land; so he has sent lions among them, and behold, they kill them because they do not know the custom of the god of the land."

27 Then the king of Assyria commanded, saying, "Take there one of the priests whom you carried away into [I]exile, and let [II]him go and live there; and let him teach them the custom of the god of the land."

28 So one of the priests whom they had carried away into exile from Samaria came and lived at Bethel, and taught them how they should fear[3372] the LORD.

29 But every nation[1471] still made gods of its own and put them [a]in the houses of the high places which the people of Samaria had made, every nation in their cities in which they lived.

30 And [a]the men of Babylon made Succoth-benoth, the men of Cuth made Nergal, the men of Hamath made Ashima,

31 and the Avvites made Nibhaz and Tartak; and [a]the Sepharvites burned[8313]

---

13 [c]1Sam. 9:9 [d]Jer. 7:3-7; 18:11; Ezek. 18:31

14 [I]Lit., *like the neck of* [a]Ex. 32:9; 33:3; Acts 7:51

15 [a]Jer. 8:9 [b]Ex. 24:6-8; Deut. 29:25 [c]Deut. 32:21 [d]Jer. 2:5; Rom. 1:21-23 [e]Deut. 12:30, 31

16 [I]I.e., a wooden symbol of a female deity [a]1Kin. 12:28 [b]1Kin. 14:15, 23 [c]Deut. 4:19; 2Kin. 21:3 [d]1Kin. 16:31

17 [a]2Kin. 16:3 [b]Lev. 19:26; Deut. 18:10-12 [c]1Kin. 21:20

18 [I]Lit., *face* [a]2Kin. 17:6 [b]1Kin. 11:13, 32, 36

19 [I]Lit., *statutes* [II]Lit., *of Israel which they* [III]Lit., *made* [a]1Kin. 14:22, 23 [b]2Kin. 16:3

20 [I]Lit., *seed* [II]Lit., *from His face* [a]2Kin. 15:29

21 [I]Lit., *sin* [a]1Kin. 11:11, 31 [b]1Kin. 12:20 [c]1Kin. 12:28-33

23 [a]2Kin. 17:6 [b]2Kin. 17:13 [c]2Kin. 17:6

24 [I]In 2Kin. 18:34, *Ivvah* [a]Ezra 4:2, 10 [b]2Kin. 18:34 [c]1Kin. 8:65

25 [a]2Kin. 17:32-41

27 [I]Lit., *exile from there* [II]Lit., *them*

29 [a]1Kin. 12:31; 13:32

30 [a]2Kin. 17:24

31 [a]2Kin. 17:17

their children in the fire to [b]Adramme-
lech and Anammelech the gods of
[c]Sepharvaim.
32 [a]They also feared[3373] the LORD
and [I][b]appointed from among themselves
priests of the high places, who acted
for them in the houses of the high places.
33 They feared the LORD and served
their own gods according to the custom
of the nations from among whom they
had been carried away into exile.
34 To this day they do according
to the earlier[7223] customs: they do not
fear[3373] the LORD, nor do they [I]follow
their statutes or their ordinances or the
law, or the commandments[4687] which the
LORD commanded the sons of Jacob,
[a]whom He named Israel;
35 with whom the LORD made a covenant and commanded them, saying,
"[a]You shall not fear other gods, nor
[b]bow down yourselves to them nor
[c]serve them nor sacrifice to them.
36 "But the LORD, [a]who brought you
up from the land of Egypt with great
power and with [b]an outstretched arm,
[c]Him you shall fear, and to Him you
shall bow[7812] yourselves down, and to
Him you shall sacrifice.
37 "And the statutes and the ordinances and the law and the commandment, which He wrote for you, [a]you
shall observe to do forever; and you
shall not fear other gods.
38 "And the covenant that I have
made with you, [a]you shall not forget,
nor shall you fear other gods.
39 "But the LORD your God you shall
fear; and He will deliver[5537] you from
the hand of all your enemies."
40 However, they did not listen, but
they did[6213] according to their earlier
custom.
🔑41 [a]So while these nations feared
the LORD, they also served their
[I]idols; their children likewise and their
grandchildren, as their fathers did, so
they do to this day.

31 [b]2Kin. 19:37 [c]2Kin. 17:24

32 [I]Lit., *made for themselves from among* [a]Zeph. 1:5 [b]1Kin. 12:31

34 [I]Lit., *do according to* [a]Gen. 32:28; 35:10

35 [a]Judg. 6:10 [b]Ex. 20:5 [c]Deut. 5:9

36 [a]Ex. 14:15-30 [b]Ex. 6:6; 9:15 [c]Lev. 19:32; Deut. 6:13

37 [a]Deut. 5:32

38 [a]Deut. 4:23; 6:12

41 [I]Or, *graven images* [a]Zeph. 1:5; Matt. 6:24

1 [a]2Kin. 16:2; 17:1 [b]2Chr. 28:27

2 [a]2Chr. 29:1, 2

3 [a]2Kin. 20:3; 2Chr. 31:20

4 [I]I.e., a wooden symbol of a female deity [II]I.e., a piece of bronze [a]2Kin. 18:22; 2Chr. 31:1 [b]Num. 21:8, 9

5 [a]2Kin. 19:10 [b]2Kin. 23:25

6 [a]Deut. 10:20; Josh. 23:8

7 [a]Gen. 39:2, 3; 1Sam. 18:14 [b]2Kin. 16:7

8 [I]Lit., *smote* [a]2Chr. 28:18; Is. 14:29 [b]2Kin. 17:9

9 [a]2Kin. 17:3-7

Hezekiah Reigns over Judah

18 🔑Now it came about [a]in the
third year of Hoshea, the son
of Elah king[4428] of Israel, that [b]Hezekiah
the son of Ahaz king of Judah became
king.
2 He was [a]twenty-five years old
when he became king, and he reigned
twenty-nine years in Jerusalem; and his
mother's name was Abi the daughter
of Zechariah.
3 [a]And he did[6213] right in the sight
of the LORD, according to all that his
father[1] David had done.
🔑4 [a]He removed the high places and
broke down the *sacred* pillars[4676] and
cut down[3772] the [I]Asherah.[842] He also
broke[7665] in pieces [b]the bronze serpent
that Moses had made, for until those
days[3117] the sons[1121] of Israel burned
incense[6999] to it; and it was called[7121]
[II]Nehushtan.
5 [a]He trusted in the LORD, the
God[430] of Israel; [b]so that after him there
was none like him among all the kings[4428]
of Judah, nor *among those* who were
before him.
6 For he [a]clung to the LORD; he did
not depart[5493] from following Him, but
kept[8104] His commandments,[4687] which
the LORD had commanded[6680] Moses.

Hezekiah Victorious

7 [a]And the LORD was with him;
wherever he went he prospered. And
[b]he rebelled against the king of Assyria
and did not serve him.
8 [a]He [I]defeated the Philistines as
far as Gaza and its territory, from
[b]watchtower[5341] to fortified city.
9 Now it came about in the fourth
year of King Hezekiah, which was the
seventh year of Hoshea son of Elah king
of Israel, that [a]Shalmaneser king of Assyria came up against Samaria and besieged it.

🔑 **17:41** These people became known as the Samaritans.
🔑 **18:1-12** See II Chr. 29:1,2; 31:1.
🔑 **18:4** See note on Num. 21:4-9.

10 And at the end of three years they captured it; in the sixth year of Hezekiah, which was [a]the ninth year of Hoshea king of Israel, Samaria was captured.

11 Then the king of Assyria carried Israel away into exile to Assyria, and put them in [a]Halah and on the Habor, the river of Gozan, and in the cities of the Medes,

12 because they [a]did not obey the voice of the LORD their God, but transgressed His covenant,[1285] even all that Moses the servant of the LORD commanded; they would neither listen, nor do[6213] *it.*

Invasion of Judah

13 [a]Now in the fourteenth year of King Hezekiah, Sennacherib king of Assyria came up against all the fortified cities of Judah and seized them.

14 Then Hezekiah king of Judah sent to the king of Assyria at Lachish, saying, "[a]I have done wrong. [I]Withdraw from me; whatever you [II]impose on me I will bear."[5375] So the king of Assyria [III]required[7760] of Hezekiah king of Judah three hundred talents of silver and thirty talents of gold.

15 And [a]Hezekiah gave *him* all the silver which was found in the house of the LORD, and in the treasuries of the king's[4428] house.

16 At that time Hezekiah cut off *the gold from* the doors of the temple of the LORD, and *from* the doorposts which Hezekiah king of Judah had overlaid, and gave it to the king of Assyria.

17 Then the king of Assyria sent [a]Tartan and Rab-saris and Rabshakeh from Lachish to King Hezekiah with a large army to Jerusalem. So they went up and came to Jerusalem. And when they went up, they came and stood by the [b]conduit of the upper[5945] pool, which is on the highway of the [I]fuller's[3526] field.[7704]

18 When they called to the king, [a]Eliakim the son of Hilkiah, who was over the household, and [b]Shebnah the scribe and Joah the son of Asaph the recorder, came out to them.

19 Then Rabshakeh said to them, "Say now to Hezekiah, 'Thus says the great king, the king of Assyria, "[a]What is this confidence[986] that you [I]have?

20 "You say (but *they are* [I]only empty[8193] words),[1697] '*I have* counsel[6098] and strength for the war.' Now on whom do you rely, [a]that you have rebelled against me?

21 "Now behold, you [I][a]rely on the staff of this crushed reed, *even* on Egypt; on which if a man leans, it will go into his [II]hand and pierce[5344] it. So is Pharaoh king of Egypt to all who rely on him.

22 "But if you say to me, 'We trust in the LORD our God,' is it not He whose high places and [a]whose altars[4196] Hezekiah has taken away, and has said to Judah and to Jerusalem, 'You shall worship[7812] before this altar[4196] in Jerusalem'?

23 "Now therefore, [I]come, make a bargain with my master[113] the king of Assyria, and I will give you two thousand horses, if you are able on your part to set riders on them.

24 "How then can you [I]repulse one [II]official[6346] of the least of my master's servants, and [III]rely on Egypt for chariots and for horsemen?

25 "Have I now come up [I]without the LORD's approval against this place to destroy[7843] it? The LORD said to me, 'Go up against this land and destroy it.' " ' "

26 Then Eliakim the son of Hilkiah, and Shebnah and Joah, said to Rabshakeh, "Speak now to your servants in Aramaic, for we [I]understand[8085] *it;* and do not speak with us in [II][a]Judean, in the

10 [a]2Kin. 17:6
11 [a]1Chr. 5:26
12 [a]1Kin. 9:6; Dan. 9:6, 10
13 [a]2Chr. 32:1; Is. 36:1-39:8
14 [I]Lit., *Return* [II]Lit., *give* [III]Lit., *put on* [a]2Kin. 18:7
15 [a]1Kin. 15:18, 19; 2Kin. 12:18; 16:8
17 [I]I.e., launderer's [a]Is. 20:1 [b]2Kin. 20:20; Is. 7:3
18 [a]2Kin. 19:2; Is. 22:20 [b]Is. 22:15
19 [I]Lit., *trust* [a]2Chr. 32:10
20 [I]Lit., *a word of the lips* [a]2Kin. 18:7
21 [I]Lit., *rely for yourself* [II]Lit., *palm* [a]Is. 30:2, 3, 7; Ezek. 29:6, 7
22 [a]2Kin. 18:4; 2Chr. 31:1
23 [I]Lit., *please exchange pledges*
24 [I]Lit., *turn away the face of* [II]Or, *governor* [III]Lit., *rely for yourself*
25 [I]Lit., *without the LORD*
26 [I]Lit., *hear* [II]I.e., Hebrew [a]Ezra 4:7; Dan. 2:4

18:13-37 See II Chr. 32:1-19; Isa. 36:1-22.

18:22 This was a false statement. Hezekiah had destroyed the Canaanite high places and altars in order to honor the true God.

hearing[241] of the people[5971] who are on the wall."

27 But Rabshakeh said to them, "Has my master sent me only to your master and to you to speak these words, *and* not to the men who sit on the wall, *doomed* to eat their own dung and drink their own urine with you?"

28 Then Rabshakeh stood and cried[7121] with a loud voice in Judean, [I]saying, "Hear the word[1697] of the great king, the king of Assyria.

29 "Thus says the king, '[a]Do not let Hezekiah deceive you, for he will not be able to deliver[5337] you from [I]my hand;

30 nor let Hezekiah make you trust in the LORD, saying, "The LORD will surely deliver us, and this city shall not be given into the hand of the king of Assyria."

31 'Do not listen to Hezekiah, for thus says the king of Assyria, "[I]Make your peace with me and come out to me, and eat [a]each of his vine and each of his fig tree and drink each of the waters of his own cistern,[953]

32 until I come and take you away [a]to a land like your own land, a land of grain and new wine, a land of bread and vineyards, a land of olive trees and honey, that you may live[2421] and not die." But do not listen to Hezekiah, when he misleads you, saying, "The LORD will deliver us."

33 '[a]Has any one of the gods[430] of the nations[1471] delivered[5337] his land from the hand of the king of Assyria?

34 '[a]Where are the gods of Hamath and [b]Arpad? Where are the gods of Sepharvaim, Hena and [I][c]Ivvah? Have they delivered Samaria from my hand?

35 'Who among all the gods of the lands[776] [I]have delivered their land[776]

28 [I]Lit., *and spoke, saying,*

29 [I]Heb., *his* [a]2Chr. 32:15

31 [I]Lit., *Make with me a blessing* [a]1Kin. 4:20, 25

32 [a]Deut. 8:7-9; 11:12

33 [a]2Kin. 19:12; Is. 10:10,11

34 [I]In 2Kin. 17:24, *Avva* [a]2Kin. 19:13 [b]Is. 10:9 [c]2Kin. 17:24

35 [I]Lit., *who have* [a]Ps. 2:1-3; 59:7

37 [a]2Kin. 18:26 [b]2Kin. 6:30

1 [a]2Chr. 32:20-22; Is. 37:1 [b]2Kin. 18:37 [c]1Kin. 21:27

2 [a]2Sam. 3:31 [b]Is. 1:1; 2:1

4 [a]Josh. 14:12; 2Sam. 16:12 [b]2Kin. 18:35 [c]Is. 1:9

6 [a]2Kin. 18:17 [b]2Kin. 18:22-25; 30:35

from my hand, [a]that the LORD should deliver Jerusalem from my hand?'"

36 But the people were silent and answered him not a word, for the king's commandment[4687] was, "Do not answer him."

37 Then [a]Eliakim the son of Hilkiah, who was over the household, and Shebna the scribe and Joah the son of Asaph, the recorder, came to Hezekiah [b]with their clothes torn and told him the words of Rabshakeh.

Isaiah Encourages Hezekiah

19 🔑 [a]And when King[4428] Hezekiah heard *it,* he [b]tore his clothes, [c]covered[3680] himself with sackcloth and entered the house of the LORD.

2 Then he sent Eliakim who was over the household with Shebna the scribe and the elders[2205] of the priests, [a]covered with sackcloth, to [b]Isaiah the prophet the son of Amoz.

3 And they said to him, "Thus says Hezekiah, 'This day[3117] is a day of distress, rebuke, and rejection;[5007] for children[1121] have come to birth, and there is no strength to *deliver.*

4 '[a]Perhaps the LORD your God[430] will hear all the words[1697] of Rabshakeh, whom his master the king of Assyria has sent [b]to reproach the living[2416] God, and will rebuke the words which the LORD your God has heard. Therefore, offer a prayer[8605] for [c]the remnant that is left.'"

5 So the servants of King Hezekiah came to Isaiah.

6 And Isaiah said to them, "Thus you shall say to your master, 'Thus says the LORD, "Do not be afraid[3372] because of the words that you have heard, with which the [a]servants of the king of Assyria [b]have blasphemed[1442] Me.

🔑 **19:1-37** This passage is virtually identical to Isa. 37:1-38. Why would God include both passages? The passages are repeated to emphasize different things in different contexts. The inclusion of the passage in Isaiah marks the transition from Assyrian prominence (Isa. 8:7; 20:1-6) to Babylonian supremacy (Isa. 39:5-7). Here, the passage illustrates God's miraculous intervention on Judah's behalf. Compare with II Kgs. 7:5-7.

7 "Behold, I will put a spirit[7307] in
him so that [a]he shall hear a rumor and
return to his own land. And [b]I will make
him fall by the sword in his own land." ' "

Sennacherib Defies God

8 Then Rabshakeh returned and
found the king of Assyria fighting against
[a]Libnah, for he had heard that [I]the king
had left [b]Lachish.
9 When he heard *them* say concerning Tirhakah king of [I]Cush, "Behold, he
has come out to fight against you," he
sent messengers again to Hezekiah saying,
10 "Thus you shall say to Hezekiah
king of [I]Judah, 'Do not [a]let your God
in whom you trust deceive you saying,
"[b]Jerusalem shall not be given into the
hand of the king of Assyria."
11 'Behold, you have heard what the
kings[4428] of Assyria have done[6213] to all
the lands,[776] destroying[2763] them completely. So will you be [I]spared?[5337]
12 '[a]Did the gods[430] of [I]those
nations[1471] which my fathers[1] destroyed
deliver them, *even* [b]Gozan and [c]Haran
and Rezeph and [d]the sons of Eden who
were in Telassar?
13 '[a]Where is the king of Hamath,
the king of Arpad, the king of the city
of Sepharvaim, and *of* Hena and Ivvah?' "

Hezekiah's Prayer

14 Then [a]Hezekiah took the
[I]letter from the hand of the messengers
and read it, and he went up to the house
of the LORD and [II]spread it out before
the LORD.
15 And Hezekiah prayed[6419] before
the LORD and said, "O LORD, the God
of Israel, [a]who art [I]enthroned *above* the
cherubim,[3742] [b]Thou art the God, Thou
alone, of all the kingdoms[4467] of the
earth. Thou hast made heaven and
earth.[776]
16 "[a]Incline Thine ear,[241] O LORD,
and hear; [b]open Thine eyes, O LORD,
and see; and listen to the words of Sennacherib, which he has sent [c]to reproach
the living God.
17 "Truly, O LORD, the kings of Assyria have devastated[2717] the nations and
their lands
18 and have cast their gods into the
fire, [a]for they were not gods but the
work of men's hands, wood and stone.
So they have destroyed[6] them.
19 "And now, O LORD our God, I
pray,[4994] deliver us from his hand
[a]that all the kingdoms of the earth may
know[3045] that Thou alone, O [b]LORD, art
God."

God's Answer through Isaiah

20 Then Isaiah the son of Amoz
sent to Hezekiah saying, "Thus says
the LORD, the God of Israel, 'Because
you have prayed to Me about Sennacherib king of Assyria, [a]I have
heard *you*.'
21 "This is the word[1697] that the
LORD has spoken against him:
'She has despised you and
mocked you,
[a]The virgin[1330] daughter of Zion;
She [b]has shaken *her* head behind
you,
The daughter of Jerusalem!
22 'Whom have you [a]reproached and
[b]blasphemed?
And against whom have you
raised *your* voice,
And [I]haughtily lifted up your
eyes?
Against the [c]Holy One of Israel!
23 "[a]Through your messengers you
have reproached the Lord,
And you have said, "With my
many chariots I came up to
the heights of the mountains,
To the remotest parts of
Lebanon;
And I [I]cut down[3772] its tall cedars
and its choice cypresses.
And I [I]entered its farthest
lodging place, its [b]thickest
forest.
24 "I dug *wells* and drank foreign
waters,

7 [a]2Kin. 7:6 [b]2Kin. 19:37
8 [I]Lit., *he* [a]Josh. 10:29 [b]2Kin. 18:14
9 [I]Or, *Ethiopia*
10 [I]Lit., *Judah, saying,* [a]2Kin. 18:5 [b]2Kin. 18:30
11 [I]Lit., *delivered*
12 [I]Lit., *the* [a]2Kin. 18:33 [b]2Kin. 17:6 [c]Gen. 11:31 [d]Is. 37:12
13 [a]2Kin. 18:34
14 [I]Lit., *letters ... read them* [II]Lit., *Hezekiah spread* [a]Is. 37:14
15 [I]Lit., *seated* [a]Ex. 25:22; Is. 37:14 [b]2Kin. 5:15
16 [a]Ps. 31:2; Is. 37:17 [b]1Kin. 8:29; 2Chr. 6:40 [c]2Kin. 19:4
18 [a]Is. 44:9-20; Acts 17:29
19 [a]1Kin. 8:42, 43 [b]2Kin. 19:15
20 [a]2Kin. 20:5
21 [a]Jer. 14:17; Lam. 2:13 [b]Ps. 109:25; Matt. 27:39
22 [I]Lit., *on high* [a]2Kin. 19:4 [b]2Kin. 19:6 [c]Is. 5:24; 30:11-15
23 [I]So with some ancient versions; M.T., *will cut ... will enter* [a]2Kin. 18:17 [b]2Chr. 26:10; Is. 10:18

And with the sole of my feet I
[I][a]dried up
All the rivers of [II]Egypt."
25 '[a]Have you not heard?
Long ago I did it;
From ancient[6924] times I
planned[3335] it.
[b]Now I have brought it to pass,
That you should turn fortified
cities into ruinous heaps.
26 'Therefore their inhabitants were
short of strength,[3027]
They were dismayed[2865] and put
to shame;[954]
They were [a]as the vegetation
of the field[7704] and as the
green herb,
As grass on the housetops is
scorched before it is grown
up.
27 'But [a]I know your sitting down,
And your going out and your
coming in,
And your raging against Me.
28 'Because of your raging against
Me,
And because your [I]arrogance
has come up to My ears,[241]
Therefore I [a]will put My hook
in your nose,[639]
And My bridle in your lips,[8193]
And [b]I will turn you back by the
way[1870] which you came.
29 'Then this shall be [a]the sign for
you: [I]you shall eat this year what grows
of itself, in the second year what springs
from the same, and in the third year
sow, reap, plant vineyards, and eat their
fruit.
30 '[a]And the surviving[6413] remnant
of the house of Judah shall again take
root downward and bear fruit upward.
31 'For out of Jerusalem shall go
forth a remnant, and [a]out of Mount Zion
[I]survivors.[6413] [b]The zeal[7068] of [II]the LORD
shall perform[6213] this.
32 'Therefore thus says the LORD
concerning the king of Assyria, "[a]He
shall not come to this city or shoot an
arrow there; neither shall he come before it with a shield, nor throw up[8210]
a mound against it.
33 "[a]By the way that he came, by
the same he shall return, and he shall
not come to this city,"' declares the
LORD.
34 '[a]For I will defend this city to
save it for My own sake and [b]for My
servant David's sake.'"
35 [a]Then it happened that night[3915]
that the angel[4397] of the LORD went out,
and struck 185,000 in the camp[4264] of
the Assyrians; and when [I]men rose early
in the morning, behold, all of them were
[II]dead.[4191]
36 So [a]Sennacherib king of Assyria
departed and returned *home,* and lived
at [b]Nineveh.
37 And it came about as he was
worshiping[7812] in the house of Nisroch
his god, that [I][a]Adrammelech and Sharezer killed him with the sword; and
they escaped[4422] into [b]the land of Ararat.
And [c]Esarhaddon his son became king
in his place.

Hezekiah's Illness and Recovery

20 [a]In those days[3117] Hezekiah
became [I]mortally[4191] ill. And Isaiah the prophet the son of Amoz came
to him and said to him, "Thus says the
LORD, '[b]Set your house in order, for
you shall die[4191] and not live.'"[2421]
2 Then he turned his face to the
wall, and prayed[6419] to the LORD, saying,
3 "[a]Remember now, O LORD, I
beseech[577] Thee, [b]how I have walked
before Thee in truth and with a whole[8003]
heart, and have done[6213] what is good[2896]
in Thy sight." And [c]Hezekiah wept
[I]bitterly.
4 And it came about before Isaiah
had gone out of the middle court, that
the word[1697] of the LORD came to him,
saying,
5 "Return and say to [a]Hezekiah the
leader[5057] of My people,[5971] 'Thus says

24 [I]So with some ancient versions; M.T., *will dry up* [II]Lit., *the besieged place* [a]Is. 19:6
25 [a]Is. 45:7 [b]Is. 10:5
26 [a]Ps. 129:6
27 [a]Ps. 139:1
28 [I]Lit., *complacency* [a]Ezek. 19:9; 29:4 [b]2Kin. 19:33, 36
29 [I]Lit., *eating* [a]Ex. 3:12; 2Kin. 20:8, 9
30 [a]2Kin. 19:4; 2Chr. 32:22, 23
31 [I]Lit., *those who escape* [II]Some ancient mss. read *the LORD of hosts* [a]Is. 10:20 [b]Is. 9:7
32 [a]Is. 8:7-10
33 [a]2Kin. 19:28
34 [a]2Kin. 20:6; Is. 31:5 [b]1Kin. 11:12, 13
35 [I]Lit., *they* [II]Lit., *dead bodies* [a]2Sam. 24:16; 2Chr. 32:21
36 [a]2Kin. 19:7, 28, 33 [b]Jon. 1:2
37 [I]Some ancient mss. read *Adrammelech and Sharezer his sons smote him* [a]2Kin. 19:17, 31 [b]Gen. 8:4; Jer. 51:27 [c]Ezra 4:2
1 [I]Lit., *sick to the point of death* [a]2Chr. 32:24; Is. 38:1-22 [b]2Sam. 17:23
3 [I]Lit., *great weeping* [a]Neh. 5:19; 13:14, 22, 31 [b]2Kin. 18:3-6 [c]2Sam. 12:21,22
5 [a]1Sam. 9:16; 10:1

20:1-11 See II Chr. 32:24-26; Isa. 38:1-8,21,22.

the LORD, the God[430] of your father[1]
David, "[b]I have heard your prayer,[8605]
[c]I have seen your tears; behold, I will
heal you. On the third day[3117] you shall
go up to the house of the LORD.
6 "And I will add fifteen years to
your [I]life, and I will deliver[5337] you and
this city from the hand of the king[4428]
of Assyria; and [a]I will defend this city
for My own sake and for My servant
David's sake."'"
7 Then Isaiah said, "Take a cake
of figs." And they took and laid[7760] *it*
on the boil, and he recovered.
8 Now Hezekiah said to Isaiah,
"What will be the sign that the LORD
will heal me, and that I shall go up to
the house of the LORD the third day?"
9 And Isaiah said, "[a]This shall be
the sign to you from the LORD, that the
LORD will do[6213] the thing that He has
spoken: shall the shadow go forward
ten steps or go back ten steps?"
10 So Hezekiah [I]answered,[559] "It is
easy for the shadow to decline ten steps;
no, but let the shadow turn backward
ten steps."
11 And Isaiah the prophet cried[7121]
to the LORD, and [a]He brought the
shadow on the [I]stairway back ten steps
by which it had gone down on the
[I]stairway of Ahaz.

Hezekiah Shows Babylon His Treasures

12 [a]At that time [I]Berodach-baladan
a son of Baladan, king of Babylon, sent
letters[5612] and a present to Hezekiah,
for he heard that Hezekiah had been
sick.
13 And Hezekiah listened to them,
and showed them [a]all his treasure house,
the silver and the gold and the spices
and the precious oil and the house of
his armor and all that was found in his
treasuries. There was nothing[3808,1697] in
his house, nor in all his dominion, that
Hezekiah did not show them.
14 Then Isaiah the prophet came to
King Hezekiah and said to him, "What
did these men say, and from where have
they come to you?" And Hezekiah said,
"They have come from a far country,[776]
from Babylon."
15 And he said, "What have they
seen in your house?" So Hezekiah
[I]answered, "They have seen all that is
in my house; there is nothing among
my treasures that I have not shown
them."
16 Then Isaiah said to Hezekiah,
"Hear the word of the LORD.
17 'Behold, the days are coming
when [a]all that is in your house, and all
that your fathers[1] have laid up in store
to this day shall be carried[5375] to Babylon; nothing shall be left,'[3498] says the
LORD.
18 'And some [a]of your sons who
shall issue from you, whom you shall
beget, shall be taken away; and they
shall become [b]officials[5631] in the
palace[1964] of the king of Babylon.'"
19 Then Hezekiah said to Isaiah,
"The word of the LORD which you have
spoken is [a]good." For he [I]thought, "Is
it not so, if there shall be peace[7965] and
truth in my days?"
20 [a]Now the rest of the acts[1697] of
Hezekiah and all his might, and how
he [b]made the pool and the conduit,
and brought water into the city, are
they not written in the Book[5612] of the
Chronicles of the Kings[4428] of Judah?
21 [a]So Hezekiah slept with his fathers, and Manasseh his son became
king in his place.

5 [b]2Kin. 19:20 [c]Ps. 39:12
6 [I]Lit., *days* [a]2Kin. 19:34
9 [a]Is. 38:7
10 [I]Lit., *said*
11 [I]Lit., *steps* [a]Josh. 10:12-14; Is. 38:8
12 [I]Many mss. and ancient versions read *Merodach-baladan;* cf. Is. 39:1 [a]2Chr. 32:31; Is. 39:1-8
13 [a]2Chr. 32:27
15 [I]Lit., *said*
17 [a]2Kin. 24:13; 25:13-15; 2Chr. 36:10; Jer. 52:17-19
18 [a]2Kin. 24:12; 2Chr. 33:11 [b]Dan. 1:3-7
19 [I]Lit., *said* [a]1Sam. 3:18
20 [a]2Chr. 32:32 [b]Neh. 3:16
21 [a]2Chr. 32:33

20:12-19 See Isa. 39:1-8.
20:20 "The pool" is probably a reference to the pool of Siloam which was fed by a conduit from the spring of Gihon (II Chr. 32:30). Perhaps the conduit was at first a surface aqueduct which Hezekiah replaced with a tunnel to assure that the supply of water would not be interrupted. A tunnel has been found in that area along with an inscription describing its construction.
20:20,21 See II Chr. 32:32,33.

Manasseh Succeeds Hezekiah

21 [a]Manasseh was twelve years
old when he became king, and
he reigned fifty-five years in Jerusalem;
and his mother's name was Hephzibah.
2 And [a]he did[6213] evil[7451] in the sight
of the LORD, [b]according to the abominations of the nations whom the LORD
dispossessed[3423] before the sons[1121] of
Israel.
3 For [a]he rebuilt the high places
which Hezekiah his father had destroyed;[6] and [b]he erected altars[4196]
for Baal and made an [I]Asherah,[842] as
Ahab king[4428] of Israel had done, and
[c]worshiped[7812] all the host of heaven and
served them.
4 And [a]he built altars in the house
of the LORD, of which the LORD had
said, "[b]In Jerusalem I will put My name."
5 For he built altars for [a]all the host
of heaven in [b]the two courts of the house
of the LORD.
6 And [a]he made his son pass through
the fire, [b]practiced witchcraft and used
divination,[5172] and dealt[6213] with mediums and spiritists.[3049] He did much
evil[7451] in the sight of the LORD provoking *Him to* anger.[3707]
7 Then [a]he set the carved image
of Asherah that he had made, in the
house of which the LORD said to David
and to his son Solomon, "[b]In this house
and in Jerusalem, which I have chosen[977]
from all the tribes of Israel, I will put
My name forever.
8 "And I [a]will not make the feet of
Israel wander anymore from the land[127]
which I gave their fathers,[1] if only they
will observe to do[6213] according to all
that I have commanded[6680] them, and
according to all the law[8451] that My servant Moses commanded them."
9 But they did not listen, and Manasseh [a]seduced them to do evil more
than the nations[1471] whom the LORD
destroyed[8045] before the sons of Israel.

1 [a]2Chr. 33:1-9

2 [a]Jer. 15:4 [b]2Kin. 16:3

3 [I]I.e., a wooden symbol of a female deity [a]2Kin. 18:4 [b]1Kin. 16:31-33 [c]Deut. 17:2-5; 2Kin. 17:16; 23:5

4 [a]2Kin. 16:10-16 [b]2Sam. 7:13; 1Kin. 8:29

5 [a]2Kin. 23:4, 5 [b]1Kin. 7:12; 2Kin. 23:12

6 [a]Lev. 18:21; 2Kin. 16:3; 17:17 [b]Lev. 19:26, 31; Deut. 18:10-14

7 [a]Deut. 16:21; 2Kin. 23:6 [b]1Kin. 8:29; 9:3; 2Chr. 7:12, 16

8 [a]2Sam. 7:10; 2Kin. 18:11, 12

9 [a]Prov. 29:12

11 [a]2Kin. 21:2; 24:3, 4 [b]Gen. 15:16; 1Kin. 21:26 [c]2Kin. 21:16 [d]2Kin. 21:21

12 [a]1Sam. 3:11; Jer. 19:3

13 [a]Is. 34:11; Amos 7:7, 8

16 [a]2Kin. 24:4 [b]2Kin. 21:11

17 [I]Lit., *sinned* [a]2Chr. 33:11-19

18 [a]2Chr. 33:20 [b]2Kin. 21:26

The King's Idolatries Rebuked

10 Now the LORD spoke through
His servants the prophets, saying,
11 "[a]Because Manasseh king of
Judah has done these abominations,
[b]having done[6213] wickedly more than all
the Amorites did who *were* before him,
and [c]has also made Judah sin [d]with his
idols;[1544]
12 therefore thus says the LORD,
the God[430] of Israel, 'Behold, I am bringing *such* calamity on Jerusalem and Judah, that whoever hears of it, [a]both his
ears[241] shall tingle.
13 '[a]And I will stretch over Jerusalem the line of Samaria and the
plummet[4949] of the house of Ahab, and
I will wipe Jerusalem as one wipes[4229]
a dish, wiping it and turning it upside
down.
14 'And I will abandon the remnant
of My inheritance[5159] and deliver them
into the hand of their enemies, and they
shall become[1961] as plunder and spoil
to all their enemies;
15 because they have done evil in
My sight, and have been provoking
Me to anger, since the day[3177] their fathers came from Egypt, even to this
day.' "
16 [a]Moreover, Manasseh shed
very much innocent[5355] blood[1818] until
he had filled Jerusalem from one end
to another; besides his sin [b]with which
he made Judah sin, in doing[6213] evil in
the sight of the LORD.
17 [a]Now the rest of the acts[1697]
of Manasseh and all that he did and
his sin which he [I]committed, are
they not written in the Book[5612] of
the Chronicles of the Kings[4428] of Judah?
18 [a]And Manasseh slept with his fathers and was buried[6912] in the garden
of his own house, [b]in the garden of Uzza,
and Amon his son became king in his
place.

21:1-18 See II Chr. 33:1-20.
21:6 See note on Lev. 18:21.
21:17 II Chr. 33:10-13 relates his imprisonment and conversion.

Amon Succeeds Manasseh

19 [a]Amon was twenty-two years
old when he became king, and he reigned
two years in Jerusalem; and his mother's
name *was* Meshullemeth the daughter
of Haruz of Jotbah.
20 And he did evil in the sight of
the LORD, [a]as Manasseh his father had
done.
21 For he walked in all the way[1870]
that his father had walked, and served
the idols that his father had served and
worshiped them.
22 So [a]he forsook[5800] the LORD, the
God of his fathers, and did not walk in
the way[1870] of the LORD.
23 And [a]the servants of Amon conspired against him and killed the king
in his own house.
24 Then [a]the people[5971] of the land
[I]killed all those who had conspired
against King[4428] Amon, and the people
of the land made Josiah his son king in
his place.
25 Now the rest of the acts of Amon
which he did, are they not written in
the Book of the Chronicles of the Kings
of Judah?
26 And he was buried in his
grave[6900] [a]in the garden of Uzza, and
Josiah his son became king in his place.

Josiah Succeeds Amon

22 [a]Josiah was eight years old
when he became king, and he
reigned thirty-one years in Jerusalem; and his mother's name *was* Jedidah the daughter of Adaiah of [b]Boz-
kath.
2 And he did[6213] right in the sight
of the LORD and walked in all the way[1870]
of his father[1] David, nor did he [a]turn
aside to the right or to the left.
3 Now [a]it came about in the eighteenth year of King[4428] Josiah that the
king sent Shaphan, the son of Azaliah
the son of Meshullam the scribe, to
the house of the LORD saying,
4 "[a]Go up to Hilkiah the high priest
that he may [I]count the money brought
in to the house of the LORD which the
doorkeepers[8104] have gathered[622] from
the people.[5971]
5 "[a]And let them deliver it into the
hand of the workmen[4399] who have the
oversight of the house of the LORD, and
let them give it to the workmen who
are in the house of the LORD to repair
the [I]damages of the house,
6 to the carpenters and the
builders[1129] and the masons and for buying timber and hewn[4274] stone to repair
the house.
7 "Only [a]no accounting shall be
made with them for the money delivered
into their hands, for they deal[6213]
faithfully."[530]

The Lost Book

8 Then Hilkiah the high priest said
to Shaphan the scribe, "I have found
the book[5612] of the law[8451] in the house
of the LORD." And Hilkiah gave the book
to Shaphan who read it.
9 And Shaphan the scribe came to
the king and brought back word[1697] to
the king and said, "Your servants have
emptied out the money that was found
in the house, and have delivered it into
the hand of the workmen[6213,4399] who
have the oversight of the house of the
LORD."
10 Moreover, Shaphan the scribe
told the king saying, "Hilkiah the priest
has given me a book." And Shaphan read
it in the presence of the king.
11 And it came about when the king
heard the words[1697] of the book of the
law, that [a]he tore his clothes.
12 Then the king commanded[6680]
Hilkiah the priest, [a]Ahikam the son of
Shaphan, [Ib]Achbor the son of Micaiah,
Shaphan the scribe, and Asaiah the
king's[4428] servant saying,

19 [a]2Chr. 33:21-23
20 [a]2Kin. 21:2-6, 11, 16
22 [a]2Kin. 22:17; 1Chr. 28:9
23 [a]2Kin. 12:20; 14:19
24 [I]Lit., *smote* [a]2Kin. 14:5
26 [a]2Kin. 21:18
1 [a]2Chr. 34:1 [b]Josh. 15:39
2 [a]Deut. 5:32; Josh. 1:7
3 [a]2Chr. 34:8
4 [I]Or, *total* [a]2Kin. 12:4, 9, 10
5 [I]Lit., *breach* [a]2Kin. 12:11-14
7 [a]2Kin. 12:15; 1Cor. 4:2
8 [a]Deut. 31:24-26; 2Chr. 34:14, 15
11 [a]Gen. 37:34; Josh. 7:6
12 [I]In 2Chr. 34:20, *Abdon, son of Micah* [a]2Kin. 25:22; Jer. 26:24 [b]2Chr. 34:20

21:19-26 See II Chr. 33:21-25.
22:1,2 See II Chr. 34:1,2.
22:3-20 See II Chr. 34:8-28.

13 "Go, inquire of the LORD for me and the people and all Judah concerning the words of this book that has been found, for [a]great is the wrath of the LORD that burns against us, because our fathers[1] have not listened to the words of this book, to do according to all that is written concerning us."

Huldah Predicts

14 So Hilkiah the priest, Ahikam, Achbor, Shaphan, and Asaiah went to Huldah the prophetess, the wife[802] of Shallum the son of [I][a]Tikvah, the son of Harhas, keeper[8104] of the wardrobe (now she lived in Jerusalem in the [b]Second Quarter); and they spoke to her.

15 And she said to them, "Thus says the LORD God[430] of Israel, 'Tell the man who sent you to me,

16 thus says the LORD, "Behold, I [a]bring evil[7451] on this place and on its inhabitants, *even* all the words of the book which the king of Judah has read.

17 "[a]Because they have forsaken[5800] Me and have burned incense[6999] to other gods[430] that they might provoke Me to anger[3707] with all the work of their hands, therefore My wrath burns against this place, and it shall not be quenched."'

18 "But to [a]the king of Judah who sent you to inquire of the LORD thus shall you say to him, 'Thus says the LORD God of Israel, "*Regarding* the words which you have heard,

19 [a]because your heart was tender and [b]you humbled yourself before the LORD when you heard what I spoke against this place and against its inhabitants that they should become[1961] [c]a desolation[8047] and a [d]curse,[7045] and you have [e]torn your clothes and wept before Me, I truly have heard you," declares the LORD.

20 "Therefore, behold, I will gather[622] you to your fathers, and [a]you shall be gathered to your grave in peace,[7965] neither shall your eyes see all the evil which I will bring on this place."'" So they brought back word to the king.

Josiah's Covenant

23 🗝 [a]Then the king[4428] sent, and they gathered[622] to him all the elders[2205] of Judah and of Jerusalem.

2 And the king went up to the house of the LORD and all the men of Judah and all the inhabitants of Jerusalem with him, and the priests and the prophets and all the people,[5971] both small and great; and [a]he read in their hearing[241] all the words[1697] of the book[5612] of the covenant,[1285] [b]which was found in the house of the LORD.

3 And [a]the king stood by the pillar and made a covenant before the LORD, [b]to walk after the LORD, and to keep[8104] His commandments[4687] and His testimonies and His statutes with all *his* heart and all *his* soul, to carry out the words of this covenant that were written in this book. And all the people [I]entered into the covenant.

Reforms under Josiah

🗝 4 Then the king commanded[6680] Hilkiah the high priest and [a]the priests of the second order and the [I]doorkeepers,[8104] [b]to bring out of the temple of the LORD all the vessels that were made for Baal, for [II]Asherah,[842] and for all the host of heaven; and [c]he burned[8313] them outside Jerusalem in the fields of the Kidron, and carried their ashes[6083] to Bethel.

5 And he did away with the idolatrous priests whom the kings[4428] of Judah had appointed to burn incense[6999] in the

---

13 [a]Deut. 29:23-28; 31:17,18

14 [I]In 2Chr. 34:22, *Tokhath, son of Hasrah* [a]2Chr. 34:22 [b]Zeph. 1:10

16 [a]Deut. 29:27; Dan. 9:11-14

17 [a]Deut. 29:25, 26; 2Kin. 21:22

18 [a]2Chr. 34:26

19 [a]1Sam. 24:5; Ps. 51:17 [b]Ex. 10:3; 1Kin. 21:29 [c]Lev. 26:31 [d]Jer. 26:6 [e]2Kin. 22:11

20 [a]2Kin. 23:30

1 [a]2Chr. 34:29-32

2 [a]Deut. 31:10-13 [b]2Kin. 22:8

3 [I]Lit., *took a stand in* [a]2Kin. 11:14, 17 [b]Deut. 13:4

4 [I]Lit., *keepers of the threshold* [II]I.e., a wooden symbol of a female deity, and so throughout the ch. [a]2Kin. 25:18; Jer. 52:24 [b]2Kin. 21:37; 2Chr. 33:3 [c]2Kin. 23:15

🗝 **23:1-20** See II Chr. 34:3-7,29-33.
🗝 **23:4-20** See note on Zeph. 1:4,5.

high places in the cities of Judah and in the surrounding area of Jerusalem, also those who burned incense[6999] to Baal, to the sun and to the moon and to the constellations and to all the [a]host of heaven.

6 And he brought out the Asherah from the house of the LORD outside Jerusalem to the brook Kidron, and burned it at the brook Kidron, and [a]ground *it* to dust,[6083] and [b]threw its dust on the graves[6913] of the [I]common people.

7 He also broke down the houses of the [a]*male* cult prostitutes[6945] which *were* in the house of the LORD, where [b]the women[802] were weaving [I]hangings for the Asherah.

8 Then he brought all the priests from the cities of Judah, and defiled[2930] the high places where the priests had burned incense, from [a]Geba to Beersheba; and he broke down the high places of the gates which *were* at the entrance of the gate of Joshua the governor of the city, which *were* on one's left at the city gate.

9 Nevertheless [a]the priests of the high places did not go up to the altar[4196] of the LORD in Jerusalem, but they ate unleavened[4682] bread among their brothers.[251]

10 [a]He also defiled [I]Topheth, which is in the valley of the son of Hinnom, [b]that no man might make his son or his daughter pass through the fire for [c]Molech.

11 And he did away with the horses which the kings of Judah had given to the [a]sun, at the entrance of the house of the LORD, by the chamber of Nathan-melech the official,[5631] which *was* in the precincts; and he burned the chariots of the sun with fire.

12 And [a]the altars[4196] which *were* on the roof, the upper chamber of Ahaz, which the kings of Judah had made, and [b]the altars which Manasseh had made in the two courts of the house of the LORD, the king broke down; and he [I]smashed them there, and [c]threw their dust[6083] into the brook Kidron.

13 And the high places which *were* before Jerusalem, which *were* on the right of [a]the mount of destruction[4889] which Solomon the king of Israel had built for [b]Ashtoreth the abomination[8251] of the Sidonians, and for [c]Chemosh the abomination[8441] of Moab, and for Milcom the abomination of the sons of Ammon, the king defiled.[2930]

14 And [a]he broke[7665] in pieces the *sacred* pillars[4676] and cut down[3772] the Asherim[842] and [b]filled their places with human bones.[6106]

15 Furthermore, [a]the altar that *was* at Bethel *and* the [b]high place which Jeroboam the son of Nebat, who made Israel sin, had made, even that altar and the high place he broke down. Then he [I][c]demolished its stones, ground them to dust, and burned the Asherah.

16 Now when Josiah turned, he saw the graves[6913] that *were* there on the mountain, and he sent and took the bones from the graves and burned *them* on the altar and defiled[2930] it [a]according to the word[1697] of the LORD which the man of God[430] proclaimed, who proclaimed these things.

17 Then he said, "What is this monument that I see?" And the men of the city told him, "[a]It is the grave[6913] of the man of God who came from Judah and proclaimed these things which you have done[6213] against the altar of Bethel."

18 And he said, "Let him alone; let no one disturb his bones." So they [I]left his bones undisturbed [a]with the bones of the prophet who came from Samaria.

19 And Josiah also removed all the houses of the high places which *were* [a]in the cities of Samaria, which the kings of Israel had made provoking [I]the LORD; and he did[6213] to them [II]just as he had done in Bethel.

20 And all the priests of the high places who *were* there [a]he slaughtered on the altars and burned human bones on them; then he returned to Jerusalem.

5 [a]2Kin. 21:3

6 [I]Lit., *sons of the people* [a]2Kin. 23:15 [b]2Chr. 34:4

7 [I]Or, *tents;* lit., *houses* [a]1Kin. 14:24; 15:12 [b]Ex. 35:25, 26; Ezek. 16:16

8 [a]Josh. 21:17; 1Kin. 15:22

9 [a]Ezek. 44:10-14

10 [I]I.e., place of burning [a]Is. 30:33; Jer. 7:31, 32; 19:4-6 [b]Lev. 18:21 [c]1Kin. 11:7

11 [a]Deut. 4:19; Job 31:26; Ezek. 8:16

12 [I]Or, *ran from there* [a]Jer. 19:13; Zeph. 1:5 [b]2Kin. 21:5; 2Chr. 33:5 [c]2Kin. 23:4, 6

13 [a]1Kin. 11:7 [b]1Kin. 11:5 [c]Num. 21:29

14 [a]Deut. 7:5, 25 [b]2Kin. 23:16

15 [I]So the Gr.; Heb., *burned the high place* [a]1Kin. 13:1 [b]1Kin. 12:28-33 [c]2Kin. 23:6

16 [a]1Kin. 13:2

17 [a]1Kin. 13:1, 30, 31

18 [I]Lit., *let his bones escape with* [a]1Kin. 13:11, 31

19 [I]So with ancient versions [II]Lit., *according to all the acts* [a]2Chr. 34:6, 7

20 [a]2Kin. 10:25; 11:18

Passover Reinstituted

21 Then the king commanded all the
people saying, "[a]Celebrate[6213] the
Passover[6453] to the LORD your God
[b]as it is written in this book of the covenant."
22 [a]Surely such a Passover had not
been celebrated[6213] from the days[3117]
of the judges[8199] who judged[8199] Israel,
nor in all the days of the kings of Israel
and of the kings of Judah.
23 But in the eighteenth year of
King Josiah, this Passover was observed[6213] to the LORD in Jerusalem.
24 Moreover, Josiah [I]removed
[a]the mediums and the spiritists[3049] and
the [b]teraphim[8655] and [c]the idols[1544] and
all the abominations[8251] that were seen
in the land of Judah and in Jerusalem,
[d]that he might [II]confirm the words of
the law[8451] which were written [e]in the
book that Hilkiah the priest found in the
house of the LORD.
25 And before him there was no king
[a]like him who turned to the LORD with
all his heart and with all his soul and
with all his might, according to all the
law of Moses; nor did any like him arise
after him.
26 However, the LORD did not turn
from the fierceness of His great wrath[639]
with which His anger[639] burned[2734]
against Judah, [a]because of all the provocations with which Manasseh had provoked Him.
27 And the LORD said, "I will remove Judah also from My sight, [a]as I
have removed Israel. And [b]I will cast
off Jerusalem, this city which I have chosen,[977] and the [I]temple of which I said,
'My name shall be there.' "

Jehoahaz Succeeds Josiah

28 Now the rest of the acts[1697] of
Josiah and all that he did, are they not
written in the Book of the Chronicles
of the Kings of Judah?
29 [a]In his days [b]Pharaoh Neco king
of Egypt went up to the king of Assyria
to the river Euphrates. And King Josiah
went to meet him, and when *Pharaoh
Neco* saw him he killed him at [c]Megiddo.
30 And [a]his servants drove [I]his
body[4191] in a chariot from Megiddo, and
brought him to Jerusalem and buried[6912]
him in his own tomb.[6900] [b]Then the people of the land took Jehoahaz the son
of Josiah and anointed[4886] him and made
him king[4427] in place of his father.[1]
31 [a]Jehoahaz was twenty-three
years old when he became king, and
he reigned three months in Jerusalem;
and his mother's name was [b]Hamutal
the daughter of Jeremiah of Libnah.
32 And he did evil[7451] in the sight
of the LORD, [a]according to all that his
fathers[1] had done.
33 And [a]Pharaoh Neco imprisoned
him at [b]Riblah in the land of [c]Hamath,
that he might not reign in Jerusalem;
and he imposed on the land a fine of
one hundred talents of silver and a talent
of gold.

Jehoiakim Made King by Pharaoh

34 And Pharaoh Neco made
[a]Eliakim the son of Josiah king in the
place of Josiah his father,[1] and [b]changed
his name to Jehoiakim. But he took Jehoahaz away and [I][c]brought *him* to Egypt,
and he died[4191] there.
35 So Jehoiakim [a]gave the silver and
gold to Pharaoh, but he taxed the land
in order to give the money at the
[I]command of Pharaoh. He exacted the
silver and gold from the people of
the land, each according to his valuation, to give it to Pharaoh Neco.
36 [a]Jehoiakim was twenty-five
years old when he became king, and

21 [a]2Chr. 35:1-17 [b]Num. 9:2-4; Deut. 16:2-8
22 [a]2Chr. 35:18, 19
24 [I]Lit., *consumed* [II]Or, *perform* [a]Lev. 19:31; 2Kin. 21:6 [b]Gen. 31:19 mg. [c]2Kin. 21:11, 21 [d]Deut. 18:10-22 [e]2Kin. 22:8
25 [a]2Kin. 18:5
26 [a]2Kin. 21:11-13; Jer. 15:4
27 [I]Lit., *house* [a]2Kin. 18:11 [b]2Kin. 21:13,14
29 [a]2Chr. 35:20-24 [b]Jer. 46:2 [c]Judg. 5:19
30 [I]Lit., *him, dead* [a]2Kin. 9:28 [b]2Chr. 36:1-4
31 [a]1Chr. 3:15; Jer. 22:11 [b]2Kin. 24:18
32 [a]2Kin. 21:2-7
33 [a]2Kin. 23:29 [b]2Kin. 25:6 [c]1Kin. 8:65
34 [I]So with Gr.; Heb., *he came* [a]1Chr. 3:15 [b]2Kin. 24:17; 2Chr. 36:4 [c]Jer. 22:11, 12; Ezek. 19:3, 4
35 [I]Lit., *mouth* [a]2Kin. 23:33
36 [a]2Chr. 36:5; Jer. 22:18, 19; 26:1

23:21-23 See II Chr. 35:1-19.
23:28-30 See II Chr. 35:20—36:1.
23:31-34 See II Chr. 36:2-4.
23:35—24:7 See II Chr. 36:5-8.

he reigned eleven years in Jerusalem; and his mother's name *was* Zebidah the daughter of Pedaiah of Rumah.

37 And he did evil in the sight of the LORD, [a]according to all that his fathers had done.

Babylon Controls Jehoiakim

24 [a]In his <u>days</u>[3117] Nebuchadnezzar <u>king</u>[4428] of Babylon came up, and Jehoiakim became his servant *for* three years; then he turned and rebelled against him.

2 And the LORD sent against him [a]bands of Chaldeans, [b]bands of Arameans, [c]<u>bands</u>[1416] of Moabites, and bands of Ammonites. So He sent them against Judah to <u>destroy</u>[6] it, [d]according to the <u>word</u>[1697] of the LORD, which He had spoken through His servants the prophets.

3 [a]Surely at the [1]command of the LORD it came upon Judah, to remove *them* from His sight [b]because of the sins of Manasseh, according to all that he had <u>done</u>,[6213]

4 and [a]also for the <u>innocent</u>[5355] <u>blood</u>[1818] which he shed, for he filled Jerusalem with innocent blood; and the LORD <u>would</u>[14] not <u>forgive</u>.[5545]

5 Now the rest of the <u>acts</u>[1697] of Jehoiakim and all that he did, are they not written in the <u>Book</u>[5612] of the Chronicles of the <u>Kings</u>[4428] of Judah?

Jehoiachin Reigns

6 So [a]Jehoiakim slept with his <u>fathers</u>,[1] and Jehoiachin his son became king in his place.

7 And [a]the king of Egypt did not come out of his land again, [b]for the king of Babylon had taken all that belonged to the king of Egypt from [c]the brook of Egypt to the river Euphrates.

8 [a]Jehoiachin was [b]eighteen years old when he became king, and he reigned three months in Jerusalem; and his mother's name *was* Nehushta the daughter of Elnathan of Jerusalem.

9 And he did <u>evil</u>[7451] in the sight of the LORD, [a]according to all that his <u>father</u>[1] had <u>done</u>.[6213]

Deportation to Babylon

10 At that time the servants of Nebuchadnezzar king of Babylon went up to Jerusalem, and the city came under siege.

11 And Nebuchadnezzar the king of Babylon came to the city, while his servants were besieging it.

12 And [a]Jehoiachin the king of Judah went out to the king of Babylon, he and his mother and his servants and his captains and his officials. So [b]the king of Babylon took him captive in the eighth year of his reign.

13 And [a]he carried out from there all the treasures of the house of the LORD, and the treasures of the <u>king's</u>[4428] house, and [b]cut in pieces all the vessels of gold [c]which Solomon king of Israel had made in the temple of the LORD, just as the LORD had said.

14 Then [a]he led away into exile all Jerusalem and all the captains and all the mighty men of <u>valor</u>,[2428] [b]ten thousand <u>captives</u>,[1540] and [c]all the craftsmen and the smiths. None remained [d]except the poorest <u>people</u>[5971] of the land.

15 So [a]he led Jehoiachin away into exile to Babylon; also the king's mother and the king's <u>wives</u>[802] and his officials and the leading men of the land, he led away into <u>exile</u>[1473] from Jerusalem to Babylon.

16 And all the men of valor, [a]seven thousand, and the craftsmen and the

37 [a]2Kin. 23:32
1 [a]2Chr. 36:6; Jer. 25:1; Dan. 1:1, 2
2 [a]Jer. 35:11f. [b]2Kin. 6:23 [c]2Kin. 13:20 [d]2Kin. 23:27
3 [1]Lit., *mouth* [a]2Kin. 18:25 [b]2Kin. 23:26
4 [a]2Kin. 21:16
6 [a]Jer. 22:18, 19
7 [a]Jer. 37:5-7 [b]Jer. 46:2 [c]Gen. 15:18
8 [a]1Chr. 3:16 [b]2Chr. 36:9
9 [a]2Kin. 21:2-7
12 [a]Jer. 22:24-30; 24:1; 29:1, 2 [b]2Chr. 36:10
13 [a]2Kin. 20:17; Is. 39:6 [b]2Kin. 25:13-15 [c]1Kin. 7:48-50
14 [a]Jer. 24:1 [b]2Kin. 24:16; Jer. 52:28 [c]Jer. 24:1; 29:2 [d]2Kin. 25:12
15 [a]2Chr. 36:10; Jer. 22:24-28; Ezek. 17:12
16 [a]2Kin. 24:14

24:1 Babylonia had conquered Assyria and taken over its empire.

24:4 According to II Chr. 33:12,13. Manasseh himself had personally repented and found mercy from God. However, that did not remove the consequences of what he had done.

24:7 As Babylonia grew stronger and stronger, the power of Egypt waned.

24:8-17 See II Chr. 36:9,10.

smiths, one thousand, all strong and
fit[6213] for war, and these the king of
Babylon brought into exile to Babylon.

Zedekiah Made King

17 [a]Then the king[4428] of Babylon
made [I]his uncle Mattaniah, king in his
place, and changed his name to Zedekiah.
🔑 **18** [a]Zedekiah was twenty-one years
old when he became king, and he reigned
eleven years in Jerusalem; and his
mother's name *was* [b]Hamutal the daughter of Jeremiah of Libnah.
19 And he did evil in the sight of
the LORD, [a]according to all that Jehoiakim had done.
20 For [a]through the anger[639] of the
LORD *this* came about in Jerusalem and
Judah until He cast them out from His
presence. And [b]Zedekiah rebelled
against the king of Babylon.

Nebuchadnezzar Besieges Jerusalem

25 🔑 [a]Now it came about in the
ninth year of his reign, on the
tenth day of the tenth month, that
[b]Nebuchadnezzar king[4428] of Babylon
came, he and all his army, against Jerusalem, camped against it, and [c]built a
siege wall all around [I]it.
2 So the city was under siege until
the eleventh year of King Zedekiah.
🔑 3 On the ninth day of the *fourth*
month [a]the famine was so severe in the
city that there was no food for the
people[5971] of the land.
4 [a]Then the city was broken into,
and all the men of war *fled* by night[3915]
by way[1870] of the gate between the two
walls beside [b]the king's[4428] garden,
though the Chaldeans were all around
the city. And [I]they went by way of the
Arabah.[6160]
5 But the army[2428] of the Chaldeans
pursued the king and overtook him in
the plains[6160] of Jericho and all his army
was scattered from him.
6 Then [a]they captured the king and
[b]brought[5927] him to the king of Babylon
at [c]Riblah, and [I]he passed sentence[4941]
on him.
7 And [a]they slaughtered the sons
of Zedekiah before his eyes, then
[b]put out the eyes of Zedekiah and bound
him with bronze fetters and brought him
to Babylon.

Jerusalem Burned and Plundered

🔑 **8** [a]Now on the seventh day of the
[b]fifth month, which was the nineteenth
year of King Nebuchadnezzar, king of
Babylon, Nebuzaradan the captain of the
guard, a servant of the king of Babylon,
came to Jerusalem.
9 And [a]he burned[8313] the house of
the LORD, [b]the king's house, and all the
houses of Jerusalem; even every great
house he burned with fire.
10 So all the army of the Chaldeans
who *were with* the captain of the guard
[a]broke down the walls around Jerusalem.
11 Then [a]the rest of the people who
were left[7604] in the city and the
deserters[5307] who had deserted[5307] to
the king of Babylon and the rest of the
multitude, Nebuzaradan the captain of
the guard carried away into exile.
12 But the captain of the guard left
some of [a]the poorest of the land to be
vinedressers and plowmen.[1461]
13 [a]Now the bronze pillars which
were in the house of the LORD, and the
stands and [b]the bronze sea which were
in the house of the LORD, the Chaldeans

17 [I]I.e., Jehoiachin's uncle [a]2Chr. 36:10-13; Jer. 37:1
18 [a]Jer. 27:1; 28:1; 52:1 [b]2Kin. 23:31
19 [a]2Kin. 23:37
20 [a]Deut. 4:24; 29:27; 2Kin. 23:26 [b]2Chr. 36:13; Ezek. 17:15
1 [I]Lit., *against it* [a]2Chr. 36:17-20; Jer. 39:1-7 [b]Jer. 21:2; 34:1, 2; Ezek. 24:2 [c]Ezek. 21:22
3 [a]2Kin. 6:24, 25; Lam. 4:9, 10
4 [I]So some ancient mss. and versions; M.T., *he* [a]Ezek. 33:21 [b]Neh. 3:15
6 [I]Lit., *they spoke judgment with him* [a]Jer. 34:21, 22 [b]Jer. 32:4 [c]2Kin. 23:33
7 [a]Jer. 39:6, 7 [b]Ezek. 12:13
8 [a]Jer. 52:12 [b]Jer. 39:8-12
9 [a]1Kin. 9:8; 2Chr. 36:19; Ps. 74:3-7 [b]Amos 2:5
10 [a]2Kin. 14:13; Neh. 1:3
11 [a]2Chr. 36:20
12 [a]2Kin. 24:14; Jer. 40:7
13 [a]1Kin. 7:15-22; 2Kin. 20:17; 2Chr. 3:15-17; 36:18 [b]1Kin. 7:23-26; 2Chr. 4:2-4

🔑 **24:18-20** See II Chr. 36:11,12; Jer. 52:1-3.
🔑 **25:1-7** See II Chr. 36:13-21; Jer. 52:3-11.
🔑 **25:3** Compare Jer. 39:2,4; 52:6,7. One should read Jer. 39 and 40 to understand these critical events better.
🔑 **25:8-17** See Jer. 52:12-23.

broke[7665] in pieces and carried[5375] the [I]bronze to Babylon.

14 [a]And they took away the pots, the shovels, the snuffers, the spoons, and all the bronze vessels which were used in *temple* service.

15 The captain of the guard also took away the firepans and the basins, what was fine gold and what was fine silver.

16 The two pillars, the one sea, and the stands which Solomon had made for the house of the LORD—[a]the bronze of all these vessels was beyond weight.

17 [a]The height of the one pillar was eighteen [I]cubits, and a bronze capital was on it; the height of the capital was three [I]cubits, with a network[7639] and pomegranates on the capital all around, all of bronze. And the second pillar was like these with network.

🔑**18** Then the captain of the guard took [a]Seraiah the chief[7218] priest and [b]Zephaniah the second priest, with the three [I]officers[8104] of the temple.

19 And from the city he took one official who was overseer of the men of war, and [a]five [I]of the king's advisers who were found in the city; and the [II]scribe of the captain of the army, who mustered the people of the land; and sixty men of the people of the land who were found in the city.

20 And Nebuzaradan the captain of the guard took them and brought them to the king of Babylon at [a]Riblah.

21 Then the king of Babylon struck them down and put them to death at Riblah in the land of Hamath. [a]So Judah was led away into exile from its land.[127]

Gedaliah Made Governor

🔑**22** Now *as for* the people who were left in the land of Judah, whom Nebuchadnezzar king of Babylon had left, he appointed [a]Gedaliah the son of Ahikam, the son of Shaphan over them.

23 [a]When all the captains[8269] of the forces,[2428] they and *their* men, heard that the king of Babylon had appointed Gedaliah *governor*,[6485] they came to Gedaliah to [b]Mizpah, namely, Ishmael the son of Nethaniah, and Johanan the son of Kareah, and Seraiah the son of Tanhumeth the Netophathite, and Jaazaniah the son of the Maacathite, they and their men.

24 And Gedaliah swore to them and their men and said to them, "Do not be afraid[3372] of the servants of the Chaldeans; live in the land and serve the king of Babylon, and it will be well[3190] with you."

25 [a]But it came about in the seventh month, that Ishmael the son of Nethaniah, the son of Elishama, of the royal [I]family, came [II]with ten men and struck Gedaliah down so that he died[4191] along with the Jews and the Chaldeans who were with him at Mizpah.

26 [a]Then all the people, both small and great, and the captains of the forces arose and went to Egypt; for they were afraid[3372] of the Chaldeans.

🔑**27** [a]Now it came about in the thirty-seventh year of [b]the exile[1546] of Jehoiachin king of Judah, in the twelfth month, on the twenty-seventh *day* of the month, that Evil-merodach king of Babylon, in the year that he became king, [I][c]released Jehoiachin king of Judah from prison;

13 [I]Lit., *bronze of them*
14 [a]Ex. 27:3; 1Kin. 7:47-50; 2Chr. 4:16
16 [a]1Kin. 7:47
17 [I]I.e., One cubit equals approx. 18 in. [a]1Kin. 7:15-22
18 [I]Lit., *keepers of the door* [a]1Chr. 6:14; Ezra 7:1 [b]Jer. 21:1; 29:25, 29
19 [I]Lit., *men of those seeing the king's face* [II]Or, *scribe, a captain* [a]Esth. 1:14
20 [a]2Kin. 23:33
21 [a]Deut. 28:64; 2Kin. 23:27
22 [a]Jer. 39:14; 40:7-9
23 [a]Jer. 40:7-9 [b]Josh. 18:26
25 [I]Lit., *seed* [II]Lit., *and ten men with him* [a]Jer. 41:1, 2
26 [a]Jer. 43:4-7
27 [I]Lit., *lifted up the head of* [a]Jer. 52:31-34 [b]2Kin. 24:12, 15 [c]Gen. 40:13, 20

🔑**25:18-21** See Jer. 52:24-27.

🔑**25:22** Shaphan had been King Josiah's secretary. The book which was found in the temple was handed to him. After he read it, he took it to King Josiah (II Kgs. 22:8-13).

🔑**25:22-26** See Jer. 40:7-9; 41:1-3.

🔑**25:27** Evil-merodach was the son of Nebuchadnezzar and reigned from 561 to 560 B.C. His Babylonian name was Amel-Marduk meaning "man of Marduk." The prefix "Evil" has nothing to do with the modern English term. The Babylonians respected Jehoiachin as the rightful king of Judah. Cuneiform tablets of that period have been found mentioning the provisions which were supplied to Jehoiachin and his five sons.

🔑**25:27-30** See Jer. 52:31-34.

28 and he [a]spoke kindly[2896] to him and set his throne above the throne of the kings[4428] who *were* with him in Babylon.

🗝 29 And [I]Jehoiachin changed his prison clothes, and [II][a]had his meals in [III]the king's presence regularly all the days[3117] of his life;[2416]

30 and for his [a]allowance, a regular[8548] allowance was given him by the king, a portion for each day,[3117] all the days of his life

28 [a]Dan. 2:37; 5:18, 19
29 [I]Lit., *he* [II]Lit., *ate bread* [III]Lit., *his presence* [a]2Sam. 9:7
30 [a]Neh. 11:23; 12:47

🗝 **25:29** Evil-Merodach ruled for only two years. His brother-in-law assassinated him in 560 B.C.

The First Book of the

CHRONICLES

The name "Chronicles" was coined by Jerome, the famous Latin Bible translator. The Jews called I and II Chronicles by another name—"the words of the days." Originally appearing in the Hebrew Bible as one volume, they constitute a recapitulation of everything which preceded them. (The Books of Chronicles are the last books in the Hebrew Bible.) They retell the same story and end with the same conclusions. However, special attention is given to the rule of David, Solomon, and the kings of the southern kingdom (Judah). I Chronicles is similar to II Samuel except that I Chronicles is prefaced by massive genealogies from the beginning of time until the Babylonian Captivity. Jewish tradition says that the author was Ezra, who led them back from exile. Whoever the author was, he had access to many historical archives which have not been preserved. Guided under the inspiration of God, the writer penned what suited his purpose. Though there is much repetitive material and some double narratives, we must not be lulled into thinking that these accounts are not an important part of God's revelation. God is constantly involved with His people. When they obey, God blesses them. When they disobey, God cancels their spiritual privileges. We must be faithful to God. I Chronicles is not to be confused with the lost chronicles of Israel mentioned in I and II Kings. The Books of Chronicles were written after the Books of Kings. I and II Chronicles were compiled after the Jews returned from the Babylonian exile (II Chr. 36:21-23) in the priestly and legal spirit of Ezra.

Genealogy from Adam

1 [a]Adam, Seth, Enosh,
2 Kenan, Mahalalel, Jared,
3 Enoch, Methuselah, Lamech,
4 Noah, Shem, Ham and Japheth.
5 [a]The sons of Japheth *were* Gomer,
Magog, Madai, Javan, Tubal, Meshech,
and Tiras.
6 And the sons of Gomer *were*
Ashkenaz, [I]Diphath, and Togarmah.
7 And the sons of Javan *were* Elishah, Tarshish, Kittim, and [I]Rodanim.
8 The sons of Ham *were* Cush,
Mizraim, Put, and Canaan.
9 And the sons of Cush *were* Seba,
Havilah, Sabta, Raama, and Sabteca; and
the sons of Raamah *were* Sheba and Dedan.
10 And Cush [I]became the father of
Nimrod; he began to be a mighty one
in the earth.[776]
11 [a]And Mizraim became the father
of the people of Lud, Anam, Lehab,
Naphtuh,
12 Pathrus, Casluh, from which the
[I]Philistines came, and Caphtor.
13 And Canaan became the father
of Sidon, his first-born, Heth,
14 and the Jebusites, the Amorites,
the Girgashites,
15 the Hivites, the Arkites, the
Sinites,
16 the Arvadites, the Zemarites,
and the Hamathites.
17 [a]The sons of Shem *were* Elam,
Asshur, Arpachshad, Lud, Aram, Uz,
Hul, Gether, and [I]Meshech.
18 And Arpachshad became the father of Shelah and Shelah became the
father of Eber.
19 And two sons were born to Eber,
the name of the one was Peleg, for in
his days[3117] the earth was divided,[6385]
and his brother's[251] name was Joktan.
20 And Joktan became the father
of Almodad, Sheleph, Hazarmaveth,
Jerah,
21 Hadoram, Uzal, Diklah,
22 [I]Ebal, Abimael, Sheba,

1 [a]Gen. 4:25-5:32
5 [a]Gen. 10:2-4
6 [I]In Gen. 10:3, *Riphath*
7 [I]In Gen. 10:4, *Dodanim*
10 [I]Lit., *begot,* and so through out the ch.
11 [a]Gen. 10:13-18
12 [I]Or, *people of Pelisht*
17 [I]In Gen. 10:23, *Mash* [a]Gen. 10:22-29
22 [I]In Gen. 10:28, *Obal*

1:1-4 See Gen. 5:1-32.
1:5-23 See Gen. 10:1-32.

23 Ophir, Havilah, and Jobab; all these *were* the sons of Joktan.
🔑 **24** [a]Shem, Arpachshad, Shelah,
25 Eber, Peleg, Reu,
26 Serug, Nahor, Terah,
27 Abram, that is Abraham.

Descendants of Abraham

🔑 **28** The sons of Abraham *were* Isaac and Ishmael.
29 [a]These are their genealogies:[8535] the first-born of Ishmael *was* Nebaioth, then Kedar, Adbeel, Mibsam,
30 Mishma, Dumah, Massa, Hadad, Tema,
31 Jetur, Naphish and Kedemah; these *were* the sons of Ishmael.
32 [a]And the sons of Keturah, Abraham's concubine, *whom* she bore, *were* Zimran, Jokshan, Medan, Midian, Ishbak, and Shuah. And the sons of Jokshan *were* Sheba and Dedan.
33 And the sons of Midian *were* Ephah, Epher, Hanoch, Abida, and Eldaah. All these were the sons of Keturah.
🔑 34 And [a]Abraham became the father of Isaac. The sons of Isaac *were* [b]Esau and Israel.
35 [a]The sons of Esau *were* Eliphaz, Reuel, Jeush, Jalam, and Korah.
36 The sons of Eliphaz *were* Teman, Omar, [I]Zephi, Gatam, Kenaz, Timna, and Amalek.
37 The sons of Reuel *were* Nahath, Zerah, Shammah, and Mizzah.
🔑 38 [a]And the sons of Seir *were* Lotan, Shobal, Zibeon, Anah, Dishon, Ezer, and Dishan.
39 And the sons of Lotan *were* Hori and [I]Homam; and Lotan's sister[269] *was* Timna.
40 The sons of Shobal *were* [I]Alian, Manahath, Ebal, [II]Shephi, and Onam.

24 [a]Gen. 11:10-26; Luke 3:34-36
29 [a]Gen. 25:13-16
32 [a]Gen. 25:1-4
34 [a]1Chr. 1:28 [b]Gen. 25:25, 26; 32:28
35 [a]Gen. 36:4-10
36 [I]In Gen. 36:11, *Zepho*
38 [a]Gen. 36:20-28
39 [I]In Gen. 36:22, *Hemam*
40 [I]In Gen. 36:23, *Alvan* [II]In Gen. 36:23, *Shepho*
41 [I]Lit., *sons* [II]In Gen. 36:26, *Hemdan*
42 [I]Or, *Akan*, as in Gen. 36:27
43 [a]Gen. 36:31-43
44 [a]Is. 34:6
45 [a]Job 2:11
46 [I]Lit., *smote*
50 [I]In Gen. 36:39, *Hadar* [II]In Gen. 36:39, *Pau*
51 [I]In Gen. 36:40, *Alvah*

And the sons of Zibeon *were* Aiah and Anah.
41 The [I]son of Anah *was* Dishon. And the sons of Dishon *were* [II]Hamran, Eshban, Ithran, and Cheran.
42 The sons of Ezer *were* Bilhan, Zaavan and [I]Jaakan. The sons of Dishan *were* Uz and Aran.
43 [a]Now these are the kings[4428] who reigned in the land[776] of Edom before any king[4428] of the sons[1121] of Israel reigned. Bela *was* the son of Beor, and the name of his city was Dinhabah.
44 When Bela died,[4191] Jobab the son of Zerah of [a]Bozrah became king in his place.
45 When Jobab died, Husham of the land of [a]the Temanites became king in his place.
46 When Husham died, Hadad the son of Bedad, who [I]defeated Midian in the field[7704] of Moab, became king in his place; and the name of his city *was* Avith.
47 When Hadad died, Samlah of Masrekah became king in his place.
48 When Samlah died, Shaul of Rehoboth by the River became king in his place.
49 When Shaul died, Baal-hanan the son of Achbor became king in his place.
50 When Baal-hanan died, [I]Hadad became king in his place; and the name of his city was [II]Pai, and his wife's[802] name was Mehetabel, the daughter of Matred, the daughter of Mezahab.
51 Then Hadad died.[4191] Now the chiefs of Edom were: chief Timna, chief [I]Aliah, chief Jetheth,
52 chief Oholibamah, chief Elah, chief Pinon,
53 chief Kenaz, chief Teman, chief Mibzar,
54 chief Magdiel, chief Iram. These *were* the chiefs of Edom.

🔑 **1:24-27** See Gen. 11:10-26.
🔑 **1:28-33** See Gen. 25:1-6,12-18.
🔑 **1:34-54** See Gen. 36:1-43.
🔑 **1:38** Seir belonged to the Horites (Gen. 36:20). They were an important people who dwelled among the rocks. Some of them settled in Edom before the arrival of Esau (Deut. 2:12,22).

Genealogy: Twelve Sons of Jacob (Israel)

2 🔑 [a]These are the sons of Israel: Reuben, Simeon, Levi, Judah, Issachar, Zebulun,

2 Dan, Joseph, Benjamin, Naphtali, Gad, and Asher.

3 [a]The sons of Judah *were* Er, Onan, and Shelah; *these* three were born to him by Bath-shua the Canaanitess. And Er, Judah's first-born, was wicked[7451] in the sight of the LORD, so He put him to death.

🔑 4 And [a]Tamar his daughter-in-law bore him Perez and Zerah. Judah had five sons in all.

5 The sons of Perez *were* Hezron and Hamul.

6 And the sons of Zerah *were* [I]Zimri, Ethan, Heman, Calcol, and [II]Dara; five of them in all.

7 And the [I]son of Carmi *was* [II][a]Achar, the troubler of Israel, who violated the ban.[2764]

8 And the [I]son of Ethan *was* Azariah.

Genealogy of David

9 Now the sons of Hezron, who were born to him *were* Jerahmeel, Ram, and Chelubai.

10 And Ram [I]became the father of Amminadab, and Amminadab became the father of Nahshon, leader of the sons[1121] of Judah;

11 Nahshon became the father of Salma, Salma became the father of Boaz,

12 Boaz became the father of Obed, and Obed became the father of Jesse;

13 and Jesse became the father of Eliab his first-born, then Abinadab the second, [I]Shimea the third,

14 Nethanel the fourth, Raddai the fifth,

🔑 15 Ozem the sixth, David the seventh;

🔑 16 and their sisters[269] *were* Zeruiah and Abigail. And the three sons of Zeruiah *were* [I]Abshai, Joab, and Asahel.

17 And Abigail bore Amasa, and the father[1] of Amasa was [I]Jether the Ishmaelite.

18 Now Caleb the son of Hezron had sons by Azubah *his* wife,[802] and by Jerioth; and these were her sons: Jesher, Shobab, and Ardon.

19 When Azubah died,[4191] Caleb married Ephrath, who bore him Hur.

20 And Hur became the father of Uri, and Uri became the father of Bezalel.

21 Afterward Hezron went in to the daughter of Machir the father of Gilead, whom he married when he was sixty years old; and she bore him Segub.

22 And Segub became the father of Jair, who had twenty-three cities in the land[776] of Gilead.

🔑 23 But Geshur and Aram took [I]the towns of Jair from them, with Kenath and its villages, *even* sixty cities. All these were the sons of Machir, the father of Gilead.

24 And after the death[4194] of Hezron in Caleb-ephrathah, Abijah, Hezron's wife, bore him Ashhur the father of Tekoa.

25 Now the sons of Jerahmeel the first-born of Hezron *were* Ram the first-born, then Bunah, Oren, Ozem, *and* Ahijah.

26 And Jerahmeel had another wife, whose name was Atarah; she was the mother[517] of Onam.

27 And the sons of Ram, the first-born of Jerahmeel, were Maaz, Jamin, and Eker.

28 And the sons of Onam were Shammai and Jada. And the sons of Shammai *were* Nadab and Abishur.

---

1 [a]Gen. 35:22-26; 46:8-25

3 [a]Gen. 38:2-10

4 [a]Gen. 38:13-30

6 [I]In Josh. 7:1, *Zabdi* [II]In 1Kin. 4:31, *Darda*

7 [I]Lit., *sons* [II]In Josh. 7:18, *Achan* [a]Josh. 7:1

8 [I]Lit., *sons*

10 [I]Lit., *begot,* and so through out the ch.

13 [I]In 1Sam. 16:9, *Shammah;* in 2Sam. 13:3, *Shimeah*

16 [I]In 2Sam. 2:18, *Abishai*

17 [I]In 2Sam. 17:25, *Ithra the Israelite*

23 [I]Or, *Havvoth-jair*

🔑 **2:1,2** See Gen. 35:22-26.

🔑 **2:4** See Gen. 38 for more details.

🔑 **2:15** There was a seventh son who was not named (I Sam. 16:10; 17:12). Actually, David was the eighth son.

🔑 **2:16** These two sisters were half-sisters, apparently by a different father (II Sam. 17:25).

🔑 **2:23** See Num. 32:41,42; Deut. 3:14.

29 And the name of Abishur's wife *was* Abihail, and she bore him Ahban and Molid.

30 And the sons of Nadab *were* Seled and Appaim, and Seled died[4191] without sons.

31 And the [I]son of Appaim *was* Ishi. And the [I]son of Ishi *was* Sheshan. And the [I]son of Sheshan *was* Ahlai.

32 And the sons of Jada the brother[251] of Shammai *were* Jether and Jonathan, and Jether died without sons.

33 And the sons of Jonathan *were* Peleth and Zaza. These were the sons of Jerahmeel.

34 Now Sheshan had no sons, only daughters. And Sheshan had an Egyptian servant whose name was Jarha.

35 And Sheshan gave his daughter to Jarha his servant in marriage, and she bore him Attai.

36 And Attai became the father of Nathan, and Nathan became the father of Zabad,

37 and Zabad became the father of Ephlal, and Ephlal became the father of Obed,

38 and Obed became the father of Jehu, and Jehu became the father of Azariah,

39 and Azariah became the father of Helez, and Helez became the father of Eleasah,

40 and Eleasah became the father of Sismai, and Sismai became the father of Shallum,

41 and Shallum became the father of Jekamiah, and Jekamiah became the father of Elishama.

42 Now the sons of Caleb, the brother of Jerahmeel, *were* Mesha his first-born, who was the father of Ziph; and [I]his son was Mareshah, the father of Hebron.

43 And the sons of Hebron *were* Korah and Tappuah and Rekem and Shema.

31 [I]Lit., *sons*

42 [I]Lit., *the sons of*

50 [I]Lit., *son*

44 And Shema became the father of Raham, the father of Jorkeam; and Rekem became the father of Shammai.

45 And the son of Shammai was Maon, and Maon *was* the father of Bethzur.

46 And Ephah, Caleb's concubine, bore Haran, Moza, and Gazez; and Haran became the father of Gazez.

47 And the sons of Jahdai *were* Regem, Jotham, Geshan, Pelet, Ephah, and Shaaph.

48 Maacah, Caleb's concubine, bore Sheber and Tirhanah.

🔑 49 She also bore Shaaph the father of Madmannah, Sheva the father of Machbena and the father of Gibea; and the daughter of Caleb *was* Achsah.

50 These were the sons of Caleb.
The [I]sons of Hur, the first-born of Ephrathah, *were* Shobal the father of Kiriath-jearim,

51 Salma the father of Bethlehem *and* Hareph the father of Bethgader.

52 And Shobal the father of Kiriath-jearim had sons: Haroeh, half of the Manahathites,

53 and the families[4940] of Kiriath-jearim: the Ithrites, the Puthites, the Shumathites, and the Mishraites; from these came the Zorathites and the Eshtaolites.

54 The sons of Salma *were* Bethlehem and the Netophathites, Atroth-beth-joab and half of the Manahathites, the Zorites.

🔑 55 And the families of scribes who lived at Jabez *were* the Tirathites, the Shimeathites, *and* the Sucathites. Those are the Kenites who came from Hammath, the father of the house of Rechab.

🔑 **2:49** Achsah was actually a distant descendant of this Caleb, son of Hezron, and an immediate daughter of Caleb, the faithful spy, son of Jephunneh. She was made famous as the bride of Othniel, because she had been given to him because of his conquest of Debir (Josh. 15:15-19; Judg. 1:11-15).

🔑 **2:55** The Kenites were from the family of Hobab, the brother-in-law of Moses. They became incorporated by marriage (or adoption) into the tribe of Judah (Judg. 1:16). Jehonadab (Jonadab), a later descendant of Rechab, was noted as a reformer who kept himself pure (II Kgs. 10:15,23-28; Jer. 35).

Family of David

3 🔑 [a]Now these were the sons of
David who were born to him in Hebron: the first-born *was* Amnon, by
Ahinoam the Jezreelitess; the second
was Daniel, by Abigail the Carmelitess;
2 the third *was* Absalom the son of
Maacah, the daughter of Talmai king[4428]
of Geshur; the fourth *was* Adonijah the
son of Haggith;
3 the fifth *was* Shephatiah, by Abital;
the sixth *was* Ithream, by his wife[802]
Eglah.
4 Six were born to him in Hebron,
and [a]there he reigned seven years and
six months. And in Jerusalem he reigned
thirty-three years.
🔑 5 [a]And these were born to him in
Jerusalem: Shimea, Shobab, Nathan,
and [b]Solomon, four, by [c]Bath-shua the
daughter of Ammiel;
6 and Ibhar, Elishama, Eliphelet,
7 Nogah, Nepheg, and Japhia,
8 Elishama, Eliada, and Eliphelet,
nine.
🔑 9 All *these were* the sons of David,
besides the sons of the concubines; and
[a]Tamar *was* their sister.[269]
10 Now Solomon's son *was* Rehoboam, Abijah *was* his son, Asa his son,
Jehoshaphat his son,
11 Joram his son, Ahaziah his son,
Joash his son,
12 Amaziah his son, Azariah his son,
Jotham his son,
13 Ahaz his son, Hezekiah his son,
Manasseh his son,
14 Amon his son, Josiah his son.
🔑 15 And the sons of Josiah *were* Johanan the first-born, and the second *was*
Jehoiakim, the third Zedekiah, the fourth
Shallum.
🔑 16 And the sons of Jehoiakim *were*
Jeconiah his son, Zedekiah his son.
🔑 17 And the sons of Jeconiah, the
prisoner, *were* Shealtiel his son,
18 and Malchiram, Pedaiah, Shenazzar, Jekamiah, Hoshama, and Nedabiah.
🔑 19 And the sons of Pedaiah *were*
Zerubbabel and Shimei. And the [I]sons
of Zerubbabel *were* Meshullam and
Hananiah, and Shelomith *was* their sister;
20 and Hashubah, Ohel, Berechiah,
Hasadiah, and Jushab-hesed, five.
21 And the [I]sons of Hananiah *were*
Pelatiah and Jeshaiah, the sons of Rephaiah, the sons of Arnan, the sons of
Obadiah, the sons of Shecaniah.
22 And the [I]son of Shecaniah *was*
Shemaiah, and the sons of Shemaiah
were Hattush, Igal, Bariah, Neariah, and
Shaphat, six.
23 And the [I]sons of Neariah *were*
Elioenai, Hizkiah, and Azrikam, three.
24 And the sons of Elioenai *were*
Hodaviah, Eliashib, Pelaiah, Akkub,
Johanan, Delaiah, and Anani, seven.

1 [a]2Sam. 3:2-5
4 [a]2Sam. 2:11; 5:4, 5; 1Kin. 2:11; 1Chr. 29:27
5 [a]2Sam. 5:14-16; 1Chr. 14:4-7 [b]2Sam. 12:24, 25 [c]2Sam. 11:3
9 [a]2Sam. 13:1
19 [I]Lit., *son*
21 [I]Lit., *son*
22 [I]Lit., *sons*
23 [I]Lit., *son*

Line of Hur, Asher

4 [a]The sons of Judah *were* Perez,
Hezron, Carmi, Hur, and Shobal.
2 And Reaiah the son of Shobal
[I]became the father of Jahath, and Jahath
became the father of Ahumai and Lahad.
These *were* the families[4940] of the Zorathites.
3 And these *were* the [I]sons of Etam:

1 [a]1Chr. 2:3
2 [I]Lit., *begot*, and so through out the ch.
3 [I]So with some ancient versions; Heb., *father*

🔑 **3:1-9** See II Sam. 3:2-5; 5:13-16; I Chr. 14:3-7.
🔑 **3:5** Bath-shua is the same as Bathsheeba. This list occurs in I Chr. 14:4-7 and II Sam. 5:14-16.
🔑 **3:9** Tamar was raped by Amnon and avenged by Absalom (see II Sam. 13).
🔑 **3:15** Shallum was also called Jehoahaz (II Kgs. 23:31; II Chr. 36:2; cf. Jer. 22:11). Actually, he was older than Zedekiah (II Kings. 24:18), but he ruled for a shorter time.
🔑 **3:16** Jeconiah was also called Coniah (Jer. 22:24,28; 37:1) and Jehoiachin (II Kgs. 24:8,12; II Chr. 36:9).
🔑 **3:17** Shealtiel may have been a legal son. Lk. 3:27 says that he was the son of Neri.
🔑 **3:19** Zerubbabel was reckoned as a son of Pedaiah's brother, Shealtiel (Ezr. 3:2; Hag. 1:1,12; Mt. 1:12; Lk. 3:27). Perhaps this occurred through the custom of levirate marriage (Deut. 25:5-10). He was a leader in the return of the Jews to Palestine after the exile in 538 B.C. (Ezr. 2:2; 3:2) and an heir to the throne of David.

Jezreel, Ishma, and Idbash; and the name of their sister[269] *was* Hazzelelponi.

4 And Penuel *was* the father of Gedor, and Ezer the father of Hushah. These *were* the sons of Hur, the firstborn of Ephrathah, the father of Bethlehem.

5 And Ashhur, the father of Tekoa, had two wives,[802] Helah and Naarah.

6 And Naarah bore him Ahuzzam, Hepher, Temeni, and Haahashtari. These were the sons of Naarah.

7 And the sons of Helah *were* Zereth, [I]Izhar and Ethnan.

8 And Koz became the father of Anub and Zobebah, and the families of Aharhel the son of Harum.

9 And Jabez was more honorable than his brothers,[251] and his mother[517] named[7121] him Jabez saying, "Because I bore *him* with pain."

10 Now Jabez called on the God[430] of Israel, saying, "Oh that Thou wouldst bless[1288] me indeed, and enlarge my border, and that Thy hand might be with me, and that Thou wouldst keep[6213] *me* from harm,[7451] that *it* may not pain[6087] me!" And God granted him what he requested.

11 And Chelub the brother[251] of Shuhah became the father of Mehir, who was the father of Eshton.

12 And Eshton became the father of Beth-rapha and Paseah, and Tehinnah the father of [I]Ir-nahash. These are the men[582] of Recah.

🔑 **13** Now the sons of Kenaz *were* Othniel and Seraiah. And the [I]son of Othniel *was* Hathath.

14 And Meonothai became the father of Ophrah, and Seraiah became the father of Joab the father of [I]Geharashim, for they were craftsmen.

🔑 15 And the sons of Caleb the son of Jephunneh *were* Iru, Elah and Naam; and the [I]son of Elah *was* [II]Kenaz.

16 And the sons of Jehallelel *were* Ziph and Ziphah, Tiria and Asarel.

17 And the [I]sons of Ezrah *were* Jether, Mered, Epher, and Jalon. ([II]And these are the sons of Bithia the daughter of Pharaoh, whom Mered took) and she conceived *and bore* Miriam, Shammai, and Ishbah the father of Eshtemoa.

18 And his Jewish wife[802] bore Jered the father of Gedor, and Heber the father of Soco, and Jekuthiel the father of Zanoah.

19 And the sons of the wife of Hodiah, the sister of Naham, *were* the [I]fathers of Keilah the Garmite and Eshtemoa the Maacathite.

20 And the sons of Shimon *were* Amnon and Rinnah, Benhanan and Tilon. And the sons of Ishi *were* Zoheth and Ben-zoheth.

21 The sons of Shelah the son of Judah *were* Er the father of Lecah and Laadah the father of Mareshah, and the families of the house of the linen workers[5656] at Beth-ashbea;

22 and Jokim, the men of Cozeba, Joash, Saraph, who ruled[1166] in Moab, and Jashubi-lehem. And the [I]records are ancient.

23 These were the potters and the inhabitants of Netaim and Gederah; they lived there with the king[4428] for his work.[4399]

Descendants of Simeon

24 The sons of Simeon *were* [I]Nemuel and Jamin, [II]Jarib, [III]Zerah, Shaul;

25 Shallum his son, Mibsam his son, Mishma his son.

26 And the sons of Mishma *were* Hammuel his son, Zaccur his son, Shimei his son.

27 Now Shimei had sixteen sons and six daughters; but his brothers did not have many sons,[1121] nor did all their family[4940] multiply like the sons of Judah.

28 And they lived at Beersheba, Moladah, and Hazar-shual,

7 [I]Another reading is *Zohar*

12 [I]Or, *the city of Nahash*

13 [I]Lit., *sons*

14 [I]Or, *valley of craftsmen*

15 [I]Lit., *sons* [II]Lit., *and Kenaz*

17 [I]Lit., *son* [II]In the Heb. the words in () are at the end of v. 18

19 [I]Lit., *father*

22 [I]Lit., *words*

24 [I]In Gen. 46:10 and Ex. 6:15, *Jemuel* [II]In Num. 26:12, *Jachin* [III]In Gen. 46:10 and Ex. 6:15, *Zohar*

🔑 **4:13** Othniel was the first of the judges (Judg. 3:9,10), about 1381 B.C.

🔑 **4:15** Caleb was the faithful spy (see Num. 13 and 14).

29 at Bilhah, Ezem, Tolad,
30 Bethuel, Hormah, Ziklag,
31 Beth-marcaboth, Hazar-susim, Beth-biri, and Shaaraim. These *were* their cities until the reign of David.
32 And their villages *were* Etam, Ain, Rimmon, Tochen, and Ashan, five cities;
33 and all their villages that *were* around the same cities as far as [I]Baal. These *were* their settlements, and they have their genealogy.
34 And Meshobab and Jamlech and Joshah the son of Amaziah,
35 and Joel and Jehu the son of Joshibiah, the son of Seraiah, the son of Asiel,
36 and Elioenai, Jaakobah, Jeshohaiah, Asaiah, Adiel, Jesimiel, Benaiah,
37 Ziza the son of Shiphi, the son of Allon, the son of Jedaiah, the son of Shimri, the son of Shemaiah;
38 these mentioned by name *were* leaders in their families; and their fathers'[1] houses increased greatly.
39 And they went to the entrance of Gedor, even to the east side of the valley, to seek pasture for their flocks.
40 And they found rich and good[2896] pasture, and [a]the land[776] was broad and quiet and peaceful; for those who lived there formerly *were* Hamites.
41 And [a]these, recorded by name, came in the days[3117] of Hezekiah king of Judah, and [I]attacked their tents, and the Meunites who were found there, and destroyed[2763] them utterly to this day,[3117] and lived in their place; because there was pasture there for their flocks.
42 And from them, from the sons of Simeon, five hundred men went to [a]Mount Seir, with Pelatiah, Neariah, Rephaiah, and Uzziel, the sons of Ishi, as their leaders.[7218]
🔑43 And [a]they [I]destroyed the remnant of the Amalekites who escaped,[6413] and have lived there to this day.

33 [I]In Josh. 19:8, *Baalath*
40 [a]Judg. 18:7-10
41 [I]Lit., *smote* [a]1Chr. 4:33-38
42 [a]Gen. 36:8, 9
43 [I]Lit., *smote* [a]1Sam. 15:7, 8; 30:17
1 [a]Gen. 29:32; 1Chr. 2:1 [b]Gen. 35:22; 49:4 [c]Gen. 48:15-22
2 [a]Gen. 49:8-10; Ps. 60:7; 108:8 [b]Mic. 5:2; Matt. 2:6
3 [a]Gen. 46:9; Ex. 6:14; Num. 26:5-9
4 [a]1Chr. 5:8
6 [I]In 2Kin. 15:29, *Tiglath-pileser*
7 [I]Lit., *brothers* [a]1Chr. 5:17
8 [a]Num. 32:34; Josh. 12:2
9 [a]Josh. 22:8, 9
10 [I]Lit., *dwelt in* [II]Lit., *all the face of the east* [a]1Chr. 5:18-21

Genealogy from Reuben

5 Now the sons of Reuben the first-born of Israel (for [a]he was the first-born, but because [b]he defiled[2490] his father's[1] bed, [c]his birthright[1062] was given to the sons of Joseph the son of Israel; so that he is not enrolled in the genealogy according to the birthright.
2 [a]Though Judah prevailed over his brothers,[251] and [b]from him *came* the leader, yet the birthright belonged to Joseph),
3 [a]the sons of Reuben the first-born of Israel *were* Hanoch and Pallu, Hezron and Carmi.
4 The sons of Joel *were* Shemaiah his son, Gog his son, [a]Shimei his son,
5 Micah his son, Reaiah his son, Baal his son,
🔑6 Beerah his son, whom [I]Tilgath-pilneser king[4428] of Assyria carried away into exile;[1540] he was leader of the Reubenites.
7 And his [I]kinsmen by their families,[4940] [a]in the genealogy of their generations,[8435] *were* Jeiel the chief,[7218] then Zechariah
8 and Bela the son of Azaz, the son of Shema, the son of Joel, who lived in [a]Aroer, even to Nebo and Baal-meon.
9 And to the east he settled as far as the entrance of the wilderness from the river Euphrates, [a]because their cattle had increased in the land[776] of Gilead.
🔑10 And in the days[3117] of Saul [a]they made[6213] war with the Hagrites, who fell[5307] by their hand, so that they [I]occupied their tents throughout [II]all the land east of Gilead.
11 Now the sons[1121] of Gad lived

🔑**4:43** Both Saul and David had won great victories over the Amalekites (I Sam. 14:48; 15:7; II Sam. 8:12).
🔑**5:6** Elsewhere it is spelled Tiglath-pileser. This probably refers to the preliminary captivity of the two and one-half tribes of the other side of the Jordan River in 733 B.C. (see v. 26 and II Kgs. 15:29). It is not referring to the final fall of Samaria in 722 B.C.
🔑**5:10** In 1050-1010 B.C.

opposite them in the land of [a]Bashan as far as [b]Salecah.

12 Joel *was* the chief, and Shapham the second, then Janai and Shaphat in Bashan.

13 And their [I]kinsmen of their fathers'[1] households *were* Michael, Meshullam, Sheba, Jorai, Jacan, Zia, and Eber, seven.

14 These *were* the sons of Abihail, the son of Huri, the son of Jaroah, the son of Gilead, the son of Michael, the son of Jeshishai, the son of Jahdo, the son of Buz;

15 Ahi the son of Abdiel, the son of Guni, *was* head of their fathers' households.

16 And they lived in Gilead, in Bashan and in its towns, and in all the pasture lands of [a]Sharon, as far as their [I]borders.

🔑 17 All of these were enrolled in the genealogies in the days of [a]Jotham king of Judah and in the days of [b]Jeroboam king of Israel.

18 The sons of Reuben and the Gadites and the half-tribe of Manasseh, *consisting* of valiant men,[582] men who bore[5375] shield[4043] and sword and shot with bow, and *were* skillful in battle,[6635] *were* 44,760, who [a]went to war.

19 And they made war against [a]the Hagrites, [b]Jetur, Naphish, and Nodab.

20 And they were helped against them, and the Hagrites and all who *were* with them were given into their hand; for [a]they cried[2199] out to God[430] in the battle, and He was entreated[6279] for them, because [b]they trusted in Him.

21 And they took away their cattle: their 50,000 camels, 250,000 sheep, 2,000 donkeys, and 100,000 [I]men.[120]

11 [a]Josh. 13:11 [b]Deut. 3:10
13 [I]Lit., *brother*
16 [I]Lit., *goings out* [a]1Chr. 27:29; Song 2:1; Is. 35:2; 65:10
17 [a]2Kin. 15:5, 32 [b]2Kin. 14:16, 28
18 [a]Num. 1:3
19 [a]1Chr. 5:10 [b]Gen. 25:15; 1Chr. 1:31
20 [a]2Chr. 14:11-13 [b]Ps. 9:10; 20:7, 8; 22:4, 5
21 [I]Lit., *souls of men*
22 [a]Josh. 23:10; 2Chr. 32:8; Rom. 8:31 [b]1Chr. 4:41 [c]2Kin. 15:29; 17:6
23 [a]Deut. 3:9
25 [a]Deut. 32:15-18 [b]Ex. 34:15 [c]2Kin. 17:7
26 [I]In 2Kin. 15:29, *Tiglath-pileser* [a]2Kin. 15:19, 29; 2Chr. 28:20 [b]2Kin. 17:6
1 [I]Ch. 5:27 in Heb. [II]In v. 16, *Gershom* [a]Gen. 46:11; Ex. 6:16-25
4 [I]Lit., *begot*, and so through out the ch.

22 For many fell slain,[2491] because [a]the war *was* of God. And [b]they settled in their place until the [c]exile.[1473]

23 Now the sons of the half-tribe of Manasseh lived in the land; from Bashan to Baal-hermon and [a]Senir and Mount Hermon they were numerous.

24 And these were the heads of their fathers' households, even Epher, Ishi, Eliel, Azriel, Jeremiah, Hodaviah, and Jahdiel, mighty men of valor,[2428] famous men, heads of their fathers' households.

25 But they [a]acted treacherously against the God of their fathers, and [b]played the harlot [c]after the gods[430] of the peoples of the land, whom God had destroyed[8045] before them.

26 So the God of Israel stirred up the spirit of [a]Pul, king of Assyria, even the spirit of [I]Tilgath-pilneser king of Assyria, and he [b]carried them away into exile, namely the Reubenites, the Gadites, and the half-tribe of Manasseh, and brought them to Halah, Habor, Hara, and to the river of Gozan, to this day.[3117]

Genealogy: The Priestly Line

6 [I][a]The sons of Levi *were* [II]Gershon, Kohath and Merari.

2 And the sons of Kohath *were* Amram, Izhar, Hebron, and Uzziel.

🔑 3 And the children[1121] of Amram *were* Aaron, Moses, and Miriam. And the sons of Aaron *were* Nadab, Abihu, Eleazar, and Ithamar.

4 Eleazar [I]became the father of Phinehas, *and* Phinehas became the father of Abishua,

5 and Abishua became the father of Bukki, and Bukki became the father of Uzzi,

---

🔑 **5:17** Respectively, in 751-736 B.C. and 793-753 B.C.

🔑 **6:3** Note that Nadab and Abihu left no descendants. They were killed in the wilderness for their irreverent behavior (Lev. 10:1,2; Num. 3:4). The list of high priests which follows for the 860 years between the exodus and the fall of Jerusalem doesn't include the descendants of Ithamar who held the office under the last judges and the early kingdom: Eli, Phinehas II, Ahitub I, Ahimelech I (Ahiah), Abiathar, and Ahimelech II, (I Sam. 14:3; 22:20; II Sam. 8:17); nor certain other high priests who are mentioned elsewhere—Amariah II (II Chr. 19:11), Jehoida (II Kgs. 11:9), Zechariah (II Chr. 24:20), Urijah (II Kgs. 16:10), Azariah III (II Chr. 31:10), and Meraioth (I Chr. 9:11).

6 and Uzzi became the father of Zerahiah, and Zerahiah became the father of Meraioth,

7 Meraioth became the father of Amariah, and Amariah became the father of Ahitub,

8 and [a]Ahitub became the father of Zadok, and Zadok [b]became the father of Ahimaaz,

9 and Ahimaaz became the father of Azariah, and Azariah became the father of Johanan,

10 and Johanan became the father of Azariah ([a]it was he who served as the priest in the house [b]which Solomon built in Jerusalem),

11 and [a]Azariah became the father of Amariah, and Amariah became the father of Ahitub,

12 and Ahitub became the father of Zadok, and Zadok became the father of [I]Shallum,

13 and Shallum became the father of Hilkiah, and Hilkiah became the father of Azariah,

14 and Azariah became the father of [a]Seraiah, and Seraiah became the father of Jehozadak;

15 and Jehozadak went *along* when the LORD carried Judah and Jerusalem away into exile [I]by Nebuchadnezzar.

16 [Ia]The sons of Levi *were* [II]Gershom, Kohath, and Merari.

17 And these are the names of the sons of Gershom: Libni and Shimei.

18 And the sons of Kohath *were* Amram, Izhar, Hebron, and Uzziel.

19 The sons of [a]Merari *were* Mahli and Mushi. And these are the families[4940] of the Levites according to their fathers'[1] *households.*

20 Of Gershom: Libni his son, Jahath his son, Zimmah his son,

21 Joah his son, Iddo his son, Zerah his son, Jeatherai his son.

22 The sons of Kohath *were* Amminadab his son, Korah his son, Assir his son,

23 Elkanah his son, Ebiasaph his son, and Assir his son,

24 Tahath his son, Uriel his son, Uzziah his son, and Shaul his son.

25 And the sons of Elkanah *were* Amasai and Ahimoth.

26 *As for* Elkanah, the sons of Elkanah *were* Zophai his son and Nahath his son,

27 Eliab his son, Jeroham his son, Elkanah his son.

28 And the sons of Samuel *were* [a]Joel, the first-born and Abijah, the second.

29 The sons of Merari *were* Mahli, Libni his son, Shimei his son, Uzzah his son,

30 Shimea his son, Haggiah his son, Asaiah his son.

31 [a]Now these are those whom David appointed over the service of song in the house of the LORD, [b]after the ark[727] rested *there.*

32 And they ministered[8334] with song before the tabernacle of the tent of meeting,[4150] until Solomon had built the house of the LORD in Jerusalem; and they [I]served in their office according to their order.[4941]

33 And these are those who [I]served with their sons. From the sons of the Kohathites *were* Heman the singer, the son of Joel, the son of Samuel,

34 the son of Elkanah, the son of Jeroham, the son of Eliel, the son of Toah,

35 the son of Zuph, the son of Elkanah, the son of Mahath, the son of Amasai,

36 the son of Elkanah, the son of Joel, the son of Azariah, the son of Zephaniah,

37 the son of Tahath, the son of Assir, the son of Ebiasaph, the son of Korah,

38 the son of Izhar, the son of Kohath, the son of Levi, the son of Israel.

8 [a]2Sam. 8:17 [b]2Sam. 15:27

10 [a]2Chr. 26:17 [b]1Kin. 6:1; 2Chr. 3:1

11 [a]Ezra 7:3

12 [I]In ch. 9:11, *Meshullam*

14 [a]Neh. 11:11

15 [I]Lit., *by the hand of*

16 [I]Ch. 6:1 in Heb. [II]In v. 1, *Gershon* [a]Gen. 46:11; Ex. 6:16

19 [a]Num. 3:33; 1Chr. 23:21

28 [a]1Sam. 8:2; 1Chr. 6:33

31 [a]1Chr. 15:16-22, 27; 16:4-6 [b]2Sam. 6:17; 1Kin. 8:4; 1Chr. 15:25-16:1

32 [I]Lit., *stood over*

33 [I]Lit., *stood*

6:22 Korah was swallowed by the earth for rebelling against Moses (see Num. 16).

6:27 Elkanah IV was the husband of Hannah and the father of Samuel (I Sam. 1:1).

39 And *Heman's* brother[251] Asaph
stood at his right hand, even Asaph the
son of Berechiah, the son of Shimea,
40 the son of Michael, the son of
Baaseiah, the son of Malchijah,
41 the son of Ethni, the son of
Zerah, the son of Adaiah,
42 the son of Ethan, the son of Zimmah, the son of Shimei,
43 the son of Jahath, the son of Gershom, the son of Levi.
44 And on the left hand *were* their
[I]kinsmen[251] the sons of Merari: Ethan
the son of Kishi, the son of Abdi, the
son of Malluch,
45 the son of Hashabiah, the son
of Amaziah, the son of Hilkiah,
46 the son of Amzi, the son of Bani,
the son of Shemer,
47 the son of Mahli, the son of Mushi, the son of Merari, the son of Levi.
48 And their [I]kinsmen the Levites
were [II]appointed for all the service of
the tabernacle of the house of God.[430]
49 But Aaron and his sons [Ia]offered
on the altar[4196] of burnt offering and
[b]on the altar of incense,[7004] for all the
work[4399] of the most holy place, and
[c]to make atonement[3722] for Israel, according to all that Moses the servant
of God had commanded.[6680]
50 [a]And these are the sons of Aaron:
Eleazar his son, Phinehas his son,
Abishua his son,
51 Bukki his son, Uzzi his son, Zerahiah his son,
52 Meraioth his son, Amariah his
son, Ahitub his son,
53 Zadok his son, Ahimaaz his son.
54 Now these are their settlements[4186] according to their camps within their borders. To the sons of
Aaron of the families of the Kohathites
(for theirs was the [a]*first* lot),
55 to them they gave [a]Hebron in
the land[776] of Judah, and its pasture lands
around it;

44 [I]Lit., *brothers*
48 [I]Lit., *brothers* [II]Lit., *given*
49 [I]Lit., *offered up in smoke* [a]Ex. 27:1-8 [b]Ex. 30:1-7 [c]Ex. 30:10-16
50 [a]1Chr. 6:4-8; Ezra 7:5
54 [a]Josh. 21:4, 10
55 [a]Josh. 14:13; 21:11f.
56 [a]Josh. 15:13
57 [a]Josh. 21:13, 19
58 [I]In Josh. 21:15, *Holon*
59 [I]In Josh. 21:16, *Ain*
60 [I]In Josh. 21:18, *Almon*
61 [a]Josh. 21:5; 1Chr. 6:66-70
63 [a]Josh. 21:7, 34-40
64 [a]Num. 35:1-8; Josh. 21:3, 41, 42
65 [a]1Chr. 6:57-60
66 [a]Josh. 21:20-26

56 [a]but the fields[7704] of the city and
its villages, they gave to Caleb the son
of Jephunneh.
57 And [a]to the sons of Aaron they
gave the *following* cities of refuge: Hebron, Libnah also with its pasture lands,
Jattir, Eshtemoa with its pasture lands,
58 [I]Hilen with its pasture lands, Debir with its pasture lands,
59 [I]Ashan with its pasture lands, and
Beth-shemesh with its pasture lands;
60 and from the tribe of Benjamin:
Geba with its pasture lands, [I]Allemeth
with its pasture lands, and Anathoth with
its pasture lands. All their cities throughout their families were thirteen cities.
61 [a]Then to the rest[3498] of the sons
of Kohath *were given* by lot, from the
family[4940] of the tribe, from the half-
tribe, the half of Manasseh, ten cities.
62 And to the sons of Gershom, according to their families, *were given* from
the tribe of Issachar and from the tribe
of Asher, the tribe of Naphtali, and the
tribe of Manasseh, thirteen cities in
Bashan.
63 [a]To the sons of Merari *were given*
by lot, according to their families, from
the tribe of Reuben, the tribe of Gad,
and the tribe of Zebulun, twelve cities.
64 [a]So the sons of Israel gave to
the Levites the cities with their pasture
lands.
65 And they gave by lot from the
tribe of the sons of Judah, the tribe of
the sons of Simeon, and the tribe of
the sons of Benjamin, [a]these cities which
are mentioned[7121] by name.
66 [a]Now some of the families of the
sons of Kohath had cities of their territory from the tribe of Ephraim.
67 And they gave to them the *following* cities of refuge: Shechem in the hill
country of Ephraim with its pasture
lands, Gezer also with its pasture lands,
68 Jokmeam with its pasture lands,
Beth-horon with its pasture lands,

6:54-81 The Aaronic group had won the first lot in the distribution of the land (Josh. 21:10). See Josh. 21:1-42.

6:56 This was promised by Moses and Joshua (Josh. 14:6-15).

6:57 See Num. 35:9-34; Deut. 19:1-10, and Josh. 20:1-9 concerning these six cities of refuge.

69 Aijalon with its pasture lands, and Gath-rimmon with its pasture lands;

70 and from the half-tribe of Manasseh: Aner with its pasture lands and Bileam with its pasture lands, for the rest of the family of the sons of Kohath.

71 To the sons of Gershom *were given,* from the family of the half-tribe of Manasseh: Golan in Bashan with its pasture lands and Ashtaroth with its pasture lands;

72 and from the tribe of Issachar: Kedesh with its pasture lands, Daberath with its pasture lands,

73 and Ramoth with its pasture lands, Anem with its pasture lands;

74 and from the tribe of Asher: Mashal with its pasture lands, Abdon with its pasture lands,

75 Hukok with its pasture lands, and Rehob with its pasture lands;

76 and from the tribe of Naphtali: Kedesh in Galilee with its pasture lands, Hammon with its pasture lands, and Kiriathaim with its pasture lands.

77 To the rest of *the Levites,* the sons of Merari, *were given,* from the tribe of Zebulun: Rimmono with its pasture lands, Tabor with its pasture lands;

78 and beyond the Jordan at Jericho, on the east side of the Jordan, *were given them,* from the tribe of Reuben: Bezer in the wilderness with its pasture lands, Jahzah with its pasture lands,

79 Kedemoth with its pasture lands, and Mephaath with its pasture lands;

80 and from the tribe of Gad: Ramoth in Gilead with its pasture lands, Mahanaim with its pasture lands,

81 Heshbon with its pasture lands, and Jazer with its pasture lands.

Genealogy from Issachar

7 Now the sons of Issachar *were* four: Tola, [I]Puah, [II]Jashub, and Shimron.

2 And the sons of Tola *were* Uzzi, Rephaiah, Jeriel, Jahmai, Ibsam, and Samuel, heads of their fathers'[1] households. *The sons* of Tola *were* mighty[2428] men of valor in their generations;[8435] [a]their number in the days[3117] of David was 22,600.

3 And the [I]son of Uzzi *was* Izrahiah. And the sons of Izrahiah *were* Michael, Obadiah, Joel, Isshiah; all five of them *were* [a]chief[7218] men.

4 And with them by their generations according to their fathers'[1] households were 36,000 [I]troops of the army for war, for they had many wives[802] and sons.

5 And their [I]relatives[251] among all the families[4940] of Issachar *were* mighty men of valor, enrolled by genealogy, in all 87,000.

Descendants of Benjamin

6 [a]*The sons of* Benjamin *were* three: Bela and Becher and Jediael.

7 And the sons of Bela were five: Ezbon, Uzzi, Uzziel, Jerimoth, and Iri. They *were* heads of fathers' households, mighty men of valor,[2428] and were 22,034 enrolled by genealogy.

8 And the sons of Becher *were* Zemirah, Joash, Eliezer, Elioenai, Omri, Jeremoth, Abijah, Anathoth, and Alemeth. All these *were* the sons of Becher.

9 And they were enrolled by genealogy, according to their generations, heads of their fathers' households, 20,200 mighty men of valor.

10 And the [I]son of Jediael *was* Bilhan. And the sons of Bilhan *were* Jeush, Benjamin, Ehud, Chenaanah, Zethan, Tarshish, and Ahishahar.

11 All these *were* sons of Jediael, according to the heads of their fathers' households, 17,200 mighty men of valor, who were [I]ready to go out with the army to war[6635].

12 And [I]Shuppim and [II]Huppim *were* the sons[1121] of [III]Ir; Hushim *was* the [IV]son of [V]Aher.

Sons of Naphtali

13 The sons of Naphtali *were* [I]Jahziel, Guni, Jezer, and [II]Shallum, the sons of Bilhah.

1 [I]In Gen. 46:13, *Puvvah;* in Num. 26:23, *Puvah* [II]In Gen. 46:13, *Iob*

2 [a]2Sam. 24:1-9

3 [I]Lit., *sons* [a]1Chr. 5:24

4 [I]Or, *bands*

5 [I]Lit., *brothers,* and so throughout the ch.

6 [a]1Chr. 8:1-40

10 [I]Lit., *sons*

11 [I]Lit., *going out*

12 [I]In Num. 26:39, *Shephupham* [II]In Num. 26:39, *Hupham* [III]In v. 7, *Iri* [IV]Lit., *sons* [V]In Num. 26:38, *Ahiram*

13 [I]In Gen. 46:24, *Jahzeel* [II]In Gen. 46:24 and Num. 26:49, *Shillem*

Descendants of Manasseh

14 The sons of Manasseh *were* Asriel, whom his Aramean concubine bore;
she bore Machir the father[1] of Gilead.
15 And Machir took a wife[802] for
Huppim and Shuppim, [I]whose sister's
name was Maacah. And the name of
the second was Zelophehad, and Zelophehad had daughters.
16 And Maacah the wife of Machir
bore a son, and she named[7121] him Peresh; and the name of his brother[251]
was Sheresh, and his sons *were* Ulam
and Rakem.
17 And the [I]son of Ulam *was* Bedan.
These *were* the sons of Gilead the son
of Machir, the son of Manasseh.
18 And his sister Hammolecheth
bore Ishhod and [I]Abiezer and Mahlah.
19 And the sons of Shemida were
Ahian and Shechem and Likhi and
Aniam.

Descendants of Ephraim

20 And [a]the sons of Ephraim *were*
Shuthelah and [I]Bered his son, Tahath
his son, Eleadah his son, Tahath his
son,
21 Zabad his son, Shuthelah his son,
and Ezer and Elead whom the men[582]
of Gath who were born in the land[776]
killed, because they came down to take
their livestock.
22 And their father Ephraim
[a]mourned many days, and his relatives
[b]came to comfort[5162] him.
23 Then he went in to his wife, and
she conceived and bore a son, and he
named him [I]Beriah, because misfortune[7451] had come upon his house.
24 And his daughter was Sheerah,
[a]who built lower[8481] and upper[5945] Beth-
horon, also Uzzen-sheerah.
25 And Rephah was his son *along*
with Resheph, Telah his son, Tahan his
son,
26 Ladan his son, Ammihud his son,
Elishama his son,
27 [I]Non his son, and [a]Joshua his son.
28 And [a]their possessions and
settlements *were* Bethel with its towns,
and to the east [I]Naaran, and to the west
Gezer with its towns, and Shechem with
its towns as far as [II]Ayyah with its
towns,
29 and along the borders of the sons
of Manasseh, Beth-shean with its
towns, Taanach with its towns, Megiddo
with its towns, Dor with its towns. In
these lived the [a]sons of Joseph the son
of Israel.

Descendants of Asher

30 [a]The sons of Asher *were* Imnah,
Ishvah, Ishvi and Beriah, and Serah their
sister.
31 And the sons of Beriah *were* Heber and Malchiel, who was the father
of Birzaith.
32 And Heber [I]became the father
of Japhlet, [II]Shomer and Hotham, and
Shua their sister.
33 And the sons of Japhlet *were* Pasach, Bimhal, and Ashvath. These were
the sons of Japhlet.
34 And the sons of [I]Shemer *were*
Ahi and Rohgah, Jehubbah and Aram.
35 And the [I]sons of his brother Helem *were* Zophah, Imna, Shelesh, and
Amal.
36 The sons of Zophah *were* Suah,
Harnepher, Shual, Beri, and Imrah,
37 Bezer, Hod, Shamma, Shilshah,
Ithran, and Beera.
38 And the sons of Jether *were* Jephunneh, Pispa, and Ara.
39 And the sons of Ulla *were* Arah,
Hanniel, and Rizia.
40 All these *were* the sons of Asher,
heads of the fathers' houses, choice[1305]
and mighty men of valor, heads of the
princes. And the number of them enrolled by genealogy for service in war
was 26,000 men.

Genealogy from Benjamin

8 And [a]Benjamin [I]became the father
of Bela his first-born, Ashbel the
second, [b]Aharah the third,

15 [I]Lit., *and his*
17 [I]Lit., *sons*
18 [I]In Num. 26:30, *Iezer*
20 [I]In Num. 26:35, *Becher* [a]Num. 26:35, 36
22 [a]Gen. 37:34 [b]Job 2:11; John 11:19
23 [I]I.e., on misfortune
24 [a]Josh. 16:3, 5; 2Chr. 8:5
27 [I]In Ex. 33:11, *Nun* [a]Ex. 17:9-14; 24:13
28 [I]In Josh. 16:7, *Naarah* [II]Many mss. read *Azzah* [a]Josh. 16:2
29 [a]Judg. 1:22-29
30 [a]Gen. 46:17; Num. 26:44-46
32 [I]Lit., *begot* [II]In v. 34, *Shemer*
34 [I]In v. 32, *Shomer*
35 [I]Lit., *son*
1 [I]Lit., *begot*, and so through out the ch. [a]Gen. 46:21; 1Chr. 7:6-12 [b]1Chr. 7:12

2 Nohah the fourth, and Rapha the
fifth.
3 And Bela had sons: [I]Addar, Gera,
Abihud,
4 Abishua, Naaman, Ahoah,
5 Gera, Shephuphan, and Huram.
6 And these are the sons of Ehud:
these are the heads of fathers'[1] *households* of the inhabitants of Geba, and
they carried them into exile to Manahath,
7 namely, Naaman, Ahijah, and
Gera—he carried them into exile; and
he became the father of Uzza and Ahihud.
8 And Shaharaim became the father
of children in the [I]country[7704] of Moab,
after he had [II]sent away Hushim and
Baara his wives.[802]
9 And by Hodesh his wife[802] he became the father of Jobab, Zibia, Mesha,
Malcam,
10 Jeuz, Sachia, Mirmah. These
were his sons, heads of fathers' *households.*
11 And by Hushim he became the
father of Abitub and Elpaal.
12 And the sons of Elpaal *were* Eber,
Misham, and Shemed, who built Ono
and Lod, with its towns;
13 and Beriah and Shema, who were
heads of fathers' *households* of the inhabitants of Aijalon, who put to flight
the inhabitants of Gath;
14 and [I]Ahio, Shashak, and Jeremoth.
15 And Zebadiah, Arad, Eder,
16 Michael, Ishpah, and Joha *were*
the sons of Beriah.
17 And Zebadiah, Meshullam, Hizki,
Heber,
18 Ishmerai, Izliah, and Jobab *were*
the sons of Elpaal.
19 And Jakim, Zichri, Zabdi,
20 Elienai, Zillethai, Eliel,
21 Adaiah, Beraiah, and Shimrath
were the sons of [I]Shimei.
22 And Ishpan, Eber, Eliel,
23 Abdon, Zichri, Hanan,
24 Hananiah, Elam, Anthothijah,
25 Iphdeiah, and Penuel *were* the
sons of Shashak.
26 And Shamsherai, Shehariah,
Athaliah,
27 Jaareshiah, Elijah, and Zichri *were*
the sons of Jeroham.
28 These were heads of the fathers'
households according to their generations,[8435] chief[7218] men, [I]who lived in
Jerusalem.
29 [a]Now in Gibeon, *Jeiel,* the father
of Gibeon lived, and his wife's[802] name
was Maacah;
30 and his first-born son *was* Abdon,
then Zur, Kish, Baal, Nadab,
31 Gedor, Ahio, and [I]Zecher.
32 And Mikloth became the father
of [I]Shimeah. And they also lived with
their [II]relatives[251] in Jerusalem opposite
their *other* [II]relatives.

Genealogy from King Saul

33 [a]And Ner became the father of
Kish, and Kish became the father of
Saul, and Saul became the father
of Jonathan, Malchi-shua, [I]Abinadab,
and [II]Eshbaal.
34 And the son of Jonathan *was*
[I]Merib-baal, and Merib-baal became the
father of Micah.
35 And the sons of Micah *were* Pithon, Melech, [I]Tarea, and Ahaz.
36 And Ahaz became the father of
[I]Jehoaddah, and Jehoaddah became the
father of Alemeth, Azmaveth, and Zimri;
and Zimri became the father of Moza.
37 And Moza became the father of
Binea; [I]Raphah *was* his son, Eleasah his
son, Azel his son.
38 And Azel had six sons, and these
were their names: Azrikam, Bocheru,
Ishmael, Sheariah, Obadiah and Hanan.
All these *were* the sons of Azel.
39 And the sons of Eshek his
brother[251] *were* Ulam his first-born,
Jeush the second, and Eliphelet the
third.
40 And the sons of Ulam were
mighty men[582] of valor,[2428] archers, and
had many sons and grandsons, 150 *of
them.* All these *were* of the sons of Benjamin.

3 [I]In Gen. 46:21 and Num. 26:40, *Ard*

8 [I]Lit., *field* [II]Lit., *sent them away*

14 [I]Or, *his brothers*

21 [I]In v. 13, *Shema*

28 [I]Lit., *these*

29 [a]1Chr. 9:35-38

31 [I]In ch. 9:37, *Zechariah*

32 [I]In ch. 9:38, *Shimeam* [II]Lit., *brothers*

33 [I]1Sam. 14:49, *Ishvi* [II]In 2Sam. 2:8, *Ish-bosheth* [a]1Chr. 9:39-44

34 [I]In 2Sam. 4:4, *Mephibosheth*

35 [I]In 9:41, *Tahrea*

36 [I]In 9:42, *Jarah*

37 [I]In 9:43, *Rephaiah*

People of Jerusalem

9 So all Israel was enrolled by genealogies; and behold, they are written in the Book[5612] of the Kings[4428] of
Israel. And [a]Judah was carried away into
exile to Babylon for their unfaithfulness.
2 [a]Now the first[7223] who lived in
their possessions in their cities *were* Israel, the priests, the Levites and
[b]the [I]temple servants.
3 And some of the sons of Judah,
of the sons[1121] of Benjamin, and of the
sons of Ephraim and Manasseh lived in
[a]Jerusalem:
4 Uthai the son of Ammihud, the
son of Omri, the son of Imri, the son
of Bani, from the sons of Perez the
[a]son of Judah.
5 And from the Shilonites *were*
Asaiah the first-born and his sons.
6 And from the sons of Zerah *were*
Jeuel and their [I]relatives,[251] 690 *of them.*
7 And from the sons of Benjamin
were Sallu the son of Meshullam, the
son of Hodaviah, the son of Hassenuah,
8 and Ibneiah the son of Jeroham,
and Elah the son of Uzzi, the son of
Michri, and Meshullam the son of
Shephatiah, the son of Reuel, the son
of Ibnijah;
9 and their relatives according to
their generations,[8435] [a]956. All these
were heads[7218] of fathers'[1] *households*
according to their fathers' houses.
10 [a]And from the priests *were* Jedaiah, Jehoiarib, Jachin,
11 and [I]Azariah the son of Hilkiah,
the son of Meshullam, the son of Zadok,
the son of Meraioth, the son of Ahitub,
[a]the chief officer of the house of God;[430]
12 and Adaiah the son of Jeroham,
the son of Pashhur, the son of Malchijah,
and Maasai the son of Adiel, the son
of Jahzerah, the son of Meshullam, the
son of Meshillemith, the son of Immer;
13 and their relatives, heads of their
fathers' households, 1,760 very able[2428]
men for the work[4399] of the service of
the house of God.
14 [a]And of the Levites *were* Shemaiah the son of Hasshub, the son of
Azrikam, the son of Hashabiah, of the
sons of Merari;
15 and Bakbakkar, Heresh and Galal
and Mattaniah the son of Mica, the son
of [I]Zichri, the son of Asaph,
16 and [I]Obadiah the son of [II]Shem-
aiah, the son of Galal, the son of Jeduthun, and Berechiah the son of Asa, the
son of Elkanah, who lived in the villages
of the Netophathites.
17 Now the gatekeepers[7778] *were*
[I]Shallum and Akkub and Talmon and Ahiman and their relatives (Shallum the
chief
18 *being stationed* until now at
[a]the king's[4428] gate to the east). These
were the gatekeepers for the camp[4264]
of the sons of Levi.
19 And Shallum the son of Kore,
the son of [I]Ebiasaph, the son of Korah,
and his relatives, of his father's[1] house,
the Korahites, *were* over the work of
the service, keepers[8104] of the thresholds of the tent; and their fathers had
been over the camp of the LORD,
keepers of the entrance.
20 And [a]Phinehas the son of Eleazar
was ruler over them previously, *and*
the LORD was with him.
21 [a]Zechariah the son of Meshelemiah was gatekeeper of the entrance
of the tent of meeting.[4150]
22 All these who were chosen[1305]
to be gatekeepers in the thresholds
were 212. These were enrolled by genealogy in their villages, [a]whom David
and Samuel the seer appointed[3245]
[b]in their office of trust.

1 [a]1Chr. 5:25, 26
2 [I]Heb., *Nethinim* [a]Ezra 2:70; Neh. 7:73; 11:3-22 [b]Ezra 2:43, 58; 8:20
3 [a]Neh. 11:1
4 [a]Gen. 46:12; Num. 26:20
6 [I]Lit., *brothers,* and so throughout the ch.
9 [a]Neh. 11:8
10 [a]Neh. 11:10-14
11 [I]In Neh. 11:11, *Seraiah* [a]Jer. 20:1
14 [a]Neh. 11:15-19
15 [I]In Neh. 11:17, *Zabdi*
16 [I]In Neh. 11:17, *Abda* [II]In Neh. 11:17, *Shammua*
17 [I]In v. 21, *Meshelemiah;* in 26:14, *Shelemiah;* in Neh. 12:25, *Meshullam*
18 [a]Ezek. 44:1; 46:1, 2
19 [I]In Ex. 6:24, *Abiasaph*
20 [a]Num. 25:7-13
21 [a]1Chr. 26:2, 14
22 [a]1Chr. 26:1 [b]2Chr. 31:15, 18

9:1-34 See Neh. 11:1-24.

9:10 These appear to be the names of the second, first, and twenty-first courses (shifts) of the twenty-four priestly courses which David had established (I Chr. 24:7-18) rather than the names of individuals.

9:19 Though Korah himself was destroyed (Num. 16), his clan continued as an important part of the Kohath division of Levi. Before the permanent temple was built by Solomon, the tabernacle was a movable, flexible structure.

23 So they and their sons [I]had charge of the gates of the house of the LORD, *even* the house of the tent, as guards.*4931*

24 The gatekeepers were [I]on the four sides, to the east, west, north, and south.

25 And their relatives in their villages [a]*were* to come in every seven days*3117* from time to time *to be* with [I]them;

26 for the four chief gatekeepers who *were* Levites, were in an office of trust, and were over the chambers and over the treasuries in the house of God.

27 And they spent the night around the house of God, [a]because the watch was [I]committed to them; and they *were* [II]in charge*4931* of opening *it* morning by morning.

28 Now some of them [I]had charge of the utensils of service,*5656* for [II]they counted them when they brought them in and when they took them out.

29 Some of them also were appointed over the furniture and over all the utensils of the sanctuary and [a]over the fine flour and the wine and the oil*8081* and the frankincense3828 and the spices.

30 And some of [a]the sons of the priests prepared the mixing of the spices.

🗝 31 And Mattithiah, one of the Levites, who was the first-born of Shallum the Korahite, had [a]the [I]responsibility over the things which were baked in pans.

🗝 32 And some of their relatives of the sons of the Kohathites [a]*were* over the showbread to prepare it every sabbath.*7676*

33 Now these are [a]the singers, heads of fathers' *households* of the Levites, *who lived* in the chambers *of the temple* free *from other service;* for they were [I]engaged [b]in their work day*3119* and night.

34 These were heads of fathers' *households* of the Levites according to their generations, chief men, [I]who lived in Jerusalem.

Ancestry and Descendants of Saul

35 [a]And in Gibeon Jeiel the father of Gibeon lived, and his wife's*802* name was Maacah,

36 and his first-born son *was* Abdon, then Zur, Kish, Baal, Ner, Nadab,

37 Gedor, Ahio, Zechariah, and Mikloth.

38 And Mikloth became the father of Shimeam. And they also lived with their relatives in Jerusalem opposite their *other* relatives.

39 [a]And Ner became the father of Kish, and Kish became the father of Saul, and Saul became the father of Jonathan, Malchi-shua, Abinadab, and Eshbaal.

40 And the son of Jonathan *was* Merib-baal; and Merib-baal became the father of Micah.

41 And the sons of Micah *were* Pithon, Melech, Tahrea, [a]*and Ahaz.*

42 And Ahaz became the father of Jarah, and Jarah became the father of Alemeth, Azmaveth, and Zimri; and Zimri became the father of Moza,

43 and Moza became the father of Binea and Rephaiah his son, Eleasah his son, Azel his son.

44 And Azel had six sons whose names are these: Azrikam, Bocheru and Ishmael and Sheariah and Obadiah and Hanan. These were the sons of Azel.

Defeat and Death of Saul and His Sons

10 🗝 [a]Now the Philistines fought against Israel; and the men*376* of

23 [I]Lit., *were over the gates*
24 [I]Lit., *to the four winds*
25 [I]Lit., *these* [a]2Kin. 11:5, 7; 2Chr. 23:8
27 [I]Lit., *on them* [II]Lit., *over the opening* [a]1Chr. 23:30-32
28 [I]Lit., *were over the* [II]Lit., *by count they brought them in and by count they took them out*
29 [a]1Chr. 23:29
30 [a]Ex. 30:23-25
31 [I]Lit., *office of trust* [a]1Chr. 9:22
32 [a]Lev. 24:5-8
33 [I]Lit., *over them in the work* [a]1Chr. 6:31-47; 25:1 [b]Ps. 134:1
34 [I]Lit., *these*
35 [a]1Chr. 8:29-32
39 [a]1Chr. 8:33-38
41 [a]1Chr. 8:35-37
1 [a]1Sam. 31:1-13

🗝 **9:31** The flat cakes were for meal offerings (Lev. 2:4-7).
🗝 **9:32** This was the showbread (Lev. 24:5,6).
🗝 **10:1** This chapter is almost identical with I Sam. 31.
🗝 **10:1-12** See I Sam. 31:1-13.

Israel fled before the Philistines, and
fell[5307] slain on Mount Gilboa.
2 And the Philistines closely pursued Saul and his sons, and the Philistines struck down Jonathan, [1][a]Abinadab
and Malchi-shua, the sons of Saul.
3 And the battle became heavy
against Saul, and the archers[3384] [1]over-
took him; and he was wounded[2342] by
the archers.
4 Then Saul said[559] to his armor
bearer, "Draw your sword and thrust
me through with it, lest these uncircumcised[6189] come and abuse me." But
his armor bearer would[14] not, for
he was greatly afraid.[3372] [a]Therefore
Saul took his sword and fell on it.
5 And when his armor bearer saw
that Saul was dead,[4191] he likewise fell
on his sword and died.[4191]
6 [a]Thus Saul died with his three
sons, and all *those* of his house died together.
7 When all the men of Israel who
were in the valley saw that they had
fled, and that Saul and his sons were
dead, they forsook[5800] their cities and
fled; and the Philistines came and lived
in them.
8 And it came about the next day,
when the Philistines came to strip the
slain, that they found Saul and his sons
fallen[5307] on Mount Gilboa.
9 [a]So they stripped him and took
his head and his armor and sent *messen-*
gers around the land[776] of the Philistines,
to carry the good news to their idols[6091]
and to the people.
10 And they put his armor in the
house of their gods[430] and fastened[8628]
his head in the house of Dagon.

Jabesh-gilead's Tribute to Saul

11 When all Jabesh-gilead heard all
that the Philistines had done[6213] to Saul,
12 [a]all the valiant men arose and
took away the body[1480] of Saul and the
bodies of his sons, and brought them
to Jabesh and buried[6912] their bones[6106]
under the oak in Jabesh, and fasted
seven days.[3117]
13 [a]So Saul died for his trespass
which he committed[4603] against the
LORD, because of the word[1697] of the
LORD which he did not keep;[8104] and
also [b]because he asked[7592] counsel of a
medium, making inquiry *of it,*
14 and did not inquire of the LORD.
Therefore He killed him, and [a]turned
the kingdom to David the son of Jesse.

David Made King over All Israel

11 ⊶ [a]Then all Israel gathered[6908]
to David at Hebron [1]and said,
"Behold, we are your bone[6106] and your
flesh.[1320]
2 "In times past, even when Saul
was king,[4428] you *were* the one who led
out and brought in Israel; and the LORD
your God[430] said[559] to you, '[a]You shall
shepherd My people Israel, and you shall
be prince over My people Israel.' "
3 So all the elders[2205] of Israel came
to the king at Hebron, and David
made[3772] a covenant[1285] with them in
Hebron before the LORD; and [a]they
anointed[4886] David king over Israel,
[b]according to the word[1697] of the LORD
through Samuel.

Jerusalem, Capital City

4 Then David and all Israel went
to Jerusalem ([a]that is, Jebus); and the
Jebusites, the inhabitants of the land,[776]
were there.
5 And the inhabitants of Jebus said
to David, "You shall not enter here."
Nevertheless David captured the
stronghold of Zion (that is, the city of
David).
6 Now David had said, "Whoever

2 [1]In 1Sam. 14:49, *Ishvi* [a]1Sam. 31:2
3 [1]Lit., *found him*
4 [a]1Sam. 31:4
6 [a]1Sam. 31:6
9 [a]1Sam. 31:9
12 [a]1Sam. 31:12f.
13 [a]1Sam. 13:13, 14; 15:23 [b]Lev. 19:31; 20:6; 1Sam. 28:7
14 [a]1Sam. 15:28; 1Chr. 12:23

1 [1]Lit., *saying* [a]2Sam. 5:1, 3, 6-10
2 [a]2Sam. 5:2; 7:7
3 [a]2Sam. 2:4; 5:3, 5 [b]1Sam. 16:1, 3, 12, 13
4 [a]Josh. 15:8, 63; Judg. 1:21

⊶ **11:1** David ruled at Hebron only over Judah for seven and a half years, from 1010 to 1003 B.C. (II Sam. 2—4). This is not mentioned here. Verses 1-9 are parallel to II Sam. 5:1-10.
⊶ **11:1-9** See II Sam. 5:1-10.

strikes down a Jebusite first[7223] shall be
chief[7218] and commander."[8269] [a]And Joab
the son of Zeruiah went up first, so he
became chief.
7 Then David dwelt in the stronghold; therefore it was called[7121] the city
of David.
8 And he [I]built the city all around,
from the [II]Millo even to the surrounding
area; and Joab [III]repaired the rest of the
city.
9 And [a]David became greater and
greater, for the LORD of hosts *was* with
him.

David's Mighty Men

🗝 **10** [a]Now these are the heads of the
mighty men whom David had, who gave
him strong support in his kingdom,[4438]
together with all Israel, to make him
king,[4427] [b]according to the word of the
LORD concerning Israel.
11 And these *constitute* the list of
the mighty men whom David had:
[a]Jashobeam, the son of a Hachmonite,
[b]the chief of the thirty;[7991] he lifted up
his spear against three hundred [I]whom
he killed at one time.
12 And after him was Eleazar the
son of [a]Dodo, the Ahohite, who *was*
[I]one of the three mighty men.
13 He was with David at [I]Pasdam-
mim [a]when the Philistines were gathered[622] together there to battle, and
there was a plot of ground[7704] full of
barley; and the people fled before the
Philistines.
14 And they took their stand in the
midst of the plot, and defended[5337] it,
and struck down the Philistines; and the
LORD saved them by a great [I]victory.[8668]
15 Now three of the thirty chief
men went down to the rock to David,
into the cave of Adullam, while [a]the army
of the Philistines was camping in the
valley of Rephaim.
16 And David was then in the
stronghold, while [a]the garrison of the
Philistines *was* then in Bethlehem.

17 And David had a craving[183] and
said, "Oh that someone would give me
water to drink from the well[953] of Bethlehem, which is by the gate!"
18 So the three broke through the
camp of the Philistines, and drew water
from the well of Bethlehem which *was*
by the gate, and took *it* and brought *it*
to David; nevertheless David would[14]
not drink it, but poured it out to the
LORD;
19 and he said, "Be it far from me
before my God that I should do[6213] this.
Shall I drink the blood[1818] of these men[582]
who went [I]at the risk of their lives?[5315]
For at the risk of their lives they brought
it." Therefore he would not drink it.
These things the three mighty men
did.[6213]
20 As for [I]Abshai the brother[251] of
Joab, he was chief of the [II]thirty, and
he swung his spear against three hundred [III]and killed them; and he had a
name as well as the [II]thirty.
21 Of the three in the second *rank*
he was the most honored, and became
their commander; however, he did not
attain to the *first* three.
22 [a]Benaiah the son of Jehoiada, the
son of a valiant man[376] of Kabzeel,
mighty in deeds, struck down the
[I]two *sons of* Ariel of Moab. He also went
down and [II]killed a lion inside a pit on
a snowy day.[3117]
23 And he [I]killed an Egyptian, a man
of *great* stature five [II]cubits tall. Now
in the Egyptian's hand *was* [a]a spear like
a weaver's beam, but he went down
to him with a club and snatched the spear
from the Egyptian's hand, and [I]killed him
with his own spear.
24 These *things* Benaiah the son of
Jehoiada did, and had a name as well
as the three mighty men.
25 Behold, he was honored among
the thirty, but he did not attain to the
three; and David appointed him over
his guard.[4928]
26 Now the mighty men of the
armies[2428] *were* Asahel the brother of

6 [a]2Sam. 8:16

8 [I]Or, *fortified* [II]I.e., citadel [III]Lit., *revived*

9 [a]2Sam. 3:1

10 [a]2Sam. 23:8-39 [b]1Chr. 11:3

11 [I]Lit., *slain ones* [a]2Sam. 23:8 [b]1Chr. 12:18

12 [I]Lit., *among* [a]1Chr. 27:4

13 [I]In 1Sam. 17:1, *Ephes-dammim* [a]2Sam. 23:11, 12

14 [I]Or, *salvation*

15 [a]1Chr. 14:9

16 [a]1Sam. 10:5

19 [I]Lit., *with their souls*

20 [I]In 2Sam. 23:18, *Abishai* [II]So Syriac; M.T., *three* [III]Lit., *slain ones*

22 [I]Or, *two lion-like heroes of* [II]Lit., *smote* [a]2Sam. 8:18

23 [I]Lit., *smote* [II]I.e., One cubit equals approx. 18 in. [a]1Sam. 17:7

🗝 **11:10-47** See II Sam. 23:8-39.

Joab, Elhanan the son of Dodo of Bethlehem,

27 [I]Shammoth the Harorite, Helez the [II]Pelonite,

28 Ira the son of Ikkesh the Tekoite, Abiezer the Anathothite,

29 [I]Sibbecai the Hushathite, [II]Ilai the Ahohite,

30 Maharai the Netophathite, [I]Heled the son of Baanah the Netophathite,

31 Ithai the son of Ribai of Gibeah of the <u>sons</u>[1121] of Benjamin, Benaiah the Pirathonite,

32 [I]Hurai of the brooks of Gaash, [II]Abiel the Arbathite,

33 Azmaveth the Baharumite, Eliahba the Shaalbonite,

34 the sons of [I]Hashem the Gizonite, Jonathan the son of Shagee the Hararite,

35 Ahiam the son of [I]Sacar the Hararite, [II]Eliphal the son of Ur,

36 Hepher the Mecherathite, Ahijah the Pelonite,

37 Hezro the Carmelite, [I]Naarai the son of Ezbai,

38 Joel the brother of Nathan, Mibhar the son of Hagri,

39 Zelek the Ammonite, Naharai the Berothite, the armor bearer of Joab the son of Zeruiah,

40 Ira the Ithrite, Gareb the Ithrite,

41 Uriah the Hittite, Zabad the son of Ahlai,

42 Adina the son of Shiza the Reubenite, a chief of the Reubenites, and thirty with him,

43 Hanan the son of Maacah and Joshaphat the Mithnite,

44 Uzzia the Ashterathite, Shama and Jeiel the sons of Hotham the Aroerite,

45 Jediael the son of Shimri and Joha his brother, the Tizite,

46 Eliel the Mahavite and Jeribai and Joshaviah, the sons of Elnaam, and Ithmah the Moabite,

47 Eliel and Obed and Jaasiel the Mezobaite.

David's Supporters in Ziklag

12 [a]Now these are the ones who came to David at Ziklag, while he was still restricted because of Saul the son of Kish; and they were among the mighty men who helped *him* in war.

2 They were <u>equipped</u>[5401] with bows, [a]using both the right hand and the left *to sling* stones and *to shoot* arrows from the bow; [b]*they were* Saul's <u>kinsmen</u>[251] from Benjamin.

3 The chief was Ahiezer, then Joash, the sons of Shemaah the Gibeathite; and Jeziel and Pelet, the sons of Azmaveth, and <u>Beracah</u>[1294] and Jehu the Anathothite,

4 and Ishmaiah the Gibeonite, a mighty man among the thirty, and over the thirty. [I]Then Jeremiah, Jahaziel, Johanan, Jozabad the Gederathite,

5 [I]Eluzai, Jerimoth, Bealiah, Shemariah, Shephatiah the Haruphite,

6 Elkanah, Isshiah, Azarel, Joezer, Jashobeam, the Korahites,

7 and Joelah and Zebadiah, the sons of Jeroham of Gedor.

8 And from the Gadites there [I]came over to David in the stronghold in the wilderness, mighty <u>men</u>[582] of <u>valor,</u>[2428] men trained for <u>war,</u>[6635] who could handle shield and <u>spear,</u>[7420] and whose faces were like the faces of lions, and [a]*they were* as swift as the <u>gazelles</u>[6643] on the mountains.

9 Ezer *was* the <u>first,</u>[7218] Obadiah the second, Eliab the third,

10 Mishmannah the fourth, Jeremiah the fifth,

11 Attai the sixth, Eliel the seventh,

12 Johanan the eighth, Elzabad the ninth,

27 [I]In 2Sam. 23:25, *Shammah the Harodite* [II]In 2Sam. 23:26, *Paltite*

29 [I]In 2Sam. 23:27, *Mebunnai* [II]In 2Sam. 23:28, *Zalmon*

30 [I]In 2Sam. 23:29, *Heleb*

32 [I]In 2Sam. 23:30, *Hiddai* [II]In 2Sam. 23:31, *Abi-albon*

34 [I]In 2Sam. 23:32, *Jashen*

35 [I]In 2Sam. 23:33, *Sharar* [II]In 2Sam. 23:34, *Eliphelet the son of Ahasbai*

37 [I]In 2Sam. 23:35, *Paarai the Arbite*

1 [a]1Sam. 27:2-6

2 [a]Judg. 3:15; 20:16 [b]1Chr. 12:29

4 [I]In Heb. the beginning of v. 5, making 41 vv. in ch.

5 [I]V. 6 in Heb.

8 [I]Lit., *separated themselves* [a]2Sam. 2:18

11:41 See II Sam. 11 regarding Uriah the Hittite.

12:8 This may refer to the Cave of Adullam. Compare 1 Chr. 11:15 with I Sam. 22:1.

13 Jeremiah the tenth, Machbannai the eleventh.

14 These of the sons of Gad were [I]captains of the army; [a]he who was least was equal to a hundred and the greatest to a thousand.

15 [a]These are the ones who crossed the Jordan in the first[7223] month when it was overflowing all its banks and they put to flight all those in the valleys, both to the east and to the west.

16 Then some of the sons[1121] of Benjamin and Judah came to the stronghold to David.

17 And David went out to meet them, and answered and said[559] to them, "If you come peacefully to me to help me, my heart shall be united with you; but if to betray me to my adversaries, since there is no [I]wrong[2555] in my hands, may the God[430] of our fathers[1] look on *it* and decide."

18 Then [a]the Spirit [I]came upon [b]Amasai, who was the chief of the thirty,[7991] *and he said,*

> "*We* are yours, O David,
> And with you, O son of Jesse!
> [c]Peace, peace to you,
> And peace to him who helps you;
> Indeed, your God helps you!"

Then David received them and made them [II]captains of the band.[1416]

19 [a]From Manasseh also some defected[5307] to David, when he was about to go to battle with the Philistines against Saul. But they did not help them, for the lords[5633] of the Philistines after consultation[6098] sent him away, saying, "At *the cost of* our heads he may defect to his master[113] Saul."

20 As he went to Ziklag, there defected to him from Manasseh: Adnah, Jozabad, Jediael, Michael, Jozabad, Elihu, and Zillethai, [I]captains of thousands who belonged to Manasseh.

21 And they helped David against [a]the band of raiders, for they were all mighty men of valor,[2428] and were captains[8269] in the army.

22 For day[3117] by day *men* came to David to help him, until there was a great army [a]like the army of God.

14 [I]Or, *chiefs* [a]Deut. 32:30
15 [a]Josh. 3:15; 4:18
17 [I]Lit., *violence*
18 [I]Lit., *clothed* [II]Or, *chiefs* [a]Judg. 3:10; 6:34 [b]1Chr. 2:17 [c]1Sam. 25:5, 6
19 [a]1Sam. 29:2-9
20 [I]Or, *chiefs*
21 [a]1Sam. 30:1
22 [a]Gen. 32:2; Josh. 5:13-15
23 [I]Lit., *heads* [II]Lit., *mouth* [a]2Sam. 2:3, 4 [b]1Chr. 10:14 [c]1Chr. 11:10
28 [a]2Sam. 8:17; 1Chr. 6:8, 53
29 [a]1Chr. 12:2 [b]2Sam. 2:8, 9
32 [a]Esth. 1:13
33 [I]Lit., *not of double heart* [a]Ps. 12:2

Supporters Gathered at Hebron

23 Now these are the numbers of the [I]divisions equipped for war, [a]who came to David at Hebron, [b]to turn the kingdom[4438] of Saul to him, [c]according to the [II]word of the LORD.

24 The sons of Judah who bore[5375] shield and spear *were* 6,800, equipped for war.

25 Of the sons of Simeon, mighty men of valor for war, 7,100.

26 Of the sons of Levi 4,600.

27 Now Jehoiada was the leader[5057] of *the house of* Aaron, and with him were 3,700,

28 also [a]Zadok, a young man mighty of valor, and of his father's[1] house twenty-two captains.

29 And of the sons of Benjamin, [a]Saul's kinsmen, 3,000; for until now [b]the greatest part of them had kept[8104] their allegiance[4931] to the house of Saul.

30 And of the sons of Ephraim 20,800, mighty men of valor, famous men in their fathers' households.

31 And of the half-tribe of Manasseh 18,000, who were designated[5344] by name to come and make David king.[4427]

32 And of the sons of Issachar, [a]men who understood[998] the times, with knowledge[3045] of what Israel should do,[6213] their chiefs were two hundred; and all their kinsmen were at their command.[6310]

33 Of Zebulun, there were 50,000 who went out in the army, who could draw up in battle[6635] formation with all kinds of weapons of war and helped *David* [I]with [a]an undivided heart.

34 And of Naphtali *there were* 1,000 captains, and with them 37,000 with shield and spear.

35 And of the Danites who could draw up in battle formation, *there were* 28,600.

36 And of Asher *there were* 40,000 who went out in the army to draw up in battle formation.

37 And from the other side of the Jordan, of the Reubenites and the Gadites and of the half-tribe of Manasseh,

there were 120,000 with all *kinds* of
weapons of war for the battle.
38 All these, being men of war, who
could draw up in battle formation, came
to Hebron with [a]a perfect heart, to make
David king over all Israel; and all the
rest also of Israel were of one mind to
make David king.
39 And they were there with David
three days,[3117] eating and drinking; for
their kinsmen had prepared for them.
40 Moreover those who were near
to them, *even* as far as Issachar and
Zebulun and Naphtali, [a]brought food on
donkeys, camels, mules, and on oxen,
great quantities of flour cakes, fig cakes
and bunches of raisins, wine, oil,[8081]
oxen and sheep. There was joy indeed
in Israel.

Peril in Transporting the Ark

13 Then David consulted[3289] with
the captains[8269] of the thousands
and the hundreds, even with every
leader.[5057]
2 And David said[559] to all the
assembly[6951] of Israel, "If it seems
good[2895] to you, and if it is from the
LORD our God,[430] let us send everywhere to our kinsmen[251] who remain[7604]
in all the land[776] of Israel, also to the
priests and Levites who are with them
in their cities with pasture lands, that
they may meet[6908] with us;
3 and let us bring back the ark[727]
of our God to us, [a]for we did not seek
it in the days[3117] of Saul."
4 Then all the assembly said that
they would do[6213] so, for the thing was
right in the eyes of all the people.
5 [a]So David assembled[6950] all Israel
together, from the Shihor of Egypt even
to the entrance of Hamath, [b]to bring
the ark of God from Kiriath-jearim.
6 [a]And David and all Israel went up
to [b]Baalah, *that is,* to Kiriath-jearim,
which belongs to Judah, to bring up from
there the ark of God, the LORD [c]who
is enthroned *above* the cherubim,[3742]
where His name is called.[7121]
7 And they [I]carried the ark of God
on a new cart from [a]the house of Abinadab, and Uzza and Ahio drove the cart.
8 And David and all Israel were celebrating before God with all *their* might,
[a]even with songs and with lyres, harps,
tambourines,[8596] cymbals, and with
trumpets.
9 When they came to [a]the threshing
floor of Chidon, Uzza put out his hand
to hold the ark, because the oxen nearly
upset *it.*
10 And the anger[639] of the LORD
burned[2734] against Uzza, so He struck
him down [a]because he put out his hand
to the ark; [b]and he died[4191] there before
God.
11 Then David became angry[2734]
because [I]of the LORD's outburst against
Uzza; and he called that place [II]Perez-
uzza to this day.[3117]
12 And David was afraid[3372] of God

38 [a]2Sam. 5:1-3; 1Chr. 12:33
40 [a]1Sam. 25:18
3 [a]1Sam. 7:1, 2
5 [a]2Sam. 6:1; 1Kin. 8:65; 1Chr. 15:3 [b]1Sam. 6:21; 7:1
6 [a]2Sam. 6:2-11 [b]Josh. 15:9 [c]Ex. 25:22; 2Kin. 19:15
7 [I]Lit., *caused to ride* [a]1Sam. 7:1
8 [a]1Chr. 15:16
9 [a]2Sam. 6:6
10 [a]1Chr. 15:13, 15 [b]Lev. 10:2
11 [I]Lit., *the LORD had broken through a break-through* [II]I.e., the breakthrough of Uzza

13:3 See notes on I Sam. 14:8.
13:5-14 See II Sam. 6:1-11.
13:9,10 Uzza was from the tribe of Levi which had the responsibility for the tabernacle and its contents including the ark. The ark had rested for twenty years in the house of his father Abinadab. It is generally thought that Uzza was stricken down here because only the priests, i.e., those of the house of Aaron were to touch the ark. In fact the priests were responsible for covering the ark (as well as all the utensils and furniture of the sanctuary) for travel (Num. 4:5-14), and it would appear from the context that they were not to touch the ark while doing so. The Kohathites were in charge of carrying the ark (using the rings and poles provided (Ex. 25:14), but were promised sure death if they touched it (Num. 4:15). It was not to be carried on wagons, but on human shoulders (Num. 7:9). A flagrant disregard for the ark was displayed by all because it was traveling uncovered and open to the gaze of all, as well as being carried upon a wagon. It appears that there was no priest in charge of its transporting (Num. 3:32). Certainly Uzza's death followed the warning to the Kohathites. Perhaps Uzza was also possessed of a reckless and sacrilegious spirit because of his familiarity with it. It certainly stood out as an example to check effectively the evil spreading among the people (I Chr. 15:2-13).

that day, saying, "How can I bring the ark of God *home* to me?"

13 So David did not take the ark with him to the city of David, but took it aside [a]to the house of Obed-edom the Gittite.

🔑14 Thus the ark of God remained with the family[4940] of Obed-edom in his house three months; and [a]the LORD blessed[1288] the family of Obed-edom with all that he had.

David's Family Enlarged

14 🔑 [a]Now Hiram king[4428] of Tyre sent messengers[4397] to David with cedar trees, masons, and carpenters, to build a house for him.

2 And David realized that the LORD had established[3559] him as king over Israel, *and* that his kingdom[4438] was highly exalted, for the sake of His people Israel.

🔑3 Then David took more wives[802] at Jerusalem, and David [I]became the father of more sons and daughters.

4 [a]And these are the names of the children [I]born *to him* in Jerusalem: Shammua, Shobab, Nathan, Solomon,

5 Ibhar, Elishua, Elpelet,

6 Nogah, Nepheg, Japhia,

7 Elishama, Beeliada and Eliphelet.

Philistines Defeated

🔑8 When the Philistines heard that David had been anointed[4886] king over all Israel, all the Philistines went up in search of David; and David heard of it and went out against them.

9 Now the Philistines had come and [a]made a raid in the valley of Rephaim.

10 And David inquired[7592] of God,[430] saying, "Shall I go up against the Philistines? And wilt Thou give them into my hand?" Then the LORD said[559] to him, "Go up, for I will give them into your hand."

11 So they came up to Baal-perazim, and David [I]defeated them there; and David said, "God has broken through my enemies by my hand, like the breakthrough of waters." Therefore they named[7121] that place [II]Baal-perazim.

🔑12 And they abandoned[5800] their gods[430] there; so David gave the order[559] and they were burned[8313] with fire.

13 And the Philistines made [a]yet another raid in the valley.

14 And David inquired again of God, and God said to him, "You shall not go up after them; circle around [I]behind them, and come at them in front of the [II]balsam trees.

15 "And it shall be when you hear the sound of marching in the tops of the balsam trees, then you shall go out to battle, for God will have gone out before you to strike the army of the Philistines."

16 And David did[6213] just as God had commanded[6680] him, and they struck down the army of the Philistines from [I]Gibeon even as far as Gezer.

17 Then the fame of David went out into all the lands;[776] and [a]the LORD brought the fear[6343] of him on all the nations.

Plans to Move the Ark to Jerusalem

15 🔑Now *David* built[6213] houses for himself in the city of David; and he prepared a place for the ark[727] of God,[430] and [a]pitched a tent for it.

13 [a]1Chr. 15:25
14 [a]1Chr. 26:4, 5
1 [a]2Sam. 5:11
3 [I]Lit., *begot*
4 [I]Lit., *were to* [a]1Chr. 3:5-8
9 [a]1Chr. 11:15; 14:13
11 [I]Lit., *smote* [II]I.e., the master of breakthrough
13 [a]1Chr. 14:9
14 [I]Lit., *from upon* [II]Or, *baka shrubs*
16 [I]In 2Sam. 5:25, *Geba*
17 [a]Ex. 15:14-16; Deut. 2:25
1 [a]1Chr. 15:3; 16:1; 17:1-5

🔑 **13:14** Obed-edom was a Levite of the family of Korah in the clan of Kohath (I Chr. 26:1,4). Therefore, this met the requirement for a valid caretaker of the ark of the covenant.
🔑 **14:1,2** II Sam. 5:11,12.
🔑 **14:3-7** See II Sam. 5:13-16; I Chr. 3:5-9.
🔑 **14:8-17** See II Sam. 5:17-25.
🔑 **14:12** This was required by the Law of Moses (Deut. 7:5,25).
🔑 **15:1-29** II Sam. 6:12-23 abbreviates this and the following chapter.

2 Then David said,[559] "[a]No one is to carry[5375] the ark of God but the Levites; for the LORD chose[977] them to carry the ark of God, and to minister[8334] to Him forever."

3 And [a]David assembled all Israel at Jerusalem, to bring up the ark of the LORD [b]to its place, which he had prepared for it.

4 And David gathered[6950] together the sons[1121] of Aaron, and [a]the Levites:

5 of the sons of Kohath, Uriel the chief, and 120 of his [1]relatives;[251]

6 of the sons of Merari, Asaiah the chief, and 220 of his relatives;

7 of the sons of Gershom, Joel the chief, and 130 of his relatives;

8 of the sons of Elizaphan, Shemaiah the chief, and 200 of his relatives;

9 of the sons of Hebron, Eliel the chief, and 80 of his relatives;

10 of the sons of Uzziel, Amminadab the chief, and 112 of his relatives.

11 Then David called[7121] for [a]Zadok and [b]Abiathar the priests, and for the Levites, for Uriel, Asaiah, Joel, Shemaiah, Eliel, and Amminadab,

12 and said to them, "You are the heads[7218] of the fathers'[1] *households* of the Levites; [a]consecrate yourselves both you and your relatives, that you may bring up the ark of the LORD God of Israel, [b]to *the place* that I have prepared for it.

13 "[a]Because you did not *carry it* at the first,[7223] the LORD our God made an outburst on us, for we did not seek Him according to the ordinance."[4941]

14 [a]So the priests and the Levites consecrated themselves to bring up the ark of the LORD God of Israel.

15 And the sons of [a]the Levites carried[5375] the ark of God on their shoulders, with the poles thereon as Moses had commanded[6680] according to the word[1697] of the LORD.

16 Then David spoke to the chiefs of the Levites [a]to appoint their relatives the singers, with instruments of music,[7892] harps, lyres, loud-sounding cymbals, to raise sounds of joy.

17 So [a]the Levites appointed Heman the son of Joel, and from his relatives, Asaph the son of Berechiah; and from the sons of Merari their relatives, Ethan the son of Kushaiah,

18 and with them their relatives of the second rank, Zechariah, [1]Ben, Jaaziel, Shemiramoth, Jehiel, Unni, Eliab, Benaiah, Maaseiah, Mattithiah, Eliphelehu, Mikneiah, Obed-edom, and Jeiel, the gatekeepers.[7778]

19 So the singers, Heman, Asaph, and Ethan *were appointed* to sound aloud cymbals of bronze;

20 and Zechariah, Aziel, Shemiramoth, Jehiel, Unni, Eliab, Maaseiah, and Benaiah, with [1]harps *tuned* to [a]alamoth;

21 and Mattithiah, Eliphelehu, Mikneiah, Obed-edom, Jeiel, and Azaziah, to lead with [1]lyres tuned to [a]the sheminith.

22 And Chenaniah, chief of the Levites, was *in charge of* the singing; he gave instruction[3256] in singing because he was skillful.

23 And Berechiah and Elkanah were gatekeepers for the ark.

24 And Shebaniah, Joshaphat, Nethanel, Amasai, Zechariah, Benaiah, and Eliezer, the priests, [a]blew the trumpets before the ark of God. Obed-edom and Jehiah also *were* gatekeepers for the ark.

25 [a]So *it was* David, with the elders[2205] of Israel and the captains[8269] over thousands, who went to bring up the ark of the covenant[1285] of the LORD from [b]the house of Obed-edom with joy.

26 And it came about because God was helping the Levites who were carrying the ark of the covenant of the LORD, that they sacrificed[2076] [a]seven bulls and seven rams.

27 Now David was clothed with a robe of fine linen with all the Levites who were carrying the ark, and the

2 [a]Num. 4:15; Deut. 10:8
3 [a]1Kin. 8:1; 1Chr. 13:5 [b]Ex. 40:20f.; 2Sam. 6:12, 17; 1Chr. 15:1, 12
4 [a]1Chr. 6:16-30; 12:26
5 [1]Lit., *brothers;* i.e., fellow tribesmen, and so through out the ch.
11 [a]1Chr. 12:28 [b]1Sam. 22:20-23; 1Kin. 2:26, 35
12 [a]Ex. 19:14, 15; 2Chr. 35:6 [b]1Chr. 15:1, 3
13 [a]2Sam. 6:3; 1Chr. 13:7
14 [a]1Chr. 15:12
15 [a]Ex. 25:14; Num. 4:5f.
16 [a]1Chr. 13:8; 25:1
17 [a]1Chr. 25:1
18 [1]Omitted in Gr. and many mss.
20 [1]Or, *harps of maiden-like tone* [a]Ps. 46:title
21 [1]Or, *octave harps* [a]Ps. 6:title
24 [a]1Chr. 15:28; 16:6
25 [a]2Sam. 6:12, 15 [b]1Chr. 13:13
26 [a]Num. 23:1-4, 29

15:2-13 See note on I Chr. 13:9,10.

15:25 Psalm 24 seems to have been written and set to music for that occasion. It proved to be prophetic of Christ's triumphal entry into Jerusalem.

singers and Chenaniah the leader[8269] of
the singing *with* the singers. [a]David also
wore an ephod of linen.
28 Thus all Israel brought[5927] up the
ark of the covenant of the LORD with
shouting, and with sound of the horn,
with trumpets, with loud-sounding cymbals, with harps and lyres.
29 And it happened when the ark
of the covenant of the LORD came to
the city of David, that [a]Michal the daughter of Saul looked out of the window,
and saw King[4428] David leaping and making merry; and she despised him in her
heart.

A Tent for the Ark

16 And they brought in the ark[727]
of God[430] and [a]placed it inside
the tent which David had pitched for
it, and they offered[7126] burnt offerings
and peace offerings before God.
2 When David had finished[3615]
offering[5927] the burnt offering and the
peace offerings, he blessed[1288] the people in the name of the LORD.
3 And he distributed to everyone
of Israel, both man[376] and woman,[802]
to everyone[376] a loaf of bread and a portion *of meat* and a raisin cake.[809]
4 And he appointed some of the
Levites *as* ministers[8334] before the ark
of the LORD, even to celebrate and to
thank and praise the LORD God of Israel:
5 Asaph the chief,[7218] and second
to him Zechariah, *then* [I]Jeiel, Shemiramoth, Jehiel, Mattithiah, Eliab, Benaiah,
Obed-edom, and Jeiel, with musical instruments, harps, lyres; also Asaph
played loud-sounding cymbals,
6 and Benaiah and Jahaziel the
priests *blew* trumpets continually[8548] before the ark of the covenant[1285] of God.
🗝 **7** Then on that day[3117] David
[a]first[7218] assigned [I]Asaph and his [II]rela-
tives[251] to give thanks to the LORD.

Psalm of Thanksgiving

8 [a]Oh give thanks to the LORD,
call[7121] upon His name;
[b]Make known[3045] His deeds
among the peoples.
9 Sing to Him, sing praises to
Him;
[I]Speak of all His [II]wonders.
10 [I]Glory[1984] in His holy name;
Let the heart of those who seek
the LORD be glad.
11 [a]Seek the LORD and His
strength;
Seek His face continually.
12 [a]Remember His wonderful[6381]
deeds which He has done,[6213]
[b]His marvels[4159] and the
judgments[4941] from His
mouth,[6310]
13 O seed of Israel His servant,
Sons[1121] of Jacob, His chosen
ones!
14 He is the LORD our God;
[a]His judgments are in all the
earth.[776]
15 Remember[2142] His covenant
forever,[5769]
The word[1697] which He
commanded[6680] to a thousand
generations,[1755]
16 [a]*The covenant* which He
made[3772] with Abraham,
And His oath[7621] to Isaac.
17 [a]He also confirmed it to Jacob
for a statute,[2706]
To Israel as an everlasting[5769]
covenant,
18 Saying, "[a]To you I will give the
land[776] of Canaan,
As the portion of your
inheritance."[5159]
19 [a]When they were only a few
in number,
Very few, and strangers in it,
20 And they wandered about from
nation to nation,

27 [a]2Sam. 6:14
29 [a]2Sam. 3:13f.; 6:16
1 [a]1Chr. 15:1
5 [I]In 1Chr. 15:18, *Jaaziel*
7 [I]Lit., *by the hand of Asaph* [II]Lit., *brothers* [a]2 Sam. 22:1; 23:1
8 [a]1Chr. 16:8-36; Ps. 105:1-15 [b]1Kin. 8:43; 2Kin. 19:19
9 [I]Or, *Meditate on* [II]I.e., wonderful acts
10 [I]Or, *Boast*
11 [a]Ps. 24:6
12 [a]Ps. 103:2 [b]Ps. 78:43-68
14 [a]Ps. 48:10
16 [a]Gen. 12:7; 17:2; 22:16-18; 26:3
17 [a]Gen. 35:11, 12
18 [a]Gen. 13:15
19 [a]Gen. 34:30; Deut. 7:7

🗝 **16:7** Twelve psalms were written by Asaph and his descendants (Ps. 50,73–83).
🗝 **16:7-36** David's model songs consisted of Ps. 105:1-45; 96:1-13; 106:1-48. Although these three psalms are listed as anonymous in the Book of Psalms, it appears that David wrote them.

And from *one* kingdom[4467] to
another people,
21 He permitted no man to oppress
them,
And [a]He reproved kings[4428] for
their sakes, *saying,*
22 "Do not touch My anointed[4899]
ones,
And [a]do My prophets no harm."
23 [a]Sing to the LORD, all the earth;
Proclaim good tidings of His
salvation[3444] from day to day.
24 Tell[5608] of His glory[3519] among
the nations,
His wonderful deeds among all
the peoples.
25 For [a]great is the LORD, and
greatly to be praised;
He also is [b]to be feared[3372] above
all gods.[430]
26 For all the gods of the peoples
are [I][a]idols,[457]
[b]But the LORD made[6213] the
heavens.
27 Splendor and majesty are before
Him,
Strength and joy are in His
place.
28 Ascribe to the LORD, O families
of the peoples,
Ascribe to the LORD glory and
strength.
29 Ascribe to the LORD the glory
due His name;
Bring[5375] an [I]offering,[4503] and
come before Him;
[a]Worship[7812] the LORD in
[II]holy array.[1927]
30 Tremble[2342] before Him, all the
earth;
Indeed, the world[8398] is firmly
established, it will not be
moved.
31 [a]Let the heavens be glad, and
let the earth rejoice;
And let them say among the
nations, "[b]The LORD reigns."
32 [a]Let the sea [I]roar, and
[II]all it contains;
Let the field[7704] exult, and all
that is in it.
33 Then the trees of the forest
will sing for joy before the
LORD;
For He is coming to judge[8199]
the earth.
34 [a]O give thanks to the LORD,
for *He is* good;[2896]
For His lovingkindness[2617] is
everlasting.
35 [a]Then say, "Save us, O God
of our salvation,
And gather[6908] us and deliver[5337]
us from the nations,
To give thanks to Thy holy
name,
And [I]glory[7623] in Thy praise."
36 [a]Blessed be the LORD, the God
of Israel,
From everlasting even to
everlasting.
Then all the people [b]said,[559] "Amen,"[543]
and praised the LORD.

Worship before the Ark

37 So he left[5800] Asaph and his
[I]relatives there [a]before the ark of the
covenant of the LORD, to minister before
the ark continually, [b]as every day's work
required;
38 and [a]Obed-edom with [I]his 68 relatives; Obed-edom, also the son of Jeduthun, and [b]Hosah as gatekeepers.[7778]
39 And *he left* [a]Zadok the priest and
his [I]relatives the priests [b]before the
[II]tabernacle of the LORD in the high place
which *was* at Gibeon,
40 to offer burnt offerings to the
LORD on the altar[4196] of burnt offering
continually morning and evening,
[a]even according to all that is written in
the law[8451] of the LORD, which He commanded Israel.
41 And with them *were* [a]Heman and
Jeduthun, and [b]the rest who were chosen,[1305] who were designated[5344] by
name, to [c]give thanks to the LORD, because His lovingkindness is everlasting.
42 And with them *were* Heman and
Jeduthun *with* trumpets and cymbals for
those who should sound aloud, and *with*
instruments *for* [a]the songs[7892] of God,
and the sons of Jeduthun for the gate.[8179]

21 [a]Gen. 12:17; 20:3; Ex. 7:15-18
22 [a]Gen. 20:7
23 [a]Ps. 96:1-13
25 [a]Ps. 144:3-6 [b]Ps. 89:7
26 [I]Or, *non-existent things* [a]Lev. 19:4 [b]Ps. 102:25
29 [I]Or, *a grain offering* [II]Or, *the splendor of holiness* [a]Ps. 29:2
31 [a]Is. 44:23; 49:13 [b]Ps. 93:1; 96:10
32 [I]Or, *thunder* [II]Lit., *its fulness* [a]Ps. 98:7
34 [a]2Chr. 5:13; 7:3; Ezra 3:11; Ps. 106:1; 136:1; Jer. 33:11
35 [I]Lit., *boast* [a]Ps. 106:47, 48
36 [a]1Kin. 8:15, 56; Ps. 72:18 [b]Deut. 27:15; Neh. 8:6
37 [I]Lit., *brothers* [a]1Chr. 16:4, 5 [b]2Chr. 8:14; Ezra 3:4
38 [I]Lit., *their brothers, 68* [a]1Chr. 13:14 [b]1Chr. 26:10
39 [I]Lit., *brothers* [II]Lit., *dwelling place* [a]1Chr. 15:11 [b]1Kin. 3:4
40 [a]Ex. 29:38-42; Num. 28:3, 4
41 [a]1Chr. 6:33 [b]1Chr. 25:1-6 [c]2Chr. 5:13
42 [a]1Chr. 25:7; 2Chr. 7:6; 29:27

43 [a]Then all the people departed
each to his house, and David returned
to bless[1288] his household.

God's Covenant with David

17 🔑 [a]And it came about, when David dwelt in his house, that David
said[559] to Nathan the prophet, "Behold,
I am dwelling in a house of cedar, but
the ark[727] of the covenant[1285] of the LORD
is under curtains."
2 Then Nathan said to David,
"Do[6213] all that is in your heart, for
God[430] is with you."
3 And it came about the same night,
that the word[1697] of God came to Nathan,
saying,
🔑 4 "Go and tell David My servant,
'Thus says[559] the LORD, [a]"You shall not
build a house for Me to dwell in;
5 for I have not dwelt in a house
since the day[3117] that I brought[5927] up
Israel to this day, [a]but I have [l]gone from
tent to tent and from *one* dwelling place
to another.
6 "In all places where I have walked
with all Israel, have I spoken a word
[a]with any of the judges[8199] of Israel,
whom I commanded[6680] to shepherd My
people, saying, 'Why have you not built
for Me a house of cedar?' "'
7 "Now, therefore, thus shall you
say to My servant David, 'Thus says
the LORD of hosts, "I took you from
the pasture,[5116] from following the
sheep, that you should be leader over
My people Israel.
8 "And I have been with you wherever you have gone, and have cut
off[3772] all your enemies from before you;
and I will make[6213] you a name like the
name of the great ones who are in the
earth.[776]
🔑 9 "And I will appoint[7760] a place for
My people Israel, and will plant them,

43 [a]2Sam. 6:19
1 [a]2Sam. 7:1-29
4 [a]1Chr. 28:2, 3
5 [l]Lit., *been* [a]Ex. 40:2, 3; 2Sam. 7:6
6 [a]2Sam. 7:7
9 [l]Lit., *sons of wickedness*
11 [l]Lit., *seed*
13 [a]2Cor. 6:18; Heb. 1:5 [b]1Chr. 10:14
16 [a]2Sam. 7:18

that they may dwell[7931] in their own place
and be moved no more; neither shall
the [l]wicked[5766] waste them anymore as
formerly,[7223]
10 even from the day that I commanded judges *to be* over My people
Israel. And I will subdue all your enemies. Moreover, I tell you that the LORD
will build a house for you.
11 "And it shall come about when
your days[3117] are fulfilled that you must
go *to be* with your fathers,[1] that I will
set up *one of* your [l]descendants after
you, who shall be of your sons; and I
will establish his kingdom.[4438]
🔑 12 "He shall build for Me a house,
and I will establish his throne forever.
13 "[a]I will be his father, and he shall
be My son; and I will not take My
lovingkindness[2617] away from him, [b]as
I took it from him who was before you.
14 "But I will settle him in My house
and in My kingdom forever, and his
throne shall be established[3559] forever." ' "[5769]
15 According to all these words[1697]
and according to all this vision,[2377] so
Nathan spoke to David.

David's Prayer in Response

16 Then David the king[4428] went
in and sat before the LORD and said,
"[a]Who am I, O LORD God, and what is
my house that Thou hast brought me
this far?
17 "And this was a small thing in
Thine eyes, O God; but Thou hast spoken of Thy servant's house for a great
while to come, and hast regarded me
according to the standard of a man[120]
of high degree, O LORD God.
18 "What more can David still *say*
to Thee concerning the honor *bestowed*
on Thy servant? For Thou knowest[3045]
Thy servant.

🔑 **17:1-27** See II Sam. 7:1-29.
🔑 **17:4** David was disqualified because of his warfare (I Chr. 22:8; 28:3).
🔑 **17:9** The Israelites were oppressed in Egypt and harassed by the Amalekites, Ammonites, Midianites, and Philistines.
🔑 **17:12** This was accomplished by Solomon (I Kgs. 5:5).

19 "O LORD, [a]for Thy servant's
sake, and according to Thine own heart,
Thou hast wrought[6213] all this greatness, to make known[3045] all these great
things.
20 "O LORD, there is none like
Thee, neither is there any God besides
Thee, according to all that we have
heard with our ears.[241]
21 "And what one nation in the earth
is like Thy people Israel, whom God
went to redeem for Himself *as* a people,
to make[7760] Thee a name by great and
terrible things, in driving out nations
from before Thy people, whom Thou
didst redeem out of Egypt?
🔑22 "[a]For Thy people Israel Thou
didst make Thine own people forever,
and Thou, O LORD, didst become their
God.
23 "And now, O LORD, let the word
that Thou hast spoken concerning Thy
servant and concerning his house, be
established[539] forever, and do as Thou
hast spoken.[1696]
24 "And let Thy name be established and magnified forever, saying,
'The LORD of hosts is the God of Israel,
even a God to Israel; and the house of
David Thy servant is established before
Thee.'
🔑25 "For Thou, O my God, hast revealed to Thy servant that Thou wilt
build for him a house; therefore Thy
servant hath found *courage* to pray before Thee.
26 "And now, O LORD, Thou art
God, and hast [I]promised this good thing
to Thy servant.
27 "And now it hath pleased Thee
to bless[1288] the house of Thy servant,
that it may [I]continue forever before
Thee; for Thou, O LORD, hast blessed,
and it is blessed[1288] forever."

19 [a]2Sam. 7:21; Is. 37:35
22 [a]Ex. 19:5, 6
26 [I]Lit., *said*
27 [I]Lit., *be*
1 [I]Lit., *smote*, and so in vv. 1-3 [a]2Sam. 8:1-18
3 [I]Lit., *hand*
5 [I]Heb., *Darmeseq* [II]Lit., *smote* [a]1Chr. 19:6
6 [I]Heb., *Darmeseq*
7 [I]Lit., *on*
8 [I]In 2Sam. 8:8, *Betah* [a]1Kin. 7:40-47; 2Chr. 4:11-18
9 [I]In 2Sam. 8:9, *Toi* [II]Lit., *smitten*
10 [I]In 2Sam. 8:10, *Joram* [II]Lit., *ask him of his welfare* [III]Lit., *smitten*

David's Kingdom Strengthened

18 🔑Now after this [a]it came about
that David [I]defeated the Philistines and subdued them and took Gath
and its towns from the hand of the Philistines.
2 And he defeated Moab, and the
Moabites became servants to David,
bringing[5375] tribute.
🔑3 David also defeated Hadadezer
king[4428] of Zobah *as far as* Hamath, as
he went to establish his [I]rule to the
Euphrates River.
4 And David took from him 1,000
chariots and 7,000 horsemen and 20,000
foot soldiers, and David hamstrung[6131]
all the chariot horses, but reserved
enough of them for 100 chariots.
5 When the Arameans of [I]Damascus
came to help Hadadezer king [a]of Zobah,
David [II]killed 22,000 men[376] of the Arameans.
6 Then David put *garrisons* among
the Arameans of [I]Damascus; and the
Arameans became servants to David,
bringing tribute. And the LORD helped
David wherever he went.
7 And David took the shields of gold
which were [I]carried by the servants of
Hadadezer, and brought them to Jerusalem.
🔑8 Also from [I]Tibhath and from Cun,
cities of Hadadezer, David took a very
large amount of bronze, with which
[a]Solomon made[6213] the bronze sea and
the pillars and the bronze utensils.
9 Now when [I]Tou king of Hamath
heard that David had [II]defeated all the
army of Hadadezer king of Zobah,
10 he sent [I]Hadoram his son to King
David, to [II]greet[7592] him and to bless[1288]
him, because he had fought against
Hadadezer and had [III]defeated him; for

🔑 **17:22** These last few words are the central promise of God's covenant (Gen. 17:7; Ex. 6:7; Rev. 21:3).

🔑 **17:25** "House" here does not refer to a building, but to a dynasty.

🔑 **18:1-13** See II Sam. 8:1-14.

🔑 **18:3** See I Chr. 19:16-18, the second defeat of the Syrians.

🔑 **18:8** This was collected for the temple. Notice what David had accumulated for Solomon's temple in I Chr. 22:2-5,14,15.

Hadadezer had been at war with Tou.
And *Hadoram brought* all kinds of articles of gold and silver and bronze.
🔑 11 King David also dedicated[6942]
these to the LORD with the silver and
the gold which he had carried away from
all the nations: from Edom, Moab, the
sons[1121] of Ammon, the Philistines, and
from Amalek.
🔑 **12** Moreover Abishai the son of
Zeruiah [I]defeated 18,000 Edomites in
the Valley of Salt.
13 Then he put garrisons in Edom,
and all the Edomites became servants
to David. And the LORD helped David
wherever he went.
🔑 **14** So David reigned over all Israel;
and he [I]administered[6213] justice[4941] and
righteousness[6666] for all his people.
15 And [a]Joab the son of Zeruiah *was*
over the army, and Jehoshaphat the son
of Ahilud *was* recorder;
16 and Zadok the son of Ahitub
and Abimelech the son of Abiathar
were priests, and Shavsha *was* secretary;
17 and Benaiah the son of Jehoiada
was over the Cherethites and the Pelethites, and the sons of David *were*
chiefs[7223] at the king's side.

David's Messengers Abused

19 🔑 [a]Now it came about after this,
that Nahash the king[4428] of the
sons[1121] of Ammon died,[4191] and his son
became king in his place.
🔑 2 Then David said,[559] "I will show
kindness[2617] to Hanun the son of Nahash, because his father showed kindness to me." So David sent messengers[4397] to console[5162] him concerning
his father. And David's servants came
into the land[776] of the sons of Ammon
to Hanun, to console him.
3 But the princes of the sons of Ammon said to Hanun, "[I]Do you think that
David is honoring your father, in that
he has sent comforters[5162] to you? Have
not his servants come to you to search
and to overthrow[2015] and to spy out the
land?"
4 So Hanun took David's servants
and shaved them, and cut off[3772] their
garments in the middle as far as their
hips, and sent them away.
5 Then *certain persons* went and told
David about the men.[582] And he sent
to meet them, for the men were greatly
humiliated. And the king said, "[I]Stay at
Jericho until your beards[2206] grow, and
then return."
6 When the sons of Ammon saw
that they had made themselves odious[887]
to David, Hanun and the sons of Ammon
sent 1,000 talents of silver to hire for
themselves chariots and horsemen from
Mesopotamia, from Aram-maacah, and
[a]from Zobah.
7 So they hired for themselves
32,000 chariots, and the king of Maacah
and his people, who came and camped
before [a]Medeba. And the sons of Ammon gathered[622] together from their cities and came to battle.
8 When David heard *of it,* he sent
Joab and all the army, the mighty men.
9 And the sons of Ammon came out
and drew up in battle array at the entrance of the city, and the kings[4428] who
had come were by themselves in the
field.[7704]

Ammon and Aram Defeated

10 Now when Joab saw that the
[I]battle was set against him in front and

12 [I]Lit., *smote*
14 [I]Lit., *was doing*
15 [a]1Chr. 11:6
1 [a]2Sam. 10:1-19
3 [I]Lit., *In your eyes is David honoring your father because*
5 [I]Lit., *Return to*
6 [a]1Chr. 18:5, 9
7 [a]Num. 21:30; Josh. 13:9, 16
10 [I]Lit., *the face of the battle*

🔑 **18:11** The Philistines were Europeans. According to Amos 9:7, they had originally come from Caphtor (Crete). They were greatly reinforced by refugees from Crete when the island fell to Greek invaders about 1200 B.C. (Jer. 47:4). At the time of the rise of Saul, 1048 B.C., the Philistines were dominating Israel and using Hebrews as mercenary troops (I Sam. 14:21), but David's victories reversed the situation.
🔑 **18:12** See note on II Sam. 8:13.
🔑 **18:14-17** See II Sam. 8:15-18; 20:23-26.
🔑 **19:1-19** See II Sam. 10:1-19.
🔑 **19:2** This would hardly be the same Nahash whom Saul fought some fifty-five years before (I Sam. 11). Perhaps he was a son.

in the rear, he selected[977] from all the
choice men of Israel and they arrayed
themselves against the Arameans.
11 But the remainder of the people
he placed in the hand of [I]Abshai his
brother;[251] and they arrayed themselves
against the sons of Ammon.
12 And he said, "If the Arameans
are too strong for me, then you shall
help me; but if the sons of Ammon are
too strong for you, then I will help you.
13 "Be strong,[2388] and let us show
ourselves courageous[2388] for the sake
of our people and for the cities of our
God;[430] and may the LORD do[6213] what
is good in His sight."
14 So Joab and the people who were
with him drew near to the battle against
the Arameans, and they fled before him.
15 When the sons of Ammon saw
that the Arameans fled, they also fled
before Abshai his brother, and entered
the city. Then Joab came to Jerusalem.
🔑 **16** When the Arameans saw that
they had been [I]defeated by Israel, they
sent messengers, and brought out the
Arameans who were beyond the
[II]River, with Shophach the commander[8269] of the army of Hadadezer
[III]leading them.
17 When it was told David, he gathered all Israel together and crossed the
Jordan, and came upon them and drew
up in formation against them. And when
David drew up in battle array against
the Arameans, they fought against
him.
18 And the Arameans fled before
Israel, and David killed of the Arameans
7,000 charioteers and 40,000 foot soldiers, and put to death[4191] Shophach the
commander of the army.
19 So when the servants of Hadadezer saw that they were [I]defeated by
Israel, they made peace with David and
served him. Thus the Arameans were
not willing[14] to help the sons of Ammon
anymore.

War with Philistine Giants

20 🔑 [a]Then it happened [I]in the
spring, at the time when
kings[4428] go out *to battle*, that Joab led
out the army[6635] and ravaged[7843] the
land[776] of the sons[1121] of Ammon, and
came and besieged Rabbah. But David
stayed at Jerusalem. And [b]Joab struck
Rabbah and overthrew[2040] it.
2 [a]And David took the crown of
[I]their king[4428] from his head, and he
found it to weigh a talent of gold, and
there was a precious stone in it; and it
was placed on David's head. And he
brought out the spoil of the city, a very
great amount.
3 And he brought out the people
who *were* in it, [a]and cut *them* with saws
and with sharp instruments[2757] and with
axes. And thus David did[6213] to all the
cities of the sons of Ammon. Then David
and all the people returned *to* Jerusalem.
🔑 **4** [a]Now it came about after this, that
war [I]broke out at [II]Gezer with the Philistines; then Sibbecai the Hushathite
[III]killed Sippai, one of the descendants
of the [IV]giants, and they were subdued.
5 And there was war with the Philistines again, and Elhanan the son of
[a]Jair [I]killed Lahmi the brother[251] of Goliath the Gittite, the [b]shaft of whose
spear *was* like a weaver's beam.
6 And again there was war at Gath,
where there was a man[376] of *great* stature who had twenty-four fingers and
toes, six *fingers on each hand* and six
toes on each foot; and he also was descended from the giants.
7 And when he taunted[2778] Israel,
Jonathan the son of Shimea, David's

11 [I]In 2Sam. 10:10, *Abishai*
16 [I]Lit., *smitten before* [II]I.e., Euphrates [III]Lit., *before*
19 [I]Lit., *smitten before*
1 [I]Lit., *at the return of the year* [a]2Sam. 11:1 [b]2Sam. 12:26
2 [I]In Zeph. 1:5, *Malcam* [a]2Sam. 12:30, 31
3 [a]2Sam. 12:31
4 [I]Lit., *stood up* [II]In 2Sam. 21:18, *Gob* [III]Lit., *smote* [IV]Heb., *Raphah*, and so in vv. 6, 8 [a]2Sam. 21:18-22
5 [I]Lit., *smote* [a]2Sam. 21:19 [b]1Sam. 17:7; 1Chr. 11:23

🔑 **19:16** East of the Euphrates.
🔑 **20:1-3** See II Sam. 12:26-31.
🔑 **20:4** The Rephaim were an ancient people who were renowned for their size (Gen. 14:5). Except for Og's kingdom in Bashan, they had died out by the time of Moses (Deut. 3:11).
🔑 **20:4-8** See II Sam. 21:18-22.
🔑 **21:1-27** See II Sam. 24:1-25.

brother, [I]killed him.
8 These were descended from the giants in Gath, and they fell[5307] by the hand of David and by the hand of his servants.

Census Brings Pestilence

21 🔑 [a]Then Satan stood up against Israel and moved David to number Israel.
2 So David said[559] to Joab and to the princes of the people, "[a]Go, number Israel from Beersheba even to Dan, and bring me *word* that I may know[3045] their number."
3 And Joab said,[559] "[a]May the LORD add to His people a hundred times as many as they are! But, my lord[113] the king,[4428] are they not all my lord's servants? Why does my lord seek this thing? Why should he be a cause of guilt to Israel?"
4 Nevertheless, the king's[4428] word[1697] prevailed against Joab. Therefore, Joab departed and went throughout all Israel, and came to Jerusalem.
5 And Joab gave the number of the [I]census of *all* the people to David. And [a]all Israel were 1,100,000 men[376] who drew the sword; and Judah *was* 470,000 men who drew the sword.
6 [a]But he did not [I]number[6485] Levi and Benjamin among them, for the king's [II]command was abhorrent[8581] to Joab.
7 And [I]God[430] was displeased[3415] with this thing, so He struck Israel.
8 And David said to God, "I have sinned greatly, in that I have done[6213] this thing. [a]But now, please[4994] take away the iniquity[5771] of Thy servant, for I have done very foolishly."
9 And the LORD spoke to [a]Gad, David's [b]seer, saying,
10 "Go and speak to David, saying, 'Thus says[559] the LORD, "I [I]offer you three things; choose[977] for yourself one of them, that I may do[6213] *it* to you." ' "
11 So Gad came to David and said to him, "Thus says the LORD, 'Take for yourself
12 [a]either three years of famine, or three months to be swept away[5595] before your foes, while the sword of your enemies overtakes *you,* or else three days[3117] of the sword of the LORD, even pestilence in the land,[776] and the angel[4397] of the LORD destroying[7843] throughout all the territory of Israel.' Now, therefore, consider what answer I shall return to Him who sent me."
13 And David said to Gad, "I am in great distress;[6887] please let me fall into the hand of the LORD, [a]for His mercies are very great. But do not let me fall into the hand of man."[120]
14 [a]So the LORD [I]sent a pestilence on Israel; 70,000 men of Israel fell.[5307]
15 And God sent an angel to Jerusalem to destroy[7843] it; but as he was about to destroy *it,* the LORD saw[7200] and [a]was sorry over the calamity,[7451] and said to the destroying[7843] angel, "It is enough; now relax your hand." And the angel of the LORD was standing by the threshing floor of [I]Ornan the Jebusite.
16 Then David lifted up his eyes and saw the angel of the LORD standing between earth[776] and heaven, with his drawn sword in his hand stretched out over Jerusalem. Then David and the elders,[2205] [a]covered with sackcloth, fell on their faces.
17 And David said to God, "Is it not I who [I]commanded[559] to count the people? Indeed, I am the one who has sinned and done very wickedly,[7489] [a]but these sheep, what have they done?[6213] O LORD my God, please let Thy hand be against me and my father's[1] household, but not against Thy people that they should be plagued."

7 [I]Lit., *smote*
1 [a]2Sam. 24:1-25
2 [a]1Chr. 27:23, 24
3 [a]Deut. 1:11
5 [I]Lit., *muster* [a]2Sam. 24:9
6 [I]Lit., *muster* [II]Lit., *word* [a]1Chr. 27:24
7 [I]Lit., *it was evil in the sight of God*
8 [a]2Sam. 12:13
9 [a]2Sam. 24:11; 1Chr. 29:29 [b]1Sam. 9:9
10 [I]Lit., *stretch out to*
12 [a]2Sam. 24:13
13 [a]Ps. 51:1; 130:4, 7
14 [I]Lit., *gave* [a]1Chr. 27:24
15 [I]In 2Sam. 24:16, *Araunah* [a]Ex. 32:14; 1Sam. 15:11; Jon. 3:10
16 [a]1Kin. 21:27
17 [I]Lit., *said* [a]2Sam. 7:8; Ps. 74:1

🔑 **21:1** This is the only reference to Satan, by that specific name, in the historical books of the O.T. He is further mentioned only in the Books of Job, Psalms (once), and Zechariah. The parallel record in II Sam. 24 shows that Satan was the instrument of God to execute punishment upon Israel for their sins (cf. Job 1:6-12; I Kgs. 22:20-22).

David's Altar

18 [a]Then the angel of the LORD
[I]commanded Gad to say to David, that
David should go up and build an altar[4196]
to the LORD on the threshing floor of
Ornan the Jebusite.
19 So David went up at the word
of Gad, which he spoke in the name of
the LORD.
20 Now Ornan turned back and saw
the angel, and his four sons *who were*
with him hid themselves. And Ornan
was threshing wheat.
21 And as David came to Ornan,
Ornan looked and saw David, and went
out from the threshing floor, and prostrated[7812] himself [I]before David with his
face[629] to the ground.[776]
22 Then David said to Ornan, "Give
me the [I]site of *this* threshing floor, that
I may build on it an altar to the LORD;
for the full price you shall give it to me,
that the plague may be restrained from
the people."
23 And Ornan said to David, "Take
it for yourself; and let my lord the king
do what is good[2896] in his sight. See, I
will give the oxen for burnt offerings
and the threshing sledges for wood and
the wheat for the grain offering;[4503] I
will give *it* all."
24 But King David said to Ornan,
"No, but I will surely buy *it* for the full
price; for I will not take what is yours
for the LORD, or offer a burnt offering
[I]which costs me nothing."
25 So [a]David gave Ornan 600 shekels of gold by weight for the [I]site.
🔑 26 Then David built an altar to the
LORD there, and offered[5927] burnt offerings and peace offerings. And he
called[7121] to the LORD and [a]He answered
him with fire from heaven on the altar
of burnt offering.

18 [I]Lit., *said to* [a]2 Chr. 3:1
21 [I]Lit., *to*
22 [I]Lit., *place*
24 [I]Lit., *gratuitously*
25 [I]Lit., *place* [a]2Sam. 24:24
26 [a]Lev. 9:24; Judg. 6:21
29 [a]1Kin. 3:4; 1Chr. 16:39

27 And the LORD commanded the
angel, and he put his sword back in its
sheath.
🔑 **28** At that time, when David saw
that the LORD had answered him on the
threshing floor of Ornan the Jebusite,
he offered sacrifice[2076] there.
29 [a]For the tabernacle of the LORD,
which Moses had made[6213] in the wilderness, and the altar of burnt offering *were*
in the high place at Gibeon at that time.
30 But David could not go before
it to inquire of God, for he was terrified[1204] by the sword of the angel of
the LORD.

David Prepares for Temple Building

22 Then David said,[559] "[a]This is the
house of the LORD God,[430] and
this is the altar[4196] of burnt offering for
Israel."
2 So David [I]gave orders[559] to
gather[3644] [a]the foreigners who were in
the land[776] of Israel, and [b]he set stonecutters to hew out stones to build the
house of God.
3 And David [a]prepared large quantities of iron [I]to make the nails for the
doors of the gates and for the clamps,
and more [b]bronze than could be
weighed;
4 and timbers of cedar logs beyond
number, for [a]the Sidonians and Tyrians
brought large quantities of cedar timber
to David.
🔑 5 And David said, "My son [a]Solo-
mon is young and inexperienced, and the
house that is to be built for the LORD
shall be exceedingly magnificent,[1431] famous and glorious[8597] throughout all
lands.[776] *Therefore* now I will make preparation for it." So David made ample
preparations before his death.[4194]

1 [a]1Chr. 21:18-28; 2Chr. 3:1
2 [I]Lit., *said to* [a]1Kin. 9:20, 21; 2Chr. 2:17 [b]1Kin. 5:17, 18
3 [I]Lit., *for* [a]1Chr. 29:2, 7 [b]1Chr. 22:14
4 [a]1Kin. 5:6-10
5 [a]1Kin. 3:7; 1Chr. 29:1

🔑 **21:26-28** See II Sam. 24:16-25.
🔑 **21:28** The threshing-floor of Ornan was on Mount Moriah, where Abraham had attempted to offer Isaac to God. The temple was soon built by Solomon (II Chr. 3:1) there. Ps. 30:5,6 describes David's situation at this point.
🔑 **22:5** If Solomon were born about 990 B.C., he would have been twenty years old at his accession to the throne of David.

Solomon Charged with the Task

6 Then [a]he called[7121] for his son Solomon, and charged[6680] him to build a house for the LORD God of Israel.

7 And David said to Solomon, "[a]My son, [I]I had intended[3824] to build a house to the name of the LORD my God.

⊶ 8 "But the word[1697] of the LORD came to me, saying, '[a]You have shed much blood,[1818] and have [I]waged[6213] great wars; you shall not build a house to My name, because you have shed *so* much blood on the earth[776] before Me.

⊶ 9 'Behold, a son shall be born to you, who shall be a man[376] of rest; and [a]I will give him rest from all his enemies on every side; for [b]his name shall be [I]Solomon, and I will give peace and quiet to Israel in his days.[3117]

10 '[a]He shall build a house for My name, and he shall be My son, and I will be his father; and I will establish the throne of his kingdom[4438] over Israel forever.'

11 "Now, my son, [a]the LORD be with you that you may be successful, and build the house of the LORD your God just as He has spoken[1696] concerning you.

12 "[a]Only the LORD give you discretion[7922] and understanding,[998] and give you charge[6680] over Israel, so that you may [b]keep[8104] the law[8451] of the LORD your God.

13 "[a]Then you shall prosper, if you are careful to observe the statutes and the ordinances[4941] which the LORD commanded Moses concerning Israel. [b]Be strong and courageous, do not fear nor be dismayed.[2865]

14 "Now behold, [I]with great pains I have prepared for the house of the LORD [a]100,000 talents of gold and 1,000,000 talents of silver, and [b]bronze and iron beyond weight, for [II]they are in great quantity; also timber and stone I have prepared, and you may add to them.

15 "Moreover, there are many workmen with you, stonecutters[2672] and masons of stone and carpenters, and all men who are skillful[2450] in every kind of work.[4399]

16 "Of the gold, the silver and the bronze and the iron, there is no limit. Arise and work,[6213] and may [a]the LORD be with you."

17 [a]David also commanded[6680] all the leaders of Israel to help his son Solomon, *saying,*

18 "Is not the LORD your God with you? And [a]has He not given you rest on every side? For He has given the inhabitants of the land into my hand, and the land is subdued before the LORD and before His people.

19 "Now [a]set your heart and your soul to seek the LORD your God; arise, therefore, and build the sanctuary of the LORD God, [b]so that you may bring the ark[727] of the covenant[1285] of the LORD, and the holy vessels of God into the house that is to be built [c]for the name of the LORD."

Solomon Reigns

23 [a]Now when David [I]reached old age,[3117] [b]he made his son Solomon king[4427] over Israel.

2 And he gathered[622] together all the leaders of Israel with the priests and the Levites.

Offices of the Levites

3 And [a]the Levites were numbered from thirty years old and upward, and [b]their number by [I]census of men[1397] was 38,000.

4 Of these, 24,000 were [a]to oversee the work[4399] of the house of the LORD; and 6,000 *were* [b]officers[7860] and judges,

5 and 4,000 *were* gatekeepers,[7778]

---

6 [a]1Kin. 2:1

7 [I]Lit., *as for me, it was in my heart* [a]2Sam. 7:2, 3; 1Chr. 17:1

8 [I]Lit., *made* [a]1Chr. 28:3

9 [I]I.e., peaceful [a]1Kin. 4:20, 25 [b]2Sam. 12:24, 25

10 [a]2Sam. 7:13, 14; 1Chr. 17:12

11 [a]1Chr. 22:16

12 [a]1Kin. 3:9-12; 2Chr. 1:10 [b]1Kin. 2:3

13 [a]1Chr. 28:7 [b]Josh. 1:6-9

14 [I]Lit., *in my affliction* [II]Lit., *it is* [a]1Chr. 29:4 [b]1Chr. 22:3

16 [a]1Chr. 22:11

17 [a]1Chr. 28:1-6

18 [a]1Chr. 22:9; 23:25

19 [a]1Chr. 28:9 [b]1Kin. 8:6, 21; 2Chr. 5:7 [c]1Chr. 22:7

1 [I]Lit., *became old and sated with days* [a]1Chr. 29:28 [b]1Kin. 1:1-40; 2:12; 1Chr. 28:5; 29:22

3 [I]Lit., *their heads* [a]Num. 4:3-49 [b]Num. 4:48; 1Chr. 23:24

4 [a]Ezra 3:8, 9 [b]1Chr. 26:29

⊶ **22:8** See note on II Sam. 7:4-16.

⊶ **22:9** In Hebrew the name Solomon means "peaceful."

and [a]4,000 *were* praising the LORD with the instruments which [I]David made[6213] for giving praise.

6 And David divided them into divisions [a]according to the sons of Levi: Gershon, Kohath, and Merari.

Gershonites

7 Of the Gershonites *were* [I]Ladan and Shimei.

8 The sons of Ladan *were* Jehiel the first[7218] and Zetham and Joel, three.

9 The sons of Shimei *were* Shelomoth and Haziel and Haran, three. These were the heads of the fathers'[1] *households* of Ladan.

10 And the sons of Shimei *were* Jahath, [I]Zina, Jeush, and Beriah. These four *were* the sons of Shimei.

11 And Jahath was the first, and Zizah the second; but Jeush and Beriah did not have many sons, so they became a father's[1] household, one [I]class.

Kohathites

12 The sons of Kohath were four: Amram, Izhar, Hebron and Uzziel.

13 [a]The sons of Amram were Aaron and Moses. And [b]Aaron was set apart to sanctify him as most holy, he and his sons forever, [c]to burn incense[6999] before the LORD, to minister[8334] to Him and to bless[1288] in His name forever.

14 But *as for* [a]Moses the man[376] of God,[430] his sons were named among the tribe of Levi.

15 The sons of Moses *were* Gershom and Eliezer.

16 The [I]son of Gershom *was* [II]Shebuel the chief.

17 And the [I]son of Eliezer was Rehabiah the chief; and Eliezer had no other sons, but the sons of Rehabiah were very many.

18 The [I]son of Izhar was [II]Shelomith the chief.

19 The sons of Hebron *were* Jeriah the first, Amariah the second, Jahaziel the third and Jekameam the fourth.

20 The sons of Uzziel *were* Micah the first and Isshiah the second.

Merarites

21 The sons of Merari were Mahli and Mushi. The sons of Mahli *were* Eleazar and Kish.

22 And Eleazar died[4191] and had no sons, but daughters only, so their brothers,[251] the sons of Kish, took them *as wives*.

23 The sons of Mushi *were* three: Mahli, Eder, and Jeremoth.

Duties Revised

24 [a]These were the sons of Levi according to their fathers' households, *even* the heads of the fathers' *households* of those of them who were [I]counted,[6485] in the number of names by their [II]census, doing[6213] the work for the service of the house of the LORD, [b]from twenty years old and upward.

25 For David said,[559] "The LORD God of Israel [a]has given rest to His people, and He dwells[7931] in Jerusalem forever.

26 "And also, [a]the Levites will no longer need to carry[5375] the tabernacle and all its utensils for its service."

27 For by the last words[1697] of David the sons of Levi *were* numbered, from twenty years old and upward.

28 For their office is [I]to assist the sons of Aaron with the service of the house of the LORD, in the courts and in the chambers and in the purifying of all holy things, even the work of the service of the house of God,

5 [I]Lit., *I made* [a]1Chr. 15:16
6 [a]1Chr. 6:1
7 [I]In Ex. 6:17, *Libni*
10 [I]In v. 11, *Zizah*
11 [I]Lit., *mustering*
13 [a]Ex. 6:20 [b]Ex. 28:1 [c]Ex. 30:6-10
14 [a]Deut. 33:1; Ps. 90:title
16 [I]Lit., *sons* [II]In ch. 24:20, *Shubael*
17 [I]Lit., *sons . . . were*
18 [I]Lit., *sons* [II]In ch. 24:22, *Shelomoth*
24 [I]Lit., *mustered* [II]Lit., *heads* [a]Num. 10:17, 21 [b]1Chr. 23:3
25 [a]1Chr. 22:18
26 [a]Num. 4:5, 15; 7:9; Deut. 10:8
28 [I]Lit., *at the hand of*

23:9 This Shimei could hardly be the Shimei, son of Gershon, who is listed in vv. 7, 10. It is probable that he and Laadan were sons of Libni, the older son of Gershon and brother of Shimei (see I Chr. 6:17). Thus, the clans of Gershon totaled nine; six for Ladan and three for Shimei, on the basis of the combination of Jeush and Beriah in v. 11.

29 [a]and with the showbread, and
[b]the fine flour for a grain offering,[4503]
and unleavened[4682] wafers, or [c]*what is*
baked in the pan, or [d]what is well-mixed,
and [e]all measures of volume and size.
30 And they are to stand every
morning to thank and to praise the LORD,
and likewise at evening,
31 and to offer all burnt offerings
to the LORD, [a]on the sabbaths,[7676] the
new moons and [b]the fixed festivals[4150]
in the number *set* by the ordinance[4941]
concerning them, continually[8548] before
the LORD.
32 Thus [a]they are to keep[8104] charge
of the tent of meeting,[4150] and charge[4931]
of the holy place, and [b]charge of the
sons of Aaron their [I]relatives, for the
service of the house of the LORD.

Divisions of Levites

24 Now the divisions of the [I]de-
scendants of Aaron *were these:*
[a]the sons of Aaron *were* Nadab, Abihu,
Eleazar, and Ithamar.
2 [a]But Nadab and Abihu died[4191] before their father and had no [I]sons.[1121]
So Eleazar and Ithamar served as
priests.
3 And David, with [a]Zadok of the
sons of Eleazar and Ahimelech of the
sons of Ithamar, divided them according
to their offices[6486] [I]for their ministry.
4 Since more chief[7218] men[1397] were
found from the [I]descendants of Eleazar
than the [I]descendants of Ithamar, they
divided them thus: *there were* sixteen
heads of fathers' households of the
[I]descendants of Eleazar, and eight of
the [I]descendants of Ithamar according
to their fathers'[1] households.
5 [a]Thus they were divided by lot,
the one as the other; for they were
officers[8269] of the sanctuary and officers

29 [a]Lev. 24:5-9 [b]Lev. 6:20 [c]1Chr. 9:31 [d]Lev. 6:21 [e]Lev. 19:35, 36
31 [a]Is. 1:13, 14 [b]Lev. 23:2-4
32 [I]Lit., *brothers* [a]Num. 1:53; 1Chr. 9:27 [b]Num. 3:6-9, 38
1 [I]Lit., *sons* [a]Ex. 6:23
2 [I]Or, *children* [a]Lev. 10:2
3 [I]Lit., *in their service* [a]1Chr. 6:8
4 [I]Lit., *sons*
5 [I]Lit., *sons* [a]1Chr. 24:31
6 [a]1Chr. 18:16
10 [a]Neh. 12:4; Luke 1:5
19 [a]1Chr. 9:25
20 [I]In 23:16, *Shebuel*

of God,[430] both from the [I]descendants
of Eleazar and the [I]descendants of Ithamar.
6 And Shemaiah, the son of Nethanel the scribe, from the Levites, recorded them in the presence of the
king,[4428] the princes, Zadok the priest,
[a]Ahimelech the son of Abiathar, and the
heads of the fathers' *households* of the
priests and of the Levites; one father's
household taken for Eleazar and one
taken for Ithamar.
7 Now the first[7223] lot came out for
Jehoiarib, the second for Jedaiah,
8 the third for Harim, the fourth for
Seorim,
9 the fifth for Malchijah, the sixth
for Mijamin,
10 the seventh for Hakkoz, the
eighth for [a]Abijah,
11 the ninth for Jeshua, the tenth
for Shecaniah,
12 the eleventh for Eliashib, the
twelfth for Jakim,
13 the thirteenth for Huppah, the
fourteenth for Jeshebeab,
14 the fifteenth for Bilgah, the sixteenth for Immer,
15 the seventeenth for Hezir, the
eighteenth for Happizzez,
16 the nineteenth for Pethahiah, the
twentieth for Jehezkel,
17 the twenty-first for Jachin, the
twenty-second for Gamul,
18 the twenty-third for Delaiah, the
twenty-fourth for Maaziah.
19 [a]These were their offices[6486] for
their ministry, when *they* came in to the
house of the LORD according to the
ordinance[4941] *given* to them through
Aaron their father, just as the LORD God
of Israel had commanded[6680] him.
20 Now for the rest of the sons of
Levi: of the sons of Amram, [I]Shubael;
of the sons of Shubael, Jehdeiah.

24:4 The twenty-four classes contined as the basis for rotating the priestly duties into N.T. times. Although some of these classes died out or had to be consolidated with others, new ones were formed to take their places. In the return from exile, in 538 B.C., four registered classes were represented: David's second, third, and sixteenth, and a new class. Pashhur (Ezra 2:36-39); and by 520 B.C. twenty-two of them were operational again (Neh. 12:1-7. Cf. vv. 12-21 and 10:2-8).

24:10 Zacharias, the father of John the Baptist, belonged to the course of Abijah (Lk. 1:5).

21 Of Rehabiah: of the sons of Rehabiah, Isshiah the first.[7218]

22 Of the Izharites, [I]Shelomoth; of the sons of Shelomoth, Jahath.

23 And the sons [a]*of Hebron:* Jeriah *the first,* Amariah the second, Jahaziel the third, Jekameam the fourth.

24 *Of* the sons of Uzziel, Micah; of the sons of Micah, Shamir.

25 The brother of Micah, Isshiah; of the sons of Isshiah, Zechariah.

26 The sons of Merari, Mahli and Mushi; the sons of Jaaziah, Beno.

27 The sons of Merari: by Jaaziah *were* Beno, Shoham, Zaccur, and Ibri.

28 By Mahli: Eleazar, who had no sons.

29 By Kish: the sons of Kish, Jerahmeel.

30 And the sons of Mushi: Mahli, Eder, and Jerimoth. These *were* the sons of the Levites according to their fathers' households.

31 [a]These also cast[5307] lots just as their [I]relatives[251] the sons of Aaron in the presence of David the king, [b]Zadok, Ahimelech, and the heads of the fathers' *households* of the priests and of the Levites—the head of fathers' *households* as well as those of his younger brother.

Number and Services of Musicians

25 Moreover, David and the commanders[8269] of the army set apart for the service *some* of the sons of [a]Asaph and of Heman and of Jeduthun, who *were* to [b]prophesy with lyres, [c]harps, and cymbals; and the number of [I]those who performed their service was:

2 Of the sons of Asaph: Zaccur, Joseph, Nethaniah, and [I]Asharelah; the sons of Asaph *were* under the [II]direction of Asaph, who prophesied under the [II]direction of the king.[4428]

3 [a]Of Jeduthun, the sons of Jeduthun: Gedaliah, [I]Zeri, Jeshaiah, [II]Shimei, Hashabiah, and Mattithiah, six, under the [III]direction of their father Jeduthun with the harp, who prophesied in giving thanks and praising the LORD.

4 Of Heman, the sons of Heman: Bukkiah, Mattaniah, [I]Uzziel, [II]Shebuel and Jerimoth, Hananiah, Hanani, Eliathah, Giddalti and Romamti-ezer, Joshbekashah, Mallothi, Hothir, Mahazioth.

5 All these *were* the sons of Heman [a]the king's[4428] seer to [I]exalt him according to the words[1697] of God,[430] for God gave fourteen sons and three daughters to Heman.

6 All these were under the [I]direction of their father to sing in the house of the LORD, [a]with cymbals, harps and lyres, for the service of the house of God. [b]Asaph, Jeduthun and Heman *were* under the [I]direction of the king.

7 And their number who were trained[3925] in singing to the LORD, with their [I]relatives,[251] all who were skillful,[995] *was* [a]288.

Divisions of Musicians

8 And [a]they cast[5307] lots for their duties,[4931] all alike, the small as well as the great, the teacher *as well* as the pupil.

9 Now the first[7223] lot came out for Asaph to Joseph, the second for Gedaliah, he with his relatives and sons *were* twelve;

10 the third to Zaccur, his sons and his relatives, twelve;

11 the fourth to [I]Izri, his sons and his relatives, twelve;

12 the fifth to Nethaniah, his sons and his relatives, twelve;

13 the sixth to Bukkiah, his sons and his relatives, twelve;

14 the seventh to [I]Jesharelah, his sons and his relatives, twelve;

15 the eighth to Jeshaiah, his sons and his relatives, twelve;

16 the ninth to Mattaniah, his sons and his relatives, twelve;

17 the tenth to Shimei, his sons and his relatives, twelve;

18 the eleventh to Azarel, his sons and his relatives, twelve;

19 the twelfth to Hashabiah, his sons and his relatives, twelve;

22 [I]In 23:18, *Shelomith*

23 [a]1Chr. 23:19

31 [I]Lit., *brothers* [a]1Chr. 24:5, 6 [b]1Chr. 24:6

1 [I]Lit., *workmen according to their service* [a]1Chr. 6:33, 39 [b]2Kin. 3:15 [c]1Chr. 15:16

2 [I]In v. 14, *Jesharelah* [II]Lit., *hand*(s)

3 [I]In v. 11, *Izri* [II]So with mss. and ancient versions, cf. v. 17 [III]Lit., *hands* [a]1Chr. 16:41, 42

4 [I]In v. 18, *Azarel* [II]In v. 20, *Shubael*

5 [I]Lit., *lift up the horn* [a]2Sam. 24:11; 1Chr. 21:9

6 [I]Lit., *hands* [a]1Chr. 15:16 [b]1Chr. 15:19

7 [I]Lit., *brothers,* and so throughout the ch. [a]1Chr. 23:5

8 [a]1Chr. 26:13

11 [I]In v. 3, *Zeri*

14 [I]In v. 2, *Asharelah*

20 for the thirteenth, Shubael, his sons and his relatives, twelve;
21 for the fourteenth, Mattithiah, his sons and his relatives, twelve;
22 for the fifteenth to Jeremoth, his sons and his relatives, twelve;
23 for the sixteenth to Hananiah, his sons and his relatives, twelve;
24 for the seventeenth to Joshbekashah, his sons and his relatives, twelve;
25 for the eighteenth to Hanani, his sons and his relatives, twelve;
26 for the nineteenth to Mallothi, his sons and his relatives, twelve;
27 for the twentieth to Eliathah, his sons and his relatives, twelve;
28 for the twenty-first to Hothir, his sons and his relatives, twelve;
29 for the twenty-second to Giddalti, his sons and his relatives, twelve;
30 for the twenty-third to Mahazioth, his sons and his relatives, twelve;
31 for the twenty-fourth to Romamti-ezer, his sons and his relatives, twelve.

Divisions of the Gatekeepers

26 🔑 For the divisions of the gatekeepers *there were* of the Korahites, [I]Meshelemiah the son of Kore, of the sons of [II]Asaph.
2 And Meshelemiah had sons: Zechariah the first-born, Jediael the second, Zebadiah the third, Jathniel the fourth,
3 Elam the fifth, Johanan the sixth, Eliehoenai the seventh.
🔑 4 And [a]Obed-edom had sons: Shemaiah the first-born, Jehozabad the second, Joah the third, Sacar the fourth, Nethanel the fifth,
5 Ammiel the sixth, Issachar the seventh, *and* Peullethai the eighth; God[430] had indeed blessed him.
6 Also to his son Shemaiah sons were born who ruled over the house of their father, for they were mighty men of valor.[2428]
7 The sons of Shemaiah *were* Othni, Rephael, Obed, and Elzabad, whose brothers,[251] Elihu and Semachiah, were valiant men.
8 All these *were* of the sons of Obed-edom; they and their sons and their [I]relatives *were* able[2428] men[376] with strength for the service, 62 from Obed-edom.
9 And Meshelemiah had sons and relatives, 18 valiant men.
10 Also [a]Hosah, *one* of the sons[1121] of Merari had sons: Shimri the first[7218] (although he was not the first-born, his father made[7760] him first),
11 Hilkiah the second, Tebaliah the third, Zechariah the fourth; all the sons and relatives of Hosah *were* 13.
12 To these divisions of the gatekeepers, the chief men,[1397] *were given* duties[4931] like their relatives to minister[8334] in the house of the LORD.
13 [a]And they cast[5307] lots, the small and the great alike, according to their fathers'[1] households, for every gate.
14 And the lot to the east fell[5307] to [I]Shelemiah. Then they cast lots *for* his son Zechariah, a counselor[3289] with insight,[7922] and his lot came out to the north.
15 For Obed-edom *it fell* to the south, and to his sons went the storehouse.
16 For Shuppim and Hosah *it was* to the west, by the gate of Shallecheth, on the ascending highway. Guard corresponded to guard.
17 On the east there were six Levites, on the north four daily,[3117] on the south four daily, and at the storehouse two by two.
18 At the [Ia]Parbar on the west *there*

1 [I]In v. 14, *Shelemiah* [II]In 9:19, *Ebiasaph*
4 [a]2Sam. 6:11; 1Chr. 13:14
8 [I]Lit., *brothers,* and so throughout the ch.
10 [a]1Chr. 16:38
13 [a]1Chr. 24:5, 31; 25:8
14 [I]In 9:17, *Shallum*
18 [I]Possibly *court* or *colonnade* [a]2Kin. 23:11

🔑 **26:1** From I Chr. 9:19 it appears that the full spelling of Kore's father's name was Ebiasaph. "Asaph" could not be the famous musician of that name who belonged to the clan of Gershon, becasuse Korah and his descendants, who were to guard the temple gates, belonged to the clan of Kohath.
🔑 **26:4** Obed-edom was the Levite who had received God's blessing when he maintained the ark of the covenant after the death of Uzza (I Chr. 13:13,14). See his appointment in I Chr. 15:24,25; 16:38.

were four at the highway and two at the Parbar.

19 These were the divisions of the gatekeepers of the sons of Korah and of the sons of Merari.

Keepers of the Treasure

20 [I]And the Levites, their relatives, [II]had [a]charge of the treasures of the house of God, and of the treasures of the dedicated gifts.[6944]

21 The sons of Ladan, the sons of the Gershonites belonging to Ladan, *namely,* the Jehielites, *were* the heads of the fathers' *households,* belonging to Ladan the Gershonite.

22 The sons of Jehieli, Zetham and Joel his brother,[251] [I]had charge of the treasures of the house of the LORD.

23 As for the Amramites, the Izharites, the Hebronites, and the Uzzielites,

24 Shebuel the son of Gershom, the son of Moses, was officer over the treasures.

25 And his relatives by Eliezer *were* Rehabiah his son, Jeshaiah his son, Joram his son, Zichri his son, and Shelomoth his son.

26 This Shelomoth and his relatives [I]had charge of all the treasures of the dedicated[6942] gifts, [a]which King[4428] David and the heads of the fathers' *households,* the commanders[8269] of thousands and hundreds, and commanders of the army, had dedicated.

27 They dedicated[6942] [I]part of the spoil won in battles to repair[2388] the house of the LORD.

28 And all that Samuel the seer had dedicated and Saul the son of Kish, Abner the son of Ner and Joab the son of Zeruiah, everyone who had dedicated *anything, all of this* was [I]in the care of [II]Shelomoth and his relatives.

Outside Duties

29 As for the Izharites, Chenaniah and his sons [a]were *assigned* to outside duties[4399] for Israel, as [b]officers[7860] and judges.

30 As for the Hebronites, [a]Hashabiah and his relatives, 1,700 capable men, had charge of the affairs of Israel [I]west of the Jordan, for all the work of the LORD and the service of the king.

31 As for the Hebronites, [a]Jerijah the chief [I](these Hebronites were investigated according to their genealogies[8435] and fathers' *households,* in the fortieth year of David's reign, and men of outstanding capability were found among them at [b]Jazer of Gilead)

32 and his relatives, capable men, *were* 2,700 in number, heads of fathers' *households.* And King David made them overseers of the Reubenites, the Gadites and the half-tribe of the Manassites [a]concerning [I]all the affairs[1697] of God and of the king.

Commanders of the Army

27 Now *this is* the enumeration of the sons[1121] of Israel, the heads[7218] of fathers'[1] *households,* the commanders[8269] of thousands and of hundreds, and their officers[7860] who served the king[4428] in all the affairs[1697] of the divisions which came in and went out month by month throughout all the months of the year, each division *numbering* 24,000.

2 Jashobeam the son of Zabdiel [I][a]had charge of the first[7223] division for the first month; and in his division *were* 24,000.

3 *He was* from the sons of Perez, *and was* chief of all the commanders of the army for the first month.

4 Dodai the Ahohite and his division had charge of the division for the second month, Mikloth *being* the chief officer; and in his division *were* 24,000.

5 The third commander[8269] of the army for the third month *was* Benaiah, the son of Jehoiada the priest, *as* chief; and in his division *were* 24,000.

20 [I]So Gr.; Heb., *As for the Levites, Ahijah had* [II]Lit., *were over* [a]1Chr. 26:22, 24, 26; 28:12; Ezra 2:69

22 [I]Lit., *were over*

26 [I]Lit., *were over* [a]2Sam. 8:11

27 [I]Heb., *from the battles and from the spoil*

28 [I]Lit., *under the hand* [II]Heb., *Shelomith*

29 [a]Neh. 11:16 [b]1Chr. 23:4

30 [I]Lit., *beyond the Jordan westward* [a]1Chr. 27:17

31 [I]Heb., *according to the Hebronites . . . father's households* [a]1Chr. 23:19 [b]1Chr. 6:81

32 [I]Lit., *every matter of God and matter of the king.* [a]2Chr. 19:11

2 [I]Lit., *was over, and so throughout the ch.* [a]2Sam. 23:8-30; 1Chr. 11:11-31

26:25 Shelomoth was a descendant of Moses.

6 This Benaiah *was* the mighty man of the thirty, and had charge of thirty; and over his division was Ammizabad his son.

7 The fourth for the fourth month *was* Asahel the brother[251] of Joab, and Zebadiah his son after him; and in his division *were* 24,000.

8 The fifth for the fifth month *was* the commander Shamhuth the Izrahite; and in his division *were* 24,000.

9 The sixth for the sixth month *was* Ira the son of Ikkesh the Tekoite; and in his division *were* 24,000.

10 The seventh for the seventh month *was* Helez the Pelonite of the sons of Ephraim; and in his division *were* 24,000.

11 The eighth for the eighth month *was* Sibbecai the Hushathite of the Zerahites; and in his division *were* 24,000.

12 The ninth for the ninth month *was* Abiezer the Anathothite of the Benjamites; and in his division *were* 24,000.

13 The tenth for the tenth month *was* Maharai the Netophathite of the Zerahites; and in his division *were* 24,000.

14 The eleventh for the eleventh month *was* Benaiah the Pirathonite of the sons of Ephraim; and in his division *were* 24,000.

15 The twelfth for the twelfth month *was* Heldai the Netophathite of Othniel; and in his division *were* 24,000.

Chief Officers of the Tribes

16 Now in charge of the tribes of Israel: chief officer for the Reubenites was Eliezer the son of Zichri; for the Simeonites, Shephatiah the son of Maacah;

17 for Levi, Hashabiah the son of Kemuel; for Aaron, Zadok;

18 for Judah, Elihu, *one* of David's brothers;[251] for Issachar, Omri the son of Michael;

19 for Zebulun, Ishmaiah the son of Obadiah; for Naphtali, Jeremoth the son of Azriel;

20 for the sons of Ephraim, Hoshea the son of Azaziah; for the half-tribe of Manasseh, Joel the son of Pedaiah;

21 for the half-tribe of Manasseh in Gilead, Iddo the son of Zechariah; for Benjamin, Jaasiel the son of Abner;

22 for Dan, Azarel the son of Jeroham. [a]These *were* the princes of the tribes of Israel.

23 But David did not [I]count those twenty years of age and under, [a]because the LORD had said[559] He would multiply Israel [b]as the stars of heaven.

24 Joab the son of Zeruiah had begun to count *them,* but did not finish;[3615] and because of [a]this, wrath[7110] came[1961] upon Israel, and the number was not included in the account of the chronicles of King David.

Various Overseers

25 Now Azmaveth the son of Adiel had charge of the king's[4428] storehouses. And Jonathan the son of Uzziah had charge of the storehouses in the country,[7704] in the cities, in the villages, and in the towers.

26 And Ezri the son of Chelub had charge of the [I]agricultural[7704] workers who tilled the soil.[127]

27 And Shimei the Ramathite had charge of the vineyards; and Zabdi the Shiphmite had charge of the [I]produce of the vineyards *stored* in the wine cellars.

28 And Baal-hanan the Gederite had charge of the olive and [a]sycamore trees in the [I]Shephelah; and Joash had charge of the stores of oil.[8081]

29 And Shitrai the Sharonite had charge of the cattle which were grazing in [a]Sharon; and Shaphat the son of Adlai had charge of the cattle in the valleys.

30 And Obil the Ishmaelite had charge of the camels; and Jehdeiah the Meronothite had charge of the donkeys.

31 And Jaziz the [a]Hagrite had charge of the flocks. All these were [I]overseers of the property which belonged to King David.

22 [a]1Chr. 28:1

23 [I]Lit., *take their number from* [a]1Chr. 21:2-5 [b]Gen. 15:5; 22:17; 26:4

24 [a]2Sam. 24:12-15; 1Chr. 21:1-7

26 [I]Lit., *doers of the work of the field for the tilling of. . . .*

27 [I]Lit., *what was in the vineyards of the storehouses of wine*

28 [I]Or, *lowlands* [a]1Kin. 10:27; 2Chr. 1:15

29 [a]1Chr. 5:16

31 [I]Or, *rulers* [a]1Chr. 5:10

Counselors

32 Also Jonathan, David's uncle,
was a counselor,[3289] a man[376] of understanding,[995] and a scribe; and Jehiel the
son of Hachmoni [I]tutored the king's
sons.
33 And [a]Ahithophel was counselor
to the king; and [b]Hushai the Archite was
the king's friend.
🗝 34 And Jehoiada the son of [a]Benaiah,
and [b]Abiathar [I]succeeded Ahithophel;
and Joab was the [c]commander[8269] of the
king's army.[6635]

David's Address about the Temple

28 Now [a]David assembled[6950] at Jerusalem all the officials of Israel,
the princes of the tribes, and the
commanders[8269] of the divisions that
served[8334] the king,[4428] and the commanders of thousands, and the commanders of hundreds, and the overseers
of all the property and livestock belonging to the king and his sons, with the
officials[5631] and [b]the mighty men, even
all the valiant men.
2 Then King David rose to his feet
and said,[559] "Listen to me, my
brethren[251] and my people; I [a]*had*
[I]intended to build a [II]permanent home
for the ark[727] of the covenant[1285] of the
LORD and for [b]the footstool of our
God.[430] So I had made preparations to
build *it.*
3 "But God said to me, '[a]You shall
not build a house for My name because
you are a man[376] of war and have shed
blood.'[1818]
4 "Yet, the LORD, the God of Israel,
[a]chose[977] me from all the house of my
father to be king[4427] over Israel [b]forever.
For [c]He has chosen[977] Judah to be a
leader; and [d]in the house of Judah, my
father's house, and among the sons of
my father He took pleasure[7521] in me
to make *me* king over all Israel.
5 "And [a]of all my sons (for the LORD
has given me many sons), [b]He has chosen my son Solomon to sit on the throne
of the kingdom[4438] of the LORD over Israel.
6 "And He said to me, 'Your son
[a]Solomon is the one who shall build My
house and My courts; for I have chosen
him to be a son to Me, and I will be a
father to him.
7 'And I will establish his kingdom
forever, [a]if he resolutely[2388] performs[6213] My commandments[4687] and My
ordinances,[4941] as [I]is done now.'[3117]
8 "So now, in the sight of all Israel,
the assembly[6951] of the LORD, and in
the hearing[241] of our God, observe[8104]
and seek after all the commandments
of the LORD your God in order that you
may possess the good[2896] land[776] and
bequeath[5157] *it* to your sons[1121] after you
forever.
9 "As for you, my son Solomon,
know[3045] the God of your father, and
[a]serve Him with [I]a whole heart and a
willing[2655] [II]mind;[5315] [b]for the LORD
searches all hearts, and understands[995]
every intent[3336] of the thoughts.
[c]If you seek Him, He will let you find
Him; but if you forsake[5800] Him, He will
reject you forever.
10 "Consider now, for the LORD has
chosen you to build a house for the sanctuary; [a]be courageous and act."
11 Then David gave to his son Solomon [a]the plan of [b]the porch *of the temple,*
its buildings, its storehouses, its upper
rooms, its inner rooms, and [c]the room
for the mercy[3727] seat;
12 and the plan of all that he had
in [I]mind, for the courts of the house of
the LORD, and for all the surrounding
rooms, for [a]the storehouses of the house
of God, and for the storehouses of the
dedicated things;[6944]
13 also for [a]the divisions of the
priests and [b]the Levites and for all the
work[4399] of the service of the house of
the LORD and for all the utensils of service in the house of the LORD;

32 [I]Lit., *was with*
33 [a]2Sam. 15:12 [b]2Sam. 15:32, 37
34 [I]Lit., *after* [a]1Chr. 27:5 [b]1Kin. 1:7 [c]1Chr. 11:6
1 [a]1Chr. 23:2; 27:1-31 [b]1Chr. 11:10-47
2 [I]Lit., *in my heart* [II]Lit., *house of rest* [a]1Chr. 17:1, 2 [b]Ps. 132:7; Is. 66:1
3 [a]1Chr. 22:8
4 [a]1Sam. 16:6-13 [b]1Chr. 17:23, 27 [c]Gen. 49:8-10; 1Chr. 5:2 [d]1Sam. 16:1
5 [a]1Chr. 3:1-9; 14:3-7 [b]1Chr. 22:9, 10
6 [a]2Sam. 7:13, 14
7 [I]Lit., *at this day* [a]1Chr. 22:13
9 [I]Or, *the same* [II]Lit., *soul* [a]1Kin. 8:61; 1Chr. 29:17-19 [b]1Sam. 16:7 [c]2Chr. 15:2; Jer. 29:13
10 [a]1Chr. 22:13
11 [a]Ex. 25:40; 1Chr. 28:12, 19 [b]1Kin. 6:3 [c]Ex. 25:17-22
12 [I]Lit., *the spirit with him* [a]1Chr. 26:20, 28
13 [a]1Chr. 24:1 [b]1Chr. 23:6

🗝 **27:34** Ahithophel had deserted David for Absalom (II Sam. 15:12,31; 16:20-23), but when thwarted by Hushai (15:32,37; 17:1-16), he committed suicide (17:23).

14 for the golden *utensils,* the
weight of gold for all utensils for every
kind of service; for the silver utensils,
the weight *of silver* for all utensils for
every kind of service;
15 and the weight *of gold* for the
[a]golden lampstands and their golden
lamps,[5216] with the weight of each lampstand and its lamps; and *the weight of*
silver for the silver lampstands, with the
weight of each lampstand and its lamps
according to the use[5656] of each lampstand;
16 and the gold by weight for the
tables of showbread, for each table; and
silver for the silver tables;
17 and the forks, the basins, and
the pitchers of pure gold; and for the
golden bowls[3713] with the weight for
each bowl; and for the silver bowls with
the weight for each bowl;
🔑 18 and for [a]the altar[4196] of incense[7004] refined gold by weight; and
gold for the model of the chariot, *even*
[b]the cherubim,[3742] that spread out *their*
wings, and covered the ark of the covenant of the LORD.
19 "All *this,*" *said David,* "the LORD
made me understand[7919] in writing by
His hand upon me, [a]all the [I]details of
this pattern."
20 Then David said to his son Solomon, "[a]Be strong and courageous, and
act; do not fear[3372] nor be dismayed,[2865]
for the LORD God, my God, is with
you. [b]He will not fail[7503] you nor for
sake you until all the work for the
service of the house of the LORD is
finished.[3615]
21 "Now behold, [a]*there are* the divisions of the priests and the Levites for
all the service of the house of God, and
[b]every willing[5081] man of any skill will
be with you in all the work for all kinds
of service. The officials also and all the
people will be entirely at your
command."[1697]

Offerings for the Temple

29 Then King[4427] David said[559] to
the entire assembly,[6951] "My son
Solomon, whom alone God[430] has chosen,[977] [a]is still young and inexperienced
and the work[4399] is great; for [b]the
[I]temple is not for man,[120] but for the
LORD God.
2 "Now [a]with all my ability I have
provided for the house of my God the
gold for the *things of* gold, and the silver
for the *things of* silver, and the bronze
for the *things of* bronze, the iron for
the *things of* iron, and wood for the *things*
of wood, onyx stones and inlaid *stones,*
stones of antimony,[6320] and stones of
various colors, and all kinds of precious
stones, and alabaster in abundance.
3 "And moreover, in my delight in
the house of my God, the treasure I
have of gold and silver, I give to the
house of my God, over and above all
that I have already provided for the holy
[I]temple,
4 *namely,* [a]3,000 talents of gold, of
[b]the gold of Ophir, and 7,000 talents
of refined silver, to overlay the walls
of the [I]buildings;
5 of gold for the *things of* gold, and
of silver for the *things of* silver, that
is, for all the work [I]done by the
craftsmen.[2796] Who then is willing[5068]
[II]to consecrate himself this day[3117] to
the LORD?"
6 Then [a]the rulers of the fathers'[1]
households, and the princes of the tribes
of Israel, and the commanders[8269] of
thousands and of hundreds, with
[b]the overseers over the king's[4428] work,
offered willingly;[5068]
7 and for the service for the house
of God they gave 5,000 talents and
10,000 [a]darics[150] of gold, and 10,000 talents of silver, and 18,000 talents of
brass, and 100,000 talents of iron.
8 And [I]whoever possessed *precious*

15 [a]Ex. 25:31-39
18 [a]Ex. 30:1-10 [b]Ex. 25:18-22
19 [I]Lit., *works* [a]1Chr. 28:11, 12
20 [a]1Chr. 22:13 [b]Josh. 1:5; Heb. 13:5
21 [a]1Chr. 28:13 [b]Ex. 35:25-35; 36:1, 2
1 [I]Lit., *palace* [a]1Chr. 22:5 [b]1Chr. 29:19
2 [a]1Chr. 22:3-5
3 [I]Lit., *house*
4 [I]Lit., *houses* [a]1Chr. 22:14 [b]1Kin. 9:28
5 [I]Lit., *by the hand of the craftsmen* [II]Lit., *to fill his hand*
6 [a]1Chr. 27:1; 28:1 [b]1Chr. 27:25-31
7 [a]Ezra 2:69; Neh. 7:70
8 [I]Lit., *those with whom were found*

🔑 **28:18** Cherubim were angelic beings who appeared in human form, but they had wings (Ezek. 1:5,6; cf. 10:12). God is said to have ridden upon them (II Sam. 22:11). This probably means that God's glorious presence was between the cherubim on top of the ark (see I Chr. 13:6; Ex. 25:22).

stones gave them to the treasury of the house of the Lord, [II]in care of [a]Jehiel the Gershonite.

9 Then the people rejoiced because they had offered so willingly, for they made their offering to the Lord [a]with a whole heart, and King David also rejoiced greatly.

David's Prayer

10 So David blessed the Lord in the sight of all the assembly; and David said, "Blessed art Thou, O Lord God of Israel our father, forever and ever.

11 "[a]Thine, O Lord, is the greatness and the power and the glory[8597] and the victory[5331] and the majesty,[1935] indeed everything that is in the heavens and the earth;[776] Thine is the dominion,[4467] O Lord, and Thou dost exalt Thyself as head over all.

12 "[a]Both riches and honor *come* from Thee, and Thou dost rule over all, and [b]in Thy hand is power and might; and it lies in Thy hand to make great, and to strengthen everyone.

13 "Now therefore, our God, we thank Thee, and praise Thy glorious[8597] name.

14 "But who am I and who are my people that we should [I]be able to offer as generously as this? For all things come from Thee, and from Thy hand we have given Thee.

15 "For [a]we are sojourners before Thee, and tenants, as all our fathers were; [b]our days[3117] on the earth are like a shadow, and there is no hope.

16 "O Lord our God, all this abundance that we have provided to build Thee a house for Thy holy name, it is from Thy hand, and all is Thine.

17 "Since I know,[3045] O my God, that [a]Thou triest the heart and [b]delightest in uprightness,[3476] I, in the integrity[4334] of my heart, have willingly offered all these *things;* so now with joy I have seen Thy people, who are present here, make *their* offerings willingly to Thee.

18 "O Lord, the God of Abraham, Isaac, and Israel, our fathers, preserve[8104] this forever in the [I]intentions[3336] of the heart of Thy people, and direct their heart to Thee;

19 "and [a]give to my son Solomon a perfect heart to keep Thy commandments,[4687] Thy testimonies, and Thy statutes, and to do[6213] *them* all, and [b]to build the [I]temple, for which I have made provision."

20 Then David said to all the assembly, "Now bless[1288] the Lord your God." And [a]all the assembly blessed the Lord, the God of their fathers, and [b]bowed low and did homage[7812] to the Lord and to the king.

Sacrifices

21 And on the next day [a]they [I]made[2076] sacrifices[2077] to the Lord and offered[5927] burnt offerings to the Lord, 1,000 bulls, 1,000 rams *and* 1,000 lambs, with their libations and sacrifices in abundance for all Israel.

22 So they ate and drank that day before the Lord with great gladness.

Solomon Again Made King

And they made Solomon the son of David king[4427] [a]a second time, and they [b]anointed[4886] *him* as ruler[5057] for the Lord and Zadok as priest.

23 Then [a]Solomon sat on the throne of the Lord as king instead of David his father; and he prospered, and all Israel obeyed[8085] him.

24 And all the officials, the mighty men, and also all the sons of King David [I]pledged allegiance to King Solomon.

25 And [a]the Lord highly exalted Solomon in the sight of all Israel, and [b]bestowed on him royal majesty which had not been on any king before him in Israel.

🔑 **26** Now [a]David the son of Jesse reigned over all Israel.

27 [a]And the period which he reigned

8 [II]Lit., *under the hand of* [a]1Chr. 23:8

9 [a]1Kin. 8:61; 2Cor. 9:7

11 [a]Matt. 6:13; Rev. 5:13

12 [a]2Chr. 1:12 [b]2Chr. 20:6

14 [I]Lit., *retain strength*

15 [a]Lev. 25:23 [b]Job 14:2, 10-12

17 [a]1Chr. 28:9 [b]Ps. 15:2

18 [I]Lit., *intent of the thoughts of the heart*

19 [I]Lit., *palace* [a]1Chr. 28:9; Ps. 72:1 [b]1Chr. 29:1, 2

20 [a]Josh. 22:33 [b]Ex. 4:31

21 [I]Lit., *sacrificed* [a]1Kin. 8:62, 63

22 [a]1Chr. 23:1 [b]1Kin. 1:33-39

23 [a]1Kin. 2:12

24 [I]Lit., *put a hand under Solomon*

25 [a]2Chr. 1:1 [b]1Kin. 3:13; 2Chr. 1:12

26 [a]1Chr. 18:14

27 [a]2Sam. 5:4, 5; 1Kin. 2:11; 1Chr. 3:4

🔑 **29:26-30** See I Kgs. 2:10-12.

over Israel *was* forty years; he reigned
in Hebron seven years and [I]in Jerusalem
thirty-three *years*.

Death of David

28 Then he died[4191] in [a]a [I]ripe old
age, [b]full of days, riches and honor; and
his son Solomon reigned in his place.

29 Now the acts[1697] of King David,
from first[7223] to last, are written in the
chronicles of [a]Samuel the seer, in the
chronicles of [b]Nathan the prophet, and
in the chronicles of [c]Gad the seer,
30 with all his reign, his power, and
the circumstances which came on him,
on Israel, and on all the kingdoms[4667]
of the lands.[776]

27 [I]Lit., *he reigned in*

28 [I]Lit., *good* [a]Gen. 15:15; Acts 13:36 [b]1Chr. 23:1

29 [a]1Sam. 9:9 [b]2Sam. 7:2-4; 12:1-7 [c]1Sam. 22:5

29:29 If the Chronicles of Samuel the seer, Nathan the prophet, and Gad the seer were intended here as actual books from which the historic events during the reign of David were taken, they have not come down to us in modern times. On the other hand, they may be understood as sections of the large historical compilations already represented in the Books of Samuel and Kings.

The Second Book of the

CHRONICLES

The Second Book of Chronicles continues the story of I Chronicles. They were originally one book in the Hebrew Bible. They encompassed most of the history of the Old Testament before the Babylonian Exile. Ezra the priest is believed to be the author, but we cannot be absolutely certain. Generally speaking, II Chronicles covers the same events of I Kings and II Kings, except that it omits the narratives concerning the kings of the apostate northern kingdom (Israel). The Books of Kings were clearly written before the captivity and the Books of Chronicles were written afterward. The former traces the same history from a prophetic point of view, while the latter stresses the viewpoint of the priests. The northern kingdom is hardly given honorable mention because they were not considered true Israelites. They had not only defected from the kingdom of David, but also from God's law. II Chronicles states that the principal reason for the deportation of the southern kingdom (Judah) was their refusal to conform to the Law of Moses. The author condemns empty ritualism; God deserves to be recognized both formally and with sincerity. The great temple of Solomon had become only a vacuous symbol for the people. Few took this holy place seriously. Although Jeroboam, the founder of the northern kingdom (Israel), substituted a false form of religion which may have appeared more responsive to the needs of the people, and Rehoboam, Solomon's headstrong son, retained the original outward form of Jewish religion with little or no spirituality, the influence of both men doomed succeeding generations to rootlessness. II Chronicles teaches that the path back to God begins with genuine repentance and a desire to restore God's original pattern.

Solomon Worships at Gibeon

1 Now [a]Solomon the son of David established himself securely over his kingdom,[4438] and the LORD his God[430] *was* with him and [b]exalted him greatly.

2 And Solomon spoke to all Israel, [a]to the commanders[8269] of thousands and of hundreds and to the judges[8199] and to every leader in all Israel, the heads[7218] of the fathers'[1] *households.*

3 Then Solomon, and all the assembly[6951] with him, went to [a]the high place which was at Gibeon; [b]for God's tent of meeting[4150] was there, which Moses the servant of the LORD had made in the wilderness.

4 However, David had brought[5927] up [a]the ark[727] of God from Kiriath-jearim [I]to [b]the place he had prepared for it; for he had pitched a tent for it in Jerusalem.

5 Now [a]the bronze altar,[4196] which Bezalel the son of Uri, the son of Hur, had made, [I]was there before the tabernacle of the LORD, and Solomon and the assembly sought it out.

6 And Solomon went up there before the LORD to the bronze altar which *was* at the tent of meeting, and [a]offered a thousand burnt offerings on it.

7 [a]In that night[3915] God appeared[7200] to Solomon and said to him, "Ask[7592] what I shall give you."

Solomon's Prayer for Wisdom

8 And Solomon said to God, "Thou hast dealt with my father David with

1 [a]1Kin. 2:12, 46 [b]1Chr. 29:25
2 [a]1Chr. 28:1
3 [a]1Kin. 3:4 [b]Ex. 36:8
4 [I]Lit., *where David had prepared for it* [a]1Chr. 15:25-28 [b]2Chr. 6:2
5 [I]Lit., *he put* [a]Ex. 31:9; 38:1-7
6 [a]1Kin. 3:4
7 [a]1Kin. 3:5-14

1:1-13 See I Kgs. 3:3-15.

1:4 The old tabernacle and the bronze altar were still at Gibeon, although David had prepared a place in Jerusalem for the ark (I Chr. 15).

great lovingkindness, and [a]hast made me king in his place.

9 "Now, O LORD God, [a]Thy [I]promise to my father David is fulfilled;[539] for Thou hast made me king[4427] over [b]a people[5971] as numerous as the dust[6083] of the earth.[776]

10 "[a]Give me now wisdom[2451] and knowledge, [b]that I may go out and come in before this people; for who can rule[8199] this great people of Thine?"

11 [a]And God said to Solomon, "Because [I]you had this in mind, and did not ask[7592] for riches, wealth, or honor, or the life[5315] of those who hate[8130] you, nor have you even asked for long life,[3117] but you have asked for yourself wisdom and knowledge, that you may rule My people, over whom I have made you king,

12 wisdom and knowledge have been granted to you. And [a]I will give you riches and wealth and honor, [I]such as none of the kings[4428] who were before you has possessed, nor those who will [II]come after you."

13 [a]So Solomon went [I]from the high place which was at Gibeon, from the tent of meeting, to Jerusalem, and he reigned over Israel.

Solomon's Wealth

14 [a]And Solomon amassed[622] chariots and horsemen. [b]He had 1,400 chariots, and 12,000 horsemen, and he stationed them in [c]the chariot cities and with the king[4428] at Jerusalem.

15 And [a]the king made [b]silver and gold as plentiful in Jerusalem as stones, and he made cedars as plentiful as sycamores in the [I]lowland.[8219]

16 And Solomon's [a]horses were imported from Egypt and from Kue; the king's[4428] traders procured them from Kue for a price.

17 And they [I]imported chariots from Egypt for 600 *shekels* of silver apiece, and horses for 150 apiece, and [II]by the same means they [III]exported them to all the kings of the Hittites and the kings of Aram.

Solomon Will Build a Temple and Palace

2 [Ia]Now Solomon [II]decided[559] to build a house for the name of the LORD, and a [III]royal palace for himself.[4438]

2 [I]So [a]Solomon [II]assigned 70,000 men to carry loads, and 80,000 men to quarry[2672] *stone* in the mountains, and 3,600 to supervise them.

3 [a]Then Solomon sent *word* to [I]Huram the king[4428] of Tyre, saying, "[b]As you dealt[6213] with David my father, and sent him cedars to build him a house to dwell in, so do for me.

4 "Behold, I am about to build a house for the name of the LORD my God,[430] dedicating[6942] it to Him, [a]to burn fragrant incense[7004] before Him, and *to set out* [b]the showbread continually,[8548] and to offer [c]burnt offerings morning and evening, [d]on sabbaths and on new moons and on the appointed feasts[4150] of the LORD our God, this *being required* forever in Israel.

5 "And the house which I am about to build *will be* great; for [a]greater is our God than all the gods.[430]

6 "But [a]who is able to build a house for Him, for the heavens and the highest heavens cannot contain Him? So who am I, that I should build a house for Him, except to [I]burn *incense* before Him?

7 "And now [a]send me a skilled[2450] man to work[6213] in gold, silver, brass and iron, and in purple, crimson and vio-

---

8 [a]1Chr. 28:5
9 [I]Lit., *word* [a]2Sam. 7:12-16 [b]Gen. 13:16; 22:17; 28:14
10 [a]1Kin. 3:9 [b]Num. 27:17; 2Sam. 5:2
11 [I]Lit., *this was in your heart* [a]1Kin. 3:11
12 [I]Lit., *which was not so to the kings who were before you* [II]Lit., *be* [a]1Chr. 29:25; 2Chr. 9:22
13 [I]Lit., *to* [a]2Chr. 1:3
14 [a]1Kin. 10:26-29 [b]1Kin. 4:26 [c]1Kin. 9:19
15 [I]Heb., *shephelah* [a]1Kin. 10:27 [b]Deut. 17:17
16 [a]Deut. 17:16
17 [I]Lit., *brought up and brought out* [II]Lit., *and in like manner by their hand* [III]Lit., *brought out*

1 [I]Ch. 1:18 in Heb. [II]Lit., *said* [III]Lit., *house for his royalty* [a]1 Kin. 5:5
2 [I]Ch. 2:1 in Heb. [II]Lit., *numbered* [a]1Kin. 5:15, 16; 2Chr. 2:18
3 [I]In 1Kin. 5:18, *Hiram* [a]1Kin. 5:2-11 [b]1Chr. 14:1
4 [a]Ex. 30:7 [b]Ex. 25:30 [c]Ex. 29:38-42 [d]Num. 28:9, 10
5 [a]Ex. 15:11; 1Chr. 16:25
6 [I]Lit., *offer up in smoke* [a]1Kin. 8:27; 2Chr. 6:18
7 [a]Ex. 31:3-5; 2Chr. 2:13, 14

1:9 This promise was recorded in I Chr. 22:9,10.
1:14 This was forbidden by Deut. 17:16.
1:14-17 See I Kgs. 10:26-29; II Chr. 9:25-28.
2:1-18 See I Kgs. 5:1-18; 7:13,14.
2:3 Huram is called Hiram throughout I Kings. He is to be distinguished from Huram, the master craftsman, who was also referred to as Hiram in the Books of Kings.

let *fabrics,* and who knows how to make engravings, to *work* with the skilled men [I][b]whom I have in Judah and Jerusalem, whom David my father provided.

8 "[a]Send me also cedar, cypress and algum[418] timber from Lebanon, for I know[3045] that your servants know how to cut[3772] timber of Lebanon; and indeed, [b]my servants *will work* with your servants,

9 to prepare timber in abundance for me, for the house which I am about to build *will be* great and wonderful.[6381]

10 "Now behold, [a]I will give to your servants, the woodsmen[2404] who cut the timber, 20,000 [I]kors of crushed[4347] wheat, and 20,000 [I]kors of barley, and 20,000 baths of wine, and 20,000 baths of oil."

Huram to Assist

11 Then Huram, king of Tyre, [I]answered[559] in a letter sent to Solomon: "[a]Because the LORD loves[160] His people,[5971] He has made you king over them."

12 Then Huram [I]continued, "Blessed[1288] be [a]the LORD, the God of Israel, who has made heaven and earth,[776] who has given King David a wise[2450] son, [II]endowed with discretion and understanding,[998] [b]who will build a house for the LORD and a [III]royal palace for himself.

13 "And now I am sending a skilled man, [I]endowed with understanding, Huram-abi,

⊶ 14 [a]the son of a [I]Danite woman[802] and [II]a Tyrian father, who knows how to work in gold, silver, bronze, iron, stone and wood, *and* in purple, violet, linen and crimson fabrics, and *who knows how* to make all kinds of engravings[6603] and to [III]execute any design[4284] which may be assigned to him, *to work* with your skilled men, and with [IV]those of my lord[113] David your father.

15 "Now then, let my lord send to his servants wheat and barley, oil and wine, of [a]which he has spoken.

16 "And [a]we will cut whatever timber you need from Lebanon, and bring it to you on rafts[7513] by sea to Joppa, so that you may carry it up to Jerusalem."

17 And Solomon numbered[5608] all the aliens who *were* in the land[776] of Israel, [a]following the [I]census which his father David had [II]taken; and 153,600 were found.

18 [a]And he appointed 70,000 of them to carry loads, and 80,000 to quarry[2672] *stones* in the mountains, and 3,600 supervisors to make the people work.[5647]

The Temple Construction in Jerusalem

3 ⊶ [a]Then Solomon began to build the house of the LORD in Jerusalem on Mount Moriah, where *the Lord* had appeared[7200] to his father David, at the place that David had prepared, [b]on the threshing floor of [I]Ornan the Jebusite.

2 And he began to build on the second *day* in the second month [I]of the fourth year of his reign.

Dimensions and Materials of the Temple

3 Now these are the [I]foundations which [a]Solomon laid[3245] for building the house of God.[430] The length[753] in [II]cubits, according to the old[7223] standard *was* sixty cubits, and the width twenty cubits.

4 And the porch which was in front of the house [a]was as long as the width of the house, twenty cubits, and the

7 [I]Lit., *who are with me* [b]1Chr. 22:15

8 [a]1Kin. 5:6 [b]2Chr. 9:10, 11

10 [I]I.e., A kor equals approx. 10 bu. [a]1Kin. 5:11

11 [I]Lit., *said . . . and he sent* [a]1Kin. 10:9; 2Chr. 9:8

12 [I]Lit., *said* [II]Lit., *knowing discretion* [III]Lit., *house for his royalty* [a]Ps. 33:6; 102:25 [b]2Chr. 2:1

13 [I]Lit., *knowing understanding*

14 [I]Lit., *a woman of the daughters of Dan* [II]Lit., *whose father is a Tyrian man* [III]Lit., *devise any device* [IV]Lit., *skilled men* [a]1Kin. 7:14

15 [a]2Chr. 2:10

16 [a]1Kin. 5:8, 9

17 [I]Lit., *numbering* [II]Lit., *numbered of them* [a]1Chr. 22:2

18 [a]2Chr. 2:2

1 [I]In 2 Sam. 24:18, *Araunah* [a]1Kin. 6:1 [b]1Chr. 21:18

2 [I]Lit., *in*

3 [I]Lit., *founding of Solomon to build* [II]I.e., One cubit equals approx. 18 in. [a]1Kin. 6:2

4 [a]1Kin. 6:3

⊶ **2:14** Probably of Dan by birth, though a widow of a man of Naphtali (I Kgs. 7:14). Undoubtedly Solomon's choice of a man who was half-Hebrew was popular with his people.

⊶ **3:1** See II Sam. 24:16-25. This is where David sacrificed (I Chr. 21:18-30) and was the probable site where Abraham attempted to offer Isaac (Gen. 22:2ff.).

⊶ **3:1-14** See I Kgs. 6:1-38.

height 120; and inside he overlaid it with pure gold.

5 And he overlaid[2645] [a]the [I]main room with cypress wood and overlaid it with fine gold, and [II]ornamented it with palm trees and chains.

6 Further, he [I]adorned[6823] the house with precious[8597] stones; and the gold was gold from [II]Parvaim.

7 [a]He also overlaid the house with gold—the beams, the thresholds, and its walls, and its doors; and he [b]carved[6605] cherubim[3742] on the walls.

8 Now he made [a]the [I]room of the holy of holies: its length, across the width of the house, *was* twenty cubits, and its width *was* twenty cubits; and he overlaid it with fine gold, *amounting* to 600 talents.

9 And the weight of the nails was fifty shekels of gold. He also overlaid [a]the upper rooms with gold.

10 [a]Then he made two [I]sculptured cherubim in the room of the holy of holies and overlaid them with gold.

11 And the wingspan of the cherubim[3742] *was* twenty cubits; the wing of one, of five cubits, touched the wall of the house, and *its* other wing, of five cubits, touched the wing of the other cherub.

12 And the wing of the other cherub, of five cubits, touched the wall of the house; and *its* other wing of five cubits, was attached to the wing of the [I]first cherub.

13 The wings of these cherubim extended twenty cubits, and they stood on their feet [I]facing the *main* room.

14 [a]And he made the veil of violet, purple, crimson and fine linen, and he worked cherubim on it.

🔑 **15** [a]He also made two pillars for the front of the house, thirty-five cubits [I]high, and the capital on the top of each *was* five cubits.

16 And he made chains in the inner sanctuary, and placed *them* on the tops of the pillars; and he made one hundred pomegranates and placed *them* on the chains.

17 [a]And he erected the pillars in front of the temple, one on the right and the other on the left, and named[7121] the one on the right Jachin and the one on the left Boaz.

Furnishings of the Temple

4 🔑 Then [a]he made a bronze altar,[4196] twenty cubits in length[753] and twenty cubits in width and ten cubits in height.

2 [a]Also he made the cast *metal* sea, ten cubits from brim to brim,[8193] circular in form, and its height *was* five cubits and [I]its circumference thirty cubits.

3 Now figures like oxen *were* under it *and* all around it, ten cubits, entirely encircling[5362] the sea. The oxen *were* in two rows, cast [I]in one piece.

4 It stood on twelve oxen, three facing the north, three facing west, three facing south, and three facing east; and the sea *was set* on top of them, and all their hindquarters turned inwards.[1004]

5 And it was a handbreadth thick, and its brim was made like the brim of a cup, *like* a lily blossom; it [a]could hold 3,000 baths.

6 [a]He also made ten basins[3595] in which to wash,[7364] and he set five on the right side and five on the left, [I]to rinse[1740] things for the burnt offering; but the sea *was* for the priests to wash in.

7 Then [a]he made the ten golden lampstands in the way prescribed[4941] for them, and he set them in the temple, five on the right side and five on the left.

8 He also made [a]ten tables and placed them in the temple, five on the right side and five on the left. And he made one hundred golden bowls.[4219]

9 Then he made [a]the court of the priests and [b]the great court and doors

5 [I]Lit., *great house* [II]Lit., *put on it palm trees* [a]1Kin. 6:17
6 [I]Lit., *overlaid . . . for beauty* [II]Or, *country of gold*
7 [a]1Kin. 6:20-22 [b]1Kin. 6:29-35
8 [I]Lit., *house* [a]Ex. 26:33; 1Kin. 6:16
9 [a]1Chr. 28:11
10 [I]Lit., *cherubim of sculptured work* [a]Ex. 25:18-20; 1Kin. 6:23-28
12 [I]Lit., *other*
13 [I]Lit., *and their faces to*
14 [a]Ex. 26:31
15 [I]Lit., *long* [a]1Kin. 7:15-20
17 [a]1Kin. 7:21
1 [a]Ex. 27:1, 2; 2Kin. 16:14
2 [I]Lit., *a line of 30 cubits encircling it round about* [a]1Kin. 7:23-26
3 [I]Lit., *in its casting*
5 [a]1Kin. 7:26
6 [I]Lit., *in which to* [a]Ex. 30:17-21; 1Kin. 7:38, 40
7 [a]Ex. 25:31-40; 1Kin. 7:49
8 [a]1Kin. 7:48
9 [a]1Kin. 6:36 [b]2Kin. 21:5

🔑 **3:15-17** See I Kgs. 7:15-22.
🔑 **4:1—5:1** See I Kgs. 7:23-51.

for the court, and overlaid their doors
with bronze.
10 And [a]he set the sea on the right
[I]side *of the house* toward the southeast.
11 [a]Huram also made the pails, the
shovels, and the bowls. So Huram
finished[3615] doing the work[4399] which he
performed for King[4428] Solomon in the
house of God:[430]
12 the two pillars, the bowls[1543] and
the two capitals on top of the pillars,
and the two networks to cover[3680] the
two bowls of the capitals which were
on top of the pillars,
13 and [a]the four hundred pomegranates for the two networks, two
rows of pomegranates for each network
to cover the two bowls of the capitals
which were on the pillars.
14 [a]He also made the stands and
he made the basins on the stands,
15 *and* the one sea with the twelve
oxen under it.
16 And the pails, the shovels, the
forks, and all its utensils, [a]Huram-abi
made of polished bronze for King Solomon for the house of the LORD.
17 On the plain of the Jordan the
king cast them, in the clay ground[127]
between Succoth and Zeredah.
18 [a]Thus Solomon made all these
utensils in great quantities, for the
weight of the bronze could not be found
out.
19 Solomon also made all the things
that *were* in the house of God: even
the golden altar, [a]the tables with the
bread of the Presence on them,
20 the lampstands with their
lamps[5216] of pure gold, [a]to burn in front
of the inner sanctuary in the way prescribed;
21 the flowers, the lamps, and the
tongs of gold, of purest gold;
22 and the snuffers, the bowls, the
spoons, and the firepans of pure gold;
and the entrance of the house, its inner
doors for the holy of holies, and the
doors of the house, *that is,* of the nave,
of gold.

10 [I]Lit., *shoulder* [a]1Kin. 7:39
11 [a]1Kin. 7:40-51
13 [a]1Kin. 7:20
14 [a]1Kin. 7:27-43
16 [a]1Kin. 7:14; 2Chr. 2:13
18 [a]1Kin. 7:47
19 [a]2Chr. 4:8
20 [a]Ex. 25:31-37; 2Chr. 5:7
1 [I]Lit., *dedicated things of David,* [a]1Kin. 7:51 [b]2Sam. 8:11; 1Chr. 18:11
2 [a]1Kin. 8:1-9 [b]2Sam. 6:12-15; 1Chr. 15:25-28; 2Chr. 1:4
3 [a]1Kin. 8:2 [b]2Chr. 7:8-10
4 [a]Josh. 3:6; 2Chr. 5:7
6 [I]Lit., *sheep . . . numbered for multitude*
8 [I]Lit., *poles above*
9 [a]1Kin. 8:8, 9

The Ark Is Brought into the Temple

5 [a]Thus all the work[4399] that Solomon
performed for the house of the LORD
was finished.[7999] And Solomon brought
in the [I][b]things that David his father had
dedicated,[6944] even the silver and the
gold and all the utensils, *and* put *them*
in the treasuries of the house of God.[430]
🔑**2** [a]Then Solomon assembled[6950] to
Jerusalem the elders[2205] of Israel and
all the heads of the tribes, the leaders[5387]
of the fathers'[1] *households* of the sons[1121]
of Israel, [b]to bring up the ark[727] of the
covenant[1285] of the LORD out of the city
of David, which is Zion.
3 And [a]all the men of Israel assembled themselves to the king[4428] at [b]the
feast,[2282] that is *in* the seventh month.
4 Then all the elders of Israel came,
and [a]the Levites took up the ark.
🔑5 And they brought[5927] up the ark
and the tent of meeting[4150] and all the
holy utensils which *were* in the tent; the
Levitical priests brought them up.
6 And King Solomon and all the
congregation[5712] of Israel who were
assembled[3259] with him before the ark
were sacrificing [I]so many sheep and
oxen, that they could not be counted
or numbered.
7 Then the priests brought the ark
of the covenant of the LORD to its place,
into the inner sanctuary of the house,
to the holy of holies, under the wings
of the cherubim.[3742]
8 For the cherubim spread their
wings over the place of the ark, so that
the cherubim made a covering[3680] over
the ark and its [I]poles.
9 And the poles were so long that
[a]the ends of the poles of the ark could
be seen in front of the inner sanctuary, but they could not be seen outside;

🔑**5:2-14** See I Kgs. 8:1-11.
🔑**5:5** Levites were forbidden to touch the ark (Num. 4:15). Failure to observe this caused the death of Uzza (I Chr. 13:1-10). Thereafter, David and Solomon observed this rule strictly.

and [I]they are there to this <u>day</u>.[3117]

10 [a]There was nothing in the ark except the two tablets which Moses put *there* at Horeb, where the LORD made a covenant with the sons of Israel, when they came out of Egypt.

The Glory of God Fills the Temple

11 And when the priests came forth from the holy place (for all the priests who were present had sanctified themselves, without <u>regard</u>[8104] [a]to divisions),

12 and all the Levitical singers, [a]Asaph, Heman, Jeduthun, and their sons and <u>kinsmen</u>,[251] clothed in fine linen, [b]with cymbals, harps, and lyres, standing east of the <u>altar</u>,[4196] and with them one hundred and twenty priests [c]blowing trumpets

13 in unison when the trumpeters and the singers were to make themselves heard with one voice to <u>praise</u>[1984] and to glorify the LORD, and when they lifted up their voice [a]accompanied by trumpets and cymbals and instruments of music, and when they <u>praised</u>[1984] the LORD *saying,* "[b]*He* indeed is <u>good</u>[2896] for His lovingkindness is everlasting," then the house, the house of the LORD, was filled with a <u>cloud</u>,[6051]

14 so that the priests could not stand to minister because of the cloud, for [a]the <u>glory</u>[3519] of the LORD filled the house of God.

Solomon's Dedication

6 [a]Then Solomon said,
"The LORD has said that He would
<u>dwell</u>[7931] in the thick
<u>cloud</u>.[6205]

2 "I have built Thee a lofty house,
And a place for Thy dwelling
forever."

3 Then the <u>king</u>[4428] [I]faced about and <u>blessed</u>[1288] all the <u>assembly</u>[6951] of Israel, while all the assembly of Israel was standing.

4 And he said, "Blessed be the LORD, the <u>God</u>[430] of Israel, who spoke with His mouth to my father David and has fulfilled *it* with His hands, saying,

5 'Since the <u>day</u>[3117] that I brought My <u>people</u>[5971] from the <u>land</u>[776] of Egypt, I <u>did</u> not <u>choose</u>[977] a city out of all the tribes of Israel *in which* to build a house that My name might be there, nor did I choose any man for a leader over My people Israel;

6 but [a]I have <u>chosen</u>[977] Jerusalem that My name might be there, and I [b]have chosen David to be over My people Israel.'

7 "[a]Now it was [I]in the heart of my father David to build a house for the name of the LORD, the God of Israel.

8 "But the LORD said to my father David, 'Because it was [I]in your heart to build a house for My name, you did <u>well</u>[2895] that it was [I]in your heart.

9 'Nevertheless you shall not build the house, but your son who [I]shall be born to you, he shall build the house for My name.'

10 "Now the LORD has fulfilled His <u>word</u>[1697] which He spoke; for I have risen in the place of my father David and sit on the throne of Israel, as the LORD [I]promised, and have built the house for the name of the LORD, the God of Israel.

11 "And there I have set the <u>ark</u>,[727] [a]in which is the <u>covenant</u>[1285] of the LORD, which He made with the <u>sons</u>[1121] of Israel."

Solomon's Prayer of Dedication

12 Then he stood before the <u>altar</u>[4196] of the LORD in the presence of all the assembly of Israel and spread out his hands.

---

9 [I]Lit., *it is*
10 [a]Deut. 10:2-5; Heb. 9:4
11 [a]1Chr. 24:1-5
12 [a]1Chr. 25:1-4 [b]1Chr. 13:8; 15:16, 24 [c]2Chr. 7:6
13 [a]1Chr. 16:42 [b]1Chr. 16:34; 2Chr. 7:3; Ezra 3:11; Ps. 100:5; Jer. 33:11
14 [a]Ex. 40:35; 1Kin. 8:11
1 [a]1Kin. 8:12-50
3 [I]Lit., *turned his face about*
6 [a]2Chr. 12:13 [b]1Chr. 28:4
7 [I]Lit., *with* [a]1Kin. 5:3; 1Chr. 28:2
8 [I]Lit., *with*
9 [I]Lit., *is to come forth from your loins*
10 [I]Lit., *spoke*
11 [a]2Chr. 5:7, 10

5:10 See Ex. 25:16; 40:20. Aaron's rod and the manna disappeared over the years. No one knows what happened to them.

6:1 This was mentioned in Ex. 19:9; Lev. 16:2.

6:1—7:10 See I Kgs. 8:12-66.

6:6 See I Chr. 17:4-14.

13 [a]Now Solomon had made a
bronze platform, five cubits long,[753] five
cubits wide, and three cubits high, and
had set it in the midst of the court; and
he stood on it, [b]knelt[1288] on his knees
in the presence of all the assembly of
Israel, and spread out his hands toward
heaven.
14 And he said, "O LORD, the God
of Israel, [a]there is no god like Thee in
heaven or on earth,[776] [b]keeping[8104] covenant and *showing* lovingkindness to Thy
servants who walk before Thee with
all their heart;
15 [a]who has kept[8104] with Thy servant David, my father, that which Thou
hast [I]promised him; indeed, Thou hast
spoken with Thy mouth, and hast fulfilled it with Thy hand, as it is this day.
16 "Now therefore, O LORD, the
God of Israel, keep[8104] with Thy servant
David, my father, that which Thou hast
[I]promised him, saying, '[II][a]You shall not
lack a man to sit on the throne of Israel,
if only your sons take heed to their
way,[1870] to walk in My law[8451] as you
have walked before Me.'
17 "Now therefore, O LORD, the
God of Israel, let Thy word be confirmed[539] which Thou hast spoken to
Thy servant David.
18 "But [a]will God indeed dwell with
mankind on the earth? Behold, [b]heaven
and the [I]highest heaven cannot contain
Thee; how much less this house which
I have built.
19 "Yet have regard to the
prayer[8605] of Thy servant and to his supplication, O LORD my God, to listen to
the cry and to the prayer which Thy
servant prays before Thee;
20 that Thine [a]eyes may be open
toward this house day and night,[3915]
toward [b]the place of which Thou hast
said that *Thou wouldst* put Thy name
there, to listen to the prayer which Thy
servant shall pray toward this place.
21 "And listen to the supplications
of Thy servant and of Thy people Israel,
when they pray toward this place; hear
Thou from Thy dwelling place, from
heaven; [a]hear Thou and forgive.[5545]
22 "If a man sins against his neighbor,[7453] and is made to take an oath,
and he comes *and* takes an oath before
Thine altar in this house,
23 then hear Thou from heaven and
act[6213] and judge[8199] Thy servants,
[I][a]punishing the wicked[7563] by bringing
his way on his own head and justifying[6663]
the righteous by giving him according
to his righteousness.
24 "And if Thy people Israel [I]are
defeated before an enemy, because
[a]they have sinned against Thee, and they
return *to Thee* and confess[3034] Thy
name, and pray and make supplication
before Thee in this house,
25 then hear Thou from heaven and
forgive the sin of Thy people Israel, and
bring them back to the land[127] which
Thou hast given to them and to their
fathers.[1]
26 "When the [a]heavens are shut up
and there is no rain because they have
sinned against Thee, and they pray toward this place and confess Thy name,
and turn from their sin when Thou dost
afflict them;
27 then hear Thou in heaven and
forgive the sin of Thy servants and Thy
people Israel, indeed, [a]teach them the
good[2896] way in which they should walk.
And send rain on Thy land, which Thou
hast given to Thy people for an inheritance.[5159]
28 "If there is [a]famine in the land,
if there is pestilence,[1698] if there is blight
or mildew, if there is locust or grasshopper, if their enemies besiege them in
the land of their [I]cities, whatever plague
or whatever sickness *there is*,

13 [a]Neh. 8:4 [b]1Kin. 8:54
14 [a]Ex. 15:11; Deut. 3:24 [b]Deut. 7:9
15 [I]Lit., *spoken to* [a]1Chr. 22:9, 10
16 [I]Lit., *spoken to* [II]Lit., *There shall not be cut off to you a man from before Me* [a]1Kin. 2:4; 2Chr. 7:18
18 [I]Lit., *heaven of heavens* [a]Ps. 113:5, 6 [b]2Chr. 2:6; Is. 66:1; Acts 7:49
20 [a]Ps. 33:18; 34:15 [b]Deut. 12:11
21 [a]Is. 43:25; 44:22; Mic. 7:18
23 [I]Lit., *returning* [a]Is. 3:11; Rom. 2:8, 9
24 [I]Lit., *smitten* [a]Ps. 51:4
26 [a]1Kin. 17:1
27 [a]Ps. 94:12
28 [I]Lit., *gates* [a]2Chr. 20:9

6:14 This is one of the most beautiful prayers in Scripture. It shows great familiarity and reverence for the warnings of God, which were given to all Israel through Moses in Lev. 26 and Deut. 28.
6:16 Solomon seemed conscious of the condition which was required for blessings from God (see I Kgs. 2:4; 6:12,13; cf. Ex. 32:13; Num. 14:18; Neh. 1:8,9; Dan. 9:13).
6:18 See note on Isa. 66:1,2.

29 whatever prayer or supplication is made by any man or by all Thy people Israel, [I]each knowing[3045] his own affliction and his own pain, and spreading his hands toward this house,

30 then hear Thou from heaven Thy dwelling place, and forgive, and render to each according to all his ways,[1870] whose heart Thou knowest[3045] [a]for Thou alone dost know the hearts of the sons of men,

31 that they may [I]fear[3372] Thee, to walk in Thy ways [II]as long as they live[2416] in the land which Thou hast given to our fathers.

32 "Also concerning [a]the foreigner who is not from Thy people Israel, when he comes from a far country for Thy great name's sake and Thy mighty hand and Thine outstretched arm, when they come and pray toward this house,

33 then hear Thou from heaven, from Thy dwelling place, and do according to all for which the foreigner calls[7121] to Thee, in order that all the peoples of the earth may know Thy name, and [I]fear Thee, as *do* Thy people Israel, and that they may know that [II]this house which I have built is [a]called[7121] by Thy name.

34 "When Thy people go out to battle against their enemies, by whatever way Thou shalt send them, and they pray to Thee toward this city which Thou hast chosen, and the house which I have built for Thy name,

35 then hear Thou from heaven their prayer and their supplication, and maintain their cause.[4941]

36 "When they sin against Thee ([a]for there is no man who does not sin) and Thou art angry[599] with them and dost deliver them to an enemy, so that [I]they take them away captive[7617] to a land far off or near,

37 if they [I]take thought[7725] in the land where they are taken captive,[7617] and repent and make supplication to Thee in the land of their captivity,[7633] saying, 'We have sinned, we have committed iniquity,[5753] and have acted wickedly';[7561]

38 [a]if they return to Thee with all their heart and with all their soul in the land of their captivity, where they have been taken captive, and pray toward their land which Thou hast given to their fathers, and the city which Thou hast chosen, and toward the house which I have built for Thy name,

39 then hear from heaven, from Thy dwelling place, their prayer and supplications, and maintain their cause, and forgive Thy people who have sinned against Thee.

40 "Now, O my God, I pray Thee, [a]let Thine eyes be open, and [b]Thine ears[241] attentive[7183] to the prayer *offered* in this place.

41 "[a]Now therefore arise, O LORD God, to Thy resting place, Thou and the ark of Thy might; let Thy priests, O LORD God, be clothed with salvation, and let Thy godly ones rejoice in what is good.

42 "O LORD God, do not turn away the face of Thine anointed;[4899] [a]remember *Thy* lovingkindness to Thy servant David."

The Shekinah Glory

7 [a]Now when Solomon had finished[3615] praying, [b]fire came down from heaven and consumed the burnt offering and the sacrifices; and the glory[3519] of the LORD filled the house.

2 And [a]the priests could not enter into the house of the LORD, because the glory of the LORD filled the LORD's house.

3 And all the sons[1121] of Israel, seeing the fire come down and the glory of the LORD upon the house, bowed[3766]

29 [I]Lit., *whoever shall know*

30 [a]1Sam. 16:7; 1Chr. 28:9

31 [I]Or, *reverence* [II]Lit., *all the days that they live on the face of the land*

32 [a]Is. 56:3-8

33 [I]Or, *reverence* [II]Lit., *Thy name is called upon this house* [a]2Chr. 7:14

36 [I]Lit., *their captors take them captive* [a]Job 15:14-16; James 3:2; 1John 1:8-10

37 [I]Lit., *return to their heart*

38 [a]Jer. 29:12, 13

40 [a]2Chr. 7:15; Neh. 1:6, 11 [b]Ps. 17:1

41 [a]Ps. 132:8, 9

42 [a]Ps. 89:24, 28; 132:10-12; Is. 55:3

1 [a]1Kin. 8:54 [b]Lev. 9:23f.; 1Kin. 18:24, 38

2 [a]2Chr. 5:14

6:37 Compare Ps. 106; Dan. 9:5.

6:42 This is the formula which was used when the ark of the covenant was moved during the wilderness journey (Num. 10:35,36). It was preserved in Ps. 132:8-10.

7:2 This was similar to the occurrence at the dedication of the tabernacle (Ex. 40:34,35).

down on the pavement with their faces
to the ground,[776] and they worshiped[7812]
and gave praise[3035] to the LORD, *saying,*
“[a]Truly He is good,[2896] truly His lovingkindness is everlasting.”

Sacrifices Offered

4 [a]Then the king[4428] and all the
people[5971] offered sacrifice before the
LORD.
5 And King Solomon offered a sacrifice of 22,000 oxen, and 120,000 sheep.
Thus the king and all the people
dedicated[2596] the house of God.[430]
6 And the priests stood at their
posts and [a]the Levites, with the instruments of music to the LORD, which King
David had made for giving praise[3034]
to the LORD—“for His lovingkindness
is everlasting”—whenever [I]he gave
praise[1984] by their [II]means, while
[b]the priests on the other side blew trumpets; and all Israel was standing.
7 [a]Then Solomon consecrated the
middle of the court that *was* before the
house of the LORD, for there he offered
the burnt offerings and the fat of the
peace offerings, because the bronze
altar[4196] which Solomon had made was
not able to contain the burnt offering,
the grain offering, and the fat.

The Feast of Dedication

8 So [a]Solomon observed[6213] the
feast[2282] at that time for seven days,[3117]
and all Israel with him, a very great
assembly, *who came* from the entrance
of Hamath to the [b]brook of Egypt.
9 And on the eighth day[3117] they
held [a]a solemn assembly,[6116] for the
dedication[2598] of the altar they observed
seven days, and the feast seven days.
10 Then on the twenty-third day of
the seventh month he sent the people
to their tents, rejoicing and happy of
heart because of the goodness that the
LORD had shown to David and to Solomon and to His people Israel.

God’s Promise and Warning

🔑**11** [a]Thus Solomon finished[3615] the
house of the LORD and the king’s[4428]
palace, and successfully completed all
that [I]he had planned on doing in the
house of the LORD and in his palace.
🔑12 Then the LORD appeared[7200] to
Solomon at night[3915] and said to him,
“I have heard your prayer,[8605] and
[a]have chosen[977] this place for Myself
as a house of sacrifice.
13 “[a]If I shut up the heavens so that
there is no rain, or if I command[6680]
the locust to devour the land,[776] or if I
send pestilence[1698] among My people,
14 [a]and My people [I]who are
called[7121] by My name humble themselves and pray, and seek My face and
turn from their wicked[7451] ways,[1870] then
I will hear from heaven, will forgive[5545]
their sin, and will heal their land.
15 “[a]Now My eyes shall be open
and My ears[241] attentive[7183] to the
[I]prayer *offered* in this place.
16 “For [a]now I have chosen and consecrated this house that My name may
be there forever, and My eyes and My
heart will be there perpetually.
17 “And as for you, if you walk before Me as your father David walked
even to do[6213] according to all that I
have commanded[6680] you and will keep
My statutes and My ordinances,[4941]
18 then I will establish your royal[4438]
throne as I covenanted[3772] with your father David, saying, ‘[I][a]You shall not lack
a man *to be* ruler in Israel.’
19 “[a]But if you turn away and
forsake[5800] My statutes and My commandments[4687] which I have set before you and shall go and serve other
gods[430] and worship[7812] them,
20 [a]then I will uproot you from My
land[127] which I have given [I]you, and this
house which I have consecrated for My
name I will cast out of My sight, and I
will make it [b]a proverb and a byword
among all peoples.[5971]

3 [a]2Chr. 5:13; 20:21
4 [a]1Kin. 8:62, 63
6 [I]Lit., *David* [II]Lit., *hand* [a]1Chr. 15:16-21 [b]2Chr. 5:12
7 [a]1Kin. 8:64-66
8 [a]1Kin. 8:65 [b]Gen. 15:18
9 [a]Lev. 23:36
11 [I]Lit., *came upon the heart of Solomon to do* [a]1Kin. 9:1-9
12 [a]Deut. 12:5, 11
13 [a]2Chr. 6:26-28
14 [I]Lit., *over whom My name is called* [a]2Chr. 6:37-39; James 4:10
15 [I]Lit., *prayer of this place* [a]2Chr. 6:20, 40
16 [a]2Chr. 7:12
18 [I]Lit., *There shall not be cut off to you a man* [a]1Kin. 2:4; 2Chr. 6:16
19 [a]Lev. 26:14, 33; Deut. 28:15
20 [I]Ancient versions and Heb. read *them* [a]Deut. 29:28; 1Kin. 14:15 [b]Deut. 28:37

🔑**7:11-22** See I Kgs. 9:1-9.
🔑**7:12** Sacrifice had a very central position in worship (Lev. 17:11; Heb. 9:22).

21 "As for this house, which was
exalted, everyone who passes[5674] by it
will be astonished[8074] and say, '[a]Why
has the LORD done thus to this land and
to this house?'
22 "And they will say,[559] 'Because
[a]they forsook[5800] the LORD, the God of
their fathers,[1] who brought them from
the land of Egypt, and they adopted
other gods and worshiped them and
served them, therefore He has brought
all this adversity[7451] on them.' "

Solomon's Activities and Accomplishments

8 ⚿[a]Now it came about at the end
of the twenty years in which Solomon had built the house of the LORD
and his own house
2 that he built the cities which Huram had given to [I]him, and settled the
sons[1121] of Israel there.
3 Then Solomon went to Hamath-
zobah and captured it.
4 And he built Tadmor in the wilderness and all the storage cities which he
had built in Hamath.
5 He also built upper[5945] [a]Beth-
horon and lower Beth-horon, [b]forti-
fied[8481] cities *with* walls, gates, and bars;
6 and Baalath and all the storage cities that Solomon had, and all the cities
for [I]his chariots and cities for [I]his horsemen, and all that it pleased Solomon
to build in Jerusalem, in Lebanon, and
in all the land[776] [II]under his rule.[4475]
7 [a]All of the people[5971] who were
left[3498] of the Hittites, the Amorites,
the Perizzites, the Hivites, and the Jebusites, who were not of Israel,
8 namely, from their descendants
who were left after them in the land
whom the sons of Israel had not
destroyed,[3615] [a]them Solomon raised as
forced laborers to this day.[3117]
9 But Solomon did not make slaves
for his work[4399] from the sons of Israel;
they were men of war, his chief captains,[7991] and commanders[8269] of his
chariots and his horsemen.
10 And these were the chief
[I]officers of King[4428] Solomon, two hundred and fifty who ruled over the people.
11 [a]Then Solomon brought[5927] Pharaoh's daughter up from the city of
David to the house which he had built
for her; for he said, "My wife[802] shall
not dwell in the house of David king of
Israel, because [I]the places are holy
where the ark[727] of the LORD has entered."
12 Then Solomon offered burnt offerings to the LORD on [a]the altar[4196] of
the LORD which he had built before the
porch;
13 and [a]*did so* according to the daily
rule, offering *them* up [b]according to the
commandment[4687] of Moses, for [c]the
sabbaths, [d]the new moons, and the
[e]three annual feasts[4150]—the Feast of
Unleavened[4682] Bread, the Feast of
Weeks, and the Feast of Booths.
14 Now according to the ordinance
of his father David, he appointed
[a]the divisions of the priests for their service, and [b]the Levites for their duties
of praise[1984] and ministering before the
priests according to the daily rule,[1697]
and [c]the gatekeepers[7778] by their divisions at every gate; for [d]David the man
of God[430] had so commanded.
15 And they did not depart[5493] from
the commandment of the king to the
priests and Levites in any manner or
concerning the storehouses.
16 Thus all the work of Solomon
was carried out [I]from the day of the
foundation[4143] of the house of the LORD,
and until it was finished.[3615] So the house
of the LORD was completed.[8003]
17 Then Solomon went to [a]Ezion-
geber and to [b]Eloth on the seashore in
the land of Edom.
18 And Huram by his servants sent
him ships and servants who knew[3045]

21 [a]Deut. 29:24-27
22 [a]Judg. 2:13
1 [a]1Kin. 9:10-28
2 [I]Lit., *Solomon*
5 [a]1Chr. 7:24 [b]2Chr. 14:7
6 [I]Lit., *the* [II]Lit., *of*
7 [a]Gen. 15:18-21; 1Kin. 9:20
8 [a]1Kin. 4:6; 9:21
10 [I]Or, *deputies*
11 [I]Lit., *they are* [a]1Kin. 3:1; 7:8
12 [a]2Chr. 4:1
13 [a]Ex. 29:38-42 [b]Num. 28:3 [c]Num. 28:9, 10 [d]Num. 28:11 [e]Ex. 23:14-17; 34:22, 23; Deut. 16:16
14 [a]1Chr. 24:1 [b]1Chr. 25:1 [c]1Chr. 26:1 [d]Neh. 12:24, 36
16 [I]So ancient versions; M.T., *as far as*
17 [a]1Kin. 9:26 [b]2Kin. 14:22

⚿ **8:1** Seven years were spent on the temple (I Kgs. 6:37,38) and thirteen years on Solomon's palace (I Kgs. 7:1).

⚿ **8:1-18** See I Kgs. 9:10-28.

the sea; and they went with Solomon's
servants to Ophir, and [a]took from there
four hundred and fifty talents of gold,
and brought them to King Solomon.

Visit of the Queen of Sheba

9 🔑 [a]Now when the queen[4436] of
Sheba heard of the fame[8088] of Solomon, she came to Jerusalem to test Solomon with difficult questions. She had a
very large retinue,[2428] with camels
carrying[5375] spices, and a large amount
of gold and precious stones; and when
she came to Solomon, she spoke with
him about all that was on her heart.
2 And Solomon [I]answered all her
questions;[1697] nothing[1697] was hidden
from Solomon which he did not [II]explain
to her.
3 And when the queen of Sheba had
seen the wisdom[2451] of Solomon, the
house which he had built,
4 the food at his table, the seating
of his servants, the attendance of his
ministers and their attire, his cupbearers
and their attire, and [I]his stairway by
which he went up to the house of the
LORD, she was breathless.
5 Then she said to the king,[4428] "It
was a true report which I heard in my
own land[776] about your words[1697] and
your wisdom.
6 "Nevertheless I did not believe[539]
their reports[1697] until I came and my
eyes had seen it. And behold, the half
of the greatness of your wisdom was
not told me. You surpass the report that
I heard.
7 "How [I]blessed are your men, how
[I]blessed are these your servants who
stand before you continually[8548] and hear
your wisdom.
8 "Blessed[1288] be the LORD your
God[430] who delighted[2654] in you, [a]set-
ting you on His throne as king for
the LORD your God; [b]because your God
loved[160] Israel establishing them forever, therefore He made you king over
them, to do[6213] justice[4941] and righteousness."[6666]
9 Then she gave the king one hundred and twenty talents of gold, and a
very great *amount of* spices and precious
stones; there had never been spice like
that which the queen of Sheba gave to
King Solomon.
10 And the servants of Huram and
the servants of Solomon [a]who brought
gold from Ophir, also brought algum[418]
trees and precious stones.
11 And from the algum the king
made steps for the house of the LORD
and for the king's[4428] palace, and lyres
and harps for the singers; and none like
that was seen before in the land of Judah.
12 And King Solomon gave to the
queen of Sheba all her desire[2656] which
she requested besides *a return for* what
she had brought to the king. Then she
turned and went to her own land with
her servants.

Solomon's Wealth and Power

🔑 **13** [a]Now the weight of gold which
came to Solomon in one year was 666
talents of gold,
14 besides that which the traders
and merchants brought; and all [a]the
kings[4428] of Arabia and the governors[6346]
of the country brought gold and silver
to Solomon.
15 And King Solomon made 200
large shields of beaten[7820] gold, [I]using
600 *shekels of* beaten gold on each large
shield.
16 And *he made* 300 shields of
beaten gold, [I]using three hundred shekels of gold on each shield, and the king
put them in the house of the forest of
Lebanon.
17 Moreover, the king made a great
throne of ivory and overlaid it with pure
gold.
18 And *there were* six steps to the
throne and a footstool in gold attached

18 [a]2Chr. 9:10, 13
1 [a]1Kin. 10:1-13; Matt. 12:42; Luke 11:31
2 [I]Lit., *told her all her words* [II]Lit., *tell*
4 [I]Or, *his burnt offering which he offered*
7 [I]Or, *happy*
8 [a]1Chr. 28:5; 29:23 [b]Deut. 7:8; 2Chr. 2:11
10 [a]1Kin. 10:11; 2Chr. 8:18
13 [a]1Kin. 10:14-28
14 [a]Ps. 68:29; 72:10
15 [I]Lit., *he brought up*
16 [I]Lit., *he brought up*

🔑 **9:1-12** See I Kgs. 10:1-13.
🔑 **9:13-28** See I Kgs. 10:14-29; II Chr. 1:14-17.

to the throne, and [I]arms [II]on each side
of the seat, and two lions standing beside
the [I]arms.
19 And twelve lions were standing
there on the six steps on the one side
and on the other; nothing like *it* was
made for any *other* kingdom.[4467]
20 And all King Solomon's drinking
vessels *were* of gold, and all the vessels
of the house of the forest of Lebanon
were of pure gold; silver was not considered [I]valuable[2803] in the days[3117] of Solomon.
21 [a]For the king had ships which
went to Tarshish with the servants of
Huram; once every three years the
ships of Tarshish came bringing[5375] gold
and silver, ivory and apes and peacocks.
22 [a]So King Solomon became
greater than all the kings of the earth[776]
in riches and wisdom.
23 And all the kings of the earth
were seeking the presence of Solomon,
to hear his wisdom which God had put
in his heart.
24 And [a]they brought every man his
gift, articles of silver and gold, garments, weapons, spices, horses, and
mules, so much year by year.
25 Now Solomon had [a]4,000 stalls
for horses and chariots and 12,000
horsemen, and he stationed them in the
chariot cities and with the king in Jerusalem.
26 [a]And he was the ruler over all
the kings from the Euphrates River even
to the land of the Philistines, and as
far as the border of Egypt.
27 [a]And the king made silver *as common* as stones in Jerusalem, and he made
cedars as plentiful as sycamore trees
that are in the [I]lowland.
28 [a]And they were bringing horses
for Solomon from Egypt and from all
countries.[776]
🔑 **29** [a]Now the rest of the acts of Solomon, from first[7223] to last, [b]are they not
written in the [I]records of Nathan the
prophet, and in the prophecy of Ahijah
the Shilonite, and in the visions[2378] of
[II]Iddo the seer concerning Jeroboam the
son of Nebat?
30 And [a]Solomon reigned forty
years in Jerusalem over all Israel.

Death of Solomon

31 And Solomon slept with his fathers[1] and was buried[6912] in [a]the city
of his father David; and his son Rehoboam reigned in his place.

Rehoboam's Reign of Folly

10 🔑 [a]Then Rehoboam went to
Shechem, for all Israel had come
to Shechem to make him king.[4427]
🔑 2 And it came about when Jeroboam
the son of Nebat heard *of it* (for [a]he
was in Egypt where he had fled from
the presence of King[4428] Solomon), that
Jeroboam returned from Egypt.
3 So they sent and summoned[7121]
him. When Jeroboam and all Israel came,
they spoke to Rehoboam, saying,
4 "Your father made our [a]yoke hard;
now therefore lighten the hard[7186] service of your father and his heavy yoke
which he put on us, and we will serve
you."
5 And he said to them, "Return to
me again in three days."[3117] So the
people[5971] departed.
6 Then King Rehoboam [a]con-
sulted[3289] with the elders who had
[I]served his father Solomon while he was
still alive,[2416] saying, "How do you counsel *me* to answer[1697] this people?"
7 And they spoke to him, saying, "If
you will be kind[2896] to this people and
please[7521] them and [a]speak good[2896]
words[1697] to them, then they will be
your servants forever."
8 But he [a]forsook[5800] the counsel[6098]

18 [I]Lit., *hands* [II]Lit., *on this side and on this at the place of the seat*
20 [I]Lit., *anything*
21 [a]2Chr. 20:36, 37
22 [a]1Kin. 3:13; 2Chr. 1:12
24 [a]Ps. 72:10
25 [a]Deut. 17:16; 1Kin. 4:26; 10:26; 2Chr. 1:14
26 [a]Gen. 15:18; 1Kin. 4:21, 24
27 [I]Heb., *shephelah* [a]2Chr. 1:15-17
28 [a]2Chr. 1:16
29 [I]Lit., *words* [II]Heb., *Jedo* [a]1Kin. 11:41-43 [b]1Chr. 29:29
30 [a]1Kin. 11:42, 43
31 [a]1Kin. 2:10
1 [a]1Kin. 12:1-20
2 [a]1Kin. 11:40
4 [a]1Kin. 5:13-16
6 [I]Lit., *stood before* [a]Job 8:8, 9; 32:7
7 [a]Prov. 15:1
8 [a]2Sam. 17:14; Prov. 13:20

🔑 **9:29-31** See I Kgs. 11:41-43.
🔑 **10:1—11:4** See I Kgs. 12:1-24.
🔑 **10:2** See I Kgs. 11:40.

of the elders which they had given him, and consulted with the young men who grew up with him [I]and served him.

9 So he said to them, "What counsel do you give that we may answer this people, who have spoken to me, saying, 'Lighten the yoke which your father put on us'?"

10 And the young men who grew up with him spoke to him, saying, "Thus you shall say[559] to the people who spoke to you, saying, 'Your father made our yoke heavy, but you make it lighter[7043] for us.' Thus you shall say to them, 'My little finger is thicker than my father's[1] loins!

11 'Whereas my father loaded you with a heavy yoke, I will add to your yoke; my father disciplined[3256] you with whips, but I *will discipline you* with scorpions.' "

12 So Jeroboam and all the people came to Rehoboam on the third day[3117] as the king had [I]directed, saying, "Return to me on the third day."

13 And the king answered them harshly, and King Rehoboam forsook the counsel of the elders.

14 And he spoke to them according to the advice[6098] of the young men, saying, "[I]My father made your yoke heavy, but I will add to it; my father disciplined you with whips, but I *will discipline you* with scorpions."

🔑 15 So the king did not listen to the people, [a]for it was a turn *of events* from God[430] [b]that the LORD might establish His word,[1697] which He spoke through Ahijah the Shilonite to Jeroboam the son of Nebat.

🔑 **16** And when all Israel *saw* that the king did not listen to them the people answered the king, saying,

"[a]What portion do we have in
David?
We have no inheritance[5159] in
the son of Jesse.
Every man to your tents,
O Israel;
Now look after your own house,
David."

[b]So all Israel departed to their tents.

17 But as for the sons[1121] of Israel who lived in the cities of Judah, Rehoboam reigned over them.

18 Then King Rehoboam sent Hadoram, who was [a]over the forced labor, and the sons of Israel stoned him [I]to death. And King Rehoboam made haste to mount his chariot to flee to Jerusalem.

19 So [a]Israel has been in rebellion against the house of David to this day.

Rehoboam Reigns over Judah and Builds Cities

11 [a]Now when Rehoboam had come to Jerusalem, he assembled[6950] the house of Judah and Benjamin, 180,000 chosen men who were warriors, to fight against Israel to restore the kingdom[4467] to Rehoboam.

2 But the word[1697] of the LORD came to [a]Shemaiah the man of God,[430] saying,

3 "Speak to Rehoboam the son of Solomon, king[4428] of Judah, and to all Israel in Judah and Benjamin, saying,

4 'Thus says the LORD, "You shall not go up or fight against [a]your [I]relatives;[251] return every man to his house, [b]for this thing is from Me." ' " So they listened to the words[1697] of the LORD and returned from going against Jeroboam.

5 Rehoboam lived in Jerusalem and [a]built cities for defense in Judah.

6 Thus he built Bethlehem, Etam, Tekoa,

7 Beth-zur, Soco, Adullam,

8 Gath, Mareshah, Ziph,

9 Adoraim, Lachish, Azekah,

10 Zorah, Aijalon, and Hebron, which are fortified cities in Judah and in Benjamin.

11 He also strengthened[2388] the fortresses and put officers in them

8 [I]Lit., *who stood before*
12 [I]Lit., *spoken*
14 [I]Many mss. read *I have made*
15 [a]2Chr. 25:16-20 [b]1Kin. 11:29-39
16 [a]2Sam. 20:1 [b]2Chr. 10:19
18 [I]Lit., *with stones that he died* [a]1Kin. 4:6; 5:14
19 [a]1Kin. 12:19
1 [a]1Kin. 12:21-24
2 [a]2Chr. 12:5-7, 15
4 [I]Lit., *brothers* [a]2Chr. 28:8-11 [b]2Chr. 10:15
5 [a]2Chr. 8:2-6; 11:23

🔑 **10:15** See I Kgs. 11:30,31.
🔑 **10:16** This slogan was used by Sheba in rebellion against David (II Sam. 20:1).

and stores of food,[3978] oil and wine.

12 And *he put* shields and spears in every city and strengthened them greatly. So he held Judah and Benjamin.

13 Moreover, the priests and the Levites who were in all Israel stood with him from all their districts.

Jeroboam Appoints False Priests

14 For [a]the Levites left[5800] their pasture lands and their property[272] and came to Judah and Jerusalem, for [b]Jeroboam and his sons had excluded[6213] them from serving as priests to the LORD.

15 And [a]he set up priests of his own for the high places, for the satyrs,[8163] and for the calves which he had made.

16 And [a]those from all the tribes of Israel who set their hearts on seeking the LORD God of Israel, [I]followed them to Jerusalem to sacrifice to the LORD God of their fathers.[1]

17 [a]And they strengthened the kingdom[4438] of Judah and supported Rehoboam the son of Solomon for three years, for they walked in the way[1870] of David and Solomon for three years.

Rehoboam's Family

18 Then Rehoboam took as a wife[802] Mahalath the daughter of Jerimoth the son of David *and of* Abihail the daughter of [a]Eliab the son of Jesse,

19 and she bore him sons:[1121] Jeush, Shemariah, and Zaham.

20 And after her he took [a]Maacah the daughter of [I]Absalom, and she bore him Abijah, Attai, Ziza, and Shelomith.

21 And Rehoboam loved[157] Maacah the daughter of Absalom more than all his *other* wives and concubines. For [a]he had taken eighteen wives[802] and sixty concubines and fathered twenty-eight sons and sixty daughters.

22 And [a]Rehoboam appointed Abijah the son of Maacah as head[7218] and leader among his brothers, for he *intended* to make him king.[4427]

23 And he acted wisely and distributed [I]some of his sons through all the territories[776] of Judah and Benjamin to all the fortified cities, and he gave them food[4202] in abundance. And he sought[7592] many wives *for them.*

Shishak of Egypt Invades Judah

12 It took place [a]when the kingdom[4438] of Rehoboam was established[3559] and strong that [b]he and all Israel with him forsook[5800] the law[8451] of the LORD.

2 [a]And it came about in King[4428] Rehoboam's fifth year, because they had been unfaithful to the LORD, that [b]Shishak king of Egypt came up against Jerusalem

3 with 1,200 chariots and 60,000 horsemen. And the people[5971] who came with him from Egypt were without number: [a]the Lubim, the Sukkiim, and the Ethiopians.

4 And he captured [a]the fortified cities of Judah and came as far as Jerusalem.

5 Then [a]Shemaiah the prophet came to Rehoboam and the princes of Judah who had gathered[622] at Jerusalem because of Shishak, and he said to them, "Thus says the LORD, '[b]You have forsaken[5800] Me, so I also have forsaken[5800] you [I]to Shishak.'"

6 So the princes of Israel and the king humbled themselves and said, "The [a]LORD is righteous."

7 And when the LORD saw that they humbled themselves, the word[1697] of the LORD came to Shemaiah, saying, "[a]They have humbled themselves so I will not destroy[7843] them, but I will grant them some *measure* of deliverance,[6413] and [b]My wrath[2534] shall not be poured out on Jerusalem by means of Shishak.

---

14 [a]Num. 35:2-5 [b]1Kin. 12:28-33; 2Chr. 13:9
15 [a]1Kin. 12:31; 13:33
16 [I]Lit., *came after* [a]2Chr. 15:9
17 [a]2Chr. 12:1
18 [a]1Sam. 16:6
20 [I]In 1Kin. 15:2, *Abishalom* [a]1Kin. 15:2; 2 Chr. 13:2
21 [a]Deut. 17:17
22 [a]Deut. 21:15-17
23 [I]Lit., *from all*
1 [a]2Chr. 11:17; 12:13 [b]2Chr. 26:13-16
2 [a]1Kin. 14:25 [b]1Kin. 11:40
3 [a]2Chr. 16:8; Nah. 3:9
4 [a]2Chr. 11:5-12
5 [I]Lit., *in the hand of* [a]2Chr. 11:2 [b]Deut. 28:15; 2Chr. 15:2
6 [a]Ex. 9:27; Dan. 9:14
7 [a]1Kin. 21:29 [b]2Chr. 34:25-27; Ps. 78:38

11:20-22 See note on I Kgs. 15:2-10.
11:23 Perhaps a lesson was learned from David's sad experience (II Sam. 13:26,27).
12:1-16 See I Kgs. 14:21-31.

8 "But they will become his slaves so [a]that they may learn[3045] *the difference between* My service and the service of the kingdoms[4467] of the countries."[776]

Plunder Impoverishes Judah

9 [a]So Shishak king of Egypt came up against Jerusalem, and took the treasures of the house of the LORD and the treasures of the king's[4428] palace. He took everything; [b]he even took the golden shields which Solomon had made.

10 Then King Rehoboam made shields of bronze in their place, and committed[6485] them to the [I]care of the commanders[5387] of the [II]guard who guarded[8104] the door of the king's house.

11 And it happened as often as the king entered the house of the LORD, the [I]guards came and carried them and *then* brought them back into the [I]guards' room.

12 And [a]when he humbled himself, the anger of the LORD turned away from him, so as not to destroy *him* completely; and also conditions [b]were good in Judah.

13 [a]So King Rehoboam strengthened himself in Jerusalem, and reigned. Now Rehoboam was forty-one years old when he began to reign, and he reigned seventeen years in Jerusalem, the city which the LORD had chosen[977] from all the tribes of Israel, to put His name there. And his mother's name was Naamah the Ammonitess.

14 And he did[6213] evil[7451] [a]because he did not set his heart to seek the LORD.

15 [a]Now the acts[1697] of Rehoboam, from first[7223] to last, are they not written in the [I]records of [b]Shemaiah the prophet and of [c]Iddo the seer, according to genealogical enrollment? And *there were* wars between Rehoboam and Jeroboam continually.

16 And Rehoboam slept with his fathers,[1] and was buried[6912] in the city of David; and his son [a]Abijah became king in his place.

Abijah Succeeds Rehoboam

13 🔑 [a]In the eighteenth year of King[4428] Jeroboam, Abijah became king over Judah.

🔑 2 He reigned three years in Jerusalem; and his mother's name was Micaiah the daughter of Uriel of Gibeah. [a]And there was war between Abijah and Jeroboam.

3 And Abijah began the battle with an army[2428] of valiant warriors, 400,000 chosen men, while Jeroboam drew up in battle formation against him with 800,000 chosen men *who were* valiant[2428] warriors.

Civil War

4 Then Abijah stood on Mount [a]Zemaraim, which is in the hill country of Ephraim, and said, "Listen to me, Jeroboam and all Israel:

🔑 5 "Do you not know[3045] that [a]the LORD God[430] of Israel gave the rule[4467] over Israel forever to David [I]and his sons by [b]a covenant[1285] of salt?

🔑 6 "Yet [a]Jeroboam the son of Nebat, the servant of Solomon the son of David, rose up and rebelled against his [I]master,

7 and worthless men gathered[6908] about him, scoundrels,[1121,1100] who proved too strong for Rehoboam, the son of Solomon, when [Ia]he was young and timid and could not hold his own against[2388] them.

8 "So now you intend to resist the kingdom of the LORD [I]through the sons

8 [a]Deut. 28:47, 48
9 [a]1Kin. 14:26-28 [b]1Kin. 10:16, 17; 2Chr. 9:15, 16
10 [I]Lit., *hands* [II]Lit., *runners*
11 [I]Lit., *runners*
12 [a]2Chr. 12:6, 7 [b]2Chr. 19:3
13 [a]1Kin. 14:21
14 [a]2Chr. 19:3
15 [I]Lit., *words* [a]1Kin. 14:29 [b]2Chr. 12:5 [c]2Chr. 9:29
16 [a]2Chr. 11:20
1 [a]1Kin. 15:1, 2
2 [a]1Kin. 15:7
4 [a]Josh. 18:22
5 [I]Lit., *to him and to his sons* [a]2Sam. 7:12-16 [b]Lev. 2:13; Num. 18:19
6 [I]Or, *lord* [a]1Kin. 11:26
7 [I]Lit., *Rehoboam* [a]2Chr. 12:13
8 [I]Lit., *in the hands of*

🔑 **13:1-22** See I Kgs. 15:1-8.
🔑 **13:2** Micaiah was called Maacah in II Chr. 11:20. She was related to Absalom, whose only daughter, Tamar (II Sam. 14:27), married Uriel.
🔑 **13:5** Eating salt together signified an unbreakable friendship. Salt was used as a preservative. Therefore, it was an appropriate symbol for eternity. The covenant must not be changed (cf. Num. 18:19).
🔑 **13:6** Jeroboam was mentioned in I Kgs. 11:28.

of David, [II]being a great multitude and *having* with you [a]the golden calves which Jeroboam made for gods[430] for you.

9 "[a]Have you not driven out the priests of the LORD, the sons of Aaron and the Levites, and made for yourselves priests like the peoples[5971] of *other* lands?[776] Whoever comes [b]to consecrate himself with a young[1121] bull and seven rams, even he may become a priest of *what are* [c]no gods.

10 "But as for us, the LORD is our God, and we have not forsaken[5800] Him; and the sons of Aaron are ministering to the LORD as priests, and the Levites [I]attend to their work.[4399]

11 "And every morning and evening [a]they [I]burn[6999] to the LORD burnt offerings and fragrant incense,[7004] and [b]the showbread is *set* on the clean table, and the golden lampstand with its lamps[5216] is *ready* to light every evening; for we keep[8104] the charge[4931] of the LORD our God, but you have forsaken Him.

12 "Now behold, God is with us at *our* head and [a]His priests with the signal trumpets to sound the alarm against you. O sons of Israel, do not fight against the LORD God of your fathers,[1] for you will not succeed."

13 But Jeroboam [a]had set an ambush to come from the rear, so that *Israel* was in front of Judah, and the ambush was behind them.

14 When Judah turned around, behold, [I]they were attacked both front and rear; so [a]they cried to the LORD, and the priests blew the trumpets.

15 Then the men of Judah raised a war cry, and when the men of Judah raised the war cry, then it was that God [I][a]routed Jeroboam and all Israel before Abijah and Judah.

16 And when the sons of Israel fled before Judah, [a]God gave them into their hand.

17 And Abijah and his people[5971] defeated them with a great slaughter, so that 500,000 chosen men of Israel fell[5307] slain.

18 Thus the sons of Israel were subdued at that time, and the sons of Judah [I]conquered [a]because they trusted in the LORD, the God of their fathers.

19 And Abijah pursued Jeroboam, and captured from him *several* cities, Bethel with its villages, Jeshanah with its villages, and [I]Ephron with its villages.

Death of Jeroboam

20 And Jeroboam did not again recover strength in the days[3117] of Abijah; and the [a]LORD struck him and [b]he died.

21 But Abijah became powerful, and took fourteen wives[802] to himself; and became the father of twenty-two sons and sixteen daughters.

22 Now the rest of the acts[1697] of Abijah, and his ways[1870] and his words are written in [a]the [I]treatise of [b]the prophet Iddo.

Asa Succeeds Abijah in Judah

14 [I][a]So Abijah slept with his fathers,[1] and they buried[6912] him in the city of David, and his son Asa became king in his place. The land[776] was undisturbed[8252] for ten years during his days.[3117]

2 [I]And Asa did[6213] good[2896] and right in the sight of the LORD his God,[430]

3 for he removed [a]the foreign altars[4196] and [b]high places, tore[7665] down the *sacred* pillars,[4676] cut down the [I][c]Asherim,[842]

4 and commanded[559] Judah to seek the LORD God of their fathers and to observe[6213] the law[8451] and the commandment.[4687]

5 He also removed the high places and the [a]incense altars[2553] from all the cities of Judah. And the kingdom[4467] was undisturbed under him.

6 And [a]he built fortified cities in Judah, since the land was undisturbed, and

8 [II]Lit., *and you are a* [a]1Kin. 12:28; 2Chr. 11:15

9 [a]2Chr. 11:14, 15 [b]Ex. 29:29-33 [c]Jer. 2:11; 5:7

10 [I]Lit., *in the work*

11 [I]Lit., *offer up in smoke* [a]Ex. 29:38; 2Chr. 2:4 [b]Ex. 25:30-39; Lev. 24:5-9

12 [a]Num. 10:8, 9

13 [a]Josh. 8:4-9

14 [I]Lit., *the battle was before and behind them* [a]2Chr. 14:11

15 [I]Lit., *smote* [a]2Chr. 14:12

16 [a]2Chr. 16:8

18 [I]Lit., *were strong* [a]2Chr. 14:11

19 [I]Another reading is *Ephrain*

20 [a]1Sam. 25:38 [b]1Kin. 14:20

22 [I]Heb., *midrash* [a]2Chr. 24:27 [b]2Chr. 9:29

1 [I]Ch. 13:23 in Heb. [a]1Kin. 15:8

2 [I]Ch. 14:1 in Heb.

3 [I]I.e., wooden symbols of a female deity [a]Deut. 7:5 [b]1Kin. 15:12-14 [c]Ex. 34:13

5 [a]2Chr. 34:4, 7

6 [a]2Chr. 11:5

14:1-15 See I Kgs. 15:9-12.

[I]there was no one at war with him during
those years, [b]because the LORD had
given him rest.
7 For he said to Judah, "[a]Let us build
these cities and surround *them* with walls
and towers, gates and bars. The land
is still [I]ours, because we have sought
the LORD our God; we have sought Him,
and He has given us rest on every side."
So they built and prospered.
8 Now Asa had an army[2428] of
[a]300,000 from Judah, bearing[5375] large
shields and spears, and 280,000 from
Benjamin, bearing shields and wielding
bows; all of them were valiant[2428] warriors.
🔑 9 Now Zerah the Ethiopian [a]came
out against them with an army of a million
men and 300 chariots, and he came to
[b]Mareshah.
10 So Asa went out [I]to meet him,
and they drew up in battle formation
in the valley of Zephathah at Mareshah.
11 Then Asa [a]called[7121] to the LORD
his God, and said, "LORD, there is no
one besides Thee to help *in the battle*
between the powerful and those who
have no strength; so help us, O LORD
our God, [b]for we trust in Thee, and in
Thy name have come against this multitude.
O LORD, Thou art our God; let
not man prevail against Thee."
12 So [a]the LORD [I]routed the Ethiopians
before Asa and before Judah, and
the Ethiopians fled.
13 And Asa and the people[5971] who
were with him pursued them as far as
[a]Gerar; and so many Ethiopians fell that
[I]they could not recover, for they were
shattered[7665] before the LORD, and before
His army. And they carried[5375] away
very much plunder.
14 And they [I]destroyed all the cities
around Gerar, [a]for the dread[6343] of the
LORD had fallen on them; and they despoiled
all the cities, for there was much
plunder in them.
15 They also struck down [I]those

6 [I]Lit., *there was not with him war* [b]2Chr. 15:15
7 [I]Lit., *before us* [a]2Chr. 8:5
8 [a]2Chr. 13:3
9 [a]2Chr. 12:2, 3; 16:8 [b]2Chr. 11:8
10 [I]Lit., *before him*
11 [a]2Chr. 13:14 [b]2Chr. 13:18
12 [I]Lit., *struck* [a]2Chr. 13:15
13 [I]Or, *there was none left alive* [a]Gen. 10:19
14 [I]Lit., *smote* [a]2Chr. 17:10
15 [I]Lit., *tents of livestock*
1 [a]2Chr. 20:14; 24:20
2 [I]Lit., *before Asa* [a]2Chr. 20:17 [b]2Chr. 15:4, 15
3 [a]1Kin. 12:28-33 [b]Lev. 10:8-11; 2Chr. 17:9
4 [a]Deut. 4:29
5 [I]Lit., *were on* [a]Judg. 5:6
6 [a]Matt. 24:7
7 [I]Lit., *let your hands drop* [a]Josh. 1:7, 9 [b]Ps. 58:11
8 [I]With several ancient versions; Heb., *the prophecy, Oded the prophet* [a]2Chr. 13:19 [b]2Chr. 4:1; 8:12

who owned livestock, and they carried
away large numbers of sheep and camels.
Then they returned to Jerusalem.

The Prophet Azariah Warns Asa

15 🔑 Now [a]the Spirit of God[430]
came on Azariah the son of Oded,
2 and he went out [I]to meet Asa and
said to him, "Listen to me, Asa, and
all Judah and Benjamin: [a]the LORD is
with you when you are with Him. And
[b]if you seek Him, He will let you find
Him; but if you forsake[5800] Him, He will
forsake you.
3 "And [a]for many days Israel was
without the true God and without
[b]a teaching priest and without law.[8451]
4 "But [a]in their distress they turned
to the LORD God of Israel, and they
sought Him, and He let them find Him.
5 "[a]And in those times there was
no peace[7965] to him who went out or
to him who came in, for many disturbances[4103]
[I]afflicted all the inhabitants
of the lands.[776]
6 "And [a]nation[1471] was crushed[3807]
by nation, and city by city, for God
troubled[2000] them with every kind of distress.
7 "But you, [a]be strong and do not
[I]lose courage,[7503,3027] for there is
[b]reward for your work."

Asa's Reforms

8 Now when Asa heard these
words[1697] and the [I]prophecy which Azariah
the son of Oded the prophet spoke,
he took courage[2388] and removed the
abominable idols from all the land[776] of
Judah and Benjamin and from [a]the cities
which he had captured in the hill country
of Ephraim. [b]He then restored the
altar[4196] of the LORD which was in front
of the porch of the LORD.
9 And he gathered[6908] all Judah and
Benjamin and those from Ephraim,

🔑 **14:9** Zerah was probably Osorkon I, successor to Sheshenk I (or, Shishak of II Chr. 12:2) and the second ruler of the twenty-second dynasty of Egypt, a period of revived power.
🔑 **15:1-18** See I Kgs. 15:13-15.

Manasseh, and Simeon [a]who resided with them, for many defected[5307] to him from Israel when they saw that the LORD his God was with him.

10 So they assembled at Jerusalem in the third month of the fifteenth year of Asa's reign.

11 And [a]they sacrificed to the LORD that day 700 oxen and 7,000 sheep from the spoil they had brought.

12 And [a]they entered into the covenant[1285] to seek the LORD God of their fathers[1] with all their heart and soul;

13 and whoever would not seek the LORD God of Israel [a]should be put to death,[4191] whether small or great, man or woman.[802]

14 Moreover, they made an oath to the LORD with a loud voice, with shouting, with trumpets, and with horns.

15 And all Judah rejoiced concerning the oath, for they had sworn with their whole heart and had sought Him [I]earnestly,[7522] and He let them find Him. So [a]the LORD gave them rest on every side.

🔑 **16** [a]And he also removed Maacah, the mother of King[4428] Asa, from the *position of* queen mother, because she had made a horrid image[4656] [I]as [b]an Asherah, and [c]Asa cut down[3772] her horrid image, crushed *it* and burned[8313] *it* at the brook Kidron.

17 But the high places were not removed from Israel; nevertheless Asa's heart was blameless[8003] all his days.[3117]

18 And he brought into the house of God the dedicated[6944] things of his father and his own dedicated things: silver and gold and utensils.

🔑 19 And there was no more war until the thirty-fifth year of Asa's reign.

Asa Wars against Baasha

16 🔑 In the thirty-sixth year of Asa's reign [a]Baasha king of Israel came up against Judah and [I]fortified Ramah in order to prevent *anyone* from going out or coming in to Asa king[4428] of Judah.

2 Then Asa brought out silver and gold from the treasuries of the house of the LORD and the king's[4428] house, and sent them to Ben-hadad king of Aram, who lived in Damascus, saying,

3 "*Let there be* a treaty[1285] between [I]you and me, *as* between my father and your father. Behold, I have sent you silver and gold; go, break[6565] your treaty with Baasha king of Israel so that he will withdraw from me."

4 So Ben-hadad listened to King Asa and sent the commanders[8269] of his armies[2428] against the cities of Israel, and they [I]conquered Ijon, Dan, Abel-maim, and all [a]the [II]store cities of Naphtali.

5 And it came about when Baasha heard *of it* that he ceased [I]fortifying Ramah and stopped[7673] his work.[4399]

6 Then King Asa brought all Judah, and they carried[5375] away the stones of Ramah and its timber with which Baasha had been building, and with them he [I]fortified Geba and Mizpah.

Asa Imprisons the Prophet

7 At that time [a]Hanani the seer came to Asa king of Judah and said to him, "[b]Because you have relied on the king of Aram and have not relied on the LORD your God,[430] therefore the army of the king of Aram has escaped[4422] out of your hand.

8 "Were not [a]the Ethiopians and the Lubim [b]an immense army with very many chariots and horsemen? Yet, [c]because you relied on the LORD, He delivered them into your hand.

9 "For [a]the eyes of the LORD move to and fro throughout the earth[776] that He may strongly support those [b]whose heart is completely[8003] His. You have

9 [a]2Chr. 11:16
11 [a]2Chr. 14:13-15
12 [a]2Chr. 23:16
13 [a]Ex. 22:20; Deut. 13:6-9
15 [I]Lit., *with their whole desire* [a]2Chr. 14:7
16 [I]Or, *for Asherah* [a]1Kin. 15:13-15 [b]Ex. 34:13 [c]2Chr. 14:2-5
1 [I]Lit., *built* [a]1Kin. 15:17-22
3 [I]Lit., *me and you*
4 [I]Lit., *smote* [II]Lit., *storage places of the cities* [a]Ex. 1:11
5 [I]Lit., *building*
6 [I]Lit., *built*
7 [a]1Kin. 16:1; 2Chr. 19:2 [b]2Chr. 14:11; 32:7, 8
8 [a]2Chr. 14:9 [b]2Chr. 12:3 [c]2Chr. 13:16, 18
9 [a]Prov. 15:3; Jer. 16:17; Zech. 4:10 [b]2Chr. 15:17

🔑 **15:16** She was Absalom's daughter, the queen grandmother (cf. II Chr. 11:20,21).
🔑 **15:19** Dated from the division of Israel from Judah in 930 B.C.
🔑 **16:1-14** See I Kgs. 15:16-24.

acted foolishly in this. Indeed, from now
on you will surely have wars."
10 Then Asa was angry[3707] with the
seer and put him in [I]prison, for he was
enraged at him for this. And Asa oppressed some of the people[5971] at the
same time.
11 [a]And now, the acts[1697] of Asa
from first[7223] to last, behold, they are
written in the Book[5612] of the Kings[4428]
of Judah and Israel.
12 And in the thirty-ninth year of
his reign Asa became diseased[2470] in his
feet. His disease[2483] was severe, yet
even in his disease he [a]did not seek the
LORD, but the physicians.
13 So Asa slept with his fathers,[1]
[I]having died in the forty-first year of
his reign.
14 And they buried[6912] him in his
own tomb[6913] which he had cut out for
himself in the city of David, and they
laid him in the resting place which he
had filled [a]with spices of various kinds
blended by the perfumers'[4842] art; and
[b]they made a very great fire[8316] for him.

Jehoshaphat Succeeds Asa

17 [a]Jehoshaphat his son then became king in his place, and made
his position over Israel firm.
2 He placed troops in all [a]the fortified cities of Judah, and set garrisons
in the land[776] of Judah, and in the cities
of Ephraim [b]which Asa his father had
captured.

His Good Reign

3 And the LORD was with Jehosha-
phat because he [I]followed the example[1870]
of his father David's earlier[7223] days and
did not seek the Baals,
4 but sought the God[430] of his father,
[I]followed His commandments,[4687] [a]and
did not act as Israel did.
5 So the LORD established[3559] the
kingdom[4467] in his [I]control, and all Judah
brought tribute to Jehoshaphat, and
[a]he had great riches and honor.
6 And [I]he took great pride in the
ways of the LORD and again [a]removed
the high places and the Asherim[842] from
Judah.
7 Then in the third year of his reign
he sent his officials, Ben-hail, Obadiah,
Zechariah, Nethanel, and Micaiah,
[a]to teach in the cities of Judah;
8 and with them [a]the Levites, Shemaiah, Nethaniah, Zebadiah, Asahel,
Shemiramoth, Jehonathan, Adonijah,
Tobijah, and Tobadonijah, the Levites;
and with them Elishama and Jehoram,
the priests.
9 And they taught in Judah, *having*
[a]the book[5612] of the law[8451] of the LORD
with them; and they went throughout
all the cities of Judah and taught among
the people.[5971]
10 Now [a]the dread[6343] of the LORD
was[1961] on all the kingdoms[4467] of the
lands[776] which *were* around Judah, so
that they did not make war against Jehoshaphat.
11 And some of the Philistines
[a]brought gifts and silver as tribute to
Jehoshaphat; the Arabians also brought
him flocks, 7,700 rams and 7,700 male
goats.
12 So Jehoshaphat grew greater and
greater, and he built fortresses and
store cities in Judah.
13 And he had large supplies[4399] in
the cities of Judah, and warriors, valiant[2428] men, in Jerusalem.
14 And this was their muster according to their fathers'[1] households: of
Judah, commanders[8269] of thousands,
Adnah *was* the commander,[8269] and with
him 300,000 valiant warriors;
15 and next to him *was* Johanan the
commander,[8269] and with him 280,000;
16 and next to him Amasiah the son
of Zichri, [a]who volunteered[5071] for the
LORD, and with him 200,000 valiant warriors;
17 and of Benjamin, Eliada a valiant
warrior, and with him 200,000 armed[5401]
with bow and shield;
18 and next to him Jehozabad, and
with him 180,000 equipped for war.[6635]
19 These are they who served the
king,[4428] apart from [a]those whom the

10 [I]Lit., *the house of the stocks*
11 [a]1Kin. 15:23, 24
12 [a]Jer. 17:5
13 [I]Lit., *and*
14 [a]Gen. 50:2; John 19:39, 40 [b]2Chr. 21:19
1 [a]1Kin. 15:24
2 [a]2Chr. 11:5 [b]2Chr. 15:8
3 [I]Lit., *walked in the earlier ways of his father*
4 [I]Lit., *walked in* [a]1Kin. 12:28
5 [I]Lit., *hand* [a]2Chr. 18:1
6 [I]Lit., *his heart was high* [a]2Chr. 15:17
7 [a]2Chr. 15:3; 35:3
8 [a]2Chr. 19:8
9 [a]Deut. 6:4-9
10 [a]2Chr. 14:14
11 [a]2Chr. 9:14; 26:8
16 [a]Judg. 5:2, 9; 1Chr. 29:9
19 [a]2Chr. 17:2

king put in the fortified cities through all Judah.

Jehoshaphat Allies with Ahab

18 🔑 Now [a]Jehoshaphat had great riches and honor; and he allied himself by marriage[2859] with Ahab.

2 [a]And some years later he went down to *visit* Ahab at Samaria. And Ahab slaughtered many sheep and oxen for him and the people[5971] who were with him, and induced him to go up against Ramoth-gilead.

3 And Ahab king[4428] of Israel said to Jehoshaphat king of Judah, "Will you go with me *against* Ramoth-gilead?" And he said[559] to him, "I am as you are, and my people as your people, and *we will be* with you in the battle."

4 Moreover, Jehoshaphat said to the king of Israel, "Please inquire [I]first for the word[1697] of the LORD."

🔑 5 Then the king of Israel assembled[6908] the prophets, four hundred men, and said to them, "Shall we go against Ramoth-gilead to battle, or shall I refrain?" And they said, "Go up, for God[430] will give *it* into the hand of the king."[4428]

6 But Jehoshaphat said, "Is there not yet a prophet of the LORD here that we may inquire of him?"

7 And the king of Israel said to Jehoshaphat, "There is yet one man by whom we may inquire of the LORD, but I hate him, for he never prophesies good[2896] concerning me but always evil.[7451] He is Micaiah, son of Imla." But Jehoshaphat said, "Let not the king say so."

1 [a]2Chr. 17:5
2 [a]1Kin. 22:2-35
4 [I]Lit., *as the day*
8 [I]Lit., *Hasten*
9 [a]Ruth 4:1
13 [a]Num. 22:18-20, 35

Ahab's False Prophets Assure Victory

8 Then the king of Israel called[7121] an officer and said, "[I]Bring quickly Micaiah, Imla's son."

9 Now the king of Israel and Jehoshaphat the king of Judah were sitting each on his throne, arrayed in *their* robes, and *they* were sitting [a]at the threshing floor at the entrance of the gate of Samaria; and all the prophets were prophesying before them.

10 And Zedekiah the son of Chenaanah made horns of iron for himself and said, "Thus says the LORD, 'With these you shall gore the Arameans, until they are consumed.' "[3615]

11 And all the prophets were prophesying thus, saying, "Go up to Ramoth-gilead and succeed, for the LORD will give *it* into the hand of the king."

Micaiah Brings Word from God

12 Then the messenger who went to summon[7121] Micaiah spoke to him saying, "Behold, the words[1697] of the prophets are uniformly favorable to the king. So please let your word be like one of them and speak favorably."

🔑 13 But Micaiah said, "As the LORD lives,[2416] [a]what my God says, that I will speak."

🔑 14 And when he came to the king, the king said to him, "Micaiah, shall we go to Ramoth-gilead to battle, or shall I refrain?" He said, "Go up and succeed, for they will be given into your hand."

🔑 15 Then the king said to him, "How

🔑 **18:1** Jehoshaphat's son, Jehoram, was given in marriage to Athaliah, Ahab and Jezebel's daughter (II Chr. 21:6). This very unwise alliance was rebuked in II Chr. 19:2. It graphically illustrates the truth of Amos 3:3; I Cor. 7:39; and II Cor. 6:14.

🔑 **18:1-34** See I Kgs. 22:1-40.

🔑 **18:5** These prophets were probably connected with the calf worship which was established by Jeroboam in Dan and Bethel. It was carried on in the name of the Lord (I Kgs. 12:28).

🔑 **18:13** Similar to Baalam's resolve (Num. 22:18-20,38; 24:13).

🔑 **18:14** Micah was the short form of Micaiah. In the N.T., Silas was the abbreviated form of Silvanus, and Prisca was short for Priscilla.

🔑 **18:15** King Ahab sensed that Micaiah was being sarcastic.

many times must I adjure[7650] you to
speak to me nothing but the truth in
the name of the LORD?"
16 So he said,
"I saw all Israel
Scattered on the mountains,
[a]Like sheep which have no
shepherd;
And the LORD said,
'These have no master.
Let each of them return to his
house in peace.' "[7965]
17 Then the king of Israel said to
Jehoshaphat, "Did I not tell you that
he would not prophesy good concerning
me, but evil?"
18 And Micaiah said, "Therefore,
hear the word of the LORD. [a]I saw the
LORD sitting on His throne, and all the
host of heaven standing on His right
and on His left.
19 "And the LORD said, 'Who will
entice[6601] Ahab king of Israel to go up
and fall at Ramoth-gilead?' And one said
this while another said that.
20 "Then a [a]spirit came forward and
stood before the LORD and said, 'I will
entice him.' And the LORD said to him,
'How?'
21 "And he said, 'I will go and be
[a]a deceiving spirit in the mouth of all
his prophets.' Then He said, 'You are
to entice *him* and prevail also. Go and
do[6213] so.'
22 "Now therefore, behold, [a]the
LORD has put a deceiving spirit in the
mouth of these your prophets; for
the LORD has proclaimed disaster
against you."
23 Then Zedekiah the son of Chenaanah came near[5066] and [a]struck Micaiah on the cheek and said, "[I]How[1823]
did the Spirit of the LORD pass from
me to speak to you?"
24 And Micaiah said, "Behold, you
shall see on that day, when you enter
an inner room to hide yourself."
25 Then the king of Israel said,
"[a]Take Micaiah and return him to Amon
[b]the governor[8269] of the city, and to
Joash the king's son;
26 and say, 'Thus says the king,
"[a]Put this *man* in prison, and feed him
[I]sparingly with bread and water until I
return safely." ' "
27 And Micaiah said, "If you indeed
return safely, the LORD has not spoken
by me." And he said, "[a]Listen, all you
people."

Ahab's Defeat and Death

28 So the king of Israel and Jehoshaphat king of Judah went up against
Ramoth-gilead.
29 And the king of Israel said to Jehoshaphat, "I will disguise myself and
go into battle, but you put on your
robes." So the king of Israel disguised
himself, and they went into battle.
30 Now the king of Aram had
commanded[6680] the captains[8269] of his
chariots, saying, "Do not fight with small
or great, but with the king of Israel
alone."
31 So it came about when the captains of the chariots saw Jehoshaphat,
that they said, "It is the king of Israel,"
and they turned aside to fight against
him. But Jehoshaphat [a]cried[2199] out, and
the LORD helped him, and God diverted
them from him.
32 Then it happened when the captains of the chariots saw[7200] that it was
not the king of Israel, that they turned
back from pursuing him.
33 And a certain man drew his bow
at random[8537] and struck the king of Israel [I]in a joint of the armor. So he said
to the driver of the chariot, "Turn
[II]around, and take me out of the [III]fight;
for I am severely wounded."
34 And the battle raged[5927] that day,
and the king of Israel propped himself
up in his chariot in front of the Arameans
until the evening; and at sunset he
died.

16 [a]Num. 27:17; 1Kin. 22:17; Ezek. 34:5; 35:4-8; Matt. 9:36; Mark 6:34
18 [a]Is. 6:1-5; Dan. 7:9, 10
20 [a]Job 1:6; 2 Thess. 2:9
21 [a]John 8:44
22 [a]Is. 19:14; Ezek. 14:9
23 [I]Lit., *Which way* [a]Jer. 20:2; Mark 14:65; Acts 23:2
25 [a]2Chr. 18:8 [b]2Chr. 34:8
26 [I]Lit., *with bread of affliction and water of affliction* [a]2Chr. 16:10
27 [a]Mic. 1:2
31 [a]2Chr. 13:14, 15
33 [I]Lit., *between the scale-armor and the breastplate* [II]Lit., *your hand* [III]Lit., *camp*

18:20 Possibly this spirit was "the accuser" (Satan) of Job 1:6,7.

Jehu Rebukes Jehoshaphat

19 Then Jehoshaphat the king[4428] of Judah returned in safety[7965] to his house in Jerusalem.

2 And [a]Jehu the son of Hanani the seer went out to meet him and said to King Jehoshaphat, "[b]Should you help the wicked[7563] and love[157] those who hate the LORD and [I][c]so *bring* wrath[7110] on yourself from the LORD?

3 "But [I][a]there is *some* good[2896] in you, for [b]you have removed the [II]Asheroth[842] from the land[776] and you [c]have set your heart to seek God."[430]

4 So Jehoshaphat lived in Jerusalem and went out again among the people[5971] from Beersheba to the hill country of Ephraim and [a]brought them back to the LORD, the God of their fathers.[1]

Reforms Instituted

5 And he appointed [a]judges[8199] in the land in all the fortified cities of Judah, city by city.

6 And he said to the judges, "Consider what you are doing,[6213] for [a]you do not judge[8199] for man but for the LORD who is with you [I]when you render judgment.[4941]

7 "Now then let the fear[6343] of the LORD be upon you; [I]be very careful what you do, for [II]the LORD our God will [a]have no part in unrighteousness,[5766] [b]or partiality, or the taking of a bribe."

8 And in Jerusalem also Jehoshaphat appointed some [a]of the Levites and priests, and some of the heads[7218] of the fathers' *households* of Israel, for the judgment of the LORD and to judge [I]disputes[7379] among the inhabitants of Jerusalem.

9 Then he charged[6680] them saying, "Thus you shall do in the fear[3374] of the LORD, faithfully[530] and wholeheartedly.[8003]

10 "[a]And whenever any dispute[7379] comes to you from your brethren[251] who live in their cities, between blood[1818] and blood, between law[8451] and commandment,[4687] statutes and ordinances,[4941] you shall warn them that they may not be guilty before the LORD, and [b]wrath may *not* come on you and your brethren. Thus you shall do and you will not be guilty.

11 "And behold, Amariah the chief priest will be over you in [I][a]all that pertains to the LORD; and Zebadiah the son of Ishmael, the ruler of the house of Judah, in [I]all that pertains to the king.[4428] Also the Levites shall be officers before you. [II][b]Act[6213] resolutely,[2388] and the LORD be with the upright."

Judah Invaded

20 Now it came about after this that the sons[1121] of Moab and the sons of Ammon, together with some of the [I][a]Meunites, came to make war against Jehoshaphat.

🔑2 Then some came and reported to Jehoshaphat, saying, "A great multitude is coming against you from beyond the sea, out of [I]Aram and behold, they are in [a]Hazazon-tamar (that is Engedi)."

3 And Jehoshaphat was afraid and [I][a]turned his attention to seek the LORD; and [b]proclaimed a fast throughout all Judah.

4 So Judah gathered[6908] together to [a]seek help from the LORD; they even came from all the cities of Judah to seek the LORD.

Jehoshaphat's Prayer

5 Then Jehoshaphat stood in the assembly of Judah and Jerusalem, in the house of the LORD before the new court,

6 and he said, "O LORD, the God[430] of our fathers,[1] [a]art Thou not God in the heavens? And [b]art Thou not ruler over all the kingdoms[4467] of the nations? Power and might are in Thy hand so that no one can stand against Thee.

7 "Didst Thou not, O our God, drive

---

2 [I]Lit., *by this* [a]1Kin. 16:1; 2Chr. 20:34 [b]2Chr. 18:1, 3 [c]2Chr. 24:18

3 [I]Lit., *good things are found* [II]I.e., wooden pillars [a]2Chr. 12:12 [b]2Chr. 17:6 [c]2Chr. 12:14

4 [a]2Chr. 15:8-13

5 [a]Deut. 16:18-20

6 [I]Lit., *in the word of judgment* [a]Lev. 19:15; Deut. 1:17

7 [I]Lit., *be careful and do* [II]Lit., *there is not with the LORD our God* [a]Gen. 18:25; Deut. 32:4 [b]Deut. 10:17, 18

8 [I]So the versions; Heb. reads *disputes. And they returned to Jerusalem. Or, And they lived in Jerusalem* [a]2Chr. 17:8, 9

10 [a]Deut. 17:8 [b]2Chr. 19:2

11 [I]Lit., *every matter of* [II]Lit., *Be strong and do* [a]2Chr. 19:8 [b]1Chr. 28:20

1 [I]So with Gr.; Heb., *Ammonites* [a]1Chr. 4:41; 2Chr. 26:7

2 [I]Another reading is *Edom* [a]Gen. 14:7

3 [I]Lit., *set his face* [a]2Chr. 19:3 [b]1Sam. 7:6; Ezra 8:21

4 [a]Joel 1:14

6 [a]Deut. 4:39 [b]1Chr. 29:11

🔑 **20:2** The sea referred to here is the Dead Sea.

out the inhabitants of this land[776] before Thy people[5971] Israel, and [a]give it to the descendants of [b]Abraham Thy friend[157] forever?

8 "And they lived in it, and have built Thee a sanctuary there for Thy name, saying,

9 '[a]Should evil[7451] come upon us, the sword, *or* judgment, or pestilence,[1698] or famine, we will stand before this house and before Thee (for [b]Thy name is in this house) and cry[2199] to Thee in our distress, and Thou wilt hear and deliver *us*.'

🔑 10 "And now behold, [a]the sons of Ammon and Moab and [1]Mount Seir, [b]whom Thou didst not let Israel invade when they came out of the land of Egypt (they turned aside from them and did not destroy[8045] them),

11 behold *how* they are rewarding us, by [a]coming to drive us out from Thy possession[3425] which Thou hast given us as an inheritance.[3423]

🔑 12 "O our God, [a]wilt Thou not judge[8199] them? For we are powerless before this great multitude who are coming against us; nor do we know[3045] what to do, but [b]our eyes are on Thee."

13 And all Judah was standing before the LORD, with their infants, their wives,[802] and their children.

Jahaziel Answers the Prayer

🔑 **14** Then in the midst of the assembly [a]the Spirit of the LORD came upon Jahaziel the son of Zechariah, the son of Benaiah, the son of Jeiel, the son of Mattaniah, the Levite of the sons of Asaph;

🔑 15 and he said, "Listen, all Judah and the inhabitants of Jerusalem and King[4428] Jehoshaphat: thus says the LORD to you, '[a]Do not fear[3372] or be dismayed[2865] because of this great multitude, for [b]the battle is not yours but God's.

16 'Tomorrow go down against them. Behold, they will come up by the ascent of Ziz, and you will find them at the end of the valley in front of the wilderness of Jeruel.

🔑 17 'You *need* not fight in this *battle;* station yourselves, [a]stand and see the salvation of the LORD on your behalf, O Judah and Jerusalem.' Do not fear[3372] or be dismayed; tomorrow go out to face them, [b]for the LORD is with you."

18 And Jehoshaphat [a]bowed his head with *his* face[639] to the ground,[776] and all Judah and the inhabitants of Jerusalem fell down before the LORD, worshiping[7812] the LORD.

19 And the Levites, from the sons of the Kohathites and of the sons of the Korahites, stood up to praise[1984] the LORD God of Israel, with a very loud voice.

Enemies Destroy Themselves

20 And they rose early in the morning and went out to the wilderness of Tekoa; and when they went out, Jehoshaphat stood and said, "Listen to me, O Judah and inhabitants of Jerusalem, [a]put your trust[539] in the LORD your God, and you will be established.[539] Put your trust in His prophets and succeed."

21 And when he had consulted[3289] with the people, he appointed those who sang to the LORD and those who [a]praised[3034] *Him* in holy attire,[1927] as they went out before the army and said, "[b]Give thanks to the LORD, for His lovingkindness is everlasting."

22 And when they began singing and praising,[8416] the LORD [a]set ambushes against the sons of [b]Ammon, Moab, and

7 [a]Is. 41:8 [b]James 2:23
9 [a]2Chr. 6:28-30 [b]2Chr. 6:20
10 [1]I.e., Edom [a]2Chr. 20:1, 22 [b]Num. 20:17-21
11 [a]Ps. 83:12
12 [a]Judg. 11:27 [b]Ps. 25:15; 121:1, 2
14 [a]2Chr. 15:1; 24:20
15 [a]Ex. 14:13; Deut. 20:1-4; 2Chr. 32:7, 8 [b]1Sam. 17:47
17 [a]Ex. 14:13 [b]2Chr. 15:2
18 [a]Ex. 4:31
20 [a]Is. 7:9
21 [a]1Chr. 16:29; Ps. 29:2 [b]1Chr. 16:34
22 [a]2Chr. 13:13 [b]2Chr. 20:10

🔑 **20:10** This was quoted from Deut. 2:4,5,9,19.
🔑 **20:12** Compare Ps. 123:2.
🔑 **20:14** Jahaziel may be the inspired descendant of the psalmist Asaph, the specific author of Psalm 83. The military situation was very similar.
🔑 **20:15** This is what David said when he faced Goliath (I Sam. 17:47).
🔑 **20:17** At the Red Sea, God ordered Moses to do the same thing (Ex. 14:13).

Mount Seir, who had come against Judah; so they were [I]routed.
23 For the sons of Ammon and
Moab rose up against the inhabitants
of Mount Seir destroying[8045] *them* completely, and when they had finished[2615]
with the inhabitants of Seir, [a]they helped
to destroy[4889] one another.[7453]
24 When Judah came to the lookout
of the wilderness, they looked toward
the multitude; and behold, they *were*
corpses lying[5307] on the ground,[776] and
no one had escaped.[6413]
25 And when Jehoshaphat and his
people came to take their spoil, they
found much among them, *including*
goods, [I]garments, and valuable things
which they took for themselves, more
than they could carry. And they were
three days[3117] taking the spoil because
there was so much.

Triumphant Return to Jerusalem

26 Then on the fourth day[3117] they
assembled[6950] in the valley of Bera-
cah,1294 for there they blessed[1288] the
LORD. Therefore they have named[7121]
that place "The Valley of [I]Beracah"
until today.
27 And every man of Judah and Jerusalem returned with Jehoshaphat at their
head, returning to Jerusalem with joy,
[a]for the LORD had made them to rejoice
over their enemies.
28 And they came to Jerusalem with
harps, lyres, and trumpets to the house
of the LORD.
29 And [a]the dread[6343] of God was
on all the kingdoms of the lands[776] when
they heard that the LORD had fought
against the enemies of Israel.
30 So the kingdom of Jehoshaphat
was at peace,[8252] [a]for his God gave him
rest on all sides.
⊶ **31** [a]Now Jehoshaphat reigned over
Judah. He *was* thirty-five years old when
he became king, and he reigned in Jerusalem twenty-five years. And his mother's name *was* Azubah the daughter of
Shilhi.
32 And he walked in the way[1870] of
his father Asa and did not depart[5493] from
it, doing[6213] right in the sight of the
LORD.
33 [a]The high places, however, were
not removed; [b]the people had not yet
directed their hearts to the God of their
fathers.
34 Now the rest of the acts[1697] of
Jehoshaphat, first[7223] [I]to last, behold,
they are written in the annals of [a]Jehu
the son of Hanani, which is [II]recorded
in the Book[5612] of the Kings[4428] of Israel.

Alliance Displeases God

35 [a]And after this Jehoshaphat king
of Judah allied himself with Ahaziah king
of Israel. He acted wickedly[7561] [I]in so
doing.
36 So he allied himself with him to
make ships to go [a]to Tarshish, and they
made the ships in Ezion-geber.
37 Then Eliezer the son of Doda-
vahu of Mareshah prophesied against
Jehoshaphat saying, "Because you have
allied yourself with Ahaziah, the LORD
has destroyed your works." So the ships
were broken[7665] and could not go to
Tarshish.

Jehoram Succeeds Jehoshaphat in Judah

21 ⊶ [a]Then Jehoshaphat slept with
his fathers and was buried[6912]
with his fathers[1] in the city of David,
and Jehoram his son became king in his
place.
2 And he had brothers,[251] the sons
of Jehoshaphat: Azariah, Jehiel, Zechariah, [I]Azaryahu, Michael, and Shephatiah. All these *were* the sons of Jehoshaphat king[4428] [a]of Israel.
3 And their father gave them many
gifts of silver, gold and precious things,
[a]with fortified cities in Judah, but he gave

22 [I]Lit., *struck down*
23 [a]Judg. 7:22; 1Sam. 14:20
25 [I]So several ancient mss.; others read *corpses*
26 [I]I.e., blessing
27 [a]Neh. 12:43
29 [a]2Chr. 14:14; 17:10
30 [a]2Chr. 14:6, 7; 15:15
31 [a]1Kin. 22:41-43
33 [a]2Chr. 17:6 [b]2Chr. 19:3
34 [I]Lit., *and* [II]Lit., *taken up* [a]2Chr. 19:2
35 [I]Lit., *to do* [a]1Kin. 22:48, 49
36 [a]2Chr. 9:21
1 [a]1Kin. 22:50
2 [I]Or, *Azariah* [a]2Chr. 12:6; 23:2
3 [a]2Chr. 11:5

⊶ **20:31-37** See I Kgs. 22:41-50.
⊶ **21:1-20** See II Kgs. 8:16-24.

the kingdom[4467] to Jehoram because he was the first-born.

4 Now when Jehoram had [I]taken over the kingdom of his father and made himself [II]secure, he [a]killed all his brothers with the sword, and some of the rulers of Israel also.

5 [a]Jehoram *was* thirty-two years old when he became king, and he reigned eight years in Jerusalem.

6 [a]And he walked in the way[1870] of the kings[4428] of Israel, just as the house of Ahab did[6213] ([b]for Ahab's daughter was his wife),[802] and he did evil[7451] in the sight of the LORD.

7 Yet the LORD was not willing[14] to destroy[7843] the house of David because of the covenant[1285] which He had made with David, [a]and since He had promised to give a lamp[5216] to him and his sons forever.

Revolt against Judah

8 In his days[3117] [a]Edom revolted [I]against the rule[3027] of Judah, and set up a king over themselves.

9 Then Jehoram crossed over with his commanders and all his chariots with him. And it came about that he arose by night[3915] and struck down the Edomites who were surrounding him and the commanders[8269] of the chariots.

10 So Edom revolted [I]against Judah to this day.[3117] Then Libnah revolted at the same time [II]against his rule, because he had forsaken[5800] the LORD God[430] of his fathers.

11 Moreover, [a]he made high places in the mountains of Judah, and caused the inhabitants of Jerusalem [b]to play[2181] the harlot and led Judah astray.

12 Then a letter came to him from Elijah the prophet saying, "Thus says the LORD God of your father David, 'Because [a]you have not walked in the ways[1870] of Jehoshaphat your father [b]and the ways of Asa king of Judah,

13 but [a]have walked in the way of the kings of Israel, and have caused Judah and the inhabitants of Jerusalem to play the harlot [b]as the house of Ahab played the harlot, and you [c]have also killed your brothers, [I]your own family, who were better[2896] than you,

14 behold, the LORD is going to strike your people,[5971] your sons,[1121] your wives,[802] and all your possessions with a great [I]calamity;

15 and [a]you will suffer [I]severe sickness, a disease[4245] of your bowels,[4578] until your bowels come out because of the sickness, day by day.' "

16 Then [a]the LORD stirred up against Jehoram the spirit of the Philistines and [b]the Arabs who [I]bordered the Ethiopians;

17 and they came against Judah and invaded it, and carried away all the possessions found in the king's[4428] house together with his sons and his wives, so that no son was left[7604] to him except [Ia]Jehoahaz, the youngest of his sons.

18 So after all this the LORD smote him [a]in his bowels with an incurable sickness.

🔑 19 Now it came about in the course of time, at the end of two years, that his bowels came out because of his sickness and he died in great pain.[8463] And his people made no fire for him like [a]the fire[8316] for his fathers.

20 He was thirty-two years old when he became king, and he reigned in Jerusalem eight years; and he departed [Ia]with no one's regret, and they buried him in the city of David, [b]but not in the tombs[6913] of the kings.

Ahaziah Succeeds Jehoram in Judah

22 🔑 [a]Then the inhabitants of Jerusalem made [I]Ahaziah, his youngest son, king[4427] in his place, for the band[1416] of men who came with [b]the Arabs to the camp had slain all the older

4 [I]Lit., *risen up* [II]Lit., *strong* [a]Gen. 4:8; Judg. 9:5
5 [a]2Kin. 8:17-22
6 [a]1Kin. 12:28-30 [b]2Chr. 18:1
7 [a]2Sam. 7:12-17; 1Kin. 11:13, 36
8 [I]Lit., *from under the hand of* [a]2Chr. 20:22, 23; 21:10
10 [I]Lit., *from under the hand of* [II]Lit., *from under his hand*
11 [a]1Kin. 11:7 [b]Lev. 20:5
12 [a]2Chr. 17:3, 4 [b]2Chr. 14:2-5
13 [I]Lit., *your father's house* [a]2Chr. 21:6 [b]1Kin. 16:31-33 [c]2Chr. 21:4
14 [I]Lit., *blow*
15 [I]Lit., *in many sicknesses* [a]2Chr. 21:18, 19
16 [I]Lit., *were at the hand of* [a]2Chr. 33:11 [b]2Chr. 17:11; 22:1
17 [I]In 2Chr. 22:1, *Ahaziah* [a]2Chr. 25:23
18 [a]2Chr. 21:15
19 [a]2Chr. 16:14
20 [I]Lit., *without desire* [a]Jer. 22:18, 28 [b]2Chr. 24:25; 28:27
1 [I]In 2Chr. 21:17, *Jehoahaz* [a]2Kin. 8:24-29 [b]2Chr. 21:16

🔑 **21:19** An example of such a burning is recorded in II Chr. 16:14.
🔑 **22:1-6** See II Kgs. 8:25-29.

sons. So Ahaziah the son of Jehoram king[4428] of Judah began to reign.

🔑2 Ahaziah *was* [I]twenty-two years old when he became king, and he reigned one year in Jerusalem. And his mother's name was Athaliah, the [II]granddaughter of Omri.

3 He also walked in the ways[1870] of the house of Ahab, for his mother was his counselor[3289] to do wickedly.[7561]

4 And he did[6213] evil[7451] in the sight of the LORD like the house of Ahab, for they were his counselors after the death[4194] of his father, to [a]his destruction.[4889]

Ahaziah Allies with Jehoram of Israel

🔑5 He also walked according to their counsel,[6098] and went with Jehoram the son of Ahab king of Israel to wage war against Hazael king of Aram at Ramoth-gilead. But the [I][a]Arameans [II]wounded [III]Joram.

6 So he returned to be healed in Jezreel of the wounds[4347] [I]which they had inflicted[5221] on him at Ramah, when he fought against Hazael king of Aram. And [II]Ahaziah, the son of Jehoram king of Judah, went down to see Jehoram the son of Ahab in Jezreel, because he was sick.

🔑**7** Now [a]the destruction[8395] of Ahaziah was from God,[430] in that [I]he went to Joram. For when he came, [b]he went out with Jehoram against Jehu the son of Nimshi, [c]whom the LORD had anointed[4886] to cut off[3772] the house of Ahab.

Jehu Murders Princes of Judah

8 [a]And it came about when Jehu was executing[6213] judgment[8199] on the house of Ahab, he found the princes of Judah and the sons of Ahaziah's brothers,[251] ministering to Ahaziah, and slew them.

9 [a]He also sought Ahaziah, and they caught him while he was hiding in Samaria; they brought him to Jehu, put him to death, [b]and buried[6912] him. For they said, "He is the son of Jehoshaphat, [c]who sought the LORD with all his heart." So there was no one of the house of Ahaziah to retain the power of the kingdom.[4467]

🔑**10** [a]Now when Athaliah the mother of Ahaziah saw that her son was dead,[4191] she rose and destroyed all the royal [I]offspring of the house of Judah.

11 But Jehoshabeath the king's daughter took Joash the son of Ahaziah, and stole him from among the king's[4428] sons who were being put to death, and placed him and his nurse in the bedroom. So Jehoshabeath, the daughter of King Jehoram, the wife[802] of Jehoiada the priest (for she was the sister of Ahaziah), hid him from Athaliah so that she would not put him to death.

12 And he was hidden with them in the house of God six years while Athaliah reigned over the land.[776]

Jehoiada Sets Joash on the Throne of Judah

23 [a]Now in the seventh year Jehoiada strengthened himself, and took captains[8269] of hundreds: Azariah the son of Jeroham, Ishmael the son of Johanan, Azariah the son of Obed, Maaseiah the son of Adaiah, and Elishaphat the son of Zichri, *and they entered* into a covenant[1285] with him.

2 And they went throughout Judah and gathered[6908] the Levites from all the cities of Judah, and the heads[7218]

2 [I]So some versions and 2Kin. 8:26; Heb., *42 years* [II]Lit., *daughter*
4 [a]Prov. 13:20
5 [I]Heb., *archers* [II]Lit., *smote* [III]I.e., Jehoram [a]2Kin. 8:28
6 [I]Lit., *with which . . . smitten* [II]So with 2Kin. 8:29; Heb., *Azariah*
7 [I]Lit., *to go* [a]2Chr. 10:15 [b]2Kin. 9:21 [c]2Kin. 9:6, 7
8 [a]2Kin. 10:11-14
9 [a]2Kin. 9:27 [b]2Kin. 9:28 [c]2Chr. 17:4
10 [I]Lit., *seed* [a]2Kin. 11:1-3
1 [a]2Kin. 11:4-20

🔑**22:2** Athaliah was the daughter of Ahab and Jezebel.
🔑**22:5** Joram is a shortened form of Jehoram. The longer form is used in vv. 5, 5b, and 7b in the Hebrew text. It is important to distinguish the Jehoram of Judah and the Jehoram (Joram) of Israel.
🔑**22:7** See II Kgs. 9:6,7.
🔑**22:7-9** See II Kgs. 9:27-29.
🔑**22:10—23:21** See II Kgs. 11:1-21.

of the fathers'[1] *households* of [a]Israel, and
they came to Jerusalem.
3 Then all the assembly made a covenant with the king[4428] in the house of
God.[430] And [I]Jehoiada said to them, "Behold, the king's[4428] son shall reign,
[a]as the LORD has spoken concerning the
sons of David.
4 "This is the thing which you shall
do:[6213] one third of you, of the priests
and Levites [a]who come in on the sabbath, *shall be* gatekeepers,[7778]
5 and one third *shall be* at the king's
house, and a third at the Gate of the
Foundation;[3247] and all the people[5971]
shall be in the courts of the house of
the LORD.
6 "But let no one enter the house
of the LORD except the priests and
[a]the ministering Levites; they may enter, for they are holy. And let all the
people keep[8104] the charge[4931] of the
LORD.
7 "And the Levites will surround[5362]
the king, each man with his weapons
in his hand; and whoever enters the
house, let him be killed.[4191] Thus be
with the king when he comes in and
when he goes out."
8 So the Levites and all Judah did[6213]
according to all that Jehoiada the priest
commanded.[6680] And each one of them
took his men who were to come in on
the sabbath, with those who were to
go out on the sabbath, for Jehoiada the
priest did not dismiss *any of* [a]the divisions.
9 Then Jehoiada the priest gave to
the captains of hundreds the spears and
the large and small shields[4043] which had
been King David's, which *were* in the
house of God.
10 And he stationed all the people,
each man with his weapon in his hand,
from the right [I]side of the house to the
left [I]side of the house, by the altar[4196]
and by the house, around the king.
🔑 11 Then they brought out the king's
son and put the crown[5145] on him, and
gave him [a]the testimony, and made him
king.[4427] And Jehoiada and his sons
anointed[4886] him and said, "[b]*Long* live
the king!"

Athaliah Murdered

12 When Athaliah heard the noise
of the people running and praising[1984]
the king, she came into the house of
the LORD to the people.
13 And she looked,[7200] and behold,
the king was standing by his pillar at
the entrance, and the captains and the
[I]trumpeters *were* beside the king. And
all the people of the land[776] rejoiced
and blew trumpets, the singers with
their musical instruments [II]leading the
praise.[1984] Then Athaliah tore her
clothes and said, "Treason! Treason!"
14 And Jehoiada the priest brought
out the captains of hundreds who were
appointed over the army, and said to
them, "Bring her out [I]between the
ranks; and whoever follows her, put to
death with the sword." For the priest
said, "Let her not be put to death in
the house of the LORD."
15 So they [I]seized[7760] her, and when
she arrived at the entrance of [a]the Horse
Gate of the king's house, they [b]put her
to death there.

Reforms Carried Out

16 Then [a]Jehoiada made a covenant
between himself and all the people and
the king, that they should be the LORD's
people.
17 And all the people went to the
house of Baal, and tore[7665] it down, and
they broke in pieces his altars[4196] and
his images,[6754] and [a]killed Mattan the
priest of Baal before the altars.
18 Moreover, Jehoiada placed[7760]
the offices of the house of the LORD
under the [I]authority of [a]the Levitical
priests, [b]whom David had assigned over
the house of the LORD, to offer the burnt

2 [a]2Chr. 11:13-17; 21:2
3 [I]Lit., *he* [a]2Sam. 7:12; 2Chr. 21:7
4 [a]1Chr. 9:25
6 [a]1Chr. 23:28-32
8 [a]1Chr. 24:1
10 [I]Lit., *shoulder*
11 [a]Ex. 25:16, 21 [b]1Sam. 10:24
13 [I]Lit., *trumpets* [II]Lit., *and leading for praising*
14 [I]Lit., *from within*
15 [I]Lit., *placed hands to her* [a]Neh. 3:28; Jer. 31:40 [b]2Chr. 22:10
16 [a]2Kin. 11:17
17 [a]Deut. 13:6-9; 1Kin. 18:40
18 [I]Lit., *hand* [a]2Chr. 5:5 [b]1Chr. 23:6, 25-31

🔑 **23:11** He was given the Law of Moses (Ex. 25:21), which was to be his constant guide (Deut. 17:18-20).

offerings of the LORD, as it is written in the law[8451] of Moses—[c]with rejoicing and singing according to the [II]order of David.

19 And he stationed [a]the gatekeepers of the house of the LORD, so that no one should enter *who was* in any way unclean.[2931]

20 And [a]he took the captains of hundreds, the nobles,[117] the rulers[4910] of the people, and all the people of the land, and brought the king down from the house of the LORD, and came through the upper gate to the king's house. And they placed the king upon the royal[4467] throne.

21 So [a]all of the people of the land rejoiced and the city was quiet.[8252] For they had put Athaliah to death with the sword.

Young Joash Influenced by Jehoiada

24 🗝 [a]Joash *was* seven years old when he became king, and he reigned forty years in Jerusalem; and his mother's name *was* Zibiah from Beersheba.

2 And [a]Joash did[6213] what was right in the sight of the LORD all the days[3117] of Jehoiada the priest.

3 And Jehoiada took two wives[802] for him, and he became the father of sons and daughters.

Faithless Priests

4 Now it came about after this that Joash [I]decided [a]to restore the house of the LORD.

5 And he gathered[6908] the priests and Levites, and said to them, "Go out to the cities of Judah, and collect[6908] money from all [a]Israel to [I]repair the house of your God[430] [II]annually, and you shall do the matter quickly." But the Levites did not act quickly.

🗝 6 So the king[4428] summoned[7121] Jehoiada the chief[7218] *priest* and said to him, "Why have you not required the Levites to bring in from Judah and from Jerusalem [a]the levy[4864] *fixed by* Moses the servant of the LORD on the congregation of Israel [b]for the tent of the testimony?"[5715]

7 For [a]the sons of the wicked Athaliah had broken into the house of God and even [I]used the holy[6944] things of the house of the LORD for the Baals.

Temple Repaired

8 So the king[4428] commanded,[559] and [a]they made a chest[727] and set it outside by the gate of the house of the LORD.

9 And [a]they made a proclamation in Judah and Jerusalem to bring to the LORD [b]the levy *fixed by* Moses the servant of God on Israel in the wilderness.

10 And all the officers and all the people[5971] rejoiced and brought in their levies and [I]dropped *them* into the chest until they had finished.[3615]

11 And it came about whenever the chest was brought in to the king's officer by the Levites, and when [a]they saw that there was much money, then the king's scribe and the chief priest's officer would come, empty the chest, take it, and return it to its place. Thus they did daily[3117] and collected[622] much money.

12 And the king and Jehoiada gave it to those who did the work[4399] of the service of the house of the LORD; and they hired masons and carpenters to restore the house of the LORD, and also workers in iron and bronze to [I]repair the house of the LORD.

13 So the workmen labored, and the repair work progressed[724] in their hands, and they [I]restored the house of God [II]according to its specifications,[4971] and strengthened it.

18 [II]Lit., *hands of* [c]1Chr. 25:1
19 [a]1Chr. 9:22
20 [a]2Kin. 11:19
21 [a]2Kin. 11:20
1 [a]2Kin. 11:21; 12:1-15
2 [a]2Chr. 26:4, 5
4 [I]Lit., *was with a heart* [a]2Chr. 24:7
5 [I]Lit., *to strengthen* [II]Lit., *from year to year* [a]2Chr. 21:2
6 [a]Ex. 30:12-16 [b]Num. 1:50
7 [I]Lit., *made* [a]2Chr. 21:17
8 [a]2Kin. 12:9
9 [a]2Chr. 36:22 [b]2Chr. 24:6
10 [I]Lit., *threw*
11 [a]2Kin. 12:10
12 [I]Lit., *to strengthen*
13 [I]Lit., *set up* [II]Lit., *upon its proportion*

🗝 **24:1-27** See II Kgs. 12:1-21.

🗝 **24:6** See Ex. 30:15,16. Because the tabernacle housed the tables of the law or testimony (Ex. 25:16), it was sometimes called "the tent of the testimony" (Num. 9:15).

14 And when they had finished,[3615]
they brought the rest of the money before the king and Jehoiada; and it was
made into utensils for the house of the
LORD, utensils for the service and the
burnt offering, and pans and utensils of
gold and silver. And they offered burnt
offerings in the house of the LORD
continually[8548] all the days of Jehoiada.
15 Now when Jehoiada [I]reached a
ripe old age he died; he was one hundred
and thirty years old at his death.[4194]
16 And they buried[6912] him [a]in the
city of David among the kings,[4428] because he had done[6213] well in [b]Israel and
[I]to God[430] and His house.
17 But after the death[4194] of Jehoiada the officials of Judah came and bowed
down[7812] to the king, and the king listened to them.
18 And they abandoned[5800] [a]the
house of the LORD, the God of their
fathers,[1] and [b]served the [I]Asherim[842]
and the idols;[6091] so [c]wrath[7110] came
upon Judah and Jerusalem for this their
guilt.
🔑 19 Yet [a]He sent prophets to them
to bring them back to the LORD; though
they testified against them, they would
not listen.

Joash Murders Son of Jehoiada

20 [a]Then the Spirit of God [I]came
on Zechariah the son of Jehoiada the
priest; and he stood above the people
and said to them, "Thus God has said,
'[b]Why do you transgress the commandments[4687] of the LORD and do
not prosper? [c]Because you have forsaken[5800] the LORD, He has also forsaken you.'"
🔑 21 So [a]they conspired against him
and at the command of the king they
stoned him [I]to death in the court of the
house of the LORD.

15 [I]Lit., *became old and satisfied with days*

16 [I]Lit., *with* [a]2Chr. 21:20 [b]2Chr. 21:2

18 [I]I.e., wooden symbols of a female deity [a]2Chr. 24:4 [b]Ex. 34:12-14 [c]Josh. 22:20

19 [a]Jer. 7:25

20 [I]Lit., *clothed* [a]2Chr. 20:14 [b]Num. 14:41 [c]2Chr. 15:2

21 [I]Lit., *with stones* [a]Neh. 9:26; Matt. 23:34, 35

22 [I]Lit., *seek*, or *require* [a]Gen. 9:5

23 [a]2Kin. 12:17

24 [a]2Chr. 16:7, 8 [b]2Chr. 24:20

25 [I]So some ancient versions; Heb., *sons* [a]2Kin. 12:20, 21

27 [I]Or, *burdens upon* [II]Lit., *founding* [III]Heb., *midrash* [a]2Chr. 24:12 [b]2Chr. 13:22

1 [a]2Kin. 14:1-6

22 Thus Joash the king did not remember the kindness[2617] which his father Jehoiada had shown him, but he
murdered his son. And as he died he
said, "May [a]the LORD see and [I]avenge!"

Aram Invades and Defeats Judah

23 Now it came about at the turn
of the year that [a]the army of the Arameans came up against him; and they came
to Judah and Jerusalem, destroyed[7843]
all the officials of the people from among
the people, and sent all their spoil to
the king of Damascus.
24 Indeed the army[2428] of the Arameans came with a small number of men;
yet [a]the LORD delivered a very great
army into their hands, [b]because they
had forsaken the LORD, the God of their
fathers. Thus they executed[6213] judgment[8201] on Joash.
25 [a]And when they had departed
from him (for they left him very sick),[4251]
his own servants conspired against him
because of the blood[1818] of the [I]son of
Jehoiada the priest, and murdered him
on his bed. So he died, and they buried
him in the city of David, but they did not
bury him in the tombs[6913] of the kings.
26 Now these are those who conspired against him: Zabad the son of
Shimeath the Ammonitess, and Jehozabad the son of Shimrith the Moabitess.
27 As to his sons and the many
[I]oracles[4853] against him and [a]the [II]re-
building of the house of God, behold,
they are written in the [III][b]treatise of the
Book[5612] of the Kings. Then Amaziah
his son became king in his place.

Amaziah Succeeds Joash in Judah

25 🔑 [a]Amaziah was twenty-five
years old when he became king,
and he reigned twenty-nine years in

🔑 **24:19** Compare II Chr. 30:6,10.

🔑 **24:21** This passage was referred to by Jesus in Mt. 23:35 where Berechiah is another name for Jehoiada. This priest should not be confused with the prophet Zechariah, the son of Berechiah and the author of the book of Zechariah (Zech. 1:1).

🔑 **25:1-28** See II Kgs. 14:1-22.

Jerusalem. And his mother's name was Jehoaddan of Jerusalem.

2 And he did[6213] right in the sight of the LORD, [a]yet not with a whole[8003] heart.

3 Now [a]it came about as soon as the kingdom[4467] was [I]firmly in his grasp, that he killed[5221] his servants who had slain his father the king.[4428]

🔑4 However, he did not put their children[1121] to death, but *did* as it is written in the law[8451] in the book[5612] of Moses, which the LORD commanded,[6680] saying, "[a]Fathers[1] shall not be put to death[4191] for sons, nor sons be put to death for fathers, but each shall be put to death for his own sin."

Amaziah Defeats Edomites

5 Moreover, Amaziah assembled[6908] Judah and appointed them according to *their* fathers' households under commanders[8269] of thousands and commanders of hundreds throughout Judah and Benjamin; and he [I]took a census[6485] of those [a]from twenty years old and upward, and found them to be [b]300,000 choice men, *able* to go to war[6635] *and* handle spear and shield.

6 He hired also 100,000 valiant[2428] warriors out of Israel for one hundred talents of silver.

7 But [a]a man of God[430] came to him saying, "O king, do not let the army[6635] of Israel go with you, for the LORD is not with Israel *nor with* any of the sons of Ephraim.

8 "But if you do go, do[6213] *it,* be strong for the battle; *yet* God[430] will [I]bring you down[3782] before the enemy, [a]for God has power to help and to [I]bring down."

🔑9 And Amaziah said to the man of God, "But what *shall we* do for the hundred talents which I have given to the troops[1416] of Israel?" And the man of God answered,[559] "[a]The LORD has much more to give you than this."

10 Then Amaziah [I]dismissed them, the troops which came to him from Ephraim, to go home; so their anger[639] burned[2734] against Judah and they returned [II]home in fierce[2750] anger.

11 Now Amaziah strengthened himself, and led his people[5971] forth, and went to [a]the Valley of Salt, and struck down 10,000 of the sons of Seir.

12 The sons of Judah also captured[7617] 10,000 alive[2416] and brought them to the top of the cliff, and threw them down from the top of the cliff so that they were all dashed to pieces.

13 But the [I]troops whom Amaziah sent back from going with him to battle, raided the cities of Judah, from Samaria to Beth-horon, and struck down 3,000 of them, and plundered much spoil.

Amaziah Rebuked for Idolatry

14 Now it came about after Amaziah came from slaughtering the Edomites that [a]he brought the gods[430] of the sons of Seir, set them up as his gods, bowed[7812] down before them, and burned incense[6999] to them.

15 Then the anger of the LORD burned against Amaziah, and He sent him a prophet who said to him, "Why have you sought the gods of the people [a]who have not delivered[5337] their own people from your hand?"

16 And it came about as he was talking with him that [I]the king said to him, "Have we appointed you a royal[4428] counselor?[3289] Stop! Why should you be struck down?" Then the prophet stopped and said, "I know[3045] that God has planned[3289] to destroy[7843] you, because you have done[6213] this, and have not listened to my counsel."[6098]

Amaziah Defeated by Joash of Israel

17 [a]Then Amaziah king of Judah took counsel and sent to Joash the son

2 [a]2Chr. 25:14
3 [I]Lit., *firm upon him* [a]2Kin. 14:5
4 [a]Deut. 24:16
5 [I]Lit., *mustered* [a]Num. 1:3 [b]2Chr. 26:13
7 [a]2Kin. 4:9
8 [I]Lit., *cause to stumble* [a]2Chr. 14:11; 20:6
9 [a]Deut. 8:18; Prov. 10:22
10 [I]Lit., *separated* [II]Lit., *to their own place*
11 [a]2Kin. 14:7
13 [I]Lit., *sons of the troops*
14 [a]2Chr. 28:23
15 [a]2Chr. 25:11, 12
16 [I]Lit., *he*
17 [a]2Kin. 14:8-14

🔑**25:4** See Deut. 24:16.
🔑**25:9** The latter part of this verse is a beautiful O.T. combination of Mt. 6:33 and Eph. 3:20.

of Jehoahaz the son of Jehu, the king
of Israel, saying, "Come, let us face
each other."
18 And Joash the king of Israel sent
to Amaziah king of Judah, saying, "[a]The
thorn bush which was in Lebanon sent
to the cedar which was in Lebanon, saying, 'Give your daughter to my son in
marriage.'[802] But there passed[5674] by a
wild beast[2416] that was in Lebanon, and
trampled the thorn bush.
19 "You said, 'Behold, you have
[I]defeated Edom.' And [a]your heart has
[II]become proud in boasting.[3513] Now
stay at home; for why should you provoke trouble that you, even you, should
fall and Judah with you?"
20 But Amaziah would not listen,
for it was from God, that He might deliver them into the hand *of Joash* because
they had sought the gods of Edom.
21 So Joash king of Israel went up,
and he and Amaziah king of Judah faced
each other at Beth-shemesh, which belonged to Judah.
22 And Judah was defeated [I]by Israel, and they fled each to his tent.
23 Then Joash king of Israel captured Amaziah king of Judah, the son
of Joash the son of [a]Jehoahaz, at Beth-
shemesh, and brought him to Jerusalem,
and tore down the wall of Jerusalem from
the Gate of Ephraim to the Corner Gate,
400 [I]cubits.
24 And *he took* all the gold and silver,
and all the utensils which were found
in the house of God with [a]Obed-edom,
and the treasures of the king's house,
the hostages also, and returned to Samaria.
25 [a]And Amaziah, the son of Joash
king of Judah, lived[2421] fifteen years after
the death[4194] of Joash, son of Jehoahaz,
king of Israel.
26 Now the rest of the acts[1697] of
Amaziah, from first[7223] to last, behold,
are they not written in the Book of the
Kings[4428] of Judah and Israel?
27 And from the time that Amaziah
turned away from following the LORD

18 [a]Judg. 9:8-15

19 [I]Lit., *smitten* [II]Lit., *lifted you up to boast* [a]2Chr. 26:16; 32:25

22 [I]Lit., *before*

23 [I]I.e., One cubit equals approx. 18 in. [a]2Chr. 21:17; 22:1

24 [a]1Chr. 26:15

25 [a]2Kin. 14:17-22

1 [I]In 2Kin. 14:21, *Azariah*

3 [I]In 2Kin. 15:2, *Jecoliah* [a]2Kin. 15:2, 3

5 [I]Many mss. read *in the fear of God* [II]Lit., *in the days of his seeking* [a]2Chr. 24:2 [b]Dan. 1:17 [c]2Chr. 15:2

6 [a]Is. 14:29

7 [a]2Chr. 21:16

8 [I]Lit., *name went to the entering of Egypt* [a]2Chr. 17:11

9 [a]2Chr. 25:23 [b]Neh. 2:13, 15; 3:13

they conspired against him in Jerusalem,
and he fled to Lachish; but they sent
after him to Lachish and killed him there.
28 Then they brought[5375] him on
horses and buried[6912] him with his fathers in the city of Judah.

Uzziah Succeeds Amaziah in Judah

26 ⊶ And all the people[5971] of Judah
took [I]Uzziah, who *was* sixteen
years old, and made him king[4427] in the
place of his father Amaziah.
2 He built Eloth and restored it to
Judah after the king[4428] slept with his
fathers.[1]
3 Uzziah was [a]sixteen years old
when he became king, and he reigned
fifty-two years in Jerusalem; and his
mother's name was [I]Jechiliah of Jerusalem.
4 And he did[6213] right in the sight
of the LORD according to all that his father Amaziah had done.
5 And [a]he continued to seek God[430]
in the days[3117] of Zechariah, [b]who had
understanding[995] [I]through the vision[7200]
of God; and [II][c]as long as he sought the
LORD, God prospered him.

Uzziah Succeeds in War

6 Now he went out and [a]warred
against the Philistines, and broke down
the wall of Gath and the wall of Jabneh
and the wall of Ashdod; and he built
cities in *the area of* Ashdod and among
the Philistines.
7 And [a]God helped him against the
Philistines, and against the Arabians who
lived in Gur-baal, and the Meunites.
8 The Ammonites also gave [a]trib-
ute[4503] to Uzziah, and his [I]fame extended to the border of Egypt, for he
became very strong.
9 Moreover, Uzziah built towers in
Jerusalem at [a]the Corner Gate and at
the [b]Valley Gate and at the corner but-
tress and fortified[2388] them.
10 And he built towers in the

⊶ **26:1-23** See II Kgs. 15:1-7.

wilderness and [a]hewed many cisterns,[953] for he had much livestock, both
in the [I]lowland and in the plain. *He also*
had plowmen[406] and vinedressers in the
hill country and the fertile fields, for he
loved[157] the soil.
11 Moreover, Uzziah had an army
ready for battle, which [I]entered combat[1416] by divisions, according to the number of their muster,[6486] [II]prepared by
Jeiel the scribe and Maaseiah the official, under the direction of Hananiah,
one of the king's[4428] officers.[8269]
12 The total number of the heads[7218]
of the [I]households, of valiant[2428] warriors, was 2,600.
13 And under their direction was an
[I]elite army[6635] of [a]307,500, who could
wage war with great power, to help the
king against the enemy.
14 Moreover, Uzziah prepared [I]for
all the army shields, spears, helmets,
body armor,[8302] bows and sling stones.
15 And in Jerusalem he made en-
gines[2810] *of war* invented by skillful[2803]
men to be on the towers and on the
corners, for the purpose of shooting arrows and great stones. Hence his
[I]fame spread afar, for he was marvelously helped until he *was* strong.

Pride Is Uzziah's Undoing

16 But [a]when he became strong,
his heart was so [I]proud[7843] that he acted
corruptly, and he was unfaithful to the
LORD his God, for [b]he entered the temple of the LORD to burn incense[6999] on
the altar[4196] of incense.[7004]
17 Then [a]Azariah the priest entered
after him and with him eighty priests
of the LORD, valiant men.
18 And [a]they opposed Uzziah the
king and said to him, "[b]It is not for you,
Uzziah, to burn incense to the LORD,
[c]but for the priests, the sons of Aaron
who are consecrated[6942] to burn incense. Get out of the sanctuary, for you
have been unfaithful, and will have no
honor from the LORD God."
19 But Uzziah, with a censer in his
hand for burning incense, was enraged;[2196] and while he was enraged
with the priests, [a]the leprosy broke out
on his forehead before the priests in
the house of the LORD, beside the altar
of incense.
20 And Azariah the chief priest and
all the priests looked at him, and behold,
he *was* leprous on his forehead; and they
hurried him out of there, and he himself
also hastened to get out because the
LORD had smitten him.
21 [a]And King Uzziah was a leper
to the day[3117] of his death;[4194] and he
lived in [b]a separate house, being a leper,
for he was cut off from the house of
the LORD. And Jotham his son *was* over
the king's house judging[8199] the people
of the land.[776]
22 Now the rest of the acts[1697] of
Uzziah, first[7223] to last, the prophet
[a]Isaiah, the son of Amoz, has written.
23 So Uzziah slept with his fathers,
and they buried[6912] him with his fathers
[a]in the field[7704] of the grave[6900] which
belonged to the kings,[4428] for they said,
"He is a leper." And Jotham his son
became king in his place.

Jotham Succeeds Uzziah in Judah

27 [a]Jotham was twenty-five
years old when he became king,
and he reigned sixteen years in Jerusalem. And his mother's name was Jerushah the daughter of Zadok.
2 And he did[6213] right in the sight
of the LORD, according to all that his
father Uzziah had done; [a]however he
did not enter the temple of the LORD.
But the people[5971] continued acting
corruptly.[7843]
3 He built the upper gate of the

10 [I]Heb., *shephelah* [a]Gen. 26:18-21
11 [I]Lit., *goes out to* [II]Lit., *by the hand of*
12 [I]Lit., *fathers*
13 [I]Lit., *powerful* [a]2Chr. 25:5
14 [I]Lit., *for them, for all*
15 [I]Lit., *name*
16 [I]Lit., *lifted up* [a]Deut. 32:15; 2Chr. 25:19 [b]1Kin. 13:1-4
17 [a]1Chr. 6:10
18 [a]2Chr. 19:2 [b]Num. 3:10; 16:39, 40 [c]Ex. 30:7, 8
19 [a]2Kin. 5:25-27
21 [a]2Kin. 15:5-7 [b]Lev. 13:46
22 [a]Is. 1:1
23 [a]2Chr. 21:20; 28:27; Is. 6:1
1 [a]2Kin. 15:33-35
2 [a]2Chr. 26:16

26:18 See Num. 16:40.
26:19 Compare the punishments of Miriam (Num. 12:10) and of Gehazi (II Kgs. 5:27).
27:1-9 See II Kgs. 15:32-38.
27:2 This was described in more detail in II Kgs. 15:35.

house of the LORD, and he built extensively the wall of [a]Ophel.

4 Moreover, he built [a]cities in the hill country of Judah, and he built fortresses and towers on the wooded *hills*.

5 He fought also with the king[4428] of the Ammonites and prevailed over them so that the Ammonites[1121] gave him during that year one hundred talents of silver, ten thousand [I]kors of wheat and ten thousand of barley. The Ammonites also paid him this *amount* in the second and in the third year.

6 [a]So Jotham became mighty because he ordered his ways[1870] before the LORD his God.[430]

7 [a]Now the rest of the acts[1697] of Jotham, even all his wars and his acts, behold, they are written in the Book[5612] of the Kings[4428] of Israel and Judah.

8 He was [a]twenty-five years old when he became king, and he reigned sixteen years in Jerusalem.

9 And Jotham slept with his fathers,[1] and they buried[6912] him in the city of David; and Ahaz his son became king in his place.

Ahaz Succeeds Jotham in Judah

28 🔑 [a]Ahaz *was* twenty years old when he became king, and he reigned sixteen years in Jerusalem; and [b]he did not do[6213] right in the sight of the LORD as David his father *had done*.

2 [a]But he walked in the ways[1870] of the kings[4428] of Israel; he also [b]made molten images for the Baals.

🔑 3 Moreover, [a]he burned incense[6999] in the valley of Ben-hinnom, and [b]burned his sons[1121] in fire, [c]according to the abominations[8441] of the nations whom the LORD had driven out[3423] before the sons of Israel.

4 And he sacrificed and [a]burned incense on the high places, on the hills, and under every green tree.

Judah Is Invaded

5 Wherefore, [a]the LORD his God[430] delivered him into the hand of the king[4428] of Aram; and they [I]defeated him and carried away from him a great number of captives,[7633] and brought *them* to Damascus. And he was also delivered into the hand of the king of Israel, who [II]inflicted him with heavy casualties.

6 For [a]Pekah the son of Remaliah slew in Judah 120,000 in one day,[3117] all valiant men, because they had forsaken[5800] the LORD God of their fathers.[1]

🔑 7 And Zichri, a mighty man of Ephraim, slew Maaseiah the king's[4428] son, and Azrikam the ruler of the house and Elkanah the second to the king.

8 And [a]the sons of Israel carried away captive[7617] of [b]their brethren[251] 200,000 women,[802] sons, and daughters; and [I]took also a great deal of spoil from them, and they brought the spoil to Samaria.

9 But a prophet of the LORD was there, whose name *was* Oded; and [a]he went out to meet the army which came to Samaria and said to them, "Behold, because the LORD, the God of your fathers, [b]was angry with Judah, He has delivered them into your hand, and you have slain them in a rage [c]*which* has even reached heaven.

10 "And now you are proposing to [a]subjugate for yourselves the people of Judah and Jerusalem for male and female slaves.[5650] Surely, *do* you not *have* transgressions of your own against the LORD your God?

11 "Now therefore, listen to me and return[7725] the captives [a]whom you captured from your brothers, [b]for the

---

3 [a]2Chr. 33:14; Neh. 3:26
4 [a]2Chr. 11:5
5 [I]I.e., A kor equals approx. 10 bu.
6 [a]2Chr. 26:5
7 [a]2Kin. 15:36
8 [a]2Chr. 27:1
1 [a]2Kin. 16:2-4 [b]2Chr. 27:2
2 [a]2Chr. 22:3 [b]Ex. 34:17
3 [a]Josh. 15:8 [b]Lev. 18:21; 2Chr. 33:6 [c]2Chr. 33:2
4 [a]2Chr. 28:25
5 [I]Lit., *smote* [II]Lit., *smote him with a great smiting* [a]2Kin. 16:5; 2 Chr. 24:24; Is. 7:1
6 [a]2Kin. 16:5
8 [I]Lit., *plundered* [a]Deut. 28:25, 41 [b]2Chr. 11:4
9 [a]2Chr. 25:15 [b]Is. 47:6 [c]Ezra 9:6; Rev. 18:5
10 [a]Lev. 25:39
11 [a]2Chr. 28:8 [b]James 2:13

🔑 **28:1-27** See II Kgs. 16:1-20.

🔑 **28:3** Human sacrifice was forbidden by the Law of Moses (Deut. 18:10) and condemned by the prophets (Ezek. 23:37,39). God clearly disapproved of it as early as Gen. 22:12,13, the incident of Abraham and Isaac. See Micah 6:6-8.

🔑 **28:7** "Son" here means "close male relative." Ahaz was barely old enough to have had a son this old.

burning anger of the LORD is against you."

12 Then some[582] of the heads of the sons of Ephraim—Azariah the son of Johanan, Berechiah the son of Meshillemoth, Jehizkiah the son of Shallum, and Amasa the son of Hadlai—arose against those who were coming from the battle,[6635]

13 and said to them, "You must not bring the captives in here, for you are proposing[559] *to bring* upon us guilt against the LORD adding to our sins and our guilt; for our guilt is great so that *His* burning anger is against Israel."

14 So the armed men left[5800] the captives and the spoil before the officers and all the assembly.

🔑 15 Then [a]the men who were designated[5344] by name arose, took the captives, and they clothed all their naked ones from the spoil; and they gave them clothes and sandals,[5274] fed them and [b]gave them drink, anointed[4886] them *with oil,* led all their feeble ones on donkeys, and brought them to Jericho, [c]the city of palm trees, to their brothers; then they returned to Samaria.

Compromise with Assyria

16 [a]At that time King Ahaz sent to the [I]kings of Assyria for help.

17 [a]For again the Edomites had come and attacked Judah, and carried away captives.[7628]

🔑 18 [a]The Philistines also had invaded the cities of the [I]lowland and of the Negev of Judah, and had taken Beth-shemesh, Aijalon, Gederoth, and Soco with its villages, Timnah with its villages, and Gimzo with its villages, and they settled there.

19 For the LORD humbled Judah because of Ahaz king of [a]Israel, for he had brought about a lack of restraint[6544] in Judah and was very unfaithful to the LORD.

20 So [a]Tilgath-pilneser king of Assyria came against him and afflicted him instead of strengthening him.

21 [a]Although Ahaz took a portion out of the house of the LORD and out of the palace of the king and of the princes, and gave *it* to the king of Assyria, it did not help him.

22 Now in the time of his distress this same King Ahaz [a]became yet more unfaithful to the LORD.

23 [a]For he sacrificed to the gods[430] of Damascus which had [I]defeated him, and said, "[b]Because the gods of the kings of Aram helped them, I will sacrifice to them that they may help me." But they became the [II]downfall of him and all Israel.

24 Moreover, when Ahaz gathered[622] together the utensils of the house of God, he [a]cut the utensils of the house of God in pieces; and he [b]closed the doors of the house of the LORD, and [c]made altars[4196] for himself in every corner of Jerusalem.

25 And in every city of Judah he made high places to burn incense[6999] to other gods, and provoked the LORD, the God of his fathers, to anger.[3707]

26 [a]Now the rest of his acts[1697] and all his ways, from first[7223] to last, behold, they are written in the Book[5612] of the Kings of Judah and Israel.

27 [a]So Ahaz slept with his fathers, and they buried[6912] him in the city, in Jerusalem, for they did not bring him into the tombs[6913] of the kings of [b]Israel; and Hezekiah his son reigned in his place.

Hezekiah Succeeds Ahaz in Judah

29 🔑 [a]Hezekiah became king *when he was* twenty-five years old; and

15 [a]2Chr. 28:12 [b]2Kin. 6:22; Prov. 25:21, 22 [c]Deut. 34:3

16 [I]Ancient versions read *king* [a]2Kin. 16:7

17 [a]Obad. 10, 14

18 [I]Heb., *shephelah* [a]Ezek. 16:57

19 [a]2Chr. 21:2

20 [a]1Chr. 5:26

21 [a]2Kin. 16:8, 9

22 [a]Is. 1:5; Jer. 5:3; Rev. 16:11

23 [I]Lit., *smitten* [II]Lit., *stumbling* [a]2Chr. 25:14 [b]Jer. 44:17, 18

24 [a]2Kin. 16:17 [b]2Chr. 29:7 [c]2Chr. 30:14; 33:3-5

26 [a]2Kin. 16:19, 20

27 [a]2Kin. 16:20; 2Chr. 24:25; Is. 14:28 [b]2Chr. 21:2

1 [a]2Kin. 18:1-3

🔑 **28:15** Anointing was for medical purposes. They could have used oil (Isa. 1:6), wine (Lk. 10:34), or salve (Rev. 3:18). See note on Js. 15:14,15.

🔑 **28:18** This situation fits the prophecies of Joel 3:4 and Oba. 10. Perhaps these two prophets could then be dated about 735 B.C. Isaiah warned Ahaz to trust God (Isa. 7:9), but Ahaz relied upon Assyria, to his regret.

🔑 **29:1,2** See II Kgs. 18:1-3.

he reigned twenty-nine years in Jerusalem. And his mother's name *was* Abijah,
the daughter of Zechariah.
2 And [a]he did[6213] right in the sight
of the LORD, according to all that his
father David had done.[6213]
3 In the first[7223] year of his reign,
in the first month, he [a]opened the doors
of the house of the LORD and repaired
them.
4 And he brought in the priests and
the Levites, and gathered[622] them into
the square on the east.

Reforms Begun

5 Then he said to them, "Listen to
me, O Levites. [a]Consecrate yourselves
now, and consecrate the house of the
LORD, the God[430] of your fathers,[1] and
carry the uncleanness out from the holy
place.
6 "For our fathers have been unfaithful and have done evil[7451] in the sight
of the LORD our God, and have forsaken[5800] Him and [a]turned their faces
away from the dwelling place of the
LORD, and have [I]turned *their* backs.
7 "They have also [a]shut the doors
of the porch and put out the lamps,[5216]
and have not burned incense[6999] or offered burnt offerings in the holy place
to the God of Israel.
8 "Therefore [a]the wrath[7110] of the
LORD was against Judah and Jerusalem,
and He has made them an object of terror, of horror,[8074] and of [b]hissing, as
you see with your own eyes.
9 "For behold, [a]our fathers have
fallen[5307] by the sword, and our sons
and our daughters and our wives[802] are
in captivity[7628] for this.
10 "Now it is in my heart [a]to make
a covenant[1285] with the LORD God of
Israel, that His burning anger may turn
away from us.
11 "My sons, do not be negligent[7952]
now, for [a]the LORD has chosen you to
stand before Him, to minister to Him,
and to be His ministers and burn
incense."[6999]
12 Then the Levites arose: [a]Ma-
hath, the son of Amasai and Joel the
son of Azariah, from the sons of
[b]the Kohathites; and from the sons of
Merari, Kish the son of Abdi and Azariah
the son of Jehallelel; and from the Gershonites, Joah the son of Zimmah and
Eden the son of Joah;
13 and from the sons of Elizaphan,
Shimri and [I]Jeiel; and from the sons of
Asaph, Zechariah and Mattaniah;
14 and from the sons of Heman,
[I]Jehiel and Shimei; and from the sons
of Jeduthun, Shemaiah and Uzziel.
15 And they assembled their brothers,[251] [a]consecrated themselves, and
went in [b]to cleanse[2891] the house of
the LORD, according to the commandment[4687] of the king[4428] [c]by the
words[1697] of the LORD.
16 So the priests went in to the inner
part of the house of the LORD to cleanse
it, and every unclean thing[2932] which
they found in the temple of the LORD
they brought out to the court of the
house of the LORD. Then the Levites
received *it* to carry out to [a]the Kidron
[I]valley.
17 Now they began [I]the consecration [a]on the first *day* of the first month,
and on the eighth day[3117] of the month
they entered the porch of the LORD.
Then they consecrated the house of the
LORD in eight days,[3117] and finished[3615]
on the sixteenth day of the first month.
18 Then they went in to King Hezekiah and said, "We have cleansed[2891]
the whole house of the LORD, the
altar[4196] of burnt offering with all of its
utensils, and the table of showbread with
all of its utensils.
19 "Moreover, [a]all the utensils
which King Ahaz had discarded during
his reign in his unfaithfulness, we have
prepared and consecrated; and behold,
they are before the altar of the LORD."

Hezekiah Restores Temple Worship

20 Then King Hezekiah arose early
and assembled the princes of the city
and went up to the house of the LORD.

2 [a]2Chr. 28:1; 34:2
3 [a]2Chr. 28:24; 29:7
5 [a]2Chr. 29:15, 34; 35:6
6 [I]Lit., *given* [a]Ezek. 8:16
7 [a]2Chr. 28:24
8 [a]2Chr. 24:20 [b]Jer. 25:9, 18
9 [a]2Chr. 28:5-8, 17
10 [a]2Chr. 23:16
11 [a]Num. 3:6; 8:6
12 [a]2Chr. 31:13 [b]Num. 3:19, 20
13 [I]Or, *Jeuel*
14 [I]Or, *Jehuel,* 1Chr. 15:18, 20
15 [a]2Chr. 29:5 [b]1Chr. 23:28 [c]2Chr. 30:12
16 [I]Or, *wadi* [a]2Chr. 15:16
17 [I]Lit., *to consecrate* [a]2Chr. 29:3
19 [a]2Chr. 28:24

🔑 21 And they brought seven bulls,
seven rams, seven lambs, and seven
male goats [a]for a sin offering for the
kingdom, the sanctuary, and Judah. And
he ordered[559] the priests, the sons of
Aaron, to offer *them* on the altar of the
LORD.
22 So they slaughtered[7819] the bulls,
and the priests took the blood[1818] and
sprinkled it on the altar. They also
slaughtered the rams and sprinkled the
blood on the altar; they slaughtered the
lambs also and [a]sprinkled the blood on
the altar.
23 Then they brought[5066] the male
goats of the sin offering before the king
and the assembly, and [a]they laid their
hands on them.
24 And the priests slaughtered them
and purged the altar with their blood
[a]to atone[3722] for all Israel, for the king
ordered the burnt offering and the sin
offering for all Israel.
🔑 **25** [a]He then stationed the Levites
in the house of the LORD with cymbals,
with harps, and with lyres, [b]according
to the command of David and of [c]Gad
the king's[4428] seer, and of [d]Nathan the
prophet; for the command was from the
LORD through His prophets.
26 And the Levites stood with
[a]the *musical* instruments of David, and
[b]the priests with the trumpets.
27 Then Hezekiah gave the order
to offer the burnt offering on the altar.
When the burnt offering began, [a]the
song to the LORD also began with the
trumpets, [I]*accompanied* by the instruments of David, king of Israel.
28 While the whole assembly worshiped,[7812] the singers also sang and the
trumpets sounded; all this *continued* until the burnt offering was finished.[3615]

21 [a]Lev. 4:3-14
22 [a]Lev. 4:18
23 [a]Lev. 4:15
24 [a]Lev. 4:26
25 [a]1Chr. 25:6 [b]2Chr. 8:14 [c]2Sam. 24:11 [d]2Sam. 7:2
26 [a]1Chr. 23:5 [b]2Chr. 5:12
27 [I]Lit., *and according to the authority of the instruments* [a]2Chr. 23:18
29 [a]2Chr. 20:18
30 [a]Ps. 100:1; 106:12
31 [I]Lit., *filled your hands* [II]Lit., *willing of heart* [a]2Chr. 13:9 [b]Ex. 35:5, 22
34 [I]Lit., *upright of heart* [a]2Chr. 35:11 [b]2Chr. 30:3
35 [I]Lit., *the burnt offerings to an abundance* [a]2Chr. 29:32 [b]Lev. 3:16 [c]Num. 15:5-10

29 Now at the completion of the
burnt offerings, [a]the king and all who
were present with him bowed down[3766]
and worshiped.
🔑 30 Moreover, King Hezekiah and
the officials ordered the Levites to sing
praises[1984] to the LORD with the words
of David and Asaph the seer. [a]So they
sang praises with joy, and bowed down
and worshiped.
31 Then Hezekiah answered and
said, "[a]Now *that* you have [I]consecrated
yourselves to the LORD, come near[5066]
and bring sacrifices and thank offerings
to the house of the LORD." And the assembly brought sacrifices and thank offerings, and [b]all those who were
[II]willing *brought* burnt offerings.
32 And the number of the burnt offerings which the assembly brought was
70 bulls, 100 rams, and 200 lambs; all
these were for a burnt offering to the
LORD.
33 And the consecrated things were
600 bulls and 3,000 sheep.
🔑 34 But the priests were too few,
so that they were unable to skin6584 all
the burnt offerings; [a]therefore their
brothers the Levites helped them until
the work[4399] was completed,[3615] and until the *other* priests had consecrated
themselves. For [b]the Levites were
more [I]conscientious[3477] to consecrate
themselves than the priests.
35 And there *were* also [Ia]many burnt
offerings with [b]the fat of the peace offerings and with [c]the libations for the burnt
offerings. Thus the service of the house
of the LORD was established *again*.
36 Then Hezekiah and all the people
rejoiced over what God had prepared
for the people,[5971] because the thing
came about suddenly.

🔑 **29:21** He did not want them to offer sacrifices upon any of the false altars, like those of Ahaz (II Chr. 28:24).

🔑 **29:25** This refers to I Chr. 15:16. This verse states a principle of inspiration: God is the primary Source who speaks through an agent, such as a prophet, a writer, a king, etc. (See Amos 3:7; Acts 1:16; Heb. 1:1).

🔑 **29:30** David and Asaph were the two principal authors of the Book of Psalms. David appointed Asaph for the regular praising of God with music (I Chr. 16:5,37).

🔑 **29:34** Neither the Levites nor the priests had received enough support from tithes and offerings for long periods of time in order to sustain their lives and their families.

All Israel Invited to the Passover

30 Now Hezekiah sent to all Israel
and Judah and wrote letters also
to Ephraim and Manasseh, that they
should come to the house of the LORD
at Jerusalem to [I]celebrate[6213] the Passover[6453] to the LORD God[430] of Israel.
2 For the king[4428] and his princes
and all the assembly in Jerusalem had
decided[3289] [a]to celebrate the Passover
in the second month,
3 since they could not celebrate it
[a]at that time, because the priests had
not consecrated themselves in sufficient
numbers, nor had the people[5971] been
gathered[622] to Jerusalem.
4 Thus the thing was right[3474] in
the sight of the king and [I]all the assembly.
5 So they established a decree to
circulate a [I]proclamation throughout all
Israel [a]from Beersheba even to Dan,
that they should come to celebrate the
Passover to the LORD God of Israel at
Jerusalem. For they had not celebrated[6213] *it* in great numbers as it was
[II]prescribed.
6 And [a]the [I]couriers went throughout all Israel and Judah with the letters
from the hand of the king and his princes,
even according to the command[4687] of
the king, saying, "O sons[1121] of Israel,
return to the LORD God of Abraham,
Isaac, and Israel, that He may return
to those of you who escaped[6413] *and*
are left from [b]the [II]hand of the kings[4428]
of Assyria.
7 "[a]And do not be like your fathers[1]
and your brothers,[251] who were unfaithful to the LORD God of their fathers,
so that [b]He made them a horror, as
you see.
8 "Now do not [a]stiffen your neck
like your fathers, but [I]yield to the LORD
and enter His sanctuary which He has
consecrated forever, and serve the
LORD your God, [b]that His burning anger
may turn away from you.
9 "For [a]if you return to the LORD,
your brothers and your sons *will find*
compassion[7356] before those who led
them captive,[7617] and will return to this
land.[776] [b]For the LORD your God is
gracious[2587] and compassionate, and will
not turn *His* face away from you if you
return to Him."
10 So the [I]couriers passed[5674] from
city to city through the country of
Ephraim and Manasseh, and as far as
Zebulun, but [a]they laughed them to
scorn, and mocked them.
11 Nevertheless [a]some men of
Asher, Manasseh, and Zebulun humbled
themselves and came to Jerusalem.
12 The [a]hand of God was also on
Judah to give them one heart to do[6213]
what the king and the princes commanded by the word[1697] of the LORD.

Passover Reinstituted

13 Now many people were gathered[622] at Jerusalem to celebrate the
Feast[2282] of Unleavened[4682] Bread [a]in
the second month, a very large assembly.
14 And they arose and removed the
altars[4196] which *were* in Jerusalem; they
also [a]removed all the incense altars[6999]
and [b]cast *them* into the brook Kidron.
15 Then [a]they slaughtered[7819] the
Passover *lambs* on the fourteenth of the
second month. And [b]the priests and Levites were ashamed of themselves and
consecrated themselves, and brought
burnt offerings to the house of the LORD.
16 And [a]they stood at their stations
after their custom, according to the
law[8451] of Moses the man of God; the
priests sprinkled the blood[1818] *which they*
received from the hand of the Levites.
17 For *there were* many in the assembly who had not consecrated

1 [I]Lit., *do*, so in vv. 2, 3, 5, 13, 21, 23
2 [a]Num. 9:10, 11; 2Chr. 30:13, 15
3 [a]2Chr. 29:17, 34
4 [I]Lit., *in the sight of all*
5 [I]Lit., *voice* [II]Lit., *written* [a]Judg. 20:1
6 [I]Lit., *runners* [II]Lit., *palm* [a]Esth. 8:14; Job 9:25; Jer. 51:31 [b]2Chr. 28:20
7 [a]Ezek. 20:13 [b]2Chr. 29:8
8 [I]Lit., *give a hand* [a]Ex. 32:9 [b]2Chr. 29:10
9 [a]Deut. 30:2 [b]Ex. 34:6, 7; Mic. 7:18
10 [I]Lit., *runners* [a]2Chr. 36:16
11 [a]2Chr. 30:18, 21, 25
12 [a]2Cor. 3:5; Phil. 2:13; Heb. 13:20, 21
13 [a]2Chr. 30:2
14 [a]2Chr. 28:24 [b]2Chr. 29:16
15 [a]2Chr. 30:2, 3 [b]2Chr. 29:34
16 [a]2Chr. 35:10, 15

30:2 This was not the first month, as prescribed in the Law of Moses (Ex. 12:18), because the temple was in the process of being cleansed (II Chr. 29:17). However, this exception was allowed by Num. 9:9-11.

30:11 Humility must precede access to God (cf. Isa. 57:15; Lk. 18:13,14).

themselves; therefore, [a]the Levites *were* over the slaughter of the Passover[6453] *lambs* for everyone who *was* unclean,3808,[2889] in order to consecrate *them* to the LORD.

18 For a multitude of the people, [a]*even* many from Ephraim and Manasseh, Issachar and Zebulun, had not purified[2891] themselves, [b]yet they ate the Passover [c]otherwise than [I]prescribed. For Hezekiah prayed[6419] for them, saying, "May the good[2896] LORD pardon[3722]

🔑 19 [a]everyone who prepares his heart to seek God, the LORD God of his fathers, though not according to the purification *rules* of the sanctuary."

20 So the LORD heard Hezekiah and [a]healed the people.

21 And the sons of Israel present in Jerusalem [a]celebrated[6213] the Feast of Unleavened Bread *for* seven days[3117] with great joy, and the Levites and the priests praised[1984] the LORD day[3117] after day with loud instruments to the LORD.

🔑 22 Then Hezekiah [a]spoke [I]encouragingly[3820] to all the Levites who showed good insight *in the things* of the LORD. So they ate for the appointed seven days, sacrificing peace offerings and [b]giving thanks[3034] to the LORD God of their fathers.

23 Then the whole assembly[6951] [a]decided to celebrate *the feast* another seven days, so they celebrated the seven days with joy.

24 For [a]Hezekiah king of Judah had contributed to the assembly 1,000 bulls and 7,000 sheep, and the princes had contributed to the assembly 1,000 bulls and 10,000 sheep; and [b]a large number of priests consecrated themselves.

25 And all the assembly of Judah rejoiced, with the priests and the Levites, and [a]all the assembly that came from Israel, both the sojourners who came from the land of Israel and those living in Judah.

26 So there was great joy in Jerusalem, because there was nothing like this in Jerusalem [a]since the days of Solomon the son of David, king of Israel.

27 Then [a]the Levitical priests arose and [b]blessed[1288] the people; and their voice was heard and their prayer[8605] came to [c]His holy dwelling place, to heaven.

Idols Are Destroyed

31 Now when all this was finished,[3615] all Israel who were present went out to the cities of Judah, [a]broke[7665] the pillars[4676] in pieces, cut down the [I]Asherim,[842] and pulled down the high places and the altars[4196] throughout all Judah and Benjamin, as well as in Ephraim and Manasseh, [II]until they had destroyed them all. Then all the sons[1121] of Israel returned to their cities, each to his possession.[272]

2 And Hezekiah appointed [a]the divisions of the priests and the Levites by their divisions, each according to his service, *both* the priests and the Levites, [b]for burnt offerings and for peace offerings, to minister and to give thanks and to praise[1984] in the gates of the camp of the LORD.

Reforms Continued

🔑 3 *He* also *appointed* [a]the king's[4428] portion of his goods for the burnt offerings, *namely,* for the morning and evening burnt offerings, and the burnt offerings for the sabbaths and for the new moons and for the fixed festivals,[4150] [b]as it is written in the law[8451] of the LORD.

17 [a]2Chr. 29:34
18 [I]Lit., *written* [a]2Chr. 30:11, 25 [b]Num. 9:10 [c]Ex. 12:43-49
19 [a]2Chr. 19:3
20 [a]James 5:16
21 [a]Ex. 12:15; 13:6
22 [I]Lit., *to the heart of* [a]2Chr. 32:6 [b]Ezra 10:11
23 [a]1Kin. 8:65
24 [a]2Chr. 35:7, 8 [b]2Chr. 29:34; 30:3
25 [a]2Chr. 30:11, 18
26 [a]2Chr. 7:8-10
27 [a]2Chr. 23:18 [b]Num. 6:23 [c]Deut. 26:15; Ps. 68:5
1 [I]I.e., wooden symbols of a female deity [II]Lit., *even to completion* [a]2Kin. 18:4
2 [a]1Chr. 24:1 [b]1Chr. 23:28-31
3 [a]2Chr. 35:7 [b]Num. 28:1-29:40

🔑 **30:19** This clearly stresses the spirit of law, not merely the letter of the law (cf. Mt. 23:23; Lk. 14:1-6).
🔑 **30:22** As specified in Ex. 12:16-18.
🔑 **31:3** See Num. 28 and 29.

🔑 4 Also he [I]commanded[559] the people[5971] who lived in Jerusalem to give
[a]the portion due to the priests and the
Levites, that they might devote[2388]
themselves to [b]the law of the LORD.
5 And as soon as the [I]order[1697]
spread, the sons of Israel provided in
abundance the first fruits[7225] of grain,
new wine, oil, honey, and of all the produce of the field;[7704] and they brought
in abundantly [a]the tithe of all.
6 And the sons of Israel and Judah
who lived in the cities of Judah, also
brought in the tithe of oxen and sheep,
and [a]the tithe of [I]sacred gifts which were
consecrated to the LORD their God,[430]
and placed *them* in heaps.
7 In the third month they began to
[I]make the heaps,[3245] and finished *them*
by the seventh month.
8 And when Hezekiah and the rulers came and saw the heaps, they
blessed[1288] the LORD and [a]His people
Israel.
9 Then Hezekiah questioned the
priests and the Levites concerning the
heaps.
10 And Azariah the chief[7218] priest
[a]of the house of Zadok said[559] to
[I]him, "[b]Since the contributions began to
be brought into the house of the LORD,
we have had enough to eat with plenty
left[3498] over, for the LORD has blessed
His people, and this great quantity is
left over."
11 Then Hezekiah commanded
them to prepare [a]rooms in the house
of the LORD, and they prepared *them*.
12 And they faithfully[530] brought in
the contributions and the tithes and the
consecrated[6944] things; and Conaniah
the Levite *was* the officer in charge
[a]of them and his brother[251] Shimei *was*
second.
13 And Jehiel, Azaziah, Nahath, Asahel, Jerimoth, Jozabad, Eliel, Ismachiah, Mahath, and Benaiah *were* overseers [I]under the authority of Conaniah
and Shimei his brother by the
appointment[4662] of King[4428] Hezekiah,
and [a]Azariah *was* the *chief* officer of the
house of God.
14 And Kore the son of Imnah the
Levite, the keeper[7778] of the eastern
gate, was over the freewill offerings of
God, to apportion the contributions[8641]
for the LORD and the most holy things.
15 And [I]under his authority *were*
[a]Eden, Miniamin, Jeshua, Shemaiah,
Amariah, and Shecaniah in [b]the cities
of the priests, to distribute faithfully *their*
portions to their brothers[251] by divisions,
whether great or small,
16 without regard to their genealogical enrollment, to the males from
[Ia]thirty years old and upward—everyone
who entered the house of the LORD
[b]for his daily[3117] obligations[1697]—for
their work in their duties according to
their divisions;
17 as well as the priests who were
enrolled genealogically according to
their fathers'[1] households, and the Levites [a]from twenty years old and upwards, by their duties *and* their divisions.
18 And the genealogical enrollment
included [I]all their little children, their
wives,[802] their sons, and their daughters, for the whole assembly, for they
consecrated themselves [II]faithfully in
holiness.
19 Also for the sons of Aaron the
priests *who were* in [a]the pasture lands[7704]
their cities, or in each and every city,
[b]*there were* men who were designated[5344]
by name to distribute portions to every
male among the priests and to everyone
genealogically enrolled among the Levites.
20 And thus Hezekiah did[6213]
throughout all Judah; and [a]he did what
was good,[2896] right, and true before the
LORD his God.

4 [I]Lit., *said to* [a]Num. 18:8 [b]Mal. 2:7
5 [I]Lit., *word* [a]Neh. 13:12
6 [I]Lit., *consecrated things* [a]Lev. 27:30; Deut. 14:28
7 [I]Lit., *found*
8 [a]Deut. 33:29; Ps. 33:12; 144:15
10 [I]Lit., *him, and he said* [a]1Chr. 6:8, 9 [b]Mal. 3:10
11 [a]1Kin. 6:5, 8
12 [a]2Chr. 35:9
13 [I]Lit., *from the hand of* [a]2Chr. 31:10
15 [I]Lit., *under his hand* [a]2Chr. 29:12 [b]Josh. 21:9-19
16 [I]Heb., *three* [a]1Chr. 23:3 [b]Ezra 3:4
17 [a]1Chr. 23:24
18 [I]Lit., *with all* [II]Lit., *in their faithfulness*
19 [a]Lev. 25:34; Num. 35:2-5 [b]2Chr. 31:12-15
20 [a]2Kin. 20:3; 22:2

🔑 **31:4** The priests and the Levites depended on the gifts of the people of their livelihood (Num. 18:12,21,24). Therefore, in times of backsliding, the priests and the Levites were tempted to use other means to make a living, e.g., Judg. 17:10; 18:19. It was essential to restore proper tithing for a consecrated priesthood.

21 And every work which he began
in the service of the house of God in
law and in commandment,[4687] seeking
his God, he did with all his heart and
[a]prospered.

Sennacherib Invades Judah

32 After these [I]acts of faithfulness [a]Sennacherib king[4428] of Assyria came and invaded Judah and besieged the fortified cities, and [II]thought
to break into them for himself.
2 Now when Hezekiah saw that Sennacherib had come, and that [I]he intended
to make war on Jerusalem,
3 he decided[3289] with his officers and
his warriors to cut off the *supply of* water
from the springs which *were* outside the
city, and they helped him.
4 So many people[5971] assembled[6908]
[a]and stopped up all the springs and
[b]the stream which flowed [I]through the
region,[776] saying, "Why should the
kings[4428] of Assyria come and find abundant water?"
5 And he took courage and [a]rebuilt
all the wall that had been broken down,
and [I]erected towers on it, and *built*
[b]another outside wall, and strengthened
the [c]Millo *in* the city of David, and made
weapons and shields in great number.
6 And he appointed military officers[8269] over the people, and gathered them to him in the square at the
city gate, and [a]spoke [I]encouragingly[3824]
to them, saying,
7 "[a]Be strong and courageous, do
not fear[3372] or be dismayed[2865] because
of the king of Assyria, nor because of
all the multitude which is with him;
[b]for the one with us is greater than the
one with him.
8 "With him is *only* [a]an arm of
flesh,[1320] but [b]with us is the LORD our
God[430] to help us and to fight our battles." And the people relied on the
words[1697] of Hezekiah king of Judah.

Sennacherib Undermines Hezekiah

9 After this [a]Sennacherib king of Assyria sent his servants to Jerusalem
while he *was* [I]besieging Lachish with
all his forces[4475] with him, against Hezekiah king of Judah and against all Judah
who *were* at Jerusalem, saying,
10 "Thus says Sennacherib king of
Assyria, 'On what are you trusting that
you are remaining in Jerusalem under
siege?
11 'Is not Hezekiah misleading you
to give yourselves over to die[4191] by
hunger and by thirst, saying, "The LORD
our God will deliver[5337] us from the
[I]hand of the king of Assyria"?
12 '[a]Has not the same Hezekiah
taken away His high places and His
altars,[4196] and said[559] to Judah and [I]Je-
rusalem, "You shall worship[7812] before one altar,[4196] and on it you shall
[II]burn incense"?[6999]
13 'Do you not know[3045] what I and
my fathers[1] have done[6213] to all the peoples of the lands?[776] [a]Were the gods[430]
of the nations[1471] of the lands able at
all[3605] to deliver their land from my hand?
14 '[a]Who *was there* among all the
gods of those nations which my fathers
utterly destroyed[2763] who could deliver
his people out of my hand, that your
God should be able to deliver you from
my hand?
15 'Now therefore, do not let Hezekiah deceive you or mislead you like
this, and do not believe[539] him, for
[a]no god[433] of any nation[1471] or kingdom[4467] was able to deliver his people
from my hand or from the hand of

21 [a]Deut. 29:9; Prov. 3:9, 10

1 [I]Lit., *things and this faithfulness* [II]Lit., *said* [a]2Kin. 18:13-19, 37; Is. 36:1-37:38

2 [I]Lit., *his face for war against*

4 [I]Lit., *in the midst of the land* [a]2Kin. 20:20 [b]2Chr. 32:30

5 [I]Lit., *raised on the towers* [a]2Chr. 25:23 [b]2Kin. 25:4 [c]1Kin. 9:24

6 [I]Lit., *upon their hearts* [a]2Chr. 30:22

7 [a]1Chr. 22:13 [b]2Kin. 6:16

8 [a]Jer. 17:5 [b]2Chr. 20:17

9 [I]Lit., *against* [a]2Kin. 18:17

11 [I]Lit., *palm*

12 [I]Lit., *Jerusalem, saying,* [II]Lit., *offer up in smoke* [a]2Chr. 31:1

13 [a]2Kin. 18:33-35

14 [a]Is. 10:9-11

15 [a]Ex. 5:2; Is. 36:18-20; Dan. 3:15

32:1 The siege of Sennacherib and Hezekiah's sickness and pride are mentioned in detail in II Kgs. 18—20 and Isa. 36—39. Much of it is verbatim.

32:1-19 See II Kgs. 18:13-37; Isa. 36:1-22.

32:5 Millo was a particular stronghold in Jerusalem which was used by David (II Sam. 5:9) and Solomon (I Kgs. 11:27), and it was apparently part of the old Jebusite fortress (II Sam. 5:7).

32:7 See II Kgs. 6:16.

my fathers. How much less shall your
God deliver you from my hand?' "
16 And his servants spoke further
against the LORD God and against His
servant Hezekiah.
17 He also wrote letters[5612] to insult[2778] the LORD God of Israel, and to
speak against Him, saying, "[a]As the
gods of the nations of the lands [I]have
not delivered[5337] their people from my
hand, so the God of Hezekiah shall not
deliver His people from my hand."
18 And [a]they called[7121] this out with
a loud voice in the language of Judah
to the people of Jerusalem who were
on the wall, to frighten[3372] and terrify
them, so that they might take the city.
19 And they spoke [I]of the God of
Jerusalem as of [a]the gods of the peoples
of the earth,[776] the work of men's hands.

Hezekiah's Prayer Is Answered

🔑 **20** But King Hezekiah and Isaiah
the prophet, the son of Amoz, prayed[6419]
about this and cried[2199] out to heaven.
21 And the LORD sent an angel[4397]
who destroyed every mighty warrior,
commander and officer in the camp of
the king of Assyria. So he returned
[I]in shame to his own land. And when
he had entered the temple of his god,
some of his own children killed him there
with the sword.
22 So the LORD [a]saved Hezekiah and
the inhabitants of Jerusalem from the
hand of Sennacherib the king of Assyria,
and from the hand of all *others,* and
[I]guided them on every side.
23 And [a]many were bringing
gifts[4503] to the LORD at Jerusalem and
choice presents to Hezekiah king of Judah, so that [b]he was exalted in the sight
of all nations thereafter.
🔑 **24** [a]In those days[3117] Hezekiah became [I]mortally[4191] ill; and he prayed to
the LORD, and [II]the LORD spoke to him
and gave him a sign.
25 But Hezekiah gave no return for
the benefit [I]he received, [a]because his
heart was [II]proud; [b]therefore wrath[7110]
came on him and on Judah and Jerusalem.
26 However, [a]Hezekiah [I]humbled
the pride of his heart, both he and the
inhabitants of Jerusalem, so that the
wrath of the LORD did not come on them
in the days of Hezekiah.
🔑 **27** Now Hezekiah had immense
riches and honor; and he made for himself treasuries for silver, gold, precious
stones, spices, shields and all kinds of
valuable articles,
28 storehouses also for the produce
of grain, wine and oil, pens for all kinds
of cattle and [I]sheepfolds for the flocks.
29 And he made cities for himself,
and acquired flocks and herds in abundance; for [a]God had given him very great
[I]wealth.
🔑 30 It was Hezekiah who [a]stopped
the upper[5945] outlet of the waters of
[b]Gihon and directed them to the west
side of the city of David. And Hezekiah
prospered in all that he did.
31 And even *in the matter of*
[a]the envoys[3887] of the rulers of Babylon,
who sent to him to inquire of [b]the wonder
that had happened in the land, God
left[5800] him *alone only* [c]to test him, that
He might know all that was in his heart.
🔑 **32** Now the rest of the acts[1697] of

17 [I]Lit., *who have* [a]2Chr. 32:14
18 [a]2Kin. 18:28
19 [I]Lit., *to* [a]Ps. 115:4-8
21 [I]Lit., *in shame of face*
22 [I]Another reading is *gave them rest* [a]Is. 31:5
23 [a]2Sam. 8:10 [b]2Chr. 1:1
24 [I]Lit., *sick to the point of death* [II]Lit., *He* [a]2Kin. 20:1-11; Is. 38:1-8
25 [I]Lit., *to him* [II]Lit., *high* [a]2Chr. 26:16; 32:31 [b]2Chr. 24:18
26 [I]Lit., *humbled himself in* [a]Jer. 26:18, 19
28 [I]So ancient versions; Heb., *flocks for the sheepfolds*
29 [I]Lit., *possessions, property* [a]1Chr. 29:12
30 [a]2Kin. 20:20 [b]1Kin. 1:33
31 [a]2Kin. 20:12; Is. 39:1 [b]2Chr. 32:24; Is. 38:7, 8 [c]Deut. 8:16

🔑 **32:20-23** See II Kgs. 19:1-37; Isa. 37:1-38. This is a practical example of how righteousness exalts a nation (Prov. 14:34).
🔑 **32:24** The "sign" refers to the sundial. See Isa. 38:7,8; II Kgs. 20:8-11.
🔑 **32:24-26** See II Kgs. 20:1-11; Isa. 38:1-22.
🔑 **32:27-31** See II Kgs. 20:12-19; Isa. 39:1-8.
🔑 **32:30** This and the conduit of II Kgs. 20:20 refer to the remarkable tunnel which connects the Virgin's Well with the Pool of Siloam. Archeological discoveries show that the Siloam Inscription, on the wall of the tunnel, tells the story of how the boring was accomplished (in a pre-engineering age)!
🔑 **32:32,33** See II Kgs. 20:20,21. The portion of Isaiah which is being referred to was in the "Book of the Kings of Judah and Israel" (II Chr. 16:11) which is now lost.

Hezekiah and his deeds[2617] of devotion,
behold, they are written in the vision[2377]
of Isaiah the prophet, the son of Amoz,
in the Book[5612] of the Kings of Judah
and Israel.
33 So Hezekiah slept with his fathers, and they buried[6912] him in the
[I]upper section of the tombs[6913] of the
sons of David; and all Judah and the
inhabitants of Jerusalem [a]honored[6213]
him at his death. And his son Manasseh
became king in his place.

Manasseh Succeeds Hezekiah in Judah

33 ⊶ [a]Manasseh was twelve years
old when he became king, and
he reigned fifty-five years in Jerusalem.
2 And [a]he did[6213] evil[7451] in the sight
of the LORD according to the abominations[8441] of the nations whom the
LORD dispossessed[3423] before the
sons[1121] of Israel.
⊶ 3 For [a]he rebuilt the high places
which Hezekiah his father had broken
down; [b]he also erected altars[4196] for the
Baals and made [I]Asherim,[842] and
worshiped[7812] all the host of heaven and
served them.
⊶ 4 And [a]he built altars in the house
of the LORD of which the LORD had said,
"My name shall be [b]in Jerusalem forever."
5 For he built altars for all the host
of heaven in [a]the two courts of the house
of the LORD.
6 And [a]he made his sons pass
through the fire in the valley of Ben-
hinnom; and he practiced witchcraft,
used divination,[5172] practiced sorcery,
and [b]dealt[6213] with mediums[3049] and spiritists. He did much evil in the sight of
the LORD, provoking Him *to anger.*
⊶ 7 Then he put [a]the carved image
of the idol[5566] which he had made in the
house of God,[430] of which God had said
to David and to Solomon his son, "[b]In
this house and in Jerusalem, which I
have chosen from all the tribes of Israel,
I will put My name forever;
⊶ 8 and I will not again remove the
foot of Israel from the land[127] [a]which I
have appointed for your fathers,[1] if only
they will observe to do[6213] all that I have
commanded[6680] them according to all the
law,[8451] the statutes, and the ordinances
given through Moses."
9 Thus Manasseh misled[8582] Judah
and the inhabitants of Jerusalem to do
more evil[7451] than the nations whom the
LORD destroyed[8045] before the sons[1121]
of Israel.

Manasseh's Idolatry Rebuked

10 And the LORD spoke to Manasseh and his people,[5971] but [a]they paid
no attention.
11 [a]Therefore the LORD brought the
commanders[8269] of the army of the
king[4428] of Assyria against them, and
they captured Manasseh with [I]hooks,
[b]bound him with bronze *chains,* and took
him to Babylon.
12 And when [a]he was in distress,
he entreated the LORD his God and
[b]humbled himself greatly before the God
of his fathers.
13 When he prayed[6419] to Him,
[a]He was moved[6279] by his entreaty and
heard his supplication, and brought him
again to Jerusalem to his kingdom.[4438]
Then Manasseh [b]knew[3045] that the LORD
was God.
14 Now after this he built the outer
wall of the city of David on the west
side of [a]Gihon, in the valley, even to
the entrance of the [b]Fish[1709] Gate; and
he encircled the [c]Ophel *with it* and made
it very high. Then he put army com-

---

33 [I]Or, *ascent to* [a]Ps. 112:6; Prov. 10:7
1 [a]2Kin. 21:1-9
2 [a]2Chr. 28:3; Jer. 15:4
3 [I]I.e., wooden symbols of a female deity [a]2Chr. 31:1 [b]Deut. 16:21; 2Kin. 23:5, 6
4 [a]2Chr. 28:24 [b]2Sam. 7:13; 2Chr. 7:16
5 [a]2Chr. 4:9
6 [a]2Chr. 28:3 [b]Lev. 19:31; 20:27
7 [a]2Chr. 33:15 [b]1Kin. 9:3-5; 2Chr. 7:16; 33:4
8 [a]2Sam. 7:10
10 [a]Neh. 9:29; Jer. 25:4
11 [I]I.e., thongs put through the nose [a]Deut. 28:36 [b]2Chr. 36:6
12 [a]Ps. 118:5; 120:1; 130:1, 2 [b]2Chr. 32:26
13 [a]1Chr. 5:20; Ezra 8:23 [b]Dan. 4:32
14 [a]1Kin. 1:33 [b]Neh. 3:3 [c]2Chr. 27:3

⊶ **33:1-25** See II Kgs. 21:1-26.
⊶ **33:3** Worshiping the stars was expressly forbidden in Deut. 4:19; 17:3.
⊶ **33:4** See II Chr. 6:6.
⊶ **33:7** See II Chr. 7:16.
⊶ **33:8** See II Sam. 7:10.

manders in all the fortified cities of Judah.

15 He also [a]removed the foreign gods[430] and the idol from the house of the LORD, as well as all the altars which he had built on the mountain of the house of the LORD and in Jerusalem, and he threw *them* outside the city.

16 And he set up the altar[4196] of the LORD and sacrificed [a]peace offerings and thank offerings on it; and he ordered[559] Judah to serve the LORD God of Israel.

🔑17 Nevertheless [a]the people still sacrificed in the high places, *although* only to the LORD their God.

18 Now the rest of the acts[1697] of Manasseh even [a]his prayer[8605] to his God, and the words[1697] of [b]the seers who spoke to him in the name of the LORD God of Israel, behold, they are among the records of the kings[4428] of [c]Israel.

19 His prayer also and [a]*how God* was entreated by him, and all his sin, his unfaithfulness, and [b]the sites on which he built high places and erected the Asherim and the carved images, before he humbled himself, behold, they are written in the records of the [1]Hozai.

20 So Manasseh slept with his fathers, and they buried[6912] him in his own house. And Amon his son became king in his place.

Amon Becomes King in Judah

21 [a]Amon *was* twenty-two years old when he became king, and he reigned two years in Jerusalem.

22 And he did evil in the sight of the LORD as Manasseh his father [a]had done, and Amon sacrificed to all [b]the carved images which his father[1] Manasseh had made, and he served them.

23 Moreover, he did not humble himself before the LORD [a]as his father Manasseh had [1]done, but Amon multiplied guilt.

24 Finally [a]his servants conspired against him and put him to death in his own house.

25 But the people of the land[776] [1]killed all the conspirators against King[4428] Amon, and the people of the land made Josiah his son king in his place.

Josiah Succeeds Amon in Judah

34 🔑[a]Josiah *was* eight years old when he became king, and he reigned thirty-one years in Jerusalem.

2 And [a]he did[6213] right in the sight of the LORD, and walked in the ways[1870] of his father[1] David and did not turn[5493] aside to the right or to the left.

🔑3 For in the eighth year of his reign while he was still a youth, he began to [a]seek the God[430] of his father David; and in the twelfth year he began [b]to purge Judah and Jerusalem of the high places, the Asherim,[842] the carved images, and the molten images.

4 And they tore[7665] down the altars[4196] of the Baals in his presence, and [a]the incense altars[2553] high above them he chopped down; also the Asherim, the carved images,[2553] and the molten images he broke in pieces and [b]ground to powder and scattered[2236] *it* on the graves[6913] of those who had sacrificed to them.

🔑5 Then [a]he burned[8313] the bones[6101] of the priests on their altars, and purged[2891] Judah and Jerusalem.

6 And [a]in the cities of Manasseh, Ephraim, Simeon, even as far as Naphtali, in their surrounding ruins,

7 he also tore down the altars and [a]beat[3807] the Asherim and the carved images into powder, and chopped down all the incense altars[2553] throughout the land of Israel. Then he returned to Jerusalem.

15 [a]2Chr. 33:3-7
16 [a]Lev. 7:11-18
17 [a]2Chr. 32:12
18 [a]2Chr. 33:12, 13 [b]2Chr. 33:10 [c]2Chr. 21:2
19 [1]Gr. reads *seers* [a]2Chr. 33:13 [b]2Chr. 33:3
21 [a]2Kin. 21:19-24
22 [a]2Chr. 33:2-7 [b]2Chr. 34:3, 4
23 [1]Lit., *humbled himself* [a]2Chr. 33:12, 19
24 [a]2Chr. 25:27
25 [1]Lit., *smote*
1 [a]2Kin. 22:1, 2; Jer. 1:2; 3:6
2 [a]2Chr. 29:2
3 [a]2Chr. 15:2; Prov. 8:17 [b]1Kin. 13:2; 2Chr. 33:22
4 [a]2Kin. 23:4, 5, 11 [b]Ex. 32:20
5 [a]1Kin. 13:2; 2Kin. 23:20
6 [a]2Kin. 23:15, 19
7 [a]2Chr. 31:1

🔑**33:17** This was a pitfall of other kings, e.g., Asa (I Kgs. 15:14) and even Solomon (I Kgs. 3:3).
🔑**34:1,2** See II Kgs. 22:1,2.
🔑**34:3-7** See II Kgs. 23:4-20.
🔑**34:5** So was fulfilled the prophecy to Jeroboam, the founder of the false altars (I Kgs. 13:2).

Josiah Repairs the Temple

8 [a]Now in the eighteenth year of his reign, when he had purged the land and the house, he sent Shaphan the son of Azaliah, and Maaseiah [b]an official[2587] of the city, and Joah the son of Joahaz the recorder, to repair the house of the LORD his God.

9 And they came to [a]Hilkiah the high priest and delivered the money that was brought into the house of God, which the Levites, the [I]doorkeepers,[8104] had collected[622] [II]from [b]Manasseh and Ephraim, and from all the remnant of Israel, and from all Judah and Benjamin and the inhabitants of Jerusalem.

10 Then they gave *it* into the hands of the workmen who had the oversight of the house of the LORD, and the workmen who were working in the house of the LORD [I]used it to restore and repair[2388] the house.

11 They in turn gave *it* to the carpenters[2796] and to the builders[1129] to buy quarried[4274] stone and timber for couplings and to make beams for the houses [a]which the kings[4428] of Judah had let go to ruin.[7843]

12 And [a]the men did the work[4399] faithfully[530] with foremen over them to supervise: Jahath and Obadiah, the Levites of the sons of Merari, Zechariah and Meshullam of the sons of the Kohathites, and [b]the Levites, all who were skillful with musical instruments.

13 *They were* also over [a]the burden bearers, and supervised all the workmen from job to job; and *some* of the Levites *were* scribes and officials and gatekeepers.[7778]

Hilkiah Discovers Lost Book of the Law

14 When they were bringing out the money which had been brought into the house of the LORD, [a]Hilkiah the priest found the book[5612] of the law[8451] of the LORD *given* by Moses.

15 And Hilkiah responded and said to Shaphan the scribe, "I have found the book of the law in the house of the LORD." And Hilkiah gave the book to Shaphan.

16 Then Shaphan brought the book to the king[4428] and [I]reported further word[1697] to the king, saying, "Everything that was [II]entrusted to your servants they are doing.[6213]

17 "They have also emptied out the money which was found in the house of the LORD, and have delivered it into the hands of the supervisors and the workmen."

18 Moreover, Shaphan the scribe told the king saying, "Hilkiah the priest gave me a book." And Shaphan read from it in the presence of the king.

19 And it came about when the king heard [a]the words[1697] of the law that [b]he tore his clothes.

20 Then the king commanded[6680] Hilkiah, Ahikam the son of Shaphan, [I]Abdon the son of Micah, Shaphan the scribe, and Asaiah the king's[4428] servant, saying,

21 "Go, inquire of the LORD for me and for those who are left[7604] in Israel and in Judah, concerning the words of the book which has been found; for [a]great is the wrath[2524] of the LORD which is poured out on us because our fathers[1] have not observed the word of the LORD, to do according to all that is written in this book."

Huldah, the Prophetess, Speaks

22 So Hilkiah and *those* whom the king [I]had told went to Huldah the prophetess, the wife[802] of Shallum the son of [II]Tokhath, the son of Hasrah, the keeper[8104] of the wardrobe (now she lived in Jerusalem in the Second Quar-

8 [a]2Kin. 22:3-20 [b]2Chr. 18:25
9 [I]Lit., *guardians of the threshold* [II]Lit., *from the hand of* [a]2Chr. 35:8 [b]2Chr. 30:10, 18
10 [I]Lit., *gave*
11 [a]2Chr. 33:4-7
12 [a]2Kin. 12:15 [b]1Chr. 25:1
13 [a]Neh. 4:10
14 [a]2Chr. 34:9
16 [I]Lit., *returned* [II]Lit., *given into the hand of*
19 [a]Deut. 28:3-68 [b]Josh. 7:6
20 [I]In 2Kin. 22:12, *Achbor, son of Micaiah*
21 [a]2Chr. 29:8
22 [I]So with Gr. [II]In 2Kin. 22:14 *Tikvah, son of Harhas*

34:8-33 See II Kgs. 22:3—23:3.
34:19 Rom. 3:20 says that the knowledge of sin comes through the law. It was probably Deut. 28—30 which brough about an immediate change in Josiah's attitude and subsequent reforms.

ter); and they spoke to her regarding
this.
23 And she said[559] to them, "Thus
says the LORD, the God of Israel, 'Tell
the man who sent you to Me,
24 thus says the LORD, "Behold,
[a]I am bringing evil[7451] on this place and
on its inhabitants, *even* all [b]the curses[423]
written in the book which they have read
in the presence of the king of Judah.
25 "[a]Because they have forsaken[5800] Me and have burned incense[6999] to other gods,[430] that they
might provoke Me to anger[3707] with all
the works of their hands, therefore My
wrath will be poured out on this place,
and it shall not be quenched." '
26 "But to the king of Judah who
sent you to inquire of the LORD, thus
you will say to him, 'Thus says the LORD
God of Israel *regarding* the words which
you have heard,
27 "[a]Because your heart was tender
and you humbled yourself before God,
when you heard His words against this
place and against its inhabitants, and *because* you humbled yourself before Me,
tore[7167] your clothes, and wept before
Me, I truly have heard you," declares
the LORD.
28 "Behold, I will gather[622] you to
your fathers and you shall be gathered
to your grave[6913] in peace,[7965] so your
eyes shall not see all the evil which I
will bring on this place and on its inhabitants." ' " And they brought back word
to the king.
29 [a]Then the king sent and gathered all the elders[2205] of Judah and Jerusalem.
30 And the king went up to the
house of the LORD and [a]all the men of
Judah, the inhabitants of Jerusalem, the
priests, the Levites, and all the people,[5971] from the greatest to the least;
and he read in their hearing[241] all the
words of the book of the covenant[1285]
which was found in the house of the
LORD.

Josiah's Good Reign

31 Then the king [a]stood in his place
and [b]made a covenant before the LORD
to walk after the LORD, and to keep[8104]
His commandments[4687] and His testimonies and His statutes with all his heart
and with all his soul, to perform[6213] the
words of the covenant written in this
book.
32 Moreover, he made all who were
present in Jerusalem and Benjamin to
stand *with him*. So the inhabitants of
Jerusalem did according to the covenant
of God, the God of their fathers.
33 And Josiah [a]removed all the
abominations[8441] from all the lands[776] belonging to the sons[1121] of Israel, and
made all who were present in Israel to
serve the LORD their God. Throughout
his [1]lifetime[3117] they did not turn[5493] from
following the LORD God of their fathers.

The Passover Observed Again

35 Then Josiah [a]celebrated[6213]
the Passover[6453] to the LORD in
Jerusalem, and [b]they slaughtered[7819] the
Passover *animals* on the fourteenth *day*
of the first[7223] month.
2 And he set the priests in their offices and [a]encouraged[2388] them in the
service of the house of the LORD.
3 He also said to [a]the Levites who

24 [a]2Chr. 36:14-20 [b]Deut. 28:15-68
25 [a]2Chr. 33:3
27 [a]2Kin. 22:19; 2Chr. 12:7; 32:26
29 [a]2Kin. 23:1-3
30 [a]Neh. 8:1-3
31 [a]2Kin. 11:14; 23:3; 2Chr. 30:16 [b]2Chr. 23:16; 29:10
33 [1]Lit., *days* [a]2Chr. 34:3-7
1 [a]2Kin. 23:21 [b]Ex. 12:6; Num. 9:3
2 [a]2Chr. 29:11
3 [a]2Chr. 17:8, 9; Neh. 8:7

34:25 This type of language was often used to refer to idols with contempt (cf. Deut. 4:28; II Chr. 32:19).
35:1-19 See II Kgs. 23:21-23.
35:3 No mention is made of the ark after this time, when Josiah ordered it to be restored to the temple. It may have been carried away by Nebuchadnezzar along with the other sacred articles, when he plundered the temple. Since no reference is made to the ark by Ezra, Nehemiah, or even Josephus after the captivity, it is believed that there was no ark in the second temple and that the Holy of Holies stood empty. There is a Jewish tradition that, before Nebuchadnezzar plundered the temple, the priests hid the ark and that its hiding place will be revealed by the Messiah at His coming. His knowledge of it will, they declare, be proof of His claims.

taught all Israel *and* who were holy to the LORD, "Put the holy ark[727] in the house which Solomon the son of David king[4428] of Israel built; [b]it will be a burden[4853] on *your* shoulders no longer. Now serve the LORD your God[430] and His people[5971] Israel.

4 "And [a]prepare *yourselves* by your fathers'[1] households in your divisions, according to the writing of David king of Israel and [b]according to the writing of his son Solomon.

5 "Moreover, [a]stand in the holy place according to the sections[6391] of the fathers' households of your brethren[251] the [I]lay people, and according to the Levites, by division of a father's household.

6 "Now [a]slaughter[7819] the Passover *animals*, [b]sanctify yourselves, and prepare for your brethren to do[6213] according to the word[1697] of the LORD by Moses."

7 And Josiah contributed to the lay people, to all who were present, flocks of lambs and kids, all for the Passover offerings, numbering 30,000 plus 3,000 bulls; these were from the king's[4428] possessions.

8 His officers also contributed a freewill[5068] offering to the people, the priests, and the Levites. Hilkiah and Zechariah and Jehiel, [a]the officials of the house of God, gave to the priests for the Passover offerings 2,600 *from the flocks* and 300 bulls.

9 [a]Conaniah also, and Shemaiah and Nethanel, his brothers, and Hashabiah and Jeiel and Jozabad, the officers[5387] of the Levites, contributed to the Levites for the Passover offerings 5,000 *from the flocks* and 500 bulls.

10 So the service was prepared, and [a]the priests stood at their stations and the Levites by their divisions according to the king's command.[4687]

11 And [I][a]they slaughtered the Passover *animals*, and while [b]the priests sprinkled [II]the blood[1818] *received* from their hand, [c]the Levites skinned[6584] *them*.

12 Then they removed the burnt offerings that *they* might give them to the sections[4653] of the fathers' households of the lay people to present to the LORD, as it is written in the book[5612] of Moses. *They did* this also with the bulls.

13 So [a]they roasted the Passover *animals* on the fire according to the ordinance, and they boiled[1310] [b]the holy things in pots, in kettles, in pans, and carried *them* speedily to all the lay people.

14 And afterwards they prepared for themselves and for the priests, because the priests, the sons of Aaron, *were* offering the burnt offerings and the fat until night;[3915] therefore the Levites prepared for themselves and for the priests, the sons of Aaron.

15 The singers, the sons of Asaph, *were* also at their stations [a]according to the command of David, Asaph, Heman, and Jeduthun the king's seer; and [b]the gatekeepers[7778] at each gate did not have to depart[5493] from their service, because the Levites their brethren prepared for them.

16 So all the service of the LORD was prepared on that day[3117] to celebrate[6213] the Passover, and to offer burnt offerings on the altar[4196] of the LORD according to the command of King Josiah.

17 Thus [a]the sons[1121] of Israel who were present celebrated the Passover at that time, and the Feast[2282] of Unleavened[4682] Bread seven days.[3117]

18 And [a]there had not been celebrated a Passover like it in Israel since the days of Samuel the prophet; nor had any of the kings[4428] of Israel celebrated such a Passover as Josiah did with the priests, the Levites, all Judah and Israel who were present, and the inhabitants of Jerusalem.

19 In the eighteenth year of Josiah's reign this Passover was celebrated.

3 [b]1Chr. 23:26
4 [a]1Chr. 9:10-13 [b]2Chr. 8:14
5 [I]Lit., *sons of the people*, and so throughout the ch. [a]Ezra 6:18
6 [a]2Chr. 35:1 [b]2Chr. 29:5
8 [a]2Chr. 31:13
9 [a]2Chr. 31:12
10 [a]2Chr. 35:5
11 [I]I.e., the Levites [II]So with Gr. [a]2Chr. 35:1, 6 [b]2Chr. 29:22 [c]2Chr. 29:34
13 [a]Ex. 12:8, 9 [b]Lev. 6:28
15 [a]1Chr. 25:1 [b]1Chr. 26:12-19
17 [a]Ex. 12:1-20; 2Chr. 30:21
18 [a]2Kin. 23:21; 2Chr. 30:5

35:4 The list is partially preserved in I Chr. 23—26.
35:12 Compare Hezekiah's Passover (II Chr. 30:15-18).

Josiah Dies in Battle

🔑 **20** [a]After all this, when Josiah had set the [1]temple in order, Neco king of Egypt came up to make war at [b]Carchemish on the Euphrates, and Josiah went out to engage him.

🔑 21 But [1]Neco sent messengers[4397] to him, saying, "[a]What have we to do with each other, O King of Judah? *I am* not *coming* against you today but against the house with which I am at war, and God has ordered[559] me to hurry. Stop for your own sake from *interfering with* God who is with me, that He may not destroy[7843] you."

22 However, Josiah would not turn [1]away from him, but [a]disguised himself in order to make war with him; nor did he listen to the words[1697] of Neco [b]from the mouth of God, but came to make war on the plain of [c]Megiddo.

23 And the archers[3384] shot King Josiah, and the king said to his servants, "Take me away, for I am badly wounded."

24 So his servants took him out of the chariot and carried him in the second chariot which he had, and brought him to Jerusalem [1]where he died and was buried[6912] in the tombs[6913] of his fathers. [a]And all Judah and Jerusalem mourned for Josiah.

25 Then [a]Jeremiah chanted a lament for Josiah. And all the male and female[802] singers speak about Josiah in their lamentations to this day. And they made them an ordinance in Israel; behold, they are also written in the Lamentations.

26 Now the rest of the acts[1697] of Josiah and his deeds[2617] of devotion as written in the law[8451] of the LORD,

27 and his acts,[1697] first to last, behold, they are written in the Book of the Kings of Israel and Judah.

Jehoahaz, Jehoiakim, then Jehoiachin Rule

36 🔑 [a]Then the people[5971] of the land[776] took [1b]Joahaz the son of Josiah, and made him king[4427] in place of his father[1] in Jerusalem.

2 Joahaz was twenty-three years old when he became king, and he reigned three months in Jerusalem.

3 Then the king[4428] of Egypt deposed him at Jerusalem, and imposed[6064] on the land a fine of one hundred talents of silver and one talent of gold.

4 And the king of Egypt made Eliakim his brother[251] king over Judah and Jerusalem, and changed his name to Jehoiakim. But [a]Neco took Joahaz his brother and brought him to Egypt.

🔑 5 [a]Jehoiakim was twenty-five years old when he became king, and he reigned eleven years in Jerusalem; and he did[6213] evil[7451] in the sight of the LORD his God.[430]

🔑 6 Nebuchadnezzar king of Babylon came up [a]against him and [b]bound him with bronze *chains* to take him to Babylon.

7 [a]Nebuchadnezzar also brought *some* of the articles of the house of the LORD to Babylon and put them in his temple at Babylon.

8 [a]Now the rest of the acts[1697] of Jehoiakim and [1]the abominations[8441] which he did, and what was found against him, behold, they are written in the Book[5612] of the Kings[4428] of Israel and Judah. And Jehoiachin his son became king in his place.

🔑 **9** [a]Jehoiachin was eight years old

---

20 [1]Lit., *house* [a]2Kin. 23:29, 30 [b]Is. 10:9; Jer. 46:2

21 [1]Lit., *he* [a]2Chr. 25:19

22 [1]Lit., *his face* [a]2Chr. 18:29 [b]2Chr. 35:21 [c]Judg. 5:19

24 [1]Lit., *and* [a]Zech. 12:11

25 [a]Jer. 22:10; Lam. 4:20

1 [1]I.e., short form of Jehoahaz [a]2Kin. 23:30-34 [b]Jer. 22:11

4 [a]Jer. 22:10-12

5 [a]2Kin. 23:36, 37; Jer. 22:13-19; 26:1; 35:1

6 [a]2Kin. 24:1; Jer. 25:1-9 [b]2Chr. 33:11

7 [a]2Kin. 24:13

8 [1]Lit., *his* [a]2Kin. 24:5

9 [a]2Kin. 24:8-17

🔑 **35:20-27** See II Kgs. 23:28-30.

🔑 **35:21** Pharaoh Neco was attempting to defeat Babylon who was the chief contender for world power following the decline of Assyrian supremacy.

🔑 **36:1-4** See II Kgs. 23:31-34.

🔑 **36:5-8** See II Kgs. 23:36—24:7.

🔑 **36:6** Neco was defeated at Carchemish by Nebuchadnezzar who took Daniel and other captives to Babylon as part of his occupation tactics.

🔑 **36:9,10** See II Kgs. 24:8-17. Many manuscripts read "eight years old," but "eighteen years old is given by several ancient manuscripts, and this agrees with II Kgs. 24:8.

when he became king, and he reigned
three months and ten days[3117] in Jerusalem, and he did evil in the sight of the
LORD.

Captivity in Babylon Begun

⊶10 And [a]at the turn of the year King
Nebuchadnezzar sent and brought him
to Babylon with the valuable articles of
the house of the LORD, and he made
his kinsman [b]Zedekiah king over Judah
and Jerusalem.

Zedekiah Rules in Judah

⊶11 [a]Zedekiah was twenty-one years
old when he became king, and he reigned
eleven years in Jerusalem.
12 And he did evil in the sight of
the LORD his God; [a]he did not humble
himself [b]before Jeremiah the prophet
[1]who spoke for the LORD.
13 And [a]he also rebelled against
King Nebuchadnezzar who had made
him swear *allegiance* by God. But
[b]he stiffened his neck and hardened his
heart against turning to the LORD God
of Israel.
14 Furthermore, all the officials[5387]
of the priests and the people were very
unfaithful *following* all the abominations
of the nations; and they defiled the house
of the LORD which He had sanctified in
Jerusalem.
⊶15 And the LORD, the God of their
fathers,[1] [a]sent *word* to them again and
again by His messengers, because He
had compassion on His people and on
His dwelling place;
16 but they *continually* [a]mocked the
messengers of God, [b]despised His
words[1697] and scoffed at His prophets,
[c]until the wrath[2534] of the LORD arose[5927]
against His people, until there was no
remedy.
⊶17 [a]Therefore He brought[5927] up
against them the king of the Chaldeans
who slew their young men with the
sword in the house of their sanctuary,
and had no compassion on young man
or virgin, old man or infirm; He gave
them all into his hand.
18 And [a]all the articles of the house
of God, great and small, and the treasures of the house of the LORD, and
the treasures of the king and of his officers, he brought *them* all to Babylon.
19 Then [a]they burned[8313] the house
of God, and broke down the wall of Jerusalem and burned all its fortified buildings[759] with fire, and destroyed[7843] all
its valuable articles.
20 And those who had escaped from
the sword he [a]carried away to Babylon;
and [b]they were servants to him and to
his sons until the rule of the kingdom[4438]
of Persia,
⊶21 [a]to fulfill the word[1697] of the LORD
by the mouth of Jeremiah, until [b]the
land had enjoyed its sabbaths. [c]All the
days of its desolation[8074] it kept sabbath [1][d]until seventy years were complete.

Cyrus Permits Return

⊶**22** [a]Now in the first year of Cyrus
king of Persia—in order to fulfill[3615] the
word of the LORD [b]by the mouth of Jere-

10 [a]2Sam. 11:1; Jer. 22:25; 24:1; 29:1; Ezek. 17:12 [b]Jer. 37:1

11 [a]2Kin. 24:18-20; Jer. 27:1; 28:1; 52:1

12 [1]Lit., *from the mouth of the LORD* [a]2Chr. 33:23 [b]Jer. 21:3-7

13 [a]Jer. 52:3; Ezek. 17:15 [b]2Chr. 30:8

15 [a]Jer. 7:13; 25:3

16 [a]2Chr. 30:10; Jer. 5:12, 13 [b]Prov. 1:24-32 [c]Ezra 5:12

17 [a]2Kin. 25:1-7; Jer. 21:1-10

18 [a]2Chr. 36:7, 10

19 [a]1Kin. 9:8; 2Kin. 25:9; Jer. 52:13

20 [a]2Kin. 25:11 [b]Jer. 27:7

21 [1]Lit., *to fulfill seventy years* [a]Jer. 29:10 [b]Lev. 26:34 [c]Lev. 25:4 [d]Jer. 25:11

22 [a]Ezra 1:1-3 [b]Jer. 25:12; 29:10

⊶ **36:10** Although the Hebrew text has "kinsman," it means "uncle," according to II Kgs. 24:17.

⊶ **36:11-16** See II Kgs. 24:18-20; Jer. 52:1-3.

⊶ **36:15** God tried to communicate to them early and late, and time and again. The phrase is used in Jer. 25:4 and Jer. 44:4. Jer. 35:15 summarizes the message.

⊶ **36:17-21** See II Kgs. 25:8-21; Jer. 39:8-10; 52:12-30.

⊶ **36:21** The cause of the Jews' captivity and exile by Babylon was spiritual rather than political. The forsaking of the Sabbatic years mentioned here is but one of their many provocations of the Lord. This is mentioned as a lesson coming to them from the Lord. What they would not do voluntarily was done when they were carried away and the land "rested" for seventy years. See Jer. 29:10.

⊶ **36:22** See Jer. 25:12.

⊶ **36:22,23** The last two verses are almost identical to the introductory verses of Ezra. See Ezra 1:1,2. Perhaps this means that Ezra was the author of the Books of Chronicles.

miah—the LORD [c]stirred up the spirit
of Cyrus king of Persia, so that he sent
a proclamation throughout his kingdom,
and also *put it* in writing, saying,
23 "Thus says Cyrus king of Persia,
'The LORD, the God of heaven, has given
me all the kingdoms[4467] of the earth,[776]
and He has appointed[6485] me to build
Him a house in Jerusalem, which is in
Judah. Whoever there is among you of
all His people, may the LORD his God
be with him, and let him go up!' "

22 [c]Is. 44:28

The Book of
EZRA

The Book of Ezra was formerly associated with the Book of Nehemiah. Both books were treated as one book. They give an account of the return of the Jewish exiles from Babylonia to Jerusalem. They tell of the restablishment of the temple, their worship, and national life in their original homeland. Ezra, whose name means "help," was a priest who led the people home. He wrote a very simply history and did not give much direct teaching. He made no effort to tell a continuous story. In fact, between Ezra 6 and Ezra 7 almost sixty years passed. One should read the contemporaneous Book of Esther to discover what was happening elsewhere during this time period. It would also be helpful to read the Books of Haggai, Zechariah, and Malachi, who lived and preached during this restoration age. The two prophets, Haggai and Zechariah, were closely connected with the first return of Zerubbabel in 536 B.C. God encouraged the Jews to complete His temple through these men despite much opposition. Actually, there were three groups which returned to Palestine. They were led respectively by Zerubbabel, Ezra, and Nehemiah. Ezra's group went in 457 B.C., taking four months for travel. It is not known whether any women or children made the trip. Nehemiah came later as governor in 444 B.C. The Books of Ezra, Nehemiah, and Esther cover about 100 years (536—432 B.C.). The main message of Ezra is: God uses whomever suits His purpose, whether Cyrus and Artaxerxes or Ezra, Zerubbabel, and Nehemiah. God empowered His chosen people to overcome all opposition, even against impossible odds.

Cyrus' Proclamation

1 🔑 [a]Now in the first year of Cyrus
king of Persia, in order to fulfill[3615]
the word[1697] of the LORD by the
mouth[6310] of Jeremiah, the LORD stirred
up the spirit[7307] of Cyrus king[4428] of Persia,
so that he [b]sent a proclamation[5674]
throughout all his kingdom,[4438] and also
put it in writing, saying,
2 "Thus says[559] Cyrus king of Persia,
'The LORD, the God[430] of heaven,[8064]
has given me all the kingdoms[4467] of the
earth,[776] and [a]He has appointed[6485] me
to build Him a house[1004] in Jerusalem,
which is in Judah.
3 'Whoever there is among you of
all His people,[5971] may his God be with
him! Let him go up to Jerusalem which
is in Judah, and rebuild the house of
the LORD, the God of Israel; [a]He is the
God who is in Jerusalem.
4 'And every survivor,[7604] at whatever
place he may [I]live,[1481] let the
men[582] of [II]that place support him with
silver and gold, with goods and cattle,
together with a freewill offering[5071] for
the house of God which is in Jerusalem.'"

Holy Vessels Restored

5 Then the heads[7218] of fathers'[1]
households of Judah and Benjamin and
the priests[3548] and the Levites arose,
[a]even everyone whose spirit God had
stirred to go up and rebuild the house
of the LORD which is in Jerusalem.
6 And all those about them [I][a]encouraged[2388]
them with articles of silver,
with gold, with goods, with cattle, and
with valuables, aside from all that was
given as a freewill[5068] offering.
7 [a]Also King Cyrus brought out the
articles of the house of the LORD,
[b]which Nebuchadnezzar had carried
away from Jerusalem and put in the
house of his gods;

1 [a]2Chr. 36:22; Jer. 25:12; 29:10 [b]Ezra 5:13
2 [a]Is. 44:28; 45:1, 12, 13
3 [a]1Kin. 8:23; 18:39; Is. 37:16; Dan. 6:26
4 [I]Or, *reside as an alien* [II]Lit., *his*
5 [a]Ezra 1:1, 2
6 [I]Lit., *strengthened their hands* [a]Neh. 6:9; Is. 35:3
7 [a]Ezra 5:14; 6:5 [b]2Kin. 24:13; 2Chr. 36:7

🔑 **1:1** "The first year of Cyrus" would have been 539 B.C. His reign in Persia began in 559 B.C. but he did not conquer Babylon until 539. His reign ended in 530 B.C.
🔑 **1:1-3** See II Chr. 36:22,23.

8 and Cyrus, king of Persia, had them brought out by the hand[3027] of Mithredath the treasurer, and he counted[5608] them out to [a]Sheshbazzar, the prince[5387] of Judah.
9 Now this *was* their number: 30 [a]gold dishes, 1,000 silver dishes, 29 [I]duplicates;
10 30 gold bowls,[3713] 410 silver bowls of a second *kind, and* 1,000 other articles.
11 All the articles of gold and silver *numbered* 5,400. Sheshbazzar brought them all up[5927] with the exiles[1473] who went up[5927] from Babylon to Jerusalem.

Number of Those Returning

2 [a]Now these are the [I]people[1121] of the province who came up[5927] out of the captivity[7628] of the exiles whom Nebuchadnezzar the king[4428] of Babylon had carried away[1540] to Babylon, and returned to Jerusalem and Judah, each[376] to his city.
2 [I]These came with Zerubbabel, Jeshua, Nehemiah, [II]Seraiah, [III]Reelaiah, Mordecai, Bilshan, [IV]Mispar, Bigvai, [V]Rehum, and Baanah.
The number of the men[582] of the people[5971] of Israel:
3 the sons of Parosh, 2,172;
4 the sons of Shephatiah, 372;
5 the sons of [a]Arah, 775;
6 the sons of [a]Pahath-moab of the sons of Jeshua *and* Joab, 2,812;
7 the sons of Elam, 1,254;
8 the sons of Zattu, 945;
9 the sons of Zaccai, 760;
10 the sons of [I]Bani, 642;
11 the sons of Bebai, 623;
12 the sons of Azgad, 1,222;
13 the sons of [a]Adonikam, 666;
14 the sons of Bigvai, 2,056;
15 the sons of Adin, 454;
16 the sons of Ater of Hezekiah, 98;
17 the sons of Bezai, 323;
18 the sons of [I]Jorah, 112;
19 the sons of Hashum, 223;
20 the sons of [I]Gibbar, 95;
21 the [I]men of [a]Bethlehem, 123;
22 the men of Netophah, 56;
23 the men of Anathoth, 128;
24 the sons of [I]Azmaveth, 42;
25 the sons of [I]Kiriath-arim, Chephirah, and Beeroth, 743;
26 the sons of [a]Ramah and Geba, 621;
27 the men of Michmas, 122;
28 the men of Bethel and Ai, 223;
29 the sons of Nebo, 52;
30 the sons of Magbish, 156;
31 the sons of the other Elam, 1,254;
32 the sons of Harim, 320;
33 the sons of Lod, Hadid, and Ono, 725;
34 the [I]men of [a]Jericho, 345;
35 the sons of Senaah, 3,630.

Priests Returning

36 [a]The priests:[3548] the sons of Jedaiah of the house[1004] of Jeshua, 973;
37 the sons of [a]Immer, 1,052;
38 [a]the sons of Pashhur, 1,247;
39 the sons of [a]Harim, 1,017.

Levites Returning

40 The Levites: the sons of Jeshua and Kadmiel, of the sons of [I]Hodaviah, 74.
41 The singers:[7891] the sons of Asaph, 128.
42 The sons of the gatekeepers:[7778] the sons of Shallum, the sons of Ater, the sons of Talmon, the sons of Akkub,

8 [a]Ezra 5:14
9 [I]Heb. obscure; other possible meanings are *knives, censers* [a]Ezra 8:27
1 [I]Lit., *sons* [a]2Kin. 24:14-16; 25:11; 2Chr. 36:20; Neh. 7:6-73
2 [I]Lit., *who* [II]In Neh. 7:7, *Azariah* [III]In Neh. 7:7, *Raamiah* [IV]In Neh. 7:7, *Mispereth* [V]In Neh. 7:7, *Nehum*
5 [a]Neh. 7:10
6 [a]Neh. 7:11
10 [I]In Neh. 7:15, *Binnui*
13 [a]Ezra 8:13
18 [I]In Neh. 7:24, *Hariph*
20 [I]In Neh. 7:25, *Gibeon*
21 [I]Lit., *sons* [a]Gen. 35:19; Matt. 2:6
24 [I]In Neh. 7:28, *Beth-azmaveth*
25 [I]In Neh. 7:29, *Kiriath-jearim*
26 [a]Josh. 18:25
34 [I]Lit., *sons* [a]1Kin. 16:34; 2Chr. 28:15
36 [a]1Chr. 24:7-18
37 [a]1Chr. 24:14
38 [a]1Chr. 9:12
39 [a]1Chr. 24:8
40 [I]In Ezra 3:9, *Judah;* in Neh. 7:43, *Hodevah*

1:8 "Sheshbazzar" is thought to be the Chaldean name of Zerubbabel. Sheshbazzar means "joy in affliction," while Zerubbabel means "stranger in Babylon." Since Zerubbabel was the grandson of Jehoiachin (see Ezra 3:2; I Chr. 3:17-19), who was popular in Babylon, it is quite possible that he was the one to whom the treasures of the temple were entrusted. Other scholars have sought to identify Sheshbazzar as the officially appointed leader of the group returning to Jerusalem, while Zerubbabel was the unofficial, popular leader. Yet others have identified Sheshbazzar with Shenazzar of I Chr. 3:18.

the sons of Hatita, the sons of Shobai, in all 139.

43 The [a]temple servants: the sons of Ziha, the sons of Hasupha, the sons of Tabbaoth,

44 the sons of Keros, the sons of [I]Siaha, the sons of Padon,

45 the sons of Lebanah, the sons of Hagabah, the sons of Akkub,

46 the sons of Hagab, the sons of Shalmai, the sons of Hanan,

47 the sons of Giddel, the sons of Gahar, the sons of Reaiah,

48 the sons of Rezin, the sons of Nekoda, the sons of Gazzam,

49 the sons of Uzza, the sons of Paseah, the sons of Besai,

50 the sons of Asnah, the sons of Meunim, the sons of [I]Nephisim,

51 the sons of Bakbuk, the sons of Hakupha, the sons of Harhur,

52 the sons of [I]Bazluth, the sons of Mehida, the sons of Harsha,

53 the sons of Barkos, the sons of Sisera, the sons of Temah,

54 the sons of Neziah, the sons of Hatipha.

55 The sons of [a]Solomon's servants:[5650] the sons of Sotai, the sons of [I]Hassophereth, the sons of [II]Peruda,

56 the sons of Jaalah, the sons of Darkon, the sons of Giddel,

57 the sons of Shephatiah, the sons of Hattil, the sons of Pochereth-hazzebaim, the sons of [I]Ami.

58 All the [a]temple servants, and the sons of [b]Solomon's servants, were 392.

59 Now these are those who came up from Tel-melah, Tel-harsha, Cherub, [I]Addan, *and* Immer, but they were not able to [II]give evidence[5046] of their fathers'[1] households, and their [III]descendants,[2233] whether they were of Israel:

60 the sons of Delaiah, the sons of Tobiah, the sons of Nekoda, 652.

Priests Removed

61 And of the sons of the priests: the sons of [I]Habaiah, the sons of Hakkoz, the sons of [a]Barzillai, who took a wife[802] from the daughters of Barzillai the Gileadite, and he was called[7121] by their name.

62 These searched *among* their ancestral registration, but they could not be located; [a]therefore they were considered unclean *and excluded* from the priesthood.[3550]

63 And the [I]governor said[559] to them [a]that they should not eat from the most holy things[6944] until a priest[3548] stood up with [b]Urim[217] and Thummim.[8537]

64 The whole assembly[6951] [I]numbered 42,360,

65 besides their male and female servants, [I]who numbered 7,337; and they had 200 [a]singing men[7891] and women.[7891]

66 Their horses were 736; their mules, 245;

67 their camels, 435; *their* donkeys, 6,720.

68 And some of the heads[7218] of fathers'[1] *households,* when they arrived at the house of the LORD which is in Jerusalem, offered willingly[5068] for the house of God[430] to [I]restore it on its foundation.

69 According to their ability they gave [a]to the treasury for the work[4399] 61,000 gold drachmas,[1871] and 5,000 silver minas, and 100 priestly [I]garments.

70 [a]Now the priests and the Levites, some of the people, the singers, the gatekeepers, and the temple servants lived in their cities, and all Israel in their cities.

Altar and Sacrifices Restored

3 Now when the seventh month came,[5060] and [a]the sons[1121] of Israel *were* in the cities, the people[5971] gathered together as one man to Jerusalem.

43 [a]1Chr. 9:2
44 [I]In Neh. 7:47, *Sia*
50 [I]In Neh. 7:52, *Nephushesim*
52 [I]In Neh. 7:54, *Bazlith*
55 [I]In Neh. 7:57, *Sophereth* [II]In Neh. 7:57, *Perida* [a]1Kin. 9:21
57 [I]In Neh. 7:59, *Amon*
58 [a]1Chr. 9:2 [b]1Kin. 9:21
59 [I]In Neh. 7:61, *Addon* [II]Lit., *tell* [III]Lit., *seed*
61 [I]In Neh. 7:63, *Hobaiah* [a]2Sam. 17:27; 1Kin. 2:7
62 [a]Num. 16:39, 40
63 [I]Heb., *Tirshatha*, a Persian title [a]Lev. 2:3, 10 [b]Ex. 28:30; Num. 27:21
64 [I]Lit., *together was*
65 [I]Lit., *they were* [a]2Chr. 35:25
68 [I]Lit., *establish*
69 [I]Or, *tunics* [a]Ezra 8:25-34
70 [a]1Chr. 9:2; Neh. 11:3
1 [a]Neh. 7:73; 8:1

2:63 "Governor" is applied here to Zerubbabel. Concerning "Urim and Thummim," see note on Ex. 28:30. They are mentioned for the last time in Neh. 7:65.

🔑2 Then [a]Jeshua the son[1121] of Jozadak and his brothers[251] the priests,[3548]
and [b]Zerubbabel the son [c]of Shealtiel,
and his brothers arose and [d]built the
altar[4196] of the God[430] of Israel, to offer
burnt offerings[5928] on it, [e]as it is written
in the law[8451] of Moses, the man of God.
3 So they set up the altar on its
foundation, for [Ia]they were terrified[367]
because of the peoples of the lands;[776]
and they [b]offered[5927] burnt offerings[5930]
on it to the LORD, burnt offerings morning and evening.
4 And they celebrated[6213] the
[a]Feast[2282] of [I]Booths, [b]as it is written,
and *offered* [II]the fixed number of burnt
offerings daily,[3117] [c]according to the ordinance,[4941] as each day[3117] required;
5 and afterward *there was* a [a]con-
tinual[8548] burnt offering,[5930] also [b]for the
new moons and [c]for all the fixed
festivals[4150] of the LORD that were consecrated,[6942] and from everyone who
offered[5068] a freewill offering[5071] to the
LORD.
6 From the first day of the seventh
month they began to offer burnt offerings to the LORD, but the foundation[3245]
of the temple[1964] of the LORD had not
been laid.
7 Then they gave money to the
masons and carpenters, and [a]food,
drink,[4960] and oil to the Sidonians and
to the Tyrians, [b]to bring cedar wood
from Lebanon to the sea at [c]Joppa, according to the permission they had
[I]from [d]Cyrus king[4428] of Persia.

Temple Restoration Begun

8 Now in the second year of their
coming to the house[1004] of God at Jerusalem in the second month, [a]Zerubbabel
the son of Shealtiel and Jeshua the son
of Jozadak and the rest[7605] of their brothers the priests and the Levites, and all
who came from the captivity[7628] to Jerusalem, began *the work* and [b]appointed
the Levites from twenty years and older

2 [a]Neh. 12:1, 8 [b]Ezra 2:2; Hag. 1:1; 2:2 [c]1Chr. 3:17 [d]Ex. 27:1 [e]Deut. 12:5, 6

3 [I]Lit., *terror was upon them* [a]Ezra 4:4 [b]Num. 28:2

4 [I]Or, *Tabernacles* [II]Lit., *by number* [a]Neh. 8:14; Zech. 14:16 [b]Ex. 23:16 [c]Num. 29:12

5 [a]Ex. 29:38; Num. 28:3 [b]Num. 28:11 [c]Num. 29:39

7 [I]Lit., *of* [a]2Chr. 2:10; Acts 12:20 [b]2Chr. 2:16 [c]Acts 9:36 [d]Ezra 1:2; 6:3

8 [a]Ezra 3:2; 4:3 [b]1Chr. 23:4, 24

9 [I]In Ezra 2:40, *Hodaviah* [a]Ezra 2:40

10 [I]So with the Gr. and some mss.; M.T., *they set the priests* [II]Lit., *hands* [a]Zech. 4:6-10 [b]1Chr. 6:31; 25:1

11 [a]2Chr. 7:3; Neh. 12:24, 40 [b]1Chr. 16:34; 2 Chr. 5:13; Ps. 100:5; 106:1; 107:1; 118:1; 131:1; Jer. 33:11

12 [I]Lit., *house* [a]Hag. 2:3

1 [a]Ezra 4:7-10 [b]Ezra 1:11

2 [a]2Kin. 17:32 [b]2Kin. 19:37

to oversee the work[4399] of the house
of the LORD.
9 Then [a]Jeshua *with* his sons[1121] and
brothers stood united *with* Kadmiel and
his sons, the sons of [I]Judah *and* the
sons of Henadad *with* their sons and
brothers the Levites, to oversee the
workmen in the temple of God.
10 Now when the builders[1129] had
[a]laid the foundation of the temple of the
LORD, [I]the priests stood in their apparel
with trumpets, and the Levites, the sons
of Asaph, with cymbals, to praise[1984]
the LORD [b]according to the [II]directions
of King David of Israel.
11 And [a]they sang, praising[1984] and
giving thanks[3034] to the LORD, *saying,*
"[b]For He is good,[2896] for His lovingkindness[2617] is upon Israel forever."[5769]
And all the people shouted[7321] with a
great shout when they praised[1984] the
LORD because the foundation of the
house of the LORD was laid.
12 Yet many of the priests and Levites and heads[7218] of fathers'[1] *households,* [a]the old men[2204] who had seen[7200]
the first[7223] [I]temple, wept with a loud
voice when the foundation of this house
was laid before their eyes, while many
shouted aloud for joy;
13 so that the people could not
distinguish[5234] the sound of the shout
of joy from the sound of the weeping
of the people, for the people shouted
with a loud shout, and the sound was
heard[8085] far away.

Adversaries Hinder the Work

4 Now when [a]the enemies of Judah
and Benjamin heard[8085] that [b]the
people[1121] of the exile[1473] were building
a temple[1964] to the LORD God[430] of Israel,
2 they approached Zerubbabel and
the heads[7218] of fathers'[1] *households,* and
said[559] to them, "Let us build with you,
for we, like you, seek your God;
[a]and we have been sacrificing[2076] to Him
since the days[3117] of [b]Esarhaddon

🔑**3:2** See Ezra. 2:63; I Chr. 3:17.

king[4428] of Assyria, who brought[5927] us up here."

3 But Zerubbabel and Jeshua and the rest[7605] of the heads of fathers' *households* of Israel said to them, "[a]You have nothing in common with us in building a house[1004] to our God; but we ourselves will together build to the LORD God of Israel, [b]as King Cyrus, the king of Persia has commanded[6680] us."

4 Then [a]the people[5971] of the land[776] [I]discouraged[7503] the people of Judah, and frightened them from building,

🔑 5 and hired counselors[3289] against them to frustrate[6565] their counsel all the days of Cyrus king of Persia, even until the reign[4438] of Darius king of Persia.

🔑 **6** Now in the reign of [Ia]Ahasuerus, in the beginning of his reign, they wrote an accusation[7855] against the inhabitants of Judah and Jerusalem.

7 And in the days of [I]Artaxerxes, Bishlam, Mithredath, Tabeel, and the rest of his colleagues, wrote to Artaxerxes king of Persia; and the [II]text of the letter was written in Aramaic and translated [a]*from* Aramaic.

The Letter to King Artaxerxes

🔑 8 [I]Rehum the commander[1169] and Shimshai the scribe[5613] wrote a letter against Jerusalem to King[4430] Artaxerxes, as follows—

9 then *wrote* Rehum the commander and Shimshai the scribe and [a]the rest[7606] of their colleagues, the judges and [b]the lesser governors, the officials, the secretaries, the men of Erech, the Babylonians, the men of Susa, that is, the Elamites,

10 and the rest of the nations[524] which the great and honorable [I]Osnappar deported[1451] and settled in the city of Samaria, and in the rest of the region beyond the [II]River. [a]And now

11 this is the copy of the letter which they sent to him: "To King Artaxerxes: Your servants,[5649] the men[606] in the region beyond the River, and now

12 let it be known[3046] to the king, that the Jews who came up from you have come to us at Jerusalem; they are rebuilding [a]the rebellious[4779] and evil city, and [b]are finishing[3635] the walls and repairing the foundations.

13 "Now let it be known to the king, that if that city is rebuilt and the walls are finished, [a]they will not pay tribute, custom, or toll, and it will damage the revenue of the kings.[4430]

14 "Now because we [I]are in the service of the palace,[1964] and it is not fitting for us to see[2370] the king's dishonor, therefore we have sent and informed the king,

15 so that a search may be made in the record books[5609] of your fathers.[1] And you will discover in the record books, and learn[3046] that that city is a rebellious city and damaging to kings and provinces, and that they have incited revolt within it in past[5957] days;[3118] therefore that city was laid waste.[2718]

16 "We inform[3046] the king that, if that city is rebuilt and the walls finished, as a result you will have no possession in *the province* beyond the River."

The King Replies and Work Stops

17 *Then* the king sent an answer[6600] to Rehum the commander, to Shimshai the scribe, and to the rest of their colleagues who live in Samaria and in the rest of *the provinces* beyond the River: "Peace.[8001] And now

18 the document which you sent to us has been [Ia]translated and read before me.

19 "And a decree[2942] has been [I]issued by me, and a search has been made and it has been discovered that

3 [a]Neh. 2:20 [b]Ezra 1:1, 2

4 [I]Lit., *weakened the hands of* [a]Ezra 3:3

6 [I]Or, *Xerxes;* Heb., *Ahashverosh* [a]Esth. 1:1; Dan. 9:1

7 [I]Heb., *Artahshashta* [II]Lit., *writing* [a]2Kin. 18:26; Dan. 2:4

8 [I]Ch. 4:8-6:18 is in Aram.

9 [a]2Kin. 17:24 [b]Ezra 5:6; 6:6

10 [I]I.e., probably Ashurbanipal [II]I.e., Euphrates River, and so throughout the ch. [a]Ezra 4:11, 17; 7:12

12 [a]2Chr. 36:13 [b]Ezra 5:3, 9

13 [a]Ezra 4:20; 7:24

14 [I]Lit., *eat the salt*

18 [I]Lit., *plainly read before* [a]Neh. 8:8

19 [I]Lit., *put forth*

🔑 **4:5** Darius reigned from 522 B.C. to 486 B.C.

🔑 **4:6** Ahasuerus is better known as Xerxes, who reigned from 486 B.C. to 465 B.C. See note on Esth. 1:1.

🔑 **4:8—6:18** See note on Dan. 2:4b-7:28.

that city has risen up against the kings
in past days, that rebellion[4776] and revolt
have been perpetrated in it,
20 [a]that mighty kings have [I]ruled[7990]
over Jerusalem, governing all *the prov-*
inces [b]beyond the River, and that
[c]tribute, custom, and toll were paid to
them.
21 "So, now issue a decree[2942] to
make these men[1400] stop *work,* that the
city may not be rebuilt until a decree[2442]
is issued by me.
22 "And beware[2095] of being negligent in carrying out this *matter;* why
should damage increase to the detriment
of the kings?"
23 Then as soon as the copy of King
Artaxerxes' document was read before
Rehum and Shimshai the scribe and their
colleagues, they went in haste to Jerusalem to the Jews and stopped them by
force of arms.[2429]
24 Then work on the house of
God[426] in Jerusalem ceased, and it was
stopped until the second year of the
reign[4437] of Darius king of Persia.

Temple Work Resumed

5 When the prophets,[5029] [a]Haggai the
prophet[5029] and [b]Zechariah the son
of Iddo, prophesied[5013] to the Jews who
were in Judah and Jerusalem, in the
name of the God[426] of Israel, who was
over them,
2 then [a]Zerubbabel the son of Shealtiel and Jeshua the son of Jozadak arose
and began to rebuild the house of God
which is in Jerusalem; and [b]the prophets
of God were with them supporting them.
3 At that time[2116] [a]Tattenai, the
governor[6347] of *the province* beyond the
[I]River, and Shethar-bozenai and their
colleagues came to them and spoke[560]
to them thus, "[b]Who issued you a
decree[2942] to rebuild this [II]temple and
to finish[3635] this structure?"
4 [a]Then we told them accordingly
what the names of the men[1400] were
who were reconstructing this building.
5 But [a]the eye of their God was on
the elders[7868] of the Jews, and they did
not stop them until a report[2941] should
come to Darius, and then a written reply
be returned concerning it.

Adversaries Write to Darius

6 *This is* the copy of the letter which
[a]Tattenai, the governor of *the province*
beyond the River, and Shethar-bozenai
and his colleagues [b]the officials, who
were beyond the River, sent to Darius
the king.[4430]
7 They sent a report[6600] to him in
which it was written thus: "To Darius
the king, all peace.[8001]
8 "Let it be known[3046] to the king,
that we have gone to the province of
Judah, to the house of the great God,
which is being built with huge stones,
and [I]beams are being laid in the walls;
and this work is going on with great
care and is succeeding in their hands.[3028]
9 "Then we asked[7993] those elders
and said to them thus, 'Who issued you
a decree to rebuild this temple and to
finish this structure?'
10 "We also asked them their names
so as to inform[3046] you, and that we
might write down the names of the men
who were at their head.[7217]
11 "And thus they [I]answered[6600] us,
saying, 'We are the servants[5649] of the
God of heaven[8065] and earth and are rebuilding the temple that was built many
years ago,[6928] [a]which a great king of
Israel built and finished.
12 'But [a]because our fathers[2] had
provoked[7265] the God of heaven to
wrath, [b]He gave them into the hand[3038]
of Nebuchadnezzar king of Babylon, the
Chaldean, *who* destroyed[5642] this temple
and deported the people[5972] to Babylon.
13 'However, [a]in the first year of
Cyrus king of Babylon, King Cyrus
[b]issued a decree[2942] to rebuild this house
of God.
14 'And also [a]the gold and silver
utensils of the house of God which Nebuchadnezzar had taken from the temple[1965] [I]in Jerusalem, and brought them
to the temple of Babylon, these King
Cyrus took from the temple[1965] of Babylon,

20 [I]Lit., *been* [a]1Kin. 4:21; 1Chr. 18:3 [b]Gen. 15:18; Josh. 1:4 [c]Ezra 4:13; 7:24

1 [a]Hag. 1:1 [b]Zech. 1:1

2 [a]Ezra 3:2; Hag. 1:12; Zech. 4:6-9 [b]Ezra 6:14; Hag. 2:4; Zech. 3:1

3 [I]I.e., Euphrates River, and so throughout the ch. [II]Lit., *house,* and so in vv. 9, 11, 12 [a]Ezra 6:6, 13 [b]Ezra 1:3; 5:9

4 [a]Ezra 5:10

5 [a]Ezra 7:6, 28

6 [a]Ezra 5:3 [b]Ezra 4:9

8 [I]Lit., *timber is*

11 [I]Lit., *returned us the word* [a]1Kin. 6:1, 38

12 [a]2Chr. 36:16, 17 [b]2Kin. 25:8-11; Jer. 52:12-15

13 [a]Ezra 1:1 [b]Ezra 1:1-4

14 [I]Lit., *that was in* [a]Ezra 1:7; 6:5; Dan. 5:2

and they were given to one [b]whose
name was Sheshbazzar, whom he had
appointed governor.
15 ‘And he said to him, “Take these
utensils, go *and* deposit them in the temple [I]in Jerusalem, and let the house of
God be rebuilt in its place.”
16 ‘Then that Sheshbazzar came
and [a]laid the foundations of the house
of God [I]in Jerusalem; and from then until
now it has been under construction, and
it is [b]not *yet* completed.’[8000]
17 “And now, if it pleases the king
[a]let a search be conducted in the
king’s[4430] treasure house, which is there
in Babylon, if it be that a decree was
issued by King Cyrus to rebuild this
house of God at Jerusalem; and let the
king send to us his decision concerning
this *matter*.”

Darius Finds Cyrus’ Decree

6 Then King[4430] Darius issued a decree,[2942] and [a]search was made in
the [I]archives, where the treasures were
stored in Babylon.
2 And in [I]Ecbatana in the fortress,
which is [a]in the province of Media, a
scroll[4040] was found and there was written in it as follows: “Memorandum—
3 “[a]In the first year of King Cyrus,
Cyrus the king issued a decree: *‘Concerning* the house of God[426] at Jerusalem, let the temple, the place where
sacrifices[1685] are offered,[1684] be rebuilt
and let its foundations be [I]retained, its
height being 60 cubits and its width 60
cubits;
4 [a]with three layers of huge stones,
and [I]one layer of timbers. And let the
cost be paid from the [II]royal[4430] treasury.
5 ‘And also let [a]the gold and silver
utensils of the temple of God, which
Nebuchadnezzar took from the temple[1965] in Jerusalem and brought to
Babylon, be returned and [I]brought to
their places in the temple in Jerusalem;
and you shall put *them* in the house of
God.’
6 “Now *therefore,* [a]Tattenai, governor[6347] of *the province* beyond the
[I]River, Shethar-bozenai, and [II]your colleagues, the officials of *the provinces* beyond the [I]River, [III]keep away from there.
7 “Leave this work on the house
of God alone; let the governor of the
Jews and the elders[7868] of the Jews rebuild this house of God on its site.
8 “Moreover, [a]I issue a decree concerning what you are to do for these
elders of Judah in the rebuilding of this
house of God: the full cost is to be paid
to these people[1400] from the royal treasury out of the taxes of *the provinces*
beyond the River, and that without delay.
9 “And whatever is needed, both
young[1123] bulls, rams, and lambs for a
burnt offering[5928] to the God of heav-
en,[8065] and wheat, salt, wine, and anointing oil,[4887] as the priests in Jerusalem
request,[3983] *it* is to be given to them
daily[3118] without fail,
10 that they may offer [I]acceptable
sacrifices to the God of heaven and
[a]pray[6739] for the life[2417] of the king and
his sons.[1123]
11 “And I issued a decree that
[a]any man who violates[8133] this edict,[6600]
a timber shall be drawn[5256] from his
house and he shall be impaled on it and
[b]his house shall be made a refuse heap
on account of this.
12 “And may the God who [a]has
caused His name to dwell there
overthrow[4049] any king[4430] or people[5972]
who [I]attempts[3028] to change *it,* so as
to destroy[2255] this house of God in Jerusalem. I, Darius, have issued *this* decree, let *it* be carried out with all diligence!”

The Temple Completed and Dedicated

13 Then [a]Tattenai, the governor of
the province beyond the River, Shethar-
bozenai, and their colleagues carried out
the decree with all diligence, just as King
Darius had sent.
14 And [a]the elders of the Jews
[I]were successful in building through the
prophesying[5017] of Haggai the proph-

14 [b]Ezra 1:8; 5:16

15 [I]Lit., *that is in*

16 [I]Lit., *that is in* [a]Ezra 3:8, 10 [b]Ezra 6:15

17 [a]Ezra 6:1, 2

1 [I]Lit., *house of the books* [a]Ezra 5:17

2 [I]Aram., *Achmetha* [a]2Kin. 17:6

3 [I]Or, *fixed, laid* [a]Ezra 1:1; 5:13

4 [I]So Gr.; Aram., *a layer of new timber* [II]Lit., *king's house* [a]1Kin. 6:36

5 [I]Lit., *go* [a]Ezra 1:7; 5:14

6 [I]I.e., Euphrates River, and so throughout the ch. [II]Aram., *their* [III]Lit., *be distant* [a]Ezra 5:3; 6:13

8 [a]Ezra 6:4; 7:14-22

10 [I]Lit., *pleasing;* or, *sweet-smelling sacrifices* [a]Ezra 7:23; Jer. 29:7; 1Tim. 2:1, 2

11 [a]Ezra 7:26 [b]Dan. 2:5; 3:29

12 [I]Lit., *sends his hand* [a]Deut. 12:5, 11; 1Kin. 9:3

13 [a]Ezra 6:6

14 [I]Lit., *were building and succeeding* [a]Ezra 5:1, 2

et[5029] and Zechariah the son of Iddo.
And [II]they finished[3635] building according
to the command[2941] of the God of Israel
and the decree[2942] [b]of Cyrus, [c]Darius,
and [d]Artaxerxes king of Persia.
15 And this temple was completed
[I]on the third day of the [a]month Adar;
it was the sixth year of the reign[4437] of
King Darius.
🔑 16 And the sons[1121] of Israel, the
priests, the Levites, and the rest[7606]
of the [I]exiles,[1547] [a]celebrated the dedication of this house of God with joy.
17 And they offered for the dedication of this temple of God 100 bulls,
200 rams, 400 lambs, and as a sin offering for all Israel [a]12 male goats, corresponding to the number of the tribes[7625]
of Israel.
18 Then they appointed the priests
to [a]their divisions[6392] and the Levites
in [b]their orders for the service of God
[I]in Jerusalem, [c]as it is written in the
book[5609] of Moses.

The Passover Observed

19 And [a]the exiles[1547] observed[6213]
the Passover[6453] on [b]the fourteenth of
the first[7223] month.
20 [a]For the priests[3548] and the Levites had purified[2891] themselves together; all of them were pure.[2889] Then
[b]they slaughtered[7819] the Passover *lamb*
for all the exiles, both for their
brothers[251] the priests and for themselves.
21 And the sons of Israel who returned from exile and [a]all those who
had separated themselves from [b]the
impurity[2932] of the nations[1471] of the
land[776] to *join* them, to seek the LORD
God[430] of Israel, ate *the Passover*.
22 And [a]they observed the Feast[2282]
of Unleavened[4682] Bread seven days[3117]
with joy, for the LORD had caused them
to rejoice, and [b]had turned the heart[3820]
of [c]the king[4428] of Assyria toward them
to [I]encourage[2388] them[3027] in the
work[4399] of the house[1004] of God, the
God of Israel.

Ezra Journeys from Babylon to Jerusalem

7 [a]Now after these things,[1697] in the
reign[4438] of [b]Artaxerxes king[4428] of
Persia, *there went up* Ezra son of
Seraiah, son[1121] of Azariah, son of Hilkiah,
2 son of Shallum, son of Zadok, son
of Ahitub,
3 son of Amariah, son of Azariah,
son of Meraioth,
4 son of Zerahiah, son of Uzzi, son
of Bukki,
5 son of Abishua, son of Phinehas,
son of Eleazar, son of Aaron the chief[7218]
priest.[3548]
6 This Ezra went up[5927] from Babylon, and he was a [a]scribe skilled in the
law[8451] of Moses, which the LORD God[430]
of Israel had given; and the king granted
him all [I]he requested [b]because the
hand[3027] of the LORD his God *was* upon
him.
7 And [a]some of the sons[1121] of Israel
and some of the priests,[3548] the Levites,
the singers,[7891] the gatekeepers,[7778] and
the temple servants went up to Jerusalem in the seventh year of King Artaxerxes.
8 And he came to Jerusalem in the
fifth month, which was in the seventh
year of the king.
9 For on the first[7223] of the first
month [I]he began to go up from Babylon;
and on the first of the fifth month he
came to Jerusalem, [a]because the
good[2896] hand of his God *was* upon him.
10 For Ezra had set[3559] his heart[3824]
to [I]study the law of the LORD, and to
practice[6213] *it*, and [a]to teach[3925] *His*
statutes[2706] and ordinances[4941] in Israel.

14 [II]Lit., *built and finished* [b]Ezra 1:1; 5:13 [c]Ezra 4:24; 6:12 [d]Ezra 7:1
15 [I]Lit., *until* [a]Esth. 3:7
16 [I]Lit., *sons of the captivity* [a]1Kin. 8:63; 2Chr. 7:5
17 [a]Ezra 8:35
18 [I]Lit., *which is in* [a]1Chr. 24:1; 2Chr. 35:5 [b]1Chr. 23:6 [c]Num. 3:6; 8:9
19 [a]Ezra 1:11 [b]Ex. 12:6
20 [a]2Chr. 29:34; 30:15 [b]2Chr. 35:11
21 [a]Neh. 9:2; 10:28 [b]Ezra 9:11
22 [I]Lit., *strengthen their hands* [a]Ex. 12:15 [b]Ezra 7:27; Prov. 21:1 [c]Ezra 1:1; 6:1
1 [a]1Chr. 6:4-14 [b]Ezra 7:12, 21; Neh. 2:1
6 [I]Lit., *his request* [a]Ezra 7:11, 12, 21 [b]Ezra 7:9, 28; 8:22
7 [a]Ezra 8:1-20
9 [I]Lit., *was the foundation* [a]Ezra 7:6; Neh. 2:8
10 [I]Lit., *seek* [a]Deut. 33:10; Ezra 7:25; Neh. 8:1

🔑 **6:16** This probably occurred in 515 B.C. After the temple was rebuilt, it never did rise to the glory of the temple of Solomon. Nothing is said of it being filled with the glory of God as Solomon's temple or the tabernacle before it had been. It was later enlarged and further beautified by Herod the Great. This was the temple which was finally destroyed in A.D. 70 by Titus of Rome.

King's Decree on Behalf of Ezra

11 Now this is the copy of the decree which King Artaxerxes gave to
Ezra the priest, the scribe, [I]learned in
the words[1697] of the commandments[4687]
of the LORD and His statutes to Israel:
🔑 12 "[I]Artaxerxes, [a]king[4430] of kings,
to Ezra the priest, the scribe of the
law[1882] of the God[426] of heaven,[8065]
perfect[1585] *peace.* And now
13 [a]I have issued a decree[2942] that
any of the people[5972] of Israel and their
priests and the Levites in my kingdom[4437] who are willing[5069] to go to Jerusalem, may go with you.
14 "Forasmuch as you are sent
[I]by the king and his [a]seven counselors
to inquire concerning Judah and Jerusalem according to the law of your God
which is in your hand,[3028]
15 and to bring the silver and gold,
which the king and his counselors have
freely offered[5069] to the God of Israel,
[a]whose dwelling is in Jerusalem,
16 with [a]all the silver and gold which
you shall find in the whole province of
Babylon, along [b]with the freewill offering[5069] of the people and of the priests,
who [c]offered willingly[5069] for the house
of their God which is in Jerusalem;
17 with this money, therefore, you
shall diligently buy bulls, rams, and
lambs, [a]with their grain offerings[4504] and
their libations[5261] and [b]offer them on the
altar of the house of your God which
is in Jerusalem.
18 "And whatever seems good to
you and to your brothers[252] to do with
the rest[7606] of the silver and gold, you
may do according to the will of your
God.
19 "Also the utensils which are
given to you for the service of the house
of your God, deliver[8000] in full before
the God of Jerusalem.
20 "And the rest of the needs for
the house of your God, for which you
may have occasion[5308] to provide,
[a]provide *for it* from the royal[4430] treasury.
21 "And I, even I King Artaxerxes,
issue a decree to all the treasurers who
are *in the provinces* beyond the [I]River,
that whatever Ezra the priest,[3548]
[a]the scribe of the law of the God of
heaven, may require[7593] of you, it shall
be done diligently,
22 *even* up to 100 talents of silver,
100 [I]kors of wheat, 100 baths of wine,
100 baths of oil,[4887] and salt [II]as needed.
23 "Whatever is [I]commanded by the
God of heaven, let it be done with zeal
for the house of the God of heaven,
[a]lest there be wrath[7109] against the kingdom of the king and his sons.
24 "We also inform[3046] you that
[a]it is not allowed to [I]impose tax, tribute
or toll [b]*on* any of the priests, Levites,
singers, doorkeepers,[8652] Nethinim, or
servants[6399] of this house of God.
25 "And you, Ezra, according to the
wisdom[2452] of your God which is in your
hand, [a]appoint magistrates[8200] and
judges[1782] that they may judge[1778] all the
people who are in *the province* beyond
the River, *even* all those who know[3046]
the laws of your God; and you may
[b]teach anyone who is ignorant *of them.*
26 "And [a]whoever will not observe
the law of your God and the law of the
king, let judgment[1780] be executed upon
him strictly, whether for death[4193] or
for [I]banishment or for confiscation[6065]
of goods or for imprisonment."

The King's Kindness

27 Blessed[1288] be the LORD, the
God of our fathers,[1] [a]who has put *such
a thing* as this in the king's[4428] heart,
to adorn[6286] the house[1004] of the LORD
which is in Jerusalem,
28 and [a]has extended lovingkindness[2617] to me before the king and his
counselors[3289] and before all the king's
mighty princes.[8269] Thus I was strengthened[2388] according to [b]the hand of the

11 [I]Lit., *the scribe of*
12 [I]Ch. 7:12-26 is in Aram. [a]Ezek. 26:7; Dan. 2:37
13 [a]Ezra 6:1
14 [I]Lit., *from before* [a]Ezra 7:15, 28; 8:25
15 [a]2Chr. 6:2; Ezra 6:12; Ps. 135:21
16 [a]Ezra 8:25 [b]Ezra 1:4, 6 [c]1Chr. 29:6
17 [a]Num. 15:4-13 [b]Deut. 12:5-11
20 [a]Ezra 6:4
21 [I]I.e., Euphrates River, and so throughout the ch. [a]Ezra 7:6
22 [I]I.e., One kor equals approx. ten bu. [II]Lit., *without prescription*
23 [I]Lit., *from the decree of* [a]Ezra 6:10
24 [I]Lit., *throw on them* [a]Ezra 4:13, 20 [b]Ezra 7:7
25 [a]Ex. 18:21; Deut. 16:18 [b]Ezra 7:10; Mal. 2:7; Col. 1:28
26 [I]Lit., *rooting out* [a]Ezra 6:11, 12
27 [a]Ezra 6:22
28 [a]Ezra 9:9 [b]Ezra 5:5

🔑 **7:12-26** See note on Dan. 2:4b-7:28.

LORD my God upon me, and I gathered[6908] [I]leading men from Israel to go up with me.

People Who Went with Ezra

8 Now these are the heads[7218] of their fathers'[1] *households* and the genealogical enrollment of those who went up[5927] with me from Babylon in the reign[4438] of King[4428] Artaxerxes:

2 of the sons[1121] of Phinehas, Gershom; of the sons of Ithamar, Daniel; of the sons of David, [a]Hattush;

3 of the sons of Shecaniah *who was* of the sons of [a]Parosh, Zechariah and with him 150 males[2145] *who were in* the genealogical list;

4 of the sons of Pahath-moab, Eliehoenai the son[1121] of Zerahiah and 200 males with him;

5 of the sons of Shecaniah, the son of Jahaziel and 300 males with him;

6 and of the sons of [a]Adin, Ebed the son of Jonathan and 50 males with him;

7 and of the sons of Elam, Jeshaiah the son of Athaliah and 70 males with him;

8 and of the sons of Shephatiah, Zebadiah the son of Michael and 80 males with him;

9 of the sons of Joab, Obadiah the son of Jehiel and 218 males with him;

10 and of the sons of Shelomith, the son of Josiphiah and 160 males with him;

11 and of the sons of Bebai, Zechariah the son of Bebai and 28 males with him;

12 and of the sons of Azgad, Johanan the son of Hakkatan and 110 males with him;

13 and of the sons of Adonikam, the last ones, these being their names, Eliphelet, Jeuel, and Shemaiah and 60 males with them;

14 and of the sons of Bigvai, Uthai and [I]Zabbud and 70 males with [II]them.

Ezra Sends for Levites

15 Now I assembled[6908] them at [a]the river that runs to Ahava, where we camped for three days;[3117] and when I observed the people[5971] and the priests,[3548] I [b]did not find any Levites there.

16 So I sent for Eliezer, Ariel, Shemaiah, Elnathan, Jarib, Elnathan, Nathan, Zechariah, and Meshullam, [I]leading men,[1400] and for Joiarib and Elnathan, teachers.[995]

17 And I sent them to Iddo the [I]leading man at the place Casiphia; and I [II]told them what to say[1696] to [III]Iddo *and* his brothers,[251] [a]the temple servants at the place Casiphia, *that is,* to bring ministers to us for the house[1004] of our God.[430]

18 And [a]according to the good[2896] hand[3027] of our God upon us they brought us a [b]man of insight[7922] of the sons of Mahli, the son of Levi, the son of Israel, namely Sherebiah, and his sons and brothers, 18 men;

19 and Hashabiah and [I]Jeshaiah of the sons of Merari, with his brothers and their sons, 20 men;

20 and 220 of [a]the temple servants, whom David and the princes[8269] had given for the service[5656] of the Levites, all of them designated by name.

Protection of God Invoked

21 Then I proclaimed [a]a fast there at [b]the river of Ahava, that we might [c]humble ourselves before our God to seek from Him a [I]safe[3477] journey[1870] for us, our little ones,[2945] and all our possessions.

22 For I was ashamed[954] to request from the king troops and horsemen to [I]protect us from the enemy on the way, because we had said[559] to the king, "[a]The hand of our God is [II]favorably disposed to all those who seek Him, but [b]His power and His anger[639] are against all those who [c]forsake[5800] Him."

23 So we fasted and sought our God concerning this *matter,* and He [I][a]listened to our entreaty.[6279]

24 Then I set apart[914] twelve of the leading priests, [a]Sherebiah, Hashabiah, and with them ten of their brothers;

---

28 [I]Lit., *heads*

2 [a]1Chr. 3:22

3 [a]Ezra 2:3

6 [a]Ezra 2:15; Neh. 7:20; 10:16

14 [I]Or, *Zakkur* [II]Or, *him*

15 [a]Ezra 8:21, 31 [b]Ezra 7:7; 8:2

16 [I]Lit., *heads*

17 [I]Lit., *head* [II]Lit., *put words in their mouth to say* [III]So Gr.; Heb., *Iddo his brother* [a]Ezra 2:43

18 [a]Ezra 7:6, 28 [b]2Chr. 30:22

19 [I]So Gr.; Heb., *with him Jeshaiah*

20 [a]Ezra 2:43; 7:7

21 [I]Lit., *straight way* [a]1Sam. 7:6; 2Chr. 20:3 [b]Ezra 8:15, 31 [c]Lev. 16:29; 23:29; Is. 58:3, 5

22 [I]Lit., *help* [II]Lit., *upon all . . . for good* [a]Ezra 7:6, 9, 28 [b]Josh. 22:16 [c]2Chr. 15:2

23 [I]Lit., *was entreated by us* [a]1Chr. 5:20; 2Chr. 33:13

24 [a]Ezra 8:18, 19

25 and I [a]weighed out to them [b]the silver, the gold, and the utensils, the offering[8641] for the house of our God which the king and [c]his counselors[3289] and his princes, and all Israel present *there,* had offered.

26 [a]Thus I weighed into their hands 650 talents of silver, and silver utensils *worth* 100 talents, *and* 100 gold talents,

27 and 20 gold bowls,[3713] *worth* 1,000 darics;[150] and two utensils of fine shiny bronze, precious as gold.

28 Then I said[559] to them, "[a]You are holy[6944] to the LORD, and the [b]utensils are holy; and the silver and the gold are a freewill offering[5071] to the LORD God of your fathers.

29 "Watch and keep[8104] *them* [a]until you weigh *them* before the leading priests, the Levites, and the heads of the fathers' *households* of Israel at Jerusalem, *in* the chambers of the house of the LORD."

30 So the priests and the Levites [a]accepted the weighed out silver and gold and the utensils, to bring *them* to Jerusalem to the house of our God.

31 Then we journeyed from [a]the river Ahava on [b]the twelfth of the first[7223] month to go to Jerusalem; and [c]the hand of our God was over us, and He delivered[5337] us from the hand[3709] of the enemy and the ambushes by the way.

32 [a]Thus we came to Jerusalem and remained there three days.

Treasure Placed in the Temple

33 And on the fourth day[3117] the silver and the gold and the utensils [a]were weighed out in the house of our God into the hand of [b]Meremoth the son of Uriah the priest,[3548] and with him *was* Eleazar the son of Phinehas; and with them *were* the Levites, Jozabad the son of Jeshua and Noadiah the son of Binnui.

34 Everything *was* numbered and weighed, and all the weight was recorded at that time.[6256]

35 [a]The exiles[1473,1121] who had come from the captivity[7628] offered[7126] burnt offerings[5930] to the God of Israel: [b]12 bulls for all Israel, 96 rams, 77 lambs, 12 male goats for a sin[2403] offering, all as a burnt offering[5930] to the LORD.

36 Then [a]they delivered the king's[4428] edicts[1881] to [b]the king's satraps, and to the governors[6346] *in the provinces* beyond the [I]River, and they supported[5375] the people and the house of God.

Mixed Marriages

9 Now when these things had been completed,[3615] the princes[8269] approached me, saying, "The people of Israel and the priests[3548] and the Levites have not [a]separated[914] themselves from the peoples[5971] of the lands,[776] [b]according to their abominations,[8441] *those* of the Canaanites, the Hittites, the Perizzites, the Jebusites, the Ammonites, the Moabites, the Egyptians, and the Amorites.

2 "For [a]they have taken[5375] some of their daughters *as wives* for themselves and for their sons,[1121] so that [b]the holy[6944] [I]race[2233] has [c]intermingled with the peoples of the lands; indeed, the hands[3927] of the princes and the rulers[5461] have been foremost[7223] in this unfaithfulness."[4604]

3 And when I heard[8085] about this matter,[1697] I [a]tore my garment and my robe,[4598] and pulled some of the hair from my head[7218] and my beard,[2206] and [b]sat down appalled.[8074]

4 Then [a]everyone who trembled[2730] at the words[1697] of the God[430] of Israel on account of the unfaithfulness[4604] of the exiles[1473] gathered[622] to me, and I sat appalled until [b]the evening offering.[4503]

Prayer of Confession

5 But at the evening offering I arose from my [I]humiliation, even with my garment and my robe torn, and I fell[3766] on my knees and [a]stretched out my [II]hands[3709] to the LORD my God;

25 [a]Ezra 8:33 [b]Ezra 7:15, 16 [c]Ezra 7:14
26 [a]Ezra 1:9-11
28 [a]Lev. 21:6-8 [b]Lev. 22:2, 3
29 [a]Ezra 8:33, 34
30 [a]Ezra 1:9
31 [a]Ezra 8:15, 21 [b]Ezra 7:9 [c]Ezra 8:22
32 [a]Neh. 2:11
33 [a]Ezra 8:30 [b]Neh. 3:4, 21
35 [a]Ezra 2:1 [b]Ezra 6:17
36 [I]I.e., Euphrates River [a]Ezra 7:21-24 [b]Ezra 4:7; 5:6
1 [a]Ezra 6:21; Neh. 9:2 [b]Lev. 18:24-30
2 [I]Lit., *seed* [a]Deut. 7:3; Ezra 10:2, 18 [b]Ex. 22:31; Deut. 14:2; 2Cor. 6:14 [c]Neh. 13:3
3 [a]2Kin. 18:37 [b]Neh. 1:4
4 [a]Ezra 10:3; Is. 66:2 [b]Ex. 29:39
5 [I]Or, *fasting* [II]Lit., *palms* [a]Ex. 9:29

6 and I said,[559] "O my God, I am ashamed[954] and embarrassed to lift up my face to Thee, my God, for our iniquities[5771] have [I]risen above our heads, and our [a]guilt[819] has grown even to the heavens.[8064]

7 "[a]Since the days[3117] of our fathers[1] to this day[3117] we *have been* in great guilt, and on account of our iniquities we, our kings *and* our priests have been given into the hand of the kings of the lands, to the sword,[2719] to captivity,[7628] and to plunder and to [I][b]open shame, as *it is* this day.

8 "But now for a brief moment grace[8467] has been *shown* from the LORD our God, [a]to leave us an escaped[6413] remnant and to give us a [b]peg in His holy place, that our God may [c]enlighten our eyes and grant us a little reviving[4241] in our bondage.[5659]

9 "[a]For we are slaves;[5650] yet in our bondage, our God has not forsaken[5800] us, but [b]has extended lovingkindness[2617] to us in the sight of the kings of Persia, to give us reviving to raise up the house[1004] of our God, to restore its ruins,[2723] and to give us a wall in Judah and Jerusalem.

10 "And now, our God, what shall we say[559] after this? For we have forsaken Thy commandments,[4687]

11 which Thou hast commanded[6680] by Thy servants[5690] the prophets,[5030] saying, 'The land[776] which you are entering to possess[3423] is an unclean land with the uncleanness of the peoples of the lands, with their abominations which have filled it from end to end[6310] *and* [a]with their impurity.[2932]

12 'So now do not [a]give your daughters to their sons nor take[5375] their daughters to your sons, and [b]never seek their peace or their prosperity,[2896] that you may be strong[2388] and eat the good *things* of the land and [c]leave *it* as an inheritance[3423] to your sons[1121] forever.'[5769]

13 "And after all that has come upon us for our evil[7451] deeds and [a]our great guilt, since Thou our God hast requited *us* less than our iniquities *deserve,* and hast given us [b]an escaped remnant as this,

14 [a]shall we again break Thy commandments and intermarry[2859] with the peoples [I]who commit these abominations? [b]Wouldst Thou not be angry[559] with us [II]to the point of destruction,[3615] until there is no remnant[7611] nor any who escape?[6413]

15 "O LORD God of Israel, [a]Thou art righteous,[6662] for we have been left an escaped[6413] remnant, as *it is* this day; behold, we are before Thee in [b]our guilt,[819] for [c]no one can stand before Thee because of this."

Reconciliation with God

10 Now [a]while Ezra was praying[6419] and making confession,[3034] weeping and prostrating himself [b]before the house[1004] of God,[430] a very large assembly,[6951] men,[582] women,[802] and children, gathered[6908] to him from Israel; for the people[5971] wept bitterly.

2 And Shecaniah the son[1121] of Jehiel, one of the sons[1121] of Elam, answered and said[559] to Ezra, "[a]We have been unfaithful[4603] to our God, and have [I]married foreign[5237] women[802] from the peoples of the land;[776] yet now there is hope[4723] for Israel in spite of this.

3 "So now [a]let us make a covenant[1285] with our God to put away all the wives and [I][b]their children, according to the counsel[6098] of [II]my lord[136] and of [c]those who tremble at the commandment[4687] of our God; and let it be done[6213] [d]according to the law.[8451]

4 "Arise! For *this* matter[1697] is [I]your responsibility, but we will be with you; [a]be courageous[2388] and act."[6213]

5 Then Ezra rose and [a]made the leading priests,[3548] the Levites, and all Israel, take oath[7650] that they would do according to this [I]proposal;[1697] so they took the oath.[7650]

6 Then Ezra [a]rose from before the house of God and went into the chamber of Jehohanan the son of Eliashib. Although he went there, [b]he did not eat bread, nor drink water, for he was

6 [I]Lit., *multiplied over the head* [a]2Chr. 28:9; Ezra 9:13, 15; Rev. 18:5

7 [I]Lit., *shame of faces* [a]2Chr. 29:6; Ps. 106:6 [b]Dan. 9:7

8 [a]Ezra 9:13-15 [b]Is. 22:23 [c]Ps. 13:3

9 [a]Neh. 9:36 [b]Ezra 7:28

11 [a]Ezra 6:21

12 [a]Ex. 34:15, 16; Deut. 7:3; Ezra 9:2 [b]Deut. 23:6 [c]Prov. 13:22

13 [a]Ezra 9:6, 7 [b]Ezra 9:8

14 [I]Lit., *of these abominations* [II]Lit., *to destroy* [a]Ezra 9:2 [b]Deut. 9:8, 14

15 [a]Neh. 9:33; Dan. 9:7 [b]Ezra 9:6 [c]Job 9:2; Ps. 130:3

1 [a]Dan. 9:4, 20 [b]2Chr. 20:9

2 [I]Lit., *given dwelling to* [a]Ezra 9:2; Neh. 13:27

3 [I]Lit., *that which is born of them* [II]Or, *the Lord* [a]2Chr. 34:31 [b]Ezra 10:44 [c]Ezra 9:4 [d]Deut. 7:2, 3

4 [I]Lit., *upon you* [a]1Chr. 28:10

5 [I]Lit., *word, thing* [a]Neh. 5:12; 13:25

6 [a]Ezra 10:1 [b]Deut. 9:18

mourning over the unfaithfulness[4604] of
the exiles.[1473]
7 And they made a proclamation[5674]
throughout Judah and Jerusalem to all
the exiles,[1473] that they should assemble[6908] at Jerusalem,
8 and that whoever would not come
within three days,[3117] according to the
counsel of the leaders[8269] and the elders,[2205] all his possessions should be
forfeited[2763] and he himself excluded[914]
from the assembly of the exiles.
9 So all the men of Judah and Benjamin assembled[6908] at Jerusalem within
the three days. It was the ninth month
on the twentieth of the month, and all
the people sat in the open square *before*
the house of God, [a]trembling[7460] because
of this matter and the heavy rain.
10 Then Ezra the priest[3548] stood
up and said to them, "You have been
unfaithful[4603] and have married foreign
wives adding to the guilt[819] of Israel.
11 "Now, therefore, [a]make confession[8426] to the LORD God of your fathers,[1] and [b]do His will;[7522] and
[c]separate[914] yourselves from the peoples of the land and from the foreign
wives."
12 Then all the assembly answered
and said with a loud voice, "That's right!
As you have said, so it is [I]our duty to
do.
13 "But there are many people, it
is the rainy season,[6256] and we are not
able to stand in the open. Nor *can* the
task[4399] *be done* in one or two days,[3117]
for we have transgressed[6586] greatly in
this matter.[1697]
14 "Let our leaders[8269] [I]represent
the whole assembly and let all those in
our cities who have married foreign
wives come at appointed[2163] times,[6256]
together with the elders and judges[8199]
of each city, until the [a]fierce anger[639]
of our God on account of this matter
is turned away from us."
15 Only Jonathan the son of Asahel
and Jahzeiah the son of Tikvah [I]opposed
this, with Meshullam and Shabbethai the
Levite supporting them.
16 But the exiles did[6213] so. And
[I]Ezra the priest selected men *who were*
heads of fathers' *households* for *each of*
their father's households, all of them
by name. So they [II]convened on the first
day of the tenth month to investigate
the matter.
17 And they finished[3615] *investigat-*
ing all the men who had married foreign
wives by the first[7223] of the first month.

List of Offenders

18 And among the sons of the
priests who had married foreign wives
were found of the sons of [a]Jeshua the
son of Jozadak, and his brothers:[251]
Maaseiah, Eliezer, Jarib, and Gedaliah.
19 And they [I]pledged[3027] to put
away their wives, and being guilty,[816]
[a]*they offered* a ram of the flock for their
offense.
20 And of the sons of Immer *there*
were Hanani and Zebadiah;
21 and of the sons of Harim: Maaseiah, Elijah, Shemaiah, Jehiel, and Uzziah;
22 and of the sons of Pashhur: Elioenai, Maaseiah, Ishmael, Nethanel, Jozabad, and Elasah.
23 And of Levites *there were* Jozabad, Shimei, Kelaiah (that is, Kelita),
Pethahiah, Judah, and Eliezer.
24 And of the singers[7891] *there was*
Eliashib; and of the gatekeepers:[7778]
Shallum, Telem, and Uri.
25 And of Israel, of the sons of
[a]Parosh *there were* Ramiah, Izziah, Malchijah, Mijamin, Eleazar, Malchijah, and
Benaiah;
26 and of the sons of Elam: Mattaniah, Zechariah, Jehiel, Abdi, Jeremoth,
and Elijah;
27 and of the sons of [a]Zattu: Elioenai, Eliashib, Mattaniah, Jeremoth, Zabad, and Aziza;
28 and of the sons of Bebai: Jehohanan, Hananiah, Zabbai, *and* Athlai;
29 and of the sons of Bani: Meshullam, Malluch, and Adaiah, Jashub,
Sheal, *and* Jeremoth;
30 and of the sons of Pahath-moab:
Adna, Chelal, Benaiah, Maaseiah,

9 [a]1Sam. 12:18; Ezra 9:4; 10:3
11 [a]Lev. 26:40; Prov. 28:13 [b]Rom. 12:2 [c]Ezra 10:3
12 [I]Lit., *upon us*
14 [I]Lit., *stand for* [a]2Kin. 23:26; 2Chr. 28:11-13; 29:10; 30:8
15 [I]Lit., *stood against*
16 [I]Heb. reads *there were set apart Ezra the priest, men* [II]Lit., *sat*
18 [a]Ezra 5:2; Hag. 1:1, 12; 2:4; Zech. 3:1; 6:11
19 [I]Lit., *gave their hand* [a]Lev. 5:15; 6:6
25 [a]Ezra 2:3; 8:3; Neh. 7:8
27 [a]Ezra 2:8; Neh. 7:13

Mattaniah, Bezalel, Binnui, and Manasseh;
31 and *of* the sons of Harim: Eliezer, Isshijah, [a]Malchijah, Shemaiah, Shimeon,
32 Benjamin, Malluch, *and* Shemariah;
33 of the sons of Hashum: Mattenai, Mattattah, Zabad, Eliphelet, Jeremai, Manasseh, *and* Shimei;
34 of the sons of Bani: Maadai, Amram, Uel,
35 Benaiah, Bedeiah, Cheluhi,
36 Vaniah, Meremoth, Eliashib,
37 Mattaniah, Mattenai, Jaasu,
38 Bani, Binnui, Shimei,
39 Shelemiah, Nathan, Adaiah,
40 Machnadebai, Shashai, Sharai,
41 Azarel, Shelemiah, Shemariah,
42 Shallum, Amariah, *and* Joseph.
43 Of the sons of [a]Nebo *there were* Jeiel, Mattithiah, Zabad, Zebina, Jaddai, Joel, *and* Benaiah.
44 All these had married[5375] [a]foreign wives, and some of them had wives *by whom* they had children.

31 [a]Neh. 3:11
43 [a]Num. 32:38; Ezra 2:29
44 [a]1Kin. 11:1-3; Ezra 10:3

The Book of

NEHEMIAH

Although the current Books of Ezra and Nehemiah were originally one book, and later came to be known as I Ezra and II Ezra, Jerome was the first man to call the second portion by the name of "Nehemiah." The names of "Ezra" and "Nehemiah" were first printed in an English edition in the Geneva Bible in 1560. Nehemiah means "Jehovah comforts." Nehemiah was the principal character of the book and probably wrote it. The book recounts the rebuilding of Jerusalem as a fortified city and the establishment of civil authority there. Nehemiah was appointed by the Persians to be governor. He came with an army escort at government expense to accomplish God's purpose. The Book of Nehemiah is a natural sequel to the Book of Ezra. It focuses much attention upon their efforts to rebuild the walls of Jerusalem, despite fierce opposition from unfriendly neighbors. The Persian kings were humane rulers, unlike their predecessors, the Assyrians. The Persian Empire (539—331 B.C.) was established upon a more benign policy of returning displaced ethnic groups to their homelands. Nehemiah was a remarkable spiritual leader who could perform in practical ways. He was very sad to learn of the terrible condition of Jerusalem, but he believed that God, working through pagan kings, could bring about full restoration. He trusted God completely and would not be intimidated by anyone. The Book of Nehemiah covers about twenty-five years (457—432 B.C.). The prophet Malachi was active during this time.

Nehemiah's Grief for the Exiles

1 The words[1697] of [a]Nehemiah the
son[1121] of Hacaliah.
Now it happened in [b]the month Chislev, [c]*in* the twentieth year, while I was
in [d]Susa the [I]capitol,
2 that [a]Hanani, one of my brothers,[251] and [I]some men[582] from Judah
came; and I asked[7592] them concerning
the Jews who had escaped[6413] *and* had
survived[7604] the captivity,[7628] and about
Jerusalem.
3 And they said to me, "The remnant there in the [a]province who survived
the captivity are in great distress[7451] and
[b]reproach,[2781] and [c]the wall of Jerusalem
is broken down and [d]its gates are burned
with fire."
4 Now it came about when I
heard[8085] these words, [a]I sat down and
wept and mourned for days;[3117] and I
was fasting and praying[6419] before
[b]the God[430] of heaven.[8064]
5 And I said, "I beseech[577] Thee,
O LORD God of heaven, [a]the great and
awesome[3372] God,[410] [b]who preserves[8104] the covenant[1285] and lovingkindness[2617] for those who love[157] Him
and keep[8104] His commandments,[4687]
6 [a]let Thine ear[241] now be attentive
and Thine eyes open to hear[8085] the
prayer[8605] of Thy servant[5650] which I
am praying[6419] before Thee now, day[3119]
and night,[3915] on behalf of the sons[1121]
of Israel Thy servants,[5650] [b]confess-
ing[3034] the sins of the sons of Israel
which we have sinned[2398] against Thee;
[c]I and my father's[1] house[1004] have
sinned.
7 "[a]We have acted very corruptly[2254] against Thee and have not
kept[8104] the commandments, nor the
statutes,[2706] nor the ordinances[4941]
[b]which Thou didst command[6680] Thy servant Moses.
8 "Remember[2142] the word[1697]
which Thou didst command Thy servant
Moses, saying, '[a]If you are unfaithful[4603]
I will scatter you among the peoples;[5971]
9 [a]but if you return[7725] to Me and
keep[8104] My commandments and do[6213]
them, though those of you who have
been scattered were in the most remote
part of the heavens, I [b]will gather[6908]
them from there and will bring them
[c]to the place where I have chosen[977]
to cause My name to dwell.'

1 [I]Or, *palace* or *citadel* [a]Neh. 10:1 [b]Zech. 7:1 [c]Neh. 2:1 [d]Esth. 1:2; Dan. 8:2
2 [I]Lit., *he and some* [a]Neh. 7:2
3 [a]Neh. 7:6 [b]Neh. 2:17 [c]Neh. 2:17 [d]Neh. 2:3
4 [a]Ezra 9:3; 10:1 [b]Neh. 2:4
5 [a]Neh. 4:14; 9:32; Dan. 9:4 [b]Ex. 20:6; Ps. 89:2, 3
6 [a]Dan. 9:17 [b]Ezra 10:1; Dan. 9:20 [c]2Chr. 29:6
7 [a]Dan. 9:5 [b]Deut. 28:14
8 [a]Lev. 26:33
9 [a]Deut. 30:2, 3 [b]Deut. 30:4 [c]Deut. 12:5

10 "And [a]they are Thy servants and
Thy people[5971] whom Thou didst
redeem[6299] by Thy great power and by
Thy strong[2389] hand.[3027]
🔑 11 "O Lord,[136] I beseech Thee,
[a]may Thine ear be attentive to the
prayer of Thy servant and the prayer
of Thy servants who delight[2655] to
[I]revere[3372] Thy name, and make Thy
servant successful today,[3117] and grant
him compassion[7356] before this man."[376]
Now I was the [b]cupbearer to the
king.[4428]

Nehemiah's Prayer Answered

2 And it came about in the month Nisan, [a]in the twentieth year of King
[b]Artaxerxes, that wine *was* before him,
and [c]I took up[5375] the wine and gave it
to the king.[4428] Now I had not been sad
in his presence.
2 So the king said to me, "Why is
your face sad though you are not sick?
[a]This is nothing but sadness of
heart."[3820] Then I was very much
afraid.
3 And I said[559] to the king, "[a]Let
the king live[2421] forever.[5769] Why should
my face not be sad [b]when the city, the
place of my fathers'[1] tombs,[6913] lies
desolate[2720] and its gates have been consumed by fire?"
4 Then the king said to me, "What
would you request?" [a]So I prayed[6419]
to the God[430] of heaven.[8064]
5 And I said to the king, "If it
please[2898] the king, and if your
servant[5650] has found favor before you,
send me to Judah, to the city of my
fathers' tombs, that I may rebuild it."
6 Then the king said to me, the
queen[7694] sitting beside him, "How long
will your journey be, and when will you
return?"[7725] So it pleased the king to
send me, and [a]I gave him a definite
time.[2165]
7 And I said to the king, "If it please
the king, let letters be given me
[a]for the governors[6346] *of the provinces*
beyond the River, that they may
allow[5674] me to pass through until I come
to Judah,
8 and a letter to Asaph the
keeper[8104] of the king's[4428] [a]forest, that
he may give me timber to make beams
for the gates of [b]the fortress which is
by the [I]temple,[1004] for the wall of the
city, and for the house to which I will
go." And the king granted *them* to me
because [c]the good[2896] hand[3027] of my
God *was* on me.
9 Then I came to [a]the governors
of the provinces beyond the River and
gave them the king's letters. Now
[b]the king had sent with me officers[8269]
of the army[2428] and horsemen.
🔑 10 And when [a]Sanballat the Horonite and Tobiah the Ammonite [I]official
heard[8085] *about it,* it was very displeasing
to them that someone[120] had come to
seek the welfare of the sons[1121] of Israel.

Nehemiah Inspects Jerusalem's Walls

11 So I [a]came to Jerusalem and was
there three days.[3117]

10 [a]Ex. 32:11; Deut. 9:29
11 [I]Or, *fear* [a]Neh. 1:6 [b]Gen. 40:21; Neh. 2:1
1 [a]Neh. 1:1 [b]Ezra 7:1 [c]Neh. 1:11
2 [a]Prov. 15:13
3 [a]Dan. 2:4 [b]2Kin. 25:8-10; 2Chr. 36:19; Neh. 1:3; Jer. 52:12-14
4 [a]Neh. 1:4
6 [a]Neh. 13:6
7 [a]Ezra 7:21; 8:36
8 [I]Lit., *house* [a]Eccl. 2:5, 6 [b]Neh. 7:2 [c]Ezra 7:6; Neh. 2:18
9 [a]Neh. 2:7 [b]Ezra 8:22
10 [I]Lit., *servant* [a]Neh. 2:19; 4:1
11 [a]Ezra 8:32

🔑 **1:11** The position of cupbearer was one of complete trust; it gave one access to the king. The cupbearer's main responsibility was to taste wine from the king's cup to insure that he would not be poisoned. Since cupbearers were usually eunuchs, some scholars have noted that no mention is made of Nehemiah being married, and therefore they have concluded that he also must have been a eunuch. This may be true since he also had contact with the queen (Neh. 2:6).

🔑 **2:10** Sanballat was a Horonite indicating he was either from Beth-horon in Ephraim or from Horonaim. The names of his two sons, Delaiah and Shelemiah (also mentioned in the papyri), would seem to indicate that he worshiped Yahweh (Jehovah). The Elephantine papyri mention him as the governor of Samaria. Therefore, his opposition was politically motivated, since Samaria would no longer have control of the region of Judea. Tobiah, being an Ammonite, probably governed the area of east of Judea. He was either a subordinate of Sanballat (note he is called "official") or in very close collaboration with him.

12 And I arose in the night,[3915] I and a few men[582] with me. I did not tell[5046] anyone what my God was putting into my [I]mind to do[6213] for Jerusalem and there was no animal with me except the animal on which I was riding.

13 So I went out at night by [a]the Valley Gate in the direction of the Dragon's[8577] Well and *on* to the [I]Refuse Gate, inspecting the walls of Jerusalem [b]which were broken down and its [c]gates which were consumed by fire.

14 Then I passed on to [a]the Fountain Gate and [b]the King's Pool, but there was no place for [I]my mount to pass.

15 So I went up at night by the [a]ravine and inspected[7665] the wall. Then I entered the Valley Gate again and returned.[7725]

16 And the officials[5461] did not know[3045] where I had gone or what I had done; nor had I as yet told the Jews, the priests,[3548] the nobles,[2715] the officials, or the rest[3499] who did the work.[4399]

17 Then I said to them, "You see the bad situation[7451] we are in, that [a]Jerusalem is desolate and its gates burned by fire. Come, let us rebuild the wall of Jerusalem that we may no longer be a reproach."[2781]

18 And I told them how the hand of my God had been favorable to me, and also about the king's words[1697] which he had spoken to me. Then they said, "Let us arise and build." [a]So they put[2388] their hands[3027] to the good *work.*

19 But when Sanballat the Horonite, and Tobiah the Ammonite [I]official, and [a]Geshem the Arab heard *it,* [b]they mocked us and despised us and said, "What is this thing[1697] you are doing? [c]Are you rebelling[4775] against the king?"

20 So I answered them and said to them, "[a]The God of heaven will give us success; therefore we His servants[5650] will arise and build, [b]but you have no portion, right,[6666] or memorial[2146] in Jerusalem."

12 [I]Lit., *heart*
13 [I]Lit., *Gate of Ash-heaps* [a]Neh. 3:13 [b]Neh. 1:3 [c]Neh. 2:3, 17
14 [I]Lit., *the animal under me* [a]Neh. 3:15 [b]2Kin. 20:20
15 [a]John 18:1
17 [a]Neh. 1:3
18 [a]2Sam. 2:7
19 [I]Lit., *servant* [a]Neh. 6:6 [b]Neh. 4:1 [c]Neh. 6:6
20 [a]Ezra 4:3 [b]Neh. 2:4; Acts 8:21
1 [I]Lit., *it* [a]Neh. 3:20; 13:28 [b]Neh. 3:32; 12:39 [c]Neh. 6:1; 7:1 [d]Neh. 12:39 [e]Jer. 31:38
2 [I]Lit., *him* [a]Neh. 7:36
3 [a]Neh. 12:39
4 [I]Lit., *them*
5 [I]Lit., *them* [II]Lit., *bring their neck to*
6 [a]Neh. 12:39
7 [I]Or, *which was under the jurisdiction of the governor* of the province *beyond the River, also made repairs* [a]Neh. 2:7
8 [a]Neh. 3:31, 32 [b]Neh. 12:38
9 [a]Neh. 3:12, 17

Builders of the Walls

3 Then [a]Eliashib the high priest[3548] arose with his brothers[251] the priests[3548] and built [b]the Sheep Gate; they consecrated it and [c]hung its doors. They consecrated[6942] [I]the wall to [d]the Tower of the Hundred *and* [e]the Tower of Hananel.

2 And next to him [a]the men[582] of Jericho built, and next to [I]them Zaccur the son[1121] of Imri built.

3 Now the sons[1121] of Hassenaah built [a]the Fish[1709] Gate; they laid its beams and hung its doors with its bolts and bars.

4 And next to them Meremoth the son of Uriah the son of Hakkoz made repairs.[2388] And next to him Meshullam the son of Berechiah the son of Meshezabel made repairs. And next to [I]him Zadok the son of Baana also made repairs.

5 Moreover, next to [I]him the Tekoites made repairs, but their nobles[117] did not [II]support the work[5656] of their masters.[113]

6 And Joiada the son of Paseah and Meshullam the son of Besodeiah repaired [a]the Old Gate; they laid its beams and hung its doors, with its bolts and its bars.

7 Next to them Melatiah the Gibeonite and Jadon the Meronothite, the men of Gibeon and of Mizpah, [I]also made repairs for the official seat[3678] of the [a]governor[6346] *of the province* beyond the River.

8 Next to him Uzziel the son of Harhaiah of the [a]goldsmiths[6884] made repairs. And next to him Hananiah, one of the perfumers,[7543] made repairs, and they restored Jerusalem as far as [b]the Broad Wall.

9 And next to them Rephaiah the son of Hur, [a]the official[8269] of half the district of Jerusalem, made repairs.

10 Next to them Jedaiah the son of Harumaph made repairs opposite his house.[1004] And next to him Hattush the son of Hashabneiah made repairs.

11 Malchijah the son of Harim and

Hasshub the son of Pahath-moab repaired another section and [a]the Tower of Furnaces.

12 And next to him Shallum the son of Hallohesh, [a]the official of half the district of Jerusalem, made repairs, he and his daughters.

13 Hanun and the inhabitants of Zanoah repaired [a]the Valley Gate. They built it and hung its doors with its bolts and its bars, and a thousand cubits of the wall to the [I]Refuse Gate.

14 And Malchijah the son of Rechab, the official of the district of [a]Beth-haccherem repaired the [Ib]Refuse Gate. He built it and hung its doors with its bolts and its bars.

15 Shallum the son of Col-hozeh, the official of the district of Mizpah, [a]repaired the Fountain Gate. He built it, covered it, and hung its doors with its bolts and its bars, and the wall of the Pool of Shelah at [b]the king's[4428] garden as far as [c]the steps that descend from the city of David.

16 After him Nehemiah the son of Azbuk, [a]official of half the district of Beth-zur, made[6213] repairs as far as *a point* opposite the tombs[6913] of David, and as far as [b]the artificial pool and the house of the mighty men.

17 After him the Levites carried out repairs *under* Rehum the son of Bani. Next to him Hashabiah, the official of half the district of Keilah, carried out repairs for his district.

18 After him their brothers carried out repairs *under* Bavvai the son of Henadad, official of *the other* half of the district of Keilah.

19 And next to him Ezer the son of Jeshua, [a]the official of Mizpah, repaired [I]another section, in front of the ascent of the armory[5402] [b]at the Angle.

20 After him Baruch the son of Zabbai zealously[2734] repaired another section, from the Angle to the door way of the house of [a]Eliashib the high priest.

21 After him Meremoth the son of Uriah the son of Hakkoz repaired another section, from the doorway of Eliashib's house even as far as the end of [I]his house.

22 And after him the priests, [a]the men of the [I]valley, carried out repairs.

23 After [I]them Benjamin and Hasshub carried out repairs in front of their house. After [I]them Azariah the son of Maaseiah, son of Ananiah carried out repairs beside his house.

24 After him Binnui the son of Henadad repaired another section, from the house of Azariah as far as [a]the Angle and as far as the corner.

25 Palal the son of Uzai *made repairs* in front of the Angle and the tower projecting from the upper[5945] house of the king, which is by [a]the court of the guard. After him Pedaiah the son of Parosh *made repairs.*

26 And [a]the temple servants living in [b]Ophel *made repairs* as far as the front of [c]the Water Gate toward the east and the projecting tower.

27 After him [a]the Tekoites repaired another section in front of the great projecting tower and as far as the wall of Ophel.

28 Above [a]the Horse Gate the priests carried out repairs, each[376] in front of his house.

29 After [I]them Zadok the son of Immer carried out repairs in front of his house. And after him Shemaiah the son of Shecaniah, the keeper[8104] of the East Gate, carried out repairs.

30 After him Hananiah the son of Shelemiah, and Hanun the sixth son of Zalaph, repaired another section. After him Meshullam the son of Berechiah carried out repairs in front of his own [I]quarters.

31 After him Malchijah [I]one of [a]the goldsmiths, carried out repairs as far as the house of the temple servants and of the merchants, in front of the [II]Inspection Gate and as far as the upper room of the corner.

32 And between the upper room of the corner and [a]the Sheep Gate the goldsmiths and the merchants carried out repairs.

11 [a]Neh. 12:38
12 [a]Neh. 3:9
13 [I]Lit., *Gate of Ash-heaps* [a]Neh. 2:13
14 [I]Lit., *Gate of Ash-heaps* [a]Jer. 6:1 [b]Neh. 2:13
15 [a]Neh. 2:17 [b]2Kin. 25:4 [c]Neh. 12:37
16 [a]Neh. 3:9, 12, 17 [b]2Kin. 20:20; Is. 7:3
19 [I]Lit., *a second measure,* and so in vv. 20, 21, 24, 30 [a]Neh. 3:15 [b]2Chr. 26:9
20 [a]Neh. 3:1
21 [I]Lit., *Eliashib's*
22 [I]Lit., *circle;* i.e., lower Jordan valley [a]Neh. 12:28
23 [I]Lit., *him*
24 [a]Neh. 3:19
25 [a]Jer. 32:2
26 [a]Neh. 7:46 [b]Neh. 11:21 [c]Neh. 8:1
27 [a]Neh. 3:5
28 [a]2Kin. 11:16; 2Chr. 23:15; Jer. 31:40
29 [I]Lit., *him*
30 [I]Or, *cell*
31 [I]Lit., *son of* [II]Or, *Mustering* [a]Neh. 3:8, 32
32 [a]Neh. 3:1; 12:39

Work Is Ridiculed

4 [I]Now it came about that when
[a]Sanballat heard[8085] that we were
rebuilding the wall, he became furious[2734] and very angry[3707] and mocked
the Jews.
2 And he spoke[559] in the presence
of his brothers[251] and [a]the [I]wealthy[2428]
men of Samaria and said,[559] "What are
these feeble Jews doing?[6213] Are they
going to restore *it* for themselves? Can
they offer sacrifices?[2076] Can they finish
in a day?[3117] Can they revive[2421] the
stones from the [IIb]dusty rubble[6083] even
the burned[8313] ones?"
3 Now Tobiah the Ammonite *was*
near him and he said, "Even what they
are building—[a]if a fox should [I]jump on
it, he would break their stone wall
down!"
4 [a]Hear,[8085] O our God,[430] how we
are despised! [b]Return[7725] their reproach[2781] on their own heads[7218] and
give them up for plunder in a land[776]
of captivity.[7633]
5 Do not [Ia]forgive[3680] their iniquity[5771] and let not their sin be blotted
out[4229] before Thee, for they have
[II]demoralized[3707] the builders.[1129]
6 So we built the wall and the whole
wall was joined together to half its *height,*
for the people[5971] had a [I]mind[3820] to
work.[6213]
7 [I]Now it came about when Sanballat, Tobiah, the Arabs, the Ammonites,
and the Ashdodites heard that the
[II]repair of the walls of Jerusalem went
on,[724] *and* that the breaches began to
be closed, they were very angry.
8 And all of them [a]conspired together to come *and* fight against Jerusalem and to cause a disturbance in it.

Discouragement Overcome

9 But we prayed to our God,[430] and
because of them we [a]set up a guard
against them day[3119] and night.[3915]
10 Thus [I]in Judah it was said,
"The strength of the burden
bearers is failing,[3782]
Yet there is much [II]rubbish;
And we ourselves are unable
To rebuild the wall."
11 And our enemies said, "They will
not know[3045] or see until we come among
them, kill[2026] them, and put a stop[7673]
to the work."[4399]
12 And it came about when the Jews
who lived near them came and told us
ten times, "[I]They will come up against
us from every place where you may
turn,"[7725]
13 then I stationed *men* in the lowest parts of the space behind the wall,
the [I]exposed places, and I [a]stationed
the people in families[4940] with their
swords,[2719] spears, and bows.
14 When I saw *their fear,* I rose and
spoke to the nobles,[2715] the officials,[5461]
and the rest[3499] of the people: "[a]Do not
be afraid of them; remember[2142] the
Lord[136] who is great and awesome,[3372]
and [b]fight for your brothers, your
sons,[1121] your daughters, your wives,[802]
and your houses."[1004]
15 And it happened when our enemies heard that it was known[3045] to us,
and that [a]God had frustrated[6565] their
plan,[6098] then all of us returned[7725] to
the wall, each one[376] to his work.
16 And it came about from that
day[3117] on, that half of my servants carried on the work while half of them
held[2388] the spears, the shields, the
bows, and the breastplates;[8302] and the
captains[8269] *were* behind the whole
house[1004] of Judah.
17 Those who were rebuilding the
wall and those who carried[5375] burdens
took *their* load with one hand[3027] doing
the work and the other holding a
weapon.
18 As for the builders, each *wore*
his sword[2719] girded at his side as he
built, while [I]the trumpeter[8628] *stood* near
me.
19 And I said to the nobles, the officials, and the rest of the people, "The
work is great and extensive, and we
are separated on the wall far from one
another.
20 "At whatever place you hear the

1 [I]Ch. 3:33 in Heb. [a]Neh. 2:10
2 [I]Or, *army* [II]Lit., *heaps of dust* [a]Ezra 4:9, 10 [b]Neh. 4:10
3 [I]Lit., *go up* [a]Lam. 5:18
4 [a]Ps. 123:3, 4 [b]Ps. 79:12
5 [I]Lit., *cover* [II]Lit., *offended against* [a]Ps. 69:27, 28; Jer. 18:23
6 [I]Lit., *heart*
7 [I]Ch. 4:1 in Heb. [II]Lit., *healing*
8 [a]Ps. 83:3
9 [a]Neh. 4:11
10 [I]Lit., *Judah said* [II]Lit., *dust*
12 [I]So Gr.; Heb. omits *they . . . up*
13 [I]Lit., *bare* [a]Neh. 4:17, 18
14 [a]Num. 14:9; Deut. 1:29, 30 [b]2Sam. 10:12
15 [a]2Sam. 17:14
18 [I]Lit., *he who sounded the trumpet*

sound of the trumpet, [I]rally[6908] to us there. [a]Our God will fight for us.”

21 So we carried on the work with half of them holding spears from [I]dawn[5927] until the stars [II]appeared.

22 At that time[6256] I also said to the people, “Let each man with his servant spend the night within Jerusalem so that they may be a guard for us by night and a laborer[4399] by day.”

23 So neither I, my brothers, my servants, nor the men[582] of the guard who followed me, none of us removed our clothes, each *took* his weapon *even to* the water.

Usury Abolished

5 Now [a]there was a great outcry of the people[5971] and of their wives[802] against their [b]Jewish brothers.[251]

2 For there were those who said, “We, our sons[1121] and our daughters, are many; therefore let us [a]get grain that we may eat and live.”[2421]

3 And there were others who said, “We are mortgaging[6148] our fields, our vineyards, and our houses[1004] that we might get grain because of the famine.”

4 Also there were those who said, “We have borrowed money [a]for the king's[4428] tax *on* our fields and our vineyards.

5 “And now [a]our flesh[1320] is like the flesh of our brothers, our children[1121] like their children. Yet behold, [b]we are forcing our sons and our daughters to be slaves,[5650] and some of our daughters are forced into bondage *already,* and [I]we are helpless because our fields and vineyards belong to others.”[582]

6 Then I was very [a]angry[2734] when I had heard[8085] their outcry and these words.[1697]

7 And I consulted with myself, and contended with the nobles[2715] and the rulers[5461] and said to them, “[a]You are exacting usury, each[376] from his brother!”[251] Therefore, I held a great assembly[6952] against them.

8 And I said to them, “We according to our ability [a]have [I]redeemed our Jewish brothers who were sold to the nations;[1471] now would you even sell your brothers that they may be sold to us?” Then they were silent and could not find a word *to say.*

9 Again I said, “The thing which you are doing[6213] is not good;[2896] should you not walk in the fear[3374] of our God because of [a]the reproach[2781] of the nations, our enemies?

10 “And likewise I, my brothers and my servants, are lending them money and grain. Please,[4994] let us leave off[5800] this usury.

11 “Please, give back[7725] to them this very day[3117] their fields, their vineyards, their olive groves, and their houses, also the hundredth *part* of the money and of the grain, the new wine, and the oil[3323] that you are exacting from them.”

12 Then they said, “We [a]will give *it* back and [b]will require nothing from them; we will do exactly as you say.”[559] So I called[7121] the priests[3548] and [c]took an oath[7650] from them that they would do according to this [I]promise.[1697]

13 I [a]also shook out the [I]front of my garment and said, “Thus may God shake out every man[376] from his house[1004] and from his possessions who does not fulfill this [II]promise; even thus may he be shaken out and emptied.” And [b]all the assembly[6951] said, “Amen!”[543] And they praised[1984] the LORD. Then the people did according to this [II]promise.

Nehemiah's Example

14 Moreover, from the day[3117] that I was appointed[6680] to be their governor[6346] in the land[776] of Judah, from [a]the twentieth year to the [b]thirty-second year of King[4428] Artaxerxes, *for* twelve years, neither I nor my [I]kinsmen have eaten the governor's food *allowance.*

15 But the former[7223] governors[6346] who were before me [I]laid burdens[3513] on the people and took from them bread and wine besides forty shekels of silver; even their servants domineered[7980] the

20 [I]Lit., *assemble yourselves* [a]Ex. 14:14; Deut. 1:30

21 [I]Lit., *rising of the dawn* [II]Lit., *came out*

1 [a]Lev. 25:35 [b]Deut. 15:7

2 [a]Hag. 1:6

4 [a]Ezra 4:13; 7:24

5 [I]Lit., *there is not the power in our hands* [a]Gen. 37:27 [b]Lev. 25:39

6 [a]Ex. 11:8

7 [a]Ex. 22:25; Lev. 25:36; Deut. 23:19, 20

8 [I]Lit., *bought* [a]Lev. 25:48

9 [a]Neh. 4:4

12 [I]Lit., *word* [a]2Chr. 28:15 [b]Neh. 10:31 [c]Ezra 10:5

13 [I]Lit., *bosom* [II]Lit., *word* [a]Acts 18:6 [b]Neh. 8:6

14 [I]Lit., *brothers* [a]Neh. 1:1 [b]Neh. 13:6

15 [I]Lit., *made heavy*

people. But I did not do so [a]because
of the fear of God.
16 And I also [I]applied[2388] myself to
the work[4399] on this wall; we did not
buy any land, and all my servants were
gathered[6908] there for the work.
17 Moreover, [a]*there were* at my table one hundred and fifty Jews and officials, besides those who came to us from
the nations that were around us.
18 Now [a]that which was prepared
for each day[3117] was one ox *and* six
choice[1305] sheep, also birds were prepared for me; and once in ten days[3117]
all sorts of wine *were furnished* in abundance. Yet for all this [b]I did not demand
the governor's food *allowance,* because
the servitude[5656] was heavy[3513] on this
people.
19 [a]Remember[2142] me, O my God,
for good, *according to* all that I have
done[6213] for this people.

The Enemy's Plot

6 Now it came about when it was
reported[8085] to Sanballat, Tobiah,
to Geshem the Arab, and to the rest[3499]
of our enemies that I had rebuilt the
wall, and *that* no breach remained[3498]
in it, [a]although at that time[6256] I had
not set up the doors in the gates,
2 that Sanballat and Geshem sent
a message to me, saying, "Come, let
us meet[3259] together at [I]Chephirim in
the plain of [a]Ono." But they were
planning[2803] to [II]harm me.
3 So I sent messengers[4397] to them,
saying, "I am doing[6213] a great work[4399]
and I cannot come down. Why should
the work stop[7673] while I leave it and
come down to you?"
4 And they sent *messages* to me four
times in this manner, and I answered
them in the same way.
5 Then Sanballat sent his servant
to me in the same manner a fifth time
with an open letter in his hand.[3027]
6 In it was written, "It is reported[8085] among the nations,[1471] and
[I]Gashmu says,[559] that [a]you and the Jews
are planning[2803] to rebel;[4775] therefore
you are rebuilding[1129] the wall. And you
are to be their king,[4428] according to
these reports.[1697]
7 "And you have also appointed
prophets[5030] to proclaim in Jerusalem
concerning [I]you, 'A king is in Judah!'
And now it will be reported to the king
according to these reports. So come
now, let us take counsel[3289] together."
8 Then I sent *a message* to him saying, "Such things[1697] as you are saying[559]
have not been done, but you are
[a]inventing[908] them [I]in your own
mind."[3820]
9 For all of them were *trying* to
frighten us, [I]thinking, "[II]They will become discouraged[7503] with the work and
it will not be done."[6213] But now,
[a]*O God,* strengthen[2388] my hands.
10 And when I entered the
house[1004] of Shemaiah the son[1121] of
Delaiah, son of Mehetabel, [a]who was
[I]confined at home, he said, "Let us meet
together in the house of God, within
the temple,[1964] and let us close the doors
of the temple, for they are coming to
kill[2026] you, and they are coming to kill
you at night."[3915]
11 But I said, "[a]Should a man[376] like
me flee? And could one such as I go
into the temple [I]to save his life?[2425] I
will not go in."
12 Then I perceived[5234] [I]that surely
God had not sent him, but he uttered[1696]
his prophecy[5016] against me because Tobiah and Sanballat had hired him.
13 He was hired for this reason,
[a]that I might become frightened and act
accordingly and sin,[2398] so that they
might have an evil[7451] report in order
that they could reproach me.
14 [a]Remember, O my God, Tobiah
and Sanballat according to these works
of theirs, and also Noadiah [b]the prophetess[5031] and the rest of the prophets
who were *trying* to frighten[3372] me.

The Wall Is Finished

15 So [a]the wall was completed[7555]
on the twenty-fifth of *the month* Elul,
in fifty-two days.[3117]

15 [a]Neh. 5:9; Job 31:23
16 [I]Or, *held fast*
17 [a]1Kin. 18:19
18 [a]1Kin. 4:22, 23 [b]2Thess. 3:8
19 [a]Neh. 13:14, 22, 31

1 [a]Neh. 3:1, 3
2 [I]Another reading is, one of *the villages* [II]Lit., *do evil to me* [a]1Chr. 8:12
6 [I]In v. 1 and elsewhere, *Geshem* [a]Neh. 2:19
7 [I]Lit., *you, saying*
8 [I]Lit., *from your heart* [a]Job 13:4; Ps. 52:2
9 [I]Lit., *saying,* [II]Lit., *Their hands will drop from* [a]Ps. 138:3
10 [I]Lit., *shut up* [a]Jer. 36:5
11 [I]Lit., *and live* [a]Prov. 28:1
12 [I]Lit., *and behold God*
13 [a]Neh. 6:6
14 [a]Neh. 13:29 [b]Ezek. 13:17
15 [a]Neh. 4:1, 2

16 And it came about [a]when all our
enemies heard *of it,* and all the nations
surrounding us saw[7200] *it,* they [I]lost their
confidence;[5307] for [b]they recognized[3045]
that this work had been accomplished
[II]with the help of our God.
17 Also in those days many letters
went from the nobles[2715] of Judah to
Tobiah, and Tobiah's *letters* came to
them.
18 For many in Judah were bound
by oath to him because he was the son-
in-law of Shecaniah the son of Arah, and
his son Jehohanan had married the
daughter of Meshullam the son of Berechiah.
19 Moreover, they were speaking[559] about his good deeds[2896] in
my presence and reported my words
to him. Then Tobiah sent letters to
frighten me.

Census of First Returned Exiles

7 Now it came about when [a]the wall
was rebuilt and I had set up the
doors, and the gatekeepers[7778] and the
singers[7891] and the Levites were appointed,
2 that I put [a]Hanani my brother,[251]
and [b]Hananiah the commander[8269] of
[c]the fortress, in charge[6680] of Jerusalem,
for he was [d]a faithful[571] man[376] and feared
God[430] more than many.
3 Then I said to them, "Do not let
the gates of Jerusalem be opened until
the sun is hot, and while they are standing *guard,* let them shut and bolt the
doors. Also appoint guards[4931] from the
inhabitants of Jerusalem, each at his
post, and each[376] in front of his own
house."[1004]
4 Now the city was large and spacious, but the people[5971] in it were few
and the houses were not built.
5 [a]Then my God put it into my
heart[3820] to assemble[6908] the nobles,[2715]
the officials,[5461] and the people to be
enrolled by genealogies. Then I found
the book of the genealogy of those who
came up[5927] first[7223] [I]in which I found
the following record:

6 [a]These are the [I]people[1121] of the
province who came up[5927] from the
captivity[7628] of the exiles[1473] whom
Nebuchadnezzar the king[4428] of Babylon
had carried away,[1540] and who returned
to Jerusalem and Judah, each to his city,
7 who came with Zerubbabel,
Jeshua, Nehemiah, [I]Azariah, [II]Raamiah,
Nahamani, Mordecai, Bilshan, [III]Mis-
pereth, Bigvai, [IV]Nehum, Baanah.
The number of men[582] of the people
of Israel:
8 the sons of Parosh, 2,172;
9 the sons of Shephatiah, 372;
10 the sons of Arah, 652;
11 the sons of Pahath-moab of the
sons of Jeshua and Joab, 2,818;
12 the sons of Elam, 1,254;
13 the sons of Zattu, 845;
14 the sons of Zaccai, 760;
15 the sons of [I]Binnui, 648;
16 the sons of Bebai, 628;
17 the sons of Azgad, 2,322;
18 the sons of Adonikam, 667;
19 the sons of Bigvai, 2,067;
20 the sons of Adin, 655;
21 the sons of Ater, of Hezekiah,
98;
22 the sons of Hashum, 328;
23 the sons of Bezai, 324;
24 the sons of [I]Hariph, 112;
25 the sons of [I]Gibeon, 95;
26 the men of Bethlehem and Netophah, 188;
27 the men of Anathoth, 128;
28 the men of [I]Beth-azmaveth, 42;
29 the men of [I]Kiriath-jearim, Chephirah, and Beeroth, 743;
30 the men of Ramah and Geba,
621;
31 the men of Michmas, 122;
32 the men of Bethel and Ai, 123;
33 the men of the other Nebo, 52;
34 the sons of the other Elam,
1,254;
35 the sons of Harim, 320;
36 the [I]men of Jericho, 345;
37 the sons of Lod, Hadid, and Ono,
721;
38 the sons of Senaah, 3,930.
39 The priests:[3548] the sons of Jedaiah of the house of Jeshua, 973;

16 [I]Lit., *fell exceedingly in their own eyes* [II]Lit., *from our God* [a]Neh. 2:10; 4:1, 7 [b]Ex. 14:25

1 [a]Neh. 6:1, 15

2 [a]Neh. 1:2 [b]Neh. 10:23 [c]Neh. 2:8 [d]Neh. 13:13

5 [I]Lit., *and I found written in it* [a]Prov. 2:6; 3:6

6 [I]Lit., *sons* [a]Ezra 2:1-70

7 [I]In Ezra 2:2, *Seraiah* [II]In Ezra 2:2, *Reelaiah* [III]In Ezra 2:2, *Mispar* [IV]In Ezra 2:2, *Rehum*

15 [I]In Ezra 2:10, *Bani*

24 [I]In Ezra 2:18, *Jorah*

25 [I]In Ezra 2:20, *Gibbar*

28 [I]In Ezra 2:24, *Azmaveth*

29 [I]In Ezra 2:25, *Kiriath-arim*

36 [I]Lit., *sons*

40 the sons of Immer, 1,052;

41 the sons of Pashhur, 1,247;

42 the sons of Harim, 1,017.

43 The Levites: the sons of Jeshua, of Kadmiel, of the sons of [I]Hodevah, 74.

44 The singers: the sons of Asaph, 148.

45 The gatekeepers: the sons of Shallum, the sons of Ater, the sons of Talmon, the sons of Akkub, the sons of Hatita, the sons of Shobai, 138.

46 The temple servants: the sons of Ziha, the sons of Hasupha, the sons of Tabbaoth,

47 the sons of Keros, the sons of [I]Sia, the sons of Padon,

48 the sons of Lebana, the sons of Hagaba, the sons of Shalmai,

49 the sons of Hanan, the sons of Giddel, the sons of Gahar,

50 the sons of Reaiah, the sons of Rezin, the sons of Nekoda,

51 the sons of Gazzam, the sons of Uzza, the sons of Paseah,

52 the sons of Besai, the sons of Meunim, the sons of [I]Nephushesim,

53 the sons of Bakbuk, the sons of Hakupha, the sons of Harhur,

54 the sons of [I]Bazlith, the sons of Mehida, the sons of Harsha,

55 the sons of Barkos, the sons of Sisera, the sons of Temah,

56 the sons of Neziah, the sons of Hatipha.

57 The sons of Solomon's servants:[5650] the sons of Sotai, the sons of [I]Sophereth, the sons of [II]Perida,

58 the sons of Jaala, the sons of Darkon, the sons of Giddel,

59 the sons of Shephatiah, the sons of Hattil, the sons of Pochereth-hazzebaim, the sons of [I]Amon.

60 All the temple servants and the sons of Solomon's servants *were* 392.

61 And these *were* they who came up from Tel-melah, Tel-harsha, Cherub, [I]Addon, and Immer; but they could not show[5046] their fathers' houses or their [II]descendants,[2233] whether they were of Israel:

62 the sons of Delaiah, the sons of Tobiah, the sons of Nekoda, 642.

63 And of the priests: the sons of [I]Hobaiah, the sons of Hakkoz, the sons of Barzillai, who took a wife[802] of the daughters of Barzillai, the Gileadite, and was named[7121] after them.

64 These searched *among* their ancestral registration, but it could not be located; therefore they were considered unclean *and excluded* from the priesthood.[3550]

🗝 65 And [a]the [I]governor said to them that they should not eat from the most holy things[6944] until a priest[3548] arose with [b]Urim[217] and Thummim.[8537]

Total of People and Gifts

66 The whole assembly[6951] together *was* 42,360,

67 besides their male and their female servants, [I]of whom *there were* 7,337; and they had 245 male and female singers.[7891]

68 [Ia]Their horses were 736; their mules, 245;

69 *their* camels, 435; *their* donkeys, 6,720.

70 And some from among the heads[7218] of fathers'[1] *households* gave to the work.[4399] The [Ia]governor gave to the treasury 1,000 gold drachmas,[1871] 50 basins, 530 priests'[3548] garments.

71 And some of the heads of fathers' *households* gave into the treasury of the work 20,000 gold drachmas, and 2,200 silver minas.

72 And that which the rest[7611] of the people gave was 20,000 gold drachmas and 2,000 silver minas, and 67 priests' garments.

73 Now [a]the priests, the Levites, the gatekeepers, the singers, some of the people, the temple servants, and all Israel, lived in their cities.

[b]And when the seventh month

43 [I]In Ezra 2:40, *Hodaviah*

47 [I]In Ezra 2:44, *Siaha*

52 [I]In Ezra 2:50, *Nephisim*

54 [I]In Ezra 2:52, *Bazluth*

57 [I]In Ezra 2:55, *Hassophereth* [II]In Ezra 2:55, *Peruda*

59 [I]In Ezra 2:57, *Ami*

61 [I]In Ezra 2:59, *Addan* [II]Lit., *seed*

63 [I]In Ezra 2:61, *Habaiah*

65 [I]Heb., *Tirshatha,* a Persian title [a]Neh. 8:9; 10:1 [b]Ex. 28:30; Deut. 33:8

67 [I]Lit., *these*

68 [I]So with some ancient mss. and Gr. [a]Ezra 2:66

70 [I]Heb., *Tirshatha,* a Persian title [a]Neh. 7:65; 8:9

73 [a]1Chr. 9:2 [b]Ezra 3:1

🗝 **7:65** The Urim and the Thummim are mentioned here for the last time in the O.T. See Ezra 2:63; note on Ex. 28:30.

came,[5060] the sons of Israel *were* in their cities.

Ezra Reads the Law

8 And all the people[5971] gathered[622] as one man[376] at the square which was in front of [a]the Water Gate, and they [I]asked[559] [b]Ezra the scribe[5608] to bring [c]the book[5612] of the law[8451] of Moses which the LORD had [II]given[6680] to Israel.

2 Then [a]Ezra the priest[3548] brought the law before the assembly[6951] of men,[376] women,[802] and all who *could* listen[8085] with understanding,[995] on [b]the first day[3117] of the seventh month.

3 And he read[7121] from it before the square which was in front of [a]the Water Gate from [I]early morning until midday, in the presence of men[582] and women, those who could understand;[995] and all the people were attentive to the book of the law.

4 And Ezra the scribe stood at a wooden podium which they had made[6213] for the purpose.[1697] And beside him stood Mattithiah, Shema, Anaiah, Uriah, Hilkiah, and Maaseiah on his right hand; and Pedaiah, Mishael, Malchijah, Hashum, Hashbaddanah, Zechariah, *and* Meshullam on his left hand.

5 And Ezra opened [a]the book in the sight of all the people for he was standing above all the people; and when he opened it, all the people [b]stood up.

6 Then Ezra blessed[1288] the LORD the great God.[430] And all the people answered, "[a]Amen,[543] Amen!" while lifting up their hands;[3027] then [b]they bowed low and worshiped[7812] the LORD with *their* faces to the ground.[776]

7 Also Jeshua, Bani, Sherebiah, Jamin, Akkub, Shabbethai, Hodiah, Maaseiah, Kelita, Azariah, Jozabad, Hanan, Pelaiah, and the Levites, explained the law to the people while the people *remained* in their place.

8 And they read from the book, from the law of God, [I]translating to give the sense[7922] so that they understood the reading.[4744]

"This Day Is Holy"

9 Then Nehemiah, who was the [I][a]governor, and Ezra [b]the priest *and* scribe, and the Levites who taught the people said[559] to all the people, "[c]This day is holy[6918] to the LORD your God; [d]do not mourn or weep." For all the people were weeping when they heard[8085] the words[1697] of the law.

10 Then he said to them, "Go, eat of the fat, drink of the sweet, and [a]send portions to him who has nothing prepared;[3559] for this day is holy to our Lord.[113] Do not be grieved,[6087] for the joy of the LORD is your strength."

11 So the Levites calmed all the people, saying, "Be still, for the day is holy; do not be grieved."

12 And all the people went away to eat, to drink, [a]to send portions and to [I]celebrate[6213] a great festival, [b]because they understood[995] the words which had been made known[3045] to them.

Feast of Booths Restored

13 Then on the second day the heads[7218] of fathers'[1] *households* of all the people, the priests,[3548] and the Levites were gathered to Ezra the scribe

1 [I]Lit., *said to* [II]Lit., *commanded* [a]Neh. 3:26 [b]Ezra 7:6 [c]2Chr. 34:15

2 [a]Deut. 31:9-11; Neh. 8:9 [b]Lev. 23:24

3 [I]Lit., *the light* [a]Neh. 8:1

5 [a]Neh. 8:3 [b]Judg. 3:20; 1Kin. 8:12-14

6 [a]Neh. 5:13 [b]Ex. 4:31

8 [I]Or, *explaining*

9 [I]Heb., *Tirshatha*, a Persian title [a]Neh. 7:65, 70 [b]Neh. 12:26 [c]Neh. 8:2 [d]Deut. 12:7, 12

10 [a]Deut. 26:11-13

12 [I]Lit., *make a great rejoicing* [a]Neh. 8:10 [b]Neh. 8:7, 8

8:8 Possibly some of the people no longer understood Hebrew because they spoke only Aramaic. It is probable that this is a reference to an extemporaneous translation of the reading of the law into Aramaic so that the people could clearly understand it. Later, written translations called Targums were made of the Scriptures into the Aramaic language. See note on Dan. 2:4b—7:28.

8:9 Ezra and Nehemiah were contemporaries during a part of their activities. They had both led groups of pilgrims from Babylon at different times, Ezra in 458 B.C. and Nehemiah in 444 B.C. Ezra was associated with the rebuilding of the temple and Nehemiah was in charge of rebuilding the walls of Jerusalem. Nehemiah was the governor while Ezra was the priest. The title of governor is applied to Zerubbabel (Ezra 2:63).

that they might gain insight[7919] into the
words of the law.
14 And they found written in the
law how the LORD had commanded
through Moses that the sons[1121] of Israel
[a]should live in booths during the feast[2282]
of the seventh month.
15 [Ia]So they proclaimed[8085] and circulated a proclamation in all their cities
and [b]in Jerusalem, saying, "[c]Go out
to the hills, and bring olive branches,
and [II]wild olive[8081] branches, myrtle
branches, palm branches, and branches
of *other* leafy trees, to make booths,
as it is written."
16 So the people went out and
brought *them* and made booths for themselves, each[376] [a]on his roof, and in their
courts, and in the courts of the house
of God, and in the square at [b]the Water
Gate, and in the square at [c]the Gate
of Ephraim.
17 And the entire assembly of those
who had returned from the captivity[7628]
made booths and lived in [I]them. The
sons of Israel [a]had indeed not done[6213]
so from the days[3117] of Joshua the son[1121]
of Nun to that day. And [b]there was great
rejoicing.
18 And [a]he read from the book of
the law of God daily,[3117] from the first[7223]
day to the last day. And they [b]cele-
brated[6213] the feast seven days, and on
[c]the eighth day *there was* a solemn
assembly[6116] according to the ordinance.[4941]

The People Confess Their Sin

9 Now on the twenty-fourth day[3117]
of [a]this month the sons[1121] of Israel
assembled[622] [b]with fasting, in sackcloth,[8242] and with [c]dirt[127] upon them.
2 And the [Ia]descendants[2233] of Israel
separated[914] themselves from all foreigners, and stood and [b]confessed[3034]
their sins and the iniquities[5771] of their
fathers.[1]
3 While [a]they stood in their place,
they read[7121] from the book[5612] of the
law[8451] of the LORD their God[430] for a
fourth of the day; and for *another* fourth
they confessed and worshiped[7812] the
LORD their God.
4 [a]Now on the Levites' platform
stood Jeshua, Bani, Kadmiel, Shebaniah,
Bunni, Sherebiah, Bani, *and* Chenani,
and they cried[2199] with a loud voice to
the LORD their God.
5 Then the Levites, Jeshua, Kadmiel, Bani, Hashabneiah, Sherebiah,
Hodiah, Shebaniah, *and* Pethahiah,
said,[559] "Arise, bless[1288] the LORD your
God forever[5769] and ever!
O may Thy glorious[3519] name be
blessed[1288]
And exalted above all
blessing[1293] and praise![8416]
6 "[a]Thou alone art the LORD.
[b]Thou hast made[6213] the
heavens,[8064]
The heaven of heavens[8064] with
all their host,[6635]
The earth[776] and all that is on
it,
The seas and all that is in them.
[c]Thou dost give life[2421] to all of
them
And the heavenly host bows
down before[7812] Thee.
7 "Thou art the LORD God,
[a]Who chose[977] Abram
And brought him out from
[b]Ur of the Chaldees,
And [c]gave[7760] him the name
Abraham.
8 "And Thou didst find [a]his heart[3824]
faithful[539] before Thee,
And didst make[3772] a
covenant[1285] with him
To give *him* the land[776] of the
Canaanite,
Of the Hittite and the Amorite,
Of the Perizzite, the Jebusite,
and the Girgashite—
To give *it* to his [I]descendants.
And Thou [b]hast fulfilled Thy
promise,[1697]
For Thou art righteous.[6662]
9 "[a]Thou didst see the affliction of
our fathers in Egypt,
And didst [b]hear[8085] their cry by
the [I]Red Sea.
10 "Then Thou didst perform

14 [a]Lev. 23:34, 40, 42

15 [I]Lit., *And that they will cause to be heard* [II]Lit., *oil tree,* species unknown [a]Lev. 23:4 [b]Deut. 16:16 [c]Lev. 23:40

16 [a]Jer. 32:29 [b]Neh. 8:1 [c]2Kin. 14:13; Neh. 12:39

17 [I]Lit., *the booths* [a]2Chr. 7:8; 8:13 [b]2Chr. 30:21

18 [a]Deut. 31:11 [b]Lev. 23:36 [c]Num. 29:35

1 [a]Neh. 8:2 [b]Ezra 8:23 [c]1Sam. 4:12

2 [I]Lit., *seed* [a]Ezra 10:11; Neh. 13:3 [b]Prov. 28:13; Jer. 3:13

3 [a]Neh. 8:4

4 [a]Neh. 8:7

6 [a]Deut. 6:4; 2Kin. 19:15 [b]Gen. 1:1 [c]Col. 1:16f.

7 [a]Gen. 12:1 [b]Gen. 11:31 [c]Gen. 17:5

8 [I]Lit., *seed* [a]Gen. 15:6, 18-21 [b]Josh. 21:43-45

9 [I]Lit., *Sea of Reeds* [a]Ex. 3:7 [b]Ex. 14:10-14, 31

[a]signs[226] and wonders[4159]
against Pharaoh,
Against all his servants[5650]
and all the people[5971] of his
land;
For Thou didst know[3045] that
[b]they acted arrogantly toward
them,
And [c]didst make a name for
Thyself as *it is* this day.
11 "And [a]Thou didst divide the sea
before them,
So they passed through the
midst of the sea on dry[3004]
ground;
And [b]their pursuers Thou didst
hurl into the depths,
Like a stone into [I]raging waters.
12 "And with a pillar of cloud
[a]Thou didst lead[5148] them by
day,[3119]
And with a pillar of fire by
night[3915]
To light[216] for them the way[1870]
In which they were to go.
13 "Then [a]Thou didst come down on
Mount Sinai,
And didst [b]speak[1696] with them
from heaven;
Thou didst give to them
[c]just[3477] ordinances[4941] and
true[571] laws,[8451]
Good[2896] statutes[2706] and
commandments.[4687]
14 "So Thou didst make known[3045]
to them [a]Thy holy[6944]
sabbath,[7676]
And didst lay down[6680] for them
commandments,[4687]
statutes, and law,
Through[3027] Thy servant[5650]
Moses.
15 "Thou didst [a]provide bread from
heaven for them for their
hunger,
Thou didst [b]bring forth water
from a rock for them for their
thirst,
And Thou didst [c]tell them to
enter in order to possess[3423]
The land which Thou didst
[I]swear to give them.

16 "But they, our fathers,
[a]acted arrogantly;
They [I][b]became stubborn and
would not listen[8085] to Thy
commandments.
17 "And they refused[3985] to listen,
And [a]did not remember[2142] Thy
wondrous deeds[6381] which
Thou hadst performed[6213]
among them;
So they became stubborn[4805] and
[b]appointed a leader to
return[7725] to their slavery[5659]
[I]in Egypt.
But Thou art a God [c]of
forgiveness,[5547]
Gracious[2587] and compassionate,
Slow[750] to anger,[639] and
abounding in
lovingkindness;[2617]
And Thou didst not forsake
them.
18 "Even when they [a]made for
themselves
A calf of molten[4541] metal
And said, 'This is your God
Who brought[5927] you up from
Egypt,'
And committed great
[I]blasphemies,
19 [a]Thou, in Thy great
compassion,[7356]
Didst not forsake them in the
wilderness;
[b]The pillar of cloud[6051] did not
leave[5493] them by day,[3119]
To guide[5148] them on their way,
Nor the pillar of fire by night,
to light[5046] for them the way
in which they were to go.
20 "And [a]Thou didst give Thy
good Spirit[7307] to instruct
them,
Thy manna[4478] Thou didst not
withhold from their
mouth,[6310]
And Thou didst give them water
for their thirst.
21 "Indeed, [a]forty years Thou didst
provide for them in the
wilderness *and* they were not
in want;

10 [a]Ex. 7:8-12:32 [b]Ex. 5:2 [c]Ex. 9:16

11 [I]Lit., *strong, mighty* [a]Ex. 14:21 [b]Ex. 15:1, 5, 10

12 [a]Ex. 13:21, 22

13 [a]Ex. 19:11, 18-20 [b]Ex. 20:1 [c]Ps. 19:7-9

14 [a]Ex. 16:23; 20:8

15 [I]Lit., *lift up Thy hand* [a]Ex. 16:4, 14, 15 [b]Ex. 17:6; Num. 20:7-13 [c]Deut. 1:8, 21

16 [I]Lit., *stiffened their neck;* so also v. 17 [a]Neh. 9:10 [b]Deut. 1:26-33; 31:27; Neh. 9:29

17 [I]So Gr. and some Heb. mss.; Heb. reads *in their rebellion* [a]Ps. 78:11, 42-55 [b]Num. 14:4 [c]Ex. 34:6, 7; Num. 14:18

18 [I]Lit., *acts of contempt* [a]Ex. 32:4-8, 31

19 [a]Deut. 8:2-4; Neh. 9:27, 31 [b]Neh. 9:12

20 [a]Num. 11:17; Neh. 9:30; Is. 63:11-14

21 [a]Deut. 2:7

Their clothes did not wear out,
nor did their feet swell.
22 "Thou didst also give them
kingdoms[4467] and
peoples,[5971]
And Thou didst allot *them* to
them as a [I]boundary.
[a]And they took possession[3423] of
the land of Sihon [II]the king
of Heshbon,
And the land of Og the king[4428]
of Bashan.
23 "And Thou didst make their sons
numerous as [a]the stars of
heaven,
And Thou didst bring them into
the land
Which Thou hadst told[559] their
fathers to enter and possess.
24 "[a]So their sons entered and
possessed the land.
And [b]Thou didst subdue before
them the inhabitants of the
land, the Canaanites,
And Thou didst give them into
their hand,[3027] with their
kings,[4428] and the peoples of
the land,
To do[6213] with them [I]as they
desired.[7522]
25 "And [a]they captured fortified
cities and a [Ib]fertile land.
They took possession of
[c]houses[1004] full of every good
thing,[2898]
Hewn cisterns,[953] vineyards,
olive groves,
Fruit trees in abundance.
So they ate, were filled, and
[d]grew fat,
And [e]reveled in Thy great
goodness.
26"[a]But they became
disobedient[4784] and
rebelled[4775] against Thee,
And [b]cast Thy law behind their
backs
And [c]killed[2026] Thy prophets[5030]
who had [d]admonished[5149]
them
So that they might return[7725] to
Thee,
And [e]they committed great
[I]blasphemies.
27 "Therefore Thou didst
[a]deliver[5414]
them into the hand of their
oppressors who
oppressed[6687] them,
But when they cried to Thee
[b]in the time[6256] of their
distress,
Thou didst hear from heaven,
and according to Thy great
compassion
Thou didst [c]give them
deliverers[3467] who
delivered[3467] them from the
hand of their oppressors.
28 "But [a]as soon as they had rest,
they did evil[7451] again before
Thee;
Therefore Thou didst
abandon[5800] them to the hand
of their enemies, so that they
ruled[7287] over them.
When they cried again[7725] to
Thee, Thou didst hear from
heaven,
And [b]many times[6256] Thou didst
rescue[5337] them according to
Thy compassion,
29 And [a]admonished them in order
to turn them back to Thy law.
Yet [b]they acted arrogantly and
did not listen to Thy
commandments but
sinned[2398] against Thine
ordinances,
By [c]which if a man[120] observes
them he shall live.[2421]
And they [Id]turned[5637] a stubborn
shoulder and stiffened their
neck, and would not
listen.[8085]
30 "[a]However, Thou didst bear with
them for many years,
And [b]admonished them by
[c]Thy Spirit through Thy
prophets,
Yet they would not give ear.
Therefore Thou didst give them
into the hand of the peoples
of the lands.[776]

22 [I]Lit., *side, corner* [II]So the Gr. and the Latin; Heb. reads *and the land of the king of Heshbon* [a]Num. 21:21-35

23 [a]Gen. 15:5; 22:17

24 [I]Lit., *according to their desire* [a]Josh. 11:23; 21:43 [b]Josh. 18:1

25 [I]Lit., *fat* [a]Deut. 3:5 [b]Num. 13:27 [c]Deut. 6:11 [d]Deut. 32:15 [e]1Kin. 8:66

26 [I]Lit., *acts of contempt* [a]Judg. 2:11 [b]1Kin. 14:9 [c]2Chr. 36:16 [d]Neh. 9:30 [e]Neh. 9:18

27 [a]Judg. 2:14 [b]Deut. 4:29 [c]Judg. 2:16

28 [a]Judg. 3:11 [b]Ps. 106:43

29 [I]Lit., *gave* [a]Neh. 9:26, 30 [b]Neh. 9:10, 16 [c]Lev. 18:5 [d]Zech. 7:11

30 [a]Ps. 95:10; Acts 13:18 [b]2Kin. 17:13-18; 2Chr. 36:15, 16; Neh. 9:26, 29 [c]Neh. 9:20

31 "Nevertheless, in Thy great
compassion Thou [a]didst not
make an end[3617] of them or
forsake[5800] them,
For Thou art [b]a gracious and
compassionate God.
32 "Now therefore, our God,
[a]the great, the mighty, and
the awesome[3372] God, who
dost keep[8104] covenant and
lovingkindness,[2617]
Do not let all the hardship seem
insignificant before Thee,
Which has come upon us, our
kings, our princes,[8269] our
priests,[3548] our prophets, our
fathers, and on all Thy
people,
[b]From the days[3117] of the kings
of Assyria to this day.
33 "However, [a]Thou art just[6662] in
all that has come upon us;
For Thou hast dealt[6213]
faithfully,[571] but we have
acted wickedly.[7561]
34 "For our kings, our leaders, our
priests, and our fathers have
not kept[6213] Thy law
Or paid attention[7181] to Thy
commandments and Thine
[I]admonitions[5715] with which
Thou hast [II]admonished[5749]
them.
35 "But [a]they, in their own
kingdom,[4438]
[b]With Thy great goodness which
Thou didst give them,
With the broad and rich land
which Thou didst set before
them,
Did not serve[5647] Thee or turn
from their evil[7451] deeds.
36 "Behold, [a]we are slaves today,
And as to the land which Thou
didst give to our fathers to
eat of its fruit and its
bounty,[2898]
Behold, we are slaves on it.
37 "And [a]its abundant produce is for
the kings
Whom Thou hast set over us
because of our sins;
They also rule[4910] over our
bodies[1472]
And over our cattle as they
please,[7522]
So we are in great distress.

A Covenant Results

38 "[I]Now because of all this
[a]We are making an agreement[548]
in writing;
And on the [b]sealed document *are
the names of* our leaders, our
Levites *and* our priests."

Signers of the Document

10 [I]Now on the [a]sealed document
were the names of: Nehemiah the
[II]governor, the son[1121] of Hacaliah, and
Zedekiah,
2 Seraiah, Azariah, Jeremiah,
3 Pashhur, Amariah, Malchijah,
4 Hattush, Shebaniah, Malluch,
5 Harim, Meremoth, Obadiah,
6 Daniel, Ginnethon, Baruch,
7 Meshullam, Abijah, Mijamin,
8 Maaziah, Bilgai, Shemaiah. These
were the priests.[3548]
9 And the Levites: Jeshua the son
of Azaniah, Binnui of the sons[1121] of
Henadad, Kadmiel;
10 also their brothers Shebaniah,
Hodiah, Kelita, Pelaiah, Hanan,
11 Mica, Rehob, Hashabiah,
12 Zaccur, Sherebiah, Shebaniah,
13 Hodiah, Bani, Beninu.
14 The leaders[7218] of the people:[5971]
Parosh, Pahath-moab, Elam, Zattu,
Bani,
15 Bunni, Azgad, Bebai,
16 Adonijah, Bigvai, Adin,
17 Ater, Hezekiah, Azzur,
18 Hodiah, Hashum, Bezai,
19 Hariph, Anathoth, Nebai,
20 Magpiash, Meshullam, Hezir,
21 Meshezabel, Zadok, Jaddua,
22 Pelatiah, Hanan, Anaiah,
23 Hoshea, Hananiah, Hasshub,
24 Hallohesh, Pilha, Shobek,
25 Rehum, Hashabnah, Maaseiah,
26 Ahiah, Hanan, Anan,
27 Malluch, Harim, Baanah.

31 [a]Jer. 4:27 [b]Neh. 9:17

32 [a]Neh. 1:5 [b]2Kin. 15:19, 29; 2Kin. 17:3-6; Ezra 4:2, 10

33 [a]Gen. 18:25; Jer. 12:1

34 [I]Lit., *testimonies* [II]Or, *witnessed*

35 [a]Deut. 28:47 [b]Neh. 9:25

36 [a]Deut. 28:48

37 [a]Deut. 28:33

38 [I]Ch. 10:1 in Heb. [a]Neh. 10:29 [b]Neh. 10:1

1 [I]Ch. 10:2 in Heb. [II]Heb., *Tirshatha*, a Persian title [a]Neh. 9:38

Obligations of the Document

28 Now [a]the rest[7605] of the people, the priests, the Levites, the gatekeepers,[7778] the singers,[7891] the temple servants, and [b]all those who had separated[914] themselves from the peoples of the lands[776] to the law[8451] of God,[430] their wives,[802] their sons and their daughters, all those who had knowledge[3045] and understanding,[995]

29 are joining with their [I]kinsmen, their nobles,[117] and are [II][a]taking on themselves a curse[423] and an oath[7621] to walk in God's law, which was given through Moses, God's servant,[5650] and to keep[8104] and to observe[6213] all the commandments[4687] of [III]GOD our Lord,[113] and His ordinances[4941] and His statutes;[2706]

30 and [a]that we will not give our daughters to the peoples of the land[776] or take their daughters for our sons.

31 As [a]for the peoples of the land who bring wares[4728] or any grain[7668] on the sabbath[7676] day[3117] to sell, we will not buy from them on the sabbath or a holy[6944] day; and we will forego[5203] *the crops* the [b]seventh year and the [c]exaction of every debt.

32 We also [I]placed ourselves under obligation to contribute yearly [a]one third of a shekel for the service[5656] of the house[1004] of our God:

33 for the [a]showbread,[4635] for the continual[8548] grain offering,[4503] for the continual burnt offering,[5930] the sabbaths,[7676] the new moon, for the appointed times,[4150] for the holy things and for the sin[2403] offerings to make atonement[3722] for Israel, and all the work[4399] of the house of our God.

34 Likewise [a]we cast[5307] lots [b]for the supply[7133] of wood *among* the priests, the Levites, and the people in order that they might bring it to the house[1004] of our God, according to our fathers'[1] households, at fixed times[6256] annually, to burn on the altar[4196] of the LORD our God as it is written in the law;

35 and in order that they might bring the first fruits of our ground[127] and [a]the first fruits of all the fruit of every tree to the house of the LORD annually,

36 and [a]bring to the house of our God the first-born of our sons and of our cattle, and the first-born of our herds and our flocks as it is written in the law, for the priests who are ministering[8334] in the house of our God.

37 [a]We will also bring the first[7225] of our [I]dough, our contributions,[8641] the fruit of every tree, the new wine and the oil[3323] [b]to the priests at the chambers of the house of our God, and the [c]tithe[4643] of our ground to the Levites, for the Levites are they who receive the tithes[6237] in all the rural towns.

38 And [a]the priest,[3548] the son of Aaron, shall be with the Levites when the Levites receive tithes,[6237] and the Levites shall bring up[5927] the tenth[4643] of the tithes to the house of our God, to the chambers of [b]the storehouse.

39 For the sons[1121] of Israel and the sons of Levi shall bring the [a]contribution[8641] of the grain, the new wine and the oil, to the chambers; there are the utensils of the sanctuary,[4720] the priests who are ministering, the gatekeepers, and the singers. Thus [b]we will not [I]neglect[5800] the house of our God.

Time Passes
Heads of Provinces

11 Now [a]the leaders[8269] of the people[5971] lived in Jerusalem, but the rest[7605] of the people [b]cast[5307] lots to bring one out of ten to live in Jerusalem, [c]the holy[6944] city, while nine-tenths[3027] [8672] *remained* in the *other* cities.

2 And the people blessed[1288] all the men[582] who [a]volunteered to live in Jerusalem.

3 [a]Now these are the heads[7218] of the provinces who lived in Jerusalem, but in the cities of Judah [b]each[376] lived on his own property[272] in their cities—the [I]Israelites, the priests,[3548] the Levites, the [II][c]temple servants and the [III][d]descendants[1121] of Solomon's servants.

---

28 [a]Ezra 2:36-58 [b]Neh. 9:2

29 [I]Lit., *brothers* [II]Lit., *entering into a* [III]Heb., *YHWH*, usually rendered LORD [a]Neh. 5:12

30 [a]Ex. 34:16; Deut. 7:3

31 [a]Neh. 13:15-22 [b]Ex. 23:10, 11; Lev. 25:1-7 [c]Deut. 15:1, 2

32 [I]Lit., *imposed commandments on us* [a]Ex. 30:11-16; Matt. 17:24

33 [a]Lev. 24:5, 6; 2Chr. 2:4

34 [a]Neh. 11:1 [b]Neh. 13:31

35 [a]Ex. 23:19; 34:26; Deut. 26:2

36 [a]Ex. 13:2

37 [I]Or, *coarse meal* [a]Lev. 23:17 [b]Neh. 13:5, 9 [c]Lev. 27:30; Num. 18:21

38 [a]Num. 18:26 [b]Neh. 13:12, 13

39 [I]Lit., *forsake* [a]Deut. 12:6 [b]Neh. 13:10, 11

1 [a]Neh. 7:4 [b]Neh. 10:34 [c]Neh. 11:18; Is. 48:2

2 [a]Judg. 5:9

3 [I]Lit., *Israel* [II]Heb., *Nethinim* [III]Lit., *sons* [a]1Chr. 9:2-34 [b]Neh. 7:73; 11:20 [c]Ezra 2:43 [d]Neh. 7:57

4 And some of the sons of Judah and some of the sons of Benjamin lived in Jerusalem. From the sons of Judah: Athaiah the son[1121] of Uzziah, the son of Zechariah, the son of Amariah, the son of Shephatiah, the son of Mahalalel, of the sons of Perez;

5 and Maaseiah the son of Baruch, the son of Col-hozeh, the son of Hazaiah, the son of Adaiah, the son of Joiarib, the son of Zechariah, the son of the Shilonite.

6 All the sons[1121] of Perez who lived in Jerusalem were 468 able men.

7 Now these are the sons of Benjamin: Sallu the son of Meshullam, the son of Joed, the son of Pedaiah, the son of Kolaiah, the son of Maaseiah, the son of Ithiel, the son of Jeshaiah;

8 and after him Gabbai *and* Sallai, 928.

9 And Joel the son of Zichri was their overseer, and Judah the son of Hassenuah was second [I]in command of the city.

10 From the priests: Jedaiah the son of Joiarib, Jachin,

11 Seraiah the son of Hilkiah, the son of Meshullam, the son of Zadok, the son of Meraioth, the son of Ahitub, the leader[5057] of the house[1004] of God,[430]

12 and their [I]kinsmen who performed the work[4399] of the [II]temple, 822; and Adaiah the son of Jeroham, the son of Pelaliah, the son of Amzi, the son of Zechariah, the son of Pashhur, the son of Malchijah,

13 and his kinsmen, heads of fathers'[1] *households,* 242; and Amashsai the son of Azarel, the son of Ahzai, the son of Meshillemoth, the son of Immer,

14 and their brothers, valiant warriors,[2428, 1368] 128. And their overseer was Zabdiel, the son of [I]Haggedolim.

15 Now from the Levites: Shemaiah the son of Hasshub, the son of Azrikam, the son of Hashabiah, the son of Bunni;

16 and Shabbethai and Jozabad, from the [I]leaders of the Levites, who were [II]in charge of [a]the outside work[4399] of the house of God;

17 and Mattaniah the son of Mica, the son of [I]Zabdi, the son of Asaph, who was the [II]leader[7218] in beginning the thanksgiving[3034] at prayer,[8605] and Bakbukiah, the second among his brethren; and [III]Abda the son of [IV]Shammua, the son of Galal, the son of Jeduthun.

18 All the Levites in [a]the holy city *were* 284.

19 Also the gatekeepers,[7778] Akkub, Talmon, and their brethren, who kept[8104] watch at the gates, *were* 172.

Outside Jerusalem

20 And the rest[7605] of Israel, of the priests, *and* of the Levites, *were* in all the cities of Judah, each [a]on his own inheritance.[5159]

21 But [a]the temple servants were living in Ophel, and Ziha and Gishpa were [I]in charge of the temple servants.

22 Now [a]the overseer of the Levites in Jerusalem was Uzzi the son of Bani, the son of Hashabiah, the son of Mattaniah, the son of Mica, from the sons of Asaph, who were the singers[7891] for the [I]service of the house of God.

23 [a]For *there was* a commandment[4687] from the king[4428] concerning them and a firm regulation[548] for the song leaders [b]day by day.[3117]

24 And Pethahiah the son of Meshezabel, of the sons [a]of Zerah the son of Judah, was the [b]king's [I]representative[3027] in all matters concerning the people.

25 Now as for the villages with their fields,[7704] some of the sons of Judah lived in [a]Kiriath-arba and its [I]towns, in [b]Dibon and its [I]towns, and in Jekabzeel and its villages,

26 and in Jeshua, in Moladah and Beth-pelet,

27 and in Hazar-shual, in Beersheba and its towns,

28 and in Ziklag, in Meconah and in its towns,

29 and in En-rimmon, in Zorah and in Jarmuth,

30 Zanoah, Adullam, and their villages, Lachish and its fields, Azekah and

9 [I]Lit., *over*
12 [I]Lit., *brothers,* and so throughout the ch. [II]Lit., *house*
14 [I]Or, *the great ones*
16 [I]Lit., *heads* [II]Lit., *over* [a]1Chr. 26:29
17 [I]In 1Chr. 9:15, *Zichri* [II]Lit., *head* [III]In 1Chr. 9:16, *Obadiah* [IV]In 1Chr. 9:16, *Shemaiah*
18 [a]Neh. 11:1
20 [a]Neh. 11:3
21 [I]Lit., *over* [a]Neh. 3:26
22 [I]Or, *work* [a]Neh. 11:9, 14
23 [a]Ezra 6:8; 7:20 [b]Neh. 12:47
24 [I]Lit., *hand* [a]Gen. 38:30 [b]1Chr. 18:17
25 [I]Lit., *daughters,* and so throughout the ch. [a]Josh. 14:15 [b]Josh. 13:9, 17

its towns. So they encamped from
Beersheba as far as the valley of Hinnom.
31 The sons of Benjamin also *lived*
from Geba *onward,* at Michmash and
Aija, at Bethel and its towns,
32 at Anathoth, Nob, Ananiah,
33 Hazor, Ramah, Gittaim,
34 Hadid, Zeboim, Neballat,
35 Lod and Ono, the valley of craftsmen.
36 And from the Levites, *some*
divisions in Judah belonged to Benjamin.

Priests and Levites Who Returned to Jerusalem with Zerubbabel

12 Now these are [a]the priests[3548]
and the Levites who came up[5927]
with Zerubbabel the son[1121] of Shealtiel,
and Jeshua: Seraiah, Jeremiah, Ezra,
2 Amariah, Malluch, Hattush,
3 Shecaniah, Rehum, Meremoth,
4 Iddo, Ginnethoi, Abijah,
5 Mijamin, Maadiah, Bilgah,
6 Shemaiah and Joiarib, Jedaiah,
7 Sallu, Amok, Hilkiah, and Jedaiah.
These were the heads[7218] of the priests
and their [I]kinsmen in the days[3117] of
Jeshua.
8 And the Levites *were* Jeshua, Binnui,
Kadmiel, Sherebiah, Judah, *and*
Mattaniah *who was* [I]in charge of the
songs of thanksgiving, he and his brothers.
9 Also Bakbukiah and Unni, their
brothers, stood opposite them [a]in *their*
service divisions.[4931]
10 And Jeshua [I]became the father
of Joiakim, and Joiakim [I]became the father
of Eliashib, and Eliashib [I]became
the father of Joiada,
11 and Joiada became the father of
Jonathan, and Jonathan became the father
of Jaddua.
12 Now in the days of Joiakim the
priests, the heads of fathers'[1] *households*
were: of Seraiah, Meraiah; of Jeremiah,
Hananiah;
13 of Ezra, Meshullam; of Amariah,
Jehohanan;

1 [a]Ezra 2:1; 7:7
7 [I]Lit., *brothers*
8 [I]Lit., *over*
9 [a]Neh. 12:24
10 [I]Lit., *begot,* and so in vv. 11, 12
14 [I]In Neh. 12:2, *Malluch*
24 [I]Lit., *in the commandment of* [a]Neh. 11:17 [b]Neh. 12:9
25 [a]1Chr. 26:15
26 [a]Neh. 8:9

14 of [I]Malluchi, Jonathan; of Shebaniah,
Joseph;
15 of Harim, Adna; of Meraioth,
Helkai;
16 of Iddo, Zechariah; of Ginnethon,
Meshullam;
17 of Abijah, Zichri; of Miniamin, of
Moadiah, Piltai;
18 of Bilgah, Shammua; of Shemaiah,
Jehonathan;
19 of Joiarib, Mattenai; of Jedaiah,
Uzzi;
20 of Sallai, Kallai; of Amok, Eber;
21 of Hilkiah, Hashabiah; of Jedaiah,
Nethanel.

The Chief Levites

22 As for the Levites, the heads
of fathers' *households* were registered
in the days of Eliashib, Joiada, and Johanan,
and Jaddua; so *were* the priests
in the reign[4438] of Darius the Persian.
23 The sons[1121] of Levi, the heads
of fathers' *households,* were registered
in the Book[5612] of the Chronicles up to
the days of Johanan the son of Eliashib.
24 And the heads of the Levites *were*
Hashabiah, Sherebiah, and Jeshua the
son of Kadmiel, with their brothers opposite
them, [a]to praise[1984] *and* give
thanks,[3034] [I]as prescribed[4687] by David
the man[376] of God,[430] [b]division corresponding
to division.
25 Mattaniah, and Bakbukiah, Obadiah,
Meshullam, Talmon, *and* Akkub
were gatekeepers[7778] keeping[8104] watch
at [a]the storehouses[624] of the gates.
26 These *served* in the days of
Joiakim the son of Jeshua, the son of
Jozadak, and in the days of [a]Nehemiah
the governor[6346] and of Ezra the
priest[3548] *and* scribe.[5608]

Dedication of the Wall

27 Now at the dedication[2598] of the
wall of Jerusalem they sought out the
Levites from all their places, to bring
them to Jerusalem so that they might
celebrate[6213] the dedication with gladness,
with hymns of thanksgiving and

with songs[7892] [a]*to the accompaniment* of
cymbals, harps, and lyres.
28 So the sons of the singers[7891]
were assembled[622] from the district
around Jerusalem, and from [a]the villages
of the Netophathites,
29 from Beth-gilgal, and from *their*
fields[7704] in Geba and Azmaveth, for the
singers had built themselves villages
around Jerusalem.
30 And the priests and the Levites
[a]purified themselves; they also purified
the people,[5971] the gates, and the wall.

Procedures for the Temple

31 Then I had the leaders[8269] of Judah come up[5927] on top of the wall, and
I appointed two great [I]choirs, [II][a]the first
proceeding to the right on top of the
wall toward [b]the Refuse Gate.
32 Hoshaiah and half of the leaders
of Judah followed them,
33 with Azariah, Ezra, Meshullam,
34 Judah, Benjamin, Shemaiah,
Jeremiah,
35 and some of the sons of the
priests[3548] with trumpets; *and* Zechariah
the son of Jonathan, the son of Shemaiah, the son of Mattaniah, the son of
Micaiah, the son of Zaccur, the son of
Asaph,
36 and his [I]kinsmen, Shemaiah, Azarel, Milalai, Gilalai, Maai, Nethanel, Judah *and* Hanani, [a]with the musical[7892]
instruments of David the man of God.
And Ezra the scribe went before them.
37 And at [a]the Fountain Gate they
went directly up [b]the steps of the city
of David by the stairway of the wall
above the house of David to [c]the Water
Gate on the east.
38 [a]The second [I]choir proceeded to
the [II]left, while I followed them with
half of the people on the wall, [b]above
the Tower of Furnaces, to [c]the Broad
Wall,
39 and above [a]the Gate of Ephraim,
by [b]the Old Gate, by the [c]Fish[1709] Gate,
[d]the Tower of Hananel, and the Tower
of the Hundred, as far as the Sheep
Gate, and they stopped at [e]the Gate of
the Guard.
40 Then the two choirs took their
stand in the house of God. So did I and
half of the officials[5461] with me;
41 and the priests, Eliakim, Maaseiah, Miniamin, Micaiah, Elioenai,
Zechariah, and Hananiah, with the trumpets;
42 and Maaseiah, Shemaiah, Eleazar, Uzzi, Jehohanan, Malchijah, Elam,
and Ezer. And the singers [I]sang,[8085] with
Jezrahiah *their* leader,
43 and on that day[3117] they
offered[2076] great sacrifices[2077] and rejoiced because [a]God had given them
great joy, even the women[802] and children rejoiced, so that the joy of Jerusalem was heard[8085] from afar.
44 On that day[3117] [a]men were also
appointed over the chambers for the
stores, the contributions,[8641] the first
fruits,[7225] and the tithes, to gather[3664]
into them from the fields of the cities
the portions required by the law[8451] for
the priests and Levites; for Judah rejoiced over the priests and Levites who
[I]served.
45 For they performed[8104] the
[I]worship[4931] of their God and the service
of purification,[2893] together with the
singers and the gatekeepers [a]in accordance with the command of David
and of his son Solomon.
46 For in the days of David and
[a]Asaph, in ancient[6924] times, *there were*
[I][b]leaders of the singers, songs[7892] of
praise[8416] and hymns of thanksgiving to
God.
47 And so all Israel in the days of
Zerubbabel and Nehemiah gave the portions due the singers and the gatekeepers [a]as each day[3117] required, and
[b]set apart the consecrated *portion* for
the Levites, and the Levites set apart
the consecrated[6942] *portion* for the
sons[1121] of Aaron.

Foreigners Excluded

13 On that day[3117] [a]they read[7121]
aloud from the book[5612] of Moses
in the hearing[241] of the people;[5971] and
there was found written in it that

27 [a]1Chr. 15:16, 28
28 [a]1Chr. 9:16
30 [a]Neh. 13:22, 30
31 [I]Lit., *thanksgiving choirs* [II]Heb., *and processions to the right* [a]Neh. 12:38 [b]Neh. 2:13
36 [I]Lit., *brothers* [a]Neh. 12:24
37 [a]Neh. 2:14 [b]Neh. 3:15 [c]Neh. 3:26
38 [I]Lit., *thanksgiving choir* [II]Lit., *front* [a]Neh. 12:31 [b]Neh. 3:11 [c]Neh. 3:8
39 [a]Neh. 8:16 [b]Neh. 3:6 [c]Neh. 3:3 [d]Neh. 3:1 [e]Neh. 3:25
42 [I]Lit., *caused their voices to be heard*
43 [a]Ps. 9:2; 92:4
44 [I]Lit., *stood* [a]Neh. 13:4, 5, 12, 13
45 [I]Lit., *service* [a]1Chr. 25:1
46 [I]Lit., *heads* [a]2Chr. 29:30 [b]1Chr. 9:33
47 [a]Neh. 11:23 [b]Num. 18:21
1 [a]Neh. 9:3

[b]no Ammonite or Moabite should ever[5769] enter the assembly[6951] of God,[430]

2 because they did not meet the sons[1121] of Israel with bread and water, but [a]hired Balaam against them to curse[7043] them. However, [b]our God turned[2015] the curse[7045] into a blessing.[1293]

3 So it came about, that when they heard[8085] the law,[8451] [a]they excluded[914] [b]all foreigners[6154] from Israel.

Tobiah Expelled and the Temple Cleansed

4 Now prior to this, Eliashib the priest,[3548] [a]who was appointed over the chambers of the house[1004] of our God, being [I]related to [b]Tobiah,

5 had prepared a large [I]room for him, where formerly they put the grain offerings,[4503] the frankincense,[3828] the utensils, and the tithes of grain, wine and oil[3323] [a]prescribed for the Levites, the singers[7891] and the gatekeepers,[7778] and the [II]contributions for the priests.[3548]

6 But during all this *time* I was not in Jerusalem, for in [a]the thirty-second year of [b]Artaxerxes king[4428] of Babylon I had gone to the king. After some time,[3117] however, I asked leave[7592] from the king,

7 and I came to Jerusalem and [I]learned[995] about the evil[7451] that Eliashib had done for Tobiah, [a]by preparing[6213] a [II]room for him in the courts of the house of God.

8 And it was very displeasing to me, so I [a]threw all of Tobiah's household[1004] goods out of the room.

9 Then I gave an order[559] and [a]they cleansed[2891] the rooms; and I returned there the utensils of the house of God with the grain offerings[4503] and the frankincense.

Tithes Restored

10 I also [I]discovered[3045] that [a]the portions of the Levites had not been given *them*, so that the Levites and the singers who performed the service[4399] had [II]gone away, [b]each[376] to his own field.[7704]

11 So I [I][a]reprimanded the officials[5461] and said,[559] "[b]Why is the house of God forsaken?"[5800] Then I gathered[6908] them together and restored them to their posts.

12 All Judah then brought [a]the tithe[4643] of the grain, wine, and oil into the storehouses.

13 And in charge of the storehouses I appointed Shelemiah the priest, Zadok the scribe, and Pedaiah of the Levites, and in addition to them was Hanan the son[1121] of Zaccur, the son of Mattaniah; for [a]they were considered[2803] reliable,[539] and it was [I]their task to distribute to their [II]kinsmen.

14 [a]Remember[2142] me for this, O my God, and do not blot out my loyal deeds[2617] which I have performed[6213] for the house of my God and its services.

Sabbath Restored

15 In those days I saw[7200] in Judah some who were treading wine presses [a]on the sabbath,[7676] and bringing in sacks of grain and loading *them* on donkeys, as well as wine, grapes, figs, and all kinds of loads,[4853] [b]and they brought *them* into Jerusalem on the sabbath day. So [c]I admonished[5749] *them* on the day they sold food.[6718]

16 Also men of Tyre were living [I]there *who* imported fish[1709] and all kinds of merchandise,[4377] and sold *them* to the sons of Judah on the sabbath, even in Jerusalem.

17 Then [a]I [I]reprimanded the nobles[2715] of Judah and said to them, "What is this evil thing[1697] you are doing,[6213] [II]by profaning the sabbath day?

18 "[a]Did not your fathers[1] do the same so that our God brought on us, and on this city, all this trouble? Yet you are adding to the wrath on Israel by profaning[2490] the sabbath."

19 [a]And it came about that just as it grew dark[6751] at the gates of Jerusalem

1 [b]Deut. 23:3-5; Neh. 13:23
2 [a]Num. 22:3-11 [b]Deut. 23:5
3 [a]Neh. 9:2; 10:28 [b]Ex. 12:38
4 [I]Lit., *close to* [a]Neh. 12:44 [b]Neh. 2:10; 6:1, 17, 18
5 [I]Or, *chamber* [II]Lit., *heave offerings* [a]Num. 18:21
6 [a]Neh. 5:14 [b]Ezra 6:22
7 [I]Or, *understood* [II]Or, *chamber, and so in vv. 8, 9* [a]Neh. 13:5
8 [a]John 2:13-16
9 [a]2Chr. 29:5, 15, 16
10 [I]Or, *knew* [II]Lit., *fled* [a]Deut. 12:19; Neh. 10:37 [b]Neh. 12:28, 29
11 [I]Or, *contended with* [a]Neh. 13:17, 25 [b]Neh. 10:39
12 [a]Neh. 10:37; 12:44; Mal. 3:10
13 [I]Lit., *on them to* [II]Lit., *brothers* [a]Neh. 7:2
14 [a]Neh. 5:19; 13:22, 31
15 [a]Ex. 20:8; 34:21; Deut. 5:12-14; Jer. 17:22 [b]Neh. 10:31; Jer. 17:21 [c]Neh. 9:29; 13:21
16 [I]Lit., *in it*
17 [I]Or, *contended with* [II]Lit., *and* [a]Neh. 13:11, 25
18 [a]Ezra 9:13; Jer. 17:21
19 [a]Lev. 23:32

before the sabbath, I commanded that
the doors should be shut [I]and that they
should not open them until after the sabbath. Then I stationed some of my
servants[5650] at the gates *that* no load[4853]
should enter on the sabbath day.
20 Once or twice the traders and
merchants of every kind of merchandise[4465] spent the night outside Jerusalem.
21 Then [a]I [I]warned them and said
to them, "Why do you spend the night
in front of the wall? If you do so again,
I will [II]use force[3027] against you." From
that time[6256] on they did not come on
the sabbath.
22 And I commanded the Levites
that [a]they should purify[2891] themselves
and come as gatekeepers[8104] to sanctify[6942] the sabbath day. *For* this also
[b]remember me, O my God, and have
compassion on me according to the
greatness of Thy lovingkindness.[2617]

Mixed Marriages Forbidden

23 In those days I also saw that
the Jews had [Ia]married women[802] from
[b]Ashdod, [c]Ammon, *and* Moab.
24 As for their children, half
spoke[1696] in the language of Ashdod, and
none of them was able to speak[1696] the
language of Judah, but [I]the language of
his own people.
25 So [a]I contended with them and
cursed[7043] them and [b]struck[5221] some
of them and pulled out their hair, and
[c]made them swear[7650] by God, "You
shall not give your daughters to their
sons,[1121] nor take[5375] of their daughters
for your sons or for yourselves.
26 "[a]Did not Solomon king of Israel
sin[2398] regarding these things? [b]Yet
among the many nations[1471] there was
no king like him, and [c]he was loved by
his God, and God made him king over
all Israel; nevertheless the foreign[5237]
women[802] caused even him to sin.[2398]
27 "[I]Do we then hear[8085] about you
that you have committed all this great
evil [a]by acting unfaithfully[4603] against our
God by [II]marrying foreign[5237] women?"
⊶ 28 Even one of the sons of Joiada,
the son of Eliashib the high priest, was
a son-in-law of [a]Sanballat the Horonite,
so I drove him away from me.
29 [a]Remember them, O my God,
[I]because they have defiled the priesthood[3550] and the [b]covenant[1285] of the
priesthood and the Levites.
30 [a]Thus I purified them from
everything foreign and appointed
duties[4931] for the priests and the Levites, each in his task,[4399]
31 and *I arranged* [a]for the supply[7133]
of wood at appointed[2163] times[6256] and
for the first fruits. [b]Remember me, O
my God, for good.[2896]

19 [I]Lit., *and commanded*
21 [I]Lit., *witnessed against* [II]Lit., *send a hand against* [a]Neh. 13:15
22 [a]1Chr. 15:12; Neh. 12:30 [b]Neh. 13:14, 31
23 [I]Lit., *given dwelling to* [a]Ex. 34:11-16; Deut. 7:1-5; Ezra 9:2; Neh. 10:30 [b]Neh. 4:7 [c]Ezra 9:1; Neh. 13:1
24 [I]Lit., *according to the tongue of people and people*
25 [a]Neh. 13:11, 17 [b]Deut. 25:2 [c]Neh. 10:29, 30
26 [a]1Kin. 11:1 [b]1Kin. 3:13; 2Chr. 1:12 [c]2Sam. 12:24, 25
27 [I]Or, *Is it reported* [II]Lit., *giving dwelling to* [a]Ezra 10:2; Neh. 13:23
28 [a]Neh. 2:10, 19; 4:1
29 [I]Lit., *for the defilings of* [a]Neh. 6:14 [b]Num. 25:13
30 [a]Neh. 10:30
31 [a]Neh. 10:34 [b]Neh. 13:14, 22

⊶ **13:28** Joiada, even though he was a priest, was expelled from the Jewish community because he had married outside the family of Israel. Josephus used an event which was quite similar to this to explain the complete break between Jews and Samaritans. This climaxed in the building of the rival Samaritan temple on Mount Gerizim. Josephus' date is 100 years too late for this incident, though he was probably correct in his dating of the Samaritan temple. One might correctly assume that Joiada was induced by this father-in-law to join him in Samaria with the promise of being the high priest in the new temple to be built there. He evidently took with him a copy of the law which is the basis of the Samaritan Pentateuch.

The Book of
ESTHER

The name of this book comes from its main character, Esther, a young Jewish girl who later became Queen of the Persian Empire. Through the providence of God, she was in position (Esth. 4:14) to prevent the annihilation of her entire nation. The Feast of Purim commemorates the deliverance of the Jewish people on that occasion. There is no organic connection between the Book of Esther and the rest of the Bible, but scholars believe that this book is our only glimpse of Jewish life under the Persians during the period between the first and second returns of Jerusalem. Although there is no mention in the Book of Esther of Palestine, Jerusalem, the temple, or the Law of Moses, the events took place within the general timeframe of officially-approved migrations of Jewish exiles back to their homeland. Esther lived during the reign of Ahasuerus (Xerxes I) in 486—465 B.C. Early in his rule, his armies fought the Greeks for the first time. His empire extended from India to Ethiopia and included twenty satrapies, which were divided into many provinces. Jerusalem was only a tiny outpost in his kingdom. Though the name of God never appears in Esther, God's power is implied everywhere in the book. The Book of Esther teaches that God's providence is active in every facet of human life. We cannot escape Him. His purposes, though sometimes hidden, are far-reaching. We can be confident of God's care and protection.

The Banquets of the King

1 🔑 Now it took place in the days[3117]
of [a]Ahasuerus, the Ahasuerus who
reigned[4427] [b]from India to [I]Ethiopia over
[c]127 provinces,
2 in those days as King[4428] Ahasuerus [a]sat on his royal[4438] throne[3678]
which *was* in [b]Susa the capital,
3 in the third year of his reign,[4427]
[a]he gave[6213] a banquet[4960] for all his
princes[8269] and attendants,[5650] the army
officers[2428] of Persia and Media, the nobles,[6579] and the princes of his provinces
being in his presence.
4 [I]And he displayed[7200] the riches
of his royal glory and the splendor of
his great majesty for many days, 180
days.
5 And when these days were completed, the king gave a banquet lasting
seven days for all the people[5971] who
were present in Susa the capital, from
the greatest to the least, in the court
of [a]the garden of the king's[4428] palace.
6 *There were hangings of* fine white
and violet linen held by cords of fine
purple linen on silver rings and marble
columns, *and* [a]couches of gold and silver
on a mosaic pavement of porphyry, marble, mother-of-pearl, and precious
stones.
7 Drinks were served in golden vessels of various kinds, and the royal[4438]
wine was plentiful [a]according to the
king's [I]bounty.[3027]
8 And the drinking was *done* according to the law,[1881] there was no compulsion,[597] for so the king had given
orders[3245] to each official of his
household[1004] that he should do[6213] according to the desires[7522] of each person.
9 Queen[4436] Vashti also gave a banquet for the women[802] in the [I]palace
which belonged to King Ahasuerus.

Queen Vashti's Refusal

10 On the seventh day,[3117] when
the heart[3820] of the king was [a]merry[2896]
with wine, he commanded[559] Mehuman,
Biztha, Harbona, Bigtha, Abagtha, Zethar, and Carkas, the seven eunuchs[5631]

1 [I]Lit., *Cush* [a]Ezra 4:6; Dan. 9:1 [b]Esth. 8:9 [c]Esth. 9:30

2 [a]1Kin. 1:46 [b]Neh. 1:1; Dan. 8:2

3 [a]Esth. 2:18

4 [I]Lit., *When*

5 [a]Esth. 7:7, 8

6 [a]Ezek. 23:41; Amos 6:4

7 [I]Lit., *hand* [a]Esth. 2:18

9 [I]Lit., *royal house*

10 [a]Judg. 16:25

🔑 **1:1** "Ahasuerus" is the Hebrew transliteration of the Persian name Khshayarsha. He is better known to us in history as Xerxes which is the Greek form of the name.

who served[8334] in the presence of King Ahasuerus,

11 to bring Queen Vashti before the king with *her* royal [a]crown in order to display[7200] her beauty to the people and the princes, for she was beautiful.[2896]

12 But Queen Vashti refused[3985] to come at the king's command[1697] delivered by the eunuchs. Then the king became very angry[7107] and his wrath burned within him.

13 Then the king said to [a]the wise[2450] men [b]who understood[5234] the times—[6256] for it was the custom of the king so *to speak* before all who knew law and justice,[1779]

14 and were close to him: Carshena, Shethar, Admatha, Tarshish, Meres, Marsena, and Memucan, the seven princes of Persia and Media [a]who [I]had access[7200] to the king's presence and sat in the first[7223] place in the kingdom—

15 "According to law, what is to be done with Queen Vashti, because she did not [I]obey the command[3982] of King Ahasuerus *delivered* by the eunuchs?"

16 And in the presence of the king and the princes, Memucan said,[559] "Queen Vashti has wronged not[5753] only the king but *also* all the princes, and all the peoples who are in all the provinces of King Ahasuerus.

17 "For the queen's conduct will [I]become known to all the women causing them [II]to look with contempt on their husbands by saying,[559] 'King Ahasuerus commanded Queen Vashti to be brought in to his presence, but she did not come.'

18 "And this day the ladies[8282] of Persia and Media who have heard[8085] of the queen's conduct will speak[559] in *the same way* to all the king's princes, and there will be plenty of contempt and anger.[7110]

19 "If it pleases[2895] the king, let a royal [I]edict be issued by him and let it be written in the laws[1881] of Persia and Media so [a]that it cannot [II]be repealed, that Vashti should come no more into the presence of King Ahasuerus, and let the king give her royal position to [III]another[7468] who is more worthy[2896] than she.

20 "And when the king's edict[6599] which he shall make[6213] is heard[8085] throughout all his kingdom,[4438] [I]great as it is, then [a]all women[802] will give honor to their husbands, great and small."

21 And *this* word[1697] pleased the king and the princes, and the king did[6213] [I]as Memucan proposed.[1697]

22 So he sent letters[5612] to all the king's provinces, [a]to each province according to its script and to every people according to their language, that every man[376] should [b]be the master[8323] in his own house and the one who speaks[1696] in the language of his own people.

Vashti's Successor Sought

2 After these things[1697] [a]when the anger[2534] of King[4428] Ahasuerus had subsided, he remembered[2142] Vashti and what she had done[6213] and [b]what had been decreed[1504] against her.

2 Then the king's[4428] attendants, who served[8334] him, said, "[a]Let beautiful young virgins[1330] be sought for the king.

3 "And let the king appoint[6485] overseers[6496] in [a]all the provinces of his kingdom[4438] that they may gather[6908] every beautiful young virgin to Susa the capital, to the harem,[1004,802] into the custody[3027] of [b]Hegai, the king's eunuch,[5631] who was in charge[8104] of the women;[802] and [c]let their cosmetics[8562] be given *them*.

4 "Then let the young lady who pleases the king be queen[4427] in place of Vashti." And the matter[1697] pleased the king, and he did[6213] accordingly.

5 *Now* there was a Jew in Susa the capital whose name was [a]Mordecai, the son[1121] of Jair, the son of Shimei, the son of Kish, a Benjamite,

6 [a]who had been taken into exile[1540] from Jerusalem with the captives[1473] who had been exiled with Jeconiah king of Judah, whom Nebuchadnezzar the king of Babylon had exiled.

---

11 [a]Esth. 2:17; 6:8

13 [a]Jer. 10:7; Dan. 2:2 [b]1Chr. 12:32

14 [I]Lit., *saw the face of the king* [a]2Kin. 25:19; Matt. 18:10

15 [I]Lit., *do*

17 [I]Lit., *go forth* [II]Lit., *to despise . . . in their eyes*

19 [I]Lit., *word go forth from* [II]Lit., *pass away* [III]Lit., *her neighbor* [a]Esth. 8:8; Dan. 6:8

20 [I]Lit., *for great is it* [a]Eph. 5:22; Col. 3:18

21 [I]Lit., *according to the word of*

22 [a]Esth. 3:12; 8:9 [b]Eph. 5:22-24

1 [a]Esth. 7:10 [b]Esth. 1:19, 20

2 [a]1Kin. 1:2

3 [a]Esth. 1:1, 2 [b]Esth. 2:8, 15 [c]Esth. 2:9, 12

5 [a]Esth. 3:2

6 [a]2Kin. 24:14, 15; 2Chr. 36:10

🔑 7 And he was bringing up Hadassah, that is [a]Esther, his uncle's daughter, for she had neither father[1] nor mother.[517] Now the young lady was beautiful[2896] of form and [I]face, and when her father and her mother died,[4194] Mordecai took her as his own daughter.

Esther Finds Favor

8 So it came about when the command[1697] and decree[1881] of the king were heard[8085] and [a]many young ladies were gathered[6908] to Susa the capital into the custody of [b]Hegai, that Esther was taken to the king's [I]palace into the custody of Hegai, who was in charge of the women.

9 Now the young lady pleased him and found[5375] favor[2617] with him. So he quickly provided her with her [a]cosmetics and [I]food, gave her seven choice maids from the king's palace, and transferred her and her maids to the best[2896] place in the harem.

10 [a]Esther did not make known[5046] her people[5971] or her kindred, for Mordecai had instructed[6680] her that she should not make *them* known.[5046]

11 And every day[3117] Mordecai walked back and forth in front of the court of the harem to learn[3045] how Esther was and how she fared.[6213]

12 Now when the turn of each young lady came[5060] to go in to King Ahasuerus, after the end of her twelve months under the regulations[1881] for the women—for the days[3117] of their beautification[4795] were completed[4390] as follows: six months with oil[8081] of myrrh[4753] and six months with spices and the cosmetics for women—

13 the young lady would go in to the king in this way: anything that she [I]desired was given her to take with her from the harem to the king's palace.

14 In the evening she would go in and in the morning she would return[7725] to the second harem, to the [I]custody of Shaashgaz, the king's eunuch who was in charge[8104] of the concubines. She would not again go in to the king unless the king delighted[2654] in her and she was summoned by name.

15 Now when the turn of Esther, [a]the daughter of Abihail the uncle of Mordecai who had taken her as his daughter, came to go in to the king, she did not request anything[1697] except what [b]Hegai, the king's eunuch who was in charge of the women, [I]advised.[559] And Esther found favor[2580] in the eyes of all who saw her.

16 So Esther was taken to King Ahasuerus to his royal[4438] palace in the tenth month which is the month Tebeth, in the seventh year of his reign.[4438]

Esther Becomes Queen

17 And the king loved[157] Esther more than all the women, and she found favor[2580] and kindness[2617] with him more than all the virgins, so that [a]he set[7760] the royal crown on her head[7218] and made her queen instead of Vashti.

18 Then [a]the king gave[6213] a great banquet,[4960] Esther's banquet, for all his princes[8269] and his servants;[5650] he also made a holiday for the provinces and gave gifts[4864] [b]according to the king's bounty.[3027]

19 And [a]when the virgins were gathered together[6908] the second time, then Mordecai [b]was sitting at the king's gate.

20 [a]Esther had not yet made known her kindred or her people, even as Mordecai had commanded[3982] her, for Esther did [I]what Mordecai told her as she had done [b]when under his care.

Mordecai Saves the King

21 In those days, while Mordecai was sitting at the king's gate, [a]Bigthan

7 [I]Lit., *good of appearance* [a]Esth. 2:15
8 [I]Lit., *house* [a]Esth. 2:3 [b]Esth. 2:3, 15
9 [I]Lit., *portions* [a]Esth. 2:3, 12
10 [a]Esth. 2:20
13 [I]Lit., *said*
14 [I]Lit., *hand*
15 [I]Lit., *said* [a]Esth. 2:7; 9:29 [b]Esth. 2:3, 8
17 [a]Esth. 1:11
18 [a]Esth. 1:3 [b]Esth. 1:7
19 [a]Esth. 2:3, 4 [b]Esth. 2:21; 3:2
20 [I]Lit., *the word of Mordecai* [a]Esth. 2:10 [b]Esth. 2:7
21 [a]Esth. 6:2

🔑 **2:7** Esther's Hebrew name was Hadassah which means "myrtle." "Esther" probably comes from the Persian word for "star," though some scholars have made a connection between it and the Babylonian goddess Ishtar. It appears that Esther had been orphaned and subsequently adopted by her cousin, Mordecai.

and Teresh, two of the king's officials[5631] from those who guarded the door, became angry[7107] and sought to [I]lay hands[3027] on King Ahasuerus.

22 But the [I]plot became known[3045] to Mordecai, and [a]he told[5046] Queen[4436] Esther, and Esther [II]informed the king in Mordecai's name.

23 Now when the plot[1697] was investigated[1245] and found *to be so,* they were both hanged on a [I]gallows; and it was written in [a]the Book[5612] of the Chronicles in the king's presence.

Haman's Plot against the Jews

3 After these events[1697] King[4428] Ahasuerus [a]promoted Haman, the son[1121] of Hammedatha [b]the Agagite, and [c]advanced[5357] him and [I]established[7760] his authority[3678] over all the princes[8269] who *were* with him.

2 And all the king's[4428] servants who were at the king's gate bowed[3766] down [I]and paid homage[7812] to Haman; for so the king had commanded[6680] concerning him. But [a]Mordecai neither bowed down nor paid homage.[7812]

3 Then the king's servants who were at [a]the king's gate said to Mordecai, "[b]Why are you transgressing the king's command?"[4687]

4 Now it was when they had spoken[559] daily[3117] to him and he would not listen[8085] to them, that they told[5046] Haman to see whether Mordecai's reason would stand; for he had told them that he was a Jew.

5 When Haman saw[7200] that [a]Mordecai neither bowed down nor paid homage to him, Haman was filled with rage.[2534]

6 But he [I]disdained to [II]lay hands[3027] on Mordecai alone, for they had told[5046] him *who* the people[5971] of Mordecai *were;* therefore Haman [a]sought to destroy[8045] all the Jews, the people of Mordecai, who *were* throughout the whole kingdom[4438] of Ahasuerus.

7 In the first[7223] month, which is the month Nisan, in the twelfth year of King Ahasuerus, [I]Pur, that is the lot, was [a]cast before Haman from day[3117] to day and from month *to month,* [II]until the twelfth month, that is [b]the month Adar.

8 Then Haman said to King Ahasuerus, "There is a certain people scattered and dispersed among the peoples in all the provinces of your kingdom; [a]their laws[1881] are different from *those* of all *other* people, and they do not observe[6213] the king's laws, so it is not in the king's interest to let them remain.

9 "If it is pleasing[2895] to the king, let it be [I]decreed that they be destroyed,[6] and I will pay ten thousand talents of silver into the hands of those who carry on the *king's* business,[4399] to put into the king's treasuries."

10 Then [a]the king took his signet ring from his hand[3027] and gave it to Haman, the son of Hammedatha [b]the Agagite, [c]the enemy of the Jews.

11 And the king said to Haman, "The silver is [I]yours, and the people *also,* to do[6213] with them as you please."[2896]

12 [a]Then the king's scribes[5608] were summoned[7121] on the thirteenth day of the first month, and it was written just as Haman commanded to [b]the king's satraps, to the governors[6346] who were over each province, and to the princes[8269] of each people, each province according to its script, each people according to its language, being written [c]in the name of King Ahasuerus and sealed with the king's signet ring.

21 [I]Lit., *send a hand against*
22 [I]Lit., *matter,* so also v. 23 [II]Lit., *told* [a]Esth. 6:1, 2
23 [I]Lit., *tree* [a]Esth. 10:2
1 [I]Lit., *set his seat* [a]Esth. 5:11 [b]Esth. 3:10; 8:3 [c]Esth. 5:11
2 [I]Lit., *and prostrated themselves before* [a]Esth. 2:19; 5:9
3 [a]Esth. 2:19 [b]Esth. 3:2
5 [a]Esth. 5:9
6 [I]Lit., *despised in his eyes* [II]Lit., *send a hand against* [a]Ps. 83:4
7 [I]Lit., *he cast Pur . . . before* [II]Gr., *and the lot fell on the thirteenth day of* [a]Esth. 9:24-26 [b]Ezra 6:15
8 [a]Ezra 4:12-15; Acts 16:20, 21
9 [I]Lit., *written*
10 [a]Gen. 41:42; Esth. 8:2 [b]Esth. 3:1 [c]Esth. 7:6
11 [I]Lit., *given to you*
12 [a]Esth. 8:9 [b]Ezra 8:36 [c]1Kin. 21:8; Esth. 8:8, 10

3:1-6 Haman is called a descendant of the Agagites. Agag was a king of the Amalekites in I Sam. 15. Agag was probably a title of the king of the Amalekites rather than the name of an individual. He was promoted to position of prime minister by Ahasuerus. This was probably unexpected because of the reluctance of the people to bow down to him, which is implied by the king's command in v. 2. The Israelites, those who were subjects, were required to prostrate themselves before the king (II Sam. 9:8) and other leaders (II Sam. 18:21). The reason stated by Mordecai for not bowing was that he was a Jew. This probably suggests that Haman was demanding worship and not mere allegiance.

13 And letters[5612] were sent by [a]couriers to all the king's provinces [b]to destroy, to kill,[2026] and to annihilate[6] all the Jews, both young and old,[2205] women[802] and children,[2945] [c]in one day, the thirteenth *day* of the twelfth month, which is the month Adar, and to [d]seize their possessions as plunder.

14 [a]A copy of the edict to be [I]issued as law in every province was published[1540] to all the peoples so that they should be ready for this day.

15 The couriers went out impelled by the king's command[1697] while the decree[1881] was [I]issued in Susa the capital; and while the king and Haman sat down to drink, [a]the city of Susa was in confusion.

Esther Learns of Haman's Plot

4 When Mordecai learned[3045] [a]all that had been done,[6213] [I]he tore his clothes, put on sackcloth and ashes, and went out into the midst of the city and wailed[2199] loudly and bitterly.[4751]

2 And he went as far as the king's[4428] gate, for no one was to enter the king's gate clothed in sackcloth.

3 And in each and every province where the command[1697] and decree[1881] of the king came,[5060] there was great mourning among the Jews, with [a]fasting, weeping, and wailing; and many lay on sackcloth and ashes.

4 Then Esther's maidens and her eunuchs[5631] came and told[5046] her, and the queen[4436] writhed in great anguish.[2342] And she sent garments to clothe Mordecai that he might remove his sackcloth from him, but he did not accept *them.*

5 Then Esther summoned[7121] Hathach from the king's eunuchs, whom [I]the king had appointed to attend her, and ordered him *to go* to Mordecai to learn[3045] what this *was* and why it *was.*

6 So Hathach went out to Mordecai to the city square in front of the king's gate.

7 And Mordecai told him all that had happened to him, and [a]the exact amount of money that Haman had promised[559] to pay to the king's treasuries for the destruction[6] of the Jews.

8 He also gave him [a]a copy of the text of the edict which had been issued in Susa for their destruction,[8045] that he might show[7200] Esther and inform[5046] her, and to order[6680] her to go in to the king[4428] to implore[2603] his favor and to plead with him for her people.[5971]

9 And Hathach came back and related Mordecai's words[1697] to Esther.

10 Then Esther spoke[559] to Hathach and ordered him *to reply* to Mordecai:

11 "All the king's servants[5650] and the people of the king's provinces know that for any man[376] or woman[802] who [a]comes to the king to the inner court who is not summoned, [b]he has but one law,[1881] that he be put to death,[4191] unless the king holds out [c]to him the golden scepter[8275] so that he may live.[2421] And I have not been summoned to come to the king for these thirty days."[3117]

12 And they related Esther's words to Mordecai.

13 Then Mordecai told[559] *them* to reply[7725] to Esther, "Do not imagine that you in the king's palace[1004] can escape[4422] any more than all the Jews.

14 "For if you remain silent at this time,[6256] relief[7305] and [a]deliverance will arise for the Jews from another place and you and your father's[1] house will perish.[6] And who knows whether you have not attained[5060] royalty[4438] for such a time as this?"

Esther Plans to Intercede

15 Then Esther told *them* to reply[7725] to Mordecai,

16 "Go, assemble[3664] all the Jews who are found in Susa, and fast for me; [a]do not eat or drink for [b]three days,[3117] night[3915] or day. I and my maidens also will fast in the same way. And thus I will go in to the king, which is not according to the law; and if I perish,[6] I perish."

17 So Mordecai went away and did[6213] just as Esther had commanded[6680] him.

---

13 [a]2Chr. 30:6; Esth. 8:10, 14 [b]Esth. 7:4 [c]Esth. 8:12 [d]Esth. 8:11; 9:10

14 [I]Lit., *given* [a]Esth. 8:13, 14

15 [I]Lit., *given* [a]Esth. 8:15

1 [I]Lit., *Mordecai* [a]2Sam. 1:11; Esth. 3:8-10; Jon. 3:5,6

3 [a]Esth. 4:16

5 [I]Lit., *he*

7 [a]Esth. 3:9

8 [a]Esth. 3:14

11 [a]Esth. 5:1; 6:4 [b]Dan. 2:9 [c]Esth. 5:2; 8:4

14 [a]Lev. 26:42; 2Kin. 13:5

16 [a]Joel 1:14; 2:12 [b]Esth. 5:1

Esther Plans a Banquet

5 Now it came about [a]on the third day[3117] that Esther put on her royal[4438] robes and stood [b]in the inner court of the king's[4428] palace[1004] in front of the king's [I]rooms, and the king[4428] was sitting on his royal throne in the [II]throne[3678] room, opposite the entrance to the palace.

2 And it happened when the king saw[7200] Esther the queen[4436] standing in the court, [a]she obtained[5375] favor[2580] in his sight; and [b]the king extended to Esther the golden scepter[8275] which was in his hand.[3027] So Esther came near and touched[5060] the top of the scepter.

3 Then the king said[559] to her, "What is *troubling* you, Queen Esther? And what is your request? [a]Even to half of the kingdom[4438] it will be given to you."

4 And Esther said,[559] "If it please[2895] the king, may the king and Haman come this day to the banquet[4960] that I have prepared[6213] for him."

5 Then the king said, "[a]Bring Haman quickly that we may do[6213] [I]as Esther desires." So the king and Haman came to the banquet which Esther had prepared.

6 And, [I]as they drank their wine at the banquet, [a]the king said to Esther, "[b]What is your petition,[7596] for it shall be granted to you. And what is your request? Even to half of the kingdom it shall be done."

7 So Esther answered and said, "My petition and my request is:

8 [a]if I have found favor in the sight of the king, and if it please[2895] the king to grant my petition and do[6213] [I]what I request, may the king and Haman come to [b]the banquet which I shall prepare for them, and tomorrow I will do [II]as the king says."

Haman's Pride

9 Then Haman went out that day glad[2896] and pleased of heart;[3820] but when Haman saw Mordecai [a]in the king's gate, and [b]that he did not stand up or [I]tremble[2111] before him, Haman was filled with anger against Mordecai.

10 Haman controlled himself, however, went to his house,[1004] and [I]sent for his friends[157] and his wife[802] [a]Zeresh.

11 Then Haman recounted[5608] to them the glory[3519] of his riches, and the [I][a]number of his sons,[1121] and every *instance* where the king had magnified him, and how he had [II][b]promoted[5375] him above the princes[8269] and servants[5650] of the king.

12 Haman also said, "Even Esther the queen let no one but me come with the king to the banquet which she had prepared; and [a]tomorrow also I am [I]invited[7121] by her with the king.

13 "Yet all of this [I]does not satisfy[7737] me every time I see Mordecai the Jew sitting at [a]the king's gate."

14 Then Zeresh his wife and all his friends said to him, "[a]Have a [I]gallows fifty cubits high made[6213] and in the morning ask[559] the king to have Mordecai hanged on it, then go joyfully with the king to the banquet." And the [II]advice[1697] pleased[3190] Haman, so he had the gallows made.

The King Plans to Honor Mordecai

6 During that night[3915] [I]the king[4428] [a]could not sleep so he gave an order[559] to bring [b]the book[5612] of records,[2146] the chronicles, and they were read[7121] before the king.

2 And it was found written what [a]Mordecai had reported[5046] concerning Bigthana and Teresh, two of the king's[4428] eunuchs[5631] who were doorkeepers,[8104] that they had sought to lay hands[3027] on King Ahasuerus.

3 And the king said, "What honor or dignity has been bestowed[6213] on Mordecai for this?" Then the king's servants[5650] who attended[8334] him said,[559] "Nothing[1697] has been done for him."

4 So the king said, "Who is in the court?" Now Haman had just [a]entered

---

5:1 [I]Lit., *house* [II]Lit., *royal house* [a]Esth. 4:16 [b]Esth. 4:11; 6:4
2 [a]Esth. 2:9 [b]Esth. 4:11; 8:4
3 [a]Esth. 7:2; Mark 6:23
5 [I]Lit., *the word of Esther* [a]Esth. 6:14
6 [I]Lit., *at the banquet of wine* [a]Esth. 7:2 [b]Esth. 5:3
8 [I]Lit., *my request* [II]Lit., *according to the word of the king* [a]Esth. 7:3; 8:5 [b]Esth. 6:14
9 [I]Or, *move for* [a]Esth. 2:19 [b]Esth. 3:5
10 [I]Lit., *sent and brought* [a]Esth. 6:13
11 [I]Lit., *multitude* [II]Lit., *lifted* [a]Esth. 9:7-10 [b]Esth. 3:1
12 [I]Lit., *summoned to her* [a]Esth. 5:8
13 [I]Lit., *is not suitable to me* [a]Esth. 5:9
14 [I]Lit., *tree* [II]Lit., *thing* [a]Esth. 6:4; 7:9, 10
6:1 [I]Lit., *the king's sleep fled* [a]Dan. 6:18 [b]Esth. 2:23; 10:2
2 [a]Esth. 2:21, 22
4 [a]Esth. 4:11

the outer court of the king's palace[1004] in order to speak[559] to the king about [b]hanging Mordecai on the gallows which he had prepared[3559] for him.

5 And the king's servants said to him, "Behold, Haman is standing in the court." And the king said, "Let him come in."

6 So Haman came in and the king said to him, "What is to be done for the man[376] [a]whom the king desires[2654] to honor?" And Haman said[559] [I]to himself,[3820] "Whom would the king desire[2654] to honor more than me?"

7 Then Haman said[559] to the king, "For the man whom the king desires to honor,

8 let them bring a royal[4438] robe which the king has worn, and [a]the horse on which the king has ridden, and on whose head[7218] [b]a royal crown has been placed;

9 and let the robe and the horse be handed over to one[376] of the king's most noble[6579] princes[8269] and let them array the man whom the king desires to honor and lead him on horseback through the city square, [a]and proclaim[7121] before him, 'Thus it shall be done to the man whom the king desires to honor.' "

Haman Must Honor Mordecai

10 Then the king said[1696] to Haman, "Take quickly the robes and the horse as you have said, and do so for Mordecai the Jew, who is sitting at the king's gate; do not fall short in anything of all that you have said."[1696]

11 So Haman took the robe and the horse, and arrayed Mordecai, and led him *on horseback* through the city square, and proclaimed before him, "Thus it shall be done to the man whom the king desires to honor."

12 Then Mordecai returned to the king's gate. But Haman hurried home, mourning, [a]with *his* head covered.

13 And Haman recounted[5608] [a]to Zeresh his wife[802] and all his friends[157] everything that had happened to him. Then his wise men[2450] and Zeresh his wife said to him, "If Mordecai, before whom you have begun to fall, is [I]of Jewish origin,[2233] you will not overcome him, but will surely fall before him."

14 While they were still talking with him, the king's eunuchs arrived and hastily[926] [a]brought Haman to the banquet[4960] which Esther had prepared.[6213]

Esther's Plea

7 Now the king[4428] and Haman came to drink *wine* with Esther the queen.[4436]

2 And the king said[559] to Esther on the second day[3117] also [I]as they drank their wine at the banquet,[4960] "[a]What is your petition,[7596] Queen Esther? It shall be granted you. And what is your request? [b]Even to half of the kingdom[4438] it shall be done."

3 Then Queen Esther answered and said, "[a]If I have found favor[2580] in your sight, O king, and if it please[2895] the king, let my life[5315] be given me as my petition, and my people[5971] as my request;

4 for [a]we have been sold, I and my people, to be destroyed,[8045] [b]to be killed and to be annihilated.[6] Now if we had only been sold as slaves,[5650] men and women, I would have remained silent, for the [I]trouble would not be commensurate[7737] with the [II]annoyance to the king."[4428]

5 Then King Ahasuerus [I]asked[559] Queen Esther, "Who is he, and where is he, [II]who would presume[3820] to do[6213] thus?"

6 And Esther said, "[a]A foe and an enemy, is this wicked[7451] Haman!" Then Haman became terrified[1204] before the king and queen.

Haman Is Hanged

7 And the king arose [a]in his anger[2534] from [I]drinking wine *and went* into [b]the palace garden; but Haman stayed to beg for his life from Queen Esther,

---

4 [b]Esth. 5:14

6 [I]Lit., *in his heart* [a]Esth. 6:7, 9, 11

8 [a]1Kin. 1:33 [b]Esth. 1:11; 2:17

9 [a]Gen. 41:43

12 [a]2Sam. 15:30

13 [I]Lit., *from the seed of the Jews* [a]Esth. 5:10

14 [a]Esth. 5:8

2 [I]Lit., *at the banquet of wine* [a]Esth. 5:6; 9:12 [b]Esth. 5:3

3 [a]Esth. 5:8; 8:5

4 [I]Or, *enemy could not compensate for the loss* [II]Or, *damage* [a]Esth. 3:9 [b]Esth. 3:13

5 [I]Lit., *said and said to* [II]Lit., *whose heart has been filled*

6 [a]Esth. 3:10

7 [I]Lit., *the banquet of wine* [a]Esth. 1:12 [b]Esth. 1:5

for he saw[7200] that harm[7451] had been
determined[3615] against him by the king.
8 Now when the king returned[7725]
from the palace garden into the [I]place
where they were drinking wine, Haman
was falling[5307] on [a]the couch where
Esther was. Then the king said, "Will
he even assault the queen with me in
the house?"[1004] As the word[1697] went
out of the king's[4428] mouth,[6310] they covered Haman's face.
9 Then Harbonah, one of the
eunuchs[5631] who *were* before the king
said, "Behold indeed, [a]the gallows standing at Haman's house fifty cubits high,
which Haman made[6213] for Mordecai
[b]who spoke[1696] good[2896] on behalf of the
king!" And the king said, "Hang him
on it."
10 [a]So they hanged Haman on the
[I]gallows which he had prepared[3559] for
Mordecai, [b]and the king's anger subsided.

Mordecai Promoted

8 On that day[3117] King[4428] Ahasuerus
gave the house[1004] of Haman,
[a]the enemy of the Jews, to Queen[4436]
Esther; and Mordecai came before the
king, for Esther had disclosed[5046]
[b]what he was to her.
2 [a]And the king took off[5493] his signet
ring which he had taken away from Haman, and gave it to Mordecai. And
Esther set[7760] Mordecai over the house
of Haman.
3 Then Esther spoke[1696] again to
the king, fell at his feet,[5307] wept, and
implored[2603] him to avert[5674] the evil
scheme[7451] of Haman the Agagite and
his plot[4284] which he had devised[2803]
against the Jews.
4 [a]And the king extended the golden
scepter[8275] to Esther. So Esther arose
and stood before the king.
5 Then she said,[559] "[a]If it pleases[2896]
the king and if I have found favor[2580]
before him and the matter[1697] *seems*
proper[3787] to the king and I am
pleasing[2896] in his sight, let it be written
to revoke[7725] the [b]letters[5612] devised[4284]
by Haman, the son[1121] of Hammedatha
the Agagite, which he wrote to destroy[6]
the Jews who are in all the king's[4428]
provinces.
6 "For [a]how can I endure to see
the calamity[7451] which shall befall my
people,[5971] and how can I endure to see
the destruction[13] of my kindred?"
7 So King Ahasuerus said to Queen
Esther and to Mordecai the Jew, "Behold, [a]I have given the house of Haman
to Esther, and him they have hanged
on the gallows because he had stretched
out his hands[3027] against the Jews.

The King's Decree Avenges the Jews

8 "Now you write to the Jews
[I]as you see fit,[2896] in the king's name,
and [a]seal *it* with the king's signet ring;
for a decree which is written in the name
of the king and sealed with the king's
signet ring [b]may not be revoked."
9 [a]So the king's scribes[5608] were
called[7121] at that time[6256] in the third
month (that is, the month Sivan), on
the twenty-third [I]day; and it was written
according to all that Mordecai commanded[6680] to the Jews, the satraps,
the governors,[6346] and the princes[8269]
of the provinces which *extended* [b]from
India to [II]Ethiopia, 127 provinces, to
[c]every province according to its script,
and to every people according to their
language, as well as to the Jews according to their script and their language.
10 And he wrote in the name of King
Ahasuerus, and sealed it with the king's
signet ring, and sent letters by couriers
on [a]horses, riding on steeds sired by
the royal stud.
11 [I]In them the king granted the
Jews who were in each and every city
the right [a]to assemble and to defend their
lives,[5315] [b]to destroy,[8045] to kill,[2026] and
to annihilate[6] the entire army[2428] of any
people or province which might attack
them, including children[2945] and wom-
en,[802] and [c]to plunder their spoil,
12 on [a]one day in all the provinces
of King Ahasuerus, the thirteenth *day*

8 [I]Lit., *house of the banquet of wine* [a]Esth. 1:6
9 [a]Esth. 5:14 [b]Esth. 2:22
10 [I]Lit., *tree* [a]Ps. 7:16; 94:23 [b]Esth. 7:7, 8
1 [a]Esth. 7:6 [b]Esth. 2:7, 15
2 [a]Esth. 3:10
4 [a]Esth. 4:11; 5:2
5 [a]Esth. 5:8; 7:3 [b]Esth. 3:13
6 [a]Esth. 7:4; 9:1
7 [a]Esth. 8:1
8 [I]Lit., *according to the good in your eyes* [a]Esth. 3:12; 8:10 [b]Esth. 1:19
9 [I]Lit., *in it* [II]Lit., *Cush* [a]Esth. 3:12 [b]Esth. 1:1 [c]Esth. 1:22; 3:12
10 [a]1Kin. 4:28
11 [I]Lit., *Which* [a]Esth. 9:2 [b]Esth. 3:13 [c]Esth. 9:10
12 [a]Esth. 3:13; 9:1

of the twelfth month (that is, the month Adar).

13 [a]A copy of the edict to be [I]issued as law in each and every province, was published[1540] to all the peoples, so that the Jews should be ready for this day to avenge[5358] themselves on their enemies.

14 The couriers, hastened and impelled by the king's command,[1697] went out, riding on the royal steeds; and the decree[1881] was given out in Susa the capital.

15 Then Mordecai went out from the presence of the king [a]in royal[4438] robes of [I]blue and white, with a large crown of gold and [b]a garment of fine linen and purple; and [c]the city of Susa shouted and rejoiced.

16 For the Jews there was [a]light[219] and gladness and joy and honor.

17 And in each and every province, and in each and every city, wherever the king's commandment and his decree arrived,[5060] there was gladness and joy for the Jews, a feast[4960] and a [I][a]holiday.[2896] And [b]many among the peoples of the land[776] became Jews, for the dread[6343] of the Jews had fallen on them.

The Jews Destroy Their Enemies

9 Now [a]in the twelfth month (that is, the month Adar), on [b]the thirteenth [I]day[3117] [c]when the king's[4428] command[1697] and edict[1881] [II]were about to[5060] be executed,[6213] on the day when the enemies of the Jews hoped to gain the mastery[7980] over them, it was turned[2015] to the contrary so that the Jews themselves gained the mastery[7980] over those who hated[8130] them.

2 [a]The Jews assembled[6950] in their cities throughout all the provinces of King[4428] Ahasuerus to lay hands[3027] on those who sought their harm;[7451] and no one[376] could stand before them, [b]for the dread[6343] of them had fallen[5307] on all the peoples.[5971]

3 Even all the princes[8269] of the provinces, [a]the satraps, the governors,[6346] and those who were doing the king's business [I]assisted[5375] the Jews, because the dread of Mordecai had fallen on them.

4 Indeed, Mordecai was great in the king's house,[1004] and his fame spread throughout all the provinces; for the man Mordecai [a]became greater and greater.

5 Thus [a]the Jews struck[5221] all their enemies with [I]the sword,[2719] killing[2027] and destroying;[12] and they did[6213] what they pleased[7522] to those who hated them.

6 And in Susa the capital the Jews killed[2026] and destroyed[6] five hundred men,[376]

7 and Parshandatha, Dalphon, Aspatha,

8 Poratha, Adalia, Aridatha,

9 Parmashta, Arisai, Aridai, and Vaizatha,

10 [a]the ten sons of Haman the son[1121] of Hammedatha, the Jews' enemy; but [b]they did not lay their hands on the plunder.

11 On that day the number of those who were killed in Susa the capital [I]was reported to the king.

12 And the king said[559] to Queen[4436] Esther, "The Jews have killed and destroyed five hundred men and the ten sons[1121] of Haman in Susa the capital. What then have they done[6213] in the rest[7605] of the king's provinces! [a]Now what is your petition?[7596] It shall even be granted you. And what is your further request? It shall also be done."

13 Then said Esther, "If it pleases[2896] the king, [a]let tomorrow also be granted to the Jews who are in Susa to do[6213] according to the edict of today; and let Haman's ten sons be hanged on the gallows."

14 So the king commanded[559] that it should be done so; and an edict was issued in Susa, and Haman's ten sons were hanged.

15 And the Jews who were in Susa assembled also on the fourteenth day of the month Adar and killed [a]three hundred men in Susa, but [b]they did not lay their hands on the plunder.

---

13 [I]Lit., *given* [a]Esth. 3:14

15 [I]Or, *violet* [a]Esth. 5:11 [b]Gen. 41:42 [c]Esth. 3:15

16 [a]Ps. 97:11; 112:4

17 [I]Lit., *good day* [a]Esth. 9:19 [b]Esth. 9:27

1 [I]Lit., *day in it* [II]Lit., *drew near* [a]Esth. 8:12 [b]Esth. 9:17 [c]Esth. 3:13

2 [a]Esth. 8:11; 9:15-18 [b]Esth. 8:17

3 [I]Lit., *lifted up* [a]Ezra 8:36

4 [a]2Sam. 3:1; 1Chr. 11:9

5 [I]Lit., *the stroke of* [a]Esth. 3:13

10 [a]Esth. 5:11 [b]Esth. 8:11

11 [I]Lit., *came*

12 [a]Esth. 5:6; 7:2

13 [a]Esth. 8:11; 9:15

15 [a]Esth. 9:12 [b]Esth. 9:10

🔑 **16** Now [a]the rest of the Jews who *were* in the king's provinces [b]assembled, to defend their lives[5315] and [I]rid themselves of their enemies, and kill 75,000 of those who hated[8130] them; but they did not lay their hands[3027] on the plunder.

17 *This was done* on [a]the thirteenth day of the month Adar, and [b]on the fourteenth [I]day they rested and made[6213] it a day of feasting[4960] and rejoicing.

18 But the Jews who were in Susa [a]assembled[6950] on the thirteenth and [b]the fourteenth [I]of the same month, and they rested on the fifteenth [I]day and made it a day of feasting and rejoicing.

19 Therefore the Jews of the rural areas, who live in [a]the rural towns, make the fourteenth day of the month Adar a [I][b]holiday[2896] for rejoicing and feasting and [c]sending portions *of food* to one[376] another.[7453]

The Feast of Purim Instituted

20 Then Mordecai recorded these events,[1697] and he sent letters[5612] to all the Jews who were in all the provinces of King Ahasuerus, both near and far,

21 obliging them to celebrate[6213] the fourteenth day of the month Adar, and the fifteenth day [I]of the same month, annually,

22 because on those days[3117] the Jews [I]rid themselves of their enemies, and *it was a* month which was [a]turned for them from sorrow into gladness and from mourning into a [II]holiday; that they should make[6213] them days of feasting and rejoicing and [b]sending portions *of food* to one another and gifts to the poor.

23 Thus the Jews undertook what they had started to do, and what Mordecai had written to them.

24 For Haman the son of Hammedatha, the Agagite, the adversary of all the Jews, had schemed[2803] against the Jews to destroy[6] them, and [a]had cast Pur, that is the lot, to disturb[2000] them and destroy them.

25 But [a]when it came [I]to the king's attention, he commanded by letter [b]that his wicked[7451] scheme[4284] which he had [II]devised against the Jews, [c]should return[7725] on his own head,[7218] and that he and his sons should be hanged on the [III]gallows.

26 Therefore they called[7121] these days Purim after the name of Pur. [I]And [a]because of the instructions[1697] in this letter, both what they had seen[7200] in this regard and what had happened[5060] to them,

27 the Jews established and [I]made a custom for themselves, and for their [II]descendants,[2233] and for [a]all those who allied themselves with them, so that [III]they should not fail[5647] [b]to celebrate these two days according to their [IV]regulation, and according to their appointed time[2165] annually.

28 So these days were to be remembered[2142] and celebrated[6213] throughout every generation,[1755] every family,[4940] every province, and every city; and these days of Purim were not to [I]fail from among the Jews, or their memory[2143] [II]fade[5486] from their [III]descendants.

29 Then Queen Esther, [a]daughter of Abihail, with Mordecai the Jew, wrote with full authority[8633] to confirm [b]this second letter about Purim.

30 And he sent letters to all the Jews, [a]to the 127 provinces of the kingdom[4438] of Ahasuerus, namely, words of peace and truth,[571]

31 to establish these days of Purim at their appointed times,[2165] just as Mordecai the Jew and Queen Esther had

16 [I]Lit., *have rest from* [a]Esth. 9:2 [b]Lev. 26:7, 8; Esth. 8:11
17 [I]Lit., *in it* [a]Esth. 9:1 [b]Esth. 9:21
18 [I]Lit., *in it* [a]Esth. 8:11; 9:2 [b]Esth. 9:21
19 [I]Lit., *rejoicing and feasting and a good day and sending* [a]Deut. 3:5; Zech. 2:4 [b]Esth. 9:22 [c]Neh. 8:10
21 [I]Lit., *in it*
22 [I]Lit., *had rest from* [II]Lit., *good day* [a]Ps. 30:11 [b]Neh. 8:12
24 [a]Esth. 3:7
25 [I]Lit., *before the king, he* [II]Lit., *schemed* [III]Lit., *tree* [a]Esth. 7:4-10 [b]Esth. 3:6-15 [c]Ps. 7:16
26 [I]Lit., *Therefore because of all the words* [a]Esth. 9:20
27 [I]Lit., *received* [II]Lit., *seed* [III]Lit., *it should not pass away* [IV]Lit., *writing* [a]Esth. 8:17 [b]Esth. 9:20, 21
28 [I]Lit., *pass away* [II]Lit., *end* [III]Lit., *seed*
29 [a]Esth. 2:15 [b]Esth. 9:20, 21
30 [a]Esth. 1:1

🔑 **9:16-32** *Purim* is the plural form of Pur (see v. 26), which means "lot" in the sense of something which has been crushed, broken, or destroyed. This feast was instituted by Mordecai. It began the fourteenth day of the twelfth month and was held to commemorate the defeat of Haman's evil plan (See Esth. 5:9—7:10; 8:15—9:15). It lasted two days and was made the occasion of much joy, of rest, and of sending presents. After it was confirmed by King Ahasuerus, the Jews bound themselves to keep the feast. It may be that there is a reference to this feast in Jn. 5:1.

established[6965] for them, and just as they
had established for themselves and for
their [I]descendants with [II]instructions
[a]for their times of fasting and their
lamentations.
32 And the command[3982] of Esther
established these [I]customs for [a]Purim,
and it was written in the book.[5612]

Mordecai's Greatness

10 Now King[4428] Ahasuerus laid[7760]
a tribute on the land[776] and on
the [a]coastlands of the sea.
2 And all the [I]accomplishments of
his authority and strength, and the full
account of the greatness of Mordecai,
[a]to which the king [II]advanced him, are
they not written in [b]the Book[5612] of the
Chronicles of the Kings[4428] of Media and
Persia?
3 For Mordecai the Jew was
[a]second *only* to King Ahasuerus and
great among the Jews, and in favor[7521]
with the multitude of his kinsmen,[251]
[b]one who sought the good of his
people[5971] and one who spoke[1696] for
the welfare of his whole nation.[2233]

31 [I]Lit., *seed* [II]Lit., *words* [a]Esth. 4:3

32 [I]Lit., *words* [a]Esth. 9:26

1 [a]Is. 11:11; 24:15

2 [I]Lit., *doings* [II]Lit., *made him great* [a]Esth. 8:15; 9:4 [b]Esth. 2:23

3 [a]Gen. 41:43, 44 [b]Neh. 2:10

The Book of
JOB

We do not know precisely where these historical events took place. The Land of Uz (Job 1:1) may have been somewhere between Palestine and Arabia. The exact time is also unknown, but many believe that Job lived at the same time as Abraham, in the Patriarchal Age. Nowhere is the Law of Moses or the nation of Israel mentioned. The Book of Job was an early part of the wisdom literature of the Old Testament, but it was not connected with Psalms, Proverbs, the Song of Solomon, Ecclesiastes or any other biblical book. Job is recognized even by secular literary critics as being among the world's most magnificent dramatic pieces. It is comprised mostly of poetic passages. Hebrew poetry did not have Western-style meter or rhyme. It was composed of parallel thoughts which were synonymous or contrasting. Only the first and second chapters and the last chapter are prose.

Job is the most ancient statement which addresses the perennial, multitudinous questions of the problem of evil and human suffering: How could such a good God make such an evil world? Why should we do good? What reward is there for living right? Why do some righteous people suffer and why does sin sometimes go unpunished? How does this square with the concept of a fair, holy, loving God? Does God really care for and protect His people who revere Him? Are adversity and affliction a sign that a sufferer is wicked? If God is good, why does He allow the suffering of the innocent?

The story begins with a very prosperous, respected, and good man who was devastated in just one day. He lost everything he had, including all of his ten children. However, he refused to blame God for his troubles. Later Job was stricken with a terrible disease and he suffered excruciating pain for a long time. Then, in three series of dialogues, some of his friends (Eliphaz, Bildad, and Zophar) came to comfort him, but later they began to criticize him unmercifully along traditional lines of religious thought. They were certain that all of these horrible things which had happened to Job were due to his own sin. They simplistically taught that all suffering is *always* the result of sin. Therefore, if Job would only repent of his sins, all would be well again. Job knew better. He was sure that he did not deserve this alleged cruel punishment, but he could not understand how God could let this happen to him. And so he was faced with the dilemma that God must be dealing unfairly with him or there was some other unknown explanation. He desired to regain the honor that he once had as a good man. He boldly challenged God to allow him to plead his own case (chapters 29–31). He struggled on with the confidence that he would eventually be vindicated. Job never did lose his faith.

Another friend, Elihu, appeared (Job 32:1—37:24) and declared that afflictions sometimes do come from God in order to purify the righteous and that this, in no way, indicates that God is unloving. It is only His way of calling us back to Him, like a father chastening his children. Suffering sometimes instructs us in righteousness and prevents us from sinning. Elihu cautioned Job not to question God or accuse Him. He told Job to humbly submit himself to God's will.

Then God spoke in chapters 38—41. God chose not to answer any of Job's penetrating questions. Instead, God overwhelmed Job with a panoramic view of His creative power and divine wisdom. Then God reprimanded the friends of Job for not understanding the true meaning of Job's suffering. Job was truly humbled and felt foolish (Job 42:1–6). Unless you can canvass your own world, how can you presume to tell God how to run His world? Finally, God restored Job twofold (Job 42:7–17).

Do we understand the enigmas of life any better than Job did? We did not ask to be born, and we are just as bewildered about the prosperity of evil men and the calamities of good men. But now that Jesus has come, we can understand the mystery much better. He suffered much and was unjustly condemned and executed, yet He too was victorious. Surely we can see that all things do work together for good to those who love God (see Rom. 8:28).

Job's Character and Wealth

1 There was a man[376] in the
[a]land[776] of Uz, whose name was
[b]Job, and that man was [c]blameless,[8535]
upright,[3477] [d]fearing[3373] God,[430] and
[e]turning away[5493] from evil.[7451]
2 [a]And seven sons[1121] and three
daughters were born to him.
3 [a]His possessions also were 7,000
sheep, 3,000 camels, 500 yoke of oxen,
500 female donkeys, and very many
servants;[5657] and that man was [b]the
greatest of all the [I]men of the east.
4 And his sons used to go and hold
a feast in the house[1004] of each one[376]
on his day,[3117] and they would send and
invite[7121] their three sisters[269] to eat
and drink with them.
5 And it came about, when the days
of feasting[4960] had completed their cycle,[5362] that Job would send and
consecrate[6942] them, rising up early in
the morning and offering[5927] [a]burnt
offerings[5930] *according to* the number of
them all; for Job said,[559] "[b]Perhaps my
sons have sinned[2398] and [c]cursed God
in their hearts."[3824] Thus Job did[6213] continually.
6 [a]Now there was a day when the
[b]sons of God came to present themselves before the LORD, and [I]Satan[7854]
also came among them.
7 And the LORD said to Satan,
"From where do you come?" Then Satan
answered the LORD and said, "[a]From
roaming about on the earth[776] and walking around on it."
8 And the LORD said to Satan, "Have
you [I]considered [a]My servant[5650] Job?
For there is no one like him on the earth,
[b]a blameless and upright man, [II]fearing
God and turning away[5493] from evil."
9 Then [a]Satan answered the [I]LORD,
"Does Job fear[3372] God for nothing?[2600]
10 "[a]Hast Thou not made a hedge
about him and his house[1004] and all that
he has, on every side? [b]Thou hast
blessed[1288] the work of his hands,[3027]
and his [c]possessions have increased in
the land.
11 "[a]But put forth Thy hand[3027] now
and [b]touch[5060] all that he has; he will
surely curse Thee to Thy face."
12 Then the LORD said to Satan,
"Behold, all that he has is in your
[I]power,[3027] only do not put forth your
hand on him." So Satan departed from
the presence of the LORD.

Satan Allowed to Test Job

13 Now it happened on the day
when his sons and his daughters were
eating and drinking wine in their oldest
brother's[251] house,
14 that a messenger[4397] came to Job
and said, "The oxen were plowing and
the [I]donkeys feeding beside them,
15 and [I]the [a]Sabeans [II]attacked[5307]
and took them. They also [III]slew[5221] the
servants with the edge[6310] of the

1 [a]Jer. 25:20; Lam. 4:21 [b]Ezek. 14:14, 20; James 5:11 [c]Gen. 6:9; 17:1; Deut. 18:13 [d]Gen. 22:12; 42:18; Ex. 18:21; Prov. 8:13 [e]Job 28:28
2 [a]Job 42:13
3 [I]Lit., *sons* [a]Job 42:12 [b]Job 29:25
5 [a]Gen. 8:20; Job 42:8 [b]Job 8:4 [c]1Kin. 21:10, 13
6 [I]I.e., the adversary, and so throughout chs. 1 and 2 [a]Job 2:1 [b]Job 38:7
7 [a]1Pet. 5:8
8 [I]Lit., *set your heart to* [II]Or, *revering* [a]Num. 12:7; Josh. 1:2, 7; Job 42:7, 8 [b]Job 1:1
9 [I]Lit., *LORD and said* [a]Rev. 12:9f.
10 [a]Job 29:2-6; Ps. 34:7 [b]Job 31:25 [c]Job 1:3; 31:25
11 [a]Job 2:5 [b]Job 19:21
12 [I]Lit., *hand*
14 [I]Lit., *female donkeys*
15 [I]Lit., *Sheba* [II]Lit., *fell upon* [III]Lit., *smote* [a]Gen. 10:7; Job 6:19

1:1 "The land of Uz" cannot be located exactly. It was probably located to the east of Palestine, near Arabia and Edom (Jer. 25:20; Lam. 4:21). That Job is described, among other things, as a blameless man does not indicate that he was sinlessly perfect. This was never claimed of Job. He was a man of integrity, and moral and spiritual stability.

1:6-12 Satan is introduced here as the force behind all the calamities which came upon Job. Though he is mentioned only in these verses and a few times in chapter 2, his presence and influence pervade the major part of the Book of Job. This passage is important for the Christian to understand. It shows how Satan works to trap and ensnare people. God does not "build hedges around" His people so that Satan cannot approach them. However, He does not leave us defenseless, just as He did not leave Job to his own resources. The Christian has the additional power which Christ has made available to him through the Holy Spirit to fend off the discouragements and enticements of the devil (Eph. 6:13).

1:14—2:8 The first attack which Satan makes on Job is physical. He causes Job to lose the three things in life which are considered signs of a man's well-being. First, he lost his wealth (vv. 14-17). Second, all of his children perished (vv. 18,19). In the third place he lost his good health (2:1-8). Men have cursed God when any of the three things have happened to them, but Job did not do so when all three happened to him.

sword,[2719] and [IV]I alone have escaped[4422]
to tell[5046] you."
16 While he was still speaking,[1696]
another also came and said, "[a]The fire
of God fell[5307] from heaven[8064] and
burned up the sheep and the servants
and consumed them, and I alone have
escaped to tell you."
17 While he was still speaking, another also came and said, "The [a]Chal-
deans formed[7760] three bands and made
a raid on the camels and took them and
[I]slew the servants with the edge of the
sword; and I alone have escaped to tell
you."
18 While he was still speaking, another also came and said, "Your sons
and your daughters were eating and
drinking wine in their oldest brother's
house,
19 and behold, a great wind[7307]
came from across the wilderness and
struck[5060] the four corners of the house,
and it fell on the young people and they
died;[4191] and I alone have escaped to
tell you."
20 Then Job arose and [a]tore his
robe[4598] and shaved his head,[7218] and
he fell[5307] to the ground[776] and worshiped.[7812]
21 And he said,
"[a]Naked[6174] I came from my
mother's[517] womb,[990]
And naked I shall return[7725]
there.
The [b]LORD gave and the LORD
has taken away.
Blessed be the name of the
LORD."
22 [a]Through all this Job did not sin
nor did he [I]blame God.

Job Loses His Health

2 [a]Again there was a day[3117] when
the sons[1121] of God[430] came to present themselves before the LORD, and
Satan[7854] also came among them to present himself before the LORD.
2 And the LORD said[559] to Satan,
"Where have you come from?" Then
Satan answered the LORD and said,
"From roaming about on the earth,[776]
and walking around on it."
3 And the LORD said to Satan, "Have
you [I]considered My servant[5650] Job? For
there is no one like him on the earth,
a blameless[8535] and upright[3477] man[376]
[II]fearing God and turning away[5493] from
evil.[7451] And he still [a]holds fast[2388] his
integrity,[8538] although you incited Me
against him, to [III]ruin[1104] him without
cause."
4 And Satan answered the LORD and
said, "Skin[5785] for skin! Yes, all that a
man has he will give for his life.[5315]
5 "[a]However, put forth Thy
hand,[3027] now, and [b]touch[5060] his
bone[6106] and his flesh;[1320] he will curse
Thee to Thy face."
6 So the LORD said to Satan, "Behold, he is in your [I]power, only spare
his life."
7 Then Satan went out from the
presence of the LORD, and smote[5221]
Job with [a]sore[7451] boils from the sole[3709]
of his foot to the crown of his head.
8 And he took a potsherd[2789] to
scrape himself while [a]he was sitting
among the ashes.
9 Then his wife[802] said to him, "Do
you still hold fast your integrity? Curse
God and die!"[4191]
10 But he said to her, "You speak
as one of the foolish women speaks.
[a]Shall we indeed accept good[2896] from
God and not accept adversity?" [b]In all
this Job did not sin[2398] with his lips.[8193]
🔑 **11** Now when Job's three
friends[7453] heard[8085] of all this adversity
that had come upon him, they came each
one[376] from his own place, Eliphaz the
[a]Temanite, Bildad the [b]Shuhite, and

15 [IV]Lit., *only I alone,* and so also vv. 16, 17, 19
16 [a]Gen. 19:24; Lev. 10:2; Num. 11:1-3
17 [I]Lit., *smote* [a]Gen. 11:28, 31
20 [a]Gen. 37:29, 34; Josh. 7:6
21 [a]Eccl. 5:15 [b]1Sam. 2:7, 8; Job 2:10
22 [I]Lit., *ascribe unseemliness to* [a]Job 2:10
1 [a]Job 1:6-8
3 [I]Lit., *set your heart to* [II]Or, *re-vering* [III]Lit., *swallow him up* [a]Job 27:5, 6
5 [a]Job 1:11 [b]Job 19:20
6 [I]Lit., *hand*
7 [a]Deut. 28:35; Job 7:5; 13:28; 30:17, 18, 30
8 [a]Job 42:6; Jer. 6:26; Ezek. 27:30; Jon. 3:6
10 [a]Job 1:21 [b]Job 1:22; Ps. 39:1; James 1:12
11 [a]Gen. 36:11; Job 6:19; Jer. 49:7 [b]Gen. 25:2

🔑 **2:11** The second means which Satan used to attack Job was his friends. However, let us be fair with Eliphaz, Bildad, and Zophar. They were not "fair weather friends." They were truly concerned for their friend Job in his time of personal loss and suffering. It would have been much easier for them to have gone their own ways and to have ignored Job. Their intention was to help Job straighten out his

(continued on next page)

Zophar the Naamathite; and they made
an appointment[3259] together to come to
[c]sympathize with him and comfort[5162]
him.
12 And when they lifted up[5375] their
eyes at a distance, and did not recognize
him, they raised their voices and wept.
And each of them [a]tore his robe,[4598]
and they [b]threw[2236] dust[6083] over their
heads[7218] toward the sky.[8064]
13 [a]Then they sat down on the
ground[776] with him for seven days
and seven nights[3915] with no one
speaking[1696] a word[1697] to him, for they
saw[7200] that *his* pain was very great.

Job's Lament

3 Afterward Job opened his mouth[6310]
and cursed[7043] [I]the day[3117] of his
birth.
2 And Job [I]said,[559]
3 "[a]Let the day perish[6] on which I
was to be born,
And the night[3915] *which* said, 'A
[I]boy[1397] is conceived.'
4 "May that day be darkness;[2822]
Let not God[433] above care for it,
Nor light shine on it.
5 "Let [a]darkness and black
gloom[6757] claim it;
Let a cloud settle[7931] on it;
Let the blackness[3650] of the day
terrify[1204] it.
6 "*As for* that night, let darkness[652]
seize it;
Let it not rejoice among the days
of the year;
Let it not come into the number
of the months.
7 "Behold, let that night be barren;
Let no joyful shout enter it.
8 "Let those curse[5344] it who
curse[779] the day,
Who are [I]prepared to [a]rouse
Leviathan.
9 "Let the stars of its twilight be
darkened;[2821]
Let it wait for light[216] but have
none,
Neither let it see the [I]breaking
dawn;
10 Because it did not shut the
opening of my *mother's*
womb,[990]
Or hide trouble from my eyes.
11 "[a]Why did I not die[4191] [I]at birth,
Come forth from the womb[990]
and expire?[1478]
12 "Why did the knees receive me,
And why the breasts, that I
should suck?
13 "For now I [a]would have lain down
and been quiet;[8252]
I would have slept then, I would
have been at rest,
14 With [a]kings[4428] and *with*
[b]counselors[3289] of the
earth,[776]
Who rebuilt [c]ruins[2723] for
themselves;
15 Or with [a]princes[8267] [b]who had
gold,
Who were filling their houses[1004]
with silver.
16 "Or like a miscarriage[5309] which
is [I]discarded, I would not be,
As infants that never saw[7200]
light.
17 "There the wicked[7563] cease from
raging,[7267]
And there the [I]weary are at
[a]rest.
18 "The prisoners are at ease
together;
They do not hear[8085] the voice
of the taskmaster.
19 "The small and the great are
there,
And the slave[5650] is free from
his master.[113]
20 "Why is [a]light given to him who
suffers,[6001]
And life[2416] to the bitter[4751] of
soul;[5315]

11 [c]Job 42:11; Rom. 12:15
12 [a]Job 1:20 [b]Josh. 7:6; Neh. 9:1; Lam. 2:10; Ezek. 27:30
13 [a]Gen. 50:10; Ezek. 3:15
1 [I]Lit., *his day*
2 [I]Lit., *answered and said*
3 [I]Lit., *man-child* [a]Jer. 20:14-18
5 [a]Jer. 13:16
8 [I]Or, *skillful* [a]Job 41:1, 25
9 [I]Lit., *eyelids*
11 [I]Lit., *from the womb* [a]Job 10:18, 19
13 [a]Job 3:13-19; 7:8-10, 21; 10:21, 22; 14:10-15, 20-22; 16:22; 17:13-16; 19:25-27; 21:13, 23-26; 24:19, 20; 26:5, 6; 34:22
14 [a]Job 12:18 [b]Job 12:17 [c]Job 15:28; Is. 58:12
15 [a]Job 12:21 [b]Job 27:16, 17
16 [I]Lit., *hidden*
17 [I]Lit., *weary of strength* [a]Job 17:16
20 [a]Jer. 20:18

(continued from previous page)
life and recover from the disasters which had fallen upon him. What follows is a true record of what they said, but what they said was not always right (see Job 4:1—31:40). However, some of their statements were correct and quoted as Scripture in the N.T. (compare Job 5:11-13 with I Cor. 3:19).

21 Who [Ia]long for death,[4194] but
there is none,
And dig for it more than for
[b]hidden treasures;
22 Who rejoice greatly,
They exult when they find the
grave?[6913]
23 "*Why is light given* to a man
[a]whose way[1870] is hidden,
And whom [b]God has hedged in?
24 "For [a]my groaning comes at the
sight of my food,
And [b]my cries pour out like
water.
25 "For [Ia]what I fear[6342] comes upon
me,
And what I dread[3025] befalls me.
26 "I [a]am not at ease, nor am I quiet,
And I am not at rest,[8252] but
turmoil[7267] comes."

Eliphaz: Innocent Do Not Suffer

4 🗝 Then Eliphaz the Temanite [I]answered,[559]
2 "If one ventures[5254] a word with
you, will you become
impatient?
But [a]who can refrain [I]from
speaking?[4405]
3 "Behold [a]you have
admonished[3256] many,
And you have strengthened[2388]
weak hands.[3027]
4 "Your words[4405] have [I]helped[6965]
the tottering to stand,
And you have strengthened
[II]feeble[3766] knees.
5 "But now it has come to you, and
you [a]are impatient;
It [b]touches[5060] you, and you are
dismayed.[926]
6 "Is not your [Ia]fear[3374] *of God*
[b]your confidence,[3690]
And the integrity[8537] of your
ways[1870] your hope?
7 "Remember[2142] now, [a]who
ever perished[6] being
innocent?[5355]
Or where were the upright[6662]
destroyed?
8 "According to what I have
seen,[7200] [a]those who plow
iniquity[205]
And those who sow trouble
harvest it.
9 "By [a]the breath of God[433] they
perish,[6]
And [b]by the [I]blast[7307] of His
anger[639] they come to an
end.[3615]
10 "The [a]roaring of the lion and the
voice of the *fierce* lion,
And the teeth of the young lions
are broken.
11 "The [a]lion perishes[6] for lack of
prey,
And the [b]whelps[1121] of the
lioness are scattered.
12 "Now a word[1697] [a]was brought to
me stealthily,
And my ear[241] received a
[b]whisper of it.
13 "Amid disquieting [a]thoughts from
the visions[2384] of the
night,[3915]

21 [I]Lit., *wait* [a]Rev. 9:6 [b]Prov. 2:4
23 [a]Job 19:6, 8, 12 [b]Job 19:8; Ps. 88:8; Lam. 3:7
24 [a]Job 6:7; 33:20 [b]Job 30:16; Ps. 42:4
25 [I]Lit., *the fear I fear and* [a]Job 9:28; 30:15
26 [a]Job 7:13, 14

1 [I]Lit., *answered and said*
2 [I]Lit., *in words* [a]Job 32:18-20
3 [a]Job 4:3, 4; 29:15, 16, 21, 25
4 [I]Lit., *caused* [II]Lit., *bowing*
5 [a]Job 6:14 [b]Job 19:21
6 [I]Or, *reverence* [a]Job 1:1 [b]Prov. 3:26
7 [a]Job 8:20; 36:6, 7; Ps. 37:25
8 [a]Job 15:31, 35; Prov. 22:8; Hos. 10:13; Gal. 6:7
9 [I]Lit., *wind* [a]Job 15:30; Is. 11:4; 30:33; 2Thess. 2:8 [b]Job 40:11-13
10 [a]Job 5:15; Ps. 58:6
11 [a]Job 29:17; Ps. 34:10 [b]Job 5:4; 20:10; 27:14
12 [a]Job 4:12-17; 33:15-18 [b]Job 26:14
13 [a]Job 33:15

🗝 **4:1—31:40** Job's friends' counsel to him is presented in three cycles of speeches in which each friend presents his view of Job's problems. Job answers each proposal that is made. In the third cycle Bildad has almost given up on his friend and Zophar does not bother to speak at all. In the first cycle of discussions (chapters 4—14), Eliphaz points out that Job is obviously guilty of sin, Bildad accuses him of being a hypocrite and Zophar tells him he is both a hypocrite and a liar; all of which Job denies and pleads for their mercy, stating that he is well aware of God's power as well as his own innocence. In the second cycle (chapters 15—21) his friends repeat their accusations that he is a sinner, justly pointed out by his denial of any wrongdoing. They add to this vivid pictures of the punishment of wicked men in order to bring Job to repentance. Job claims that they are simply confusing him with words and only interested in persecuting him. In the third cycle (chapters 22—31) his friends point out that the things which have fallen upon him are just the kinds of things that come to men who give in to temptation and beg him to repent. At the end Job goes into detail about his life to defend his blamelessness, insisting that he is telling the truth and that the full knowledge of the truth lies with God and not with men.

When deep sleep falls[5307] on men,[582]
14 Dread[6343] came upon me, and trembling,[7461]
And made [I]all my bones[6106] shake.[6342]
15 "Then a [I]spirit[7307] passed by my face;
The hair of my flesh[1320] bristled up.
16 "It stood still, but I could not discern its appearance;
A form[8544] *was* before my eyes;
There was silence, then I heard[8085] a voice:
17 'Can [a]mankind[582] be just[6663] [I]before God?
Can a man be pure [I]before his [b]Maker?[6213]
18 '[a]He puts no trust[539] even in His servants;[5650]
And against His angels He charges error.
19 'How much more those who dwell[7931] in [a]houses[1004] of clay,
Whose [b]foundation[3247] is in the dust,[6083]
Who are crushed[1792] before the moth!
20 '[a]Between morning and evening they are broken[3807] in pieces;
Unobserved,[7760] they [b]perish forever.[5331]
21 'Is not their [a]tent-cord plucked up within them?
They die,[4191] yet [b]without wisdom.'[2451]

God Is Just

5 "Call[7121] now, is there anyone who will answer you?
And to which of the [a]holy ones[6918] will you turn?
2 "For [a]vexation[3708] slays the foolish man,
And anger[7068] kills[4191] the simple.
3 "I have seen[7200] the [a]foolish taking root,
And I [b]cursed[5344] his abode immediately.
4 "His [a]sons[1121] are far from safety,[3468]
They are even [I]oppressed[1792] in the gate,
Neither is there a deliverer.[5337]
5 "[I]His harvest the hungry devour,
And take it to a *place of* thorns;
And the [II][a]schemer is eager for their wealth.[2428]
6 "For [a]affliction[205] does not come from the dust,[6083]
Neither does trouble[5999] sprout from the ground,[127]
7 For [a]man[120] is born for trouble,
As sparks fly upward.
8 "But as for me, I would [a]seek God,[410]
And I would place[7760] my cause[1700] before God;[430]
9 Who [a]does[6213] great and unsearchable things,
[I]Wonders[6381] without number.
10 "He [a]gives rain on the earth,[776]
And sends water on the fields,
11 So that [a]He sets[7760] on high those who are lowly,
And those who mourn[6937] are lifted to safety.
12 "He [a]frustrates[6565] the plotting[4284] of the shrewd,[6175]
So that their hands[3027] cannot attain success.[8454]
13 "He [a]captures the wise[2450] by their own shrewdness[6193]
And the advice[6098] of the cunning[6617] is quickly thwarted.
14 "By day[3119] they [a]meet with darkness,[2822]
And grope at noon as in the night.[3915]
15 "But He saves[3467] from [a]the sword[2719] of their mouth,[6310]
And [b]the poor from the hand[3027] of the mighty.[2389]
16 "So the helpless has hope,
And [a]unrighteousness[5766] must shut its mouth.
17 "Behold, how [a]happy[835] is the

14 [I]Lit., *the multitude of*
15 [I]Or, *breath passed over*
17 [I]Lit., *from* [a]Job 9:2; 25:4 [b]Job 31:15; 32:22; 35:10; 36:3
18 [a]Job 15:15
19 [a]Job 10:9; 33:6 [b]Gen. 2:7; 3:19; Job 22:16
20 [a]Job 14:2 [b]Job 14:20; 20:7
21 [a]Job 8:22 [b]Job 18:21; 36:12

1 [a]Job 15:15
2 [a]Prov. 12:16; 27:3
3 [a]Jer. 12:2 [b]Job 24:18; 31:30
4 [I]Lit., *crushed* [a]Job 4:11
5 [I]Lit., *Whose* [II]Ancient versions read *thirsty* [a]Job 18:8-10; 22:10
6 [a]Job 15:35
7 [a]Job 14:1
8 [a]Job 13:2, 3; Ps. 50:15
9 [I]Or, *Miracles* [a]Job 9:10; 37:14, 16; 42:3
10 [a]Job 36:27-29; 37:6-11; 38:26
11 [a]Job 22:29; 36:7
12 [a]Ps. 33:10
13 [a]Job 37:24; 1Cor. 3:19
14 [a]Job 12:25; 15:30; 18:18; 20:26; 24:13
15 [a]Job 4:10, 11; Ps. 35:10 [b]Job 29:17; 34:28; 36:6, 15; 38:15
16 [a]Ps. 107:42
17 [a]Ps. 94:12

man[582] whom God[433]
reproves,[3198]
So do not despise[3988] the
[b]discipline[4148] of [I]the
Almighty.[7706]
18 "For [a]He inflicts pain, and
[I]gives relief;[2280]
He wounds,[4272] and His hands
also heal.
19 "[I]From six troubles [a]He will
deliver you,
Even in seven [b]evil[7451] will not
touch[5060] you.
20 "In [a]famine He will redeem[6299]
you from death,[4194]
And [b]in war from the power[3027]
of the sword.
21 "You will be [a]hidden from the
scourge[7752] of the tongue,
[b]Neither will you be afraid[3372] of
violence[7701] when it comes.
22 "You will [a]laugh at violence and
famine,
[b]Neither will you be afraid of
[I]wild beasts.[2416]
23 "For you will be in league[1285] with
the stones of the field;[7704]
And [a]the beasts of the field will
be at peace[7999] with you.
24 "And you will know[3045] that your
[a]tent[168] is secure,
For you will visit[6485] your abode
and fear no loss.[2398]
25 "You will know also that your
[Ia]descendants[2233] will be
many,
And [b]your offspring as the grass
of the earth.
26 "You will [a]come to the grave[6913]
in full vigor,
Like the stacking of grain in its
season.[6256]
27 "Behold this, we have
investigated it, thus it is;
Hear[8085] it, and know for
yourself."

Job's Friends Are No Help

6 Then Job [I]answered,[559]
2 "[a]Oh that my vexation[3708] were
actually weighed,
And laid in the balances together
with my iniquity![1942]
3 "For then it would be [a]heavier[3513]
than the sand of the seas,
Therefore my words[1697] have
been rash.
4 "For the [a]arrows of the
Almighty[7706] are within me;
[I]Their [b]poison[2534] my spirit[7307]
drinks;
The [c]terrors of God[433] are
arrayed against me.
5 "Does the [a]wild donkey bray over
his grass,
Or does the ox low[1600] over his
fodder?
6 "Can something tasteless be
eaten without salt,
Or is there any taste[2940] in the
[I]white of an egg?
7 "My soul[5315] [a]refuses[3985] to
touch[5060] *them;*
They are like loathsome food to
me.
8 "Oh that my request[7596] might
come to pass,
And that God would grant my
longing!
9 "Would that God were [a]willing[2974]
to crush[1792] me;
That He would loose His
hand[3027] and cut me off![1214]
10 "But it is still my consolation,[5165]
And I rejoice in unsparing pain,
That I [a]have not [I]denied the
words[561] of the Holy One.[6918]
11 "What is my strength, that I
should wait?[3176]
And what is my end, that I should
[Ia]endure?[748]
12 "Is my strength the strength of
stones,
Or is my flesh[1320] bronze?
13 "Is it that my [a]help is not within
me,
And that [Ib]deliverance[8454] is
driven from me?
14 "For the [a]despairing man *there*
should be kindness[2617] from
his friend;[7453]
Lest he [b]forsake[5800] the
[I]fear[3374] of the Almighty.

17 [I]Heb., *Shaddai,* and so throughout ch. 6 [b]Job 36:15, 16; Prov. 3:11; Heb. 12:5-11; James 1:12
18 [I]Lit., *binds* [a]Deut. 32:39; 1Sam. 2:6; Is. 30:26; Hos. 6:1
19 [I]Lit., *In* [a]Ps. 34:19 [b]Ps. 91:10
20 [a]Ps. 33:19; 37:19 [b]Ps. 144:10
21 [a]Job 5:15; Ps. 31:20 [b]Ps. 91:5, 6
22 [I]Lit., *beasts of the earth* [a]Job 8:21 [b]Ps. 91:13; Ezek. 34:25; Hos. 2:18
23 [a]Is. 11:6-9; 65:25
24 [a]Job 8:6
25 [I]Lit., *seed* [a]Ps. 112:2 [b]Is. 44:3, 4; 48:19
26 [a]Job 42:17

1 [I]Lit., *answered and said*
2 [a]Job 31:6
3 [a]Job 23:2
4 [I]Lit., *Whose* [a]Job 16:13; Ps. 38:2 [b]Job 20:16; 21:20 [c]Job 30:15
5 [a]Job 39:5-8
6 [I]Heb., *hallamuth,* meaning uncertain. Perhaps the juice of a plant.
7 [a]Job 3:24; 33:20
9 [a]Num. 11:15; 1Kin. 19:4; Job 7:16; 9:21; 10:1
10 [I]Lit., *hidden* [a]Job 22:22; 23:11, 12
11 [I]Lit., *prolong my soul* [a]Job 21:4
13 [I]So ancient versions [a]Job 26:2 [b]Job 26:3
14 [I]Or, *reverence* [a]Job 4:5 [b]Job 1:5; 15:4

15 "My brothers[251] have acted
[a]deceitfully[898] like a [I]wadi,
Like the torrents of [I]wadis which
vanish,[5674]
16 Which are turbid[6937] because of
ice,
And into which the snow
[I]melts.
17 "When[6256] [a]they become
waterless, they [I]are silent,
When it is hot, they vanish[6789]
from their place.
18 "The [I]paths[734] of their course[1870]
wind along,
They go up into nothing[8414] and
perish.[6]
19 "The caravans[734] of [a]Tema
looked,
The travelers of [b]Sheba
hoped[6960] for them.
20 "They [a]were [I]disappointed[954] for
they had trusted,[682]
They came there and were
confounded.
21 "Indeed, you have now become
such,
[a]You see a terror and are
afraid.[3372]
22 "Have I said,[559] 'Give me
something,'
Or, 'Offer a bribe for me from
your wealth,'
23 Or, 'Deliver me from the hand
of the adversary,'
Or, 'Redeem[6299] me from the
hand of the tyrants'?
24 "Teach[3384] me, and [a]I will be
silent;
And show[995] me how I have
erred.[7683]
25 "How painful are honest[3476]
words!
But what does your
argument[3198] prove?[3198]
26 "Do you intend[2803] to reprove *my*
words,[4405]
When the [a]words[561] of one in
despair[2976] belong to the
wind?[7307]
27 "You would even [a]cast *lots* for
[b]the orphans,
And [c]barter over your friend.
28 "And now please[2974] look at me,
And *see* if I [a]lie[3576] to your face.
29 "Desist[7725] now, let there be no
injustice;[5766]
Even desist, [a]my
righteousness[6664] is yet in it.
30 "Is there injustice on my tongue?
Cannot [a]my palate discern[995]
[I]calamities?[1942]

Job's Life Seems Futile

7 "[I]Is not man[582] [a]forced to
labor[6635] on earth,[776]
And *are not* his days like the days
of [b]a hired man?
2 "As a slave[5650] who pants for the
shade,
And as a hired man who eagerly
waits[6960] for his wages,
3 So am I allotted[5157] months of
vanity,[7723]
And [a]nights[3915] of trouble are
appointed me.
4 "When I [a]lie down I say,[559]
'When shall I arise?'
But the night continues,
And I am [I]continually tossing
until dawn.
5 "My [a]flesh[1320] is clothed with
worms and a crust of dirt;[6083]
My skin[5785] hardens and runs.
6 "My days are [a]swifter[7043] than a
weaver's shuttle,
And come to an end[3615]
[b]without hope.
7 "Remember[2142] that my life[2416]
[a]is *but* breath,[7307]
My eye will [b]not again see
good.[2896]
8 "The [a]eye of him who sees[7210]
me will behold me no more;
Thine eyes *will be* on me, but
[b]I will not be.
9 "When a [a]cloud[6051] vanishes,[3615]
it is gone,
So [b]he who goes down to
[c]Sheol[7585] does not come
up.[5927]
10 "He will not return[7725] again to
his house,[1004]
Nor will [a]his place know[5234] him
anymore.

15 [I]Or, *brooks* [a]Jer. 15:18
16 [I]Lit., *hides itself*
17 [I]Or, *cease* [a]Job 24:19
18 [I]Or, *caravans turn from their course, they go up into the waste and perish.*
19 [a]Gen. 25:15; Is. 21:14; Jer. 25:23 [b]Job 1:15
20 [I]Lit., *ashamed* [a]Jer. 14:3
21 [a]Ps. 38:11
24 [a]Ps. 39:1
26 [a]Job 8:2; 15:2; 16:3
27 [a]Joel 3:3; Nah. 3:10 [b]Job 22:9; 24:3, 9 [c]2Pet. 2:3
28 [a]Job 27:4; 33:3; 36:4
29 [a]Job 13:18; 19:6; 23:10; 27:5, 6; 34:5; 42:1-6
30 [I]Or, *words* [a]Job 12:11
1 [I]Lit., *Has not man compulsory labor* [a]Job 5:7; 10:17; 14:1, 14 [b]Job 14:6
3 [a]Job 16:7
4 [I]Lit., *sated with* [a]Deut. 28:67; Job 7:13, 14
5 [a]Job 2:7; 17:14
6 [a]Job 9:25 [b]Job 13:15; 14:19; 17:15, 16; 19:10
7 [a]Job 7:16; Ps. 78:39; James 4:14 [b]Job 9:25
8 [a]Job 8:18; 20:9 [b]Job 7:21
9 [a]Job 30:15 [b]Job 3:13-19 [c]2Sam. 12:23; Job 11:8; 14:13; 17:13, 16
10 [a]Job 8:18; 20:9; 27:21, 23

11 "Therefore, [a]I will not restrain
my mouth;[6310]
I will speak[1696] in the anguish[6862]
of my spirit,[7307]
I will complain[7878] in the
bitterness[4751] of my soul.[5315]
12 "Am I the sea, or [a]the sea
monster,[8577]
That Thou dost set[7760] a guard
over me?
13 "If I say, '[a]My bed will comfort[5162]
me,
My couch will [I]ease[5375] my
complaint,'[7878]
14 Then Thou dost frighten[2865] me
with dreams
And terrify[1204] me by visions;[2384]
15 So that my soul would choose[977]
suffocation,
Death[4194] rather than my
[I]pains.
16 "I [I][a]waste away;[3988] I will not
live[2421] forever.
Leave me alone, [b]for my days
are *but* a breath.
17 "[a]What is man that Thou dost
magnify him,
And that Thou [I]art concerned[3820]
about him,
18 That [a]Thou dost examine[6485]
him every morning,
And try[974] him every moment?
19 "[I][a]Wilt Thou never turn Thy gaze
away from me,
Nor let me alone[7503] until I
swallow[1104] my spittle?
20 "[a]Have I sinned?[2398] What have
I done to Thee,
O [b]watcher[5341] of men?[120]
Why hast Thou set[7760] me as
Thy target,
So that I am a burden[4853] to
myself?
21 "Why then [a]dost Thou not
pardon[5375] my
transgression[6588]
And take away[5674] my
iniquity?[5771]
For now I will [b]lie down in the
dust;
And Thou wilt seek me,
[c]but I will not be."

Bildad Says God Rewards the Good

8 Then Bildad the Shuhite [I]answered,[559]
2 "How long will you say[4448] these
things,
And the [a]words[561] of your
mouth[6310] be a mighty
wind?[7307]
3 "Does [a]God[410] pervert[5791]
justice[4941]
Or does [I]the Almighty[7706]
pervert what is right?[6664]
4 "[a]If your sons[1121] sinned[2398]
against Him,
Then He delivered them into the
[I]power of their
transgression.[6588]
5 "If you would [a]seek[7836] God
And implore the compassion[2603]
of [I]the Almighty,
6 If you are pure[2134] and
upright,[3477]
Surely now [a]He would rouse
Himself for you
And restore your righteous[6664]
[I][b]estate.[7999]
7 "Though your beginning[7225] was
insignificant,
Yet your [a]end[319] will increase
greatly.
8 "Please[4994] [a]inquire[7592] of past[7223]
generations,[1755]
And consider[3559] the things
searched out by their
fathers.[1]
9 "For we are *only* of yesterday
and know[3045] nothing,
Because [a]our days on earth[776]
are as a shadow.
10 "Will they not teach[3384] you *and*
tell[559] you,
And bring forth words[4405] from
their minds?[3820]
11 "Can the papyrus grow up[1342]
without marsh?
Can the rushes[260] grow without
water?
12 "While it is still green *and* not
cut down,
Yet it withers[3001] before any
other [I]plant.

11 [a]Job 10:1; 21:4; 23:2; Ps. 40:9
12 [a]Ezek. 32:2, 3
13 [I]Lit., *bear* [a]Job 7:4; Ps. 6:6
15 [I]Lit., *bones*
16 [I]Or, *loathe* [a]Job 6:9; 9:21; 10:1 [b]Job 7:7
17 [I]Lit., *shouldst set Thy heart on* [a]Job 22:2; Ps. 8:4; 144:3; Heb. 2:6
18 [a]Job 14:3
19 [I]Lit., *How long wilt Thou not* [a]Job 9:18; 10:20; 14:6
20 [a]Job 35:3, 6 [b]Ps. 36:6
21 [a]Job 9:28; 10:14 [b]Job 10:9 [c]Job 7:8

1 [I]Lit., *answered and said*
2 [a]Job 6:26
3 [I]Heb., *Shaddai* [a]Gen. 18:25; Deut. 32:4; 2Chr. 19:7; Job 34:10, 12; 36:23; 37:23; Rom. 3:5
4 [I]Lit., *hand* [a]Job 1:5, 18, 19
5 [I]Heb., *Shaddai* [a]Job 5:17-27
6 [I]Lit., *place* [a]Job 22:27; 34:28; Ps. 7:6 [b]Job 5:24
7 [a]Job 42:12
8 [a]Deut. 4:32; 32:7; Job 15:18; 20:4
9 [a]Job 14:2
12 [I]Lit., *reed*

13 "So are the paths[734] of [a]all who
forget God,
And the [b]hope of the godless[2611]
will perish,[6]
14 Whose confidence[3689] is fragile,
And whose trust a [a]spider's
[I]web.
15 "He [I]trusts[8172] in his [a]house,[1004]
but it does not stand;
He holds fast to it, but it does
not endure.
16 "He [Ia]thrives before the sun,
And his [b]shoots spread out over
his garden.
17 "His roots wrap around a rock
pile,
He [I]grasps[2372] a house of stones.
18 "If he is [I]removed[1104] from
[a]his place,
Then it will deny him, *saying,*
'[b]I never saw[7200] you.'
19 "Behold, [a]this is the joy of His
way;[1870]
And out of the dust[6083] others
will spring.
20 "Lo, [a]God will not reject[3988] *a
man of* integrity,[8535]
Nor [b]will He [I]support[2388] the
evildoers.[7489]
21 "He will yet fill [a]your mouth with
laughter,
And your lips[8193] with shouting.
22 "Those who hate[8130] you will be
[a]clothed with shame;
And the [b]tent[168] of the
wicked[7563] will be no
more."[369]

Job Says There Is No Arbitrator between God and Man

9 Then Job [I]answered,[559]
2 "In truth[551] I know[3045] that this
is so,
But how can a [a]man[582] be in the
right[6663] [I]before God?[410]
3 "If one wished to [a]dispute[7378] with
Him,
He could not answer Him once
in a thousand *times.*
4 "[a]Wise[2450] in heart[3824] and
[b]mighty in strength,
Who has [Ic]defied Him [II]without
harm?[7999]
5 "[a]*It is God* who removes the
mountains, they know not
how,
When He overturns[2015] them in
His anger;[639]
6 Who [a]shakes the earth[776] out
of its place,
And its [b]pillars tremble;
7 Who commands[559] the
[a]sun [I]not to shine,
And sets a seal upon the stars;
8 Who alone [a]stretches out the
heavens,[8064]
And [Ib]tramples down the waves
of the sea;
9 Who makes[6213] the [a]Bear,
Orion, and the Pleiades,
And the [b]chambers of the south;
10 Who [a]does[6213] great things,
[I]unfathomable,
And wondrous[6381] works
without number.
11 "Were He to pass by me,
[a]I would not see Him;
Were He to move past *me,* I
would not perceive[995] Him.
12 "Were He to snatch away, who
could [a]restrain Him?
Who could say[559] to Him, '[b]What
art Thou doing?'[6213]
13 "God[433] will not turn back His
anger;
Beneath Him crouch the helpers
of [a]Rahab.
14 "How then can [a]I [I]answer Him,
And choose[977] my words[1697]
[II]before Him?
15 "For [a]though I were right,[6663] I
could not [I]answer;
I would have to [b]implore the
mercy[2603] of my judge.[8199]
16 "If I called[7121] and He answered
me,
I could not believe[539] that He
was listening[238] to my voice.
17 "For He [a]bruises me with a
tempest,

13 [a]Ps. 9:17 [b]Job 11:20; 13:16; 15:34; 20:5; 27:8
14 [I]Lit., *house* [a]Is. 59:5, 6
15 [I]Lit., *leans on* [a]Job 8:22; 27:18; Ps. 49:11
16 [I]Lit., *is lush* [a]Ps. 37:35; Jer. 11:16 [b]Ps. 80:11
17 [I]Heb., *sees*
18 [I]Lit., *swallowed up* [a]Job 7:10 [b]Job 7:8
19 [a]Job 20:5
20 [I]Lit., *strengthen the hand of* [a]Job 4:7 [b]Job 21:30
21 [a]Job 5:22; Ps. 126:1, 2
22 [a]Ps. 132:18 [b]Job 8:15; 15:34; 18:14; 21:28

1 [I]Lit., *answered and said*
2 [I]Lit., *with* [a]Job 4:17; 25:4
3 [a]Job 10:2; 13:19; 23:6; 40:2
4 [I]Lit., *stiffened his neck against* [II]Lit., *and remained safe* [a]Job 11:6; 12:13; 28:23; 38:36, 37 [b]Job 9:19; 23:6 [c]2Chr. 13:12; Prov. 29:1
5 [a]Job 9:5-10; 26:6-14; 41:11
6 [a]Is. 2:19, 21; 13:13; Hag. 2:6 [b]Ps. 75:3
7 [I]Lit., *and it does not shine* [a]Is. 13:10; Ezek. 32:7, 8
8 [I]Lit., *treads upon the heights of* [a]Gen. 1:1; Job 37:18; Ps. 104:2; Is. 40:22 [b]Job 38:16; Ps. 77:19
9 [a]Job 38:31, 32; Amos 5:8 [b]Job 37:9
10 [I]Lit., *until there is no searching out* [a]Job 5:9
11 [a]Job 23:8, 9; 35:14
12 [a]Job 10:7; 11:10 [b]Is. 45:9
13 [a]Job 26:12; Ps. 89:10; Is. 30:7; 51:9
14 [I]Or, *plead my case* [II]Lit., *with* [a]Job 9:3, 32
15 [I]Or, *plead my case* [a]Job 9:20, 21; 10:15 [b]Job 8:5
17 [a]Job 16:12, 14; 30:22

And multiplies my wounds
without cause.
18 "He will [a]not allow me to get my
breath,[7307]
But saturates me with
[b]bitterness.
19 "If *it is a matter* of power,
[a]behold, *He is* the strong one!
And if *it is a matter* of justice,[4941]
who can summon[3259]
[I]Him?
20 "[a]Though I am righteous,[6663] my
mouth[6310] will [b]condemn[7561]
me;
Though I am guiltless,[8535] He
will declare me guilty.
21 "I am [a]guiltless;
I do not take notice of myself;[5315]
I [b]despise[3988] my life.[2416]
22 "It is *all* one; therefore I say,
'He [a]destroys[3615] the guiltless
and the wicked.'[7563]
23 "If the scourge[7752] kills[4191]
suddenly,
He [a]mocks the despair[4531] of the
innocent.[5355]
24 "The earth [a]is given into the
hand[3027] of the wicked;
He [b]covers the faces of its
judges.[8199]
If *it is* not *He,* then who is it?
25 "Now [a]my days are swifter[7043]
than a runner;
They flee away, [b]they see no
good.[2896]
26 "They slip by like [a]reed boats,
Like an [b]eagle that swoops on
[I]its prey.
27 "Though I say, 'I will forget
[a]my complaint,[7878]
I will leave off my *sad*
countenance and be cheerful,'
28 I am [a]afraid[3025] of all my
pains,[6094]
I know that [b]Thou wilt not
acquit[5352] me.
29 "I am accounted [a]wicked,[7561]
Why then should I toil in vain?
30 "If I should [a]wash[7364] myself with
snow
And cleanse[2141] [b]my hands[3709]
with lye,

18 [a]Job 7:19; 10:20 [b]Job 13:26; 27:2
19 [I]So with Gr.; Heb., *me* [a]Job 9:4
20 [a]Job 9:15 [b]Job 9:29; 15:6
21 [a]Job 1:1; 12:4; 13:18 [b]Job 7:16
22 [a]Job 10:7, 8
23 [a]Job 24:12
24 [a]Job 10:3; 12:6; 16:11 [b]Job 12:17
25 [a]Job 7:6 [b]Job 7:7
26 [I]Lit., *food* [a]Is. 18:2 [b]Job 39:29; Hab. 1:8
27 [a]Job 7:11
28 [a]Job 3:25 [b]Job 7:21; 10:14
29 [a]Job 10:2; Ps. 37:33
30 [a]Jer. 2:22 [b]Job 31:7
32 [I]Lit., *judgment* [a]Eccl. 6:10 [b]Job 9:3; Rom. 9:20
33 [a]1Sam. 2:25; Job 9:19; Is. 1:18
34 [a]Job 13:21
35 [a]Job 13:22
1 [I]Lit., *My soul loathes* [a]Job 7:16 [b]Job 7:11
2 [a]Job 9:29
3 [I]Lit., *good* [II]Lit., *you shine forth* [a]Job 9:22-24; 16:11; 19:6; 27:2 [b]Job 10:8; 14:15; Ps. 138:8; Is. 64:8 [c]Job 21:16; 22:18
4 [a]1Sam. 16:7; Job 28:24; 34:21
5 [a]Job 36:26
6 [a]Job 14:16
7 [a]Job 9:21; 13:18 [b]Job 9:12; 23:13; 27:22

31 Yet Thou wouldst plunge[2881] me
into the pit,[7845]
And my own clothes would
abhor[8581] me.
32 "For [a]*He is* not a man[376] as I am
that [b]I may answer Him,
That we may go to [I]court
together.
33 "There is no [a]umpire[3198] between
us,
Who may lay his hand upon us
both.
34 "Let Him [a]remove His rod from
me,
And let not dread[367] of Him
terrify[1204] me.
35 "*Then* I [a]would speak and not
fear[3372] Him;
But I am not like that in myself.

Job Despairs of God's Dealings

10 "[I][a]I loathe my own[5315] life;[2416]
I will give full vent[5800] to
[b]my complaint;[7878]
I will speak[1696] in the
bitterness[4751] of my soul.
2 "I will say[559] to God,[433] '[a]Do not
condemn[7561] me;
Let me know[3045] why Thou dost
contend[7378] with me.
3 'Is it [I]right[2896] for Thee indeed
to [a]oppress,
To reject[3988] [b]the labor of Thy
hands,[3709]
And [II]to look favorably on
[c]the schemes[6098] of the
wicked?[7563]
4 'Hast Thou eyes of flesh?[1320]
Or dost Thou [a]see as a man[582]
sees?[7200]
5 'Are Thy days as the days of a
mortal,
Or [a]Thy years as man's[1397]
years,
6 That [a]Thou shouldst seek for
my guilt,[5771]
And search after my sin?[2403]
7 'According to Thy knowledge[1847]
[a]I am indeed not guilty;[7561]
Yet there is [b]no deliverance[5337]
from Thy hand.[3027]

8 '[a]Thy hands[3027] fashioned[6087] and
made[6213] me [I]altogether,
[b]And wouldst Thou destroy[1104]
me?
9 '[a]Remember[2142] now, that Thou
hast made[6213] me as [a]clay;
And wouldst Thou [b]turn me into
dust[6083] again?
10 'Didst Thou not pour me out like
milk,
And curdle me like cheese;
11 Clothe me with skin[5785] and
flesh,
And knit me together with
bones[6106] and sinews?
12 'Thou hast [a]granted[6213] me life
and lovingkindness;[2617]
And Thy care[6486] has
preserved[8104] my spirit.[7307]
13 'Yet [a]these things Thou hast
concealed in Thy heart;[3824]
I know[3045] that this is within
Thee:
14 If I sin, then Thou wouldst
[a]take note[8104] of me,
And [b]wouldst not acquit[5352] me
of my guilt.
15 'If [a]I am wicked, woe to me!
And [b]if I am righteous,[6663] I
dare not lift up[5375] my
head.[7218]
I am sated with disgrace and
[I]conscious of my misery.
16 'And should *my head* be lifted
up,[1342] [a]Thou wouldst hunt
me like a lion;
And again Thou wouldst show
Thy [b]power[6381] against me.
17 'Thou dost renew [a]Thy
witnesses against me,
And increase Thine anger
toward me,
[I][b]Hardship after hardship[6635] is
with me.
18 '[a]Why then hast Thou brought
me out of the womb?
Would that I had died[1478] and no
eye had seen[7200] me!
19 'I should have been as though I
had not been,
Carried from womb[990] to
tomb.'[6913]
20 "Would He not let [a]my few days
alone?
[I][b]Withdraw from me that I may
have a little cheer
21 Before I go—[a]and I shall not
return—[7725]
[b]To the land[776] of darkness[2822]
and [c]deep shadow;[6757]
22 The land of utter gloom[5890] as
darkness[652] *itself,*
Of deep shadow without order,
And which shines as the
darkness."

Zophar Rebukes Job

11 Then Zophar the Naamathite
[I]answered,[559]
2 "Shall a multitude of words[1697] go
unanswered,
And a [a]talkative man[376] be
acquitted?[6663]
3 "Shall your boasts silence men?
And shall you [a]scoff and none
rebuke?
4 "For [a]you have said, 'My
teaching[3948] is pure,[2134]
And [b]I am innocent[1249] in your
eyes.'
5 "But would that God[433] might
speak,[1696]
And open His lips[8193] against
you,
6 And show[5046] you the secrets
of wisdom![2451]
For sound wisdom [I][a]has two
sides.
Know[3045] then that God
[II]forgets a part of [b]your
iniquity.[5771]
7 "[a]Can you discover the depths of
God?
Can you discover the limits of
the Almighty?[7706]
8 "*They are* [a]high as [I]the
heavens,[8064] what can you
do?
Deeper than [II][b]Sheol,[7585] what
can you know?
9 "Its measure is longer[752] than the
earth,[776]
And broader than the sea.

8 [I]Lit., *together round about* [a]Job 10:3; Ps. 119:73 [b]Job 9:22

9 [a]Job 4:19; 33:6 [b]Job 7:21

12 [a]Job 33:4

13 [a]Job 23:13

14 [a]Job 7:20 [b]Job 7:21; 9:28

15 [I]Lit., *see* [a]Job 10:7; Is. 3:11 [b]Job 6:29

16 [a]Is. 38:13; Lam. 3:10; Hos. 13:7 [b]Job 5:9

17 [I]Lit., *Changes and warfare are with me* [a]Ruth 1:21; Job 16:8 [b]Job 7:1

18 [a]Job 3:11-13

20 [I]Lit., *Put* [a]Job 14:1 [b]Job 7:16, 19

21 [a]2Sam. 12:23; Job 3:13-19; 16:22 [b]Ps. 88:12 [c]Job 10:22; 34:22; 38:17; Ps. 23:4

1 [I]Lit., *answered and said*

2 [a]Job 8:2; 15:2; 18:2

3 [a]Job 17:2; 21:3

4 [a]Job 6:10 [b]Job 10:7

6 [I]Lit., *is double* [II]Lit., *causes to be forgotten for you* [a]Job 9:4 [b]Job 15:5; 22:5

7 [a]Job 33:12, 13; 36:26; 37:5, 23; Rom. 11:33

8 [I]Lit., *the heights of heaven* [II]I.e., the nether world [a]Job 22:12; 35:5 [b]Job 26:6; 38:17

10 "If He passes by or shuts up,
Or calls an assembly,[6950]
[a]who can restrain Him?
11 "For [a]He knows false[7723] men,
And He [b]sees[7200] iniquity[205]
[I]without investigating.[995]
12 "And [I][a]an idiot will become
intelligent[3823]
When the [II]foal of a [b]wild donkey
is born a man.[120]
13 "[a]If you would [b]direct[3559] your
heart[3820] right,
And [c]spread out your hand[3709]
to Him;
14 If iniquity[205] is in your hand,[3027]
[a]put it far away,
And do not let wickedness[5766]
dwell[7931] in your tents.[168]
15 "Then, indeed, you could
[a]lift up[5375] your face without
moral defect,[3971]
And you would be steadfast and
[b]not fear.[3372]
16 "For you would [a]forget *your*
trouble,[5999]
As [b]waters that have passed
by,[5674] you would
remember[2142] *it.*
17 "And your [I]life[2465] would be
[II][a]brighter than noonday;
Darkness would be like the
morning.
18 "Then you would trust,[982]
because there is hope;
And you would look around and
rest securely.
19 "You would [a]lie down and none
would disturb[2729] *you,*
And many would [b]entreat your
[I]favor.
20 "But the [a]eyes of the wicked[7563]
will fail,[3615]
And [I]there will [b]be no
escape[6] [4499] for them;
And their [c]hope is [II][d]to
breathe [5313] their last."[4646]

Job Chides His Accusers

12 Then Job [I]responded,[559]
2 "Truly[551] then [a]you are the
people,[5971]
And with you wisdom[2451] will
die![4191]
3 "But [a]I have intelligence[3824] as
well as you;
I am not inferior[5307] to you.
And [I]who does not know such
things as these?
4 "I am a [a]joke to [I]my friends.[7453]
The one who called[7121] on
God,[433] and He answered
him;
The just *and* [b]blameless[8549] *man*
is a joke.
5 "[I]He who is at ease holds calamity
in contempt,
As prepared[3559] for those whose
feet slip.
6 "The [a]tents[168] of the
destroyers[7703] prosper,
And those who provoke God[410]
[b]are secure,[987]
[I]Whom God brings [c]into their
power.[3027]
7 "But now ask[7592] the beasts, and
let them teach[3384] you;
And the birds of the heavens,[8064]
and let them tell[5046] you.
8 "Or speak[7878] to the earth,[776] and
let it teach you;
And let the fish[1709] of the sea
declare[5608] to you.
9 "Who among all these does not
know
That [a]the hand of the LORD has
done this,
10 [a]In whose hand is the life[5315]
of every living thing,[2416]
And [b]the breath[7307] of all
mankind?
11 "Does not [a]the ear[241] test[974]
words,[4405]
As the palate [I]tastes its
food?
12 "Wisdom is with [a]aged[3453] men,
With [I]long[753] life is
understanding.[8394]

Job Speaks of the Power of God

13 "With Him are [a]wisdom and
[a]might;

10 [a]Job 9:12
11 [I]Or, *even He does not consider* [a]Job 34:21-23 [b]Job 24:23; 28:24; 31:4
12 [I]Lit., *a hollow man* [II]Lit., *donkey* [a]Ps. 39:5, 11; 62:9; 144:4; Eccl. 1:2; 11:10 [b]Job 39:5
13 [a]Job 5:17-27; 11:13-20 [b]1Sam. 7:3; Ps. 78:8 [c]Job 22:27; Ps. 88:9; 143:6
14 [a]Job 22:23
15 [a]Job 22:26 [b]Ps. 27:3; 46:2
16 [a]Is. 65:16 [b]Job 22:11
17 [I]Lit., *duration of life* [II]Lit., *above noonday* [a]Job 22:26
19 [I]Lit., *face* [a]Lev. 26:6; Is. 17:2; Mic. 4:4; Zeph. 3:13 [b]Is. 45:14
20 [I]Lit., *escape has perished from them* [II]Lit., *the expiring of the soul* [a]Deut. 28:65; Job 17:5 [b]Job 27:22; 34:22 [c]Job 8:13 [d]Job 6:9

1 [I]Lit., *answered and said*
2 [a]Job 17:10
3 [I]Lit., *with whom is there not like these?* [a]Job 13:2
4 [I]Lit., *his* [a]Job 17:6; 30:1, 9, 10; 34:7 [b]Job 6:29
5 [I]Lit., *Contempt for calamity is the thought of him who is at ease*
6 [I]Or, *He who brings God into his hand* [a]Job 9:24; 21:7-9 [b]Job 24:23 [c]Job 22:18
9 [a]Is. 41:20
10 [a]Acts 17:28 [b]Job 27:3; 33:4
11 [I]Lit., *tastes food for itself* [a]Job 34:3
12 [I]Lit., *length of days* [a]Job 15:10; 32:7
13 [a]Job 9:4

To Him belong counsel[6098] and
[b]understanding.
14 "Behold, He [a]tears[2040] down, and
it cannot be rebuilt;
He [Ib]imprisons a man,[376] and
[II]there can be no release.
15 "Behold, He [a]restrains the
waters, and they dry up;[3001]
And He [b]sends them out, and
they [I]inundate[2015] the earth.
16 "With Him are strength and sound
wisdom,[8454]
The [a]misled[7683] and the
misleader[7686] belong to Him.
17 "He makes [a]counselors[3289] walk
[I]barefoot,
And makes fools[1984] of
[b]judges.[8199]
18 "He [a]loosens the [I]bond[4148] of
kings,[4428]
And binds their loins with a
girdle.[232]
19 "He makes priests[3548] walk
[I]barefoot,
And overthrows [a]the secure
ones.
20 "He deprives[5493] the trusted[539]
ones of speech,[8193]
And [a]takes away the
discernment[2940] of the
elders.[2205]
21 "He [a]pours[8210] contempt on
nobles,[5081]
And [b]loosens[7503] the belt of the
strong.
22 "He [a]reveals mysteries from the
darkness,[2822]
And brings the deep
darkness[6757] into light.[216]
23 "He [a]makes the nations[1471] great,
then destroys[6] them;
He [I]enlarges the nations, then
leads[5148] them away.
24 "He [a]deprives of intelligence[3820]
the chiefs[7218] of the earth's
people,
And makes them wander[8582] in
a pathless[1870,3808] waste.[8414]
25 "They [a]grope in darkness[2822] with
no light,
And He makes them [b]stagger[8582]
like a drunken man.

Job Says His Friends' Proverbs Are Ashes

13 "[a]Behold, my eye has seen[7200]
all *this,*
My ear[241] has heard[8085] and
understood[995] it.
2 "[a]What you know[1847] I also
know.[3045]
I am not inferior[5307] to you.
3 "But [a]I would speak[1696] to
[I]the Almighty,[7706]
And I desire[2654] to [b]argue[3198]
with God.[410]
4 "But you [a]smear with lies;[8267]
You are all [b]worthless
physicians.
5 "O that you would [a]be completely
silent,
And that it would become your
wisdom![2451]
6 "Please hear[8085] my
argument,[8433]
And listen[7181] to the contentions
of my lips.[8193]
7 "Will you [a]speak what is unjust
for God,
And speak[1696] what is deceitful
for Him?
8 "Will you [a]show partiality[5375] for
Him?
Will you contend[7378] for God?
9 "Will it be well[2896] when He
examines you?
Or [a]will you deceive Him as one
deceives a man?[582]
10 "He will surely reprove[3198] you,
If you secretly [a]show partiality.
11 "Will not [a]His [I]majesty terrify[1204]
you,
And the dread[6343] of Him fall on
you?
12 "Your memorable sayings are
proverbs of ashes,
Your defenses are defenses of
clay.

Job Is Sure He Will Be Vindicated

13 "[a]Be silent before me so that I
may speak;
Then let come on me what may.

13 [b]Job 11:6; 26:12; 32:8; 36:5; 38:36
14 [I]Lit., *shuts against* [II]Lit., *it is not opened* [a]Job 19:10; Is. 25:2 [b]Job 37:7
15 [I]Lit., *overturn* [a]Deut. 11:17; 1Kin. 8:35; 17:1 [b]Gen. 7:11-24
16 [a]Job 13:7, 9
17 [I]Or, *stripped* [a]Job 3:14 [b]Job 9:24
18 [I]Or, *discipline* [a]Ps. 116:16
19 [I]Or, *stripped* [a]Job 24:22; 34:24-28; 35:9
20 [a]Job 17:4; 32:9
21 [a]Job 34:19; Ps. 107:40 [b]Job 12:18
22 [a]Dan. 2:22; 1Cor. 4:5
23 [I]Or, *spreads out* [a]Is. 9:3; 26:15
24 [a]Job 12:20
25 [a]Job 5:14 [b]Is. 24:20
1 [a]Job 12:9
2 [a]Job 12:3
3 [I]Heb., *Shaddai* [a]Job 13:22; 23:4 [b]Job 13:15
4 [a]Ps. 119:69 [b]Jer. 23:32
5 [a]Job 13:13; 21:5; Prov. 17:28
7 [a]Job 27:4
8 [a]Lev. 19:15; Prov. 24:23
9 [a]Job 12:16
10 [a]Job 13:8; 32:21; 34:19
11 [I]Lit., *exaltation* [a]Job 31:23
13 [a]Job 13:5

14 "Why should I take[5375] my
flesh[1320] in my teeth,
And [a]put my life[5315] in my
[I]hands?[3709]
15 "[a]Though He slay me,
I will hope[3176] in Him.
Nevertheless I [b]will argue[3198]
my ways[1870] [I]before Him.
16 "This also will be my
[a]salvation,[3444]
For [b]a godless man[2611] may not
come before His presence.
17 "Listen carefully[8085] to my
speech,
And let my declaration *fill* your
ears.[241]
18 "Behold now, I have [a]prepared
my case;[4941]
I know that [b]I will be
vindicated.[6663]
19 "[a]Who will contend[7378] with me?
For then I would be silent and
[b]die.[1478]
20 "Only two things do not do to
me,
Then I will not hide from Thy
face:
21 [a]Remove Thy [I]hand from me,
And let not the dread[367] of Thee
terrify me.
22 "Then call,[7121] and [a]I will answer;
Or let me speak, then reply[7725]
to me.
23 "[a]How many are my iniquities[5771]
and sins?
Make known to me my
[I]rebellion[6588] and my sin.[2403]
24 "Why dost Thou [a]hide Thy face,
And consider[2803] me [b]Thine
enemy?
25 "Wilt Thou cause a [a]driven leaf
to tremble?[6206]
Or wilt Thou pursue the dry[3002]
[b]chaff?
26 "For Thou dost write [a]bitter
things against me,
And dost [b]make me to inherit[3423]
the iniquities of my youth.
27 "Thou [a]dost put[7760] my feet in the
stocks,
And dost watch[8104] all my
paths;[734]
Thou dost [I]set a limit for the
soles of my feet,
28 While [I]I am decaying like a
[a]rotten thing,
Like a garment that is moth-
eaten.

Job Speaks of the Finality of Death

14 "[a]Man,[120] who is born of
woman,[802]
Is [I]short-lived and [b]full of
turmoil.[7267]
2 "[a]Like a flower he comes forth
and withers.
He also flees like [b]a shadow and
does not remain.
3 "Thou also dost [a]open Thine eyes
on him,
And [b]bring [I]him into
judgment[4941] with Thyself.
4 "[a]Who can make the clean[2889] out
of the unclean?[2931]
No one!
5 "Since his days are determined,
The [a]number of his months is
with Thee,
And his limits Thou hast
[I]set so that he cannot pass.
6 "[a]Turn Thy gaze from him that
he may [I]rest,
Until he [II]fulfills[7521] his day[3117]
like a hired man.
7 "For there is hope for a tree,
When it is cut down,[3772] that it
will sprout again,
And its shoots will not
[I]fail.
8 "Though its roots grow old[2204] in
the ground,[776]
And its stump dies[4191] in the dry
soil,[6083]
9 At the scent of water it will
flourish
And put forth[6213] sprigs like a
plant.
10 "But [a]man[1397] dies[4191] and lies
prostrate.
Man [b]expires,[1478] and where is
he?
11 "*As* [a]water [I]evaporates from the
sea,

14 [I]Lit., *palm* [a]Ps. 119:109
15 [I]Lit., *to His face* [a]Job 7:6 [b]Job 27:5
16 [a]Job 23:7; Is. 12:1, 2 [b]Job 34:21-23
18 [a]Job 23:4 [b]Job 9:21; 10:7; 12:4
19 [a]Is. 50:8 [b]Job 7:21; 10:8
21 [I]Lit., *palm* [a]Job 9:34; Ps. 39:10
22 [a]Job 9:16; 14:15
23 [I]Or, *transgression* [a]Job 7:21
24 [a]Ps. 13:1; 44:24; 88:14; Is. 8:17 [b]Job 19:11; 33:10; Lam. 2:5
25 [a]Lev. 26:36 [b]Job 21:18
26 [a]Job 9:18 [b]Ps. 25:7
27 [I]Lit., *carve for* [a]Job 33:11
28 [I]Lit., *he is* [a]Job 2:7

1 [I]Lit., *short of days* [a]Job 5:7 [b]Eccl. 2:23
2 [a]Ps. 90:5, 6; 103:15; Is. 40:6, 7; James 1:10; 1Pet. 1:24 [b]Job 8:9
3 [I]So with some ancient versions; M.T., *me* [a]Ps. 8:4; 144:3 [b]Ps. 143:2
4 [a]Job 15:14; 25:4; Ps. 51:5
5 [I]Lit., *made* [a]Job 21:21
6 [I]Lit., *cease* [II]Lit., *makes acceptable* [a]Job 7:19; Ps. 39:13
7 [I]Or, *cease*
10 [a]Job 3:13; 14:10-15 [b]Job 13:9
11 [I]Lit., *disappears* [a]Is. 19:5

And a river becomes parched[2717]
and dried up,[3001]
12 So [a]man[376] lies down and does
not rise.
Until the heavens[8064] be no
more,
[I]He will not awake nor be
aroused out of [II]his sleep.
13 "Oh that Thou wouldst hide me
in [I]Sheol,[7585]
That Thou wouldst conceal me
[a]until Thy wrath[639] returns *to*
Thee,
That Thou wouldst set a limit
for me and remember[2142] me!
14 "If a man dies, will he live[2421]
again?
All the days of my struggle[6635]
I will wait,[3176]
Until my change comes.
15 "Thou wilt call,[7121] and I will
answer Thee;
Thou wilt long for [a]the work of
Thy hands.[3027]
16 "For now Thou dost [a]number my
steps,
Thou dost not [b]observe my
sin.[2403]
17 "My transgression[6588] is
[a]sealed up in a bag,
And Thou dost [I]wrap up my
iniquity.[5771]
18 "But the falling mountain
[I]crumbles away,[5034]
And the rock moves from its
place;
19 Water wears[7833] away stones,
Its torrents wash away[7857] the
dust[6083] of the earth;
So Thou dost [a]destroy[6] man's[582]
hope.
20 "Thou dost forever[5331]
overpower him and he
[a]departs;
Thou dost change his
appearance and send him
away.
21 "His sons[1121] achieve honor,[3513]
but [a]he does not know *it;*
Or they become insignificant,
but he does not perceive[995]
it.
22 "But his [I]body[1320] pains him,
And he mourns only for
himself."[5315]

Eliphaz Says Job Presumes Much

15 Then Eliphaz the Temanite
[I]responded,[559]
2 "Should a wise[2450] man answer
with windy[7307]
knowledge,[1847]
[a]And fill [I]himself[990] with the east
wind?[7307]
3 "Should he argue[3198] with useless
talk,
Or with words[4405] which are not
profitable?
4 "Indeed, you do away[6565] with
[I]reverence,[3374]
And hinder meditation[7881] before
God.[410]
5 "For [a]your guilt[5771] teaches[502]
your mouth,[6310]
And you choose[977] the language
of [b]the crafty.[6175]
6 "Your [a]own mouth condemns[7561]
you, and not I;
And your own lips[8193] testify
against you.
7 "Were you the first[7223] man[120] to
be born,
Or [a]were you brought forth[2342]
before the hills?
8 "Do you hear[8085] the [a]secret[5475]
counsel of God,
And limit wisdom[2451] to
yourself?
9 "[a]What do you know[3045] that we
do not know?
What do you understand[995] that
[I]we do not?
10 "Both the [a]gray-haired[7867] and
the aged[3453] are among
us,
Older than your father.[1]
11 "Are [a]the consolations[8575] of God
too small for you,
Even the [b]word[1697] *spoken*
gently with you?
12 "Why does your [a]heart[3820] carry
you away?

12 [I]Lit., *They* [II]Lit., *their* [a]Job 3:13
13 [I]I.e., the nether world [a]Is. 26:20
15 [a]Job 10:3
16 [a]Job 31:4; 34:21; Ps. 139:1-3; Prov. 5:21 [b]Job 10:6
17 [I]Lit., *plaster; or, glue together* [a]Deut. 32:32-34
18 [I]Lit., *withers*
19 [a]Job 7:6
20 [a]Job 4:20; 20:7
21 [a]Eccl. 9:5
22 [I]Lit., *flesh*
1 [I]Lit., *answered and said*
2 [I]Lit., *his belly* [a]Job 6:26
4 [I]Lit., *fear*
5 [a]Job 22:5 [b]Job 5:12, 13
6 [a]Job 18:7
7 [a]Job 38:4, 21; Prov. 8:25
8 [a]Job 29:4; Rom. 11:34; 1Cor. 2:11
9 [I]Lit., *is not within us?* [a]Job 12:3; 13:2
10 [a]Job 12:12; 32:6, 7
11 [a]Job 5:17-19; 36:15, 16 [b]Job 6:10; 23:12
12 [a]Job 11:13; 36:13

And why do your eyes flash,7335
13 That you should turn[7725] your
spirit[7307] against God,
And allow *such* words to go out
of your mouth?
14 "What is man,[582] that [a]he should
be pure,[2135]
Or [b]he who is born of a
woman,[802] that he should be
righteous?[6663]
15 "Behold, He puts no trust[539] in
His [a]holy ones,[6918]
And the [b]heavens[8064] are not
pure[2141] in His sight;
16 How much less one who is
[a]detestable[8581] and
corrupt,
Man,[376] who [b]drinks iniquity[5766]
like water!

What Eliphaz Has Seen of Life

17 "I will tell you, listen[8085] to me;
And what I have seen[2372] I will
also declare;[5608]
18 What wise men have told,[5046]
And have not concealed from
[a]their fathers,[1]
19 To whom alone the land[776] was
given,
And no alien[2114] passed[5674]
among them.
20 "The wicked[7563] man writhes[2342]
[a]in pain all *his* days,
And [I]numbered are the years
[b]stored up for the ruthless.
21 "[I]Sounds of [a]terror[6343] are in his
ears,[241]
[b]While at peace[7965] the
destroyer[7703] comes upon
him.
22 "He does not believe[539] that he
will [a]return[7725] from
darkness,[2822]
And he is destined for
[b]the sword.[2719]
23 "He wanders about for food,
saying, 'Where is it?'
He knows that a day[3117] of
[a]darkness is [I]at hand.[3027]

14 [a]Job 14:4; Prov. 20:9; Eccl. 7:20 [b]Job 25:4
15 [a]Job 5:1 [b]Job 25:5
16 [a]Ps. 14:1 [b]Job 34:7; Prov. 19:28
18 [a]Job 8:8; 20:4
20 [I]Lit., *the number of years are* [a]Job 15:24 [b]Job 24:1; 27:13
21 [I]Lit., *A sound of terrors is* [a]Job 15:24; 18:11; 20:25; 24:17; 27:20 [b]Job 20:21; 1Thess. 5:3
22 [a]Job 15:30 [b]Job 19:29; 27:14; 33:18; 36:12
23 [I]Lit., *ready at his hand* [a]Job 15:22, 30
25 [I]Heb., *Shaddai* [a]Job 36:9
26 [I]Lit., *with a stiff neck* [II]Lit., *the thick-bossed shields*
27 [a]Ps. 73:7; 119:70
28 [I]Or, *heaps* [a]Job 3:14; Is. 5:8,9
29 [a]Job 27:16, 17
30 [I]Lit., *turn aside* [a]Job 5:14; 15:22 [b]Job 15:34; 20:26; 22:20; 31:12 [c]Job 4:9
31 [I]Lit., *exchange* [a]Job 35:13; Is. 59:4
32 [a]Job 22:16; Eccl. 7:17 [b]Job 18:16
33 [a]Job 14:2
34 [I]Lit., *a bribe* [a]Job 8:13 [b]Job 8:22
35 [I]Or, *pain* [II]Lit., *belly* [a]Ps. 7:14; Is. 59:4

24 "Distress and anguish4691
terrify[1204] him,
They overpower him like a
king[4428] ready for the attack,
25 Because he has stretched out
his hand against God,
And conducts himself
[a]arrogantly against [I]the
Almighty.[7706]
26 "He rushes [I]headlong at Him
With [II]his massive shield.4043
27 "For he has [a]covered[3680] his face
with his fat,
And made[6213] his thighs
heavy6371 with flesh.
28 "And he has [a]lived[7931] in desolate
cities,
In houses[1004] no one would
inhabit,
Which are destined to become
[I]ruins.
29 "He [a]will not become rich, nor
will his wealth[2428] endure;
And his grain will not bend down
to the ground.
30 "He will [a]not [I]escape[5493] from
darkness;
The [b]flame will wither[3001] his
shoots,
And by [c]the breath[7307] of His
mouth he will go away.
31 "Let him not [a]trust in
emptiness,[7723] deceiving[8582]
himself;
For emptiness will be his
[I]reward.[8545]
32 "It will be accomplished4390
[a]before his time,[3117]
And his palm [b]branch will not
be green.
33 "He will drop off[2554] his unripe
grape like the vine,
And will [a]cast off his flower like
the olive tree.
34 "For the company[5712] of
[a]the godless[2611] is barren,
And fire consumes [b]the tents[168]
of [I]the corrupt.
35 "They [a]conceive [I]mischief[5999] and
bring forth iniquity,[205]
And their [II]mind prepares
deception."[4820]

Job Says Friends Are Sorry Comforters

16 Then Job [I]answered,[559]
2 "I have heard[8085] many
such things;
[Ia]Sorry[5999] comforters[5162] are
you all.
3 "Is there *no* limit to [a]windy[7307]
words?[1697]
Or what plagues you that you
answer?
4 "I too could speak[1696] like you,
If [I]I were in your place.
I could compose words[4405]
against you,
And [a]shake my head[7218] at you.
5 "I could strengthen you with my
mouth,[6310]
And the solace of my lips[8193]
could lessen[2820] *your pain.*

Job Says God Shattered Him

6 "If I speak, [a]my pain is not
lessened,[2820]
And if I hold back, what has left
me?
7 "But now He has [a]exhausted me;
Thou hast laid [b]waste[8074] all my
company.[5712]
8 "And Thou hast shriveled me up,
[a]It has become a witness;
And my [b]leanness rises up
against me,
It testifies to my face.
9 "His anger[639] has [a]torn me and
[I]hunted[7852] me down,
He has [b]gnashed[2786] at me with
His teeth;
My [c]adversary [II]glares at me.
10 "They have [a]gaped at me with
their mouth,
They have [Ib]slapped[5221] me
on the cheek with
contempt;[2781]
They have [c]massed themselves
against me.
11 "God[410] hands me over to
ruffians,[5760]
And tosses me into the hands[3027]
of the wicked.[7563]
12 "I was at ease, but [a]He
shattered[6565] me,
And He has grasped me by the
neck and shaken me to
pieces;
He has also set me up as His
[b]target.
13 "His [a]arrows surround me.
Without mercy He splits my
kidneys[3629] open;
He pours[8210] out [b]my gall[4845] on
the ground.[776]
14 "He [a]breaks through me with
breach after breach;
He [b]runs at me like a warrior.
15 "I have sewed [a]sackcloth over my
skin,[1539]
And [b]thrust my horn in the
dust.[6083]
16 "My face is flushed from
[a]weeping,
[b]And deep darkness[6757] is on my
eyelids,
17 Although there is no
[a]violence[2555]
in my hands,[3709]
And [b]my prayer[8605] is pure.[2134]
18 "O earth,[776] do not cover[3680] my
blood,[1818]
And let there be no *resting* place
for my cry.
19 "Even now, behold, [a]my witness
is in heaven,[8064]
And my [I]advocate is [b]on high.
20 "My friends[7453] are my
scoffers;[3887]
[a]My eye [I]weeps to God.[433]
21 "O that a man[1397] might plead[3198]
with God
As a man[120] with his
neighbor![7453]
22 "For when a few years are past,
I shall go the way[734] [a]of no
return.[7725]

Job Says He Has Become a Byword

17 "My spirit[7307] is broken,[2254] my
days are extinguished,
The [Ia]grave[6913] is *ready* for me.
2 "[a]Surely mockers are with me,

1 [I]Lit., *answered and said*
2 [I]Lit., *Comforters of trouble* [a]Job 13:4; 21:34
3 [a]Job 6:26
4 [I]Lit., *your soul were in place of my soul* [a]Ps. 22:7; 109:25; Zeph. 2:15; Matt. 27:39
6 [a]Job 9:27, 28
7 [a]Job 7:3 [b]Job 16:20; 19:13-15
8 [a]Job 10:17 [b]Job 19:20; Ps. 109:24
9 [I]Lit., *borne a grudge against me* [II]Lit., *sharpens his eyes* [a]Job 19:11; Hos. 6:1 [b]Ps. 35:16; Lam. 2:16; Acts 7:54 [c]Job 13:24; 33:10
10 [I]Lit., *struck* [a]Ps. 22:13 [b]Is. 50:6; Lam. 3:30; Acts 23:2 [c]Job 30:12; Ps. 35:15
12 [a]Job 9:17 [b]Job 7:20; Lam. 3:12
13 [a]Job 6:4; 19:12; 25:3 [b]Job 20:25
14 [a]Job 9:17 [b]Joel 2:7
15 [a]Gen. 37:34; Ps. 69:11 [b]Ps. 7:5
16 [a]Job 16:20 [b]Job 24:17
17 [a]Is. 59:6; Jon. 3:8 [b]Job 27:4
19 [I]Or, *witness* [a]Gen. 31:50; Job 19:25-27; Rom. 1:9; Phil. 1:8; 1Thess. 2:5 [b]Job 31:2
20 [I]Or, *drips* [a]Job 17:7
22 [a]Job 3:13
1 [I]Lit., *graves* [a]Ps. 88:3, 4
2 [a]Job 12:4; 17:6

And my eye [I]gazes on their
provocation.[4784]
3 "Lay down,[7760] now, a pledge[6148]
[a]for me with Thyself;
Who is there that will [I]be my
guarantor?[8628]
4 "For Thou hast [Ia]kept their
heart[3820] from
understanding;[7922]
Therefore Thou wilt not exalt
them.
5 "He who [a]informs[5046] against
friends[7453] for a share *of the
spoil,*
The [b]eyes of his children[1121] also
shall languish.[3615]
6 "But He has made me a
[a]byword of the people,[5971]
And I am [I]one at whom men
[b]spit.[8611]
7 "My eye has also grown
[a]dim because of grief,[3708]
And all my [b]members are as a
shadow.
8 "The upright[3477] shall be
appalled[8074] at this,
And the [a]innocent[5355] shall stir
up himself against the
godless.[2611]
9 "Nevertheless [a]the righteous[6662]
shall hold to his way,[1870]
And [b]he who has clean[2891] hands
shall grow stronger and
stronger.
10 "But come again[7725] all of
[I]you now,
For I [a]do not find a wise[2450] man
among you.
11 "My [a]days are past,[5674] my
plans[2154] are torn apart,
Even the wishes of my heart.[3824]
12 "They make night[3915] into day,[3117]
saying,
'The light[216] is near,' in the
presence of darkness.[2822]
13 "If I look[6960] for [a]Sheol[7585] as my
home,[1004]
I [I]make my bed in the darkness;
14 If I call to the [a]pit,[7845] 'You are
my father';[1]
To the [b]worm, 'my mother[517]
and my sister';[269]
15 Where now is [a]my hope?
And who regards my hope?
16 "[I]Will it go down with me to
Sheol?[7585]
Shall we together [a]go down into
the dust?"[6083]

Bildad Speaks of the Wicked

18 Then Bildad the Shuhite [I]responded,[559]
2 "How long will you hunt[7760] for
words?[4405]
Show understanding and then
we can talk.[1696]
3 "Why are we [a]regarded[2803] as
beasts,
As stupid[2933] in your eyes?
4 "O [I]you who tear yourself in your
anger—[639]
For your sake is the earth[776] to
be abandoned,[5800]
Or the rock to be moved from
its place?
5 "Indeed, the [a]light[216] of the
wicked[7563] goes out,
And the [I]flame of his fire gives
no light.
6 "The light in his tent[168] is
[a]darkened,[2821]
And his lamp[5216] goes out above
him.
7 "His [I]vigorous stride is
shortened,[3334]
And his [a]own scheme[6098] brings
him down.
8 "For he is [a]thrown into the net
by his own feet,
And he steps on the webbing.
9 "A snare[6341] seizes *him* by the
heel,[6119]
And a trap snaps[2388] shut on him.
10 "A noose for him is hidden in the
ground,[776]
And a trap[4434] for him on the
path.
11 "All around [a]terrors frighten[1204]
him,
And [b]harry him at every step.
12 "His strength is [a]famished,[7457]
And calamity[343] is ready[3559] at
his side.

2 [I]Lit., *lodges*
3 [I]Lit., *strike hands with me* [a]Ps. 119:122; Is. 38:14
4 [I]Lit., *hidden* [a]Job 12:20
5 [a]Lev. 19:13, 16 [b]Job 11:20
6 [I]Lit., *a spitting to the faces* [a]Job 17:2 [b]Job 30:10
7 [a]Job 16:16 [b]Job 16:8
8 [a]Job 22:19
9 [a]Prov. 4:18 [b]Job 22:30; 31:7
10 [I]With some ancient mss. and versions; M.T., *them* [a]Job 12:2
11 [a]Job 7:6
13 [I]Lit., *spread out* [a]Job 3:13
14 [a]Job 7:5; 13:28; 30:30 [b]Job 21:26; 25:6
15 [a]Job 7:6
16 [I]So the Gr.; Heb. possibly, *Let my limbs sink down to Sheol, since there is rest in the dust for all.* [a]Job 3:17; 21:33

1 [I]Lit., *answered and said*
3 [a]Ps. 73:22
4 [I]Lit., *he-. . .tears himself. . .his*
5 [I]Lit., *spark* [a]Job 21:17; Prov. 13:9; 20:20; 24:20
6 [a]Job 12:25
7 [I]Lit., *steps of his strength* [a]Job 15:6
8 [a]Job 22:10; Ps. 9:15; 35:8; Is. 24:17, 18
11 [a]Job 15:21 [b]Job 18:18; 20:8
12 [a]Is. 8:21

13 "[I]His skin[5785] is devoured by
disease,
The first-born of death[4194]
[a]devours his [II]limbs.
14 "He is [a]torn from [I]the security
of his tent,
And [II]they march him before the
king[4428] of [b]terrors.
15 "[I]There dwells[7931] in his tent
nothing of his;
[a]Brimstone[1614] is scattered on
his habitation.
16 "His [a]roots are dried[3001] below,
And his [b]branch is cut off above.
17 "[a]Memory[2143] of him perishes[6]
from the earth,
And he has no name abroad.
18 "[I]He is driven from light
[a]into darkness,[2822]
And [b]chased from the inhabited
world.[8398]
19 "He has no [a]offspring or posterity
among his people,[5971]
Nor any survivor[8300] where he
sojourned.[4033]
20 "Those [I]in the west are
appalled[8074] at [a]his [II]fate,[3117]
And those [III]in the east are
seized with horror.[8178]
21 "Surely such are the
[a]dwellings[4908]
of the wicked,[5767]
And this is the place of him who
does not know God."[410]

Job Feels Insulted

19 Then Job [I]responded,[559]
2 "How long will you
torment[3013] [I]me,[5315]
And crush[1792] me with
words?[4405]
3 "These ten times you have
insulted me,
You are not ashamed[954] to wrong
me.
4 "Even if I have truly[551] erred,[7683]
My error[4879] lodges with me.
5 "If indeed you [a]vaunt[3198]
yourselves against me,
And prove my disgrace[2781] to
me,
6 Know[3045] then that [a]God[433] has
wronged[5791] me,
And has closed[5362] [b]His net[4685]
around me.

Everything Is against Him

7 "Behold, [a]I cry, 'Violence!'[2555] but
I get no answer;
I shout for help, but there is no
justice.[4941]
8 "He has [a]walled up my way[734] so
that I cannot pass;
And He has put[7760] [b]darkness[2822]
on my paths.
9 "He has [a]stripped my honor[3519]
from me,
And removed the [b]crown from
my head.[7218]
10 "He [a]breaks me down on every
side, and I am gone;
And He has uprooted my
[b]hope [c]like a tree.
11 "He has also [a]kindled[2374] His
anger[639] against me,
And [b]considered[2803] me as His
enemy.
12 "His [a]troops[1416] come together,
And [b]build up their [I]way[1870]
against me,
And camp around my tent.[168]
13 "He has [a]removed my brothers[251]
far from me,
And my [b]acquaintances[3045] are
completely estranged[2114]
from me.
14 "My relatives have failed,
And my [a]intimate[3045] friends
have forgotten me.
15 "Those who live[1481] in my
house[1004] and my maids
consider me a stranger.[2114]
I am a foreigner[5237] in their sight.
16 "I call[7121] to my servant,[5650] but
he does not answer,
I have to implore[2603] him with
my mouth.[6310]
17 "My breath[7307] is [I]offensive[2114] to
my wife,[802]
And I am loathsome to my own
brothers.[990]
18 "Even young children[1121]
despise[3988] me;

13 [I]Heb., *It eats parts of his skin* [II]Or, *parts* [a]Zech. 14:12
14 [I]Lit., *his tent his trust* [II]Or, *you or she shall march* [a]Job 8:22; 18:6 [b]Job 15:21
15 [I]A suggested reading is *Fire dwells in his tent* [a]Ps. 11:6
16 [a]Is. 5:24; Hos. 9:16; Amos 2:9; Mal. 4:1 [b]Job 15:30, 32
17 [a]Job 24:20; Ps. 34:16; Prov. 10:7
18 [I]Lit., *They drive him . . . And chase him* [a]Job 5:14; Is. 8:22; 15:30 [b]Job 20:8; 27:21-23
19 [a]Job 27:14, 15; Is. 14:22
20 [I]Lit., *who come after* [II]Lit., *day* [III]Lit., *who have gone before* [a]Ps. 37:13; Jer. 50:27; Obad. 12
21 [a]Job 21:28

1 [I]Lit., *answered and said*
2 [I]Lit., *my soul*
5 [a]Ps. 35:26; 38:16; 55:12, 13
6 [a]Job 16:11; 27:2 [b]Job 18:8-10; Ps. 66:11; Lam. 1:13
7 [a]Job 9:24; 30:20, 24; Hab. 1:2
8 [a]Job 3:23; Lam. 3:7, 9 [b]Job 30:26
9 [a]Job 12:17, 19; Ps. 89:44 [b]Job 16:15; Ps. 89:39; Lam. 5:16
10 [a]Job 12:14 [b]Job 7:6 [c]Job 24:20
11 [a]Job 16:9 [b]Job 13:24; 33:10
12 [I]I.e., siege-work [a]Job 16:13 [b]Job 30:12
13 [a]Job 16:7; Ps. 69:8 [b]Job 16:20; Ps. 88:8, 18
14 [a]Job 19:19
17 [I]Lit., *strange*

I rise up and they speak[1696]
against me.
19 "All [I]my [a]associates abhor[8581] me,
And those I love[157] have
turned[2015] against me.
20 "My [a]bone[6106] clings to my
skin[5785] and my flesh,[1320]
And I have escaped[4422] *only* by
the skin of my teeth.
21 "Pity[3603] me, pity me, O you my
friends,[7453]
For the [a]hand[3027] of God has
struck[5060] me.
22 "Why do you [a]persecute me as
God[410] *does,*
And are not satisfied with my
flesh?

Job Says, "My Redeemer Lives"

23 "Oh that my words were written!
Oh that they were [a]inscribed[2710]
in a book![5612]
24 "That with an iron stylus and lead
They were engraved in the rock
forever![5703]
🗝 25 "And as for me, I know that
[a]my [I]Redeemer[1350] lives,[2416]
And [II]at the last He will take His
stand on the [III]earth.[6083]
26 "Even after my skin [I]is
destroyed,[5362]
Yet from my flesh I shall
[a]see[2372] God;
27 Whom I [I]myself shall behold,[7200]
And whom my eyes shall see
and not another.[2114]
My [II]heart[3629] [a]faints[3615]
[III]within me.
28 "If you say,[559] 'How shall we
[a]persecute him?'
And '[I]What pretext[1697] for a case
against him can we find?'

19 [I]Lit., *the men of my council* [a]Ps. 38:11; 55:12, 13
20 [a]Job 16:8; 33:21; Ps. 102:5; Lam. 4:8
21 [a]Job 1:11; Ps. 38:2
22 [a]Job 13:24, 25; 16:11; 19:6; Ps. 69:26
23 [a]Is. 30:8; Jer. 36:2
25 [I]Or, *Vindicator, defender;* lit., *kinsman* [II]Or, *as the Last* [III]Lit., *dust* [a]Job 16:19; Ps. 78:35; Prov. 23:11; Is. 43:14; Jer. 50:34
26 [I]Lit., *which they have cut off* [a]Ps. 17:15; Matt. 5:8; 1Cor. 13:12; 1John 3:2
27 [I]Or, *on my side* [II]Lit., *kidneys* [III]Lit., *in my loins* [a]Ps. 73:26
28 [I]Or, *the root of the matter is found in him* [a]Job 19:22
29 [a]Job 15:22 [b]Job 22:4; Ps. 1:5; 9:7; Eccl. 12:14

1 [I]Lit., *answered and said*
2 [I]Lit., *return* [II]Lit., *haste within me*
3 [a]Job 19:3
4 [a]Job 8:8
5 [a]Job 8:12, 13; Ps. 37:35, 36 [b]Job 8:13
6 [I]Lit., *goes up to* [a]Is. 14:13, 14; Obad. 3, 4
7 [a]Job 4:20; 14:20 [b]Job 7:10; 8:18
8 [a]Ps. 73:20; 90:5 [b]Job 18:18; 27:21-23

29 "*Then* be afraid[1481] of [a]the
sword[2719] for yourselves,
For wrath[2534] *brings* the
punishment[5771] of the sword,
So that you may know
[b]there is judgment."[1779]

Zophar Says, "The Triumph of the Wicked Is Short"

20 Then Zophar the Naamathite
[I]answered,[559]
2 "Therefore my disquieting
thoughts make me
[I]respond,[7725]
Even because of my [II]inward
agitation.
3 "I listened[8085] to [a]the reproof[4148]
which insults me,
And the spirit[7307] of my
understanding[998] makes me
answer.
4 "Do you know[3045] this from
[a]of old,
From the establishment[7760] of
man[120] on earth,[776]
5 That the [a]triumphing of the
wicked[7563] is short,
And [b]the joy of the godless[2611]
momentary?
6 "Though his loftiness
[I][a]reaches[5927]
the heavens,[8064]
And his head[7218] touches[5060] the
clouds,
7 He [a]perishes[6] forever[5331] like
his refuse;
Those who have seen[7200] him
[b]will say,[559] 'Where is he?'
8 "He flies away like a [a]dream, and
they cannot find him;
Even like a vision[2384] of the
night[3915] he is [b]chased away.

🗝 **19:25** "I know that may Redeemer lives" are familar words to the Christian because of their adaptation to Christ in several well-known hymns. However, the sense here is different from that which is usually understood when applied to Christ. The Christian idea of "Redeemer" is of one who is deliverer from sin. The Hebrew word *go'el* (1350) should more appropriately be translated "Vindicator," i.e., one who delivers from affliction and wrong which is not due to sin (see entry in Lexical Aids). Job, unable to convince his friends of his innocence, was leaving it in God's hands to prove to them that he was not guilty of the sin of which they accused him. This is the high point in Job's stated trust in God and dependence upon Him.

9 "The [a]eye which saw him sees
him no more,
And [b]his place no longer beholds
him.
10 "His [a]sons[1121] [I]favor[7521] the poor,
And his hands[3027] [b]give back[7725]
his wealth.
11 "His [a]bones[6106] are full of his
youthful vigor,
But it lies down with him
[I]in the dust.[6083]
12 "Though [a]evil[7451] is sweet in his
mouth,[6310]
And he hides it under his tongue,
13 *Though* he [I]desires it and will
not let it go,[5800]
But holds it [a]in his [II]mouth,
14 *Yet* his food in his stomach[4578]
is changed[2015]
To the [I]venom[4846] of cobras[6620]
within[7130] him.
15 "He swallows[1104] riches,[2428]
But will [a]vomit them up;
God[410] will expel[3423] them from
his belly.[990]
16 "He sucks [a]the poison of cobras;
The viper's tongue slays[2026]
him.
17 "He does not look at [a]the
streams,[6390]
The rivers flowing with honey
and curds.
18 "He [a]returns what he has attained
And cannot swallow[1104] *it;*
As to the riches[2428] of his
trading,[8545]
He cannot even enjoy *them.*
19 "For he has [a]oppressed *and*
forsaken[5800]
the poor;
He has seized a house[1004] which
he has not built.
20 "Because he knew no quiet
[I]within him
He does [a]not retain[4422] anything
he desires.
21 "Nothing remains[8300] [I]for him to
devour,
Therefore [a]his prosperity[2898]
does not endure.
22 "In the fulness of his plenty he
will be cramped;
The [a]hand[3027] of everyone who
suffers will come *against*
him.
23 "When he [a]fills his belly,
God will send His fierce anger[639]
on him
And will [b]rain *it* on him
[I]while he is eating.[3894]
24 "He may [a]flee from the iron
weapon,[5402]
But the bronze bow will pierce
him.
25 "It is drawn forth and comes out
of his back,
Even the glittering point from
[a]his gall.
[b]Terrors[367] come upon him,
26 Complete [a]darkness[2822] is held
in reserve for his treasures,
And unfanned [b]fire will devour
him;
It will consume[3415] the survivor
in his tent.[168]
27 "The [a]heavens[8064] will reveal[1540]
his iniquity,[5771]
And the earth will rise up against
him.
28 "The [a]increase of his house will
depart;[1540]
His possessions will flow away
[b]in the day[3117] of His anger.
29 "This is the wicked man's
[a]portion from God,[430]
Even the heritage[5159] decreed[561]
to him by God."[410]

Job Says God Will Deal with the Wicked

21 Then Job [I]answered,[559]
2 "Listen carefully[8085] to my
speech,
And let this be your *way of*
consolation.[8575]
3 "Bear[5375] with me that I may
speak;[1696]
Then after I have spoken,[1696]
you may [a]mock.
4 "As for me, is [a]my complaint[7878]
[I]to man?[120]
And [b]why should [II]I not be
impatient?

9 [a]Job 7:8; 8:18 [b]Job 7:10
10 [I]Or, *seek the favor of* [a]Job 5:4; 27:14 [b]Job 20:18; 27:16, 17
11 [I]Lit., *on* [a]Job 21:23, 24
12 [a]Job 15:16
13 [I]Lit., *has compassion on* [II]Lit., *palate* [a]Num. 11:18-20, 33; Job 20:23
14 [I]Lit., *gall*
15 [a]Job 20:10, 20, 21
16 [a]Deut. 32:24, 33
17 [a]Deut. 32:13, 14; Job 29:6
18 [a]Job 20:10, 15
19 [a]Job 24:2-4; 35:9
20 [I]Lit., *in his belly* [a]Eccl. 5:13-15
21 [I]Or, *of what he devours* [a]Job 15:29
22 [a]Job 5:5
23 [I]Or, *as his food* [a]Job 20:13, 14 [b]Num. 11:18-20, 33; Ps. 78:30, 31
24 [a]Is. 24:18; Amos 5:19
25 [a]Job 16:13 [b]Job 18:11, 14
26 [a]Job 18:18 [b]Job 15:30; Ps. 21:9
27 [a]Deut. 31:28; Is. 26:21
28 [a]Deut. 28:31 [b]Job 20:15; 21:30
29 [a]Job 27:13; 31:2, 3
1 [I]Lit., *answered and said*
3 [a]Job 11:3; 17:2
4 [I]Or, *against* [II]Lit., *my spirit* [a]Job 7:11 [b]Job 6:11

5 "Look at me, and be astonished,[8074]
And [a]put[7760] *your* hand[3027] over *your* mouth.[6310]
6 "Even when I remember,[2142] I am disturbed,[926]
And [a]horror[6427] takes hold of my flesh.[1320]
7 "Why [a]do the wicked[7563] *still* live,[2421]
Continue on, also become very [b]powerful?[2428]
8 "Their [I][a]descendants[2233] are established[3559] with them in their sight,
And their offspring before their eyes,
9 Their houses[1004] [a]are safe[7965] from fear,[6343]
Neither is the rod of God[433] on them.
10 "His ox mates[5674] [I]without fail;
His cow calves and does not abort.
11 "They send forth their little ones like the flock,
And their children skip about.
12 "They [I]sing to the timbrel[8596] and harp
And rejoice at the sound of the flute.
13 "They [a]spend[3615] their days in prosperity,
And [I]suddenly they go down[2865] to [II]Sheol.[7585]
14 "And they say[559] to God,[410] '[a]Depart[5493] from us!
We do not even desire[2654] the knowledge[1847] of Thy ways.[1870]
15 '[I]Who is [II]the Almighty,[7706] that we should serve[5647] Him,
And [a]what would we gain if we entreat Him?'
16 "Behold, their prosperity[2898] is not in their hand;
The [a]counsel[6098] of the wicked is far from me.
17 "How often is [a]the lamp[5216] of the wicked put out,
Or *does* their [b]calamity[343] fall on them?
Does [I]God apportion destruction[2256] in His anger?[639]
18 "Are they as [a]straw before the wind,[7307]
And like [b]chaff which the storm carries away?
19 "*You say,* '[a]God stores away [I]a man's iniquity[205] for his sons.'[1121]
Let [II]God repay[7999] him so that he may know[3045] *it.*
20 "Let his [a]own eyes see his decay,[3589]
And let him [b]drink of the wrath[2534] of [I]the Almighty.
21 "For what does he care[2656] for his household[1004] [I]after him,
When the number of his months is cut off?
22 "Can anyone [a]teach[3925] God knowledge,
In that He [b]judges[8199] those on high?
23 "One [a]dies[4191] in his full[8537] strength,[6106]
Being wholly at ease and [I]satisfied;
24 His [I]sides are filled out with fat,
And the [a]marrow of his bones[6106] is moist,
25 While another dies with a bitter[4751] soul,[5315]
Never even [I]tasting *anything* good.[2896]
26 "Together they [a]lie down in the dust,[6083]
And [b]worms cover[3680] them.
27 "Behold, I know your thoughts,[4284]
And the plans[4209] by which you would wrong me.
28 "For you say, 'Where is the house of [a]the nobleman,[5081]
And where is the [b]tent, the dwelling places of the wicked?'
29 "Have you not asked[7592] wayfaring[1870] men,

5 [a]Judg. 18:19; Job 13:5; 29:9; 40:4
6 [a]Ps. 55:5
7 [a]Job 9:24; Ps. 73:3; Jer. 12:1; Hab. 1:13 [b]Job 12:19
8 [I]Lit., *seed* [a]Ps. 17:14
9 [a]Job 12:6
10 [I]Lit., *and does not fail*
12 [I]Lit., *lifted up the voice*
13 [I]So with most versions; M.T., *are shattered by Sheol.* [II]I.e., the nether world [a]Job 21:23; 36:11
14 [a]Job 22:17
15 [I]Lit., *What* [II]Heb., *Shaddai* [a]Job 22:17; 34:9
16 [a]Job 22:18
17 [I]Lit., *He* [a]Job 18:5, 6 [b]Job 31:2, 3
18 [a]Job 13:25; Ps. 83:13 [b]Ps. 1:4; 35:5; Is. 17:13; Hos. 13:3
19 [I]Lit., *his* [II]Lit., *Him* [a]Ex. 20:5; Jer. 31:29; Ezek. 18:2
20 [I]Heb., *Shaddai* [a]Num. 14:28-32; Jer. 31:30; Ezek. 18:4 [b]Ps. 60:3; Is. 51:17; Jer. 25:15; Rev. 14:10
21 [I]I.e., after he dies
22 [a]Job 35:11; 36:22; Is. 40:14; Rom. 11:34 [b]Job 4:18; 15:15; Ps. 82:1
23 [I]Or, *quiet* [a]Job 20:11; 21:13
24 [I]So with Syr.; Heb. uncertain. Some render as, *his pails are full of milk* [a]Prov. 3:8
25 [I]Lit., *eating*
26 [a]Job 3:13; 20:11; Eccl. 9:2 [b]Job 24:20; Is. 14:11
28 [a]Job 1:3; 31:37 [b]Job 8:22; 18:21

And do you not recognize[5234]
their [I]witness?[226]
30 "For the [a]wicked[7451] is reserved
for the day[3117] of calamity;[343]
They will be led forth at
[b]the day of fury.[5678]
31 "Who will [I]confront[5046] him with
his actions,
And who will repay[7999] him for
what he has done?[6213]
32 "While he is carried to the
grave,[6913]
Men will keep watch over *his*
tomb.
33 "The [a]clods of the valley will
[I]gently cover him;
Moreover, [b]all men will
[II]follow after him,
While countless ones *go* before
him.
34 "How then will you vainly
[a]comfort[5162] me,
For your answers remain[7604] *full*
of [I]falsehood?"

Eliphaz Accuses and Exhorts Job

22 Then Eliphaz the Temanite
[I]responded,[559]
2 "Can a vigorous [a]man[1397] be of
use to God,[410]
Or a wise[7919] man be useful to
himself?
3 "Is there any pleasure[2656] to
[I]the Almighty[7706] if you are
righteous,[6663]
Or profit if you make your
ways[1870] perfect?[8552]
4 "Is it because of your
[I]reverence[3374]
that He reproves[3198] you,
That He [a]enters into
judgment[4941] against you?
5 "Is not [a]your wickedness[7451]
great,
And your iniquities[5771] without
end?
6 "For you have [a]taken pledges[2254]
of your brothers[251] without
cause,[2600]
And [b]stripped [I]men naked.[6174]
7 "To the weary you have
[a]given no water to drink,
And from the hungry you have
[b]withheld[4513] bread.
8 "But the earth[776] [a]belongs to the
[b]mighty man,[376]
And [c]the honorable man dwells
in it.
9 "You have sent [a]widows away
empty,
And the [I]strength of the
[b]orphans has been
crushed.[1792]
10 "Therefore [a]snares[6341] surround
you,
And sudden [b]dread[6343]
terrifies[926] you,
11 Or [a]darkness,[2822] so that you
cannot see,
And an [b]abundance of water
covers[3680] you.
12 "Is not God[433] [a]*in* the height of
heaven?[8064]
Look[7200] also at the [I]distant[7218]
stars, how high they are!
13 "And you say,[559] '[a]What does God
know?[3045]
Can He judge[8199] through the
thick darkness?[6205]
14 '[a]Clouds are a hiding place for
Him, so that He cannot
see;[7200]
And He walks on the [I]vault of
heaven.'
15 "Will you keep[8104] to the
ancient[5769] path[734]
Which [a]wicked[205] men have trod,
16 Who were snatched away
[a]before their time,[6256]
Whose [b]foundations[3247] were
[I]washed away by a river?
17 "They [a]said to God, 'Depart[5493]
from us!'
And 'What can [I]the Almighty do
to them?'
18 "Yet He [a]filled their houses[1004]
with good[2896] *things;*
But [b]the counsel[6098] of the
wicked[7563] is far from me.
19 "The [a]righteous[6662] see and are
glad,
And the innocent[5355] mock them,

29 [I]Lit., *signs*
30 [a]Job 20:29; Prov. 16:4; 2Pet. 2:9 [b]Job 21:17, 20; 40:11
31 [I]Lit., *declare his way to his face*
33 [I]Lit., *be sweet to him* [II]Lit., *draw* [a]Job 3:22; 17:16 [b]Job 3:19; 24:24
34 [I]Or, *faithlessness* [a]Job 16:2

1 [I]Lit., *answered and said*
2 [a]Job 35:7; Luke 17:10
3 [I]Heb., *Shaddai*
4 [I]Or, *fear* [a]Job 14:3; 19:29
5 [a]Job 11:6; 15:5
6 [I]Lit., *clothing of the naked* [a]Ex. 22:26; Deut. 24:6, 17; Job 24:3, 9; Ezek. 18:16 [b]Job 31:19, 20
7 [a]Job 31:16, 17 [b]Job 31:31
8 [a]Job 9:24 [b]Job 12:19 [c]Is. 3:3; 9:15
9 [I]Lit., *arms* [a]Job 24:3, 21; 29:13; 31:16, 18 [b]Job 6:27
10 [a]Job 18:8 [b]Job 15:21
11 [a]Job 5:14 [b]Job 38:34; Ps. 69:2; 124:5; Lam. 3:54
12 [I]Lit., *head, topmost* [a]Job 11:7-9
13 [a]Ps. 10:11; 59:7; 64:5; 94:7; Is. 29:15; Ezek. 8:12
14 [I]Lit., *circle* [a]Job 26:9
15 [a]Job 34:36
16 [I]Lit., *poured out* [a]Job 15:32; 21:13, 18 [b]Job 14:19; Ps. 90:5; Is. 28:2; Matt. 7:26, 27
17 [I]Heb., *Shaddai* [a]Job 21:14, 15
18 [a]Job 12:6 [b]Job 21:16
19 [a]Ps. 52:6; 58:10; 107:42

20 *Saying,* 'Truly our adversaries
are cut off,
And their [I]abundance[3499]
[a]the fire has consumed.'
21 "[Ia]Yield[5532] now and be at
peace[7999] with Him;
Thereby good will come to you.
22 "Please[4994] receive
[Ia]instruction[8451] from His
mouth,[6310]
And establish[7760] His words[561]
in your heart.[3824]
23 "If you [a]return[7725] to [I]the
Almighty, you will be
[II]restored;
If you [b]remove
unrighteousness[5766] far from
your tent,[168]
24 And [a]place *your* [I]gold in the
dust,[6083]
And *the gold of* Ophir among the
stones of the brooks,
25 Then [I]the Almighty will be your
[II]gold
And choice silver to you.
26 "For then you will [a]delight in
[I]the Almighty,
And lift up[5375] your face to God.
27 "You will [a]pray[6279] to Him, and
[b]He will hear[8085] you;
And you will pay your vows.[5088]
28 "You will also decree a thing,[562]
and it will be established for
you;
And [a]light[216] will shine on your
ways.
29 "When [I]you are cast down, you
will speak[559] with [II]confidence
And the [IIIa]humble person He will
save.[3467]
30 "He will deliver[4422] one who is
not innocent,
And he will be [a]delivered through
the cleanness of your
hands."[3709]

Job Says He Longs for God

23 Then Job [I]replied,[559]
2 "Even today[3117] my
[a]complaint[7878] is
rebellion;[4805]
[I]His hand[3027] is [b]heavy[3513]
despite my groaning.
3 "Oh that I knew[3045] where I might
find Him,
That I might come to His seat!
4 "I would [a]present *my* case[4941]
before Him
And fill my mouth[6310] with
arguments.[8433]
5 "I would learn[3045] the words[4405]
which He would [I]answer,
And perceive[995] what He would
say[559] to me.
6 "Would He contend[7379] with me
by [a]the greatness of *His*
power?
No, surely He would pay
attention to me.
7 "There the upright[3477] would
[a]reason[3198] with Him;
And I [I]would be [b]delivered
forever[5331] from my
Judge.[8199]
8 "Behold, I go forward[6924] but He
is not *there,*
And backward, but I [a]cannot
perceive[995] Him;
9 When He acts[6213] on the left,
I cannot behold[2372] *Him;*
He turns on the right, I cannot
see Him.
10 "But He knows the [I]way[1870] I
take;
When He has [a]tried[974] me, I shall
come forth as gold.
11 "My foot has [a]held fast to His
path;
I have kept[8104] His way and not
turned aside.
12 "I have not departed from the
command[4687] of His lips;[8193]
I have treasured the [a]words[561]
of His mouth [I]more than my
[II]necessary food.
13 "But He is unique and who can
turn[7725] Him?
And *what* His soul[5315] desires,[183]
that He does.[6213]
14 "For He performs[7999] what is
appointed[2706] for me,
And many such *decrees* are with
Him.

---

20 [I]Or, *excess* [a]Job 15:30
21 [I]Or, *Know intimately* [a]Ps. 34:10
22 [I]Or, *law* [a]Job 6:10; 23:12; Prov. 2:6
23 [I]Heb., *Shaddai* [II]Lit., *built up* [a]Job 8:5; 11:13; Is. 19:22; 31:6; Zech. 1:3 [b]Job 11:14
24 [I]Lit., *ore* [a]Job 31:24, 25
25 [I]Heb., *Shaddai* [II]Lit., *ore*
26 [I]Heb., *Shaddai* [a]Job 27:10; Ps. 37:4; Is. 58:14
27 [a]Job 11:13; 33:26; Is. 58:9 [b]Job 34:28
28 [a]Job 11:17; Ps. 112:4
29 [I]Lit., *they cast you down* [II]Lit., *pride* [III]Lit., *lowly of eyes* [a]Job 5:11; 36:7; Matt. 23:12; James 4:6; 1Pet. 5:5
30 [a]Job 42:7, 8; Ps. 18:20; 24:3, 4

1 [I]Lit., *answered and said*
2 [I]So with Gr. and Syr.; M.T., *My* [a]Job 7:11 [b]Job 6:2, 3; Ps. 32:4
4 [a]Job 13:18
5 [I]Lit., *answer me*
6 [a]Job 9:4
7 [I]Or, *bring forth my justice forever* [a]Job 13:3 [b]Job 13:16; 23:10
8 [a]Job 9:11; 35:14
10 [I]Lit., *way with me* [a]Job 7:18; Ps. 7:9; 11:5; 66:10; Zech. 13:9; 1Pet. 1:7
11 [a]Job 31:7; Ps. 17:5; 44:18
12 [I]Or, with some versions, *in my breast* [II]Lit., *prescribed portion* [a]Job 6:10; 22:22

15 "Therefore, I would be dismayed[926] at His presence;
When I consider,[995] I am terrified[6342] of Him.
16 "*It is* God[410] *who* has made my [a]heart[3820] faint,
And the Almighty[7706] *who* has dismayed[926] me,
17 But I [a]am not silenced by the darkness,[2822]
Nor [b]deep gloom[652] *which* covers[3680] *me.*

Job Says God Seems to Ignore Wrongs

24 "[a]Why are [I]times[6256] not stored up by the Almighty,[7706]
And why do those who know[3045] Him not see[2372] [b]His days?
2 "[I]Some [a]remove the landmarks;
They seize and [II]devour flocks.
3 "They drive away the donkeys of the [a]orphans;
They take the [b]widow's ox for a pledge.[2254]
4 "They push [a]the needy aside from the road;[1870]
The [b]poor of the land[776] are made to hide themselves altogether.
5 "Behold, as [a]wild donkeys in the wilderness
They [b]go forth seeking[7836] food in their activity,
As [I]bread for *their* children in the desert.[6160]
6 "They harvest their fodder in the field,[7704]
And they glean[3953] the vineyard of the wicked.[7563]
7 "[a]They spend the night naked,[6174] without clothing,
And have no covering against the cold.
8 "They are wet with the mountain rains,
And they hug the rock for want of a shelter.
9 "[I]Others snatch the [a]orphan from the breast,
And against the poor they take a pledge.[2254]
10 "They cause *the poor* to go about naked without clothing,
And they take away[5375] the sheaves from the hungry.
11 "Within the walls they produce oil;
They tread wine presses but thirst.
12 "From the city men groan,
And the souls[5315] of the wounded[2491] cry out;
Yet God[433] [a]does not pay attention[7760] to folly.
13 "[I]Others have been with those who rebel[4775] against the light;[216]
They do not want to know[5234] its ways,[1870]
Nor abide in its paths.
14 "The murderer[7523] [a]arises at dawn;
He [b]kills the poor and the needy,
And at night[3915] he is as a thief.
15 "And the eye of the [a]adulterer[5003] waits for[8104] the twilight,
Saying, 'No eye will see me.'
And he [I]disguises his face.
16 "In the dark[2822] they [a]dig into houses,[1004]
They [b]shut themselves up by day;[3119]
They do not know the light.
17 "For the morning is the same to him as thick darkness,[6751]
For he is familiar with the [a]terrors of thick darkness.
18 "They are [Ia]insignificant on the surface of the water;
Their portion is [b]cursed[7043] on the earth.
They do not turn [II]toward the [c]vineyards.
19 "Drought and heat [Ia]consume the snow waters,
So does [IIb]Sheol[7585] *those who* have sinned.[2398]
20 "A [Ia]mother will forget him;
The [b]worm feeds sweetly till he is remembered[2142] [c]no more.

16 [a]Deut. 20:3; Job 27:2; Jer. 51:46
17 [a]Job 10:18, 19 [b]Job 19:8
1 [I]I.e., times of judgment [a]Acts 1:7 [b]Is. 2:12; Jer. 46:10; Obad. 15; Zeph. 1:7
2 [I]Lit., *They* [II]Or, *pasture* [a]Deut. 19:14; 27:17; Prov. 23:10
3 [a]Job 6:27 [b]Deut. 24:17; Job 22:9
4 [a]Job 24:14; 29:16; 30:25; 31:19 [b]Job 29:12; Ps. 41:1; Prov. 14:31; 28:28; Amos 8:4
5 [I]Lit., *his bread* [a]Job 39:5-8 [b]Ps. 104:23
7 [a]Ex. 22:26; Job 22:6
9 [I]Lit., *They* [a]Job 6:27
12 [a]Job 9:23, 24
13 [I]Lit., *They*
14 [a]Mic. 2:1 [b]Ps. 10:8
15 [I]Or, *puts a covering on his face* [a]Prov. 7:9
16 [a]Ex. 22:2; Matt. 6:19 [b]John 3:20
17 [a]Job 15:21
18 [I]Or, *light* or *swift* [II]Lit., *to the path of* [a]Job 22:11, 16; 27:20 [b]Job 5:3 [c]Job 24:6, 11
19 [I]Lit., *seize* [II]I.e., nether world [a]Job 6:16, 17 [b]Job 21:13
20 [I]Lit., *womb* [a]Is. 49:15 [b]Job 21:26 [c]Job 18:17; Ps. 34:16; Prov. 10:7

And wickedness[5766] will be
broken [d]like a tree.
21 "He wrongs the [I]barren6135
woman,
And does no good[3190] for
[a]the widow.
22 "But He drags off the valiant[47]
by [a]His power;
He rises, but [b]no one has
assurance[539] of life.[2416]
23 "He provides them [a]with
security, and they are
supported;[8172]
And His [b]eyes are on their
ways.
24 "They are exalted a [a]little while,
then they are gone;
Moreover, they are [b]brought
low and like everything
gathered up;
Even like the heads[7218] of grain
they are cut off.
25 "Now if it is not so, [a]who can
prove[7760] me a liar,[3576]
And make my speech
worthless?"

Bildad Says Man Is Inferior

25 Then Bildad the Shuhite [I]an-
swered,[559]
2 "[a]Dominion and awe[6343]
[I]belong to Him
Who establishes[6213] peace in
[b]His heights.
3 "Is there any number to
[a]His troops?[1416]
And upon whom does His light[216]
not rise?
4 "How then can a man[582] be
[a]just[6663] with God?[410]
Or how can he be [b]clean[2135] who
is born of woman?[802]
5 "If even [a]the moon has no
brightness
And the [b]stars are not pure[2141]
in His sight,
6 How much less [a]man, *that*
[b]maggot,
And the son[1121] of man,[120] *that*
worm!"

Job Rebukes Bildad

26 Then Job [I]responded,[559]
2 "What a help you are to
[I][a]the weak!
How you have saved[3467] the arm
[b]without strength!
3 "What counsel[3289] you have given
to *one* without wisdom![2451]
What helpful insight you have
abundantly [I]provided!
4 "To whom have you uttered[5046]
words?[4405]
And whose [I]spirit was expressed
through you?

The Greatness of God

5 "The [I][a]departed[7496] spirits
tremble[2342]
Under the waters and their
inhabitants.[7931]
6 "Naked[6174] is [I][a]Sheol[7585] before
Him
And [II][b]Abaddon[11] has no
covering.
7 "He [a]stretches out the north over
empty space,[8414]
And hangs the earth[776] on
nothing.
8 "He [a]wraps up the waters in His
clouds;
And the cloud[6051] does not burst
under them.
9 "He [I][a]obscures the face of the
[II]full moon,[3678]
And spreads His cloud over
it.
10 "He has inscribed a [a]circle on the
surface of the waters,
At the [b]boundary of light and
darkness.
11 "The pillars of heaven[8064]
tremble,
And are amazed at His
rebuke.[1606]
12 "He [a]quieted the sea with His
power,
And by His [b]understanding[8394]
He shattered[4272] [c]Rahab.
13 "By His breath[7307] the
[a]heavens[8064] are [I]cleared;8231

20 [d]Job 19:10; Dan. 4:14
21 [I]Lit., *barren who does not bear* [a]Job 22:9
22 [a]Job 9:4 [b]Job 18:20
23 [a]Job 12:6 [b]Job 10:4; 11:11
24 [a]Ps. 37:10 [b]Job 14:21
25 [a]Job 6:28; 27:4

1 [I]Lit., *answered and said*
2 [I]Lit., *are with Him* [a]Job 9:4; 36:5, 22; 37:23; 42:2 [b]Job 16:19; 31:2
3 [a]Job 16:13
4 [a]Job 4:17; 9:2 [b]Job 14:4
5 [a]Job 31:26 [b]Job 15:15
6 [a]Job 7:17 [b]Job 17:14

1 [I]Lit., *responded and said*
2 [I]Lit., *no power* [a]Job 6:11, 12 [b]Ps. 71:9
3 [I]Lit., *made known*
4 [I]Lit., *breath has gone forth*
5 [I]Or, *shades;* Heb., *Rephaim* [a]Job 3:13; Ps. 88:10
6 [I]I.e., the nether world [II]I.e., place of destruction [a]Job 9:5-10; 26:6-14; 38:17; 41:11 [b]Job 28:22; 31:12
7 [a]Job 9:8
8 [a]Job 37:11; Prov. 30:4
9 [I]Lit., *covers* [II]Or, *throne* [a]Job 22:14; Ps. 97:2; 105:39
10 [a]Job 38:1-11; Prov. 8:29 [b]Job 38:19, 20, 24
12 [a]Is. 51:15; Jer. 31:35 [b]Job 12:13 [c]Job 9:13
13 [I]Lit., *made beautiful* [a]Job 9:8

His hand[3027] has pierced
[b]the fleeing serpent.[5175]
14 "Behold, these are the fringes of
His ways;[1870]
And how faint [a]a word[1697] we
hear[8085] of Him!
But His mighty [b]thunder, who
can understand?"[995]

Job Affirms His Righteousness

27 Then Job [I]continued his [a]discourse and said,[559]
2 "As God[410] lives,[2416] [a]who has
taken away[5493] my right,[4941]
And the Almighty,[7706] [b]who has
embittered[4843] my soul,[5315]
3 For as long as [I]life[5397] is in
me,
And the [II][a]breath[7307] of God[433]
is in my nostrils,[639]
4 My lips[8193] certainly will not
speak[1696] unjustly,[5766]
Nor will [a]my tongue mutter
deceit.
5 "Far be it from me that I should
declare you right;[6663]
Till I die[1478] [a]I will not put away
my integrity[8538] from me.
6 "I [a]hold fast[2388] my
righteousness[6666] and will not
let it go.
My heart[3824] does not reproach
any of my days.

The State of the Godless

7 "May my enemy be as the
wicked,[7563]
And [I]my opponent as the
unjust.[5767]
8 "For what is [a]the hope of the
godless[2611] [I]when he is cut
off,[1214]
When God requires [b]his
[II]life?
9 "Will God [a]hear[8085] his cry,
When [b]distress comes upon
him?
10 "Will he take [a]delight in the
Almighty,
Will he call[7121] on God at all
times?[6256]
11 "I will instruct[3384] you in the
[I]power[3027] of God;
What is with the Almighty I will
not conceal.
12 "Behold, all of you have seen[2372]
it;
Why then do you [I]act foolishly?
13 "This is [a]the portion of a wicked
man[120] from God,
And the inheritance[5159] *which*
[b]tyrants receive from the
Almighty.
14 "Though his sons[1121] are many,
[I]they are destined [a]for the
sword;[2719]
And his [b]descendants will not be
satisfied with bread.
15 "His survivors[8300] will be
buried[6912] because of the
plague,[4194]
And [I]their [a]widows will not be
able to weep.
16 "Though he piles up silver like
dust,[6083]
And prepares[3559] garments as
plentiful as the clay;
17 He may prepare *it,* [a]but the just
will wear *it,*
And the innocent[5355] will divide
the silver.
18 "He has built his [a]house[1004] like
the [I]spider's web,
Or as a hut[5521] *which* the
watchman has made.[6213]
19 "He lies down rich, but never
[I]again;[622]
He opens his eyes, and
[a]it is no more.
20 "[a]Terrors overtake him like a
flood;
A tempest steals him away
[b]in the night.[3915]
21 "The east [a]wind carries him away,
and he is gone,
For it whirls[8175] him [b]away from
his place.
22 "For it will hurl at him [a]without
sparing;
He will surely[1272] try to
[b]flee from its [I]power.

13 [b]Is. 27:1
14 [a]Job 4:12 [b]Job 36:29; 37:4,5
1 [I]Or, *again took up* [a]Job 13:12; 29:1
2 [a]Job 16:11; 34:5 [b]Job 9:18
3 [I]Lit., *breath* [II]Or, *spirit* [a]Job 32:8; 33:4
4 [a]Job 6:28; 33:3
5 [a]Job 6:29
6 [a]Job 2:3; 13:18
7 [I]Lit., *he who rises up against me*
8 [I]Or, *though he gains* [II]Lit., *soul* [a]Job 8:13; 11:20 [b]Job 12:10
9 [a]Job 35:12, 13; Ps. 18:41; Prov. 1:28; Is. 1:15; Jer. 14:12; Mic. 3:4 [b]Prov. 1:27
10 [a]Job 22:26, 27; Ps. 37:4; Is. 58:14
11 [I]Lit., *hand*
12 [I]Or, *speak vanity*
13 [a]Job 20:29 [b]Job 15:20
14 [I]Lit., *the sword is for them* [a]Job 15:22; 18:19 [b]Job 20:10
15 [I]So ancient versions; Heb., *his* [a]Ps. 78:64
17 [a]Job 20:18-21
18 [I]So ancient versions; Heb., *moth* [a]Job 8:15; 18:14
19 [I]So ancient versions; Heb., *will be gathered* [a]Job 7:8, 21; 20:7
20 [a]Job 15:21 [b]Job 20:8; 34:20
21 [a]Job 21:18 [b]Job 7:10
22 [I]Lit., *hand* [a]Jer. 13:14; Ezek. 5:11; 24:14 [b]Job 11:20

23 "*Men* will clap[5606] their hands[3709]
at him,
And will [a]hiss him from his
place.

Job Tells of Earth's Treasures

28 "Surely there is a [I]mine for
silver,
And a place [II]where they
refine[2212] gold.
2 "Iron is taken from the dust,[6083]
And from rock copper is
smelted.
3 "*Man* puts an end to
darkness,[2822]
And [a]to the farthest limit he
searches out
The rock in gloom[652] and deep
shadow.[6757]
4 "He [I]sinks a shaft far from
[II]habitation,
Forgotten by the foot;
They hang and swing to and fro
far from men.[582]
5 "The earth,[776] from it comes
food,
And underneath it is turned[2015]
up as fire.
6 "Its rocks are the [I]source of
sapphires,
And its dust[6083] *contains* gold.
7 "The path no bird of prey knows,
Nor has the falcon's eye caught
sight of it.
8 "The [I]proud beasts[1121] have not
trodden it,
Nor has the *fierce* lion passed
over it.
9 "He puts his hand[3027] on the
flint;
He overturns[2015] the mountains
at the [I]base.
10 "He hews out channels through
the rocks;
And his eye sees[7200] anything
precious.
11 "He dams up[2280] the streams
from [I]flowing;
And what is hidden he brings
out to the light.[216]

The Search for Wisdom Is Harder

12 "But [a]where can wisdom[2451] be
found?
And where is the place of
understanding?[998]
13 "[a]Man[582] does not know its value,
Nor is it found in the land[776] of
the living.[2416]
14 "The deep says,[559] 'It is not in
me';
And the sea says, 'It is not with
me.'
15 "[a]Pure gold cannot be given in
exchange for it,
Nor can silver be weighed as
its price.
16 "It cannot be valued in the gold
of Ophir,
In precious onyx, or sapphire.
17 "[a]Gold or glass cannot equal it,
Nor can it be exchanged for
articles of fine gold.
18 "Coral and crystal are not to be
mentioned;
And the acquisition of [a]wisdom
is above *that of* pearls.
19 "The topaz of Ethiopia cannot
equal it,
Nor can it be valued in
[a]pure gold.
20 "[a]Where then does wisdom come
from?
And where is the place of
understanding?
21 "Thus it is hidden from the eyes
of all living,
And concealed from the birds of
the sky.[8064]
22 "[Ia]Abaddon[11] and Death[4194]
say,[559]
'With our ears[241] we have
heard[8085] a report[8088] of it.'
23 "[a]God[430] understands[995] its
way;[1870]
And He knows its place.
24 "For He [a]looks to the ends of the
earth,
And sees everything under the
heavens.[8064]
25 "When He imparted[6213]
[a]weight to the wind,[7307]

---

23 [a]Job 18:18; 20:8
1 [I]Or, *source* [II]Lit., *for gold they refine*
3 [a]Eccl. 1:13
4 [I]Lit., *breaks open* [II]Lit., *sojourning*
6 [I]Or, *place*
8 [I]Lit., *sons of pride*
9 [I]Lit., *roots*
11 [I]Lit., *weeping*
12 [a]Job 28:23, 28; Eccl. 7:24
13 [a]Matt. 13:44-46
15 [a]Prov. 3:13, 14; 8:10, 11; 16:16
17 [a]Prov. 8:10; 16:16
18 [a]Prov. 8:11
19 [a]Prov. 8:19
20 [a]Job 28:23, 28
22 [I]I.e., Destruction [a]Job 26:6; Prov. 8:32-36
23 [a]Job 9:4; Prov. 8:22-36
24 [a]Ps. 11:4; 33:13, 14; 66:7; Prov. 15:3
25 [a]Ps. 135:7

And [b]meted out the waters by
measure,
26 When He set[6213] a [a]limit[2706] for
the rain,
And a course for the
[b]thunderbolt,
27 Then He saw it and declared[5608]
it;
He established[3559] it and also
searched it out.
28 "And to man[120] He said,[559]
'Behold, the [a]fear[3374] of the
Lord,[136] that is wisdom;
And to depart[5493] from evil[7451]
is understanding.'"

Job's Past Was Glorious

29 And Job again took up his
[a]discourse and said,[559]
2 "Oh that I were as in months gone
by,
As in the days when God[433]
[a]watched over[8104] me;
3 When [a]His lamp[5216] shone[1984]
over my head,[7218]
And [b]by His light[216] I walked
through darkness;[2822]
4 As I was in [I]the prime of my
days,
When the [IIa]friendship[5475] of God
was over my tent;[168]
5 When [I]the Almighty[7706] was yet
with me,
And my children were around
me;
6 When my steps were bathed[7364]
in [a]butter,
And the [b]rock poured out for me
streams of oil![8081]
7 "When I went out to [a]the gate
of the city,
When I [I]took[3559] my seat[4186] in
the square;
8 The young men saw[7200] me and
hid themselves,
And the old men[3453] arose *and*
stood.
9 "The princes[8269] [a]stopped
talking,[4405]
And [b]put[7760] *their* hands[3709] on
their mouths;[6310]

10 The voice of the nobles was
[Ia]hushed,
And their [b]tongue stuck to their
palate.
11 "For when [a]the ear[241] heard,[8085]
it called me blessed;[833]
And when the eye saw, it gave
witness[5749] of me,
12 Because I delivered[4422]
[a]the poor who cried for help,
And the [b]orphan who had no
helper.
13 "The blessing[1293] of the one
[a]ready to perish[6] came upon
me,
And I made the [b]widow's
heart[3820] sing for joy.
14 "I [a]put on righteousness,[6664] and
it clothed me;
My justice[4941] was like a robe
and a turban.[6797]
15 "I was [a]eyes to the blind,
And feet to the lame.
16 "I was a father[1] to [a]the needy,
And I investigated the case[7379]
which I did not know.[3045]
17 "And I [a]broke[7665] the jaws of the
wicked,[5767]
And snatched the prey from his
teeth.
18 "Then I [I]thought, 'I shall die[1478]
[II]in my nest,
And I shall multiply *my* days as
the sand.
19 'My [a]root is spread out to the
waters,
And [b]dew lies all night on my
branch.
20 'My glory[3519] is *ever* new with
me,
And my [a]bow is renewed in my
hand.'[3027]
21 "To me [a]they listened and
waited,[3176]
And kept silent for my
counsel.[6098]
22 "After my words[1697] they did not
[a]speak again,
And [b]my speech dropped[5197] on
them.
23 "And they waited for me as for
the rain,

25 [b]Job 12:15; 38:8-11
26 [a]Job 37:6, 11, 12; 38:26-28 [b]Job 37:3; 38:25
28 [a]Ps. 111:10; Prov. 1:7; 9:10; Eccl. 12:13

1 [a]Num. 23:7; 24:3; Job 13:12; 27:1
2 [a]Jer. 31:28
3 [a]Job 18:6 [b]Job 11:17
4 [I]Lit., *the days of my autumn* [II]Lit., *counsel* [a]Job 15:8; Ps. 25:14; Prov. 3:32
5 [I]Heb., *Shaddai*
6 [a]Deut. 32:14; Job 20:17 [b]Deut. 32:13; Ps. 81:16
7 [I]Lit., *set up* [a]Job 31:21
9 [a]Job 29:21 [b]Job 21:5
10 [I]Lit., *hidden* [a]Job 29:22 [b]Ps. 137:6
11 [a]Job 4:3, 4
12 [a]Job 24:4, 9; 34:28; Ps. 72:12; Prov. 21:13 [b]Job 31:17, 21
13 [a]Job 31:19 [b]Job 22:9
14 [a]Job 27:5, 6; Ps. 132:9; Is. 59:17; 61:10; Eph. 6:14
15 [a]Num. 10:31
16 [a]Job 24:4; Prov. 29:7
17 [a]Ps. 3:7
18 [I]Lit., *said* [II]Lit., *with*
19 [a]Jer. 17:8 [b]Hos. 14:5
20 [a]Gen. 49:24; Ps. 18:34
21 [a]Job 4:3; 29:9
22 [a]Job 29:10 [b]Deut. 32:2

And opened their mouth as for the spring rain.
24 "I smiled on them when they did not believe,[539]
And the light of my face they did not cast down.[5307]
25 "I chose[977] a way[1870] for them and sat as [a]chief,[7218]
And dwelt[7931] as a king[4428] among the troops,[1416]
As one who [b]comforted[5162] the mourners.

Job's Present State Is Humiliating

30 "But now those younger than I [a]mock me,
Whose fathers[1] I disdained[3988] to put with the dogs of my flock.
2 "Indeed, what *good was* the strength of their hands[3027] to me?
Vigor had perished[6] from them.
3 "From want and famine they are gaunt
Who gnaw the dry ground by night in waste and desolation,[7728]
4 Who pluck [I]mallow[4408] by the bushes,[7880]
And whose food is the root of the broom shrub.
5 "They are driven from the community;
They shout[7321] against them as *against* a thief,
6 So that they dwell[7931] in dreadful [I]valleys,
In holes of the earth[6083] and of the rocks.
7 "Among the bushes they [I]cry out;
Under the nettles they are gathered together.
8 "[I]Fools, even [II]those without a name,
They were scourged[5217] from the land.[776]
9 "And now I have become their [I][a]taunt,
I have even become a [b]byword[4405] to them.
10 "They abhor[8581] me *and* stand aloof from me,
And they do not [I]refrain from [a]spitting at my face.
11 "Because [I]He has loosed [II]His [III]bowstring and [a]afflicted me,
They have cast off [b]the bridle before me.
12 "On the right hand their [I]brood arises;
They [a]thrust aside my feet
[b]and build up against me their ways[734] of destruction.[343]
13 "They [a]break up my path,
They profit [I]from my destruction,[1942]
No one restrains them.
14 "As *through* a wide breach they come,
[I]Amid the tempest[7722] they roll[1556] on.
15 "[a]Terrors are turned[2015] against me,
They pursue my [I]honor as the wind,[7307]
And my [II]prosperity[3444] has passed away[5674] [b]like a cloud.
16 "And now [a]my soul[5315] is poured out[8210] [I]within me;
Days of affliction have seized me.
17 "At night[3915] it pierces [a]my bones[6106] [I]within me,
And my gnawing *pains* take no rest.
18 "By a great force my garment is [a]distorted;
It binds me about as the collar[6310] of my coat.
19 "He has cast[3384] me into the [a]mire,
And I have become like dust[6083] and ashes.
20 "I [a]cry out to Thee for help, but Thou dost not answer me;
I stand up, and Thou dost turn[995] Thy attention against me.
21 "Thou hast [I]become cruel to me;

25 [a]Job 1:3; 31:37 [b]Job 4:4; 16:5
1 [a]Job 12:4
4 [I]I.e., plant of the salt marshes
6 [I]Or, *wadis*
7 [I]Or, *bray*
8 [I]Lit., *Sons of fools* [II]Lit., *sons*
9 [I]Lit., *song* [a]Job 12:4 [b]Job 17:6; Ps. 69:11; Lam. 3:14, 63
10 [I]Lit., *withhold spit from my face* [a]Num. 12:14; Deut. 25:9; Job 17:6; Is. 50:6; Matt. 26:67
11 [I]Or, *they* [II]Some mss. read *my* [III]Or, *cord* [a]Ruth 1:21; Ps. 88:7 [b]Ps. 32:9
12 [I]Possibly, *sprout* or *offspring* [a]Ps. 140:4, 5 [b]Job 19:12
13 [I]Lit., *for* [a]Is. 3:12
14 [I]Lit., *Under*
15 [I]Or, *nobility* [II]Or, *welfare* [a]Job 3:25; 31:23; Ps. 55:3-5 [b]Job 7:9; Hos. 13:3
16 [I]Lit., *upon* [a]1 Sam. 1:15; Job 3:24; Ps. 22:14; 42:4; Is. 53:12
17 [I]Lit., *from upon* [a]Job 30:30
18 [a]Job 2:7
19 [a]Ps. 69:2, 14
20 [a]Job 19:7
21 [I]Lit., *turned to be*

With the might of Thy hand[3027]
Thou dost [a]persecute[7852] me.
22 "Thou dost [a]lift me up to the wind
and cause me to ride;
And Thou dost dissolve me in
a storm.[7738]
23 "For I know[3045] that Thou
[a]wilt bring me to death[4194]
And to the [b]house[1004] of
meeting[4150] for all living.[2416]
24 "Yet does not one in a heap of
ruins[1164] stretch out *his* hand,
Or in his disaster[6365] therefore
[a]cry out for help?
25 "Have I not [a]wept for the
[I]one whose life is hard?[7186]
Was not my soul grieved for
[b]the needy?
26 "When I [a]expected[6960] good,[2896]
then evil[7451] came;
When I waited[3176] for light,[216]
[b]then darkness[652] came.
27 "[I]I am seething[4578] [a]within, and
cannot relax;
Days of affliction confront me.
28 "I go about [Ia]mourning[6937] without
comfort;
I stand up in the assembly[6951]
and [b]cry out for help.
29 "I have become a brother[251] to
[a]jackals,[8577]
And a companion of ostriches.
30 "My [a]skin[5785] turns black
[I]on me,
And my [b]bones burn[2787] with
[II]fever.
31 "Therefore my [a]harp [I]is turned
to mourning,
And my flute to the sound of
those who weep.

Job Asserts His Integrity

31 "I have made[3772] a covenant[1285]
with my [a]eyes;
How then could I gaze at a
virgin?[1330]
2 "And what is [a]the portion of
God[433] from above
Or the heritage[5159] of the
Almighty[7706] from on
high?
3 "Is it not [a]calamity[343] to the
unjust,[5767]
And disaster[5235] to [b]those who
work iniquity?[205]
4 "Does He not [a]see my ways,[1870]
And [b]number[5608] all my steps?
5 "If I have [a]walked with
falsehood,[7723]
And my foot has hastened after
deceit,[4820]
6 Let Him [a]weigh me with
[I]accurate scales,
And let God know[3045] [b]my
integrity.[3887]
7 "If my step has [a]turned from the
way,[1870]
Or my heart[3820] [I]followed my
eyes,
Or if any [b]spot[3971] has stuck to
my hands,[3709]
8 Let me [a]sow and another eat,
And let my [Ib]crops be uprooted.
9 "If my heart has been [a]enticed
by a woman,[802]
Or I have lurked at my
neighbor's[7453] doorway,
10 May my wife[802] [a]grind for
another,
And let [b]others [I]kneel down[3766]
over her.
11 "For that would be a [a]lustful
crime;[2154]
Moreover, it would be
[b]an iniquity[5771] *punishable by
judges.*[6414]
12 "For it would be [a]fire that
consumes to [Ib]Abaddon,[11]
And would [c]uproot all my
[II]increase.
13 "If I have [a]despised[3988] the
claim[4941] of my male or female
slaves[5650]
When they filed a complaint[7379]
against me,
14 What then could I do when
God[410] arises,
And when He calls me to
account, what will I
answer[7725] Him?
15 "Did not [a]He who made[6213] me
in the womb[990] make[6213]
him,

21 [a]Job 10:3; 16:9, 14; 19:6, 22
22 [a]Job 9:17; 27:21
23 [a]Job 9:22; 10:8 [b]Job 3:19; Eccl. 12:5
24 [a]Job 19:7
25 [I]Lit., *hard of day* [a]Ps. 35:13, 14; Rom. 12:15 [b]Job 24:4
26 [a]Job 3:25, 26; Jer. 8:15 [b]Job 19:8
27 [I]Lit., *My inward parts are boiling* [a]Lam. 2:11
28 [I]Or, *blackened, but not by the heat of the sun* [a]Job 30:31; Ps. 38:6; 42:9; 43:2 [b]Job 19:7
29 [a]Ps. 44:19; Mic. 1:8
30 [I]Lit., *from upon* [II]Lit., *heat* [a]Job 2:7 [b]Ps. 102:3
31 [I]Lit., *becomes* [a]Is. 24:8

1 [a]Matt. 5:28
2 [a]Job 20:29
3 [a]Job 18:12; 21:30 [b]Job 34:22
4 [a]2Chr. 16:9; Job 24:23; 28:24; 34:21; 36:7; Prov. 5:21; 15:3 [b]Job 14:16; 31:37
5 [a]Job 15:31; Mic. 2:11
6 [I]Lit., *just* [a]Job 6:2, 3 [b]Job 23:10; 27:5, 6
7 [I]Lit., *walked after* [a]Job 23:11 [b]Job 9:30
8 [I]Or, *offspring* [a]Lev. 26:16; Job 20:18; Mic. 6:15 [b]Job 31:12
9 [a]Job 24:15; 31:1
10 [I]I.e., sexual relations [a]Is. 47:2 [b]Deut. 28:30; Jer. 8:10
11 [a]Lev. 20:10; Deut. 22:24 [b]Job 31:28
12 [I]I.e., place of destruction [II]Or, *yield* [a]Job 15:30 [b]Job 26:6 [c]Job 20:28; 31:8
13 [a]Deut. 24:14, 15
15 [a]Job 10:3

And the same one fashion[3559] us
in the womb?
16"If I have kept [a]the poor from
their desire,[2656]
Or have caused the eyes of
[b]the widow to fail,[3615]
17 Or have [a]eaten my morsel alone,
And [b]the orphan has not
[I]shared it
18 (But from my youth he grew
up with me as with a father,[1]
And from [I]infancy I guided[5148]
her),
19 If I have seen[7200] anyone perish[6]
[a]for lack of clothing,
Or that [b]the needy had no
covering,
20 If his loins have not [I]thanked[1288]
me,
And if he has not been warmed
with the fleece of my sheep,
21 If I have lifted up[5130] my hand[3027]
against [a]the orphan,
Because I saw[7200] [I]I had support
[b]in the gate,
22 Let my shoulder fall from the
[I]socket,
And my [a]arm be broken[7665] off
[II]at the elbow.
23"For [a]calamity from God is a
terror[6343] to me,
And because of [b]His [I]majesty I
can do nothing.
24"If I have put my confidence[3689]
in [a]gold,
And called[559] fine gold my trust,
25 If I have [a]gloated because my
wealth[2428] was great,
And because my hand had
secured *so* much;
26 If I have [a]looked[7200] at the
[I]sun when it shone,[1984]
Or the moon going in splendor,
27 And my heart became secretly
enticed,6601
And my hand [I]threw a kiss[5401]
from my mouth,[6310]
28 That too would have been
[a]an iniquity *calling for*
[I]judgment,
For I would have [b]denied3584 God
above.

16 [a]Job 5:16; 20:19 [b]Ex. 22:22-24; Job 22:9
17 [I]Lit., *eaten from it* [a]Job 22:7 [b]Job 29:12
18 [I]Lit., *my mother's womb*
19 [a]Job 22:6; 29:13 [b]Job 24:4
20 [I]Lit., *blessed*
21 [I]Lit., *my help* [a]Job 29:12; 31:17 [b]Job 29:7
22 [I]Lit., *shoulder; or, back* [II]Lit., *from the bone of the upper arm* [a]Job 38:15
23 [I]Lit., *exaltation* [a]Job 31:3 [b]Job 13:11
24 [a]Job 22:24; Mark 10:23-25
25 [a]Job 1:3, 10; Ps. 62:10
26 [I]Lit., *light* [a]Deut. 4:19; 17:3; Ezek. 8:16
27 [I]Lit., *kissed my mouth*
28 [I]Lit., *judges* [a]Deut. 17:2-7; Job 31:11 [b]Josh. 24:27; Is. 59:13
29 [I]Lit., *lifted myself up* [a]Prov. 17:5; 24:17; Obad. 12
30 [I]Lit., *And* [II]Lit., *given my palate* [a]Ps. 7:4 [b]Job 5:3
31 [I]Lit., *give* [a]Job 22:7
32 [I]M.T., *way*
33 [I]Or, *mankind* [a]Gen. 3:10; Prov. 28:13
34 [a]Ex. 23:2
35 [I]Lit., *mark* [a]Job 19:7; 30:20, 24, 28; 35:14 [b]Job 27:7
37 [a]Job 31:4 [b]Job 1:3; 29:25
38 [a]Job 24:2
39 [I]Lit., *strength* [II]Lit., *the soul of its owners to expire* [a]Job 24:6, 10-12; James 5:4 [b]1Kin. 21:19

29"Have I [a]rejoiced at the
extinction[6365] of my
enemy,[8130]
Or [I]exulted when evil[7451] befell
him?
30 "[I]No, [a]I have not [II]allowed my
mouth to sin[2398]
By asking[7592] for his life[5315] in
[b]a curse.[423]
31"Have the men of my tent[168] not
said,
'Who can [I]find one who has not
been [a]satisfied with his
meat'?[1320]
32"The alien[1616] has not lodged
outside,
For I have opened my doors to
the [I]traveler.[734]
33"Have I [a]covered[3680] my
transgressions[6588] like
[I]Adam,
By hiding my iniquity in my
bosom,
34 Because I [a]feared[6206] the great
multitude,
And the contempt of families[4940]
terrified[2865] me,
And kept silent and did not go
out of doors?
35 "Oh that I had one to hear[8085]
me!
Behold, here is my [I]signature;
[a]Let the Almighty answer
me!
And the indictment which my
[b]adversary[7379] has written,
36 Surely I would carry it on my
shoulder;
I would bind it to myself like a
crown.
37 "I would declare[5046] to Him
[a]the number of my steps;
Like [b]a prince[5057] I would
approach[7126] Him.
38"If my [a]land[127] cries[2199] out
against me,
And its furrows8525 weep
together;
39 If I have [a]eaten its [I]fruit without
money,
Or have [b]caused [II]its owners[1167]
to lose their lives,[5315]

40 Let [a]briars [I]grow instead of
wheat,
And stinkweed[890] instead of
barley."
The words[1697] of Job are ended.[8552]

Elihu in Anger Rebukes Job

32 Then these three men[582]
ceased[7673] answering Job, because he was [a]righteous[6662] in his own
eyes.
2 But the anger of Elihu the son[1121]
of Barachel the [a]Buzite, of the family[4950]
of Ram burned;[2374] against Job his
anger[639] burned, [b]because he
justified[6663] himself [Ic]before God.[430]
3 And his anger burned against his
three friends[7453] because they had found
no answer, and yet had condemned Job.
4 Now Elihu had waited [I]to speak
to Job because they were years older
than he.
5 And when Elihu saw[7200] that there
was no answer in the mouth[6310] of the
three men his anger burned.
6 So Elihu the son of Barachel the
Buzite [I]spoke out and said,[559]
"I am young in years and you are
[a]old;[3453]
Therefore I was shy and
afraid[2119] to tell you [II]what I
think.[1843]
7 "I [I]thought [IIa]age should
speak,[1696]
And [III]increased years should
teach[3045] wisdom.[2451]
8 "But it is a spirit[7307] in man,
And the [a]breath of the
Almighty[7706] gives them
[b]understanding.[995]
9 "The [I]abundant *in years* may not
be wise,[2449]
Nor may [a]elders[2205]
understand[995] justice.[4941]
10 "So I [I]say, 'Listen[8085] to me,
I too will tell [II]what I think.'
11 "Behold, I waited[3176] for your
words,[1697]
I listened[238] to your
reasonings,[8394]
While you [I]pondered what to
say.
12 "I even paid close attention[995] to
you,
[I]Indeed, there was no one who
refuted[3198] Job,
Not one of you who answered
his words.[561]
13 "[I]Do not say,[559]
'[a]We have found wisdom;
God[410] will [II]rout him, not
man.'[376]
14 "For he has not arranged *his*
words[4405] against me;
Nor will I reply[7725] to him with
your [I]arguments.[561]
15 "They are dismayed,[2865] they
answer no more;
Words have [I]failed[4405] them.
16 "And shall I wait, because they
do not speak,[1696]
Because they [I]stop *and* answer
no more?
17 "I too will answer my share,
I also will tell my opinion.
18 "For I am full of words;[4405]
The spirit within me constrains
me.
19 "Behold, my belly[990] is like
unvented wine,
Like new wineskins it is about
to burst.
20 "Let me speak that I may get
relief;[7304]
Let me open my lips[8193] and
answer.
21 "Let me now [a]be partial[5375] to no
one;
Nor flatter *any* man.[120]

40 [I]Lit., *come forth* [a]Job 32:13; Is. 5:6

1 [a]Job 10:7; 13:18; 27:5, 6; 31:6

2 [I]Or, *more than* [a]Gen. 22:21 [b]Job 27:5, 6 [c]Job 30:21

4 [I]Lit., *for Job with words;* or possibly, *while they were speaking with Job*

6 [I]Lit., *answered* [II]Lit., *my knowledge* [a]Job 15:10

7 [I]Lit., *said* [II]Lit., *days* [III]Lit., *many* [a]Job 8:8, 9

8 [a]Job 33:4 [b]Job 38:36

9 [I]Or, *nobles* [a]Job 32:7

10 [I]Or, *said* [II]Lit., *my knowledge*

11 [I]Lit., *searched out words*

12 [I]Lit., *Behold*

13 [I]Lit., *Lest you say* [II]Lit., *drive away* [a]Jer. 9:23

14 [I]Lit., *words*

15 [I]Lit., *moved away from*

16 [I]Lit., *stand*

21 [a]Lev. 19:15; Job 13:8, 10; 34:19

32:1—37:24 Elihu was probably present for the discussions between Job, Eliphaz, Bildad and Zophar, but because of his youth compared to their age and wisdom, he had hesitated to speak. Becoming impatient with the inability of the other three not only to convince Job of his error but even to understand the real problem, he now stepped in to set all things right. In defending himself Job had unjustly accused God. He needed to understand that God had permitted suffering in order to bring him to righteousness and prevent him from sinning. Elihu was only partially correct in his assessment of Job and his circumstances, though he understood a great deal about suffering and God's justice and righteousness.

22 "For I do not know[3045] how to
flatter,
Else my Maker[6213] would soon
take me away.

Elihu Claims to Speak for God

33 "However now, Job, please[4994]
[a]hear[8085] my speech,[4405]
And listen[238] to all my words.[1697]
2 "Behold now, I open my
mouth,[6310]
My tongue in my [I]mouth
speaks.[1696]
3 "My words[561] are *from* the
uprightness[3476] of my
heart;[3820]
And my lips[8193] speak[4448]
[a]knowledge[1847] sincerely.[1305]
4 "The [a]Spirit[7307] of God[410] has
made[6213] me,
And the [b]breath[5397] of
[I]the Almighty[7706] gives me
life.[2421]
5 "[a]Refute[7725] me if you can;
Array yourselves before me,
take your stand.
6 "Behold, I belong to God like you;
I too have been [I]formed out of
the [a]clay.
7 "Behold, [a]no fear[367] of me should
terrify[1204] you,
Nor should my pressure weigh
heavily[3513] on you.
8 "Surely you have spoken[559] in my
hearing,[241]
And I have heard[8085] the sound
of *your* words:[4405]
9 'I am [a]pure,[2134] [b]without
transgression;[6588]
I am innocent and there
[c]is no guilt[5771] in me.
10 'Behold, He [I]invents pretexts
against me;
He [a]counts[2803] me as His enemy.
11 'He [a]puts[7760] my feet in the
stocks;
He watches[8104] all my paths.'[734]
12 "Behold, let me [I]tell you,
[a]you are not right[6663] in this,
For God[433] is greater than
man.[582]
13 "Why do you [a]complain[7378] against
Him,
That He does not give an
account of all His doings?
14 "Indeed [a]God speaks[1696] once,
Or twice, *yet* no one notices it.
15 "In a [a]dream, a vision[2384] of the
night,[3915]
When sound sleep falls[5307] on
men,[582]
While they slumber in their
beds,
16 Then [a]He opens[1540] the ears[241]
of men,
And seals their instruction,
17 That He may turn[5493] man[120]
aside *from his* conduct,
And [I]keep[3680] man[1397] from
pride;
18 He [a]keeps back his soul[5315] from
the pit,[7845]
And his life[2416] from [I]passing[5674]
over [b]into Sheol.
19 "[I]Man is also chastened[3198] with
[a]pain on his bed,
And with unceasing[7379]
complaint in his bones;[6106]
20 So that his life [a]loathes[2092]
bread,
And his soul favorite food.
21 "His [a]flesh[1320] wastes[3615] away
from sight,[7210]
And his [b]bones which were not
seen[7200] stick out.[8205]
22 "Then [a]his soul draws near[7126] to
the pit,[7845]
And his life to those who bring
death.
23 "If there is an angel[4397] *as*
[a]mediator[3887] for him,
One out of a thousand,
To remind[5046] a man what is
[I]right for him,
24 Then let him be gracious[2603] to
him, and say,[559]
'Deliver[6308] him from [a]going
down to the pit,
I have found a [b]ransom';[3724]
25 Let his flesh become fresher
than in youth,
Let him return[7725] to the days
of his youthful vigor;

1 [a]Job 13:6
2 [I]Lit., *palate*
3 [a]Job 6:28; 27:4; 36:4
4 [I]Heb., *Shaddai* [a]Gen. 2:7; Job 10:3; 32:8 [b]Job 27:3
5 [a]Job 33:32
6 [I]Lit., *cut out of* [a]Job 4:19
7 [a]Job 13:21
9 [a]Job 9:21; 10:7; 13:18; 16:17 [b]Job 7:21; 13:23; 14:17 [c]Job 10:14
10 [I]Lit., *finds* [a]Job 13:24
11 [a]Job 13:27
12 [I]Lit., *answer* [a]Eccl. 7:20
13 [a]Job 40:2; Is. 45:9
14 [a]Job 33:29; 40:5; Ps. 62:11
15 [a]Job 4:12-17; 33:15-18
16 [a]Job 36:10, 15
17 [I]Lit., *hide*
18 [I]M.T., *perishing by the sword* [a]Job 33:22, 24, 28, 30 [b]Job 15:22
19 [I]Lit., *He* [a]Job 30:17
20 [a]Job 3:24; 6:7; Ps. 107:18
21 [a]Job 16:8 [b]Job 19:20; Ps. 22:17; 102:5
22 [a]Job 33:18, 28
23 [I]Lit., *his uprightness* [a]Gen. 40:8
24 [a]Job 33:18, 28; Is. 38:17 [b]Job 36:18; Ps. 49:7

26 Then he will [a]pray[6279] to God,[433]
and He will accept[7521] him,
That [b]he may see His face with
joy,
And He may restore[7725] His
righteousness[6666] to man.
27 "He will sing to men and say,[559]
'I [a]have sinned[2398] and
perverted[5753] what is
right,[3477]
And it is not [b]proper for me.
28 'He has redeemed[6299] my soul
from going to the pit,
And my life shall [a]see the
light.'[216]
29 "Behold, God does [a]all these
[I]oftentimes with men,
30 To [a]bring back his soul from
the pit,
That he may be enlightened with
the light of life.[2416]
31 "Pay attention, O Job, listen[8085]
to me;
Keep silent and let me speak.[1696]
32 "*Then* if [I]you have anything to
say,[4405] answer me;
Speak, for I desire[2654] to
justify[6663] you.
33 "If not, [a]listen to me;
Keep silent, and I will teach[502]
you wisdom."[2451]

Elihu Vindicates God's Justice

34 Then Elihu continued and said,
2 "Hear[8085] my words,[4405] you
wise[2450] men,
And listen[238] to me, you who
know.[3045]
3 "For [a]the ear tests[974] words,
As the palate tastes food.
4 "Let us choose[977] for ourselves
what is right;[4941]
Let us know[3045] among
ourselves what is good.[2896]
5 "For Job has said, '[a]I am
righteous,[6663]
But [b]God[410] has taken away[5493]
my right;
6 [I]Should I lie[3576] concerning my
right?[4941]
My [II][a]wound is incurable, *though
I am* without transgres-
sion.'[6588]
7 "What man[1397] is like Job,
Who [a]drinks up derision like
water,
8 Who goes [a]in company with the
workers of iniquity,[205]
And walks with wicked[7562]
men?[582]
9 "For he has said, '[a]It profits a
man nothing
When he [I]is pleased[7521] with
God.'[430]
10 "Therefore, listen[8085] to me, you
men of understanding.
Far be it from God to
[a]do wickedness,[7562]
And from the Almighty[7706] to do
wrong.[5766]
11 "For He pays[7999] a man[120]
according to [a]his work,
And makes [I]him find it according
to his way.[734]
12 "Surely,[551] [a]God will not act
wickedly,[7561]
And the Almighty will not
pervert[5791] justice.
13 "Who [a]gave Him authority over
the earth?[776]
And who [b]has laid[7760] *on Him*
the whole world?[8398]
14 "If He should [I]determine[3820] to
do so,
If He should [a]gather[622] to
Himself His spirit[7307] and His
breath,[5397]
15 All [a]flesh would perish[1478]
together,
And man would [b]return[7725] to
dust.[6083]
16 "But if *you have* understanding,[998]
hear[238] this;
Listen to the sound of my
words.
17 "Shall [a]one who hates[8130] justice
rule?[2280]
And [b]will you condemn[7561] a
righteous mighty one,
18 Who says[559] to a king,[4428]
'Worthless one,'[1100]
To nobles,[5081] 'Wicked ones';[7563]

26 [a]Job 22:27; 34:28; Ps. 50:14, 15 [b]Job 22:26
27 [a]2Sam. 12:13; Luke 15:21 [b]Rom. 6:21
28 [a]Job 22:28
29 [I]Lit., *twice, three times* [a]Eph. 1:11; Phil. 2:13
30 [a]Job 33:18; Zech. 9:11
32 [I]Lit., *there are words*
33 [a]Ps. 34:11
3 [a]Job 12:11
5 [a]Job 13:18; 33:9 [b]Job 27:2
6 [I]Or, *Although I am right I am accounted a liar* [II]Lit., *arrow* [a]Job 6:4
7 [a]Job 15:16
8 [a]Job 22:15
9 [I]Or, *takes delight in God* [a]Job 21:15; 35:3; Ps. 50:18
10 [a]Gen. 18:25; Deut. 32:4; Job 8:3; 34:12; Rom. 9:14
11 [I]Lit., *a man* [a]Job 34:25; Ps. 62:12; Prov. 24:12; Jer. 32:19; Ezek. 33:20; Matt. 16:27; Rom. 2:6; 2Cor. 5:10; Rev. 22:12
12 [a]Job 34:10
13 [a]Job 38:4 [b]Job 38:5
14 [I]Lit., *set His mind on Himself* [a]Job 12:10; Ps. 104:29; Eccl. 12:7
15 [a]Gen. 7:21; Job 9:22 [b]Gen. 3:19; Job 10:9
17 [a]2Sam. 23:3; Job 34:30 [b]Job 40:8

19 Who shows no [a]partiality[5375][6440]
to princes,[8269]
Nor regards the rich above the
poor,
For they all are the [b]work of
His hands?[3027]
20 "In a moment they die,[4191] and
[a]at midnight
People[5971] are shaken and pass
away,[5674]
And [b]the mighty[47] are taken
away without a hand.[3027]
21 "For [a]His eyes are upon the
ways[1870] of a man,
And He sees[7200] all his steps.
22 "There is [a]no darkness[2822] or
deep shadow[6757]
Where the workers of iniquity
may hide themselves.
23 "For He does not [a]*need to*
consider[7760] a man further,
That he should go before God
in judgment.
24 "He breaks in pieces[7489]
[a]mighty men without inquiry,
And sets others in their place.
25 "Therefore He [a]knows their
works,
And [b]He overthrows[2015] *them* in
the night,[3915]
And they are crushed.[1792]
26 "He [a]strikes[5606] them like the
wicked[7563]
[I]In a public place,
27 Because they [a]turned aside from
following Him,
And [b]had no regard[7919] for any
of His ways;
28 So that they caused [a]the cry
of the poor to come to Him,
And that He might [b]hear[8085] the
cry of the afflicted—
29 When He keeps quiet,[8252] who
then can condemn?[7561]
And when He hides His face,
who then can behold Him,
That is, in regard to both
nation[1471] and man?—
30 So that [a]godless[2611] men should
not rule,[4427]
Nor be snares[4170] of the people.
31 "For has anyone said to God,
'I have borne[5375] *chastisement;*
I will not offend[2254] *anymore;*
32 Teach[3384] Thou me what I do
not see;
If I have [a]done iniquity,
I will do it no more'?
33 "Shall He [a]recompense[7999] on
your terms, because you
have rejected *it?*
For you must choose, and
not I;
Therefore declare[1696] what you
know.[3045]
34 "Men of understanding will say[559]
to me,
And a wise man who hears me,
35 'Job [a]speaks[1696] without
knowledge,[1847]
And his words[1697] are without
wisdom.[7919]
36 'Job ought to be tried[974]
[I]to the limit,[5331]
Because he answers [a]like
wicked[205] men.
37 'For he adds [a]rebellion to his
sin;[2403]
He [b]claps[5606] his hands among
us,
And multiplies his words[561]
against God.' "

Elihu Sharply Reproves Job

35 Then Elihu continued and said,
2 "Do you think[2803] this is
according to [a]justice?[4941]
Do you say,[559] 'My
righteousness[6664] is more
than God's'?
3 "For you say, '[a]What
advantage[5532] will it be to
[I]You?
[b]What profit shall I have, more
than if I had sinned?'[2403]
4 "I will answer[7725] you,
And your friends with you.
5 "[a]Look at the heavens[8064] and
see;
And behold [b]the clouds—[7834]
they are higher than you.
6 "If you have sinned, [a]what do you
accomplish[6213] against Him?

19 [a]Lev. 19:15; Deut. 10:17; 2Chr. 19:7; Acts 10:34; Rom. 2:11; Gal. 2:6; Eph. 6:9; Col. 3:25; 1Pet. 1:17 [b]Job 10:3
20 [a]Ex. 12:29; Job 34:25; 36:20 [b]Job 12:19
21 [a]Job 24:23; 31:4; Prov. 5:21; 15:3; Jer. 16:17
22 [a]Ps. 139:11, 12; Amos 9:2, 3
23 [a]Job 11:11
24 [a]Job 12:19
25 [a]Job 34:11 [b]Job 34:20
26 [I]Lit., *In the place of the ones seeing* [a]Ps. 9:5; 11:5
27 [a]1Sam. 15:11 [b]Job 21:14
28 [a]Job 35:9; James 5:4 [b]Ex. 22:23; Job 22:27
30 [a]Job 5:15; 20:5; 34:17; Prov. 29:2-12
32 [a]Job 33:27
33 [a]Job 41:11
35 [a]Job 35:16; 38:2
36 [I]Or, *to the end* [a]Job 22:15
37 [a]Job 23:2 [b]Job 27:23
2 [a]Job 27:2
3 [I]Or, *you* [a]Job 34:9 [b]Job 9:30, 31
5 [a]Gen. 15:5; Ps. 8:3 [b]Job 22:12
6 [a]Job 7:20; Prov. 8:36; Jer. 7:19

And if your transgressions[6588]
are many, what do you do
to Him?
7 "If you are righteous,[6663]
[a]what do you give to Him?
Or what does He receive from
your hand?[3027]
8 "Your wickedness[7562] is for a
man[376] like yourself,
And your righteousness[6666] is for
a son[1121] of man.[120]
9 "Because of the [a]multitude of
oppressions they cry[2199] out;
They cry for help because of the
arm [b]of the mighty.
10 "But [a]no one says,[559] 'Where is
God[433] my Maker,[6213]
Who [b]gives songs in the
night,[3915]
11 Who [a]teaches[502] us more than
the beasts of the earth,[776]
And makes us wiser[2449] than the
birds of the heavens?'[8064]
12 "There [a]they cry out, but He does
not answer
Because of the pride of evil[7451]
men.
13 "Surely [a]God[410] will not listen[8085]
to [1]an empty[7723] *cry,*
Nor will the Almighty[7706] regard
it.
14 "How much less when [a]you say[559]
you do not behold Him,
The [b]case[1779] is before Him, and
you must wait[2342] for Him!
15 "And now, because He has not
visited[6485] *in* His anger,[639]
Nor has He acknowledged
[1]transgression well,
16 So Job opens his mouth[6310]
[1]emptily;
He multiplies words[4405]
[a]without knowledge."[1847]

Elihu Speaks of God's Dealings with Men

36 Then Elihu continued and said,
2 "Wait for me a little, and
I will show you
That there [1]is yet more to be
said in God's behalf.
3 "I will fetch my knowledge[1843]
from afar,
And I will ascribe
[a]righteousness[6664] to my
Maker.
4 "For truly[551] [a]my words[4405] are
not false;[8267]
One who is [b]perfect[8549] in
knowledge[1844] is with you.
5 "Behold, God[410] is mighty but
does not [a]despise[3988] *any;*
He is [b]mighty in strength of
understanding.[3820]
6 "He does not [a]keep the wicked[7563]
alive,
But gives justice[4941] to
[b]the afflicted.
7 "He does not [a]withdraw His eyes
from the righteous;[6662]
But [b]with kings[4428] on the
throne[3678]
He has seated them forever,[5331]
and they are exalted.
8 "And if they are bound in fetters,
And are caught[3920] in the cords
of [a]affliction,
9 Then He declares[5046] to them
their work
And their transgressions,[6588]
that they have [a]magnified
themselves.
10 "And [a]He opens[1540] their ear[241]
to instruction,[4148]
And [b]commands[559] that they
return[7725] from evil.[205]
11 "If they hear and serve[5647] *Him,*
They shall [a]end[3615] their days in
prosperity,[2896]
And their years in [b]pleasures.
12 "But if they do not hear, they
shall [1]perish [a]by the sword,
And they shall [b]die[1478] without
knowledge.[1847]
13 "But the godless[2611] in heart[3820]
lay up anger;[639]
They do not cry for help when
He binds them.
14 "[1]They die[4191] in youth,
And their life *perishes* among the
[a]cult prostitutes.[6945]
15 "He delivers[2502] the afflicted in
[1]their [a]affliction,

7 [a]Job 22:2, 3; Prov. 9:12; Luke 17:10; Rom. 11:35
9 [a]Ex. 2:23 [b]Job 12:19
10 [a]Job 21:14; 27:10; 36:13; Is. 51:13 [b]Job 8:21; Ps. 42:8; 77:6; 149:5; Acts 16:25
11 [a]Job 36:22; Ps. 94:12; Jer. 32:33
12 [a]Prov. 1:28
13 [1]Or, *falsehood* [a]Job 27:9; Prov. 15:29; Is. 1:15; Jer. 11:11; Mic. 3:4
14 [a]Job 9:11; 23:8, 9 [b]Job 31:35
15 [1]Or, *arrogance*
16 [1]Lit., *vainly* [a]Job 34:35; 38:2
2 [1]Lit., *are yet words for God*
3 [a]Job 8:3; 37:23
4 [a]Job 33:3 [b]Job 37:16
5 [a]Ps. 22:24; 69:33; 102:17 [b]Job 12:13
6 [a]Job 8:22; 34:26 [b]Job 5:15
7 [a]Ps. 33:18; 34:15 [b]Job 5:11; Ps. 113:8
8 [a]Job 36:15, 21
9 [a]Job 15:25
10 [a]Job 33:16; 36:15 [b]2Kin. 17:13; Job 36:21; Jon. 3:8
11 [a]1Tim. 4:8 [b]Ps. 16:11
12 [1]Lit., *pass away* [a]Job 15:22 [b]Job 4:21
14 [1]Or, *Their soul dies* [a]Deut. 23:17
15 [1]Lit., *his* [a]Job 36:8, 21

And [b]opens their ear[241]
[II]in *time of* oppression.
16 "Then indeed, He [a]enticed you
from the mouth of
distress,6862
Instead of it, a broad place with
no constraint;
And that which was set on your
table was full of [I]fatness.
17 "But you were full of [a]judgment
on the wicked;
Judgment[1779] and justice take
hold *of you.*
18 "*Beware* lest [a]wrath[2534] entice
you to scoffing;
And do not let the greatness of
the [b]ransom[3724] turn you
aside.
19 "Will your [I]riches keep *you* from
distress,
Or all the forces of *your*
strength?
20 "Do not long for [a]the night,[3915]
When people[5971] [I]vanish in their
place.
21 "Be careful,[8104] do [a]not turn to
evil;
For you have preferred[977] this
to [b]affliction.
22 "Behold, God is exalted7682 in His
power;
Who is a [a]teacher[3384] like Him?
23 "Who has appointed[6485] Him His
way,[1870]
And who has said,[559] '[a]Thou hast
done wrong'?[5766]
24 "Remember[2142] that you should
[a]exalt His work,
Of which men[582] have
[b]sung.[7891]
25 "All men[120] have seen it;
Man[582] beholds from afar.
26 "Behold, God is [a]exalted, and
[b]we do not know[3045]
Him;
The [c]number of His years is
unsearchable.
27 "For [a]He draws up the drops of
water,
They distill[2212] rain from
[I]the [II]mist,
28 Which the clouds pour down,
They drip7491 upon man
abundantly.
29 "Can anyone understand[995]
the [a]spreading of the
clouds,
The [b]thundering of His
[I]pavilion?[5521]
30 "Behold, He spreads His
[I]lightning[216] about Him,
And He covers[3680] the depths
of the sea.
31 "For by these He [a]judges
peoples;
He [b]gives food in abundance.
32 "He covers *His* hands[3709] with the
[I]lightning,
And [a]commands[6680] it to strike
the mark.
33 "Its [a]noise declares [I]His
presence;
The cattle also, concerning what
is coming up.

Elihu Says God Is Back of the Storm

37 "At this also my heart[3820]
trembles,[2729]
And leaps from its place.
2 "Listen closely[8085] to the
[a]thunder[7267] of His voice,
And the rumbling[1899] that goes
out from His mouth.[6310]
3 "Under the whole heaven[8064] He
lets it loose,[3474]
And His [I]lightning to the
[a]ends of the earth.[776]
4 "After it, a voice roars;
He thunders with His majestic
voice;
And He does not restrain[6117]
[I]the lightnings when His voice
is heard.[8085]
5 "God[410] [a]thunders with His voice
wondrously,[6381]
Doing[6213] [b]great things which we
cannot comprehend.[3045]
6 "For to [a]the snow He says,[559]
'Fall on the earth,'
And to the [I][b]downpour and the
rain, 'Be strong.'

---

15 [II]Or, *in adversity* [b]Job 36:10
16 [I]Or, *rich food* [a]Hos. 2:14
17 [a]Job 22:5, 10, 11
18 [a]Jon. 4:4, 9 [b]Job 33:24
19 [I]Or, *cry*
20 [I]Lit., *go up* [a]Job 34:20, 25
21 [a]Job 36:10; Ps. 31:6; 66:18 [b]Job 36:8, 15; Heb. 11:25
22 [a]Job 35:11
23 [a]Deut. 32:4; Job 8:3
24 [a]Ps. 92:5; Rev. 15:3 [b]Ex. 15:1; Judg. 5:1; 1Chr. 16:9; Ps. 59:16; 138:5
26 [a]Job 11:7-9; 37:23 [b]1Cor. 13:12 [c]Job 10:5; Ps. 90:2; 102:24, 27; Heb. 1:12
27 [I]Lit., *its* [II]Or, *flood* [a]Job 5:10; 36:26-29; 37:6, 11; 38:28; Ps. 147:8
29 [I]Lit., *booth* [a]Job 37:11, 16 [b]Job 26:14
30 [I]Lit., *light*
31 [a]Job 37:13 [b]Ps. 104:27; 136:25; Acts 14:17
32 [I]Lit., *light* [a]Job 37:11, 12, 15
33 [I]Lit., *concerning Him* [a]Job 37:2
2 [a]Job 36:33; 37:4, 5; Ps. 29:3-9
3 [I]Lit., *light* [a]Job 28:24; 37:11, 12; 38:13
4 [I]Lit., *them*
5 [a]Job 26:14 [b]Job 5:9; 37:14, 16, 23
6 [I]Lit., *shower of rain and shower of rains* [a]Job 38:22 [b]Job 36:27

7 "He [a]seals the hand[3027] of every
man,[120]
That [b]all men[582] may know[3045]
His work.
8 "Then the beast[2416] goes into its
[a]lair,
And remains in its [I]den.
9 "Out of the [Ia]south comes the
storm,
And out of the [II]north the cold.
10 "From the breath[5397] of God
[a]ice is made,
And the expanse of the waters
is frozen.[4164]
11 "Also with moisture He
[a]loads the thick cloud;
He [b]disperses [c]the cloud[6051] of
His [I]lightning.[216]
12 "And it changes direction,
turning[2015] around by His
guidance,
That [I]it may do whatever He
[a]commands[6680] [II]it
On the [b]face of the inhabited
earth.[8398]
13 "Whether for [Ia]correction, or for
[b]His world,[776]
Or for [c]lovingkindness,[2617] He
causes it to [II]happen.
14 "Listen[238] to this, O Job,
Stand and consider[995] the
wonders[6381] of God.
15 "Do you know how God[433]
establishes[7760] them,
And makes the [I]lightning[216] of
His cloud to shine?
16 "Do you know about the layers
of the thick clouds,
The [a]wonders of one [b]perfect[8549]
in knowledge,[1843]
17 You whose garments are hot,
When the land is still[8252] because
of the south wind?

7 [a]Job 12:14 [b]Ps. 111:2
8 [I]Lit., *dens* [a]Job 38:40; Ps. 104:21, 22
9 [I]Lit., *chamber* [II]Lit., *scattering winds* [a]Job 9:9
10 [a]Job 38:29; Ps. 147:17
11 [I]Lit., *light* [a]Job 36:27 [b]Job 36:29 [c]Job 37:15
12 [I]Lit., *they* [II]Lit., *them* [a]Job 36:32; Ps. 148:8 [b]Is. 14:21; 27:6
13 [I]Lit., *the rod* [II]Lit., *be found* [a]Ex. 9:18, 23; 1Sam. 12:18, 19 [b]Job 38:26, 27 [c]1Kin. 18:41-46
15 [I]Lit., *light*
16 [a]Job 37:5, 14, 23 [b]Job 36:4
18 [a]Job 9:8; Ps. 104:2; Is. 44:24; 45:12; Jer. 10:12; Zech. 12:1
19 [a]Job 9:14; Rom. 8:26
20 [I]Or, *If a man speak, surely he shall be swallowed up*
21 [I]Lit., *they*
23 [a]Job 11:7, 8; Rom. 11:33; 1Tim. 6:16 [b]Job 9:4; 36:5 [c]Is. 63:9; Lam. 3:33; Ezek. 18:23, 32; 33:11 [d]Job 8:3
24 [a]Matt. 10:28 [b]Job 5:13; Matt. 11:25; 1Cor. 1:26

1 [a]Job 40:6
2 [a]Job 35:16; 42:3
3 [a]Job 40:7

18 "Can you, with Him, [a]spread[7554]
out the skies,[7834]
Strong[2389] as a molten
mirror?[7209]
19 "Teach[3045] us what we shall say[559]
to Him;
We [a]cannot arrange *our case*
because of darkness.[2822]
20 "Shall it be told[5608] Him that I
would speak?[1696]
[I]Or should a man[376] say[559] that
he would be swallowed
up?[1104]
21 "And now [I]men do not see the
light which is bright in the
skies;[7834]
But the wind[7307] has passed[5674]
and cleared[2891] them.
22 "Out of the north comes golden
splendor;
Around God is awesome[3372]
majesty.[1935]
23 "The Almighty—[7706] [a]we cannot
find Him;
He is [b]exalted in power;
And [c]He will not do violence
[d]to justice[4941] and abundant
righteousness.[6666]
24 "Therefore men [a]fear[3372] Him;
He does not [b]regard any who
are wise[2450] of heart."

God Speaks Now to Job

38 🗝 Then the LORD [a]answered
Job out of the whirlwind and
said,[559]
2 "Who is this that [a]darkens[2821]
counsel[6098]
By words[4405] without
knowledge?[1847]
3 "Now [a]gird up your loins like a
man,[1397]

🗝 **38:1—41:34** In making his defense, Job, though innocent of the sin of which he had been accused, had presumed to be able to explain God's actions. God stated that he had spoken "without knowledge," and proceeded to ask Job a series of rhetorical questions, as if to say, "Who are you to explain why I do things in a certain way? Were you there?" It is interesting to note that He makes no mention of the foregoing discussion about suffering and innocence. Perhaps God used the rhetorical question to emphasize the distance between man and his Creator and, therefore, man's inability to understand even if God explained it to man. Though man cannot understand, there is one thing he can do—he can trust his Creator.

And [b]I will ask[7592] you, and you
instruct Me!
4 "Where were you [a]when I laid
the foundation[3245] of the
earth?[776]
Tell[5046] *Me,* if you [I]have
understanding,[998]
5 Who set[7760] its [a]measurements,
since you know?[3045]
Or who stretched the line on it?
6 "On what [a]were its bases sunk?
Or who laid[3384] its cornerstone,
7 When the morning stars sang
together,
And all the [a]sons[1121] of God[430]
shouted for joy?[7321]
8 "Or *who* [a]enclosed the sea with
doors,
When, bursting forth, it went out
from the womb;
9 When I made[7760] a cloud[6051] its
garment,
And thick darkness[6205] its
swaddling band,2854
10 And I [Ia]placed boundaries on
it,
And I set[7760] a bolt and doors,
11 And I said, 'Thus far you shall
come, but no farther;
And here shall your proud waves
stop'?

God's Mighty Power

12 "Have you [I]ever in your life
commanded[6680] the morning,
And caused the dawn to
know[3045] its place;
13 That it might take hold of
[a]the ends of the earth,
And [b]the wicked[7563] be shaken
out of it?
14 "It is changed[2015] like clay *under*
the seal;
And they stand forth like a
garment.
15 "And [a]from the wicked their
light[216] is withheld,4513
And the [b]uplifted arm is
broken.[7665]
16 "Have you entered into
[a]the springs of the sea?

3 [b]Job 42:4
4 [I]Lit., *know understanding* [a]Job 15:7; Ps. 104:5; Prov. 8:29; 30:4
5 [a]Prov. 8:29; Is. 40:12
6 [a]Job 26:7
7 [a]Job 1:6
8 [a]Gen. 1:9; Ps. 104:6-9; Prov. 8:29; Jer. 5:22
10 [I]Lit., *broke My decree on it* [a]Gen. 1:9; Ps. 33:7; 104:9; Prov. 8:29; Jer. 5:22
12 [I]Lit., *from your days*
13 [a]Job 28:24; 37:3 [b]Job 34:25, 26; 36:6
15 [a]Job 5:14 [b]Num. 15:30; Ps. 10:15; 37:17
16 [I]Or, *in search of* [a]Gen. 7:11; 8:2; Prov. 8:24, 28
17 [a]Job 10:21; 26:6; 34:22
18 [I]Or, *width* [a]Job 28:24
20 [I]Lit., *house* [a]Job 26:10
21 [a]Job 15:7
22 [a]Job 37:6 [b]Ex. 9:18; Josh. 10:11; Is. 30:30; Ezek. 13:11, 13; Rev. 16:21
24 [a]Job 26:10
26 [I]Lit., *man* [a]Job 36:27
27 [I]Or, *growth* [a]Ps. 104:13, 14; 107:35
28 [a]Job 36:27, 28; Ps. 147:8; Jer. 14:22
29 [a]Job 37:10; Ps. 147:17
30 [I]Lit., *hides itself*

Or have you walked [I]in the
recesses of the deep?
17 "Have the gates of death[4194] been
revealed to you?
Or have you seen[7200] the gates
of [a]deep darkness?[6757]
18 "Have you understood[995] the
[I]expanse of [a]the earth?
Tell *Me,* if you know all
this.
19 "Where is the way[1870] to the
dwelling[7931] of light?
And darkness,[2822] where is its
place,
20 That you may take it to
[a]its territory,
And that you may discern[995] the
paths to its [I]home?[1004]
21 "You know, for [a]you were born
then,
And the number of your days
is great!
22 "Have you entered the
storehouses [a]of the snow,
Or have you seen the
storehouses of the [b]hail,
23 Which I have reserved for the
time[6256] of distress,
For the day[3117] of war and battle?
24 "Where is the way that
[a]the light is divided,
Or the east wind scattered on
the earth?
25 "Who has cleft[6385] a channel for
the flood,[7858]
Or a way for the thunderbolt;
26 To bring [a]rain on a land without
[I]people,[376]
On a desert without a man[120]
in it,
27 To [a]satisfy the waste[7722] and
desolate land,
And to make the [I]seeds of grass
to sprout?
28 "Has [a]the rain a father?[1]
Or who has begotten3205 the
drops of dew?
29 "From whose womb[990] has come
the [a]ice?
And the frost3713 of heaven,[8064]
who has given it birth?
30 "Water [I]becomes hard like stone,

And the surface of the deep is
imprisoned.
31 "Can you bind the chains of the
[a]Pleiades,
Or loose the cords of Orion?
32 "Can you lead forth a
[I]constellation in its
season,[6256]
And guide[5148] the Bear with her
[II]satellites?
33 "Do you know the [a]ordinances[2708]
of the heavens,
Or fix their rule over the earth?
34 "Can you lift up your voice to the
clouds,
So that an [a]abundance of water
may cover[3680] you?
35 "Can you [a]send forth lightnings
that they may go
And say[559] to you, 'Here we
are'?
36 "Who has [a]put wisdom[2451] in the
innermost being,
Or has given [b]understanding to
the [I]mind?[7907]
37 "Who can count[5608] the clouds[7834]
by wisdom,
Or [a]tip the water jars of the
heavens,
38 When the dust[6083] hardens into
a mass,
And the clods stick together?
39 "Can you hunt the [a]prey for the
lion,
Or satisfy the appetite of the
young lions,
40 When they [a]crouch in *their* dens,
And lie in wait in *their* lair?[5521]
41 "Who prepares for [a]the raven its
nourishment,
When its young cry to God,[410]
And wander[8582] about without
food?

God Speaks of Nature and Its Beings

39 "Do you know[3045] the time[6256]
the [Ia]mountain goats give
birth?
Do you observe[8104] the
calving[2342] of the [b]deer?[355]
2 "Can you count[5608] the months
they fulfill,
Or do you know the time they
give birth?
3 "They kneel down,[3766] they bring
forth their young,
They get rid of their labor pains.
4 "Their offspring[1121] become
strong, they grow up in the
open field;
They leave and do not return[7725]
to them.
5 "Who sent out the [a]wild donkey
free?
And who loosed the bonds of
the swift donkey,
6 To whom I gave[7760] [a]the
wilderness[6160] for a home,[1004]
And the salt[4420] land for his
dwelling place?[4908]
7 "He scorns the tumult of the city,
The shoutings of the driver he
does not hear.
8 "He explores the mountains for
his pasture,
And he searches after every
green thing.
9 "Will the [a]wild ox consent[14] to
serve[5647] you?
Or will he spend the night at
your manger?[18]
10 "Can you bind the wild ox in a
furrow[8525] with [I]ropes?
Or will he harrow[7702] the valleys
after you?
11 "Will you trust[982] him because his
strength is great
And leave[5800] your labor to him?
12 "Will you have faith[539] in him
that he will return your
[I]grain,[2233]
And gather[622] *it from* your
threshing floor?
13 "The ostriches' wings flap
joyously
With the pinion and plumage of
[I]love,
14 For she abandons her eggs to
the earth,[776]
And warms them in the dust,[6083]
15 And she forgets that a foot may
crush [I]them,

31 [a]Job 9:9; Amos 5:8
32 [I]Heb., *Mazzaroth* [II]Lit., *sons*
33 [a]Ps. 148:6; Jer. 31:35, 36
34 [a]Job 22:11; 36:27, 28; 38:37
35 [a]Job 36:32; 37:3
36 [I]Or, *cock* [a]Job 9:4; Ps. 51:6; Eccl. 2:26 [b]Job 32:8
37 [a]Job 38:34
39 [a]Ps. 104:21
40 [a]Job 37:8
41 [a]Ps. 147:9; Matt. 6:26; Luke 12:24
1 [I]Lit., *goats of the rock* [a]Deut. 14:5; 1Sam. 24:2; Ps. 104:18 [b]Ps. 29:9
5 [a]Job 6:5; 11:12; 24:5; Ps. 104:11
6 [a]Job 24:5; Jer. 2:24; Hos. 8:9
9 [a]Num. 23:22; Deut. 33:17; Ps. 22:21; 29:6; 92:10; Is. 34:7
10 [I]Lit., *his rope*
12 [I]Lit., *seed*
13 [I]Or, *a stork*
15 [I]Lit., *it*

Or that a wild beast[2416] may
trample [I]them.
16 "She treats her young
[a]cruelly,[7188] as if *they* were
not hers;
Though her labor be in vain, *she*
is [I]unconcerned;[1097,6343]
17 Because God[433] has made her
forget wisdom,[2451]
And has not given her a share
of understanding.[998]
18 "When she lifts[5375] herself
[I]on high,
She laughs at the horse and his
rider.
19 "Do you give the horse *his* might?
Do you clothe his neck with a
mane?
20 "Do you make him [a]leap[7493] like
the locust?
His majestic[1935] [b]snorting is
terrible.[367]
21 "[I]He paws in the valley, and
rejoices in *his* strength;
He [a]goes out to meet the
weapons.
22 "He laughs at fear and is not
dismayed;[2865]
And he does not turn back from
the sword.[2719]
23 "The quiver rattles against
him,
The flashing spear and javelin.
24 "With shaking and rage[7267] he
[I]races over the ground;[776]
And he does not stand still[539]
at the voice of the trumpet.
25 "As often as the trumpet *sounds*
he says,[559] 'Aha!'
And he scents[7306] the battle from
afar,
And thunder of the captains,[8269]
and the war cry.
26 "Is it by your understanding[998]
that the hawk soars,
Stretching his wings toward the
south?
27 "Is it at your [I]command that the
eagle mounts up,
And makes [a]his nest on high?
28 "On the cliff he dwells[7931] and
lodges,
Upon the rocky crag, an
inaccessible place.
29 "From there he [a]spies out food;
His eyes see *it* from afar.
30 "His young ones also suck up
blood;[1818]
And [a]where the slain[2491] are,
there is he."

Job: What Can I Say?

40 Then the LORD said[559] to Job,
2 "Will the faultfinder
[a]contend[7378] with the
Almighty?[7706]
Let him who [b]reproves[3198]
God[433] answer it."
3 Then Job answered the LORD and
said,
4 "Behold, I am insignificant;[7043]
what can I reply[7725] to Thee?
I [a]lay[7760] my hand[3027] on my
mouth.[6310]
5 "Once I have spoken,[1696] and
[a]I will not answer;
Even twice, and I will add no
more."

God Questions Job

6 Then the [a]LORD answered Job out
of the storm, and said,
7 "Now [a]gird up your loins like a
man;[1397]
I will [b]ask[7592] you, and you
instruct Me.
8 "Will you really [a]annul[6565] My
judgment?[4941]
Will you [b]condemn[7561] Me
[c]that you may be justified?[6663]
9 "Or do you have an arm like
God,[410]
And can you [a]thunder with a
voice like His?
10 "[a]Adorn yourself with eminence
and dignity;
And clothe yourself with
honor[1935] and majesty.[1926]
11 "Pour out [a]the overflowings[5678]
of your anger;[639]
And look[7200] on everyone who
is [b]proud, and make him
low.[8213]

---

15 [I]Lit., *it*
16 [I]Lit., *without fear* [a]Lam. 4:3
18 [I]Or, *to flee*
20 [a]Joel 2:5 [b]Jer. 8:16
21 [I]Lit., *They paw* [a]Jer. 8:6
24 [I]Or, *swallows up*
27 [I]Lit., *mouth* [a]Jer. 49:16; Obad.4
29 [a]Job 9:26
30 [a]Matt. 24:28; Luke 17:37
2 [a]Job 9:3; 10:2; 33:13; Is. 45:9 [b]Job 13:3; 23:4; 31:35
4 [a]Job 21:5; 29:9
5 [a]Job 9:3, 15
6 [a]Job 38:1
7 [a]Job 38:3 [b]Job 38:3; 42:4
8 [a]Rom. 3:4 [b]Job 10:3, 7; 16:11; 19:6; 27:2 [c]Job 13:18; 27:6
9 [a]Job 37:5; Ps. 29:3
10 [a]Ps. 93:1; 104:1
11 [a]Is. 42:25; Nah. 1:6, 8 [b]Is. 2:12; Dan. 4:37

12 "Look on everyone who is proud, *and* [a]humble him;
And [b]tread down the wicked[7563] [I]where they stand.
13 "[a]Hide them in the dust[6083] together;
Bind[2280] [I]them in the hidden *place.*
14 "Then I will also [I]confess[3034] to you,
That your own right hand can save[3467] you.

God's Power Shown in Creatures

15 "Behold now, [I]Behemoth, which [a]I made[6213] [II]as well as you;
He eats grass like an ox.
16 "Behold now, his strength in his loins,
And his power in the muscles of his belly.[990]
17 "He bends his tail like a cedar;
The sinews of his thighs are knit together.
18 "His bones[6106] are tubes of bronze;
His [I]limbs are like bars of iron.
19 "He is the [a]first of the ways[1870] of God;
Let his [b]maker bring near[5066] his sword.[2719]
20 "Surely the mountains [a]bring[5375] him food,
And all the beasts[2416] of the field[7704] [b]play there.
21 "Under the lotus plants he lies down,
In the covert[5643] of the reeds and the marsh.[1207]
22 "The lotus plants cover him with [I]shade;[6752]
The willows of the brook surround him.
23 "If a river [I]rages, he is not alarmed;
He is confident,[982] though the [a]Jordan rushes to his mouth.
24 "Can anyone capture him [I]when he is on watch,
With [II]barbs[4170] can anyone pierce[5344] *his* nose?[639]

12 [I]Lit., *under them* [a]1Sam. 2:7; Is. 2:12; 13:11; Dan. 4:37 [b]Is. 63:3
13 [I]Or, *their faces* [a]Is. 2:10-12
14 [I]Or, *praise you*
15 [I]Or, *the hippopotamus* [II]Lit., *with* [a]Job 40:19
18 [I]Lit., *bones*
19 [a]Job 41:33 [b]Job 40:15
20 [a]Ps. 104:14 [b]Ps. 104:26
22 [I]Lit., *his shade*
23 [I]Or, *oppresses* [a]Gen. 13:10
24 [I]Lit., *in his eyes* [II]Lit., *snares*
1 [I]Ch. 40:25 in Heb. [II]Or, *the crocodile* [a]Job 3:8; Ps. 74:14; 104:26; Is. 27:1
2 [I]Lit., *rope of rushes* [II]Or, *thorn* or *ring* [a]2Kin. 19:28; Is. 37:29
6 [I]Lit., *partners*
8 [I]Lit., *do not add*
9 [I]Ch. 41:1 in Heb. [II]Lit., *his* [III]Lit., *he*
10 [a]Job 3:8
11 [I]Lit., *anticipated* [a]Rom. 11:35 [b]Ex. 19:5; Deut. 10:14; Job 9:5-10; 26:6-14; 28:24; Ps. 24:1; 50:12; 1Cor. 10:26
12 [I]Or, *graceful*
13 [I]Lit., *uncover the face of his garment*

God's Power Shown in Creatures

41 "[I]Can you draw out [II][a]Leviathan with a fishhook?
Or press down his tongue with a cord?[2256]
2 "Can you [a]put a [I]rope in his nose?[639]
Or pierce his jaw with a [II]hook?
3 "Will he make many supplications[8469] to you?
Or will he speak[1696] to you soft words?
4 "Will he make a covenant[1285] with you?
Will you take him for a servant[5650] forever?[5769]
5 "Will you play with him as with a bird?
Or will you bind him for your maidens?
6 "Will the [I]traders bargain over him?
Will they divide him among the merchants?
7 "Can you fill his skin[5785] with harpoons,
Or his head[7218] with fishing[1709] spears?
8 "Lay[7760] your hand[3709] on him;
Remember[2142] the battle;
[I]you will not do it again!
9 "[I]Behold, [II]your expectation[8431] is false;[3576]
Will [III]you be laid low even at the sight of him?
10 "No one is so fierce that he dares to [a]arouse him;
Who then is he that can stand before Me?
11 "Who has [I][a]given to Me that I should repay[7999] *him?*
Whatever is [b]under the whole heaven[8064] is Mine.
12 "I will not keep silence concerning his limbs,
Or his mighty strength, or his [I]orderly[2433] frame.
13 "Who can [I]strip off[1540] his outer armor?

Who can come within his double
[II]mail?
14 "Who can open the doors of his
face?
Around his teeth there is
terror.[367]
15 "*His* [I]strong scales are *his* pride,
Shut up *as with* a tight seal.
16 "One is so near[5066] to another,
That no air can come between
them.
17 "They are joined one[376] to
another;
They clasp each other and
cannot be separated.6504
18 "His sneezes flash forth light,[216]
And his eyes are like the
[a]eyelids of the morning.
19 "Out of his mouth[6310] go burning
torches;
Sparks of fire leap forth.[4422]
20 "Out of his nostrils smoke goes
forth,
As *from* a boiling pot and *burning*
rushes.
21 "His breath[5315] kindles coals,
And a flame goes forth from his
mouth.
22 "In his neck lodges strength,
And dismay leaps before
him.
23 "The folds of his flesh[1320] are
joined together,
Firm on him and immovable.
24 "His heart[3820] is as hard as a
stone;
Even as hard as a lower8482
millstone.
25 "When he raises himself up, the
[I]mighty[410] fear;[1481]
Because of the crashing[7667] they
are bewildered.[2398]
26 "The sword[2719] that reaches him
cannot avail;
Nor the spear, the dart, or the
javelin.8302
27 "He regards[2803] iron as straw,
Bronze as rotten wood.
28 "The [I]arrow cannot make him
flee;
Slingstones are turned[2015] into
stubble for him.

13 [II]So Gr.; Heb., *bridle*

15 [I]Lit., *rows of shields*

18 [a]Job 3:9

25 [I]Or, *gods*

28 [I]Lit., *son of the bow*

30 [I]Or, *moves across*

33 [I]Lit., *dust* [a]Job 40:19

34 [I]Ch. 41:26 in Heb. [a]Job 28:8

2 [a]Gen. 18:14; Matt. 19:26

3 [a]Job 38:2 [b]Ps. 40:5; 131:1; 139:6

4 [a]Job 38:3; 40:7

5 [a]Job 26:14; Rom. 10:17 [b]Is. 6:5; Eph. 1:17, 18

29 "Clubs are regarded[2803] as
stubble;
He laughs at the rattling of the
javelin.
30 "His underparts are *like* sharp
potsherds;[2789]
He [I]spreads out *like* a threshing
sledge on the mire.
31 "He makes the depths boil like
a pot;
He makes[7760] the sea like a jar
of ointment.
32 "Behind him he makes a wake
to shine;
One would think[2803] the deep to
be gray-haired.[7872]
33 "[a]Nothing on [I]earth[6083] is like
him,
One made[6213] without fear.
34 "[I]He looks[7200] on everything that
is high;
He is king[4428] over all the
[a]sons[1121] of pride."

Job's Confession

42 Then Job answered the LORD,
and said,[559]
2 "I know[3045] that [a]Thou canst do
all things,
And that no purpose[4209] of Thine
can be thwarted.1219
3 'Who is this that [a]hides
counsel[6098] without
knowledge?'[3045]
"Therefore I have declared[5046]
that which I did not
understand,[995]
Things [b]too wonderful[6381] for
me, which I did not
know."[3045]
4 'Hear,[8085] now, and I will
speak;[1696]
I will [a]ask[7592] Thee, and do Thou
instruct me.'
5 "I have [a]heard[8085] of Thee by the
hearing[8088] of the ear;[241]
But now my [b]eye sees[7200] Thee;
6 Therefore I retract,
And I repent[5162] in dust[6083] and
ashes."

God Displeased with Job's Friends

7 And it came about after the LORD had spoken[1696] these words[1697] to Job, that the LORD said to Eliphaz the Temanite, "My wrath[639] is kindled[2734] against you and against your two friends,[7453] because you have not spoken of Me what is right [a]as My servant[5650] Job has.

8 "Now therefore, take for yourselves [a]seven bulls and seven rams, and go to My servant Job, and offer up a [b]burnt offering[5930] for yourselves, and My servant Job will [c]pray[6419] for you. [d]For I will [I]accept[5375] him so that I may not do[6213] with you *according to your* folly, because you have not spoken of Me what is right, as My servant Job has."

9 So Eliphaz the Temanite and Bildad the Shuhite *and* Zophar the Naamathite went and did[6213] as the LORD told[1696] them; and the LORD [I]accepted[5375] Job.

God Restores Job's Fortunes

10 And the LORD [a]restored the fortunes[7622] of Job when he prayed[6419] for his friends, and the LORD increased all that Job had twofold.

11 Then all his [a]brothers,[251] and all his sisters,[269] and all who had known him[3045] before, came to him, and they ate bread with him in his house;[1004] and they [b]consoled him and comforted[5162] him for all the evil[7451] that the LORD had brought on him. And each one[376] gave him one [I]piece of money, and each[376] a ring of gold.

12 [a]And the LORD blessed[1288] the latter[319] *days* of Job more than his beginning,[7225] [b]and he had 14,000 sheep, and 6,000 camels, and 1,000 yoke of oxen, and 1,000 female donkeys.

13 And [a]he had seven sons[1121] and three daughters.

14 And he named[7121] the first[7223] Jemimah, and the second Keziah, and the third Keren-happuch.

15 And in all the land[776] no women[802] were found so fair as Job's daughters; and their father[1] gave them inheritance[5159] among their brothers.

16 And after this Job lived[2421] 140 years, and saw[7200] his sons, and his grandsons, four generations.[1755]

17 [a]And Job died,[4191] an old[2205] man and full of days.

7 [a]Job 40:3-5; 42:1-6
8 [I]Lit., *lift up his face* [a]Num. 23:1 [b]Job 1:5 [c]Gen. 20:17; James 5:16; 1John 5:16 [d]Job 22:30
9 [I]Lit., *lifted up the face of*
10 [a]Deut. 30:3; Job 1:2, 3; Ps. 14:7; 85:1-3; 126:1-6
11 [I]Heb., *qesitah* [a]Job 19:13 [b]Job 2:11
12 [a]Job 1:10; 8:7; James 5:11 [b]Job 1:3
13 [a]Job 1:2
17 [a]Gen. 15:15; 25:8; Job 5:26

THE PSALMS

The name "Psalms" comes from the Greek *Psalmoi* which means "songs." Sometimes the book is called the Psalter. It has been called the "Hebrew Prayer and Praise Book." It was the first book in the third main division of the Old Testament which is called the Writings (see Lk. 24:44).

The Book of Psalms may very well be the most beloved book of the Old Testament! It was the hymnbook and prayer book of Israel and later of the early Christians. It has provided people with much comfort in times of trouble, as well as in private and public worship.

The Psalms were written by different authors over a long period of time. Of the 150 Psalms, seventy-three were ascribed to David, forty-nine are anonymous, twelve were written by Asaph, twelve by the sons of Korah, two by Solomon, one by Moses, and one by Ethan.

The collection is arranged in five books: Book I (Ps. 1—41); Book II (Ps. 42—72); Book III (Ps. 73—89); Book IV (Ps. 90—106); Book V (Ps. 107—150). There are sub-groups here and there within Psalms: the psalms of Korah's sons (Ps. 42—49); the michtam psalms (Ps. 56—60); the psalms of Asaph (Ps. 73—83); and the songs of degrees (Ps. 120—134). The longest psalm is Psalm 119 with 176 verses. It is also the longest chapter in the entire Bible. In this particular psalm, each character of the Hebrew alphabet (from aleph to tau) begins a verse in each section of eight verses. The shortest psalm is Psalm 117.

There was a wide variety of purposes and occasions which prompted the writing of the various types of psalms. Some are national in scope and some are intimately personal. Some are exultant and some are forlorn. Seeing that there is a tremendous range of human emotion expressed in the Psalms (both collectively and individually), it is no wonder that Psalms has been so popular through the ages. There is something there for everyone: temple hymns, royal psalms which anticipated Christ as Messianic King, imprecatory wishes, aspirations, struggles, deep contrition, feelings of deliverance, outpourings of prayer to God, worship, confession, inner conflicts, pleas for help and protection, and songs of thanksgiving for God's blessings.

In the New Testament there are 283 quotations from the Old Testament; 116 of them are from the Book of Psalms alone! Jesus loved the Psalms. Even while dying on the cross, Jesus quoted from them (Mt. 27:46; Lk. 23:46). Messianic predictions abound regarding His suffering, death, resurrection, and final victory in glory.

The Psalms are especially useful for all of us today. The book emphasizes the following things: There is only one God. He is ever-present, all-powerful, and infinitely wise.

We must all recognize the universality of God's love, His providence, and His goodness. He is sovereign and we must obey Him unfalteringly with reverence. Idols are empty, false, and abominable. Sin is horrible and God hates it. He will execute judgment upon sinners. But God is also merciful and forgiving, and if man is truly penitent and submissive great joy will result. Some psalms stress the beauty of God's holiness and a deep personal relationship with God.

The following expressions occur often in the Psalms:

Selah	May mean *Pause, Crescendo* or *Musical Interlude*
Maskil	Possibly, *Contemplative,* or *Didactic,* or *Skillful Psalm*
Mikhtam	Possibly, *Epigrammatic Poem,* or *Atonement Psalm*
Sheol	The nether world

BOOK 1

The Righteous and the Wicked Contrasted

1 🔑 How blessed[835] is the man[376]
who [a]does not walk in the
[b]counsel of the wicked,[7563]
Nor stand in the [Ic]path[1870] of
sinners,[2400]
Nor [d]sit in the seat[4186] of
scoffers![3887]
2 But his [a]delight[2656] is [b]in the
law[8451] of the LORD,
And in His law he meditates[1897]
[c]day[3119] and [d]night.[3915]
3 And he will be like [a]a tree *firmly*
planted by [I]streams of water,
Which yields its fruit in its
season,[6256]
And its [II]leaf does not wither;
And [III]in whatever he does,[6213]
[b]he prospers.
4 The wicked are not so,
But they are like [a]chaff which
the wind[7307] drives away.
5 Therefore [a]the wicked will not
stand in the [b]judgment,[4941]
Nor sinners in [c]the assembly[5712]
of the righteous.[6662]
6 For the LORD [Ia]knows the way
of the righteous,
But the way of [b]the wicked will
perish.[6]

The Reign of the LORD's Anointed

2 🔑 Why are [a]the [I]nations[1471] in an
uproar,[7283]
And the peoples[3816] [b]devising[1897]
a vain thing?
2 The [a]kings[4428] of the earth[776]
take their stand,

1 [I]Or, *way* [a]Prov. 4:14 [b]Ps. 5:9, 10; 10:2-11; 36:1-4 [c]Ps. 17:4; 119:104 [d]Ps. 26:4, 5; Jer. 15:17
2 [a]Ps. 119:14, 16, 35 [b]Josh. 1:8 [c]Ps. 25:5 [d]Ps. 63:5, 6
3 [I]Or, *canals* [II]Or, *foliage* [III]Or, *all that he does prospers* [a]Ps. 92:12-14; Jer. 17:8; Ezek. 19:10 [b]Gen. 39:2, 3, 23; Ps. 128:2
4 [a]Job 21:18; Ps. 35:5; Is. 17:13
5 [a]Ps. 5:5 [b]Ps. 9:7, 8, 16 [c]Ps. 89:5, 7
6 [I]Or, *approves* or *has regard to* [a]Ps. 37:18; Nah. 1:7; John 10:14; 2Tim. 2:19 [b]Ps. 9:5, 6; 11:6

1 [I]Or, *Gentiles* [a]Ps. 46:6; 83:2-5; Acts 4:25, 26 [b]Ps. 21:11
2 [I]Or, *Messiah* [a]Ps. 48:4-6 [b]Ps. 74:18, 23 [c]John 1:41
3 [a]Jer. 5:5
4 [I]Or, *is enthroned* [a]Ps. 37:13 [b]Ps. 59:8
5 [a]Ps. 21:8, 9; 76:7 [b]Ps. 78:49, 50
6 [I]Or, *consecrated* [a]Ps. 45:6 [b]Ps. 48:1, 2
7 [I]Or, *decree: The LORD said to Me* [a]Acts 13:33; Heb. 1:5; 5:5
8 [I]Or, *Gentiles* [a]Ps. 21:1, 2 [b]Ps. 22:27 [c]Ps. 67:7
9 [I]Another reading is *rule* [II]Or, *scepter* or *staff* [III]Lit., *potter's ware*

And the rulers[7336] take
counsel[3245] together
[b]Against the LORD and against
His [Ic]Anointed:[4899]
3 "Let us [a]tear their fetters apart,
And cast away their cords from
us!"
4 He who [I]sits in the heavens[8064]
[a]laughs,
The Lord[136] [b]scoffs at them.
5 Then He will speak[1696] to them
in His [a]anger[639]
And [b]terrify[926] them in His fury:
6 "But as for Me, I have
[I]installed[5258] [a]My King[4428]
Upon Zion, [b]My holy[6944]
mountain."
🔑 7 "I will surely tell[5608] of the
[I]decree of the LORD:
He said to Me, 'Thou art [a]My
Son,[1121]
Today[3117] I have begotten[3205]
Thee.
8 'Ask[7592] of Me, and [a]I will surely
give [b]the [I]nations as Thine
inheritance,[5159]
And the *very* [c]ends of the earth
as Thy possession.[272]
🔑 9 'Thou shalt [Ia]break[7489] them with
a [II]rod[7626] of iron,
Thou shalt [b]shatter them like
[III]earthenware.'"[3335]
10 Now therefore, O kings,
[a]show discernment;[7919]
Take warning,[3256] O [I]judges[8199]
of the earth.
11 [I]Worship[5647] the LORD with
[IIa]reverence,[3374]

[a]Ps. 89:23; 110:5, 6; Rev. 2:26, 27; 12:5; 19:15 [b]Ps. 28:5; 52:5; 72:4 **10** [I]Or, *leaders* [a]Prov. 8:15; 27:11
11 [I]Or, *Serve* [II]Or, *fear* [a]Ps. 5:7

🔑 **1:1** There is no conflict between the "blessed" of this verse and the "blessed" of Ps. 32:1. "Blessed" means a joyful mental state of contentment, a joy, a condition of comfort and security for which a person is to be admired. Both of these individuals are in this state of blessedness. Both of them are in a state of forgiveness. See note on Mt. 5:1-12.

🔑 **2:1,2** See Acts 4:25,26.

🔑 **2:7** See Acts 13:33; Heb. 1:5; 5:5.

🔑 **2:9** This passage presents the Messiah in a different manner from that of Isa. 42:3. Here Christ has an attitude of strength toward the proud and rebellious, but He has a gentle attitude toward the penitent and the humble. Jesus could say either Mt. 11:28-30 or Mt. 23:2-39.

And rejoice with [b]trembling.[7460]
12 [I]Do homage[5401] to [a]the Son, lest
He become angry,[599] and you
perish[6] *in* the way,[1870]
For [b]His wrath may [II]soon be
kindled.
How blessed[835] are all who
[c]take refuge[2620] in Him!

Morning Prayer of Trust in God

A Psalm of David, when [+]he fled from Absalom his son.

3 O LORD, how [a]my adversaries have
increased!
Many are rising up against
me.
2 Many are saying[559] [I]of my
soul,[5315]
"There is no [II][a]deliverance[3444] for
him in God."[430] [III]Selah.
3 But Thou, O LORD, art [a]a
shield about me,
My [b]glory,[3519] and the One who
[c]lifts my head.
4 I was crying[7121] to the LORD with
my voice,
And He [a]answered me from
[b]His holy[6944] [I]mountain.
Selah.
5 [I]I [a]lay down and slept;
I awoke, for the LORD sustains
me.
6 I will [a]not be afraid[3372] of ten
thousands of people[5971]
Who have [b]set themselves
against me round about.
7 [a]Arise, O LORD; [b]save[3467] me,
O my God!
For Thou [I]hast [c]smitten[5221] all
my enemies on the [II]cheek;
Thou [III]hast [d]shattered[7665] the
teeth of the wicked.[7563]
8 [I][a]Salvation[3444] belongs to the
LORD;

11 [b]Ps. 119:119, 120
12 [I]Lit., *Kiss;* some ancient versions read *Do homage purely,* or, *Lay hold of instruction* [II]Or, *quickly, suddenly, easily* [a]Ps. 2:7 [b]Rev. 6:16, 17 [c]Ps. 5:11; 34:22

[+]2Sam. 15:13-17, 29
1 [a]2Sam. 15:12; Ps. 69:4
2 [I]Or, *to* [II]Or, *salvation* [III]*Selah* may mean: *Pause, Crescendo* or *Musical interlude* [a]Ps. 22:7, 8; 71:11
3 [a]Ps. 5:12; 28:7 [b]Ps. 62:7 [c]Ps. 9:13; 27:6
4 [I]Or, *hill* [a]Ps. 4:3; 34:4 [b]Ps. 2:6; 15:1; 43:3
5 [I]Or, *As for me, I* [a]Lev. 26:6; Ps. 4:8; Prov. 3:24
6 [a]Ps. 23:4; 27:3 [b]Ps. 118:10-13
7 [I]Or, *dost smite* [II]Or, *jaw* [III]Or, *dost shatter* [a]Ps. 7:6 [b]Ps. 6:4; 22:21 [c]Job 16:10 [d]Ps. 57:4; 58:6
8 [I]Or, *Deliverance* [II]Or, *is* [a]Ps. 28:8; 35:3; Is. 43:11 [b]Ps. 29:11

[+]I.e., Belonging to the choir director's anthology
1 [I]I.e., who maintainest my right [II]Lit., *made room for* [a]Ps. 3:4; 17:6 [b]Ps. 18:6 [c]Ps. 18:18, 19 [d]Ps. 25:16 [e]Ps. 17:6; 39:12
2 [I]Or, *glory* [II]*Selah* may mean: *Pause, Crescendo* or *Musical interlude* [a]Ps. 3:3 [b]Ps. 69:7-10, 19, 20 [c]Ps. 12:2; 31:6 [d]Ps. 31:18

Thy [b]blessing[1293] [II]*be* upon Thy
people! Selah.

Evening Prayer of Trust in God

[+]For the choir director; on stringed instruments. A Psalm of David.

4 [a]Answer me when [b]I call,[7121] O
God[430] [I]of my
righteousness![6664]
Thou hast [II][c]relieved me in my
distress;
Be [d]gracious[2603] to me and
[e]hear[8085] my prayer.[8605]
2 O sons[1121] of men,[376] how long
will [a]my [I]honor[3519] become
[b]a reproach?
How long will you love[157]
[c]what is worthless and aim
at [d]deception?[3577] [II]Selah.
3 But know that the LORD has
[I][a]set apart[6395] the [b]godly[2623]
man for Himself;
The LORD [c]hears when I call to
Him.
4 [I][a]Tremble, [II][b]and do not
sin;[2398]
[III][c]Meditate in your heart[3824]
upon your bed, and be still.
Selah.
5 Offer[2076] [I]the [a]sacrifices[2077] of
righteousness,
And [b]trust[982] in the LORD.
6 Many are saying,[559] "[a]Who will
show[7200] us *any* good?"[2896]
[b]Lift up the light[216] of Thy
countenance upon us, O
LORD!
7 Thou hast put [a]gladness in my
heart,[3820]

3 [I]Another reading is *dealt wonderfully with* [a]Ps. 135:4 [b]Ps. 31:23; 50:5; 79:2 [c]Ps. 6:8, 9; 17:6
4 [I]I.e., with anger or fear [II]Or, *but* [III]Lit., *Speak* [a]Ps. 99:1 [b]Ps. 119:11; Eph. 4:26 [c]Ps. :6 5 [I]Or, *righteous sacrifices* [a]Deut. 33:19; Ps. 51:19 [b]Ps. 37:3, 5; 62:8
6 [a]Job 7:7; 9:25 [b]Num. 6:26; Ps. 80:3, 7, 19
7 [a]Ps. 97:11, 12; Is. 9:3; Acts 14:17

3:2 The word "Selah" occurs a number of times in the Psalms. It was a musical or liturgical sign, the meaning of which is not entirely understood today. Some regard it as a pause in the music to mark a transition in the theme or composition. It seems to have no grammatical connection with the sentence after which it appears. Therefore, it was not an integral part of each psalm. It was probably a note to the singers of the psalms or perhaps to those who were accompanying the singers with instruments.

More than when[6256] their grain
and new wine abound.
8 In peace I will [I]both [a]lie down
and sleep,
For Thou alone, O LORD, dost
make me to [b]dwell in safety.

Prayer for Protection from the Wicked

For the choir director; for [+]flute accompaniment. A Psalm of David.

5 [a]Give ear[238] to my words,[561] O
LORD,
Consider[995] my [I][b]groaning.
2 Heed[7181] [a]the sound of my cry
for help, [b]my King[4428] and my
God,[430]
For to Thee do I pray.[6419]
3 In the morning, O LORD,
[I]Thou wilt hear[8085] my voice;
In the [a]morning I will order *my*
[II]*prayer* to Thee and *eagerly*
[b]watch.
4 For Thou art not a God[410]
[a]who takes pleasure[2655] in
wickedness;[7562]
[b]No evil[7451] [I]dwells[1481] with
Thee.
5 The [a]boastful[1984] shall not
[b]stand before Thine eyes;
Thou [c]dost hate[8130] all who do
iniquity.[205]
6 Thou [a]dost destroy[6] those who
speak[1696] falsehood;[3577]
The LORD abhors[8581] [b]the man[376]
of bloodshed[1818] and
deceit.[4820]
7 But as for me, [a]by Thine
abundant lovingkindness[2617] I
will enter Thy house,[1004]
[I]At Thy holy[6944] temple[1964] I will
[b]bow[7812] in [c]reverence[3374] for
Thee.
8 O LORD, [a]lead[5148] me [b]in Thy
righteousness[6666] [c]because of
[I]my foes;
Make Thy way[1870] [II]straight[3474]
before me.
9 There is [a]nothing [I]reliable[3559] in
[II]what they say;[6310]
Their [b]inward part[7130] is
destruction[1942] *itself;*
Their [c]throat is an open
grave;[6913]
They [III]flatter with their tongue.
10 Hold them guilty,[816] O God;
[a]By their own devices let them
fall!
In the multitude of their
transgressions[6588] [b]thrust
them out,
For they are [c]rebellious[4784]
against Thee.
11 But let all who [a]take refuge[2620]
in Thee [b]be glad,
Let them ever sing for joy;
And [I]mayest Thou [c]shelter
them,
That those who [d]love[157] Thy
name may exult in Thee.
12 For it is Thou who dost
[a]bless[1288] the righteous[6662]
man, O LORD,
Thou dost [b]surround him with
favor[7522] as with a shield.

Prayer for Mercy in Time of Trouble

For the choir director; with stringed instruments, [+]upon an eight-string lyre. A Psalm of David.

6 O LORD, [a]do not rebuke[3198] me in
Thine anger,[639]
Nor chasten me in Thy
wrath.[2534]
2 Be gracious[2603] to me, O LORD,
for I *am* [a]pining away;
[b]Heal me, O LORD, for
[c]my bones[6106] are
dismayed.[926]
3 And my [a]soul[5315] is greatly
dismayed;

---

8 [I]Or, *at the same time* [a]Job 11:19; Ps. 3:5 [b]Lev. 25:18; Deut. 12:10; Ps. 16:9

[+]Heb., *Nehiloth*

1 [I]Or, *meditation* [a]Ps. 54:2 [b]Ps. 104:34

2 [a]Ps. 140:6 [b]Ps. 84:3

3 [I]Or, *mayest Thou hear* [II]Or, *sacrifice* [a]Ps. 88:13 [b]Ps. 130:5

4 [I]Lit., *sojourns* [a]Ps. 11:5; 34:16 [b]Ps. 92:15

5 [a]Ps. 73:3; 75:4 [b]Ps. 1:5 [c]Ps. 11:5; 45:7

6 [a]Ps. 52:4, 5 [b]Ps. 55:23

7 [I]Or, *Toward* [a]Ps. 69:13 [b]Ps. 138:2 [c]Ps. 115:11, 13

8 [I]Or, *those who lie in wait for me* [II]Or, *smooth* [a]Ps. 31:3 [b]Ps. 31:1 [c]Ps. 27:11

9 [I]Or, *true* [II]Lit., *his mouth* [III]Or, *make their tongue smooth* [a]Ps. 52:3 [b]Ps. 7:14 [c]Rom. 3:13

10 [a]Ps. 9:16 [b]Ps. 36:12 [c]Ps. 107:10, 11

11 [I]Or, *Thou dost shelter* [a]Ps. 2:12 [b]Ps. 33:1; 64:10 [c]Ps. 12:7 [d]Ps. 69:36

12 [a]Ps. 29:11 [b]Ps. 32:7, 10

[+]Or, *according to a lower octave* (Heb., *Sheminith*)

1 [a]Ps. 38:1; 118:18

2 [a]Ps. 102:4, 11 [b]Ps. 41:4; 147:3; Hos. 6:1 [c]Ps. 22:14; 31:10

3 [a]Ps. 88:3; John 12:27

5:8-10 Cf. Ps. 7:11-17; 25:1-22; 88:10; 69:1-36; 137:8,9. How can "a man after God's heart" say such things? First, we must remember that these particular imprecatory psalms were expressions of his innermost feelings at a time of great distress. Also, the outpouring of the "curses" were not within *(continued on next page)*

But Thou, O LORD—[b]how long?
4 Return,7725 O LORD, [a]rescue2502 my [I]soul;
Save3467 me because of Thy lovingkindness.
5 For [a]there is no [I]mention2143 of Thee in death;4194
In [II]Sheol7585 who will give Thee thanks?
6 I am [a]weary with my sighing;
Every night3915 I make my bed swim,
I dissolve my couch with [b]my tears.
7 My [a]eye has wasted away with grief;3708
It has become old because of all my adversaries.
8 [a]Depart5493 from me, all you who do iniquity,205
For the LORD [b]has heard8005 the voice of my weeping.
9 The LORD [a]has heard my supplication,8467
The LORD [b]receives my prayer.8605
10 All my enemies shall [a]be ashamed954 and greatly dismayed;
They shall [I]turn back, they shall [b]suddenly be ashamed.954

The LORD Implored to Defend the Psalmist against the Wicked

A +Shiggaion of David, which he sang to the LORD •concerning Cush, a Benjamite.

7 O LORD my God,430 [a]in Thee I have taken refuge;2620
Save3467 me from all those who pursue me, and [b]deliver5337 me,
2 Lest he tear [I]my soul5315 [a]like a lion,
[II]Dragging6561 me away, while there is none to deliver.
3 O LORD my God, if I have done6213 this,
If there is [a]injustice5766 in my hands,3709
4 If I have [a]rewarded1580 evil7451 to [I]my friend,7999
Or have [b]plundered2502 [II]him who without cause was my adversary,
5 Let the enemy pursue [I]my soul and overtake [II]*it;*
And let him trample my life2416 down to the ground,776
And lay my glory3519 in the dust.6083 [III]Selah.
6 [a]Arise, O LORD, in Thine anger;639
[b]Lift up5375 Thyself against [c]the rage5678 of my adversaries,
And [d]arouse Thyself [I]for me;
Thou hast appointed6680 judgment.4941
7 And let the assembly5712 of the [a]peoples3816 encompass Thee;
And over [I]them return7725 Thou on high.
8 The LORD [a]judges1777 the peoples;5971

3 [b]Ps. 90:13
4 [I]Or, *life* [a]Ps. 17:13
5 [I]Or, *remembrance* [II]I.e., the nether world [a]Ps. 30:9; 88:10-12; 115:17; Eccl. 9:10; Is. 38:18
6 [a]Ps. 69:3 [b]Ps. 42:3
7 [a]Job 17:7; Ps. 31:9; 38:10
8 [a]Ps. 119:115; Matt. 7:23; Luke 13:27 [b]Ps. 3:4; 28:6
9 [a]Ps. 116:1 [b]Ps. 66:19, 20
10 [I]Or, *again be ashamed suddenly* [a]Ps. 71:13, 24 [b]Ps. 73:19

+I.e., Dithyrambic rhythm; or, wild passionate song •Or, *concerning the words of*
1 [a]Ps. 31:1; 71:1 [b]Ps. 31:15
2 [I]Or, *me* [II]Or, *Rending it in pieces, while* [a]Ps. 57:4; Is. 38:13
3 [a]1Sam. 24:11
4 [I]Lit., *him who was at peace with me* [II]Or, *my adversary without cause* [a]Ps. 109:4, 5 [b]1Sam. 24:7; 26:9
5 [I]Or, *me* [II]Or, me [III]*Selah may mean: Pause, Crescendo or Musical interlude*
6 [I]One ancient version reads *O my God* [a]Ps. 3:7 [b]Ps. 94:2 [c]Ps. 138:7 [d]Ps. 35:23; 44:23
7 [I]Lit., *it* [a]Ps. 22:27
8 [a]Ps. 96:13; 98:9

(continued from previous page)
earshot of David's enemies; they were directed to God. God listens to us as we really are. Sometimes we have terrible feelings towards others. God wants us to tell Him everything, good or bad. He truly understands how bad we feel and how much we need His help against those who plot to hurt us. We need to be completely open to God, even in the sharing of our faults and weaknesses, and no matter how desperate our situation is. David was not a Christian; he was a Jewish man who lived under the Law of Moses. We should not read the Sermon on the Mount into the O.T. (cf. Mt. 5:43,44). David was merely appealing to God for His justice.

6:5 David's words are highly poetic and figurative, representing the dead as entirely separated from earthly scenes, employments, and society. As far as visible and material perspectives are concerned, there *is* no evidence of sensation or emotion shown. This passage, along with Ecc. 9:5,6 and Isa. 38:18, speaks of death in its earthly aspect, in relation to this present life. Compare Gen. 37:35; I Sam. 28:15,19; II Sam. 12:23; Lk. 16:27,28,30; I Pet. 4:6.

[I][b]Vindicate[8199] me, O LORD,
according to my
righteousness[6664] and my
integrity[8537] that is in
me.
9 O let [a]the evil[7451] of the
wicked[7563] come to an
end,[1584] but [b]establish the
righteous;[6662]
For the righteous[6662] God
[c]tries[974] the hearts[3826] and
[I]minds.3629
10 My [a]shield is [I]with God,
Who [b]saves[3467] the upright[3477]
in heart.[3820]
🔑 11 God[410] is a [a]righteous judge,[8199]
And a God who has
[b]indignation[2194] every
day.[3117]
12 If [I]a man [a]does not repent,[7725]
He will [b]sharpen His
sword;[2719]
He has [c]bent His bow and
[II]made it ready.[3559]
13 He has also prepared[3559]
[I]for Himself deadly[4194]
weapons;
He makes His [a]arrows fiery
shafts.
14 Behold, he travails[2254] with
wickedness,[205]
And he [a]conceives mischief,[5999]
and brings forth falsehood.
15 He has dug a pit[953] and hollowed
it out,
And has [a]fallen[5307] into the
hole[7845] which he made.
16 His [a]mischief will return upon his
own head,[7218]
And his [b]violence[2555] will
descend upon [I]his own
pate.6936
17 I will give thanks[3034] to the LORD
[a]according to His
righteousness,
And will [b]sing praise to the
name of the LORD Most
High.[5945]

8 [I]Lit., *Judge* [b]Ps. 18:20; 26:1; 35:24; 43:1
9 [I]Lit., *kidneys, figurative for inner man* [a]Ps. 34:21; 94:23 [b]Ps. 37:23; 40:2 [c]Ps. 11:4, 5; Jer. 11:20; Rev. 2:23
10 [I]Lit., *upon* [a]Ps. 18:2, 30 [b]Ps. 97:10, 11; 125:4
11 [a]Ps. 50:6 [b]Ps. 90:9
12 [I]Lit., *he* [II]Lit., *fixed it* [a]Ps. 58:5 [b]Deut. 32:41 [c]Ps. 64:7
13 [I]Or, *His deadly weapons* [a]Ps. 18:14; 45:5
14 [a]Job 15:35; Is. 59:4; James 1:15
15 [a]Job 4:8; Ps. 57:6
16 [I]I.e., the crown of his own head [a]Esth. 9:25; Ps. 140:9 [b]Ps. 140:11
17 [a]Ps. 71:15, 16 [b]Ps. 9:2; 66:1, 2, 4

1 [I]Or, *set* [a]Ps. 57:5, 11; 113:4; 148:13
2 [I]Or, *a bulwark* [a]Matt. 21:16; 1 Cor. 1:27 [b]Ps. 29:1; 118:14 [c]Ps. 44:16
3 [I]Or, *see* [II]Or, *appointed, fixed* [a]Ps. 111:2 [b]Ps. 89:11; 144:5 [c]Ps. 136:9
4 [I]Or, *dost remember him* [a]Job 7:17; Ps. 144:3; Heb. 2:6-8
5 [I]Or, *the angels;* Heb., *Elohim* [a]Gen. 1:26; Ps. 82:6 [b]Ps. 103:4 [c]Ps. 21:5
6 [a]Gen. 1:26, 28 [b]1Cor. 15:27; Eph. 1:22; Heb. 2:8
7 [I]Or, *animals*
9 [a]Ps. 8:1

The LORD's Glory and Man's Dignity

For the choir director; on the Gittith. A Psalm of David.

8 O LORD, our Lord,[113]
How majestic[117] is Thy name in
all the earth,[776]
Who hast [I][a]displayed Thy
splendor[1935] above the
heavens![8064]
2 [a]From the mouth[6310] of
infants5768 and nursing
babes Thou hast
established[3245] [I][b]strength,
Because of Thine adversaries,
To make [c]the enemy and the
revengeful[5358] cease.
3 When I [I][a]consider[7200] [b]Thy
heavens, the work of Thy
fingers,
The [c]moon and the stars, which
Thou hast [II]ordained;
🔑 4 [a]What is man,[582] that Thou
[I]dost take thought[2142] of
him?
And the son[1121] of man,[120] that
Thou dost care[6485] for him?
5 Yet Thou hast made him a
[a]little lower than [I]God,
And [b]dost crown him with
[c]glory[3519] and majesty!
6 Thou dost make him to
[a]rule[4910] over the works of
Thy hands;[3027]
Thou hast [b]put all things under
his feet,
7 All sheep and oxen,
And also the [I]beasts of the
field,[7704]
8 The birds of the heavens,[8064] and
the fish[1709] of the sea,
Whatever passes[5674] through
the paths[734] of the seas.
9 [a]O LORD, our Lord,
How majestic is Thy name in
all the earth!

🔑 **7:11-17** See note on Ps. 5:8-10.
🔑 **8:4,5** See Heb. 2:6-8.

A Psalm of Thanksgiving for God's Justice

For the choir director; on [+]Muth-labben. A Psalm of David.

9 I will give thanks[3034] to the LORD
with all [a]my heart;[3820]
I will [b]tell of[5608] all Thy
[I]wonders.[6381]
2 I will be glad and [a]exult in
Thee;
I will [b]sing praise to Thy name,
O [c]Most High.[5945]
3 When my enemies turn
back,
They stumble[3782] and [a]perish[6]
before Thee.
4 For Thou hast [a]maintained[6213]
[I]my just[4941] cause;[1779]
Thou dost sit on the throne[3678]
[IIb]judging[8199] righteously.[6664]
5 Thou hast [a]rebuked[1605] the
nations;[1471] Thou hast
destroyed[6] the wicked;[7563]
Thou hast [b]blotted out[4229] their
name forever and
ever.[5703]
6 [I]The enemy has come to an
end[8552] in perpetual[5331]
ruins,[2723]
And Thou hast uprooted the
cities;
The very [a]memory[2143] of them
has perished.[6]
7 But the [a]LORD [I]abides forever;
He has established[3559] His
[b]throne for judgment,[4941]
8 And He will [a]judge[8199] the
world[8398] in
righteousness;[6664]
He will execute judgment[1777] for
the peoples[3816] with
equity.[4334]
9 [I]The LORD also will be a
[a]stronghold for the
oppressed,
A stronghold in times[6256] of
trouble,
10 And [I]those who [a]know Thy
name will put their trust[982]
in Thee;
For Thou, O LORD, hast not
[b]forsaken[5800] those who seek
Thee.
11 Sing praises to the LORD, who
[a]dwells in Zion;
[b]Declare[5046] among the
peoples[5971] His deeds.
12 For [a]He who [I]requires[1875]
blood[1818] remembers[2142]
them;
He does not forget [b]the cry of
the afflicted.
13 Be gracious[2603] to me, O
LORD;
Behold[7200] my affliction from
those [a]who hate[8130] me,
Thou who [b]dost lift me up from
the gates of death;[4194]
14 That I may tell of [a]all Thy
praises,[8416]
That in the gates of the daughter
of Zion
I may [b]rejoice in Thy
[I]salvation.[3444]
15 The nations have sunk down
[a]in the pit[7845] which they have
made;[6213]
In the [b]net which they hid,
their own foot has been
caught.
16 The LORD has [a]made Himself
known;[3045]
He has [b]executed[6213] judgment.
In the work of his own hands[3709]
the wicked is snared.
[I]Higgaion [II]Selah.
17 The wicked will [Ia]return to
[II]Sheol,[7585]
Even all the nations[1471] who
[b]forget God.[430]
18 For the [a]needy will not
always[5331] be forgotten,
Nor the [b]hope of the afflicted
perish forever.
19 [a]Arise, O LORD, do not let man[582]
prevail;
Let the nations be [b]judged[8199]
before Thee.
20 Put them [a]in fear,[4172] O LORD;
Let the nations know that
they are [b]but men.[582]
Selah.

[+]I.e., "Death to the Son"
1 [I]Or, *miracles* [a]Ps. 86:12 [b]Ps. 26:7
2 [a]Ps. 5:11; 104:34 [b]Ps. 66:2, 4 [c]Ps. 83:18; 92:1
3 [a]Ps. 27:2
4 [I]Lit., *my right and my cause* [II]Or, *a righteous Judge* [a]Ps. 140:12 [b]Ps. 50:6
5 [a]Ps. 119:21 [b]Ps. 69:28; Prov. 10:7
6 [I]Or, *O enemy, desolations are finished forever; And their cities Thou hast plucked up.* [a]Ps. 34:16
7 [I]Or, *sits as king* [a]Ps. 10:16 [b]Ps. 89:14
8 [a]Ps. 96:13; 98:9
9 [I]Or, *Let the LORD also be* [a]Ps. 32:7; 59:9, 16, 17
10 [I]Or, *let those . . . name put* [a]Ps. 91:14 [b]Ps. 37:28; 94:14
11 [a]Ps. 76:2 [b]Ps. 105:1; 107:22
12 [I]I.e., avenges bloodshed [a]Gen. 9:5; Ps. 72:14 [b]Ps. 9:18
13 [a]Ps. 38:19 [b]Ps. 30:3; 86:13
14 [I]Or, *deliverance* [a]Ps. 106:2 [b]Ps. 13:5; 20:5; 35:9; 51:12
15 [a]Ps. 7:15, 16 [b]Ps. 57:6
16 [I]Perhaps, resounding music or meditation [II]*Selah* may mean: *Pause, Crescendo* or *Musical interlude* [a]Ex. 7:5 [b]Ps. 9:4
17 [I]Or, *turn* [II]I.e., the nether world [a]Ps. 49:14 [b]Job 8:13; Ps. 50:22
18 [a]Ps. 9:12; 12:5 [b]Ps. 62:5; 71:5; Prov. 23:18
19 [a]Num. 10:35 [b]Ps. 9:5
20 [a]Ps. 14:5 [b]Ps. 62:9

A Prayer for the Overthrow of the Wicked

10 Why [a]dost Thou stand afar
off, O LORD?
Why [b]dost Thou hide [I]*Thyself* in
times[6256] of trouble?
2 In [a]pride the wicked[7563]
[I]hotly pursue the afflicted;
[II]Let them be [b]caught in the
plots[4209] which they have
devised.[2803]
3 For the wicked [a]boasts[1984] of his
[b]heart's desire,
And [I]the greedy[1214] man
curses[1288] *and* [c]spurns[5006] the
LORD.
4 The wicked, in the haughtiness
of his countenance,[639] [a]does
not seek *Him*.
All his [I]thoughts[4209] are, "[b]There
is no God."
5 His ways[1870] [I][a]prosper[2342] at all
times;[6256,3605]
Thy judgments[4941] are on high,
[b]out of his sight;
As for all his adversaries, he
snorts[6315] at them.
6 He says to himself,[3820] "[a]I shall
not be moved;
[I]Throughout all generations [b]I
shall not be in adversity."[7451]
7 His [a]mouth[6310] is full of curses[423]
and deceit[4820] and
[b]oppression;
[c]Under his tongue is mischief[5999]
and wickedness.[205]
8 He sits in the [a]lurking places of
the villages;
In the hiding places he
[b]kills[2026] the innocent;[5355]
His eyes [I]stealthily[6845] watch for
the [II][c]unfortunate.
9 He lurks in a hiding place as [a]a
lion in his [I]lair;
He [b]lurks to catch [c]the afflicted;
He catches the afflicted when he
draws him into his [d]net.
10 He [I]crouches, he [II]bows down,
And the [III]unfortunate fall
[IV]by his mighty ones.
11 He [a]says to himself, "God[410] has
forgotten;
He has hidden His face; He will
never see it."
12 Arise, O LORD; O God,
[a]lift up[5375] Thy hand.[3027]
[b]Do not forget the afflicted.
13 Why has the wicked [a]spurned[5006]
God?
He has said to himself, "Thou
wilt not require *it*."
14 Thou hast seen[7200] *it*, for Thou
hast beheld [a]mischief and
vexation[3708] to [I]take it into
Thy hand.
The [II][b]unfortunate commits[5800]
himself to Thee;
Thou hast been the [c]helper of
the orphan.
15 [a]Break[7665] the arm of the wicked
and the evildoer,[7451]
[I][b]Seek out his wickedness[7562]
until Thou dost find none.
16 The LORD is [a]King[4428]
forever[5769] and ever;[5703]
[b]Nations[1471] have perished[6] from
His land.[776]
17 O LORD, Thou hast heard[8085] the
[a]desire of the [I]humble;
Thou wilt [b]strengthen[3559] their
heart, [c]Thou wilt incline
Thine ear[241]
18 To [I]vindicate[8199] the [a]orphan and
the [b]oppressed,
That man[582] who is of the
earth[776] may cause [c]terror[6206]
no more.

The LORD a Refuge and Defense

For the choir director. *A Psalm* of David.

11 In the LORD I [a]take refuge;[2620]
How can you say[559] to my
soul,[5315] "Flee *as* a bird to
your [b]mountain;
2 For, behold, the wicked[7563]
[a]bend the bow,

1 [I]Or, *Thine eyes* [a]Ps. 22:1 [b]Ps. 13:1; 55:1
2 [I]Lit., *burn* [II]Or, *They will be caught* [a]Ps. 73:6, 8 [b]Ps. 7:16; 9:16
3 [I]Or, *blesses the greedy man* [a]Ps. 49:6; 94:3, 4 [b]Ps. 112:10 [c]Ps. 10:13
4 [I]Or, *plots* [a]Ps. 10:13; 36:2 [b]Ps. 14:1; 36:1
5 [I]Lit., *are strong* [a]Ps. 52:7 [b]Ps. 28:5
6 [I]Lit., *To* [a]Ps. 49:11; Eccl. 8:11 [b]Rev. 18:7
7 [a]Rom. 3:14 [b]Ps. 73:8 [c]Job 20:12; Ps. 140:3
8 [I]Lit., *lie in wait* [II]Or, *poor* [a]Ps. 11:2 [b]Ps. 94:6 [c]Ps. 72:12
9 [I]Or, *thicket* [a]Ps. 17:12 [b]Ps. 59:3; Mic. 7:2 [c]Ps. 10:2 [d]Ps. 140:5
10 [I]Or, *is crushed* [II]Or, *is bowed down* [III]Or, *poor* [IV]Or, *into his claws*
11 [a]Ps. 10:4
12 [a]Ps. 17:7; Mic. 5:9 [b]Ps. 9:12
13 [a]Ps. 10:3
14 [I]Lit., *put, give* [II]Or, *poor* [a]Ps. 10:7 [b]Ps. 22:11 [c]Ps. 68:5
15 [I]Or, *Mayest Thou seek* [a]Ps. 37:17 [b]Ps. 140:11
16 [a]Ps. 29:10 [b]Deut. 8:20
17 [I]Or, *afflicted* [a]Ps. 9:18 [b]1Chr. 29:18 [c]Ps. 34:15
18 [I]Lit., *judge* [a]Ps. 146:9 [b]Ps. 9:9; 74:21 [c]Is. 29:20

1 [a]Ps. 2:12 [b]Ps. 121:1
2 [a]Ps. 7:12; 37:14

10:1 See note on Ps. 46:1.

They [I][b]make ready[3559] their
arrow upon the string,
To [c]shoot[3384] in darkness[652] at
the upright[3477] in heart.[3820]
3 If the [a]foundations are
destroyed,[2040]
What can the righteous[6662] do?"
4 The LORD is in His [a]holy[6944]
temple;[1964] the [I]LORD's
[b]throne[3678] is in heaven;[8064]
His [c]eyes behold,[2372] His eyelids
test[974] the sons[1121] of men.[120]
5 The LORD [a]tests[974] the righteous
and [b]the wicked,
And the one who loves[157]
violence[2555] His soul
hates.[8130]
6 Upon the wicked He will [a]rain
[I]snares;
[b]Fire and brimstone[1614] and
[c]burning[2152] wind[7307] will be
the portion of [d]their cup.
7 For the LORD is [a]righteous;
[b]He loves [I]righteousness;[6666]
The upright will [c]behold His face.

God, a Helper against the Treacherous

For the choir director; [+]upon an eight-stringed lyre. A Psalm of David.

12 Help,[3467] LORD, for [a]the godly
man[2623] ceases[1584] to be,
For the faithful[539] disappear
from among the sons[1121] of
men.[120]
2 They [a]speak[1696] [I]falsehood[7723] to
one[376] another;[7453]
With [b]flattering [II]lips[8193] and with
a double heart[3820] they speak.
3 May the LORD cut off[3772] all
flattering lips,
The tongue that [a]speaks great
things;
4 Who [a]have said, "With our
tongue we will prevail;
Our lips are [I]our own; who is
lord[113] over us?"
5 "Because of the [a]devastation[7701]
of the afflicted, because of the
groaning of the needy,
Now [b]I will arise," says the
LORD; "I will [c]set him in the
safety[3468] for which he
longs."[6315]
6 The [a]words[565] of the LORD are
pure words;
As silver [b]tried[6884] in a furnace
on the earth,[776] refined[2212]
seven times.
7 Thou, O LORD, wilt keep[8104]
them;
Thou wilt [a]preserve[5341] him from
this generation[1755]
forever.[5769]
8 The [a]wicked[7563] strut about on
every side,
When [I][b]vileness[2149] is exalted
among the sons of men.

Prayer for Help in Trouble

For the choir director. A Psalm of David.

13 How long, O LORD? Wilt Thou
[a]forget me forever?[5331]
How long [b]wilt Thou hide Thy
face from me?
2 How long shall I [a]take counsel[6098]
in my soul,[5315]
Having [b]sorrow in my heart[3824]
all the day?
How long will my enemy be
exalted over me?
3 [a]Consider *and* answer me, O
LORD, my God;[430]
[b]Enlighten my eyes, lest I
[c]sleep the *sleep of* death,[4194]
4 Lest my enemy [a]say,[559] "I have
overcome him,"
Lest [b]my adversaries rejoice
when I am shaken.
5 But I have [a]trusted[982] in Thy
lovingkindness;[2617]
My heart[3820] shall [b]rejoice in Thy
salvation.[3444]
6 I will [a]sing[7891] to the LORD,
Because He has [b]dealt
bountifully[1580] with me.

Folly and Wickedness of Men

For the choir director. *A Psalm* of David.

14 The fool has [a]said in his heart,[3820]
"There is no God."[430]

2 [I]Or, *fixed* [b]Ps. 64:3 [c]Ps. 64:4
3 [a]Ps. 82:5; 87:1; 119:152
4 [I]Lit., *LORD, His throne* [a]Ps. 18:6; Mic. 1:2; Hab. 2:20 [b]Ps. 103:19; Is. 66:1; Matt. 5:34; Rev. 4:2 [c]Ps. 33:18; 34:15, 16
5 [a]Gen. 22:1; Ps. 34:19; James 1:12 [b]Ps. 5:5
6 [I]Or, *coals of fire* [a]Ps. 18:13, 14 [b]Gen. 19:24; Ezek. 38:22 [c]Jer. 4:11, 12 [d]Ps. 75:8
7 [I]Or, *righteous deeds* [a]Ps. 7:9, 11 [b]Ps. 33:5; 45:7 [c]Ps. 16:11; 17:15

[+]Or, *according to a lower octave* (Heb., *Sheminith*)
1 [a]Is. 57:1; Mic. 7:2
2 [I]Or, *emptiness* [II]Lit., *lip* [a]Ps. 10:7; 41:6 [b]Ps. 28:3; 55:21; Jer. 9:8; Rom. 16:18
3 [a]Dan. 7:8; Rev. 13:5
4 [I]Lit., *with us* [a]Ps. 73:8, 9
5 [a]Ps. 9:9; 10:18 [b]Is. 33:10 [c]Ps. 34:6; 35:10
6 [a]2Sam. 22:31; Ps. 18:30; 19:8, 10; 119:140 [b]Prov. 30:5
7 [a]Ps. 37:28; 97:10
8 [I]Or, *worthlessness* [a]Ps. 55:10, 11 [b]Is. 32:5

1 [a]Ps. 44:24 [b]Job 13:24; Ps. 89:46
2 [a]Ps. 42:4 [b]Ps. 42:9
3 [a]Ps. 5:1 [b]1Sam. 14:29; Ezra 9:8; Job 33:30; Ps. 18:28 [c]Jer. 51:39
4 [a]Ps. 12:4 [b]Ps. 25:2; 38:16
5 [a]Ps. 52:8 [b]Ps. 9:14
6 [a]Ps. 96:1, 2 [b]Ps. 116:7; 119:17; 142:7

1 [a]Ps. 10:4; 53:1

They are corrupt,[7843] they have
committed abominable[8581]
[I]deeds;
There is [b]no one who does[6213]
good.[2896]
🔑 2 The LORD has [a]looked down from
heaven[8064] upon the sons[1121]
of men,[120]
To see if there are any who
[Ib]understand,[7919]
Who [c]seek after God.
3 They have all [a]turned aside;[5493]
together they have become
corrupt;
There is [b]no one who does good,
not even one.
4 Do all the workers of
wickedness[205] [a]not know,[3045]
Who [b]eat up my people[5971] *as*
they eat bread,
And [c]do not call[7121] upon the
LORD?
5 There they are in great
dread,[6342]
For God is with the
[a]righteous[6662] generation.[1755]
6 You would put to shame the
counsel[6098] of the afflicted,
But the LORD is his [a]refuge.
7 Oh, that [a]the salvation[3444] of
Israel [I]would come out of
Zion!
When the LORD [IIb]restores[7725]
His captive[7622] people,
Jacob will rejoice, Israel will be
glad.

1 [I]Lit., *doings* [b]Ps. 14:1-3; 130:3; Rom. 3:10-12
2 [I]Or, *act wisely* [a]Ps. 33:13, 14; 102:19 [b]Ps. 92:6 [c]1Chr. 22:19
3 [a]Ps. 58:3 [b]Ps. 143:2
4 [a]Ps. 82:5 [b]Ps. 27:2; Jer. 10:25; Mic. 3:3 [c]Ps. 79:6; Is. 64:7
5 [a]Ps. 73:15; 112:2
6 [a]Ps. 9:9; 40:17; 46:1; 142:5
7 [I]Lit., *would be* [II]Or, *restores the fortunes of His people* [a]Ps. 53:6 [b]Ps. 85:1, 2

Description of a Citizen of Zion

A Psalm of David.

15 O LORD, who may [I]abide[1481]
[a]in Thy tent?[168]
Who may dwell[7931] on Thy
[b]holy[6944] hill?
2 He who [a]walks with integrity,
and works righteousness,[6664]
And [b]speaks truth[571] in his
heart.[3824]
3 He [a]does not slander[7270]
[I]with his tongue,
Nor [b]does[6213] evil[7451] to his
neighbor,[7453]
Nor [c]takes up[5375] a reproach[2781]
against his friend;
4 In [I]whose eyes a reprobate[3988]
is despised,[959]
But [II]who [a]honors[3413] those who
fear[3373] the LORD;
He [b]swears[7650] to his own
hurt,[7489] and does not
change;
5 He [a]does not put out his money
[I]at interest,
Nor [b]does he take a bribe against
the innocent.[5355]
[c]He who does these things will
never be shaken.

1 [I]Lit., *sojourn* [a]Ps. 27:5, 6; 61:4 [b]Ps. 24:3
2 [a]Ps. 24:4; Is. 33:15 [b]Zech. 8:16; Eph. 4:25
3 [I]Lit., *according to* [a]Ps. 50:20 [b]Ps. 28:3 [c]Ex. 23:1
4 [I]Lit., *his* [II]Lit., *he* [a]Acts 28:10 [b]Judg. 11:35
5 [I]I.e., to a fellow Israelite [a]Ex. 22:25; Lev. 25:36; Deut. 23:20; Ezek. 18:8 [b]Ex. 23:8; Deut. 16:19 [c]2Pet. 1:10

The LORD the Psalmist's Portion in Life and Deliverer in Death

A [+]Mikhtam of David.

16 [a]Preserve me, O God,[410] for
[b]I take refuge[2620] in Thee.
2 [I]I said to the LORD, "Thou art
[II]my Lord;[136]
I [a]have no good[2896] besides
Thee."
3 As for the [Ia]saints[6918] who are
in the earth,[776]
[II]They are the majestic[117] ones
[b]in whom is all my delight.[2656]

[+]Possibly, *Epigrammatic Poem or Atonement Psalm*
1 [a]Ps. 17:8 [b]Ps. 7:1
2 [I]Or, O my soul, *you said* [II]Or, *the Lord* [a]Ps. 73:25
3 [I]Lit., *holy ones;* i.e., the godly [II]Lit., *And the majestic ones . . . delight*
[a]Ps. 101:6 [b]Ps. 119:63

🔑 **14:2,3** Cf. I Kgs. 8:46; Prov. 20:9; Ecc. 7:20; Mk. 10:18; Rom. 3:18,23; I Jn. 1:8. On the other hand, see Gen. 6:9; Job 1:1; Ps. 24:3,4; 86:2; Lk. 6:45; I Jn. 2:1; 3:6,9. Is man without sin or are some people sinless? Is there a contradiction in the Bible? The first series of passages contemplates men in their unregenerate state. These texts teach the undeniable truth that no mere human being has ever reached the age of accountability without violating the moral law, without sinning. However, if we say that we have not sinned, then we begin to believe that we do not need pardon. That is false; we all need God's forgiveness. The citations in the second series (except for I Jn. 3:6,9) refer to men who possess relative goodness. Only God is good in the absolute sense, i.e., underived goodness, but men are "good" only in the derived sense, "good" only in relationship to "bad" men. I Jn. 3:6,9 refer to habitual sin (see the exegetical note there).

4 The [I][a]sorrows[6094] of those who
have [II]bartered for another
god will be multiplied;
I shall not pour out[5258] their
libations[5262] of [b]blood,[1818]
Nor shall I [c]take[5375] their names
upon my lips.[8193]

5 The LORD is the [a]portion of my
inheritance and my [b]cup;
Thou dost support my [c]lot.

6 The [a]lines[2256] have fallen[5307] to
me in pleasant places;
Indeed, my heritage[5159] is
[b]beautiful to me.

7 I will bless[1288] the LORD who has
[a]counseled[3289] me;
Indeed, my [I][b]mind[3629]
instructs[3256] me in the
night.[3915]

🗝 8 [a]I have [b]set the LORD
continually[8548] before me;
Because He is [c]at my right hand,
[d]I will not be shaken.

9 Therefore [a]my heart[3820] is glad,
and [b]my glory[3519] rejoices;
My flesh[1320] also will [c]dwell
securely.[983]

10 For Thou [a]wilt not abandon[5800]
my soul to [I]Sheol;[7585]
Neither wilt Thou [II][b]allow Thy
[III]Holy One[2623] to [IV]undergo
decay.[7845]

11 Thou wilt make known[3045] to me
[a]the path[734] of life;[2416]
In [b]Thy presence is fulness of
joy;
In Thy right hand there are
[c]pleasures forever.

Prayer for Protection against Oppressors

A Prayer of David.

17 Hear[8085] a [a]just[6664] cause, O
LORD, [b]give heed to my cry;
[c]Give ear[238] to my prayer,[8605]
which is not from
[d]deceitful[4820] lips.[8193]

2 Let [a]my [I]judgment come forth
from Thy presence;
Let Thine eyes look[2372] with
[b]equity.

3 Thou hast [a]tried[974] my heart;[3820]
Thou hast visited[6485] *me* by
night;[3915]
Thou hast [b]tested[6884] me and
[c]dost find [I]nothing;
I have [d]purposed[2161] that my
mouth[6310] will not
transgress.[5674]

4 As for the deeds of men,[120]
[a]by the word[1697] of Thy
lips
I have kept[8104] from the
[b]paths[734] of the violent.[6530]

5 My [a]steps have held fast to Thy
[I]paths.
My [b]feet have not slipped.

6 I have [a]called upon[7121] Thee, for
Thou wilt answer me, O
God;[410]
[b]Incline Thine ear[241] to me, hear
my speech.[565]

7 [a]Wondrously show Thy
lovingkindness,
O [b]Savior[3467] of those who take
refuge[2620] [I]at Thy right hand
From those who rise up *against
them.*

8 Keep[8104] me as [I]the [a]apple of the
eye;
Hide me [b]in the shadow of Thy
wings,

9 From the [a]wicked[7563] who
despoil[7703] me,
My [b]deadly[5315] enemies, who
surround[5362] me.

10 They have [a]closed their
[I]unfeeling *heart*;
With their mouth they
[b]speak[1696] proudly.

11 They have now [a]surrounded us
in our steps;

4 [I]I.e., sorrows due to idolatry [II]Or, *hastened to* [a]Ps. 32:10 [b]Ps. 106:37, 38 [c]Ex. 23:13; Josh. 23:7
5 [a]Ps. 73:26; 119:57; 142:5; Lam. 3:24 [b]Ps. 23:5 [c]Ps. 125:3mg.
6 [a]Ps. 78:55 [b]Jer. 3:19
7 [I]Lit., *kidneys,* figurative for inner man [a]Ps. 73:24 [b]Ps. 77:6
8 [a]Ps. 16:8-11; Acts 2:25-28 [b]Ps. 27:8; 123:1, 2 [c]Ps. 73:23; 110:5; 121:5 [d]Ps. 112:6
9 [a]Ps. 4:7; 13:5 [b]Ps. 30:12; 57:8; 108:1 [c]Ps. 4:8
10 [I]I.e., the nether world [II]Lit., *give* [III]Or, *godly one* [IV]Or, *see corruption* or *the pit* [a]Ps. 49:15; 86:13 [b]Acts 13:35
11 [a]Ps. 139:24; Matt. 7:14 [b]Ps. 21:6; 43:4 [c]Job 36:11; Ps. 36:7, 8; 46:4

1 [a]Ps. 9:4 [b]Ps. 61:1; 142:6 [c]Ps. 88:2 [d]Is. 29:13
2 [I]I.e., vindication [a]Ps. 103:6 [b]Ps. 98:9; 99:4
3 [I]Or, *no evil device in me; My mouth* [a]Ps. 26:1, 2 [b]Job 23:10; Ps. 66:10; Zech. 13:9; 1Pet. 1:7 [c]Jer. 50:20 [d]Ps. 39:1
4 [a]Ps. 119:9, 101 [b]Ps. 10:5-11
5 [I]Lit., *tracks* [a]Job 23:11; Ps. 44:18; 119:133 [b]Ps. 18:36; 37:31
6 [a]Ps. 86:7; 116:2 [b]Ps. 88:2
7 [I]Or, *from those who rise up at Thy right hand* [a]Ps. 31:21 [b]Ps. 20:6
8 [I]Lit., *the pupil, the daughter of the eye* [a]Deut. 32:10; Zech. 2:8 [b]Ruth 2:12; Ps. 36:7; 57:1; 61:4; 63:7; 91:1, 4 **9** [a]Ps. 31:20 [b]Ps. 27:12
10 [I]Lit., *fat* [a]Job 15:27; Ps. 73:7 [b]1Sam. 2:3; Ps. 31:18; 73:8 **11** [a]Ps. 88:17

🗝 **16:8-11** See Acts 2:25-28; 13:35.

They set their eyes [b]to cast *us*
down to the ground.[776]
12 He is [a]like a lion that is eager
to tear,
And as a young lion [b]lurking in
hiding places.
13 [a]Arise, O LORD, confront him,
[b]bring him low;
[c]Deliver my soul[5315] from the
wicked with [d]Thy sword,[2719]
🔑14 From men with [a]Thy hand,[3027]
O LORD,
From men [I]of the world,[2465]
[b]whose portion is in *this*
life;[2416]
And whose belly[990] Thou
[c]dost fill with Thy treasure;
They are satisfied with
children,[1121]
And leave their abundance[3499] to
their babes.
🔑15 As for me, I shall [a]behold Thy
face in righteousness;[6664]
[b]I will be satisfied [I]with Thy
[c]likeness[8544] when I awake.

The LORD *Praised for Giving Deliverance*

For the choir director. *A Psalm* of David the servant of the LORD, [+]who spoke to the LORD the words of this song in the day that the LORD delivered him from the hand of all his enemies and from the hand of Saul. And he said,

18 "I love[7355] Thee, O LORD,
[a]my strength."[2391]
2 The LORD is [a]my [I]rock and
[b]my fortress and my
[c]deliverer,
My God,[410] my rock, in whom
I take refuge;[2620]
My [d]shield[4043] and the [e]horn of
my salvation,[3468] my
[f]stronghold.
3 I call[7121] upon the LORD, who
is [a]worthy to be praised,[1984]
And I am [b]saved[3467] from my
enemies.
4 The [a]cords[2256] of death[4194]
encompassed me,
And the [b]torrents of [I]ungodliness
[II]terrified[1204] me.
5 The [a]cords of [I]Sheol[7585]
surrounded me;
The snares[4170] of death
confronted me.
6 In my [a]distress I called upon[7121]
the LORD,
And cried to my God[430] for help;
He heard[8085] my voice [b]out of
His temple,[1964]
And my [c]cry for help before Him
came into His ears.[241]
7 Then the [a]earth[776] shook[1607] and
quaked;[7493]
And the [b]foundations[4146] of the
mountains were trembling
And were shaken, because He
was angry.[2734]
8 Smoke went up[5927] [I]out of His
nostrils,[639]
And [a]fire from His mouth[6310]
devoured;
Coals were kindled by it.

11 [b]Ps. 37:14
12 [a]Ps. 7:2 [b]Ps. 10:9
13 [a]Ps. 3:7 [b]Ps. 55:23 [c]Ps. 22:20 [d]Ps. 7:12
14 [I]Or, *whose portion in life is of the world* [a]Ps. 17:7 [b]Ps. 73:3-7; Luke 16:25 [c]Ps. 49:6
15 [I]Or, *with beholding* [a]Ps. 11:7; 16:11; 140:13; 1John 3:2 [b]Ps. 4:6, 7 [c]Num. 12:8

[+]2Sam. 22:1-51
1 [a]Ps. 59:17
2 [I]Or, *crag* [a]Deut. 32:18; 1Sam. 2:2; Ps. 18:31, 46; 28:1; 31:3; 42:9; 71:3; 78:15 [b]Ps. 144:2 [c]Ps. 19:14 [d]Ps. 28:7; 33:20; 59:11; 84:9, 11; Prov. 30:5 [e]Ps. 75:10 [f]Ps. 59:9
3 [a]Ps. 48:1; 96:4; 145:3 [b]Ps. 34:6
4 [I]Or, *destruction;* Heb., *Belial* [II]Or, *were assailing or terrifying* [a]Ps. 116:3 [b]Ps. 69:2; 124:3, 4
5 [I]I.e., the nether world [a]Ps. 116:3
6 [a]Ps. 50:15; 120:1 [b]Ps. 3:4 [c]Ps. 34:15
7 [a]Judg. 5:4; Ps. 68:7, 8; Is. 13:13; Hag. 2:6 [b]Ps. 114:4, 6
8 [I]Or, *in His wrath* [a]Ps. 50:3

🔑 **17:14** See note on Ps. 34:21.

🔑 **17:15** The reward of saints prepared by God and Christ for the servants of Christ is of God's good pleasure, not given us on merit, but by grace (Mt. 20:14; Jn. 14:2; Rom. 2:7; Col. 3:24; Heb. 11:16). It is described as being with Christ, beholding the glory of Christ and of God, and of being glorified with Christ (Mt. 5:8; Jn. 12:26; 17:24; Rom. 8:17,18; Col. 3:4). In this state we shall sit in judgment and reign with Christ forever and ever (Dan. 7:22; Mt. 19:28; II Tim. 2:12; Rev. 22:5). This reward is an incorruptible crown of righteousness, glory, and life with Christ and all the saints of an immovable kingdom and all things (Mt. 25:34; Acts 20:32; Rom. 8:17; I Cor. 9:25; II Tim. 4:8; Heb. 9:15; 12:28; Js. 1:12; I Pet. 1:4; 5:4; Rev. 21:7). In this glorious state we will shine as the stars with everlasting light and live in an eternal home in the heavens and in a city which has solid foundations, enter rest and fullness of joy (Ps. 16:11; Dan. 12:3; Isa. 60:19; Mt. 25:21; Lk. 18:30; II Cor. 5:1; Heb. 4:9; 10:34; 11:10). Such reward is great, full, sure, satisfying, and inestimable. Saints may feel confident of attaining it, but they should be careful not to lose it (Prov. 11:18; Isa. 64:4; Mt. 5:12; II Jn. 8). Therefore, we must be diligent to press forward, to endure suffering for Christ, and be faithful until death (II Cor. 4:16-18; Phil. 3:14; Rev. 2:10).

9 He [a]bowed the heavens[8064] also,
and came down
With thick [b]darkness[6205] under
His feet.
10 And He rode upon a [a]cherub[3742]
and flew;
And He sped upon the [b]wings
of the wind.[7307]
11 He made [a]darkness[2822] His
hiding place, [b]His [I]canopy
around Him,
Darkness[2824] of waters, thick
clouds of the skies.[7834]
12 From the [a]brightness before
Him passed[5674] His thick
clouds,
Hailstones and [b]coals of fire.
13 The LORD also [a]thundered in the
heavens,
And the Most High[5945] uttered
His voice,
Hailstones and coals of fire.
14 And He [a]sent out His arrows,
and scattered them,
And lightning flashes in
abundance, and [I]routed them.
15 Then the [a]channels of water
appeared,[7200]
And the foundations of the
world[8398] were [I]laid bare
At Thy [b]rebuke,[1606] O LORD,
At the blast of the [c]breath[7307]
of Thy nostrils.
16 He [a]sent from on high, He took
me;
He drew me out of [b]many
waters.
17 He [a]delivered[5337] me from my
strong enemy,
And from those who hated[8130]
me, for they were [b]too
mighty for me.
18 They confronted me in
[a]the day[3117] of my calamity,[343]
But [b]the LORD was my stay.
19 He brought me forth also into
a [a]broad place;
He rescued[2502] me, because
[b]He delighted[2654] in me.
20 The LORD has [a]rewarded[1580] me
according to my
righteousness;[6664]
According to the [b]cleanness[1252]
of my hands[3027] He has
recompensed[7725] me.
21 For I have [a]kept[8104] the ways[1870]
of the LORD,
And have [b]not wickedly
departed[7561] from my God.
22 For all [a]His ordinances[4941] were
before me,
And I did not put away[5493] His
[b]statutes[2708] from me.
23 I was also [Ia]blameless[8549] with
Him,
And I [b]kept myself from my
iniquity.[5771]
24 Therefore the LORD has
[a]recompensed me according
to my righteousness,
According to the cleanness of
my hands in His eyes.
25 With [a]the kind[2623] Thou dost
show Thyself kind;
With the [I]blameless[8552]
[b]Thou dost show Thyself
blameless;
26 With the pure[1305] Thou dost
show Thyself [a]pure;
And with the crooked[6141]
[b]Thou dost show Thyself
[I]astute.[6617]
27 For Thou dost [a]save[3467] an
afflicted people;[5971]
But [b]haughty eyes Thou dost
abase.
28 For Thou dost [a]light my
lamp;[5216]
The LORD my God [b]illumines my
darkness.
29 For by Thee I can [Ia]run upon a
troop;[1416]
And by my God I can [b]leap over
a wall.
30 As for God, His way[1870] is
[Ia]blameless;[8549]
The [b]word[565] of the LORD is
tried;[6884]
He is a [c]shield to all who take
refuge in Him.
31 For [a]who is God,[433] but the
LORD?
And who is a [b]rock, except our
God,

9 [a]Ps. 144:5 [b]Ps. 97:2
10 [a]Ps. 80:1; 99:1 [b]Ps. 104:3
11 [I]Or, *pavilion* [a]Deut. 4:11 [b]Ps. 97:2
12 [a]Ps. 104:2 [b]Ps. 97:3; 140:10; Hab. 3:4
13 [a]Ps. 29:3; 104:7
14 [I]Lit., *confused* [a]Ps. 144:6; Hab. 3:11
15 [I]Or, *uncovered* [a]Ps. 106:9 [b]Ps. 76:6 [c]Ps. 18:8
16 [a]Ps. 144:7 [b]Ps. 32:6
17 [a]Ps. 59:1 [b]Ps. 35:10; 142:6
18 [a]Ps. 59:16 [b]Ps. 16:8
19 [a]Ps. 4:1; 31:8; 118:5 [b]Ps. 37:23; 41:11
20 [a]1Sam. 24:19; Job 33:26; Ps. 7:8 [b]Job 22:30; Ps. 24:4
21 [a]Ps. 37:34; 119:33; Prov. 8:32 [b]2Chr. 34:33; Ps. 119:102
22 [a]Ps. 119:30 [b]Ps. 119:83
23 [I]Lit., *complete;* or, *having integrity;* or, *perfect* [a]Ps. 18:32 [b]Ps. 19:12, 13; 25:11; 66:18
24 [a]1Sam. 26:23; Ps. 18:20
25 [I]V. 23, note 1 [a]1Kin. 8:32; Ps. 62:12; Matt. 5:7 [b]Ps. 18:30
26 [I]Lit., *twisted* [a]Job 25:5; Hab. 1:13 [b]Lev. 26:23, 24, 27, 28; Prov. 3:34
27 [a]Ps. 72:12 [b]Ps. 101:5; Prov. 6:17
28 [a]1Kin. 15:4; Job 18:6; Ps. 132:17 [b]Ps. 27:1
29 [I]Or, *crush a troop* [a]Ps. 118:10-12 [b]Ps. 18:33; 40:2
30 [I]V. 23, note 1 [a]Deut. 32:4; Ps. 19:7; 145:17; Rev. 15:3 [b]Ps. 12:6 [c]Ps. 17:7; 91:4
31 [a]Deut. 32:39; 1Sam. 2:2; Ps. 86:8-10; Is. 45:5 [b]Deut. 32:31; Ps. 18:2; 62:2

32 The God who [a]girds me with strength,2428
And [I]makes my way [IIb]blameless?
33 He [a]makes my feet like hinds' 355 *feet*,
And [b]sets me upon my high places.1116
34 He [a]trains3925 my hands for battle,
So that my arms can [b]bend a bow of bronze.
35 Thou hast also given me [a]the shield of Thy salvation,
And Thy [b]right hand upholds5582 me;
And [c]Thy [I]gentleness makes me great.
36 Thou dost [a]enlarge my steps under me,
And my [Ib]feet have not slipped.
37 I [a]pursued my enemies and overtook them,
And I did not turn back7725 [b]until they were consumed.3615
38 I shattered4272 them, so that they were [a]not able to rise;
They fell5307 [b]under my feet.
39 For Thou hast [a]girded me with strength for battle;
Thou hast [Ib]subdued3766 under me those who rose up against me.
40 Thou hast also made my enemies [a]turn their backs to me,
And I [Ib]destroyed6789 those who hated8130 me.
41 They cried for help, but there was [a]none to save,
Even to the LORD, but [b]He did not answer them.
42 Then I beat7833 them fine as the [a]dust6083 before the wind;
I emptied them out as the mire of the streets.
43 Thou hast delivered me from the [a]contentions7379 of the people;
Thou hast placed7760 me as [b]head7218 of the nations;1471
A [c]people whom I have not known3045 serve5647 me.
44 As soon as they hear,8085 they obey me;
Foreigners [Ia]submit to me.
45 Foreigners [a]fade away,
And [b]come trembling2727 out of their [I]fortresses.
46 The LORD [a]lives,2416 and blessed1288 be [b]my rock;
And exalted be [c]the God of my salvation,
47 The God who [a]executes vengeance5360 for me,
And [b]subdues1696 peoples under me.
48 He [a]delivers me from my enemies;
Surely Thou [b]dost lift me above those who rise up against me;
Thou dost rescue me from the [c]violent2555 man.376
49 Therefore I will [a]give thanks3034 to Thee among the nations, O LORD,
And I will [b]sing praises to Thy name.
50 He gives great [Ia]deliverance3444 to His king,4428
And shows6213 lovingkindness2617 to [b]His anointed,4899
To David and [c]his [II]descendants2233 forever.5769

The Works and the Word of God

For the choir director. A Psalm of David.

19 The [a]heavens8064 are telling5608 of the glory3519 of God;410
And their [b]expanse7549 is declaring5046 the work of His hands.
2 Day3117 to [a]day pours forth speech,562
And [b]night3915 to night reveals knowledge.1847
3 There is no speech, nor are there words;
Their voice is not heard.8065

---

32 [I]Or, *has made* [II]Lit., *complete;* or, *having integrity* [a]Ps. 18:39; Is. 45:5 [b]Ps. 18:23
33 [a]Hab. 3:19 [b]Deut. 32:13
34 [a]Ps. 144:1 [b]Job 29:20
35 [I]Or, *condescension* [a]Ps. 33:20 [b]Ps. 63:8; 119:117 [c]Ps. 138:6
36 [I]Lit., *ankles* [a]Ps. 18:33 [b]Ps. 66:9; Prov. 4:12
37 [a]Ps. 44:5 [b]Ps. 37:20
38 [a]Ps. 36:12 [b]Ps. 47:3
39 [I]Lit., *caused to bow down* [a]Ps. 18:32 [b]Ps. 18:47
40 [I]Or, *silenced* [a]Ps. 21:12 [b]Ps. 94:23
41 [a]Ps. 50:22 [b]Job 27:9; Prov. 1:28
42 [a]Ps. 83:13
43 [a]2Sam. 3:1; 19:9; Ps. 35:1 [b]2Sam. 8:1-18; Ps. 89:27 [c]Is. 55:5
44 [I]Lit., *deceive me;* i.e., give feigned obedience [a]Ps. 66:3
45 [I]Lit., *fastnesses* [a]Ps. 37:2 [b]Mic. 7:17
46 [a]Job 19:25 [b]Ps. 18:2 [c]Ps. 51:14
47 [a]Ps. 94:1 [b]Ps. 18:43; 47:3; 144:2
48 [a]Ps. 3:7 [b]Ps. 27:6; 59:1 [c]Ps. 11:5
49 [a]Rom. 15:9 [b]Ps. 108:1
50 [I]I.e., victories; lit., *salvations* [II]Lit., *seed* [a]Ps. 21:1; 144:10 [b]Ps. 28:8 [c]Ps. 89:4
1 [a]Ps. 8:1; 50:6; Rom. 1:19, 20 [b]Gen. 1:6, 7
2 [a]Ps. 74:16 [b]Ps. 139:12

4 Their [I][a]line has gone out through all the earth,[776]
And their utterances[4405] to the end of the world.[8398]
In them He has [b]placed[7760] a tent[168] for the sun,
5 Which is as a bridegroom coming out of his chamber;
It rejoices as a strong man to run his course.[734]
6 Its [a]rising is from [I]one end of the heavens,[8064]
And its circuit to the [II]other end of them;
And there is nothing hidden from its heat.
7 [a]The law[8451] of the LORD is [I][b]perfect,[8549] [c]restoring[7725] the soul;[5315]
The testimony[5715] of the LORD is [d]sure,[539] making [e]wise[2449] the simple.
8 The precepts[6490] of the LORD are [a]right,[3477] [b]rejoicing the heart;[3820]
The commandment[4687] of the LORD is [c]pure, [d]enlightening the eyes.
9 The fear[3374] of the LORD is clean,[2889] enduring[5975] forever;[5703]
The judgments[4941] of the LORD are [a]true;[571] they are [b]righteous[6663] altogether.
10 They are more desirable than [a]gold, yes, than much fine gold;
[b]Sweeter also than honey and the drippings of the honeycomb.
11 Moreover, by them [a]Thy servant[5650] is warned;[2094]
In keeping[8104] them there is great [b]reward.
12 Who can [a]discern[995] *his* errors?[7691] [b]Acquit[5352] me of [c]hidden *faults.*
13 Also keep back Thy servant [a]from presumptuous[2086] *sins;*
Let them not [b]rule[4910] over me;
Then I shall be [I][c]blameless,[8552]
And I shall be acquitted[5352] of [d]great transgression.[6588]
14 Let the words[561] of my mouth[6310] and [a]the meditation of my heart
Be acceptable[7522] in Thy sight,
O LORD, [b]my rock and my [c]Redeemer.[1350]

4 [I]Another reading is *sound* [a]Rom. 10:18 [b]Ps. 104:2
6 [I]Lit., *the* [II]Lit., *the ends* [a]Ps. 113:3; Eccl. 1:5
7 [I]I.e., blameless [a]Ps. 111:7 [b]Ps. 119:160 [c]Ps. 23:3 [d]Ps. 93:5 [e]Ps. 119:98-100
8 [a]Ps. 119:128 [b]Ps. 119:14 [c]Ps. 12:6 [d]Ps. 36:9
9 [a]Ps. 119:142 [b]Ps. 119:138
10 [a]Ps. 119:72, 127 [b]Ps. 119:103
11 [a]Ps. 17:4 [b]Ps. 24:5, 6; Prov. 29:18
12 [a]Ps. 40:12; 139:6 [b]Ps. 51:1, 2 [c]Ps. 90:8; 139:23, 24
13 [I]Lit., *complete* [a]Num. 15:30 [b]Ps. 119:133 [c]Ps. 18:32 [d]Ps. 25:11
14 [a]Ps. 104:34 [b]Ps. 18:2 [c]Ps. 31:5; Is. 47:4

Prayer for Victory over Enemies

For the choir director. A Psalm of David.

20 May the LORD answer you [a]in the day[3117] of trouble!
May the [b]name of the [c]God[430] of Jacob set you *securely* on high!
2 May He send you help [a]from the sanctuary,[6944]
And [b]support you from Zion!
3 May He [a]remember[2142] all your meal offerings,[4503]
And [b]find your burnt offering[5930] [I]acceptable![1878] [II]Selah.
4 May He grant you your [a]heart's[3824] desire,
And [b]fulfill all your [I]counsel![6098]
5 [I]We will [a]sing for joy over your [II]victory,[3444]
And in the name of our God we will [b]set[7760] up our banners.
May the LORD [c]fulfill all your petitions.
6 Now [a]I know that the LORD saves[3467] His anointed;[4899]
He will [b]answer him from His holy[6944] heaven,[8064]
With the [I][c]saving[3468] strength of His right hand.

1 [a]Ps. 50:15 [b]Ps. 91:14 [c]Ps. 46:7, 11
2 [a]Ps. 3:4 [b]Ps. 110:2
3 [I]Lit., *fat* [II]*Selah* may mean: *Pause, Crescendo* or *Musical interlude* [a]Acts 10:4 [b]Ps. 51:19
4 [I]Or, *purpose* [a]Ps. 21:2 [b]Ps. 145:19
5 [I]Or, *Let us sing* [II]Or, *salvation* [a]Ps. 9:14 [b]Ps. 60:4 [c]1Sam. 1:17
6 [I]Or, *mighty deeds of the victory of His right hand* [a]Ps. 41:11 [b]Is. 58:9 [c]Ps. 28:8

19:13 "Presumptuous sins" are arrogant and irreverent moral actions. Some people, even religious people, have a bold and daring confidence in God's goodness, but they do not obey Him or heed His warnings because they rationalize that He will always forgive them later. We cannot invoke God's blessing and continue to live in sin! We must not be complacent about our spiritual condition. Instead, we ought to search deeply in our hearts for the possibility of hidden, selfish causes of our misfortunes.

7 Some [I]*boast* in chariots, and
some in [a]horses;
But [b]we [II]will boast in the name
of the LORD, our God.
8 They have [a]bowed down[3766] and
fallen;[5307]
But we have [b]risen and stood
upright.
9 [Ia]Save,[3467] O LORD;
May the [b]King[4428] answer us in
the day we call.[7121]

Praise for Deliverance

For the choir director. A Psalm of David.

21 O LORD, in Thy strength the
king[4428] will [a]be glad,
And in Thy [I]salvation[3444] how
greatly he will rejoice!
2 Thou hast [a]given him his
heart's[3820] desire,
And Thou hast not withheld[4513]
the request of his lips.[8193]
[I]Selah.
3 For Thou [a]dost meet him with
the blessings[1293] of good[2896]
things;
Thou dost set a [b]crown of fine
gold on his head.[7218]
4 He asked[7592] life[2416] of Thee,
Thou [a]didst give it to him,
[b]Length[753] of days[3117]
forever[5769] and ever.[5703]
5 His [a]glory[3519] is great through
Thy [I]salvation,
[b]Splendor[1935] and majesty[1926]
Thou dost place upon him.
6 For Thou dost make him
[I]most [a]blessed forever;
Thou dost make him joyful
[b]with gladness in Thy
presence.
7 For the king [a]trusts[982] in the
LORD,
And through the
lovingkindness[2617] of the
Most High[5945] [b]he will not be
shaken.
8 Your hand[3027] will [a]find out all
your enemies;
Your right hand will find out
those who hate[8130] you.
9 You will make them [a]as a fiery
oven in the time[6256] [I]of your
anger;
The LORD will [b]swallow[1104] them
up in His wrath,[639]
And [c]fire will devour them.
10 Their [I]offspring Thou wilt
destroy[6] from the earth,[776]
And their [IIa]descendants[2233]
from among the sons[1121] of
men.[120]
11 Though they [Ia]intended evil[7451]
against Thee,
And [b]devised[2803] a plot,[4209]
They will not succeed.
12 For Thou wilt [a]make them turn
their back;
Thou wilt [I]aim[3559] [b]with Thy
bowstrings at their faces.
13 Be Thou exalted, O LORD, in
Thy strength;
We will [a]sing[7891] and praise Thy
power.

A Cry of Anguish and a Song of Praise

For the choir director; upon +Aijeleth Hashshahar. A Psalm of David.

22 ⊶ [a]My God,[410] my God, why
hast Thou forsaken[5800] me?
[Ib]Far from my deliverance are
the words[1697] of my
[IIc]groaning.
2 O my God,[430] I [a]cry[7121] by
day,[3119] but Thou dost not
answer;
And by night,[3915] but [I]I have no
rest.

---

7 [I]Or, praise *chariots*, or, trust, or, are strong *through* [II]Lit., *make mention of;* or, *praise the name* [a]Ps. 33:17 [b]2Chr. 32:8
8 [a]Is. 2:11, 17 [b]Ps. 37:24; Mic. 7:8
9 [I]Or, *O LORD, save the king; answer us* [a]Ps. 3:7 [b]Ps. 17:6

1 [I]Or, *victory* [a]Ps. 59:16, 17
2 [I]*Selah* may mean: *Pause, Crescendo* or *Musical interlude* [a]Ps. 20:4; 37:4
3 [a]Ps. 59:10 [b]2Sam. 12:30
4 [a]Ps. 61:6; 133:3 [b]Ps. 91:16
5 [I]Or, *victory* [a]Ps. 9:14; 20:5 [b]Ps. 8:5; 96:6
6 [I]Lit., *blessings* [a]1Chr. 17:27 [b]Ps. 43:4
7 [a]Ps. 125:1 [b]Ps. 112:6
8 [a]Is. 10:10
9 [I]Or, *of your presence* [a]Mal. 4:1 [b]Lam. 2:2 [c]Ps. 50:3
10 [I]Lit., *fruit* [II]Lit., *seed* [a]Ps. 37:28
11 [I]Lit., *stretched out* [a]Ps. 2:1-3 [b]Ps. 10:2
12 [I]Lit., *make ready* [a]Ps. 18:40 [b]Ps. 7:12, 13
13 [a]Ps. 59:16; 81:1

+Lit., *the hind of the morning*
1 [I]Or, Why art Thou so *far from helping me,* and from *the words of my groaning?* [II]Lit., *roaring* [a]Matt. 27:46; Mark 15:34 [b]Ps. 10:1 [c]Job 3:24; Ps. 6:6; 32:3; 38:8
2 [I]Lit., *there is no silence for me* [a]Ps. 42:3; 88:1

⊶ **22:1** Jesus quoted this in the original language (Mt. 27:46; Mk. 15:34), while dying on the cross. It was the crisis of His sufferings, the moment when He paid the debt of the world's sin. Contrast the statement, "It is finished" (Jn. 19:30), where the mighty voice of a dying Savior exults in the accomplishment of His mission.

3 Yet [a]Thou art holy,[6918]
O Thou who [I]art enthroned upon
[b]the praises[8416] of Israel.
4 In Thee our fathers[1] [a]trusted;[982]
They trusted, and Thou didst
[b]deliver them.
5 To Thee they cried[2199] out, and
were delivered;[4422]
[a]In Thee they trusted, and were
not [I]disappointed.[954]
6 But I am a [a]worm, and not a
man,[376]
A [b]reproach[2781] of men,[120] and
[c]despised by the people.[5971]
🗝 7 All who see me [Ia]sneer at me;
They [II]separate with the lip, they
[b]wag the head,[7218] *saying,*
8 "[I]Commit[1556] *yourself* to the
LORD; [a]let Him deliver him;
Let Him rescue[5337] him, because
He delights[2654] in him."
9 Yet Thou art He who [a]didst bring
me forth from the womb;[990]
Thou didst make me trust[982]
when upon my mother's[517]
breasts.
10 Upon Thee I was cast [a]from
[I]birth;
Thou hast been my God from
my mother's womb.[990]
11 [a]Be not far from me, for
[I]trouble is near;
For there is [b]none to help.
12 Many [a]bulls have surrounded
me;
Strong[47] *bulls* of [b]Bashan have
encircled me.
13 They [a]open wide their mouth[6310]
at me,
As a ravening and a roaring
[b]lion.
14 I am [a]poured out[8210] like water,
And all my [b]bones[6106] are out
of joint;
My [c]heart[3820] is like wax;
It is melted within [I]me.[4578]
15 My [a]strength is dried up[3001] like
a potsherd,[2789]

3 [I]Or, *dost inhabit the praises* [a]Ps. 99:9 [b]Deut. 10:21; Ps. 148:14
4 [a]Ps. 78:53 [b]Ps. 107:6
5 [I]Or, *ashamed* [a]Is. 49:23
6 [a]Job 25:6; Is. 41:14 [b]Ps. 31:11 [c]Is. 49:7; 53:3
7 [I]Or, *mock me* [II]I.e., make mouths at me [a]Ps. 79:4; Is. 53:3; Luke 23:35 [b]Matt. 27:39; Mark 15:29
8 [I]Lit., *Roll;* another reading is *He committed himself* [a]Ps. 91:14; Matt. 27:43
9 [a]Ps. 71:5, 6
10 [I]Lit., *a womb* [a]Is. 46:3; 49:1
11 [I]Or, *distress* [a]Ps. 71:12 [b]2Kin. 14:26; Ps. 72:12; Is. 63:5
12 [a]Ps. 22:21; 68:30 [b]Deut. 32:14; Amos 4:1
13 [a]Job 16:10; Ps. 35:21; Lam. 2:16; 3:46 [b]Ps. 10:9; 17:12
14 [I]Lit., *my inward parts* [a]Job 30:16 [b]Ps. 31:10; Dan. 5:6 [c]Josh. 7:5; Job 23:16; Ps. 73:26; Nah. 2:10
15 [I]Lit., *to* [a]Ps. 38:10 [b]John 19:28 [c]Ps. 104:29
16 [I]Or, *An assembly* [II]Another reading is *Like a lion, my. . .* [a]Ps. 59:6, 7 [b]Matt. 27:35; John 20:25
17 [a]Luke 23:27, 35
18 [a]Matt. 27:35; Mark 15:24; Luke 23:34; John 19:24
19 [a]Ps. 22:11 [b]Ps. 70:5
20 [I]Or, *life* [II]Lit., *paw* [a]Ps. 37:14 [b]Ps. 35:17
21 [a]Ps. 22:13 [b]Ps. 22:12

And [b]my tongue cleaves to my
jaws;
And Thou dost [c]lay me [I]in the
dust[6083] of death.[4194]
🗝 16 For [a]dogs have surrounded me;
[I]A band[5712] of evildoers[7489] has
encompassed[5362] me;
[II]They [b]pierced my hands[3027] and
my feet.
17 I can count[5608] all my bones.
[a]They look, they stare at me;
🗝 18 They [a]divide my garments
among them,
And for my clothing they cast[5307]
lots.
19 But Thou, O LORD, [a]be not far
off;
O Thou my help, [b]hasten to my
assistance.
20 Deliver my [I]soul[5315] from [a]the
sword,[2719]
My [b]*only life*[3173] from the
[II]power[3027] of the dog.
21 Save[3467] me from the [a]lion's
mouth;[6310]
And from the horns of the [b]wild
oxen Thou dost [c]answer me.
22 I will [a]tell[5608] of Thy name to
my brethren;[251]
In the midst of the assembly[6951]
I will praise[1984] Thee.
23 [a]You who fear[3373] the LORD,
praise Him;
All you [I]descendants[2233] of
Jacob, [b]glorify[3513] Him,
And [c]stand in awe of[1481] Him,
all you [I]descendants of Israel.
24 For He has [a]not despised nor
abhorred[8262] the affliction of
the afflicted;
Neither has He [b]hidden His face
from him;
But [c]when he cried to Him for
help, He heard.[8085]

[c]Ps. 34:4; 118:5; 120:1 **22** [a]Ps. 40:10; Heb. 2:12
23 [I]Lit., *seed* [a]Ps. 135:19, 20 [b]Ps. 86:12 [c]Ps. 33:8
24 [a]Ps. 69:33 [b]Ps. 27:9; 69:17; 102:2 [c]Ps. 31:22; Heb. 5:7

🗝 **22:7,8** See Mt. 27:39,43; Mk. 15:29.
🗝 **22:16** See Mt. 27:35.
🗝 **22:18** See Mt. 27:35; Lk. 23:34; Jn. 19:24.

25 From Thee *comes* [a]my praise[8416]
in the great assembly;
I shall [b]pay my vows[5088] before
those who fear Him.
26 The [I]afflicted shall eat and
[a]be satisfied;
Those who seek Him will
[b]praise the LORD.
Let your [c]heart[3824] live[2421]
forever![5703]
27 All the [a]ends of the earth will
remember[2142] and turn[7725] to
the LORD,
And all the [b]families of the
nations[1471] will worship[7812]
before [I]Thee.
28 For the [a]kingdom is the LORD's,
And He [b]rules[4910] over the
nations.
29 All the [Ia]prosperous of the
earth[776] will eat and worship,
All those who [b]go down to the
dust will bow[3766] before Him,
Even he who [IIc]cannot keep his
soul alive.[2421]
30 [Ia]Posterity will serve[5647] Him;
It will be told[5608] of the Lord[136]
to [b]the *coming*
generation.[1755]
31 They will come and [a]will
declare[5046] His
righteousness[6666]
To a people [b]who will be born,
that He has performed[6213] *it.*

The LORD, the Psalmist's Shepherd

A Psalm of David.

23 🗝 The LORD is my [a]shepherd,
I [I]shall [b]not want.

25 [a]Ps. 35:18; 40:9, 10 [b]Ps. 61:8; Eccl. 5:4
26 [I]Or, *poor* [a]Ps. 107:9 [b]Ps. 40:16 [c]Ps. 69:32
27 [I]Some versions read *Him* [a]Ps. 2:8; 82:8 [b]Ps. 86:9
28 [a]Ps. 47:7; Obad. 21; Zech. 14:9; Matt. 6:13 [b]Ps. 47:8
29 [I]Lit., *fat ones* [II]Or, *did not* [a]Ps. 17:10; 45:12; Hab. 1:16 [b]Ps. 28:1; Is. 26:19 [c]Ps. 89:48
30 [I]Lit., *A seed* [a]Ps. 102:28 [b]Ps. 102:18
31 [a]Ps. 40:9; 71:18 [b]Ps. 78:6

1 [I]Or, *do* [a]Ps. 78:52; 80:1; Is. 40:11; Jer. 31:10; Ezek. 34:11-13; John 10:11; 1Pet. 2:25 [b]Ps. 34:9, 10; Phil. 4:19
2 [I]Lit., *waters of rest* [a]Ps. 65:11-13; Ezek. 34:14 [b]Rev. 7:17 [c]Ps. 36:8; 46:4
3 [I]Lit., *tracks* [a]Ps. 19:7 [b]Ps. 5:8; 31:3 [c]Ps. 85:13; Prov. 4:11; 8:20
4 [I]Or, *valley of deep darkness* [II]Or, *harm* [a]Job 10:21, 22; Ps. 107:14 [b]Ps. 3:6; 27:1 [c]Ps. 16:8; Is. 43:2 [d]Mic. 7:14
5 [I]Or, *dost anoint* [a]Ps. 78:19 [b]Ps. 92:10; Luke 7:46 [c]Ps. 16:5
6 [I]Or, *Only* [II]Another reading is *return to*

2 He makes me lie down in
[a]green pastures;[4999]
He [b]leads me beside [Ic]quiet
waters.
3 He [a]restores[7725] my soul;[5315]
He [b]guides me in the [Ic]paths of
righteousness[6664]
For His name's sake.
4 Even though I [a]walk through the
[I]valley of the shadow of
death,[6757]
I [b]fear[3372] no [II]evil;[7451] for
[c]Thou art with me;
Thy [d]rod[7626] and Thy staff, they
comfort[5162] me.
5 Thou dost [a]prepare a table
before me in the presence of
my enemies;
Thou [I]hast [b]anointed[1878] my
head[7218] with oil;[8081]
My [c]cup overflows.
6 [I]Surely [a]goodness[2896] and
lovingkindness[2617] will follow
me all the days[3117] of my
life,[2416]
And I will [IIb]dwell in the house[1004]
of the LORD [III]forever.

The King of Glory Entering Zion

A Psalm of David.

24 The [a]earth[776] is the LORD's, and
[I]all it contains,
The [b]world,[8398] and those who
dwell in it.
2 For He has [a]founded[3245] it upon
the seas,
And established[3559] it upon the
rivers.

[III]Lit., *for length of days* [a]Ps. 25:7, 10 [b]Ps. 27:4-6
1 [I]Lit., *its fulness* [a]1Cor. 10:26 [b]Ps. 89:11
2 [a]Ps. 104:3, 5; 136:6

🗝 **23:1-6** This Psalm was written by David during a time when he was fleeing from Saul. He had been wandering from place to place. He was in exile from his own people and constantly living among strangers, even enemies. His life was continually being threatened. It is an outpouring of David's confidence in the Lord and trust in His care for him in every moment of his life even to the point of death. With His loving care and concern there could be no reason to fear even before his enemies. We can well imagine, from the imagery, that David's thoughts had returned to the secure time of his boyhood when he himself was a shepherd who totally cared for his sheep and in whom his sheep had complete trust. What a vivid, comforting thought for him to conceive of the Lord as his Shepherd and then to sum up the whole thought of the psalm with the words, "I shall not want." The thought is just as vivid and comforting today to the Christian who, in the midst of the turmoil and frustrations of life fully understands that the Lord is his Shepherd also and, therefore, he shall not want.

3 Who may [a]ascend[5927] into the
[b]hill of the LORD?
And who may stand in His
holy[6944] [c]place?
4 He who has [a]clean hands[3709] and
a [b]pure[1249] heart,[3824]
Who has not [c]lifted up[5375] his
soul[5315] [I]to falsehood,[7723]
And has not [d]sworn
deceitfully.[4820]
5 He shall receive[5375] a
[a]blessing[1293] from the LORD
And [I][b]righteousness[6666] from the
God[430] of his salvation.[3468]
6 [I]This is the generation[1755] of
those who [a]seek Him,
Who seek Thy face—*even* Jacob.
[II]Selah.
7 [a]Lift up[5375] your heads,[7218] O
gates,
And be lifted up, O [I]ancient[5769]
doors,
That the King[4428] of [b]glory[3519]
may come in!
8 Who is the King of glory?
The LORD [a]strong and
mighty,
The LORD [b]mighty in battle.
9 Lift up your heads, O gates,
And lift *them* up, O [I]ancient
doors,
That the King of [a]glory may
come in!
10 Who is this King of glory?
The LORD of [a]hosts,[6635]
He is the King of glory. Selah.

Prayer for Protection, Guidance and Pardon

A Psalm of David.

25 To Thee, O LORD, I [a]lift up[5375]
my soul.[5315]
2 O my God,[430] in Thee [a]I
trust,[982]
Do not let me [b]be ashamed;[954]
Do not let my [c]enemies exult
over me.
3 Indeed, [a]none of those who
wait for[6960] Thee will be
ashamed;
[I]Those who [b]deal treacherously
without cause will be
ashamed.
4 [a]Make me know[3045] Thy
ways,[1870] O LORD;
Teach[3925] me Thy paths.[734]
5 Lead me in [a]Thy truth[571] and
teach me,
For Thou art the [b]God of my
salvation;[3468]
For Thee I [c]wait all the day.[3117]
6 [a]Remember,[2142] O LORD, Thy
compassion[7356] and Thy
lovingkindnesses,
For they have been [I][b]from of old.
7 Do not remember the [a]sins of
my youth or my
transgressions;[6588]
[b]According to Thy
lovingkindness[2617] remember
Thou me,
For Thy [c]goodness' sake, O
LORD.
8 [a]Good[2896] and [b]upright[3477] is the
LORD;
Therefore He [c]instructs[3384]
sinners[2400] in the way.[1870]
9 He [a]leads the [I]humble in
justice,[4941]
And He [b]teaches the [I]humble His
way.
10 All the paths of the LORD
are [a]lovingkindness and
truth
To [b]those who keep[5341] His
covenant[1285] and His
testimonies.[5713]
11 For [a]Thy name's sake, O LORD,
[b]Pardon[5545] my iniquity,[5771] for
it is great.
12 Who is the man[376] who [a]fears the
LORD?
He will [b]instruct[3384] him in the
way he should choose.[977]
13 His soul will [a]abide in
[I]prosperity,[2896]
And his [II]descendants[2233] will
[b]inherit[3423] the [III]land.[776]
14 The [I][a]secret[5475] of the LORD is
for those who fear[3373] Him,

3 [a]Ps. 15:1 [b]Ps. 2:6 [c]Ps. 65:4
4 [I]Or, *in vain* [a]Job 17:9; Ps. 22:30; 26:6 [b]Ps. 51:10; 73:1; Matt. 5:8 [c]Ezek. 18:15 [d]Ps. 15:4
5 [I]I.e., as vindicated [a]Ps. 115:13 [b]Ps. 36:10
6 [I]Or, *Such* [II]*Selah* may mean: *Pause, Crescendo* or *Musical interlude* [a]Ps. 27:4, 8
7 [I]Lit., *everlasting* [a]Ps. 118:20; Is. 26:2 [b]Ps. 29:2, 9; 97:6; Acts 7:2; 1Cor. 2:8
8 [a]Deut. 4:34; Ps. 96:7 [b]Ex. 15:3, 6; Ps. 76:3-6
9 [I]Lit., *everlasting* [a]Ps. 26:8; 57:11
10 [a]Gen. 32:2; Josh. 5:14; 2Sam. 5:10; Neh. 9:6

1 [a]Ps. 86:4; 143:8
2 [a]Ps. 31:1 [b]Ps. 25:20; 31:1 [c]Ps. 13:4; 41:11
3 [I]Or, *Let those . . .be ashamed* [a]Ps. 37:9; 40:1; Is. 49:23 [b]Ps. 119:158; Is. 21:2; Hab. 1:13
4 [a]Ex. 33:13; Ps. 27:11; 86:11
5 [a]Ps. 25:10; 43:3 [b]Ps. 79:9 [c]Ps. 40:1
6 [I]Or, *everlasting* [a]Ps. 98:3 [b]Ps. 103:17
7 [a]Job 13:26; 20:11 [b]Ps. 51:1 [c]Ps. 31:19
8 [a]Ps. 86:5 [b]Ps. 92:15 [c]Ps. 32:8
9 [I]Or, *afflicted* [a]Ps. 23:3 [b]Ps. 27:11
10 [a]Ps. 40:11 [b]Ps. 103:18
11 [a]Ps. 31:3; 79:9 [b]Ex. 34:9
12 [a]Ps. 31:19 [b]Ps. 25:8; 37:23
13 [I]Lit., *good* [II]Lit., *seed* [III]Or, *earth* [a]Prov. 1:33; Jer. 23:6 [b]Ps. 37:11; 69:36; Matt. 5:5

14 [I]Or, *counsel* or *intimacy* [a]Prov. 3:32; John 7:17

[II]And He will [b]make them know
His covenant.
15 My [a]eyes are continually[8548]
toward the LORD,
For He will [I][b]pluck my feet out
of the net.
16 [a]Turn to me and be gracious[2603]
to me,
For I am [b]lonely[3173] and afflicted.
17 [I]The [a]troubles of my heart[3824]
are enlarged;
Bring me [b]out of my
distresses.[4691]
18 [a]Look upon[7200] my affliction and
my [I]trouble,[5999]
And [b]forgive[5375] all my sins.
19 Look upon[7200] my enemies, for
they [a]are many;
And they [b]hate[8130] me with
violent hatred.[8135]
20 [a]Guard[8104] my soul and
deliver[5337] me;
Do not let me [b]be ashamed, for
I take refuge[2620] in Thee.
21 Let [a]integrity[8537] and
uprightness[3476] preserve[5341]
me,
For [b]I wait for Thee.
22 [a]Redeem[6299] Israel, O God,
Out of all his troubles.

Protestation of Integrity and Prayer for Protection

A Psalm of David.

26 [I][a]Vindicate[8199] me, O LORD, for
I have [b]walked in my
integrity;[8537]
And I have [c]trusted[982] in the
LORD [II][d]without wavering.
2 [a]Examine[974] me, O LORD, and
try[5254] me;
[b]Test[6884] my [I]mind[3629] and my
heart.[3820]
3 For Thy [a]lovingkindness is
before my eyes,
And I have [b]walked in Thy
[I]truth.[571]
4 I do not [a]sit with [I]deceitful[7723]
men,
Nor will I go with [II][b]pretenders.
5 I [a]hate the assembly[6951] of
evildoers,
And I will not sit with the
wicked.[7563]
6 I shall [a]wash[7364] my hands[3709] in
innocence,[5356]
And I will go about [b]Thine
altar,[4196] O LORD,
7 That I may proclaim[8085] with the
voice of [a]thanksgiving,[8425]
And declare[5608] all Thy
[I]wonders.[6381]
8 O LORD, I [a]love[157] the habitation
of Thy house,[1004]
And the place [I]where Thy
[b]glory[3519] dwells.[4908]
9 [a]Do not [I]take[622] my soul[5315] away
along with sinners,[2400]
Nor my life[2416] with [b]men[582] of
bloodshed,[1818]
10 In whose hands[3027] is a
[a]wicked scheme,
And whose right hand is full of
[b]bribes.
11 But as for me, I shall [a]walk in
my integrity;
[b]Redeem[6299] me, and be
gracious[2603] to me.
12 [a]My foot stands on a [b]level place;
In the [c]congregations I shall
bless[1288] the LORD.

A Psalm of Fearless Trust in God

A Psalm of David.

27 The LORD is my [a]light[216] and my
[b]salvation;[3468]
Whom shall I fear?[3372]
The LORD is the [I][c]defense of my
life;[2416]
[d]Whom shall I dread?[6342]
2 When evildoers[7489] came upon
me to [a]devour my flesh,[1320]
My adversaries and my
enemies, they [b]stumbled[3782]
and fell.[5307]
3 Though a [a]host[4264] encamp
against me,
My heart[3820] will not fear;

14 [II]Or, *And His covenant, to make them know it.* [b]Gen. 17:1, 2
15 [I]Lit., *bring out* [a]Ps. 123:2; 141:8 [b]Ps. 31:4; 124:7
16 [a]Ps. 69:16 [b]Ps. 143:4
17 [I]Some commentators read *Relieve the troubles of my heart* [a]Ps. 40:12 [b]Ps. 107:6
18 [I]Lit., *toil* [a]2Sam. 16:12; Ps. 31:7 [b]Ps. 103:3
19 [a]Ps. 3:1 [b]Ps. 9:13
20 [a]Ps. 86:2 [b]Ps. 25:2
21 [a]Ps. 41:12 [b]Ps. 25:3
22 [a]Ps. 130:8

1 [I]Lit., *Judge* [II]Lit., *I do not slide* [a]Ps. 7:8 [b]2Kin. 20:3; Prov. 20:7 [c]Ps. 13:5; 28:7 [d]Heb. 10:23
2 [I]Lit., *kidneys*, figurative for inner man [a]Ps. 17:3; 139:23 [b]Ps. 7:9
3 [I]Or, *faithfulness* [a]Ps. 48:9 [b]2Kin. 20:3; Ps. 86:11
4 [I]Or, *worthless men; lit., men of falsehood* [II]Or, *dissemblers, hypocrites* [a]Ps. 1:1 [b]Ps. 28:3
5 [a]Ps. 31:6; 139:21
6 [a]Ps. 73:13 [b]Ps. 43:3, 4
7 [I]Or, *miracles* [a]Ps. 9:1
8 [I]Lit., *of the tabernacle of Thy glory* [a]Ps. 27:4 [b]Ps. 24:7
9 [I]Lit., *gather* [a]Ps. 28:3 [b]Ps. 139:19
10 [a]Ps. 37:7 [b]Ps. 15:5
11 [a]Ps. 26:1 [b]Ps. 44:26; 69:18
12 [a]Ps. 40:2 [b]Ps. 27:11 [c]Ps. 22:22

1 [I]Or, *refuge* [a]Ps. 18:28; Is. 60:20; Mic. 7:8 [b]Ex. 15:2; Ps. 62:7; 118:14; Is. 33:2; Jon. 2:9 [c]Ps. 28:8 [d]Ps. 118:6

2 [a]Ps. 14:4 [b]Ps. 9:3 **3** [a]Ps. 3:6

Though war arise against me,
In *spite of* this I [I]shall be
[b]confident.[982]
4 [a]One thing I have asked[7592] from
the LORD, that I shall seek:
That I may [b]dwell in the
house[1004] of the LORD all the
days[3117] of my life,
To behold[2372] [c]the [I]beauty of the
LORD,
And to [II][d]meditate in His
temple.[1964]
5 For in the [a]day[3117] of trouble[7451]
He will [b]conceal me in His
[I]tabernacle;
In the secret place of His tent[168]
He will [c]hide me;
He will [d]lift me up on a rock.
6 And now [a]my head[7218] will be
lifted up above my enemies
around me;
And I will offer[2076] in His tent
[b]sacrifices[2077] [I]with shouts of
joy;
I will [c]sing,[7891] yes, I will sing
praises[2167] to the LORD.
7 [a]Hear,[8085] O LORD, when I
cry[7121] with my voice,
And be gracious[2603] to me and
[b]answer me.
8 *When Thou didst say,* "[a]Seek My
face," my heart said to Thee,
"Thy face, O LORD, [b]I shall
seek."
9 [a]Do not hide Thy face from me,
Do not turn Thy servant[5650]
away in [b]anger;[639]
Thou hast been [c]my help;
[d]Do not abandon[5203] me nor
[e]forsake[5800] me,
O God[430] of my salvation!
10 [I]For my father[1] and [a]my
mother[517] have forsaken
me,
But [b]the LORD will take me up.
11 [a]Teach[3384] me Thy way,[1870] O
LORD,
And lead[5148] me in a [b]level
path,[734]
Because of [I]my foes.
12 Do not deliver me over to the
[I][a]desire of my adversaries;
For [b]false[8267] witnesses have
risen against me,
And such as [c]breathe out
violence.[2555]
13 [I]*I would have despaired* unless
I had believed[539] that I would
see the [a]goodness of the
LORD
In the [b]land[776] of the living.[2416]
14 [a]Wait for[6960] the LORD;
Be [b]strong,[2388] and let your
heart take courage;
Yes, wait for the LORD.

A Prayer for Help, and Praise for Its Answer

A Psalm of David.

28 To Thee, O LORD, I call;[7121]
My [a]rock, do not be deaf to me,
Lest, if Thou [b]be silent to me,
I become like those who
[c]go down to the pit.[953]
2 Hear[8085] the [a]voice of my
supplications[8469] when I cry
to Thee for help,
When I [b]lift up[5375] my hands[3027]
[c]toward [I]Thy holy[6944]
[d]sanctuary.[1687]
3 [a]Do not drag me away with the
wicked[7563]
And with those who work
iniquity;[205]
Who [b]speak[1696] peace with their
neighbors,[7453]
While evil[7451] is in their
hearts.[3824]
4 Requite them [a]according to their
work and according to the
evil[7455] of their practices;
Requite them according to the
deeds of their hands;
Repay[7725] them their
[I]recompense.
5 Because they [a]do not regard[995]
the works of the LORD
Nor the deeds of His hands,
He will tear them down[2040] and
not build them up.
6 Blessed[1288] be the LORD,

3 [I]Lit., *am confident* [b]Job 4:6
4 [I]Lit., *delightfulness* [II]Lit., *inquire* [a]Ps. 26:8 [b]Ps. 23:6 [c]Ps. 90:17 [d]Ps. 18:6
5 [I]Or, *shelter* [a]Ps. 50:15 [b]Ps. 31:20 [c]Ps. 17:8 [d]Ps. 40:2
6 [I]Lit., *of shouts* [a]Ps. 3:3 [b]Ps. 107:22 [c]Ps. 13:6
7 [a]Ps. 4:3; 61:1 [b]Ps. 13:3
8 [a]Ps. 105:4; Amos 5:6 [b]Ps. 34:4
9 [a]Ps. 69:17 [b]Ps. 6:1 [c]Ps. 40:17 [d]Ps. 94:14 [e]Ps. 37:28
10 [I]Or, *If my father. . .forsake me, Then the LORD* [a]Is. 49:15 [b]Is. 40:11
11 [I]Or, *those who lie in wait for me* [a]Ps. 25:4; 86:11 [b]Ps. 5:8; 26:12
12 [I]Lit., *soul* [a]Ps. 41:2 [b]Deut. 19:18; Ps. 35:11; Matt. 26:60 [c]Acts 9:1
13 [I]Or, *Surely I believed* [a]Ps. 31:19 [b]Job 28:13; Ps. 52:5; 116:9; 142:5; Is. 38:11; Jer. 11:19; Ezek. 26:20
14 [a]Ps. 25:3; 37:34; 40:1; 62:5; 130:5; Prov. 20:22; Is. 25:9 [b]Ps. 31:24

1 [a]Ps. 18:2 [b]Ps. 35:22; 39:12; 83:1 [c]Ps. 88:4; 143:7; Prov. 1:12
2 [I]Lit., *the innermost place of Thy sanctuary* [a]Ps. 140:6 [b]Ps. 134:2; 141:2; Lam. 2:19; 1Tim. 2:8 [c]Ps. 5:7; 138:2 [d]1Kin. 6:5
3 [a]Ps. 26:9 [b]Ps. 12:2; 55:21; 62:4; Jer. 9:8
4 [I]Or, *dealings* [a]Ps. 62:12; 2Tim. 4:14; Rev. 18:6; 22:12
5 [a]Is. 5:12

Because He [a]has heard[8085] the
voice of my supplication.
7 The LORD is my [a]strength and
my [b]shield;
My heart[3820] [c]trusts[982] in Him,
and I am helped;
Therefore [d]my heart exults,
And with [e]my song[7892] I shall
thank[3034] Him.
8 The LORD is [I]their [a]strength,
And He is a [IIb]saving[3444] defense
to His anointed.[4899]
9 [a]Save[3467] Thy people,[5971] and
bless[1288] [b]Thine
inheritance;[5159]
Be their [c]shepherd also, and
[d]carry them forever.[5769]

The Voice of the LORD in the Storm

A Psalm of David.

29 [a]Ascribe to the LORD, O [I]sons
of the mighty,[410]
Ascribe to the LORD glory[3519]
and strength.
2 Ascribe to the LORD the glory
[I]due to His name;
Worship[7812] the LORD [a]in
[II]holy[6944] array.[1927]
3 The [a]voice of the LORD is upon
the waters;
The God[410] of glory [b]thunders,
The LORD is over [Ic]many waters.
4 The voice of the LORD is
[a]powerful,
The voice of the LORD is
majestic.[1926]
5 The voice of the LORD breaks[7665]
the cedars;
Yes, the LORD breaks in pieces
[a]the cedars of Lebanon.
6 And He makes Lebanon
[a]skip[7540] like a calf,
And [b]Sirion like a young[1121] wild
ox.
7 The voice of the LORD hews out
[I]flames of fire.
8 The voice of the LORD
[I]shakes[2342] the wilderness;
The LORD shakes the wilderness
of [a]Kadesh.

6 [a]Ps. 28:2
7 [a]Ps. 18:2; 59:17 [b]Ps. 3:3 [c]Ps. 13:5; 112:7 [d]Ps. 16:9 [e]Ps. 40:3; 69:30
8 [I]A few mss. and ancient versions read *the strength of His people* [II]Or, *refuge of salvation* [a]Ps. 20:6; 89:17 [b]Ps. 27:1; 140:7
9 [a]Ps. 106:47 [b]Deut. 9:29; 32:9; 1Kin. 8:51; Ps. 33:12; 106:40 [c]Ps. 80:1 [d]Deut. 1:31; Is. 40:11; 46:3; 63:9

1 [I]Or, *sons of gods* [a]1Chr. 16:28, 29; Ps. 96:7-9
2 [I]Lit., *of His name* [II]Or, *the majesty of holiness* [a]2Chr. 20:21; Ps. 110:3
3 [I]Or, *great* [a]Ps. 104:7 [b]Job 37:4, 5; Ps. 18:13 [c]Ps. 18:16; 107:23
4 [a]Ps. 68:33
5 [a]Judg. 9:15; 1Kin. 5:6; Ps. 104:16; Is. 2:13; 14:8
6 [a]Ps. 114:4, 6 [b]Deut. 3:9
7 [I]I.e., lightning
8 [I]Or, *causes . . . to whirl* [a]Num. 13:26
9 [a]Job 39:1 [b]Ps. 26:8
10 [a]Gen. 6:17 [b]Ps. 10:16
11 [I]Or, *May the LORD give* [II]Or, *May the LORD bless* [a]Ps. 28:8; 68:35; Is. 40:29 [b]Ps. 37:11; 72:3

1 [a]Ps. 118:28; 145:1 [b]Ps. 3:3 [c]Ps. 25:2; 35:19, 24
2 [a]Ps. 88:13 [b]Ps. 6:2; 103:3; Is. 53:5
3 [I]I.e., the nether world [II]Some mss. read *from among those who go down* [a]Ps. 86:13 [b]Ps. 28:1
4 [I]Lit., *memorial* [a]Ps. 149:1 [b]Ps. 50:5 [c]Ps. 97:12 [d]Ex. 3:15; Ps. 135:13; Hos. 12:5
5 [a]Ps. 103:9; Is. 26:20; 54:7, 8 [b]Ps. 118:1 [c]Ps. 126:5; 2Cor. 4:17
6 [a]Ps. 10:6; 62:2, 6

9 The voice of the LORD makes
[a]the deer[355] to calve,[2342]
And strips the forests bare,
And [b]in His temple[1964]
everything says,[559] "Glory!"
10 The LORD sat *as King* at the
[a]flood;
Yes, the LORD sits as [b]King[4428]
forever.[5769]
11 [I]The LORD will give [a]strength to
His people;[5971]
[II]The LORD will bless[1288] His
people with [b]peace.

Thanksgiving for Deliverance from Death

A Psalm; a Song at the Dedication of the House. *A Psalm* of David.

30 I will [a]extol Thee, O LORD, for
Thou hast [b]lifted me up,
And hast not let my [c]enemies
rejoice over me.
2 O LORD my God,[430]
I [a]cried to Thee for help, and
Thou didst [b]heal me.
3 O LORD, Thou hast [a]brought
up[5927] my soul[5315] from
[I]Sheol;[7585]
Thou hast kept me alive,
[II]that I should not [b]go down
to the pit.[953]
4 [a]Sing[2167] praise to the LORD, you
[b]His godly ones,[2623]
And [c]give thanks[3034] to His
holy[6944] [Id]name.
5 For [a]His anger[639] is but for a
moment,
His [b]favor[7522] is for a lifetime;[2416]
Weeping may [c]last for the night,
But a shout of joy *comes* in the
morning.
6 Now as for me, I said in my
prosperity, "I will [a]never be
moved."
7 O LORD, by Thy favor Thou hast
made my mountain to stand
strong;

Thou didst [a]hide Thy face, I was dismayed.[926]
8 To Thee, O LORD, I called,[7121]
And to the Lord I made supplication:[2603]
9 "What profit is there in my blood,[1818] if I [a]go down to the pit?[7845]
Will the [b]dust[6083] praise[3034] Thee? Will it declare[5046] Thy faithfulness?[571]
10 "[a]Hear,[8085] O LORD, and be gracious[2603] to me;
O LORD, be Thou my [b]helper."
11 Thou hast turned[2015] for me [a]my mourning into dancing;
Thou hast [b]loosed my sackcloth and girded me with [c]gladness;
12 That *my* [1a]soul[3519] may sing praise[2167] to Thee, and not be silent.
O LORD my God, I will [b]give thanks to Thee forever.[5769]

A Psalm of Complaint and of Praise

For the choir director. A Psalm of David.

31 [a]In Thee, O LORD, I have taken refuge;[2620]
Let me never [b]be ashamed;[954]
[c]In Thy righteousness[6666] deliver me.
2 [a]Incline Thine ear[241] to me, rescue[5337] me quickly;
Be Thou to me a [b]rock of [1]strength,
A stronghold[1004,4686] to save[3467] me.
3 For Thou art my [1]rock and [a]my fortress;
For [b]Thy name's sake Thou wilt lead[5148] me and guide me.
4 Thou wilt [a]pull me out of the net which they have secretly[2934] laid for me;
For Thou art my [b]strength.
5 [a]Into Thy hand[3027] I commit my spirit;[7307]
Thou hast [b]ransomed[6299] me, O LORD, [c]God[410] of [1]truth.[571]
6 I hate those who [a]regard[8104] [1]vain[7723] idols;
But I [b]trust[982] in the LORD.
7 I will [a]rejoice and be glad in Thy lovingkindness,[2617]
Because Thou hast [b]seen[7200] my affliction;
Thou hast known[3045] the troubles of my soul,[5315]
8 And Thou hast not [a]given me over into the hand of the enemy;
Thou hast set my feet in a large place.
9 Be gracious[2603] to me, O LORD, for [a]I am in distress;
My [b]eye is wasted away from grief,[3708] [c]my soul and my body[990] *also.*
10 For my life[2416] is spent[3615] with [a]sorrow,
And my years with sighing;
My [b]strength has failed[3782] because of my iniquity,[5771]
And [c]my [1]body[6106] has wasted away.
11 Because of all my adversaries, I have become a [a]reproach,[2781]
Especially to my [b]neighbors,[7934]

7 [a]Deut. 31:17; Ps. 104:29; 143:7
9 [a]Ps. 28:1 [b]Ps. 6:5
10 [a]Ps. 4:1; 27:7 [b]Ps. 27:9; 54:4
11 [a]Eccl. 3:4; Jer. 31:4, 13 [b]Is. 20:2 [c]Ps. 4:7
12 [1]Lit., *glory* [a]Ps. 16:9; 57:8; 108:1 [b]Ps. 44:8

1 [a]Ps. 31:1-3; 71:1-3 [b]Ps. 25:2 [c]Ps. 143:1
2 [1]Or, *refuge, protection* [a]Ps. 17:6; 71:2; 86:1; 102:2 [b]Ps. 18:2; 71:3
3 [1]Or, *crag* [a]Ps. 18:2 [b]Ps. 23:3; 25:11
4 [a]Ps. 25:15 [b]Ps. 46:1
5 [1]Or, *faithfulness* [a]Luke 23:46; Acts 7:59 [b]Ps. 55:18; 71:23 [c]Deut. 32:4; Ps. 71:22
6 [1]Lit., *empty vanities* [a]Jon. 2:8 [b]Ps. 52:8
7 [a]Ps. 90:14 [b]Ps. 10:14
8 [a]Deut. 32:30; Ps. 37:33
9 [a]Ps. 66:14; 69:17 [b]Ps. 6:7 [c]Ps. 63:1
10 [1]Or, *bones, substance* [a]Ps. 13:2 [b]Ps. 39:11 [c]Ps. 32:3; 38:3; 102:3
11 [a]Ps. 69:19 [b]Job 19:13; Ps. 38:11; 88:8, 18

31:5 See Lk. 23:46. Redemption is defined by Paul (I Cor. 6:20; 7:23) as being bought with a price. It is of God by the blood of Christ, who was sent on earth to effect it for us (Isa. 44:22; Mt. 20:28; Acts 20:28; Gal. 4:4,5; Heb. 9:12; I Pet. 1:19). And from what are we redeemed? From the bondage of the law and its curse, the power of sin, and the grave; all troubles, iniquity, evil, enemies, death, and destruction (Gal 4:5; 3:13; Rom. 6:18,22; Ps. 49:15; 25:22; 103:4; 130:8; Gen. 48:16; Jer. 15:21; Hos. 13:14). Because of our redemption, we have justification, forgiveness, adoption, and purification (Ps. 49:8; Rom. 3:24; Gal. 4:4,5; Eph. 1:7; Tit. 2:14). Through redemption God manifests His power, grace, love, and mercy (Isa. 50:2; 52:3; 63:9; Jn. 3:16). When we have been redeemed, we become God's property, His first-fruits, a special people, sealed until the great day, zealous of good works and living in holiness, committing ourselves to God while awaiting the completion of our redemption (II Sam. 7:23; Job 19:25; Isa. 35:10; 43:1; Rom. 8:23; Eph. 2:10; 4:30).

And an object of dread[6343] to my
acquaintances;[3045]
Those who see me in the street
flee from me.
12 I am [a]forgotten as a dead[4191]
man, out of mind,[3820]
I am like a broken vessel.
13 For I have heard[8085] the
[I][a]slander of many,
[b]Terror[4032] is on every side;
While they [c]took counsel[3245]
together against me,
They [d]schemed[2161] to take away
my life.[5315]
14 But as for me, I trust[982] in Thee,
O LORD,
I say, "[a]Thou art my God."[430]
15 My [a]times[6256] are in Thy hand;
[b]Deliver me from the hand of
my enemies, and from those
who persecute me.
16 Make Thy [a]face to shine upon
Thy servant;[5650]
[b]Save me in Thy lovingkindness.
17 Let me not be [a]put to shame,
O LORD, for I call upon[7121]
Thee;
Let the [b]wicked[7563] be put to
shame, let them [c]be silent in
[I]Sheol.[7585]
18 Let the [a]lying lips[8193] be dumb,
Which [b]speak[1696] arrogantly
against the righteous[6662]
With pride and contempt.
19 How great is Thy [a]goodness,
Which Thou hast stored up for
those who fear[3373] Thee,
Which Thou hast wrought for
those who [b]take refuge in
Thee,
[c]Before the sons[1121] of men![120]
20 Thou dost hide them in the
[a]secret place of Thy presence
from the [b]conspiracies of
man;[376]
Thou dost keep them secretly
in a [I]shelter from the
[c]strife[7379] of tongues.
21 [a]Blessed[1288] be the LORD,
For He has made [b]marvelous[6381]
His lovingkindness[2617] to me
in a besieged [c]city.

12 [a]Ps. 88:5
13 [I]Lit., *whispering* [a]Ps. 50:20; Jer. 20:10 [b]Lam. 2:22 [c]Ps. 62:4; Matt. 27:1 [d]Ps. 41:7
14 [a]Ps. 140:6
15 [a]Job 14:5; 24:1 [b]Ps. 143:9
16 [a]Num. 6:25; Ps. 4:6; 80:3 [b]Ps. 6:4
17 [I]I.e., the nether world [a]Ps. 25:2, 20 [b]Ps. 25:3 [c]1Sam. 2:9; Ps. 94:17; 115:17
18 [a]Ps. 109:2; 120:2 [b]1Sam. 2:3; Ps. 94:4; Jude 15
19 [a]Ps. 65:4; 145:7; Is. 64:4; Rom. 2:4; 11:22 [b]Ps. 5:11 [c]Ps. 23:5
20 [I]Or, *pavilion* [a]Ps. 27:5 [b]Ps. 37:12 [c]Job 5:21; Ps. 31:13
21 [a]Ps. 28:6 [b]Ps. 17:7 [c]1Sam. 23:7; Ps. 87:5
22 [a]Ps. 116:11 [b]Ps. 88:5; Is. 38:11, 12; Lam. 3:54 [c]Ps. 18:6; 66:19; 145:19
23 [a]Ps. 30:4; 37:28; 50:5 [b]Ps. 145:20; Rev. 2:10 [c]Deut. 32:41; Ps. 94:2
24 [I]Or, *wait for* [a]Ps. 27:14

+Possibly, *Contemplative*, or *Didactic*, or *Skillful Psalm*
1 [a]Ps. 85:2; 103:3; Rom. 4:7, 8
2 [a]2Cor. 5:19 [b]John 1:47
3 [I]Or, *bones, substance* [II]Lit., *roaring* [a]Ps. 39:2, 3 [b]Ps. 31:10 [c]Ps. 38:8
4 [I]Lit., *life juices were turned into the drought of summer* [II]*Selah* may mean: *Pause, Crescendo* or *Musical interlude* [a]1Sam. 5:6; Job 23:2; 33:7; Ps. 38:2; 39:10 [b]Ps. 22:15
5 [I]Or, *iniquity* [a]Lev. 26:40 [b]Job 31:33 [c]Ps. 38:18; Prov. 28:13; 1John 1:9 [d]Ps. 103:12

22 As for me, [a]I said in my alarm,
"I am [b]cut off from before
Thine eyes";
Nevertheless Thou didst
[c]hear[8085] the voice of my
supplications[8469]
When I cried to Thee.
23 O love[157] the LORD, all you
[a]His godly ones![2623]
The LORD [b]preserves[5341] the
faithful,[539]
And fully [c]recompenses[7999] the
proud doer.[6213]
24 [a]Be strong,[2388] and let your
heart[3824] take courage,
All you who [I]hope[3176] in the
LORD.

Blessedness of Forgiveness and of Trust in God

A Psalm of David. A +Maskil.

32

[a]How blessed[835] is he whose
transgression[6588] is
forgiven,[5375]
Whose sin[2401] is covered![3680]
2 How blessed is the man[120] to
whom the LORD [a]does not
impute[2803] iniquity,[5771]
And in whose spirit[7307] there is
[b]no deceit!
3 When [a]I kept silent *about my sin*,
[b]my [I]body[6106] wasted away
Through my [II][c]groaning all
day[3117] long.
4 For day[3119] and night[3915]
[a]Thy hand[3027] was heavy[3513]
upon me;
My [I][b]vitality was drained[2015]
away *as* with the fever heat
of summer. [II]Selah.
5 I [a]acknowledged[3045] my sin to
Thee,
And my iniquity I [b]did not hide;
I said, "[c]I will confess[3034] my
transgressions[6588] to the
LORD";
And Thou [d]didst forgive[5375] the
[I]guilt of my sin.[2403] Selah.

6 Therefore, let everyone who is godly[2623] pray[6419] to Thee
[I][a]in a time[6256] when Thou mayest be found;
Surely [b]in a flood[7858] of great waters they shall not reach[5060] him.
7 Thou art [a]my hiding place; Thou [b]dost preserve[5341] me from trouble;
Thou dost surround me with [I][c]songs of deliverance. Selah.
8 I will [a]instruct you and teach[3384] you in the way[1870] which you should go;
I will counsel[3289] you [b]with My eye upon you.
9 Do not be [a]as the horse or as the mule which have no understanding,[995]
Whose trappings include bit and bridle to hold them in check,
Otherwise they will not come near[7126] to you.
10 Many are the [a]sorrows of the wicked;[7563]
But [b]he who trusts[982] in the LORD, lovingkindness[2617] shall surround him.
11 Be [a]glad in the LORD and rejoice, you righteous[6662] ones,
And shout for joy, all you who are [b]upright[3477] in heart.[3820]

Praise to the Creator and Preserver

33 [a]Sing for joy in the LORD, O you righteous[6662] ones;
Praise[8416] is [b]becoming[5000] to the upright.[3477]
2 Give thanks[3034] to the LORD with the [a]lyre;
Sing praises[2167] to Him with a [b]harp of ten strings.
3 Sing[7891] to Him a [a]new song;[7892]
Play skillfully[3190] with [b]a shout of joy.
4 For the word[1697] of the LORD [a]is upright;[3477]
And all His work is *done* [b]in faithfulness.[530]
5 He [a]loves[157] righteousness[6666] and justice;[4941]
The [b]earth[776] is full of the lovingkindness[2617] of the LORD.
6 By the [a]word of the LORD the heavens[8064] were made,[6213]
And [b]by the breath[7307] of His mouth[6310] [c]all their host.[6635]
7 He gathers[3664] the [a]waters of the sea together [I]as a heap;
He lays up the deeps in storehouses.
8 Let [a]all the earth fear[3372] the LORD;
Let all the inhabitants of the world[8398] [b]stand in awe of Him.
9 For [a]He spoke,[559] and it was done;
He commanded,[6680] and it [I]stood fast.
10 The LORD [a]nullifies[6331] the counsel[6098] of the nations;[1471]
He frustrates the plans[4284] of the peoples.[5971]
11 The [a]counsel of the LORD stands forever,[5769]
The [b]plans[4284] of His heart[3820] from generation to generation.[1755]
12 Blessed[835] is the [a]nation[1471] whose God[430] is the LORD,
The people whom He has [b]chosen for His own inheritance.[5159]
13 The LORD [a]looks from heaven;[8064]
He [b]sees[7200] all the sons[1121] of men;[120]
14 From [a]His dwelling place He looks out
On all the inhabitants of the earth,
15 He who [a]fashions[3335] [I]the hearts[3820] of them all,
He who [b]understands[995] all their works.
16 [a]The king[4428] is not saved[3467] by a mighty army;[2428]

---

6 [I]Lit., *in a time of finding out* [a]Ps. 69:13; Is. 55:6 [b]Ps. 46:1-3; 69:1; 124:5; 144:7; Is. 43:2
7 [I]Or, *shouts* [a]Ps. 9:9; 31:20; 91:1; 119:114 [b]Ps. 121:7 [c]Ex. 15:1; Judg. 5:1; Ps. 40:3
8 [a]Ps. 25:8 [b]Ps. 33:18
9 [a]Prov. 26:3
10 [a]Ps. 16:4; Prov. 13:21; Rom. 2:9 [b]Ps. 5:11, 12; Prov. 16:20
11 [a]Ps. 64:10; 68:3; 97:12 [b]Ps. 7:10; 64:10

1 [a]Ps. 32:11; Phil. 3:1; 4:4 [b]Ps. 92:1; 147:1
2 [a]Ps. 71:22; 147:7 [b]Ps. 144:9
3 [a]Ps. 40:3; 96:1; 98:1; 144:9; Is. 42:10; Rev. 5:9 [b]Ps. 98:4
4 [a]Ps. 19:8 [b]Ps. 119:90
5 [a]Ps. 11:7; 37:28 [b]Ps. 119:64
6 [a]Gen. 1:6; Ps. 148:5; Heb. 11:3 [b]Ps. 104:30 [c]Gen. 2:1
7 [I]Some versions read *in a water skin;* i.e., container [a]Ex. 15:8; Josh. 3:16; Ps. 78:13
8 [a]Ps. 67:7 [b]Ps. 96:9
9 [I]Or, *stood forth* [a]Gen. 1:3; Ps. 148:5
10 [a]Ps. 2:1-3; Is. 8:10; 19:3
11 [a]Job 23:12; Prov. 19:21 [b]Ps. 40:5; 92:5; 139:17; Is. 55:8
12 [a]Ps. 144:15 [b]Ex. 19:5; Deut. 7:6; Ps. 28:9
13 [a]Job 28:24; Ps. 14:2 [b]Ps. 11:4
14 [a]1Kin. 8:39, 43; Ps. 102:19
15 [I]Or, *their heart together* [a]Job 10:8; Ps. 119:73 [b]2Chr. 16:9; Job 34:21; Jer. 32:19
16 [a]Ps. 44:6; 60:11

A warrior is not delivered[5337] by great strength.
17 A [a]horse is a false hope[8267] for victory;[8668]
Nor does it deliver anyone by its great strength.[2428]
18 Behold, [a]the eye of the LORD is on those who fear[3373] Him,
On those who [1b]hope[3176] for His lovingkindness,[2617]
19 To [a]deliver[5337] their soul[5315] from death,[4194]
And to keep them alive [b]in famine.
20 Our soul [a]waits for the LORD;
He is our [b]help and our shield.
21 For our [a]heart rejoices in Him,
Because we trust[982] in His holy[6944] name.
22 Let Thy lovingkindness, O LORD, be upon us,
According as we have [1]hoped in Thee.

The LORD a Provider and Deliverer

A Psalm of David when he +feigned madness before •Abimelech, who drove him away and he departed.

34 I will [a]bless[1288] the LORD at all times;[6256]
His [b]praise[8416] shall continually[8548] be in my mouth.[6310]
2 My soul[5315] shall [a]make its boast[1984] in the LORD;
The [b]humble shall hear[8085] it and rejoice.
3 O [a]magnify the LORD with me,
And let us [b]exalt His name together.
4 I [a]sought the LORD, and He answered me,
And [b]delivered[5337] me from all my fears.[4035]
5 They [a]looked to Him and were radiant,
And their faces shall [b]never be ashamed.
6 This [1]poor man cried[7121] and [a]the LORD heard[8085] him,
And saved[3467] him out of all his troubles.
7 The [a]angel[4397] of the LORD encamps around those who fear[3373] Him,
And rescues[2502] them.
8 O [a]taste and see that the LORD is good;[2896]
How [b]blessed[835] is the man[1397] who takes refuge[2620] in Him!
9 O fear[3372] the LORD, you [a]His saints;[6918]
For to those who fear[3373] Him, there is [b]no want.
10 The young lions do lack and suffer hunger;
But they who seek the LORD shall [a]not be in want of any good thing.
11 [a]Come, you children,[1121] listen[8085] to me;
[b]I will teach[3925] you [c]the fear[3374] of the LORD.
12 [a]Who is the man[376] who desires[2655] life,[2416]
And loves[157] *length of* days[3117] that he may [b]see good?
13 Keep[5341] [a]your tongue from evil,[7451]
And your lips[8193] from speaking[1696] [b]deceit.[4820]
14 [a]Depart[5493] from evil, and do[6213] good;
Seek peace, and [b]pursue it.
15 The [a]eyes of the LORD are toward the righteous,[6662]
And His ears[241] are *open* to their cry.
16 The [a]face of the LORD is against evildoers,
To [b]cut off[3772] the memory[2143] of them from the earth.[776]
17 *The righteous* [a]cry and the LORD hears,[8085]
And delivers[5337] them out of all their troubles.
18 The LORD [a]is near to the [b]brokenhearted,[7665,3820]
And saves[3467] those who are [1c]crushed[1793] in spirit.[7307]

17 aPs. 20:7; 147:10; Prov. 21:31
18 1Or, *wait* aJob 36:7; Ps. 32:8; 34:15; 1Pet. 3:12 bPs. 32:10; 147:11
19 aPs. 56:13; Acts 12:11 bJob 5:20; Ps. 37:19
20 aPs. 62:1; 130:6; Is. 8:17 bPs. 115:9
21 aPs. 13:5; 28:7; Zech. 10:7; John 16:22
22 1Or, *waited for*

+Or, *changed his behavior*
•Possibly a title of King Achish of Gath. See 1Sam. 21:10-15
1 aEph. 5:20; 1Thess. 5:18 bPs. 71:6
2 aPs. 44:8; Jer. 9:24; 1Cor. 1:31 bPs. 69:32
3 aPs. 35:27; 69:30; Luke 1:46 bPs. 18:46
4 a2Chr. 15:2; Ps. 9:10; Matt. 7:7 bPs. 34:6, 17, 19
5 aPs. 36:9; Is. 60:5 bPs. 25:3
6 1Or, *afflicted* aPs. 34:4
7 aPs. 91:11; Dan. 6:22
8 aPs. 119:103; Heb. 6:5; 1Pet. 2:3 bPs. 2:12
9 aPs. 31:23 bPs. 23:1
10 aPs. 84:11
11 aPs. 66:16 bPs. 32:8 cPs. 111:10
12 aPs. 34:12-16; 1Pet. 3:10-12 bEccl. 3:13
13 aPs. 141:3; Prov. 13:3; James 1:26 b1Pet. 2:22
14 aPs. 37:27; Is. 1:16, 17 bRom. 14:19; Heb. 12:14
15 aJob 36:7; Ps. 33:18
16 aLev. 17:10; Jer. 44:11; Amos 9:4 bJob 18:17; Ps. 9:6; 109:15; Prov. 10:7
17 aPs. 34:6; 145:19
18 1Or, *contrite* aPs. 145:18 bPs. 147:3; Is. 61:1 cPs. 51:17; Is. 57:15

19 [a]Many are the [b]afflictions[7451] of
the righteous;
But the LORD [c]delivers him out
of them all.
20 He keeps[8104] all his bones;[6106]
[a]Not one of them is broken.
21 [a]Evil shall slay[4191] the
wicked;[7563]
And those who hate[8130] the
righteous will be
[I]condemned.
22 The LORD [a]redeems[6299] the soul
of His servants;[5650]
And none of those who [b]take
refuge[2620] in Him will be
[I]condemned.

Prayer for Rescue from Enemies

A Psalm of David.

35 Contend,[7378] O LORD, with those
who [a]contend with me;
Fight against those who
[b]fight against me.
2 Take hold of [Ia]buckler[6793] and
shield,
And rise up for [b]my help.
3 Draw also the spear and [I]the
battle-axe to meet those who
pursue me;
Say[559] to my soul,[5315] "I am
[a]your salvation."[3444]
4 Let those be [a]ashamed[954] and
dishonored who seek my
[I]life;
Let those be [b]turned back and
humiliated who devise[2803]
evil[7451] against me.
5 Let them be [a]like chaff before
the wind,[7307]
With the angel[4397] of the LORD
driving *them* on.
6 Let their way be dark[2822] and
[a]slippery,
With the angel of the LORD
pursuing them.
7 For [a]without cause they [b]hid
their net for me;
Without cause they dug a
[I]pit[7845] for my soul.
8 Let [a]destruction come upon him
unawares;[3045]
And [b]let the net which he hid
catch himself;
Into that very [c]destruction let
him fall.
9 And my soul shall [a]rejoice in the
LORD;
It shall [b]exult in His salvation.
10 All my [a]bones[6106] will say,
"LORD, [b]who is like Thee,
Who delivers[5337] the afflicted
from him [c]who is too
strong[2389] for him,
And [d]the afflicted and the needy
from him who robs him?"
11 [a]Malicious[2555] witnesses rise
up;
They ask me of things that I do
not know.[3045]
12 They [a]repay[7999] me evil[7451] for
good,[2896]
To the bereavement[7908] of my
soul.
13 But as for me, [a]when they were
sick, my [b]clothing was
sackcloth;
I [c]humbled my soul with fasting;
And my [d]prayer[8605] kept
returning[7725] to my bosom.
14 I went about as though it were
my friend[7453] or brother;[251]
I [a]bowed down [I]mourning,[6937] as
one who sorrows for a
mother.[517]
15 But [a]at my [I]stumbling they
rejoiced, and gathered[622]
themselves together;
The [IIb]smiters[5522] whom I did not

34:19 [a]Prov. 24:16 [b]Ps. 71:20; 2Tim. 3:11f. [c]Ps. 34:4, 6, 17
20 [a]John 19:33, 36
21 [I]Or, *held guilty* [a]Ps. 94:23; 140:11; Prov. 24:16
22 [I]V. 21, note 1 [a]1Kin. 1:29; Ps. 71:23 [b]Ps. 37:40

35:1 [a]Ps. 18:43; Is. 49:25 [b]Ps. 56:2
2 [I]I.e., small shield [a]Ps. 91:4 [b]Ps. 44:26
3 [I]Or, *close up the path against those* [a]Ps. 62:2
4 [I]Or, *soul* [a]Ps. 70:2 [b]Ps. 40:14; 129:5
5 [a]Job 21:18; Ps. 83:13; Is. 29:5
6 [a]Ps. 73:18; Jer. 23:12
7 [I]*Pit* has been transposed from line above [a]Ps. 69:4; 109:3; 140:5 [b]Ps. 9:15
8 [a]Ps. 55:23; Is. 47:11; 1Thess. 5:3 [b]Ps. 9:15 [c]Ps. 73:18
9 [a]Is. 61:10 [b]Ps. 9:14; 13:5; Luke 1:47
10 [a]Ps. 51:8 [b]Ex. 15:11; Ps. 86:8; Mic. 7:18 [c]Ps. 18:17 [d]Ps. 37:14; 109:16
11 [a]Ps. 27:12
12 [a]Ps. 38:20; 109:5; Jer. 18:20; John 10:32
13 [a]Job 30:25 [b]Ps. 69:11 [c]Ps. 69:10 [d]Matt. 10:13; Luke 10:6
14 [I]Or, *dressed in black* [a]Ps. 38:6
15 [I]Or, *limping* [II]Or, *smitten ones* [a]Obad. 12 [b]Job 30:1, 8, 12

34:20 See Jn. 19:36.
34:21 Cf. Job 12:6; Ps. 17:14; 73:7,12; Jer. 12:1. These five texts refer to the temporary prosperity which the wicked frequently enjoy. The transitory nature of this prosperity was not understood by the psalmist until he entered the sanctuary of God. Then he perceived that they were on slippery ground (Ps. 73:16-18). It is not asserted that harm will pursue and kill the wicked without a moment's delay; however, *ultimately* that will be the case.

know gathered together
against me,
They [III][c]slandered me without
ceasing.
16 Like godless[2611] jesters at a
feast,
They [a]gnashed[2786] at me with
their teeth.
17 Lord,[136] [a]how long wilt Thou
look on?
Rescue[7725] my soul [b]from their
ravages,[7722]
My [c]only *life*[3173] from the lions.
18 I will [a]give Thee thanks in the
great congregation;[6951]
I will [b]praise[1984] Thee among a
mighty throng.[5971]
🔑 19 [a]Do not let those who are
wrongfully[8267] [b]my enemies
rejoice over me;
Neither let those [c]who hate[8130]
me without cause [I][d]wink[7169]
maliciously.
20 For they do not speak[1696] peace,
But they devise [a]deceitful[4820]
words against those who are
quiet in the land.[776]
21 And they [a]opened their
mouth[6310] wide against me;
They said, "[b]Aha, aha, our eyes
have seen[7200] it!"
22 [a]Thou hast seen it, O LORD,
[b]do not keep silent;
O Lord, [c]do not be far from me.
23 [a]Stir up Thyself, and awake to
my right,[4941]
And to my cause,[7379] my God[430]
and my Lord.
24 [a]Judge[8199] me, O LORD my God,
according to Thy
righteousness;[6664]
And [b]do not let them rejoice over
me.
25 Do not let them say in their
heart, "[a]Aha, our desire!"
Do not let them say, "We have
[b]swallowed[1104] him up!"
26 Let [a]those be ashamed[954] and
humiliated altogether who
rejoice at my distress;
Let those be [b]clothed with
shame and dishonor who
[c]magnify themselves over
me.
27 Let them [a]shout for joy and
rejoice, who favor[2655] [b]my
vindication;[6664]
And [c]let them say
continually,[8548] "The LORD be
magnified,
Who [d]delights[2655] in the
prosperity[7965] of His
servant."[5650]
28 And [a]my tongue shall declare[1897]
Thy righteousness
And Thy praise[8416] all day[3117]
long.

Wickedness of Men and Lovingkindness of God

For the choir director. *A Psalm* of David the servant of the LORD.

36 Transgression[6588] speaks[5001] to
the ungodly[7563] within[7130]
[I]his heart;[3820]
There is [a]no fear[6343] of God[430]
before his eyes.
2 For [I]it [a]flatters him in his *own*
eyes,
Concerning the discovery of his
iniquity[5771] *and* the hatred *of*
it.
3 The [a]words[1697] of his mouth[6310]
are wickedness[205] and
deceit;[4820]
He has [b]ceased to [I]be wise[7919]
and to do good.[3190]
4 He [a]plans[2803] wickedness upon
his bed;
He sets himself on a [b]path[1870]
that is not good;[2896]
He [c]does not despise[3988]
evil.[7451]
5 Thy [a]lovingkindness,[2617] O
LORD, [I]extends to the
heavens,[8064]
Thy faithfulness[530] *reaches* to the
skies.[7834]

15 [III]Lit., *tore* [c]Ps. 7:2
16 [a]Job 16:9; Ps. 37:12; Lam. 2:16
17 [a]Ps. 13:1; Hab. 1:13 [b]Ps. 35:7 [c]Ps. 22:20, 21
18 [a]Ps. 22:22 [b]Ps. 22:25
19 [I]Or, *wink the eye* [a]Ps. 13:4; 30:1; 38:16 [b]Ps. 38:19; 69:4 [c]John 15:25 [d]Prov. 6:13; 10:10
20 [a]Ps. 55:21; Jer. 9:8; Mic. 6:12
21 [a]Job 16:10; Ps. 22:13 [b]Ps. 40:15; 70:3
22 [a]Ex. 3:7; Ps. 10:14 [b]Ps. 28:1 [c]Ps. 10:1; 22:11; 38:21; 71:12
23 [a]Ps. 7:6; 44:23; 59:4; 80:2
24 [a]Ps. 9:4; 26:1; 43:1 [b]Ps. 35:19
25 [a]Ps. 35:21 [b]Ps. 56:1; 124:3; Prov. 1:12; Lam. 2:16
26 [a]Ps. 40:14 [b]Ps. 109:29 [c]Job 19:5; Ps. 38:16
27 [a]Ps. 32:11 [b]Ps. 9:4 [c]Ps. 40:16; 70:4 [d]Ps. 147:11; 149:4
28 [a]Ps. 51:14; 71:15, 24

1 [I]Another reading is *my heart* [a]Rom. 3:18
2 [I]Or, *he flatters himself* [a]Deut. 29:19; Ps. 10:11; 49:18
3 [I]Or, *understand to do good* [a]Ps. 10:7; 12:2 [b]Ps. 94:8; Jer. 4:22
4 [a]Prov. 4:16; Mic. 2:1 [b]Is. 65:2 [c]Ps. 52:3; Rom. 12:9
5 [I]Lit., *is in* [a]Ps. 57:10; 103:11; 108:4

🔑 **35:19** See Jn. 15:25.

6 Thy [a]righteousness[6666] is like the [I]mountains of God;
Thy [b]judgments[4941] are *like* a great deep.
O LORD, Thou [c]preservest[3467] man[120] and beast.

7 How [a]precious is Thy lovingkindness, O God!
And the children[1121] of men[120] [b]take refuge[2620] in the shadow of Thy wings.

8 They [a]drink their fill of the [I]abundance of Thy house;[1004]
And Thou dost give them to drink of the [b]river of Thy delights.

9 For with Thee is the [a]fountain of life;[2416]
In Thy light we see light.[216]

10 O continue Thy lovingkindness to [a]those who know Thee,
And Thy [b]righteousness to the upright[3477] in heart.

11 Let not the foot of pride come upon me,
And let not the hand[3027] of the wicked drive me away.

12 There the doers of iniquity have fallen;[5307]
They have been thrust down and [a]cannot rise.

Security of Those Who Trust in the LORD, and Insecurity of the Wicked

A Psalm of David.

37 [a]Do not fret[2734] because of evildoers,[7489]
Be not [b]envious toward wrongdoers.[6213,5766]

2 For they will [a]wither quickly like the grass,
And [b]fade like the green herb.

3 [a]Trust[982] in the LORD, and do[6213] good;[2896]
[b]Dwell[7931] in the land[776] and [I][c]cultivate faithfulness.[530]

4 [a]Delight yourself in the LORD;
And He will [b]give you the desires[4862] of your heart.[3820]

5 [a]Commit[1556] your way[1870] to the LORD,
Trust also in Him, and He will do it.

6 And He will bring forth [a]your righteousness[6664] as the light,[216]
And your judgment[4941] [b]as the noonday.

7 [I]Rest in the LORD and [a]wait [II]patiently[2342] for Him;
[b]Do not fret because of him who [c]prospers in his way,
Because of the man[376] who carries out wicked schemes.[4209]

8 Cease[7503] from anger,[639] and [a]forsake wrath;[2534]
Do not fret, *it leads* only to evildoing.[7489]

9 For [a]evildoers will be cut off,[3772]
But those who wait for[6960] the LORD, they will [b]inherit[3423] the land.[776]

10 Yet [a]a little while and the wicked[7563] man will be no more;
And you will look carefully[995] for [b]his place, and he will not be *there.*

11 But [a]the humble will inherit the land,
And will delight themselves in [b]abundant prosperity.

12 The wicked [a]plots[2161] against the righteous,
And [b]gnashes[2786] at him with his teeth.

13 The Lord[136] [a]laughs at him;
For He sees[7200] [b]his day[3117] is coming.

14 The wicked have drawn the sword[2719] and [a]bent their bow,
To cast down[5307] the [b]afflicted and the needy,
To [c]slay[2873] those who are upright[8549] in conduct.[1870]

15 Their sword will enter their own heart,
And their [a]bows will be broken.[7665]

---

6 [I]Or, *mighty mountains* [a]Ps. 71:19 [b]Job 11:8; Ps. 77:19; Rom. 11:33 [c]Neh. 9:6; Ps. 104:14, 15; 145:16
7 [a]Ps. 40:5; 139:17 [b]Ruth 2:12; Ps. 17:8; 57:1; 91:4
8 [I]Lit., *fatness* [a]Ps. 63:5; 65:4; Is. 25:6; Jer. 31:12-14 [b]Job 20:17; Ps. 46:4; Rev. 22:1
9 [a]Jer. 2:13
10 [a]Jer. 22:16 [b]Ps. 24:5
12 [a]Ps. 140:10; Is. 26:14

1 [a]Prov. 23:17; 24:19 [b]Ps. 73:3; Prov. 3:31
2 [a]Job 14:2; Ps. 90:6; 92:7; James 1:11 [b]Ps. 129:6
3 [I]Or, *feed securely* or *feed on His faithfulness* [a]Ps. 62:8 [b]Deut. 30:20 [c]Is. 40:11; Ezek. 34:13, 14
4 [a]Job 22:26; Ps. 94:19; Is. 58:14 [b]Ps. 21:2; 145:19; Matt. 7:7, 8
5 [a]Ps. 55:22; Prov. 16:3; 1Pet. 5:7
6 [a]Ps. 97:11; Is. 58:8, 10; Mic. 7:9 [b]Job 11:17
7 [I]Or, *Be still* [II]Or, *longingly* [a]Ps. 40:1; 62:5; Lam. 3:26 [b]Ps. 37:1, 8 [c]Jer. 12:1
8 [a]Eph. 4:31; Col. 3:8
9 [a]Ps. 37:2, 22 [b]Ps. 25:13; Prov. 2:21; Is. 57:13; 60:21; Matt. 5:5
10 [a]Job 24:24 [b]Job 7:10; Ps. 37:35, 36
11 [a]Matt. 5:5 [b]Ps. 72:7
12 [a]Ps. 31:13, 20 [b]Ps. 35:16
13 [a]Ps. 2:4 [b]1Sam. 26:10; Job 18:20
14 [a]Ps. 11:2; Lam. 2:4 [b]Ps. 35:10; 86:1 [c]Ps. 11:2
15 [a]1Sam. 2:4; Ps. 46:9

16 [a]Better[2896] is the little of the righteous[6662]
Than the abundance of many wicked.
17 For the [a]arms of the wicked will be broken;
But the LORD [b]sustains[5564] the righteous.
18 The LORD [a]knows the days[3117] of the [I]blameless;[8549]
And their [b]inheritance[5159] will be forever.[5769]
19 They will not be ashamed[954] in the time[6256] of evil;[7451]
And [a]in the days of famine they will have abundance.
20 But the [a]wicked will perish;[6]
And the enemies of the LORD will be like the [I]glory of the pastures,[3733]
They vanish—[b]like smoke they vanish away.
21 The wicked borrows and does not pay[7999] back,
But the righteous [a]is gracious[2603] and gives.
22 For [a]those blessed[1288] by Him will [b]inherit the land;
But those [c]cursed[7043] by Him will be cut off.
23 [a]The steps of a man[1397] are established[3359] by the LORD;
And He [b]delights[2654] in his way.
24 When [a]he falls, he shall not be hurled headlong;
Because [b]the LORD is the One [I]who holds his hand.[3027]
🔑25 I have been young, and now I am old;[2204]
Yet [a]I have not seen[7200] the righteous forsaken,[5800]
Or [b]his [I]descendants[2233] begging[1245] bread.
26 All day long [a]he is gracious[2603] and lends;
And [b]his [I]descendants are a blessing.
27 [a]Depart[5493] from evil, and do good,
[I]So you will abide [b]forever.[5769]
28 For the LORD [a]loves[157] [I]justice,
And [b]does not forsake[5800] His godly ones;[2623]
They are [c]preserved[8104] forever;
But the [II][d]descendants of the wicked will be cut off.
29 The righteous will [a]inherit the land,
And [b]dwell in it forever.[5703]
30 The mouth[6310] of the righteous [a]utters[1897] wisdom,[2451]
And his tongue [b]speaks justice.
31 The [a]law[8451] of his God[430] is in his heart;
His [b]steps do not slip.
32 The [a]wicked spies upon the righteous,
And [b]seeks to kill[4191] him.
33 The LORD will [a]not leave[5800] him in his hand,
Or [b]let him be condemned[7561] when he is judged.[8199]
34 [a]Wait for[6960] the LORD, and keep[8104] His way,
And He will exalt you to inherit the land;
When the [b]wicked are cut off, you will see it.
35 I have [a]seen a violent, wicked man
Spreading himself like a [b]luxuriant [I]tree in its native soil.

16 [a]Prov. 15:16; 16:8 **17** [a]Job 38:15; Ps. 10:15; Ezek. 30:21 [b]Ps. 71:6; 145:14 **18** [I]Lit., *complete*; or, *perfect* [a]Ps. 1:6; 31:7 [b]Ps. 37:27, 29 **19** [a]Job 5:20; Ps. 33:19 **20** [I]I.e., *flowers* [a]Ps. 73:27 [b]Ps. 68:2; 102:3 **21** [a]Ps. 112:5, 9 **22** [a]Prov. 3:33 [b]Ps. 37:9 [c]Job 5:3 **23** [a]1Sam. 2:9; Ps. 40:2; 66:9; 119:5 [b]Ps. 147:11 **24** [I]Or, *who sustains him with His hand* [a]Ps. 145:14; Prov. 24:16; Mic. 7:8 [b]Ps. 147:6 **25** [I]Lit., *seed* [a]Ps. 37:28; Is. 41:17; Heb. 13:5 [b]Ps. 109:10 **26** [I]Lit., *seed* [a]Deut. 15:8; Ps. 37:21 [b]Ps. 147:13 **27** [I]Or, *And dwell forever* [a]Ps. 34:14 [b]Ps. 37:18; 102:28 **28** [I]Lit., *judgment* [II]Lit., *seed* [a]Ps. 11:7; 33:5 [b]Ps. 37:25 [c]Ps. 31:23 [d]Ps. 21:10; 37:9; Prov. 2:22; Is. 14:20 **29** [a]Ps. 37:9; Prov. 2:21 [b]Ps. 37:18 **30** [a]Ps. 49:3; Prov. 10:13 [b]Ps. 101:1; 119:13 **31** [a]Deut. 6:6; Ps. 40:8; 119:11; Is. 51:7; Jer. 31:33 [b]Ps. 26:1; 37:23 **32** [a]Ps. 10:8; 17:11 [b]Ps. 37:14 **33** [a]Ps. 31:8; 2Pet. 2:9 [b]Ps. 34:22; 109:31

34 [a]Ps. 27:14; 37:9 [b]Ps. 52:5, 6; 91:8 **35** [I]Lit., *native*; Heb. obscure [a]Job 5:3; Jer. 12:2 [b]Job 8:16

🔑**37:25** The psalmist merely stated his own experience. He personally had never seen "the righteous forsaken or his descendants begging bread." It does not say that it never occurs. God takes care of His people. There is enough wealth in the world to provide food, clothing, and shelter for all. However, some do get more than their share and others suffer. If a good man is wasteful, acts unwisely, or speculates unduly, then God will not intervene to keep him from ruin. We must learn the general lesson well.

36 Then [I]he passed[5674] away, and
lo, he [a]was no more;
I sought for him, but he could
not be found.
37 Mark[8104] the [Ia]blameless[8535]
man, and behold[7200] the
[b]upright;
For the man of peace will have
a [IIc]posterity.[319]
38 But transgressors[6586] will be
altogether [a]destroyed;[8045]
The [I]posterity of the wicked will
be [b]cut off.
39 But the [a]salvation[8668] of the
righteous is from the LORD;
He is their strength [b]in time of
trouble.
40 And [a]the LORD helps them, and
delivers them;
He [b]delivers them from the
wicked, and saves[3467] them,
Because they [c]take refuge[2620] in
Him.

Prayer of a Suffering Penitent

A Psalm of David, for a memorial.

38 O LORD, [a]rebuke[3198] me not in
Thy wrath;[7110]
And chasten me not in Thy
burning anger.[2534]
2 For Thine [a]arrows have sunk
deep into me,
And [b]Thy hand[3027] has pressed
down on me.
3 There is [a]no soundness in my
flesh[1320] [b]because of Thine
indignation;[2195]
There is no health [c]in my
bones[6106] because of my
sin.[2403]
4 For my [a]iniquities[5771] are gone
over my head;[7218]
As a heavy burden[4853] they
weigh too much[3513] for
me.
5 My [I]wounds grow foul[887] *and*
fester.
Because of [a]my folly,
6 I am bent[5753] over and [a]greatly
bowed down;
I [b]go mourning[6937] all day[3117]
long.
7 For my loins are filled with
[a]burning;
And there is [b]no soundness in
my flesh.
8 I am [a]benumbed and [I]badly
crushed;
I [IIb]groan because of the
[III]agitation of my heart.[3820]
9 Lord,[136] all [a]my desire is
[I]before Thee;
And my [b]sighing is not hidden
from Thee.
10 My heart throbs, [a]my strength
fails[5800] me;
And the [b]light[216] of my eyes,
even [I]that [II]has gone from
me.
11 My [Ia]loved ones[157] and my
friends[7453] stand aloof from
my plague;[5061]
And my kinsmen [b]stand afar
off.
12 Those who [a]seek my life[5315]
[b]lay snares[5367] *for me;*
And those who [c]seek to
injure[7451] me have
[I]threatened[1696]
destruction,[1942]
And they [d]devise[1897] treachery
all day long.
13 But I, like a deaf man, do not
hear;[8085]
And I am like a [a]dumb man who
does not open his mouth.[6310]
14 Yes, I am like a man[376] who does
not hear,[8085]
And in whose mouth are no
arguments.[8433]
15 For [a]I [I]hope[3176] in Thee, O LORD;
Thou [b]wilt answer, O Lord my
God.[430]
16 For I said, "May they not rejoice
over me,
Who, when my foot slips,
[a]would magnify themselves
against me."

36 [I]Ancient versions read *I passed by* [a]Job 20:5; Ps. 37:10
37 [I]Lit., *complete;* or, *perfect* [II]Lit., *an end* [a]Ps. 37:18 [b]Ps. 7:10 [c]Is. 57:1, 2
38 [I]Lit., *end* [a]Ps. 1:4-6; 37:20, 28 [b]Ps. 37:9; 73:17
39 [a]Ps. 3:8; 62:1 [b]Ps. 9:9; 37:19
40 [a]Ps. 54:4 [b]Ps. 22:4; Is. 31:5; Dan. 3:17; 6:23 [c]1Chr. 5:20; Ps. 34:22

1 [a]Ps. 6:1
2 [a]Job 6:4 [b]Ps. 32:4
3 [a]Is. 1:6 [b]Ps. 102:10 [c]Job 33:19; Ps. 6:2; 31:10
4 [a]Ezra 9:6; Ps. 40:12
5 [I]Or, *stripes* [a]Ps. 69:5
6 [a]Ps. 35:14 [b]Job 30:28; Ps. 42:9; 43:2
7 [a]Ps. 102:3 [b]Ps. 38:3
8 [I]Or, *greatly* [II]Lit., *roar* [III]Lit., *growling* [a]Lam. 1:13, 20f.; 2:11; 5:17 [b]Job 3:24; Ps. 22:1; 32:3
9 [I]Or, known *to Thee* [a]Ps. 10:17 [b]Ps. 6:6; 102:5
10 [I]Lit., *they have* [II]Lit., *is not with me* [a]Ps. 31:10 [b]Ps. 6:7; 69:3; 88:9
11 [I]Or, *lovers* [a]Ps. 31:11; 88:18 [b]Luke 23:49
12 [I]Lit., *spoken* [a]Ps. 54:3 [b]Ps. 140:5 [c]Ps. 35:4 [d]Ps. 35:20
13 [a]Ps. 39:2, 9
15 [I]Or, *wait for* [a]Ps. 39:7 [b]Ps. 17:6
16 [a]Ps. 35:26

38:11 See Lk. 23:49.

17 For I am [a]ready[3559] to fall,
And [b]my [I]sorrow is
continually[8548] before me.
18 For I [I][a]confess[5046] my
iniquity;[5771]
I am full of [b]anxiety because of
my sin.
19 But my [a]enemies are vigorous
and [I]strong;
And many are those who
[b]hate[8130] me wrongfully.[8267]
20 And those who [a]repay[7999] evil[7451]
for good,[2896]
They [b]oppose[7853] me, because
I follow what is good.
21 Do not forsake[5800] me, O LORD;
O my God, [a]do not be far from
me!
22 Make [a]haste to help me,
O Lord, [b]my salvation![8668]

The Vanity of Life

For the choir director, for [+]Jeduthun. A Psalm of David.

39 I said, "I will [a]guard[8104] my
ways,[1870]
That I [b]may not sin[2398] with my
tongue;
I will guard[8104] [c]my mouth[6310] as
with a muzzle,
While the wicked[7563] are in my
presence."
2 I was [a]dumb [I]and silent,
I [II]refrained *even* from good;[2896]
And my [III]sorrow grew worse.
3 My [a]heart[3820] was hot within[7130]
me;
While I was musing[1901] the fire
burned;
Then I spoke[1696] with my
tongue:
4 "LORD, make me to know [a]my
end,
And what is the extent of my
days,[3117]
Let me know how [b]transient I
am.
5 "Behold, Thou hast made
[a]my days *as* handbreadths,
And my [b]lifetime[2465] as nothing
in Thy sight,
Surely every man[120] [I]at his
best[5324] is [II]a mere [c]breath.
[III]Selah.
6 "Surely every man[376] [a]walks
about as [I]a phantom;
Surely they make an [b]uproar for
nothing;
He [c]amasses *riches*, and does not
know who will gather[622]
them.
7 "And now, Lord,[136] for what do
I wait?[6960]
My [a]hope[8431] is in Thee.
8 "[a]Deliver[5337] me from all my
transgressions;[6588]
Make[7760] me not the
[b]reproach[2781] of the foolish.
9 "I have become [a]dumb, I do not
open my mouth,
Because it is [b]Thou who hast
done[6213] *it.*
10 "[a]Remove Thy plague[5061] from
me;
Because of [b]the opposition of
Thy hand,[3027] I am
[I]perishing.[3615]
11 "With [a]reproofs[8433] Thou dost
chasten[3256] a man for
iniquity;[5771]
Thou dost [b]consume as a
moth what is precious[2530] to
him;
Surely [c]every man is a mere
breath. Selah.
12 "[a]Hear[8085] my prayer,[8605] O
LORD, and give ear[238] to my
cry;
Do not be silent [b]at my tears;
For I am [c]a stranger with
Thee,
A [d]sojourner[8453] like all my
fathers.[1]
13 "[a]Turn Thy gaze away from
me, that I may [I]smile
again,
Before I depart and am no
more."

---

17 [I]Lit., *pain* [a]Ps. 35:15 [b]Ps. 13:2
18 [I]Or, *declare* [a]Ps. 32:5 [b]2Cor. 7:9, 10
19 [I]Or, *numerous* [a]Ps. 18:17 [b]Ps. 35:19
20 [a]Ps. 35:12 [b]Ps. 109:5; 1John 3:12
21 [a]Ps. 22:19; 35:22
22 [a]Ps. 40:13, 17 [b]Ps. 27:1

[+]1Chr. 16:41
1 [a]1Kin. 2:4; 2Kin. 10:31; Ps. 119:9 [b]Job 2:10; Ps. 34:13; James 3:5-12 [c]Ps. 141:3; James 3:2
2 [I]Lit., *with silence* [II]Lit., *kept silence* [III]Lit., *pain* [a]Ps. 38:13
3 [a]Ps. 32:4; Jer. 20:9; Luke 24:32
4 [a]Job 6:11; Ps. 90:12; 119:84 [b]Ps. 78:39; 103:14
5 [I]Lit., *standing firm* [II]Or, *altogether vanity* [III]*Selah* may mean: *Pause, Crescendo* or *Musical interlude* [a]Ps. 89:47 [b]Ps. 144:4 [c]Job 14:2; Ps. 62:9; Eccl. 6:12
6 [I]Lit., *an image* [a]1Cor. 7:31; James 1:10, 11; 1Pet. 1:24 [b]Ps. 127:2; Eccl. 5:17 [c]Ps. 49:10; Eccl. 2:26; 5:14; Luke 12:20
7 [a]Ps. 38:15
8 [a]Ps. 51:9, 14; 79:9 [b]Ps. 44:13; 79:4; 119:22
9 [a]Ps. 39:2 [b]2Sam. 16:10; Job 2:10
10 [I]Or, *wasting away* [a]Job 9:34; 13:21 [b]Ps. 32:4
11 [a]Ezek. 5:15; 2Pet. 2:16 [b]Job 13:28; Ps. 90:7; Is. 50:9 [c]Ps. 39:5
12 [a]Ps. 102:1; 143:1 [b]2Kin. 20:5; Ps. 56:8 [c]Lev. 25:23; 1Chr. 29:15; Ps. 119:19; Heb. 11:13; 1Pet. 2:11 [d]Gen. 47:9
13 [I]Or, *become cheerful* [a]Job 7:19; 10:20, 21; 14:6; Ps. 102:24

God Sustains His Servant

For the choir director. A Psalm of David.

40 I [a]waited [I]patiently6960 for the
LORD;
And He inclined to me, and
[b]heard8085 my cry.
2 He brought5927 me up out of the
[a]pit953 of destruction,7588 out
of the [I]miry3121 clay;
And [b]He set my feet upon a rock
[c]making my footsteps
firm.3559
3 And He put a [a]new song7892 in
my mouth,6310 a song of
praise8416 to our God;430
Many will [b]see and fear,3372
And will trust982 in the LORD.
4 How [a]blessed835 is the man1397
who has made7760 the LORD
his trust,
And [b]has not [I]turned to the
proud, nor to those who
[c]lapse into falsehood.3577
5 Many, O LORD my God, are
[a]the wonders6381 which Thou
hast done,6213
And Thy [b]thoughts4284 toward
us;
There is none to compare with
Thee;
If I would declare5046 and
speak1696 of them,
They [c]would be too
numerous5608 to count.
🔑 6 [I][a]Sacrifice2077 and meal
offering4503 Thou hast not
desired;2654
My ears241 Thou hast [II]opened;
Burnt offering5930 and sin
offering2401 Thou hast not
required.7592
7 Then I said, "Behold, I come;
In the scroll4039 of the book5612
it is [I]written of me;
8 [a]I delight2654 to do6213 Thy
will,7522 O my God;
[b]Thy Law8451 is within my
heart."4578
9 I have [a]proclaimed1319 glad
tidings of righteousness6664 in
the great congregation;6951
Behold, I will [b]not restrain my
lips,8193
O LORD, [c]Thou knowest.3045
10 I have [a]not hidden Thy
righteousness6666 within my
heart;3820
I have [b]spoken559 of Thy
faithfulness30 and Thy
salvation;8668
I have not concealed Thy
lovingkindness and Thy
truth571 from the great
congregation.
11 Thou, O LORD, wilt not withhold
Thy compassion7356 from me;
[I]Thy [a]lovingkindness and Thy
truth will continually8548
preserve5341 me.
12 For evils beyond number have
[a]surrounded me;
My [b]iniquities5771 have
overtaken me, so that I am
not able to see;7200
They are [c]more numerous than
the hairs of my head;7218
And my [d]heart has [I]failed5800 me.
13 [a]Be pleased, O LORD, to
deliver5337 me;
Make [b]haste, O LORD, to help
me.
14 Let those be [a]ashamed954 and
humiliated together
Who [b]seek my [I]life5315 to
destroy5595 it;
Let those be turned back and
dishonored
Who delight2655 [II]in my hurt.7451
15 Let those [a]be [I]appalled8074
because of their shame
Who [b]say559 to me, "Aha, aha!"
16 [a]Let all who seek Thee rejoice
and be glad in Thee;
Let those who love157 Thy
salvation [b]say continually,
"The LORD be magnified!"
17 Since [a]I am afflicted and needy,
[I][b]Let the Lord136 be mindful2803
of me;

1 [I]Or, *intently* [a]Ps. 25:5; 27:14; 37:7 [b]Ps. 34:15
2 [I]Lit., *mud of the mire* [a]Ps. 69:2, 14; Jer. 38:6 [b]Ps. 27:5 [c]Ps. 37:23
3 [a]Ps. 32:7; 33:3 [b]Ps. 52:6; 64:9
4 [I]Lit., *regard* [a]Ps. 34:8; 84:12 [b]Job 37:24 [c]Ps. 125:5
5 [a]Job 5:9; Ps. 136:4 [b]Ps. 139:17; Is. 55:8 [c]Ps. 71:15; 139:18
6 [I]I.e., Blood sacrifice [II]Lit., *dug; or possibly, pierced* [a]1Sam. 15:22; Ps. 51:16; Is. 1:11; Jer. 6:20; 7:22, 23; Amos 5:22; Mic. 6:6-8; Heb. 10:5-7
7 [I]Or, *prescribed for*
8 [a]John 4:34 [b]Ps. 37:31; Jer. 31:33; 2Cor. 3:3
9 [a]Ps. 22:22, 25 [b]Ps. 119:13 [c]Josh. 22:22; Ps. 139:4
10 [a]Acts 20:20, 27 [b]Ps. 89:1
11 [I]Or, *May. . . preserve* [a]Ps. 43:3; 57:3; 61:7; Prov. 20:28
12 [I]Lit., *forsaken* [a]Ps. 18:5; 116:3 [b]Ps. 38:4; 65:3 [c]Ps. 69:4 [d]Ps. 73:26
13 [a]Ps. 70:1 [b]Ps. 22:19; 71:12
14 [I]Or, *soul* [II]Or, *to injure me* [a]Ps. 35:4, 26; 70:2; 71:13 [b]Ps. 63:9
15 [I]Or, *desolated* [a]Ps. 70:3 [b]Ps. 35:21; 70:3
16 [a]Ps. 70:4 [b]Ps. 35:27
17 [I]Or, *The Lord is mindful* [a]Ps. 70:5; 86:1; 109:22 [b]Ps. 40:5; 1Pet. 5:7

🔑 **40:6-8** See Heb. 10:5-7.

Thou art my help and my
deliverer;
Do not delay, O my God.

The Psalmist in Sickness Complains of Enemies and False Friends

For the choir director. A Psalm of David.

41 How blessed[835] is he who
[a]considers[7919] the [I]helpless;
The LORD will deliver him
[b]in a day[3117] of [II]trouble.[7451]
2 The LORD will [a]protect[8104] him,
and keep him alive,
And he shall [I]be called
[b]blessed[833] upon the earth;[776]
And [c]do not give him over to
the desire of his enemies.
3 The LORD will sustain him upon
his sickbed;
In his illness, Thou dost
[I]restore him to health.
4 As for me, I said, "O LORD, be
gracious[2603] to me;
[a]Heal my soul,[5315] for [b]I have
sinned[2398] against Thee."
5 My enemies [a]speak[559] evil[7451]
against me,
"When will he die,[4191] and his
name perish?"[6]
6 And [I]when he comes to see *me*,
he [a]speaks [II]falsehood;[7723]
His heart[3820] gathers[6908]
wickedness[205] to itself;
When he goes outside, he
tells[1696] it.
7 All who hate[8130] me whisper[3907]
together against me;
Against me they [a]devise[2803] my
hurt,[7451] *saying,*
8 "A wicked[1100] thing[1697] is poured
out [I]upon him,
That when he lies down, he will
[a]not rise up again."
🔑9 Even my [a]close friend,[7965] in
whom I trusted,[982]
Who ate my bread,
Has lifted up his heel[6119] against
me.
10 But Thou, O LORD, be gracious
to me, and [a]raise me up,
That I may repay them.
11 By this I know that [a]Thou art
pleased with[2654] me,
Because [b]my enemy does not
shout in triumph[7321] over me.
12 As for me, [a]Thou dost uphold[8551]
me in my integrity,[8537]
And Thou dost set[5324] me
[b]in Thy presence forever.[5769]
13 [a]Blessed[1288] be the LORD, the
God[430] of Israel,
From everlasting[5769] to
everlasting.
Amen, and Amen.[543]

BOOK 2

Thirsting for God in Trouble and Exile

For the choir director. A +Maskil of the sons of Korah.

42 As the deer [I]pants for the water
brooks,
So my soul[5315] [Ia]pants for Thee,
O God.[430]
2 My soul [a]thirsts for God, for the
[b]living[2416] God;[410]
When shall I come and
[Ic]appear[7200] before God?
3 My [a]tears have been my food
day[3119] and night,[3915]
While *they* [b]say[559] to me all
day[3119] long, "Where is your
God?"
4 These things I remember,[2142]
and I [a]pour out[8210] my soul
within me.
For I [b]used to go along with the
throng *and* [I]lead them in
procession to the house[1004]
of God,
With the voice of [c]joy and
thanksgiving,[8426] a multitude
keeping festival.

1 [I]Or, *poor* [II]Or, *evil* [a]Ps. 82:3, 4; Prov. 14:21 [b]Ps. 27:5; 37:19
2 [I]Or, *be blessed* [a]Ps. 37:28 [b]Ps. 37:22 [c]Ps. 27:12
3 [I]Lit., *turn all his bed*
4 [a]Ps. 6:2; 103:3; 147:3 [b]Ps. 51:4
5 [a]Ps. 38:12
6 [I]Or, *if he* [II]Or, *emptiness* [a]Ps. 12:2; 62:4; Prov. 26:24-26
7 [a]Ps. 56:5
8 [I]Or, *within* [a]Ps. 71:10, 11
9 [a]2Sam. 15:12; Job 19:13, 19; Ps. 55:12, 13, 20; Jer. 20:10; Mic. 7:5; Matt. 26:23; Luke 22:21; John 13:18
10 [a]Ps. 3:3
11 [a]Ps. 37:23; 147:11 [b]Ps. 25:2
12 [a]Ps. 18:32; 37:17; 63:8 [b]Job 36:7; Ps. 21:6
13 [a]Ps. 72:18, 19; 89:52; 106:48; 150:6

+Possibly, *Contemplative,* or *Didactic,* or *Skillful Psalm*
1 [I]Lit., *longs for* [a]Ps. 119:131
2 [I]Some mss. read *see the face of God* [a]Ps. 63:1; 84:2; 143:6 [b]Josh. 3:10; Ps. 84:2; Jer. 10:10; Dan. 6:26; Matt. 26:63; Rom. 9:26; 1Thess. 1:9 [c]Ex. 23:17; Ps. 43:4; 84:7
3 [a]Ps. 80:5; 102:9 [b]Ps. 79:10; 115:2; Joel 2:17; Mic. 7:10
4 [I]Or, *move slowly with them* [a]1Sam. 1:15; Job 30:16; Ps. 62:8; Lam. 2:19 [b]Ps. 55:14; 122:1; Is. 30:29 [c]Ps. 100:4

🔑 **41:9** See Jn. 13:18.

5 [a]Why are you [I][b]in despair, O my soul?
And *why* have you become [c]disturbed within me?
[II][d]Hope[3176] in God, for I shall [III]again praise[3034] [IV]Him
For the [V][e]help[3444] of His presence.
6 O my God, my soul is [I]in despair within me;
Therefore I [a]remember Thee from [b]the land[776] of the Jordan,
And the [II]peaks of [c]Hermon, from Mount Mizar.
7 Deep calls[7121] to deep at the sound of Thy waterfalls;
All Thy [a]breakers and Thy waves have rolled over[5674] me.
8 The LORD will [a]command[6680] His lovingkindness in the daytime;[3119]
And His song[7892] will be with me [b]in the night,
A prayer[8605] to [c]the God of my life.[2416]
9 I will say to God [a]my rock, "Why hast Thou forgotten me?
Why do I go [b]mourning[6937] [I]because of the [c]oppression of the enemy?"
10 As a shattering of my bones,[6106] my adversaries revile me,
While they [a]say to me all day[3117] long, "Where is your God?"
11 [a]Why are you [I]in despair, O my soul?
And why have you become disturbed within me?
[II]Hope in God, for I shall yet praise Him,
The [III]help of my countenance, and my God.

Prayer for Deliverance

43 [a]Vindicate[8199] me, O God,[430] and [b]plead my case[7379] against an ungodly nation;[1471]
[I]O deliver me from [c]the deceitful[4820] and unjust[5766] man![376]
2 For Thou art the [a]God of my strength; why hast Thou [b]rejected me?
Why do I go [c]mourning[6937] [I]because of the oppression of the enemy?
3 O send out Thy [a]light[216] and Thy truth,[571] let them lead[5148] me;
Let them bring me to Thy [b]holy[6944] hill,
And to Thy [c]dwelling places.[4908]
4 Then I will go to [a]the altar[4196] of God,[410]
To God [I]my exceeding [b]joy;
And upon the [c]lyre I shall praise[3044] Thee, O God, my God.
5 [a]Why are you [I]in despair, O my soul?[5315]
And why are you disturbed within me?
[II]Hope[3176] in God, for I shall [III]again praise Him,
The [IV]help of my countenance, and my God.

Former Deliverances and Present Troubles

For the choir director. A [+]Maskil of the sons of Korah.

44 O God,[430] we have heard[8085] with our ears,[241]
Our [a]fathers[1] have told[5608] us,
The [b]work that Thou didst in their days,[3117]
In the [c]days of old.[6924]
2 Thou with Thine own hand[3027] didst [a]drive out[3423] the nations;[1471]
Then Thou didst [b]plant them;
Thou didst [c]afflict the peoples,[3816]
Then Thou didst [d]spread them abroad.

42:5 [I]Or, *sunk down* [II]Or, *Wait for* [III]Or, *still* [IV]Some ancient versions read *Him, the help of my countenance and my God* [V]Or, *saving acts of* [a]Ps. 42:11; 43:5 [b]Ps. 38:6; Matt. 26:38 [c]Ps. 77:3 [d]Ps. 71:14; Lam. 3:24 [e]Ps. 44:3
6 [I]Or, *sunk down* [II]Lit., *Hermons* [a]Ps. 61:2 [b]2Sam. 17:22 [c]Deut. 3:8
7 [a]Ps. 69:1, 2; 88:7; Jon. 2:3
8 [a]Ps. 57:3; 133:3 [b]Job 35:10; Ps. 16:7; 63:6; 77:6; 149:5 [c]Eccl. 5:18; 8:15
9 [I]Or, *while the enemy oppresses* [a]Ps. 18:2 [b]Ps. 38:6 [c]Ps. 17:9
10 [a]Ps. 42:3; Joel 2:17
11 [I]Or, *sunk down* [II]Or, *Wait for* [III]Or, *saving acts of* [a]Ps. 42:5; 43:5

43:1 [I]Or, *Mayest Thou* [a]Ps. 26:1; 35:24 [b]1Sam. 24:15; Ps. 35:1 [c]Ps. 5:6; 38:12
2 [I]Or, *while the enemy oppresses* [a]Ps. 18:1; 28:7; 31:4 [b]Ps. 44:9; 88:14 [c]Ps. 42:9
3 [a]Ps. 36:9 [b]Ps. 2:6; 3:4; 42:4; 46:4 [c]Ps. 84:1
4 [I]Lit., *the gladness of my joy* [a]Ps. 26:6 [b]Ps. 21:6 [c]Ps. 33:2; 49:4; 57:8; 71:22
5 [I]Or, *sunk down* [II]Or, *Wait for* [III]Or, *still* [IV]Or, *saving acts of* [a]Ps. 42:5, 11

[+]Possibly, *Contemplative*, or *Didactic*, or *Skillful Psalm*
44:1 [a]Ex. 12:26, 27; Deut. 6:20; Judg. 6:13; Ps. 78:3 [b]Ps. 78:12 [c]Deut. 32:7; Ps. 77:5; Is. 51:9; 63:9
2 [a]Josh. 3:10; Neh. 9:24; Ps. 78:55; 80:8 [b]Ex. 15:17; 2Sam. 7:10; Jer. 24:6; Amos 9:15 [c]Ps. 135:10-12 [d]Ps. 80:9-11; Zech. 2:6

3 For by their own sword[2719] they
[a]did not possess the land;[776]
And their own arm did not
save[3467] them;
But Thy right hand, and Thine
[b]arm, and the [c]light[216] of Thy
presence,
For Thou didst [d]favor them.
4 Thou art [a]my King,[4428] O God;
[b]Command[6680] [I]victories[3444] for
Jacob.
5 Through Thee we will [a]push
back our adversaries;
Through Thy name we will
[b]trample[947] down those who
rise up against us.
6 For I will [a]not trust[982] in my bow,
Nor will my sword save me.
7 But Thou [a]hast saved[3467] us from
our adversaries,
And Thou hast [b]put to shame[654]
those who hate us.
8 In God we have [a]boasted[1984] all
day[3117] long,
And we will [b]give thanks[3034] to
Thy name forever.[5769]
[I]Selah.
9 Yet Thou [a]hast rejected *us* and
brought us to [b]dishonor,
And [c]dost not go out with our
armies.[6635]
10 Thou dost cause us to
[a]turn[7725] back from the
adversary;
And those who hate[8130] us
[b]have taken spoil[8154] for
themselves.
11 Thou dost give us as [a]sheep
[I]to be eaten,
And hast [b]scattered us among
the nations.
12 Thou dost [a]sell Thy people[5971]
[I]cheaply,[1952]
And hast not [II]profited by their
sale.
13 Thou dost make[6213] us a
[a]reproach[2781] to our
neighbors,[7934]
A scoffing and a [b]derision to
those around us.
14 Thou dost make us [a]a byword
among the nations,
A [I][b]laughingstock[7218] among the
peoples.
15 All day long my dishonor is
before me,
And [I]my [a]humiliation has
overwhelmed[3680] me,
16 Because of the voice of him who
[a]reproaches and reviles,[1442]
Because of the presence of the
[b]enemy and the avenger.[5358]
17 All this has come upon us, but
we have [a]not forgotten Thee,
And we have not [b]dealt falsely
with Thy covenant.[1285]
18 Our heart[3820] has not [a]turned
back,
And our steps [b]have not deviated
from Thy way,[734]
19 Yet Thou hast [a]crushed us in a
place of [b]jackals,[8577]
And covered us with [c]the
shadow of death.[6757]
20 If we had [a]forgotten the name
of our God,
Or extended our [I]hands[3709] to
[b]a strange[2114] god;[410]
21 Would not God [a]find this out?
For He knows the secrets of the
heart.
22 But [a]for Thy sake we are
killed[2026] all day long;
We are considered[2803] as
[b]sheep to be slaughtered.[2878]
23 [a]Arouse Thyself, why [b]dost
Thou sleep, O Lord?[136]
Awake, [c]do not reject us
forever.[5331]
24 Why dost Thou [a]hide Thy face,
And [b]forget our affliction and our
oppression?
25 For our [a]soul[5315] has sunk down
into the dust;[6083]
Our body[990] cleaves to the
earth.[776]
26 [a]Rise up, be our help,
And [b]redeem[6299] us for the sake
of Thy lovingkindness.

3 [a]Deut. 8:17, 18; Josh. 24:12 [b]Ps. :15 [c]Ps. 4:6; 89:15 [d]Deut. 4:37; 7:7, 8; 10:15; Ps. 106:4
4 [I]Lit., *salvation* [a]Ps. 74:12 [b]Ps. 42:8
5 [a]Deut. 33:17; Ps. 60:12; Dan. 8:4 [b]Ps. 108:13; Zech. 10:5
6 [a]1Sam. 17:47; Ps. 33:16; Hos. 1:7
7 [a]Ps. 136:24 [b]Ps. 53:5
8 [I]*Selah* may mean: *Pause, Crescendo* or *Musical interlude* [a]Ps. 34:2 [b]Ps. 30:12
9 [a]Ps. 43:2; 60:1, 10; 74:1; 89:38; 108:11 [b]Ps. 69:19 [c]Ps. 60:10; 108:11
10 [a]Lev. 26:17; Josh. 7:8, 12; Ps. 89:43 [b]Ps. 89:41
11 [I]Lit., *for food* [a]Ps. 44:22; Rom. 8:36 [b]Lev. 26:33; Deut. 4:27; 28:64; Ps. 106:27; Ezek. 20:23
12 [I]Lit., *for no wealth* [II]Or, *set a high price on them* [a]Deut. 32:30; Judg. 2:14; 3:8; Is. 52:3, 4; Jer. 15:13
13 [a]Deut. 28:37; Ps. 79:4; 89:41 [b]Ps. 80:6; Ezek. 23:32
14 [I]Lit., *shaking of the head* [a]Job 17:6; Ps. 69:11; Jer. 24:9 [b]2Kin. 19:21; Ps. 109:25
15 [I]Lit., *the shame of my face has covered me* [a]2Chr. 32:21; Ps. 69:7
16 [a]Ps. 74:10 [b]Ps. 8:2
17 [a]Ps. 78:7; 119:61, 83, 109, 141, 153, 176 [b]Ps. 78:57
18 [a]Ps. 78:57 [b]Job 23:11; Ps. 119:51, 157
19 [a]Ps. 51:8; 94:5 [b]Job 30:29; Is. 13:22; Jer. 9:11 [c]Job 3:5; Ps. 23:4

20 [I]Lit., *palms* [a]Ps. 78:11 [b]Deut. 6:14; Ps. 81:9
21 [a]Ps. 139:1, 2; Jer. 17:10 **22** [a]Rom. 8:36 [b]Is. 53:7; Jer. 12:3 **23** [a]Ps. 7:6 [b]Ps. 78:65 [c]Ps. 77:7 **24** [a]Job 13:24; Ps. 88:14 [b]Ps. 42:9; Lam. 5:20 **25** [a]Ps. 119:25 **26** [a]Ps. 35:2 [b]Ps. 6:4; 25:22

A Song Celebrating the King's Marriage

For the choir director; according to the +Shoshannim. A •Maskil of the sons of Korah. A Song of Love.

45 My heart3820 [I]overflows with a good2896 theme;1697
I [II]address559 my [III]verses to the [IV]King;4428
My tongue is the pen of
[a]a ready writer.5608
2 Thou art fairer than the sons1121 of men;120
[a]Grace2580 is poured [I]upon Thy lips;8193
Therefore God430 has
[b]blessed1288 Thee forever.5769
3 Gird [a]Thy sword2719 on *Thy* thigh,3409 O [I][b]Mighty One,
In Thy splendor1935 and Thy majesty!1926
4 And in Thy majesty ride on victoriously,
For the cause of truth571 and
[a]meekness *and* righteousness;6664
Let Thy [b]right hand teach3384 Thee [I]awesome things.3372
5 Thine [a]arrows are sharp;8150
The [b]peoples5971 fall under Thee;
Thine arrows are [c]in the heart of the King's4428 enemies.
6 [a]Thy throne,3678 O God, is forever5769 and ever;5703
A scepter7626 of [b]uprightness is the scepter7626 of Thy kingdom.4438
7 Thou hast [a]loved157 righteousness, and hated wickedness;7562
Therefore God, Thy God, has
[b]anointed4886 Thee
With the oil8081 of joy above Thy fellows.
8 All Thy garments are *fragrant with* [a]myrrh4753 and aloes174 *and* cassia;7102
Out of ivory palaces1964
[b]stringed instruments have made Thee glad.
9 Kings' daughters are among
[a]Thy noble ladies;
At Thy [b]right hand stands5324 the queen7694 in [c]gold from Ophir.
10 Listen,8085 O daughter, give attention7200 and incline your ear;241
[a]Forget your people and your father's1 house;1004
11 Then the King will desire183 your beauty;
Because He is your
[a]Lord,113 [b]bow down7812 to Him.
12 And the daughter of [a]Tyre *will come* with a gift;
The [b]rich among the people will entreat your favor.
13 The King's daughter is all glorious within;
Her clothing is [a]interwoven with gold.
14 She will be [a]led to the King
[b]in embroidered work;
The [c]virgins,1330 her companions who follow her,
Will be brought to Thee.
15 They will be led forth with gladness and rejoicing;
They will enter into the King's palace.1964
16 In place of your fathers1 will be your sons;
You shall make them princes8269 in all the earth.776
17 I will cause [a]Thy name to be remembered2142 in all generations;1755
Therefore the peoples
[b]will give Thee thanks3034 forever5769 and ever.5703

+Or possibly, *Lilies* •Possibly, *Contemplative*, or *Didactic*, or *Skillful Psalm*

1 [I]Lit., *is astir* [II]Lit., *am saying* [III]Lit., *works* [IV]Probably refers to Solomon as a type of Christ. [a]Ezra 7:6

2 [I]Or, *through* [a]Luke 4:22 [b]Ps. 21:6

3 [I]Or, *warrior* [a]Heb. 4:12; Rev. 1:16 [b]Is. 9:6

4 [I]Or, *fearful* [a]Zeph. 2:3 [b]Ps. 21:8

5 [a]Ps. 18:14; 120:4; Is. 5:28; 7:13 [b]Ps. 92:9 [c]2Sam. 18:14

6 [a]Ps. 93:2; Heb. 1:8, 9 [b]Ps. 98:9

7 [a]Ps. 11:7; 33:5 [b]Ps. 2:2

8 [a]Song 4:14; John 19:39 [b]Ps. 150:4

9 [a]Song 6:8 [b]1Kin. 2:19 [c]1Kin. 9:28; Is. 13:12

10 [a]Deut. 21:13; Ruth 1:16, 17

11 [a]Gen. 18:12; 1Pet. 3:6 [b]Eph. 5:33

12 [a]Ps. 87:4 [b]Ps. 22:29; 68:29; 72:10, 11; Is. 49:23

13 [a]Ex. 39:2, 3

14 [a]Song 1:4 [b]Judg. 5:30; Ezek. 16:10 [c]Ps. 45:9

17 [a]Mal. 1:11 [b]Ps. 138:4

45:6,7 See Heb. 1:8,9.

God the Refuge of His People

For the choir director. *A Psalm* of the sons of Korah, +set to Alamoth. A Song.

46 ⊶ God[430] is our [a]refuge and strength,
[I]A very [b]present help [c]in [II]trouble.
2 Therefore we will [a]not fear,[3372]
though [b]the earth[776] should change,
And though [c]the mountains slip into the heart of the [I]sea;
3 Though its [a]waters roar *and* foam,
Though the mountains quake[7493] at its swelling pride. [I]Selah.
4 There is a [a]river whose streams make glad the [b]city of God,
The holy[6918] [c]dwelling places[4908] of the Most High.[5945]
5 God is [a]in the midst[7130] of her, she will not be moved;
God will [b]help her [I]when morning dawns.
6 The [I]nations[1471] [a]made an uproar, the kingdoms[4467] tottered;
He [II][b]raised His voice, the earth [c]melted.
7 The LORD of hosts[6635] [a]is with us;
The God of Jacob is [b]our stronghold. Selah.
8 Come, [a]behold[2372] the works of the LORD,
[I]Who has wrought[7760] [b]desolations[8047] in the earth.
9 He [a]makes wars to cease[7673] to the end of the earth;
He [b]breaks[7665] the bow and cuts the spear in two;
He [c]burns[8313] the chariots with fire.
10 "[I]Cease *striving* and [a]know that I am God;
I will be [b]exalted among the [II]nations, I will be exalted in the earth."
11 The LORD of hosts is with us;
The God of Jacob is our stronghold. Selah.

+Possibly, *for soprano voices*
1 [I]Or, *Abundantly available for help* [II]Or, *tight places* [a]Ps. 14:6; 62:7, 8 [b]Deut. 4:7; Ps. 145:18 [c]Ps. 9:9
2 [I]Lit., *seas* [a]Ps. 23:4; 27:1 [b]Ps. 82:5 [c]Ps. 18:7
3 [I]*Selah* may mean: *Pause, Crescendo* or *Musical interlude* [a]Ps. 93:3, 4; Jer. 5:22
4 [a]Ps. 36:8; 65:9; Is. 8:6; Rev. 22:1 [b]Ps. 48:1; 87:3; 101:8; Is. 60:14; Rev. 3:12 [c]Ps. 43:3
5 [I]Lit., *at the turning of the morning* [a]Deut. 23:14; Is. 12:6; Ezek. 43:7, 9; Hos. 11:9; Joel 2:27; Zech. 2:5 [b]Ps. 37:40; Is. 41:14; Luke 1:54
6 [I]Or, *Gentiles* [II]Lit., *gave forth* [a]Ps. 2:1, 2 [b]Ps. 18:13; 68:33; Jer. 25:30; Joel 2:11; Amos 1:2 [c]Amos 9:5; Mic. 1:4; Nah. 1:5
7 [a]Num. 14:9; 2Chr. 13:12 [b]Ps. 9:9; 48:3
8 [I]Or, *Which He has wrought as desolations* [a]Ps. 66:5 [b]Is. 61:4; Jer. 51:43
9 [a]Is. 2:4; Mic. 4:3 [b]1Sam. 2:4; Ps. 76:3 [c]Is. 9:5; Ezek. 39:9
10 [I]Or, *Let go, relax* [II]Or, *Gentiles* [a]Ps. 100:3 [b]Is. 2:11, 17

God the King of the Earth

For the choir director. A Psalm of the sons of Korah.

47 O [a]clap[8628] your hands,[3709] all peoples;[5971]
[b]Shout[7321] to God[430] with the voice of [I]joy.
2 For the LORD Most High[5945] is to be [a]feared,[3372]
A [b]great King[4428] over all the earth.[776]
3 He [a]subdues[1696] peoples under us,
And nations[3816] under our feet.
4 He chooses[977] our [a]inheritance[5159] for us,
The [b]glory of Jacob whom He loves.[157] [I]Selah.
5 God has [a]ascended[5927] [I]with a shout,
The LORD, [I]with the [b]sound of a trumpet.
6 [a]Sing praises[2167] to God, sing praises;
Sing praises to [b]our King, sing praises.
7 For God is the [a]King of all the earth;
Sing praises [b]with a [I]skillful psalm.
8 God [a]reigns[4427] over the nations,[1471]
God [I]sits on [b]His holy[6944] throne.[3678]

1 [I]Or, *a ringing cry* [a]Ps. 98:8 [b]Ps. 106:47
2 [a]Deut. 7:21; Neh. 1:5; Ps. 66:3, 5; 68:35 [b]Mal. 1:14
3 [a]Ps. 18:47
4 [I]*Selah* may mean: *Pause, Crescendo* or *Musical interlude* [a]1Pet. 1:4 [b]Amos 6:8; 8:7; Nah. 2:2
5 [I]Or, *amid* [a]Ps. 68:18 [b]Ps. 98:6
6 [a]Ps. 68:4 [b]Ps. 89:18
7 [I]Heb., *Maskil* [a]Zech. 14:9 [b]1Cor. 14:15
8 [I]Or, *has taken His seat* [a]1Chr. 16:31; Ps. 22:28 [b]Ps. 97:2

⊶ **46:1** Cf. Ps. 10:1; Isa. 45:15; Lam. 3:44; Ezek. 20:3; I Tim. 6:16; Js. 4:8; all of which indicate that God is not so accessible. However, since God is an omnipresent Being, there is no place which is not as near as another to Him. Though it may sometimes seem that He is far away, Paul said that He is not far from anyone (Acts 17:27). We must want the contact.

9 The [I][a]princes[5081] of the people
have assembled[622]
themselves *as* the [b]people of
the God of Abraham;
For the [c]shields of the earth
belong to God;
He [II]is [d]highly exalted.[5927]

The Beauty and Glory of Zion

A Song; a Psalm of the sons of Korah.

48 [a]Great is the LORD, and greatly
to be praised,[1984]
In the [b]city of our God,[430] His
[c]holy[6944] mountain.
2 [a]Beautiful in elevation,[5131]
[b]the joy of the whole earth,[776]
Is Mount Zion *in* the far north,
The [c]city of the great King.[4428]
3 God, in her palaces,[759]
Has made Himself known[3045] as
a [a]stronghold.
4 For, lo, the [a]kings[4428]
assembled[3259] themselves,
They passed by[5674] together.
5 They saw[7200] *it,* then they were
amazed;
They were [a]terrified,[926] they
[I]fled in alarm.
6 [I]Panic[7461] seized them there,
Anguish, as of [a]a woman in
childbirth.
7 With the [a]east wind[7307]
Thou [b]dost break the [c]ships of
Tarshish.
8 As we have heard,[8085] so have
we seen[7200]
In the city of the LORD of
hosts,[6635] in the city of our
God;
God will [a]establish her
forever.[5769] [I]Selah.
9 We have thought on [a]Thy
lovingkindness, O God,
In the midst[7130] of Thy
temple.[1964]
10 As is Thy [a]name, O God,
So is Thy [b]praise[8416] to the ends
of the earth;
Thy [c]right hand is full of
righteousness.[6664]
11 Let Mount [a]Zion be glad,
Let the [a]daughters of Judah
rejoice,
Because of Thy judgments.[4941]
12 Walk about Zion, and go
around[5362] her;
Count[5608] her [a]towers;
13 Consider her [a]ramparts;
Go through her palaces;
That you may [b]tell *it* to the next
generation.[1755]
14 For [I]such is God,
Our God forever[5769] and
ever;[5703]
He will [a]guide us [II]until death.[4192]

The Folly of Trusting in Riches

For the choir director. A Psalm of the sons of Korah.

49 [a]Hear[8085] this, all peoples;[5971]
Give ear,[238] all [b]inhabitants of
the world,[2465]
2 Both [a]low and high,[376]
Rich and poor together.
3 My mouth[6310] will [a]speak[1696]
wisdom;[2454]
And the meditation[1900] of my
heart[3820] *will be*
[b]understanding.[8394]
4 I will incline my ear[241] to [a]a
proverb;
[b]I will [I]express my [c]riddle[2420] on
the harp.
5 Why should I [a]fear[3372] in days[3117]
of adversity,
When the iniquity of my [I]foes
surrounds me,
6 Even those who [a]trust[982] in their
wealth,[2428]
And boast[1984] in the abundance
of their riches?
7 No man can by any means
[a]redeem[6299] *his* brother,[251]
Or give to God[430] a [b]ransom[3724]
for him—
8 For [a]the redemption of [I]his
soul[5315] is costly,
And he should cease *trying*
forever—[5769]

9 [I]Or, *nobles* [II]Lit., *has greatly exalted Himself* [a]Ps. 72:11; 102:22; Is. 49:7, 23 [b]Rom. 4:11, 12 [c]Ps. 89:18 [d]Ps. 97:9

1 [a]1Chr. 16:25; Ps. 96:4; 145:3 [b]Ps. 46:4 [c]Ps. 2:6; 87:1; Is. 2:3; Mic. 4:1; Zech. 8:3
2 [a]Ps. 50:2 [b]Lam. 2:15 [c]Matt. 5:35
3 [a]Ps. 46:7
4 [a]2Sam. 10:6-19
5 [I]Lit., *were hurried away* [a]Ex. 15:15
6 [I]Lit., *Trembling* [a]Is. 13:8
7 [a]Jer. 18:17 [b]1Kin. 22:48 [c]1Kin. 10:22; Ezek. 27:25
8 [I]*Selah* may mean: *Pause, Crescendo* or *Musical interlude* [a]Ps. 87:5
9 [a]Ps. 26:3; 40:10
10 [a]Deut. 28:58; Josh. 7:9; Mal. 1:11 [b]Ps. 65:1, 2; 100:1 [c]Is. 41:10
11 [a]Ps. 97:8
12 [a]Neh. 3:1, 11, 25-27
13 [a]Ps. 122:7 [b]Ps. 78:5-7
14 [I]Lit., *this* [II]Lit., *upon;* some mss. and the Gr. read *forever.* [a]Ps. 23:4; Is. 58:11

1 [a]Ps. 78:1; Is. 1:2; Mic. 1:2 [b]Ps. 33:8
2 [a]Ps. 62:9
3 [a]Ps. 37:30 [b]Ps. 119:130
4 [I]Lit., *open up* [a]Ps. 78:2 [b]2Kin. 3:15 [c]Num. 12:8
5 [I]Lit., *supplanters* [a]Ps. 23:4; 27:1
6 [a]Job 31:24; Ps. 52:7; Prov. 11:28; Mark 10:24
7 [a]Matt. 25:8, 9 [b]Job 36:18, 19
8 [I]Lit., *their* [a]Matt. 16:26

9 That he should [a]live[2421] on
eternally;[5703]
That he should not [I][b]undergo
decay.[7845]
10 For he sees[7200] *that even*
[a]wise men[2450] die;[4191]
The [b]stupid and the senseless
alike perish,[6]
And [c]leave[5800] their wealth to
others.
11 Their [I][a]inner thought[7130] is,
that their houses[1004] [b]are
forever,
And their dwelling places[4908] to
all generations;[1755]
They have [c]called[7121] their lands
after their own names.
12 But [a]man[120] in *his* [I]pomp will not
endure;
He is like the [II]beasts that
[III]perish.[1820]
13 This is the [a]way[1870] of those who
are foolish,[3689]
And of those after them who
[b]approve[7520] their words.
[I]Selah.
14 As sheep they are appointed
[a]for [I]Sheol;[7585]
Death[4194] shall be their
shepherd;
And the [b]upright shall rule[7287]
over them in the morning;
And their form[6736] shall be for
[I]Sheol [c]to consume,
[II]So that they have no habitation.
15 But God will [a]redeem my soul
from the [I]power[3027] of
[II]Sheol;
For [b]He will receive me. Selah.
16 Do not be afraid[3372] [a]when a
man[376] becomes rich,
When the [I]glory[3519] of his
house[1004] is increased;
17 For when he dies[4194] he will
[a]carry nothing away;
His [I]glory will not descend after
him.
18 Though while he lives[2416] he
[a]congratulates[1288] [I]himself—
And though *men* praise[3034] you
when you do well[3190] for
yourself—

9 [I]Or, *see corruption or the pit* [a]Ps. 22:29 [b]Ps. 16:10; 89:48
10 [a]Eccl. 2:16 [b]Ps. 92:6; 94:8 [c]Ps. 39:6; Eccl. 2:18, 21; Luke 12:20
11 [I]Some versions read *graves are their houses* [a]Ps. 64:6 [b]Ps. 10:6 [c]Gen. 4:17; Deut. 3:14
12 [I]Lit., *honor* [II]Or, *animals* [III]Lit., *are destroyed* [a]Ps. 49:20
13 [I]*Selah* may mean: *Pause, Crescendo* or *Musical interlude* [a]Jer. 17:11 [b]Ps. 49:18
14 [I]I.e., the nether world [II]Lit., *Away from his habitation* [a]Ps. 9:17 [b]Dan. 7:18; Mal. 4:3; 1Cor. 6:2; Rev. 2:26 [c]Job 24:19
15 [I]Lit., *hand* [II]I.e., the nether world [a]Ps. 16:10; 56:13; Hos. 13:14 [b]Gen. 5:24; Ps. 16:11; 73:24
16 [I]Or, *wealth* [a]Ps. 37:7
17 [I]Or, *wealth* [a]Ps. 17:14; 1Tim. 6:7
18 [I]Lit., *his soul* [a]Deut. 29:19; Ps. 10:3, 6; Luke 12:19
19 [I]Lit., *You;* or, *It* [a]Gen. 15:15 [b]Job 33:30; Ps. 56:13
20 [I]Lit., *honor* [II]Or, *animals* [III]Lit., *are destroyed* [a]Ps. 49:12 [b]Eccl. 3:19
+1Chr. 15:17; 2Chr. 29:30
1 [a]Josh. 22:22 [b]Ps. 113:3
2 [a]Ps. 48:2; Lam. 2:15 [b]Deut. 33:2; Ps. 80:1; 94:1
3 [a]Ps. 96:13 [b]Lev. 10:2; Num. 16:35; Ps. 97:3; Dan. 7:10 [c]Ps. 18:12, 13
4 [a]Deut. 4:26; 31:28; 32:1; Is. 1:2

19 [I]He shall [a]go to the
generation[1755] of his fathers;[1]
They shall never see [b]the
light.[216]
20 [a]Man in *his* [I]pomp, yet without
understanding,[995]
Is [b]like the [II]beasts that
[III]perish.

God the Judge of the Righteous and the Wicked

A Psalm of +Asaph.

50 [a]The Mighty[410] One, God,[430] the
LORD, has spoken,[1696]
And summoned[7121] the earth[776]
[b]from the rising of the sun
to its setting.
2 Out of Zion, [a]the perfection of
beauty,
God [b]has shone forth.
3 May our God [a]come and not keep
silence;
[b]Fire devours before Him,
And it is very [c]tempestuous[8175]
around Him.
4 He [a]summons[7121] the
heavens[8064] above,
And the earth, to judge[177] His
people:[5971]
5 "Gather[622] My [a]godly ones[2623] to
Me,
Those who have made[3772] a
[b]covenant[1285] with Me by
[c]sacrifice."[2077]
6 And the [a]heavens declare[5066] His
righteousness,[6664]
For [b]God Himself is judge.[8199]
[I]Selah.
7 "[a]Hear,[8085] O My people, and I
will speak;[1696]
O Israel, I will testify[5749]
[I]against you;
I am God, [b]your God.
8 "I do [a]not reprove[3198] you for your
sacrifices,[2077]

5 [a]Ps. 30:4; 37:28; 52:9 [b]Ex. 24:7; 2Chr. 6:11; Ps. 25:10 [c]Ps. 50:8 **6** [I]*Selah* may mean: *Pause, Crescendo* or *Musical interlude* [a]Ps. 89:5; 97:6 [b]Ps. 75:7; 96:13 **7** [I]Or, *to* [a]Ps. 49:1; 81:8 [b]Ex. 20:2; Ps. 48:14
8 [a]Ps. 40:6; 51:16; Is. 1:11; Hos. 6:6

And your burnt offerings[5930] are
continually[8548] before Me.
9 "I shall take no [a]young bull out
of your house,[1004]
Nor male goats out of your folds.
10 "For [a]every beast[2416] of the forest
is Mine,
The cattle on a thousand hills.
11 "I know every [a]bird of the
mountains,
And everything that moves in
the field[7704] is [I]Mine.
12 "If I were hungry, I would not
tell[559] you;
For the [a]world[8398] is Mine, and
[I]all it contains.
13 "Shall I eat the flesh[1320] of
[Ia]bulls,[47]
Or drink the blood[1818] of male
goats?
14 "Offer[2076] to God [a]a sacrifice of
thanksgiving,[8426]
And [b]pay your vows[5088] to the
Most High;[5945]
15 And [a]call upon Me in the day[3117]
of trouble;
I shall [b]rescue[2502] you, and you
will [c]honor[3513] Me."
16 But to the wicked[7563] God
says,[559]
"What right have you to tell[5608]
of My statutes,[2706]
And to take[5375] [a]My covenant in
your mouth?[6310]
17 "For you [a]hate discipline,[4148]
And you [b]cast My words[1697]
behind you.
18 "When you see[7200] a thief,
you [Ia]are pleased[7521] with
him,
And [II]you [b]associate with
adulterers.[5003]

9 [a]Ps. 69:31
10 [a]Ps. 104:24
11 [I]Or, *in My mind;* lit., *with Me* [a]Matt. 6:26
12 [I]Lit., *its fulness* [a]Ex. 19:5; Deut. 10:14; Ps. 24:1; 1Cor. 10:26
13 [I]Lit., *strong ones* [a]Ps. 50:9
14 [a]Ps. 27:6; 69:30; 107:22; 116:17; Hos. 14:2; Rom. 12:1; Heb. 13:15 [b]Num. 30:2; Deut. 23:21; Ps. 22:25; 56:12; 61:8; 65:1; 76:11
15 [a]Ps. 91:15; 107:6, 13; Zech. 13:9 [b]Ps. 81:7 [c]Ps. 22:23
16 [a]Is. 29:13
17 [a]Prov. 5:12; 12:1; Rom. 2:21, 22 [b]1Kin. 14:9; Neh. 9:26
18 [I]Some ancient versions read *run together* [II]Lit., *your part is with* [a]Rom. 1:32 [b]1Tim. 5:22
19 [I]Lit., *send* [a]Ps. 10:7 [b]Ps. 36:3; 52:2
20 [a]Job 19:18; Matt. 10:21
21 [a]Eccl. 8:11; Is. 42:14; 57:11 [b]Ps. 90:8
22 [a]Job 8:13; Ps. 9:17 [b]Ps. 7:2
23 [I]Lit., *sets* [a]Ps. 50:14 [b]Ps. 85:13 [c]Ps. 91:16

[+]2Sam. 12:1
1 [a]Ps. 4:1; 109:26 [b]Ps. 69:16; 106:45 [c]Ps. 51:9; Is. 43:25; 44:22; Acts 3:19; Col. 2:14
2 [a]Ps. 51:7; Is. 1:16; 4:4; Jer. 4:14; Acts 22:16; Rev. 1:5

19 "You [Ia]let your mouth loose in
evil,[7451]
And your [b]tongue frames
deceit.[4820]
20 "You sit and [a]speak[1696] against
your brother;[251]
You slander your own
mother's[517] son.[1121]
21 "These things you have done,[6213]
and [a]I kept silence;
You thought that I was just like
you;
I will [b]reprove you, and state
the case in order before your
eyes.
22 "Now consider[995] this, you who
[a]forget God,[433]
Lest I [b]tear *you* in pieces, and
there be none to deliver.[5337]
23 "He who [a]offers a sacrifice of
thanksgiving[8426] honors [3513]
Me;
And to him who [Ib]orders *his*
way[1870] *aright*
I shall [c]show[7200] the salvation[3468]
of God."

A Contrite Sinner's Prayer for Pardon

For the choir director. A Psalm of David, when [+]Nathan the prophet came to him, after he had gone in to Bathsheba.

51 🗝 [a]Be gracious[2603] to me, O
God,[430] according to Thy
lovingkindness;
According to the greatness
of [b]Thy compassion[7356]
[c]blot out[4229] my
transgressions.[6588]
🗝 2 [a]Wash[3526] me thoroughly from
my iniquity,

🗝 **51:1-19** This is one of the greatest passages in the entire Bible concerning confession and forgiveness. It was written after David had committed adultery with Bathsheba and subsequently had her husband Uriah killed in battle (see II Sam. 11:2-17). David's repentance included: (1) a godly sorrow for his sin (cf. II Cor. 7:10); (2) verbal confession; (3) a turning away from sin, a renouncing; (4) forgiveness; (5) restoration to God's favor; (6) rejoicing in salvation; (7) a willingness to testify to others about the grace of God.

🗝 **51:2** Cf. Deut. 30:6; Ezek. 36:25,26; Lam. 5:21; Eph. 2:5,6,10 show that man should voluntarily receive God's salvation. Deut. 10:16; Isa. 1:16; Jer. 4:14; Ezek. 18:31; Zech. 1:3; Eph. 5:14 all indicate

(continued on next page)

And [b]cleanse5352 me from my sin.2403
3 For [I]I [a]know3045 my transgressions,6588
And my sin is ever8548 before me.
4 [a]Against Thee, Thee only, I have sinned,2398
And done6213 what is [b]evil7451 in Thy sight,
So that [c]Thou [I]art justified6663
[II]when Thou dost speak,1696
And [III]blameless when Thou dost judge.8199
5 Behold, I was [a]brought forth2342 in iniquity,
And in sin2399 my mother517 conceived me.
6 Behold, Thou dost desire2654 [a]truth571 in the [I]innermost being,
And in the hidden part Thou wilt [b]make me know wisdom.2451
7 [I]Purify2398 me [a]with hyssop,231 and I shall be clean;2891
[II]Wash me, and I shall be [b]whiter than snow.
8 [I]Make me to hear8085 [a]joy and gladness,
Let the [b]bones6106 which Thou hast broken rejoice.
9 [a]Hide Thy face from my sins,2399
And blot out all my iniquities.5771
10 [a]Create1254 [I]in me a [b]clean2889 heart,3820 O God,
And renew [II]a [c]steadfast spirit7307 within7130 me.
11 [a]Do not cast me away from Thy presence,
And do not take Thy [b]Holy6944 Spirit from me.

2 [b]Jer. 33:8; Ezek. 36:33; Heb. 9:14; 1John 1:7, 9
3 [I]Or, *I myself know* [a]Is. 59:12
4 [I]Or, *mayest be in the right* [II]Many mss. read *in Thy words* [III]Lit., *pure* [a]Gen. 20:6; 39:9; 2Sam. 12:13; Ps. 41:4 [b]Luke 15:21 [c]Rom. 3:4
5 [a]Job 14:4; 15:14; Ps. 58:3; Eph. 2:3
6 [I]Or, *inward parts* [a]Job 38:36; Ps. 15:2 [b]Prov. 2:6; Eccl. 2:26; James 1:5
7 [I]Or, *Mayest Thou purify. . . that I may be clean* [II]Or, *Mayest Thou wash* [a]Ex. 12:22; Lev. 14:4; Num. 19:18; Heb. 9:19 [b]Is. 1:18
8 [I]Or, *Mayest Thou make* [a]Is. 35:10; Joel 1:16 [b]Ps. 35:10
9 [a]Jer. 16:17
10 [I]Lit., *for* [II]Or, *an upright* [a]Ezek. 18:31; Eph. 2:10 [b]Ps. 24:4; Matt. 5:8; Acts 15:9 [c]Ps. 78:37
11 [a]2Kin. 13:23; 24:20; Jer. 7:15 [b]Is. 63:10, 11
12 [a]Ps. 13:5 [b]Ps. 110:3
13 [I]Or, *turn back* [a]Acts 9:21, 22 [b]Ps. 22:27

12 Restore7725 to me the [a]joy of Thy salvation,3468
And sustain me with a [b]willing spirit.
13 *Then* I will [a]teach3925 transgressors6586 Thy ways,1870
And sinners2400 will [I]be [b]converted7725 to Thee.
14 Deliver5337 me from [a]bloodguiltiness,1818 O God, Thou [b]God of my salvation;8668
Then my [c]tongue will joyfully sing of Thy righteousness.6666
15 O Lord, [I][a]open my lips,8193
That my mouth may [b]declare5046 Thy praise.
16 For Thou [a]dost not delight in sacrifice,2077 otherwise I would give it;
Thou art not pleased7521 with burnt offering.5930
17 The sacrifices2077 of God are a [a]broken7665 spirit;
A broken and a contrite1794 heart, O God, Thou wilt not despise.
18 [a]By Thy favor7522 do good3190 to Zion;
[I][b]Build the walls2426 of Jerusalem.
19 Then Thou wilt delight2654 in [I][a]righteous6664 sacrifices,
In [b]burnt offering and whole burnt offering;3632

14 [a]2Sam. 12:9; Ps. 26:9 [b]Ps. 25:5 [c]Ps. 35:28; 71:15
15 [I]Or, *mayest Thou open* [a]Ex. 4:15 [b]Ps. 9:14
16 [a]1Sam. 15:22; Ps. 40:6 17 [a]Ps. 34:18
18 [I]Or, *Mayest Thou build* [a]Ps. 69:35; Is. 51:3 [b]Ps. 102:16; 147:2 19 [I]Or, *sacrifices of righteousness* [a]Ps. 4:5 [b]Ps. 66:13, 15

(continued from previous page)
that man is passive in the regeneration process. The simple truth is that man is both passive and active. Man is active in thinking upon the truth, in exercising his sensibilities in relation to it, and in giving up his heart to God, but man is passive in that he is acted upon by the truth and the Holy Spirit. God does not regenerate indifferent individuals. They must respond from their hearts! There is a divine *and* human cooperation. It may be slowed by human resistance or accelerated by obedience to God. God will not force Himself upon us. He wants us to love Him back having first accepted His love and redemption.

Then [II]young bulls will be offered
on Thine altar.4196

Futility of Boastful Wickedness

For the choir director. A +Maskil of David, •when Doeg the Edomite came and told Saul, and said to him, "David has come to the house of Ahimelech."

52 Why do you [a]boast1984 in evil,7451
O mighty man?
The [b]lovingkindness2617 of
God410 *endures* all day
long.
2 Your tongue devises2803
[a]destruction,1942
Like a [b]sharp razor, [c]O worker
of deceit.
3 You [a]love157 evil7451 more than
good,2896
[b]Falsehood more than
speaking1696 what is right.6664
[I]Selah.
4 You love all words1697 that
devour,1105
O [a]deceitful4820 tongue.
5 [I]But God will break you down5422
forever;5331
He will snatch you up, and
[a]tear5255 you away from *your*
tent,168
And [b]uproot you from the
[c]land776 of the living.2416
Selah.
6 And the righteous6662 will
[a]see and fear,3372
And will [b]laugh at him, *saying,*
7 "Behold, the man1397 who would
not make7760 God430 his
refuge,
But [a]trusted982 in the abundance
of his riches,
And [b]was strong in [I]his *evil*
desire."1942
8 But as for me, I am like a
[a]green olive tree in the
house1004 of God;
I [b]trust982 in the
lovingkindness2617 of God
forever5769 and ever.5703
9 I will [a]give Thee thanks3034

19 [II]Lit., *they will offer young bulls*

+Possibly, *Contemplative*, or *Didactic*, or *Skillful Psalm* •1Sam. 22:9

1 [a]Ps. 94:4 [b]Ps. 52:8

2 [a]Ps. 5:9 [b]Ps. 57:4; 59:7 [c]Ps. 101:7

3 [I]*Selah* may mean: *Pause, Crescendo* or *Musical interlude* [a]Ps. 36:4 [b]Ps. 58:3; Jer. 9:5

4 [a]Ps. 120:3

5 [I]Or, *Also* [a]Is. 22:18, 19 [b]Prov. 2:22 [c]Ps. 27:13

6 [a]Ps. 37:34; 40:3 [b]Job 22:19

7 [I]Or, *his destruction* [a]Ps. 49:6 [b]Ps. 10:6

8 [a]Ps. 92:12; 128:3; Jer. 11:16 [b]Ps. 13:5

9 [a]Ps. 30:12 [b]Ps. 54:6

+I.e., sickness, a sad tone •Possibly, *Contemplative*, or *Didactic*, or *Skillful Psalm*

1 [a]Ps. 10:4; 14:1-7; 53:1-6 [b]Rom. 3:10

2 [I]Or, *acts wisely* [a]Rom. 3:11 [b]2Chr. 15:2

3 [a]Rom. 3:12

4 [a]Jer. 4:22

5 [I]Or, *dread* [II]Or possibly, *those* [a]Lev. 26:17, 36; Prov. 28:1 [b]Ps. 141:7; Jer. 8:1, 2; Ezek. 6:5 [c]Ps. 44:7 [d]2Kin. 17:20; Jer. 6:30; Lam. 5:22

6 [I]Lit., *would be* [II]Or, *restores the fortunes of His people* [III]Or, *Jacob will rejoice, Israel will be glad* [a]Ps. 14:7

forever, because Thou hast
done6213 *it,*
And I will wait on6960 Thy name,
[b]for *it is* good, in the presence
of Thy godly ones.2623

Folly and Wickedness of Men

For the choir director; according to +Mahalath. A •Maskil of David.

53 [a]The fool has said in his heart,3820
"There is no God,"430
They are corrupt, and have
committed abominable8581
injustice;5766
[b]There is no one who does6213
good.2896
2 God has looked down from
heaven8064 upon the sons1121
of men,120
To see if there is [a]anyone who
[I]understands,7919
Who [b]seeks after God.
3 [a]Every one of them has turned
aside; together they have
become corrupt;
There is no one who does good,
not even one.
4 Have the workers of
wickedness205 [a]no
knowledge,3045
Who eat up My people5971 *as*
though they ate bread,
And have not called upon7121
God?
5 There they were in great
[I]fear6343 [a]*where* no [I]fear had
been;
For God [b]scattered the
bones6106 of [II]him who
encamped against you;
You [c]put *them* to shame,954
because [d]God had
rejected3988 them.
6 Oh, that [a]the salvation3444 of
Israel [I]would come out of
Zion!
When God [II]restores7725 His
captive7622 people,
[III]Let Jacob rejoice, let Israel be
glad.

Prayer for Defense against Enemies

For the choir director; on stringed instruments. A +Maskil of David, •when the Ziphites came and said to Saul, "Is not David hiding himself among us?"

54 Save[3467] me, O God,[430] by
[a]Thy name,
And [I]vindicate[1777] me by [b]Thy
power.
2 [a]Hear[8085] my prayer,[8605] O God;
[b]Give ear[238] to the words[561] of
my mouth.[6310]
3 For strangers[2114] have [a]risen
against me,
And [b]violent men have [c]sought
my [I]life;[5315]
They have [d]not set[7760] God
before them. [II]Selah.
4 Behold, [a]God is my helper;
The Lord is [I]the [b]sustainer of
my soul.
5 [I]He will [a]recompense[7725] the
evil[7451] to [II]my foes;
[III][b]Destroy them [c]in Thy
[IV]faithfulness.[571]
6 [I][a]Willingly[5071] I will sacrifice[2076]
to Thee;
I will give [b]thanks[3034] to Thy
name, O LORD, for it is
good.[2896]
7 For [I]He has [a]delivered[5337] me
from all [II]trouble;
And my eye has [b]looked[7200] *with
satisfaction* upon my
enemies.

Prayer for the Destruction of the Treacherous

For the choir director; on stringed instruments. A +Maskil of David.

55 [a]Give ear[238] to my prayer,[8605] O
God;[430]
And [b]do not hide Thyself from
my supplication.[8467]
2 Give [a]heed to me, and answer
me;
I am restless in my
[b]complaint[7878] and [I][c]am
surely distracted,[1949]

+Possibly, *Contemplative,* or *Didactic,* or *Skillful Psalm* •1Sam. 23:19; 26:1
1 [I]Lit., *judge* [a]Ps. 20:1 [b]2Chr. 20:6
2 [a]Ps. 17:6; 55:1 [b]Ps. 5:1
3 [I]Or, *soul* [II]*Selah* may mean: *Pause, Crescendo* or *Musical interlude* [a]Ps. 86:14 [b]Ps. 18:48; 86:14; 140:1, 4, 11 [c]1Sam. 20:1; 25:29; Ps. 40:14; 63:9; 70:2 [d]Ps. 36:1
4 [I]Lit., *as those who sustain* [a]Ps. 30:10; 37:40; 118:7 [b]Ps. 37:17, 24; 41:12; 51:12; 145:14; Is. 41:10
5 [I]Lit., *The evil will return* [II]Or, *those who lie in wait for me* [III]Or, *Put to silence* [IV]Or, *truth* [a]Ps. 94:23 [b]Ps. 143:12 [c]Ps. 89:49; 96:13; Is. 42:3
6 [I]Or, *With a freewill offering* [a]Num. 15:3; Ps. 116:17 [b]Ps. 50:14
7 [I]Or, *it;* i.e., His name [II]Or, *distress* [a]Ps. 34:6 [b]Ps. 59:10; 92:11; 112:8; 118:7

+Possibly, *Contemplative,* or *Didactic,* or *Skillful Psalm*
1 [a]Ps. 54:2; 61:1; 86:6 [b]Ps. 27:9
2 [I]Or, *I must moan* [a]Ps. 66:19; 86:6, 7 [b]1Sam. 1:16; Job 9:27; Ps. 64:1; 77:3; 142:2 [c]Is. 38:14; 59:11; Ezek. 7:16
3 [I]Or, *wickedness* [a]Ps. 17:9 [b]2Sam. 16:7, 8 [c]Ps. 71:11; 143:3
4 [a]Ps. 38:8 [b]Ps. 18:4, 5; 116:3
5 [I]Lit., *shuddering* [a]Ps. 119:120 [b]Job 21:6; Is. 21:4; Ezek. 7:18
6 [I]Lit., *settle down* [a]Job 3:13

3 Because of the voice of the
enemy,
Because of the [a]pressure of the
wicked;[7563]
For they [b]bring down [I]trouble[205]
upon me,
And in anger[639] they [c]bear a
grudge against me.
4 My [a]heart[3820] is in anguish[2342]
within[7130] me,
And the terrors[367] of [b]death[4194]
have fallen[5307] upon me.
5 Fear[3374] and [a]trembling[7460] come
upon me;
And [I][b]horror[6427] has
overwhelmed[3680] me.
6 And I said, "Oh, that I had wings
like a dove!
I would fly away and [I][a]be at rest.
7 "Behold, I would wander far
away,
I would [a]lodge in the wilderness.
[I]Selah.
8 "I would hasten to my place of
refuge
From the [a]stormy wind *and*
tempest."
9 [I]Confuse,[1104] O Lord,[136]
[a]divide[6385] their tongues,
For I have seen[7200] [b]violence[2555]
and strife in the city.
10 Day[3119] and night[3915] they go
around her upon her
walls;[2426]
And iniquity and mischief are in
her midst.[7130]
11 [a]Destruction is in her midst;
[b]Oppression and deceit[4820] do
not depart from her [I]streets.
12 For it is [a]not an enemy who
reproaches me,
Then I could bear[5375] *it;*
Nor is it one who hates me who
[b]has exalted himself against
me,
Then I could hide myself from
him.

7 [I]*Selah* may mean: *Pause, Crescendo* or *Musical interlude* [a]1Sam. 23:14 **8** [a]Is. 4:6; 25:4; 29:6
9 [I]Lit., *Swallow up* [a]Gen. 11:9 [b]Ps. 11:5; Jer. 6:7
11 [I]Or, *plaza* [a]Ps. 5:9 [b]Ps. 10:7; 17:9 **12** [a]Ps. 41:9 [b]Ps. 35:26

13 But it is you, a man[582] [I]my equal,
My [a]companion and my
[IIb]familiar friend.[3045]
14 We who had sweet
[I]fellowship[5475] together,
[a]Walked in the house[1004] of God
in the throng.[7285]
15 Let [I]death come [a]deceitfully
upon them;
Let them [b]go down alive[2416] to
[II]Sheol,[7585]
For evil[7451] is in their
dwelling,[4033] in their
midst.[7130]
16 As for me, I shall [a]call[7121] upon
God,
And the LORD will save[3467] me.
17 [a]Evening and [b]morning and at
[c]noon, I will complain[7878] and
murmur,
And He will hear[8085] my voice.
18 He will [a]redeem[6299] my soul[5315]
in peace [I]from the battle
which is against me,
For they are [b]many *who strive*
with me.
19 God[410] will [a]hear and [I]answer
them—
Even the one [b]who [II]sits
enthroned from of old—[6924]
Selah.
With whom there [III]is no change,
And who [c]do not fear[3372] God.
20 He has put forth his hands[3027]
against [a]those who were at
peace[7965] with him;
He has [Ib]violated[2490] his
covenant.[1285]
21 His [I]speech[6310] was [a]smoother
than butter,
But his heart was war;
His words[1697] were [b]softer than
oil,[8081]
Yet they were drawn [c]swords.
22 [a]Cast [I]your burden upon the
LORD, and He will sustain
you;
[b]He will never allow the
righteous[6662] to [IIc]be shaken.
23 But Thou, O God, wilt bring
them down to the [Ia]pit of
destruction;[7845]

13 [I]Lit., *according to my valuation* [II]Or, *acquaintance* [a]2Sam. 15:12 [b]Job 19:14; Ps. 41:9
14 [I]Lit., *counsel;* or, *intimacy* [a]Ps. 42:4
15 [I]Another reading is *desolations be upon them* [II]I.e., the nether world [a]Ps. 64:7; Prov. 6:15; Is. 47:11; 1Thess. 5:3 [b]Num. 16:30, 33
16 [a]Ps. 57:2, 3
17 [a]Ps. 141:2; Dan. 6:10; Acts 3:1; 10:3, 30 [b]Ps. 5:3; 88:13; 92:2 [c]Acts 10:9
18 [I]Or, *so that none may approach me* [a]Ps. 103:4 [b]Ps. 56:2
19 [I]Or, *afflict* [II]Or, *abides from* [III]Lit., *are no changes* [a]Ps. 78:59 [b]Deut. 33:27; Ps. 90:2; 93:2 [c]Ps. 36:1
20 [I]Lit., *profaned* [a]Ps. 7:4; 120:7 [b]Num. 30:2; Ps. 89:34
21 [I]Lit., *mouth* [a]Ps. 12:2; 28:3; Prov. 5:3, 4 [b]Ps. 57:4; 59:7
22 [I]Or, *what He has given you* [II]Or, *totter* [a]Ps. 37:5; 1Pet. 5:7 [b]Ps. 37:24 [c]Ps. 15:5; 112:6
23 [I]Or, *lowest pit* [a]Ps. 73:18; Is. 38:17; Ezek. 28:8 [b]Ps. 5:6 [c]Job 15:32; Prov. 10:27 [d]Ps. 25:2; 56:3

+Or, *The silent dove of those who are far off,* or, *The dove of the distant terebinths.* •Possibly, *Epigrammatic Poem,* or *Atonement Psalm* Δ1Sam. 21:10, 11
1 [I]Or, *snapped at* [II]Or, *A fighting man* [a]Ps. 57:3 [b]Ps. 17:9
2 [I]Or, *snapped at* [II]Or, *many are fighting* [a]Ps. 35:25; 57:3; 124:3 [b]Ps. 35:1
3 [I]Lit., *In the day* [II]Or, *I am one*

[b]Men of bloodshed[1818] and
deceit[4820] will [c]not live out half
their days.[3117]
But I will [d]trust[982] in Thee.

Supplication for Deliverance, and Grateful Trust in God

For the choir director; according to +Jonath elem rehokim. A •Mikhtam of David, Δwhen the Philistines seized him in Gath.

56 Be gracious[2603] to me, O God,[430]
for man[582] has [Ia]trampled
upon me;
[II]Fighting all day[3117] long he
[b]oppresses me.
2 My foes have [Ia]trampled upon
me all day long,
For [II]they are many who
[b]fight proudly against me.
3 [I]When[3117] I am [a]afraid,[3372]
[II]I will [b]put my trust[982] in Thee.
4 [a]In God, whose word[1697] I
praise,[1984]
In God I have put my trust;
I shall not be afraid.[3372]
[b]What can *mere* [I]man[1320] do[6213]
to me?
5 All day long[3117] they [Ia]distort[6087]
my words;[1697]
All their [IIb]thoughts[4284] are
against me for evil.[7451]
6 They [Ia]attack,[1481] they lurk,
They [b]watch[8104] my [II]steps,[6119]
As they have [c]waited[6960] *to take*
my [III]life.[5315]
7 Because of wickedness,[205]
[Ia]cast them forth,
In anger[639] [b]put down the
peoples,[5971] O God!
8 Thou [a]hast taken account[5608] of
my wanderings;
Put my [b]tears in Thy bottle;
Are *they* not in [c]Thy book?[5612]
9 Then my enemies will

who puts [a]Ps. 55:4, 5 [b]Ps. 11:1 **4** [I]Lit., *flesh* [a]Ps. 56:10, 11 [b]Ps. 118:6; Heb. 13:6 **5** [I]Or, *trouble my affairs* [II]Or, *purposes* [a]2Pet. 3:16 [b]Ps. 41:7 **6** [I]Or, *stir up strife* [II]Lit., *heels* [III]Lit., *soul* [a]Ps. 59:3; 140:2; Is. 54:15 [b]Ps. 17:11 [c]Ps. 71:10 **7** [I]Or, *will they have escape?* [a]Ps. 36:12; Prov. 19:5; Ezek. 17:15; Rom. 2:3 [b]Ps. 55:23 **8** [a]Ps. 139:3 [b]2Kin. 20:5; Ps. 39:12 [c]Mal. 3:16

[a]turn[7725] back [b]in the day
when I call;[7121]
This I know, [I]that [c]God is for
me.
10 In God, *whose* word I praise,
In the LORD, *whose* word I
praise,
11 In God I have put my [I]trust, I
shall not be afraid.
What can man[120] do to me?
12 Thy [a]vows[5088] are *binding* upon
me, O God;
I will render[7999] thank
offerings[8426] to Thee.
13 For Thou hast [a]delivered[5337] my
soul from death,[4194]
[I]Indeed [b]my feet from stumbling,
So that I may [c]walk before God
In the [d]light[216] of the [II]living.[2416]

Prayer for Rescue from Persecutors

For the choir director; *set to* [+]Al-tashheth. A [•]Mikhtam of David, [Δ]when he fled from Saul, in the cave.

57 Be gracious[2603] to me, O God,[430]
be gracious to me,
For my soul[5315] [a]takes refuge[2620]
in Thee;
And in the [b]shadow of Thy wings
I will take refuge,
Until destruction [c]passes by.[5674]
2 I will cry[7121] to God Most
High,[5945]
To God[410] who
[a]accomplishes[1584] *all things*
for me.
3 He will [a]send from heaven[8064]
and save[3467] me;
He reproaches him who
[I][b]tramples upon me. [II]Selah.
God will send forth His
[c]lovingkindness[2617] and His
[III]truth.[571]
4 My soul is among [a]lions;
I must lie among those who
breathe forth fire,
Even the sons[1121] of men,[120]
whose [b]teeth are spears and
arrows,

9 [I]Or, *because* [a]Ps. 9:3 [b]Ps. 102:2 [c]Ps. 41:11; 118:6; Rom. 8:31
11 [I]Or, *trust without fear*
12 [a]Ps. 50:14
13 [I]Or, *Hast Thou not delivered* [II]Or, *life* [a]Ps. 33:19; 49:15; 86:13 [b]Ps. 116:8 [c]Ps. 116:9 [d]Job 33:30

[+]Lit., *Do Not Destroy* [•]Possibly, *Epigrammatic Poem* or *Atonement Psalm* [Δ]1Sam. 22:1; 24:3
1 [a]Ps. 2:12; 34:22 [b]Ruth 2:12; Ps. 17:8; 36:7; 63:7; 91:4 [c]Is. 26:20
2 [a]Ps. 138:8
3 [I]Or, *snaps at* [II]*Selah* may mean: *Pause, Crescendo* or *Musical interlude* [III]Or, *faithfulness* [a]Ps. 18:16; 144:5, 7 [b]Ps. 56:2 [c]Ps. 25:10; 40:11
4 [a]Ps. 35:17; 58:6 [b]Prov. 30:14 [c]Ps. 55:21; 59:7; 64:3; Prov. 12:18
5 [a]Ps. 57:11; 108:5
6 [I]Or, *spread* [a]Ps. 10:9; 31:4; 35:7; 140:5 [b]Ps. 145:14 [c]Ps. 7:15 [d]Prov. 26:27; 28:10; Eccl. 10:8
7 [a]Ps. 57:7-11; 108:1-5 [b]Ps. 112:7
8 [a]Ps. 16:9; 30:12 [b]Ps. 150:3
9 [I]Lit., *peoples* [a]Ps. 108:3
10 [I]Or, *faithfulness* [a]Ps. 36:5; 103:11; 108:4
11 [a]Ps. 57:5; 108:5

[+]Lit., *Do Not Destroy* [•]Possibly, *Epigrammatic Poem* or *Atonement Psalm*
1 [I]Another reading is *speak righteousness in silence* [II]Or, *mighty ones* or *judges* [III]Or, *uprightly the sons of men* [a]Ps. 82:2 **2** [a]Mal. 3:15 [b]Ps. 94:20; Is. 10:1 **3** [a]Ps. 51:5; Is. 48:8

And their [c]tongue a sharp
sword.[2719]
5 [a]Be exalted above the
heavens,[8064] O God;
Let Thy glory[3519] *be* above all
the earth.[776]
6 They have [I]prepared[3559] a
[a]net for my steps;
My soul is [b]bowed down;
They [c]dug a pit before me;
They *themselves* have [d]fallen[5307]
into the midst of it. Selah.
7 [a]My [b]heart[3820] is steadfast,[3559]
O God, my heart is steadfast;
I will sing,[7891] yes, I will sing
praises!
8 Awake, [a]my glory;
Awake, [b]harp and lyre,
I will awaken the dawn!
9 [a]I will give thanks[3034] to Thee,
O Lord,[136] among the
peoples;[5971]
I will sing[2167] praises to Thee
among the [I]nations.[3816]
10 For Thy [a]lovingkindness is great
to the heavens,
And Thy [I]truth to the clouds.[7834]
11 [a]Be exalted above the heavens,
O God;
Let Thy glory *be* above all the
earth.

Prayer for the Punishment of the Wicked

For the choir director; *set to* [+]Al-tashheth. A [•]Mikhtam of David.

58 Do you indeed[552] [I]speak[1696]
righteousness,[6664] O [II]gods?
Do you [a]judge[8199] [III]uprightly,[4334]
O sons[1121] of men?[120]
2 No, in heart[3820] you [a]work
unrighteousness;[5766]
On earth[776] you [b]weigh out the
violence[2555] of your
hands.[3027]
3 The wicked[7563] are
estranged[2114] [a]from the
womb;

These who speak[1696] lies[3577]
[b]go astray[8582] from [I]birth.[990]
4 They have venom like the
[a]venom[2534] of a serpent;[5175]
Like a deaf cobra[6620] that stops
up its ear,[241]
5 So that it [a]does not hear[8085] the
voice of [Ib]charmers,[3907]
Or a skillful[2449] caster of spells.
6 O God,[430] [a]shatter[2040] their teeth
in their mouth;[6310]
Break out[5422] the fangs of the
young lions, O LORD.
7 Let them [a]flow away like water
that runs off;
When he [Ib]aims his arrows, let
them be as [II]headless
shafts.[4135]
8 *Let them be* as a snail which
[I]melts away as it goes along,
Like the [a]miscarriages[5309] of a
woman[802] which never
see[2372] the sun.
9 Before your [a]pots can feel[995] *the*
fire of thorns,
He will [b]sweep them away with
a whirlwind,[8175] the
[I]green[2416] and the burning
alike.
10 The [a]righteous[6662] will rejoice
when he [b]sees[2372] the
vengeance;[5359]
He will [c]wash[7364] his feet in the
blood[1818] of the wicked.
11 And men[120] will say,[559] "Surely
there is a [Ia]reward for the
righteous;
Surely there is a God who
[b]judges[8199] [II]on earth!"

Prayer for Deliverance from Enemies

For the choir director; *set to* [+]Al-tashheth. A [•]Mikhtam of David, [Δ]when Saul sent *men,* and they watched the house in order to kill him.

59 [a]Deliver[5337] me from my
enemies, O my God;[430]
[Ib]Set me *securely* on high away
from those who rise up
against me.
2 Deliver me from [a]those who do
iniquity,[205]
And save[3467] me from [b]men[582]
of bloodshed.[1818]
3 For behold, they [a]have [I]set an
ambush for my [II]life;[5315]
[III]Fierce men [IVa]launch an attack
against me,
[b]Not for my transgression nor
for my sin,[2403] O LORD,
4 [Ia]For no guilt of *mine,* they run
and set[3559] themselves
against me.
[b]Arouse Thyself to [II]help me,
and see![7200]
5 And Thou, [a]O LORD God
of hosts,[6635] the God of
Israel,
Awake to [Ib]punish[6485] all the
nations;[1471]
[c]Do not be gracious[2603] to any
who are treacherous[205] in
iniquity.[898] [II]Selah.
6 They [a]return[7725] at evening,
they howl like a [b]dog,
And go around the city.
7 Behold, they [a]belch forth with
their mouth;[6310]
[b]Swords[2719] are in their lips,[8193]
For, *they say,* "Who hears?"[8085]
8 But Thou, O LORD, dost
[a]laugh at them;
Thou dost [b]scoff at all the
nations.
9 *Because of* [I]his [a]strength I will
watch for Thee,
For God is my [b]stronghold.
10 [I]My God [a]in His
lovingkindness[2617] will meet
me;
God will let me [b]look
triumphantly upon [II]my
foes.
11 Do not slay[2026] them, [a]lest my
people[5971] forget;

3 [I]Lit., *the womb* [b]Ps. 53:3
4 [a]Deut. 32:33; Ps. 140:3
5 [I]Or, *whisperers* [a]Jer. 8:17 [b]Eccl. 10:11
6 [a]Job 4:10; Ps. 3:7
7 [I]Lit., *bends* [II]Lit., *though they were cut off* [a]Josh. 2:11; 7:5; Ps. 112:10; Is. 13:7; Ezek. 21:7 [b]Ps. 64:3
8 [I]I.e., secretes slime [a]Job 3:16; Eccl. 6:3
9 [I]Lit., *living* [a]Ps. 118:12; Eccl. 7:6 [b]Job 27:21; Ps. 83:15; Prov. 10:25
10 [a]Job 22:19; Ps. 32:11; 64:10; 107:42 [b]Deut. 32:43; Ps. 91:8; Jer. 11:20; 20:12 [c]Ps. 68:23
11 [I]Lit., *fruit* [II]Or, *in* [a]Ps. 18:20; 19:11; Is. 3:10; Luke 6:23, 35 [b]Ps. 9:8; 67:4; 75:7; 94:2

[+]Lit., *Do Not Destroy* [•]Possibly, *Epigrammatic Poem* or *Atonement Psalm* [Δ]1Sam. 19:11
1 [I]Or, *Mayest Thou put me in an inaccessibly high place* [a]Ps. 143:9 [b]Ps. 20:1; 69:29
2 [a]Ps. 28:3; 36:12; 53:4; 92:7; 94:16 [b]Ps. 26:9; 139:19; Prov. 29:10
3 [I]Or, *lain in wait* [II]Lit., *soul* [III]Or, *Strong* [IV]Or, *stir up strife* [a]Ps. 56:6 [b]1Sam. 24:11; Ps. 7:3, 4; 69:4
4 [I]Lit., *Without guilt* [II]Lit., *meet* [a]Ps. 35:19 [b]Ps. 7:6; 35:23
5 [I]Lit., *visit* [II]*Selah* may mean: *Pause, Crescendo* or *Musical interlude* [a]Ps. 69:6; 80:4; 84:8 [b]Ps. 9:5; Is. 26:14 [c]Is. 2:9; Jer. 18:23
6 [a]Ps. 59:14 [b]Ps. 22:16

7 [a]Ps. 94:4; Prov. 15:2, 28 [b]Ps. 57:4; Prov. 12:18 [c]Job 22:13; Ps. 10:11; 73:11; 94:7 **8** [a]Ps. 37:13; Prov. 1:26 [b]Ps. 2:4 **9** [I]Many mss. and some ancient versions read *My strength* [a]Ps. 18:17 [b]Ps. 9:9; 62:2 **10** [I]Many mss. and some ancient versions read *The God of my lovingkindness* [II]Lit., *those who lie in wait for me* [a]Ps. 21:3 [b]Ps. 54:7 **11** [a]Deut. 4:9; 6:12

[Ib]Scatter them by Thy power,[2428] and bring them down,
O Lord,[136] [c]our shield.
12 [I]*On account of* the [a]sin of their mouth *and* the words[1697] of their lips,
Let them even be [b]caught in their pride,
And on account of [c]curses[423] and [II]lies which they utter.
13 [Ia]Destroy *them* in wrath,[2534] [I]destroy *them*, that they may be no more;
That *men* may [b]know that God [II]rules[4910] in Jacob,
To the ends of the earth.[776] Selah.
14 And they [a]return at evening, they howl like a dog,
And go around the city.
15 They [a]wander about [I]for food,
And [II]growl if they are not satisfied.
16 But as for me, I shall [a]sing[7891] of Thy strength;
Yes, I shall [b]joyfully sing of Thy lovingkindness in the [c]morning,
For Thou hast been my [d]stronghold,
And a [e]refuge in the day[3117] of my distress.
17 [a]O my strength, I will sing[2167] praises to Thee;
For God is my [b]stronghold, the [I]God who shows me lovingkindness.

Lament over Defeat in Battle, and Prayer for Help

For the choir director; according to [+]Shushan Eduth. A [•]Mikhtam of David, to teach; [Δ]when he struggled with Aram-naharaim and with Aram-zobah, and Joab returned, and smote twelve thousand of Edom in the Valley of Salt.

60 O God,[430] [a]Thou hast rejected us. Thou hast [Ib]broken us;
Thou hast been [c]angry;[599] O, [d]restore[7725] us.
2 Thou hast made the [Ia]land[776] quake,[7463] Thou hast split it open;
[b]Heal its breaches,[7667] for it totters.
3 Thou hast [Ia]made Thy people[5971] experience hardship;[7186]
Thou hast given us [II]wine to [b]drink that makes us stagger.
4 Thou hast given a [a]banner to those who fear[3373] Thee,
That it may be displayed because of the truth.[7189] [I]Selah.
5 [a]That Thy [b]beloved[3039] may be delivered,[2502]
[c]Save[3467] with Thy right hand, and answer [I]us!
6 God has spoken[1696] in His [Ia]holiness:[6944]
"I will exult, I will portion out [b]Shechem and measure out[4058] the valley of [c]Succoth.
7 "[a]Gilead is Mine, and Manasseh is Mine;
[b]Ephraim also is the [I]helmet of My head;[7218]
Judah is My [IIc]scepter.[2710]
8 "[a]Moab is My washbowl;[7366]
Over [b]Edom I shall throw My shoe;
Shout loud,[7321] O [c]Philistia, because of Me!"
9 Who will bring me into the besieged city?
Who [I]will lead[5148] me to Edom?
10 Hast not Thou Thyself, O God, [a]rejected us?
And [b]wilt Thou not go forth with our armies,[6635] O God?
11 O give us help[8668] against the adversary,
For [a]deliverance [I]by man[120] is in vain.[7723]
12 [I]Through God we shall [a]do[6213] valiantly,[2428]
And it is He who will [b]tread down[947] our adversaries.

11 [I]Or, *Make them wander* [b]Ps. 106:27; 144:6; Is. 33:3 [c]Ps. 84:9
12 [I]Or, *The sin of their mouth is the word of their lips*, [II]Lit., *lying* [a]Prov. 12:13 [b]Zeph. 3:11 [c]Ps. 10:7
13 [I]Lit., *Bring to an end* [II]Or, *is Ruler* [a]Ps. 104:35 [b]Ps. 83:18
14 [a]Ps. 59:6
15 [I]Or, *to devour* [II]Another reading is *tarry all night* [a]Job 15:23
16 [a]Ps. 21:13 [b]Ps. 101:1 [c]Ps. 5:3; 88:13 [d]Ps. 59:9 [e]2Sam. 22:3; Ps. 46:1
17 [I]Lit., *God of my lovingkindness* [a]Ps. 59:9 [b]Ps. 59:10

[+]Lit., *The lily of testimony* [•]Possibly, *Epigrammatic Poem* or *Atonement Psalm* [Δ]2Sam. 8:3, 13; 1Chr. 18:3, 12
1 [I]Or, *broken out upon us* [a]Ps. 44:9 [b]2Sam. 5:20 [c]Ps. 79:5 [d]Ps. 80:3
2 [I]Or, *earth* [a]Ps. 18:7 [b]2Chr. 7:14; Is. 30:26
3 [I]Lit., *caused Thy people to see* [II]Lit., *wine of staggering* [a]Ps. 66:12; 71:20 [b]Ps. 75:8; Is. 51:17, 22; Jer. 25:15
4 [I]*Selah* may mean: *Pause, Crescendo* or *Musical interlude* [a]Ps. 20:5; Is. 5:26; 11:12; 13:2
5 [I]Some authorities read *me* [a]Ps. 60:5-12; 108:6-13 [b]Deut. 33:12; Ps. 127:2; Is. 5:1; Jer. 11:15 [c]Ps. 17:7
6 [I]Or, *sanctuary* [a]Ps. 89:35 [b]Gen. 12:6; 33:18; Josh. 17:7 [c]Gen. 33:17; Josh. 13:27
7 [I]Lit., *protection* [II]Or, *lawgiver* [a]Josh. 13:31 [b]Deut. 33:17 [c]Gen. 49:10
8 [a]2Sam. 8:2 [b]2Sam. 8:14 [c]2Sam. 8:1
9 [I]Or, *has led*
10 [a]Ps. 60:1; 108:11 [b]Josh. 7:12; Ps. 44:9
11 [I]Lit., *of* [a]Ps. 146:3
12 [I]Or, *In* or *With* [a]Num. 24:18; Ps. 118:16 [b]Ps. 44:5; Is. 63:3

Confidence in God's Protection

For the choir director; on a stringed instrument.
A Psalm of David.

61 [a]Hear[8085] my cry, O God;[430]
[b]Give heed to my prayer.[8605]
2 From the [a]end of the earth[776] I
call[7121] to Thee, when my
heart is [b]faint;
Lead[5148] me to [c]the rock that
is higher than I.
3 For Thou hast been a
[a]refuge for me,
A [b]tower of strength [I]against the
enemy.
4 Let me [Ia]dwell[1481] in Thy tent[168]
forever;[5769]
Let me [b]take refuge[2620] in the
shelter5643 of Thy wings.
[II]Selah.
5 For Thou hast heard[8085] my
[a]vows,[5088] O God;
Thou hast given *me* the
inheritance[3425] of those who
[b]fear[3373] Thy name.
6 Thou wilt [Ia]prolong the king's[4428]
[II]life;[3117]
His years will be as many
generations.[1755]
7 He will [I]abide [a]before God
forever;
Appoint [b]lovingkindness[2617] and
truth,[571] that they may
preserve[5341] him.
8 So I will [a]sing praise[2167] to Thy
name forever,[5703]
That I may [b]pay[7999] my vows
day by day.[3117]

God Alone a Refuge from Treachery and Oppression

For the choir director; +according to Jeduthun.
A Psalm of David.

62 [a]My soul[5315] *waits* in silence for
God[430] only;
From Him [b]is my salvation.[3444]
2 He only is my [a]rock and my
salvation,
My [b]stronghold; I shall not be
greatly shaken.
3 How long will you assail a
man,[376]
That you may murder[7523] *him,*
all of you,
Like a [a]leaning wall, like a
tottering fence?
4 They have counseled[3289] only to
thrust him down from his high
position;
They [a]delight[7521] in
falsehood;[3577]
They [b]bless[1288] with [I]their
mouth,[6310]
But inwardly they curse.[7043]
[II]Selah.
5 My soul, [a]wait in silence for God
only,
For my hope is from Him.
6 He only is [a]my rock and my
salvation,
My stronghold; I shall not be
shaken.
7 On God my [a]salvation[3468] and my
glory[3519] *rest;*
The rock of my strength, my
[b]refuge is in God.
8 [a]Trust[982] in Him at all times,[6256]
O people;[5971]
[b]Pour out[8210] your heart[3824]
before Him;
God is a refuge for us. Selah.
9 Men[120] of [a]low degree are only
[b]vanity, and men of
rank[376,1121] are a [c]lie;[3576]
In the [d]balances they go up;
They are together lighter than
breath.
10 [a]Do not trust in oppression,
And do not [I]vainly hope in
[b]robbery;
If riches[2428] increase, [c]do not
set *your* heart[3820] *upon
them.*
11 [I]Once God has [a]spoken;[1696]
[II]Twice I have heard[8085] this:
That [b]power belongs to
God;
12 And lovingkindness[2617] [a]is
Thine, O Lord,

Psalm 61
1 [a]Ps. 64:1 [b]Ps. 86:6
2 [a]Ps. 42:6 [b]Ps. 77:3 [c]Ps. 18:2; 94:22
3 [I]Lit., *from* [a]Ps. 62:7 [b]Ps. 59:9; Prov. 18:10
4 [I]Or, *sojourn* [II]*Selah* may mean: *Pause, Crescendo* or *Musical interlude* [a]Ps. 23:6; 27:4 [b]Ps. 17:8; 91:4
5 [a]Job 22:27; Ps. 56:12 [b]Deut. 28:58; Neh. 1:11; Ps. 86:11; 102:15; Is. 59:19; Mal. 2:5; 4:2
6 [I]Lit., *add days to* [II]Lit., *days* [a]Ps. 21:4
7 [I]Or, *sit enthroned* [a]Ps. 41:12 [b]Ps. 40:11
8 [a]Judg. 5:3; Ps. 30:4; 33:2; 71:22 [b]Ps. 65:1; Is. 19:21

Psalm 62
+Cf. 1Chr. 16:41; 25:1; Ps. 39 and 77 titles
1 [a]Ps. 33:20 [b]Ps. 37:39
2 [a]Ps. 89:26 [b]Ps. 59:17; 62:6
3 [a]Is. 30:13
4 [I]Lit., *his* [II]*Selah* may mean: *Pause, Crescendo* or *Musical interlude* [a]Ps. 4:2 [b]Ps. 28:3; 55:21
5 [a]Ps. 62:1
6 [a]Ps. 62:2
7 [a]Ps. 85:9; Jer. 3:23 [b]Ps. 46:1
8 [a]Ps. 37:3, 5; 52:8; Is. 26:4 [b]1Sam. 1:15; Ps. 42:4; Lam. 2:19
9 [a]Ps. 49:2 [b]Job 7:16; Ps. 39:5; Is. 40:17 [c]Ps. 116:11 [d]Is. 40:15
10 [I]Lit., *become vain in robbery* [a]Is. 30:12 [b]Is. 61:8; Ezek. 22:29; Nah. 3:1 [c]Job 31:25; Ps. 49:6; 52:7; Mark 10:24; Luke 12:15; 1Tim. 6:10
11 [I]Or, *One thing* [II]Or, *These two things I have heard* [a]Job 33:14; 40:5 [b]Ps. 59:17; Rev. 19:1
12 [a]Ps. 86:5; 103:8; 130:7

For Thou [b]dost recompense[7999]
a man according to his work.

The Thirsting Soul Satisfied in God

A Psalm of David, [+]when he was in the wilderness of Judah.

63 O God,[430] [a]Thou art my God;[410]
I shall seek Thee [I]earnestly;
My soul[5315] [b]thirsts for Thee,
my flesh[1320] [II]yearns for Thee,
In a [c]dry and weary land[776]
where there is no water.
2 Thus I have [a]beheld[2372] Thee in the sanctuary,[6944]
To see[7200] Thy power and Thy glory.[3519]
3 Because Thy [a]lovingkindness is better[2896] than life,[2416]
My lips[8193] will praise[7623] Thee.
4 So I will bless[1288] Thee [a]as long as I live;[2416]
I will [b]lift up[5375] my hands[3709] in Thy name.
5 My soul is [a]satisfied as with [I]marrow and fatness,
And my mouth[6310] offers [b]praises[1984] with joyful lips.
6 When I remember[2142] Thee [a]on my bed,
I meditate[1897] on Thee in the [b]night watches,
7 For [a]Thou hast been my help,
And in the [b]shadow of Thy wings I sing for joy.
8 My soul [a]clings [I]to Thee;
Thy [b]right hand upholds[8551] me.
9 But those who [a]seek my [I]life, to destroy[7722] it,
Will go into the [II][b]depths of the earth.[776]
10 [I]They will be [II][a]delivered over to the power of the sword;[2719]
They will be a [III][b]prey for foxes.
11 But the [a]king[4428] will rejoice in God;
Everyone who [b]swears[7650] by Him will glory,[1984]
For the [c]mouths of those who speak[1696] lies[8267] will be stopped.

Prayer for Deliverance from Secret Enemies

For the choir director. A Psalm of David.

64 Hear[8085] my voice, O God,[430] in [a]my [I]complaint;[7879]
[b]Preserve[5341] my life[2416] from dread[6343] of the enemy.
2 Hide me from the [a]secret counsel[5475] of evildoers,[7489]
From the tumult[7285] of [b]those who do iniquity,[205]
3 Who [a]have sharpened[8150] their tongue like a sword.[2719]
They [b]aimed bitter[4751] speech[1697] *as* their arrow,
4 To [a]shoot[3384] [I]from concealment at the blameless;[8535]
Suddenly they shoot at him, and [b]do not fear.[3372]
5 They [I]hold fast[2388] to themselves an evil[7451] purpose;[1697]
They [II]talk of [a]laying snares[4170] secretly;[2934]
They say,[559] "[b]Who can see them?"
6 They [I]devise injustices, *saying,*
"We are [II]ready[8552] with a well-conceived plot";
For the [III][a]inward thought[7130] and the heart[3820] of a man[376] are [IV]deep.
7 But [a]God [I]will shoot at them with an arrow;
Suddenly [II]they will be wounded.[4347]
8 So [I]they [II]will [a]make him stumble;
[b]Their own tongue is against them;
All who see them will [c]shake the head.
9 Then all men[120] [I]will [a]fear,

12 [b]Job 34:11; Ps. 28:4; Jer. 17:10; Matt. 16:27; Rom. 2:6; 1Cor. 3:8; Rev. 2:23

[+]1Sam. 22:5; 23:14
1 [I]Lit., *early* [II]Lit., *faints* [a]Ps. 118:28 [b]Ps. 42:2; 84:2; Matt. 5:6 [c]Ps. 143:6
2 [a]Ps. 27:4
3 [a]Ps. 69:16
4 [a]Ps. 104:33; 146:2 [b]Ps. 28:2; 143:6
5 [I]Lit., *fat* [a]Ps. 36:8 [b]Ps. 71:23
6 [a]Ps. 4:4 [b]Ps. 16:7; 42:8; 119:55
7 [a]Ps. 27:9 [b]Ps. 17:8
8 [I]Lit., *after* [a]Num. 32:12; Deut. 1:36; Hos. 6:3 [b]Ps. 18:35; 41:12
9 [I]Lit., *soul* [II]Lit., *lowest places* [a]Ps. 40:14 [b]Ps. 55:15
10 [I]Lit., *They will pour him out* [II]Lit., *poured out by* [III]Lit., *portion* [a]Jer. 18:21; Ezek. 35:5 [b]Lam. 5:18
11 [a]Ps. 21:1 [b]Deut. 6:13; Is. 45:23; 65:16 [c]Job 5:16; Ps. 107:42; Rom. 3:19

1 [I]Or, *concern* [a]Ps. 55:2 [b]Ps. 140:1
2 [a]Ps. 56:6 [b]Ps. 59:2
3 [a]Ps. 140:3 [b]Ps. 58:7
4 [I]Lit., *in* [a]Ps. 10:8; 11:2 [b]Ps. 55:19
5 [I]Lit., *make firm* [II]Lit., *tell of* [a]Ps. 140:5 [b]Job 22:13; Ps. 10:11
6 [I]Or, *search out* [II]Lit., *complete* [III]Or, *inward part* [IV]Or, *unsearchable* [a]Ps. 49:11
7 [I]Or, *shot* [II]Or, *they were wounded;* lit., *their wounds occurred* [a]Ps. 7:12, 13

8 [I]Or, *they make their tongue a stumbling for themselves* [II]Or, *made* [a]Ps. 9:3 [b]Prov. 12:13; 18:7 [c]Ps. 22:7; 44:14; Jer. 18:16; 48:27; Lam. 2:15 9 [I]Or, *feared* [a]Ps. 40:3

And [II]will [b]declare[5046] the work
of God,
And [III]will consider[7919]
[IV]what He has done.
10 The righteous[6662] man will be
[a]glad in the LORD, and will
[b]take refuge[2620] in Him;
And all the upright in heart will
glory.[1984]

God's Abundant Favor to Earth and Man

For the choir director. A Psalm of David. A Song.

65 There will be silence [I]before
Thee, *and* praise[8416] in Zion,
O God;[430]
And to Thee the [a]vow will be
performed.[7999]
2 O Thou who dost hear[8085]
prayer,[8605]
To Thee [a]all [I]men[1320] come.
3 [Ia]Iniquities[5771] prevail against
me;
As for our transgressions,[6588]
Thou dost [IIb]forgive them.
4 How [a]blessed[835] is the one whom
Thou dost [b]choose,[977] and
bring near[7126] *to Thee,*
To dwell in Thy courts.
We will be [c]satisfied with the
goodness of Thy house,[1004]
Thy holy[6918] temple.[1964]
5 By [a]awesome *deeds*[3372] Thou
dost answer us in
righteousness,[6664] O [b]God of
our salvation,
Thou who art the trust of all the
[c]ends of the earth[776] and of
the farthest [Id]sea;
6 Who dost [a]establish[3559] the
mountains by His strength,
Being [b]girded with might;
7 Who dost [a]still[7623] the roaring[7588]
of the seas,
The roaring of their waves,
And the [b]tumult of the
peoples.[3816]
8 And they who dwell in the
[a]ends *of the earth* stand in
awe[3372] of Thy signs;[226]
Thou dost make the [I]dawn and
the sunset shout for joy.
9 Thou dost visit[6485] the earth, and
[a]cause it to overflow;
Thou dost greatly [b]enrich it;
The [Ic]stream of God is full of
water;
Thou dost prepare[3559] their
[d]grain, for thus Thou dost
prepare [II]the earth.
10 Thou dost water its furrows
abundantly;
Thou dost [I]settle its ridges;[1418]
Thou dost soften it [a]with
showers;
Thou dost bless its growth.
11 Thou hast crowned the year
[I]with Thy [IIa]bounty,[2896]
And Thy [III]paths [b]drip *with*
fatness.
12 [a]The pastures[4999] of the
wilderness drip,
And the [b]hills gird themselves
with rejoicing.
13 The meadows[3733] are [a]clothed
with flocks,
And the valleys are [b]covered
with grain;
They [c]shout for joy,[7321] yes,
they sing.[7891]

Praise for God's Mighty Deeds and for His Answer to Prayer

For the choir director. A Song. A Psalm.

66 [a]Shout joyfully[7321] to God,[430] all
the earth;[776]
2 Sing[2167] the [a]glory[3519] of His
name;
Make[7760] His [b]praise[8416]
glorious.[3519]
3 Say[559] to God, "How
[a]awesome[3372] are Thy
works!
Because of the greatness of Thy
power Thine enemies will
[Ib]give feigned obedience to
Thee.

9 IIOr, *declared* IIIOr, *considered* IVLit., *His work* [b]Jer. 51:10
10 [a]Job 22:19; Ps. 32:11 [b]Ps. 11:1; 25:20
1 ILit., *to* [a]Ps. 116:18
2 ILit., *flesh* [a]Ps. 86:9; 145:21; Is. 66:23
3 ILit., *Words of iniquities* IILit., *cover over, atone for* [a]Ps. 38:4; 40:12 [b]Ps. 79:9
4 [a]Ps. 33:12; 84:4 [b]Ps. 4:3 [c]Ps. 36:8
5 IOr, *seas* [a]Ps. 45:4; 66:3 [b]Ps. 85:4 [c]Ps. 22:27; 48:10 [d]Ps. 107:23
6 [a]Ps. 95:4 [b]Ps. 93:1
7 [a]Ps. 89:9; 93:3, 4; 107:29; Matt. 8:26 [b]Ps. 2:1; 74:23; Is. 17:12, 13
8 ILit., *the outgoings of the morning and evening* [a]Ps. 2:8; 139:9; Is. 24:16
9 IOr, *channel* IILit., *it* [a]Lev. 26:4; Job 5:10; Ps. 68:9; 104:13; 147:8; Jer. 5:24 [b]Ps. 104:24 [c]Ps. 46:4 [d]Ps. 104:14; 147:14
10 IOr, *smooth* [a]Deut. 32:2; Ps. 72:6; 147:8
11 ILit., *of* IIOr, *goodness* IIII.e., wagon tracks [a]Ps. 104:28 [b]Job 36:28; Ps. 147:14
12 [a]Job 38:26, 27; Joel 2:22 [b]Ps. 98:8; Is. 55:12
13 [a]Ps. 144:13; Is. 30:23 [b]Ps. 72:16 [c]Ps. 98:8; Is. 44:23; 55:12

1 [a]Ps. 81:1; 95:1; 98:4; 100:1
2 [a]Ps. 79:9; Is. 42:8 [b]Is. 42:12
3 ILit., *deceive* [a]Ps. 47:2; 65:5; 145:6 [b]Ps. 18:44; 81:15

4 "[a]All the earth[776] will worship[7812]
Thee,
And will [b]sing praises to Thee;
They will sing praises to Thy
name." [I]Selah.
5 [a]Come and see the works of
God,
Who is [b]awesome in *His* deeds
toward the sons[1121] of
men.[120]
6 He [a]turned[2015] the sea into
dry[3004] land;
They passed through [b]the river
on foot;
There let us [c]rejoice in Him!
7 He [a]rules[4910] by His might
forever;[5769]
His [b]eyes keep watch on the
nations;[1471]
Let not the rebellious[5637]
[c]exalt themselves. Selah.
8 Bless[1288] our God, O
peoples,[5971]
And [Ia]sound[8085] 6963 His praise
abroad,
9 Who [Ia]keeps[7760] us in life,[2416]
And [b]does not allow5414 our feet
to [II]slip.
10 For Thou hast [a]tried[974] us, O
God;
Thou hast [b]refined us as silver
is refined.[6884]
11 Thou [a]didst bring us into the
net;[4685]
Thou didst lay[7760] an oppressive
burden upon our loins.
12 Thou didst make men[582]
[a]ride over our heads;[7218]
We went through [b]fire and
through water;
Yet Thou [c]didst bring us out into
a place of abundance.
13 I shall [a]come into Thy
house[1004] with burnt
offerings;[5930]
I shall [b]pay Thee my vows,[5088]
14 Which my lips[8193] uttered
And my mouth[6310] spoke[1696]
when I was [a]in distress.
15 I shall [a]offer to Thee burnt
offerings[5930] of fat beasts,
With the smoke[7004] of [b]rams;
I shall make *an offering of*
[I]bulls with male goats.
Selah.
16 [a]Come *and* hear,[8085] all who
[I]fear[3373] God,
And I will [b]tell[5608] of what He
has done[6213] for my soul.
17 I cried[7121] to Him with my
mouth,
And [I]He was [a]extolled with my
tongue.
18 If I [Ia]regard[7200] wickedness[205] in
my heart,[3820]
The [b]Lord[136] [II]will not [III]hear;
19 But certainly [a]God has heard;
He has given heed[7181] to the
voice of my prayer.[8605]
20 [a]Blessed[1288] be God,
Who [b]has not turned away my
prayer,
Nor His lovingkindness[2617] from
me.

4 [I]*Selah* may mean: *Pause, Crescendo* or *Musical interlude* [a]Ps. 22:27; 67:7; 86:9; 117:1; Zech. 14:16 [b]Ps. 67:4
5 [a]Ps. 46:8 [b]Ps. 106:22
6 [a]Ex. 14:21; Ps. 106:9 [b]Josh. 3:16; Ps. 114:3 [c]Ps. 105:43
7 [a]Ps. 145:13 [b]Ps. 11:4 [c]Ps. 140:8
8 [I]Lit., *cause to hear the sound of His praise* [a]Ps. 98:4
9 [I]Lit., *puts our soul in life* [II]Or, *dodder, stumble* [a]Ps. 30:3 [b]Ps. 121:3
10 [a]Job 23:10; Ps. 7:9; 17:3; 26:2 [b]Is. 48:10; Zech. 13:9; Mal. 3:3; 1Pet. 1:7
11 [a]Lam. 1:13; Ezek. 12:13
12 [a]Is. 51:23 [b]Ps. 78:21; Is. 43:2 [c]Ps. 18:19
13 [a]Ps. 96:8; Jer. 17:26 [b]Ps. 22:25; 116:14; Eccl. 5:4
14 [a]Ps. 18:6
15 [I]Or, *cattle* [a]Ps. 51:19 [b]Num. 6:14
16 [I]Or, *revere* [a]Ps. 34:11 [b]Ps. 71:15, 24
17 [I]Or, *praise was under my tongue* [a]Ps. 30:1
18 [I]Or, *had regarded* [II]Or, *would* [III]Or, *have heard* [a]Job 36:21; John 9:31 [b]Job 27:9; Ps. 18:41; Prov. 1:28; 28:9; Is. 1:15; James 4:3
19 [a]Ps. 18:6; 116:1, 2
20 [a]Ps. 68:35 [b]Ps. 22:24

The Nations Exhorted to Praise God

For the choir director; with stringed instruments. A Psalm. A Song.

67 God[430] be gracious[2603] to us and
[a]bless[1288] us,
And [b]cause His face to shine
[I]upon us— [II]Selah.
2 That [a]Thy way[1870] may be
known[3045] on the earth,[776]
[b]Thy salvation[3468] among all
nations.[1471]
3 Let the [a]peoples[5971] praise[3034]
Thee, O God;
Let all the peoples praise Thee.
4 Let the [a]nations[3816] be glad and
sing for joy;
For Thou wilt [b]judge[8199] the
peoples with uprightness,[4334]
And [c]guide[5148] the nations on the
earth. Selah.
5 Let the [a]peoples praise Thee,
O God;
Let all the peoples praise Thee.

1 [I]Lit., *with* [II]*Selah* may mean: *Pause, Crescendo* or *Musical interlude* [a]Num. 6:25 [b]Ps. 4:6; 31:16; 80:3, 7, 19; 119:135
2 [a]Ps. 98:2; Acts 18:25; Titus 2:11 [b]Is. 52:10
3 [a]Ps. 66:4

4 [a]Ps. 100:1, 2 [b]Ps. 9:8; 96:10, 13; 98:9 [c]Ps. 47:8
5 [a]Ps. 67:3

6 The [a]earth has yielded its produce;
God, our God, [b]blesses us.
7 God blesses us,
[I]That [a]all the ends of the earth may fear[3372] Him.

The God of Sinai and of the Sanctuary

For the choir director. A Psalm of David. A Song.

68 Let [a]God[430] arise, [II]let His enemies be scattered;
And [III]let those who hate[8130] Him flee before Him.
2 As [a]smoke is driven away, *so* drive *them* away;
As [b]wax melts before the fire,
So let the [c]wicked[7563] perish[6] before God.
3 But let the [a]righteous[6662] be glad; let them exult before God;
Yes, let them rejoice with gladness.
4 Sing[7891] to God, [a]sing praises[2167] to His name;
[I][b]Lift up *a song* for Him who [c]rides through the deserts,[6160]
Whose [d]name is [II]the LORD, and exult before Him.
5 A [a]father[1] of the fatherless and a [b]judge[1781] [I]for the widows,
Is God in His [c]holy[6944] habitation.
6 God [I][a]makes a home for the lonely;[3173]
He [b]leads out the prisoners into prosperity,
Only [c]the rebellious[5637] dwell[7931] in a parched land.
7 O God, when Thou [a]didst go forth before Thy people,[5971]
When Thou didst [b]march through the wilderness, [I]Selah.
8 The [a]earth[776] quaked;[7493]
The [b]heavens[8064] also dropped[5197] *rain* at the presence of God;

6 [a]Lev. 26:4; Ps. 85:12; Ezek. 34:27; Zech. 8:12 [b]Ps. 29:11; 115:12
7 [I]Or, *And let all . . . earth fear Him* [a]Ps. 22:27; 33:8
1 [I]Or, *God shall* [II]Or, *His enemies shall* [III]Or, *those who hate Him shall* [a]Num. 10:35; Ps. 12:5; 132:8
2 [a]Ps. 37:20; Is. 9:18; Hos. 13:3 [b]Ps. 22:14; 97:5; Mic. 1:4 [c]Ps. 9:3; 37:20; 80:16
3 [a]Ps. 32:11; 64:10; 97:12
4 [I]Or, *Cast up a highway* [II]Heb., YAH [a]Ps. 66:2 [b]Is. 57:14; 62:10 [c]Deut. 33:26; Ps. 18:10; 68:33; Is. 40:3 [d]Ex. 6:3; Ps. 83:18
5 [I]Lit., *of* [a]Ps. 10:14; 146:9 [b]Deut. 10:18 [c]Deut. 26:15
6 [I]Lit., *makes the solitary to dwell in a house* [a]Ps. 107:4-7; 113:9 [b]Ps. 69:33; 102:20; 107:10, 14; 146:7; Acts 12:7; 16:26 [c]Ps. 78:17; 107:34, 40
7 [I]*Selah* may mean: *Pause, Crescendo* or *Musical interlude* [a]Ex. 13:21; Ps. 78:14; Hab. 3:13 [b]Judg. 5:4; Ps. 78:52
8 [I]Lit., *This is Sinai which* [a]Ex. 19:18; Judg. 5:4; 2Sam. 22:8; Ps. 77:18; Jer. 10:10 [b]Judg. 5:4; Ps. 18:9; Is. 45:8 [c]Ex. 19:18; Judg. 5:5
9 [I]Lit., *weary* [a]Lev. 26:4; Deut. 11:11; Job 5:10; Ezek. 34:26
10 [a]Ps. 65:9; 74:19; 78:20; 107:9
11 [I]Lit., *word* [a]Ex. 15:20; 1Sam. 18:6

[I][c]Sinai itself *quaked* at the presence of God, the God of Israel.
9 Thou didst [a]shed abroad[5130] a plentiful rain, O God;
Thou didst confirm Thine inheritance,[5159] when it was [I]parched.
10 Thy creatures[2416] settled in it;
Thou didst [a]provide[3559] in Thy goodness[2896] for the poor, O God.
11 The Lord gives the [I]command;[562]
The [a]women who proclaim[1319] the *good* tidings are a great host:[6635]
12 "[a]Kings[4428] of armies[6635] flee, they flee,
And she who remains at home[1004] will [b]divide the spoil!"
13 [I]When you lie down [a]among the [II]sheepfolds,
You are like the wings of a dove covered with silver,
And its pinions with glistening gold.
14 When the Almighty[7706] [a]scattered the kings [I]there,
It was snowing in [b]Zalmon.
15 A [I][a]mountain of God is the mountain of Bashan;
A mountain *of many* peaks is the mountain of Bashan.
16 Why do you look with envy, O mountains with *many* peaks,
At the mountain which God has [a]desired[2530] for His abode?
Surely, [b]the LORD will dwell *there* forever.[5331]
17 The [a]chariots of God are [I]myriads, [b]thousands[505] upon thousands;

12 [a]Josh. 10:16; Judg. 5:19; Ps. 135:11 [b]Judg. 5:30; 1Sam. 30:24 13 [I]Lit., *If* [II]Or, *cooking stones* or *saddle bags* [a]Gen. 49:14; Judg. 5:16 14 [I]Lit., *in it* [a]Josh. 10:10 [b] Judg. 9:48 15 [I]Or, *mighty mountain is* [a]Ps. 36:6 16 [a]Deut. 12:5; Ps. 87:1, 2; 132:13 [b]Ps. 132:14 17 [I]Lit., *twice ten thousand* [a]2Kin. 6:17; Hab. 3:8 [b]Deut. 33:2; Dan. 7:10

[II]The Lord[136] is among them *as*
at Sinai, in holiness.
18 Thou hast [a]ascended on high,
Thou hast [b]led captive[7617]
Thy captives;[7628]
Thou hast received gifts among
men,[120]
Even *among* the rebellious also,
that [I]the LORD God may dwell
there.
19 Blessed[1288] be the Lord, who
daily[3117] [a]bears our burden,
[b]The God[430] *who* is our
salvation.[3444] Selah.
20 God is to us a [a]God of
deliverances;[4190]
And [b]to [I]GOD the Lord
belong escapes [II]from
death.[4194]
21 Surely God will [a]shatter[4272] the
head[7218] of His enemies,
The hairy crown of him who goes
on in his guilty deeds.
22 The Lord [I]said, "[a]I will bring
them back[7725] from Bashan.
I will bring *them* back from the
depths of the sea;
23 That [I][a]your foot may shatter[4272]
them in blood,[1818]
The tongue of your [b]dogs *may*
have its portion from *your*
enemies."
24 They have seen[7200] [a]Thy
[I]procession, O God,
The [I]procession of my God, my
King,[4428] [II][b]into the
sanctuary.[6944]
25 The [a]singers[7891] went on, the
musicians after *them*,
[I]In the midst of the [b]maidens[5959]
beating tambourines.[8606]
26 [a]Bless[1288] God in the
congregations,
Even the LORD, *you who are* of
the [b]fountain of Israel.
27 There is [a]Benjamin, the
[I]youngest, [II]ruling[7287] them,
The princes of Judah *in* their
throng,

17 [II]Another reading is *The Lord came from Sinai into the sanctuary*
18 [I]Heb., YAH [a]Ps. 7:7; 47:5; Eph. 4:8 [b]Judg. 5:12
19 [a]Ps. 55:22; Is. 46:4 [b]Ps. 65:5
20 [I]Heb., *YHWH*, usually rendered *LORD* [II]I.e., in view of; lit., *for* [a]Ps. 106:43 [b]Deut. 32:39; Ps. 49:15; 56:13
21 [a]Ps. 110:6; Hab. 3:13
22 [I]Or, *says* [a]Num. 21:33; Amos 9:1-3
23 [I]Some versions render, you may *bathe your foot in blood* [a]Ps. 58:10 [b]1Kin. 21:19; Jer. 15:3
24 [I]Lit., *goings* [II]Lit., *in the sanctuary;* or, *in holiness* [a]Ps. 77:13 [b]Ps. 63:2
25 [I]Or, *The maidens in the midst* [a]1Chr. 13:8; 15:6; Ps. 47:6 [b]Ex. 15:20; Judg. 11:34
26 [a]Ps. 22:22, 23; 26:12 [b]Deut. 33:28; Is. 48:1
27 [I]Or, *smallest* [II]Or, *their ruler* [a]Judg. 5:14; 1Sam. 9:21 [b]Judg. 5:18
28 [I]Some mss. read *Command, God* [II]Lit., *for us* [a]Ps. 29:11; 44:4 [b]Is. 26:12
29 [I]Or, *From Thy temple* [a]1Kin. 10:10, 25; 2Chr. 32:23; Ps. 45:12; 72:10; Is. 18:7
30 [I]Lit., *of* [a]Job 40:21; Ezek. 29:3 [b]Ps. 22:12 [c]Ps. 18:14; 89:10
31 [I]Lit., *Cush* [a]Is. 19:19, 21 [b]Is. 45:14; Zeph. 3:10

The princes of [b]Zebulun, the
princes[8269] of Naphtali.
28 [I]Your God has [a]commanded[6680]
your strength;
Show Thyself strong, O God,
[b]who hast acted [II]on our
behalf.
29 [I]Because of Thy temple[1964] at
Jerusalem
[a]Kings will bring gifts to
Thee.
30 Rebuke[1605] the [a]beasts[2416] [I]in
the reeds,
The herd[5712] of [b]bulls[47] with the
calves of the peoples,
Trampling under foot the pieces
of silver;
He has [c]scattered the peoples
who delight[2654] in war.
31 Envoys[2831] will come out of
[a]Egypt;
[I][b]Ethiopia will quickly stretch out
her hands[3027] to God.
32 Sing to God, O [a]kingdoms[4467] of
the earth;
[b]Sing praises to the Lord,
Selah.
33 To Him who [a]rides upon the
[I][b]highest heavens, which are
from ancient times;[6924]
Behold, [c]He [II]speaks forth
with His voice, a [d]mighty
voice.
34 [a]Ascribe strength to God;
His majesty is over Israel,
And [b]His strength is in the
[I]skies.[7834]
35 [I]O God, *Thou art* [a]awesome[3372]
from Thy [II]sanctuary.
The God of Israel Himself
[b]gives strength and power to
the people.
[c]Blessed be God!

32 [a]Ps. 102:22 [b]Ps. 67:4 **33** [I]Lit., *heaven of heavens of old* [II]Lit., *gives forth* [a]Deut. 33:26; Ps. 18:10; 104:3 [b]Deut. 10:14; 1Kin. 8:27 [c]Ps. 46:6 [d]Ps. 29:4
34 [I]Lit., *clouds* [a]Ps. 29:1 [b]Ps. 150:1 **35** [I]Or, *Awesome is God from your sanctuary* [II]Lit., *holy places* [a]Deut. 7:21; 10:17; Ps. 47:2; 66:5 [b]Ps. 29:11; Is. 40:29 [c]Ps. 66:20; 2Cor. 1:3

68:18 See Eph. 4:8.

A Cry of Distress and Imprecation on Adversaries

For the choir director; according to +Shoshannim. *A Psalm* of David.

69 Save[3467] me, O God,[430]
For the [a]waters have [I]threatened my life.[5315]
2 I have sunk in deep [a]mire, and there is no foothold;
I have come into deep waters, and a [Ib]flood overflows[7857] me.
3 I am [a]weary with my crying;[7121] my throat is parched;[2787]
My [b]eyes fail[3615] while I wait[3176] for my God.
4 Those [a]who hate[8130] me without a cause are more than the hairs of my head;[7218]
Those who would [I]destroy[6789] me [b]are powerful, being wrongfully my enemies,
[c]What I did not steal, I then have to restore.[7725]
5 O God, it is Thou who dost know[3045] [a]my folly,
And [b]my wrongs[819] are not hidden from Thee.
6 May those who wait for[6960] Thee not [a]be ashamed[954] through me, O Lord[136] [I]GOD of hosts;[6635]
May those who seek Thee not be dishonored through me, O God of Israel,
7 Because [a]for Thy sake I have borne[5375] reproach;[2781]
[b]Dishonor has covered[3680] my face.
8 I have become[1961] [a]estranged[2114] [I]from my brothers,[251]
And an alien[5237] to my mother's[517] sons.[1121]
9 For [a]zeal[7068] for Thy house[1004] has consumed me,
And [b]the reproaches[2781] of those who reproach Thee have fallen[5307] on me.
10 When I wept [a]in my soul with fasting,
It became my reproach.
11 When I made [a]sackcloth my clothing,
I became [b]a byword to them.
12 Those who [a]sit in the gate talk[7878] about me,
And I *am* the [Ib]song of the drunkards.
13 But as for me, my prayer[8605] is to Thee, O LORD, [a]at an acceptable[7522] time;[6256]
O God, in the [b]greatness of Thy lovingkindness,[2617]
Answer me with [I]Thy saving[3468] truth.[571]
14 Deliver[5337] me from the [a]mire, and do not let me sink;
May I be [b]delivered from [I]my foes, and from the [IIc]deep waters.
15 May the [Ia]flood of water not overflow me,
And may the deep not swallow[1104] me up,
And may the [b]pit not shut its mouth[6310] on me.
16 Answer me, O LORD, for [a]Thy lovingkindness is good;[2896]
[b]According to the greatness of Thy compassion,[7356] [c]turn to me,
17 And [a]do not hide Thy face from Thy servant,[5650]
For I am [b]in distress; answer me quickly.
18 Oh draw near to my soul *and* [a]redeem[1350] it;
[b]Ransom[6299] me because of my enemies!
19 Thou dost know[3045] my [a]reproach and my shame and my dishonor;

+Or possibly, *Lilies*
1 [I]Lit., *come to the soul* [a]Job 22:11; Ps. 32:6; 42:7; 69:14, 15; Jon. 2:5
2 [I]Lit., *flowing stream* [a]Ps. 40:2 [b]Jon. 2:3
3 [a]Ps. 6:6 [b]Deut. 28:32; Ps. 38:10; 119:82, 123; Is. 38:14
4 [I]Or, *silence* [a]Ps. 35:19; John 15:25 [b]Ps. 35:19; 38:19; 59:3 [c]Ps. 35:11; Jer. 15:10
5 [a]Ps. 38:5 [b]Ps. 44:21
6 [I]Heb., *YHWH,* usually rendered LORD [a]2Sam. 12:14
7 [a]Jer. 15:15 [b]Ps. 44:15; Is. 50:6; Jer. 51:51
8 [I]Lit., *to* [a]Job 19:13-15; Ps. 31:11; 38:11
9 [a]Ps. 119:139; John 2:17 [b]Ps. 89:41, 50; Rom. 15:3
10 [a]Ps. 35:13
11 [a]1Kin. 20:31; Ps. 35:13 [b]1Kin. 9:7; Job 17:6; Ps. 44:14; Jer. 24:9
12 [I]Lit., *songs* [a]Gen. 19:1; Ruth 4:1 [b]Job 30:9
13 [I]Or, *the faithfulness of Thy salvation* [a]Ps. 32:6; Is. 49:8; 2Cor. 6:2 [b]Ps. 51:1
14 [I]Lit., *those who hate me* [II]Lit., *deep places of water* [a]Ps. 69:2 [b]Ps. 144:7 [c]Ps. 69:2
15 [I]Lit., *stream* [a]Ps. 124:4, 5 [b]Num. 16:33; Ps. 28:1; 141:7
16 [a]Ps. 63:3; 109:21 [b]Ps. 51:1; 106:45 [c]Ps. 25:16; 86:16
17 [a]Ps. 27:9; 102:2; 143:7 [b]Ps. 31:9; 66:14
18 [a]2Sam. 4:9; Ps. 26:11; 49:15 [b]Ps. 119:134
19 [a]Ps. 22:6; 31:11

69:1-36 See note on Ps. 5:8-10.
69:4 See Jn. 15:25.
69:9 See Jn. 2:17; Rom. 15:3.

All my adversaries are [I]before
Thee.
20 Reproach has [a]broken[7665] my
heart,[3820] and I am so sick.
And [b]I looked[6960] for sympathy,
but there was none,
And for [c]comforters,[5162] but I
found none.
21 They also gave me [Ia]gall[7219]
[II]for my food,
And for my thirst they [b]gave me
vinegar to drink.
22 May [a]their table before them
become a snare;[6341]
And [Ib]when they are in
peace,[7965] *may it become* a
trap.[4170]
23 May their [a]eyes grow dim[2821] so
that they cannot see,
And make their [b]loins shake
continually.[8548]
24 [a]Pour out[8210] Thine
indignation[2195] on them,
And may Thy burning anger[639]
overtake them.
25 May their [Ia]camp be
desolate;[8074]
May none dwell in their tents.[168]
26 For they have [a]persecuted him
whom [b]Thou Thyself hast
smitten,[5221]
And they tell[5608] of the pain of
those whom [c]Thou hast
[I]wounded.[2491]
27 Do Thou add [a]iniquity[5771] to their
iniquity,
And [b]may they not come into
[c]Thy righteousness.[6666]
28 May they be [a]blotted out[4229] of
the [b]book[5612] of life,[2416]
And may they not be [Ic]recorded
with the righteous.[6662]
29 But I am [a]afflicted and in
pain;
[I]May Thy salvation,[3444] O God,
[b]set me *securely* on high.
30 I will [a]praise[1984] the name of God
with song,
And shall [b]magnify Him with
[c]thanksgiving.[8426]

19 [I]Or, known *to Thee*
20 [a]Jer. 23:9 [b]Ps. 142:4; Is. 63:5 [c]Job 16:2
21 [I]Or, *poison* [II]Or, *in* [a]Deut. 29:18 [b]Matt. 27:34, 48; Mark 15:23, 36; Luke 23:36; John 19:28-30
22 [I]Lit., *for those who are secure* [a]Rom. 11:9, 10 [b]1Thess. 5:3
23 [a]Is. 6:10 [b]Dan. 5:6
24 [a]Ps. 79:6; Jer. 10:25; Ezek. 20:8; Hos. 5:10
25 [I]Lit., *encampment* [a]Matt. 23:38; Luke 13:35; Acts 1:20
26 [I]Lit., *pierced* [a]2Chr. 28:9; Zech. 1:15 [b]Is. 53:4 [c]Ps. 109:22
27 [a]Neh. 4:5; Ps. 109:14; Rom. 1:28 [b]Is. 26:10 [c]Ps. 103:17
28 [I]Lit., *written* [a]Ex. 32:32, 33; Rev. 3:5 [b]Phil. 4:3; Rev. 13:8; 17:8; 20:15 [c]Ps. 87:6; Ezek. 13:9; Luke 10:20; Heb. 12:23
29 [I]Or, *Thy salvation, O God, will set. . .* [a]Ps. 70:5 [b]Ps. 20:1; 59:1
30 [a]Ps. 28:7 [b]Ps. 34:3 [c]Ps. 50:14
31 [a]Ps. 50:13, 14; 51:16
32 [I]Some mss. and ancient versions read *will see* [II]Or, *live* [a]Ps. 34:2 [b]Ps. 22:26
33 [a]Ps. 12:5 [b]Ps. 68:6
34 [a]Ps. 96:11; 98:7; 148:1-13; Is. 44:23; 49:13 [b]Is. 55:12
35 [a]Ps. 46:5; 51:18 [b]Ps. 147:2; Is. 44:26 [c]Obad. 17
36 [I]Lit., *seed* [a]Ps. 25:13; 102:28 [b]Ps. 37:29

31 And it will [a]please[3190] the LORD
better than an ox
Or a young bull with horns and
hoofs.
32 The [a]humble [I]have seen *it and*
are glad;
You who seek God, [b]let your
heart[3824] [II]revive.[2421]
33 For [a]the LORD hears[8085] the
needy,
And [b]does not despise His *who*
are prisoners.
34 Let [a]heaven[8064] and earth[776]
praise Him,
The seas and [b]everything that
moves in them.
35 For God will [a]save Zion and
[b]build the cities of Judah,
That they may dwell there and
[c]possess it.
36 And the [Ia]descendants[2233] of His
servants[5650] will inherit[5157]
it,
And those who love[157] His name
[b]will dwell[7931] in it.

Prayer for Help against Persecutors

For the choir director. *A Psalm* of David; for a memorial.

70 [a]O God,[430] *hasten* to deliver[5337]
me;
O LORD, hasten to my help!
2 [a]Let those be ashamed[954] and
humiliated
Who seek my [I]life;[5315]
Let those be turned back and
dishonored
Who delight[2655] [II]in my hurt.[7451]
3 [a]Let those be [I]turned back
because of their shame
Who say,[559] "Aha, aha!"
4 Let all who seek Thee rejoice
and be glad in Thee;

1 [a]Ps. 40:13-17; 70:1-5 **2** [I]Or, *soul* [II]Or, *to injure me* [a]Ps. 35:4, 26 **3** [I]Some mss. read *appalled* [a]Ps. 40:15

69:21 See Mt. 27:34,48; Mk. 15:23; Lk. 23:36; Jn. 19:28-30.

And let those who love[157] Thy salvation say continually,[8548]
"Let God be magnified."
5 But [a]I am afflicted and needy;
[b]Hasten to me, O God!
Thou art my help and my deliverer;
O LORD, do not delay.

Prayer of an Old Man for Deliverance

71 [a]In Thee, O LORD, I have taken refuge;[2620]
Let me never be ashamed.[954]
2 [a]In Thy righteousness[6666] deliver[5337] me, and rescue me;
[b]Incline Thine ear[241] to me, and save[3467] me.
3 [a]Be Thou to me a rock of [b]habitation, to which I may continually[8548] come;
Thou hast given [c]commandment to save me,
For Thou art [d]my [I]rock and my fortress.
4 [a]Rescue me, O my God,[430] out of the hand[3027] of the wicked,[7563]
Out of the [I]grasp of the wrongdoer[5765] and ruthless[2556] man,
5 For Thou art my [a]hope;
O Lord[136] [I]GOD, *Thou art* my [b]confidence from my youth.
6 [I]By Thee I have been [a]sustained[5564] from *my* birth;[990]
Thou art He who [b]took me from my mother's[517] womb;[4578]
My [c]praise[8416] is continually [II]of Thee.
7 I have become a [a]marvel to many;
For Thou art [b]my strong refuge.
8 My [a]mouth[6310] is filled with Thy praise,
And with [b]Thy glory[8597] all day[3117] long.
9 Do not cast me off in the [a]time[6256] of old age;[2209]
Do not forsake[5800] me when my strength fails.[3615]
10 For my enemies have spoken[559] [I]against me;
And those who [a]watch[8104] for my [II]life[5315] [b]have consulted[3289] together,
11 Saying, "[a]God has forsaken[5800] him;
Pursue and seize him, for there is [b]no one to deliver."
12 O God, [a]do not be far from me;
O my God, [b]hasten to my help!
13 Let those who are adversaries[7853] of my soul be [a]ashamed[954] *and* consumed;[3615]
Let them be [b]covered with reproach[2781] and dishonor, who [c]seek [I]to injure[7451] me.
14 But as for me, I will [a]hope[3176] continually,
And will [I][b]praise Thee yet more and more.
15 My [a]mouth shall tell[5608] of Thy righteousness,
And of [b]Thy salvation[8668] all day long;
For I [c]do not know the [I]sum *of them.*
16 I will come [a]with the mighty deeds of the Lord [I]GOD;
I will [b]make mention of Thy righteousness, Thine alone.
17 O God, Thou [a]hast taught[3925] me from my youth;
And I still [b]declare[5046] Thy wondrous deeds.[6381]
18 And even when *I am* [a]old and gray, O God, do not forsake me,
Until I [b]declare[5046] Thy [I]strength to *this* generation,[1755]
Thy power to all who are to come.
19 [I]For Thy [a]righteousness, O God, *reaches* to the [II]heavens,
Thou who hast [b]done[6213] great things;
O God, [c]who is like Thee?

---

5 [a]Ps. 40:17 [b]Ps. 141:1
1 [a]Ps. 25:2, 3; 31:1-3; 71:1-3
2 [a]Ps. 31:1 [b]Ps. 17:6
3 [I]Or, *crag* [a]Ps. 31:2, 3 [b]Deut. 33:27; Ps. 90:1; 91:9 [c]Ps. 7:6; 42:8 [d]Ps. 18:2
4 [I]Lit., *palm* [a]Ps. 140:1, 4
5 [I]Heb., *YHWH*, usually rendered LORD [a]Ps. 39:7; Jer. 14:8; 17:7, 13, 17; 50:7 [b]Ps. 22:9
6 [I]Lit., *Upon Thee I have been supported* [II]Lit., *in* [a]Ps. 22:10; Is. 46:3 [b]Job 10:18; Ps. 22:9 [c]Ps. 34:1
7 [a]Is. 8:18; 1Cor. 4:9 [b]Ps. 61:3
8 [a]Ps. 35:28; 63:5 [b]Ps. 96:6; 104:1
9 [a]Ps. 71:18; 92:14; Is. 46:4
10 [I]Lit., *with reference to* [II]Lit., *soul* [a]Ps. 56:6 [b]Ps. 31:13; 83:3; Matt. 27:1
11 [a]Ps. 3:2 [b]Ps. 7:2
12 [a]Ps. 10:1; 22:11; 35:22; 38:21 [b]Ps. 38:22; 40:13; 70:1, 5
13 [I]Lit., *my injury* [a]Ps. 35:4, 26; 40:14 [b]Ps. 109:29 [c]Esth. 9:2; Ps. 71:24
14 [I]Lit., *add upon all Thy praise* [a]Ps. 130:7 [b]Ps. 71:8
15 [I]Lit., *numbers* [a]Ps. 35:28 [b]Ps. 96:2 [c]Ps. 40:5
16 [I]Heb., *YHWH*, usually rendered LORD [a]Ps. 106:2 [b]Ps. 51:14
17 [a]Deut. 4:5; 6:7 [b]Ps. 26:7; 40:5; 119:27
18 [I]Lit., *arm* [a]Ps. 71:9 [b]Ps. 22:31; 78:4, 6
19 [I]Or, *And* [II]Lit., *height* [a]Ps. 36:6; 57:10 [b]Ps. 126:2; Luke 1:49 [c]Deut. 3:24; Ps. 35:10

20 Thou, who hast [a]shown[7200]
[I]me many troubles and
distresses,[7451]
Wilt [b]revive[2421] [I]me again,
And wilt bring [I]me up again
[c]from the depths of the
earth.[776]
21 Mayest Thou increase my
[a]greatness,
And turn *to* [b]comfort[5162] me.
22 I will also praise[3034] Thee with
[Ia]a harp,
Even Thy [II]truth,[571] O my God;
To Thee I will sing praises[2167]
with the [b]lyre,
O Thou [c]Holy One[6918] of Israel.
23 My lips[8193] will [a]shout for joy
when I sing praises to Thee;
And my [b]soul, which Thou hast
redeemed.[6299]
24 My [a]tongue also will utter[1897]
Thy righteousness all day
long;
For they are [b]ashamed, for they
are humiliated who seek
[I]my hurt.

The Reign of the Righteous King

A Psalm of Solomon.

72 Give the king[4428] [a]Thy
judgments,[4941] O God,[430]
And [b]Thy righteousness[6666] to
the king's[4428] son.[1121]
2 [I]May [II]he [a]judge[177] Thy
people[5971] with
righteousness,[6664]
And [III][b]Thine afflicted with
justice.[4941]
3 [I]Let the mountains bring[5375]
[II][a]peace to the people,
And the hills in righteousness.
4 [I]May he [a]vindicate[8199] the
[II]afflicted of the people,
Save[3467] the children[1121] of the
needy,
And crush[1792] the oppressor.
5 [I]Let them fear[3372] Thee
[a]while the sun *endures*,
And [II]as long as the moon,
throughout all
generations.[1755]
6 [I]May he come down [a]like rain
upon the mown grass,
Like [b]showers that water the
earth.[776]
7 In his days[3117] [I]may the
[a]righteous[6662] flourish,
And [b]abundance of peace till the
moon is no more.
8 May he also rule[7287] [a]from sea
to sea,
And from the River to the ends
of the earth.
9 [I]Let [a]the nomads of the desert
[b]bow[3766] before him;
And his enemies [c]lick the
dust.[6083]
10 [I]Let the kings[4428] of [a]Tarshish
and of the [IIb]islands bring
presents;[4503]
The kings of [c]Sheba and
[d]Seba [e]offer[7126] [III]gifts.
11 [I]And let all [a]kings bow down[7812]
before him,
All [b]nations[1471] serve[5647] him.
12 For he will [a]deliver[5337] the
needy when he cries for
help,
The [I]afflicted also, and him who
has no helper.
13 He will have [a]compassion on the
poor and needy,
And the [I]lives[5315] of the needy
he will save.
14 He will [Ia]rescue[1350] their
[II]life[5315] from oppression and
violence;[2555]
And their blood[1818] will be
[b]precious in his sight;
15 So may he live;[2421] and may the
[a]gold of Sheba be given to
him;
And let [I]them pray for him
continually;[8548]
Let [I]them bless[1288] him all day
long.[3117]

20 [I]Another reading is *us* [a]Ps. 60:3 [b]Ps. 80:18; 85:6; 119:25; 138:7; Hos. 6:1, 2 [c]Ps. 86:13
21 [a]Ps. 18:35 [b]Ps. 23:4; 86:17; Is. 12:1; 49:13
22 [I]Lit., *an instrument of a harp* [II]Or, *faithfulness* [a]Ps. 33:2; 81:2; 92:1-3; 144:9 [b]Ps. 33:2; 147:7 [c]2Kin. 19:22; Ps. 78:41; 89:18; Is. 1:4
23 [a]Ps. 5:11; 32:11; 132:9, 16 [b]Ps. 34:22; 55:18; 103:4
24 [I]Or, *to injure me* [a]Ps. 35:28 [b]Ps. 71:13

1 [a]1Kin. 3:9; 1Chr. 22:13 [b]Ps. 24:5
2 [I]Or, *He will judge* [II]Many of the pronouns in this Psalm may be rendered *He* since the typical reference is to the Messiah. [III]Or, *Thy humble* [a]Is. 9:7; 11:2-5; 32:1 [b]Ps. 82:3
3 [I]Or, *The mountains will bring* [II]Or, *prosperity* [a]Is. 2:4; 9:5, 6; Mic. 4:3, 4; Zech. 9:10
4 [I]Or, *He will vindicate* [II]Or, *humble* [a]Is. 11:4
5 [I]Or, *They will fear* [II]Lit., *before the moon* [a]Ps. 72:17; 89:36, 37
6 [I]Or, *He will come down* [a]Deut. 32:2; 2Sam. 23:4; Hos. 6:3 [b]Ps. 65:10
7 [I]Or, *the righteous will flourish* [a]Ps. 92:12 [b]Is. 2:4
8 [a]Ex. 23:31; Zech. 9:10
9 [I]Or, *The nomads. . . will bow* [a]Ps. 74:14; Is. 23:13 [b]Ps. 22:29 [c]Is. 49:23; Mic. 7:17
10 [I]Or, *The kings . . . will bring* [II]Or, *coastlands* [III]Or, *tribute* [a]2Chr. 9:21; Ps. 48:7 [b]Ps. 97:1; Is. 42:4, 10; Zeph. 2:11 [c]1Kin. 10:1; Job 6:19; Is. 60:6 [d]Gen. 10:7; Is. 43:3 [e]Ps. 45:12; 68:29
11 [I]Or, *All kings will bow down* [a]Ps. 138:4; Is. 49:23 [b]Ps. 86:9 **12** [I]Or, *humble* [a]Job 29:12; Ps. 72:4
13 [I]Lit., *souls* [a]Prov. 19:17; 28:8 **14** [I]Lit., *redeem* [II]Lit., *soul* [a]Ps. 69:18 [b]1Sam. 26:21; Ps. 116:15
15 [I]Lit., *him* [a]Is. 60:6

16 May there be abundance of grain
in the earth on top of the
mountains;
Its fruit will wave[7463] like *the*
cedars of [a]Lebanon;
And may those from the city
flourish like [b]vegetation of the
earth.
17 May his [a]name endure
forever;[5769]
May his name [I]increase
[IIb]as long as the sun
shines;
And let *men* [c]bless[1288]
themselves by him;
[d]Let all nations call him
blessed.[833]
18 [a]Blessed be the LORD God, the
God of Israel,
Who alone [b]works[6213]
wonders.[6381]
19 And blessed be His [a]glorious[3519]
name forever;
And may the whole [b]earth be
filled with His glory.[3519]
[c]Amen, and Amen.[543]
20 The prayers[8605] of David the son
of Jesse are ended.[3615]

BOOK 3

The End of the Wicked Contrasted with That of the Righteous

A Psalm of Asaph.

73 Surely God[430] is [a]good[2896] to
Israel,
To those who are [b]pure[1249] in
heart![3824]
2 But as for me, [a]my feet came
close to stumbling;
My steps [I]had almost
slipped.[8210]
3 For I was [a]envious of the
[I]arrogant,[1984]
As I saw[7200] the [b]prosperity[7965]
of the wicked.[7563]

4 For there are no pains in their
death;[4194]
And their [I]body is fat.
5 They are [a]not [I]in trouble[5999] *as*
other [II]men;[582]
Nor are they [b]plagued[5060]
[III]like mankind.[120]
6 Therefore pride is [a]their
necklace;
The [b]garment of violence[2555]
covers them.
7 Their eye [I]bulges from
[a]fatness;
The imaginations[4906] of *their*
heart [II]run riot.
8 They [a]mock,[4167] and
[I]wickedly[7451] speak[1696] of
oppression;
They [b]speak from on high.
9 They have [a]set their
mouth[6310] [I]against the
heavens,[8064]
And their tongue [II]parades
through the earth.[776]
10 Therefore [I]his people[5971]
return[7725] to this place;
And waters of [a]abundance are
[II]drunk by them.
11 And they say,[559] "[a]How does
God[410] know?
And is there knowledge[1844]
[I]with the Most High?"[5945]
12 Behold, [a]these are the
wicked;[7563]
And always [b]at ease, they have
increased *in* wealth.[2428]
13 Surely [a]in vain I have [I]kept my
heart pure,[2135]
And [b]washed[7364] my hands[3709] in
innocence;[5356]
14 For I have been stricken [a]all
day[3117] long,
And [Ib]chastened[8433] every
morning.
15 If I had said, "I will speak thus,"
Behold, I should have
betrayed[898] the
[a]generation[1755] of Thy
children.[1121]

16 [a]Ps. 104:16 [b]Job 5:25
17 [I]Or, *sprout forth* [II]Lit., *before the sun* [a]Ex. 3:15; Ps. 135:13 [b]Ps. 89:36 [c]Gen. 12:3; 22:18 [d]Luke 1:48
18 [a]1Chr. 29:10; Ps. 41:13; 89:52; 106:48 [b]Ex. 15:11; Job 5:9; Ps. 77:14; 86:10; 136:4
19 [a]Neh. 9:5; Ps. 96:8 [b]Num. 14:21 [c]Ps. 41:13

1 [a]Ps. 86:5 [b]Ps. 24:4; 51:10; Matt. 5:8
2 [I]Lit., *were caused to slip* [a]Ps. 94:18
3 [I]Or, *boasters* [a]Ps. 37:1; Prov. 23:17 [b]Job 21:7; Ps. 37:7; Jer. 12:1
4 [I]Or, *belly*
5 [I]Lit., *in the trouble of men* [II]Or, *mortals* [III]Lit., *with* [a]Job 21:9; Ps. 73:12 [b]Ps. 73:14
6 [a]Gen. 41:42; Prov. 1:9 [b]Ps. 109:18
7 [I]Lit., *goes forth* [II]Lit., *overflow* [a]Job 15:27; Ps. 17:10; Jer. 5:28
8 [I]Or, *they speak in wickedness; From on high they speak of oppression.* [a]Ps. 1:1 [b]Ps. 17:10; 2Pet. 2:18; Jude 16
9 [I]Or, *in* [II]Lit., *walks* [a]Rev. 13:6
10 [I]Or, *His* [II]Lit., *drained out* [a]Ps. 23:5
11 [I]Lit., *in* [a]Job 22:13
12 [a]Ps. 49:6; 52:7 [b]Jer. 49:31; Ezek. 23:42
13 [I]Or, *cleansed my heart* [a]Job 21:15; 34:9; 35:3 [b]Ps. 26:6
14 [I]Lit., *my chastening* [a]Ps. 38:6 [b]Job 33:19; Ps. 118:18
15 [a]Ps. 14:5

73:7,12 See note on Ps. 34:21.

16 When I [a]pondered[2803] to
understand this,
It was [I]troublesome[5999] in my
sight
17 Until I came into the
[I][a]sanctuary[4720] of God;
Then I perceived[995] their
[b]end.[319]
18 Surely Thou dost set them in
[a]slippery places;
Thou dost cast them down to
[I][b]destruction.[4876]
19 How they are [I][a]destroyed[8047] in
a moment!
They are utterly swept away[8552]
by [b]sudden terrors!
20 Like a [a]dream when one awakes,
O Lord,[136] when [b]aroused,
Thou wilt [c]despise their
[I]form.[6754]
21 When my [a]heart was
embittered,[2556]
And I was [b]pierced[8150] [I]within,
22 Then I was [a]senseless and
ignorant;
I was *like* [I]a [b]beast [II]before Thee.
23 Nevertheless [a]I am
continually[8548] with Thee;
Thou hast taken hold[270] of my
right hand.[3027]
24 With Thy counsel[6098] Thou wilt
[a]guide[5148] me,
And afterward [b]receive me [I]to
glory.[3519]
25 [a]Whom have I in heaven[8064] *but*
Thee?
And [I]besides Thee, I desire[2654]
nothing on earth.
26 My [a]flesh and my heart may
fail,[65]
But God is the [I]strength of my
heart and my [b]portion
forever.[5769]
27 For, behold, [a]those who are far
from Thee will [b]perish;[6]
Thou hast [I]destroyed[6789] all
those who [II][c]are unfaithful[2181]
to Thee.
28 But as for me, [a]the nearness of
God is my good;
I have made the Lord
[I]GOD my [b]refuge,

16 [I]Lit., *labor, trouble* [a]Eccl. 8:17
17 [I]Lit., *sanctuaries* [a]Ps. 27:4; 77:13 [b]Ps. 37:38
18 [I]Lit., *ruins* [a]Ps. 35:6 [b]Ps. 35:8; 36:12
19 [I]Lit., *become a desolation* [a]Num. 16:21; Is. 47:11 [b]Job 18:11
20 [I]Or, *image* [a]Job 20:8 [b]Ps. 78:65 [c]1Sam. 2:30
21 [I]Lit., *in my kidneys* [a]Judg. 10:16 [b]Acts 2:37
22 [I]Or, *an animal* [II]Lit., *with Thee* [a]Ps. 49:10; 92:6 [b]Job 18:3; Ps. 49:20; Eccl. 3:18
23 [a]Ps. 16:8
24 [I]Or, *with honor* [a]Ps. 32:8; 48:14; Is. 58:11 [b]Gen. 5:24; Ps. 49:15
25 [I]Or, *with* [a]Ps. 16:2; Phil. 3:8
26 [I]Lit., *rock* [a]Ps. 38:10; 40:12; 84:2; 119:81 [b]Ps. 16:5
27 [I]Or, *silenced* [II]Lit., *go to a whoring from* [a]Ps. 119:155 [b]Ps. 37:20 [c]Ex. 34:15; Num. 15:39; Ps. 106:39; Hos. 4:12; 9:1
28 [I]Heb., *YHWH,* usually rendered *LORD* [a]Ps. 65:4; Heb. 10:22; James 4:8 [b]Ps. 14:6; 71:7 [c]Ps. 40:5; 107:22; 118:17

+Possibly, *Contemplative,* or *Didactic,* or *Skillful Psalm*
1 [I]Or, *pasturing* [a]Ps. 44:9; 77:7 [b]Deut. 29:20; Ps. 18:8; 89:46 [c]Ps. 79:13; 95:7; 100:3
2 [a]Ex. 15:16; Deut. 32:6 [b]Ex. 15:13; Ps. 77:15; 106:10; Is. 63:9 [c]Deut. 32:9; Is. 63:17; Jer. 10:16; 51:19 [d]Ps. 9:11; 68:16

That I may [c]tell[5608] of all Thy
works.

An Appeal against the Devastation of the Land by the Enemy

A +Maskil of Asaph.

74

O God,[430] why hast Thou
[a]rejected *us* forever?[5331]
Why does Thine anger[639]
[b]smoke[6225] against the
[c]sheep of Thy [I]pasture?
2 Remember[2142] Thy
congregation,[5712] which
Thou hast [a]purchased of
old,[6924]
Which Thou hast [b]redeemed[1350]
to be the [c]tribe[7626] of Thine
inheritance;[5159]
And this Mount [d]Zion, where
Thou hast dwelt.[7931]
3 [I]Turn Thy footsteps toward the
[a]perpetual ruins;
The enemy [b]has damaged[7489]
everything within the
sanctuary.[6944]
4 Thine adversaries have
[a]roared in the midst[7130] of
Thy meeting place;
They have set up[7760] their
[b]own [I]standards [c]for signs.[226]
5 It seems as if one had lifted
up
His [I][a]axe in a [II]forest of trees.
6 And now [I]all its [a]carved work
They smash with hatchet and
[II]hammers.
7 They have [I][a]burned Thy
sanctuary[4720] [II]to the
ground;[776]
They have [b]defiled[2490] the
dwelling place of Thy name.
8 They [a]said in their heart,[3820]
"Let us [I]completely
[II]subdue[3238] them."
They have burned[8313] all the

3 [I]Lit., *Lift up* [a]Is. 61:4 [b]Ps. 79:1 **4** [I]Lit., *signs* [a]Lam. 2:7 [b]Num. 2:2 [c]Ps. 74:9 **5** [I]Lit., *axes* [II]Lit., *thicket* [a]Jer. 46:22 **6** [I]Lit., *altogether* [II]Or, *axes* [a]1Kin. 6:18, 29, 32, 35 **7** [I]Lit., *set on fire* [II]Or, *To the ground they. . .* [a]2Kin. 25:9 [b]Ps. 89:39; Lam. 2:2 **8** [I]Lit., *altogether* [II]Or, *oppress* [a]Ps. 83:4

meeting places of God[410] in
the land.[776]
9 We do not see our [a]signs;
There is [b]no longer any
prophet,[5030]
Nor is there any among us who
knows [c]how long.
10 How long, O God, will the
adversary [a]revile,
And the enemy [b]spurn[5006] Thy
name forever?
11 Why [a]dost Thou withdraw[7725]
Thy hand,[3027] even Thy right
hand?
From within Thy bosom,
[b]destroy *them*!
12 Yet God is [a]my king[4428] from of
old,
Who works deeds of
deliverance[3444] in the midst
of the earth.[776]
13 [I]Thou didst [a]divide[6565] the sea
by Thy strength;
[I]Thou [b]didst break[7665] the
heads[7218] of the [c]sea
monsters[8577] [II]in the waters.
14 [I]Thou didst crush the heads of
[II][a]Leviathan;
[I]Thou didst give him as food for
the [III]creatures[5971] [b]of the
wilderness.
15 [I]Thou didst [a]break open springs
and torrents;
[I]Thou didst [b]dry up ever-flowing
streams.
16 Thine is the day,[3117] Thine also
is the night;[3915]
[I]Thou hast [a]prepared[3559] the
[II]light[3974] and the sun.
17 [I]Thou hast [a]established all the
boundaries of the earth;
[I]Thou hast [II]made[3335] [b]summer
and winter.
18 Remember this, [I]O LORD, that
the enemy has [a]reviled;
And a [b]foolish people has
spurned[5006] Thy name.
19 Do not deliver the soul[5315] of Thy
[a]turtledove to the wild
beast;[2416]
[b]Do not forget the life[2416] of
Thine afflicted forever.
20 Consider the [a]covenant;[1285]
For the [b]dark places[4285] of the
land are full of the
habitations[4999] of
violence.[2555]
21 Let not the [a]oppressed
return[7725] dishonored;
Let the [b]afflicted and needy
praise[1984] Thy name.
22 Do arise, O God, *and*
[a]plead Thine own cause;[7379]
Remember [I]how the [b]foolish man
reproaches Thee all day
long.[3117]
23 Do not forget the voice of Thine
[a]adversaries,
The [b]uproar[7588] of those who
rise against Thee which
ascends continually.[8548]

God Abases the Proud, but Exalts the Righteous

For the choir director; *set to* [+]Al-tashheth.
A Psalm of Asaph, a Song.

75 We [a]give thanks to Thee, O
God,[430] we give thanks,[3034]
For Thy name is [b]near;
Men declare[5608] [c]Thy wondrous
works.[6381]
2 "When I select an [a]appointed
time,[4150]
It is I who [b]judge[8199] with
equity.[4334]
3 "The [a]earth[776] and all who dwell
in it [I]melt;[4127]
It is I who have firmly set its
[b]pillars. [II]Selah.
4 "I said to the boastful,[1984] 'Do not
boast,'[1984]
And to the wicked,[7563] '[a]Do not
lift up the horn;
5 Do not lift up your horn on high,
[a]Do not speak[1696] with insolent
[I]pride.' "
6 For not from the east, nor from
the west,

9 [a]Ps. 78:43 [b]1Sam. 3:1; Lam. 2:9; Ezek. 7:26; Amos 8:11 [c]Ps. 6:3; 79:5; 80:4
10 [a]Ps. 44:16; 79:12; 89:51 [b]Lev. 24:16
11 [a]Lam. 2:3 [b]Ps. 59:13
12 [a]Ps. 44:4
13 [I]Or, *Thou Thyself* [II]Lit., *on* [a]Ex. 14:21; Ps. 78:13 [b]Is. 51:9 [c]Ps. 148:7; Jer. 51:34
14 [I]Or, *Thou Thyself* [II]Or, *sea monster* [III]Lit., *people* [a]Job 41:1; Ps. 104:26; Is. 27:1 [b]Ps. 72:9
15 [I]Or, *Thou Thyself* [a]Ex. 17:5, 6; Num. 20:11; Ps. 78:15; 105:41; 114:8; Is. 48:21 [b]Ex. 14:21, 22; Josh. 2:10; 3:13; Ps. 114:3
16 [I]Or, *Thou Thyself* [II]Or, *luminary* [a]Gen. 1:14-18; Ps. 104:19; 136:7,8
17 [I]Or, *Thou Thyself* [II]Or, *formed* [a]Deut. 32:8; Acts 17:26 [b]Gen. 8:22; Ps. 147:16-18
18 [I]Or, *that the enemy has reviled the LORD* [a]Ps. 74:10 [b]Deut. 32:6; Ps. 14:1; 39:8; 53:1
19 [a]Song 2:14 [b]Ps. 9:18
20 [a]Gen. 17:7; Ps. 106:45 [b]Ps. 88:6; 143:3
21 [a]Ps. 103:6 [b]Ps. 35:10; Is. 41:17
22 [I]Lit., *Thy reproach from the foolish man* [a]Ps. 43:1; Is. 3:13; 43:26; Ezek. 20:35 [b]Ps. 14:1; 53:1; 74:18
23 [a]Ps. 74:10 [b]Ps. 65:7

[+]Lit., *Do Not Destroy*
1 [a]Ps. 79:13 [b]Ps. 145:18 [c]Ps. 26:7; 44:1; 71:17
2 [a]Ps. 102:13 [b]Ps. 9:8; 67:4; Is. 11:4

3 [I]Or, *totter* [II]*Selah* may mean: *Pause, Crescendo* or *Musical interlude* [a]Ps. 46:6; Is. 24:19 [b]1Sam. 2:8
4 [a]Zech. 1:21 5 [I]Lit., *neck* [a]1Sam. 2:3; Ps. 94:4

Nor from the [Ia]desert *comes*
exaltation;
7 But [a]God is the Judge;
He [b]puts down one, and exalts
another.
8 For a [a]cup is in the hand[3027] of
the LORD, and the wine
foams;
It is [Ib]well mixed, and He pours
out of this;
Surely all the wicked of the earth
must drain *and* [c]drink down
its dregs.[8105]
9 But as for me, I will [a]declare[5046]
it forever;[5769]
I will sing praises to the God
of Jacob.
10 And all the [a]horns of the wicked
[I]He will cut off,
But [b]the horns of the
righteous[6662] will be lifted up.

The Victorious Power of the God of Jacob

For the choir director; on stringed instruments. A Psalm of Asaph, a Song.

76 God[430] is [a]known[3045] in Judah;
His name is [b]great in Israel.
2 And His [Ia]tabernacle is in
[b]Salem;
His [c]dwelling place also is in
Zion.
3 There He [a]broke[7665] the
[I]flaming arrows,
The shield, and the sword,[2719]
and the [II]weapons of war.
[III]Selah.
4 Thou art resplendent,
[I]More majestic[117] than the
mountains of prey.
5 The [a]stouthearted were
plundered;
[I]They sank into sleep;
And none of the [II]warriors[582,2428]
could use his hands.[3027]
6 At Thy [a]rebuke,[1606] O God of
Jacob,
Both [Ib]rider and horse were cast
into a dead sleep.

7 Thou, even Thou, art [a]to be
feared;[3372]
And [b]who may stand in Thy
presence when once[227]
[I]Thou art angry?[639]
8 Thou didst cause judgment[1779]
to be heard[8085] from
heaven;[8064]
The earth[776] [a]feared, and was
still,[8252]
9 When God [a]arose to
judgment,[4941]
To save[3467] all the humble of the
earth. Selah.
10 For the [Ia]wrath[2534] of man[120]
shall praise[3034] Thee;
With a remnant[7611] of wrath
Thou shalt gird Thyself.
11 [a]Make vows[5087] to the LORD
your God and [b]fulfill *them*;
Let all who are around Him
[c]bring gifts to Him who is to
be feared.[4172]
12 He will cut off the spirit[7307] of
princes;[5057]
He is [Ia]feared[3372] by the kings[4428]
of the earth.

Comfort in Trouble from Recalling God's Mighty Deeds

For the choir director; +according to Jeduthun. A Psalm of Asaph.

77 My voice *rises* to God, and I will
[a]cry aloud;
My voice *rises* to God,[430] and
He will hear[238] me.
2 In the [a]day[3117] of my trouble I
sought the Lord;[136]
[b]In the night[3915] my [c]hand was
stretched out [I]without
weariness;
My soul[5315] [d]refused[3985] to be
comforted.[5162]
3 *When* I remember[2142] God, then
I am [a]disturbed;
When I [b]sigh,[7878] then

6 [I]Or, *mountainous desert* [a]Ps. 3:3
7 [a]Ps. 50:6 [b]1Sam. 2:7; Ps. 147:6; Dan. 2:21
8 [I]Lit., *full of mixture* [a]Job 21:20; Ps. 11:6; 60:3; Jer. 25:15 [b]Prov. 23:30 [c]Obad. 16
9 [a]Ps. 22:22; 40:10
10 [I]Heb., *I* [a]Ps. 101:8; Jer. 48:25 [b]1Sam. 2:1; Ps. 89:17; 92:10; 148:14

1 [a]Ps. 48:3 [b]Ps. 99:3
2 [I]Lit., *shelter* [a]Ps. 27:5; Lam. 2:6 [b]Gen. 14:18 [c]Ps. 9:11; 132:13; 135:21
3 [I]Lit., *fiery shafts of the bow* [II]Lit., *battle* [III]*Selah* may mean: *Pause, Crescendo* or *Musical interlude* [a]Ps. 46:9
4 [I]Or, *Majestic from the mountains*
5 [I]Lit., *They slumbered their sleep* [II]Lit., *men of might have found their hands* [a]Is. 10:12; 46:12
6 [I]Lit., *chariot* [a]Ps. 80:16 [b]Ex. 15:1, 21; Ps. 78:53
7 [I]Lit., *Thine anger is* [a]1Chr. 16:25; Ps. 89:7; 96:4 [b]Ezra 9:15; Ps. 130:3; Nah. 1:6; Mal. 3:2; Rev. 6:17
8 [a]1Chr. 16:30; 2Chr. 20:29, 30; Ps. 33:8
9 [a]Ps. 9:7, 8; 74:22; 82:8
10 [I]Lit., *wraths* [a]Ex. 9:16; Rom. 9:17
11 [a]Eccl. 5:4-6 [b]Ps. 50:14 [c]2Chr. 32:23; Ps. 68:29
12 [I]Lit., *awesome to* [a]Ps. 47:2

+1Chr. 16:41
1 [a]Ps. 3:4; 142:1
2 [I]Lit., *and did not grow numb* [a]Ps. 50:15; 86:7 [b]Ps. 63:6; Is. 26:9 [c]Job 11:13; Ps. 88:9 [d]Gen. 37:35

3 [a]Ps. 42:5, 11; 43:5 [b]Ps. 55:2; 142:2

[c]my spirit[7307] grows faint.
[I]Selah.
4 Thou hast held my eyelids *open*;
I am so troubled that I
[a]cannot speak.[1696]
5 I have considered[2803] the
[a]days[3117] of old,[6924]
The years of long ago.[5769]
6 I will remember[2142] my
[a]song in the night;
I [b]will meditate[7878] with my
heart;[3824]
And my spirit [I]ponders.
7 Will the Lord [a]reject forever?[5769]
And will He [b]never be
favorable[7521] again?
8 Has His [a]lovingkindness[2617]
ceased forever?[5331]
Has *His* [Ib]promise[562] come to an
end[1584] [II]forever?
9 Has God[410] [a]forgotten to be
gracious?
Or has He in anger[639]
[I]withdrawn His
[b]compassion?[7356] Selah.
10 Then I said,[559] "[a]It is my [I]grief,
That the [b]right hand of the Most
High[5945] has changed."
11 I shall remember the [a]deeds of
[I]the LORD;
Surely I will [a]remember Thy
wonders[6382] of old.
12 I will [a]meditate[1897] on all Thy
work,
And muse[7878] on Thy deeds.
13 Thy way,[1870] O God, is
[a]holy;[6944]
[b]What god[410] is great like our
God?
14 Thou art the [a]God who
workest[6213] wonders;
Thou hast [b]made known[3045] Thy
strength among the
peoples.[5971]
15 Thou hast by Thy [I]power
[a]redeemed[1350] Thy people,
The sons[1121] of Jacob and
[b]Joseph. Selah.
16 The [a]waters saw[7200] Thee, O
God;
The waters saw Thee, they
were in anguish;[2342]
The deeps also trembled.
17 The [a]clouds poured out water;
The skies[7834] [b]gave forth a
sound;
Thy [c]arrows [I]flashed here and
there.
18 The [a]sound of Thy thunder was
in the whirlwind;[1534]
The [b]lightnings lit up the
world;[8398]
The [c]earth[776] trembled and
shook.
19 Thy [a]way was in the sea,
And Thy paths in the mighty
waters,
And Thy footprints[6119] may not
be known.[3045]
20 Thou [a]didst lead[5148] Thy people
like a flock,
By the hand[3027] of [b]Moses and
Aaron.

God's Guidance of His People in Spite of Their Unfaithfulness

A [+]Maskil of Asaph.

78 [a]Listen,[238] O my people,[5971] to
my [I]instruction;[8451]
[b]Incline your ears to the
words[561] of my mouth.[6310]
🗝 2 I will [a]open my mouth in a
parable;
I will utter [b]dark sayings[2420] of
old,[6924]
3 Which we have heard[8085] and
known,[3045]
And [a]our fathers[1] have told[5608]
us.
4 We will [a]not conceal them from
their children,[1121]
But [b]tell to the generation[1755] to
come the praises[8416] of the
LORD,
And His strength and His

3 [I]*Selah* may mean: *Pause, Crescendo* or *Musical interlude* [c]Ps. 61:2; 143:4
4 [a]Ps. 39:9
5 [a]Deut. 32:7; Ps. 44:1; 143:5; Is. 51:9
6 [I]Lit., *searched* [a]Ps. 42:8 [b]Ps. 4:4
7 [a]Ps. 44:9 [b]Ps. 85:1, 5
8 [I]Lit., *word* [II]Lit., *from generation to generation* [a]Ps. 89:49 [b]2Pet. 3:9
9 [I]Lit., *shut up* [a]Is. 49:15 [b]Ps. 25:6; 40:11; 51:1
10 [I]Or, *infirmity, the years of the right hand of the Most High* [a]Ps. 31:22; 73:14 [b]Ps. 44:2, 3
11 [I]Heb., YAH [a]Ps. 105:5; 143:5
12 [a]Ps. 145:5
13 [a]Ps. 63:2; 73:17 [b]Ex. 15:11; Ps. 71:19; 86:8
14 [a]Ps. 72:18 [b]Ps. 106:8
15 [I]Lit., *arm* [a]Ex. 6:6; Deut. 9:29; Ps. 74:2; 78:42 [b]Ps. 80:1
16 [a]Ex. 14:21; Ps. 114:3; Hab. 3:8, 10
17 [I]Lit., *went* [a]Judg. 5:4 [b]Ps. 68:33 [c]Ps. 18:14
18 [a]Ps. 18:13; 104:7 [b]Ps. 97:4 [c]Judg. 5:4; Ps. 18:7
19 [a]Is. 51:10; Hab. 3:15
20 [a]Ex. 13:21; 14:19; Ps. 78:52; 80:1; Is. 63:11-13 [b]Ex. 6:26; Ps. 105:26

[+]Possibly, *Contemplative*, or *Didactic*, or *Skillful Psalm*
1 [I]Or, *law, teaching* [a]Is. 51:4 [b]Is. 55:3
2 [a]Ps. 49:4; Matt. 13:35 [b]Prov. 1:6
3 [a]Ps. 44:1
4 [a]Ex. 12:26; Deut. 6:7; 11:19; Job 15:18; Ps. 145:4; Is. 38:19; Joel 1:3 [b]Ex. 13:8, 14; Ps. 22:30

🗝 **78:2** See Mt. 13:35.

[c]wondrous works**6381** that He
has done.**6213**
5 For He established a
[a]testimony**5715** in Jacob,
And appointed**7760** a [b]law in
Israel,
Which He [c]commanded**6680** our
fathers,
That they should [I][d]teach them
to their children,
6 [a]That the generation to come
might know, *even* [b]the
children *yet* to be born,
That they may arise and
[c]tell**5608** *them* to their
children,
7 That they should put**7760** their
confidence**3689** in God,**430**
And [a]not forget the works of
God,**410**
But [b]keep**5341** His
commandments,**4687**
8 And [a]not be like their fathers,
A [b]stubborn**5637** and rebellious
generation,
A generation that [c]did not
[I]prepare its heart,**3820**
And whose spirit**7307** was not
[d]faithful**539** to God.
9 The sons of Ephraim [I]were
[a]archers equipped**5401** with
bows,
Yet [b]they turned back**2015** in the
day**3117** of battle.
10 They [a]did not keep**8104** the
covenant**1285** of God,
And refused**3985** to [b]walk in His
law;
11 And they [a]forgot His deeds,
And His [I]miracles**6381** that He had
shown**7200** them.
12 [a]He wrought**6213** wonders before
their fathers,
In the land**776** of Egypt, in the
[b]field**7704** of Zoan.
13 He [a]divided the sea, and caused
them to pass through;**5674**
And He made the waters
stand [b]up**5324** like a heap.
14 Then He led**5148** them with the
cloud**6051** by [a]day,**3119**
And all the night**3915** with a
[b]light**216** of fire.
🔑 15 He [a]split the rocks in the
wilderness,
And gave *them* abundant drink
like the ocean depths.
16 He [a]brought forth streams also
from the rock,
And caused waters to run down
like rivers.
17 Yet they still continued to sin**2398**
against Him,
To [a]rebel**4784** against the Most
High**5945** in the desert.
18 And in their heart**3824** they [a]put
God to the test**5254**
By asking**7592** [b]food according to
their desire.**5315**
19 Then they spoke**1696** against
God;
They said,**559** "[a]Can God prepare
a table in the wilderness?
20 "Behold, He [a]struck**5221** the rock,
so that waters gushed out,
And streams were
overflowing;**7857**
Can He give bread also?
Will He provide [I][b]meat for His
people?"
21 Therefore the LORD heard and
[I]was [a]full of wrath,**5674**
And a fire was kindled against
Jacob,
And anger**639** also mounted**5927**
against Israel;
22 Because they [a]did not believe**539**
in God,
And did not trust**982** in His
salvation.**3444**
23 Yet He commanded the
clouds**7834** above,
And [a]opened the doors of
heaven;**8064**

4 [c]Job 37:16; Ps. 26:7; 71:17
5 [I]Lit., *make them known* [a]Ps. 19:7; 81:5; Is. 8:20 [b]Ps. 147:19 [c]Deut. 6:4-9 [d]Deut. 4:9
6 [a]Ps. 102:18 [b]Ps. 22:31 [c]Deut. 11:19
7 [a]Deut. 4:9; 6:12; 8:14 [b]Deut. 4:2; 5:1, 29; 27:1; Josh. 22:5
8 [I]Or, *put right* [a]2Kin. 17:14; 2Chr. 30:7; Ezek. 20:18 [b]Ex. 32:9; Deut. 9:7, 24; 31:27; Judg. 2:19; Is. 30:9 [c]Job 11:13; Ps. 78:37 [d]Ps. 51:10
9 [I]Or, *being* [a]1Chr. 12:2 [b]Judg. 20:39; Ps. 78:57
10 [a]Judg. 2:20; 1Kin. 11:11; 2Kin. 17:15; 18:12 [b]Ps. 119:1; Jer. 32:23; 44:10, 23
11 [I]Or, *wonderful works* [a]Ps. 106:13
12 [a]Ex. chs. 7-12; Ps. 106:22 [b]Num. 13:22; Ps. 78:43; Is. 19:11; 30:4; Ezek. 30:14
13 [a]Ex. 14:21; Ps. 74:13; 136:13 [b]Ex. 15:8; Ps. 33:7
14 [a]Ex. 13:21; Ps. 105:39 [b]Ex. 14:24
15 [a]Ex. 17:6; Num. 20:11; Ps. 105:41; 114:8; Is. 48:21; 1Cor. 10:4
16 [a]Num. 20:8, 10, 11
17 [a]Deut. 9:22; Is. 63:10; Heb. 3:16
18 [a]Ex. 17:6; Deut. 6:16; Ps. 78:41, 56; 95:9; 106:14; 1Cor. 10:9 [b]Num. 11:4
19 [a]Ex. 16:3; Num. 11:4; 20:3; 21:5; Ps. 23:5

20 [I]Lit., *flesh* [a]Num. 20:11; Ps. 78:15, 16 [b]Num. 11:18
21 [I]Or, *became infuriated* [a]Num. 11:1 **22** [a]Deut. 1:32; 9:23; Heb. 3:18 **23** [a]Gen. 7:11; Mal. 3:10

🔑 **78:15,16** See note on Ex. 17:6.

24 And He [a]rained down manna[4478]
upon them to eat,
And gave them [Ib]food from
heaven.
25 Man[376] did eat the bread of
[I]angels;[47]
He sent them [II]food [IIIa]in
abundance.
26 He [a]caused the east wind to blow
in the heavens;
And by His [I]power He directed
the south wind.
27 When He rained [I]meat upon
them like the dust,[6083]
Even [a]winged fowl like the sand
of the seas,
28 Then He let *them* fall in the
midst[7130] of [I]their camp,
Round about their dwellings.[4908]
29 So they [a]ate and were well
filled;
And their desire He gave to
them.
30 [I]Before they had satisfied[2114]
their desire,
[a]While their food was in their
mouths,[6310]
31 The [a]anger[639] of God rose
against them,
And killed[2026] [I]some of their
[b]stoutest ones,
And [II]subdued[3766] the choice
men of Israel.
32 In spite of all this they [a]still
sinned,
And [b]did not believe in His
wonderful works.[6381]
33 So He brought [a]their days[3117] to
an end in [I]futility,
And their years in sudden terror.
34 When He killed them, then they
[a]sought Him,
And returned[7725] and searched
[b]diligently for God;
35 And they remembered[2142] that
God was their [a]rock,
And the Most High God their
[b]Redeemer.[1350]
36 But they [a]deceived Him with
their mouth,
And [b]lied[3576] to Him with their
tongue.
37 For their heart was not
[a]steadfast toward Him,
Nor were they faithful in His
covenant.
38 But He, being [a]compassionate,
[Ib]forgave *their* iniquity,[5771]
and did not destroy[7843] *them*;
And often He [IIc]restrained His
anger,
And did not arouse all His
wrath.[2534]
39 Thus [a]He remembered that they
were but [b]flesh,[1320]
A [Ic]wind[7307] that passes and does
not return.
40 How often they [a]rebelled[4784]
against Him in the
wilderness,
And [b]grieved[6087] Him in the
[c]desert!
41 And again and again they
[Ia]tempted God,
And pained the [b]Holy One[6918] of
Israel.
42 They [a]did not remember [b]His
[I]power,[3027]
The day when He [c]redeemed[6299]
them from the adversary,
43 When He performed His
[a]signs[226] in Egypt,
And His [b]marvels[4159] in the field
of Zoan,
44 And [a]turned their rivers to
blood,[1818]
And their streams, they could
not drink.
45 He sent among them swarms of
[a]flies, which devoured them,
And [b]frogs which destroyed
them.
46 He gave also their crops to the
[a]grasshopper,
And the product of their labor
to the [b]locust.
47 He [I]destroyed[2026] their vines
with [a]hailstones,
And their sycamore trees with
frost.

24 [I]Lit., *grain* [a]Ex. 16:4 [b]Ps. 105:40; John 6:31
25 [I]Lit., *mighty ones* [II]Or, *provision* [III]Lit., *to satiation* [a]Ex. 16:3
26 [I]Or, *strength* [a]Num. 11:31
27 [I]Lit., *flesh* [a]Ex. 16:13; Ps. 105:40
28 [I]Lit., *His*
29 [a]Num. 11:19, 20
30 [I]Lit., *They were not estranged from* [a]Num. 11:33
31 [I]Lit., *among their fat ones* [II]Lit., *caused to bow down* [a]Num. 11:33, 34; Job 20:23 [b]Is. 10:16
32 [a]Num. chs. 14, 16, 17 [b]Num. 14:11; Ps. 78:11
33 [I]Lit., *vanity, a mere breath* [a]Num. 14:29, 35
34 [a]Num. 21:7; Hos. 5:15 [b]Ps. 63:1
35 [a]Deut. 32:4 [b]Ex. 15:13; Deut. 9:26; Ps. 74:2; Is. 41:14
36 [a]Ex. 24:7, 8; Ezek. 33:31 [b]Ex. 32:7, 8; Is. 57:11
37 [a]Ps. 51:10; 78:8; Acts 8:21
38 [I]Lit., *covered over, atoned for* [II]Lit., *turned away* [a]Ex. 34:6 [b]Num. 14:18-20 [c]Is. 48:9
39 [I]Or, *breath* [a]Job 10:9; Ps. 103:14 [b]Gen. 6:3 [c]Job 7:7, 16; Ps. 103:14; James 4:14
40 [a]Ps. 95:8, 9; 106:43; 107:11; Heb. 3:16 [b]Ps. 95:10; Is. 63:10; Eph. 4:30 [c]Ps. 106:14
41 [I]Or, *put God to the test* [a]Num. 14:22 [b]2Kin. 19:22; Ps. 89:18
42 [I]Lit., *hand* [a]Judg. 8:34 [b]Ps. 44:3 [c]Ps. 106:10
43 [a]Ps. 105:27 [b]Ex. 4:21; 7:3
44 [a]Ex. 7:20; Ps. 105:29
45 [a]Ex. 8:24; Ps. 105:31 [b]Ex. 8:6; Ps. 105:30
46 [a]1Kin. 8:37; Ps. 105:34 [b]Ex. 10:14
47 [I]Lit., *was killing* [a]Ex. 9:23-25; Ps. 105:32

48 He gave over their [a]cattle also
to the hailstones,
And their herds to bolts of
lightning.
49 He [a]sent upon them His burning
anger,
Fury,[5678] and indignation,[2195]
and trouble,
[I]A band of destroying[7451]
angels.[4397]
50 He leveled a path for His anger;
He did not spare their soul[5315]
from death,[4194]
But [a]gave over their life[2416] to
the plague,[1698]
51 And [a]smote all the first-born in
Egypt,
The [b]first[7225] *issue* of their virility
in the tents[168] of [c]Ham.
52 But He [a]led forth His own people
like sheep,
And guided them in the
wilderness [b]like a flock;
53 And He led them [a]safely,[983] so
that they did not fear;[6342]
But [b]the sea engulfed[3680] their
enemies.
54 So [a]He brought them to His holy
[I]land,[6944]
To this [II][b]hill country [c]which His
right hand had gained.
55 He also [a]drove out the
nations[1471] before them,
And He [b]apportioned them for
an inheritance[5159] by
measurement,[2256]
And made the tribes[7626] of Israel
dwell[7931] in their tents.[168]
56 Yet they [I][a]tempted and
[b]rebelled[4784] against the Most
High God,
And did not keep His
testimonies,[5713]
57 But turned back and [a]acted
treacherously[898] like their
fathers;
They [b]turned aside like a
treacherous bow.
58 For they [a]provoked[3707] Him with
their [b]high places,[1116]
And [c]aroused His jealousy with
their [d]graven images.

59 When God heard, He [I]was filled
with [a]wrath,
And greatly [b]abhorred[3988] Israel;
60 So that He [a]abandoned the
[b]dwelling place[4908] at Shiloh,
The tent[168] [I]which He had
pitched[7931] among men,[120]
61 And gave up His [a]strength to
captivity,[7628]
And His glory[8597] [b]into the hand
of the adversary.
62 He also [a]delivered His people to
the sword,[2719]
And [I]was filled with wrath at His
inheritance.
63 [a]Fire devoured [I]His young men;
And [I]His [b]virgins[1330] had no
wedding songs.
64 [I]His [a]priests[3548] fell[5307] by the
sword;
And [I]His [b]widows could not
weep.
65 Then the Lord[136] [a]awoke as *if
from* sleep,
Like a [b]warrior [I]overcome by
wine.
66 And He [I][a]drove His adversaries
backward;
He put on them an
everlasting[5769] reproach.[2781]
67 He also [a]rejected the tent[168] of
Joseph,
And did not choose[977] the tribe
of Ephraim,
68 But chose the tribe[7626] of Judah,
Mount [a]Zion which He loved.[157]
69 And He [a]built His sanctuary[4720]
like the heights,
Like the earth[776] which He has
founded[3245] forever.[5769]
70 He also [a]chose David His
servant,[5650]
And took him from the
sheepfolds;
71 From [I][a]the care of the
[II]ewes[5763] [b]with suckling
lambs He brought him,

48 [a]Ex. 9:19
49 [I]Lit., *A deputation of angels of evil* [a]Ex. 15:7
50 [a]Ex. 12:29, 30
51 [a]Ex. 12:29; Ps. 105:36; 135:8; 136:10 [b]Gen. 49:3 [c]Ps. 105:23, 27; 106:22
52 [a]Ex. 15:22 [b]Ps. :20
53 [a]Ex. 14:19, 20 [b]Ex. 14:27, 28; Ps. 106:11
54 [I]Lit., *border, territory* [II]Or, *mountain* [a]Ex. 15:17 [b]Ps. 68:16; Is. 11:9 [c]Ps. 44:3
55 [a]Josh. 11:16-23; Ps. 44:2 [b]Josh. 13:7; 23:4; Ps. 105:11; 135:12
56 [I]Or, *put to the test* [a]Ps. 78:18 [b]Judg. 2:11-13; Ps. 78:40
57 [a]Ezek. 20:27, 28 [b]Hos. 7:16
58 [a]Deut. 4:25; Judg. 2:12; 1Kin. 14:9; Is. 65:3 [b]Lev. 26:30; 1Kin. 3:2; 2Kin. 16:4; Jer. 17:3 [c]Deut. 32:16, 21; 1Kin. 14:22 [d]Ex. 20:4; Lev. 26:1; Deut. 4:25
59 [I]Or, *became infuriated* [a]Deut. 1:34; 9:19; Ps. 106:40 [b]Lev. 26:30; Deut. 32:19; Amos 6:8
60 [I]Some ancient versions read *where He dwelt* [a]1Sam. 4:11; Ps. 78:67; Jer. 7:12, 14; 26:6 [b]Josh. 18:1
61 [a]Ps. 63:2; 132:8 [b]1Sam. 4:17
62 [I]Or, *became infuriated* [a]Judg. 20:21; 1Sam. 4:10
63 [I]Or, *their* [a]Num. 11:1; 21:28; Is. 26:11; Jer. 48:45 [b]Jer. 7:34; 16:9; Lam. 2:21
64 [I]Or, *their* [a]1Sam. 4:17; 22:18 [b]Job 27:15; Ezek. 24:23
65 [I]Or, *sobered up from* [a]Ps. 44:23; 73:20 [b]Is. 42:13

66 [I]Lit., *smote* [a]1Sam. 5:6 **67** [a]Ps. 78:60
68 [a]Ps. 87:2; 132:13 **69** [a]1Kin. 6:1-38
70 [a]1Sam. 16:11, 12 **71** [I]Lit., *following* [II]Lit., *ewes which gave suck, He. . .* [a]2Sam. 7:8; Is. 40:11 [b]Gen. 33:13

To [c]shepherd Jacob His people,
And Israel [d]His inheritance.
72 So he shepherded them according to the [a]integrity[8537] of his heart,
And guided[5148] them with his skillful[8394] hands.[3709]

A Lament over the Destruction of Jerusalem, and Prayer for Help

A Psalm of Asaph.

79 O God,[430] the [a]nations[1471] have [I]invaded [b]Thine inheritance;[5159]
They have defiled[2930] Thy [c]holy[6944] temple;[1964]
They have [d]laid[7760] Jerusalem in ruins.
2 They have given the [a]dead bodies[5038] of Thy servants[5650] for food to the birds of the heavens,[8064]
The flesh[1320] of Thy godly ones[2623] to the beasts[2416] of the earth.[776]
3 They have poured out[8210] their blood[1818] like water round about Jerusalem;
And there was [a]no one to bury[6912] them.
4 We have become[1961] a [a]reproach[2781] to our neighbors,[7934]
A scoffing and derision to those around us.
5 [a]How long, O LORD? Wilt Thou be angry[599] forever?[5331]
Will Thy [b]jealousy[7068] [c]burn like fire?
6 [a]Pour out[8210] Thy wrath[2534] upon the nations which [b]do not know[3045] Thee,
And upon the kingdoms[4467] which [c]do not call upon[7121] Thy name.
7 For they have [a]devoured Jacob,
And [b]laid waste[8074] his [I]habitation.
8 [a]Do not remember[2142] [I]the iniquities[5771] of *our* forefathers[7223] against us;
Let Thy compassion[7356] come quickly to [b]meet us;
For we are [c]brought very low.
9 [a]Help us, O God of our salvation,[3468] for the glory[3519] of [b]Thy name;
And deliver[5337] us, and [I][c]forgive[3722] our sins, [d]for Thy name's sake.
10 [a]Why should the nations say,[559] "Where is their God?"
Let there be known[3045] among the nations in our sight,
[b]Vengeance[5360] for the blood of Thy servants, which has been shed.
11 Let [a]the groaning of the prisoner come before Thee;
According to the greatness of Thy [I]power preserve[3498] [II]those who are [a]doomed to die.[1121,8546]
12 And return[7725] to our neighbors [a]sevenfold [b]into their bosom
[I]The [c]reproach with which they have reproached Thee, O Lord.[136]
13 So we Thy people[5971] and the [a]sheep of Thy [I]pasture
Will [b]give thanks to Thee forever;[5769]
To all generations[1755] we will [c]tell[5608] of Thy praise.[8416]

God Implored to Rescue His People from Their Calamities

For the choir director; *set to* +El Shoshannim; •Eduth. A Psalm of Asaph.

80 Oh, give ear,[238] [a]Shepherd of Israel,
Thou who dost lead [b]Joseph like a flock;
Thou who [c]art enthroned *above* the cherubim,[3742] shine forth!
2 Before [a]Ephraim and Benjamin

71 [c]2Sam. 5:2; 1Chr. 11:2; Ps. 28:9 [d]1Sam. 10:1
72 [a]1Kin. 9:4
1 [I]Lit., *come into* [a]Lam. 1:10 [b]Ps. 74:2 [c]Ps. 74:3, 7 [d]2Kin. 25:9, 10; 2Chr. 36:17-19; Jer. 26:18; 52:12-14; Mic. 3:12
2 [a]Deut. 28:26; Jer. 7:33; 16:4; 19:7; 34:20
3 [a]Jer. 14:16; 16:4
4 [a]Ps. 44:13; 80:6; Dan. 9:16
5 [a]Ps. 13:1; 74:1, 9, 10; 85:5; 89:46 [b]Deut. 29:20; Ezek. 36:5; 38:19 [c]Ps. 89:46; Zeph. 3:8
6 [a]Ps. 69:24; Jer. 10:25; Ezek. 21:31; Zeph. 3:8 [b]1Thess. 4:5; 2Thess. 1:8 [c]Ps. 14:4; 53:4
7 [I]Lit., *pasture* [a]Ps. 53:4 [b]2Chr. 36:19; Jer. 39:8
8 [I]Or, our *former iniquities* [a]Ps. 106:6; Is. 64:9 [b]Ps. 21:3 [c]Deut. 28:43; Ps. 116:6; 142:6; Is. 26:5
9 [I]Lit., *cover over, atone for* [a]2Chr. 14:11 [b]Ps. 31:3 [c]Ps. 25:11; 65:3 [d]Jer. 14:7
10 [a]Ps. 42:10; 115:2 [b]Ps. 94:1, 2
11 [I]Lit., *arm* [II]Lit., *the children of death* [a]Ps. 102:20
12 [I]Lit., *Their* [a]Gen. 4:15; Lev. 26:21, 28; Ps. 12:6; 119:164; Prov. 6:31; 24:16; Is. 30:26 [b]Ps. 35:13; Is. 65:6, 7; Jer. 32:18; Luke 6:38 [c]Ps. 74:10, 18, 22
13 [I]Or, *pasturing* [a]Ps. 74:1; 95:7; 100:3 [b]Ps. 44:8 [c]Ps. 89:1; Is. 43:21

+Possibly, *to the Lilies* •Lit., *A testimony*

1 [a]Ps. 23:1 [b]Ps. :15; 78:67; Amos 5:15 [c]Ex. 25:22; 1Sam. 4:4; 2Sam. 6:2; Ps. 99:1 2 [a]Num. 2:18-24

and Manasseh, [b]stir up Thy
power,
And come to save us!
3 O God,[430] [a]restore[7725] us,
And [b]cause Thy face to shine
upon us, [I]and we will be
saved.[3467]
4 O [a]LORD God *of* hosts,[6635]
[b]How long wilt Thou [I]be
angry[6225] with the prayer[8605]
of Thy people?[5971]
5 Thou hast fed them with the
[a]bread of tears,
And Thou hast made them to
drink tears in [I]large
measure.[7991]
6 Thou dost make us [I]an object
of contention [a]to our
neighbors;[7934]
And our enemies laugh among
themselves.
7 O God *of* hosts, restore us,
And cause Thy face to shine
upon us, [I]and we will be
saved.
8 Thou didst remove a [a]vine from
Egypt;
Thou didst [b]drive out the
[I]nations,[1471] and didst [c]plant
it.
9 Thou didst [a]clear *the ground*
before it,
And it [b]took deep root and filled
the land.[776]
10 The mountains were covered[3680]
with its shadow;
And [I]the cedars of God[410] with
its [a]boughs.
11 It was sending out its branches
[a]to the sea,
And its shoots to the River.
12 Why hast Thou [a]broken down
its [I]hedges,
So that all who pass *that* way[1870]
pick its *fruit*?
13 A boar from the forest [a]eats it
away,
And whatever moves in the
field[7704] feeds on it.
14 O God *of* hosts, [a]turn again[7725]
now, we beseech[4994] Thee;
[b]Look down from heaven[8064] and
see,[7200] and take care[6485] of
this vine,
15 Even the [Ia]shoot which Thy right
hand has planted,
And on the [II]son whom Thou
hast [III]strengthened for
Thyself.
16 It is [a]burned[8313] with fire, it is
cut down;
They perish[6] at the [b]rebuke[1606]
of Thy countenance.
17 Let [a]Thy hand be upon the
man[376] of Thy right hand,[3027]
Upon the son[1121] of man[120]
whom Thou [b]didst make
strong for Thyself.
18 Then we shall not [a]turn back
from Thee;
[b]Revive[2421] us, and we will
call[7121] upon Thy name.
19 O LORD God of hosts,
[a]restore us;
Cause Thy face to shine *upon*
us, [I]and we will be saved.

God's Goodness and Israel's Waywardness

For the choir director; [+]on the Gittith. *A Psalm* of Asaph.

81 [a]Sing for joy to God[430] our
[b]strength;
Shout [c]joyfully[7321] to the [d]God of
Jacob.
2 Raise[5375] a song, strike [a]the
timbrel,[8596]
The sweet sounding [b]lyre with
the [c]harp.
3 Blow[8628] the trumpet at the
[a]new moon,
At the full moon, on our
[b]feast[2282] day.[3117]
4 For it is a statute[2706] for Israel,
An ordinance[4941] of the God of
Jacob.
5 He established[7760] it for a
testimony[5715] in Joseph,
When he [Ia]went throughout the
land[776] of Egypt.
I heard[8085] a [b]language[8193] that
I did not know:[3045]

2 [b]Ps. 35:23
3 [I]Or, *that we may,* [a]Ps. 60:1; 80:7, 19; 85:4; 126:1; Lam. 5:21 [b]Num. 6:25; Ps. 4:6; 31:16
4 [I]Lit., *smoke against* [a]Ps. 59:5; 84:8 [b]Ps. 79:5; 85:5
5 [I]Lit., *a third part of a* [a]Ps. 42:3; 102:9; Is. 30:20
6 [I]Lit., *a strife to* [a]Ps. 44:13; 79:4
7 [I]Or, *that we may*
8 [I]Or, *Gentiles* [a]Ps. 80:15; Is. 5:1, 2, 7; Jer. 2:21; 12:10; Ezek. 17:6; 19:10 [b]Josh. 13:6; 2Chr. 20:7; Ps. 44:2; Acts 7:45 [c]Jer. 11:17; 32:41; Ezek. 17:23; Amos 9:15
9 [a]Ex. 23:28; Josh. 24:12; Is. 5:2 [b]Hos. 14:5
10 [I]Or, *its boughs are like the cedars of God* [a]Gen. 49:22
11 [a]Ps. 72:8
12 [I]Or, *walls, fences* [a]Ps. 89:40; Is. 5:5
13 [a]Jer. 5:6
14 [a]Ps. 90:13 [b]Ps. 102:19; Is. 63:15
15 [I]Or, *root* [II]Or, figuratively: *branch* [III]Or, *secured* [a]Ps. 80:8
16 [a]2Chr. 36:19; Ps. 74:8; Jer. 52:13 [b]Ps. 39:11; 76:6
17 [a]Ps. 89:21 [b]Ps. 80:15
18 [a]Is. 50:5 [b]Ps. 71:20
19 [I]Or, *that we may* [a]Ps. 80:3

[+]Or, *according to*
1 [a]Ps. 51:14; 59:16; 95:1 [b]Ps. 46:1 [c]Ps. 66:1; 95:2; 98:4 [d]Ps. 84:8
2 [a]Ex. 15:20; Ps. 149:3 [b]Ps. 92:3; 98:5; 147:7 [c]Ps. 108:2; 144:9
3 [a]Num. 10:10 [b]Lev. 23:24
5 [I]Lit., *went out over* [a]Ex. 11:4 [b]Deut. 28:49; Ps. 114:1; Jer. 5:15

6 "I [I][a]relieved[5493] his shoulder of the
burden,
His hands[3709] were freed from
the [II]basket.
7 "You [a]called[7121] in trouble, and I
rescued[2502] you;
I [b]answered you in the hiding
place of thunder;
I proved[974] you at the [c]waters
of Meribah. [I]Selah.
8 "[a]Hear,[8085] O My people,[5971] and
I will [I]admonish[5749] you;
O Israel, if you [b]would listen[8085]
to Me!
9 "Let there be no [a]strange[2114]
god[410] among you;
Nor shall you worship[7812] any
foreign[5236] god.
10 "[a]I, the LORD, am your God,
Who brought you up[5937] from the
land of Egypt;
[b]Open your mouth[6310] wide and
I will [c]fill it.
11 "But My people [a]did not listen
to My voice;
And Israel did not [I]obey[14] Me.
12 "So I [a]gave [I]them over to the
stubbornness[8307] of their
heart,
To walk in their own devices.
13 "Oh that My people [a]would
listen[8085] to Me,
That Israel would [b]walk in My
ways![1870]
14 "I would quickly [a]subdue their
enemies,
And [b]turn My hand[3027] against
their adversaries.
15 "[a]Those who hate the LORD would
[b]pretend obedience to Him;
And their time[2656] *of punishment*
would be forever.[5769]
16 "[I]But I would feed you with the
[II][a]finest of the wheat;
And with [b]honey from the rock
I would satisfy you."

Unjust Judgments Rebuked

A Psalm of Asaph.

82 God[430] takes His [a]stand[5324] in
[I]His own congregation;[5712]
He [b]judges[8199] in the midst of
the [II][c]rulers.[430]
2 How long will you [a]judge[8199]
unjustly,[5766]
And [b]show partiality[5375][6440] to the
wicked?[7563] [I]Selah.
3 [a]Vindicate[8199] the weak and
fatherless;
Do justice[6663] to the afflicted and
destitute.
4 [a]Rescue the weak and needy;
Deliver[5337] *them* out of the
hand[3027] of the wicked.
5 They [a]do not know nor do they
understand;[995]
They [b]walk about in
darkness;[2825]
All the [c]foundations[4146] of the
earth[776] are shaken.
6 [I]I [a]said,[559] "You are gods,
And all of you are [b]sons[1121] of
the Most High.[5945]
7 "Nevertheless [a]you will die[4191]
like men,[8947]
And fall like *any* [b]one of the
princes."[8269]
8 [a]Arise, O God, [b]judge the earth!
For it is Thou who dost
[c]possess[5157] all the
nations.[1471]

God Implored to Confound His Enemies

A Song, a Psalm of Asaph.

83 O God,[430] [a]do not remain quiet;
[b]Do not be silent and, O God,[410]
do not be still.[8252]
2 For, behold, Thine enemies
[a]make an uproar;
And [b]those who hate[8130] Thee
have [I][c]exalted[5375]
themselves.[7218]
3 They [a]make shrewd[6191]
plans[5475] against Thy
people,[5971]

6 [I]Lit., *removed his shoulder from* [II]Or, *brick load* [a]Is. 9:4; 10:27
7 [I]*Selah* may mean: *Pause, Crescendo* or *Musical interlude* [a]Ex. 2:23; 14:10; Ps. 50:15 [b]Ex. 19:19; 20:18 [c]Ex. 17:6, 7; Num. 20:13; Ps. 95:8
8 [I]Or, *bear witness against* [a]Ps. 50:7 [b]Ps. 95:7
9 [a]Ex. 20:3; Deut. 5:7; 32:12; Ps. 44:20; Is. 43:12
10 [a]Ex. 20:2; Deut. 5:6 [b]Job 29:23 [c]Ps. 37:4; 78:25; 107:9
11 [I]Lit., *yield to* [a]Deut. 32:15; Ps. 106:25
12 [I]Lit., *him* [a]Job 8:4; Acts 7:42; Rom. 1:24, 26
13 [a]Deut. 5:29; Ps. 81:8; Is. 48:18 [b]Ps. 128:1; Is. 42:24; Jer. 7:23
14 [a]Ps. 18:47; 47:3 [b]Amos 1:8
15 [a]Rom. 1:30 [b]Ps. 18:44; 66:3
16 [I]Lit., *He would feed him* [II]Lit., *fat* [a]Deut. 32:14; Ps. 147:14 [b]Deut. 32:13

1 [I]Lit., *the congregation of God* [II]Lit., *gods* [a]Is. 3:13 [b]2Chr. 19:6; Ps. 58:11 [c]Ex. 21:6; 22:8, 28
2 [I]*Selah* may mean: *Pause, Crescendo* or *Musical interlude* [a]Ps. 58:1 [b]Deut. 1:17; Prov. 18:5
3 [a]Deut. 24:17; Ps. 10:18; Is. 11:4; Jer. 22:16
4 [a]Job 29:12
5 [a]Ps. 14:4; Jer. 4:22; Mic. 3:1 [b]Prov. 2:13; Is. 59:9; Jer. 23:12 [c]Ps. 11:3
6 [I]Lit., *I, on my part* [a]Ps. 82:1; John 10:34 [b]Ps. 89:26
7 [a]Job 21:32; Ps. 49:12; Ezek. 31:14 [b]Ps. 83:11
8 [a]Ps. 12:5 [b]Ps. 58:11; 96:13 [c]Ps. 2:8; Rev. 11:15

1 [a]Ps. 28:1; 35:22 [b]Ps. 109:1 **2** [I]Lit., *lifted up the head* [a]Ps. 2:1; Is. 17:12 [b]Ps. 81:15 [c]Judg. 8:28; Zech. 1:21 **3** [a]Ps. 64:2; Is. 29:15

And [I]conspire together[3289]
against [b]Thy [II]treasured
ones.
4 They have said,[559] "Come, and
[a]let us wipe them out [I]as a
nation,[1471]
That the [b]name of Israel be
remembered[2142] no more."
5 For they have [Ia]conspired
together with one mind;
Against Thee do they make a
covenant:
6 The tents[168] of [a]Edom and the
[b]Ishmaelites;
[c]Moab, and the [d]Hagrites;
7 [a]Gebal, and [b]Ammon, and
[c]Amalek;
[d]Philistia with the inhabitants of
[e]Tyre;
8 [a]Assyria also has joined with
them;
They have become [I]a help[2220]
to the [b]children[1121] of Lot.[2256]
[II]Selah.
9 Deal[6213] with them [a]as with
Midian,
As [b]with Sisera *and* Jabin, at the
torrent of Kishon,
10 Who were destroyed[8045] at
En-dor,
Who [a]became as dung for the
ground.[127]
11 Make their nobles[5081] like
[a]Oreb and Zeeb,
And all their princes[5257] like
[b]Zebah and Zalmunna,
12 Who said, "[a]Let us possess for
ourselves
The [b]pastures[4999] of God."
13 O my God, make them like the
[Ia]whirling dust;[1534]
Like [b]chaff before the wind.[7307]
14 Like [a]fire that burns the forest,
And like a flame that [b]sets the
mountains on fire,
15 So pursue them [a]with Thy
tempest,
And terrify[926] them with Thy
storm.
16 [a]Fill their faces with dishonor,
That they may seek Thy name,
O LORD.
17 Let them be [a]ashamed[954] and
dismayed[926] forever;[5703]
And let them be humiliated and
perish,[6]
18 That they may [a]know that
[b]Thou alone, whose name is
the LORD,
Art the [c]Most High[5945] over all
the earth.[776]

Longing for the Temple Worship

For the choir director; [+]on the Gittith. A Psalm of the sons of Korah.

84 How lovely[3039] are Thy [a]dwelling
places,[4908]
O LORD of hosts![6635]
2 My [a]soul[5315] longed and even
yearned[3615] for the courts of
the LORD;
My heart[3820] and my flesh[1320]
sing for joy to the [b]living[2416]
God.[410]
3 The bird also has found a
house,[1004]
And the swallow a nest for
herself, where she may lay
her young,
Even Thine [a]altars,[4196] O LORD
of hosts,
[b]My King[4428] and my God.[430]
4 How [a]blessed[835] are those who
dwell in Thy house!
They are [b]ever praising[1984]
Thee. [I]Selah.
5 How blessed is the man[120]
whose [a]strength is in Thee;
In [I]whose heart[3824] are the
[b]highways *to Zion*!
6 Passing through[5674] the valley of
[I]Baca, they make[6213] it a
[II]spring,
The [a]early rain also covers it
with blessings.
7 They [a]go from strength[2428] to
strength,
[I]*Every one of them* [b]appears[7200]
before God in Zion.

3 [I]Or, *consult* [II]Or, *hidden ones* [b]Ps. 27:5; 31:20
4 [I]Lit., *from* [a]Esth. 3:6; Ps. 74:8; Jer. 48:2 [b]Ps. 41:5; Jer. 11:19
5 [I]Or, *consulted* [a]Ps. 2:2; Dan. 6:7
6 [a]2Chr. 20:10; Ps. 137:7 [b]Gen. 25:12-16 [c]2Chr. 20:10 [d]1Chr. 5:10
7 [a]Josh. 13:5; Ezek. 27:9 [b]2Chr. 20:10 [c]1Sam. 15:2 [d]1Sam. 4:1; 29:1 [e]Ezek. 27:3; Amos 1:9
8 [I]Lit., *an arm* [II]*Selah* may mean: *Pause, Crescendo* or *Musical interlude* [a]2Kin. 15:19 [b]Deut. 2:9
9 [a]Judg. 7:1-24 [b]Judg. 4:7, 15, 21-24
10 [a]Zeph. 1:17
11 [a]Judg. 7:25 [b]Judg. 8:12, 21
12 [a]2Chr. 20:11 [b]Ps. 132:13
13 [I]Or, *tumble-weed* [a]Is. 17:13 [b]Job 21:18; Ps. 35:5; Is. 40:24; Jer. 13:24
14 [a]Is. 9:18 [b]Ex. 19:18; Deut. 32:22
15 [a]Job 9:17; Ps. 58:9
16 [a]Job 10:15; Ps. 109:29; 132:18
17 [a]Ps. 35:4; 70:2
18 [a]Ps. 59:13 [b]Ps. 86:10; Is. 45:21 [c]Ps. 9:2; 18:13; 97:9

[+]Or, *according to*
1 [a]Ps. 43:3; 132:5
2 [a]Ps. 42:1, 2; 63:1 [b]Ps. 42:2
3 [a]Ps. 43:4 [b]Ps. 5:2
4 [I]*Selah* may mean: *Pause, Crescendo* or *Musical interlude* [a]Ps. 65:4 [b]Ps. 42:5, 11
5 [I]Lit., *their* [a]Ps. 81:1 [b]Ps. 86:11; 122:1; Jer. 31:6
6 [I]Probably, *Weeping;* or, *Balsam trees* [II]Or, *place of springs* [a]Ps. 107:35; Joel 2:23
7 [I]Some ancient versions read *The God of gods will be seen in Zion.* [a]Prov. 4:18; Is. 40:31; John 1:16; 2Cor. 3:18 [b]Ex. 34:23; Deut. 16:16; Ps. 42:2

8 O [a]LORD God of hosts, hear[8085]
my prayer;[8605]
Give ear,[238] O [b]God of Jacob!
Selah.
9 Behold[7200] our [a]shield, O God,
And look upon the face of
[b]Thine anointed.[4899]
10 For [a]a day[3117] in Thy courts is
better[2896] than a thousand
outside.
I would rather stand at the
threshold of the house of my
God,
Than dwell in the tents[168] of
wickedness.[7562]
11 For the LORD God is [a]a sun and
[b]shield;
The LORD gives grace[2580] and
[c]glory;[3519]
[d]No good thing[2896] does He
withhold [I]from those who
walk [II]uprightly.
12 O LORD of hosts,
How [a]blessed is the man who
trusts[982] in Thee!

Prayer for God's Mercy upon the Nation

For the choir director. A Psalm of the sons of Korah.

85 O LORD, Thou didst show
[a]favor to Thy land;[776]
Thou didst [Ib]restore the
captivity[7622] of Jacob.
2 Thou didst [a]forgive[5375] the
iniquity[5771] of Thy people;[5971]
Thou didst [b]cover[3680] all their
sin.[2403] [I]Selah.
3 Thou didst [a]withdraw[5375] all Thy
fury;[5678]
Thou didst [b]turn away from Thy
burning anger.[639]
4 [a]Restore[7725] us, O God[430] of our
salvation,[3468]
And [b]cause Thine indignation
toward us to cease.
5 Wilt [a]Thou be angry[559] with us
forever?[5769]
Wilt Thou prolong Thine anger
to [I]all generations?[1755]

8 [a]Ps. 59:5; 80:4; 84:1 [b]Ps. 81:1
9 [a]Gen. 15:1; Ps. 3:3; 28:7; 59:11; 115:9-11 [b]1Sam. 16:6; 2Sam. 19:21; Ps. 2:2; 132:17
10 [a]Ps. 27:4
11 [I]Lit., *with regard to* [II]Lit., *with integrity* [a]Is. 60:19, 20; Mal. 4:2; Rev. 21:23 [b]Gen. 15:1 [c]Ps. 85:9 [d]Ps. 34:9, 10
12 [a]Ps. 2:12; 40:4

1 [I]Or, *restore the fortunes* [a]Ps. 77:7; 106:4 [b]Ezra 1:11; Ps. 14:7; 126:1; Jer. 30:18; Ezek. 39:25; Hos. 6:11; Joel 3:1
2 [I]*Selah* may mean: *Pause, Crescendo* or *Musical interlude* [a]Num. 14:19; 1Kin. 8:34; Ps. 78:38; 103:3; Jer. 31:34 [b]Ps. 32:1
3 [a]Ps. 78:38; 106:23 [b]Ex. 32:12; Deut. 13:17; Ps. 106:23; Jon. 3:9
4 [a]Ps. 80:3,7 [b]Dan. 9:16
5 [I]Lit., *generation and generation* [a]Ps. 74:1; 79:5; 80:4
6 [I]Or, *bring to life* [a]Ps. 71:20; 80:18 [b]Ps. 33:1; 90:14; 149:2
7 [a]Ps. 106:4
8 [I]Or, *Let me hear* [II]Lit., *even to* [III]Or, *stupidity* [a]Ps. 29:11; Hag. 2:9; Zech. 9:10 [b]Ps. 78:57; 2Pet. 2:21
9 [I]Or, *reverence* [a]Ps. 34:18; Is. 46:13 [b]Ps. 84:11; Hag. 2:7; Zech. 2:5; John 1:14
10 [I]Or, *faithfulness* [a]Ps. 25:10; 89:14; Prov. 3:3 [b]Ps. 72:3; Is. 32:17
11 [I]Or, *Faithfulness* [a]Is. 45:8
12 [a]Ps. 84:11; James 1:17 [b]Lev. 26:4; Ps. 67:6; Ezek. 34:27; Zech. 8:12
13 [a]Ps. 89:14

6 Wilt Thou not Thyself
[Ia]revive[2421] us again,
That Thy people may [b]rejoice
in Thee?
7 Show[7200] us Thy
lovingkindness,[2617] O LORD,
And [a]grant us Thy salvation.
8 [I]I will hear[8085] what God[410] the
LORD will say;[1696]
For He will [a]speak peace to His
people, [II]to His godly
ones;[2623]
But let them not [b]turn back to
[III]folly.[3690]
9 Surely [a]His salvation is near to
those who [I]fear[3373] Him,
That [b]glory[3519] may dwell[7931] in
our land.
10 [a]Lovingkindness and [I]truth[571]
have met together;
[b]Righteousness[6664] and peace
have kissed[5401] each other.
11 [I]Truth [a]springs from the
earth;[776]
And righteousness looks down
from heaven.[8064]
12 Indeed, [a]the LORD will give what
is good;[2896]
And our [b]land will yield its
produce.
13 [a]Righteousness will go before
Him,
And will make[7760] His footsteps
into a way.[1870]

A Psalm of Supplication and Trust

A Prayer of David.

86 [a]Incline Thine ear,[241] O LORD,
and answer me;
For I am [b]afflicted and needy.
2 [a]Do preserve[8104] my [I]soul,[5315]
for I am a [b]godly[2623] man;
O Thou my God,[430] save[3467] Thy
servant[5650] who [c]trusts[982] in
Thee.
3 Be [a]gracious[2603] to me, O
Lord,[136]

1 [a]Ps. 17:6; 31:2; 71:2 [b]Ps. 40:17; 70:5 **2** [I]Or, *life* [a]Ps. 25:20 [b]Ps. 4:3; 50:5 [c]Ps. 25:2; 31:14; 56:4
3 [a]Ps. 4:1; 57:1

For [b]to Thee I cry[7121] all day
long.[3117]
4 Make glad the soul of Thy
servant,
For to Thee, O Lord, [a]I lift
up[5375] my soul.
5 For Thou, Lord, art [a]good,[2896]
and [b]ready to forgive,[5546]
And [c]abundant in
lovingkindness[2617] to all who
call[7121] upon Thee.
6 [a]Give ear,[238] O LORD, to my
prayer;[8605]
And give heed to the voice of
my supplications![8469]
7 In [a]the day[3117] of my trouble I
shall call upon Thee,
For [b]Thou wilt answer me.
8 There is [a]no one like Thee
among the gods,[430] O
Lord;
Nor are there any works
[b]like Thine.
9 [a]All nations[1471] whom Thou hast
made[6213] shall come and
worship[7812] before Thee, O
Lord;
And they shall glorify[3513] Thy
name.
10 For Thou art [a]great and
[b]doest[6213] [I]wondrous
deeds;[6381]
Thou alone [c]art God.
11 [a]Teach[3384] me Thy way,[1870] O
LORD;
I will walk in Thy truth;[571]
[b]Unite my heart[3824] to fear[3372]
Thy name.
12 I will [a]give thanks[3034] to Thee,
O Lord my God, with all my
heart,
And will glorify Thy name
forever.[5769]
13 For Thy lovingkindness toward
me is great,
And Thou hast [a]delivered[5337] my
soul from the [I]depths of
[II]Sheol.[7585]
14 O God, arrogant men[2086] have
[a]risen up against me,
And [I]a band of violent men have
sought my [II]life,
And they have not set[7760] Thee
before them.
15 But Thou, O Lord, art a God[410]
[a]merciful and gracious,[2587]
Slow to anger and abundant in
lovingkindness and [I]truth.
16 [a]Turn to me, and be gracious[2603]
to me;
Oh [b]grant Thy strength to Thy
servant,
And save the [c]son[1121] of Thy
handmaid.
17 [a]Show[6213] me a sign[226] for good,
That those who hate[8130] me may
[b]see *it,* and be ashamed,[954]
Because Thou, O LORD,
[c]hast helped[5826] me and
comforted[5162] me.

The Privileges of Citizenship in Zion

A Psalm of the sons of Korah. A Song.

87

His [a]foundation[3248] is in the
holy[6944] mountains.
2 The LORD [a]loves[157] the gates of
Zion
More than all the *other*
dwelling places[4908] of Jacob.
3 [a]Glorious things[2513] are
spoken[1696] of you,
O [b]city of God.[430] [I]Selah.
4 "I shall mention [Ia]Rahab and
Babylon [II]among those who
know Me;
Behold, Philistia and [b]Tyre with
[IIIc]Ethiopia:
'This one was born there.'"
5 But of Zion it shall be said,[559]
"This one and that one[376]
were born in her";
And the Most High[5945] Himself
will [a]establish her.
6 The LORD shall count[5608] when
He [a]registers the peoples,[5971]
"This one was born there."
Selah.
7 Then those who [a]sing[7891] as well
as those who [Ib]play the flutes
shall say,
"All my [c]springs *of joy* are in you."

---

3 [b]Ps. 25:5; 88:9
4 [a]Ps. 25:1; 143:8
5 [a]Ps. 25:8 [b]Ps. 130:4 [c]Ex. 34:6; Neh. 9:17; Ps. 103:8; 145:8; Joel 2:13; Jon. 4:2
6 [a]Ps. 55:1
7 [a]Ps. 50:15; 77:2 [b]Ps. 17:6
8 [a]Ex. 15:11; 2Sam. 7:22; 1Kin. 8:23; Ps. 89:6; Jer. 10:6 [b]Deut. 3:24
9 [a]Ps. 22:27; 66:4; Is. 66:23; Rev. 15:4
10 [I]Or, *miracles* [a]Ps. 77:13 [b]Ex. 15:11; Ps. 72:18; :14; 136:4 [c]Deut. 6:4; 32:39; Ps. 83:18; Is. 37:16; 44:6, 8; Mark 12:29; 1Cor. 8:4
11 [a]Ps. 25:5 [b]Jer. 32:39
12 [a]Ps. 111:1
13 [I]Lit., *lowest Sheol* [II]I.e., the nether world [a]Ps. 30:3
14 [I]Or, *an assembly* [II]Lit., *soul* [a]Ps. 54:3
15 [I]Or, *faithfulness* [a]Ps. 86:5
16 [a]Ps. 25:16 [b]Ps. 68:35 [c]Ps. 116:16
17 [a]Judg. 6:17; Ps. 119:122 [b]Ps. 112:10 [c]Ps. 118:13

1 [a]Ps. 78:69; Is. 28:16
2 [a]Ps. 78:67, 68
3 [I]*Selah* may mean: *Pause, Crescendo* or *Musical interlude* [a]Is. 60:1 [b]Ps. 46:4; 48:8
4 [I]I.e., Egypt [II]Or, *as* [III]Lit., *Cush* [a]Job 9:13; Ps. 89:10; Is. 19:23-25 [b]Ps. 45:12 [c]Ps. 68:31
5 [a]Ps. 48:8
6 [a]Ps. 69:28; Is. 4:3; Ezek. 13:9
7 [I]Or, *dance* [a]Ps. 68:25; 149:3 [b]2Sam. 6:14; Ps. 30:11 [c]Ps. 36:9

A Petition to Be Saved from Death

A Song. A Psalm of the sons of Korah. For the choir director; according to Mahalath Leannoth. A •Maskil of Heman +the Ezrahite.

88 O LORD, the [a]God[430] of my
salvation,[3444]
I have [b]cried out by day[3117] and
in the night[3915] before Thee.
2 Let my prayer[8605] [a]come before
Thee;
[b]Incline Thine ear[241] to my cry!
3 For my [a]soul[5315] has [I]had enough
troubles,[7451]
And [b]my life[2416] has drawn
near[5060] to [II]Sheol.[7585]
4 I am reckoned[2803] among those
who [a]go down to the pit;[953]
I have become like a man[1397]
[b]without strength,
5 [I]Forsaken [a]among the dead,[4191]
Like the slain[2491] who lie in the
grave,[6913]
Whom Thou dost remember[2142]
no more,
And they are [b]cut off from Thy
hand.[3027]
6 Thou hast put me in [a]the lowest
pit,
In [b]dark places,[4285] in the
[c]depths.
7 Thy wrath[2534] [a]has rested upon
me,
And Thou hast afflicted me with
[b]all Thy waves. [I]Selah.
8 Thou hast removed [a]my
acquaintances[3045] far from
me;
Thou hast made me an [Ib]object
of loathing[8441] to them;
I am [c]shut up and cannot go
out.
9 My [a]eye has wasted away
because of affliction;
I have [b]called[7121] upon Thee
every day,[3117] O LORD;
I have [c]spread out my
[I]hands[3709] to Thee.
🔑 **10** Wilt Thou perform[6213]
wonders[6382] for the dead?
Will [a]the [I]departed spirits[7496] rise
and praise[3034] Thee? Selah.
11 Will Thy lovingkindness be
declared[5608] in the grave,
Thy faithfulness[530] in
[I]Abaddon?[11]
12 Will Thy wonders be made
known[3045] in the
[a]darkness?[2822]
And Thy [I]righteousness[6666] in
the land[776] of forgetfulness?
13 But I, O LORD, have cried out
[a]to Thee for help,
And [b]in the morning my prayer
comes before Thee.
14 O LORD, why [a]dost Thou reject
my soul?
Why dost Thou [b]hide Thy face
from me?
15 I was afflicted and [a]about to
die[1478] from my youth on;
I suffer[5375] [b]Thy terrors;[367] I am
[I]overcome.
16 Thy [a]burning anger has passed
over me;
Thy terrors have [Ib]destroyed
me.
17 They have [a]surrounded me
[b]like water all day long;
They have [c]encompassed[5362] me
altogether.
18 Thou hast removed [a]lover and
friend[7453] far from me;
My acquaintances are *in*
darkness.

•Possibly, *Contemplative*, or *Didactic*, or *Skillful Psalm* +1Kin. 4:31; 1Chr. 2:6; Ps. 89:title
1 [a]Ps. 24:5; 27:9 [b]Ps. 22:2; 86:3; Luke 18:7
2 [a]Ps. 18:6 [b]Ps. 31:2; 86:1
3 [I]Or, *been satisfied with* [II]I.e., the nether world [a]Ps. 107:26 [b]Ps. 107:18; 116:3
4 [a]Ps. 28:1; 143:7 [b]Job 29:12; Ps. 22:11
5 [I]Lit., *A freed one among the dead* [a]Ps. 31:12 [b]Ps. 31:22; Is. 53:8
6 [a]Ps. 86:13; Lam. 3:55 [b]Ps. 143:3 [c]Ps. 69:15
7 [I]*Selah* may mean: *Pause, Crescendo* or *Musical interlude* [a]Ps. 32:4; 39:10 [b]Ps. 42:7
8 [I]Lit., *abomination to them* [a]Job 19:13, 19; Ps. 31:11; 142:4 [b]Job 30:10 [c]Ps. 142:7; Jer. 32:2; 36:5
9 [I]Lit., *palms* [a]Ps. 6:7; 31:9 [b]Ps. 22:2; 86:3 [c]Job 11:13; Ps. 143:6
10 [I]Or, *ghosts, shades* [a]Ps. 6:5; 30:9
11 [I]I.e., place of destruction
12 [I]I.e., faithfulness to His gracious promises [a]Job 10:21; Ps. 88:6
13 [a]Ps. 30:2 [b]Ps. 5:3; 119:147
14 [a]Ps. 43:2; 44:9 [b]Job 13:24; Ps. 13:1; 44:24
15 [I]Or, *embarrassed* [a]Prov. 24:11 [b]Job 6:4; 31:23
16 [I]Or, *silenced* [a]2Chr. 28:11; Is. 13:13; Lam. 1:12 [b]Lam. 3:54; Ezek. 37:11

The LORD's Covenant with David, and Israel's Afflictions

A •Maskil of [Δ]Ethan +the Ezrahite.

89 I will [a]sing of the
lovingkindness[2617] of the
LORD forever;[5769]

17 [a]Ps. 118:10-12 [b]Ps. 124:4 [c]Ps. 17:11; 22:12, 16
18 [a]Job 19:13; Ps. 88:8; 31:11; 38:11 •Possibly, *Contemplative*, or *Didactic*, or *Skillful Psalm* [Δ]1Kin. 4:31 +Ps. 88:title **1** [a]Ps. 59:16; 101:1

🔑 **88:10** See note on Ps. 5:8-10.

To all generations[1755] I will [b]make known[3045] Thy [c]faithfulness[530] with my mouth.[6310]
2 For I have said,[559]
"[a]Lovingkindness[2617] will be built up forever;
In the heavens[8064] Thou wilt establish Thy [b]faithfulness."
3 "I have made[3772] a covenant[1285] with [a]My chosen;
I have [b]sworn to David My servant,[5650]
4 I will establish your [a]seed[2233] forever,
And build up your [b]throne[3678] to all generations." [I]Selah.
5 And the [a]heavens will praise[3034] Thy wonders, O LORD;
Thy faithfulness also [b]in the assembly[6951] of the [c]holy ones.[6918]
6 For [a]who in the skies[7834] is comparable to the LORD?
Who among the [Ib]sons[1121] of the mighty[410] is like the LORD,
7 A God[410] [a]greatly feared[6206] in the council[5475] of the [b]holy ones,
And [c]awesome[3372] above all those who are around Him?
8 O LORD God[430] of hosts,[6635] [a]who is like Thee, O mighty [I]LORD?
Thy faithfulness also surrounds Thee.
9 Thou dost rule[4910] the swelling of the sea;
When its waves rise, Thou [a]dost still[7623] them.
10 Thou Thyself didst crush[1792] [Ia]Rahab like one who is slain;[2491]
Thou didst [b]scatter Thine enemies with [II]Thy mighty arm.
11 The [a]heavens are Thine, the earth[776] also is Thine;
The [b]world[8398] and [I]all it contains, Thou hast founded[3245] them.
12 The [a]north and the south, Thou hast created[1254] them;
[b]Tabor and [c]Hermon [d]shout for joy at Thy name.
13 Thou hast [I]a strong arm;
Thy hand[3027] is mighty, Thy [a]right hand is exalted.
14 [a]Righteousness[6664] and justice[4941] are the foundation of Thy throne;
[b]Lovingkindness and [I]truth[571] go before Thee.
15 How blessed[835] are the people[5971] who know the [Ia]joyful sound!
O LORD, they walk in the [b]light[216] of Thy countenance.
16 In [a]Thy name they rejoice all the day,[3117]
And by Thy righteousness[6666] they are exalted.
17 For Thou art the glory[8597] of [a]their strength,
And by Thy favor[7522] [I]our [b]horn is exalted.
18 For our [a]shield belongs to the LORD,
[I]And our king[4428] to the [b]Holy One[6918] of Israel.
19 [I]Once Thou didst speak[1696] in vision[2377] to Thy godly [II]ones,[2623]
And didst say, "I have [III]given help to one who is [a]mighty;
I have exalted one [b]chosen from the people.
20 "I have [a]found David My servant;
With My holy[6944] [b]oil I have anointed[4886] him,
21 With whom [a]My hand will be established;[3559]
My arm also will [b]strengthen him.
22 "The enemy will not [I]deceive him,
Nor the [IIa]son[1121] of wickedness[5766] afflict him.

1 [b]Ps. 40:10 [c]Ps. 36:5; 88:11; 89:5, 8, 24, 33, 49; 92:2; 119:90; Is. 25:1; Lam. 3:23
2 [a]Ps. 103:17 [b]Ps. 36:5; 119:90
3 [a]1Kin. 8:16 [b]Ps. 132:11
4 [I]*Selah may mean: Pause, Crescendo* or *Musical interlude* [a]2Sam. 7:16 [b]2Sam. 7:13; Is. 9:7; Luke 1:33
5 [a]Ps. 19:1; 97:6 [b]Ps. 149:1 [c]Job 5:1
6 [I]Or, *sons of gods* [a]Ps. 86:8; 113:5 [b]Ps. 29:1; 82:1
7 [a]Ps. 47:2; 68:35; 76:7, 11 [b]Ps. 89:5 [c]Ps. 96:4
8 [I]Heb. *YAH* [a]Ps. 35:10; 71:19
9 [a]Ps. 65:7; 107:29
10 [I]I.e., Egypt [II]Lit., *the arm of Thy might* [a]Ps. 87:4; Is. 30:7; 51:9 [b]Ps. 18:14; 68:1; 144:6
11 [I]Lit., *its fulness* [a]Gen. 1:1; 1Chr. 29:11; Ps. 96:5 [b]Ps. 24:1
12 [a]Job 26:7 [b]Josh. 19:22; Judg. 4:6; Jer. 46:18 [c]Deut. 3:8; Josh. 11:17; 12:1; Ps. 133:3; Song 4:8 [d]Ps. 98:8
13 [I]Lit., *an arm with strength* [a]Ps. 98:1; 118:16
14 [I]Or, *faithfulness* [a]Ps. 97:2 [b]Ps. 85:13
15 [I]Or, *blast of the trumpet, shout of joy* [a]Lev. 23:24; Num. 10:10; Ps. 98:6 [b]Ps. 4:6; 44:3; 67:1; 80:3; 90:8
16 [a]Ps. 105:3
17 [I]Another reading is *Thou dost exalt our horn* [a]Ps. 28:8 [b]Ps. 75:10; 92:10; 148:14
18 [I]Or, *Even to the Holy One of Israel our King* [a]Ps. 47:9 [b]Ps. 71:22; 78:41

19 [I]Or, *At that time* [II]Some mss. read *one* [III]Lit., *placed help upon* [a]2Sam. 17:10 [b]1Kin. 11:34; Ps. 78:70
20 [a]1Sam. 13:14; 16:1-12; Acts 13:22 [b]1Sam. 16:13
21 [a]Ps. 18:35; 80:17 [b]Ps. 18:32 **22** [I]Or, *exact usury from him* [II]Or, *wicked man* [a]2Sam. 7:10; Ps. 125:3

23 "But I shall [a]crush[3807] his
adversaries before him,
And strike[5063] those who
hate[8130] him.
24 "And My [a]faithfulness and My
lovingkindness will be with
him,
And in My name his [b]horn will
be exalted.
25 "I shall also set[7760] his hand [a]on
the sea,
And his right hand on the rivers.
26 "He will cry[7121] to Me, 'Thou art
[a]my Father,[1]
My God, and the [b]rock of my
salvation.'[3444]
27 "I also shall make him *My*
[a]first-born,
The [b]highest[5945] of the kings[4428]
of the earth.
28 "My [a]lovingkindness I will
keep[8104] for him forever,[5769]
And My [b]covenant shall be
confirmed to him.
29 "So I will establish[7760] his
[I][a]descendants forever,[5703]
And his [b]throne [c]as the days[3117]
of heaven.[8064]
30 "If his sons[1121] [a]forsake[5800] My
law,[8451]
And do not walk in My
judgments,
31 If they [I]violate[2490] My
statutes,[2708]
And do not keep My
commandments,[4687]
32 Then I will visit[6485] their
transgression[6588] with the
[a]rod,[7626]
And their iniquity[5771] with
stripes.
33 "But I will not break off
[a]My lovingkindness from
him,
Nor deal falsely[8266] in My
faithfulness.
34 "My [a]covenant I will not
[I]violate,
Nor will I [b]alter[8138] [II]the
utterance of My lips.
35 "[I]Once I have [a]sworn by My
holiness;[6944]

23 [a]2Sam. 7:9; Ps. 18:40
24 [a]Ps. 89:1 [b]Ps. 132:17
25 [a]Ps. 72:8
26 [a]2Sam. 7:14; 1Chr. 22:10; Jer. 3:19 [b]2Sam. 22:47; Ps. 95:1
27 [a]Ex. 4:22; Ps. 2:7; Jer. 31:9; Col. 1:15, 18 [b]Num. 24:7; Ps. 72:11; Rev. 19:16
28 [a]Ps. 89:33 [b]Ps. 89:3, 34
29 [I]Lit., *seed* [a]Ps. 18:50; 89:4, 36 [b]1Kin. 2:4; Ps. 89:4; 132:12; Is. 9:7; Jer. 33:17 [c]Deut. 11:21
30 [a]2Sam. 7:14; Ps. 119:53
31 [I]Lit., *profane*
32 [a]Job 9:34; 21:9
33 [a]2Sam. 7:15
34 [I]Lit., *profane* [II]Lit., *that which goes forth* [a]Deut. 7:9; Jer. 33:20, 21 [b]Num. 23:19
35 [I]Or, *One thing* [a]Ps. 60:6; Amos 4:2
36 [I]Lit., *seed* [a]Ps. 89:29; Luke 1:33 [b]Ps. 72:5 [c]Ps. 72:17
37 [I]*Selah* may mean: *Pause, Crescendo* or *Musical interlude* [a]Ps. 72:5 [b]Job 16:19
38 [I]Lit., *with* [a]Ps. 44:9 [b]Deut. 32:19; 1Chr. 28:9 [c]Ps. 20:6; 89:20, 51
39 [I]Lit., *to the ground* [a]Ps. 78:59; Lam. 2:7 [b]Ps. 74:7 [c]Lam. 5:16
40 [a]Ps. 80:12 [b]Lam. 2:2, 5
41 [a]Ps. 80:12 [b]Ps. 44:13; 69:9, 19; 79:4
42 [a]Ps. 13:2 [b]Ps. 80:6
43 [a]Ps. 44:10
44 [I]Lit., *clearness, luster* [a]Ezek. 28:7
45 [a]Ps. 102:23 [b]Ps. 44:15; 71:13; 109:29

I will not lie[3576] to David.
36 "His [I][a]descendants shall endure
forever,
And his [b]throne [c]as the sun
before Me.
37 "It shall be established forever
[a]like the moon,
And the [b]witness in the sky is
faithful."[539] [I]Selah.
38 But Thou hast [a]cast off and
[b]rejected,[3988]
Thou hast been full of wrath[5674]
[I]against Thine [c]anointed.[4899]
39 Thou hast [a]spurned the covenant
of Thy servant;
Thou hast [b]profaned[2490]
[c]his crown[5145] [I]in the
dust.[776]
40 Thou hast [a]broken down all his
walls;
Thou hast [b]brought[7760] his
strongholds to ruin.[4288]
41 [a]All who pass along the way[1870]
plunder him;
He has become a [b]reproach[2781]
to his neighbors.[7934]
42 Thou hast [a]exalted the right hand
of his adversaries;
Thou hast [b]made all his enemies
rejoice.
43 Thou dost also turn back the
edge of his sword,[2719]
And hast [a]not made him stand
in battle.
44 Thou hast made his
[I][a]splendor[2892] to cease,[7673]
And cast his throne to the
ground.
45 Thou hast [a]shortened the days
of his youth;
Thou hast [b]covered him with
shame.[955] Selah.
46 [a]How long, O LORD?
Wilt Thou hide Thyself
forever?[5331]
Will Thy [b]wrath[2534] burn like
fire?
47 [a]Remember[2142] [I]what my span
of life[2465] is;

46 [a]Ps. 13:1; 44:24 [b]Ps. 79:5; 80:4
47 [I]Lit., *of what duration I am* [a]Job 7:7; 10:9; 14:1

For what [b]vanity[7723] [II]Thou hast
created all the sons of men![120]
48 What man[1397] can live and not
[a]see death?[4194]
Can he [b]deliver his soul[5315] from
the [I]power of [II]Sheol?[7585]
Selah.
49 Where are Thy former[7223]
lovingkindnesses, O Lord,[136]
Which Thou didst [a]swear[7650] to
David in Thy faithfulness?[530]
50 Remember, O Lord, the
[a]reproach of Thy
servants;[5650]
[I]How I do bear[5375] in my bosom
the reproach of all the many
peoples,
51 With which [a]Thine enemies have
reproached, O LORD,
With which they have
reproached the footsteps[6119]
of [b]Thine anointed.
52 [a]Blessed[1288] be the LORD
forever!
Amen and Amen.[543]

BOOK 4

God's Eternity and Man's Transitoriness

A Prayer of +Moses the man of God.

90 LORD,[136] Thou hast been our
[Ia]dwelling place in all
generations.[1755]
2 Before [a]the mountains were
born,
[I]Or Thou [b]didst give birth[2342] to
the earth[776] and the
world,[8398]
Even [c]from everlasting[5769] to
everlasting, Thou art God.[410]
3 Thou dost [a]turn man[582] back into
dust,[1793]
And dost say,[559] "Return,[7725] O
children[1121] of men."[120]
4 For [a]a thousand years in Thy
sight
Are like [b]yesterday when it
passes by,[5674]
[I]Or *as* a [c]watch in the night.[3915]

47 [II]Or, *hast Thou . . . men* [b]Ps. 39:5; 62:9; Eccl. 1:2; 2:11
48 [I]Lit., *hand* [II]I.e., the nether world [a]Ps. 22:29; 49:9 [b]Ps. 49:15
49 [a]2Sam. 7:15; Jer. 30:9; Ezek. 34:23
50 [I]Lit., *My bearing in my bosom* [a]Ps. 69:9; 74:18, 22
51 [a]Ps. 74:10, 18, 22 [b]Ps. 89:38
52 [a]Ps. 41:13; 72:19; 106:48
+Deut. 33:1
1 [I]Or, *hiding place;* some ancient mss. read *place of refuge* [a]Deut. 33:27; Ps. 71:3; 91:1; Ezek. 11:16
2 [I]Or, *And* [a]Job 15:7; Prov. 8:25 [b]Gen. 1:1; Ps. 102:25; 104:5 [c]Ps. 93:2; 102:24, 27; Jer. 10:10
3 [a]Gen. 3:19; Job 34:14, 15; Ps. 104:29
4 [I]Or, *And* [a]2Pet. 3:8 [b]Ps. 39:5 [c]Ex. 14:24; Judg. 7:19
5 [I]Or, *flooded* [II]Lit., *become asleep* [III]Or, *passes away* [a]Job 22:16; 27:20 [b]Job 14:12; 20:8; Ps. 76:5 [c]Ps. 103:15; Is. 40:6
6 [I]Or, *passes away* [a]Job 14:2 [b]Ps. 92:7; Matt. 6:30 [c]James 1:11
7 [I]Or, *terrified* [a]Ps. 39:11
8 [a]Ps. 50:21; Jer. 16:17 [b]Ps. 19:12; Eccl. 12:14
9 [I]Or, *whisper* [a]Ps. 78:33
10 [I]Lit., *years* [II]Lit., *in them are* [a]2Kin. 19:35 [b]Eccl. 12:2-7; Jer. 20:18 [c]Job 20:8; Ps. 78:39
11 [I]Or, *knows* [II]Lit., *of Thee* [a]Ps. 76:7 [b]Neh. 5:9

5 Thou [a]hast [I]swept them away
like a flood, they [IIb]fall asleep;
In the morning they are like
[c]grass which [III]sprouts anew.
6 In the morning it [a]flourishes, and
[I]sprouts anew;
Toward evening it [b]fades,[4135]
and [c]withers away.[3001]
7 For we have been [a]consumed[3615]
by Thine anger,[639]
And by Thy wrath[2534] we have
been [I]dismayed.[926]
8 Thou hast [a]placed our
iniquities[5771] before Thee,
Our [b]secret *sins* in the light[3974]
of Thy presence.
9 For [a]all our days[3117] have
declined in Thy fury;[5678]
We have finished[3615] our years
like a [I]sigh.[1899]
10 As for the days of our [I]life,
[II]they contain seventy years,
Or if due to strength, [a]eighty
years,
Yet their pride is *but* [b]labor[5999]
and sorrow;[205]
For soon it is gone[1504] and we
[c]fly away.
11 Who [I]understands the [a]power of
Thine anger,
And Thy fury, according to the
[b]fear[3374] [II]that is due Thee?
12 So [a]teach[3045] us to number our
days,
That we may [Ib]present to Thee
a heart[3824] of wisdom.[2451]
13 Do [a]return, O LORD; [b]how long
will it be?
And [I]be [c]sorry[5162] for Thy
servants.[5650]
14 O [a]satisfy us in the morning with
Thy lovingkindness,[2617]
That we may [b]sing for joy and
be glad all our days.
15 [a]Make us glad [I]according to the
days Thou hast afflicted us,

12 [I]Or, *gain, bring in* [a]Deut. 32:29; Ps. 39:4 [b]Prov. 2:1-6 13 [I]Or, *repent in regard to* [a]Ps. 6:4; 80:14 [b]Ps. 6:3; 74:10 [c]Ex. 32:12; Deut. 32:36; Ps. 106:45; 135:14; Amos 7:3, 6; Jon. 3:9 14 [a]Ps. 36:8; 65:4; 103:5; Jer. 31:14 [b]Ps. 31:7; 85:6 15 [I]Or, *as many days as* [a]Ps. 86:4

And the [b]years we have seen[7200]
[II]evil.[7451]
16 Let Thy [a]work appear[7200] to Thy
servants,
And Thy [b]majesty[1926] [I]to their
children.
17 And let the [a]favor of the Lord
our God[430] be upon us;
And do [I][b]confirm for us the work
of our hands;[3027]
Yes, [I]confirm the work of our
hands.

Security of the One Who Trusts in the Lord

91 He who dwells in the [a]shelter
of the Most High[5945]
Will abide in the [b]shadow of the
Almighty.[7706]
2 I will say[559] to the Lord, "My
[a]refuge and my [b]fortress,
My God,[430] in whom I
[c]trust!"[982]
3 For it is He who delivers[5337] you
from the [a]snare[6341] of the
trapper,
And from the deadly[1942]
[b]pestilence.[1698]
4 He will [a]cover you with His
pinions,
And [b]under His wings you may
seek refuge;[2620]
His [c]faithfulness[571] is a [d]shield
and bulwark.[5507]
5 You [a]will not be afraid[3372] of the
[b]terror[6343] by night,[3915]
Or of the [c]arrow that flies by
day;[3119]
6 Of the [a]pestilence that
[I]stalks in darkness,[652]
Or of the [b]destruction[6986] that
lays waste at noon.
7 A thousand may fall at your side,
And ten thousand at your right
hand;
But [a]it shall not approach[5066]
you.
8 You will only look on with your
eyes,
And [a]see the recompense[8011] of
the wicked.[7563]
9 [I]For you have made[7760] the
Lord, [a]my refuge,
Even the Most High, [b]your
dwelling place.
10 [a]No evil[7451] will befall you,
Nor will any plague[5061] come
near your [I]tent.
11 For He will give [a]His angels[4397]
charge[6680] concerning you,
To guard[8104] you in all your
ways.[1870]
12 They will [a]bear[5375] you up in their
hands,[3709]
Lest you strike[5062] your foot
against a stone.
13 You will [a]tread upon the lion and
cobra,[6620]
The young lion and the
[I]serpent[8577] you will trample
down.
14 "[a]Because he has loved[2836] Me,
therefore I will deliver him;
I will [b]set him *securely* on high,
because he has [c]known[3045]
My name.
15 "He will [a]call[7121] upon Me, and I
will answer him;
I will be with him in [I]trouble;
I will rescue[2502] him, and
[b]honor[3513] him.
16 "With [I]a [a]long[753] life[3117] I will
satisfy him,
And [II][b]let him behold[7200] My
salvation."[3444]

Praise for the Lord*'s Goodness*

A Psalm, a Song for the Sabbath day.

92 It is [a]good[2896] to give thanks[3034]
to the Lord,
And to [b]sing praises[2167] to Thy
name, O Most High;[5945]
2 To [a]declare[5046] Thy
lovingkindness in the
morning,
And Thy [b]faithfulness[530]
[I]by night,[3915]

15 [II]Or, *trouble* [b]Deut. 2:14-16; Ps. 31:10
16 [I]Or, *upon* [a]Deut. 32:4; Ps. 44:1; 77:12; 92:4; Hab. 3:2 [b]1Kin. 8:11; Is. 6:3
17 [I]Or, *give permanence to* [a]Ps. 27:4 [b]Ps. 37:23; Is. 26:12; 1Cor. 3:7

1 [a]Ps. 27:5; 31:20; 32:7 [b]Ps. 17:8; 121:5; Is. 25:4; 32:2
2 [a]Ps. 14:6; 91:9; 94:22; 142:5 [b]Ps. 18:2; 31:3; Jer. 16:19 [c]Ps. 25:2; 56:4
3 [a]Ps. 124:7; Prov. 6:5 [b]1Kin. 8:37; 2Chr. 20:9; Ps. 91:6
4 [a]Is. 51:16 [b]Ps. 17:8; 36:7; 57:1; 63:7 [c]Ps. 40:11 [d]Ps. 35:2
5 [a]Job 5:19-23; Ps. 23:4; 27:1 [b]Song 3:8 [c]Ps. 64:4
6 [I]Or, *walks* [a]2Kin. 19:35; Ps. 91:10 [b]Job 5:22
7 [a]Gen. 7:23; Josh. 14:10
8 [a]Ps. 37:34; 58:10
9 [I]Or, *For Thou O* Lord *art my Refuge; You have made the Most High your dwelling place.* [a]Ps. 91:2 [b]Ps. 90:1
10 [I]Or, *dwelling* [a]Prov. 12:21
11 [a]Ps. 34:7; Matt. 4:6; Luke 4:10, 11; Heb. 1:14
12 [a]Matt. 4:6; Luke 4:11
13 [I]Or, *dragon* [a]Judg. 14:6; Dan. 6:22; Luke 10:19
14 [a]Ps. 145:20 [b]Ps. 59:1 [c]Ps. 9:10
15 [I]Or, *distress* [a]Job 12:4; Ps. 50:15 [b]1Sam. 2:30; John 12:26
16 [I]Lit., *length of days* [II]Or, *cause him to feast his eyes on* [a]Deut. 6:2; Ps. 21:4; Prov. 3:1, 2 [b]Ps. 50:23

1 [a]Ps. 147:1 [b]Ps. 135:3 **2** [I]Lit., *nights* [a]Ps. 59:16 [b]Ps. 89:1

3 [I]With the [a]ten-stringed lute, and
[I]with the [b]harp;
[I]With resounding music [II]upon
the [c]lyre.
4 For Thou, O LORD, hast made
me glad by [I]what Thou
[a]hast done,
I will [b]sing for joy at the
[c]works of Thy hands.[3027]
5 How [a]great are Thy works, O
LORD!
Thy [Ib]thoughts[4284] are very
[c]deep.
6 A [a]senseless man[376] has no
knowledge;
Nor does a [b]stupid man
understand[995] this:
7 That when the wicked[7563]
[a]sprouted up like grass,
And all [b]who did iniquity[205]
flourished,
It *was only* that they might be
[c]destroyed[8045]
forevermore.[5703]
8 But Thou, O LORD, art
[a]on high forever.[5769]
9 For, behold, Thine enemies, O
LORD,
For, behold, [a]Thine enemies will
perish;[6]
All who do iniquity will be
[b]scattered.
10 But Thou hast exalted my
[a]horn like *that of* the wild ox;
I have [I]been [b]anointed[1101] with
fresh oil.[8081]
11 And my eye has [a]looked
exultantly upon [I]my foes,
My ears[241] hear[8085] of the
evildoers[7489] who rise up
against me.
12 The [a]righteous[6662] man will
[I]flourish like the palm
tree,
He will grow like a [b]cedar in
Lebanon.
13 [a]Planted in the house[1004] of the
LORD,
They will flourish [b]in the courts
of our God.[430]
14 They will still [Ia]yield fruit in old
age;[7872]
They shall be [II]full of sap and
very green,
15 To [I]declare that [a]the LORD is
upright;
He is my [b]rock, and there is
[c]no unrighteousness[5766] in
Him.

The Majesty of the LORD

93 [a]The LORD [I]reigns,[4427] He is
[b]clothed with majesty;
The LORD has [c]clothed and
girded Himself with strength;
Indeed, the [d]world[8398] is firmly
established,[3559] it will not be
moved.
2 Thy [a]throne[3678] is
established[3559] from of old;[227]
Thou [b]art from everlasting.[5769]
3 The [a]floods have lifted up,[5375]
O LORD,
The floods have lifted up their
voice;
The floods lift up[5375] their
pounding waves.
4 More than the sounds of many
waters,
Than the mighty[117] breakers of
the sea,
The LORD [a]on high is mighty.[117]
5 Thy [a]testimonies[5713] are fully
confirmed;[539]
[b]Holiness[6944] befits Thy
house,[1004]
O LORD, [I]forevermore.

The LORD Implored to Avenge His People

94 O LORD, God[410] of
[Ia]vengeance;[5360]
God of [I]vengeance, [IIb]shine
forth!
2 [a]Rise up,[5375] O [b]Judge[8199] of the
earth;[776]
Render[7725] recompense [c]to the
proud.

3 [I]Lit., *Upon* [II]Lit., *by means of* [a]1Sam. 10:5; 1Chr. 13:8; Neh. 12:27; Ps. 33:2
4 [I]Lit., *Thy working* [a]Ps. 40:5; 90:16 [b]Ps. 106:47 [c]Ps. 8:6; 111:7; 143:5
5 [I]Or, *purposes* [a]Ps. 40:5; 111:2; Rev. 15:3 [b]Ps. 33:11; 40:5; 139:17 [c]Ps. 36:6; Rom. 11:33
6 [a]Ps. 49:10; 73:22; 94:8
7 [a]Job 12:6; Ps. 90:5 [b]Ps. 94:4 [c]Ps. 37:38
8 [a]Ps. 83:18; 93:4; 113:5
9 [a]Ps. 37:20 [b]Ps. 68:1; 89:10
10 [I]Or, *become moist* [a]Ps. 75:10; 89:17; 112:9 [b]Ps. 23:5; 45:7
11 [I]Or, *those who lie in wait for me* [a]Ps. 54:7; 91:8
12 [I]Lit., *sprout* [a]Num. 24:6; Ps. 1:3; 52:8; 72:7; Jer. 17:8; Hos. 14:5, 6 [b]Ps. 104:16; Ezek. 31:3
13 [a]Ps. 80:15; Is. 60:21 [b]Ps. 100:4; 116:19
14 [I]Or, *thrive in* [II]Lit., *fat and* [a]Prov. 11:30; Is. 37:31; John 15:2; James 3:18
15 [I]Or, *show forth* [a]Job 34:10; Ps. 25:8 [b]Deut. 32:4; Ps. 18:2; 94:22 [c]Rom. 9:14

1 [I]Or, *has assumed kingship* [a]Ps. 96:10; 97:1; 99:1 [b]Ps. 104:1 [c]Ps. 65:6; Is. 51:9 [d]Ps. 96:10
2 [a]Ps. 45:6; Lam. 5:19 [b]Ps. 90:2
3 [a]Ps. 96:11; 98:7, 8
4 [a]Ps. 65:7; 89:6, 9; 92:8
5 [I]Lit., *for length of days* [a]Ps. 19:7 [b]Ps. 29:2; 96:9; 1Cor. 3:17

1 [I]Or, *avenging acts* [II]Or, *has shone forth* [a]Deut. 32:35; Is. 35:4; Nah. 1:2; Rom. 12:19 [b]Ps. 50:2; 80:1
2 [a]Ps. 7:6 [b]Gen. 18:25 [c]Ps. 31:23

3 How long shall the wicked,[7563]
O LORD,
How long shall the [a]wicked
exult?
4 They pour forth *words,* they
[a]speak[1696] arrogantly;
All who do wickedness[205]
[b]vaunt[559] themselves.
5 They [a]crush[1792] Thy people,[5971]
O LORD,
And [b]afflict Thy heritage.[5159]
6 They [a]slay[2026] the widow and the
[I]stranger,[1616]
And murder[7523] the orphans.
7 And [a]they have said,[559] "[I]The
LORD does not see,
Nor does the God[430] of Jacob
pay heed."[995]
8 Pay heed,[995] you [a]senseless
among the people;
And when will you
understand,[7919] [b]stupid ones?
9 He who [a]planted the ear,[241]
[I]does He not hear?[8085]
He who formed[3335] the eye,
[I]does He not see?
10 He who [Ia]chastens[3256] the
nations,[1471] will He not
rebuke,[3198]
Even He who [b]teaches[3925]
man[120] knowledge?[1847]
11 The LORD [a]knows the
thoughts[4284] of man,
[I]That they are a *mere* breath.
12 Blessed[835] is the man[1397] whom
[a]Thou dost chasten,[3256] O
[I]LORD,
And [b]dost teach[3925] out of Thy
law;[8451]
13 That Thou mayest grant him
[a]relief[8252] from the [b]days[3117]
of adversity,[7451]
Until [c]a pit[7845] is dug for the
wicked.
14 For [a]the LORD will not
abandon[5203] His people,
Nor will He [b]forsake[5800] His
inheritance.[5159]
15 For [Ia]judgment[4941] [II]will again
be[7725] righteous;
And all the upright in heart[3820]
[III]will follow it.

3 [a]Job 20:5
4 [a]Ps. 31:18; 75:5 [b]Ps. 10:3; 52:1
5 [a]Is. 3:15 [b]Ps. 79:1
6 [I]Or, *sojourner* [a]Is. 10:2
7 [I]Heb., YAH [a]Job 22:13; Ps. 10:11
8 [a]Ps. 92:6
9 [I]Or, *can* [a]Ex. 4:11; Prov. 20:12
10 [I]Or, *instructs* [a]Ps. 44:2 [b]Job 35:11; Is. 28:26
11 [I]Or, *For* [a]Job 11:11; 1Cor. 3:20
12 [I]Heb., YAH [a]Deut. 8:5; Job 5:17; Ps. 119:71; Prov. 3:11, 12; Heb. 12:5, 6 [b]Ps. 119:171
13 [a]Job 34:29; Hab. 3:16 [b]Ps. 49:5 [c]Ps. 9:15; 55:23
14 [a]1Sam. 12:22; Lam. 3:31; Rom. 11:2 [b]Ps. 37:28
15 [I]I.e., administration of justice [II]Lit., *will return to righteousness* [III]Lit., *will be after it* [a]Ps. 97:2; Is. 42:3; Mic. 7:9
16 [a]Num. 10:35; Is. 28:21; 33:10 [b]Ps. 17:13; 59:2
17 [a]Ps. 124:1, 2
18 [a]Ps. 38:16; 73:2
19 [I]Or, *are many* [a]Is. 57:18; 66:13
20 [I]Or, *tribunal* [II]Or, *trouble, misfortune* [a]Amos 6:3 [b]Ps. 50:16; 58:2
21 [I]Or, *soul* [II]Lit., *innocent blood* [a]Ps. 56:6; 59:3 [b]Ex. 23:7; Ps. 106:38; Prov. 17:15; Matt. 27:4
22 [a]Ps. 9:9; 59:9 [b]Ps. 18:2; 71:7
23 [I]Or, *silence* [a]Ps. 7:16; 140:9, 11 [b]Gen. 19:15

1 [a]Ps. 66:1; 81:1 [b]Ps. 89:26
2 [I]Or, *a song of thanksgiving* [a]Mic. 6:6 [b]Ps. 100:4; 147:7; Jon. 2:9

16 Who will [a]stand up for me against
evildoers?[7489]
Who will take his stand for me
[b]against those who do
wickedness?
17 If [a]the LORD had not been my
help,
My soul[5315] would soon have
dwelt[7931] in *the abode of*
silence.
18 If I should say,[559] "[a]My foot has
slipped,"
Thy lovingkindness,[2617] O LORD,
will hold me up.
19 When my anxious thoughts[8312]
[I]multiply within[7130] me,
Thy [a]consolations[8575] delight my
soul.
20 Can a [Ia]throne[3678] of
destruction[1942] be allied with
Thee,
One [b]which devises[3335]
[II]mischief[5999] by decree?[2706]
21 They [a]band[1413] themselves
together against the [I]life of
the righteous,[6662]
And [b]condemn[7561] [II]the
innocent[5355] to death.[1818]
22 But the LORD has been my
[a]stronghold,
And my God the [b]rock of my
refuge.
23 And He has [a]brought back
their wickedness upon
them,
And will [Ib]destroy them in their
evil;[7451]
The LORD our God will
[I]destroy them.

Praise to the LORD, and Warning against Unbelief

95 O come, let us [a]sing for joy to
the LORD;
Let us shout joyfully[7321] to
[b]the rock of our
salvation.[3468]
2 Let us [a]come before His
presence [b]with
[I]thanksgiving;[8426]

Let us shout joyfully to Him
[c]with [II]psalms.
3 For the LORD is a [a]great
God,410
And a great King4428 [b]above all
gods,430
4 In whose hand3027 are the
[a]depths of the earth;776
The peaks of the mountains are
His also.
5 [I]The sea is His, for it was He
[a]who made6213 it;
And His hands3027 formed3335 the
dry3006 land.
6 Come, let us [a]worship7812 and
bow down;3766
Let us [b]kneel1288 before the
LORD our [c]Maker.6213
7 For He is our God,430
And [a]we are the people5971 of
His [Ib]pasture, and the sheep
of His hand.
[c]Today,3117 [II]if you would
hear8085 His voice,
8 Do not harden your hearts,3824
as at [Ia]Meribah,
As in the day of [IIb]Massah4531
in the wilderness;
9 "When your fathers1 [a]tested5254
Me,
They tried974 Me, though they
had seen7200 My work.
10 "For [a]forty years I loathed *that*
generation,1755
And said559 they are a people
who err8582 in their heart,
And they do not know3045 My
ways.1870
11 "Therefore I [a]swore7650 in My
anger,639
Truly they shall not enter into
My [b]rest."

A Call to Worship the LORD the Righteous Judge

96 [a]Sing7891 to the LORD a [b]new
song;
Sing to the LORD, all the earth.776
2 Sing to the LORD, bless1288 His
name;
[a]Proclaim good tidings of His
salvation3444 from day to
day.3117
3 Tell5608 of [a]His glory3519 among
the nations,1471
His wonderful deeds6381 among
all the peoples.5971
4 For [a]great is the LORD, and
[b]greatly to be praised;1984
He is to be [c]feared3372 [d]above
all gods.430
5 For [a]all the gods of the
peoples5971 are [I]idols,457
But [b]the LORD made6213 the
heavens.8064
6 [a]Splendor1935 and majesty1926
are before Him,
Strength and beauty8597 are in
His sanctuary.4720
7 [I]Ascribe to the LORD, O
[a]families of the peoples,
[Ib]Ascribe to the LORD glory and
strength.
8 [I]Ascribe to the LORD the
[a]glory of His name;
Bring5375 an [IIb]offering,4503 and
come into His courts.
9 [a]Worship7812 the LORD in
[I]holy6944 attire;1927
[b]Tremble before Him, all the
earth.
10 Say559 among the nations, "[a]The
LORD reigns;4427
Indeed, the [a]world8398 is firmly
established,3559 it will not be
moved;
He will [b]judge1777 the peoples
with [I]equity."
11 Let the [a]heavens be glad, and
let the [b]earth rejoice;
Let [c]the sea [I]roar, and [II]all it
contains;

2 [II]Or, *songs* (with instrumental accompaniment) [c]Ps. 81:2; Eph. 5:19; James 5:13
3 [a]Ps. 48:1; 135:5; 145:3 [b]Ps. 96:4; 97:9
4 [a]Ps. 135:6
5 [I]Lit., *Who has the sea* [a]Gen. 1:9, 10; Ps. 146:6; Jon. 1:9
6 [a]Ps. 96:9; 99:5, 9 [b]2Chr. 6:13; Dan. 6:10; Phil. 2:10 [c]Ps. 100:3; 149:2; Is. 17:7; Hos. 8:14
7 [I]Lit., *pasturing* [II]Or, *O that you would obey* [a]Ps. 79:13 [b]Ps. 74:1 [c]Heb. 3:7-11, 15; 4:7
8 [I]Or, *place of strife* [II]Or, *temptation* [a]Ex. 17:2-7; Num. 20:13 [b]Ex. 17:7; Deut. 6:16
9 [a]Num. 14:22; Ps. 78:18; 1Cor. 10:9
10 [a]Acts 7:36; 13:18; Heb. 3:10, 17
11 [a]Num. 14:23, 28-30; Deut. 1:35; Heb. 4:3, 5 [b]Deut. 12:9

1 [a]1Chr. 16:23-33 [b]Ps. 40:3
2 [a]Ps. 71:15
3 [a]Ps. 145:12
4 [a]Ps. 48:1; 145:3 [b]Ps. 18:3 [c]Ps. 89:7 [d]Ps. 95:3
5 [I]Or, *non-existent things* [a]1Chr. 16:26; Jer. 10:11 [b]Ps. 115:15; Is. 42:5
6 [a]Ps. 104:1
7 [I]Lit., *Give* [a]Ps. 22:27 [b]1Chr. 16:28, 29; Ps. 29:1, 2
8 [I]Lit., *Give* [II]Or, *meal offering* [a]Ps. 79:9; 115:1 [b]Ps. 45:12; 72:10
9 [I]Or, *the splendor of holiness* [a]1Chr. 16:29; 2Chr. 20:21; Ps. 29:2; 110:3 [b]Ps. 33:8; 114:7
10 [I]Or, *uprightness* [a]Ps. 93:1; 97:1 [b]Ps. 9:8; 58:11; 67:4; 98:9
11 [I]Or, *thunder* [II]Lit., *its fulness* [a]Ps. 69:34; Is. 49:13 [b]Ps. 97:1 [c]Ps. 98:7

95:7b-11 See note on Num. 13:26.

12 Let the [a]field[7704] exult, and all
that is in it.
Then all the [b]trees of the forest
will sing for joy
13 Before the LORD, [a]for He is
coming;
For He is coming to judge the
earth.
[b]He will judge[8199] the world in
righteousness,[6664]
And the peoples in His
faithfulness.[530]

The LORD's Power and Dominion

97 [a]The LORD [I]reigns;[4427] let the
[b]earth[776] rejoice;
Let the many [IIc]islands be glad.
2 [a]Clouds[6051] and thick
darkness[6205] surround Him;
[b]Righteousness[6664] and
justice[4941] are the foundation
of His throne.[3678]
3 [a]Fire goes before Him,
And [b]burns up His adversaries
round about.
4 His [a]lightnings lit up the
world;[8398]
The earth saw[7200] and
[b]trembled.
5 The mountains [a]melted like wax
at the presence of the LORD,
At the presence of the
[b]Lord[113] of the whole earth.
6 The [a]heavens[8064] declare[5046] His
righteousness,
And [b]all the peoples[5971] have
seen His glory.[3519]
🔑 7 Let all those be ashamed[954] who
serve[5647] [a]graven images,
Who boast[1984] themselves of
[b]idols;[457]
[Ic]Worship[7812] Him, all you
[II]gods.[430]
8 Zion [I]heard[8085] *this* and [a]was
glad,
And the daughters of Judah have
rejoiced
Because of Thy judgments,[4941]
O LORD.
9 For Thou art the LORD [a]Most
High[5945] over all the earth;
Thou art exalted[5927] far
[b]above all [I]gods.
10 [a]Hate[8130] evil,[7451] you who
love[157] the LORD,
Who [b]preserves[8104] the souls[5315]
of His godly ones;[2623]
He [c]delivers[5337] them from the
hand[3027] of the wicked.[7563]
11 [a]Light[216] is sown *like seed* for
the righteous,[6662]
And [b]gladness for the upright in
heart.[3820]
12 Be [a]glad in the LORD, you
righteous ones;
And [b]give thanks[3034] [I]to His
holy[6944] name.[2143]

A Call to Praise the LORD for His Righteousness

A Psalm.

98 O sing[7891] to the LORD a [a]new
song,
For He has done[6213]
[b]wonderful[6381] things,
His [c]right hand and His
[d]holy[6944] arm have [I]gained the
victory for Him.
2 [a]The LORD has made known[3045]
His salvation;[3444]
He has [b]revealed His
[I]righteousness[6666] in the
sight of the nations.[1471]
3 He has [a]remembered[2142] His
lovingkindness[2617] and His
faithfulness[530] to the
house[1004] of Israel;
[b]All the ends of the earth[776] have
seen[7200] the salvation of our
God.[430]

12 [a]Ps. 65:13; Is. 35:1; 55:12, 13 [b]Is. 44:23
13 [a]Ps. 98:9 [b]Rev. 19:11
1 [I]Or, *has assumed Kingship* [II]Or, *coastlands* [a]Ps. 96:10 [b]Ps. 96:11 [c]Is. 42:10, 12
2 [a]Ex. 19:9; Deut. 4:11; 1Kin. 8:12; Ps. 18:11 [b]Ps. 89:14
3 [a]Ps. 18:8; 50:3; Dan. 7:10; Hab. 3:5 [b]Mal. 4:1; Heb. 12:29
4 [a]Ex. 19:16; Ps. 77:18 [b]Ps. 96:9; 104:32
5 [a]Ps. 46:6; Amos 9:5; Mic. 1:4; Nah. 1:5 [b]Josh. 3:11
6 [a]Ps. 19:1; 50:6 [b]Ps. 98:2; Is. 6:3; 40:5; 66:18
7 [I]Or, *All the gods have worshiped Him* [II]Or, *supernatural powers* [a]Ps. 78:58; Is. 42:17; 44:9, 11; Jer. 10:14 [b]Ps. 106:36; Jer. 50:2; Hab. 2:18 [c]Heb. 1:6
8 [I]Or possibly, *hears and is glad* [a]Ps. 48:11; Zeph. 3:14
9 [I]Or, *supernatural powers* [a]Ps. 83:18 [b]Ex. 18:11; Ps. 95:3; 96:4; 135:5
10 [a]Ps. 34:14; Prov. 8:13; Amos 5:15; Rom. 12:9 [b]Ps. 31:23; 145:20; Prov. 2:8 [c]Ps. 37:40; Jer. 15:21; Dan. 3:28
11 [a]Job 22:28; Ps. 112:4; Prov. 4:18 [b]Ps. 64:10
12 [I]Lit., *for the memory of His holiness* [a]Ps. 32:11 [b]Ps. 30:4
1 [I]Or, *accomplished salvation* [a]Ps. 33:3 [b]Ps. 40:5; 96:3 [c]Ex. 15:6 [d]Is. 52:10

2 [I]I.e., faithfulness to His gracious promises [a]Is. 52:10 [b]Is. 62:2; Rom. 3:25 3 [a]Luke 1:54, 72 [b]Ps. 22:27

🔑 **97:7b** See Heb. 1:6.

4 [a]Shout joyfully[7321] to the LORD,
all the earth;
[b]Break forth and sing for joy and
sing praises.[2167]
5 Sing praises to the LORD with
the [a]lyre;
With the lyre and the [Ib]sound
of melody.
6 With [a]trumpets and the sound
of the horn
[b]Shout joyfully before [c]the
King,[4428] the LORD.
7 Let the [a]sea roar and [I]all it
contains,
The [b]world[8398] and those who
dwell in it.
8 Let the [a]rivers clap their
hands;[3709]
Let the [b]mountains sing together
for joy
9 Before the LORD; for He is
coming to [a]judge the earth;
He will judge[8199] the world with
righteousness,[6664]
And [b]the peoples[5971] with
[I]equity.[4339]

Praise to the LORD for His Fidelity to Israel

99 [a]The LORD reigns,[4427] let the
peoples[5971] tremble;
He [Ib]is enthroned *above* the
cherubim,[3742] let the earth[776]
shake!
2 The LORD [I]is [a]great in Zion,
And He is [b]exalted above all the
peoples.
3 Let them praise[3034] Thy [a]great
and awesome[3372] name;
[b]Holy[6918] is [I]He.
4 And the [I]strength of the King[4428]
[a]loves[157] [II]justice;[4941]
Thou hast established
[IIIb]equity;[4339]
Thou hast [c]executed[6213]
[II]justice and
righteousness[6666] in Jacob.
5 [Ia]Exalt the LORD our God,[430]
And [b]worship[7812] at His
footstool;
[c]Holy is He.
6 [a]Moses and Aaron were among
His [b]priests,[3548]
And [c]Samuel was among those
who [d]called[7121] on His name;
They [e]called upon[7121] the LORD,
and He answered them.
7 He [a]spoke[1696] to them in the
pillar of cloud;
They [b]kept[8104] His
testimonies,[5713]
And the statute[2706] that He gave
them.
8 O LORD our God,[410] Thou didst
[a]answer them;
Thou wast a [b]forgiving[5375] God
to them,
And *yet* an [c]avenger[5358] of their
evil deeds.
9 Exalt the LORD our God,
And worship at His holy hill;
For holy[6944] is the LORD our
God.

All Men Exhorted to Praise God

A Psalm for [+]Thanksgiving.

100 [a]Shout joyfully[7321] to the
LORD, all the earth.[776]
2 [a]Serve[5647] the LORD with
gladness;
[b]Come before Him with joyful
singing.
3 Know that [a]the LORD [I]Himself
is God;[430]
It is He who has [b]made[6213] us,
and [II]not we ourselves;
We are [c]His people[5971] and the
sheep of His pasture.
4 Enter His gates [a]with
[I]thanksgiving,[8426]
And His courts with praise.[8416]
Give thanks to Him; [b]bless[1288]
His name.
5 For [a]the LORD is good;[2896]
[b]His lovingkindness[2617] is
everlasting,[5769]

4 [a]Ps. 100:1 [b]Is. 44:23
5 [I]Or, *voice of song* (accompanied by music) [a]Ps. 92:3 [b]Is. 51:3
6 [a]Num. 10:10; 2Chr. 15:14 [b]Ps. 66:1 [c]Ps. 47:7
7 [I]Lit., *its fulness* [a]Ps. 96:11 [b]Ps. 24:1
8 [a]Ps. 93:3; Is. 55:12 [b]Ps. 65:12; 89:12
9 [I]Or, *uprightness* [a]Ps. 96:13 [b]Ps. 96:10

1 [I]Lit., *sits* [a]Ps. 97:1 [b]Ex. 25:22; 1Sam. 4:4; Ps. 80:1
2 [I]Or, *in Zion is great* [a]Ps. 48:1; Is. 12:6 [b]Ps. 97:9; 113:4
3 [I]Or, *it* [a]Deut. 28:58; Ps. 76:1 [b]Lev. 19:2; Josh. 24:19; 1Sam. 2:2; Ps. 22:3; Is. 6:3
4 [I]Or, *Thou hast established in equity the strength of the King who loves justice* [II]Or, *judgment* [III]Or, *uprightness* [a]Ps. 11:7; 33:5 [b]Ps. 17:2; 98:9 [c]Ps. 103:6; 146:7; Jer. 23:5
5 [I]The verb is plural. [a]Ps. 34:3; 107:32; 118:28 [b]Ps. 132:7 [c]Ps. 99:3
6 [a]Jer. 15:1 [b]Ex. 24:6-8; 29:26; 40:23-27; Lev. 8:1-30 [c]Jer. 15:1 [d]1Sam. 7:9; 12:18; Ps. 22:4, 5 [e]Ex. 15:25; 32:30-34
7 [a]Ex. 33:9; Num. 12:5 [b]Ps. 105:28
8 [a]Ps. 106:44 [b]Num. 14:20; Ps. 78:38 [c]Ex. 32:28; Num. 20:12; Ps. 95:11; 107:12

[+]Or, *thank offering*
1 [a]Ps. 95:1; 98:4, 6
2 [a]Deut. 12:11, 12; 28:47 [b]Ps. 95:2
3 [I]Or, *He* [II]Some mss. read *His we are* [a]Deut. 4:35; 1Kin. 18:39; Ps. 46:10 [b]Job 10:3, 8; Ps. 95:6; 119:73 [c]Ps. 74:1, 2; 95:7; Is. 40:11; Ezek. 34:30, 31
4 [I]Or, *a thank offering* [a]Ps. 95:2; 116:17 [b]Ps. 96:2
5 [a]1Chr. 16:34; 2Chr. 5:13; 7:3; Ezra 3:11; Ps. 25:8; 86:5; 106:1; 107:1; 118:1; Jer. 33:11; Nah. 1:7 [b]Ps. 136:1

And His [c]faithfulness[530] to all generations.[1755]

The Psalmist's Profession of Uprightness

A Psalm of David.

101 I will [a]sing[7891] of lovingkindness[2617] and [I]justice,[4941]
To Thee, O LORD, I will sing praises.[2167]
2 I will [Ia]give heed[7919] to the [II]blameless[8549] way.[1870]
When wilt Thou come to me?
I will walk within[7130] my house[1004] in the [IIIb]integrity[8537] of my heart.[3824]
3 I will set no [a]worthless[1100] thing[1697] before my eyes;
I hate the [I]work[6213] of those who [b]fall away;
It shall not fasten its grip on me.
4 A [a]perverse[6141] heart shall depart[5493] from me;
I will know no evil.[7451]
5 Whoever secretly[5643] [a]slanders his neighbor,[7453] him I will [I]destroy;[6789]
No one who has a [b]haughty look and an arrogant heart will I endure.
6 My eyes shall be upon the faithful[539] of the land,[776] that they may dwell with me;
He who walks in a [Ia]blameless way is the one who will minister[8334] to me.
7 He who [a]practices[6213] deceit shall not dwell within my house;
He who speaks[1696] falsehood[8267] [b]shall not [I]maintain his position before me.
8 [a]Every morning I will [Ib]destroy[6789] all the wicked[7563] of the land,
So as to [c]cut off[3772] from the [d]city of the LORD all those who do iniquity.[205]

Prayer of an Afflicted Man for Mercy on Himself and on Zion

A Prayer of the Afflicted, when he is faint, and +pours out his complaint before the LORD.

102 [a]Hear[8085] my prayer,[8605] O LORD!
And let my cry for help [b]come to Thee.
2 [a]Do not hide Thy face from me in the day[3117] of my distress;
[b]Incline Thine ear[241] to me;
In the day when I call[7121] [c]answer me quickly.
3 For my days[3117] [a]have been [I]consumed[3615] in smoke,
And my [b]bones[6106] have been scorched[2787] like a hearth.
4 My heart[3824] [a]has been smitten[5221] like [I]grass and has [b]withered[3001] away,
Indeed, I [c]forget to eat my bread.
5 Because of the [I]loudness of my groaning
My [a]bones [II]cling to my flesh.
6 I [I]resemble a [a]pelican of the wilderness;
I have become like an owl of the waste places.[2723]
7 I [a]lie awake,
I have become like a lonely bird on a housetop.
8 My enemies [a]have reproached me all day long;
Those who [Ib]deride me [II]have used my *name* as a [c]curse.
9 For I have eaten ashes like bread,
And [a]mingled my drink with weeping,
10 [a]Because of Thine indignation[2195] and Thy wrath;[7110]
For Thou hast [b]lifted me up and cast me away.
11 My days are like a [Ia]lengthened shadow;
And [II]I [b]wither away like [III]grass.

---

5 [c]Ps. 119:90
1 [I]Or, *judgment* [a]Ps. 51:14; 89:1; 145:7
2 [I]Or, *behave prudently in* [II]Or, *way of integrity* [III]Or, *blamelessness* [a]1Sam. 18:5, 14 [b]1Kin. 9:4
3 [I]Or, *practice of apostasy* [a]Deut. 15:9 [b]Josh. 23:6; Ps. 40:4
4 [a]Prov. 11:20
5 [I]Or, *silence* [a]Ps. 50:20; Jer. 9:4 [b]Ps. 10:4; 18:27; Prov. 6:17
6 [I]Or, *way of integrity* [a]Ps. 119:1
7 [I]Lit., *be established before my eyes* [a]Ps. 43:1; 52:2 [b]Ps. 52:4, 5
8 [I]Or, *silence* [a]Jer. 21:12 [b]Ps. 75:10 [c]Ps. 118:10-12 [d]Ps. 46:4; 48:2, 8

+Ps. 142:2
1 [a]Ps. 39:12; 61:1 [b]Ex. 2:23; 1Sam. 9:16
2 [a]Ps. 69:17 [b]Ps. 31:2 [c]Ps. 69:17
3 [I]Or, *finished* [a]Ps. 37:20; James 4:14 [b]Job 30:30; Lam. 1:13
4 [I]Lit., *herbage* [a]Ps. 90:5, 6 [b]Ps. 37:2; Is. 40:7 [c]1Sam. 1:7; 2Sam. 12:17; Ezra 10:6; Job 33:20
5 [I]Lit., *voice* [II]Lit., *have cleaved* [a]Job 19:20; Lam. 4:8
6 [I]Lit., *have become similar to* [a]Is. 34:11; Zeph. 2:14
7 [a]Ps. 77:4
8 [I]Or, *made a fool of* [II]Lit., *have sworn by me* [a]Ps. 31:11 [b]Acts 26:11 [c]2Sam. 16:5; Is. 65:15; Jer. 29:22
9 [a]Ps. 42:3; 80:5
10 [a]Ps. 38:3 [b]Job 27:21; 30:22
11 [I]Lit., *stretched out* [II]Or, *as for me, I* [III]Lit., *herbage* [a]Job 14:2; Ps. 109:23 [b]Ps. 102:4

12 But Thou, O LORD, dost
[Ia]abide forever;[5769]
And Thy [IIb]name[2143] to all
generations.[1755]
13 Thou wilt [a]arise *and* have
[b]compassion[7355] on Zion;
For [c]it is time[6256] to be
gracious[2603] to her,
For the [d]appointed time has
come.
14 Surely Thy servants[5650] [I]find
pleasure[7521] in her stones,
And feel pity for her dust.[6083]
15 [I]So the [IIa]nations[1471] will fear[3372]
the name of the LORD,
And [b]all the kings[4428] of the
earth[776] Thy glory.[3519]
16 For the LORD has [a]built up Zion;
He has [b]appeared[7200] in His
glory.
17 He has [a]regarded the prayer of
the [I]destitute,
And has not despised their
prayer.
18 [I]This will be [a]written for the
[b]generation[1755] to come;
[II]That [c]a people[5971] yet to be
created[1254] [III]may praise[1984]
[IV]the LORD.
19 For He [a]looked down from His
holy height;[6944]
[b]From heaven[8064] the LORD
gazed [I]upon the earth,
20 To hear the [a]groaning of the
prisoner;
To [b]set free [I]those who were
doomed[1121] to death;[8546]
21 That *men* may [a]tell[5608] of the
name of the LORD in Zion,
And His praise[8416] in Jerusalem;
22 When [a]the peoples are gathered
together,[6908]
And the kingdoms,[4467] to
serve[5647] the LORD.
23 He has weakened my strength
in the way;[1870]
He has [a]shortened my days.
24 I say,[559] "O my God,[410]
[a]do not take me away in the
[I]midst of my days,
Thy [b]years are throughout all
generations.
25 "Of old Thou didst [a]found[3245] the
earth;
And the [b]heavens[8064] are the
work of Thy hands.[3027]
26 "[I]Even they will [a]perish,[6] but
Thou dost endure;
And all of them will wear out
like a garment;
Like clothing Thou wilt change
them, and they will be
changed.
27 "But Thou art [Ia]the same,
And Thy years will not come to
an end.[8552]
28 "The [a]children[1121] of Thy
servants will continue,[7931]
And their [Ib]descendants[2233] will
be established[3559] before
Thee."

Praise for the LORD's Mercies

A Psalm of David.

103

[a]Bless[1288] the LORD, O my
soul;[5315]
And all that is within[7130] me, *bless*
His [b]holy[6944] name.
2 Bless the LORD, O my soul,
And [a]forget none of His benefits;
3 Who [a]pardons[5545] all your
iniquities;[5771]
Who [b]heals all your diseases;[8463]
4 Who [a]redeems[1350] your life[2416]
from the pit;[7845]
Who [b]crowns you with
lovingkindness and
compassion;[7356]
5 Who [a]satisfies your [I]years with
good[2896] things,
So that your youth is [b]renewed
like the eagle.
6 The LORD [a]performs[6213]
[I]righteous[6666] deeds,

102:12 [I]Or, *sit enthroned* [II]Lit., *memorial* [a]Ps. 9:7; 10:16; Lam. 5:19 [b]Ex. 3:15; Ps. 135:13
13 [a]Ps. 12:5; 44:26 [b]Is. 60:10; Zech. 1:12 [c]Ps. 119:126 [d]Ps. 75:2; Dan. 8:19
14 [I]Or, *have found*
15 [I]Or, *And* [II]Or, *Gentiles, heathen* [a]1Kin. 8:43; Ps. 67:7 [b]Ps. 138:4
16 [a]Ps. 147:2 [b]Is. 60:1, 2
17 [I]Or, *naked* [a]Neh. 1:6; Ps. 22:24
18 [I]Or, *Let this be written* [II]Or, *And* [III]Or, *will* [IV]Heb., YAH [a]Deut. 31:19; Rom. 15:4; 1Cor. 10:11 [b]Ps. 22:30; 48:13 [c]Ps. 22:31; 78:6f.
19 [I]Lit., *toward* [a]Deut. 26:15; Ps. 14:2; 53:2 [b]Ps. 33:13
20 [I]Lit., *the sons of death* [a]Ps. 79:11 [b]Ps. 146:7
21 [a]Ps. 22:22
22 [a]Ps. 22:27; 86:9; Is. 49:22, 23; 60:3; Zech. 8:20-23
23 [a]Ps. 39:5
24 [I]Lit., *half* [a]Ps. 39:13; Is. 38:10 [b]Job 36:26; Ps. 90:2; 102:12; Hab. 1:12
25 [a]Gen. 1:1; Neh. 9:6; Heb. 1:10-12 [b]Ps. 96:5
26 [I]Lit., *They themselves* [a]Is. 34:4; 51:6; Matt. 24:35; 2Pet. 3:10; Rev. 20:11
27 [I]Lit., *He* [a]Is. 41:4; 43:10; Mal. 3:6; James 1:17
28 [I]Lit., *seed* [a]Ps. 69:36 [b]Ps. 89:4

103:1 [a]Ps. 104:1, 35 [b]Ps. 33:21; 105:3; 145:21; Ezek. 36:21; 39:7
2 [a]Deut. 6:12; 8:11 **3** [a]Ex. 34:7; Ps. 86:5; 130:8; Is. 43:25 [b]Ex. 15:26; Ps. 30:2; Jer. 30:17 **4** [a]Ps. 49:15 [b]Ps. 5:12 **5** [I]Or, *desire* [a]Ps. 107:9; 145:16 [b]Is. 40:31 **6** [I]Or, *deeds of vindication* [a]Ps. 99:4; 146:7

102:25-27 See note on Gen. 8:21,22. Also, compare Heb. 1:10-12.

And judgments[4941] for all who
are [b]oppressed.
7 He [a]made known[3045] His
ways[1870] to Moses,
His [b]acts to the sons[1121] of
Israel.
8 The LORD is [a]compassionate and
gracious,[2587]
[b]Slow[750] to anger[639] and
abounding in
lovingkindness.[2617]
9 He [a]will not always[5331] strive[7378]
with us;
Nor will He [b]keep *His anger*
forever.[5769]
10 He has [a]not dealt with[6213] us
according to our sins,[2399]
Nor rewarded[1580] us according
to our iniquities.
11 For as high [a]as the heavens[8064]
are above the earth,[776]
So great is His lovingkindness
toward those who [I]fear[3373]
Him.
12 As far as the east is from the
west,
So far has He [a]removed our
transgressions from us.
13 Just [a]as a father[1] has compassion
on *his* children,
So the LORD has compassion
on[7355] those who [I]fear Him.
14 For [a]He Himself knows [I]our
frame;[3336]
He [b]is mindful[2142] that we are
but [c]dust.[6083]
15 As for man,[582] his days[3117] are
[a]like grass;
As a [b]flower of the field,[7704] so
he flourishes.
16 When the [a]wind[7307] has passed
over[5674] it, it is no more;
And its [b]place acknowledges it
no longer.
17 But the [a]lovingkindness of the
LORD is from everlasting[5769]
to everlasting on those who
[I]fear Him,
And His [II]righteousness [b]to
children's children,
18 To [a]those who keep[8104] His
covenant,[1285]
And who remember[2142] His
precepts[6490] to do[6213] them.
19 The LORD has established[3559]
His [a]throne[3678] in the
heavens;[8064]
And His [I][b]sovereignty[4438]
rules[4910] over [II]all.
20 Bless the LORD, you [a]His
angels,[4397]
[b]Mighty in strength, who
[c]perform His word,[1697]
[d]Obeying the voice of His
word![1697]
21 Bless the LORD, all you
[a]His hosts,[6635]
You [b]who serve[8334] Him, doing
His will.[7522]
22 Bless the LORD, [a]all you works
of His,
In all places of His dominion;[4475]
Bless the LORD, O my soul!

The LORD's Care over All His Works

104 [a]Bless[1288] the LORD, O my
soul![5315]
O LORD my God,[430] Thou art
very great;
Thou art [b]clothed with
splendor[1935] and majesty,[1926]
2 Covering Thyself with
[a]light[216] as with a cloak,
[b]Stretching out heaven[8064] like
a *tent* curtain.
3 [I]He [a]lays[7760] the beams of His
upper chambers in the
waters;
[I]He makes[7760] the [b]clouds His
chariot;
[I]He walks upon the [c]wings of the
wind;[7307]
4 [I]He makes[6213] [II][a]the winds[7307]
His messengers,[4397]
[III]Flaming [b]fire His ministers.[8334]
5 He [a]established the earth[776]
upon its foundations,
So that it will not [I]totter
forever[5769] and ever.[5703]

6 [b]Ps. 12:5
7 [a]Ex. 33:13; Ps. 99:7; 147:19 [b]Ps. 78:11; 106:22
8 [a]Ex. 34:6; Num. 14:18; Neh. 9:17; Ps. 86:15; Jon. 4:2; James 5:11 [b]Ps. 145:8; Joel 2:13; Nah. 1:3
9 [a]Ps. 30:5; Is. 57:16 [b]Jer. 3:5, 12; Mic. 7:18
10 [a]Ezra 9:13; Lam. 3:22
11 [I]Or, *revere* [a]Ps. 36:5; 57:10
12 [a]2Sam. 12:13; Is. 38:17; 43:25; Zech. 3:9; Heb. 9:26
13 [I]Or, *revere* [a]Mal. 3:17
14 [I]I.e., what we are made of [a]Is. 29:16 [b]Ps. 78:39 [c]Gen. 3:19; Eccl. 12:7
15 [a]Ps. 90:5; Is. 40:6; 1Pet. 1:24 [b]Job 14:2; James 1:10, 11
16 [a]Is. 40:7 [b]Job 7:10; 8:18; 20:9
17 [I]Or, *revere* [II]I.e., faithfulness to His gracious promises [a]Ps. 25:6 [b]Ex. 20:6; Deut. 5:10; Ps. 105:8
18 [a]Deut. 7:9; Ps. 25:10
19 [I]Or, *kingdom* [II]I.e., the universe [a]Ps. 11:4 [b]Ps. 47:2, 8; Dan. 4:17, 25
20 [a]Ps. 148:2 [b]Ps. 29:1; 78:25 [c]Matt. 6:10 [d]Ps. 91:11; Heb. 1:14
21 [a]1Kin. 22:19; Neh. 9:6; Ps. 148:2; Luke 2:13 [b]Ps. 104:4
22 [a]Ps. 145:10

1 [a]Ps. 103:22 [b]Ps. 93:1
2 [a]Dan. 7:9 [b]Is. 40:22
3 [I]Lit., *The one who* [a]Amos 9:6 [b]Is. 19:1 [c]Ps. 18:10
4 [I]Lit., *Who* [II]Or, *His angels, spirits* [III]Or, *His ministers flames of fire* [a]Ps. 148:8; Heb. 1:7 [b]2Kin. 2:11; 6:17

5 [I]Or, *move out of place* [a]Job 38:4; Ps. 24:2

6 Thou [a]didst cover[3680] it with the
deep as with a garment;
The waters were standing above
the mountains.
7 At Thy [a]rebuke[1606] they fled;
At the [b]sound of Thy thunder
they hurried away.
8 The mountains rose; the valleys
sank down
To the [a]place which Thou didst
establish[3245] for them.
9 Thou didst set[7760] a [a]boundary
that they may not pass
over;[5674]
That they may not return[7725] to
cover[3680] the earth.
10 [I]He sends forth [a]springs in the
valleys;
They flow between the
mountains;
11 They [a]give drink to every
beast[2416] of the field;[7704]
The [b]wild donkeys quench[7665]
their thirst.
12 [I]Beside them the birds of the
heavens[8064] [a]dwell;[7931]
They [II]lift up *their* voices among
the branches.
13 [I]He [a]waters the mountains from
His upper chambers;
[b]The earth is satisfied with the
fruit of His works.
14 [I]He causes the [a]grass to grow
for the [II]cattle,
And [b]vegetation for the
[III]labor[5656] of man,[120]
So that [IV]he may bring forth
[V]food [c]from the earth,
15 And [a]wine which makes man's[582]
heart[3824] glad,
[b]So that he may make *his* face
glisten with oil,[8081]
And [I]food which [c]sustains man's
heart.
16 The trees of the LORD [I]drink
their fill,
The cedars of Lebanon which
He planted,
17 Where the [a]birds build their
nests,
And the [b]stork, whose home[1004]
is the [I]fir trees.
18 The high mountains are for the
[a]wild goats;
The [b]cliffs are a refuge for the
[c]rock badgers.[8227]
19 He made[6213] the moon [a]for the
seasons;[4150]
The [b]sun knows the place of its
setting.
20 Thou [a]dost appoint darkness[2822]
and it becomes night,[3915]
In which all the [b]beasts[2416] of
the forest [I]prowl about.
21 The [a]young lions roar after their
prey,
[I]And [b]seek their food from
God.[410]
22 *When* the sun rises they
withdraw,[622]
And lie down in their [a]dens.
23 Man goes forth to [a]his work
And to his labor until evening.
24 O LORD, how [a]many are Thy
works!
[I]In [b]wisdom[2451] Thou hast
made[6213] them all;
The [c]earth is full of Thy
[II]possessions.
25 [I]There is the [a]sea, great and
[II]broad,
In which are swarms without
number,
Animals both small and great.
26 There the [a]ships move along,
And [Ib]Leviathan, which Thou
hast formed[3335] to sport in it.
27 They all [a]wait for Thee,
To [b]give them their food in
[I]due season.[6256]
28 Thou dost give to them, they
gather[3950] *it* up;
Thou [a]dost open Thy hand,[3027]
they are satisfied with
good.[2896]
29 Thou [a]dost hide Thy face, they
are dismayed;[926]
Thou [b]dost take away their
[I]spirit,[7307] they expire,[1478]
And [c]return[7725] to their dust.[6083]
30 Thou dost send forth Thy

6 [a]Gen. 1:2
7 [a]Ps. 18:15; 106:9; Is. 50:2 [b]Ps. 29:3; :18
8 [a]Ps. 33:7
9 [a]Job 38:10, 11; Jer. 5:22
10 [I]Lit., *The one who sends* [a]Ps. 107:35; Is. 41:18
11 [a]Ps. 104:13 [b]Job 39:5
12 [I]Or, *Over, Above* [II]Lit., *give forth* [a]Matt. 8:20
13 [I]Lit., *Who* [a]Ps. 65:9; 147:8 [b]Jer. 10:13
14 [I]Lit., *Who* [II]Or, *beasts* [III]Or, *cultivation by* or *service of* [IV]Or, *He* [V]Lit., *bread* [a]Job 38:27; Ps. 147:8 [b]Gen. 1:29 [c]Job 28:5
15 [I]Lit., *bread* [a]Judg. 9:13; Prov. 31:6; Eccl. 10:19 [b]Ps. 23:5; 92:10; 141:5; Luke 7:46 [c]Gen. 18:5; Judg. 19:5, 8
16 [I]Lit., *are satisfied*
17 [I]Or, *cypress* [a]Ps. 104:12 [b]Lev. 11:19
18 [a]Job 39:1 [b]Prov. 30:26 [c]Lev. 11:5
19 [a]Gen. 1:14 [b]Ps. 19:6
20 [I]Lit., *creep* [a]Ps. 74:16; Is. 45:7 [b]Ps. 50:10; Is. 56:9; Mic. 5:8
21 [I]Lit., *And to seek* [a]Job 38:39 [b]Ps. 145:15; Joel 1:20
22 [a]Job 37:8
23 [a]Gen. 3:19
24 [I]Or, *With* [II]Or, *creatures* [a]Ps. 40:5 [b]Ps. 136:5; Prov. 3:19; Jer. 10:12; 51:15 [c]Ps. 65:9
25 [I]Or, *This* [II]Or, *broad of dimensions* (lit., *hands*) [a]Ps. 8:8; 69:34
26 [I]Or, *a sea monster* [a]Ps. 107:23; Ezek. 27:9 [b]Job 41:1; Ps. 74:14; Is. 27:1
27 [I]Lit., *its appointed time* [a]Ps. 145:15 [b]Job 36:31; 38:41; Ps. 136:25; 147:9

28 [a]Ps. 145:16 **29** [I]Or, *breath* [a]Deut. 31:17; Ps. 30:7 [b]Job 34:14, 15; Ps. 146:4; Eccl. 12:7 [c]Gen. 3:19; Job 10:9; Ps. 90:3

[Ia]Spirit,7307 they are
created;1254
And Thou dost renew the face
of the ground.
31 Let the [a]glory3519 of the LORD
endure forever;
Let the LORD [b]be glad in His
works;
32 [I]He [a]looks at the earth, and it
[b]trembles;7460
He [c]touches5060 the mountains,
and they smoke.6225
33 [I]I will sing7891 to the LORD
[IIa]as long as I live;2416
[I]I will [b]sing praise2167 to my God
[III]while I have my being.
34 Let my [a]meditation7879 be
pleasing6148 to Him;
As for me, I shall [b]be glad in
the LORD.
35 Let sinners2400 be [a]consumed8552
from the earth,
And let the [b]wicked7563 be no
more.
[c]Bless the LORD, O my soul.
[Id]Praise1984 [II]the LORD!

The LORD's Wonderful Works in Behalf of Israel

105 Oh [a]give thanks3034 to the
LORD, [b]call7121 upon His
name;
[c]Make known3045 His deeds
among the peoples.5971
2 Sing7891 to Him, [a]sing praises2167
to Him;
[Ib]Speak7878 of all His
[II]wonders.6381
3 [I]Glory1984 in His holy6944 name;
Let the [a]heart3820 of those who
seek the LORD be glad.
4 Seek the LORD and [a]His
strength;
[b]Seek His face continually.8548
5 Remember2142 His [Ia]wonders6381
which He has done,6213
His marvels,4159 and the
[b]judgments4941 [II]uttered by
His mouth,6310
6 O seed2233 of [a]Abraham, His
servant,5650
O sons1121 of [b]Jacob, His
[c]chosen ones!
7 He is the LORD our God;430
His [a]judgments are in all the
earth.776
8 He has [a]remembered2142 His
covenant1285 forever,5769
The word1697 which He
commanded to a [b]thousand
generations,1755
9 *The* [a]*covenant* which He
made3772 with Abraham,
And His [b]oath7621 to Isaac.
10 Then He [a]confirmed it to Jacob
for a statute,2706
To Israel as an everlasting5769
covenant,
11 Saying, "[a]To you I will give the
land776 of Canaan
As the [Ib]portion of your
inheritance,"5159
12 When they were only a
[a]few men in number,
Very few, and [b]strangers1481 in
it.
13 And they wandered about from
nation to nation,1471
From *one* kingdom4467 to another
people.
14 He [a]permitted no man120 to
oppress them,
And He [b]reproved3198 kings4428
for their sakes:
15 "[a]Do not touch5060 My anointed
ones,4899
And do7489 My prophets5030 no
harm."7489
16 And He [a]called7121 for a famine
upon the land;
He [b]broke the whole staff4294 of
bread.
17 He [a]sent a man376 before them,
Joseph, *who* was [b]sold as a
slave.
18 They afflicted his [a]feet with
fetters,
[I]He himself was laid in irons;
19 Until the time6256 that his
[a]word came to pass,

30 [I]Or, *breath* [a]Job 33:4; Ezek. 37:9
31 [a]Ps. 86:12; 111:10 [b]Gen. 1:31
32 [I]Lit., *The one who* [a]Judg. 5:5; Ps. 97:4, 5; 114:7 [b]Hab. 3:10 [c]Ex. 19:18; Ps. 144:5
33 [I]Or, *Let me sing* [II]Lit., *in my lifetime* [III]Lit., *while I still am* [a]Ps. 63:4 [b]Ps. 146:2
34 [a]Ps. 19:14 [b]Ps. 9:2
35 [I]Or, *Hallelujah!* [II]Heb., YAH [a]Ps. 59:13 [b]Ps. 37:10 [c]Ps. 104:1 [d]Ps. 105:45; 106:48

1 [a]1Chr. 16:8-22, 34; Ps. 106:1; Is. 12:4 [b]Ps. 99:6 [c]Ps. 145:12
2 [I]Or, *Meditate on* [II]I.e., wonderful acts [a]Ps. 96:1; 98:5 [b]Ps. 77:12; 119:27; 145:5
3 [I]Or, *Boast* [a]Ps. 33:21
4 [a]Ps. 63:2 [b]Ps. 27:8
5 [I]I.e., wonderful acts [II]Lit., *of His mouth* [a]Ps. 40:5; :11 [b]Ps. 119:13
6 [a]Ps. 105:42 [b]Ps. 135:4 [c]1Chr. 16:13; Ps. 106:5; 135:4
7 [a]Is. 26:9
8 [a]Ps. 105:42; 106:45; Luke 1:72 [b]Deut. 7:9
9 [a]Gen. 12:7; 17:2, 8; 22:16-18; Gal. 3:17 [b]Gen. 26:3
10 [a]Gen. 28:13-15
11 [I]Lit., *measuring line* [a]Gen. 13:15; 15:18 [b]Josh. 23:4; Ps. 78:55
12 [a]Gen. 34:30; Deut. 7:7 [b]Gen. 23:4; Heb. 11:9
14 [a]Gen. 20:7; 35:5 [b]Gen. 12:17; 20:3, 7
15 [a]Gen. 26:11
16 [a]Gen. 41:54 [b]Lev. 26:26; Is. 3:1; Ezek. 4:16
17 [a]Gen. 45:5 [b]Gen. 37:28, 36; Acts 7:9

18 [I]Lit., *His soul came into* [a]Gen. 39:20; 40:15
19 [a]Gen. 40:20, 21

The word[565] of the LORD
[Ib]tested[6884] him.
20 The [a]king[4428] sent and released
him,
The ruler[4910] of peoples, and set
him free.
21 He [a]made[7760] him lord[113] of his
house,[1004]
And ruler over all his
possessions,
22 To [I]imprison his princes[8269]
[IIa]at will,[5315]
That he might teach his
elders[2205] wisdom.[2449]
23 [a]Israel also came into Egypt;
Thus Jacob [b]sojourned[1481] in the
land of Ham.
24 And He [a]caused His people to
be very fruitful,
And made them stronger than
their adversaries.
25 He [a]turned[2015] their heart to
hate[8130] His people,
To [b]deal craftily with His
servants.[5650]
26 He [a]sent Moses His servant,
And [b]Aaron whom He had
chosen.[977]
27 They [Ia]performed[7760] His
wondrous acts among
them,
And miracles in the land of
Ham.
28 He [a]sent darkness[2822] and made
it dark;[2821]
And they did not [b]rebel[4784]
against His words.
29 He [a]turned their waters into
blood,[1818]
And caused their fish[1710] to
die.[4191]
30 Their land swarmed with
[a]frogs
Even in the [b]chambers of their
kings.
31 He spoke,[559] and there came a
[a]swarm of flies
And [b]gnats in all their
territory.
32 He [I]gave them [a]hail for rain,
And flaming fire in their
land.
33 He [a]struck down[5221] their vines
also and their fig trees,
And shattered the trees of their
territory.
34 He spoke, and [a]locusts came,
And young locusts, even without
number,
35 And ate up all vegetation in their
land,
And ate up the fruit of their
ground.[127]
36 He also [a]struck down all the first-
born in their land,
The [b]first fruits[7225] of all their
vigor.
37 Then He brought them out with
[a]silver and gold;
And among His tribes[7626] there
was not one who
stumbled.[3782]
38 Egypt was [a]glad when they
departed;
For the [b]dread[6343] of them had
fallen[5307] upon them.
39 He spread a [a]cloud[6051] for a
[I]covering,
And [b]fire to illumine[216] by
night.[3915]
40 [I]They [a]asked,[7592] and He
brought [b]quail,
And satisfied them with the
[IIc]bread of heaven.[8064]
41 He opened the [I]rock, and
[a]water flowed out;
[II]It ran in the dry places *like* a
river.
42 For He [a]remembered His holy
word[1697]
With Abraham His servant;
43 And He brought forth His people
with joy,
His chosen ones with a joyful
[a]shout.
44 He [a]gave them also the lands[776]
of the [I]nations,[1471]
That they [b]might take
possession[3423] of *the fruit of*
the peoples'[3816] labor,[5999]
45 So that they might [a]keep[8104] His
statutes,[2706]
And observe[5341] His laws,[8451]
[I]Praise[1984] [II]the LORD!

19 [I]Or, *refined* [b]Ps. 66:10
20 [a]Gen. 41:14
21 [a]Gen. 41:40-44
22 [I]Lit., *bind* [II]Lit., *at his* [a]Gen. 41:44
23 [a]Gen. 46:6; Acts 7:15 [b]Acts 13:17
24 [a]Ex. 1:7, 9
25 [a]Ex. 1:8; 4:21 [b]Ex. 1:10; Acts 7:19
26 [a]Ex. 3:10; 4:12 [b]Ex. 4:14; Num. 16:5; 17:5-8
27 [I]Lit., *set the words of His signs* [a]Ps. 78:43-51; 105:27-36
28 [a]Ex. 10:21, 22 [b]Ps. 99:7
29 [a]Ex. 7:20, 21
30 [a]Ex. 8:6 [b]Ex. 8:3
31 [a]Ex. 8:21 [b]Ex. 8:16, 17
32 [I]Or, *made their rain hail* [a]Ex. 9:23-25
33 [a]Ps. 78:47
34 [a]Ex. 10:12-15
36 [a]Ex. 12:29; 13:15; Ps. 135:8; 136:10 [b]Gen. 49:3
37 [a]Ex. 12:35, 36
38 [a]Ex. 12:33 [b]Ex. 15:16
39 [I]Or, *curtain* [a]Ex. 13:21; Neh. 9:12; Ps. 78:14; Is. 4:5 [b]Ex. 40:38
40 [I]Or, *One* [II]Or, *food* [a]Ex. 16:12; Ps. 78:18 [b]Ex. 16:13; Num. 11:31; Ps. 78:27 [c]Ex. 16:15; Neh. 9:15; Ps. 78:24; John 6:31
41 [I]Or, *boulder* [II]Lit., *They went* [a]Ex. 17:6; Num. 20:11; Ps. 78:15; 114:8; Is. 48:21; 1Cor. 10:4
42 [a]Gen. 15:13, 14; Ps. 105:8
43 [a]Ex. 15:1; Ps. 106:12
44 [I]Or, *Gentiles* [a]Josh. 11:16-23; 13:7; Ps. 78:55 [b]Deut. 6:10, 11
45 [I]Or, *Hallelujah!* [II]Heb., *YAH* [a]Deut. 4:1, 40

Israel's Rebelliousness and the LORD's Deliverances

106 [I]Praise[1984] [II]the LORD!
Oh [a]give thanks[3034] to the LORD, for He [b]is good;[2896]
For [c]His lovingkindness[2617] is everlasting.[5769]
2 Who can speak[4448] of the [a]mighty deeds of the LORD,
Or can show forth[8085] all His praise?[8416]
3 How blessed[835] are those who keep[8104] [I]justice,[4941]
[II]Who [a]practice[6213] righteousness[6666] at all times![6256]
4 Remember[2142] me, O LORD, in *Thy* [a]favor[7522] [I]toward Thy people;[5971]
Visit[6485] me with Thy salvation,[3444]
5 That I may see the [a]prosperity of Thy chosen ones,
That I may [b]rejoice in the gladness of Thy nation,[1471]
That I may [c]glory[1984] with Thine [I]inheritance.
6 [a]We have sinned[2398] [I][b]like our fathers,[1]
We have committed iniquity,[5753] we have behaved[6213] wickedly.[7561]
7 Our fathers in Egypt did not understand[7919] Thy [I]wonders;[6381]
They [a]did not remember[2142] [II]Thine abundant kindnesses,[2617]
But [b]rebelled[4784] by the sea, at the [III]Red Sea.
8 Nevertheless He saved[3467] them [a]for the sake of His name,
That He might [b]make His power known.[3045]
9 Thus He [a]rebuked[1605] the [I]Red Sea and it [b]dried up;[2717]
And He [c]led them through the deeps, as through the wilderness.
10 So He [a]saved them from the [I]hand[3027] of the one who hated *them,*
And [b]redeemed[1350] them from the [I]hand of the enemy.
11 And [a]the waters covered[3680] their adversaries;
Not one of them was left.[3498]
12 Then they [a]believed[539] His words;[1697]
They [b]sang His praise.
13 They quickly [a]forgot His works;
They [b]did not wait for His counsel,[6098]
14 But [a]craved[183] intensely in the wilderness,
And [I][b]tempted[5254] God[410] in the desert.
15 So He [a]gave them their request,[7596]
But [b]sent a [I]wasting disease among them.
16 When they became [a]envious[7065] of Moses in the camp,
And of Aaron, the holy one[6918] of the LORD,
17 The [a]earth[776] opened and swallowed up[1104] Dathan,
And engulfed the [I]company[5712] of Abiram.
18 And a [a]fire blazed up in their [I]company;
The flame consumed the wicked.[7563]
19 They [a]made[6213] a calf in Horeb,
And worshiped[7812] a molten[4541] image.[6754]
20 Thus they [a]exchanged their glory[3519]
For the image[8403] of an ox that eats grass.
21 They [a]forgot God their Savior,[3467]
Who had done [b]great things in Egypt,
22 [I][a]Wonders[6381] in the land[776] of Ham,
And awesome things[3372] by the [II]Red Sea.

1 [I]Or, *Hallelujah!* [II]Heb., *YAH* [a]Ps. 105:1; 107:1; 118:1; 136:1; Jer. 33:11 [b]2Chr. 5:13; 7:3; Ezra 3:11; Ps. 100:5 [c]1Chr. 16:34, 41
2 [a]Ps. 145:4, 12; 150:2
3 [I]Or, *judgment* [II]Many Heb. mss. read *The one who performs* [a]Ps. 15:2
4 [I]Lit., *of* [a]Ps. 44:3; 119:132
5 [I]I.e., people [a]Ps. 1:3 [b]Ps. 118:15 [c]Ps. 105:3
6 [I]Lit., *with* [a]1Kin. 8:47; Ezra 9:7; Neh. 1:7; Jer. 3:25; Dan. 9:5 [b]2Chr. 30:7; Neh. 9:2; Ps. 78:8, 57; Zech. 1:4
7 [I]I.e., wonderful acts [II]Lit., *the multitude of Thy lovingkindnesses* [III]Lit., *Sea of Reeds* [a]Judg. 3:7; Ps. 78:11, 42 [b]Ex. 14:11, 12; Ps. 78:17
8 [a]Ezek. 20:9 [b]Ex. 9:16
9 [I]Lit., *Sea of Reeds* [a]Ps. 18:15; 78:13; Is. 50:2; Nah. 1:4 [b]Ex. 14:21; Is. 51:10 [c]Is. 63:11-13
10 [I]Or, *power* [a]Ex. 14:30 [b]Ps. 78:42; 107:2
11 [a]Ex. 14:27, 28; 15:5; Ps. 78:53
12 [a]Ex. 14:31 [b]Ex. 15:1-21; Ps. 105:43
13 [a]Ex. 15:24; 16:2; 17:2 [b]Ps. 107:11
14 [I]Or, *put God to the test* [a]Num. 11:4; Ps. 78:18; 1Cor. 10:6 [b]Ex. 17:2; 1Cor. 10:9
15 [I]Or, *leanness into their soul* [a]Num. 11:31; Ps. 78:29 [b]Is. 10:16
16 [a]Num. 16:1-3
17 [I]Or, *assembly, band* [a]Num. 16:32; Deut. 11:6
18 [I]Or, *assembly, band* [a]Num. 16:35
19 [a]Ex. 32:4; Deut. 9:8; Acts 7:41
20 [a]Jer. 2:11; Rom. 1:23
21 [a]Ps. 78:11; 106:7, 13 [b]Deut. 10:21
22 [I]I.e., Wonderful acts [II]Lit., *Sea of Reeds* [a]Ps. 105:27

23 Therefore [a]He said[559] that He
would destroy[8045] them,
Had not [b]Moses His chosen one
stood in the breach before
Him,
To turn away[7725] His wrath[2534]
from destroying[7843] *them*.
24 Then they [a]despised[3988] the
[b]pleasant land;
They [c]did not believe in His
word,[1697]
25 But [a]grumbled in their tents;[168]
They did not listen[8085] to the
voice of the LORD.
26 Therefore He [I][a]swore[5375] to
them,
That He would cast them
down[5307] in the wilderness,
27 And that He would [a]cast their
seed[2233] among the
nations,[1471]
And [b]scatter them in the
lands.[776]
28 They [a]joined themselves also to
[I]Baal-peor,
And ate [b]sacrifices[2077] offered to
the dead.[4191]
29 Thus they [a]provoked *Him* to
anger[3707] with their deeds;
And the plague broke out among
them.
30 Then Phinehas [a]stood up and
interposed;[6419]
And so the [b]plague was
stayed.
31 And it was [a]reckoned[2803] to him
for righteousness,
To all generations[1755]
forever.[5769]
32 They also [a]provoked[7107] *Him* to
wrath at the waters of
[I]Meribah,
So that it [b]went hard[3415] with
Moses on their account;
33 Because they [a]were rebellious
against [I]His Spirit,[7307]
He spoke rashly[981] with his
lips.[8413]
34 They [a]did not destroy the
peoples,[5971]
As [b]the LORD commanded[559]
them,
35 But [a]they mingled[6148] with the
nations,[1471]
And learned[3925] their
[I]practices,
36 And [a]served their idols,[6091]
[b]Which became a snare[4170] to
them.
37 They even [a]sacrificed[2076] their
sons[1121] and their daughters
to the [b]demons,[7700]
38 And shed[8210] [a]innocent[5355]
blood,[1818]
The blood of their [b]sons and their
daughters,
Whom they sacrificed to the
idols of Canaan;
And the land was [c]polluted[2610]
with the blood.
39 Thus they became [a]unclean[2930]
in their [I]practices,
And [b]played the harlot[2181] in
their deeds.
40 Therefore the [a]anger[639] of the
LORD was kindled[2734] against
His people,
And He [b]abhorred[8581] His
[I][c]inheritance.
41 Then [a]He gave them into the
hand of the [I]nations;
And those who hated them
ruled[4910] over them.
42 Their enemies also [a]oppressed
them,
And they were subdued under
their [I]power.
43 Many times He would
[a]deliver[5337] them;

23 [a]Ex. 32:10; Deut. 9:14; Ezek. 20:8, 13 [b]Ex. 32:11-14; Deut. 9:25-29
24 [a]Num. 14:31 [b]Deut. 8:7; Jer. 3:19; Ezek. 20:6 [c]Deut. 1:32; 9:23; Heb. 3:19
25 [a]Num. 14:2; Deut. 1:27
26 [I]Lit., *lifted up His hand* [a]Num. 14:28-35; Ps. 95:11; Ezek. 20:15; Heb. 3:11
27 [a]Deut. 4:27 [b]Lev. 26:33; Ps. 44:11
28 [I]Or, *Baal of Peor* [a]Num. 25:3; Deut. 4:3; Hos. 9:10 [b]Num. 25:2
29 [a]Num. 25:4
30 [a]Num. 25:7 [b]Num. 25:8
31 [a]Gen. 15:6; Num. 25:11-13
32 [I]Lit., *strife* [a]Num. 20:2-13; Ps. 81:7; 95:9 [b]Num. 20:12
33 [I]Or, *his spirit* [a]Num. 20:3, 10; Ps. 78:40; 107:11
34 [a]Judg. 1:21, 27-36 [b]Deut. 7:2, 16
35 [I]Lit., *works* [a]Judg. 3:5, 6
36 [a]Judg. 2:12 [b]Deut. 7:16
37 [a]Deut. 12:31; 32:17; 2Kin. 16:3;17:17; Ezek. 16:20, 21; 1Cor. 10:20 [b]Lev. 17:7
38 [a]Ps. 94:21 [b]Deut. 18:10 [c]Num. 35:33; Is. 24:5; Jer. 3:1, 2
39 [I]Lit., *works* [a]Lev. 18:24; Ezek. 20:18 [b]Lev. 17:7; Num. 15:39; Judg. 2:17; Hos. 4:12
40 [I]I.e., people [a]Judg. 2:14; Ps. 78:59 [b]Lev. 26:30; Deut. 32:19 [c]Deut. 9:29; 32:9
41 [I]Or, *Gentiles* [a]Judg. 2:14; Neh. 9:27 **42** [I]Lit., *hand* [a]Judg. 4:3; 10:12 **43** [a]Judg. 2:16-18

106:37,38 This passage shows that some lives were actually sacrificed and not merely made to pass between two burning pyres as a purification rite. It was a heathen form of worship to Molech, Milcom, or Chemosh, which the Israelites had borrowed from the Moabites and Ammonites. See Jer. 7:31. It was assumed that the victims were purged from the body's dross and then attained union with the deity.

They, however, were rebellious
in their [b]counsel,
And *so* [c]sank down in their
iniquity.[5771]
44 Nevertheless He looked[7200]
upon their distress,
When He [a]heard[8085] their cry;
45 And He [a]remembered[5162] His
covenant[1285] for their sake,
And [I][b]relented [c]according to the
greatness of His
lovingkindness.
46 He also made them [a]*objects* of
compassion[7356]
In the presence of all their
captors.[7617]
47 [a]Save[3467] us, O LORD our God,[430]
And [b]gather[6908] us from among
the nations,
To give thanks to Thy holy[6944]
name,
And [I][c]glory[7623] in Thy praise.
48 [a]Blessed[1288] be the LORD, the
God of Israel,
From everlasting[5769] even to
everlasting.
And let all the people say,[559]
"Amen."[543]
[I]Praise [II]the LORD!

BOOK 5

The LORD Delivers Men from Manifold Troubles

107 Oh [a]give thanks[3034] to the
LORD, for [b]He is good;[2896]
For His lovingkindness[2617] is
everlasting.[5769]
2 Let [a]the redeemed[1350] of the
LORD say[559] *so,*
Whom He has [b]redeemed from
the hand[3027] of the adversary,
3 And [a]gathered[6908] from the
lands,[776]
From the east and from the
west,
From the north and from the
[I]south.
4 They [a]wandered[8582] in the
wilderness in a [I]desert
region;
They did not find a way[1870] to
[II]an inhabited [b]city.
5 *They were* hungry [I]and thirsty;
Their [a]soul fainted within
them.
6 Then they [a]cried out to the LORD
in their trouble;[7451]
He delivered[5337] them out of
their distresses.[4691]
7 He led them also by a
[I][a]straight[3477] way,
To go to [II][b]an inhabited city.
8 [a]Let them give thanks[3034] to the
LORD for His
lovingkindness,[2617]
And for His [I]wonders[6381] to the
sons[1121] of men![120]
9 For He has [a]satisfied the
[I]thirsty soul,
And the [b]hungry soul He has
filled with what is good.[2896]
10 There were those who
[a]dwelt in darkness[2822] and in
the shadow of death,[6757]
[b]Prisoners in [I]misery and
[II]chains,
11 Because they had [a]rebelled[4784]
against the words[561] of
God,[410]
And [b]spurned[5006] the
[c]counsel[6098] of the Most
High.[5945]
12 Therefore He humbled their
heart[3820] with labor;[5999]
They stumbled[3782] and there
was [a]none to help.
13 Then they [a]cried out[2199] to the
LORD in their trouble;
He saved[3467] them out of their
distresses.
14 He [a]brought them out of
darkness and the shadow of
death,
And [b]broke their bands apart.
15 [a]Let them give thanks to the
LORD for His lovingkindness,
And for His [I]wonders to the sons
of men!

43 [b]Ps. 81:12 [c]Judg. 6:6 **44** [a]Judg. 3:9; 6:7; 10:10 **45** [I]Lit., *was sorry* [a]Lev. 26:42; Ps. 105:8 [b]Judg. 2:18 [c]Ps. 69:16 **46** [a]1Kin. 8:50; 2Chr. 30:9; Ezra 9:9; Neh. 1:11; Jer. 42:12 **47** [I]Lit., *boast* [a]1Chr. 16:35, 36 [b]Ps. 147:2 [c]Ps. 47:1 **48** [I]Or, *Hallelujah!* [II]Heb., *YAH* [a]Ps. 41:13; 72:18; 89:52

1 [a]1Chr. 16:34; Ps. 106:1; 118:1; 136:1; Jer. 33:11 [b]2Chr. 5:13; 7:3; Ezra 3:11; Ps. 100:5 **2** [a]Is. 35:9, 10; 62:12; 63:4 [b]Ps. 78:42; 106:10 **3** [I]Lit., *sea* [a]Deut. 30:3; Neh. 1:9; Ps. 106:47; Is. 11:12; 43:5; 56:8; Ezek. 11:17; 20:34 **4** [I]Lit., *waste* [II]Or, *a habitable city; lit., a city of habitation* [a]Num. 14:33; 32:13; Deut. 2:7; 32:10; Josh. 5:6; 14:10 [b]Ps. 107:7, 36 **5** [I]Lit., *also* [a]Ps. 77:3 **6** [a]Ps. 50:15; 107:13, 19, 28 **7** [I]Or, *level* [II]Or, *a habitable city; lit., a city of habitation* [a]Ezra 8:21; Ps. 5:8; Jer. 31:9 [b]Ps. 107:4, 36 **8** [I]I.e., wonderful acts [a]Ps. 107:15, 21, 31 **9** [I]Or, *parched* [a]Ps. 22:26; 34:10; 63:5; 103:5 [b]Ps. 146:7; Matt. 5:6; Luke 1:53 **10** [I]Lit., *affliction* [II]Lit., *irons* [a]Ps. 143:3; Is. 42:7; Mic. 7:8; Luke 1:79 [b]Job 36:8; Ps. 102:20 **11** [a]Ps. 78:40; 106:7; Lam. 3:42 [b]Num. 15:31; 2Chr. 36:16; Prov. 1:25; Is. 5:24 [c]Ps. 73:24

12 [a]Ps. 22:11; 72:12 **13** [a]Ps. 107:6 **14** [a]Ps. 86:13; 107:10 [b]Ps. 116:16; Jer. 2:20; 30:8; Nah. 1:13; Luke 13:16; Acts 12:7 **15** [I]I.e., wonderful acts [a]Ps. 107:8, 21, 31

16 For He has [a]shattered[7665] gates
of bronze,
And cut bars of iron asunder.
17 Fools, because of [I]their
rebellious[6588] way,
And [a]because of their
iniquities,[5771] were afflicted.
18 Their [a]soul abhorred[8581] all kinds
of food;
And they [b]drew near to the
[c]gates of death.[4194]
19 Then they cried out[2199] to the
LORD in their trouble;
He saved[3467] them out of their
distresses.
20 He [a]sent His word[1697] and
[b]healed them,
And [c]delivered[4422] *them* from
their [I]destructions.[7825]
21 [a]Let them give thanks to the
LORD for His lovingkindness,
And for His [I]wonders to the sons
of men!
22 Let them also offer[2076]
[a]sacrifices[2077] of
thanksgiving,[8426]
And [b]tell[5608] of His works with
joyful singing.
23 Those who [a]go down to the sea
in ships,
Who do[6213] business[4399] on great
waters;
24 They have seen the works of
the LORD,
And His [I]wonders in the deep.
25 For He [a]spoke[559] and raised up
a [b]stormy wind,[7307]
Which [c]lifted up the waves
[I]of the sea.
26 They rose up[5927] to the
heavens,[8064] they went down
to the depths;
Their soul [a]melted away in *their*
misery.
27 They reeled and [a]staggered like
a drunken man,
And [I]were at their wits'[2451] end.
28 Then they cried to the LORD in
their trouble,
And He brought them out of
their distresses.
29 He [a]caused the storm to be still,
So that the waves [I]of the sea
were hushed.
30 Then they were glad because
they were quiet;
So He guided[5148] them to their
desired haven.
31 [a]Let them give thanks to the
LORD for His lovingkindness,
And for His [Ib]wonders to the
sons of men!
32 Let them [a]extol Him also
[b]in the congregation[6951] of the
people,[5971]
And [c]praise[1984] Him at the
seat[4186] of the elders.[2205]
33 He [Ia]changes[7760] rivers into a
[II]wilderness,
And springs of water into a
thirsty ground;[127]
34 A [a]fruitful land[776] into a
[b]salt waste,
Because of the wickedness[7451]
of those who dwell in it.
35 He [Ia]changes a [II]wilderness into
a pool of water,
And a dry land into springs of
water;
36 And there He makes the hungry
to dwell,
So that they may establish[3559]
[Ia]an inhabited city,
37 And sow fields,[7704] and
[a]plant vineyards,
And [I]gather[6213] a fruitful harvest.
38 Also He blesses[1288] them and
they [a]multiply greatly;
And He [b]does not let their cattle
decrease.
39 When they are [a]diminished and
[b]bowed down
Through oppression,
misery,[7451] and sorrow,
40 He [a]pours[8210] contempt upon
[I]princes,[5081]
And [b]makes them wander[8582]
[c]in a pathless waste.[8414]
41 But He [a]sets the needy

16 [a]Is. 45:1, 2
17 [I]Lit., *the way of their transgression* [a]Is. 65:6, 7; Jer. 30:14, 15; Lam. 3:39; Ezek. 24:23
18 [a]Job 33:20; Ps. 102:4 [b]Job 33:22; Ps. 88:3 [c]Job 38:17; Ps. 9:13
20 [I]Or, *pits* [a]Ps. 147:15, 18; Matt. 8:8 [b]2Kin. 20:5; Ps. 30:2; 103:3; 147:3 [c]Job 33:28, 30; Ps. 30:3; 49:15; 56:13; 103:4
21 [I]I.e., wonderful acts [a]Ps. 107:8, 15, 31
22 [a]Lev. 7:12; Ps. 50:14; 116:17 [b]Ps. 9:11; 73:28; 118:17
23 [a]Is. 42:10; Jon. 1:3
24 [I]I.e., wonderful acts
25 [I]Lit., *of it* [a]Ps. 105:31, 34 [b]Ps. 148:8; Jon. 1:4 [c]Ps. 93:3,4
26 [a]Ps. 22:14; 119:28
27 [I]Lit., *all their wisdom was swallowed up* [a]Job 12:25; Is. 24:20
29 [I]Lit., *of it* [a]Ps. 65:7; 89:9; Matt. 8:26; Luke 8:24
31 [I]I.e., wonderful acts [a]Ps. 107:8, 15, 21 [b]Ps. 78:4; 111:4
32 [a]Ps. 34:3; 99:5; Is. 25:1 [b]Ps. 22:22, 25 [c]Ps. 35:18
33 [I]Or, *turns* [II]Or, *desert* [a]1Kin. 17:1, 7; Ps. 74:15; Is. 42:15; 50:2
34 [a]Gen. 13:10; 14:3; 19:24, 25; Deut. 29:23 [b]Job 39:6; Jer. 17:6
35 [I]Or, *turns* [II]Or, *desert* [a]Ps. 105:41; 114:8; Is. 35:6, 7; 41:18
36 [I]Or, *a habitable city;* lit., *a city of habitation* [a]Ps. 107:4, 7
37 [I]Lit., *acquire fruits of yield* [a]2Kin. 19:29; Is. 65:21; Amos 9:14
38 [a]Gen. 12:2; 17:20; Ex. 1:7; Deut. 1:10 [b]Deut. 7:14
39 [a]2Kin. 10:32; Ezek. 5:11; 29:15 [b]Ps. 38:6; 44:25; 57:6
40 [I]Or, *nobles* [a]Job 12:21 [b]Job 12:24 [c]Deut. 32:10
41 [a]1Sam. 2:8; Ps. 59:1; 113:7, 8

[I]securely on high away from
affliction,
And [b]makes[7760] *his* families[4940]
like a flock.
42 The [a]upright[3477] see it, and are
glad;
But all [b]unrighteousness[5766]
shuts its mouth.[6310]
43 Who is [a]wise?[2450] Let him give
heed[8104] to these things;
And consider[995] the
[b]lovingkindnesses of the
LORD.

God Praised and Supplicated to Give Victory

A Song, a Psalm of David.

108 [a]My heart[3820] is steadfast,[3559]
O God;[430]
I will sing,[7891] I will sing praises,
even with my [I]soul.[3519]
2 Awake, harp and lyre;
I will awaken the dawn!
3 I will give thanks[3034] to Thee,
O LORD, among the
peoples;[5971]
And I will sing praises[2167] to
Thee among the nations.[3816]
4 For Thy [a]lovingkindness[2617] is
great [b]above the heavens;[8064]
And Thy truth[571] *reaches* to the
skies.[7834]
5 [a]Be exalted, O God, above the
heavens,
And Thy glory above all the
earth.[776]
6 [a]That Thy beloved[3039] may be
delivered,[2502]
Save[3467] with Thy right hand,
and answer me!
7 God has spoken[1696] in His
[I]holiness:[6944]
"I will exult, I will portion out
Shechem,
And measure out[4058] the valley
of Succoth.
8 "Gilead is Mine, Manasseh is
Mine;
Ephraim also is the [I]helmet of
My head;[7218]
[a]Judah is My [II]scepter.[2710]
9 "Moab is My washbowl;[7366]
Over Edom I shall throw My
shoe;
Over Philistia I will shout
aloud."[7321]
10 [a]Who will bring me into the
besieged city?
Who [I]will lead[5148] me to Edom?
11 Hast not Thou Thyself, O God,
[a]rejected us?
And wilt Thou not go forth with
our armies,[6635] O God?
12 Oh give us help[8668] against the
adversary,
For [a]deliverance [I]by man[120] is
in vain.[7723]
13 [I]Through God we shall do[6213]
valiantly;[2428]
And [a]it is He who will tread
down[947] our adversaries.

Vengeance Invoked upon Adversaries

For the choir director. A Psalm of David.

109 O [a]God[430] of my praise,[8416]
[b]Do not be silent!
2 For they have opened the
[I]wicked[7563] and [a]deceitful[4820]
mouth[6310] against me;
They have spoken[1696] [II]against
me with a [b]lying tongue.
3 They have also surrounded
me with words[1697] of
hatred,[8135]
And fought against me
[a]without cause.
4 In return [a]for my love[160] they
act as my accusers;[7853]
But [b]I am *in* prayer.[8605]
5 Thus they have [I][a]repaid me
evil[7451] for good,[2896]
And [b]hatred for my love.
6 Appoint a wicked man over him;
And let an [I][a]accuser[7854] stand at
his right hand.
7 When he is judged,[8199] let him
[a]come forth guilty;[7563]
And let his [b]prayer become[1961]
sin.[2401]
8 Let [a]his days[3117] be few;
Let [b]another take his office.[6486]

41 [I]Lit., *in an inaccessibly high place* [b]Job 21:11; Ps. 78:52; 113:9
42 [a]Job 22:19; Ps. 52:6 [b]Job 5:16; Ps. 63:11; Rom. 3:19
43 [a]Ps. 64:9; Jer. 9:12; Hos. 14:9 [b]Ps. 107:1
1 [I]Lit., *glory* [a]Ps. 57:7-11; 108:1-5
4 [a]Num. 14:18; Deut. 7:9; Ps. 36:5; 100:5; Mic. 7:18-20 [b]Ps. 113:4
5 [a]Ps. 57:5
6 [a]Ps. 60:5-12; 108:6-13
7 [I]Or, *sanctuary*
8 [I]Lit., *protection* [II]Or, *lawgiver* [a]Gen. 49:10
10 [I]Or, *has led* [a]Ps. 60:9
11 [a]Ps. 44:9
12 [I]Lit., *of* [a]Is. 30:3
13 [I]Or, *In* or *With* [a]Is. 60:12; 63:1-4
1 [a]Deut. 10:21 [b]Ps. 28:1; 83:1
2 [I]Lit., *wicked mouth and the deceitful* [II]Lit., *with* [a]Ps. 10:7; 52:4 [b]Ps. 120:2
3 [a]Ps. 35:7; 69:4; John 15:25
4 [a]Ps. 38:20 [b]Ps. 69:13; 141:5
5 [I]Lit., *laid upon me* [a]Ps. 35:12; 38:20 [b]John 7:7; 10:32
6 [I]Or, *adversary, Satan* [a]Zech. 3:1
7 [a]Ps. 1:5 [b]Prov. 28:9
8 [a]Ps. 55:23 [b]Acts 1:20

9 Let his [a]children[1121] be
fatherless,
And his [b]wife[802] a widow.
10 Let his [a]children wander about
and beg;[7592]
And let them [b]seek *sustenance*
[I]far from their ruined
homes.[2723]
11 Let [a]the creditor [I]seize[5367] all
that he has;
And let [b]strangers[2114] plunder
the product of his labor.
12 Let there be none to [Ia]extend
lovingkindness[2617] to him,
Nor [b]any to be gracious[2603] to
his fatherless children.
13 Let his [a]posterity[319] be
[I]cut off;[3772]
In a following generation[1755] let
their [b]name be blotted
out.[4229]
14 Let [a]the iniquity[5771] of his
fathers[1] be remembered[2142]
[I]before the LORD,
And do not let the sin[2403] of his
mother[517] be [b]blotted out.
15 Let [a]them be before the LORD
continually,
That He may [b]cut off their
memory[2143] from the
earth;[776]
16 Because he did not remember
to show[6213] lovingkindness,
But persecuted the [a]afflicted and
needy man,[376]
And the [b]despondent in
heart,[3824] to [c]put *them* to
death.[4191]
17 He also loved[157] cursing,[7045] so
[a]it came to him;
And he did not delight[2654] in
blessing,[1293] so it was far
from him.
18 But he [a]clothed himself with
cursing as with his garment,
And it [b]entered into [I]his body[7130]
like water,
And like oil[8081] into his bones.[6106]
19 Let it be to him as [a]a garment
with which he covers himself,
And for a belt[4206] with which he
constantly [b]girds himself.

9 [a]Ex. 22:24 [b]Jer. 18:21
10 [I]Or, *out of their desolate places* [a]Gen. 4:12; Job 30:5-8; Ps. 59:15 [b]Ps. 37:25
11 [I]Lit., *ensnare, strike at* [a]Neh. 5:7; Job 5:5; 20:15 [b]Is. 1:7; Lam. 5:2; Ezek. 7:21
12 [I]Lit., *continue* [a]Ezra 7:28; 9:9 [b]Job 5:4; Is. 9:17
13 [I]Lit., *for cutting off* [a]Job 18:19; Ps. 21:10; 37:28 [b]Ps. 9:5; Prov. 10:7
14 [I]Lit., *to* [a]Ex. 20:5; Num. 14:18; Is. 65:6, 7; Jer. 32:18 [b]Neh. 4:5; Jer. 18:23
15 [a]Ps. 90:8; Jer. 16:17 [b]Job 18:17; Ps. 34:16
16 [a]Ps. 37:14 [b]Ps. 34:18 [c]Ps. 37:32; 94:6
17 [a]Prov. 14:14; Ezek. 35:9; Matt. 7:2
18 [I]Lit., *his inward parts* [a]Ps. 73:6; 109:29; Ezek. 7:27 [b]Num. 5:22
19 [a]Ps. 73:6; 109:29; Ezek. 7:27 [b]2Sam. 22:40; Ps. 30:11; Is. 11:5
20 [I]Lit., *This is* [a]Ps. 54:5; 94:23; Is. 3:11; 2Tim. 4:14 [b]Ps. 41:5; 71:10
21 [I]Heb., *YHWH*, usually rendered LORD [a]Ps. 23:3; 25:11; 79:9; 106:8; Ezek. 36:22 [b]Ps. 69:16
22 [I]Lit., *one has pierced my heart within me* [a]Ps. 40:17; 86:1 [b]Job 24:12; Ps. 143:4; Prov. 18:14
23 [a]Ps. 102:11 [b]Ex. 10:19; Job 39:20
24 [I]Or, *totter* [a]Heb. 12:12 [b]Ps. 35:13
25 [a]Ps. 22:6 [b]Ps. 22:7; Jer. 18:16; Lam. 2:15; Matt. 27:39; Mark 15:29
26 [a]Ps. 119:86

20 [I]Let this be the [a]reward of my
accusers from the LORD,
And of those who [b]speak[1696] evil
against my soul.
21 But Thou, O [I]GOD, the Lord,[136]
deal[6213] *kindly* with me
[a]for Thy name's sake;
Because [b]Thy lovingkindness is
good, deliver[5337] me;
22 For [a]I am afflicted and needy,
And [I]my heart[3820] is
[b]wounded[2490] within[7130] me.
23 I am passing [a]like a shadow when
it lengthens;
I am shaken off [b]like the locust.
24 My [a]knees [I]are weak[3782] from
[b]fasting;
And my flesh[1320] has grown lean,
without fatness.[8081]
25 I also have become a
[a]reproach[2781] to them;
When they see[7200] me, they
[b]wag their head.[7218]
26 [a]Help me, O LORD my God;
Save[3467] me according to Thy
lovingkindness.
27 [I]And let them [a]know that this
is Thy hand;[3027]
Thou, LORD, hast done[6213] it.
28 [a]Let them curse,[7043] but do Thou
bless;[1288]
When they arise, they shall be
ashamed,[954]
But Thy [b]servant[5650] shall be
glad.
29 [I]Let [a]my accusers be clothed
with dishonor,
And [II]let them [b]cover
themselves with their own
shame as with a robe.[4598]
30 With my mouth I will give
thanks[3034] abundantly to the
LORD;
And in the midst of many
[a]I will praise[1984] Him.
31 For He stands [a]at the right hand
of the needy,

27 [I]Or, *That they may know* [a]Job 37:7 **28** [a]2Sam. 16:11, 12 [b]Is. 65:14 **29** [I]Or, *My accusers will be* [II]Or, *they will cover* [a]Job 8:22; Ps. 132:18 [b]Job 8:22; Ps. 35:26 **30** [a]Ps. 22:22; 35:18; 111:1 **31** [a]Ps. 16:8; 73:23; 110:5; 121:5

To save him from those who
[b]judge[8199] his soul.

The LORD Gives Dominion to the King

A Psalm of David.

110 🔑 [a]The LORD says[5002] to my
Lord:[113]
"[b]Sit at My right hand,
Until I make [c]Thine enemies a
footstool for Thy feet."
2 The LORD will stretch forth Thy
strong [a]scepter[4294] from
Zion, *saying*,
"[b]Rule[7287] in the midst[7130] of
Thine enemies."
3 Thy [a]people[5971] [I]will volunteer
freely in the day[3117] of Thy
[II]power;[2428]
[b]In [III]holy[6944] array,[1926] from the
womb of the dawn,
[IV]Thy youth are to Thee *as* the
[c]dew.
🔑 4 [a]The LORD has sworn and will
[b]not [I]change His mind,[5162]
"Thou art a [c]priest[3548]
forever[5769]
According to the order[1700] of
Melchizedek."
5 The Lord[136] is [a]at Thy right
hand;
He [I]will [b]shatter[4212] kings[4428]
in the [c]day of His
wrath.[639]
6 He will [a]judge[1777] among the
nations,[1471]
He [I]will fill *them* with
[b]corpses,[1472]
He [II]will [c]shatter[4272] the
[III]chief[7218] men over a broad
country.[776]
7 He will [a]drink from the brook
by the wayside;[1870]
Therefore He will [b]lift up *His*
head.[7218]

31 [b]Ps. 37:33

1 [a]Matt. 22:44; Mark 12:36; Luke 20:42, 43; Acts 2:34, 35; Heb. 1:13 [b]Matt. 26:64; Eph. 1:20; Col. 3:1; Heb. 1:3; 8:1; 10:12; 12:2 [c]1Cor. 15:25; Eph. 1:22
2 [a]Ps. 45:6; Jer. 48:17; Ezek. 19:14 [b]Ps. 2:9; 72:8; Dan. 7:13, 14
3 [I]Lit., *will be free-will offerings* [II]Or, *army* [III]Or, *the splendor of holiness* [IV]Or, *The dew of Thy youth is Thine.* [a]Judg. 5:2; Neh. 11:2 [b]1Chr. 16:29; Ps. 96:9 [c]2Sam. 17:12; Mic. 5:7
4 [I]Lit., *be sorry* [a]Heb. 7:21 [b]Num. 23:19 [c]Zech. 6:13; Heb. 5:6, 10; 6:20; 7:17, 21
5 [I]Or, *has shattered* [a]Ps. 16:8; 109:31 [b]Ps. 68:14; 76:12 [c]Ps. 2:5, 12; Rom. 2:5; Rev. 6:17
6 [I]Or, *has filled* [II]Or, *has shattered* [III]Lit., *head over* [a]Is. 2:4; Joel 3:12; Mic. 4:3 [b]Is. 66:24 [c]Ps. 68:21
7 [a]Judg. 7:5, 6 [b]Ps. 27:6

1 [I]Or, *Hallelujah! I will* [II]Heb., YAH [a]Ps. 35:18; 138:1 [b]Ps. 89:7; 149:1
2 [I]Lit., *sought out* [a]Ps. 92:5 [b]Ps. 143:5
3 [I]Lit., *Splendor and majesty* [a]Ps. 96:6; 145:5 [b]Ps. 112:3, 9; 119:142
4 [I]I.e., wonderful acts [II]Lit., *a memorial* [a]Ps. 86:5, 15; 103:8; 145:8
5 [I]Lit., *prey*

The LORD Praised for His Goodness

111 [I]Praise[1984] [II]the LORD!
I [a]will give thanks[3034] to
the LORD with all *my*
heart,[3824]
In the [b]company[5475] of the
upright and in the
assembly.[5712]
2 [a]Great are the works of the
LORD;
They are [I][b]studied by all who
delight[2656] in them.
3 [I][a]Splendid and majestic is His
work;
And [b]His righteousness[6666]
endures forever.[5703]
4 He has made[6213] His
[I]wonders[6381] [II]to be
remembered;
The LORD is [a]gracious[2587] and
compassionate.
5 He has [a]given [I]food to those who
[II]fear[3373] Him;
He will [b]remember[2143] His
covenant[1285] forever.
6 He has made known[5046] to His
people[5971] the power of His
works,
In giving them the heritage[5159]
of the nations.[1471]
7 The works of His hands[3027] are
[I][a]truth[571] and justice;[4941]
All His precepts[6490] [b]are
[II]sure.[539]
8 They are [a]upheld forever[5703] and
ever;[5769]
They are performed[6213] in
[I][b]truth[571] and uprightness.[3477]
9 He has sent [a]redemption[6304] to
His people;
He has [I]ordained[6680] His
covenant forever;

[II]Or, *revere* [a]Matt. 6:31-33 [b]Ps. 105:8 **7** [I]Or, *faithfulness* [II]Or, *trustworthy* [a]Rev. 15:3 [b]Ps. 19:7; 93:5
8 [I]Or, *faithfulness* [a]Ps. 119:160; Is. 40:8; Matt. 5:18 [b]Ps. 19:9 **9** [I]Lit., *commanded* [a]Luke 1:68

🔑 **110:1** See Mt. 22:44; 26:64; Mk. 12:36; Lk. 20:42,43; Acts 2:34,35; I Cor. 15:25; Eph. 1:20,22; Col. 3:1; Heb. 1:3,13; 8:1; 10:12; 12:2.
🔑 **110:4** See Heb. 5:6,10; 6:20; 7:17,21.

[b]Holy[6918] and [II]awesome[3372] is
His name.
10 The [Ia]fear[3374] of the LORD is the
beginning[7225] of wisdom;[2451]
A [b]good[2896] understanding[792]
have all those who [II]do[6213] *His*
commandments;
His [c]praise[8416] endures forever.

Prosperity of the One Who Fears the LORD

112 [I]Praise[1984] [II]the LORD!
How [a]blessed[835] is the
man[376] who [III]fears the
LORD,
Who greatly [b]delights[2654] in His
commandments.[4687]
🔑2 His [Ia]descendants[2233] will be
mighty [II]on earth;[776]
The generation[1755] of the
[b]upright will be blessed.[1288]
3 [a]Wealth and riches are in his
house,[1004]
And his righteousness[6666]
endures forever.[5703]
4 Light[216] arises in the
darkness[2822] [a]for the upright;
He is [b]gracious[2587] and
compassionate and
righteous.[6662]
5 It is well[2896] with the man who
[a]is gracious[2603] and lends;
He will [I]maintain his cause[1697]
in judgment.[4941]
6 For he will [a]never[5769] [3808] be shaken;
The [b]righteous will be
[I]remembered[2143] forever.[5769]
7 He will not fear[3372] [a]evil[7451]
tidings;
His [b]heart[3820] is steadfast,[3559]
[c]trusting[982] in the LORD.
8 His [a]heart is upheld, he
[b]will not fear,
Until he [c]looks *with satisfaction*
on his adversaries.
9 [I]He [a]has given freely to the poor;
His righteousness endures
forever;
His [b]horn will be exalted in
honor.[3519]
10 The [a]wicked[7563] will see it and
be [I]vexed;[3707]
He will [b]gnash[2786] his teeth and
[c]melt away;
The [d]desire of the wicked will
perish.[6]

The LORD Exalts the Humble

113 [I]Praise[1984] [II]the LORD!
[a]Praise, O [b]servants[5650] of
the LORD.
Praise the name of the LORD.
2 [a]Blessed[1288] be the name of the
LORD
From this time forth and
forever.[5769]
3 [a]From the rising of the sun to
its setting
The [b]name of the LORD is to be
praised.[1984]
4 The LORD is [a]high above all
nations;[1471]
His [b]glory[3519] is above the
heavens.[8064]
5 [a]Who is like the LORD our
God,[430]
Who [b]is enthroned on high,
6 Who [Ia]humbles Himself to
behold[7200]
The things that are in heaven[8064]
and in the earth?[776]
7 He [a]raises the poor from the
dust,[6083]
And lifts the needy from the ash
heap,
8 To make *them* [a]sit with
[I]princes,[5081]
With the [I]princes of His
people.[5971]
9 He [a]makes the barren[6135] woman
abide in the house[1004]

9 [II]I.e., inspiring reverence [b]Ps. 99:3; Luke 1:49
10 [I]Or, *reverence for* [II]Lit., *do them* [a]Job 28:28; Prov. 1:7; 9:10; Eccl. 12:13 [b]Ps. 119:98; Prov. 3:4 [c]Ps. 145:2

1 [I]Or, *Hallelujah! Blessed* [II]Heb., YAH [III]Or, *reveres* [a]Ps. 128:1 [b]Ps. 1:2; 119:14, 16
2 [I]Lit., *seed* [II]Or, *in the land* [a]Ps. 102:28; 127:4 [b]Ps. 128:4
3 [a]Prov. 3:16; 8:18; Matt. 6:33
4 [a]Job 11:17; Ps. 97:11 [b]Ps. 37:26
5 [I]Or, *conduct his affairs with justice* [a]Ps. 37:21
6 [I]Lit., *for an eternal remembrance* [a]Ps. 15:5; 55:22 [b]Prov. 10:7
7 [a]Prov. 1:33 [b]Ps. 57:7; 108:1 [c]Ps. 56:4
8 [a]Heb. 13:9 [b]Ps. 27:1; 56:11; Prov. 1:33; 3:24; Is. 12:2 [c]Ps. 54:7; 59:10
9 [I]Lit., *He has scattered, he has given to...* [a]2Cor. 9:9 [b]Ps. 75:10; 89:17; 92:10; 148:14
10 [I]Or, *angry* [a]Ps. 86:17 [b]Ps. 35:16; 37:12; Matt. 8:12; 25:30; Luke 13:28 [c]Ps. 58:7 [d]Job 8:13; Prov. 10:28; 11:7

1 [I]Or, *Hallelujah! Praise* [II]Heb., YAH [a]Ps. 135:1 [b]Ps. 34:22; 69:36; 79:10; 90:13
2 [a]Ps. 145:21; Dan. 2:20
3 [a]Ps. 50:1; Is. 59:19; Mal. 1:11 [b]Ps. 18:3; 48:1, 10
4 [a]Ps. 97:9; 99:2 [b]Ps. 8:1; 57:11; 148:13

5 [a]Ex. 15:11; Ps. 35:10; 89:6 [b]Ps. 103:19 **6** [I]Or, *looks far below in the heavens and on the earth?* [a]Ps. 11:4; 138:6; Is. 57:15 **7** [a]1Sam. 2:8; Ps. 107:41 **8** [I]Or, *nobles* [a]Job 36:7 **9** [a]1Sam. 2:5; Ps. 68:6; Is. 54:1

🔑 **112:2,3** Cf. Job 22:23,24; Prov. 15:6. See also Mt. 6:19,21; Lk. 6:20,24; 12:21; Js. 5:1-3. Neither the acquisition nor the possession of earthly riches is forbidden, but the worshiping of wealth is prohibited.

As a joyful mother[517] of children.[1121]
[I]Praise [II]the LORD!

God's Deliverance of Israel from Egypt

114 When Israel went forth [a]from Egypt,
The house[1004] of Jacob from a people[5971] of [b]strange language,[3937]
2 Judah became [a]His sanctuary,[6944]
Israel, [b]His dominion.[4475]
3 The [a]sea looked[7200] and fled;
The [b]Jordan turned back.
4 The mountains [a]skipped[7540] like rams,
The hills, like lambs.
5 What [a]ails you, O sea, that you flee?
O Jordan, that you turn back?
6 O mountains, that you skip like rams?
O hills, like lambs?
7 [a]Tremble,[2342] O earth,[776] before the Lord,[113]
Before the God[433] of Jacob,
8 Who [a]turned[2015] the rock into a [b]pool of water,
The [c]flint into a fountain of water.

Heathen Idols Contrasted with the LORD

115 [a]Not to us, O LORD, not to us,
But [b]to Thy name give glory[3519]
Because of Thy lovingkindness,[2617] because of Thy [I]truth.
2 [a]Why should the nations[1471] say,[559]
"[b]Where, now, is their God?"[430]
3 But our [a]God is in the heavens;[8064]
He [b]does[6213] whatever He pleases.[2654]

9 [I]Or, *Hallelujah!* [II]Heb., YAH
1 [a]Ex. 12:51; 13:3 [b]Ps. 81:5
2 [a]Ex. 15:17; 29:45, 46; Ps. 78:68, 69 [b]Ex. 19:6
3 [a]Ex. 14:21; Ps. 77:16 [b]Josh. 3:13, 16
4 [a]Ex. 19:18; Judg. 5:5; Ps. 18:7; 29:6; Hab. 3:6
5 [a]Hab. 3:8
7 [a]Ps. 96:9
8 [a]Ex. 17:6; Num. 20:11; Ps. 78:15; 105:41 [b]Ps. 107:35 [c]Deut. 8:15
1 [I]Or, *faithfulness* [a]Is. 48:11; Ezek. 36:22 [b]Ps. 29:2; 96:8
2 [a]Ps. 79:10 [b]Ps. 42:3, 10
3 [a]Ps. 103:19 [b]Ps. 135:6; Dan. 4:35
4 [a]Ps. 115:4-8; 135:15-18; Jer. 10:4 [b]Deut. 4:28; 2Kin. 19:18; Is. 37:19; 44:10, 20; Jer. 10:3
5 [a]Jer. 10:5
7 [I]Lit., *Their hands* [II]Lit., *Their feet*
8 [I]Or, *are like them* [a]Ps. 135:18; Is. 44:9-11
9 [a]Ps. 118:2; 135:19 [b]Ps. 37:3; 62:8 [c]Ps. 33:20
10 [a]Ps. 118:3; 135:19
11 [I]Or, *revere* [a]Ps. 22:23; 103:11; 135:20
12 [a]Ps. 98:3
13 [I]Or, *revere* [a]Ps. 103:11; 112:1; 128:1 [b]Rev. 11:18; 19:5
14 [a]Deut. 1:11
15 [a]Gen. 1:1; Neh. 9:6; Ps. 96:5; 102:25; 121:2; 124:8; 134:3; 146:6; Acts 14:15; Rev. 14:7
16 [a]Ps. 89:11 [b]Ps. 8:6
17 [I]Heb., YAH [a]Ps. 6:5; 88:10-12; Is. 38:18 [b]Ps. 31:17

4 Their [a]idols[6091] are silver and gold,
The [b]work of man's[120] hands.[3027]
5 They have mouths,[6310] but they [a]cannot speak;[1696]
They have eyes, but they cannot see;
6 They have ears,[241] but they cannot hear;[8085]
They have noses, but they cannot smell;[7306]
7 [I]They have hands, but they cannot feel;
[II]They have feet, but they cannot walk;
They cannot make a sound[1897] with their throat.
8 [a]Those who make[6213] them [I]will become like them,
Everyone who trusts[982] in them.
9 O [a]Israel, [b]trust[982] in the LORD;
He is their [c]help and their shield.
10 O house[1004] of [a]Aaron, trust in the LORD;
He is their help and their shield.
11 You who [Ia]fear[3373] the LORD, trust in the LORD;
He is their help and their shield.
12 The LORD [a]has been mindful[2142] of us; He will bless *us;*
He will bless[1288] the house of Israel;
He will bless the house of Aaron.
13 He will [a]bless those who [I]fear the LORD,
[b]The small together with the great.
14 May the LORD [a]give you increase,
You and your children.[1121]
15 May you be blessed[1288] of the LORD,
[a]Maker[6213] of heaven[8064] and earth.[776]
16 The heavens are [a]the heavens of the LORD;
But [b]the earth He has given to the sons of men.[120]
17 The [a]dead[4191] do not praise[1984] [I]the LORD,
Nor *do* any who go down into [b]silence;

18 But as for us, we will [a]bless
[I]the LORD
From this time forth and
forever.[5769]
[II]Praise [I]the LORD!

Thanksgiving for Deliverance from Death

116 [a]I love[157] the LORD, because
He [b]hears[8085]
My voice *and* my
supplications.[8469]
2 Because He has [a]inclined His
ear[241] to me,
Therefore I shall call *upon Him*
as long as[3117] I live.
3 The [a]cords[2256] of death[4194]
encompassed me,
And the [I]terrors of [II]Sheol[7585]
[III]came upon me;
I found distress and sorrow.
4 Then [a]I called[7121] upon the name
of the LORD:
"O LORD, I beseech[577] Thee,
[I][b]save my life!"[5315]
5 [a]Gracious[2587] is the LORD, and
[b]righteous;[6662]
Yes, our God[430] is
[c]compassionate.
6 The LORD preserves[8104]
[a]the simple;
I was [b]brought low, and He
saved[3467] me.
7 Return[7725] to your [a]rest, O my
soul,
For the LORD has [b]dealt
bountifully[1580] with you.
8 For Thou hast [a]rescued[2502] my
soul from death,
My eyes from tears,
My feet from stumbling.
9 I shall walk before the LORD
In the [I][a]land[776] of the living.[2416]
10 I [a]believed[539] when I said,[1696] "I
am [b]greatly afflicted."
11 I [a]said[559] in my alarm,
"[b]All men[120] are liars."[3576]
12 What shall I [a]render[7725] to the
LORD
For all His [b]benefits [I]toward
me?

18 [I]Heb., YAH [II]Or, *Hallelujah!* [a]Ps. 113:2; Dan. 2:20

1 [a]Ps. 18:1 [b]Ps. 6:8; 66:19; Is. 37:17; Dan. 9:18
2 [a]Ps. 17:6; 31:2; 40:1
3 [I]Lit., *straits* [II]I.e., the nether world [III]Lit., *found me* [a]Ps. 18:4, 5
4 [I]Or, *deliver my soul* [a]Ps. 18:6; 118:5 [b]Ps. 17:13; 22:20
5 [a]Ps. 86:15; 103:8 [b]Ezra 9:15; Neh. 9:8; Ps. 119:137; 145:17; Jer. 12:1; Dan. 9:14 [c]Ex. 34:6
6 [a]Ps. 19:7; Prov. 1:4 [b]Ps. 79:8; 142:6
7 [a]Jer. 6:16; Matt. 11:29 [b]Ps. 13:6; 142:7
8 [a]Ps. 49:15; 56:13; 86:13
9 [I]Lit., *lands* [a]Ps. 27:13
10 [a]2Cor. 4:13 [b]Ps. 88:7
11 [a]Ps. 31:22 [b]Ps. 62:9; Rom. 3:4
12 [I]Lit., *upon* [a]2Chr. 32:25; 1Thess. 3:9 [b]Ps. 103:2
13 [a]Ps. 16:5 [b]Ps. 80:18; 105:1
14 [a]Ps. 50:14; 116:18 [b]Ps. 22:25
15 [a]Ps. 72:14
16 [I]Or, *because* [a]Ps. 86:16; 119:125; 143:12 [b]Ps. 86:16 [c]Ps. 107:14
17 [a]Lev. 7:12; Ps. 50:14 [b]Ps. 116:13
18 [a]Ps. 116:14
19 [I]Or, *Hallelujah!* [II]Heb., YAH [a]Ps. 92:13; 96:8; 135:2 [b]Ps. 102:21

1 [a]Rom. 15:11
2 [I]Lit., *prevails over us* [II]Or, *faithfulness* [III]Or, *Hallelujah!* [IV]Heb., YAH [a]Ps. 103:11 [b]Ps. 100:5; 146:6

1 [a]1Chr. 16:8, 34; Ps. 106:1; 107:1; Jer.

13 I shall lift up[5375] the [a]cup of
salvation,[3444]
And [b]call[7121] upon the name of
the LORD.
14 I shall [a]pay my vows[5088] to the
LORD,
Oh *may it be* [b]in the presence
of all His people.[5971]
15 [a]Precious in the sight of the LORD
Is the death of His godly
ones.[2623]
16 O LORD, [I]surely I am [a]Thy
servant,[5650]
I am Thy servant, the
[b]son[1121] of Thy handmaid,
Thou hast [c]loosed my bonds.
17 To Thee I shall offer[2076]
[a]a sacrifice[2077] of
thanksgiving,[8426]
And [b]call upon the name of the
LORD.
18 I shall [a]pay my vows to the LORD,
Oh *may it be* in the presence of
all His people,
19 In the [a]courts of the LORD's
house,[1004]
In the midst of you, O
[b]Jerusalem.
[I]Praise[1984] [II]the LORD!

A Psalm of Praise

117 [a]Praise[1984] the LORD, all
nations;[1471]
Laud[7623] Him, all peoples![523]
2 For His [a]lovingkindness[2617]
[I]is great toward us,
And the [II][b]truth[571] of the LORD
is everlasting.[5769]
[III]Praise [IV]the LORD!

Thanksgiving for the LORD's Saving Goodness

118 [a]Give thanks[3034] to the LORD,
for [b]He is good;[2896]
For His lovingkindness[2617] is
everlasting.[5769]
2 Oh let [a]Israel say,[559]

33:11 [b]2Chr. 5:13; 7:3; Ezra 3:11; Ps. 100:5; 136:1-26 **2** [a]Ps. 115:9

"His lovingkindness is
everlasting."
3 Oh let the [a]house[1004] of Aaron
say,
"His lovingkindness is
everlasting."
4 Oh let those [a]who [I]fear[3373] the
LORD say,
"His lovingkindness is
everlasting."
5 From *my* [a]distress I called
upon[7121] [I]the LORD;
[I]The LORD answered me *and*
[b]*set me* in a large place.
6 The LORD is [a]for me; I will
[b]not fear;[3372]
[c]What can man[120] do[6213] to
me?
7 The LORD is for me [a]among those
who help me;
Therefore I shall [b]look *with*
satisfaction on those who
hate[8130] me.
8 It is [a]better[2896] to take refuge[2620]
in the LORD
Than to trust[982] in man.
9 It is [a]better[2896] to take refuge
in the LORD
Than to trust in princes.[5081]
10 All nations[1471] [a]surrounded me;
In the name of the LORD I will
surely [b]cut them off.[4135]
11 They [a]surrounded me, yes, they
surrounded me;
In the name of the LORD I will
surely cut them off.
12 They surrounded me [a]like bees;
They were extinguished as a
[b]fire of thorns;
In the name of the LORD I will
surely cut them off.
13 You [a]pushed me violently so that
I [I]was falling,
But the LORD [b]helped me.
14 [I][a]The LORD is my strength and
song,
And He has become[1961] [b]my
salvation.[3444]
15 The sound of [a]joyful shouting and
salvation is in the tents[168] of
the righteous;[6662]
The [b]right hand of the LORD
does[6213] valiantly.[2428]
16 The [a]right hand of the LORD is
exalted;
The right hand of the LORD does
valiantly.
17 I [a]shall not die,[4191] but live,[2421]
And [b]tell[5608] of the works of
[I]the LORD.
18 [I]The LORD has [a]disciplined me
severely,[3256]
But He has [b]not given me over
to death.[4194]
19 [a]Open to me the gates of
righteousness;[6664]
I shall enter through them, I shall
give thanks[3034] to [I]the LORD.
20 This is the gate of the LORD;
The [a]righteous will enter
through it.
21 I shall give thanks to Thee, for
Thou hast [a]answered me;
And Thou hast [b]become my
salvation.
🗝 **22** The [a]stone which the
builders[1129] rejected
Has become the chief[7218] corner
stone.
23 This is [I]the LORD's doing;
It is marvelous[6381] in our eyes.
24 This is the day[3117] which the
LORD has made;[6213]
Let us [a]rejoice and be glad in
it.
25 O LORD, [a]do save,[3467] we
beseech[577] Thee;
O LORD, we beseech Thee, do
send [b]prosperity!
26 [a]Blessed[1288] is the one who
comes in the name of the
LORD;
We have [b]blessed you from the
house of the LORD.
27 [a]The LORD is God,[410] and He has
given us [b]light;[216]

3 [a]Ps. 115:10
4 [I]Or, *revere* [a]Ps. 115:11
5 [I]Heb., YAH [a]Ps. 18:6; 86:7; 120:1 [b]Ps. 18:19
6 [a]Job 19:27; Ps. 56:9; Heb. 13:6 [b]Ps. 23:4; 27:1 [c]Ps. 56:4, 11
7 [a]Ps. 54:4 [b]Ps. 54:7; 59:10
8 [a]2Chr. 32:7, 8; Ps. 40:4; 108:12; Is. 31:1, 3; 57:13; Jer. 17:5
9 [a]Ps. 146:3
10 [a]Ps. 3:6; 88:17 [b]Ps. 18:40
11 [a]Ps. 88:17
12 [a]Deut. 1:44 [b]Ps. 58:9; Nah. 1:10
13 [I]Or, *fell* [a]Ps. 140:4 [b]Ps. 86:17
14 [I]Heb., YAH [a]Ex. 15:2; Is. 12:2 [b]Ps. 27:1
15 [a]Ps. 68:3 [b]Ex. 15:6; Ps. 89:13; Luke 1:51
16 [a]Ex. 15:6; Ps. 89:13
17 [I]Heb., YAH [a]Ps. 6:5; 116:8, 9; Hab. 1:12 [b]Ps. 73:28; 107:22
18 [I]Heb., YAH [a]Ps. 73:14; Jer. 31:18; 1Cor. 11:32; 2Cor. 6:9 [b]Ps. 86:13
19 [I]Heb., YAH [a]Is. 26:2
20 [a]Ps. 15:1, 2; 24:3-6; 140:13; Is. 35:8; Rev. 22:14
21 [a]Ps. 116:1; 118:5 [b]Ps. 118:14
22 [a]Matt. 21:42; Mark 12:10, 11; Luke 20:17; Acts 4:11; Eph. 2:20; 1Pet. 2:7
23 [I]Lit., *from the* LORD
24 [a]Ps. 31:7
25 [a]Ps. 106:47 [b]Ps. 122:6, 7
26 [a]Matt. 21:9; 23:39; Mark 11:9; Luke 13:35; 19:38; John 12:13 [b]Ps. 129:8
27 [a]1Kin. 18:39 [b]Esth. 8:16; Ps. 18:28; 27:1; 1Pet. 2:9

🗝 **118:22** See note on Isa. 8:14.
🗝 **118:22,23** Mt. 21:42; Mk. 12:10,11; Lk. 20:17; Acts 4:11; Eph. 2:20; I Pet. 2:7.

Bind the festival sacrifice with
cords [I]to the [c]horns of the
altar.[4196]
28 [a]Thou art my God, and I give
thanks to Thee;
Thou art my God,[430] [b]I extol
Thee.
29 [a]Give thanks to the LORD, for
He is good;
For His lovingkindness is
everlasting.

Meditations and Prayers Relating to the Law of God

א Aleph.

119 How blessed[835] are those
whose way[1870] is
[Ia]blameless,[8549]
Who [b]walk in the law[8451] of the
LORD.
2 How blessed are those who
[a]observe[5341] His
testimonies,[5713]
Who [b]seek Him [c]with all *their*
heart.[3820]
3 They also [a]do no
unrighteousness;[5766]
They walk in His ways.[1870]
4 Thou hast [Ia]ordained[6680] Thy
precepts,[6490]
[II]That we should keep[8104] *them*
diligently.
5 Oh that my [a]ways may be
established
To [b]keep Thy statutes![2706]
6 Then I [a]shall not be ashamed[954]
When I look [I]upon all Thy
commandments.[4687]
7 I shall [a]give thanks[3034] to Thee
with uprightness[3476] of
heart,[3824]
When I learn[3925] Thy
righteous[6664] judgments.[4941]
8 I shall keep Thy statutes;
Do not [a]forsake[5800] me utterly!

ב Beth.

9 How can a young man keep his
way[734] pure?
By [a]keeping *it* according to Thy
word.[1697]
10 With [a]all my heart I have sought
Thee;
Do not let me [b]wander[7686] from
Thy commandments.
11 Thy word[565] I have [a]treasured
in my heart,
That I may not sin[2398] against
Thee.
12 Blessed[1288] art Thou, O LORD;
[a]Teach[3925] me Thy statutes.
13 With my lips[8193] I have
[a]told[5608] of
All the [b]ordinances of Thy
mouth.[6310]
14 I have [a]rejoiced in the way of
Thy testimonies,[5715]
[I]As much as in all riches.
15 I will [a]meditate[7878] on Thy
precepts,
And [I]regard [b]Thy ways.[734]
16 I shall [Ia]delight in Thy
statutes;[2708]
I shall [b]not forget Thy word.

ג Gimel.

17 [a]Deal bountifully[1580] with Thy
servant,[5650]
That I may live[2421] and keep
Thy word.
18 Open[1540] my eyes, that I may
behold
Wonderful things[6381] from Thy
law.
19 I am a [a]stranger in the earth;[776]
Do not hide Thy
commandments from me.
20 My soul[5315] is crushed
[Ia]with longing
After Thine ordinances at all
times.[6256]
21 Thou dost [a]rebuke[1605] the
arrogant,[2086] [I]the
[b]cursed,[779]
Who [c]wander[7686] from Thy
commandments.
22 [a]Take away[1556] reproach[2781]
and contempt from me,

27 [I]Lit., unto [c]Ex. 27:2
28 [a]Ps. 63:1; 140:6 [b]Ex. 15:2; Is. 25:1
29 [a]Ps.118:1

1 [I]Lit., *complete;* or, *having integrity* [a]Ps. 101:2, 6; Prov. 11:20; 13:6 [b]Ps. 128:1; Ezek. 11:20; 18:17; Mic. 4:2
2 [a]Ps. 25:10; 99:7; 119:22, 168 [b]Deut. 4:29; Ps. 119:10 [c]Deut. 6:5; 10:12; 11:13; 13:3; 30:2
3 [a]1John 3:9; 5:18
4 [I]Lit., *commanded* [II]Lit., *To keep* [a]Deut. 4:13; Neh. 9:13
5 [a]Ps. 40:2; Prov. 4:26 [b]Deut. 12:1; 2Chr. 7:17
6 [I]Lit., *to* [a]Job 22:26; Ps. 119:80
7 [a]Ps. 119:62
8 [a]Ps. 38:21; 71:9, 18
9 [a]1Kin. 2:4; 8:25; 2Chr. 6:16
10 [a]2Chr. 15:15; Ps. 119:2, 145 [b]Ps. 119:21, 118
11 [a]Ps. 37:31; 40:8; Luke 2:19, 51
12 [a]Ps. 119:26, 64, 108, 124, 135, 171
13 [a]Ps. 40:9 [b]Ps. 119:72
14 [I]Lit., *As over all* [a]Ps. 119:111, 162
15 [I]Or, *look upon* [a]Ps. 1:2; 119:23, 48, 78, 97, 148 [b]Ps. 25:4; 27:11; Is. 58:2
16 [I]Lit., *delight myself* [a]Ps. 1:2; 119:24, 35, 47, 70, 77, 92, 143, 174 [b]Ps. 119:93
17 [a]Ps. 13:6; 116:7
19 [a]Gen. 47:9; Lev. 25:23; 1Chr. 29:15; Ps. 39:12; 119:54; Heb. 11:13
20 [I]Lit., *for* [a]Ps. 42:1, 2; 63:1; 84:2; 119:40, 131
21 [I]Or, *Cursed are those who wander. . .* [a]Ps. 68:30 [b]Deut. 27:26; Ps. 37:22 [c]Ps. 119:10, 118
22 [a]Ps. 39:8; 119:39

For I [b]observe[5341] Thy
testimonies.
23 Even though [a]princes[8269] sit
and talk[1696] against me,
Thy servant [b]meditates on Thy
statutes.
24 Thy testimonies also are my
[a]delight;
They are [I]my counselors.

ד Daleth.

25 My [a]soul cleaves to the
dust;[6083]
[b]Revive[2421] me [c]according to
Thy word.
26 I have told of my ways, and
Thou hast answered me;
[a]Teach me Thy statutes.
27 Make me understand[995] the
way of Thy precepts,
So I will [a]meditate[7878] on Thy
wonders.[6381]
28 My [a]soul [I]weeps because of
grief;
[b]Strengthen me according to
Thy word.
29 Remove the false way from me,
And graciously grant me Thy
law.
30 I have chosen[977] the faithful[530]
way;
I have [I]placed Thine ordinances
before me.
31 I [a]cleave to Thy testimonies;
O LORD, do not put me to
shame![954]
32 I shall run the way of Thy
commandments,
For Thou wilt [a]enlarge my
heart.

ה He.

33 [a]Teach[3384] me, O LORD, the
way of Thy statutes,
And I shall observe it to the
end.
34 [a]Give me understanding,[995]
that I may [b]observe[8104] Thy
law,
And keep it [c]with all *my* heart.

22 [b]Ps. 119:2
23 [a]Ps. 119:161 [b]Ps. 119:15
24 [I]Lit., *the men of my counsel* [a]Ps. 119:16
25 [a]Ps. 44:25 [b]Ps. 119:37, 40, 88, 93, 107, 149, 154, 156, 159; 143:11 [c]Ps. 119:65
26 [a]Ps. 25:4; 27:11; 86:11; 119:12
27 [a]Ps. 105:2; 145:5
28 [I]Lit., *drops* [a]Ps. 22:14; 107:26 [b]Ps. 20:2; 1Pet. 5:10
30 [I]Or, *accounted Thine ordinances worthy*
31 [a]Deut. 11:22
32 [a]1Kin. 4:29; Is. 60:5; 2Cor. 6:11, 13
33 [a]Ps. 119:5, 12
34 [a]Ps. 119:27, 73, 125, 144, 169 [b]1Chr. 22:12; Ezek. 44:24 [c]Ps. 119:2, 69
35 [a]Ps. 25:4; Is. 40:14 [b]Ps. 112:1; 119:16
36 [a]1Kin. 8:58 [b]Ezek. 33:31; Mark 7:21, 22; Luke 12:15; Heb. 13:5
37 [a]Is. 33:15 [b]Ps. 71:20; 119:25
38 [I]Or, *promise* [II]Lit., *Which is for the fear of Thee* [a]2Sam. 7:25
39 [a]Ps. 119:22
40 [a]Ps. 119:20
41 [I]Or, *promise* [a]Ps. 119:77 [b]Ps. 119:58, 76, 116, 170
42 [a]Prov. 27:11 [b]Ps. 102:8; 119:39
43 [I]Or, *hope in* [a]Ps. 119:49, 74, 81, 114, 147
44 [a]Ps. 119:33
45 [I]Lit., *in a wide place* [a]Prov. 4:12 [b]Ps. 119:94, 155
46 [a]Matt. 10:18; Acts 26:1, 2
47 [I]Lit., *delight myself* [a]Ps. 119:16 [b]Ps. 119:97, 127, 159

35 Make me walk in the
[a]path of Thy
commandments,
For I [b]delight[2654] in it.
36 [a]Incline my heart to Thy
testimonies,
And not to [b]*dishonest* gain.[1215]
37 Turn away[5674] my [a]eyes from
looking[7200] at vanity,[7723]
And [b]revive me in Thy
ways.
38 [a]Establish Thy [I]word to Thy
servant,
[II]As that which produces
reverence[3374] for Thee.
39 [a]Turn away my reproach which
I dread,[3025]
For Thine ordinances are
good.[2896]
40 Behold, I [a]long for Thy
precepts;
Revive me through Thy
righteousness.[6666]

ו Vav.

41 May Thy [a]lovingkindnesses[2617]
also come to me, O LORD,
Thy salvation[8668] [b]according to
Thy [I]word;
42 So I shall have an [a]answer for
him who [b]reproaches me,
For I trust[982] in Thy word.
43 And do not take the word of
truth[571] utterly out of my
mouth,
For I [Ia]wait[3176] for Thine
ordinances.
44 So I will [a]keep Thy law
continually,[8548]
Forever[5769] and ever.[5703]
45 And I will [a]walk [I]at liberty,
For I [b]seek Thy precepts.
46 I will also speak of Thy
testimonies [a]before
kings,[4428]
And shall not be ashamed.
47 And I shall [Ia]delight in Thy
commandments,
Which I [b]love.[157]
48 And I shall lift up[5375] my

119:46 See Jn. 18:33-37; Acts 24:25; 26:1-23.

hands[3709] to Thy
commandments,
Which I [a]love;
And I will [b]meditate on Thy
statutes.

ז Zayin.

49 Remember[2142] the word to Thy
servant,
[I]In which Thou hast made me
hope.[3176]
50 This is my [a]comfort[5162] in my
affliction,
That Thy word has [I]revived[2421]
me.
51 The arrogant [a]utterly deride[3887]
me,
Yet I do not [b]turn aside from
Thy law.
52 I have [a]remembered[2142] Thine
ordinances from [I]of old, O
LORD,
And comfort[5162] myself.
53 Burning [a]indignation[2152] has
seized me because of the
wicked,[7563]
Who [b]forsake Thy law.
54 Thy statutes are my songs
In the house[1004] of my
[a]pilgrimage.[4033]
55 O LORD, I [a]remember Thy
name [b]in the night,[3915]
And keep[8104] Thy law.
56 This has become mine,
[I]That I [a]observe Thy
precepts.

ח Heth.

57 The LORD is my [a]portion;
I have [I]promised[559] to
[b]keep Thy words.[1697]
58 I [a]entreated Thy favor
[b]with all *my* heart;
[c]Be gracious[2603] to me
[d]according to Thy [I]word.
59 I [a]considered[2803] my ways,
And turned my feet to Thy
testimonies.
60 I hastened and did not delay
To keep Thy commandments.
61 The [a]cords[2256] of the wicked
have encircled[5749] me,

48 [a]Ps. 119:97, 127, 159 [b]Ps. 119:15
49 [I]Lit., *On*
50 [I]Or, *preserved me alive* [a]Job 6:10; Rom. 15:4
51 [a]Job 30:1; Jer. 20:7 [b]Job 23:11; Ps. 44:18; 119:157
52 [I]Or, *everlasting* [a]Ps. 103:18
53 [a]Ex. 32:19; Ezra 9:3; Neh. 13:25; Ps. 119:158 [b]Ps. 89:30
54 [a]Gen. 47:9; Ps. 119:19
55 [a]Ps. 63:6 [b]Ps. 42:8; 92:2; 119:62; Is. 26:9; Acts 16:25
56 [I]Or, *Because* [a]Ps. 119:22, 69, 100
57 [I]Lit., *said that I would keep* [a]Ps. 16:5; Lam. 3:24 [b]Deut. 33:9
58 [I]Or, *promise* [a]1Kin. 13:6 [b]Ps. 119:2 [c]Ps. 41:4; 56:1; 57:1 [d]Ps. 119:41
59 [a]Mark 14:72; Luke 15:17
61 [a]Job 36:8; Ps. 140:5 [b]Ps. 119:83, 141, 153, 176
62 [a]Ps. 119:55 [b]Ps. 119:7
63 [I]Or, *revere* [a]Ps. 101:6
64 [a]Ps. 33:5 [b]Ps. 119:12
66 [I]Or, *judgment* [a]Phil. 1:9
67 [a]Ps. 119:71, 75; Jer. 31:18, 19; Heb. 12:5-11
68 [a]Ps. 86:5; 100:5; 106:1; 107:1; Matt. 19:17 [b]Deut. 8:16; 28:63; 30:5; Ps. 125:4 [c]Ps. 119:12
69 [I]Lit., *besmear me with lies* [a]Job 13:4; Ps. 109:2 [b]Ps. 119:56
70 [I]Lit., *gross like fat* [a]Deut. 32:15; Job 15:27; Ps. 17:10; Is. 6:10; Jer. 5:28; Acts 28:27 [b]Ps. 119:16
71 [a]Ps. 119:67, 75
72 [a]Ps. 19:10; 119:127; Prov. 8:10, 11, 19
73 [I]Lit., *established* [a]Job 10:8; 31:15; Ps. 100:3; 138:8; 139:15, 16

But I have [b]not forgotten Thy
law.
62 At [a]midnight I shall rise to give
thanks[3034] to Thee
Because of Thy [b]righteous
ordinances.
63 I am a [a]companion of all those
who [I]fear[3372] Thee,
And of those who keep Thy
precepts.
64 [a]The earth is full of Thy
lovingkindness,[2617] O LORD;
[b]Teach me Thy statutes.

ט Teth.

65 Thou hast dealt[6213] well with
Thy servant,
O LORD, according to Thy
word.
66 Teach me good[2898]
[Ia]discernment[2940]
and knowledge,[1847]
For I believe[539] in Thy
commandments.
67 [a]Before I was afflicted I went
astray,[7683]
But now I keep Thy word.
68 Thou art [a]good[2895] and
[b]doest good;
[c]Teach me Thy statutes.
69 The arrogant [I]have [a]forged a
lie against me;
With all *my* heart I will
[b]observe Thy precepts.
70 Their heart is [Ia]covered with
fat,
But I [b]delight in Thy law.
71 It is [a]good for me that I was
afflicted,
That I may learn[3925] Thy
statutes.
72 The [a]law of Thy mouth is
better[2896] to me
Than thousands[505] of gold and
silver *pieces*.

י Yodh.

73 [a]Thy hands[3027] made[6213] me and
[I]fashioned[3559] me;

[b]Give me understanding, that
I may learn Thy
commandments.
74 May those who [I]fear[3373] Thee
[a]see me and be glad,
Because I [IIb]wait for Thy word.
75 I know, O LORD, that Thy
judgments are
[a]righteous,[6664]
And that [b]in faithfulness[530]
Thou hast afflicted me.
76 O may Thy lovingkindness[2617]
[I]comfort me,
According to Thy [II]word to Thy
servant.
77 May [a]Thy compassion[7356] come
to me that I may live,
For Thy law is my [b]delight.
78 May [a]the arrogant be ashamed,
for they subvert[5791] me
[b]with a lie;[8267]
But I shall [c]meditate on Thy
precepts.
79 May those who [I]fear Thee
turn[7725] to me,
Even those who know[3045] Thy
testimonies.
80 May my heart be
[Ia]blameless[8549] in Thy
statutes,
That I may not [b]be ashamed.

כ Kaph.

81 My [a]soul languishes[3615] for Thy
salvation;
I [Ib]wait for Thy word.
82 My [a]eyes fail[3615] *with longing*
for Thy [I]word,
[II]While I say, "When wilt Thou
comfort me?"
83 Though I have [a]become[1961] like
a wineskin in the smoke,
I do [b]not forget Thy statutes.
84 How many are the [a]days[3117] of
Thy servant?
When wilt Thou [b]execute
judgment[4941] on those who
persecute me?
85 The arrogant have [a]dug pits[7882]
for me,
Men who are not [I]in accord with
Thy law.

73 [b]Ps. 119:34
74 [I]Or, *revere* [II]Or, *hope in* [a]Ps. 34:2; 35:27; 107:42 [b]Ps. 119:43
75 [a]Ps. 119:138 [b]Heb. 12:10
76 [I]Lit., *be for my comfort* [II]Or, *promise*
77 [a]Ps. 119:41 [b]Ps. 119:16
78 [a]Jer. 50:32 [b]Ps. 119:86 [c]Ps. 119:15
79 [I]Or, *revere*
80 [I]Lit., *complete;* or, *having integrity* [a]Ps. 119:1 [b]Ps. 119:46
81 [I]Or, *hope in* [a]Ps. 84:2 [b]Ps. 119:43
82 [I]Or, *promise* [II]Lit., *Saying* [a]Ps. 69:3; 119:123; Is. 38:14; Lam. 2:11
83 [a]Job 30:30 [b]Ps. 119:61
84 [a]Ps. 39:4 [b]Rev. 6:10
85 [I]Lit., *according to Thy law* [a]Ps. 7:15; 35:7; 57:6; Jer. 18:22
86 [a]Ps. 119:138 [b]Ps. 35:19; 119:78, 161 [c]Ps. 109:26
87 [I]Lit., *in the earth* [a]Is. 58:2
89 [I]Lit., *stands firm* [a]Ps. 89:2; 119:160; Is. 40:8; Matt. 24:35; 1Pet. 1:25
90 [I]Lit., *to* [a]Ps. 36:5; 89:1, 2 [b]Ps. 148:6 [c]Eccl. 1:4
91 [a]Jer. 31:35; 33:25 [b]Ps. 104:2-4
92 [a]Ps. 119:16 [b]Ps. 119:50
93 [I]Or, *kept me alive* [a]Ps. 119:16, 83 [b]Ps. 119:25
94 [a]Ps. 119:146 [b]Ps. 119:45
95 [a]Ps. 40:14; Is. 32:7
96 [I]Lit., *an end of*
97 [a]Ps. 119:47, 48, 127, 163, 165 [b]Ps. 1:2; 119:15

86 All Thy commandments are
[a]faithful;[530]
They have [b]persecuted me with
a lie;[8267] [c]help me!
87 They almost destroyed[3615] me
[I]on earth,
But as for me, I [a]did not
forsake[5800] Thy precepts.
88 Revive me according to Thy
lovingkindness,
So that I may keep the
testimony[5715] of Thy
mouth.

ל Lamedh.

89 [a]Forever,[5769] O LORD,
Thy word [I]is settled[5324] in
heaven.[8064]
90 Thy [a]faithfulness *continues*
[I]throughout all
generations;[1755]
Thou didst [b]establish[3559] the
earth, and it [c]stands.
91 They stand this day[3117]
according to Thine
[a]ordinances,[4941]
For [b]all things are Thy
servants.[5650]
92 If Thy law had not been my
[a]delight,
Then I would have perished[6]
[b]in my affliction.
93 I will [a]never forget Thy
precepts,
For by them Thou hast
[Ib]revived me.
94 I am Thine, [a]save[3467] me;
For I have [b]sought Thy
precepts.
95 The wicked [a]wait[6960] for me to
destroy[6] me;
I shall diligently consider[995] Thy
testimonies.
96 I have seen[7200] [I]a limit to all
perfection;
Thy commandment[4687] is
exceedingly broad.

מ Mem.

97 O how I [a]love[157] Thy law!
It is my [b]meditation[7881] all the
day.

98 Thy [a]commandments make me wiser[2449] than my enemies,
For they are ever [I]mine.
99 I have more insight than all my teachers,[3925]
For Thy testimonies are my [a]meditation.
100 I understand [a]more than the aged,[2204]
Because I have [b]observed Thy precepts.
101 I have [a]restrained my feet from every evil[7451] way,
That I may keep Thy word.
102 I have not [a]turned aside[5493] from Thine ordinances,
For Thou Thyself hast taught[3384] me.
103 How [a]sweet are Thy [I]words[565] to my [II]taste!
Yes, sweeter than honey to my mouth!
104 From Thy precepts I [a]get understanding;
Therefore I [b]hate[8130] every false[8267] way.

נ Nun.

105 Thy word is a [a]lamp[5216] to my feet,
And a light[216] to my path.
106 I have [a]sworn, and I will confirm it,
That I will keep Thy righteous ordinances.
107 I am exceedingly [a]afflicted;
[Ib]Revive me, O LORD, according to Thy word.
108 O accept[7521] the [a]freewill offerings[5071] of my mouth, O LORD,
And [b]teach me Thine ordinances.
109 My [Ia]life is continually [II]in my hand,
Yet I do not [b]forget Thy law.
110 The wicked have [a]laid a snare[6341] for me,
Yet I have not [b]gone astray[8582] from Thy precepts.
111 I have [a]inherited[5157] Thy testimonies forever,
For they are the [b]joy of my heart.
112 I have [a]inclined my heart to perform[6213] Thy statutes
Forever, *even* [b]to the end.

ס Samekh.

113 I hate those who are [a]double-minded,
But I love Thy [b]law.
114 Thou art my [a]hiding place and my [b]shield;
I [Ic]wait for Thy word.
115 [a]Depart[5493] from me, evildoers,[7489]
That I may [b]observe the commandments of my God.[430]
116 [a]Sustain me according to Thy [I]word, that I may live;
And [b]do not let me be [II]ashamed of my hope.
117 Uphold me that I may be [a]safe,[3467]
That I may [b]have regard for Thy statutes continually.
118 Thou hast [I]rejected all those [a]who wander from Thy statutes,
For their deceitfulness is [II]useless.
119 Thou hast [I]removed[7673] all the wicked of the earth *like* [a]dross;
Therefore I [b]love Thy testimonies.
120 My flesh[1320] [Ia]trembles for fear of Thee,
And I am [b]afraid[3372] of Thy judgments.

ע Ayin.

121 I have [a]done[6213] justice and righteousness;[6664]
Do not leave me to my oppressors.
122 Be [a]surety[6148] for Thy servant for good;
Do not let the arrogant [b]oppress me.

---

98 [I]Or, *with me* [a]Deut. 4:6; Ps. 119:130
99 [a]Ps. 119:15
100 [a]Job 32:7-9 [b]Ps. 119:22, 56
101 [a]Prov. 1:15
102 [a]Deut. 17:20; Josh. 23:6; 1Kin. 15:5
103 [I]Or, *promises* [II]Lit., *palate* [a]Ps. 19:10; Prov. 8:11; 24:13, 14
104 [a]Ps. 119:130 [b]Ps. 119:128
105 [a]Prov. 6:23
106 [a]Neh. 10:29
107 [I]Or, *Keep me alive* [a]Ps. 119:25, 50 [b]Ps. 119:25
108 [a]Hos. 14:2; Heb. 13:15 [b]Ps. 119:12
109 [I]Lit., *soul* [II]I.e., in danger [a]Judg. 12:3; Job 13:14 [b]Ps. 119:16
110 [a]Ps. 91:3; 140:5; 141:9 [b]Ps. 119:10
111 [a]Deut. 33:4 [b]Ps. 119:14, 162
112 [a]Ps. 119:36 [b]Ps. 119:33
113 [a]1Kin. 18:21; James 1:8; 4:8 [b]Ps. 119:47
114 [I]Or, *hope in* [a]Ps. 31:20; 32:7; 61:4; 91:1 [b]Ps. 84:9 [c]Ps. 119:74
115 [a]Ps. 6:8; 139:19; Matt. 7:23 [b]Ps. 119:22
116 [I]Or, *promise* [II]Lit., *put to shame because of* [a]Ps. 37:17, 24; 54:4 [b]Ps. 25:2, 20; 31:1, 17; Rom. 5:5; 9:33; Phil. 1:20
117 [a]Ps. 12:5; Prov. 29:25 [b]Ps. 119:6, 15
118 [I]Lit., *made light of* [II]Lit., *falsehood* [a]Ps. 119:10, 21
119 [I]Lit., *caused to cease* [a]Is. 1:22, 25; Ezek. 22:18, 19 [b]Ps. 119:47
120 [I]Lit., *bristles up from* [a]Job 4:14; Hab. 3:16 [b]Ps. 119:161
121 [a]2Sam. 8:15; Job 29:14
122 [a]Job 17:3; Heb. 7:22 [b]Ps. 119:134

123 My [a]eyes fail *with longing* for
Thy salvation,[3444]
And for Thy righteous[6664]
[I]word.
124 Deal[6213] with Thy servant
[a]according to Thy
lovingkindness,
And [b]teach me Thy statutes.
125 [a]I am Thy servant; [b]give me
understanding,
That I may know Thy
testimonies.
126 It is time[6256] for the LORD to
[a]act,[6213]
For they have broken[6565] Thy
law.
127 Therefore I [a]love Thy
commandments
Above gold, yes, above fine
gold.
128 Therefore I esteem right[3474] all
Thy [a]precepts concerning
everything,
I [b]hate every false way.

פ Pe.

129 Thy testimonies are
[a]wonderful;[6382]
Therefore my soul [b]observes
them.
130 The [a]unfolding of Thy words
gives light;
It gives [b]understanding to the
simple.
131 I [a]opened my mouth wide and
[b]panted,
For I [c]longed for Thy
commandments.
132 [a]Turn to me and be gracious
to me,
After Thy manner [I]with those
who love Thy name.
133 Establish[3559] my [a]footsteps in
Thy [I]word,
And do not let any iniquity[205]
[b]have dominion[7980] over me.
134 [a]Redeem[6299] me from the
oppression of man,[120]
That I may keep Thy precepts.
135 [a]Make Thy face shine upon Thy
servant,
And [b]teach me Thy statutes.
136 My eyes [I]shed [a]streams of
water,
Because they [b]do not keep Thy
law.

צ Tsadhe.

137 [a]Righteous[6662] art Thou, O
LORD,
And upright are Thy
judgments.
138 Thou hast commanded Thy
testimonies in
[a]righteousness
And exceeding [b]faithfulness.
139 My [a]zeal[7068] has [I]consumed[6789]
me,
Because my adversaries have
forgotten Thy words.
140 Thy [Ia]word is very [II]pure,[6884]
Therefore Thy servant
[b]loves[157] it.
141 I am small and [a]despised,
Yet I do not [b]forget Thy
precepts.
142 Thy righteousness is an
everlasting[5769]
righteousness,
And [a]Thy law is truth.
143 Trouble and anguish[4689] have
[I]come upon me;
Yet Thy commandments are my
[a]delight.
144 Thy [a]testimonies are righteous
forever;
[b]Give me understanding that I
may live.

ק Qoph.

145 I cried[7121] [a]with all my
heart; answer[8085] me, O
LORD!
I will [b]observe Thy statutes.
146 I cried to Thee; [a]save me,
And I shall keep Thy
testimonies.
147 I [Ia]rise before dawn and cry for
help;
I [II]wait for Thy words.
148 My eyes anticipate the
[a]night watches,
That I may [b]meditate on Thy
[I]word.

123 [I]Or, *promise* [a]Ps. 119:82
124 [a]Ps. 51:1; 106:45; 109:26; 119:88, 149, 159 [b]Ps. 119:12
125 [a]Ps. 116:16 [b]Ps. 119:27
126 [a]Jer. 18:23; Ezek. 31:11
127 [a]Ps. 19:10; 119:47
128 [a]Ps. 19:8 [b]Ps. 119:104
129 [a]Ps. 119:18 [b]Ps. 119:22
130 [a]Prov. 6:23 [b]Ps. 19:7
131 [a]Job 29:23; Ps. 81:10 [b]Ps. 42:1 [c]Ps. 119:20
132 [I]Lit., *to* [a]Ps. 25:16; 106:4
133 [I]Or, *promise* [a]Ps. 17:5 [b]Ps. 19:13; Rom. 6:12
134 [a]Ps. 119:84; 142:6; Luke 1:74
135 [a]Num. 6:25; Ps. 4:6; 31:16; 67:1; 80:3, 7, 19 [b]Ps. 119:12
136 [I]Lit., *run down* [a]Jer. 9:1, 18; 14:17; Lam. 3:48 [b]Ps. 119:158
137 [a]Ezra 9:15; Neh. 9:33; Ps. 116:5; 129:4; 145:17; Jer. 12:1; Lam. 1:18; Dan. 9:7, 14
138 [a]Ps. 19:7-9; 119:144, 172 [b]Ps. 119:86, 90
139 [I]Lit., *put an end to* [a]Ps. 69:9; John 2:17
140 [I]Or, *promise* [II]Lit., *refined* [a]Ps. 12:6; 19:8 [b]Ps. 119:47
141 [a]Ps. 22:6 [b]Ps. 119:61
142 [a]Ps. 19:9; 119:151, 160
143 [I]Lit., *found me* [a]Ps. 119:24
144 [a]Ps. 19:9 [b]Ps. 119:27
145 [a]Ps. 119:10 [b]Ps. 119:22, 55
146 [a]Ps. 3:7
147 [I]Lit., *anticipate the dawn* [II]Or, *hope in* [a]Ps. 5:3; 57:8; 108:2
148 [I]Or, *promise* [a]Ps. 63:6 [b]Ps. 119:15

149 Hear my voice [a]according to
Thy lovingkindness;
[b]Revive me, O Lord, according
to Thine ordinances.
150 Those who follow after
wickedness draw near;
They are far from Thy law.
151 Thou art [a]near, O Lord,
And all Thy commandments are
[b]truth.
152 Of old[6924] I have [a]known from
Thy testimonies,
That Thou hast founded[3245]
them [b]forever.

ר Resh.

153 [a]Look[7200] upon my [b]affliction
and rescue[2502] me,
For I do not [c]forget Thy
law.
154 [a]Plead my cause[7379] and
[b]redeem me;
Revive me according to Thy
[1]word.
155 Salvation is [a]far from the
wicked,
For they [b]do not seek Thy
statutes.
156 [1a]Great are Thy mercies, O
Lord;
Revive me according to Thine
ordinances.
157 Many are my [a]persecutors and
my adversaries,
Yet I do not [b]turn aside from
Thy testimonies.
158 I behold the [a]treacherous[898]
and [b]loathe *them*,
Because they do not keep Thy
[1]word.
159 Consider how I [a]love Thy
precepts;
[b]Revive me, O Lord, according
to Thy lovingkindness.
160 The [a]sum[7218] of Thy word is
[b]truth,[571]
And every one of Thy righteous
ordinances [c]is everlasting.

ש Shin.

161 [a]Princes persecute me without
cause,
But my heart [b]stands in awe[6342]
of Thy words.
162 I [a]rejoice at Thy [1]word,
As one who [b]finds great spoil.
163 I [a]hate and despise[8581]
falsehood,
But I [b]love Thy law.
164 Seven times a day I praise[1984]
Thee,
Because of Thy [a]righteous
ordinances.
165 Those who love Thy law have
[a]great peace,
And [1b]nothing causes[4383] them
to stumble.
166 I [a]hope for Thy salvation, O
Lord,
And do Thy commandments.
167 My [a]soul keeps Thy
testimonies,
And I [b]love them exceedingly.
168 I [a]keep Thy precepts and Thy
testimonies,
For all my [b]ways are before
Thee.

ת Tav.

169 Let my [a]cry [1]come[7126] before
Thee, O Lord;
[b]Give me understanding
[c]according to Thy word.
170 Let my [a]supplication come
before Thee;
[b]Deliver[5337] me according to
Thy [1]word.
171 Let my [a]lips utter praise,[8416]
For Thou [b]dost teach[3925] me
Thy statutes.
172 Let my [a]tongue sing of Thy
[1]word,
For all Thy [b]commandments
are righteousness.
173 Let Thy [a]hand[3027] be
[1]ready to help me,
For I have [b]chosen Thy
precepts.
174 I [a]long for Thy salvation, O
Lord,

149 [a]Ps. 119:124 [b]Ps. 119:25 **151** [a]Ps. 34:18; 145:18; Is. 50:8 [b]Ps. 119:142 **152** [a]Ps. 119:125 [b]Ps. 119:89; Luke 21:33 **153** [a]Lam. 5:1 [b]Ps. 119:50 [c]Ps. 119:16; Prov. 3:1; Hos. 4:6 **154** [1]Or, *promise* [a]1Sam. 24:15; Ps. 35:1; Mic. 7:9 [b]Ps. 119:134 **155** [a]Job 5:4 [b]Ps. 119:45, 94 **156** [1]Or, *Many* [a]2Sam. 24:14 **157** [a]Ps. 7:1; 119:86, 161 [b]Ps. 119:51 **158** [1]Or, *promise* [a]Is. 21:2; 24:16 [b]Ps. 139:21 **159** [a]Ps. 119:47 [b]Ps. 119:25 **160** [a]Ps. 139:17 [b]Ps. 119:142 [c]Ps. 119:89, 152 **161** [a]1Sam. 24:11; 26:18; Ps. 119:23 [b]Ps. 119:120 **162** [1]Or, *promise* [a]Ps. 119:14, 111 [b]1Sam. 30:16; Is. 9:3 **163** [a]Ps. 31:6; 119:104, 128; Prov. 13:5 [b]Ps. 119:47 **164** [a]Ps. 119:7, 160 **165** [1]Lit., *they have no stumbling block* [a]Ps. 37:11; Prov. 3:2; Is. 26:3; 32:17 [b]Prov. 3:23; Is. 63:13; 1John 2:10 **166** [a]Gen. 49:18; Ps. 119:81, 174 **167** [a]Ps. 119:129 [b]Ps. 119:47 **168** [a]Ps. 119:22 [b]Job 24:23; Ps. 139:3; Prov. 5:21 **169** [1]Lit., *come near before* [a]Job 16:18; Ps. 18:6; 102:1 [b]Ps. 119:27, 144 [c]Ps. 119:65, 154 **170** [1]Or, *promise* [a]Ps. 28:2; 130:2; 140:6; 143:1 [b]Ps. 22:20; 31:2; 59:1 **171** [a]Ps. 51:15; 63:3 [b]Ps. 94:12; 119:12; Is. 2:3; Mic. 4:2 **172** [1]Or, *promise* [a]Ps. 51:14 [b]Ps. 119:138 **173** [1]Lit., *to help me* [a]Ps. 37:24; 73:23 [b]Josh. 24:22; Luke 10:42 **174** [a]Ps. 119:166

And Thy law is my [b]delight.
175 Let my [a]soul live that it may praise Thee,
And let Thine ordinances help me.
176 I have [a]gone astray[8582] like a lost[6] sheep; seek Thy servant,
For I do [b]not forget Thy commandments.

Prayer for Deliverance from the Treacherous

A Song of [+]Ascents.

120 [a]In my trouble I cried[7121] to the LORD,
And He answered me.
2 Deliver[5337] my soul,[5315] O LORD, from [a]lying lips,[8193]
From a [b]deceitful tongue.
3 What shall be given to you, and what more shall be done to you,
You [a]deceitful tongue?
4 [a]Sharp arrows of the warrior,
With the *burning* [b]coals of the broom tree.
5 Woe is me, for I sojourn[1481] in [a]Meshech,
For I dwell[7931] among the [b]tents[168] of [c]Kedar!
6 Too long has my soul had its dwelling[7931]
With those who [a]hate peace.
7 I [a]am *for* peace, but when I speak,[1696]
They are [b]for war.

The LORD the Keeper of Israel

A Song of Ascents.

121 I will [a]lift up[5375] my eyes to [b]the mountains;
From whence shall my help come?
2 My [a]help *comes* from the LORD,
Who [b]made[6213] heaven[8064] and earth.[776]
3 He will not [a]allow your foot to slip;
He who [b]keeps[8104] you will not slumber.
4 Behold, He who keeps Israel
Will neither slumber nor sleep.
5 The LORD is your [a]keeper;[8104]
The LORD is your [b]shade on your right hand.[3027]
6 The [a]sun will not smite[5221] you by day,[3119]
Nor the moon by night.[3915]
7 The LORD will [I][a]protect[8104] you from all evil;[7451]
He will keep your soul.[5315]
8 The LORD will [I][a]guard your going out and your coming in
[b]From this time forth and forever.[5769]

Prayer for the Peace of Jerusalem

A Song of Ascents, of David.

122 I was glad when they said[559] to me,
"Let us [a]go to the house[1004] of the LORD."
2 Our feet are standing
Within your [a]gates, O Jerusalem,
3 Jerusalem, that is [a]built
As a city that is [b]compact together;
4 To which the tribes[7626] [a]go up, even the tribes of [I]the LORD—
[II]An ordinance[5715] for Israel—
To give thanks[3034] to the name of the LORD.
5 For there [a]thrones[3678] were set for judgment,
The thrones of the house of David.
6 Pray for the [a]peace of Jerusalem:
"May they prosper who [b]love[157] you.
7 "May peace be within your [a]walls,
And prosperity within your [b]palaces."[759]
8 For the sake of my [a]brothers[251] and my friends,

174 [b]Ps. 119:16, 24
175 [a]Is. 55:3
176 [a]Is. 53:6; Jer. 50:6; Matt. 18:12; Luke 15:4 [b]Ps. 119:16

[+]Ex. 34:24; 1Kin. 12:27
1 [a]Ps. 18:6; 66:14; 102:2; Jon. 2:2
2 [a]Ps. 109:2; Prov. 12:22 [b]Ps. 52:4; Zeph. 3:13
3 [a]Ps. 52:4; Zeph. 3:13
4 [a]Ps. 45:5; Prov. 25:18; Is. 5:28 [b]Ps. 140:10
5 [a]Gen. 10:2; 1Chr. 1:5; Ezek. 27:13; 38:2, 3; 39:1 [b]Song 1:5 [c]Gen. 25:13; Is. 21:16; 60:7; Jer. 2:10; 49:28; Ezek. 27:21
6 [a]Ps. 35:20
7 [a]Ps. 109:4 [b]Ps. 55:21

1 [a]Ps. 123:1; Is. 40:26 [b]Ps. 87:1
2 [a]Ps. 124:8 [b]Ps. 115:15
3 [a]1Sam. 2:9; Ps. 66:9 [b]Ps. 41:2; 127:1; Is. 27:3
5 [a]Ps. 91:4 [b]Ps. 16:8; 91:1; Is. 25:4
6 [a]Ps. 91:5; Is. 49:10; Jon. 4:8; Rev. 7:16
7 [I]Or, *keep* [a]Ps. 41:2; 91:10-12
8 [I]Or, *keep* [a]Deut. 28:6 [b]Ps. 113:2; 115:18

1 [a]Ps. 42:4; Is. 2:3; Mic. 4:2; Zech. 8:21
2 [a]Ps. 9:14; 87:2; 116:19; Jer. 7:2
3 [a]Ps. 48:13; 147:2 [b]2Sam. 5:9; Neh. 4:6
4 [I]Heb., *YAH* [II]Or, *A testimony* [a]Ex. 23:17; Deut. 16:16; Ps. 84:5
5 [a]Deut. 17:8; 2Chr. 19:8; Ps. 89:29
6 [a]Ps. 29:11; Jer. 29:7 [b]Ps. 102:14

7 [a]Ps. 51:18; Is. 62:6 [b]Ps. 48:3, 13; Jer. 17:27
8 [a]Ps. 133:1

I will now say,[1696] "[b]May peace
be within you."
9 For the sake of the house of the
LORD our God[430]
I will [a]seek your good.[2896]

Prayer for the LORD's Help

A Song of Ascents.

123 To Thee I [a]lift up my eyes,
O Thou who [b]art enthroned
in the heavens![8064]
2 Behold, as the eyes of
[a]servants[5650] *look* to the
hand[3027] of their master,[113]
As the eyes of a maid to the
hand of her mistress;[1404]
So our [b]eyes *look* to the LORD
our God,[430]
Until He shall be gracious[2603] to
us.
3 [a]Be gracious to us, O LORD, be
gracious to us;
For we are greatly filled
[b]with contempt.
4 Our soul[5315] is greatly filled
With the [a]scoffing of [b]those who
are at ease,
And with the [c]contempt of the
proud.[3238]

Praise for Rescue from Enemies

A Song of Ascents, of David.

124 "[a]Had it not been the LORD
who was on our side,"
[b]Let Israel now say,[559]
2 "Had it not been the LORD who
was on our side,
When men[120] rose up against us;
3 Then they would have
[a]swallowed[1104] us alive,[2416]
When their [b]anger[639] was
kindled[2734] against us;
4 Then the [a]waters would have
engulfed[7857] us,
The stream would have
[I]swept over our soul;[5315]
5 Then the [a]raging waters would
have [I]swept over our soul."
6 Blessed[1288] be the LORD,
Who has not given us [I]to be
[a]torn by their teeth.
7 Our soul has [a]escaped[4422] [b]as a
bird out of the [c]snare[6341] of
the trapper;[3369]
The snare is broken[7665] and we
have escaped.
8 Our [a]help is in the name of the
LORD,
Who [b]made[6213] heaven[8064] and
earth.[776]

The LORD Surrounds His People

A Song of Ascents.

125 Those who trust[982] in the
LORD
Are as Mount Zion, which
[a]cannot be moved, but
[b]abides forever.[5769]
2 As the mountains surround
Jerusalem,
So [a]the LORD surrounds His
people[5971]
[b]From this time forth and
forever.
3 For the [a]scepter of
wickedness[7562] shall not rest
upon the [I]land of the
righteous;[6662]
That the righteous [b]may not put
forth their hands[3027] to do
wrong.[5766]
4 [a]Do good,[2895] O LORD, to those
who are good,[2896]
And to those who are
[b]upright in their hearts.[3826]
5 But as for those who [a]turn aside
to their [b]crooked ways,
The LORD will lead them away
with the [c]doers of iniquity.[205]
[d]Peace be upon Israel.

Thanksgiving for Return from Captivity

A Song of Ascents.

126 When the LORD [a]brought
back[7725] [I]the captive[7622]
ones of Zion,
We were [b]like those who dream.

---

8 [b]1Sam. 25:6; John 20:19
9 [a]Neh. 2:10; Esth. 10:3

1 [a]Ps. 121:1; 141:8 [b]Ps. 2:4; 11:4
2 [a]Prov. 27:18; Mal. 1:6 [b]Ps. 25:15
3 [a]Ps. 4:1; 51:1 [b]Neh. 4:4; Ps. 119:22
4 [a]Neh. 2:19; Ps. 79:4 [b]Job 12:5; Is. 32:9, 11; Amos 6:1 [c]Neh. 4:4; Ps. 119:22

1 [a]Ps. 94:17 [b]Ps. 129:1
3 [a]Num. 16:30; Ps. 35:25; 56:1; 57:3; Prov. 1:12 [b]Gen. 39:19; Ps. 138:7
4 [I]Or, *passed over* [a]Job 22:11; Ps. 18:16; 32:6; 69:2; 144:7
5 [I]Or, *passed over* [a]Job 38:11
6 [I]Lit., *as a prey to* [a]Ps. 27:2; Prov. 30:14
7 [a]Ps. 141:10; 2Cor. 11:33; Heb. 11:34 [b]Prov. 6:5 [c]Ps. 91:3; Hos. 9:8
8 [a]Ps. 121:2 [b]Gen. 1:1; Ps. 134:3

1 [a]Ps. 46:5 [b]Ps. 61:7; Eccl. 1:4
2 [a]Zech. 2:5 [b]Ps. 121:8
3 [I]Lit., *lot* [a]Ps. 89:22; Prov. 22:8; Is. 14:5 [b]1Sam. 24:10; Ps. 55:20; Acts 12:1
4 [a]Ps. 119:68 [b]Ps. 7:10; 11:2; 32:11; 36:10; 94:15
5 [a]Job 23:11; Ps. 40:4; 101:3 [b]Prov. 2:15; Is. 59:8 [c]Ps. 92:7; 94:4 [d]Ps. 128:6; Gal. 6:16

1 [I]Or, *those who returned to* [a]Ps. 85:1; Jer. 29:14; Hos. 6:11 [b]Acts 12:9

2 Then our [a]mouth[6310] was filled
with laughter,
And our [b]tongue with joyful
shouting;
Then they said[559] among the
nations,[1471]
"The LORD has [c]done[6213] great
things for them."
3 The LORD has done great things
for us;
We are [a]glad.
4 Restore[7725] our captivity, O
LORD,
As the [I][a]streams in the
[II]South.
5 Those who sow in [a]tears shall
reap with [b]joyful shouting.
6 He who goes to and fro weeping,
carrying[5375] *his* bag of
seed,[2233]
Shall indeed come again with a
shout of joy, bringing[5375] his
sheaves *with him.*

Prosperity Comes from the LORD

A Song of Ascents, of Solomon.

127 Unless the LORD [a]builds the
house,[1004]
They labor in vain[7723] who build
it;
Unless the LORD [b]guards[8104] the
city,
The watchman[8104] keeps awake
in vain.
2 It is vain for you to rise up early,
To [I]retire late,
To [a]eat the bread of [II]painful
labors;[6089]
For He gives to His [b]beloved[3039]
[c]*even in his* sleep.
3 Behold, [a]children[1121] are a
[I]gift[5159] of the LORD;
The [b]fruit of the womb[990] is a
reward.
4 Like arrows in the hand[3027] of
a [a]warrior,
So are the children of one's
youth.
5 How [a]blessed[835] is the man[1397]
whose quiver is full of them;
[b]They shall not be ashamed,[954]
When they [c]speak[1696] with their
enemies [d]in the gate.

Blessedness of the Fear of the LORD

A Song of Ascents.

128 [a]How blessed[835] is everyone
who fears the LORD,
Who [b]walks in His ways.[1870]
2 When you shall [a]eat of the
[I][b]fruit of your hands,[3709]
You will be happy[835] and
[c]it will be well with you.
3 Your wife[802] shall be like a
[a]fruitful vine,
[I]Within your house,[1004]
Your children[1121] like [b]olive
plants
Around your table.
4 Behold, for thus shall the
man[1397] be blessed[1288]
Who fears the LORD.
5 [a]The LORD bless[1288] you
[b]from Zion,
And may you see the
prosperity[2898] of Jerusalem all
the days[3117] of your life.[3576]
6 Indeed, may you see your
[a]children's children.
[b]Peace be upon Israel!

Prayer for the Overthrow of Zion's Enemies

A Song of Ascents.

129 "[I]Many times they have
[II][a]persecuted me from
my [b]youth up,"
[c]Let Israel now say,[559]
2 "[I]Many times they have
[II]persecuted me from my
youth up;
Yet they have [a]not prevailed
against me.
3 "The plowers plowed upon my
back;
They lengthened[748] their
furrows." 4618

---

2 [a]Job 8:21 [b]Ps. 51:14; Is. 35:6 [c]1Sam. 12:24; Ps. 71:19; Luke 1:49
3 [a]Is. 25:9; Zeph. 3:14
4 [I]Lit., *stream-beds* [II]Heb., *Negev* [a]Is. 35:6; 43:19
5 [a]Ps. 80:5; Jer. 31:9, 16; Lam. 1:2 [b]Is. 35:10; 51:11; 61:7; Gal. 6:9

1 [a]Ps. 78:69 [b]Ps. 121:4
2 [I]Lit., *delay sitting* [II]Lit., *toils* [a]Gen. 3:17, 19 [b]Ps. 60:5 [c]Job 11:18, 19; Prov. 3:24; Eccl. 5:12
3 [I]Or, *heritage* [a]Gen. 33:5; 48:4; Josh. 24:3, 4; Ps. 113:9 [b]Deut. 7:13; 28:4; Is. 13:18
4 [a]Ps. 112:2; 120:4
5 [a]Ps. 128:2, 3 [b]Prov. 27:11 [c]Is. 29:21; Amos 5:12 [d]Gen. 34:20

1 [a]Ps. 112:1; 119:1 [b]Ps. 119:3
2 [I]Lit., *labor* [a]Is. 3:10 [b]Ps. 109:11; Hag. 2:17 [c]Eccl. 8:12; Eph. 6:3
3 [I]Lit., *In the innermost parts of* [a]Ezek. 19:10 [b]Ps. 52:8; 144:12
5 [a]Ps. 134:3 [b]Ps. 20:2; 135:21
6 [a]Gen. 48:11; 50:23; Job 42:16; Ps. 103:17; Prov. 17:6 [b]Ps. 125:5

1 [I]Lit., *Much* [II]Lit., *showed hostility toward* [a]Ex. 1:11; Judg. 3:8; Ps. 88:15 [b]Is. 47:12; Jer. 2:2; 22:21; Ezek. 16:22; Hos. 2:15; 11:1 [c]Ps. 124:1
2 [I]Lit., *Much* [II]Lit., *showed hostility toward* [a]Jer. 1:19; 15:20; 20:11; Matt. 16:18; 2Cor. 4:8,9

4 The LORD [a]is righteous;[6662]
He has cut in two the
[b]cords of the wicked.[7563]
5 May all who [a]hate[8130] Zion,
Be [b]put to shame[954] and turned
backward,
6 Let them be like [a]grass upon the
housetops,
Which withers[3001] before[6924] it
[I]grows up;
7 With which the reaper does not
fill his [I]hand,
Or the binder of sheaves his
[a]bosom;
8 Nor do those who pass by say,
"The [a]blessing[1293] of the LORD be
upon you;
We bless[1288] you in the name
of the LORD."

Hope in the LORD's Forgiving Love

A Song of Ascents.

130 Out of the [a]depths I have
cried[7121] to Thee, O LORD.
2 Lord,[136] [a]hear[8085] my voice!
Let [b]Thine ears[241] be attentive
To the [c]voice of my
supplications.[8469]
3 If Thou, [I]LORD, shouldst
mark[8104] iniquities,[5771]
O Lord, who could [a]stand?
4 But there is [a]forgiveness[5547]
with Thee,
That Thou mayest be
[b]feared.[3372]
5 I wait[6960] for the LORD, my
[a]soul[5315] does wait,
And [I][b]in His word[1697] do I
hope.[3176]
6 My soul *waits* for the Lord
More than the watchmen[8104]
[a]for the morning;
Indeed, more than the watchmen
for the morning.
7 O Israel, [a]hope in the LORD;
For with the LORD there is
[b]lovingkindness,[2617]
And with Him is [c]abundant
redemption.[6304]
8 And He will [a]redeem[6299] Israel
From all his iniquities.

4 [a]Ps. 119:137 [b]Ps. 140:5
5 [a]Mic. 4:11 [b]Ps. 70:3; 71:13
6 [I]Lit., *draws out* [a]2Kin. 19:26; Ps. 37:2; Is. 37:27
7 [I]Lit., *palm* [a]Ps. 79:12
8 [a]Ruth 2:4; Ps. 118:26

1 [a]Ps. 42:7; 69:2; Lam. 3:55
2 [a]Ps. 64:1; 119:149 [b]2Chr. 6:40; Neh. 1:6, 11 [c]Ps. 28:2; 140:6
3 [I]Heb., *YAH* [a]Ps. 76:7; 143:2; Nah. 1:6; Mal. 3:2; Rev. 6:17
4 [a]Ex. 34:7; Neh. 9:17; Ps. 86:5; Is. 55:7; Dan. 9:9 [b]1Kin. 8:39, 40; Jer. 33:8,9
5 [I]Lit., *for* [a]Ps. 27:14; 33:20; 40:1; 62:1, 5; Is. 8:17; 26:8 [b]Ps. 119:74, 81
6 [a]Ps. 63:6; 119:147
7 [a]Ps. 131:3 [b]Ps. 86:5; 103:4 [c]Ps. 111:9; Rom. 3:24; Eph. 1:7
8 [a]Ps. 103:3, 4; Luke 1:68; Titus 2:14

1 [I]Or, *lofty* [II]Lit., *go after, walk* [III]Or, *marvelous* [a]2Sam. 22:28; Ps. 101:5; Is. 2:12; Zeph. 3:11 [b]Prov. 30:13; Is. 5:15 [c]Jer. 45:5; Rom. 12:16 [d]Job 42:3; Ps. 139:6
2 [I]Or, *upon* [a]Ps. 62:1 [b]Matt. 18:3; 1Cor. 14:20
3 [a]Ps. 130:7 [b]Ps. 113:2

1 [a]Gen. 49:24; 2Sam. 16:12
2 [a]Gen. 49:24; Is. 49:26; 60:16
3 [I]Lit., *come into the tabernacle of* [II]Lit., *go up into the couch of* [a]Job 21:28
4 [a]Prov. 6:4
5 [I]Lit., *Dwelling places* [a]1Kin. 8:17; 1Chr. 22:7; Ps. 26:8; Acts 7:46 [b]Ps. 132:2

Childlike Trust in the LORD

A Song of Ascents, of David.

131 O LORD, my heart[3820] is
not [a]proud, nor my eyes
[I][b]haughty;
Nor do I [II]involve myself in
[c]great matters,
Or in things [d]too [III]difficult for
me.
2 Surely I have [a]composed and
quieted my soul;
Like a weaned [b]child *rests*
[I]against his mother,[517]
My soul[5315] is like a weaned child
[I]within me.
3 O Israel, [a]hope[3176] in the LORD
[b]From this time forth and
forever.[5769]

Prayer for the LORD's Blessing upon the Sanctuary

A Song of Ascents.

132 Remember,[2142] O LORD, on
David's behalf,
All [a]his affliction;
2 How he swore[7650] to the LORD,
And vowed[5087] to [a]the Mighty
One[430] of Jacob,
3 "Surely I will not [I]enter
[a]my house,[1004]
Nor [II]lie on my bed;
4 I will not [a]give sleep to my eyes,
Or slumber to my eyelids;
5 Until I find a [a]place for the LORD,
[I]A dwelling place[4908] for
[b]the Mighty One of Jacob."
6 Behold, we heard[8085] of it in
[a]Ephrathah;
We found it in the [b]field[7704] of
[I]Jaar.
7 Let us go into His [I][a]dwelling
place;[4908]
Let us [b]worship[7812] at His
[c]footstool.
8 [a]Arise, O LORD, to Thy
[b]resting place;

6 [I]Or, *the wood* [a]Gen. 35:19; 1Sam. 17:12 [b]1Sam. 7:1
7 [I]Lit., *dwelling places* [a]Ps. 43:3 [b]Ps. 5:7; 99:5 [c]1Chr. 28:2
8 [a]Num. 10:35; 2Chr. 6:41; Ps. 68:1 [b]Ps. 132:14

Thou and the ark[727] of Thy
[c]strength.
9 Let Thy priests[3548] be [a]clothed
with righteousness;[6664]
And let Thy [b]godly ones[2623] sing
for joy.
10 For the sake of David Thy
servant,[5650]
Do not turn[7725] away the face
of Thine [a]anointed.[4899]
11 The LORD has [a]sworn to David,
A truth[571] from which He will
not turn back;
"[b]Of the fruit of your body[990] I
will set upon your throne.[3678]
12 "If your sons[1121] will keep[8104] My
covenant,[1285]
And My testimony[5713] which I
will teach[3925] them,
Their sons also shall [a]sit upon
your throne forever."[5703]
13 For the LORD has [a]chosen[977]
Zion;
He has [b]desired it for His
habitation.
14 "This is My [a]resting place
forever;[5703]
Here I will [b]dwell, for I have
desired it.
15 "I will abundantly [a]bless[1288] her
provision;
I will [b]satisfy her needy with
bread.
16 "Her [a]priests also I will clothe
with salvation;[3468]
And her [a]godly ones will sing
aloud for joy.
17 "There I will cause the
[a]horn of David to spring
forth;
I have prepared a [b]lamp[5216] for
Mine anointed.
18 "His enemies I will [a]clothe with
shame;
But upon himself his [b]crown[5145]
shall shine."

The Excellency of Brotherly Unity

A Song of Ascents, of David.

133 Behold, how good[2896] and
how pleasant it is
For [a]brothers[251] to dwell
together in unity!
2 It is like the precious[2896]
[a]oil[8081] upon the head,[7218]
Coming down upon the
beard,[2206]
Even Aaron's beard,
Coming down upon the
[b]edge of his robes.
3 It is like the [a]dew of [b]Hermon,
Coming down upon the
[c]mountains of Zion;
For there the LORD
[d]commanded[6680] the
blessing—[1293] [e]life[2416]
forever.[5769]

Greetings of Night Watchers

A Song of Ascents.

134 Behold, [a]bless[1288] the LORD,
all [b]servants[5650] of the
LORD,
Who [I][c]serve [d]by night[3915] in the
house[1004] of the LORD!
2 [a]Lift up[5375] your hands[3027] to the
[b]sanctuary,[6944]
And bless the LORD.
3 May the LORD [a]bless you from
Zion,
He who [b]made[6213] heaven[8064]
and earth.[776]

Praise the LORD's Wonderful Works. Vanity of Idols

135 [I][a]Praise[1984] [II]the LORD!
Praise the name of the
LORD;
Praise *Him*, O [b]servants[5650] of
the LORD,
2 You who stand in the house[1004]
of the LORD,
In the [a]courts of the house of
our God![430]
3 [I]Praise [II]the LORD, for
[a]the LORD is good;[2896]
[b]Sing praises[2167] to His name,
[c]for it is lovely.
4 For [I]the LORD has [a]chosen[977]
Jacob for Himself,

---

8 [c]Ps. 78:61
9 [a]Job 29:14 [b]Ps. 30:4; 132:16; 149:5
10 [a]Ps. 2:2; 132:17
11 [a]Ps. 89:3, 35 [b]2Sam. 7:12-16; 1Chr. 17:11-14; 2Chr. 6:16; Ps. 89:4; Acts 2:30
12 [a]Luke 1:32; Acts 2:30
13 [a]Ps. 48:1, 2; 78:68 [b]Ps. 68:16
14 [a]Ps. 132:8 [b]Ps. 68:16; Matt. 23:21
15 [a]Ps. 147:14 [b]Ps. 107:9
16 [a]2Chr. 6:41; Ps. 132:9
17 [a]Ezek. 29:21; Luke 1:69 [b]1Kin. 11:36; 15:4; 2Kin. 8:19; 2Chr. 21:7; Ps. 18:28
18 [a]Job 8:22; Ps. 35:26; 109:29 [b]Ps. 21:3

1 [a]Gen. 13:8; Heb. 13:1
2 [a]Ex. 29:7; 30:25, 30; Lev. 8:12 [b]Ex. 28:33; 39:24
3 [a]Prov. 19:12; Hos. 14:5; Mic. 5:7 [b]Deut. 3:9; 4:48 [c]Ps. 48:2; 74:2; 78:68 [d]Lev. 25:21; Deut. 28:8; Ps. 42:8 [e]Ps. 21:4

1 [I]Lit., *stand* [a]Ps. 103:21 [b]Ps. 135:1, 2 [c]Deut. 10:8; 1Chr. 23:30; 2Chr. 29:11 [d]1Chr. 9:33
2 [a]Ps. 28:2; 1Tim. 2:8 [b]Ps. 63:2
3 [a]Ps. 128:5 [b]Ps. 124:8

1 [I]Or, *Hallelujah!* [II]Heb., *YAH* [a]Ps. 113:1 [b]Ps. 134:1
2 [a]Ps. 92:13; 116:19
3 [I]Or, *Hallelujah!* [II]Heb., *YAH* [a]Ps. 100:5; 119:68 [b]Ps. 68:4 [c]Ps. 147:1
4 [I]Heb., *YAH* [a]Deut. 7:6; 10:15; Ps. 105:6

Israel for His [II][b]own possession.[5459]
5 For I know that [a]the LORD is great,
And that our Lord[113] is [b]above all gods.[430]
6 [a]Whatever the LORD pleases,[2654] He does,[6213]
In heaven[8064] and in earth,[776] in the seas and in all deeps.
7 [I]He [a]causes the [II]vapors to ascend[5927] from the ends of the earth;
Who [b]makes[6213] lightnings for the rain;
Who [c]brings forth the wind[7307] from His treasuries.
8 [I]He [a]smote[5221] the first-born of Egypt,
[II]Both of man[120] and beast.
9 [I]He sent [a]signs[226] and wonders[4159] into your midst, O Egypt,
Upon [b]Pharaoh and all his servants.
10 [I][a]He [b]smote many nations,[1471]
And slew[2026] mighty kings,[4428]
11 [a]Sihon, king[4428] of the Amorites,
And [b]Og, king of Bashan,
And [c]all the kingdoms[4467] of Canaan;
12 And He [a]gave their land[776] as a heritage,[5159]
A heritage to Israel His people.[5971]
13 Thy [a]name, O LORD, is everlasting,[5769]
Thy [I]remembrance,[2143] O LORD, [II]throughout all generations.[1755]
14 For the LORD will [a]judge[1777] His people,
And [b]will have compassion[5162] on His servants.
15 The [a]idols[6091] of the nations[1471] are *but* silver and gold,
The work of man's[120] hands.[3027]
16 They have mouths,[6310] but they do not speak;[1696]
They have eyes, but they do not see;
17 They have ears,[241] but they do not hear;[238]
Nor is there any breath[7307] at all in their mouths.
18 Those who make[6213] them will be like them,
Yes, everyone who trusts[982] in them.
19 O house of [a]Israel, bless[1288] the LORD;
O house of Aaron, bless the LORD;
20 O house of Levi, bless the LORD;
You [a]who [I]revere[3373] the LORD, bless the LORD.
21 Blessed[1288] be the LORD [a]from Zion,
Who [b]dwells[7931] in Jerusalem.
[I]Praise [II]the LORD!

Thanks for the LORD's Goodness to Israel

136 [a]Give thanks[3034] to the LORD, for [b]He is good;[2896]
For [c]His lovingkindness is everlasting.[5769]
2 Give thanks to the [a]God[430] of gods,[430]
For His lovingkindness is everlasting.
3 Give thanks to the [a]Lord[113] of lords,
For His lovingkindness is everlasting.
4 To Him who [a]alone does[6213] great [I]wonders,[6381]
For His lovingkindness is everlasting;
5 To Him who [a]made[6213] the heavens[8064] [I][b]with skill,[8394]
For His lovingkindness is everlasting;
6 To Him who [a]spread out[7554] the earth[776] above the waters,
For His lovingkindness is everlasting;
7 To Him who [a]made *the* great lights,

4 [II]Or, *special treasure* [b]Ex. 19:5; Mal. 3:17; Titus 2:14; 1Pet. 2:9
5 [a]Ps. 48:1; 95:3; 145:3 [b]Ps. 97:9
6 [a]Ps. 115:3
7 [I]Lit., *The one who* [II]I.e., clouds [a]Jer. 10:13; 51:16 [b]Job 28:25, 26; 38:25, 26; Zech. 10:1 [c]Jer. 10:13; 51:16
8 [I]Lit., *The one who* [II]Lit., *From man to beast* [a]Ex. 12:12; Ps. 78:51; 105:36
9 [I]Lit., *The one who* [a]Ex. 7:10; Deut. 6:22; Ps. 78:43 [b]Ps. 136:15
10 [I]Lit., *The one who* [a]Num. 21:24; Ps. 135:10-12; 136:17-21 [b]Ps. 44:2
11 [a]Num. 21:21-26; Deut. 29:7 [b]Num. 21:33-35 [c]Josh. 12:7-24
12 [a]Deut. 29:8; Ps. 78:55; 136:21, 22
13 [I]Or, *memorial* [II]Lit., *to* [a]Ex. 3:15; Ps. 102:12
14 [a]Deut. 32:36; Ps. 50:4 [b]Ps. 90:13; 106:46
15 [a]Ps. 115:4-8; 135:15-18
19 [a]Ps. 115:9
20 [I]Lit., *fear* [a]Ps. 118:4
21 [I]Or, *Hallelujah!* [II]Heb., YAH [a]Ps. 128:5; 134:3 [b]Ps. 132:14

1 [a]1Chr. 16:34; Ps. 106:1; 107:1; 118:1; Jer. 33:11 [b]2Chr. 5:13; 7:3; Ezra 3:11; Ps. 100:5 [c]1Chr. 16:41; 2Chr. 20:21; Ps. 118:1-4
2 [a]Deut. 10:17
3 [a]Deut. 10:17
4 [I]I.e., wonderful acts [a]Deut. 6:22; Job 9:10; Ps. 72:18
5 [I]Lit., *with understanding* [a]Gen. 1:1 [b]Ps. 104:24; Prov. 3:19; Jer. 10:12; 51:15
6 [a]Gen. 1:2, 6, 9; Ps. 24:2; Is. 42:5; 44:24; Jer. 10:12
7 [a]Gen. 1:14-18; Ps. 74:16

For His lovingkindness is
everlasting:
8 The [a]sun4475 to rule [I]by day,3117
For His lovingkindness is
everlasting,
9 The [a]moon and stars to rule
[I]by night,3915
For His lovingkindness is
everlasting.
10 To Him who [a]smote5221 [I]the
Egyptians in their first-born,
For His lovingkindness is
everlasting,
11 And [a]brought Israel out from
their midst,
For His lovingkindness is
everlasting,
12 With a [a]strong2389 hand3027 and
an [b]outstretched arm,
For His lovingkindness is
everlasting;
13 To Him who [a]divided1504 the
[I]Red Sea [II]asunder,1506
For His lovingkindness2617 is
everlasting,
14 And [a]made Israel pass
through5674 the midst of it,
For His lovingkindness is
everlasting;
15 But [a]He [I]overthrew Pharaoh and
his army in the [II]Red Sea,
For His lovingkindness is
everlasting.
16 To Him who [a]led His people5971
through the wilderness,
For His lovingkindness is
everlasting;
17 To Him who [a]smote great
kings,4428
For His lovingkindness is
everlasting,
18 And [a]slew2026 [I]mighty117 kings,
For His lovingkindness is
everlasting:
19 [a]Sihon, king4428 of the Amorites,
For His lovingkindness is
everlasting,
20 And [a]Og, king of Bashan,
For His lovingkindness is
everlasting,
21 And [a]gave their land776 as a
heritage,5159

8 [I]Or, *over the* [a]Gen. 1:16
9 [I]Or, *over the* [a]Gen. 1:16
10 [I]Lit., *Egypt* [a]Ex. 12:29; Ps. 78:51; 135:8
11 [a]Ex. 12:51; 13:3; Ps. 105:43
12 [a]Ex. 6:1; 13:9; 1Kin. 8:42; Neh. 1:10; Ps. 44:3; Jer. 32:21 [b]Ex. 6:6; Deut. 4:34; 5:15; 7:19; 9:29; 11:2; 2Kin. 17:36; 2Chr. 6:32; Jer. 32:17
13 [I]Lit., *Sea of Reeds* [II]Lit., *in parts* [a]Ex. 14:21; Ps. 66:6; 78:13
14 [a]Ex. 14:22; Ps. 106:9
15 [I]Lit., *shook off* [II]Lit., *Sea of Reeds* [a]Ex. 14:27; Ps. 78:53; 106:11
16 [a]Ex. 13:18; 15:22; Deut. 8:15; Ps. 78:52
17 [a]Ps. 135:10-12; 136:17-22
18 [I]Lit., *majestic* [a]Deut. 29:7
19 [a]Num. 21:21-24
20 [a]Num. 21:33-35
21 [a]Josh. 12:1
22 [a]Ps. 105:6; Is. 41:8; 44:1; 45:4
23 [a]Ps. 9:12; 103:14; 106:45
24 [a]Judg. 6:9; Neh. 9:28; Ps. 107:2
25 [a]Ps. 104:27; 145:15
26 [a]Gen. 24:3, 7; 2Chr. 36:23; Ezra 1:2; 5:11; Neh. 1:4

1 [a]Ezek. 1:1, 3 [b]Neh. 1:4
2 [I]Or, *poplars* [II]Lit., *lyres* [a]Lev. 23:40; Is. 44:4 [b]Job 30:31; Is. 24:8; Ezek. 26:13
3 [I]Lit., *asked* [II]Lit., *words of song* [a]Ps. 80:6 [b]Is. 49:17
4 [a]2Chr. 29:27; Neh. 12:46
5 [I]I.e., become lame [a]Is. 65:11
6 [I]Lit., *cause to ascend* [a]Job 29:10; Ps. 22:15; Ezek. 3:26 [b]Neh. 2:3

For His lovingkindness is
everlasting,
22 Even a heritage to Israel His
[a]servant,5650
For His lovingkindness is
everlasting.
23 Who [a]remembered2142 us in our
low estate,
For His lovingkindness is
everlasting,
24 And has [a]rescued us from our
adversaries,
For His lovingkindness is
everlasting;
25 Who [a]gives food to all flesh,
For His lovingkindness is
everlasting.
26 Give thanks to the [a]God410 of
heaven,8064
For His lovingkindness is
everlasting.

An Experience of the Captivity

137 By the [a]rivers of Babylon,
There we sat down and
[b]wept,
When we remembered2142
Zion.
2 Upon the [Ia]willows in the midst
of it
We [b]hung our [II]harps.
3 For there our captors7617
[Ia]demanded7592 of us
[II]songs,7892
And [b]our tormentors mirth,
saying,
"Sing7891 us one of the songs7892
of Zion."
4 How can we sing [a]the LORD'S
song
In a foreign5236 land?127
5 If I [a]forget you, O Jerusalem,
May my right hand [I]forget *her*
skill.
6 May my [a]tongue cleave to the
roof of my mouth,
If I do not remember2142
you,
If I do not [Ib]exalt5927 Jerusalem
Above my chief7218 joy.

7 Remember, O LORD, against the sons[1121] of [a]Edom
The day[3117] of Jerusalem,
Who said,[559] "Raze[6168] it, raze it,
[b]To its very foundation."[3247]
8 O daughter of Babylon, you [I][a]devastated one,
How blessed[835] will be the one who [b]repays[7999] you
With [II]the recompense with which you have repaid us.
9 How blessed will be the one who seizes and [a]dashes your little ones
Against the rock.

7 [a]Ps. 83:4-8; Is. 34:5, 6; Jer. 49:7-22; Lam. 4:21; Ezek. 25:12-14; 35:2; Amos 1:11; Obad. 10-14 [b]Ps. 74:7; Hab. 3:13
8 [I]Or, *devastator* [II]Lit., *your recompense* [a]Is. 13:1-22; 47:1-15; Jer. 25:12; 50:1-46; 51:1-64 [b]Jer. 50:15; 51:24, 35, 36, 49; Rev. 18:6
9 [a]2Kin. 8:12; Is. 13:16; Hos. 13:16; Nah. 3:10

Thanksgiving for the LORD's Favor

A Psalm of David.

138 [a]I will give Thee thanks[3034] with all my heart;[3820]
I will sing praises[2167] to Thee before the [b]gods.[430]
2 I will bow down[7812] [a]toward Thy holy[6944] temple,[1964]
And [b]give thanks to Thy name for Thy lovingkindness and Thy [I]truth;[571]
For Thou hast [c]magnified Thy [II]word[565] [III]according to all Thy name.
3 On the day[3117] I [a]called[7121] Thou didst answer me;
Thou didst make me bold with [b]strength in my soul.[5315]
4 [a]All the kings[4428] of the earth[776] will give thanks to Thee, O LORD,
When they have heard[8085] the words[561] of Thy mouth.[6310]
5 And they will [a]sing[7891] of the ways[1870] of the LORD.
For [b]great is the glory[3519] of the LORD.
6 For [a]though the LORD is exalted,
Yet He [b]regards[7200] the lowly;
But the [c]haughty He knows from afar.
7 Though I [a]walk in the midst[7130] of trouble, Thou wilt [I][b]revive[2421] me;
Thou wilt [c]stretch forth Thy hand against the wrath[639] of my enemies,
And Thy right hand[3027] will [d]save[3467] me.
8 The LORD will [a]accomplish[1584] what concerns me;
Thy [b]lovingkindness,[2617] O LORD, is everlasting;[5769]
[c]Do not forsake[7503] the [d]works of Thy hands.[3027]

1 [a]Ps. 111:1 [b]Ps. 95:3; 96:4; 97:7
2 [I]Or, *faithfulness* [II]Or, *promise* [III]Or, *together with* [a]1Kin. 8:29; Ps. 5:7; 28:2 [b]Ps. 140:13 [c]Is. 42:21
3 [a]Ps. 118:5 [b]Ps. 28:7; 46:1
4 [a]Ps. 72:11; 102:15
5 [a]Ps. 145:7 [b]Ps. 21:5
6 [a]Ps. 113:4-7 [b]Prov. 3:34; Is. 57:15; Luke 1:48; James 4:6; 1Pet. 5:5 [c]Ps. 40:4; 101:5
7 [I]Or, *keep me alive* [a]Ps. 23:4; 143:11 [b]Ezra 9:8, 9; Ps. 71:20; Is. 57:15 [c]Ex. 7:5; 15:12; Is. 5:25; Jer. 51:25; Ezek. 6:14; 25:13 [d]Ps. 20:6; 60:5
8 [a]Ps. 57:2; Phil. 1:6 [b]Ps. 136:1 [c]Job 10:8; Ps. 27:9; 71:9; 119:8 [d]Job 10:3; 14:15; Ps. 100:3

God's Omnipresence and Omniscience

For the choir director. A Psalm of David.

139 O LORD, Thou hast [a]searched me and known[3045] *me.*
2 Thou [a]dost know[3045] [I]when I sit down and [II]when I rise up;[6965]
Thou [b]dost understand[995] my thought from afar.
3 Thou [a]dost [I]scrutinize my [II]path[734] and my lying down,
And art intimately acquainted[5532] with all my ways.[1870]
4 [I]Even before there is a word[4405] on my tongue,
Behold, O LORD, Thou [a]dost know it all.
5 Thou hast [a]enclosed me behind and before,

1 [a]Ps. 17:3; 44:21; Jer. 12:3
2 [I]Lit., *my sitting* [II]Lit., *my rising* [a]2Kin. 19:27 [b]Ps. 94:11; Is. 66:18; Matt. 9:4
3 [I]Lit., *winnow* [II]Or, *journeying* [a]Job 14:16; 31:4
4 [I]Lit., *For there is not* [a]Heb. 4:13
5 [a]Ps. 34:7; 125:2

139:2-4 How does one reconcile this passage (and Jer. 17:10; Acts 1:24; Heb. 4:13) with Gen. 22:12 and Deut. 8:2; 13:3? Does God know everything or not? In the latter passages, the language is accommodative. God merely conducted an experiment with Abraham to prove that the result would be the same every time, much as a physics professor knows the outcome of the same experiment year after year. Still, it must be demonstrated. The Lord dealt with the Israelites *as if* He were ignorant and wished to ascertain their sentiments toward Him.

And [b]laid Thy hand upon me.
6 *Such* [a]knowledge[1847] is [b]too wonderful[6383] for me;
It is *too* high, I cannot attain to it.
7 [a]Where can I go from Thy Spirit?[7307]
Or where can I flee from Thy presence?
8 [a]If I ascend[5927] to heaven,[8064] Thou art there;
If I make my bed in [I]Sheol,[7585] behold, [b]Thou art there.
9 If I take[5375] the wings of the dawn,
If I dwell[7931] in the remotest part[319] of the sea,
10 Even there Thy hand[3027] will [a]lead[5148] me,
And Thy right hand will lay hold of me.
11 If I say,[559] "Surely the [a]darkness[2822] will [I]overwhelm me,
And the light[216] around me will be night,"[3915]
12 Even the [a]darkness is not dark[2821] [I]to Thee,
And the night is as bright as the day.[3117]
[b]Darkness[2825] and light[219] are alike *to Thee.*
13 For Thou didst [a]form my [I]inward parts;[3629]
Thou didst [b]weave me in my mother's[517] womb.[990]
14 I will give thanks[3034] to Thee, for [I]I am fearfully[3372] and wonderfully made;
[a]Wonderful[6381] are Thy works,
And my soul[5315] knows it very well.
15 My [Ia]frame was not hidden from Thee,
When I was made[6213] in secret,
And skillfully wrought in the [b]depths of the earth.[776]
16 Thine [a]eyes have seen my unformed substance;
And in [b]Thy book[5612] they were all written,

5 [b]Job 9:33
6 [a]Rom. 11:33 [b]Job 42:3
7 [a]Jer. 23:24
8 [I]I.e., the nether world [a]Amos 9:2-4 [b]Job 26:6; Prov. 15:11
10 [a]Ps. 23:2, 3
11 [I]Lit., *bruise;* some commentators read *cover* [a]Job 22:13
12 [I]Lit., *from* [a]Job 34:22; Dan. 2:22 [b]1John 1:5
13 [I]Lit., *kidneys* [a]Ps. 119:73; Is. 44:24 [b]Job 10:11
14 [I]Some ancient versions read *Thou art fearfully wonderful* [a]Ps. 40:5
15 [I]Lit., *bones were* [a]Job 10:8-10; Eccl. 11:5 [b]Ps. 63:9
16 [a]Job 10:8-10; Eccl. 11:5 [b]Ps. 56:8 [c]Job 14:5
17 [a]Ps. 40:5; 92:5
18 [a]Ps. 40:5 [b]Ps. 3:5
19 [a]Is. 11:4 [b]Ps. 6:8; 119:115 [c]Ps. 5:6; 26:9
20 [I]Or, *of* [II]Some mss. read *lift themselves up against Thee* [a]Jude 15 [b]Ex. 20:7; Deut. 5:11
21 [a]2Chr. 19:2; Ps. 26:5; 31:6 [b]Ps. 119:158
23 [a]Job 31:6; Ps. 26:2 [b]Ps. 7:9; Prov. 17:3; Jer. 11:20; 1Thess. 2:4
24 [I]Lit., *way of pain* [a]Ps. 146:9; Prov. 15:9; 28:10; Jer. 25:5; 36:3 [b]Ps. 5:8; 143:10 [c]Ps. 16:11

1 [a]Ps. 17:13; 59:2; 71:4 [b]Ps. 18:48; 86:14; 140:11
2 [a]Ps. 7:14; 36:4; 52:2; Prov. 6:14; Is. 59:4; Hos. 7:15 [b]Ps. 56:6

The [c]days[3117] that were ordained[3335] *for me,*
When as yet there was not one of them.
17 How precious also are Thy [a]thoughts to me, O God![410]
How vast is the sum[7218] of them!
18 If I should count[5608] them, they would [a]outnumber the sand.
When [b]I awake, I am still with Thee.
19 O that Thou wouldst [a]slay the wicked,[7563] O God;[433]
[b]Depart[5493] from me, therefore, [c]men[582] of bloodshed.[1818]
20 For they [a]speak[559] [I]against Thee wickedly,[4209]
And Thine enemies [IIb]take *Thy name* in vain.
21 Do I not [a]hate those who hate[8130] Thee, O LORD?
And do I not [b]loathe those who rise up against Thee?
22 I hate them with the utmost hatred;[8135]
They have become my enemies.
23 [a]Search me, O God, and know[3045] my heart;[3824]
[b]Try[974] me and know my anxious thoughts;[8312]
24 And see if there be any [Ia]hurtful[6090] way[1870] in me,
And [b]lead me in the [c]everlasting[5769] way.

Prayer for Protection against the Wicked

For the choir director. A Psalm of David.

140 [a]Rescue[2502] me, O LORD, from evil[7451] men;[120]
Preserve[5341] me from [b]violent[2555] men,[376]
2 Who [a]devise[2803] evil things[7451] in *their* hearts;[3820]
They [b]continually stir up wars.

3 They [a]sharpen[8150] their tongues
as a serpent;[5175]
[b]Poison[2534] of a viper[5919] is under
their lips.[8193] [I]Selah.
4 [a]Keep[8104] me, O LORD, from the
hands[3027] of the wicked;[7563]
[b]Preserve me from violent
men,
Who have [I]purposed[2803] to
[IIc]trip up my feet.
5 The proud have [a]hidden a
trap[6341] for me, and cords;
They have spread a [b]net by the
[I]wayside;
They have set [c]snares[4170] for
me. Selah.
6 I [a]said[559] to the LORD, "Thou art
my God;[410]
[b]Give ear,[238] O LORD, to the
[c]voice of my supplications.
7 "O [I]GOD the Lord,[136] [a]the
strength of my salvation,[3444]
Thou hast [b]covered my head[7218]
in the day[3117] of [II]battle.[5402]
8 "Do not grant, O LORD, the
[a]desires[3970] of the wicked;
Do not promote [b]his *evil*
device,[2162] *lest* they be
exalted. Selah.
9 "As for the head of those who
surround me,
May the [a]mischief[5999] of their lips
cover[3680] them.
10 "May [a]burning coals fall upon
them;
May they be [b]cast[5307] into the
fire,
Into [I]deep pits from which they
[c]cannot rise.
11 "May a [I]slanderer not be
established[3559] in the
earth;[776]
[a]May evil hunt the violent man
[II]speedily."
12 I know[3045] that the LORD will
[a]maintain[6213] the cause[1779] of
the afflicted,
And [b]justice[4941] for the poor.
13 Surely the [a]righteous[6662] will
give thanks[3034] to Thy name;
The [b]upright will dwell in Thy
presence.

3 [I]*Selah* may mean: *Pause, Crescendo* or *Musical interlude* [a]Ps. 57:4; 64:3 [b]Ps. 58:4; Rom. 3:13; James 3:8
4 [I]Or, *devised* [II]Lit., *push violently* [a]Ps. 71:4 [b]Ps. 140:1 [c]Ps. 36:11
5 [I]Lit., *track* [a]Job 18:9; Ps. 35:7; 141:9; 142:3 [b]Ps. 31:4; 57:6; Lam. 1:13 [c]Ps. 141:9; Is. 8:14; Amos 3:5
6 [a]Ps. 16:2; 31:14 [b]Ps. 143:1 [c]Ps. 116:1; 130:2
7 [I]Heb., *YHWH*, usually rendered *LORD* [II]Lit., *weapons* [a]Ps. 28:8; 118:14 [b]Ps. 144:10
8 [a]Ps. 112:10 [b]Esth. 9:25; Ps. 10:2, 3
9 [a]Ps. 7:16; Prov. 18:7
10 [I]Lit., *watery* [a]Ps. 11:6 [b]Ps. 21:9; Matt. 3:10 [c]Ps. 36:12
11 [I]Lit., *man of tongue* [II]Lit., *thrust upon thrust* [a]Ps. 34:21
12 [a]1Kin. 8:45, 49; Ps. 9:4; 18:27; 82:3 [b]Ps. 12:5; 35:10
13 [a]Ps. 97:12 [b]Ps. 11:7; 16:11; 17:15

1 [a]Ps. 22:19; 38:22; 70:5 [b]Ps. 5:1; 143:1
2 [I]Lit., *fixed* [a]Ex. 30:8; Luke 1:10; Rev. 5:8; 8:3, 4 [b]1Tim. 2:8 [c]Ex. 29:39, 41; 1Kin. 18:29, 36; Dan. 9:21
3 [I]Lit., *to* [a]Ps. 34:13; 39:1; Prov. 13:3; 21:23 [b]Mic. 7:5
4 [I]Lit., *in* [a]Ps. 119:36 [b]Is. 32:6; Hos. 6:8; Mal. 3:15 [c]Prov. 23:6
5 [I]Or, *lovingly* [II]Lit., *And my prayer* [III]Or, *in spite of their calamities* [a]Prov. 9:8; 19:25; 25:12; 27:6; Eccl. 7:5; Gal. 6:1 [b]Ps. 23:5; 133:2 [c]Ps. 35:14

An Evening Prayer for Sanctification and Protection

A Psalm of David.

141 O LORD, I call[7121] upon Thee;
[a]hasten to me!
[b]Give ear[238] to my voice when
I call to Thee!
2 May my prayer[8605] be
[I]counted[3559] as [a]incense[7004]
before Thee;
The [b]lifting up of my hands[3709]
as the [c]evening offering.[4503]
3 Set a [a]guard, O LORD,
[I]over my mouth;[6310]
Keep[5341] watch over the
[b]door of my lips.[8193]
4 [a]Do not incline my heart[3820] to
any evil[7451] thing,
To practice deeds [I]of
wickedness[7562]
With men[376] who [b]do iniquity;[205]
And [c]do not let me eat of their
delicacies.
5 Let the [a]righteous[6662] smite[1986]
me [I]in kindness[2617] and
reprove[3198] me;
It is [b]oil[8081] upon the head;[7218]
Do not let my head refuse it,
[II]For still my prayer [c]is
[III]against their wicked deeds.
6 Their judges[8199] are [a]thrown
down by the sides of the rock,
And they hear[8085] my words,[561]
for they are pleasant.
7 As when one [a]plows and breaks
open the earth,[776]
Our [b]bones[6106] have been
scattered at the [c]mouth of
[I]Sheol.[7585]
8 For my [a]eyes are toward Thee,
O [I]GOD, the Lord;[136]
In Thee I [b]take refuge;[2620]
[c]do not [II]leave me
defenseless.
9 Keep[8104] me from the
[Ia]jaws[6341] of the trap which

6 [a]2Chr. 25:12 7 [I]I.e., the nether world [a]Ps. 129:3 [b]Ps. 53:5 [c]Num. 16:32, 33; Ps. 88:3-5
8 [I]Heb., *YHWH*, usually rendered *LORD* [II]Lit., *pour out my soul* [a]Ps. 25:15; 123:2 [b]Ps. 2:12; 11:1 [c]Ps. 27:9 9 [I]Lit., *hands of the trap* [a]Ps. 38:12; 64:5; 91:3; 119:110

they have set[3369] for me,
And from the [b]snares[4170] of
those who do iniquity.
10 Let the wicked[7563] [a]fall into their
own nets,
While I pass by [I][b]safely.

Prayer for Help in Trouble

+Maskil of David, when he was •in the cave. A Prayer.

142 I [a]cry aloud[2199] with my voice
to the LORD;
I [b]make supplication[2603] with my
voice to the LORD.
2 I [a]pour[8210] out my complaint[7878]
before Him;
I declare[5046] my [b]trouble before
Him.
3 When [a]my spirit[7307] [I]was
overwhelmed within me,
Thou didst know my path.
In the way[734] where I walk
They have [b]hidden[2934] a trap[6341]
for me.
4 Look to the right and see;
For there is [a]no one who
regards[5234] me;
[I]There is no [b]escape for me;
[c]No one cares for my soul.[5315]
5 I cried out to Thee, O LORD;
I said,[559] "Thou art [a]my refuge,
My [b]portion in the [c]land[776] of the
living.[2416]
6 "[a]Give heed to my cry,
For I am [b]brought very low;
Deliver[5337] me from my
persecutors,
For they are too [c]strong for me.
7 "[a]Bring my soul out of prison,
So that I may give thanks[3034] to
Thy name;
The righteous[6662] will surround
me,
For Thou wilt [b]deal
bountifully[1580] with me."

9 [b]Ps. 140:5
10 [I]Lit., *altogether* [a]Ps. 7:15; 35:8; 57:6 [b]Ps. 124:7

+Possibly, *Contemplative*, or *Didactic*, or *Skillful Psalm* •1Sam. 22:1; 24:3
1 [a]Ps. 77:1 [b]Ps. 30:8
2 [a]Ps. 102:title [b]Ps. 77:2
3 [I]Lit., *fainted* [a]Ps. 77:3; 143:4 [b]Ps. 140:5
4 [I]Lit., *Escape has perished from me* [a]Ps. 31:11; 88:8, 18 [b]Job 11:20; Jer. 25:35 [c]Jer. 30:17
5 [a]Ps. 91:2, 9 [b]Ps. 16:5; 73:26 [c]Ps. 27:13
6 [a]Ps. 17:1 [b]Ps. 79:8; 116:6 [c]Ps. 18:17
7 [a]Ps. 143:11; 146:7 [b]Ps. 13:6

1 [a]Ps. 140:6 [b]Ps. 89:1, 2 [c]Ps. 71:2
2 [a]Job 14:3; 22:4 [b]1Kin. 8:46; Job 4:17; 9:2; 25:4; Ps. 130:3; Eccl. 7:20; Rom. 3:10, 20; Gal. 2:16
3 [a]Ps. 44:25 [b]Ps. 88:6; Lam. 3:6
4 [I]Lit., *faints* [II]Or, *desolate* [a]Ps. 77:3; 142:3 [b]Lam. 3:11
5 [a]Ps. 77:5, 10, 11 [b]Ps. 77:12 [c]Ps. 105:2
6 [I]Lit., *weary* [II]*Selah* may mean: *Pause, Crescendo* or *Musical interlude* [a]Job 11:13; Ps. 88:9 [b]Ps. 42:2; 63:1
7 [a]Ps. 69:17 [b]Ps. 73:26; 84:2; Jer. 8:18; Lam. 1:22 [c]Ps. 27:9; 69:17; 102:2 [d]Ps. 28:1; 88:4
8 [a]Ps. 90:14 [b]Ps. 46:5 [c]Ps. 25:2 [d]Ps. 27:11; 32:8; 86:11 [e]Ps. 25:1; 86:4

Prayer for Deliverance and Guidance

A Psalm of David.

143 Hear[8085] my prayer,[8605] O
LORD,
[a]Give ear[238] to my
supplications![8469]
Answer me in Thy
[b]faithfulness,[530] in Thy
[c]righteousness![6666]
2 And [a]do not enter into
judgment[4941] with Thy
servant,[5650]
For in Thy sight [b]no man
living[2416] is righteous.[6663]
3 For the enemy has persecuted
my soul;[5315]
He has crushed[1792] my life[2416]
[a]to the ground;[776]
He [b]has made me dwell in dark
places,[4285] like those who
have long[5769] been dead.[4191]
4 Therefore [a]my spirit[7307] [I]is
overwhelmed within me;
My heart[3820] is [II][b]appalled[8074]
within me.
5 I [a]remember[2142] the days[3117] of
old;[6924]
I [b]meditate[1897] on all Thy doings;
I [c]muse[7878] on the work of Thy
hands.[3027]
6 I [a]stretch out my hands to Thee;
My [b]soul *longs* for Thee, as a
[I]parched land.[776] [II]Selah.
7 [a]Answer me quickly, O LORD,
my [b]spirit fails;[3615]
[c]Do not hide Thy face from me,
Lest I become like [d]those who
go down to the pit.[953]
8 Let me hear Thy [a]lovingkindness
[b]in the morning;
For I trust[982] [c]in Thee;
Teach[3045] me the [d]way[1870] in
which I should walk;
For to Thee I [e]lift up[5375] my
soul.

142:7 "Bring my soul out of prison" probably refers to the prison house of trouble and affliction (see Ps. 143:11). There are several passages throughout Psalms where this same figure of speech is employed.

9 [a]Deliver[5337] me, O LORD, from
my enemies;
[I]I take refuge[3680] in Thee.
10 [a]Teach[3925] me to do[6213] Thy
will,[7522]
For Thou art my God;[430]
Let [b]Thy good[2896] Spirit
[c]lead[5148] me on level [I]ground.
11 [a]For the sake of Thy name, O
LORD, [b]revive[2421] me.
[c]In Thy righteousness bring my
soul out of trouble.
12 And in Thy lovingkindness[2617]
[Ia]cut off[6789] my enemies,
And [b]destroy[6] all those who
afflict my soul;
For [c]I am Thy servant.

Prayer for Rescue and Prosperity

A Psalm of David.

144 Blessed[1288] be the LORD, [a]my
rock,
Who [b]trains[3925] my hands[3027] for
war,
And my fingers for battle;
2 My lovingkindness[2617] and
[a]my fortress,
My [b]stronghold and my
deliverer;
My [c]shield and He in whom I
take refuge;[2620]
Who [d]subdues [I]my people[5971]
under me.
3 O LORD, [a]what is man,[120] that
Thou dost take
knowledge[3045] of him?
Or the son[1121] of man,[582] that
Thou dost think of him?
4 [a]Man is like a mere breath;
His [b]days[3117] are like a
passing[5674] shadow.
5 [a]Bow Thy heavens,[8064] O LORD,
and [b]come down;
[c]Touch[5060] the mountains, that
they may smoke.[6225]
6 Flash forth [a]lightning and scatter
them;
Send out Thine [b]arrows and
confuse[1949] them.

9 [I]Lit., *To Thee have I hidden* [a]Ps. 31:15; 59:1
10 [I]Lit., *land* [a]Ps. 25:4, 5; 119:12 [b]Neh. 9:20 [c]Ps. 23:3
11 [a]Ps. 25:11 [b]Ps. 119:25 [c]Ps. 31:1; 71:2
12 [I]Or, *silence* [a]Ps. 54:5 [b]Ps. 52:5 [c]Ps. 116:16

1 [a]Ps. 18:2 [b]2Sam. 22:35; Ps. 18:34
2 [I]Another reading is *peoples* [a]Ps. 18:2; 91:2 [b]Ps. 59:9 [c]Ps. 3:3; 28:7; 84:9 [d]Ps. 18:39
3 [a]Job 7:17; Ps. 8:4; Heb. 2:6
4 [a]Ps. 39:11 [b]Job 8:9; 14:2; Ps. 102:11; 109:23
5 [a]Ps. 18:9 [b]Is. 64:1 [c]Ps. 104:32
6 [a]Ps. 18:14 [b]Ps. 7:13; 58:7; Hab. 3:11; Zech. 9:14
7 [a]Ps. 18:16 [b]Ps. 69:1, 14 [c]Ps. 18:44; 54:3
8 [a]Ps. 12:2; 41:6 [b]Gen. 14:22; Deut. 32:40; Ps. 106:26; Is. 44:20
9 [a]Ps. 33:3; 40:3 [b]Ps. 33:2
10 [a]Ps. 18:50 [b]2Sam. 18:7; Ps. 140:7
11 [a]Ps. 18:44; 54:3 [b]Ps. 12:2; 41:6 [c]Gen. 14:22; Deut. 32:40; Ps. 106:26; Is. 44:20
12 [I]Lit., *cut after the pattern of* [a]Ps. 92:12-14; 128:3 [b]Song 4:4; 7:4
13 [I]Lit., *outside* [a]Prov. 3:9, 10
14 [I]Lit., *be laden* [II]Lit., *bursting forth* [III]Lit., *going out* [a]Prov. 14:4 [b]2Kin. 25:10, 11 [c]Amos 5:3 [d]Is. 24:11; Jer. 14:2
15 [a]Ps. 33:12

1 [a]Ps. 30:1; 66:17 [b]Ps. 5:2 [c]Ps. 34:1

7 Stretch forth Thy hand[3027]
[a]from on high;
Rescue me and [b]deliver[5337] me
out of great waters,
Out of the hand of [c]aliens[1121]
8 Whose mouths[6310] [a]speak
deceit,[7723]
And whose [b]right hand is a right
hand of falsehood.
9 I will sing[2167] a [a]new song[7892]
to Thee, O God;[430]
Upon a [b]harp of ten strings I
will sing praises[2167] to Thee,
10 Who dost [a]give salvation[8668] to
kings;[4428]
Who [b]dost rescue David His
servant[5650] from the evil[7451]
sword.[2719]
11 Rescue me, and deliver me out
of the hand of [a]aliens,
Whose mouth [b]speaks deceit,
And whose [c]right hand is a right
hand of falsehood.
12 Let our sons[1121] in their youth
be as [a]grown-up plants,
And our daughters as [b]corner
pillars [I]fashioned as for[8403] a
palace;[1964]
13 *Let* our [a]garners[4200] be full,
furnishing every kind of
produce,
And our flocks bring forth
thousands and ten thousands
in our [I]fields;
14 *Let* our [a]cattle [I]bear,
Without [IIb]mishap and without
[IIIc]loss,
Let there be no [d]outcry in our
streets!
15 How blessed[835] are the people
who are so situated;
How [a]blessed are the people
whose God is the LORD!

The LORD Extolled for His Goodness

A Psalm of Praise, of David.

145 I will [a]extol Thee, [b]my
God,[430] O King;[4428]
And I will [c]bless[1288] Thy name
forever and ever.[5769,5703]

2 Every day[3117] I will bless Thee,
And I will [a]praise[1984] Thy name
forever and ever.[5769,5703]
3 [a]Great is the LORD, and highly
to be praised;[1984]
And His [b]greatness is
unsearchable.
4 One [a]generation[1755] shall
praise[7623] Thy works to
another,
And shall declare[5046] Thy mighty
acts.
5 On the [a]glorious[3519] [I]splendor[1926]
of Thy majesty,[1935]
And [b]on Thy wonderful
works,[6381] I will meditate.[7878]
6 And men shall speak[559] of the
[I]power of Thine [a]awesome
acts;[3372]
And I will [b]tell[5608] of Thy
greatness.
7 They shall [I]eagerly utter the
memory[2143] of Thine
[a]abundant goodness,
And shall [b]shout joyfully of Thy
righteousness.[6666]
8 The LORD is [a]gracious[2587] and
merciful;
Slow to anger[639] and great in
lovingkindness.[2617]
9 The LORD is [a]good[2896] to all,
And His [b]mercies[7356] are over
all His works.
10 [a]All Thy works shall give
thanks[3034] to Thee, O LORD,
And Thy [b]godly ones[2623] shall
bless Thee.
11 They shall speak of the
[a]glory[3519] of Thy kingdom,[4438]
And talk[1696] of Thy power;
12 To [a]make known[3045] to the
sons[1121] of men[120] [I]Thy
mighty acts,
And the [b]glory of the majesty[1926]
of [I]Thy kingdom.
13 Thy kingdom is [I]an
[a]everlasting[5769] kingdom,
And Thy dominion[4475] *endures*
throughout all
generations.[1755]
14 The LORD [a]sustains[5564] all who
fall,
And [b]raises up all who are bowed
down.
15 The eyes of all [I]look to Thee,
And Thou [a]dost give them their
food in due time.[6256]
16 Thou [a]dost open Thy hand,[3027]
And dost satisfy the desire[7522]
of every living thing.[2416]
17 The LORD is [a]righteous[6662] in all
His ways,[1870]
And kind[2623] in all His deeds.
18 The LORD is [a]near to all who
call[7121] upon Him,
To all who call upon Him
[b]in truth.[571]
19 He will [a]fulfill the desire of those
who fear[3373] Him;
He will also [b]hear[8085] their cry
and will save[3467] them.
20 The LORD [a]keeps[8104] all who
love[157] Him;
But all the [b]wicked,[7563] He will
destroy.[8045]
21 My [a]mouth[6310] will speak[1696] the
praise[8416] of the LORD;
And [b]all flesh[1320] will [c]bless His
holy[6944] name forever[5769] and
ever.[5703]

The LORD an Abundant Helper

146 [I]Praise[1984] [II]the LORD!
[a]Praise the LORD, O my
soul![5315]
2 I will praise the LORD [a]while I
live;[2416]
I will [b]sing praises[2167] to my
God[430] while I have my being.
3 [a]Do not trust[982] in princes,[5081]
In [I]mortal [b]man,[1121,120] in whom
there is [c]no salvation.[8668]
4 His [a]spirit[7307] departs, he
[b]returns[7725] to [I]the earth;[127]
In that very day[3117] his
[c]thoughts perish.[6]
5 How [a]blessed[835] is he whose
help is the God[410] of Jacob,
Whose [b]hope is in the LORD his
God;

2 [a]Ps. 71:6
3 [a]Ps. 48:1; 86:10; 147:5 [b]Job 5:9; 9:10; 11:7; Is. 40:28; Rom. 11:33
4 [a]Ps. 22:30, 31; Is. 38:19
5 [I]Or, *majesty of Thy splendor* [a]Ps. 145:12 [b]Ps. 119:27
6 [I]Or, *strength* [a]Deut. 10:21; Ps. 66:3; 106:22 [b]Deut. 32:3
7 [I]Or, *bubble over with* [a]Ps. 31:19; Is. 63:7 [b]Ps. 51:14
8 [a]Ex. 34:6; Num. 14:18; Ps. 86:5, 15; 103:8
9 [a]Ps. 100:5; 136:1; Jer. 33:11; Nah. 1:7; Matt. 19:17; Mark 10:18 [b]Ps. 145:15
10 [a]Ps. 19:1; 103:22 [b]Ps. 68:26
11 [a]Jer. 14:21
12 [I]Lit., *His* [a]Ps. 105:1 [b]Ps. 145:5; Is. 2:10, 19, 21
13 [I]Lit., *a kingdom of all ages* [a]Ps. 10:16; 29:10; 1Tim. 1:17; 2Pet. 1:11
14 [a]Ps. 37:24 [b]Ps. 146:8
15 [I]Lit., *wait;* or, *hope for* [a]Ps. 104:27; 136:25
16 [a]Ps. 104:28
17 [a]Ps. 116:5
18 [a]Deut. 4:7; Ps. 34:18; 119:151 [b]John 4:24
19 [a]Ps. 21:2; 37:4 [b]Ps. 10:17; Prov. 15:29; 1John 5:14
20 [a]Ps. 31:23; 91:14; 97:10 [b]Ps. 9:5; 37:38
21 [a]Ps. 71:8 [b]Ps. 65:2; 150:6 [c]Ps. 145:1, 2

1 [I]Or, *Hallelujah!* [II]Heb., *YAH* [a]Ps. 103:1
2 [a]Ps. 63:4 [b]Ps. 104:33
3 [I]Lit., *a son of a man* [a]Ps. 118:9 [b]Ps. 118:8; Is. 2:22 [c]Ps. 60:11; 108:12
4 [I]Lit., *his earth* [a]Ps. 104:29 [b]Eccl. 12:7 [c]Ps. 33:10; 1Cor. 2:6

5 [a]Ps. 144:15; Jer. 17:7 [b]Ps. 71:5

6 Who [a]made[6213] heaven[8064] and earth,[776]
The [b]sea and all that is in them;
Who [c]keeps[8104] [I]faith[571] forever;[5769]
7 Who [a]executes[6213] justice[4941] for the oppressed;
Who [b]gives food to the hungry.
The LORD [c]sets the prisoners free.
8 The LORD [a]opens *the eyes of* the blind;
The LORD [b]raises up those who are bowed down;
The LORD [c]loves[157] the righteous;[6662]
9 The LORD [Ia]protects[8104] the [II]strangers;[1616]
He [IIIb]supports the fatherless and the widow;
But He [IV]thwarts[5791] [c]the way[1870] of the wicked.[7563]
10 The LORD will [a]reign[4427] forever,
Thy God, O Zion, to all generations.[1755]
[I]Praise [II]the LORD!

Praise for Jerusalem's Restoration and Prosperity

147 [I]Praise[1984] [II]the LORD!
For [a]it is good[2896] to sing praises[2167] to our God;[430]
For [III]it is pleasant *and* praise[8416] is [b]becoming.[5000]
2 The LORD [a]builds up Jerusalem;
He [b]gathers[3664] the outcasts of Israel.
3 He heals the [a]brokenhearted,[7665,3820]
And [b]binds up[2280] their [I]wounds.[6094]
4 He [a]counts the number of the stars;
He [Ib]gives[7121] names to all of them.
5 [a]Great is our Lord,[113] and abundant in strength;
His [b]understanding[8394] is [I]infinite.
6 The LORD [Ia]supports the afflicted;
He brings down the wicked[7563] to the ground.[776]
7 [a]Sing to the LORD with thanksgiving;[8426]
Sing praises[2167] to our God on the lyre,
8 Who [a]covers[3680] the heavens[8064] with clouds,
Who [b]provides rain for the earth,[776]
Who [c]makes grass to [I]grow on the mountains.
9 He [a]gives to the beast its food,
And to the [b]young[1121] ravens which cry.[7121]
10 He does not delight[2654] in the strength of the [a]horse;
He [b]does not take pleasure in the legs of a man.[376]
11 The LORD [a]favors those who fear[3373] Him,
[b]Those who wait[3176] for His lovingkindness.[2617]
12 Praise[7623] the LORD, O Jerusalem!
Praise your God, O Zion!
13 For He has strengthened[2388] the [a]bars of your gates;
He has [b]blessed[1288] your sons[1121] within[7130] you.
14 He [a]makes[7760] [I]peace in your borders;
He [b]satisfies you with [c]the [II]finest of the wheat.
15 He sends forth His [a]command[565] to the earth;
His [b]word[1697] runs very swiftly.
16 He gives [a]snow like wool;
He scatters the [b]frost[3713] like ashes.
17 He casts forth His [a]ice as fragments;
Who can stand before His [b]cold?
18 He [a]sends forth His word and melts them;
He [b]causes His wind[7307] to blow and the waters to flow.

6 [I]Or, *truth* [a]Ps. 115:15; Rev. 14:7 [b]Acts 14:15 [c]Ps. 117:2
7 [a]Ps. 103:6 [b]Ps. 107:9; 145:15 [c]Ps. 68:6; Is. 61:1
8 [a]Matt. 9:30; John 9:7 [b]Ps. 145:14 [c]Ps. 11:7
9 [I]Or, *keeps* [II]Or, *sojourners* [III]Or, *relieves* [IV]Lit., *makes crooked* [a]Ex. 22:21; Lev. 19:34 [b]Deut. 10:18; Ps. 68:5 [c]Ps. 147:6
10 [I]Or, *Hallelujah!* [II]Heb., YAH [a]Ex. 15:18; Ps. 10:16

1 [I]Or, *Hallelujah!* [II]Heb., YAH [III]Or, *He is gracious* [a]Ps. 92:1; 135:3 [b]Ps. 33:1
2 [a]Ps. 51:18; 102:16 [b]Deut. 30:3; Ps. 106:47; Is. 11:12; 56:8; Ezek. 39:28
3 [I]Lit., *sorrows* [a]Ps. 34:18; 51:17; Is. 61:1 [b]Job 5:18; Is. 30:26; Ezek. 34:16
4 [I]Or, *calls them all by their names* [a]Gen. 15:5 [b]Is. 40:26
5 [I]Lit., *innumerable* [a]Ps. 48:1; 145:3 [b]Is. 40:28
6 [I]Or, *relieves* [a]Ps. 37:24; 146:8, 9
7 [a]Ps. 33:2; 95:1, 2
8 [I]Lit., *spring forth* [a]Job 26:8 [b]Job 5:10; 38:26; Ps. 104:13 [c]Job 38:27; Ps. 104:14
9 [a]Ps. 104:27, 28; 145:15 [b]Job 38:41; Matt. 6:26
10 [a]Ps. 33:17 [b]1Sam. 16:7
11 [a]Ps. 149:4 [b]Ps. 33:18
13 [a]Neh. 3:3; 7:3 [b]Ps. 37:26
14 [I]Lit., *your borders peace* [II]Lit., *fat* [a]Ps. 29:11; Is. 54:13; 60:17, 18 [b]Ps. 132:15 [c]Deut. 32:14; Ps. 81:16

15 [a]Job 37:12; Ps. 148:5 [b]Ps. 104:4 16 [a]Job 37:6; Ps. 148:8 [b]Job 38:29 17 [a]Job 37:10 [b]Job 37:9
18 [a]Ps. 33:9; 107:20; 147:15 [b]Ps. 107:25

19 He [a]declares5046 His words to
Jacob,
His [b]statutes2706 and His
ordinances4941 to Israel.
20 He [a]has not dealt6213 thus with
any nation;1471
And as for His ordinances, they
have [b]not known3045 them.
[I]Praise [II]the LORD!

The Whole Creation Invoked to Praise the LORD

148 [I]Praise1984 [II]the LORD!
Praise the LORD [a]from the
heavens;8064
Praise Him [b]in the heights!
2 Praise Him, [a]all His angels;4397
Praise Him, [b]all His hosts!6635
3 Praise Him, sun and moon;
Praise Him, all stars of light!216
4 Praise Him, [I][a]highest heavens,
And the [b]waters that are above
the heavens!
5 Let them praise the name of the
LORD,
For [a]He commanded6680 and
they were created.1254
6 He has also [a]established5975
them forever and
ever;5703,5769
He has made a [b]decree which
will not pass away.
7 Praise the LORD from the
earth,776
[a]Sea monsters8577 and all
[b]deeps;
8 [a]Fire and hail, [b]snow and
[c]clouds;
[d]Stormy wind,7307 [e]fulfilling His
word;1697
9 [a]Mountains and all hills;
Fruit [b]trees and all cedars;
10 [a]Beasts2416 and all cattle;
[b]Creeping things and winged
fowl;
11 [a]Kings4428 of the earth and all
peoples;3816
Princes and all judges8199 of the
earth;
12 Both young men and virgins;1330
Old men2205 and children.

19 [a]Deut. 33:3, 4 [b]Mal. 4:4
20 [I]Or, *Hallelujah!* [II]Heb., *YAH* [a]Deut. 4:7, 8, 32-34; Rom. 3:1, 2 [b]Ps. 79:6; Jer. 10:25

1 [I]Or, *Hallelujah!* [II]Heb., *YAH* [a]Ps. 69:34 [b]Job 16:19; Ps. 102:19; Matt. 21:9
2 [a]Ps. 103:20 [b]Ps. 103:21
4 [I]Lit., *heavens of heavens* [a]Deut. 10:14; 1Kin. 8:27; Neh. 9:6; Ps. 68:33 [b]Gen. 1:7
5 [a]Gen. 1:1; Ps. 33:6, 9
6 [a]Ps. 89:37; Jer. 31:35, 36; 33:20, 25 [b]Job 38:33
7 [a]Gen. 1:21; Ps. 74:13 [b]Gen. 1:2; Deut. 33:13; Hab. 3:10
8 [a]Ps. 18:12 [b]Ps. 147:16 [c]Ps. 135:7 [d]Ps. 107:25 [e]Job 37:12; Ps. 103:20
9 [a]Is. 44:23; 49:13 [b]Is. 55:12
10 [a]Is. 43:20 [b]Hos. 2:18
11 [a]Ps. 102:15
13 [a]Is. 12:4 [b]Ps. 8:1; 113:4
14 [I]Or, *Hallelujah!* [II]Heb., *YAH* [a]1Sam. 2:1; Ps. 75:10 [b]Deut. 10:21; Ps. 109:1; Jer. 17:14 [c]Lev. 10:3; Eph. 2:17

1 [I]Or, *Hallelujah!* [II]Heb., *YAH* [a]Ps. 33:3 [b]Ps. 35:18; 89:5
2 [a]Ps. 95:6 [b]Judg. 8:23; Ps. 47:6; Zech. 9:9
3 [a]2Sam. 6:14; Ps. 150:4 [b]Ex. 15:20; Ps. 81:2
4 [a]Job 36:11; Ps. 16:11; 35:27; 147:11 [b]Ps. 132:16; Is. 61:3
5 [a]Ps. 132:16 [b]Job 35:10; Ps. 42:8
6 [I]Lit., *throat* [a]Ps. 66:17 [b]Heb. 4:12 [c]Neh. 4:17
7 [a]Ezek. 25:17; Mic. 5:15

13 Let them praise the name of the
LORD,
For His [a]name alone is exalted;
His [b]glory1935 is above earth and
heaven.8064
14 And He has [a]lifted up7311 a horn
for His people,5971
[b]Praise8416 for all His godly
ones;2623
Even for the sons1121 of Israel,
a people [c]near to Him.
[I]Praise [II]the LORD!

Israel Invoked to Praise the LORD

149 [I]Praise1984 [II]the LORD!
Sing7891 to the LORD a
[a]new song,7892
And His praise8416 [b]in the
congregation6951 of the godly
ones.2623
2 Let Israel be glad in [a]his
Maker;6213
Let the sons1121 of Zion rejoice
in their [b]King.4428
3 Let them praise His name with
[a]dancing;
Let them sing praises2167 to Him
with [b]timbrel8596 and lyre.
4 For the LORD [a]takes pleasure in
His people;5971
He will [b]beautify the afflicted
ones with salvation.3444
5 Let the [a]godly ones exult in
glory;3519
Let them [b]sing for joy on their
beds.
6 *Let* the [a]high praises of God410
be in their [I]mouth,
And a [b]two-edged [c]sword2719 in
their hand,3027
7 To [a]execute vengeance5360 on
the nations,1471
And punishment8433 on the
peoples;3816
8 To bind their kings4428 [a]with
chains,
And their [b]nobles with fetters
of iron;

8 [a]Job 36:8 [b]Nah. 3:10

9 To [a]execute on them the judgment[4941] written;
This is an [b]honor for all His godly ones.
[I]Praise [II]the LORD!

A Psalm of Praise

150 [I]Praise[1984] [II]the LORD!
Praise God[410] in His [a]sanctuary;[6944]
Praise Him in His mighty [III][b]expanse.[7549]
2 Praise Him for His [a]mighty deeds;
Praise Him according to His excellent [b]greatness.
3 Praise Him with [a]trumpet sound;
Praise Him with [b]harp and lyre.
4 Praise Him with [a]timbrel[8596] and dancing;
Praise Him with [b]stringed instruments and [c]pipe.
5 Praise Him with loud[8088] [a]cymbals;
Praise Him with resounding cymbals.
6 Let [a]everything that has breath[5397] praise [I]the LORD.
[II]Praise [I]the LORD!

9 [I]Or, *Hallelujah!* [II]Heb., YAH [a]Deut. 7:12; Ezek. 28:26 [b]Ps. 112:9; 148:14

1 [I]Or, *Hallelujah!* [II]Heb., YAH [III]Or, *firmament* [a]Ps. 73:17; 102:19 [b]Ps. 19:1

2 [a]Ps. 145:12 [b]Deut. 3:24; Ps. 145:3

3 [a]Ps. 98:6 [b]Ps. 33:2

4 [a]Ps. 149:3 [b]Ps. 45:8; Is. 38:20 [c]Gen. 4:21; Job 21:12

5 [a]2Sam. 6:5; 1Chr. 13:8; 15:16; Ezra 3:10; Neh. 12:27 103:22; 145:21

6 [I]Heb., YAH [II]Or, *Hallelujah!* [a]Ps. 150:6

THE PROVERBS

The term "Proverbs," which could also be translated "similies" or "parables," is used in this book more generally to include various other types of short, pithy statements as well. Although the book itself does have a clear order and proverbs are sometimes grouped by subject matter, each proverb generally stands on its own and is without context. Proverbs, then, are timeless words of wise men concerning the way to conduct one's life, both in terms of what is right and what is prudent. Hence, Proverbs is the best Old Testament example of wisdom literature. Wisdom sayings are markedly practical, rather than abstract or theoretical. Since the focus is about everyday life, the scope of subjects treated is quite wide. The authors of Proverbs thus did not concern themselves much with overtly sacred or religious matters, but that in no way diminishes the religious character of the book. There is a distinct optimism about the world and its workings, because God is in control. Because of this the reader is assured repeatedly that he will reap what he has sown. God cannot be left out of the picture, because knowledge and wisdom begin with reverence for the Lord (Prov. 1:7; 9:10). Numerous passages from Proverbs are reflected in the New Testament and are otherwise well known, but perhaps the most beautiful is the classical Old Testament description of ideal womanhood in Prov. 31:10-31. Solomon, who is known to have spoken 3,000 proverbs (I Kgs. 4:32), is the principal author of the book, but others, both anonymous and identified, also have their maxims included. Proverbs reached its final form well beyond Solomon's day. Work was still being done on it in Hezekiah's time (Prov. 25:1), and it is generally thought that its final editing occurred just after the return from the Babylonian exile.

The Usefulness of Proverbs

1 ⚷ The [a]proverbs of Solomon [b]the son[1121] of David, king[4428] of Israel:

2 To know[3045] [a]wisdom[2451] and instruction,[4148]
To discern the sayings[561] of [b]understanding,[998]
3 To [a]receive instruction in wise behavior,[7919]
[b]Righteousness,[6664] justice[4941] and equity;[4339]
4 To give [a]prudence[6195] to the [I]naive,
To the youth [b]knowledge[1847] and discretion,[4209]
5 A wise[2450] man will hear[8085] and [a]increase in learning,[3948]
And a [b]man of understanding[995] will acquire wise counsel,
6 To understand[995] a proverb and a figure,
The words[1697] of the wise and their [a]riddles.[2420]
7 [a]The fear[3374] of the LORD is the beginning[7225] of knowledge;
Fools despise wisdom and instruction.

The Enticement of Sinners

⚷ 8 [a]Hear, my son, your father's[1] instruction,
And [b]do not forsake[5203] your mother's[517] teaching;[8451]
9 Indeed, they are a [a]graceful[2580] wreath to your head,[7218]
And [I][b]ornaments about your neck.

1 [a]1Kin. 4:32; Prov. 10:1; 25:1; Eccl. 12:9 [b]Eccl. 1:1
2 [a]Prov. 15:33 [b]Prov. 4:1
3 [a]Prov. 2:1; 19:20 [b]Prov. 2:9
4 [I]Lit., *simple ones* [a]Prov. 8:5, 12 [b]Prov. 2:10, 11; 3:21
5 [a]Prov. 9:9 [b]Prov. 14:6; Eccl. 9:11
6 [a]Num. 12:8; Ps. 49:4; 78:2; Dan. 8:23
7 [a]Job 28:28; Ps. 111:10; Prov. 9:10; 15:33; Eccl. 12:13
8 [a]Prov. 4:1 [b]Prov. 6:20
9 [I]Lit., *necklaces* [a]Prov. 4:9 [b]Gen. 41:42; Dan. 5:29

⚷ **1:1** Solomon is generally recognized to be the author of the Book of Proverbs. However, he did not write all of them (See Prov. 30:1; 31:1).

⚷ **1:8** Proverbs are frequently addressed to the young to warn them of dangers that they, by reason of their inexperience, know nothing about. Here and in the following verses the emphasis is upon training in the home as a means of moral protection. It will prepare the young person against the temptations from immoral people and the end which results.

10 My son, if sinners[2400] [a]entice[6601]
you,
[b]Do not consent.[14]
11 If they say,[559] "Come with us,
Let us [a]lie in wait for blood,[1818]
Let us [b]ambush the innocent[5355]
without cause;
12 Let us [a]swallow[1104] them
alive[2416] like Sheol,[7585]
Even whole,[8549] as those who
[b]go down to the pit;[953]
13 We shall find all *kinds* of precious
wealth,
We shall fill our houses[1004] with
spoil;
14 Throw in[5307] your lot [I]with us,
We shall all have one purse,"
15 My son, [a]do not walk in the
way[1870] with them.
[b]Keep your feet from their path,
16 For [a]their feet run to evil,[7451]
And they hasten to shed[8210]
blood.
17 Indeed, it is [I]useless to spread
the net
In the eyes of any [II]bird;
18 But they [a]lie in wait for their
own blood;
They ambush their own
lives.[5315]
19 So are the ways[734] of everyone
who [a]gains[1214] by violence;
It takes away the life[5315] of its
possessors.[1167]

Wisdom Warns

20 [a]Wisdom[2454] shouts in the
street,
She [I]lifts her voice in the square;
21 At the head[7218] of the noisy
streets she cries out;
At the entrance of the gates in
the city, she utters her
sayings:
22 "How long, O [I][a]naive ones, will
you love[157] [II]simplicity?
And [b]scoffers[3887] delight
themselves in scoffing,
And fools [c]hate[8130] knowledge?
23 "Turn[7725] to my reproof,[8433]

10 [a]Prov. 16:29 [b]Gen. 39:7-10; Deut. 13:8; Ps. 50:18; Eph. 5:11
11 [a]Prov. 12:6; Jer. 5:26 [b]Ps. 10:8; Prov. 1:18
12 [a]Ps. 124:3 [b]Ps. 28:1
14 [I]Lit., *in the midst of us*
15 [a]Ps. 1:1; Prov. 4:14 [b]Ps. 119:101
16 [a]Prov. 6:17, 18; Is. 59:7
17 [I]Lit., *in vain* [II]Lit., *possessor of wing*
18 [a]Prov. 11:19
19 [a]Prov. 15:27
20 [I]Lit., *gives* [a]Prov. 8:1-3; 9:3
22 [I]Lit., *simple ones* [II]Or, *naivete* [a]Prov. 1:4, 32; 8:5; 9:4; 22:3 [b]Ps. 1:1 [c]Prov. 1:29; 5:12
23 [a]Is. 32:15; Joel 2:28; John 7:39
24 [a]Is. 65:12; 66:4; Jer. 7:13 [b]Zech. 7:11 [c]Is. 65:2; Rom. 10:21
25 [a]Ps. 107:11; Luke 7:30 [b]Prov. 15:10
26 [a]Ps. 2:4 [b]Prov. 6:15 [c]Prov. 10:24
27 [a]Prov. 10:25
28 [a]1 Sam. 8:18; Job 27:9; 35:12; Ps. 18:41; Is. 1:15; Jer. 11:11; 14:12; Ezek. 8:18; Mic. 3:4; Zech. 7:13; James 4:3 [b]Prov. 8:17
29 [a]Job 21:14; Prov. 1:22
30 [a]Ps. 81:11; Prov. 1:25
31 [a]Job 4:8; Prov. 5:22, 23; 22:8; Is. 3:11; Jer. 6:19 [b]Prov. 14:14
32 [I]Lit., *simple ones* [a]Jer. 2:19
33 [I]Lit., *dwell* [a]Ps. 25:12, 13; Prov. 3:24-26
1 [a]Prov. 4:10 [b]Prov. 3:1

Behold, I will [a]pour out my
spirit[7307] on you;
I will make my words known[3045]
to you.
24 "Because [a]I called,[7121] and you
[b]refused;[3985]
I [c]stretched out my hand,[3027] and
no one paid attention;
25 And you [a]neglected[6544] all my
counsel,[6098]
And did not [b]want[14] my reproof;
26 I will even [a]laugh at your
[b]calamity;[343]
I will mock when your
[c]dread[6343] comes,
27 When your dread comes like a
storm,[7584]
And your calamity[343] comes on
like a [a]whirlwind,
When distress *and* anguish[6695]
come on you.
28 "Then they will [a]call[7121] on me,
but I will not answer;
They will [b]seek me diligently,
but they shall not find me,
29 Because they [a]hated[8130]
knowledge,
And did not choose[977] the fear
of the LORD.
30 "They [a]would not accept my
counsel,
They spurned[5006] all my reproof.
31 "So they shall [a]eat of the fruit of
their own way,
And be [b]satiated with their own
devices.
32 "For the [a]waywardness of the
[I]naive shall kill[2026] them,
And the complacency of fools
shall destroy[6] them.
33 "But [a]he who listens to me shall
[I]live[7931] securely,[983]
And shall be at ease from the
dread of evil."

The Pursuit of Wisdom Brings Security

2 My son,[1121] if you will [a]receive my
sayings,[561]
And [b]treasure my

commandments[4687] within
you,
2 [a]Make your ear[241] attentive[7181]
to wisdom,[2451]
Incline your heart[3820] to
understanding;[8394]
3 For if you cry[7121] for
discernment,
[I]Lift your voice for
understanding;
4 If you seek her as [a]silver,
And search for her as for
[b]hidden treasures;
5 Then you will discern[995] the
[a]fear[3374] of the LORD,
And discover the knowledge[1847]
of God.[430]
6 For [a]the LORD gives wisdom;
From His mouth[6310] *come*
knowledge and
understanding.
7 He stores up sound wisdom[8454]
for the upright;[3477]
He is a [a]shield4043 to those who
walk in integrity,[8537]
8 Guarding[5341] the paths[734] of
justice,[4941]
And He [a]preserves[8104] the
way[1870] of His godly ones.[2623]
9 Then you will discern
[a]righteousness[6664] and justice
And equity[4339] *and* every
[b]good[2896] course.
10 For [a]wisdom will enter your
heart,
And [b]knowledge will be pleasant
to your soul;[5315]
11 Discretion[4209] will [a]guard[8104]
you,
Understanding will watch
over[5341] you,
12 To [a]deliver[5337] you from the way
of evil,[7451]
From the man[376] who speaks
[b]perverse things;8419
13 From those who [a]leave[5800] the
paths of uprightness,[3476]
To walk in the [b]ways[1870] of
darkness;[2822]
14 Who [a]delight in doing[6213] evil,
And rejoice in the perversity8419
of evil;[7451]

2 [a]Prov. 22:17
3 [I]Lit., *Give*
4 [a]Prov. 3:14 [b]Job 3:21; Matt. 13:44
5 [a]Prov. 1:7
6 [a]1Kin. 3:12; Job 32:8; James 1:5
7 [a]Ps. 84:11; Prov. 30:5
8 [a]1Sam. 2:9; Ps. 66:9
9 [a]Prov. 8:20 [b]Prov. 4:18
10 [a]Prov. 14:33 [b]Prov. 22:18
11 [a]Prov. 4:6; 6:22
12 [a]Prov. 28:26 [b]Prov. 6:12
13 [a]Prov. 21:16 [b]Ps. 82:5; Prov. 4:19; John 3:19, 20
14 [a]Prov. 10:23; Jer. 11:15
15 [a]Ps. 125:5; Prov. 21:8
16 [I]Lit., *strange woman* [a]Prov. 6:24; 7:5 [b]Prov. 23:27
17 [a]Mal. 2:14, 15 [b]Gen. 2:24
18 [I]Lit., *bows down* [II]Lit., *departed spirits* [a]Prov. 7:27
19 [a]Eccl. 7:26 [b]Ps. 16:11; Prov. 5:6
20 [a]Heb. 6:12 [b]Prov. 4:18
21 [I]Or, *dwell* [a]Ps. 37:9, 29; Prov. 10:30 [b]Prov. 28:10
22 [a]Ps. 37:38; Prov. 10:30 [b]Prov. 11:3 [c]Deut. 28:63; Ps. 52:5

1 [I]Or, *law* [a]Ps. 119:61; Prov. 4:5 [b]Ex. 20:6; Deut. 30:16
2 [a]Ps. 91:16; Prov. 3:16; 4:10; 9:11; 10:27
3 [a]2Sam. 15:20; Prov. 14:22 [b]Deut. 6:8; 11:18; Prov. 1:9; 6:21 [c]Prov. 7:3; Jer. 17:1; 2Cor. 3:3
4 [I]Lit., *understanding* [a]1Sam. 2:26; Prov. 8:35; Luke 2:52 [b]Ps. 111:10
5 [a]Ps. 37:3, 5; Prov. 22:19

15 Whose paths[734] are [a]crooked,
And who are devious[3868] in their
ways;
16 To [a]deliver you from the strange
woman,[2114]
From the [I][b]adulteress who
flatters with her words;
17 That leaves[5800] the [a]companion
of her youth,
And forgets the [b]covenant[1285] of
her God;
18 For [a]her house[1004] [I]sinks down
to death,[4194]
And her tracks *lead* to the
[II]dead;[7496]
19 None [a]who go to her return[7725]
again,
Nor do they reach the
[b]paths of life.[2416]
20 So you will [a]walk in the way of
good men,
And keep[8104] to the [b]paths of the
righteous.[6662]
21 For [a]the upright[3477] will
[I]live[7931] in the land,[776]
And [b]the blameless[8549] will
remain[3498] in it;
22 But [a]the wicked[7563] will be cut
off[3772] from the land,[776]
And [b]the treacherous will be
[c]uprooted[5255] from it.

The Rewards of Wisdom

3 My son,[1121] [a]do not forget my
[I]teaching,[8451]
But let your heart[3820] [b]keep[5341]
my commandments;[4687]
2 For [a]length[753] of days[3117] and
years of life,[2416]
And peace they will add to you.
3 Do not let [a]kindness[2617] and
truth[571] leave[5800] you;
[b]Bind them around your neck,
[c]Write them on the tablet of your
heart.
4 So you will [a]find favor[2580] and
[b]good[2896] [I]repute[7922]
In the sight of God[430] and
man.[120]
5 [a]Trust[982] in the LORD with all
your heart,

And [b]do not lean[8172] on your own
understanding.[998]
6 In all your ways[1870]
[a]acknowledge[3045] Him,
And He will [b]make your paths[734]
straight.[3474]
7 [a]Do not be wise[2450] in your own
eyes;
[b]Fear[3372] the LORD and turn
away[5493] from evil.[7451]
8 It will be [a]healing to your
[I]body,
And [b]refreshment to your
bones.[6106]
9 [a]Honor[3513] the LORD from your
wealth,
And from the [b]first[7225] of all your
produce;
10 So your [a]barns will be filled with
plenty,
And your [b]vats will overflow with
new wine.
11 [a]My son, do not reject[3988] the
[I]discipline[4148] of the LORD,
Or loathe[6973] His reproof,[8433]
12 For [a]whom the LORD loves[157] He
reproves,[3198]
Even [b]as a father,[1] the son in
whom he delights.[7521]
13 [a]How blessed[835] is the man who
finds wisdom,[2451]
And the man who gains
understanding.[8394]
14 For its [a]profit is better[2896] than
the profit of silver,
And its gain than fine gold.
15 She is [a]more precious than
[I]jewels;
And nothing you desire[2656]
compares with her.
16 [Ia]Long life is in her right hand;
In her left hand are [b]riches and
honor.[3519]
17 Her [a]ways are pleasant ways,
And all her paths are [b]peace.
18 She is a [a]tree of life to those
who take hold[2388] of her,
And happy[833] are all who hold
her fast.
19 The LORD [a]by wisdom
founded[3245] the earth;[776]
By understanding He
[b]established[3559] the
heavens.[8064]
20 By His knowledge[1847] the
[a]deeps were broken up,
And the [b]skies[7834] drip with dew.
21 My son, [a]let them not depart
from your sight;
Keep sound wisdom[8454] and
discretion,[4209]
22 So they will be [a]life to your
soul,[5315]
And [b]adornment[2580] to your
neck.
23 Then you will [a]walk in your
way[1870] securely,[983]
And your foot will not
[b]stumble.[5062]
24 When you [a]lie down, you will not
be afraid;[6342]
When you lie down, your sleep
will be sweet.[6148]
25 [a]Do not be afraid[3372] of sudden
fear,[6343]
Nor of the [Ib]onslaught[7722] of the
wicked[7563] when it comes;
26 For the LORD will be [I]your
confidence,[3689]
And will [a]keep[8104] your foot from
being caught.
27 [a]Do not withhold good from
[I]those to whom it is due,
When it is in your power[410] to
do[6213] *it.*
28 [a]Do not say[559] to your
neighbor,[7453] "Go, and come
back,
And tomorrow I will give *it,*"
When you have it with you.
29 [a]Do not devise harm against your
neighbor,
While he lives in security[983]
beside you.

5 [b]Prov. 23:4; Jer. 9:23
6 [a]1Chr. 28:9; Prov. 16:3; Phil. 4:6; James 1:5 [b]Is. 45:13; Jer. 10:23
7 [a]Rom. 12:16 [b]Job 1:1; 28:28; Prov. 8:13; 16:6
8 [I]Lit., *navel* [a]Prov. 4:22 [b]Job 21:24
9 [a]Is. 43:23 [b]Ex. 23:19; Deut. 26:2; Mal. 3:10
10 [a]Deut. 28:8 [b]Joel 2:24
11 [I]Or, *instruction* [a]Job 5:17; Heb. 12:5, 6
12 [a]Rev. 3:19 [b]Deut. 8:5; Prov. 13:24
13 [a]Prov. 8:32, 34
14 [a]Job 28:15-19; Prov. 8:10, 19; 16:16
15 [I]Lit., *corals* [a]Job 28:18; Prov. 8:11
16 [I]Lit., *Length of days* [a]Prov. 3:2 [b]Prov. 8:18; 22:4
17 [a]Matt. 11:29 [b]Ps. 119:165; Prov. 16:7
18 [a]Gen. 2:9; Prov. 11:30; 13:12; 15:4; Rev. 2:7
19 [a]Ps. 104:24; Prov. 8:27 [b]Prov. 8:27, 28
20 [a]Gen. 7:11 [b]Deut. 33:28; Job 36:28
21 [a]Prov. 4:21
22 [a]Deut. 32:47; Prov. 4:22; 8:35; 16:22; 21:21 [b]Prov. 1:9
23 [a]Prov. 4:12; 10:9 [b]Ps. 91:12; Is. 5:27; 63:13
24 [a]Job 11:19; Ps. 3:5; Prov. 1:33; 6:22
25 [I]Lit., *storm* [a]Ps. 91:5; 1Pet. 3:14 [b]Job 5:21
26 [I]Or, *at your side* [a]1Sam. 2:9
27 [I]Lit., *its owners* [a]Rom. 13:7; Gal. 6:10
28 [a]Lev. 19:13; Deut. 24:15
29 [a]Prov. 6:14; 14:22

3:13-18 Real wealth is not measured by the material things which a man is able to accumulate but by acquiring true happiness through the quality of life which belongs to one who follows wisdom.

3:21-35 Through wisdom one learns to place his confidence and trust in God. It is the trust that brings peace of mind for which all men are searching so earnestly.

30 [a]Do not contend[7378] with a man
without cause,
If he has done you no harm.[7451]
31 [a]Do not envy[7065] a man of
violence,
And do not choose[977] any of his
ways.
32 For the [a]crooked[3868] *man* is an
abomination[8441] to the LORD;
But [I]He is [b]intimate[5475] with the
upright.[3477]
33 The [a]curse of the LORD is on
the house[1004] of the wicked,
But He [b]blesses[1288] the dwelling
of the righteous.
34 Though [a]He scoffs[3887] at the
scoffers,[3887]
Yet [b]He gives grace to the
afflicted.
35 [a]The wise will inherit[5157]
honor,[3519]
But fools [I]display dishonor.

A Father's Instruction

4 Hear,[8005] *O* sons,[1121] the
[a]instruction[4148] of a father,[1]
And [b]give attention that you may
[I]gain[3045] understanding,[998]
2 For I give you [I]sound[2896]
[a]teaching;[3948]
[b]Do not abandon[5800] my
[II]instruction.[8451]
3 When I was a son[1121] to my
father,[1]
[a]Tender and [b]the only[3173] son in
the sight of my mother,[517]
4 Then he [a]taught[3384] me and
said[559] to me,
"Let your heart[3820] [b]hold fast my
words;[1697]
[c]Keep[8104] my
commandments[4687] and
live;[2421]
5 [a]Acquire wisdom![2451] [b]Acquire
understanding!
Do not forget, nor turn away
from the words[561] of my
mouth.[6310]
6 "Do not forsake her, and she will
guard[8104] you;

30 [a]Prov. 26:17; Rom. 12:18
31 [a]Ps. 37:1; Prov. 24:1
32 [I]Lit., *His private counsel is* [a]Prov. 11:20 [b]Job 29:4; Ps. 25:14
33 [a]Lev. 26:14, 16; Deut. 11:28; Zech. 5:3, 4; Mal. 2:2 [b]Job 8:6; Ps. 1:3
34 [a]James 4:6 [b]1Pet. 5:5
35 [I]Lit., *raise high* [a]Dan. 12:3

1 [I]Lit., *know* [a]Ps. 34:11; Prov. 1:8 [b]Prov. 1:2; 2:2
2 [I]Lit., *good* [II]Or, *law* [a]Deut. 32:2; Job 11:4 [b]Ps. 89:30; 119:87; Prov. 3:1
3 [a]1Chr. 22:5; 29:1 [b]Zech. 12:10
4 [a]Eph. 6:4 [b]Ps. 119:168 [c]Prov. 7:2
5 [a]Prov. 4:7 [b]Prov. 16:16
6 [a]2Thess. 2:10
7 [I]Or, *the primary thing is wisdom* [a]Prov. 8:23 [b]Prov. 23:23
8 [a]1Sam. 2:30
9 [a]Prov. 1:9
10 [a]Prov. 2:1 [b]Prov. 3:2
11 [a]1Sam. 12:23
12 [a]Job 18:7; Ps. 18:36 [b]Ps. 91:11; Prov. 3:23
13 [a]Prov. 3:18 [b]Prov. 3:22; John 6:63
14 [a]Ps. 1:1; Prov. 1:15
16 [I]Lit., *their sleep is robbed* [a]Ps. 36:4; Mic. 2:1
17 [a]Prov. 13:2
18 [a]Is. 26:7; Matt. 5:14; Phil. 2:15 [b]2Sam. 23:4 [c]Dan. 12:3 [d]Job 11:17
19 [a]Job 18:5, 6; Prov. 2:13; Is. 59:9, 10; Jer. 23:12; John 12:35

[a]Love[157] her, and she will watch
over[5341] you.
7 "[a]The [I]beginning of wisdom *is:*
[b]Acquire wisdom;
And with all your acquiring, get
understanding.
8 "[a]Prize her, and she will exalt
you;
She will honor[3513] you if you
embrace her.
9 "She will place [a]on your head[7218]
a garland of grace;[2580]
She will present you with a
crown of beauty."[8597]
10 Hear, my son, and [a]accept my
sayings,[561]
And the [b]years of your life[2416]
will be many.
11 I have [a]directed you in the
way[1870] of wisdom;
I have led you in upright[3476]
paths.
12 When you walk, your [a]steps will
not be impeded;[3334]
And if you run, you [b]will not
stumble.[3782]
13 [a]Take hold[2388] of instruction; do
not let go.
Guard her, for she is your
[b]life.
14 [a]Do not enter the path[734] of the
wicked,[7563]
And do not proceed in the way
of evil[7451] men.
15 Avoid[6544] it, do not pass by it;
Turn away from it and pass
on.
16 For they [a]cannot sleep unless
they do evil;[7489]
And [I]they are robbed of sleep
unless they make *someone*
stumble.[3782]
17 For they [a]eat the bread of
wickedness,[7562]
And drink the wine of violence.[2555]
18 But the [a]path of the righteous
is like the [b]light[216] of dawn,
That [c]shines brighter and
brighter until the [d]full day.[3117]
19 The [a]way of the wicked is like
darkness;[653]

They do not know over what
they [I][b]stumble.
20 My son, [a]give attention to my
words;
[b]Incline your ear[241] to my
sayings.
21 [a]Do not let them depart from
your sight;
[b]Keep them in the midst of your
heart.[3824]
22 For they are [a]life to those who
find them,
And [b]health to all [I]their whole
body.[1320]
23 Watch over your heart with all
diligence,
For [a]from it *flow* the springs of
life.
24 Put away[5493] from you a
[a]deceitful[6143] mouth,
And [b]put devious lips[8193] far from
you.
25 Let your eyes look directly
ahead,
And let your [I]gaze be fixed
straight[3474] in front of you.
26 [a]Watch the path of your feet,
And all your [b]ways[1870] will be
established.[3559]
27 [a]Do not turn to the right nor to
the left;
[b]Turn your foot from evil.

Pitfalls of Immorality

5

My son,[1121] [a]give attention to my
wisdom,[2451]
[b]Incline your ear[241] to my
understanding;[8394]
2 That you may [a]observe[8104]
discretion,[4209]
And your [b]lips[8193] may
reserve[5341] knowledge.[1847]
3 For the lips of an [Ia]adulteress[2114]
[b]drip[5197] honey,
And [c]smoother than oil[8081] is her
[II]speech;
4 But in the end[319] she is
[a]bitter[4751] as wormwood,[3939]
[b]Sharp as a two-edged[6310]
sword.[2719]
5 Her feet [a]go down to death,[4194]

19 [I]Or, *may stumble* [b]John 11:10
20 [a]Prov. 5:1 [b]Prov. 2:2
21 [a]Prov. 3:21 [b]Prov. 7:1, 2
22 [I]Lit., *his* [a]Prov. 3:22 [b]Prov. 3:8; 12:18
23 [a]Matt. 12:34; 15:18, 19; Mark 7:21; Luke 6:45
24 [a]Prov. 6:12; 10:32 [b]Prov. 19:1
25 [I]Or, *eyelids*
26 [a]Prov. 5:21; Heb. 12:13 [b]Ps. 119:5
27 [a]Deut. 5:32; 28:14 [b]Prov. 1:15; Is. 1:16
1 [a]Prov. 4:20 [b]Prov. 22:17
2 [a]Prov. 3:21 [b]Mal. 2:7
3 [I]Lit., *strange woman* [II]Lit., *palate* [a]Prov. 2:16; 5:20; 7:5; 22:14 [b]Song 4:11 [c]Ps. 55:21
4 [a]Eccl. 7:26 [b]Ps. 57:4; Heb. 4:12
5 [a]Prov. 7:27
6 [I]Lit., *Lest she watch* [a]Prov. 4:26; 5:21 [b]2Pet. 2:14 [c]Prov. 30:20
7 [a]Prov. 7:24 [b]Ps. 119:102
8 [a]Prov. 7:25 [b]Prov. 9:14
12 [a]Prov. 1:7, 22, 29 [b]Prov. 1:25; 12:1
13 [a]Prov. 1:8
15 [I]Lit., *flowing*
16 [a]Prov. 5:18; 9:17; Song 4:12, 15
18 [a]Prov. 9:17; Song 4:12, 15 [b]Eccl. 9:9 [c]Mal. 2:14
19 [I]Lit., *intoxicated* [a]Song 2:9, 17; 4:5; 7:3

Her steps lay hold of Sheol.[7585]
6 [I]She does not ponder the
[a]path[734] of life;[2416]
Her ways are [b]unstable, she
[c]does not know[3045] *it*.
7 [a]Now then, *my* sons,[1121]
listen[8085] to me,
And [b]do not depart[5493] from the
words[561] of my mouth.[6310]
8 [a]Keep your way[1870] far from her,
And do not go near the
[b]door of her house,[1004]
9 Lest you give your vigor[1935] to
others,
And your years to the cruel one;
10 Lest strangers[2114] be filled with
your strength,
And your hard-earned goods[6089]
go to the house of an alien;
11 And you groan at your latter end,
When your flesh[1320] and your
body[7607] are consumed;[3615]
12 And you say,[559] "How I have
[a]hated[8130] instruction![4148]
And my heart[3820] [b]spurned[5006]
reproof!
13 "And I have not listened[8085] to
the voice of my [a]teachers,
Nor inclined my ear to my
instructors![3925]
14 "I was almost in utter ruin[7451]
In the midst of the assembly[5712]
and congregation."[6951]
15 Drink water from your own
cistern,[953]
And [I]fresh water from your own
well.
16 Should your [a]springs be
dispersed abroad,
Streams of water in the streets?
17 Let them be yours alone,
And not for strangers with you.
18 Let your [a]fountain be
blessed,[1288]
And [b]rejoice in the [c]wife[802] of
your youth.
19 *As* a loving[158] [a]hind[365] and a
graceful[2580] doe,
Let her breasts satisfy you at
all times;[6256]
Be [I]exhilarated[7686] always[8548]
with her love.[160]

20 For why should you, my son,
be exhilarated with an
[Ia]adulteress,
And embrace the bosom of a
[b]foreigner?
21 For the [a]ways[1870] of a man[376]
are before the eyes of the
LORD,
And He [b]watches all his paths.
22 His [a]own iniquities[5771] will
capture the wicked,[7563]
And he will be held[8551] with the
cords of his sin.
23 He will [a]die for lack of
instruction,
And in the greatness of his folly
he will go astray.[7686]

Parental Counsel

6 My son,[1121] if you have become
[a]surety[6148] for your
neighbor,[7453]
Have [I]given a pledge[8628,3709] for
a stranger,[2114]
2 *If* you have been snared[3369] with
the words[561] of your
mouth,[6310]
Have been caught with the
words of your mouth,
3 Do[6213] this then, my son, and
deliver[5337] yourself;
Since you have come into the
[I]hand of your neighbor,
Go, humble yourself, and
importune your neighbor.
4 Do not give [a]sleep to your eyes,
Nor slumber to your eyelids;
5 Deliver yourself like a gazelle
from *the hunter's* hand,[3027]
And like a [a]bird from the hand[3027]
of the fowler.
6 Go to the [a]ant, O [b]sluggard,[6102]
Observe[7200] her ways[1870] and be
wise,[2449]
7 Which, having [a]no chief,[7101]
Officer[7860] or ruler,
8 Prepares her food [a]in the
summer,
And gathers her provision in the
harvest.
9 How long will you lie down, O
sluggard?
When will you arise from your
sleep?
10 "[a]A little sleep, a little slumber,
A little folding of the hands[3027]
to [I]rest"—
11 [a]And your poverty will come in
like a [I]vagabond,
And your need like [II]an armed
man.[376]
12 A [a]worthless[1100] person, a
wicked[205] man,
Is the one who walks with a
[b]false[6143] mouth,
13 Who [a]winks[7169] with his eyes,
who [I]signals[4448] with his
feet,
Who [II]points[3384] with his fingers;
14 Who *with* [a]perversity[8419] in his
heart[3820] [b]devises evil[7451]
continually,
Who [Ic]spreads strife.
15 Therefore [a]his calamity[343] will
come suddenly;
[b]Instantly he will be broken,[7665]
and there will be [c]no healing.
16 There are six things which the
LORD hates,[8130]
Yes, seven which are an
abomination[8441] [I]to Him:
17 [a]Haughty eyes, a [b]lying tongue,
And hands that [c]shed[8210]
innocent[5355] blood,[1818]
18 A heart that devises [a]wicked
plans,[4284]
[b]Feet that run rapidly to evil,
19 A [a]false[8267] witness *who*
utters[6315] lies,[3577]
And one who [Ib]spreads strife
among brothers.[251]
20 [a]My son, observe[5341] the
commandment[4687] of your
father,[1]
And do not forsake[5203] the
[I]teaching[8451] of your
mother;[517]
21 [a]Bind them continually[8548] on
your heart;
Tie them around your neck.
22 When you [a]walk about,
[I]they will guide[5148] you;
When you sleep, [I]they will watch
over you;

---

20 [I]Lit., *strange woman* [a]Prov. 5:3 [b]Prov. 2:16; 6:24; 7:5; 23:27
21 [a]Job 14:16; 31:4; 34:21; Ps. 119:168; Prov. 15:3; Jer. 16:17; 32:19; Hos. 7:2; Heb. 4:13 [b]Prov. 4:26
22 [a]Num. 32:23; Ps. 7:15; 9:15; 40:12; Prov. 1:31, 32
23 [a]Job 4:21; 36:12

1 [I]Lit., *clapped your palms* [a]Prov. 11:15; 17:18; 20:16; 22:26; 27:13
3 [I]Lit., *palm*
4 [a]Ps. 132:4
5 [a]Ps. 91:3; 124:7
6 [a]Prov. 30:24, 25 [b]Prov. 6:9; 10:26; 13:4; 20:4; 26:16
7 [a]Prov. 30:27
8 [a]Prov. 10:5
10 [I]Lit., *lie down* [a]Prov. 24:33
11 [I]Lit., *one who walks* [II]Lit., *a man with a shield* [a]Prov. 24:34
12 [a]Prov. 16:27 [b]Prov. 4:24; 10:32
13 [I]Lit., *scrapes* [II]Lit., *instructs with* [a]Job 15:12; Ps. 35:19; Prov. 10:10
14 [I]Lit., *sends out* [a]Prov. 17:20 [b]Prov. 3:29; Mic. 2:1 [c]Prov. 6:19; 16:28
15 [a]Prov. 24:22 [b]Is. 30:13, 14; Jer. 19:11 [c]2Chr. 36:16
16 [I]Lit., *of His soul*
17 [a]Ps. 18:27; 101:5; Prov. 21:4; 30:13 [b]Ps. 31:18; 120:2; Prov. 12:22; 17:7 [c]Deut. 19:10; Prov. 28:17; Is. 1:15; 59:7
18 [a]Gen. 6:5; Prov. 24:2 [b]Prov. 1:16; Is. 59:7; Rom. 3:15
19 [I]Lit., *sends out* [a]Ps. 27:12; Prov. 12:17; 19:5, 9; 21:28 [b]Prov. 6:14
20 [I]Or, *law* [a]Eph. 6:1
21 [a]Prov. 3:3
22 [I]Lit., *she* [a]Prov. 3:23

And when you awake,
[I]they will talk[7878] to you.
23 For [a]the commandment is a
lamp,[5216] and the [I]teaching is
light;[216]
And reproofs[8433] for
discipline[4148] are the way[1870]
of life,[2416]
24 To [a]keep you from the evil[7451]
woman,[802]
From the smooth tongue of the
[I]adulteress.[5237]
25 [a]Do not desire[2530] her beauty in
your heart,[3824]
Nor let her catch you with her
[b]eyelids.
26 For [a]on account of a harlot[2181]
one is reduced to a loaf of
bread,
And [I]an adulteress[802] [b]hunts for
the precious life.[5315]
27 Can a man [I]take fire in his
bosom,
And his clothes not be
burned?[8313]
28 Or can a man[376] walk on hot
coals,
And his feet not be scorched?
29 So is the one who [a]goes in
to his neighbor's[7453]
wife;[802]
Whoever touches[5060] her
[b]will not [I]go unpunished.[5352]
30 [I]Men do not despise a thief if
he steals
To [a]satisfy [II]himself[5315] when he
is hungry;
31 But when he is found, he must
[a]repay[7999] sevenfold;
He must give all the [I]substance
of his house.[1004]
32 The one who commits
adultery[5003] with a woman is
[a]lacking [I]sense;[3820]
He who would [b]destroy[7843]
[II]himself does[6213] it.
33 Wounds[5061] and disgrace he will
find,
And his reproach[2781] will not be
blotted out.[4229]
34 For [a]jealousy[7068] [I]enrages a
man,[1397]
And he will not spare in the
[b]day[3117] of vengeance.[5359]
35 He will not [I]accept[5375] any
ransom,[3724]
Nor will he be [II]content[14] though
you give many [III]gifts.

The Wiles of the Harlot

7 My son,[1121] [a]keep[8104] my words,[561]
And treasure my command-
ments[4687] within you.
2 [a]Keep my commandments and
live,[2421]
And my [I]teaching[8451] [b]as the
[II]apple of your eye.
3 [a]Bind them on your fingers;
[b]Write them on the tablet of your
heart.[3820]
4 Say[559] to wisdom,[2451] "You are
my sister,"[269]
And call[7121] understanding[998]
your intimate friend;
5 That they may keep you from
an [I]adulteress,[2114]
From the foreigner who
[II]flatters with her words.
6 For [a]at the window of my
house[1004]
I looked out [b]through my
lattice,[822]
7 And I saw[7200] among the
[I][a]naive,
I discerned[995] among the
[II]youths,
A young man [b]lacking
[III]sense,[3820]
8 Passing[5674] through the street
near [a]her corner;
And he [I]takes the way[1870] to
[b]her house,
9 In the [a]twilight, in the
[I]evening,
In the [II]middle of the night[3915]
and *in* the darkness.[653]
10 And behold, a woman *comes* to
meet him,
[a]Dressed as a harlot[2181] and
cunning of heart.
11 She is [a]boisterous and
rebellious;[5637]
Her [b]feet do not remain at home;

22 [I]Lit., *she*
23 [I]Or, *law* [a]Ps. 19:8; 119:105
24 [I]Lit., *foreign woman* [a]Prov. 5:3; 7:5, 21
25 [a]Matt. 5:28 [b]2Kin. 9:30; Jer. 4:30; Ezek. 23:40
26 [I]Lit., *a man's wife* [a]Prov. 5:9, 10; 29:3 [b]Prov. 7:23; Ezek. 13:18
27 [I]Lit., *snatch up*
29 [I]Lit., *be innocent* [a]Ezek. 18:6; 33:26 [b]Prov. 16:5
30 [I]Lit., *They do not;* or, *Do not men. . .?* [II]Lit., *his soul* [a]Job 38:39
31 [I]Or, *wealth* [a]Ex. 22:1-4
32 [I]Lit., *heart* [II]Lit., *his soul* [a]Prov. 7:7; 9:4, 16; 10:13, 21; 11:12; 12:11 [b]Prov. 7:22, 23
34 [I]Lit., *is the rage of* [a]Prov. 27:4; Song 8:6 [b]Prov. 11:4
35 [I]Lit., *lift up the face of any* [II]Lit., *willing* [III]Or, *bribes*

1 [a]Prov. 2:1; 6:20
2 [I]Or, *law* [II]Lit., *pupil* [a]Prov. 4:4 [b]Deut. 32:10; Ps. 17:8; Zech. 2:8
3 [a]Deut. 6:8; 11:18; Prov. 6:21 [b]Prov. 3:3
5 [I]Lit., *strange woman* [II]Lit., *is smooth*
6 [a]Judg. 5:28 [b]Song 2:9
7 [I]Lit., *simple ones* [II]Lit., *sons* [III]Lit., *heart* [a]Prov. 1:22 [b]Prov. 6:32; 9:4
8 [I]Lit., *steps* [a]Prov. 7:12 [b]Prov. 7:27
9 [I]Lit., *evening of the day* [II]Lit., *pupil* (of the eye) [a]Job 24:15
10 [a]Gen. 38:14, 15; 1Tim. 2:9
11 [a]Prov. 9:13 [b]1Tim. 5:13; Titus 2:5

12 *She is* now in the streets, now
[a]in the squares,
And [b]lurks by every corner.
13 So she seizes[2388] him and
kisses[5401] him,
[I]And with a [a]brazen face she
says[559] to him:
14 "[I]I was due to offer [a]peace
offerings;[8002]
Today[3117] I have [b]paid[7999] my
vows.[5088]
15 "Therefore I have come out to
meet you,
To seek your presence
earnestly, and I have found
you.
16 "I have spread my couch with
[a]coverings,
With colored [b]linens of Egypt.
17 "I have sprinkled[5130] my bed
With [a]myrrh,[4753] aloes[174] and
[b]cinnamon.
18 "Come, let us drink our fill of
love[1730] until morning;
Let us delight[5965] ourselves with
caresses.[159]
19 "For [I]the man[376] is not at
home,[1004]
He has gone on a long
journey;[1870]
20 He has taken a [a]bag of money
[I]with him,
At full moon he will come
home."
21 With her many persuasions[3948]
she entices him;
With her [Ia]flattering lips[8193] she
seduces him.
22 Suddenly[6597] he follows her,
As an ox goes to the
slaughter,[2874]
Or as [I]*one in* fetters to the
discipline[4148] of a fool,
23 Until an arrow pierces through
his liver;
As a [a]bird hastens to the snare,
So he does not know that it *will
cost him* his life.[5315]
24 Now therefore, *my* sons,[1121]
[a]listen[8085] to me,
And pay attention to the words
of my mouth.[6310]
25 Do not let your heart [a]turn aside
to her ways,[1870]
Do not stray[8582] into her paths.
26 For many are the [I]victims[2491] she
has cast down,[5307]
And [a]numerous are all her
slain.[2026]
27 Her [a]house is the way to
Sheol,[7585]
Descending to the chambers of
death.[4194]

The Commendation of Wisdom

8 Does not [a]wisdom[2451] call,[7121]
And understanding[8394] [I]lift up
her voice?
2 On top[7218] of [a]the heights beside
the way,[1870]
Where the paths meet, she
takes her stand;[5324]
3 Beside the [a]gates, at the opening
to the city,
At the entrance of the doors,
she cries out:
4 "To you, O men,[376] I call,[7121]
And my voice is to the sons[1121]
of men.[120]
5 "O [Ia]naive ones, discern[995]
prudence;[6195]

12 [a]Prov. 9:14 [b]Prov. 23:28
13 [I]Lit., *She makes bold her face and says* [a]Prov. 21:29
14 [I]Lit., *Sacrifices of peace offerings are with me* [a]Lev. 7:11 [b]Lev. 7:16
16 [a]Prov. 31:22 [b]Is. 19:9; Ezek. 27:7
17 [a]Ps. 45:8 [b]Ex. 30:23
19 [I]I.e., my husband
20 [I]Lit., *in his hand* [a]Gen. 42:35
21 [I]Lit., *smooth* [a]Prov. 5:3; 6:24
22 [I]Or, *as a stag goes into a trap;* so some ancient versions
23 [a]Eccl. 9:12
24 [a]Prov. 5:7
25 [a]Prov. 5:8
26 [I]Lit., *mortally wounded* [a]Prov. 9:18
27 [a]Prov. 2:18; 5:5; 9:18; 1Cor. 6:9, 10; Rev. 22:15
1 [I]Lit., *give* [a]Prov. 1:20, 21; 8:1-3; 9:3; 1Cor. 1:24
2 [a]Prov. 9:3, 14
3 [a]Job 29:7
5 [I]Lit., *simple* [a]Prov. 1:4

8:1 Wisdom is a recurring theme throughout Proverbs. In this chapter and the one following we have a description of Wisdom as a person, her origin, and, as it were, her family tree and her dwelling place. She now appears as a preacher, speaking forth in all the places where men congregate. After proclaiming in various ways the excellence of the gifts she is able to provide, she asserts that she was the first of all God's creatures, who stood at His side when He formed our world, and she took part in His work as a master workman whose delight has always been in the lives and affairs of men. In the fourth century A.D., theologians of opposing schools used this chapter to a great extent in the controversies concerning Christ. However, the object of the writer seems only to recommend wisdom, which reveals itself in the right conduct of life, by showing that it is exhibited and exemplified in the wonders of nature and in the creation of the world.

And, O [b]fools, discern[995]
[II]wisdom.
6 "Listen,[8085] for I shall speak[1696]
[a]noble things;[5057]
And the opening of my lips[8193]
will produce [b]right things.[4334]
7 "For my [a]mouth will utter[1897]
truth;[571]
And wickedness[7562] is an
abomination[8441] to my lips.
8 "All the utterances[561] of my
mouth[6310] are in
righteousness;[6664]
There is nothing [a]crooked[6617] or
perverted in them.
9 "They are all [a]straightforward[5228]
to him who understands,[995]
And right[3477] to those who
[b]find knowledge.[1847]
10 "Take my [a]instruction,[4148] and not
silver,
And knowledge rather than
choicest[977] gold.
11 "For wisdom is [a]better[2896] than
[I]jewels;
And [b]all desirable things can not
compare with her.
12 "I, wisdom, [a]dwell[7931] with
prudence,[6195]
And I find [b]knowledge *and*
discretion.[4209]
13 "The [a]fear[3374] of the LORD is to
hate[8130] evil;[7451]
[b]Pride and arrogance and
[c]the evil way,
And the [d]perverted[8419] mouth,
I hate.
14 "[a]Counsel[6098] is mine and
[b]sound wisdom;[8454]
I am understanding,[998]
[c]power is mine.
15 "By me [a]kings[4428] reign,[4427]
And rulers[5081] decree[2710]
justice.[6664]
16 "By me princes[8269] rule,[8323] and
nobles,[5081]
All who judge[8199] rightly.
17 "I [a]love[157] those who love me;
And [b]those who diligently seek
me will find me.
18 "[a]Riches and honor[3519] are with
me,
Enduring [b]wealth and
righteousness.[6666]
19 "My fruit is [a]better than gold,
even pure gold,
And my yield than [b]choicest
silver.
20 "I walk in the way[734] of
righteousness,
In the midst of the paths of
justice,[4941]
21 To endow[5157] those who love me
with wealth,
That I may [a]fill their treasuries.
22 "The LORD possessed me
[a]at the beginning[7225] of His
way,
Before His works [I]of old.[227]
23 "From everlasting[5769] I was
[Ia]established,[5258]
From the beginning,[7218]
[b]from the earliest times of the
earth.
24 "When there were no [a]depths I
was [I]brought forth,[2342]
When there were no springs
abounding[3513] with water.
25 "[a]Before the mountains were
settled,
Before the hills I was [I]brought
forth;[2342]
26 While He had not yet made[6213]
the earth and the [I]fields,
Nor the first dust[6083] of the
world.[8398]
27 "When He [a]established[3559] the
heavens,[8064] I was there,
When [b]He inscribed[2710] a circle
on the face of the deep,
28 When He made firm the skies[7834]
above,
When the springs of the deep
became [I]fixed,
29 When [a]He set for the sea its
boundary,[2706]
So that the water should not
transgress His [I]com-
mand,[6310]
When He marked out[2710]
[b]the foundations[4146] of the
earth;
30 Then [a]I was beside Him, *as* a
master workman;

5 [II]Lit., *heart* [b]Prov. 1:22, 32; 3:35
6 [a]Prov. 22:20 [b]Prov. 23:16
7 [a]Ps. 37:30; John 8:14; Rom. 15:8
8 [a]Deut. 32:5; Prov. 2:15; Phil. 2:15
9 [a]Prov. 14:6 [b]Prov. 3:13
10 [a]Prov. 3:14, 15; 8:19
11 [I]Lit., *corals* [a]Job 28:15, 18; Ps. 19:10 [b]Prov. 3:15
12 [a]Prov. 8:5 [b]Prov. 1:4
13 [a]Prov. 3:7; 16:6 [b]1Sam. 2:3; Prov. 16:18; Is. 13:11 [c]Prov. 15:9 [d]Prov. 6:12
14 [a]Prov. 1:25; 19:20; Is. 28:29; Jer. 32:19 [b]Prov. 2:7; 3:21; 18:1 [c]Eccl. 7:19; 9:16
15 [a]2Chr. 1:10; Prov. 29:4; Dan. 2:21; Matt. 28:18; Rom. 13:1
17 [a]1Sam. 2:30; Prov. 4:6; John 14:21 [b]Prov. 2:4, 5; John 7:37; James 1:5
18 [a]Prov. 3:16 [b]Ps. 112:3; Matt. 6:33
19 [a]Job 28:15; Prov. 3:14 [b]Prov. 10:20
21 [a]Prov. 24:4
22 [I]Lit., *from then* [a]Job 28:26-28; Ps. 104:24; Prov. 3:19
23 [I]Or, *consecrated* [a]John 1:1-3 [b]John 17:5
24 [I]Or, *born* [a]Gen. 1:2; Ex. 15:5; Job 38:16; Prov. 3:20
25 [I]Or, *born* [a]Job 15:7; Ps. 90:2
26 [I]Lit., *outside places*
27 [a]Prov. 3:19 [b]Job 26:10
28 [I]Lit., *strong*
29 [I]Lit., *mouth* [a]Job 38:10; Ps. 104:9 [b]Job 38:6; Ps. 104:5
30 [a]John 1:2, 3

And I was daily[3117] *His* delight,
[I]Rejoicing always[6256] before Him,
31 [I]Rejoicing in the world,[8398] His earth,
And *having* [a]my delight in the sons of men.[120]
32 "Now therefore, *O* sons,[1121] [a]listen[8085] to me,
For [b]blessed[835] are they who keep[8104] my ways.[1870]
33 "[a]Heed instruction and be wise,[2449]
And do not neglect *it*.
34 "[a]Blessed is the man who listens[8085] to me,
Watching daily at my gates,
Waiting at my doorposts.
35 "For [a]he who finds me finds life,[2416]
And [b]obtains favor[7522] from the LORD.
36 "But he who [I]sins[2398] against me [a]injures[2554] himself;[5315]
All those who [b]hate me [c]love death."[4194]

Wisdom's Invitation

9 Wisdom[2454] has [a]built her house,[1004]
She has hewn out[2672] her seven pillars;
2 She has [I][a]prepared[2873] her food,[2874] she has [b]mixed her wine;
She has also [c]set her table;
3 She has [a]sent out her maidens, she [b]calls
From the [c]tops of the heights of the city:
4 "[a]Whoever is [I]naive, let him turn in here!"
To him who [b]lacks [II]understanding[3820] she says,[559]
5 "Come, [a]eat of my food,
And drink of the wine I have mixed.
6 "[I]Forsake[5800] *your* folly and [a]live,[2421]
And [b]proceed in the way[1870] of understanding."[998]
7 He who [a]corrects[3256] a scoffer[3887] gets dishonor for himself,
And he who reproves[3198] a wicked[7563] man *gets* [I]insults[3971] for himself.
8 [a]Do not reprove[3198] a scoffer, lest he hate[8130] you,
[b]Reprove[3198] a wise[2450] man, and he will love[157] you.
9 Give *instruction* to a wise man, and he will be still wiser,[2449]
Teach[3045] a righteous man, and he will [a]increase *his* learning.[3948]
10 The [a]fear[3374] of the LORD is the beginning of wisdom,[2451]
And the knowledge[1847] of the Holy One[6918] is understanding.
11 For [a]by me your days[3117] will be multiplied,
And years of life[2416] will be added to you.
12 If you are wise, you are wise[2449] [a]for yourself,
And if you [b]scoff,[3887] you alone will bear[5375] it.
13 The [I]woman[802] of folly[3687] is [a]boisterous,
She is [II]naive, and [b]knows nothing.
14 And she sits at the doorway of her house,
On a seat[3678] by [a]the high places of the city,
15 Calling[7121] to those who pass by,
Who are making[3474] their paths[734] straight:[3474]
16 "[a]Whoever is [I]naive, let him turn in here,"
And to him who lacks [II]understanding she says,
17 "Stolen water is sweet;
And [a]bread *eaten* in secret is pleasant."
18 But he does not know that the [I]dead[7496] are there,
That her guests[7121] are in the [a]depths of Sheol.[7585]

---

30 [I]Or, *Playing*
31 [I]Or, *Playing* [a]Ps. 16:3; John 13:1
32 [a]Prov. 5:7; 7:24 [b]Ps. 119:1, 2; 128:1; Prov. 29:18; Luke 11:28
33 [a]Prov. 4:1
34 [a]Prov. 3:13, 18
35 [a]Prov. 4:22; John 17:3 [b]Prov. 3:4; 12:2
36 [I]Or, *misses me* [a]Prov. 1:31, 32; 15:32 [b]Prov. 5:12; 12:1 [c]Prov. 21:6

1 [a]1Cor. 3:9, 10; Eph. 2:20-22; 1Pet. 2:5
2 [I]Lit., *slaughtered her slaughter* [a]Matt. 22:4 [b]Song 8:2 [c]Luke 14:16, 17
3 [a]Ps. 68:11; Matt. 22:3 [b]Prov. 8:1, 2 [c]Prov. 9:14
4 [I]Lit., *simple* [II]Lit., *heart* [a]Prov. 8:5; 9:16 [b]Prov. 6:32
5 [a]Song 5:1; Is. 55:1; John 6:27
6 [I]Or, *Forsake the simple ones* [a]Prov. 8:35; 9:11 [b]Ezek. 11:20; 37:24
7 [I]Lit., *a blemish* [a]Prov. 23:9
8 [a]Prov. 15:12; Matt. 7:6 [b]Ps. 141:5; Prov. 10:8
9 [a]Prov. 1:5
10 [a]Job 28:28; Ps. 111:10; Prov. 1:7
11 [a]Prov. 3:16; 10:27
12 [a]Job 22:2; Prov. 14:14 [b]Prov. 19:29
13 [I]Or, *foolish woman* [II]Lit., *simple* [a]Prov. 7:11 [b]Prov. 5:6
14 [a]Prov. 9:3
16 [I]Lit., *simple* [II]Lit., *heart* [a]Prov. 9:4
17 [a]Prov. 20:17
18 [I]Lit., *departed spirits* [a]Prov. 7:27

Contrast of the Righteous and the Wicked

10 The [a]proverbs of Solomon.
[b]A wise[2450] son[1121] makes a
father[1] glad,
But [c]a foolish son is a grief to
his mother.[517]
2 [Ia]Ill-gotten[7562] gains do not
profit,
But righteousness[6666]
delivers[5337] from death.4197
3 The LORD [a]will not allow the
[I]righteous[6662] to hunger,
But He [b]will thrust *aside* the
craving of the wicked.[7563]
4 Poor is he who works with a
negligent7423 hand,[3709]
But the [a]hand[3027] of the diligent
makes rich.
5 He who gathers in summer is
a son who acts wisely,[7919]
But he who sleeps in harvest
is a son who acts
shamefully.[954]
6 [a]Blessings[1293] are on the
head[7218] of the righteous,
But [b]the mouth[6310] of the wicked
conceals[3680] violence.[2555]
7 The [a]memory[2143] of the
righteous is blessed,
But [b]the name of the wicked will
rot.
8 The [a]wise of heart[3820] will
receive commands,[4687]
But [I]a babbling[8193] fool will be
thrown down.
9 He [a]who walks in integrity[8537]
walks securely,
But [b]he who perverts his
ways[1870] will be found out.[3045]
10 He [a]who winks7169 the eye
causes trouble,
And [Ib]a babbling fool will be
thrown down.
11 The [a]mouth of the righteous is
a fountain of life,[2416]
But [b]the mouth of the wicked
conceals violence.
12 Hatred[8135] stirs up strife,
But [a]love[160] covers all
transgressions.[6588]
13 On [a]the lips[8193] of the
discerning,[995] wisdom[2451] is
found,
But [b]a rod[7626] is for the back[1460]
of him who lacks
[I]understanding.[3820]
14 Wise men [a]store up
knowledge,[1847]
But with [b]the mouth of the
foolish, ruin[4288] is at hand.
15 The [a]rich man's wealth is his
[I]fortress,
The [b]ruin of the poor is their
poverty.
16 The [Ia]wages of the righteous is
life,
The income of the wicked,
punishment.[2403]
17 He [a]is *on* the path[734] of life who
heeds[8104] instruction,[4148]
But he who forsakes reproof
goes astray.[8582]
18 He [a]who conceals hatred *has*
lying lips,
And he who spreads slander is
a fool.
19 When there are [a]many
words,[1697] transgression is
unavoidable,
But [b]he who restrains his lips
is wise.
20 The tongue of the righteous is
as [a]choice[977] silver,
The heart of the wicked is *worth*
little.
21 The [a]lips of the righteous feed
many,
But fools [b]die for lack of
[I]understanding.[3820]
22 It is the [a]blessing[1295] of the LORD
that makes rich,
And He adds no sorrow[6089] to
it.
23 Doing[6213] wickedness is like
[a]sport to a fool;
And *so is* wisdom to a man[376]
of understanding.[8394]
24 What [a]the wicked fears[4034] will
come upon him,

1 [a]Prov. 1:1 [b]Prov. 15:20; 29:3 [c]Prov. 17:25; 29:15 **2** [I]Lit., *Treasures of wickedness* [a]Ps. 49:7; Prov. 11:4; 21:6; Ezek. 7:19; Luke 12:19, 20 **3** [I]Lit., *soul of the righteous* [a]Ps. 34:9, 10; 37:25; Prov. 28:25; Matt. 6:33 [b]Ps. 112:10; Prov. 28:9 **4** [a]Prov. 13:4; 21:5 **6** [a]Prov. 28:20 [b]Prov. 10:11; Obad. 10 **7** [a]Ps. 112:6 [b]Ps. 9:5, 6; 109:13; Eccl. 8:10 **8** [I]Lit., *the foolish of lips* [a]Prov. 9:8; Matt. 7:24 **9** [a]Ps. 23:4; Prov. 3:23; 28:18; Is. 33:15, 16 [b]Prov. 26:26; Matt. 10:26; 1Tim. 5:25 **10** [I]Lit., *the foolish of lips* [a]Ps. 35:19; Prov. 6:13 [b]Prov. 10:8 **11** [a]Ps. 37:30; Prov. 13:14; 18:4 [b]Prov. 10:6 **12** [a]Prov. 17:9; 1Cor. 13:4-7; James 5:20; 1Pet. 4:8 **13** [I]Lit., *heart* [a]Prov. 10:31 [b]Prov. 19:29; 26:3 **14** [a]Prov. 9:9 [b]Prov. 10:8, 10; 13:3; 18:7 **15** [I]Lit., *strong city* [a]Job 31:24; Ps. 52:7; Prov. 18:11 [b]Prov. 19:7 **16** [I]Or, *work* [a]Prov. 11:18, 19 **17** [a]Prov. 6:23 **18** [a]Prov. 26:24 **19** [a]Job 11:2; Prov. 18:21; Eccl. 5:3 [b]Prov. 17:27; James 1:19; 3:2 **20** [a]Prov. 8:19 **21** [I]Lit., *heart* [a]Prov. 10:11 [b]Prov. 5:23; Hos. 4:6 **22** [a]Gen. 24:35; 26:12; Deut. 8:18; Prov. 8:21 **23** [a]Prov. 2:14; 15:21 **24** [a]Job 15:21; Prov. 1:27; Is. 66:4

And the [b]desire of the righteous
will be granted.
25 When the [a]whirlwind passes,[5674]
the wicked is no more,
But the [b]righteous *has* an
everlasting[5769] foundation.
26 Like vinegar to the teeth and
smoke to the eyes,
So is the [a]lazy one[6102] to those
who send him.
27 The [a]fear[3374] of the LORD
prolongs [I]life,[3117]
But the [b]years of the wicked will
be shortened.
28 The [a]hope[8431] of the righteous
is gladness,
But the [b]expectation of the
wicked perishes.[6]
29 The [a]way[1870] of the LORD is a
stronghold to the upright,[8537]
But [b]ruin to the workers of
iniquity.[205]
30 The [a]righteous will never be
shaken,
But [b]the wicked will not dwell[7931]
in the land.[776]
31 The [a]mouth of the righteous
flows with wisdom,
But the [b]perverted[8419] tongue
will be cut out.[3772]
32 The lips of the righteous bring
forth[3045] [a]what is
acceptable,[7522]
But the [b]mouth of the wicked,
what is perverted.[8419]

Contrast the Upright and the Wicked

11 A [a]false[4820] balance is an
abomination[8441] to the LORD,
But a [b]just[8003] weight is His
delight.[7522]
2 When [a]pride[2087] comes, then
comes dishonor,
But with the humble is
wisdom.[2451]
3 The [a]integrity[8538] of the
upright[3477] will guide[5148]
them,
But the [b]falseness of the
treacherous will destroy[7703]
them.
4 [a]Riches do not profit in the
day[3117] of wrath,[5678]
But [b]righteousness[6666]
delivers[5337] from death.[4194]
5 The [a]righteousness of the
blameless[8549] will smooth[3474]
his way,[1870]
But [b]the wicked[7563] will fall by
his own wickedness.[7564]
6 The righteousness of the upright
will deliver[5337] them,
But the treacherous will
[a]be caught by *their own*
greed.[1942]
7 When a wicked man[120] dies, *his*
[a]expectation will perish,[6]
And the [b]hope[8431] of strong men
perishes.[6]
8 The righteous[6662] is
delivered[2502] from trouble,
But the wicked [I]takes his place.
9 With *his* [a]mouth[6310] the
godless[2611] man destroys[7843]
his neighbor,[7453]
But through knowledge[1847] the
[b]righteous will be delivered.
10 When it [a]goes well[2898] with the
righteous, the city rejoices,
And when the wicked perish,
there is glad shouting.
11 By the blessing[1295] of the upright
a city is exalted,
But by the mouth of the wicked
it is torn down.
12 He who despises his neighbor
lacks [I]sense,[3820]
But a man[376] of understanding
keeps silent.
13 He [a]who goes about as a
talebearer reveals[1540]
secrets,[5475]
But he who is
[I]trustworthy[539,7307]
[b]conceals[3680] a matter.[1697]
14 Where there is no [a]guidance, the
people[5971] fall,
But in abundance of
counselors[3289] there is
[I]victory.[8668]
15 He who is [a]surety[6148] for a

24 [b]Ps. 145:19; Prov. 15:8; Matt. 5:6; 1John 5:14, 15
25 [a]Job 21:18; Ps. 58:9; Prov. 12:7 [b]Ps. 15:5; Prov. 12:3; Matt. 7:24, 25
26 [a]Prov. 26:6
27 [I]Lit., *days* [a]Prov. 3:2; 9:11; 14:27 [b]Job 15:32, 33; 22:16; Ps. 55:23
28 [a]Prov. 11:23 [b]Job 8:13; 11:20; Prov. 11:7
29 [a]Prov. 13:6 [b]Prov. 21:15
30 [a]Ps. 37:29; 125:1; Prov. 2:21 [b]Prov. 2:22
31 [a]Ps. 37:30; Prov. 10:13 [b]Prov. 17:20
32 [a]Eccl. 12:10 [b]Prov. 2:12; 6:12

1 [a]Lev. 19:35, 36; Deut. 25:13-16; Prov. 20:10, 23; Mic. 6:11 [b]Prov. 16:11
2 [a]Prov. 16:18; 18:12; 29:23
3 [a]Prov. 13:6 [b]Prov. 19:3; 22:12
4 [a]Prov. 10:2; Ezek. 7:19; Zeph. 1:18 [b]Gen. 7:1
5 [a]Prov. 3:6 [b]Prov. 5:22
6 [a]Ps. 7:15, 16; 9:15; Eccl. 10:8
7 [a]Prov. 10:28 [b]Job 8:13, 14
8 [I]Lit., *enters*
9 [a]Prov. 16:29 [b]Prov. 11:6
10 [a]Prov. 28:12
12 [I]Lit., *heart*
13 [I]Lit., *faithful of spirit* [a]Lev. 19:16; Prov. 20:19; 1Tim. 5:13 [b]Prov. 19:11
14 [I]Lit., *deliverance* [a]Prov. 15:22; 20:18; 24:6
15 [a]Prov. 6:1; 27:13

stranger[2114] will surely
suffer[7321] for it,
But he who hates[8130] [I]going
surety[8628] is safe.
16 A [a]gracious woman[802] attains
honor,[3519]
And violent men attain riches.
17 The [a]merciful[2617] man does
[I]himself[5315] good,
But the cruel man [II]does
himself[7607] harm.
18 The wicked earns[6213]
deceptive[8267] wages,
But he who [a]sows righteousness
gets a true reward.
19 He who is steadfast in
[a]righteousness *will attain* to
life,[2416]
And [b]he who pursues evil[7451] *will*
bring about his own death.
20 The perverse[6141] in heart[3820] are
an abomination to the LORD,
But the [a]blameless[8549] in *their*
[I]walk are His [b]delight.
21 [I]Assuredly, the evil[7451] man will
not go unpunished,[5352]
But the [II]descendants[2233] of the
righteous will be
delivered.[4422]
22 *As* a [a]ring of gold in a swine's
snout,
So is a beautiful woman who
lacks [I]discretion.[2940]
23 The desire of the righteous is
only good,[2896]
But the [a]expectation of the
wicked is wrath.
24 There is one who scatters, yet
increases all the more,
And there is one who withholds
what is justly due,[3476] but *it*
results only in want.
25 The [Ia]generous man will be
[II]prosperous,[1878]
And he who [b]waters will himself
be watered.
26 He who withholds grain, the
[a]people[3816] will curse[5344] him,
But [b]blessing will be on the
head[7218] of him who [c]sells *it.*
27 He who diligently seeks good
seeks favor,[7522]
But [a]he who searches after
evil,[7451] it will come to him.
28 He who [a]trusts[982] in his riches
will fall,
But [b]the righteous will flourish
like the *green* leaf.
29 He who [a]troubles his own
house[1004] will [b]inherit[5157]
wind,[7307]
And [c]the foolish will be
servant[5650] to the
wisehearted.[2450]
30 The fruit of the righteous is
[a]a tree of life,
And [b]he who is wise [I]wins
souls.[5315]
31 If [a]the righteous will be
rewarded[7999] in the earth,[776]
How much more the wicked and
the sinner![2398]

Contrast the Upright and the Wicked

12 Whoever loves[157] [I]discipline[4148]
loves knowledge,[1847]
But he who hates[8130] reproof is
stupid.
2 A [a]good[2896] man will obtain
favor[7522] from the LORD,
But He will condemn[7561] a
man[376] [I]who devises evil.[4209]
3 A man[120] will [a]not be
established[3559] by
wickedness,[7562]
But the root of the [b]righteous[6662]
will not be moved.
4 An [Ia]excellent[2428] wife[802] is the
crown of her husband,[1167]
But she who shames[954] *him* is
as [b]rottenness in his
bones.[6106]
5 The thoughts[4284] of the
righteous are just,[4941]
But the counsels of the
wicked[7563] are deceitful.[4820]
6 The [a]words[1697] of the wicked lie
in wait for blood,[1818]
But the [b]mouth[6310] of the
upright[3477] will deliver[5337]
them.

15 [I]Lit., *those who strike hands*
16 [a]Prov. 31:28, 30
17 [I]Lit., *good to his own soul* [II]Lit., *troubles his flesh* [a]Matt. 5:7; 25:34-36
18 [a]Hos. 10:12; Gal. 6:8, 9; James 3:18
19 [a]Prov. 10:16; 12:28; 19:23 [b]Prov. 21:16; Rom. 6:23; James 1:15
20 [I]Lit., *way* [a]Ps. 119:1; Prov. 13:6 [b]1Chr. 29:17
21 [I]Lit., *Hand to hand* [II]Lit., *seed*
22 [I]Lit., *taste* [a]Gen. 24:47
23 [a]Prov. 10:28; Rom. 2:8, 9
25 [I]Lit., *soul of blessing* [II]Lit., *made fat* [a]Prov. 3:9, 10; 2Cor. 9:6, 7 [b]Matt. 5:7
26 [a]Prov. 24:24 [b]Job 29:13 [c]Gen. 42:6
27 [a]Esth. 7:10; Ps. 7:15, 16; 57:6
28 [a]Ps. 49:6; Mark 10:25; 1Tim. 6:17 [b]Ps. 1:3; 92:12; Jer. 17:8
29 [a]Prov. 15:27 [b]Eccl. 5:16 [c]Prov. 14:19
30 [I]Lit., *takes* [a]Prov. 3:18 [b]Prov. 14:25; Dan. 12:3; 1Cor. 9:19-22; James 5:20
31 [a]2Sam. 22:21, 25; Prov. 13:21; 1Pet. 4:18 Prov. 12

1 [I]Or, *instruction*
2 [I]Lit., *of evil devices* [a]Prov. 3:4; 8:35
3 [a]Prov. 11:5 [b]Prov. 10:25
4 [I]Or, *virtuous* [a]Prov. 31:11; 1Cor. 11:7 [b]Prov. 14:30; Hab. 3:16
6 [a]Prov. 1:11, 16 [b]Prov. 14:3

7 The [a]wicked are overthrown2013
and are no more,
But the [b]house1004 of the
righteous will stand.
8 A man will be praised6310
according to his insight,7922
But one of perverse5753
[I]mind3820 will be despised.
9 Better2896 is he who is lightly
esteemed and has a
servant,5650
Than he who honors3513 himself
and lacks bread.
10 A [a]righteous man has regard3045
for the life5315 of his beast,
But the compassion7356 of the
wicked is cruel.
11 He [a]who tills5647 his land127 will
have plenty of bread,
But he who pursues vain *things*
lacks [I]sense.3820
12 The [a]wicked desires2530 the
[I]booty of evil7451 men,
But the root of the righteous
[b]yields *fruit.*
13 [I]An evil7451 man is ensnared4170
by the transgression6588 of his
lips,8193
But the [a]righteous will escape
from trouble.
14 A man will be [a]satisfied with good
by the fruit of his [I]words,
And the [b]deeds of a man's120
hands3027 will return7725 to
him.
15 The [a]way1870 of a fool is right3477
in his own eyes,
But a wise2450 man is he who
listens to counsel.6098
16 A [a]fool's vexation3708 is
known3045 at once,3117
But a prudent6175 man
conceals3680 dishonor.
17 He who [I]speaks6315 truth530
tells5046 what is right,6664
But a false8267 witness,
deceit.
18 There is one who [a]speaks981
rashly like the thrusts of a
sword,2719
But the [b]tongue of the wise
brings healing.

7 [a]Job 34:25; Prov. 10:25 [b]Matt. 7:24-27
8 [I]Lit., *heart*
10 [a]Deut. 25:4
11 [I]Lit., *heart* [a]Prov. 28:19
12 [I]Lit., *net* [a]Prov. 21:10 [b]Prov. 11:30
13 [I]Lit., *In the transgression of the lips is an evil snare* [a]Prov. 11:8; 21:23; 2Pet. 2:9
14 [I]Lit., *mouth* [a]Prov. 13:2; 15:23; 18:20 [b]Job 34:11; Prov. 1:31; 24:12; Is. 3:10, 11; Hos. 4:9
15 [a]Prov. 14:12; 16:2; 21:2
16 [a]Prov. 14:33; 27:3; 29:11
17 [I]Lit., *breathes*
18 [a]Ps. 57:4 [b]Prov. 4:22; 15:4
19 [a]Ps. 52:4, 5; Prov. 19:9
21 [a]Ps. 91:10; 121:7; Prov. 1:33; 1Pet. 3:13
22 [a]Rev. 22:15
23 [a]Prov. 10:14; 11:13; 13:16; 15:2; 29:11
24 [I]Lit., *slackness* [a]Gen. 49:15; Judg. 1:28; 1Kin. 9:21
25 [a]Prov. 15:13 [b]Is. 50:4
27 [I]Lit., *slackness* [II]Or, *catch* [a]Prov. 10:4; 13:4
28 [a]Deut. 30:15f.; 32:46f.; Jer. 21:8
1 [a]Prov. 10:1; 15:20 [b]Prov. 9:7, 8; 15:12
2 [I]Lit., *eats* [II]Lit., *soul* [a]Prov. 12:14 [b]Prov. 1:31; Hos. 10:13

19 Truthful571 lips will be
established forever,5703
But a [a]lying tongue is only for
a moment.
20 Deceit is in the heart of those
who devise evil,
But counselors3289 of peace have
joy.
21 [a]No harm befalls the righteous,
But the wicked are filled with
trouble.7451
22 [a]Lying lips are an
abomination8441 to the LORD,
But those who deal6213 faithfully
are His delight.7522
23 A [a]prudent man conceals3680
knowledge,
But the heart of fools
proclaims7121 folly.
24 The hand3027 of the diligent will
rule,4910
But the [I]slack *hand* will be
[a]put to forced labor.
25 [a]Anxiety1674 in the heart of a man
weighs it down,7812
But a [b]good word1697 makes it
glad.
26 The righteous is a guide to his
neighbor,7453
But the way of the wicked leads
them astray.8582
27 A [I]slothful man does not
[II]roast his prey,
But the [a]precious possession of
a man *is* diligence.
28 [a]In the way734 of righteous-
ness6666 is life,2416
And in *its* pathway there is no
death.4194

Contrast the Upright and the Wicked

13 A [a]wise2450 son1121 *accepts his*
father's1 discipline,4148
But a [b]scoffer3887 does not listen
to rebuke.1606
2 From the fruit of a man's376
mouth6310 he [Ia]enjoys
good,2896
But the [II]desire of the
treacherous is [b]violence.2555

3 The one who [a]guards[5341] his mouth preserves[8104] his life;[5315]
The one who [b]opens wide his lips[8193] [I]comes to ruin.[4288]
4 The soul of the sluggard[6102] craves[183] and *gets* nothing,
But the soul of the diligent is made fat.[1878]
5 A righteous[6662] man [a]hates[8130] falsehood,
But a wicked[7563] man [I][b]acts disgustingly[887] and shamefully.
6 Righteousness[6666] [a]guards the [I]one whose way[1870] is blameless,[8537]
But wickedness[7564] subverts the [II]sinner.
7 There is one who [a]pretends to be rich, but has nothing;
Another [I]pretends to be [b]poor, but has great wealth.
8 The ransom[3724] of a man's life is his riches,
But the poor hears no rebuke.
9 The [a]light[216] of the righteous [I]rejoices,
But the [b]lamp[5216] of the wicked goes out.
10 Through presumption[2087] [I]comes nothing but strife,
But with those who receive counsel[3289] is wisdom.[2451]
11 Wealth *obtained* by [I]fraud dwindles,
But the one who gathers[6908] [II]by labor increases *it.*
12 Hope[8431] deferred makes the heart[3820] sick,
But desire [I]fulfilled is a tree of life.[2416]
13 The one who [a]despises the word[1697] will be [I]in debt[2254] to it,
But the one who fears the commandment[4687] will be [b]rewarded.[7999]
14 The [I]teaching[8451] of the wise is a [a]fountain of life,
To turn aside[5493] from the [b]snares of death.[4194]

15 [a]Good understanding[7922] produces favor,[2580]
But the way of the treacherous is hard.
16 Every [a]prudent[6175] man acts with knowledge,[1847]
But a fool [I]displays folly.
17 A wicked messenger[4397] falls[5307] into adversity,[7451]
But [a]a faithful[529] envoy[6735] *brings* healing.
18 Poverty and shame *will come* to him who [a]neglects[6544] [I]discipline,
But he who regards[8104] reproof will be honored.
19 Desire realized[1961] is sweet[6148] to the soul,
But it is an abomination[8441] to fools to depart from evil.[7451]
20 [a]He who walks with wise[2449] men will be wise,
But the companion of fools will suffer harm.[7321]
21 [a]Adversity pursues sinners,[2400]
But the [b]righteous will be rewarded with prosperity.
22 A good man [a]leaves an inheritance[5157] to his [I]children's children,[1121]
And the [b]wealth[2428] of the sinner[2398] is stored up for the righteous.
23 [a]Abundant food *is in* the fallow ground of the poor,
But [I]it is swept away[5595] by injustice.[4941]
24 He who [a]spares his rod[7626] hates his son,
But he who loves[157] him [I][b]disciplines him diligently.[7836]
25 The [a]righteous [I]has enough to satisfy his appetite,
But the stomach[990] of the [b]wicked is in want.

Contrast the Upright and the Wicked

14 The [a]wise woman[802] builds her house,[1004]

3 [I]Lit., *ruin is his* [a]Prov. 18:21; 21:23; James 3:2 [b]Prov. 18:7; 20:19
5 [I]Lit., *causes a bad odor and causes shame* [a]Col. 3:9 [b]Prov. 3:35
6 [I]Lit., *blame lessness of way* [II]Lit., *sin* [a]Prov. 11:3
7 [I]Lit., *impoverishes himself* [a]Prov. 11:24; Luke 12:20, 21 [b]Luke 12:33; 2Cor. 6:10; James 2:5
9 [I]I.e., shines brightly [a]Job 29:3; Prov. 4:18 [b]Job 18:5; Prov. 24:20
10 [I]Lit., *gives*
11 [I]Lit., *vanity* [II]Or, *gradually;* lit., *on the hand*
12 [I]Lit., *coming*
13 [I]Lit., *pledged to it* [a]Num. 15:31; 2Chr. 36:16 [b]Prov. 13:21
14 [I]Or, *law* [a]Prov. 10:11; 14:27 [b]Ps. 18:5
15 [a]Ps. 111:10; Prov. 3:4
16 [I]Lit., *spreads out* [a]Prov. 12:23
17 [a]Prov. 25:13
18 [I]Or, *instruction* [a]Prov. 15:5, 32
20 [a]Prov. 2:20; 15:31
21 [a]Ps. 32:10; 54:5; Is. 47:11 [b]Prov. 11:31; 13:13; Is. 3:10
22 [I]Lit., *sons' sons* [a]Ezra 9:12; Ps. 37:25 [b]Job 27:16, 17; Prov. 28:8; Eccl. 2:26
23 [I]Lit., *there is what is swept* [a]Prov. 12:11
24 [I]Lit., *seeks him diligently with discipline* [a]Prov. 19:18; 22:15; 23:13, 14; 29:15, 17 [b]Deut. 8:5; Prov. 3:12; Heb. 12:7
25 [I]Lit., *eats to the satisfaction of his soul* [a]Ps. 34:10; 103:5; 132:15; Prov. 10:3 [b]Prov. 13:18; Luke 15:14

1 [a]Ruth 4:11; Prov. 31:10-27

But the foolish tears it down[2040]
with her own hands.[3027]
2 He who [a]walks in his
uprightness[3476] fears the
LORD,
But he who is [b]crooked in his
ways[1870] despises Him.
3 In the mouth[6310] of the foolish
is a rod [I]for *his* back,
But [a]the lips[8193] of the wise[2450]
will preserve[8104] them.
4 Where no oxen are, the
manger[18] is clean,[1249]
But much increase *comes* by the
strength of the ox.
5 A [a]faithful[529] witness will not
lie,[3576]
But a [b]false[8267] witness
[Ic]speaks lies.[3577]
6 A scoffer[3887] seeks wisdom,[2451]
and *finds* none,
But knowledge[1847] is easy[7043] to
him who has
understanding.[995]
7 Leave the [a]presence of a fool,
Or you will not [I]discern[3045]
[II]words of knowledge.
8 The wisdom of the prudent[6175]
is to understand[995] his
way,[1870]
But [a]the folly of fools is
deceit.[4820]
9 Fools mock[3887] at [I]sin,[817]
But [a]among the upright[3477] there
is [II]good will.[7522]
10 The heart[3820] knows its own
[a]bitterness,[4751]
And a stranger[2114] does not
share[6148] its joy.
11 The [a]house of the wicked[7563] will
be destroyed,[8045]
But the tent[168] of the upright[3477]
will flourish.
12 There [a]is a way *which seems*
right[3477] to a man,
But its [b]end[319] is the way of
death.[4194]
13 Even in laughter the heart may
be in pain,
And the [a]end of joy may be grief.
14 The backslider[5472] in heart will
have his [a]fill of his own ways,

2 [a]Prov. 19:1; 28:6 [b]Prov. 2:15

3 [I]Lit., *of pride* [a]Prov. 12:6

5 [I]Lit., *breathes out* [a]Rev. 1:5; 3:14 [b]Ex. 23:1; Deut. 19:16; Prov. 6:19; 12:17 [c]Prov. 19:5

7 [I]Lit., *know* [II]Lit., *lips* [a]Prov. 23:9

8 [a]1Cor. 3:19

9 [I]Lit., *guilt* [II]Or, *the favor of God* [a]Prov. 3:34; 11:20

10 [a]1Sam. 1:10; Job 21:25

11 [a]Job 8:15

12 [a]Prov. 12:15; 16:25 [b]Rom. 6:21

13 [a]Eccl. 2:1, 2

14 [I]Lit., *from himself* [a]Prov. 1:31; 12:21 [b]Prov. 12:14; 18:20

15 [I]Lit., *simple*

16 [I]Lit., *fears* [a]Job 28:28; Ps. 34:14; Prov. 3:7; 22:3

18 [I]Lit., *simple*

19 [a]1Sam. 2:36; Prov. 11:29

20 [a]Prov. 19:7

21 [I]Or, *afflicted* [a]Prov. 11:12 [b]Ps. 41:1; Prov. 19:17; 28:8

22 [a]Ps. 36:4; Prov. 3:29; 12:2; Mic. 2:1

23 [I]Lit., *word of lips*

24 [a]Prov. 10:22; 13:8; 21:20

25 [I]Lit., *breathes out* [II]Lit., *treachery* [a]Prov. 14:5

26 [I]Or, *reverence* [II]Or, *His* [a]Prov. 18:10; 19:23; Is. 33:6

27 [I]Or, *reverence*

But a good[2896] man will
[b]*be satisfied* [I]with his.
15 The [I]naive believes[539]
everything,[1697,3605]
But the prudent man
considers[995] his steps.
16 A wise man [I]is cautious and
[a]turns away from evil,[7451]
But a fool is arrogant[5674] and
careless.
17 A quick-tempered[639] man acts
foolishly,
And a man of evil devices[4209] is
hated.[8130]
18 The [I]naive inherit[5157] folly,
But the prudent are crowned
with knowledge.
19 The [a]evil will bow down before
the good,
And the wicked at the gates of
the righteous.[6662]
20 The [a]poor is hated even by his
neighbor,[7453]
But those who love[157] the rich
are many.
21 He who [a]despises his neighbor
sins,[2398]
But [b]happy[835] is he who is
gracious[2603] to the [I]poor.
22 Will they not go astray[8582] who
[a]devise evil?
But kindness[2617] and truth[571] *will*
be to those who devise good.
23 In all labor[6089] there is profit,
But [I]mere talk *leads* only to
poverty.[4270]
24 The [a]crown of the wise is their
riches,
But the folly of fools is
foolishness.
25 A truthful[571] witness saves[5337]
lives,[5315]
But he who [Ia]speaks lies[4820] is
[II]treacherous.
26 In the [Ia]fear[3374] of the LORD there
is strong confidence,
And [II]his children[1121] will have
refuge.
27 The [I]fear of the LORD is a
fountain of life,[2416]
That one may avoid[5493] the
snares of death.

28 In a multitude of people[5971] is a
king's[4428] glory,[1927]
But in the dearth of people[3816]
is a prince's[7333] ruin.[4288]
29 He who is [a]slow[750] to anger[639]
has great understanding,[8394]
But he who is [I]quick-
tempered[7307] exalts[7311] folly.
30 A [a]tranquil heart is life to the
body,[1320]
But passion[7068] is [b]rottenness to
the bones.[6106]
31 He [a]who oppresses the poor
reproaches [b]his Maker,[6213]
But he who is gracious to the
needy honors[3513] Him.
32 The wicked is [a]thrust down by
his [I]wrongdoing,[7561]
But the [b]righteous has a
refuge[2620] when he dies.
33 Wisdom rests in the heart of one
who has understanding,[995]
But in the [I]bosom[7130] of fools it
is made known.[3045]
34 Righteousness[6666] exalts a
nation,[1471]
But sin[2403] is a disgrace[2617] to
any people.
35 The king's favor is toward a
[a]servant[5650] who acts
wisely,[7919]
But his anger[5678] is toward him
who acts shamefully.[954]

Contrast the Upright and the Wicked

15 A [a]gentle answer[639] turns
away[7725] wrath,[2534]
But a [I][b]harsh[6089] word[1697] stirs
up anger.
2 The [a]tongue of the wise[2450]
makes knowledge[1847]
[I]acceptable,
But the [b]mouth[6310] of fools
spouts folly.
3 The [a]eyes of the LORD are in
every place,
Watching[6822] the evil[7451] and the
good.[2896]
4 A [I]soothing tongue is a tree of
life,[2416]
But perversion in it [II]crushes[7667]
the spirit.[7307]
5 A fool [I]rejects[5006] his father's[1]
discipline,[4148]
But he who regards[8104] reproof
is prudent.[6191]
6 Much wealth is *in* the house[1004]
of the [a]righteous,[6662]
But trouble is in the income of
the wicked.[7563]
7 The lips[8193] of the wise spread
knowledge,
But the hearts[3820] of fools are
not so.
8 The [a]sacrifice[2077] of the wicked
is an abomination[8441] to the
LORD,
But [b]the prayer[8605] of the
upright[3477] is His delight.[7522]
9 The way[1870] of the wicked is an
abomination to the LORD,
But He loves[157] him who
[a]pursues righteousness.[6666]
10 Stern[7451] discipline[4148] is for him
who forsakes[5800] the way;[734]
He who hates[8130] reproof will
die.
11 [I][a]Sheol[7585] and [II]Abaddon[11] *lie*
open before the LORD,
How much more the [b]hearts[3826]
of [III]men![120]
12 A [a]scoffer[3887] does not love one
who reproves[3198] him,
He will not go to the wise.
13 A [a]joyful heart makes a
[I]cheerful[3190] face,
But [II]when the heart is
[b]sad, the [c]spirit is broken.
14 The [a]mind of the intelligent[995]
seeks knowledge,
But the mouth of fools feeds on
folly.
15 All the days[3117] of the afflicted
are bad,
But a [I]cheerful[2896] heart *has* a
continual[8548] feast.[4960]
16 [a]Better[2896] is a little with the
[I]fear[3374] of the LORD,
Than great treasure and
turmoil[4103] with it.
17 [a]Better is a [I]dish of [II]vegetables
where love[160] is,

29 [I]Lit., *short of spirit* [a]Prov. 16:32; 19:11; Eccl. 7:9; James 1:19
30 [a]Prov. 15:13 [b]Prov. 12:4; Hab. 3:16
31 [a]Prov. 17:5; Matt. 25:40; 1John 3:17 [b]Job 31:15; Prov. 22:2
32 [I]Or, *calamity* [a]Prov. 6:15; 24:16 [b]Gen. 49:18; Ps. 16:11; 17:15; 37:37; 73:24; 2Cor. 1:9; 5:8; 2Tim. 4:18
33 [I]Lit., *midst*
35 [a]Matt. 24:45, 47; 25:21, 23

1 [I]Lit., *painful* [a]Judg. 8:1-3; Prov. 15:18; 25:15 [b]1Sam. 25:10-13
2 [I]Lit., *good* [a]Prov. 15:7 [b]Prov. 12:23; 13:16; 15:28
3 [a]2Chr. 16:9; Job 31:4; Jer. 16:17; Zech. 4:10; Heb. 4:13
4 [I]Lit., *healing* [II]Lit., *is the crushing of the spirit*
5 [I]Or, *despises*
6 [a]Prov. 8:21
8 [a]Prov. 21:27; Eccl. 5:1; Is. 1:11; Jer. 6:20; Mic. 6:7 [b]Prov. 15:29
9 [a]1Tim. 6:11
11 [I]I.e., the nether world [II]I.e., place of destruction [III]Lit., *sons of Adam* [a]Job 26:6; Ps. 139:8 [b]1Sam. 16:7; 2Chr. 6:30; Ps. 44:21; Acts 1:24
12 [a]Prov. 13:1; Amos 5:10
13 [I]Lit., *good* [II]Lit., *in sadness of heart* [a]Prov. 17:22 [b]Prov. 12:25 [c]Prov. 17:22; 18:14
14 [a]Prov. 18:15
15 [I]Lit., *good*
16 [I]Or, *reverence* [a]Ps. 37:16; Prov. 16:8; Eccl. 4:6; 1Tim. 6:6
17 [I]Or, *portion* [II]Or, *herbs* [a]Prov. 17:1

Than a [b]fattened ox and hatred[8135] with it.
18 A [a]hot-tempered[2534] man[376] stirs up strife,
But the [b]slow[750] to anger [c]pacifies[8252] contention.[7379]
19 The way of the sluggard is as a hedge of thorns,
But the path of the upright[3477] is a highway.
20 A [a]wise son[1121] makes a father[1] glad,
But a foolish man[120] [b]despises his mother.[517]
21 Folly is joy to him who lacks [1]sense,[3820]
But a man of understanding[8394] [a]walks straight.[3474]
22 Without consultation,[5475] plans[4284] are frustrated,[6565]
But with many counselors[3289] they [1]succeed.
23 A [a]man has joy in an [1]apt answer,
And how delightful is a timely[6256] [b]word![1697]
24 The [a]path of life *leads* upward for the wise,[7919]
That he may keep away[5493] from [1]Sheol below.
25 The LORD will [a]tear down[5255] the house of the proud,
But He will [b]establish[5324] the boundary of the [c]widow.
26 Evil[7451] plans[4284] are an abomination to the LORD,
But pleasant words are pure.[2889]
27 He who [a]profits illicitly[1214] troubles his own house,
But he who [b]hates bribes will live.[2421]
28 The heart of the righteous [a]ponders[1897] how to answer,
But the [b]mouth of the wicked pours out evil things.
29 The LORD is [a]far from the wicked,
But He [b]hears[8085] the prayer of the righteous.
30 [1]Bright[3974] eyes gladden the heart;
Good news puts fat[1878] on the bones.[6106]
31 He whose ear[241] listens to the life-giving reproof
Will dwell among[7130] the wise.
32 He who [a]neglects[6544] discipline [b]despises[3988] himself,
But he who [c]listens to reproof acquires [1]understanding.[3820]
33 The [1]fear of the LORD is the instruction for wisdom,[2451]
And before honor[3519] *comes* humility.

Contrast the Upright and the Wicked

16 The [a]plans of the heart[3820] belong to man,[120]
But the answer of the tongue is from the LORD.
2 All the ways[1870] of a man[376] are clean[2134] in his own sight,
But the [a]LORD weighs the [1]motives.
3 [1a]Commit your works to the LORD,
And your plans[4284] will be established.[3559]
4 The LORD [a]has made everything for [1]its own purpose,
Even the [b]wicked[7563] for the day[3117] of evil.[7451]
5 Everyone who is proud in heart is an abomination[8441] to the LORD;
Assuredly, he will not be unpunished.[5352]
6 By [a]lovingkindness[2617] and truth[571] iniquity[5771] is atoned for,[3722]
And by the [1b]fear[3374] of the LORD one keeps away[5493] from evil.
7 When a man's ways are pleasing[7521] to the LORD,
He [a]makes even his enemies to be at peace[7999] with him.
8 Better[2896] is a little with righteousness[6666]
Than great income with injustice.[4941]
9 The mind of [a]man[120] plans[2803] his way,[1870]

17 [b]Matt. 22:4; Luke 15:23
18 [a]Prov. 16:28; 26:21; 29:22 [b]Prov. 14:29 [c]Gen. 13:8; Prov. 16:14; Eccl. 10:4
20 [a]Prov. 10:1; 29:3 [b]Prov. 30:17
21 [1]Lit., *heart* [a]Prov. 14:8; Eph. 5:15
22 [1]Or, *are established*
23 [1]Lit., *answer of his mouth* [a]Prov. 12:14 [b]Prov. 25:11; Is. 50:4
24 [1]I.e., the nether world [a]Prov. 4:18
25 [a]Prov. 12:7; 14:11 [b]Deut. 19:14; Prov. 23:10 [c]Ps. 68:5; 146:9
27 [a]Prov. 1:19; 28:25; 1Tim. 6:10 [b]Ex. 23:8; Deut. 16:19; 1Sam. 12:3; Is. 33:15
28 [a]1Pet. 3:15 [b]Prov. 10:32; 15:2
29 [a]Ps. 18:41; Prov. 1:28 [b]Ps. 145:18, 19
30 [1]Lit., *The light of the eyes gladdens*
32 [1]Lit., *heart* [a]Prov. 1:7; 8:33 [b]Prov. 8:36 [c]Prov. 15:5
33 [1]Or, *reverence*

1 [a]Prov. 16:9; 19:21
2 [1]Lit., *spirits* [a]1Sam. 16:7; Dan. 5:27
3 [1]Lit., *Roll* [a]Ps. 37:5; 55:22; Prov. 3:6; 1Pet. 5:7
4 [1]Or, *His* [a]Gen. 1:31; Eccl. 3:11 [b]Rom. 9:22
6 [1]Or, *reverence* [a]Dan. 4:27; Luke 11:41 [b]Prov. 8:13; 14:16
7 [a]Gen. 33:4; 2Chr. 17:10
9 [a]Prov. 16:1; 19:21

But [b]the LORD directs[3559] his steps.
10 A divine[7081] [a]decision is in the lips[8193] of the king;[4428]
His mouth[6310] should not [I]err[4603] in judgment.[4941]
11 A [a]just[4941] balance and scales belong to the LORD;
All the [I]weights of the bag are His [II]concern.
12 It is an abomination for kings[4428] to commit[6213] wickedness,[7562]
For a [a]throne[3678] is established on righteousness.
13 Righteous[6664] lips are the delight[7522] of kings,
And he who speaks right[3477] is loved.[157]
14 The wrath[2534] of a king is *as* messengers[4397] of death,[4194]
But a wise[2459] man will appease[3722] it.
15 In the light[216] of a king's[4428] face is life,[2416]
And his favor[7522] is like a cloud with the [Ia]spring rain.
16 How much [a]better it is to get wisdom[2451] than gold!
And to get understanding[998] is to be chosen[977] above silver.
17 The [a]highway of the upright[3477] is to depart[5493] from evil;
He who watches[5341] his way preserves[8104] his [I]life.[5315]
18 [a]Pride *goes* before destruction,[7667]
And a haughty spirit[7307] before stumbling.
19 It is better to be of a [a]humble spirit with the lowly,
Than to [b]divide the spoil with the proud.
20 He who gives attention[7919] to the word[1697] shall [a]find good,[2896]
And [b]blessed[835] is he who trusts[982] in the LORD.
21 The [a]wise in heart will be called[7121] discerning,[995]
And sweetness of [I]speech [b]increases [II]persuasiveness.[3948]

9 [b]Ps. 37:23; Prov. 20:24; Jer. 10:23
10 [I]Lit., *be unfaithful* [a]1Kin. 3:28
11 [I]Lit., *stones* [II]Lit., *work* [a]Prov. 11:1
12 [a]Prov. 25:5
15 [I]Lit., *latter* [a]Job 29:23
16 [a]Prov. 8:10, 19
17 [I]Lit., *soul* [a]Is. 35:8
18 [a]Prov. 11:2; 18:12; Jer. 49:16; Obad. 3, 4
19 [a]Prov. 3:34; 29:23; Is. 57:15 [b]Ex. 15:9; Judg. 5:30; Prov. 1:13, 14
20 [a]Prov. 19:8 [b]Ps. 2:12; 34:8; Jer. 17:7
21 [I]Lit., *lips* [II]Or, *learning* [a]Hos. 14:9 [b]Prov. 16:23
23 [I]Or, *learning* [a]Ps. 37:30; Prov. 15:28; Matt. 12:34
24 [a]Ps. 19:10; Prov. 15:26; 24:13, 14 [b]Prov. 4:22; 17:22
25 [a]Prov. 12:15; 14:12
26 [I]Lit., *mouth*
27 [I]Lit., *on his lips* [a]Prov. 6:12, 14, 18 [b]James 3:6
29 [a]Prov. 1:10; 12:26
31 [a]Prov. 20:29 [b]Prov. 3:1, 2
33 [a]Prov. 18:18 [b]Prov. 29:26
1 [I]Lit., *sacrifices of strife* [a]Prov. 15:17

22 Understanding[7922] is a fountain of life to him who has it,
But the discipline[4148] of fools is folly.
23 The [a]heart of the wise teaches[7919] his mouth,
And adds [I]persuasiveness to his lips.
24 [a]Pleasant words[561] are a honeycomb,
Sweet to the soul and [b]healing to the bones.[6106]
25 [a]There is a way *which seems* right to a man,
But its end[319] is the way of death.
26 A worker's[6001] appetite works for him,
For his [I]hunger urges him *on*.
27 A [a]worthless man digs up evil,
While [I]his words are as a [b]scorching fire.
28 A perverse[8419] man spreads strife,
And a slanderer separates intimate friends.
29 A man of violence[2555] [a]entices[6601] his neighbor,[7453]
And leads him in a way that is not good.
30 He who winks his eyes *does so* to devise[2803] perverse things;
He who compresses his lips brings evil to pass.
31 A [a]gray head[7872] is a crown of glory;[8597]
It [b]is found in the way of righteousness.
32 He who is slow[750] to anger[639] is better than the mighty,
And he who rules[4910] his spirit, than he who captures a city.
33 The [a]lot is cast into the lap,
But its every [b]decision is from the LORD.

Contrast the Upright and the Wicked

17 [a]Better[2896] is a dry[2720] morsel and quietness with it
Than a house[1004] full of [I]feasting[2077] with strife.[7379]

2 A servant[5650] who acts wisely[7919]
will rule[4910] over a son[1121]
who acts shamefully,[954]
And will share in the
inheritance[5159] among
brothers.[251]
3 The [a]refining pot is for silver and
the furnace for gold,
But [b]the LORD tests[974]
hearts.[3826]
4 An [a]evildoer[7489] listens[7181] to
wicked[205] lips,[8193]
A [I]liar[8267] pays attention[238] to a
destructive[1942] tongue.
5 He who mocks the [a]poor
reproaches his Maker;[6213]
He who [b]rejoices at calamity will
not go unpunished.[5352]
6 [a]Grandchildren[1121,1121] are the
crown of old men,[2205]
And the [b]glory[8597] of sons is their
fathers.[1]
7 [I][a]Excellent speech[8193] is not
fitting for a fool;
Much less are [b]lying lips to a
prince.[5081]
8 A [a]bribe is a [I]charm[2580] in the
sight of its owner;
Wherever he turns, he
prospers.
9 He who [a]covers[3680] a
transgression[6588] seeks
love,[160]
But he who repeats a matter[1697]
[b]separates intimate friends.
10 A rebuke[1606] goes deeper into
one who has understanding[995]
Than a hundred blows[5221] into
a fool.
11 A rebellious[4805] man seeks only
evil,[7451]
So a cruel messenger[4397] will be
sent against him.
12 Let a [a]man[376] meet a [b]bear
robbed of her cubs,[7909]
Rather than a fool in his folly.
13 He who [a]returns[7725] evil for
good,[2896]
[b]Evil will not depart from his
house.
14 The beginning[7225] of strife is *like*
letting out water,
So [a]abandon[5203] the quarrel[7379]
before it breaks out.
15 He who [a]justifies[6663] the
wicked,[7563] and he who
condemns[7561] the righteous,
Both of them alike are an
abomination[8441] to the LORD.
16 Why is there a price in the
hand[3027] of a fool to [a]buy
wisdom,[2451]
When [I]he has no sense?[3820]
17 A [a]friend[7453] loves[157] at all
times,[6256]
And a brother[251] is born for
adversity.
18 A man[120] lacking in [I]sense[3820]
[II][a]pledges,[8628,3709]
And becomes surety[6161] in the
presence of his neighbor.
19 He who [a]loves transgression
loves strife;
He who [b]raises his door seeks
destruction.[7667]
20 He who has a crooked[6141]
[I]mind [a]finds no good,
And he who is [b]perverted in his
language falls[5307] into evil.[7451]
21 He who [a]begets a fool *does so*
to his sorrow,
And the father[1] of a fool has no
joy.
22 A [a]joyful heart [I]is good[3190]
medicine,
But a broken spirit[7307]
[b]dries up[3001] the bones.
23 A wicked man receives a
[a]bribe from the bosom
To [b]pervert the ways[734] of
justice.[4941]
24 Wisdom is in the presence of
the one who has
understanding,[995]
But the [a]eyes of a fool are on
the ends of the earth.[776]
25 A [a]foolish son is a grief[3708] to
his father,
And [b]bitterness to her who bore
him.
26 It is also not good to [a]fine[6064]
the righteous,
Nor to strike[5221] the noble[5081]
for *their* uprightness.[3476]

3 [a]Prov. 27:21 [b]1Chr. 29:17; Ps. 26:2; Prov. 15:11; Jer. 17:10; Mal. 3:3
4 [I]Lit., *falsehood* [a]Prov. 14:15
5 [a]Prov. 14:31 [b]Job 31:29; Prov. 24:17; Obad. 12
6 [a]Gen. 48:11; Prov. 13:22 [b]Ex. 20:12; Mal. 1:6
7 [I]Lit., *A lip of abundance* [a]Prov. 24:7 [b]Ps. 31:18; Prov. 12:22
8 [I]Lit., *stone of favor* [a]Prov. 21:14; Is. 1:23; Amos 5:12
9 [a]Prov. 10:12; James 5:20; 1Pet. 4:8 [b]Prov. 16:28
12 [a]Prov. 29:9 [b]2Sam. 17:8; Hos. 13:8
13 [a]Ps. 35:12; 109:5; Jer. 18:20 [b]2Sam. 12:10; 1Kin. 21:22; Prov. 13:21
14 [a]Prov. 20:3; 25:8; 1Thess. 4:11
15 [a]Ex. 23:7; Prov. 18:5; 24:24; Is. 5:23
16 [I]Lit., *there is no heart* [a]Prov. 23:23
17 [a]Ruth 1:16; Prov. 18:24
18 [I]Lit., *heart* [II]Lit., *shakes hands* [a]Prov. 6:1; 11:15; 22:26
19 [a]Prov. 29:22 [b]Prov. 16:18; 29:23
20 [I]Lit., *heart* [a]Prov. 24:20 [b]James 3:8
21 [a]Prov. 10:1; 17:25; 19:13
22 [I]Lit., *causes good healing* [a]Prov. 15:13 [b]Ps. 22:15
23 [a]Prov. 17:8 [b]Ex. 23:8; Mic. 3:11; 7:3
24 [a]Eccl. 2:14
25 [a]Prov. 19:13 [b]Prov. 10:1
26 [a]Prov. 17:15; 18:5

27 He who [a]restrains his words[561]
[I]has knowledge,[1847]
And he who has a [b]cool spirit
is a man of understanding.[8394]
28 Even a fool, when he [a]keeps
silent, is considered[2803]
wise;[2450]
When he closes his lips, he is
counted prudent.

Contrast the Upright and the Wicked

18 He who separates himself seeks
his own desire,
He [Ia]quarrels against all sound
wisdom.[8454]
2 A fool does not delight[2654] in
understanding,[8394]
But only [a]in revealing[1540] his own
[I]mind.[3820]
3 When a wicked[7563] man comes,
contempt also comes,
And with dishonor *comes*
reproach.[2781]
4 The words[1697] of a man's
mouth[6310] are [a]deep waters;
[I]The fountain of wisdom[2451] is
a bubbling brook.
5 To [a]show partiality[5375,6440] to the
wicked is not good,[2896]
Nor to [b]thrust aside the
righteous[6662] in judgment.[4941]
6 A fool's lips[8193] [I]bring strife,[7379]
And his mouth calls[7121] for
[a]blows.
7 A [a]fool's mouth is his ruin,[4288]
And his lips are the snare[4170] of
his soul.[5315]
8 The words of a whisperer are
like dainty morsels,
And they go down into the
[I]innermost parts of the
body.[990]
9 He also who is [a]slack[7503] in his
work[4399]
[b]Is brother[251] to him who
destroys.[7843]
10 The [a]name of the LORD is a
[b]strong tower;
The righteous runs into it and
[c]is [I]safe.

11 A [a]rich man's wealth is his strong
city,
And like a high wall in his own
imagination.[4906]
12 [a]Before destruction[7667] the heart
of man is haughty,
But [b]humility *goes* before
honor.[3519]
13 He who [a]gives an answer[7725]
before he hears,[8085]
It is folly and shame to
him.
14 The [a]spirit[7307] of a man can
endure his sickness,
But a [b]broken spirit who can
bear?[5375]
15 The [Ia]mind of the prudent[995]
acquires knowledge,[1847]
And the [b]ear[241] of the wise[2450]
seeks knowledge.
16 A man's[120] [a]gift makes room for
him,
And brings[5148] him before great
men.
17 The first[7223] [I]to plead his case[7379]
seems just,
Until [II]another[7453] comes and
examines him.
18 The [a]lot puts an end[7673] to
contentions,
And [I]decides between the
mighty.
19 A brother offended[6586] *is harder
to be won* than a strong city,
And contentions are like the bars
of a castle.[759]
20 With the [Ia]fruit of a man's mouth
his stomach will be satisfied;
[b]He will be satisfied *with* the
product of his lips.
21 [a]Death[4194] and life[2416] are in the
[I]power[3027] of the tongue,
And those who love[157] it will eat
its [b]fruit.
22 He who finds a [a]wife[802] finds a
good thing,
And [b]obtains favor[7522] from the
LORD.
23 The [a]poor man utters supplications,[8469]
But the [b]rich man [c]answers
roughly.

27 [I]Lit., *knows* [a]Prov. 10:19; James 1:19 [b]Prov. 14:29
28 [a]Job 13:5
1 [I]Lit., *breaks out* [a]Prov. 3:21; 8:14
2 [I]Lit., *heart* [a]Prov. 12:23; 13:16; Eccl. 10:3
4 [I]Or, *A bubbling brook, a fountain of wisdom* [a]Prov. 20:5
5 [a]Lev. 19:15; Deut. 1:17; 16:19; Ps. 82:2; Prov. 17:15; 24:23; 28:21 [b]Ex. 23:2, 6; Prov. 17:26; 31:5; Mic. 3:9
6 [I]Lit., *come with* [a]Prov. 19:29
7 [a]Ps. 64:8; 140:9; Prov. 10:14; 12:13; 13:3; Eccl. 10:12
8 [I]Lit., *chambers of the belly*
9 [a]Prov. 10:4 [b]Prov. 28:24
10 [I]Lit., *set on high* [a]Ex. 3:15 [b]2Sam. 22:2, 3, 33; Ps. 18:2; 61:3; 91:2; 144:2 [c]Prov. 29:25
11 [a]Prov. 10:15
12 [a]Prov. 11:2; 16:18; 29:23 [b]Prov. 15:33
13 [a]Prov. 20:25; John 7:51
14 [a]Prov. 17:22 [b]Prov. 15:13
15 [I]Lit., *heart* [a]Prov. 15:14; Eph. 1:17 [b]Prov. 15:31
16 [a]Gen. 32:20; 1Sam. 25:27
17 [I]Lit., *in his plea* [II]Lit., *his neighbor*
18 [I]Lit., *makes a division* [a]Prov. 16:33
20 [I]I.e., speech [a]Prov. 12:14 [b]Prov. 14:14
21 [I]Lit., *hand* [a]Prov. 12:13; 13:3; Matt. 12:37 [b]Prov. 13:2; Is. 3:10; Hos. 10:13
22 [a]Gen. 2:18; Prov. 12:4; 19:14; 31:10-31 [b]Prov. 8:35
23 [a]Prov. 19:7 [b]James 2:3, 6 [c]1Kin. 12:13; 2Chr. 10:13

24 A man of *many* friends[7453] *comes*
to [I]ruin,
But there is [a]a [II]friend[157] who
sticks closer than a brother.

On Life and Conduct

19 [a]Better[2896] is a poor man who
[b]walks in his integrity[8537]
Than he who is perverse in
[I]speech[8193] and is a fool.
2 Also it is not good[2896] for a
person[5315] to be without
knowledge,[1847]
And he who makes [a]haste with
his feet [I]errs.[2398]
3 The [a]foolishness of man[120]
subverts his way,[1870]
And his heart[3820] [b]rages[2196]
against the LORD.
4 [a]Wealth adds many friends,[7453]
But a poor man is separated from
his friend.[7453]
5 A [a]false[8267] witness will not go
unpunished,[5352]
And he who [Ib]tells[6315] lies[3577] will
not escape.[4422]
6 [a]Many will entreat the favor of
a [I]generous man,[5081]
And every man is a friend[7453]
to him who [b]gives gifts.
7 All the brothers[251] of a poor man
hate[8130] him;
How much more do his
[a]friends go far from him!
He [b]pursues *them with* words,[561]
but they are [I]gone.
8 He who gets [I]wisdom[3820]
loves[157] his own soul;
He who keeps[8104] understanding[8394] will [a]find good.
9 A [a]false witness will not go
unpunished,
And he who [I]tells lies will
perish.[6]
10 Luxury is [a]not fitting for a fool;
Much less for a [b]slave[5650] to
rule[4910] over princes.[8269]
11 A man's [a]discretion[7922] makes
him slow[748] to anger,[639]
And it is his glory[8597] [b]to
overlook a transgression.[6588]

24 [I]Lit., *be broken in pieces* [II]Or, *lover* [a]Prov. 17:17; John 15:14, 15
1 [I]Lit., *his lips* [a]Prov. 28:6 [b]Ps. 26:11; Prov. 14:2; 20:7
2 [I]Lit., *sins* [a]Prov. 21:5; 28:20; 29:20
3 [a]Prov. 11:3 [b]Is. 8:21
4 [a]Prov. 14:20
5 [I]Lit., *breathes* [a]Ex. 23:1; Deut. 19:16-19; Prov. 19:9; 21:28 [b]Prov. 6:19
6 [I]Or, *noble* [a]Prov. 29:26 [b]Prov. 18:16; 21:14
7 [I]Lit., *not* [a]Ps. 38:11 [b]Prov. 18:23
8 [I]Lit., *heart* [a]Prov. 16:20
9 [I]Lit., *breathes* [a]Prov. 19:5; Dan. 6:24
10 [a]Prov. 17:7; 26:1; Eccl. 10:6, 7 [b]Prov. 30:22
11 [a]Prov. 14:29; 16:32 [b]Matt. 5:44; Eph. 4:32; Col. 3:13
12 [a]Prov. 16:14 [b]Gen. 27:28; Deut. 33:28; Ps. 133:3; Hos. 14:5; Mic. 5:7
13 [a]Prov. 17:25 [b]Prov. 21:9, 19; 27:15
14 [a]2Cor. 12:14
15 [I]Lit., *soul* [a]Prov. 6:9, 10; 24:33
16 [I]Lit., *despises* [a]Prov. 13:13; 16:17; Luke 10:28; 11:28
17 [I]Or, *benefits* [a]Deut. 15:7, 8; Prov. 14:31; 28:27; Eccl. 11:1, 2; Matt. 10:42; 25:40; 2Cor. 9:6-8; Heb. 6:10 [b]Prov. 12:14; Luke 6:38
18 [I]Lit., *causing him to die* [a]Prov. 13:24; 23:13; 29:15, 17
20 [I]Lit., *in your latter end* [a]Prov. 4:1; 8:33; 12:15
21 [a]Prov. 16:1, 9 [b]Ps. 33:10, 11; Is. 14:26, 27
22 [I]Or, *loyalty*

12 The [a]king's[4428] wrath[2197] is like
the roaring of a lion,
But his favor[7522] is like
[b]dew on the grass.
13 A [a]foolish son[1121] is
destruction[1942] to his father,[1]
And the [b]contentions of a
wife[802] are a constant
dripping.
14 House[1004] and wealth are an
[a]inheritance[5159] from
fathers,[1]
But a prudent wife is from the
LORD.
15 [a]Laziness casts into a deep
sleep,
And an idle [I]man will suffer
hunger.
16 He who [a]keeps the
commandment[4687] keeps his
soul,
But he who [I]is careless of his
ways[1870] will die.
17 He who [a]is gracious[2603] to a poor
man lends to the LORD,
And He will repay him for his
[Ib]good deed.
18 [a]Discipline your son while there
is hope,
And do not desire[5375] [I]his
death.[4191]
19 *A man of* great anger[2534] shall
bear[5375] the penalty,[6066]
For if you rescue[5337] *him,* you
will only have to do it again.
20 [a]Listen[8085] to counsel[6098] and
accept discipline,[4148]
That you may be wise[2449]
[I]the rest of your days.[319]
21 Many are the [a]plans[4284] in a
man's heart,
But the [b]counsel of the LORD,
it will stand.
22 What is desirable in a man is
his [I]kindness,[2617]
And *it is* better to be a poor
man than a liar.[3576]
23 The [Ia]fear[3374] of the LORD *leads*
to life,[2416]

23 [I]Or, *reverence* [a]Prov. 14:27; 1Tim. 4:8

So that one may sleep
[b]satisfied, [IIc]untouched[6485][1077]
by evil.
24 The [a]sluggard buries his hand[3027]
[b]in the dish,
And will not even bring it back
to his mouth.[6310]
25 [a]Strike[5221] a scoffer[3887] and the
[I]naive may become
shrewd,[6191]
But [b]reprove[3198] one who has
understanding[995] and he will
[II]gain[995] knowledge.
26 He [a]who assaults[7703] *his* father
and drives *his* mother[517]
away
Is a shameful[954] and disgraceful
son.
27 Cease listening, my son, to
discipline,
And you will stray[7686] from the
words of knowledge.
28 A rascally witness makes a
mockery[3887] of justice,[4941]
And the mouth of the wicked[7563]
[Ia]spreads[1104] iniquity.[205]
29 [I]Judgments[8201] are prepared[3559]
for [a]scoffers,[3887]
And [b]blows for the back[1460] of
fools.

On Life and Conduct

20 [a]Wine is a mocker,[3887] [b]strong
drink a brawler,
And whoever [I]is intoxicated[7686]
by it is not wise.
2 The terror[367] of a king[4428] is like
the growling of a lion;
He who provokes[5674] him to
anger [Ia]forfeits[2398] his own
life.[5315]
3 [Ia]Keeping away from strife[7379] is
an honor[3519] for a man,[376]
But any fool will [II]quarrel.
4 The [a]sluggard[6102] does not plow
after the autumn,
So he [I]begs[7592] during the
harvest and has nothing.
5 A plan[6098] in the heart[3820] of a
man is *like* deep water,
But a man of understanding[8394]
draws it out.
6 Many a man[120] [a]proclaims[7121] his
own loyalty[2617],
But who can find a [b]trust-
worthy[529] man?
7 A righteous man who [a]walks in
his integrity—[8537]
[b]How blessed[835] are his sons[1121]
after him.
8 [a]A king who sits on the
throne[3678] of justice[1779]
[I]Disperses all evil[7451] with his
eyes.
9 [a]Who can say,[559] "I have
cleansed[2135] my heart,
I am pure from my sin"?[2403]
10 [Ia]Differing weights and differing
measures,
Both of them are abominable[8441]
to the LORD.
11 It is by his deeds that a lad
[Ia]distinguishes[5234] himself
If his conduct is pure[2134] and
right.[3477]
12 The hearing[8085] [a]ear[241] and the
seeing[7200] eye,
The LORD has made[6213] both of
them.
13 [a]Do not love[157] sleep, lest you
become poor;[3423]
Open your eyes, *and* you will
be satisfied with [I]food.
14 "Bad,[7451] bad," says[559] the
buyer;
But when he goes his way, then
he boasts.[1984]
15 There is gold, and an abundance
of [I]jewels;
But the lips[8193] of knowledge[1847]
are a more precious thing.
16 Take his garment when he
becomes surety[6148] for a
stranger;[2114]
And for foreigners,[5237] hold him
in pledge.[2254]
17 [a]Bread obtained by falsehood is
sweet to a man,
But afterward his mouth[6310] will
be filled with gravel.
18 Prepare[3559] [a]plans[4284] by
consultation,

23 [II]Lit., *not visited* [b]Ps. 25:13 [c]Ps. 91:10; Prov. 12:21
24 [a]Prov. 26:15 [b]Matt. 26:23; Mark 14:20
25 [I]Lit., *simple* [II]Lit., *discern* [a]Prov. 21:11 [b]Prov. 9:8
26 [a]Prov. 28:24
28 [I]Or, *swallows* [a]Job 15:16; 20:12, 13; 34:7
29 [I]Gr., *Rods* [a]Ps. 1:1; Prov. 9:12 [b]Prov. 10:13; 18:6; 26:3

1 [I]Lit., *errs* [a]Gen. 9:21; Prov. 23:29, 30; Is. 28:7; Hos. 4:11 [b]Prov. 31:4; Is. 5:22; 56:12
2 [I]Lit., *sins against* [a]Num. 16:38; 1Kin. 2:23; Prov. 8:36; Hab. 2:10
3 [I]Lit., *Ceasing* [II]Lit., *burst out* [a]Gen. 13:7f.; Prov. 17:14
4 [I]Lit., *asks* [a]Prov. 13:4; 21:25
6 [a]Prov. 25:14; Matt. 6:2; Luke 18:11 [b]Ps. 12:1; Luke 18:8
7 [a]Prov. 19:1 [b]Ps. 37:26; 112:2
8 [I]Or, *Sifts* [a]Prov. 20:26; 25:5
9 [a]1Kin. 8:46; 2Chr. 6:36; Job 14:4; Eccl. 7:20; Rom. 3:9; 1John 1:8
10 [I]Lit., *A stone and a stone, an ephah and an ephah* [a]Prov. 11:1; 20:23
11 [I]Or, *makes himself known* [a]Matt. 7:16
12 [a]Ex. 4:11; Ps. 94:9
13 [I]Lit., *bread* [a]Prov. 6:9, 10; 19:15; 24:33
15 [I]Or, *corals*
17 [a]Prov. 9:17
18 [a]Prov. 11:14; 15:22

And [b]make[6213] war by wise[2896] guidance.

19 He who [a]goes about as a slanderer reveals[1540] secrets,[5475]
Therefore do not associate[2019] with [Ib]a gossip.

20 He who [a]curses[7043] his father[1] or his mother,[517]
His [b]lamp[5216] will go out in [I]time of darkness.[2822]

21 An inheritance[5159] gained hurriedly[973] at the beginning,[7223]
Will not be blessed[1288] in the end.[319]

22 [a]Do not say, "I will repay[7999] evil";
[b]Wait for[6960] the LORD, and He will save[3467] you.

23 [Ia]Differing weights are an abomination to the LORD,
And a [IIb]false[4820] scale is not good.

24 [a]Man's[1397] steps are *ordained* by the LORD,
How then can man[120] understand[995] his way?[1870]

25 It is a snare[4190] for a man to say rashly, "It is holy!"[6944]
And [a]after the vows[5088] to make inquiry.

26 A [a]wise[2450] king winnows the wicked,[7563]
And [I]drives the [b]*threshing* wheel[212] over them.

🔑 27 The [Ia]spirit[5397] of man is the lamp[5216] of the LORD,
Searching all the [II]innermost parts of his being.[990]

28 [I]Loyalty[2617] and [a]truth[571] preserve[5341] the king,
And he upholds[5582] his throne by [I]righteousness.

29 The glory[8597] of young men is their strength,
And the [Ia]honor[1926] of old men[2205] is their gray hair.[7872]

30 [a]Stripes that wound scour away[8562] evil,
And strokes[4347] *reach* the [I]innermost parts.

18 [b]Prov. 24:6; Luke 14:31
19 [I]Lit., *one who opens his lips* [a]Prov. 11:13 [b]Prov. 13:3
20 [I]Lit., *pupil* (of eye) [a]Ex. 21:17; Lev. 20:9; Prov. 30:11; Matt. 15:4 [b]Job 18:5; Prov. 13:9; 24:20
22 [a]Prov. 24:29; Matt. 5:39; Rom. 12:17, 19; 1Thess. 5:15; 1Pet. 3:9 [b]Ps. 27:14
23 [I]Lit., *A stone and a stone* [II]Lit., *balance of deceit* [a]Prov. 20:10 [b]Prov. 11:1
24 [a]Prov. 16:9
25 [a]Eccl. 5:4, 5
26 [I]Lit., *turns* [a]Prov. 20:8 [b]Is. 28:27
27 [I]Lit., *breath* [II]Lit., *chambers of the body* [a]1Cor. 2:11
28 [I]Lit., *Covenant loyalty* [a]Prov. 29:14
29 [I]Or, *splendor* [a]Prov. 16:31
30 [I]Lit., *chambers of the body* [a]Ps. 89:32; Prov. 22:15; Is. 53:5; 1Pet. 2:24

On Life and Conduct

21 The king's[4428] heart[3820] is *like* channels of water in the hand[3027] of the LORD;
He [a]turns it wherever He wishes.[2654]

2 [a]Every man's[376] way[1870] is right[3477] in his own eyes,
But the LORD [b]weighs the hearts.[3826]

3 To do[6213] [a]righteousness[6666] and justice[4941]
Is desired[977] by the LORD rather than sacrifice.[2077]

🔑 4 Haughty eyes and a proud heart,
The [a]lamp of the wicked,[7563] is sin.[2403]

5 The plans[4284] of the [a]diligent *lead* surely to advantage,
But everyone [b]who is hasty *comes* surely to poverty.

6 The [a]getting of treasures by a lying tongue

1 [a]Ezra 6:22
2 [a]Prov. 16:2 [b]Prov. 16:2; 24:12; Luke 16:15
3 [a]1Sam. 15:22; Prov. 15:8; Is. 1:11, 16, 17; Hos. 6:6; Mic. 6:7, 8
4 [a]Prov. 24:20; Luke 11:34
5 [a]Prov. 10:4; 13:4 [b]Prov. 28:22
6 [a]Prov. 13:11; 20:21

🔑 **20:27** "The spirit of man" distinguishes him from animals. An animal has a soul (in Hebrew, *nephesh* [5315], which expresses life and vitality; see Deut. 12:23 where "life" is from the same Hebrew word). But God breathed the "spirit" or "breath" of life into man's nostrils (Gen. 2:7, where "breath" is from the Hebrew *ruach* [7307], elsewhere translated "spirit"). Even within man who has fallen into sin, God has placed His lamp by which He is able to search the inner self (See I Cor. 2:11). The full meaning of the statement is that God has given man his conscience as a light to aid in distinguishing between good and evil.

🔑 **21:4** "Lamp" could be compared to Prov. 20:27 in which the spirit is God's lamp to search the inward parts of man. Here by contrast "haughty eyes and a proud heart" are a lamp of the wicked man showing what is within him. In the King James this word is translated "plowing." If this is correct, then it is a reference to the way that wicked men deal with others. In either case, it constitutes sin.

Is a fleeting vapor, the
[I]pursuit of [b]death.[4194]
7 The violence[7701] of the wicked
will drag them away,[1641]
Because they [a]refuse[3985] to act
with justice.
8 The way of a guilty[2054] man is
[a]crooked,[2019]
But as for the pure,[2134] his
conduct is upright.
9 It is better[2896] to live in a corner
of a roof,
Than [I]in a house[1004] shared with
a contentious woman.[802]
10 The soul[5315] of the wicked
desires[183] evil;[7451]
His [a]neighbor[7453] finds no
favor[2603] in his eyes.
11 When the [a]scoffer[3887] is
punished, the [I]naive becomes
wise;[2449]
But when the wise[2450] is
instructed,[7191] he receives
knowledge.[1847]
12 The righteous[6662] one
considers[7919] the house of the
wicked,
Turning the [a]wicked to ruin.[7451]
13 He who [a]shuts his ear[241] to the
cry[7121] of the poor
Will also cry himself and not be
[b]answered.
14 A [a]gift in secret subdues
anger,[639]
And a bribe in the bosom, strong
wrath.[2534]
15 The execution of justice is joy
for the righteous,
But is [a]terror[4288] to the workers
of iniquity.[205]
16 A man[120] who wanders[8582] from
the way of understanding
Will [a]rest in the assembly[6951] of
the [I]dead.[7496]
17 He who [a]loves[157] pleasure *will
become* a poor man;
He who loves wine and oil[8081]
will not become rich.
18 The wicked is a [a]ransom[3724] for
the righteous,
And the [b]treacherous[898] is in the
place of the upright.[3477]

6 [I]Lit., *seekers* [b]Prov. 8:36
7 [a]Amos 5:7; Mic. 3:9
8 [a]Prov. 2:15
9 [I]Lit., *with a woman of contentions and a house of association*
10 [a]Ps. 52:3; Prov. 2:14; 14:21
11 [I]Lit., *simple* [a]Prov. 19:25
12 [a]Prov. 14:11
13 [a]Matt. 18:30-34; 1John 3:17 [b]James 2:13
14 [a]Prov. 18:16; 19:6
15 [a]Prov. 10:29
16 [I]Lit., *departed spirits* [a]Ps. 49:14
17 [a]Prov. 23:21
18 [a]Is. 43:3 [b]Prov. 11:8
19 [a]Prov. 21:9
20 [a]Ps. 112:3; Prov. 8:21; 22:4 [b]Job 20:15, 18
21 [a]Prov. 15:9; Matt. 5:6; 1Cor. 15:58
22 [I]Lit., *strength of trust* [a]2Sam. 5:6-9; Prov. 24:5; Eccl. 7:19; 9:15, 16
23 [a]Prov. 12:13; 13:3; 18:21; James 3:2
24 [a]Ps. 1:1; Prov. 1:22; 3:34; 24:9; Is. 29:20 [b]Is. 16:6; Jer. 48:29
25 [a]Prov. 13:4
26 [I]Lit., *desires desire* [a]Ps. 37:26; 112:5, 9; Matt. 5:42; Eph. 4:28
27 [a]Prov. 15:8; Is. 66:3; Jer. 6:20; Amos 5:22
28 [a]Prov. 19:5, 9
29 [I]Lit., *makes firm with his face* [a]Eccl. 8:1 [b]Ps. 119:5; Prov. 11:5
30 [a]Jer. 9:23; Acts 5:38, 39; 1Cor. 3:19, 20
31 [a]Ps. 20:7; 33:17; Is. 31:1 [b]Ps. 3:8; Jer. 3:23; 1Cor. 15:57

19 [a]It is better to live in a desert
land,
Than with a contentious and
vexing woman.
20 There is precious [a]treasure and
oil in the dwelling of the
wise,
But a foolish man [b]swallows it
up.
21 He who [a]pursues
righteousness[6666] and
loyalty[2617]
Finds life,[2416] righteousness and
honor.[3519]
22 A [a]wise man scales[5927] the city
of the mighty,
And brings down the [I]stronghold
in which they trust.
23 He who [a]guards[8104] his
mouth[6310] and his tongue,
Guards his soul from troubles.
24 "Proud,"[2086] "Haughty,"
"[a]Scoffer," are his names,
Who acts with [b]insolent
pride.
25 The [a]desire of the sluggard puts
him to death,[4191]
For his hands[3027] refuse to
work;
26 All day[3117] long he [I]is craving,[183]
While the righteous [a]gives and
does not hold back.
27 The [a]sacrifice of the wicked is
an abomination,[8441]
How much more when he brings
it with evil intent![2154]
28 A [a]false witness will perish,[6]
But the man who listens[8085] *to
the truth* will speak
forever.[5331]
29 A wicked man [Ia]shows a bold
face,
But as for the [b]upright, he makes
his way sure.[3559]
30 There is [a]no wisdom[2451] and no
understanding[8394]
And no counsel[6098] against the
LORD.
31 The [a]horse is prepared[3559] for
the day of battle,
But [b]victory[8668] belongs to the
LORD.

On Life and Conduct

22 A [a]*good* name is to be more desired[977] than great riches,
Favor[2580] is better than silver and gold.
2 The rich and the poor [I]have a common bond,
The LORD is the [a]maker[6213] of them all.
3 The [a]prudent[6175] sees the evil[7451] and hides himself,
But the [I]naive go on,[5674] and are punished[6064] for it.
4 The reward of humility *and* the [I]fear[3374] of the LORD
Are riches, honor[3519] and life.[2416]
5 [a]Thorns *and* snares[6341] are in the way[1870] of the perverse;[6141]
He who guards[8104] himself[5315] will be far from them.
6 [a]Train up[2596] a child [I]in the way he should go,
Even when he is old[2204] he will not depart[5493] from it.
7 The [a]rich rules[4910] over the poor,
And the borrower *becomes* the lender's slave.[5650]
8 He who [a]sows iniquity[5766] will reap vanity,[205]
And the [b]rod[7626] of his fury[5678] will perish.[3615]
9 He who [I]is [a]generous[2896 5869] will be blessed,[1288]
For he [b]gives some of his food to the poor.
10 [a]Drive out the scoffer,[3887] and contention will go out,
Even strife[1779] and dishonor will cease.[7673]
11 He who loves[157] [a]purity[2889] of heart[3820]
And [I]whose speech[8193] is [b]gracious,[2580] the king[4428] is his friend.[7453]
12 The eyes of the LORD preserve[5341] knowledge,[1847]
But He overthrows the words[1697] of the treacherous man.[898]
13 The [a]sluggard says,[559] "There is a lion outside;
I shall be slain[7523] in the streets!"
14 The mouth[6310] of [I][a]an adulteress[2114] is a deep pit;[7745]
He who is [b]cursed[2194] of the LORD will fall [II]into it.
15 Foolishness is bound up in the heart of a child;
The [a]rod of discipline[4148] will remove it far from him.
16 He [a]who oppresses the poor to make much for himself
Or who gives to the rich, [b]*will* only *come to* poverty.
17 [a]Incline your ear[241] and hear[8085] the words of the wise,[2450]
And apply your mind to my knowledge;
18 For it will be [a]pleasant if you keep them within you,
[I]That they may be ready[3559] on your lips.
19 So that your [a]trust may be in the LORD,
I have [I]taught[3045] you today,[3117] even you.
20 Have I not written to you [I][a]excellent[7991] things
Of counsels and knowledge,
21 To make you [a]know[3045] the [I]certainty of the words[561] of truth[7189]
That you may [II][b]correctly answer[7725] to him who sent you?
22 [a]Do not rob the poor because he is poor,
Or [b]crush[1792] the afflicted at the gate;
23 For the LORD will [a]plead[7378] their case,[7379]
And [I]take the life of those who rob them.
24 Do not associate with a man[376] *given* to anger;[639]
Or go with a [a]hot-tempered[2534] man,
25 Lest you [a]learn[502] his ways,[734]
And [I]find a snare[4170] for yourself.
26 Do not be among those who [a]give[8628] [I]pledges,[3709]

1 [a]Prov. 10:7; Eccl. 7:1
2 [I]Lit., *meet together* [a]Job 31:15; Prov. 14:31
3 [I]Lit., *simple* [a]Prov. 14:16; 27:12; Is. 26:20
4 [I]Or, *reverence*
5 [a]Prov. 15:19
6 [I]Lit., *according to his way* [a]Eph. 6:4
7 [a]Prov. 18:23; James 2:6
8 [a]Job 4:8 [b]Ps. 125:3
9 [I]Lit., *has a good eye* [a]Prov. 19:17; 2Cor. 9:6 [b]Luke 14:13
10 [a]Gen. 21:9, 10; Prov. 18:6; 26:20
11 [I]Lit., *has grace on his lips* [a]Ps. 24:4; Matt. 5:8 [b]Prov. 14:35; 16:13
13 [a]Prov. 26:13
14 [I]Lit., *strange woman* [II]Lit., *there* [a]Prov. 2:16; 5:3; 7:5; 23:27 [b]Eccl. 7:26
15 [a]Prov. 13:24; 23:14
16 [a]Eccl. 5:8; James 2:13 [b]Prov. 28:22
17 [a]Prov. 5:1
18 [I]Lit., *They together* [a]Prov. 2:10
19 [I]Lit., *made you know* [a]Prov. 3:5
20 [I]Or, *previous* [a]Prov. 8:6
21 [I]Lit., *truth* [II]Lit., *return words of truth* [a]Luke 1:3, 4 [b]Prov. 25:13; 1Pet. 3:15
22 [a]Ex. 23:6; Job 31:16; Prov. 22:16 [b]Zech. 7:10; Mal. 3:5
23 [I]Lit., *rob the soul* [a]1Sam. 25:39; Ps. 12:5; 35:10; 140:12; Prov. 23:11; Jer. 51:36
24 [a]Prov. 29:22
25 [I]Lit., *take* [a]1Cor. 15:33
26 [I]Lit., *strike hands* [a]Prov. 17:18

Among those who become sureties[6148] for debts.
27 If you have nothing with which to pay,
Why should he [a]take your bed from under you?
28 [a]Do not move the ancient[5769] boundary
Which your fathers[1] have set.
29 Do you see[2372] a man skilled in his work?[4399]
He will [a]stand before kings;[4428]
He will not stand before obscure men.

On Life and Conduct

23 When you sit down to dine with a ruler,
Consider[995] carefully [I]what is before you;
2 And put a knife to your throat,
If you are a [a]man of *great* appetite.[5315]
3 Do not [a]desire[183] his delicacies,
For it is deceptive[3577] food.
4 [a]Do not weary yourself to gain wealth,
[b]Cease from your [I]consideration[998] *of it.*
5 [I]When you set your eyes on it, it is gone.
For [a]*wealth* certainly[7189] makes[6213] itself wings,
Like an eagle that flies *toward* the heavens.[8064]
6 [a]Do not eat the bread of [I]a [b]selfish[7451] man,
Or desire[183] his delicacies;
7 For as he [I]thinks[8176] within himself,[5315] so he is.
He says[559] to you, "Eat and drink!"
But [a]his heart[3820] is not with you.
8 You will [a]vomit up [I]the morsel you have eaten,
And waste[7843] your [II]compliments.[1697]

9 [a]Do not speak[1696] in the [I]hearing[241] of a fool,
For he will [b]despise the wisdom[7922] of your words.[4405]
10 Do not move the ancient[5769] boundary,
Or [a]go into the fields[7704] of the fatherless;
11 For their [a]Redeemer[1350] is strong;[2389]
[b]He will plead[7378] their case[7379] against you.
12 Apply your heart to discipline,[4148]
And your ears to words[561] of knowledge.[1847]
13 [a]Do not hold back discipline[4148] from the child,
Although you [I]beat[5221] him with the rod,[7626] he will not die.
14 You shall [I]beat[5221] him with the rod,
And [a]deliver[5337] his soul[5315] from Sheol.[7585]
15 My son,[1121] if your heart is [a]wise,[2449]
My own heart also will be glad;
16 And my [I]inmost being[3629] will rejoice,
When your lips[8193] speak [a]what is right.[4334]
17 [a]Do not let your heart envy[7065] sinners,[2400]
But *live* in the [I][b]fear[3374] of the LORD [II]always.[3117][3605]
18 Surely there is a [I][a]future,[319]
And your [b]hope will not be cut off.[3772]
19 Listen,[8085] my son, and [a]be wise,
And [b]direct your heart in the way.[1870]
20 Do not be with [a]heavy drinkers[5433] of wine,[3196]
Or with [b]gluttonous eaters of meat;[1320]

27 [a]Ex. 22:26; Prov. 20:16
28 [a]Deut. 19:14; 27:17; Job 24:2; Prov. 23:10
29 [a]Gen. 41:46; 1Kin. 10:8

1 [I]Or, *who*
2 [a]Prov. 23:20
3 [a]Ps. 141:4; Prov. 23:6; Dan. 1:5, 8, 13, 15, 16
4 [I]Or, *understanding* [a]Prov. 15:27; 28:20; Matt. 6:19; 1Tim. 6:9; Heb. 13:5 [b]Prov. 3:5, 7
5 [I]Lit., *Will your eyes fly upon it and it is not?* [a]Prov. 27:24; 1Tim. 6:17
6 [I]Lit., *an evil eye* [a]Ps. 141:4 [b]Deut. 15:9; Prov. 28:22
7 [I]Lit., *reckons in his soul* [a]Prov. 26:24, 25
8 [I]Lit., *your* [II]Lit., *pleasant words* [a]Prov. 25:16
9 [I]Lit., *ears* [a]Matt. 7:6 [b]Prov. 1:7
10 [a]Jer. 22:3; Zech. 7:10
11 [a]Job 19:25; Jer. 50:34 [b]Prov. 22:23
13 [I]Lit., *smite* [a]Prov. 13:24; 19:18
14 [I]Lit., *smite* [a]1Cor. 5:5
15 [a]Prov. 23:24f.; 27:11; 29:3
16 [I]Lit., *kidneys* [a]Prov. 8:6
17 [I]Or, *reverence* [II]Lit., *all the day* [a]Ps. 37:1; Prov. 24:1, 19 [b]Prov. 28:14
18 [I]Lit., *latter end* [a]Ps. 19:11; 58:11; Prov. 24:14 [b]Ps. 9:18
19 [a]Prov. 6:6 [b]Prov. 4:23; 9:6
20 [a]Prov. 20:1; 23:29, 30; Is. 5:22; Matt. 24:49; Luke 21:34; Rom. 13:13; Eph. 5:18 [b]Deut. 21:20; Prov. 28:7

23:11 "Redeemer" is more properly "vindicator" (See note on Job 19:25). He is the kinsman who, by law, had the right to redeem property which had been sold (see Lev. 25:25; Ruth 3:12; 4:4).

21 For the [a]heavy drinker and the glutton will come to poverty,[3423]
And [b]drowsiness will clothe *a man* with rags.
22 [a]Listen[8085] to your father[1] who begot you,
And [b]do not despise your mother[517] when she is old.[2204]
23 [a]Buy truth,[571] and do not sell *it,*
Get wisdom[2451] and instruction and understanding.[998]
24 The father of the righteous[6662] will greatly rejoice,
And [a]he who begets a wise[2450] son will be glad in him.
25 Let your [a]father and your mother be glad,
And let her rejoice who gave birth to you.
26 [a]Give me your heart, my son,
And let your eyes [I][b]delight[7521] in my ways.[1870]
27 For a harlot[2181] is a [a]deep pit,[7745]
And an [I][b]adulterous woman[5237] is a narrow well.
28 Surely she [a]lurks as a robber,
And increases the [I]faithless among men.[120]
29 Who has [a]woe? Who has sorrow?
Who has contentions? Who has complaining?[7879]
Who has wounds without cause?
Who has redness of eyes?
30 Those who [a]linger long over wine,
Those who go to [I]taste [b]mixed wine.
31 Do not look on the wine when it is red,[119]
When it [I]sparkles in the cup,
When it [a]goes down smoothly;
32 At the last it [a]bites like a serpent,[5175]
And stings like a [b]viper.6848
33 Your eyes will see[7200] strange[2114] things,
And your [I]mind will [a]utter perverse things.
34 And you will be like one who lies down in the [I]middle of the sea,
Or like one who lies down on the top[7218] of a [II]mast.
35 "They [a]struck me, *but* I did not become ill;
They beat[1986] me, *but* I did not know *it.*
When shall I awake?
I will [b]seek [I]another drink."

Precepts and Warnings

24

Do not be [a]envious of evil[7451] men,[582]
Nor desire[183] to [b]be with them;
2 For their [I]minds[3820] devise[1897] [a]violence,[7701]
And their lips[8193] [b]talk[1696] of trouble.[5999]
3 [a]By wisdom[2451] a house[1004] is built,
And by understanding[8394] it is established;[3559]
4 And by knowledge[1847] the rooms are [a]filled
With all precious and pleasant riches.
5 A [a]wise[2450] man[1397] is [I]strong,
And a man[376] of knowledge [II]increases power.
6 For [a]by wise guidance you will [I]wage war,
And [b]in abundance of counselors[3289] there is victory.[8668]
7 Wisdom[2454] is [a]too high for a fool,
He does not open his mouth[6310] [b]in the gate.
8 He who [a]plans[2803] to do evil,[7489]
Men will call[7121] him a [I]schemer.[4209]
9 The [a]devising[2154] of folly is sin,[2403]
And the scoffer[3887] is an abomination[8441] to men.[120]
10 If you [a]are slack[7503] in the day[3117] of distress,
Your strength is limited.
11 [a]Deliver[5337] those who are being taken away to death,[4194]

21 [a]Prov. 21:17 [b]Prov. 6:10, 11
22 [a]Prov. 1:8; Eph. 6:1 [b]Prov. 15:20; 30:17
23 [a]Prov. 4:7; 18:15; Matt. 13:44
24 [a]Prov. 10:1; 15:20; 29:3
25 [a]Prov. 27:11
26 [I]Another reading is *observe* [a]Prov. 3:1; 4:4 [b]Ps. 1:2; 119:24
27 [I]Lit., *strange* [a]Prov. 22:14 [b]Prov. 5:20
28 [I]Lit., *treacherous* [a]Prov. 6:26; 7:12; Eccl. 7:26
29 [a]Is. 5:11, 22
30 [I]Or, *search out* [a]1Sam. 25:36; Prov. 20:1; Is. 5:11; 28:7; Eph. 5:18 [b]Ps. 75:8
31 [I]Lit., *gives its eye* [a]Song 7:9
32 [a]Job 20:16; Prov. 20:1; Eph. 5:18 [b]Ps. 91:13; Is. 11:8
33 [I]Lit., *heart* [a]Prov. 2:12
34 [I]Lit., *heart* [II]Or, *lookout*
35 [I]Lit., *it yet again* [a]Prov. 27:22; Jer. 5:3 [b]Prov. 26:11; Is. 56:12

1 [a]Ps. 37:1; Prov. 3:31; 23:17; 24:19 [b]Ps. 1:1; Prov. 1:15
2 [I]Lit., *hearts* [a]Is. 30:12; Jer. 22:17 [b]Job 15:35; Ps. 10:7; 38:12
3 [a]Prov. 9:1; 14:1
4 [a]Prov. 8:21
5 [I]Lit., *in strength* [II]Lit., *strengthens power* [a]Prov. 21:22
6 [I]Lit., *make battle for yourself* [a]Prov. 20:18 [b]Prov. 11:14
7 [a]Ps. 10:5; Prov. 14:6; 17:16 [b]Job 5:4; Ps. 127:5
8 [I]Or, *deviser of evil* [a]Prov. 6:14; 14:22; Rom. 1:30
9 [a]Matt. 15:19; Acts 8:22
10 [a]Deut. 20:8; Job 4:5; Jer. 51:46; Heb. 12:3
11 [a]Ps. 82:4; Is. 58:6, 7

And those who are staggering
to slaughter,[2027] O hold *them*
back.
12 If you say,[559] "See, we did not
know[3045] this,"
Does He not [a]consider[995] *it*
[b]who weighs the hearts?[3826]
And [c]does He not know[3045] *it*
who [d]keeps[5341] your soul?[5315]
And will He not [Ie]render[7725] to
man[120] according to his work?
13 My son,[1121] eat [a]honey, for it
is good,[2896]
Yes, the [b]honey from the comb
is sweet to your taste;
14 Know[3045] *that* [a]wisdom is thus
for your soul;
If you find *it,* then there will be
a [Ib]future,[319]
And your hope will not be cut
off.[3772]
15 [a]Do not lie in wait, O wicked[7563]
man, against the dwelling of
the righteous;[6662]
Do not destroy[7703] his resting
place;
16 For a [a]righteous man falls[5307]
seven times, and rises
again,
But the [b]wicked stumble[3782] in
time of calamity.[7451]
17 [a]Do not rejoice when your
enemy falls,
And do not let your heart be
glad when he stumbles;
18 Lest the LORD see *it* and
[I]be displeased,
And He turn away[7725] His
anger[639] from him.
19 [a]Do not fret[2734] because of
evildoers,
Or be [b]envious of the wicked;
20 For [a]there will be no [Ib]future for
the evil man;
The [c]lamp[5216] of the wicked will
be put out.
21 My son, [Ia]fear[3372] the LORD and
the king;[4428]
Do not associate[6148] with those
who are given to change;
22 For their [a]calamity[343] will rise
suddenly,

And who knows the ruin[6365] *that
comes* from both of them?
23 These also are [a]sayings of the
wise.
To [Ib]show partiality[5234][6440] in
judgment[4941] is not good.
24 He [a]who says[559] to the wicked,
"You are righteous,"
[b]Peoples[5971] will curse[5344] him,
nations[3816] will abhor[2194]
him;
25 But [a]to those who rebuke[3198] the
wicked will be delight,
And a good blessing[1293] will
come upon them.
26 He kisses[5401] the lips
Who gives [I]a right[5228]
answer.[1697]
27 Prepare[3559] your work[4399]
outside,
And [a]make it ready for yourself
in the field;[7704]
Afterwards, then, build your
house.
28 Do not be a [a]witness against your
neighbor[7453] without cause,
And [b]do not deceive with your
lips.
29 [a]Do not say,[559] "Thus I shall
do[6213] to him as he has done
to me;
I will [I]render to the man
according to his work."
30 I passed by the field of the
sluggard,
And by the vineyard of the man
[a]lacking [I]sense;[3820]
31 And behold, it was completely
[a]overgrown with thistles,
Its surface was covered[3680] with
[Ib]nettles,
And its stone [c]wall was broken
down.
32 When I saw,[2372] I [I]reflected upon
it;
I looked,[7200] *and* received
instruction.[4148]
33 "[a]A little sleep, a little slumber,
A little folding of the hands[3027]
to rest,"
34 Then your poverty will come *as*
[I]a robber,

12 [I]Lit., *bring back* [a]Eccl. 5:8 [b]1Sam. 16:7; Prov. 21:2 [c]Ps. 94:9-11 [d]Ps. 121:3-8 [e]Job 34:11; Prov. 12:14
13 [a]Ps. 19:10; 119:103; Prov. 25:16; Song 5:1 [b]Prov. 16:24; 27:7; Song 4:11
14 [I]Lit., *latter end* [a]Prov. 2:10 [b]Prov. 23:18
15 [a]Ps. 10:9, 10
16 [a]Job 5:19; Ps. 37:24; Mic. 7:8 [b]Prov. 6:15; 14:32; 24:22; Jer. 18:17
17 [a]Job 31:29; Ps. 35:15, 19; Prov. 17:5; Obad. 12
18 [I]Lit., *it is evil in His eyes*
19 [a]Ps. 37:1 [b]Prov. 23:17; 24:1
20 [I]Lit., *latter end* [a]Job 15:31 [b]Prov. 23:18 [c]Job 18:5, 6; 21:17; Prov. 13:9; 20:20
21 [I]Or, *reverence* [a]Rom. 13:1-7; 1Pet. 2:17
22 [a]Prov. 24:16
23 [I]Lit., *regard the face* [a]Prov. 1:6; 22:17 [b]Prov. 18:5; 28:21
24 [a]Prov. 17:15; Is. 5:23 [b]Prov. 11:26
25 [a]Prov. 28:23
26 [I]Or, *an honest*
27 [a]Prov. 27:23-27
28 [a]Prov. 25:18 [b]Lev. 6:2, 3; 19:11; Eph. 4:25
29 [I]Lit., *bring back* [a]Prov. 20:22; Matt. 5:39; Rom. 12:17
30 [I]Lit., *heart* [a]Prov. 6:32
31 [I]I.e., a kind of weed [a]Gen. 3:18 [b]Job 30:7 [c]Is. 5:5
32 [I]Lit., *set my heart*
33 [a]Prov. 6:10
34 [I]Or, *a vagabond;* lit., *one who walks*

And your want like [II]an armed
man.

Similitudes, Instructions

25 These also are [a]proverbs of Solomon which the men[582] of Hezekiah, king[4428] of Judah, transcribed.
2 It is the glory[3519] of God[430] to
[a]conceal a matter,[1697]
But the glory[3519] of [b]kings[4428] is
to search out a matter.[1697]
3 *As* the heavens[8064] for height and
the earth[776] for depth,
So the heart[3820] of kings is
unsearchable.
4 Take away the [a]dross[5509] from
the silver,
And there comes out a vessel
for the [b]smith;[6884]
5 Take away the [a]wicked[7563] *from*
before the king,
And his [b]throne[3678] will be
established[3559] in
righteousness.[6664]
6 Do not claim honor in the
presence of the king,
And do not stand in the place
of great men;
7 For [a]it is better[2896] that it be
said to you, "Come up[5927]
here,"
Than that you should be put
lower in the presence of the
prince,[5081]
Whom your eyes have seen.[7200]
8 Do not go out [a]hastily to
[I]argue[7378] *your case;*
[II]Otherwise, what will you do[6213]
in [III]the end,[319]
When your neighbor[7453] puts you
to shame?
9 [Ia]Argue[7378] your case[7379] with
your neighbor,
And [b]do not reveal[1540] the
secret[5475] of another,
10 Lest he who hears[8085] *it*
reproach[2616]
you,
And the evil report about you
not [I]pass away.[7725]

11 *Like* apples of gold in settings[4906]
of silver
Is a [a]word[1697] spoken[1696] in
[I]right circumstances.
12 *Like* [I]an [a]earring of gold and an
[b]ornament of [c]fine gold
Is a wise[2450] reprover[3198] to a
[d]listening[8085] ear.[241]
13 Like the cold of snow in the
[I]time[3117] of harvest
Is a [a]faithful[539] messenger to
those who send him,
For he refreshes the soul[5315] of
his masters.[113]
14 *Like* [a]clouds[5387] and [b]wind[7307]
without rain
Is a man who boasts[1984]
[I]of his gifts falsely.[8267]
15 By [Ia]forbearance a ruler[7101] may
be persuaded,
And a soft tongue breaks[7665] the
bone.
16 Have you [a]found honey? Eat *only*
[I]what you need,
Lest you have it in excess and
vomit it.
17 Let your foot rarely be in your
neighbor's[7453] house,[1004]
Lest he become [I]weary of you
and hate[8130] you.
18 *Like* a club and a [a]sword[2719] and
a sharp[8150] [b]arrow
Is a man who bears [c]false
witness against his
neighbor.
19 *Like* a bad tooth and [I]an unsteady
foot
Is confidence in a [a]faithless[898]
man in time of trouble.
20 *Like* one who takes off a garment
on a cold day, *or like* vinegar
on [I]soda,[5427]
Is he who sings[7891] songs[7892] to
[II]a troubled heart.
21 [a]If [I]your enemy[8130] is hungry,
give him food to eat;
And if he is thirsty, give him
water to drink;
22 For you will [I]heap burning coals
on his head,[7218]
And [a]the LORD will reward[7999]
you.

34 [II]Lit., *a man with a shield*

1 [a]Prov. 1:1

2 [a]Deut. 29:29; Rom. 11:33 [b]Ezra 6:1

4 [a]Prov. 26:23; Ezek. 22:18 [b]Mal. 3:2, 3

5 [a]Prov. 20:8 [b]Prov. 16:12

7 [a]Luke 14:7-11

8 [I]Lit., *contend* [II]Lit., *Lest* [III]Lit., *its* [a]Prov. 17:14; Matt. 5:25

9 [I]Lit., *Contend* [a]Matt. 18:15 [b]Prov. 11:13

10 [I]Lit., *return*

11 [I]Lit., *its* [a]Prov. 15:23

12 [I]Or, *a nose ring* [a]Ex. 32:2; 35:22; Ezek. 16:12 [b]2Sam. 1:24 [c]Job 28:17 [d]Prov. 15:31; 20:12

13 [I]Lit., *day* [a]Prov. 13:17

14 [I]Lit., *in a gift of falsehood* [a]Jude 12 [b]Jer. 5:13; Mic. 2:11

15 [I]Lit., *length of anger* [a]Gen. 32:4; 1Sam. 25:24; Eccl. 10:4

16 [I]Lit., *your sufficiency* [a]Judg. 14:8; 1Sam. 14:25

17 [I]Lit., *surfeited with*

18 [a]Ps. 57:4; Prov. 12:18 [b]Jer. 9:8 [c]Ex. 20:16; Prov. 24:28

19 [I]Lit., *a slipping foot* [a]Job 6:15; Is. 36:6

20 [I]I.e., natron [II]Lit., *an evil*

21 [I]Lit., *one who hates you* [a]Ex. 23:4, 5; 2Kin. 6:22; 2Chr. 28:15; Matt. 5:44; Rom. 12:20

22 [I]Lit., *snatch up* [a]2Sam. 16:12; Matt. 6:4, 6

23 The north wind brings forth[2342] rain,
And a [I][a]backbiting[5643] tongue, an angry[2194] countenance.
24 It is [a]better to live in a corner of the roof
Than [I]in a house shared with a contentious woman.[802]
25 *Like* cold water to a weary soul,
So is [a]good[2896] news from a distant land.[776]
26 *Like* a [a]trampled[7843] spring and a [I]polluted well
Is a righteous[6662] man who gives way before the wicked.
27 It is not good to eat much honey,
Nor is it glory to [a]search out [I]one's own glory.
28 *Like* a [a]city that is broken into *and* without walls
Is a man [b]who has no control[4623] over his spirit.[7307]

Similitudes, Instructions

26 Like snow in summer and like [a]rain in harvest,
So honor[3519] is not [b]fitting for a fool.
2 Like a [a]sparrow in *its* [I]flitting, like a swallow in *its* flying,
So a [b]curse[7045] without cause does not [II]alight.
3 A [a]whip is for the horse, a bridle for the donkey,
And a [b]rod[7626] for the back[1460] of fools.
4 [a]Do not answer a fool according to his folly,
Lest you also be like him.
5 [a]Answer a fool as his folly *deserves*,
Lest he be [b]wise[2450] in his own eyes.
6 He cuts off *his own* feet, *and* drinks violence[2555]
Who sends a message by the hand[3027] of a fool.
7 *Like* the legs *which* hang down from the lame,
So is a proverb in the mouth[6310] of fools.
8 Like [I]one who binds a stone in a sling,
So is he who gives honor to a fool.
9 *Like* a thorn *which* [I]falls into the hand of a drunkard,
So is a proverb in the mouth of fools.
10 [I]*Like* an archer who wounds[2342] everyone,
So is he who hires a fool or who hires those who pass by.
11 Like [a]a dog that returns[7725] to its vomit
Is a fool who [b]repeats [I]his folly.
12 Do you see a man[376] [a]wise in his own eyes?
[b]There is more hope for a fool than for him.
13 The [a]sluggard says,[559] "There is a lion in the road![1870]
A lion is [I]in the open square!"
14 *As* the door turns on its hinges,
So *does* the [a]sluggard on his bed.
15 The [a]sluggard buries his hand in the dish;
He is weary of bringing it to his mouth again.
16 The sluggard[6102] is [a]wiser[2450] in his own eyes
Than seven men who can [I]give[7725] a discreet answer.[2940]
17 *Like* one who takes[2388] a dog by the ears[241]
Is he who passes[5674] by *and* [I]meddles[5674] with [a]strife[7379] not belonging to him.
18 Like a madman who throws[3384]
[a]Firebrands, arrows and death,[4194]
19 So is the man who [a]deceives his neighbor,[7453]
And says, "[b]Was I not joking?"
20 For lack of wood the fire goes out,
And where there is no [a]whisperer, [b]contention quiets down.
21 *Like* charcoal to hot embers and wood to fire,

23 [I]Lit., *tongue of secrecy* [a]Ps. 101:5
24 [I]Lit., *with a woman of contentions and a house of association* [a]Prov. 21:9
25 [a]Prov. 15:30
26 [I]Lit., *ruined* [a]Ezek. 32:2; 34:18, 19
27 [I]Lit., *their* [a]Prov. 27:2; Luke 14:11
28 [a]Prov. 16:32 [b]2Chr. 32:5; Neh. 1:3

1 [a]1Sam. 12:17 [b]Prov. 17:7
2 [I]Lit., *wandering* [II]Lit., *come* [a]Prov. 27:8; Is. 16:2 [b]Num. 23:8; Deut. 23:5; 2Sam. 16:12
3 [a]Ps. 32:9 [b]Prov. 10:13; 19:29
4 [a]Prov. 23:9; 29:9; Is. 36:21; Matt. 7:6
5 [a]Matt. 16:1-4; 21:24-27 [b]Prov. 3:7; 28:11; Rom. 12:16
8 [I]Lit., *the binding of*
9 [I]Lit., *goes up*
10 [I]Or, *A master workman produces all things, But he who hires a fool is like one who hires those who pass by.*
11 [I]Lit., *with his* [a]2Pet. 2:22 [b]Ex. 8:15
12 [a]Prov. 3:7; 26:5 [b]Prov. 29:20
13 [I]Lit., *within* [a]Prov. 22:13
14 [a]Prov. 6:9
15 [a]Prov. 19:24
16 [I]Lit., *return discreetly* [a]Prov. 27:11
17 [I]Lit., *infuriates himself* [a]Prov. 3:30
18 [a]Is. 50:11
19 [a]Prov. 24:28 [b]Eph. 5:4
20 [a]Prov. 16:28 [b]Prov. 22:10

So is a [a]contentious man to
kindle[2787] strife.
22 The [a]words[1697] of a whisperer
are like dainty morsels,
And they go down into the
[I]innermost parts of the
body.[990]
23 *Like* an earthen [a]vessel[2789]
overlaid with silver [b]dross[5509]
Are burning lips[8193] and a
wicked[7451] heart.[3820]
24 He who [a]hates[8130] disguises[5234]
it with his lips,
But he lays up [b]deceit[4820] in[7130]
his [I]heart.
25 When [I]he [a]speaks graciously,[2603]
do not believe[539] him,
For there are seven
abominations[8441] in his heart.
26 *Though his* hatred[8135]
[a]covers[3680] itself with guile,
His wickedness will be
[b]revealed before the
assembly.[6951]
27 He who [a]digs a pit[7845] will fall
into it,
And he who rolls[1556] a stone, it
will come back[7725] on him.
28 A lying tongue hates [I]those it
crushes,
And a [a]flattering mouth
works[6213] ruin.

Warnings and Instructions

27 [a]Do not boast[1984] about
tomorrow,
For you [b]do not know[3045] what
a day[3117] may bring forth.
2 Let [a]another[2114] praise[1984] you,
and not your own mouth;[6310]
A stranger, and not your own
lips.[8193]
3 A stone is heavy and the sand
weighty,
But the provocation[3708] of a fool
is heavier[8513] than both of
them.
4 Wrath[2534] is fierce and anger[639]
is a flood,[7858]
But [a]who can stand before
jealousy?[7068]
5 Better is [a]open[1540] rebuke[8433]
Than love[160] that is concealed.
6 Faithful[539] are the [a]wounds of a
friend,[157]
But [I]deceitful are the [b]kisses of
an enemy.[8130]
7 A sated [I]man[5315] [II]loathes[947]
honey,
But to a famished [I]man any
bitter[4751] thing is sweet.
8 Like a [a]bird that wanders from
her nest,
So is a man[376] who [b]wanders
from his [I]home.
9 [a]Oil[8081] and perfume[7004] make
the heart[3820] glad,
So a [I]man's counsel[6098] is sweet
to his friend.[7453]
10 Do not forsake[5800] your own
[a]friend or [b]your father's[1]
friend,
And do not go to your brother's
house[1004] in the day of your
calamity;[343]
Better is a neighbor[7934] who is
near than a brother[251] far
away.
11 [a]Be wise,[2449] my son,[1121] and
make my heart glad,
That I may [b]reply[7725,1697] to him
who reproaches me.
12 A prudent[6175] man sees evil[7451]
and hides himself,
The [I]naive proceed[5674] *and* pay
the penalty.[6064]
13 [a]Take his garment when he
becomes surety[6148] for a
stranger;[2114]
And for an [I]adulterous
woman[5237] hold him in
pledge.[2254]
14 [a]He who blesses[1288] his friend
with a loud voice early in the
morning,
It will be reckoned[2803] a curse[7045]
to him.
15 A [a]constant dripping on a day
of steady rain
And a contentious woman[802] are
alike;
16 He who would [I]restrain her
[I]restrains the wind,[7307]

---

21 [a]Prov. 15:18; 29:22
22 [I]Lit., *chambers of the belly* [a]Prov. 18:8
23 [a]Matt. 23:27; Luke 11:39 [b]Prov. 25:4
24 [I]Lit., *inward part* [a]Ps. 41:6; Prov. 10:18 [b]Prov. 12:20
25 [I]Lit., *his voice is gracious* [a]Ps. 28:3; Prov. 26:23; Jer. 9:8
26 [a]Matt. 23:28 [b]Luke 8:17
27 [a]Esth. 7:10; Prov. 28:10
28 [I]Lit., *its crushed ones* [a]Prov. 29:5

1 [a]James 4:13-16 [b]Luke 12:19, 20; James 4:14
2 [a]Prov. 25:27; 2Cor. 10:12, 18; 12:11
4 [a]Prov. 6:34; 1John 3:12
5 [a]Prov. 28:23; Gal. 2:14
6 [I]Or, *excessive* [a]Ps. 141:5; Prov. 20:30 [b]Matt. 26:49
7 [I]Lit., *soul* [II]Lit., *tramples on*
8 [I]Lit., *place* [a]Prov. 26:2; Is. 16:2 [b]Gen. 21:14
9 [I]Lit., *soul's* [a]Ps. 23:5; 141:5
10 [a]Prov. 18:24 [b]1Kin. 12:6-8; 2Chr. 10:6-8
11 [a]Prov. 10:1; 23:15; 29:3 [b]Ps. 119:42
12 [I]Lit., *simple*
13 [I]Lit., *strange* [a]Prov. 20:16
14 [a]Ps. 12:2
15 [a]Prov. 19:13
16 [I]Lit., *hide(s)*

And [II]grasps oil with his right
hand.
17 Iron sharpens iron,
So one man sharpens another.
18 He who tends[5341] the [a]fig tree
will eat its fruit;
And he who [b]cares for his
master[113] will be honored.
19 As in water face *reflects* face,
So the heart of man[120] *reflects*
man.
20 [Ia]Sheol[7585] and [II]Abaddon[10] are
[b]never satisfied,
Nor are the [c]eyes of man ever
satisfied.
21 The [a]crucible is for silver and
the furnace for gold,
And a man [b]*is tested* by the praise
accorded him.
22 Though you [a]pound a fool in a
mortar with a pestle[5940] along
with crushed grain,
Yet his folly will not depart[5493]
from him.
23 [a]Know[3045] well the [I]condition[6440]
of your flocks,
And pay attention to your herds;
24 For riches are not forever,[5769]
Nor does a [a]crown[5145] *endure* to
all generations.[1755]
25 *When* the grass disappears, the
new growth is seen,[7200]
And the herbs of the mountains
are [a]gathered[622] in,
26 The lambs *will be* for your
clothing,
And the goats *will bring* the price
of a field,[7704]
27 And *there will be* goats' milk
enough for your food,
For the food of your
household,[1004]
And sustenance for your
maidens.

Warnings and Instructions

28 The wicked[7563] [a]flee when no one
is pursuing,
But the righteous[6662] are
[I]bold as a lion.
2 By the transgression[6588] of a
land[776] [a]many are its
princes,[8269]
But [b]by a man[120] of
understanding[995] *and*
knowledge,[3045] so it
endures.[748]
3 A [a]poor man[1397] who oppresses
the lowly
Is *like* a driving rain [I]which
leaves no food.
4 Those who forsake[5800] the
law[8451] [a]praise[1984] the
wicked,
But those who keep[8104] the law
[b]strive with them.
5 Evil[7451] men[582] [a]do not
understand[995] justice,[4941]
But those who seek the LORD
[b]understand all things.
6 [a]Better[2896] is the poor who walks
in his integrity,[8537]
Than he who is [I]crooked though
he be rich.
7 He who keeps[5341] the law is a
discerning[995] son,[1121]
But he who is a companion of
[a]gluttons humiliates his
father.[1]
8 He who increases his wealth by
[a]interest and usury,
Gathers it [b]for him who is
gracious to the poor.
9 He who turns away his ear[241]
from listening[8085] to the law,
Even his [a]prayer[8605] is an
abomination.[8441]
10 He who leads the upright[3477]
astray[7686] in an evil way[1870]
Will [a]himself fall into his own
pit,[7816]
But the [b]blameless will inherit
good.
11 The rich man[376] is [a]wise[2450] in
his own eyes,
But the poor who has
understanding [I]sees through
him.
12 When the [a]righteous triumph,
there is great glory,[8597]
But [b]when the wicked rise, men
[I]hide themselves.

16 [II]Lit., *encounters*
18 [a]2Kin. 18:31; Song 8:12; Is. 36:16; 1Cor. 3:8; 9:7; 2Tim. 2:6 [b]Luke 12:42-44; 19:17
20 [I]I.e., The nether world [II]I.e., the place of destruction [a]Job 26:6; Prov. 15:11 [b]Prov. 30:15, 16; Hab. 2:5 [c]Eccl. 1:8; 4:8
21 [a]Prov. 17:3 [b]Luke 6:26
22 [a]Prov. 23:35; 26:11; Jer. 5:3
23 [I]Lit., *face* [a]Jer. 31:10; Ezek. 34:12; John 10:3
24 [a]Job 19:9; Ps. 89:39; Jer. 13:18; Lam. 5:16; Ezek. 21:26
25 [a]Is. 17:5; Jer. 40:10, 12

1 [I]Lit., *confident* [a]Lev. 26:17, 36; Ps. 53:5
2 [a]1Kin. 16:8-28; 2Kin. 15:8-15 [b]Prov. 11:11
3 [I]Lit., *and there is no bread* [a]Matt. 18:28
4 [a]Ps. 49:18; Rom. 1:32 [b]1Kin. 18:18; Neh. 13:11, 15; Matt. 3:7; 14:4; Eph. 5:11
5 [a]Ps. 92:6; Is. 6:9; 44:18 [b]Ps. 119:100; Prov. 2:9; John 7:17; 1Cor. 2:15; 1John 2:20, 27
6 [I]Lit., *perverse of two ways* [a]Prov. 19:1
7 [a]Prov. 23:20
8 [a]Ex. 22:25; Lev. 25:36 [b]Job 27:17; Prov. 13:22; 14:31
9 [a]Ps. 66:18; 109:7; Prov. 15:8; 21:27
10 [a]Ps. 7:15; Prov. 26:27 [b]Matt. 6:33; Heb. 6:12; 1Pet. 3:9
11 [I]Lit., *examines him* [a]Prov. 3:7; 26:5, 12
12 [I]Lit., *will be searched for* [a]Prov. 11:10; 29:2 [b]Prov. 28:28; Eccl. 10:5, 6

13 He who [a]conceals[3680] his
transgressions[6588] will not
prosper,
But he who [b]confesses[3034] and
forsakes[5800] *them* will find
compassion.[7355]
14 How blessed[835] is the man who
[a]fears[6342] always,[8548]
But he who [b]hardens his
heart[3820] will fall into
calamity.[7451]
15 *Like* a [a]roaring lion and a rushing
bear
Is a [b]wicked ruler over a poor
people.[5971]
16 A [a]leader[5057] who is a great
oppressor lacks
understanding,[8394]
But he who hates[8130] unjust
gain[1215] will prolong[748] *his*
days.[3117]
17 A man who is [a]laden with the
guilt of human[5315] blood[1818]
Will [I]be a fugitive until death;[953]
let no one support him.
18 He who walks blamelessly[8549]
will be delivered,[3467]
But he who is [Ia]crooked will fall
all at once.
19 [a]He who tills[5647] his land[127] will
[b]have plenty of food,
But he who follows empty
pursuits will have poverty in
plenty.
20 A [a]faithful[530] man will abound[7227]
with blessings,[1293]
But he who [b]makes haste to be
rich will not go
unpunished.[5352]
21 To [Ia]show partiality[5234][6440] is not
good,[2896]
[b]Because for a piece of bread a
man will transgress.[6586]
22 A man with an [a]evil eye
[b]hastens[926] after wealth,
And does not know[3045] that want
will come upon him.
23 He who [a]rebukes[3198] a man
will afterward find *more*
favor[2580]
Than he who [b]flatters with the
tongue.

13 [a]Job 31:33; Ps. 32:3 [b]Ps. 32:5; 1John 1:9
14 [a]Prov. 23:17 [b]Ps. 95:8; Rom. 2:5
15 [a]Prov. 19:12; 1Pet. 5:8 [b]Ex. 1:14; Prov. 29:2; Matt. 2:16
16 [a]Eccl. 10:16; Is. 3:12
17 [I]Lit., *flee to the pit* [a]Gen. 9:6; Ex. 21:14
18 [I]Lit., *perverse of two ways* [a]Prov. 10:27
19 [a]Prov. 12:11 [b]Prov. 20:13
20 [a]Prov. 10:6; Matt. 24:45; 25:21 [b]Prov. 20:21; 28:22; 1Tim. 6:9
21 [I]Lit., *regard the face* [a]Prov. 24:23 [b]Ezek. 13:19
22 [a]Prov. 23:6 [b]Prov. 21:5
23 [a]Prov. 27:5, 6 [b]Prov. 29:5
24 [a]Prov. 19:26 [b]Prov. 18:9
25 [I]Lit., *broad soul* [II]Lit., *be made fat* [a]Prov. 15:18 [b]Prov. 29:25; 1Tim. 6:6 [c]Prov. 11:25
26 [a]Prov. 3:5
27 [I]Lit., *hides* [a]Prov. 11:24; 19:17

1 [I]Lit., *and there is no remedy* [a]1Sam. 2:25; 2Chr. 36:16; Prov. 1:24-31 [b]Prov. 6:15
2 [I]Or, *become great* [a]Esth. 8:15; Prov. 11:10; 28:12
3 [a]Prov. 10:1; 15:20; 27:11; 28:7 [b]Prov. 5:10; 6:26; Luke 15:30
4 [a]2Chr. 9:8; Prov. 8:15; 29:14
5 [a]Ps. 5:9
6 [a]Prov. 22:5; Eccl. 9:12 [b]Ex. 15:1
7 [I]Lit., *knows the cause* [a]Job 29:16; Ps. 41:1; Prov. 31:8, 9

24 He who [a]robs his father or his
mother,[517]
And says,[559] "It is not a
transgression,"
Is the [b]companion of a man[376]
who destroys.[7843]
25 An [I]arrogant man [a]stirs up strife,
But he who [b]trusts[982] in the
LORD [c]will [II]prosper.[1878]
26 He who [a]trusts[982] in his own
heart is a fool,
But he who walks wisely will be
delivered.[4422]
27 He who [a]gives to the poor will
never want,
But he who [I]shuts his eyes will
have many curses.
28 When the wicked rise, men[120]
hide themselves;
But when they perish,[6] the
righteous increase.

Warnings and Instructions

29 A man who hardens *his* neck
after [a]much reproof[8433]
Will [b]suddenly be broken[7665]
[I]beyond remedy.
2 When the [a]righteous[6662]
[I]increase,[7235] the people[5971]
rejoice,
But when a wicked[7563] man
rules,[4910] people groan.
3 A man who [a]loves[157] wisdom[2451]
makes his father[1] glad,
But he who [b]keeps company
with harlots wastes *his*
wealth.
4 The [a]king[4428] gives stability[5975]
to the land[776] by justice,[4941]
But a man who takes bribes
overthrows it.
5 A man[1397] who [a]flatters his
neighbor[7453]
Is spreading a net for his steps.
6 By transgression[6588] an evil[7451]
man[376] is [a]ensnared,[4170]
But the righteous [b]sings and
rejoices.
7 The [a]righteous [I]is concerned[3045]
for the rights[1779] of the poor,

The wicked does not understand[1847] *such* [II]concern.
8 Scorners [a]set a city aflame,[6315]
But [b]wise[2450] men[582] turn away[7725] anger.[639]
9 When a wise man has a controversy[8199] with a foolish man,
[I]The foolish man either rages or laughs, and there is no rest.
10 Men of [a]bloodshed[1818] hate[8130] the blameless,[8535]
But the upright[3477] [I]are concerned for his life.[5315]
11 A [a]fool [I]always loses his temper,
But a [b]wise man holds[7623] it back.
12 If a [a]ruler pays attention[7181] to falsehood,[8267]
All his ministers *become* wicked.
13 The [a]poor man and the oppressor [I]have this in common:
The LORD gives [b]light to the eyes of both.
14 If a [a]king judges[8199] the poor with truth,[571]
His [b]throne[3678] will be established[3559] forever.[5703]
15 The [a]rod[7626] and reproof[8433] give wisdom,
But a child [I]who gets his own way [b]brings shame[954] to his mother.[517]
16 When the wicked [I]increase, transgression increases;
But the [a]righteous will see their fall.[4658]
17 [a]Correct[3256] your son,[1121] and he will give you comfort;
He will also [Ib]delight your soul.
18 Where there is [a]no [I]vision,[2377] the people [b]are unrestrained,[6544]
But [c]happy[835] is he who keeps[8104] the law.[8451]
19 A slave[5650] will not be instructed[3256] by words[1697] *alone;*
For though he understands,[995] there will be no response.

20 Do you see[2372] a man who is [a]hasty in his words?
There is [b]more hope for a fool than for him.
21 He who pampers his slave from childhood
Will in the end find him to be a son.
22 An [a]angry[639] man stirs up strife,
And a hot-tempered[2534] man abounds[7227] in transgression.
23 A man's[120] [a]pride will bring him low,
But a [b]humble spirit[7307] will obtain honor.[3519]
24 He who is a partner with a thief hates[8130] his own life;
He [a]hears[8085] the oath[423] but tells[5046] nothing.
25 The [a]fear[2731] of man[120] [I]brings a snare,
But he who [b]trusts in the LORD will be exalted.
26 [a]Many seek the ruler's [I]favor,
But [b]justice for man *comes* from the LORD.
27 An [a]unjust[5766] man is abominable[8441] to the righteous,
And he who is [b]upright[3477] in the way[1870] is abominable to the wicked.

The Words of Agur

30 The words[1697] of Agur the son[1121] of Jakeh, the [I]oracle.[4853]
The man[1397] declares[5001] to Ithiel, to Ithiel and Ucal:
2 Surely I am more [a]stupid than any man,[376]
And I do not have the understanding[998] of a man.[120]
3 Neither have I learned[3925] wisdom,[2451]
Nor do I have the [a]knowledge[1847] of the Holy One.[6918]

7 [II]Lit., *knowledge* 8 [a]Prov. 11:11 [b]Prov. 16:14 9 [I]Lit., *He* 10 [I]Lit., *seek his soul* [a]Gen. 4:5-8; 1John 3:12 11 [I]Lit., *sends forth all his spirit* [a]Prov. 12:16; 14:33 [b]Prov. 19:11 12 [a]1Kin. 12:14 13 [I]Lit., *meet together* [a]Prov. 22:2 [b]Ezra 9:8; Ps. 13:3 14 [a]Ps. 72:4; Is. 11:4 [b]Prov. 16:12; 25:5 15 [I]Lit., *left to himself* [a]Prov. 13:24; 22:15 [b]Prov. 10:1; 17:25 16 [I]Or, *become great* [a]Ps. 37:34, 36; 58:10; 91:8; 92:11; Prov. 21:12 17 [I]Lit., *give delight to* [a]Prov. 13:24; 29:15 [b]Prov. 10:1 18 [I]Or, *revelation* [a]1Sam. 3:1; Ps. 74:9; Amos 8:11, 12 [b]Ex. 32:25 [c]Ps. 1:1, 2; 106:3; 119:2; Prov. 8:32; John 13:17 20 [a]James 1:19 [b]Prov. 26:12 22 [a]Prov. 15:18; 26:21 23 [a]Prov. 11:2; 16:18; Dan. 4:30, 31; Matt. 23:12; James 4:6 [b]Prov. 15:33; 18:12; 22:4; Is. 66:2; Luke 14:11; 18:14; James 4:10 24 [a]Lev. 5:1 25 [I]Lit., *gives* [a]Gen. 12:12; 20:2; Luke 12:4; John 12:42, 43 [b]Ps. 91:1-16; Prov. 18:10; 28:25 26 [I]Lit., *face* [a]Prov. 19:6 [b]Is. 49:4; 1Cor. 4:4 27 [a]Ps. 6:8; 139:21, 22; Prov. 12:8 [b]Ps. 69:4; Prov. 29:10; Matt. 10:22; 24:9; John 15:18; 17:14; 1John 3:13

1 [I]Or, *burden*

2 [a]Ps. 49:10; 73:22; Prov. 12:1 3 [a]Prov. 9:10

4 Who has [a]ascended[5927] into
heaven[8064] and descended?
Who has gathered[622] the
[b]wind[7307] in His fists?
Who has [c]wrapped the waters
in [I]His garment?
Who has [d]established all the ends
of the earth?[776]
What is His [e]name or His son's
name?
Surely you know![3045]
5 Every [a]word[565] of God[430] is
tested;[6884]
He is a [b]shield to those who take
refuge[2620] in Him.
6 [a]Do not add to His words
Lest He reprove[3198] you, and
you be proved a liar.[3576]
7 Two things I asked[7592] of
Thee,
Do not refuse me before I die:
8 Keep deception[7723] and
[I]lies[3577] far from me,
Give me neither poverty nor
riches;
Feed me with the [a]food that is
my portion,[2706]
9 Lest I be [a]full and deny
[b]*Thee* and say,[559] "Who is the
LORD?"
Or lest I be [c]in want and
steal,
And [d]profane the name of my
God.[430]
10 Do not slander[3960] a slave[5650] to
his master,[113]
Lest he [a]curse[7043] you and you
be found guilty.[816]
11 There is a [I]kind[1755] of *man* who
[a]curses[7043] his father,[1]
And does not bless[1288] his
mother.[517]
12 There is a [I]kind who is
[a]pure[2889] in his own eyes,
Yet is not washed[7364] from his
filthiness.
13 There is a [I]kind—oh how
[a]lofty are his eyes!
And his eyelids are raised[5375] *in
arrogance.*
14 There is a [I]kind of *man* whose
[a]teeth are *like* swords,[2719]

4 [I]Lit., *the* [a]Ps. 68:18; John 3:13; Eph. 4:8 [b]Ex. 15:10; Ps. 135:7 [c]Job 26:8; 38:8, 9 [d]Ps. 24:2; Is. 45:18 [e]Rev. 19:12

5 [a]Ps. 12:6; 18:30 [b]Ps. 3:3; 84:11; Prov. 2:7

6 [a]Deut. 4:2; 12:32; Rev. 22:18

8 [I]Lit., *words of falsehood* [a]Job 23:12; Matt. 6:11

9 [a]Deut. 8:12; 31:20; Neh. 9:25; Hos. 13:6 [b]Josh. 24:27; Job 31:28 [c]Prov. 6:30 [d]Ex. 20:7

10 [a]Eccl. 7:21

11 [I]Or, *generation* [a]Ex. 21:17; Prov. 20:20

12 [I]Or, *generation* [a]Prov. 16:2; Is. 65:5; Luke 18:11; Titus 1:15, 16

13 [I]Or, *generation* [a]Prov. 6:17; Is. 2:11; 5:15

14 [I]Or, *generation* [a]Ps. 57:4 [b]Job 29:17 [c]Ps. 14:4; Amos 8:4

16 [I]I.e., The nether world [a]Prov. 27:20 [b]Gen. 30:1

17 [I]Lit., *despises to obey* [a]Gen. 9:22 [b]Prov. 15:20 [c]Deut. 28:26

19 [a]Deut. 28:49; Jer. 48:40; 49:22

20 [a]Prov. 5:6

22 [a]Prov. 19:10; Eccl. 10:7

And his [b]jaw teeth *like* knives,
To [c]devour the afflicted from the
earth,
And the needy from among
men.[120]
15 The leech has two daughters,
"Give," "Give."
There are three things that will
not be satisfied,
Four that will not say,
"Enough":
16 [I][a]Sheol,[7585] and the [b]barren[6115]
womb,
Earth that is never satisfied with
water,
And fire that never says,[559]
"Enough."
17 The eye that [a]mocks a
father,
And [I][b]scorns a mother,
The [c]ravens of the valley will
pick it out,
And the young[1121] [c]eagles will
eat it.
18 There are three things which are
too wonderful[6381] for me,
Four which I do not
understand:[3045]
19 The way[1870] of an [a]eagle in the
sky,[8064]
The way of a serpent[5175] on a
rock,
The way of a ship in the middle
of the sea,
And the way of a man with a
maid.[5959]
20 This is the way of an
[a]adulterous[5003] woman:[802]
She eats and wipes[4229] her
mouth,[6310]
And says, "I have done no
wrong."[205]
21 Under three things the earth
quakes,
And under four, it cannot bear
up:[5375]
22 Under a [a]slave when he becomes
king,[4427]
And a fool when he is satisfied
with food,
23 Under an unloved[8130] woman
when she gets a husband,[1166]

And a maidservant when she
supplants[3423] her
mistress.[1404]
24 Four things are small on the
earth,
But they are exceedingly
wise:[2450]
25 The [a]ants are not a strong
folk,[5971]
But they prepare[3559] their food
in the summer;
26 The [a]badgers[8226] are not mighty
folk,
Yet they make[7760] their houses
in the rocks;
27 The locusts have no king,[4428]
Yet all of them go out in
[a]ranks;
28 The lizard you may grasp with
the hands,[3027]
Yet it is in kings' palaces.[1964]
29 There are three things which are
stately[3190] in *their* march,
Even four which are stately[3190]
when they walk:
30 The lion *which* is [a]mighty among
beasts
And does not [Ib]retreat[7725] before
any,
31 The [I]strutting cock, the male
goat also,
And a king *when his* army is with
him.
32 If you have been foolish in
exalting[5375] yourself
Or if you have plotted *evil*,[2161]
[a]*put your* hand[3027] on your
mouth.
33 For the [I]churning of milk
produces butter,
And pressing the nose[639] brings
forth blood;[1818]
So the [I]churning of [a]anger[639]
produces strife.[7379]

25 [a]Prov. 6:6

26 [a]Lev. 11:5; Ps. 104:18

27 [a]Joel 2:7

30 [I]Lit., *turn back* [a]Judg. 14:18; 2Sam. 1:23 [b]Mic. 5:8

31 [I]Lit., *girt in the loins*

32 [a]Job 21:5; 40:4; Mic. 7:16

33 [I]Lit., *pressing* [a]Prov. 10:12; 29:22

1 [I]Or, *burden*

2 [a]Is. 49:15 [b]1Sam. 1:11

3 [a]Prov. 5:9 [b]Deut. 17:17; 1Kin. 11:1; Neh. 13:26

4 [a]Eccl. 10:17 [b]Prov. 20:1; Is. 5:22; Hos. 4:11

5 [I]Lit., *judgment* [II]Lit., *sons of affliction* [a]Ex. 23:6; Deut. 16:19; Prov. 17:15

6 [I]Lit., *bitter of soul* [a]Job 29:13 [b]Job 3:20; Is. 38:15

8 [I]Lit., *judgment* [II]Lit., *sons of passing away* [a]Job 29:12-17; Ps. 82

9 [I]Lit., *judge the afflicted* [a]Lev. 19:15; Deut. 1:16 [b]Is. 1:17; Jer. 22:16

10 [a]Ruth 3:11; Prov. 12:4; 19:14 [b]Job 28:18; Prov. 8:11

The Words of Lemuel

31 The words[1697] of King[4428] Lemuel, the [I]oracle[4853] which his
mother[517] taught[3256] him.
2 What, O my son?
And what, O [a]son of my
womb?[990]
And what, O son of my
[b]vows?[5088]
3 [a]Do not give your strength[2428]
to women,[802]
Or your ways[1870] to that which
[b]destroys[4229] kings.[4428]
4 It is not for [a]kings, O Lemuel,
It is not for kings to [b]drink wine,
Or for rulers[7336] to desire strong
drink,
5 Lest they drink and forget what
is decreed,[2710]
And [a]pervert the [I]rights[1779] of
all the [II]afflicted.
6 Give strong drink to him who
is [a]perishing,[6]
And wine to him [Ib]whose life is
bitter.[4751]
7 Let him drink and forget his
poverty,
And remember[2142] his
trouble[5999] no more.
8 [a]Open your mouth[6310] for the
dumb,
For the [I]rights[1779] of all the
[II]unfortunate.
9 Open your mouth, [a]judge[8199]
righteously,[6664]
And [I]defend the [b]rights[1777] of the
afflicted and needy.

Description of a Worthy Woman

10 An [a]excellent[2428] wife,[802] who
can find?
For her worth is far [b]above
jewels.

31:10-31 These verses are an acrostic, i.e., each verse begins with a different Hebrew letter according to the order of the Hebrew alphabet. The most famous acrostic is Psalm 119, which has every one of the twenty-two Hebrew characters highlighted by repeating it eight times. This passage sings the praises of a good wife. It is an anonymous appendix to the book, extolling the honor and dignity of women and the importance of the mother in the home. She is completely trusted by her husband and becomes a source of honor not only to him, but to the whole family. The secret to her dignity and the place of honor which she has attained is that she "fears the Lord" (v. 30).

11 The heart[3820] of her husband[1167]
trusts[982] in her,
And he will have no lack of gain.
12 She does[1580] him good[2896] and
not evil[7451]
All the days[3117] of her life.[2416]
13 She looks for wool and flax,
And works[6213] with her
[I]hands[3709] [II]in delight.[2656]
14 She is like [a]merchant ships;
She brings her food from afar.
15 She [a]rises also while it is still
night,[3915]
And [b]gives food to her
household,[1004]
And [I]portions[2706] to her
maidens.
16 She considers[2161] a field[7704] and
buys it;
From [I]her earnings she plants
a vineyard.
17 She [a]girds [I]herself with strength,
And makes her arms strong.
18 She senses that her gain is good;
Her lamp[5216] does not go out at
night.
19 She stretches out her hands[3027]
to the distaff,
And her [I]hands grasp the
spindle.[6418]
20 She [Ia]extends her hand[3709] to the
poor;
And she stretches out her hands
to the needy.
21 She is not afraid[3372] of the snow
for her household,
For all her household are
[a]clothed with scarlet.
22 She makes[6213] [a]coverings for
herself;
Her clothing is [b]fine linen and
[c]purple.
23 Her husband is known[3045]
[a]in the gates,
When he sits among the
elders[2205] of the land.[776]
24 She makes [a]linen garments and
sells *them,*
And [I]supplies belts[2289] to the
[II]tradesmen.
25 Strength and [a]dignity are her
clothing,
And she smiles at the
[I]future.
26 She [a]opens her mouth in
wisdom,[2451]
And the [I]teaching[8451] of
kindness[2617] is on her
tongue.
27 She looks well to the ways of
her household,
And does not eat the [a]bread of
idleness.
28 Her children[1121] rise up and
bless[833] her;
Her husband *also,* and
he praises[1984] her,
saying:
29 "Many daughters have done
nobly,
But you excel them all."
30 Charm[2580] is deceitful[8267] and
beauty is vain,
But a woman who [Ia]fears the
LORD, she shall be
praised.[1984]
31 Give her the [I]product of her
hands,
And let her works praise[1984] her
in the gates.

---

13 [I]Lit., *palms* [II]Or, *willingly*

14 [a]Ezek. 27:25

15 [I]Or, *prescribed tasks* [a]Prov. 20:13; Rom. 12:11 [b]Luke 12:42

16 [I]Lit., *the fruit of her palms*

17 [I]Lit., *her loins* [a]1Kin. 18:46; 2Kin. 4:29; Job 38:3

19 [I]Lit., *palms*

20 [I]Lit., *spreads out her palm* [a]Deut. 15:11; Job 31:16-20; Prov. 22:9; Rom. 12:13; Eph. 4:28

21 [a]2Sam. 1:24

22 [a]Prov. 7:16 [b]Gen. 41:42; Rev. 19:8, 14 [c]Judg. 8:26; Luke 16:19

23 [a]Deut. 16:18; Ruth 4:1, 11

24 [I]Lit., *gives* [II]Lit., *Canaanite* [a]Judg. 14:12

25 [I]Lit., *latter days* [a]1Tim. 2:9, 10

26 [I]Or, *law* [a]Prov. 10:31

27 [a]Prov. 19:15

30 [I]Or, *reverences* [a]Ps. 112:1; Prov. 22:4

31 [I]Lit., *fruit*

The Book of

ECCLESIASTES

The superscription identifies the author as the "Preacher," which is a loose translation of the Hebrew text. Based on this, the Septuagint, the ancient Greek translation of the Old Testament, gives the book the name from which our "Ecclesiastes" is derived. The identity of the author is problematic, although the traditional ascription has been to Solomon. The strongest evidence in the text against Solomon as the writer is the allusion to a line of kings over Jerusalem prior to the author's time (Ecc. 1:16). Hence, it is best to treat the book as anonymous, and this is consistent with the fact that Solomon's name nowhere appears in the work. Ecclesiastes gives us a glimpse into the life of one who had the means to pursue happiness through any avenue. He tried wisdom, pleasure, alcohol, human achievement, the fruits of great riches, and sex, but he concluded that all of this was emptiness (Ecc. 2:11). He was deeply troubled by injustice in this life. Many good men suffer and the wicked prosper in their wickedness. Regardless of how righteously a man tries to live, he ends up in the same grave as any other man—or beast! A man can do all the right things, but chance can cancel it all out. The pessimism of this book is as pronounced as is the optimism of Proverbs. Only at the end does the author tell us what he found to be the real source of meaning in life—reverence for God (Ecc. 12:13-14). He had left God out of the picture in his search for happiness. This is the book for the secular humanist to read, because it shows how utterly meaningless and unjust life is in a closed system where God does not play an effective part. The author's solution is that happiness is found only when we revere God as the center of our lives.

The Futility of All Endeavor

1 The <u>words</u>**[1697]** of the [a]<u>Preacher</u>,**[6953]**
the <u>son</u>**[1121]** of David, <u>king</u>**[4428]** in Jerusalem.

🗝 2 "[Ia]Vanity of vanities," <u>says</u>**[559]** the
Preacher, "[I]Vanity of vanities! All is [II]vanity."

3 [a]What advantage does <u>man</u>**[120]**
have in all his <u>work</u>**[5999]**
Which he does under the sun?

4 A <u>generation</u>**[1755]** goes and a
generation comes,
But the [a]<u>earth</u>**[776]** [I]remains
<u>forever</u>.**[5769]**

5 Also, [a]the sun rises and the sun
sets;
And [I]hastening to its place it
rises there *again.*

6 [Ia]Blowing toward the south,
Then turning toward the
north,
The <u>wind</u>**[7307]** continues
[II]swirling along;
And on its circular courses the
wind <u>returns</u>.**[7725]**

7 All the rivers [I]flow into the
sea,
Yet the sea is not full.
To the place where the rivers
[I]flow,
There they [I]<u>flow again</u>.**[7725]**

8 All <u>things</u>**[1697]** are wearisome;
<u>Man</u>**[376]** is not able to tell *it.*
[a]The eye is not satisfied with
<u>seeing</u>,**[7200]**
Nor is the <u>ear</u>**[241]** filled with
<u>hearing</u>.**[8085]**

1 [a]Eccl. 1:12; 7:27; 12:8-10

2 [I]Or, *Futility of futilities* [II]Or, *futile* [a]Ps. 39:5, 6; 62:9; 144:4; Eccl. 12:8; Rom. 8:20

3 [a]Eccl. 2:11; 3:9; 5:16

4 [I]Lit., *stands* [a]Ps. 104:5; 119:90

5 [I]Lit., *panting* [a]Ps. 19:6

6 [I]Lit., *Going* [II]Lit., *turning* [a]Eccl. 11:5; John 3:8

7 [I]Lit., *go*

8 [a]Prov. 27:20; Eccl. 4:8

🗝 **1:2** The theme of Ecclesiastes is stated in the words "vanity of vanities," literally "breath of breaths." This was the Hebrew means of expressing the superlative degree. This is a forceful statement which carries the meaning, "All is utter emptiness." The word "vanity" occurs thirty-eight times throughout the book and is obviously the key word. It is used to indicate the emptiness and worthlessness of outward appearances (Ecc. 2:15,19; 8:10,14) as well as the emptiness and futility of man's inward thoughts and struggles (Ecc. 1:14; 2:11). All material things are temporary and transitory.

9 [a]That which has been is that
which will be,
And that which has been done
is that which will be done.
So, there is nothing new under
the sun.
10 Is there anything[1697] of which
one might say,[559]
"See this, it is new"?
Already it has existed for
ages[5769]
Which were before us.
11 There is [a]no remembrance[2146]
of [I]earlier[7223] things;
And also of the [II]later things
which will occur,
There will be for them no
remembrance
Among those who will come
[II]later *still*.

The Futility of Wisdom

12 I, the [a]Preacher, have been king
over Israel in Jerusalem.
13 And I [a]set my [I]mind[3820] to seek
and [b]explore by wisdom[2451] concerning
all that has been done under heaven.[8064]
It is [II]a grievous[7451] [c]task *which* God[430]
has given to the sons[1121] of men to be
afflicted with.
14 I have seen[7200] all the works
which have been done under the sun,
and behold, all is [Ia]vanity and striving[7469]
after wind.[7307]
15 What is [a]crooked[5791] cannot be
straightened, and what is lacking cannot
be counted.
16 I [I]said to myself, "Behold, I have
magnified and increased [a]wisdom more
than all who were over Jerusalem before
me; and my [II]mind has observed[7200]
[IIIa] wealth of wisdom and knowledge."[1847]
17 And I [a]set my [I]mind to know[3045]
wisdom and to [b]know madness and folly;
I realized[3045] that this also is [c]striving[7475]
after wind.
18 Because [a]in much wisdom there
is much grief,[3708] and increasing knowledge *results in* increasing pain.

9 [a]Eccl. 1:10; 2:12; 3:15; 6:10
11 [I]Lit., *first* or *former* [II]Lit., *latter* or *after* [a]Eccl. 2:16; 9:5
12 [a]Eccl. 1:1; 7:27; 12:8-10
13 [I]Lit., *heart* [II]Lit., *an evil* [a]Eccl. 1:17 [b]Eccl. 3:10, 11; 7:25; 8:17 [c]Eccl. 2:23, 26; 3:10; 4:8
14 [I]Or, *futility* [a]Eccl. 2:11, 17; 4:4; 6:9
15 [a]Eccl. 7:13
16 [I]Lit., *spoke with my heart, saying* [II]Lit., *heart* [III]Lit., *an abundance* [a]1Kin. 3:12; 4:30; 10:23; Eccl. 2:9
17 [I]Lit., *heart* [a]Eccl. 1:13; 7:25 [b]Eccl. 2:12; 7:25 [c]Eccl. 1:14; 2:11, 17, 28; 4:4, 6, 16; 6:9
18 [a]Eccl. 2:23; 12:12

1 [I]Lit., *in my heart* [II]Lit., *consider with goodness* [a]Eccl. 7:4; 8:15
2 [a]Prov. 14:13; Eccl. 7:3, 6
3 [I]Lit., *heart* [II]Lit., *which they do* [III]Lit., *days* [a]Judg. 9:13; Ps. 104:15; Eccl. 10:19 [b]Eccl. 7:25 [c]Eccl. 2:24; 3:12, 13; 5:18; 6:12; 8:15; 12:13
4 [a]1Kin. 7:1-12 [b]Song 8:11
5 [a]Song 4:16; 5:1 [b]Neh. 2:8
6 [a]Neh. 2:14; 3:15, 16
7 [I]Lit., *sons of the house* [a]Gen. 14:14; 15:3 [b]1Kin. 4:23
8 [a]1Kin. 9:28; 10:10, 14, 21 [b]2Sam. 19:35
9 [a]1Chr. 29:25; Eccl. 1:16
10 [a]Eccl. 6:2 [b]Eccl. 3:22; 5:18; 9:9
11 [I]Lit., *labored to do* [II]Or, *futility, and so throughout the ch.* [a]Eccl. 1:14; 2:22, 23

The Futility of Pleasure and Possessions

2 I said[559] [I]to myself,[3820] "Come now,
I will test[5254] you with [a]pleasure.[2896]
So [II]enjoy[7200] yourself." And behold, it
too was futility.
2 [a]I said of laughter, "It is madness,"[1984] and of pleasure, "What
does[6213] it accomplish?"
3 I explored with my [I]mind *how* to
[a]stimulate my body with wine while my
[I]mind was guiding[5090] *me* wisely,[2451] and
how to take hold of [b]folly, until I could
see [c]what good[2896] there is for the
sons[1121] of men[120] [II]to do[6213] under
heaven[8064] the few [III]years[3117] of their
lives.[2416]
4 I enlarged my works: I [a]built
houses[1004] for myself, I planted [b]vine-
yards for myself;
5 I made[6213] [a]gardens and [b]parks for
myself, and I planted in them all kinds
of fruit trees;
6 I made [a]ponds of water for myself
from which to irrigate a forest of growing
trees.
7 I bought male and female slaves,
and I had [Ia]homeborn[1004] slaves. Also
I possessed flocks and [b]herds larger
than all who preceded me in Jerusalem.
8 Also, I collected[3664] for myself silver and [a]gold, and the treasure[5459] of
kings[4428] and provinces. I provided for
myself [b]male and female singers[7891] and
the pleasures of men—many concubines.
9 Then I became [a]great and increased more than all who preceded me
in Jerusalem. My wisdom also stood by
me.
10 And [a]all that my eyes desired I
did not refuse them. I did not withhold
my heart from any pleasure, for my
heart was pleased because of all my labor
and this was my [b]reward for all my
labor.[5999]
11 Thus I considered all my activities which my hands[3027] had done and
the labor which I had [I]exerted, and behold all was [IIa]vanity and striving[7469] afte

wind[7307] and there was [b]no profit under the sun.

Wisdom Excels Folly

12 So I turned to [a]consider[7200] wisdom, madness and folly, for what *will* the man[120] *do* who will come after the king[4428] *except* [b]what has already been done?

13 And I saw[7200] that [a]wisdom excels folly as light[216] excels darkness.[2822]

14 The wise[2450] man's eyes are in his head,[7218] but the [a]fool walks in darkness. And yet I know[3045] that [b]one fate befalls them both.

15 Then I said [I]to myself, "[a]As is the fate of the fool, it will also befall me. [b]Why then have I been extremely wise?"[2449] So [II]I said[1696] to myself, "This too is vanity."

16 For there is [a]no [I]lasting[5769] remembrance[2146] of the wise man *as* with the fool, inasmuch as *in* the coming days all will be forgotten. And [b]how the wise man and the fool alike die![4191]

17 So I [a]hated[8130] life, for the work which had been done under the sun was [I]grievous[7451] to me; because everything is futility and striving after wind.

The Futility of Labor

18 Thus I hated [a]all the fruit of my labor for which I had labored[6001] under the sun, for I must [b]leave it to the man who will come after me.

19 And who knows whether he will be a wise man or [a]a fool? Yet he will have [I]control[7980] over all the fruit of my labor for which I have labored by acting wisely under the sun. This too is [b]vanity.

20 Therefore I [I]completely despaired[2976] of all the fruit of my labor for which I had labored under the sun.

21 When there is a man who has labored with wisdom, knowledge[1847] and [a]skill, then he [b]gives his [I]legacy to one who has not labored with them. This too is vanity and a great evil.[7451]

22 For what does a man get in [a]all his labor and in [I]his striving[7475] with which he labors[6001] under the sun?

23 Because all his days his task is painful and [a]grievous;[3708] even at night[3915] his [I]mind [b]does not rest. This too is vanity.

24 There is [a]nothing better[2896] for a man *than* to eat and drink and [I]tell himself[5315] that his labor is good. This also I have seen, that it is [b]from the hand[3027] of God.[430]

25 For who can eat and who can have enjoyment without [I]Him?

26 For to a person who is good in His sight [a]He has given wisdom and knowledge and joy, while to the sinner[2398] He has given the task of gathering[622] and collecting[3664] so that he may [b]give to one who is good in God's sight. This too is [c]vanity and striving[7469] after wind.

A Time for Everything

3 There is an appointed time[2165] for everything. And there is a [a]time[6256] for every [I]event[2656] under heaven—[8064]

2 A time to give birth, and a
[a]time to die;[4191]
A time to plant, and a time to
uproot what is planted.

3 A [a]time to kill,[2026] and a time
to heal;
A time to tear down, and a time
to build up.

4 A time to [a]weep, and a time to
[b]laugh;
A time to mourn, and a time to
[c]dance.

5 A time to throw stones, and
a time to gather[3664]
stones;
A time to embrace, and a time
to shun embracing.

6 A time to search, and a time
to give up as lost;
A time to keep,[8104] and a time
to throw away.

7 A time to tear apart,[7167] and a
time to sew together;
A time to [a]be silent, and a time
to speak.[1696]

---

11 [b]Eccl. 1:3; 3:9; 5:16
12 [a]Eccl. 1:17 [b]Eccl. 1:9, 10; 3:15
13 [a]Eccl. 7:11, 12, 19; 9:18; 10:10
14 [a]1John 2:11 [b]Ps. 49:10; Eccl. 3:19; 6:6; 7:2; 9:2,3
15 [I]Lit., *in my heart* [II]Lit., *I spoke in my heart* [a]Eccl. 2:16 [b]Eccl. 6:8, 11
16 [I]Lit., *forever* [a]Eccl. 1:11; 9:5 [b]Eccl. 2:14
17 [I]Lit., *evil* [a]Eccl. 4:2, 3
18 [a]Eccl. 1:3; 2:11 [b]Ps. 39:6; 49:10
19 [I]Lit., *dominion* [a]1Kin. 12:13 [b]1Tim. 6:10
20 [I]Lit., *turned aside my heart to despair*
21 [I]Lit., *share* [a]Eccl. 4:4 [b]Eccl. 2:18
22 [I]Lit., *the striving of his heart* [a]Eccl. 1:3; 2:11
23 [I]Lit., *heart* [a]Job 5:7; 14:1; Eccl. 1:18; 5:17 [b]Ps. 127:2
24 [I]Lit., *cause his soul to see good in his labor* [a]Eccl. 2:3; 3:12, 13, 22; 5:18; 6:12; 8:15; 9:7; Is. 56:12; Luke 12:19; 1Cor. 15:32; 1Tim. 6:17 [b]Eccl. 3:13
25 [I]So Gr.; Heb., *me*
26 [a]Job 32:8; Prov. 2:6 [b]Job 27:16, 17; Prov. 13:22 [c]Eccl. 1:14

1 [I]Lit., *delight* [a]Eccl. 3:17; 8:6
2 [a]Job 14:5; Heb. 9:27
3 [a]Gen. 9:6; 1Sam. 2:6; Hos. 6:1, 2
4 [a]Rom. 12:15 [b]Ps. 126:2 [c]Ex. 15:20
7 [a]Amos 5:13

8 A time to love,[157] and a time to [a]hate;[8130]
A time for war, and a time for peace.
9 [a]What profit is there to the worker[6213] from that in which he toils?[6001]
10 I have seen[7200] the [a]task which God[430] has given the sons[1121] of men[120] with which to occupy themselves.

God Set Eternity in the Heart of Man

11 He has [a]made everything [I]appropriate in its time. He has also set eternity[5769] in their heart,[3820] [II]yet so that man[120] [b]will not find out the work which God has done[6213] from the beginning[7218] even to the end.
12 I know[3045] that there is [a]nothing better for them than to rejoice and to do[6213] good in one's lifetime;[2416]
13 moreover, that every man who eats and drinks sees[7200] good in all his labor—[5999] it is the [a]gift of God.
14 I know that everything God does[6213] will remain forever;[5769] there is nothing to add to it and there is nothing to take from it, for God has *so* worked that men should [Ia]fear[3372] Him.
15 That [a]which is has been already, and that which will be has already been, for God seeks what has passed by.
16 Furthermore, I have seen[7200] under the sun *that* in the place of justice[4941] there is [a]wickedness,[7562] and in the place of righteousness[6664] there is wickedness.[7562]
17 I said[559] [I]to myself, "[a]God will judge[8199] both the righteous[6662] man and the wicked[7563] man," for a [b]time for every [II]matter and for every deed is there.
18 I said [I]to myself concerning the sons of men, "God has surely tested[1305] them in order for them to see that they are but [a]beasts."
19 [a]For the fate of the sons of men and the fate of beasts [I]is the same. As one dies so dies[4194] the other; indeed, they all have the same breath[7307] and there is no advantage for man over beast, for all is [II]vanity.
20 All go to the same place. All came from the [a]dust[6083] and all return[7725] to the dust.
21 Who knows that the [a]breath[7307] of man ascends upward and the breath of the beast descends downward to the earth?[776]
22 And I have seen[7200] that [a]nothing is better[2896] than that man should be happy in his activities, for that is his lot. For who will bring him to see [b]what will occur after him?

The Evils of Oppression

4 Then I looked again[7200] at all the acts of [a]oppression which were being done under the sun. And behold *I saw* the tears of the oppressed and *that* they had [b]no one to comfort[5162] *them;* and on the side[3027] of their oppressors was power, but they had no one to comfort *them.*
2 So [a]I congratulated[7623] the dead[4191] who are already dead more than the living[2416] who are still living.[2416]
3 But [a]better[2896] *off* than both of them is the one who has never existed, who has never seen[7200] the evil[7451] activity that is done under the sun.
4 And I have seen that every labor[5999] and every [a]skill which is done is *the result of* rivalry[7068] between a man[376] and his neighbor.[7453] This too is [Ib]vanity and striving[7465] after wind.[7307]
5 The fool [a]folds his hands[3027] and [b]consumes his own flesh.[1320]
6 One hand full of rest is [a]better than two fists full of labor and striving after wind.
7 Then I looked[7200] again at vanity under the sun.
8 There was a certain man without a [I]dependent, having neither a son[1121] nor a brother,[251] yet there was no end to all his labor.[5999] Indeed, [a]his eyes were not satisfied with riches *and he never asked,* "And [b]for whom am I laboring[6001] and depriving myself[5315] of

8 [a]Ps. 101:3; Prov. 13:5
9 [a]Eccl. 1:3; 2:11; 5:16
10 [a]Eccl. 1:13; 2:26
11 [I]Lit., *beautiful* [II]Or, *without which man* [a]Gen. 1:31 [b]Job 5:9; Eccl. 7:23; 8:17; Rom. 11:33
12 [a]Eccl. 2:24
13 [a]Eccl. 2:24; 5:19
14 [I]Or, *be in awe before Him* [a]Eccl. 5:7; 7:18; 8:12, 13; 12:13
15 [a]Eccl. 1:9; 6:10
16 [a]Eccl. 4:1; 5:8; 8:9
17 [I]Lit., *in my heart* [II]Or, *delight* [a]Gen. 18:25; Ps. 96:13; 98:9; Eccl. 11:9; Matt. 16:27; Rom. 2:6-10; 2Thess. 1:6-9 [b]Eccl. 3:1; 8:6
18 [I]Lit., *in my heart* [a]Ps. 49:12, 20; 73:22
19 [I]Lit., *and they have one fate* [II]Or, *futility* [a]Ps. 49:12; Eccl. 9:12
20 [a]Gen. 3:19; Ps. 103:14; Eccl. 12:7
21 [a]Eccl. 12:7
22 [a]Eccl. 2:24 [b]Eccl. 2:18; 6:12; 8:7; 10:14

1 [a]Job 35:9; Ps. 12:5; Eccl. 3:16; 5:8; Is. 5:7 [b]Jer. 16:7; Lam. 1:9
2 [a]Job 3:11-26; Eccl. 2:17; 7:1
3 [a]Job 3:11-22; Eccl. 6:3; Luke 23:29
4 [I]Or, *futility,* and so throughout the ch. [a]Eccl. 2:21 [b]Eccl. 1:14
5 [a]Prov. 6:10; 24:33 [b]Is. 9:20
6 [a]Prov. 15:16, 17; 16:8
8 [I]Lit., *second* [a]Prov. 27:20; Eccl. 1:8; 5:10 [b]Eccl. 2:21

pleasure?"[2896] This too is vanity and it is a [c]grievous[7451] task.

9 Two are better than one because they have a good return for their labor.

10 For if [I]either of them falls, the one will lift up his companion. But woe to the one who falls[5307] when there is not [II]another to lift him up.

11 Furthermore, if two lie down together they [I]keep warm, but [a]how can one be warm *alone?*

12 And if [I]one can overpower him who is alone, two can resist him. A cord[2256] of three *strands* is not quickly torn apart.

13 A [a]poor, yet wise[2450] lad is better than an old[2205] and foolish king[4428] who no longer knows *how* to receive [I]instruction.[2094]

14 For he has come [a]out of prison to become king,[4427] even though he was born poor in his kingdom.[4438]

15 I have seen all the living under the sun throng to the side of the second lad who [I]replaces him.

16 There is no end to all the people,[5971] to all who were before them, and even the ones who will come later will not be happy with him, for this too is [a]vanity and striving[7475] after wind.

Your Attitude Toward God

5 [I][a]Guard[8104] your steps as you go to the house[1004] of God,[430] and draw near to listen[8085] rather than to offer the [b]sacrifice[2077] of fools; for they do not know[3045] they are doing[6213] evil.[7451]

2 [I]Do not be [a]hasty[926] [II]in word[6310] or [III]impulsive in thought[3820] to bring up a matter[1697] in the presence of God. For God is in heaven[8064] and you are on the earth;[776] therefore let your [b]words[1697] be few.

3 For the dream comes through much [I]effort, and the voice of a [a]fool through many words.

4 When you [a]make a vow[5087] to God, do not be late in paying it, for *He takes* no delight[2656] in fools. [b]Pay what you vow![5087]

5 It is [a]better[2896] that you should not vow[5087] than that you should vow and not pay.

6 Do not let your [I]speech cause [II]you to sin[2398] and do not say[559] in the presence of the messenger[4397] *of God* that it was a [a]mistake.[7684] Why should God be angry[7107] on account of your voice and destroy[2254] the work of your hands?[3027]

7 For in many dreams and in many words there is [I]emptiness. Rather, [II][a]fear[3372] God.

8 If you see [a]oppression of the poor and [b]denial of justice[4941] and righteousness[6664] in the province, do not be [c]shocked at the [I]sight, for one [II]official watches[8104] over another [II]official, and there are higher [III]officials over them.

9 After all, a king[4428] who cultivates the field is an advantage[5647] to the land.[7704]

The Folly of Riches

10 [a]He who loves[157] money will not be satisfied with money, nor he who loves abundance *with its* income. This too is [I]vanity.

11 [a]When good things increase, those who consume them increase. So what is the advantage[3788] to their owners[1167] except to [I]look on?[7200]

12 The sleep of the working[5647] man is [a]pleasant, whether he eats little or much. But the [I]full stomach of the rich man does not allow him to sleep.

13 There is a grievous evil *which* I have seen[7200] under the sun: [a]riches being [I]hoarded[8104] by their owner to his hurt.[7451]

14 When those riches were lost[6] through [I]a bad investment and he had fathered a son,[1121] then there was nothing [II]to support him.[3027]

15 [a]As he had come naked[6174] from his mother's[517] womb,[990] so will he return[7725] as he came. He will [b]take[5375] nothing from the fruit of his labor[5999] that he can carry in his hand.

16 And this also is a grievous evil—exactly as a man [I]is born, thus will he

---

8 [c]Eccl. 1:13
10 [I]Lit., *they fall* [II]Lit., *a second*
11 [I]Lit., *have warmth* [a]1Kin. 1:1-4
12 [I]Lit., *he*
13 [I]Or, *warning* [a]Eccl. 7:19; 9:15
14 [a]Gen. 41:14, 41-43
15 [I]Lit., *stands in his stead*
16 [a]Eccl. 1:14

1 [I]Ch. 4:17 in Heb. [a]Ex. 3:5; 30:18-20; Is. 1:12 [b]1Sam. 15:22; Prov. 15:8; 21:27
2 [I]Ch. 5:1 in Heb. [II]Lit., *with your mouth* [III]Lit., *hurry your heart* [a]Prov. 20:25 [b]Prov. 10:19; Matt. 6:7
3 [I]Lit., *task* [a]Job 11:2; Prov. 15:2; Eccl. 10:14
4 [a]Num. 30:2; Ps. 50:14; 76:11 [b]Ps. 66:13, 14
5 [a]Prov. 20:25; Acts 5:4
6 [I]Lit., *mouth* [II]Lit., *your body* [a]Lev. 4:2, 22; Num. 15:25
7 [I]Lit., *vanity* [II]Or, *revere* [a]Eccl. 3:14; 7:18; 8:12, 13; 12:13
8 [I]Lit., *delight* [II]Lit., *high one* [III]Lit., *ones* [a]Eccl. 4:1 [b]Ezek. 18:18 [c]1Pet. 4:12
10 [I]Or, *futility* [a]Eccl. 1:8; 2:10, 11; 4:8
11 [I]Lit., *see with their eyes* [a]Eccl. 2:9
12 [I]Lit., *satiety* [a]Prov. 3:24
13 [I]Lit., *guarded* [a]Eccl. 6:2
14 [I]Lit., *an evil task* [II]Lit., *in his hand*
15 [a]Job 1:21 [b]Ps. 49:17; 1Tim. 6:7
16 [I]Lit., *comes*

[II]die. So, [a]what is the advantage to him
who [b]toils for the wind?[7307]
17 Throughout his life[3117] [a]*he* also
eats in darkness[2822] with [b]great vexation,[3707] sickness and anger.[7110]
18 Here is what I have seen to be
[a]good[2896] and [I]fitting:[3303] to eat, to drink
and [II]enjoy[7200] oneself in all one's labor
in which he toils under the sun *during*
the few [III]years of his life[2416] which God
has given him; for this is his [IV][b]reward.
19 Furthermore, as for every
man[120] to whom [a]God has given riches
and wealth, He has also [b]empowered[7980]
him to eat from them and to receive
his [I]reward and rejoice in his labor; this
is the [c]gift of God.
20 For he will not often [I]consider[2142]
the [II]years of his life, because [a]God
keeps [III]him occupied with the gladness
of his heart.

The Futility of Life

6 There is an [a]evil[7451] which I have
seen[7200] under the sun and it is prevalent [I]among men—[120]
2 a man[376] to whom God[430] has
[a]given riches and wealth and honor[3519]
so that his soul[5315] [b]lacks nothing of all
that he desires,[183] but God has not empowered[7980] him to eat from them, for
a foreigner [I]enjoys them. This is
[II]vanity and a severe affliction.[2483]
3 If a man fathers a hundred *children*
and lives[2421] many years, however many
[I]they be, but his soul is not satisfied
with good[2896] things, and he does not
even have a *proper* [a]burial,[6900] *then* I
say,[559] "Better[2896] [b]the miscarriage[5309]
than he,
4 for it comes in futility and goes
into obscurity;[2822] and its name is
covered[3680] in obscurity.
5 "It never sees the sun and it never
knows[3045] *anything;* [I]it is better off than
he.
6 "Even if the *other* man lives a thousand years twice and does not [I]enjoy
good things—[a]do not all go to one
place?"

16 [II]Lit., *go* [a]Eccl. 1:3; 2:11; 3:9 [b]Prov. 11:29
17 [a]Ps. 127:2 [b]Eccl. 2:23
18 [I]Lit., *beautiful* [II]Lit., *see good* [III]Or, *days* [IV]Or, *share* [a]Eccl. 2:24 [b]Eccl. 2:10
19 [I]Or, *share* [a]2Chr. 1:12; Eccl. 6:2 [b]Eccl. 6:2 [c]Eccl. 3:13
20 [I]Lit., *remember* [II]Or, *days* [III]So with Gr. [a]Ex. 23:25

1 [I]Lit., *upon* [a]Eccl. 5:13
2 [I]Lit., *eats from them* [II]Or, *futility* [a]1Kin. 3:13 [b]Ps. 17:14; 73:7; Eccl. 2:10
3 [I]Lit., *the days of his years* [a]Is. 14:20; Jer. 8:2; 22:19 [b]Job 3:16; Eccl. 4:3
5 [I]Lit., *more rest has this one than that*
6 [I]Lit., *see* [a]Eccl. 2:14
7 [I]Lit., *soul* [II]Lit., *filled* [a]Prov. 16:26
8 [a]Eccl. 2:15
9 [I]Lit., *goes after* [a]Eccl. 11:9 [b]Eccl. 1:14
10 [a]Eccl. 1:9; 3:15 [b]Job 9:32; 40:2; Prov. 21:30; Is. 45:9
12 [I]Lit., *days* [II]Lit., *do* [a]Eccl. 3:22

1 [a]Prov. 22:1 [b]Eccl. 4:2; 7:8
2 [I]I.e., death [II]Lit., *gives* [III]Lit., *his heart* [a]Eccl. 2:14, 16; 3:19, 20; 6:6; 9:2, 3 [b]Ps. 90:12
3 [a]Eccl. 2:2 [b]2Cor. 7:10
4 [I]Lit., *heart*
5 [a]Ps. 141:5; Prov. 6:23; 13:18; 15:31, 32; 25:12; Eccl. 9:17

7 [a]All a man's[120] labor[5999] is for his
mouth[6310] and yet the [I]appetite[5315] is not
[II]satisfied.
8 For [a]what advantage does the
wise[2450] man have over the fool? What
advantage does the poor man have,
knowing *how* to walk before the
living?[2416]
9 What the eyes [a]see is better
than what the soul [I]desires.[5315] This
too is [b]futility and a striving[7469] after
wind.[7307]
10 Whatever [a]exists has already
been named,[7121] and it is known what
man is; for he [b]cannot dispute[1777] with
him who is stronger than he is.
11 For there are many words[1697]
which increase futility. What *then* is the
advantage to a man?
12 For who knows what is good for
a man during *his* lifetime,[2416] *during* the
few [I]years of his futile life? He will
[II]spend[6213] them like a shadow. For who
can tell[5046] a man [a]what will be after
him under the sun?

Wisdom and Folly Contrasted

7 A [a]good[2896] name is better[2896] than
a good[2896] ointment,[8081]
And the [b]day[3117] of *one's*
death[4194] is better than the
day of one's birth.
2 It is better to go to a house[1004]
of mourning
Than to go to a house of
feasting,[4960]
Because [I]that is the [a]end of
every man,[120]
And the living[2416] [II][b]takes *it* to
[III]heart.[3820]
3 [a]Sorrow[3708] is better than
laughter,
For [b]when a face is sad[7455] a
heart may be happy.[3190]
4 The [I]mind of the wise[2450] is in
the house of mourning,
While the [I]mind of fools is in the
house of pleasure.
5 It is better to [a]listen to[8085] the
rebuke[1606] of a wise man

Than for one[376] to listen to the
song[7892] of fools.
6 For as the [I]crackling of
[a]thorn bushes under a pot,
So is the [b]laughter of the
fool,
And this too is futility.
7 For [a]oppression makes a wise
man mad,[1984]
And a [b]bribe [I]corrupts[6] the
heart.
8 The [a]end[319] of a matter[1697] is
better than its beginning;[7225]
[b]Patience[750] of spirit[7307] is
better than haughtiness of
spirit.
9 Do not be [Ia]eager[926] in your heart
to be angry,[3707]
For anger resides in the bosom
of fools.
10 Do not say,[559] "Why is it that
the former[7223] days[3117] were
better than these?"
For it is not from wisdom that
you ask[7592] about this.
11 Wisdom[2451] along with an
inheritance[5159] is good
And an [a]advantage to those who
see the sun.
12 For [a]wisdom is [I]protection *just*
as money is [I]protection.
But the advantage of
knowledge[1847] is that
[b]wisdom preserves the
lives[2421] of its possessors.
13 Consider[7200] the [a]work of
God,[430]
For who is [b]able to straighten
what He has bent?[5791]
14 [a]In the day of prosperity[2896] be
happy,[2896]
But [b]in the day of adversity[7451]
consider—
God has made the one as well
as the other

So that man[120] may [c]not discover
anything *that will be* after
him.

15 I have seen[7200] everything during my [Ia]lifetime of futility; there is [b]a righteous man who perishes[6] in his righteousness,[6664] and there is [c]a wicked[7563] man who prolongs[748] *his life* in his wickedness.[7451]

🔑16 Do not be excessively [a]righteous,[6662] and do not [b]be overly wise.[2449] Why should you ruin[8074] yourself?

17 Do not be excessively wicked, and do not be a fool. Why should you [a]die[4191] before your time?[6256]

18 It is good that you grasp one thing, and also not [I]let go of the other; for the one who [a]fears God comes forth with [II]both of them.

19 [a]Wisdom strengthens a wise man more than ten rulers[7989] who are in a city.

20 Indeed, [a]there is not a righteous man on earth[776] who *continually* does[6213] good and who never sins.[2398]

21 Also, do not [I]take seriously all words[1697] which are spoken,[1696] lest you hear your servant[5650] [a]cursing[7043] you.

22 For [I]you also have realized that you likewise have many times cursed[7043] others.

23 I tested[5254] all this with wisdom, *and* I said,[559] "I will be wise," [a]but it was far from me.

24 What has been is remote and [a]exceedingly [I]mysterious. [b]Who can discover it?

25 I [Ia]directed my [II]mind to know,[3045] to investigate, and to seek wisdom and an explanation, and to know the evil[7562] of folly[3689] and the foolishness of madness.

26 And I discovered more [a]bitter[4751]

6 [I]Lit., *voice* [a]Ps. 58:9; 118:12 [b]Eccl. 2:2
7 [I]Lit., *destroys* [a]Eccl. 4:1; 5:8 [b]Ex. 23:8; Deut. 16:19; Prov. 17:8, 23
8 [a]Eccl. 7:1 [b]Prov. 14:29; 16:32; Gal. 5:22; Eph. 4:2
9 [I]Lit., *hasty in your spirit* [a]Prov. 14:17; James 1:19
11 [a]Prov. 8:10, 11; Eccl. 2:13
12 [I]Lit., *in a shadow* [a]Eccl. 7:19; 9:18 [b]Prov. 3:18; 8:35
13 [a]Eccl. 3:11; 8:17 [b]Eccl. 1:15
14 [a]Deut. 26:11; Eccl. 3:22; 9:7; 11:9 [b]Deut. 8:5; Job 2:10 [c]Eccl. 3:22
15 [I]Lit., *days* [a]Eccl. 6:12; 9:9 [b]Eccl. 8:14 [c]Eccl. 8:12, 13
16 [a]Prov. 25:16; Phil. 3:6 [b]Rom. 12:3
17 [a]Job 22:16; Ps. 55:23; Prov. 10:27
18 [I]Lit., *rest your hand* [II]Lit., *all* [a]Eccl. 3:14; 5:7; 8:12, 13; 12:13
19 [a]Eccl. 7:12; 9:13-18
20 [a]1Kin. 8:46; 2Chr. 6:36; Ps. 143:2; Prov. 20:9; Rom. 3:23
21 [I]Lit., *give your heart to* [a]Prov. 30:10
22 [I]Lit., *your heart knows also*
23 [a]Eccl. 3:11; 8:17
24 [I]Lit., *deep* [a]Rom. 11:33 [b]Job 11:7; 37:23; Eccl. 8:17
25 [I]Lit., *turned about* [II]Lit., *heart* [a]Eccl. 1:15, 17; 10:13
26 [a]Prov. 5:4

🔑 **7:16** Is it posssible for one to be over-righteous? The phrase "excessively righteous" is very descriptive of religious presumption, of that self-made righteousness which would lay the greatest stress upon outward performances and would claim personal credit for results which the true believer recognizes to be the gift of divine grace alone. Pharisaism, with its hypocritical assumptions of superior virtue, its multitudinous observances, and its devotion to outward ceremonial form, forgetting weightier spiritual matters, was precisely this type of supercilious "righteousness." Cf. Lk. 18:9-14; Gal. 6:13; Phil. 3:2,3,9.

than death the woman802 whose heart
is [b]snares4685 and nets,2764 whose
hands3027 are chains. [c]One who is
pleasing2896 to God will escape4422 from
her, but [d]the sinner2398 will be captured
by her.
27 "Behold,7200 I have discovered
this," says559 the Preacher,6953 "*adding*
one thing to another to find an explanation,
28 which [I]I am still seeking but have
not found. I have found one man among
a thousand, but I have not found a
[a]woman among all these.
29 "Behold, I have found only this,
that [a]God made6213 men upright,3476
but they have sought out many devices."

Obey Rulers

8 Who is like the wise2450 man and
who knows the interpretation of a
matter?1697 A man's120 wisdom2451 [a]il-
lumines [I]him and causes his [b]stern face to
[II]beam.
2 I say, "Keep8104 the [I]command6310
of the king4428 because of the [a]oath7621
[II]before God.430
3 "Do not be in a hurry926 [Ia]to
leave him. Do not join in an evil7451
matter, for he will do6213 whatever he
pleases."
4 Since the word1697 of the king4428
is authoritative,7983 [a]who will say559 to
him, "What are you doing?"6213
5 He who [a]keeps8104 a *royal* com-
mand4687 [b]experiences no [I]trouble, for
a wise heart3820 knows3045 the proper
time6256 and procedure.4941
6 For [a]there is a proper time and
procedure for every delight,2656 when
a man's120 trouble is heavy upon
him.
7 If no one [a]knows what will happen,
who can tell5046 him when it will happen?
8 [a]No man has authority7989 to restrain the wind7307 with the wind, or
authority7983 over the day3117 of
death;4194 and there is no discharge in

26 [b]Prov. 7:23 [c]Prov. 6:23, 24 [d]Prov. 22:14
28 [I]Lit., *my soul still seeks* [a]1Kin. 11:3
29 [a]Gen. 1:27
1 [I]Lit., *his face* [II]Or, *change* [a]Ex. 34:29, 30 [b]Deut. 28:50
2 [I]Lit., *mouth* [II]Lit., *of* [a]Ex. 22:11; 2Sam. 21:7; Ezek. 17:18
3 [I]Lit., *to go out from his presence* [a]Eccl. 10:4
4 [a]Job 9:12; Dan. 4:35
5 [I]Lit., *evil thing* [a]Eccl. 12:13 [b]Prov. 12:21
6 [a]Eccl. 3:1, 17
7 [a]Eccl. 3:22; 6:12; 7:14; 9:12
8 [I]Lit., *its possessors* [a]Ps. 49:7 [b]Eccl. 8:13
9 [I]Lit., *heart* [a]Eccl. 4:1; 5:8; 7:7
10 [a]Eccl. 1:11; 2:16; 9:5, 15
11 [a]Ex. 34:6; Ps. 86:15; Rom. 2:4; 2Pet. 3:9 [b]Eccl. 9:3
12 [I]Lit., *before Him* [a]Eccl. 7:15 [b]Deut. 4:40; 12:25; Ps. 37:11; Prov. 1:33; Is. 3:10
13 [a]Eccl. 8:8; Is. 3:11 [b]Job 14:2; Eccl. 6:12
14 [I]Lit., *strikes* [a]Ps. 73:14; Eccl. 7:15 [b]Job 21:7; Ps. 73:3, 12; Jer. 12:1; Mal. 3:15
15 [I]Lit., *labor* [a]Eccl. 2:24; 3:12, 13; 5:18; 9:7
16 [I]Lit., *see no sleep in his eyes* [a]Eccl. 1:13, 14 [b]Eccl. 2:23
17 [a]Eccl. 3:11

the time of war, and [b]evil7562 will not
deliver [I]those who practice it.
9 All this I have seen and applied
my [I]mind to every deed that has been
done under the sun wherein a man has
exercised [a]authority4980 over *another*
man to his hurt.
10 So then, I have seen7200 the
wicked7563 buried,6912 those who used
to go in and out from the holy6918 place,
and they are [a]*soon* forgotten in the
city where they did thus. This too is
futility.
11 Because the [a]sentence6599
against an evil deed is not executed6213
quickly, therefore [b]the hearts of the
sons1121 of men120 among them are given
fully to do6213 evil.
12 Although a sinner2398 does evil
a hundred *times* and may [a]lengthen748
his *life,* still I know3045 that it will be
[b]well for those who fear God, who
fear3372 [I]Him openly.
13 But it will [a]not be well for the
evil man and he will not lengthen748 his
days3117 like a [b]shadow, because he does
not fear God.
14 There is futility which is done
on the earth,776 that is, there are
[a]righteous men to whom it [I]happens5060
according to the deeds of the wicked.
On the other hand, there are [b]evil men
to whom it [I]happens according to the
deeds of the righteous.6662 I say559 that
this too is futility.
15 So I commended7623 pleasure,
for there is nothing good2896 for [a]a man
under the sun except to eat and to drink
and to be merry, and this will stand by
him in his [I]toils5999 *throughout* the days
of his life which God has given him under
the sun.
16 When I [a]gave my heart to know
wisdom and to see the task which has
been done on the earth (even though
one should [Ib]never sleep day or
night),3915
17 and I saw7200 every work of God,
I concluded that [a]man cannot discover
the work which has been done under
the sun. Even though man should seek
laboriously, he will not discover; and

[b]though the wise man should say, "I know," he cannot discover.

Men Are in the Hand of God

9 For I have taken all this to my heart[3820] and explain [I]it that righteous[6662] men, wise[2450] men, and their deeds are [a]in the hand[3027] of God.[430] [b]Man[120] does not know whether *it will be* [c]love[160] or hatred;[8135] anything [II]awaits him.

2 [a]It is the same for all. There is [b]one fate for the righteous and for the wicked;[7563] for the good,[2896] for the clean,[2889] and for the unclean;[2931] for the man who offers a sacrifice[2076] and for the one who does not sacrifice. As the good man is, so is the sinner;[2398] as the swearer[7650] is, so is the one who [I]is afraid to swear.[7621]

3 This is an evil[7451] in all that is done under the sun, that there is [a]one fate for all men. Furthermore, [b]the hearts of the sons[1121] of men[120] are full of evil, and [c]insanity is in their hearts[3824] throughout their lives.[2416] Afterwards they *go* to the dead.[4191]

4 For whoever is joined with all the living,[2416] there is hope;[986] surely a live dog is better[2896] than a dead lion.

5 For the living know[3045] they will die;[4191] but the dead [a]do not know anything, nor have they any longer a reward, for their [b]memory[2143] is forgotten.

6 Indeed their love, their hate, and their zeal[7068] have already perished,[6] and they will no longer have a [a]share in all that is done under the sun.

7 Go *then,* [a]eat your bread in happiness, and drink your wine with a cheerful[2896] heart; for God has already approved[7521] your works.

8 Let your [a]clothes be white all the time, and let not [b]oil[8081] be lacking on your head.[7218]

9 Enjoy[7200] life with the woman[802] whom you love[157] all the days[3117] of your [I][a]fleeting life which He has given to you under the sun[II]; for this is your [b]reward in life, and in your toil[5999] in which you have labored[6001] under the sun.

Whatever Your Hand Finds to Do

10 Whatever your hand finds to do,[6213] verily, [a]do *it* with all your might; for there is no [b]activity or planning[1847] or knowledge or wisdom[2451] in [c]Sheol[7585] where you are going.

11 I again[7725] saw[7200] under the sun that the [a]race is not to the swift, and the [b]battle is not to the warriors, and neither is bread to the wise, nor [c]wealth to the discerning,[995] nor favor[2580] to men of ability;[3045] for time[6256] and [d]chance overtake them all.

12 Moreover, man does not [a]know his time: like fish[1709] caught in a treacherous net, and [b]birds trapped in a snare,[6341] so the sons of men are [c]ensnared[3369] at an evil time when it [d]suddenly falls[5307] on them.

13 Also this I came to see[7200] as wisdom under the sun, and [I]it impressed me.

14 There [a]was a small city with few men[582] in it and a great king[4428] came to it, surrounded it, and constructed large siegeworks[4685] against it.

15 But there was found in it a [a]poor wise man[376] and he [I]delivered the city [b]by his wisdom. Yet [c]no one remembered[2142] that poor man.

16 So I said,[559] "[a]Wisdom is better than strength." But the wisdom of the poor man is despised and his words[1697] are not heeded.[8085]

17 The [a]words of the wise heard in quietness are *better* than the shouting of a ruler[4910] among fools.

18 [a]Wisdom is better than weapons of war, but [b]one sinner destroys[6] much good.

A Little Foolishness

10 Dead[4194] flies make a [a]perfumer's[7543] oil[8081] stink, so a little fool-

17 [b]Ps. 73:16; Eccl. 7:23; Rom. 11:33

1 [I]Lit., *all this* [II]Lit., *is before them* [a]Deut. 33:3; Job 12:10; Ps. 119:109 [b]Eccl. 10:14 [c]Eccl. 9:6

2 [I]Lit., *fears an oath* [a]Job 9:22; Eccl. 9:11 [b]Eccl. 2:14; 3:19; 6:6; 7:2

3 [a]Eccl. 9:2; Jer. 17:10 [b]Eccl. 8:11 [c]Eccl. 1:17

5 [a]Job 14:21 [b]Ps. 88:12; Eccl. 1:11; 2:16; 8:10; Is. 26:14

6 [a]Eccl. 2:10; 3:22

7 [a]Eccl. 2:24; 8:15

8 [a]Rev. 3:4 [b]Ps. 23:5

9 [I]Lit., *life of vanity* [II]Heb. adds *all the days of your vanity* [a]Eccl. 6:12; 7:15 [b]Eccl. 2:10

10 [a]Eccl. 11:6; Rom. 12:11; Col. 3:23 [b]Eccl. 9:5 [c]Gen. 37:35; Job 21:13; Is. 38:10

11 [a]Amos 2:14, 15 [b]2Chr. 20:15; Ps. 76:5; Zech. 4:6 [c]Deut. 8:17, 18 [d]1Sam. 6:9

12 [a]Eccl. 8:7 [b]Prov. 7:23 [c]Prov. 29:6; Is. 24:18; Hos. 9:8 [d]Luke 21:34, 35

13 [I]Lit., *great it was to me*

14 [a]2Sam. 20:16-22

15 [I]Or, *might have delivered* [a]Eccl. 4:13 [b]2Sam. 20:22 [c]Eccl. 2:16; 8:10

16 [a]Prov. 21:22; Eccl. 7:12, 19

17 [a]Eccl. 7:5; 10:12

18 [a]Eccl. 9:16 [b]Josh. 7:1-26; 2Kin. 21:2-17

1 [a]Ex. 30:25

ishness is weightier than wisdom[2451] *and*
honor.[3519]
2 A wise[2450] man's heart[3820] *directs*
him toward the right, but the foolish
[a]man's heart *directs him* toward the
left.
3 Even when the fool walks along
the road[1870] his [I]sense[3820] is lacking, and
he [IIa]demonstrates[559] to everyone *that*
he is a fool.
4 If the ruler's [I]temper[7307] rises[5927]
against you, [a]do not abandon your position, because [b]composure allays great
offenses.
5 There is an evil[7451] I have seen[7200]
under the sun, like an error[7684] which
goes forth from the ruler—[7989]
6 [a]folly is set in many exalted
places while rich men sit in humble
places.
7 I have seen [a]slaves *riding* [b]on
horses and princes[8269] walking like
slaves on the land.[776]
8 [a]He who digs a pit[1475] may fall
into it, and a [b]serpent[5175] may bite him
who breaks through a wall.
9 He who quarries stones may be
hurt[6087] by them, and he who splits logs
may be endangered by them.
10 If the [I]axe is dull and he does
not sharpen[7043] *its* edge, then he must
[II]exert more strength.[2428] Wisdom has
the advantage of giving success.[3787]
11 If the serpent bites [Ia]before being
charmed,[3908] there is no profit for the
charmer.[1167,3956]
12 [a]Words[1697] from the mouth[6310] of
a wise man are gracious, while the
lips[8193] of a [b]fool consume[1104] him;
13 the beginning of [I]his talking is
folly, and the end[319] of [II]it is wicked[7451]
[a]madness.
14 Yet the [a]fool multiplies words.
No man[120] knows what will happen, and
who can tell[5046] him [b]what will come after
him?
15 The toil[5999] of [I]a fool *so* wearies
him that he does not *even* know how
to go to a city.
16 Woe to you, O land,[776] whose
[a]king[4428] is a lad and whose princes
[I]feast in the morning.
17 Blessed[835] are you, O land,
whose king is of nobility[2715] and whose
princes eat at the appropriate time—[6256]
for strength, and not for [a]drunken-
ness.[8358]
18 Through [a]indolence the rafters
sag, and through slackness the house[1004]
leaks.
19 *Men* prepare[6213] a meal for enjoyment, and [a]wine makes life merry, and
[b]money [I]is the answer to everything.
20 Furthermore, [a]in your bedchamber do not [b]curse[7043] a king, and in your
sleeping rooms do not curse a rich man,
for a bird of the heavens[8064] will carry
the sound, and the winged creature will
make the matter[1697] known.

Cast Your Bread on the Waters

11 Cast your bread on the surface
of the waters, for you [a]will find
it [I]after many days.[3117]
2 [a]Divide your portion to seven, or
even to eight, for you do not know[3045]
what [b]misfortune[7451] may occur on the
earth.[776]
3 If the clouds are full, they pour
out rain upon the earth; and whether a
tree falls toward the south or toward
the north, wherever the tree falls,[5307]
there it [I]lies.
4 He who watches[8104] the wind[7307]
will not sow and he who looks[7200] at
the clouds will not reap.
5 Just as you do not [a]know [I]the
path[1870] of the wind[7307] and [b]how
bones[6106] *are formed* in the womb[990] of
the [II]pregnant woman, so you do not
[c]know the activity of God[432] who
makes[6213] all things.
6 Sow your seed[2233] [a]in the morning,
and do not [I]be idle in the evening, for
you do not know whether [II]morning or
evening sowing will succeed,[3787] or
whether both of them alike will be
good.[2896]
7 The light[216] is pleasant,[2896] and
it is good for the eyes to [a]see[7200] the
sun.

2 [a]Matt. 6:33; Col. 3:1
3 [I]Lit., *heart* [II]Lit., *says* [a]Prov. 13:16; 18:2
4 [I]Lit., *spirit* [a]Eccl. 8:3 [b]1Sam. 25:24-33; Prov. 25:15
6 [a]Esth. 3:1, 5f.; Prov. 28:12; 29:2
7 [a]Prov. 19:10 [b]Esth. 6:8-10
8 [a]Ps. 7:15; Prov. 26:27 [b]Amos 5:19
10 [I]Lit., *iron* [II]Lit., *strengthen*
11 [I]Lit., *without enchantment* [a]Ps. 58:4, 5; Jer. 8:17
12 [a]Prov. 10:32; 22:11; Luke 4:22 [b]Prov. 10:14; 18:7; Eccl. 4:5
13 [I]Lit., *the words of his mouth* [II]Lit., *his mouth* [a]Eccl. 7:25
14 [a]Prov. 15:2; Eccl. 5:3 [b]Eccl. 3:22; 6:12; 7:14; 8:7
15 [I]Lit., *fools*
16 [I]Lit., *eat* [a]Is. 3:4, 12
17 [a]Prov. 31:4; Is. 5:11
18 [a]Prov. 24:30-34
19 [I]Lit., *answers all* [a]Judg. 9:13; Ps. 104:15; Eccl. 2:3 [b]Eccl. 7:12
20 [a]2Kin. 6:12; Luke 12:3 [b]Ex. 22:28; Acts 23:5

1 [I]Lit., *in, within* [a]Deut. 15:10; Prov. 19:17; Matt. 10:42; Gal. 6:9; Heb. 6:10
2 [a]Ps. 112:9; Matt. 5:42; Luke 6:30; 1Tim. 6:18, 19 [b]Eccl. 11:8; 12:1
3 [I]Lit., *is*
5 [I]Or, with many mss., *how the spirit enters the bones in the womb* [II]Lit., *full* [a]John 3:8 [b]Ps. 139:13-16 [c]Eccl. 1:13; 3:10, 11; 8:17
6 [I]Lit., *let down your hand* [II]Lit., *this or that* [a]Eccl. 9:10
7 [a]Eccl. 6:5; 7:11

8 Indeed, if a man[120] should live[2421] many years, let him [a]rejoice in them all, and let him remember[2142] the [b]days of darkness,[2822] for they shall be many. Everything that is to come *will be* futility.

9 Rejoice, young man, during your childhood, and let your heart[3820] be pleasant[2895] during the days of young manhood. And follow the [I]impulses[1870] of your heart and the [IIa]desires of your eyes. Yet know[3045] that [b]God will bring you to judgment[4941] for all these things.

10 So, remove vexation[3708] from your heart and put away[5674] [Ia]pain from your body,[1320] because childhood and the prime of life are fleeting.

Remember God in Your Youth

12 [a]Remember[2142] also your Creator[1254] in the days[3117] of your youth, before the [b]evil[7451] days come and the years draw near[5060] when you will say,[559] "I have no delight in them";

2 before the [a]sun, the light,[216] the moon, and the stars are darkened,[2821] and clouds return[7725] after the rain;

3 in the day[3117] that the watchmen[8104] of the house[1004] tremble,[2111] and mighty men[582] [a]stoop,[5791] the grinding ones stand idle because they are few, and [b]those who look through[7200] [I]windows grow dim;

4 and the doors on the street are shut as the [a]sound of the grinding mill is low, and one will arise at the sound of the bird, and all the [b]daughters of song[7892] will [I]sing softly.

5 Furthermore, [I]men are afraid[3372] of a high place and of terrors[2489] on the road;[1870] the almond tree blossoms,[5006] the grasshopper drags himself along, and the caperberry is ineffective.[6565] For man[120] goes to his eternal[5769] [a]home[1004] while [b]mourners go about in the street.

6 *Remember Him* before the silver cord is [I]broken[7665] and the [a]golden bowl is crushed, the pitcher by the well is shattered and the wheel[1534] at the cistern[953] is crushed;

7 then the [a]dust[6083] will return to the earth[776] as it was, and the [Ib]spirit[7307] will return to [c]God[430] who gave it.

8 "[a]Vanity of vanities," says[559] the Preacher,[6953] "all is vanity!"

Purpose of the Preacher

9 In addition to being a wise[2450] man, the Preacher also taught[3925] the people[5971] knowledge;[1847] and he pondered,[238] searched out and arranged [a]many proverbs.

10 The Preacher sought to find [a]delightful[2656] words[1697] and to write [b]words of truth[571] correctly.

11 The [a]words of wise men are like [b]goads,[1861] and masters[1167] of *these* collections[627] are like [I]well-driven [c]nails; they are given by one Shepherd.

12 But beyond this, my son,[1121] be warned:[2094] the [I]writing of [a]many books is endless, and excessive [b]devotion *to books* is wearying to the body.[1320]

8 [a]Eccl. 9:7 [b]Eccl. 12:1
9 [I]Lit., *ways* [II]Lit., *sights* [a]Num. 15:39; Job 31:7; Eccl. 2:10 [b]Eccl. 3:17; 12:14; Rom. 14:10
10 [I]Lit., *evil* [a]2Cor. 7:1; 2Tim. 2:22

1 [a]Deut. 8:18; Neh. 4:14; Ps. 63:6; 119:55 [b]Eccl. 11:8
2 [a]Is. 5:30; 13:10; Ezek. 32:7, 8; Joel 3:15; Matt. 24:29
3 [I]Or, *holes* [a]Ps. 35:14; 38:6 [b]Gen. 27:1; 48:10; 1Sam. 3:2
4 [I]Lit., *be brought low* [a]Jer. 25:10; Rev. 18:22 [b]2Sam. 19:35
5 [I]Lit., *they* [a]Job 17:13; 30:23 [b]Gen. 50:10; Jer. 9:17
6 [I]So with Gr.; Heb., *removed* [a]Zech. 4:2, 3
7 [I]Or, *breath* [a]Gen. 3:19; Job 34:15; Ps. 104:29; Eccl. 3:20 [b]Job 34:14; Eccl. 3:21; Luke 23:46; Acts 7:59 [c]Num. 16:22; 27:16; Is. 57:16; Zech. 12:1
8 [a]Eccl. 1:2
9 [a]1Kin. 4:32
10 [a]Prov. 10:32 [b]Prov. 22:20, 21
11 [I]Lit., *planted* [a]Prov. 1:6; 22:17; Eccl. 7:5; 10:12 [b]Acts 2:37 [c]Ezra 9:8; Is. 22:23
12 [I]Lit., *making* [a]1Kin. 4:32 [b]Eccl. 1:18

12:7 From the first mention of the tree of life in paradise, the eating of which would make one immortal, the idea of a continued existence has a place in Jewish theology. Many passages could be quoted to show this belief. See the Mosaic injunction against necromancy, i.e., invoking the dead (Deut. 18:9-12; cf. I Sam. 28:7,8; Ps. 106:28). Moses wrote that God "took" Enoch (Gen. 5:24), because he had lived a pious life. David spoke of his child as being in another life when he said, "I shall go to him, but he will not return to me" (II Sam. 12:23). Job said that he would see God for himself and not another (Job 19:26,27). Here Ecclesiastes echoes faithfully the theology of that day, the belief that there is an afterlife. Compare the passages in Psalms (17:15; 49:15; 73:24,26) which reflect expectations of reward and punishment after death. The ancient Jews did believe in a future life, but they had only blurred views on the subject before Jesus rose from the grave. He brought life and immortality to light (II Tim. 1:10).

🗝 13 The conclusion, when all has been heard,[8085] *is:* [a]fear[3372] God and [b]keep[8104] His commandments,[4687] because this *applies to* [c]every person.

14 For [a]God will bring every act to judgment,[4941] everything which is hidden, whether it is good or evil.

13 [a]Eccl. 3:14; 5:7; 7:18; 8:12 [b]Deut. 4:2; Eccl. 8:5 [c]Deut. 10:12; Mic. 6:8
14 [a]Eccl. 3:17; 11:9; Matt. 10:26; Rom. 2:16; 1Cor. 4:5

🗝 **12:13,14** In the printed Hebrew text, verse 13 begins with an enlarged Hebrew character, no doubt emphasizing the importance of this statement. The Preacher has taken us on a journey through all types of doubts and fears which man may encounter during a lifetime. His theme has been that all the things which now seem so important are utterly empty in the final analysis. In conclusion, here is the remedy for all the despondency that comes from observing human misery, the real answer which will remove all the perplexities—"*fear God and keep His commandments.*" Man has no other responsibility than this. A person does not want to be found before God in judgment, weighed down with the excess baggage of so many things which he thought were so important in life, but which will be utterly empty, worthless, and futile, when he had but one responsibility.

The Song of SOLOMON

This book has come to be known in English as "The Song of Solomon," but in the original Hebrew, and hence in the Greek and Latin versions, the title is "The Song of Songs," in the superlative sense of the best of songs. The question of authorship is closely connected with that of the meaning of the book, but it has traditionally been attributed to Solomon, who figures prominently in the work. The Song of Solomon is best described as love poetry. Because of its explicitly erotic character, ancient Jews and Christians alike rejected its literal interpretation and allegorized it. For the Jews it referred to God's dealings with his bride, Israel. The early Christians saw it as representing the relationship between Christ and His bride, the Church. Vestiges of this type of interpretation can even be found in modern Christian hymns, such as "Jesus Rose of Sharon" and "I Have Found a Friend in Jesus" (see Song of Solomon 2:1; 5:10). The early Christian inability to deal with this book at the literal level was influenced more by the Greek philosophy of the time than by the Bible itself. If, as seems justified by the text, we take the Song of Solomon as the words of a couple anticipating an imminent wedding, the book serves as a useful corrective to unbiblical marital asceticism. It shows that God intended married couples to enjoy a wide range of sexual pleasure when it expresses the love between them.

The Young Shulammite Bride and Jerusalem's Daughters

1 ⊶ The [I]Song*7892* of [a]Songs,*7892*
which is Solomon's.
2 "[I]May he kiss*5401* me with the
kisses of his mouth!*6310*
For your [a]love*1730* is better*2896*
than wine.
3 "Your [a]oils*8081* have a pleasing*2896*
fragrance,
Your [b]name is *like* [I]purified
oil;*8081*
Therefore the [IIc]maidens*5959*
love*157* you.
4 "Draw me after you *and* let us
run *together!*
The [a]king*4428* has brought me
into his chambers."
"[I]We will rejoice in you and be
glad;
We will [II]extol*2142* your [b]love
more than wine.
Rightly*4334* do they love
you."
5 "[I]I am black but [a]lovely,5000
O [b]daughters of Jerusalem,
Like the [c]tents*168* of [d]Kedar,
Like the curtains of Solomon.
6 "Do not stare at me because I
am [I]swarthy,
For the sun has burned me.
My [a]mother's*517* sons*1121* were
angry*2734* with me;
They made*7760* me [b]caretaker of
the vineyards,
But I have not taken care of my
own vineyard.
7 "Tell*5046* me, O you [a]whom my
soul*5315* loves,*157*
Where do you [b]pasture *your*
flock,

1 [I]Or, *Best of the Songs* [a]1Kin. 4:32
2 [I]BRIDE [a]Song 1:4; 4:10
3 [I]Lit., *oil which is emptied* (from one vessel to another) [II]Or, *virgins* [a]Song 4:10; John 12:3 [b]Eccl. 7:1 [c]Ps. 45:14
4 [I]CHORUS [II]Lit., *mention with praise* [a]Ps. 45:14, 15 [b]Song 1:4; 4:10
5 [I]BRIDE [a]Song 2:14; 4:3; 6:4 [b]Song 2:7; 3:5, 10; 5:8, 16; 8:4 [c]Ps. 120:5 [d]Is. 60:7
6 [I]Or, *black* [a]Ps. 69:8 [b]Song 8:11
7 [a]Song 3:1-4 [b]Song 2:16; 6:3

⊶ **1:1** There is no book of Scripture which generates more diversity of strong opinion than the Song of Solomon, a short poem of only eight chapters. There is a scarcity of tangible evidence within the book itself for anyone to be dogmatic about his conclusions. The N.T. never quotes from it and early Jewish and Christian writers were silent. However, there is no doubt that it was part of the Hebrew canon. The erotic nature of the book was probably a source of embarrassment, but these legal God-ordained gaieties should not be shunned, only properly understood within a Jewish context. The traditional position attributes the book to Solomon because of several references to him (1:1,5; 3:7,9,11; 8:11). See Eph. 5:23-33 for the same type of symbolic thought concerning Christ and His people.

Where do you make *it* [c]lie
down at noon?
For why should I be like one
who [I]veils herself
Beside the flocks of your
[d]companions?"

Solomon, the Lover, Speaks

8 "[I]If you yourself do not know,[3045]
[a]Most beautiful among
women,[802]
Go forth on the trail of the flock,
And pasture your young goats
By the tents of the shepherds.
9 "[I]To me, [a]my darling, you are like
My [b]mare among the chariots
of Pharaoh.
10 "Your [a]cheeks are lovely[4998] with
ornaments,
Your neck with strings of
[b]beads."
11 "[I]We will make[6213] for you
ornaments of gold
With beads of silver."
12 "[I]While the king was at his
[II]table,
My [III][a]perfume[5373] gave forth its
fragrance.
13 "My beloved is to me a pouch
of [a]myrrh[4753]
Which lies all night between my
breasts.
14 "My beloved[1730] is to me a cluster
of [a]henna blossoms
In the vineyards of [b]Engedi."
15 "[I,II][a]How beautiful you are, my
darling,
[II]How beautiful you are!
Your [b]eyes are *like* doves."
16 "[I,II]How handsome you are,
[a]my beloved,
And so pleasant!
Indeed, our couch is luxuriant!
17 "The beams of our houses[1004] are
[a]cedars,
Our rafters, [I][b]cypresses.

The Bride's Admiration

2 "I am the [II][a]rose of [b]Sharon,
The [c]lily of the valleys."
2 "[I]Like a lily among the thorns,
So is [a]my darling among the
[II]maidens."
3 "[I]Like an [II][a]apple tree among the
trees of the forest,
So is my beloved[1730] among the
[III]young men.[1121]
In his shade I took great
delight[2530] and sat down,
And his [b]fruit was sweet to my
[IV]taste.
4 "He has [a]brought me to *his*
[I]banquet hall,[1004]
And his [b]banner over me is
love.[160]
5 "Sustain me with [a]raisin cakes,[809]
Refresh me with [I][b]apples,
Because [c]I am lovesick.
6 "*Let* [a]his left hand be under my
head[7218]
And [b]his right hand [c]embrace
me."
7 "I [a]adjure you, O [b]daughters of
Jerusalem,
By the [c]gazelles[6643] or by the
[d]hinds[355] of the field,[7704]
That you will not arouse or
awaken *my* love,
Until [II]she pleases."[2654]
8 "[I]Listen! My beloved!
Behold, he is coming,
Climbing [a]on the mountains,
Leaping[7072] on the hills!
9 "My beloved is like a [a]gazelle or
a [b]young [I]stag.
Behold, he is standing behind
our wall,
He is looking through the
windows,
He is peering [c]through the
lattice.[2762]
10 "My beloved responded and
said[559] to me,
'[a]Arise, my darling, my beautiful
one,
And come along.
11 'For behold, the winter is
past,[5674]

7 [I]Some versions read *wanders* [c]Is. 13:20; Jer. 33:12 [d]Song 8:13
8 [I]BRIDEGROOM [a]Song 5:9; 6:1
9 [I]Lit., *I have compared you to* [a]Song 1:15; 2:2, 10, 13 [b]2Chr. 1:16, 17
10 [a]Song 5:13 [b]Gen. 24:53; Is. 61:10
11 [I]CHORUS
12 [I]BRIDE [II]Or, *couch* [III]Lit., *nard* [a]Song 4:14; Mark 14:3; John 12:3
13 [a]Ps. 45:8; John 19:39
14 [a]Song 4:13 [b]1Sam. 23:29
15 [I]BRIDEGROOM [II]Lit., *Behold* [a]Song 1:16; 2:10, 13; 4:1, 7; 6:4, 10 [b]Song 4:1; 5:12
16 [I]BRIDE [II]Lit., *Behold* [a]Song 2:3, 9, 17; 5:2, 5, 6, 8
17 [I]Or, *junipers* [a]1Kin. 6:9, 10; Jer. 22:14 [b]2Chr. 3:5

1 [I]BRIDE [II]Lit., *crocus* [a]Is. 35:1 [b]Is. 33:9; 35:2 [c]Song 5:13; 7:2; Hos. 14:5
2 [I]BRIDEGROOM [II]Lit., *daughters* [a]Song 1:9
3 [I]BRIDE [II]Or, *apricot* [III]Lit., *sons* [IV]Lit., *palate* [a]Song 8:5 [b]Song 4:13, 16; 8:11, 12
4 [I]Lit., *house of wine* [a]Song 1:4 [b]Ps. 20:5
5 [I]Or, *apricots* [a]2Sam. 6:19; 1Chr. 16:3; Hos. 3:1 [b]Song 7:8 [c]Song 5:8
6 [a]Song 8:3 [b]Prov. 4:8
7 [I]BRIDEGROOM [II]Or, *it* [a]Song 3:5; 5:8, 9; 8:4 [b]Song 1:5 [c]Prov. 6:5; Song 2:9, 17; 3:5; 8:14 [d]Gen. 49:21; Ps. 18:33; Hab. 3:19
8 [I]BRIDE [a]Song 2:17; Is. 52:7
9 [I]Lit., *of the stags* [a]Prov. 6:5; Song 2:17; 3:5; 8:14 [b]Song 2:17; 8:14 [c]Judg. 5:28 **10** [a]Song 2:13

The rain is over *and* gone.
12 'The flowers have *already*
appeared[7200] in the land;[776]
The time[6256] has arrived[5060] for
[I]pruning *the vines,*
And the voice of the [a]turtledove
has been heard[8085] in our
land.[776]
13 'The [a]fig tree has ripened its figs,
And the [b]vines in blossom have
given forth *their* fragrance.
Arise, my darling, my beautiful
one,
And come along!' "
14 "[I]O [a]my dove, [b]in the clefts of
the [II]rock,
In the secret place of the steep
[III]pathway,
Let me see your [IV]form,
[c]Let me hear[8085] your voice;
For your voice is sweet,
And your [IV]form is [d]lovely."[5000]
15 "[I][a]Catch the foxes for us,
The [II]little foxes that are
ruining[2254] the vineyards,
While our [b]vineyards are in
blossom."
16 "[I][a]My beloved is mine, and I am
his;
He [b]pastures *his flock* among the
lilies.
17 "[a]Until [I]the cool of the day[3117]
when the shadows[6752] flee
away,
Turn, my beloved, and be like
a [b]gazelle
Or a young stag [c]on the
mountains of [II]Bether."

The Bride's Troubled Dream

3 "[I]On my bed night[3915] after night I
sought him
[a]Whom my soul[5315] loves;[157]
I [b]sought him but did not find
him.
2 '[I]I must arise now and [I]go about
the city;
In the [a]streets and in the squares
[II]I must seek him whom my soul
loves.'
I sought him but did not find him.
3 "[a]The watchmen[8104] who make
the rounds in the city found
me,
And I said, 'Have you seen[7200]
him whom my soul loves?'
4 "[a]Scarcely had I [I]left[5674] them
When I found him whom my soul
loves;
I [b]held on to him and would not
let him go,
Until I had [c]brought him to my
mother's[517] house,[1004]
And into the room of her who
conceived me."
5 "I [a]adjure you, O daughters of
Jerusalem,
By the [b]gazelles[6643] or by the
hinds[355] of the field,[7704]
That you will not arouse or
awaken *my* love,[160]
Until [II]she pleases."[2654]

Solomon's Wedding Day

6 "[I,II][a]What is this coming up from
the wilderness
Like [b]columns of smoke,
Perfumed[6999] with [c]myrrh[4753]
and [d]frankincense,[3828]
With all scented powders of the
merchant?
7 "Behold, it is the *traveling* couch
of Solomon;
Sixty mighty men around it,
Of the mighty men of Israel.
8 "All of them are wielders of the
sword,[7219]
[a]Expert in war;
Each man[376] has his [b]sword[7219]
at his side,
Guarding against the
[I][c]terrors[6343] of the night.
9 "King[4428] Solomon has made[6213]
for himself a sedan chair
From the timber of Lebanon.
10 "He made its posts of silver,
Its [I]back of gold
And its seat of purple fabric,
With its interior lovingly fitted
out
By the [a]daughters of Jerusalem.

12 [I]Or, *singing* [a]Gen. 15:9; Ps. 74:19; Jer. 8:7
13 [a]Matt. 24:32 [b]Song 7:12
14 [I]BRIDEGROOM [II]Or, *crag* [III]Or, *cliff* [IV]Lit., *appearance* [a]Song 5:2; 6:9 [b]Jer. 48:28 [c]Song 8:13 [d]Song 1:5
15 [I]CHORUS [II]Or, *young* [a]Ezek. 13:4; Luke 13:32 [b]Song 2:13
16 [I]BRIDE [a]Song 6:3; 7:10 [b]Song 4:5; 6:2, 3
17 [I]Lit., *the day blows* [II]Or, *cleavage or a kind of spice* [a]Song 4:6 [b]Song 2:9 [c]Song 2:8
1 [I]BRIDE [a]Song 1:7 [b]Song 5:6
2 [I]Or, *Let me arise* [II]Or, *Let me seek* [a]Jer. 5:1
3 [a]Song 5:7; Is. 21:6-8, 11, 12
4 [I]Lit., *passed* [a]Prov. 8:17 [b]Prov. 4:13; Rom. 8:35, 39 [c]Song 8:2
5 [I]BRIDEGROOM [II]Or, *it* [a]Song 2:7; 5:8; 8:4 [b]Song 2:7
6 [I]CHORUS [II]Lit., *Who* [a]Song 8:5 [b]Ex. 13:21; Joel 2:30 [c]Song 1:13; 4:6, 14; Matt. 2:11 [d]Ex. 30:34; Rev. 18:13
8 [I]Lit., *terror in the nights* [a]Jer. 50:9 [b]Ps. 45:3 [c]Ps. 91:5
10 [I]Or, *support* [a]Song 1:5

11 "Go forth, O [a]daughters of Zion,
And gaze[7200] on King Solomon
with the [I]crown
With which his mother[517] has
crowned him
On the [b]day[3117] of his
wedding,[2861]
And on the day of his gladness
of heart."[3820]

Solomon's Love Expressed

4 "[I,II]How beautiful [a]you are, my
darling,
[II]How beautiful you are!
Your [b]eyes are *like* doves
[c]behind your veil;
Your [d]hair is like a flock of
goats
That have descended from
Mount [e]Gilead.
2 "Your [a]teeth are like a flock of
newly shorn ewes
Which have come up[5927] from
their washing,[7367]
All of which bear twins,
And not one among them has
[I]lost her young.[7909]
3 "Your lips[8193] are like a
[a]scarlet thread,
And your [b]mouth is lovely.[5000]
Your [c]temples are like a slice
of a pomegranate
Behind your veil.
4 "Your [a]neck is like the tower of
David
Built [I]with rows of stones,
On which are [b]hung a thousand
shields,[4043]
All the round [c]shields[7982] of the
mighty men.
5 "Your [a]two breasts are like two
fawns,[6646]
Twins of a gazelle,
Which [b]feed among the lilies.
6 "[a]Until [I]the cool of the day[3117]

3:11 [I]Or, *wreath* [a]Is. 3:16, 17; 4:4 [b]Is. 62:5

4:1 [I]BRIDEGROOM [II]Lit., *Behold* [a]Song 1:15 [b]Song 1:15; 5:12 [c]Song 6:7 [d]Song 6:5 [e]Mic. 7:14

2 [I]Or, *miscarried* [a]Song 6:6

3 [a]Josh. 2:18 [b]Song 5:16 [c]Song 6:7

4 [I]Or, *for an arsenal* [a]Song 7:4 [b]Ezek. 27:10, 11 [c]2Sam. 1:21

5 [a]Song 7:3 [b]Song 2:16; 6:2, 3

6 [I]Lit., *the day blows* [a]Song 2:17 [b]Song 4:14

7 [a]Song 1:15; Eph. 5:27

8 [I]Or, *Look* [a]1Kin. 4:33; Ps. 72:16 [b]Song 5:1; Is. 62:5 [c]2Kin. 5:12 [d]Deut. 3:9; 1Chr. 5:23; Ezek. 27:5

9 [a]Song 4:10, 12; 5:1, 2 [b]Gen. 41:42; Prov. 1:9; Ezek. 16:11; Dan. 5:7

10 [I]Or, *balsam odors* [a]Song 7:6 [b]Song 1:2, 4 [c]Song 1:3

11 [a]Prov. 5:3 [b]Ps. 19:10; Prov. 24:13 [c]Gen. 27:27; Hos. 14:6

12 [I]Lit., *stone heap* [a]Prov. 5:15-18 [b]Gen. 29:3

When the shadows[6752] flee
away,
I will go my way to the mountain
of [b]myrrh[4753]
And to the hill of
[b]frankincense.[3828]
7 "[a]You are altogether beautiful, my
darling,
And there is no blemish[3971] in
you.
8 "*Come* with me from [a]Lebanon,
my [b]bride,
May you come with me from
Lebanon.
[I]Journey down from the
summit[7218] of [c]Amana,
From the summit of [d]Senir and
Hermon,
From the dens of lions,
From the mountains of
leopards.
9 "You have made my heart beat
faster,[3823] [a]my sister,[269] *my*
bride;
You have made my heart beat
faster with a single *glance* of
your eyes,
With a single strand of your
[b]necklace.
10 "[a]How beautiful is your love,[1730]
my sister, *my* bride!
How much [b]better[2896] is your
love than wine,
And the [c]fragrance of your
oils[8081]
Than all *kinds* of [I]spices!
11 "Your lips, *my* bride, [a]drip
[b]honey;
Honey and milk are under your
tongue,
And the fragrance of your
garments is like the
[c]fragrance of Lebanon.
12 "A garden locked is my sister,
my bride,
A [I]rock garden locked, a
[a]spring [b]sealed up.

3:11 Zion is another name for Jerusalem here and about 150 times in the O.T. "Daughters of Zion" is thought to refer to the women of the entire city.

4:1 This was a famous feeding ground. The goats of that region were well known for their shiny, black hair. See Mic. 7:14 and Num. 32:1.

13 "Your shoots are an [Ia]orchard of
[b]pomegranates
With [c]choice fruits, [d]henna with
nard plants,[5373]
14 [a]Nard and saffron,[3750]
calamus[7070] and [b]cinnamon,
With all the trees of
[c]frankincense,
[d]Myrrh and aloes,[174] along with
all the finest[7218] [I]spices.
15 "*You are* a garden spring,
A well of [Ia]fresh[2416] water,
And streams *flowing* from
Lebanon."
16 "[I]Awake, O north *wind,*
And come, *wind of* the south;
Make my [a]garden breathe[6315]
out *fragrance,*
Let its [II]spices [III]be wafted
abroad.
May [b]my beloved[1730] come into
his garden
And eat its [c]choice fruits!"

The Torment of Separation

5 "I have [a]come into my garden,
[b]my sister,[269] *my* bride;
I have gathered my [c]myrrh[4753]
along with my balsam.
I have eaten my honeycomb
[II]and my [d]honey;
I have [e]drunk my wine
[II]and my milk.
Eat, [f]friends;[7453]
Drink and [III]imbibe deeply, O
lovers."[1730]
2 "I was asleep, but my heart[3820]
was awake.
A voice! My beloved was
knocking:
'Open to me, [a]my sister, my
darling,
[b]My dove, my perfect one![8535]
For my head[7218] is [II]drenched
with dew,
My [c]locks with the [III]damp of the
night.'[3915]
3 "I have [a]taken off my dress,
How can I put it on *again?*
I have [b]washed[7364] my feet,
How can I dirty them *again?*
4 "My beloved extended his
hand[3027] through the opening,
And my [Ia]feelings[4578] were
aroused for him.
5 "I arose to open to my beloved;
And my hands[3027] [a]dripped[5197]
with myrrh,
And my fingers with [I]liquid
myrrh,
On the handles[3709] of the bolt.
6 "I opened to my beloved,
But my beloved had [a]turned
away *and* had gone!
My [I]heart[5315] went out *to him*
as he [b]spoke.[1696]
I [c]searched for him, but I did
not find him;
I [d]called[7121] him, but he did not
answer me.
7 "The [a]watchmen[8104] who make
the rounds in the city found
me,
They struck[5221] me *and*
wounded me;
The guardsmen[8104] of the walls
took away[5375] my shawl from
me.
8 "I [a]adjure you, O daughters of
Jerusalem,
If you find my beloved,
As to what you will tell[5046] him:
For [b]I am lovesick."[760]
9 "[I,II]What kind of beloved is your
beloved,
O [a]most beautiful among
women?[802]
[II]What kind of beloved is your
beloved,
That thus you adjure us?"

Admiration by the Bride

10 "[I]My beloved is dazzling and
[a]ruddy,[122]
[IIb]Outstanding among ten
thousand.
11 "His head is *like* gold, pure
gold;

13 [I]Or, *park* or *paradise* [a]Eccl. 2:5 [b]Song 6:11; 7:12 [c]Song 2:3; 4:16; 7:13 [d]Song 1:14
14 [I]Or, *balsam odors* [a]Song 1:12 [b]Ex. 30:23 [c]Song 4:6 [d]Ps. 45:8; Song 3:6; John 19:39
15 [I]Lit., *living* [a]Zech. 14:8; John 4:10
16 [I]BRIDE [II]Or, *balsam odors* [III]Lit., *flow forth* [a]Song 5:1; 6:2 [b]Song 1:13; 2:3, 8; 6:2 [c]Song 4:13
1 [I]BRIDEGROOM [II]Lit., *with* [III]Or, *become drunk* [a]Song 6:2 [b]Song 4:9 [c]Song 1:13; 4:14 [d]Song 4:11 [e]Prov. 9:5; Is. 55:1 [f]Judg. 14:11, 20; John 3:29
2 [I]BRIDE [II]Lit., *filled* [III]Lit., *drops* [a]Song 4:9 [b]Song 2:14; 6:9 [c]Song 5:11
3 [a]Luke 11:7 [b]Gen. 19:2
4 [I]Lit., *bowels* [a]Jer. 31:20
5 [I]Lit., *passing* [a]Song 5:13
6 [I]Lit., *soul* [a]Song 6:1 [b]Song 5:2 [c]Song 3:1 [d]Prov. 1:28
7 [a]Song 3:3
8 [a]Song 2:7; 3:5 [b]Song 2:5
9 [I]CHORUS [II]Or, *What is your beloved more than another beloved* [a]Song 1:8; 6:1
10 [I]BRIDE [II]Lit., *Lifted up banner* [a]1 Sam. 16:12 [b]Ps. 45:2

🗝 **5:1** Jonathan ate honey from a stick dipped in honeycomb (I Sam. 14:27).

His [a]locks are *like* clusters of
dates,
And black as a raven.
12 "His [a]eyes are like doves,
Beside streams of water,
Bathed in milk,
And [I]reposed in *their* [b]setting.
13 "His cheeks are like a [a]bed of
balsam,
Banks of sweet-scented herbs;
His lips[8193] are [b]lilies,
[c]Dripping[5197] with liquid myrrh.
14 "His hands are rods of gold
Set with [a]beryl;
His abdomen[4578] is carved ivory
Inlaid with [Ib]sapphires.
15 "His legs are pillars of alabaster
Set on pedestals of pure gold;
His appearance is like
[a]Lebanon,
Choice[977] as the [b]cedars.
16 "His [Ia]mouth is *full of* sweetness.
And he is wholly [b]desirable.
This is my beloved and this is
my friend,[7453]
O daughters of Jerusalem."

Mutual Delight in Each Other

6 "[Ia]Where has your beloved[1730]
gone,
O [b]most beautiful among
women?[802]
Where has your beloved turned,
That we may seek him with
you?"
2 "[I]My beloved has gone down to
his [a]garden,
To the [b]beds of balsam,
To [c]pasture *his flock* in the
gardens
And gather[3950] [d]lilies.
3 "[a]I am my beloved's[1730] and my
beloved is mine,
He who [b]pastures *his flock*
among the lilies."
🔑4 "[Ia]You are as beautiful as
[b]Tirzah, my darling,
As [c]lovely[5000] as [d]Jerusalem,

11 [a]Song 5:2
12 [I]Lit., *sitting upon* [a]Song 1:15; 4:1 [b]Ex. 25:7
13 [a]Song 6:2 [b]Song 2:1 [c]Song 5:5
14 [I]Lit., *lapis lazuli* [a]Ex. 28:20; 39:13; Ezek. 1:16; Dan. 10:6 [b]Ex. 24:10; 28:18; Job 28:16; Is. 54:11
15 [a]Song 7:4 [b]1Kin. 4:33; Ps. 80:10; Ezek. 17:23; 31:8
16 [I]Lit., *palate* [a]Song 7:9 [b]2Sam. 1:23

1 [I]CHORUS [a]Song 5:6 [b]Song 1:8
2 [I]BRIDE [a]Song 4:16; 5:1 [b]Song 5:13 [c]Song 1:7 [d]Song 2:1; 5:13
3 [a]Song 2:16; 7:10 [b]Song 2:16; 4:5
4 [I]BRIDEGROOM [II]Lit., *bannered ones* [a]Song 1:15 [b]1Kin. 14:17 [c]Song 1:5 [d]Ps. 48:2; 50:2 [e]Song 6:10
5 [a]Song 4:1
6 [I]Or, *miscarried* [a]Song 4:2
7 [a]Song 4:3
8 [I]Or, *virgins* [a]1Kin. 11:3 [b]Song 1:3
9 [I]Lit., *one* [II]Lit., *daughters* [a]Song 2:14; 5:2 [b]Gen. 30:13 [c]1Kin. 11:3
10 [I]Lit., *looks down* [II]Lit., *bannered ones* [a]Job 31:26 [b]Matt. 17:2; Rev. 1:16 [c]Song 6:4
11 [a]Song 7:12 [b]Song 4:13

As [e]awesome as [II]an army with
banners.
5 "Turn your eyes away from me,
For they have confused me;
[a]Your hair is like a flock of goats
That have descended from
Gilead.
6 "[a]Your teeth are like a flock of
ewes
Which have come up from *their*
washing,[7367]
All of which bear twins,
And not one among them has
[I]lost her young.[7909]
7 "[a]Your temples are like a slice
of a pomegranate
Behind your veil.
8 "There are sixty [a]queens[4436] and
eighty concubines,
And [Ib]maidens[5959] without
number;
9 *But* [a]my dove, my perfect
one,[8535] is [I]unique:
She is her mother's[517] [I]only
daughter;
She is the pure[1249] *child* of the
one who bore her.
The [IIb]maidens saw[7200] her and
called her blessed,[833]
The [c]queens and the concubines
also, and they praised[1984]
her, *saying,*
10 'Who is this that [I]grows like the
dawn,
As beautiful as the full
[a]moon,
As pure[1249] [b]as the sun,
As [c]awesome as [II]an army with
banners?'
11 "I went down to the orchard of
nut trees
To see the blossoms of the
valley,
To see whether [a]the vine had
budded
Or the [b]pomegranates had
bloomed.
12 "Before I was aware,[3045] my
soul[5315] set[7760] me

🔑 **6:4** Tirzah was an ancient Canaanite city which was conquered by Joshua (Josh. 12:24). It became the first capital of the northern kingdom (I Kgs. 15:21,33; 16:8,15,23).

Over the chariots of [I]my noble people."

13 "[I,II]Come back,[7725] come back, O Shulammite;
Come back, come back, that we may gaze[2372] at you!"
"[III]Why should you gaze[2372] at the Shulammite,
As at the [a]dance of [IV][b]the two companies?[4264]

12 [I]Another reading is *Ammi-nadib*

13 [I]CHORUS [II]Ch. 7:1 in Heb. [III]BRIDEGROOM [IV]Or, *Mahanaim* [a]Judg. 21:21 [b]Gen. 32:2; 2Sam. 17:24

Admiration by the Bridegroom

7 "[I]How beautiful are your [II]feet in sandals,
O [III][a]prince's daughter!
The curves of your hips are like [IV]jewels,
The work of the hands[3027] of an artist.
2 "Your navel is *like* a round goblet
Which never lacks mixed wine;
Your belly[990] is like a heap of wheat
Fenced about with lilies.
3 "Your [a]two breasts are like two fawns,[6646]
Twins of a gazelle.
4 "Your [a]neck is like a tower of ivory,
Your eyes *like* the pools in [b]Heshbon
By the gate of Bath-rabbim;
Your nose[639] is like the tower of Lebanon,
Which faces toward Damascus.
5 "Your head[7218] [I]crowns you like [a]Carmel,
And the flowing locks of your head are like purple threads;
The king[4428] is captivated by *your* tresses.[7298]
6 "How [a]beautiful and how delightful you are,
[I]*My* love,[160] with *all* your charms!
7 "[I]Your stature is like a palm tree,
And your breasts are *like its* clusters.
8 "I said,[559] 'I will climb the palm tree,
I will take hold of its fruit stalks.'
Oh, may your breasts be like clusters of the vine,
And the fragrance of your [I]breath like [II][a]apples,
9 And your [I][a]mouth like the best[2896] wine!"
"[II]It [b]goes *down* smoothly[4334] for my beloved,
Flowing gently *through* the lips[8193] of those who fall asleep.

1 [I]Ch. 7:2 in Heb. [II]Lit., *footsteps* [III]Or, *nobleman's* [IV]Or, *ornaments* [a]Ps. 45:13

3 [a]Song 4:5

4 [a]Song 4:4 [b]Num. 21:26

5 [I]Lit., *is upon* [a]Is. 35:2

6 [I]Or, With *love among your delights* [a]Song 1:15, 16; 4:10

7 [I]Lit., *This stature of yours*

8 [I]Lit., *nose* [II]Or, *apricots* [a]Song 2:5

9 [I]Lit., *palate* [II]BRIDE [a]Song 5:16 [b]Prov. 23:31

The Union of Love

10 "[a]I am my beloved's,[1730]
And his [b]desire[8669] is for me.
11 "Come, my beloved, let us go out into the [I]country,[7704]
Let us spend the night in the villages.
12 "Let us rise early *and go* to the vineyards;
Let us [a]see whether the vine has budded
And its blossoms have opened,
And whether the pomegranates have bloomed.
There I will give you my love.
13 "The [a]mandrakes[1736] have given forth fragrance;
And over our doors are all [b]choice *fruits,*
Both new and old,
Which I have saved up for you, my beloved.

10 [a]Song 2:16; 6:3 [b]Ps. 45:11; Gal. 2:20

11 [I]Lit., *field*

12 [a]Song 6:11

13 [a]Gen. 30:14 [b]Song 2:3; 4:13, 16; Matt. 13:52

The Lovers Speak

8 "Oh that you were like a brother[251] to me
Who nursed at my mother's[517] breasts.
If I found you outdoors, I would kiss[5401] you;
No one would despise me, either.

7:13 Cf. Gen. 30:14-16.

2 "I would lead you *and* [a]bring you
Into the house[1004] of my
mother,[517] who used to
instruct me;
I would give you spiced wine to
drink from the juice of my
pomegranates.
3 "Let [a]his left hand be under my
head,[7218]
And his right hand embrace me."
4 "[I][a]I want you to swear, O
daughters of Jerusalem,
[II]Do not arouse or awaken *my*
love,[160]
Until [III]she pleases."[2654]
5 "[I][a]Who is this coming up[5927] from
the wilderness,
Leaning on her beloved?"[1730]
"[II]Beneath the [III][b]apple tree I
awakened you;
There your mother was in labor
with you,
There she was in labor *and* gave
you birth.
6 "Put[7760] me like a [I]seal over your
heart,[3820]
Like a [a]seal on your arm.
For love is as strong as
death,[4194]
[II][b]Jealousy[7068] is as severe as
Sheol;[7585]
Its flashes are flashes of fire,
[III]The *very* flame of the LORD.[3050]
7 "Many waters cannot quench
love,
Nor will rivers overflow[7857] it;
[a]If a man[376] were to give all the
riches of his house for love,

2 [a]Song 3:4
3 [a]Song 2:6
4 [I]BRIDEGROOM [II]Or, *Why should you arouse* [III]Or, *it* [a]Song 2:7; 3:5
5 [I]CHORUS [II]BRIDE [III]Or, *apricot* [a]Song 3:6 [b]Song 2:3
6 [I]Or, *signet* [II]Or, Its *ardor is as inflexible* [III]Another reading is *A vehement flame* [a]Is. 49:16; Jer. 22:24; Hag. 2:23 [b]Prov. 6:34
7 [a]Prov. 6:35
8 [I]CHORUS [a]Ezek. 16:7
9 [a]1Kin. 6:15
10 [I]BRIDE [a]Ezek. 16:7
11 [a]Eccl. 2:4 [b]Matt. 21:33 [c]Song 1:6 [d]Is. 7:23 [e]Song 2:3; 8:12
12 [I]Lit., *before me*
13 [I]BRIDEGROOM [a]Song 1:7 [b]Song 2:14
14 [I]BRIDE [II]Lit., *Flee* [III]Lit., *of the stags* [a]Song 2:7, 9, 17 [b]Song 4:6

It would be utterly despised."[936]
8 "[I]We have a little sister,[269]
And she [a]has no breasts;
What shall we do for our sister
On the day[3117] when she is
spoken[1696] for?
9 "If she is a wall,
We shall build on her a
battlement of silver;
But if she is a door,
We shall barricade her with
[a]planks of cedar."
10 "[I]I was a wall, and [a]my breasts
were like towers;
Then I became in his eyes as
one who finds
peace.[7965]
11 "Solomon had a [a]vineyard at Baal-
hamon;
He [b]entrusted the vineyard to
[c]caretakers;
Each one[376] was to bring a
[d]thousand *shekels* of silver for
its [e]fruit.
12 "My very own vineyard is [I]at
my disposal;
The thousand *shekels* are for
you, Solomon,
And two hundred are for those
who take care of its fruit."
13 "[I]O you who sit in the gardens,
My [a]companions are listening[7181]
for your voice—
[b]Let me hear[8085] it!"
14 "[I,II]Hurry, my beloved,
And be [a]like a gazelle or a young
[III]stag
On the [b]mountains of spices."

8:6 See Jer. 22:24.
8:12 This means one-fifth in cash, besides what they ate and drank from the vineyard and adjoining vegetable gardens. Twenty percent was a common interest rate in the ancient Near East.
8:14 At first, it may seem strange that such a book is in the Bible, but it certainly shows the spiritual nature, dignity, and sanctity of love within marriage. This is a fact which has not always been sufficiently emphasized. The Song of Solomon is instructive and moral in its purpose. It comes to us in this world of sin, where lust and passion are on every hand, where fierce temptations assail us and try to turn us aside from the God-given standards of holy matrimony. It reminds us in a beautiful way of how pure and noble true love really is. Though the Song of Solomon is expressed in bold language, it provides a wholesome balance between the extremes of sexual perversion and of ascetic denial (cf. I Tim. 4:3).

The Book of

ISAIAH

Isaiah is one of the longest and most important books of the Old Testament. The prophet began his career during a time of relative peace and prosperity under Judah's kings, Uzziah and Jotham, but before long, conditions deteriorated, especially on the international scene. During Ahaz's reign Assyria became a superpower and deported Judah's sister kingdom, Israel, in 722 B.C., but Ahaz saw Syria and Israel as greater threats. Isaiah tried to reassure Ahaz, asking only that he have faith in God, but Ahaz refused, Later, in 701 B.C., during Hezekiah's reign, Assyria ravaged the Judean countryside, and Jerusalem itself almost fell. Again, Isaiah preached a message of hope for a repentant Judah who would trust in the Lord. Exactly when Isaiah's career ended is not known, but a Jewish tradition, which may be reflected in Heb. 11:37, says that he was martyred by King Manasseh, Hezekiah's son. To view Isaiah merely as a preacher about events during his lifetime is to have only half of the picture, because he is perhaps best known for his prophecies about the intermediate and distant future. Isaiah 1—39 deals primarily with events during the prophet's lifetime, but the latter part of the book is all concerned with the future. Isaiah 40 begins a major section that looks ahead to Judah's return from Babylonian exile in the sixth century B.C. The later chapters also peer beyond Isaiah's day, but the time period covered is more difficult to determine. The New Testament finds in many of these passages, including some in the first part of the book, prophecies about the Messiah. The most striking of these relate to Jesus' miraculous birth (Isa. 7:14) and His suffering and death (Isa. 53). Christians, therefore, have found Isaiah to be one of the most valuable books of the Old Testament.

Rebellion of God's People

1 The vision[2377] of Isaiah the son[1121]
of Amoz, concerning [a]Judah and Jerusalem which he saw[2372] during the
[I]reigns[3117] of [b]Uzziah, [c]Jotham, [d]Ahaz,
and [e]Hezekiah, kings of Judah.

2 [a]Listen,[8085] O heavens,[8064] and
hear,[238] O [b]earth;[776]
For the LORD speaks,[1696]
"[c]Sons[1121] I have reared and
brought up,
But they have [d]revolted[6586]
against Me.

3 "An ox knows its owner,
And a donkey its master's
manger,[18]
But Israel [a]does not know,[3045]
My people[5971] [b]do not
understand."[995]

4 Alas, sinful nation,[1471]
People weighed down with
iniquity,[5771]
[I][a]Offspring[2233] of evildoers,[7489]
Sons who [b]act corruptly![7843]
They have [c]abandoned[5800] the
LORD,
They have [d]despised[5006] the
Holy One[6918] of Israel,
They have turned away[2114]
[II]from Him.

5 Where will you be stricken
again,
As you [a]continue in *your*
rebellion?[5627]
The whole head[7218] is [b]sick,
And the whole heart[3824] is
faint.

6 [a]From the sole[3709] of the foot
even to the head
There is [b]nothing sound in it,
Only bruises, welts, and raw
wounds,
[c]Not pressed out or bandaged,
Nor softened with oil.[8081]

7 Your [a]land[776] is desolate,[8077]
Your cities are burned[8313] with
fire,
Your fields—[127] strangers[2114]
are devouring them in your
presence;
[I]It is desolation, as overthrown
by strangers.

8 And the daughter of Zion is

1 [I]Lit., *days* [a]Is. 2:1; 40:9 [b]2Kin. 15:1-7, 13; 2Chr. 26:1-23 [c]2Kin. 15:32-38; 2Chr. 27:1-9 [d]2Kin. 16:1-20; 2Chr. 28:1-27; Is. 7:1 [e]2Kin. 18:1-20:21; 2Chr. 29:1-32:33

2 [a]Deut. 32:1 [b]Mic. 1:2 [c]Jer. 3:22 [d]Is. 30:1, 9; 65:2

3 [a]Jer. 9:3, 6 [b]Is. 44:18

4 [I]Lit., *Seed* [II]Lit., *backward* [a]Is. 14:20 [b]Neh. 1:7 [c]Is. 1:28 [d]Is. 5:24

5 [a]Is. 31:6 [b]Is. 33:24; Ezek. 34:4, 16

6 [a]Job 2:7 [b]Ps. 38:3 [c]Jer. 8:22

7 [I]Lit., *And* [a]Lev. 26:33; Jer. 44:6

left[3498] like a shelter[5521] in a
vineyard,
Like a watchman's hut in a
cucumber field, like a
besieged[5341] city.
9 [a]Unless the LORD of hosts[6635]
Had left us a few [b]survivors,[8300]
We would be like [c]Sodom,
We would be like Gomorrah.

God Has Had Enough

10 Hear [a]the word[1697] of the LORD,
You rulers[7101] of [b]Sodom;
Give ear to the instruction[8451]
of our God,
You people of Gomorrah.
11 "[a]What are your multiplied
sacrifices[2077] to Me?"
Says[559] the LORD.
"I [I]have had enough of burnt
offerings[5930] of rams,
And the fat of fed cattle.
And I take no pleasure in the
blood[1818] of bulls, lambs, or
goats.
12 "When you come [a]to appear[7200]
before Me,
Who requires [I]of you this
trampling of My courts?
13 "Bring your worthless[7723]
offerings[4503] no longer,
[a]Incense[7004] is an abomination to
Me.
[b]New moon and sabbath,[7676] the
[c]calling[7121] of
assemblies—[4744]
I cannot [d]endure iniquity[205] and
the solemn assembly.[6116]
14 "I[5315] hate[8130] your new moon
festivals and your
[a]appointed[4150] feasts,
They have become a burden to
Me.
I am [b]weary of bearing[5375] *them.*
15 "So when you [a]spread out your
hands[3709] *in prayer,*
[b]I will hide My eyes from you,
Yes, even though you
[c]multiply prayers,[8605]
I will not listen.
[d]Your hands[3027] are [I]covered
with blood.
16 "[a]Wash[7364] yourselves,
[b]make yourselves clean;[2135]
[c]Remove[5493] the evil[7455] of your
deeds from My sight.
[d]Cease to do evil,[7489]
17 Learn[3925] to do good;[3190]
[a]Seek justice,[4941]
Reprove the ruthless;
[I][b]Defend[8199] the orphan,
Plead[7378] for the widow.

"Let Us Reason"

18 "Come now, and [a]let us reason[3198]
together,"
Says the LORD, "[b]Though your
sins[2399] are as scarlet,
They will be as white as snow;
Though they are red[119] like
crimson,
They will be like wool.
19 "[a]If you consent[14] and obey,[8085]
You will [b]eat the best[2893] of the
land;[776]
20 "But if you refuse[3985] and
rebel,[4784]
You will be [a]devoured by the
sword."[2719]
Truly, [b]the mouth[6310] of the
LORD has spoken.

Zion Corrupted, to be Redeemed

21 How the faithful[539] city has
become[1961] a [a]harlot,[2181]
She *who* was full of justice!
Righteousness[6664] once lodged
in her,
But now murderers.[7523]
22 Your silver has become
dross,[5509]
Your drink diluted with water.
23 Your [a]rulers[8269] are rebels,[5637]
And companions of thieves;
Everyone [b]loves[157] a bribe,
And chases after rewards.[8021]
They [c]do not [I]defend the
[II]orphan,

9 [a]Rom. 9:29 [b]Is. 10:20-22; 11:11, 16; 37:4, 31, 32; 46:3 [c]Gen. 19:24

10 [a]Is. 8:20; 28:14 [b]Is. 3:9; Ezek. 16:49; Rom. 9:29; Rev. 11:8

11 [I]Or, *am sated with* [a]Ps. 50:8; Jer. 6:20; Amos 5:21, 22; Mal. 1:10

12 [I]Lit., *of your hand* [a]Ex. 23:17

13 [a]Is. 66:3 [b]1Chr. 23:31 [c]Ex. 12:16 [d]Jer. 7:9, 10

14 [a]Is. 29:1, 2 [b]Is. 7:13; 43:24

15 [I]Lit., *full of* [a]1Kin. 8:22; Lam. 1:17 [b]Is. 8:17; 59:2 [c]Mic. 3:4 [d]Is. 59:3

16 [a]Ps. 26:6 [b]Is. 52:11 [c]Is. 55:7 [d]Jer. 25:5

17 [I]Or, *Vindicate the fatherless* [a]Jer. 22:3; Zeph. 2:3 [b]Ps. 82:3

18 [a]Is. 41:1, 21; 43:26; Mic. 6:2 [b]Ps. 51:7; Is. 43:25; 44:22; Rev. 7:14

19 [a]Deut. 28:1; 30:15, 16 [b]Is. 55:2

20 [a]Is. 3:25; 65:12 [b]Is. 40:5; 58:14; Mic. 4:4; Titus 1:2

21 [a]Is. 57:3-9; Jer. 2:20

23 [I]Or, *vindicate* [II]Or, *fatherless* [a]Hos. 5:10; Mic. 7:3 [b]Ex. 23:8; Mic. 7:3 [c]Is. 10:2; Jer. 5:28; Ezek. 22:7; Zech. 7:10

Nor does the widow's plea[7379]
come before them.
24 Therefore the Lord[113]
[I]GOD of hosts,
The [a]Mighty One of Israel
declares,[5001]
"Ah, I will be relieved of My
adversaries,
And [b]avenge[5358] Myself on My
foes.
25 "I will also turn[7725] My hand
against you,
And will [a]smelt away[6884] your
dross as with lye,
And will remove all your alloy.
26 "Then I will restore[7725] your
[a]judges[8199] as at the first,[7223]
And your counselors[3289] as at the
beginning;
After that you will be called[7121]
the [b]city of righteousness,
A faithful city."
27 Zion will be [a]redeemed[6299] with
justice,
And her [I]repentant ones[7725] with
righteousness.[6666]
28 But [I]transgressors[6586] and
sinners[2400] will be
[a]crushed[7667] together,
And those who forsake[5800] the
LORD shall come to an
end.[3615]
29 Surely, [I]you will be ashamed[954]
of the [II][a]oaks which you have
desired,
And you will be embarrassed at
the [b]gardens which you have
chosen.[977]
30 For you will be like an
[I]oak whose [a]leaf fades away,
Or as a garden that has no
water.
31 And the strong man will become
tinder,
His work also a spark.
Thus they shall both [a]burn
together,
And there will be [b]none to
quench *them*.

God's Universal Reign

2 The word[1697] which [a]Isaiah the
son[1121] of Amoz saw[2372] concerning
Judah and Jerusalem.
2 Now it will come about that
[a]In the last days,[3117]
The [b]mountain of the house[1004]
of the LORD
Will be established[3559] [I]as the
chief[7218] of the mountains,
And will be raised above the
hills;
And [c]all the nations[1471] will
stream to it.
3 And many peoples[5971] will come
and say,[559] "Come, let us go
up to the mountain of the
LORD,
To the house of the God of
Jacob;
That He may teach us [I]con-
cerning His ways,[1870]
And that we may walk in His
paths."[734]
For the [II]law[8451] will go forth
[a]from Zion,
And the word of the LORD from
Jerusalem.
4 And He will judge[8199] between
the nations,
And will [I]render decisions[3198] for
many peoples;
And [a]they will hammer[3807] their
swords[2719] into plowshares,
and their spears into pruning
hooks.
[b]Nation[1471] will not lift up[5375]
sword[2719] against nation,
And never again will they
learn[3925] war.
5 Come, [a]house of Jacob, and let
us walk in the [b]light[216] of the
LORD.
6 For Thou hast [a]abandoned[5203]
Thy people, the house of
Jacob,
Because they are filled *with*
influences from the east,

24 [I]Heb., *YHWH*, usually rendered *LORD* [a]Ps. 132:2; Is. 49:26; 60:16 [b]Deut. 28:63; Is. 35:4; 59:18; 61:2; 63:4

25 [a]Ezek. 22:19-22; Mal. 3:3

26 [a]Is. 60:17 [b]Is. 33:5; 60:14; 62:1, 2; Zech. 8:3

27 [I]Or, *returnees* [a]Is. 35:9f.; 62:12; 63:4

28 [I]Lit., *the crushing of transgressors and sinners shall be together* [a]Ps. 9:5; Is. 66:24; 2Thess. 1:8, 9

29 [I]So with some mss.; M.T., *they* [II]Or, *terebinths* [a]Is. 57:5 [b]Is. 65:3; 66:17

30 [I]Or, *terebinth* [a]Is. 64:6

31 [a]Is. 5:24; 9:19; 26:11; 33:11-14 [b]Is. 66:24; Matt. 3:12; Mark 9:43

1 [a]Is. 1:1

2 [I]Lit., *on* [a]Mic. 4:1-3 [b]Is. 27:13; 66:20 [c]Is. 56:7

3 [I]Or, *some of* [II]Or, *instruction* [a]Is. 51:4, 5; Luke 24:47

4 [I]Or, *reprove many* [a]Is. 32:17, 18; Joel 3:10 [b]Is. 9:5, 7; 11:6-9; Hos. 2:18; Zech. 9:10

5 [a]Is. 58:1 [b]Is. 60:1, 2, 19, 20; 1John 1:5

6 [a]Deut. 31:17

2:2-4 This is known as a floating oracle, because it also appears, with only minor differences, in Mic. 4:1-3. Micah and Isaiah were contemporaries.

And *they are* soothsayers*6049*
[b]like the Philistines,
And they [c]strike *bargains* with
the children of foreigners.*5237*
7 Their land*776* has also been filled
with silver and gold,
And there is no end to their
treasures;
Their land has also been filled
with [a]horses,
And there is no end to their
chariots.
8 Their land has also been
[a]filled with idols;*457*
They worship the [b]work of their
hands,*3027*
That which their fingers have
made.*6213*
9 So [a]the *common* man has been
humbled,
And the man*376* *of importance* has
been abased,
But [b]do not forgive*5375* them.
10 [a]Enter the rock and hide in the
dust*6083*
[b]From the terror*6343* of the LORD
and from the splendor*1926* of
His majesty.
11 The [Ia]proud look of man*120* will
be abased,
And the [b]loftiness of man*582* will
be humbled,
And the LORD alone will be
exalted in that day.*3117*

A Day of Reckoning Coming

12 For the LORD of hosts*6635* will
have a day *of reckoning*
Against [a]everyone who is proud
and lofty,
And against everyone who is
lifted up,*5375*
That he may be abased.
13 And *it will be* against all the
cedars of Lebanon that are
lofty and lifted up,
Against all the [a]oaks of
Bashan,
14 Against all the [a]lofty mountains,
Against all the hills that are lifted
up,

6 [b]2Kin. 1:2 [c]2Kin. 16:7, 8; Prov. 6:1

7 [a]Deut. 17:16; Is. 30:16; 31:1; Mic. 5:10

8 [a]Is. 10:11 [b]Ps. 115:4-8; Is. 17:8; 37:19; 40:19; 44:17

9 [a]Ps. 49:2; 62:9; Is. 5:15 [b]Neh. 4:5

10 [a]Is. 2:19, 21; Rev. 6:15, 16 [b]2Thess. 1:9

11 [I]Lit., *eyes of the loftiness of men* [a]Is. 5:15; 37:23 [b]Ps. 18:27; Is. 13:11; 23:9; 2Cor. 10:5

12 [a]Job 40:11, 12; Is. 24:4, 21; Mal. 4:1

13 [a]Zech. 11:2

14 [a]Is. 40:4

15 [a]Is. 25:12

16 [a]1Kin. 10:22; Is. 23:1, 14; 60:9

18 [a]Is. 21:9; Mic. 1:7

19 [I]Lit., *dust* [a]Is. 2:10 [b]Ps. 18:7; Is. 2:21; 13:13; 24:1, 19, 20; Hag. 2:6, 7; Heb. 12:26

20 [a]Is. 30:22; 31:7 [b]Lev. 11:19

21 [a]Is. 2:19

22 [I]Lit., *Cease from man* [II]Lit., *in what* [a]Ps. 146:3; Jer. 17:5 [b]Ps. 8:4; 144:3, 4; Is. 40:15, 17; James 4:14

1 [I]Heb., *YHWH*, usually rendered LORD [II]Lit., *staff* [a]Lev. 26:26; Is. 5:13; 9:20; Ezek. 4:16

15 Against every [a]high tower,
Against every fortified wall,
16 Against all the [a]ships of
Tarshish,
And against all the beautiful
craft.
17 And the pride of man will be
humbled,
And the loftiness of men will be
abased,
And the LORD alone will be
exalted in that day.
18 But the [a]idols will completely*3632*
vanish.
19 And *men* will [a]go into caves of
the rocks,
And into holes of the [I]ground*6083*
Before the terror of the LORD,
And before the splendor of His
majesty,
When He arises [b]to make the
earth*776* tremble.*6206*
20 In that day men will [a]cast
away to the moles and the
[b]bats
Their idols of silver and their
idols of gold,
Which they made for themselves
to worship,
21 In order to [a]go into the caverns
of the rocks and the clefts
of the cliffs,
Before the terror of the LORD
and the splendor of His
majesty,
When He arises to make the
earth tremble.
22 [Ia]Stop regarding man, whose
breath*5397* *of life* is in his
nostrils;*639*
For [IIb]why should he be
esteemed?*2803*

God Will Remove the Leaders

3 For behold, the Lord*113*
[I]GOD of hosts*6635* [a]is going to
remove from Jerusalem and
Judah
Both [II]supply*8172* and support,
the whole [II]supply of bread,
And the whole [II]supply of water;

2 [a]The mighty man and the warrior,[376]
The judge[8199] and the prophet,[5030]
The diviner[7080] and the elder,[2204]
3 The captain[8269] of fifty and the honorable man,
The counselor[3289] and the expert[2450] artisan,[2796]
And the skillful[995] enchanter.[3908]
4 And I will make mere [a]lads their princes[8269]
And [I]capricious children[8586] will rule[4910] over them,
5 And the people[5971] will be [a]oppressed,
Each one[376] by another, and each one by his [b]neighbor;[7453]
The youth will storm against the elder,
And the inferior against the honorable.
6 When a man [a]lays hold of his brother[251] in his father's[1] house,[1004] *saying,*
"You have a cloak, you shall be our ruler,[7101]
And these ruins[4384] will be under your [I]charge,"[3027]
7 On that day[3117] will he [I]protest, saying,
"I will not be *your* [IIa]healer,[2280]
For in my house there is neither bread nor cloak;
You should not appoint[7760] me ruler of the people."
8 For [a]Jerusalem has stumbled,[3782] and Judah has fallen,[5307]
Because their [Ib]speech and their actions are against the LORD,
To [c]rebel[4784] against [II]His glorious[3519] presence.
9 [I]The expression of their faces bears witness against them.
And they display[5046] their sin like [a]Sodom;
They do not *even* conceal *it.*
Woe to [II]them![5315]
For they have [b]brought[1580] evil[7451] on themselves.

2 [a]2Kin. 24:14; Is. 9:14, 15; Ezek. 17:12, 13

4 [I]Lit., *arbitrary power will rule* [a]Eccl. 10:16

5 [a]Mic. 7:3-6 [b]Is. 9:19; Jer. 9:3-8

6 [I]Lit., *hand* [a]Is. 4:1

7 [I]Lit., *lift up his voice* [II]Lit., *binder of wounds* [a]Ezek. 34:4; Hos. 5:13

8 [I]Lit., *tongue* [II]Lit., *the eyes of His glory* [a]Is. 1:7; 6:11 [b]Ps. 73:9-11; Is. 9:17; 59:3 [c]Is. 65:3

9 [I]Or, *Their partiality bears* [II]Lit., *their soul* [a]Gen. 13:13; Is. 1:10-15 [b]Prov. 8:36; 15:32; Rom. 6:23

10 [a]Deut. 28:1-14; Eccl. 8:12; Is. 54:17

11 [I]Lit., *the dealing of his hands* [a]Deut. 28:15-68; Is. 65:6, 7

12 [I]Or, *deal severely* [a]Is. 3:4 [b]Is. 9:16; 28:14, 15

13 [a]Is. 66:16; Hos. 4:1; Mic. 6:2

14 [a]Job 22:4; Ps. 143:2; Ezek. 20:35, 36 [b]Ps. 14:4; Mic. 3:3 [c]Job 24:9, 14; Ps. 10:9; Prov. 30:14; Is. 10:1, 2; Ezek. 18:12; James 2:6

15 [I]Heb., *YHWH,* usually rendered *LORD* [a]Ps. 94:5

16 [I]Lit., *outstretched necks* [a]Song 3:11; Is. 3:16-4:1, 4; 32:9-15

10 Say[559] to the [a]righteous[6662] that *it will go* well *with them,*
For they will eat the fruit of their actions.
11 Woe to the wicked![7563] *It will go* badly *with him,*
For [Ia]what he deserves[3027] will be done to him.
12 O My people! Their oppressors [I]are [a]children,
And women[802] rule over them.
O My people! [b]Those who guide[833] you lead *you* astray,[8582]
And confuse[1104] the direction[1870] of your paths.[734]

God Will Judge

13 [a]The LORD arises[5324] to contend,[7378]
And stands to judge[1777] the people.
14 The LORD [a]enters into judgment[4941] with the elders[2204] and princes of His people,
"It is you who have [b]devoured the vineyard;
The [c]plunder of the poor is in your houses.[1004]
15 "What do you mean by [a]crushing My people,
And grinding the face of the poor?"
Declares[5001] the Lord[136] [I]GOD of hosts.

Judah's Women Denounced

16 Moreover, the LORD said,[559]
"Because the [a]daughters of Zion are proud,
And walk with [I]heads held high and seductive eyes,
And go along with mincing steps,
And tinkle the bangles on their feet,
17 Therefore the Lord will afflict the scalp of the daughters of Zion with scabs,

And the LORD will make their
foreheads bare."

18 In that day the Lord will take
away the beauty[8597] of *their* anklets,
headbands,[7636] [a]crescent ornaments,
19 dangling earrings, bracelets,
veils,
20 [a]headdresses, ankle chains,
sashes, perfume boxes,[1004,5315] amulets,
21 [I]finger rings, [a]nose[639] rings,
22 festal robes, outer tunics,[4595]
cloaks,[4304] money purses,[2754]
23 hand mirrors, undergarments,
turbans, and veils.

24 Now it will come about that
instead of [I]sweet [a]perfume
there will be putrefaction;
Instead of a belt,[2290] a rope;
Instead of [b]well-set hair, a
[c]plucked-out scalp;
Instead of fine clothes, a
[d]donning of sackcloth;
And branding instead of beauty.
25 Your men will [a]fall by the
sword,[2719]
And your [I]mighty ones in battle.
26 And her [I][a]gates will lament and
mourn;
And deserted[5352] she will
[b]sit on the ground.[776]

A Remnant Prepared

4 For seven women[802] will take hold
of [a]one man[376] in that day,[3117] saying, "We will eat our own bread and
wear our own clothes, only let us be
called[7121] by your name; [b]take away our
reproach!"[2781]
2 In that day the [a]Branch of the
LORD will be beautiful[6643] and glorious,[3519] and the [b]fruit of the earth[776]
will be the pride and the adornment[8597]
of the [c]survivors[6413] of Israel.
3 And it will come about that he who
is [a]left[7604] in Zion and remains[3498] in
Jerusalem will be called [b]holy—[6918]
everyone who is [c]recorded for life[2416]
in Jerusalem.

18 [a]Judg. 8:21, 26
20 [a]Ex. 39:28
21 [I]Or, *signet rings* [a]Gen. 24:47; Ezek. 16:12
24 [I]Or, *balsam oil* [a]Esth. 2:12 [b]1Pet. 3:3 [c]Is. 22:12; Ezek. 27:31; Amos 8:10 [d]Is. 15:3; Lam. 2:10
25 [I]Lit., *strength* [a]Is. 1:20; 65:12
26 [I]Lit., *entrances* [a]Jer. 14:2; Lam. 1:4 [b]Lam. 2:10

1 [a]Is. 13:12 [b]Gen. 30:23; Is. 54:4
2 [a]Is. 11:1; 53:2; Jer. 23:5; 33:15; Zech. 3:8; 6:12 [b]Ps. 72:16 [c]Is. 10:20; 37:31, 32; Joel 2:32; Obad. 17
3 [a]Is. 28:5; 46:3; Rom. 11:4, 5 [b]Is. 52:1; 62:12 [c]Ex. 32:32; Ps. 69:28; Luke 10:20
4 [I]Lit., *rinsed away* [a]Is. 3:16 [b]Is. 1:15 [c]Is. 28:6 [d]Is. 1:31; 9:19; Matt. 3:11
5 [a]Ex. 13:21, 22; 24:16; Num. 9:15-23 [b]Is. 60:1, 2
6 [I]Lit., *a hiding place* [a]Ps. 27:5; Is. 25:4; 32:1, 2

1 [I]Lit., *a horn, the son of fatness* [a]Ps. 80:8; Jer. 12:10; Matt. 21:33; Mark 12:1; Luke 20:9
2 [I]Lit., *a bright red grape* [II]Or, *wine press* [III]Or, *wild grapes* [a]Jer. 2:21 [b]Matt. 21:19; Mark 11:13; Luke 13:6
3 [a]Matt. 21:40
4 [I]Lit., *and I have not done* [II]Or, *wild grapes* [a]2Chr. 36:16; Jer. 2:5; 7:25, 26; Mic. 6:3; Matt. 23:37

4 When the Lord[136] has washed[7364]
away the filth of the [a]daughters of Zion,
and [I]purged[1740] the [b]bloodshed[1818] of Jerusalem from her midst,[7130] by the
[c]spirit[7307] of judgment[4941] and the
[d]spirit of burning,
5 then the LORD will create[1254] over
the whole area of Mount Zion and over
her assemblies[4744] [a]a cloud[6051] by
day,[3119] even smoke, and the brightness
of a flaming fire by night;[3915] for over
all the [b]glory[3519] will be a canopy.
6 And there will be a [a]shelter[5521]
to *give* shade from the heat by day,[3119]
and refuge[4563] and [I]protection from the
storm and the rain.

Parable of the Vineyard

5 🔑 Let me sing now for my
well-beloved[3039]
A song[7892] of my beloved[1730]
concerning His vineyard.
My well-beloved had a
[a]vineyard on [I]a fertile[8081] hill.
2 And He dug it all around,
removed its stones,
And planted it with [I]the
[a]choicest vine.
And He built a tower in the
middle of it,
And hewed out a [II]wine vat in
it;
Then He [b]expected[6960] *it* to
produce[6213] *good* grapes,
But it produced *only* [III]worthless
ones.
3 "And now, O inhabitants of
Jerusalem and men[376] of
Judah,
[a]Judge[8199] between Me and My
vineyard.
4 "[a]What more was there to do for
My vineyard [I]that I have not
done in it?
Why, when I expected *it* to
produce *good* grapes did it
produce [II]worthless ones?
5 "So now let Me tell[3045] you what

🔑 **5:1-7** This famous Song of the Vineyard formed the backdrop against which Jesus set His parable of the wicked tenants (Mt. 21:33-41; Mk. 12:1-9).

I am going to do[6213] to My
vineyard:
I will [a]remove its hedge and it
will be consumed;
I will [b]break down its wall and
it will become [c]trampled
ground.
6 "And I will [a]lay it waste;
It will not be pruned or hoed,
But briars and thorns will come
up.[5927]
I will also charge[6680] the clouds
to [b]rain no rain on it."
7 For the [a]vineyard of the LORD
of hosts[6635] is the house[1004]
of Israel,
And the men of Judah His
delightful plant.
Thus He looked for justice,[4941]
but behold, [b]bloodshed;
For righteousness,[6666] but
behold, a cry of distress.

Woes for the Wicked

8 Woe to those who [a]add house
to house *and* join field[7704] to
field,
Until there is no more room,
So that you have to live alone
in the midst[7130] of the land![776]
9 In my ears[241] the LORD of hosts
has sworn, "Surely, [a]many
houses[1004] shall become
[b]desolate,[8047]
Even great and fine[2896] ones,
without occupants.
10 "For [a]ten acres of vineyard will
yield *only* one [I]bath *of wine,*
And a [b]homer[2563] of seed[2233] will
yield[6213] *but* an [II]ephah of
grain."
11 Woe to those who rise early in
the morning that they may
pursue [a]strong drink;
Who stay up late in the evening
that wine may inflame them!
12 And their banquets[4960] are
accompanied by lyre and
[a]harp, by tambourine[8596] and
flute, and by wine;
But they [b]do not pay attention
to the deeds of the LORD,
Nor do they consider[7200] the
work of His hands.[3027]
13 Therefore My people[5971] go into
exile[1540] for their [a]lack of
knowledge;
And [I]their [b]honorable men are
famished,
And their multitude is parched
with thirst.
14 Therefore [a]Sheol[7585] has
enlarged its [I]throat and
opened its mouth[6310] without
measure;
And [II]Jerusalem's splendor,[1926]
her multitude, her din[7588] *of
revelry,* and the jubilant within
her, descend *into it.*
15 So the *common* man[120] will be
humbled, and the man[376] of
importance abased,
[a]The eyes of the proud also will
be abased.
16 But the [a]LORD of hosts will be
[b]exalted in judgment,
And the holy[6918] God[410] will
show Himself [c]holy[6942] in
righteousness.
17 [a]Then the lambs will graze as
in their pasture,
And strangers[1481] will eat in the
waste places[2723] of the
[I]wealthy.
18 Woe to those who drag
[a]iniquity[5771] with the cords of
[I]falsehood,[7723]
And sin as if with cart ropes;
19 [a]Who say,[559] "Let Him make
speed, let Him hasten His
work, that we may see *it;*
And let the purpose[6098] of the
Holy One of Israel draw
near
And come to pass, that we may
know[3045] *it!"*
20 Woe to those who [a]call[559] evil[7451]
good,[2896] and good evil;
Who [I][b]substitute darkness[2822]
for light[216] and light for
darkness;
Who [I]substitute bitter[4571] for
sweet, and sweet for bitter!

5 [a]Ps. 89:40 [b]Ps. 80:12 [c]Is. 10:6; 28:18; Lam. 1:15; Luke 21:24; Rev. 11:2

6 [a]2Chr. 36:19-21; Is. 7:19-25; 24:1, 3; Jer. 25:11 [b]1Kin. 8:35; 17:1; Jer. 14:1-22

7 [a]Ps. 80:8-11 [b]Is. 3:14, 15; 30:12; 59:13

8 [a]Jer. 22:13-17; Mic. 2:2; Hab. 2:9-12

9 [a]Is. 6:11, 12 [b]Matt. 23:38

10 [I]I.e., Approx. 10½ gal. [II]I.e., Approx. one bu. [a]Lev. 26:26; Is. 7:23; Hag. 1:6; 2:16 [b]Ezek. 45:11

11 [a]Prov. 23:29, 30; Eccl. 10:16, 17; Is. 5:22; 22:13; 28:1, 3, 7, 8

12 [a]Amos 6:5, 6 [b]Job 34:27; Ps. 28:5

13 [I]Lit., *their glory are men of famine* [a]Is. 1:3; 27:11; Hos. 4:6 [b]Is. 3:3

14 [I]Or, *appetite* [II]Lit., *her* [a]Prov. 30:16; Hab. 2:5

15 [a]Is. 2:11; 10:33

16 [a]Is. 28:17; 30:18; 61:8 [b]Is. 2:11, 17; 33:5, 10 [c]Is. 8:13; 29:23; 1Pet. 3:15

17 [I]Lit., *the fat* [a]Is. 7:25; Mic. 2:12; Zeph. 2:6

18 [I]Or, *worthlessness* [a]Is. 59:4-8; Jer. 23:10-14

19 [a]Ezek. 12:22; 2Pet. 3:4

20 [I]Lit., *set* [a]Prov. 17:15; Amos 5:7 [b]Job 17:12; Matt. 6:22, 23; Luke 11:34, 35

21 Woe to those who are
[a]wise[2450] in their own eyes,
And clever[995] in their own sight!
22 [a]Woe to those who are heroes
in drinking wine,
And valiant[2428] men[582] in mixing
strong drink;
23 [a]Who justify[6663] the wicked[7563]
for a bribe,
And [b]take away the [I]rights of the
ones who are in the right![6662]
24 Therefore, [a]as a tongue of fire
consumes stubble,
And dry grass collapses[7503] into
the flame,
So their [b]root will become
[c]like rot and their blossom
[I]blow away as dust;[80]
For they have [d]rejected[3988] the
law[8451] of the LORD of hosts,
And despised[5006] the word[565] of
the Holy One of Israel.
25 On this account the [a]anger[639] of
the LORD has burned[2734]
against His people,
And He has stretched out His
hand[3027] against them and
struck them down,[5221]
And the [b]mountains quaked; and
their [c]corpses[5038] [I]lay like
refuse in the middle of the
streets.
[d]For all this His anger [II]is not
spent,
But His [e]hand is still stretched
out.
26 He will also lift up[5375] a
[a]standard to the [I]distant
nation,[1471]
And will [b]whistle for it
[c]from the ends of the earth;
And behold, it will [d]come with
speed swiftly.

21 [a]Prov. 3:7; Rom. 12:16; 1Cor. 3:18-20
22 [a]Prov. 23:20; Is. 5:11; 56:12; Hab. 2:15
23 [I]Lit., *righteousness* [a]Ex. 23:8; Is. 1:23; 10:1, 2; Mic. 3:11; 7:3 [b]Ps. 94:21; James 5:6
24 [I]Lit., *ascend* [a]Is. 9:18, 19; Joel 2:5 [b]Job 18:16 [c]Hos. 5:12 [d]Is. 8:6; 30:9, 12; Acts 13:41
25 [I]Lit., *were* [II]Lit., *has not turned away* [a]2Kin. 22:13, 17; Is. 66:15 [b]Ps. 18:7; Is. 64:3; Jer. 4:24; Nah. 1:5 [c]2Kin. 9:37; Is. 14:19; Jer. 16:4 [d]Is. 9:12, 17, 19, 21; 10:4; Jer. 4:8; Dan. 9:16 [e]Ex. 7:19; Is. 23:11
26 [I]Lit., *nations;* probably Assyria [a]Is. 13:2, 3 [b]Is. 7:18; Zech. 10:8 [c]Deut. 28:49 [d]Is. 13:4, 5
27 [a]Joel 2:7, 8 [b]Job 12:18
28 [I]Lit., *Which, its arrows* [II]Lit., *are regarded as* [a]Ps. 7:12, 13; 45:5; Is. 13:18 [b]Is. 21:1; Jer. 4:13
29 [a]Jer. 51:38; Zeph. 3:3; Zech. 11:3 [b]Is. 10:6; 49:24, 25; Mic. 5:8 [c]Is. 42:22
30 [a]Is. 17:12; Jer. 6:23; Luke 21:25 [b]Is. 8:22; Jer. 4:23-28; Joel 2:10; Luke 21:25, 26

27 [a]No one in it is weary or
stumbles,[3782]
None slumbers or sleeps;
Nor is the [b]belt[232] at its waist
undone,
Nor its sandal strap[8288] broken.
28 [I][a]Its arrows are sharp,[8150] and
all its bows are bent;
The hoofs of its horses
[II]seem[2803] like flint, and its
chariot [b]wheels[1534] like a
whirlwind.
29 Its [a]roaring is like a lioness,
and it roars like young
lions;
It growls as it [b]seizes the prey,
And carries *it* off with
[c]no one to deliver[5337] *it.*
30 And it shall [a]growl over it in that
day[3117] like the roaring of the
sea.
If one [b]looks to the land,[776]
behold, there is darkness *and*
distress;
Even the light is darkened[2821]
by its clouds.[6183]

Isaiah's Vision

6 ⊶ In the year of [a]King[4428] Uzziah's
death,[4194] [b]I saw[7200] the Lord[136]
sitting on a throne,[3678] lofty and
exalted,[5375] with the train of His robe
filling the temple.[1964]
2 Seraphim[8314] stood above Him,
[a]each having six wings; with two he
covered[3680] his face, and with two[8147]
he covered his feet, and with two
he flew.

1 [a]2Kin. 15:7; 2Chr. 26:23; Is. 1:1 [b]John 12:41; Rev. 4:2, 3; 20:11 **2** [a]Rev. 4:8

⊶ **6:1-13** This is the classic prophetic call account in the O.T. It occurred in 740 B.C., the year in which King Uzziah died. Isaiah was in the temple and was permitted to see the Lord in some unspecified manner, but the experience struck fear into him, because of the impurity of his own sins and those of the people. He was cleansed by a seraph, an awesome creature with six wings and a burning appearance. To the Lord's request for someone to go on a mission for Him, Isaiah issued one of the most famous statements in the prophets: "Here am I; send me" (see v. 8). God's mission was to a people who would not listen and was to continue until great desolation had occurred; yet, Isaiah faithfully executed

(continued on next page)

3 And one called out[7121] to another
and said,[559]

"[a]Holy,[6918] Holy, Holy, is the
LORD of hosts,[6635]
The [Ib]whole earth[776] is full of His
glory."[3519]

4 And the [I]foundations of the thresholds trembled at the voice of him who
called out, while the [IIa]temple[1004] was
filling with smoke.

5 Then I said,

"[a]Woe is me, for I am ruined![1820]
Because I am a man[376] of
[b]unclean[2931] lips,[8193]
And I live among a [c]people[5971]
of unclean lips;
For my eyes have seen[7200] the
[d]King, the LORD of hosts."

6 Then one of the seraphim flew
to me, with a burning coal in his hand[3027]
which he had taken from the [a]altar[4196]
with tongs.

7 And he [a]touched my mouth[6310]
with it and said, "Behold, this has
touched[5060] your lips; and [b]your iniquity[5771] is taken away,[5493] and your
sin[2403] is [I]forgiven."[3722]

Isaiah's Commission

8 Then I heard[8085] the [a]voice of the
Lord, saying, "Whom shall I send, and
who will go for Us?" Then [b]I said, "Here
am I. Send me!"

9 And He said, "Go, and tell[559] this
people:

'Keep on [a]listening,[8085] but do not
perceive;[995]
Keep on looking, but do not
understand.'[3045]

10 "[a]Render the hearts[3820] of this
people [Ib]insensitive,
Their ears[241] [II]dull,[3513]
And their eyes [III]dim,
[c]Lest they see with their
eyes,
Hear with their ears,
Understand with their
hearts,[3824]
And return[7725] and be healed."

11 Then I said, "Lord, [a]how long?"
And He answered,[559]
"Until [b]cities are devastated *and*
without inhabitant,
Houses[1004] are without
people,[120]
And the land[127] is utterly
desolate,[8077]

12 "The LORD has [a]removed men[120]
far away,
And the [Ib]forsaken places are
many in the midst[7130] of the
land.[776]

13 "Yet there will be a tenth portion
in it,
And it will again[7725] be *subject*
to burning,
Like a terebinth or an [a]oak
Whose stump[4678] remains when
it is felled.
The [b]holy[6944] seed[2233] is its
stump."

War against Jerusalem

7 Now it came about in the days[3117]
of [a]Ahaz, the son[1121] of Jotham, the
son of Uzziah, king[4428] of Judah, that
[b]Rezin the king of Aram and [c]Pekah the
son of Remaliah, king of Israel, went
up[5927] to Jerusalem to *wage* war against
it, but [d]could not [I]conquer it.

2 When it was reported[5046] to the
[a]house[1004] of David, saying, "The Arameans [Ib]have camped in [c]Ephraim," his
heart[3824] and the hearts of his people[5971]

3 [I]Lit., *fulness of the whole earth is His glory* [a]Rev. 4:8 [b]Num. 14:21; Ps. 72:19

4 [I]Lit., *door sockets* [II]Lit., *house* [a]Rev. 15:8

5 [a]Ex. 33:20; Luke 5:8 [b]Ex. 6:12, 30 [c]Is. 59:3; Jer. 9:3-8 [d]Jer. 51:57

6 [a]Rev. 8:3

7 [I]Lit., *atoned for* [a]Jer. 1:9; Dan. 10:16 [b]Is. 40:2; 53:5, 6, 11; 1John 1:7

8 [a]Ezek. 10:5; Acts 9:4 [b]Acts 26:19

9 [a]Is. 43:8; Matt. 13:14; Mark 4:12; Luke 8:10; John 12:40; Acts 28:26; Rom. 11:8

10 [I]Lit., *fat* [II]Lit., *heavy* [III]Lit., *besmeared* [a]Matt. 13:15 [b]Deut. 31:20; 32:15 [c]Jer. 5:21

11 [a]Ps. 79:5 [b]Lev. 26:31; Is. 1:7; 3:8, 26

12 [I]Or, *forsakenness will be great* [a]Deut. 28:64 [b]Jer. 4:29

13 [a]Job 14:7 [b]Deut. 7:6; Ezra 9:2

1 [I]Lit., *fight against* [a]2Kin. 16:1; Is. 1:1 [b]2Kin. 15:37 [c]2Kin. 15:25; 2Chr. 28:6 [d]Is. 7:6, 7

2 [I]Lit., *has settled down on* [a]Is. 7:13; 22:22 [b]Is. 8:12 [c]Is. 9:9

(continued from previous page)
his charge for forty to fifty years. Later, Jesus used Isa. 6:9,10 to explain His use of the parable as a teaching technique (Mt. 13:14,15; Mk. 4:12; Lk. 8:10). As John was summing up Jesus' ministry before the last week of His life, he cited Isa. 6:10 to explain why so few Jews had responded to Jesus' message (Jn. 12:40). In Acts 28:26,27, Paul used the verses to give the reason why he redirected his ministry from the Jews to the Gentiles. The point of all this was that the Jews, as a whole, in the first century A.D., were no different from the unresponsive nation which Isaiah had addressed in the eighth century B.C. See note on Jer. 1:5.

shook as the trees of the forest shake
[II]with the wind.[7307]
🔑 **3** Then the LORD said[559] to Isaiah,
"Go out now to meet Ahaz, you and
your son [I]Shear-jashub, at the end of
the [a]conduit of the upper[5945] pool, on
the highway to the [II]fuller's[3526] field,[7704]
4 and say[559] to him, 'Take care,[8104]
and be [a]calm,[8252] have no [b]fear[3372] and
[c]do not be fainthearted because of these
two stubs of smoldering [d]firebrands, on
account of the fierce[2750] anger[639] of
Rezin and Aram, and the [e]son of Remaliah.
5 'Because [a]Aram, *with* Ephraim
and the son of Remaliah, has planned[3289]
evil[7451] against you, saying,
6 "Let us go up against Judah and
[I]terrorize[6973] it, and make for ourselves
a breach in [II]its walls, and set up the
son of Tabeel as king in the midst of
it,"
7 thus says[559] the Lord[136] [I]GOD, "[a]It
shall not stand nor shall it come to pass.
8 "For the head[7218] of Aram is
[a]Damascus and the head of Damascus
is Rezin (now within another 65 years
Ephraim will be shattered, *so that it is*
no longer a people),
9 and the head of Ephraim is Samaria
and the head of Samaria is the son of
Remaliah. [a]If you will not believe,[539] you
surely shall not [I]last." ' "[539]

The Child Immanuel

10 Then the LORD spoke[1696] again
to Ahaz, saying,
11 "Ask[7592] a [a]sign for yourself from
the LORD your God;[430] [I]make *it* deep
as Sheol or high as [II]heaven."
12 But Ahaz said, "I will not ask,
nor will I test[5254] the LORD!"
13 Then he said, "Listen[8085] now,
O [a]house of David! Is it too slight a
thing for you to try the patience of
men,[582] that you will [b]try the patience
of [c]my God as well?
🔑 14 "Therefore the Lord Himself will
give you a sign: Behold, [a]a [I]virgin[5959]
will be with child and bear a son, and
she will call[7121] His name [II][b]Immanuel.
15 "He will eat [a]curds and honey
[I]at the time He knows[3045] *enough* to refuse evil and choose[977] good.[2896]

2 [II]Lit., *from before*
3 [I]I.e., a remnant shall return [II]I.e., laundryman's [a]2Kin. 18:17; Is. 36:2
4 [a]Ex. 14:13; Is. 30:15; Lam. 3:26 [b]Is. 10:24; Matt. 24:6 [c]Deut. 20:3; 1Sam. 17:32; Is. 35:4 [d]Amos 4:11; Zech. 3:2 [e]Is. 7:1, 9
5 [a]Is. 7:2
6 [I]Lit., *cause it a sickening dread* [II]Lit., *it*
7 [I]Heb., *YHWH*, usually rendered LORD [a]Is. 8:10; 28:18; Acts 4:25, 26
8 [a]Gen. 14:15; Is. 17:1-3
9 [I]Or, *be established* [a]2Chr. 20:20; Is. 5:24; 8:6-8; 30:12-14
11 [I]So with the versions; M.T., *make the request deep or high* [II]Lit., *heights* [a]2Kin. 19:29; Is. 37:30; 38:7, 8; 55:13
13 [a]Is. 7:2 [b]Is. 1:14; 43:24 [c]Is. 25:1
14 [I]Or, *maiden* [II]I.e., God is with us [a]Matt. 1:23 [b]Is. 8:8, 10

15 [I]Lit., *with respect to his knowing* [a]Is. 7:22

🔑 **7:3** See note on Isa. 8:1-4.

🔑 **7:14** Since Matthew first applied this verse to the virginal conception of Jesus (Mt. 1:23), it has been one of the key passages in the Christian collection of O.T. prophecies of Jesus. So effective were the early Christians in using this verse, and a few others from the Septuagint (the Greek, O.T. originally done by Jews in Egypt), that the Jews found it necessary to modify the translation and even produce another Greek O.T. Matthew applied it to Jesus on the basis of an interpretive principle which saw equally God-given deeper meanings for O.T. passages. In the context of the eighth century B.C., Isaiah was offering Judah's king, Ahaz, a sign of encouragement and perhaps even of punishment, should he not act on faith. Ahaz was concerned with pressure being put on him by Rezin of Damascus and Pekah of Israel, so he wanted to appeal for help from Tiglath-pileser III of Assyria (II Kgs. 16:5-7). Isaiah directed Ahaz to trust in the Lord, not in a foreign king, and offered him a sign of God's help. A woman was to conceive and bear a son, whom she would name Immanuel, which means "God with us." While the child was still young, the crisis would end. Whether or not the woman was a virgin when she conceived had nothing to do with the sign to Ahaz. The sign was in the meaning of the boy's name and in how soon the problem would be over, as indicated by his young age. Ahaz did not heed Isaiah's words and appealed to the Assyrian king, plundering the temple and his own treasury to pay for his help (II Kgs. 16:7,8). Tiglath-pileser defeated Damascus and killed Rezin (II Kgs. 16:9). In 732 B.C. he captured and exiled northern Israel, and Pekah was assassinated (II Kgs. 15:29,30). God had already determined to solve Ahaz' problem, but Ahaz foolishly took matters into his own hands and paid dearly for it. Since Matthew's use of this passage was based on the Greek O.T., not the Hebrew, and since he was deriving a deeper meaning than the one at the historical level which applied to Isaiah's day, whether the Hebrew word in Isa. 7:14 should be translated, "young woman" or "virgin" has no real bearing on the issue of Jesus' virgin birth. Matthew settled the question by choosing to follow a translation which made His virgin birth explicit. See *bethulah* (1330) and *'almah* (5959) in the Hebrew Lexical Aids section.

16 "[a]For before the boy will know *enough* to refuse evil and choose good, [b]the land[127] whose two kings[4428] you dread[6973] will be forsaken.[5800]

Trials to Come for Judah

17 "The LORD will bring on you, on your people, and on your father's[1] house such days as have never come since the day[3117] that [a]Ephraim separated from Judah, the [b]king of Assyria."

18 And it will come about in that day, that the LORD will [a]whistle for the fly that is in the [Ib]remotest part of the rivers of Egypt, and for the bee that is in the land[776] of Assyria.

19 And they will all come and settle on the steep [I]ravines, on the [a]ledges of the cliffs, [b]on all the thorn bushes, and on all the [II]watering places.

20 In that day the Lord will [a]shave with a [b]razor, [c]hired from regions beyond [d]the [I]Euphrates (*that is,* with the king of Assyria), the head and the hair of the legs; and it will also remove[5595] the beard.[2206]

21 Now it will come about in that day that a man[376] may keep alive a [a]heifer and a pair of sheep;

22 and it will happen that because of the abundance of the milk produced he will eat curds, for everyone that is left within the land will eat [a]curds and honey.

23 And it will come about in that day, [a]that every place where there used to be a thousand vines, *valued* at a thousand *shekels* of silver, will become [b]briars and thorns.

24 *People* will come there with bows and arrows because all the land will be[1961] briars and thorns.

25 And as for all the hills which used to be cultivated with the hoe,[4576] you will not go there for fear[3374] of briars and thorns; but they will become a place for [Ia]pasturing oxen and for sheep to trample.

Damascus and Samaria Fall

8 🗝 Then the LORD said[599] to me, "Take for yourself a large tablet and [a]write on it [I]in ordinary letters:[2747] [IIb]Swift is the booty, speedy is the prey.

2 "And [I]I will take to Myself faithful[539] witnesses for testimony, [a]Uriah the priest[3548] and Zechariah the son[1121] of Jeberechiah."

3 So I approached the prophetess,[5031] and she conceived and gave birth to a son. Then the LORD said to me, "Name[7121] him [Ia]Maher-shalal-hash-baz;

4 for [a]before the boy knows[3045] how to cry out[7121] 'My father'[1] or 'My mother,'[517] the wealth[2428] of [b]Damascus and the spoil of Samaria will be carried away[5375] before the king[4428] of Assyria."

5 And again the LORD spoke[1696] to me further, saying,

6 "Inasmuch as these people[5971]
have [a]rejected[3488] the gently
flowing waters of Shiloah,
And rejoice in [b]Rezin and the
son of Remaliah;
7 "Now therefore, behold, the
Lord[136] is about to bring
on[5927] them the [a]strong and
abundant waters of the
[Ib]Euphrates,
Even the [c]king of Assyria and
all his glory;[3519]
And it will [d]rise up[5927] over all
its channels and go over[5674]
all its banks.

16 [a]Is. 8:4 [b]Is. 8:14; 17:3; Jer. 7:15; Hos. 5:3, 9, 14; Amos 1:3-5
17 [a]1Kin. 12:16 [b]2Chr. 28:20; Is. 8:7, 8; 10:5, 6
18 [I]Or, *mouth of the rivers;* i.e., the Nile Delta [a]Is. 5:26 [b]Is. 13:5
19 [I]Or, *wadis* [II]Or, *pastures* [a]Is. 2:19; Jer. 16:16 [b]Is. 7:24,25
20 [I]Lit., *River* [a]2Kin. 18:13-16; Is. 24:1 [b]Ezek. 5:1-4 [c]Is. 10:5, 15 [d]Is. 8:7; 11:15; Jer. 2:18
21 [a]Is. 14:30; 27:10; Jer. 39:10
22 [a]Is. 8:15
23 [a]Is. 5:10; 32:13, 14 [b]Is. 5:6
25 [I]Lit., *sending* [a]Is. 5:17
1 [I]Lit., *with the stylus of man* [II]Heb., *Maher-shalal-hash-baz* [a]Is. 30:8; Hab. 2:2 [b]Is. 8:3
2 [I]Another reading is *take for me* [a]2Kin. 16:10, 11, 15, 16
3 [I]I.e., swift is the booty, speedy is the prey [a]Is. 8:1
4 [a]Is. 7:16 [b]Is. 7:8, 9
6 [a]Is. 1:20; 5:24; 7:9; 30:12 [b]Is. 7:1
7 [I]Lit., *River* [a]Is. 17:12, 13 [b]Is. 7:20; 11:15 [c]Is. 7:17; 10:5 [d]Amos 8:8; 9:5

🗝 **8:1-4** Scholars are divided on whether the child in this sign is the same as in the preceding chapter (7:14-16). There are several similarities between the two, but the differences suggest that probably two different children were involved. In this case, the child is Isaiah's own. Isaiah took the precaution of validating the sign ahead of time. The prophetic sign was in the name of the child, Maher-shalal-hash-baz, which means "the spoil speeds, the prey hastens," indicating the fate of Damascus and Samaria. Isaiah's other son, Shear-jashub, also bore a prophetic name, meaning, "a remnant will return" (Isa. 7:3). See note on Ezek. 24:15-24.

🔑 8 "Then [a]it will sweep on into Judah,
it will overflow[7857] and pass
through,
It will [b]reach[5060] even to the
neck;
And the spread of its wings will
[I]fill the breadth of [II]your
land,[776] O [c]Immanuel.

A Believing Remnant

9 "[a]Be broken, O peoples, and be
[Ib]shattered;
And give ear,[238] all remote
places of the earth.[776]
Gird yourselves, yet be
[I]shattered;
Gird yourselves, yet be
[I]shattered.
10 "[a]Devise a plan[6098] but it will be
thwarted;[6565]
State[1696] a [I]proposal,[1697] but
[b]it will not stand,
For [IIc]God[410] is with us."
11 For thus the LORD spoke[559] to
me [I]with [a]mighty[2393] power[3027] and
instructed[3256] me [b]not to walk in the
way[1870] of this people, saying,
12 "You are not to say,[559] '*It is* a
[a]conspiracy!'
In regard to all that this people
call a conspiracy,
And [b]you are not to fear[3372]
[I]what they fear[4172] or be in
dread[6206] of *it.*
13 "It is the [a]LORD of hosts[6635]
[b]whom you should regard as
holy.[6942]
And He shall be your fear,
And He shall be your dread.[6206]
🔑 14 "Then He shall become a
[a]sanctuary;[4720]
But to both the houses[1004] of
Israel, a [b]stone to strike[5063]
and a rock to stumble[4383]
over,
And a snare[6341] and a [c]trap[4170]
for the inhabitants of
Jerusalem.
15 "And many [a]will stumble[3782] over
them,
Then they will fall and be
broken;[7665]
They will even be snared[3369] and
caught."
🔑 **16** [a]Bind up the testimony,[8584]
[b]seal the [I]law[8451] among [c]my disciples.[3928]
17 And I will [a]wait for the LORD
[b]who is hiding His face from the
house[1004] of Jacob; I will even look eagerly for Him.
18 [a]Behold, I and the children whom
the LORD has given me are for [b]signs
and wonders[4159] in Israel from the LORD
of hosts, who [c]dwells[7931] on Mount Zion.
19 And when they say to you,
"[a]Consult the mediums[178] and the
spiritists[3049] who whisper and mutter,"
should not a people [b]consult their
God?[430] *Should they* [c]*consult* the dead[4191]
on behalf of the living?[2416]
20 To the [Ia]law and to the testimony! If they do not speak[559] according
to this word, it is because [b]they have
no dawn.
21 And they will pass through[5674]
[I]the land [a]hard-pressed and famished,

8 [I]Lit., *be the fulness of* [II]Or, *Your* [a]Is. 10:6 [b]Is. 30:28 [c]Is. 7:14
9 [I]Or, *dismayed* [a]Is. 17:12-14 [b]Dan. 2:34, 35
10 [I]Lit., *word* [II]Heb., *Immanuel* [a]Job 5:12; Is. 28:18 [b]Is. 7:7 [c]Is. 8:8; Rom. 8:31
11 [I]Lit., *with strength of the hand* [a]Ezek. 3:14 [b]Ezek. 2:8
12 [I]Lit., *their fear* [a]Is. 7:2; 30:1 [b]1Pet. 3:14, 15
13 [a]Is. 5:16; 29:23 [b]Num. 20:12
14 [a]Is. 4:6; 25:4; Ezek. 11:16 [b]Luke 2:34; Rom. 9:33; 1Pet. 2:8 [c]Is. 24:17, 18
15 [a]Is. 28:13; 59:10; Luke 20:18; Rom. 9:32
16 [I]Or, *teaching* [a]Is. 8:1, 2; 29:11, 12 [b]Dan. 12:4 [c]Is. 50:4
17 [a]Is. 25:9; 30:18; Hab. 2:3 [b]Deut. 31:17; Is. 1:15; 45:15; 54:8
18 [a]Heb. 2:13 [b]Luke 2:34 [c]Ps. 9:11; Zech. 8:3
19 [a]Lev. 20:6; 2Kin. 21:6; 23:24; Is. 19:3; 29:4; 47:12, 13 [b]Is. 30:2; 45:11 [c]1Sam. 28:8-11
20 [I]Or, *teaching* [a]Is. 1:10; 8:16; Luke 16:29 [b]Is. 8:22; Mic. 3:6
21 [I]Lit., *it* [a]Is. 9:20, 21

🔑 **8:8** Ahaz refused to heed Isaiah's two signs, so in this oracle the consequences are spelled out. The words "even to the neck" probably refer to the fact that when Sennacherib devastated Judah in 701 B.C., Jerusalem herself did not fall. See note on Mic. 1:9.

🔑 **8:14** This is one of a group of three "stone" passages which are seen in various combinations in the N.T. as prophecies of Jesus (see also Isa. 28:16; Ps. 118:22). Jesus, Himself, used them to refer to the Jewish leaders who had rejected Him (Mt. 21:42; Mk. 12:10,11; Lk. 20:17). Peter, addressing some of the same group, employed one of the verses to explain who Jesus was (Acts 4:11), and later he connected all three with the fact that Christians are living stones in a spiritual house (I Pet. 2:6-8). Paul referred to two of the passages to give the reason why the Jews as a rule missed out on righteousness, but many Gentiles did not (Rom. 9:33). Significantly, the One referred to in Isa. 8:14 is Yahweh (Jehovah), so the application to Jesus of an O.T. passage which refers to Yahweh is evidence of the fact that the early Christians regarded Jesus as a part of the Godhead, not simply as a man.

🔑 **8:16** See note on Jer. 36:2.

and it will turn out that when they are hungry, they will be enraged[7107] and curse [II]their king and their God as they face upward.

22 Then they will [a]look to the earth,[776] and behold, distress and darkness,[2825] the gloom of anguish;6695 and *they will be* [b]driven away into darkness.[653]

Birth and Reign of the Prince of Peace

9 [I]But there will be no *more* [a]gloom for her who was in anguish;4164 in earlier times[7723] He [b]treated[7043] the [c]land[776] of Zebulun and the land of Naphtali with contempt,[7043] but later on He shall make *it* glorious,[3513] by the way[1870] of the sea, on the other side of Jordan, Galilee of the [II]Gentiles.[1471]

2 [I][a]The people[5971] who walk in
darkness[2822]
Will see[7200] a great light;[216]
Those who live in a dark land,[6757]
The light will shine on them.
3 [a]Thou shalt multiply the
nation,[1471]
Thou [b]shalt [I]increase [II]their
gladness;
They will be glad in Thy
presence
As with the gladness [III]of
harvest,
As [IV][c]men rejoice when they
divide the spoil.
4 For [a]Thou shalt break[2865] the
yoke of their burden and the
staff[4294] on their shoulders,
The rod[7626] of their [b]oppressor,
as [I]at the battle[3117] of [c]Midian.
5 For every boot of the booted
warrior in the *battle* tumult,
And cloak rolled[1556] in blood,[1818]
will be for burning,[8316] fuel
for the fire.
6 For a [a]child will be born to us,
a [b]son[1121] will be given to us;
And the [c]government will
[I]rest [d]on His shoulders;
And His name will be called[7121]
[e]Wonderful[6382]
Counselor,[3289] [f]Mighty
God,[410]
Eternal[5703] [g]Father,[1] Prince[8269]
of [h]Peace.
7 There will be [a]no end to the
increase of *His* government
or of peace,
On the [b]throne[3678] of David and
over his kingdom,[4467]
To establish[3589] it and to uphold
it with [c]justice[4941] and
righteousness[6666]
From then on and
forevermore.[5769]
[d]The zeal[7068] of the LORD of
hosts6625 will accomplish[6213]
this.

God's Anger with Israel's Arrogance

8 The Lord[136] sends a
[I]message[1697] against Jacob,
And it falls[5307] on Israel.
9 And all the people know[3045] *it,*
That is, [a]Ephraim and the
inhabitants of Samaria,
Asserting[559] in pride and in
[b]arrogance of heart:[3824]
10 "The bricks have fallen[5307] down,
But we will [a]rebuild with
smooth[1496] stones;
The sycamores have been cut
down,
But we will replace *them* with
cedars."
11 Therefore the LORD raises
against them adversaries
from [a]Rezin,
And spurs their enemies on,
12 The Arameans on the east and
the [a]Philistines on the west;
And they [b]devour Israel with
[I]gaping jaws.[6310]
[c]In *spite of* all this His anger[639]
does not turn away,
And His hand[3027] is still
stretched out.
13 Yet the people [a]do not turn[7725]
back to Him who struck
them,

21 [II]Or, *by their king*

22 [a]Is. 5:30; 59:9; Jer. 13:16; Amos 5:18, 20; Zeph. 1:14, 15 [b]Is. 8:20

1 [I]Ch. 8:23 in Heb. [II]Or, *nations* [a]Is. 8:22 [b]2Kin. 15:29; 2Chr. 16:4 [c]Matt. 4:15, 16

2 [I]Ch. 9:1 in Heb. [a]Matt. 4:16; Luke 1:79; Eph. 5:8

3 [I]Another reading is *not increase* [II]Lit., *the* [III]Lit., *in* [IV]Lit., *they* [a]Is. 26:15 [b]Is. 35:10; 65:14, 18, 19; 66:10 [c]1Sam. 30:16

4 [I]Lit., *in the day of Midian* [a]Is. 10:27; 14:25 [b]Is. 14:4; 49:26; 51:13; 54:14 [c]Judg. 7:25; Is. 10:26

6 [I]Lit., *be* [a]Is. 7:14; 11:1, 2; 53:2; Luke 2:11 [b]John 3:16 [c]Matt. 28:18; 1Cor. 15:25 [d]Is. 22:22 [e]Is. 28:29 [f]Deut. 10:17; Neh. 9:32; Is. 10:21 [g]Is. 63:16; 64:8 [h]Is. 26:3, 12; 54:10; 66:12

7 [a]Dan. 2:44; Luke 1:32, 33 [b]Is. 16:5 [c]Is. 11:4, 5; 32:1; 42:3, 4; 63:1 [d]Is. 37:32; 59:17

8 [I]Lit., *word*

9 [a]Is. 7:8, 9; 28:1, 3 [b]Is. 46:12

10 [a]Mal. 1:4

11 [a]Is. 7:1, 8

12 [I]Lit., *the whole mouth* [a]2Chr. 28:18 [b]Ps. 79:7; Jer. 10:25 [c]Is. 5:25

13 [a]Jer. 5:3; Hos. 7:10

Nor do they [b]seek the LORD of
hosts.
14 So the LORD cuts off[3772]
[a]head[7218] and tail from Israel,
Both palm branch and bulrush
[b]in a single day.
15 The head is [a]the elder[2204] and
honorable man,
And the prophet[5030] who
teaches[3384] [b]falsehood[8267] is
the tail.
16 [a]For those who guide[833] this
people are leading *them*
astray;[8582]
And those who are guided[833] by
them are [I]brought to
confusion.[1104]
17 Therefore the Lord does
[a]not take pleasure in their
young men,
[b]Nor does He have pity[7355] on
their [I]orphans or their
widows;
For every one of them is
[c]godless[2611] and an
[d]evildoer,[7489]
And every [e]mouth is speaking
foolishness.
[f]In *spite of* all this His anger does
not turn away,
And His hand is still stretched
out.
18 [a]For wickedness[7564] burns like
a fire;
It consumes briars and thorns;
It even sets the thickets of the
forest aflame,
And they roll upward in a column
of smoke.
19 By the [a]fury[5678] of the LORD of
hosts the [b]land is burned
up,
And the [c]people are like fuel for
the fire;
No [d]man[376] spares his
brother.[251]
20 And [I]they slice off *what is* on
the right hand but *still* are
[a]hungry,
And [II]they eat *what is* on the
left hand but they are not
satisfied;

13 [b]Is. 31:1; Hos. 3:5

14 [a]Is. 19:15 [b]Rev. 18:8

15 [a]Is. 3:2, 3 [b]Is. 28:15; 59:3, 4; Jer. 23:14, 32; Matt. 24:24

16 [I]Or, *swallowed up* [a]Is. 3:12; Matt. 15:14; 23:16, 24

17 [I]Or, *fatherless* [a]Jer. 18:21; Amos 4:10; 8:13 [b]Is. 27:11 [c]Is. 10:6; 32:6 [d]Is. 1:4; 14:20; 31:2 [e]Matt. 12:34 [f]Is. 5:25

18 [a]Ps. 83:14; Is. 1:7; Nah. 1:10; Mal. 4:1

19 [a]Is. 10:6; 13:9, 13; 42:25 [b]Joel 2:3 [c]Is. 1:31; 24:6 [d]Mic. 7:2, 6

20 [I]Lit., *he slices* [II]Lit., *he eats* [a]Is. 8:21, 22 [b]Is. 49:26

21 [a]2Chr. 28:6, 8; Is. 11:13 [b]Is. 5:25

1 [I]Lit., *mischief* or *misfortune* [a]Ps. 94:20; Is. 29:21; 59:4, 13

2 [I]Lit., *turn aside from* [II]Or, *fatherless* [a]Is. 5:23 [b]Is. 1:23; 3:14, 15

3 [I]Lit., *glory* [a]Job 31:14 [b]Is. 13:6; 26:14, 21; 29:6; Jer. 9:9; Hos. 9:7; Luke 19:44 [c]Is. 5:26 [d]Is. 20:6; 30:5, 7; 31:3

4 [I]Lit., *under* [a]Is. 24:22 [b]Is. 22:2; 34:3; 66:16 [c]Is. 5:25

5 [a]Is. 7:17; 8:7; 14:24-27; Zeph. 2:13-15 [b]Jer. 51:20 [c]Is. 13:5; 30:30; 34:2; 66:14

6 [I]Lit., *make them a trampled place* [a]Is. 9:17 [b]Is. 9:19 [c]Is. 5:29 [d]Is. 5:25

Each of them[376] eats the
[b]flesh[1320] of his own arm.
21 Manasseh *devours* Ephraim, and
Ephraim Manasseh,
[a]*And* together they are against
Judah.
[b]In *spite of* all this His anger does
not turn away,
And His hand is still stretched
out.

Assyria Is God's Instrument

10 Woe to those who [a]enact[2710] evil
statutes,[2711]
And to those who constantly
record [I]unjust[5999] decisions,
2 So as [a]to [I]deprive the needy of
justice,[1779]
And rob the poor of My
people[5971] of *their* rights,[4941]
In order [b]that widows may be
their spoil,
And that they may plunder the
[II]orphans.
3 Now [a]what will you do[6213] in the
[b]day[3117] of punishment,[6486]
And in the devastation[7722] which
will come [c]from afar?
[d]To whom will you flee for help?
And where will you leave[5800]
your [I]wealth?[3519]
4 Nothing *remains* but to
crouch[3766] [I]among the
[a]captives
Or fall [I]among the [b]slain.[2026]
[c]In *spite of* all this His anger[639]
does not turn away,
And His hand[3027] is still
stretched out.
5 Woe to [a]Assyria, the [b]rod[7626] of
My anger
And the staff[4294] in whose hands
is [c]My indignation,[2195]
6 I send it against a [a]godless[2611]
nation[1471]
And commission[6680] it against
the [b]people of My fury[5678]
To capture booty and [c]to seize
plunder,
And to [I]trample them down like
[d]mud in the streets.

7 Yet it [a]does not so intend
Nor does [I]it plan[2803] so in its heart,
But rather it is [II]its purpose[3824] to destroy,[8045]
And to cut off[3772] [III]many nations.[1471]
8 For it says,[559] "Are not my princes[8269] [I]all kings?[4428]
9 "Is not [a]Calno like [b]Carchemish,
Or [c]Hamath like Arpad,
Or [d]Samaria like [e]Damascus?
10 "As my hand has reached to the [a]kingdoms[4467] of the idols,[457]
Whose graven images *were* greater than those of Jerusalem and Samaria,
11 Shall I not [I]do to Jerusalem and her images
Just as I have done to Samaria and [a]her idols?"[6091]

12 So it will be that when the
Lord[136] has completed[1214] all His [a]work
on Mount Zion and on Jerusalem, *He*
will say, "I will [I]punish[6485] the fruit of
the arrogant heart of the king[4428] of
Assyria and [b]the pomp of [II]his haughtiness."

13 For [a]he has said,
"By the power of my hand and by my wisdom[2451] I did *this,*
For I have understanding;[995]
And I [b]removed[5493] the boundaries of the peoples,
And plundered[8154] their treasures,
And like a mighty man I brought down [I]*their* inhabitants,
14 And my hand reached to the riches[2428] of the peoples like a [a]nest,
And as one gathers[622] abandoned[5800] eggs, I gathered[622] all the earth;[776]
And there was not one that flapped its wing or opened *its* beak[6310] or chirped."

15 Is the [a]axe to [b]boast[6286] itself over the one who chops[2672] with it?
Is the saw to exalt itself over the one who wields[5130] it?
That would be like [c]a [I]club wielding[5130] those who lift it,
Or like [d]a rod lifting *him who* is not wood.
16 Therefore the Lord,[136] the [I]GOD of hosts,[6625] will send
a [a]wasting disease among his [b]stout warriors;
And under his [c]glory a fire will be kindled like a burning flame.
17 And the [a]light[216] of Israel will become a fire and his [b]Holy One[6918] a flame,
And it will [c]burn and devour his thorns and his briars in a single day.
18 And He will [a]destroy[3615] the glory of his forest and of his fruitful garden, both soul[5315] and body;
And it will be as when a sick man wastes away.
19 And the [a]rest[7605] of the trees of his forest will be so small in number
That a child could write them down.

A Remnant Will Return

20 Now it will come about in that
day that the [a]remnant[7605] of Israel, and
those of the house[1004] of Jacob [b]who
have escaped,[6413] will never again rely
on the one who struck[5221] them, but
will truly[571] [c]rely[8172] on the LORD, the
Holy One of Israel.

21 A [a]remnant will return,[7725] the remnant of Jacob, to the [b]mighty God.
22 For [a]though your people, O Israel, may be like the sand of the sea,
Only a remnant within them will return;
A [b]destruction is determined, overflowing[7857] with righteousness.[6666]

23 For a complete destruction,[3617]
one that is decreed, [a]the Lord [I]GOD of

---

7 [I]Lit., *its heart so plan* [II]Lit., *in its heart* [III]Lit., *not a few* [a]Gen. 50:20; Mic. 4:11, 12; Acts 2:23, 24
8 [I]Lit., *altogether*
9 [a]Gen. 10:10; Amos 6:2 [b]2Chr. 35:20 [c]Num. 34:8 [d]2Kin. 17:6 [e]2Kin. 16:9
10 [a]2Kin. 19:17, 18
11 [I]Lit., *do thus* [a]Is. 2:8
12 [I]Lit., *visit* [II]Lit., *haughtiness of his eyes* [a]2 Kin. 19:31; Is. 28:21, 22; 29:14; 65:7 [b]Is. 37:23
13 [I]Or, *those who sit* on thrones [a]2Kin. 19:22-24; Is. 37:24-27; Ezek. 28:4; Dan. 4:30 [b]Hab. 2:6-11
14 [a]Jer. 49:16; Obad. 4
15 [I]Lit., *staff* [a]Jer. 51:20 [b]Is. 29:16; 45:9; Rom. 9:20, 21 [c]Is. 10:5 [d]Is. 10:5
16 [I]Heb., *YHWH,* usually rendered LORD [a]Ps. 106:15 [b]Is. 17:4 [c]Is. 8:7; 10:18
17 [a]Is. 30:33; 31:9 [b]Is. 37:23 [c]Num. 11:1-3; Is. 27:4; 33:12; Jer. 4:4; 7:20
18 [a]Is. 10:33, 34
19 [a]Is. 21:17
20 [a]Is. 1:9; 11:11, 16; 46:3 [b]Is. 4:2; 37:31, 32 [c]2 Chr. 14:11; Is. 17:7, 8; 50:10
21 [a]Is. 7:3 [b]Is. 9:6
22 [a]Rom. 9:27, 28 [b]Is. 28:22; Dan. 9:27; Rom. 9:28
23 [I]Heb., *YHWH,* usually rendered LORD [a]Is. 28:22; Dan. 9:27; Rom. 9:28

hosts will execute[6213] in the midst[7130] of the whole land.[776]

24 Therefore thus says the Lord [I]GOD of hosts, "O My people who dwell in [a]Zion, [b]do not fear[3372] the Assyrian [II]who [c]strikes[5221] you with the rod and lifts up[5375] his staff against you, the way[1870] Egypt *did.*

25 "For in a very [a]little while [b]My indignation *against you* will be spent, and My anger *will be directed* to their destruction."[8399]

26 And the LORD of hosts will [a]arouse a scourge[7752] against him like the slaughter[4347] of [b]Midian at the rock of Oreb; and His [c]staff[4294] will be over the sea, and He will lift it up [d]the way *He did* in Egypt.

27 So it will be in that day, that [I]his [a]burden will be removed[5493] from your shoulders and his yoke from your neck, and the yoke will be broken[2254] because [b]of fatness.[8081]

28 He has come against Aiath,
He has passed[5674] through
[a]Migron;
At [b]Michmash he deposited his
[c]baggage.
29 They have gone through[5674]
[a]the pass, *saying,*
"[b]Geba will be our lodging place."
[c]Ramah is terrified,[2729] and
[d]Gibeah of Saul has fled away.
30 Cry aloud with your voice, O
daughter of [a]Gallim!
Pay attention, Laishah *and*
[I]wretched [b]Anathoth!
31 Madmenah has fled.
The inhabitants of Gebim have
sought refuge.
32 Yet today he will halt at [a]Nob;
He [b]shakes his fist at the
mountain of the [I][c]daughter of
Zion, the hill of Jerusalem.
33 Behold, the Lord, the [I]GOD of
hosts, will lop off the boughs
with a terrible crash;
Those also who are [a]tall in
stature will be cut down,[1438]
And those who are lofty will be
abased.
34 And He will cut down[5362] the
thickets of the forest with an
iron *axe,*
And [a]Lebanon will fall [I]by the
Mighty[117] One.

Righteous Reign of the Branch

11 Then a [a]shoot will spring from
the [b]stem of Jesse,
And a [c]branch from [d]his roots
will bear fruit.
2 And the [a]Spirit[7307] of the LORD
will rest on Him,
The spirit of [b]wisdom[2451] and
understanding,[998]
The spirit of counsel[6098] and
[c]strength,
The spirit of knowledge[1847] and
the fear[3374] of the LORD.
3 And He will delight in the fear
of the LORD,
And He will not judge[8199] by what
His eyes [a]see,
Nor make a decision[3198] by what
His ears[241] hear;
4 But with [a]righteousness[6664] He
will judge the [b]poor,
And decide with fairness[4334] for
the [c]afflicted of the earth;[776]
And He will strike[5221] the earth
with the [d]rod[7626] of His
mouth,[6310]
And with the [e]breath[7307] of His
lips[8193] He will slay[4191] the
wicked.[7563]
5 Also [a]righteousness will be the
belt[232] about His loins,
And [b]faithfulness[530] the belt
about His waist.[2504]
6 And the [a]wolf will dwell[1481] with
the lamb,
And the leopard will lie down
with the kid,
And the calf and the young lion
[I]and the fatling together;
And a little boy will lead them.
7 Also the cow and the bear will
graze;
Their young will lie down
together;

24 [I]Heb., *YHWH,* usually rendered LORD [II]Lit., *he* [a]Ps. 87:5, 6 [b]Is. 7:4; 12:2; 37:6 [c]Ex. 5:14-16
25 [a]Is. 17:14; Hag. 2:6 [b]Is. 10:5; 26:20; Dan. 11:36
26 [a]Is. 37:36-38 [b]Judg. 7:25; Is. 9:4 [c]Ex. 14:16 [d]Ex. 14:27
27 [I]I.e., the Assyrian [a]Is. 9:4; 14:25 [b]Is. 30:23; 55:2
28 [a]1Sam. 14:2 [b]1Sam. 13:2, 5 [c]Judg. 18:21; 1Sam. 17:22
29 [a]1Sam. 13:23 [b]Josh. 21:17; 1Sam. 13:16 [c]Josh. 18:25; 1Sam. 7:17 [d]1Sam. 10:26
30 [I]An ancient version reads *Answer her, O Anathoth* [a]1Sam. 25:44 [b]Josh. 21:18; Jer. 1:1
32 [I]Another reading is *house of* [a]1Sam. 21:1; 22:9 [b]Is. 19:16; Zech. 2:9 [c]Is. 1:8; Jer. 6:23
33 [I]Heb., *YHWH,* usually rendered LORD [a]Is. 37:24, 36-38; Ezek. 31:3; Amos 2:9
34 [I]Or, *as a mighty one* [a]Is. 2:13; 33:9; 37:24

1 [a]Is. 4:2; 53:2 [b]Is. 9:7; 11:10; Acts 13:23 [c]Is. 6:13; Jer. 23:5; Zech. 3:8 [d]Rev. 5:5; 22:16
2 [a]Is. 42:1; 48:16; 61:1; Matt. 3:16; John 1:32 [b]John 16:13; 1Cor. 1:30; Eph. 1:17, 18 [c]2Tim. 1:7
3 [a]John 2:25; 7:24
4 [a]Is. 9:7; 16:5; 32:1 [b]Ps. 72:2, 13, 14; Is. 3:14 [c]Is. 29:19; 32:7; 61:1 [d]Ps. 2:9; Is. 49:2; Mal. 4:6 [e]Job 4:9; Is. 30:28, 33; 2Thess. 2:8
5 [a]Eph. 6:14 [b]Is. 25:1

6 [I]Some versions read *will feed together* [a]Is. 65:25

And the [a]lion will eat straw like
the ox.
8 And the nursing child will play
by the hole of the cobra,[6620]
And the weaned child will put
his hand[3027] on the viper's[6848]
den.
9 They will [a]not hurt[7489] or
destroy[7843] in all My holy[6944]
mountain,
For the [b]earth will be full of the
knowledge[1844] of the LORD
As the waters cover[3680] the sea.
10 Then it will come about in that
day[3117]
That the [a]nations[1471] will resort
to the [b]root of Jesse,
Who will stand as a [Ic]signal for
the peoples;[5971]
And His [d]resting place will be
[II]glorious.[3519]

The Restored Remnant

11 Then it will happen on that day
that the Lord[136]
Will again recover the second
time with His hand
The [a]remnant[7605] of His people,
who will remain,[7604]
From [b]Assyria, [c]Egypt, Pathros,
Cush, [d]Elam, Shinar,
Hamath,
And from the [Ie]islands of the sea.
12 And He will lift up[5375] a
[a]standard for the nations,[1471]
And will [b]assemble[622] the
banished ones of Israel,
And will gather[6908] the dispersed
of Judah
From the four corners of the
earth.
13 Then the [a]jealousy[7068] of
Ephraim will depart,[5493]
And those who harass Judah will
be cut off;[3772]
Ephraim will not be jealous[7065]
of Judah,
And Judah will not harass[6887]
Ephraim.
14 And they will [a]swoop down on
the slopes of the Philistines
on the [b]west;
Together they will [c]plunder the
sons of the east;
[I]They will possess [d]Edom and
[e]Moab;
And the sons[1121] of Ammon will
be [II]subject[4928] to them.
15 And the LORD will [Ia]utterly
destroy[2763]
The tongue of the [II]Sea of Egypt;
And He will [b]wave His hand over
the [IIIc]River
With His scorching wind;[7307]
And He will strike[5130] it into
seven streams,
And make *men* walk over
[IV]dry-shod.
16 And there will be a [a]highway
from Assyria
For the [b]remnant of His people
who will be left,
Just as there was for Israel
In [c]the day that they came up[5927]
out of the land[776] of Egypt.

Thanksgiving Expressed

12

Then you will say[559] on that
day,[3117]
"[a]I will give thanks[3034] to Thee,
O LORD;
For [b]although Thou wast
angry[599] with me,
Thine anger[639] is turned away,
And Thou dost comfort[5162] me.
2 "Behold, [a]God[410] is my
salvation,[3444]
I will [b]trust[982] and not be
afraid;[6342]
For [c]the LORD GOD is my
strength and song,
And He has become[1961] my
salvation."
3 Therefore you will joyously
[a]draw water
From the [b]springs of salvation.
4 And in that day you will
[a]say,

7 [a]Is. 65:25
9 [a]Job 5:23; Is. 65:25; Ezek. 34:25; Hos. 2:18 [b]Ps. 98:2, 3; Is. 45:6; 52:10; 66:18-23; Hab. 2:14
10 [I]Or, *standard* [II]Lit., *glory* [a]Luke 2:32; Acts 11:18 [b]Is. 11:1; Rom. 15:12 [c]Is. 11:12; 49:22; 62:10; John 3:14, 15; 12:32 [d]Is. 14:3; 28:12; 32:17, 18
11 [I]Or, *coastlands* [a]Is. 10:20-22; 37:4, 31, 32; 46:3 [b]Is. 19:23-25; Hos. 11:11; Zech. 10:10 [c]Is. 19:21, 22; Mic. 7:12 [d]Gen. 10:22; 14:1 [e]Is. 24:15; 42:4, 10, 12; 49:1; 51:5; 60:9; 66:19
12 [a]Is. 11:10 [b]Is. 56:8; Zeph. 3:10; Zech. 10:6
13 [a]Is. 9:21; Jer. 3:18; Ezek. 37:16, 17, 22; Hos. 1:11
14 [I]Lit., *Edom and Moab will be the outstretching of their hand* [II]Lit., *their obedience* [a]Jer. 48:40; 49:22; Hab. 1:8 [b]Is. 9:12 [c]Jer. 49:28 [d]Is. 63:1; Dan. 11:41; Joel 3:19; Amos 9:12 [e]Is. 16:14; 25:10
15 [I]Another reading is *dry up the tongue* [II]Perhaps the Red Sea [III]I.e., Euphrates [IV]Lit., *in sandals* [a]Is. 43:16; 44:27; 50:2; 51:10, 11 [b]Is. 19:16 [c]Is. 7:20; 8:7; Rev. 16:12
16 [a]Is. 19:23; 35:8; 40:3; 62:10 [b]Is. 11:11 [c]Ex. 14:26-29

1 [a]Ps. 9:1; Is. 25:1 [b]Ps. 30:5; Is. 40:1, 2; 54:7-10
2 [a]Is. 32:2; 45:17; 62:11 [b]Is. 26:3 [c]Ex. 15:2; Ps. 118:14
3 [a]John 4:10; 7:37, 38 [b]Is. 41:18; Jer. 2:13
4 [a]Is. 24:15; 42:12; 48:20

"[b]Give thanks to the LORD, call[7121] on His name.
[c]Make known His deeds among the peoples;[5971]
[I]Make *them* remember that His name is exalted."
5 [a]Praise the LORD in song, for He has done [I]excellent things;
Let this be known[3045] throughout the earth.[776]
6 [a]Cry aloud and shout for joy, O inhabitant of Zion,
For [b]great in your midst[7130] is the Holy One[6918] of Israel.

Prophecies about Babylon

13 The [Ia]oracle[4853] concerning [b]Babylon which [c]Isaiah the son[1121] of Amoz saw.[2372]
2 [a]Lift up a standard on the [Ib]bare hill,
Raise your voice to them,
[c]Wave[5130] the hand[3027] that they may [d]enter the doors of the nobles.[5081]
3 I have commanded[6680] My consecrated ones,[6942]
I have even called[7121] My [a]mighty warriors,
My proudly exulting ones,
To *execute* My anger.[639]
4 A [a]sound of tumult on the mountains,
Like that of many people![5971]
A sound of the uproar[7588] of kingdoms,[4467]
Of nations[1471] gathered together!
The LORD of hosts[6635] is mustering[6485] the army[6635] for battle.
5 They are coming from a far country[776]
From the [Ia]farthest horizons,[8064]
The LORD and His instruments of [b]indignation,[2195]
To [c]destroy[2254] the whole land.[776]

4 [I]Or, *Proclaim to them that* [b]Ps. 105:1 [c]Ps. 145:4
5 [I]Or, *gloriously* [a]Ex. 15:1; Ps. 98:1; Is. 24:14; 42:10, 11; 44:23
6 [a]Is. 52:9; 54:1; Zeph. 3:14 [b]Is. 1:24; 49:26; 60:16; Zeph. 3:15-17; Zech. 2:5, 10, 11

1 [I]Or, *burden of* [a]Is. 14:28; 15:1 [b]Is. 13:19; 14:4; 47:1-15; Jer. 24:1; 50:1-51:64; Matt. 1:11; Rev. 14:8 [c]Is. 1:1
2 [I]Or, *wind-swept mountain* [a]Is. 5:26; Jer. 50:2 [b]Jer. 51:25 [c]Is. 10:32; 19:16 [d]Is. 45:1-3; Jer. 51:58
3 [a]Joel 3:11
4 [a]Is. 5:30; 17:12; Joel 3:14
5 [I]Lit., *end of heaven* [a]Is. 5:26; 7:18 [b]Is. 10:5 [c]Is. 24:1
6 [I]Heb., *Shaddai* [a]Is. 2:12; 10:3; 13:9; 34:2, 8; 61:2; Ezek. 30:3; Amos 5:18; Zeph. 1:7 [b]Is. 10:25; 14:23; Joel 1:15
7 [a]Ezek. 7:17 [b]Is. 19:1; Ezek. 21:7; Nah. 2:10
8 [a]2Kin. 19:26; Is. 21:3; Jer. 46:5 [b]Is. 26:17; Jer. 4:31; John 16:21
9 [a]Is. 13:6
10 [a]Is. 5:30; Ezek. 32:7; Joel 2:10; Matt. 24:29; Mark 13:24; Luke 21:25; Rev. 6:13; 8:12 [b]Is. 24:23; 50:3; Ezek. 32:7; Acts 2:20; Rev. 6:12
11 [I]Or, *tyrants, despots* [a]Is. 26:21 [b]Is. 3:11; 11:4; 14:5 [c]Is. 2:11; 23:9; Dan. 5:22, 23 [d]Jer. 48:29 [e]Is. 25:3; 29:5, 20
12 [I]Lit., *more precious* [a]Is. 4:1; 6:11, 12 [b]1Kin. 9:28; Job 28:16; Ps. 45:9

Judgment on the Day of the Lord

6 Wail, for the [a]day[3117] of the LORD is near!
It will come as [b]destruction[7701] from [I]the Almighty.[7706]
7 Therefore [a]all hands[3027] will fall limp,[7503]
And every man's [b]heart[3824] will melt.
8 And they will be [a]terrified,[926]
Pains and anguish[2256] will take hold of *them;*
They will [b]writhe[2342] like a woman in labor,[3205]
They will look at one[376] another[7453] in astonishment,
Their faces aflame.
9 Behold, [a]the day of the LORD is coming,
Cruel, with fury[5678] and burning anger,
To make[7760] the land a desolation;[8047]
And He will exterminate[8045] its sinners[2400] from it.
10 For the [a]stars of heaven and their constellations
Will not flash forth their light;[216]
The [b]sun will be dark[2821] when it rises,
And the moon will not shed its light.
11 Thus I will [a]punish[6485] the world[8398] for its evil,[7451]
And the [b]wicked[7563] for their iniquity;[5771]
I will also put an end[7673] to the [c]arrogance of the proud,[2086]
And abase the [d]haughtiness of the [Ie]ruthless.
12 I will make mortal man[582] [Ia]scarcer than pure gold,
And mankind[120] than the [b]gold of Ophir.
13 Therefore I shall make the [a]heavens[8064] tremble,
And [b]the earth[776] will be shaken[7493] from its place
At the fury of the LORD of hosts

13 [a]Is. 34:4; 51:6 [b]Ps. 18:7; Is. 2:19; 24:1, 19, 20; Hag. 2:6

In [c]the day of His burning anger.
14 And it will be that like a hunted gazelle,
Or like [a]sheep with none to gather *them,*
They will each[376] turn to his own people,
And each[376] one flee to his own land.
15 Anyone who is found will be [a]thrust through,
And anyone who is captured will fall by the sword.[2719]
16 Their [a]little ones also will be dashed to pieces
Before their eyes;
Their houses[1004] will be plundered
And their wives[802] ravished.

Babylon Will Fall to the Medes

17 Behold, I am going to [a]stir up the Medes against them,
Who will not value[2803] silver or [b]take pleasure in gold,
18 And *their* bows will [I]mow down the [a]young men,
They will not even have compassion[7355] on the fruit of the womb,[990]
Nor will their [b]eye pity [II]children.[1121]
19 And [a]Babylon, the [b]beauty[6643] of kingdoms, the glory[8597] of the Chaldeans' pride,
Will be as when God[430] [c]overthrew Sodom and Gomorrah.
20 It will [a]never be inhabited or lived in from generation[1755] to generation;
Nor will the [b]Arab pitch *his* tent there,
Nor will shepherds make *their flocks* lie down there.
21 But [a]desert creatures will lie down there,
And their houses will be full of [I]owls,[255]
Ostriches also will live[7931] there,
And [II]shaggy goats[8163] will frolic there.
22 And [I]hyenas will howl in their fortified towers[490]
And jackals[8577] in their luxurious [a]palaces.[1964]
Her *fateful* time[6256] also [II]will soon come
And her days[3117] will not be prolonged.

Israel's Taunt

14 When the LORD will [a]have compassion[7355] on Jacob, and again
[b]choose[974] Israel, and settle them in
their own land,[127] then [c]strangers[1616]
will join them and attach themselves to
the house[1004] of Jacob.
2 And the peoples[5971] will take them
along and bring them to their place, and
the [a]house of Israel will possess[5157] them
as an inheritance in the land of the LORD
[b]as male servants[5650] and female servants; and [I]they will take their captors
captive,[7617] and will rule[7287] over their
oppressors.
3 And it will be in the day[3117] when
the LORD gives you [a]rest from your
pain[6090] and turmoil[7267] and harsh[7186]
service[5656] in which you have been enslaved,[5647]
4 that you will [a]take[5375] up this
[I]taunt against the king[4428] of Babylon,
and say,[559]
"How [b]the oppressor has ceased,[7673]
And how [II]fury has ceased!
5 "The LORD has broken[7665] the staff[4294] of the wicked,[7563]
The scepter[7626] of rulers[4910]
6 [a]Which used to strike[5221] the peoples in fury[5678] with unceasing strokes,[4347]
Which [I]subdued[7287] the nations[1471] in anger[639] with unrestrained persecution.
7 "The whole earth[776] is at rest *and* is quiet;[8252]
They [a]break forth into shouts of joy.
8 "Even the [a]cypress trees rejoice

---

13 [c]Lam. 1:12
14 [a]1Kin. 22:17; Matt. 9:36; Mark 6:34; 1Pet. 2:25
15 [a]Is. 14:19; Jer. 50:25; 51:3, 4
16 [a]Ps. 137:8, 9; Is. 13:18; 14:21; Hos. 10:14; Nah. 3:10
17 [a]Jer. 51:11; Dan. 5:28 [b]Prov. 6:34, 35
18 [I]Lit., *dash in pieces* [II]Lit., *sons* [a]2Kin. 8:12; 2Chr. 36:17 [b]Ezek. 9:5, 10
19 [a]Is. 21:9; 48:14 [b]Dan. 4:30; Rev. 18:11-16, 19, 21 [c]Gen. 19:24; Deut. 29:23; Jer. 49:18; Amos 4:11
20 [a]Is. 14:23; 34:10-15; Jer. 51:37-43 [b]2Chr. 17:11
21 [I]Or, *howling creatures* [II]Or, *goat demons* [a]Is. 34:11-15; Zeph. 2:14; Rev. 18:2
22 [I]Or, *howling creatures* [II]Lit., *is near to come* [a]Is. 25:2; 32:14; 34:13

1 [a]Ps. 102:13; Is. 49:13, 15; 54:7, 8 [b]Is. 41:8, 9; 44:1; 49:7; Zech. 1:17; 2:12 [c]Is. 56:3, 6; Eph. 2:12-19
2 [I]Lit., *the captors will become their captives* [a]Is. 45:14; 49:23; 54:3 [b]Is. 60:10; 61:5; Dan. 7:18, 27
3 [a]Ezra 9:8, 9; Is. 11:10; 40:2; Jer. 30:10; 46:27
4 [I]Or, *proverb* [II]Amended from the meaningless *medhebah* to *marhebah* [a]Hab. 2:6 [b]Is. 9:4; 16:4; 49:26; 51:13; 54:14
6 [I]Or, *ruled* [a]Is. 10:14; 47:6
7 [a]Ps. 47:1-3; 98:1-9; 126:1-3
8 [a]Is. 55:12; Ezek. 31:16

over you, *and* the cedars of
Lebanon, *saying,*
'Since you were laid low, no *tree*
cutter comes up[5927] against
us.'
9 "[a]Sheol[7585] from beneath is
excited over you to meet you
when you come;
It arouses for you the [I]spirits of
the dead,[7496] all the [II]leaders
of the earth;
It raises all the kings[4428] of the
nations from their
thrones.[3678]
10 "[a]They will all respond and say
to you,
'Even you have been made weak
as we,
You have become like us.
11 'Your [a]pomp *and* the music of
your harps[5035]
Have been brought down to
Sheol;[7585]
Maggots are spread out *as your
bed* beneath you,
And worms are your covering.'
12 "How you have [a]fallen[5307] from
heaven,[8064]
O [I][b]star of the morning, son[1121]
of the dawn!
You have been cut down to the
earth,[776]
You who have weakened the
nations!
13 "But you said[559] in your heart,[3824]
'I will [a]ascend[5927] to heaven;
I will [b]raise my throne[3678] above
the stars of God,[410]
And I will sit on the mount of
assembly[4150]
In the recesses of the north.
14 'I will ascend above the heights
of the clouds;
[a]I will make myself like the Most
High.'[5945]
15 "Nevertheless you [a]will be thrust
down to Sheol,
To the recesses of the pit.[953]
16 "Those who see you will gaze at
you,
They will [I]ponder[995] over you,
saying,

'Is this the man[376] who made the
earth tremble,
Who shook[7493] kingdoms,[4467]
17 Who made[7760] the world[8398] like
a [a]wilderness
And overthrew[2040] its cities,
Who [b]did not [I]allow his prisoners
to *go* home?'
18 "All the kings of the nations lie
in glory,[3519]
Each[376] in his own [I]tomb.
19 "But you have been [a]cast out of
your tomb[6913]
Like [I]a rejected[8581] branch,
[II]Clothed with the slain[2026] who
are pierced with a sword,[2719]
Who go down to the stones of
the [b]pit,
Like a [c]trampled corpse.[6297]
20 "You will not be united with them
in burial,[6900]
Because you have ruined[7843]
your country,
You have slain your people.
May the [a]offspring[2233] of
evildoers[7489] not be
mentioned[7121] forever.
21 "Prepare[3559] for his sons[1121] a
place of slaughter
Because of the [a]iniquity[5771] of
their fathers.[1]
They must not arise and take
possession[3423] of the earth
And fill the face of the world with
cities."
22 "And I will rise up against them,"
declares[5001] the LORD of hosts,[6635] "and
will cut off[3772] from Babylon [a]name and
survivors,[7605] [b]offspring and posterity,"
declares the LORD.
23 "I will also make[7760] it a possession for the [a]hedgehog, and swamps of
water, and I will sweep it with the
broom[4292] of [b]destruction,"[8045] declares
the LORD of hosts.

Judgment on Assyria

24 The LORD of hosts has sworn
saying, "Surely, [a]just as I have intended
so it has happened, and just as I have
planned[3289] so it will stand,

9 [I]Or, *shades* (Heb., *Repha'im*) [II]Lit., *male goats* [a]Is. 5:14
10 [a]Ezek. 32:21
11 [a]Is. 5:14
12 [I]Heb., *Helel;* i.e., shining one [a]Is. 34:4; Luke 10:18; Rev. 8:10; 9:1 [b]2Pet. 1:19; Rev. 2:28; 22:16
13 [a]Ezek. 28:2 [b]Dan. 5:22, 23; 8:10; 2Thess. 2:4
14 [a]Is. 47:8; 2Thess. 2:4
15 [a]Ezek. 28:8; Matt. 11:23; Luke 10:15
16 [I]Lit., *show themselves attentive to*
17 [I]Lit., *open* [a]Joel 2:3 [b]Is. 45:13
18 [I]Lit., *house*
19 [I]Lit., *an abhorred branch* [II]Or, *As the clothing of those who are slain* [a]Is. 22:16-18 [b]Jer. 41:7, 9 [c]Is. 5:25
20 [a]Job 18:16, 19; Ps. 21:10; 37:28; Is. 1:4; 31:2
21 [a]Ex. 20:5; Lev. 26:39; Is. 13:16; Matt. 23:35
22 [a]Prov. 10:7 [b]Job 18:19; Is. 47:9
23 [a]Is. 34:11; Zeph. 2:14 [b]1Kin. 14:10; Is. 13:6
24 [a]Job 23:13; Is. 46:11; 55:8, 9; Acts 4:28

25 to [a]break[7665] Assyria in My land,
and I will trample[947] him on My mountains. Then his [b]yoke will be removed
from them, and his burden removed[5493]
from their shoulder.
26 "This is the [a]plan [I]devised against
the whole earth; and this is the [b]hand[3027]
that is stretched out against all the nations.
27 "For [a]the LORD of hosts has
planned, and who can frustrate[6565] *it*?
And as for His stretched-out hand, who
can turn it back?"[7725]
28 In the [a]year that King Ahaz
died[4194] this [I][b]oracle[4853] came:

Judgment on Philistia

29 "Do not rejoice, O [a]Philistia, all
of you,
Because the rod[7626] that
[b]struck you is broken;
For from the serpent's[5175] root
a [c]viper[6848] will come out,
And its fruit will be a [d]flying
serpent.[8314]

30 "And [I]those who are most
[a]helpless will eat,
And the needy will lie down in
security;
I will [II]destroy[4191] your root with
[b]famine,
And it will kill[2026] off your
survivors.[7611]

31 "Wail, O [a]gate; cry,[2199] O city;
[I]Melt away,[4127] O [b]Philistia, all
of you;
For smoke comes from the
[c]north,
And [d]there is no straggler in his
ranks.[4151]

32 "How then will one answer the
[a]messengers[4397] of the
nation?[1471]
That [b]the LORD has founded[3245]
Zion,
And [c]the afflicted of His people
will seek refuge[2620] in it."

Judgment on Moab

15 The [I]oracle[4853] concerning
[a]Moab.

25 [a]Is. 10:12; 30:31; 31:8 [b]Is. 9:4; 10:27; Nah. 1:13
26 [I]Lit., *planned* [a]Is. 23:9; Zeph. 3:6, 8 [b]Ex. 15:12
27 [a]2Chr. 20:6; Is. 43:13; Dan. 4:31, 35
28 [I]Or, *burden* [a]2Kin. 16:20; 2Chr. 28:27 [b]Is. 13:1
29 [a]Is. 2:6; 11:14; Jer. 47:1-7; Ezek. 25:15-17; Joel 3:4-8; Amos 1:6-8; Zeph. 2:4-7; Zech. 9:5-7 [b]2Chr. 26:6 [c]Is. 11:8 [d]Is. 30:6
30 [I]Lit., *the first-born of the helpless* [II]Lit., *put to death* [a]Is. 3:14, 15; 7:21, 22; 11:4 [b]Is. 8:21; 9:20; 51:19
31 [I]Or, *Become demoralized* [a]Is. 3:26; 24:12; 45:2 [b]Is. 14:29 [c]Jer. 1:14 [d]Is. 34:16
32 [a]Is. 37:9 [b]Ps. 87:1, 5; 102:16; Is. 28:16; 44:28; 54:11 [c]Is. 4:6; 25:4; 57:13; Zeph. 3:12; Heb. 11:10; James 2:5

1 [I]Or, *burden of* [a]Is. 11:14; 25:10; Jer. 48:1; Ezek. 25:8-11; Amos 2:1-3; Zeph. 2:8-11 [b]Num. 21:28
2 [I]Lit., *house* [a]Jer. 48:18, 22 [b]Lev. 21:5; Jer. 48:37
3 [I]Lit., *going down in weeping* [a]Jon. 3:6-8 [b]Jer. 48:38 [c]Is. 22:4
4 [I]Another reading is *the loins of* [a]Num. 21:28; 32:3; Jer. 48:34
5 [a]Jer. 48:34 [b]Jer. 48:5 [c]Is. 59:7; Jer. 4:20
6 [I]Lit., *desolations* [II]Lit., *come to an end* [a]Is. 19:5-7; Jer. 48:34 [b]Joel 1:10-12; 2:3

Surely in a night[3915] [b]Ar of Moab
is devastated[7703] *and* ruined;
Surely in a night Kir of Moab
is devastated *and* ruined.
2 They have gone up[5927] to the
[I]temple and *to* [a]Dibon, *even*
to the high places[1116] to
weep.
Moab wails over Nebo and
Medeba;
Everyone's head[7218] is [b]bald *and*
every beard[2206] is cut off.
3 In their streets they have girded
themselves with [a]sackcloth;
[b]On their housetops and in their
squares
Everyone is wailing, [I][c]dissolved
in tears.
4 [a]Heshbon and Elealeh also cry
out,
Their voice is heard[8085] all the
way to Jahaz;
Therefore the [I]armed men of
Moab cry aloud;[2199]
His soul[5315] trembles[3415] within
him.
5 My heart[3820] cries out for Moab;
His fugitives are as far as
[a]Zoar *and* Eglath-shelishiyah,
For they go up the [b]ascent of
Luhith weeping;
Surely on the road[1870] to
Horonaim they raise a cry of
distress [c]over *their* ruin.[7667]
6 For the [a]waters of Nimrim are
[I]desolate.
Surely the grass is withered,[3001]
the tender grass [II]died out,
There is [b]no green thing.
7 Therefore the [a]abundance *which*
they have acquired[6213] and
stored up[6486]
They carry off[5375] over the brook
of [I]Arabim.
8 For the cry of distress has gone
around[5362] the territory of
Moab,
Its wail *goes* as far as Eglaim
and its wailing even to Beer-
elim.

7 [I]Or, *the poplars* [a]Is. 30:6; Jer. 48:36

9 For the waters of Dimon are full
of [I]blood;[1818]
Surely I will bring added *woes*
upon Dimon,
A [a]lion upon the fugitives[6413] of
Moab and upon the
remnant[7611] of the land.[127]

Prophecy of Moab's Devastation

16 [a]Send the *tribute* lamb[3733] to the
ruler[4910] of the land,[776]
From [I][b]Sela by way of the
wilderness to the [c]mountain
of the daughter of Zion.
2 Then, like [I][a]fleeing birds *or*
scattered [II]nestlings,
The daughters of [b]Moab will be
at the fords of the [c]Arnon.
3 "[I]Give *us* advice,[6098] make a
decision;[6413]
[II]Cast your [a]shadow like night[3915]
[III]at high noon;
[b]Hide the outcasts, do not
betray[1540] the fugitive.
4 "Let the [I]outcasts of Moab
stay[1481] with you;
Be a hiding place[5643] to them
from the destroyer."[7703]
For the extortioner has come
to an end, destruction[7701] has
ceased,
[a]Oppressors have completely
disappeared from the land.
5 A [a]throne[3678] will even be
established[3559] in
lovingkindness,[2617]
And a judge will sit on it in
faithfulness[571] in the tent[168]
of [b]David;
Moreover, he will seek
justice[4941]
And be prompt in
righteousness.[6664]
6 [a]We have heard[8085] of the pride
of Moab, an excessive pride;
Even of his arrogance, pride, and
fury;[5678]
[b]His idle boasts are [I]false.
7 Therefore Moab shall wail;
everyone of Moab shall wail.
You shall moan[1897] for the

9 [I]Heb., *dam* (a wordplay) [a]2Kin. 17:25; Jer. 50:17

1 [I]I.e., Petra in Edom [a]2Kin. 3:4; Ezra 7:17 [b]2 Kin. 14:7; Is. 42:11 [c]Is. 10:32

2 [I]Or, *fluttering* [II]Lit., *nest* [a]Prov. 27:8 [b]Jer. 48:20, 46 [c]Num. 21:13, 14

3 [I]Lit., *Bring* [II]Lit., *Set* [III]Lit., *in the midst of the noon* [a]Is. 25:4; 32:2 [b]1Kin. 18:4

4 [I]So the versions; M.T., *My outcasts, as for Moab* [a]Is. 9:4; 14:4; 49:26; 51:13; 54:14

5 [a]Is. 9:6, 7; 32:1; 55:4; Dan. 7:14; Mic. 4:7; Luke 1:33 [b]Is. 9:7

6 [I]Lit., *not so* [a]Jer. 48:29; Amos 2:1; Obad. 3, 4; Zeph. 2:8, 10 [b]Jer. 48:30

7 [a]1Chr. 16:3 [b]2Kin. 3:25; Jer. 48:31

8 [I]Or, *languished* [a]Is. 15:4 [b]Num. 32:38 [c]Jer. 48:32

9 [a]Jer. 48:32 [b]Is. 15:4 [c]Jer. 40:10, 12; 48:32

10 [a]Is. 24:8; Jer. 48:33 [b]Judg. 9:27; Is. 24:7; Amos 5:11, 17 [c]Job 24:11; Amos 9:13

11 [I]Lit., *entrails murmur* [II]Lit., *inward part* [a]Is. 15:5; 63:15; Jer. 48:36; Hos. 11:8; Phil. 2:1

12 [a]Num. 22:39-41; Jer. 48:35 [b]1Kin. 18:29 [c]Is. 15:2

14 [I]Lit., *the years of a hireling* [a]Job 7:1; 14:6; Is. 21:16 [b]Is. 25:10; Jer. 48:42

[a]raisin cakes of [b]Kir-hareseth
As those who are utterly
stricken.
8 For the fields of [a]Heshbon have
[I]withered, the vines of
[b]Sibmah *as well;*
The lords[1162] of the nations[1471]
have trampled down[1986] its
choice clusters
Which reached[5060] as far as Jazer
and wandered[8582] to the
deserts;
[c]Its tendrils spread themselves
out[5203] *and* passed over[5674]
the sea.
9 Therefore I will [a]weep
bitterly[1058] for Jazer, for the
vine of Sibmah;
I will drench you with my tears,
O [b]Heshbon and Elealeh;
For the shouting over your
[c]summer fruits and your
harvest has fallen[5307] away.
10 And [a]gladness and joy are taken
away[622] from the fruitful
field;
In the [b]vineyards also there will
be no cries of joy or jubilant
shouting,[7321]
No [c]treader treads out wine in
the presses,
For I have made the shouting
to cease.[7673]
11 Therefore my [I][a]heart[4578] intones
like a harp for Moab,
And my [II]inward feelings[7130] for
Kir-hareseth.
12 So it will come about when Moab
[a]presents himself,[7200]
When he [b]wearies himself upon
his [c]high place,[1116]
And comes to his sanctuary[4720]
to pray,[6419]
That he will not prevail.
13 This is the word[1697] which the
LORD spoke[1696] earlier[227] concerning
Moab.
14 But now the LORD speaks, saying, "Within three years, as [I][a]a hired
man would count them, the glory[3519] of
[b]Moab will be degraded[7034] along with
all *his* great population, and *his*

remnant[7605] will be very small *and* [II]impotent."

Prophecy about Damascus

17 The [Ia]oracle[4853] concerning [b]Damascus.
"Behold, Damascus is about to be [c]removed[5493] from being a city,
And it will become a [d]fallen ruin.
2 "The cities [I]of [a]Aroer are forsaken;[5800]
They will be for [b]flocks [II]to lie down in,
And there will be [c]no one to frighten[2729] *them.*
3 "The [Ia]fortified city will disappear[7673] from Ephraim,
And [II]sovereignty[4467] from Damascus
And the remnant[7605] of Aram;
They will be like the [b]glory[3519] of the sons of Israel,"
Declares[5001] the LORD of hosts.[6635]
4 Now it will come about in that day[3117] that the [a]glory of Jacob will [I]fade,
And [b]the fatness of his flesh[1320] will become lean.
5 It will be [a]even like the [I]reaper gathering[622] the standing grain,
As his arm harvests the ears,
Or it will be like one gleaning[3950] ears of grain
In the [b]valley of Rephaim.[7497]
6 Yet [a]gleanings will be left[7604] in it like the [I]shaking of an olive tree,
Two *or* three olives on the topmost[7218] bough,
Four *or* five on the branches of a fruitful tree,
Declares the LORD, the God[430] of Israel.
7 In that day man[120] will [a]have regard for his Maker,[6213]
And his eyes will look[7200] to the Holy One[6918] of Israel.
8 And he will not have regard for the [a]altars,[4196] the work of his hands,[3027]
Nor will he look to that which his [b]fingers have made,[6213]
Even the [Ic]Asherim[842] and [II]incense stands.[2553]
9 In that day [I]their strong cities will be like [II]forsaken places in the forest,
Or like [III]branches which they abandoned[5800] before the sons of Israel;
And [IV]the land will be a desolation.[8077]
10 For [a]you have forgotten the [b]God of your salvation[3468]
And have not remembered[2142] the [c]rock of your refuge.
Therefore you plant delightful plants
And set them with vine slips of a strange[2114] *god.*
11 In the day that you plant *it* you carefully fence *it* in,
And in the [a]morning you bring your seed[2233] to blossom;
But the harvest will [b]be a heap
In a day of sickliness and incurable pain.
12 Alas, the uproar of many peoples[5971]
[a]Who roar like the roaring of the seas,
And the rumbling[3816] of nations
Who rush on like the [b]rumbling of mighty waters!
13 The [a]nations rumble on like the rumbling of many waters,
But He will [b]rebuke[1605] them and they will flee far away,
And be chased [c]like chaff in the mountains before the wind,[7307]
Or like whirling dust[1534] before a gale.
14 At evening time,[6153] behold, *there is* terror!

14 [II]Lit., *not mighty*

1 [I]Or, *burden of* [a]Is. 13:1 [b]Gen. 14:15; 15:2; 2Kin. 16:9; Jer. 49:23; Amos 1:3-5; Zech. 9:1; Acts 9:2 [c]Is. 7:16; 8:4; 10:9 [d]Is. 25:2; Jer. 49:2; Mic. 1:6

2 [I]Gr. reads *forever and ever* [II]Lit., *and they will lie down* [a]Num. 32:34 [b]Is. 7:21, 22; Ezek. 25:5; Zeph. 2:6 [c]Mic. 4:4

3 [I]Or, *fortification* [II]Or, *royal power, kingdom* [a]Is. 7:8, 16; 8:4 [b]Is. 17:4; Hos. 9:11

4 [I]Lit., *become thin* [a]Is. 10:3 [b]Is. 10:16

5 [I]Lit., *gathering of the harvest, the standing grain* [a]Is. 17:11; Jer. 51:33; Joel 3:13; Matt. 13:30 [b]2Sam. 5:18, 22

6 [I]Lit., *striking* [a]Deut. 4:27; Is. 24:13; 27:12; Obad. 5

7 [a]Is. 10:20; Hos. 3:5; 6:1; Mic. 7:7

8 [I]I.e., wooden symbols of a female deity [II]Or, *sun pillars* [a]2 Chr. 34:7; Is. 27:9 [b]Is. 2:8, 20; 30:22; 31:7 [c]Ex. 34:13; Deut. 7:5; Mic. 5:14

9 [I]I.e., man's [II]Gr. reads *the deserted places of the Amorites and the Hivites which they abandoned* [III]Or, *the treetop* [IV]Lit., *it*

10 [a]Is. 51:13 [b]Ps. 68:19; Is. 12:2; 33:2; 61:10; 62:11 [c]Deut. 32:4, 18, 31; Is. 26:4; 30:29; 44:8

11 [a]Ps. 90:6 [b]Job 4:8; Hos. 8:7; 10:13

12 [a]Is. 5:30; Jer. 6:23; Ezek. 43:2; Luke 21:25 [b]Ps. 18:4

13 [a]Is. 33:3 [b]Ps. 9:5; Is. 41:11 [c]Job 21:18; Ps. 1:4; 83:13; Is. 29:5; 41:15, 16

Before morning [a]they are no more.
[I]Such *will be* the portion of those who plunder[8154] us,
And the lot of those who pillage us.

Message to Ethiopia

18 Alas, oh land[776] of whirring wings
Which lies beyond the rivers of [Ia]Cush,
2 Which sends envoys6735 by the sea,
Even in [a]papyrus vessels on the surface of the waters.
Go, swift messengers,[4397] to a nation [Ib]tall and smooth,4803
To a people[5971] [c]feared[3372] [II]far and wide,
A powerful6978 and oppressive nation[1471]
Whose land the rivers divide.
3 [a]All you inhabitants of the world[8398] and dwellers[7931] on earth,
As soon as a standard is raised on the mountains, [b]you will see *it,*
And as soon as the trumpet is blown,[8628] you will hear[8085] *it.*
4 For thus the LORD has told[559] me,
"I will look [I]from My [a]dwelling place quietly[8252]
Like dazzling heat in the [IIb]sunshine,
Like a cloud of [c]dew in the heat of harvest."
5 For [a]before the harvest, as soon as the bud [I]blossoms[8552]
And the flower becomes a ripening grape,
Then He will cut off[3772] the sprigs with pruning knives
And remove *and* cut away the spreading branches.
6 They will be left[5800] together for mountain birds [a]of prey,
And for the beasts of the earth;
And the birds of prey will spend the summer *feeding* on them,

14 [I]Lit., *This* [a]2 Kin. 19:35; Is. 41:12

1 [I]Or, *Ethiopia* [a]2Kin. 19:9; Is. 20:3-5; Ezek. 30:4, 5, 9; Zeph. 2:12; 3:10

2 [I]Lit., *drawn out* [II]Lit., *from it and beyond* [a]Ex. 2:3 [b]Is. 18:7 [c]Gen. 10:8, 9; 2Chr. 12:2-4; 14:9; 16:8

3 [a]Ps. 49:1; Mic. 1:2 [b]Is. 26:11

4 [I]Lit., *in* [II]Lit., *light* [a]Is. 26:21; Hos. 5:15 [b]2Sam. 23:4 [c]Prov. 19:12; Is. 26:19; Hos. 14:5

5 [I]Lit., *is finished* [a]Is. 17:10, 11; Ezek. 17:6-10

6 [a]Is. 46:11; 56:9; Jer. 7:33; Ezek. 32:4-6; 39:17-20

7 [I]So with some ancient versions and DSS; M.T. implies *Consisting of a people* [II]Lit., *drawn out* [III]Lit., *from it and beyond* [a]Ps. 68:31; Is. 45:14; Zeph. 3:10; Acts 8:27-38 [b]Zech. 14:16, 17

1 [I]Or, *burden of* [a]Is. 13:1 [b]Joel 3:19 [c]Ps. 18:9, 10; 104:3; Matt. 26:64; Rev. 1:7 [d]Ex. 12:12; Jer. 43:12; 44:8 [e]Josh. 2:11; Is. 13:7

2 [a]Judg. 7:22; 1Sam. 14:20; 2Chr. 20:23; Matt. 10:21, 36

3 [I]Or, *ghosts and spirits* [a]1Chr. 10:13; Is. 8:19; Dan. 2:2

4 [I]Or, *fierce* [a]Is. 20:4; Jer. 46:26; Ezek. 29:19

And all the beasts of the earth will spend harvest time on them.
7 At that time[6256] a gift of homage will be brought to the LORD of hosts[6635]
[I]From a [a]people [II]tall and smooth,
Even from a people feared [III]far and wide,
A powerful and oppressive nation,
Whose land the rivers divide—
To the [b]place of the name of the LORD of hosts, *even* Mount Zion.

Message to Egypt

19 The [Ia]oracle[4853] concerning [b]Egypt.
Behold, the LORD is [c]riding on a swift cloud, and is about to come to Egypt;
The [d]idols[457] of Egypt will tremble at His presence,
And the [e]heart[3824] of the Egyptians will melt within[7130] them.
2 "So I will incite Egyptians against Egyptians;
And they will [a]each[376] fight against his brother,[251] and each[376] against his neighbor,[7453]
City against city, *and* kingdom[4467] against kingdom.
3 "Then the spirit[7307] of the Egyptians will be demoralized within them;
And I will confound[1104] their strategy,[6098]
So that [a]they will resort to idols and ghosts[328] of the dead,
And to [I]mediums[128] and spiritists.[3049]
4 "Moreover, I will deliver the Egyptians into the hand[3027] of a [a]cruel[7186] master,[113]
And a [I]mighty king[4428] will rule[4910] over them,"

declares[5001] the Lord [II]GOD
of hosts.[6635]
5 [a]And the waters from the sea
will dry up,
And the river will be parched[2717]
and dry.[3001]
6 And the [Ia]canals will emit a
stench,
The [IIb]streams of Egypt will thin
out and dry up;[2717]
[c]The reeds and rushes[5488] will
rot away.
7 The bulrushes by the [a]Nile, by
the [I]edge[6310] of the Nile
And all the sown fields by the
Nile
Will become dry,[3001] be driven
away, and be no more.
8 And the [a]fishermen will lament,
And all those who cast a [I]line
into the Nile will mourn,
And those who spread nets on
the waters will [II]pine away.
9 Moreover, the
manufacturers[5647] of linen
made from combed flax
And the weavers of white [a]cloth
will be [I]utterly dejected.[954]
10 And [I]the [a]pillars *of Egypt* will be
crushed;[1792]
All the hired laborers[6213] will be
grieved in soul.[5315]
11 The princes[8269] of [Ia]Zoan are
mere fools;
The advice of Pharaoh's
wisest[2450] advisers[3289] has
become [II]stupid.
How can you *men* say[559] to
Pharaoh,
"I am a son[1121] of the [b]wise, a
son of ancient[6924] kings"?[4428]
12 Well then, where are your wise
men?
Please let them tell[5046] you,
And let them [I]understand[3045]
what the LORD of hosts
Has [a]purposed[3289] against
Egypt.
13 The princes of [I]Zoan have acted
foolishly,
The princes of [a]Memphis are
deluded;
Those who are the [b]cornerstone
of her tribes[7626]
Have [II]led Egypt astray.[8582]
14 The LORD has mixed within her
a spirit of [a]distortion;
[b]They have led Egypt astray[8582]
in all [I]that it does,
As a [c]drunken man [II]staggers[8582]
in his vomit.
15 And there will be no work for
Egypt
[a]Which *its* head[7218] or tail, *its*
palm branch or bulrush, may
do.[6213]

16 In that day[3117] the Egyptians will
become like women,[802] and they will
tremble[2729] and be in [a]dread[6342] because
of the [b]waving[8573] of the hand of the
LORD of hosts, which He is going to
wave[5130] over them.

17 And the land[127] of Judah will become a [I]terror[2283] to Egypt; everyone
[II]to whom it is mentioned will be in
dread[6342] of it, because of the [a]purpose
of the LORD of hosts which He is
purposing[3289] against them.

18 In that day five cities in the
land[776] of Egypt will be speaking[1696] the
language[8193] of Canaan and [a]swearing[7650]
allegiance to the LORD of hosts; one will
be called the City of [I]Destruction.

19 In that day there will be an
[a]altar[4196] to the LORD in the midst of
the land of Egypt, and a [b]pillar[4676] to
the LORD near its border.

20 And it will become a sign and a
witness to the LORD of hosts in the land
of Egypt; for they will cry to the LORD
because of oppressors, and He will send
them a [a]Savior[3467] and a [Ib]Champion, and
He will deliver[5337] them.

21 Thus the LORD will make Himself
known[3045] to Egypt, and the Egyptians
will know the LORD in that day. They
will[5647] even worship with [a]sacrifice[2077]
and offering,[4503] and will make a vow[5087]
to the LORD and perform it.

22 And the LORD will strike[5062]
Egypt, striking but [a]healing; so they will
[b]return[7725] to the LORD, and He will respond to them and will heal them.

23 In that day there will be a

---

4 [II]Heb., *YHWH,* usually rendered LORD
5 [a]Is. 50:2; Jer. 51:36; Ezek. 30:12
6 [I]Lit., *rivers* [II]Or, *Nile branches;* i.e., the delta [a]Ex. 7:18 [b]Is. 37:25 [c]Ex. 2:3; Job 8:11; Is. 15:6
7 [I]Or, *mouth* [a]Is. 23:3, 10
8 [I]Lit., *hook* [II]Or, *languish* [a]Ezek. 47:10; Hab. 1:15
9 [I]Lit., *ashamed* [a]Prov. 7:16; Ezek. 27:7
10 [I]Lit., *her pillars* or, *her weavers* [a]Ps. 11:3
11 [I]Or, *Tanis* [II]Or, *brutish* [a]Num. 13:22; Ps. 78:12, 43; Is. 30:4 [b]Gen. 41:38, 39; 1Kin. 4:30; Acts 7:22
12 [I]Or, *know* [a]Is. 14:24; Rom. 9:17
13 [I]Or, *Tanis* [II]Or, *have caused Egypt to stagger* [a]Jer. 2:16; 46:14, 19; Ezek. 30:13 [b]Zech. 10:4
14 [I]Lit., *its work* [II]Or, *goes astray* [a]Prov. 12:8; Matt. 17:17 [b]Is. 3:12; 9:16 [c]Is. 28:7
15 [a]Is. 9:14, 15
16 [a]2Cor. 5:11; Heb. 10:31 [b]Is. 11:15
17 [I]Or, *cause of shame* [II]Lit., *who mentions it will be in dread to it* [a]Is. 14:24; Dan. 4:35
18 [I]Some ancient mss. and versions read *the Sun* [a]Is. 45:23; 65:16
19 [a]Is. 56:7; 60:7 [b]Gen. 28:18; Ex. 24:4; Josh. 22:10, 26, 27
20 [I]Lit., *Mighty One* [a]Is. 43:3, 11; 45:15, 21; 49:26; 60:16; 63:8 [b]Is. 49:25
21 [a]Is. 56:7; 60:7; Zech. 14:16-18
22 [a]Deut. 32:39; Is. 30:26; 57:18; Heb. 12:11 [b]Is. 27:13; 45:14; Hos. 14:1

[a]highway from Egypt to Assyria, and
the Assyrians will come into Egypt and
the Egyptians into Assyria, and the
Egyptians will [b]worship[5647] with the Assyrians.

24 In that day Israel will be the third
party with Egypt and Assyria, a
blessing[1293] in the midst of the earth,
25 whom the LORD of hosts has
blessed,[1288] saying, "Blessed[1288] is
[a]Egypt My people,[5971] and Assyria
[b]the work of My hands,[3027] and Israel
My inheritance."[5159]

Prophecy about Egypt and Ethiopia

20 In the year that the [I][a]commander
came to [b]Ashdod, when Sargon
the king[4428] of Assyria sent him and he
fought against Ashdod and captured it,
🔑 2 at that time[6256] the LORD spoke[1696]
through [a]Isaiah the son[1121] of Amoz, saying, "Go and loosen the [b]sackcloth from
your hips, and take your [c]shoes off your
feet." And he did[6213] so, going [d]naked[6174]
and barefoot.
3 And the LORD said,[559] "Even as
My servant[5650] Isaiah has gone naked
and barefoot three years as a [I][a]sign and
token against Egypt and [II][b]Cush,
4 so the [a]king of Assyria will lead
away the captives[7628] of Egypt and the
exiles[1546] of Cush, [b]young and old,[2205]
naked and barefoot with buttocks uncovered, to the [I]shame[6172] of Egypt.
5 "Then they shall be [a]dismayed[2865]
and ashamed[954] because of Cush their
hope and Egypt their [b]boast.[8597]
6 "So the inhabitants of this coastland will say[559] in that day,[3117] 'Behold,
such is our hope, where we fled
[a]for help to be delivered[5337] from the
king of Assyria; and we, [b]how shall we
escape?' "[4422]

God Commands That Babylon Be Taken

21 The [I][a]oracle[4853] concerning the
[II][b]wilderness of the sea.

23 [a]Is. 11:16; 35:8; 49:11; 62:10 [b]Is. 27:13
25 [a]Is. 45:14 [b]Ps. 100:3; Is. 29:23; 45:11; 60:21; 64:8; Eph. 2:10

1 [I]Heb., *Tartan* [a]2Kin. 18:17 [b]1Sam. 5:1
2 [a]Is. 1:1; 13:1 [b]Zech. 13:4; Matt. 3:4 [c]Ezek. 24:17, 23 [d]1Sam. 19:24; Mic. 1:8
3 [I]Or, *wonder* [II]Or, *Ethiopia*, so in vv. 4, 5 [a]Is. 8:18 [b]Is. 37:9; 43:3
4 [I]Lit., *nakedness* [a]Is. 19:4 [b]Is. 47:2,3
5 [a]2Kin. 18:21; Is. 30:3-5; 31:1; Ezek. 29:6, 7 [b]Jer. 9:23, 24; 17:5; 1Cor. 3:21
6 [a]Is. 10:3; 30:7; 31:3; Jer. 30:1, 7, 15-17; 31:1-3 [b]Matt. 23:33; 1Thess. 5:3; Heb. 2:3

1 [I]Or, *burden of* [II]Or, *sandy wastes, sea country* [III]I.e., South country [a]Is. 13:1 [b]Is. 13:20-22; 14:23; Jer. 51:42 [c]Zech. 9:14
2 [I]Lit., *her groaning* [a]Ps. 60:3 [b]Is. 24:16; 33:1 [c]Is. 22:6; Jer. 49:34
3 [a]Is. 13:8; 16:11 [b]Ps. 48:6; Is. 13:8; 26:17; 1Thess. 5:3
4 [I]Lit., *heart has wandered* [II]Lit., *shuddering* [a]Deut. 28:67
5 [I]Or, *spread out the rugs* or possibly, *they arranged the seating* [a]Jer. 51:39, 57; Dan. 5:1-4
6 [a]2Kin. 9:17-20
7 [a]Is. 21:9
8 [I]So DSS; M.T., *he called* like a *lion* [a]Hab. 2:1

As [c]windstorms in the [III]Negev
sweep on,
It comes from the wilderness,
from a terrifying[3372] land.[776]
2 A [a]harsh[7186] vision[2380] has been
shown[5046] to me;
The [b]treacherous[898] one still
deals treacherously,[898] *and*
the destroyer[7703] still
destroys.[7703]
Go up, [c]Elam, lay siege, Media;
I have made an end[7673] of all
[I]the groaning she has caused.
3 For this reason my [a]loins are full
of anguish;
Pains have seized me like the
pains of a [b]woman in labor.[3205]
I am so bewildered I cannot
hear,[8085] so terrified I cannot
see.[7200]
4 My [I]mind[3824] reels,[8582]
[II]horror[6427] overwhelms[1204]
me;
The twilight I longed for[2837] has
been [a]turned for me into
trembling.
5 They [a]set the table, they
[I]spread out the cloth, they
eat, they drink;
"Rise up, captains,[8269] oil[4886] the
shields,"
6 For thus the Lord[136] says[559] to
me,
"Go, station the lookout, let
him [a]report[5046] what he
sees.[7200]
7 "When he sees[7200] [a]riders,
horsemen in pairs,
A train of donkeys, a train of
camels,
Let him pay close attention,[7181]
very close attention."
8 Then [I]the lookout called,[7121]
"[a]O Lord, I stand continually[8548]
by day[3119] on the
watchtower,
And I am stationed[5324] every
night[3915] at my guard
post.[4931]
9 "Now behold, here comes a troop

🔑 **20:2,3** See note on Mic. 1:8.

of riders,[376] horsemen in pairs."
And one answered and said,
"[a]Fallen,[5307] fallen is Babylon;
And all the [b]images of her gods[430] [I]are shattered[7665] on the ground."[776]
10 O my [a]threshed *people,* and my [I]afflicted[1121] of the threshing floor!
What I have heard[8085] from the LORD of hosts,[6635]
The God[430] of Israel, I make known to you.

Oracles about Edom and Arabia

11 The [I]oracle concerning [II][a]Edom.
One keeps calling[7121] to me from [b]Seir,
"Watchman,[8104] [III]how far gone is the night?[3915]
Watchman, [III]how far gone is the night?"
12 The watchman says,
"Morning comes but also night.
If you would inquire,[1158] inquire;
Come back[7725] again."
13 The [I]oracle about [a]Arabia.
In the thickets of Arabia you [II]must spend the night,
O caravans of [b]Dedanites.
14 Bring water [I]for the thirsty,
O inhabitants of the land of [a]Tema,
Meet the fugitive with bread.
15 For they have [a]fled from the swords,[2719]
From the drawn[5203] sword,[2719] and from the bent bow,
And from the press of battle.

16 For thus the Lord said to me,
"In a [a]year, as [I]a hired man would count
it, all the splendor[3519] of [b]Kedar will
terminate;[3615]

17 and the [a]remainder[7605] of the
number of bowmen, the mighty men
of the sons[1121] of Kedar, will be
few; for the LORD God of Israel [b]has
spoken."[1696]

9 [I]Lit., *he has shattered to the earth* [a]Is. 13:19; 47:5, 9; 48:14; Jer. 51:8; Rev. 14:8; 18:2 [b]Is. 46:1; Jer. 50:2; 51:44
10 [I]Lit., *son* [a]Jer. 51:33; Mic. 4:13
11 [I]Or, *burden* [II]So the Gr.; Heb., *Dumah, silence* [III]Lit., *what is the time of the night?* [a]Gen. 25:14 [b]Gen. 32:3
13 [I]Or, *burden* [II]Or, *will spend* [a]Jer. 25:23, 24; 49:28 [b]Gen. 10:7; Ezek. 27:15
14 [I]Lit., *to meet* [a]Gen. 25:15; Job 6:19
15 [a]Is. 13:14, 15; 17:13
16 [I]Lit., *the years of a hireling* [a]Is. 16:14 [b]Ps. 120:5; Song 1:5; Is. 42:11; 60:7; Ezek. 27:21
17 [a]Is. 10:19 [b]Num. 23:19; Zech. 1:6

1 [I]Or, *burden of* [a]Ps. 125:2; Jer. 21:13; Joel 3:12, 14 [b]Is. 15:3
2 [I]Lit., *dead in battle* [a]Is. 23:7; 32:13 [b]Jer. 14:18; Lam. 2:20
3 [I]Lit., *from a bow* [II]So with ancient versions; Heb., *They fled far away* [a]Is. 21:15
4 [I]Lit., *insist* [a]Is. 15:3; Jer. 9:1; Luke 19:41
5 [I]Heb., *YHWH*, usually rendered LORD [II]Or, *against* [a]Lam. 1:5; 2:2 [b]Is. 37:3 [c]Is. 10:6; 63:3 [d]Is. 22:1
6 [I]Lit., *man* [a]Is. 21:2; Jer. 49:35 [b]2Kin. 16:9; Amos 1:5; 9:7
8 [I]Lit., *screen, covering* [II]Or, *looked to, considered* [a]1Kin. 7:2; 10:17

The Valley of Vision

22 The [I]oracle[4853] concerning the [a]valley of vision.[2384]
What is the matter with you now, that you have all gone up[5927] to the [b]housetops?
2 You who were full of noise,
You boisterous town, you [a]exultant city;
Your slain[2491] were [b]not slain with the sword,[2719]
Nor [I]did they die[4191] in battle.
3 [a]All your rulers[7101] have fled together,
And have been captured [I]without the bow;
All of you who were found were taken captive together,
[II]Though they had fled far away.
4 Therefore I say,[559] "Turn your eyes away from me,
Let me [a]weep bitterly,
Do not [I]try to comfort[5162] me concerning the destruction[7701] of the daughter of my people."[5971]
5 [a]For the Lord[136] [I]GOD of hosts[6635] has a [b]day[3117] of panic,[4103] [c]subjugation, and confusion
[d]In the valley of vision,
A breaking down of walls
And a crying [II]to the mountain.
6 And [a]Elam took up[5375] the quiver
With the chariots, [I]infantry,[120] *and* horsemen;
And [b]Kir uncovered the shield.
7 Then your choicest valleys were full of chariots,
And the horsemen took up fixed positions at the gate.
8 And He removed the [I]defense of Judah.
In that day you [II]depended on the weapons[5402] of the [a]house[1004] of the forest,
9 And you saw[7200] that the breaches
In the *wall* of the city of David were many;

And you [a]collected[6908] the
waters of the lower pool.
10 Then you counted[5608] the
houses[1004] of Jerusalem,
And you tore down[5422] houses
to fortify the wall.
11 And you made[6213] a reservoir
[a]between the two walls
For the waters of the [b]old pool.
But you did not [I]depend on Him
who made it,
Nor did you [II]take into
consideration[7200] Him who
planned[3335] it long ago.
12 Therefore in that day the Lord
[I]GOD of hosts, called[7121] *you*
to [a]weeping, to wailing,
To [b]shaving the head, and to
wearing sackcloth.
13 Instead, there is [a]gaiety and
gladness,
Killing[7819] of cattle and
slaughtering of sheep,
Eating of meat[1320] and drinking
of wine:
"[b]Let us eat and drink, for
tomorrow we may die."[4191]
14 But the LORD of hosts
revealed[1540] Himself [I]to
me,[241]
"Surely this [a]iniquity[5771] [b]shall not
be [II]forgiven[3722] you
[c]Until you die," says[559] the Lord
[III]GOD of hosts.
15 Thus says the Lord [I]GOD of
hosts,
"Come, go to this steward,
To [a]Shebna, who is in charge
of the *royal* household,
16 'What right do you have here,
And whom do you have here,
That you have [a]hewn[2672] a tomb
for yourself here,
You who hew a tomb[6913] on the
height,
You who carve[2710] a resting
place[4908] for [I]yourself in the
rock?
17 'Behold, the LORD is about to hurl
you headlong, O man.[1397]
And He is about to grasp you
firmly,

9 [a]2Kin. 20:20; Neh. 3:16
11 [I]Or, *look to, consider* [II]Lit., *see. . .Him* [a]2Kin. 25:4; Jer. 39:4 [b]2Kin. 20:20; 2Chr. 32:3, 4
12 [I]Heb., *YHWH,* usually rendered LORD [a]Is. 32:11; Joel 1:13; 2:17 [b]Mic. 1:16
13 [a]Is. 5:11, 22; 28:7, 8; Luke 17:26-29 [b]Is. 56:12; 1Cor. 15:32
14 [I]Lit., *in my ears* [II]Lit., *atoned for* [III]Heb., *YHWH,* usually rendered LORD [a]Is. 13:11; 26:21; 30:13; 65:7 [b]1Sam. 3:14; Ezek. 24:13 [c]Is. 65:20
15 [I]Heb., *YHWH,* usually rendered LORD [a]2Kin. 18:18, 26, 37; Is. 36:3, 11, 22; 37:2
16 [I]Lit., *himself* [a]2Sam. 18:18; 2Chr. 16:14; Matt. 27:60
18 [a]Job 18:18; Is. 17:13
19 [I]So with many ancient versions; Heb., *He* [a]Job 40:11, 12; Ezek. 17:24
20 [a]2Kin. 18:18; Is. 36:3, 22; 37:2
21 [I]Lit., *rule* [a]Gen. 45:8; Job 29:16
22 [a]Rev. 3:7 [b]Is. 7:2, 13 [c]Job 12:14
23 [a]Ezra 9:8; Zech. 10:4 [b]1Sam. 2:8; Job 36:7
24 [I]Or perhaps, *leaf*
25 [a]Is. 22:23 [b]Esth. 9:24, 25 [c]Is. 46:11; Mic. 4:4
1 [I]Or, *burden of* [a]Josh. 19:29; 1Kin. 5:1; Jer. 25:22; 47:4; Ezek. 26:1-27:36; Joel 3:4-8; Amos 1:9; Zech. 9:2-4 [b]Is. 2:16 [c]Gen. 10:4; 1Kin 10:22

18 *And* roll you tightly like a ball,
To be [a]*cast* into a vast country;[776]
There you will die,
And there your splendid[3519]
chariots will be,
You shame of your master's
house.'
19 "And I will [a]depose you from your
office,
And [I]I will pull[2040] you down from
your station.[4612]
20 "Then it will come about in that
day,
That I will summon My
servant[5650] [a]Eliakim the
son[1121] of Hilkiah
21 And I will clothe him with your
tunic,
And tie your sash[73] securely[2388]
about him,
I will entrust him[3027] with your
[I]authority,[4475]
And he will become a [a]father[1]
to the inhabitants of
Jerusalem and to the house
of Judah.
22 "Then I will set [a]the key of the
[b]house of David on his
shoulder,
When he opens no one will shut,
When he shuts no one will
[c]open.
23 "And I will drive[8628] him *like* a
[a]peg in a firm[539] place,
And he will become a [b]throne[3678]
of glory[3519] to his father's[1]
house.
24 "So they will hang on him all the
glory of his father's house, offspring and
[I]issue, all the least of vessels, from
bowls to all the jars.[5035]
25 "In that day," declares[5001] the
LORD of hosts, "the [a]peg driven[8628] in
a firm place will give way; it will even
[b]break off[3772] and fall, and the load hanging on it will be cut off,[3772] for the
[c]LORD has spoken."[1696]

The Fall of Tyre

23 The [I]oracle[4853] concerning [a]Tyre.
Wail, O [b]ships of [c]Tarshish,

For *Tyre* is destroyed,[7703]
without house[1004] *or*
[IId]harbor;
It is reported[1540] to them from
the land[776] of [IIIe]Cyprus.
2 [a]Be silent, you inhabitants of the
coastland,
You merchants of Sidon;
[I]Your messengers crossed[5674]
the sea
3 And *were* on many waters.
[a]The grain[2233] of the [Ib]Nile, the
harvest of the River was her
revenue;
And she was the [c]market of
nations.[1471]
4 Be ashamed,[954] O [a]Sidon;
For the sea speaks,[559] the
stronghold of the sea,
saying,
"I have neither travailed[2342] nor
given birth,
I have neither brought up young
men *nor* reared virgins."[1330]
5 When the report[8088] *reaches*
Egypt,
They will be in [a]anguish[2342] at
the report of Tyre.
6 Pass over to [a]Tarshish;
Wail, O inhabitants of the
coastland.
7 Is this your [a]jubilant *city,*
Whose origin[6927] is from
antiquity,[6924]
Whose feet used to carry her
to [I]colonize[1481] distant
places?
8 Who has planned[3289] this against
Tyre, [a]the bestower of
crowns,
Whose merchants were
princes,[8269] whose
traders3669 were the
honored[3513] of the earth?[776]
9 [a]The LORD of hosts[6635] has
planned[3289] it to [b]defile the
pride of all beauty,[6643]
To despise all the [c]honored of
the earth.
10 [I]Overflow your land like the Nile,
O daughter of Tarshish,
There is no more [II]restraint.

11 He has [a]stretched His hand[3027]
out [b]over the sea,
He has [c]made the kingdoms[4467]
tremble;
The LORD has given a
command[4687] concerning
Canaan to [d]demolish[8045] its
strongholds.
12 And He has said,[559] "[a]You shall
exult no more, O crushed
virgin[1330] daughter of Sidon.
Arise, pass over to [Ib]Cyprus;
even there you will find no
rest."
13 Behold, the land of the Chaldeans—this is the people[5971] *which* was
not; [a]Assyria appointed[3245] it for [b]desert
creatures—they erected their siege
towers, they stripped its palaces,[759]
[c]they made[7760] it a ruin.
14 Wail, O [a]ships of Tarshish,
For your stronghold is
destroyed.
15 Now it will come about in that
day[3117] that Tyre will be forgotten for
[a]seventy years like the days of one
king.[4428] At the end of seventy years
it will happen to Tyre as *in* the song
of the harlot:[2181]
16 Take *your* harp, walk about the
city,
O forgotten harlot;
Pluck the strings skillfully,[3190]
sing many songs,[7892]
That you may be
remembered.[2142]
17 And it will come about at [a]the
end of seventy years that the LORD will
visit[6485] Tyre. Then she will go back[7725]
to her harlot's wages, and will [b]play the
harlot[2181] with all the kingdoms [I]on the
face of the earth.[127]
18 And her [a]gain and her harlot's
wages will be [b]set apart[6944] to the LORD;
it will not be stored up or hoarded, but
her gain will become sufficient food and
choice attire for those who dwell in the
presence of the LORD.

Judgment on the Earth

24 Behold, the LORD [a]lays the
earth[776] waste, devastates it,

1 [II]Lit., *entering* [III]Heb., *Kittim* [d]Is. 24:10 [e]Gen. 10:4; Is. 23:12; Ezek. 27:6

2 [I]So DSS; M.T., *Who passed over the sea, they replenished you.* [a]Is. 47:5

3 [I]Heb., *Shihor* [a]Is. 19:7-9 [b]Josh. 13:3; 1Chr. 13:5; Jer. 2:18 [c]Ezek. 27:3-23

4 [a]Gen. 10:15, 19; Josh. 11:8; Judg. 10:6; Jer. 25:22; 27:3; 47:4; Ezek. 28:21, 22

5 [a]Ex. 15:14-16; Josh. 2:9-11

6 [a]Is. 23:1

7 [I]Lit., *sojourn afar off* [a]Is. 22:2; 32:13

8 [a]Ezek. 28:2

9 [a]Is. 2:11; 13:11 [b]Job 40:11, 12; Dan. 4:37 [c]Is. 5:13; 9:15

10 [I]Lit., *Pass over* [II]Perhaps *girdle* or *shipyard*

11 [a]Ex. 14:21; Is. 14:26 [b]Is. 19:5; 50:2 [c]Is. 13:13 [d]Is. 25:2; Zech. 9:3, 4

12 [I]Heb., *Kittim* [a]Ezek. 26:13, 14; Rev. 18:22 [b]Is. 23:1

13 [a]Is. 10:5 [b]Is. 13:21; 18:6 [c]Is. 10:7

14 [a]Is. 2:16; Ezek. 27:25, 26

15 [a]Jer. 25:11, 22

17 [I]Lit., *of the earth on the face of the land* [a]Is. 23:15 [b]Ezek. 16:25-29; Nah. 3:4

18 [a]Ps. 72:10, 11; Is. 60:5-9; Mic. 4:13 [b]Ex. 28:36; Zech. 14:20

1 [a]Is. 2:19; 13:13; 24:19, 20; 30:32; 33:9

distorts[5753] its surface, and scatters its
inhabitants.
2 And the people[5971] will be like the
priest,[3548] the servant[5650] like his master,[113] the maid like her mistress,[1404]
the buyer like the seller, the lender like
the borrower, the [a]creditor like the
debtor.
3 The earth[776] will be completely
laid waste and completely despoiled, for
the LORD has spoken[1696] this word.[1697]
4 The [a]earth mourns *and* withers,
the world[8398] fades *and* withers, the
[b]exalted of the people of the earth fade
away.
5 The earth is also [a]polluted[2610]
[I]by its inhabitants, for they transgressed[5674] laws, violated statutes,[2706]
[b]broke[6565] the everlasting[5769] covenant.[1285]
6 Therefore, a [a]curse[423] devours
the earth, and those who live in it are
held guilty.[816] Therefore, the [b]inhabi-
tants of the earth are burned,[2787] and
few men[582] are left.[7604]

7 The [a]new wine mourns,
The vine decays,
All the merry-hearted sigh.
8 The [a]gaiety of tambourines[8596]
ceases,[7673]
The noise[7588] of revelers stops,
The gaiety of the harp ceases.
9 They do not drink wine with
song;[7892]
[a]Strong drink is [b]bitter to those
who drink it.
10 The [a]city of chaos[8414] is
broken[7665] down;
[b]Every house[1004] is shut up so
that none may enter.
11 There is an [a]outcry in the streets
concerning the wine;
[b]All joy [I]turns to gloom.
The gaiety of the earth is
banished.
12 Desolation[8047] is left in the
city,
And the [a]gate is battered[3807] to
ruins.[7591]
13 For [a]thus it will be in the
midst[7130] of the earth among
the peoples,
As the [I]shaking of an olive tree,
As the gleanings when the grape
harvest is over.[3615]
14 [a]They raise[5375] their voices, they
shout for joy.
They cry out from the
[I]west concerning the majesty
of the LORD.
15 Therefore [a]glorify[3513] the LORD
in the [I]east,[217]
The [b]name of the LORD, the
God[430] of Israel
In the [II][c]coastlands of the sea.
16 From the [a]ends of the earth we
hear[8085] songs, "[b]Glory to the
Righteous[6662] One,"
But I say,[559] "[I][c]Woe to me!
[I]Woe to me! Alas for me!
The [d]treacherous[898] deal
treacherously,[898]
And the treacherous deal very
treacherously."
17 [a]Terror[6343] and pit[6354] and
snare[6341]
[I]Confront you, O inhabitant of
the earth.
18 Then it will be that he who flees
the [I]report of disaster will fall
into the pit,
And he who [II]climbs out[5927] of
the pit will be caught in the
snare;
For the [a]windows [III]above are
opened, and the
[b]foundations[4146] of the earth
shake.[7493]
19 [a]The earth is broken
asunder,[7489]
The earth is [b]split
through,[6565]
The earth is shaken violently.
20 The earth [a]reels to and fro like
a drunkard,
And it totters like a [I]shack,
For its [b]transgression[6588] is
heavy[3513] upon it,
And it will fall, [c]never to rise
again.
21 So it will happen in that day,[3117]
That the LORD will [a]punish[6485]
the host[6635] of [I]heaven, on
high,

2 [a]Lev. 25:36, 37; Deut. 23:19, 20
4 [a]Is. 33:9 [b]Is. 2:12; 24:21
5 [I]Lit., *under* [a]Gen. 3:17; Num. 35:33; Is. 9:17; 10:6 [b]Is. 33:8
6 [a]Josh. 23:15; Is. 34:5; 43:28; Zech. 5:3,4 [b]Is. 1:31; 5:24; 9:19
7 [a]Is. 16:10; Joel 1:10, 12
8 [a]Is. 5:12, 14; Ezek. 26:13; Hos. 2:11; Rev. 18:22
9 [a]Is. 5:11, 22 [b]Is. 5:20
10 [a]Is. 34:11 [b]Is. 23:1
11 [I]Lit., *is darkened* [a]Jer. 14:2; 46:12 [b]Is. 16:10; 32:13
12 [a]Is. 14:31; 45:2
13 [I]Lit., *striking* [a]Is. 17:6; 27:12
14 [I]Lit., *sea* [a]Is. 12:6; 48:20; 52:8; 54:1
15 [I]Lit., *region of light* [II]Or, *islands* [a]Is. 25:3 [b]Mal. 1:11 [c]Is. 11:11; 42:4, 10, 12; 49:1; 51:5; 60:9; 66:19
16 [I]Lit., *Wasting to me!* [a]Is. 11:12; 42:10 [b]Is. 28:5; 60:21 [c]Lev. 26:39 [d]Is. 21:2; 33:1; Jer. 3:20; 5:11
17 [I]Lit., *Are upon you* [a]Jer. 48:43; Amos 5:19
18 [I]Lit., *sound of terror* [II]Lit., *goes up from the midst of* [III]Lit., *from the height;* i.e., heaven [a]Gen. 7:11 [b]Ps. 18:7; 46:2; Is. 2:19, 21; 13:13
19 [a]Is. 24:1 [b]Num. 16:31, 32; Deut. 11:6
20 [I]Or, *hut* [a]Is. 19:14; 24:1; 28:7 [b]Is. 1:28; 43:27; 66:24 [c]Dan. 11:19; Amos 8:14
21 [I]Lit., *the height in the height* [a]Is. 10:12; 13:11

And the [b]kings[4428] of the
earth,[127] on earth.
22 And they will be gathered
together[626]
Like [a]prisoners in the
[I]dungeon,[953]
And will be confined in prison;
And after many days[3117] they will
[b]be punished.[6485]
23 Then the [a]moon will be abashed
and the sun ashamed,[954]
For the [b]LORD of hosts[6635] will
reign[4427] on [c]Mount Zion and
in Jerusalem,
And *His* glory will be before His
elders.[2204]

Song of Praise for God's Favor

25 O LORD, Thou art [a]my God;[430]
I will exalt Thee, I will give
thanks[3034] to Thy name;
For Thou hast [b]worked[6213]
wonders,[6382]
[c]Plans *formed* long ago, with
perfect faithfulness.[530]
2 For Thou hast made[7760] a city
into a [a]heap,
A [b]fortified city into a ruin;
A [c]palace[759] of strangers[2114] is
a city no more,
It will never be rebuilt.
3 Therefore a strong people[5971]
will [a]glorify[3513] Thee;
[b]Cities of ruthless nations[1471] will
revere[3372] Thee.
4 For Thou hast been a
[a]defense for the helpless,
A defense for the needy in his
distress,
A [b]refuge from the storm, a
shade from the heat;
For the breath[7307] of the
[c]ruthless
Is like a *rain* storm *against* a
wall.
5 Like heat in drought, Thou dost
subdue the [a]uproar[7588] of
aliens;
Like heat by the shadow of a
cloud, the song of the
ruthless is [I]silenced.

6 And [a]the LORD of hosts[6635] will
prepare[6213] a [I]lavish[8081]
banquet[4960] for [b]all peoples on
this mountain;
A banquet of [II]aged wine,
[III]choice pieces with marrow,
And [IV]refined,[2212] aged[8105]
wine.
7 And on this mountain He will
swallow up[1104] the [Ia]covering
which is over all peoples,
Even the veil which is
[II]stretched over all nations.
8 He will [a]swallow up death[4194] for
all time,[5331]
And the Lord[136] [I]GOD will
[b]wipe tears away from all
faces,
And He will remove the
[c]reproach[2781] of His people
from all the earth;[776]
For the LORD has spoken.[1696]
9 And it will be said[569] in that
day,[3117]
"Behold, [a]this is our God for
whom we have [b]waited[6960]
that [c]He might save[3467]
us.
This is the LORD for whom we
have waited;
[d]Let us rejoice and be glad in
His salvation."[3444]
10 For the hand[3027] of the LORD will
rest on this mountain,
And [a]Moab will be trodden down
in his place
As straw is trodden down in the
water of a manure pile.
11 And he will [a]spread out his
hands[3027] in the middle[7130]
of it
As a swimmer spreads out *his*
hands to swim,
But *the Lord* will [b]lay low his
pride together with the
trickery of his hands.
12 And the [a]unassailable
fortifications of your walls He
will bring down,
Lay low, *and* cast to the
ground,[776] even to the
dust.[6083]

21 [b]Ps. 76:12
22 [I]Lit., *pit* [a]Is. 10:4; 42:22 [b]Ezek. 38:8; Zech. 9:11, 12
23 [a]Is. 13:10 [b]Is. 60:19, 20; Zech. 14:6, 7; Rev. 21:23; 22:5 [c]Mic. 4:7; Heb. 12:22

1 [a]Ex. 15:2; Ps. 118:28; Is. 7:13; 49:4, 5; 61:10 [b]Ps. 40:5; 98:1 [c]Eph. 1:11
2 [a]Is. 17:1; 26:5; 27:10; 32:19 [b]Is. 17:3; 25:12 [c]Is. 13:22; 32:14; 34:13
3 [a]Is. 24:15 [b]Is. 13:11
4 [a]Is. 14:32; 17:10; 27:5; 33:16 [b]Is. 4:6; 32:2 [c]Is. 29:5, 20; 49:25
5 [I]Lit., *humbled* [a]Jer. 51:54-56
6 [I]Lit., *feast of fat things;* i.e., abundance [II]Lit., *wine on the lees* [III]Lit., *fat pieces* [IV]Lit., *wine refined on the lees* [a]Is. 1:19 [b]Is. 2:2-4; 56:7
7 [I]Lit., *face of the covering* [II]Lit., *woven* [a]2Cor. 3:15, 16; Eph. 4:18
8 [I]Heb., *YHWH*, usually rendered LORD [a]Hos. 13:14; 1Cor. 15:54 [b]Is. 30:19; 35:10; 51:11; 65:19; Rev. 7:17; 21:4 [c]Ps. 69:9; 89:50, 51; Is. 51:7; 54:4; Matt. 5:11; 1Pet. 4:14
9 [a]Is. 35:2; 40:9; 52:10 [b]Is. 8:17; 30:18; 33:2 [c]Is. 33:22; 35:4; 49:25, 26; 60:16 [d]Ps. 20:5; Is. 35:1, 2, 10; 65:18; 66:10
10 [a]Is. 16:14; Jer. 48:1-47; Ezek. 25:8-11; Amos 2:1-3; Zeph. 2:9
11 [a]Is. 5:25; 14:26 [b]Job 40:11; Is. 2:10-12, 15-17; 16:6, 14
12 [a]Is. 15:1; 25:2; 26:5

Song of Trust in God's Protection

26 [a]In that day[3117] this song[7892] will be sung[7891] in the land[776] of Judah:
"We have a [b]strong city;
He[430] sets up walls and ramparts for [I][c]security.[3444]
2 "Open the [a]gates, that the [b]righteous[6662] nation[1471] may enter,
The one that [I]remains[8104] faithful.[529]
3 "The steadfast of mind[3336] Thou wilt keep[5341] in perfect [a]peace,
Because he trusts[982] in Thee.
4 "[a]Trust[982] in the LORD forever,[5957]
For in [I]GOD the LORD, *we have* an everlasting[5769] [b]Rock.
5 "For He has brought low those who dwell on high, the [a]unassailable city;
[b]He lays it low, He lays it low to the ground,[776] He casts it to the dust.[6083]
6 "[a]The foot will trample it,
The feet of the [b]afflicted, the steps of the helpless."
7 The [a]way[734] of the righteous is smooth;[4334]
O Upright[3477] One, [b]make the path of the righteous level.
8 Indeed, *while following* the way of [a]Thy judgments,[4941] O LORD,
We have waited[6960] for Thee eagerly;
[b]Thy name, even Thy [c]memory,[2143] is the desire of *our* souls.[5315]
9 [a]At night[3915] [I]my soul longs for Thee,
Indeed, [II]my spirit[7307] within[7130] me [b]seeks Thee diligently;
For when the earth[776] [III]experiences Thy judgments
The inhabitants of the world[8398] [c]learn[3925] righteousness.[6664]
10 *Though* the wicked[7563] is shown favor,[2603]
He does not [a]learn righteousness;
He [b]deals unjustly[5765] in the land of uprightness,
And does not perceive[7200] the majesty of the LORD.
11 O LORD, Thy hand[3027] is lifted up *yet* they [a]do not see[2372] it.
[I]They see [b]*Thy* zeal for the people[5971] and are put to shame;[954]
Indeed, [II][c]fire will devour Thine enemies.
12 LORD, Thou wilt establish [a]peace for us,
Since Thou hast also performed for us all our works.
13 O LORD our God, [a]other masters besides Thee have ruled[1166] us;
But through Thee alone we [I][b]confess Thy name.
14 [a]The dead[4191] will not live,[2421] the [I]departed spirits[7496] will not rise;
Therefore Thou hast [b]punished[6485] and destroyed[8045] them,
And Thou hast wiped out[6] all remembrance[2143] of them.
15 [a]Thou hast increased the nation, O LORD,
Thou hast increased the nation, Thou art glorified;[3513]
Thou hast [b]extended all the borders of the land.
16 O LORD, they sought Thee [a]in distress;
They [I]could only whisper a prayer,[3908]
Thy chastening[4148] was upon them.
17 [a]As the pregnant woman approaches *the time* to give birth,
She writhes[2342] *and* cries out in her labor pains,[2256]
Thus were we before Thee, O LORD.
18 We were pregnant, we writhed *in labor*,

1 [I]Or, *salvation* [a]Is. 4:2; 12:1 [b]Is. 14:31; 31:5, 9; 33:5, 6, 20-24 [c]Is. 60:18
2 [I]Lit., *keeps faithfulness* [a]Is. 60:11, 18; 62:10 [b]Is. 45:25; 54:14, 17; 58:8; 60:21; 61:3; 62:1, 2
3 [a]Is. 26:12; 27:5; 57:19; 66:12
4 [I]Heb., YAH, usually rendered LORD [a]Is. 12:2; 50:10; 51:5 [b]Is. 17:10; 30:29; 44:8
5 [a]Is. 25:12 [b]Job 40:11-13
6 [a]Is. 28:3 [b]Is. 3:14, 15; 11:4; 29:19
7 [a]Is. 57:2 [b]Ps. 25:4, 5; 27:11; Is. 42:16; 52:12
8 [a]Is. 51:4; 56:1 [b]Is. 12:4; 24:15; 25:1; 26:13 [c]Ex. 3:15
9 [I]Lit., with *my soul I long* [II]Lit., with *my spirit. . . I seek* [III]Lit., *has* [a]Ps. 63:5, 6; 77:2; 119:62; Is. 50:10; Luke 6:12 [b]Ps. 63:1; 78:34; Matt. 6:33 [c]Is. 55:6; Hos. 5:15
10 [a]Is. 22:12, 13; 32:6, 7 [b]Hos. 11:7; John 5:37, 38
11 [I]Or, *Let them see. . . and be* [II]Or, *let the fire for Thine adversaries devour them* [a]Is. 44:9, 18 [b]Is. 9:7; 37:32; 59:17 [c]Is. 5:24; 9:18, 19; 10:17; 66:15, 24; Heb. 10:27
12 [a]Is. 26:3
13 [I]Or, *cause to be remembered* [a]Is. 2:8; 10:11 [b]Is. 63:7
14 [I]Or, *shades* [a]Deut. 4:28; Ps. 135:17; Is. 8:19; Hab. 2:19 [b]Is. 10:3
15 [a]Is. 9:3 [b]Is. 33:17; 54:2, 3
16 [I]Lit., *sound forth a whisper* [a]Is. 37:3; Hos. 5:15
17 [a]Is. 13:8; 21:3; John 16:21

We [a]gave birth, as it were, *only*
to wind.*7307*
We could not accomplish
deliverance*3444* for the earth
Nor were [b]inhabitants of the
world [I]born.*5307*

19 Your [a]dead*7496* will live;
[I]Their corpses*5038* will rise.
You who lie*7931* in the dust,
[b]awake and shout for joy,
For your dew is as the dew of
the [II]dawn,
And the earth will [III]give birth*5307*
to the [IV]departed spirits.

20 Come, my people, [a]enter into
your rooms,
And close your doors behind
you;
Hide for a little [Ib]while,
Until [c]indignation*2195* [II]runs *its*
course.*5674*

21 For behold, the LORD is about
to [a]come out from His place
To [b]punish*6485* the inhabitants of
the earth for their
iniquity;*5771*
And the earth will [c]reveal*1540* her
bloodshed,*1818*
And will no longer cover*3680* her
slain.*2026*

The Deliverance of Israel

27 [a]In that day*3117* the LORD will
punish*6485* [Ib]Leviathan the
fleeing serpent,*5175*
With His fierce*7186* and great and
mighty*2389* sword,*2719*
Even [I]Leviathan the twisted
serpent;
And [c]He will kill*2026* the
dragon*8577* who *lives* in the
sea.

2 In that day,
"A [Ia]vineyard of wine, sing of it!

3 "I, the LORD, am its keeper;*5341*
[a]I water it every moment.
Lest anyone [I]damage it,
I [b]guard it night*3915* and day.

4 "I have no wrath.
Should [I]someone give Me
[a]briars *and* thorns in battle,
Then I would step on them,
[b]I would burn them
[II]completely.

5 "Or let him [Ia]rely on My
protection,
Let him make*6213* peace with
Me,
Let him [b]make peace with
Me."

6 [I]In the days to come Jacob
[a]will take root,
Israel will [b]blossom and sprout;
And they will fill the [II]whole
world*8398* with [c]fruit.

7 Like the striking*5221* of Him who
has struck*4347* them, has
[a]He struck*5221* them?
Or like the slaughter*2027* of His
slain,*2026* [I]have they been
slain?

8 Thou didst contend*7378* with
them [I]by banishing them, by
[a]driving them away.
With His fierce*7186* wind*7307* He
has expelled *them* on the day
of the [b]east wind.

9 Therefore through this Jacob's
iniquity*5771* will be
[a]forgiven;*3722*
And this will be [I]the full price
of the [IIb]pardoning of his
sin:*2403*
When he makes*7760* all the
[c]altar*4196* stones like
pulverized chalk stones;
When [III]Asherim*842* and incense
altars*2553* will not stand.

10 For the fortified city is
[a]isolated,
A [I]homestead forlorn and
forsaken*5800* like the desert;
[b]There the calf will graze,
And there it will lie down and
[II]feed*3615* on its branches.

18 [I]Lit., *fallen* [a]Is. 33:11; 59:4 [b]Ps. 17:14
19 [I]So with some ancient versions; Heb., *My* [II]Lit., *lights* [III]Lit., *cause to fall* [IV]Or, *shades* [a]Is. 25:8; Ezek. 37:1-14; Dan. 12:2; Hos. 13:14 [b]Eph. 5:14
20 [I]Lit., *moment* [II]Lit., *passes over* [a]Ex. 12:22, 23; Ps. 91:1, 4 [b]Ps. 30:5; Is. 54:7, 8; 2Cor. 4:17 [c]Is. 10:5, 25; 13:5; 34:2; 66:14
21 [a]Mic. 1:3; Jude 14 [b]Is. 13:11; 30:12-14; 65:6, 7 [c]Job 16:18; Luke 11:50

1 [I]Or, *sea monster* [a]Is. 66:16 [b]Job 3:8; 41:1; Ps. 74:14; 104:26 [c]Is. 51:9
2 [I]Some mss. read *a vineyard of delight* [a]Ps. 80:8; Is. 5:7; Jer. 2:21
3 [I]Lit., *punish* [a]Is. 58:11 [b]1Sam. 2:9; Is. 31:5; John 10:28
4 [I]Lit., *who* [II]Lit., *altogether* [a]2Sam. 23:6; Is. 10:17 [b]Is. 33:12; Matt. 3:12; Heb. 6:8
5 [I]Lit., *take hold of* [a]Is. 12:2; 25:4 [b]Job 22:21; Is. 26:3, 12; Rom. 5:1; 2Cor. 5:20
6 [I]Lit., *Those coming* [II]Lit., *face of* [a]Is. 37:31 [b]Is. 35:1, 2; Hos. 14:5, 6 [c]Is. 4:2
7 [I]Lit., *he was slain* [a]Is. 10:12, 17; 30:31-33; 31:8, 9; 37:36-38
8 [I]Some ancient versions read *by exact measure* [a]Is. 50:1; 54:7 [b]Jer. 4:11; Ezek. 19:12; Hos. 13:15
9 [I]Lit., *all the fruit* [II]Lit., *removing* [III]I.e., wooden symbols of a female deity [a]Is. 1:25; 48:10; Dan. 11:35 [b]Rom. 11:27 [c]Ex. 34:13; Deut. 12:3; 2Kin. 10:26; Is. 17:8
10 [I]Lit., *pasture* [II]Lit., *consume* [a]Is. 32:13, 14 [b]Is. 17:2

🔑 **26:19** See note on Dan. 12:2.

11 When its [a]limbs are dry,[3001] they
are broken[7665] off;
Women[802] come *and* make a fire
with them.
For they are not a people[5971] of
[b]discernment,
Therefore [c]their Maker[6213]
[d]will not have compassion[7355]
on them.
And their Creator[3335] will not be
gracious[2603] to them.

12 And it will come about in that
day, that the LORD [a]will start *His* threshing from the flowing stream of the
[b]Euphrates to the brook of Egypt; and
you will be [c]gathered[3950] up one by one,
O sons[1121] of Israel.
13 It will come about also in that
day that a great [a]trumpet will be
blown;[8628] and those who were perishing[6] in the land[776] of [b]Assyria and
who were scattered in the land of Egypt
will come and [c]worship[7812] the LORD in
the holy[6944] mountain at Jerusalem.

Ephraim's Captivity Predicted

28 Woe to the proud crown of the
[a]drunkards of [b]Ephraim,
And to the fading flower of its
glorious[6643] beauty,[8597]
Which is at the head[7218] of the
[I]fertile[8081] valley
Of those who are [II]overcome[1986]
with wine!
2 Behold, the Lord[136] has a
strong[2389] and [a]mighty *agent;*
As a storm of [b]hail, a tempest[8178]
of destruction,[6986]
Like a storm of [c]mighty
overflowing[7857] waters,
He has cast *it* down to the
earth[776] with *His* hand.[3027]
3 The proud crown of the
drunkards of Ephraim is
[a]trodden under foot.
4 And the fading flower of its
glorious beauty,
Which is at the head of the
[I]fertile valley,
Will be like the [a]first-ripe fig prior
to summer;
Which [II]one sees,[7200]
And [III]as soon as it is in his
[IV]hand,[3709]
He swallows it.
5 In that day[3117] the [a]LORD of
hosts[6635] will become a
beautiful [b]crown
And a glorious diadem[6843] to the
remnant[7605] of His people;[5971]
6 A [a]spirit[7307] of justice[4941] for him
who sits in judgment,
A [b]strength to those who
repel[7725] the [I]onslaught at the
gate.
7 And these also [a]reel[7686] with
wine and stagger[8582] from
strong drink:
[b]The priest[3548] and [c]the
prophet[5030] reel[7686] with
strong drink,
They are confused[1104] by wine,
they stagger from [d]strong
drink;
They reel[7686] while [I]having
[e]visions,[7203]
They totter *when rendering*
judgment.
8 For all the tables are full of filthy
[a]vomit, without a *single clean*
place.
9 "To [a]whom would He teach[3384]
knowledge?
And to whom would He
interpret[995] the message?[8052]
Those *just* [b]weaned from milk?
Those *just* taken from the
breast?
10 "For *He says,*
'[I][a]Order on order, order on
order,
Line on line, line on line,
A little here, a little there.' "
11 Indeed, He will speak[1696] to this
people
Through [a]stammering lips[8193]
and a foreign tongue,
12 He who said[559] to them, "Here
is [a]rest, give rest to the
weary,"

11 [a]Is. 18:5 [b]Deut. 32:28; Is. 1:3; 5:13; Jer. 8:7 [c]Deut. 32:18; Is. 43:1, 7; 44:2, 21, 24 [d]Is. 9:17
12 [a]Is. 11:11; 17:6; 24:13; 56:8 [b]Gen. 15:18 [c]Deut. 30:3, 4; Neh. 1:9
13 [a]Lev. 25:9; 1Chr. 15:24; Matt. 24:31; Rev. 11:15 [b]Is. 19:24, 25 [c]Is. 19:21, 23; 49:7; 66:23; Zech. 14:16; Heb. 12:22

1 [I]Lit., *valley of fatness* [II]Lit., *smitten* [a]Is. 28:7; Hos. 7:5 [b]Is. 9:9
2 [a]Is. 8:7; 40:10 [b]Is. 28:17; 30:30; 32:19; Ezek. 13:11 [c]Is. 8:6, 7; 30:28; Nah. 1:8
3 [a]Is. 26:6; 28:18
4 [I]Lit., *valley of fatness* [II]Lit., *the one seeing sees* [III]Lit., *while it is yet* [IV]Lit., *palm* [a]Hos. 9:10; Mic. 7:1; Nah. 3:12
5 [a]Is. 41:16; 45:25; 60:1, 19 [b]Is. 62:3
6 [I]Lit., *battle* [a]1Kin. 3:28; Is. 11:2; 32:15, 16; John 5:30 [b]2Chr. 32:6-8; Is. 25:4
7 [I]Lit., *seeing* [a]Is. 5:11, 22; 22:13; 56:12; Hos. 4:11 [b]Is. 24:2 [c]Is. 9:15 [d]Hab. 2:15, 16 [e]Is. 29:11
8 [a]Jer. 48:26
9 [a]Is. 2:3; 28:26; 30:20; 48:17; 50:4; 54:13 [b]Ps. 131:2
10 [I]Heb., *Sav lasav, sav lasav, Kav lakav, kav lakav, Ze'er sham, ze'er sham.* These Hebrew monosyllables, imitating the babbling of a child, mock the prophet's preaching [a]2Chr. 36:15; Neh. 9:30

11 [a]Is. 33:19; 1Cor. 14:21 12 [a]Is. 11:10; 30:15; 32:17, 18; Jer. 6:16; Matt. 11:28, 29

And, "Here is repose," but they would[14] not listen.[8085]
13 So the word[1697] of the LORD to them will be,
"[I]Order on order, order on order,
Line on line, line on line,
A little here, a little there,"
That they may go and [a]stumble[3782] backward, be broken,[7665] snared,[3369] and taken captive.

Judah Is Warned

14 Therefore, [a]hear the word of the LORD, O [b]scoffers,[582]
Who rule[4910] this people who are in Jerusalem,
15 Because you have said, "We have made[3772] a [a]covenant[1285] with death,[4194]
And with [I]Sheol[7585] we have made a [II]pact.[2374]
[b]The overwhelming [III]scourge[7885] will not reach us when it passes by,
For we have made[7760] [c]falsehood[3577] our refuge and we have [d]concealed ourselves with deception."
16 Therefore thus says[559] the Lord [I]GOD,
"[a]Behold, I am laying in Zion a stone, a tested[976] [b]stone,
A costly cornerstone *for* the foundation,[4143] [II]firmly placed.[3245]
He who believes[539] *in it* will not be [III]disturbed.
17 "And I will make[7760] [a]justice the measuring line,
And righteousness[6666] the level;[4949]
Then [b]hail shall sweep away the refuge of lies,
And the waters shall overflow[7857] the secret place.
18 "And your [a]covenant with death shall be [I][b]canceled,[3722]
And your pact[2380] with Sheol shall not stand;
When the [c]overwhelming scourge[7752] passes through,
Then you become its [d]trampling *place*.
19 "As [a]often as it passes through,[5674] it will [I]seize you.
For [b]morning after morning it will pass through,[5674] *anytime* during the day or night.[3915]
And it will be [II]sheer [c]terror[2113] to understand [III]what it means."
20 The bed is too short on which to stretch out,
And the [a]blanket[4541] is too [I]small to wrap[3664] oneself in.
21 For the LORD will rise up as *at* Mount [a]Perazim,
He will be stirred up as in the valley of [b]Gibeon;
To do[6213] His [c]task, His [I][d]unusual[2114] task,
And to work[5647] His work,[5656] His [II]extraordinary[5237] work.
22 And now do not carry on as [a]scoffers,[3887]
Lest your fetters be made stronger;[2388]
For I have heard[8085] from the Lord [I]GOD of hosts,
Of decisive [b]destruction[3617] on all the earth.
23 Give ear and hear my voice,
Listen[7181] and hear my words.[565]
24 Does the [I]farmer plow [II]continually to plant seed?
Does he *continually* [III]turn and harrow the ground?[127]
25 Does he not level its surface,
And sow dill[7100] and scatter [a]cummin,[3646]
And [I]plant [b]wheat in rows,
Barley in its place, and rye within its [II]area?

13 [I]V. 10, note 1. The Lord responds to their scoffing by imitating their mockery, to represent the unintelligible language of a conqueror. [a]Is. 8:15; Matt. 21:44
14 [a]Is. 1:10; 28:22 [b]Is. 29:20
15 [I]I.e., the nether world [II]So some ancient versions; Heb., *seer* [III]Or, *flood* [a]Is. 28:18 [b]Is. 8:8; 28:2; 30:28; Dan. 11:22 [c]Is. 9:15; 30:9; 44:20; 59:3, 4; Ezek. 13:22 [d]Is. 29:15
16 [I]Heb., *YHWH*, usually rendered LORD [II]Lit., *well-laid* [III]Lit., *in a hurry* [a]Rom. 9:33; 10:11; 1Pet. 2:6 [b]Ps. 118:22; Is. 8:14, 15; Matt. 21:42; Mark 12:10; Luke 20:17; Acts 4:11; Eph. 2:20
17 [a]2Kin. 21:13; Is. 5:16; 30:18; 61:8; Amos 7:7-9 [b]Is. 28:2
18 [I]Lit., *covered over* [a]Is. 28:15 [b]Is. 7:7; 8:10 [c]Is. 28:15 [d]Is. 28:3; Dan. 8:13
19 [I]Lit., *take* [II]Lit., *only* [III]Lit., *the report,* or, *the message* [a]2Kin. 24:2 [b]Is. 50:4 [c]Job 6:4; 18:11; 24:17; Ps. 55:4; 88:15; Lam. 2:22
20 [I]Lit., *narrow* [a]Is. 59:6
21 [I]Lit., *task is strange* [II]Lit., *work is alien* [a]2Sam. 5:20; 1Chr. 14:11 [b]Josh. 10:10, 12; 2Sam. 5:25; 1Chr. 14:16 [c]Is. 10:12; 29:14; 65:7 [d]Lam. 2:15; 3:33; Luke 19:41-44
22 [I]Heb., *YHWH*, usually rendered LORD [a]Is. 28:14 [b]Is. 10:22, 23
24 [I]Lit., *plowman* [II]Lit., *all day* [III]Lit., *open*
25 [I]Lit., *put* [II]Lit., *region* [a]Matt. 23:23 [b]Ex. 9:32

28:16 See note on Isa. 8:14.

26 For his God[430] instructs[3256] and
teaches him properly.[4941]
27 For dill is not threshed with a
[a]threshing sledge,
Nor is the cartwheel[212] [5699]
[I]driven over cummin;
But dill is beaten out with a
rod,[4294] and cummin with a
club.[7626]
28 *Grain for* bread is crushed,
Indeed, he does not continue to
thresh it forever.
Because the wheel[1536] of *his* cart
and his horses *eventually*
[I]damage *it,*
He does not thresh it longer.
29 This also comes from the LORD
of hosts,
Who has made *His* counsel[6098]
[a]wonderful[6381] and *His*
wisdom[8454] [b]great.

Jerusalem Is Warned

29 Woe, O [I]Ariel, [I]Ariel the city
where David *once* [a]camped!
Add year to year, [II][b]observe *your*
feasts on schedule.
2 And I will bring distress to Ariel,
And she shall be *a city of*
lamenting and [a]mourning;
And she shall be like an Ariel
to me.
3 And I will [a]camp against you
[I]encircling *you,*
And I will set siegeworks against
you,
And I will raise up battle towers
against you.
4 Then you shall [a]be brought low;
From the earth[776] you shall
speak,[1696]
And from the dust[6083] *where* you
are prostrate,
Your words[565] *shall come.*
Your voice shall also be like that
of a [I]spirit[178] from the ground,
And your speech shall whisper
from the dust.
5 But the multitude of your
[I]enemies[2114] shall become
like fine [a]dust,[80]
And the multitude of the
[b]ruthless ones like the chaff
which [II]blows away;[5674]
And it shall happen [c]instantly,
suddenly.
6 From the LORD of hosts[6635] you
will be [a]punished[6485] with
[b]thunder and earthquake[7494]
and loud noise,
With whirlwind and tempest and
the flame of a consuming
fire.
7 And the [a]multitude of all the
nations[1471] who wage war[6633]
against [I]Ariel,
Even all who wage war against
her and her stronghold, and
who distress her,
Shall be like a dream, a
[b]vision[2377] of the night.[3915]
8 And it will be as when a hungry
man dreams—
And behold, he is eating;
But when he awakens, his
[I]hunger[5315] is not satisfied,
Or as when a thirsty man
dreams—
And behold, he is drinking,
But when he awakens, behold,
he is faint,
And his [I]thirst is not quenched.
[a]Thus the multitude of all the
nations shall be,
Who wage war against Mount
Zion.
9 [a]Be delayed and wait.
Blind yourselves and be blind.
They [b]become drunk, but not
with wine;
They stagger, but not with
strong drink.
10 For the LORD has poured
over[5258] you a spirit[7307] of
deep [a]sleep,
He has [b]shut your eyes, the
prophets;[5030]
And He has covered[3680] your
heads,[7218] the seers.[2374]
11 And the entire vision[2380] shall
be[1961] to you like the words[1697] of a
sealed [I][a]book,[5612] which when they give
it to the one who [II]is literate,[3045] saying,

27 [I]Lit., *rolled* [a]Amos 1:3

28 [I]Lit., *discomfit*

29 [a]Is. 9:6 [b]Is. 31:2; Rom. 11:33

1 [I]I.e., Lion of God, or, Jerusalem [II]Lit., *let your feasts run their round* [a]2Sam. 5:9 [b]Is. 1:14; 5:12; 22:12, 13; 29:9, 13

2 [a]Is. 3:26; Lam. 2:5

3 [I]Lit., *like a circle* [a]Luke 19:43, 44

4 [I]Or, *ghost* [a]Is. 8:19

5 [I]Lit., *strangers* [II]Lit., *passes away* [a]Is. 17:13; 41:15, 16 [b]Is. 13:11; 25:3; 29:20 [c]Is. 17:14; 30:13; 47:11; 1Thess. 5:3

6 [a]Is. 10:3; 26:14, 21 [b]1Sam. 2:10; Matt. 24:7; Mark 13:8; Luke 21:11; Rev. 11:13, 19; 16:18

7 [I]V. 1, note 1 [a]Mic. 4:11, 12; Zech. 12:9 [b]Job 20:8; Ps. 73:20; Is. 17:14

8 [I]Lit., *soul* [a]Is. 54:17

9 [a]Is. 29:1 [b]Is. 51:17, 21, 22; 63:6

10 [a]Ps. 69:23; Is. 6:9, 10; Mic. 3:6; Rom. 11:8 [b]Is. 44:18; 2Thess. 2:9-12

11 [I]Or, *scroll* [II]Lit., *knows books* [a]Is. 8:16; Dan. 12:4, 9; Matt. 13:11

"Please[4994] read[7121] this," he will say,[559]
"I cannot, for it is sealed."

12 Then the [I]book will be given to
the one who [II]is illiterate, saying,
"Please read this." And he will say, "I
[III]cannot read."

13 Then the Lord[136] said,[559]
"Because [a]this people[5971] draw
near[5066] with their [I]words[6310]
And honor[3513] Me with their
[II]lip[8193] service,
But they remove their hearts[3820]
far from Me,
And their [III]reverence[3374] for Me
[IV]consists of [V]tradition[4687]
learned[3925] *by rote,*

14 Therefore behold, I will once
again deal [a]marvelously with
this people, wondrously
marvelous;[6381]
And [b]the wisdom[2451] of their
wise[2450] men shall perish,[6]
And the discernment[998] of their
discerning[995] men shall be
concealed."

15 Woe to those who deeply
[a]hide their [I]plans[6098] from the
LORD,
And whose [b]deeds are *done* in
a dark[4285] place,
And they say,[559] "[c]Who sees[7200]
us?" or "Who knows us?"

16 You turn *things* around!
Shall the potter[3335] be
considered[2803] [I]as equal with
the clay,
That [a]what is made[6213] should
say to its maker, "He did not
make me";
Or what is formed[3336] say to him
who formed it, "He has no
understanding"?[995]

Blessing after Discipline

17 Is it not yet just a little while
[I]Before Lebanon will be turned
into a [a]fertile field,
And the fertile field will be
considered as a forest?

18 And on that day[3117] the
[a]deaf shall hear[8085] [b]words of
a book,
And out of *their* gloom[652] and
darkness[2822] the [c]eyes of the
blind shall see.

19 The [a]afflicted also shall increase
their gladness in the LORD,
And the [b]needy of mankind[120]
shall rejoice in the Holy
One[6918] of Israel.

20 For the [a]ruthless will come
to an end,[656] and the
[b]scorner[3887] will be
finished,[3615]
Indeed [c]all who [I]are intent on
doing evil[205] will be cut off;[3772]

21 Who [I]cause a person[120] to be
indicted[2398] by a word,[1697]
And [a]ensnare[6983] him who
adjudicates[3198] at the gate,
And [II][b]defraud the one in the
right with [III]meaningless
arguments.[8414]

22 Therefore thus says the LORD,
who redeemed[6299] [a]Abraham, concerning the house[1004] of Jacob,
"Jacob [b]shall not now be
ashamed,[954] nor shall his face
now turn pale;

23 But when [I]he sees his
[a]children, the [b]work of My
hands,[3027] in his midst,[7130]
They will sanctify[6942] My name;
Indeed, they will [c]sanctify the
Holy One of Jacob,
And will stand in awe[6206] of the
God[430] of Israel.

24 "And those who [a]err[8582] in
[I]mind will [b]know [II]the truth,
And those who [III]criticize will
[IV][c]accept[3925] instruction.[3948]

Judah Warned against Egyptian Alliance

30 "Woe to the [a]rebellious[5637]
children,"[1121] declares[5001]
the LORD,

12 [I]Or, *scroll* [II]Lit., *does not know books* [III]Lit., *do not know books*
13 [I]Lit., *mouth* [II]Lit., *lips* [III]Lit., *fear of Me* [IV]Lit., *is* [V]Lit., *commandment of rulers* [a]Ezek. 33:31; Matt. 15:8, 9; Mark 7:6, 7
14 [a]Is. 6:9, 10; 28:21; 65:7; Hab. 1:5 [b]Is. 44:25; Jer. 8:9; 49:7; 1Cor. 1:19
15 [I]Lit., *counsel* [a]Ps. 10:11, 13; Is. 28:15; 30:1 [b]Job 22:13; Is. 57:12; Ezek. 8:12 [c]Ps. 94:7; Is. 47:10; Mal. 2:17
16 [I]Lit., *like* [a]Is. 45:9; 64:8; Jer. 18:1-6; Rom. 9:19-21
17 [I]Lit., *And* [a]Ps. 84:6; 107:33, 35; Is. 32:15
18 [a]Is. 35:5; 42:18, 19; 43:8; Matt. 11:5; Mark 7:37 [b]Is. 29:11 [c]Ps. 119:18; Prov. 20:12; Is. 32:3
19 [a]Ps. 25:9; 37:11; Is. 11:4; 61:1; Matt. 5:5; 11:29 [b]Is. 3:14, 15; 11:4; 14:30, 32; 25:4; 26:6; Matt. 11:5; James 1:9; 2:5
20 [I]Lit., *watch evil* [a]Is. 29:5 [b]Is. 28:14 [c]Is. 59:4; Mic. 2:1
21 [I]Lit., *bring a person under condemnation* [II]Lit., *turn aside* [III]Lit., *confusion* [a]Amos 5:10 [b]Is. 32:7; Amos 5:12
22 [a]Is. 41:8; 51:2; 63:16 [b]Is. 45:17; 49:23; 50:7; 54:4
23 [I]Or, *his children see* [a]Is. 49:20-26 [b]Is. 26:12; 45:11; Eph. 2:10 [c]Is. 5:16; 8:13
24 [I]Lit., *spirit* [II]Lit., *understanding* [III]Lit., *murmur* [IV]Lit., *learn* [a]Is. 30:21; Heb. 5:2 [b]Is. 41:20; 60:16 [c]Is. 54:13

1 [a]Is. 1:2, 23; 30:9; 65:2

"Who [b]execute a plan,6098 but not
Mine,
And [Ic]make an alliance,5258,4541
but not of My Spirit,7307
In order to add sin2403 to sin;
2 Who [a]proceed down to Egypt,
Without [b]consulting7592 [I]Me,
[c]To take refuge in the safety of
Pharaoh,
And to seek shelter2620 in the
shadow of Egypt!
3 "Therefore the safety of Pharaoh
will be [a]your shame,
And the shelter2622 in the
shadow of Egypt, your
humiliation.
4 "For [a]their princes8269 are at
Zoan,
And their ambassadors4397
arrive5060 at Hanes.
5 "Everyone will be [a]ashamed954
because of a people5971 who
cannot profit them,
Who are [b]not for help or profit,
but for shame and also for
reproach."2781

6 The [I]oracle4853 concerning the
[a]beasts of the [b]Negev.
Through a land776 of [c]distress
and anguish,6695
From [II]where *come* lioness and
lion, viper and [d]flying
serpent,
They [e]carry5375 their riches2428
on the [III]backs of young
donkeys
And their treasures on [f]camels'
humps,
To a people who cannot profit
them;
7 Even Egypt, whose [a]help is vain
and empty.
Therefore, I have called7121 [I]her
"[IIb]Rahab who has been
exterminated."7673
8 Now go, [a]write it on a tablet
before them
And inscribe2710 it on a scroll,5612
That it may [I]serve in the time3117
to come
[II]As a witness forever.5703
9 For this is a [a]rebellious4805
people, [b]false3586 sons,
Sons who [I]refuse to [c]listen8085
To the [II]instruction8451 of the
LORD;
10 Who say559 to the [a]seers, "You
must not see *visions";*
And to the prophets,2374 "You
must not [b]prophesy5012 to us
what is right,5128
[c]Speak1696 to us [I]pleasant words,
Prophesy illusions.
11 "Get out of the way,1870 [a]turn
aside from the path,734
[Ib]Let us hear no more7673 about
the Holy One6918 of Israel."
12 Therefore thus says559 the Holy
One of Israel,
"[a]Since you have rejected3988 this
word,1697
And have put your trust982 in
[b]oppression and guile, and
have relied8172 on them,
13 Therefore this [a]iniquity5771 will
be to you
Like a [b]breach about to fall,5307
A bulge in a high wall,
Whose collapse comes
[c]suddenly in an instant.
14 "And whose collapse7665 is like
the smashing of a [a]potter's
jar;
[I]So ruthlessly shattered3807
That a sherd2789 will not be found
among its pieces
To [II]take fire from a hearth,
Or to scoop water from a
cistern."
15 For thus the Lord136 [I]GOD,
the Holy One of Israel, has
said,
"In [II]repentance and [a]rest you
shall be saved,3467
In [b]quietness8252 and trust985 is
your strength."
But you were not willing,14

1 [I]Lit., *pour out a drink offering* [b]Is. 29:15 [c]Is. 8:11, 12
2 [I]Lit., *My mouth* [a]Is. 31:1; Jer. 43:7 [b]Is. 8:19 [c]Is. 36:9
3 [a]Is. 20:5, 6; 36:6; Jer. 42:18, 22
4 [a]Is. 19:11
5 [a]Jer. 2:36 [b]Is. 10:3; 30:7; 31:3
6 [I]Or, *burden of* [II]Lit., *them* [III]Lit., *shoulders* [a]Is. 46:1, 2 [b]Gen. 12:9 [c]Ex. 5:10, 21; Deut. 4:20; 8:15; Is. 5:30; 8:22; Jer. 11:4 [d]Deut. 8:15; Is. 14:29 [e]Is. 15:7; 46:1, 2 [f]1Kin. 10:2
7 [I]Lit., *this one* [II]M.T. reads *They are Rahab* (or *arrogance*), *to remain* [a]Is. 30:5 [b]Job 9:13; Ps. 87:4; 89:10; Is. 51:9
8 [I]Lit., *be* [II]So the versions; Heb., *Forever and ever* [a]Is. 8:1
9 [I]Lit., *are not willing* [II]Or, *law* [a]Is. 30:1 [b]Is. 28:15; 59:3, 4 [c]Is. 1:10; 5:24; 24:5
10 [I]Lit., *smooth things* [a]Is. 29:10 [b]Is. 5:20; Jer. 11:21; Amos 2:12; 7:13 [c]1Kin. 22:8, 13; Jer. 6:14; 23:17, 26; Ezek. 13:7; Rom. 16:18; 2Tim. 4:3, 4
11 [I]Lit., *Cause to cease from our presence the* [a]Acts 13:8 [b]Job 21:14
12 [a]Is. 5:24; 7:9; 8:6 [b]Is. 3:14, 15; 5:7; 59:13
13 [a]Is. 26:21 [b]1Kin. 20:30; Ps. 62:4; Is. 58:12 [c]Is. 29:5; 47:11
14 [I]Lit., *Crushed, it will not be spared* [II]Lit., *snatch up* [a]Ps. 2:9; Jer. 19:10, 11
15 [I]Heb., *YHWH,* usually rendered LORD [II]Lit., *returning* [a]Ps. 116:7; Is. 28:12 [b]Is. 7:4; 32:17

30:10 See note on Amos 2:12.

16 And you said,[559] "No, for we will
flee on [a]horses,"
Therefore you shall flee! "And
we will ride on swift *horses,*"
Therefore those who pursue you
shall be swift.
17 [a]One thousand *shall flee* at the
threat[1606] of one *man,*
You shall flee at the threat of
five;
Until you are left[3498] as a [I]flag
on a mountain top,[7218]
And as a signal on a hill.

God Is Gracious and Just

18 Therefore the LORD [Ia]longs to
be gracious[2603] to you,
And therefore He [II]waits on
[b]high to have compassion[7355]
on you.
For the LORD is a [c]God[430] of
justice;[4941]
How blessed[835] are all those who
[IIId]long for Him.

19 [I]O people in Zion, [a]inhabitant in
Jerusalem, you will [b]weep no longer.
He will surely be gracious to you at the
sound of your cry; when He hears it,
He will [c]answer you.

20 Although the Lord has given you
[a]bread of privation and water of oppression, *He,* your Teacher will no longer
[b]hide Himself, but your eyes will behold
your Teacher.

21 And your ears[241] will hear a word
behind you, [I]"This is the [a]way, walk in
it," whenever you [b]turn to the right[541]
or to the left.

22 And you will defile[2930] your
graven [a]images, overlaid with silver, and
your molten [a]images[4541] plated with
gold. You will scatter them as an impure
thing; *and* say to [I]them, "[b]Be gone!"

23 Then He will [a]give *you* rain for
[I]the seed[2233] which you will sow in the
ground,[127] and bread *from* the yield of
the ground,[127] and it will be [II]rich and
[III]plenteous; on that day[3117] [b]your livestock will graze in a roomy pasture.[3733]

24 Also the oxen and the donkeys
which work[5647] the ground will eat salted
fodder,[1098] which [I]has been [a]win-
nowed[2219] with shovel and fork.

25 And on every lofty mountain and
on [a]every high[5375] hill there will be
[I]streams running with water on the day
of the great [b]slaughter,[2027] when the
towers fall.

26 And [a]the light[216] of the moon will
be as the light of the sun, and the light
of the sun will be seven times *brighter,*
like the light of seven days,[3117] on the
day [b]the LORD binds up[2280] the [c]frac-
ture[7667] of His people and [d]heals the
bruise[4273] [I]He has inflicted.[4347]

27 Behold, [a]the name of the LORD
comes from a [I]remote place;
[b]Burning is His anger,[639] and
[II]dense is *His* [III]smoke;
His lips[8193] are filled with
[c]indignation,[2195]
And His tongue is like a
[d]consuming fire;
28 And His [a]breath[7307] is like an
overflowing[7857] torrent,
Which [b]reaches to the neck,
To [c]shake the nations[1471] back
and forth in a [I]sieve,
And to *put* in the jaws of the
peoples [d]the bridle which
[II]leads to ruin.[8582]
29 You will have [I]songs[7892] as in the
night[3915] when you keep the
festival;
And gladness of heart[3824] as
when one marches to *the
sound of* the flute,
To go to the mountain of the
LORD, to the Rock of Israel.
30 And the LORD will cause
[I]His voice of authority to be
heard,[8085]
And the [II]descending of His arm
to be seen[7200] in fierce
anger,[2197]
And *in* the flame of a consuming
fire,
In cloudburst, downpour, and
hailstones.
31 For [a]at the voice of the LORD

16 [a]Is. 2:7; 31:1,3
17 [I]Lit., *pole* [a]Lev. 26:36; Deut. 28:25; 32:30; Josh. 23:10; Prov. 28:1
18 [I]Lit., *waits* [II]Lit., *is on high* [III]Lit., *wait* [a]Is. 42:14, 16; 48:9; Jon. 3:4, 10; 2Pet. 3:9, 15 [b]Is. 2:11, 17; 33:5 [c]Is. 5:16; 28:17; 61:8 [d]Is. 8:17; 25:9; 26:8; 33:2
19 [I]M.T. reads *A people will inhabit Zion, Jerusalem.* [a]Is. 65:9; Ezek. 37:25, 28 [b]Is. 25:8; 60:20; 61:1-3 [c]Ps. 50:15; Is. 58:9; 65:24; Matt. 7:7-11
20 [a]1Kin. 22:27; Ps. 80:5 [b]Ps. 74:9; Amos 8:11
21 [I]Lit., *saying, "This* [a]Ps. 25:8, 9; Prov. 3:6; Is. 35:8, 9; 42:16 [b]Is. 29:24
22 [I]Lit., *it "Go out"* [a]Ex. 32:2, 4; Judg. 17:3, 4; Is. 46:6 [b]Matt. 4:10
23 [I]Lit., *your* [II]Lit., *fatness* [III]Lit., *fat* [a]Ps. 65:9-13; 104:13, 14 [b]Ps. 144:13; Is. 32:20; Hos. 4:16
24 [I]Lit., *one winnows* [a]Matt. 3:12; Luke 3:17
25 [I]Lit., *canals, streams of water* [a]Is. 35:6, 7; 41:18; 43:19, 20 [b]Is. 34:2
26 [I]Lit., *of His blow* [a]Is. 24:23; 60:19, 20; Rev. 21:23; 22:5 [b]Is. 61:1 [c]Is. 1:6; 30:13, 14 [d]Deut. 32:39; Job 5:18; Is. 33:24; Jer. 33:6; Hos. 6:1, 2
27 [I]Lit., *distance* [II]Lit., *heaviness* [III]Lit., *uplifting* [a]Is. 59:19 [b]Is. 10:17 [c]Is. 10:5; 13:5; 66:14 [d]Is. 66:15
28 [I]Lit., *sifting of the worthless* [II]Lit., *misleads* [a]Is. 11:4; 30:33; 2Thess. 2:8 [b]Is. 8:8 [c]Amos 9:9 [d]2Kin. 19:28; Is. 37:29
29 [I]Lit., *the song*
30 [I]Lit., *the majesty of His voice* [II]Lit., *descent*
31 [a]Is. 11:4

[b]Assyria will be terrified,[2865]
When He strikes[5221] with the
[c]rod.[7626]
32 And every [I]blow[4145] of the
[IIa]rod[4294] of punishment,
Which the LORD will lay on him,
Will be with *the music of*
[b]tambourines[8596] and lyres;
And in battles, [c]brandishing[8573]
weapons, He will fight them.
33 For [Ia]Topheth has long been
ready,
Indeed, it has been prepared[3559]
for the king.[4428]
He has made it deep and large,
[II]A pyre of fire with plenty of
wood;
The [b]breath[5397] of the LORD, like
a torrent of [c]brimstone,[1614]
sets it afire.

Help Not in Egypt but in God

31 Woe to those who go down to
[a]Egypt for help,
And [b]rely[8172] on horses,
And trust[982] in chariots because
they are many,
And in horsemen because they
are very strong,
But they do not [c]look to the
[d]Holy One[6918] of Israel, nor
seek the LORD!
2 Yet He also is [a]wise[2450] and will
[b]bring disaster,[7451]
And does [c]not retract His
words,[1697]
But will arise against the
house[1004] of [d]evildoers,[7489]
And against the help of the
[e]workers[6213] of iniquity.[205]
3 Now the Egyptians are
[a]men, and not God,[410]
And their [b]horses are flesh[1320]
and not spirit;[7307]
So the LORD will [c]stretch out His
hand,[3027]
And [d]he who helps will
stumble[3782]
And he who is helped[5826] will fall,
And all of them will come to an
end[3615] together.

4 For thus says[559] the LORD to me,
"As the [a]lion or the young lion
growls[1897] over his prey,
Against which a band of
shepherds is called out,[7121]
Will not be terrified[2865] at their
voice, nor disturbed[6031] at
their noise,
So will the LORD of hosts[6635]
come down to wage [b]war[6633]
on Mount Zion and on its hill."
5 Like [I]flying [a]birds so the LORD
of hosts will protect
Jerusalem.
He will [b]protect and deliver[5337]
it;
He will pass[5674] over and
rescue[4422] *it.*
6 [a]Return[7725] to Him from whom
[I]you have [b]deeply defected, O sons[1121]
of Israel.
7 For in that day[3117] every man[376]
will [a]cast away[3988] his silver idols[457] and
his gold idols, which your hands[3027] have
made[6213] as [b]a sin.[2399]
8 And the [a]Assyrian will fall by a
sword[2719] not of man,
And a [b]sword not of man[120] will
devour him.
So he will [Ic]not escape the
sword,
And his young men will become
[d]forced laborers.
9 "And his [a]rock will pass away[5674]
because of panic,[4032]
And his princes[8269] will be
terrified at the [b]standard,"
Declares[5001] the LORD, whose
[c]fire[217] is in Zion and whose
furnace is in Jerusalem.

The Glorious Future

32 Behold, a [a]king[4428] will reign[4427]
righteously,[6664]
And princes[8269] will rule[8323]
justly.[4941]
2 And each[376] will be like a
[a]refuge from the wind,

31 [b]Is. 10:12; 14:25; 31:8 [c]Is. 10:26; 11:4
32 [I]Lit., *passing* [II]Lit., *staff of foundation* [a]Is. 10:24 [b]1Sam. 18:6; Jer. 31:4 [c]Ezek. 32:10
33 [I]I.e., the place of human sacrifice to Molech [II]Lit., *Its pile* [a]2Kin. 23:10; Jer. 7:31; 19:6 [b]Is. 11:4; 30:28 [c]Gen. 19:24; Is. 34:9

1 [a]Is. 30:2, 7; 36:6 [b]Deut. 17:16; Ps. 20:7; 33:17; Is. 2:7; 30:16 [c]Is. 9:13; Dan. 9:13; Amos 5:4-8 [d]Is. 10:17; 43:15; Hos. 11:9; Hab. 1:12; 3:3
2 [a]Is. 28:29; Rom. 16:27 [b]Is. 45:7 [c]Num. 23:19; Jer. 44:29 [d]Is. 1:4; 9:17; 14:20 [e]Is. 22:14; 32:6
3 [a]Ezek. 28:9; 2Thess. 2:4 [b]Is. 36:9 [c]Is. 9:17; Jer. 15:6; Ezek. 20:33, 34 [d]Is. 30:5, 7; Matt. 15:14
4 [a]Num. 24:9; Hos. 11:10; Amos 3:8 [b]Is. 42:13; Zech. 12:8
5 [I]Or, *hovering* [a]Deut. 32:11; Ps. 91:4 [b]Is. 37:35; 38:6
6 [I]Lit., *they* [a]Is. 44:22; 55:7; Jer. 3:10, 14, 22; Ezek. 18:31, 32 [b]Is. 1:2, 5
7 [a]Is. 2:20; 30:22 [b]1Kin. 12:30
8 [I]Lit., *flee* [a]Is. 10:12; 14:25; 30:31-33; 37:7, 36-38 [b]Is. 66:16 [c]Is. 21:15 [d]Gen. 49:15; Is. 14:2
9 [a]Deut. 32:31, 37 [b]Is. 5:26; 13:2; 18:3 [c]Is. 10:16, 17; 30:33; Zech. 2:5

1 [a]Ps. 72:1-4; Is. 9:6, 7; 11:4, 5; Jer. 23:5; 33:15; Ezek. 37:24; Zech. 9:9 2 [a]Is. 4:6; 25:4

And a shelter[5643] from the storm,
Like [I][b]streams of water in a dry country,
Like the [a]shade of a [II]huge rock in [III]a parched land.[776]
3 Then [a]the eyes of those who see will not be [I]blinded,
And the ears[241] of those who hear[8085] will listen.[7181]
4 And the [I]mind[3824] of the [a]hasty will discern[995] the [II]truth,[1847]
And the tongue of the stammerers will hasten to speak[1696] clearly.
5 No longer will the [a]fool[5036] be called[7121] noble,[5081]
Or the rogue[3596] be spoken[559] of *as* generous.
6 For a fool speaks nonsense,[5039]
And his heart[3820] [I][a]inclines toward wickedness,[205]
To practice [b]ungodliness[2612] and to speak error[8432] against the LORD,
To [II][c]keep the hungry person[5315] unsatisfied
And [III]to withhold drink from the thirsty.
7 As for a rogue, his weapons are evil;[7451]
He [a]devises[3289] wicked schemes
To [b]destroy[2254] *the* afflicted with [I]slander,[561]
[c]Even though *the* needy one speaks [II]what is right.[4941]
8 But [a]the noble man devises noble plans;
And by noble plans he stands.
9 Rise up you [a]women[802] who are at ease,
And hear my voice;
[b]Give ear[238] to my word,[565]
You complacent daughters.
10 Within a year and *a few* days,[3117]
You will be troubled, O complacent daughters;
[a]For the vintage is ended,[3615]
And the *fruit* gathering[625] will not come.
11 Tremble,[2729] you *women* who are at ease;
[a]Be troubled, you complacent *daughters;*
[b]Strip, undress, and put *sackcloth* on *your* waist,
12 [a]Beat your breasts for the pleasant fields,[7704] for the fruitful vine,
13 [a]For the land[127] of my people[5971] *in which* thorns *and* briars shall come up;[5927]
Yea, for all the joyful houses,[1004] *and for* the [b]jubilant city.
14 Because [a]the palace[759] has been abandoned,[5203] the [I]populated [b]city forsaken.[5800]
[II]Hill and watch-tower have become [c]caves forever,[5769]
A delight for [d]wild donkeys, a pasture for flocks;
15 Until the [a]Spirit[7307] is poured out upon us from on high,
And the wilderness becomes a [b]fertile field
And the fertile field is considered[2803] as a forest.
16 Then [a]justice will dwell[7931] in the wilderness,
And righteousness[6666] will abide in the fertile field.
17 And the [a]work of righteousness will be peace,
And the service[5656] of righteousness, [b]quietness[8252] and [I]confidence[983] forever.
18 Then my people will live in a [a]peaceful habitation,
And in secure dwellings[4908] and in undisturbed [b]resting places;
19 And it will [a]hail when the [b]forest comes down,
And [c]the city will be utterly laid low.
20 How [a]blessed[835] will you be, you who sow beside all waters,
Who [I]let out freely the ox and the donkey.

The Judgment of God

33 Woe [a]to you, O destroyer,[7703]
While you were not destroyed;[7703]

2 [I]Lit., *canals* [II]Lit., *heavy* [III]Lit., *an exhausted* [b]Is. 35:6; 41:18; 43:19, 20
3 [I]Or, *turned away* [a]Is. 29:18
4 [I]Lit., *heart* [II]Lit., *knowledge* [a]Is. 29:24
5 [a]1Sam. 25:25
6 [I]Or, *does* [II]Lit., *make empty the hungry soul* [III]Lit., *he causes to lack* [a]Prov. 19:3; 24:7-9; Is. 59:7, 13 [b]Is. 9:17; 10:6 [c]Is. 3:15; 10:2
7 [I]Lit., *words of falsehood* [II]Lit., *justly* [a]Jer. 5:26-28; Mic. 7:3 [b]Is. 11:4; 61:1 [c]Is. 5:23
8 [a]Prov. 11:25
9 [a]Is. 47:8; Amos 6:1; Zeph. 2:15 [b]Is. 28:23
10 [a]Is. 5:5, 6; 7:23; 24:7
11 [a]Is. 22:12 [b]Is. 47:2
12 [a]Nah. 2:7
13 [a]Is. 5:6, 10, 17; 27:10 [b]Is. 22:2; 23:9
14 [I]Lit., *multitude of the* [II]Or, *Ophel* [a]Is. 13:22; 25:2; 34:13 [b]Is. 6:11; 22:2; 24:10, 12 [c]Is. 13:21; 34:13 [d]Ps. 104:11; Jer. 14:6
15 [a]Is. 11:2; 44:3; 59:21; Ezek. 39:29; Joel 2:28 [b]Ps. 107:35; Is. 29:17; 35:1, 2
16 [a]Is. 33:5; Zech. 8:3
17 [I]Or, *security* [a]Ps. 72:2, 3; 85:8; 119:165; Is. 2:4; Rom. 14:17; James 3:18 [b]Is. 30:15
18 [a]Is. 26:3, 12 [b]Is. 11:10; 14:3; 30:15; Hos. 2:18-23; Zech. 2:5; 3:10
19 [a]Is. 28:2, 17; 30:30 [b]Is. 10:18, 19, 34 [c]Is. 24:10, 12; 26:5; 27:10; 29:4
20 [I]Lit., *send out the foot of the ox* [a]Eccl. 11:1; Is. 30:23, 24
1 [a]Is. 10:6; 21:2

And he [b]who is treacherous,*898*
while *others* did not deal
treacherously with him.
As soon as you shall finish*8552*
destroying,*7703* [c]you shall be
destroyed;
As soon as you shall cease to
deal treacherously, *others*
shall [d]deal treacherously with
you.
2 O LORD, [a]be gracious to us;
we have [b]waited*6960* for
Thee.
Be Thou [I]their [IIc]strength every
morning,
Our salvation*3444* also in the
[d]time*6256* of distress.
3 At the sound of the tumult
[a]peoples*5971* flee;
At the [b]lifting up of Thyself
nations*1471* disperse.
4 And your spoil is gathered *as*
the caterpillar gathers;*625*
As locusts rushing about, men
rush about on it.
5 The LORD is [a]exalted, for He
dwells*7931* on high;
He has [b]filled Zion with
justice*4941* and
righteousness.*6666*
6 And He shall be the [Ia]stability*530*
of your times,*6256*
A [b]wealth of salvation,*5307*
wisdom,*2451* and [c]knowledge;
The [d]fear*3374* of the LORD is his
treasure.
7 Behold, their brave men cry in
[I]the streets,
The [IIa]ambassadors*4397* of peace
weep bitterly.*4751*
8 The highways are desolate,*8074*
[I]the [a]traveler*5674* has
ceased,*7673*
He has [b]broken*6565* the
covenant,*1285* he has
despised*3988* the cities,
He has no regard*2803* for man.*582*
9 [a]The land*776* mourns and pines
away,
[b]Lebanon is shamed and
withers;7060
[c]Sharon is like a desert*6160* plain,

1 [b]Is. 24:16; 48:8 [c]Is. 10:12; 14:25; 31:8 Hab. 2:8 [d]Jer. 25:12-14; Matt. 7:2
2 [I]Some versions read *our* [II]Lit., *arm* [a]Is. 30:18, 19 [b]Is. 25:9 [c]Is. 40:10; 51:5; 59:16 [d]Is. 37:3
3 [a]Is. 17:13; 21:15 [b]Is. 10:33; 17:13; 59:16-18; Jer. 25:30, 31
5 [a]Ps. 97:9 [b]Is. 1:26; 28:6; 32:16
6 [I]Or, *faithfulness* [a]Is. 33:20 [b]Is. 45:17; 51:6 [c]Is. 11:9 [d]2Kin. 18:7; Ps. 112:1-3; Is. 11:3; Matt. 6:33
7 [I]Lit., *the outside* [II]Lit., *messengers* [a]2Kin. 18:18, 37
8 [I]Lit., *he who passes along the way* [a]Is. 35:8 [b]Is. 24:5
9 [I]Lit., *shake off* [a]Is. 3:26; 24:4; 29:2 [b]Is. 2:13; 10:34 [c]Is. 35:2; 65:10
10 [a]Ps. 12:5; Is. 2:19, 21
11 [I]Lit., *dry grass* [II]So one ancient version; M.T. reads *Your breath will* [a]Ps. 7:14; Is. 26:18; 59:4; James 1:15 [b]Is. 1:31
12 [a]2Sam. 23:6, 7; Is. 10:17; 27:4
13 [I]Lit., *know* [a]Ps. 48:10; Is. 49:1
14 [I]Lit., *everlasting* [a]Is. 1:28 [b]Is. 32:11 [c]Is. 30:27, 30; Heb. 12:29 [d]Is. 9:18, 19; 10:16; 47:14
15 [I]Lit., *gain of extortioners* [a]Ps. 15:2; 24:4; Is. 58:6-11 [b]Ps. 119:37
16 [I]Lit., *stronghold of rock* [a]Is. 25:4 [b]Is. 49:10
17 [a]Is. 6:5; 24:23; 33:21, 22 [b]Is. 26:15
18 [a]Is. 17:14 [b]1Cor. 1:20

And Bashan and Carmel
[I]lose *their foliage.*
10 "Now [a]I will arise," says*559* the
LORD,
"Now I will be exalted, now I will
be lifted up.*5375*
11 "You have [a]conceived [I]chaff, you
will give birth to stubble;
[II]My [b]breath*7309* will consume
you like a fire.
12 "And the peoples will be burned
to lime,
[a]Like cut thorns which are
burned in the fire.
13 "You who are far away,
[a]hear*8085* what I have
done;*6213*
And you who are near,
[I]acknowledge*3045* My might."
14 [a]Sinners*2400* in Zion are
terrified;*6342*
[b]Trembling*7461* has seized the
godless.*2611*
"Who among us can live*1481* with
[c]the consuming fire?
Who among us can live with
[I]continual*5769* [d]burning?"
15 He who [a]walks righteously, and
speaks with sincerity,*4334*
He who rejects*3988* [I]unjust gain,
And shakes his hands*3709* so that
they hold no bribe;
He who stops his ears*241* from
hearing*8085* about
bloodshed,*1818*
And [b]shuts his eyes from
looking*7200* upon evil;*7451*
16 He will dwell*7931* on the heights;
[a]His refuge will be the
[I]impregnable rock;
[b]His bread will be given *him;*
His water will be sure.*539*
17 Your eyes will see*2372*
[a]the King*4428* in His beauty;
They will behold*7200* [b]a far-
distant land.*776*
18 Your heart*3820* will meditate*1897*
on [a]terror:*367*
"Where is [b]he who counts?*5608*
Where is he who weighs?
Where is he who counts the
towers?"

19 You will no longer see a fierce people,
A people of [I][a]unintelligible[6012] speech[8193] [II]which no one comprehends,
Of a stammering tongue [III]which no one understands.[998]
20 [a]Look upon[2372] Zion, the city of our appointed feasts;[4150]
Your eyes shall see Jerusalem an [b]undisturbed habitation,
[c]A tent[168] which shall not be folded,
Its stakes shall never be pulled up
Nor any of its cords be torn apart.
21 But there the majestic[117] *One,* the LORD, shall be for us
A place of [a]rivers *and* wide canals,
On which no boat with oars shall go,
And on which no mighty[117] ship shall pass—[5674]
22 For the LORD is our [a]judge,[8199]
The LORD is [b]our lawgiver,[2710]
The LORD is [c]our king;
[d]He will save[3467] us—
23 Your tackle[2256] hangs slack;[5203]
It cannot hold the base of its mast firmly,[2388]
Nor spread out the sail.
Then the [a]prey of an abundant spoil will be divided;
[b]The lame will take the plunder.
24 And no resident[7934] will say,[559] "I am [a]sick";
The people who dwell [I]there will be [b]forgiven[5375] *their* iniquity.[5771]

God's Wrath against Nations

34 Draw near,[7126] [a]O nations,[1471] to hear;[8085] and listen,[7181] O peoples![3817]
[b]Let the earth[776] and [I]all it contains hear, and the world[8393] and all that springs from it.

2 For the LORD's [a]indignation[7110] is against all the nations,
And *His* wrath against all their armies;[6635]
He has [I][b]utterly destroyed[2763] them,
He has given them over to [c]slaughter.[2874]
3 So their slain[2491] will be [a]thrown out,
And their corpses[6297] [I]will give off[5927] their [b]stench,
And the mountains will [II]be drenched with their [c]blood.[1818]
4 And [a]all the host[6635] of heaven[8064] will [I]wear away,[4743]
And the [b]sky[8064] will be rolled[1556] up like a scroll;
All their hosts will also wither away
As a leaf withers from the vine,
Or as *one* withers from the fig tree.
5 For [a]My sword[2719] is satiated in heaven,
Behold it shall descend for judgment upon [b]Edom,
And upon the people[5971] whom I have [c]devoted[2764] to destruction.[4941]
6 The sword of the LORD is filled with blood,
It is [I]sated with fat,[1878] with the blood of lambs[3733] and goats,
With the fat of the kidneys of rams.
For the LORD has a sacrifice[2077] in [a]Bozrah,
And a great slaughter in the land[776] of [b]Edom.
7 [a]Wild oxen shall also [I]fall with them,
And [b]young bulls with strong ones;[47]
Thus their land shall be [c]soaked with blood,
And their dust[6083] [II]become greasy with fat.
8 For the LORD has a day[3117] of [a]vengeance,[5359]

33:19 [I]Lit., *deepness of lip* [II]Lit., *from hearing* [III]Lit., *there is no understanding* [a]Deut. 28:49, 50; Is. 28:11; Jer. 5:15
20 [a]Ps. 48:12 [b]Ps. 46:5; 125:1, 2; Is. 32:18 [c]Is. 54:2
21 [a]Is. 41:18; 43:19, 20; 48:18; 66:12
22 [a]Is. 2:4; 11:4; 16:5; 51:5 [b]Is. 1:10; 51:4, 7; James 4:12 [c]Ps. 89:18; Is. 33:17; Zech. 9:9 [d]Is. 25:9; 35:4; 49:25, 26; 60:16
23 [a]2Kin. 7:16 [b]2Kin. 7:8; Is. 35:6
24 [I]Lit., *in it* [a]Is. 30:26; 58:8; Jer. 30:17 [b]Is. 40:2; 44:22; Jer. 50:20; Mic. 7:18, 19; 1John 1:7-9

34:1 [I]Lit., *its fulness* [a]Ps. 49:1; Is. 41:1; 43:9 [b]Deut. 32:1; Is. 1:2
2 [I]Lit., *put under the ban* [a]Is. 26:20 [b]Is. 13:5; 24:1 [c]Is. 30:25; 63:6; 65:12
3 [I]Lit., *their stench will go up* [II]Lit., *dissolve* [a]Is. 14:19 [b]Joel 2:20; Amos 4:10 [c]Ezek. 14:19; 35:6; 38:22
4 [I]Lit., *rot* [a]Is. 13:13; 51:6; Ezek. 32:7, 8; Joel 2:31; Matt. 24:29; 2Pet. 3:10 [b]Rev. 6:12-14
5 [a]Deut. 32:41, 42; Jer. 46:10; Ezek. 21:3-5 [b]Is. 63:1; Jer. 49:7, 8, 20; Ezek. 25:12-14; 35:1-15; Amos 1:11, 12; Obad. 1-14; Mal. 1:4 [c]Is. 24:6; 43:28
6 [I]Lit., *made fat* [a]Is. 63:1; Jer. 49:13 [b]Is. 63:1
7 [I]Lit., *go down* [II]Lit., *made fat* [a]Num. 23:22; Ps. 22:21 [b]Ps. 68:30; Jer. 50:27 [c]Is. 63:6
8 [a]Is. 13:6; 35:4; 47:3; 61:2; 63:4

A year of recompense[7966] for the [I]cause[7379] of Zion.
9 And [I]its streams shall be turned[2015] into pitch,
And its loose earth into [a]brimstone,[1614]
And its land shall become[1961] burning pitch.
10 It shall [a]not be quenched night[3915] or day;[3119]
Its [b]smoke shall go up forever;[5769]
From [c]generation[1755] to generation it shall be desolate;[2717]
[d]None shall pass through[5674] it forever[5331] and ever.
11 But [Ia]pelican and hedgehog shall possess[3423] it,
And [II]owl and raven shall dwell[7931] in it;
And He shall stretch over it the [b]line of [III]desolation[8414]
And the [IV]plumb line of emptiness.
12 Its nobles—[2715]there is [a]no one there
Whom they may proclaim[7121] king—
And all its princes[8269] shall be [b]nothing.
13 And thorns shall come up in its [a]fortified towers,[759]
Nettles and thistles in its fortified cities;
It shall also be a haunt of [b]jackals[8577]
And an abode of ostriches.
14 And the desert [a]creatures shall meet with the [I]wolves,
The [IIb]hairy goat[8163] also shall cry[7121] to its kind;[7453]
Yes, the [III]night monster shall settle there
And shall find herself a resting place.
15 The tree snake shall make its nest and lay *eggs* there,
And it will hatch and gather *them* under its [I]protection.
Yes, [a]the [II]hawks shall be gathered[6908] there,

8 [I]Or, *controversy*
9 [I]I.e., Edom's [a]Deut. 29:23; Ps. 11:6; Is. 30:33
10 [a]Is. 1:31; 66:24 [b]Rev. 14:11; 19:3 [c]Is. 13:20-22; 24:1; 34:10-15; Mal. 1:3, 4 [d]Ezek. 29:11
11 [I]Or, *owl or jackdaw* [II]Or, *great horned owl* [III]Or, *formlessness* [IV]Lit., *stones of void* [a]Zeph. 2:14 [b]2Kin. 21:13; Is. 24:10; Lam. 2:8
12 [a]Jer. 27:20; 39:6 [b]Is. 41:11, 12
13 [a]Is. 13:22; 25:2; 32:13 [b]Ps. 44:19; Jer. 9:11; 10:22
14 [I]Or, *howling creatures* [II]Or, *demon* [III]Heb., *Lilith* [a]Is. 13:21 [b]Is. 13:21
15 [I]Lit., *shade* [II]Or, *kites* [a]Deut. 14:13
16 [I]So DSS; M.T., *My* [a]Is. 30:8 [b]Is. 1:20; 40:5; 58:14
17 [a]Is. 17:13, 14; Jer. 13:25 [b]Is. 34:11 [c]Is. 34:10

1 [I]Or, *desert* [a]Is. 6:11; 7:21-25; 27:10; 41:18; 55:12, 13 [b]Is. 41:19; 51:3
2 [a]Is. 27:6; 32:15 [b]Is. 25:9; 35:10; 55:12, 13; 66:10, 14 [c]Is. 60:13 [d]Song 7:5 [e]Is. 25:9
3 [I]Lit., *slack hands* [II]Lit., *tottering knees* [a]Job 4:3, 4; Heb. 12:12
4 [a]Is. 32:4 [b]Is. 1:24; 47:3; 61:2; 63:4 [c]Is. 34:8; 59:18 [d]Ps. 145:19; Is. 33:22; 35:4
5 [a]Is. 29:18; 32:3, 4; 42:7, 16; 50:4; Matt. 11:5; John 9:6, 7
6 [a]Matt. 15:30; John 5:8, 9; Acts 3:8

Every one[802] with its kind.[7468]
16 Seek from the [a]book[5612] of the LORD, and read:[7121]
Not one of these will be missing;
None[802] will lack its mate.
For [Ib]His mouth[6310] has commanded,[6680]
And His Spirit[7307] has gathered them.
17 And He has cast[5307] the [a]lot for them,
And His hand[3027] has divided it to them by [b]line.
They shall possess it forever;
From [c]generation to generation they shall dwell in it.

Zion's Happy Future

35 The [a]wilderness and the desert will be glad,
And the [Ib]Arabah[6160] will rejoice and blossom;
Like the crocus
2 It will [a]blossom profusely
And [b]rejoice with rejoicing and shout of joy.
The [c]glory[3519] of Lebanon will be given to it,
The majesty[1926] of [d]Carmel and Sharon.
They will see the [e]glory of the LORD,
The majesty of our God.[430]
3 [a]Encourage[2388] the [I]exhausted,[3027,7504] and strengthen the [II]feeble.[3782,1290]
4 Say[559] to those with [a]anxious heart,[3820]
"Take courage, fear[3372] not.
Behold, your God will come *with* [b]vengeance;[5359]
The [c]recompense of God will come,
But He will [d]save[3467] you."
5 Then the [a]eyes of the blind will be opened,
And the ears[241] of the deaf will be unstopped.
6 Then the [a]lame will leap like a deer,

And the [b]tongue of the dumb will
shout for joy.
For waters will break forth in
the [c]wilderness
And streams in the [I]Arabah.
7 And the [I]scorched land will
become[1961] a pool,
And the thirsty ground[776]
[a]springs of water;
In the [b]haunt of jackals,[8577] its
resting place,
Grass *becomes* reeds and rushes.
8 And [a]a highway will be there,
[b]a roadway,[1870]
And it will be called[7121] the
Highway of [c]Holiness.[6944]
The unclean[2931] will not travel
on[5674] it,
But it *will* be for him who
walks[1980] *that* way,
And [d]fools will not wander[8582]
on it.
9 No [a]lion will be there,
Nor will any vicious[6530] beast[2416]
go up on it;
[I]These will not be found there.
But [b]the redeemed[1350] will walk
there,
10 And [a]the ransomed[6299] of the
LORD will return,[7725]
And come with joyful shouting
to Zion,
With everlasting[5769] joy upon
their heads.[7218]
They will [I]find gladness and joy,
And [b]sorrow and sighing will flee
away.

Sennacherib Invades Judah

36 [a]Now it came about in the fourteenth year of King[4428] Hezekiah, [b]Sennacherib king of Assyria came up[5927] against all the fortified cities of Judah and seized them.

2 And the [a]king of Assyria sent Rabshakeh from Lachish to Jerusalem to King Hezekiah with a large army.[2426] And he stood by the [b]conduit of the upper[5945] pool on the highway of the [I]fuller's[3526] field.[7704]

3 Then [a]Eliakim the son[1121] of Hilkiah, who was over the household,[1004] and [b]Shebna the scribe,[5608] and Joah the son of Asaph, the recorder,[2142] came out to him.

4 Then [a]Rabshakeh said[559] to them, "Say[559] now to Hezekiah, 'Thus says[559] the great king, the king of Assyria, "What is this confidence[986] that you [I]have?[982]

5 "I say, 'Your counsel[6098] and strength for the war are only [I]empty[8193] words.'[1697] Now on whom do you rely,[982] that [a]you have rebelled[4775] against me?

6 "Behold, you rely on the [a]staff of this crushed reed, *even* on Egypt; on which if a man[376] leans, it will go into his [I]hand[3709] and pierce[5344] it. [b]So is Pharaoh king of Egypt to all who rely on him.

7 "But if you say to me, 'We trust in the LORD our God,'[430] is it not He [a]whose high places and whose altars[4196] Hezekiah has taken away,[5493] and has said to Judah and to Jerusalem, 'You shall worship[7812] before this altar'?[4196]

8 "Now therefore, [I]come make a bargain[6145] with my master[113] the king of Assyria, and I will give you two thousand horses, if you are able on your part to set riders on them.

9 "How then can you [I]repulse[7725] one [II]official[6346] of the least of my master's[113] servants,[5650] and [III][a]rely on Egypt for chariots and for horsemen?

10 "And have I now come up[5927] [I]without the LORD's approval against this land[776] to destroy[7843] it? [a]The LORD said to me, 'Go up against this land, and destroy it.'" ' "

11 Then Eliakim and Shebna and Joah said to Rabshakeh, "Speak[1696] now to your servants in [a]Aramaic, for we [I]understand[8085] *it;* and do not speak with us in [II][b]Judean,[8193] in the hearing[241] of the people[5971] who are on the wall."

12 But Rabshakeh said, "Has my master sent me only to your master and to you to speak these words, *and* not to the men[582] who sit on the wall, *doomed* to eat their own dung and drink their own urine with you?"

---

6 [I]Or, *desert* [b]Matt. 9:32; Luke 11:14 [c]Is. 35:1; 41:18; 43:19; 49:10; 51:3; John 7:38

7 [I]Or, *mirage* [a]Is. 49:10 [b]Is. 13:22; 34:13

8 [a]Is. 11:16; 19:23; 40:3; 49:11; 62:10 [b]Is. 30:21; 51:10 [c]Is. 4:3; 52:1; Matt. 7:13, 14; 1Pet. 1:15, 16 [d]Is. 33:8

9 [I]Lit., *It* [a]Is. 5:29; 30:6 [b]Is. 51:10; 62:12; 63:4

10 [I]Lit., *overtake* [a]Is. 1:27; 51:11 [b]Is. 25:8; 30:19; 65:19; Rev. 7:17; 21:4

1 [a]2Kin. 18:13 [b]2Chr. 32:1

2 [I]I.e., launderer's [a]2 Kin. 18:17-20:11; 2Chr. 32:9-24; Is. 36:2-38:8 [b]Is. 7:3

3 [a]Is. 22:20 [b]Is. 22:15

4 [I]Lit., *trust* [a]2Kin. 18:19

5 [I]Lit., *words of lips* [a]2Kin. 18:7

6 [I]Lit., *palm* [a]Ezek. 29:6, 7 [b]Ps. 146:3; Is. 30:3, 5, 7

7 [a]Deut. 12:2-5; 2Kin. 18:4, 5

8 [I]Lit., *please exchange pledges*

9 [I]Lit., *turn away the face of* [II]Or, *governor* [III]Lit., *rely on for yourself* [a]Is. 20:5; 30:2-5, 7; 31:3

10 [I]Lit., *without the LORD* [a]1Kin. 13:18; 22:6, 12

11 [I]Lit., *hear* [II]I.e., Hebrew [a]Ezra 4:7; Dan. 2:4 [b]Is. 36:13

13 Then Rabshakeh stood and [a]cried[7121] with a loud voice in Judean, and said, "Hear[8085] the words of the great king, the king of Assyria.

14 "Thus says the king, 'Do not let Hezekiah [a]deceive you, for he will not be able to deliver[5337] you;

15 nor let Hezekiah make you [a]trust in the LORD, saying, "The LORD will surely deliver us, this city shall not be given into the hand[3027] of the king of Assyria."

16 'Do not listen[8085] to Hezekiah,' for thus says the king of Assyria, '[1]Make[6213] your peace with me and come out to me, and eat each[376] of his [a]vine and each of his fig tree and drink each of the [b]waters of his own cistern,[953]

17 until I come and take you away to a land like your own land, a land of grain and new wine, a land of bread and vineyards.

18 '*Beware* lest Hezekiah misleads you, saying, "[a]The LORD will deliver[5337] us." Has any one of the gods[430] of the nations[1471] delivered his land from the hand of the king of Assyria?

19 'Where are the gods of [a]Hamath and Arpad? Where are the gods of [a]Sepharvaim? And when have they [b]delivered Samaria from my hand?

20 'Who among all the [a]gods of these lands[776] have delivered their land from my hand, that the [b]LORD should deliver Jerusalem from my hand?' "

21 But they were silent and [a]answered him not a word;[1697] for the king's[4428] commandment was, "Do not answer him."

22 Then [a]Eliakim the son of Hilkiah, who was over the household,[1004] and [b]Shebna the scribe and Joah the son of Asaph, the recorder, came to Hezekiah with their clothes torn and told[5046] him the words of Rabshakeh.

Hezekiah Seeks Isaiah's Help

37 And [a]when King[4428] Hezekiah heard[8085] *it,* he tore his clothes, covered[3680] himself with sackcloth and entered the house[1004] of the LORD.

2 Then he sent [a]Eliakim who was over the household[1004] with [b]Shebna the scribe[5608] and the elders[2205] of the priests,[3548] covered with sackcloth, to [c]Isaiah the prophet,[5030] the son[1121] of Amoz.

3 And they said[559] to him, "Thus says[559] Hezekiah, 'This day[3117] is a [a]day of distress, rebuke,[8433] and rejection;[5007] for [b]children[1121] have come to birth, and there is no strength to [1]deliver.

4 'Perhaps the LORD your God[430] will hear[8085] the words[1697] of Rabshakeh, whom his master[113] the king of Assyria has sent to [a]reproach the living[2416] God, and will rebuke[3198] the words which the LORD your God has heard. Therefore, offer[5375] a prayer[8605] for [b]the remnant[7611] that is left.' "

5 So the servants[5650] of King Hezekiah came to Isaiah.

6 And Isaiah said to them, "Thus you shall say[559] to your master, 'Thus says the LORD, "[a]Do not be afraid[3372] because of the words that you have heard, with which the servants of the king of Assyria have blasphemed[1442] Me.

7 "Behold, I will put a spirit[7307] in him so that he shall [a]hear a rumor and [b]return[7725] to his own land. And I will make him fall by the sword[2719] in his own land." ' "[776]

8 Then Rabshakeh returned[7725] and found the king of Assyria fighting against [a]Libnah, for he had heard that [1]the king had left [b]Lachish.

9 When he [a]heard *them* say concerning Tirhakah king of [1b]Cush, "He has come out to fight against you," and when he heard *it* he sent messengers[4397] to Hezekiah, saying,

10 "Thus you shall say[559] to Hezekiah king of [1]Judah, '[a]Do not let your God in whom you trust[982] deceive you, saying, "Jerusalem shall not be given into the hand[3027] of the king of Assyria."

11 '[a]Behold, you have heard what the kings[4428] of Assyria have done[6213] to all the lands,[776] destroying[2763] them completely. So will you be [1]spared?[5337]

12 'Did the gods[430] of [1]those

13 [a]2Chr. 32:18
14 [a]Is. 37:10
15 [a]Is. 36:18, 20; 37:10, 11
16 [1]Lit., *Make with me a blessing* [a]1Kin. 4:25; Mic. 4:4; Zech. 3:10 [b]Prov. 5:15
18 [a]Is. 36:15
19 [a]Is. 10:9-11; 37:11-13; Jer. 49:23 [b]2Kin. 17:6
20 [a]1Kin. 20:23, 28 [b]Is. 36:15
21 [a]Prov. 9:7, 8; 26:4
22 [a]Is. 22:20; 36:3 [b]Is. 22:15
1 [a]2Kin. 19:1-37; Is. 37:1-38
2 [a]Is. 22:20 [b]Is. 22:15 [c]Is. 1:1; 20:2
3 [1]Lit., *give birth* [a]Is. 22:5; 26:16; 33:2 [b]Is. 26:17, 18; 66:9; Hos. 13:13
4 [a]Is. 36:13-15, 18, 20 [b]Is. 1:9; 10:20-22; 37:31, 32; 46:3
6 [a]Is. 7:4; 35:4
7 [a]Is. 37:9 [b]Is. 37:37, 38
8 [1]Lit., *he* [a]Num. 33:20; Josh. 10:29 [b]Josh. 10:31, 32
9 [1]Or, *Ethiopia* [a]Is. 37:7 [b]Is. 18:1; 20:5
10 [1]Lit., *Judah, saying* [a]Is. 36:15
11 [1]Lit., *delivered* [a]Is. 10:9-11; 36:18-20
12 [1]Lit., *the*

nations[1471] which my fathers[1] have destroyed[7843] deliver them, *even* [a]Gozan and [b]Haran and Rezeph and the sons of Eden who *were* in Telassar?

13 'Where is the king of Hamath, the king of Arpad, the king of the city of Sepharvaim, *and of* Hena and Ivvah?' "

Hezekiah's Prayer in the Temple

14 Then Hezekiah took the [I]letter[5612] from the hand of the messengers and read[7121] it, and he went up[5927] to the house of the LORD and [II]spread it out before the LORD.

15 And Hezekiah prayed[6419] to the LORD saying,

16 "O LORD of hosts,[6635] the God of Israel, [a]who art enthroned *above* the cherubim,[3742] Thou art the [b]God, Thou alone, of all the kingdoms[4467] of the earth. [c]Thou hast made[2613] heaven[8064] and earth.[776]

17 "[a]Incline Thine ear,[241] O LORD, and hear; open Thine eyes, O LORD, and see; and [b]listen to all the words of Sennacherib, who sent *them* to [c]reproach the living God.

18 "Truly,[551] O LORD, the [a]kings of Assyria have devastated[2717] all the countries and their lands,[776]

19 and have cast their gods into the fire, for they were not gods but the [a]work of men's[120] hands,[3027] wood and stone. So they have [b]destroyed[6] them.

20 "And now, O LORD our God, [a]deliver[3467] us from his hand that [b]all the kingdoms of the earth may know[3045] that Thou alone, LORD, [I]art God."

God Answers through Isaiah

21 Then [a]Isaiah the son of Amoz sent *word* to Hezekiah, saying, "Thus says the LORD, the God of Israel, 'Because you have prayed to Me about Sennacherib king of Assyria,

22 this is the word[1697] that the LORD has spoken[1697] against him:

"She[1330] has despised you and
mocked you,
The [a]virgin [b]daughter of Zion;
She has [c]shaken *her* head[7218]
behind you,
The daughter of Jerusalem!

23 "Whom have you [a]reproached and
blasphemed?
And against whom have you
raised *your* voice,
And [I]haughtily [b]lifted up[5375] your
eyes?
Against the [c]Holy One[6918] of
Israel!

24 "Through your servants you have
reproached the Lord,[136]
And you have said, 'With my
many chariots I came up to
the heights of the mountains,
To the remotest parts of
[a]Lebanon;
And I cut down[3772] its tall
[b]cedars *and* its choice
cypresses.
And I will go to its [I]highest peak,
its thickest [c]forest.

25 'I dug *wells* and drank waters,
And [a]with the sole[3709] of my feet
I dried up
All the rivers of [I]Egypt.'

26 "[a]Have you not heard?
Long ago I did it,
From ancient[6924] times I
[b]planned[3335] it.
Now [c]I have brought it to
pass,
That [d]you should turn fortified
cities into [e]ruinous heaps.

27 "Therefore their inhabitants were
short of strength,[3027]
They were dismayed[2865] and put
to shame;[954]
They were *as* the [a]vegetation
of the field[7704] and *as* the
green herb,
As [b]grass on the housetops
[I]is scorched before it is grown
up.

28 "But I [a]know your sitting down,
And your going out and your
coming in,
And your raging against Me.

12 [a]2Kin. 17:6; 18:11 [b]Gen. 11:31; 12:1-4; Acts 7:2

14 [I]Lit., *letters,* [II]Lit., *Hezekiah spread*

16 [a]Ex. 25:22; 1Sam. 4:4; Ps. 80:1; 99:1 [b]Deut. 10:17; Ps. 86:10; 136:2, 3 [c]Is. 42:5; 45:12; Jer. 10:12

17 [a]2Chr. 6:40; Ps. 17:6; Dan. 9:18 [b]Ps. 74:22 [c]Is. 37:4

18 [a]2Kin. 15:29; 16:9; 17:6, 24; 1Chr. 5:26

19 [a]Is. 2:8; 17:8; 41:24, 29 [b]Is. 26:14

20 [I]So DSS and 2Kin. 19:19; M.T. omits *God* [a]Is. 25:9; 33:22; 35:4 [b]1Kin. 18:36, 37; Ps. 46:10; Is. 37:16; Ezek. 36:23

21 [a]Is. 37:2

22 [a]Jer. 14:17; Lam. 2:13 [b]Ps. 9:14; Zeph. 3:14; Zech. 2:10 [c]Job 16:4

23 [I]Lit., *on high* [a]Is. 37:4 [b]Is. 2:11; 5:15, 21 [c]Ezek. 39:7; Hab. 1:12

24 [I]Lit., *farthest height* [a]Is. 10:33, 34 [b]Is. 14:8 [c]Is. 10:18

25 [I]Or, *the besieged place* [a]Deut. 11:10; 1Kin. 20:10

26 [a]Is. 40:21, 28 [b]Acts 2:23; 4:27, 28; 1Pet. 2:8 [c]Is. 46:11 [d]Is. 10:6 [e]Is. 17:1; 25:2

27 [I]So DSS and 2Kin. 19:26; M.T., *as a plowed field* [a]Is. 40:7 [b]Ps. 129:6

28 [a]Ps. 139:1

29 "Because of your raging against
Me,
And because your [I][a]arrogance
has come up[5927] to My
ears,[241]
Therefore I will put My
[b]hook in your nose,[639]
And My [c]bridle in your lips,[8193]
And I will turn you back[7725]
[d]by the way[1870] which you
came.
30 "Then this shall be the sign for
you: [I]you shall eat this year what
[a]grows of itself, in the second year what
springs from the same, and in the third
year sow, reap, plant vineyards, and
eat their fruit.
31 "And the [a]surviving[6413] [b]remnant
of the house of Judah shall again [c]take
root downward and bear fruit upward.
32 "For out of Jerusalem shall go
forth a [a]remnant, and out of Mount Zion
[I]survivors.[6413] The [b]zeal[7068] of the LORD
of hosts shall perform[6213] this." '
33 "Therefore, thus says the LORD
concerning the king of Assyria, 'He shall
not come to this city, or shoot an arrow
there; neither shall he come before it
with a shield, nor throw up[8210] a
[a]mound against it.
34 "[a]By the way that he came, by
the same he shall return, and he shall
not come to this city,' declares[5001] the
LORD.
35 'For I will [a]defend this city to
save it [b]for My own sake and for My
servant[5650] David's sake.' "

Assyrians Destroyed

36 Then the [a]angel[4397] of the LORD
went out, and struck[5221] 185,000 in the
camp[4264] of the Assyrians; and when
[I]men arose early in the morning, behold,
all of these were [II]dead.[4191]
37 So Sennacherib, king of Assyria,
departed and [I]returned *home,* and lived
at [a]Nineveh.
38 And it came about as he was
worshiping[7812] in the house of Nisroch
his god, that Adrammelech and Sharezer
his sons[1121] killed him with the sword;
and they escaped[4422] into the land of
[a]Ararat. And [b]Esarhaddon his son became king[4427] in his place.

Hezekiah Healed

38 [a]In those days[3117] Hezekiah became [I]mortally[4191] ill. And
[b]Isaiah the prophet[5030] the son[1121] of
Amoz came to him and said[559] to him,
"Thus says[559] the LORD, '[c]Set your
house[1004] in order, for you shall die[4191]
and not live.' "[2421]
2 Then Hezekiah turned his face to
the wall, and prayed[6419] to the LORD,
3 and said, "[a]Remember[2142] now, O
LORD, I beseech[577] Thee, how I have
[b]walked before Thee in truth[571] and with
a [c]whole[8003] heart,[3820] and [d]have
done[6213] what is good[2896] in Thy sight."
And Hezekiah [e]wept [I]bitterly.
4 Then the word[1697] of the LORD
came to Isaiah, saying,
5 "Go and say[559] to Hezekiah, 'Thus
says the LORD, the God[430] of your
father[1] David, "I have heard[8085] your
prayer,[8605] I have seen[7200] your tears;
behold, I will add [a]fifteen years to your
[I]life.
6 "And I will [a]deliver[5337] you and
this city from the hand[3709] of the king[4428]
of Assyria; and I will defend this city." '
🗝 7 "And this shall be the [a]sign to you
from the LORD, that the LORD will do[6213]
this thing[1697] that He has spoken:[1696]
8 "Behold, I will [a]cause[7725] the
shadow on the stairway, which has gone
down with the sun on the stairway of
Ahaz, to go back ten steps." So the
[b]sun's *shadow* went back[7725] ten steps
on the stairway on which it had gone
down.
9 A writing of Hezekiah king of Judah, after his illness and [I]recovery:
10 I said, "[a]In the middle of my
[I]life
I am to enter the [b]gates of
Sheol;[7585]

29 [I]Lit., *complacency* [a]Is. 10:12 [b]Ezek. 29:4; 38:4 [c]Is. 30:28 [d]Is. 37:34
30 [I]Lit., *eating* [a]Lev. 25:5, 11
31 [a]Is. 4:2; 10:20 [b]Is. 37:4 [c]Is. 27:6
32 [I]Lit., *those who escape* [a]Is. 37:4 [b]2Kin. 19:31; Is. 9:7; 59:17; Joel 2:18; Zech. 1:14
33 [a]Jer. 6:6; 32:24
34 [a]Is. 37:29
35 [a]2Kin. 20:6; Is. 31:5; 38:6 [b]Is. 43:25; 48:9, 11
36 [I]Lit., *they* [II]Lit., *dead bodies* [a]2Kin. 19:35; Is. 10:12, 33, 34
37 [I]Lit., *went and returned* [a]Gen. 10:11; Jon. 1:2; 3:3; 4:11; Zeph. 2:13
38 [a]Gen. 8:4; Jer. 51:27 [b]Ezra 4:2

1 [I]Lit., *sick to the point of death* [a]2Kin. 20:1-6, 9-11; 2Chr. 32:24; Is. 38:1-8 [b]Is. 1:1; 37:2 [c]2Sam. 17:23
3 [I]Lit., *great weeping* [a]Neh. 13:14 [b]2Kin. 18:5, 6; Ps. 26:3 [c]1Chr. 28:9; 29:19 [d]Deut. 6:18 [e]Ps. 6:6-8
5 [I]Lit., *days* [a]2Kin. 18:2, 13
6 [a]Is. 31:5; 37:35
7 [a]Judg. 6:17, 21, 36-40; Is. 7:11, 14; 37:30
8 [a]2Kin. 20:9-11 [b]Josh. 10:12-14
9 [I]Lit., *he lived after his illness*
10 [I]Lit., *days* [a]Ps. 102:24 [b]Ps. 107:18

🗝 **38:7,8** See note on Josh. 10:12-14.

I am to be [c]deprived[6485] of the rest[3499] of my years."
11 I said, "I shall not see the LORD,
The LORD [a]in the land[776] of the living;[2416]
I shall look on[7200] man[120] no more among the inhabitants of the world.[2309]
12 "Like a shepherd's [a]tent[168] my dwelling is pulled up[1755] and removed from me;
As a [b]weaver I [c]rolled up[1214] my life.[2416]
He [d]cuts me off from the loom;[1803]
From [e]day[3117] until night[3915] Thou dost make an end of me.
13 "I composed *my soul* until morning.
[a]Like a lion—so He [b]breaks[7665] all my bones,[6106]
From [c]day until night Thou dost make an end of me.
14 "[a]Like a swallow, *like* a crane, so I twitter;
I [b]moan[1897] like a dove;
My [c]eyes look wistfully to the heights;
O Lord, I am oppressed, be my [d]security.[6148]
15 "[a]What shall I say?[1696]
[I]For He has spoken[559] to me, and He Himself has done it;
I shall [b]wander about all my years because of the [c]bitterness[4751] of my soul.[5315]
16 "O Lord,[136] [a]by *these* things *men* live;
And in all these is the life of my spirit;[7307]
[I][b]O restore me to health, and [c]let me live!
17 "Lo, for *my own* welfare I had great[4751] bitterness;
It is Thou who hast [I][a]kept[2836] my soul from the pit[7845] of [II]nothingness,
For Thou hast [b]cast all my sins[2399] behind Thy back.[1460]
18 "For [a]Sheol cannot thank[3034] Thee,
Death[4194] cannot praise[1984] Thee;
Those who go down [b]to the pit[953] cannot hope for Thy faithfulness.
19 "It is the [a]living who give thanks to Thee, as I do today;
A [b]father tells[3045] his sons[1121] about Thy faithfulness.
20 "The LORD will surely save[3467] me;
So we will [a]play my songs on stringed instruments
[b]All *the* days of our life [c]at the house of the LORD."
21 Now [a]Isaiah had said, "Let them
take[5375] a cake of figs, and apply it to
the boil, that he may recover."[2421]
22 Then Hezekiah had said, "What
is the [a]sign that I shall go up to the
house of the LORD?"

Hezekiah Shows His Treasures

39 [a]At that time[6256] Merodach-baladan son[1121] of Baladan, king[4428]
of Babylon, sent letters[5612] and a
present[4503] to Hezekiah, for he heard[8085]
that he had been sick and had recovered.[2388]
2 And Hezekiah [I]was [a]pleased, and
showed[7200] them all his treasure[5238]
house,[1004] the [b]silver and the gold and
the spices and the precious oil[8081] and
his whole armory and all that was found
in his treasuries. There was nothing[1697]
in his house, nor in all his dominion,[4475]
that Hezekiah did not show them.
3 Then Isaiah the [a]prophet[5030] came
to King Hezekiah and said[559] to him,
"What did these men[582] say, and from
where have they come to you?" And
Hezekiah said, "They have come to me
from a far [b]country,[776] from Babylon."
4 And he said, "What have they
seen[7200] in your house?" So Hezekiah
[I]answered,[559] "They have seen all that
is in my house; there is nothing among
my treasuries that I have not shown
them."
5 Then Isaiah said to Hezekiah,

---

10 [c]Job 17:11, 15; 2Cor. 1:9
11 [a]Ps. 27:13; 116:9
12 [a]2Cor. 5:1, 4; 2Pet. 1:13, 14 [b]Job 7:6 [c]Heb. 1:12 [d]Job 6:9 [e]Job 4:20; Ps. 73:14
13 [a]Job 10:16 [b]Ps. 51:8; Dan. 6:24 [c]Ps. 32:4
14 [a]Job 30:29; Ps. 102:6 [b]Is. 59:11; Ezek. 7:16; Nah. 2:7 [c]Ps. 119:123 [d]Job 17:3; Ps. 119:122
15 [I]Targum and DSS read *And what shall I say for He* [a]Ps. 39:9 [b]1Kin. 21:27 [c]Job 7:11; 10:1; Is. 38:17
16 [I]Lit., *Thou wilt* [a]Ps. 119:71, 75 [b]Ps. 39:13 [c]Ps. 119:25
17 [I]So some versions; Heb., *loved* [II]Or, *destruction* [a]Ps. 30:3; 86:13; Jon. 2:6 [b]Is. 43:25; Jer. 31:34; Mic. 7:19
18 [a]Ps. 6:5; 30:9; 88:11; Eccl. 9:10 [b]Num. 16:33; Ps. 28:1
19 [a]Ps. 118:17; 119:175 [b]Deut. 6:7; 11:19; Ps. 78:5-7
20 [a]Ps. 33:1-3; 68:24-26 [b]Ps. 104:33; 116:2; 146:2 [c]Ps. 116:17-19
21 [a]2Kin. 20:7, 8
22 [a]Is. 38:7
1 [a]2Kin. 20:12-19; 2Chr. 32:31; Is. 39:1-8
2 [I]Lit., *rejoiced over them* [a]2Chr. 32:25, 31; Job 31:25 [b]2Kin. 18:15, 16
3 [a]2Sam. 12:1; 2Chr. 16:7 [b]Deut. 28:49; Jer. 5:15
4 [I]Lit., *said*

"Hear[8085] the [a]word[1697] of the LORD of
hosts,[6635]
6 'Behold, the days[3117] are coming
when [a]all that is in your house, and all
that your fathers[1] have laid up in store
to this day[3117] shall be carried[5375] to
Babylon; nothing shall be left,'[3498]
says[559] the LORD.
7 'And *some* of your sons[1121] who
shall issue from you, whom you shall
beget, [a]shall be taken away; and
[b]they shall become officials[5631] in the
palace[1964] of the king of Babylon.' "
8 [a]Then Hezekiah said to Isaiah,
"The word of the LORD which you have
spoken[1696] is good."[2896] For he [I]thought,
"For there will be peace and truth[571]
[b]in my days."

The Greatness of God

40 "[a]Comfort,[5162] O comfort My
people,"[5971] says[559] your
God.[430]
2 "[a]Speak[1696] [I]kindly[3820] to
Jerusalem;
And call out[7121] to her, that her
[II][b]warfare[6635] has ended,[4390]
That her [III][c]iniquity[5771] has been
removed,
That she has received of the
LORD'S hand[3027]
[d]Double for all her sins."
3 [a]A voice [I]is calling,
"[b]Clear the way[1870] for the LORD
in the wilderness;
Make smooth[3474] in the
desert[6160] a highway for our
God.
4 "Let every valley be lifted up,
And every mountain and hill be
made low;
And let the rough[6121] ground
become a plain,
And the rugged terrain a broad
valley;
5 [I]Then the [a]glory[3519] of the LORD
will be revealed,[1540]
And [b]all flesh[1320] will see *it*
together;
For the [c]mouth[6310] of the LORD
has spoken."[1696]
6 A voice says,[559] "Call out."
Then [I]he answered, "What shall
I call out?"
[a]All flesh is grass, and all its
[II]loveliness is like the flower
of the field.[7704]
7 The [a]grass withers,[3001] the
flower fades,
[I]When the [b]breath[7307] of the
LORD blows[5380] upon it;
Surely the people are grass.
8 The grass withers, the flower
fades,
But [a]the word[1697] of our God
stands forever.[5769]
9 Get yourself up on a [a]high
mountain,
O Zion, bearer of [b]good
news,[1319]
Lift up your voice mightily,
O Jerusalem, bearer of good
news;
Lift *it* up, do not fear.[3372]
Say[559] to the [c]cities of Judah,
"[d]Here is your God!"
10 Behold, the Lord[136] [I]GOD will
come [a]with might,[2389]
With His [b]arm ruling[4910] for Him.
Behold, His [c]reward is with Him,
And His recompense before
Him.
11 Like a shepherd He will [a]tend
His flock,
In His arm He will gather[6908] the
lambs,
And carry[5375] *them* in His bosom;
He will gently lead the nursing
ewes.

5 [a]1Sam. 13:13, 14; 15:16
6 [a]2Kin. 24:13; 25:13-15; Jer. 20:5
7 [a]2Kin. 24:10-16; 2Chr. 36:10 [b]Dan. 1:1-7
8 [I]Lit., *said* [a]2Chr. 32:26 [b]2Chr. 34:28

1 [a]Is. 12:1; 49:13; 51:3, 12; 52:9; 61:2; 66:13; Jer. 31:10-14; Zeph. 3:14-17; 2Cor. 1:4
2 [I]Lit., *to the heart of* [II]Or, *hard service* [III]Or, *penalty of iniquity accepted as paid off* [a]Is. 35:4; Zech. 1:13 [b]Is. 41:11-13; 49:25; 54:15, 17 [c]Is. 33:24; 53:5, 6, 11 [d]Jer. 16:18; Zech. 9:12; Rev. 18:6
3 [I]Or, *of one calling out* [a]Matt. 3:3; Mark 1:3; Luke 3:4-6; John 1:23 [b]Mal. 3:1; 4:5, 6
5 [I]Or, *In order that the* [a]Is. 6:3; Hab. 2:14 [b]Is. 52:10; Joel 2:28 [c]Is. 1:20; 34:16; 58:14
6 [I]Another reading is *I said* [II]Or, *constancy* [a]Job 14:2; Ps. 102:11; 103:15; 1Pet. 1:24, 25
7 [I]Or, *Because* [a]Ps. 90:5, 6; James 1:10, 11 [b]Job 4:9; 41:21; Is. 40:24; 11:4
8 [a]Is. 55:11; 59:21; Matt. 5:18
9 [a]Is. 52:7 [b]Is. 61:1 [c]Is. 44:26 [d]Is. 25:9; 35:2
10 [I]Heb., *YHWH*, usually rendered *LORD* [a]Is. 9:6, 7 [b]Is. 59:16, 18 [c]Is. 62:11; Rev. 22:12
11 [a]Jer. 31:10; Ezek. 34:12-14, 23, 31; Mic. 5:4; John 10:11, 14-16

40:3 This well-known passage was seen in the N.T. as referring to John the Baptist. Not only did the first three Gospel writers make this connection (Mt. 3:3; Mk. 1:3; Lk. 3:4), but John himself did (Jn. 1:23).

40:6-8 Peter quoted these verses in I Pet. 1:24,25 to emphasize the enduring nature of God's Word as it is connected with the new birth.

12 Who has [a]measured the
[I]waters in the hollow of His
hand,
And marked[8505] off the
heavens[8064] by the [II]span,
And [III]calculated[3557] the dust[6083]
of the earth[776] by the
measure,[7991]
And weighed the mountains in
a balance,
And the hills in a pair of scales?
13 [a]Who has [I]directed the Spirit of
the LORD,
Or as His [b]counselor has
informed[3045] Him?
14 [a]With whom did He consult[3289]
and *who* [b]gave Him
understanding?[995]
And *who* taught[3925] Him in the
path[734] of justice[4941] and
taught Him knowledge,
And informed[3045] Him of the way
of understanding?[8394]
15 Behold, the [a]nations[1471] are like
a drop from a bucket,
And are regarded[2803] as a speck
of [b]dust[7834] on the scales;
Behold, He lifts up the [I]islands
like fine dust.
16 Even Lebanon is not enough to
burn,
Nor its [a]beasts[2416] enough for a
burnt offering.[5930]
17 [a]All the nations are as nothing
before Him,
They are regarded by Him as
less than nothing[8414] and
[I]meaningless.[8414]
18 [a]To whom then will you liken
God?[410]
Or what likeness[1823] will you
compare[6186] with Him?
19 *As for* the [Ia]idol, a craftsman
casts[5258] it,
A goldsmith[6884] [b]plates it with
gold,
And a silversmith *fashions* chains
of silver.
20 He who is too impoverished for
such an offering[8641]
Selects[977] a [a]tree that does not
rot;
He seeks out for himself a
skillful[2450] craftsman
To [I]prepare[3559] [II]an idol that
[b]will not totter.
21 [a]Do you not know?[3045] Have you
not heard?[8085]
Has it not been declared[5046] to
you from the beginning?[7218]
Have you not understood[995]
[b]from the foundations[4146] of
the earth?
22 It is He who [I]sits above the
[IIa]vault of the earth,
And its inhabitants are like
[b]grasshoppers,
Who [c]stretches out the
heavens[8064] like a [d]curtain
And spreads them out like a
[e]tent[168] to dwell in.
23 He *it is* who reduces [a]rulers[7336]
to nothing,
Who [b]makes[6213] the judges[8199]
of the earth [I]meaningless.
24 [I]Scarcely have they been
planted,
[I]Scarcely have they been
sown,
[I]Scarcely has their stock taken
root in the earth,
But He merely blows on them,
and they wither,[3001]
And the [a]storm carries[5375] them
away like stubble.
25 "[a]To whom then will you liken
Me
That I should be *his* equal?" says
the Holy One.[6918]
26 [a]Lift up[5375] your eyes on high
And see[7200] [b]who has created[1254]
these *stars,*
The [c]One who leads forth their
host[6635] by number,
He calls[7121] them all by name;
Because of the [d]greatness of His
might and the [I]strength of *His*
power
[e]Not one[376] *of them* is
missing.
27 [a]Why do you say,[559] O Jacob,
and assert,[1696] O Israel,
"My way is [b]hidden from the
LORD,

12 [I]DSS reads *waters of the sea* [II]Or, *half cubit;* i.e., 9 in. [III]Lit., *contained* or *comprehended* [a]Job 38:8-11; Ps. 102:25, 26; Is. 48:13; Heb. 1:10-12
13 [I]Or, *measured, marked off* [a]Rom. 11:34; 1Cor. 2:16 [b]Is. 41:28
14 [a]Job 38:4 [b]Job 21:22; Col. 2:3
15 [I]Or, *coastlands* [a]Jer. 10:10 [b]Is. 17:13; 29:5
16 [a]Ps. 50:9-11; Mic. 6:6, 7; Heb. 10:5-9
17 [I]Or, *void* [a]Is. 29:7
18 [a]Ex. 8:10; 15:11; 1Sam. 2:2; Is. 40:25; 46:5; Mic. 7:18; Acts 17:29
19 [I]Or, *graven image* [a]Ps. 115:4-8; Is. 41:7; 44:10; Hab. 2:18, 19 [b]Is. 2:20; 30:22
20 [I]Or, *set up* [II]Or, *a graven image* [a]Is. 44:14 [b]1Sam. 5:3, 4; Is. 41:7; 46:7
21 [a]Ps. 19:1; 50:6; Is. 37:26; Acts 14:17; Rom. 1:19 [b]Is. 48:13; 51:13
22 [I]Or, *is enthroned* [II]Or, *circle* [a]Job 22:14; Prov. 8:27 [b]Num. 13:33 [c]Job 9:8; Is. 37:16; 42:5; 44:24 [d]Ps. 104:2 [e]Job 36:29; Ps. 18:11; 19:4
23 [I]Or, *void* [a]Job 12:21; Ps. 107:40; Is. 34:12 [b]Is. 5:21; Jer. 25:18-27
24 [I]Or, *Not even* [a]Is. 17:13; 41:16
25 [a]Is. 40:18
26 [I]So DSS and ancient versions; M.T., *strong* [a]Is. 51:6 [b]Is. 42:5; 48:12, 13 [c]Ps. 147:4 [d]Ps. 89:11-13 [e]Is. 34:16; 48:13
27 [a]Is. 49:4, 14 [b]Is. 54:8

And the [c]justice due me
[I]escapes[5674] the notice of
[d]my God"?
28 [a]Do you not know? Have you
not heard?
The [b]Everlasting[5769] God, the
LORD, the Creator[1254] of the
ends of the earth
Does not become weary or
tired.
His understanding is
[c]inscrutable.
29 He gives strength to the
[a]weary,
And to *him who* lacks might He
[b]increases power.
30 Though [a]youths grow weary and
tired,
And vigorous [b]young men
stumble[3782] badly,
31 Yet those who [I]wait for[6960] the
LORD
Will [a]gain new strength;
They will [II][b]mount up[5927] *with*
[III]wings like eagles,
They will run and not get tired,
They will walk and not become
weary.

Israel Encouraged

41 "[a]Coastlands, listen to Me [b]in
silence,
And let the peoples[3816] [c]gain
new strength;
[d]Let them come forward,[5066]
then let them speak;[1696]
[e]Let us come[7126] together for
judgment.[4941]
2 "[a]Who has aroused one from the
east
Whom He [b]calls[7121] in
righteousness[6664] to His
[I]feet?
He [c]delivers up nations[1471]
before him,
And subdues[7287] kings.[4428]
He makes them like [d]dust[6083]
with his sword,[2719]
As the wind-driven [e]chaff with
his bow.

27 [I]Lit., *passes by my God* [c]Job 27:2; 34:5; Luke 18:7, 8 [d]Is. 25:1
28 [a]Is. 40:21 [b]Gen. 21:33; Ps. 90:2 [c]Ps. 147:5; Rom. 11:33
29 [a]Is. 50:4; Jer. 31:25 [b]Is. 41:10
30 [a]Jer. 6:11; 9:21 [b]Is. 9:17
31 [I]Or, *hope in* [II]Or, *sprout wings* [III]Or, *pinions* [a]Job 17:9; Ps. 103:5; 2Cor. 4:8-10, 16 [b]Ex. 19:4; Deut. 32:11; Luke 18:1; 2Cor. 4:1, 16; Gal. 6:9; Heb. 12:3

1 [a]Is. 11:11 [b]Hab. 2:20; Zech. 2:13 [c]Is. 40:31 [d]Is. 34:1; 48:16 [e]Is. 1:18; 43:26; 50:8
2 [I]Lit., *foot* [a]Is. 41:25; 45:1-3; 46:11 [b]Is. 42:6 [c]2Chr. 36:23; Ezra 1:2 [d]2Sam. 22:43 [e]Is. 40:24
3 [I]Lit., *going*
4 [a]Is. 41:26; 44:7; 46:10 [b]Is. 43:10; 44:6; Rev. 1:8, 17; 22:13 [c]Is. 43:13; 46:4; 48:12
5 [a]Is. 41:1; Ezek. 26:15, 16 [b]Josh. 5:1; Ps. 67:7
7 [a]Is. 44:12, 13 [b]Is. 40:19 [c]Is. 40:20; 46:7
8 [a]Is. 42:19; 43:10; 44:1, 2, 21 [b]Is. 29:22; 51:2; 63:16 [c]2Chr. 20:7; James 2:23
9 [I]Or, *taken hold of* [a]Is. 11:11 [b]Is. 43:5-7 [c]Is. 42:1; 44:1 [d]Deut. 7:6; 14:2; Ps. 135:4
10 [a]Deut. 20:1; 31:6; Josh. 1:9; Ps. 27:1; Is. 41:13, 14; 43:2, 5; Rom. 8:31 [b]Is. 41:14; 44:2; 49:8 [c]Ps. 89:13, 14
11 [a]Is. 45:24

3 "He pursues them, passing on[5674]
in safety,[7965]
By a way[734] he had not been
[I]traversing with his feet.
4 "[a]Who has performed and
accomplished[6213] *it,*
Calling[7121] forth the
generations[1755] from the
beginning?[7218]
'[b]I, the LORD, am the first,[7223]
and with the last. [c]I am He.' "
5 The [a]coastlands have seen[7200]
and are afraid;[3372]
The [b]ends of the earth[776]
tremble;[2729]
They have drawn near and have
come.
6 Each one[376] helps his
neighbor,[7453]
And says[559] to his brother,[251]
"Be strong!"[2388]
7 So the [a]craftsman
encourages[2388] the
[b]smelter,[6884]
And he who smooths *metal* with
the hammer *encourages* him
who beats[1986] the anvil,
Saying of the soldering,[1694] "It
is good";
And he fastens[2388] it with nails,
[c]*That* it should not totter.
8 "But you, Israel, [a]My servant,[5650]
Jacob whom I have chosen,[977]
Descendant[2233] of [b]Abraham My
[c]friend,[157]
9 You whom I have [I][a]taken[2388]
from the ends of the earth,
And called from its [b]remotest
parts,[6787]
And said to you, 'You are [c]My
servant,
I have [d]chosen you and not
rejected you.
10 'Do not [a]fear,[3372] for I am with
you;
Do not anxiously look about you,
for I am your God.[430]
I will strengthen you, surely
[b]I will help you,
Surely I will uphold you with My
righteous[6662] [c]right hand.'
11 "Behold, [a]all those who are

angered2732 at you will be shamed954 and dishonored;
[b]Those who contend with you will be as nothing, and will perish.6
12 "[a]You will seek those who quarrel with you, but will not find them,
Those who war with you will be as nothing, and non-existent.657
13 "For I am the LORD your God, [a]who upholds your right hand,
Who says to you, '[b]Do not fear, I will help you.'
14 "Do not fear, you [a]worm Jacob, you men of Israel;
I will help you," declares5001 the LORD, "[I]and [b]your Redeemer1350 is the Holy One6918 of Israel.
15 "Behold, I have made7760 you a new, sharp threshing sledge with double edges;
[a]You will thresh the [b]mountains, and pulverize *them,*
And will make the hills like chaff.
16 "You will [a]winnow them, and the wind7307 will carry5375 them away,
And the storm will scatter them;
But you will [b]rejoice in the LORD,
You will glory1984 in the Holy One of Israel.
17 "The [I]afflicted and needy are seeking [a]water, but there is none,
And their tongue is parched with thirst;
I, the LORD, [b]will answer them Myself,
As the God of Israel I [c]will not forsake5800 them.
18 "I will open [a]rivers on the bare heights,
And springs in the midst of the valleys;
I will make [b]the wilderness a pool of water,
And the dry land776 fountains of water.

11 [b]Is. 17:13; 29:5, 7, 8
12 [a]Job 20:7-9; Ps. 37:35, 36; Is. 17:14
13 [a]Is. 42:6; 45:1 [b]Is. 41:10
14 [I]Or, *even your Redeemer, the Holy One* [a]Job 25:6; Ps. 22:6 [b]Is. 35:10; 43:14; 44:6, 22-24
15 [a]Mic. 4:13; Hab. 3:12 [b]Is. 42:15; 64:1; Jer. 9:10; Ezek. 33:28
16 [a]Jer. 51:2 [b]Is. 25:9; 35:10; 51:3; 61:10
17 [I]Or, *poor* [a]Is. 43:20; 44:3; 49:10; 55:1 [b]Is. 30:19; 65:24 [c]Is. 42:16; 62:12
18 [a]Is. 30:25; 43:19 [b]Ps. 107:35; Is. 35:6, 7
19 [I]Or, *oleaster* [a]Is. 35:1; 55:13; 60:13
20 [a]Is. 40:5; 43:10 [b]Job 12:9; Is. 66:14
21 [I]Lit., *Bring near* [a]Is. 44:6
22 [a]Is. 44:7; 45:21; 46:10 [b]Is. 43:9
23 [a]Is. 42:9; 44:7, 8; 45:3; John 13:19 [b]Jer. 10:5
24 [I]Lit., *nothing* [a]Ps. 115:8; Is. 44:9; 1Cor. 8:4 [b]Is. 37:19; 41:29 [c]Prov. 3:32; 28:9
25 [a]Is. 41:2; Jer. 50:3 [b]2Sam. 22:43; Is. 10:6; Mic. 7:10; Zech. 10:5
26 [a]Is. 41:22; 44:7; 45:21

19 "I will put the cedar in the wilderness,
The acacia, and the [a]myrtle, and the [I]olive8081 tree;
I will place7760 the [a]juniper in the desert,6160
Together with the box tree and the cypress,8410
20 That [a]they may see and recognize,3045
And consider7760 and gain insight7919 as well,
That the [b]hand3027 of the LORD has done this,
And the Holy One of Israel has created1254 it.
21 "[I]Present7126 your case,"7379 the LORD says.559
"Bring forward5066 your strong *arguments,"*
The [a]King4428 of Jacob says.
22 [a]Let them bring forth and declare5046 to us what is going to take place;
As for the [b]former7223 *events,* declare what they *were,*
That we may consider them, and know their outcome;319
Or announce8085 to us what is coming.
23 [a]Declare the things that are going to come afterward,
That we may know that you are gods;430
Indeed, [b]do good or evil,7489 that we may anxiously look about us and fear together.
24 Behold, [a]you are of [I]no account,
And [b]your work amounts to nothing;659
He who chooses977 you is an [c]abomination.
25 "I have aroused [a]one from the north, and he has come;
From the rising of the sun he will call7121 on My name;
And he will come upon rulers5461 as *upon* [b]mortar,
Even as the potter treads clay."
26 Who has [a]declared5046 *this* from the beginning, that we might know?

Or from former times, that we
may say,559 "*He is*
right!"?6662
Surely there was [b]no one who
declared,5046
Surely there was no one who
proclaimed,5046
Surely there was no one
who heard8085 your
words.561
27 "[a]Formerly *I said* to Zion,
'Behold, here they are.'
And to Jerusalem, 'I will give a
[b]messenger of good
news.'1319
28 "But [a]when I look,7200 there is
no one,376
And there is no [b]counselor3289
[I]among them
Who, if I ask,7592 can [c]give an
answer.7725,1697
29 "Behold, all of them are
[I]false;205
Their [a]works are [b]worthless,
Their molten images5262 are
[c]wind and emptiness.8414

God's Promise concerning His Servant

42 "[a]Behold, My [b]Servant,5650
whom I [I]uphold;
My [c]chosen one972 *in whom* My
[d]soul5315 delights.7521
I have put My [e]Spirit7307 upon
Him;
He will bring forth [f]justice4941 to
the [II]nations.1471
2 "He will not cry out or raise5375
His voice,

26 [b]Hab. 2:18, 19
27 [a]Is. 48:3-8 [b]Is. 40:9; 44:28; 52:7; Nah. 1:15
28 [I]Lit., *out of those* [a]Is. 50:2; 59:16; 63:5 [b]Is. 40:13, 14 [c]Is. 46:7
29 [I]Another reading is *nothing* [a]Is. 2:8; 17:8; 41:24 [b]Is. 44:9 [c]Jer. 5:13

1 [I]Or, *hold fast* [II]Or, *Gentiles* [a]Matt. 12:18-21 [b]Is. 41:8; 43:10; 49:3-6; 52:13; 53:11; Matt. 12:18-21; Phil. 2:7 [c]Luke 9:35; 1Pet. 2:4, 6 [d]Matt. 3:17; 17:5; Mark 1:11; Luke 3:22 [e]Is. 11:2; 59:21; 61:1; Matt. 3:16; Luke 4:18, 19, 21 [f]Is. 2:4
3 [a]Ps. 72:2, 4; 96:13
4 [I]Or, *instruction* [a]Is. 40:28 [b]Is. 11:11; 24:15; 42:10, 12; 49:1; 51:5; 60:9; 66:19
5 [I]Or, *vegetation* [a]Ps. 102:25, 26; Is. 45:18 [b]Ps. 104:2; Is. 40:22 [c]Ps. 24:1, 2; 136:6 [d]Job 12:10; 33:4; Is. 57:16; Dan. 5:23; Acts 17:25
6 [a]Is. 41:2; Jer. 23:5, 6 [b]Is. 41:13; 45:1 [c]Is. 26:3; 27:3 [d]Is. 49:8 [e]Is. 49:6; 51:4; 60:1, 3; Luke 2:32; Acts 13:47; 26:23
7 [a]Is. 29:18; 35:5 [b]Is. 49:9; 61:1
8 [a]Is. 43:3, 11, 15 [b]Ex. 3:15; Ps. 83:18

Nor make His voice heard8085
in the street.
3 "A bruised reed He will not
break,7665
And a dimly burning wick He will
not extinguish;
He will faithfully571 bring forth
[a]justice.
4 "He will not be [a]disheartened or
crushed,7533
Until He has established7760
justice in the earth;776
And the [b]coastlands will wait3176
expectantly for His [I]law."8451
5 Thus says559 God410 the LORD,
Who [a]created1254 the
heavens8064 and [b]stretched
them out,
Who spread out7554 the
[c]earth and its [I]offspring,
Who [d]gives breath5397 to the
people5971 on it,
And spirit to those who walk in
it,
6 "I am the LORD, I have
[a]called7121 you in
righteousness,6664
I will also [b]hold you by the
hand3027 and [c]watch over5341
you,
And I will appoint you as a
[d]covenant1285 to the people,
As a [e]light216 to the nations,
7 To [a]open blind eyes,
To [b]bring out prisoners from the
dungeon,
And those who dwell in
darkness2822 from the
prison.
8 "[a]I am the LORD, that is [b]My
name;

42:1-4 This is the first of several servant songs in this section of Isaiah (see also 49:1-6; 50:4-11; 52:13—53:12). The identity of the servant has been a matter of dispute. Jewish scholarship, probably somewhat influenced by the Christian insistence that Jesus was the servant, has generally regarded Israel herself as the servant. Even Christian scholarship is not in agreement, and the texts themselves justify some of this disagreement. For example, the servant clearly is Israel in 41:8 and 49:3 but not in 49:6, because in 49:6 Israel is the beneficiary of the servant's action. The N.T. identification of Jesus with the servant is quite clear (Mt. 12:18-21; Acts 26:23). This comes out particularly in the several passages of which identify Jesus with the figure in Isa. 52:13—53:12. See note on that passage. Paul applied Isaiah 49:6 to Christians (Acts 13:47), which may simply be by way of extension from Jesus Himself (see Acts 26:23), much like Jesus, the Light of the world (Jn. 8:12; 9:5), could call His disciples the light of the world (Mt. 5:14).

I will not give My [c]glory[3519] to
another,
Nor My praise[8416] to [I]graven
images.
9 "Behold, the [a]former[7223] things
have come to pass,
Now I declare[5046] [b]new things;
Before they spring forth I
proclaim *them* to you."
10 Sing to the LORD a [a]new
song,[7892]
Sing His praise from the
[b]end of the earth!
[c]You who go down to the sea,
and [d]all that is in it.
You [e]islands and those who dwell
on them.
11 Let the [a]wilderness and its cities
lift up *their voices,*
The settlements where [b]Kedar
inhabits.
Let the inhabitants of [c]Sela sing
aloud,
Let them shout for joy from the
tops[7218] of the [d]mountains.
12 Let them [a]give[7760] glory to the
LORD,
And declare His praise in the
[b]coastlands.
13 [a]The LORD will go forth like a
warrior,[376]
He will arouse *His* [b]zeal[7068] like
a man of war.
He will utter a shout, yes, He
will raise a war cry.
He will [c]prevail against His
enemies.

The Blindness of the People

14 "[a]I have kept silent[2814] for a
long[5769] time,
I have kept still and restrained
Myself.
Now like a woman in labor I will
groan,
I will both gasp[5395] and pant.
15 "I will [a]lay waste[2717] the
mountains and hills,
And wither[3001] all their
vegetation;
I will [b]make the rivers into
coastlands,
And dry up the ponds.
16 "And I will [a]lead the blind by
a way[1870] they do not
know,[3045]
In paths they do not know[3045] I
will guide them.
I will [b]make darkness[4285] into
light before them
And [c]rugged places[1697] into
plains.
These are the things I will do,[6213]
And I will [d]not leave[5800] them
undone."
17 They shall be turned back and
be [a]utterly put to shame,[954]
Who trust[982] in [I]idols,
Who say[559] to molten
images,[4541]
"You are our gods."[430]
18 [a]Hear,[8085] you deaf!
And look, you blind, that you
may see.
19 Who is blind but My [a]servant,
Or so deaf as My [b]messenger[4397]
whom I send?
Who is so blind as he that is
[Ic]at peace[7999] *with Me,*
Or so blind as the servant of
the LORD?
20 [a]You have seen[7200] many things,
but you do not observe[8104]
them;
Your ears[241] are open, but none
hears.[8085]
21 The LORD was pleased[2654] for
His righteousness' sake
To make the law [a]great and
glorious.[142]
22 But this is a people plundered
and despoiled;[8154]
All of them are [a]trapped in
[I]caves,
Or are [b]hidden away in
prisons;[1004] [3608]
They have become a prey with
none to deliver[5337] *them,*
And a spoil, with none to say,
"Give *them* back!"[7725]
23 Who among you will give ear[238]
to this?
Who will give heed[7181] and listen
hereafter?

---

8 [I]Or, *idols* [c]Ex. 20:3-5; Is. 48:11
9 [a]Is. 48:3 [b]Is. 43:19; 48:6
10 [a]Ps. 33:3; 40:3; 98:1 [b]Is. 49:6; 62:11 [c]Ps. 65:5; 107:23 [d]Ex. 20:11; 1Chr. 16:32; Ps. 96:11 [e]Is. 42:4
11 [a]Is. 32:16; 35:1, 6 [b]Is. 21:16; 60:7 [c]Is. 16:1 [d]Is. 52:7; Nah. 1:15
12 [a]Is. 24:15 [b]Is. 42:4
13 [a]Ex. 15:3 [b]Is. 9:7; 26:11; 37:32; 59:17 [c]Is. 66:14-16
14 [a]Ps. 50:21; Is. 57:11
15 [a]Is. 2:12-16; Ezek. 38:19, 20 [b]Is. 44:27; 50:2; Nah. 1:4-6
16 [a]Is. 29:18; 30:21; 32:3; Jer. 31:8, 9; Luke 1:78, 79 [b]Is. 29:18; Eph. 5:8 [c]Is. 40:4; Luke 3:5 [d]Josh. 1:5; Ps. 94:14; Is. 41:17; Heb. 13:5
17 [I]Or, *graven images* [a]Ps. 97:7; Is. 1:29; 44:9, 11; 45:16
18 [a]Is. 29:18; 35:5
19 [I]Or, *the devoted one* [a]Is. 41:8 [b]Is. 44:26 [c]Is. 26:3; 27:5
20 [a]Rom. 2:21
21 [a]Is. 42:4; 51:4
22 [I]Or, *holes* [a]Is. 24:18 [b]Is. 24:22

24 Who gave Jacob up for spoil, and
Israel to plunderers?
Was it not the LORD, against
whom we have sinned,[2398]
And in whose ways[1870] they
[a]were not willing[14] to walk,
And whose law they did not
[b]obey?[8085]
25 So He poured[8210] out on him the
heat of His anger[639]
And the [a]fierceness of battle;
And it set him aflame all around,
Yet he did not recognize *it;*
And it burned him, but he
[1b]paid[7760] no attention.[3820]

Israel Redeemed

43 But now, thus says[559] the LORD,
your [a]Creator,[1254] O Jacob,
And He who [b]formed[3335] you,
O Israel,
"Do not [c]fear,[3372] for I have
[d]redeemed[1350] you;
I have [e]called[7121] you by name;
you are [f]Mine!
2 "When you [a]pass[5674] through the
waters, [b]I will be with you;
And through the rivers, they will
not overflow[7857] you.
When you [c]walk through the fire,
you will not be scorched,
Nor will the flame burn you.
3 "For [a]I am the LORD your God,[430]
The Holy One[6918] of Israel, your
[b]Savior;[3467]
I have given Egypt as your
ransom,[3724]
[1c]Cush and Seba in your place.
4 "Since you are [a]precious in My
sight,
Since you are [b]honored[3513] and
I [c]love[157] you,
I will give *other* men[120] in your
place and *other* peoples[3816]
in exchange for your
life.[5315]
5 "Do not fear, for [a]I am with you;
I will bring [b]your offspring[2233]
from the east,
And [c]gather[6908] you from the
west.

24 [a]Is. 30:15 [b]Is. 48:18; 57:17
25 [1]Lit., *did not lay it to heart* [a]Is. 5:25; 9:19 [b]Is. 29:13; 47:7; 57:1; Hos. 7:9
1 [a]Is. 43:15 [b]Is. 43:7, 21; 44:2, 21, 24 [c]Is. 43:5 [d]Is. 44:22, 23; 48:20 [e]Gen. 32:28; Is. 43:7; 45:3, 4 [f]Is. 43:21
2 [a]Ps. 66:12; Is. 8:7, 8 [b]Deut. 31:6, 8 [c]Is. 29:6; 30:27-29; Dan. 3:25, 27
3 [1]Or, *Ethiopia* [a]Ex. 20:2 [b]Is. 19:20; 43:11; 45:15, 21; 49:26; 60:16; 63:8 [c]Is. 20:3-5
4 [a]Ex. 19:5, 6 [b]Is. 49:5 [c]Is. 63:9
5 [a]Is. 8:10; 43:2 [b]Is. 41:8; 49:12; 61:9 [c]Is. 49:12
6 [a]Ps. 107:3 [b]2Cor. 6:18 [c]Is. 45:22
7 [a]Is. 56:5; 62:2; James 2:7 [b]Ps. 100:3; Is. 29:23; Eph. 2:10 [c]Is. 44:23; 46:13 [d]Is. 43:1
8 [a]Is. 6:9; 42:19; Ezek. 12:2
9 [a]Is. 34:1; 41:1 [b]Is. 41:22, 23, 26 [c]Is. 44:9 [d]Is. 43:26
10 [a]Is. 44:8 [b]Is. 41:8 [c]Is. 41:4 [d]Is. 45:5, 6
11 [a]Is. 43:3; 45:21; Hos. 13:4 [b]Is. 44:6, 8
12 [a]Deut. 32:16; Ps. 81:9

6 "I will say[559] to the [a]north, 'Give
them up!'
And to the south, 'Do not hold
them back.'
Bring My [b]sons[1121] from afar,
And My daughters from the
[c]ends of the earth,[776]
7 Everyone who is [a]called by My
name,
And whom I have [b]created for
My [c]glory,[3519]
[d]Whom I have formed, even
whom I have made."[6213]

Israel Is God's Witness

8 Bring out the people[5971] who are
[a]blind, even though they have
eyes,
And the deaf, even though they
have ears.[241]
9 All the nations[1471] have
[a]gathered together[6908]
In order that the peoples may
be assembled.[622]
Who among them can
[b]declare[5046] this
And proclaim to us the
former[7223] things?
Let them present [c]their
witnesses [d]that they may be
justified,[6663]
Or let them hear[8085] and say,
"It is true."[571]
10 "You are [a]My witnesses,"
declares[5001] the LORD,
"And [b]My servant[5650] whom I
have chosen,[977]
In order that you may know[3045]
and believe[539] Me,
And understand[995] that [c]I am
He.
[d]Before Me there was no God[410]
formed,
And there will be none after Me.
11 "I, even I, am the LORD;
And there is no [a]savior
[b]besides Me.
12 "It is I who have declared[5046] and
saved[3467] and proclaimed,[8085]
And there was no [a]strange[2114]
god among you;

So you are My witnesses,"
declares the LORD,
"And I am God.
13 "Even [I][a]from eternity[3117] [b]I am He;
And there is [c]none who can deliver[5337] out of My hand;[3027]
[d]I act and who can reverse it?"

Babylon to Be Destroyed

14 Thus says the LORD your [a]Redeemer,[1350] the Holy One of Israel,
"For your sake I have sent to Babylon,
And will bring them all down as fugitives,
[I]Even the [b]Chaldeans, into the [c]ships [II]in which they rejoice.
15 "I am the LORD, your Holy One,
[a]The Creator[1254] of Israel, your [b]King."[4428]
16 Thus says the LORD,
Who [a]makes a way[1870] through the sea
And a path through the mighty waters,
17 Who brings forth the [a]chariot and the horse,
The army[2428] and the mighty man
(They will lie down together *and* not rise again;
They have been [b]quenched *and* extinguished like a wick):
18 "[a]Do not call to mind[2142] the former things,
Or ponder[995] things of the past.
19 "Behold, I will do[6213] something [a]new,
Now it will spring forth;
Will you not be aware of it?
I will even [b]make[7760] a roadway in the wilderness,
Rivers in the desert.
🔑 20 "The beasts[2416] of the field[7704] will glorify[3513] Me;
The [a]jackals[8577] and the ostriches;
Because I have [b]given waters in the wilderness
And rivers in the desert,
To give drink to My chosen people.
21 "The people whom [a]I formed for Myself,
[b]Will declare[5608] My praise.[8416]

The Shortcomings of Israel

22 "Yet you have not called on[7121] Me, O Jacob;
But you have become [a]weary of Me, O Israel.
23 "You have [a]not brought to Me the sheep of your burnt offerings;[5930]
Nor have you [b]honored Me with your sacrifices.[2077]
I have not [c]burdened[5647] you with [I]offerings,[4503]
Nor wearied you with [d]incense.
24 "You have bought Me no [I][a]sweet cane with money,
Neither have you [II]filled Me with the fat of your sacrifices;
Rather you have burdened Me with your sins,
You have [b]wearied Me with your iniquities.[5771]
25 "I, even I, am the one who [a]wipes[4229] out your transgressions[6588] [b]for My own sake;
And I will [c]not remember your sins.
26 "[I]Put Me in remembrance;[2142]
[a]let us argue our case together,
State[5608] your *cause,* [b]that you may be proved right.
27 "Your [a]first[7223] [I]forefather[1] sinned,[2398]
And your [II][b]spokesmen[3887] have [III]transgressed[6586] against Me.

---

13 [I]So with Gr.; Heb., *from the day* [a]Ps. 90:2; Is. 48:16 [b]Is. 41:4 [c]Ps. 50:22 [d]Job 9:12; Is. 14:27
14 [I]Another reading is *As for the Chaldeans, their rejoicing* is turned *into lamentations* [II]Lit., *of their rejoicing* [a]Is. 41:14 [b]Is. 23:13 [c]Jer. 51:13
15 [a]Is. 43:1 [b]Is. 41:20; 44:6
16 [a]Ex. 14:21, 22; Ps. 77:19; Is. 11:15; 44:27; 50:2; 51:10; 63:11, 12
17 [a]Ex. 15:19 [b]Ps. 118:12; Is. 1:31
18 [a]Is. 65:17; Jer. 23:7
19 [a]Is. 42:9; 48:6; 2Cor. 5:17 [b]Ex. 17:6; Num. 20:11; Deut. 8:15; Ps. 78:16; Is. 35:1, 6; 41:18, 19; 49:10; 51:3
20 [a]Is. 13:22; 35:7 [b]Is. 41:17, 18; 48:21
21 [a]Is. 43:1 [b]Ps. 102:18; Is. 42:12; Luke 1:74, 75; 1Pet. 2:9
22 [a]Mic. 6:3; Mal. 1:13; 3:14
23 [I]Or, *a meal offering* [a]Amos 5:25 [b]Zech. 7:5, 6; Mal. 1:6-8 [c]Jer. 7:21-26 [d]Ex. 30:34; Lev. 2:1; 24:7
24 [I]Or, *calamus* [II]Or, *saturated* [a]Ex. 30:23; Jer. 6:20 [b]Ps. 95:10; Is. 1:14; 7:13; Ezek. 6:9; Mal. 2:17
25 [a]Is. 44:22; 55:7; Jer. 50:20 [b]Is. 37:35; 48:9, 11; Ezek. 36:22 [c]Is. 38:17; Jer. 31:34
26 [I]Or, *Report to Me* [a]Is. 1:18; 41:1; 50:8 [b]Is. 43:9
27 [I]Lit., *father* [II]Or, *interpreters* [III]Or, *rebelled* [a]Is. 51:2; Ezek. 16:3 [b]Is. 9:15; 28:7; 29:10; Jer. 5:31

🔑 **43:20,21** See note on Ex. 19:5,6.

28 "So I will [I]pollute[2490] the
[II]princes[8269] of the
sanctuary;[6944]
And I will consign Jacob to the
[a]ban,[2764] and Israel to
[b]revilement.

The Blessings of Israel

44 "But now listen,[8085] O Jacob, My
[a]servant;[5650]
And Israel, whom I have
chosen:[977]
2 Thus says[559] the LORD who
made[6213] you
And [a]formed[3335] you from the
womb,[990] who [b]will help
you,
'[c]Do not fear,[3372] O Jacob My
servant;
And you [d]Jeshurun whom I have
chosen.
3 'For [a]I will pour out water on
[I]the thirsty *land*
And streams on the dry
ground;[3004]
I will [b]pour out My Spirit on your
[c]offspring,[2233]
And My blessing[1293] on your
descendants;
4 And they will spring up [I]among
the grass
Like [a]poplars by streams of
water.'
5 "This one will say,[559] 'I am the
LORD'S';
And that one [I]will call[7121] on the
name of Jacob;
And another will [a]write [II]*on* his
hand,[3027] 'Belonging to the
LORD,'
And will name Israel's name with
honor.
6 "Thus says the LORD, the
[a]King[4428] of Israel
And his [b]Redeemer,[1350] the
LORD of hosts:[6635]
'I am the [c]first[7223] and I am the
last,
And there is no God[430]
[d]besides Me.
7 'And who is like Me? [a]Let him
proclaim and declare[5046] it;
Yes, let him recount it to Me
in order,
[I]From the time that I
established[7760] the
ancient[5769] [II]nation.[5971]
And let them declare[5046] to them
the things that are coming
And the events that are going
to take place.
8 'Do not tremble[6342] and do not
be afraid;[7297]
[a]Have I not long since[227]
announced[8085] it to you and
declared[5046] it?
And [b]you are My witnesses.
Is there any God[433] [c]besides Me,
Or is there any *other* [d]Rock?
I know[3045] of none.' "

The Folly of Idolatry

9 Those who fashion[3335] [I]a graven
image are all of them futile,[8414] and their
precious things[2530] are of no profit; even
their own witnesses fail to see or know,
so that they will be [a]put to shame.[954]
10 Who has fashioned a god[410] or
cast[5258] [I]an idol to [a]no profit?
11 Behold, all his companions will
be [a]put to shame, for the craftsmen
themselves are mere men.[120] Let them
all assemble[6908] themselves, let them
stand up, let them tremble, let
them together be put to shame.
12 The [a]man shapes iron into a cutting tool, and does his work over the
coals, [I]fashioning[3335] it with hammers,
and working it with his strong arm. He
also gets hungry and [II]his strength fails;
he drinks no water and becomes weary.
13 [a]*Another* shapes wood, he extends a measuring line; he outlines it
with red chalk. He works it with planes,
and outlines it with a compass, and
makes[6213] it like the form[8403] of a man,
like the beauty[8597] of [b]man,[120] so that
it may sit in a [c]house.[1004]
14 Surely he cuts[3772] cedars for himself, and takes a [I]cypress or an oak,
and [II]raises *it* for himself among the trees

28 [I]Or, *pierce through* [II]Or, *holy princes* [a]Is. 24:6; 34:5; Jer. 24:9; Dan. 9:11; Zech. 8:13 [b]Ps. 79:4; Ezek. 5:15
1 [a]Is. 41:8; Jer. 30:10; 46:27, 28
2 [a]Is. 44:21, 24 [b]Is. 41:10 [c]Is. 43:5 [d]Deut. 32:15; 33:5, 26
3 [I]Or, *him who is thirsty* [a]Is. 41:17; Ezek. 34:26; Joel 3:18 [b]Is. 32:15; Joel 2:28 [c]Is. 61:9; 65:23
4 [I]Another reading is *like grass among the waters* [a]Lev. 23:40; Job 40:22
5 [I]Another reading is *will be called by the name of Jacob* [II]Or, *with* [a]Ex. 13:9; Neh. 9:38
6 [a]Is. 41:21; 43:15 [b]Is. 41:14; 43:1, 14 [c]Is. 41:4; 43:10; 48:12; Rev. 1:8, 17; 22:13 [d]Is. 43:11; 44:8; 45:5, 6, 21
7 [I]Lit., *From My establishing of* [II]Or, *people* [a]Is. 41:22, 26
8 [a]Is. 42:9; 48:5 [b]Is. 43:10 [c]Deut. 4:35, 39; 1Sam. 2:2; Is. 45:5; Joel 2:27 [d]Is. 17:10; 26:4; 30:29
9 [I]Or, *an idol* [a]Ps. 97:7; Is. 42:17; 44:11; 45:16
10 [I]Or, *a graven image* [a]Is. 41:29; Jer. 10:5; Hab. 2:18; Acts 19:26
11 [a]Ps. 97:7; Is. 42:17; 44:9; 45:16
12 [I]Lit., *and fashions* [II]Lit., *there is no strength* [a]Is. 40:19, 20; 41:6, 7; 46:6, 7; Jer. 10:3-5; Hab. 2:18
13 [a]Is. 41:7 [b]Ps. 115:5-7 [c]Judg. 17:4, 5; Ezek. 8:10, 11
14 [I]Or, *holm-oak* [II]Lit., *makes strong*

of the forest. He plants a fir, and the rain makes it grow.

15 Then it becomes *something* for a man to burn, so he takes one of them and warms himself; he also makes a fire to bake bread. He also [a]makes a god and worships[7812] it; he makes it a graven image, and [b]falls down before it.

16 Half of it he burns[8313] in the fire; over *this* half he eats meat[1320] as he roasts a roast, and is satisfied. He also warms himself and says, "Aha! I am warm, I have seen[7200] the fire."[217]

17 But the rest[7611] of it he [a]makes into a god, his graven image. He falls down before it and worships; he also [b]prays[6419] to it and says, "Deliver[5337] me, for thou art my god."

18 They do not [a]know,[3045] nor do they understand,[995] for He has [b]smeared over their eyes so that they cannot see and their hearts[3826] so that they cannot comprehend.[7919]

19 And no one [I]recalls,[7725] nor is there [a]knowledge or understanding[8394] to say, "I have burned half of it in the fire, and also have baked bread over its coals. I roast meat and eat *it*. Then [II]I make[6213] the rest[3499] of it into an [b]abomination, [III]I fall down[5456] before a block of wood!"

20 He [I][a]feeds on ashes; a [b]deceived heart has turned him aside. And he cannot deliver [II]himself,[5315] nor say, "[c]Is there not a lie in my right hand?"

God Forgives and Redeems

21 "[a]Remember[2142] these things, O
Jacob,
And Israel, for you are [b]My
servant;
I have formed you, you are My
servant,
O Israel, you will [c]not be
forgotten by Me.
22 "I have [a]wiped out[4229] your
transgressions[6588] like a thick
cloud,[6051]
And your sins like a [I]heavy mist.
[b]Return[7725] to Me, for I have
[c]redeemed[1350] you."
23 [a]Shout for joy, O heavens,[8064]
for the LORD has done[6213] *it*!
Shout[7321] joyfully, you lower
parts of the earth;[776]
[b]Break forth into a shout of joy,
you mountains,
O forest, and every tree in it;
For [c]the LORD has redeemed
Jacob
And in Israel He [d]shows forth
His glory.[6286]

24 Thus says the LORD, your [a]Redeemer, and the one who [b]formed you from the womb,

"I, the LORD, am the maker of
all things,
[c]Stretching out the heavens by
Myself,
And spreading out the earth
[I]all alone,
25 [a]Causing[6565] the [I]omens[226] of
boasters to fail,[6565]
[II]Making fools out of diviners,[7080]
[b]Causing wise[2450] men to draw
back,[7725]
And [III]turning their knowledge
into foolishness,
26 [a]Confirming the word[1697] of His
servant,
And [I]performing[7999] the
purpose[6098] of His
messengers.[4426]
It is I who says of Jerusalem,
'She shall be inhabited!'
And of the [b]cities of Judah,
'[c]They shall be built.'
And I will raise up her ruins[2723]
again.
27 "*It is I* who says to the depth of
the sea, 'Be dried up!'[2717]
And I will make your rivers
[a]dry.[3001]
28 "*It is I* who says of [a]Cyrus, '*He
is* My shepherd!

15 [a]Is. 44:17 [b]2Chr. 25:14
17 [a]Is. 44:15 [b]1Kin. 18:26, 28; Is. 45:20
18 [a]Is. 1:3; Jer. 10:8, 14 [b]Ps. 81:12; Is. 6:9, 10; 29:10
19 [I]Lit., *returns to his heart* [II]Or, *shall I make. . .?* [III]Or, *shall I fall. . .?* [a]Is. 5:13; 44:18, 19; 45:20 [b]Deut. 27:15; 1Kin. 11:5, 7; 2Kin. 23:13, 14
20 [I]Or, *is a companion of ashes* [II]Lit., *his soul* [a]Ps. 102:9 [b]Job 15:31; Hos. 4:12; Rom. 1:21, 22; 2Thess. 2:11; 2Tim. 3:13 [c]Is. 57:11; 59:3, 4, 13; Rom. 1:25
21 [a]Is. 46:8; Zech. 10:9 [b]Is. 44:1, 2 [c]Is. 49:15
22 [I]Or, *cloud* [a]Ps. 51:1, 9; Is. 43:25; Acts 3:19 [b]Is. 31:6; 55:7 [c]Is. 43:1; 48:20; 1Cor. 6:20; 1Pet. 1:18, 19
23 [a]Ps. 69:34; 96:11, 12; Is. 42:10; 49:13 [b]Ps. 98:7, 8; 148:7, 9; Is. 55:12 [c]Is. 43:1 [d]Is. 49:3; 61:3
24 [I]Or, *who was with Me?* [a]Is. 41:14; 43:14 [b]Is. 44:2 [c]Is. 40:22; 42:5; 45:12, 18; 51:13
25 [I]Lit., *signs* [II]Lit., *He makes* [III]Lit., *He turns* [a]Is. 47:13 [b]2Sam. 15:31; Job 5:12-14; Ps. 33:10; Is. 29:14; Jer. 51:57; 1Cor. 1:20, 27
26 [I]Lit., *He performs* [a]Zech. 1:6; Matt. 5:18 [b]Is. 40:9 [c]Jer. 32:15, 44
27 [a]Is. 42:15; 50:2; Jer. 50:38; 51:36
28 [a]Is. 45:1

44:28 Cyrus was the Medo-Persian king who overthrew Babylon in 539 B.C. and freed the Jews
(continued on next page)

And he will perform all My
desire.'[2656]
And [I]he declares of Jerusalem,
"[b]She will be built,'
And of the temple,[1964] '[II]Your
foundation[3245] will be laid.' "

God Uses Cyrus

45 Thus says[559] the LORD to [a]Cyrus His anointed,[4899]
Whom I have taken[2388] by the
right [b]hand,
To [c]subdue nations[1471] before
him,
And [I]to [d]loose the loins of
kings;[4428]
To open doors before him so
that gates will not be shut:
2 "I will go before you and [a]make
the [I]rough places[1921]
smooth;[3474]
I will [b]shatter[7665] the doors of
bronze, and cut through their
iron [c]bars.
3 "And I will give you the
[I][a]treasures of darkness,[2822]
And hidden wealth of secret
places,
In order that you may know[3045]
that it is I,
The LORD, the God[430] of Israel,
who [b]calls[7121] you by your
name.
4 "For the sake of [a]Jacob My
servant,
And Israel My chosen[972] *one,*
I have also [b]called[7121] you by
your name;
I have given you a title of honor
Though you have [c]not known[3045]
Me.
5 "I am the LORD, and [a]there is no
other;
[b]Besides Me there is no God.
I will [I][c]gird you, though you have
not known Me;
6 That [I][a]men may know from the
rising to the setting of the
sun
That there is [b]no one besides
Me.
I am the LORD, and there is no
other,
7 The One [a]forming light[216] and
[b]creating darkness,
Causing [I]well-being[7965] and
[c]creating[1254] calamity;[7451]
I am the LORD who does[6213] all
these.

God's Supreme Power

8 "[a]Drip down, O heavens,[8064] from
above,
And let the clouds[7834] pour down
righteousness;[6664]
Let the [b]earth[776] open up and
salvation[3468] bear fruit,
[c]And righteousness[6666] spring up
with it.
I, the LORD, have created[1254] it.
9 "Woe to *the one* who [a]quarrels[7378]
with his [I]Maker—[3335]
An earthenware vessel[2789]
[II]among the vessels[2789] of
earth![127]
Will the [b]clay say[559] to the
[I]potter,[3335] 'What are you
doing?'[6213]
Or the thing you are making *say,*
'He has no hands'?[3027]
10 "Woe to him who says to a
father,[1] 'What are you
begetting?'
Or to a woman,[802] 'To what are
you [I]giving birth?' "[2342]
11 Thus says the [a]LORD, the Holy

28 [I]Lit., *to say* [II]Lit., *You will be founded* [b]2Chr. 36:22, 23; Ezra 1:1; Is. 14:32; 45:13; 54:11
1 [I]Lit., *I will loose* [a]Is. 44:28 [b]Ps. 73:23; Is. 41:13; 42:6 [c]Is. 41:2, 25; Jer. 50:3, 35; 51:11, 20, 24 [d]Job 12:21; Is. 45:5
2 [I]Another reading is *mountains* [a]Is. 40:4 [b]Ps. 107:16 [c]Jer. 51:30
3 [I]Or, *hoarded treasures* [a]Jer. 41:8; 50:37 [b]Ex. 33:12, 17; Is. 43:1; 49:1
4 [a]Is. 41:8, 9; 44:1 [b]Is. 43:1 [c]Acts 17:23
5 [I]Or, *arm* [a]Is. 45:6, 14, 18, 21; 46:9 [b]Is. 44:6, 8 [c]Ps. 18:39
6 [I]Lit., *they* [a]Ps. 102:15; Mal. 1:11 [b]Is. 45:5
7 [I]Or, *peace* [a]Is. 42:16 [b]Ps. 104:20; 105:28 [c]Is. 31:2; 47:11; Amos 3:6
8 [a]Ps. 72:6; Hos. 10:12; 14:5; Joel 3:18 [b]Ps. 85:11 [c]Is. 60:21; 61:11
9 [I]Lit., *Fashioner* [II]Lit., *with* [a]Job 15:25; 40:8, 9; Ps. 2:2, 3; Prov. 21:30; Jer. 50:24 [b]Is. 29:16; 64:8; Jer. 18:6; Rom. 9:20, 21
10 [I]Lit., *in labor pains with*
11 [a]Is. 43:15; 48:17; Ezek. 39:7

(continued from previous page)
from their exile, so they could return to their land. In this remarkable passage Isaiah was able to look ahead a century and a half to two centuries and give the exact name of a then unborn deliverer. This pagan king is referred to as both God's shepherd (44:28) and His anointed (45:1), terms which would later be applied to Jesus. "Messiah" simply means "anointed," and in Isaiah several figures were anointed, including kings and priests. What the Jews were looking for, and many of them found in Jesus' day, was the special one anointed by God, *the* Messiah.

One[6918] of Israel, and his [Ib]Maker:
"[IIc]Ask[7592] Me about the things
to come [III]concerning My
[d]sons,[1121]
And you shall commit[6680] to Me
[e]the work of My hands.
12 "It is I who [a]made[6213] the earth,
and created man upon it.
I [b]stretched out the heavens
with My hands,
And I [I]ordained[6680] [c]all their
host.[6635]
13 "I have aroused him in
[a]righteousness,
And I will [b]make all his ways[1870]
smooth;[3474]
He will [c]build My city, and will
let My exiles[1546] go [d]free,
Without any payment or
reward," says the LORD of
hosts.[6635]
14 Thus says the LORD,
"The [I]products of [a]Egypt and the
merchandise of [IIb]Cush
And the Sabeans, men[582] of
stature,
Will [c]come over to you and will
be yours;
They will walk behind you, they
will come over in [d]chains
And will [e]bow down[7812] to you;
They will make supplication[6419]
to you:
'[III]Surely, [f]God[410] is [IV]with you,
and [g]there is none else,
No other God.' "
15 Truly, Thou art a God[410] who
[a]hides Himself,
O God of Israel, [b]Savior![3467]
16 They will be [a]put to shame[954]
and even humiliated, all of
them;
The [b]manufacturers of idols[6736]
will go away together in
humiliation.
17 Israel has been saved[3467] by the
LORD
With an [a]everlasting[5769]
salvation;[8668]
You [b]will not be put to shame
or humiliated
To all eternity.[5769]

18 For thus says the LORD, who
[a]created the heavens
(He is the God who [b]formed[3335]
the earth and made it,
He established[3559] it and did
not create it [I]a [c]waste
place,[8414]
But formed it to be [d]inhabited),
"I am the LORD, and [e]there
is none else.
19 "[a]I have not spoken[1696] in secret,
In [I]some dark[2822] land;
I did not say[559] to the
[IIb]offspring[2233] of Jacob,
'[c]Seek Me in [III]a waste place';
I, the LORD, [d]speak[1696]
righteousness
[e]Declaring[5046] things that are
upright.[4334]
20 "[a]Gather[6908] yourselves and
come;
Draw near[5066] together, you
fugitives of the nations;
[b]They have no knowledge,[3045]
Who [c]carry[5375] about [I]their
wooden idol,
And [d]pray[6419] to a god who
cannot save.[3467]
21 "[a]Declare[3045] and set forth[5066]
your case;
Indeed, let them consult[3289]
together.
[b]Who has announced[8085] this
from of old?[6924]
Who has long since[227]
declared[5046] it?
Is it not I, the LORD?
And there is [c]no other God
besides Me,
A righteous God and a
[d]Savior;
There is none except Me.
22 "[a]Turn to Me, and [b]be saved, all
the ends of the earth;
For I am God, and there is no
other.
23 "[a]I have sworn by Myself,
The [b]word[1697] has gone forth
from My mouth[6310] in
righteousness

11 [I]Lit., *Fashioner* [II]Or, *Will you ask* [III]Or, *upon* [b]Is. 44:2; 54:5 [c]Is. 8:19 [d]Jer. 31:9 [e]Is. 19:25; 29:23; 60:21; 64:8
12 [I]Or, *commanded* [a]Is. 42:5; 45:18; Jer. 27:5 [b]Ps. 104:2; Is. 42:5; 44:24 [c]Gen. 2:1; Neh. 9:6
13 [a]Is. 41:2 [b]Is. 45:2 [c]2Chr. 36:22, 23; Is. 44:28 [d]Is. 52:3
14 [I]Lit., *labor* [II]Or, *Ethiopia* [III]Or, *God is with you alone* [IV]Or, *in* [a]Ps. 68:31; Is. 19:21 [b]Is. 18:1; 43:3 [c]Is. 14:1, 2; 49:23; 54:3 [d]Ps. 149:8 [e]Is. 49:23; 60:14 [f]Jer. 16:19; Zech. 8:20-23; 1Cor. 14:25 [g]Is. 45:5
15 [a]Ps. 44:24; Is. 1:15; 8:17; 57:17 [b]Is. 43:3
16 [a]Is. 42:17; 44:9 [b]Is. 44:11
17 [a]Is. 26:4; 51:6; Rom. 11:26 [b]Is. 49:23; 50:7; 54:4
18 [I]Or, *in vain* [a]Is. 42:5 [b]Is. 45:12 [c]Gen. 1:2 [d]Gen. 1:26; Ps. 115:16 [e]Is. 45:5
19 [I]Lit., *a place of a land of darkness* [II]Lit., *seed* [III]Or, *vain* [a]Is. 48:16 [b]Is. 45:25; 65:9 [c]2Chr. 15:2; Ps. 78:34; Jer. 29:13, 14 [d]Ps. 19:8; Is. 45:23; 63:1 [e]Is. 43:12; 44:8
20 [I]Lit., *the wood of their graven image* [a]Is. 43:9 [b]Is. 44:18, 19; 48:5-7 [c]Is. 46:1, 7; Jer. 10:5 [d]Is. 44:17; 46:6, 7
21 [a]Is. 41:23; 43:9 [b]Is. 41:26; 44:7; 48:14 [c]Is. 45:5 [d]Is. 43:3, 11
22 [a]Num. 21:8, 9; 2Chr. 20:12; Mic. 7:7; Zech. 12:10 [b]Is. 30:15; 49:6, 12; 52:10

23 [a]Gen. 22:16; Is. 62:8; Heb. 6:13 [b]Is. 55:11

And will not turn back,[7725]
That to Me [c]every knee will
bow,[3766] every tongue will
[d]swear[7650] *allegiance.*
24 "They will say of Me, 'Only
[a]in the LORD are
righteousness and strength.'
Men will come to Him,
And [b]all who were angry[2734] at
Him shall be put to shame.
25 "In the LORD all the offspring of
Israel
Will be [a]justified,[6663] and will
[b]glory."[1984]

Babylon's Idols and the True God

46 [a]Bel has bowed down,[3766] Nebo
stoops over;
Their images are *consigned* to
the beasts[2416] and the cattle.
The things [I]that you carry are
burdensome,
A load[4853] for the weary *beast.*
2 They stooped over, they have
bowed down[3766] together;
They could not rescue the
burden,
But [I]have themselves [a]gone into
captivity.[7628]
3 "[a]Listen[8085] to Me, O house of
Jacob,
And all [b]the remnant[7611] of the
house[1004] of Israel,
You who have been [c]borne by
Me from [I]birth,
And have been carried[5375] from
the womb;
4 Even to your old age,[2209]
[a]I [I]shall be the same,
And even to your [IIb]graying
years[7822] I shall bear *you!*
I have [III]done[6213] *it,* and I shall
carry *you;*
And I shall bear *you,* and I shall
deliver *you.*
5 "[a]To whom would you liken Me,
And make Me equal and
compare[4911] Me,
That we should be alike?
6 "Those who [a]lavish gold from the
purse
And weigh silver on the scale
Hire a goldsmith,[6884] and he
makes[6213] it *into* a god;
They [b]bow down,[5456] indeed
they worship[7812] it.
7 "They [a]lift it upon the shoulder
and carry it;
They set it in its place and it
stands *there.*
[b]It does not move from its place.
Though one may cry to it, it
[c]cannot answer;
It [d]cannot deliver[3467] him from
his distress.
8 "[a]Remember[2142] this, and be
[I]assured;
[b]Recall it to [II]mind,[3820] you
[c]transgressors.[6586]
9 "Remember the [a]former[7223]
things long past,[5769]
For I am God, and there is
[b]no other;
I am God,[430] and there is [c]no
one like Me,
10 Declaring[5046] the end[319] from the
beginning[7225]
And from ancient times[6924]
things which have not been
done,[6213]
Saying, '[a]My purpose[6098] will be
established,
And I will accomplish[6213] all My
good pleasure';[2656]
11 Calling[7121] a [a]bird of prey from
the [b]east,
The man[376] of [I]My purpose from
a far country.[776]
Truly I have [c]spoken;[1696] truly
I will bring it to pass.
I have planned[3335] *it, surely* I will
do it.
12 "[a]Listen to Me, you [b]stubborn-
minded,
Who are [c]far from
righteousness.[6666]
13 "I [a]bring near[7126] My
righteousness, it is not far off;
And My salvation[8668] will not
delay.
And I will grant [b]salvation in
Zion,
And My [c]glory for Israel.

23 [c]Rom. 14:11; Phil. 2:10 [d]Deut. 6:13; Ps. 63:11; Is. 19:18; 65:16

24 [a]Jer. 33:16 [b]Is. 41:11

25 [a]1Kin. 8:32; Is. 53:11 [b]Is. 41:16; 60:19

1 [I]Lit., *carried by you* [a]Is. 2:18; 21:9; Jer. 50:2-4; 51:44

2 [I]Or, *their soul has* [a]Judg. 18:17, 18, 24; 2Sam. 5:21; Jer. 43:12, 13; 48:7; Hos. 10:5, 6

3 [I]Lit., *the belly* [a]Is. 46:12 [b]Is. 10:21, 22 [c]Ps. 71:6; Is. 49:1

4 [I]Lit., *I am He* [II]Lit., *gray hairs* [III]Or, *made you* [a]Is. 41:4; 43:13; 48:12 [b]Ps. 71:18

5 [a]Is. 40:18, 25

6 [a]Is. 40:19; 41:7; 44:12-17; Jer. 10:4 [b]Is. 44:15, 17

7 [a]Is. 45:20; 46:1; Jer. 10:5 [b]Is. 40:20; 41:7 [c]Is. 41:28 [d]Is. 45:20

8 [I]Lit., *firm* [II]Lit., *heart* [a]Is. 44:21 [b]Is. 44:19 [c]Is. 50:1

9 [a]Deut. 32:7; Is. 42:9; 65:17 [b]Is. 45:5, 21 [c]Is. 41:26, 27

10 [a]Ps. 33:11; Prov. 19:21; Is. 14:24; 25:1; 40:8; Acts 5:39

11 [I]Lit., *His* [a]Is. 18:6 [b]Is. 41:2 [c]Num. 23:19; Is. 14:24; 37:26

12 [a]Is. 46:3 [b]Ps. 76:5; Is. 48:4; Zech. 7:11, 12; Mal. 3:13 [c]Ps. 119:150; Is. 48:1; Jer. 2:5

13 [a]Is. 51:5; 61:11; Rom. 3:21 [b]Is. 61:3; 62:11; Joel 3:17; 1Pet. 2:6 [c]Is. 43:7; 44:23

Lament for Babylon

47 "[a]Come down and sit in the
dust,[6083]
O [b]virgin[1330] [c]daughter of
Babylon;
Sit on the ground[776] without a
throne,[3678]
O daughter of the Chaldeans.
For you shall no longer be
called[7121] [d]tender and
delicate.
2 "Take the [a]millstones and [b]grind
meal.
Remove[1540] your [c]veil, [d]strip off
the skirt,
Uncover the leg, cross[5674] the
rivers.
3 "Your [a]nakedness[6172] will be
uncovered,[1540]
Your shame also will be
exposed;[7200]
I will [b]take vengeance[5359] and
will not [I]spare a man."[120]
4 Our [a]Redeemer,[1350] the LORD of
hosts[6635] is His name,
The Holy One[6918] of Israel.
5 "[a]Sit silently, and go into
[b]darkness,[2822]
O daughter of the Chaldeans;
For you will no more be
called
The [c]queen[1404] of [d]kingdoms.[4467]
6 "I was angry[7107] with My
people,[5971]
I profaned[2490] My heritage,[5159]
And gave them into your
hand[3027]
You did not show[7760] mercy[7356]
to them,
On the [a]aged[2204] you made your
yoke very heavy.
7 "Yet you said,[559] 'I shall be a
[a]queen forever.'[5769]
These things you did not
[b]consider,[7760]
Nor remember[2142] the
[c]outcome[319] of [I]them.
8 "Now, then, hear[8085] this, you
[a]sensual one,
Who [b]dwells securely,[983]
Who says[559] in [I]your heart,[3824]
'[c]I am, and there is no one
besides me.
I shall [d]not sit as a widow,
Nor shall I know[3045] loss of
children.'[1121]
9 "But these [a]two things shall come
on you [b]suddenly in one
day:[3117]
Loss of children[7908] and
widowhood.
They shall come on you in full
measure[1214]
In spite of your many
[c]sorceries,[3785]
In spite of the great power of
your spells.[2267]
10 "And you felt [a]secure[982] in your
wickedness[7451] and said,[559]
'[b]No one sees[7200] me,'
Your [c]wisdom[2451] and your
knowledge,[1847] [I]they have
deluded[7725] you;
For you have said in your heart,
'[d]I am, and there is no one
besides me.'
11 "But [a]evil[7451] will come on you
Which you will not know how
to charm away;
And disaster[1943] will fall on you
For which you cannot atone,[3722]
And [b]destruction[7722] about which
you do not know
Will come on you [c]suddenly.
12 "Stand *fast* now in your [a]spells
And in your many sorceries
With which you have labored
from your youth;
Perhaps you will be able to
profit,
Perhaps you may cause
trembling.[6206]
13 "You are [a]wearied with your many
counsels;
Let now the [b]astrologers,[8064]
Those who prophesy by the
stars,[2374]
Those who predict[3045] by the
new moons,
Stand up and [c]save[3467] you from
what will come upon you.
14 "Behold, they have become
[a]like stubble,

1 [a]Is. 3:26; Jer. 48:18 [b]Is. 23:12; 37:22; Jer. 46:11 [c]Ps. 137:8; Jer. 50:42; 51:33; Zech. 2:7 [d]Deut. 28:56

2 [a]Ex. 11:5; Jer. 25:10 [b]Job 31:10; Eccl. 12:4; Matt. 24:41 [c]Gen. 24:65; Is. 3:23; 1Cor. 11:5 [d]Is. 32:11

3 [I]Lit., *meet* [a]Ezek. 16:37; Nah. 3:5 [b]Is. 34:8; 63:4

4 [a]Is. 41:14

5 [a]Is. 23:2; Jer. 8:14; Lam. 2:10 [b]Is. 13:10 [c]Is. 47:7 [d]Is. 13:19; Dan. 2:37

6 [a]Deut. 28:50

7 [I]Lit., *it* [a]Is. 47:5 [b]Is. 42:25; 57:11 [c]Deut. 32:29; Jer. 5:31; Ezek. 7:2, 3

8 [I]Lit., *her* [a]Is. 22:13; 32:9; Jer. 50:11 [b]Is. 32:9, 11; Zeph. 2:15 [c]Is. 45:5, 6, 18; 47:10; Zeph. 2:15 [d]Rev. 18:7

9 [a]Is. 13:16, 18; 14:22 [b]Ps. 73:19; 1Thess. 5:3; Rev. 18:8, 10 [c]Is. 47:13; Nah. 3:4; Rev. 18:23

10 [I]Lit., *it has* [a]Ps. 52:7; 62:10; Is. 59:4 [b]Is. 29:15; Ezek. 8:12; 9:9 [c]Is. 5:21; 44:20 [d]Is. 47:8

11 [a]Is. 57:1 [b]Is. 13:6; Jer. 51:8, 43; Luke 17:27; 1Thess. 5:3 [c]Is. 47:9

12 [a]Is. 47:9

13 [a]Jer. 51:58, 64 [b]Is. 8:19; 44:25; 47:9; Dan. 2:2, 10 [c]Is. 47:15

14 [a]Is. 5:24; Nah. 1:10; Mal. 4:1

[b]Fire burns[8313] them;
They cannot deliver[5337]
themselves from the
power[3027] of the flame;
There will be [c]no coal to warm
by,
Nor a fire[217] to sit before!
15 "So have those become to you
with whom you have labored,
Who have [a]trafficked with you
from your youth;
Each[376] has wandered[8582] in his
own [I]way.
There is [b]none to save you.

Israel's Obstinacy

48 "[a]Hear[8085] this, O house[1004] of
Jacob, who are named Israel
And who came forth[7121] from the
[Ib]loins of Judah,
Who [c]swear[7650] by the name of
the LORD
And invoke the God[430] of Israel,
But not in truth[571] nor in
[d]righteousness.[6666]
2 "For they call[7121] themselves
after the [a]holy[6944] city,
And [b]lean on the God of Israel;
The LORD of hosts[6635] is His
name.
3 "I [a]declared[5046] the former[7223]
things long ago[227]
And they went forth from My
mouth,[6310] and I
proclaimed[8085] them.
[b]Suddenly I acted,[6213] and they
[c]came to pass.
4 "Because I know that you are
[Ia]obstinate,[7186]
And your [b]neck is an iron sinew,
And your [c]forehead bronze,
5 Therefore I declared *them* to you
long ago,
Before [I]they took place I
proclaimed *them* to you,
Lest you should say,[559] 'My
[a]idol[6090] has done[6213] them,
And my graven image and my
molten image[5262] have
commanded[6680] them.'

14 [b]Is. 10:17; Jer. 51:30, 32, 58 [c]Is. 44:16
15 [I]Lit., *side, region* [a]Rev. 18:11 [b]Is. 5:29; 43:13; 46:7

1 [I]Lit., *waters* [a]Is. 46:12 [b]Num. 24:7; Deut. 33:28; Ps. 68:26 [c]Deut. 6:13; Is. 45:23; 65:16 [d]Is. 58:2; Jer. 4:2
2 [a]Is. 52:1; 64:10 [b]Is. 10:20; Jer. 7:4; 21:2; Mic. 3:11; Rom. 2:17
3 [a]Is. 41:22; 42:9; 43:9; 44:7, 8; 45:21; 46:10 [b]Is. 29:5; 30:13 [c]Josh. 21:45; Is. 42:9
4 [I]Or, *harsh* [a]Ex. 32:9; Deut. 31:27; Ezek. 2:4; 3:7 [b]2Chr. 36:13; Prov. 29:1; Acts 7:51 [c]Ezek. 3:7-9
5 [I]Lit., *it* [a]Jer. 44:15-18
6 [a]Is. 42:9; 43:19
8 [I]Or, *transgressor* [II]Lit., *the belly* [a]Is. 42:25; 47:11; Hos. 7:9 [b]Deut. 9:7, 24; Ps. 58:3; Is. 46:8
9 [a]Is. 48:11 [b]Neh. 9:30, 31; Ps. 78:38; 103:8-10; Is. 30:18; 65:8
10 [a]Jer. 9:7; Ezek. 22:18-22 [b]Deut. 4:20; 1Kin. 8:51; Jer. 11:4
11 [a]1Sam. 12:22; Ps. 25:11; 106:8; Is. 37:35; 43:25; Jer. 14:7; Ezek. 20:9, 14, 22, 44; Dan. 9:17-19 [b]Deut. 32:26, 27; Is. 42:8
12 [I]Lit., *My called one* [a]Is. 41:4; 43:10-13; 46:4 [b]Is. 44:6; Rev. 1:17; 22:13
13 [a]Ex. 20:11; Ps. 102:25; Is. 42:5; 45:12, 18; Heb. 1:10-12 [b]Is. 40:26
14 [a]Is. 43:9; 45:20

6 "You have heard;[8085] look at[2372]
all this.
And you, will you not declare[5046]
it?
I proclaim to you [a]new things
from this time,
Even hidden things which you
have not known.[3045]
7 "They are created[1254] now and
not long ago;
And before today[3117] you have
not heard[8085] them,
Lest you should say, 'Behold, I
knew[3045] them.'
8 "You have not [a]heard, you have
not known.[3045]
Even from long ago[227] your
ear[241] has not been open,
Because I knew that you would
deal very treacherously;[898]
And you have been called a
[Ib]rebel from [II]birth.[990]
9 "[a]For the sake of My name I
[b]delay[748] My wrath,[639]
And *for* My praise[8416] I restrain
it for you,
In order not to cut you off.[3772]
10 "Behold, I have refined[6884] you,
but [a]not as silver;
I have tested[977] you in the
[b]furnace of affliction.
11 "[a]For My own sake, for My own
sake, I will act;[6213]
For how can *My name* be
profaned?[2490]
And My [b]glory[3519] I will not give
to another.

Deliverance Promised

12 "Listen[8085] to Me, O Jacob, even
Israel [I]whom I called;
[a]I am He, [b]I am the first,[7223] I
am also the last.
13 "Surely My hand[3027] [a]founded[3245]
the earth,[776]
And My right hand spread out
the heavens;[8064]
When I [b]call to them, they stand
together.
14 "[a]Assemble,[6908] all of you, and
listen!

[b]Who among them has declared
these things?
The LORD loves[157] him; he shall
[c]carry out His good
pleasure[2656] on [d]Babylon,
And His arm *shall be against* the
Chaldeans.
15 "I, even I, have spoken;[1696]
indeed I have [a]called him,
I have brought him, and He will
make his ways[1870] successful.
16 "[a]Come near to Me, listen to
this:
From the first[7218] I have [b]not
spoken in secret,
[c]From the time[6256] it took place,
I was there.
And now [d]the Lord[136] [I]GOD has
sent Me, and His Spirit."[7307]
17 Thus says[559] the LORD, your
[a]Redeemer,[1350] the Holy One[6918] of Israel;
"I am the LORD your God, who
teaches[3925] you to profit,
Who [b]leads you in the way you
should go.
18 "If only you had [a]paid attention[7181]
to My commandments![4687]
Then your [I][b]well-being would
have been like a river,
And your [c]righteousness like the
waves of the sea.
19 "Your [I][a]descendants[2233] would
have been like the sand,
And [II]your offspring like its
grains;
[b]Their name would never be cut
off[3772] or destroyed[8045] from
My presence."
20 [a]Go forth from Babylon! Flee
from the Chaldeans!
Declare with the sound of
[b]joyful shouting, proclaim
this,
[c]Send it out to the end of the
earth;
Say, "[d]The LORD has
redeemed[1350] His servant[5650]
Jacob."
21 And they did not [a]thirst when
He led them through the
deserts.[2723]
He [b]made the water flow out of
the rock for them;
He split the rock, and [c]the water
gushed forth.
22 "[a]There is no peace for the
wicked,"[7563] says the LORD.

Salvation Reaches to the End of the Earth

49 Listen[8085] to Me, O [a]islands,
And pay attention,[7181] you
peoples[3816] from afar.
[b]The LORD called[7121] Me from
the womb;[990]
From the [I]body[4578] of My
mother[517] He named Me.
2 And He has made[7760] My
[a]mouth[6310] like a sharp
sword;[2719]
In the [b]shadow of His hand[3027]
He has concealed Me,
And He has also made Me a
[I]select [c]arrow;
He has hidden Me in His quiver.
3 And He said[559] to Me, "[a]You are
My Servant,[5650] Israel,
[b]In Whom I will [I]show My
glory."[6286]
4 But I said, "I have [a]toiled in vain,
I have spent[3615] My strength for
nothing[8414] and vanity;
Yet surely the justice[4941] *due* to
Me is with the LORD,
And My [b]reward with My
God."[430]
5 And now says[559] [a]the LORD, who
formed[3335] Me from the
womb to be His Servant,
To bring Jacob back to Him, in
order that [b]Israel might be
gathered to Him
(For I am [c]honored in the sight
of the LORD,
And My God is My [d]strength),
6 He says, "It is too [I]small a
thing[7043] that You should be
My Servant

---

14 [b]Is. 45:21 [c]Is. 46:10, 11 [d]Is. 13:4, 5, 17-19; Jer. 50:21-29; 51:24
15 [a]Is. 41:2; 45:1, 2
16 [I]Heb., *YHWH, usually rendered* LORD [a]Is. 34:1; 41:1; 57:3 [b]Is. 45:19 [c]Is. 43:13 [d]Zech. 2:9, 11
17 [a]Is. 41:14; 43:14; 49:7, 26; 54:5, 8 [b]Ps. 32:8; Is. 30:21; 49:9, 10
18 [I]Or, *peace* [a]Deut. 5:29; 32:29; Ps. 81:13-16 [b]Ps. 119:165; Is. 32:16-18; 66:12 [c]Is. 45:8; 61:10, 11; 62:1; Hos. 10:12; Amos 5:24
19 [I]Lit., *seed* [II]Lit., *the offspring of your inward parts* [a]Gen. 22:17; Is. 10:22; 44:3, 4; 54:3; Jer. 33:22 [b]Is. 56:5; 66:22
20 [a]Jer. 50:8; 51:6, 45; Zech. 2:6, 7; Rev. 18:4 [b]Is. 42:10; 49:13; 52:9 [c]Is. 62:11; Jer. 31:10; 50:2 [d]Is. 43:1; 52:9; 63:9
21 [a]Is. 30:25; 35:6, 7; 41:17, 18; 43:19, 20; 49:10 [b]Ex. 17:6; Ps. 78:15, 16 [c]Ps. 78:20; 105:41
22 [a]Is. 57:21

1 [I]Lit., *inward parts* [a]Is. 42:4 [b]Is. 44:2, 24; 46:3; Jer. 1:5
2 [I]Or, *sharpened* [a]Is. 11:4; Heb. 4:12; Rev. 1:16; 2:12, 16 [b]Is. 51:16 [c]Hab. 3:11
3 [I]Or, *glorify Myself* [a]Zech. 3:8 [b]Is. 44:23
4 [a]Is. 65:23 [b]Is. 35:4; 59:18
5 [a]Is. 44:2 [b]Is. 11:12; 27:12 [c]Is. 43:4 [d]Is. 12:2
6 [I]Lit., *light*

49:1-6 See note on Isa. 42:1-4.

To raise up the tribes[7626] of
Jacob, and to restore[7725] the
[a]preserved ones of Israel;
I will also make You a [b]light[216]
[II]of the nations[1471]
So that My salvation[3444] may
[III]reach to the [c]end of the
earth."[776]
7 Thus says the LORD, the
[a]Redeemer[1350] of Israel, *and*
its Holy One,[6918]
To the [b]despised One,
To the One abhorred[8581] by the
nation,[1471]
To the Servant of rulers,[4910]
"[c]Kings[4428] shall see and arise,
Princes[8269] shall also [d]bow
down;[7812]
Because of the LORD who is
faithful,[539] the Holy One of
Israel who has chosen[977]
You."
8 Thus says the LORD,
"In a [a]favorable[7522] time[6256] I have
answered You,
And in a day[3117] of salvation I
have helped You;
And I will [b]keep[5341] You and
[c]give You for a covenant[1285]
of the people,[5971]
To [I][d]restore the land, to make
them inherit[5157] the
desolate[8076] heritages;
9 Saying[559] to those who are
[a]bound, 'Go forth,'
To those who are in
darkness,[2822] 'Show[1540]
yourselves.'
Along the roads[1870] they will
feed,
And their pasture will be on all
[b]bare heights.
10 "They will [a]not hunger or thirst,
Neither will the scorching
[b]heat or sun strike them
down;[5221]
For [c]He who has compassion on
them will [d]lead them,
And will guide them to
[e]springs of water.
11 "And I will make[7760] all [a]My
mountains a road,[1870]
And My [b]highways will be raised
up.
12 "Behold, these shall come
[a]from afar;
And lo, these *will come* from the
[b]north and from the west,
And these from the land[776] of
Sinim."
13 [a]Shout for joy, O heavens![8064]
And rejoice, O earth!
Break forth into joyful shouting,
O mountains!
For the [b]LORD has comforted[5162]
His people,
And will [c]have compassion[7355] on
His afflicted.

Promise to Zion

14 But Zion said, "The LORD has
forsaken[5800] me,
And the Lord[136] has forgotten
me."
15 "Can a woman[802] forget her
nursing child,
And have no compassion[7355] on
the son[1121] of her womb?
Even these may forget, but
[a]I will not forget you.
16 "Behold, I have [a]inscribed[2710] you
on the palms *of My hands;*[3709]
Your [b]walls are continually[8548]
before Me.
17 "Your [I]builders[1121] hurry;
Your [a]destroyers[2040] and
devastators[2717]
Will depart from you.
18 "[a]Lift up[5375] your eyes and look
around;[7200]
[b]All of them gather[6908] together,
[c]they come to you.
[d]As I live,"[2416] declares[5001] the
LORD,
"You shall surely [e]put on all of
them as [I]jewels, and bind
them on as a bride.
19 "For [a]your waste[2723] and
desolate[8074] places, and your
destroyed land—
Surely now you will be [b]too
cramped for the inhabitants,

6 [II]Or, *to* [III]Lit., *be* [a]Ps. 37:28; 97:10 [b]Is. 42:6; 51:4; Luke 2:32; Acts 13:47; 26:23 [c]Is. 48:20

7 [a]Is. 48:17 [b]Ps. 22:6-8; 69:7-9; Is. 53:3 [c]Is. 52:15 [d]Is. 19:21, 23; 27:13; 66:23

8 [I]Lit., *establish* [a]Ps. 69:13; 2Cor. 6:2 [b]Is. 26:3; 27:3; 42:6 [c]Is. 42:6 [d]Is. 44:26

9 [a]Is. 42:7; 61:1; Luke 4:18 [b]Is. 41:18

10 [a]Is. 33:16; 48:21; Rev. 7:16 [b]Ps. 121:6 [c]Is. 14:1 [d]Ps. 23:2; Is. 40:11 [e]Is. 35:7; 41:17

11 [a]Is. 40:4 [b]Is. 11:16; 19:23; 35:8; 62:10

12 [a]Is. 49:1; 60:4 [b]Is. 43:5, 6

13 [a]Is. 44:23 [b]Is. 40:1; 51:3, 12 [c]Is. 54:7, 8, 10

15 [a]Is. 44:21

16 [a]Song 8:6; Hag. 2:23 [b]Ps. 48:12, 13; Is. 62:6, 7

17 [I]So ancient versions and DSS; M.T. reads *sons* [a]Is. 10:6; 37:18

18 [I]Lit., *an ornament* [a]Is. 60:4; John 4:35 [b]Is. 43:5; 54:7; 60:4 [c]Is. 49:12 [d]Is. 45:23; 54:9 [e]Is. 52:1; 61:10

19 [a]Is. 1:7; 3:8; 5:6; 51:3 [b]Is. 54:1, 2; Zech. 10:10

And those who [c]swallowed[1104]
you will be far away.
20 "The [a]children of [I]whom you were
bereaved will yet say in your
ears,[241]
'The place is too cramped[6862] for
me;
Make room[5066] for me that I may
live *here*.'
21 "Then you will [a]say in your
heart,[3824]
'Who has begotten[3205] these for
me,
Since I have been bereaved of
my children,
And am [b]barren, an [c]exile and
a wanderer?
And who has reared these?
Behold, I was [d]left[7604] alone;
[I][e]From where did these
come?' "
22 Thus says the Lord [I]GOD,
"Behold, I will lift up My hand
to the nations,
And set up My [a]standard to the
peoples;
And they will [b]bring your
sons[1121] in *their* bosom,
And your daughters will be
carried[5375] on *their* shoulders.
23 "And [a]kings will be your
guardians,
And their princesses[8282] your
nurses.
They will [b]bow down to you
with their faces[639] to the
earth,
And [c]lick the dust[6083] of your
feet;
And *you* will [d]know[3045] that I am
the LORD;
Those who hopefully [e]wait
for[6960] Me will [f]not be put to
shame.[954]
24 "[a]Can the prey be taken from the
mighty man,
Or the captives[7628] of [I]a tyrant
be rescued?"[4422]
25 Surely, thus says the LORD,
"Even the [a]captives[7628] of the
mighty man will be taken
away,
And the prey of the tyrant will
be rescued;
For I will contend[7378] with the
one who contends with
you,
And I will [b]save[3467] your sons.
26 "And I will feed your
[a]oppressors[3238] with their
[b]own flesh,[1320]
And they will become drunk with
their own blood[1818] as with
sweet wine;
And [c]all flesh will know that I,
the LORD, am your
[d]Savior,[3467]
And your [e]Redeemer, the
Mighty One of Jacob."

God Helps His Servant

50 Thus says[559] the LORD,
"Where is the [a]certificate[5612] of
divorce,[3748]
By which I have [b]sent your
mother[517] away?
Or to whom of My creditors did
I [c]sell you?
Behold, you were sold for your
[d]iniquities,[5771]
And for your [e]transgressions[6588]
your mother[517] [f]was sent
away.
2 "Why was there [a]no man[376] when
I came?
When I called,[7121] *why* was there
none to answer?
Is My [b]hand[3027] so short that it
cannot ransom?[6304]
Or have I no power to
deliver?[5337]
Behold, I [c]dry up[2717] the sea with
My rebuke,[1606]
I [d]make[7760] the rivers a
wilderness;
Their fish stink[887] for lack of
water,
And die[4191] of thirst.
3 "I [a]clothe the heavens[8064] with
blackness,[6940]
And I make sackcloth their
covering."

19 [c]Ps. 56:1, 2

20 [I]Lit., *your bereavement* [a]Is. 54:1-3

21 [I]Lit., *These, where are they?* [a]Is. 29:23; 54:6, 7 [b]Is. 27:10; Lam. 1:1 [c]Is. 5:13 [d]Is. 1:8 [e]Is. 60:8

22 [I]Heb., *YHWH*, usually rendered *LORD* [a]Is. 11:10, 12; 18:3; 62:10 [b]Is. 14:2; 43:6; 60:4

23 [a]Is. 14:1, 2; 60:3, 10, 11 [b]Is. 45:14; 60:14 [c]Ps. 72:9; Mic. 7:17 [d]Is. 41:20; 43:10; 60:16 [e]Ps. 37:9; Is. 25:9; 26:8 [f]Ps. 25:3; Is. 45:17; Joel 2:27

24 [I]So ancient versions and DSS; M.T. reads *the righteous*, cf. v. 25 [a]Matt. 12:29; Luke 11:21

25 [a]Is. 10:6; 14:1, 2; Jer. 50:33, 34 [b]Is. 25:9; 33:22; 35:4

26 [a]Is. 9:4; 14:4; 16:4; 51:13; 54:14 [b]Is. 9:20 [c]Is. 45:6; Ezek. 39:7 [d]Is. 43:3 [e]Is. 49:7

1 [a]Deut. 24:1, 3; Jer. 3:8 [b]Is. 54:6, 7 [c]Deut. 32:30; 2Kin. 4:1; Neh. 5:5 [d]Is. 52:3; 59:2 [e]Is. 1:28; 43:27 [f]Jer. 3:8

2 [a]Is. 41:28; 59:16; 66:4 [b]Gen. 18:14; Num. 11:23; Is. 59:1 [c]Ex. 14:21; Is. 19:5; 43:16; 44:27 [d]Josh. 3:16; Is. 42:15

3 [a]Is. 13:10; Rev. 6:12

4 The Lord[136] [I]GOD has given Me
the tongue of [a]disciples,[3928]
That I may know[3045] how to
[b]sustain[5790] the weary one
with a word.[1697]
He awakens *Me* [c]morning by
morning,
He awakens My ear[241] to
listen[8085] as a disciple.
5 The Lord GOD has [a]opened My
ear;
And I was [b]not disobedient,
Nor did I turn back.
6 I [a]gave My back[1460] to those who
strike[5221] *Me,*
And My cheeks to those who
pluck out the beard;
I did not cover My face from
humiliation and spitting.
7 For the Lord GOD [a]helps Me,
Therefore, I am [b]not disgraced;
Therefore, I have set[7760] My
face like [c]flint,
And I know that I shall not be
ashamed.[954]
8 He who [a]vindicates[6663] Me is
near;
Who will contend[7378] with Me?
Let us [b]stand up to each other;
Who has a case against Me?
Let him draw near[5066] to Me.
9 Behold, [a]the Lord GOD helps
Me;
[b]Who is he who condemns[7561]
Me?
Behold, [c]they will all wear out
like a garment;
The moth will eat them.
10 Who is among you that fears the
LORD,
That obeys[8085] the voice of His
[a]servant,[5650]
That [b]walks in darkness[2825] and
has no light?
Let him [c]trust[982] in the name of
the LORD and rely[8172] on his
God.[430]
11 Behold, all you who [a]kindle a fire,
Who [I]encircle yourselves with
firebrands,
Walk in the light[217] of your fire
And among the brands you have
set ablaze.
This you will have from My
hand;
And you will [b]lie down in
torment.

Israel Exhorted

51 "[a]Listen[8085] to me, you who
[b]pursue righteousness,[6666]
Who seek the LORD:
Look to the [c]rock from which
you were hewn,[2672]
And to the [I]quarry[953] from which
you were dug.
2 "Look to [a]Abraham your father,[1]
And to Sarah who gave birth to
you in pain;
When *he* [b]*was* one I called[7121]
him,
Then I blessed[1288] him and
multiplied him."
3 Indeed, [a]the LORD will
comfort[5162] Zion;
He will comfort all her
[b]waste places.[2723]
And her [c]wilderness He will
make[7760] like [d]Eden,
And her desert[6160] like the
[e]garden of the LORD;
[f]Joy and gladness will be found
in her,
Thanksgiving[8426] and sound of a
melody.
4 "[a]Pay attention[7181] to Me, O My
people;[5971]
And give ear[238] to Me, O My
[I]nation;
For a [b]law[8451] will go forth from
Me,
And I will [II]set My [c]justice[4941]
for a [d]light[216] of the peoples.
5 "My [a]righteousness is near, My
salvation[3468] has gone forth,
And My [b]arms will judge[8199] the
peoples;
The [c]coastlands will wait[6960] for
Me,

---

4 [I]Heb., *YHWH,* usually rendered LORD, and so throughout the ch. [a]Is. 8:16; 54:13 [b]Is. 57:19; Jer. 31:25 [c]Ps. 5:3; 88:13; 119:147; 143:8
5 [a]Ps. 40:6; Is. 35:5 [b]Matt. 26:39; John 8:29; 14:31; 15:10; Acts 26:19; Phil. 2:8; Heb. 5:8; 10:7
6 [a]Matt. 26:67; 27:30; Mark 14:65; 15:19; Luke 22:63
7 [a]Is. 42:1; 49:8 [b]Is. 45:17; 54:4 [c]Ezek. 3:8, 9
8 [a]Is. 45:25; Rom. 8:33, 34 [b]Is. 1:18; 41:1; 43:26
9 [a]Is. 41:10 [b]Is. 54:17 [c]Job 13:28; Is. 51:8
10 [a]Is. 49:2, 3; 50:4 [b]Is. 9:2; 26:9; Eph. 5:8 [c]Is. 12:2; 26:4
11 [I]Lit., *gird* [a]Prov. 26:18; Is. 9:18; James 3:6 [b]Is. 8:22; 65:13-15; Amos 4:9, 10

1 [I]Lit., *excavation of a pit* [a]Is. 46:3; 48:12; 51:7 [b]Ps. 94:15; Prov. 15:9 [c]Gen. 17:15-17
2 [a]Is. 29:22; 41:8; 63:16 [b]Gen. 12:1; 15:5; Deut. 1:10; Ezek. 33:24
3 [a]Is. 40:1; 49:13 [b]Is. 52:9 [c]Is. 35:1; 41:19 [d]Gen. 2:8; Joel 2:3 [e]Gen. 13:10 [f]Is. 25:9; 41:16; 65:18; 66:10
4 [I]Or, *people* [II]Lit., *cause to rest* [a]Ps. 50:7; 78:1 [b]Deut. 18:18; Is. 2:3; Mic. 4:2 [c]Is. 1:27; 42:4 [d]Is. 42:6; 49:6
5 [a]Is. 46:13; 54:17 [b]Is. 40:10 [c]Is. 42:4; 60:9

50:4-11 See note on Isa. 42:1-4.

And for My [d]arm they will wait
expectantly.[3176]
6 "[a]Lift up[5375] your eyes to the
sky,[8064]
Then look to the earth[776]
beneath;
For the [b]sky will vanish like
smoke,
And the [b]earth will wear out like
a garment,
And its inhabitants will die[4191]
[I]in like manner,
But My [c]salvation[3444] shall be
forever,[5769]
And My righteousness[6666] shall
not [II]wane.[2865]
7 "[a]Listen to Me, you who know[3045]
righteousness,
A people in whose [b]heart[3820] is
My law;
Do not fear[3372] the [c]reproach[2781]
of man,[582]
Neither be dismayed[2865] at their
revilings.
8 "For the [a]moth will eat them like
a garment,
And the [b]grub will eat them like
wool.
But My [c]righteousness shall be
forever,
And My salvation to all
generations."[1755]
9 [a]Awake, awake, put on strength,
O arm of the LORD;
Awake as in the [b]days[3117] of
old,[6924] the generations[1755] of
long ago.[5769]
[c]Was it not Thou who cut Rahab
in pieces,
Who pierced[2490] the [d]dragon?[8577]
10 Was it not Thou who [a]dried up
the sea,
The waters of the great
deep;
Who made[7760] the depths of the
sea a pathway[1870]
For the [b]redeemed[1350] to cross
over?[5674]
11 So the [a]ransomed[6299] of the
LORD will return,[7725]
And come with joyful shouting
to Zion;

5 [d]Is. 59:16; 63:5
6 [I]Or, *like gnats* [II]Lit., *be broken* [a]Is. 40:26 [b]Ps. 102:25, 26; Is. 13:13; 34:4; Matt. 24:35; Heb. 1:10-12; 2Pet. 3:10 [c]Is. 45:17; 51:8
7 [a]Is. 51:1 [b]Ps. 37:31 [c]Is. 25:8; 54:4; Matt. 5:11; Acts 5:41
8 [a]Is. 50:9 [b]Is. 14:11; 66:24 Is. 51:6
9 [a]Is. 51:17; 52:1 [b]Ex. 6:6; Deut. 4:34 [c]Job 26:12; Ps. 89:10; Is. 30:7 [d]Ps. 74:13; Is. 27:1
10 [a]Is. 11:15, 16; 50:2; 63:11, 12 [b]Ex. 15:13; Ps. 106:10; Is. 63:9
11 [a]Is. 35:10; Jer. 31:11, 12 [b]Is. 60:19; 61:7 [c]Is. 25:8; 60:20; 65:19; Rev. 7:17; 21:1, 4; 22:3
12 [a]Is. 51:3 [b]Ps. 118:6; Is. 2:22 [c]Is. 40:6, 7; 1Pet. 1:24
13 [a]Deut. 6:12; 8:11; Is. 17:10 [b]Job 9:8; Ps. 104:2; Is. 40:22; 45:12, 18; 48:13 [c]Is. 7:4; 10:24 [d]Is. 49:26; 54:14
14 [I]Lit., *one in chains* [a]Is. 48:20; 52:2 [b]Is. 33:6; 49:10
15 [a]Ps. 107:25; Jer. 31:35
16 [I]Lit., *plant* [a]Deut. 18:18; Is. 59:21 [b]Ex. 33:22; Is. 49:2 [c]Is. 66:22
17 [I]Lit., *bowl of the cup of reeling* [II]Lit., *drunk* [a]Is. 51:9; 52:1 [b]Job 21:20; Is. 29:9; 63:6; Jer. 25:15; Rev. 14:10; 16:19
18 [a]Ps. 88:18; 142:4; Is. 49:21

And [b]everlasting[5769] joy *will be*
on their heads.[7218]
They will obtain gladness and
joy,
And [c]sorrow and sighing will flee
away.
12 "I, even I, am He who
[a]comforts[5162] you.
Who are you that you are
afraid[3372] of [b]man[582] who dies,
And of the son[1121] of man[120] who
is made [c]like grass;
13 That you have [a]forgotten the
LORD your Maker,[6213]
Who [b]stretched out the heavens,
And laid the foundations[3245] of
the earth;
That you [c]fear[6342] continually[8548]
all day[3117] long because of the
fury of the oppressor,
As he makes ready[3559] to
destroy?[7843]
But where is the fury of the
[d]oppressor?
14 "The [I][a]exile will soon be set free,
and will not die in the dungeon,[7845]
[b]nor will his bread be lacking.
15 "For I am the LORD your God,[430]
who [a]stirs up the sea and its waves roar
(the LORD of hosts[6635] is His name).
16 "And I have [a]put My words[1697]
in your mouth,[6310] and have [b]covered[3680]
you with the shadow of My hand,[3027]
to [I][c]establish the heavens, to found the
earth, and to say[559] to Zion, 'You are
My people.' "
17 [a]Rouse yourself! Rouse
yourself! Arise, O Jerusalem,
You who have [b]drunk from the
LORD's hand the cup of His
anger;
The [I]chalice of reeling you have
[II]drained to the dregs.[6907]
18 There is [a]none to guide her
among all the sons[1121] she has
borne;
Nor is there one to take[2388] her
by the hand among all the
sons she has reared.
19 These two things have befallen
you;
Who will mourn for you?

The [a]devastation[7701] and destruction,[7667] famine and sword;[2719]
How shall I comfort you?
20 Your sons have fainted,
They [a]lie *helpless* at the head of every street,
Like an [b]antelope in a net,
Full of the wrath of the LORD,
The [c]rebuke[1606] of your God.
21 Therefore, please hear[8085] this, you [a]afflicted,
Who are [b]drunk, but not with wine:
22 Thus says[559] your Lord,[113] the LORD, even your God
Who [a]contends[7378] for His people,
"Behold, I have taken out of your hand the [b]cup of reeling;
The [I]chalice of My anger,
You will never drink it again.
23 "And I will [a]put it into the hand of your tormentors,
Who have said[559] to [I]you,[5315]
'[b]Lie down that we may walk over[5674] you.'
You have even made[7760] your back[1460] like the ground,[776]
And like the street for those who walk over[5674] *it*."

Cheer for Prostrate Zion

52 [a]Awake, awake,
Clothe yourself in your strength, O Zion;
Clothe yourself in your [b]beautiful[8597] garments,
O Jerusalem, the [c]holy[6944] city.
For the uncircumcised[6189] and the [d]unclean[2931]
Will no more come into you.
2 Shake yourself [a]from the dust,[6083] [b]rise up,
O captive Jerusalem;
[c]Loose yourself from the chains around your neck,
O captive[7628] daughter of Zion.
3 For thus says[559] the LORD, "You
were [a]sold for nothing[2600] and you will
be [b]redeemed[1350] [c]without money."

19 [a]Is. 8:21; 9:20; 14:30
20 [a]Is. 5:25; Jer. 14:16 [b]Deut. 14:5 [c]Is. 66:15
21 [a]Is. 54:11 [b]Is. 29:9; 51:17; 63:6
22 [I]Lit., *bowl of the cup of* [a]Is. 3:12, 13; 49:25; Jer. 50:34 [b]Is. 51:17
23 [I]Lit., *your soul* [a]Is. 49:26; Jer. 25:15-17, 26, 28; Zech. 12:2 [b]Josh. 10:24

1 [a]Is. 51:9, 17 [b]Ex. 28:2, 40; 1Chr. 16:29; Ps. 110:3; Is. 49:18; 61:3, 10; Zech. 3:4 [c]Neh. 11:1; Is. 48:2; 64:10; Zech. 14:20, 21; Matt. 4:5; Rev. 21:2-27 [d]Is. 35:8
2 [a]Is. 29:4 [b]Is. 60:1 [c]Is. 9:4; 10:27; 14:25; Zech. 2:7
3 [a]Ps. 44:12; Jer. 15:13 [b]Is. 1:27; 62:12; 63:4 [c]Is. 45:13
4 [I]Heb., *YHWH*, usually rendered *LORD* [a]Gen. 46:6
5 [a]Ezek. 36:20, 23; Rom. 2:24
6 [a]Is. 49:23
7 [I]Or, *well-being* [II]Lit., *good* [III]Or, *is King* [a]Is. 40:9; 61:1; Nah. 1:15; Rom. 10:15; Eph. 6:15 [b]Ps. 93:1; Is. 24:23
8 [I]Lit., *eye to eye* [a]Is. 62:6
9 [a]Ps. 98:4; Is. 44:23 [b]Is. 44:26; 51:3; 61:4 [c]Is. 43:1; 48:20
10 [I]Lit., *And ... earth will see* [a]Ps. 98:1-3; Is. 51:9; 66:18, 19 [b]Is. 45:22; 48:20
11 [a]Is. 48:20; Jer. 50:8; Zech. 2:6, 7; 2Cor. 6:17 [b]Num. 19:11, 16 [c]Lev. 22:2; Is. 1:16

4 For thus says the Lord[136] [I]GOD,
"My people[5971] [a]went down at the first
into Egypt to reside there, then the
Assyrian oppressed them without
cause.
5 "Now therefore, what do I have
here," declares[5001] the LORD, "seeing
that My people have been taken away
without cause?" *Again* the LORD declares, "Those who rule[4910] over them
howl, and My [a]name is continually[8548]
blasphemed[5006] all day[3117] long.
6 "Therefore My people shall
[a]know My name; therefore in that day
I am the one who is speaking,[1696] 'Here
I am.' "
7 How lovely on the mountains
Are the feet of him who brings[1319] [a]good[2896] news,[1319]
Who announces[8085] [I]peace
And brings good news of [II]happiness,
Who announces salvation,[3444]
And says to Zion, "Your [b]God[430] [III]reigns!"[4427]
8 Listen! Your watchmen lift up *their* [a]voices,
They shout joyfully together;
For they will see [I]with their own eyes
When the LORD restores[7725] Zion.
9 [a]Break forth, shout joyfully together,
You [b]waste places[2723] of Jerusalem;
For the LORD has comforted[5162] His people,
He has [c]redeemed Jerusalem.
10 The LORD has bared His holy [a]arm
In the sight of all the nations,[1471]
[I]That [b]all the ends of the earth[776] may see
The salvation of our God.
11 [a]Depart,[5493] depart, go out from there,
[b]Touch[5060] nothing unclean;
Go out of the midst of her,
[c]purify[1305] yourselves,
You who carry[5375] the vessels of the LORD.

12 But you will not go out in [a]haste,
Nor will you go [I]as fugitives;
For the [b]LORD will go before you,
And [c]the God of Israel *will be* your rear guard.*622*

The Exalted Servant

🗝 13 Behold, My [a]servant*5650* will prosper,*7919*
He will be high and lifted up, and [I]greatly [b]exalted.
14 Just as many were astonished*8074* at you, *My people,*
So His [a]appearance*4758* was marred more than any man,*376*
And His form more than the sons*1121* of men.*120*
15 Thus He will [a]sprinkle*5137* many nations,
Kings*4428* will [b]shut their mouths*6310* on account of Him;
For [c]what had not been told*5608* them they will see,
And what they had not heard*8085* they will understand.*995*

The Suffering Servant

53 [a]Who has believed*539* our message?
And to whom has the arm of the LORD been revealed?*1540*
2 For He grew up before Him like a [a]tender [I]shoot,
And like a root out of parched ground;*776*
He has [b]no *stately* form or majesty*1926*
That we should look upon Him,
Nor appearance that we should [II]be attracted*2530* to Him.
3 He was [a]despised and forsaken of men,*376*
A man*376* of [I]sorrows, and [b]acquainted*3045* with [II]grief;
And like one from whom men hide their face,
He was [c]despised, and we did not [d]esteem*2803* Him.
4 Surely our [I]griefs He Himself [a]bore,*5375*
And our [II]sorrows He carried;
Yet we ourselves esteemed*2803* Him stricken,*5060*
[III]Smitten*5221* of [b]God,*430* and afflicted.
5 But He was [I]pierced through*2490* for [a]our transgressions,*6588*
He was crushed*1792* for [b]our iniquities;*5771*
The [c]chastening*4148* for our [II]well-being *fell* upon Him,
And by [d]His scourging we are healed.
6 All of us like sheep have gone astray,*8582*
Each*376* of us has turned to his own way;*1870*
But the LORD has caused the iniquity*5771* of us all
To [I]fall on Him.
7 He was oppressed and He was afflicted,
Yet He did not [a]open His mouth;*6310*
[b]Like a lamb that is led to slaughter,*2874*
And like a sheep that is silent before its shearers,
So He did not open His mouth.
8 By oppression and judgment*4941* He was taken away;

52:12 [I]Lit., *in flight* [a]Ex. 12:11, 33; Deut. 16:3 [b]Is. 26:7; 42:16; 49:10, 11 [c]Ex. 14:19, 20; Is. 58:8

13 [I]Or, *very high* [a]Is. 42:1; 49:1-7; 53:11 [b]Is. 57:15; Phil. 2:9

14 [a]Is. 53:2, 3

15 [a]Num. 19:18-21; Ezek. 36:25 [b]Job 21:5 [c]Rom. 15:21; Eph. 3:5

53:1 [a]John 12:38; Rom. 10:16

2 [I]Lit., *suckling* [II]Lit., *desire* [a]Is. 11:1 [b]Is. 52:14

3 [I]Or, *pains* [II]Or, *sickness* [a]Ps. 22:6; Is. 49:7; Luke 18:31-33 [b]Is. 53:10 [c]Mark 10:33, 34 [d]John 1:10, 11

4 [I]Or, *sickness* [II]Or, *pains* [III]Or, *Struck down by* [a]Matt. 8:17 [b]John 19:7

5 [I]Or, *wounded* [II]Or, *peace* [a]Is. 53:8; Heb. 9:28 [b]Is. 53:10; Rom. 4:25; 1Cor. 15:3 [c]Deut. 11:2; Heb. 5:8 [d]1Pet. 2:24, 25

6 [I]Lit., *encounter Him*

7 [a]Matt. 26:63; 27:12-14; Mark 14:61; 15:5; Luke 23:9; John 19:9 [b]Acts 8:32, 33; Rev. 5:6

🗝 **52:13—53:12** This servant song makes some of the clearest references to the work of Jesus to be found in the O.T. Jesus, Himself, taught His disciples that He fulfilled at least part of it (Lk. 22:37), and several N.T. writers took their cue from Him. Matthew connected Isa. 53:4 with Jesus' healing ministry (Mt. 8:17). John used Isa. 53:1 to explain why not many of the Jews became Jesus' disciples during His ministry (Jn. 12:38). The writer of Hebrews (Heb. 9:28) and John (Rev. 5:6,12; 13:8) made references to Jesus' death by drawing on the words and phrases of the passage. The most extensive use in the N.T., however, is in I Pet. 2:22-25, where Peter completely wove the language of several verses of Isa. 53 into his own sentence structure.

And as for His generation,[1755]
who considered[7878]
That He was cut[1504] off out of
the land[776] of the [I]living,[2416]
[a]For the transgression[6588] of my
people[5971] to whom the
stroke[5061] *was due?*
9 His grave[6913] was assigned with
wicked[7563] men,
Yet He was with a [a]rich man in
His death,[4194]
[b]Because He had [c]done[6213] no
violence,[2555]
Nor was there any deceit[4820] in
His mouth.
10 But the LORD was pleased[2654]
To [a]crush[1792] Him, [Ib]putting *Him*
to grief;
If [II]He would render[7760]
Himself[5315] *as* a guilt
[c]offering,[817]
He will see [d]*His* [III]offspring,[2233]
He will prolong[748] *His* days,[3117]
And the [IV]good [e]pleasure[2656] of
the LORD will prosper in His
hand.[3027]
11 As a result of the [I]anguish[5999]
of His soul,
He will [a]see [II]*it* and be satisfied;
By His [b]knowledge the
Righteous[6662] One,
My Servant,[5650] will justify[6663]
the many,
As He will [c]bear their iniquities.
12 Therefore, I will allot Him a
[a]portion with the great,
And He will divide the booty with
the strong;
Because He poured out
[Ib]Himself to death,
And was [c]numbered with the
transgressors;[6586]
Yet He Himself [d]bore[5375] the
sin[2399] of many,
And interceded for the
transgressors.

The Fertility of Zion

54 "[a]Shout for joy, O barren[6135] one,
you who have borne no *child;*
Break forth into joyful shouting
and cry aloud, you who have
not travailed;[2342]
For the sons[1121] of the
[b]desolate[8074] one *will be*
[c]more numerous
Than the sons of the married
woman,"[1166] says[559] the
LORD.
2 "[a]Enlarge the place of your
tent;[168]
[I]Stretch out the curtains of your
dwellings,[4908] spare not;
Lengthen[748] your [b]cords,
And strengthen[2388] your [c]pegs.
3 "For you will [a]spread abroad to
the right and to the left.
And your [I]descendants[2233] will
[b]possess[3423] nations,[1471]
And they will [c]resettle the
desolate[8077] cities.
4 "Fear[3372] not, for you will
[a]not be put to shame;[954]
Neither feel humiliated, for you
will not be disgraced;
But you will forget the [b]shame
of your youth,
And the [c]reproach[2781] of your
widowhood you will
remember[2192] no more.
5 "For your [a]husband[1166] is your
Maker,
Whose name is the LORD of
hosts;[6635]
And your [b]Redeemer[1350] is the
Holy One[6918] of Israel,
Who is called[7121] the [c]God[430] of
all the earth.[776]
6 "For the LORD has called you,
Like a wife[802] [a]forsaken[5800] and
grieved in spirit,[7307]
Even like a wife[802] of *one's* youth
when she is rejected,"
Says your God.
7 "[I]For a [a]brief moment I forsook
you,
But with great compassion[7356]
I will [b]gather[6908] you.
8 "In an [Ia]outburst of anger[7110]
I hid My face from you for a
moment;
But with everlasting[5769]
[b]lovingkindness[2617] I will

8 [I]Or, *life* [a]Is. 53:5, 12

9 [a]Matt. 27:57-60 [b]Is. 42:1-3 [c]1Pet. 2:22

10 [I]Lit., *He made Him sick* [II]Lit., *His soul* [III]Lit., *seed* [IV]Or, *will of* [a]Is. 53:5 [b]Is. 53:3, 4 [c]Is. 53:6, 12; John 1:29 [d]Ps. 22:30; Is. 54:3; 61:9; 66:22 [e]Is. 46:10

11 [I]Or, *toilsome labor* [II]Another reading is *light* [a]John 10:14-18 [b]Is. 45:25; Rom. 5:18, 19 [c]Is. 53:5, 6

12 [I]Lit., *His soul* [a]Is. 52:13; Phil. 2:9-11 [b]Matt. 26:38, 39, 42 [c]Mark 15:28; Luke 22:37 [d]Is. 53:6, 11; 2Cor. 5:21

1 [a]Gal. 4:27 [b]Is. 62:4 [c]1Sam. 2:5; Is. 49:20

2 [I]Lit., *Let them stretch out* [a]Is. 33:20; 49:19, 20 [b]Ex. 35:18; 39:40

3 [I]Lit., *seed* [a]Gen. 28:14; Is. 43:5, 6; 60:3 [b]Is. 14:1, 2 [c]Is. 49:19

4 [a]Is. 45:17 [b]Jer. 31:19 [c]Is. 4:1; 25:8; 51:7

5 [a]Jer. 3:14; Hos. 2:19 [b]Is. 43:14; 48:17 [c]Is. 6:3; 11:9; 65:16

6 [a]Is. 49:14-21; 50:1, 2; 62:4

7 [I]Lit., *in* [a]Is. 26:20 [b]Is. 11:12; 43:5; 49:18

8 [I]Lit., *overflowing* [a]Is. 60:10 [b]Is. 54:10; 63:7

[c]have compassion[7355] on
you,"
Says the LORD your [d]Redeemer.
9 "For [I]this is like the days of Noah
to Me;
When I swore that the waters
of Noah
Should [a]not [II]flood[5674] the earth
again,
So I have sworn that I will
[b]not be angry[7107] with
you,
Nor will I rebuke[1605] you.
10 "For the [a]mountains may be
removed and the hills may
shake,
But My lovingkindness will not
be removed from you,
And My [b]covenant[1285] of peace
will not be shaken,"
Says [c]the LORD who has
compassion on you.
11 "O [a]afflicted one, storm-tossed,
and [b]not comforted,[5162]
Behold, I will set your stones
in antimony,
And your foundations[3245] I will
[c]lay in [I][d]sapphires.
12 "Moreover, I will make[7760] your
battlements of [I]rubies,
And your gates of [II]crystal,
And your entire [III]wall of
precious[2656] stones.
13 "And [a]all your sons will be
[I]taught[3928] of the LORD;
And the well-being of your sons
will be [b]great.
14 "In [a]righteousness[6666] you will be
established;[3559]
You will be far from [b]oppression,
for you will [c]not fear;
And from [d]terror,[4288] for it will
not come near[7126] you.
15 "If anyone fiercely assails[1481] *you*
it will not be from Me.
[a]Whoever assails you will fall
because of you.
16 "Behold, I Myself have
created[1254] the smith who
blows[5301] the fire of coals,
And brings out a weapon for its
work;
And I have created the
destroyer[7843] to ruin.[2254]
17 "[a]No weapon that is formed[3335]
against you shall prosper;
And [b]every tongue that
[I]accuses you in judgment[4941]
you will condemn.[7561]
This is the heritage[5199] of the
servants[5650] of the LORD,
And their [c]vindication is from
Me," declares[5001] the LORD.

The Free Offer of Mercy

55 "Ho! Every one who [a]thirsts,
come to the waters;
And you who have [b]no
[I]money come, buy and eat.
Come, buy [c]wine and milk
[d]Without money and without
cost.
2 "Why do you [I]spend money for
what is [a]not bread,
And your wages for what does
not satisfy?
Listen carefully[8085] to Me, and
[b]eat what is good,[2896]
And [c]delight yourself[5315] in
abundance.
3 "[a]Incline your ear[241] and come to
Me.
Listen,[8085] that [I]you may
[b]live;[2421]
And I will make [c]an
everlasting[5769] covenant[1285]
with you,
According to the [d]faithful[539]
mercies[2617] [II]shown to David.
4 "Behold, I have made [a]him a
witness to the peoples,[3816]
A [b]leader and commander[6680] for
the peoples.
5 "Behold, you will call[7121] a
[a]nation[1471] you do not
know,[3045]
And a nation[1471] which knows[3045]
you not will [b]run to you,
Because of the LORD your
God,[430] even the Holy
One[6918] of Israel;
For He has [c]glorified[6286] you."

8 [c]Is. 49:10, 13 [d]Is. 54:5
9 [I]Some mss. read *the waters of Noah this is to me* [II]Lit., *cross over* [a]Gen. 9:11 [b]Is. 12:1; Ezek. 39:29
10 [a]Ps. 102:26; Is. 51:6 [b]2Sam. 23:5; Ps. 89:34; Is. 55:3; 59:21; 61:8 [c]Is. 54:8
11 [I]Or, *lapis lazuli* [a]Is. 51:21 [b]Is. 51:18, 19 [c]Is. 14:32; 28:16; 44:28 [d]Job 28:16; Rev. 21:19
12 [I]I.e., bright red [II]Or, *carbuncles* [III]Lit., *border, boundary*
13 [I]Or, *disciples* [a]John 6:45 [b]Is. 48:18; 66:12
14 [a]Is. 1:26, 27; 9:7; 62:1 [b]Is. 9:4; 14:4 [c]Is. 54:4 [d]Is. 33:18
15 [a]Is. 41:11-16
17 [I]Lit., *rises against* [a]Is. 17:12-14; 29:8 [b]Is. 50:8, 9 [c]Is. 45:24; 46:13

1 [I]Lit., *silver* [a]Ps. 42:1, 2; 63:1; 143:6; Is. 41:17; 44:3; John 4:14; 7:37; Rev. 21:6 [b]Lam. 5:4 [c]Song 5:1; Joel 3:18 [d]Hos. 14:4; Matt. 10:8
2 [I]Lit., *weigh out silver* [a]Eccl. 6:2; Hos. 8:7 [b]Ps. 22:26; Is. 1:19; 62:8, 9 [c]Is. 25:6; Jer. 31:14
3 [I]Lit., *your soul* [II]Lit., *of David* [a]Is. 51:4 [b]Lev. 18:5; Rom. 10:5 [c]Is. 61:8 [d]Acts 13:34
4 [a]Ps. 18:43; Jer. 30:9; Hos. 3:5 [b]Ezek. 34:24; 37:24, 25; Dan. 9:25; Mic. 5:2
5 [a]Is. 45:14, 22-24; 49:6, 12, 23 [b]Zech. 8:22 [c]Is. 60:9

6 [a]Seek the LORD while He may
be found;
[b]Call upon Him while He is near.
7 [a]Let the wicked[7563] forsake[5800]
his way,[1870]
And the unrighteous man[376] his
[b]thoughts;[4284]
And let him [c]return[7725] to the
LORD,
And He will have
[d]compassion[7355] on him;
And to our God,
For He will [e]abundantly
pardon.[5545]
8 "For My thoughts are not [a]your
thoughts,
Neither are [b]your ways[1870] My
ways," declares the LORD.
9 "For [a]*as* the heavens[8064] are
higher than the earth,[776]
So are My ways higher than your
ways,
And My thoughts than your
thoughts.
10 "For as the [a]rain and the snow
come down from heaven,[8064]
And do not return[7725] there
without watering the earth,
And making it bear and sprout,
And furnishing [b]seed[2233] to the
sower and bread to the eater;
11 So shall My [a]word[1697] be which
goes forth from My
mouth;[6310]
It shall [b]not return to Me empty,
Without [c]accomplishing[6213] what
I desire,[2654]
And without succeeding *in the
matter* for which I sent it.
12 "For you will go out with [a]joy,
And be led forth with [b]peace;
The [c]mountains and the hills will
break forth into shouts of joy
before you,
And all the [d]trees of the field[7704]
will clap *their* hands.[3709]
13 "Instead of the [a]thorn bush the
[b]cypress will come up;[5927]
And instead of the [c]nettle the
myrtle will come up;
And [I]it will be a [II][d]memorial to
the LORD,
For an everlasting [e]sign which
[f]will not be cut off."[3772]

Rewards for Obedience to God

56 Thus says[559] the LORD,
"[a]Preserve[8104] justice,[4941] and
do[6213] righteousness,[6666]
For My [b]salvation[3444] is about
to come
And My righteousness[6666] to be
revealed.[1540]
2 "How [a]blessed[835] is the man[582]
who does[6213] this,
And the son[1121] of man[120] who
[b]takes hold of it;
Who [c]keeps[8104] from
profaning[2490] the sabbath,[7676]
And keeps his hand[3027] from
doing[6213] any evil."[7451]
3 Let not the [a]foreigner[5236] who
has joined himself to the LORD
say,[559]
"The LORD will surely separate[914]
me from His people."[5971]
Neither let the [b]eunuch[5631] say,
"Behold, I am a dry tree."
4 For thus says the LORD,
"To the eunuchs[5631] who [a]keep
My sabbaths,[7676]
And choose[977] what pleases[2654]
Me,
And [b]hold fast My covenant,[1285]
5 To them I will give in My
[a]house[1004] and within My
[b]walls a memorial,
And a name better[2896] than that
of sons[1121] and daughters;
I will give [I]them an
everlasting[5769] [c]name which
[d]will not be cut off.[3772]
6 "Also the [a]foreigners who join
themselves to the LORD,
To minister[8334] to Him, and to
love[157] the name of the LORD,
To be His servants,[5650] every
one who [b]keeps from
profaning the sabbath,
And holds fast[2388] My covenant;
7 Even [a]those I will bring to My
[b]holy[6944] mountain,
And [c]make them joyful in

6 [a]Ps. 32:6; Is. 45:19; 22; 49:8; Amos 5:6 [b]Is. 58:9; 65:24

7 [a]Is. 1:16, 19; 58:6 [b]Is. 32:7; 59:7 [c]Is. 31:6; 44:22 [d]Is. 14:1; 54:8, 10 [e]Is. 1:18; 40:2; 43:25; 44:22

8 [a]Is. 65:2; 66:18 [b]Is. 53:6

9 [a]Ps. 103:11

10 [a]Is. 30:23 [b]2Cor. 9:10

11 [a]Is. 45:23; Matt. 24:35 [b]Is. 44:26; 59:21 [c]Is. 46:10; 53:10

12 [a]Ps. 105:43; Is. 51:11; 52:9 [b]Is. 54:10, 13; Jer. 29:11 [c]Is. 44:23; 49:13 [d]1Chr. 16:33

13 [I]I.e., the transformation of the desert [II]Lit., *name* [a]Is. 7:19 [b]Is. 60:13 [c]Is. 5:6; 7:24; 32:13 [d]Is. 63:12, 14; Jer. 33:9 [e]Is. 19:20 [f]Is. 56:5

1 [a]Is. 1:17; 33:5; 61:8 [b]Ps. 85:9; Is. 46:13; 51:5

2 [a]Ps. 112:1; 119:1, 2 [b]Is. 56:4, 6 [c]Ex. 20:8-11; 31:13-17; Is. 56:6; 58:13; Jer. 17:21, 22; Ezek. 20:12, 20

3 [a]Is. 14:1; 56:6 [b]Deut. 23:1; Jer. 38:7; Acts 8:27

4 [a]Is. 56:2, 6 [b]Is. 56:6

5 [I]So DSS; M.T. reads *him* [a]Is. 2:2, 3; 56:7; 66:20 [b]Is. 26:1; 60:18 [c]Is. 62:2 [d]Is. 48:19; 55:13

6 [a]Is. 56:3; 60:10; 61:5 [b]Is. 56:2, 4

7 [a]Is. 2:2, 3; 60:11; Mic. 4:1, 2 [b]Is. 11:9; 65:25 [c]Is. 61:10

My house of prayer.[8605]
Their burnt offerings[5930] and their sacrifices[2077] will be acceptable[7522] on [d]My altar;[4196]
For [e]My house will be called[7121] a house of prayer for all the peoples."
8 The Lord[136] [I]GOD, who [a]gathers[6908] the dispersed of Israel, declares,[5001]
"Yet [b]*others* I will gather[6908] to [II]them, to those *already* gathered."[6908]
9 All you [a]beasts[2416] of the field,[7704]
All you beasts in the forest,
Come to eat.
10 His [a]watchmen are [b]blind,
All of them know nothing.
All of them are dumb dogs unable to bark,
[I]Dreamers lying down, who love to slumber;
11 And the dogs are [I][a]greedy, they [II]are not satisfied.
And they are shepherds who have [b]no understanding;[995]
They have all [c]turned to their own way,[1870]
Each one[376] to his unjust gain, to the last one.
12 "Come," *they say,* "let [I]us get [a]wine, and let us drink heavily of strong drink;
And [b]tomorrow will be like today,[3117] only more so."[1419]

Evil Leaders Rebuked

57 The righteous[6662] man perishes,[6] and no man[376] [a]takes[7760] it to heart;[3820]
And devout[2617] men[582] are taken away, while no one understands.[995]
For the righteous man is taken away[622] from [b]evil,[7451]
2 He enters into peace;
They rest in their [I]beds,
Each one who [a]walked in his upright[5228] way.
3 "But come here,[7126] you sons[1121] of a [a]sorceress,[6049]
[b]Offspring[2233] of an adulterer[5003] and [I]a [c]prostitute.[2181]
4 "Against whom do you jest?
Against whom do you open wide your mouth[6310]
And stick out[748] your tongue?
Are you not children of [a]rebellion,[6588]
Offspring of deceit,
5 *Who* inflame yourselves among the [I][a]oaks,
[b]Under every luxuriant tree,
Who [c]slaughter the children in the [II]ravines,
Under the clefts of the crags?
6 "Among the [I][a]smooth *stones* of the [II]ravine
Is your portion, [III]they are your lot;
Even to them you have [b]poured out[8210] a libation,[5262]
You have made[5927] a grain offering.[4503]
Shall I [IV][c]relent[5162] concerning these things?
7 "Upon a [a]high and lofty[5375] mountain
You have [b]made[7760] your bed.
You also went up there to offer[2076] sacrifice.[2077]
8 "And behind the door and the doorpost
You have set up your sign;[2146]
Indeed, far removed from Me, you have [a]uncovered yourself;
And have gone up[5927] and made your bed wide.
And you have made[3772] an agreement[1285] for yourself with them,
You have loved[157] their [I]bed,
You have looked on *their* [II]manhood.
9 "And you have journeyed to the king[4428] with oil[8081]
And increased your perfumes;
You have [a]sent your envoys a great distance,

7 [d]Is. 60:7 [e]Matt. 21:13; Mark 11:17; Luke 19:46
8 [I]Heb., *YHWH,* usually rendered LORD [II]Lit., *him* [a]Is. 11:12 [b]Is. 60:3-11; 66:18-21; John 10:16
9 [a]Is. 18:6; 46:11
10 [I]So DSS; M. T., *Ravers* [a]Ezek. 3:17 [b]Is. 29:9-14; Jer. 14:13, 14
11 [I]Lit., *strong of soul / appetite* [II]Lit., *do not know satisfaction* [a]Is. 28:7; Ezek. 13:19; Mic. 3:5, 11 [b]Is. 1:3 [c]Is. 57:17; Jer. 22:17
12 [I]So DSS and many versions; M. T., *me* [a]Is. 5:11, 12, 22 [b]Ps. 10:6; Luke 12:19, 20
1 [a]Is. 42:25; 47:7 [b]2Kin. 22:20; Is. 47:11; Jer. 18:11
2 [I]I.e., graves [a]Is. 26:7
3 [I]So ancient versions; Heb., *she prostitutes herself* [a]Mal. 3:5 [b]Is. 1:4; Matt. 16:4 [c]Is. 1:21; 57:7-9
4 [a]Is. 48:8
5 [I]Or, *terebinths* [II]Or, *wadis* [a]Is. 1:29 [b]2Kin. 16:4; Jer. 2:20; 3:13 [c]2Kin. 23:10; Ps. 106:37, 38; Jer. 7:31
6 [I]I.e., symbols of fertility gods [II]Or, *wadi* [III]Lit., *they, they* [IV]Or, *repent* [a]Jer. 3:9; Hab. 2:19 [b]Jer. 7:18 [c]Jer. 5:9, 29; 9:9
7 [a]Jer. 3:6; Ezek. 16:16 [b]Ezek. 23:41
8 [I]Or, *lying down* [II]Lit., *hand* [a]Ezek. 23:18
9 [a]Ezek. 23:16, 40

And made *them* go down to
[I]Sheol.[7585]
10 "You were tired out by the length
of your road,[1870]
Yet you did not say,[559] '[a]It is
hopeless.'
You found [I]renewed[2416]
strength,[3027]
Therefore you did not
[II]faint.
11 "Of [a]whom were you worried[1672]
and fearful,[3372]
When you lied,[3576] and did
[b]not remember[2142] Me,
[I]Nor [c]give[7760] *Me* a thought?
Was I not silent even for a long
time[5769]
So you do not fear Me?
12 "I will [a]declare[5046] your
righteousness[6666] and your
[b]deeds,
But they will not profit you.
13 "When you cry out, [a]let your
collection *of idols* deliver[5337]
you.
But the wind will carry all of
them up,[5375]
And a breath will take *them*
away.
But he who [b]takes refuge[2620] in
Me shall [c]inherit[5157] the
land,[776]
And shall [d]possess[3423] My
holy[6944] mountain."
14 And it shall be said,[559]
"[a]Build up, build up, prepare the
way,
Remove *every* obstacle[4383] out
of the way of My
people."[5971]
15 For thus says[559] the [a]high and
exalted[5375] One
Who [I][b]lives[7931] forever,[5703]
whose name is Holy,[6918]
"I [c]dwell[7931] *on* a high and holy
place,
And *also* with the [d]contrite[1793]
and lowly of spirit[7307]
In order to [e]revive[2421] the spirit
of the lowly
And to revive the heart of the
contrite.[1792]

16 "For I will [a]not contend[7378]
forever,[5769]
[b]Neither will I always[5331] be
angry;[7107]
For the spirit would grow faint
before Me,
And the [c]breath[5397] *of those*
whom I have made.[6213]
17 "Because of the iniquity[5771] of his
[a]unjust gain[1215] I was angry
and struck[5221] him;
I hid *My face* and was angry,
And he went on [b]turning
away,[7726] in the way of his
heart.
18 "I have seen[7200] his ways,[1870] but
I will [a]heal him;
I will [b]lead[5148] him and
[c]restore[7999] comfort[5150] to
him and to his mourners,
19 Creating[1254] the [I][a]praise of the
lips.[8193]
[b]Peace, peace to him who is
[c]far and to him who is near,"
Says the LORD, "and I will heal
him."
20 But the [a]wicked[7563] are like the
tossing sea,
For it cannot be quiet,[8252]
And its waters toss up refuse
and mud.
21 "[a]There is no peace," says
[b]my God,[430] "for the wicked."

Observances of Fasts

58 "[a]Cry[7121] loudly, do not hold
back;
Raise your voice like a trumpet,
And declare[5046] to My people[5971]
their [b]transgression,[6588]
And to the house[1004] of Jacob
their sins.
2 "Yet they [a]seek Me day by
day,[3117] and delight to
know[1847] My ways,[1870]
As a nation[1471] that has done[6213]
[b]righteousness,[6666]
And [c]has not forsaken[5800] the
ordinance[4941] of their God.[430]
They ask[7592] Me *for* just[6664]
decisions,[4941]

9 [I]I.e., the nether world

10 [I]Lit., *the life of your hand* [II]Or, *become sick* [a]Jer. 2:25; 18:12

11 [I]Lit., *You did not set it upon your heart* [a]Prov. 29:25; Is. 51:12, 13 [b]Jer. 2:32; 3:21 [c]Ps. 50:21; Is. 42:14

12 [a]Is. 58:1, 2 [b]Is. 29:15; 59:6; 65:7; 66:18; Mic. 3:2-4

13 [a]Jer. 22:20; 30:14 [b]Ps. 37:3, 9; Is. 25:4 [c]Is. 49:8; 60:21 [d]Is. 65:9

14 [a]Is. 62:10; Jer. 18:15

15 [I]Or, *dwells in eternity* [a]Is. 52:13 [b]Deut. 33:27; Is. 40:28 [c]Is. 33:5; 66:1 [d]Ps. 34:18; 51:17; Is. 66:2 [e]Ps. 147:3; Is. 61:1-3

16 [a]Gen. 6:3 [b]Ps. 85:5; 103:9; Mic. 7:18 [c]Is. 42:5

17 [a]Is. 2:7; 56:11; Jer. 6:13 [b]Is. 1:4; Jer. 3:14, 22

18 [a]Is. 19:22; 30:26; 53:5 [b]Is. 52:12 [c]Is. 61:1-3

19 [I]Lit., *fruit of the lips* [a]Is. 6:7; 51:16; 59:21; Heb. 13:15 [b]Is. 26:12; 32:17 [c]Acts 2:39; Eph. 2:17

20 [a]Job 18:5-14; Is. 3:9, 11

21 [a]Is. 48:22; 59:8 [b]Is. 49:4

1 [a]Is. 40:6 [b]Is. 43:27; 50:1; 59:12

2 [a]Is. 1:11; Titus 1:16 [b]Is. 48:1; Jer. 7:9, 10 [c]Is. 1:4, 28; 59:13

They delight[2654] [d]in the nearness
of God.
3 'Why have we [a]fasted and Thou
dost not see?
Why have we humbled
ourselves[5315] and Thou dost
not [I]notice?'[3045]
Behold, on the [b]day of your fast
you find *your* desire,[2656]
And drive hard all your
workers.[6092]
4 "Behold, you fast for
contention[7379] and [a]strife and
to strike[5221] with a wicked[7562]
fist.
You do not fast like *you do* today
to [b]make your voice heard[8085]
on high.
5 "Is it a fast like this which I
choose,[977] a day for a man[120]
to humble himself?
Is it for bowing [I]one's head[7218]
like a reed,
And for spreading out
[a]sackcloth and ashes as a
bed?
Will you call[7121] this a fast, even
an [b]acceptable[7522] day to the
LORD?
6 "Is this not the fast which I
choose,
To [a]loosen the bonds of
wickedness,
To undo the bands of the
yoke,
And to [b]let the oppressed go
free,
And [c]break every yoke?
7 "Is it not to [a]divide your bread
[I]with the hungry,
And [b]bring the homeless poor
into the house;
When you see the [c]naked,[6174]
to cover[3680] him;
And not to [d]hide yourself from
your own flesh?[1320]
8 "Then your [a]light[216] will break out
like the dawn,
And your [b]recovery[724] will
speedily spring forth;
And your [c]righteousness[6664] will
go before you;

2 [d]Ps. 119:151; Is. 29:13; 57:3; James 4:8
3 [I]Lit., *know* [a]Mal. 3:14; Luke 18:12 [b]Is. 22:12, 13; Zech. 7:5, 6
4 [a]Is. 3:14, 15; 59:6 [b]Is. 1:15; 59:2; Joel 2:12-14
5 [I]Lit., *his* [a]1Kin. 21:27 [b]Is. 49:8; 61:2
6 [a]Neh. 5:10-12; Jer. 34:8 [b]Is. 1:17 [c]Is. 58:9
7 [I]Lit., *for* [a]Job 31:19, 20; Is. 58:10; Ezek. 18:7, 16 [b]Is. 16:3, 4; Heb. 13:2 [c]Matt. 25:35, 36; Luke 3:11 [d]Deut. 22:1-4; Luke 10:31, 32
8 [a]Is. 58:10 [b]Is. 30:26; 33:24; Jer. 30:17; 33:6 [c]Ps. 85:13; Is. 62:1 [d]Ex. 14:19; Is. 52:12
9 [I]Lit., *sending out* [a]Ps. 50:15; Is. 55:6; 65:24 [b]Is. 58:6 [c]Prov. 6:13 [d]Ps. 12:2; Is. 59:13
10 [I]Lit., *furnish* [II]Or, *soul* [a]Deut. 15:7; Is. 58:7 [b]Job 11:17; Ps. 37:6; Is. 42:16; 58:8
11 [I]Or, *soul* [II]Or, *deceive* [a]Is. 49:10; 57:18 [b]Ps. 107:9; Is. 41:17 [c]Is. 66:14 [d]Song 4:15; Is. 27:3; Jer. 31:12 [e]John 4:14; 7:38
12 [I]Lit., *paths* [a]Is. 49:8; 61:4; Ezek. 36:10 [b]Is. 44:28 [c]Is. 30:13; Amos 9:11
13 [a]Ex. 31:16, 17; 35:2, 3; Is. 56:2, 4, 6; Jer. 17:21-27 [b]Ps. 27:4; 42:4; 84:2, 10 [c]Is. 55:8

The glory[3519] of the [d]LORD will
be your rear guard.[622]
9 "Then you will [a]call, and the LORD
will answer;
You will cry, and He will say,[559]
'Here I am.'
If you [b]remove the yoke from
your midst,
The [I][c]pointing of the finger, and
[d]speaking[1696] wickedness,[205]
10 And if you [I][a]give yourself to the
hungry,
And satisfy the [II]desire of the
afflicted,
Then your [b]light will rise in
darkness,[2822]
And your gloom[653] *will become*
like midday.
11 "And the [a]LORD will
continually[8548] guide[5148] you,
And [b]satisfy your [I]desire in
scorched places,
And [c]give strength to your
bones;[6106]
And you will be like a [d]watered
garden,
And like a [e]spring of water whose
waters do not [II]fail.[3576]
12 "And those from among you will
[a]rebuild the ancient[5769]
ruins;[2723]
You will [b]raise up the age-old[1755]
foundations;[4146]
And you will be called[7121] the
repairer of the [c]breach,
The restorer[7725] of the
[I]streets in which to dwell.

Keeping the Sabbath

13 "If because of the sabbath,[7676]
you [a]turn[7725] your foot
From doing[6213] your *own*
pleasure on My holy[6944]
day,[3117]
And call the sabbath a
[b]delight, the holy[6918] *day* of
the LORD honorable,[3513]
And shall honor[3513] it, desisting
from your [c]*own* ways,
From seeking your *own*
pleasure,

And [d]speaking *your own*
word,[1697]
14 Then you will take [a]delight in
the LORD,
And I will make you ride
[b]on the heights[1116] of the
earth;[776]
And I will feed you *with* the
heritage[5814] of Jacob your
father,[1]
For the [c]mouth[6310] of the LORD
has spoken."[1696]

Separation from God

59 Behold, [a]the LORD's hand[3027] is
not so short
That it cannot save;[3467]
[b]Neither is His ear[241] so dull[3513]
That it cannot hear.[8085]
2 But your [a]iniquities[5771] have
made a separation[914]
between you and your
God,[430]
And your sins have hidden *His*
[I]face from you, so that He
does [b]not hear.
3 For your [a]hands[3709] are defiled
with blood,[1818]
And your fingers with
iniquity;[5771]
Your lips[8193] have spoken[1696]
[b]falsehood,[8267]
Your tongue mutters[1897]
wickedness.[5766]
4 [a]No one sues[7121] righteously[6664]
and [b]no one pleads[8199]
[I]honestly.[530]
They [c]trust[982] in confusion,[8414]
and speak[1696] lies;[7723]
They [d]conceive mischief,[5999] and
bring forth iniquity.[205]
5 They hatch adders'[6848] eggs and
[a]weave the spider's web;
He who eats of their eggs
dies,[4191]
And *from* that which is crushed
a snake breaks forth.
6 Their webs will not become[1961]
clothing,
Nor will they [a]cover[3680]
themselves with their works;
Their [b]works are works of
iniquity,
And an [c]act of violence[2555] is in
their [I]hands.
7 [a]Their feet run to evil,[7451]
And they hasten to shed[8210]
innocent[5355] blood;
[b]Their thoughts[4284] are thoughts
of iniquity;
Devastation[7701] and
destruction[7667] are in their
highways.
8 They do not know[3045] the
[a]way[1870] of peace,
And there is [b]no justice[4941] in
their tracks;
They have made their paths
crooked;
[c]Whoever treads on [I]them does
not know peace.

A Confession of Wickedness

9 Therefore, [a]justice is far from
us,
And righteousness[6666] does not
overtake us;
We [b]hope for[6960] light,[216] but
behold, darkness;[2822]
For brightness, but we walk in
gloom.[653]
10 We [a]grope along the wall like
blind men,
We grope like those who have
no eyes;
We [b]stumble[3782] at midday as in
the twilight,
Among those who are vigorous
we are [c]like dead[4191] men.
11 All of us growl like bears,
And [a]moan[1897] sadly like doves;
We hope for [b]justice, but there
is none,
For salvation,[3444] *but* it is far
from us.
12 For our [a]transgressions[6588] are
multiplied before Thee,
And our [b]sins [I]testify against us;
For our transgressions are with
us,
And [II]we know our iniquities:

13 [d]Is. 59:13

14 [a]Job 22:26; Is. 61:10 [b]Deut. 32:13; 33:29; Is. 33:16; Hab. 3:19 [c]Is. 1:20; 40:5

1 [a]Num. 11:23; Is. 50:2; Jer. 32:17 [b]Is. 58:9; 65:24; Ezek. 8:18

2 [I]So versions; M. T., *faces* [a]Is. 1:15; 50:1 [b]Is. 58:4

3 [a]Is. 1:15, 21; Jer. 2:30, 34; Ezek. 7:23; Hos. 4:2 [b]Is. 28:15; 30:9; 59:13

4 [I]Lit., *in truth* [a]Is. 5:7; 59:14 [b]Is. 59:14, 15 [c]Is. 30:12; Jer. 7:4, 8 [d]Job 15:35; Ps. 7:14; Is. 33:11

5 [a]Job 8:14

6 [I]Lit., *palms* [a]Is. 28:20 [b]Is. 57:12; Jer. 6:7 [c]Is. 58:4; Ezek. 7:11

7 [a]Prov. 1:16; 6:17; Rom. 3:15-17 [b]Is. 65:2; 66:18; Mark 7:21, 22

8 [I]Lit., *it* [a]Luke 1:79 [b]Is. 59:9, 11; Hos. 4:1 [c]Is. 57:20, 21

9 [a]Is. 59:14 [b]Is. 5:30; 8:21, 22

10 [a]Deut. 28:29; Job 5:14 [b]Is. 8:14, 15; 28:13 [c]Lam. 3:6

11 [a]Is. 38:14; Ezek. 7:16 [b]Is. 59:9, 14

12 [I]Lit., *answer* [II]Lit., *our iniquities we know them* [a]Ezra 9:6; Is. 58:1 [b]Is. 3:9; Jer. 14:7; Hos. 5:5

13 Transgressing[6586] and [a]denying the LORD,
And turning away from our God,
Speaking[1696] [b]oppression and revolt,[5627]
Conceiving *in* and [c]uttering[1897] from the heart[3820] lying words.[1697]
14 And [a]justice is turned back,
And [b]righteousness stands far away;
For truth[571] has stumbled[3782] in the street,
And uprightness[5229] cannot enter.
15 Yes, truth is lacking;
And he who turns aside from evil [a]makes himself a prey.
Now the LORD saw,[7200]
And it was [I]displeasing[7489] in His sight [b]that there was no justice.
16 And He saw that there was [a]no man,[376]
And was astonished[8074] that there was no one to intercede;
Then His [b]own arm brought salvation to Him;
And His righteousness[6666] upheld Him.
17 And He put on [a]righteousness like a breastplate,
And a [b]helmet of salvation on His head;[7218]
And He put on [c]garments of vengeance[5359] for clothing,
And wrapped Himself with [d]zeal[7068] as a mantle.
18 [a]According to *their* [I]deeds, [II]so He will repay,[7999]
Wrath to His adversaries, recompense to His enemies;
To the coastlands He will [III]make recompense.
19 So they will fear[3372] the name of the LORD from the [a]west
And His glory[3519] from the [b]rising of the sun,
For He will [c]come like a [I]rushing stream,
Which the wind of the LORD drives.
20 "And a [a]Redeemer[1350] will come to Zion,
And to those who [b]turn[7725] from transgression[6588] in Jacob,"
declares[5001] the LORD.

21 "And as for Me, this is My
[a]covenant[1285] with them," says[559] the
LORD: "My [b]Spirit which is upon you,
and My [c]words which I have put in your
mouth,[6310] shall not depart from your
mouth, nor from the mouth of
your [I]offspring,[2233] nor from the mouth
of your [I]offspring's[2233] offspring," says
the LORD, "from now and forever."[5769]

A Glorified Zion

60

"[a]Arise, shine; for your [b]light[216] has come,
And the [c]glory[3519] of the LORD has risen upon you.
2 "For behold, [a]darkness[2822] will cover[3680] the earth,[776]
And deep darkness[6205] the peoples;[3816]
But the LORD will rise upon you,
And His [b]glory will appear[7200] upon you.
3 "And [a]nations[1471] will come to your light,
And kings[4428] to the brightness of your rising.
4 "[a]Lift up[5375] your eyes round about, and see;
They all gather[6908] together, they [b]come to you.
Your sons[1121] will come from afar,
And your [c]daughters will be [I]carried[539] in the arms.
5 "Then you will see and be [a]radiant,
And your heart[3824] will [I]thrill[6342] and rejoice;
Because the [b]abundance of the sea will be turned[2015] to you,
The [c]wealth[2428] of the nations will come to you.
6 "A multitude of camels will cover you,

13 [a]Josh. 24:27; Prov. 30:9; Matt. 10:33; Titus 1:16 [b]Is. 5:7; 30:12; Jer. 9:3, 4 [c]Is. 59:3, 4; Mark 7:21, 22

14 [a]Is. 1:21; 5:7 [b]Is. 46:12; Hab. 1:4

15 [I]Or, *evil* [a]Is. 5:23; 10:2; 29:21; 32:7 [b]Is. 1:21-23

16 [a]Is. 41:28; 63:5; Ezek. 22:30 [b]Ps. 98:1; Is. 52:10; 63:5

17 [a]Eph. 6:14 [b]Eph. 6:17; 1Thess. 5:8 [c]Is. 63:2, 3 [d]Is. 9:7; 37:32; Zech. 1:14

18 [I]Lit., *recompense* [II]Lit., *accordingly* [III]Lit., *repay* [a]Job 34:11; Is. 65:6, 7; 66:6; Jer. 17:10

19 [I]Lit., *narrow* [a]Is. 49:12 [b]Ps. 113:3 [c]Is. 30:28; 66:12

20 [a]Rom. 11:26 [b]Ezek. 18:30, 31; Acts 2:38, 39

21 [I]Lit., *seed* [a]Jer. 31:31-34; Rom. 11:27 [b]Is. 11:2; 32:15; 44:3 [c]Is. 55:11

1 [a]Is. 52:2 [b]Is. 60:19, 20 [c]Is. 24:23; 35:2; 58:8

2 [a]Is. 58:10; Jer. 13:16; Col. 1:13 [b]Is. 4:5

3 [a]Is. 2:3; 45:14, 22-25; 49:23

4 [I]Lit., *nursed upon the side* [a]Is. 11:12; 49:18 [b]Is. 49:20-22 [c]Is. 43:6; 49:22

5 [I]Lit., *tremble and be enlarged* [a]Ps. 34:5 [b]Is. 23:18; 24:14 [c]Is. 61:6

The young camels of Midian and
[a]Ephah;
All those from [b]Sheba will come;
They will bring[5375] [c]gold and
frankincense,
And will [d]bear[1319] good news of
the praises[8416] of the LORD.
7 "All the flocks of [a]Kedar will be
gathered[6908] together to
you,
The rams of Nebaioth will
minister[8334] to you;
They will go up[5927] with
acceptance[7522] on My
[b]altar,[4196]
And I shall [Ic]glorify[6286] My
[II]glorious[8597] house.[1004]
8 "[a]Who are these who fly like a
cloud,
And like the doves to their
[I]lattices?
9 "Surely the [a]coastlands will wait
for[6960] Me;
And the [b]ships of Tarshish *will*
come first,[7223]
To [c]bring your sons from afar,
Their silver and their gold with
them,
For the name of the LORD your
God,[430]
And for the Holy One[6918] of
Israel because He has
[Id]glorified[6286] you.
10 "And [a]foreigners will build up your
walls,
And their [b]kings will minister to
you;
For in My [c]wrath[7110] I struck[5221]
you,
And in My favor[7522] I have had
compassion on you.
11 "And your [a]gates will be open
continually;[8548]
They will not be closed day[3119]
or night,[3915]
So that *men* may [b]bring to you
the wealth of the nations,
With [c]their kings led in
procession.
12 "For the [a]nation[1471] and the
kingdom[4467] which will not
serve[5647] you will perish,[6]
And the nations[1471] will be
utterly ruined.[2717]
13 "The [a]glory of Lebanon will come
to you,
The [b]juniper, the box tree,[8410]
and the cypress together,
To beautify[6286] the place of My
sanctuary;[4720]
And I shall make[7760] the
[c]place of My feet glorious.[3513]
14 "And the [a]sons of those who
afflicted you will come bowing
to you,
And all those who despised[5006]
you will bow themselves at
the soles[3709] of your feet;
And they will call[7121] you the
[b]city of the LORD,
The [c]Zion of the Holy One of
Israel.
15 "Whereas you have been
[a]forsaken[5800] and [b]hated[8130]
With no one passing through,
I will make you an everlasting[5769]
[c]pride,
A joy from generation to
generation.[1755]
16 "You will also [a]suck the milk of
nations,
And will suck the breast of kings;
Then you will know[3045] that I,
the LORD, am your
[b]Savior,[3467]
And your [c]Redeemer,[1350] the
Mighty One of Jacob.
17 "Instead of bronze I will bring
gold,
And instead of iron I will bring
silver,
And instead of wood, bronze,
And instead of stones, iron.
And I will make peace your
administrators,
And righteousness[6666] your
overseers.
18 "[a]Violence[2555] will not be
heard[8085] again in your
land,[776]
Nor [b]devastation[7701] or
destruction[7667] within your
borders;
But you will call your [c]walls

6 [a]Gen. 25:4 [b]Gen. 25:3; Ps. 72:10 [c]Is. 60:9; Matt. 2:11 [d]Is. 42:10
7 [I]Or, *beautify* [II]Or, *beautiful* [a]Gen. 25:13 [b]Is. 19:19; 56:7 [c]Is. 60:13; Hag. 2:7, 9
8 [I]Or, *dovecotes, windows* [a]Is. 49:21
9 [I]Lit., *beautified* [a]Is. 11:11; 24:15; 42:4, 10, 12; 49:1; 51:5; 66:19 [b]Ps. 48:7; Is. 2:16 [c]Is. 14:2; 43:6; 49:22 [d]Is. 55:5
10 [a]Is. 14:1, 2; 61:5; Zech. 6:15 [b]Is. 49:23; Rev. 21:24 [c]Is. 54:8
11 [a]Is. 26:2; 60:18; 62:10; Rev. 21:25, 26 [b]Is. 60:5 [c]Ps. 149:8; Is. 24:21
12 [a]Is. 14:2; Zech. 14:17
13 [a]Is. 35:2 [b]Is. 41:19 [c]1Chr. 28:2; Ps. 99:5; 132:7
14 [a]Is. 14:1, 2; 45:14, 23; 49:23; Rev. 3:9 [b]Is. 1:26 [c]Heb. 12:22
15 [a]Is. 1:7-9; 6:11-13; Jer. 30:17 [b]Is. 66:5 [c]Is. 4:2; 65:18
16 [a]Is. 66:11 [b]Is. 19:20; 43:3, 11; 45:15, 21; 63:8 [c]Is. 59:20; 63:16
18 [a]Is. 54:14 [b]Is. 51:19 [c]Is. 26:1

salvation,[3468] and your
[d]gates praise.[8416]
19 "No longer will you have the
[a]sun for light by day,[3119]
Nor for brightness will the moon
give you light;
But you will have the [b]LORD for
an everlasting[5769] light,
And your [c]God for your
[I]glory.
20 "Your [a]sun will set no more,
Neither will your moon wane;[622]
For you will have the LORD for
an everlasting light,
And the days[3117] of your
[b]mourning will be
finished.[7999]
21 "Then all your [a]people[5971] *will be*
righteous;[6662]
They will [b]possess[3423] the land
forever,[5769]
The branch of [I]My planting,
The [c]work of My hands,[3027]
That I may be [d]glorified.
22 "The [a]smallest one will
become[1961] a [I]clan,
And the least one a mighty
nation.
I, the LORD, will hasten it in its
time."[6256]

Exaltation of the Afflicted

61 The [a]Spirit[7307] of the Lord[136]
[I]GOD is upon me,
Because the LORD has
anointed[4886] me
To [b]bring good news[1319] to the
[II][c]afflicted;
He has sent me to [d]bind[2280] up
the brokenhearted,
To [e]proclaim[7121] liberty to
captives,[7628]
And [III]freedom to prisoners;
2 To [a]proclaim the favorable[7522]
year of the LORD,
And the [b]day[3117] of
vengeance[5359] of our God;[430]
To [c]comfort[5162] all who mourn,
3 To [a]grant[776] those who mourn
in Zion,
Giving them a garland instead
of ashes,
The [b]oil[8086] of gladness instead
of mourning,
The mantle of praise[8416] instead
of a spirit of fainting.
So they will be called[7121]
[I][c]oaks of righteousness,[6664]
The planting of the LORD, that
He may be glorified.[6286]
4 Then they will [a]rebuild the
ancient[5769] ruins,[2723]
They will raise up the former[7223]
devastations,[8074]
And they will repair the ruined
cities,
The desolations of many
generations.[1755]
5 And [a]strangers[2114] will stand and
pasture your flocks,
And [I]foreigners[5236] will be your
farmers and your
vinedressers.
6 But you will be called[4121] the
[a]priests[3548] of the LORD;
You will be spoken[7121] of *as*
[b]ministers[8334] of our God.
You will eat the [c]wealth of
nations,[1471]
And in their [I]riches[3519] you will
boast.[3235]
7 Instead of your [a]shame *you will*
have a [b]double *portion,*
And *instead of* humiliation they
will shout for joy over their
portion.
Therefore they will possess[3423]
a double *portion* in their
land,[776]
[c]Everlasting[5769] joy will be
theirs.
8 For I, the LORD, [a]love[157]
justice,[4941]
I hate[8130] robbery [I]in the burnt
offering;[5930]
And I will faithfully[571] give them
their recompense,
And I will make an [b]everlasting
covenant[1285] with them.
9 Then their offspring[2233] will
be known[3045] among the
nations,

18 [d]Is. 60:11
19 [I]Or, *beauty* [a]Rev. 21:23; 22:5 [b]Is. 2:5; 9:2 [c]Is. 41:16; 45:25; Zech. 2:5
20 [a]Is. 30:26 [b]Is. 35:10; 65:19; Rev. 21:4
21 [I]Lit., *His* [a]Is. 45:24, 25; 52:1 [b]Ps. 37:11, 22; Is. 57:13; 61:7 [c]Is. 19:25; 29:23; 45:11; 64:8 [d]Is. 61:3
22 [I]Or, *thousand* [a]Is. 10:22; 51:2
1 [I]Heb., *YHWH,* usually rendered LORD [II]Or, *humble* [III]Lit., *opening to those who are bound* [a]Is. 11:2; 48:16; Luke 4:18 [b]Matt. 11:5; Luke 7:22 [c]Is. 11:4; 29:19; 32:7 [d]Is. 57:15 [e]Is. 42:7; 49:9
2 [a]Is. 49:8; 60:10 [b]Is. 2:12; 13:6; 34:2, 8 [c]Is. 57:18; Jer. 31:13; Matt. 5:4
3 [I]Or, *terebinths* [a]Is. 60:20 [b]Ps. 23:5; 45:7; 104:15 [c]Is. 60:21; Jer. 17:7, 8
4 [a]Is. 49:8; 58:12; Ezek. 36:33; Amos 9:14
5 [I]Lit., *sons of the foreigner* [a]Is. 14:2; 60:10
6 [I]Or, *glory* [a]Is. 66:21 [b]Is. 56:6 [c]Is. 60:5, 11
7 [a]Is. 54:4 [b]Is. 40:2; Zech. 9:12 [c]Ps. 16:11
8 [I]Or, *with iniquity* [a]Is. 5:16; 28:17; 30:18 [b]Gen. 17:7; Ps. 105:10; Is. 55:3; Jer. 32:40

And their descendants in the
midst of the peoples.[5971]
All who see them will
recognize[5234] them
Because they are the [a]offspring
whom the LORD has
blessed.[1288]
10 I will [a]rejoice greatly in the LORD,
My soul[5315] will exult in [b]my
God;
For He has [c]clothed me with
garments of salvation,[3468]
He has wrapped me with a robe
of righteousness,[6666]
As a bridegroom decks[3547]
himself with a garland,
And [d]as a bride adorns herself
with her jewels.
11 For as the [a]earth[776] brings forth
its sprouts,
And as a garden causes the
things sown in it to spring
up,
So the Lord [I]GOD will [b]cause
[c]righteousness and praise
To spring up before all the
nations.[1471]

Zion's Glory and New Name

62 For Zion's sake I will not keep
silent,
And for Jerusalem's sake I will
not keep quiet,[8252]
Until her [a]righteousness[6664]
goes forth like brightness,
And her [b]salvation[3444] like a
torch that is burning.
2 And the [a]nations[1471] will see your
righteousness,
And all kings[4428] your glory;[3519]
And you will be called[7121] by a
new [b]name,
Which the mouth of the LORD
will designate.
3 You will also be a [a]crown of
beauty[8597] in the hand[3027] of
the LORD,
And a royal [I]diadem[6797] in the
hand[3709] of your God.[430]
4 It will no longer be said[559] to
you, "[I][a]Forsaken,"[5800]

9 [a]Is. 44:3

10 [a]Is. 12:1, 2; 25:9; 41:16; 51:3 [b]Is. 49:4 [c]Is. 49:18; 52:1 [d]Rev. 21:2

11 [I]Heb., *YHWH,* usually rendered LORD [a]Is. 4:2; 55:10 [b]Is. 45:23, 24; 60:18, 21 [c]Ps. 72:3; 85:11

1 [a]Is. 1:26; 58:8; 61:11 [b]Is. 46:13; 52:10

2 [a]Is. 60:3 [b]Is. 56:5; 62:4, 12; 65:15

3 [I]Lit., *turban* [a]Is. 28:5; Zech. 9:16; 1Thess. 2:19

4 [I]I.e., Azubah [II]I.e., Shemamah [III]I.e., Hephzibah [IV]I.e., Beulah [a]Is. 54:6, 7; 60:15, 18 [b]Hos. 2:19, 20 [c]Jer. 32:41; Zeph. 3:17

5 [I]Lit., *exultation of the bridegroom* [a]Is. 65:19

6 [a]Is. 52:8; Jer. 6:17; Ezek. 3:17; 33:7 [b]Ps. 74:2; Jer. 14:21; Lam. 5:1, 20

7 [a]Luke 18:1-8 [b]Is. 60:18; Jer. 33:9; Zeph. 3:19, 20

8 [I]Lit., *sons of foreigners* [a]Is. 45:23; 54:9 [b]Lev. 26:16; Deut. 28:31, 33; Judg. 6:3-6; Is. 1:7; Jer. 5:17

9 [a]Is. 65:13, 21-23

10 [I]Lit., *of* [a]Is. 26:1; 60:11, 18 [b]Is. 57:14 [c]Is. 11:16; 19:23; 35:8; 49:11 [d]Is. 11:10, 12; 49:22

Nor to your land[776] will it any
longer be said,
"[II]Desolate";[8077]
But you will be called, "[III]My
delight is in her,"
And your land, "[IV][b]Married";[1166]
For the [c]LORD delights[2654] in
you,
And *to Him* your land will be
married.[1166]
5 For *as* a young man marries a
virgin,[1330]
So your sons[1121] will marry[1166]
you;
And *as* the [I]bridegroom rejoices
over the bride,
So your [a]God will rejoice over
you.
6 On your walls, O Jerusalem, I
have appointed
[a]watchmen;[8104]
All day[3117] and all night[3915] they
will never keep silent.
You who [b]remind the LORD, take
no rest for yourselves;
7 And [a]give Him no rest until He
establishes
And makes[7760] [b]Jerusalem a
praise[8416] in the earth.[776]
8 [a]The LORD has sworn by His
right hand and by His strong
arm,
"I will [b]never again give your grain
as food for your enemies;
Nor will [I]foreigners[5236] drink
your new wine, for which you
have labored."
9 But those who [a]garner it will
eat it, and praise[1984] the
LORD;
And those who gather it will
drink it in the courts of My
sanctuary.[6944]
10 Go through, [a]go through the
gates;
Clear the way[1870] [I]for the
people;[5971]
[b]Build up, build up the
[c]highway;
Remove the stones, lift up a
[d]standard over the peoples.
11 Behold, the LORD has

proclaimed to the [a]end of the earth,
[b]Say[559] to the daughter of Zion,
"Lo, your [c]salvation[3468] comes;
[d]Behold His reward is with Him, and His recompense before Him."
12 And they will call[7121] them, "[a]The holy[6944] people,
The [b]redeemed[1350] of the LORD";
And you will be called, "Sought out, a city [c]not forsaken."

God's Vengeance on the Nations

63 Who is this who comes from [a]Edom,
With [b]garments of [I]glowing colors from [c]Bozrah,
This One who is majestic[1921] in His apparel,
[II]Marching in the greatness of His strength?
"It is I who speak[1696] in righteousness,[6666] [d]mighty to save."[3467]
2 Why is Your apparel red,[122]
And Your garments like the one who [a]treads in the wine press?
3 "[a]I have trodden the wine trough alone,
And from the peoples[5971] there was no man with Me.
I also [b]trod them in My anger,[639]
And [c]trampled them in My wrath;
And [d]their [I]lifeblood[5332] is sprinkled[5137] on My garments,
And I [II]stained all My raiment.
4 "For the [a]day[3117] of vengeance[5359] was in My heart,[3820]
And My year of redemption[1350] has come.
5 "And I looked, and there was [a]no one to help,
And I was astonished[8074] and there was no one to uphold;
So My [b]own arm brought salvation to Me;
And My wrath upheld Me.
6 "And I [a]trod[947] down the peoples in My anger,
And made them [b]drunk in My wrath,
And I [I]poured out their lifeblood[5332] on the earth."[776]

God's Ancient Mercies Recalled

7 I shall make mention of the [a]lovingkindnesses of the LORD, the praises[8416] of the LORD,
According to all that the LORD has granted[1580] us,
And the great [b]goodness toward the house[1004] of Israel,
Which He has granted them according to His [c]compassion,[7356]
And according to the multitude of His lovingkindnesses.
8 For He said,[559] "Surely, they are [a]My people,
Sons[1121] who will not deal falsely."[8266]
So He became their [b]Savior.[3467]
9 In all their affliction [I][a]He was afflicted,
And the [b]angel[4397] of His presence saved[3467] them;
In His [c]love[160] and in His mercy[2551] He [d]redeemed them;
And He [e]lifted them and carried[5375] them all the days[3117] of old.[5769]
10 But they [a]rebelled[4784]
And grieved[6087] His [b]Holy[6944] Spirit;[7307]
Therefore, He turned[2015] Himself to become their enemy,
He fought against them.
11 Then [a]His people remembered[2142] the days of old, of Moses.
Where is [b]He who brought[5927] them up out of the sea with

11 [a]Is. 42:10; 49:6 [b]Matt. 21:5; Zech. 9:9 [c]Is. 51:5 [d]Is. 40:10; Rev. 22:12

12 [a]Deut. 7:6; Is. 4:3; 1Pet. 2:9 [b]Is. 35:9; 51:10 [c]Is. 41:17; 42:16; 62:4

1 [I]Or, *crimson* [II]Lit., *Inclining* [a]Ps. 137:7; Is. 34:5, 6; Ezek. 25:12-14; 35:1-15; Obad. 1-14; Mal. 1:2-5 [b]Is. 63:2 [c]Is. 34:6; Jer. 49:13; Amos 1:12 [d]Zeph. 3:17

2 [a]Rev. 19:13, 15

3 [I]Lit., *juice* [II]Lit., *defiled* [a]Rev. 14:20; 19:15 [b]Is. 22:5; 28:3 [c]Mic. 7:10 [d]Rev. 19:13

4 [a]Is. 34:8; 35:4; 61:2; Jer. 51:6

5 [a]Is. 59:16 [b]Ps. 44:3; Is. 40:10; 52:10

6 [I]Lit., *brought down their juice to the earth* [a]Is. 22:5; 34:2; 65:12 [b]Is. 29:9; 51:17, 21

7 [a]Ps. 25:6; 92:2; Is. 54:8, 10 [b]1Kin. 8:66; Neh. 9:25, 35 [c]Ps. 51:1; 86:5, 15; Is. 54:7, 8; Eph. 2:4

8 [a]Ex. 6:7; Is. 3:15; 51:4 [b]Is. 60:16

9 [I]Another reading is *He was not an adversary.* [a]Judg. 10:16 [b]Ex. 23:20-23; 33:14, 15 [c]Deut. 7:7, 8 [d]Is. 43:1; 52:9 [e]Deut. 1:31; 32:10-12; Is. 46:3

10 [a]Ps. 78:40; 106:33; Acts 7:51; Eph. 4:30 [b]Ps. 51:11; Is. 63:11

11 [a]Ps. 106:44, 45 [b]Is. 51:10

the [I]shepherds of His flock?
Where is He who [c]put His Holy
Spirit in the midst[7130] of
[II]them,
12 Who caused His [a]glorious[8597]
arm to go at the right hand
of Moses,
Who [b]divided the waters before
them to make[6213] for Himself
an everlasting[5769] name,
13 Who led them through the
depths?
Like the horse in the wilderness,
they did not [a]stumble;[3782]
14 As the cattle which go down into
the valley,
The Spirit of the [a]LORD gave
[I]them rest.
So didst Thou [b]lead Thy people,
To make for Thyself a glorious
name.

"Thou Art Our Father"

15 [a]Look down from heaven,[8064]
and see[7200] from Thy holy[6944]
and glorious[8597] [b]habitation;
Where are Thy [c]zeal[7068] and Thy
mighty deeds?
The [d]stirrings of Thy heart[4578]
and Thy compassion are
restrained toward me.
16 For Thou art our [a]Father,[1]
though [b]Abraham does not
know us,
And Israel does not
recognize[5234] us.
Thou, O LORD, art our Father,
Our [c]Redeemer[1350] from of old
is Thy name.
17 Why, O LORD, dost Thou
[a]cause us to stray[8582] from
Thy ways,[1870]
And [b]harden[7188] our heart from
fearing[3374] Thee?
[c]Return[7725] for the sake of Thy
servants, the tribes[7626] of
Thy heritage.[5159]
18 Thy holy people possessed[3423]
Thy sanctuary[4720] for a little
while,

11 [I]Some mss. read *shepherd* [II]Lit., *him* [c]Num. 11:17, 25, 29; Hag. 2:5
12 [a]Ex. 6:6; 15:16 [b]Ex. 14:21, 22; Is. 11:15; 51:10
13 [a]Jer. 31:9
14 [I]Lit., *him* [a]Josh. 21:44; 23:1 [b]Deut. 32:12
15 [a]Deut. 26:15; Ps. 80:14 [b]Ps. 68:5; 123:1 [c]Is. 9:7; 26:11; 37:32; 42:13; 59:17 [d]Jer. 31:20; Hos. 11:8
16 [a]Is. 1:2; 64:8 [b]Is. 29:22; 41:8; 51:2 [c]Is. 41:14; 44:6; 60:16
17 [a]Is. 30:28; Ezek. 14:7-9 [b]Is. 29:13, 14 [c]Num. 10:36
18 [a]Ps. 74:3-7; Is. 64:11
1 [I]Ch. 63:19b in Heb. [a]Ex. 19:18; Ps. 18:9; 144:5; Mic. 1:3, 4; Hab. 3:13 [b]Judg. 5:5; Ps. 68:8; Nah. 1:5
2 [I]Ch. 64:1 in Heb. [a]Ps. 99:1; Jer. 5:22; 33:9
3 [a]Ps. 65:5; 66:3, 5; 106:22
4 [a]1Cor. 2:9 [b]Is. 25:9; 30:18; 40:31
5 [a]Ex. 20:24 [b]Is. 56:1 [c]Is. 26:13; 63:7 [d]Is. 12:1
6 [a]Is. 6:5 [b]Is. 46:12; 48:1 [c]Ps. 90:5, 6; Is. 1:30 [d]Is. 50:1

Our adversaries have [a]trodden
it down.[947]
19 We have become *like* those over
whom Thou hast never
ruled,[4910]
Like those who were not
called[7121] by Thy name.

Prayer for Mercy and Help

64 [I]Oh, that Thou wouldst rend[7167]
the heavens[8064] *and* [a]come
down,
That the mountains might
[b]quake at Thy presence—
2 [I]As fire kindles the brushwood,
as fire causes water to
boil—[1158]
To make Thy name known[3045]
to Thine adversaries,
That the [a]nations[1471] may
tremble at Thy presence!
3 When Thou didst[6213] [a]awesome
things[3372] which we did not
expect,[6960]
Thou didst come down, the
mountains quaked at Thy
presence.
4 For from of old[5769] [a]they have
not heard[8085] nor perceived
by ear,[238]
Neither has the eye seen[7200] a
God[430] besides Thee,
Who acts in behalf of the one
who [b]waits for Him.
5 Thou dost [a]meet[6293] him who
rejoices in [b]doing[6213]
righteousness,[6664]
Who [c]remembers[2142] Thee in
Thy ways.[1870]
Behold, [d]Thou wast angry,[7107]
for we sinned,[2398]
We continued in them a long
time;[5769]
And shall we be saved?[3467]
6 For all of us have become like
one who is [a]unclean,[2931]
And all our [b]righteous deeds are
like a filthy garment;
And all of us [c]wither like a leaf,
And our [d]iniquities,[5771] like the
wind, take[5375] us away.

7 And there is [a]no one who calls[7121]
on Thy name,
Who arouses himself to take hold
of Thee;
For Thou hast [b]hidden Thy face
from us,
And hast [I]delivered us into the
power of our iniquities.
8 But now, O LORD, [a]Thou art our
Father,[1]
We are the [b]clay, and Thou our
potter;
And all of us are the [c]work of
Thy hand.[3027]
9 Do not be [a]angry beyond
measure, O LORD,
[b]Neither remember iniquity[5771]
forever;[5957]
Behold, look now,[4994] all of us
are [c]Thy people.[5971]
10 Thy [a]holy[6944] cities have become
a [b]wilderness,
Zion has become a wilderness,
Jerusalem a desolation.[8077]
11 Our holy and beautiful[8597]
[a]house,[1004]
Where our fathers[1] praised[1984]
Thee,
Has been burned[8316] *by* fire;
And [b]all our precious things have
become a ruin.[2723]
12 Wilt Thou [a]restrain Thyself at
these things, O LORD?
Wilt Thou keep silent and afflict
us beyond measure?

A Rebellious People

65 "I permitted Myself to be sought
by [a]those who did not
ask[7592] *for Me;*
I permitted Myself to be found
by those who did not seek
Me.
I said,[559] 'Here am I, here am
I,'
To a nation[1471] which [b]did not
call[7121] on My name.
2 "[a]I have spread out My hands[3027]
all day[3117] long to a
[b]rebellious[5637] people,[5971]
Who walk *in* the way[1870] which
is not good,[2896] [I]following
their own [c]thoughts,[4284]
3 A people who continually[8548]
[a]provoke[3707] Me to My face,
Offering sacrifices[2076] in
[b]gardens and [c]burning
incense[6999] on bricks;
4 Who sit among graves,[6913] and
spend the night in secret
places;[5341]
Who [a]eat swine's flesh,[1320]
And the broth of unclean
meat[6292] is *in* their pots.
5 "Who say,[559] '[a]Keep to yourself,
do not come near[5066] me,
For I am holier[6942] than you!'
These are smoke in My
[I]nostrils,[639]
A fire that burns all the day.
6 "Behold, it is written before Me,
I will [a]not keep silent, but
[b]I will repay;[7999]
I will even repay into their
bosom,
7 Both [I]their own [a]iniquities[5771]
and the iniquities of their
fathers[1] together," says[559]
the LORD.
"Because they have [b]burned
incense[6999] on the mountains,
And [c]scorned[2778] Me on the hills,
Therefore I will [d]measure their
former[7223] work into their
bosom."
8 Thus says the LORD,
"As the new wine is found in the
cluster,
And one says, 'Do not
destroy[7843] it, for there is
[I]benefit[1293] in it,'
So I will act[6213] on behalf of My
servants
In order [a]not to destroy
[II]all of them.
9 "And I will bring forth
[a]offspring[2233] from Jacob,
And an [b]heir of My mountains
from Judah;
Even [c]My chosen[972] ones shall
inherit[3423] it,
And [d]My servants[5650] shall
dwell[7931] there.

7 [I]Reading with the DSS and versions; M.T., *melted* [a]Is. 59:4; Ezek. 22:30 [b]Deut. 31:18; Is. 1:15; 54:8

8 [a]Is. 63:16 [b]Is. 29:16; 45:9 [c]Ps. 100:3; Is. 60:21

9 [a]Is. 57:17; 60:10 [b]Is. 43:25; Mic. 7:18 [c]Ps. 79:13; Is. 63:8

10 [a]Is. 48:2; 52:1 [b]Is. 1:7; 6:11

11 [a]2Kin. 25:9; Ps. 74:5-7; Is. 63:18 [b]Lam. 1:7, 10, 11

12 [a]Ps. 74:10, 11, 18, 19; Is. 42:14; 63:15

1 [a]Rom. 9:24-26; 10:20 [b]Is. 63:19; Hos. 1:10

2 [I]Lit., *after* [a]Rom. 10:21 [b]Is. 1:2, 23; 30:1, 9 [c]Ps. 81:11, 12; Is. 59:7; 66:18

3 [a]Job 1:11; 2:5; Is. 3:8 [b]Is. 1:29; 66:17 [c]Is. 66:3

4 [a]Lev. 11:7; Is. 66:3, 17

5 [I]Lit., *nose* [a]Matt. 9:11; Luke 7:39; 18:9-12

6 [a]Ps. 50:3, 21; Is. 42:14; 64:12 [b]Jer. 16:18

7 [I]Lit., *your* [a]Is. 13:11; 22:14; 26:21; 30:13, 14 [b]Is. 57:7; Hos. 2:13 [c]Ezek. 20:27, 28 [d]Jer. 5:29; 13:25

8 [I]Lit., *blessing* [II]Lit., *the whole* [a]Is. 1:9; 10:21, 22; 48:9

9 [a]Is. 45:19, 25; Jer. 31:36, 37 [b]Is. 49:8; 60:21; Amos 9:11-15 [c]Is. 57:13 [d]Is. 32:18

10 "And [a]Sharon shall be a pasture
land for flocks,
And the [b]valley of Achor a
resting place for herds,
For My people who [c]seek
Me.
11 "But you who [a]forsake5800 the
LORD,
Who forget My [b]holy6944
mountain,
Who set a table for [I]Fortune,
And who fill *cups* with mixed
wine for [II]Destiny,
12 I will destine you for the
[a]sword,2719
And all of you shall bow down3766
to the [b]slaughter.2874
Because I called, but you
[c]did not answer;
I spoke,1696 but you did not
hear.8085
And you did evil7451 in My sight,
And chose977 that in which I
did6213 not delight."2654
13 Therefore, thus says the Lord136
[I]GOD,
"Behold, My servants shall
[a]eat, but you shall be [b]hungry.
Behold, My servants shall
[c]drink, but you shall be
[d]thirsty.
Behold, My servants shall
[e]rejoice, but you shall be
[f]put to shame.954
14 "Behold, My servants shall
[a]shout joyfully2898 with a glad
heart,
But you shall [b]cry out with a
[I]heavy heart,3820
And you shall wail with a
broken7667 spirit.7307
15 "And you will leave your name
for a [a]curse7621 to My chosen
ones,
And the Lord [I]GOD will slay4191
you.
But [II]My servants will be
called7121 by [b]another name.

10 [a]Is. 33:9; 35:2 [b]Josh. 7:24, 26; Hos. 2:15 [c]Is. 51:1; 55:6
11 [I]Heb., *Gad* [II]Heb., *Meni* [a]Deut. 29:24, 25; Is. 1:4, 28 [b]Is. 2:2, 3; 66:20
12 [a]Is. 27:1; 34:5, 6; 66:16 [b]Is. 63:6 [c]2Chr. 36:15, 16; Prov. 1:24; Is. 41:28; 50:2; 66:4; Jer. 7:13
13 [I]Heb., *YHWH*, usually rendered LORD [a]Is. 1:19 [b]Is. 8:21 [c]Is. 41:17, 18; 49:10 [d]Is. 5:13 [e]Is. 61:7; 66:14 [f]Is. 42:17; 44:9, 11; 66:5
14 [I]Lit., *pain of* [a]Ps. 66:4; Is. 51:11; James 5:13 [b]Is. 13:6; Matt. 8:12
15 [I]Heb., *YHWH*, usually rendered LORD [II]So with Gr.; Heb., *He will call His servants* [a]Jer. 24:9; 25:18; Zech. 8:13 [b]Is. 62:2
16 [I]Or, *bless(es) himself* [a]Ex. 34:6; Ps. 31:5 [b]Is. 19:18; 45:23
17 [I]Lit., *heart* [a]Is. 66:22; 2Pet. 3:13; Rev. 21:1 [b]Is. 43:18; Jer. 3:16
18 [a]Ps. 98; Is. 12:1, 2; 25:9; 35:10; 41:16; 51:3; 61:10
19 [a]Is. 62:4, 5; Jer. 32:41 [b]Is. 25:8; 30:19; 35:10; 51:11; Rev. 7:17; 21:4
20 [I]Lit., *from there* [II]Lit., *fill out* [III]Lit., *one who misses the mark* [a]Deut. 4:40; Job 5:26; Ps. 34:12 [b]Eccl. 8:12, 13; Is. 3:11; 22:14
21 [a]Is. 32:18; Amos 9:14 [b]Is. 30:23; 37:30; Jer. 31:5

16 "Because he who [I]is blessed1288
in the earth776
Shall [I]be blessed1288 by the
[a]God430 of truth;543
And he who swears7650 in the
earth
Shall [b]swear7650 by the God of
truth;
Because the former troubles are
forgotten,
And because they are hidden
from My sight!

New Heavens and a New Earth

🔑 **17** "For behold, I create [a]new
heavens8064 and a new
earth;
And the [b]former things shall not
be remembered2142 or come
to [I]mind.3820
18 "But be [a]glad and rejoice
forever5957 in what I create;
For behold, I create Jerusalem
for rejoicing,
And her people *for* gladness.
19 "I will also [a]rejoice in Jerusalem,
and be glad in My people;
And there will no longer be
heard8085 in her
The voice of [b]weeping and the
sound of crying.
20 "No longer will there be
[I]in it an infant *who lives but
a few* days,3117
Or an old man2205 who does
[a]not [II]live out his days;
For the youth will die4191 at the
age of one hundred
And the [III][b]one2398 who does not
reach the age1121 of one
hundred
Shall be *thought* accursed.7043
21 "And they shall [a]build houses1004
and inhabit *them;*
They shall also [b]plant vineyards
and eat their fruit.

🔑 **65:17** Peter drew on this graphic language as he described what is in store for God's people after the total destruction of the universe following Jesus' second coming (II Pet. 3:13). Further, John's apocalyptic vision of the new Jerusalem was enhanced by allusions to this verse (Rev. 21:1-4).

22 "They shall not build, and
[a]another inhabit,
They shall not plant, and another
eat;
For [b]as the [I]lifetime of a tree,
so shall be the days of My
people,
And My chosen ones shall
[c]wear out the work of their
hands.
23 "They shall [a]not labor in vain,
Or bear *children* for calamity;[928]
For they are the [Ib]offspring of
those blessed[1288] by the
LORD,
And their descendants with
them.
24 "It will also come to pass that
before they call, I will [a]answer; and while
they are still speaking,[1696] I will hear.
25 "The [a]wolf and the lamb shall
graze together, and the [b]lion shall eat
straw like the ox; and [c]dust[6083] shall be
the serpent's[5175] food. They shall
[d]do no evil[7489] or harm in all My [e]holy
mountain," says the LORD.

Heaven Is God's Throne

66 Thus says[559] the LORD,
"[a]Heaven[8064] is My throne,[3678]
and the earth[776] is My
footstool.
Where then is a [b]house[1004] you
could build for Me?
And where is a place that
[I]I may rest?
2 "For [a]My hand[3027] made[6213] all
these things,
Thus all these things came into
being," declares[5001] the
LORD.
"But to this one I will look,

22 [I]Lit., *days* [a]Is. 62:8, 9 [b]Ps. 92:12-14 [c]Ps. 21:4; 91:16

23 [I]Lit., *seed* [a]Deut. 28:3-12; Is. 55:2 [b]Is. 61:9; Jer. 32:38, 39; Acts 2:39

24 [a]Ps. 91:15; Is. 55:6; 58:9; Dan. 9:20-23; 10:12

25 [a]Is. 11:6 [b]Is. 11:7 [c]Gen. 3:14; Mic. 7:17 [d]Is. 11:9; Mic. 4:3 [e]Is. 65:11

1 [I]Lit., *is My resting place?* [a]1Kin. 8:27; Ps. 11:4; Matt. 5:34, 35; 23:22 [b]2Sam. 7:5-7; Jer. 7:4; John 4:20, 21; Acts 7:48-50

2 [a]Is. 40:26 [b]Ps. 34:18; Is. 57:15; Matt. 5:3, 4; Luke 18:13, 14 [c]Ps. 119:120; Is. 66:5

3 [I]Lit., *offers a memorial of incense* [a]Is. 65:4 [b]Lev. 2:2; Is. 1:13 [c]Is. 57:17; 65:2 [d]Is. 44:19

4 [I]Lit., *ill treatments* [a]Prov. 1:31, 32; Is. 65:7 [b]Prov. 10:24 [c]Prov. 1:24; Is. 65:12; Jer. 7:13 [d]2Kin. 21:2, 6; Is. 59:7; 65:12; Jer. 7:30

5 [a]Is. 66:2 [b]Ps. 38:20; Is. 60:15 [c]Matt. 5:10-12; 10:22; John 9:34; 15:18-20

To him who is humble and
[b]contrite[5223] of spirit,[7307] and
who [c]trembles[2730] at My
word.[1697]

Hypocrisy Rebuked

3 "*But* he who kills[7819] an ox is
like one who slays[5221] a
man;[376]
He who sacrifices[2076] a lamb is
like the one who breaks a
dog's neck;
He who offers[5927] a grain
offering[4503] *is like one who
offers* [a]swine's blood;[1818]
He who [Ib]burns[2142] incense is
like the one who blesses[1288]
an idol.
As they have chosen[977] their
[c]*own* ways,[1870]
And their soul[5315] delights[2654] in
their [d]abominations,[8251]
4 So I will [a]choose[977] their
[I]punishments,[8586]
And I will [b]bring on them what
they dread.[4035]
Because I called,[7121] but [c]no one
answered;
I spoke,[1696] but they did not
listen.[8085]
And they did[6213] [d]evil[7451] in My
sight,
And chose[977] that in which I did
not delight."[2654]
5 Hear the word of the LORD, you
who [a]tremble[2730] at His word:
"Your brothers[251] who
[b]hate[8130] you, who [c]exclude
you for My name's sake,
Have said,[559] 'Let the LORD be
glorified,[3513] that we may
see[7200] your joy.'

66:1,2 One of the mistakes which Israel made at times was to place too great an importance on the temple. This was particularly the case during Jermiah's day, when the people's belief in the indestructibility of the temple nearly led them to murder Jeremiah for his oracle against the temple (Jer. 7:2-15; 26:4-9). Jesus later issued His own oracle against the improper use of the temple, drawing on Jeremiah's denunciation (Jer. 7:11), and it contributed to the death plot against Him (Mk. 11:18). These verses in Isaiah help put the temple in proper perspective, something which Solomon had already done in his prayer at the temple's dedication (I Kgs. 8:27; II Chr. 6:18). Stephen, the first Christian martyr, was accused of speaking against the temple (Acts 6:13), so he clarified his position by quoting from Isa. 66:1,2 (Acts 7:49,50), but the Sanhedrin was not receptive to his words.

But [d]they will be put to shame.[954]
6 "A voice of uproar[7588] from the city, a voice from the temple,[1964]
The voice of the LORD who is [a]rendering recompense to His enemies.
7 "Before she travailed, [a]she brought forth;
Before her pain came, [b]she gave birth to a boy.
8 "[a]Who has heard[8085] such a thing? Who has seen[7200] such things?
Can a land be [I]born in one day?[3117]
Can a nation[1471] be brought forth all at once?
As soon as Zion travailed,[2342] she also brought forth her sons.[1121]
9 "Shall I bring to the point of birth, and [a]not give delivery?" says the LORD.
"Or shall I who gives delivery shut *the womb?*" says your God.[430]

Joy in Jerusalem's Future

10 "Be [a]joyful with Jerusalem and rejoice for her, all you who [b]love[157] her;
Be exceedingly [c]glad with her, all you who mourn over her,
11 That you may nurse and [a]be satisfied with her comforting[8575] breasts,
That you may suck and be delighted with her [b]bountiful bosom."[3519]
12 For thus says the LORD, "Behold, I extend [a]peace to her like a river,
And the [b]glory of the nations[1471] like an overflowing[7857] stream;
And you shall [I]be nursed, you shall be [c]carried[5375] on the [II]hip and fondled on the knees.

5 [d]Luke 13:17
6 [a]Is. 59:18; 65:6; Joel 3:7
7 [a]Is. 37:3; 54:1 [b]Rev. 12:5
8 [I]Lit., *travailed with* [a]Is. 64:4
9 [a]Is. 37:3
10 [a]Deut. 32:43; Is. 65:18; Rom. 15:10 [b]Ps. 26:8; 122:6 [c]Ps. 137:6
11 [a]Is. 49:23; 60:16; Joel 3:18 [b]Is. 60:1, 2; 62:2
12 [I]Lit., *nurse* [II]Lit., *side* [a]Ps. 72:3, 7; Is. 48:18 [b]Is. 60:5; 61:6 [c]Is. 60:4
13 [a]Is. 12:1; 40:1, 2; 49:13; 51:3; 2Cor. 1:3, 4
14 [a]Is. 33:20 [b]Zech. 10:7 [c]Prov. 3:8; Is. 58:11 [d]Ezra 7:9; 8:31 [e]Is. 10:5; 13:5; 34:2
15 [a]Is. 10:17; 30:27, 33; 31:9 [b]Ps. 68:17; Is. 5:28; Hab. 3:8
16 [a]Is. 30:30; Ezek. 38:22 [b]Is. 65:12; Ezek. 38:21
17 [I]Lit., *After* [a]Is. 1:29; 65:3 [b]Lev. 11:7; Is. 65:4 [c]Is. 1:28, 31
18 [I]So with Gr.; Heb. omits *know* [II]Lit., *it is coming* [a]Is. 59:7; 65:2 [b]Is. 45:22-25; Jer. 3:17
19 [I]So with Gr.; Heb., *Pul* [II]So with Gr.; Heb., *those who draw the bow* [III]I.e., Greece [a]Is. 11:10, 12; 49:22; 62:10 [b]Is. 2:16; 60:9 [c]Ezek. 27:10 [d]Gen. 10:2 [e]Is. 11:11; 24:15; 60:9 [f]1Chr. 16:24; Is. 42:12
20 [a]Is. 43:6; 49:22; 60:4

13 "As one[376] whom his mother[5172] comforts,[5162] so I will [a]comfort[5162] you;
And you shall be comforted[5162] in Jerusalem."
14 Then you shall [a]see *this,* and your [b]heart[3820] shall be glad,
And your [c]bones[6106] shall flourish like the new grass;
And the [d]hand of the LORD shall be made known[3045] to His servants,[5650]
But He shall be [e]indignant[2194] toward His enemies.
15 For behold, the LORD will come in [a]fire
And His [b]chariots like the whirlwind,
To render[7725] His anger[639] with fury,
And His rebuke[1606] with flames of fire.
16 For the LORD will execute judgment by [a]fire
And by His [b]sword[2719] on all flesh,[1320]
And those slain[2491] by the LORD will be many.
17 "Those who sanctify[6942] and purify[2891] themselves *to go* to the [a]gardens,
[I]Following one in the center,
Who eat [b]swine's flesh, detestable things,[8263] and mice,
Shall [c]come to an end[5486] altogether," declares the LORD.
18 "For I [I]know[3045] their works
and their [a]thoughts;[4284] [II]the time is
coming to [b]gather[6908] all nations[1471] and
tongues. And they shall come and see
My glory.
19 "And I will set[7760] a [a]sign among
them and will send survivors from them
to the nations: [b]Tarshish, [I]Put, [c]Lud,
[II]Meshech, Rosh, [d]Tubal, and [III]Javan,
to the distant [e]coastlands that have neither heard My fame nor seen My glory.
And they will [f]declare[5046] My glory
among the nations.
20 "Then they shall [a]bring all your

brethren from all the nations as a grain offering[4503] to the LORD, on horses, in chariots, in litters, on mules, and on camels, to My [b]holy[6944] mountain Jerusalem," says the LORD, "just as the sons of Israel bring their grain offering in a [c]clean[2889] vessel to the house of the LORD.

21 "I will also take some of them for [a]priests[3548] *and* for Levites," says the LORD.

22 "For just as the [a]new heavens[8064]
and the new earth
Which I make[6213] will endure
before Me," declares the
LORD,
"So your [b]offspring[2233] and your
[c]name will endure.

20 [b]Is. 2:2, 3; 11:9; 56:7; 65:11, 25 [c]Is. 52:11
21 [a]Ex. 19:6; Is. 61:6; 1Pet. 2:5, 9
22 [a]Is. 65:17; Heb. 12:26, 27; 2Pet. 3:13; Rev. 21:1 [b]Is. 61:8, 9; 65:22, 23; John 10:27-29; 1Pet. 1:4, 5 [c]Is. 56:5
23 [I]Lit., *flesh* [a]Is. 1:13, 14; Ezek. 46:1, 6 [b]Is. 19:21, 23; 27:13; 49:7
24 [I]Or, *rebelled* [II]Lit., *flesh* [a]Is. 5:25; 34:3 [b]Is. 1:28; 24:20 [c]Is. 14:11; Mark 9:48 [d]Is. 1:31; Matt. 3:12 [e]Dan. 12:2

23 "And it shall be from [a]new moon
to new moon
And from sabbath[7676] to sabbath,
All [I]mankind will come to
[b]bow down[7812] before Me,"
says the LORD.
24 "Then they shall go forth and
look
On[7200] the [a]corpses[6297] of the
men[582]
Who have [I][b]transgressed[6586]
against Me.
For their [c]worm shall not die,[4191]
[d]And their fire shall not be
quenched;
And they shall be an
[e]abhorrence[1860] to all
[II]mankind."

The Book of JEREMIAH

Jeremiah came from a priestly family in Anathoth, a suburb of Jerusalem. As the author of the longest prophetic book, his career spanned more than forty years during the reigns of Judah's last five kings and beyond. Jeremiah was called by God when he was still a young man, and throughout his long, turbulent life constantly had to confront a people who had rejected God for false gods. He warned them that this would cause their destruction, but they refused to repent, so Jerusalem and the temple were destroyed and the people were deported to Babylon. In his famous temple sermon, he told the people that the temple was vulnerable and nearly lost his life for it. Jesus later drew from this sermon. Before Jerusalem fell, Jeremiah had to deal with lying prophets predicting deliverance and was treated as a traitor. In a letter to those already in exile, he warned about the false prophets in Babylon and told the people to settle down for a long stay, giving them instructions for preserving their identity. When the city fell, the Babylonians gave Jeremiah the option of remaining in Judah. He chose to stay, but a band of Jews forced him to go to Egypt, where tradition has it that he died. Even in Egypt he had to prophesy against worshiping other gods. Jeremiah was one of the most colorful of the prophets, using visual aids to reinforce his messages. He was also one of the saddest, because his burden was so heavy. The people would not listen to him, and even some of his own townspeople and relatives, opposed him and tried to kill him. He had periods of depression over his failure. He did not want to be a prophet in the first place, but the urgency of his message was like a fire raging within him, and he could not contain it (20:9). His life is an example of total faithfulness to God, regardless of personal desires or circumstances.

Jeremiah's Call and Commission

1 🔑 The words[1697] of [a]Jeremiah, the son[1121] of Hilkiah, of the priests[3548] who were in [b]Anathoth in the land[776] of Benjamin,

2 to whom the word[1697] of the LORD came in the days[3117] of [a]Josiah, the son of [b]Amon, king[4428] of Judah, in the [c]thirteenth year of his reign.[4427]

3 It came also in the days of [a]Jehoiakim, the son of Josiah, king of Judah, until the end of the eleventh year of [b]Zedekiah, the son of Josiah, king of Judah, until the exile[1540] of Jerusalem in the fifth month.

4 Now the word of the LORD came to me saying,

🔑 5 "Before I [a]formed you in the
womb I knew[3045] you,
And [b]before you were born I
consecrated[6942] you;
I have [c]appointed you a
prophet[5030] to the
nations."[1471]

1 [a]2Chr. 35:25; 36:12, 21, 22; Ezra 1:1; Dan. 9:2; Matt. 2:17; 16:14; 27:9 [b]Josh. 21:18; 1Kin. 2:26; 1Chr. 6:60; Is. 10:30; Jer. 11:21; 32:7
2 [a]1Kin. 13:2; 2Kin. 21:24; 22:3; 2Chr. 34:1; Jer. 3:6; 36:2 [b]2Kin. 21:18, 24 [c]Jer. 25:3
3 [a]2Kin. 23:34; 1Chr. 3:15; 2Chr. 36:5-8; Jer. 25:1 [b]2Kin. 24:17; 1Chr. 3:15; 2Chr. 36:11-13; Jer. 39:2
5 [a]Ps. 139:15, 16 [b]Is. 49:1, 5; Luke 1:15 [c]Jer. 1:10; 25:15-26

🔑 **1:1** Anathoth was about three miles northeast of Jerusalem and was one of the cities originally given to the priests after the conquest of Canaan (Josh. 21:18). It had been the home of Abiathar, the priest and close associate of King David, and he was banished there by Solomon because he had backed the unsuccessful attempt by Adonijah to succeed David (I Kgs. 2:26).

🔑 **1:5** This verse forms part of the important O.T. background for Paul's call to be an apostle to the Gentiles (Gal. 1:15,16). Both Paul and Jeremiah were selected for their ministries before their births, and both had a specific mission to the Gentiles. Jeremiah's call is also reminiscent of two others in the O.T. His reluctance because he did not know how to speak (1:6) sounds somewhat like that of Moses at the burning bush (Ex. 4:10), although Moses was an eighty-year-old man, whereas Jeremiah attributed his inability to his young age. At Isaiah's call, a seraph touched his mouth with a hot coal to cleanse him (Isa. 6:6,7). In Jeremiah's case, the Lord touched his mouth to deposit His message (1:9).

6 Then [a]I said,[559] "Alas, Lord[136]
[I]GOD!
Behold, I do not know how to
speak,[1696]
Because [b]I am a youth."
7 But the LORD said to me,
"Do not say,[559] 'I am a youth,'
[a]Because everywhere I send
you, you shall go,
And [b]all that I command[6680] you,
you shall speak.
8 "[a]Do not be afraid[3372] of them,
For [b]I am with you to deliver[5337]
you," declares[5001] the LORD.
9 Then the LORD stretched out His
hand[3027] and [a]touched[5060] my mouth,[6310]
and the LORD said to me,
"Behold, I have [b]put My words
in your mouth.
10 "See, [a]I have appointed you this
day[3117] over the nations and
over the kingdoms,[4467]
[b]To pluck up and to break
down,[5422]
To destroy[6] and to
overthrow,[2040]
[c]To build and to plant."

The Almond Rod and Boiling Pot

11 And the word of the LORD came
to me saying, "What do you see,
[a]Jeremiah?" And I said, "I see a rod of
an [I]almond tree."
12 Then the LORD said to me, "You
have seen[7200] well,[3190] for [a]I am [I]watch-
ing over My word to perform[6213] it."
13 And the word of the LORD came
to me a second time saying, "[a]What do
you see?" And I said, "I see a boiling
[b]pot, facing away from the north."
14 Then the LORD said to me, "[a]Out
of the north the evil[7451] [I]will break forth
on all the inhabitants of the land.
15 "For, behold, I am calling[7121]
[a]all the families[4940] of the kingdoms of
the north," declares the LORD; "and they
will come, and they will [b]set each one[376]
his throne[3678] at the entrance of the
gates of Jerusalem, and against all its
walls round about, and against all the
[c]cities of Judah.
16 "And I will [I]pronounce My
judgments[4941] on them concerning all
their wickedness,[7451] whereby they
have [a]forsaken[5800] Me and have [II][b]of-
fered sacrifices[6999] to other gods,[430] and
worshiped[7812] the [c]works of their own
hands.[3027]
17 "Now, [a]gird up your loins, and
arise, and speak to them all which I command you. [b]Do not be dismayed[2865] before them, lest I dismay[2865] you before
them.
18 "Now behold, I have made you
today as a fortified city, and as a pillar
of iron and as walls of bronze against
the whole land, to the kings[4428] of Judah,
to its princes,[8269] to its priests and to
the people[5971] of the land.
19 "And they will fight against you,
but they will not overcome you, for
[a]I am with you to deliver you," declares
the LORD.

Judah's Apostasy

2 Now the word[1697] of the LORD came
to me saying,
🔑 2 "Go and [a]proclaim[2199] in the
ears[241] of Jerusalem, saying, 'Thus
says[559] the LORD,
"I remember[2142] concerning you
the [I][b]devotion[2617] of your
youth,
The love[160] of your
betrothals,[3623]
[c]Your following after Me in the
wilderness,
Through a land[776] not sown.

6 [I]Heb., *YHWH*, usually rendered LORD [a]Ex. 4:10 [b]1Kin. 3:7
7 [a]Ezek. 2:3, 4 [b]Num. 22:20; Jer. 1:17
8 [a]Ex. 3:12; Deut. 31:6; Josh. 1:5; Jer. 15:20 [b]Ezek. 2:6
9 [a]Is. 6:7; Mark 7:33-35 [b]Ex. 4:11-16; Deut. 18:18; Is. 51:16
10 [a]Rev. 11:3-6 [b]Jer. 18:7-10; Ezek. 32:18; 2Cor. 10:4 [c]Is. 44:26-28; Jer. 24:6; 31:28, 40
11 [I]Heb., *shaqed* [a]Jer. 24:3; Amos 7:8
12 [I]Heb., *shoqed* [a]Jer. 31:28
13 [a]Zech. 4:2 [b]Ezek. 11:3, 7
14 [I]Lit., *will be opened* [a]Is. 41:25; Jer. 4:6; 10:22
15 [a]Jer. 25:9 [b]Is. 22:7; Jer. 39:3 [c]Jer. 4:16; 9:11
16 [I]Lit., *speak* [II]Or, *burned incense* [a]Deut. 28:20 [b]Jer. 7:9; 19:4; 44:17 [c]Is. 2:8; 37:19; Jer. 10:3-5
17 [a]1Kin. 18:46; Job 38:3 [b]Ezek. 2:6; 3:16-18
19 [a]Num. 14:9; Jer. 1:8; 20:11

2 [I]Or, *lovingkindness* [a]Is. 58:1; Jer. 7:2; 11:6 [b]Ezek. 16:8; Hos. 2:15 [c]Deut. 2:7; Jer. 2:6

🔑 **2:2** This verse offers one of the most telling commentaries on how low the people of Jeremiah's day had sunk. God looked back longingly to the period of Israel's wandering in the wilderness, as if it were a honeymoon with His bride. The passage is very similar to one written a little more than 100 years earlier to Israel, the northern kingdom, who was also God's bride (Hos. 2:15). In the next chapter Jeremiah depicted Israel and Judah as sisters, both of them married to the Lord. Israel had played the harlot, and God divorced her. Now Judah's guilt was worse than hers (3:6-11).

3 "Israel was [a]holy to the LORD,
The [b]first[7235] of His harvest;
[c]All who ate of it became guilty;[816]
Evil[7451] came upon them,"
declares[5001] the LORD.' "

4 Hear[8085] the word of the LORD,
O house[1004] of Jacob, and all the
families[4940] of the house of Israel.

5 Thus says the LORD,
"[a]What injustice[5766] did your fathers[1] find in Me,
That they went far from Me
And walked after [b]emptiness and became empty?
6 "And they did not say,[559] 'Where is the LORD
Who [a]brought us up[5927] out of the land of Egypt,
Who [b]led us through the wilderness,
Through a land of deserts and of pits,[7745]
Through a land of drought and of [I]deep darkness,[6757]
Through a land that no one[376] crossed[5674]
And where no man[120] dwelt?'
7 "And I brought you into the [a]fruitful land,[776]
To eat its fruit and its good things.
But you came and [b]defiled[2930] My land,
And My inheritance[5159] you made[7760] an abomination.[8441]
8 "The [a]priests[3548] did not say,
'Where is the LORD?'
And those who handle the law[8451] [b]did not know[3045] Me;
The [I]rulers also transgressed[6586] against Me,
And the [c]prophets[5030] prophesied[5012] by Baal
And walked after [d]things that did not profit.

9 "Therefore I will yet [a]contend[7378] with you," declares the LORD,
"And with your sons' sons[1121] I will contend.
10 "For [a]cross to[5674] the coastlands of [I]Kittim and see,
And send to [b]Kedar and observe[995] closely,
And see if there has been such *a thing* as this!
11 "Has a nation[1471] changed gods,[430]
When [a]they were not gods?
But My people[5971] have [b]changed their glory[3519]
For that which does not profit.
12 "Be appalled,[8074] [a]O heavens,[8064] at this,
And shudder,[8175] be very desolate,"[2717] declares the LORD.
13 "For My people have committed[6213] two evils:
They have forsaken[5800] Me,
The [a]fountain of living[2416] waters,
To hew[2672] for themselves [b]cisterns,
Broken[7665] cisterns,
That can hold no water.

14 "Is Israel [a]a slave?[5650] Or is he a homeborn servant?
Why has he become a prey?
15 "The young [a]lions have roared at him,
They have [I]roared loudly.
And they have [b]made his land a waste;[8047]
His cities have been destroyed, without inhabitant.
16 "Also the [I]men of [a]Memphis and Tahpanhes
Have [II]shaved the [b]crown of your head.
17 "Have you not [a]done[6213] this to yourself,
By your forsaking the LORD your God,[430]
When He [a]led you in the way?[1870]
18 "But now what are you doing [a]on the road to Egypt,
To drink the waters of the [I][b]Nile?
Or what are you doing on the road to Assyria,

3 [a]Ex. 19:5, 6; Deut. 7:6; 14:2 [b]James 1:18; Rev. 14:4 [c]Is. 41:11; Jer. 30:16; 50:7
5 [a]Is. 5:4; Mic. 6:3 [b]2Kin. 17:15; Jer. 8:19; Rom. 1:21
6 [I]Or, *the shadow of death* [a]Ex. 20:2; Is. 63:11 [b]Deut. 8:15; 32:10
7 [a]Deut. 8:7-9; 11:10-12 [b]Ps. 106:38; Jer. 3:2; 16:18
8 [I]Lit., *shepherds* [a]Jer. 10:21 [b]Jer. 4:22; Mal. 2:7, 8 [c]Jer. 23:13 [d]Jer. 16:19; Hab. 2:18
9 [a]Jer. 2:35; Ezek. 20:35, 36
10 [I]I.e., Cyprus and other islands [a]Is. 23:12 [b]Ps. 120:5; Is. 21:16; Jer. 49:28
11 [a]Is. 37:19; Jer. 5:7; 16:20 [b]Ps. 106:20; Rom. 1:23
12 [a]Is. 1:2; Jer. 4:23
13 [a]Ps. 36:9; Jer. 17:13; John 4:14 [b]Jer. 14:3
14 [a]Jer. 5:19; 17:4
15 [I]Lit., *given their voice* [a]Jer. 50:17 [b]Jer. 4:7
16 [I]Or, *sons* [II]Lit., *grazed* [a]Is. 19:13; Jer. 44:1; Hos. 9:6 [b]Deut. 33:20; Jer. 48:45
17 [a]Deut. 32:10; Jer. 4:18
18 [I]Heb., *Shihor* [a]Is. 30:2 [b]Josh. 13:3

To drink the waters of the
[II]Euphrates?
19 "[a]Your own wickedness[7451] will
correct[3256] you,
And your [b]apostasies[4878] will
reprove[3198] you;
Know[3045] therefore and see that
it is evil and [c]bitter[4751]
For you to forsake the LORD
your God,
And [d]the dread[6345] of Me is not
in you," declares the Lord[136]
[I]GOD of hosts.[6635]
20 "For long ago[5769] [I][a]I broke your
yoke
And tore off your bonds;
But you said,[559] 'I will not
serve!'[5647]
For on every [b]high hill
And under every green tree
You have lain down as a
harlot.[2181]
21 "Yet I [a]planted you a choice vine,
A completely faithful[571] seed.[2233]
How then have you turned
yourself before Me
Into the [b]degenerate shoots of
a foreign vine?
22 "Although you [a]wash[3526] yourself
with lye[5427]
And [I]use much soap,
The [b]stain of your iniquity[5771] is
before Me," declares the
Lord [II]GOD.
23 "[a]How can you say,[559] 'I am not
defiled,[2930]
I have not gone after the
[b]Baals'?
Look at your way in the
[c]valley!
Know what you have done![6213]
You are a swift young camel
[d]entangling her ways,[1870]
24 A [a]wild donkey accustomed to
the wilderness,
That sniffs the wind[7307] in her
passion.[5315]
In *the time of* her [I]heat who can
turn her away?[7725]
All who seek her will not become
weary;
In her month they will find her.

25 "Keep your feet from being
unshod[3182]
And your throat from thirst;
But you said, '[a]It is [I]hopeless!
No! For I have [b]loved[157]
strangers,[2114]
And after them I will walk.'
26 "As the [a]thief is shamed when
he is discovered,
So the house of Israel is
shamed;[954]
They, their kings,[4428] their
princes,[8269]
And their priests, and their
prophets,
27 Who say to a tree, 'You are my
father,'[1]
And to a stone, 'You gave me
birth.'
For they have turned *their*
[a]back to Me,
And not *their* face;
But in the [b]time[6256] of their
[I]trouble[7451] they will say,
'Arise and save[3467] us.'
28 "But where are your [a]gods
Which you made[6213] for
yourself?
Let them arise, if they can
[b]save you
In the time of your [I]trouble;
For [c]*according to* the number of
your cities
Are your gods, O Judah.
29 "Why do you contend with Me?
You have [a]all transgressed
against Me," declares the
LORD.
30 "[a]In vain[7723] I have struck[5221] your
sons;
They accepted no
chastening.[4148]
Your [b]sword[2719] has devoured
your prophets
Like a destroying[7843] lion.
31 "O generation,[1755] heed the word
of the LORD.
Have I been a wilderness to
Israel,
Or a [a]land of thick darkness?
Why do My people say, '[b]We
are free to roam;[7300]

18 [II]Lit., *River*

19 [I]Heb., *YHWH*, usually rendered LORD [a]Is. 3:9; Jer. 4:18; Hos. 5:5 [b]Jer. 3:6, 8, 11, 14; Hos. 11:7 [c]Job 20:12-16; Amos 8:10 [d]Ps. 36:1; Jer. 5:24

20 [I]Or, *you* [a]Lev. 26:13 [b]Deut. 12:2; Is. 57:5, 7; Jer. 3:2, 6; 17:2

21 [a]Ex. 15:17; Ps. 44:2; 80:8; Is. 5:2 [b]Is. 5:4

22 [I]Lit., *cause to be great to you* [II]Heb., *YHWH*, usually rendered LORD [a]Jer. 4:14 [b]Job 14:17; Hos. 13:12

23 [a]Prov. 30:12 [b]Jer. 9:14 [c]Jer. 7:31 [d]Jer. 2:33, 36; 31:22

24 [I]Lit., *occasion* [a]Jer. 14:6

25 [I]Or, *desperate* [a]Jer. 18:12 [b]Deut. 32:16; Jer. 14:10

26 [a]Jer. 48:27

27 [I]Or, *evil* [a]Jer. 18:17; 32:33 [b]Judg. 10:10; Is. 26:16

28 [I]Or, *evil* [a]Deut. 32:37; Judg. 10:14; Is. 45:20; Jer. 1:16 [b]Jer. 11:12 [c]2Kin. 17:30, 31; Jer. 11:13

29 [a]Jer. 5:1; 6:13; Dan. 9:11

30 [a]Is. 1:5; Jer. 5:3; 7:28 [b]Neh. 9:26; Jer. 26:20-24; Acts 7:52; 1Thess. 2:15

31 [a]Is. 45:19 [b]Deut. 32:15; Jer. 2:20, 25

We will come no more to Thee'?
32 "Can a virgin[1330] forget her
ornaments,
Or a bride her attire?
Yet My people have [a]forgotten
Me
Days[3117] without number.
33 "How well you prepare[3190] your
way
To seek love!
Therefore even [I]the wicked[7451]
women
You have taught[3925] your ways.
34 "Also on your skirts is found
The [a]lifeblood[1818,5315] of the
innocent poor;
You did not find them [b]breaking
in.
But in spite of all these things,
35 Yet you said,[559] 'I am
innocent;[5352]
Surely His anger[639] is turned
away from me.'
Behold, I will [a]enter into
judgment[8199] with you
Because you [b]say, 'I have not
sinned.'[2398]
36 "Why do you [a]go around so much
Changing your way?
Also, [b]you shall be put to shame
by Egypt
As you were put to shame by
[c]Assyria.
37 "From this *place* also you shall
go out
With [a]your hands[3027] on your
head;[7218]
For the LORD has rejected[3988]
[b]those in whom you trust,
And you shall not prosper with
them."

The Polluted Land

3 *God* [I]says,[559] "[a]If a husband[376]
divorces his wife,[802]
And she goes from him,
And belongs[1961] to another man,
Will he still return[7725] to her?

32 [a]Ps. 106:21; Is. 17:10; Jer. 3:21; 13:25; Hos. 8:14

33 [I]Or, *in wickedness*

34 [a]2Kin. 21:16; 24:4; Ps. 106:38; Jer. 7:6; 19:4 [b]Ex. 22:2

35 [a]Jer. 25:31 [b]Prov. 28:13; 1John 1:8, 10

36 [a]Jer. 2:23; 31:22; Hos. 12:1 [b]Is. 30:3 [c]2Chr. 28:16, 20, 21

37 [a]2Sam. 13:19; Jer. 14:3, 4 [b]Jer. 37:7-10

1 [I]Lit., *saying* [II]Or, *alienated* [III]Lit., *companions* [a]Deut. 24:1-4 [b]Jer. 2:20; Ezek. 16:26, 28, 29 [c]Jer. 4:1; Zech. 1:3

2 [a]Deut. 12:2; Jer. 2:20; 3:21; 7:29 [b]Gen. 38:14; Ezek. 16:25 [c]Jer. 2:7

3 [a]Lev. 26:19; Jer. 14:3-6 [b]Jer. 6:15; 8:12

4 [I]Lit., *leader* [a]Jer. 3:19; 31:9 [b]Ps. 71:17; Prov. 2:17 [c]Jer. 2:2; Hos. 2:15

5 [I]Lit., *keep it* [II]Lit., *been able* [a]Ps. 103:9; Is. 57:16; Jer. 3:12

6 [a]Jer. 17:2; Ezek. 23:4-10

7 [I]Lit., *said* [a]2Kin. 17:13 [b]Jer. 3:11; Ezek. 16:47

Will not that land[776] be
completely [II]polluted?[2610]
But you [b]are a harlot[2181] *with*
many [III]lovers;
Yet you [c]turn to Me,"
declares[5001] the LORD.
2 "Lift up[5375] your eyes to the
[a]bare heights[8205] and see;
Where have you not been
violated?
By the roads[1870] you have
[b]sat for them
Like an Arab in the desert,
And you have [c]polluted a land
With your harlotry[2184] and with
your wickedness.[7451]
3 "Therefore the [a]showers have
been withheld,[4513]
And there has been no spring
rain.
Yet you had a [b]harlot's[2181]
forehead;
You refused[3985] to be ashamed.
4 "Have you not just now called[2199]
to Me,
'[a]My Father,[1] Thou art the
[I][b]friend of my [c]youth?
5 '[a]Will He be angry forever?
Will He [I]be indignant to the
end?'[5531]
Behold, you have spoken[1696]
And have done[6213] evil[7451]
things,
And you have [II]had your way."

Faithless Israel

6 Then the LORD said[559] to me in
the days[3117] of Josiah the king,[4428] "Have
you seen[7200] what faithless[4878] Israel
did? She [a]went up on every high hill
and under every green tree, and she
was a harlot there.
7 "And [a]I [I]thought, 'After she has
done all these things, she will return[7725]
to Me'; but she did not return,[7725] and
her [b]treacherous sister[269] Judah saw[7200]
it.
8 "And I saw that for all the
adulteries[5003] of faithless Israel, I had

3:6-11 See note on Jer. 2:2.

sent her away and [a]given her a writ[5612]
of divorce,[3748] yet her [b]treacherous[898]
sister Judah did not fear;[3372] but she
went and was a harlot also.
9 "And it came about because of the
lightness of her harlotry,[2184] that she
[a]polluted[2610] the land and committed
adultery with [b]stones and trees.
10 "And yet in spite of all this her
treacherous sister Judah did not return
to Me with all her heart,[3820] but rather
in [a]deception,"[8267] declares the LORD.

God Invites Repentance

11 And the LORD said to me,
"[a]Faithless Israel has proved herself
more righteous[6663] than treacherous Judah.

12 "Go, and proclaim[7121] these
words[1697] toward the north
and say,
'[a]Return, faithless Israel,'
declares the LORD;
'[b]I will not [I]look upon you in
anger.
For I am [c]gracious,'[2623] declares
the LORD;
'I will not be angry forever.[5769]
13 'Only [Ia]acknowledge[3045] your
iniquity,[5771]
That you have transgressed[6586]
against the LORD your God[430]
And have [b]scattered your
[II]favors to the strangers[2114]
[c]under every green tree,
And you have not obeyed[8085] My
voice,' declares the LORD.
14 'Return, O faithless[7726] sons,'[1121]
declares the LORD;
'For I am a [a]master[1166] to you,
And I will take you one from a
city and two from a family,[4940]
And [b]I will bring you to Zion.'

15 "Then I will give you [a]shepherds
after My own heart, who will [b]feed you
on knowledge[1844] and understanding.
16 "And it shall be in those days
when you are multiplied and increased
in the land," declares the LORD, "they
shall [a]say no more, 'The ark[727] of the
covenant[1285] of the LORD.' And it shall
not come to mind,[3820] nor shall they
remember[2142] it, nor shall they miss[6485]
it, nor shall it be made again.
17 "At that time[6256] they shall
call[7121] Jerusalem 'The [a]Throne[3676] of
the LORD,' and [b]all the nations[1471] will
be gathered to it, to Jerusalem, for the
[c]name of the LORD; nor shall they
[d]walk anymore after the stubbornness[8307] of their evil heart.
18 "[a]In those days the house[1004] of
Judah will walk with the house of Israel,
and they will come together [b]from the
land of the north to the [c]land that I
gave[5157] your fathers[1] as an inheritance.[5157]

19 "Then I said,
'How I would set you among
[I]My sons,
And give you a pleasant land,
The most [a]beautiful
inheritance[5159] of the
nations!'[6635,1471]
And I said, 'You shall call Me,
[b]My Father,
And not turn away[7725] from
following Me.'
20 "Surely, as a woman
treacherously[898] departs
from her [I]lover,[7453]
So you have [a]dealt
treacherously[898] with Me,
O house of Israel," declares the
LORD.
21 A voice is heard[8085] on the
[a]bare heights,
The weeping *and* the
supplications[8469] of the sons
of Israel;
Because they have
perverted[5753] their way,
They have [b]forgotten the LORD
their God.
22 "Return, O faithless sons,
[a]I will heal your
faithlessness."[4878]
"Behold, we come to Thee;
For Thou art the LORD our God.
23 "Surely, [a]the hills are a
deception,[8267]
A tumult *on* the mountains.
Surely, in the [b]LORD our God
Is the salvation[6942] of Israel.

8 [a]Deut. 24:1, 3; Is. 50:1 [b]Ezek. 16:46, 47; 23:11
9 [a]Jer. 2:7; 3:2 [b]Is. 57:6; Jer. 2:27; 10:8
10 [a]Jer. 12:2; Hos. 7:14
11 [a]Ezek. 16:51, 52; 23:11
12 [I]Lit., *cause My countenance to fall* [a]Jer. 3:14, 22; Ezek. 33:11 [b]Jer. 3:5 [c]Ps. 86:15; Jer. 12:15; 31:20; 33:26
13 [I]Lit., *know* [II]Lit., *ways* [a]Deut. 30:1-3; Jer. 3:25; 14:20; 1John 1:9 [b]Jer. 2:20, 25; 3:2, 6 [c]Deut. 12:2
14 [a]Jer. 31:32; Hos. 2:19 [b]Jer. 31:6, 12
15 [a]Jer. 23:4; 31:10; Ezek. 34:23; Eph. 4:11 [b]Acts 20:28
16 [a]Is. 65:17
17 [a]Jer. 17:12; Ezek. 43:7 [b]Jer. 3:19; 4:2; 12:15, 16; 16:19 [c]Is. 60:9 [d]Jer. 11:8
18 [a]Is. 11:13; Jer. 50:4, 5; Hos. 1:11 [b]Jer. 16:15; 31:8 [c]Amos 9:15
19 [I]Lit., *the* [a]Ps. 16:6 [b]Is. 63:16; Jer. 3:4
20 [I]Or, *companion* [a]Is. 48:8
21 [a]Is. 15:2; Jer. 3:2; 7:29 [b]Is. 17:10; Jer. 2:32; 13:25
22 [a]Jer. 30:17; 33:6; Hos. 6:1; 14:4
23 [a]Jer. 17:2 [b]Ps. 3:8; Jer. 17:14; 31:7

24 "But [a]the shameful thing has consumed the labor of our fathers since
our youth, their flocks and their herds,
their sons[1121] and their daughters.
25 "Let us lie down in our [a]shame,
and let our humiliation cover[3680] us; for
we have sinned[2398] against the LORD our
God, we and our fathers, [b]since our
youth even to this day.[3117] And we have
not obeyed the voice of the LORD our
God."

Judah Threatened with Invasion

4 "If you will [a]return,[7725] O Israel,"
declares the LORD,
"*Then* you should return to Me.
And [b]if you will put away[5493] your
detested things[8251] from My
presence,
And will not waver,
2 And you will [a]swear,[7650] 'As the
LORD lives,'[2416]
[b]In truth,[571] in justice,[4941] and
in righteousness;[6666]
Then the [c]nations[1471] will
bless[1288] themselves in Him,
And [d]in Him they will glory."[1984]
3 For thus says[559] the LORD to the
men[376] of Judah and to Jerusalem,
"[I][a]Break up your fallow ground,[776]
And [b]do not sow among thorns.
4 "[a]Circumcise[4135] yourselves to
the LORD
And remove the foreskins[6190] of
your heart,[3824]
Men of Judah and inhabitants of
Jerusalem,
Lest My [b]wrath go forth like fire
And burn with [c]none to quench
it,
Because of the evil[7455] of your
deeds."
5 Declare[5046] in Judah and
proclaim[8085] in Jerusalem,
and say,[559]
"[a]Blow[8628] the trumpet in the
land;[776]
Cry[2199] aloud and say,
'[b]Assemble[622] yourselves, and
let us go
Into the fortified cities.'

6 "Lift up[5375] a [a]standard toward
Zion!
Seek refuge, do not stand *still,*
For I am bringing [b]evil[7451] from
the north,
And great destruction.[7667]
7 "A [a]lion has gone up[5927] from his
thicket,
And a [b]destroyer[7893] of
nations[1471] has set out;
He has gone out from his place
To [c]make[7760] your land a
waste.[8047]
Your cities will be ruins
Without inhabitant.
8 "For this, [a]put on sackcloth,
Lament and wail;
For the [b]fierce anger[639] of the
LORD
Has not turned back from us."
9 "And it shall come about in that
day,"[3117] declares[5001] the LORD, "that
the [a]heart[3820] of the king[4428] and the
heart of the princes[8269] will fail;[6] and
the priests[3548] will be appalled,[8074] and
the [b]prophets[5030] will be astounded."
10 Then I said,[559] "Ah, Lord
[I]GOD! Surely Thou hast utterly [a]de-
ceived this people[5971] and Jerusalem,
saying, '[b]You will have peace'; whereas
a sword[2719] touches[5060] the [II]throat."[5315]
11 In that time[6256] it will be said
to this people and to Jerusalem, "A
[a]scorching wind[7307] from the bare
heights[8205] in the wilderness in the direction of the daughter of My people—not
to winnow, and not to cleanse,[1305]
12 a wind too strong for [I]this—will
come [II]at My command; now I will also
pronounce judgments against them.
13 "Behold, he [a]goes up like clouds,
And his [b]chariots like the
whirlwind;
His horses are [c]swifter[7043] than
eagles.
Woe to us, for [d]we are
ruined!"[7703]
14 Wash[3526] your heart from
evil,[7451] O Jerusalem,
That you may be saved.[3467]
How long will your [a]wicked
thoughts[4284]

24 [a]Hos. 9:10
25 [a]Ezra 9:6, 7 [b]Jer. 22:21
1 [a]Jer. 3:22; 15:19; Joel 2:12 [b]Jer. 7:3, 7; 35:15
2 [a]Deut. 10:20; Is. 45:23; 65:16; Jer. 12:16 [b]Is. 48:1 [c]Gen. 22:18; Jer. 3:17; 12:15, 16; Gal. 3:8 [d]Is. 45:25; Jer. 9:24; 1Cor. 1:31
3 [I]Lit., *Plow for yourselves plowed ground* [a]Hos. 10:12 [b]Matt. 13:7
4 [a]Deut. 10:16; 30:6; Jer. 9:25, 26; Rom. 2:28, 29; Col. 2:11 [b]Is. 30:27, 33; Jer. 21:12; Zeph. 2:2 [c]Amos 5:6; Mark 9:43, 48
5 [a]Jer. 6:1; Hos. 8:1 [b]Josh. 10:20; Jer. 8:14
6 [a]Is. 62:10; Jer. 4:21; 50:2 [b]Jer. 1:14, 15; 6:1, 22
7 [a]Jer. 5:6; 25:38; 50:17 [b]Jer. 25:9; Ezek. 26:7-10 [c]Is. 1:7; 6:11; Jer. 2:15
8 [a]Is. 22:12; Jer. 6:26 [b]Is. 5:25; 10:4; Jer. 30:24
9 [a]Is. 22:3-5; Jer. 48:41 [b]Is. 29:9, 10; Ezek. 13:9-16
10 [I]Heb., *YHWH,* usually rendered LORD [II]Or, *life* [a]Ezek. 14:9; 2Thess. 2:11 [b]Jer. 5:12; 14:13
11 [a]Jer. 13:24; 51:1; Ezek. 17:10; Hos. 13:15
12 [I]Lit., *these* [II]Lit., *for Me*
13 [a]Is. 19:1; Nah. 1:3 [b]Is. 5:28; 66:15 [c]Lam. 4:19; Hab. 1:8 [d]Is. 3:8
14 [a]Prov. 1:22; Jer. 6:19; 13:27; James 4:8

Lodge within[7130] you?
15 For a voice declares[5046] from
[a]Dan,
And proclaims[8085] wickedness[205]
from Mount Ephraim.
16 "Report *it* to the nations, now!
Proclaim over Jerusalem,
'Besiegers[5341] come from a
[a]far country,[776]
And [b]lift their voices against the
cities of Judah.
17 'Like watchmen[8104] of a field[7704]
they are [a]against her round
about,
Because she has [b]rebelled
against Me,' declares the
LORD.
18 "Your [a]ways[1870] and your deeds
Have [I]brought[6213] these things
to you.
This is your evil. How
[b]bitter![4751]
How it has touched your heart!"

Lament over Judah's Devastation

19 [a]My [I]soul,[4578] my [I]soul! I am in
anguish![3176] [II]Oh, my heart!
My [b]heart is pounding in me;
I cannot be silent,
Because [III]you have heard,[8085]
O my soul,
The [c]sound of the trumpet,
The alarm of war.
20 [a]Disaster on disaster is
proclaimed,[7121]
For the [b]whole land is
devastated;
Suddenly my [c]tents[168] are
devastated,
My curtains in an instant.
21 How long must I see the
standard,
And hear[8085] the sound of the
trumpet?
22 "[a]For My people are foolish,
They know[3045] Me not;
They are stupid[5530] children,[1121]
And they have no
understanding.[995]
They are shrewd[2450] to
[b]do evil,[7489]
But to do good[3190] they do not
know."[3045]
23 I looked[7200] on the earth,[776] and
behold, *it was* [Ia] formless[8414]
and void;
And to the heavens,[8064] and they
had no light.[216]
24 I looked on the mountains, and
behold, they were
[a]quaking,[7493]
And all the hills [I]moved to and
fro.[7043]
25 I looked, and behold, there was
no man,[120]
And all the [a]birds of the heavens
had fled.
26 I looked, and behold,
[I]the [a]fruitful land was a
wilderness,
And all its cities were pulled
down[5422]
Before the LORD, before His
fierce anger.
27 For thus says the LORD,
"The [a]whole land shall be a
desolation,[8077]
Yet I will [b]not execute[6213] a
complete destruction.[3617]
28 "For this the [a]earth shall mourn,
And the [b]heavens above be
dark,[6937]
Because I have [c]spoken,[1696] I
have purposed,[2161]
And I will not [I]change My
mind,[5162] nor will I turn[7725]
from it."
29 At the sound of the horseman
and bowman [a]every city
flees;
They [b]go into the thickets and
climb among the rocks;
[c]Every city is forsaken,[5800]
And no man[376] dwells in them.
30 And you, O desolate one,
[a]what will you do?[6213]
Although you dress in scarlet,
Although you decorate *yourself*
with ornaments of gold,
Although you [b]enlarge[7167] your
eyes with paint,
In vain[7723] you make yourself
beautiful;

15 [a]Jer. 8:16
16 [a]Is. 39:3; Jer. 5:15 [b]Ezek. 21:22
17 [a]2Kin. 25:1, 4 [b]Is. 1:20, 23; Jer. 5:23
18 [I]Lit., *done* [a]Ps. 107:17; Is. 50:1; Jer. 2:17, 19 [b]Jer. 2:19
19 [I]Lit., *inward parts* [II]Lit., *The walls of my heart* [III]Or, *I, my soul, heard* [a]Is. 15:5; 16:11; 21:3; 22:4; Jer. 9:1, 10; 20:9 [b]Hab. 3:16 [c]Num. 10:9
20 [a]Ps. 42:7; Ezek. 7:26 [b]Jer. 4:27 [c]Jer. 10:20
22 [a]Jer. 5:4, 21; 10:8; Rom. 1:22 [b]Jer. 9:3; 13:23; Rom. 16:19; 1Cor. 14:20
23 [I]Or, *a waste and emptiness* [a]Gen. 1:2; Is. 24:19
24 [I]Lit., *moved lightly* [a]Is. 5:25; Jer. 10:10; Ezek. 38:20
25 [a]Jer. 9:10; 12:4; Zeph. 1:3
26 [I]Or, *Carmel* [a]Jer. 9:10
27 [a]Jer. 12:11, 12; 25:11 [b]Jer. 5:10, 18; 30:11; 46:28
28 [I]Lit., *be sorry* [a]Jer. 12:4, 11; 14:2; Hos. 4:3 [b]Is. 5:30; 50:3; Joel 2:30, 31 [c]Num. 23:19; Jer. 23:20; 30:24
29 [a]2Kin. 25:4 [b]Is. 2:19-21; Jer. 16:16 [c]Jer. 4:7
30 [a]Is. 10:3; 20:6; Jer. 13:21 [b]2Kin. 9:30; Ezek. 23:40

Your [I][c]lovers[5689] despise[3988]
you;
They seek your life.[5315]
31 For I heard a [I]cry as of a woman
in labor,
The anguish[6869] as of one giving
birth to her first child,
The [I]cry of the daughter of Zion
[a]gasping for breath,
[b]Stretching out her [II]hands,[3709]
saying,
"Ah, woe is me, for [III]I faint
before murderers."[2026]

Jerusalem's Godlessness

5 "[a]Roam to and fro through the
streets of Jerusalem,
And look now, and take note.[3045]
And seek in her open squares,
If you can [b]find a man,[376]
[c]If there is one who does[6213]
justice,[4941] who seeks
[I]truth,[530]
Then I will pardon[5545] her.
2 "And [a]although they say,[559] 'As
the LORD lives,'[2416]
Surely they swear[7650]
falsely."[8267]
3 O LORD, do not [a]Thine eyes
look for [I]truth?
Thou hast [b]smitten them,
But they did not [II]weaken;[2342]
Thou hast consumed[3615] them,
But they [c]refused[3985] to take
correction.[4148]
They have [d]made their faces
harder than rock;
They have refused to repent.[7725]
4 Then I said,[559] "They are only
the poor,
They are foolish;
For they [a]do not know the
way[1870] of the LORD
Or the ordinance of their God.[430]
5 "I will go to the great
And will speak[1696] to them,
For [a]they know[3045] the way of
the LORD,
And the ordinance of their God."
But they too, with one accord,
have [b]broken[7665] the yoke
And burst the bonds.
6 Therefore [a]a lion from the forest
shall slay[5221] them,
A [b]wolf of the deserts[6160] shall
destroy[7703] them,
A [c]leopard is watching their
cities.
Everyone who goes out of them
shall be torn in pieces,
Because their
[d]transgressions[6588] are
many,
Their apostasies[4878] are
numerous.
7 "Why should I pardon you?
Your sons[1121] have forsaken[5800]
Me
And [a]sworn by those who are
[b]not gods.[430]
When I had fed them to the full,
They [c]committed adultery[5003]
And trooped[1413] to the harlot's
house.[1004]
8 "They were well-fed lusty
horses,
Each one[376] neighing after his
[a]neighbor's[7453] wife.[802]
9 "Shall I not punish[6485] [I]these
people," declares[5001] the
LORD,
"And on a nation[1471] such as this
[a]Shall I not avenge[5358]
Myself?[5315]
10 "Go up through her vine rows
and destroy,
But do not execute[6213] a
complete destruction;[3617]
Strip away her branches,
For they are not the LORD's.
11 "For the [a]house[1004] of Israel and
the house of Judah
Have dealt very
treacherously[898] with Me,"
declares the LORD.
12 They have [a]lied about the LORD
And said, "[I][b]Not He;
Misfortune[7451] will [c]not come on
us;
And we [d]will not see sword[2719]
or famine.
13 "And the [a]prophets[5030] are[1961] *as*
wind,[7307]

30 [I]Lit., *paramours* [c]Jer. 22:20, 22; Lam. 1:2, 19; Ezek. 23:9, 10, 22
31 [I]Lit., *sound* [II]Lit., *palms* [III]Lit., *my soul faints* [a]Is. 42:14 [b]Is. 1:15; Lam. 1:17
1 [I]Lit., *faithfulness* [a]2Chr. 16:9; Dan. 12:4 [b]Ezek. 22:30 [c]Gen. 18:26, 32
2 [a]Is. 48:1; Titus 1:16
3 [I]Lit., *faithfulness* [II]Or, *become sick* [a]2Chr. 16:9 [b]Is. 1:5; 9:13; Jer. 2:30 [c]Jer. 7:28; 8:5; Zeph. 3:2 [d]Jer. 7:26; 19:15; Ezek. 3:8
4 [a]Is. 27:11; Jer. 8:7; Hos. 4:6
5 [a]Mic. 3:1 [b]Ex. 32:25; Ps. 2:3; Jer. 2:20
6 [a]Jer. 4:7 [b]Ezek. 22:27; Hab. 1:8; Zeph. 3:3 [c]Hos. 13:7 [d]Jer. 30:14, 15
7 [a]Josh. 23:7; Jer. 12:16; Zeph. 1:5 [b]Deut. 32:21; Jer. 2:11; Gal. 4:8 [c]Jer. 7:9
8 [a]Jer. 13:27; 29:23; Ezek. 22:11
9 [I]Or, *for these things* [a]Jer. 9:9
11 [a]Jer. 3:6, 7, 20
12 [I]Lit., *He is not* [a]2Chr. 36:16 [b]Prov. 30:9; Jer. 14:22; 43:1-4 [c]Jer. 23:17 [d]Jer. 14:13
13 [a]Job 8:2; Jer. 14:13, 15; 22:22

And the word is not in them.
Thus it will be done[6213] to
them!"

Judgment Proclaimed

14 Therefore, thus says[559] the
LORD, the God of hosts,[6635]
"Because you have spoken this
word,[1697]
Behold, I am [a]making My
words[1697] in your mouth[6310]
fire
And this people[5971] wood, and
it will consume them.
15 "Behold, I am [a]bringing a nation
against you from afar, O
house of Israel," declares the
LORD.
"It is an enduring nation,
It is an ancient[5769] nation,
A nation whose [b]language you
do not know,[3045]
Nor can you understand what
they say.[1696]
16 "Their [a]quiver is like an
[b]open grave,[6913]
All of them are mighty men.
17 "And they will [a]devour your
harvest and your food;
They will devour your sons[1121]
and your daughters;
They will devour your flocks and
your herds;
They will devour your
[b]vines and your fig trees;
They will demolish with the
sword your [c]fortified cities in
which you trust.[982]
18 "Yet even in those days,"[3117] declares the LORD, "I will not make you
a complete destruction.
19 "And it shall come about [a]when
[I]they say, 'Why has the LORD our God
done[6213] all these things to us?' then
you shall say[559] to them, 'As you have
forsaken Me and served[5647] foreign[5236]
gods in your land,[776] so you shall
[b]serve[5647] strangers[2114] in a land that
is not yours.'
20 "Declare[5046] this in the house of
Jacob
And proclaim[8085] it in Judah,
saying,
21 'Hear[8085] this, O foolish and
[I]senseless[3820] people,
Who have [a]eyes, but see not;
Who have ears,[241] but hear
not.
22 'Do you not [a]fear[3372] Me?'
declares the LORD.
'Do you not tremble[2342] in My
presence?
For I have [b]placed the sand as
a boundary for the sea,
An eternal[5769] decree,[2706] so it
cannot cross over it.
Though the waves toss, yet they
cannot prevail;
Though they roar, yet they
cannot cross over[5674] it.
23 'But this people has a
[a]stubborn[5637] and rebellious
heart;[3820]
They have turned aside and
departed.
24 'They do not say in their
heart,[3824]
"Let us now fear the LORD our
God,
Who [a]gives rain in its season,[6256]
Both [b]the autumn rain and the
spring rain,
Who keeps[8104] for us
The [c]appointed weeks of the
harvest."
25 'Your [a]iniquities[5771] have turned
these away,
And your sins have withheld[4513]
good[2896] from you.
26 'For wicked[7563] men are found
among My people,
They [a]watch like fowlers [I]lying
in wait;
They set[5324] a trap,[4889]
They catch men.[582]
27 'Like a cage full of birds,
So their houses are full of
[a]deceit;[4820]
Therefore they have become
great and rich.
28 'They are [a]fat, they are sleek,
They also [I]excel[5674] in deeds[1697]
of wickedness;[7451]

14 [a]Is. 24:6; Jer. 1:9; 23:29; Hos. 6:5; Zech. 1:6
15 [a]Deut. 28:49; Is. 5:26; Jer. 4:16 [b]Is. 28:11
16 [a]Is. 5:28; 13:18 [b]Ps. 5:9
17 [a]Lev. 26:16; Deut. 28:31, 33; Jer. 8:16; 50:7, 17 [b]Jer. 8:13 [c]Hos. 8:14
19 [I]Or, *you* [a]Deut. 29:24-26; 1Kin. 9:8, 9; Jer. 13:22; 16:10-13 [b]Deut. 28:48; Jer. 16:13
21 [I]Lit., *without heart* [a]Is. 6:9; 43:8; Ezek. 12:2; Matt. 13:14; Mark 8:18; John 12:40; Acts 28:26; Rom. 11:8
22 [a]Deut. 28:58; Ps. 119:120; Jer. 2:19; 10:7; Rev. 15:4 [b]Job 38:8-11; Ps. 104:9; Prov. 8:29
23 [a]Deut. 21:18; Ps. 78:8; Jer. 4:17; 6:28
24 [a]Ps. 147:8; Jer. 3:3; Matt. 5:45; Acts 14:17 [b]Joel 2:23 [c]Gen. 8:22
25 [a]Jer. 2:17; 4:18
26 [I]Perhaps, *crouching down* [a]Ps. 10:9; Prov. 1:11; Jer. 18:22; Hab. 1:15
27 [a]Jer. 9:6
28 [I]Lit., *pass over,* or, *overlook deeds* [a]Deut. 32:15

They do not plead[1777] the
cause,[1779]
The cause of the [IIb]orphan, that
they may prosper;
And they do not [III]defend[8199] the
rights[4941] of the poor.
29 '[a]Shall I not punish [I]these *people?*'
declares the LORD,
'On a nation such as this
Shall I not avenge Myself?'
30 "An appalling[8047] and [a]horrible
thing[8186]
Has happened[1961] in the land:
31 The [a]prophets prophesy[5012]
falsely,
And the priests[3548] rule[7287]
[I]on their *own* authority;[3027]
And My people [b]love[157] it so!
But what will you do[6213] at the
end[319] of it?

Destruction of Jerusalem Impending

6 "Flee for safety, O sons[1121] of
[a]Benjamin,
From the midst[7130] of Jerusalem!
Now blow[8628] a trumpet in
Tekoa,
And raise[5375] a signal over
[Ib]Beth-haccerem;
For evil[7451] looks down from the
[c]north,
And a great destruction.[7667]
2 "The comely[5000] and [a]dainty one,
[b]the daughter of Zion, I will
cut off.
3 "[a]Shepherds and their flocks will
come to her,
They will [b]pitch[8628] *their* tents[168]
[I]around her,
They will pasture each[376] in his
[II]place.
4 "[Ia]Prepare[6942] war against her;
Arise, and let us [II]attack at
[b]noon.
Woe to us, for the day[3117]
declines,
For the shadows[6752] of the
evening lengthen!
5 "Arise, and let us [I]attack by
night[3915]
And [a]destroy her [II]palaces!"[759]
6 For thus says[559] the LORD of
hosts,[6635]
"[a]Cut[3772] down her trees,
And cast[8210] up a [b]siege against
Jerusalem.
This is the city to be
punished,[6485]
In whose midst there is only
[c]oppression.
7 "[a]As a well[953] [I]keeps its waters
fresh,
So she [I]keeps fresh her
wickedness.[7451]
[b]Violence[2555] and destruction[7701]
are heard[8085] in her;
[c]Sickness and wounds[4347] are
ever[8548] before Me.
8 "[a]Be warned,[3256] O Jerusalem,
Lest [Ib]I[5315] be alienated from
you;
Lest I make[7760] you a
desolation,[8077]
A land[776] not inhabited."
9 Thus says[559] the LORD of hosts,
"They will [a]thoroughly glean as
the vine the [b]remnant[7611] of
Israel;
Pass[7725] your hand[3027] again like
a grape gatherer
Over the branches."
10 To whom shall I speak[1696] and
give warning,
That they may hear?[8085]
Behold, their [a]ears[241] are
[I]closed,[6189]
And they cannot listen.[7181]
Behold, [b]the word[1697] of the
LORD has become a
reproach[2781] to them;
They have no delight[2654] in it.
11 But I am [a]full of the wrath of
the LORD:
I am [b]weary with holding *it* in.
"[c]Pour[8210] *it* out on the children
in the street,
And on the [I]gathering[5475] of
young men together;
For both husband[376] and wife[802]
shall be taken,
The aged [II]and the very
old.[4293,3117]

---

28 [II]Or, *fatherless* [III]Lit., *judge* [b]Is. 1:23; Jer. 7:6; 22:3; Zech. 7:10

29 [I]Or, *for these things* [a]Jer. 5:9; Mal. 3:5

30 [a]Jer. 23:14; Hos. 6:10

31 [I]Lit., *over their own hands* [a]Ezek. 13:6 [b]Mic. 2:11

1 [I]I.e., house of the vineyard [a]Josh. 18:28 [b]Neh. 3:14 [c]Jer. 1:14; 4:6; 6:22

2 [a]Deut. 28:56 [b]Is. 1:8; Jer. 4:31

3 [I]Lit., *against her round about* [II]Lit., *hand* [a]Jer. 12:10 [b]2Kin. 25:1; Jer. 4:17; Luke 19:43

4 [I]Lit., *Sanctify* [II]Lit., *go up* [a]Jer. 6:23; Joel 3:9 [b]Jer. 15:8; Zeph. 2:4

5 [I]Lit., *go up* [II]Or, *fortified towers* [a]Is. 32:14; Jer. 52:13

6 [a]Deut. 20:19, 20 [b]Jer. 32:24; 33:4 [c]Jer. 22:17

7 [I]Lit., *keeps cold* [a]James 3:11f. [b]Jer. 20:8; Ezek. 7:11, 23 [c]Jer. 30:12, 13

8 [I]Lit., *my soul* [a]Jer. 7:28; 17:23 [b]Ezek. 23:18; Hos. 9:12

9 [a]Jer. 16:16; 49:9; Obad. 5, 6 [b]Jer. 8:3; 11:23

10 [I]Lit., *uncircumcised* [a]Jer. 5:21; 7:26; Acts 7:51 [b]Jer. 20:8

11 [I]Lit., *council* [II]Lit., *with fulness of days* [a]Job 32:18, 19; Mic. 3:8 [b]Jer. 15:6; 20:9 [c]Jer. 7:20; 9:21

12 "And their [a]houses[1004] shall be
turned over to others,
Their fields[7704] and their
wives[802] together;
For I will [b]stretch out My hand
Against the inhabitants of the
land," declares[5001] the LORD.
13 "For [a]from the least of them even
to the greatest of them,
Everyone is [b]greedy1215 for gain,
And from the prophet[5030] even
to the priest[3548]
Everyone [I]deals falsely.[8267]
14 "And they have [a]healed the
brokenness[7667] of My
people[5971] superficially,
Saying, 'Peace, peace,'
But there is no peace.
15 "Were they [a]ashamed[954] because
of the abomination[8441] they
have done?[6213]
They were not even ashamed
at all;
They did not even know how
to blush.
Therefore they shall fall among
those who fall;
At the time[6256] that I punish[6485]
them,
They shall be cast down,"[3782]
says the LORD.
16 Thus says the LORD,
"Stand by the ways[1870] and see
and ask[7592] for the
[a]ancient[5769] paths,
Where the good[2896] way[1870] is,
and walk in it;
And [b]you shall find rest for your
souls.[5315]
But they said, 'We will not walk
in it.'
17 "And I set [a]watchmen over you,
saying,
'Listen to the sound of the
trumpet!'
But they said, 'We will not
listen.'
18 "Therefore hear, O nations,[1471]
And know,[3045]
O congregation,[5712] what is
among them.
19 "[a]Hear, O earth:[776] behold, I am
bringing disaster on this
people,
The [b]fruit of their [I]plans,[4284]
Because they have not
listened[7181] to My words,[1697]
And as for My law,[8451] they have
[c]rejected[3988] it also.
20 "[a]For what purpose does
[b]frankincense come to Me
from Sheba,
And the [I][c]sweet cane from a
distant land?[776]
[d]Your burnt offerings[5930] are not
acceptable,[7522]
And your sacrifices[2077] are not
pleasing[6148] to Me."
21 Therefore, thus says the LORD,
"Behold, [a]I am [I]laying stumbling
blocks[4383] before this people.
And they will stumble[3782] against
them,
[b]Fathers[1] and sons[1121] together;
Neighbor[7934] and [II]friend will
perish."[6]

The Enemy from the North

22 Thus says the LORD,
"Behold, [a]a people is coming from
the north land,
And a great nation[1471] will be
aroused from the [b]remote
parts of the earth.
23 "They seize[2388] [a]bow and spear;
They are [b]cruel and have no
mercy;
Their voice [c]roars like the sea,
And they ride on horses,
Arrayed as a man[376] for the
battle
Against you, O daughter of
Zion!"
24 We have [a]heard the report of
it;
Our hands[3027] are limp.[7503]
[b]Anguish6869 has seized[2388] us,
Pain as of a woman in childbirth.
25 [a]Do not go out into the field,[7704]
And [b]do not walk on the road,
For the enemy has a sword,[2719]
[c]Terror[4032] is on every side.

12 [a]Deut. 28:30; Jer. 8:10; 38:22, 23 [b]Jer. 15:6
13 [I]Or, *makes lies* [a]Jer. 8:10 [b]Is. 56:11; 57:17; Jer. 8:10; 22:17
14 [a]Jer. 8:11; Ezek. 13:10
15 [a]Jer. 3:3; 8:12
16 [a]Is. 8:20; Jer. 12:16; 18:15; 31:21; Mal. 4:4; Luke 16:29 [b]Matt. 11:29
17 [a]Is. 21:11; 58:1; Jer. 25:4; Ezek. 3:17; Hab. 2:1
19 [I]Or, *devices* [a]Is. 1:2; Jer. 19:3, 15; 22:29 [b]Prov. 1:31 [c]Jer. 8:9
20 [I]Lit., *good* [a]Ps. 50:7-9; Is. 1:11; 66:3; Mic. 6:6 [b]Is. 60:6 [c]Ex. 30:23 [d]Ps. 40:6; Amos 5:22
21 [I]Lit., *giving* [II]Lit., *his friend* [a]Is. 8:14; Jer. 13:16 [b]Is. 9:14-17; Jer. 9:21, 22
22 [a]Jer. 1:15; 10:22; 50:41-43 [b]Neh. 1:9
23 [a]Is. 13:18; Jer. 4:29 [b]Jer. 50:42 [c]Is. 5:30
24 [a]Is. 28:19; Jer. 4:19-21 [b]Is. 21:3; Jer. 4:31; 13:21; 30:6; 49:24; 50:43
25 [a]Jer. 14:18 [b]Judg. 5:6 [c]Jer. 20:10; 46:5; 49:29

26 O daughter of my people,
[a]put on sackcloth
And [b]roll in ashes;
[1c]Mourn as for an only[3173] son,
A lamentation most bitter.
For suddenly the destroyer[7703]
Will come upon us.
27 "I have [a]made you an assayer *and*
a tester among My people,
That you may know and assay[974]
their way."
28 All of them are stubbornly[5493]
rebellious,[5637]
[a]Going about as a talebearer.
They are [b]bronze and iron;
They, all of them, are
corrupt.[7843]
29 The bellows blow fiercely,[2787]
The lead is consumed[8552] by the
fire;
In vain the refining[6884] goes on,
But the [a]wicked[7451] are not
[1]separated.
30 [a]They call[7121] them rejected[3988]
silver,
Because the [b]LORD has rejected
them.

Message at the Temple Gate

7 The word[1697] that came to Jeremiah
from the LORD, saying,
2 "[a]Stand in the gate of the LORD's
house[1004] and proclaim[7121] there this
word, and say,[559] 'Hear[8085] the word
of the LORD, all you of Judah, who enter
by these gates to worship[7812] the
LORD!' "
3 Thus says[559] the LORD of
hosts,[6635] the God[430] of Israel,
"[a]Amend[3190] your ways[1870] and your
deeds, and I will let you dwell[7931] in
this place.
4 "[a]Do not trust[982] in deceptive
words,[1697] saying, '[1]This is the
temple[1964] of the LORD, the temple of
the LORD, the temple of the LORD.'
5 "For [a]if you truly amend your ways
and your deeds, if you truly [b]practice
justice[4941] between a man[376] and his
neighbor,[7453]
6 *if* you do not oppress the alien,[1616]
the [1a]orphan, or the widow, and do not
shed[8210] [b]innocent[5355] blood[1818] in this
place, nor [c]walk after other gods[430] to
your own ruin,[7451]
7 then I will let you [a]dwell in this
place, in the [b]land[776] that I gave to your
fathers[1] forever and ever.
8 "Behold, you are trusting in
[a]deceptive words to no avail.
9 "Will you steal, murder,[7523] and
commit adultery,[5003] and swear[7650]
falsely,[8267] and [1a]offer sacrifices[6999] to
Baal, and walk after [b]other gods that
you have not known,[3045]
10 then [a]come and stand before Me
in [b]this house, which is called[7121] by My
name, and say, 'We are delivered!'—
that you may do[6213] all these
abominations?[8441]
11 "Has [a]this house, which is called
by My name, become a [b]den of robbers[6530] in your sight? Behold, [c]I, even
I, have seen[7200] *it*," declares[5001] the
LORD.
12 "But go now to My place which
was in [a]Shiloh, where I [b]made[7931] My
name dwell at the first,[7223] and [c]see what
I did[6213] to it because of the wickedness[7451] of My people[5971] Israel.
13 "And now, because you have
done[6213] all these things," declares the
LORD, "and I spoke[1696] to you, [a]rising
up early and [b]speaking,[1696] but you did
not hear,[8085] and I [c]called you but you
did not answer,
14 therefore, I will do to the
[a]house which is called by My name,
[b]in which you trust, and to the place
which I gave you and your fathers, as
I [c]did to Shiloh.
15 "And I will [a]cast you out of My
sight, as I have cast out all your brothers,[251] all the [1]offspring[2233] of [b]Ephraim.
16 "As for you, [a]do not pray[6419] for
this people, and do not lift up[5375] cry
or prayer[8605] for them, and do not intercede with Me; for I do not hear you.

26 [1]Lit., *Make for yourself mourning* [a]Jer. 4:8 [b]Jer. 25:34; Mic. 1:10 [c]Amos 8:10; Zech. 12:10
27 [a]Jer. 1:18; 15:20
28 [a]Jer. 9:4 [b]Ezek. 22:18
29 [1]Or, *drawn off* [a]Jer. 15:19
30 [a]Ps. 119:119; Is. 1:22 [b]Jer. 7:29; Hos. 9:17; Zech. 11:8

2 [a]Jer. 17:19; 26:2
3 [a]Jer. 4:1; 7:5; 18:11; 26:13
4 [1]Lit., *They are* [a]Jer. 7:8; Mic. 3:11
5 [a]Is. 1:19; Jer. 4:1, 2 [b]1Kin. 6:12; Jer. 21:12; 22:3
6 [1]Or, *fatherless* [a]Ex. 22:21-24; Jer. 5:28 [b]Jer. 2:34; 19:4 [c]Deut. 6:14, 15; 8:19; 11:28; Jer. 13:10
7 [a]Deut. 4:40 [b]Jer. 3:18
8 [a]Jer. 7:4; 28:15
9 [1]Or, *burn incense* [a]Jer. 11:13, 17 [b]Ex. 20:3; Jer. 7:6; 19:4
10 [a]Ezek. 23:39 [b]Jer. 7:11, 14, 30; 32:34
11 [a]Is. 56:7 [b]Matt. 21:13; Mark 11:17; Luke 19:46 [c]Jer. 29:23
12 [a]Judg. 18:31; Jer. 26:6 [b]Josh. 18:1, 10 [c]1Sam. 4:10, 11, 22; Ps. 78:60-64
13 [a]Jer. 7:25 [b]Jer. 35:17 [c]Prov. 1:24; Is. 65:12; 66:4
14 [a]Deut. 12:5; 1Kin. 9:7 [b]Jer. 7:4 [c]Jer. 7:12
15 [1]Lit., *seed* [a]Jer. 15:1; 52:3 [b]Ps. 78:67; Hos. 7:13; 9:13; 12:1
16 [a]Ex. 32:10; Deut. 9:14; Jer. 11:14

7:2-15 See note on Isa. 66:1,2.

17 "Do you not see what they are
doing in the cities of Judah and in the
streets of Jerusalem?
18 "The [I]children[1121] gather[3950]
wood, and the fathers kindle the fire,
and the women[802] knead dough to
make[6213] cakes for the queen[4446] of
heaven;[8064] and *they* [a]pour[5258] out
libations[5262] to other gods in order to
[b]spite[3707] Me.
19 "[a]Do they spite Me?" declares
the LORD. "Is it not themselves *they*
spite, to [I]their own [b]shame?"
20 Therefore thus says the Lord
[I]GOD, "Behold, My [a]anger[639] and My
wrath will be poured out on this place,
on man[120] and on beast and on the
[b]trees of the field[7704] and on the fruit
of the ground;[127] and it will burn and
not be quenched."
21 Thus says the LORD of hosts,
the God of Israel, "Add your [a]burnt
offerings[5930] to your sacrifices[2077] and
[b]eat flesh.[1320]
22 "For I did not [a]speak to your fathers, or command[6680] them in the
day[3117] that I brought them out of the
land of Egypt, concerning burnt offerings
and sacrifices.
23 "But this is [I]what[1697] I commanded them, saying, '[a]Obey[8085] My
voice, and [b]I will be your God, and you
will be My people; and you will walk
in all the way which I command you,
that it may [c]be well[3190] with you.'
24 "Yet they [a]did not obey[8085] or
incline their ear,[241] but walked in *their*
own counsels *and* in the stubbornness[8307] of their evil[7451] heart,[3820] and
[I][b]went backward and not forward.
25 "Since the day that your fathers
came out of the land of Egypt until this
day, I have [a]sent you all My servants[5650]
the prophets,[5030] daily[3117] rising early
and sending *them.*
26 "Yet they did not listen to Me
or incline their ear, but [a]stiffened their
neck; they [b]did evil[7489] more than their
fathers.
27 "And you shall [a]speak[1696] all
these words to them, but they will not
listen[8085] to you; and you shall call[7121]
to them, but they will [b]not answer
you.
28 "And you shall say to them, 'This
is the nation[1471] that [a]did not obey[8085]
the voice of the LORD their God or accept correction; [I][b]truth[530] has perished[6]
and has been cut off[3772] from their
mouth.[6310]
29 '[a]Cut off [I]your hair and cast *it*
away,
And [b]take[5375] up a lamentation
on the bare heights;[8205]
For the LORD has [c]rejected[3988]
and forsaken[5203]
The generation[1755] of His
wrath.'[5678]
30 "For the sons of Judah have done
that which is evil in My sight," declares
the LORD, "they have [a]set[7760] their detestable things[8251] in the house which
is called by My name, to defile it.
31 "And they have [a]built the high
places[1116] of Topheth, which is in the
valley of the son[1121] of Hinnom, to
[b]burn[8313] their sons[1121] and their daughters in the fire, which I [c]did not command, and it did not come into My
[I]mind.
32 "[a]Therefore, behold, days[3117]
are coming," declares the LORD, "when
it will no more be called Topheth, or
the valley of the son of Hinnom, but
the valley of the Slaughter;[2028] for they
will [b]bury[6912] in Topheth [I]because there
is no *other* place.
33 "And the [a]dead bodies[5038] of this
people will be food for the birds of the
sky, and for the beasts of the earth;[776]
and no one will frighten[2729] *them away.*
34 "Then I will make to [a]cease[7673]
from the cities of Judah and from the
streets of Jerusalem the voice of joy

18 [I]Lit., *sons* [a]Jer. 19:13 [b]Deut. 32:16, 21; 1Kin. 14:9; 16:2; Jer. 11:17; Ezek. 8:17
19 [I]Lit., *their faces'* [a]Job 35:6; 1Cor. 10:22 [b]Jer. 9:19; 15:9; 22:22
20 [I]Heb., *YHWH,* usually rendered LORD [a]Is. 42:25; Jer. 6:11, 12; 42:18; Lam. 2:3-5; 4:11 [b]Jer. 8:13; 11:16
21 [a]Is. 1:11; Jer. 6:20; 14:12; Amos 5:22 [b]Ezek. 33:25; Hos. 8:13
22 [a]1Sam. 15:22; Ps. 51:16; Hos. 6:6
23 [I]Lit., *the word which* [a]Ex. 15:26; 16:32; Deut. 6:3 [b]Ex. 19:5, 6; Lev. 26:12; Jer. 11:4; 13:11 [c]Is. 3:10; Jer. 38:20; 42:6
24 [I]Lit., *they were* [a]Deut. 29:19; Ps. 81:11; Jer. 11:8; Ezek. 20:8, 13, 16, 21 [b]Jer. 15:6
25 [a]2Chr. 36:15; Jer. 25:4; 29:19; Luke 11:49
26 [a]Neh. 9:16; Jer. 17:23; 19:15 [b]Jer. 16:12; Matt. 23:32
27 [a]Jer. 1:7; 26:2; Ezek. 2:7 [b]Is. 50:2; 65:12; Zech. 7:13
28 [I]Lit., *faithfulness* [a]Jer. 6:17; 11:10 [b]Is. 59:14, 15; Jer. 9:5
29 [I]Lit., *your crown* [a]Job 1:20; Is. 15:2; 22:12; Jer. 16:6; Mic. 1:16 [b]Jer. 3:21; 9:17, 18 [c]Jer. 6:30; 14:19
30 [a]2Kin. 21:3f.; 2Chr. 33:3-5, 7; Jer. 32:34, 35; Ezek. 7:20; Dan. 9:27; 11:31
31 [I]Lit., *heart* [a]2Kin. 23:10; Jer. 19:5; 32:35 [b]Lev. 18:21; 2Kin. 17:17; Ps. 106:38 [c]Deut. 17:3 **32** [I]Or, *until there is no place left* [a]Jer. 19:6, 11 [b]2Kin. 23:10
33 [a]Deut. 28:26; Ps. 79:2; Jer. 12:9; 19:7 **34** [a]Is. 24:7, 8; Jer. 16:9; 25:10; Ezek. 26:13; Hos. 2:11; Rev. 18:23

7:31 See note on Lev. 18:21.

and the voice of gladness, the voice of
the bridegroom and the voice of the
bride; for the [b]land will become a ruin.

The Sin and Treachery of Judah

8 "At that time,"[6256] declares the
LORD, "they will [a]bring out the
bones[6196] of the kings[4428] of Judah, and
the bones of its princes,[8269] and the
bones of the priests,[3548] and the bones
of the prophets,[5030] and the bones of
the inhabitants of Jerusalem from their
graves.[6913]
2 "And they will spread them out
to the sun, the moon, and to all the
[a]host[6635] of heaven,[8064] which they have
loved,[157] and which they have
served,[5647] and which they have gone
after, and which they have sought, and
which they have worshiped.[7812] They
will not be gathered [b]or buried;[6912]
[c]they will be as dung on the face of the
ground.[127]
3 "And [a]death[4194] will be chosen[977]
rather than life[2416] by all the remnant[7611]
that remains of this evil[7451] family,[4940]
that remains in all the [b]places to which
I have driven them," declares the LORD
of hosts.[6635]
4 "And you shall say[559] to them,
'Thus says[559] the LORD,

"Do *men* [a]fall and not get up again?
Does one turn away[7725] and not
[I]repent?[7725]
5 "Why then has this people,[5971]
Jerusalem,
[a]Turned away in continual[5331]
apostasy?[4878]
They [b]hold fast[2388] to deceit,
They [c]refuse[3985] to return.
6 "I [a]have listened[7181] and
heard,[8085]
They have spoken[1696] what is
not right;
[b]No man[376] repented[5162] of his
wickedness,[7451]
Saying, 'What have I done?'[6213]
Everyone turned to his course,
Like a [c]horse charging[7857] into
the battle.
7 "Even the stork in the sky
[a]Knows her seasons;[4150]
And the [b]turtledove and the swift
and the thrush
Observe[8104] the time of their
[I]migration;
But [c]My people do not know[3045]
The ordinance[4941] of the LORD.
8 "[a]How can you say, 'We are
wise,[802]
And the law[8451] of the LORD is
with us'?
But behold, the lying pen of the
scribes[5608]
Has made[6213] *it* into a lie.[8267]
9 "The wise men are [a]put to
shame,[954]
They are dismayed[2865] and
caught;
Behold, they have [b]rejected[3988]
the word[1697] of the LORD,
And what kind of wisdom[2451] do
they have?
10 "Therefore I will [a]give their
wives[802] to others,
Their fields[7704] to [I]new
owners;[3423]
Because from the least even to
the greatest
Everyone is [b]greedy for gain;[1215]
From the prophet[5030] even to the
priest[3548]
Everyone practices deceit.[8267]
11 "And they [a]heal the
brokenness[7667] of the
daughter of My people
superficially,
Saying, 'Peace, peace,'
But there is no peace.
12 "Were they [a]ashamed because of
the abomination[8441] they had
done?[6213]
They certainly were not
ashamed,
And they did not know how to
blush;
Therefore they shall [b]fall among
those who fall;
At the [c]time of their
punishment[6486] they shall be
brought down,"[3782]
Declares the LORD.

24 [b]Lev. 26:33; Is. 1:7; Jer. 4:27

1 [a]Ezek. 6:5

2 [a]2Kin. 23:5; Jer. 19:13; Zeph. 1:5; Acts 7:42 [b]Jer. 22:19; 36:30 [c]2Kin. 9:37; Ps. 83:10; Jer. 9:22

3 [a]Job 3:21, 22; 7:15, 16; Jon. 4:3; Rev. 9:6 [b]Deut. 30:1, 4; Jer. 23:3, 8; 29:14

4 [I]Lit., *turn back* [a]Prov. 24:16; Amos 5:2; Mic. 7:8

5 [a]Jer. 5:6; 7:24 [b]Jer. 5:27; 9:6 [c]Jer. 5:3

6 [a]Ps. 14:2; Mal. 3:16 [b]Ezek. 22:30; Mic. 7:2; Rev. 9:20 [c]Job 39:21-25

7 [I]Lit., *coming* [a]Prov. 6:6-8; Is. 1:3 [b]Song 2:12 [c]Jer. 5:4

8 [a]Job 5:12, 13; Jer. 4:22; Rom. 1:22

9 [a]Is. 19:11; Jer. 6:15; 1Cor. 1:27 [b]Jer. 6:19

10 [I]Lit., *possessing ones* [a]Deut. 28:30; Jer. 6:12, 13; 38:22f. [b]Is. 56:11; 57:17; Jer. 6:13

11 [a]Jer. 6:14; 14:13, 14; Lam. 2:14; Ezek. 13:10

12 [a]Ps. 52:1, 7; Is. 3:9; Jer. 3:3; 6:15; Zeph. 3:5 [b]Is. 9:14; Jer. 6:21; Hos. 4:5 [c]Deut. 32:35; Jer. 10:15

13 "I will [a]surely snatch[5486] them
away," declares[5001] the
LORD;
"There will be [b]no grapes on the
vine,
And [c]no figs on the fig tree,
And the leaf shall wither;
And what I have given them shall
pass away." ' "
14 Why are we sitting still?
[a]Assemble[622] yourselves, and let
us [b]go into the fortified cities,
And let us perish there,
Because the LORD our God[430]
has doomed us
And given us [c]poisoned[7219] water
to drink,
For [d]we have sinned[2398] against
the LORD.
15 *We* [a]waited for peace, but no
good[2896] *came;*
For a time of healing, but behold,
terror!
16 From [a]Dan is heard the snorting
of his horses;
At the sound of the neighing of
his [b]stallions[47]
The whole land[776] quakes;[7493]
For they come and [c]devour the
land and its fulness,
The city and its inhabitants.
17 "For behold, I am [a]sending
serpents[5175] against you,
Adders,[6848] for which there is
[b]no charm,[3908]
And they will bite you," declares
the LORD.
18 [I]My [a]sorrow is beyond healing,
My [b]heart[3820] is faint *within me!*
19 Behold, listen! The cry of the
daughter of my people from
a [a]distant land:[776]
"Is the LORD not in Zion? Is her
King[4428] not within her?"
"Why have they [b]provoked[3707]
Me with their graven images,
with foreign[5236] [I][c]idols?"
20 "Harvest is past,[5674] summer is
ended,[3645]
And we are not saved."[3467]
21 For the [a]brokenness of the
daughter of my people
I am broken;[7665]
I [b]mourn,[6937] dismay[8047] has
taken hold[2388] of me.
22 Is there no [a]balm in Gilead?
Is there no physician there?
[b]Why then has not the
[I]health[724] of the daughter of
my people [II]been
restored?[5927]

A Lament over Zion

9 [I][a]Oh, that my head[7218] were waters,
And my eyes a fountain of tears,
That I might weep day[3119] and
night[3915]
For the slain[2491] of the
[b]daughter of my people![5971]
2 [I][a]O that I had in the desert
A wayfarers'[732] lodging place;
That I might leave[5800] my
people,
And go from them!
For all of them are
[b]adulterers,[5003]
An assembly[6116] of
[c]treacherous[898] men.
3 "And they [a]bend their tongue *like*
their bow;
Lies[8267] and not truth[530] prevail
in the land;[776]
For they [b]proceed from evil[7451]
to evil,
And they [c]do not know[3045] Me,"
declares the LORD.
4 "Let everyone[376] [a]be on guard
against his neighbor,[7453]
And [b]do not trust[982] any
brother;[251]
Because every [c]brother deals
[I]craftily,[6117]
And every neighbor [d]goes about
as a slanderer.
5 "And everyone [a]deceives his
neighbor,
And does not speak[1696] the
truth,[571]
They have taught[3925] their
tongue to speak lies;
They [b]weary themselves
committing iniquity.[5753]
6 "Your [a]dwelling is in the midst
of deceit;[4820]

13 [a]Jer. 14:12; Ezek. 22:20, 21 [b]Jer. 5:17; 7:20; Joel 1:7 [c]Matt. 21:19; Luke 13:6
14 [a]Jer. 4:5 [b]2Sam. 20:6; Jer. 35:11 [c]Deut. 29:18; Ps. 69:21; Jer. 9:15; 23:15; Lam. 3:19; Matt. 27:34 [d]Jer. 3:25; 14:20
15 [a]Jer. 8:11; 14:19
16 [a]Judg. 18:29; Jer. 4:15 [b]Judg. 5:22 [c]Jer. 3:24; 10:25
17 [a]Num. 21:6; Deut. 32:24 [b]Ps. 58:4, 5
18 [I]So Gr. and versions [a]Is. 22:4; Lam. 1:16, 17 [b]Jer. 23:9; Lam. 5:17
19 [I]Lit., *vanities* [a]Is. 13:5; 39:3; Jer. 4:16; 9:16 [b]Deut. 32:21; Jer. 7:19 [c]Ps. 31:6
21 [a]Jer. 4:19; 9:1; 14:17 [b]Jer. 14:2; Joel 2:6; Nah. 2:10
22 [I]Or, *healing* [II]Lit., *gone up* [a]Gen. 37:25; Jer. 46:11 [b]Jer. 14:19; 30:13

1 [I]Ch. 8:23 in Heb. [a]Is. 22:4; Jer. 8:18; 13:17; Lam. 2:18 [b]Jer. 6:26; 8:21, 22
2 [I]Ch. 9:1 in Heb. [a]Ps. 55:6, 7; 120:5, 6 [b]Jer. 5:7, 8; 23:10; Hos. 4:2 [c]Jer. 5:11; 12:1, 6
3 [a]Ps. 64:3; Is. 59:4; Jer. 9:8 [b]Jer. 4:22 [c]Judg. 2:10; 1Sam. 2:12; Jer. 4:22; 5:4, 5; Hos. 4:1; 1Cor. 15:34
4 [I]I.e., like Jacob (a play on words) [a]Ps. 12:2; Prov. 26:24, 25; Jer. 9:8; Mic. 7:5, 6 [b]Jer. 12:6 [c]Gen. 27:35 [d]Ps. 15:3; Prov. 10:18; Jer. 6:28
5 [a]Mic. 6:12 [b]Jer. 12:13; 51:58, 64
6 [a]Ps. 120:5, 6; Jer. 5:27; 8:5

Through deceit they [b]refuse[3985]
to know Me," declares the
LORD.

7 Therefore thus says[559] the LORD
of hosts,[6635]
"Behold, I will refine them and
[a]assay[974] them;
For [b]what *else* can I do,[6213]
because of the daughter of
My people?

8 "Their [a]tongue is a deadly[7819]
arrow;
It speaks deceit;
With his mouth[6310] one
[b]speaks peace[7965] to his
neighbor,
But inwardly he [c]sets[7760] an
ambush for him.

9 "[a]Shall I not punish[6485] them for
these things?" declares[5001]
the LORD.
"On a nation[1471] such as this
Shall I not avenge[5358]
Myself?[5315]

10 "For the [a]mountains I will take
up[5375] a weeping and wailing,
And for the pastures of the
[b]wilderness a dirge,
Because they are [c]laid waste,
so that no one passes
through,[5674]
And the lowing of the cattle is
not heard;[8085]
Both the [d]birds of the sky[8064]
and the beasts have fled; they
are gone.

11 "And I will make Jerusalem a
[a]heap of ruins,
A haunt of [b]jackals;[8577]
And I will make the cities of
Judah a [c]desolation,[8077]
without inhabitant."

12 Who is the [a]wise[2450] man[376] that
may understand[995] this? And *who is* he
to whom [b]the mouth of the LORD has
spoken,[1696] that he may declare[5046] it?
[c]Why is the land[776] ruined,[6] laid waste
like a desert, so that no one passes
through?[5674]

13 And the LORD said, "Because
they have [a]forsaken[5800] My law[8451]
which I set before them, and have not
obeyed[8085] My voice nor walked according
to it,

14 but have [a]walked after the
stubbornness[8307] of their heart[3820] and
after the [b]Baals, as their [c]fathers[1] taught
them,"

15 therefore thus says the LORD of
hosts, the God[430] of Israel, "behold,
[a]I will feed them, this people, with
wormwood[3939] and give them [b]poisoned[7219] water to drink.

16 "And I will [a]scatter them among
the nations,[1471] whom neither they nor
their fathers have known;[3045] and I will
send the [b]sword[2719] after them until[5647]
I have annihilated[3615] them."

17 Thus says the LORD of hosts,
"Consider[995] and call[7121] for the
[a]mourning women, that they
may come;
And send for the [1b]wailing
women, that they may
come!

18 "And let them make haste, and
take up a wailing for us,
That our [a]eyes may shed tears,
And our eyelids flow with water.

19 "For a voice of [a]wailing is
heard[8085] from Zion,
'[b]How are we ruined![7703]
We are put to great shame,[954]
For we have [c]left the land,
Because they have cast down
our dwellings.' "[4908]

20 Now hear the word[1697] of the
LORD, O you [a]women,[802]
And let your ear[241] receive the
word of His mouth;
Teach[3925] your daughters
wailing,
And everyone[802] her
neighbor[7468] a dirge.

21 For [a]death[4194] has come up[5927]
through our windows;
It has entered our palaces[759]
To cut off[3772] the [b]children from
the streets,
The young men from the town
squares.

22 Speak, "Thus declares the
LORD,
'The corpses[5038] of men[120] will

---

6 [b]Job 21:14, 15; Prov. 1:24; Jer. 11:10; 13:10; John 3:19, 20

7 [a]Is. 1:25; Jer. 6:27; Mal. 3:3 [b]Hos. 11:8

8 [a]Jer. 9:3 [b]Ps. 28:3 [c]Jer. 5:26

9 [a]Is. 1:24; Jer. 5:9, 29

10 [a]Jer. 4:24; 7:29 [b]Jer. 4:26; Hos. 4:3 [c]Jer. 12:4, 10; Ezek. 14:15; 29:11; 33:28 [d]Jer. 4:25; 12:4; Hos. 4:3

11 [a]Is. 25:2; Jer. 51:37 [b]Is. 13:22; 34:13 [c]Jer. 4:27; 26:9

12 [a]Ps. 107:43; Is. 42:23; Hos. 14:9 [b]Jer. 9:20; 23:16 [c]Ps. 107:34; Jer. 23:10

13 [a]2Chr. 7:19; Ps. 89:30; Jer. 5:19; 22:9

14 [a]Jer. 7:24; 11:8; Rom. 1:21-24 [b]Jer. 2:8, 23; 23:27 [c]Gal. 1:14; 1Pet. 1:18

15 [a]Ps. 80:5 [b]Deut. 29:18; Jer. 8:14; 23:15; Lam. 3:15

16 [a]Lev. 26:33; Deut. 28:64; Jer. 13:24 [b]Jer. 44:27; Ezek. 5:2, 12

17 [1]Lit., *skilled* [a]2Chr. 35:25; Eccl. 12:5 [b]Amos 5:16

18 [a]Is. 22:4; Jer. 9:1; 14:17

19 [a]Jer. 7:29; Ezek. 7:16-18 [b]Deut. 28:29; Jer. 4:13 [c]Jer. 7:15; 15:1

20 [a]Is. 32:9

21 [a]2Chr. 36:17; Jer. 15:7; 18:21; Ezek. 9:5, 6; Amos 6:9, 10 [b]Jer. 6:11

fall [a]like dung on the open
field,[7704]
And like the sheaf after the
reaper,
But no one will gather[622] *them.*' "

23 Thus says the LORD, "[a]Let not a wise man boast of his wisdom,[2451] and let not the [b]mighty man boast[1984] of his might, let not a [c]rich man boast of his riches;

24 but let him who boasts [a]boast of this, that he understands[7919] and knows Me, that I am the LORD who [b]exercises[6213] lovingkindness, justice,[4941] and righteousness[6666] on earth; for I [c]delight[2654] in these things," declares the LORD.

25 "Behold, the days[3117] are coming," declares the LORD, "that I will punish[6485] all who are circumcised[4135] and yet [a]uncircumcised—[6190]

26 Egypt, and Judah, and Edom, and the sons[1121] of Ammon, and Moab, and [a]all those inhabiting the desert who clip the hair on their temples; for all the nations[1471] are uncircumcised,[6189] and all the house[1004] of Israel are [b]uncircumcised of heart."

A Satire on Idolatry

10 Hear[8085] the word[1697] which the LORD speaks to you, O house[1004] of Israel.

2 Thus says[559] the LORD,
"[a]Do not learn[3925] the way[1870] of
the nations,[1471]
And do not be terrified[2865] by
the signs[226] of the
heavens[8064]
Although the nations are
terrified by them;
3 For the customs of the
peoples[5971] are [I][a]delusion;
Because [b]it is wood cut[3772] from
the forest,
The work of the hands[3027] of a
craftsman with a cutting tool.
4 "They [a]decorate *it* with silver and
with gold;
They [b]fasten[2388] it with nails and
with hammers
So that it will not totter.
5 "Like a scarecrow in a cucumber
field are they,
And they [a]cannot speak;[1696]
They must be [b]carried,[5375]
Because they cannot walk!
Do not fear[3372] them,
For they [c]can do no harm,[7489]
Nor can they do any good."[3190]
6 [a]There is none like Thee, O
LORD;
Thou art [b]great, and great is Thy
name in might.
7 [a]Who would not fear[3372] Thee,
O [b]King[4428] of the nations?[1471]
Indeed it is Thy due!
For among all the [c]wise men[2450]
of the nations,
And in all their kingdoms,[4467]
There is none like Thee.
8 But they are altogether
[a]stupid and foolish[3688]
In their discipline[4148] of
[I]delusion—[II]their idol is
wood!
9 Beaten[7554] [a]silver is brought
from [b]Tarshish,
And [c]gold from Uphaz,
The work of a craftsman and
of the hands of a
goldsmith;[6884]
Violet and purple are their
clothing;
They are all the [d]work of
skilled[2450] men.
10 But the LORD is the [a]true[571]
God;[430]
He is the [b]living[2416] God and the
[c]everlasting[5769] King.
At His wrath[7110] the [d]earth[776]
quakes,[7493]
And the nations cannot
[e]endure His indignation.[2195]

11 [I]Thus you shall say[560] to them, "The [a]gods[426] that did not make the heavens[8065] and the earth[778] shall [b]perish[7] from the earth and from under the [II]heavens."

12 *It is* [a]He who made[6213] the earth
by His power,
Who [b]established[3559] the
world[8398] by His wisdom;[2451]

22 [a]Ps. 83:10; Is. 5:25; Jer. 8:2; 16:4; 25:33

23 [a]Eccl. 9:11; Is. 47:10; Ezek. 28:3-7 [b]1Kin. 20:10, 11; Is. 10:8-12 [c]Job 31:24, 25; Ps. 49:6-9

24 [a]Ps. 20:7; 44:8; Is. 41:16; Jer. 4:2; 1Cor. 1:31; 2Cor. 10:17; Gal. 6:14 [b]Ex. 34:6, 7; Ps. 36:5, 7; 51:1 [c]Is. 61:8; Mic. 7:18

25 [a]Jer. 4:4; Rom. 2:28, 29

26 [a]Jer. 25:23 [b]Lev. 26:41; Jer. 4:4; 6:10; Ezek. 44:7; Rom. 2:28

2 [a]Lev. 18:3; 20:23; Deut. 12:30

3 [I]Lit., *vanity* [a]Jer. 14:22 [b]Is. 44:9-20

4 [a]Is. 40:19 [b]Is. 40:20; 41:7

5 [a]Ps. 115:5; Is. 46:7; Jer. 10:14; 1Cor. 12:2 [b]Ps. 115:7; Is. 46:1, 7 [c]Is. 41:23, 24

6 [a]Ex. 15:11; Deut. 33:26; Ps. 86:8, 10; Jer. 10:16 [b]Ps. 48:1; 96:4; Is. 12:6; Jer. 32:18

7 [a]Rev. 15:4 [b]Ps. 22:28 [c]Dan. 2:27, 28; 1Cor. 1:19, 20

8 [I]Lit., *vanities*, or *idols* [II]Lit., *it is* [a]Jer. 4:22; 5:4; 10:14

9 [a]Is. 40:19 [b]Ps. 72:10; Is. 23:6 [c]Dan. 10:5 [d]Ps. 115:4

10 [a]Is. 65:16 [b]Jer. 4:2 [c]Ps. 10:16; 29:10 [d]Jer. 4:24; 50:46 [e]Ps. 76:7

11 [I]This verse is in Aram. [II]Or, *these heavens* [a]Ps. 96:5 [b]Is. 2:18; Zeph. 2:11

12 [a]Gen. 1:1, 6; Job 38:4-7; Ps. 136:5; 148:4, 5; Jer. 51:15, 19 [b]Ps. 78:69; Is. 45:18

And by His understanding8394 He
has [c]stretched out the
heavens.8064
13 When He utters His [a]voice, *there*
is a tumult of waters in the
heavens,
And He causes the [b]clouds to
ascend5927 from the end of the
earth;
He makes6213 lightning for the
rain,
And brings out the [c]wind7307
from His storehouses.
14 Every man120 is [a]stupid, devoid
of knowledge;1847
Every goldsmith is put to shame
by his [I]idols;6459
For his molten images5262 are
deceitful,
And there is no breath7307 in
them.
15 They are [a]worthless, a work
of mockery;8595
In the [b]time6256 of their
punishment6486 they will
perish.6
16 The [a]portion of Jacob is not like
these;
For the [Ib]Maker3335 of all is He,
And [c]Israel is the tribe7626 of His
inheritance;5159
The [d]LORD of hosts6635 is His
name.
17 [a]Pick up622 your bundle3666 from
the ground,776
You who dwell under siege!
18 For thus says the LORD,
"Behold, I am [a]slinging out the
inhabitants of the land
At this time,
And will cause them distress,
That they may [I]be found."
19 [a]Woe is me, because of my
[I]injury!7667
My [b]wound4347 is incurable.
But I said,559 "Truly this is a
sickness,
And I [c]must bear5375 it."
20 My [a]tent168 is destroyed,7703
And all my ropes are broken;
My [b]sons1121 have gone from me
and are no more.
There is [c]no one to stretch out
my tent168 again
Or to set up my curtains.
21 For the shepherds have become
stupid
And [a]have not sought the LORD;
Therefore they have not
prospered,7919
And [b]all their flock is scattered.
22 The sound of a [a]report! Behold,
it comes—
A great commotion [b]out of the
land776 of the north—
To [c]make7760 the cities of Judah
A desolation,8077 a haunt of
jackals.8577
23 I know,3045 O LORD, that
[a]a man's way is not in himself;
[b]Nor is it in a man who walks
to direct3559 his steps.
24 [a]Correct3256 me, O LORD, but
with justice;4941
Not with Thine anger,639 lest
Thou [I]bring me to nothing.
25 [a]Pour out8210 Thy wrath on the
nations that [b]do not know
Thee,
And on the families4940 that
[c]do not call7121 Thy name;
For they have devoured Jacob;
They have [d]devoured him and
consumed3615 him,
And have laid waste8074 his
[I]habitation.

The Broken Covenant

11 The word1697 which came to
Jeremiah from the LORD, saying,
2 "[a]Hear8085 the words1697 of this
[b]covenant,1285 and speak1696 to the
men376 of Judah and to the inhabitants
of Jerusalem;
3 and say559 to them, 'Thus says559
the LORD, the God430 of Israel,
"[a]Cursed779 is the man376 who does not
heed8085 the words of this covenant
4 which I commanded6680 your
forefathers1 in the [a]day3117 that I brought
them out of the land776 of Egypt, from
the [b]iron furnace, saying, "[c]Listen8085 to
My voice, and [I]do6213 according to all

12 [c]Job 9:8; Is. 40:22
13 [a]Ps. 29:3-9 [b]Job 36:27-29 [c]Ps. 135:7
14 [I]Or, *graven image* [a]Jer. 10:8; 51:17, 18
15 [a]Is. 41:24; Jer. 8:19; 14:22 [b]Jer. 8:12; 51:18
16 [I]Lit., *Fashioner* [a]Ps. 16:5; 73:26; 119:57; Jer. 51:19; Lam. 3:24 [b]Is. 45:7; Jer. 10:12 [c]Deut. 32:9; Ps. 74:2 [d]Jer. 31:35; 32:18
17 [a]Ezek. 12:3-12
18 [I]Lit., *find* [a]1Sam. 25:29
19 [I]Lit., *breaking* [a]Jer. 4:31 [b]Jer. 14:17 [c]Mic. 7:9
20 [a]Jer. 4:20; Lam. 2:4 [b]Jer. 31:15; Lam. 1:5 [c]Is. 51:18
21 [a]Jer. 2:8 [b]Jer. 23:2
22 [a]Jer. 4:15 [b]Jer. 1:14; 25:9 [c]Jer. 9:11; 49:33
23 [a]Prov. 16:1; 20:24 [b]Is. 26:7
24 [I]Lit., *diminish me* [a]Ps. 6:1; 38:1
25 [I]Or, *pasture* [a]Ps. 79:6, 7; Zeph. 3:8 [b]Job 18:21; 1Thess. 4:5; 2Thess. 1:8 [c]Zeph. 1:6 [d]Jer. 8:16; 50:7, 17
2 [a]Jer. 11:6 [b]Ex. 19:5
3 [a]Deut. 27:26; Jer. 17:5; Gal. 3:10
4 [I]Lit., *do them* [a]Ex. 24:3-8; Jer. 31:32 [b]Deut. 4:20; 1Kin. 8:51 [c]Lev. 26:3; Deut. 11:27; Jer. 7:23; 26:13

which I command[6680] you; so you shall
be [d]My people,[5971] and I will be your
God,'
5 in order to confirm the [a]oath[7621]
which I swore to your forefathers, to
give them a land flowing with milk and
honey, as *it is* this day."'" Then I answered and said,[559] "[b]Amen, O LORD."
6 And the LORD said to me,
"[a]Proclaim[7121] all these words in the cities of Judah and in the streets of Jerusalem, saying, '[b]Hear the words of this
covenant and [c]do them.
7 'For I solemnly [a]warned[5749] your
fathers in the [b]day that I brought them
up[5927] from the land of Egypt, even
to this day, [Ic]warning persistently, saying, "[d]Listen to My voice."
8 'Yet they [a]did not obey[8085] or incline their ear,[241] but walked, each
one,[376] in the stubbornness[8307] of his
evil[7451] heart;[3820] therefore I brought on
them all the [b]words of this covenant,
which I commanded[6680] *them* to do, but
they did[6213] not.'"
9 Then the LORD said to me, "A
[a]conspiracy has been found among the
men of Judah and among the inhabitants
of Jerusalem.
10 "They have [a]turned back to the
iniquities[5771] of their [I]ancestors who
[b]refused[3985] to hear My words, and they
[c]have gone after other gods[430] to
serve[5647] them; the house[1004] of Israel
and the house of Judah have [d]broken[6565]
My covenant which I made[3772] with their
fathers."
11 Therefore thus says the LORD,
"Behold I am [a]bringing disaster on them
which they will [b]not be able to escape;
though they will [c]cry[2199] to Me, yet I
will not listen[8085] to them.
12 "Then the cities of Judah and the
inhabitants of Jerusalem will [a]go and cry
to the gods to whom they burn incense,[6999] but they surely will not
save[3467] them in the time[6256] of their
disaster.[7451]
13 "For your gods are [Ia]as many as
your cities, O Judah; and [I]as many as
the streets of Jerusalem are the
altars[4196] you have set up[7760] to the
[b]shameful thing, altars to [c]burn incense[6999] to Baal.
14 "Therefore [a]do not pray[6419] for
this people, nor lift up[5375] a cry[7121] or
prayer[8605] for them; for I will [b]not listen
when they call to Me because of their
disaster.
15 "What right has My [a]beloved[3039]
in My house
When [b]she has done many vile
deeds?[4209]
Can the sacrificial[6944] flesh[1320]
take away[5674] from you your
disaster,
[I]So *that* you can rejoice?"
16 The LORD called[7121] your name,
"A [a]green olive tree, beautiful in
fruit and form";
With the [b]noise of a great
tumult[1999]
He has [c]kindled fire on it,
And its branches are
worthless.[7489]
17 And the LORD of hosts,[6635] who
[a]planted you, has [b]pronounced evil
against you because of the evil of the
house of Israel and of the house of Judah,
which they have [I]done[6213] to provoke[3707]
Me by [IIc]offering up sacrifices to Baal.

Plots against Jeremiah

18 Moreover, the LORD [a]made it
known[3045] to me and I
knew[3045] it;
Then Thou didst show[7200] me
their deeds.
19 But I was like a gentle
[a]lamb led to the slaughter;[2873]
And I did not know[3045] that they
had [b]devised[2803] plots[4284]
against me, *saying,*
"Let us destroy the tree with its
[I]fruit,
And [c]let us cut him off[3772] from
the [d]land of the living,[2416]
That his [e]name be
remembered[2142] no more."

4 [d]Jer. 24:7; Zech. 8:8
5 [a]Ex. 13:5; Deut. 7:12; Ps. 105:9; Jer. 32:22 [b]Jer. 28:6
6 [a]Jer. 3:12; 7:2 [b]Jer. 11:2 [c]John 13:17; Rom. 2:13; James 1:22
7 [I]Lit., *rising early and warning* [a]1Sam. 8:9 [b]Jer. 11:4 [c]Ex. 15:26; 2Chr. 36:15; Jer. 7:25 [d]Jer. 11:7
8 [a]Jer. 7:24; 9:14; 35:15; Ezek. 20:8 [b]Lev. 26:14-43
9 [a]Ezek. 22:25; Hos. 6:9
10 [I]Lit., *former fathers* [a]1Sam. 15:11; Jer. 3:10, 11; Ezek. 20:18 [b]Deut. 9:7; Ps. 78:8-10; Jer. 13:10 [c]Judg. 2:11-13 [d]Jer. 3:6-11; Ezek.16:59
11 [a]2Kin. 22:16; Jer. 6:19; 11:17 [b]Is. 24:17; Jer. 25:35 [c]Ps. 18:41; Prov. 1:28; Is. 1:15; Jer. 11:14; 14:12; Ezek. 8:18; Mic. 3:4; Zech. 7:13
12 [a]Deut. 32:37; Jer. 44:17
13 [I]Lit., *the number of* [a]2Kin. 23:13; Jer. 2:28 [b]Jer. 3:24 [c]Jer. 7:9
14 [a]Ex. 32:10; Jer. 7:16; 14:11; 1John 5:16 [b]Ps. 66:18; Jer. 11:11; Hos. 5:6
15 [I]Lit., *Then* [a]Jer. 13:27 [b]Ezek. 16:25
16 [a]Ps. 52:8; Rom. 11:17 [b]Ps. 83:2 [c]Ps. 80:16; Is. 27:11; Jer. 21:14
17 [I]Or, *done for themselves* [II]Or, *burning incense* [a]Is. 5:2; Jer. 2:21; 12:2 [b]Jer. 1:14; 16:10; 19:15 [c]Jer. 7:9; 11:13; 32:29

18 [a]1Sam. 23:11, 12; 2Kin. 6:9, 10; Ezek. 8:6
19 [I]Lit., *bread* [a]Is. 53:7 [b]Jer. 18:18; 20:10 [c]Ps. 83:4; Is. 53:8 [d]Job 28:13; Ps. 52:5 [e]Ps. 109:13

20 But, O LORD of hosts, who
[a]judges[8199] righteously,[6664]
Who [b]tries the [I]feelings3629 and
the heart,
Let me see Thy vengeance[5360]
on them,
For to Thee have I
[II]committed[1540] my
cause.[7379]

🔑 21 Therefore thus says the LORD
concerning the men[582] of [a]Anathoth, who
[b]seek your life,[5315] saying, "[c]Do not
prophesy[5012] in the name of the LORD,
that you might not [d]die[4191] at our
hand";[3027]
22 therefore, thus says the LORD
of hosts, "Behold, I am about to
[a]punish[6485] them! The [b]young men will
die by the sword,[2719] their sons[1121] and
daughters will die by famine;
23 and a remnant[7611] [a]will not be left
to them, for I will [b]bring disaster on
the men of Anathoth—[c]the year of their
punishment."6489

Jeremiah's Prayer

12 [a]Righteous[6662] art Thou, O
LORD, that I would plead[7378]
my case with Thee;
Indeed I would [b]discuss[1696]
matters of justice[4941] with
Thee:
Why has the [c]way[1870] of the
wicked[7563] prospered?
Why are all those who [d]deal in
treachery[898] at ease?
2 Thou hast [a]planted them, they
have also taken root;
They grow, they have even
produced[6213] fruit.
Thou art [b]near [I]to their lips[6310]
But far from their [II]mind.3629
3 But Thou [a]knowest[3045] me, O
LORD;
Thou seest[7200] me;
And Thou dost [b]examine[974] my
heart's[3820] *attitude* toward
Thee.

20 [I]Lit., *kidneys* [II]Lit., *revealed* [a]Gen. 18:25; Ps. 7:8; Jer. 20:12 [b]1Sam. 16:7; Ps. 7:9; Jer. 17:10
21 [a]Jer. 1:1 [b]Jer. 12:5, 6; 20:10 [c]Amos 2:12 [d]Jer. 26:8; 38:4
22 [a]Jer. 21:14 [b]2Chr. 36:17; Jer. 18:21
23 [a]Jer. 6:9 [b]Jer. 23:12; Hos. 9:7; Mic. 7:4 [c]Luke 19:44

1 [a]Ezra 9:15; Ps. 51:4; 129:4; Jer. 11:20 [b]Job 13:3 [c]Job 12:6; Jer. 5:27, 28; Hab. 1:4; Mal. 3:15 [d]Jer. 3:7, 20; 5:11
2 [I]Lit., *in their mouth* [II]Lit., *kidneys* [a]Jer. 11:17; 45:4; Ezek. 17:5-10 [b]Is. 29:13; Jer. 3:10; Ezek. 33:31; Titus 1:16
3 [I]Lit., *sanctify them* [a]Ps. 139:1-4 [b]Ps. 7:9; 11:5; Jer. 11:20 [c]Jer. 17:18; 50:27; James 5:5
4 [a]Jer. 4:28; 9:10; 23:10 [b]Joel 1:10-17 [c]Ps. 107:34 [d]Jer. 4:25; 7:20; 9:10; Hos. 4:3; Hab. 3:17 [e]Jer. 5:31; Ezek. 7:2
5 [I]Lit., *pride* [a]Jer. 49:19; 50:44
6 [a]Gen. 37:4-11; Job 6:15; Ps. 69:8; Jer. 9:4, 5 [b]Ps. 12:2; Prov. 26:25
7 [a]Is. 2:6; Jer. 7:29; 23:39 [b]Jer. 11:15; Hos. 11:1-8
8 [I]Lit., *raised her voice* [a]Is. 59:13 [b]Hos. 9:15; Amos 6:8

Drag them off like sheep for the
slaughter[2873]
And [I]set them apart[6942] for a
[c]day[3117] of carnage![2028]
4 How long is the [a]land[776] to
mourn
And the [b]vegetation of the
countryside[7704] to wither?[3001]
For the [c]wickedness[7451] of those
who dwell in it,
[d]Animals and birds have been
snatched away,[5595]
Because *men* have said,[559] "He
will not see our latter
[e]ending."[319]
5 "If you have run with footmen
and they have tired you out,
Then how can you compete[2734]
with horses?
If you fall down in a land of
peace,
How will you do[6213] in the
[Ia]thicket of the Jordan?
6 "For even your [a]brothers[251] and
the household[1004] of your
father,[1]
Even they have dealt
treacherously[898] with you,
Even they have cried[7121] aloud
after you.
Do not believe[539] them, although
they may say[1696] [b]nice
things[2896] to you."

God's Answer

7 "I have [a]forsaken[5800] My house,
I have abandoned[5203] My
inheritance;[5159]
I have given the [b]beloved[3033] of
My soul[5315]
Into the hand[3709] of her enemies.
8 "My inheritance has become to
Me
Like a lion in the forest;
She has [Ia]roared against Me;
Therefore I have come to
[b]hate her.
9 "Is My inheritance like a speckled
bird of prey to Me?

🔑 **11:21** See note on Amos 2:12.

Are the [a]birds of prey against
her on every side?
Go, gather[622] all the [b]beasts[4216]
of the field,
Bring them to devour!
10 "Many [a]shepherds have
ruined[7843] My [b]vineyard,
They have [c]trampled down My
field;
They have made My [d]pleasant
field
A desolate[8077] wilderness.
11 "[I]It has been made[7760] a
desolation,[8074]
Desolate, it [a]mourns [II]before
Me;
The [b]whole land has been made
desolate,[8074]
Because no man[376] [c]lays[7760] it
to heart.
12 "On all the [I][a]bare heights[8205] in
the wilderness
Destroyers[7703] have come,
For a [b]sword[2719] of the LORD is
devouring
From one end of the land even
to the [II]other;
There is [c]no peace for
[III]anyone.[1320]
13 "They have [a]sown wheat and
have reaped thorns,
They have [b]strained themselves
[I]to no profit.
But be ashamed[954] of your
[II][c]harvest
Because of the [d]fierce anger[639]
of the LORD."

14 Thus says[559] the LORD concerning all My [a]wicked[7451] neighbors[7934] who
[b]strike[5060] at the inheritance[5159] with
which I have endowed[5157] My people[5971]
Israel, "Behold I am about to uproot
them from their land[127] and will [c]up-
root the house of Judah from among
them.

15 "And it will come about that after
I have uprooted them, I will [a]again[7725]
have compassion[7355] on them; and I will
[b]bring them back, each one[376] to his inheritance and each one to his land.

16 "Then it will come about that if
they will really [a]learn[3925] the ways[1870]
of My people, to [b]swear[7650] by My name,
'As the LORD lives,'[2416] even as they
taught[3925] My people to [c]swear by Baal,
then they will be [d]built up in the midst
of My people.

17 "But if they will not listen,[8085]
then I will [a]uproot that nation,[1471] uproot
and destroy[6] it," declares[5001] the LORD.

The Ruined Waistband

13 Thus the LORD said[559] to me,
"Go and [a]buy yourself a linen
waistband,[232] and put it around your
waist, but do not put it in water."

2 So I bought the waistband in accordance with the [a]word[1697] of the LORD
and put it around my waist.

3 Then the word of the LORD came
to me a second time, saying,

4 "Take the waistband that you have
bought, which is around your waist, and
arise, go to [I]the [a]Euphrates and hide it
there in a crevice of the rock."

5 So I went and hid it by the Euphrates, [a]as the LORD had commanded
me.

6 And it came about after many
days[3117] that the LORD said[559] to me,
"Arise, go to the Euphrates and take
from there the waistband which I commanded you to hide there."

7 Then I went to the Euphrates and
dug, and I took the waistband from the
place where I had hidden it; and lo, the
waistband was ruined,[7843] it was totally
worthless.

8 Then the word of the LORD came
to me, saying,

9 "Thus says the LORD, 'Just so will
I destroy[7843] the [a]pride of Judah and the
great pride of Jerusalem.

10 'This wicked[7451] people,[5971] who
[a]refuse[3987] to listen[8085] to My words,[1697]
who [b]walk in the stubbornness[8307] of
their hearts[3820] and have gone after
other gods[430] to serve[5647] them and to
bow down[7812] to them, let them be just
like this waistband, which is totally
worthless.

11 'For as the waistband clings to
the waist of a man,[376] so I made the

9 [a]2Kin. 24:2; Ezek. 23:22-25 [b]Is. 56:9; Jer. 7:33; 15:3; 34:20

10 [a]Jer. 6:3; 23:1 [b]Ps. 80:8-16; Is. 5:1-7 [c]Is. 63:18 [d]Jer. 3:19

11 [I]Lit., *One has made it* [II]Or, *upon* [a]Jer. 12:4; 14:2; 23:10 [b]Jer. 4:20, 27; 25:11 [c]Is. 42:25

12 [I]Or, *caravan trails* [II]Lit., *other end of the land* [III]Lit., *all flesh* [a]Jer. 3:2, 21 [b]Is. 34:6; Jer. 47:6; Amos 9:4 [c]Jer. 16:5; 30:5

13 [I]Lit., *they do not profit* [II]Lit., *products* [a]Lev. 26:16; Deut. 28:38; Mic. 6:15; Hag. 1:6 [b]Is. 55:2; Jer. 9:5 [c]Jer. 17:10 [d]Jer. 4:26; 25:37, 38

14 [a]Jer. 49:1, 7; Zeph. 2:8-10 [b]Jer. 2:3; 50:11, 12; Zech. 2:8 [c]Deut. 30:3; Ps. 106:47; Is. 11:11-16

15 [a]Jer. 48:47; 49:6, 39 [b]Amos 9:14

16 [a]Is. 42:6; 49:6 [b]Jer. 4:2; Zeph. 1:5 [c]Josh. 23:7; Jer. 5:7 [d]Jer. 3:17; 4:2; 16:19

17 [a]Ps. 2:8-12; Is. 60:12

1 [a]Jer. 13:11

2 [a]Is. 20:2; Ezek. 2:8

4 [I]Or, *Parah*, cf. Josh. 18:23; so through v. 7 [a]Jer. 51:63

5 [a]Ex. 39:42, 43; 40:16

9 [a]Lev. 26:19; Is. 2:10-17; 23:9; Jer. 13:15-17; Zeph. 3:11

10 [a]Num. 14:11; 2Chr. 36:15, 16; Jer. 11:10 [b]Jer. 9:14; 11:8; 16:12

whole household[1004] of Israel and the whole household of Judah [a]cling to Me,' declares[5001] the LORD, 'that they might be for Me a people, for [1b]renown, for [c]praise,[8416] and for glory;[8597] but they [d]did not listen.'

Captivity Threatened

12 "Therefore you are to speak[559] this word to them, 'Thus says the LORD, the God[430] of Israel, "Every jug is to be filled with wine."' And when they say[559] to you, 'Do we not very well know[3045] that every jug is to be filled with wine?'

13 then say to them, 'Thus says the LORD, "Behold I am about to fill all the inhabitants of this land—[776] the kings[4428] that sit for David on his throne,[3678] the priests,[3548] the prophets[5030] and all the inhabitants of Jerusalem—with [a]drunkenness![7943]

14 "And I will [a]dash them against each[376] other, both the [b]fathers[1] and the sons[1121] together," declares the LORD. "I will [c]not show pity nor be sorry nor have compassion[7355] that I should not destroy them."'"

15 Listen and give heed,[238] do not
be [a]haughty,
For the LORD has spoken.[1696]
16 [a]Give glory[3511] to the LORD your
God,
Before He brings [b]darkness
And before your [c]feet
stumble[5062]
On the dusky mountains,
And while you are hoping for
light[216]
He makes it into [d]deep
darkness,[6757]
And turns *it* into gloom.[6205]
17 But [a]if you will not listen to it,
My soul[5315] will [b]sob in secret
for *such* pride;
And my eyes will bitterly weep
And flow down with tears,
Because the [c]flock of the LORD
has been taken captive.[7617]
18 Say to the [a]king[4428] and the
queen mother,

11 [1]Lit., *a name* [a]Ex. 19:5, 6; Deut. 32:10, 11 [b]Jer. 32:20 [c]Is. 43:21; Jer. 33:9 [d]Ps. 81:11; Jer. 7:13, 24, 26
13 [a]Ps. 60:3; 75:8; Is. 51:17; 63:6; Jer. 25:27; 51:7, 57
14 [a]Is. 9:20, 21; Jer. 19:9-11 [b]Jer. 6:21; Ezek. 5:10 [c]Deut. 29:20; Is. 27:11; Jer. 16:5; 21:7
15 [a]Prov. 16:5; Is. 28:14-22
16 [a]Josh. 7:19; Ps. 96:8 [b]Is. 5:30; 8:22; 59:9; Amos 5:18; 8:9 [c]Prov. 4:19; Jer. 23:12 [d]Ps. 44:19; 107:10, 14; Jer. 2:6
17 [a]Mal. 2:2 [b]Ps. 119:136; Jer. 9:1; 14:17; Luke 19:41, 42 [c]Ps. 80:1; Jer. 23:1, 2
18 [a]2Kin. 24:12, 15; Jer. 22:26 [b]2Chr. 33:12, 19 [c]Ex. 39:28; Is. 3:20; Ezek. 24:17, 23; 44:18
19 [a]Jer. 32:44 [b]Jer. 20:4; 52:27-30
20 [a]Jer. 1:15; 6:22; Hab. 1:6 [b]Jer. 13:17; 23:2
21 [1]Or, *chieftains* [a]Jer. 2:25; 38:22 [b]Is. 13:8; Jer. 4:31
22 [1]Or, *suffered violence* [a]Deut. 7:17 [b]Jer. 5:19; 16:10 [c]Jer. 2:17-19; 9:2-9 [d]Is. 47:2; Ezek. 16:37; Nah. 3:5
23 [a]Prov. 27:22; Is. 1:5 [b]Jer. 4:22; 9:5
24 [a]Lev. 26:33; Jer. 9:16; Ezek. 5:2, 12 [b]Jer. 4:11; 18:17
25 [a]Job 20:29; Ps. 11:6; Matt. 24:51 [b]Ps. 9:17; Jer. 2:32; 3:21
26 [a]Lam. 1:8; Ezek. 23:29; Hos. 2:10

"[b]Take a lowly seat,
For your beautiful [c]crown
Has come down from your
head."[4761]
19 The [a]cities of the Negev have
been locked up,
And there is no one to open
them;
All [b]Judah has been carried into
exile,[1540]
Wholly[7965] carried into exile.
20 "Lift up[5375] your eyes and see[7200]
Those coming [a]from the north.
Where is the [b]flock that was
given you,
Your beautiful[8597] sheep?
21 "What will you say when He
appoints over[6485] you—
And you yourself had taught[3925]
them—
Former [1a]companions to be
head[7218] over you?
Will not [b]pangs[2256] take hold of
you,
Like a woman[802] in childbirth?
22 "And if you [a]say in your heart,[3824]
'[b]Why have these things
happened to me?'
Because of the [c]magnitude of
your iniquity[5771]
[d]Your skirts have been
removed,
And your heels[6119] have [1]been
exposed.[2554]
23 "[a]Can the Ethiopian change his
skin[5785]
Or the leopard his spots?
Then you also can [b]do good[3190]
Who are accustomed[3928] to doing
evil.[7489]
24 "Therefore I will [a]scatter them
like drifting[5674] straw
To the desert [b]wind.[7307]
25 "This is your [a]lot, the portion
measured to you
From Me," declares the LORD,
"Because you have [b]forgotten Me
And trusted[982] in falsehood.
26 "So I Myself have also [a]stripped
your skirts off over your face,
That your shame may be
seen.[7200]

27 "As for your [a]adulteries[5004] and
your *lustful* neighings,
The [b]lewdness[2154] of your
prostitution[2184]
On the [c]hills in the field,[7704]
I have seen[7200] your
abominations.[8251]
Woe to you, O Jerusalem!
[d]How long will you remain
unclean?"[2891]

Drought and a Prayer for Mercy

14 That which came as the word[1697] of the LORD to Jeremiah in regard to the [a]drought:

2 "Judah mourns,
And [a]her gates languish;
They sit on the ground[776] [b]in
mourning,[6937]
And the [c]cry of Jerusalem has
ascended.[5674]
3 "And their nobles[117] have
[a]sent their [I]servants for
water;
They have come to the
[b]cisterns and found no water.
They have returned[7725] with
their vessels empty;
They have been [c]put to shame[954]
and humiliated,
And they [d]cover their heads.[7218]
4 "Because the [a]ground[127] is
[I]cracked,
For there has been [b]no rain on
the land;[776]
The [c]farmers have been put to
shame,
They have covered their heads.
5 "For even the doe[365] in the
field[7704] has given birth only
to abandon[5800] *her young,*
Because there is [a]no grass.
6 "And the [a]wild donkeys stand on
the bare heights;[8205]
They pant for air[7307] like
jackals,[8577]
Their eyes fail[3615]
For there is [b]no vegetation.
7 "Although our [a]iniquities[5771]
testify against us,
O LORD, act[6213] [b]for Thy name's
sake!
Truly our [c]apostasies[4878] have
been many,
We have [d]sinned[2398] against
Thee.
8 "Thou [a]Hope[4723] of Israel,
Its [b]Savior[3467] in [c]time[6256] of
distress,
Why art Thou like a stranger[1616]
in the land[776]
Or like a traveler[732] who has
pitched his *tent* for the night?
9 "Why art Thou like a man[376]
dismayed,[1724]
Like a mighty man who
[a]cannot save?[3467]
Yet [b]Thou art in our midst,[7130]
O LORD,
And we are [c]called[7121] by Thy
name;
Do not forsake us!"

10 Thus says[559] the LORD to this people,[5971] "Even so they have [a]loved[157] to wander; they have not [b]kept their feet in check. Therefore the LORD does [c]not accept[7521] them; now He will [d]remember[2142] their iniquity[5771] and call[6485] their sins to account."

11 So the LORD said[559] to me, "[a]Do not pray[6419] for the welfare[2896] of this people.

12 "When they fast, I am [a]not going to listen[8085] to their cry; and when they offer [b]burnt offering[5930] and grain offering,[4503] I am not going to accept them. Rather I am going to [c]make an end of them by the [d]sword,[2719] famine and pestilence."[1698]

False Prophets

13 But, "Ah, Lord[136] [I]GOD!" I said, "Look, the prophets[5030] are telling[559] them, 'You [a]will not see the sword nor will you have famine, but I will give you [II]lasting[571] [b]peace in this place.' "

14 Then the LORD said to me, "The [a]prophets are prophesying[5012] falsehood[8267] in My name. [b]I have neither sent them nor commanded[6680] them nor spoken[1696] to them; they are prophesy-

---

27 [a]Jer. 5:7, 8 [b]Jer. 11:15 [c]Is. 65:7; Jer. 2:20; Ezek. 6:13 [d]Prov. 1:22; Hos. 8:5

1 [a]Jer. 17:8

2 [a]Is. 3:26 [b]Jer. 8:21 [c]1Sam. 5:12; Jer. 11:11; 46:12; Zech. 7:13

3 [I]Lit., *little ones* [a]1Kin. 18:5 [b]2Kin. 18:31; Jer. 2:13 [c]Job 6:20; Ps. 40:14 [d]2Sam. 15:30

4 [I]Lit., *shattered* [a]Joel 1:19, 20 [b]Jer. 3:3 [c]Joel 1:11

5 [a]Is. 15:6

6 [a]Job 39:5, 6; Jer. 2:24 [b]Joel 1:18

7 [a]Is. 59:12; Hos. 5:5 [b]Ps. 25:11; Jer. 14:21 [c]Jer. 5:6; 8:5 [d]Jer. 3:25; 8:14; 14:20

8 [a]Jer. 17:13 [b]Is. 43:3; 63:8 [c]Ps. 9:9; 50:15

9 [a]Num. 11:23; Is. 50:2; 59:1 [b]Ex. 29:45; Ps. 46:5; Jer. 8:19 [c]Is. 63:19; Jer. 15:16

10 [a]Jer. 2:25; 3:13 [b]Ps. 119:101 [c]Jer. 6:20; Amos 5:22 [d]Jer. 44:21-23; Hos. 8:13; 9:9

11 [a]Ex. 32:10; Jer. 7:16; 11:14

12 [a]Prov. 1:28; Is. 1:15; Jer. 11:11; Ezek. 8:18; Mic. 3:4; Zech. 7:13 [b]Jer. 6:20; 7:21 [c]Jer. 8:13 [d]Jer. 21:9

13 [I]Heb., *YHWH,* usually rendered LORD [II]Lit., *peace of truth* [a]Jer. 5:12; 23:17 [b]Jer. 6:14; 8:11

14 [a]Jer. 5:31; 23:25 [b]Jer. 23:21

ing to you a [c]false[8267] vision,[2377] divination,[7081] futility[457] and the deception of
their own [I]minds.[3820]
15 "Therefore thus says the LORD
concerning the prophets who are prophesying in My name, although it was
not I who sent them—yet they keep
saying, 'There shall be no sword or famine in this land'—[a]by sword and famine those prophets shall [I]meet their
end![8552]
16 "The people also to whom they
are prophesying will be [a]thrown out into
the streets of Jerusalem because of the
famine and the sword; and there will
be no one to [b]bury[6912] them—*neither*
them, *nor* their wives,[802] nor their
sons,[1121] nor their daughters—for I shall
[c]pour out[8210] their *own* wickedness[7451]
on them.

17 "And you will say this word to
them,
'[a]Let my eyes flow down with
tears night[3915] and day,[3119]
And let them not cease;[1820]
For the virgin[1330] [b]daughter of
my people has been
crushed[7655] with a mighty
blow,[4347]
With a sorely [c]infected wound.
18 'If I [a]go out to the country,
Behold, those [I]slain[2491] with the
sword!
Or if I enter the city,
Behold, diseases of famine!
For [b]both prophet[5030] and
priest[3548]
Have [II]gone roving about in the
land that they do not
know.' "[3045]
19 Hast Thou completely
[a]rejected[3988] Judah?
Or hast [I]Thou[5315] loathed Zion?
Why hast Thou stricken[5221] us
so that we [b]are beyond
healing?
We [c]waited for peace, but
nothing good *came;*
And for a time of healing, but
behold, terror!
20 We [a]know[3045] our
wickedness,[7562] O LORD,
The iniquity of our fathers,[1] for
[b]we have sinned against
Thee.
21 Do not despise[5006] *us,*
[a]for Thine own name's sake;
Do not disgrace[5034] the
[b]throne[3678] of Thy glory;[3519]
Remember *and* do not annul[6565]
Thy covenant[1285] with us.
22 Are there any among the
[Ia]idols of the nations[1471] who
[b]give rain?
Or can the heavens[8064] grant
showers?
Is it not Thou, O LORD our
God?[430]
Therefore we [IIc]hope in[6960]
Thee,
For Thou art the one who hast
done[6213] all these things.

Judgment Must Come

15 Then the LORD said[559] to me,
"Even [a]though [b]Moses and
[c]Samuel were to [d]stand before Me, My
[I]heart[5315] would not be [II]with this
people;[5971] [e]send them away from My
presence and let them go!
2 "And it shall be that when they
say[559] to you, 'Where should we go?'
then you are to tell[559] them, 'Thus says
the LORD:
"Those *destined* [a]for death,[4194] to
death;
And those *destined* for the
sword,[2719] to the sword;
And those *destined* for famine,
to famine;
And those *destined* for
captivity,[7628] to captivity." '
3 "And I shall [a]appoint[6485] over them
four kinds[4940] *of doom,*" declares[5001] the
LORD: "the sword to slay,[2026] the
[b]dogs to drag off, and the [c]birds of the
sky[8064] and the beasts of the earth[776]
to devour and destroy.
4 "And I shall [a]make them an object
of horror among all the kingdoms[4467] of
the earth because of [b]Manasseh, the
son[1121] of Hezekiah, the king[4428] of Judah, for what he did[6213] in Jerusalem.

14 [I]Lit., *hearts* [c]Jer. 23:16, 26; 27:9, 10; Ezek. 12:24
15 [I]Lit., *be finished* [a]Jer. 23:15; Ezek. 14:10
16 [a]Ps. 79:2, 3; Jer. 7:33; 15:2, 3 [b]Jer. 8:1, 2 [c]Prov. 1:31; Jer. 13:22-25
17 [a]Jer. 9:1; 13:17; Lam. 1:16 [b]Is. 37:22; Jer. 8:21; Lam. 1:15; 2:13 [c]Jer. 10:19; 30:14
18 [I]Lit., *pierced* [II]Or, *gone around trading* [a]Jer. 6:25; Lam. 1:20; Ezek. 7:15 [b]Jer. 6:13; 8:10
19 [I]Lit., *Thy soul* [a]Jer. 6:30; 7:29; 12:7; Lam. 5:22 [b]Jer. 30:13 [c]Job 30:26; Jer. 8:15; 1Thess. 5:3
20 [a]Neh. 9:2; Ps. 32:5; Jer. 3:25 [b]Jer. 8:14; 14:7; Dan. 9:8
21 [a]Ps. 25:11; Jer. 14:7 [b]Jer. 3:17; 17:12
22 [I]Lit., *vanities* [II]Or, *wait for* [a]Is. 41:29; Jer. 10:3 [b]1Kin. 17:1; Jer. 5:24 [c]Lam. 3:26

1 [I]Lit., *soul* [II]Lit., *toward* [a]Ps. 99:6; Ezek. 14:14, 20 [b]Ex. 32:11-14; Num. 14:13-20; Ps. 99:6; 106:23 [c]1Sam. 7:9; 12:23 [d]Jer. 15:19; 18:20; 35:19 [e]2Kin. 17:20; Jer. 7:15; 10:18; 52:3
2 [a]Jer. 14:12; 24:10; 43:11; Ezek. 5:2, 12; Zech. 11:9; Rev. 13:10
3 [a]Lev. 26:16, 22, 25; Ezek. 14:21 [b]1Kin. 21:23, 24 [c]Deut. 28:26; Is. 18:6; Jer. 7:33
4 [a]Lev. 26:33; Jer. 24:9; 29:18; Ezek. 23:46 [b]2Kin. 21:1-18; 23:26, 27; 24:3, 4; 2Chr. 33:1-9

5 "Indeed, who will have [a]pity on
you, O Jerusalem,
Or who will [b]mourn for you,
Or who will turn aside to ask[7592]
about your welfare?
6 "You who have [a]forsaken[5203]
Me," declares the LORD,
"You keep [b]going backward.
So I will [c]stretch out My hand[3027]
against you and destroy you;
I am [d]tired of relenting!
7 "And I will [a]winnow them with a
winnowing fork
At the gates of the land;[776]
I will [b]bereave *them* of
children,[1121] I will destroy[6]
My people;
[c]They did not [1]repent[7725] of their
ways.[1870]
8 "Their [a]widows will be more
numerous before Me
Than the sand of the seas;
I will bring against them, against
the mother[517] of a young man,
A [b]destroyer[7703] at noonday;
I will suddenly bring down on
her
Anguish and dismay.[928]
9 "She who [a]bore seven *sons* pines
away;
[1]Her breathing[5315] is labored.
Her [b]sun has set while it was
yet day;[3119]
She has been [c]shamed[954] and
humiliated.
So I shall [d]give over their
survivors[7611] to the sword
Before their enemies," declares
the LORD.
10 [a]Woe to me, my mother, that
you have borne me
As a [b]man[376] of strife[7379] and a
man of contention to all the
land!
I have neither [c]lent, nor have
men lent money to me,
Yet everyone curses[7043] me.
11 The LORD said, "Surely I will
[a]set you free[8293] for *purposes
of* good;
Surely I will cause the [b]enemy
to make supplication to you
In a time[6256] of disaster[7451] and
a time of distress.
12 "Can anyone smash[7489] iron,
[a]Iron from the north, or bronze?
13 "Your [a]wealth[2428] and your
treasures
I will give for booty [b]without
cost,
Even for all your sins
And within all your borders.
14 "Then I will cause your enemies
to bring [1]*it*
Into a [a]land you do not know;[3045]
For a [b]fire has been kindled in
My anger,[639]
It will burn upon you."

Jeremiah's Prayer and God's Answer

15 [a]Thou who knowest, O LORD,
Remember[2142] me, take
notice[6485] of me,
And [b]take vengeance for me on
my persecutors.
Do *not,* in view of Thy patience,
take me away;
Know[3045] that [c]for Thy sake I
endure reproach.[2781]
16 Thy words[1697] were found and
I [a]ate them,
And Thy [b]words[1697] became for
me a joy and the delight of
my heart;[3824]
For I have been [c]called[7181] by
Thy name,
O LORD God[430] of hosts.[6635]
17 I [a]did not sit in the circle[5475]
of merrymakers,
Nor did I exult.
Because of Thy hand *upon me*
I sat [b]alone,
For Thou didst [c]fill me with
indignation.[2195]
18 Why has my pain been
perpetual[5331]
And my [a]wound[4347] incurable,
refusing[3985] to be healed?
Wilt Thou indeed be to me
[b]like a deceptive *stream*
With water that is unreliable?[539]

5 [a]Ps. 69:20; Is. 51:19; Jer. 13:14; 21:7 [b]Nah. 3:7

6 [a]Jer. 6:19; 8:9 [b]Is. 1:4; Jer. 7:24 [c]Jer. 6:12; Zeph. 1:4 [d]Jer. 6:11; 7:16

7 [1]Lit., *turn back from* [a]Ps. 1:4; Jer. 51:2 [b]Jer. 18:21; Hos. 9:12-16 [c]Is. 9:13

8 [a]Is. 3:25, 26; 4:1 [b]Jer. 22:7

9 [1]Or, *She has breathed out her soul* [a]1Sam. 2:5; Is. 47:9 [b]Jer. 6:4; Amos 8:9 [c]Jer. 50:12 [d]Jer. 21:7

10 [a]Job 3:1, 3; Jer. 20:14 [b]Jer. 1:18, 19; 15:20; 20:7, 8 [c]Ex. 22:25; Lev. 25:36, 37; Deut. 23:19

11 [a]Ps. 138:3; Is. 41:10 [b]Jer. 21:2; 37:3; 38:14; 42:2

12 [a]Jer. 28:14

13 [a]Jer. 17:3; 20:5 [b]Ps. 44:12; Is. 52:3

14 [1]I. e., your possessions [a]Deut. 28:36, 64; Jer. 16:13 [b]Deut. 32:22; Ps. 21:9; Jer. 17:4

15 [a]Jer. 12:3 [b]Jer. 11:20 [c]Ps. 44:22; 69:7-9; Jer. 20:8

16 [a]Ezek. 3:3 [b]Job 23:12; Ps. 119:103 [c]Jer. 14:9

17 [a]Ps. 1:1; Jer. 16:8; 2Cor. 6:17 [b]Ps. 102:7; Jer. 13:17; Lam. 3:28; Ezek. 3:24, 25 [c]Jer. 6:11

18 [a]Job 34:6; Jer. 30:12, 15; Mic. 1:9 [b]Job 6:15, 20; Jer. 14:3

19 Therefore, thus says[559] the LORD,
"[a]If you return, then I will restore
you—
[b]Before Me you will stand;
And [c]if you extract the
precious from the
worthless,[2151]
You will become [I]My
spokesman.[6310]
They for their part may turn to
you,
But as for you, you must not
turn to them.
20 "Then I will [a]make you to this
people
A fortified wall of bronze;
And though they fight against
you,
They will not prevail over you;
For [b]I am with you to save[3467]
you
And deliver[5337] you," declares
the LORD.
21 "So I will [a]deliver you from
the hand[3709] of the
wicked,[7451]
And I will [b]redeem[6299] you from
the [I]grasp of the violent."

Distresses Foretold

16 The word[1697] of the LORD also came to me saying,

🔑 2 "You shall not take a wife[802] for yourself nor have sons[1121] or daughters in this place."

3 For thus says[559] the LORD concerning the sons and daughters born in this place, and concerning their [a]mothers[517] who bear them, and their [b]fathers[1] who beget them in this land:[776]

4 "They will [a]die[4191] of deadly diseases, they [b]will not be lamented or buried;[6912] they will be as [c]dung on the surface of the ground[127] and come to an end[3615] by sword[2719] and famine, and their carcasses[5038] will become food for the [d]birds of the sky[8064] and for the beasts of the earth."[776]

5 For thus says[5001] the LORD, "Do not enter a house[1004] of [I][a]mourning, or go to lament or to console them; for I have [b]withdrawn[622] My peace from this people,"[5971] declares the LORD, "*My* [c]lovingkindness and compassion.[7356]

6 "Both [a]great men and small will die in this land; they will not be buried, they will not be lamented, nor will anyone [b]gash[1413] himself or [c]shave his head for them.

7 "Neither will men [a]break *bread* in mourning for them, to comfort[5162] anyone for the dead,[4191] nor give them a cup of consolation[8575] to drink for anyone's father[1] or mother.[517]

8 "Moreover you shall [a]not go into a house of feasting[4960] to sit with them to eat and drink."

9 For thus says the LORD of hosts,[6635] the God[430] of Israel: "Behold, I am going to [I][a]eliminate[7673] from this place, before your eyes and in your time,[3117] the voice of rejoicing and the voice of gladness, the voice of the groom and the voice of the bride.

10 "Now it will come about when you tell[5046] this people all these words[1697] that they will say[559] to you, '[a]For what reason has the LORD declared all this great calamity[7451] against us? And what is our iniquity,[5771] or what is our sin[2403] which we have committed[2398] against the LORD our God?'

11 "Then you are to say to them, '*It is* [a]because your forefathers have forsaken[5800] Me,' declares the LORD, 'and have followed [b]other gods[430] and served[5647] them and bowed down[7812] to them; but Me they have forsaken and have not kept[8104] My law.[8451]

12 'You too have done[6213] evil,[7489] *even* [a]more than your forefathers; for behold, you are each one[376] walking according to the [b]stubbornness[8307] of his own [c]evil heart,[3820] without listening[8085] to Me.

19 [I]Lit., *as My mouth* [a]Jer. 4:1; Zech. 3:7 [b]1Kin. 17:1; Jer. 15:1; 35:19 [c]Jer. 6:29; Ezek. 22:26; 44:23
20 [a]Jer. 1:18, 19; Ezek. 3:9 [b]Ps. 46:7; Is. 41:10; Jer. 1:8, 19; 15:15; 20:11
21 [I]Lit., *palm* [a]Ps. 37:40; Is. 49:25; Jer. 20:13; 39:11, 12 [b]Gen. 48:16; Is. 49:26; 60:16; Jer. 31:11; 50:34
3 [a]Jer. 15:8 [b]Jer. 6:21
4 [a]Jer. 15:2 [b]Jer. 25:33 [c]Ps. 83:10; Jer. 9:22; 25:33 [d]Ps. 79:2; Is. 18:6; Jer. 15:3; 34:20
5 [I]Or, *banqueting* [a]Ezek. 24:16-23 [b]Jer. 12:12; 15:1-4 [c]Ps. 25:6; Is. 27:11; Jer. 13:14
6 [a]2Chr. 36:17; Ezek. 9:6 [b]Deut. 14:1; Jer. 41:5; 47:5 [c]Is. 22:12
7 [a]Deut. 26:14; Ezek. 24:17; Hos. 9:4
8 [a]Eccl. 7:2-4; Is. 22:12-14; Jer. 15:17; Amos 6:4-6
9 [I]Lit., *cause to cease* [a]Jer. 7:34; 25:10; Ezek. 26:13; Hos. 2:11; Rev. 18:23
10 [a]Deut. 29:24; 1Kin. 9:8; Jer. 5:19; 13:22; 22:8
11 [a]Deut. 29:25; 1Kin. 9:9; 2Chr. 7:22; Neh. 9:26-29; Jer. 22:9 [b]Deut. 29:26; 1Kin. 9:9; Ps. 106:35-41; Jer. 5:7-9; 8:2; Ezek. 11:21; 1Pet. 4:3
12 [a]Jer. 7:26 [b]1Sam. 15:23; Jer. 7:24; 9:14; 13:10 [c]Eccl. 9:3; Mark 7:21

🔑 **16:2** See note on Ezek. 24:15-24.

13 'So I will [a]hurl you out of this land into the [b]land which you have not known,[3045] neither you nor your fathers; and there you will [c]serve[5647] other gods day[3119] and night,[3915] for I shall grant you no favor.'

God Will Restore Them

14 "[a]Therefore behold, days are coming," declares the LORD, "when it will no longer be said,[559] 'As the LORD lives,[2416] who [b]brought up[5927] the sons[1121] of Israel out of the land of Egypt,'

15 but, 'As the LORD lives, who brought up the sons of Israel from the [a]land[127] of the north and from all the countries[776] where He had banished them.' For I will restore them to their own land which I gave to their fathers.

16 "Behold, I am going to send for many [a]fishermen," declares the LORD, "and they will fish for them; and afterwards I shall send for many hunters, and they will [b]hunt them [c]from every mountain and every hill, and from the clefts of the rocks.

17 "[a]For My eyes are on all their ways;[1870] they are not hidden from My face, [b]nor is their iniquity concealed from My eyes.

18 "And I will first[7223] [a]doubly repay[7999] their iniquity and their sin, because they have [b]polluted[2490] My land; they have filled My inheritance[5159] with the carcasses of their [c]detestable[8251] idols and with their abominations."[8441]

19 O LORD, my [a]strength and my stronghold,
And my [b]refuge in the day[3117] of distress,
To Thee the [c]nations[1471] will come
From the ends of the earth and say,
"Our fathers have inherited nothing but [d]falsehood,[8267]
Futility and [1e]things of no profit."
20 Can man[120] make[6213] gods for himself?
Yet they are [a]not gods!

21 "Therefore behold, I am going to make them know—
This time I will [a]make them know
My [1]power[3027] and My might;
And they shall [b]know that My name is the LORD."

The Deceitful Heart

17 The [a]sin[2403] of Judah is written down with an [b]iron stylus;
With a diamond point it is [c]engraved upon the tablet of their heart,[3820]
And on the horns of [1]their altars,[4196]
2 As they remember[2142] their [a]children,[1121]
So they *remember* their altars and their [1b]Asherim[842]
By [c]green trees on the high hills.
3 O [a]mountain of Mine in the countryside,[7704]
I will [b]give over your wealth[2428] and all your treasures for booty,
Your high places[1116] for sin throughout your borders.
4 And you will, even of yourself, [a]let go of your inheritance[5159]
That I gave you;
And I will make you serve[5647] your [b]enemies
In the [c]land[776] which you do not know;[3045]
For you have [d]kindled a fire in My anger[639]
Which will burn forever.[5769]
5 Thus says[559] the LORD,
"[a]Cursed[779] is the man[1397] who trusts[982] in mankind[120]
And makes [b]flesh[1320] his [1]strength,
And whose heart turns away from the LORD.
6 "For he will be like a [a]bush[6176] in the desert[6160]

---

13 [a]Deut. 4:26, 27; 2Chr. 7:20; Jer. 15:1 [b]Jer. 15:14; 17:4 [c]Deut. 4:28; 28:36; Jer. 5:19
14 [a]Is. 43:18; Jer. 23:7 [b]Ex. 20:2; Deut. 15:15
15 [a]Ps. 106:47; Is. 11:11-16; 14:1; Jer. 3:18; 23:8; 24:6
16 [a]Amos 4:2; Hab. 1:14, 15 [b]1Sam. 26:20; Mic. 7:2 [c]Is. 2:21; Amos 9:3
17 [a]2Chr. 16:9; Job 34:21; Ps. 90:8; Prov. 5:21; 15:3; Jer. 23:24; 32:19; Zech. 4:10; Luke 12:2; 1Cor. 4:5; Heb. 4:13 [b]Jer. 2:22
18 [a]Jer. 17:18; Rev. 18:6 [b]Num. 35:33, 34; Jer. 2:7; 3:9 [c]Jer. 7:30; Ezek. 11:18, 21
19 [1]Lit., *there is nothing profitable in them* [a]Ps. 18:1, 2; Is. 25:4 [b]Nah. 1:7 [c]Ps. 22:27; Is. 2:2; Jer. 3:17; 4:2 [d]Is. 44:20; Hab. 2:18 [e]Is. 44:10
20 [a]Ps. 115:4-8; Is. 37:19; Jer. 2:11; 5:7; Hos. 8:4-6; Gal. 4:8
21 [1]Lit., *hand* [a]Ps. 9:16 [b]Ps. 83:18; Is. 43:3; Jer. 33:2; Amos 5:8

1 [1]So ancient versions; M.T., *your* [a]Jer. 2:22; 4:14 [b]Job 19:24 [c]Prov. 3:3; 7:3; Is. 49:16; 2Cor. 3:3
2 [1]I.e., wooden symbols of a female deity [a]Jer. 7:18 [b]Ex. 34:13; 2Chr. 24:18; 33:3; Is. 17:8 [c]Jer. 3:6
3 [a]Jer. 26:18; Mic. 3:12 [b]2Kin. 24:13; Is. 39:4-6; Jer. 15:13; 20:5
4 [a]Jer. 12:7; Lam. 5:2 [b]Deut. 28:48; Is. 14:3; Jer. 15:14; 27:12, 13 [c]Jer. 16:13 [d]Is. 5:25; Jer. 7:20; 15:14
5 [1]Lit., *arm* [a]Ps. 146:3; Is. 2:22; 30:1; Ezek. 29:7 [b]2Chr. 32:8; Is. 31:3
6 [a]Jer. 48:6

And will not see when
prosperity[2896] comes,
But will live[7931] in stony
wastes[2788] in the wilderness,
A [b]land of salt [I]without
inhabitant.
7 "[a]Blessed[1288] is the man who
trusts in the LORD
And whose [b]trust is the LORD.
8 "For he will be like a [a]tree planted
by the water,
That extends its roots by a
stream
And will not fear when the heat
comes;
But its leaves will be green,
And it will not be anxious in a
year of [b]drought
Nor cease to yield[6213] fruit.
9 "The [a]heart is more [b]deceitful[6121]
than all else
And is desperately [c]sick;
Who can understand[3045] it?
10 "I, the LORD, [a]search the heart,
I test[974] the [I]mind,[3629]
Even [b]to give to each man[376]
according to his ways,[1870]
According to the [II]results of his
deeds.
11 "As a partridge that hatches eggs
which it has not laid,
So is he who [a]makes[6213] a
fortune, but unjustly;[4941,3808]
In the midst of his days[3117] it
will forsake[5800] him,
And in [I]the end[319] he will be a
[b]fool."
12 [a]A glorious[3519] throne[3678] on
high from the beginning[7223]
Is the place of our sanctuary.[4720]
13 O LORD, the [a]hope[4723] of
Israel,
All who [b]forsake[5800] Thee will
be put to shame.[954]
Those who turn [I]away on
earth[776] will be [c]written
down,
Because they have forsaken[5800]
the fountain of living[2416]
water, even the LORD.
14 [a]Heal me, O LORD, and I will
be healed;

6 [I]Lit., *and is not inhabited* [b]Deut. 29:23; Job 39:6
7 [a]Ps. 2:12; 34:8; 84:12; Prov. 16:20 [b]Ps. 40:4
8 [a]Ps. 1:3; 92:12-14; Ezek. 31:3-9 [b]Jer. 14:1-6
9 [a]Eccl. 9:3; Mark 7:21, 22 [b]Rom. 7:11; Eph. 4:22 [c]Is. 1:5, 6; 6:10; Matt. 13:15; Mark 2:17; Rom. 1:21
10 [I]Lit., *kidneys* [II]Lit., *fruit* [a]1Sam. 16:7; 1Chr. 28:9; Ps. 139:23; Prov. 17:3; Jer. 11:20; 20:12; Rom. 8:27; Rev. 2:23 [b]Ps. 62:12; Jer. 32:19; Rom. 2:6
11 [I]Lit., *his* [a]Jer. 6:13; 8:10; 22:13, 17 [b]Luke 12:20
12 [a]Jer. 3:17; 14:21
13 [I]Lit., *away from Me* [a]Jer. 14:8; 50:7 [b]Is. 1:28 [c]Luke 10:20
14 [a]Jer. 30:17; 33:6 [b]Ps. 54:1; 60:5 [c]Deut. 10:21; Ps. 109:1
15 [a]Is. 5:19; 2Pet. 3:4
16 [a]Jer. 12:3
17 [a]Ps. 88:15 [b]Jer. 16:19; Nah. 1:7
18 [a]Ps. 35:4, 26; Jer. 17:13; 20:11 [b]Jer. 1:17 [c]Ps. 35:8
19 [I]Lit., *gate of the sons of the people*
20 [a]Ezek. 2:7 [b]Ps. 49:1, 2; Jer. 19:3, 4
21 [a]Deut. 4:9, 15, 23; Mark 4:24 [b]Num. 15:32-36; Neh. 13:15-21; John 5:9-12
22 [I]Lit., *fathers* [a]Ex. 16:23-29; 20:8-10; Deut. 5:12-14; Is. 56:2-6; 58:13 [b]Ex. 31:13-17; Ezek. 20:12; Zech. 1:4
23 [a]Jer. 7:24, 28; 11:10

[b]Save[3467] me and I will be
saved,[3467]
For Thou art my [c]praise.[8416]
15 Look, they keep [a]saying[559] to
me,
"Where is the word[1697] of the
LORD?
Let it come now!"
16 But as for me, I have not hurried
away from *being* a shepherd
after Thee,
Nor have I longed for the woeful
day;[3117]
[a]Thou Thyself knowest the
utterance of my lips[8193]
Was in Thy presence.
17 Do not be a [a]terror[4288] to me;
Thou art my [b]refuge in the day
of disaster.[7451]
18 Let those who persecute me
be [a]put to shame,[954] but as
for me, [b]let me not be put
to shame;
Let them be dismayed,[2865] but
let me not be dismayed.
[c]Bring on them a day of disaster,
And crush[7665] them with twofold
destruction![7670]

The Sabbath Must Be Kept

19 Thus the LORD said[559] to me, "Go and stand in the [I]public[1121,5971] gate, through which the kings[4428] of Judah come in and go out, as well as in all the gates of Jerusalem;

20 and say to them, '[a]Listen[8085] to the word of the LORD, [b]kings of Judah, and all Judah, and all inhabitants of Jerusalem, who come in through these gates:

21 'Thus says the LORD, "[a]Take heed[8104] for yourselves, and [b]do not carry[5375] any load[4853] on the sabbath[7676] day or bring anything in through the gates of Jerusalem.

22 "And you shall not bring a load out of your houses[1004] on the sabbath day [a]nor do[6213] any work,[4399] but keep the sabbath day holy,[6942] as I [b]commanded[6680] your [I]forefathers.[1]

23 "Yet they [a]did not listen[8085] or

incline their ears,[241] but [b]stiffened their necks in order not to listen or take correction.[4148]

24 "But it will come about, if you [a]listen[8085] attentively to Me," declares[5001] the LORD, "to [b]bring no load in through the gates of this city on the sabbath day, [c]but to keep the sabbath day holy by doing no work on it,

25 [a]then there will come in through the gates of this city kings and princes[8269] [b]sitting on the throne of David, riding in chariots and on horses, they and their princes, the men[376] of Judah, and the inhabitants of Jerusalem; and this [c]city will be inhabited forever.

26 "They will come in from the [a]cities of Judah and from the environs of Jerusalem, from the land of Benjamin, from the [b]lowland, from the hill country, and from the [c]Negev, bringing burnt offerings,[5930] sacrifices,[2077] grain offerings[4503] and incense, and bringing sacrifices of thanksgiving[8426] to the house[1004] of the LORD.

27 "But [a]if you do not listen to Me to keep the sabbath day holy by not carrying a load and coming in through the gates of Jerusalem on the sabbath day, then [b]I shall kindle a fire in its gates, and it will [c]devour the palaces[759] of Jerusalem and [d]not be quenched."'"

The Potter and the Clay

18 The word[1697] which came to Jeremiah from the LORD saying,

2 "Arise and [a]go down to the potter's[3335] house,[1004] and there I shall announce[8085] My words[1697] to you."

3 Then I went down to the potter's house, and there he was, making something[4399] on the [I]wheel.

4 But the vessel that he was making[6213] of clay was spoiled[7843] in the hand[3027] of the potter; so he remade it into another vessel, as it pleased[3474] the potter to make.[6213]

5 Then the word of the LORD came to me saying,

6 "Can I not, O house of Israel, deal[6213] with you as this potter *does?*" declares the LORD. "Behold, like the [a]clay in the potter's hand, so are you in My hand, O house of Israel.

🔑 7 "At one moment I might speak[1696] concerning a nation[1471] or concerning a kingdom[4467] to [a]uproot, to pull down,[5422] or to destroy[6] *it;*

8 [a]if that nation against which I have spoken turns[7725] from its evil,[7451] I will [Ib]relent[5162] concerning the calamity I planned[2803] to bring on it.

9 "Or at another moment I might speak concerning a nation or concerning a kingdom to [a]build up or to plant *it;*

10 if it does [a]evil in My sight by not obeying[8085] My voice, then I will [Ib]think better of the good[2896] with which I had promised[559] to [II]bless[3190] it.

11 "So now then, speak[559] to the men[376] of Judah and against the inhabitants of Jerusalem saying, 'Thus

23 [b]Prov. 29:1; Jer. 7:26; 19:15
24 [a]Ex. 15:26; Deut. 11:13; Is. 21:7; 55:2 [b]Jer. 17:21, 22 [c]Ex. 20:8-11; Ezek. 20:20
25 [a]Jer. 22:4 [b]2Sam. 7:16; Is. 9:7; Jer. 33:15, 17, 21; Luke 1:32 [c]Ps. 132:13, 14; Heb. 12:22
26 [a]Jer. 32:44; 33:13 [b]Zech. 7:7 [c]Ps. 107:22; Jer. 33:11
27 [a]Is. 1:20; Jer. 22:5; 26:4; Zech. 7:11-14 [b]Lam. 4:11 [c]2Kin. 25:9; Jer. 39:8; Amos 2:5 [d]Jer. 7:20; Ezek. 20:47

2 [a]Jer. 19:1, 2
3 [I]Lit., *pair of stone discs*
6 [a]Is. 45:9; 64:8; Matt. 20:15; Rom. 9:21
7 [a]Jer. 1:10
8 [I]Lit., *repent of* [a]Jer. 7:3-7; 12:16; Ezek. 18:21 [b]Ps. 106:45; Jer. 26:3, 13, 19; Hos. 11:8; Joel 2:13, 14; Jon. 3:10
9 [a]Jer. 1:10; 31:28; Amos 9:11-15
10 [I]Lit., *repent* [II]Lit., *do it good* [a]Ps. 125:5; Jer. 7:24-28; Ezek. 33:18 [b]1Sam. 2:30; 13:13

🔑 **18:7-10** This is the clearest statement in the O.T. of the conditional nature of prophecy and of God's promises. God is free to revoke any promise or threat, because He chooses to consider man's conduct as a factor in whether it is carried out or not. For example, He promised that His people would never again return to Egypt, but He warned them through Moses that their action could nullify that promise (Deut. 28:68). Through Jonah He threatened to overthrow Nineveh. Though He stated no condition for reversing Himself, He still accepted the city's repentance and revoked the threat (Jon. 3:4-10). Yet, the fact that physical Israel never realized some of the prophecies about themselves and promises to them does not mean that they never will be fulfilled. According to Paul, Christians now constitute God's special people (Gal. 6:16), and the true Jew is not measured by outward or physical standards (Rom. 2:28,29). Abraham's offspring, and therefore the heirs of God's promise to him, are people who have faith in Christ (Gal. 3:7,9,29), not those who can trace their genealogical line to him. On this basis, many of the prophecies and promises in the O.T. found their fulfillment in the Church. For example, the new covenant promise of Jer. 31:31-34, which was addressed to "the house of Israel and the house of Judah," reached its fulfillment in Christians, not in physical Israel (Heb. 8—9). Of course, God's unconditional promise to Israel will yet be fulfilled (Ezek. 37:15-28; Amos 9:13-15; Mic. 7:20; Zeph. 3:14-20).

says[559] the LORD, "Behold, I am
[a]fashioning[3335] calamity against you and
devising[4284] a plan[2803] against you. Oh
[b]turn back,[7725] each of you from his evil
way,[1870] and [I]reform[3190] your ways[1870]
and your deeds." '
12 "But [a]they will say, 'It's hopeless![2976] For we are going to follow our
own plans,[4284] and each of us will act
according to the [b]stubbornness[8307] of his
evil heart.'[3820]
13 "Therefore thus says the LORD,

'[a]Ask[7592] now among the
nations,[1471]
Who ever heard[8085] the like of
[I]this?
The [b]virgin[1330] of Israel
Has done[6213] a most [c]appalling
thing.[8186]
14 'Does the snow of Lebanon
forsake[5800] the rock of the
open country?[7704]
Or is the cold flowing water *from*
a foreign[2114] *land* ever
snatched away?
15 'For [a]My people[5971] have
forgotten Me,
[b]They burn incense[6999] [I]to
worthless[7723] gods
And they [II]have stumbled[3784]
[III]from their ways,
[III]From the [c]ancient[5769] paths,
To walk in bypaths,
Not on a [d]highway,
16 To make[7760] their land[776] a
[a]desolation,[8047]
An object of perpetual[5769]
[b]hissing;
Everyone who passes[5674] by it
will be astonished[8074]
And [c]shake[5110] his head.[7218]
17 'Like an [a]east wind[7307] I will
[b]scatter them
Before the enemy;
I will [I]show[7200] them [c]My back
and not *My* face
[d]In the day[3117] of their
calamity.' "[343]

18 Then they said, "Come and let
us [a]devise plans against Jeremiah. Surely
the [b]law[8451] is not going to be lost[6] to
the priest,[3548] nor [c]counsel[6098] to the
sage,[2450] nor the *divine* [d]word to the
prophet![5030] Come on and let us
[e]strike[5221] at him with *our* tongue, and
let us [f]give no heed[7181] to any of his
words."

19 Do give heed to me, O LORD,
And listen[8085] to [I]what my
opponents are saying!
20 [a]Should good be repaid[7999] with
evil?
For they have [b]dug a pit[7745] for
[I]me.[5315]
Remember[2142] how I [c]stood
before Thee
To speak good on their
behalf,
So as to turn away[7725] Thy
wrath[2534] from them.
21 Therefore, [a]give their
children[1121] over to famine,
And deliver them up to the
[I]power of the sword;[2719]
And let their wives[802] become
[b]childless[7909] and [c]widowed.
Let their men[582] also be smitten
to death,[4194]
Their [d]young men struck
down[5221] by the sword in
battle.
22 May an [a]outcry be heard from
their houses,[1004]
When Thou suddenly bringest
raiders[1416] upon them;
[b]For they have dug a pit[7882] to
capture me
And [c]hidden snares[6341] for my
feet.
23 Yet Thou, O LORD, knowest[3045]
All their [I]deadly designs against
me;
[a]Do not [II]forgive[3722] their
iniquity[5771]
Or blot out[4229] their sin[2403] from
Thy sight.
But may they be
[III][b]overthrown[3782] before
Thee;
Deal[6213] with them in the
[c]time[6256] of Thine anger![639]

11 [I]Lit., *make good* [a]Is. 5:5; Jer. 4:6; 11:11 [b]2Kin. 17:13; Is. 1:16-19; Jer. 4:1; Acts 26:20
12 [a]Is. 57:10; Jer. 2:25 [b]Deut. 29:19; Jer. 7:24; 16:12
13 [I]Lit., *these* [a]Is. 66:8; Jer. 2:10, 11 [b]Jer. 14:17; 31:4 [c]Jer. 5:30; 23:14; Hos. 6:10
15 [I]Lit., *to worthlessness* [II]So ancient versions; Heb., *caused them to* [III]Or, *in* [a]Jer. 2:32; 3:21 [b]Is. 65:7; Jer. 7:9; 10:15; 44:17 [c]Jer. 6:16 [d]Is. 57:14; 62:10
16 [a]Jer. 25:9; 49:13; 50:13; Ezek. 33:28, 29 [b]1Kin. 9:8; Lam. 2:15; Mic. 6:16 [c]Ps. 22:7; Is. 37:22; Jer. 48:27
17 [I]So ancient versions; M.T. reads *look them in the back and not in the face* [a]Ps. 48:7 [b]Job 27:21; Jer. 13:24 [c]Jer. 2:27; 32:33 [d]Jer. 46:21
18 [a]Jer. 11:19; 18:11 [b]Jer. 2:8; Mal. 2:7 [c]Job 5:13; Jer. 8:8 [d]Jer. 5:13 [e]Ps. 52:2; Jer. 20:10 [f]Jer. 43:2
19 [I]Lit., *the voice of my opponents*
20 [I]Lit., *my soul* [a]Ps. 109:4 [b]Ps. 35:7; 57:6; Jer. 5:26; 18:22 [c]Ps. 106:23
21 [I]Lit., *hands of* [a]Ps. 109:9-20; Jer. 11:22; 14:16 [b]1Sam. 15:33; Is. 13:18 [c]Jer. 15:8; Ezek. 22:25 [d]Jer. 9:21; 11:22
22 [a]Jer. 6:26; 25:34, 36 [b]Jer. 18:20 [c]Ps. 140:5
23 [I]Lit., *unto death* [II]Lit., *cover over, atone for* [III]Lit., *ones made to stumble* [a]Neh. 4:5; Ps. 109:14; Is. 2:9 [b]Jer. 6:15, 21 [c]Jer. 7:20; 17:4

The Broken Jar

19 Thus says[559] the LORD, "Go and buy a [a]potter's[3335] earthenware[2789] [b]jar, and *take* some of the [c]elders[2204] of the people[5971] and some of the [1d]senior priests.[3548]

2 "Then go out to the [a]valley of Ben-hinnom, which is by the entrance of the potsherd gate; and [b]proclaim[7121] there the words[1697] that I shall tell[1696] you,

3 and say,[559] 'Hear[8085] the word[1697] of the LORD, O [a]kings[4428] of Judah and inhabitants of Jerusalem: thus says the LORD of hosts,[6635] the God[430] of Israel, "Behold I am about to bring a [b]calamity[7451] upon this place, at which the [c]ears[241] of everyone that hears[8085] of it will tingle.

4 "Because they have [a]forsaken[5800] Me and have [b]made this an alien[5234] place and have burned [1]sacrifices[6999] in it to [c]other gods[430] that neither they nor their forefathers[1] nor the kings of Judah had *ever* known,[3045] and *because* they have filled this place with the [d]blood[1818] of the innocent

5 and have built the [a]high places[1116] of Baal to burn[8313] their [b]sons[1121] in the fire as burnt offerings to Baal, a thing which I never commanded[6680] or spoke[1696] of, nor did it *ever* enter My [1]mind;[3820]

6 therefore, behold, [a]days[3117] are coming," declares[5001] the LORD, "when this place will no longer be called[7121] [b]Topheth or [c]the valley of Ben-hinnom, but rather the valley of Slaughter.[2028]

7 "And I shall [a]make void the counsel[6098] of Judah and Jerusalem in this place, and [b]I shall cause them to fall by the sword[2719] before their enemies and by the hand[3027] of those who seek their life;[5315] and I shall give over their [c]carcasses[5038] as food for the birds of the sky[8064] and the beasts of the earth.[776]

8 "I shall also make[7760] this city a [a]desolation[8047] and an *object of* hissing; [b]everyone who passes[5674] by it will be astonished[8074] and hiss because of all its [1]disasters.[4347]

9 "And I shall make them [a]eat the flesh[1320] of their sons and the flesh of their daughters, and they will eat one another's[376] flesh in the siege and in the distress with which their enemies and those who seek their life will distress[6693] them." '

10 "Then you are to break[7665] the [a]jar in the sight of the men[582] who accompany you

11 and say to them, 'Thus says the LORD of hosts, "Just so shall I [a]break this people and this city, even as one breaks[7665] a potter's vessel, which cannot again be repaired; and they will [b]bury[6912] in Topheth [1]because there is no *other* place for burial.

12 "This is how I shall treat[6213] this place and its inhabitants," declares the LORD, "so as to make this city like Topheth.

13 "And the [a]houses[1004] of Jerusalem and the houses of the kings of Judah will be [b]defiled[2931] like the place Topheth, because of all the [c]houses on whose rooftops they burned [1]sacrifices to [d]all the heavenly host[6635] and [e]poured out[5258] libations[5262] to other gods." ' "

14 Then Jeremiah came from Topheth, where the LORD had sent him to prophesy;[5012] and he stood in the [a]court of the LORD's house[1004] and said[559] to all the people:

15 "Thus says the LORD of hosts, the God of Israel, 'Behold, I am about to bring on this city and all its towns the entire calamity that I have declared against it, because they have [a]stiffened their necks so [b]as not to heed My words.' "

Pashhur Persecutes Jeremiah

20 When Pashhur the priest,[3548] the son[1121] of [a]Immer, who was [b]chief officer[5057] in the house[1004] of the LORD, heard[8085] Jeremiah prophesying[5012] these things,[1697]

2 Pashhur had Jeremiah the

---

1 [1]Or, *elders of* [a]Jer. 18:2 [b]Jer. 19:10 [c]Num. 11:16 [d]2Kin. 19:2; Ezek. 8:11
2 [a]Josh. 15:8; 2Kin. 23:10; Jer. 7:31, 32; 32:35 [b]Prov. 1:20
3 [a]Jer. 17:20 [b]Jer. 6:19; 19:15 [c]1Sam. 3:11
4 [1]Or, *incense* [a]Deut. 28:20; Is. 65:11; Jer. 2:13, 17, 19; 17:13 [b]Ezek. 7:22; Dan. 11:31 [c]Jer. 7:9; 11:13 [d]2Kin. 21:6, 16; Jer. 2:34; 7:6
5 [1]Lit., *heart* [a]Num. 22:41; Jer. 32:35 [b]Lev. 18:21; 2Kin. 17:17; Ps. 106:37, 38
6 [a]Jer. 7:32 [b]Is. 30:33 [c]Josh. 15:8
7 [a]Ps. 33:10, 11; Is. 28:17, 18; Jer. 8:8, 9 [b]Lev. 26:17; Deut. 28:25; Jer. 15:2, 9 [c]Ps. 79:2; Jer. 16:4
8 [1]Lit., *blows* [a]Jer. 18:16; 49:13; 50:13 [b]1Kin. 9:8; 2Chr. 7:21
9 [a]Lev. 26:29; Deut. 28:53, 55; Is. 9:20; Lam. 4:10; Ezek. 5:10
10 [a]Jer. 19:1
11 [1]Or, *until there is no place left to bury* [a]Ps. 2:9; Is. 30:14; Lam. 4:2; Rev. 2:27 [b]Jer. 7:32
13 [1]Or, *incense* [a]Jer. 52:13 [b]2Kin. 23:10; Ps. 74:7; 79:1; Ezek. 7:21, 22 [c]Jer. 32:29; Zeph. 1:5 [d]Deut. 4:19; 2Kin. 17:16; Jer. 8:2 [e]Jer. 7:18; 44:18; Ezek. 20:28
14 [a]2Chr. 20:5; Jer. 26:2
15 [a]Neh. 9:17, 29; Jer. 7:26; 17:23 [b]Ps. 58:4

1 [a]1Chr. 24:14; Ezra 2:37, 38 [b]2Kin. 25:18

prophet[5030] [a]beaten,[5221] and put him in
the [b]stocks that were at the upper[5945]
[c]Benjamin Gate, which was by the house
of the LORD.
3 Then it came about on the next
day, when Pashhur released Jeremiah
from the stocks, that Jeremiah said[559]
to him, "Pashhur is not the name the
LORD has [a]called[7121] you, but rather
[I][b]Magor-missabib.
4 "For thus says[559] the LORD, 'Behold,[7200] I am going to make you a
[a]terror[4032] to yourself and to all your
friends;[157] and while [b]your eyes look on,
they will fall by the sword[2719] of their
enemies. So I shall [c] give over all Judah
to the hand[3027] of the king[4428] of Babylon,
and he will carry them away as [d]exiles[1540]
to Babylon and will slay[5221] them with
the sword.
5 'I shall also give over all the
[a]wealth of this city, all its produce, and
all its costly things; even all the treasures of the kings[4428] of Judah I shall
give over to the [b]hand of their enemies,
and they will plunder them, take them
away, and bring them to Babylon.
6 'And you, [a]Pashhur, and all who
live in your house will go into captivity;[7628] and you will enter Babylon,
and there you will die,[4191] and there you
will be buried,[6912] you and all your
[b]friends to whom you have [c]falsely[8267]
prophesied.' "

Jeremiah's Complaint

7 O LORD, Thou hast deceived me
and I was deceived;
Thou hast [a]overcome[2388] me and
prevailed.
I have become a [b]laughingstock
all day long;[3117]
Everyone [c]mocks me.
8 For each time I speak,[1696] I
cry[2199] aloud;
I [a]proclaim[7121] violence[2555] and
destruction,[7701]
Because for me the [b]word[1697]
of the LORD has [I]resulted
In reproach[2781] and derision all
day long.
9 But if I say, "I will not
[a]remember Him
Or speak[1696] anymore in His
name,"
Then in [b]my heart[3820] it becomes
like a burning fire
Shut up in my bones;[6106]
And I am weary of holding *it* in,
And [c]I cannot endure *it.*
10 For [a]I have heard the whispering
of many,
"[b]Terror[4032] on every side!
[c]Denounce[5046] *him;* yes, let us
denounce him!"
[I]All my [d]trusted friends,
Watching for my fall, say:
"Perhaps[194] he will be
[II]deceived,[6601] so that we
may [e]prevail against him
And take our revenge[5360] on
him."
11 But the [a]LORD is with me like
a dread champion;
Therefore my [b]persecutors
will stumble[3782] and not
prevail.
They will be utterly ashamed,[954]
because they have [I]failed,
With an [c]everlasting[5769] disgrace
that will not be forgotten.
12 Yet, O LORD of hosts,[6635] Thou
who dost [a]test the
righteous,[6662]
Who seest the [I]mind[3629] and the
heart;
Let me [b]see Thy vengeance[5360]
on them;
For [c]to Thee I have set forth
my cause.[7379]
13 [a]Sing[7891] to the LORD, praise[1984]
the LORD!
For He has [b]delivered the
soul[5315] of the needy one
From the hand of evildoers.[7489]

2 [a]1Kin. 22:27; 2Chr. 16:10; 24:21; Jer. 1:19; Amos 7:10-13 [b]Job 13:27; 33:11 [c]Jer. 37:13; 38:7; Zech. 14:10
3 [I]I.e., terror on every side [a]Is. 8:3; Hos. 1:4, 9 [b]Jer. 6:25; 20:10
4 [a]Job 18:11-21; Jer. 6:25; 46:5; Ezek. 26:21 [b]Jer. 29:21; 39:6, 7 [c]Jer. 21:4-10; 25:9 [d]Jer. 13:10; 52:27
5 [a]Jer. 15:13; 17:3 [b]2Kin. 20:17, 18; 2Chr. 36:10; Jer. 27:21, 22
6 [a]Jer. 20:1 [b]Jer. 20:4; 29:21 [c]Jer. 14:14, 15; Lam. 2:14
7 [a]Ezek. 3:14 [b]Job 12:4; Lam. 3:14 [c]Ps. 22:7; Jer. 38:19
8 [I]Lit., *become* [a]Jer. 6:7 [b]2Chr. 36:16; Jer. 6:10
9 [a]1Kin. 19:3, 4; Jon. 1:2, 3 [b]Job 32:18-20; Ps. 39:3; Jer. 4:19; 23:9; Ezek. 3:14; Acts 4:20 [c]Job 32:18-20
10 [I]Lit., *Every man of my peace* [II]Or, *persuaded* [a]Ps. 31:13 [b]Jer. 6:25 [c]Neh. 6:6-13; Is. 29:21; Jer. 18:18 [d]Ps. 41:9 [e]1Kin. 19:2
11 [I]Lit., *not succeeded;* or, *not acted wisely* [a]Jer. 1:8; 15:20; Rom. 8:31 [b]Deut. 32:35, 36; Jer. 15:15, 20; 17:18 [c]Jer. 23:40
12 [I]Lit., *kidneys* [a]Ps. 7:9; 11:5; 17:3; 139:23; Jer. 11:20; 17:10 [b]Ps. 54:7; 59:10; Jer. 11:20 [c]Ps. 62:8
13 [a]Jer. 31:7 [b]Ps. 34:6; 69:33; Jer. 15:21

20:9 This is the classic statement of prophetic urgency found in the prophets. It was impossible for Jeremiah to hold back the Lord's message, even if he had wanted to, because it was so powerful that it could not be contained.

14 Cursed[779] be the [a]day[3117] when
I was born;
Let the day not be blessed[1288]
when my mother[517] bore me!
15 Cursed be the man[376] who
brought the news[1319]
To my father,[1] saying,
"A [I][a]baby boy[1121] has been born
to you!"
And made him very happy.
16 But let that man be like the
cities
Which the LORD [a]overthrew[2015]
without [I]relenting,[5162]
And let him hear[8085] an
[b]outcry in the morning
And a [II]shout of alarm at noon;
17 Because he did not [a]kill me
[I]before birth,
So that my mother would have
been my grave,
And her womb ever[5769]
pregnant.
18 Why did I ever come forth from
the womb
To [a]look on trouble[5999] and
sorrow,
So that my [b]days[3117] have been
spent[3615] in [c]shame?

Jeremiah's Message for Zedekiah

21 The word[1697] which came to
Jeremiah from the LORD when
[a]King[4428] Zedekiah sent to him [b]Pashhur
the son[1121] of Malchijah, and [c]Zephaniah
the priest,[3548] the son of Maaseiah, saying,
2 "Please[4994] [a]inquire of the LORD
on our behalf, for [b]Nebuchadnezzar king
of [c]Babylon is warring against us; perhaps the LORD will deal[6213] with us
[d]according to all His [I]wonderful acts,[6381]
that *the enemy* may withdraw from us."
3 Then Jeremiah said[559] to them,
"You shall say[559] to Zedekiah as follows:
4 'Thus says[559] the LORD God[430] of
Israel, "Behold, I am about to [a]turn back
the weapons of war which are in your
hands,[3027] with which you are warring
against the king of Babylon and the Chaldeans who are besieging you outside
the wall; and I shall [b]gather[622] them into
the center of this city.
5 "And I [a]Myself shall war against
you with an [b]outstretched hand[3027] and
a mighty[2389] arm, even in [c]anger[639] and
wrath and great indignation.[7110]
6 "I shall also strike[5221] down the
inhabitants of this city, both man[120] and
beast; they will die[4191] of a great
[a]pestilence.[1698]
7 "Then afterwards," declares[5001]
the LORD, "[a]I shall give over Zedekiah
king of Judah and his servants[5650] and
the people,[5971] even those who survive[7604] in this city from the pestilence, the sword,[2719] and the famine,
into the hand of Nebuchadnezzar king
of Babylon, and into the hand of their
foes, and into the hand of those who
seek their lives;[5315] and he will strike
them down with the edge[6310] of the
sword. He [b]will not spare them nor have
pity nor compassion." '[7355]
8 "You shall also say to this people,
'Thus says the LORD, "Behold, I [a]set
before you the way[1870] of life[2416] and
the way of death.[4194]
9 "He who [a]dwells in this city will
die by the [b]sword and by famine and
by pestilence; but he who goes out and
falls away[5307] to the Chaldeans who are
besieging you will live,[2421] and he will
have his own life as booty.
10 "For I have [a]set[7760] My face
against this city for [I]harm[7451] and not
for good,"[2896] declares the LORD. "It
will be [b]given into the hand of the king
of Babylon, and he will [c]burn[8313] it with
fire." '
11 "Then *say* to the household[1004]
of the [a]king of Judah, 'Hear[8085] the word
of the LORD,
12 O [a]house of David, thus says the
LORD:
"[b]Administer[1777] justice[4941]
[I]every [c]morning;
And deliver[5337] the *person* who
has been robbed from the
[II]power of his oppressor,

14 [a]Job 3:3-6; Jer. 15:10
15 [I]Lit., *male child* [a]Gen. 21:6, 7
16 [I]Lit., *being sorry* [II]Or, *trumpet blast* [a]Gen. 19:25 [b]Jer. 18:22; 48:3, 4
17 [I]Lit., *from the womb* [a]Job 3:10, 11, 16; 10:18, 19
18 [a]Job 3:20; 5:7; 14:1; Jer. 15:10; Lam. 3:1 [b]Ps. 90:9; 102:3 [c]Ps. 69:19; Jer. 3:25; 1Cor. 4:9-13

1 [a]2Kin. 24:17, 18; Jer. 32:1-3; 37:1; 52:1-3 [b]1Chr. 9:12; Jer. 38:1 [c]2Kin. 25:18; Jer. 29:25, 29; 37:3; 52:24
2 [I]Or, *miracles* [a]Ex. 9:28; Jer. 37:3, 17; Ezek. 14:7; 20:1-3 [b]2Kin. 25:1 [c]Gen. 10:10; 2Kin. 17:24 [d]Ps. 44:1-3; Jer. 32:17
4 [a]Jer. 32:5; 33:5; 37:8-10; 38:2, 3, 17, 18 [b]Is. 5:5; 13:4; Jer. 39:3; Lam. 2:5, 7; Zech. 14:2
5 [a]Is. 63:10 [b]Ex. 6:6; Deut. 4:34; Jer. 6:12 [c]Is. 5:25; Jer. 32:37
6 [a]Jer. 14:12; 32:24
7 [a]2Kin. 25:5-7, 18-21; Jer. 37:17; 39:5-9; 52:9 [b]2Chr. 36:17; Jer. 13:14; Ezek. 7:9; Hab. 1:6-10
8 [a]Deut. 30:15, 19; Is. 1:19,20
9 [a]Jer. 38:2, 17-23; 39:18; 45:5 [b]Jer. 14:12; 24:10
10 [I]Lit., *evil* [a]Lev. 17:10; Jer. 44:11, 27; Amos 9:4 [b]Jer. 32:28, 29; 38:3 [c]2Chr. 36:19; Jer. 34:2; 37:10; 38:18; 39:8; 52:13
11 [a]Jer. 17:20
12 [I]Or, *in the* [II]Lit., *hand* [a]Is. 7:2, 13 [b]Ps. 72:1; Is. 1:17; Jer. 7:5; 22:3; Zech. 7:9, 10 [c]Ps. 101:8; Zeph. 3:5

[d]That My wrath may not go forth
like fire
And [e]burn with none to
extinguish *it,*
Because of the evil[7455] of their
deeds.
13 "Behold, [a]I am against you, O
[b]valley dweller,
O [1]rocky plain," declares the
LORD,
"You men who say, '[c]Who will
come down against us?
Or who will enter into our
habitations?'
14 "But I shall punish[6485] you
[a]according to the [1]results of
your deeds," declares the
LORD,
"And I shall [b]kindle a fire in its
forest
That it may devour all its
environs." ' "

Warning of Jerusalem's Fall

22 Thus says[559] the LORD, "Go
down to the house[1004] of the
king[4428] of Judah, and there speak[1696]
this word,[1697]
2 and say,[559] 'Hear[8085] the word of
the LORD, O king of Judah, who [a]sits
on David's throne,[3678] you and your
servants[5650] and your people[5971] who enter these gates.
3 'Thus says the LORD, "[a]Do
justice[4941] and righteousness,[6666] and
deliver[5337] the one who has been robbed
from the power[3027] of *his* [b]oppressor.
Also [c]do not mistreat[3238] *or* do
violence[2564] to the stranger,[1616] the orphan, or the widow; and do not [d]shed[8210]
innocent[5355] blood[1818] in this place.
4 "For if you men will indeed
perform[6213] this thing,[1697] then [a]kings[4428]
will enter the gates of this house, sitting
[1]in David's place on his throne, riding
in chariots and on horses, *even the king*
himself and his servants and his people.
5 "[a]But if you will not obey these
words,[1697] I [b]swear[7650] by Myself,"
declares[5001] the LORD, "that this house
will become[1961] a desolation." ' "[2723]

6 For thus says the LORD concerning the house of the king[4428] of Judah:
"You are *like* [a]Gilead to Me,
Like the summit[7218] of Lebanon;
Yet most assuredly I shall make
you like a [b]wilderness,
Like cities which are not
inhabited.
7 "For I shall set apart[6942]
[a]destroyers against you,
Each[376] with his weapons;
And they will [b]cut down[3772] your
choicest cedars
And [c]throw *them* on the fire.
8 "And many nations[1471] will pass
by this city; and they will [a]say to one[376]
another,[7453] 'Why has the LORD done[6213]
thus to this great city?'
9 "Then they will [1]answer,[559] 'Because they [a]forsook[5800] the covenant[1285]
of the LORD their God[430] and bowed
down[7812] to other gods[430] and served[5647]
them.' "
10 [a]Do not weep for the dead[4191]
or mourn for him,
But weep continually for the one
who goes away;
For [b]he will never return[7725]
Or see his native land.[776]
11 For thus says the LORD in regard
to [1][a]Shallum the son[1121] of Josiah, king
of Judah, who became king[4427] in the
place of Josiah his father,[1] who went
forth from this place, "He will never
return there;
12 but in the place where they led
him captive,[1540] there he will [a]die[4191] and
not see this land[776] again.

Messages about the Kings

13 "Woe to him who builds his house
[a]without righteousness
And his [1]upper rooms without
justice,
Who uses his neighbor's[7453]
services[5647] without pay
And [b]does not give him his
wages,
14 Who says, 'I will [a]build myself
a roomy house

12 [d]Jer. 4:4; 17:4; Ezek. 20:47, 48; Nah. 1:6 [e]Is. 1:31; Jer. 7:20
13 [1]Lit., *rock of the level place* [a]Jer. 23:30-32; Ezek. 13:8 [b]Ps. 125:2; Is. 22:1 [c]2Sam. 5:6, 7; Jer. 49:4; Lam. 4:12; Obad. 3, 4
14 [1]Lit., *fruit* [a]Is. 3:10, 11; Jer. 17:10; 32:19 [b]2Chr. 36:19; Is. 10:16, 18; Jer. 11:16; 17:27; 52:13; Ezek. 20:47, 48

2 [a]Is. 9:7; Jer. 17:25; 22:4, 30; Luke 1:32
3 [a]Is. 58:6, 7; Jer. 7:5, 23; 21:12; Mic. 6:8; Zech. 7:9; 8:16; Matt. 23:23 [b]Ps. 72:4 [c]Ex. 22:21-24 [d]Jer. 7:6; 19:4; 22:17
4 [1]Lit., *for David* [a]Jer. 17:25
5 [a]Jer. 17:27; 26:4 [b]Gen. 22:16; Amos 6:8; Heb. 6:13
6 [a]Gen. 37:25; Num. 32:1; Song 4:1 [b]Ps. 107:34; Is. 6:11; Jer. 7:34; Mic. 3:12
7 [a]Is. 10:3-6; Jer. 4:6, 7 [b]Is. 10:33, 34; 37:24 [c]Jer. 21:14
8 [a]Deut. 29:24-26; 1Kin. 9:8, 9; 2Chr. 7:20-22; Jer. 16:10
9 [1]Lit., *say* [a]2Kin. 22:17; 2Chr. 34:25; Jer. 11:3
10 [a]Eccl. 4:2; Is. 57:1; Jer. 16:7; 22:18 [b]Jer. 25:27; 44:14
11 [1]I.e., Jehoahaz [a]2Kin. 23:30-34; 1Chr. 3:15; 2Chr. 36:1-4
12 [a]2Kin. 23:34; Jer. 22:18
13 [1]Or, *roof chambers* [a]Jer. 17:11; Mic. 3:10; Hab. 2:9 [b]Lev. 19:13; James 5:4
14 [a]Is. 5:8

With spacious[7304] [I]upper rooms,
And cut out its windows,
[II]Paneling[5603] *it* with [b]cedar and
painting[4886] *it* [III]bright
red.'[8350]

15 "Do you become a king[4427]
because you are competing
in cedar?
Did not your father eat and
drink,
And [a]do justice and
righteousness?[6666]
Then it was [b]well with him.

16 "He pled[1777] the cause[1779] of the
[a]afflicted and needy;
Then it was well.
[b]Is not that what it means to
know[1847] Me?"
Declares the LORD.

17 "But your eyes and your heart[3820]
Are *intent* only upon your own
[a]dishonest gain,[1215]
And on [b]shedding innocent blood
And on practicing oppression
and extortion."

18 Therefore thus says the LORD
in regard to [a]Jehoiakim the son of Josiah,
king of Judah,
"They will not [b]lament for him:
'[c]Alas, my brother!'[251] or, 'Alas,
sister!'[269]
They will not lament for him:
'Alas for the master!'[113] or, 'Alas
for his splendor!'

19 "He will be [a]buried[6912] with a
donkey's burial,[6900]
Dragged off and thrown out
beyond the gates of
Jerusalem.

20 "Go up to Lebanon and cry out,
And lift up your voice in Bashan;
Cry out also from [a]Abarim,
For all your [b]lovers[157] have been
crushed.[7665]

21 "I spoke[1696] to you in your
prosperity;
But [a]you said,[559] 'I will not
listen!'
[b]This has been your practice[1870]
[c]from your youth,
That you have not obeyed[8085]
My voice.

22 "The wind[7307] will sweep away
all your [a]shepherds,
And your [b]lovers will go into
captivity;[7628]
Then you will surely be
[c]ashamed[954] and humiliated
Because of all your
wickedness.[7451]

23 "You who dwell in Lebanon,
Nested in the cedars,
How you will groan[2603] when
pangs[2256] come upon you,
[a]Pain like a woman in
childbirth!

24 "As I live,"[2416] declares the
LORD, "even though [I][a]Coniah the son
of Jehoiakim king of Judah were a
[b]signet *ring* on My right hand, yet I
would pull [I]you [II]off;
25 and I shall [a]give you over into
the hand of those who are seeking your
life,[5315] yes, into the hand of those whom
you dread, even into the hand of Nebuchadnezzar king of Babylon, and into
the hand of the Chaldeans.
26 "I shall [a]hurl you and your
[b]mother[517] who bore you into another
country where you were not born, and
there you will die.
27 "But as for the land to which they
desire[5315] to return, they will not return
to it.

28 "Is this man Coniah a despised,
shattered jar?[6089]
Or is he an [a]undesirable[2656]
vessel?
Why have he and his
descendants[2233] been [b]hurled
out
And cast into a [c]land that they
had not known?[3045]

29 "[a]O land,[776] land, land,
Hear the word of the LORD!

30 "Thus says the LORD,
'Write this man down
[a]childless,
A man[1397] who will [b]not prosper
in his days;[3117]
For no man of his [c]descendants
will prosper
Sitting on the throne of David
Or ruling again in Judah.' "

14 [I]Or, *roof chambers* [II]Or, *Paneled* [III]Or, *vermilion* [b]2Sam. 7:2; Hag. 1:4
15 [a]2Kin. 23:25; Jer. 7:5; 21:12 [b]Ps. 128:2; Is. 3:10; Jer. 42:6
16 [a]Ps. 72:1-4, 12, 13 [b]1Chr. 28:9; Jer. 9:24
17 [a]Jer. 6:13; 8:10; Luke 12:15-20 [b]2Kin. 24:4; Jer. 22:3
18 [a]2Kin. 23:36-24:6; 2Chr. 36:5 [b]Jer. 22:10; 34:5 [c]1Kin. 13:30
19 [a]1Kin. 21:23, 24; Jer. 36:30
20 [a]Num. 27:12; Deut. 32:49 [b]Jer. 2:25; 3:1
21 [a]Jer. 13:10; 19:15 [b]Jer. 3:25 [c]Jer. 3:24; 32:30
22 [a]Jer. 23:1 [b]Jer. 30:14 [c]Is. 65:13; Jer. 20:11
23 [a]Jer. 4:31; 6:24
24 [I]I.e., Jehoiachin [II]Lit., *off from there* [a]2Kin. 24:6; 1Chr. 3:16; 2Chr. 36:9; Jer. 37:1 [b]Song 8:6; Is. 49:16; Hag. 2:23
25 [a]2Kin. 24:15, 16; Jer. 21:7; 34:20, 21
26 [a]2Kin. 24:15; Jer. 10:18; 16:13 [b]2Kin. 24:8
28 [a]Ps. 31:12; Jer. 48:38; Hos. 8:8 [b]Jer. 15:1 [c]Jer. 17:4
29 [a]Deut. 4:26; Jer. 6:19; Mic. 1:2
30 [a]1Chr. 3:17; Matt. 1:12 [b]Jer. 2:37; 10:21 [c]Ps. 94:20; Jer. 36:30

The Coming Messiah: the Righteous Branch

23 "[a]Woe to the shepherds who are [b]destroying[6] and scattering the [c]sheep of My pasture!" declares[5001] the LORD.

2 Therefore thus says[559] the LORD God[430] of Israel concerning the shepherds who are [I]tending My people:[5971] "You have scattered My flock and driven them away, and have not attended[6485] to them; behold, I am about to [a]attend[6485] to you for the [b]evil[7455] of your deeds," declares the LORD.

3 "Then I Myself shall [a]gather[6908] the remnant[7611] of My flock out of all the countries[776] where I have driven them and shall bring them back to their pasture; and they will be fruitful and multiply.

4 "I shall also raise up [a]shepherds over them and they will [I]tend them; and they will [b]not be afraid[3372] any longer, nor be terrified,[2865] [c]nor will any be missing,"[6485] declares the LORD.

5 "Behold, *the* [a]days[3117] are
coming," declares the LORD,
"When I shall raise up for
David a righteous[6662]
[I][b]Branch;
And He will [c]reign[4427] as king[4428]
and [II]act wisely[7919]
And [d]do justice[4941] and
righteousness[6666] in the
land.[776]

6 "In His days Judah will be
saved,[3467]
And [a]Israel will dwell[7931]
securely;[983]
And this is His [b]name by which
He will be called,[7121]
'The [c]LORD our
righteousness.'[6664]

7 "[a]Therefore behold, *the* days are coming," declares the LORD, "when they will no longer say,[559] 'As the LORD lives,[2416] who brought up[5927] the sons[1121] of Israel from the land[776] of Egypt,'

8 [a]but, 'As the LORD lives, who [b]brought up and led back the descendants[2233] of the household[1004] of Israel from *the* north land[776] and from all the countries where I had driven them.' Then they will live on their own soil."[127]

False Prophets Denounced

⊶9 As for the prophets:[5030]
My [a]heart[3820] is broken[7665]
within[7130] me,
All my bones[6106] tremble;
I have become like a drunken
man,[376]
Even like a man[1397] overcome
with wine,
Because of the LORD
And because of His holy
words.[1697]

10 For the land is full of
[a]adulterers;[5003]
For the land [b]mourns because
of the curse.[423]
The [c]pastures[4999] of the
wilderness have dried up.[3001]
Their course also is evil,[7451]
And their might is not right.

11 "For [a]both prophet[5030] and
priest[3548] are polluted;[2610]
Even in My house I have found
their wickedness,"[7451]
declares the LORD.

12 "Therefore their way[1870] will be
like [a]slippery paths to them,
They will be driven away into
the [b]gloom[653] and fall down
in it;
For I shall bring [c]calamity upon
them,
The year of their
punishment,"[6486] declares
the LORD.

13 "Moreover, among the prophets
of Samaria I saw[7200] an
[a]offensive thing:
They [b]prophesied[5012] by Baal
and [c]led My people Israel
astray.[8582]

---

1 [a]Ezek. 13:3; 34:2; Zech. 11:17 [b]Is. 56:9-12; Jer. 10:21; 50:6 [c]Ezek. 34:31

2 [I]Lit., *shepherding* [a]Ex. 32:34 [b]Jer. 21:12; 44:22

3 [a]Is. 11:11, 12, 16; Jer. 31:7, 8; 32:37

4 [I]Or, *shepherd* [a]Jer. 3:15; 31:10; Ezek. 34:23 [b]Jer. 30:10; 46:27, 28 [c]John 6:39; 10:28; 1Pet. 1:5

5 [I]Lit., *Sprout* [II]Or, *succeed* [a]Jer. 33:14 [b]Is. 4:2; 11:1-5; 53:2; Jer. 30:9; 33:15, 16; Zech. 3:8; 6:12, 13 [c]Is. 9:7; 52:13; Luke 1:32, 33 [d]Ps. 72:2; Is. 9:7; 32:1; Dan. 9:24

6 [a]Deut. 33:28; Jer. 30:10; Zech. 14:11 [b]Is. 7:14; 9:6; Matt. 1:21-23 [c]Is. 45:24; Jer. 33:16; Dan. 9:24; Rom. 3:22; 1Cor. 1:30

7 [a]Is. 43:18, 19; Jer. 16:14, 15

8 [a]Jer. 16:15 [b]Is. 43:5, 6; Ezek. 34:13; Amos 9:14, 15

9 [a]Jer. 8:18; Hab. 3:16

10 [a]Jer. 9:2; Hos. 4:2, 3; Mal. 3:5 [b]Jer. 12:4 [c]Ps. 107:34; Jer. 9:10

11 [a]Jer. 6:13; Zeph. 3:4

12 [a]Ps. 35:6; Prov. 4:19; Jer. 13:16 [b]Is. 8:22; John 12:35 [c]Jer. 11:23

13 [a]Hos. 9:7, 8 [b]1Kin. 18:18-21; Jer. 2:8; 23:32 [c]Is. 9:16

⊶ **23:9-32** See note on Deut. 18:20-22.

14 "Also among the prophets of
Jerusalem I have seen a
[a]horrible thing:[8186]
The committing of [b]adultery[5003]
and walking in falsehood;[8267]
And they strengthen[2388] the
hands[3027] of [c]evildoers,[7489]
So that no one has turned
back[7725] from his
wickedness.
All of them have become to Me
like [d]Sodom,
And her inhabitants like
Gomorrah.
15 "Therefore thus says the LORD
of hosts[6635] concerning the prophets,
'Behold, I am going to
[a]feed them wormwood[3939]
And make them drink
poisonous[7219] water,
For from the prophets of
Jerusalem
Pollution[2613] has gone forth into
all the land.'"
16 Thus says the LORD of hosts,
"[a]Do not listen[8085] to the words
of the prophets who are
prophesying[5012] to you.
They are [b]leading you into
futility;
They speak[1696] a [c]vision[2377] of
their own [I]imagination,
Not [d]from the mouth[6310] of the
LORD.
17 "They keep saying to those who
[a]despise Me,
'The LORD has said,[1696] "[b]You will
have peace"';
And as for everyone who walks
in the [c]stubbornness[8307] of his
own heart,
They say, "[d]Calamity will not
come upon you.'
18 "But [a]who has stood in the
council[5475] of the LORD,
That he should see[7200] and
hear[8085] His word?[1697]
Who has given [b]heed to
[I]His word and listened?
19 "Behold, the [a]storm of the LORD
has gone forth in wrath,
Even a whirling[2342] tempest;
It will swirl down[2342] on the
head[7218] of the wicked.
20 "The [a]anger[639] of the LORD will
not turn back
Until[5647] He has [b]performed[6213]
and carried out the
purposes[4209] of His heart;
[c]In the last[319] days you will
clearly[998] understand[995]
it.
21 "[a]I did not send *these* prophets,
But they ran.
I did not speak[1696] to them,
But they prophesied.
22 "But if they had [a]stood in My
council,
Then they would have
[b]announced[8085] My words to
My people,
And would have turned them
back from their evil way
And from the evil of their
deeds.
23 "Am I a God who is [a]near,"
declares the LORD,
"And not a God far off?
24 "Can a man [a]hide himself in hiding
places,
So I do not see him?" declares
the LORD.
"[b]Do I not fill the heavens[8064] and
the earth?" declares the
LORD.
25 "I have [a]heard what the prophets
have said[559] who [b]prophesy falsely in
My name, saying, 'I had a [c]dream, I
had a dream!'
26 "How long? Is there *anything* in
the hearts of the prophets who prophesy
falsehood, even *these* prophets of the
[a]deception of their own heart,
27 who intend[2803] to [a]make My people forget My name by their dreams
which they relate[5608] to one[376] another,[7453] just as their fathers[1] [b]forgot
My name because of Baal?
28 "The prophet who has a dream
may relate *his* dream, but let him who
has [a]My word speak My word in truth.
[b]What does straw have *in common* with
grain?" declares the LORD.
29 "Is not My word like [a]fire?" de-

14 [a]Jer. 5:30 [b]Jer. 29:23 [c]Jer. 23:22; Ezek. 13:22, 23 [d]Gen. 18:20; Deut. 32:32; Is. 1:9, 10; Jer. 20:16; 49:18; Matt. 11:24
15 [a]Deut. 29:18; Jer. 8:14; 9:15
16 [I]Lit., *heart* [a]Jer. 27:9, 10, 14-17; 1John 4:1 [b]Matt. 7:15; 2Cor. 11:13-15; Gal. 1:8, 9 [c]Jer. 14:14; Ezek. 13:3, 6 [d]Jer. 9:12, 20
17 [a]Mic. 2:11 [b]Jer. 8:11; Ezek. 13:10 [c]Jer. 13:10; 18:12 [d]Jer. 5:12; Amos 9:10; Mic. 3:11
18 [I]Another reading is *My* [a]Job 15:8, 9; Jer. 23:22; 1Cor. 2:16 [b]Job 33:31
19 [a]Jer. 25:32; 30:23; Amos 1:14
20 [a]2Kin. 23:26, 27; Jer. 30:24 [b]Is. 55:11; Zech. 1:6 [c]Gen. 49:1
21 [a]Jer. 14:14; 23:32; 27:15
22 [a]Jer. 9:12; 23:18 [b]Jer. 35:15; Zech. 1:4
23 [a]Ps. 139:1-10
24 [a]Job 22:13, 14; 34:21, 22; Ps. 139:7-12; Is. 29:15; Jer. 49:10; Heb. 4:13 [b]1Kin. 8:27; 2Chr. 2:6; Is. 66:1
25 [a]Jer. 8:6; 1Cor. 4:5 [b]Jer. 14:14 [c]Num. 12:6; Jer. 23:28, 32; 29:8; Joel 2:28
26 [a]1Tim. 4:1, 2
27 [a]Deut. 13:1-3; Jer. 29:8 [b]Judg. 3:7; 8:33, 34
28 [a]Jer. 9:12, 20 [b]1Cor. 3:12, 13
29 [a]Jer. 5:14; 20:9

clares the LORD, "and like a [b]hammer which shatters a rock?

30 "Therefore behold, [a]I am against the prophets," declares the LORD, "who steal My words from each[376] other.

31 "Behold, I am against the prophets," declares the LORD, "who use their tongues and declare,[5001] '*The Lord* declares.'

32 "Behold, I am against those who have prophesied [a]false[8267] dreams," declares the LORD, "and related them, and led My people astray by their falsehoods and [b]reckless boasting; yet [c]I did not send them or command[6680] them, nor do they [d]furnish this people the slightest benefit," declares the LORD.

33 "Now when this people or the prophet or a priest asks[7592] you saying, 'What is the [1a]oracle[4853] of the LORD?' then you shall say to them, 'What [1]oracle?' The LORD declares, 'I shall [b]abandon[5203] you.'

34 "Then as for the prophet or the priest or the people who say, 'The [a]oracle of the LORD,' I shall bring punishment[6485] upon that man and his household.

35 "Thus shall each of you say to his neighbor and to his brother,[251] '[a]What has the LORD answered?' or, 'What has the LORD spoken?'

36 "For you will no longer remember the oracle of the LORD, because every man's own word will become the oracle, and you have [a]perverted the words of the [b]living[2416] God, the LORD of hosts, our God.

37 "Thus you will say to *that* prophet, 'What has the LORD answered you?' and, 'What has the LORD spoken?'

38 "For if you say, 'The oracle of the LORD!' surely thus says the LORD, 'Because you said this word, "The oracle of the LORD!" I have also sent to you, saying, "You shall not say, 'The oracle of the LORD!'" '

39 "Therefore behold, [a]I shall surely forget you and cast you away from My presence, along with the city which I gave you and your fathers.

40 "And I will put an everlasting[5769] [a]reproach[2781] on you and an everlasting[5769] humiliation which will not be forgotten."

Baskets of Figs and the Returnees

24 After [a]Nebuchadnezzar king of Babylon had carried away captive[1540] Jeconiah the son[1121] of Jehoiakim, king[4428] of Judah, and the officials[8269] of Judah with the craftsmen and smiths from Jerusalem and had brought them to Babylon, the LORD showed[7200] me: behold, two [b]baskets of figs set[3259] before the temple[1964] of the LORD!

2 One basket had very good[2896] figs, like [a]first-ripe figs; and the other basket had [b]very bad[7451] figs, which could not be eaten due to rottenness.[7451]

3 Then the LORD said[559] to me, "[a]What do you see, Jeremiah?" And I said, "Figs, the good figs, very good; and the bad[7451] *figs,* very bad, which cannot be eaten due to rottenness."[7455]

4 Then the word[1697] of the LORD came to me, saying,

5 "Thus says[559] the LORD God[430] of Israel, 'Like these good figs, so I will regard[5234] [a]as good the captives[1546] of Judah, whom I have sent out of this place *into* the land[776] of the Chaldeans.

6 'For I will set[7760] My eyes on them for good, and I will [a]bring them again to this land; and I will [b]build them up and not overthrow[2040] them, and I will [c]plant them and not pluck *them* up.

7 'And I will give them a [a]heart[3820] to know[3045] Me, for I am the LORD; and they will be [b]My people,[5971] and I will be their God, for they will [c]return[7725] to Me with their whole heart.

8 'But like the [a]bad figs which cannot be eaten due to rottenness—indeed, thus says the LORD—so I will [1]abandon [b]Zedekiah king of Judah and his officials, and the [c]remnant[7611] of Jerusalem who remain in this land, and the ones who dwell in the land of [d]Egypt.

9 'And I will [a]make them a terror *and an* evil[7451] for all the kingdoms[4467] of the earth, as a [b]reproach[2781] and a

29 [b]2Cor. 10:4, 5
30 [a]Deut. 18:20; Ps. 34:16; Jer. 14:14, 15; Ezek. 13:8
32 [a]Deut. 13:1, 2; Jer. 23:25 [b]Zeph. 3:4 [c]Jer. 23:21; Lam. 3:37 [d]Jer. 7:8; Lam. 2:14
33 [1]Or, *burden,* and so throughout the ch. [a]Is. 13:1; Nah. 1:1; Hab. 1:1; Zech. 9:1; Mal. 1:1 [b]Jer. 12:7; 23:39
34 [a]Lam. 2:14; Zech. 13:3
35 [a]Jer. 33:3; 42:4
36 [a]Gal. 1:7, 8; 2Pet. 3:16 [b]2Kin. 19:4; Jer. 10:10
39 [a]Jer. 7:14, 15; 23:33; Ezek. 8:18
40 [a]Jer. 20:11; 42:18; Ezek. 5:14, 15

1 [a]2Kin. 24:10-16; 2Chr. 36:10; Jer. 27:20; 29:1, 2 [b]Amos 8:1
2 [a]Mic. 7:1; Nah. 3:12 [b]Is. 5:4, 7; Jer. 29:17
3 [a]Jer. 1:11, 13; Amos 8:2; Zech. 4:2
5 [a]Nah. 1:7; Zech. 13:9
6 [a]Jer. 12:15; 29:10; 32:37; Ezek. 11:17 [b]Jer. 31:4; 32:41; 33:7; 42:10 [c]Jer. 32:41
7 [a]Deut. 30:6; Jer. 31:33; 32:40; Ezek. 11:19; 36:26 [b]Is. 51:16; Jer. 7:23; 30:22; 31:33; 32:38; Ezek. 14:11; Zech. 8:8; Heb. 8:10 [c]1Sam. 7:3; Ps. 119:2; Jer. 29:13
8 [1]Lit., *give up* [a]Jer. 29:17 [b]Jer. 39:5; Ezek. 12:12, 13 [c]Jer. 39:9 [d]Jer. 44:1, 26-30
9 [a]Jer. 15:4; 29:18; 34:17 [b]1Kin. 9:7; Ps. 44:13, 14

proverb, a taunt and a [c]curse[7045] in all
places where I shall scatter them.
10 'And I will send the [a]sword,[2719]
the famine, and the pestilence[1698] upon
them until they are destroyed[8552] from
the land[127] which I gave to them and
their forefathers.' "[1]

Prophecy of the Captivity

25 The word[1697] that came to Jeremiah concerning all the peo-
ple[5971] of Judah, in the [a]fourth year of
[b]Jehoiakim the son[1121] of Josiah,
king[4428] of Judah (that was the [c]first[7224]
year of Nebuchadnezzar king of Bab-
ylon),
2 which Jeremiah the prophet[5030]
spoke[1696] to all the [a]people of Judah and
to all the inhabitants of Jerusalem, saying,
3 "From the [a]thirteenth year of
[b]Josiah the son of Amon, king of Judah,
even to this day,[3117] [I]these [c]twenty-
three years the word of the LORD has
come to me, and I have spoken[1696] to
you [II][d]again and again, but you have not
listened.[8085]
4 "And the LORD has sent to you
all His [a]servants[5650] the prophets[5030]
[I]again and again, but you have not listened nor inclined your ear[241] to
hear,[8085]
5 saying,[559] '[a]Turn[7725] now everyone[376] from his evil[7451] way[1870] and from
the evil[7455] of your deeds, and dwell on
the land which the LORD has given to
you and your forefathers[1] [b]forever[5769]
and ever;
6 and [a]do not go after other gods[430]
to [I]serve[5647] them and to [II]worship[7812]
them, and do not provoke Me to
anger[3707] with the work of your
hands,[3027] and I will do you no harm.'[7489]
7 "Yet you have not listened to Me,"
declares[5001] the LORD, "in order that
you might [a]provoke Me to anger with
the work of your hands to your own
harm.[7451]
8 "Therefore thus says[559] the LORD
of hosts,[6635] 'Because you have not
obeyed[8085] My words,[1697]

9 [c]Is. 65:15
10 [a]Is. 51:19; Jer. 21:9; 27:8; Ezek. 5:12-17

1 [a]Jer. 36:1; 46:2 [b]2Kin. 24:1, 2; 2Chr. 36:4-6; Dan. 1:1, 2 [c]Jer. 32:1
2 [a]Jer. 18:11
3 [I]Lit., *this* [II]Lit., *rising early and speaking* [a]Jer. 1:2 [b]2Chr. 34:1-3, 8 [c]Jer. 36:2 [d]Jer. 7:25; 11:7; 26:5
4 [I]Lit., *rising early and sending* [a]2Chr. 36:15; Jer. 26:5
5 [a]2Kin. 17:13; Is. 55:6, 7; Jer. 4:1; 35:15; Ezek. 18:30; Jon. 3:8-10 [b]Gen. 17:8; Jer. 7:7; 17:25
6 [I]Or, *worship* [II]Or, *bow down to* [a]Deut. 6:14; 8:19; 2Kin. 17:35; Jer. 35:15
7 [a]2Kin. 17:17; 21:15; Jer. 7:19; 32:30-33
9 [I]Or, *put them under the ban* [a]Jer. 1:15; 6:22, 23 [b]Is. 13:3; Jer. 27:6; 43:10 [c]1Kin. 9:7, 8; Jer. 18:16; 25:18
10 [I]Lit., *cause to perish* [a]Is. 24:8-11; Jer. 7:34; 16:9; Ezek. 26:13; Rev. 18:23 [b]Eccl. 12:4; Is. 47:2
11 [a]Jer. 4:27; 12:11, 12 [b]2Chr. 36:21; Jer. 29:10; Dan. 9:2; Zech. 7:5
12 [a]Ezra 1:1; Jer. 29:10; Dan. 9:2 [b]Is. 13:14; Jer. ch. 50, 51 [c]Is. 13:19
13 [a]Jer. 36:4, 29, 32 [b]Jer. 1:5, 10; 36:2
14 [I]Or, *For they have served many nations and great kings* [a]Jer. 27:7; 50:9, 41; 51:27, 28 [b]Jer. 51:6, 24, 56
15 [a]Job 21:20; Ps. 75:8; Is. 51:17, 22; Jer. 51:7
16 [a]Nah. 3:11
17 [a]Jer. 1:10; 25:28

9 behold, I will [a]send and take all
the families[4940] of the north,' declares
the LORD, 'and *I will send* to Nebuchadnezzar king of Babylon, [b]My servant,[5650]
and will bring them against this land,[776]
and against its inhabitants, and against
all these nations[1471] round about; and I
will [I]utterly destroy[2763] them, and
[c]make[7760] them a horror,[8047] and a hissing, and an everlasting[5769] desolation.[8077]
10 'Moreover, I will [I][a]take from
them the voice of joy and the voice of
gladness, the voice of the bridegroom
and the voice of the bride, the [b]sound
of the millstones and the light[216] of the
lamp.[5216]
11 'And [a]this whole land shall be a
desolation[2723] and a horror, and these
nations shall serve the king of Babylon
[b]seventy years.

Babylon Will Be Judged

12 'Then it will be [a]when seventy
years are completed4390 I will [b]punish[6485]
the king of Babylon and that nation,'[1471]
declares the LORD, 'for their iniquity,[5771]
and the land of the Chaldeans; and
[c]I will make it an everlasting desolation.[8077]
13 'And I will bring upon that land
all My words which I have pronounced
against it, all that is written in [a]this
book,[5612] which Jeremiah has prophesied[5012] against [b]all the nations.
14 '([I]For [a]many nations and great
kings4423 shall make slaves of them, even
them; and I will [b]recompense[7999] them
according to their deeds, and according
to the work of their hands.)' "
15 For thus the LORD, the God[430]
of Israel, says to me, "Take this
[a]cup of the wine of wrath from My
hand,[3027] and cause all the nations, to
whom I send you, to drink it.
16 "And they shall [a]drink and stagger and go mad[1984] because of the
sword[2719] that I will send among them."
17 Then I took the cup from the
LORD's hand, and [a]made all the nations
drink, to whom the LORD sent me:

18 [a]Jerusalem and the cities of Judah, and its kings *and* its princes,[8269] to make them a ruin, a horror, a hissing, and a curse,[7045] as it is this day;

19 [a]Pharaoh king of Egypt, his servants, his princes, and all his people;

20 and all the [Ia]foreign people, all the kings of the [b]land of Uz, all the kings of the land of the [c]Philistines (even Ashkelon, Gaza, Ekron, and the remnant[7611] of [d]Ashdod);

21 [a]Edom, [b]Moab, and the sons[1121] of [c]Ammon;

22 and all the kings of [a]Tyre, all the kings of Sidon, and the kings of [b]the coastlands which are beyond the sea;

23 and [a]Dedan, Tema, [b]Buz, and all who [c]cut the corners *of their hair;*

24 and all the kings of [a]Arabia and all the kings of the [Ib]foreign people who dwell[7931] in the desert;

25 and all the kings of Zimri, all the kings of [a]Elam, and all the kings of [b]Media;

26 and all the kings of the north, near and far, one with another; and [a]all the kingdoms[4467] of the earth which are upon the face of the ground,[127] and the king of [Ib]Sheshach shall drink after them.

27 "And you shall say[559] to them, 'Thus says the LORD of hosts, the God of Israel, "[a]Drink, be drunk, vomit, fall, and rise no more because of the [b]sword which I will send among you."'

28 "And it will be, if they [a]refuse[3985] to take the cup from your hand to drink, then you will say to them, 'Thus says the LORD of hosts: "[b]You shall surely drink!

29 "For behold, I am [a]beginning to work calamity[7489] in *this* city which is [b]called[7121] by My name, and shall you be completely free from punishment?[5352] You will not be free from punishment; for [c]I am summoning[7121] a sword against all the inhabitants of the earth," declares the LORD of hosts.'

30 "Therefore you shall prophesy[5012] against them all these words, and you shall say to them,

'The [a]LORD will [b]roar from on high,
And utter His voice from His holy[6944] habitation;
He will roar mightily against His [I]fold.
He will shout like those who tread *the grapes,*
Against all the inhabitants of the earth.

31 'A clamor[7588] has come to the end of the earth,
Because the LORD has [a]a controversy[7379] with the nations.
He is entering into [b]judgment[8199] with all flesh;[1320]
As for the wicked,[7563] He has given them to the sword,'
declares the LORD."

32 Thus says the LORD of hosts,
"Behold, evil is going forth
From [a]nation to nation,
And a great [b]storm is being stirred up
From the remotest parts of the earth.

33 "And those [a]slain[2491] by the LORD on that day shall be from one end of the earth to the [I]other. They shall [b]not be lamented, gathered, or buried;[6912] they shall be like [c]dung on the face of the ground.[127]

34 "Wail, you shepherds, and cry;[2199]
And [a]wallow *in ashes,* you masters[117] of the flock;
For the days[3117] of your [b]slaughter[2873] and your dispersions [I]have come,
And you shall fall like a choice vessel.

35 "[a]Flight shall perish from the shepherds,
And escape[6413] from the masters of the flock.

36 "*Hear* the sound of the cry of the shepherds,
And the wailing of the masters of the flock!
For the LORD is destroying[7703] their pasture,

18 [a]Ps. 60:3; Is. 51:17
19 [a]Jer. 46:2-28; Nah. 3:8-10
20 [I]Or, *mixed multitude* [a]Jer. 25:24; 50:37; Ezek. 30:5 [b]Job 1:1; Lam. 4:21 [c]Jer. 47:1-7 [d]Is. 20:1
21 [a]Ps. 137:7; Jer. 49:7-22 [b]Jer. 48:1-47; Amos 2:1-3 [c]Jer. 49:1-6; Amos 1:13-15
22 [a]Jer. 47:4; Zech. 9:2-4 [b]Jer. 31:10
23 [a]Is. 21:13; Jer. 49:7, 8 [b]Gen. 22:21 [c]Jer. 9:26; 49:32
24 [I]Or, *mixed multitude* [a]2Chr. 9:14 [b]Jer. 25:20; 50:37; Ezek. 30:5
25 [a]Gen. 10:22; Is. 11:11; Jer. 49:34 [b]Is. 13:17; Jer. 51:11, 28
26 [I]Cryptic name for Babylon [a]Jer. 25:9; 50:9 [b]Jer. 51:41
27 [a]Jer. 25:16; Hab. 2:16 [b]Ezek. 21:4, 5
28 [a]Job 34:33 [b]Jer. 49:12
29 [a]Prov. 11:31; Is. 10:12; Jer. 13:13; Ezek. 9:6; 1Pet. 4:17 [b]1Kin. 8:43 [c]Ezek. 38:21
30 [I]Or, *pasture* [a]Is. 42:13; Jer. 25:38 [b]Joel 2:11; 3:16; Amos 1:2
31 [a]Hos. 4:1; Mic. 6:2 [b]Is. 66:16; Ezek. 20:35,36; Joel 3:2
32 [a]2Chr. 15:6; Is. 34:2 [b]Is. 30:30; Jer. 23:19
33 [I]Lit., *other end of the earth* [a]Is. 34:2, 3; 66:16 [b]Ps. 79:3; Jer. 16:4; Ezek. 39:4, 17 [c]Is. 5:25
34 [I]Lit., *are full* [a]Jer. 6:26; Ezek. 27:30 [b]Is. 34:6, 7; Jer. 50:27
35 [a]Job 11:20; Jer. 11:11; Amos 2:14

37 "And the peaceful [1][a]folds are made
silent
Because of the [b]fierce anger[639]
of the LORD.
38 "He has left[5880] His hiding
place[5520] [a]like the lion;
For their land has become a
horror[8047]
Because of the fierceness of the
[1]oppressing[3238] *sword,*
And because of His fierce
anger."

Cities of Judah Warned

26 In the beginning[7725] of the
reign[4468] of [a]Jehoiakim the
son[1121] of Josiah, king[4428] of Judah, this
word[1697] came from the LORD, saying,
2 "Thus says[559] the LORD, '[a]Stand
in the court of the LORD's house, and
speak[1696] to all the cities of Judah, who
have [b]come to worship[7812] *in* the LORD's
house,[1004] [c]all the words[1697] that I have
commanded[6680] you to speak to them.
[d]Do not omit a word!
3 '[a]Perhaps they will listen[8085] and
everyone[376] will turn[7725] from his evil[7451]
way,[1870] that [b]I may repent[5162] of the
calamity which I am planning[2803] to do[6213]
to them because of the evil[7455] of their
deeds.'
4 "And you will say[559] to them,
'Thus says the LORD, "[a]If you will not
listen to Me, to [b]walk in My law,[8451]
which I have set before you,
5 to listen to the words of [a]My
servants[5650] the prophets,[5030] whom I
have been sending to you [1]again and
again, but you have not listened;[8085]
6 then I will make this house like
[a]Shiloh, and this city I will make a
[b]curse[7045] to all the nations[1471] of the
earth." ' "[776]

A Plot to Murder Jeremiah

7 And the [a]priests[3548] and the
prophets and all the people[5971] heard[8085]
Jeremiah speaking[1696] these words in the
house of the LORD.
8 And when Jeremiah finished[3615]
speaking all that the LORD had commanded[6680] *him* to speak to all the people, the priests and the prophets and
all the people seized him, saying,
"[a]You must die![4191]
9 "Why have you prophesied[5012] in
the name of the LORD saying, 'This
house will be like Shiloh, and this city
will be [a]desolate,[2717] without inhabitant'?" And [b]all the people gathered[6950]
about Jeremiah in the house of the
LORD.
10 And when the [a]princes[8269] of Judah heard these things,[1697] they came
up[5927] from the king's[4428] house to the
house of the LORD and sat in the
[b]entrance of the New Gate of the LORD's
house.
11 Then the priests and the prophets [a]spoke[559] to the officials and to all
the people, saying, "A [b]death[4194] sentence for this man! For he has prophesied [c]against this city as you have heard
in your hearing."[241]
12 Then Jeremiah spoke to all
the officials and to all the people, saying, "[a]The LORD sent me to prophesy[5012] against this house and against
this city all the words that you have
heard.
13 "Now therefore [a]amend[3190] your
ways[1870] and your deeds, and obey[8085]
the voice of the LORD your God;[430]
and the LORD will [1]change His mind about
the misfortune which He has pronounced against you.
14 "But as for me, behold, [a]I am
in your hands;[3027] do with me as is
good[2896] and right in your sight.
15 "Only know for certain[3045] that
if you put me to death,[4191] you will bring
[a]innocent[5355] blood[1818] on yourselves,
and on this city, and on its inhabitants;
for truly[571] the LORD has sent me to
you to speak all these words in your
hearing."

37 [1]Or, *pastures* [a]Is. 27:10, 11; Jer. 5:17; 13:20 [b]Ps. 97:1-3; Is. 66:15; Heb. 12:29
38 [1]Or, *oppressor* [a]Jer. 4:7; 5:6; Hos. 5:14; 13:7, 8
1 [a]2Kin. 23:36; 2Chr. 36:4, 5
2 [a]2Chr. 24:20, 21; Jer. 7:2; 19:14 [b]Deut. 12:5 [c]Jer. 1:17; 42:4; Matt. 28:20; Acts 20:20, 27 [d]Deut. 4:2
3 [a]Is. 1:16-19; Jer. 36:3-7 [b]Jer. 18:8; Jon. 3:8
4 [a]Lev. 26:14; 1Kin. 9:6; Is. 1:20; Jer. 17:27; 22:5 [b]Jer. 32:23; 44:10, 23
5 [1]Lit., *rising early and sending* [a]2Kin. 9:7; Ezra 9:11; Jer. 7:13; 25:3, 4
6 [a]Josh. 18:1; 1Sam. 4:12; Ps. 78:60, 61; Jer. 7:12, 14 [b]2Kin. 22:19; Is. 65:15; Jer. 24:9; 25:18
7 [a]Jer. 5:31; Mic. 3:11
8 [a]Jer. 11:19; 18:23; Lam. 4:13, 14; Matt. 21:35, 36; 23:34, 35; 27:20
9 [a]Jer. 9:11; 33:10 [b]Acts 3:11; 5:12
10 [a]Jer. 26:21 [b]Jer. 36:10
11 [a]Jer. 18:23 [b]Deut. 18:20; Matt. 26:66 [c]Jer. 38:4; Acts 6:11-14
12 [a]Jer. 1:17, 18; 26:15; Amos 7:15; Acts 4:19; 5:29
13 [1]Lit., *be sorry for* [a]Jer. 7:3, 5; 18:8, 11; 26:3; 35:15; Joel 2:14; Jon. 3:9; 4:2
14 [a]Jer. 38:5
15 [a]Num. 35:33; Prov. 6:16, 17; Jer. 7:6

🗝 **26:4-9** See note on Isa. 66:1,2.

Jeremiah Is Spared

16 Then the officials and all the people [a]said[559] to the priests and to the prophets, "No [b]death sentence for this man! For he has spoken[1696] to us in the name of the LORD our God."

17 Then [a]some[582] of the elders[2205] of the land[776] rose up and spoke to all the assembly[6951] of the people, saying,

🔑 18 "[I][a]Micah of Moresheth prophesied in the days[3117] of Hezekiah king of Judah; and he spoke to all the people of Judah, saying, 'Thus the LORD of hosts[6635] has said,

"[b]Zion will be plowed *as* a field,[7704]
And Jerusalem will become[1961] ruins,
And the [c]mountain of the house as the [II]high places[1116] of a forest." '

19 "Did Hezekiah king of Judah and all Judah put him to death? Did he not [a]fear the LORD and entreat the favor of the LORD, and [b]the LORD [I]changed His mind[5162] about the misfortune which He had pronounced against them? But we are [c]committing[6213] a great evil against ourselves."[5315]

20 Indeed, there was also a man who prophesied in the name of the LORD, Uriah the son of Shemaiah from [a]Kiriath-jearim; and he prophesied against this city and against this land words similar to all those of Jeremiah.

21 When King Jehoiakim and all his mighty men and all the officials heard his words, then the [a]king sought to put him to death; but Uriah heard *it,* and he was afraid[3372] and [b]fled, and went to Egypt.

22 Then King Jehoiakim sent men[582] to Egypt: [a]Elnathan the son of Achbor and *certain* men with him *went* into Egypt.

23 And they brought Uriah from Egypt and led him to King Jehoiakim, who [a]slew[5221] him with a sword,[2719] and cast his dead body[5038] into the [I]burial place[6913] of the [II]common[1121] people.

24 But the hand of [a]Ahikam the son of Shaphan was with Jeremiah, so that he was [b]not given into the hands of the people to put him to death.

The Nations to Submit to Nebuchadnezzar

27 In the beginning[7225] of the reign of [I][a]Zedekiah the son[1121] of Josiah, king[4428] of Judah, this word[1697] came to Jeremiah from the LORD, saying—

2 thus says[559] the LORD to me—"Make[6213] for yourself [a]bonds and [b]yokes and put them on your neck,

3 and send [I]word to the king of [a]Edom, to the king of [a]Moab, to the king of the sons of [a]Ammon, to the king of [a]Tyre, and to the king of [a]Sidon [II]by the messengers who come to Jerusalem to Zedekiah king of Judah.

4 "And command[6680] them *to go* to their masters,[113] saying,[559] 'Thus says the LORD of hosts,[6635] the God[430] of Israel, thus you shall say to your masters,

5 "[a]I have made[6213] the earth,[776] the men[120] and the beasts which are on the face of the earth[776] [b]by My great power and by My outstretched arm, and I will [c]give it to the one who is [I]pleasing in My sight.

6 "And now I [a]have given all these lands[776] into the hand of Nebuchadnezzar king of Babylon, [b]My servant,[5650] and I have given him also the [c]wild animals[2416] of the field[7704] to serve[5647] him.

7 "And [a]all the nations[1471] shall serve him, and his son, and his grandson, [b]until the time[6256] of his own land[776] comes; then [c]many nations and great kings[4428] will [I]make him their servant.

8 "And it will be, *that* the nation[1471] or the kingdom[4467] which [a]will not serve him, Nebuchadnezzar king of Babylon, and which will not put its neck under

16 [a]Jer. 26:11; 36:19, 25; 38:7, 13 [b]Acts 5:34-39; 23:9, 29; 25:25; 26:31
17 [a]Acts 5:34
18 [I]Lit., *Micaiah the Morasthite* [II]Or, *a wooded height* [a]Mic. 1:1 [b]Neh. 4:2; Ps. 79:1; Jer. 9:11; Mic. 3:12 [c]Is. 2:2, 3; Jer. 17:3; Mic. 4:1; Zech. 8:3
19 [I]Lit., *was sorry for* [a]2Chr. 29:6-11; 32:26; Is. 37:1, 4, 15-20 [b]Ex. 32:14; 2Sam. 24:16 [c]Jer. 44:7; Hab. 2:10
20 [a]Josh. 9:17; 1Sam. 6:21; 7:2
21 [a]2Chr. 16:10; 24:21; Jer. 36:26; Matt. 14:5 [b]1Kin. 19:2-4; Matt. 10:23
22 [a]Jer. 36:12
23 [I]Lit., *graves* [II]Lit., *sons of the people* [a]Jer. 2:30
24 [a]2Kin. 22:12-14; Jer. 39:14; 40:5-7 [b]1Kin. 18:4; Jer. 1:18, 19

1 [I]Many mss. read *Jehoiakim* [a]2Kin. 24:18-20; 2Chr. 36:11-13
2 [a]Jer. 30:8 [b]Jer. 28:10, 13
3 [I]Lit., *them* [II]Lit., *by the hand of* [a]Jer. 25:21, 22
5 [I]Or, *upright* [a]Ps. 96:5; 146:5, 6; Is. 42:5; 45:12; Jer. 10:12; 51:15 [b]Deut. 9:29; Jer. 32:17; Dan. 4:17 [c]Ps. 115:15, 16; Acts 17:26
6 [a]Jer. 21:7; 22:25; Ezek. 29:18-20 [b]Is. 44:28; Jer. 25:9; 43:10 [c]Jer. 28:14; Dan. 2:38
7 [I]Or, *enslave him* [a]2Chr. 36:20; Jer. 44:30; 46:13 [b]Dan. 5:26; Zech. 2:8, 9 [c]Is. 14:4-6; Jer. 25:12
8 [a]Jer. 38:17-19; 42:15, 16; Ezek. 17:19-21

🔑 **26:18** Mic. 3:12.

the yoke of the king of Babylon, I will punish[6485] that nation with the [b]sword,[2719] with famine, and with pestilence,"[1698] declares[5001] the LORD, "until I have destroyed[8552] [I]it by his hand.

9 "But as for you, [a]do not listen[8085] to your prophets,[5030] your diviners,[7080] your [I]dreamers, your soothsayers,[6049] or your sorcerers,[3786] who speak[559] to you, saying, 'You shall not serve the king of Babylon.'

10 "For they prophesy[5012] a [a]lie to you, in order to [b]remove you far from your land;[127] and I will drive you out, and you will perish.[6]

11 "But the nation which will [a]bring its neck under the yoke of the king of Babylon and serve him, I will [b]let remain on its land," declares the LORD, "and they will till it and dwell in it." ' "

12 And I spoke[1696] words[1697] like all these to [a]Zedekiah king of Judah, saying, "Bring your necks under the yoke of the king of Babylon, and serve him and his people,[5971] and live![2421]

13 "Why will you [a]die,[4191] you and your people, by the sword, famine, and pestilence, as the LORD has spoken[1696] to that nation which will not serve the king of Babylon?

14 "So [a]do not listen to the words of the prophets who speak to you, saying, 'You shall not serve the king of Babylon,' for they prophesy a [b]lie to you;

15 for [a]I have not sent them," declares the LORD, "but they [b]prophesy falsely in My name, in order that I may [c]drive you out, and that you may perish, [d]you and the prophets who prophesy to you."

16 *Then* I spoke to the priests[3548] and to all this people, saying, "Thus says the LORD: Do not listen to the words of your prophets who prophesy to you, saying, 'Behold, the [a]vessels of the LORD'S house[1004] will now shortly be brought again[7725] from Babylon'; for they are prophesying a [b]lie to you.

17 "Do not listen to them; serve the king of Babylon, and live! Why should this city [a]become a ruin?[2723]

18 "But [a]if they are prophets, and if the word of the LORD is with them, let them now [b]entreat the LORD of hosts, that the vessels which are left[3498] in the house of the LORD, in the house of the king of Judah, and in Jerusalem, may not go to Babylon.

19 "For thus says the LORD of hosts concerning the [a]pillars, concerning the sea, concerning the stands, and concerning the rest[3499] of the vessels that are left[3498] in this city,

20 which Nebuchadnezzar king of Babylon did not take when he [a]carried into exile[1546] Jeconiah the son of Jehoiakim, king of Judah, from Jerusalem to Babylon, and all the nobles[2715] of Judah and Jerusalem.

21 "Yes, thus says the LORD of hosts, the God of Israel, concerning the vessels that are left in the house of the LORD, and in the house of the king of Judah, and in Jerusalem,

22 'They shall be [a]carried to Babylon, and they shall be there until the [b]day[3117] I visit[6485] them,' declares the LORD. 'Then I will [c]bring them [I]back and restore[7725] them to this place.' "

Hananiah's False Prophecy

28 Now it came about in the same year, [a]in the beginning[7225] of the reign of [b]Zedekiah king[4428] of Judah, in the fourth year, in the fifth month, that [c]Hananiah the son[1121] of Azzur, the prophet,[5030] who was from [d]Gibeon, spoke[559] to me in the house[1004] of the LORD in the presence of the priests[3548] and all the people,[5971] saying,

2 "[a]Thus says[559] the LORD of hosts,[6635] the God[430] of Israel, 'I have broken[7665] the yoke of the king of Babylon.

3 'Within two years I am going to bring back[7725] to this place [a]all the vessels of the LORD'S house, which Nebuchadnezzar king of Babylon took away from this place and carried to Babylon.

8 [I]Lit., them [b]Jer. 24:10; 27:13; 29:17, 18; Ezek. 14:21
9 [I]Lit., *dreams* [a]Ex. 22:18; Deut. 18:10; Prov. 19:27; Is. 8:19; Mal. 3:5; Eph. 5:6
10 [a]Jer. 23:25 [b]Jer. 8:19; 32:31
11 [a]Jer. 27:2, 8, 12 [b]Jer. 21:9; 38:2; 40:9-12; 42:10, 11
12 [a]Jer. 27:3; 28:1; 38:17
13 [a]Prov. 8:36; Jer. 27:8; 38:23; Ezek. 18:31
14 [a]Jer. 27:9; 2Cor. 11:13-15 [b]Jer. 14:14; 23:21; 27:10; 29:8, 9; Ezek. 13:22
15 [a]Jer. 23:21; 29:9 [b]Jer. 23:25 [c]2Chr. 25:16; Jer. 27:10 [d]Jer. 6:13-15; 14:15, 16
16 [a]2Kin. 24:13; 2Chr. 36:7, 10; Jer. 28:3; Dan. 1:2 [b]Jer. 27:10
17 [a]Jer. 7:34
18 [a]1Kin. 18:24 [b]1Sam. 7:8; 12:19, 23; Jer. 18:20
19 [a]1Kin. 7:15; 2Kin. 25:13, 17; Jer. 52:17-23
20 [a]2Kin. 24:12, 14-16; 2Chr. 36:10, 18; Jer. 22:28; 24:1
22 [I]Lit., *up* [a]Jer. 34:2, 3 [b]Jer. 25:11, 12; 27:7; 29:10; 32:5 [c]Ezra 1:7-11; 5:13-15; 7:19

1 [a]Jer. 27:1; 49:34 [b]2Kin. 24:18-20; 2Chr. 36:11-13; Jer. 27:3, 12 [c]Jer. 28:17 [d]Josh. 9:3; 10:12; 1Kin. 3:4
2 [a]Jer. 27:12; 28:11
3 [a]2Kin. 24:13; 2Chr. 36:10; Jer. 27:16; Dan. 1:2

4 'I am [a]also going to bring back to this place [b]Jeconiah the son of Jehoiakim, king of Judah, and all the [c]exiles[1546] of Judah who went to Babylon,' declares[5001] the LORD, 'for I will break[7665] the [d]yoke of the king of Babylon.' "

5 Then the prophet Jeremiah spoke[559] to the prophet Hananiah in the presence of the priests and in the presence of all the people who were standing in the [a]house of the LORD,

6 and the prophet Jeremiah said, "[a]Amen![543] May the LORD do[6213] so; may the LORD [I]confirm your words[1697] which you have prophesied[5012] to bring back the vessels of the LORD's house and all the exiles, from Babylon to this place.

7 "Yet [a]hear[8085] now this word[1697] which I am about to speak[1696] in your hearing[241] and in the hearing of all the people!

8 "The prophets[5030] who were before me and before you from ancient times[5769] [a]prophesied against many lands[776] and against great kingdoms,[4467] of war and of calamity[7451] and of pestilence.[1698]

9 "The prophet who prophesies[5012] of peace, [a]when the word of the prophet shall come to pass, then that prophet will be known[3045] *as* one whom the LORD has truly[571] sent."

10 Then Hananiah the prophet took the [a]yoke from the neck of Jeremiah the prophet and broke[7665] it.

11 And Hananiah spoke in the presence of all the people, saying, "[a]Thus says[559] the LORD, 'Even so will I break within two full years, the yoke of Nebuchadnezzar king of Babylon from the neck of all the nations.' "[1471] Then the prophet Jeremiah went his way.[1870]

4 [a]Jer. 22:26, 27 [b]2Kin. 25:27; Jer. 22:24; 24:1 [c]Jer. 22:10 [d]Jer. 27:8
5 [a]Jer. 28:1
6 [I]Or, *fulfill* [a]1Kin. 1:36; Ps. 41:13; Jer. 11:5
7 [a]1Kin. 22:28
8 [a]Lev. 26:14-39; 1Kin. 14:15; 17:1; 22:17; Is. 5:5-7; Joel 1:20; Amos 1:2; Nah. 1:2
9 [a]Deut. 18:22
10 [a]Jer. 27:2
11 [a]Jer. 14:14; 27:10; 28:15
12 [a]Jer. 1:2
13 [a]Ps. 107:16; Is. 45:2
14 [a]Deut. 28:48; Jer. 27:8 [b]Jer. 25:11 [c]Jer. 27:6
15 [a]Jer. 20:6; 29:31; Lam. 2:14; Ezek. 13:2, 3, 22; 22:28; Zech. 13:3
16 [I]Lit., *send you away* [II]Lit., *spoken* [a]Gen. 7:4; Ex. 32:12; Deut. 6:15; 1Kin. 13:34 [b]Jer. 20:6 [c]Deut. 13:5; Jer. 29:32
1 [a]2Chr. 30:1, 6; Esth. 9:20; Jer. 29:25, 29
2 [a]2Kin. 24:12-16; 2Chr. 36:9, 10; Jer. 22:24-28; 24:1; 27:20 [b]2Kin. 24:12, 15; Jer. 13:18; 22:26

12 And the [a]word of the LORD came to Jeremiah, after Hananiah the prophet had broken the yoke from off the neck of the prophet Jeremiah, saying,

13 "Go and speak[559] to Hananiah, saying, 'Thus says the LORD, "You have broken the yokes of wood, but you have made[6213] instead of them [a]yokes of iron."

14 'For thus says the LORD of hosts, the God of Israel, "I have put a [a]yoke of iron on the neck of all these nations, that they may serve[5647] Nebuchadnezzar king of Babylon; and they shall [b]serve him. And [c]I have also given him the beasts[2416] of the field." ' "[7704]

15 Then Jeremiah the prophet said to Hananiah the prophet, "Listen now, Hananiah, the LORD has not sent you, and [a]you have made this people trust[982] in a lie.

16 "Therefore thus says the LORD, '[a]Behold, I am about to [I]remove you from the face of the earth.[127] This year you are going to [b]die,[4191] because you have [II][c]counseled rebellion[5627] against the LORD.' "

17 So Hananiah the prophet died[4191] in the same year in the seventh month.

Message to the Exiles

29 Now these are the words[1697] of the [a]letter[5612] which Jeremiah the prophet[5030] sent from Jerusalem to the rest[3499] of the elders[2205] of the exile,[1473] the priests,[3548] the prophets,[5030] and all the people[5971] whom Nebuchadnezzar had taken into exile[1540] from Jerusalem to Babylon.

2 (This was after King[4428] [a]Jeconiah and the [b]queen mother, the court officials,[5631] the princes[8269] of Judah and

28:8,9 See note on Deut. 18:20-22.

28:16 See note on Deut. 18:20-22.

29:1-32 Little is known about actual conditions in Babylon during the exile, so Jeremiah's letter to the exiles provides us with some important details. Although other prophets were predicting a short stay in Babylon, Jeremiah was sticking by his prophecy of seventy years (29:10); hence, the people should adjust their lives accordingly. They were to build houses, plant gardens, marry among themselves and have children, and stay close together in the cities (29:5-7). This implies a certain amount of freedom in Babylon. In addition to the information it gives, the letter was important because it showed the exiles that it was possible to maintain their national identity, even separated from their land and the temple.

Jerusalem, the craftsmen and the smiths had departed from Jerusalem.)

3 *The letter was sent* by the hand[3027] of Elasah the son[1121] of Shaphan, and Gemariah the son of [a]Hilkiah, whom Zedekiah king of Judah sent to Babylon to Nebuchadnezzar king of Babylon, saying,

4 "Thus says[559] the LORD of hosts,[6635] the God[430] of Israel, to all the exiles whom I have [a]sent into exile[1540] from Jerusalem to Babylon,

5 '[a]Build houses[1004] and live *in them;* and plant gardens, and eat their [I]produce.

6 'Take [a]wives[802] and [I]become the fathers of sons[1121] and daughters, and take wives for your sons and give your daughters to husbands,[582] that they may bear sons and daughters; and multiply there and do not decrease.

7 'And [a]seek the [I]welfare of the city where I have sent you into exile,[1540] and [b]pray[6419] to the LORD on its behalf; for in its [I]welfare you will have [I]welfare.'

8 "For thus says the LORD of hosts, the God of Israel, 'Do not let your [a]prophets who are in your midst[7130] and your diviners[7080] [b]deceive you, and do not listen[8085] to [I][c]the dreams which [II]they dream.

9 'For they [a]prophesy[5012] falsely[8267] to you in My name; [b]I have not sent them,' declares[5001] the LORD.

10 "For thus says the LORD, 'When [a]seventy years have been completed[4390] for Babylon, I will visit[6485] you and fulfill My [b]good[2896] word[1697] to you, to bring you back[7725] to this place.

11 'For I know[3045] the [a]plans[4284] that I [I]have[2803] for you,' declares the LORD, 'plans for [b]welfare and not for calamity[7451] to give you a future[319] and a [c]hope.

12 'Then you will [a]call[7121] upon Me and come and pray to Me, and I will [b]listen to you.

13 'And you will [a]seek Me and find *Me,* when you [b]search for Me with all your heart.[3824]

14 'And I will be [a]found by you,' declares the LORD, 'and I will [b]restore[7725] your [I]fortunes[7622] and will [c]gather[6908] you from all the nations[1471] and from all the places where I have driven you,' declares the LORD, 'and I will [d]bring you back to the place from where I sent you into exile.'[1540]

15 "Because you have said,[559] 'The LORD has raised up [a]prophets for us in Babylon'—

16 for thus says the LORD concerning the king who sits on the throne[3678] of David, and concerning all the people who dwell in this city, your brothers[251] who did [a]not go with you into exile—[1473]

17 thus says the LORD of hosts, 'Behold, I am sending upon them the [a]sword,[2719] famine, and pestilence,[1698] and I will make them like [b]split-open[8182] figs that cannot be eaten due to rottenness.[7455]

18 'And I will pursue them with the sword, with famine and with pestilence; and I will [a]make them a terror to all the kingdoms[4467] of the earth,[776] to be a [b]curse,[423] and a horror,[8047] and a [c]hissing, and a reproach[2781] among all the nations where I have driven them,

19 because they have [a]not listened[8085] to My words,' declares the LORD, 'which I sent to them again and again by [b]My servants[5650] the prophets; but you did not listen,'[8085] declares the LORD.

20 "You, therefore, hear the word of the LORD, all you exiles, whom I have [a]sent away from Jerusalem to Babylon.

21 "Thus says the LORD of hosts, the God of Israel, concerning Ahab the son of Kolaiah and concerning Zedekiah the son of Maaseiah, who are [a]prophesying to you falsely in My name, 'Behold, I will deliver them into the hand of Nebuchadnezzar king of Babylon, and he shall slay[5221] them before your eyes.

22 'And because of them a [a]curse[7045] shall be [I]used by all the exiles[1546] from Judah who are in Babylon, saying, "May the LORD make[7760] you like Zedekiah and like Ahab, whom the king of Babylon [b]roasted in the fire,

3 [a]1Chr. 6:13
4 [a]Jer. 24:5
5 [I]Lit., *fruit* [a]Jer. 29:28
6 [I]Lit., *beget* [a]Jer. 16:2-4
7 [I]Or, *peace* [a]Dan. 4:27; 6:4, 5 [b]Ezra 6:10; 7:23; Dan. 4:19; 1Tim. 2:1, 2
8 [I]Lit., *your* [II]Lit., *you* [a]Jer. 27:9; 29:1 [b]Jer. 14:14; 23:21; 27:14, 15; 28:15; Eph. 5:6 [c]Jer. 23:25, 27
9 [a]Jer. 27:15; 29:21 [b]Jer. 29:31
10 [a]2Chr. 36:21-23; Jer. 25:12; 27:22; Dan. 9:2; Zech. 7:5 [b]Jer. 24:6, 7; Zeph. 2:7
11 [I]Lit., *am planning* [a]Ps. 40:5; Jer. 23:5, 6; 30:9, 10 [b]Is. 40:9-11; Jer. 30:18-22 [c]Jer. 31:17; Hos. 2:15
12 [a]Ps. 50:15; Jer. 33:3; Dan. 9:3 [b]Ps. 145:19
13 [a]Deut. 4:29; Ps. 32:6; Matt. 7:7 [b]1Chr. 22:19; 2Chr. 22:9; Jer. 24:7
14 [I]Or, *captivity* [a]Deut. 30:1-10; Ps. 32:6; Is. 55:6 [b]Jer. 30:3; 32:37-41 [c]Is. 43:5, 6; Jer. 23:8; 32:37 [d]Jer. 3:14; 12:15; 16:15
15 [a]Jer. 29:21, 24
16 [a]Jer. 38:2, 3, 17-23
17 [a]Jer. 27:8; 29:18; 32:24 [b]Jer. 24:3, 8-10
18 [a]Deut. 28:25; 2Chr. 29:8; Jer. 15:4; 24:9; 34:17; Ezek. 12:15 [b]Is. 65:15; Jer. 42:18 [c]Jer. 25:9; Lam. 2:15, 16
19 [a]Jer. 6:19 [b]Jer. 25:4; 26:5; 35:15
20 [a]Jer. 24:5; Ezek. 11:9; Mic. 4:10
21 [a]Jer. 14:14, 15; 29:8, 9; Lam. 2:14; 2Pet. 2:1
22 [I]Lit., *taken* [a]Is. 65:15 [b]Dan. 3:6, 21

23 because they have [a]acted[6213] foolishly[5039] in Israel, and [b]have committed adultery[5003] with their neighbors'[7453] wives, and have [c]spoken[1696] words in My name falsely, which I did not command[6680] them; and I am He who [d]knows, and am a witness," declares the LORD.' "

24 And to [a]Shemaiah the Nehelamite you shall speak[559], saying,

25 "Thus says[559] the LORD of hosts, the God of Israel, 'Because you have sent [a]letters[5612] in your own name to all the people who are in Jerusalem, and to [b]Zephaniah the son of Maaseiah, the priest,[3548] and to all the priests, saying,

26 "The LORD has made you priest instead of Jehoiada the priest, to be the [I][a]overseer[6496] in the house[1004] of the LORD over every [b]madman[376][7696] who [c]prophesies,[5012] to [d]put him in the stocks and in the iron collar,

27 now then, why have you not rebuked Jeremiah of [a]Anathoth who prophesies to you?

28 "For he has [a]sent to us in Babylon, saying, "*The exile* will be [b]long;[752] [c]build houses and live *in them* and plant gardens and eat their [I]produce.' " ' "

29 And [a]Zephaniah the priest read[7121] this letter [I]to Jeremiah the prophet.

30 Then came the word of the LORD to Jeremiah, saying,

31 "Send to [a]all the exiles, saying, 'Thus says the LORD concerning [b]Shemaiah the Nehelamite, "Because Shemaiah has [c]prophesied[5012] to you, although I did not send him, and he has [d]made you trust[982] in a lie,"

32 therefore thus says the LORD, "Behold,[7200] I am about to [a]punish[6485] Shemaiah the Nehelamite and his [I]descendants;[2233] he shall [b]not have anyone living among this people, [c]and he shall not see the good that I am about to do[6213] to My people," declares the LORD, "because he has [II][d]preached rebellion[5627] against the LORD." ' "

23 [a]Gen. 34:7; 2Sam. 13:12 [b]Jer. 5:8; 23:14 [c]Jer. 29:8, 9, 21 [d]Prov. 5:21; Jer. 7:11; 16:17; Mal. 3:5; Heb. 4:13
24 [a]Jer. 29:31, 32
25 [a]Jer. 29:1 [b]2Kin. 25:18; Jer. 21:1; 29:29; 37:3; 52:24
26 [I]Lit., *overseers* [a]Jer. 20:1 [b]2Kin. 9:11; Hos. 9:7; Mark 3:21; John 10:20; Acts 26:24, 25; 2Cor. 5:13 [c]Deut. 13:1-5; Zech. 13:1-5 [d]Jer. 20:1, 2; Acts 16:24
27 [a]Jer. 1:1
28 [I]Lit., *fruit* [a]Jer. 29:1 [b]Jer. 29:10 [c]Jer. 29:5
29 [I]Lit., *in the ears of* [a]Jer. 29:25
31 [a]Jer. 29:20 [b]Jer. 29:24 [c]Jer. 14:14, 15; 29:9, 23; Ezek. 13:8-16, 22, 23 [d]Jer. 28:15
32 [I]Lit., *seed* [II]Lit., *spoken* [a]Jer. 36:31 [b]1Sam. 2:30-34; Jer. 22:30 [c]2Kin. 7:2, 19, 20; Jer. 17:6; 29:10 [d]Deut. 13:5; Jer. 28:16

Deliverance from Captivity Promised

30 The word[1697] which came to Jeremiah from the LORD, saying,

2 "Thus says the LORD, the God[430] of Israel, '[a]Write all the words[1697] which I have spoken[1696] to you in a book.[5612]

3 'For, behold, [a]days[3117] are coming,' declares[5001] the LORD, 'when I will [b]restore[7725] the [I]fortunes[7622] of My people[5971] [c]Israel and Judah.' The LORD says,[559] 'I will also [d]bring them back[7725] to the land[776] that I gave to their forefathers,[1] and they shall possess[3423] it.' "

4 Now these are the words which the LORD spoke[1696] concerning Israel and concerning Judah,

5 "For thus says the LORD,
'[I]I have heard[8085] a sound of
[a]terror,[2731]
Of dread, and there is no peace.
6 'Ask[7592] now, and see,
If a male can give birth.
Why do I see every man[1397]
With his hands[3027] on his loins,
[a]as a woman in childbirth?
And *why* have all faces turned[2015]
pale?
7 'Alas! for that [a]day[3117] is great,
There is [b]none like it;
And it is the time[6256] of Jacob's
[c]distress,
But he will be [d]saved[3467] from
it.

8 'And it shall come about on that day,' declares the LORD of hosts,[6635] 'that I will [a]break[7665] his yoke from off [I]their neck, and will tear off [I]their [b]bonds; and strangers[2114] shall no longer [c]make [II]them their slaves.[5647]

9 'But they shall serve the LORD their God, and [a]David their king,[4428] whom I will raise up for them.

10 '[a]And fear[3372] not, O Jacob My
servant,'[5650] declares the
LORD,

2 [a]Is. 30:8; Jer. 25:13; 36:4, 28, 32; Hab. 2:2
3 [I]Or, *captivity* [a]Jer. 29:10 [b]Ps. 53:6; Jer. 29:14; 30:18; 32:44; Ezek. 39:25; Amos 9:14; Zeph. 3:20 [c]Jer. 3:18 [d]Jer. 16:15; 23:7, 8; Ezek. 20:42; 36:24
5 [I]Lit., *We* [a]Is. 5:30; Jer. 6:25; 8:16; Amos 5:16-18
6 [a]Jer. 4:31; 6:24; 22:23
7 [a]Is. 2:12; Hos. 1:11; Joel 2:11; Amos 5:18; Zeph. 1:14 [b]Lam. 1:12; Dan. 9:12; 12:1 [c]Jer. 2:27, 28; 14:8 [d]Jer. 30:10; 50:19
8 [I]So Gr.; Heb., *your* [II]Lit., *him their slave* [a]Is. 9:4; Jer. 2:20; Ezek. 34:27 [b]Jer. 27:2 [c]Ezek. 34:27
9 [a]Is. 55:3-5; Ezek. 34:23, 24; 37:24, 25; Hos. 3:5; Luke 1:69; Acts 2:30; 13:23, 34
10 [a]Is. 41:13; 43:5; 44:2; Jer. 46:27, 28

'And do not be dismayed,[2865] O
Israel;
For behold, I will save[3467] you
[b]from afar,
And your [I]offspring[2233] from the
land of their captivity.
And Jacob shall return, and shall
be [c]quiet[8252] and at ease,
And [d]no one shall make him
afraid.[2729]
11 'For [a]I am with you,' declares
the LORD, 'to save you;
For I will [b]destroy[6213]
completely[3617] all the
nations[1471] where I have
scattered you,
Only I will [c]not destroy you
completely.
But I will [d]chasten[3256] you
justly,[4941]
And will by no means leave you
unpunished.'[5352]
12 "For thus says the LORD,
'Your wound[7667] is incurable,
And your [a]injury[4347] is serious.
13 'There is no one to plead[1777] your
cause;[1779]
No healing for *your* sore,
[a]No recovery for you.
14 'All your [a]lovers[157] have
forgotten you,
They do not seek you;
For I have [b]wounded[5221] you
with the wound of an
enemy,
With the [c]punishment[4148] of a
[d]cruel one,
Because your [e]iniquity[5771] is
great
And your [f]sins are numerous.
15 'Why do you cry out over your
injury?[7667]
Your pain is incurable.
Because your iniquity is great
And your sins are numerous,
I have done[6213] these things to
you.
16 'Therefore all who [a]devour you
shall be devoured;
And all your adversaries, every
one of them, [b]shall go into
captivity;[7633]
And those who plunder[7701] you
shall be for plunder,
And all who prey upon you I will
give for prey.
17 'For I will [I]restore[5927] you to
[II][a]health[724]
And I will heal you of your
wounds,'[4347] declares the
LORD,
'Because they have called[7121] you
an [b]outcast, saying:
"It is Zion; no one [III]cares for
her." '

Restoration of Jacob

18 "Thus says the LORD,
'Behold, I will [a]restore the
[I]fortunes of the tents[168] of
Jacob
And [b]have compassion[7355] on his
dwelling places;
And the [c]city shall be rebuilt on
its ruin,
And the [d]palace[759] shall stand on
its rightful[4941] place.
19 'And from them shall proceed
[a]thanksgiving[8426]
And the voice of those who
[I][b]make merry;
And I will [c]multiply them, and
they shall not be diminished;
I will also [d]honor[3513] them, and
they shall not be insignificant.
20 '[I]Their children[1121] also shall be
as formerly,[6924]
And [II]their congregation[5712] shall
be [a]established[3559] before
Me;
And I will punish[6485] all
[II]their oppressors.
21 'And [I]their [a]leader[117] shall be one
of them,
And [I]their ruler shall come forth
from [I]their midst;[7130]
And I will [b]bring him near,[7126]
and he shall approach[5066] Me;
For [II]who would dare to risk his
life[3820] to [c]approach Me?'
declares the LORD.
22 'And you shall be [a]My people,
And I will be your God.' "

10 [I]Lit., *seed* [b]Is. 60:4; Jer. 23:3, 8; 29:14 [c]Is. 35:9; Jer. 33:16; Hos. 2:18 [d]Mic. 4:4
11 [a]Jer. 1:8, 19 [b]Jer. 46:28; Amos 9:8 [c]Jer. 4:27; 5:10, 18 [d]Ps. 6:1; Jer. 10:24
12 [a]2Chr. 36:16; Jer. 15:18; 30:15
13 [a]Jer. 14:19; 46:11
14 [a]Jer. 22:20, 22; Lam. 1:2 [b]Lam. 2:4,5 [c]Job 30:21 [d]Jer. 6:23; 50:42 [e]Jer. 32:30-35; 44:22 [f]Jer. 5:6
16 [a]Jer. 2:3; 8:16; 10:25 [b]Is. 14:2; Joel 3:8
17 [I]Lit., *cause to go up* [II]Or, *healing* [III]Lit., *is seeking* [a]Ex. 15:26; Ps. 107:20; Is. 30:26; Jer. 8:22; 33:6 [b]Is. 11:12; 56:8; Jer. 33:24
18 [I]Or, *captivity* [a]Jer. 30:3; 31:23 [b]Ps. 102:13 [c]Jer. 31:4, 38-40 [d]1Chr. 29:1, 19; Ps. 48:3, 13; 122:7
19 [I]Or, *dance* [a]Is. 12:1; 35:10; 51:3; Jer. 17:26; 33:11 [b]Ps. 126:1, 2; Is. 51:11; Jer. 31:4; Zeph. 3:14 [c]Jer. 33:22 [d]Is. 55:5; 60:9
20 [I]Lit., *His* [II]Lit., *his* [a]Is. 54:14
21 [I]Lit., *his* [II]Lit., *who is he that gives his heart in pledge* [a]Jer. 30:9; Ezek. 34:23, 24; 37:24 [b]Num. 16:5; Ps. 65:4 [c]Ex. 3:5; Jer. 50:44
22 [a]Ex. 6:7; Jer. 32:38; Ezek. 36:28; Hos. 2:23; Zech. 13:9

23 Behold, the [a]tempest of the
LORD!
Wrath has gone forth,
A [I]sweeping[1641] tempest;
It will burst[2342] on the head[7218]
of the wicked.[7563]
24 The [a]fierce anger[639] of the LORD
will not turn back,
Until He has performed, and
until He has accomplished
The intent[4209] of His heart;
In the [b]latter[319] days you will
understand[995] this.

Israel's Mourning Turned to Joy

31 "At that time,"[6256] declares[5001]
the LORD, "I will be the [a]God[430]
of all the [b]families[4940] of Israel, and they
shall be My people."[5971]
2 Thus says[559] the LORD,
"The people who survived[8300] the
sword[2719]
[a]Found grace[2580] in the
wilderness—
Israel, when it went to
[b]find its rest."
3 The LORD appeared[7200] to
[I]him from afar, *saying,*
"I have [a]loved[157] you with an
everlasting[5769] love;[160]
Therefore I have drawn you with
[b]lovingkindness.
4 "[a]Again I will build you, and you
shall be rebuilt,
O virgin[1330] of Israel!
Again you shall [I]take up5710 your
[b]tambourines,8596
And go forth to the dances of
the [c]merrymakers.
5 "Again you shall [a]plant vineyards
On the [I]hills of Samaria;
The planters shall plant
And shall [II]enjoy *them.*
6 "For there shall be a day[3117] when
watchmen[5341]
On the hills of Ephraim shall call
out,[7121]
'Arise, and [a]let us go up *to* Zion,
To the LORD our God.' "
7 For thus says the LORD,
"[a]Sing aloud with gladness for
Jacob,
And shout among the [I][b]chiefs[7218]
of the nations;[1471]
Proclaim,[8085] give praise,[1984] and
say,[559]
'O LORD, [c]save[3467] Thy people,
The [d]remnant[7611] of Israel.'
8 "Behold, I am [a]bringing them
from the north country,[776]
And I will [b]gather[6908] them from
the remote parts of the
earth,[776]
Among them the [c]blind and the
[d]lame,
The woman with child and she
who is in labor3205 with child,
together;
A great [I]company,[6951] they shall
return[7725] here.
9 "[a]With weeping they shall come,
And by supplication[8469] I will lead
them;
I will make them walk by
[b]streams of waters,
On a straight[3477] path[1870] in
which they shall [c]not
stumble;[3782]
For I am a [d]father[1] to Israel,
And Ephraim is [e]My first-
born."
10 Hear[8085] the word[1697] of the
LORD, O nations,
And declare[5046] in the
[a]coastlands afar off,
And say, "He who scattered
Israel will [b]gather him,
And keep[8104] him as a
[c]shepherd keeps his flock."
11 For the LORD has [a]ransomed[6299]
Jacob,
And redeemed[1350] him from the
hand[3027] of him who was
[b]stronger than he.
12 "And they shall [a]come and shout
for joy on the [b]height of Zion,
And they shall be [c]radiant over
the [I]bounty of the LORD—
Over the [d]grain, and the new
wine, and the oil,[3323]
And over the young[1121] of the
[e]flock and the herd;

23 [I]Or, *raging* [a]Jer. 23:19
24 [a]Jer. 4:8 [b]Jer. 23:20
1 [a]Jer. 30:22 [b]Gen. 17:7, 8; Is. 41:10; Rom. 11:26-28
2 [a]Num. 14:20 [b]Ex. 33:14; Num. 10:33; Deut. 1:33; Josh. 1:13
3 [I]Lit., *me* [a]Deut. 4:37; 7:8; Mal. 1:2 [b]Ps. 25:6
4 [I]Or, *be adorned with* [a]Jer. 24:6; 33:7 [b]Is. 30:32 [c]Jer. 30:19
5 [I]Or, *mountains* [II]Lit., *defile* [a]Ps. 107:37; Is. 65:21; Ezek. 28:26; Amos 9:14
6 [a]Is. 2:3; Jer. 31:12; 50:4, 5; Mic. 4:2
7 [I]Lit., *heads* [a]Ps. 14:7; Jer. 20:13 [b]Deut. 28:13; Is. 61:9 [c]Ps. 28:9 [d]Is. 37:31; Jer. 23:3
8 [I]Or, *assembly* [a]Jer. 3:18; 23:8 [b]Deut. 30:4; Is. 43:6; Ezek. 34:13 [c]Is. 42:16 [d]Is. 40:11; Ezek. 34:16; Mic. 4:6
9 [a]Ps. 126:5; Jer. 50:4 [b]Is. 43:20; 49:10 [c]Is. 63:13 [d]Is. 64:8; Jer. 3:4, 19 [e]Ex. 4:22
10 [a]Is. 66:19; Jer. 25:22 [b]Jer. 50:19 [c]Is. 40:11; Ezek. 34:12
11 [a]Is. 44:23; 48:20; Jer. 15:21; 50:34 [b]Ps. 142:6
12 [I]Lit., *goodness* [a]Jer. 31:6, 7 [b]Ezek. 17:23 [c]Is. 2:2; Mic. 4:1 [d]Hos. 2:22; Joel 3:18 [e]Jer. 31:24; 33:12, 13

And their life[5315] shall be like a
[f]watered garden,
And they shall [g]never languish
again.
13 "Then the virgin shall rejoice in
the [a]dance,
And the young men and the
old,[2205] together,
For I will [b]turn[7725] their
mourning into joy,
And will comfort[5162] them, and
give them [c]joy for their
sorrow.
14 "And I will [I]fill the soul of the
priests[3548] with [II]abundance,
And My people shall be
[a]satisfied with My
goodness," declares the
LORD.
15 Thus says the LORD,
"[a]A voice is heard[8085] in
[b]Ramah,
Lamentation *and* bitter
weeping.
Rachel is weeping for her
children;[1121]
She [c]refuses[3985] to be
comforted[5162] for her
children,
Because [d]they are no more."
16 Thus says the LORD,
"[a]Restrain your voice from
weeping,
And your eyes from tears;
For your [b]work shall be
rewarded," declares the
LORD,
"And they shall [c]return from the
land[776] of the enemy.
17 "And there is [a]hope for your
future,"[319] declares the
LORD,
"And *your* children shall return
to their own territory.
18 "I have surely heard Ephraim
[a]grieving,
'Thou hast [b]chastised[3256] me, and
I was chastised,
Like an untrained[3925] [c]calf;
[d]Bring me back[7725] that I may
be restored,
For Thou art the LORD my God.

19 'For after I turned back, I
[a]repented;[5162]
And after I was instructed, I
[b]smote[5606] on *my* thigh;[3409]
I was [c]ashamed,[954] and also
humiliated,
Because I bore[5375] the
reproach[2781] of my youth.'
20 "Is [a]Ephraim My dear son?[1121]
Is he a delightful child?
Indeed, as often as I have
spoken[1696] against him,
I certainly *still* remember[2142]
him;
Therefore My [I][b]heart[4578] yearns
for him;
I will surely [c]have mercy[7355] on
him," declares the LORD.
21 "Set[5324] up for yourself
roadmarks,[6725]
Place[7760] for yourself
guideposts;
[a]Direct your [I]mind[3820] to the
highway,
The way by which you went.
[b]Return, O virgin of Israel,
Return[7725] to these your
cities.
22 "How long will you go here and
there,
O [a]faithless[7728] daughter?
For the LORD has created[1254] a
new thing in the earth—
A woman[5347] will encompass a
man."[1397]
23 Thus says the LORD of hosts,[6635]
the God of Israel, "Once again they will
speak this word[1697] in the land of Judah
and in its cities, when I [a]restore[7725] their
[I]fortunes,[7622]
'The LORD bless[1288] you, O
[b]abode of righteousness,[6664]
O [c]holy hill!'
24 "And Judah and all its cities will
[a]dwell together in it, the farmer[406] and
they who go about with flocks.
25 "[a]For I satisfy the weary
ones and [I]refresh everyone who languishes."
26 At this I [a]awoke and looked,[7200]
and my [b]sleep was pleasant[6148] to
me.

12 [f]Is. 58:11 [g]Is. 35:10; 60:20; 65:19; John 16:22; Rev. 21:4

13 [a]Judg. 21:21; Ps. 30:11; Zech. 8:4, 5 [b]Is. 61:3 [c]Is. 51:11

14 [I]Lit., *saturate* [II]Lit., *fatness* [a]Jer. 50:19

15 [a]Matt. 2:18 [b]Josh. 18:25; Judg. 4:5; Is. 10:29; Jer. 40:1 [c]Gen. 37:35; Ps. :2 [d]Gen. 5:24; 42:13, 36; Jer. 10:20

16 [a]Is. 25:8; 30:19 [b]Ruth 2:12; Heb. 6:10 [c]Jer. 30:3; Ezek. 11:17

17 [a]Jer. 29:11

18 [a]Jer. 3:21 [b]Job 5:17; Ps. 94:12 [c]Hos. 4:16 [d]Ps. 80:3, 7, 19; Jer. 17:14; Lam. 5:21; Acts 3:26

19 [a]Ezek. 36:31; Zech. 12:10 [b]Ezek. 21:12; Luke 18:13 [c]Jer. 3:25

20 [I]Lit., *inward parts* [a]Hos. 11:8 [b]Gen. 43:30; Judg. 10:16; Is. 63:15; Hos. 11:8 [c]Is. 55:7; 57:18; Hos. 14:4; Mic. 7:18

21 [I]Lit., *heart* [a]Jer. 50:5 [b]Is. 48:20; 52:11

22 [a]Jer. 3:6; 49:4

23 [I]Or, *captivity* [a]Jer. 30:18; 32:44 [b]Is. 1:26; Jer. 50:7 [c]Ps. 48:1; 87:1; Zech. 8:3

24 [a]Jer. 31:12; Ezek. 36:10; Zech. 8:4-8

25 [I]Lit., *fill* [a]Ps. 107:9; Jer. 31:12, 14; Matt. 5:6; John 4:14

26 [a]Zech. 4:1 [b]Prov. 3:24

A New Covenant

27 "Behold, days[3117] are coming,"
declares the LORD, "when I will [a]sow
the house of Israel and the house[1004]
of Judah with the seed[2233] of man[120] and
with the seed of beast.
28 "And it will come about that as
I have [a]watched over them to [b]pluck
up, to break down, to overthrow,[2040]
to destroy,[6] and to bring disaster, so I
will watch over them to [c]build and to
plant," declares the LORD.
🔑 29 "In those days they will not say
again,
'[a]The fathers[1] have eaten sour
grapes,
And the children's teeth are
[I]set on edge.'
30 "But [a]everyone[376] will die[4191] for
his own iniquity;[5771] each man who eats
the sour grapes, his teeth will be
[I]set on edge.
🔑 31 "[a]Behold, days are coming," declares the LORD, "when I will make a
[b]new covenant[1285] with the house of Israel and with the house of Judah,
32 not like the [a]covenant which I
made[3772] with their fathers in the day I
[b]took[2388] them by the hand to bring them
out of the land of Egypt, My [c]covenant
which they broke,[6565] although I was a
husband[1166] to them," declares the
LORD.
33 "But [a]this is the covenant which
I will make with the house of Israel after
those days," declares the LORD, "[b]I will
put My law[8451] within[7130] them, and on
their heart[3820] I will write it; and
[c]I will be their God, and they shall be
My people.
34 "And they shall [a]not teach[3925]
again, each man[376] his neighbor[7453] and
each man[376] his brother,[251] saying,
'Know[3045] the LORD,' for they shall all
[b]know Me, from the least of them to
the greatest of them," declares the
LORD, "for I will [c]forgive[5545] their iniquity, and their [d]sin[2403] I will remember
no more."
35 Thus says the LORD,
Who [a]gives the sun for light[216]
by day,[3119]
And the [I]fixed order[2708] of the
moon and the stars for light
by night,[3915]
Who [b]stirs up the sea so that
its waves roar;
[c]The LORD of hosts is His name:
36 "[a]If [I]this fixed order[2706] departs
From before Me," declares the
LORD,
"Then the offspring of Israel also
shall [b]cease[7673]
From being a nation[1471] before
Me [II]forever."
37 Thus says the LORD,
"[a]If the heavens[8064] above can be
measured,
And the foundations[4146] of the
earth searched out below,
Then I will also [b]cast off[3988] all
the offspring of Israel
For all that they have done,"[6213]
declares the LORD.
38 "Behold, days are coming," declares the LORD, "when the [a]city shall
be rebuilt for the LORD from the
[b]Tower of Hananel to the [c]Corner Gate.
39 "And the [a]measuring line shall
go out farther straight ahead to the hill
Gareb; then it will turn to Goah.
40 "And [a]the whole valley of the

27 [a]Ezek. 36:9, 11; Hos. 2:23
28 [a]Jer. 44:27; Dan. 9:14 [b]Jer. 1:10; 18:7 [c]Jer. 24:6
29 [I]Or, *dull* [a]Lam. 5:7; Ezek. 18:2
30 [I]Or, *dull* [a]Deut. 24:16; Is. 3:11; Ezek. 18:4, 20
31 [a]Jer. 31:31-34; Heb. 8:8-12 [b]Jer. 32:40; 33:14; Ezek. 37:26; Luke 22:20; 1Cor. 11:25; 2Cor. 3:6; Heb. 8:8-12; 10:16, 17
32 [a]Ex. 19:5; 24:6-8; Deut. 5:2, 3 [b]Deut. 1:31; Is. 63:12 [c]Jer. 11:7, 8
33 [a]Jer. 32:40; Heb. 10:16 [b]Ps. 40:8; 2Cor. 3:3 [c]Jer. 24:7; 30:22; 32:38
34 [a]1Thess. 4:9; 1John 2:27 [b]Is. 11:9; 54:13; Jer. 24:7; Hab. 2:14; John 6:45; 1John 2:20 [c]Jer. 33:8; 50:20; Mic. 7:18; Rom. 11:27 [d]Is. 43:25; Heb. 10:17
35 [I]Lit., *statutes* [a]Gen. 1:14-18; Deut. 4:19; Ps. 19:1-6; 136:7-9 [b]Is. 51:15 [c]Jer. 10:16; 32:18; 50:34
36 [I]Lit., *these statutes* [II]Lit., *all the days* [a]Ps. 89:36, 37; 148:6; Is. 54:9, 10; Jer. 33:20-26 [b]Amos 9:8, 9
37 [a]Is. 40:12; Jer. 33:22 [b]Jer. 33:24-26; Rom. 11:2-5, 26, 27
38 [a]Jer. 30:18; 31:4 [b]Neh. 3:1; 12:39; Zech. 14:10 [c]2Kin. 14:13; 2Chr. 26:9
39 [a]Zech. 2:1
40 [a]Jer. 7:32; 8:2

🔑 **31:29,30** See note on Ezek. 18:1-4.

🔑 **31:31-34** From a Christian perspective, this is the most important passage in Jeremiah, because of the way the writer of Hebrews used it. It was quoted in its entirety in Heb. 8:8-12, the longest quotation of an O.T. text in the N.T. From the words "new covenant," the author argued that the covenant established at Jesus' death had superceded the one made with Israel at Mount Sinai (Heb. 8:6-8,13). Later, on the basis of another meaning of the Greek word for "covenant," he developed the point that Jesus' death initiated the new covenant, because a "will" or "testament," goes into effect only upon the death of the one who made it (Heb. 9:16-18). Hence, our term "New Testament" comes from the Hebrew writer's use of Jer. 31:31. See the note on Jer. 18:7-10.

dead bodies[6297] and of the ashes, and all the fields as far as the brook [b]Kidron, to the corner of the [c]Horse Gate toward the east, shall be [d]holy[6944] to the LORD; it shall not be plucked up, or overthrown[2040] anymore forever.”[5769]

Jeremiah Imprisoned

32 The word[1697] that came to Jeremiah from the LORD in the [a]tenth year of Zedekiah king[4428] of Judah, which was the eighteenth year of Nebuchadnezzar.

2 Now at that time the army[2428] of the king of Babylon was besieging Jerusalem, and Jeremiah the prophet[5030] was shut up in the [a]court of the guard, which was *in* the house[1004] of the king of Judah,

3 because Zedekiah king of Judah had [a]shut him up, saying, “Why do you [b]prophesy,[5012] saying,[559] ‘[c]Thus says[559] the LORD, “Behold, I am about to [d]give this city into the hand[3027] of the king of Babylon, and he will take it;

4 and Zedekiah king of Judah shall [a]not escape[4422] out of the hand of the Chaldeans, but he shall surely be given into the hand of the king of Babylon, and he shall [b]speak[1696] with him [1]face[6310] to face, and see[7200] him eye to eye;

5 and he shall [a]take Zedekiah to Babylon, and he shall be there until I visit[6485] him,” declares[5001] the LORD. “If you fight against the Chaldeans, you shall [b]not succeed” ’?”

6 And Jeremiah said,[559] “The word of the LORD came to me, saying,

7 ‘Behold, Hanamel the son[1121] of Shallum your uncle is coming to you, saying, “Buy for yourself my field[7704] which is at [a]Anathoth, for you have the [b]right[4941] of redemption[1353] to buy *it.*” ’

8 “Then Hanamel my uncle’s son came to me in the [a]court of the guard according to the word of the LORD, and said to me, ‘Buy my field, please,[4994] that is at [b]Anathoth, which is in the land[776] of Benjamin; for you have the right of possession[3425] and the redemption is yours; buy *it* for yourself.’ Then I knew[3045] that this was the [c]word of the LORD.

9 “And I bought the field which was at Anathoth from Hanamel my uncle’s son, and I [a]weighed out the silver for him, seventeen [b]shekels of silver.

10 “And I [1][a]signed and [b]sealed the deed,[5612] and [c]called in witnesses, and weighed out the silver on the scales.

11 “Then I took the deeds of purchase, both the sealed *copy containing* the [a]terms and conditions,[2706] and the open[1540] *copy;*

12 and I gave the deed of purchase to [a]Baruch the son of [b]Neriah, the son of Mahseiah, in the sight of Hanamel my uncle’s *son,* and in the sight of the witnesses who signed the deed[5612] of purchase, before all the Jews who were sitting in the court of the guard.

13 “And I commanded[6680] Baruch in their presence, saying,

14 ‘Thus says the LORD of hosts,[6635] the God[430] of Israel, “Take these deeds, this sealed deed of purchase, and this open deed, and put them in an earthenware[2789] jar, that they may [1]last a long time.”[3117]

15 ‘For thus says the LORD of hosts, the God of Israel, “[a]Houses[1004] and fields[7704] and vineyards shall again be bought in this land.” ’[776]

Jeremiah Prays and God Explains

16 “After I had given the deed of purchase to Baruch the son of Neriah, then I [a]prayed[6419] to the LORD, saying,

17 ‘[a]Ah Lord[136] [1]GOD! Behold, Thou hast [b]made[6213] the heavens and the earth[776] by Thy great power and by Thine outstretched arm! [c]Nothing is too difficult[6381] for Thee,

18 who [a]showest lovingkindness to thousands,[505] but [b]repayest[7999] the iniquity[5771] of fathers[1] into the bosom of their children[1121] after them, O

40 [b]2Sam. 15:23; 2Kin. 23:6, 12; John 18:1 [c]2Kin. 11:16; 2Chr. 23:15; Neh. 3:28 [d]Joel 3:17; Zech. 14:20

1 [a]2Kin. 25:1, 2; Jer. 39:1, 2

2 [a]Neh. 3:25; Jer. 33:1; 37:21; 38:6; 39:14

3 [a]2Kin. 6:32 [b]Jer. 26:8, 9 [c]Jer. 21:3-7; 34:2, 3 [d]Jer. 21:4-7; 32:28, 29; 34:2, 3

4 [1]Lit., *mouth to mouth* [a]2Kin. 25:4-7; Jer. 37:17; 38:18, 23; 39:4-7 [b]Jer. 39:5

5 [a]Jer. 27:22; 39:7; Ezek. 12:12, 13 [b]Ezek. 17:9, 10, 15

7 [a]Jer. 1:1; 11:21 [b]Lev. 25:25; Ruth 4:3, 4

8 [a]Jer. 32:2; 33:1 [b]Jer. 1:1; 32:7 [c]1Sam. 9:16, 17; 10:3-7; 1Kin. 22:25; Jer. 32:25

9 [a]Gen. 23:16; Zech. 11:12 [b]Gen. 24:22; Ex. 21:32; Neh. 5:15; Ezek. 4:10

10 [1]Or, *wrote . . . on the document* [a]Is. 44:5; Jer. 32:44 [b]Deut. 32:34; Job 14:17 [c]Ruth 4:1, 9; Is. 8:2

11 [a]Luke 2:27

12 [a]Jer. 32:16; 36:4, 5, 32; 43:3; 45:1 [b]Jer. 51:59

14 [1]Lit., *stand many days*

15 [a]Jer. 30:18; 31:5, 12, 24; 32:37, 43, 44; 33:12, 13; Amos 9:14, 15; Zech. 3:10

16 [a]Gen. 32:9-12; Jer. 12:1; Phil. 4:6, 7

17 [1]Heb., *YHWH,* usually rendered LORD [a]Jer. 1:6; 4:10 [b]2Kin. 19:15; Ps. 102:25; Is. 40:26-29; Jer. 27:5 [c]Gen. 18:14; Jer. 32:27; Zech. 8:6; Matt. 19:26; Mark 10:27; Luke 1:37; 18:27

18 [a]Ex. 20:6; 34:6, 7; Deut. 5:9, 10; 7:9, 10 [b]1Kin. 14:9, 10; 16:1-3; Matt. 23:32-36

[c]great and [d]mighty God.[410] The [e]LORD of hosts is His name;

19 [a]great in counsel[6098] and mighty in deed, whose [b]eyes are open to all the ways[1870] of the sons[1121] of men,[120] [c]giving to everyone[376] according to his ways and according to the fruit of his deeds;

20 who hast [a]set[7760] signs[226] and wonders[4159] in the land of Egypt, *and* even to this day[3119] both in Israel and among mankind; and Thou hast [b]made a name for Thyself, as at this day.

21 'And Thou didst [a]bring Thy people[5971] Israel out of the land of Egypt with signs and with wonders, and with a strong[2389] hand and with an outstretched arm, and with great terror;[4172]

22 and gavest them this land, which Thou didst [a]swear[7650] to their forefathers to give them, a land flowing with milk and honey.

23 'And they [a]came in and took possession[3423] of it, but they [b]did not obey[8085] Thy voice or [c]walk in Thy law;[8451] they have done[6213] nothing of all that Thou commandedst[6680] them to do;[6213] therefore Thou hast made [d]all this calamity[7451] come upon them.

24 'Behold, the [a]siege mounds have reached the city to take it; and the city is [b]given into the hand of the Chaldeans who fight against it, because of the [c]sword,[2719] the famine, and the pestilence;[1698] and what Thou hast spoken[1696] has [d]come to pass; and, behold, Thou seest *it.*

25 'And Thou hast said to me, O Lord [I]GOD, "Buy for yourself the field with money, and call in witnesses"—although the city is given into the hand of the Chaldeans.' "

26 Then the word of the LORD came to Jeremiah, saying,

27 "Behold, I am the LORD, the [a]God of all flesh;[1320] is anything[1697][3605] [b]too difficult for Me?"

28 Therefore thus says the LORD, "Behold, I am about to [a]give this city into the hand of the Chaldeans and into the hand of Nebuchadnezzar king of Babylon, and he shall take it.

18 [c]Ps. 145:3 [d]Ps. 50:1; Is. 9:6; Jer. 20:11 [e]Jer. 10:16; 31:35
19 [a]Is. 9:6; 28:29 [b]Job 34:21; Jer. 23:24 [c]Ps. 62:12; Jer. 17:10; 21:14; Matt. 16:27; John 5:29
20 [a]Ps. 78:43; 105:27 [b]Ex. 9:16; Is. 63:12, 14; Dan. 9:15
21 [a]Ex. 6:6; Deut. 4:34; 7:19; 26:8; 2Sam. 7:23; 1Chr. 17:21; Ps. 136:11
22 [a]Ex. 3:8, 17; 13:5; Deut. 1:8; Ps. 105:9-11; Jer. 11:5
23 [a]Ps. 44:2, 3; 78:54, 55; Jer. 2:7 [b]Neh. 9:26; Jer. 11:8; Dan. 9:10-14 [c]Ezra 9:7; Jer. 26:4; 44:10 [d]Lam. 1:18; Dan. 9:11, 12
24 [a]Jer. 33:4; Ezek. 21:22 [b]Jer. 20:5; 21:4-7; 32:5 [c]Jer. 14:12; 29:17, 18; 32:36; 34:17; Ezek. 14:21 [d]Deut. 4:26; Josh. 23:15, 16; Zech. 1:6
25 [I]Heb., *YHWH,* usually rendered LORD
27 [a]Num. 16:22; 27:16 [b]Jer. 32:17; Matt. 19:26
28 [a]2Kin. 25:11; 2Chr. 36:17-21; Jer. 19:7-12; 32:3, 24, 36; 34:2, 3
29 [a]2Chr. 36:19; Jer. 21:10; 37:8, 10; 39:8 [b]Jer. 19:13; 44:17-19, 25; 52:13
30 [a]Deut. 9:7-12; Is. 63:10; Jer. 2:7; 7:22-26 [b]Jer. 8:19; 11:17; 25:7
31 [a]1Kin. 11:7, 8; 2Kin. 21:4-7, 16; Jer. 5:9-11; 6:6, 7; Matt. 23:37 [b]2Kin. 23:27; 24:3, 4; Jer. 27:10
32 [a]Ezra 9:7; Is. 1:4-6, 23; Jer. 2:26; 44:17, 21; Dan. 9:8

29 "And the Chaldeans who are fighting against this city shall enter and [a]set this city on fire and burn[8313] it, with the [b]houses where *people* have offered incense[6999] to Baal on their roofs and poured out[5258] libations[5262] to other gods[430] to provoke Me to anger.[3707]

30 "Indeed the sons of Israel and the sons of Judah have been doing only [a]evil in My sight from their youth; for the sons of Israel have been only [b]provoking Me to anger by the work of their hands,"[3027] declares the LORD.

31 "Indeed this city has been to Me *a* [a]*provocation of* My anger[639] and My wrath from the day that they built it, even to this day, that it should be [b]removed from before My face,

32 because of all the evil of the sons of Israel and the sons of Judah, which they have done to provoke Me to anger—they, their [a]kings,[4428] their leaders,[8269] their priests,[3548] their prophets,[5030] the men[376] of Judah, and the inhabitants of Jerusalem.

33 "And they have turned *their* back to Me, and not *their* face; though *I* taught[3925] them, [I][a]teaching again and again, they would not listen[8085] [II]and receive instruction.[4148]

34 "But they [a]put[7760] their detestable things[8251] in the house which is called[7121] by My name, to defile it.

35 "And they built the [a]high places[1116] of Baal that are in the valley of Ben-hinnom to cause their sons and their daughters to pass through[5674] *the fire* to [b]Molech, which I had not commanded[6680] them nor had it [I]entered My mind[3820] that they should do this abomination,[8441] to cause Judah to sin.[2398]

36 "Now therefore thus says the LORD God of Israel concerning this city of which you say, 'It is [a]given into the

33 [I]Lit., *rising up early and teaching* [II]Lit., *to* [a]2Chr. 36:15, 16; Jer. 7:13; 25:3; 26:5; 35:15; John 8:2 **34** [a]2Kin. 21:1-7; Jer. 7:30; 19:4-6; Ezek. 8:5 **35** [I]Lit., *come up into My heart* [a]2Chr. 28:2, 3; 33:6; Jer. 7:31; 19:5 [b]Lev. 18:21; 20:2-5; 1Kin. 11:7; 2Kin. 23:10; Acts 7:43 **36** [a]Jer. 32:24

hand of the king of Babylon by sword,
by famine, and by pestilence.'
37 "Behold, I will [a]gather[6908] them
out of all the lands[776] to which I have
driven them in My anger, in My wrath,
and in great indignation;[7110] and I will
bring them back to this place and
[b]make them dwell in safety.[983]
38 "And they shall be [a]My people,
and I will be their God;
39 and I will [a]give them one heart[3820]
and one way,[1870] that they may fear[3372]
Me always, for their own [b]good,[2896] and
for *the good of* their children after them.
40 "And I will make an [a]everlast-
ing[5769] covenant[1285] with them that I will
[b]not turn away[7725] from them, to do them
good;[3190] and I will [c]put the fear[3374] of
Me in their hearts[3824] so that they will
not turn away[5493] from Me.
41 "And I will [a]rejoice over them
to do them good,[2895] and I will [I]faith-
fully[571] [b]plant them in this land with
[c]all My heart and with all My soul.[5315]
42 "For thus says the LORD, '[a]Just
as I brought all this great disaster on
this people, so I am going to [b]bring on
them all the good that I am promising[1696]
them.
43 'And [a]fields shall be bought in this
land of which you say, "[b]It is a desolation,[8077] without man[120] or beast; it is
given into the hand of the Chaldeans."
44 'Men shall buy fields for money,
[Ia]sign and seal deeds, and call in witnesses in the [b]land of Benjamin, in the
environs of Jerusalem, in the cities of
Judah, in the cities of the hill country,
in the cities of the lowland, and in the
cities of the [II]Negev; for I will [c]re-
store[7725] their [III]fortunes,'[7622] declares
the LORD."

Restoration Promised

33 Then the word[1697] of the LORD
came to Jeremiah the second
time, while he was still [Ia]confined in the
court of the guard, saying,
2 "Thus says[559] [a]the LORD who
made[6213] [I]*the earth,* the LORD who
formed it to establish it, the [b]LORD is
His name,
3 '[a]Call[7121] to Me, and I will answer
you, and I will tell[5046] you [b]great and
mighty things, [c]which you do not
know.'[3045]
4 "For thus says the LORD God[430]
of Israel concerning the [a]houses[1004] of
this city, and concerning the houses of
the kings[4428] of Judah, which are broken
down[5422] *to make a defense* against the
[b]siege mounds and against the
sword,[2719]
5 'While *they* are coming to [a]fight
with the Chaldeans, and to fill them with
the corpses[6297] of men[120] whom I have
slain[5221] in My anger[639] and in My wrath,
and I have [b]hidden My face from this
city because of all their wickedness:[7451]
6 'Behold, I will bring to it [a]health[724]
and healing,[4832] and I will heal[7495] them;
and I will reveal to them an [b]abundance
of peace and truth.
7 'And I will [a]restore[7725] the [I]for-
tunes[7622] of Judah and the fortunes of
Israel, and I will [b]rebuild them as they
were at first.[7223]
8 'And I will [a]cleanse[2891] them from
all their iniquity[5771] by which they have
sinned[2398] against Me, and I will
pardon[5545] all their iniquities[5771] by which
they have sinned against Me, and by
which they have transgressed[6586]
against Me.
9 'And [I]it shall be to Me a [a]name
of joy, praise,[8416] and glory[8597] before
[b]all the nations[1471] of the earth,[776] which
shall hear[8085] of all the [c]good[2896] that I
do[6213] for them, and they shall [d]fear
and tremble because of all the good
and all the peace[7956] that I make[6213] for
it.'
10 "Thus says the LORD, 'Yet again
there shall be heard[8085] in this place,
of which you say,[559] "It is a [a]waste,[2717]
without man[120] and without beast," *that
is,* in the cities of Judah and in the streets

37 [a]Deut. 30:3; Ps. 106:47; Is. 11:11-16; Jer. 16:14, 15; 23:3, 8; Ezek. 11:17; Hos. 1:11; Amos 9:14, 15 [b]Jer. 23:6; Ezek. 34:25, 28; Zech. 14:11
38 [a]Jer. 24:7
39 [a]2Chr. 30:12; Jer. 31:33; Ezek. 11:19; John 17:21; Acts 4:32 [b]Deut. 11:18-21; Ezek. 37:25
40 [a]Is. 55:3; Jer. 31:33, 34; 50:5; Ezek. 37:26 [b]Deut. 31:6, 8; Ezek. 39:29 [c]Jer. 24:7; 31:33
41 [I]Or, *truly* [a]Deut. 30:9; Is. 62:5; 65:19 [b]Jer. 24:6; 31:28; Amos 9:15 [c]Hos. 2:19, 20
42 [a]Jer. 31:28; Zech. 8:14,15 [b]Jer. 33:14
43 [a]Jer. 32:15, 25; Ezek. 37:11-14 [b]Jer. 33:10
44 [I]Or, *write . . . on the document* [II]I.e., South country [III]Or, *captivity* [a]Jer. 32:10 [b]Jer. 17:26; 33:13 [c]Jer. 31:23; 33:7, 11, 26

1 [I]Lit., *shut up* [a]Jer. 32:2, 8; 37:21; 38:28
2 [I]Lit., *it* [a]Jer. 51:19 [b]Ex. 3:15; 6:3; 15:3; Jer. 10:16
3 [a]Ps. 50:15; 91:15; Is. 55:6, 7; Jer. 29:12 [b]Jer. 32:17, 27 [c]Is. 48:6
4 [a]Is. 32:13, 14 [b]Jer. 32:24; Ezek. 4:2; 21:22; Hab. 1:10
5 [a]Jer. 21:4-7; 32:5 [b]Is. 8:17; Jer. 21:10; Mic. 3:4
6 [a]Jer. 17:14; 30:17; Hos. 6:1 [b]Is. 66:12; Gal. 5:22, 23
7 [I]Or, *captivity* [a]Ps. 85:1; Jer. 30:18; 32:44; 33:26; Amos 9:14 [b]Is. 1:26; Jer. 30:18; 31:4, 38; Amos 9:14, 15
8 [a]Ps. 51:2; Is. 44:22; Jer. 50:20; Ezek. 36:25, 33; Mic. 7:18, 19; Zech. 13:1; Heb. 9:11-14
9 [I]I.e., this city [a]Is. 62:2, 4, 7; Jer. 13:11 [b]Jer. 3:17, 19; 4:2; 16:19 [c]Jer. 24:6; 32:42 [d]Neh. 6:16; Ps. 40:3; Is. 60:5; Hos. 3:5
10 [a]Jer. 32:43

of Jerusalem that are [b]desolate,[8074] without man and without inhabitant and without beast,

11 the voice of [a]joy and the voice of gladness, the voice of the bridegroom and the voice of the bride, the voice of those who say,

"[b]Give thanks[3034] to the LORD of hosts,[6635]
For the LORD is good,
For His lovingkindness[2617] is everlasting";[5769]

and of those who bring a [c]thank offering[2426] into the house[1004] of the LORD. For I will restore the [I]fortunes of the land[776] as they were at first,' says the LORD.

12 "Thus says the LORD of hosts, 'There shall again be in this place which is waste, [a]without man or beast, and in all its cities, a [I]habitation of shepherds who rest their [b]flocks.

13 'In the [a]cities of the hill country, in the cities of the lowland,[8219] in the cities of the Negev, in the land of Benjamin, in the environs of Jerusalem, and in the cities of Judah, the flocks shall again [b]pass under the hands[3027] of the one who numbers them,' says the LORD.

The Davidic Kingdom

14 'Behold, [a]days[3117] are coming,' declares[5001] the LORD, 'when I will [b]fulfill the good word which I have spoken[1696] concerning the house of Israel and the house of Judah.

15 'In those days and at that time[6256] I will cause a [a]righteous[6666] Branch of David to spring forth; and He shall execute [b]justice[4941] and righteousness on the earth.

16 'In those days [a]Judah shall be saved,[3467] and Jerusalem shall dwell[7931] in safety;[983] and this is *the name* by which she shall be called:[7121] the [b]LORD is our righteousness.'[6664]

17 "For thus says the LORD, '[I]David shall [a]never lack a man[376] to sit on the throne[3678] of the house of Israel;

18 [I]and the [a]Levitical priests[3548] shall never lack a man before Me to offer burnt offerings,[5930] to burn[6999] grain offerings,[4503] and to [b]prepare sacrifices[2077] [II]continually.'"

19 And the word of the LORD came to Jeremiah, saying,

20 "Thus says the LORD, 'If you can [a]break[6565] My covenant for the day,[3117] and My covenant[1285] for the night,[3915] so that day[3119] and night will not be at their appointed time,[6256]

21 then [a]My covenant may also be broken[6565] with David My servant[5650] that he shall not have a son[1121] to reign[4427] on his throne, and with the Levitical priests, My ministers.[8334]

22 'As the [a]host[6635] of heaven[8064] cannot be counted,[5608] and the [b]sand of the sea cannot be measured, so I will [c]multiply the [I]descendants[2233] of David My servant and the [d]Levites who minister[8334] to Me.'"

23 And the word of the LORD came to Jeremiah, saying,

24 "Have you not observed[7200] what this people[5971] have spoken,[1696] saying, 'The [a]two families[4940] which the LORD chose,[977] He has [b]rejected them'? Thus they [c]despise My people, no longer are they as a nation[1471] [I]in their sight.

25 "Thus says the LORD, 'If My [a]covenant *for* day and night *stand* not, *and* the [I]fixed patterns[2708] of heaven and earth I have [b]not established,[7760]

26 then I would [a]reject[3988] the [I]descendants of Jacob and David My servant, [II]not taking from his [I]descendants [b]rulers[4910] over the [I]descendants of Abraham, Isaac, and Jacob. But I will [c]restore their [III]fortunes and will have [d]mercy[7355] on them.'"

A Prophecy against Zedekiah

34 The word[1697] which came to Jeremiah from the LORD, when [a]Nebuchadnezzar king[4428] of Babylon

10 [b]Jer. 26:9; 34:22
11 [I]Or, *captivity* [a]Is. 35:10; 51:3, 11 [b]1Chr. 16:8, 34; 2Chr. 5:13; 7:3; Ezra 3:11; Ps. 100:4, 5; 106:1; 107:1; 118:1; 136:1 [c]Lev. 7:12, 13; Ps. 107:22; 116:17; Jer. 17:26; Heb. 13:15
12 [I]Or, *pasture* [a]Jer. 32:43; 36:29; 51:62 [b]Is. 65:10; Jer. 31:12; Ezek. 34:12-15; Zeph. 2:6, 7
13 [a]Jer. 17:26; 32:44 [b]Lev. 27:32; Luke 15:4
14 [a]Jer. 23:5 [b]Is. 32:1, 2; Jer. 29:10; 32:42; 33:9; Ezek. 34:23-25; Hag. 2:6-9
15 [a]Is. 4:2; 11:1-5; Jer. 23:5, 6; 30:9; Zech. 3:8; 6:12, 13 [b]Ps. 72:1-5
16 [a]Is. 45:17, 22; Jer. 23:6 [b]Is. 45:24, 25; Jer. 23:6; 1Cor. 1:30; 2Cor. 5:21; Phil. 3:9
17 [I]Lit., *There shall not be cut off for David* [a]2Sam. 7:16; 1Kin. 2:4; 8:25; 1Chr. 17:11-14; Ps. 89:29-37
18 [I]Lit., *there shall not be cut off for the Levitical priests* [II]Lit., *all the days* [a]Num. 3:5-10; Deut. 18:1; 24:8; Josh. 3:3; Ezek. 44:15 [b]Ezra 3:5; Heb. 13:15
20 [a]Ps. 89:37; 104:19-23; Is. 54:9, 10; Jer. 31:35-37; 33:25
21 [a]2Sam. 23:5; 2Chr. 7:18; 21:7
22 [I]Lit., *seed* [a]Gen. 15:5; Jer. 31:37 [b]Gen. 22:17 [c]Ezek. 37:24-27 [d]Is. 66:21; Jer. 33:18
24 [I]Lit., *to their faces* [a]Is. 7:17; 11:13; Jer. 3:7, 8, 10, 18; 33:26; Ezek. 37:22 [b]Jer. 30:17 [c]Neh. 4:2-4; Esth. 3:6, 8, 9; Ps. 44:13, 14; 83:4
25 [I]Lit., *statutes* [a]Gen. 8:22; Jer. 31:35, 36; 33:20 [b]Ps. 74:16, 17
26 [I]Lit., *seed* [II]Lit., *from taking* [III]Or, *captivity* [a]Jer. 31:37 [b]Gen. 49:10 [c]Jer. 33:7 [d]Is. 14:1; 54:8; Jer. 31:20; Ezek. 39:25; Hos. 1:7; 2:23
1 [a]2Kin. 25:1; Jer. 32:2; 39:1; 52:4

and all his army,[2428] with [b]all the
kingdoms[4467] of the earth[776] that were
under his dominion and all the peoples,[5971] were fighting against Jerusalem
and against all its cities, saying,
2 "Thus says[559] the LORD God[430] of
Israel, "[a]Go and speak[559] to Zedekiah
king of Judah and say[559] to him: "Thus
says the LORD, 'Behold, [b]I am giving
this city into the hand[3027] of the king
of Babylon, and [c]he will burn[8313] it with
fire.
3 'And [a]you will not escape[4422] from
his hand, for you will surely be captured
and delivered into his hand; and you will
[b]see[7200] the king of Babylon eye to eye,
and he will speak[1696] with you [I]face[6310]
to face, and you will go to Babylon.' " '
4 "Yet hear[8085] the word of the
LORD, O Zedekiah king of Judah! Thus
says the LORD concerning you, 'You will
not die[4191] by the sword.[2719]
5 'You will die in peace; and as spices
were burned for your fathers,[1] the
former[7223] kings[4428] who were before
you, so they will [a]burn spices for you;
and [b]they will lament for you, "Alas,
lord!" '[113] For I have spoken the word,"
declares[5001] the LORD.

6 Then Jeremiah the prophet[5030]
spoke[1696] [a]all these words[1697] to Zedekiah king of Judah in Jerusalem
7 when the army of the king of Babylon was fighting against Jerusalem and
against all the remaining[3498] cities of Judah, *that is*, [a]Lachish and [b]Azekah, for
they *alone* remained[7604] as [c]fortified cities among the cities of Judah.

8 The word which came to Jeremiah
from the LORD, after King Zedekiah had
[a]made[3772] a covenant[1285] with all the
people who were in Jerusalem to [b]pro-
claim[7121] [I]release to them:
9 that each man[376] should set free
his male servant[5650] and each man his
female servant, a [a]Hebrew man or a
Hebrew woman; so that [b]no one should
keep[5647] them, a Jew his brother,[251] in
bondage.[5647]
10 And all the [a]officials[8269] and all
the people obeyed,[8085] who had entered
into the covenant that each man[376]
should set free his male servant and
each man his female servant, so that
no one should keep them any longer in
bondage; they obeyed,[8085] and set *them*
free.
11 But afterward they turned
around and took back[7725] the male
servants[5650] and the female servants,
whom they had set free, and brought
them into subjection for male servants
and for female servants.

12 Then the word of the LORD came
to Jeremiah from the LORD, saying,
13 "Thus says the LORD God of Israel, 'I [a]made a covenant with your forefathers in the day[3117] that I [b]brought
them out of the land[776] of Egypt, from
the house[1004] of bondage,[5650] saying,
14 "[a]At the end of seven years each
of you shall set free his Hebrew brother,
who [I]has been sold to you and has
served[5647] you six years, you shall send
him out free from you; but your forefathers [b]did not obey[8085] Me, or incline
their ear[241] to Me.
15 "Although recently you *had*
turned and [a]done[6213] what is right[3477]
in My sight, each man proclaiming
[I]release to his neighbor,[7453] and you had
[b]made a covenant before Me [c]in the
house which is called[7121] by My name.
16 "Yet you [a]turned and [b]pro-
faned[2490] My name, and each man[376]
[I]took back his male servant[5650] and each
man his female servant, whom you had
set free according to their desire,[5315]
and you brought them into subjection
to be your male servants and female
servants." '

17 "Therefore thus says the LORD,
'You have not obeyed Me in proclaiming
[I]release each man to his brother, and
each man to his neighbor. Behold, I am
[a]proclaiming a [I]release to you,' declares
the LORD, 'to the [b]sword, to the pestilence,[1698] and to the famine; and I will
make you a [c]terror to all the kingdoms
of the earth.
18 'And I will give the men[582] who
have [a]transgressed[5674] My covenant,
who have not fulfilled the words of the

1 [b]Jer. 1:15; 27:7; Dan. 2:37, 38
2 [a]2Chr. 36:11, 12; Jer. 22:1, 2; 37:1, 2 [b]Jer. 21:10; 32:3; 34:22; 37:8-10 [c]Jer. 32:29
3 [I]Lit., *mouth to mouth* [a]2Kin. 25:4, 5; Jer. 21:7; 32:4; 34:21 [b]2Kin. 25:6, 7; Jer. 39:6, 7
5 [a]2Chr. 16:14; 21:19 [b]Jer. 22:18
6 [a]1Sam. 3:18; 15:16-24
7 [a]Josh. 10:3, 5; 2Kin. 14:19; 18:14; Is. 36:2 [b]Josh. 10:10; 2Chr. 11:9 [c]2Chr. 11:5-10
8 [I]Or, *liberty* [a]2Kin. 11:17; 23:2, 3 [b]Ex. 21:2; Lev. 25:10, 39-46; Neh. 5:1-13; Is. 58:6; Jer. 34:14, 17
9 [a]Gen. 14:13; Ex. 2:6 [b]Lev. 25:39
10 [a]Jer. 26:10, 16
13 [a]Ex. 24:3, 7, 8; Deut. 5:2, 3, 27; Jer. 31:32 [b]Ex. 20:2
14 [I]Or, *has sold himself* [a]Ex. 21:2; Deut. 15:12; 1Kin. 9:22 [b]1Sam. 8:7, 8; 2Kin. 17:13, 14
15 [I]Or, *liberty* [a]Jer. 34:8 [b]2Kin. 23:3; Neh. 10:29 [c]Jer. 7:10f.; 32:34
16 [I]Lit., *caused them to return* [a]1Sam. 15:11; Jer. 34:11; Ezek. 3:20; 18:24 [b]Ex. 20:7; Lev. 19:12
17 [I]Or, *liberty* [a]Lev. 26:34, 35; Esth. 7:10; Dan. 6:24; Matt. 7:2 [b]Jer. 32:24; 38:2 [c]Deut. 28:25; Jer. 29:18
18 [a]Deut. 17:2; Hos. 6:7; 8:1; Rom. 2:8

covenant which they made before Me,
when they [b]cut[3772] the calf in two[8147]
and passed[5674] between its parts—
19 the [a]officials of Judah, and the
officials of Jerusalem, the court officers,[5631] and the priests,[3548] and all the
people of the land, who passed between
the parts of the calf—
20 and I will give them into the hand
of their enemies and into the hand of
those who [a]seek their life.[5315] And their
[b]dead bodies[5038] shall be food for the
birds of the sky[8064] and the beasts of
the earth.
21 'And [a]Zedekiah king of Judah and
his officials I will give into the hand of
their enemies, and into the hand of those
who seek their life, and into the hand
of the army of the king of Babylon which
has [b]gone away[5674] from you.
22 'Behold, I am going to com-
mand,'[6680] declares the LORD, 'and I will
bring them back to this city; and they
shall fight against it and [a]take it and burn
it with fire; and I will make the cities
of Judah a [b]desolation[8077] [c]without inhabitant.'"

The Rechabites' Obedience

35 The word[1697] which came to
Jeremiah from the LORD in the
days[3117] of [a]Jehoiakim the son[1121] of Josiah, king[4428] of Judah, saying,
2 "Go to the house[1004] of the
[a]Rechabites, and speak[1696] to them, and
bring them into the house of the LORD,
into one of the [b]chambers, and give them
wine to drink."
3 Then I took Jaazaniah the son of
Jeremiah, son of Habazziniah, and his
brothers,[251] and all his sons,[1121] and the
whole house of the Rechabites,
4 and I brought them into the house
of the LORD, into the chamber of the
sons of Hanan the son of Igdaliah, the
[a]man[376] of God,[430] which was near the
chamber of the officials,[8269] which was
above the chamber of Maaseiah the son
of Shallum, [b]the doorkeeper.[8104][5592]
5 Then I set before the [I]men of the
house of the Rechabites pitchers full of
wine, and cups; and I said[559] to them,
"[a]Drink wine!"
6 But they said, "We will not drink
wine, for [a]Jonadab the son of [b]Rechab,
our father,[1] commanded[6680] us, saying,
'You shall [c]not drink wine, you or your
sons, forever.[5769]
7 'And you shall not build a house,
and you shall not sow seed,[2233] and you
shall not plant a vineyard or own one;
but in [a]tents[168] you shall dwell all your
days, that you may live[2421] [b]many days
in the land[127] where you [c]sojourn.'[1481]
8 "And we have [a]obeyed[8085] the
voice of Jonadab the son of Rechab, our
father, in all that he commanded[6680] us,
not to drink wine all our days, we, our
wives,[802] our sons, or our daughters,
9 nor to build ourselves houses[1004]
to dwell in; and we [a]do not have vineyard
or field[7704] or seed.
10 "We have only [a]dwelt in tents,
and have obeyed, and have done[6213] according to all that [b]Jonadab our father
commanded us.
11 "But it came about, when
[a]Nebuchadnezzar king of Babylon came
up[5927] against the land,[776] that we said,
'Come and let us [b]go to Jerusalem before
the army of the Chaldeans and before
the army[2428] of the Arameans.' So we
have dwelt in Jerusalem."

Judah Rebuked

12 Then the word of the LORD came
to Jeremiah, saying,
13 "Thus says[559] the LORD of
hosts,[6635] the God of Israel, 'Go and
say[559] to the men[376] of Judah and the
inhabitants of Jerusalem, "[a]Will you not
receive instruction[4148] by listening[8085] to
My words?"[1697] declares[5001] the LORD.
14 "The [a]words of Jonadab the son
of Rechab, which he commanded his
sons not to drink wine, are observed.
So they do not drink *wine* to this day,[3117]
for they have obeyed[8085] their father's[1]
command.[4687] But I have spoken[1696] to
you [I][b]again and again; yet you have
[c]not listened[8085] to Me.
15 "Also I have sent to you all My

18 [b]Gen. 15:10
19 [a]Jer. 34:10; Ezek. 22:27; Zeph. 3:3, 4
20 [a]Jer. 11:21; 21:7; 22:25 [b]Deut. 28:26; 1Sam. 17:44, 46; 1Kin. 14:11; 16:4; Ps. 79:2; Jer. 7:33; 16:4; 19:7
21 [a]2Kin. 25:18-21; Jer. 32:3, 4; 39:6; 52:10, 24-27; Ezek. 17:16 [b]Jer. 37:5-11
22 [a]Jer. 34:2; 39:1; 2, 8; 52:7, 13 [b]Jer. 4:7; 9:11 [c]Jer. 33:10; 44:22

1 [a]2Kin. 23:34-36; 24:1; 2Chr. 36:5-7; Jer. 1:3; 27:20; Dan. 1:1
2 [a]2Kin. 10:15; 1Chr. 2:55 [b]1Kin. 6:5, 8; 1Chr. 9:26, 33
4 [a]Deut. 33:1; Josh. 14:6; 1Kin. 12:22; 2Kin. 1:9-13 [b]1Chr. 9:18f.
5 [I]Lit., *sons* [a]Amos 2:12
6 [a]2Kin. 10:15, 23 [b]1Chr. 2:55 [c]Lev. 10:9; Num. 6:2-4; Judg. 13:7, 14; Luke 1:15
7 [a]Gen. 25:27; Heb. 11:9 [b]Ex. 20:12; Eph. 6:2, 3 [c]Gen. 36:7
8 [a]Prov. 1:8, 9; 4:1, 2, 10; 6:20; Eph. 6:1; Col. 3:20
9 [a]Ps. 37:16; Jer. 35:7; 1Tim. 6:6
10 [a]Jer. 35:7 [b]Jer. 35:6
11 [a]2Kin. 24:1, 2; Dan. 1:1, 2 [b]Jer. 4:5-7; 8:14
13 [a]Is. 28:9-12; Jer. 5:3; 6:8-10; 32:33
14 [I]Lit., *rising early and speaking* [a]Jer. 35:6-10 [b]2Chr. 36:15; Jer. 7:13, 25; 11:7; 25:3, 4 [c]Is. 30:9; 50:2

[a]servants[5650] the prophets,[5030] sending
them [I]again and again, saying: '[b]Turn[7725]
now every man[376] from his evil[7451]
way,[1870] and amend[3190] your deeds, and
[c]do not go after other gods[430] to worship[5647] them, then you shall [d]dwell
in the land which I have given to you
and to your forefathers;[1] but you have
not [e]inclined your ear[241] or listened to
Me.
16 'Indeed, the sons of Jonadab the
son of Rechab have [a]observed the command of their father which he commanded them, but this people[5971] has
not listened to Me.' " '
17 "Therefore thus says the LORD,
the God of hosts, the God of Israel,
'Behold, [a]I am bringing on Judah and
on all the inhabitants of Jerusalem all
the disaster that I have pronounced
against them; because I [b]spoke to them
but they did not listen,[8085] and I have
[b]called[7121] them but they did not answer.' "
18 Then Jeremiah said to the house
of the Rechabites, "Thus says the LORD
of hosts, the God of Israel, 'Because
you have [a]obeyed the command of Jonadab your father, kept[8104] all his commands,[4687] and done according to all that
he commanded you;
19 therefore thus says the LORD of
hosts, the God of Israel, "Jonadab the
son of Rechab [a]shall not lack a man to
[b]stand before Me [I]always." ' "

Jeremiah's Scroll Read in the Temple

36 And it came about in the [a]fourth
year of Jehoiakim the son[1121] of
Josiah, king[4428] of Judah, that this
word[1697] came to Jeremiah from the
LORD, saying,
🗝 2 "Take a [Ia]scroll[4039,5612] and write
on it all the [b]words[1697] which I have
spoken[1696] to you concerning [c]Israel, and
concerning Judah, and concerning all the
[d]nations,[1471] from the [e]day[3117] I *first*
spoke[1696] to you, from the days of Josiah,
even to this day.[3117]
3 "[a]Perhaps the house[1004] of Judah
will hear[8085] all the calamity[7451] which I
plan[2803] to bring[6213] on them, in order
that every man[376] will [b]turn[7725] from his
evil way;[1870] then I will [c]forgive[5545] their
iniquity[5771] and their sin."[2403]
4 Then Jeremiah called[7121] [a]Baruch
the son of Neriah, and Baruch wrote
[I]at the dictation[6310] of Jeremiah all the
words of the LORD, which He had spoken
to him, on a [IIb]scroll.
5 And Jeremiah commanded[6680] Baruch, saying, "I am [Ia]restricted; I cannot
go into the house of the LORD.
6 "So you go and [a]read[7121] from the
scroll which you have [b]written [I]at my
dictation the words of the LORD [II]to the
people[5971] in the LORD'S house on a
[c]fast day. And also you shall read them
[II]to all *the people of* Judah who come from
their cities.
7 "[a]Perhaps their supplication[8467]
will [I]come[5307] before the LORD, and
everyone[376] will turn from his evil way,
for [b]great is the anger[639] and the wrath

15 [I]Lit., *rising early and speaking* [a]Jer. 7:25; 25:4; 26:5; 29:19; 32:33 [b]Is. 1:16, 17; Jer. 4:1; 18:11; 25:5f.; Ezek. 18:30-32; Acts 26:20 [c]Deut. 6:14; Jer. 7:6; 13:10; 25:6 [d]Jer. 7:7; 25:5, 6 [e]Jer. 7:24, 26; 11:8; 17:23; 34:14
16 [a]Jer. 35:14; Mal. 1:6
17 [a]Josh. 23:15; Jer. 19:3, 15; 21:4-10; Mic. 3:12 [b]Prov. 1:24, 25; Is. 65:12; 66:4; Jer. 7:13, 26, 27; 26:5; Luke 13:34, 35; Rom. 10:21
18 [a]Ex. 20:12; Eph. 6:1-3
19 [I]Lit., *all the days* [a]1Chr. 2:55; Jer. 33:17 [b]Jer. 15:19; Luke 21:36

1 [a]2Kin. 24:1; 2Chr. 36:5-7; Jer. 25:1, 3; 45:1; 46:2; Dan. 1:1
2 [I]Lit., *scroll of a book* [a]Ex. 17:14; Is. 8:1; Jer. 36:6, 23, 28; Zech. 5:1, 2 [b]Jer. 1:9, 10; 30:2; Hab. 2:2 [c]Jer. 3:3-10; 23:13, 14; 32:30-32 [d]Jer. 1:5, 10; 25:9-29; chs. 47-51 [e]Jer. 1:2, 3; 25:3
3 [a]Jer. 26:3; 36:7; Ezek. 12:3 [b]Deut. 30:2, 8; 1Sam. 7:3; Is. 55:7; Jer. 18:8, 11; 35:15; Jon. 3:8 [c]Jon. 3:10; Mark 4:12; Acts 3:19

4 [I]Lit., *from the mouth of* [II]Lit., *scroll of a book* [a]Jer. 32:12; 36:18; 43:3; 45:1 [b]Jer. 36:14; Ezek. 2:9 **5** [I]Lit., *shut up* [a]Jer. 32:2; 33:1; 2Cor. 11:23 **6** [I]Lit., *from my mouth* [II]Lit., *in the ears of,* and so throughout this context [a]Jer. 36:8 [b]Jer. 36:4 [c]Jer. 36:9; Zech. 8:19
7 [I]Lit., *fall* [a]1Kin. 8:33; 2Chr. 33:12, 13; Jer. 26:3; 36:3 [b]Deut. 28:15; 31:16, 17; 2Kin. 22:13, 17; Jer. 4:4; 21:5; Lam. 4:11

🗝 **36:2** Jeremiah was one of the writing prophets, as opposed to prophets like Elijah and Elisha, who left no writings bearing their names. This chapter indicates how some of the prophets may have written their books. In order to encourage Judah to repent, God wanted Jeremiah to write down all the words which He had given him since He began more than twenty years before. Instead of writing the words himself, Jeremiah dictated them to Baruch, his scribe (36:4). The scroll eventually got to King Jehoiakim, and he destroyed it piece by piece (36:23). God simply directed Jeremiah to do it again, giving him additional words, and Jeremiah and Baruch repeated the process (36:27-32). Earlier, Isaiah had written and sealed up an oracle at God's command (Isa. 8:1,16), and Habakkuk was told to write down a vision (Hab. 2:2).

that the LORD has pronounced against this people."

8 And Baruch the son of Neriah did[6213] according to all that Jeremiah the prophet[5030] commanded him, [a]reading from the book the words of the LORD in the LORD'S house.

9 Now it came about in the [a]fifth year of Jehoiakim the son of Josiah, king of Judah, in the [b]ninth month, that all the people in Jerusalem and all the people who [c]came from the cities of Judah to Jerusalem proclaimed[7121] a [d]fast before the LORD.

10 Then Baruch read from the book the words of Jeremiah in the house of the LORD in the [a]chamber of [b]Gemariah the son of Shaphan the [c]scribe,[5608] in the upper[5945] court, at the [d]entry of the New Gate of the LORD'S house, to all the people.

11 Now when [a]Micaiah the son of Gemariah, the son of Shaphan, had heard[8085] all the words of the LORD from the book,

12 he went down to the king's[4428] house, into the scribe's chamber. And, behold, all the officials[8269] were sitting there—[a]Elishama the scribe, and [b]Delaiah the son of Shemaiah, and [c]Elnathan the son of Achbor, and Gemariah the son of Shaphan, and Zedekiah the son of Hananiah, and all the *other* officials.

13 And Micaiah [a]declared to them all the words that he had heard, when Baruch read from the book to the people.

14 Then all the officials sent [a]Jehudi the son of Nethaniah, the son of Shelemiah, the son of Cushi, to Baruch, saying, "Take in your hand[3027] the scroll from which you have read to the people and come." So Baruch the son of Neriah [b]took the scroll in his hand and went to them.

15 And they said[559] to him, "Sit down please, and read it to us." So Baruch [a]read it to them.

16 Now it came about when they had heard all the words, they turned in [a]fear[6342] one[376] to another and said to Baruch, "We will surely [b]report[5046] all these words to the king."

17 And they asked[7592] Baruch, saying, "Tell us please, [a]how did you write all these words? *Was it* [1]at his dictation?"

18 Then Baruch said[559] to them, "He [a]dictated all these words to me, and I wrote them with ink on the book."

19 Then the officials said to Baruch, "Go, [a]hide yourself, you and Jeremiah, and do not let anyone know[3045] where you are."

The Scroll Is Burned

20 So they went to the [a]king in the court, but they had deposited the scroll in the chamber of [a]Elishama the scribe, and they reported[5046] all the words to the king.

21 Then the king sent Jehudi to get the scroll, and he took it out of the chamber of Elishama the scribe. And Jehudi [a]read it to the king as well as to all the officials who stood beside the king.

22 Now the king was sitting in the [a]winter house in the [b]ninth month, with *a fire* burning in the brazier before him.

23 And it came about, when Jehudi had read three or four columns, *the king* cut it with a scribe's knife and [a]threw *it* into the fire that was in the brazier, until all the scroll was consumed[8552] in the fire that was in the brazier.

24 Yet the king and all his servants[5650] who heard all these words were [a]not afraid, nor did they [b]rend their garments.

25 Even though Elnathan and Delaiah and Gemariah [a]entreated the king not to burn[8313] the scroll, he would not listen to them.

26 And the king commanded Jerahmeel the king's son, Seraiah the son of Azriel, and Shelemiah the son of Abdeel to [a]seize Baruch the scribe and Jeremiah the prophet, but the [b]LORD hid them.

8 [a]Jer. 1:17; 36:6

9 [a]Jer. 36:1 [b]Jer. 36:22 [c]Jer. 36:6 [d]Judg. 20:26; 1Sam. 7:6; 2Chr. 20:3; Esth. 4:16; Joel 1:14; 2:15; Jon. 3:5

10 [a]Jer. 35:4 [b]Jer. 36:11, 25 [c]2Sam. 8:17; Jer. 52:25 [d]Jer. 26:10

11 [a]Jer. 36:13

12 [a]Jer. 36:20 [b]Jer. 36:25 [c]Jer. 26:22

13 [a]2Kin. 22:10

14 [a]Jer. 36:21 [b]Jer. 36:2; Ezek. 2:7-10

15 [a]Jer. 36:21

16 [a]Jer. 36:24; Acts 24:25 [b]Jer. 13:18; Amos 7:10, 11

17 [1]Lit., *from his mouth,* and so throughout this context [a]John 9:10, 15, 26

18 [a]Jer. 36:4

19 [a]1 Kin. 17:3; 18:4, 10; Jer. 26:20-24; 36:26

20 [a]Jer. 36:12

21 [a]2Kin. 22:10; 2Chr. 34:18; Ezek. 2:4, 5

22 [a]Judg. 3:20; Amos 3:15 [b]Jer. 36:9

23 [a]1Kin. 22:8, 27; Prov. 1:30; Is. 5:18, 19; 28:14, 22; Jer. 36:29

24 [a]Ps. 36:1; 64:5; Jer. 36:16 [b]Gen. 37:29, 34; 2Sam. 1:11; 1Kin. 21:27; 2Kin. 19:1, 2; 22:11, 19; Is. 36:22; 37:1; Jon. 3:6

25 [a]Gen. 37:22, 26, 27; Acts 5:34-39

26 [a]1Kin. 19:1-3, 10, 14; Matt. 23:34, 37 [b]Ps. 91:1

The Scroll Is Replaced

27 Then the word of the LORD came to Jeremiah after the king had [a]burned[8313] the scroll and the words which [b]Baruch had written at the dictation of Jeremiah, saying,

28 "[a]Take again another scroll and write on it all the former[7223] words that were [b]on the first[7223] scroll which Jehoiakim the king of Judah burned.

29 "And concerning Jehoiakim king of Judah you shall say,[559] 'Thus says[559] the LORD, "You have [a]burned this scroll, saying, "[b]Why have you written on it [I]that the [c]king of Babylon shall certainly come and destroy this land,[776] and shall make[7673] man[120] and beast to cease[7673] from it?" "

30 'Therefore thus says the LORD concerning Jehoiakim king of Judah, "He shall have [a]no one to sit on the throne[3678] of David, and his [b]dead body[5038] shall be cast out to the heat of the day and the frost of the night.[3915]

31 "I shall also [a]punish[6485] him and his [I]descendants[2233] and his servants for their iniquity, and I shall [b]bring on them and the inhabitants of Jerusalem and the men[376] of Judah all the calamity that I have declared to them—but they did not listen." ' "[8085]

32 Then Jeremiah took another scroll and gave it to Baruch the son of Neraiah, the scribe, and he [a]wrote on it at the dictation of Jeremiah all the words of the book which Jehoiakim king of Judah had burned in the fire; and many [I]similar words were added to them.

Jeremiah Warns against Trust in Pharaoh

37 Now [a]Zedekiah the son[1121] of Josiah whom Nebuchadnezzar king of Babylon had [b]made king in the land[776] of Judah, reigned[4427] as king[4428] in place of [c]Coniah the son of Jehoiakim.

2 But [a]neither he nor his servants[5650] nor the people[5971] of the land listened[8085] to the words[1697] of the LORD which He spoke[1696] through Jeremiah the prophet.[5030]

3 Yet [a]King Zedekiah sent Jehucal the son of Shelemiah, and [b]Zephaniah the son of Maaseiah, the priest,[3548] to Jeremiah the prophet, saying, "[c]Please pray[6419] to the LORD our God[430] on our behalf."

4 Now Jeremiah was *still* coming in and going out among the people, for they had not *yet* [a]put him in the prison.

5 Meanwhile, [a]Pharaoh's army[2428] had set out from Egypt; and when the Chaldeans who had been besieging Jerusalem heard[8085] the report[8088] about them, they [b]lifted the *siege* from Jerusalem.

6 Then the word[1697] of the LORD came to Jeremiah the prophet, saying,

7 "Thus says[559] the LORD God of Israel, '[a]Thus you are to say[559] to the king of Judah, who sent you to Me to inquire of Me: "Behold, [b]Pharaoh's army which has come out for your assistance is going to return[7725] to its own land of Egypt.

8 "The Chaldeans will also [a]return and fight against this city, and they will capture it and burn[8313] it with fire." '

9 "Thus says the LORD, 'Do not [a]deceive yourselves, saying, "The Chaldeans will surely go away from us," for they will not go.

10 'For [a]even if you had defeated[5221] the entire army of Chaldeans who were fighting against you, and there were *only* wounded men[582] left[7604] among them, each man[376] in his tent,[168] they would rise up and [b]burn this city with fire.' "

Jeremiah Imprisoned

11 Now it happened, when the army of the Chaldeans had lifted *the siege*[5927] from Jerusalem because of Pharaoh's army,

12 that Jeremiah went out from Jerusalem to go to the land of Benjamin in order to [a]take [I]possession of *some* property there among the people.

27 [a]Jer. 36:23 [b]Jer. 36:4, 18
28 [a]Zech. 1:5, 6 [b]Jer. 36:4, 23
29 [I]Lit., *saying* [a]Deut. 29:19; Job 15:24, 25; Is. 45:9 [b]Is. 29:21; 30:10; Jer. 26:9; 32:3 [c]Jer. 25:9-11
30 [a]2Kin. 24:12-15; Jer. 22:30 [b]Jer. 22:19
31 [I]Lit., *seed* [a]Jer. 23:34 [b]Deut. 28:15; Prov. 29:1; Jer. 19:15; 35:17
32 [I]Lit., *like those* [a]Ex. 4:15, 16; 34:1; Jer. 36:4, 18, 23
1 [a]2Kin. 24:17; 1Chr. 3:15; 2Chr. 36:10 [b]Ezek. 17:12-21 [c]2Kin. 24:12; 1Chr. 3:16; 2Chr. 36:9, 10; Jer. 22:24, 28; 24:1; 52:31
2 [a]2Kin. 24:19, 20; 2Chr. 36:12-16; Prov. 29:12
3 [a]Jer. 21:1, 2 [b]Jer. 29:25; 52:24 [c]1 Kin. 13:6; Jer. 2:27; 15:11; 21:1, 2; 42:1-4, 20; Acts 8:24
4 [a]Jer. 32:2, 3; 37:15
5 [a]2Kin. 24:7; Jer. 37:7; Ezek. 17:15 [b]Jer. 37:11
7 [a]2Kin. 22:18; Jer. 21:1, 2; 37:3 [b]Is. 30:1-3; 31:1-3; Jer. 2:18, 36; Lam. 4:17; Ezek. 17:17
8 [a]Jer. 34:22; 38:23; 39:2-8
9 [a]Jer. 29:8; Obad. 3; Matt. 24:4, 5; Eph. 5:6
10 [a]Lev. 26:36-38; Is. 30:17; Jer. 21:4, 5 [b]Jer. 37:8
12 [I]Or, *part in a dividing* [a]Jer. 32:8

13 While he was at the [a]Gate of Benjamin, a captain[1167] of the guard[6488] whose name was Irijah, the son of Shelemiah the son of Hananiah was there; and he [b]arrested Jeremiah the prophet, saying, "You are [I]going over[5307] to the Chaldeans!"

14 But Jeremiah said,[559] "[a]A lie![8267] I am not [I]going over to the Chaldeans"; yet he would not listen[8085] to him. So Irijah arrested Jeremiah and brought him to the officials.[8269]

15 Then the officials were [a]angry[7107] at Jeremiah and beat[5221] him, and they [b]put him in jail in the house[1004] of Jonathan the scribe,[5608] which they had made[6213] into the prison.

16 For Jeremiah had come into the [Ia]dungeon,[953] that is, the vaulted cell; and Jeremiah stayed there many days.[3117]

17 Now King Zedekiah sent and took him *out;* and in his palace the king [a]secretly asked[7592] him and said, "Is there a [b]word from the LORD?" And Jeremiah said, "There is!" Then he said, "You will be [c]given into the hand[3027] of the king of Babylon!"

18 Moreover Jeremiah said to King Zedekiah, "[a]*In* what *way* have I sinned[2398] against you, or against your servants, or against this people, that you have put me in prison?

19 "[a]Where then are your prophets[5030] who prophesied[5012] to you, saying, 'The [b]king of Babylon will not come against you or against this land'?

20 "But now, please[4994] listen,[8085] O my lord[113] the king; please let my [a]petition[8467] [I]come[5307] before you, and do not make me return to the house of Jonathan the scribe, that I may not die[4191] there."

21 Then King Zedekiah gave commandment,[6680] and they committed Jeremiah to the [a]court of the guardhouse and gave him a loaf of [b]bread daily[3117] from the bakers' street, until all the bread in the city was [c]gone.[8552] So Jeremiah remained in the court of the guardhouse.

Jeremiah Thrown into the Cistern

38 Now Shephatiah the son[1121] of Mattan, and Gedaliah the son of Pashhur, and Jucal the [a]son of Shelemiah, and [b]Pashhur the son of Malchijah heard[8085] the words[1697] that Jeremiah was speaking[1696] to all the people,[5971] saying,

2 "Thus says[559] the LORD, 'He who [a]stays in this city will die[4191] by the [b]sword[2719] and by famine and by pestilence,[1698] but he who goes out to the Chaldeans will live[2421] and have his *own* [c]life[5315] as booty and stay alive.'[2425]

3 "Thus says the LORD, 'This city will certainly be [a]given into the hand[3027] of the army[2428] of the king[4428] of Babylon, and he will capture it.' "

4 Then the [a]officials[8269] said[559] to the king, "Now let this man[376] be put to death,[4191] inasmuch as he is [Ib]discouraging[7503] the men[582] of war who are left in this city and [II]all the people, by speaking[1696] such words to them; for this man [c]is not seeking the well-being[7965] of this people, but rather their harm."[7451]

5 So King Zedekiah said, "Behold, he is in your [I]hands; for the king [a]can *do* nothing against you."

6 Then they took Jeremiah and cast him into the [a]cistern[953] *of* Malchijah the king's son, which was in the court of the guardhouse; and they let Jeremiah down with ropes. Now in the cistern there was no water but only [b]mud, and Jeremiah sank into the mud.

7 But [a]Ebed-melech the Ethiopian, [I]a[376] [b]eunuch,[5631] while he was in the king's[4428] palace,[1004] heard that they had put Jeremiah into the cistern. Now the king was sitting in the [c]Gate of Benjamin;

8 and Ebed-melech went out from the king's palace and spoke[1696] to the king, saying,

9 "My lord[113] the king, these men have acted wickedly[7489] in all that

13 [I]Lit., *falling* [a]Jer. 38:7; Zech. 14:10 [b]Jer. 18:18; 20:10; Luke 23:2; Acts 6:11; 24:5-9,13
14 [I]Lit., *falling* [a]Ps. 27:12; 52:1, 2; Jer. 40:4-6; Matt. 5:11, 12
15 [a]Jer. 18:23; 20:1-3; 26:16; Matt. 21:35 [b]Gen. 39:20; 2Chr. 16:10; 18:26; Jer. 38:26; Acts 5:18
16 [I]Lit., *house of the cistern-pit* [a]Jer. 38:6
17 [a]1Kin. 14:1-4; Jer. 38:5, 14-16, 24-27 [b]1Kin. 22:15, 16; 2Kin. 3:11, 12; Jer. 15:11; 21:1, 2; 37:3 [c]Jer. 21:7; 24:8; Ezek. 12:12, 13; 17:19, 20
18 [a]1Sam. 24:9; 26:18; Dan. 6:22; John 10:32; Acts 25:8, 11, 25
19 [a]Deut. 32:37, 38; 2Kin. 3:13; Jer. 2:28 [b]Jer. 27:14; 28:1-4, 10-17
20 [I]Lit., *fall* [a]Jer. 36:7; 38:26
21 [a]Jer. 32:2; 38:13, 28 [b]1Kin. 17:6; Job 5:20; Ps. 33:18, 19; Is. 33:16 [c]2Kin. 25:3; Jer. 38:9; 52:6

1 [a]Jer. 37:3 [b]Jer. 21:1
2 [a]Jer. 21:9 [b]Jer. 34:17; 42:17 [c]Jer. 21:9; 39:18; 45:5
3 [a]Jer. 21:10; 32:3-5
4 [I]Lit., *weakening the hands of* [II]Lit., *the hands of all* [a]Jer. 18:23; 26:11, 21; 36:12 [b]Ex. 5:4; 1Kin. 18:17, 18; 21:20; Neh. 6:9; Amos 7:10; Acts 16:20 [c]Jer. 29:7
5 [I]Lit., *hand* [a]2Sam. 3:39
6 [a]Jer. 37:16, 21; Acts 16:24 [b]Ps. 40:2; 69:2, 14, 15; Jer. 38:22; Zech. 9:11
7 [I]Or, *an official* [a]Jer. 39:16 [b]Jer. 29:2; Acts 8:27 [c]Deut. 21:19; Job 29:7; Jer. 37:13; Amos 5:10

they have done[6213] to Jeremiah the prophet[5030] whom they have cast into the cistern; and he [I]will die right where he is because of the famine, for there is [a]no more bread in the city."

10 Then the king commanded[6680] Ebed-melech the Ethiopian, saying, "Take thirty men from here [I]under your authority, and bring up Jeremiah the prophet from the cistern before he dies."

11 So Ebed-melech took the men under his [I]authority and went into the king's palace to *a place* beneath the storeroom and took from there worn-out clothes[5499] and worn-out rags and let them down by ropes into the cistern to Jeremiah.

12 Then Ebed-melech the Ethiopian said to Jeremiah, "Now put these worn-out clothes and rags under your armpits under the ropes"; and Jeremiah did[6213] so.

13 So they pulled Jeremiah up with the ropes and lifted him out of the cistern, and Jeremiah stayed in the [a]court of the guardhouse.

14 Then King Zedekiah [a]sent and [I]had Jeremiah the prophet brought to him at the third entrance that is in the house of the LORD; and the king said to Jeremiah, "I am going to [b]ask[7592] you something; do not hide anything[1697] from me."

15 Then Jeremiah said to Zedekiah, "[a]If I tell[5046] you, will you not certainly put me to death? Besides, if I give you advice,[3289] you will not listen[8085] to me."

16 But King Zedekiah swore[7650] to Jeremiah in [a]secret saying, "As the LORD lives,[2416] who made this [I][b]life[5315] for us, surely I will not put you to death nor will I give you over to the hand of [c]these men who are seeking your [I]life."

Interview with Zedekiah

17 Then Jeremiah said to Zedekiah, "Thus says the LORD [a]God[430] of hosts,[6635] the [b]God of Israel, 'If you will indeed [c]go out to the officers of the king of Babylon, then [I]you will live, this city will not be burned[8313] with fire, and you and your household will [II]survive.

18 'But if you will [a]not go out to the officers of the king of Babylon, then this city [b]will be given over to the hand of the Chaldeans; and they will burn[8313] it with fire, and [c]you yourself will not escape[4422] from their hand.' "

19 Then King Zedekiah said to Jeremiah, "I [a]dread[1672] the Jews who have [I][b]gone over[5307] to the Chaldeans, lest they give me over into their hand and they [c]abuse me."

20 But Jeremiah said, "They will not give you over. Please [I][a]obey[8085] the LORD in what I am saying[1696] to you, that it may go [b]well[3190] with you and [II][c]you may live.

21 "But if you keep refusing[3986] to go out, this is the word[1697] which the LORD has shown[7200] me:

22 'Then behold, all of the [a]women[802] who have been left[7604] in the palace of the king of Judah are going to be brought out to the [I]officers of the king of Babylon; and those women will say,[559]

"[II]Your close friends[7965]
Have misled and overpowered you;
While your feet were sunk in the mire,
They turned back."

23 'They will also bring out all your wives[802] and your [a]sons[1121] to the Chaldeans, and [b]you yourself will not escape from their hand, but will be seized by the hand of the king of Babylon, and [c]this city will be burned with fire.' "

24 Then Zedekiah said to Jeremiah, "Let no man know[3045] about these words and you will not die.

25 "But if the [a]officials hear[8085] that I have talked[1696] with you and come to you and say to you, 'Tell us now what you said[1696] to the king, and what the king said to you; do not hide *it* from us, and we will not put you to death,'

26 then you are to say to them, 'I was [a]presenting[5307] my petition[8467] before the king, not to make me return[7725]

9 [I]M.T. reads *has died* [a]Jer. 37:21; 52:6
10 [I]Lit., *in your hand*
11 [I]Lit., *hand*
13 [a]Neh. 3:25; Jer. 32:2; 37:21; 38:6; 39:14, 15; Acts 23:35; 24:27; 28:16,30
14 [I]Lit., *took Jeremiah the prophet to him* [a]Jer. 21:1, 2; 37:17 [b]1Sam. 3:17, 18; 1Kin. 22:16; Jer. 15:11; 42:2-5, 20
15 [a]Luke 22:67, 68
16 [I]Lit., *soul* [a]Jer. 37:17; John 3:2 [b]Num. 16:22; 27:16; Is. 42:5; 57:16; Zech. 12:1; Acts 17:25, 28 [c]Jer. 34:20; 38:4-6
17 [I]Lit., *your soul* [II]Lit., *live* [a]Ps. 80:7, 14; Amos 5:27 [b]1Chr. 17:24; Ezek. 8:4 [c]2Kin. 24:12; 25:27-30; Jer. 21:8-10; 27:12, 17; 38:2; 39:3
18 [a]Jer. 27:8 [b]2Kin. 25:4-10; Jer. 24:8-10; 32:3-5; 37:8; 38:3 [c]Jer. 32:4; 34:3
19 [I]Lit., *fallen* [a]Is. 51:12, 13; 57:11; John 12:42; 19:12, 13 [b]Jer. 39:9 [c]2Chr. 30:10; Neh. 4:1; Jer. 38:22
20 [I]Lit., *listen to the voice of* [II]Lit., *your soul* [a]2Chr. 20:20; Jer. 11:4, 8; 26:13; Dan. 4:27; Acts 26:29 [b]Jer. 7:23 [c]Gen. 19:20; Is. 55:3
22 [I]Or, *princes* [II]Lit., *The men of your peace* [a]Jer. 6:12; 8:10; 43:6
23 [a]2Kin. 25:7; Jer. 39:6; 41:10 [b]Jer. 38:18
25 [a]Jer. 38:4-6, 27
26 [a]Jer. 37:20

to the house of Jonathan to die there.' "
27 Then all the officials came to
Jeremiah and questioned[7592] him. So he
reported[5046] to them in accordance with
all these words which the king had commanded; and they ceased speaking with
him, since the [I] conversation[1697] had not
been overheard.[8085]
28 So Jeremiah [a]stayed in the court
of the guardhouse until the day[3117] that
Jerusalem was captured.

Jerusalem Captured

39 [I]Now it came about when Jerusalem was captured [IIa]in the
ninth year of Zedekiah king[4428] of Judah,
in the tenth month, Nebuchadnezzar
king of Babylon and all his army[2428] came
to Jerusalem and laid siege to it;
2 in the eleventh year of Zedekiah,
in the fourth month, in the ninth *day*
of the month, the city *wall* was
[a]breached.
3 Then all the [a]officials[8269] of the king
of Babylon came in and sat down at the
[b]Middle Gate: Nergal-sar-ezer, Samgar-
nebu, Sar-sekim the [I]Rab-saris, Nergal-
sar-ezer *the* [II]Rab-mag, and all the
rest[7611] of the officials of the king of
Babylon.
4 And it came about, when Zedekiah
the king of Judah and all the men[582] of
war saw[7200] them, that they [a]fled and
went out of the city at night[3915] by
way[1870] of the king's[4428] garden through
the gate [b]between the two walls; and
he went out toward the [I]Arabah.[6160]
5 But the army of the [a]Chaldeans
pursued them and overtook Zedekiah
in the [b]plains[6160] of Jericho; and they
seized him and brought him up[5927] to
Nebuchadnezzar king of Babylon at
[c]Riblah in the land[776] of Hamath, and
he passed sentence[4941] on him.
6 Then the [a]king of Babylon slew[7809]
the sons[1121] of Zedekiah [b]before his eyes
at Riblah; the king of Babylon also slew
all the [c]nobles[2715] of Judah.
7 He then [a]blinded Zedekiah's eyes
and bound him in [b]fetters of bronze to
bring him to [c]Babylon.
8 The Chaldeans also [a]burned[8313]
with fire the king's palace[1004] and the
houses[1004] of the people,[5791] and they
[b]broke down[5422] the walls of Jerusalem.
9 And as for the rest[3499] of the people who were left[7604] in the city, the
[Ia]deserters[5307] who had gone over to
him and [b]the rest[3499] of the people who
remained, [c]Nebuzaradan the [d]captain of
the bodyguard carried *them* into exile[1540]
in Babylon.
10 But some of the [a]poorest people
who had nothing, [b]Nebuzaradan the captain of the bodyguard left[7604] behind in
the land of Judah, and gave them vineyards and fields [I]at that time.[3117]

Jeremiah Spared

11 Now Nebuchadnezzar king of
Babylon gave orders[6680] about [a]Jeremiah
through Nebuzaradan the captain of the
bodyguard, saying,
12 "Take him and [I]look after him,
and [a]do[6213] nothing harmful[7451] to him;
but rather deal with him just as he
tells[1696] you."
13 So Nebuzaradan the captain of
the bodyguard sent *word,* along with Nebushazban the [I]Rab-saris, and Nergal-
sar-ezer the [II]Rab-mag, and all the leading officers of the king of Babylon;
14 they even sent and [a]took Jeremiah out of the court of the guardhouse
and entrusted him to [b]Gedaliah, the
son[1121] of [c]Ahikam, the son of Shaphan,
to take him home.[1004] So he stayed
among the people.
15 Now the word[1697] of the LORD
had come to Jeremiah while he was
[a]confined in the court of the guardhouse,
saying,
16 "Go and speak[559] to [a]Ebed-me-
lech the Ethiopian, saying, 'Thus says[559]
the LORD of hosts,[6635] the God[430] of

27 [I]Lit., *word*
28 [a]Ps. 23:4; Jer. 15:20, 21; 37:20, 21; 38:13; 39:13, 14

1 [I]Ch. 38:28-b in Heb. [II]Ch. 39:1 in Heb. [a]2Kin. 25:1-12; Jer. 52:4; Ezek. 24:1, 2
2 [a]2Kin. 25:4; Jer. 52:7
3 [I]I.e., chief official [II]I.e., title of a high official [a]Jer. 38:17 [b]Jer. 21:4
4 [I]I.e., Jordan valley [a]2Kin. 25:4; Is. 30:16; Jer. 52:7; Amos 2:14 [b]2Chr. 32:5
5 [a]Jer. 32:4, 5; 38:18, 23; 52:8 [b]Josh. 4:13; 5:10 [c]2Kin. 23:33; Jer. 52:9, 26, 27
6 [a]2Kin. 25:7; Jer. 52:10 [b]Deut. 28:34 [c]Jer. 21:7; 24:8-10; 34:19-21
7 [a]2Kin. 25:7; Jer. 52:11; Ezek. 12:13 [b]Judg. 16:21 [c]Jer. 32:5
8 [a]2Kin. 25:9; Jer. 21:10; 38:18; 52:13 [b]2Kin. 25:10; Neh. 1:3; Jer. 52:14
9 [I]Lit., *fallers who had fallen* [a]Jer. 38:19; 52:15 [b]Jer. 24:8 [c]2Kin. 25:11, 20; Jer. 39:13; 40:1; 52:12-16, 26 [d]Gen. 37:36
10 [I]Lit., *on that day* [a]2Kin. 25:12; Jer. 52:16
11 [a]Job 5:15, 16; Jer. 1:8; 15:20, 21; Acts 24:23
12 [I]Lit., *set your eyes on* [a]Ps. 105:14, 15; Prov. 16:7; 21:1; 1Pet. 3:13
13 [I]I.e., chief official [II]I.e., title of a high official
14 [a]Jer. 38:28; 40:1-6 [b]Jer. 40:5 [c]2Kin. 22:12, 14; 2Chr. 34:20; Jer. 26:24

15 [a]Jer. 38:28 16 [a]Jer. 38:7

39:1-10 Ezekiel prophesied all of this from Babylon before it happened (Ezek. 12:8-16).

Israel, "Behold, I am about to bring My words[1697] on this city [b]for disaster[7451] and not for [I]prosperity;[2896] and they will [c]take place before you on that day.[3117]

17 "But I will [a]deliver[5337] you on that day," declares[5001] the LORD, "and you shall not be given into the hand[3027] of the men whom you dread.[3025]

18 "For I will certainly rescue you, and you will not fall by the sword;[2719] but you will have your *own* [a]life[5315] as booty, because you have [b]trusted[982] in Me," declares the LORD.'"

Jeremiah Remains in Judah

40 The word[1697] which came to Jeremiah from the LORD after [a]Nebuzaradan captain of the bodyguard had released him from [b]Ramah, when he had taken him bound in [c]chains, among all the exiles[1546] of Jerusalem and Judah, who were being exiled[1450] to Babylon.

2 Now the captain of the bodyguard had taken Jeremiah and said[559] to him, "The [a]LORD your God[430] promised this calamity[7451] against this place;

3 and the LORD has brought *it* on and done[6213] just as He promised.[1696] Because you *people* [a]sinned[2398] against the LORD and did not listen[8085] to His voice, therefore this thing has happened to you.

4 "But now, behold,[7200] I am [a]freeing you today[3117] from the chains which are on your hands.[3027] If [I]you would prefer[2896][5869] to come with me to Babylon, come *along,* and I will [II]look after you; but if [III]you would prefer not to[7451][5869] come with me to Babylon, [IV]never mind. Look, the [b]whole land[776] is before you; go wherever it seems good and right[3477] for you to go."

5 As [I]Jeremiah was still not going back,[7725] [II]*he said,* "Go on back then to [a]Gedaliah the son[1121] of Ahikam, the son of Shaphan, whom the king[4428] of Babylon has [b]appointed[6485] over the cities of Judah, and stay with him among the people;[5971] or else go anywhere it seems right for you to go." So the captain of the bodyguard gave him a [c]ration[737] and a [d]gift[4864] and let him go.

6 Then Jeremiah went to [a]Mizpah to [b]Gedaliah the son of Ahikam and stayed with him among the people who were left[7604] in the land.

7 [a]Now all the [I]commanders[8269] of the forces[2428] that were in the field,[7704] they and their men,[582] heard[8085] that the king of Babylon had appointed Gedaliah the son of Ahikam over the land and that he had put him in charge[6485] of the men, women[802] and [II]children,[2945] those of the [b]poorest of the land who had not been exiled to Babylon.

8 So they came to Gedaliah at Mizpah, along with [a]Ishmael the son of Nethaniah, and [b]Johanan and Jonathan the sons[1121] of Kareah, and Seraiah the son of Tanhumeth, and the sons of Ephai the [c]Netophathite, and [d]Jezaniah the son of the [e]Maacathite, *both* they and their men.

9 Then Gedaliah the son of Ahikam, the son of Shaphan, [a]swore[7650] to them and to their men, saying, "[b]Do not be afraid[3372] of serving[5647] the Chaldeans; stay in the land and serve the king of Babylon, that it may go well[3190] with you.

10 "Now as for me, behold, I am going to stay at Mizpah to [a]stand *for you* before the Chaldeans who come to us; but as for you, [b]gather[622] in wine and [c]summer fruit and oil,[8081] and put *them* in your *storage* vessels, and live in your cities that you have taken over."

11 Likewise also all the Jews who were in [a]Moab and among the sons of [b]Ammon and in [c]Edom, and who were in all the *other* countries,[776] heard that the king of Babylon had left a remnant[7611] for Judah and that he had appointed over[6485] them Gedaliah the son of Ahikam, the son of Shaphan.

12 Then all the Jews [a]returned[7725] from all the places to which they had been driven away and came to the land of Judah, to Gedaliah at Mizpah, and gathered[622] in wine and summer fruit in great abundance.

13 Now Johanan the son of Kareah

---

16 [I]Lit., *good* [b]Jer. 21:10; Dan. 9:12; Zech. 1:6 [c]Ps. 91:8
17 [a]Ps. 41:1, 2; 50:15
18 [a]Jer. 21:9; 38:2; 45:5 [b]Ps. 34:22; Jer. 17:7, 8

1 [a]Jer. 39:9, 11 [b]Jer. 31:15 [c]Acts 12:6, 7; 21:13; 28:20; Eph. 6:20
2 [a]Lev. 26:14-38; Deut. 28:15-68; 29:24-28; 31:17; 32:19-25; Jer. 22:8, 9
3 [a]Jer. 50:7; Dan. 9:11; Rom. 2:5
4 [I]Lit., *it is good in your eyes* [II]Lit., *set my eyes on* [III]Lit., *it is evil in your eyes* [IV]Lit., *refrain!* [a]Jer. 39:11, 12 [b]Gen. 13:9; 20:15; 47:6
5 [I]Lit., *he* [II]I.e., Nebuzaradan [a]Jer. 39:14 [b]2Kin. 25:23 [c]Jer. 52:34 [d]2Kin. 8:7-9
6 [a]Judg. 20:1; 21:1; 1Sam. 7:5; 2Chr. 16:6 [b]Jer. 39:14
7 [I]Or, *princes* [II]Lit., *infants* [a]2Kin. 25:23 [b]Jer. 39:10; 52:16
8 [a]Jer. 40:14; 41:2 [b]Jer. 40:13, 15; 42:1; 43:2 [c]2Sam. 23:28, 29; Ezra 2:22; Neh. 7:26 [d]Jer. 42:1 [e]Deut. 3:14; Josh. 12:5; 2Sam. 10:6, 8
9 [a]1Sam. 20:16, 17; 2Kin. 25:24 [b]Jer. 27:11; 38:17-20
10 [a]Deut. 1:38; 1Kin. 10:8; Jer. 35:19 [b]Deut. 16:13; Jer. 39:10 [c]Is. 16:9; Jer. 40:12; 48:32
11 [a]Num. 22:1; 25:1, 2; Is. 16:4; Jer. 9:26 [b]1Sam. 11:1; 12:12 [c]Gen. 36:8; Is. 11:14
12 [a]Jer. 43:5

and all the commanders of the forces that were in the field came to Gedaliah at Mizpah,

14 and said to him, "Are you well aware[3045] that Baalis the king of the sons of [a]Ammon has sent Ishmael the son of Nethaniah to take your life?" But Gedaliah the son of Ahikam did not believe[539] them.

15 Then Johanan the son of Kareah spoke secretly to Gedaliah in Mizpah, saying, "[a]Let me go and kill[5221] Ishmael the son of Nethaniah, and not a man[376] will know! Why should he [b]take your life, so that all the Jews who are gathered[6908] to you should be scattered and the [c]remnant of Judah perish?"[6]

16 But Gedaliah the son of Ahikam said to Johanan the son of Kareah, "[a]Do not do[6213] this thing, for you are telling[1696] a lie[8267] about Ishmael."

Gedaliah Is Murdered

41 Now it [a]came about in the seventh month that [b]Ishmael the son[1121] of Nethaniah, the son of Elishama, of the royal [1]family[2233] and *one* of the chief officers of the king,[4428] along with ten men,[582] came to Mizpah to [c]Gedaliah the son of Ahikam. While they [d]were eating bread together there in Mizpah,

2 Ishmael the son of Nethaniah and the ten men who were with him arose and [a]struck down[5221] Gedaliah the son of Ahikam, the son of Shaphan, with the sword[2719] and [b]put to death the one [c]whom the king of Babylon had appointed[6485] over the land.[776]

3 Ishmael also struck down[5221] all the Jews who were with him, *that is* with Gedaliah at Mizpah, and the Chaldeans who were found there, the men of war.

4 Now it happened on the [1]next day[3117] after the killing[4191] of Gedaliah, when no one[376] knew[3045] about *it,*

5 that eighty men[376] [a]came from [b]Shechem, from [c]Shiloh, and from [d]Samaria with [e]their beards[2206] shaved off and their clothes torn and [1]their bodies [f]gashed,[1413] having grain offerings[4503] and incense in their hands[3027] to bring to the [g]house[1004] of the LORD.

6 Then Ishmael the son of Nethaniah went out from Mizpah to meet them, [a]weeping as he went; and it came about as he met them that he said[559] to them, "Come to Gedaliah the son of Ahikam!"

7 Yet it turned out that as soon as they came inside the city, Ishmael the son of Nethaniah and the men that were with him [a]slaughtered[7819] them, *and cast them* into the cistern.[953]

8 But ten men who were found among them said to Ishmael, "Do not put us to death;[4191] for we have [a]stores of wheat, barley, oil[8081] and honey hidden in the field."[7704] So he refrained and did not put them to death along with their companions.[251]

9 Now as for the cistern where Ishmael had cast all the corpses[6297] of the men whom he had struck down[5221] [1]because of Gedaliah, it was the [a]one that King Asa had made[6213] on [b]account of Baasha, king of Israel; Ishmael the son of Nethaniah filled it with the slain.[2491]

10 Then Ishmael took captive[7617] all the [a]remnant[7611] of the people[5971] who were in Mizpah, the [b]king's[4428] daughters and all the people who were left[7604] in Mizpah, whom Nebuzaradan the captain of the bodyguard had put under the charge[6485] of Gedaliah the son of Ahikam; thus Ishmael the son of Nethaniah took them captive and proceeded to cross over[5674] to the sons of [c]Ammon.

Johanan Rescues the People

11 But Johanan the son of Kareah and all the [a]commanders[8269] of the forces[2428] that were with him heard[8085] of all the evil[7456] that Ishmael the son of Nethaniah had done.[6213]

12 So they took all the men and went to [a]fight with Ishmael the son of Nethaniah and they found him by the [b]great [1]pool that is in Gibeon.

13 Now it came about, as soon as all the people who were with Ishmael

---

14 [a]1Sam. 11:1-3; 2Sam. 10:1-6; Jer. 25:21; 41:10
15 [a]1Sam. 26:8 [b]2Sam. 21:17 [c]Jer. 42:2
16 [a]Matt. 10:16; 1Cor. 13:5
1 [1]Lit., *seed* [a]2Kin. 25:25 [b]Jer. 40:8, 14 [c]Jer. 39:14; 40:5, 6 [d]Ps. 41:9; Jer. 40:13, 14
2 [a]2Sam. 3:27; 20:9, 10; 2Kin. 25:25; Ps. 41:9; 109:5; John 13:18 [b]2Kin. 25:25 [c]Jer. 40:5
4 [1]Or, *second*
5 [1]Lit., *having cut themselves* [a]2Kin. 10:13, 14 [b]Gen. 33:18; 37:12; Judg. 9:1; 1Kin. 12:1, 25 [c]Josh. 18:1; Judg. 18:31; 1Sam. 3:21; Ps. 78:60 [d]1Kin. 16:24, 29 [e]Lev. 19:27; Deut. 14:1 [f]Deut. 14:1; Jer. 16:6 [g]1Sam. 1:7; 2Kin. 25:9
6 [a]2Sam. 3:16; Jer. 50:4
7 [a]Ps. 55:23; Is. 59:7; Ezek. 22:27; 33:24, 26
8 [a]Is. 45:3
9 [1]Or, *by the side of* [a]1Kin. 15:17-22; 2Chr. 16:1-6 [b]Judg. 6:2; 1Sam. 13:6; 2Sam. 17:9; Heb. 11:38
10 [a]Jer. 40:11, 12 [b]Jer. 43:6 [c]Neh. 2:10, 19; 4:7; Jer. 40:14
11 [a]Jer. 40:7, 8, 13-16
12 [1]Lit., *waters* [a]Gen. 14:14-16; 1Sam. 30:1-8, 18, 20 [b]2Sam. 2:13

saw[7200] Johanan the son of Kareah and the commanders of the forces that were with him, they were glad.

14 So all the people whom Ishmael had taken captive from Mizpah turned around and came back,[7725] and went to Johanan the son of Kareah.

15 But Ishmael the son of Nethaniah [a]escaped[4422] from Johanan with eight men and went to the sons of Ammon.

16 Then Johanan the son of Kareah and all the commanders of the forces that were with him took from Mizpah [a]all the remnant[7611] of the people whom he had [I]recovered[7725] from Ishmael the son of Nethaniah, after he had struck down Gedaliah the son of Ahikam, *that is,* the men who were [II]soldiers, *the* women,[802] *the* [III]children,[2945] and *the* eunuchs,[5631] whom he had brought back[7725] from Gibeon.

17 And they went and stayed in [I][a]Geruth Chimham, which is beside Bethlehem, in order to [b]proceed into Egypt

18 because of the Chaldeans; for they were [a]afraid[3372] of them, since Ishmael the son of Nethaniah had struck down Gedaliah the son of Ahikam, whom [b]the king of Babylon had appointed over the land.

Warning against Going to Egypt

42 Then all the [I]commanders[8269] of the forces,[2428] [a]Johanan the son[1121] of Kareah, Jezaniah the son[1121] of Hoshaiah, and all the people[5971] [b]both small and great approached[5066]

2 and said[559] to Jeremiah the prophet,[5030] "Please[4994] let our [a]petition[8467] [I]come[5307] before you, and [b]pray[6419] for us to the LORD your God,[430] *that is* for all this remnant;[7611] because we are left[7604] *but* a [c]few out of many, as your own eyes *now* see[7200] us,

3 that the LORD your God may tell[5046] us the [a]way[1870] in which we should walk and the thing that we should do."[6213]

4 Then Jeremiah the prophet said to them, "I have heard[8085] *you.* Behold, I am going to [a]pray to the LORD your God in accordance with your words;[1697] and it will come about that the whole [I]message which the [b]LORD will answer you I will tell[5046] you. I will [c]not keep back a word[1697] from you."

5 Then they said to Jeremiah, "May the [a]LORD be a true[571] and faithful[539] witness against us, if we do not act in accordance with the whole [I]message[1697] with which the LORD your God will send you to us.

6 "Whether *it* is [I]pleasant[2896] or [II]unpleasant,[7451] we will [a]listen[8085] to the voice of the LORD our God to whom we are sending you, in order that it may go [b]well with us when we listen to the voice of the LORD our God."

7 Now it came about at the [a]end of ten days[3117] that the word[1697] of the LORD came to Jeremiah.

8 Then he called[7121] for Johanan the son of Kareah, and all the [I]commanders of the forces that were with him, and for all the people both small and great,

9 and said to them, "Thus [a]says[559] the LORD the God of Israel, to whom you sent me to present[5307] your petition before Him:

10 'If you will indeed stay in this land,[776] then I will [a]build you up and not tear you down,[2040] and I will plant you and not uproot you; for I [I]shall [b]relent[5162] concerning the calamity that I have inflicted[6213] on you.

11 '[a]Do not be afraid[3372] of the king[4428] of Babylon, whom you are *now* fearing;[3373] do not be afraid of him,' declares[5001] the LORD, 'for [b]I am with you to save[3467] you and deliver[5337] you from his hand.[3027]

12 'I will also show you compassion,[7356] so that [a]he will have compassion[7355] on you and restore[7725] you to your own soil.[127]

13 'But if you are going to say,[559] "We will [a]not stay in this land," so as

15 [a]1Sam. 30:17; 1Kin. 20:20; Job 21:30; Prov. 28:17
16 [I]Lit., *brought back* [II]Lit., *men of war* [III]Lit., *infants* [a]Jer. 42:8; 43:4-7
17 [I]Or, *the lodging place of Chimham* [a]2Sam. 19:37, 38, 40 [b]Jer. 42:14
18 [a]Is. 51:12, 13; 57:11; Jer. 42:11, 16; 43:2, 3; Luke 12:4, 5 [b]Jer. 40:5

1 [I]Or, *princes* [a]Jer. 40:8, 13; 41:11, 18 [b]Jer. 6:13; 8:10; 42:8; 44:12; Acts 8:10
2 [I]Lit., *fall* [a]Jer. 36:7; 37:20 [b]Ex. 8:28; 1Sam. 7:8; 12:19; 1Kin. 13:6; Is. 37:4; Jer. 37:3; 42:20; Acts 8:24; James 5:16 [c]Lev. 26:22; Deut. 28:62; Is. 1:9; Lam. 1:1
3 [a]Ps. 86:11; Prov. 3:6; Jer. 6:16; Mic. 4:2
4 [I]Lit., *word* [a]Ex. 8:29; 1Sam. 12:23 [b]1Kin. 22:14; Jer. 23:28 [c]1Sam. 3:17, 18; Ps. 40:10; Acts 20:20
5 [I]Lit., *word* [a]Gen. 31:50; Judg. 11:10; Jer. 43:2; Mic. 1:2; Mal. 2:14; 3:5
6 [I]Lit., *good* [II]Lit., *evil* [a]Ex. 24:7; Deut. 5:27; Josh. 24:24 [b]Deut. 5:29, 33; 6:3; Jer. 7:23
7 [a]Ps. 27:14; Is. 30:18
8 [I]Or, *princes*
9 [a]2Kin. 19:4, 6, 20; 22:15
10 [I]Or, *shall have changed my mind about* [a]Jer. 24:6; 31:28; 33:7; Ezek. 36:36 [b]Jer. 18:7, 8; Hos. 11:8; Joel 2:13; Amos 7:3, 6; Jon. 3:10; 4:2

11 [a]Jer. 1:8; 27:12, 17; 41:18 [b]Num. 14:9; 2Chr. 32:7, 8; Ps. 46:7, 11; 118:6; Is. 8:9, 10; 43:2, 5; Jer. 1:19; 15:20; Rom. 8:31 **12** [a]Neh. 1:11; Ps. 106:46; Prov. 16:7 **13** [a]Ex. 5:2; Jer. 44:16

not to listen to the voice of the LORD
your God,
14 saying, "No, but we will [a]go to
the land of Egypt, where we shall not
see war or [b]hear[8085] the sound of a trumpet or hunger for bread, and we will
stay there";
15 then [I]in that case listen to the
word of the LORD, O remnant of Judah.
Thus says the LORD of hosts,[6635] the
God of Israel, "If you really set[7760] your
[II]mind to enter [a]Egypt, and go in to
reside[1481] there,
16 then it will come about that the
[a]sword,[2719] which you are afraid[3373] of
will overtake you there in the land of
Egypt; and the famine, about which you
are anxious,[1672] will follow closely after
you there *in* Egypt; and you will die[4191]
there.
17 "So all the men[582] who set their
[I]mind to go to Egypt to reside there
will die by the [a]sword, by famine, and
by pestilence;[1698] and they will [b]have
no survivors[8300] or refugees from the
calamity that I am going to bring on
them."'"
18 For thus says the LORD of hosts,
the God of Israel, "As My [a]anger[639] and
wrath have been poured out on the inhabitants of Jerusalem, so My wrath will
be poured out on you when you enter
Egypt. And you will become a [b]curse,[423]
an object of horror,[8047] an imprecation,[7045] and a reproach;[2781] and [c]you
will see this place no more."
19 The LORD has spoken[1696] to you,
O remnant of Judah, "Do not [a]go into
Egypt!" You should clearly [b]under-
stand[3045] that today[3117] I have [c]testi-
fied[5749] against you.
20 For you have *only* [Ia]deceived[8582]
yourselves; for it is you who sent me
to the LORD your God, saying, "Pray
for us to the LORD our God; and whatever the LORD our God says, tell us
so, and we will do it."
21 So, I have [a]told you today, but
you have [b]not [I]obeyed[8085] the LORD your
God, even in whatever He has sent me
to *tell* you.
22 Therefore you should now
clearly understand[3045] that you will
[a]die by the sword, by famine, and by
pestilence, in the [b]place where you wish
to go to reside.

In Egypt Jeremiah Warns of Judgment

43 But it came about, as soon as
Jeremiah whom the LORD their
God had sent, had [a]finished[3615] telling[1696]
all the people[5971] all the words[1697] of
the LORD their God—[430] that is, all these
words—
2 that Azariah the [a]son[1121] of Hoshaiah, and Johanan the son of Kareah,
and all the arrogant[2086] men[582] said[559]
to Jeremiah, "You are [b]telling[1696] a
lie![8267] The LORD our God has not sent
you to say,[559] 'You are not to enter
Egypt to reside[1481] there';
3 but [a]Baruch the son of Neriah is
inciting you against us to give us over
into the hand[3027] of the Chaldeans, so
they may put us to death[4191] or exile[1540]
us to Babylon."
4 So [a]Johanan the son of Kareah and
all the [I]commanders[8269] of the forces,[2428]
and all the people, [b]did not obey[8085] the
voice of the LORD, so as to [c]stay in the
land[776] of Judah.
5 But Johanan the son of Kareah and
all the [I]commanders of the forces took
the [a]entire remnant[7611] of Judah who had
returned[7725] from all the nations[1471] to
which they had been driven away, in
order to reside[1481] in the land of Judah—
6 the men,[1397] the women,[802] the
[I]children,[2945] the [a]king's[4428] daughters
and [b]every person[5315] that Nebuzaradan
the captain of the bodyguard had left
with Gedaliah the son of Ahikam
[II]and grandson of Shaphan, together with
[c]Jeremiah the prophet[5030] and Baruch
the son of Neriah—
7 and they entered the land of Egypt
(for they did not obey the voice of the
LORD) and went in as far as [a]Tahpanhes.
8 Then the word[1697] of the LORD
came to Jeremiah in [a]Tahpanhes, saying,
9 "Take *some* large stones in your
[I]hands and hide them in the mortar in

14 [a]Is. 31:1; Jer. 41:17 [b]Ex. 16:3; Num. 11:4; Jer. 4:19, 21
15 [I]Lit., *now therefore* [II]Lit., *face* [a]Deut. 17:16; Jer. 42:17; 44:12-14
16 [a]Jer. 44:13, 27; Ezek. 11:8; Amos 9:1-4
17 [I]Lit., *face* [a]Jer. 24:10; 38:2; 42:22; 44:13 [b]Jer. 44:14, 28
18 [a]2Chr. 36:16-19; Jer. 7:20; 33:5; 39:1-9 [b]Deut. 29:21; Is. 65:15; Jer. 18:16; 24:9; 29:18; 44:12 [c]Jer. 22:10, 27
19 [a]Deut. 17:16; Is. 30:1-7 [b]Ezek. 2:5 [c]Neh. 9:26, 29, 30
20 [I]Or, *acted errantly in your souls* [a]Jer. 43:2; Ezek. 14:3
21 [I]Lit., *listened to the voice of* [a]Deut. 11:26; Jer. 43:1; Ezek. 2:7; Zech. 7:11; Acts 20:26, 27 [b]Jer. 43:4
22 [a]Jer. 43:11; Ezek. 6:11 [b]Hos. 9:6

1 [a]Jer. 26:8; 51:63
2 [a]Jer. 42:1 [b]2Chr. 36:13; Is. 7:9; Jer. 5:12, 13; 42:5
3 [a]Jer. 36:4, 10, 26, 32; 43:6; 45:1-3
4 [I]Or, *princes* [a]Jer. 42:8 [b]2Chr. 25:16; Jer. 42:5, 6; 44:5 [c]Ps. 37:3; Jer. 42:10-12
5 [I]Or, *princes* [a]Jer. 40:11
6 [I]Lit., *infants* [II]Lit., *the son* [a]Jer. 41:10 [b]Jer. 39:10; 40:7 [c]Eccl. 9:1, 2; Lam. 3:1
7 [a]Jer. 2:16; 44:1
8 [a]Jer. 2:16; 44:1; 46:14; Ezek. 30:18
9 [I]Lit., *hand*

the [II]brick *terrace* which is at the entrance of Pharaoh's [III]palace[1004] in Tahpanhes, in the sight of [IV]some *of the*
Jews;
10 and say to them, 'Thus says[559]
the LORD of hosts,[6635] the God of Israel,
"Behold, I am going to send and get
[a]Nebuchadnezzar the king[4428] of Babylon, [b]My servant,[5650] and I am going
to set[7760] his throne[3678] *right* over these
stones that I have hidden; and he will
spread his [c]canopy over them.
11 "He will also come and [a]strike[5221]
the land of Egypt; those who are *meant*
for death *will be given over* to death,[4194]
and those for captivity[7628] to captivity,
and [b]those for the sword[2719] to the
sword.
12 "And [I]I shall set fire to the
temples[1004] of the [a]gods[430] of Egypt, and
he will burn[8313] them and take them
captive.[7617] So he will [b]wrap himself with
the land of Egypt as a shepherd wraps
himself with his garment, and he will
depart from there safely.
13 "He will also shatter[7665] the
[I]obelisks[4676] of [II]Heliopolis, which is in
the land of Egypt; and the temples of
the gods of Egypt he will burn with
fire." ' "

Conquest of Egypt Predicted

44 The word[1697] that came to Jeremiah for all the Jews living in
the land[776] of Egypt, those who were
living in [a]Migdol, [b]Tahpanhes, [c]Mem-
phis, and the land[776] of [d]Pathros, saying,
2 "Thus says[559] the LORD of
hosts,[6635] the God[430] of Israel, 'You
yourselves have seen[7200] all the
calamity[7451] that I have brought on Jerusalem and all the cities of Judah; and
behold, this day[3117] they are in [a]ruins[2723]
and no one lives in them,
3 [a]because of their wickedness[7451]
which they committed[6213] so as to
[b]provoke Me to anger[3707] by continuing
to [c]burn [I]sacrifices[6999] *and* to [d]serve[5647]
other gods[430] whom they had not
known,[3045] *neither* they, you, nor your
fathers.[1]
4 'Yet I [a]sent you all My servants[5650]
the prophets,[5030] [I]again and again, saying, "Oh, do[6213] not do this [b]abomin-
able[8441] thing[1697] which I hate."[8130]
5 'But [a]they did not listen[8085] or incline their ears[241] to turn[7725] from their
wickedness, so as not to burn [I]sacrifices
to other gods.
6 'Therefore My [a]wrath and My
anger[639] were poured out and burned
in the [b]cities of Judah and in the streets
of Jerusalem, so they have become a
ruin[2723] and a [c]desolation[8077] as it is this
day.
7 'Now then thus says the LORD God
of hosts, the God of Israel, "Why are
you [a]doing[6213] great harm to yourselves,[5315] so as to [b]cut off[3772] from you
man[376] and woman,[802] child and infant,
from among Judah, leaving[3498] yourselves without remnant,[7611]
8 [a]provoking Me to anger[3707] with
the works of your hands,[3027] [b]burning
[I]sacrifices to other gods in the land of
Egypt, where you are entering to reside,[1481] so that you might be cut off
and become a [c]curse[7045] and a reproach[2781] among all the nations[1471]
of the earth?[776]
9 "Have you forgotten the [a]wicked-
ness of your fathers, the wickedness of
the kings[4428] of Judah, and the wickedness of their wives,[802] your own wickedness, and the wickedness of your
wives, which they committed in the
land of Judah and in the streets of
Jerusalem?

9 [II]Or, *brickwork* [III]Lit., *house* [IV]Lit., *men*
10 [a]Jer. 25:9, 11 [b]Is. 44:28; 45:1; Jer. 25:9; 27:6 [c]Ps. 18:11; 27:5; 31:20
11 [a]Is. 19:1-25; Jer. 25:15-19; 44:13; 46:1, 2, 13-26; Ezek. 29:19, 20 [b]Jer. 15:2
12 [I]Some ancient versions read *He will set* [a]Ex. 12:12; Is. 19:1; Jer. 46:25; Ezek. 30:13 [b]Ps. 104:2; 109:18, 19; Is. 49:18
13 [I]Or, *stone pillars* [II]Heb., *Beth-shemesh;* i.e., the house of the sun-god

1 [a]Ex. 14:2; Jer. 46:14 [b]Jer. 43:7; Ezek. 30:18 [c]Is. 19:13; Jer. 2:16; 46:14; Ezek. 30:13, 16; Hos. 9:6 [d]Is. 11:11; Ezek. 29:14; 30:14
2 [a]Is. 6:11; Jer. 4:7; 9:11; 34:22; Mic. 3:12
3 [I]Or, *incense* [a]Neh. 9:33; Jer. 2:17-19; 44:23; Ezek. 8:17, 18; Dan. 9:5 [b]Is. 3:8; Jer. 7:19; 32:30-32; 44:8 [c]Jer. 19:4 [d]Deut. 13:6; 29:26; 32:17
4 [I]Lit., *rising early and sending* [a]Jer. 7:13, 25; 25:4; 26:5; 29:19; 35:15; Zech. 7:7 [b]Jer. 16:18; 32:34, 35; Ezek. 8:10
5 [I]Or, *incense* [a]Jer. 11:8, 10; 13:10
6 [a]Is. 51:17-20; Jer. 42:18; Ezek. 8:18 [b]Jer. 7:17, 34 [c]Jer. 4:27; 34:22

7 [a]Num. 16:38; Jer. 26:19; Ezek. 33:11; Hab. 2:10 [b]Jer. 3:24; 9:21; 51:22 **8** [I]Or, *incense* [a]2Kin. 17:15-17; Jer. 25:6, 7; 44:3; 1Cor. 10:21, 22 [b]Jer. 7:9; 11:12, 17; 44:3; Hos. 4:13; Hab. 1:16 [c]1Kin. 9:7, 8; 2Chr. 7:20; Jer. 42:18 **9** [a]Jer. 7:9, 10, 17, 18; 44:17, 21

44:8 Incredibly, the group of Jews who kidnapped Jeremiah and escaped to Egypt after Jerusalem fell were still worshiping foreign deities, so the Lord gave Jeremiah an oracle against them. Their response showed remarkably twisted thinking, because they reasoned that everything was fine while they were in Judah worshiping the queen of heaven, but when they stopped, times became very hard (vv. 17,18).

10 “But they [a]have not become
[I]contrite[1792] even to this day, nor have
they feared[3372] nor [b]walked in My law[8451]
or My statutes,[2708] wwich I have set
before you and before your fathers.” ’
11 “Therefore thus says the LORD
of hosts, the God of Israel, ‘Behold, I
am going to [a]set[7760] My face against you
for [I]woe, even to cut off all Judah.
12 ‘And I will [a]take away the
remnant[7611] of Judah who have set their
[I]mind on entering the land of Egypt to
reside[1481] there, and they will all
[IIb]meet their end[8552] in the land of Egypt;
they will fall by the sword *and* meet
their end by famine. Both small and great
will die[4191] by the sword[2719] and famine;
and they will become a [c]curse,[423] an object of horror,[8047] an imprecation and a
reproach.
13 ‘And I will [a]punish[6485] those who
live in the land of Egypt, as I have punished Jerusalem, with the sword, with
famine, and with pestilence.[1698]
14 ‘So there will be [a]no refugees
or survivors for the remnant of Judah
who have entered the land of Egypt to
reside[8300] there and then to return[7725]
to the land of Judah, to which they are
[Ib]longing[5315] to return and live; for none
will [c]return except *a few* refugees.’ ”
15 Then [a]all the men[582] who were
aware that their wives were burning
[I]sacrifices[6999] to other gods, along with
all the women who were standing by,
as a large assembly,[6951] [II]including all
the people[5971] who were living in Pathros
in the land of Egypt, responded to Jeremiah, saying,
16 “As for the [Ia]message that you
have spoken[1696] to us in the name of
the LORD, [b]we are not going to listen[8085]
to you!
17 “But rather we will certainly
[a]carry out every word that has proceeded from our mouths,[6310] [I]by burning [II]sacrifices to the [b]queen[4446] of
heaven[8064] and pouring out[5258] libations[5262] to her, just as [c]we ourselves,
our forefathers, our kings and our
princes[8269] did[6213] in the cities of Judah
and in the streets of Jerusalem; for *then*
we had [d]plenty of [III]food,[3899] and were
well off, and saw[7200] no [IV]misfortune.
18 “But since we stopped burning
[I]sacrifices to the queen of heaven and
pouring out libations to her, we have
[a]lacked everything and have [II]met our
end by the sword and by famine.”
19 “And,” *said the women,* “when
we were [a]burning [I]sacrifices to the
queen of heaven, and [II]were pouring
out[5258] libations[5262] to her, was it
[b]without our husbands that we made[6213]
for her *sacrificial* cakes [III]in her image[6087]
and poured out libations to her?”

Calamity for the Jews

20 Then Jeremiah said[559] to all the
people, to the men[1397] and women—
even to all the people who were giving
him *such* an answer—saying,
21 “As for the [Ia]smoking sacrifices
that you burned in the cities of Judah
and in the [b]streets of Jerusalem, you
and your forefathers, your kings and
your princes, and the people of the land,
did not the LORD [c]remember[2142] them,
and did not *all this* come into His
[II]mind?[3820]
22 “So the LORD was [a]no longer able
to endure[5375] *it,* [b]because of the evil[7455]
of your deeds, because of the abominations[8441] which you have committed;
thus your land has become a [c]ruin, an
object of horror and a curse, without
an inhabitant, as *it is* this day.
23 “Because you have burned
[I]sacrifices and have sinned[2398] against
the LORD and [a]not obeyed[8085] the voice
of the LORD or [b]walked in His law, His
statutes or His testimonies,[5715] therefore this [c]calamity has befallen you, as
it has this day.”
24 Then Jeremiah said to all the people, including all the women, “[a]Hear[8085]
the word of the LORD, all Judah who
are [b]in the land of Egypt,
25 thus says the LORD of hosts, the

10 [I]Lit., *crushed* [a]Jer. 6:15; 8:12 [b]Jer. 26:4; 32:23; 44:23
11 [I]Lit., *evil* [a]Lev. 17:10; 20:5, 6; 26:17; Jer. 21:10; Amos 9:4
12 [I]Lit., *face* [II]Lit., *be finished* [a]Jer. 42:15-18, 22 [b]Is. 1:28; Jer. 16:4; 44:7 [c]Is. 65:15; Jer. 18:16; 24:9; 26:6; 29:18; 42:18; Zech. 8:13
13 [a]Jer. 11:22; 44:27, 28
14 [I]Lit., *lifting up their soul* [a]Jer. 22:10; 44:27 [b]Jer. 22:26, 27 [c]Is. 4:2; 10:20; Jer. 44:28; Rom. 9:27
15 [I]Or, *incense* [II]Lit., *and* [a]Prov. 11:21; Is. 1:5; Jer. 5:1-5
16 [I]Lit., *word* [a]Jer. 43:2 [b]Prov. 1:24-27; Jer. 11:8, 10; 13:10
17 [I]Or, *so as to burn* [II]Or, *incense* [III]Lit., *bread* [IV]Lit., *evil* [a]Num. 30:12; Deut. 23:23 [b]2Kin. 17:16; Jer. 7:18 [c]Neh. 9:34; Jer. 32:32; 44:21 [d]Ex. 16:3; Hos. 2:5-9; Phil. 3:19
18 [I]Or, *incense* [II]Lit., *been finished* [a]Num. 11:5, 6; Jer. 40:12; Mal. 3:13-15
19 [I]Or, *incense* [II]Lit., *to pour* [III]Lit., *to make an image of her* [a]Jer. 7:18 [b]Num. 30:6, 7; Jer. 44:15
21 [I]Or, *incense* [II]Lit., *heart* [a]Ezek. 8:10, 11 [b]Jer. 11:13; 44:9, 17 [c]Ps. 79:8; Is. 64:9; Jer. 14:10; Hos. 7:2; Amos 8:7
22 [a]Is. 7:13; 43:24; Mal. 2:17 [b]Jer. 4:4; 21:12; 30:14 [c]Gen. 19:13; Ps. 107:33, 34; Jer. 25:11, 18, 38; 29:18; 42:18; 44:12
23 [I]Or, *incense* [a]Jer. 7:13-15; 40:3 [b]Jer. 44:10; Ps. 119:136, 150 [c]1Kin. 9:9; Neh. 13:18; Jer. 44:2; Dan. 9:11, 12
24 [a]Jer. 42:15; 44:16 [b]Jer. 43:7; 44:15, 26

God of Israel, as follows: 'As for you and your wives, you have spoken with your mouths[6310] and fulfilled *it* with your hands,[3027] saying, "We will [a]certainly perform[6213] our vows[5088] that we have vowed,[5087] to burn [I]sacrifices to the queen of heaven and pour out libations to her." [II][b]Go ahead and confirm[6965] your vows, and certainly perform your vows!'

26 "[I]Nevertheless hear the word of the LORD, all Judah who are living in the land of Egypt, 'Behold, I have [a]sworn by My great name,' says the LORD, '[b]never shall My name be invoked[7121] again by the mouth of any man of Judah in all the land of Egypt, saying, "[c]As the Lord[136] [II]GOD lives."[2416]

27 'Behold, I am watching over them [a]for harm and not for good,[2896] and [b]all the men[376] of Judah who are in the land of Egypt will [I]meet their end by the sword and by famine until they [II]are completely gone.[3615]

28 '[a]And those who escape the sword will return out of the land of Egypt to the land of Judah [I][b]few in number. Then all the remnant of Judah who have gone to the land of Egypt to reside there will know[3045] [c]whose word[1697] will stand, Mine or theirs.

29 'And this will be the [a]sign[226] to you,' declares[5001] the LORD, 'that I am going to punish you in this place, so that you may know that [b]My words will surely stand against you for harm.'

30 "Thus says the LORD, 'Behold, I am going to give over [a]Pharaoh Hophra king[4428] of Egypt to the hand of his enemies, to the hand of those who seek his life,[5315] just as I gave over [b]Zedekiah king of Judah to the hand of Nebuchadnezzar king of Babylon, *who was* his enemy and was seeking his life.' "

Message to Baruch

45 *This is* the message[1697] which Jeremiah the prophet[5030] spoke[1696] to [a]Baruch the son[1121] of Neriah, when he had [b]written down these words[1697] in a book[5612] [I]at Jeremiah's dictation,[6310] in the [c]fourth year of Jehoiakim the son of Josiah, king[4428] of Judah, saying:

2 "Thus says[559] the LORD the God[430] of Israel to you, O Baruch:

3 'You said,[559] "Ah, woe is me! For the LORD has added sorrow to my pain; I am [a]weary with my groaning and have found no rest." '

4 "Thus you are to say to him, 'Thus says the LORD, "Behold, [a]what I have built I am about to tear down,[2040] and what I have planted I am about to uproot, that is, the whole land."[776]

5 'But you, are you [a]seeking great things for yourself? Do not seek *them;* for behold, I am going to [b]bring disaster[7451] on all flesh,'[1320] declares[5001] the LORD, 'but I will [c]give your life[5315] to you as booty in all the places where you may go.' "

Defeat of Pharaoh Foretold

46 That which came as the word[1697] of the LORD to Jeremiah the prophet[5030] [a]concerning the nations.[1471]

2 To [a]Egypt, concerning the army[2428] of [b]Pharaoh Neco king[4428] of Egypt, which was by the Euphrates River at [c]Carchemish, which Nebuchadnezzar king of Babylon defeated[5221] in the [d]fourth year of Jehoiakim the son[1121] of Josiah, king of Judah:

3 "[a]Line up the shield[4043] and
[I]buckler,
And draw near[5066] for the battle!
4 "Harness the horses,
And [I]mount the steeds,
And take your stand with
helmets *on!*
[a]Polish[4838] the spears,
Put on the [b]scale-armor![5630]
5 "Why have I seen[7200] *it?*
They are terrified,
They are [a]drawing back,
And their [b]mighty men are
defeated[3807]

25 [I]Or, *incense* [II]Lit., *Surely cause to stand* [a]Jer. 44:17; Matt. 14:9; Acts 23:12 [b]Ezek. 20:39
26 [I]Lit., *Therefore* [II]Heb., *YHWH,* usually rendered *LORD* [a]Gen. 22:16; Deut. 32:40, 41; Jer. 22:5; Amos 6:8; Heb. 6:13 [b]Ps. 50:16; Ezek. 20:39 [c]Is. 48:1, 2; Jer. 5:2
27 [I]Lit., *be finished* [II]Lit., *come to an end* [a]Jer. 1:10; 31:28; 39:16 [b]2 Kin. 21:14; Jer. 44:14
28 [I]Lit., *men of number* [a]Jer. 44:14 [b]Is. 10:19; 27:12, 13 [c]Ps. 33:11; Is. 14:27; 46:10, 11; Zech. 1:6
29 [a]Is. 7:11, 14; 8:18; Jer. 44:30; Matt. 24:15, 16, 32 [b]Prov. 19:21; Is. 40:8
30 [a]Jer. 43:9-13; 46:25; Ezek. 29:3; 30:21 [b]2Kin. 25:4-7; Jer. 34:21; 39:5-7

1 [I]Lit., *from the mouth of Jeremiah* [a]Jer. 32:12, 16; 43:3, 6 [b]Jer. 36:4, 18, 32 [c]2Kin. 24:1; 2Chr. 36:5-7; Jer. 25:1; 36:1; 46:2; Dan. 1:1
3 [a]Ps. 6:6; 69:3; 2Cor. 4:1, 16; Gal. 6:9
4 [a]Is. 5:5; Jer. 1:10; 11:17; 18:7-10; 31:28
5 [a]1Kin. 3:9, 11; 2Kin. 5:26; Matt. 6:25, 32; Rom. 12:16 [b]Is. 66:16; Jer. 25:31 [c]Jer. 21:9; 38:2; 39:18

1 [a]Jer. 1:10; 25:15-38
2 [a]Jer. 46:14; Ezek. chs. 29-32 [b]2Kin. 18:21; 23:29, 33-35; Jer. 25:19 [c]2Chr. 35:20; Is. 10:9 [d]Jer. 45:1

3 [I]I.e., small shield [a]Is. 21:5; Jer. 51:11; Joel 3:9; Nah. 2:1; 3:14 **4** [I]Or, *go up, you horsemen* [a]Ezek. 21:9-11 [b]1Sam. 17:5, 38; 2Chr. 26:14; Neh. 4:16; Jer. 51:3
5 [a]Is. 42:17; Jer. 46:21 [b]Is. 5:25; Ezek. 39:18

And have taken refuge in flight,
Without facing back;
[Ic]Terror4032 is on every side!"
Declares the LORD.
6 Let not the [a]swift man flee,
Nor the mighty man escape;4422
In the north beside the river Euphrates
They have [b]stumbled3782 and fallen.
7 Who is this that [a]rises5927 like the Nile,
Like the rivers whose waters surge about?
8 Egypt rises5927 like the Nile,
Even like the rivers whose waters surge about;
And He has said,559 "I will [a]rise and cover3680 *that* land;776
I will surely [b]destroy6 the city and its inhabitants."
9 Go up,5927 you horses, and [Ia]drive madly,1984 you chariots,
That the mighty men may [II]march forward:
Ethiopia and [IIIb]Put, that handle the shield,
And the [IVc]Lydians, that handle *and* bend the bow.
10 For [a]that day3117 belongs to the Lord136 [I]GOD of hosts,6635
A day of [b]vengeance,5360 so as to avenge5358 Himself on His foes;
And the [c]sword2719 will devour and be satiated
And [II]drink its fill of their blood;1818
For there will be a [d]slaughter2077 for the Lord [I]GOD of hosts,
In the land776 of the north by the river Euphrates.
11 Go [a]up to Gilead and obtain balm,
[b]O virgin1330 daughter of Egypt!
In vain7723 have you multiplied [I]remedies;
There is [c]no healing8585 for you.
12 The nations1471 have heard8085 of your [a]shame,
And the earth776 is full of your [b]cry *of distress;*
For one [c]warrior has stumbled3782 over [I]another,
And both of them have fallen5307 down together.
13 *This is* the [I]message which the
LORD spoke1696 to Jeremiah the prophet
about the [a]coming of Nebuchadnezzar
king of Babylon to [b]smite5221 the land
of Egypt:
14 "Declare5046 in Egypt and proclaim8085 in [a]Migdol,
Proclaim also in Memphis and [b]Tahpanhes;
Say,559 'Take your stand and get yourself ready,3559
For the [c]sword has devoured those around you.'
15 "Why have your [a]mighty47 ones become prostrate?
They do not stand because the LORD has [b]thrust them down.
16 "They have repeatedly [a]stumbled;3782
Indeed, they have fallen5307 one376 against another.7453
Then they said,559 'Get up! And [b]let us go back7725
To our own people5971 and our native land
Away from the [Ic]sword of the oppressor.'3238
17 "[I]They cried7121 there, 'Pharaoh king of Egypt *is but* [a]a big noise;7588
He has let the appointed time4150 pass by!'5674
18 "As I live,"2416 declares5001 the [a]King
Whose name is the LORD of hosts,
"Surely one shall come *who looms up* like [b]Tabor among the mountains,
Or like [c]Carmel by the sea.
19 "Make your baggage ready for [a]exile,1473
O [b]daughter dwelling in Egypt,
For [c]Memphis will become a desolation;8047

5 [I]Heb., *Magor-missabib;* i.e., Terror is on every side [c]Jer. 6:25; 20:3; 49:29
6 [a]Is. 30:16 [b]Jer. 46:12, 16; Dan. 11:19
7 [a]Jer. 47:2
8 [a]Is. 37:24 [b]Is. 10:13
9 [I]Lit., *act like madmen* [II]Lit., *go forth* [III]I.e., Libya (or Somaliland) [IV]Heb., *Ludim* [a]Jer. 47:3; Nah. 2:4 [b]Nah. 3:9 [c]Is. 66:19
10 [I]Heb., *YHWH,* usually rendered LORD [II]Lit., *be saturated with* [a]Joel 1:15 [b]Jer. 50:15, 18 [c]Deut. 32:42; Is. 31:8; Jer. 12:12 [d]Is. 34:6; Zeph. 1:7
11 [I]Lit., *healings* [a]Jer. 8:22 [b]Is. 47:1; Jer. 31:4, 21 [c]Jer. 30:13; Mic. 1:9; Nah. 3:19
12 [I]Lit., *warrior* [a]Jer. 2:36; Nah. 3:8-10 [b]Jer. 14:2 [c]Is. 19:2
13 [I]Lit., *word* [a]Jer. 43:10-13 [b]Is. 19:1
14 [a]Jer. 44:1 [b]Jer. 43:8 [c]Is. 1:20; Jer. 2:30; 46:10; Nah. 2:13
15 [a]Is. 66:15, 16; Jer. 46:5 [b]Ps. 18:14, 39; 68:1, 2
16 [I]Lit., *oppressing sword* [a]Lev. 26:36, 37; Jer. 46:6 [b]Jer. 51:9 [c]Jer. 50:16
17 [I]Some ancient versions read *Call the name of Pharaoh a big noise* [a]Ex. 15:9, 10; 1Kin. 20:10, 11; Is. 19:11-16
18 [a]Jer. 48:15; Mal. 1:14 [b]Josh. 19:22; Judg. 4:6; Ps. 89:12 [c]Josh. 12:22; 1Kin. 18:42
19 [a]Is. 20:4 [b]Jer. 48:18 [c]Jer. 46:14; Ezek. 30:13

It will even be burned down *and*
[I]bereft of inhabitants.
20 "Egypt is a pretty [a]heifer,
But a [I]horsefly[7171] is coming
[b]from the north—it is coming!
21 "Also her [a]mercenaries in her
midst[7130]
Are like [I]fattened [b]calves,
For even they too have turned
back *and* have fled away
together;
They did not stand *their ground.*
For the day of their calamity[343]
has come upon them,
The time[6256] of their
[c]punishment.[6489]
22 "Its sound moves along like a
serpent;[5175]
For they move on [I]like an army
And come to her as
woodcutters[2404] with axes.
23 "They have cut down[3772] her
[a]forest," declares the LORD;
"Surely it will no *more* be found,
Even though [I]they are *now* more
numerous than [b]locusts
And are without number.
24 "The daughter of Egypt has been
put to shame,
Given over to the [I]power[3027] of
the [a]people of the north."
25 The LORD of hosts, the God[430]
of Israel, says, "Behold, I am going to
punish[6485] Amon of [a]Thebes, and
[b]Pharaoh, and Egypt along with her
[c]gods[430] and her kings,[4428] even Pharaoh
and those who [d]trust[982] in him.
26 "And I shall give them over to
the [I]power of those who are [a]seeking
their lives,[5315] even into the hand of
Nebuchadnezzar king of Babylon and
into the hand of his [II]officers. [b]After-
wards, however, it will be inhabited[4626]
as in the days[3117] of old,"[6924] declares
the LORD.
27 "But as for you, O Jacob My
servant,[5650] [a]do not fear,[3372]
Nor be dismayed,[2865] O Israel!
For, see, I am going to
[b]save[3467] you from afar,
And your descendants[2233] from
the land of their captivity;[7633]
And Jacob shall return[7725] and
be [c]undisturbed[8252]
And secure, with no one making
him tremble.[2729]
28 "O Jacob My servant, do not
fear," declares the LORD,
"For [a]I am with you.
For I shall make[6213] a full end[3617]
of all the nations
Where I have driven you,
Yet I shall [b]not make a full end
of you;
But I shall [c]correct[3256] you
properly[4941]
And by no means leave you
unpunished."[5352]

Prophecy against Philistia

47 That which came as the word[1697]
of the LORD to Jeremiah the
prophet[5030] concerning the [a]Philistines,
before Pharaoh [I]conquered[5221] [b]Gaza.
2 Thus says[559] the LORD:
"Behold, waters are going to
rise[5927] from [a]the north
And become an overflowing[7857]
torrent,
And [b]overflow[7857] the land[776] and
all its fulness,
The city and those who live in
it;
And the men[120] will [c]cry[2199] out,
And every inhabitant of the land
will wail.
3 "Because of the noise of the
[Ia]galloping hoofs of his
[II]stallions,
The tumult of his chariots, *and*
the rumbling of his
wheels,[1534]
The fathers[1] have not turned
back for *their* children,[1121]
Because of the limpness of *their*
hands,[3027]
4 On account of the day[3117] that
is coming
To [a]destroy[7703] all the
Philistines,
To cut off[3772] from [b]Tyre and
Sidon
Every ally that is left;[8300]

19 [I]Lit., *without*
20 [I]Or possibly, *mosquito* [a]Hos. 10:11 [b]Jer. 1:14; 47:2
21 [I]Lit., *of the stall* [a]2Sam. 10:6; 2Kin. 7:6; Jer. 46:5 [b]Is. 34:7 [c]Jer. 48:44; Hos. 9:7; Obad. 13; Mic. 7:4
22 [I]Or, *in force*
23 [I]I.e., trees of the forest, the Egyptians [a]Jer. 21:14 [b]Judg. 6:5; 7:12; Joel 2:25
24 [I]Lit., *hand* [a]Jer. 1:15
25 [a]Ezek. 30:14-16; Nah. 3:8 [b]Jer. 44:30 [c]Ex. 12:12; Jer. 43:12, 13; Ezek. 30:13; Zeph. 2:11 [d]Is. 20:5
26 [I]Lit., *hand* [II]Lit., *servants* [a]Jer. 44:30; Ezek. 32:11 [b]Ezek. 29:8-14
27 [a]Is. 41:13, 14; Jer. 30:10, 11 [b]Is. 11:11; Jer. 23:3, 4; 29:14; Mic. 7:12 [c]Jer. 23:6; 50:19
28 [a]Ps. 46:7, 11; Is. 8:10; 43:2; Jer. 1:19 [b]Jer. 4:27; Amos 9:8, 9 [c]Jer. 10:24; Hab. 3:2

1 [I]Lit., *smote* [a]Jer. 25:20; Zech. 9:6 [b]Gen. 10:19; 1Kin. 4:24; Jer. 25:20; Amos 1:6; Zeph. 2:4
2 [a]Is. 14:31; Jer. 1:14; 6:22; 46:20, 24 [b]Is. 8:7, 8 [c]Is. 15:2-5; Jer. 46:12
3 [I]Lit., *stamping of the* [II]Lit., *mighty ones* [a]Judg. 5:22; Jer. 8:16; Nah. 3:2
4 [a]Is. 14:31 [b]Is. 23:5; Jer. 25:22; Joel 3:4; Amos 1:9, 10; Zech. 9:2-4

For the LORD is going to destroy
the Philistines,
The remnant[7611] of the coastland
of [c]Caphtor.
5 "[a]Baldness has come upon Gaza;
[b]Ashkelon has been ruined.[1820]
O remnant of their valley,
How long will you [c]gash
yourself?
6 "Ah, [a]sword[2719] of the LORD,
How long will you not[3808] be
quiet?[8252]
Withdraw into your sheath;
Be at rest and stay still.
7 "How can [I]it be quiet,
When the LORD has [a]given it an
order?[6680]
Against Ashkelon and against
the seacoast—
There He has [b]assigned[3259] it."

Prophecy against Moab

48 Concerning [a]Moab.
Thus says[559] the LORD of
hosts,[6635] the God[430] of
Israel,
"Woe to [b]Nebo, for it has been
destroyed;[7703]
[c]Kiriathaim has been put to
shame, it has been captured;
The lofty stronghold has been
put to shame and
[I]shattered.[2865]
2 "There is praise[8416] for Moab no
longer;
In [a]Heshbon they have
devised[2803] calamity[7451]
against her:
'Come and let us cut her off[3772]
from *being* a nation!'[1471]
You too, [I]Madmen, will be
silenced;
The sword[2719] will follow after
you.
3 "The sound of an outcry from
[a]Horonaim,
'Devastation[7701] and great
destruction!'[7667]
4 "Moab is broken,[7665]
Her little ones have sounded[8085]
out a cry *of distress*.
5 "For by the ascent of [a]Luhith
They will ascend with continual
weeping;
For at the descent of
Horonaim
They have heard the [I]anguished
cry of destruction.
6 "[a]Flee, save[3467] your lives,[5315]
That you may be like a
juniper[6176] in the wilderness.
7 "For because of your [a]trust[982] in
your own achievements and
treasures,
Even you yourself will be
captured;
And [b]Chemosh will go off into
exile[1473]
Together with his priests[3548] and
his princes.[8269]
8 "And a destroyer[7703] will come
to every city,
So that no city will escape;[4422]
The valley also will be ruined,[6]
And the [a]plateau will be
destroyed,[8045]
As the LORD has said.[559]
9 "Give [Ia]wings to Moab,
For she will [II]flee away;
And her cities will become a
[b]desolation,[8047]
Without inhabitants in them.
10 "[a]Cursed[779] be the one who
does[6213] the LORD' work[4399]
[b]negligently,
And cursed be the one who
restrains his [c]sword from
blood.[1818]
11 "Moab has been [a]at ease since
his youth;
He has also been
[b]undisturbed[8252] on his
lees,[8105]
Neither has he been [c]emptied
from vessel to vessel,
Nor has he gone into exile.
Therefore [I]he retains his
flavor,[2940]
And his aroma has not changed.
12 "Therefore behold, the days[3117]
are coming," declares[5001] the LORD,
"when I shall send to him those who
tip *vessels,* and they will tip him over,

4 [c]Gen. 10:14; Deut. 2:23; Amos 9:7
5 [a]Jer. 48:37; Mic. 1:16 [b]Judg. 1:18; Jer. 25:20; Amos 1:7, 8; Zeph. 2:4, 7; Zech. 9:5 [c]Jer. 16:6; 41:5
6 [a]Judg. 7:20; Jer. 12:12; Ezek. 21:3-5
7 [I]Lit., *you* [a]Is. 10:6; Ezek. 14:17 [b]Mic. 6:9
1 [I]Or, *dismayed* [a]Is. 15:1; Ezek. 25:9 [b]Num. 32:3, 38; Jer. 48:22 [c]Num. 32:37; Jer. 48:23; Ezek. 25:9
2 [I]I.e., a city of Moab [a]Num. 21:25; Jer. 48:34, 45; 49:3
3 [a]Is. 15:5; Jer. 48:5, 34
5 [I]Lit., *distresses of outcry* [a]Is. 15:5
6 [a]Jer. 51:6
7 [a]Ps. 52:7; Is. 59:4; Jer. 9:23 [b]Num. 21:29; 1Kin. 11:33; Jer. 48:13, 46
8 [a]Josh. 13:9, 17, 21
9 [I]Or, *salt* [II]Or, *fall in ruins* [a]Ps. 11:1; Is. 16:2; Jer. 48:28 [b]Jer. 44:22
10 [a]Jer. 11:3 [b]1Kin. 20:39, 40, 42; 2Kin. 13:19 [c]Jer. 47:6,7
11 [I]Lit., *his flavor has stayed in him* [a]Jer. 22:21; Ezek. 16:49; Zech. 1:15 [b]Zeph. 1:12 [c]Nah. 2:2

and they will empty his vessels and shatter [I]his jars.

13 "And Moab will be [a]ashamed[954] of [b]Chemosh, as the house[1004] of Israel was ashamed of [c]Bethel, their confidence.

14 "How can you say,[559] 'We are
[a]mighty warriors,
And men[582] valiant for battle'?
15 "Moab has been destroyed, and
[I]men have gone up to [II]his
cities;
His choicest [III][a]young men have
also gone down to the
slaughter,"[2874]
Declares the [b]King,[4428] whose
name is the LORD of
hosts.
16 "The disaster[343] of Moab will
[a]soon come,
And his calamity[7451] has swiftly
hastened.
17 "Mourn for him, all you who *live*
around him,
Even all of you who know[3045]
his name;
Say, 'How has the mighty
[I][a]scepter[4294] been broken,[7665]
A staff of splendor!'[8597]
18 "[a]Come down from your glory[3519]
And sit [I]on the parched ground,
O [b]daughter dwelling in
[c]Dibon,
For the destroyer of Moab has
come up against you,
He has ruined your strongholds.
19 "Stand by the road[1870] and keep
watch,
O inhabitant of [a]Aroer;
[b]Ask[7592] him who flees and her
who escapes[4422]
And say, 'What has happened?'
20 "Moab has been put to shame,
for it has been [I]shattered.[2865]
Wail and cry[2199] out;
Declare[5046] by the [a]Arnon
That Moab has been destroyed.

21 "Judgment[4941] has also come
upon the plain, upon Holon, [a]Jahzah, and
against [b]Mephaath,

22 against Dibon, Nebo, and Beth-
diblathaim,

23 against Kiriathaim, Beth-gamul,
and [a]Beth-meon,

24 against [a]Kerioth, Bozrah, and all
the cities of the land[776] of Moab, far
and near.

25 "The [a]horn of Moab has been
cut off, and his [b]arm broken," declares
the LORD.

26 "[a]Make him drunk, for he has
[I]become [b]arrogant toward the LORD; so
Moab will [II]wallow[5606] in his vomit, and
he also will become a laughingstock.

27 "Now was not Israel a [a]laugh-
ingstock to you? Or was he [I][b]caught
among thieves? For each time you speak
about him you [c]shake *your head in*
scorn.[5110]

28 "Leave[5800] the cities and
dwell[7931] among the [a]crags,
O inhabitants of Moab,
And be like a [b]dove that nests
Beyond the mouth[6310] of the
chasm.[6354]
29 "[a]We have heard of the pride of
Moab—he *is* very proud—
Of his haughtiness, his
[b]pride, his arrogance and
[I]his self-exaltation.[3820] [7312]
30 "I know his [a]fury," [5678] declares
the LORD,
"But it is futile;
His idle boasts have
accomplished nothing.
31 "Therefore I shall [a]wail for Moab,
Even for all Moab shall I cry out;
[I]I will moan[1897] for the men of
[b]Kir-heres.
32 "More than the [a]weeping for
[b]Jazer
I shall weep for you, O vine of
Sibmah!
Your tendrils stretched
across[5674] the sea,
They reached[5060] to the sea of
Jazer;
Upon your summer fruits and
your grape harvest
The destroyer has fallen.[5307]
33 "So [a]gladness and joy are taken
away
From the fruitful field, even from
the land of Moab.

12 [I]Lit., *their*
13 [a]Is. 45:16; Jer. 48:39 [b]Judg. 11:24 [c]1Kin. 12:29; Hos. 8:5, 6
14 [a]Ps. 33:16; Is. 10:13-16
15 [I]Lit., *one has* [II]Lit., *her* [III]I.e., warriors [a]Is. 40:30, 31; Jer. 50:27 [b]Jer. 46:18; 51:57; Mal. 1:14
16 [a]Is. 13:22
17 [I]Or, *rod* [a]Is. 9:4; 14:5
18 [I]Lit., *in thirst* [a]Is. 47:1 [b]Jer. 46:19 [c]Num. 21:30; Josh. 13:9, 17; Is. 15:2; Jer. 48:22
19 [a]Deut. 2:36; Josh. 12:2 [b]1Sam. 4:13, 14, 16
20 [I]Or, *dismayed* [a]Num. 21:13
21 [a]Num. 21:23; Is. 15:4; Jer. 48:34 [b]Josh. 13:18
23 [a]Josh. 13:17
24 [a]Jer. 48:41; Amos 2:2
25 [a]Ps. 75:10; Zech. 1:19-21 [b]Job 22:9; Ps. 10:15
26 [I]Or, *magnified himself against* [II]Or, *splash into* [a]Jer. 25:15 [b]Ex. 5:2; Jer. 48:42; Dan. 5:23
27 [I]Or, *found* [a]Lam. 2:15-17; Mic. 7:8-10 [b]Jer. 2:26 [c]Job 16:4; Jer. 18:16
28 [a]Judg. 6:2; Is. 2:19; Jer. 49:16; Obad. 3 [b]Ps. 55:6; Song 2:14
29 [I]Lit., *elevation of his heart* [a]Is. 16:6; Zeph. 2:8 [b]Job 40:11, 12; Ps. 138:6
30 [a]Is. 37:28
31 [I]Another reading is *He* [a]Is. 15:5; 16:7, 11 [b]2Kin. 3:25; Is. 16:7, 11; Jer. 48:36
32 [a]Is. 16:8, 9 [b]Num. 21:32
33 [a]Is. 16:10; Jer. 25:10; Joel 1:12

And I have made the wine to
[b]cease from the wine
presses;
No one will tread *them* with
shouting,
The shouting will not be shouts
of joy.
34 "[a]From the outcry at Heshbon
even to [b]Elealeh, even to Jahaz they
have [I]raised their voice, from [c]Zoar even
to Horonaim *and to* Eglath-shelishiyah;
for even the waters of Nimrim will become desolate.
35 "And I shall make an end[7673] of
Moab," declares the LORD, "the one who
offers[5927] *sacrifice* on the [a]high place[1116]
and the one who [I][b]burns incense[6999] to
his gods.[430]
36 "Therefore My [a]heart [I]wails for
Moab like flutes; My heart also [I]wails
like flutes for the men of Kir-heres.
Therefore they have [b]lost[6] the abundance it produced.[6213]
37 "For [a]every head[7218] is bald and
every beard[2206] cut short; there are
gashes on all the hands[3027] and [b]sack-
cloth on the loins.
38 "On all the [a]housetops of Moab
and in its streets [I]there is lamentation
everywhere; for I have broken Moab
like an undesirable [b]vessel," declares
the LORD.
39 "How [I]shattered it is! *How* they
have wailed! How Moab has turned his
back—he is ashamed![954] So Moab will
become a laughingstock and an [a]object
of terror[4288] to all around him."
40 For thus says the LORD,
"Behold, one will [a]fly swiftly like
an eagle,
And [b]spread out his wings
against Moab.
41 "Kerioth has been captured
And the strongholds have been
seized,
So the [a]hearts[3821] of the
mighty men of Moab in that
day[3117]
Will be like the heart of a
[b]woman[802] in labor.
42 "And Moab will be [a]destroyed
from *being* a people[5971]
Because he has [I]become
[b]arrogant toward the LORD.
43 "[a]Terror, pit,[6354] and snare[6341]
are *coming* upon you,
O inhabitant of Moab," declares
the LORD.
44 "The one who [a]flees from the
terror
Will fall into the pit,
And the one who climbs up[5927]
out of the pit
Will be caught in the snare;
For I shall bring upon her, *even*
upon Moab,
The year of their
[b]punishment,"[4686] declares
the LORD.
45 "In the shadow of Heshbon
The fugitives stand without
strength;
For a fire has gone forth from
Heshbon,
And a [a]flame from the midst of
[b]Sihon,
And it has devoured the
[c]forehead of Moab
And the scalps of the [I]riotous[7588]
revelers.
46 "[a]Woe to you, Moab!
The people of [b]Chemosh have
perished;[6]
For your sons[1121] have been
taken away captive,[7628]
And your daughters into
captivity.[7633]
47 "Yet I will [a]restore[7725] the
[I]fortunes[7622] of Moab
In the [II]latter[319] days," declares
the LORD.
Thus far the judgment on Moab.

Prophecy against Ammon

49 Concerning the sons of [a]Ammon.
Thus says[559] the LORD:
"Does Israel have no sons?[1121]
Or has he no heirs?[3423]
Why then has [I]Malcam[4428] taken
possession of Gad
And his people[5971] settled in its
cities?
2 "Therefore behold, the days[3117]

33 [b]Is. 5:10; Hag. 2:16
34 [I]Lit., *given forth* [a]Is. 15:4-6 [b]Num. 32:3, 37 [c]Gen. 13:10; 14:2; Is. 15:5, 6
35 [I]Or, *offers up in smoke* [a]Is. 15:2; 16:12 [b]Jer. 7:9; 11:13
36 [I]Lit., *sounds* [a]Is. 15:5; 16:11 [b]Is. 15:7
37 [a]Is. 15:2; Jer. 16:6; 41:5; 47:5 [b]Gen. 37:34; Is. 15:3; 20:2
38 [I]Lit., *all of it is lamentation* [a]Is. 22:1 [b]Jer. 19:10, 11; 22:28; 25:34
39 [I]Or, *dismayed* [a]Ezek. 26:16
40 [a]Deut. 28:49; Jer. 49:22; Hos. 8:1; Hab. 1:8 [b]Is. 8:8
41 [a]Jer. 49:22 [b]Is. 13:8; 21:3; Jer. 30:6; Mic. 4:9, 10
42 [I]Or, *magnified himself against* [a]Ps. 83:4; Jer. 48:2 [b]Is. 37:23; Jer. 48:26
43 [a]Is. 24:17, 18; Lam. 3:47
44 [a]1Kin. 19:17; Is. 24:18; Amos 5:19 [b]Jer. 46:21
45 [I]Lit., *sons of tumult* [a]Num. 21:28, 29 [b]Num. 21:21, 26; Ps. 135:11 [c]Num. 24:17
46 [a]Num. 21:29 [b]Judg. 11:24; 1Kin. 11:7; Jer. 48:7
47 [I]Or, *captivity* [II]Lit., *end of the days* [a]Jer. 12:14-17; 49:6, 39
1 [I]In 1Kin. 11:5, 33 and Zeph. 1:5, *Milcom* [a]Deut. 23:3, 4; 2Chr. 20:1; Ezek. 21:28-32; 25:2-10; Amos 1:13-15; Zeph. 2:8-11

are coming," declares[5001] the LORD,
"That I shall cause a [Ia]trumpet blast of war to be heard[8085]
Against [b]Rabbah of the sons of Ammon;
And it will become a desolate[8077] heap,
And her [c]towns will be set on fire.
Then Israel will take [d]possession of his possessors,"
Says the LORD.
3 "Wail, O [a]Heshbon, for [b]Ai has been destroyed![7703]
Cry out, O daughters of Rabbah,
[c]Gird yourselves with sackcloth and lament,
And rush back and forth inside the walls;
For [I]Malcam will [d]go into exile[1473]
Together with his priests[3548] and his princes.[8269]
4 "How [a]boastful[1984] you are about the valleys!
Your valley is flowing *away,*
O [b]backsliding[7728] daughter
Who trusts[982] in her [c]treasures, *saying,*
'[d]Who will come against me?'
5 "Behold, I am going to bring [a]terror upon you,"
Declares the Lord[136] [I]GOD of hosts,[6635]
"From all *directions* around you;
And each of you[376] will be [b]driven out [II]headlong,
With no one to gather[6908] the [c]fugitives together.
6 "But afterward I will [a]restore[7725]
The [I]fortunes[7622] of the sons[1121] of Ammon,"
Declares the LORD.

Prophecy against Edom

7 Concerning [a]Edom.
Thus says the LORD of hosts,
"Is there no longer any [b]wisdom[2451] in [c]Teman?
Has good counsel[6098] been lost[6] to the prudent?[995]
Has their wisdom decayed?
8 "Flee away, turn back, dwell in the depths,
O inhabitants of [a]Dedan,
For I [I]will bring the [b]disaster[343] of Esau upon him
At the time[6256] I [II]punish[6485] him.
9 "[a]If grape gatherers came to you,
Would they not leave[7604] gleanings?
If thieves *came* by night,[3915]
They would destroy *only* [I]until they had enough.
10 "But I have [a]stripped Esau bare,
I have uncovered[1540] his hiding places
So that he will not be able to conceal himself;
His [I]offspring[2233] has been destroyed along with his [II]relatives[251]
And his neighbors,[7934] and [b]he is no more.
11 "Leave[5800] your [Ia]orphans behind,
I will keep[2421] *them* alive;
And let your [b]widows trust[982] in Me."

12 For thus says the LORD, "Behold, those [I]who were not sentenced[4941] to drink the [a]cup will certainly drink *it,* and are you the one who will be [b]completely acquitted?[5352] You will not be acquitted, but you will certainly drink *it.*

13 "For I have [a]sworn by Myself," declares the LORD, "that [b]Bozrah will become[1961] an [c]object of horror,[8047] a reproach,[2781] a ruin and a curse;[7045] and all its cities will become perpetual[5769] ruins."[2723]

14 I have [a]heard a message from the LORD,
And an [b]envoy[6735] is sent among the nations,[1471] *saying,*
"[c]Gather yourselves together and come against her,
And rise up for battle!"
15 "For behold, I have made you small among the nations,
Despised among men.[120]
16 "As for the terror of you,

2 [I]Or, *shout of* [a]Num. 10:9; Jer. 4:19 [b]Deut. 3:11; 2Sam. 11:1; Ezek. 21:20 [c]Josh. 17:11, 16 [d]Is. 14:2
3 [I]Cf. v. 1 [a]Jer. 48:2 [b]Josh. 7:2-5; 8:1-29; Ezra 2:28 [c]Is. 32:11; Jer. 48:37 [d]Jer. 46:25; 48:7
4 [a]Jer. 9:23 [b]Jer. 31:22 [c]Ps. 62:10; Ezek. 28:4, 5; 1Tim. 6:17 [d]Jer. 21:13
5 [I]Heb., *YHWH,* usually rendered LORD [II]Lit., *before him* [a]Jer. 48:43f.; 49:29 [b]Jer. 16:16; 46:5 [c]Lam. 4:15
6 [I]Or, *captivity* [a]Jer. 48:47; 49:39
7 [a]Gen. 25:30; 32:3; Is. 34:5, 6; Jer. 25:21; Ezek. 25:12; Amos 1:11; Obad. 1-21 [b]Job 2:11; Jer. 8:9 [c]Gen. 36:11, 15, 34; Jer. 49:20
8 [I]Or, *brought* [II]Or, *punished* [a]Is. 21:13; Jer. 25:23 [b]Jer. 46:21; Mal. 1:3, 4
9 [I]Lit., *their sufficiency* [a]Obad. 5
10 [I]Lit., *seed* [II]Lit., *brothers* [a]Jer. 13:26 [b]Is. 17:14
11 [I]Or, *fatherless* [a]Ps. 68:5; Hos. 14:3 [b]Ps. 68:5; Zech. 7:10
12 [I]Lit., *whose judgment was not to* [a]Jer. 25:15 [b]Jer. 25:28, 29; 1Pet. 4:17
13 [a]Gen. 22:16; Is. 45:23; Jer. 44:26; Amos 6:8 [b]Gen. 36:33; 1Chr. 1:44; Is. 34:6; 63:1; Amos 1:12 [c]Is. 34:9-15; Jer. 18:16
14 [a]Obad. 1-4 [b]Is. 18:2; 30:4 [c]Jer. 50:14

The arrogance[2087] of your
heart[3820] has deceived you,
O you who live[7931] in the clefts
of [I]the [a]rock,
Who occupy the height of the
hill.
Though you make your nest as
[b]high as an eagle's,
I will [c]bring you down from
there," declares the LORD.
17 "And Edom will become an [a]ob-
ject of horror; everyone who passes by
it will be horrified[8074] and will [b]hiss at
all its wounds.[4347]
18 "Like the [a]overthrow of Sodom
and Gomorrah with its neighbors,"[7934]
says the LORD, "[b]no one will live there,
nor will a son[1121] of man[120] reside[1481]
in it.
19 "[a]Behold, one will come up[5927]
like a lion from the [Ib]thickets of the Jordan against [II]a perennially watered pasture; for in an instant I shall make him
run away from it, and whoever is
[c]chosen I shall appoint[6485] over it. For
who is [d]like Me, and who will summon[3259] Me *into court?* And who then
is the shepherd [e]who can stand against
Me?"
20 Therefore hear[8085] the [a]plan of
the LORD which He has planned against
Edom, and His purposes[4284] which He
has purposed[2803] against the inhabitants
of Teman: surely they will drag them
off, *even* the little ones of the flock;
surely He will make their [I]pasture
[b]desolate[8074] because of them.
21 The [a]earth[776] has quaked[7493] at
the noise of their downfall. There is an
outcry! The noise of it has been heard
at the [I]Red Sea.
22 Behold, [I]He will mount up and
[a]swoop like an eagle, and spread out
His wings [II]against Bozrah; and the
[b]hearts of the mighty men of Edom in
that day[3117] will be like the heart of a
woman[802] in labor.

Prophecy against Damascus

23 Concerning [a]Damascus.
"[b]Hamath and [c]Arpad are put to
shame,[954]
For they have heard bad[7451]
news;
They are [d]disheartened.
There is anxiety[1674] by the sea,
It [e]cannot be calmed.[8252]
24 "Damascus has become
helpless;[7503]
She has turned away to flee,
And panic[7374] has gripped her;
[a]Distress[6869] and pangs[2256] have
taken hold of her
Like a woman in childbirth.
25 "How [I]the [a]city of praise[8416] has
not been deserted,[5800]
The town of My joy!
26 "Therefore, her [a]young men will
fall in her streets,
And all the men[582] of war will
be [I]silenced in that day,"
declares the LORD of hosts.
27 "And I shall [a]set fire to the wall
of Damascus,
And it will devour the [I]fortified
towers[759] of [b]Ben-hadad."

Prophecy against Kedar and Hazor

28 Concerning [a]Kedar and the
kingdoms[4467] of Hazor, which Nebuchadnezzar king of Babylon defeated.[5221]
Thus says the LORD,
"Arise, go up to Kedar
And devastate[7703] the [Ib]men of
the east.
29 "They will take away[5375] their
tents[168] and their flocks;
They will carry off for
themselves
Their tent [a]curtains, all their
goods, and their [b]camels,
And they will call out[7121] to one
another, '[c]Terror[4032] on
every side!'
30 "Run away, flee! Dwell in the
depths,
O inhabitants of Hazor,"
declares the LORD;
"For [a]Nebuchadnezzar king of
Babylon has formed a plan
against you
And devised a scheme[4284]
against you.

16 [I]Or, *Sela* [a]2Kin. 14:7; Jer. 48:28 [b]Job 39:27; Is. 14:13-15 [c]Amos 9:2
17 [a]Jer. 18:16; 49:13; 50:13; Ezek. 35:7 [b]1Kin. 9:8; Jer. 51:37
18 [a]Gen. 19:24, 25; Deut. 29:23; Jer. 50:40; Amos 4:11; Zeph. 2:9 [b]Job 18:15-18; Jer. 49:33
19 [I]Lit., *pride* [II]Or, *an enduring habitation* [a]Jer. 50:44 [b]Josh. 3:15; Jer. 12:5 [c]Num. 16:5 [d]Ex. 15:11; Is. 46:9 [e]Job 41:10
20 [I]Or, *habitation* [a]Is. 14:24, 27; Jer. 50:45 [b]Mal. 1:3, 4
21 [I]Lit., *Sea of Reeds* [a]Jer. 50:46; Ezek. 26:15, 18
22 [I]Or, *one* [II]Or, *over* [a]Jer. 4:13; 48:40; Hos. 8:1 [b]Is. 13:8; Jer. 30:6; 48:41
23 [a]Gen. 14:15; 15:2; 2Kin. 5:12; 2Chr. 16:2; Is. 7:8; 17:1; Amos 1:3; Acts 9:2 [b]Num. 13:21; Is. 10:9; Jer. 39:5; Amos 6:2 [c]2Kin. 18:34; 19:13; Is. 10:9 [d]Ex. 15:15; Nah. 2:10 [e]Is. 57:20
24 [a]Is. 13:8
25 [I]Or, *deserted is the city of praise* [a]Jer. 33:9; 51:41
26 [I]Or, *destroyed* [a]Jer. 11:22; 50:30; Amos 4:10
27 [I]Or, *palaces* [a]Jer. 43:12; Amos 1:3-5 [b]1Kin. 15:18-20; 2Kin. 13:3
28 [I]Lit., *sons* [a]Gen. 25:13; Ps. 120:5; Is. 21:16, 17; Jer. 2:10; Ezek. 27:21 [b]Job 1:3; Is. 11:14
29 [a]Hab. 3:7 [b]1Chr. 5:21 [c]Jer. 46:5
30 [a]Jer. 25:9; 27:6

31 "Arise, go up against a nation[1471]
which is [a]at ease,
Which lives securely,"[983]
declares the LORD.
"It has [b]no gates or bars;
They [c]dwell[7931] alone.
32 "And their camels will become
plunder,[957]
And the multitude[527] of their
cattle for booty,
And I shall [a]scatter to all the
winds[7307] those who [b]cut the
corners *of their hair;*
And I shall bring their disaster
from every side," declares
the LORD.
33 "And Hazor will become a
[a]haunt of jackals,[8577]
A desolation[8077] forever;[5769]
No one will live there,
Nor will a son of man reside
in it."

Prophecy against Elam

34 That which came as the word[1697]
of the LORD to Jeremiah the prophet[5030]
concerning [a]Elam, [b]at the beginning of
the reign[4438] of Zedekiah king of Judah,
saying,
35 "Thus says the LORD of hosts,
'Behold, I am going to
[a]break[7665] the bow of Elam,
The [I]finest[7225] of their might.
36 'And I shall bring upon Elam the
[a]four winds
From the four ends of
heaven,[8064]
And shall [b]scatter them to all
these winds;
And there will be no nation
To which the outcasts of Elam
will not go.
37 'So I shall [I]shatter[2865] Elam
before their enemies
And before those who seek their
lives;[5315]
And I shall [a]bring calamity upon
them,
Even My [b]fierce anger,'[639]
declares the LORD,
'And I shall [c]send out the
sword[2719] after them
Until[5647] I have consumed[3615]
them.
38 'Then I shall set[7760] My
throne[3678] in Elam,
And I shall destroy[6] [I]out of it
king and princes,'
Declares the LORD.
39 'But it will come about in the
last[319] days
That I shall [a]restore the
[I]fortunes of Elam,' "
Declares the LORD.

Prophecy against Babylon

50 The word[1697] which the LORD
spoke[1696] concerning [a]Babylon,
the land[776] of the Chaldeans, through
Jeremiah the prophet:[5030]
2 "[a]Declare[5046] and proclaim among
the nations.[1471]
Proclaim[8085] it and [b]lift up[5375] a
standard.
Do not conceal *it but* say,[559]
'[c]Babylon has been captured,
[d]Bel has been put to shame,
[I]Marduk has been
[II]shattered;
Her [e]images[6091] have been put
to shame, her idols[1544] have
been shattered.'[2865]
3 "For a nation[1471] has come up[5927]
against her out of the [a]north; it will make
her land [b]an object of horror,[8047] and
there will be [c]no inhabitant in it. Both
man[120] and beast have wandered off,
they have gone away!
4 "In those days[3117] and at that
time,"[6256] declares[5001] the LORD, "the
sons[1121] of Israel will come, *both* they
and the sons of Judah [a]as well; they will
go along [b]weeping as they go, and it
will be [c]the LORD their God[430] they will
seek.
5 "They will [a]ask[7592] for the way[1870]
to Zion, *turning* their faces [I]in its direction; [II]they [III]will come that they may
join themselves to the LORD *in* an
[b]everlasting[5769] covenant[1285] that will not
be forgotten.

31 [a]Judg. 18:7; Is. 47:8 [b]Is. 42:11 [c]Num. 23:9; Deut. 33:28; Mic. 7:14
32 [a]Ezek. 5:10; 12:14, 15 [b]Jer. 9:26; 25:23
33 [a]Is. 13:20-22; Jer. 9:11; 10:22; 51:37; Zeph. 2:9, 13-15; Mal. 1:3
34 [a]Gen. 10:22; 14:1, 9; Is. 11:11; Jer. 25:25; Ezek. 32:24; Dan. 8:2 [b]2Kin. 24:17, 18; Jer. 28:1
35 [I]Lit., *first* [a]Ps. 46:9; Is. 22:6; Jer. 51:56
36 [a]Dan. 7:2; 8:8; Rev. 7:1 [b]Jer. 49:32; Ezek. 5:10; Amos 9:9
37 [I]Or, *dismay* [a]Jer. 6:19 [b]Jer. 30:24 [c]Jer. 9:16; 48:2
38 [I]Or, *from there*
39 [I]Or, *captivity* [a]Jer. 48:47

1 [a]Gen. 10:10; 11:9; 2Kin. 17:24; Is. 13:1; 47:1; Dan. 1:1; Rev. 14:8
2 [I]Heb., *Merodach* [II]Or, *dismayed* [a]Jer. 4:16 [b]Jer. 51:27 [c]Jer. 51:31 [d]Is. 46:1 [e]Jer. 51:47
3 [a]Is. 13:17; Jer. 50:9; 51:11, 27 [b]Is. 14:22, 23; Jer. 50:13 [c]Jer. 9:10, 11; Zeph. 1:3
4 [a]Is. 11:12, 13; Jer. 3:18; 31:31; 33:7; Hos. 1:11 [b]Ezra 3:12, 13; Ps. 126:5; Jer. 31:9 [c]Hos. 3:5
5 [I]Lit., *hither* [II]M.T. reads *come ye!* [III]Or, *will have come* [a]Is. 35:8; Jer. 6:16 [b]Is. 55:3; Jer. 32:40; Heb. 8:6-10

6 “My people[5971] have become
[a]lost[6] sheep;
[b]Their shepherds have led them astray.[8582]
They have made them turn aside *on* the [c]mountains;
They have gone along from mountain to hill
And have forgotten their [d]resting place.
7 “All who came upon them have devoured them;
And their adversaries have said,[559] ‘[a]We are not guilty,[816]
Inasmuch as they have sinned[2398] against the LORD *who is* the [b]habitation of righteousness,[6664]
Even the LORD, the [c]hope[4723] of their fathers.’[1]
8 “Wander away from the [a]midst of Babylon,
And [I]go forth from the land of the Chaldeans;
Be also like male goats [II]at the head of the flock.
9 “For behold, I am going to [a]arouse and bring up[5927] against Babylon
A horde[6957] of great nations from the land[776] of the north,
And they will draw up *their* battle lines against her;
From there she will be taken captive.
Their arrows will be like [I]an expert warrior
Who does not return[7725] empty-handed.
10 “And [Ia]Chaldea will become plunder;
All who plunder her will have enough,” declares the LORD.
11 “Because you are glad, because you are jubilant,
O you who [a]pillage[8154] My heritage,[5159]
Because you skip about [I]like a threshing [b]heifer
And neigh like [II]stallions,[47]
12 Your [a]mother[517] [I]will be greatly ashamed,[954]
She who gave you birth [I]will be humiliated.
Behold, *she will be* the least[319] of the nations,
A [b]wilderness, a parched land, and a desert.[6160]
13 “Because of the indignation[7110] of the LORD she will [a]not be inhabited,
But she will be [b]completely desolate;[8077]
Everyone who passes by Babylon [c]will be horrified[8074]
And will hiss because of all her wounds.[4347]
14 “Draw up your battle lines against Babylon on every side,
All you who [I]bend the bow;
Shoot at her, do not be sparing with *your* arrows,
For she has [a]sinned against the LORD.
15 “Raise your battle cry[7321] against her on every side!
She has [a]given [I]herself up, her pillars have fallen,[5307]
Her [b]walls have been torn down.[2040]
For this is the [c]vengeance[5360] of the LORD:
Take vengeance[5358] on her;
[d]As she has done[6213] *to others,* *so* do[6213] to her.
16 “Cut off[3772] the [a]sower from Babylon,
And the one who wields the sickle at the time of harvest;
From before [I]the [b]sword[2719] of the oppressor[3238]
[c]They will each[376] turn back to his own people,
And they will each flee to his own land.

17 “Israel is a [a]scattered [I]flock, the
[b]lions have driven *them* away. The
first[7223] one *who* devoured him was the
[c]king[4428] of Assyria, and this last one
who has broken his bones[6106] is [d]Nebu-
chadnezzar king of Babylon.
18 “Therefore thus says[559] the
LORD of hosts,[6635] the God of Israel:
‘Behold, I am going to punish[6485] the

6 [a]Is. 53:6; Ezek. 34:15, 16; Matt. 9:36; 10:6 [b]Jer. 23:11-14 [c]Jer. 13:16; Ezek. 34:6 [d]Jer. 33:12; 50:19

7 [a]Jer. 2:3; Zech. 11:5 [b]Jer. 31:23; 40:2, 3 [c]Ps. 22:4; Jer. 14:8; 17:13

8 [I]Another reading is *let them go forth* [II]Or, *in front of* [a]Is. 48:20; Jer. 51:6; Rev. 18:4

9 [I]So some mss. and versions; M.T. reads *a warrior who makes childless* [a]Jer. 51:1

10 [I]Or, *the Chaldeans* [a]Jer. 51:24, 35; Ezek. 11:24

11 [I]Another reading is *in the grass* [II]Lit., *mighty ones* [a]Jer. 12:14 [b]Jer. 46:20

12 [I]Or, *has become* [a]Jer. 15:9 [b]Jer. 22:6; 51:43

13 [a]Jer. 34:22 [b]Jer. 51:26 [c]Jer. 18:16; 49:17

14 [I]Lit., *tread* (in order to string) [a]Hab. 2:8, 17

15 [I]Lit., *her hand* [a]1Chr. 29:24; 2Chr. 30:8; Lam. 5:6 [b]Jer. 50:44, 58; 51:58 [c]Jer. 46:10 [d]Ps. 137:8; Rev. 18:6

16 [I]Or, *the oppressing sword* [a]Joel 1:11 [b]Jer. 25:38; 46:16 [c]Is. 13:14

17 [I]Lit., *sheep* [a]Joel 3:2 [b]Jer. 2:15; 4:7 [c]2Kin. 15:19; 17:6; 18:9-13 [d]2Kin. 24:1, 10-12; 25:1-7

king of Babylon and his land, just as I
[a]punished the king of Assyria.
19 'And I shall [a]bring Israel back to
his pasture, and he will graze on Carmel
and Bashan, and his [I]desire[5315] will be
satisfied in the [b]hill country of Ephraim
and Gilead.
20 'In those days and at that time,'
declares the LORD, 'search will be made
for the iniquity[5771] of Israel, but [a]there
will be none; and for the sins of Judah,
but they will not be found; for I shall
pardon[5545] those [b]whom I leave as a remnant.'

21 "Against the land of [I]Merathaim,
go up against it,
And against the inhabitants of
[II][a]Pekod.
Slay[2717] and [III]utterly destroy[2763]
them," declares the LORD,
"And do according to all that I
have commanded[6680] you.
22 "The [a]noise of battle is in the land,
And great destruction.[7667]
23 "How the [a]hammer of the whole
earth[776]
Has been cut off and broken!
How Babylon has become[1961]
An object of horror[8047] among
the nations!
24 "I [a]set a snare for you, and you
were also [b]caught, O
Babylon,
While you yourself were not
aware;[3045]
You have been found and also
seized
Because you have engaged in
[c]conflict with the LORD."
25 The LORD has opened His
armory
And has brought forth the
[a]weapons of His
indignation,[2195]
For it is a [b]work[4399] of the
Lord[136] [I]GOD of hosts
In the land of the Chaldeans.
26 Come to her from the
[I]farthest border;
[a]Open up her barns,
Pile her up like heaps
And [II][b]utterly destroy her,
Let nothing be left to her.
27 [a]Put all her young bulls to the
sword;[2717]
Let them [b]go down to the
slaughter![2874]
Woe be upon them, for their
[c]day[3117] has come,
The time of their
punishment.[6486]
28 There is a [a]sound of fugitives
and refugees from the land
of Babylon,
To declare in Zion the
[b]vengeance of the LORD our
God,
Vengeance for His [c]temple.[1964]
29 "Summon[8085] [I]many against
Babylon,
All those who [II]bend the bow:
Encamp against her on every
side,
Let there be no [III]escape.[6413]
Repay[7999] her according to her
work;
[a]According to all that she has
done, *so* do to her;
For she has become [b]arrogant
against the LORD,
Against the Holy One[6918] of
Israel.
30 "Therefore her [a]young men will
fall in her streets,
And all her men[582] of war will
be [I][b]silenced in that day,"
declares the LORD.
31 "Behold, [a]I am against you, O
[I]arrogant[2087] one,"
Declares the Lord [II]GOD of
hosts,
"For your day has come,
The time [III]when I shall
punish[6485] you.
32 "And the [I][a]arrogant one will
stumble[3782] and fall
With no one to raise him up;
And I shall [b]set fire to his
cities,
And it will devour all his
environs."
33 Thus says the LORD of hosts,
"The sons of Israel are
oppressed,

18 [a]Is. 10:12; Ezek. 31:3, 11, 12; Nah. 3:7, 18, 19
19 [I]Lit., *soul* [a]Is. 65:10; Jer. 31:10; 33:12; Ezek. 34:13 [b]Jer. 31:6
20 [a]Is. 43:25; Jer. 31:34; Mic. 7:19 [b]Is. 1:9
21 [I]Or, *Double Rebellion* [II]Or, *Punishment* [III]Lit., *put under the ban* [a]Ezek. 23:23
22 [a]Jer. 4:19-21; 51:54-56
23 [a]Jer. 51:20-24
24 [a]Jer. 48:43, 44 [b]Jer. 51:31; Dan. 5:30, 31 [c]Job 9:4; 40:2,9
25 [I]Heb., *YHWH*, usually rendered *LORD* [a]Is. 13:5 [b]Jer. 50:15; 51:12, 25, 55
26 [I]Lit., *end* [II]Lit., *put under the ban* [a]Is. 45:3; Jer. 50:10 [b]Is. 14:23
27 [a]Is. 34:7 [b]Jer. 48:10 [c]Ps. 37:13; Jer. 46:21; 48:44; Ezek. 7:7
28 [a]Is. 48:20 [b]Ps. 149:6-9; Jer. 50:15; 51:10 [c]Lam. 1:10; 2:6, 7
29 [I]Another reading is *archers* [II]Lit., *tread* (in order to string) [III]Some mss. add *to her* [a]Ps. 137:8; Jer. 50:15; 51:56; 2Thess. 1:6 [b]Ex. 10:3; Jer. 49:16; Dan. 4:37
30 [I]Or, *made lifeless* or *destroyed* [a]Is. 13:17, 18; Jer. 9:21; 18:21; 49:26; 51:4 [b]Jer. 51:57
31 [I]Lit., *arrogance* [II]Heb., *YHWH*, usually rendered *LORD* [III]Another reading is *of your punishment* [a]Jer. 21:13; Nah. 2:13
32 [I]Lit., *arrogance* [a]Is. 10:12-15 [b]Jer. 21:14; 49:27

And the sons of Judah as well;
And [a]all who took them captive[7617] have held[2388] them fast,
They have refused[3985] to let them go.
34 "Their [a]Redeemer[1350] is strong,[2389] [b]the LORD of hosts is His name;
He will vigorously [c]plead[7378] their case,[7379]
So that He may [d]bring rest to [I]the earth,
But turmoil to the inhabitants of Babylon.
35 "A [a]sword against the Chaldeans," declares the LORD,
"And against the inhabitants of Babylon,
And against her [b]officials[8269] and her [c]wise[2450] men!
36 "A sword against the [a]oracle priests, and they will become fools![2973]
A sword against her [b]mighty men, and they will be [Ic]shattered![2865]
37 "A sword against [I]their [a]horses and against [I]their chariots,
And against all the [IIb]foreigners who are in the midst of her,
And they will become [c]women!
A sword against her treasures, and they will be plundered!
38 "A [Ia]drought on her waters, and they will be dried up![3001]
For it is a land of [b]idols,
And they are mad[1984] over fearsome idols.[367]
39 "Therefore the [a]desert creatures will live *there* along with the jackals;
The ostriches also will live[7931] in it,
And it will [b]never again be inhabited
Or dwelt in from generation[1755] to generation.
40 "As when God overthrew [a]Sodom
And Gomorrah with its neighbors,"[7934] declares the LORD,
"No man[376] will live there,
Nor will *any* son[1121] of man reside[1481] in it.
41 "Behold, a people is coming [a]from the north,
And a great nation and many kings[4428]
Will be aroused from the remote parts of the earth.
42 "They [a]seize *their* bow and javelin;
They are [b]cruel and have no mercy.[7355]
Their [c]voice roars like the sea,
And they ride on [d]horses,
[e]Marshalled like a man for the battle
Against you, O daughter of Babylon.
43 "The [a]king of Babylon has heard[8085] the report[8088] about them,
And his hands[3027] hang limp;[7503]
[b]Distress[6869] has gripped[2388] him,
Agony like a woman in childbirth.

44 "[a]Behold, one will come up like a lion from the [I]thicket of the Jordan to [II]a perennially watered pasture; for in an instant I shall make them run away from it, and whoever is [b]chosen I shall appoint[6485] over it. For who is [c]like Me, and who will summon[3259] Me *into court?* And who then is the shepherd who can [d]stand before Me?"

45 Therefore hear[8085] the [a]plan[6098] of the LORD which He has planned against Babylon, and His purposes[4284] which He has purposed[2803] against the land of the Chaldeans: [b]surely they will drag them off, *even* the little ones of the flock; surely He will make their [I]pasture desolate[8074] because of them.

46 At the [I]shout, "Babylon has been seized!" the [a]earth is shaken, and an [b]outcry is heard among the nations.

33 [a]Is. 14:17; 58:6
34 [I]Or, their *land* [a]Prov. 23:11; Is. 43:14; Jer. 15:21; 31:11; Rev. 18:8 [b]Is. 47:4; Jer. 32:18; 51:19 [c]Jer. 51:36; Mic. 7:9 [d]Is. 14:3-7
35 [a]Jer. 47:6; Hos. 11:6 [b]Dan. 5:1, 2 [c]Dan. 5:7, 8
36 [I]Or, *dismayed* [a]Is. 44:25 [b]Jer. 49:22 [c]Nah. 3:13
37 [I]Lit., *his* [II]Lit., *mixed multitude* [a]Ps. 20:7, 8; Jer. 51:21, 22 [b]Jer. 25:20; Ezek. 30:5 [c]Jer. 48:41; 51:30; Nah. 3:13
38 [I]Another reading is *sword* [a]Is. 44:27; Jer. 51:32, 36; Rev. 16:12 [b]Is. 46:1, 6, 7
39 [a]Is. 13:21; 34:14; Rev. 18:2 [b]Is. 13:20; Jer. 25:12
40 [a]Gen. 19:24, 25; Is. 13:19; Jer. 49:18; Luke 17:28-30; 2Pet. 2:6; Jude 7
41 [a]Is. 13:2-5; Jer. 6:22; 50:3, 9; 51:27, 28
42 [a]Jer. 6:23 [b]Is. 13:17, 18; 47:6 [c]Is. 5:30 [d]Jer. 8:16; 47:3; Hab. 1:8 [e]Jer. 50:9, 14; Joel 2:5
43 [a]Jer. 51:31 [b]Jer. 30:6; 49:24
44 [I]Lit., *pride* [II]Or, *an enduring habitation* [a]Jer. 49:19-21 [b]Num. 16:5 [c]Is. 46:9 [d]Job 41:10; Jer. 30:21
45 [I]Or, *habitation* [a]Ps. 33:11; Is. 14:24; Jer. 51:10, 11 [b]Jer. 49:20
46 [I]Lit., *voice* [a]Jer. 10:10; 49:21; Ezek. 26:18; 31:16 [b]Is. 5:7; 15:5; Jer. 46:12; 51:54; Ezek. 27:28

Babylon Judged for Sins against Israel

51 Thus says[559] the LORD:
"Behold, I am going to arouse
against Babylon
And against the inhabitants of
[I]Leb-kamai
[II]The [a]spirit[7307] of a
destroyer.[7843]
2 "And I shall dispatch
[I]foreigners[2114] to Babylon
that they may [a]winnow her
And may devastate her land;[776]
For on every side they will be
opposed to her
In the day[3117] of *her* calamity.[7451]
3 "[I]Let not [II]him who [III][a]bends his
bow [III]bend *it,*
[I]Nor let him rise up in his
[b]scale-armor;[5630]
So do not spare her young men;
Devote all her army[6635] to
destruction.
4 "And they will fall down
[I]slain[2491] in the land of the
Chaldeans,
And [a]pierced through in their
streets."
5 For [a]neither Israel nor Judah
has been [I]forsaken[488]
By his God,[430] the LORD of
hosts,[6635]
Although their land is [b]full of
guilt[817]
[II]Before the Holy One[6918] of
Israel.
6 [a]Flee from the midst of Babylon,
And each of you[376] save his
life![5315]
Do not be [I][b]destroyed[3772] in her
[II]punishment,[5771]
For this is the [c]LORD's time[6256]
of vengeance;[5360]
He is going to [d]render[7999]
recompense to her.
7 Babylon has been a golden
[a]cup in the hand[3027] of the
LORD,
Intoxicating all the earth.[776]
The [b]nations[1471] have drunk of
her wine;
Therefore the nations are
[c]going mad.[1984]
8 Suddenly [a]Babylon has fallen[5307]
and been broken;[7665]
[b]Wail over her!
[c]Bring [I]balm for her pain;
Perhaps she may be healed.
9 We applied healing to Babylon,
but she was not healed;
Forsake[5800] her and [a]let us
each[376] go to his own
country,[776]
For her judgment[4941] has
[b]reached[5060] to heaven[8064]
And [I]towers[5375] up to the very
skies.[7834]
10 The LORD has [a]brought [I]about
our vindication;[6666]
Come and let us [b]recount[5608] in
Zion
The work of the LORD our God!
11 [a]Sharpen the arrows, fill the
quivers!
The LORD has aroused the
spirit[7307] of the kings[4428] of
the Medes,
Because His purpose[4209] is
against Babylon to destroy it;
For it is the [b]vengeance of the
LORD, vengeance for His
temple.[1964]
12 [a]Lift up[5375] a [I]signal against the
walls of Babylon;
Post a strong[2388] guard,
Station [II]sentries,[8104]
Place[3559] men in ambush!
For the LORD has both
[b]purposed[2161] and
performed[6213]
What He spoke[1696] concerning
the inhabitants of Babylon.
13 O you who [a]dwell[7931] by many
waters,
Abundant[7227] in [b]treasures,
Your end has come,
The [I]measure of your [II][c]end.[1215]
14 The [a]LORD of hosts has sworn
by Himself:
"Surely I will fill you with a
[I]population[120] like [b]locusts,
And they will cry out with
[II]shouts of victory over you."

1 [I]Cryptic name for Chaldea; or, *the heart of those who rise up against Me* [II]Or, *a destroying wind* [a]Jer. 4:11, 12; 23:19; Hos. 13:15
2 [I]Some versions read *winnowers* [a]Is. 41:16; Jer. 15:7; Matt. 3:12
3 [I]M.T. reads *Against him who* [II]I.e., the Chaldean defender [III]Lit., *tread(s)* (in order to string) [a]Jer. 50:14, 29 [b]Jer. 46:4
4 [I]Or, *wounded* [a]Is. 13:15; 14:19; Jer. 49:26; 50:30, 37
5 [I]Lit., *widowed* [II]Lit., *From* [a]Is. 54:7, 8; Jer. 33:24-26 [b]Hos. 4:1, 2
6 [I]Or, *silenced* or *made lifeless* [II]Or, *penalty for iniquity* [a]Jer. 50:8, 28; Rev. 18:4 [b]Num. 16:26 [c]Jer. 50:15 [d]Jer. 25:14
7 [a]Jer. 25:15; Hab. 2:16; Rev. 14:8; 17:4 [b]Rev. 14:8; 18:3 [c]Jer. 25:16
8 [I]Or, *balsam resin* [a]Is. 21:9; Jer. 50:2; Rev. 14:8; 18:2 [b]Is. 13:6; Rev. 18:9 [c]Jer. 46:11
9 [I]Lit., *is lifted* [a]Is. 13:14; Jer. 46:16; 50:16 [b]Ezra 9:6; Rev. 18:5
10 [I]Lit., *forth* [a]Ps. 37:6; Mic. 7:9 [b]Is. 40:2; Jer. 50:28
11 [a]Jer. 46:4, 9; Joel 3:9, 10 [b]Jer. 50:28
12 [I]Or, *standard* [II]Or, *watchmen* [a]Is. 13:2; Jer. 50:2; 51:27 [b]Jer. 4:28; 23:20; 51:29
13 [I]Lit., *cubit* [II]Lit., *being cut off* [a]Rev. 17:1 [b]Is. 45:3 [c]Is. 57:17; Hab. 2:9-11
14 [I]Or, *mankind* [II]I.e., like the song of grape treaders [a]Jer. 49:13 [b]Jer. 51:27; Nah. 3:15

15 *It is* [a]He who made[6213] the earth
by His power,
Who established[3559] the
world[8398] by His wisdom,[2451]
And by His understanding[8394] He
[b]stretched out the heavens.
16 When He utters His [a]voice, *there*
is a tumult[527] of waters in the
heavens,[8064]
And He causes the [b]clouds to
ascend[5927] from the end of the
earth;
He makes[6213] lightning for the
rain,
And brings forth the [c]wind from
His storehouses.
17 [a]All mankind[120] is stupid, devoid
of knowledge;[1847]
Every goldsmith[6884] is put to
shame by his [I]idols,[6459]
For his molten images[5262] are
[b]deceitful,
And there is no breath[7307] in
them.
18 They are [a]worthless, a work
of mockery;[8595]
In the time of their
punishment[6486] they will
perish.[6]
19 The [a]portion of Jacob is not like
these;
For the [I]Maker[3335] of all is He,
And of the [II]tribe[7626] of His
inheritance;[5159]
The [b]LORD of hosts is His name.
20 *He says,* "You are My [Ia]war-
club, *My* weapon of war;
And with you I [b]shatter nations,
And with you I destroy
kingdoms.[4467]
21 "And with you I [a]shatter the horse
and his rider,
22 And with you I shatter the
[a]chariot and its rider,
And with you I shatter [b]man[376]
and woman,[802]
And with you I shatter old[2205]
man and [c]youth,
And with you I shatter young
man and virgin,[1330]
23 And with you I shatter the
shepherd and his flock,

15 [a]Gen. 1:1; Jer. 10:12-16; 51:15-19 [b]Job 9:8; Ps. 146:5, 6; Jer. 32:17; Acts 14:15; Rom. 1:20
16 [a]Job 37:2-6; Ps. 18:13 [b]Ps. 135:7; Jer. 10:13 [c]Jon. 1:4
17 [I]Or, *graven images* [a]Is. 44:18-20; Jer. 10:14 [b]Hab. 2:18, 19
18 [a]Jer. 18:15
19 [I]Lit., *Fashioner* [II]Or, *Scepter;* cf. Num. 24:17 [a]Ps. 73:26; Jer. 10:16 [b]Jer. 50:34
20 [I]Lit., *shatterer* [a]Is. 10:5; 41:15, 16; Jer. 50:23 [b]Is. 8:9; 41:15, 16; Mic. 4:12, 13
21 [a]Ex. 15:1
22 [a]Ex. 15:4; Is. 43:17 [b]2Chr. 36:17; Is. 13:15, 16 [c]Is. 13:18
24 [a]Jer. 50:10 [b]Jer. 50:15, 29
25 [a]Jer. 50:31 [b]Is. 13:2; Zech. 4:7 [c]Rev. 8:8
26 [a]Is. 13:19-22; 50:13; Jer. 51:29
27 [I]Or, *standard* [a]Is. 13:2-5; 18:3; Jer. 50:2; 51:12 [b]Jer. 50:3, 9 [c]Gen. 8:4; 2Kin. 19:37; Is. 37:38 [d]Gen. 10:3 [e]Jer. 50:42
28 [I]Lit., *Her* [II]I.e., lieutenant governors [III]Lit., *his*
29 [I]Or, *An object of horror* [a]Jer. 8:16; 10:10; 50:46; Amos 8:8 [b]Is. 13:19, 20; 47:11; Jer. 50:13; 51:26, 43

And with you I shatter the
farmer[406] and his team,
And with you I shatter
governors[6346] and
prefects.[5461]
24 "But I will repay Babylon and
all the inhabitants of [a]Chaldea for [b]all
their evil[7451] that they have done in
Zion before your eyes," declares[5001] the
LORD.
25 "Behold, [a]I am against you,
[b]O destroying[4889] mountain,
Who destroys[7843] the whole
earth," declares the LORD,
"And I will stretch out My hand
against you,
And roll you down[1556] from the
crags
And I will make you a
[c]burnt[8316] out mountain.
26 "And they will not take from you
even a stone for a corner
Nor a stone for foundations,[4146]
But you will be [a]desolate[8077]
forever,"[5769] declares the
LORD.
27 [a]Lift up a [I]signal in the land,
Blow[8628] a trumpet among the
nations!
Consecrate[6942] the nations
against her,
Summon against her the
[b]kingdoms of [c]Ararat, Minni
and [d]Ashkenaz;
Appoint[6485] a marshal[2951] against
her,
Bring up[5927] the [e]horses like
bristly locusts.
28 Consecrate the nations against
her,
The kings of the Medes,
[I]Their governors and all [I]their
[II]prefects,
And every land of [III]their
dominion.
29 So the [a]land quakes[7493] and
writhes,
For the purposes[4284] of the LORD
against Babylon stand,
To make[7660] the land of Babylon
[I]A [b]desolation[8047] without
inhabitants.

30 The [a]mighty men of Babylon
have ceased fighting,
They stay in the strongholds;
[b]Their strength is [I]exhausted,
They are becoming [c]*like*
women;[802]
Their dwelling places are set on
fire,
The [c]bars of her *gates* are
broken.
31 One [Ia]courier runs to meet
[I]another,
And one [IIb]messenger[5046] to
meet [II]another,
To tell[5046] the king[4428] of Babylon
That his city has been captured
from end *to end;*
32 The fords also have been
seized,
And they have burned[8313] the
marshes with fire,
And the men[582] of war are
terrified.[926]

33 For thus says the LORD of hosts,
the God of Israel:
"The daughter of Babylon is like
a [a]threshing floor
At the time [I]it is stamped firm;
Yet in a little while the time
of [b]harvest will come for
her."
34"Nebuchadnezzar king of Babylon
has [a]devoured me *and*
crushed[2000] me,
He has set me down *like* an
[b]empty vessel;
He has [c]swallowed[1104] me like
a monster,[8577]
He has filled his stomach with
my delicacies;
He has washed[1740] me away.
35 "May the [a]violence[2555] *done* to me
and to my flesh[7607] be upon
Babylon,"
The [I]inhabitant of Zion will
say;[559]
And, "May my blood[1818] be upon
the inhabitants of Chaldea,"
Jerusalem will say.
36 Therefore thus says the LORD,
"Behold, I am going to
[a]plead[7378] your case[7379]
And [b]exact full vengeance for
you;
And [c]I shall dry up[2717] her
[I]sea
And make her fountain dry.[3001]
37 "And [a]Babylon will become[1961] a
heap *of ruins,* a haunt of
jackals,[8577]
An [b]object of horror[8047] and
hissing, without inhabitants.
38 "They will roar together like
[a]young lions,
They will growl like lions'
cubs.[1484]
39 "When they become heated up,
I shall serve *them* their
banquet
And [a]make them drunk, that
they may become jubilant
And may [b]sleep a perpetual[5769]
sleep
And not wake up," declares the
LORD.
40 "I shall bring them down like
[I]lambs[3733] [a]to the
slaughter,[2873]
Like rams together with male
goats.
41"How [Ia]Sheshak has been
captured,
And [b]the praise[8416] of the whole
earth been seized!
How Babylon has become an
object of horror among the
nations!
42 "The [Ia]sea has come up over
Babylon;
She has been engulfed[3680] with
its tumultuous waves.
43 "Her cities have become an
[a]object of horror,
A parched land and a desert,[6160]
A land in which [b]no man lives,
And through which no son[1121]
of man passes.
44 "And [a]I shall punish[6485] Bel in
Babylon,
And I shall make what he has
swallowed[1105] [b]come out of
his mouth;[6310]
And the nations will no longer
[c]stream to him.

30 [I]Lit., *dried up* [a]Ps. 76:5; Jer. 50:15, 36, 37 [b]Is. 13:7, 8; Nah. 3:13 [c]Is. 45:1, 2; Lam. 2:9; Amos 1:5; Nah. 3:13

31 [I]Lit., *runner* [II]Lit., *announcer* [a]2Chr. 30:6 [b]2Sam. 18:19-31

33 [I]Lit., *of treading it* [a]Is. 21:10; 41:15, 16; Mic. 4:13 [b]Is. 17:5; Hos. 6:11; Joel 3:13; Rev. 14:15

34 [a]Jer. 50:17 [b]Is. 24:1-3 [c]Job 20:15; Jer. 51:44

35 [I]Lit., *inhabitress* [a]Ps. 137:8

36 [I]Or, *broad river* [a]Ps. 140:12 [b]Jer. 51:6, 11; Rom. 12:19 [c]Jer. 50:38

37 [a]Rev. 18:2 [b]Jer. 25:9

38 [a]Jer. 2:15

39 [a]Jer. 25:27; 48:26; 51:57 [b]Ps. 76:5

40 [I]Or, *young rams* [a]Jer. 48:15; 50:27

41 [I]Cryptic name for Babylon [a]Jer. 25:26 [b]Jer. 49:25

42 [I]Or, *broad river* [a]Is. 8:7, 8; Jer. 51:55; Dan. 9:26

43 [a]Jer. 50:12 [b]Is. 13:20; Jer. 2:6

44 [a]Is. 46:1; Jer. 50:2 [b]Ezra 1:7, 8 [c]Is. 2:2

Even the [d]wall of Babylon has
fallen down!
45 "[a]Come forth from her midst, My
people,[5971]
And each of you [b]save
yourselves
From the fierce anger[639] of the
LORD.
46 "Now [a]lest your heart grow faint,
And you be afraid[3372] at the
[b]report that *will be* heard[8085]
in the land—
For the report will come [I]one
year,
And after that [II]another report
in [II]another year,
And violence *will be* in the land
With [c]ruler against ruler—
47 Therefore behold, days[3117] are
coming
When I shall punish[6485] the
[a]idols of Babylon;
And her whole land will be
[b]put to shame,[954]
And all her slain will fall in her
midst.
48 "Then [a]heaven and earth and all
that is in them
Will shout for joy over Babylon,
For [b]the destroyers[7703] will
come to her from the north,"
Declares the LORD.
49 [a]Indeed Babylon is to fall *for* the
slain of Israel,
As also for Babylon [b]the slain
of all the earth have fallen.
50 You [a]who have escaped the
sword,[2719]
Depart! Do not stay!
[b]Remember[2142] the LORD from
afar,
And let Jerusalem [I]come to your
mind.[3824]
51 [a]We are ashamed because we
have heard reproach;[2781]
Disgrace has covered our faces,
For [b]aliens[2114] have entered
The holy places[4720] of the LORD'S
house.[1004]
52 "Therefore behold, the days are
coming," declares the LORD,
"When I shall punish her [a]idols,
And the mortally wounded[2491]
will groan throughout her
land.
53 "Though Babylon should
[a]ascend[5927] to the heavens,
And though she should fortify
[I]her lofty stronghold,
From [b]Me destroyers will come
to her," declares the LORD.
54 The [a]sound of an outcry from
Babylon,
And of great destruction[7667]
from the land of the
Chaldeans!
55 For the LORD is going to
destroy[7703] Babylon,
And He will make *her* loud
[I]noise vanish[6] from her.
And their [a]waves will roar like
many waters;
The tumult[7588] of their voices
[II]sounds forth.
56 For the [a]destroyer[7703] is coming
against her, against Babylon,
And her mighty men will be
captured,
Their [b]bows are shattered;[2865]
For the LORD is a God[410] of
[c]recompense,
He will fully repay.[7999]
57 "And I shall [a]make her princes[8269]
and her wise[2450] men drunk,
Her governors, her prefects,[5461]
and her mighty men,
That they may sleep a
[b]perpetual sleep and not wake
up,"
[c]Declares the King, whose name
is the LORD of hosts.
58 Thus says the LORD of hosts,
"The broad [a]wall of Babylon will
be completely razed,
And her high [b]gates will be set
on fire;
So the peoples will [c]toil for
nothing,
And the nations[3816] become
[d]exhausted *only* for fire."
59 The [I]message[1697] which Jeremiah the prophet[5030] commanded[6680]
Seraiah the son of [a]Neriah, the grandson
of Mahseiah, when he went with

44 [d]Jer. 50:15; 51:58
45 [a]Is. 48:20; Jer. 50:8, 28; 51:6; Rev. 18:4 [b]Gen. 19:12-16; Acts 2:40
46 [I]Lit., *in the* [II]Lit., *the* [a]Is. 43:5; Jer. 46:27, 28 [b]2Kin. 19:7; Is. 13:3-5 [c]Is. 19:2
47 [a]Is. 21:9; 46:1, 2; Jer. 50:2; 51:52 [b]Jer. 50:12, 35-37
48 [a]Is. 44:23; 48:20; 49:13; Rev. 18:20 [b]Jer. 50:3
49 [a]Ps. 137:8; Jer. 50:29 [b]Rev. 18:24
50 [I]Lit., *come upon your heart* [a]Jer. 44:28 [b]Deut. 4:29-31; Ps. 137:6
51 [a]Ps. 44:15 [b]Ps. 74:3-8; Lam. 1:10
52 [a]Jer. 50:38
53 [I]Lit., *the height of her strength* [a]Gen. 11:4; Job 20:6; Ps. 139:8-10; Is. 14:12-14; Jer. 49:16; Amos 9:2; Obad. 4 [b]Is. 13:3
54 [a]Jer. 48:3-5; 50:22, 46
55 [I]Or, *voice* [II]Lit., *is given* [a]Ps. 18:4; 69:2; 124:2, 4, 5; Jer. 51:42
56 [a]Jer. 51:48, 53; Hab. 2:8 [b]Ps. 46:9; 76:3 [c]Deut. 32:35; Ps. 94:1, 2; Jer. 51:6, 24
57 [a]Jer. 25:27 [b]Ps. 76:5, 6 [c]Jer. 46:18; 48:15
58 [a]Jer. 50:15 [b]Is. 45:1, 2 [c]Hab. 2:13 [d]Jer. 9:5; 51:64; Lam. 5:5
59 [I]Lit., *word* [a]Jer. 32:12; 36:4; 45:1

[b]Zedekiah the king of Judah to Babylon in the fourth year of his reign.[4427] (Now Seraiah was quartermaster.)

60 So Jeremiah [a]wrote in a single [I]scroll[5612] all the calamity which would come upon Babylon, *that is,* all these words[1697] which have been written concerning Babylon.

61 Then Jeremiah said[559] to Seraiah, "As soon as you come to Babylon, then see that you read[7121] all these words aloud,

62 and say, 'Thou, O LORD, hast [I]promised[1696] concerning this place to [a]cut it off, so that there will be [b]nothing dwelling in it, [II]whether man or beast, but it will be a perpetual desolation.'

63 "And it will come about as soon as you finish[3615] reading this [I]scroll, you will tie a stone to it and [a]throw it into the middle of the Euphrates,

64 and say, 'Just so shall Babylon sink down and [a]not rise again, because of the calamity that I am going to bring upon her; and they will become [b]exhausted.' " [c]Thus far are the words of Jeremiah.

Recount the Fall of Jerusalem

52 [a]Zedekiah was twenty-one years old[1121] when he became king,[4427] and he reigned[4427] eleven years in Jerusalem; and his mother's[517] name was [I][b]Hamutal the daughter of Jeremiah of [c]Libnah.

2 And he did[6213] [a]evil[7451] in the sight of the LORD like all that [b]Jehoiakim had done.[6213]

3 For through the [a]anger[639] of the LORD *this* came about in Jerusalem and Judah until[5647] He cast them out from His presence. And Zedekiah [b]rebelled[4775] against the king[4428] of Babylon.

4 [a]Now it came about in the ninth year of his reign, on the tenth day of the tenth month, that Nebuchadnezzar king of Babylon came, he and all his army,[2428] against Jerusalem, camped against it, and built a [b]siege wall all around [I]it.

5 [a]So the city was under siege until the eleventh year of King Zedekiah.

6 On the ninth day of the [a]fourth month the [b]famine was so severe[2388] in the city that there was no food for the people[5971] of the land.[776]

7 Then the city was [a]broken into, and all the [b]men[582] of war fled and went forth from the city at night[3915] by way[1870] of the gate between the two walls which *was* by the king's[4428] garden, though the Chaldeans were [I][c]all around the city. And they went by way of the Arabah.[6160]

8 But the army of the Chaldeans pursued the king and [a]overtook Zedekiah in the [I]plains[6160] of Jericho, and all his army was scattered from him.

9 Then they captured the king and [a]brought him up to the king of Babylon at [b]Riblah in the land of [c]Hamath; and he [I]passed sentence[4941] on him.

10 And the king of Babylon [a]slaughtered[7819] the sons[1121] of Zedekiah before his eyes, and he also slaughtered all the [I]princes[8269] of Judah in Riblah.

11 Then he [a]blinded the eyes of Zedekiah; and the king of Babylon bound him with bronze fetters and brought him to Babylon, and put him in prison until the day[3117] of his death.[4194]

12 [a]Now on the tenth day of the fifth month, which was the [b]nineteenth year of King Nebuchadnezzar, king of Babylon, [c]Nebuzaradan the captain of the bodyguard, [I]who was in the service of the king of Babylon, came to Jerusalem.

13 And he [a]burned[8313] the house[1004] of the LORD, the [b]king's house, and all the houses[1004] of Jerusalem; even every large house he burned with fire.

14 So all the army of the Chaldeans who *were* with the captain of the guard [a]broke down[5422] all the walls around Jerusalem.

15 Then Nebuzaradan the captain of the guard [a]carried away into exile[1540] some of the poorest of the people, the

59 [b]Jer. 28:1; 52:1
60 [I]Or, *book* [a]Is. 30:8; Jer. 30:2, 3; 36:2, 4, 32
62 [I]Lit., *spoken* [II]Lit., *from man even to beast* [a]Is. 13:19-22; 14:22, 23; Jer. 50:3, 13, 39, 40 [b]Jer. 51:43; Ezek. 35:9
63 [I]Or, *book* [a]Jer. 19:10, 11; Rev. 18:21
64 [a]Nah. 1:8, 9 [b]Jer. 51:58 [c]Job 31:40; Ps. 72:20

1 [I]Another reading is *Hamital* [a]2Kin. 24:18; 2Chr. 36:11 [b]2Kin. 22:31; 24:18 [c]Josh. 10:29; 2Kin. 8:22; Is. 37:8
2 [a]1Kin. 14:22; 2Kin. 24:19; 2Chr. 36:12 [b]Jer. 36:30,31
3 [a]2Kin. 24:20; Is. 3:1, 4, 5 [b]2Chr. 36:13; Ezek. 17:12-16
4 [I]Lit., *against it* [a]2Kin. 25:1; Jer. 39:1; Ezek. 24:1, 2; Zech. 8:19 [b]Jer. 32:24
5 [a]2Kin. 25:2
6 [a]Jer. 39:2 [b]2Kin. 25:3; Is. 3:1; Jer. 38:9; Ezek. 4:16; 5:16; 14:13
7 [I]Lit., *against the city on every side* [a]2Kin. 25:4; Jer. 39:2 [b]Jer. 39:4-7; 51:32 [c]Ezek. 33:21
8 [I]Lit., *Arabah* [a]Jer. 21:7; 32:4; 34:21; 37:17; 38:23
9 [I]Lit., *spoke judgments with* [a]2Kin. 25:6; Jer. 32:4; 39:5 [b]Num. 34:11; Jer. 39:5 [c]Num. 13:21; Josh. 13:5
10 [I]Or, *commanders* [a]2Kin. 25:7; Jer. 22:30; 39:6
11 [a]Jer. 39:7; Ezek. 12:13
12 [I]Lit., *stood before the king* [a]2Kin. 25:8-21; Zech. 7:5; 8:19 [b]2Kin. 24:12; 25:8; Jer. 52:29 [c]Jer. 39:9
13 [a]1Kin. 9:8; 2Kin. 25:9; 2Chr. 36:19; Ps. 74:6-8; 79:1; Is. 64:10, 11; Lam. 2:7; Mic. 3:12 [b]Jer. 39:8
14 [a]2Kin. 25:10; Neh. 1:3
15 [a]2Kin. 25:11

rest[3499] of the people who were left[7604] in the city, the [I][b]deserters[5307] who had deserted to the king of Babylon, and the rest[3499] of the artisans.[527]

16 But [a]Nebuzaradan the captain of the guard left[7604] some of the poorest of the land to be vinedressers and [I]plowmen.[3009]

17 Now the bronze [a]pillars which belonged to the house of the LORD and the [b]stands and the bronze [c]sea, which were in the house of the LORD, the Chaldeans broke in pieces[7665] and carried[5375] all their bronze to Babylon.

18 And they also took away the [a]pots, the shovels, the snuffers, the basins, the [I]pans,[3709] and all the bronze vessels which were used in *temple* service.[8334]

19 The captain of the guard also took away the [a]bowls,[5592] the firepans, the basins, the pots, the lampstands, the [I]pans and the libation bowls, what was fine gold and what was fine silver.

20 The two pillars, the one sea, and the twelve bronze bulls that were under [I]the sea, *and* the stands, which King Solomon had made[6213] for the house of the LORD—the bronze of all these vessels was [a]beyond weight.

21 As for the pillars, the [a]height of each pillar was eighteen [I]cubits, and [II]it was twelve cubits in [b]circumference and four fingers in thickness, *and* hollow.

22 Now a [a]capital of bronze was on it; and the height of each capital was five cubits, with network and [b]pomegranates upon the capital all around, all of bronze. And the second pillar was like these, including pomegranates.

23 And there were ninety-six [I]exposed pomegranates; all [a]the pomegranates *numbered* a hundred on the network all around.

24 Then the captain of the guard took [a]Seraiah the chief[7218] priest[3548] and [b]Zephaniah the second priest, with the three [I][c]officers[8104] of the temple.

25 He also took from the city one official[5631] who was overseer[6496] of the men of war, and seven [I]of the [a]king's advisers who were found in the city, and the scribe[5608] of the commander[8269] of the army[6635] who mustered[6633] the people of the land, and sixty men[376] of the people of the land who were found in the midst of the city.

26 And Nebuzaradan the captain of the guard took them and [a]brought them to the king of Babylon at Riblah.

27 Then the king of Babylon [a]struck[5221] them down and put them to death[4191] at Riblah in the land[127] of Hamath. So Judah was [b]led away into exile from its land.

28 These are the people whom [a]Nebuchadnezzar carried away[1540] into exile: in the [I]seventh year 3,023 Jews;

29 in the eighteenth year of Nebuchadnezzar 832 persons[5315] from Jerusalem;

30 in the twenty-third year of Nebuchadnezzar, [a]Nebuzaradan the captain of the guard carried into exile 745 Jewish people; there were 4,600 persons in all.

31 [a]Now it came about in the thirty-seventh year of the exile[1546] of Jehoiachin king of Judah, in the twelfth month, on the twenty-fifth of the month, that [I]Evil-merodach king of Babylon, in the *first* year of his reign,[4438] [II][b]showed favor[5375] to Jehoiachin king of Judah and brought him out of prison.

32 [a]Then he spoke[1696] kindly to him and set his throne[3678] above the thrones of the kings[4428] who *were* with him in Babylon.

33 So [I]Jehoiachin [a]changed his prison clothes, and [II][b]had his meals in [III]the king's presence regularly[8548] all the days[3117] of his life.[2416]

34 And for his allowance, a [a]regular[8548] allowance was given him by the king of Babylon, a daily[3117] portion[1697] all the days of his life until the day of his death.

15 [I]Lit., *fallers who had fallen* [b]Jer. 39:9
16 [I]Or, *unpaid laborers* [a]2Kin. 25:12; Jer. 39:10; 40:2-6
17 [a]1Kin. 7:15-22; 2Kin. 25:13; Jer. 27:19-22; 52:20-23 [b]1Kin. 7:27-37 [c]1Kin. 7:23-26
18 [I]Or, *spoons for incense* [a]Ex. 27:3; 1Kin. 7:40, 45; 2Kin. 25:14
19 [I]Or, *spoons for incense* [a]1Kin. 7:49, 50; 2Kin. 25:15
20 [I]So Gr. and Syriac; Heb. omits *the sea* [a]1Kin. 7:47; 2Kin. 25:16
21 [I]I.e., One cubit equals approx. 18 in. [II]Lit., *a line of 12 cubits would encircle it* [a]1Kin. 7:15; 2Kin. 25:17; 2Chr. 3:15
22 [a]1Kin. 7:16; 2Kin. 25:17 [b]1Kin. 7:20,42
23 [I]Lit., *windward* [a]1Kin. 7:20
24 [I]Lit., *keepers of the door* [a]2Kin. 25:18; 1Chr. 6:14; Ezra 7:1 [b]2Kin. 25:18; Jer. 21:1; 29:25, 29; 37:3 [c]1Chr. 9:19; Jer. 35:4
25 [I]Lit., *men of those seeing the king's face* [a]2Kin. 25:19; Esth. 1:14
26 [a]2Kin. 25:20
27 [a]2Kin. 25:21; Ezek. 8:11-18 [b]Is. 6:11, 12; 27:10; 32:13, 14; Jer. 13:19; 20:4; 25:9-11; 39:9; Ezek. 33:28; Mic. 4:10
28 [I]Or possibly, *seventeenth* [a]2Kin. 24:2, 3, 12-16; 2Chr. 36:20; Ezra 2:1; Neh. 7:6; Dan. 1:1-3
30 [a]2Kin. 25:11; Jer. 39:9
31 [I]Or, *Awil-Marduk* ("Man of Marduk") [II]Lit., *lifted up the head of* [a]2Kin. 25:27 [b]Gen. 40:13, 20; Ps. 3:3; 27:6
32 [a]2Kin. 25:28
33 [I]Lit., *he* [II]Lit., *ate* [III]Lit., *his presence* [a]Gen. 41:14, 42; 2Kin. 25:29 [b]2Sam. 9:7, 13; 1Kin. 2:7
34 [a]2Sam. 9:10; 2Kin. 25:30

THE LAMENTATIONS

of Jeremiah

Lamentations is the work of one who had a broken heart. If, as has been the traditional view, Jeremiah was the author, it serves as a supplement to his longer work. Certainly the author was a witness to the destruction of Jerusalem and its aftermath in 586 B.C., and the book is largely comprised of elegies for Jerusalem. The author alternates between horrifying accounts of the destruction of the city and the suffering of its inhabitants, descriptions and confessions of the sins which caused it, appeals for divine help, and the holding out of hope because of God's great mercy. The overall tone is melancholy. In the midst of the gloom, the author framed the first four chapters in a beautiful literary device called an acrostic. Chapters 1, 2, and 4 each have twenty-two verses, corresponding to the twenty-two letters of the Hebrew alphabet, and the first word of each verse begins with a different letter in order through the alphabet. Chapter 3 does the same thing in blocks of three verses, for a total of sixty-six. Although chapter 5 also has twenty-two verses, no acrostic is present. To this day Jews use Lamentations in their religious calendar to mourn the destruction of Jerusalem.

The Sorrows of Zion

1 How [a]lonely sits the city
That was [b]full of people![5971]
She has become[1961] like a
[c]widow
Who was *once* [d]great among the
nations![1471]
She who was a princess[8282]
among the [I]provinces
Has become a [e]forced laborer!
2 She [a]weeps bitterly in the
night,[3915]
And her tears are on her cheeks;
She has none to comfort[5162] her
Among all her [b]lovers.[157]
All her friends[7453] have [c]dealt
treacherously[898] with her;
They have become her enemies.
3 [a]Judah has gone into exile[1540]
[I]under affliction,
And [I]under [II]harsh servitude;[5656]
She dwells [b]among the
nations,[1471]
But she has found no rest;
All [c]her pursuers have overtaken
her
In the midst of [III]distress.
4 The roads[1870] [I]of Zion are in
mourning
Because [a]no one comes to the
appointed feasts.[4150]
All her gates are [b]desolate;[8076]
Her priests[3548] are groaning,
Her [c]virgins[1330] are afflicted,
And she herself [II]is [d]bitter.
5 Her adversaries have become
[I]her masters,[7218]
Her enemies [II]prosper;
For the LORD has [a]caused her
grief
Because of the multitude of her
transgressions;[6588]
Her little ones have gone
away
As captives[7628] before the
adversary.
6 And all her [a]majesty[1926]
Has departed from the daughter
of Zion;
Her princes[8269] have become
like bucks
That have found no pasture;
And they have [I][b]fled without
strength
Before the pursuer.
7 In the days[3117] of her affliction
and homelessness
[a]Jerusalem remembers[2142] all
her precious things

1 [I]Or, *districts* [a]Is. 3:26 [b]Is. 22:2 [c]Is. 54:4 [d]1Kin. 4:21; Ezra 4:20; Jer. 31:7 [e]2Kin. 23:35; Jer. 40:9

2 [a]Ps. 6:6; 77:2-6; Lam. 1:16 [b]Jer. 2:25; 3:1; 22:20-22 [c]Job 19:13, 14; Ps. 31:11; Mic. 7:5

3 [I]Or, *by reason of* [II]Lit., *great* [III]Or, *narrow places* [a]Jer. 13:19 [b]Lev. 26:39; Deut. 28:64-67 [c]2Kin. 25:4, 5

4 [I]Or, *to* [II]Or, *suffers bitterly* [a]Is. 24:4-6; Lam. 2:6, 7 [b]Jer. 9:11; 10:22 [c]Lam. 2:10, 21 [d]Joel 1:8-13

5 [I]Lit., *head* [II]Or, *are at ease* [a]Ps. 90:7, 8; Ezek. 8:17, 18; 9:9, 10

6 [I]Lit., *gone* [a]Jer. 13:18 [b]2Kin. 25:4, 5

7 [a]Ps. 42:4; 77:5-9

1:1 See the introduction to Lamentations.

That were from the days of old[6924]
When her people fell[5307] into the hand[3027] of the adversary,
And [b]no one helped her.
The adversaries saw[7200] her,
They [c]mocked at her [I]ruin.
8 Jerusalem sinned[2398] [a]greatly,[2399]
Therefore [b]she has become an unclean thing.
All who honored her despise her
Because they have seen[7200] her nakedness;[6172]
Even [c]she herself groans and turns away.[7725]
9 Her [a]uncleanness[2932] was in her skirts;
She [I]did not consider[2142] her [b]future;
Therefore she has [II][c]fallen astonishingly;[6382]
[d]She has no comforter.[5162]
"[e]See,[7200] O LORD, my affliction,
For the enemy has [f]magnified himself!"
10 The adversary has stretched out his hand
Over all her precious things,
For she has seen the [a]nations enter her sanctuary,[4720]
The ones whom Thou didst command[6680]
That they should [b]not enter into Thy congregation.[6951]
11 All her people groan [a]seeking bread;
They have given their precious things for food
To [b]restore[7725] their [I]lives[5315] themselves.
"See, O LORD, and look,
For I am [c]despised."[2151]
12 "Is [a]it nothing to all you who pass this way?
Look and see if there is any [I]pain like my [I]pain
Which was severely dealt out to me,
Which the [b]LORD inflicted on the day[3117] of His [c]fierce anger.[639]

7 [I]Lit., *cessation* [b]Jer. 37:7; Lam. 4:17 [c]Ps. 79:4; Jer. 48:27
8 [a]Is. 59:2-13; Lam. 1:5, 20 [b]Lam. 1:17 [c]Lam. 1:11, 21, 22
9 [I]Lit., *did not remember her later end* [II]Lit., *come down* [a]Jer. 2:34; Ezek. 24:13 [b]Deut. 32:29; Is. 47:7 [c]Is. 3:8; Jer. 13:17, 18 [d]Eccl. 4:1; Jer. 16:7 [e]Ps. 25:18; 119:153 [f]Ps. 74:23; Zeph. 2:10
10 [a]Ps. 74:4-8; Is. 64:10, 11; Jer. 51:51 [b]Deut. 23:3
11 [I]Lit., *soul* [a]Jer. 38:9; 52:6 [b]1Sam. 30:12 [c]Jer. 15:19
12 [I]Or, *sorrow* [a]Jer. 18:16; 48:27 [b]Jer. 30:23, 24 [c]Is. 13:13; Jer. 4:8
13 [I]Or, *descended, overthrew* [II]Or, *Sick* [a]Job 30:30; Ps. 22:14; Hab. 3:16 [b]Job 19:6; Ps. 66:11 [c]Jer. 44:6
14 [I]Lit., *stumble* [a]Prov. 5:22; Is. 47:6 [b]Jer. 28:13, 14 [c]Jer. 32:3, 5; Ezek. 25:4, 7
15 [I]Or, *feast* [a]Is. 41:2; Jer. 13:24; 37:10 [b]Jer. 6:11; 18:21 [c]Mal. 4:3
16 [I]Lit., *My eye, my eye* [a]Jer. 14:17; Lam. 2:11, 18; 3:48, 49 [b]Ps. 69:20; Eccl. 4:1; Lam. 1:2
17 [a]Is. 1:15; Jer. 4:31 [b]2Kin. 24:2-4; Jer. 12:9 [c]Lam. 1:8
18 [I]Lit., *mouth* [II]Or, *sorrow* [a]Ps. 119:75; Jer. 12:1 [b]1Sam. 12:14, 15; Jer. 4:17 [c]Lam. 1:12 [d]Deut. 28:32, 41

13 "From on high He sent fire into my [a]bones,[6106]
And it [I]prevailed *over them;*
He has spread a [b]net for my feet;
He has turned me back;
He has made me [c]desolate,
[II]Faint all day long.
14 "The [a]yoke of my transgressions is bound;
By His hand they are knit together;
They have [b]come[5927] upon my neck;
He has made my strength [I]fail;[3782]
The Lord[136] [c]has given me into the hands[3027]
Of *those against whom* I am not able to stand.
15 "The [a]Lord has rejected all my strong[47] men
In my midst;[7130]
He has called[7121] an appointed [I]time against me
To crush[7665] my [b]young men;
The Lord has [c]trodden *as in* a wine press
The virgin[1330] daughter of Judah.
16 "For these things I [a]weep;
[I]My eyes run down with water;
Because far from me is a [b]comforter,
One who restores my soul;
My children[1121] are desolate
Because the enemy has prevailed."
17 Zion [a]stretches out her hands;
There is no one to comfort her;
The LORD has [b]commanded[6680] concerning Jacob
That the ones round about him should be his adversaries;
[c]Jerusalem has become an unclean thing among them.
18 "The LORD is [a]righteous;[6662]
For I have [b]rebelled[4784] against His [I]command;[6310]
Hear[8085] now,[4994] all peoples,
And [c]behold my [II]pain;
[d]My virgins and my young men
Have gone into captivity.

19 "I [a]called to my lovers, *but* they
deceived me;
My [b]priests and my elders[2205]
perished[1478] in the city,
While they sought food to
[c]restore [I]their strength
themselves.[5315]
20 "See, O LORD, for I am in
distress;
My [Ia]spirit[4578] is greatly
troubled;
My heart[3820] is overturned[2015]
within[7130] me,
For I have been very
[b]rebellious.
In the street the sword[2719]
[II]slays;
In the house[1004] it is like
death.[4194]
21 "They have heard[8085] that I
[a]groan;
There is no one to comfort me;
All my enemies have heard of
my [I]calamity;[7451]
They are [b]glad that Thou hast
done[6213] *it*.
Oh, that Thou wouldst bring the
day which Thou hast
proclaimed,
That they may become
[c]like me.
22 "Let all their wickedness[7451]
come before Thee;
And [a]deal with them as Thou
hast dealt with me
For all my transgressions;
For my groans are many, and
my heart is faint."

God's Anger over Israel

2 How the Lord[136] has [a]covered
the daughter of Zion
With a cloud in His anger![639]
He has [b]cast from heaven[8064] to
earth[776]
The [c]glory[8597] of Israel,
And has not remembered[2142] His
[d]footstool
In the day[3117] of His anger.

19 [I]Lit., *their soul* [a]Job 19:13-19; Lam. 1:2 [b]Jer. 14:15; Lam. 2:20 [c]Lam. 1:11

20 [I]Lit., *inward parts are in ferment* [II]Lit., *bereaves* [a]Is. 16:11; Lam. 2:11 [b]Jer. 14:20

21 [I]Lit., *evil* [a]Lam. 1:4, 8, 22 [b]Ps. 35:15; Jer. 50:11; Lam. 2:15 [c]Is. 14:5, 6; 47:6, 11; Jer. 30:16

22 [a]Neh. 4:4, 5; Ps. 137:7, 8

1 [a]Ezek. 30:18 [b]Is. 14:12-15; Ezek. 28:14-16 [c]Is. 64:11 [d]Ps. 99:5; 132:7

2 [a]Ps. 21:9; Lam. 3:43 [b]Lam. 2:5; Mic. 5:11, 14 [c]Is. 25:12; 26:5 [d]Ps. 89:39, 40; Is. 43:28

3 [I]Lit., *Every horn* [a]Ps. 75:5, 10; Jer. 48:25 [b]Ps. 74:11; Jer. 21:4, 5 [c]Is. 42:25; Jer. 21:14

4 [a]Job 6:4; 16:13; Lam. 3:12, 13 [b]Ezek. 24:25 [c]Is. 42:25; Jer. 7:20

5 [a]Jer. 30:14 [b]Lam. 2:2 [c]Jer. 52:13; Lam. 2:2 [d]Jer. 9:17-20

6 [I]Lit., *booth* [II]Or, *feast* [a]Jer. 52:13 [b]Jer. 17:27; Lam. 1:4; Zeph. 3:18

2 The Lord has [a]swallowed up;[1104]
He has not spared
All the habitations[4999] of Jacob.
In His wrath[5678] He has
[b]thrown down[2040]
The strongholds of the daughter
of Judah;
He has [c]brought *them* down to
the ground;[776]
He has [d]profaned the
kingdom[4467] and its
princes.[8269]
3 In fierce[2750] anger He has cut
off
[I]All the [a]strength of Israel;
He has [b]drawn[7725] back His right
hand
From before the enemy.
And He has [c]burned in Jacob like
a flaming fire
Consuming round about.
4 He has bent His [a]bow like an
enemy,
He has set[5324] His right hand like
an adversary
And slain[2026] all that were
[b]pleasant to the eye;
In the tent[168] of the daughter
of Zion
He has [c]poured out[8210] His wrath
like fire.
5 The Lord has become like an
[a]enemy.
He has [b]swallowed up[1104] Israel;
He has swallowed up all its
[c]palaces;[759]
He has destroyed[7843] its
strongholds
And [d]multiplied in the daughter
of Judah
Mourning and moaning.
6 And He has violently[2554] treated
His [I]tabernacle like a garden
booth;
He has [a]destroyed His appointed
[II]meeting place;
The LORD has [b]caused to be
forgotten
The appointed feast[4150] and
sabbath[7676] in Zion,

2:1 See the introduction to Lamentations.

And He has [c]despised[5006]
king[4428] and priest[3548]
In the indignation[2195] of His
anger.
7 The Lord has [a]rejected His
altar,[4196]
He has abandoned His
sanctuary;[4720]
He [b]has delivered into the
hand[3027] of the enemy
The walls of her palaces.
They have made a [c]noise in the
house[1004] of the LORD
As in the day of an appointed
feast.
8 The LORD [I]determined[2803] to
destroy[7843]
The wall of the daughter of
Zion.
He has [a]stretched out a line,
He has not restrained[7725] His
hand from [II]destroying;[1104]
And He has [b]caused rampart[2426]
and wall to lament;
They have languished together.
9 Her [a]gates have sunk into the
ground,
He has destroyed[6] and
broken[7665] her bars.
Her king and her princes are
among the nations;[1471]
The [b]law[8451] is no more;
Also, her prophets find
[c]No vision[2377] from the LORD.
10 The elders[2205] of the daughter
of Zion
[a]Sit on the ground, they
[b]are silent.
They have thrown[5927] [c]dust[6083]
on their heads;[7218]
They have girded themselves
with [d]sackcloth.
The [e]virgins[1330] of Jerusalem
Have bowed their heads to the
ground.
11 My [a]eyes fail[3615] because of
tears,
My [Ib]spirit[4578] is greatly
troubled;
My [IIc]heart is poured out on the
earth,
[d]Because of the [III]destruction of
the daughter of my
people,[5971]
When [e]little ones and infants faint
In the streets of the city.
12 They say[559] to their mothers,[517]
"[a]Where is grain and wine?"
As they faint like a wounded[2491]
man
In the streets of the city,
As their [b]life[5315] is poured out
On their mothers' bosom.
13 How shall I admonish[5749] you?
To what [a]shall I compare
you,
O daughter of Jerusalem?
To what shall I liken you as I
comfort[5162] you,
O [b]virgin[1330] daughter of Zion?
For your [I]ruin[7667] is as vast as
the sea;
Who can [c]heal you?
14 Your [a]prophets have seen[2372] for
you
False[7723] and foolish *visions;*
And they have not [b]exposed
your iniquity[5771]
So as to restore[7725] you from
captivity,[7622]
But they have [c]seen for you
false[7723] and misleading
[I]oracles.[4864]
15 All who pass along the way
[a]Clap[5606] their hands[3709] *in
derision* at you;
They [b]hiss and shake[5128] their
heads[7218]
At the daughter of Jerusalem,
"Is this the city of which they
said,[559]
'[c]The perfection[3632] of beauty,
[d]A joy to all the earth'?"
16 All [a]your enemies
Have opened their mouths[6310]
wide against you;
They hiss and [b]gnash[2786] *their*
teeth.
They say, "We have [c]swallowed
her up!
Surely this is the [d]day for which
we waited;
We have reached *it,* we have
seen[7200] *it.*"

6 [c]Lam. 4:16
7 [a]Ps. 78:59-61; Is. 64:11; Ezek. 7:20-22 [b]Jer. 33:4, 5; 52:13 [c]Ps. 74:3-8
8 [I]Lit., *thought* [II]Lit., *swallowing up* [a]2Kin. 21:13; Is. 34:11; Amos 7:7-9 [b]Is. 3:26; Jer. 14:2
9 [a]Neh. 1:3 [b]Hos. 3:4 [c]Jer. 14:14; 23:16; Ezek. 7:26
10 [a]Job 2:13; Is. 3:26; 47:1 [b]Amos 8:3 [c]Job 2:12; Ezek. 27:30 [d]Is. 15:3; Jon. 3:6-8 [e]Lam. 1:4
11 [I]Lit., *inward parts are in ferment* [II]Lit., *liver* [III]Lit., *breaking* [a]Lam. 1:16; 3:48, 51 [b]Jer. 4:19 [c]Job 16:13 [d]Is. 22:4; Lam. 4:10 [e]Jer. 44:7; Lam. 2:19
12 [a]Jer. 5:17 [b]Job 30:16; Ps. 42:4; 62:8
13 [I]Lit., *breaking* [a]Lam. 1:12 [b]Is. 37:22 [c]Jer. 8:22; 30:12-15
14 [I]Lit., *burdens* [a]Jer. 23:25-29; 29:8, 9 [b]Is. 58:1; Ezek. 23:36; Mic. 3:8 [c]Jer. 23:36; Ezek. 22:25, 28
15 [a]Job 27:23; Ezek. 25:6 [b]Ps. 22:7; Is. 37:22; Jer. 18:16; 19:8; Zeph. 2:15 [c]Ps. 50:2 [d]Ps. 48:2
16 [a]Job 16:10; Ps. 22:13; Lam. 3:46 [b]Job 16:9; Ps. 35:16; 37:12 [c]Ps. 56:2; 124:3; Jer. 51:34 [d]Obad. 12-15

17 The LORD has [a]done6213 what He purposed;2161
He has accomplished1214 His word565
Which He commanded6608 from days3117 of old.6924
He has thrown down [b]without sparing,
And He has caused the enemy to [c]rejoice over you;
He has [d]exalted the [I]might of your adversaries.
18 Their [a]heart3820 cried out to the Lord,
"O [b]wall of the daughter of Zion,
Let *your* [c]tears run down like a river day3119 and night;3915
Give yourself no relief;
Let [I]your eyes have no rest.
19 "Arise, cry aloud in the [a]night
At the beginning7218 of the night watches;
[b]Pour out8210 your heart like water
Before the presence of the Lord;
Lift up5375 your hands to Him
For the [c]life5315 of your little ones
Who are [d]faint because of hunger
At the head7218 of every street."
20 See,7200 O LORD, and look!
With [a]whom hast Thou dealt thus?
Should women802 [b]eat their [I]offspring,
The little ones who were [II]born healthy?
Should [c]priest and prophet5030 be slain2026
In the sanctuary of the Lord?
21 On the ground in the streets
Lie [a]young and old,2205
My [b]virgins and my young men
Have fallen5307 by the sword.2719
Thou hast slain *them* in the day of Thine anger,
Thou hast slaughtered, [c]not sparing.
22 Thou didst call7121 as in the day of an appointed feast
My [a]terrors4032 on every side;
And there was [b]no one who escaped or survived8300
In the day of the LORD's anger.
Those [c]whom I [I]bore2946 and reared,
My enemy annihilated3615 them.

17 [I]Lit., *horn* [a]Jer. 4:28 [b]Lam. 2:1, 2; Ezek. 5:11; 7:8, 9; 8:18 [c]Ps. 35:24, 26; 89:42; Is. 14:29 [d]Deut. 28:43, 44; Lam. 1:5
18 [I]Lit., *the daughter of your eye* [a]Ps. 119:145; Hos. 7:14 [b]Lam. 2:8; Hab. 2:11 [c]Ps. 119:136; Jer. 9:1; Lam. 1:2, 16; 3:48, 49
19 [a]Ps. 42:3; Is. 26:9 [b]1Sam. 1:15; Ps. 42:4; 62:8 [c]Lam. 2:11 [d]Is. 51:20
20 [I]Lit., *fruit* [II]Or, *tenderly cared for* [a]Ex. 32:11; Deut. 9:26 [b]Jer. 19:9; Lam. 4:10 [c]Ps. 78:64; Jer. 14:15; 23:11, 12
21 [a]2Chr. 36:17; Jer. 6:11 [b]Ps. 78:62, 63 [c]Jer. 13:14; Zech. 11:6
22 [I]Lit., *bore healthy* or, *tenderly cared for* [a]Ps. 31:13; Is. 24:17; Jer. 6:25 [b]Jer. 11:11 [c]Jer. 16:2-4; 44:7

Jeremiah Shares Israel's Affliction

3 ⊶ I am the man1397 who has [a]seen7200 affliction
Because of the rod7626 of His wrath.5678
2 He has driven me and made me walk
In [a]darkness2822 and not in light.216
3 Surely against me He has [a]turned7725 His hand3027
Repeatedly all the day.3117
4 He has caused my [a]flesh1320 and my skin5785 to waste away,
He has [b]broken7665 my bones.6106
5 He has [a]besieged and encompassed5362 me with [b]bitterness7219 and hardship.
6 In [a]dark places4285 He has made me dwell,
Like those who have long5769 been dead.4191
7 He has [a]walled *me* in so that I cannot go out;
He has made my [I][b]chain heavy.3513
8 Even when I cry2199 out and call for help,
He [a]shuts out my prayer.8605
9 He has [a]blocked my ways1870 with hewn1496 stone;
He has made my paths crooked.5753
10 He is to me like a bear lying in wait,
Like a lion in secret places.
11 He has turned aside my ways and [a]torn me to pieces;
He has made7760 me desolate.8076
12 He [a]bent His bow

1 [a]Ps. 88:7, 15, 16
2 [a]Job 30:26; Is. 59:9; Jer. 4:23
3 [a]Ps. 38:2; Is. 5:25
4 [a]Ps. 31:9, 10; 38:2-8; 102:3-5 [b]Ps. 51:8; Is. 38:13
5 [a]Job 19:8 [b]Jer. 23:15; Lam. 3:19
6 [a]Ps. 88:5, 6; 143:3
7 [I]Lit., *bronze piece* [a]Job 3:23; 19:8 [b]Jer. 40:4
8 [a]Job 30:20; Ps. 22:2
9 [a]Is. 63:17; Hos. 2:6
11 [a]Job 16:12, 13; Jer. 15:3; Hos. 6:1
12 [a]Ps. 7:12; Lam. 2:4

⊶ **3:1** See the introduction to Lamentations.

And [b]set[5324] me as a target for
the arrow.
13 He made the [I]arrows of His
[a]quiver
To enter into my [II]inward
parts.[3629]
14 I have become a [a]laughingstock
to all my people,[5971]
Their *mocking* [b]song all the day.
15 He has [a]filled me with bitterness,
He has made me drunk with
wormwood.[3939]
16 And He has [a]broken my teeth
with [b]gravel;
He has made me cower[3728] in
the [c]dust.
17 And my soul[5315] has been
rejected [a]from peace;
I have forgotten [I]happiness.[2896]
18 So I say,[559] "My strength[5331] has
perished,[6]
And *so has* my [a]hope[8431] from
the LORD."

Hope of Relief in God's Mercy

19 Remember my affliction and my
[I]wandering, the [a]wormwood
and bitterness.
20 Surely [a]my soul remembers[2142]
And is [b]bowed down within me.
21 This I recall to my mind,[3820]
Therefore I have [a]hope.[3176]
22 The LORD'S
[a]lovingkindnesses[2617] [I]indeed
never cease,[8552]
[b]For His compassions never
fail.[3615]
23 *They* are new [a]every morning;
Great is [b]Thy faithfulness.[530]
24 "The LORD is my [a]portion,"
says[559] my soul,
"Therefore I [b]have hope in Him."
25 The LORD is good[2896] to those
who [a]wait[6960] for Him,
To the [I]person who [b]seeks Him.
26 *It is* good that he [a]waits silently
For the salvation of the LORD.
27 *It is* good for a man that he
should bear[5375]
The yoke in his youth.
28 Let him [a]sit alone and be silent
Since He has laid *it* on him.
29 Let him [I]put his mouth[6310] in the
[a]dust,[6083]
Perhaps there is [b]hope.
30 Let him give his [a]cheek to
[I]the smiter;
Let him be filled with
reproach.[2781]
31 For the Lord[136] will [a]not reject
forever,[5769]
32 For if He causes grief,
Then He will have
[a]compassion[7355]
According to His abundant
lovingkindness.
33 For He [a]does not afflict
[I]willingly,[3820]
Or grieve the sons[1121] of men.[376]
34 To crush[1792] under His feet
All the prisoners of the
[I]land,[776]
35 To [I]deprive a man of [a]justice[4941]
In the presence of the Most
High,[5945]
36 To [I][a]defraud[5719] a man[120] in his
lawsuit—[7379]
Of these things the Lord does
not [II]approve.[7200]
37 Who is [I]there who speaks and
it [a]comes to pass,
Unless the Lord has
commanded[6680] *it*?
38 *Is it* not from the mouth of the
Most High
That [I][a]both good and ill[7451] go
forth?
39 Why should *any* living[2416]
[I]mortal, or *any* man,
Offer [a]complaint [II]in view of his
sins?[2399]

12 [b]Job 6:4; 7:20; Ps. 38:2
13 [I]Lit., *sons* [II]Lit., *kidneys* [a]Jer. 5:16
14 [a]Ps. 22:6, 7; 123:4; Jer. 20:7 [b]Job 30:9; Lam. 3:63
15 [a]Jer. 9:15
16 [a]Ps. 3:7; 58:6 [b]Prov. 20:17 [c]Jer. 6:26
17 [I]Lit., *good* [a]Is. 59:11; Jer. 12:12
18 [a]Job 17:15; Ezek. 37:11
19 [I]Or, *bitterness* [a]Jer. 9:15; Lam. 3:5, 15
20 [a]Job 21:6 [b]Ps. 42:5, 6, 11; 43:5; 44:25
21 [a]Ps. 130:7
22 [I]Or, *that we are not consumed* [a]Ps. 78:38; Jer. 3:12; 30:11 [b]Mal. 3:6
23 [a]Is. 33:2; Zeph. 3:5 [b]Heb. 10:23
24 [a]Ps. 16:5; 73:26 [b]Ps. 33:18
25 [I]Lit., *soul* [a]Ps. 27:14; Is. 25:9 [b]Is. 26:9
26 [a]Ps. 37:7
28 [a]Jer. 15:17
29 [I]Lit., *give* [a]Job 16:15; 40:4 [b]Jer. 31:17
30 [I]Lit., *his* [a]Job 16:10; Is. 50:6
31 [a]Ps. 77:7; 94:14; Is. 54:7-10
32 [a]Ps. 78:38; 106:43-45; Hos. 11:8
33 [I]Lit., *from His heart* [a]Ps. 119:67, 71, 75; Ezek. 33:11; Heb. 12:10
34 [I]Or, *earth*
35 [I]Or, *turn aside a man's case* [a]Ps. 140:12; Prov. 17:15
36 [I]Lit., *make crooked* [II]Lit., *see* [a]Jer. 22:3; Hab. 1:13
37 [I]Lit., *this* [a]Ps. 33:9-11
38 [I]Lit., *the evil things and the good* [a]Job 2:10; Is. 45:7; Jer. 32:42
39 [I]Or, *human being* [II]Or, *on the basis of* [a]Jer. 30:15; Mic. 7:9; Heb. 12:5, 6

3:22-24 Lamentations is the most melancholy book in the Prophets. The author was so overwhelmed by the destruction of Jerusalem, the sin which produced it, and the suffering which resulted that he found it difficult to be diverted from his somber mood. Yet, in the midst of the gloom, this passage sparkles as one of the most beautiful expressions of hope and trust in the O.T.

40 Let us [a]examine and probe our
ways,
And let us return[7725] to the
LORD.
41 We [a]lift up[5375] our heart
[I]and hands[3709]
Toward God[410] in heaven;[8064]
42 We have [a]transgressed[5060] and
rebelled,[4784]
Thou hast [b]not pardoned.[5545]
43 Thou hast covered *Thyself* with
[a]anger[639]
And [b]pursued us;
Thou hast slain[2026] *and* [c]hast
not spared.
44 Thou hast [a]covered Thyself with
a cloud[6051]
So that [b]no prayer can pass
through.[5674]
45 *Mere* [a]offscouring and refuse
Thou hast made us
In the midst[7130] of the peoples.
46 All our enemies have [a]opened
their mouths[6310] against
us.
47 [a]Panic[6343] and pitfall[6354] have
befallen us,
Devastation and destruction;
48 My [Ia]eyes run down with
streams of water
Because of the destruction of the
daughter of my people.
49 My eyes pour down
[a]unceasingly,[1820]
Without stopping,
50 Until the LORD [a]looks down
And sees[7200] from heaven.[8064]
51 My eyes bring pain to my
soul[5315]
Because of all the daughters of
my city.
52 My enemies [a]without cause
Hunted me down [b]like a bird;
53 They have silenced [I]me[2416]
[a]in the pit[953]
And have [IIb]placed a stone on
me.
54 Waters flowed [a]over my
head;[7218]
I said, "I am cut off!"[1504]

55 I [a]called on[7121] Thy name, O
LORD,
Out of the lowest pit.
56 Thou hast [a]heard[8085] my voice,
"[b]Do not hide Thine ear[241]
from my *prayer for* relief,[7309]
From my cry for help."
57 Thou didst [a]draw near when I
called on Thee;
Thou didst say,[559] "[b]Do not
fear!"[3372]
58 O Lord, Thou didst [a]plead[7378] my
soul's cause;
Thou hast [b]redeemed[1350] my
life.
59 O LORD, Thou hast [a]seen my
oppression;[5792]
[b]Judge[8199] my case.[4941]
60 Thou hast seen all their
vengeance,[5360]
All their [a]schemes[4284] against
me.
61 Thou hast heard their
[a]reproach, O LORD,
All their schemes against me.
62 The [a]lips[8193] of my assailants and
their whispering
Are against me all day long.
63 Look on their [a]sitting and their
rising;
[b]I am their mocking song.
64 Thou wilt [a]recompense[7725]
them, O LORD,
According to the work of their
hands.[3027]
65 Thou wilt give them [Ia]hardness
of heart,[3820]
Thy curse will be on them.
66 Thou wilt [a]pursue them in anger
and destroy[8045] them
From under the [b]heavens of the
LORD!

Distress of the Siege Described

4 🔑 How [a]dark the gold has become,
How the pure gold has changed!
The sacred[6944] stones are
poured out[8210]

40 aPs. 119:59; 139:23, 24; 2Cor. 13:5
41 ILit., *toward our* aPs. 25:1; 28:2; 141:2
42 aNeh. 9:26; Jer. 14:20; Dan. 9:5 b2Kin. 24:4; Jer. 5:7, 9
43 aLam. 2:21 bPs. 83:15; Lam. 3:66 cLam. 2:2, 17, 21
44 aPs. 97:2 bLam. 3:8; Zech. 7:13
45 a1Cor. 4:13
46 aJob 30:9, 10; Ps. 22:6-8; Lam. 2:16
47 aIs. 24:17, 18; Jer. 48:43,44
48 ILit., *eye brings* aPs. 119:136; Jer. 9:1, 18; Lam. 1:16; 2:11, 18
49 aPs. 77:2; Jer. 14:17
50 aPs. 80:14; Is. 63:15; Lam. 5:1
52 aPs. 35:7, 19 b1Sam. 26:20; Ps. 11:1; 124:7
53 ILit., *my life* IIOr, *cast stones* aJer. 37:16; 38:6, 9 bDan. 6:17
54 aPs. 69:2; Jon. 2:3-5
55 aPs. 130:1; Jon. 2:2
56 aJob 34:28 bPs. 55:1
57 aPs. 145:18 bIs. 41:10, 14
58 aJer. 50:34 bPs. 34:22
59 aJer. 18:19, 20 bPs. 26:1; 43:1
60 aJer. 11:19
61 aPs. 74:18; 89:50; Lam. 5:1; Zeph. 2:8
62 aPs. 59:7, 12; 140:3; Ezek. 36:3
63 aPs. 139:2 bJob 30:9; Lam. 3:14
64 aPs. 28:4; Jer. 51:6, 24, 56
65 IOr, *insolence* aEx. 14:8; Deut. 2:30; Is. 6:10
66 aLam. 3:43 bPs. 8:3
1 aEzek. 7:19-22

🔑 **4:1** See the introduction to Lamentations.

At the [I]corner[7218] of every
street.
2 The precious sons[1121] of Zion,
Weighed against fine gold,
How they are regarded[2803] as
[a]earthen[2789] jars,
The work of a potter's hands![3027]
3 Even [a]jackals[8577] offer the
breast,
They nurse their young;
But the daughter of my
people[5971] has become
[b]cruel
Like [c]ostriches in the
wilderness.
4 The [a]tongue of the infant cleaves
To the roof of its mouth because
of [b]thirst;
The little ones [c]ask[7592] for bread,
But no one breaks *it* for them.
5 Those who ate [a]delicacies
Are desolate[8074] in the streets;
Those [I]reared in purple
Embrace ash pits.
6 For the [I]iniquity[5771] of the
daughter of my people
Is greater than the [IIa]sin[2401] of
Sodom,
Which was [b]overthrown[2015] as
in a moment,
And no hands were [III]turned[2342]
toward her.
7 Her [I]consecrated ones[5139] were
[a]purer[2141] than snow,
They were whiter than milk;
They were more ruddy[119] *in*
[II]body[6106] than corals,
Their polishing *was* like [IIIb]lapis
lazuli.
8 Their appearance[8389] is
[a]blacker[2821] than soot,[7815]
They are not recognized in the
streets;
Their [b]skin[5785] is shriveled on
their bones,[6106]
It is withered,[3001] it has
become[1961] like wood.
9 Better[2896] are those [Ia]slain[2491]
with the sword[2719]
Than those [I]slain with hunger;
For they [IIb]pine[2100] away, being
stricken
For lack of the fruits of [III]the
field.[7704]
10 The hands of compassionate
women[802]
[a]Boiled[1310] their own children;
They became [b]food for them
Because of the destruction of the
daughter of my people.
11 The LORD has [a]accomplished[3615]
His wrath,
He has poured out His fierce
anger;[639]
And He has [b]kindled a fire in
Zion
Which has consumed its
foundations.[3247]
12 The kings[4428] of the earth[776] did
not believe,[539]
Nor *did* any of [a]the inhabitants
of the world,[8398]
That the adversary and the
enemy
Could [b]enter the gates of
Jerusalem.
13 Because of the sins[2399] of her
[a]prophets[5030]
And the iniquities[5771] of her
priests,[3548]
Who have shed[8210] in her
midst[7130]
The [b]blood[1818] of the righteous,
14 They wandered, [a]blind, in the
streets;
They were defiled with [b]blood
So that no one could touch[5060]
their [c]garments.
15 "Depart![5493] [a]Unclean!"[2931]
[I]they cried[7121] of themselves.
"Depart, depart, do not touch!"
So they [b]fled and wandered;
Men among the nations[1471]
said,[559]
"They shall not continue to
dwell[1481] *with us.*"
16 The presence of the LORD has
scattered them;
He will not continue to regard
them.
They did not [Ia]honor the priests,
They did not favor[2603] the
elders.[2205]
17 Yet our eyes failed;

1 [I]Lit., *head*
2 [a]Is. 30:14; Jer. 19:1, 11
3 [a]Is. 13:22; 34:13 [b]Is. 49:15; Ezek. 5:10 [c]Job 39:14-17
4 [a]Ps. 22:15 [b]Jer. 14:3 [c]Lam. 2:12
5 [I]Lit., *established in crimson* [a]Jer. 6:2; Amos 6:3-7
6 [I]Or, *punishment for iniquity* [II]Or, *punishment for sin* [III]Or, *wrung over her* [a]Gen. 19:24 [b]Gen. 19:25; Jer. 20:16
7 [I]Or, *Nazirites* [II]Lit., *bones* [III]Heb., *sappir* [a]Ps. 51:7 [b]Ex. 24:10; Job 28:16
8 [a]Job 30:30; Lam. 5:10 [b]Job 19:20; Ps. 102:3-5
9 [I]Lit., *pierced* [II]Lit., *flow away* [III]Lit., *my fields* [a]Jer. 16:4 [b]Lev. 26:39; Ezek. 24:23
10 [a]Lev. 26:29; Deut. 28:57; 2Kin. 6:29; Jer. 19:9; Lam. 2:20; Ezek. 5:10 [b]Deut. 28:53-55
11 [a]Jer. 7:20; Lam. 2:17; Ezek. 22:31 [b]Deut. 32:22; Jer. 17:27
12 [a]Deut. 29:24 [b]Jer. 21:13
13 [a]Jer. 5:31; 6:13; Lam. 2:14; Ezek. 22:26-28 [b]Jer. 2:30; 26:8, 9; Matt. 23:31
14 [a]Deut. 28:28, 29; Is. 29:10; 56:10; 59:9, 10 [b]Is. 1:15 [c]Jer. 2:34
15 [I]Or, *they* (men) *cried to them* [a]Lev. 13:45, 46 [b]Jer. 49:5
16 [I]Lit., *lift up the faces of* [a]Is. 9:14-16; Jer. 52:24-27

Looking for [I]help was [a]useless.
In our watching we have
watched
For a [b]nation[1471] that could not
save.[3467]
18 They [a]hunted our steps
So that we could not walk in our
streets;
Our [b]end drew near,
Our days[3117] were [I]finished
For our end had come.
19 Our pursuers were [a]swifter
Than the eagles of the sky.[8064]
They chased us on the
mountains;
They waited in ambush for us
in the wilderness.
20 The [a]breath[7307] of our
nostrils,[639] the [b]LORD's
anointed,[4899]
Was [c]captured in their pits,[7825]
Of whom we had said, "Under
his [d]shadow
We shall live[2421] among the
nations."
21 Rejoice and be glad, O daughter
of [a]Edom,
Who dwells in the land[776] of
Uz;
But the [b]cup will come
around[5674] to you as well,
You will become drunk and make
yourself naked.
22 *The punishment* of your iniquity
has been [a]completed[8552] O
daughter of Zion;
He will exile[1540] you no longer.
But He [b]will punish[6485] your
iniquity, O daughter of Edom;
He will expose[1540] your sins!

A Prayer for Mercy

5 Remember,[2142] O LORD, what has
befallen us;
Look, and see[7200] our
[a]reproach![2781]
2 Our inheritance[5159] has been
turned[2015] over to
[a]strangers,[2114]
Our [b]houses[1004] to aliens.[5237]
3 We have become orphans
[a]without a father,
Our mothers[517] are like widows.
4 [I]We have to pay for our drinking
[a]water,
Our wood comes *to us* at a
price.
5 [I]Our pursuers are at our necks;
We are worn out, there is
[a]no rest for us.
6 We have [I]submitted[3027] to
[a]Egypt *and* Assyria [II]to get
enough bread.
7 Our [a]fathers[1] sinned,[2398] *and* are
no more;
It is we who have borne their
iniquities.[5771]
8 [a]Slaves[5650] rule[4910] over us;
There is [b]no one to deliver us
from their hand.
9 We get our bread [I]at the
[a]risk of our lives[5315]
[II]Because of the sword[2719] in the
wilderness.
10 Our skin[5785] has become as
[a]hot as an oven,
Because of [I]the burning heat[2152]
of famine.
11 They ravished the [a]women[802] in
Zion,
The virgins[1330] in the cities of
Judah.
12 Princes[8269] were hung by their
hands;
[Ia]Elders[2205] were not
respected.[1921]
13 Young men [Ia]worked[5375] at the
grinding mill;
And youths [b]stumbled under
loads of wood.
14 Elders [I]are gone[7673] from the
gate,
Young men from their [a]music.
15 The joy of our hearts[3820] has
[a]ceased;
Our dancing has been turned into
mourning.
16 The [a]crown has fallen[5307] from
our head;[7218]
[b]Woe to us, for we have sinned!
17 Because of this our [a]heart is
faint;

17 [I]Lit., *our help* [a]Jer. 37:7; Lam. 1:7 [b]Ezek. 29:6, 7, 16
18 [I]Lit., *full* [a]Jer. 16:16 [b]Jer. 5:31; Ezek. 7:2-12; Amos 8:2
19 [a]Is. 5:26-28; 30:16, 17; Jer. 4:13; Hab. 1:8
20 [a]Gen. 2:7 [b]2Sam. 1:14; 19:21 [c]Jer. 39:5; 52:9 [d]Dan. 4:12
21 [a]Ps. 137:7; Jer. 25:21 [b]Obad. 16
22 [a]Is. 40:2; Jer. 33:7, 8 [b]Jer. 49:10; Mal. 1:3, 4

1 [a]Ps. 44:13-16
2 [a]Is. 1:7; Hos. 8:7, 8 [b]Zeph. 1:13
3 [a]Ex. 22:24; Jer. 15:8; 18:21
4 [I]Lit., *We drink our water for silver* [a]Is. 3:1
5 [I]Lit., *We have been pursued upon* [a]Neh. 9:36, 37
6 [I]Lit., *given the hand to* [II]Lit., *to be satisfied with* [a]Hos. 9:3; 12:1
7 [a]Jer. 14:20; 16:12
8 [a]Neh. 5:15 [b]Ps. 7:2; Zech. 11:6
9 [I]Lit., *with our soul* [II]Or, *In the face of* [a]Jer. 40:9-12
10 [I]Or, *the ravages of hunger* [a]Job 30:30; Lam. 4:8
11 [a]Is. 13:16; Zech. 14:2
12 [I]Lit., *The faces of elders* [a]Is. 47:6; Lam. 4:16
13 [I]Lit., *carry* [a]Judg. 16:21 [b]Jer. 7:18
14 [I]Lit., *have ceased* [a]Is. 24:8; Jer. 7:34
15 [a]Jer. 25:10; Amos 8:10
16 [a]Job 19:9; Ps. 89:39; Jer. 13:18 [b]Is. 3:9-11
17 [a]Is. 1:5

Because of these things our
[b]eyes are dim;[2821]
18 Because of [a]Mount Zion which
lies desolate,[8074]
[b]Foxes prowl in it.
19 [a]Thou, O LORD, dost [I]rule
forever;[5769]
Thy [b]throne[3678] is from
generation[1755] to generation.
20 Why dost Thou [a]forget us
forever;[5331]
Why dost Thou forsake[5800] us
[I]so long?[753,3117]
21 [a]Restore[7725] us to Thee, O
LORD, that we may be
restored;
Renew [b]our days[3117] as of
old,[6924]
22 Unless [a]Thou hast utterly
rejected[3988] us,
And art exceedingly [b]angry[7107]
with us.

17 [b]Job 17:7; Lam. 2:11
18 [a]Mic. 3:12 [b]Neh. 4:3
19 [I]Lit., *sit* [a]Ps. 102:12, 25-27 [b]Ps. 45:6
20 [I]Lit., *to length of days* [a]Ps. 13:1; 44:24
21 [a]Ps. 80:3; Jer. 31:18 [b]Is. 60:20-22
22 [a]Ps. 60:1, 2; Jer. 7:29 [b]Is. 64:9

The Book of
EZEKIEL

Ezekiel went to Babylon in the second deportation in 597 B.C. Four years later he began a prophetic career that was to last more than twenty years, all of it in Babylon. He had the helpful habit of dating many of his prophecies, and most of the messages about contemporary events were delivered before the fall of Jerusalem in 586 B.C. The New Jerusalem section in chapters 40—48 held out hope for restoration of the land and the temple after the exile. Of all the prophets, Ezekiel was probably the most colorful. He used pantomime, would cry and wail and slap his thighs, ate a scroll, and did many other unusual things to burn his messages into the minds of the people. Some of his visions are unusually arresting in their graphic details. From Ezekiel we get a picture of a holy, transcendent God whose name and glory must be protected. By contrast, Judah had sunk to the depths of depravity in national apostasy. God had to punish His people because of His hatred of idolatry, but He never ceased to love them. Not only was Judah's sin a national one, but Ezekiel stressed individual responsibility for one's own sins to an extent unparalleled in the rest of the Old Testament. Ezekiel forms the important background for many passages in the New Testament, but this is perhaps true more of Revelation than any other book. Material from most of Ezekiel's chapters is quoted or alluded to in all but one chapter in Revelation.

The Vision of Four Figures

1 Now it came about in the thirtieth
year, on the fifth *day* of the fourth
month, while I was by the [a]river Chebar
among the exiles,[1473] the [b]heavens[8064]
were opened and I saw[7200] [I][c]visions[4759]
of God.[430]
🔑2 (On the fifth of the month [I]in the
[a]fifth year of King[4428] Jehoiachin's
exile,[1546]
3 the [a]word[1697] of the LORD came
expressly to Ezekiel the priest,[3548]
son[1121] of Buzi, in the [b]land[127] of the
Chaldeans by the river Chebar; and
there [c]the hand[3027] of the LORD came
upon him.)
4 And as I looked,[7200] behold, a
[a]storm wind was coming from the north,
a great cloud[6051] with fire flashing forth
continually and a bright light around it,
and in its midst something like [b]glowing
metal in the midst of the fire.
5 And within it there were figures
resembling[1823] [a]four living beings.[2416]
And this was their appearance: they had
human[120] [b]form.
6 Each of them had [a]four faces and
[b]four wings.
7 And their legs were straight[3474]
and [I]their feet were like a calf's hoof,[3709]
and they gleamed like [a]burnished
bronze.
8 Under their wings on their [a]four
sides *were* human [b]hands.[3027] As for the
faces and wings of the four of them,
9 their wings touched one[802] another;[269] their *faces* did [a]not turn when
they moved, each[376] [b]went straight forward.
10 As for the [a]form of their faces,
each had the [b]face of a man, [I]all four
had the face of a lion on the right and
the face of a bull on the left, and [I]all
four had the face of an eagle.
11 Such were their faces. Their
wings were spread out above; each had
two touching another[376] *being,* and
[a]two covering[3680] their bodies.[1472]
12 And [a]each went straight forward;

1 [I]Some ancient mss. and versions read *a vision* [a]Ezek. 3:23; 10:15, 20 [b]Matt. 3:16; Mark 1:10; Luke 3:21; Acts 7:56; 10:11; Rev. 4:1; 19:11 [c]Ex. 24:10; Num. 12:6; Is. 1:1; 6:1; Ezek. 8:3; 11:24; 40:2; Dan. 8:1, 2
2 [I]Lit., *it was* [a]2Kin. 24:12-15; Ezek. 8:1; 20:1
3 [a]2Pet. 1:21 [b]Ezek. 12:13 [c]1Kin. 18:46; 2Kin. 3:15; Ezek. 3:14, 22
4 [a]Is. 21:1; Jer. 23:19; Ezek. 13:11, 13 [b]Ezek. 1:27; 8:2
5 [a]Ezek. 10:15, 17, 20; Rev. 4:6-8 [b]Ezek. 1:26
6 [a]Ezek. 1:10; 10:14, 21 [b]Ezek. 1:23
7 [I]Lit., *the soles of their feet* [a]Dan. 10:6; Rev. 1:15
8 [a]Ezek. 1:17; 10:11 [b]Ezek. 10:8, 21
9 [a]Ezek. 1:17 [b]Ezek. 1:12; 10:22
10 [I]Lit., *the four of them* [a]Rev. 4:7 [b]Ezek. 10:14
11 [a]Is. 6:2; Ezek. 1:23
12 [a]Ezek. 1:9

🔑 **1:2,3** The exile of King Jehoiachin was in 597 B.C., so Ezekiel's call and first dated prophecy was in the summer of 593 B.C. His entire prophetic career was spent in Babylon.

[b]wherever the spirit[7307] was about to go, they would go, without turning as they went.

13 [I]In the midst of the living beings[2416] there was something that looked like burning coals of [a]fire, [II]like torches darting back and forth among the living beings. The fire was bright, and lightning was [III]flashing from the fire.

14 And the living beings [a]ran to and fro[7725] like bolts of [b]lightning.

15 Now as I looked[7200] at the living beings,[2416] behold, there was one [a]wheel[212] on the earth[776] beside the living beings, [I]for *each of* the four of them.

16 The [a]appearance of the wheels[212] and their workmanship *was* like [I]sparkling [b]beryl, and all four of them had the same form, their appearance and workmanship *being* as if [II]one wheel were within another.

17 Whenever they [I]moved, they [I]moved in any of their four [II]directions, without [a]turning as they [I]moved.

18 As for their rims they were lofty and awesome,[3374] and the rims of all four of them were [a]full of eyes round about.

19 And [a]whenever the living beings[2416] [I]moved, the wheels [I]moved with them. And whenever the living beings [b]rose[5375] from the earth, the wheels rose *also*.

20 [a]Wherever the spirit was about to go, they would go in that direction[I]. And the wheels rose close beside them; for the spirit of the living [II]beings[2416] *was* in the wheels.

21 [a]Whenever those went, these went; and whenever those stood still, these stood still. And whenever those rose[5375] from the earth, the wheels rose close beside them; for the spirit of the living [I]beings *was* in the wheels.

Vision of Divine Glory

22 Now [a]over the heads[7218] of the living [I]beings *there was* something like an expanse,[7549] like the awesome[3372] gleam of [II]crystal, extended over their heads.

23 And under the expanse their wings *were stretched out* straight, one toward the other; each one also had [a]two wings covering their bodies on the one side and on the other.

24 I also heard[8085] the sound of their wings like the [a]sound of abundant waters as they went, like the [b]voice of [I]the Almighty,[7706] a sound of tumult[1999] like the [c]sound of an army camp;[4264] whenever they stood still, they dropped[7503] their wings.

25 And there came a voice from above the [a]expanse that was over their heads; whenever they stood still, they dropped their wings.

26 Now [a]above the expanse that was over their heads there was something [b]resembling a throne, like [I][c]lapis lazuli in appearance; and on that which resembled a throne,[3678] high up, *was* a figure with the appearance of a [d]man.

27 Then I [I]noticed from the appearance of His loins and upward something [a]like [II]glowing metal that looked like fire all around within[1004] it, and from the appearance of His loins and downward I saw something like fire; and *there was* a radiance around Him.

28 As the appearance of the [a]rainbow [I]in the clouds on a rainy day,[3117] so *was* the appearance of the surrounding radiance. Such *was* the appearance of the likeness of the [b]glory[3519] of the LORD. And when I saw *it*, I [c]fell[5307] on my face and heard a voice speaking.[1696]

The Prophet's Call

2 🔑 Then He said[559] to me, "Son[1121] of man,[120] [a]stand on your feet that I may speak[1696] with you!"

2 And as He spoke[1696] to me the [a]Spirit[7307] entered me and set me on

12 [b]Ezek. 1:20 **13** [I]So with some ancient versions; Heb., *as the likeness of the living beings.* [II]Lit., *like the appearance of* [III]Lit., *coming out* [a]Ps. 104:4; Rev. 4:5 **14** [a]Zech. 4:10 [b]Matt. 24:27; Luke 17:24 **15** [I]Lit., *for his four faces* [a]Ezek. 1:19-21; 10:9 **16** [I]Lit., *the look of beryl* [II]Lit., *the wheel in the midst of the wheel* [a]Ezek. 10:9-11 [b]Ezek. 10:9; Dan. 10:6 **17** [I]Lit., *went* [II]Lit., *sides* [a]Ezek. 1:9, 12; 10:11 **18** [a]Ezek. 10:12; Rev. 4:6, 8 **19** [I]Lit., *went* [a]Ezek. 10:16 [b]Ezek. 10:19 **20** [I]M.T. adds *the spirit to go* [II]M.T. reads *being* [a]Ezek. 1:12 **21** [I]M.T. reads *being* [a]Ezek. 10:17 **22** [I]So some ancient mss. and versions; M.T. reads *being* [II]Or, *ice* [a]Ezek. 10:1 **23** [a]Ezek. 1:6, 11 **24** [I]Heb., *Shaddai* [a]Ezek. 43:2; Rev. 1:15; 19:6 [b]Ezek. 10:5 [c]2Kin. 7:6; Dan. 10:6 **25** [a]Ezek. 1:22; 10:1 **26** [I]Heb., *eben-sappir* [a]Ezek. 1:22; 10:1 [b]Is. 6:1; Ezek. 10:1; Dan. 7:9 [c]Ex. 24:10; Is. 54:11 [d]Ezek. 43:6, 7; Rev. 1:13 **27** [I]Lit., *saw* [II]Or, *electrum* [a]Ezek. 1:4; 8:2 **28** [I]Lit., *which occurs in* [a]Gen. 9:13; Rev. 4:3; 10:1 [b]Ex. 24:16; Ezek. 8:4; 11:22, 23; 43:4, 5 [c]Gen. 17:3; Ezek. 3:23; Dan. 8:17; Rev. 1:17

1 [a]Dan. 10:11; Acts 9:6 **2** [a]Ezek. 3:24; Dan. 8:18

🔑 **2:1** God's normal way of addressing Ezekiel was with the phrase "son of man," probably to emphasize

(continued on next page)

my feet; and I heard[8085] *Him* speaking to me.

3 Then He said to me, "Son of man, I am sending you to the sons[1121] of Israel, to a rebellious people[1471] who have [a]rebelled[4775] against Me; [b]they and their fathers[1] have transgressed[6586] against Me to this very day.[3117]

4 "And I am sending you to them who are [Ia]stubborn and obstinate children; and you shall say[559] to them, 'Thus says[559] the Lord[136] [II]GOD.'

5 "As for them, [a]whether they listen[8085] or [I]not—for they are a rebellious[4805] house—[1004] they will [b]know[3045] that a prophet[5030] has been among them.

6 "And you, son of man, [a]neither fear[3373] them nor fear their words, though [b]thistles and thorns are with you and you sit on scorpions; neither fear their words[1697] nor be dismayed[2865] at their presence, for they are a rebellious house.

7 "But you shall [a]speak My words to them [b]whether they listen or [I]not, for they are rebellious.

8 "Now you, son of man, listen to what I am speaking[1696] to you; do not be rebellious like that rebellious house. Open your mouth[6310] and [a]eat what I am giving you."

9 Then I looked,[7200] behold, a [a]hand[3027] was extended to me; and lo, a [Ib]scroll[4039,5612] *was* in it.

3 [a]1Sam. 8:7, 8; Jer. 3:25 [b]Ezek. 20:18, 30
4 [I]Lit., *the sons, stiff-faced and hard-hearted* [II]Heb., *YHWH,* usually rendered LORD [a]Ps. 95:8; Is. 48:4; Jer. 5:3; 6:15; Ezek. 3:7
5 [I]Lit., *forbear* [a]Ezek. 2:7; 3:11, 27; Matt. 10:12-15; Acts 13:46 [b]Ezek. 33:33; Luke 10:10, 11; John 15:22
6 [a]Is. 51:12; Jer. 1:8, 17; Ezek. 3:9 [b]2Sam. 23:6, 7; Ezek. 28:24; Mic. 7:4
7 [I]Lit., *forbear* [a]Jer. 1:7, 17; Ezek. 3:10, 17 [b]Ezek. 2:5
8 [a]Jer. 15:16; Ezek. 3:3; Rev. 10:9
9 [I]Lit., *scroll of a book* [a]Ezek. 8:3 [b]Jer. 36:2; Ezek. 3:1; Rev. 5:1-5; 10:8-11
10 [a]Is. 3:11; Rev. 8:13

1 [a]Ezek. 2:9
2 [a]Jer. 25:17
3 [I]Lit., *inward parts* [a]Jer. 6:11; 20:9 [b]Jer. 15:16 [c]Ps. 19:10; 119:103; Rev. 10:9, 10
4 [I]Lit., *go, come*
5 [I]Lit., *deepness of lip and heaviness of tongue* [a]Jon. 1:2; Acts 14:11; 26:17 [b]Is. 28:11; 33:19
6 [I]Lit., *deepness of lip and heaviness of tongue* [II]Or, *If I had sent you to them, they would listen to you.* [III]Lit., *they*
7 [a]1Sam. 8:7

10 When He spread it out before me, it was written on the front and back; and written on it were lamentations, mourning[1899] and [a]woe.

Ezekiel's Commission

3 Then He said[559] to me, "Son[1121] of man,[120] eat what you find; [a]eat this scroll,[4040] and go, speak[1696] to the house[1004] of Israel."

2 So I [a]opened my mouth,[6310] and He fed me this scroll.

3 And He said to me, "Son of man, feed your stomach, and [a]fill your [I]body[4578] with this scroll which I am giving you." Then I [b]ate it, and it was sweet as [c]honey in my mouth.

4 Then He said to me, "Son of man, [I]go to the house of Israel and speak with My words[1697] to them.

5 "For [a]you are not being sent to a people[5971] of [Ib]unintelligible[6012] speech[8193] or difficult language, *but* to the house of Israel,

6 nor to many peoples of [I]unintelligible speech or difficult language, whose words you cannot understand.[8085] [II]But I have sent you to them [III]who should listen[8085] to you;

7 yet the house of Israel will not be willing to listen[8085] to you, since they are [a]not willing to listen to Me. Surely

---

(continued from previous page)
his humanity over against God's holiness. Jesus referred to Himself the same way, but with an entirely different meaning, so the Book of Ezekiel does not serve as the direct background for Jesus' use of the phrase. See the note on Dan. 7:13.

2:8—3:3 Of all the prophets, Ezekiel was called on by God to perform more unusual acts in connection with his message than any others. On this occasion he ate a scroll, presumably because it had on it the words he was to utter (see Rev. 10:8-10). At another time, he acted out an after dark escape of some of his fellow countrymen back in Jerusalem (12:3-7). He used a type of shadowboxing to depict the Babylonian slaughter which was coming (21:14-17). At times during his preaching he would clap his hands, stamp his feet and cry, "Alas" (6:11), or as he cried and wailed, he would slap his thighs (21:12). As a sign to the people, he used a brick to represent Jerusalem and built a model depicting its siege (4:1-3). To represent the length of Israel's and Judah's punishment, respectively, he was bound with cords and lay on his left side for 390 days and on his right for forty days (4:4-8). During that first period, he consumed only rationed food and water, to symbolize the plight of those left in Jerusalem (4:9-17). He also cut his hair, divided it into thirds and disposed of it in three different manners, to indicate the ways in which the inhabitants of Jerusalem would perish (5:1-12). All of this was at the direction of the Lord and helped reinforce his message.

the whole house of Israel is [I]stubborn
and obstinate.
8 "Behold, I have made your face
as hard as their faces, and your forehead as hard[2389] as their foreheads.
9 "Like [I]emery[8068] harder than flint
I have made your forehead. Do not be
afraid[3372] of them or be dismayed[2865] before them, though they are a rebellious[4809] house."
10 Moreover, He said to me, "Son
of man, take into your heart[3824] all My
[a]words which I shall speak to you, and
listen[8085] [I]closely.
11 "And [I]go to the exiles,[1473] to the
sons[1121] of your people, and speak to
them and tell[559] them, whether they listen or [II]not, 'Thus says[559] the Lord
[III]GOD.' "
12 Then the [a]Spirit[7307] lifted me
up,[5375] and I heard[8085] a great [b]rumbling
sound behind me, "Blessed[1288] be the
glory[3519] of the LORD [I]in His place."
13 And I *heard* the sound of the
wings of the living beings[2416] touching[5401] one[802] another,[269] and the sound
of the [a]wheels[212] beside them, even a
great rumbling sound.
14 So the Spirit lifted me up and
took me away; and I went embittered[4751]
in the rage[2534] of my spirit, and [a]the
hand[3027] of the LORD was strong[2388] on
me.
15 Then I came to the exiles who
lived beside the river Chebar at Telabib,
and I sat there [a]seven days[3117] where
they were living, causing consternation[8074] among them.
🗝 **16** Now it came about [a]at the end
of seven days that the word[1697] of the
LORD came to me, saying,
17 "Son of man, I have appointed
you a [a]watchman to the house of Israel;
whenever you hear a word from My
mouth, [b]warn[2094] them from Me.
18 "When I say[559] to the wicked,
'You shall surely die';[4191] and you do
not warn him or speak[1696] out to warn
the wicked[7563] from his wicked way[1870]
that he may live,[2421] that wicked man
shall die in his iniquity,[5771] but his
[a]blood[1818] I will require at your hand.
19 "Yet if you have [a]warned the
wicked, and he does not turn[7725] from
his wickedness[7562] or from his wicked
way, he shall die in his iniquity; but you
have [b]delivered[5337] yourself.[5315]
20 "Again, [a]when a righteous[6662]
man turns away from his righteousness[6664] and commits[6213] iniquity,[5766]
and I place an [b]obstacle[4383] before him,
he shall die; since you have not warned
him, he shall die in his sin,[2403] and his
righteous deeds[6666] which he has done[6213]
shall not be remembered;[2142] but his
blood I will require at your hand.
21 "However, if you have [a]warned
[I]the righteous man that the righteous
should not sin,[2398] and he does not sin,
he shall surely live[2421] because he took
warning;[2094] and you have delivered
yourself."
22 And the hand of the LORD was
on me there, and He said to me, "Get
up, go out to the plain, and there I will
[a]speak[1696] to you."
23 So I got up and went out to the
plain; and behold, the [a]glory of the LORD
was standing there, like the glory which
[b]I saw[7200] by the river Chebar, and I
fell[5307] on my face.
24 The [a]Spirit then entered me and
made me stand on my feet, and He
spoke[1696] with me and said to me, "Go,
shut yourself up in your house.
25 "As for you, son of man, they
will [a]put ropes on you and bind you with
them, so that you cannot go out among
them.
26 "Moreover, [a]I will make your
tongue stick to [I]the roof of your mouth
so that you will be dumb, and cannot
be a man who rebukes[3198] them, for they
are a rebellious house.
27 "But [a]when I speak to you, I will
open your mouth, and you will say to
them, 'Thus says the Lord[136] [I]GOD.' He
who hears,[8085] let him hear; and he who
refuses, let him refuse; [b]for they are a
rebellious house.

7 [I]Lit., *of a hard forehead and a stiff heart*
9 [I]Lit., *corundum*
10 [I]Lit., *with your ears* [a]Job 22:22; Ezek. 2:8; 3:1-3
11 [I]Lit., *go, come* [II]Lit., *forbear* [III]Heb., *YHWH*, usually rendered LORD
12 [I]Or, *from* [a]Ezek. 3:14; 8:3; Acts 8:39 [b]Acts 2:2
13 [a]Ezek. 1:15; 10:16, 17
14 [a]2Kin. 3:15
15 [a]Job 2:13
16 [a]Jer. 42:7
17 [a]Is. 52:8; 56:10; 62:6; Jer. 6:17; Ezek. 33:7-9 [b]2Chr. 19:10; Is. 58:1; Hab. 2:1
18 [a]Ezek. 3:20; 33:6, 8
19 [a]2Kin. 17:13, 14; Ezek. 33:3, 9 [b]Ezek. 14:14, 20; Acts 18:6; 1Tim. 4:16
20 [a]Ps. 125:5; Ezek. 18:24; 33:18; Zeph. 1:6 [b]Is. 8:14; Jer. 6:21; Ezek. 14:3, 7-9
21 [I]Lit., *him, the righteous* [a]Acts 20:31
22 [a]Acts 9:6
23 [a]Ezek. 1:28; Acts 7:55 [b]Ezek. 1:1
24 [a]Ezek. 2:2
25 [a]Ezek. 4:8
26 [I]Lit., *your palate* [a]Luke 1:20, 22
27 [I]Heb., *YHWH*, usually rendered LORD [a]Ezek. 24:27; 33:22 [b]Ezek. 12:2, 3

🗝 **3:16-21** See note on Ezek. 18:1-4.

Siege of Jerusalem Predicted

4 🔑 “Now you son[1121] of man,[120] [a]get yourself a brick, place it before you, and inscribe[2710] a city on it, Jerusalem.

2 “Then [a]lay siege against it, build a siege wall, [I]raise[8210] up a ramp, pitch camps,[4264] and place[7760] battering rams[3733] against it all around.

3 “Then get yourself an iron plate and set it up as an iron wall between you and the city, and set your face toward it so that [a]it is under siege, and besiege it. This is a [b]sign[226] to the house[1004] of Israel.

4 “As for you, lie down on your left side, and lay[7760] the iniquity[5771] of the house of Israel on it; you shall [a]bear[5375] their iniquity for the number of days[3117] that you lie on it.

5 “For I have assigned you a number of days corresponding to the years of their iniquity, three hundred and ninety days; thus [a]you shall bear the iniquity of the house of Israel.

6 “When you have completed[3615] these, you shall lie down a second time, *but* on your right side, and bear the iniquity of the house of Judah; I have assigned it to you for forty days, a day[3117] for [a]each year.

7 “Then you shall set your face toward the siege of Jerusalem with your arm bared, and [a]prophesy[5012] against it.

8 “Now behold, I will [a]put ropes on you so that you cannot turn[2015] from one side to the other, until you have completed[3615] the days of your siege.

Defiled Bread

9 “But as for you, take wheat, barley, beans, lentils, millet and [a]spelt,[3698] put them in one vessel and make[6213] them into bread for yourself; you shall eat it according to the number of the days that you lie on your side, three hundred and ninety days.

10 “And your food which you eat *shall be* [a]twenty shekels a day by weight; you shall eat it from time[6256] to time.

11 “And the water you drink will be the sixth part of a hin by measure; you shall drink it from time to time.

12 “And you shall eat it as a barley cake, having baked *it* in their sight over human [a]dung.”

13 Then the LORD said,[559] “Thus shall the sons[1121] of Israel eat their bread [a]unclean among the nations[1471] where I shall banish them.”

14 But I said, “[a]Ah, Lord[136] [I]GOD! Behold, I have [b]never been defiled;[2930] for from my youth until now I have never eaten what [c]died of itself[5038] or was torn by beasts, nor has any [d]unclean[6292] meat ever entered my mouth.”[6310]

15 Then He said to me, “See, I shall give you cow’s dung in place of human[120] dung over which you will prepare your bread.”

16 Moreover, He said to me, “Son of man, behold, I am going to [a]break[7665] the staff[4294] of bread in Jerusalem, and they will eat bread by [b]weight and with anxiety,[1674] and drink water by [c]measure and in horror,

17 because bread and water will be scarce; and they will be appalled[8074] with one[376] another and [a]waste away in their iniquity.

Jerusalem’s Desolation Foretold

5 🔑 “As for you, son[1121] of man,[120] take a [a]sharp sword;[2719] take and [I]use it *as* a barber’s razor on your head[7218] and beard.[2206] Then take [b]scales for weighing and divide [II]the hair.

2 “One third you shall burn in the fire at the center of the city, when the [a]days[3117] of the siege are completed. Then you shall take one third and strike[5221] *it* with the sword all around [I]the city, and one third you shall scatter to the wind;[7307] and I will [b]unsheathe a sword[2719] behind them.

3 “Take also a few in number from

---

1 [a]Is. 20:2; Jer. 13:1; 18:2; 19:1
2 [I]Lit., *cast* [a]Jer. 6:6; Ezek. 21:22
3 [a]Jer. 39:1, 2; Ezek. 5:2 [b]Is. 8:18; 20:3; Ezek. 12:6, 11; 24:24-27
4 [a]Lev. 10:17; 16:22; Num. 18:1
5 [a]Num. 14:34
6 [a]Num. 14:34; Dan. 9:24-26; 12:11, 12; Rev. 11:2, 3
7 [a]Ezek. 21:2
8 [a]Ezek. 3:25
9 [a]Ex. 9:32; Is. 28:25
10 [a]Ezek. 45:12
12 [a]Is. 36:12
13 [a]Dan. 1:8; Hos. 9:3
14 [I]Heb., *YHWH*, usually rendered *LORD* [a]Jer. 1:6; Ezek. 9:8; 20:49 [b]Acts 10:14 [c]Lev. 17:15; 22:8; Ezek. 44:31 [d]Deut. 14:3; Is. 65:4; 66:17
16 [a]Lev. 26:26; Is. 3:1; Ezek. 5:16; 14:13 [b]Ezek. 4:10, 11; 12:19 [c]Lam. 5:4; Ezek. 12:18, 19
17 [a]Lev. 26:39; Ezek. 24:23; 33:10

1 [I]Lit., *make it pass over your head* [II]Lit., *them* [a]Lev. 21:5; Is. 7:20; Ezek. 44:20 [b]Dan. 5:27
2 [I]Lit., *it* [a]Jer. 39:1, 2; Ezek. 4:2-8 [b]Lev. 26:33

🔑 **4:1-17** See note on Ezek. 2:8—3:3.
🔑 **5:1-12** See note on Ezek. 2:8—3:3.

[I]them and bind them in the edges of your *robes*.

4 "And take again some of them and throw them into the fire, and burn them in the fire; from it a fire will [I]spread to all the house[1004] of Israel.

5 "Thus says[559] the Lord[136] [I]GOD, 'This is [a]Jerusalem; I have set[7760] her at the [b]center of the nations,[1471] with lands[776] around her.

6 'But she has rebelled[4784] against My ordinances[4981] more wickedly[7564] than the nations and against My statutes[2708] [a]more than the lands which surround her; for they have [b]rejected My ordinances and have not walked [I]in My statutes.'

7 "Therefore, thus says the Lord GOD, 'Because you have [a]more turmoil than the nations which surround you, and have not walked in My statutes, nor observed[6213] My ordinances, nor observed[6213] the ordinances of the nations which surround you,'

8 therefore, thus says the Lord GOD, 'Behold, I, even I, am [a]against you, and I will [b]execute judgments among you in the sight of the nations.

9 'And because of all your abominations,[8441] I will do[6213] among you what I have [a]not done, and the like of which I will never do again.

10 'Therefore, [a]fathers[1] will eat *their* sons[1121] among you, and sons will eat their fathers; for I will execute judgments[8201] on you, and [b]scatter all your remnant[7611] to every wind.[7307]

11 'So as I live,'[2416] declares[5001] the Lord GOD, 'surely, because you have [a]defiled[2930] My sanctuary[4720] with all your [b]detestable idols[8251] and with all your abominations, therefore I will also withdraw, and My eye shall have no pity and I will not spare.

12 'One third of you will die[4191] by [a]plague[1698] or be consumed[3615] by famine among you, one third will fall by the sword around you, and one third I will [b]scatter to every wind, and I will [c]unsheathe a sword behind them.

13 'Thus My anger[639] will be spent,[3615] and I will [I]satisfy My wrath on them, and I shall be [IIa]appeased;[5162] then they will know[3045] that I, the LORD, have [b]spoken[1696] in My zeal[7068] when I have spent My wrath upon them.

14 'Moreover, I will make you a desolation[2723] and a [a]reproach[2781] among the nations which surround you, in the sight of all who pass by.

15 'So [I]it will be a reproach, a reviling, a [a]warning[4148] and an object of horror[8047] to the nations who surround you, when I [b]execute judgments against you in anger, wrath, and raging[2534] rebukes.[8433] I, the LORD, have spoken.

16 'When I send against them the [I]deadly[7451] arrows of famine which [II]were for the destruction[4889] of those whom I shall send to destroy[7843] you, then I shall also intensify the famine upon you, and break[7665] the staff[4294] of bread.

17 'Moreover, [a]I will send on you famine and wild beasts,[2416] and they will bereave you of children; [b]plague and bloodshed[1818] also will pass through[5674] you, and I will bring the sword on you. I, the LORD, have spoken.'"

Idolatrous Worship Denounced

6 And the word[1697] of the LORD came to me saying,

2 "Son[1121] of man,[120] set[7760] your face toward the [a]mountains of Israel, and prophesy[5012] against them,

3 and say,[559] 'Mountains of Israel, listen[8085] to the word of the Lord[136] [I]GOD! Thus says[559] the Lord [I]GOD to the mountains, the hills, the ravines and the valleys: "Behold, I Myself am going to bring a sword[2719] on you, and [a]I will destroy[6] your high places.[1116]

4 "So your [a]altars[4196] will become desolate,[8074] and your incense altars[2553] will be smashed;[7665] and I shall make your slain[2491] fall[5307] in front of your idols.[1544]

5 "I shall also lay the dead bodies[6297] of the sons[1121] of Israel in front of their idols; and I shall scatter your [a]bones[6106] around your altars.

3 [I]Lit., *there*
4 [I]Lit., *go out*
5 [I]Heb., *YHWH*, usually rendered *LORD*, and so throughout the ch. [a]Jer. 6:6; Ezek. 4:1 [b]Deut. 4:6; Lam. 1:1; Ezek. 16:14
6 [I]Lit., *in them, My statutes* [a]2Kin. 17:8-20; Ezek. 16:47, 48, 51 [b]Neh. 9:16, 17; Ps. 78:10; Jer. 11:10; Zech. 7:11
7 [a]2Kin. 21:9-11; 2Chr. 33:9; Jer. 2:10, 11
8 [a]Jer. 21:5, 13; Ezek. 15:7; 21:3; Zech. 14:2 [b]Jer. 24:9; Ezek. 5:15; 11:9
9 [a]Dan. 9:12; Amos 3:2; Matt. 24:21
10 [a]Lev. 26:29; Jer. 19:9; Lam. 4:10 [b]Ps. 44:11; Ezek. 5:2, 12; 6:8; 12:14; Amos 9:9; Zech. 2:6; 7:14
11 [a]Jer. 7:9-11; Ezek. 8:5, 6, 16 [b]Jer. 16:18; Ezek. 7:20
12 [a]Jer. 15:2; 21:9; Ezek. 5:17; 6:11, 12 [b]Ezek. 5:2, 10; Amos 9:9; Zech. 2:6 [c]Jer. 43:10, 11; 44:27; Ezek. 5:2; 12:14
13 [I]Lit., *cause to rest* [II]Lit., *comforted* [a]Is. 1:24 [b]Is. 59:17; Ezek. 36:5, 6; 38:19
14 [a]Ps. 74:3-10; 79:1-4; Ezek. 22:4
15 [I]Ancient versions read *you* [a]Is. 26:9; Jer. 22:8, 9; 1Cor. 10:11 [b]Is. 66:15, 16; Ezek. 5:8; 25:17
16 [I]Lit., *evil* [II]Or, *are for destruction, which I will send*
17 [a]Lev. 26:22; Rev. 6:8 [b]Ezek. 38:22

2 [a]Ezek. 36:1
3 [I]Heb., *YHWH*, usually rendered *LORD* [a]Lev. 26:30

4 [a]Lev. 26:30; 2Chr. 14:5; Is. 27:9; Ezek. 6:6
5 [a]2Kin. 23:14, 16, 20; Jer. 8:1, 2

6 “In all your dwellings, [a]cities will
become waste[2717] and the high places
will be desolate,[3456] that your altars may
become waste and [1]desolate,[816] your
[b]idols may be broken and brought to
an end,[7673] your incense altars may be
cut down, and your works may be blotted out.[4229]
7 “And the slain will fall among you,
and you will know[3045] that I am the LORD.
8 “However, I shall leave a [a]rem-
nant,[3498] for you will have those who
[b]escaped the sword among the
nations[1471] when you are scattered
among the countries.[776]
9 “Then those of you who escape
will [a]remember[2142] Me among the nations to which they will be carried captive,[7617] how I have [1b]been hurt by their
adulterous[2181] hearts[3820] which turned
away[5493] from Me, and by their eyes,
which played the harlot[2181] after their
idols; and they will [c]loathe themselves
in their own sight for the evils which
they have committed,[6213] for all their
abominations.[8441]
10 “Then they will know that I am
the LORD; I have not said[1696] in vain
[1]that I would inflict[6213] this disaster[7451]
on them.” ’
11 “Thus says the Lord [1]GOD,
‘Clap[5221] your hand,[3709] [a]stamp[7554] your
foot, and say, “[b]Alas, because of all the
evil abominations of the house[1004] of Israel, which will fall by [c]sword, famine,
and plague![1698]
12 “He who is [a]far off will die[4191]
by the plague, and he who is near will
fall by the sword, and he who remains[7604]
and is besieged[5341] will die by the famine.
Thus shall I [b]spend[3615] My wrath on
them.
13 “Then you will know that I am
the LORD, when their [a]slain are among
their idols around their altars, on
[b]every high hill, on all the tops[7218] of
the mountains, under every green tree,
and under every leafy oak—the places
where they offered soothing aroma to
all their idols.
14 “So throughout all their habitations[4186] I shall [a]stretch out My
hand[3027] against them and make the
land[127] more desolate[8077] and waste[8047]
than the wilderness toward Diblah; thus
they will know that I am the LORD.” ’ ”

Punishment for Wickedness Foretold

7 Moreover, the word[1697] of the LORD
came to me saying,
2 “And you, son[1121] of man,[120] thus
says[559] the Lord[136] [1]GOD to the land[776]
of Israel, ‘An [a]end! The end is coming
on the four corners of the land.
3 ‘Now the end is upon you, and I
shall send My anger[639] against you; I
shall judge[8199] you according to your
ways,[1870] and I shall bring all your
abominations[8441] upon you.
4 ‘For My eye will have no pity on
you, nor shall I spare *you,* but I shall
[a]bring your ways upon you, and your
abominations will be among you; then
you will [b]know[3045] that I am the LORD!’
5 “Thus says the Lord [1]GOD, ‘A
[a]disaster,[7451] unique disaster, behold it
is coming!
6 ‘An end is coming; the end has
come! It has [a]awakened against you; behold, it has come!
7 ‘Your doom has come to you, O
inhabitant of the land. The [a]time[6256] has
come, the [b]day[3117] is near—tumult[4103]
rather than joyful shouting on the mountains.
8 ‘Now I will shortly [a]pour out[8210]
My wrath on you, and spend[3615] My
anger against you, [b]judge you according
to your ways, and bring on you all your
abominations.
9 ‘And My eye will show no pity,
nor will I spare. I will [1]repay you according to your ways, while your abominations are in your midst; then you will

6 [1]So some ancient versions; Heb., *bear their guilt* [a]Lev. 26:31; Is. 6:11; Ezek. 5:14 [b]Ezek. 6:4; Mic. 1:7; Zech. 13:2
8 [a]Is. 6:13; Jer. 30:11 [b]Jer. 44:14, 28; Ezek. 7:16; 14:22
9 [1]Lit., *been broken,* or, *broken for Myself their* [a]Deut. 4:29; 30:2; Jer. 51:50 [b]Ps. 78:40; Is. 7:13; 43:24; Hos. 11:8 [c]Job 42:6; Ezek. 20:43; 36:31
10 [1]Lit., *to do this evil to*
11 [1]Heb., *YHWH,* usually rendered LORD [a]Ezek. 25:6 [b]Ezek. 9:4 [c]Ezek. 5:12; 7:15
12 [a]Dan. 9:7 [b]Lam. 4:11, 22; Ezek. 5:13
13 [a]Ezek. 6:4-7 [b]1Kin. 14:23; 2Kin. 16:4; Is. 57:5-7; Ezek. 20:28; Hos. 4:13
14 [a]Is. 5:25; 9:12; Ezek. 14:13; 20:33, 34

2 [1]Heb., *YHWH,* usually rendered LORD [a]Ezek. 7:3, 5, 6; 11:13; Amos 8:2, 10
4 [a]Ezek. 11:21; 22:31; Hos. 9:7 [b]Ezek. 6:7, 14; 7:27
5 [1]Heb., *YHWH,* usually rendered LORD [a]2Kin. 21:12, 13; Nah. 1:9
6 [a]Zech. 13:7
7 [a]Ezek. 7:12; 12:23-25, 28 [b]Is. 22:5
8 [a]Is. 42:25; Ezek. 9:8; 14:19; Nah. 1:6 [b]Ezek. 7:3; 33:20; 36:19
9 [1]Lit., *give*

6:8-10 One of the positive effects of the Babylonian exile was the fact that the Jews who returned to Judea were forever cured of their idolatry.
6:11 See note on Ezek. 2:8—3:3.

know that I, the LORD, do the smiting.
10 'Behold, the day! Behold, it is
coming! *Your* doom has gone forth; the
[a]rod[4294] has budded, arrogance[2087] has
blossomed.
11 'Violence[2555] [I]has grown into a
rod of [a]wickedness.[7562] None of them
shall remain, none of their multitude,
none of their [b]wealth, nor anything eminent among them.
12 'The [a]time has come, the day has
arrived. Let not the [b]buyer rejoice nor
the seller mourn; for [c]wrath is against
all their multitude.
13 'Indeed, the seller will not [I][a]re-
gain[7725] [II]what he sold as long as [III]they
both live;[2416] for the vision[2377] regarding
all their multitude will not [IV]be averted,
nor will any of them maintain[2388] his
life[2416] by his iniquity.[5771]
14 'They have [a]blown[8628] the trumpet and made everything ready,[3559] but
no one is going to the battle; for My
wrath is against all [I]their multitude.
15 'The [a]sword[2719] is outside, and
the plague[1698] and the famine are
within.[1004] He who is in the field[7704] will
die[4191] by the sword; famine and the
plague will also consume those in the
city.
16 'Even when their survivors [a]es-
cape, they will be on the mountains
like [b]doves of the valleys, all of them
[I][c]mourning, each[376] over his own iniquity.
17 'All [a]hands[3027] will hang limp,[7503]
and all knees will [I]become like water.
18 'And they will [a]gird themselves
with sackcloth, and [b]shuddering[6427] will
overwhelm[3680] them; and shame *will be*
on all faces, and [c]baldness on all their
heads.[7218]
19 'They shall [a]fling their silver into
the streets, and their gold shall become
an abhorrent thing; their [b]silver and their
gold shall not be able to deliver[5337] them
in the day of the wrath[5678] of the LORD.
They cannot satisfy their [I]appetite,[5315]
nor can they fill their stomachs,[4578] for
their iniquity has become an occasion
of stumbling.[4383]

The Temple Profaned

20 'And they transformed[7760] the
beauty[6643] of His ornaments into pride,
and [a]they made[6213] the images[6754] of
their abominations *and* their detestable
things[8251] with it; therefore I will make
it an abhorrent thing to them.
21 'And I shall give it into the hands
of the [a]foreigners as plunder and to the
wicked[7562] of the earth[776] as spoil, and
they will profane[2490] it.
22 'I shall also turn My [a]face from
them, and they will profane My secret
place; then robbers[6530] will enter and
profane[2490] it.
23 "[a]Make[6213] the chain, for the land
is full of [I][b]bloody[1818] crimes,[4941] and the
city is [c]full of violence.
24 'Therefore, I shall bring the
worst[7451] of the [a]nations,[1471] and they
will possess[3423] their houses.[1004] I shall
also make the [b]pride of the strong ones
cease,[7673] and their [c]holy[6942] places will
be profaned.
25 'When anguish[7089] comes, they
will seek [a]peace, but there will be none.
26 "[a]Disaster[1943] will come upon
disaster, and [b]rumor will be *added* to
rumor; then they will seek a [c]vision from
a prophet,[5030] but the [d]law[8451] will be
lost[6] from the priest[3548] and [e]counsel[6098]
from the elders.[2204]
27 'The king[4428] will mourn, the
prince[5387] will be [a]clothed with horror,[8077] and the hands of the people[5971]
of the land will [I]tremble.[926] According
to their conduct[1870] I shall deal[6213] with
them, and by their judgments I shall
judge them. And they will know that I
am the LORD.' "

Vision of Abominations in Jerusalem

8 And it came about in the sixth year,
on the fifth *day* of the sixth month,
as I was sitting in my house[1004] with
the elders[2205] of Judah sitting before me,

10 [a]Ps. 89:32; Is. 10:5
11 [I]Lit., *has risen* [a]Ps. 73:8; 125:3; Is. 59:6-8 [b]Zeph. 1:18
12 [a]Ezek. 7:5-7, 10; 1Cor. 7:29-31; James 5:8, 9 [b]Prov. 20:14; 1Cor. 7:30 [c]Is. 5:13, 14; Ezek. 6:11, 12; 7:14
13 [I]Lit., *return to* [II]Lit., *thing sold,* i.e., his inherited land [III]Lit., *their life among the living ones* [IV]Lit., *return* [a]Lev. 25:24-28, 31
14 [I]Lit., *her* [a]Num. 10:9; Jer. 4:5
15 [a]Jer. 14:18; Ezek. 5:12; 6:11, 12; 12:16
16 [I]Lit., *moaning* [a]Ezra 9:15; Is. 37:31; Ezek. 6:8; 14:22 [b]Is. 38:14 [c]Is. 59:11; Nah. 2:7
17 [I]Lit., *run with water* [a]Is. 13:7; Ezek. 21:7; 22:14; Heb. 12:12
18 [a]Is. 15:3; Ezek. 27:31; Amos 8:10 [b]Job 21:6; Ps. 55:5 [c]Ezek. 27:31
19 [I]Lit., *soul* [a]Is. 2:20; 30:22 [b]Prov. 11:4; Zeph. 1:18
20 [a]Jer. 7:30
21 [a]2Kin. 24:13; Ps. 74:2-8; Jer. 52:13
22 [a]Jer. 18:17; Ezek. 39:23, 24
23 [I]Lit., *judgment of blood* [a]Jer. 27:2 [b]Ezek. 9:9; Hos. 4:2 [c]Ezek. 8:17
24 [a]Ezek. 21:31; 28:7 [b]Ezek. 33:28 [c]2 Chr. 7:20; Ezek. 24:21
25 [a]Ezek. 13:10, 16
26 [a]Is. 47:11; Jer. 4:20 [b]Ezek. 21:7 [c]Jer. 21:2; 37:17 [d]Ps. 74:9; Ezek. 22:26; Mic. 3:6 [e]Jer. 18:18; Ezek. 11:2
27 [I]Lit., *be terrified*

[a]Job 8:22; Ps. 35:26; 109:18, 29; Ezek. 26:16

that the hand[3027] of the Lord[136] [I]GOD
fell[5307] on me there.
2 Then I looked,[7200] and behold, a
likeness[1823] as the appearance of [I]a
man; from His loins and downward
there was the [a]appearance of fire, and
from His loins and upward the appearance of brightness, like the appearance
[b]of [II]glowing metal.
3 And He stretched out the form[8403]
of a hand and caught me by a lock of
my head;[7218] and the [a]Spirit[7307] lifted me
up between earth[776] and heaven[8064] and
brought me in the visions[4759] of God[430]
to Jerusalem, to the entrance of the
[I]north gate of the inner *court,* where
the seat[4186] of the idol[5566] of jealousy,[7068]
which [b]provokes to jealousy, was *located.*
4 And behold, the [a]glory[3519] of the
God of Israel *was* there, like the appearance which I saw[7200] in the plain.
5 Then He said[559] to me, "Son[1121]
of man,[120] [a]raise[5375] your eyes, now,
toward the north." So I raised[5375] my
eyes toward the north, and behold, to
the north of the altar[4196] gate *was* this
[b]idol of jealousy at the entrance.
6 And He said to me, "Son of man,
do you see what they are doing,[6213] the
great [a]abominations[8441] which the house
of Israel are committing[6213] here, that
I should be far from My sanctuary?[4720]
But yet you will see still greater abominations."
🔑 **7** Then He brought me to the entrance of the court, and when I
looked,[7200] behold, a hole in the wall.
8 And He said to me, "Son of man,
now [a]dig through the wall." So I dug
through the wall, and behold, an entrance.
9 And He said to me, "Go in and
see[7200] the wicked[7451] abominations that
they are committing here."
10 So I entered and looked, and behold, every form of creeping things
and beasts *and* detestable[8263] things,
with all the idols[1544] of the house of
Israel, were carved[2707] on the wall all
around.
11 And standing in front of them
were [a]seventy [b]elders[2204] of the house
of Israel, with Jaazaniah the son of Shaphan standing among them, each man[376]
with his [c]censer in his hand, and the
fragrance of the cloud[6051] of incense[7004]
rising.[5927]
12 Then He said to me, "Son of man,
do you see[7200] what the elders of the
house of Israel are committing in the
dark,[2822] each man in the room of his
carved images?[4906] For they say,[559]
'[a]The LORD does not see[7200] us; the
LORD has [b]forsaken[5800] the land.' "
13 And He said to me, "Yet you
will see still greater abominations which
they are committing."
14 Then He brought me to the entrance of the [a]gate of the LORD's house
which *was* toward the north; and behold,
women[802] were sitting there weeping
for Tammuz.
15 And He said to me, "Do you see
this, son of man? Yet you will see still
greater abominations than these."
16 Then He brought me into the
inner court of the LORD's house. And
behold, at the entrance to the temple[1964]
of the LORD, between the porch and
the altar, *were* about twenty-five men
with their [a]backs to the temple of the
LORD and their faces toward the east;
and [b]they were [I]prostrating themselves
eastward toward the sun.
17 And He said to me, "Do you see
this, son of man? Is it too light a thing[7043]
for the house of Judah to commit[6213]
the abominations which they have committed here, that they have [a]filled the
land[776] with violence[2555] and [b]pro-
voked[3707] Me repeatedly?[7725] For be-

1 [I]Heb., *YHWH,* usually rendered LORD
2 [I]Lit., *fire* [II]Or, *electrum* [a]Ezek. 1:27 [b]Ezek. 1:4, 27
3 [I]Lit., *facing north* [a]Ezek. 3:12; 11:1 [b]Ex. 20:4; Deut. 32:16
4 [a]Ezek. 1:28; 3:22, 23
5 [a]Jer. 3:2; Zech. 5:5 [b]Ps. 78:58; Jer. 7:30; 32:34; Ezek. 8:3
6 [a]2 Kin. 23:4, 5; Ezek. 5:11; 8:9, 17
8 [a]Is. 29:15
11 [a]Num. 11:16, 25; Luke 10:1 [b]Jer. 19:1 [c]Num. 16:17, 35
12 [a]Ps. 14:1; Is. 29:15; Ezek. 9:9 [b]Ps. 10:11
14 [a]Ezek. 44:4; 46:9
16 [I]I.e., worshiping [a]2Chr. 29:6; Jer. 2:27; Ezek. 23:39 [b]Deut. 4:19; 17:3; Job 31:26-28; Jer. 44:17
17 [a]Ezek. 7:11, 23; 9:9; Amos 3:10; Mic. 2:2 [b]Jer. 7:18, 19; Ezek. 16:26

🔑 **8:7-12** Among the incredible religious corruption in the temple, Ezekiel saw animal worship, which suggests Egyptian religion, since, of all the ancient Near Eastern peoples, the Egyptians were most closely associated with this practice. God's finding elders of the nation in a dark room thinking that He could not see them recalls Zephaniah's well-known statement, "At that time I will search Jerusalem with lamps" (Zeph. 1:12).

hold, they are putting the twig to their nose.[639]

18 "Therefore, I indeed shall deal[6213] in wrath. My eye will have no pity nor shall I spare; and [a]though they cry[7121] in My ears[241] with a loud voice, yet I shall not listen[8085] to them."

The Vision of Slaughter

9 Then He cried out in my hearing[241] with a loud [a]voice saying, "Draw near,[7126] [I]O executioners[6486] of the city, each[376] with his destroying weapon in his hand."[3027]

2 And behold, six men[582] came from the direction[1870] of the upper[5945] gate which faces north, each[376] with his shattering[4460] weapon in his hand; and among them was [a]a certain man clothed in linen with a [I]writing[5608] case at his loins. And they went in and stood beside the bronze altar.[4196]

3 Then the [a]glory[3519] of the God[430] of Israel went up from the cherub[3742] on which it had been, to the threshold of the [I]temple.[1004] And He called[7123] to the man clothed in linen at whose loins was the writing case.

4 And the LORD said[559] to him, "Go through the midst of the city, *even* through the midst of Jerusalem, and put a [a]mark on the foreheads of the men who [b]sigh and groan over all the abominations[8441] which are being committed[6213] in its midst."

5 But to the others He said in my hearing,[241] "Go through the city after him and strike;[5221] do not let your eye have pity, and do not spare.

6 "[I]Utterly [a]slay[2026] old[2205] men, young men, maidens,[1330] little children, and women,[802] but do not [b]touch any man on whom is the mark; and you shall [c]start from My sanctuary."[4720] So they started with the [II]elders[2204] who *were* before the [III]temple.

7 And He said to them, "[a]Defile[2930] the [I]temple and fill the courts with the slain.[2497] Go out!" Thus they went out and struck down[5221] *the people* in the city.

8 Then it came about as they were striking and I *alone* was left,[7604] that I [a]fell[5307] on my face and cried out [I]saying, "[b]Alas, Lord[136] [II]GOD! Art Thou destroying[7843] the whole remnant[7611] of Israel [III]by pouring out[8210] Thy wrath on Jerusalem?"

9 Then He said to me, "The iniquity[5771] of the house of Israel and Judah is very, very great, and the land[776] is [a]filled with blood,[1818] and the city is [b]full of perversion;[4297] for [c]they say,[559] 'The LORD has forsaken[5800] the land,[776] and the LORD does not see!'[7200]

10 "But as for Me, [a]My eye will have no pity nor shall I spare, but [b]I shall bring their conduct upon their heads."[7218]

11 Then behold, the man clothed in linen at whose loins was the [I]writing case [II]reported, saying, "I have done just as Thou hast commanded[6680] me."

Vision of God's Glory Departing from the Temple

10 Then I looked,[7200] and behold, in the [Ia]expanse[7549] that was over the heads[7218] of the cherubim[3742] something like a [b]sapphire stone, in appearance resembling[1823] a [c]throne,[3678] appeared[7200] above them.

2 And He spoke[559] to the man[376] clothed in linen and said,[559] "Enter between the [a]whirling wheels[1534] under the [I]cherubim,[3742] and fill your hands with [b]coals of fire from between the cherubim, and scatter *them* over the city." And he entered in my sight.

3 Now the cherubim were standing on the right side of the [I]temple[1004] when the man entered, and the cloud[6051] filled the [a]inner court.

4 Then the [a]glory[3519] of the LORD went up from the cherub to the threshold of the temple, and the [b]temple was filled with the cloud, and the court was filled with the [c]brightness of the glory of the LORD.

5 Moreover, the sound of the wings of the cherubim was heard[8085] as far as the outer court, like the [a]voice of

---

18 [a]Is. 1:15; Jer. 11:11; Mic. 3:4; Zech. 7:13

1 [I]Lit., *you who punish* [a]Is. 6:8
2 [I]Or, *scribal inkhorn* [a]Lev. 16:4
3 [I]Lit., *house* [a]Ezek. 10:4; 11:22, 23
4 [a]Ex. 12:7, 13; Ezek. 9:6; 2Cor. 1:22; 2Tim. 2:19; Rev. 7:2, 3; 9:4; 14:1 [b]Ps. 119:53, 136; Jer. 13:17; Ezek. 6:11; 21:6
6 [I]Lit., To *destruction* [II]Or, *old men* [III]Lit., *house* [a]2Chr. 36:17 [b]Ex. 12:23; Rev. 9:4 [c]Jer. 25:29; Amos 3:2; Luke 12:47
7 [I]Lit., *house* [a]2 Chr. 36:17; Ezek. 7:20-22
8 [I]Lit., *and said* [II]Heb., *YHWH*, usually rendered *LORD* [III]Lit., *by Thy pouring* [a]1Chr. 21:16 [b]Ezek. 11:13; Amos 7:2-6
9 [a]2Kin. 21:16; Jer. 2:34; Ezek. 7:23; 22:2, 3 [b]Ezek. 22:29; Mic. 3:1-3; 7:3 [c]Job 22:13; Ps. 10:11; 94:7; Is. 29:15; Ezek. 8:12
10 [a]Is. 65:6; Ezek. 8:18; 24:14 [b]Ezek. 7:4; 11:21; Hos. 9:7
11 [I]Or, *inkhorn* [II]Lit., *brought back word*

1 [I]Or, *firmament* [a]Ezek. 1:22, 26 [b]Ex. 24:10 [c]Rev. 4:2, 3
2 [I]So with Gr.; Heb., *cherub* [a]Ezek. 1:15-21; 10:13 [b]Ps. 18:10-13; Is. 6:6; Ezek. 1:13; Rev. 8:5
3 [I]Lit., *house*, and so throughout the ch. [a]Ezek. 8:3, 16
4 [a]Ezek. 9:3; 11:22, 23 [b]Ex. 40:34, 35; Is. 6:1-4 [c]Ezek. 1:28
5 [a]Job 40:9; Ezek. 1:24; Rev. 10:3

[I]God[410] Almighty[7706] when He speaks.

6 And it came about when He commanded[6680] the man clothed in linen, saying, "Take fire from between the whirling wheels, from between the cherubim," he entered and stood beside a wheel.[212]

7 Then the cherub stretched out his hand[3027] from between the cherubim to the fire which *was* between the cherubim, took[5375] some and put it into the hands of the one clothed in linen, who took *it* and went out.

8 And the cherubim appeared to have the form of a man's[120] hand under their wings.

9 Then I looked, and behold, [a]four wheels beside the cherubim, one wheel[212] beside each cherub; and the appearance of the wheels *was* like the gleam of a [I][b]Tarshish stone.

10 And as for their appearance, all four of them had the same likeness, as if one wheel were within another wheel.

11 When they moved, they went [a]in *any of* their four [I]directions without turning as they went; but they followed in the direction which [II]they faced, without turning as they went.

12 And their [a]whole body, their backs, their hands,[3027] their wings, and the [b]wheels were full of eyes all around, the wheels belonging to all four of them.

13 The wheels were called in my hearing,[241] the whirling wheels.[1534]

14 And [a]each one had four faces. The first face *was* the face of a cherub, the second face *was* the face of a man,[120] the third the face of a lion, and the fourth the face of an eagle.

15 Then the cherubim rose up. They are the [a]living beings[2416] that I saw[7200] by the river Chebar.

16 Now when the cherubim moved, the wheels would go beside them; also when the cherubim lifted up[5375] their wings to rise from the ground,[776] the wheels would not turn from beside them.

17 When [I]the cherubim [a]stood still, [I]the wheels would stand still; and when they rose up, [I]the wheels would rise with them; for the spirit[7307] of the living beings *was* in them.

🔑 **18** Then the glory of the LORD departed from the threshold of the temple and stood [a]over the cherubim.

19 When [a]the cherubim departed, they lifted their wings and rose up from the earth in my sight with the wheels beside them; and they stood still at the entrance of the east gate of the LORD's house. And the glory of the God[430] of Israel [I]hovered over them.

20 These are the [a]living beings that I saw beneath the God of Israel by [b]the river Chebar; so I knew[3045] that they *were* cherubim.

21 [a]Each one had four faces and each one four wings, and beneath their wings *was* the form of human hands.

22 As for the likeness of their faces, they were the same faces whose appearance I had seen by the river Chebar. Each one[376] went straight ahead.

Evil Rulers to Be Judged

11 Moreover, the [a]Spirit[7307] lifted me up and brought me to the east gate of the LORD's house[1004] which faced eastward. And behold, *there were* twenty-five men[376] at the entrance of the gate, and among them I saw[7200] Jaazaniah son[1121] of Azzur and [b]Pelatiah son of Benaiah, leaders[8269] of the people.[5971]

2 And He said[559] to me, "Son of man,[120] these are the men[582] who devise[2803] iniquity and [a]give evil[7451] advice[6098] in this city,

3 who say,[559] '[I]Is not *the time* near to build houses?[1004] [II]This [a]*city* is the pot and we are the flesh.'

4 "Therefore, [a]prophesy[5012] against them, son of man, prophesy!"

5 Then the Spirit of the LORD fell[5307] upon me, and He said to me, "Say,[559] 'Thus says[559] the LORD, "So you think,

5 [I]Heb., *El Shaddai*
9 [I]Perhaps, *beryl* [a]Ezek. 1:15-17 [b]Dan. 10:6; Rev. 21:20
11 [I]Lit., *sides* [II]Lit., *the head turned* [a]Ezek. 1:17
12 [a]Rev. 4:6, 8 [b]Ezek. 1:18
14 [a]1 Kin. 7:29, 36; Ezek. 1:6, 10; 10:21; Rev. 4:7
15 [a]Ezek. 1:3, 5
17 [I]Lit., *they* [a]Ezek. 1:21
18 [a]Ps. 18:10
19 [I]Lit., *over them from above* [a]Ezek. 11:22
20 [a]Ezek. 1:5, 22, 26; 10:15 [b]Ezek. 1:1
21 [a]Ezek. 1:6, 8; 10:14; 41:18, 19
1 [a]Ezek. 3:12, 14; 8:3; 11:24; 43:5 [b]Ezek. 11:13
2 [a]Ps. 2:1, 2; 52:2; Is. 30:1; Jer. 5:5; Mic. 2:1
3 [I]Or, *The time is not near* [II]Or, *This is* [a]Jer. 1:13; Ezek. 11:7, 11; 24:3, 6
4 [a]Ezek. 3:4, 17

🔑 **10:18,19** See note on Ezek. 43:1-5.

house of Israel, for [a]I know[3045] [I]your [b]thoughts.[7307]

6 "You have [a]multiplied your slain[2491] in this city, filling its streets with [I]them."

7 'Therefore, thus says the Lord[136] [I]GOD, "Your [a]slain whom you have laid in the midst of [II]the city are the flesh, and this *city* is the pot; but [III]I shall [b]bring you out of it.

8 "You have [a]feared[3372] a sword;[2719] so I will [b]bring a sword upon you," the Lord GOD declares.[5001]

9 "And I shall bring you out of the midst of [I]the city, and I shall deliver you into the hands[3027] of [a]strangers and [b]execute judgments[8201] against you.

10 "You will [a]fall by the sword. I shall judge[8199] you to the [b]border of Israel; so you shall know that I am the LORD.

11 "This *city* will [a]not be a pot for you, nor will you be flesh in the midst of it, *but* I shall judge[8199] you to the border of Israel.

12 "Thus you will know that I am the LORD; for you have not walked in My statutes[2706] nor have you [a]executed[6213] My ordinances,[4941] but have acted[6213] according to the ordinances[4941] of the [b]nations[1471] around you." ' "

13 Now it came about as I prophesied,[5012] that [a]Pelatiah son of Benaiah died.[4191] Then I fell[5307] on my face and cried out with a loud voice and said, "[b]Alas, Lord GOD! Wilt Thou bring[6213] the remnant[7611] of Israel to a complete end?"[3617]

Promise of Restoration

14 Then the word[1697] of the LORD came to me, saying,

15 "Son of man, your brothers,[251] your [I]relatives, [II]your fellow exiles, and the whole house of Israel, all of them, *are those* to whom the inhabitants of Jerusalem have said, 'Go far from the LORD; this land[776] has been given [a]us as a possession.'[4181]

16 "Therefore say, 'Thus says the Lord GOD, "Though I had removed them far away among the nations, and though I had scattered them among the countries,[776] yet I was a [a]sanctuary[4720] for them a little while in the countries where they had gone." '

17 "Therefore say, 'Thus says the Lord GOD, "I shall [a]gather[6908] you from the peoples and assemble[622] you out of the countries among which you have been scattered, and I shall give you the land[127] of Israel." '

18 "When they come there, they will [a]remove all its [b]detestable things[8251] and all its abominations[8441] from it.

19 "And I shall [a]give them one heart,[3820] and shall put a new spirit within[7130] [I]them. And I shall take the [b]heart of stone out of their flesh and give them a [c]heart of flesh,

20 that they may [a]walk in My statutes[2708] and keep[8104] My ordinances,[4941] and do[6213] them. Then they will be [b]My people, and I shall be their God.[430]

21 "[I]But as for those whose hearts go after their [a]detestable things and abominations, I shall [b]bring their conduct[1870] down on their heads,"[7218] declares the Lord GOD.

🗝 **22** Then the cherubim[3742] [a]lifted up their wings with the wheels[212] beside them, and [b]the glory[3519] of the God of Israel [I]hovered over them.

23 And the [a]glory of the LORD went up[5927] from the midst of the city, and [b]stood over the mountain which is east of the city.

24 And the [a]Spirit lifted me up[5375] and brought me in a vision by the Spirit of God to the exiles[1473] [I]in Chaldea. So the vision that I had seen[7200] [II][b]left me.

5 [I]Lit., *what comes up in your spirit* [a]Jer. 11:20; 17:10 [b]Ezek. 38:10
6 [I]Lit., *the slain* [a]Is. 1:15; Ezek. 7:23; 22:2-6, 9, 12, 27
7 [I]Heb., *YHWH,* usually rendered *LORD,* and so throughout the ch. [II]Lit., *it* [III]So with Gr.; Heb., *he will bring you out* [a]Ezek. 24:3-13; Mic. 3:2, 3 [b]2Kin. 25:18-22; Jer. 52:24-27; Ezek. 11:9
8 [a]Prov. 10:24; Is. 66:4 [b]Job 3:25; Is. 24:17, 18
9 [I]Lit., *it* [a]Deut. 28:36, 49, 50; Ps. 106:41 [b]Ezek. 5:8; 16:41
10 [a]Jer. 52:9, 10 [b]2Kin. 14:25
11 [a]Ezek. 11:3, 7; 24:3, 6
12 [a]Ezek. 18:8, 9 [b]Ezek. 8:10, 14, 16
13 [a]Ezek. 11:1 [b]Ezek. 9:8
15 [I]Lit., *brothers* [II]So with Gr. and some ancient versions; Heb., *the men of your redemption* [a]Ezek. 33:24
16 [a]Ps. 31:20; 90:1; 91:9; Is. 8:14; Jer. 29:7, 11
17 [a]Is. 11:11-16; Jer. 3:12, 18; 24:5; Ezek. 20:41, 42; 28:25
18 [a]Ezek. 37:23 [b]Ezek. 5:11; 7:20
19 [I]So with Gr. and many mss.; Heb., *you* [a]Jer. 24:7; 32:39; Ezek. 18:31; 36:26 [b]Zech. 7:12; Rom. 2:4, 5 [c]2Cor. 3:3
20 [a]Ps. 105:45; Ezek. 36:27 [b]Ezek. 14:11
21 [I]Lit., *And to the heart of their detestable things and their abomination their heart goes.* [a]Jer. 16:18; Ezek.

11:18 [b]Ezek. 9:10; 16:43 **22** [I]Lit., *over them from above* [a]Ezek. 10:19 [b]Ezek. 43:2 **23** [a]Ezek. 8:4 [b]Zech. 14:4 **24** [I]I.e., Babylonia [II]Lit., *went up from* [a]Ezek. 8:3; 11:1; 37:1; 2Cor. 12:2-4 [b]Acts 10:16

🗝 **11:22,23** See note on Ezek. 43:1-5.

25 Then I [a]told[1696] the exiles all the things that the LORD had shown me.

Ezekiel Prepares for Exile

12 Then the word[1697] of the LORD came to me saying,

2 "Son[1121] of man,[120] you live in the [a]midst of the [b]rebellious[4805] house,[1004] who [c]have eyes to see but do not see, ears[241] to hear[8085] but do not hear; for they are a rebellious house.

3 "Therefore, son of man, prepare for yourself baggage for exile[1473] and go into exile[1540] by day[3119] in their sight; even go into exile from your place to another place in their sight. [a]Perhaps they will [I]understand[7200] though they are a rebellious house.

4 "And bring your baggage out by day in their sight, as baggage for exile. Then you will go out [a]at evening in their sight, as those going into exile.[1473]

5 "Dig a hole through the wall in their sight and [I]go out through it.

6 "Load[5375] *the baggage* on *your* shoulder in their sight, *and* carry *it* out in the dark. You shall [a]cover[3680] your face so that you can not see the land,[776] for I have set you as a [b]sign[4159] to the house of Israel."

7 And I [a]did[6213] so, as I had been commanded.[6680] By day I [b]brought out my baggage like the baggage of an exile. Then in the evening I dug through the wall with my[3027] hands; I went out in the dark *and* carried[5375] *the baggage* on *my* shoulder in their sight.

8 And in the morning the word of the LORD came to me, saying,

9 "Son of man, has not the house of Israel, the [a]rebellious house, said[559] to you, '[b]What are you doing?'[6213]

10 "Say[559] to them, 'Thus says[559] the Lord[136] [I]GOD, "This [IIa]burden[4853] *concerns* the prince[5387] in Jerusalem, as well as all the house of Israel who are [III]in it." '

11 "Say, 'I am [I]a [a]sign to you. As I have done,[6213] so it will be done to them; they will [b]go into exile,[1743] into captivity.'[7628]

12 "And the [a]prince who is among them will load *his baggage* on *his* shoulder in the dark and go out. [I]They will dig a hole through the wall to bring *it* out. He will cover his face so that he can not see the land with *his* eyes.

13 "I shall also spread My [a]net over him, and he will be caught in My snare. And I shall bring him to Babylon in the land[776] of the Chaldeans; yet he will [b]not see it, though he will die[4191] there.

14 "And I shall [a]scatter to every wind[7307] all who are around him, his helpers and all his troops; and I shall draw out a sword[2719] after them.

15 "So they will [a]know[3045] that I am the LORD when I scatter them among the nations,[1471] and spread them among the countries.[776]

16 "But I shall [I]spare[3498] a few of them from the [a]sword, the famine, and the pestilence[1698] that they may tell[5608] all their abominations[8441] among the nations[1471] where they go, and [II]may [b]know that I am the LORD."

17 Moreover, the word of the LORD came to me saying,

18 "Son of man, [a]eat your bread with trembling, and drink your water with quivering[7269] and anxiety.[1674]

19 "Then say to the people[5971] of the land,[127] 'Thus says the Lord GOD concerning the inhabitants of Jerusalem in the land of Israel, "They will eat their bread with anxiety and drink their water with horror, because [I]their land will be [IIa]stripped[3456] of its fulness on account of the violence[2555] of all who live in it.

20 "And the inhabited [a]cities will be laid waste,[2717] and the [b]land will be a desolation.[8077] So you will know that I am the LORD." ' "

25 [a]Ezek. 2:7; 3:4, 17, 27
2 [a]Is. 6:5 [b]Ps. 78:40; Is. 1:23; Ezek. 2:7, 8 [c]Is. 6:9f.; 43:8; Jer. 5:21; Matt. 13:13, 14; Mark 4:12; 8:18; Luke 8:10; John 9:39-41; 12:40; Acts 28:26f.; Rom. 11:8
3 [I]Or, *see that they are* [a]Jer. 26:3; 36:3, 7; Luke 20:13; 2Tim. 2:25
4 [a]2Kin. 25:4; Jer. 39:4; Ezek. 12:12
5 [I]Lit., *bring it out*
6 [a]1 Sam. 28:8; Ezek. 12:12, 13 [b]Is. 8:18; 20:3; Ezek. 4:3; 12:11; 24:24
7 [a]Ezek. 24:18; 37:7, 10 [b]Ezek. 12:3-6
9 [a]Ezek. 2:5-8; 12:1-3 [b]Ezek. 17:12; 20:49; 24:19
10 [I]Heb., *YHWH*, usually rendered *LORD*, and so throughout the ch. [II]Or, *oracle* [III]Lit., *in their midst* [a]2Kin. 9:25; Is. 13:1; Ezek. 12:3-8
11 [I]Lit., *your sign* [a]Ezek. 12:6 [b]Jer. 15:2; 52:15, 28-30; Ezek. 12:3
12 [I]I.e., the king's attendants [a]2Kin. 25:4; Jer. 39:4; 52:7; Ezek. 12:6
13 [a]Is. 24:17, 18; Ezek. 17:20; 19:8; Hos. 7:12 [b]Jer. 39:7; 52:11
14 [a]2Kin. 25:4, 5; Ezek. 5:2; 17:21
15 [a]Ezek. 6:7, 14; 12:16, 20
16 [I]Lit., *leave over* [II]Or, *they will know* [a]Ezek. 7:15; 14:21 [b]Jer. 22:8,9
18 [a]Lam. 5:9; Ezek. 4:16
19 [I]Lit., *her* [II]Lit., *desolate* [a]Jer. 10:22; Ezek. 6:6, 7, 14; Mic. 7:13; Zech. 7:14
20 [a]Is. 3:26; Jer. 4:7; Ezek. 5:14 [b]Is. 7:23, 24; Jer. 25:9; Ezek. 36:3

12:3-6 See note on Ezek. 2:8—3:3.
12:8-16 See note on Jer. 39:1-10.

🔑 **21** Then the word of the LORD came to me saying,

22 "Son of man, what is this [a]proverb you *people* have concerning the land of Israel, saying, 'The [b]days[3117] are long[748] and every [c]vision[2377] fails'?[6]

23 "Therefore say[559] to them, 'Thus says the Lord GOD, "I will make this proverb cease[7673] so that they will no longer use it as a proverb in Israel." But tell[1696] them, "[a]The days draw near[7126] as well as the [I]fulfillment of every vision.

24 "For there will no longer be any [Ia]false[7723] vision or flattering divination4738 within the house of Israel.

25 "For I the LORD shall speak,[1696] and whatever [a]word I speak will be performed.[6213] It will no longer be delayed, for in [b]your days, O [c]rebellious house, I shall speak the word and perform[6213] it," declares[5001] the Lord GOD.' "

26 Furthermore, the word of the LORD came to me saying,

27 "Son of man, behold, the house of Israel is saying, 'The vision that he sees[2372] is for [a]many [I]years *from now,* and he prophesies[5012] of times[6256] far off.'

28 "Therefore say to them, 'Thus says the Lord GOD, "None of My words will be delayed any longer. Whatever word[1697] I speak[1696] will be performed," ' " declares the Lord GOD."

False Prophets Condemned

13 🔑 Then the word[1697] of the LORD came to me saying,

2 "Son[1121] of man,[120] prophesy[5012] against the [a]prophets[5030] of Israel who prophesy, and say[559] to those who prophesy from their own [I]inspiration,[3820] '[b]Listen[8085] to the word of the LORD!

3 'Thus says[559] the Lord[136] [I]GOD, "Woe to the [a]foolish prophets who are following their own spirit[7307] and have [b]seen[7200] nothing.

4 "O Israel, your prophets have been like foxes among ruins.[2723]

5 "You have not [a]gone up[5927] into the [b]breaches, nor did you build the wall around the house[1004] of Israel to stand in the battle on the [c]day[3117] of the LORD.

6 "They see[2372] [Ia]falsehood[7723] and lying[3577] divination[7081] who are saying, 'The LORD declares,'[5001] when the LORD has not sent them; [b]yet they hope[3176] for the fulfillment of *their* word.

7 "[a]Did you not see a false[7723] vision[4236] and speak[1696] a lying divination4738 when you said, 'The LORD declares,' but it is not I who have spoken?" ' "[559]

8 Therefore, thus says the Lord GOD, "Because you have spoken [I]falsehood and seen a lie,[3577] therefore behold, [a]I am against you," declares the Lord GOD.

9 "So My hand[3027] will be against the [a]prophets who see false visions and utter lying divinations.[7080] They will [I]have no place in the council[5475] of My people,[5971] [b]nor will they be written down in the register of the house of Israel, nor will they enter the land[127] of Israel, [II]that you may know[3045] that I am the Lord GOD.

10 "It is definitely because they have [a]misled My people by saying, '[b]Peace!' when there is [c]no peace. And when anyone builds a wall, behold, they plaster it over with whitewash;8602

11 *so* tell those who plaster it over with whitewash, that it will fall. A [a]flooding[7857] rain will come, and you, O hailstones, will fall; and a violent wind[7307] will break1234 out.

12 "Behold, when the wall has fallen,[5307] will you not be asked,[559] 'Where is the plaster with which you plastered *it*?' "

22 [a]Ezek. 16:44; 18:2, 3 [b]Jer. 5:12; Ezek. 11:3; 12:27; Amos 6:3; 2Pet. 3:4 [c]Ezek. 7:26
23 [I]Lit., *word* [a]Ps. 37:13; Joel 2:1; Zeph. 1:14
24 [I]Lit., *vain* [a]Jer. 14:13-16; Ezek. 13:6, 23; Zech. 13:2-4
25 [a]Num. 14:28-34; Is. 14:24; Ezek. 6:10; 12:28 [b]Jer. 16:9; Hab. 1:5 [c]Ezek. 12:2
27 [I]Lit., *days* [a]Ezek. 12:22; Dan. 10:14
2 [I]Lit., *heart* [a]Is. 9:15; Jer. 37:19; Ezek. 22:25, 28 [b]Is. 1:10; Amos 7:16
3 [I]Heb., *YHWH,* usually rendered *LORD,* and so throughout the ch. [a]Lam. 2:14; Hos. 9:7; Zech. 11:15 [b]Jer. 23:28-32
5 [a]Ps. 106:23; Jer. 23:22; Ezek. 22:30 [b]Is. 58:12 [c]Is. 13:6, 9; Ezek. 7:19
6 [I]Lit., *vanity* [a]Jer. 29:8; Ezek. 22:28 [b]Jer. 28:15; 37:19
7 [a]Ezek. 22:28
8 [I]Lit., *vanity* [a]Ezek. 5:8; 21:3; Nah. 2:13
9 [I]Lit., *not be in* [II]Or, *and you will know* [a]Jer. 20:3-6; 28:15-17 [b]Ps. 69:28; 87:6; Jer. 17:13; Dan. 12:1
10 [a]Jer. 23:32; 50:6 [b]Jer. 6:14; 8:11; 14:13 [c]Ezek. 7:25; 13:16
11 [a]Ezek. 38:22

🔑 **12:21-25** Israel's proverb that God changed to one of His own was a challenge to the credibility of the visions He had sent. Peter encountered scoffers of the same kind as he dealt with the problem of the delay of Jesus' second coming (II Pet. 3:3-4).

🔑 **13:1-16** See note on Deut. 18:20-22.

13 Therefore, thus says the Lord GOD, "I will make a violent wind break out in My wrath. There will also be in My anger[639] a flooding rain and [a]hailstones to consume[3615] *it* in wrath.

14 "So I shall tear down[2040] the wall which you plastered over with whitewash and bring it down to the ground,[776] so that its [a]foundation[3247] is laid bare; and when it falls, you will be [b]consumed[3615] in its midst. And you will [c]know that I am the LORD.

15 "Thus I shall spend[3615] My wrath[2534] on the wall and on those who have plastered it over with whitewash; and I shall say to you, 'The wall [I]is gone and its plasterers are gone,

16 *along with* the prophets of Israel who prophesy to Jerusalem, and who [a]see visions[2377] of peace for her when there is [b]no peace,' declares the Lord GOD.

17 "Now you, son of man, set[7760] your face against the daughters of your people who are [a]prophesying [b]from their own [I]inspiration.[3820] Prophesy against them,

18 and say, 'Thus says the Lord GOD, "Woe to the women who sew *magic* bands on [I]all wrists, and make[6213] veils for the heads[7218] of *persons* of every stature to [a]hunt down [II]lives![5315] Will you hunt down the [II]lives of My people, but preserve[2421] the [II]lives *of others* for yourselves?

19 "And [a]for handfuls of barley and fragments of bread, you have profaned[2490] Me to My people to put to death[4191] [I]some who should not die[4191] and to [b]keep [I]others alive who should not live,[2421] by your lying[3576] to My people who listen to lies."'"

20 Therefore, thus says the Lord GOD, "Behold, I am against your *magic* bands by which you hunt [I]lives there as [II]birds, and I will tear them off your arms; and I will let [I]them go, even those [I]lives whom you hunt as [II]birds.

21 "I will also tear off your veils and [a]deliver[5337] My people from your hands, and they will no longer be in your hands to be hunted; and you will know that I am the LORD.

22 "Because you [a]disheartened the righteous[6662] with falsehood when I did not cause him grief, but have [Ib]encouraged[2388] the wicked[7451] not to [c]turn[7725] from his wicked[7563] way[1870] *and* preserve[2421] his life,

23 therefore, you women will no longer see[2372] [Ia]false visions or practice[7080] divination,[7081] and I will [b]deliver My people out of your hand. Thus you will [c]know that I am the LORD."

Idolatrous Elders Condemned

14 Then some[518] [a]elders[2205] of Israel came to me and [b]sat down before me.

2 And the word[1697] of the LORD came to me saying,

3 "Son[1121] of man,[120] these men[582] have [a]set up their idols[1544] in their hearts,[3820] and have [b]put right before their faces the stumbling block[4383] of their iniquity.[5771] Should I be [c]consulted by them at all?

4 "Therefore speak[1696] to them and tell[559] them, 'Thus says[559] the Lord[136] [I]GOD, "Any man[376] of the house[1004] of Israel who sets up[5927] his idols in his heart, puts[7760] right before his face the stumbling block of his iniquity, and *then* comes to the prophet,[5030] I the LORD will be brought to give him an answer in [II]the matter in view of the [a]multitude of his idols,

5 in order to lay hold of [Ia]the hearts of the house of Israel who are [IIb]estranged[2114] from Me through all their idols."'

6 "Therefore say to the house of Israel, 'Thus says the Lord GOD, "[a]Repent[7725] and turn away[7725] from your idols, and turn your faces away[7725] from all your [b]abominations.[3441]

7 "For anyone[376] of the house of Israel or of the [a]immigrants[1616] who stay[1481] in Israel who separates[5144] himself from Me, sets up his idols in his

13 [a]Ex. 9:24, 25; Ps. 18:12, 13; Is. 30:30; Rev. 11:19; 16:21
14 [a]Mic. 1:6; Hab. 3:13 [b]Jer. 6:15; 14:15 [c]Ezek. 13:9
15 [I]Lit., *is not . . . are not*
16 [a]Jer. 6:14; 8:11; Ezek. 13:10 [b]Is. 57:21
17 [I]Lit., *heart* [a]Judg. 4:4; 2Kin. 22:14; Luke 2:36; Acts 21:9 [b]Ezek. 13:2; Rev. 2:20
18 [I]Lit., *all joints of the hand;* M.T. reads *of my hands* [II]Or, *souls* [a]2Pet. 2:14
19 [I]Or, *souls* [a]Prov. 28:21; Mic. 3:5 [b]Jer. 23:14, 17
20 [I]Lit., *souls* [II]Or, *flying ones*
21 [a]Ps. 91:3; 124:7
22 [I]Lit., *strengthen the hands of* [a]Amos 5:12 [b]Jer. 23:14; 34:16, 22 [c]Ezek. 18:21, 27, 30-32; 33:14-16
23 [I]Lit., *vanity* [a]Ezek. 12:24; 13:6; Mic. 3:6; Zech. 13:3 [b]Ezek. 13:21; 34:10 [c]Ezek. 13:9, 21

1 [a]2Kin. 6:32; Ezek. 8:1; 20:1 [b]Is. 29:13; Ezek. 33:31, 32
3 [a]Ezek. 20:16 [b]Ezek. 7:19; 14:4, 7; Zeph. 1:3 [c]Is. 1:15; Jer. 11:11; Ezek. 20:3, 31
4 [I]Heb., *YHWH,* usually rendered *LORD,* and so throughout the ch. [II]Lit., *it* [a]1Kin. 21:20-24; 2Kin. 1:16; Is. 66:4
5 [I]Lit., *their* [II]Or, *all estranged from Me through their idols* [a]Jer. 17:10; Zech. 7:12 [b]Is. 1:4; Jer. 2:11; Zech. 11:8
6 [a]1Sam. 7:3; Neh. 1:9; Is. 2:20; 30:22; 55:6, 7; Ezek. 18:30 [b]Ezek. 8:6; 14:4
7 [a]Ex. 12:48; 20:10

heart, puts right before his face the stumbling block of his iniquity, and *then* comes to the prophet to inquire of Me for himself, [b]I the LORD will be brought to answer him in My own person.

8 "And I shall [a]set My face against that man and make him a [b]sign[226] and [1]a proverb, and I shall cut him off[3772] from among My people.[5971] So you will know[3045] that I am the LORD.

9 "But if the prophet is [1]prevailed upon to speak[1696] a word,[1697] it is I, the LORD, who have [1]prevailed upon that prophet, and I will stretch out My hand[3027] against him and [a]destroy[8045] him from among My people Israel.

10 "And they will bear[5375] *the punishment of* their iniquity;[5771] as the iniquity of the inquirer is, so the iniquity of the prophet will be,

11 in order that the house of Israel may no longer [a]stray from Me and no longer [b]defile[2930] themselves with all their transgressions.[6588] Thus they will be [c]My people, and I shall be their God,"[430] declares[5001] the Lord GOD."

The City Will Not Be Spared

🔑 **12** Then the word of the LORD came to me saying,

13 "Son of man, if a country[776] sins[2398] against Me by [a]committing unfaithfulness, and I stretch out My hand against it, [1]destroy[7665] its [b]supply[4294] of bread, send famine against it, and cut off[3772] from it both man and beast,

14 even [a]*though* these three men, [b]Noah, [c]Daniel, and [d]Job were in its midst, by their *own* righteousness[6666] they could *only* deliver[5337] [e]themselves,"[5315] declares the Lord GOD.

15 "If I were to cause [a]wild beasts[2416] to pass through[5674] the land, and they [1]depopulated it, and it became desolate[8077] so that no one would pass through it because of the beasts,

16 *though* these three men were in its midst, as I live,"[2416] declares the Lord GOD, "they could not deliver either *their* sons[1121] or *their* daughters. [a]They alone would be delivered,[5337] but the country would be desolate.

17 "Or *if* I should [a]bring a sword[2719] on that country and say, 'Let the sword pass through the country and [b]cut off man and beast from it,'

18 even *though* these three men were in its midst, as I live," declares the Lord GOD, "they could not deliver either *their* sons or *their* daughters, but they alone would be delivered.

19 "Or *if* I should send a [a]plague[1698] against that country and pour out[8210] My wrath in blood[1818] on it, to cut off man and beast from it,

20 even *though* Noah, Daniel, and Job were in its midst, as I live," declares the Lord GOD, "they could not deliver either *their* son or *their* daughter. They would deliver only themselves by their righteousness."

21 For thus says the Lord GOD, "How much more when [a]I send My four [1]severe[7451] judgments[8201] against Jerusalem: sword, famine, wild beasts,[2416] and plague to cut off man and beast from it!

22 "Yet, behold, [1]survivors[6413] will be left[3498] in it who will be brought out, *both* sons and daughters. Behold, they are going to come forth to you and you will [a]see their conduct[1870] and actions; then you will be [b]comforted[5162] for the calamity[7451] which I have brought against Jerusalem for everything which I have brought upon it.

23 "Then they will comfort[5162] you when you see their conduct[1870] and actions, for you will know that I have not done[6213] [a]in vain whatever I did [1]to it," declares the Lord GOD.

Jerusalem Like a Useless Vine

15 Then the word[1697] of the LORD came to me saying,

2 "Son[1121] of man,[120] how is the wood of the [a]vine *better* than any wood

7 [b]Ezek. 14:4

8 [1]Lit., *proverbs* [a]Jer. 44:11; Ezek. 15:7 [b]Is. 65:15; Ezek. 5:15

9 [1]Or, *enticed* [a]Jer. 6:14, 15; 14:15

11 [a]Ezek. 44:10, 15; 48:11 [b]Ezek. 11:18; 37:23 [c]Ezek. 11:20; 34:30; 36:28

13 [1]Lit., *break the staff* [a]Ezek. 15:8; 20:27 [b]Lev. 26:26; Is. 3:1; Ezek. 4:16

14 [a]Jer. 15:1 [b]Gen. 6:8; 7:1; Heb. 11:7 [c]Ezek. 28:3; Dan. 1:6; 9:21; 10:11 [d]Job 1:1, 5; 42:8, 9 [e]Ezek. 16:18, 20; 18:20

15 [1]Lit., *bereave of children* [a]Lev. 26:22; Num. 21:6; Ezek. 5:17; 14:21

16 [a]Gen. 19:29; Ezek. 18:20

17 [a]Lev. 26:25; Ezek. 5:12; 21:3, 4 [b]Ezek. 25:13; Zeph. 1:3

19 [a]Jer. 14:12; Ezek. 5:12; 14:21

21 [1]Lit., *evil* [a]Ezek. 5:17; 33:27; Amos 4:6-10; Rev. 6:8

22 [1]Lit., *escaped ones* [a]Ezek. 12:16; 36:20 [b]Ezek. 16:54; 31:16; 32:31

23 [1]Or, *in* [a]Jer. 22:8, 9

2 [a]Ps. 80:8-16; Is. 5:1-7; Hos. 10:1

🔑 **14:12-20** See note on Ezek. 18:1-4.

of a branch which is among the trees of the forest?

3 "Can wood be taken from it to make[6213] [I]anything,[4399] or can *men* take a peg from it on which to hang any vessel?

4 "[I]If it has been put into the [a]fire for fuel, *and* the fire has consumed both of its ends, and its middle part has been charred,[2787] is it *then* useful for [II]anything?

5 "Behold, while it is intact,[8549] it is not made into [I]anything. How much less, when the fire has consumed it and it is charred, can it still be made into [I]anything!

6 "Therefore, thus says[559] the Lord[136] [I]GOD, 'As the wood of the vine among the trees of the forest, which I have given to the fire for fuel, so have I given up the inhabitants of Jerusalem;

7 and I [a]set[7760] My face against them. *Though* they have [b]come out of the fire, yet the fire will consume them. Then you will know[3045] that I am the LORD, when I set My face against them.

8 'Thus I will make the land[776] desolate,[8077] because they have [a]acted[4603] unfaithfully,' "[4604] declares[5001] the Lord GOD.

God's Grace to Unfaithful Jerusalem

16 Then the word[1697] of the LORD came to me saying,

2 "Son[1121] of man,[120] [a]make known[3045] to Jerusalem her abominations,[8441]

3 and say,[559] 'Thus says[559] the Lord[136] [I]GOD to Jerusalem, "Your origin and your birth are from the land[776] of the Canaanite, your father[1] was an Amorite and your mother[517] a Hittite.

4 "As for your birth, [a]on the day[3117] you were born your navel cord was not cut,[3772] nor were you washed[7364] with water for cleansing; you were not rubbed with salt or even wrapped in cloths.2858

5 "No eye looked with pity on you to do[6213] any of these things for you, to have compassion on you. Rather you were thrown out into the [Ia]open field,[7704] [II]for you[5315] were abhorred on the day you were born.

6 "When I passed by[5674] you and saw[7200] you squirming[947] in your blood,[1818] I said[559] to you *while you were* in your blood, 'Live!'[2421] I said to you while you were in your blood, 'Live!'

7 "I [a]made you [I]numerous like plants of the field. Then you grew up, became tall, and reached the age for fine ornaments; *your* breasts were formed[3559] and your hair had grown. Yet you were naked and bare.[6181]

8 "Then I passed by you and saw[7200] you, and behold, [I]you were at the time[6256] for love;[1730] so I [a]spread My skirt over you and covered[3680] your nakedness.[6172] I also [b]swore[7650] to you and [c]entered into a covenant[1285] with you so that you [d]became Mine," declares[5001] the Lord GOD.

9 "Then I bathed you with water, washed off[7857] your blood from you, and [a]anointed[5480] you with oil.[8081]

10 "I also clothed you with [a]embroidered cloth, and put sandals of porpoise skin on your feet;5274 and I wrapped[2280] you with fine linen and covered you with silk.

11 "And I adorned you with ornaments, put [a]bracelets on your hands,[3027] and a [b]necklace around your neck.

12 "I also put a [a]ring in your nostril,[639] earrings in your ears,[241] and a [b]beautiful[8597] crown on your head.[7218]

13 "Thus you were adorned with [a]gold and silver, and your dress was of fine linen, silk, and embroidered cloth. You ate fine flour, honey, and oil; so you were exceedingly beautiful and advanced to [b]royalty.

14 "Then your [a]fame went forth among the nations[1471] on account of your beauty, for it was [b]perfect[3632] because of My splendor[1926] which I bestowed on you," declares the Lord GOD.

15 "But you [a]trusted[982] in your beauty and [b]played the harlot[2181] because of your fame, and you poured out

3 [I]Lit., *a work*

4 [I]Or, *Behold* [II]Lit., *a work* [a]Is. 27:11; Ezek. 15:6; 19:14

5 [I]Lit., *a work*

6 [I]Heb., *YHWH*, usually rendered LORD, and so throughout the ch.

7 [a]Lev. 26:17; Ps. 34:16; Jer. 21:10; Ezek. 14:8 [b]1Kin. 19:17; Is. 24:18; Amos 9:1-4

8 [a]Ezek. 14:13; 17:20

2 [a]Is. 58:1; Ezek. 20:4; 22:2

3 [I]Heb., *YHWH*, usually rendered LORD, and so throughout the ch.

4 [a]Hos. 2:3

5 [I]Lit., *surface* [II]Lit., *in the loathing of your soul* [a]Deut. 32:10

7 [I]Lit., *a myriad* [a]Ex. 1:7; Deut. 1:10

8 [I]Lit., *your time was* [a]Ruth 3:9; Jer. 2:2 [b]Gen. 22:16-18 [c]Ex. 24:7, 8 [d]Ex. 19:5; Ezek. 20:5; Hos. 2:19, 20

9 [a]Ruth 3:3

10 [a]Ex. 26:36; Ezek. 16:13, 18; 26:16; 27:7, 16

11 [a]Gen. 24:22, 47; Is. 3:19; Ezek. 23:42 [b]Gen. 41:42; Prov. 1:9

12 [a]Gen. 24:47; Is. 3:21 [b]Is. 28:5; Jer. 13:18; Ezek. 16:14

13 [a]Ps. 45:13, 14; Ezek. 16:17 [b]1Sam. 10:1; 1Kin. 4:21

14 [a]1Kin. 10:1, 24 [b]Ps. 50:2; Lam. 2:15

15 [a]Ezek. 16:25; 27:3 [b]Is. 57:8; Jer. 2:20

your harlotries[8457] on every passer-by [I]who might be *willing*.

16 "And you took some of your clothes, made[6213] for yourself high places[1116] of various colors, and played the harlot on them, [I]which should never come about nor happen.

17 "You also took your beautiful[8597] [Ia]jewels *made* of My gold and of My silver, which I had given you, and made for yourself male images[6754] that you might play the harlot[2181] with them.

18 "Then you took your embroidered cloth and covered them, and offered My oil and My incense[7004] before them.

19 "Also [a]My bread which I gave you, fine flour, oil, and honey with which I fed you, [I]you would offer before them for a soothing aroma; so it happened," declares the Lord GOD.

20 "Moreover, you took your sons[1121] and daughters whom you had borne to [a]Me, and you [b]sacrificed[2076] them to [I]idols to be devoured. Were your harlotries[8457] so small a matter?

21 "You slaughtered[7891] [a]My children,[1121] and offered them up to [I]idols by [b]causing them to pass through[5674] *the fire*.

22 "And besides all your abominations and harlotries you did not remember[2142] the days[3117] of [a]your youth, when you were naked and bare and squirming in your blood.

23 "Then it came about after all your wickedness[7451] ('Woe, woe to you!' declares the Lord GOD),

24 that you built yourself a [a]shrine and made[6213] yourself a [b]high place in every square.

25 "You built yourself a high place at the top of [a]every street,[1870] and made your beauty abominable;[8581] and you spread your legs to every passer-by to multiply your harlotry.

26 "You also played the harlot[2181] with the Egyptians, your [I]lustful neighbors,[7934] and multiplied your harlotry to [a]make Me angry.[3707]

27 "Behold now, I have stretched out My hand[3027] against you and diminished your rations.[2706] And I delivered you up to the desire of those who hate[8130] you, the [a]daughters of the Philistines, who are ashamed of your lewd[2154] conduct.

28 "Moreover, you played the harlot[2181] with the [a]Assyrians because you were not satisfied; you even played the harlot[2181] with them and still were not satisfied.

29 "You also multiplied your harlotry[8457] with the land of merchants, Chaldea, yet even with this you were not satisfied."'"

30 "How [a]languishing is your heart,"[3826] declares the Lord GOD, "while you do[6213] all these things, the actions of a [Ib] bold-faced harlot.[2181]

31 "When you built[1129] your shrine at the beginning of every street and made[6213] your high place in every square, in [a]disdaining money, you were not like a harlot.

32 "You adulteress[5003] wife,[802] who takes strangers instead of her husband![376]

33 "[I]Men give gifts to all harlots,[2181] but you [a]give your gifts to all your lovers[157] to bribe them to come to you from every direction for your harlotries.[8457]

34 "Thus you are different from those women[802] in your harlotries, in that no one plays the harlot [I]as you do, because you give money and no money is given you; thus you are different."

35 Therefore, O harlot, hear[8085] the word of the LORD.

36 Thus says the Lord GOD, "Because your lewdness was poured out[8210] and your nakedness uncovered through your harlotries with your lovers and with all your detestable [a]idols,[1544] and because of the blood of your sons which you gave to [I]idols,

37 therefore, behold, I shall [a]gather[6908] all your lovers with whom you took pleasure,[6148] even all those whom you loved[157] *and* all those whom you [b]hated. So I shall gather them against you from every direction and

15 [I]Lit., *to whom it might be*

16 [I]Lit., *things which had not happened nor will it be*

17 [I]Lit., *articles of beauty* [a]Ezek. 16:11, 12

19 [I]Lit., *and you. . .offer it* [a]Hos. 2:8

20 [I]Lit., *them* [a]Ex. 13:2, 12; Deut. 29:11, 12 [b]Ps. 106:37, 38; Jer. 7:31; Ezek. 20:31; 23:37

21 [I]Lit., *them* [a]Ex. 13:2 [b]2Kin. 17:17; Jer. 19:5

22 [a]Jer. 2:2

24 [a]Jer. 11:13; Ezek. 16:31, 39; 20:28, 29 [b]Ps. 78:58; Is. 57:7

25 [a]Prov. 9:14

26 [I]Lit., *great of flesh* [a]Jer. 7:18, 19; Ezek. 8:17

27 [a]Is. 9:12; Ezek. 16:57

28 [a]2Kin. 16:7, 10-18; 2Chr. 28:16, 20-23; Jer. 2:18, 36; Ezek. 23:12; Hos. 10:6

30 [I]Lit., *domineering* [a]Prov. 9:13; Is. 1:3; Jer. 4:22 [b]Is. 3:9; Jer. 3:3

31 [a]Is. 52:3

33 [I]Lit., *they* [a]Is. 57:9; Ezek. 16:41; Hos. 8:9, 10

34 [I]Lit., *after you*

36 [I]Lit., *them* [a]Jer. 19:5; Ezek. 20:31; 23:37

37 [a]Jer. 13:22, 26; Ezek. 23:9, 22; Hos. 2:3, 10; Nah. 3:5, 6 [b]Ezek. 23:17, 28

[c]expose[1540] your nakedness to them that they may see all your nakedness.

38 "Thus I shall [a]judge[8199] you, like women who commit adultery or shed[8210] blood are judged; and I shall bring on you the blood of [b]wrath and jealousy.

39 "I shall also give you into [I]the hands of your lovers, and they will teardown[2040] your shrines, demolish your high places, [a]strip you of your clothing, take away your [II]jewels, and will leave you naked and bare.

40 "They will [I]incite[5927] a [a]crowd[6951] against you, and they will stone you and cut you to pieces with their swords.[2719]

41 "And they will [a]burn your houses[1004] with fire and execute judgments[8201] on you in the sight of many women. Then I shall [b]stop[7673] you from playing the harlot, and you will also no longer pay [I]your lovers.

42 "So I [a]shall calm My fury against you, and My jealousy will depart[5493] from you, and I shall be pacified[8252] and angry[3707] [b]no more.

43 "Because you have [a]not remembered the days of your youth but [I]have [b]enraged Me by all these things, behold, I in turn will [c]bring your conduct down on your own head," declares the Lord GOD, "so that you will not commit[6213] this lewdness[2154] on top of all your *other* abominations.

44 "Behold, everyone who quotes [a]proverbs will quote *this* proverb concerning you, saying, '[I]Like mother, [I]like daughter.'

45 "You are the daughter of your mother,[517] who loathed her husband and children. You are also the [a]sister[269] of your sisters,[269] who [b]loathed their husbands[582] and children. Your mother was a Hittite and your father an Amorite.

46 "Now your [a]older sister is Samaria, who lives [I]north of you with her [II]daughters; and your younger sister, who lives [III]south of you, is [b]Sodom with her [II]daughters.

47 "Yet you have not merely walked in their ways[1870] or done[6213] according to their abominations; but, as if that were [a]too little, you acted [b]more corruptly[7843] in all your conduct than they.

48 "As I live,"[2416] declares the Lord GOD, "Sodom, your sister, and her daughters, have [a]not done as you and your daughters have done.

49 "Behold, this was the guilt[5771] of your sister Sodom: she and her daughters had [a]arrogance, [b]abundant food, and [c]careless ease,[8252] but she did not [I]help[2388] the [d]poor and needy.

50 "Thus they were haughty and committed[6213] [a]abominations[8441] before Me. Therefore I [b]removed them [I]when I saw *it*.

51 "Furthermore, Samaria did not commit[2398] half of your sins, for you have multiplied your abominations more than they. Thus you have made your sisters appear [a]righteous[6663] by all your abominations which you have committed.

52 "Also bear[5375] your disgrace in that you have [I]made judgment favorable for your sisters. Because of your sins in which you acted [a]more abominably[8581] than they, they are more in the right[6663] than you. Yes, be also ashamed[954] and bear your disgrace, in that you made your sisters appear righteous.

53 "Nevertheless, I will restore[7725] their captivity,[7622] the captivity of Sodom and her daughters, the captivity of Samaria and her daughters, and [I]along with them [II]your own captivity,

54 in order that you may bear your humiliation, and feel [a]ashamed for all that you have done when you become [b]a consolation[5162] to them.

55 "And your sisters, Sodom with her daughters and Samaria with her daughters, [I]will return[7725] to their former state,[6927] and you with your daughters will *also* return to your former state.

56 "As *the name of* your sister Sodom was not heard from your lips[6310] in your day of pride,

57 before your [a]wickedness was uncovered, [I]so now you have become the

37 [c]Is. 47:3
38 [a]Ezek. 23:45 [b]Ps. 79:3, 5; Jer. 18:21; Ezek. 23:25; Zeph. 1:17
39 [I]Lit., *their hands, and they* [II]Lit., *articles of beauty* [a]Ezek. 23:26; Hos. 2:3
40 [I]Lit., *bring up an assembly* [a]Ezek. 23:47; Hab. 1:6-10
41 [I]Lit., *a harlot's hire* [a]2Kin. 25:9; Jer. 39:8; 52:13 [b]Ezek. 23:48
42 [a]2 Sam. 24:25; Ezek. 5:13; 21:17; Zech. 6:8 [b]Is. 40:1, 2; 54:9, 10; Ezek. 39:29
43 [I]So with ancient versions; Heb., *are angry against* [a]Ps. 78:42; 106:13; Ezek. 16:22 [b]Is. 63:10; Ezek. 6:9 [c]Ezek. 11:21; 22:31
44 [I]Lit., *Her* [a]1 Sam. 24:13; Ezek. 12:22, 23; 18:2, 3
45 [a]Ezek. 23:2 [b]Is. 1:4; Ezek. 23:37-39; Zech. 11:8
46 [I]Lit., *on your left* [II]I.e., environs; so through v. 55 [III]Lit., *from your right* [a]Jer. 3:8-11; Ezek. 23:4 [b]Gen. 13:10-13; 18:20; Ezek. 16:48, 49, 53-56, 61
47 [a]1Kin. 16:31 [b]2 Kin. 21:9; Ezek. 5:6; 16:48, 51
48 [a]Matt. 10:15; 11:23, 24
49 [I]Lit., *grasp the hand of* [a]Gen. 19:9; Ps. 138:6; Is. 3:9; Ezek. 28:2, 9, 17 [b]Gen. 13:10; Is. 22:13; Amos 6:4-6 [c]Luke 12:16-20; 16:19 [d]Ezek. 18:7, 12, 16
50 [I]Many ancient mss. and versions read *as you have seen* [a]Gen. 13:13; 18:20; 19:5 [b]Gen. 19:24, 25
51 [a]Jer. 3:8-11
52 [I]Lit., *mediated for* [a]Ezek. 16:47, 48, 51
53 [I]Lit., *in their midst* [II]Lit., *the captivity of your captivity*
54 [a]Jer. 2:26 [b]Ezek. 14:22, 23
55 [I]Heb. includes *will return. . . state* after Sodom also
57 [I]Lit., *as at the time of* [a]Ezek. 16:36, 37

[b]reproach[2781] of the daughters of [II]Edom, and of all who are around her, of the daughters of the Philistines—those surrounding *you* who despise you.

58 "You have [a]borne[5375] *the penalty of* your lewdness and abominations," the LORD declares.

59 For thus says the Lord GOD, "I will also do[6213] with you as you have done, you who have [a]despised the oath[423] by breaking[6565] the covenant.

The Covenant Remembered

60 "Nevertheless, I will remember[2142] My covenant with you in the days of your youth, and I will establish an [a]everlasting[5769] covenant with you.

61 "Then you will [a]remember your ways and be ashamed when you receive your sisters, *both* your older and your younger; and I will give them to you as daughters, but not because of your covenant.

62 "Thus I will [a]establish My covenant with you, and you shall [b]know that I am the LORD,

63 in order that you may [a]remember and be ashamed, and [b]never open your mouth anymore because of your humiliation, when I have [c]forgiven[3722] you for all that you have done," the Lord GOD declares.

Parable of Two Eagles and a Vine

17 Now the word[1697] of the LORD came to me saying,

2 "Son[1121] of man,[120] propound a riddle,[2420] and speak a [a]parable to the house[1004] of Israel,

3 [I]saying,[559] 'Thus says[559] the Lord[136] [II]GOD, "A great [a]eagle with [b]great wings, long pinions and a full plumage of many colors, came to [c]Lebanon and took away the top of the cedar.

4 "He plucked off the topmost[7218] of its young twigs and brought it to a land[776] of merchants;[3667] he set[7760] it in a city of traders.

5 "He also took some of the seed[2233] of the land and planted it in [Ia]fertile soil.[7704] He [II]placed *it* beside abundant waters; he set it *like* a [b]willow.

6 "Then it sprouted and became a low, spreading vine with its branches turned toward him, but its roots remained under it. So it became a vine, and yielded[5375] shoots and sent out branches.

7 "But there was [I]another great eagle with great wings and much plumage; and behold, this vine bent its roots toward him and sent out its branches toward him from the beds[6170] where it was [a]planted, that he might water it.

8 "It was planted in good[2896] [I]soil beside abundant waters, that it might yield[6213] branches and bear[5375] fruit, *and* become a splendid vine."'

9 "Say, 'Thus says the Lord GOD, "Will it thrive? Will he not pull up its roots and cut off its fruit, so that it withers—[3001] so that all its sprouting leaves wither? And neither by great [I]strength nor by many people[5971] can it be raised from its roots *again*.

10 "Behold, though it is planted, will it thrive? Will it not [a]completely wither as soon as the east wind[7307] strikes[5060] it—wither on the beds where it grew?"'"

Zedekiah's Rebellion

11 Moreover, the word of the LORD came to me saying,

12 "Say now to the [a]rebellious[4805] house, 'Do you not [b]know[3045] what these things *mean?*' Say,[559] 'Behold, the [c]king[4428] of Babylon came to Jerusalem, took its king and princes,[8269] and brought them to him in Babylon.

13 'And he took one of the royal [Ia]family and made[3772] a covenant[1285] with him, [II]putting him under [b]oath.[423] He also took away the [c]mighty of the land,

14 that the kingdom[4467] might [a]be [I]in subjection, not exalting itself, *but* keeping[8104] his covenant, that it might continue.

15 'But he [a]rebelled[4775] against him by sending his envoys[4397] to Egypt that

---

57 [II]So with many mss. and one version; M.T., *Aram* [b]2Kin. 16:5-7; 2Chr. 28:5, 6, 18-23; Ezek. 5:14, 15; 22:4

58 [a]Ezek. 23:49

59 [a]Is. 24:5; Ezek. 17:19

60 [a]Is. 55:3; Jer. 32:38-41; Ezek. 37:26

61 [a]Jer. 50:4, 5; Ezek. 6:9

62 [a]Ezek. 20:37; 34:25; 37:26 [b]Jer. 24:7; Ezek. 20:43, 44

63 [a]Ezek. 36:31, 32; Dan. 9:7, 8 [b]Ps. 39:9; Rom. 3:19 [c]Ps. 65:3; 78:38; 79:9

2 [a]Ezek. 20:49; 24:3

3 [I]Lit., *and you shall say* [II]Heb., *YHWH*, usually rendered *LORD*, and so throughout the ch. [a]Jer. 48:40; Ezek. 17:12; Hos. 8:1 [b]Dan. 4:22 [c]Jer. 22:23

5 [I]Lit., *a field of seed* [II]Lit., *took* [a]Deut. 8:7-9 [b]Is. 44:4

7 [I]So with several ancient versions; M.T., *one* [a]Ezek. 31:4

8 [I]Lit., *field*

9 [I]Lit., *arm*

10 [a]Ezek. 19:14; Hos. 13:15

12 [a]Ezek. 2:3-5 [b]Ezek. 12:9-11; 24:19 [c]2Kin. 24:11, 12, 15; Ezek. 1:2; 17:3

13 [I]Lit., *seed* [II]Lit., *and caused him to enter into an oath* [a]2Kin. 24:17; Ezek. 17:5 [b]2Chr. 36:13 [c]2Kin. 24:15,16

14 [I]Lit., *low* [a]Ezek. 29:14

15 [a]2Kin. 24:20; 2Chr. 36:13; Jer. 52:3; Ezek. 17:7

they might give him horses and many [I]troops. Will he succeed? Will he who does[6213] such things [b]escape?[4422] Can he indeed break[6565] the covenant and escape?[4422]

16 ‘As I live,’[2416] declares[5001] the Lord GOD, ‘Surely in the [I]country of the king[4427] who [II]put him on the throne, whose oath he [a]despised, and whose covenant he broke,[6565] [IIIb]in Babylon he shall die.[4191]

17 ‘And [a]Pharaoh with *his* mighty army[2428] and great company[6951] will not [I]help[6213] him in the war, when they cast up[8210] mounds and build siege walls to cut off[3772] many lives.[5315]

18 ‘Now he despised the oath by breaking[6565] the covenant, and behold, he [Ia]pledged his allegiance,[3027] yet did[6213] all these things; he shall not escape.’ ”

19 Therefore, thus says the Lord GOD, “As I live, surely My oath which he despised and My covenant which he broke, I will [I]inflict on his head.[7218]

20 “And I will spread My [a]net over him, and he will be [b]caught in My snare. Then I will bring him to Babylon and [c]enter into judgment[8199] with him there *regarding* the unfaithful act[4604] which he has committed against Me.

21 “And all the [Ia]choice men in all his troops will fall by the sword,[2719] and the survivors will be scattered to every wind;[7307] and you will know that I, the LORD, have spoken.”[1696]

22 Thus says the Lord GOD, “I shall also take *a sprig* from the lofty top of the cedar and set *it* out; I shall pluck from the topmost of its young twigs a tender one, and I shall plant *it* on a [a]high and lofty mountain.

23 “On the high mountain of Israel I shall plant it, that it may bring[5375] forth boughs and bear fruit, and become a stately [a]cedar. And birds of every [I]kind will [II]nest[7931] under it; they will [II]nest in the shade of its branches.

24 “And all the [a]trees of the field will know that I am the LORD; I bring down the high tree, exalt the low tree, dry up[3001] the green tree, and make the dry[3002] tree [b]flourish. I am the LORD; I have spoken, and I will perform *it*.”

God Deals Justly with Individuals

18 Then the word[1697] of the LORD came to me saying,

2 “[a]What do you mean by using this proverb concerning the land[127] of Israel saying,

‘[b]The fathers[1] eat the sour
grapes,
But the children’s teeth [I]are set
on edge’?

3 “As I live,”[2416] declares[5001] the Lord[136] [I]GOD, “you are surely not going to use this proverb in Israel anymore.

4 “Behold, [a]all [I]souls[5315] are Mine; the [II]soul[5315] of the father[1] as well as the [II]soul of the son[1121] is Mine. The [III]soul who [b]sins[2398] will die.[4191]

5 “But if a man[376] is righteous, and practices[6213] justice[4941] and righteousness,[6666]

6 and does not [a]eat at the mountain *shrines* or [b]lift up[5375] his eyes to the

15 [I]Lit., *people* [b]Jer. 34:3; 38:18, 23; Ezek. 17:18
16 [I]Lit., *place* [II]Lit., *made him king* [III]Lit., *with him in Babylon* [a]2 Kin. 24:17, 20; Ezek. 16:59; 17:13, 18, 19 [b]Jer. 52:11; Ezek. 12:13
17 [I]Lit., *act with* [a]Is. 36:6; Jer. 37:5, 7; Ezek. 29:6, 7
18 [I]Lit., *gave his hand* [a]1Chr. 29:24
19 [I]Lit., *give it*
20 [a]Ezek. 12:13; 32:3 [b]Jer. 39:5-7 [c]Jer. 2:35; Ezek. 20:35, 36
21 [I]So many ancient mss. and versions; M.T., *fugitives* [a]2 Kin. 25:5, 11; Ezek. 5:2, 10, 12-14
22 [a]Ps. 72:16; Ezek. 20:40; 37:22
23 [I]Lit., *wing* [II]Lit., *dwell* [a]Ps. 92:12
24 [a]Ps. 96:12; Is. 55:12 [b]Amos 9:11

2 [I]Lit., *become dull* [a]Is. 3:15 [b]Jer. 31:29; Lam. 5:7
3 [I]Heb., *YHWH*, usually rendered *LORD*, and so throughout the ch.
4 [I]Or, *lives* [II]Or, *life* [III]Or, *person* [a]Num. 16:22; 27:16; Is. 42:5; 57:16 [b]Ezek. 18:20; Rom. 6:23
6 [a]Ezek. 6:13; 18:15; 22:9 [b]Deut. 4:19; Ezek. 18:12, 15; 20:24; 33:25

18:1-4 One of the features of the religious thought of the Book of Ezekiel which stands out is individual responsibility for one’s own actions (3:16-21; 14:12-20; 18:1-32; 33:1-20). In this passage the Lord was disapproving of an old proverb in Israel and replacing it with one of His own: “The soul who sins will die.” To a far greater extent than in the religion of the N.T., Israel had a group relationship with God. The Babylonian exile, in which Ezekiel himself was participating, was God’s judgment on a sinful nation, and many righteous people had to suffer alongside the sinners. Nevertheless, God now wanted it emphasized that individual guilt and righteousness should not be swallowed up in the group, even when the group was the family. Depending on the stress laid, the law could be read either way. In the Ten Commandments God stated that He would visit “the iniquity of the fathers on the children, on the third and fourth generations” (Ex. 20:5; Deut. 5:9), but in Deut. 24:16, fathers and children are not to be held responsible for each others’ guilt. Therefore, by rejecting the old proverb, God was settling in Ezek. 18 (and Jer. 31:29,30) any question anyone might have.

idols[1544] of the house[1004] of Israel, or [c]defile[2930] his neighbor's[7453] wife,[802] or approach[7126] a woman[802] during her menstrual period—

7 if a man does not oppress[3238] anyone, but [a]restores[7725] to the debtor his pledge,[2258] [b]does not commit robbery, *but* [c]gives his bread to the hungry, and covers[3680] the naked with clothing,

8 if he does not lend *money* on [a]interest or take [b]increase, *if* he keeps[7725] his hand[3027] from iniquity,[5766] *and* [c]executes[6213] true[571] justice[4941] between man and man,

9 *if* he walks in [a]My statutes[2708] and My ordinances[4941] so as to deal[6213] faithfully—[571] [b]he is righteous *and* will surely [c]live,"[2421] declares the Lord GOD.

10 "Then he may [I]have a violent[6530] son who sheds blood,[1818] and who does[6213] any of these things to a brother

11 (though he himself did not do any of these things), that is, he even eats at the mountain *shrines,* and [a]defiles his neighbor's wife,

12 oppresses the [a]poor and needy, [b]commits robbery, does not restore a pledge, but lifts up his eyes to the idols, *and* [c]commits[6213] abomination,[8441]

13 he [a]lends *money* on interest and takes increase; will he live?[2425] He will not live! He has committed[6213] all these abominations,[8441] he will surely be put to death;[4191] his [b]blood will be [I]on his own head.

14 "Now behold, he [I]has a son who has observed[7200] all his father's[1] sins which he committed, and [a]observing[7200] does not do likewise.

15 "He does not eat at the mountain *shrines* or lift up his eyes to the idols of the house of Israel, or defile his neighbor's wife,

16 or oppress anyone, or retain[2254] a pledge, or commit robbery, *but* he [a]gives his bread to the hungry, and covers the naked with clothing,

17 he keeps[7725] his hand from [I]the poor, does not take interest or increase, *but* executes My ordinances, and walks in My statutes; [a]he will not die for his father's iniquity,[5771] he will surely live.

18 "As for his father, because he practiced extortion, robbed *his* brother,[251] and did[6213] what was not good[2896] among his people,[5971] behold, he will die for his iniquity.

19 "Yet you say,[559] '[a]Why should the son not bear[5375] the punishment for the father's iniquity?' When the son has practiced [b]justice and righteousness, and has observed all My statutes and done them, he shall surely live.

20 "The person who [a]sins will die. The [b]son will not bear the punishment for the father's iniquity, nor will the father bear the punishment for the son's iniquity; the [c]righteousness[6666] of the righteous[6662] will be upon himself, and the wickedness[7564] of the wicked will be upon himself.

21 "But if the [a]wicked man turns[7725] from all his sins which he has committed and observes[8104] all My statutes and practices justice and righteousness, he shall surely live; he shall not die.

22 "[a]All his transgressions[6588] which he has committed will not be remembered[2142] against him; because of his [b]righteousness which he has practiced, he will live.

23 "[a]Do I have any pleasure in the death[4194] of the wicked," declares the Lord GOD, "[I]rather than that he should [b]turn[7725] from his ways[1870] and live?

24 "But when a righteous man [a]turns away[7725] from his righteousness, commits[6213] iniquity, and does according to all the abominations that a wicked man does, will he live? [b]All his righteous deeds which he has done will not be remembered for his [c]treachery[4604] which he has committed and his sin[2403] which he has committed;[2398] for them he will die.

25 "Yet you say, '[a]The way[1870] of the Lord is not right.' Hear[8085] now, O house of Israel! Is [b]My way not right? Is it not your ways that are not right?

26 "When a righteous man turns away from his righteousness, commits

6 [c]Ezek. 18:15; 22:11
7 [a]Deut. 24:13; Ezek. 33:15; Amos 2:8 [b]Lev. 19:13; Amos 3:10 [c]Deut. 15:11; Ezek. 18:16; Matt. 25:35-40; Luke 3:11
8 [a]Ex. 22:25; Deut. 23:19, 20 [b]Lev. 25:36 [c]Zech. 7:9; 8:16
9 [a]Lev. 18:5 [b]Rom. 8:1 [c]Amos 5:4; Hab. 2:4; Rom. 1:17
10 [I]Lit., *beget*
11 [a]1Cor. 6:9
12 [a]Amos 4:1; Zech. 7:10 [b]Is. 59:6, 7; Jer. 22:3, 17; Ezek. 7:23; 18:7, 16, 18 [c]2Kin. 21:11; Ezek. 8:6, 17
13 [I]Lit., *on him* [a]Ex. 22:25 [b]Ezek. 33:4, 5
14 [I]Lit., *begets* [a]2Chr. 29:6-10; 34:21
16 [a]Job 31:16, 20; Ps. 41:1; Is. 58:7, 10; Ezek. 18:7
17 [I]So M.T.; Gr. reads *iniquity* as in v. 8 [a]Rom. 2:7
19 [a]Ex. 20:5; Jer. 15:4; Ezek. 18:2 [b]Ezek. 18:9; 20:18-20; Zech. 1:3-6
20 [a]2Kin. 14:6; 22:18-20; Ezek. 18:4 [b]Deut. 24:16; Jer. 31:30 [c]1Kin. 8:32; Is. 3:10, 11; Matt. 16:27; Rom. 2:6-9
21 [a]Ezek. 18:27, 28; 33:12,19
22 [a]Is. 43:25; Jer. 50:20; Ezek. 18:24; 33:16; Mic. 7:19 [b]Ps. 18:20-24
23 [I]Lit., *is it not* [a]Ezek. 18:32; 33:11 [b]Ps. 147:11; Mic. 7:18
24 [a]1Sam. 15:11; 2Chr. 24:2, 17-22; Ezek. 3:20; 18:26; 33:18 [b]Ezek. 18:22; Gal. 3:3, 4 [c]Prov. 21:16; Ezek. 17:20; 20:27

25 [a]Ezek. 18:29; 33:17, 20; Mal. 2:17; 3:13-15 [b]Gen. 18:25; Jer. 12:1; Zeph. 3:5

iniquity, and dies[4191] because of it, for his iniquity which he has committed he will die.

27 "Again, when a wicked man turns away [a]from his wickedness which he has committed and practices justice and righteousness, he will save[2421] his life.

28 "Because he considered and turned away from all his transgressions which he had committed, he shall surely live; he shall not die.

29 "But the house of Israel says,[559] 'The way of the Lord is not right.' Are My ways not right, O house of Israel? Is it not your ways that are not right?

30 "Therefore I will judge[8199] you, O house of Israel, each[376] according to his conduct," declares the Lord GOD. "[a]Repent[7725] and turn away from all your transgressions, so that iniquity may not become a stumbling block[4383] to you.

31 "'[a]Cast away from you all your transgressions which you have committed,[6586] and make[6213] yourselves a [b]new heart[3820] and a new spirit![7307] For why will you die, O house of Israel?

32 "For I have [a]no pleasure in the death[4194] of anyone who dies," declares the Lord GOD. "Therefore, repent and live."

Lament for the Princes of Israel

19 "As for you, take up[5375] a [a]lamentation for the [b]princes[5387] of Israel,

2 and say,[559]

'[I]What was your mother?[517]
A lioness among lions!
She lay down among young lions,
She reared her cubs.[1482]

3 'When she brought up[5927] one of her cubs,
He became a lion,
And he learned[3925] to tear *his* prey;
He devoured men.[120]

4 'Then nations[1471] heard[8085] about him;
He was captured in their pit,[7845]
And they [a]brought him with hooks
To the land[776] of Egypt.

5 'When she saw,[7200] as she waited,[3176]
That her hope was lost,[6]
She took [I]another of her cubs
And made[7760] him a young lion.

6 'And he [a]walked about among the lions;
He became a young lion,
He learned to tear *his* prey;
He devoured men.

7 'And he [I]destroyed[3045] their [II]fortified towers[490]
And laid waste[2717] their cities;
And the land and its fulness were appalled[3456]
Because of the sound of his roaring.

8 'Then [a]nations set against him
On every side from *their* provinces,
And they spread their net over him;
He was captured in their pit.

9 'And [a]they put him in a cage with hooks
And [b]brought him to the king[4428] of Babylon;
They brought him in hunting nets
So that his voice should be heard no more
On the mountains of Israel.

10 'Your mother was [a]like a vine in your [I]vineyard,
Planted by the waters;
It was fruitful and full of branches
Because of abundant waters.

11 'And it had [I][a]strong branches *fit* for scepters[7626] of rulers,[4910]
And its [b]height was raised above the clouds
So that it was seen[7200] in its height with the mass of its branches.

12 'But it was [a]plucked up in fury;
It was [b]cast down to the ground;[776]
And the [c]east wind[7307] dried up[3001] its fruit.
Its [I][d]strong branch [II]was torn off
So that [III]it withered;[3001]

27 [a]Is. 1:18; 55:7
30 [a]Ezek. 14:6; 33:11; Hos. 12:6
31 [a]Is. 1:16, 17; 55:7 [b]Ps. 51:10; Ezek. 11:19; 36:26
32 [a]Ezek. 18:23; 33:11
1 [a]Ezek. 2:10; 19:14 [b]2Kin. 23:29, 30, 34; 24:6, 12; 25:5-7
2 [I]Or, *Why did your mother, a lioness, lie down among lions; among young lions rear her cubs?*
4 [a]2Kin. 23:34; 2Chr. 36:4, 6
5 [I]Lit., *one*
6 [a]2Kin. 24:9; 2Chr. 36:9
7 [I]So Targum; M.T., *knew* [II]Or, *widows*
8 [a]2Kin. 24:11
9 [a]2Chr. 36:6 [b]2Kin. 24:15
10 [I]So with some ancient mss.; M.T., *blood* [a]Ps. 80:8-11
11 [I]Lit., *rods of strength* [a]Ps. 80:15 [b]Ezek. 31:3
12 [I]Lit., *rods of her strength* [II]So Gr.; M.T., *they were* [III]So Gr.; M.T., *they* [a]Jer. 31:28 [b]Lam. 2:1; Ezek. 28:17 [c]Ezek. 17:10; Hos. 13:15 [d]Is. 27:11; Ezek. 19:11

The fire consumed it.
13 'And now it is planted in the [a]wilderness,
In a dry and thirsty land.
14 'And [a]fire has gone out from *its* branch;[4294]
It has consumed its shoots *and* fruit,
So that there is not in it a [I]strong branch,
A scepter[7626] to rule.' "
This is a lamentation, and has become a lamentation.

God's Dealings with Israel Rehearsed

20 Now it came about in the seventh year, in the fifth *month,* on the tenth of the month, that [I]certain[582] of the [a]elders[2205] of Israel came to inquire of the LORD, and sat before me.

2 And the word[1697] of the LORD came to me saying,

3 "Son[1121] of man,[120] speak[1696] to the elders of Israel, and say[559] to them, 'Thus says[559] the Lord [I]GOD, "Do you come to inquire of Me? As I live,"[2416] declares[5001] the Lord[136] GOD, "[a]I will not be inquired of by you." '

4 "Will you judge[8199] them, will you judge them, son of man? [a]Make them know[3045] the abominations[8441] of their fathers;[1]

5 and say to them, 'Thus says the Lord GOD, "On the day[3117] when I [a]chose[977] Israel and [I]swore[5375,3027] to the [II]descendants[2233] of the house[1004] of Jacob and made Myself known[3045] to them in the land[776] of Egypt, when I [I]swore to them, saying, [b]I am the LORD your God,[430]

6 on that day I swore to them, [a]to bring them out from the land of Egypt into a land that I had [I]selected for them, [b]flowing with milk and honey, which is [c]the glory[6643] of all lands.[776]

7 "And I said[559] to them, '[a]Cast away, each of you,[376] the detestable things[8251] of his eyes, and [b]do not defile[2930] yourselves with the idols[1544] of Egypt; [c]I am the LORD your God.'

8 "But they [a]rebelled[4784] against Me and were not willing[14] to listen[8085] to Me; [I]they did not cast away the detestable things of their eyes, nor did they forsake[5800] the [b]idols of Egypt.

Then I [II]resolved to [c]pour out[8210] My wrath on them, to accomplish[3615] My anger[639] against them in the midst of the land of Egypt.

9 "But I acted [a]for the sake of My name, that it should [b]not be profaned[2490] in the sight of the nations[1471] among whom they *lived,* in whose sight I made Myself known to them by bringing them out of the land of Egypt.

10 "So I took them out of the land of Egypt and brought them into the [a]wilderness.

11 "And I gave them My [a]statutes[2708] and informed[3045] them of My ordinances,[4941] by [b]which, if a man [I]observes[6213] them, he will live.[2425]

12 "And also I gave them My sabbaths[7676] to be a [a]sign[226] between Me and them, that they might know that I am the LORD who sanctifies[6942] them.

13 "But the house of Israel [a]rebelled against Me in the wilderness. They did not walk in My statutes, and they rejected[3988] My ordinances, [b]by which, if a man [I]observes them, he will live; and My [c]sabbaths they greatly profaned. Then I [II]resolved to [d]pour out My wrath on them in the wilderness, to annihilate[3615] them.

14 "But I acted for the sake of My name, that it should not be profaned in the sight of the nations, before whose sight I had brought them out.

15 "And also [a]I swore to them in the wilderness that I would not bring them into the land which I had given them, flowing with milk and honey, which is the glory of all lands,

16 because they rejected My ordinances, and as for My statutes, they did not walk in them; they even profaned My sabbaths, for their [a]heart[3820] continually went after their idols.

17 "Yet My eye spared them rather than destroying[7843] them, and I did not

---

13 [a]2Kin. 24:12-16; Ezek. 19:10; 20:35; Hos. 2:3
14 [I]Lit., *rod of strength* [a]Ezek. 15:4; 20:47, 48
1 [I]Lit., *men* [a]Ezek. 8:1, 11, 12
3 [I]Heb., *YHWH,* usually rendered LORD, and so throughout the ch. [a]Ezek. 14:3
4 [a]Ezek. 16:2; 22:2; Matt. 23:32
5 [I]Lit., *lifted up My hand,* and so throughout the ch. [II]Lit., *seed* [a]Ex. 6:6-8 [b]Ex. 6:2, 3
6 [I]Lit., *spied out* [a]Jer. 32:22 [b]Ex. 13:5; 33:3 [c]Ps. 48:2
7 [a]Ex. 20:4, 5; 22:20 [b]Lev. 18:3; Deut. 29:16-18 [c]Ex. 20:2
8 [I]Lit., *each one* [II]Lit., *said* [a]Deut. 9:7; Is. 63:10 [b]Ex. 32:1-9 [c]Ezek. 5:13; 7:8; 20:13, 21
9 [a]Ex. 32:11-14; Ezek. 20:14, 22; 36:21, 22 [b]Ezek. 39:7
10 [a]Ex. 19:1
11 [I]Lit., *does* [a]Ex. 20:1-23:33 [b]Lev. 18:5; Ezek. 20:13
12 [a]Ex. 31:13, 17; Ezek. 20:20
13 [I]Lit., *does* [II]Lit., *said* [a]Num. 14:11, 12, 22; Ezek. 20:8 [b]Lev. 18:5 [c]Is. 56:6; Ezek. 20:21 [d]Ex. 32:10; Deut. 9:8; Ezek. 20:8, 21
15 [a]Num. 14:30; Ps. 95:11; 106:26
16 [a]Ezek. 11:21; 14:3-7; 20:8

cause[6213] their [a]annihilation[3615] in the wilderness.

18 "And I said to their [I][a]children[1121] in the wilderness, '[b]Do not walk in the statutes[2706] of your fathers, or keep[8104] their ordinances, or defile yourselves with their idols.

19 '[a]I am the LORD your God; [b]walk in My statutes, and keep[8104] My ordinances, and [I]observe them.

20 'And [a]sanctify[6942] My sabbaths; and they shall be a sign between Me and you, that you may know that I am the LORD your God.'

21 "But the [a]children rebelled against Me; they did not walk in My statutes, nor were they careful to observe[8104] My ordinances, by which, *if* a man observes them, he will live; they profaned My sabbaths. So I [I]resolved to pour out My wrath on them, to accomplish My anger against them in the wilderness.

22 "But I [a]withdrew[7725] My hand and acted [b]for the sake of My name, that it should not be profaned in the sight of the nations in whose sight I had brought them out.

23 "Also I swore to them in the wilderness that I would [a]scatter them among the nations and disperse them among the lands,[776]

24 because they had not observed[6213] My ordinances, but had rejected My statutes, and had profaned My sabbaths, and [a]their eyes were [I]on the idols of their fathers.[1]

25 "And I also gave them statutes that were [a]not good[2896] and ordinances by which they could not live;[2421]

26 and I pronounced them [a]unclean[2930] because of their gifts, in that they [b]caused all [I]their first-born to pass through[5674] *the fire* so that I might make them desolate,[8074] in order that they might [c]know that I am the LORD."'

27 "Therefore, son of man, [a]speak to the house of Israel, and say to them, 'Thus says the Lord GOD, "Yet in this your fathers have [b]blasphemed[1442] Me by [c]acting treacherously[4604] against Me.

28 "When I had [a]brought them into the land which I swore to give to them, then they saw[7200] every [b]high hill and every leafy tree, and they offered[2076] there their sacrifices,[2077] and there they presented the provocation[3708] of their offering.[7133] There also they made[7760] their soothing aroma, and there they poured out[5258] their libations.[5262]

29 "Then I said to them, 'What is the high place[1116] to which you go?' So its name is called[7121] [I]Bamah[1116] to this day."'

30 "Therefore, say to the house of Israel, 'Thus says the Lord GOD, "Will you defile yourselves [I]after the manner of your [a]fathers and play the harlot[2181] after their detestable things?

31 "And [I]when you offer[5375] your gifts, when you [a]cause your sons[1121] to pass through the fire, you are defiling yourselves with all your idols to this day. And shall I be inquired of by you, O house of Israel? As I live," declares the Lord GOD, "I will not be inquired of by you.

32 "And what [a]comes [I]into your mind[7307] will not come about, when you say: 'We will be like the nations, like the tribes[4940] of the lands, [b]serving[8334] wood and stone.'

God Will Restore Israel to Her Land

33 "As I live," declares the Lord GOD, "surely with a mighty[2389] hand and with an [a]outstretched arm and with wrath poured out,[8210] I shall be [b]king[4427] over you.

34 "And I shall [a]bring you out from the peoples[5971] and gather[6908] you from the lands where you are scattered, with a mighty hand and with an outstretched arm and with [b]wrath poured out;

35 and I shall bring you into the [a]wilderness of the peoples, and there I shall enter into judgment[8199] with you face to face.

36 "As I [a]entered into judgment[8199] with your fathers in the [b]wilderness of the land of Egypt, so I will enter into

17 [a]Jer. 4:27; 5:18; Ezek. 11:13
18 [I]Lit., *sons* [a]Num. 14:31; Deut. 4:3-6 [b]Zech. 1:4
19 [I]Lit., *do* [a]Ex. 6:7; 20:2 [b]Deut. 5:32, 33; 6:1, 2; 8:1, 2; 11:1; 12:1
20 [a]Jer. 17:22
21 [I]Lit., *said* [a]Num. 21:5; 25:1-3
22 [a]Job 13:21; Ps. 78:38; Ezek. 20:17 [b]Is. 48:9-11; Jer. 14:7, 21; Ezek. 20:9, 14
23 [a]Lev. 26:33; Deut. 4:27; 28:64
24 [I]Lit., *after* [a]Ezek. 6:9
25 [a]Ps. 81:12; Is. 66:4; Rom. 1:21-25, 28
26 [I]Lit., *that which opens the womb* [a]Lev. 18:21; 20:2-5; Is. 63:17; Ezek. 20:30; Rom. 11:8 [b]Jer. 7:31; 19:4-9 [c]Ezek. 6:7; 20:12, 20
27 [a]Ezek. 2:7; 3:4, 11, 27 [b]Num. 15:30; Rom. 2:24 [c]Ezek. 18:24; 39:23, 26
28 [a]Josh. 23:3, 14; Neh. 9:22-26; Ps. 78:55; Jer. 2:7 [b]1Kin. 14:23; Ps. 78:58; Is. 57:5-7; Jer. 3:6; Ezek. 6:13
29 [I]Or, *High Place*
30 [I]Lit., *in the way of* [a]Judg. 2:19; Jer. 7:26; 16:12
31 [I]Lit., *in your lifting up* [a]Ps. 106:37-39; Jer. 7:31; Ezek. 16:20; 20:26
32 [I]Lit., *upon your spirit* [a]Ezek. 11:5 [b]Jer. 2:25; 44:17
33 [a]Jer. 21:5 [b]Jer. 51:57
34 [a]Is. 27:12, 13; Ezek. 20:38; 34:16 [b]Jer. 42:18; 44:6; Lam. 2:4
35 [a]Ezek. 19:13; 20:36; Hos. 2:14
36 [a]Num. 11:1-35; Ps. 106:15; Ezek. 20:13, 21; 1Cor. 10:5-10 [b]Deut. 32:10

judgment with you," declares the Lord GOD.

37 "And I shall make you [a]pass under the rod,[7626] and I shall bring you into the bond of the covenant;[1285]

38 and I shall [a]purge[1305] from you the rebels[4775] and those who transgress[6586] against Me; I shall bring them out of the land[776] where they sojourn,[4033] but they will [b]not enter the [I]land[127] of Israel. Thus you will know that I am the LORD.

39 "As for you, O house of Israel," thus says the Lord GOD, "[a]Go, serve[5647] everyone[376] his idols; [I]but later, you will surely listen to Me, and My holy[6944] name you will [b]profane[2490] no longer with your gifts and with your idols.

40 "For on My holy mountain, on the high mountain of Israel," declares the Lord GOD, "there the whole house of Israel, [a]all of them, will serve Me in the land; there I shall [b]accept[7521] them, and there I shall [I]seek your contributions[8641] and the choicest[7225] of your gifts,[4864] with all your holy things.

41 "[I]As a soothing aroma I shall accept you, when I [a]bring you out from the peoples and gather you from the lands where you are scattered; and I shall prove Myself [b]holy[6942] among you in the sight of the nations.

42 "And [a]you will know that I am the LORD, [b]when I bring you into the land of Israel, into the [c]land which I swore to give to your forefathers.

43 "And there you will [a]remember[2142] your ways[1870] and all your deeds, with which you have defiled[2930] yourselves; and you will [b]loathe yourselves in your own [I]sight for all the evil things that you have done.[6213]

44 "Then [a]you will know that I am the LORD when I have dealt with you [b]for My name's sake, not according to your evil[7451] ways or according to your corrupt[7843] deeds, O house of Israel," declares the Lord GOD.'"

45 [I]Now the word of the LORD came to me saying,

46 "Son of man, set[7720] your face toward[1870] [I]Teman, and speak[5197] out against the [a]south, and [b]prophesy[5012] against the [c]forest [II]land[7704] of the Negev,

47 and say to the forest of the Negev, 'Hear[8085] the word of the LORD: thus says the Lord GOD, "Behold, I am about to [a]kindle a fire in you, and it shall consume every [I]green tree in you, as well as every dry[3002] tree; the blazing flame will not be quenched, and [II][b]the whole surface from south to north will be burned by it.

48 "And all flesh will see that I, the LORD, have kindled it; it shall [a]not be quenched."'"

49 Then I said, "Ah Lord GOD! They are saying of me, 'Is he not *just* speaking [a]parables?'"

Parable of the Sword of the LORD

21 [I]And the word[1697] of the LORD came to me saying,

2 "Son[1121] of man,[120] [a]set[7760] your face toward Jerusalem, and [I][b]speak[5197] against the sanctuaries, and prophesy[5012] against the land[127] of Israel;

3 and say[559] to the land of Israel, 'Thus says[559] the LORD, "Behold, [a]I am against you; and I shall draw My sword[2719] out of its sheath and cut off[3772] from you the [b]righteous[6662] and the wicked.[7563]

4 "Because I shall cut off from you the righteous and the wicked, therefore My sword shall go forth from its sheath against [a]all flesh from south *to* north.

5 "Thus all flesh will know[3045] that I, the LORD, have drawn My sword out of its sheath. It will [a]not return[7725] *to its sheath* again."'

6 "As for you, son of man, groan with breaking[7670] [I]heart and bitter grief, groan in their sight.

7 "And it will come about when they say to you, 'Why do you groan?' that you will say,[559] 'Because of the [a]news that is coming; and [b]every heart[3820] will melt, all hands[3027] will be feeble,[7503]

37 [a]Lev. 27:32; Jer. 33:13
38 [I]Lit., *ground* or *soil* [a]Ezek. 34:17-22; Amos 9:9, 10; Zech. 13:8, 9; Mal. 3:3; 4:1-3 [b]Num. 14:29, 30; Ps. 95:11; Ezek. 13:9; 20:15, 16; Heb. 4:3
39 [I]Or, *and afterwards, if you will not listen to Me, but* [a]Jer. 44:25, 26 [b]Is. 1:13-15; Ezek. 23:38, 39; 43:7
40 [I]Or, *require* [a]Is. 66:23; Ezek. 37:22, 24 [b]Is. 56:7; 60:7; Ezek. 43:12, 27
41 [I]Lit., *With* [a]Is. 27:12, 13; Ezek. 11:17; 28:25 [b]Is. 5:16; Ezek. 28:25; 36:23
42 [a]Ezek. 36:23; 38:23 [b]Ezek. 11:17; 34:13; 36:24 [c]Ezek. 20:6, 15
43 [I]Lit., *faces* [a]Ezek. 6:9; 16:61, 63; Hos. 5:15 [b]Jer. 31:18; Ezek. 36:31; Zech. 12:10
44 [a]Ezek. 24:24 [b]Ezek. 36:22
45 [I]Ch. 21:1 in Heb.
46 [I]Or, *the South* [II]Lit., *of the field* [a]Jer. 13:19; Ezek. 21:4 [b]Ezek. 21:2; Amos 7:16 [c]Is. 30:6-11
47 [I]Lit., *moist* [II]Or, *all the faces* [a]Is. 9:18, 19; Jer. 21:14 [b]Is. 13:8
48 [a]Jer. 7:20; 17:27
49 [a]Ezek. 17:2; Matt. 13:13; John 16:25

1 [I]Ch. 21:6 in Heb.
2 [I]Lit., *flow* [a]Ezek. 20:46; 25:2; 28:21 [b]Job 29:22; Ezek. 20:46
3 [a]Jer. 21:13; Ezek. 5:8; Nah. 2:13; 3:5 [b]Is. 57:1
4 [a]Jer. 12:12; Ezek. 7:2; 20:47

5 [a]1Sam. 3:12; Jer. 23:20; Ezek. 21:30; Nah. 1:9
6 [I]Lit., *loins* 7 [a]Ezek. 7:26 [b]Is. 13:7; Nah. 2:10

every spirit[7307] will [I]faint, and all knees will [II]be weak as water. Behold, it comes and it will happen,' declares[5001] the Lord[136] [III]GOD."

8 Again the word of the LORD came to me saying,

9 "Son of man, prophesy and say, 'Thus says the LORD.' Say,
"[a]A sword, a sword sharpened
And also polished![4803]
10 'Sharpened to make a [a]slaughter,
Polished [I]to flash like lightning!'
Or shall we rejoice, the [II]rod[7626] of My son [b]despising[3988] every tree?

11 "And it is given to be polished, that it may be handled; the sword is sharpened and polished, to give it into the hand[3027] of the slayer.

12 "[a]Cry[2199] out and wail, son of man; for it is against My people,[5971] it is against all the [b]officials[5387] of Israel. They are delivered[4048] over to the sword with My people, therefore strike[5606] *your* thigh.[3409]

13 "For *there is* a testing;[974] and what if even the [I]rod which despises[3988] will be no more?" declares the Lord GOD.

14 "You therefore, son of man, prophesy, and clap[5221] *your* hands[3709] together; and let the sword be [a]doubled the third time,[6256] the sword for the slain.[2491] It is the sword for the great one slain, which surrounds them,

15 that *their* [a]hearts may melt, and many [b]fall[4383] at all their [c]gates. I have given the glittering sword. Ah! It is made *for striking* like lightning, it is wrapped up *in readiness* for slaughter.[2874]

16 "[I]Show yourself sharp, go to the right; set yourself; go to the left, wherever your [II]edge is appointed.[3259]

17 "I shall also clap My hands together, and I shall [I][a]appease My wrath; I, the LORD, have spoken."[1696]

The Instrument of God's Judgment

18 And the word of the LORD came to me saying,

19 "As for you, son of man, [I][a]make[7760] two ways[1870] for the sword of the king[4428] of Babylon to come; both[8147] of them will go out of one land.[776] And [II]make a signpost; [III]make it at the head[7218] of the way[1870] to the city.

20 "You shall [I]mark a way for the sword to come to [a]Rabbah of the sons of Ammon, and to Judah into [b]fortified Jerusalem.

21 "For the king of Babylon stands at the [I]parting of the way, at the head of the two ways, to use[7080] [a]divination;[7081] he [b]shakes[7043] the arrows, he consults[7592] the [II][c]household idols,[8655] he looks at the liver.

22 "Into his right hand came the divination, 'Jerusalem,' to [a]set battering rams, to open the mouth[6310] [I]for slaughter, to lift up the voice with a battle cry, to set battering rams[3733] against the gates, to cast up[8210] mounds, to build a siege wall.

23 "And it will be to them like a false divination[7080] in their eyes; [a]they have *sworn* solemn oaths. But he [b]brings iniquity[5771] to remembrance,[2142] that they may be seized.

24 "Therefore, thus says the Lord GOD, 'Because you have made your iniquity to be remembered,[2142] in that your transgressions[6588] are uncovered, so that in all your deeds your sins appear—[7200] because you have come to remembrance, you will be seized with the hand.

25 'And you, O slain,[2491] wicked one, the prince[5387] of Israel, whose [a]day[3117] has come, in the time of the [I]punishment of the end,'

26 thus says the Lord GOD, 'Remove the turban,[4701] and take off the [a]crown; this will *be* [I]no more the same. [b]Exalt that which is low, and abase[8213] that which is high.

27 "[a]A ruin, a ruin, a ruin, I shall make it. This also will be no more, until [b]He comes whose right[4941] it is; and I shall give it *to Him*.'

7 [I]Lit., *be dim* [II]Lit., *flow* [III]Heb., *YHWH*, usually rendered LORD, and so throughout the ch.
9 [a]Deut. 32:41
10 [I]Lit., *lightning to be to her* [II]Or, *scepter* [a]Is. 34:5, 6 [b]Ps. 110:5, 6; Ezek. 20:47
12 [a]Ezek. 21:6; Joel 1:13 [b]Ezek. 21:25; 22:6
13 [I]Or, *scepter*
14 [a]Lev. 26:21, 24; 2Kin. 24:1, 10-16; 25:1
15 [a]Josh. 2:11; 2Sam. 17:10; Ps. 22:14; Ezek. 21:7 [b]Is. 59:10; Jer. 13:16; 18:15 [c]Jer. 17:27; Ezek. 21:19
16 [I]Or, *Unite yourself* [II]Lit., *face*
17 [I]Lit., *cause to rest* [a]Ezek. 5:13
19 [I]Or, *set for yourself* [II]Lit., *cut out a hand* [III]Lit., *cut it* [a]Jer. 1:10; Ezek. 4:1-3
20 [I]Lit., *set* [a]Deut. 3:11; Jer. 49:2; Ezek. 25:5; Amos 1:14 [b]Ps. 48:12, 13; 125:1, 2
21 [I]Lit., *mother* [II]Heb., *teraphim* [a]Num. 22:7; 23:23 [b]Prov. 16:33 [c]Gen. 31:19, 30; Judg. 17:5; 18:17, 20
22 [I]Lit., *in* [a]Ezek. 4:2; 26:9
23 [a]Ezek. 17:16, 18 [b]Num. 5:15; Ezek. 21:24; 29:16
25 [I]Or, *iniquity* [a]Ps. 37:13; Ezek. 7:2, 3, 7
26 [I]Lit., *not this* [a]Jer. 13:18; Ezek. 16:12 [b]Ps. 75:7; Ezek. 17:24
27 [a]Hag. 2:21, 22 [b]Ps. 2:6; 72:7, 10; Jer. 23:5, 6; Ezek. 34:24; 37:24

21:12-17 See note on Ezek. 2:8—3:3.

28 “And you, son of man, prophesy
and say, ‘Thus says the Lord GOD concerning the sons of Ammon and concerning their [a]reproach,’[2781] and say: ‘A
sword, a sword is drawn, polished for
the slaughter, to cause it [I]to [b]consume,
that it may be like lightning—
29 while they see[2372] for you
[a]false visions,[7723] while they divine[7080]
lies[3576] for you—to place you on the
necks of the wicked who are slain,
whose day has come, in the [b]time of
the [I]punishment of the end.
30 “[a]Return *it* to its sheath. In the
[b]place where you were created,[1254] in
the land of your origin, I shall judge[8199]
you.
31 ‘And I shall [a]pour out[8210] My
indignation[2195] on you; I shall [b]blow[6315]
on you with the fire of My wrath,[5678]
and I shall give you into the hand of
brutal men,[582] [I][c]skilled in destruction.[4889]
32 ‘You will be [I][a]fuel for the fire;
your blood[1818] will be in the midst of
the land. You will [b]not be remembered,
for I, the LORD, have spoken.’ ”[1696]

The Sins of Israel

22 Then the word[1697] of the LORD
came to me saying,
2 “And you, son[1121] of man,[120] will
you judge,[8199] will you judge the
bloody[1818] city? Then cause her to know
all her abominations.[8441]
3 “And you shall say,[559] ‘Thus
says[559] the Lord[136] [I]GOD, “A city
[a]shedding[8210] blood[1818] in her midst, so
that her time[6256] will come, and that
makes[6213] idols,[1544] contrary to her *interest,* for defilement![2930]
4 “You have become [a]guilty[816] by
[I]the blood which you have shed,[8210] and
defiled[2920] by your idols which you have
made.[6213] Thus you have brought[7126]
your [II]day[3117] near[7126] and have come
to your years; therefore I have made
you a [b] reproach[2781] to the nations,[1471]
and a mocking to all the lands.[776]
5 “Those who are near and those
who are far from you will mock you,
you of ill repute, full of [a]turmoil.[4103]

6 “Behold, the [a]rulers[5387] of Israel,
each[376] according to his [I]power, have
been in you for the purpose of shedding
blood.
7 “They have [a]treated father[1] and
mother[517] lightly within you. The
[b]alien[1616] they have oppressed in your
midst; the [c]fatherless and the widow
they have wronged[3238] in you.
8 “You have [a]despised My holy
things[6944] and [b]profaned[2490] My sabbaths.[7676]
9 “Slanderous men[582] have been in
you for the purpose of shedding blood,
and in you they have eaten at the mountain *shrines.* In your midst they have
[a]committed[6213] acts of lewdness.[2154]
10 “In you [I]they have [a]uncovered
their fathers’[1] nakedness;[6172] in you they
have humbled her who was [b]unclean[5079]
in her menstrual impurity.[2931]
11 “And one has committed[6213]
abomination[8441] with his [a]neighbor’s[7453]
wife,[802] and another[376] has lewdly defiled
his [b]daughter-in-law. And another in you
has [c]humbled his sister,[269] his father’s[1]
daughter.
12 “In you they have [a]taken bribes
to shed blood; you have taken [b]interest
and profits, and you have injured[1214]
your neighbors[7453] for gain[1214] by
[c]oppression, and you have [d]forgotten
Me,” declares[5001] the Lord GOD.
13 “Behold, then, I smite[5221] My
hand at your [a]dishonest gain which you
have acquired and at [I]the bloodshed
which is among you.
14 “Can [a]your heart[3820] endure, or
can your hands[3027] be strong,[2388] in the
days that I shall deal[6213] with you?
[b]I, the LORD, have spoken[1696] and shall
act.[6213]
15 “And I shall [a]scatter you among
the nations, and I shall disperse you
through the lands, and I shall [b]consume
your uncleanness[2932] from you.
16 “And you will profane yourself
in the sight of the nations, and you will
[a]know[3045] that I am the LORD.” ’ ”

28 [I]Lit., *to finish* [a]Ezek. 36:15; Zeph. 2:8-10 [b]Is. 31:8; Jer. 12:12; 46:10, 14
29 [I]Or, *iniquity* [a]Jer. 27:9; Ezek. 13:6-9; 22:28 [b]Ezek. 21:25; 35:5
30 [a]Jer. 47:6, 7 [b]Ezek. 25:5
31 [I]Or, *artisans of* [a]Ezek. 14:19; 25:7; Nah. 1:6 [b]Ps. 18:15; Is. 30:33; Ezek. 22:20, 21; Hag. 1:9 [c]Jer. 4:7; 6:22, 23; 51:20-23; Hab. 1:6,10
32 [I]Lit., *food* [a]Ezek. 20:47, 48; Mal. 4:1 [b]Ezek. 25:10

3 [I]Heb., *YHWH,* usually rendered *LORD,* and so throughout the ch. [a]Ezek. 22:6, 27; 23:37, 45
4 [I]Lit., *your* [II]Lit., *days* [a]2Kin. 21:16; Ezek. 24:7, 8 [b]Ps. 44:13, 14; Ezek. 5:14, 15; 16:57
5 [a]Is. 22:2
6 [I]Lit., *arm* [a]Is. 1:23; Ezek. 22:27
7 [a]Ex. 20:12; Lev. 20:9; Deut. 5:16; 27:16 [b]Ex. 22:21f.; 23:9; Deut. 24:17; Jer. 7:6; Zech. 7:10 [c]Ex. 22:22; Ezek. 22:25; Mal. 3:5
8 [a]Ezek. 22:26 [b]Ezek. 20:13, 21, 24; 23:38, 39
9 [a]Ezek. 23:29; Hos. 4:2, 10, 14
10 [I]Lit., *he has* [a]Lev. 18:8 [b]Lev. 18:19; Ezek. 18:6
11 [a]Ezek. 18:11; 33:26 [b]Lev. 18:15 [c]2Sam. 13:11-14
12 [a]Ex. 23:8; Deut. 16:19; 27:25; Mic. 7:2, 3 [b]Lev. 25:36; Deut. 23:19 [c]Lev. 19:13 [d]Ps. 106:21; Ezek. 23:35
13 [I]Lit., *your* [a]Is. 33:15; Amos 2:6-8; Mic. 2:2
14 [a]Ezek. 21:7 [b]Ezek. 17:24

15 [a]Deut. 4:27; Neh. 1:8; Ezek. 20:23; Zech. 7:14 [b]Ezek. 23:27, 48 **16** [a]Ps. 83:18; Ezek. 6:7

17 And the word of the LORD came to me saying,

18 "Son of man, the house[1004] of Israel has become[1961] [a]dross[5509] to Me; all of them are [b]bronze and tin and iron and lead in the [c]furnace; they are the dross of silver.

19 "Therefore, thus says the Lord GOD, 'Because all of you have become dross, therefore, behold, I am going to gather[6908] you into the midst of Jerusalem.

20 'As they gather[6910] silver and bronze and iron and lead and tin into the [a]furnace to blow fire on it in order to melt *it,* so I shall gather *you* in My anger[639] and in My wrath, and I shall lay you *there* and melt you.

21 'And I shall gather[3664] you and blow on you with the fire of My wrath, and you will be melted in the midst of it.

22 'As silver is melted in the furnace, so you will be melted in the midst of it; and you will know that I, the LORD, have [a]poured out[8210] My wrath on you.' "

23 And the word of the LORD came to me saying,

24 "Son of man, say to her, 'You are a land[776] that is [a]not cleansed[2891] or rained on in the day[3117] of indignation.'[2195]

25 "There is a [a]conspiracy of her prophets[5030] in her midst, like a roaring lion tearing the prey. They have [b]devoured lives; they have taken treasure and precious things; they have made many [c]widows in the midst of her.

26 "Her [a]priests[3548] have done violence[2554] to My law[8451] and have [b]profaned My holy things; they have made no [c]distinction[914] between the holy and the profane,[2455] and they have not taught[3045] the difference between the [d]unclean[2931] and the clean;[2889] and they hide their eyes from My sabbaths, and I am profaned among them.

27 "Her princes[8269] within[7130] her are like wolves tearing the prey, by shedding blood *and* [a]destroying[6] lives in order to get [b] dishonest gain.

28 "And her prophets have smeared8602 whitewash for them, seeing [a]false visions[7723] and divining[7080] lies[3577] for them, saying, 'Thus says the Lord GOD,' when the LORD has not spoken.

29 "The people[5971] of the land have practiced [a]oppression and committed robbery, and they have wronged the poor and needy and have [b]oppressed the sojourner without justice.

30 "And I [a]searched for a man[376] among them who should [b]build up the wall and [c]stand in the gap before Me for the land, that I should not destroy[7843] it; but I found [1]no one.

31 "Thus I have poured out My [a]indignation on them; I have consumed[3615] them with the fire of My wrath; [b]their way[1870] I have brought upon their heads,"[7218] declares the Lord GOD.

Oholah and Oholibah's Sin and Its Consequences

23 The word[1697] of the LORD came to me again saying,

2 "Son[1121] of man,[120] there were [a]two women,[802] the daughters of one mother;[517]

3 and they played the harlot[2181] in Egypt. They [a]played the harlot in their youth; there their breasts were pressed, and there their virgin[1331] bosom was handled.[6213]

4 "And their names were Oholah the elder and Oholibah her sister.[269] And they became Mine, and they bore sons[1121] and daughters. And *as for* their names, Samaria is Oholah, and Jerusalem is Oholibah.

5 "And Oholah played the harlot[2181] [1]while she was Mine; and she lusted[5689] after her lovers,[157] after the [a]Assyrians, *her* neighbors,

6 who were clothed in purple, [a]governors[6346] and officials,[5461] all of them desirable young men, horsemen riding on horses.

7 "And she bestowed her harlotries[8457] on them, all of whom *were* the choicest [1]men of Assyria; and with all

---

18 [a]Ps. 119:119; Is. 1:22; Lam. 4:1 [b]Jer. 6:28-30 [c]Prov. 17:3; Is. 48:10
20 [a]Is. 1:25
22 [a]Ezek. 20:8, 33; Hos. 5:10
24 [a]Is. 9:13; Jer. 2:30; Ezek. 24:13; Zeph. 3:2
25 [a]Jer. 11:9; Hos. 6:9 [b]Jer. 2:34; Ezek. 13:19; 22:27 [c]Jer. 15:8; Ezek. 22:7
26 [a]Jer. 2:8, 26; Ezek. 7:26 [b]1Sam. 2:12-17, 22; Ezek. 22:8 [c]Lev. 10:10; Ezek. 44:23 [d]Hag. 2:11-14
27 [a]Ezek. 22:25 [b]Ezek. 22:13
28 [a]Jer. 23:25-32; Ezek. 13:6
29 [a]Is. 5:7; Ezek. 9:9; 22:7; Amos 3:10 [b]Ex. 23:9
30 [1]Lit., *not* [a]Is. 59:16; 63:5; Jer. 5:1 [b]Ezek. 13:5 [c]Ps. 106:23; Jer. 15:1
31 [a]Is. 10:5; 13:5; 30:27; Ezek. 22:20 [b]Ezek. 7:3, 8, 9; 9:10; 16:43; Rom. 2:8, 9
2 [a]Ezek. 16:46
3 [a]Lev. 17:7; Jer. 3:9
5 [1]Lit., *under Me* [a]2Kin. 15:19; 16:7; 17:3; Ezek. 16:28; Hos. 5:13; 8:9, 10
6 [a]Ezek. 23:12, 13
7 [1]Lit., *sons of Asshur*

whom she lusted after, with all their
idols[1544] she [a]defiled[2930] herself.
8 "And she did not forsake[5800] her
harlotries [a]from *the time in* Egypt; for
in her youth [I]men had lain with her,
and they handled her virgin bosom
and poured[8210] out their [II]lust[8457] on
her.
9 "Therefore, I gave her into the
hand[3027] of her [a]lovers, into the hand
of the [I]Assyrians, after whom she
lusted.
10 "They [a]uncovered her nakedness;[6172] they took her sons and her
daughters, but they slew her with the
sword.[2719] Thus she became a [I]byword
among women, and they executed[6213]
judgments on her.
11 "Now her sister Oholibah
saw[7200] *this,* yet she was [a]more corrupt[7843] in her lust than she, and her
harlotries were more than the harlotries[2183] of her sister.
12 "She lusted after the [Ia]Assyrians,
governors and officials, the ones near,
magnificently dressed, horsemen riding
on horses, all of them desirable young
men.
13 "And I saw that she had defiled
herself; they both took [I]the same
way.[1870]
14 "So she increased her harlotries.
And she saw men[582] [a]portrayed2707 on
the wall, images[6754] of the [b]Chaldeans
portrayed[2710] with vermilion,8350
15 girded with belts232 on their loins,
with flowing turbans on their heads,[7218]
all of them looking like officers,[7991]
[I]like the [II]Babylonians *in* Chaldea, the
land[776] of their birth.
16 "And [I]when she saw them she
[a]lusted after them and sent messengers
to them in Chaldea.
17 "And the [Ia]Babylonians came to
her to the bed of love,[1730] and they defiled her with their harlotry. And when
she had been defiled[2930] by them,
[II]she[5315] became disgusted3363 with
them.
18 "And she [a]uncovered her harlotries and uncovered her nakedness;
then [I]I became [b]disgusted with her,
as [I]I had become disgusted with her
[c]sister.
19 "Yet she multiplied her harlotries, remembering[2142] the days[3117] of
her youth, when she played the harlot
in the land of Egypt.
20 "And she [a]lusted after their
paramours,6370 whose flesh is *like* the
flesh of donkeys and whose issue is
like the issue of horses.
21 "Thus you longed for[6485] the
[a]lewdness[2154] of your youth, when
[I]the Egyptians handled your bosom because of the breasts7699 of your youth.
22 "Therefore, O Oholibah, thus
says[559] the Lord[136] [I]GOD, 'Behold I will
arouse your lovers against you, from
whom [II]you were alienated, and I will
bring them against you from every side:
23 the [Ia]Babylonians and all the
[b]Chaldeans, [c]Pekod and Shoa and Koa,
and all the [IId]Assyrians with them; desirable young men, governors and officials
all of them, officers[7991] and [III]men of renown,[7121] all of them riding on horses.
24 'And they will come against you
with weapons, [a]chariots, and [I]wag-
ons,[1534] and with a company[6951] of
peoples.[5971] They will set themselves
against you on every side with
buckler6793 and shield and helmet; and
I shall commit[7760] the [b]judgment[4941] to
them, and they will judge[8199] you according to their customs.[4941]
25 'And I will set My [a]jealousy
against you, that they may deal[6213] with
you in wrath. They will remove your
nose[639] and your ears;[241] and your
[I]survivors[319] will fall by the sword. They
will take your [b]sons and your daughters;
and your [I]survivors[319] will be consumed
by the fire.
26 'They will also [a]strip you of your
clothes and take away your [b]beautiful[8597]
jewels.
27 'Thus [a]I shall make your lewdness and your harlotry[2184] *brought* from
the land of Egypt to cease[7673] from you,
so that you will not lift up[5375] your eyes

7 [a]Ezek. 20:7; 22:3, 4; Hos. 5:3; 6:10
8 [I]Lit., *they* [II]Lit., *harlotry* [a]Ex. 32:4; 1Kin. 12:28; 2Kin. 10:29; 17:16; Ezek. 23:3, 19
9 [I]Lit., *sons of Asshur* [a]Ezek. 16:37; 23:22
10 [I]Lit., *name* [a]Ezek. 16:37, 41
11 [a]Jer. 3:8-11; Ezek. 16:51
12 [I]Lit., *sons of Asshur* [a]2Kin. 16:7
13 [I]Lit., *one*
14 [a]Ezek. 8:10 [b]Ezek. 16:29
15 [I]Lit., *the likeness of* [II]Lit., *sons of Babel*
16 [I]Lit., *at the sight of her eyes* [a]Ezek. 23:20; Matt. 5:28
17 [I]Lit., *sons of Babel* [II]Lit., *her soul* [a]2Kin. 24:17
18 [I]Lit., *My soul* [a]Jer. 8:12; Ezek. 21:24; 23:10 [b]Ps. 78:59; 106:40; Jer. 12:8 [c]Ezek. 23:9; Amos 5:21
20 [a]Ezek. 16:26; 17:15
21 [I]So two mss.; M.T., *from Egypt* [a]Jer. 3:9; Ezek. 23:3
22 [I]Heb., *YHWH,* usually rendered LORD, and so throughout the ch. [II]Lit., *your soul was alienated*
23 [I]Lit., *sons of Babylon* [II]Lit., *sons of Assyria* [III]Lit., *the called ones* [a]2Kin. 20:14-17; Ezek. 21:19; 23:14-17 [b]2Kin. 24:2; Job 1:17; Is. 23:13 [c]Jer. 50:21 [d]Gen. 2:14; 25:18; Ezra 6:22
24 [I]Lit., *wheels* [a]Jer. 47:3; Ezek. 26:10; Nah. 2:3, 4 [b]Jer. 39:5, 6; Ezek. 16:38; 23:45
25 [I]Lit., *remainder* [a]Ex. 34:14; Ezek. 5:13; 8:17, 18; Zeph. 1:18 [b]Ezek. 23:47; Hos. 2:4
26 [a]Jer. 13:22; Ezek. 16:39; 23:29 [b]Is. 3:18-23
27 [a]Ezek. 16:41

to them or remember[2142] Egypt anymore.'

28 "For thus says the Lord GOD, 'Behold, I will give you into the hand of those whom you [a]hate,[8130] into the hand of those from whom [I]you were alienated.

29 'And they will [a]deal with you in hatred,[8135] take all your property, and leave[5800] you naked and bare.[6181] And the nakedness of your harlotries shall be uncovered, both your lewdness and your harlotries.

30 'These things will be done to you because you have [a]played the harlot[2181] with the nations,[1471] because you have defiled yourself with their idols.

31 'You have walked in the way of your sister; therefore I will give [a]her cup into your hand.'

32 "Thus says the Lord GOD,

'You will [a]drink your sister's[269]
cup,
Which is deep and wide.
[I]You will be [b]laughed at and held
in derision;
It contains much.

33 'You will be filled with
[a]drunkenness[7943] and
sorrow,
The cup of horror[8047] and
desolation,[8077]
The cup of your sister Samaria.

34 'And you will [a]drink it and drain
it.
Then you will gnaw its
fragments[2789]
And tear your breasts;

for I have spoken,'[1696] declares the Lord GOD.

35 "Therefore, thus says the Lord GOD, 'Because you have [a]forgotten Me and [b]cast Me behind your back,[1458] bear[5375] now the *punishment* of your lewdness and your harlotries.' "

36 Moreover, the LORD said[559] to me, "Son of man, will you [a]judge Oholah and Oholibah? Then [b]declare[5046] to them their abominations.[8441]

37 "For they have committed adultery,[5003] and blood[1818] is on their hands.[3027] Thus they have committed adultery with their idols and even caused their sons, [a]whom they bore to Me, to pass through *the fire* to [I]them as food.

38 "Again, they have done[6213] this to Me: they have [a]defiled My sanctuary on the same day[3117] and have [b]profaned[2490] My sabbaths.[7676]

39 "For when they had slaughtered[7819] their children[1121] for their idols, they entered My [a]sanctuary[4320] on the same day to profane it; and lo, thus they did within My house.[1004]

40 "Furthermore, [I]they have even sent for men who come from afar, to whom a messenger[4397] was sent; and lo, they came—for whom you bathed,[7364] [a]painted your eyes, and [b]decorated yourselves with ornaments;

41 and you sat on a splendid [a]couch with a [b]table arranged before it, on which you had set My [c]incense[7004] and My [c]oil.[8081]

42 "And the sound of a [Ia]carefree multitude was with her; and [b]drunkards were brought from the wilderness with men of the [II]common sort. And they put [c]bracelets on [III]the hands of the women and beautiful[8597] crowns on their heads.

43 "Then I said concerning her who was [a]worn out by adulteries,[5004] '[I]Will they now commit[2181] adultery with her when she is *thus?*'

44 "[I]But they went in to her as they would go in to a harlot.[2181] Thus they went in to Oholah and to Oholibah, the lewd[2154] women.

45 "But they, righteous[6662] men, will [a]judge them with the judgment[4941] of adulteresses,[5003] and with the judgment of women who shed[8210] blood, because they are adulteresses and blood is on their hands.

46 "For thus says the Lord GOD, 'Bring up[5927] a company[6951] against them, and give them over to [a]terror and plunder.

47 'And the company will [a]stone them with stones and cut them down with their swords;[2719] they will slay[4191] their sons and their daughters and [b]burn their houses[1004] with fire.

---

28 [I]Lit., *your soul was alienated* [a]Jer. 21:7-10; 34:20; Ezek. 16:37; 23:17, 22
29 [a]Deut. 28:48; Ezek. 23:25, 26, 45-47
30 [a]Ezek. 6:9
31 [a]2Kin. 21:13; Jer. 7:14, 15; Ezek. 23:33
32 [I]Or, *It will be for jesting and deriding because of its great size* [a]Ps. 60:3; Is. 51:17; Jer. 25:15 [b]Ezek. 5:14, 15; 16:57; 22:4, 5
33 [a]Jer. 25:15, 16, 27; Hab. 2:16
34 [a]Ps. 75:8; Is. 51:17
35 [a]Is. 17:10; Jer. 3:21; Ezek. 22:12; Hos. 8:14; 13:6 [b]1Kin. 14:9; Jer. 2:27; 32:33
36 [a]Jer. 1:10; Ezek. 20:4; 22:2 [b]Is. 58:1; Ezek. 16:2; Mic. 3:8
37 [I]I.e., idols [a]Ezek. 16:20; 20:26
38 [a]2Kin. 21:4, 7; Ezek. 5:11; 7:20 [b]Jer. 17:27; Ezek. 20:13, 24
39 [a]Jer. 7:9-11
40 [I]Or, *you* (women) [a]2Kin. 9:30; Jer. 4:30 [b]Is. 3:18-23; Ezek. 16:13-16
41 [a]Esth. 1:6; Is. 57:7; Amos 6:4 [b]Is. 65:11; Ezek. 44:16 [c]Jer. 44:17; Hos. 2:8
42 [I]Lit., *at ease* [II]Lit., *multitude of mankind* [III]Lit., *their hands* [a]Ezek. 16:49; Amos 6:3-6 [b]Jer. 51:7 [c]Gen. 24:30; Ezek. 16:11, 12
43 [I]Or, *Now they will commit adultery with her, and she with them.* [a]Ezek. 23:3
44 [I]Or, *And*
45 [a]Ezek. 16:38
46 [a]Jer. 15:4; 24:9; 29:18
47 [a]Lev. 20:10; Ezek. 16:40 [b]Jer. 39:8

48 'Thus I shall make lewdness cease from the land, that all women may be admonished[3256] and not commit[6213] [I]lewdness as you have done.
49 'And your lewdness [I]will be [a]requited upon you, and you will bear *the penalty of worshiping* your idols; thus you will know[3045] that I am the Lord GOD.' "

Parable of the Boiling Pot

24 And the word[1697] of the LORD came to me in the ninth year, in the tenth month, on the tenth of the month, saying,
2 "Son[1121] of man,[120] write the name of the day,[3117] this very day. The king[4428] of Babylon [I]has [a]laid siege to Jerusalem this very day.
3 "And speak a [a]parable to the [b]rebellious[4805] house,[1004] and say[559] to them, 'Thus says[559] the Lord[136] [I]GOD,

"Put on the [c]pot, put *it* on, and
also pour water in it;
4 [Ia]Put[622] in it the pieces,
Every good[2896] piece, the
thigh,[3409] and the shoulder;
Fill *it* with choice bones.[6106]
5 "Take the [a]choicest of the flock,
And also pile [I]wood under
[II]the pot.
Make it boil vigorously.
Also seethe its bones in it."

6 'Therefore, thus says the Lord GOD,

"Woe to the [a]bloody[1818] city,
To the pot in which there is rust
And whose rust has not gone
out of it!
Take out of it piece after piece,
[I]Without making a choice.
7 "For her blood[1818] is in her midst;
She placed[7760] it on the bare
rock;
She did not [a]pour[8210] it on the
ground[776]
To cover[3680] it with dust.[6083]

48 [I]Lit., *according to your lewdness*

49 [I]Lit., *they will give* [a]Is. 59:18; Ezek. 7:4, 9; 9:10; 23:35

2 [I]Lit., *leaned on* [a]2Kin. 25:1; Jer. 39:1; 52:4

3 [I]Heb., *YHWH,* usually rendered *LORD,* and so throughout the ch. [a]Ps. 78:2; Ezek. 17:2; 20:49 [b]Is. 1:2; 30:1, 9; Ezek. 2:3, 6, 8 [c]Jer. 1:13, 14; Ezek. 11:3, 7, 11; 24:6

4 [I]Lit., *Gather her pieces* [a]Mic. 3:2, 3

5 [I]Lit., *bones* [II]Lit., *it* [a]Jer. 39:6; 52:10, 24-27

6 [I]Lit., *No lot has fallen on it* [a]2Kin. 24:3, 4; Ezek. 22:2, 3, 27; Mic. 7:2; Nah. 3:1

7 [a]Lev. 17:13; Deut. 12:16

8 [a]Is. 26:21

9 [a]Ezek. 24:6; Hab. 2:12

10 [I]Lit., *Complete*

11 [I]Lit., *become hot* [a]Jer. 21:10; Mal. 4:1 [b]Ezek. 22:15; 23:27

12 [a]Jer. 9:5

13 [I]Lit., *caused to rest* [a]Jer. 6:28-30; Ezek. 22:24 [b]Ezek. 5:13; 8:18

14 [I]So with several ancient mss. and versions; M.T., *they* [a]Ps. 33:9; Is. 55:11 [b]Jer. 13:14; Ezek. 9:10 [c]Is. 3:11; Ezek. 18:30; 36:19

16 [a]Song 7:10; Ezek. 24:18

8 "That it may [a]cause wrath to
come up[5927] to take
vengeance,[5359]
I have put her blood on the bare
rock,
That it may not be covered."
9 'Therefore, thus says the Lord
GOD,
"[a]Woe to the bloody city!
I also shall make the pile great.
10 "Heap on the wood, kindle the
fire,
[I]Boil the flesh well,
And mix in the spices,
And let the bones be burned.[2787]
11 "Then [a]set it empty on its coals,
So that it may be hot,
And its bronze may [I]glow,[2787]
And its [b]filthiness[2932] may be
melted in it,
Its rust consumed.[8552]
12 "She has [a]wearied *Me* with toil,
Yet her great rust has not gone
from her;
Let her rust *be* in the fire!
13 "In your filthiness is
lewdness.[2154]
Because I *would* have cleansed
you,
Yet you are [a]not clean,
You will not be cleansed from
your filthiness again,
Until I have [Ib]spent My wrath
on you.

14 "I, the LORD, have spoken;[1696]
it is [a]coming and I shall act.[6213] I shall
not relent,[6544] and I shall not [b]pity, and
I shall not be sorry;[5162] [c]according to
your ways[1870] and according to your
deeds [I]I shall judge[8199] you," declares[5001]
the Lord GOD.' "

Death of Ezekiel's Wife Is a Sign

⊶ **15** And the word of the LORD came to me saying,
16 "Son of man, behold, I am about to take from you the [a]desire of your

---

⊶ **24:15-24** Being a prophet often greatly affected these servants' personal family life. God could use such simple functions as the naming of a child to carry out His purposes (Isa. 8:3,4; Hos. 1:4,6,9). For *(continued on next page)*

eyes with a [b]blow; but you shall not [c]mourn, and you shall not weep, and your [d]tears shall not come.

17 "Groan silently; make[6213] [a]no mourning for the dead.[4191] Bind[2280] on your turban, and put your shoes on your feet, and do not cover *your* mustache,[8222] and [b]do not eat the bread of men."[582]

18 So I spoke[1696] to the people[5971] in the morning, and in the evening my wife[802] died.[4191] And in the morning I did[6213] as I was commanded.[6680]

19 And the people said[559] to me, "Will you not tell[5046] us what these things that you are doing[6213] mean for us?"

20 Then I said[559] to them, "The word of the LORD came to me saying,

21 'Speak[559] to the house of Israel, "Thus says the Lord GOD, 'Behold, I am about to profane My sanctuary,[4720] the pride of your power, the [a]desire of your eyes, and the delight[4263] of your soul;[5315] and your [b]sons[1121] and your daughters whom you have left[5800] behind will fall by the sword.[2719]

22 'And you will do as I have done;[6213] you will not cover *your* mustache, and you will not eat the bread of men.

23 'And your turbans will be on your heads[7218] and your shoes on your feet. You [a]will not mourn, and you will not weep; but [b]you will rot[4743] away in your iniquities,[5771] and you will groan [I]to one[376] another.

24 'Thus Ezekiel will be a [a]sign[4159] to you; according to all that he has done you will do; when it comes, then you will know[3045] that I am the Lord GOD.'"

25 'As for you, son of man, will *it* not be on the day when I take from them their [a]stronghold, the joy of their [I]pride,[8597] the desire of their eyes, and [II]their heart's delight,[5315] their sons and their daughters,

26 that on that day he who [a]escapes will come to you with information for *your* ears?[241]

27 'On that day your [a]mouth[6310] will be opened to him who escaped, and you will speak[1696] and be dumb no longer. Thus you will be a sign to them, and they will know that I am the LORD.'"

Judgment on Gentile Nations—Ammon

25 And the word[1697] of the LORD came to me saying,

2 "Son[1121] of man,[120] set[7760] your face toward the [a]sons of Ammon, and prophesy[5012] against them,

3 and say[559] to the sons of Ammon, 'Hear[8085] the word of the Lord[136] [I]GOD! Thus says[559] the Lord GOD, "Because you said,[559] '[a]Aha!' against My sanctuary[4720] when it was profaned,[2490] and against the land[127] of Israel when it was made desolate,[8074] and against the house[1004] of Judah when they went into exile,[1473]

4 therefore, behold, I am going to give you to the [a]sons of the east for a possession,[4181] and they will set their encampments among you and make their dwellings[4908] among you; they will [b]eat your fruit and drink your milk.

5 "And I shall make [a]Rabbah a pasture for camels and the sons of Ammon a resting place for flocks. Thus you will know[3045] that I am the LORD."

6 'For thus says the Lord GOD, "Because you have [a]clapped your hands[3027] and stamped[7554] your feet and [b]rejoiced with all the scorn of your soul[5315] against the land of Israel,

7 therefore, behold, I have [a]stretched out My hand[3027] against you, and I shall give you for [b]spoil to the nations.[1471] And I shall [c]cut you off[3772] from the peoples[5971] and [d]make you perish[6] from the lands;[776] I shall

16 [b]Job 23:2 [c]Jer. 16:5; 22:10 [d]Jer. 13:17

17 [a]Lev. 21:10-12 [b]Jer. 16:7; Hos. 9:4

21 [a]Ps. 27:4; 84:1; Ezek. 24:16 [b]Jer. 6:11; 16:3, 4; Ezek. 23:25, 47

23 [I]Lit., *a man to his brother* [a]Job 27:15; Ps. 78:64 [b]Lev. 26:39; Ezek. 33:10

24 [a]Ezek. 4:3; Luke 11:29, 30

25 [I]Or, *beauty* [II]Lit., *the lifting up of their soul* [a]Ps. 48:2; 50:2; Ezek. 24:21

26 [a]1Sam. 4:12; Job 1:15-19

27 [a]Ezek. 3:26; 33:22

2 [a]Jer. 49:1-6; Amos 1:13-15; Zeph. 2:9

3 [I]Heb., *YHWH,* usually rendered *LORD,* and so throughout the ch. [a]Ps. 70:2, 3; Ezek. 21:28; 25:6; 26:2; 36:2

4 [a]Judg. 6:3, 33; 1Kin. 4:30 [b]Deut. 28:33, 51; Is. 1:7

5 [a]Deut. 3:11; 2Sam. 12:26; Jer. 49:2; Ezek. 21:20

6 [a]Job 27:23; Nah. 3:19 [b]Obad. 12; Zeph. 2:8, 10

7 [a]Ezek. 25:13, 16; Zeph. 1:4 [b]Is. 33:4; Ezek. 26:5 [c]Ezek. 21:32 [d]Amos 1:14, 15

(continued from previous page)

Hosea, there was a need to have him take a wife of harlotry (Hos. 1:2), but for Jeremiah, it was best that he not marry at all (Jer. 16:2). In Ezekiel's case, he was forbidden to mourn the death of his wife publicly, as a sign to his fellow captives in Babylon that when they would get word shortly that Jerusalem had fallen, they were not to show public anguish.

destroy[8045] you. Thus you will [e]know that I am the LORD."

Moab

8 'Thus says the Lord GOD, "Because [a]Moab and Seir say, 'Behold, the house of Judah is like all the nations,'

9 therefore, behold, I am going to [I]deprive the flank of Moab of *its* cities, of its cities which are on its [II]frontiers, the glory[6643] of the land,[776] [a]Beth-jeshimoth, [b]Baal-meon, and [c]Kiriathaim,

10 and I will give it for a possession, along with the sons of Ammon, to the [a]sons of the east, that the sons of Ammon may not be remembered[2142] among the nations.[1471]

11 "Thus I will execute judgments[8201] on Moab, and they will know that I am the LORD."

Edom

12 'Thus says the Lord GOD, "Because [a]Edom has acted[6213] against the house of Judah by taking vengeance,[5359] and has incurred grievous guilt,[816] and avenged themselves upon them,"

13 therefore, thus says the Lord GOD, "I will also [a]stretch out My hand against Edom and [b]cut off[3772] man and beast from it. And I will lay it waste; from [c]Teman even to [d]Dedan they will fall by the sword.[2719]

14 "And [a]I will lay My vengeance[5360] on Edom by the hand of My people Israel. Therefore, they will act[6213] in Edom [b]according to My anger[639] and according to My wrath; thus they will know My vengeance," declares[5001] the Lord GOD.

Philistia

15 'Thus says the Lord GOD, "Because the Philistines have acted in [a]revenge[5360] and have taken vengeance with scorn[7589] of soul to destroy[4889] with everlasting[5769] enmity,"[342]

16 therefore, thus says the Lord GOD, "Behold, I will [a]stretch out My hand against the Philistines, even cut off the [b]Cherethites and destroy the remnant[7611] of the seacoast.

17 "And I will execute great vengeance on them with wrathful[2534] rebukes;[8433] and they will [a]know that I am the LORD when I lay My vengeance on them." ' "

Judgment on Tyre

26 Now it came about in the eleventh year, on the first of the month, that the word[1697] of the LORD came to me saying,

2 "Son[1121] of man,[120] because [a]Tyre has said[559] concerning Jerusalem, 'Aha, the [b]gateway of the peoples[5971] is broken;[7665] it has [Ic]opened to me. I shall be filled, *now that* she is laid waste,'[2717]

3 therefore, thus says[559] the Lord[136] [I]GOD, 'Behold, I am against you, O Tyre, and I will bring up[5927] [a]many nations[1471] against you, as the [b]sea brings up its waves.

4 'And they will [a]destroy[7843] the walls of Tyre and break down[2040] her towers; and I will scrape her debris[6083] from her and make her a bare rock.

5 'She will be a place for the spreading of nets[2764] in the midst of the sea, for I have spoken,' declares[5001] the Lord GOD, 'and she will become[1961] [a]spoil for the nations.

6 'Also her [a]daughters who are [I]on the mainland[7704] will be slain[2026] by the sword,[2719] and they will know[3045] that I am the LORD.' "

7 For thus says the Lord GOD, "Behold, I will bring upon Tyre from the north Nebuchadnezzar king[4428] of Babylon, [a]king of kings,[4428] with horses, [b]chariots, cavalry, and [I]a great army.

8 "He will slay[4191] your daughters [I]on the mainland with the sword; and he will make [a]siege walls against you, cast up[8210] a [b]mound against you, and raise up a large shield[6793] against you.

9 "And the blow of his battering rams[4239] he will direct against your walls,

---

7 [e]Ezek. 6:14

8 [a]Is. 15:1; Jer. 48:1; Amos 2:1, 2

9 [I]Lit., *open* [II]Lit., *end* [a]Num. 33:49; Josh. 12:3; 13:20 [b]Num. 32:3, 38; Josh. 13:17; 1Chr. 5:8; Jer. 48:23 [c]Num. 32:37; Josh. 13:19; Jer. 48:1, 23

10 [a]Ezek. 25:4

12 [a]2Chr. 28:17; Ps. 137:7; Jer. 49:7-22

13 [a]Jer. 49:8, 13 [b]Ezek. 29:8; Mal. 1:3, 4 [c]Gen. 36:34; Jer. 49:7; Amos 1:12 [d]Jer. 25:23; 49:8

14 [a]Is. 11:14 [b]Ezek. 35:11

15 [a]Is. 14:29-31; Ezek. 25:6, 12; Joel 3:4

16 [a]Jer. 25:20; 47:1-7 [b]1Sam. 30:14; Zeph. 2:5

17 [a]Ps. 9:16

2 [I]Lit., *turned* [a]2Sam. 5:11; Is. 23:1; Jer. 25:22 [b]Is. 62:10 [c]Ezek. 25:8; 35:10

3 [I]Heb., *YHWH*, usually rendered *LORD*, and so throughout the ch. [a]Mic. 4:11 [b]Is. 5:30; Jer. 50:42; 51:42

4 [a]Is. 23:11; Ezek. 26:9; Amos 1:10

5 [a]Ezek. 25:7; 29:19

6 [I]Lit., *in the field* [a]Ezek. 16:46, 53; 26:8

7 [I]Lit., *an assembly, even many people* [a]Ezra 7:12; Is. 10:8; Jer. 52:32; Dan. 2:37, 47 [b]Ezek. 23:24; Nah. 2:3, 4

8 [I]Lit., *in the field* [a]Jer. 52:4; Ezek. 21:22 [b]Jer. 32:24

and with his [I]axes he will break down
your towers.
10 "Because of the multitude of his
[a]horses, the dust[80] *raised by* them will
cover[3680] you; your walls will [b]shake[7493]
at the noise of cavalry and [I]wagons[1534]
and chariots, when he [c]enters your
gates as men enter a city that is
breached.
11 "With the hoofs of his [a]horses
he will trample all your streets. He will
slay your people with the sword; and
your strong pillars[4676] will [b]come down
to the ground.[776]
12 "Also they will make a spoil of
your riches[2428] and a prey of your
[a]merchandise, [b]break down your
walls and destroy[5422] your [c]pleasant
houses,[1004] and [I]throw[7760] your stones
and your timbers and your debris
[d]into the water.
13 "So I will [I]silence[7673] the sound
of your [a]songs,[7892] and the sound of your
[b]harps will be heard[8085] no more.
14 "And I will make you a bare rock;
you will be a place for the spreading of
nets. You will be [a]built no more, for I
the [b]LORD have spoken," declares the
Lord GOD.
15 Thus says the Lord GOD to
Tyre, "Shall not the [a]coastlands [b]shake
at the sound of your fall[4658] when the
wounded[2491] groan, when the slaughter[2027] occurs in your midst?
16 "Then all the princes[5387] of the
sea will [a]go down from their thrones,
remove[5493] their robes, and strip off
their embroidered garments. They will
[b]clothe themselves with [I]trembling;[2731]
they will sit on the ground, [c]tremble[2729]
every moment, and be appalled[8074] at
you.
17 "And they will take up[5375] a
[a]lamentation over you and say[559] to you,
'[b]How you have perished, O
inhabited one,
From the seas, O renowned
city,
Which was [c]mighty[2389] on the
sea,
She and her inhabitants,
Who [I]imposed [II]her terror[2851]
On all her inhabitants!
18 'Now the [a]coastlands will tremble
On the day[3117] of your fall;
Yes, the coastlands which are
by the sea
Will be terrified[926] at your
[b]passing.'"
19 For thus says the Lord GOD,
"When I shall make you a desolate[2717]
city, like the cities which are not inhabited, when I shall [a]bring up[5927] the deep
over you, and the great waters will cover
you,
20 then I shall bring you down with
those who [a]go down to the pit,[953] to
the people of old,[5769] and I shall make
you dwell in the [b]lower parts of the
earth,[776] like the ancient[5769] waste
places, with those who go down to the
pit, so that you will not [I]be inhabited;
but I shall set [c]glory[6643] in the land[776]
of the living.[2416]
21 "I shall [I]bring [a]terrors on you,
and you will be no more; though you
will be sought, [b]you will never be found
again," declares the Lord GOD.

Lament over Tyre

27 Moreover, the word[1697] of the
LORD came to me saying,
2 "And you, son[1121] of man,[120]
[a]take up[5375] a lamentation over Tyre;
3 and say[559] to Tyre, [a]who dwells
at the [I]entrance to the sea, [b]merchant
of the peoples[5971] to many coastlands,
'Thus says[559] the Lord[136] [II]GOD,
"O Tyre, you have said,[559] 'I am
perfect[3632] in beauty.'
4 "Your borders are in the heart[3820]
of the seas;
Your builders[1129] have
perfected[3634] your beauty.
5 "They have [I]made all *your*
planks of fir trees from
[a]Senir;
They have taken a cedar from
Lebanon to make[6213] a mast
for you.
6 "Of [a]oaks from [b]Bashan they have
made[6213] your oars;

---

9 [I]Lit., *swords*
10 [I]Lit., *wheels* [a]Jer. 4:13; 47:3 [b]Ezek. 26:15; 27:28 [c]Jer. 39:3
11 [a]Is. 5:28; Hab. 1:8 [b]Is. 26:5; Jer. 43:13
12 [I]Lit., *put* [a]Is. 23:8, 18; Ezek. 27:3-27; Zech. 9:3 [b]Jer. 52:14 [c]2Chr. 32:27; Amos 5:11 [d]Ezek. 27:27, 32, 34; 28:8
13 [I]Lit., *cause to cease* [a]Is. 23:16; 24:8, 9; Amos 6:5 [b]Is. 5:12; Rev. 18:22
14 [a]Deut. 13:16; Job 12:14; Mal. 1:4 [b]Is. 14:27
15 [a]Ezek. 26:18; 27:35 [b]Jer. 49:21; Ezek. 31:16
16 [I]Lit., *tremblings* [a]Jon. 3:6 [b]Job 8:22; Ps. 35:26; Ezek. 7:27; 1Pet. 5:5 [c]Ezek. 32:10; Hos. 11:10
17 [I]Lit., *put* [II]Lit., *their* [a]Ezek. 19:1, 14; 27:2, 32; 32:2, 16 [b]Is. 14:12; Jer. 48:39; 50:23 [c]Ezek. 27:3, 10, 11; 28:2
18 [a]Is. 41:5; Ezek. 26:15; 27:35 [b]Is. 23:5-7, 10, 11
19 [a]Is. 8:7, 8; Ezek. 26:3
20 [I]Or, *return* [a]Is. 14:9, 10; Ezek. 32:30 [b]Ps. 88:6; Amos 9:2; Jon. 2:2, 6 [c]Jer. 33:9; Zech. 2:8
21 [I]Lit., *give you terrors* [a]Ezek. 26:15, 16; 27:36 [b]Rev. 18:21

2 [a]Jer. 9:10, 17-20; Ezek. 28:12
3 [I]Lit., *entrances* [II]Heb., *YHWH,* usually rendered *LORD,* and so throughout the ch. [a]Ezek. 28:2 [b]Is. 23:3
5 [I]Lit., *built* [a]Deut. 3:9; 1Chr. 5:23; Song 4:8
6 [a]Is. 2:13; Zech. 11:2 [b]Num. 21:33; Is. 2:13; Jer. 22:20

With ivory they have [I]inlaid your
deck of boxwood from the
coastlands of [c]Cyprus.
7 "Your sail was of fine
embroidered linen from
Egypt
So that it became your
[I]distinguishing mark;
Your [II]awning was [III][a]blue and
purple from the coastlands of
[b]Elishah.
8 "The inhabitants of Sidon and
[a]Arvad were your rowers;
Your [b]wise men,*2450* O Tyre,
were [I]aboard; they were your
pilots.
9 "The elders*2204* of [a]Gebal and
her wise men were with
you repairing your
seams;
All the ships of the sea and their
sailors were with you in order
to deal*6148* in your
merchandise.
10 "[a]Persia and [a]Lud and [a]Put were
in your army,*2428* your men*582* of war.
They hung shield and helmet in you;
they set forth your splendor.*1926*
11 "The sons of Arvad and your
army were on your walls, *all* around,
and the [I]Gammadim were in your towers. They hung their shields*7982* on your
walls, *all* around; they perfected*3634*
your beauty.
12 "Tarshish was your customer
because of the abundance of all *kinds*
of wealth; with silver, iron, tin, and lead,
they paid for your wares.
13 "[a]Javan, [a]Tubal, and [b]Meshech,
they were your traders; with the
[c]lives*5315* of men*120* and vessels of bronze
they paid for your merchandise.
14 "Those from [a]Beth-togarmah
gave horses and war horses and mules
for your wares.
15 "The sons of [a]Dedan were your
traders. Many coastlands were [I]your
market; [b]ivory tusks and ebony they
brought as your payment.
16 "[a]Aram was your customer because of the abundance of your
[I]goods;4639 they paid for your wares with

6 [I]Lit., *made* [c]Gen. 10:4; Is. 23:1, 12; Jer. 2:10
7 [I]Or, *standard* [II]Lit., *covering* [III]Or, *violet* [a]Ex. 25:4; Jer. 10:9 [b]Gen. 10:4
8 [I]Lit., *in you* [a]Gen. 10:18; 1Chr. 1:16; Ezek. 27:11 [b]1Kin. 9:27
9 [a]Josh. 13:5; 1Kin. 5:18
10 [a]Ezek. 30:5; 38:5
11 [I]Or, *valorous ones*
13 [a]Gen. 10:2; Is. 66:19; Ezek. 27:19 [b]Gen. 10:2; Ezek. 38:2; 39:1 [c]Joel 3:3; Rev. 18:13
14 [a]Gen. 10:3; Ezek. 38:6
15 [I]Lit., *the market of your hand* [a]Jer. 25:23; Ezek. 25:13; 27:20 [b]1Kin. 10:22; Rev. 18:12
16 [I]Lit., *works* [a]Judg. 10:6; Is. 7:1-8; Ezek. 16:57 [b]Ezek. 28:13 [c]Ezek. 16:13, 18
17 [I]Heb., *pannag* [a]Judg. 11:33
18 [I]Lit., *works* [a]Gen. 14:15; Is. 7:8; Jer. 49:23; Ezek. 47:16-18
19 [I]Or, *with yarn* [II]Or, *calamus*
20 [a]Gen. 25:3
21 [I]Lit., *customers of your hand* [a]Is. 21:13 [b]Is. 60:7
22 [a]Gen. 10:7; Is. 60:6; Ezek. 38:13 [b]Gen. 43:11; 1Kin. 10:2
23 [a]2Kin. 19:12; Is. 37:12; Amos 1:5
24 [I]Or, *violet*
25 [I]Lit., *your travelers* [II]Lit., *honored* [a]Is. 2:16
26 [a]Ezek. 26:19 [b]Ps. 48:7; Jer. 18:17; Acts 27:14

[b]emeralds, purple, [c]embroidered work,
fine linen, coral, and rubies.
17 "Judah and the land*776* of Israel,
they were your traders; with the wheat
of [a]Minnith, [I]cakes, honey, oil,*8081*
and balm they paid for your merchandise.
18 "[a]Damascus was your customer
because of the abundance of your
[I]goods, because of the abundance of all
kinds of wealth, because of the wine
of Helbon and white wool.
19 "Vedan and Javan paid for your
wares [I]from Uzal; wrought iron, cassia,6916 and [II]sweet cane7070 were among
your merchandise.
20 "[a]Dedan traded with you in sad-
dlecloths for riding.
21 "[a]Arabia and all the princes*5387*
of Kedar, they were [I]your customers
for [b]lambs,*3733* rams, and goats; for
these they were your customers.
22 "The traders of [a]Sheba and
Raamah, they traded with you; they paid
for your wares with the best*7218* of all
kinds of [b]spices, and with all *kinds* of
precious stones, and gold.
23 "Haran, Canneh, [a]Eden, the
traders of Sheba, Asshur, *and* Chilmad
traded with you.
24 "They traded with you in choice
garments, in clothes of [I]blue and embroidered work, and in carpets of many colors, *and* tightly wound cords, *which were*
among your merchandise.
25 "The [a]ships of Tarshish were
[I]the carriers for your merchandise.
And you were filled and were
very [II]glorious*3519*
In the heart of the seas.
26 "Your rowers have brought you
Into [a]great waters;
The [b]east wind*7307* has
broken*7665* you
In the heart of the seas.
27 "Your wealth, your wares, your
merchandise,
Your sailors, and your pilots,
Your repairers of seams, your
dealers*6148* in merchandise,
And all your men of war who
are in you,

With all your company[6951] that
is in your midst,
Will fall into the heart of the seas
On the day[3117] of your
overthrow.[4658]
28 "At the sound of the cry of your
pilots
The pasture lands will
[a]shake.[7493]
29 "And all who handle the oar,
The [a]sailors, *and* all the pilots
of the sea
Will come down from their ships;
They will stand on the land,
30 And they will [a]make their voice
heard[8085] over you
And will cry[2199] bitterly.[4751]
They will [b]cast[5927] dust[6083] on
their heads,[7218]
They will [c]wallow in ashes.
31 "Also they will make themselves
[a]bald for you
And [b]gird themselves with
sackcloth;
And they will [c]weep for you in
bitterness[4751] of soul[5315]
With bitter[4751] mourning.
32 "Moreover, in their wailing they
will take up a [a]lamentation for
you
And lament over you:
'Who is like Tyre,
Like her who is silent[1822] in the
midst of the sea?
33 'When your wares[5801] went out
from the seas,
You satisfied many peoples;
With the [a]abundance of your
wealth and your merchandise
You enriched the kings[4428] of
earth.[776]
34 '[I]Now[6256] that you are [a]broken
by the seas
In the depths of the waters,
Your [b]merchandise and all your
company
Have fallen in the midst of you.
35 'All the [a]inhabitants of the
coastlands
Are appalled[8074] at you,
And their kings are horribly[8178]
afraid;[8175]
They are troubled in
countenance.
36 'The merchants among the
peoples [a]hiss at you;
You have become [I]terrified,
And you [b]will be no more.' " ' "

Tyre's King Overthrown

28 The word[1697] of the LORD came
again to me saying,
2 "Son[1121] of man,[120] say[559] to the
[I]leader[5057] of Tyre, 'Thus says[559] the
Lord[136] [II]GOD,
"Because your heart[3820] is lifted
up
And you have said,[559] '[a]I am a
god,[410]
I sit in the seat[4186] of [III]gods,[430]
In the heart[3820] of the seas';
Yet you are a [b]man and not God,
Although you make your heart
like the heart of God—
3 Behold, you are wiser[2450] than
[a]Daniel;
There is no secret that is a match
for you.
4 "By your wisdom[2451] and
understanding
You have acquired[6213] [a]riches[2428]
for yourself,
And have acquired gold and
silver for your treasuries.
5 "By your great wisdom, by your
[a]trade[7404]
You have increased your riches,
And your [b]heart[3824] is lifted up
because of your riches—
6 Therefore, thus says the Lord
GOD,
'Because you have [a]made your
heart
Like the heart of God,
7 Therefore, behold, I will bring
[a]strangers upon you,
The [b]most ruthless of the
nations.[1471]
And they will draw their
swords[2719]
Against the beauty of your
wisdom
And defile[2490] your splendor.

28 [a]Ezek. 26:10, 15, 18
29 [a]Rev. 18:17-19
30 [a]Is. 23:1-6; Ezek. 26:17 [b]1Sam. 4:12; 2Sam. 1:2; Lam. 2:10; Rev. 18:19 [c]Jer. 6:26; Jon. 3:6
31 [a]Is. 15:2; Ezek. 29:18 [b]Is. 22:12; Ezek. 7:18 [c]Is. 16:9; 22:4
32 [a]Ezek. 26:17; 27:2; 28:12
33 [a]Ezek. 27:12, 18; 28:4, 5
34 [I]Lit., *The time* [a]Ezek. 26:12; 27:26, 27 [b]Zech. 9:3, 4
35 [a]Is. 23:6; Ezek. 26:16
36 [I]Lit., *terrors* [a]Jer. 18:16; 19:8; 49:17; 50:13; Zeph. 2:15 [b]Ps. 37:10,36
2 [I]Or, *ruler, prince* [II]Heb., *YHWH*, usually rendered LORD, and so throughout the ch. [III]Or, *God* [a]Is. 14:14; 47:8; Ezek. 28:9; 2Thess. 2:4 [b]Ps. 9:20; 82:6, 7; Is. 31:3; Ezek. 28:9
3 [a]Dan. 1:20; 2:20-23, 28; 5:11, 12
4 [a]Ezek. 27:33; Zech. 9:2,3
5 [a]Ezek. 27:12; Hos. 12:7, 8 [b]Job 31:24, 25; Ps. 52:7; Ezek. 28:2; Hos. 13:6
6 [a]Ex. 9:17; Ezek. 28:2
7 [a]Ezek. 26:7 [b]Ezek. 30:11; 31:12; 32:12; Hab. 1:6-8

8 'They will bring you down to the
pit,[7845]
And you will die[4191] the
[a]death of those who are
slain[2491]
In the heart of the seas.
9 'Will you still say, "I am a god,"
In the presence of your
slayer,[2026]
Although you are a man and not
God,
In the hands[3027] of those who
wound you?
10 'You will die the death[4194] of the
[a]uncircumcised[6189]
By the hand of strangers,
For I have spoken!'[1696]
declares[5001] the Lord
GOD!" ' "

11 Again the word of the LORD
came to me saying,
12 "Son of man, [a]take up[5375] a lamentation over the king[4428] of Tyre,
and say to him, 'Thus says the Lord
GOD,
"You [I]had the seal of perfection,
Full of wisdom and perfect[3632]
in beauty.
13 "You were in [a]Eden, the garden
of God;
[b]Every precious stone was your
covering:
The [c]ruby, the topaz, and the
diamond;
The beryl, the onyx, and the
jasper;
The lapis lazuli, the turquoise,
and the emerald;
And the gold, the workmanship
of your [I][d]settings[8596] and
[II]sockets,
Was in you.
On the day[3117] that you were
created[1254]
They were prepared.[3559]
14 "You were the [a]anointed[4473]
cherub[3742] who [I]covers,
And I placed you *there.*
You were on the holy[6944]
[b]mountain of God;
You walked in the midst of the
[c]stones of fire.
15 "You were [a]blameless[8549] in your
ways[1870]
From the day you were created,
Until [b]unrighteousness[5766] was
found in you.
16 "By the [a]abundance of your trade
[I]You were internally [b]filled with
violence,[2555]
And you sinned;[2398]
Therefore I have cast you as
profane
From the mountain of God.
And I have destroyed[6] you, O
[II]covering cherub,
From the midst of the stones
of fire.
17 "Your heart was lifted up because
of your [a]beauty;
You [b]corrupted[7843] your wisdom
by reason of your splendor.
I cast you to the ground;[776]
I put you before [c]kings,[4428]
That they may see[7200] you.
18 "By the multitude of your
iniquities,[5771]
In the unrighteousness of your
trade,
You profaned your
sanctuaries.[4720]
Therefore I have brought
[a]fire from the midst of you;
It has consumed you,
And I have turned you to
[b]ashes on the earth[776]
In the eyes of all who see you.
19 "All who know[3045] you among the
peoples[5971]
Are appalled[8074] at you;
You have become [I][a]terrified,
And you will be [b]no more." ' "

Judgment of Sidon

20 And the word of the LORD came
to me saying,
21 "Son of man, [a]set[7760] your face
toward [b]Sidon, prophesy[5012] against her,
22 and say, 'Thus says the Lord
GOD,
"Behold, I am against you, O
Sidon,

8 [a]Ezek. 27:26, 27, 34

10 [a]1Sam. 17:26, 36; Ezek. 31:18; 32:30

12 [I]Lit., *were the one sealing a pattern* [a]Ezek. 19:1; 26:17; 27:2

13 [I]Or, *tambourines* [II]Or, *flutes* [a]Gen. 2:8; Is. 51:3; Ezek. 31:8, 9, 16; 36:35 [b]Ezek. 27:16, 22 [c]Ex. 28:17-20 [d]Is. 24:8; 30:32

14 [I]Or, *guards* [a]Ex. 25:17-20; 30:26; 40:9; Ezek. 28:16 [b]Ezek. 20:40; 28:16 [c]Ezek. 28:13, 16; Rev. 18:16

15 [a]Ezek. 27:3, 4; 28:3-6, 12 [b]Ezek. 28:17, 18

16 [I]Lit., *They filled your midst* [II]Or, *guardian* [a]Ezek. 27:12 [b]Ezek. 8:17; Hab. 2:8, 17

17 [a]Ezek. 27:3, 4; 28:7 [b]Is. 19:11 [c]Ezek. 26:16

18 [a]Amos 1:9, 10 [b]Mal. 4:3

19 [I]Lit., *terrors* [a]Ezek. 26:21; 27:36 [b]Jer. 51:64

21 [a]Ezek. 6:2; 25:2 [b]Gen. 10:15, 19; Is. 23:2, 4; Ezek. 27:8

And I shall [I]be glorified in your
midst.
Then they will know that I am
the LORD, when I
[a]execute[6213] judgments[8201] in
her,
And I shall manifest My
holiness[6942] in her.
23 "For [a]I shall send pestilence[1698]
to her
And blood[1818] to her streets,
And the [b]wounded[2491] will
[I]fall[5307] in her midst
By the sword[2713] upon her on
every side;
Then they will know that I am
the LORD.
24 "And there will be no more for
the house[1004] of Israel a [a]prickling brier
or a painful thorn from any round about
them who scorned them; then they will
know that I am the Lord GOD."

Israel Regathered

25 'Thus says the Lord GOD,
"When I [a]gather[6908] the house of Israel
from the peoples among whom they are
scattered, and shall manifest My holiness in them in the sight of the nations,[1471] then they will [b]live in their
[I]land[127] which I gave to My servant[5650]
Jacob.
26 "And they will [a]live in it
securely;[983] and they will [b]build
houses,[1004] plant vineyards, and live securely,[983] when I [c]execute judgments
upon all who scorn them round about
them. Then they will know that I am
the LORD their God." ' "

Judgment of Egypt

29 In the [a]tenth year, in the tenth
month, on the twelfth of the
month, the word[1697] of the LORD came
to me saying,
2 "Son[1121] of man,[120] set[7760] your
face against [a]Pharaoh, king[4428] of Egypt,
and prophesy[5012] against him and against
all [b]Egypt.
3 "Speak[1696] and say,[559] 'Thus
says[559] the Lord[136] [I]GOD,
"Behold, I am against you,
Pharaoh, king of Egypt,
The great [II][a]monster[8577] that lies
in the midst of his [III]rivers,
That [b]has said,[559] 'My Nile is
mine, and I myself have made
it.'
4 "And I shall put [a]hooks in your
jaws,
And I shall make the fish[1710] of
your [I]rivers cling to your
scales.
And I shall bring you up out of
the midst of your [I]rivers,
And all the fish of your [I]rivers
will cling to your scales.
5 "And I shall [a]abandon[5203] you to
the wilderness, you and all
the fish of your [I]rivers;
You will fall on the [II]open
field;[7704] you will not be
brought together or
[III][b]gathered.[6908]
I have given you for [c]food to the
beasts[2416] of the earth and to
the birds of the sky.[8064]
6 "Then all the inhabitants of Egypt
will know[3045] that I am the
LORD,
Because they have been *only* a
[a]staff *made* of reed to the
house[1004] of Israel.
7 "When they took hold of you with
the hand,[3709]
You [a]broke and tore all their
[I]hands;
And when they leaned[8172] on
you,
You broke[7665] and made all their
loins [II]quake."
8 'Therefore, thus says the Lord
GOD, "Behold, I shall [a]bring upon you
a sword,[2719] and I shall cut off[3772] from
you man and beast.
9 "And the [a]land[776] of Egypt will become a desolation[8077] and waste.[2723]
Then they will know that I am the LORD.
Because [I]you [b]said, 'The Nile is
mine, and I have made[6213] *it,*'
10 therefore, behold, I am [a]against

---

22 [I]Or, *glorify Myself* [a]Ezek. 28:26; 30:19
23 [I]Or, *be judged* [a]Ezek. 38:22 [b]Jer. 51:52
24 [a]Num. 33:55; Josh. 23:13; Is. 55:13; Ezek. 2:6
25 [I]Lit., *ground* [a]Ps. 106:47; Is. 11:12, 13; Jer. 32:37; Ezek. 20:41; 34:13, 27 [b]Jer. 23:8; 27:11
26 [a]Jer. 23:6; Ezek. 34:25-28; 38:8 [b]Jer. 32:15, 43, 44; Amos 9:13, 14 [c]Ezek. 25:11; 28:22

1 [a]Ezek. 26:1; 29:17; 30:20
2 [a]Jer. 44:30 [b]Is. 19:1-17; Jer. 46:2-26; Ezek. 30:1-32:32
3 [I]Heb., *YHWH,* usually rendered *LORD,* and so throughout the ch. [II]Lit., *tannim* [III]Or, *Nile* [a]Is. 27:1; Ezek. 32:2 [b]Ezek. 29:9; 30:12
4 [I]Or, *Nile* [a]2Kin. 19:28; Ezek. 38:4
5 [I]Or, *Nile* [II]Lit., *faces of the field* [III]Or, with several mss. and Targum, *buried* [a]Ezek. 32:4-6 [b]Jer. 8:2; 25:33 [c]Jer. 7:33; 34:20; Ezek. 39:4
6 [a]2Kin. 18:21; Is. 36:6
7 [I]So with some ancient versions; M.T., *shoulders* [II]Lit., *stand* [a]2Kin. 18:21; Is. 36:6; Ezek. 17:15-17
8 [a]Jer. 46:13; Ezek. 14:17
9 [I]Lit., *he* [a]Ezek. 29:10-12; 30:7, 8, 13-19 [b]Prov. 16:18; 18:12; Ezek. 29:3
10 [a]Ezek. 13:8; 21:3; 26:3; 29:3

you and against your [I]rivers, and I will
make the land of Egypt an utter waste
and desolation, from Migdol *to* Syene
and even to the border of [II]Ethiopia.
11 "A man's foot will [a]not pass
through[5674] it, and the foot of a beast
will not pass through it, and it will not
be inhabited for forty years.
12 "So I shall make the land of Egypt
a desolation in the [a]midst of desolated[8074]
lands.[776] And her cities, in the midst
of cities that are laid waste,[2717] will be
desolate forty years; and I shall [b]scatter
the Egyptians among the nations[1471] and
disperse them among the lands."
13 'For thus says the Lord GOD,
"At the end of forty years I shall
[a]gather[6908] the Egyptians from the
peoples[5971] [I]among whom they were
scattered.
14 "And I shall turn[7725] the fortunes[7622] of Egypt and shall make them
return[7725] to the land of [a]Pathros, to
the land of their origin; and there they
will be a lowly kingdom.[4467]
15 "It will be the [a]lowest of the
kingdoms;[4467] and it will never again lift
itself up[5375] above the nations. And
I shall make them so small that they
will not [b]rule[7287] over the nations.
16 "And it will never again be the
[a]confidence of the house of Israel,
[Ib]bringing to mind[2142] the iniquity[5771] of
their having turned [II]to Egypt. Then
they will know that I am the Lord
GOD."'"
17 Now in the [a]twenty-seventh
year, in the first[7223] *month,* on the first
of the month, the word of the LORD
came to me saying,
18 "Son of man, [a]Nebuchadnezzar
king of Babylon made his army[2428]
labor[5647] [I]hard against Tyre; every
head[7218] was made [b]bald, and every
shoulder was rubbed bare.[4803] But he
and his army had no wages from Tyre
for the labor that he had [II]performed[5647]
against it."
19 Therefore, thus says the Lord
GOD, "Behold, I [a]shall give the land of
Egypt to Nebuchadnezzar king of Babylon. And he will carry off[5375] her
[Ib]wealth, and capture her spoil and seize
her plunder; and it will be wages for
his army.
20 "I have given him the land of
Egypt *for* his labor which he [Ia]performed,
because they acted for Me," declares[5001]
the Lord GOD.
21 "On that day[3117] I shall make a
[a]horn sprout for the house of Israel, and
I shall [Ib]open your mouth[6310] in their
midst. Then they will know that I am
the LORD."

Lament over Egypt

30 The word[1697] of the LORD came
again to me saying,
2 "Son[1121] of man,[120] prophesy[5012]
and say,[559] 'Thus says[559] the Lord[136]
[I]GOD,
"[a]Wail, 'Alas for the day!'[3117]
3 "For the day is near,
Even [a]the day of the LORD is
near;
It will be a day of [b]clouds,
A time[6256] *of doom* for the
nations.[1471]
4 "And a sword[2719] will come upon
Egypt,
And anguish will be in
[I]Ethiopia,
When the slain[2491] fall in Egypt,
They [a]take away her [II]wealth,
And her foundations[3247] are torn
down.
5 "[I]Ethiopia, Put, Lud, all [IIa]Arabia,
[III]Libya, and the [IV]people[5971] of the
land[776] [V]that is in league[1285] will fall with
them by the sword."
6 'Thus says the LORD,
"Indeed, those who support
[a]Egypt will fall,
And the pride of her power will
come down;
From Migdol *to* Syene
They will fall within her by the
sword,"
Declares[5001] the Lord GOD.
7 "And they will be desolate[8074]

10 [I]Or, *Nile* [II]Lit., *Cush*
11 [a]Jer. 43:11, 12; 46:19; Ezek. 32:13
12 [a]Jer. 25:15-19; 27:6-11; Ezek. 30:7 [b]Jer. 46:19; Ezek. 30:23, 26
13 [I]Lit., *where* [a]Is. 19:22; Jer. 46:26
14 [a]Is. 11:11; Jer. 44:1, 15; Ezek. 30:14
15 [a]Ezek. 17:6, 14; 30:13; Zech. 10:11 [b]Ezek. 31:2; 32:2; Nah. 3:8-10
16 [I]Lit., *causing to remember* [II]Lit., *after them* [a]Is. 20:5; 30:1-3; 31:1; 36:6; Ezek. 17:15; 29:6, 7 [b]Is. 64:9; Jer. 14:10; Ezek. 21:23; Hos. 8:13
17 [a]Ezek. 24:1; 26:1; 29:1; 30:20; 40:1
18 [I]Lit., *a great labor* [II]Lit., *labored* [a]Jer. 25:9; 27:6; Ezek. 26:7-12 [b]Jer. 48:37; Ezek. 27:31
19 [I]Or, *multitude* [a]Ezek. 30:10, 24, 25; 32:11 [b]Jer. 43:10-13; Ezek. 30:14
20 [I]Lit., *labored* [a]Is. 10:6, 7; 45:1-3; Jer. 25:9
21 [I]Lit., *give you an opening of the mouth* [a]1 Sam. 2:10; Ps. 92:10; 132:17 [b]Ezek. 3:27; 24:27; 33:22; Amos 3:7, 8; Luke 21:15

2 [I]Heb., *YHWH,* usually rendered *LORD,* and so throughout the ch. [a]Is. 13:6; 15:2; Ezek. 21:12; Joel 1:5, 11, 13
3 [a]Ezek. 7:19; 13:5; Joel 1:15; 2:1; Obad. 15 [b]Ezek. 30:18; 32:7; 34:12
4 [I]Lit., *Cush* [II]Or, *multitude* [a]Ezek. 29:19
5 [I]Lit., *Cush* [II]Or, *the mixed people* [III]Or, *Cub* [IV]Lit., *sons* [V]Lit., *of the covenant* [a]Jer. 25:20, 24
6 [a]Is. 20:3-6

In the [a]midst of the desolated
lands;[776]
And her cities will be
In the midst of the
devastated[2717] cities.
8 "And they will [a]know[3045] that I
am the LORD,
When I set a [b]fire in Egypt
And all her helpers are
broken.[7665]
9 "On that day [a]messengers will go
forth from Me in ships to frighten[2729]
[b]secure[983] [I]Ethiopia; and [c]anguish will
be on them as on the day of Egypt;
for, behold, it comes!"
10 'Thus says the Lord GOD,
"[a]I will also make the [I]multitude
of Egypt cease[7673]
By the hand[3027] of
Nebuchadnezzar king[4428] of
Babylon.
11 "He and his people with him,
[a]The most ruthless of the
nations,[1471]
Will be brought in to destroy[7843]
the land;
And they will draw their
swords[2719] against Egypt
And fill the land with the slain.
12 "Moreover, I will make the
[a]Nile canals dry[2724]
And [b]sell the land into the hands
of evil men.[7451]
And I will make the land
desolate,[8074]
And [I]all that is in it,
By the hand of strangers; I, the
LORD, have spoken."[1696]
13 'Thus says the Lord GOD,
"I will also [a]destroy[6] the idols[1544]
And make the [I]images[457] cease
from [II][b]Memphis.
And there will no longer be a
prince[5387] in the land of
Egypt;
And I will put fear[3374] in the land
of Egypt.
14 "And I will make [a]Pathros
desolate,
Set a fire in [b]Zoan,
And execute judgments[8201] on
[I][c]Thebes.

7 [a]Jer. 25:18-26; Ezek. 29:12
8 [a]Ps. 58:11; Ezek. 29:6, 9, 16 [b]Ezek. 22:31; 30:14, 16; Amos 1:4, 7, 10, 12, 14
9 [I]Lit., *Cush* [a]Is. 18:1, 2 [b]Is. 47:8; Ezek. 38:11; 39:6 [c]Is. 19:17; 23:5; Ezek. 32:9, 10
10 [I]Or, *wealth* [a]Ezek. 29:19
11 [a]Ezek. 28:7
12 [I]Lit., *her fulness* [a]Ezek. 29:3, 9 [b]Is. 19:4
13 [I]Or, *futile ones* [II]Or, *Noph* [a]Is. 2:18 [b]Is. 19:13; Jer. 2:16; 44:1; 46:14; Ezek. 30:16
14 [I]Or, *No* [a]Is. 11:11; Jer. 44:1, 15; Ezek. 29:14 [b]Ps. 78:12, 43; Is. 19:11, 13 [c]Jer. 46:25; Ezek. 30:15, 16; Nah. 3:8
15 [I]Or, *Pelusium* [II]Or, *No*
16 [I]Or, *Pelusium* [II]Or, *No* [III]Or, *Noph* [IV]Or, *adversaries*
17 [I]Or, *Aven* [II]Lit., *they* [a]Gen. 41:45; 46:20
18 [I]So with many mss. and ancient versions; M.T., *restrain* [a]Jer. 43:8-13 [b]Ezek. 30:3 [c]Lev. 26:13; Is. 10:27; Jer. 27:2; 28:10, 13; 30:8; Ezek. 34:27
19 [a]Ps. 9:16; Ezek. 5:8, 15; 25:11; 30:14
20 [a]Ezek. 26:1; 29:1, 17; 31:1
21 [I]Lit., *to give healing* [II]Lit., *to put a bandage, to wrap it* [a]Ps. 10:15; 37:17; Ezek. 30:24 [b]Jer. 30:13; 46:11
22 [a]Jer. 46:25; Ezek. 29:3 [b]2Kin. 24:7; Jer. 37:7 [c]Jer. 46:21
23 [a]Ezek. 29:12; 30:17, 18, 26
24 [a]Neh. 6:9; Is. 45:1, 5; Ezek. 30:10, 25; Zech. 10:12

15 "And I will pour out[8210] My wrath
on [I]Sin,
The stronghold of Egypt;
I will also cut off[3772] the multitude
of [II]Thebes.
16 "And I will set a fire in Egypt;
[I]Sin will writhe in anguish,
[II]Thebes will be breached,
And [III]Memphis *will have*
[IV]distresses[6862] daily.
17 "The young men of [I][a]On[206] and
of Pi-beseth
Will fall by the sword,
And [II]the women will go into
captivity.[7628]
18 "And in [a]Tehaphnehes the day will
[I]be [b]dark[2821]
When I [c]break[7665] there the yoke
bars of Egypt.
Then the pride of her power will
cease in her;
A cloud[6051] will cover[3680] her,
And her daughters will go into
captivity.
19 "Thus I will [a]execute judgments
on Egypt,
And they will know that I am
the LORD." ' "

Victory for Babylon

20 And it came about in the
[a]eleventh year, in the first[7223] *month,*
on the seventh of the month, that the
word of the LORD came to me saying,
21 "Son of man, I have [a]broken[7665]
the arm of Pharaoh king of Egypt; and,
behold, it has not been [b]bound up
[I]for healing [II]or wrapped[2280] with a
bandage, that it may be strong[2388] to
hold the sword.
22 "Therefore, thus says the Lord
GOD, 'Behold, I am [a]against Pharaoh
king of Egypt and will break his arms,
both the strong[2389] and the [b]broken; and
I will make the sword [c]fall from his
hand.
23 'And I will [a]scatter the Egyptians
among the nations and disperse them
among the lands.
24 'For I will [a]strengthen[2388] the
arms of the king of Babylon and put

[b]My sword in his hand; and I will break
the arms of Pharaoh, so that he will
groan before him with the groanings of
a wounded[2491] man.
25 'Thus I will strengthen the arms
of the king of Babylon, but the arms
of Pharaoh will fall. Then they will know
that I am the LORD, when I put My
sword into the hand of the king of Babylon and he [a]stretches it out against the
land of Egypt.
26 'When I scatter the Egyptians
among the nations and disperse them
among the lands, then they will know
that I am the LORD.'"

Pharaoh Warned of Assyria's Fate

31 And it came about in the [a]eleventh year, in the third *month,*
on the first of the month, that the
word[1697] of the LORD came to me saying,
2 "Son[1121] of man,[120] say[559] to Pharaoh king[4428] of Egypt, and to his
[a]multitude,

'Whom are you like in your
greatness?
3 'Behold, Assyria *was* a
[a]cedar in Lebanon
With beautiful branches and
forest shade,[6751]
And [I][b]very high;
And its top was among the
[II]clouds.
4 'The [a]waters made it grow, the
[I]deep made it high.
With its rivers it continually
[II]extended all around its
planting place,
And it sent out its channels to
all the trees of the field.[7704]
5 'Therefore [a]its height was loftier
than all the trees of the field
And its boughs became many
and its branches long[748]
Because of [b]many waters
[I]as it spread them out.
6 'All the [a]birds of the heavens
nested in its boughs,
And under its branches all the
beasts[2416] of the field gave
birth,
And all great nations[1471] lived
under its shade.
7 'So it was beautiful in its
greatness, in the length[753] of
its branches;
For its [I]roots extended to many
waters.
8 'The [a]cedars in [b]God's[430] garden
[I]could not match it;
The [II]cypresses [I]could not
compare with its boughs,
And the plane trees [III]could not
match its branches.
No tree in [b]God's garden [I]could
compare with it in its
beauty.
9 'I made it beautiful with the
multitude of its branches,
And all the trees of [a]Eden, which
were in the [b]garden of God,
were jealous[7065] of it.

10 'Therefore, thus says[559] the
Lord[136] [I]GOD, "Because [II]it is high in
stature, and it has set its top among
the [III]clouds, and its [a]heart[3824] is haughty
in its loftiness,
11 therefore, I will give it into the
hand[3027] of a [I][a]despot[410] of the
nations;[1471] he will thoroughly deal[6213]
with it. According to its wickedness[7562]
I have [b]driven it away.
12 "And [a]alien [b]tyrants of the nations have cut it down[3772] and left[5203]
it; on the [c]mountains and in all the valleys
its branches have fallen,[5307] and its
boughs have been broken[7665] in all the
ravines of the land.[776] And all the
peoples[5971] of the earth[776] have [d]gone
down from its shade and left it.
13 "On its ruin[4658] all the [a]birds of
the heavens will dwell. And all the beasts
of the field will be on its *fallen* branches
14 in order that all the trees by the
waters may not be exalted in their stature, nor set their top among the
[I]clouds, nor their [II]well-watered mighty
ones stand *erect* in their height. For they
have all been given over to death,[4194]
to the [a]earth beneath,[8482] among the

24 [b]Ezek. 30:11; 25; Zeph. 2:12
25 [a]Josh. 8:18; 1Chr. 21:16; Is. 5:25

1 [a]Jer. 52:5, 6; Ezek. 30:20; 32:1
2 [a]Ezek. 29:19; 30:10; Nah. 3:9
3 [I]Lit., *high of stature* [II]So Gr.; M.T., *thick boughs* [a]Is. 10:33, 34; Ezek. 17:3, 4, 22; 31:16; Dan. 4:10, 20-23 [b]Is. 10:33; Ezek. 31:5, 10
4 [I]I.e., subterranean waters [II]Lit., *was going* [a]Ezek. 17:5, 8; Rev. 17:1, 15
5 [I]Lit., *in its sending forth* [a]Dan. 4:11 [b]Ps. 1:3; Ezek. 17:5
6 [a]Ezek. 17:23; 31:13; Dan. 4:12, 21; Matt. 13:32
7 [I]Lit., *root was*
8 [I]Lit., *did* [II]Or, *Phoenician junipers* [III]Lit., *were not like* [a]Ps. 80:10; Ezek. 31:3 [b]Gen. 2:8, 9; 13:10; Is. 51:3; Ezek. 28:13; 31:16, 18
9 [a]Gen. 2:8, 9; 13:10; Is. 51:3; Ezek. 28:13; 31:16, 18
10 [I]Heb., *YHWH,* usually rendered LORD, and so throughout the ch. [II]Lit., *you are* [III]Or, *thick boughs* [a]2Chr. 32:25; Is. 10:12; 14:13, 14; Ezek. 28:17; Dan. 5:20
11 [I]Or, *mighty one* [a]Ezek. 30:10, 11; 32:11, 12; Dan. 5:18, 19 [b]Deut. 18:12; Nah. 3:18
12 [a]Ezek. 7:21; 28:7; 30:12; Hab. 1:6 [b]Ezek. 28:7; 30:11; 32:12 [c]Ezek. 32:5; 35:8 [d]Ezek. 31:17; Dan. 4:14; Nah. 3:17, 18
13 [a]Is. 18:6; Ezek. 29:5; 31:6; 32:4

14 [I]Or, *thick boughs* [II]Lit., *drinkers of water* [a]Num. 16:30, 33; Ps. 63:9; Ezek. 26:20; 31:18; 32:24; Amos 9:2; Jon. 2:2, 6; Eph. 4:9

sons[1121] of men,[120] with those who go
down to the pit."[953]
15 'Thus says the Lord GOD, "On
the day[3117] when it went down to
Sheol[7585] I [a]caused lamentations; I
closed[3680] the [I]deep over it and held back
its rivers. And *its* many waters were
stopped up, and I made Lebanon
[II]mourn[6937] for it, and all the trees of
the field wilted away on account of it.
16 "I made the nations [a]quake[7493]
at the sound of its fall[4658] when I made
it [b]go down to Sheol[7585] with those who
go down to the pit; and all the [I]well-
watered trees of Eden, the choicest
and best[2896] of [c]Lebanon, were [d]com-
forted[5162] in the earth beneath.
17 "They also [a]went down with it
to Sheol to those who were [b]slain[2491]
by the sword;[2719] and those who were
its [I]strength lived [c]under its shade
among the nations.
18 "To which among the trees of
Eden are you thus [I]equal in glory[3519]
and greatness? Yet you will be brought
down with the trees of Eden to the earth
beneath; you will lie in the midst of the
[a]uncircumcised,[6189] with those who
were slain by the sword. [b]So is Pharaoh
and all his multitude!"' declares[5001] the
Lord GOD."

Lament over Pharaoh and Egypt

32 And it came about in the [a]twelfth
year, in the twelfth *month,* on
the first of the month, that the word[1697]
of the LORD came to me saying,
2 "Son[1121] of man,[120] take up[5375] a
[a]lamentation over Pharaoh king[4428] of
Egypt, and say[559] to him,
'You [I]compared yourself to a
young [b]lion of the nations,[1471]
Yet you are like the [c]monster
in the seas;
And you [d]burst forth in your
rivers,
And muddied the waters with
your feet,
And [II]fouled their rivers.'"
3 Thus says[559] the Lord[136]
[I]GOD,
"Now I will [a]spread My net[2764]
over you
With a company[6951] of many
peoples,[5971]
And they shall lift you up in My
net.
4 "And I will leave[5203] you on the
land;[776]
I will cast you on the [I]open
field.[7704]
And I will cause all the [a]birds
of the heavens[8064] to dwell
on you,
And I will satisfy the beasts[2416]
of the whole earth[776] [II]with
you.
5 "And I will lay your flesh [a]on the
mountains,
And fill the valleys with your
refuse.
6 "I will also make the land drink
the discharge of your
[a]blood,[1818]
As far as the mountains,
And the ravines shall be full of
you.
7 "And when *I* [a]extinguish you,
I will [b]cover the heavens, and
darken[6937] their [c]stars;
I will cover[3680] the [d]sun with a
cloud,[6051]
And the moon shall not give its
light.[216]
8 "All the shining [a]lights[3974] in the
heavens
I will darken over you
And will set darkness[2822] on your
land,"
Declares[5001] the Lord GOD.
9 "I will also [a]trouble[3707] the
hearts[3820] of many peoples, when I
[b]bring your destruction[7667] among the
nations, into lands[776] which you have
not known.[3045]
10 "And I will make many peoples
[a]appalled at you, and their kings[4428] shall
be horribly[8178] afraid[8175] of you when I
brandish My sword[2719] before them; and
[b]they shall tremble[2729] every moment,
every man[376] for his own life,[5315] on the
day[3117] of your fall."[4658]
11 For [a]thus says the Lord GOD,

15 [I]I.e., subterranean waters [II]Lit., *be darkened* [a]Ezek. 32:7; Nah. 2:10
16 [I]Lit., *drinkers of water* [a]Ezek. 26:15; 27:28; Hag. 2:7 [b]Is. 14:15; Ezek. 32:18 [c]Is. 14:8; Hab. 2:17 [d]Ezek. 14:22, 23; 32:31
17 [I]Lit., *arm* [a]Ps. 9:17 [b]Ezek. 32:20f. [c]Ezek. 31:3, 6; Dan. 4:12
18 [I]Lit., *like* [a]Jer. 9:25, 26; Ezek. 28:10; 32:19, 21 [b]Ps. 52:7; Matt. 13:19

1 [a]Ezek. 30:20; 31:1; 32:17; 33:21
2 [I]Or, *were like* [II]Lit., *fouled by stamping* [a]Ezek. 19:1; 27:2; 28:12; 32:16 [b]Jer. 4:7; Ezek. 19:2-6; Nah. 2:11-13 [c]Is. 27:1; Ezek. 29:3 [d]Jer. 46:7, 8
3 [I]Heb., *YHWH,* usually rendered LORD, and so throughout the ch. [a]Ezek. 12:13
4 [I]Lit., *surface of the field* [II]Lit., *from* [a]Is. 18:6
5 [a]Ezek. 31:12
6 [a]Ex. 7:17; Is. 34:3, 7; Ezek. 35:6; Rev. 14:20
7 [a]Job 18:5, 6; Prov. 13:9 [b]Ex. 10:21-23; Is. 34:4; Ezek. 30:3, 18; 34:12 [c]Is. 13:10 [d]Joel 2:2, 31; 3:15; Amos 8:9; Matt. 24:29; Mark 13:24f.; Luke 21:25; Rev. 6:12; 8:12
8 [a]Gen. 1:14
9 [a]Ezek. 27:29-32; 28:19; Rev. 18:10-15 [b]Ex. 15:14-16
10 [a]Ezek. 27:35 [b]Ezek. 26:16
11 [a]Jer. 46:26

"The sword of the king of Babylon shall
come upon you.
12 "By the swords[2719] of the mighty
ones I will cause your multitude to fall;
all of them are [a]tyrants of the nations,
And they shall [b]devastate[7703] the
pride of Egypt,
And all its multitude shall be
destroyed.
13 "I will also destroy[6] all its cattle
from beside many waters;
And [a]the foot of man shall not
muddy[4103] them anymore,
And the hoofs of beasts shall not
muddy them.
14 "Then I will make their waters
settle,
And will cause their rivers to
run like oil,"[8081]
Declares the Lord GOD.
15 "When I make the land of Egypt
a [a]desolation,[8077]
And the land[776] is destitute of
that which filled it,
When I smite[5221] all those who
live in it,
Then they shall [b]know[3045] that
I am the LORD.
16 "This is a [a]lamentation and they
shall [I]chant it. The daughters of the nations shall [I]chant it. Over Egypt and over
all her multitude they shall [I]chant it,"
declares the Lord GOD.
17 And it came about in the
[a]twelfth year, on the [b]fifteenth of the
month, that the word of the LORD came
to me saying,
18 "Son of man, [a]wail for the multitude of Egypt, and [b]bring it down, her
and the daughters of the powerful[117] nations, to the [c]nether[8482] world, with
those who go down to the pit;[953]
19 'Whom do you surpass in beauty?
Go down and make your bed
with the [a]uncircumcised.'[6189]
20 "They shall fall in the midst of
those who are slain[2491] by the sword.
[I]She is given over to the sword; they
have [a]drawn her and all her multitudes
away.
21 "The [a]strong[410] among the
mighty ones shall speak[1696] of him *and*
his helpers from the midst of Sheol,[7585]
'They have gone down, they lie still,
the uncircumcised, slain by the sword.'
22 "[a]Assyria is there and all her
company; [I]her graves[6913] are round
about [II]her. All of them are slain,
fallen[5307] by the sword,
23 whose [a]graves are set in the remotest parts of the pit, and her company
is round about her grave.[6900] All of them
are slain, fallen by the sword, who
[I]spread terror[2851] in the land of the
living.[2416]
24 "[a]Elam is there and all her multitude around her grave; all of them slain,
fallen by the sword, who went down
uncircumcised to the [b]lower parts of the
earth, who instilled their terror in the
[c]land of the living, and [d]bore[5375] their
disgrace with those who went down to
the pit.
25 "They have made a [a]bed for her
among the slain with all her multitude.
Her graves are around it, they are all
uncircumcised, slain by the sword (although their terror was [I]instilled in the
land of the living), and they bore their
disgrace with those who go down to
the pit; [II]they were put in the midst of
the slain.
26 "[a]Meshech, [b]Tubal and all their
multitude are there; their graves
[I]surround them. All of them were slain
by the sword [c]uncircumcised, though
they instilled their terror in the land of
the living.
27 "[a]Nor do they lie beside the fallen
[I][b]heroes of the uncircumcised, who went
down to Sheol with their weapons of
war, and whose swords were laid under
their heads;[7218] but the punishment for
their [c]iniquity[5771] rested on their
bones,[6106] though the terror of *these*
[I]heroes *was* once in the land of the living.
28 "But in the midst of the uncircumcised you will be broken[7665] and lie
with those slain by the sword.
29 "There also is [a]Edom, its kings,
and all its [I]princes,[5387] who [II]for *all* their
might are laid with those slain by the

12 [a]Ezek. 28:7 [b]Ezek. 28:19
13 [a]Ezek. 29:11
15 [a]Ps. 107:33, 34; Ezek. 29:12, 19, 20 [b]Ex. 7:5; 14:4, 18; Ps. 9:16; 83:17, 18; Ezek. 6:7; 30:19, 26
16 [I]Or, *lament* [a]2Sam. 1:17; 3:33, 34; 2Chr. 35:25; Jer. 9:17; Ezek. 26:17; 32:2
17 [a]Ezek. 31:1; 32:1; 33:21
18 [a]Is. 16:9; Ezek. 21:6; 32:2, 16; Mic. 1:8 [b]Jer. 1:10; Ezek. 43:3; Hos. 6:5 [c]Ezek. 31:14, 16, 18; 32:24
19 [a]Jer. 9:25, 26; Ezek. 31:18; 32:21, 24, 29, 30
20 [I]Or, *The sword is given* [a]Ps. 28:3
21 [a]Is. 14:9-12; Ezek. 32:27
22 [I]Lit., *his* [II]Lit., *him* [a]Ezek. 27:23; 31:3, 16
23 [I]Lit., *gave,* and so throughout the ch. [a]Is. 14:15
24 [a]Gen. 10:22; 14:1; Is. 11:11; Jer. 25:25; 49:34-39 [b]Ezek. 26:20; 31:14, 18; 32:18 [c]Job 28:13; Ps. 27:13; 52:5; 142:5; Is. 38:11; Jer. 11:19 [d]Ezek. 16:52, 54; 32:25, 30
25 [I]Lit., *given* [II]So with ancient versions; M.T. reads *he was* [a]Ps. 139:8
26 [I]Lit., *are around him* [a]Gen. 10:2; Ezek. 27:13; 38:2, 3; 39:1 [b]Gen. 10:2; Is. 66:19; Ezek. 27:13; 38:2, 3; 39:1 [c]Ezek. 32:19
27 [I]Or, *mighty ones* [a]Is. 14:18, 19 [b]Job 3:13-15; Ezek. 32:21 [c]Job 20:11; Ps. 109:18
29 [I]Or, *leaders* [II]Or, *in* [a]Is. 34:5-15; Jer. 49:7-22; Ezek. 25:13; 35:9, 15

sword; they will lie with the uncircumcised, and with those who go down to the pit.

30 "There also are the [I]chiefs[5257] of the [a]north, all of them, and all the [b]Sidonians, who in spite of the terror resulting from their might, in shame[950] went down with the slain. So they lay down uncircumcised with those slain by the sword, and bore[5375] their disgrace with those who go down to the pit.

31 "These Pharaoh will see, and he will be [a]comforted[5162] for all his multitude slain by the sword, *even* Pharaoh and all his army,"[2428] declares the Lord GOD.

32 "Though I instilled a terror of him in the land of the living, yet he will be made to lie down among *the* uncircumcised *along* with those slain by the sword, *even* Pharaoh and all his multitude," declares the Lord GOD.

The Watchman's Duty

33 🗝 And the word[1697] of the LORD came to me saying,

2 "Son[1121] of man,[120] speak[1696] to the [a]sons[1121] of your people, and say[559] to them, 'If I bring a sword[2719] upon a land,[776] and the people[5971] of the land take one man[376] from among them and make him their watchman;

3 and he sees[7200] the sword coming upon the land, and he [a]blows[8628] on the trumpet and warns the people,

4 then he who hears[8085] the sound of the trumpet and [a]does not take warning,[2094] and a sword comes and takes him away, his [b]blood[1818] will be on his *own* head.[7218]

5 'He heard[8085] the sound of the trumpet, but did not take warning; his blood will be on himself. But had he taken warning, he would have [a]delivered his life.[5315]

6 'But if the watchman sees the sword coming and does not blow the trumpet, and the people are not warned,[2094] and a sword comes and takes a person[5315] from them, he is [a]taken away [I]in his iniquity;[5771] but his [b]blood I will require from the watchman's hand.'[3027]

7 "Now as for you, son of man, I have [Ia]appointed you a watchman for the house[1004] of Israel; so you will hear[8085] a [II]message from My mouth,[6310] and give them [b]warning from Me.

8 "When I say to the wicked,[7563] 'O wicked man, you shall [a]surely die,'[4191] and you do not speak to warn the wicked from his way,[1870] that wicked man shall die in his iniquity, but his blood I will require from your hand.

9 "But if you on your part warn a wicked man to turn[7725] from his way, and he [a]does not turn from his way, he will die in his iniquity; but you have [b]delivered[5337] your life.

10 "Now as for you, son of man, say[559] to the house of Israel, 'Thus you have spoken, saying, "Surely our transgressions[6588] and our sins are upon us, and we are [a]rotting[4743] away in them; [b]how then can we [I]survive?"'[2421]

11 "Say to them, '[a]As I live!' declares the Lord[136] [I]GOD, 'I take [b]no pleasure in the death[4194] of the wicked, but rather that the wicked [c]turn from his way and live.[2416] [d]Turn back, turn back from your evil[7451] ways![1870] Why then will you die, O house of Israel?'

12 "And you, son of man, say to [I]your fellow citizens, 'The [a]righteousness[6666] of a righteous[6662] man will not deliver[5337] him in the day[3117] of his transgression,[6588] and as for the wickedness[7564] of the wicked, he will [b]not stumble[3782] because of it in the day when he turns[7725] from his wickedness;[7562] whereas a righteous man will not be able to live [II]by his righteousness on the day when he commits sin.'[2398]

13 "When I say to the righteous he will surely live, and he *so* trusts[982] in his righteousness that he [a]commits[6213] iniquity,[5766] none of his righteous deeds

30 [I]Or, *princes* [a]Jer. 1:15; 25:26; Ezek. 38:6, 15; 39:2 [b]Jer. 25:22; Ezek. 28:21-23
31 [a]Ezek. 14:22; 31:16
2 [a]Ezek. 3:11; 33:12, 17, 30; 37:18
3 [a]Neh. 4:18-20; Is. 58:1; Ezek. 33:9; Hos. 8:1; Joel 2:1
4 [a]2Chr. 25:16; Jer. 6:17; Zech. 1:4 [b]Ezek. 18:13; 33:5, 9; Acts 18:6
5 [a]Ex. 9:19-21; Heb. 11:7
6 [I]Or, *for,* and so throughout the ch. [a]Ezek. 18:20, 24; 33:8, 9 [b]Ezek. 3:18, 20
7 [I]Or, *given* [II]Lit., *word* [a]Is. 62:6; Ezek. 3:17-21 [b]Jer. 1:17; 26:2; Ezek. 2:7, 8; Acts 5:20
8 [a]Is. 3:11; Ezek. 18:4, 13, 18, 20; 33:14
9 [a]Acts 13:40, 41, 46 [b]Ezek. 3:19, 21; Acts 20:26
10 [I]Lit., *live* [a]Lev. 26:39; Ezek. 4:17; 24:23 [b]Is. 49:14; Ezek. 37:11
11 [I]Heb., *YHWH,* usually rendered *LORD,* and so throughout the ch. [a]Is. 49:18; Ezek. 5:11 [b]Ezek. 18:23, 32; Hos. 11:8 [c]Jer. 31:20; 1Tim. 2:4; 2Pet. 3:9 [d]Is. 55:6, 7; Jer. 3:22; Ezek. 18:30, 31; Hos. 14:1; Acts 3:19
12 [I]Lit., *the sons of your people* [II]Lit., *by it* [a]Ezek. 3:18; 18:24; 33:20 [b]2Chr. 7:14; Ezek. 18:21; 33:19
13 [a]Ezek. 18:26; Heb. 10:38; 2Pet. 2:20, 21

🗝 **33:1-20** See note on Ezek. 18:1-4.

will be remembered;[2142] but in that same iniquity of his which he has committed[6213] he will die.

14 "But when I say to the wicked, 'You will surely die,' and he [a]turns from his sin[2403] and practices[6213] [b]justice[4941] and righteousness,[6666]

15 *if a* wicked man restores[7725] a pledge,[2258] [a]pays back what he has taken by robbery, walks by the [b]statutes[2708] [I]which ensure life[2416] without committing iniquity, he will surely live; he shall not die.

16 "[a]None of his sins that he has committed[2398] will be remembered[2142] against him. He has practiced[6213] justice and righteousness; he will surely live.

17 "Yet [I]your fellow citizens say, 'The way of the Lord is not right,' when it is their own way that is not right.

18 "When the righteous turns from his righteousness and [a]commits[6213] iniquity, then he shall die in [I]it.

19 "But when the wicked turns from his wickedness and practices justice and righteousness, he will live by them.

20 "Yet you say, '[a]The way of the Lord is not right.' O house of Israel, I will judge[8199] each[376] of you according to his ways."

Word of Jerusalem's Capture

21 Now it [a]came about in the [b]twelfth year of our exile,[1546] on the fifth of the tenth month, that the [I]refugees from Jerusalem came to me, saying, "[c]The city has been [II]taken."[5221]

22 Now the [a]hand of the LORD had been upon me in the evening, before the [I]refugees came. And He [b]opened my mouth [II]at the time *they* came to me in the morning; so my mouth was [c]opened, and I was no longer [III]speechless.

23 Then the word of the LORD came to me saying,

24 "Son of man, they who [a]live in these waste[2723] places in the land[127] of Israel are saying, '[b]Abraham was *only* one, yet he possessed[3423] the land; so to [c]us who are many the land has been given as a possession.'[4181]

25 "Therefore, say to them, 'Thus says[559] the Lord GOD, "You eat *meat* with the [a]blood *in it,* lift up[5375] your eyes to your idols[1544] as you shed[8210] blood. [b]Should you then possess[3423] the land?

26 "You [I][a]rely on your sword, you commit[6213] abominations,[8441] and each of you defiles[2930] his neighbor's[7453] wife.[802] Should you then possess the land?" '

27 "Thus you shall say to them, 'Thus says the Lord GOD, "As I live, surely those who are in the waste places will [a]fall by the sword, and whoever is in the [I]open field[7704] I will give to the beasts[2416] to be devoured, and those who are in the strongholds and in the [b]caves will die of pestilence.[1698]

28 "And I shall [a]make the land a desolation[8077] and a waste, and the [b]pride of her power will cease;[7673] and the mountains of Israel will be desolate,[8074] so that no one will pass through.[5674]

29 "Then they will know[3045] that I am the LORD, when I make the land a desolation and a waste because of all their abominations[8441] which they have committed." '

30 "But as for you, son of man, [I]your fellow citizens who talk about you by the walls and in the doorways of the houses,[1004] speak to one another, each to his brother,[251] saying, '[a]Come now,[4994] and hear what the [II]message is which comes forth from the LORD.'

31 "And they come to you as people come, and sit before you *as* My people, and hear your words,[1697] but they do not do them, for they do[6213] the lustful desires *expressed* by their [a]mouth, *and* their heart[3820] goes after their [b]gain.[1215]

32 "And behold, you are to them like a sensual song[7892] by one who has a [a]beautiful voice and plays well[2895] on

14 [a]Is. 55:7; Jer. 18:7, 8; Ezek. 18:27; 33:8, 19; Hos. 14:1, 4 [b]Mic. 6:8
15 [I]Lit., *of life* [a]Ex. 22:1-4; Lev. 6:4, 5; Luke 19:8 [b]Ps. 119:59; 143:8; Ezek. 20:11
16 [a]Is. 1:18; 43:25; Ezek. 18:22
17 [I]Lit., *the sons of your people*
18 [I]Lit., *them* [a]Ezek. 3:20; 18:24; 33:12, 13
20 [a]Ezek. 18:25
21 [I]Or, *refugee* [II]Lit., *smitten* [a]Ezek. 31:1; 32:1, 17 [b]Jer. 39:1, 2; 40:1; 52:4-7; Ezek. 24:1, 2 [c]2Kin. 25:10; Jer. 39:8
22 [I]Lit., *refugee* [II]Lit., *until he came* [III]Or, *dumb* [a]Ezek. 1:3; 8:1; 37:1 [b]Ezek. 3:26, 27; 24:27 [c]Luke 1:64
24 [a]Jer. 39:10; 40:7; Ezek. 33:27 [b]Is. 51:2; Luke 3:8; Acts 7:5; Rom. 4:12 [c]Ezek. 11:15
25 [a]Lev. 17:10, 12, 14; Deut. 12:16, 23; 15:23 [b]Jer. 7:9, 10
26 [I]Lit., *stand* [a]Mic. 2:1, 2; Zeph. 3:3
27 [I]Lit., *surface of the field* [a]Jer. 15:2, 3; 42:22; Ezek. 5:12 [b]1Sam. 13:6; Is. 2:19
28 [a]Ezek. 5:14; 6:14; Mic. 7:13 [b]Ezek. 7:24; 24:21; 30:6
30 [I]Lit., *the sons of your people* [II]Lit., *word* [a]Is. 29:13; 58:2; Ezek. 14:3; 20:3, 31
31 [a]Ps. 78:36, 37; Is. 29:13; 1John 3:18 [b]Ezek. 22:13, 27; Luke 12:15
32 [a]Mark 6:20

33:25,26 The sins mentioned here almost exactly parallel those Gentile Christians were asked to avoid by their Jewish brethren in Jerusalem (Acts 15:20,29).

an instrument; for they hear your words, but they do not practice them.

33 "So when it [a]comes to pass—[I]as surely it will—then they will know that a prophet[5030] has been in their midst."

Prophecy against the Shepherds of Israel

34 Then the word[1697] of the LORD came to me saying,

2 "Son[1121] of man,[120] prophesy[5012] against the [a]shepherds of Israel. Prophesy and say[559] to [I]those shepherds, 'Thus says[559] the Lord[136] [II]GOD, "Woe, shepherds of Israel who have been [III][b]feeding themselves! Should not the shepherds [III][c]feed the flock?

3 "You [a]eat the fat and clothe yourselves with the wool, you [b]slaughter[2076] the fat *sheep* without [I]feeding the flock.

4 "Those who are sickly[2456] you have not strengthened,[2388] the [I]diseased you have not healed, [a]the broken[7665] you have not bound up, the scattered you have not brought back,[7725] nor have you [b]sought for the lost;[6] but with force[2394] and with severity you have dominated[7287] them.

5 "And they were [a]scattered for lack of a shepherd, and they became [b]food for every beast[2416] of the field[7704] and were scattered.

6 "My flock [a]wandered[7686] through all the mountains and on every high hill, and [b]My flock was scattered over all the surface of the earth;[776] and there was [c]no one to search or seek *for them.*"'"

7 Therefore, you shepherds, hear[8085] the word of the LORD:

8 "As I live,"[2416] declares[5001] the Lord GOD, "surely because My flock has become a [a]prey, My flock has even become food for all the beasts[2416] of the field for lack of a shepherd, and My shepherds did not search for My flock, but *rather* the shepherds fed themselves and did not feed My flock;

9 therefore, you shepherds, hear the word of the LORD:

10 'Thus says the Lord GOD, "Behold, I am [a]against the shepherds, and I shall demand My [I]sheep [II]from them and make them [b]cease[7673] from feeding [I]sheep. So the shepherds will not [III]feed themselves anymore, but I shall [c]deliver[5337] My flock from their mouth,[6310] that they may not be food for them."'"

The Restoration of Israel

11 For thus says the Lord GOD, "Behold, I Myself will [a]search for My sheep and seek them out.

12 "[a]As a shepherd [I]cares for his herd in the day[3117] when he is among his scattered [II]sheep, so I will [I][b]care for My [II]sheep and will deliver them from all the places to which they were scattered on a [c]cloudy and gloomy day.[6205]

13 "And I will bring them out from the peoples[5971] and gather[6908] them from the countries[776] and bring them to their own land;[127] and I will [a]feed them on the mountains of Israel, by the [b]streams, and in all the inhabited places[4186] of the land.[776]

14 "I will feed them in a [a]good[2896] pasture, and their grazing ground will be on the mountain heights of Israel. There they will lie down in good grazing ground, and they will feed in [I][b]rich pasture on the mountains of Israel.

15 "I will [a]feed My flock and I will [I]lead them to rest," declares the Lord GOD.

16 "I will seek the lost, bring back[7725] the scattered, bind up[2280] the broken, and strengthen[2388] the sick; but the [a]fat and the strong[2389] I will destroy.[8045] I will [b]feed them with judgment.[4941]

17 "And as for you, My flock, thus says the Lord GOD, 'Behold, I will [a]judge[8199] between one [I]sheep and another, between the rams and the male goats.

18 'Is it too [a]slight a thing for you

33 [I]Lit., *behold, it is coming* [a]Jer. 28:9; Ezek. 33:29
2 [I]Lit., *them, the shepherds* [II]Heb., *YHWH*, usually rendered LORD, and so throughout the ch. [III]Lit., *pasturing, pasture* [a]Jer. 2:8; 3:15; 10:21; 12:10 [b]Jer. 23:1; Ezek. 22:25; 34:8-10; Mic. 3:1-3, 11 [c]Ps. 78:71, 72; Is. 40:11; Ezek. 34:14, 15; John 10:11; 21:15-17
3 [I]Lit., *pasturing* [a]Zech. 11:16 [b]Ezek. 22:25,27
4 [I]Lit., *sick* [a]Zech. 11:16 [b]Matt. 9:36; 10:6; 18:12, 13; Luke 15:4
5 [a]Num. 27:17; 2Chr. 18:16; Jer. 10:21; 23:2; 50:6, 7; Matt. 9:36; Mark 6:34 [b]Ezek. 34:8, 28
6 [a]Jer. 40:11, 12; Ezek. 7:16; 1Pet. 2:25 [b]John 10:16 [c]Ps. 142:4
8 [a]Acts 20:29
10 [I]Or, (a) *flock* [II]Lit., *from their hand* [III]Lit., *pasture*, and so throughout the ch. [a]Jer. 21:13; Ezek. 5:8; 13:8; 34:2; Zech. 10:3 [b]1Sam. 2:29, 30; Jer. 52:24-27 [c]Ps. 72:12-14; Ezek. 13:23
11 [a]Ezek. 11:17; 20:41
12 [I]Or, *seek(s) out* [II]Or, *flock* [a]Jer. 31:10 [b]Is. 40:11; 56:8; Jer. 23:3; 31:8; Luke 19:10; John 10:16 [c]Jer. 13:16; Ezek. 30:3; Joel 2:2
13 [a]Ezek. 34:23; 36:29, 30; Mic. 7:14 [b]Is. 30:25
14 [I]Lit., *fat* [a]Ps. 23:2; Jer. 31:12-14, 25; John 10:9 [b]Ezek. 28:25, 26; 36:29, 30
15 [I]Lit., *cause them to lie down* [a]Ps. 23:1, 2; Ezek. 34:23
16 [a]Is. 10:16 [b]Is. 49:26
17 [I]Or, *lamb* [a]Ezek. 20:38; 34:20-22; Mal. 4:1; Matt. 25:32
18 [a]Num. 16:9, 13; 2Sam. 7:19; Is. 7:13

that you should feed in the good pasture,
that you must tread down with your feet
the rest[3499] of your pastures? Or that
you should drink of the clear waters,
that you must [I]foul the rest[3498] with your
feet?
19 'And as for My flock, they must
eat what you tread down with your feet,
and they must drink what you [I]foul with
your feet!' "
20 Therefore, thus says the Lord
GOD to them, "Behold, I, even I, will
judge between the fat sheep and the
lean sheep.
21 "Because you push with side and
with shoulder, and [a]thrust at all the
[I]weak with your horns, until you have
scattered them [II]abroad,
22 therefore, I will [a]deliver[3467] My
flock, and they will no longer be a prey;
and I will judge between one sheep and
another.
23 "Then I will [a]set over them one
[b]shepherd, My servant[5650] [c]David, and
he will feed them; he will feed them
himself and be their shepherd.
24 "And I, the LORD, will be their
God,[430] and My servant [a]David will be
prince[5387] among them; I, the LORD,
have spoken.[1696]
25 "And I will make a [a]covenant[1285]
of peace with them and [b]eliminate
harmful[7451] beasts from the land,[776]
so that they may [c]live securely[983]
in the wilderness and sleep in the
woods.
26 "And I will make them and the
places around My hill a [a]blessing.[1293]
And I will cause [b]showers to come down
in their season;[6256] they will be showers
of [c]blessing.
27 "Also the tree of the field will
yield its fruit, and the earth will yield
its increase, and they will be [a]secure[983]
on their land. Then they will know[3045]
that I am the LORD, when I have
[b]broken the bars of their yoke and have
delivered[5337] them from the hand of
those who enslaved[5647] them.
28 "And they will no longer be a
prey to the nations,[1471] and the beasts
of the earth will not devour them; but
they will [a]live securely, and no one will
make *them* afraid.[2729]
29 "And I will establish for them a
[a]renowned planting place, and they will
[b]not again be [I]victims[622] of famine in the
land, and they will not [c]endure[5375] the
insults of the nations anymore.
30 "Then they will know that
[a]I, the LORD their God, am with them,
and that they, the house[1004] of Israel,
are My people," declares the Lord GOD.
31 "As for you, My [a]sheep, the
[b]sheep of My pasture, you are men,[120]
and I am your God," declares the Lord
GOD.

Prophecy against Mount Seir

35 Moreover, the word[1697] of the
LORD came to me saying,
2 "Son[1121] of man,[120] set[7760] your
face against [a]Mount Seir, and prophesy[5012] against it,
3 and say[559] to it, 'Thus says[559] the
Lord[136] [I]GOD,
"Behold, I am against you, Mount
Seir,
And I will [a]stretch out My
hand[3027] against you,
And I will make you a
[b]desolation[8077] and a waste.
4 "I will [a]lay[7760] waste[2723] your
cities,
And you will become a
desolation.
Then you will know[3045] that I
am the LORD.
5 "Because you have had everlast-
ing[5769] [a]enmity[342] and have [I]delivered
the sons[1121] of Israel to the power of
the sword at the time[6256] of their calamity,[343] at the time of the [IIb]punish-
ment[5771] of the end,
6 therefore, as I live,"[2416] declares[5001] the Lord GOD, "I will [I]give
you over to [a]bloodshed,[1818] and bloodshed will pursue you; since you have
not hated bloodshed, therefore bloodshed will pursue you.
7 "And I will make Mount Seir a
waste and a desolation, and I will cut

18 [I]Lit., *foul by trampling*
19 [I]Lit., *foul by trampling*
21 [I]Or, *sick* [II]Lit., *to the outside* [a]Deut. 33:17; Dan. 8:4; Luke 13:14-16
22 [a]Ps. 72:12-14; Jer. 23:3; Ezek. 34:10
23 [a]Rev. 7:17 [b]Is. 40:11; John 10:11 [c]Jer. 30:9; Ezek. 37:24
24 [a]Is. 55:3; Jer. 30:9; Ezek. 37:24, 25; Hos. 3:5
25 [a]Ezek. 16:60; 20:37; 37:26 [b]Job 5:22, 23; Is. 11:6-9 [c]Jer. 33:16; Ezek. 28:26; 34:27, 28
26 [a]Gen. 12:2; Ezek. 34:14 [b]Deut. 11:13-15; 28:12 [c]Lev. 25:21; Is. 44:3
27 [a]Ezek. 38:8, 11 [b]Lev. 26:13; Is. 52:2, 3; Jer. 30:8
28 [a]Jer. 30:10; Ezek. 39:26
29 [I]Lit., *those gathered* [a]Is. 4:2; 60:21; 61:3 [b]Ezek. 34:26, 27; 36:29 [c]Ezek. 36:6,15
30 [a]Ps. 46:7, 11; Ezek. 14:11; 36:28
31 [a]Ps. 78:52; 80:1; Ezek. 36:38 [b]Ps. 100:3; Jer. 23:1

2 [a]Gen. 36:8; Ezek. 25:12; 36:5
3 [I]Heb., *YHWH*, usually rendered *LORD*, and so throughout the ch. [a]Jer. 6:12; 15:6; Ezek. 25:13 [b]Jer. 49:13, 17, 18; Ezek. 35:7
4 [a]Ezek. 6:6; 35:9; Mal. 1:3, 4
5 [I]Lit., *poured* [II]Or, *iniquity* [a]Ps. 137:7; Ezek. 25:12, 15; 36:5; Amos 1:11; Obad. 10 [b]Ezek. 7:2; 21:25, 29
6 [I]Lit., *prepare you for* [a]Is. 63:2-6; Ezek. 16:38; 32:6

off[3772] from it the one who passes[5674] through and returns.[7725]
8 "And I will [a]fill its mountains with its slain;[2491] on your hills and in your valleys and in all your ravines those slain by the sword will [I]fall.
9 "I will make you an everlasting [a]desolation, and your cities will not be inhabited. Then you will know that I am the LORD.
10 "Because you have [a]said,[559] 'These two nations[1471] and these two lands[776] will be mine, and we will possess[3423] [I]them,' although the [b]LORD was there,
11 therefore, as I live," declares the Lord GOD, "I will deal[6213] *with you* [a]according to your anger[639] and according to your envy[7068] which you showed because of your hatred[8135] against them; so I will [b]make Myself known[3045] among them when I judge[8199] you.
12 "Then you will know [I]that I, the LORD, have heard[8085] all your revilings[5007] which you have spoken[559] against the mountains of Israel saying, 'They are laid desolate;[8074] they are [a]given to us for food.'
13 "And you have [I][a]spoken arrogantly against Me and have multiplied your words[1697] against Me; [b]I have heard."
14 'Thus says the Lord GOD, "As all the [a]earth[776] rejoices, I will make[6213] you a desolation.
15 "As you [a]rejoiced over the inheritance[5159] of the house[1004] of Israel because it was desolate, [b]so I will do to you. You will be a [c]desolation,[8077] O Mount Seir, and all Edom, all of it. Then they will know that I am the LORD."'

The Mountains of Israel to Be Blessed

36 "And you, son[1121] of man,[120] prophesy[5012] to the mountains of Israel and say,[559] 'O mountains of Israel, hear[8085] the word[1697] of the LORD.
2 'Thus says[559] the Lord[136] [I]GOD, "Because the enemy has spoken[559] against you, 'Aha!' and, 'The everlasting[5769] [II][a]heights[1116] have become our possession,'[4181]
3 therefore, prophesy and say, 'Thus says the Lord GOD, "[I]For good cause they have made you [a]desolate[8074] and crushed you from every side, that you should become a possession of the rest[7611] of the nations,[1471] and you have been taken up[5927] in the [II][b]talk[8193] and the whispering of the people."' "[5971]
4 'Therefore, O [a]mountains of Israel, hear the word of the Lord GOD. Thus says the Lord GOD to the mountains and to the hills, to the ravines and to the valleys, to the desolate[8076] wastes[2723] and to the forsaken[5800] cities, which have become a [b]prey and a derision to the rest of the nations which are round about,
5 therefore, thus says the Lord GOD, "Surely in the fire of My [a]jealousy I have spoken[1696] against the [b]rest of the nations, and against all Edom, who [I]appropriated My land[776] for themselves as a possession with wholehearted[3824][3605] [c]joy *and* with scorn[7589] of soul,[5315] to drive it out for a prey."
6 'Therefore, prophesy concerning the land[127] of Israel, and say to the mountains and to the hills, to the ravines and to the valleys, "Thus says the Lord GOD, 'Behold, I have spoken in My jealousy and in My wrath because you have [a]endured[5375] the insults of the nations.'
7 "Therefore, thus says the Lord GOD, 'I have [I]sworn[5375,3027] that surely the nations which are around you will themselves endure[5375] their insults.
8 'But you, O mountains of Israel, you will [a]put forth your branches and bear your fruit for My people Israel; for they will soon[7126] come.
9 'For, behold, I am for you, and I will [a]turn to you, and you shall be [b]cultivated and sown.
10 'And I will multiply men[120] on you, [a]all the house[1004] of Israel, all of it; and the [b]cities will be inhabited, and the waste places will be rebuilt.

8 [I]Lit., *fall in them* [a]Is. 34:5, 6; Ezek. 31:12; 32:4, 5; 39:4, 5
9 [a]Jer. 49:13; Ezek. 25:13
10 [I]Lit., *it* [a]Ps. 83:4-12; Ezek. 36:2, 5 [b]Ps. 48:1-3; 132:13, 14; Is. 12:6; Ezek. 48:35; Zeph. 3:15
11 [a]Ps. 137:7; Ezek. 25:14; Amos 1:11 [b]Ps. 9:16; 73:17,18
12 [I]Or, *that I am the LORD: I have heard* [a]Jer. 50:7; Ezek. 36:2
13 [I]Lit., *made great with your mouth* [a]Is. 10:13, 14; 36:20; Jer. 48:26, 42; Dan. 11:36 [b]Jer. 7:11; 29:23
14 [a]Is. 44:23; 49:13; Jer. 51:48
15 [a]Jer. 50:11; Lam. 4:21 [b]Obad. 15 [c]Is. 34:5, 6; Ezek. 35:3, 4

2 [I]Heb., *YHWH,* usually rendered *LORD,* and so throughout the ch. [II]Heb., *Bamoth* [a]Deut. 32:13; Ps. 78:69; Is. 58:14; Hab. 3:19
3 [I]Lit., *Because;* or, *By the cause* [II]Lit., *lip of the tongue* [a]Jer. 2:15 [b]Ps. 44:13, 14; Jer. 18:16; Ezek. 35:13
4 [a]Deut. 11:11; Ezek. 36:1, 6, 8 [b]Ezek. 34:8, 28
5 [I]Lit., *gave* [a]Ezek. 5:13; 36:6; 38:19 [b]Jer. 25:9, 15-29; Ezek. 36:3 [c]Jer. 50:11; Ezek. 35:15; Mic. 7:8
6 [a]Ps. 74:10; 123:3, 4; Ezek. 34:29
7 [I]Lit., *lifted up My hand*
8 [a]Is. 4:2; 27:6; Ezek. 17:23; 34:26-29
9 [a]Lev. 26:9 [b]Ezek. 28:26; 34:14; 36:34

10 [a]Is. 27:6; 49:17-23; Ezek. 37:21, 22 [b]Jer. 31:27, 28; 33:12; Ezek. 36:33

11 'And I will multiply on you man and beast; and they will increase and be fruitful; and I will cause you to be inhabited as you were [a]formerly[6927] and will [1]treat you [b]better[2896] than at the first.[7221] Thus you will know[3045] that I am the LORD.

12 'Yes, I will cause [a]men—My people Israel—to walk on you and possess[3423] you, so that you will become their [b]inheritance[5159] and never again [c]bereave them of children.'

13 "Thus says the Lord GOD, 'Because they say to you, "You are a [a]devourer of men and have bereaved your [1]nation[1471] of children,"

14 therefore, you will no longer devour men, and no longer bereave your nation of children,' declares[5001] the Lord GOD.

15 "And I will not let you hear [a]insults from the nations anymore, nor will you bear [b]disgrace[2781] from the peoples any longer, nor will you cause your nation to [c]stumble[3782] any longer," declares the Lord GOD.'"

16 Then the word of the LORD came to me saying,

17 "Son of man, when the house of Israel was living in their own land, they [a]defiled[2930] it by their ways[1870] and their deeds; their way before Me was like [b]the uncleanness[2932] of a woman in her impurity.

18 "Therefore, I [a]poured out[8210] My wrath on them for the blood[1818] which they had shed[8210] on the land, because they had defiled[2930] it with their idols.[1544]

19 "Also I [a]scattered them among the nations, and they were dispersed throughout the lands.[776] [b]According to their ways and their deeds I judged[8199] them.

20 "When they came to the nations where they went, they [a]profaned[2490] My holy[6944] name, because it was said of them, 'These are the [b]people of the LORD; yet they have come out of His land.'

21 "But I had [1]concern for My [a]holy name, which the house of Israel had profaned among the nations where they went.

Israel to Be Renewed for His Name's Sake

22 "Therefore, say to the house of Israel, 'Thus says the Lord GOD, "It is [a]not for your sake, O house of Israel, that I am about to act,[6213] but for My holy name, which you have profaned among the nations where you went.

23 "And I will [a]vindicate[6942] the holiness of My great name which has been profaned among the nations, which you have profaned in their midst. Then the [b]nations will know that I am the LORD," declares the Lord GOD, "when I prove Myself holy[6942] among you in their sight.

24 "For I will [a]take you from the nations, gather[6908] you from all the lands, and bring you into your own land.

25 "Then I will [a]sprinkle[2236] clean[2889] water on you, and you will be clean;[2891] I will cleanse[2891] you from all your [b]filthiness[2932] and from all your [c]idols.

26 "Moreover, I will give you a [a]new heart[3820] and put a new spirit[7307] within[7130] you; and I will remove the [b]heart of stone from your flesh and give you a heart of flesh.

27 "And I will [a]put My Spirit within you and cause you to walk in My statutes,[2706] and you will be careful to observe[8104] My ordinances.[4941]

28 "And you will live in the land that I gave to your forefathers;[1] so you will be [a]My people, and I will be your God.[430]

29 "Moreover, I will save[3467] you from all your uncleanness; and I will call[7121] for the grain and multiply it, and I [a]will not [1]bring a famine on you.

30 "And I will [a]multiply the fruit of the tree and the produce of the field,[7704] that you may not receive again the disgrace of famine among the nations.

31 "Then you will [a]remember[2142] your evil[7451] ways[1870] and your deeds that were not good,[2896] and you will loathe yourselves in your own sight for

11 [1]Lit., *cause good* [a]Jer. 30:18; Ezek. 16:55; Mic. 7:14 [b]Job 42:12; Is. 51:3
12 [a]Ezek. 34:13, 14 [b]Ezek. 47:14 [c]Jer. 15:7; Ezek. 22:12, 27
13 [1]Or, *nations*, and so throughout the ch. [a]Num. 13:32
15 [a]Is. 60:14; Ezek. 34:29; 36:7 [b]Ps. 89:50; Is. 54:4; Ezek. 22:4 [c]Is. 63:13; Jer. 13:16; 18:15
17 [a]Jer. 2:7 [b]Lev. 15:19
18 [a]2Chr. 34:21, 25; Lam. 2:4; 4:11; Ezek. 22:20, 22
19 [a]Deut. 28:64; Ezek. 5:12; 22:15; Amos 9:9 [b]Ezek. 24:14; 39:24; Rom. 2:6
20 [a]Is. 52:5; Ezek. 12:16; Rom. 2:24 [b]Jer. 33:24
21 [1]Lit., *compassion* [a]Ps. 74:18; Is. 48:9; Ezek. 20:44
22 [a]Deut. 7:7, 8; 9:5, 6; Ezek. 36:32
23 [a]Is. 5:16; Ezek. 20:41; 38:23; 39:7, 25 [b]Ps. 102:15; 126:2
24 [a]Is. 43:5, 6; Ezek. 34:13; 37:21
25 [a]Num. 19:17-19; Ps. 51:7; Titus 3:5, 6; Heb. 9:13, 19; 10:22 [b]Is. 4:4; Zech. 13:1 [c]Is. 2:18, 20; Hos. 14:3, 8
26 [a]Ps. 51:10; Ezek. 11:19; 18:31; John 3:3, 5; 2Cor. 5:17 [b]Ezek. 11:19; Zech. 7:12
27 [a]Is. 44:3; 59:21; Ezek. 37:14; 39:29; Joel 2:28, 29
28 [a]Ezek. 14:11; 37:23, 27
29 [1]Lit., *put* [a]Ezek. 34:27, 29; Hos. 2:21-23
30 [a]Lev. 26:4; Ezek. 34:27
31 [a]Ezek. 16:61-63; 20:43

your iniquities[5771] and your abominations.[8441]

32 "I am not doing *this* [a]for your sake," declares the Lord GOD, "let it be known[3045] to you. Be ashamed[954] and confounded for your ways, O house of Israel!"

33 'Thus says the Lord GOD, "On the day[3117] that I cleanse[2891] you from all your iniquities, I will cause the [a]cities to be inhabited, and the [b]waste places will be rebuilt.

34 "And the desolate[8077] land will be cultivated instead of being a desolation in the sight of everyone who passed by.[5674]

35 "And they will say, 'This desolate land has become[1961] like the [a]garden of Eden; and the waste,[2720] desolate, and ruined[2040] cities are fortified *and* inhabited.'

36 "Then the nations that are left[7604] round about you will know that I, the LORD, have rebuilt the ruined places *and* planted that which was desolate; I, the LORD, have spoken and [a]will do it."

37 'Thus says the Lord GOD, "This also I will let the house of Israel ask Me to do for them: I will increase their men like a flock.

38 "Like the [a]flock [I]for sacrifices, like the flock at Jerusalem during her appointed feasts,[4150] so will the waste cities be filled with [b]flocks of men. Then they will know that I am the LORD."'"

Vision of the Valley of Dry Bones

37 The [a]hand[3027] of the LORD was upon me, and He [b]brought me out [I]by the Spirit[7307] of the LORD and set me down in the middle of the [c]valley; and it was full of bones.[6106]

2 And He caused me to pass among them round about, and behold, *there were* very many on the surface of the valley; and lo, *they were* very dry.[3002]

3 And He said to me, "Son[1121] of man,[120] [a]can these bones live?"[2421] And I answered,[559] "O Lord[136] [I]GOD, [b]Thou knowest."[3045]

4 Again He said to me, "[a]Prophesy[5012] over these bones, and say[559] to them, 'O dry bones, [b]hear[8085] the word[1697] of the LORD.'

5 "Thus says[559] the Lord GOD to these bones, 'Behold, I will cause [I][a]breath[7307] to enter you that you may come to life.

6 'And I will put sinews on you, make flesh grow[5927] back on you, cover you with skin,[5785] and put breath in you that you may come alive; and you will [a]know[3045] that I am the LORD.'"

7 So I prophesied[5012] [a]as I was commanded;[6680] and as I prophesied, there was a [I]noise, and behold, a rattling; and the bones came together, bone[6106] to its bone.

8 And I looked,[7200] and behold, sinews were on them, and flesh grew,[5927] and skin covered them; but there was no breath in them.

9 Then He said to me, "Prophesy to the breath,[7307] prophesy, son of man, and say to the breath, 'Thus says the Lord GOD, "Come from the four winds,[7307] O breath, and [a]breathe on these slain,[2027] that they [b]come to life."'"

10 So I prophesied as He commanded me, and the [a]breath came into them, and they came to life,[2421] and stood on their feet, an [b]exceedingly great army.[2428]

The Vision Explained

11 Then He said to me, "Son of man, these bones are the [a]whole house[1004] of Israel; behold, they say, 'Our [b]bones are dried up,[3001] and our hope has perished.[6] We are [I]completely [c]cut off.'[1504]

12 "Therefore prophesy, and say to them, 'Thus says the Lord GOD, "Behold, I will open your graves[6913] and [a]cause you to come up[5927] out of your graves, My people;[5971] and I will bring you into the land[127] of Israel.

13 "Then you will know that I am the LORD, when I have opened your graves and caused you to come up[5927] out of your graves, My people.

32 [a]Deut. 9:5

33 [a]Ezek. 36:10; Zech. 8:7, 8 [b]Is. 58:12

35 [a]Is. 51:3; Ezek. 31:9; Joel 2:3

36 [a]Ezek. 17:24; 22:14; 37:14; Hos. 14:4-9

38 [I]Lit., *of holy things* [a]1Kin. 8:63; 2Chr. 35:7-9; John 2:14 [b]Ps. 74:1; 100:3; Jer. 23:1; John 10:7, 9, 16

1 [I]Or, *in* [a]Ezek. 1:3; 33:22; 40:1 [b]Ezek. 8:3; 11:24; 43:5; Acts 8:39 [c]Jer. 7:32-8:2

3 [I]Heb., *YHWH*, usually rendered *LORD*, and so throughout the ch. [a]Ezek. 26:19 [b]Deut. 32:39; 1Sam. 2:6

4 [a]Ezek. 37:9, 12 [b]Jer. 22:29; Ezek. 36:1

5 [I]Or, *spirit*, and so throughout the ch. [a]Gen. 2:7; Ps. 104:29, 30; Ezek. 37:9, 10, 14

6 [a]Is. 49:23; Ezek. 35:9; 38:23; 39:6; Joel 2:27; 3:17

7 [I]Lit., *voice;* or, *thunder* [a]Jer. 13:5-7

9 [a]Ps. 104:30 [b]Hos. 13:14

10 [a]Rev. 11:11 [b]Jer. 30:19; 33:22

11 [I]Lit., *cut off to ourselves* [a]Jer. 33:24; Ezek. 36:10; 39:25 [b]Ps. 141:7 [c]Ps. 88:5; Lam. 3:54

12 [a]Deut. 32:39; 1Sam. 2:6; Is. 26:19; 66:14; Hos. 13:14

14 “And I will [a]put My [I]Spirit within you, and you will come to life, and I will place you on your own land. Then you will know that I, the LORD, have spoken[1696] and done it,” declares[5001] the LORD.’ ”

Reunion of Judah and Israel

15 The word of the LORD came again to me saying,

16 “And you, son of man, take for yourself [a]one stick and write on it, ‘For [b]Judah and for the sons[1121] of Israel, his companions’; then take another stick and write on it, ‘For [c]Joseph, the stick of Ephraim and all the house of Israel, his companions.’

17 “Then [a]join[7126] them for yourself one to another into one stick, that they may become[1961] one in your hand.

18 “And when the sons of your people speak[559] to you saying, ‘Will you not declare[5046] to us [a]what you mean by these?’

19 say[1696] to them, ‘Thus says the Lord GOD, “Behold, I will take the stick of Joseph, which is in the hand of Ephraim, and the tribes[7626] of Israel, his companions; and I will put them with it, with the stick of Judah, and make[6213] them one stick, and they will be one in My hand.” ’

20 “And the sticks on which you write will be in your hand before their eyes.

21 “And say to them, ‘Thus says the Lord GOD, “Behold, I will [a]take the sons of Israel from among the nations[1471] where they have gone, and I will gather[6908] them from every side and bring them into their own land;

22 and I will make them [a]one nation[1471] in the land,[776] on the mountains of Israel; and [b]one king[4428] will be king for all of them; and they will no longer be two nations,[1471] and they will no longer be divided into two kingdoms.[4467]

23 “And they will [a]no longer defile[2930] themselves with their idols,[1544] or with their detestable things,[8251] or with any of their transgressions;[6588] but [b]I will deliver[3467] them from all their [I]dwelling places in which they have sinned,[2398] and will cleanse[2891] them. And they will be My people, and I will be their God.[430]

The Davidic Kingdom

24 “And My servant[5650] [a]David will be king over them, and they will all have [b]one shepherd; and they will walk in My ordinances,[4941] and keep[8104] My statutes,[2708] and observe[6213] them.

25 “And they shall live on the land that I gave to Jacob My servant, in which your fathers[1] lived; and they will live on it, they, and their sons, and their sons’ sons, forever;[5769] and [a]David My servant shall be their prince[5387] forever.

26 “And I will make a [a]covenant[1285] of peace with them; it will be an [b]everlasting[5769] covenant with them. And I will [I]place them and [c]multiply them, and will set My [d]sanctuary[4720] in their midst forever.[5769]

27 “My [a]dwelling place[4908] also will be with them; and [b]I will be their God, and they will be My people.

28 “And the nations will know that I am the LORD [a]who sanctifies[6942] Israel, when My sanctuary is in their midst forever.” ’ ”

Prophecy about Gog and Future Invasion of Israel

38 And the word[1697] of the LORD came to me saying,

2 “Son[1121] of man,[120] set[7760] your face toward [a]Gog of the land[776] of [b]Magog, the [I]prince[5387] of [c]Rosh, [d]Meshech, and [e]Tubal, and prophesy[5012] against him,

3 and say,[559] ‘Thus says[559] the Lord[136] [I]GOD, “Behold, I am against you, O Gog, [II]prince of Rosh, Meshech, and Tubal.

4 “And I will turn you about,[7725] and put hooks into your jaws, and I will [a]bring you out, and all your army,[2428] [b]horses and horsemen, all of them

14 [I]Or, *breath* [a]Is. 32:15; Ezek. 11:19; 36:27; 37:6, 9; 39:29; Joel 2:28, 29; Zech. 12:10
16 [a]Num. 17:2, 3 [b]2Chr. 10:17; 11:11-17; 15:9 [c]1Kin. 12:16-20; 2Chr. 10:19
17 [a]Is. 11:13; Jer. 50:4; Ezek. 37:22-24; Hos. 1:11; Zeph. 3:9
18 [a]Ezek. 12:9; 17:12; 20:49; 24:19
21 [a]Is. 43:5, 6; Jer. 29:14; Ezek. 36:24; 39:27; Amos 9:14, 15
22 [a]Jer. 3:18; 50:4, 5; Ezek. 36:10 [b]Ezek. 34:23, 24; 37:24
23 [I]Another reading is *backslidings* [a]Ezek. 36:25 [b]Ezek. 36:28, 29
24 [a]Jer. 30:9; Ezek. 34:24; 37:25; Hos. 3:5 [b]Ps. 78:71; Is. 40:11; Ezek. 34:23
25 [a]Is. 11:1; Ezek. 37:24; Zech. 6:12
26 [I]Lit., *give* [a]Ezek. 16:62; 20:37; 34:25 [b]Ps. 89:3, 4; Is. 55:3; 59:21; Ezek. 16:60 [c]Jer. 30:19; Ezek. 36:10, 11, 37 [d]Ezek. 20:40; 43:7
27 [a]John 1:14; Rev. 21:3 [b]Ezek. 37:23; 2Cor. 6:16
28 [a]Ex. 31:13; Ezek. 20:12

2 [I]Or, *chief prince of Meshech* [a]Ezek. 38:3, 14, 16, 18; 39:1, 11; Rev. 20:8 [b]Gen. 10:2; Ezek. 39:6; Rev. 20:8 [c]Ezek. 38:3; 39:1 [d]Ezek. 27:13; 38:3; 39:1
3 [I]Heb., *YHWH*, usually rendered *LORD*, and so throughout the ch. [II]Or, *chief prince of Meshech*
4 [a]Is. 43:17 [b]Ezek. 38:15; Dan. 11:40

[I]splendidly attired, a great company[6951]
with buckler[6793] and shield, all of them
wielding swords;[2719]
5 [a]Persia, [Ib]Ethiopia, and [c]Put with
them, all of them *with* shield and helmet;
6 [a]Gomer with all its troops;
[b]Beth-togarmah *from* the remote parts
of the north with all its troops—many
peoples[5971] with you.
7 "[a]Be prepared,[3559] and prepare[3559] yourself, and all your companies that are assembled[6950] about you,
and be a guard for them.
8 "[a]After many days[3117] you will be
summoned;[6485] in the latter[319] years you
will come into the land that is restored
from the sword,[2719] *whose inhabitants*
have been [b]gathered[6908] from many
[I]nations to the [c]mountains of Israel which
had been a continual[8548] waste;[2723] but
[II]its people were brought out from the
[I]nations,[1471] and they are [d]living securely,[983] all of them.
9 "And you will go up,[5927] you will
come [a]like a storm;[7722] you will be like
a [b]cloud[6051] covering[3680] the land, you
and all your troops, and many peoples
with you."
10 'Thus says the Lord GOD, "It
will come about on that day,[3117] that
[I]thoughts[1697] will come into your
mind,[3824] and you will [a]devise[2803] an
evil[7451] plan,
11 and you will say, 'I will go up
against the land of [Ia]unwalled villages.
I will go against those who are [b]at
rest,[8252] that live securely, all of them
living without walls, and having no bars
or gates,
12 to [a]capture spoil and to seize
plunder, to turn your hand[3027] against
the waste places[2723] which are *now* inhabited, and against the people who are
gathered[622] from the nations, who have
acquired[6213] cattle and goods, who live
at the [I]center of the world.'
13 "[a]Sheba, and [b]Dedan, and the
merchants of [c]Tarshish, with all its
[I]villages, will say to you, 'Have you come
to capture spoil? Have you assembled[6950] your company to seize plunder,
to carry away[5375] silver and gold, to take
away cattle and goods, to capture great
[d]spoil?' " '
14 "Therefore, prophesy, son of
man, and say to Gog, 'Thus says the
Lord GOD, "On that day[3117] when My
people Israel are [a]living securely, will
you not know[3045] *it*?
15 "And [a]you will come from your
place out of the remote parts of the
north, you and many peoples with you,
all of them riding on horses, a great
assembly and a mighty army;
16 and you will come up[5927] against
My people Israel like a cloud to cover
the land. It will come about in the last
days that I shall bring you against My
land, in order that the nations[1471] may
[a]know Me when I shall be [b]sanctified[4720]
through you before their eyes, O
Gog."
17 'Thus says the Lord GOD, "Are
you the one of whom I spoke[1696] in former days through My servants[5650] the
prophets[5030] of Israel, who [a]proph-
esied[5012] in those days for *many* years
that I would bring you against them?
18 "And it will come about on that
day, when Gog comes against the land[127]
of Israel," declares[5001] the Lord GOD,
"that My fury will mount up[5927] in My
[a]anger.[639]
19 "And in My [a]zeal and in My blazing wrath[5678] I declare[1696] *that* on that
day there will surely be a great [Ib]earth-
quake in the land of Israel.
20 "[a]And the fish[1709] of the sea, the
birds of the heavens,[8064] the beasts[2416]
of the field,[7704] all the creeping things
that creep on the earth,[127] and all the
men[120] who are on the face of the earth
will shake[7493] at My presence; the
[b]mountains also will be thrown down,[2040]
the steep pathways will [I]collapse, and
every wall will fall to the ground.[776]
21 "And I shall call[7121] for a [a]sword
against [I]him on all My mountains," declares the Lord GOD. "[b]Every man's
sword will be against his brother.[251]
22 "And with pestilence[1698] and with
blood[1818] I shall enter into [a]judgment[8199]
with him; and I shall rain on him, and
on his troops, and on the many peoples

4 [I]Or, *clothed in full armor*
5 [I]Lit., *Cush* [a]2Chr. 36:20; Ezra 1:1; Ezek. 27:10; Dan. 8:20 [b]Gen. 10:6-8; Ezek. 30:4, 5 [c]Ezek. 27:10; 30:5
6 [a]Gen. 10:2, 3 [b]Gen. 10:3; Ezek. 27:14
7 [a]Is. 8:9
8 [I]Lit., *peoples* [II]Lit., *it was* [a]Is. 24:22 [b]Is. 11:11; Ezek. 36:24; 37:21; 38:12; 39:27, 28 [c]Ezek. 34:13; 36:1-8 [d]Ezek. 38:11, 14; 39:26
9 [a]Is. 5:28; 21:1; 25:4; 28:2; Jer. 4:13 [b]Ezek. 30:18; 38:16; Joel 2:2
10 [I]Lit., *words* [a]Ps. 36:4; Mic. 2:1
11 [I]Or, *open country* [a]Zech. 2:4 [b]Jer. 49:31
12 [I]Lit., *navel* [a]Is. 10:6; Ezek. 29:19
13 [I]Or, *young lions* [a]Ezek. 27:22, 23 [b]Ezek. 25:13; 27:15, 20 [c]Ezek. 27:12 [d]Is. 10:6; 33:23; Jer. 15:13
14 [a]Jer. 23:6; Ezek. 38:8, 11; Zech. 2:5, 8
15 [a]Ezek. 39:2
16 [a]Ps. 83:18; Ezek. 36:23; 38:23 [b]Is. 5:16; 8:13; 29:23; Ezek. 28:22
17 [a]Is. 5:26-29; 34:1-6; 63:1-6; 66:15, 16; Joel 3:9-14
18 [a]Ps. 18:8, 15
19 [I]Or, *shaking* [a]Deut. 32:22; Ps. 18:7, 8; Ezek. 5:13; 36:5, 6; Nah. 1:2; Heb. 12:29 [b]Joel 3:16; Hag. 2:6, 7, 21
20 [I]Lit., *fall* [a]Jer. 4:24, 25; Hos. 4:3; Nah. 1:4-6 [b]Zech. 14:4
21 [I]I.e., Gog [a]Ezek. 14:17 [b]Judg. 7:22; 1Sam. 14:20; 2Chr. 20:23; Hag. 2:22
22 [a]Is. 66:16; Jer. 25:31

who are with him, [I]a torrential[7857] rain, with [b]hailstones, fire, and brimstone.[1614]

23 "And I shall magnify Myself, sanctify[6942] Myself, and [a]make Myself known[3045] in the sight of many nations; and they will know that I am the LORD." '

Prophecy against Gog—Invaders Destroyed

39 "And [a]you, son[1121] of man,[120] prophesy[5012] against Gog, and say,[559] 'Thus says[559] the Lord[136] [I]GOD, "Behold, I am against you, O Gog, [II]prince[5387] of Rosh,[7218] Meshech, and Tubal;

2 and I shall turn you around,[7725] drive you on, take you up[5927] from the remotest parts of the north, and bring you against the mountains of Israel.

3 "And I shall [a]strike[5221] your bow from your left hand,[3027] and dash down your arrows from your right hand.

4 "You shall [a]fall on the mountains of Israel, you and all your troops, and the peoples[5971] who are with you; I shall give you as [b]food to every [I]kind of predatory bird and beast[2416] of the field.[7704]

5 "You will fall on the [I]open field; for it is I who have spoken,"[1696] declares[5001] the Lord GOD.

6 "And I shall send [a]fire upon Magog and those who inhabit the [b]coastlands in safety;[983] and they will know[3045] that I am the LORD.

7 "And My [a]holy[6944] name I shall make known[3045] in the midst of My people Israel; and I shall not let My holy name be [b]profaned[2490] anymore. And the [c]nations[1471] will know that I am the LORD, the [d]Holy One[6918] in Israel.

8 "Behold, it is coming and it shall be done," declares the Lord GOD. "That is the day[3117] of which I have spoken.

9 "Then those who inhabit the cities of Israel will [a]go out, and make [b]fires with the weapons[5402] and burn *them,* both shields and bucklers,[6793] bows and arrows, war clubs[4731] and spears and for seven years they will make fires of them.

10 "And they will not take[5375] wood from the field or gather firewood from the forests, for they will make fires with the weapons; and they will take the spoil of those who despoiled them, and seize the [a]plunder of those who plundered them," declares the Lord GOD.

11 "And it will come about on that day that I shall give Gog a burial ground[6913] there in Israel, the valley of those who pass by[5674] east of the sea, and it will block off the passers-by. So they will bury[6912] Gog there with all his multitude, and they will call[7121] *it* the valley of [I]Hamon-gog.

12 "For seven months the house[1004] of Israel will be burying[6912] them in order to [a]cleanse[2891] the land.[776]

13 "Even all the people of the land will bury *them;* and it will be [I]to their [a]renown *on* the day that I [b]glorify Myself," declares the Lord GOD.

14 "And they will set apart[914] men[582] who will constantly[8548] pass through[5674] the land, [a]burying those who were passing through, even those left[3498] on the surface of the ground,[776] in order to cleanse it. At the end of seven months they will make a search.

15 "And as those who pass through[5674] the land pass through and anyone sees[7200] a man's[120] bone,[6106] then he will [I]set up a marker by it until the buriers have buried[6912] it in the valley of [II]Hamon-gog.

16 "And even *the* name of *the* city will be Hamonah. So they will cleanse the land." '

17 "And as for you, son of man, thus says the Lord GOD, 'Speak[559] to every [I]kind of [a]bird and to every [a]beast[2416] of the field, "Assemble[6908] and come, gather[622] from every side to My sacrifice which I am going to [b]sacrifice[2076] for you, as a great sacrifice[2077] on the mountains of Israel, that you may eat flesh and drink blood.[1818]

18 "You shall [a]eat the flesh of mighty men, and drink the blood of the princes[5387] of the earth, as *though they were* [b]rams, lambs,[3733] goats, and [c]bulls, all of them fatlings of [d]Bashan.

22 [I]Lit., *an overflowing* [b]Ps. 11:6; 18:12-14; Is. 28:17
23 [a]Ps. 9:16; Ezek. 37:28; 38:16
1 [I]Heb., *YHWH,* usually rendered *LORD,* and so throughout the ch. [II]Or, *chief prince of Meshech* [a]Ezek. 38:2
3 [a]Ps. 76:3; Jer. 21:4, 5; Ezek. 30:21-24; Hos. 1:5
4 [I]Lit., *wing* [a]Is. 14:24, 25; Ezek. 39:17-20 [b]Ezek. 29:5; 32:4, 5; 33:27
5 [I]Lit., *face of the*
6 [a]Ezek. 30:8, 16; 38:19, 22; Amos 1:4, 7, 10; Nah. 1:6 [b]Ps. 72:10; Is. 66:19; Jer. 25:22
7 [a]Ezek. 36:20-22; 39:25 [b]Ex. 20:7; Ezek. 20:9, 14, 39 [c]Ezek. 38:16, 23 [d]Is. 12:6; 43:3, 14; 55:5; 60:9, 14
9 [a]Is. 66:24; Mal. 1:5 [b]Josh. 11:6; Ps. 46:9
10 [a]Is. 14:2; 33:1; Mic. 5:8; Hab. 2:8
11 [I]Or, *the multitude of Gog*
12 [a]Deut. 21:23; Ezek. 39:14, 16
13 [I]Or, *a memorial for them* [a]Jer. 33:9; Zeph. 3:19, 20 [b]Ezek. 28:22
14 [a]Jer. 14:16
15 [I]Lit., *build* [II]Or, *the multitude of Gog*
17 [I]Lit., *wing* [a]Is. 56:9; Jer. 12:9; Ezek. 39:4; Rev. 19:17, 18 [b]Is. 34:6, 7; Jer. 46:10; Zeph. 1:7
18 [a]Ezek. 29:5; Rev. 19:18 [b]Jer. 51:40 [c]Jer. 50:27 [d]Ps. 22:12; Amos 4:1

19 "So you will eat fat until you are glutted, and drink blood until you are drunk, from My sacrifice[2076] which I have sacrificed for you.

20 "And you will be glutted at My table with [a]horses and charioteers, with mighty men and all the men[376] of war," declares the Lord GOD.

21 "And I shall set My [a]glory[3519] among the nations; and all the nations will see My judgment[4941] which I have executed,[6213] and My hand which I have laid[7760] on them.

22 "And the house of Israel will [a]know that I am the LORD their God[430] from that day onward.

23 "And the nations will know that the house of Israel went into exile[1540] for their [a]iniquity[5771] because they acted treacherously[4603] against Me, and I [b]hid My face from them; so I gave them into the hand of their adversaries, and all of them fell[5307] by the sword.[2719]

24 "[a]According to their uncleanness[2932] and according to their transgressions[6588] I dealt[6213] with them, and I hid My face from them." ' "

Israel Restored

25 Therefore thus says the Lord GOD, "Now I shall [I][a]restore[7725] the fortunes[7622] of Jacob, and have mercy[7355] on the whole [b]house of Israel; and I shall be [c]jealous[7065] for My holy[6944] name.

26 "And they shall [I][a]forget[5375] their disgrace and all their treachery[4604] which they [II]perpetrated against Me, when they [b]live securely[983] on their *own* land[127] with [c]no one to make them afraid.[2729]

27 "When I [a]bring them back from the peoples and gather[6908] them from the lands[776] of their enemies, then I shall be [b]sanctified[6942] [I]through them in the sight of the many nations.[1471]

28 "Then they will know that I am the LORD their God because I made them go into exile[1473] among the nations, and then gathered[3664] them *again* to their own land; and I will leave[3498] none of them there any longer.

29 "And I will not hide My face from them any longer, for I shall have [a]poured out[8210] My Spirit[7307] on the house of Israel," declares the Lord GOD.

Vision of the Man with a Measuring Rod

40 In the [a]twenty-fifth year of our exile,[1546] at the beginning[7218] of the year, on the tenth of the month, in the fourteenth year after the [b]city was [I]taken,[5221] on that same day[3117] the [c]hand[3027] of the LORD was upon me and He brought me there.

2 In the [a]visions[4759] of God[430] He brought me into the land[776] of Israel, and set me on a very [b]high mountain; and on it [c]to the south *there was* a [d]structure like a city.

3 So He brought me there; and behold, there was a man[376] whose appearance was like the appearance of [a]bronze, with a [b]line of flax and a [c]measuring [I]rod in his hand; and he was standing in the gateway.

4 And the man said[1696] to me, "[a]Son[1121] of man,[120] [b]see[7200] with your eyes, hear[8085] with your ears,[241] and give[7760] attention[3820] to all that I am going to show you; for you have been brought here in order to show *it* to you. [c]Declare[5046] to the house[1004] of Israel all that you see."

Measurements Relating to the Temple

5 And behold, there was a [a]wall on the outside of the [I]temple all around, and in the man's hand was a measuring rod of six cubits, *each of which was* a cubit and a [II]handbreadth. So he measured the thickness of the [III]wall, one rod; and the height, one rod.

6 Then he went to the gate which faced[1870] [a]east, went up[5927] its steps, and measured the threshold of the gate,

20 [a]Ps. 76:5, 6; Ezek. 38:4; Hag. 2:22; Rev. 19:18
21 [a]Ex. 9:16; Is. 37:20; Ezek. 36:23; 38:16, 23; 39:13
22 [a]Jer. 24:7
23 [a]Jer. 22:8, 9; 44:22; Ezek. 36:18, 19 [b]Is. 1:15; 59:2; Ezek. 39:29
24 [a]2Kin. 17:7; Jer. 2:17, 19; 4:18; Ezek. 36:19
25 [I]Or, *return the captivity* [a]Is. 27:12, 13; Jer. 33:7; Ezek. 34:13 [b]Jer. 31:1; Ezek. 36:10; 37:21, 22; Hos. 1:11 [c]Ex. 20:5; Nah. 1:2
26 [I]Another reading is *bear* [II]Lit., *did treacherously* [a]Ezek. 16:63; 20:43; 36:31 [b]1Kin. 4:25; Ezek. 34:25-28 [c]Is. 17:2; Mic. 4:4
27 [I]Lit., *in* [a]Ezek. 36:24; 37:21 [b]Ezek. 36:23; 38:16, 23
29 [a]Is. 32:15; Ezek. 36:27; 37:14; Joel 2:28
1 [I]Lit., *struck* [a]Ezek. 32:1, 17; 33:21 [b]2Kin. 25:1-7; Jer. 39:1-9; 52:4-11; Ezek. 33:21 [c]Ezek. 1:3; 3:14, 22; 37:1
2 [a]Ezek. 1:1; 8:3; Dan. 7:1, 7 [b]Is. 2:2, 3; Ezek. 17:23; 20:40; 37:22; Mic. 4:1; Rev. 21:10 [c]Ps. 48:2; Is. 14:13 [d]1Chr. 28:12, 19
3 [I]Lit., *reed,* and so throughout the ch. [a]Ezek. 1:7; Dan. 10:6; Rev. 1:15 [b]Ezek. 47:3; Zech. 2:1, 2 [c]Rev. 11:1; 21:15
4 [a]Ezek. 2:1, 3, 6, 8; 44:5 [b]Ezek. 2:7, 8; 44:5 [c]Is. 21:10; Jer. 26:2; Acts 20:27
5 [I]Lit., *house* [II]I.e., 20.4 in.

5 [III]Lit., *building* [a]Is. 26:1; Ezek. 42:20 6 [a]Ezek. 8:16; 11:1; 40:20; 43:1

one rod [I]in width; and the other threshold *was* one rod [I]in width.

7 And the [a]guardroom *was* one rod long[753] and one rod wide; and *there were* five cubits between the guardrooms. And the threshold of the gate by the porch of the gate [I]facing inward *was* one rod.

8 Then he measured the porch of the gate [I]facing inward, one rod.

9 And he measured the porch of the gate, eight cubits; and its side pillars, two cubits. And the porch of the gate was [I]faced inward.

10 And the guardrooms of the gate toward the east *numbered* three on each side; the three of them had the same measurement. The side pillars also had the same measurement on each side.

11 And he measured the width of the [I]gateway, ten cubits, and the length[753] of the gate, thirteen cubits.

12 And *there was* a [I]barrier *wall* one cubit *wide* in front of the guardrooms on each side; and the guardrooms *were* six cubits *square* on each side.

13 And he measured the gate from the roof of the one guardroom to the roof of the other, a width of twenty-five cubits from *one* door to *the* door opposite.

14 And he made[6213] the side pillars sixty cubits *high;* the gate *extended* round about to the side pillar of the [a]courtyard.

15 And *from* the front of the entrance gate to the front of the inner porch of the gate *was* fifty cubits.

16 And *there were* [Ia]shuttered windows *looking* toward the guardrooms, and toward their side pillars within the gate all around, and likewise for the porches. And *there were* windows all around inside; and on *each* side pillar *were* [b]palm tree ornaments.

17 Then he brought me into the [a]outer court, and behold, *there were* [b]chambers and a pavement, made for the court all around; thirty chambers [I]faced the pavement.

18 And the pavement (*that is,* the lower pavement) *was* by the [I]side of the gates, corresponding to the length of the gates.

19 Then he measured the width from the front of the [a]lower gate to the front of the exterior of the inner court, a [b]hundred cubits on the east and on the north.

20 And *as for* the [a]gate of the outer court which faced the north, he measured its length and its width.

21 And [I]it had three [a]guardrooms on each side; and its [b]side pillars and its porches [II]had the same measurement as the first[7223] gate. Its length *was* [c]fifty cubits, and the width [d]twenty-five cubits.

22 And its [a]windows, and its porches, and its palm tree ornaments *had* the same measurements as the [b]gate which faced toward the east; and [I]it was reached by seven [c]steps, and its [II]porch *was* in front of them.

23 And the inner court had a gate opposite the gate on the north as well as *the gate* on the east; and he measured a [a]hundred cubits from gate to gate.

24 Then he led me toward the south, and behold, there was a [a]gate toward the south; and he measured its [b]side pillars and its porches according to [I]those same measurements.

25 And [I]the gate and its porches had [a]windows all around like [II]those other windows; the length *was* [b]fifty cubits and the width twenty-five cubits.

26 And *there were* seven [a]steps going up to it, and its porches *were* in front of them; and it had [b]palm tree ornaments on its side pillars, one on each side.

27 And the inner court had a gate toward the [a]south; and he measured from gate to gate toward the south, a [b]hundred cubits.

28 Then he brought me to the inner court by the south gate; and he measured the south gate [a]according to those same measurements.

29 Its [a]guardrooms also, its side pillars, and its [b]porches *were* according to those same measurements. And [I]the gate and its porches had [c]windows all

6 [I]Or, *in depth*
7 [I]Lit., *from the house* [a]Ezek. 40:10-16, 21, 29, 33, 36
8 [I]Lit., *from the house*
9 [I]Lit., *from the house*
11 [I]Lit., *entrance of the gate*
12 [I]Lit., *border*
14 [a]Ex. 27:9; 1Chr. 28:6; Ps. 100:4; Is. 62:9; Ezek. 8:7; 42:1
16 [I]Or, *beveled inwards* [a]1 Kin. 6:4; Ezek. 41:16, 26 [b]1Kin. 6:29, 32, 35; 2Chr. 3:5; Ezek. 40:22, 26, 31, 34, 37; 41:18-20, 25, 26
17 [I]Lit., *to* [a]Ezek. 10:5; 42:1; 46:21; Rev. 11:2 [b]2Kin. 23:11; 1Chr. 9:26; 23:28; 2Chr. 31:11; Ezek. 40:38
18 [I]Lit., *shoulder*
19 [a]Ezek. 40:23, 27; 46:1, 2 [b]Ezek. 40:23, 27
20 [a]Ezek. 40:6
21 [I]Lit., *its guardrooms were three* [II]Lit., *were* [a]Ezek. 40:7 [b]Ezek. 40:16, 30 [c]Ezek. 40:15 [d]Ezek. 40:13
22 [I]Lit., *they were going up into it* [II]Or, *porches* [a]Ezek. 40:16 [b]Ezek. 40:6 [c]Ezek. 40:26, 31, 34, 37, 49
23 [a]Ezek. 40:19, 27
24 [I]Lit., *these measurements,* and so throughout the ch. [a]Ezek. 40:6, 20, 35; 46:9 [b]Ezek. 40:21
25 [I]Lit., *it* [II]Lit., *these windows* [a]Ezek. 40:16, 22, 29 [b]Ezek. 40:21, 33
26 [a]Ezek. 40:6, 22 [b]Ezek. 40:16
27 [a]Ezek. 40:23, 32 [b]Ezek. 40:19
28 [a]Ezek. 40:32, 35
29 [I]Lit., *it* [a]Ezek. 40:7, 10, 21 [b]Ezek. 40:16, 22, 25 [c]Ezek. 40:21

around; it *was* [b]fifty cubits long and twenty-five cubits wide.

30 And *there were* [a]porches all around, twenty-five cubits long and five cubits wide.

31 And its porches *were* toward the outer court; and [a]palm tree ornaments *were* on its side pillars, and its stairway had eight [b]steps.

32 And he brought me into the [a]inner court toward the east. And he measured the gate [b]according to those same measurements.

33 Its [a]guardrooms also, its side pillars, and its porches *were* according to those same measurements. And [I]the gate and its porches had [b]windows all around; it *was* [c]fifty cubits long and twenty-five cubits wide.

34 And its [a]porches *were* toward the outer court; and [a]palm tree ornaments *were* on its side pillars, on each side, and its stairway had eight [b]steps.

35 Then he brought me to the [a]north gate; and he measured *it* according to those same measurements,

36 *with* its [a]guardrooms, its side pillars, and its [b]porches. And [I]the gate had [b]windows all around; the length *was* [c]fifty cubits and the width twenty-five cubits.

37 And its side pillars *were* toward the outer court; and [a]palm tree ornaments *were* on its side pillars on each side, and its stairway had eight [b]steps.

38 And a [a]chamber with its doorway was by the side pillars at the gates; there they [b]rinse[1740] the burnt offering.[5930]

39 And in the porch of the gate *were* two [a]tables on each side, on which to slaughter[7819] the [b]burnt offering, the sin offering, and the guilt offering.[817]

40 And on the outer [I]side, [II]as one went up to the [III]gateway toward the north, were two tables; and on the other [I]side of the porch of the gate *were* two tables.

41 Four [a]tables *were* on each side [I]next to the gate; *or,* eight tables on which they slaughter[7819] *sacrifices.*

42 And for the burnt offering[5930] *there were* four [a]tables of [b]hewn[1496] stone, a cubit and a half long, a cubit and a half wide, and one cubit high, on which they lay the instruments with which they slaughter the [c]burnt offering and the sacrifice.

43 And the double [I]hooks, one handbreadth in length, were installed [II]in the house all around; and on the tables *was* the flesh of the offering.[7133]

44 And from the outside to the [a]inner gate were [Ib]chambers for the [c]singers[7891] in the inner court, *one of* which was at the [II]side of the north gate, with [III]its front toward the south, and one at the [II]side of the [IV]east gate facing toward the north.

45 And he said to me, "This is the [a]chamber which faces toward the south, *intended* for the priests[3548] who [b]keep[8104] charge[4931] of the [I] temple;

46 but the [a]chamber which faces toward the north is for the priests who [b]keep charge of the altar.[4196] These are the [c]sons[1121] of Zadok, who from the sons of Levi [d]come near to the LORD to minister[8334] to Him."

47 And he measured the court, a *perfect* square, a [a]hundred cubits long and a hundred cubits wide; and the altar was in front of the [I]temple.

48 Then he brought me to the [a]porch of the [I]temple and measured *each* side pillar of the porch, five cubits on each side; and the width of the gate was three cubits on each side.

49 The length of the porch was twenty cubits, and the width eleven cubits; and at the [a]stairway by which it was ascended *were* [b]columns belonging to the side pillars, one on each side.

The Inner Temple

41 Then he [a]brought me to the [Ib]nave[1964] and measured the [c]side pillars; six cubits wide on each side *was* the width of the [II]side pillar.

2 And the width of the entrance *was* ten cubits, and the [I]sides of the entrance

29 [b]Ezek. 40:16, 22, 25
30 [a]Ezek. 40:16, 21
31 [a]Ezek. 40:16 [b]Ezek. 40:22, 26, 34, 37
32 [a]Ezek. 40:28-31, 35 [b]Ezek. 40:28
33 [I]Lit., *it* [a]Ezek. 40:29 [b]Ezek. 40:16 [c]Ezek. 40:21
34 [a]Ezek. 40:16 [b]Ezek. 40:22, 37
35 [a]Ezek. 40:27, 32; 44:4; 47:2
36 [I]Lit., *it* [a]Ezek. 40:7, 29 [b]Ezek. 40:16 [c]Ezek. 40:21
37 [a]Ezek. 40:16 [b]Ezek. 40:34
38 [a]1Chr. 28:12; Neh. 13:5, 9; Jer. 35:4; 36:10; Ezek. 40:17; 41:10; 42:13 [b]2Chr. 4:6
39 [a]Ezek. 40:42 [b]Lev. 1:3-17; Ezek. 46:2
40 [I]Lit., *shoulder* [II]Lit., *to the one going up* [III]Lit., *entrance of the gate*
41 [I]Lit., *by the shoulder of* [a]Ezek. 40:39, 40
42 [a]Ezek. 40:39 [b]Ex. 20:25 [c]Ezek. 40:39
43 [I]Or, *ledges* [II]Or, *inside*
44 [I]Gr. reads *in two chambers* [II]Lit., *shoulder* [III]Lit., *their* [IV]Gr. reads *south* [a]Ezek. 40:23, 27 [b]Ezek. 40:17, 38 [c]1Chr. 6:31, 32; 16:41-43; 25:1-7
45 [I]Or, *house* [a]Ezek. 40:17, 38 [b]1Chr. 9:23; Ps. 134:1
46 [a]Ezek. 40:17, 38 [b]Lev. 6:12, 13; Ezek. 44:15 [c]1Kin. 2:35; Ezek. 43:19; 48:11 [d]Lev. 10:3; Num. 16:5, 40; Ezek. 42:13; 45:4
47 [I]Lit., *house* [a]Ezek. 40:19, 23, 27
48 [I]Lit., *house* [a]1Kin. 6:3; 2Chr. 3:4
49 [a]Ezek. 40:31, 34, 37 [b]1Kin. 7:15-22; 2Chr. 3:17; Jer. 52:17-23; Rev. 3:12

1 [I]I.e., the main inner hall [II]Lit., *tent* [a]Ezek. 40:2, 3, 17 [b]Ezek. 41:21, 23 [c]Ezek. 40:9; 41:3
2 [I]Lit., *shoulders*

were five cubits on each side. And he measured [II]the length[753] of the nave, [a]forty cubits, and the width, [b]twenty cubits.

3 Then he went [Ia]inside and measured each [b]side pillar of the doorway, two cubits, and the doorway, six cubits *high;* and the width of the doorway, seven cubits.

4 And he measured its length, [a]twenty cubits, and the width, twenty cubits, before the [b]nave; and he said[559] to me, "This is the [c]most holy[6944] *place.*"

5 Then he measured the wall of the [I]temple,[1004] six cubits; and the width of the [a]side chambers, four cubits, all around about the house on every side.

6 And [a]the side chambers were in three stories, [I]one above another, and [II]thirty in each story; and [III]the side chambers [b]extended to the wall which *stood* on [IV]their inward side all around, that they might be fastened, and not be fastened into the wall of the temple *itself.*

7 And the side chambers surrounding the temple were wider at each successive story. Because the [a]structure surrounding the temple went upward by stages on all sides of the temple, therefore the width of the temple *increased* as it went higher; and thus one went up[5927] from the lowest *story* to the highest[5925] by way of the [I]second *story.*

8 I saw[7200] also that the house had a raised [I]platform all around; the foundations of the side chambers were a full rod of [a]six [II]long cubits *in height.*

9 The [I]thickness of the outer wall of the side chambers was five cubits. But the [a]free space between the side chambers belonging to the temple[1004]

10 and the *outer* [a]chambers *was* twenty cubits in width all around the temple on every side.

11 And the [I]doorways of the [II]side chambers toward the [a]free space *consisted of* one doorway toward[1870] the north and another doorway toward the south; and the width of the [a]free space was five cubits all around.

12 And the [a]building that *was* in front of the [b]separate area at the side toward the west *was* seventy cubits wide; and the wall of the building was five cubits [I]thick all around, and its length *was* ninety cubits.

13 Then he measured the temple, a [a]hundred cubits long; the [b]separate area with the [c]building and its walls *were* also a [a]hundred cubits long.[753]

14 Also the width of the front of the temple and *that of* the separate [I]areas along the east *side totaled* a hundred cubits.

15 And he measured the length of the [a]building [I]along the front of the [b]separate area behind it, with a [IIc]gallery[862] on each side, a hundred cubits; *he* also *measured* the inner nave and the porches of the court.

16 The [a]thresholds, the [Ib]latticed windows, and the [IIc]galleries[862] round about their [d]three stories, opposite the threshold, were [e]paneled[7824] with wood all around, and *from* the ground[776] to the windows (but the windows were covered),[3680]

17 over the entrance, and to the inner house, and on the outside, and on all the wall all around inside and outside, by measurement.

18 And it was [I]carved[6213] with [a]cherubim[3742] and [b]palm trees; and a palm tree was between cherub[3742] and cherub, and every cherub had two faces,

19 a [a]man's[120] face toward the palm tree on one side, and a young [a]lion's face toward the palm tree on the other side; they were [I]carved on all the house all around.

20 From the ground to above the entrance [a]cherubim and [a]palm trees were [I]carved, as well as *on* the wall of the nave.

21 The [a]doorposts of the [b]nave were square; as for the front of the sanctuary,[6944] the appearance of one doorpost was like that of the other.

22 The [a]altar[4196] *was* of wood, three cubits high, and its length two cubits;

2 [II]Lit., *its length,* [a]1Kin. 6:2, 17; 2Chr. 3:3
3 [I]I.e., of the inner sanctuary [a]Ezek. 40:16 [b]Ezek. 41:1
4 [a]1Kin. 6:20 [b]1Kin. 6:5 [c]Ex. 26:33, 34; 1Kin. 6:16; 7:50; 8:6; 2Chr. 5:7; Heb. 9:3-8
5 [I]Lit., *house,* and so throughout the ch. [a]1 Kin. 6:5; Ezek. 41:6-11
6 [I]Lit., *chamber upon chamber* [II]Lit., *thirty times* [III]Lit., they were *coming* [IV]Lit., *the inside of the side chambers* [a]1Kin. 6:5-10 [b]1Kin. 6:6, 10
7 [I]Lit., *middle* [a]1Kin. 6:8
8 [I]Lit., *height* [II]Or, *to the joint* [a]Ezek. 40:5
9 [I]Lit., *width* [a]Ezek. 41:11
10 [a]Ezek. 40:17
11 [I]Lit., *doorway* [II]Lit., *side chamber* [a]Ezek. 41:9
12 [I]Lit., *wide* [a]Ezek. 41:13, 15; 42:1 [b]Ezek. 41:14; 42:10, 13
13 [a]Ezek. 40:47 [b]Ezek. 41:13-15; 42:1, 10, 13 [c]Ezek. 41:12
14 [I]Lit., *area*
15 [I]Lit., *to* [II]Or, *passageway* [a]Ezek. 41:12, 13; 42:1 [b]Ezek. 41:14; 42:1, 10, 13 [c]Ezek. 41:16; 42:3, 5
16 [I]Or, *framed* [II]Or, *passageways* [a]Is. 6:4; Ezek. 10:18; 40:6; 41:25 [b]1Kin. 6:4; Ezek. 40:16, 25; 41:26 [c]Ezek. 41:15 [d]Ezek. 42:3 [e]1Kin. 6:15
18 [I]Lit., *made* [a]1Kin. 6:29, 32, 35; 7:36; Ezek. 41:20, 25 [b]2Chr. 3:5; Ezek. 40:16
19 [I]Lit., *made* [a]Ezek. 1:10; 10:14
20 [I]Lit., *made* [a]Ezek. 41:18
21 [a]1Kin. 6:33; Ezek. 40:9, 14, 16; 41:1 [b]Ezek. 41:1

22 [a]Ex. 30:1-3; 1Kin. 6:20; Rev. 8:3

its corners, its [I]base, and its [II]sides *were*
of wood. And he said[1696] to me, "This
is the [b]table that is before the LORD."
23 And the [a]nave and the [b]sanctuary
each had a double [c]door.
24 And each of the doors had two
leaves, two [Ia]swinging leaves; two *leaves*
for one door and two leaves for the
other.
25 Also there were [I]carved on them,
on the doors of the nave, [a]cherubim and
[a]palm trees like those [I]carved on the
walls; and *there was* a [IIb]threshold of
wood on the front of the porch outside.
26 And *there were* [Ia]latticed windows
and [b]palm trees on one side and on the
other, on the sides of the [c]porch; thus
were the [d]side chambers of the house
and the [II]thresholds.

Chambers of the Temple

42 Then he [a]brought me out into
the [b]outer court, the way[1870]
[c]toward the north; and he brought me
to the [d]chamber which *was* opposite the
[e]separate area and opposite the [f]building
toward the north.
2 Along the length,[753] *which was* a
[a]hundred cubits, *was* the north door;
the width *was* fifty cubits.
3 Opposite the [a]twenty *cubits* which
belonged to the inner court, and opposite the [b]pavement which belonged to
the outer court, *was* [Ic]gallery corresponding to [I]gallery in three stories.
4 And before the [a]chambers *was* an
inner walk ten cubits wide, a way of
one *hundred* cubits; and their openings
were on the north.
5 Now the upper[5945] chambers *were*
[I]smaller because the [II] [a]galleries[862] took
more *space* away from them than from
the lower and middle ones in the building.
6 For they *were* in [a]three stories and
had no pillars like the pillars of the
courts; therefore *the upper chambers*
were [I]set back[680] from the ground[776]
upward, more than the lower and middle
ones.
7 As for the [a]outer wall by the side
of the chambers, toward the outer court
facing the chambers, its length *was* fifty
cubits.
8 For the length of the chambers
which *were* in the outer court *was* fifty
cubits; and behold, *the length of those*
facing the temple[1964] *was* a [a]hundred cubits.
9 And below these chambers *was*
the [a]entrance on the east side, as one
enters them from the outer court.
10 In the [I]thickness of the [a]wall of
the court toward the east, facing the
[b]separate area and facing the building,
there were [c]chambers.
11 And the [a]way in front of them
was like the appearance of the chambers
which *were* on the north, according to
their length[753] so was their width; and
all their exits *were* both according
to their arrangements[4941] and openings.
12 And corresponding to the openings of the chambers which were toward
the south was an opening at the head[7218]
of the way, the way in front of the
[a]wall toward the east, as one enters
them.
13 Then he said[559] to me, "The
north chambers *and* the south chambers, which are opposite the [a]separate
area, they are the [b]holy[6944] chambers
where the priests[3548] who are [c]near to
the LORD shall eat the [d]most holy
things.[6944] There they shall lay the most
holy things, the grain offering,[4503] the
sin offering,[2403] and the guilt offering;[817]
for the place is holy.[6918]
14 "When the priests enter, then
they shall not go out into the outer court
from the sanctuary [I]without [a]laying there
their [b]garments in which they minister,[8334] for they are holy. They shall
put on other garments; then they shall
approach[7126] that which is for the
people."[5971]
15 Now when he had finished[3615]
measuring the inner house,[1004] he
brought me out by the way of the
[a]gate which faced toward the east, and
measured it all around.
16 He measured on the east side

---

22 [I]Lit., *length* [II]Lit., *walls* [b]Ex. 25:23, 30; Lev. 24:6; Ezek. 23:41; 44:16; Mal. 1:7, 12
23 [a]Ezek. 41:1 [b]Ezek. 41:4 [c]1Kin. 6:31-35
24 [I]Or, *turning* [a]1Kin. 6:34
25 [I]Lit., *made* [II]Or, *canopy of wood over* [a]Ezek. 41:18 [b]Ezek. 41:16
26 [I]Or, *framed* [II]Or, *canopies* [a]Ezek. 41:16 [b]Ezek. 40:16 [c]Ezek. 40:9, 48 [d]Ezek. 41:5
1 [a]Ezek. 40:17, 28, 48; 41:1 [b]Ezek. 40:17, 20 [c]Ezek. 40:20 [d]Ezek. 40:17; 42:4 [e]Ezek. 41:12; 42:10, 13 [f]Ezek. 41:12
2 [a]Ezek. 41:13
3 [I]Or, *passageway* [a]Ezek. 41:10 [b]Ezek. 40:17 [c]Ezek. 41:15, 16; 42:5
4 [a]Ezek. 46:19
5 [I]Lit., *shorter* [II]Or, *passageways* [a]Ezek. 42:3
6 [I]Or, *reduced* [a]Ezek. 41:6
7 [a]Ezek. 42:10, 12
8 [a]Ezek. 41:13, 14
9 [a]Ezek. 44:5; 46:19
10 [I]Lit., *width* [a]Ezek. 42:7 [b]Ezek. 42:1, 13 [c]Ezek. 40:17
11 [a]Ezek. 42:4
12 [a]Ezek. 42:7
13 [a]Ezek. 42:1, 10 [b]Ex. 29:31; Lev. 7:6; 10:13, 14, 17 [c]Lev. 10:3; Deut. 21:5; Ezek. 40:46 [d]Lev. 6:25, 29; 14:13; Num. 18:9, 10
14 [I]Lit., *but there they shall lay* [a]Ezek. 44:19 [b]Ex. 29:4-9; Lev. 8:7, 13; Is. 61:10; Zech. 3:4, 5
15 [a]Ezek. 40:6; 43:1

with the measuring reed five hundred
reeds, by the [a]measuring reed.
17 He measured on the north side
five hundred reeds by the measuring
reed.
18 On the south side he measured
five hundred reeds with the measuring
reed.
19 He turned to the west side, *and*
measured five hundred reeds with the
measuring reed.
20 He measured it [I]on the four
sides; it had a [a]wall all around, the
[b]length five hundred and the [b]width five
hundred, to [c]divide[914] between the
holy[6944] and the profane.[2455]

Vision of the Glory of God Filling the Temple

43 🗝 Then he led me to the
[a]gate, the gate facing toward[1870]
the east;
2 and behold, the [a]glory[3519] of the
God[430] of Israel was coming from the
way[1870] of the [b]east. And His [c]voice was
like the sound of many waters; and the
earth[776] [d]shone with His glory.
3 And *it was* like the appearance of
the vision which I saw,[7200] like the
[a]vision which I saw when [I]He came to
[b]destroy[7843] the city. And the visions[4579]
were like the vision which I saw by the
[c]river Chebar; and I [d]fell[5307] on my face.
4 And the glory of the LORD came
into the house[1004] by the way of the
gate facing toward the [a]east.
5 And the [a]Spirit lifted me up[5375] and
brought me into the inner court; and
behold, the [b]glory of the LORD filled the
house.
6 Then I heard[8085] one speaking[1696]
to me from the house, while a [a]man[376]
was standing beside me.
7 And He said[559] to me, "Son[1121]
of man,[120] *this is* the place of My
[a]throne and the place of the soles[3709]
of My feet, where I will [b]dwell[7931] among
the sons[1121] of Israel forever.[5769] And
the house of Israel will not again
defile[2930] My holy[6944] name, neither they
nor their kings,[4428] by their harlotry[2184]
and by the [Ic]corpses of their kings
[II]when they die,[1116]
8 by setting their threshold by My
threshold, and their door post beside
My door post, with *only* the wall between Me and them. And they have
[a]defiled[2930] My holy name by their
abominations[8441] which they have committed.[6213] So I have consumed them
in My anger.[639]
9 "Now let them [a]put away their harlotry and the [I]corpses of their kings far
from Me; and I will [b]dwell among them
forever.
10 "As for you, son of man,
[Ia]describe[5046] the [II]temple to the house
of Israel, that they may be [b]ashamed
of their iniquities;[5771] and let them
measure the [IIIc]plan.
11 "And if they are ashamed of all
that they have done,[6213] make known[3045]
to them the [I]design of the house, its
structure, its [a]exits, its entrances, all
its designs, all its statutes[II], and all its
laws. And write *it* [b]in their sight, so
that they may observe[8104] its whole
[I]design and all its statutes,[2708] and
[c]do[6213] them.
12 "This is the [I]law[8451] of the house:
its entire [II]area on the top[7218] of the
[a]mountain all around *shall be* most
holy.[6944] Behold, this is the [I]law of the
house.

The Altar of Sacrifice

13 "And these are the measurements of the [a]altar[4196] by cubits (the
[b]cubit being a cubit and a handbreadth):
the [I]base *shall be* a cubit, and the width
a cubit, and its border on its edge round
about one span; and this *shall be* the
height of the [II]base of the altar.

13 [I]Lit., *lap* [II]Or, *back* [a]Ex. 27:1-8; 2Chr. 4:1 [b]Ezek. 40:5; 41:8

16 [a]Ezek. 40:3
20 [I]Lit., *toward the four winds* [a]Is. 60:18; Ezek. 40:5; Zech. 2:5 [b]Ezek. 45:2; Rev. 21:16 [c]Ezek. 22:26; 44:23; 48:15
1 [a]Ezek. 10:19; 40:6; 42:15; 43:4; 44:1; 46:1
2 [a]Is. 6:3; Ezek. 1:28; 3:23; 10:18, 19 [b]Ezek. 11:23 [c]Ezek. 1:24; Rev. 1:15; 14:2 [d]Ezek. 1:28; 10:4; Rev. 18:1
3 [I]So with some mss. and some ancient versions; M.T., *I* [a]Ezek. 1:4-28 [b]Jer. 1:10; Ezek. 9:1, 5; 32:18 [c]Ezek. 1:3; 10:20 [d]Ezek. 1:28; 3:23
4 [a]Ezek. 10:19; 11:23; 43:2
5 [a]Ezek. 3:14; 8:3; 11:1, 24; 2Cor. 12:2-4 [b]Ezek. 10:4
6 [a]Ezek. 1:26; 40:3
7 [I]Or, *monuments* as in Ugaritic [II]Or, *in their high places* [a]Ps. 47:8; Ezek. 1:26 [b]Ezek. 37:26, 28 [c]Lev. 26:30; Ezek. 6:5, 13
8 [a]Ezek. 8:3, 16
9 [I]Or, *monuments* as in Ugaritic [a]Ezek. 18:30, 31 [b]Ezek. 37:26-28; 43:7
10 [I]Lit., *declare* [II]Lit., *house* [III]Lit., *perfection or pattern* [a]Ezek. 40:4 [b]Ezek. 16:61, 63; 43:11 [c]Ezek. 28:12
11 [I]Or, *form(s)* [II]M.T. repeats *and all its designs* after *statutes* [a]Ezek. 44:5 [b]Ezek. 12:3 [c]Ezek. 11:20; 36:27
12 [I]Or, *instruction for* [II]Lit., *border* [a]Ezek. 40:2

🗝 **43:1-5** Ezekiel here described the magnificent scene of the glory of the Lord returning to the reconstructed temple. Shortly before the earlier temple was destroyed, God's glory left the temple and city and went east (Ezek. 10:18,19; 11:22,23), so, appropriately, it returned from the east.

14 "And from the base on the ground[776] to the lower [a]ledge *shall be* two cubits, and the width one cubit; and from the smaller ledge to the larger ledge *shall be* four cubits, and the width [I]one cubit.

15 "And the [I]altar hearth *shall be* four cubits; and from the [I]altar hearth shall extend upwards four [a]horns.

16 "Now the [I]altar hearth *shall be* twelve *cubits* long[753] by twelve wide, [a]square in its four sides.

17 "And the ledge *shall be* fourteen *cubits* long by fourteen wide in its four sides, the border around it *shall be* half a cubit, and its base *shall be* a cubit round about; and its [a]steps shall [I][b]face the east."

The Offerings

18 And He said to me, "[a]Son of man, thus says[559] the Lord[136] [I]GOD, 'These are the statutes for the altar on the day[3117] it is built, to offer [b]burnt offerings[5930] on it and to [c]sprinkle[2236] blood[1818] on it.

19 'And you shall give to the Levitical priests[3548] who are from the offspring[2233] of [a]Zadok, who draw [b]near to Me to minister[8334] to Me,' declares the Lord GOD, 'a [c]young[1121] bull for a [d]sin[2403] offering.

20 'And you shall take some of its blood, and put it on its four [a]horns, and on the four corners of the [b]ledge, and on the border round about; thus you shall [c]cleanse[2398] it and make atonement[3722] for it.

21 'You shall also take the bull for the sin offering; and it *shall be* [a]burned in the appointed place of the house, outside the sanctuary.[4720]

22 'And on the second day you shall offer[7126] a [a]male[8163] goat without blemish[8549] for a sin offering; and they shall [b]cleanse the altar, as they cleansed *it* with the bull.

23 'When you have finished[3615] cleansing[2893] *it,* you shall present a [a]young bull without blemish[8549] and a [b]ram without blemish from the flock.

24 'And you shall present them before the LORD, and the priests shall throw [a]salt on them, and they shall offer them up as a burnt offering[5930] to the LORD.

25 "[a]For seven days[3117] you shall prepare daily[3117] a goat[8163] for a sin offering; also a young bull and a ram from the flock, without blemish, shall be prepared.[3559]

26 'For seven days they shall make atonement for the altar and purify[2891] it; so shall they [I]consecrate it.

27 'And when they have completed[3615] the days, it shall be that on the [a]eighth day and onward, the priests shall [I]offer your burnt offerings on the altar, and your [b]peace offerings;[8002] and I will [c]accept[7521] you,' declares the Lord GOD."

Gate for the Prince

44 Then He brought me back by the way[1870] of the [a]outer gate of the sanctuary,[4720] which faces[1870] the east; and it was shut.

2 And the LORD said[559] to me, "This gate shall be shut; it shall not be opened, and no one[376] shall enter by it, for the [a]LORD God[430] of Israel has entered by it; therefore it shall be shut.

3 "As for the [a]prince,[5387] he shall sit in it as prince to [b]eat bread before the LORD; he shall [c]enter by way of the [d]porch of the gate, and shall go out [I]by the same way."

4 Then He brought me by way of the [a]north gate to the front of the house;[1004] and I looked,[7200] and behold, the [b]glory[3519] of the LORD filled the house of the LORD, and I [c]fell[5307] on my face.

5 And the LORD said to me, "Son[1121] of man,[120] [I][a]mark well, see[7200] with your eyes, and hear[8085] with your ears[241] all that I say[1696] to you concerning all the [b]statutes[2708] of the house of the LORD and concerning all its laws; and [I]mark well the entrance of the house, with all exits of the sanctuary.

6 "And you shall say[559] to the

14 [I]Lit., *the* [a]Ezek. 43:17, 20; 45:19
15 [I]Or, *ariel* shall [a]Ex. 27:2; Lev. 9:9; 1Kin. 1:50; Ps. 118:27
16 [I]Or, *ariel* shall [a]Ex. 27:1
17 [I]Or, *be on the east side* [a]Ex. 20:26 [b]Ezek. 40:6
18 [I]Heb., *YHWH*, usually rendered *LORD*, and so throughout the ch. [a]Ezek. 2:1 [b]Ex. 40:29 [c]Lev. 1:5, 11; Heb. 9:21, 22
19 [a]1Kin. 2:35; Ezek. 40:46; 44:15 [b]Num. 16:5, 40 [c]Lev. 4:3; Ezek. 43:23; 45:18 [d]Ezek. 45:19; Heb. 7:27
20 [a]Lev. 8:15; 9:9; Ezek. 43:15 [b]Ezek. 43:14, 17 [c]Lev. 16:19; Ezek. 43:22, 26
21 [a]Ex. 29:14; Lev. 4:12; Heb. 13:11
22 [a]Ezek. 43:25 [b]Ezek. 43:20, 26
23 [a]Ex. 29:1, 10; Ezek. 45:18 [b]Ex. 29:1
24 [a]Lev. 2:13; Num. 18:19; Mark 9:49, 50; Col. 4:6
25 [a]Ex. 29:35-37; Lev. 8:33, 35
26 [I]Lit., *fill its hands*
27 [I]Lit., *make* [a]Lev. 9:1 [b]Lev. 3:1; 17:5 [c]Ezek. 20:40

1 [a]Ezek. 40:6, 17; 42:14
2 [a]Ezek. 43:2-4
3 [I]Lit., *by his way* [a]Ezek. 34:24; 37:25 [b]Gen. 31:54; Ex. 24:9-11 [c]Ezek. 46:2, 8-10 [d]Ezek. 40:9
4 [a]Ezek. 40:20, 40 [b]Is. 6:3, 4; Ezek. 1:28; 3:23; 43:4, 5; Hag. 2:7 [c]Ezek. 1:28; 43:3
5 [I]Lit., *set your heart on* [a]Deut. 32:46; Ezek. 40:4 [b]Deut. 12:32; Ezek. 43:10, 11

[I][a]rebellious ones,[4805] to the house of Israel, 'Thus says[559] the Lord[136] [II]GOD, "[b]Enough of all your abominations,[8441] O house of Israel,

7 when you brought in [a]foreigners, [b]uncircumcised[6189] in heart[3820] and uncircumcised in flesh, to be in My sanctuary to profane[2490] it, *even* My house, when you [c]offered[7126] My food, the fat and the blood;[1818] for they [d]made[6565] My covenant[1285] void—[6565] *this* in addition to all your abominations.

8 "And you have not [a]kept[8104] charge[4931] of My holy things[6944] yourselves, but you have set[7760] *foreigners* [I]to keep charge of My sanctuary."

9 'Thus says the Lord GOD, "[a]No foreigner,[5236] uncircumcised in heart and uncircumcised in flesh, of all the foreigners who are among the sons[1121] of Israel, shall enter My sanctuary.

10 "But the Levites who went far from Me, when Israel went astray, who [a]went astray from Me after their idols,[1544] shall [b]bear[5375] the punishment for their iniquity.[5771]

11 "Yet they shall be [a]ministers[8334] in My sanctuary, having [b]oversight at the gates of the house and [c]ministering[8334] in the house; they shall [d]slaughter[7819] the burnt offering[5930] and the sacrifice for the people,[5971] and they shall [e]stand before them to minister[8334] to them.

12 "Because they ministered[8334] to them [a]before their idols and became a [b]stumbling block[4383] of iniquity to the house of Israel, therefore I have [I][c]sworn[5375,3027] against them," declares[5001] the Lord GOD, "that they shall [d]bear the punishment for their iniquity.

13 "And they shall [a]not come near to Me to serve as a priest[3547] to Me, nor come near[5066] to any of My holy things, to the things that are most holy;[6944] but they shall [b]bear their shame and their abominations which they have committed.[6213]

14 "Yet I will [I]appoint them [II]to [a]keep charge of the house, of all its service,[5656] and of all that shall be done[6213] in it.

Ordinances for the Levites

15 "But the [a]Levitical priests,[3548] the sons[1121] of [b]Zadok, who [c]kept charge of My sanctuary when the sons of Israel [d]went astray from Me, shall come near[7126] to Me to minister to Me; and they shall [e]stand before Me to offer Me the [f]fat and the blood," declares the Lord GOD.

16 "They shall [a]enter My sanctuary; they shall come near to My [b]table to minister to Me and keep[8104] My charge.

17 "And it shall be that when they enter at the gates of the inner court, they shall be clothed with [a]linen garments; and wool shall not [I]be on them while they are ministering in the gates of the inner court and in the house.[1004]

18 "Linen [a]turbans shall be on their heads,[7218] and [b]linen undergarments shall be on their loins; they shall not gird themselves with *anything which makes them* sweat.

19 "And when they go out into the outer court, into the outer court to the people, they shall [a]put off their garments in which they have been ministering and lay them in the holy chambers; then they shall put on other garments that they may [b]not transmit holiness[6942] to the people with their garments.

20 "Also they shall [a]not shave their heads, yet they shall not [b]let their locks [I]grow long; they shall only trim *the hair of* their heads.

21 "[a]Nor shall any of the priests[3548] drink wine when they enter the inner court.

22 "And they shall not [I]marry a widow or a [a]divorced woman but shall [b]take virgins[1330] from the offspring[2233] of the house of Israel, or a widow who is the widow of a priest.

23 "Moreover, they shall teach[3384]

6 [I]Lit., *rebellion* [II]Heb., *YHWH*, usually rendered LORD, and so throughout the ch. [a]Ezek. 2:5-7; 3:9 [b]Ezek. 45:9; 1Pet. 4:3
7 [a]Ex. 12:43-49 [b]Lev. 26:41; Deut. 10:16; Jer. 4:4; 9:26 [c]Lev. 22:25 [d]Gen. 17:14
8 [I]Lit., *as keepers of My charge in My* [a]Lev. 22:2; Num. 18:7
9 [a]Ezek. 44:7; Joel 3:17; Zech. 14:21
10 [a]2Kin. 23:8, 9; Ezek. 22:26; 44:12 [b]Num. 18:23
11 [a]Num. 3:5-37; 4:1-33; 18:2-7 [b]1Chr. 26:1-19 [c]Ezek. 40:45; 44:14 [d]2Chr. 29:34; 30:17 [e]Num. 16:9
12 [I]Lit., *lifted up My hand* [a]2Kin. 16:10-16 [b]Ezek. 14:3, 4 [c]Ezek. 20:15, 23 [d]Ezek. 44:10
13 [a]Num. 18:3 [b]Ezek. 16:61, 63; 39:26
14 [I]Lit., *give* [II]Lit., *keepers of the charge* [a]Num. 18:4; 1Chr. 23:28-32; Ezek. 44:11
15 [a]Jer. 33:18-22 [b]Ezek. 40:46; 43:19; 48:11 [c]Num. 18:7; Ezek. 40:45 [d]Ezek. 44:10; 48:11 [e]Zech. 3:1, 7 [f]Lev. 3:16, 17; 17:5, 6; Ezek. 44:7
16 [a]Num. 18:5, 7, 8 [b]Ezek. 41:22; Mal. 1:7, 12
17 [I]Lit., *come upon* [a]Ex. 28:42, 43; 39:27-29; Rev. 19:8
18 [a]Ex. 28:40; Is. 3:20; Ezek. 24:17, 23 [b]Ex. 28:42; Lev. 16:4
19 [a]Lev. 6:10; 16:4, 23, 24; Ezek. 42:14 [b]Lev. 6:27; Ezek. 46:20
20 [I]Or, *hang loose* [a]Lev. 21:5 [b]Num. 6:5
21 [a]Lev. 10:9 **22** [I]Lit., *take as wives for themselves* [a]Lev. 21:7, 14 [b]Lev. 21:13

My people *the* [a]*difference* between the holy and the profane,[2455] and cause them to discern[3045] between the unclean[2931] and the clean.

24 "And in a dispute[7379] [a]they shall take their stand to judge;[8199] they shall judge[8199] it according to My ordinances. They shall also keep My laws and My statutes[2708] in all My [b]appointed feasts,[4150] and [c]sanctify[6942] My sabbaths.[7676]

25 "And [Ia]they shall not go to a dead[4191] person to defile[2930] *themselves;* however, for father,[1] for mother,[517] for son, for daughter, for brother,[251] or for a sister[269] who has not had a husband,[376] they may defile themselves.

26 "And after he is [a]cleansed,[2893] seven days[3117] shall [I]elapse[5608] for him.

27 "And on the day[3117] that he goes into the sanctuary,[6944] into the [a]inner court to minister in the sanctuary, he shall offer his [b]sin offering,"[2403] declares the Lord GOD.

28 "And it shall be with regard to an inheritance[5159] for them, *that* [a]I am their inheritance; and you shall give them no possession[272] in Israel—I am their possession.

29 "They shall [a]eat the grain offering,[4503] the sin offering, and the guilt offering;[817] and every [Ib]devoted thing[2764] in Israel shall be theirs.

30 "And the first[7225] of all the [a]first fruits of every kind and every [I]contribution[8641] of every kind, from all your [I]contributions,[8641] shall be for the priests;[3548] you shall also give to the priest the [b]first of your [II]dough to cause a [c]blessing[1293] to rest on your house.

31 "The priests shall not eat any bird or beast that has [a]died a natural death[5038][3605] or has been torn to pieces.

The Lord's Portion of the Land

45 "And when you shall [a]divide by lot[5307] the land[776] for inheritance,[5159] you shall offer [I]an [b]allotment[8641] to the LORD, a [c]holy portion[6944] of the land; the length shall be the length of 25,000 [d]*cubits,* and the width shall be [II]10,000. It shall be holy within all its boundary round about.

2 "Out of this there shall be for the holy place[6944] a square round about [a]five hundred by five hundred *cubits,* and fifty cubits for its [Ib]open space round about.

3 "And from this [I]area you shall measure a length[753] of 25,000 *cubits,* and a width of 10,000 *cubits;* and in it shall be the sanctuary,[4720] the most holy[6944] place.

4 "It shall be the holy portion of the land; it shall be for the [a]priests,[3548] the ministers[8334] of the sanctuary, who [b]come near to minister[8334] to the LORD, and it shall be a place for their houses[1004] and a holy place for the sanctuary.

5 "And *an area* [a]25,000 *cubits* in length and 10,000 in width shall be for the Levites, the ministers of the house,[1004] *and* for their possession[272] [I]cities to dwell in.

6 "And you shall give the [a]city possession of *an area* 5,000 *cubits* wide and 25,000 *cubits* long,[753] alongside the [I]allotment of the holy portion; it shall be for the whole house of Israel.

Portion for the Prince

7 "And the [a]prince[5387] shall have *land* on either side of the holy[6944] [I]allotment and the [II]property of the city, adjacent to the holy [I]allotment and the [II]property of the city, on the west side toward the west and on the east side toward the east, and in length comparable to one of the portions, from the west border to the east border.

8 "This shall be his land for a possession in Israel; so My princes[5387] shall no longer [a]oppress[3238] My people,[5971] but they shall give *the rest of* the land to the house of Israel [b]according to their tribes."[7626]

9 'Thus says[5001] the Lord[136] [I]GOD, "[a]Enough, you princes of Israel; put away [b]violence[2555] and destruction,[7701]

23 [a]Lev. 10:10; Ezek. 22:26; Hos. 4:6; Mic. 3:9-11; Zeph. 3:4; Hag. 2:11-13; Mal. 2:6-8
24 [a]Deut. 17:8, 9; 19:17; 21:5; 1Chr. 23:4; 2Chr. 19:8-10 [b]Lev. 23:2, 4, 44 [c]Ezek. 20:12, 20
25 [I]Lit., *he* [a]Lev. 21:1-4
26 [I]Lit., *be counted* [a]Num. 19:13-19
27 [a]Ezek. 44:17 [b]Lev. 5:3, 6; Num. 6:9-11
28 [a]Num. 18:20; Deut. 10:9; 18:1, 2; Josh. 13:33
29 [I]Or, *dedicated* [a]Num. 18:9, 14; Josh. 13:14 [b]Lev. 27:21, 28; Num. 18:14
30 [I]Or, *heave offering(s)* [II]Or, *coarse meal* [a]Num. 18:12, 13; 2Chr. 31:4-6, 10; Neh. 10:35-37 [b]Num. 15:20, 21 [c]Mal. 3:10
31 [a]Lev. 22:8; Deut. 14:21; Ezek. 4:14

1 [I]Or, *a contribution* [II]Or, with Gr., *20,000* [a]Num. 34:13; Josh. 13:7; 14:3; Ezek. 47:21; 48:29 [b]Ezek. 48:8, 9 [c]Zech. 14:20, 21 [d]Ezek. 42:16; 45:2
2 [I]Or, *pasture land* [a]Ezek. 42:20 [b]Ezek. 27:28
3 [I]Lit., *measure*
4 [a]Ezek. 48:10, 11 [b]Num. 16:5; Ezek. 40:45; 43:19
5 [I]So with Gr.; M.T., *twenty chambers* [a]Ezek. 48:13
6 [I]Or, *contribution* [a]Ezek. 48:15-18, 30-35
7 [I]Or, *contribution* [II]Lit., *possession* [a]Ezek. 34:24; 37:24; 46:16-18; 48:21
8 [a]Is. 11:3-5; Jer. 23:5; Ezek. 19:7; 22:27; 46:18 [b]Josh. 11:23
9 [I]Heb., *YHWH,* usually rendered *LORD,* and so throughout the ch. [a]Ezek. 44:6 [b]Jer. 6:7; Ezek. 7:11, 23; 8:17

and [c]practice justice[4941] and righteousness.[6666] Stop your [d]expropriations from My people," declares[559] the Lord GOD.

10 "You shall have [a]just[6664] balances, a just [b]ephah, and a just [c]bath.

11 "The ephah and the bath shall be [I]the same quantity, so that the bath may contain a tenth[4643] of a [a]homer,2563 and the ephah a tenth of a homer; [II]their standard shall be according to the homer.

12 "And the [a]shekel shall be twenty [b]gerahs;1626 twenty shekels, twenty-five shekels, *and* fifteen shekels shall be your [I]maneh.4488

13 "This is the offering that you shall offer: a sixth of an ephah from a homer of wheat; a sixth of an ephah from a homer of barley;

14 and the prescribed portion[2706] of oil[8081] (*namely,* the bath of oil), a tenth of a bath from *each* kor (*which is* ten baths *or* a homer, for ten baths are a homer);

15 and one sheep from *each* flock of two hundred from the watering places of Israel—for a [a]grain offering,[4503] for a burnt offering,[5930] and for peace offerings,[8002] to [b]make atonement[3722] for them," declares the Lord GOD.

16 "'[a]All the people of the land shall [I]give to this offering for the [b]prince in Israel.

17 "And it shall be the [a]prince's part *to provide* the [b]burnt offerings,[5930] the grain offerings,[4503] and the libations,[5262] at the [c]feasts,[2282] on the [d]new moons, and on the sabbaths,[7676] at all the appointed feasts[4150] of the house of Israel; he shall provide[3559] the sin offering,[2403] the grain offering, the burnt offering,[5930] and the [e]peace offerings, to make atonement for the house of Israel."

18 'Thus says the Lord GOD, "In the [a]first[7223] *month,* on the first of the month, you shall take a young bull [b]without blemish[8549] and [c]cleanse[2398] the sanctuary.

19 "And the priest[3548] shall take some of the blood[1818] from the sin offering and put *it* on the door posts of the house, on the [a]four corners of the [b]ledge of the altar,[4196] and on the posts of the gate of the inner court.

20 "And thus you shall do[6213] on the seventh *day* of the month for everyone[376] who goes [a]astray[7686] or is [I]naive; so you shall make [b]atonement[3722] for the house.

21 "In the [a]first[7223] *month,* on the fourteenth day[3117] of the month, you shall have the [b]Passover,[6453] a feast[2282] of seven days;[3117] unleavened[4682] bread shall be eaten.

22 "And on that day the prince shall provide for himself and all the people of the land a [a]bull for a sin offering.

23 "And *during* the [a]seven days of the feast he shall provide as a [b]burnt offering to the LORD [c]seven bulls and seven rams without blemish on every day[3117] of the seven days, and a male goat[8163] daily for a sin offering.

24 "And he shall provide as a [a]grain offering an ephah [I]with a bull, an ephah [I]with a ram, and a hin of oil [I]with an ephah.

25 "In the [a]seventh *month,* on the fifteenth day of the month, at the feast, he shall provide like this, seven days [I]for the sin offering, the burnt offering, the grain offering, and the oil."

The Prince's Offerings

46 'Thus says[559] the Lord[136] [I]GOD, "The [a]gate of the [b]inner court facing[1870] east shall be [c]shut the six [d]working days;[3117] but it shall be opened on the [e]sabbath[7676] day, and opened on the day[3117] of the [f]new moon.

2 "And the [a]prince[5387] shall enter by way[1870] of the porch of the gate from outside and stand by the [b]post of the gate. Then the priests[3548] shall provide[3559] his burnt offering[5930] and his peace offerings,[8002] and he shall worship[7812] at the threshold of the gate and then go out; but the gate shall not be [c]shut until the evening.

3 "The [a]people[5971] of the land[776] shall also worship at the doorway of that

9 [c]Jer. 22:3; Zech. 8:16 [d]Neh. 5:1-5
10 [a]Lev. 19:36; Deut. 25:15; Prov. 16:11; Amos 8:4-6; Mic. 6:10, 11 [b]Is. 5:10
11 [I]Lit., *one* [II]Lit., *its measure* [a]Is. 5:10
12 [I]Or, *mina* [a]Ex. 30:13; Lev. 27:25; Num. 3:47
15 [a]Ezek. 45:17 [b]Lev. 1:4; 6:30
16 [I]Lit., *be* [a]Ex. 30:14, 15 [b]Is. 16:1
17 [a]Ezek. 46:4-12 [b]1Kin. 8:64; 1Chr. 16:2; 2Chr. 31:3 [c]Lev. 23:1-44; Num. 28:1-29:39 [d]Is. 66:23 [e]1Kin. 8:63; Ezek. 43:27
18 [a]Ex. 12:2 [b]Lev. 22:20; Heb. 9:14 [c]Lev. 16:16, 33; Ezek. 43:22, 26
19 [a]Lev. 16:18-20; Ezek. 43:20 [b]Ezek. 43:14, 17, 20
20 [I]Lit., *simple* [a]Lev. 4:27; Ps. 19:12 [b]Lev. 16:20; Ezek. 45:15, 18
21 [a]Num. 28:16f. [b]Ex. 12:1-24; Lev. 23:5-8
22 [a]Lev. 4:14
23 [a]Lev. 23:8 [b]Num. 28:16-25 [c]Num. 23:1, 2; Job 42:8
24 [I]Lit., *for* [a]Num. 28:12-15; Ezek. 46:5-7
25 [I]Lit., *according to* [a]Lev. 23:33-43; Num. 29:12-38; 2Chr. 5:3; 7:8, 10

1 [I]Heb., *YHWH,* usually rendered *LORD,* and so throughout the ch. [a]Ezek. 45:19 [b]Ezek. 8:16; 10:3 [c]Ezek. 44:1, 2 [d]Ex. 20:9 [e]Is. 66:23; Ezek. 45:17 [f]Ezek. 45:18; 46:3, 6
2 [a]Ezek. 44:3; 46:8 [b]Ezek. 45:19 [c]Ezek. 46:12
3 [a]Luke 1:10

gate before the LORD on the sabbaths[7676]
and on the [b]new moons.
4 "And the [a]burnt offering which the
prince shall offer[7126] to the LORD on the
sabbath day shall be [b]six lambs without
blemish[8549] and a ram without blemish;
5 and the [a]grain offering[4503] shall be
an ephah [I]with the ram, and the grain
offering [I]with the lambs [II]as much as
he is [b]able[3027] to give, and a hin of oil[8081]
[I]with an ephah.
6 "And on the day of the [a]new moon
he shall offer a young bull without blemish, also six lambs and a ram, *which*
shall be without blemish.
7 "And he shall provide a [a]grain offering, an ephah [I]with the bull, and an
ephah [I]with the ram, and [I]with the lambs
as [II]much as he is [b]able, and a hin of
oil [I]with an ephah.
8 "And when the [a]prince enters, he
shall go in by way of the porch of the
gate and go out [I]by the same way.
9 "But when the people of the land
come [a]before the LORD at the appointed
feasts,[4150] he who enters by way of the
north gate to worship shall go out by
way of the south gate. And he who enters by way of the south gate shall go
out by way of the north gate. [I]No one
shall return[7725] by way of the gate by
which he entered but shall go straight
out.
10 "And when they go in, the prince
shall go in [a]among them; and when they
go out, [I]he shall go out.
11 "And at the [a]festivals[2282] and the
appointed feasts[4150] the [b]grain offering
shall be an ephah [I]with a bull and an
ephah [I]with a ram, and [I]with the lambs
as [II]much as one is able to give, and a
hin of oil [I]with an ephah.
12 "And when the prince provides
a [a]freewill offering,[5071] a burnt offering,
or peace offerings[8002] *as* a freewill
offering[5071] to the LORD, the gate facing
east shall be [b]opened for him. And he
shall provide his burnt offering and his
peace offerings as he does[6213] on the
[c]sabbath day. Then he shall go out, and
the gate shall be shut after he goes out.
13 "And you shall provide a [a]lamb
a year old[1121,8141] without blemish for a
burnt offering to the LORD daily;[3117]
[b]morning by morning you shall provide
it.
14 "Also you shall provide a grain
offering[4503] with it morning by morning,
a [a]sixth of an ephah, and a third of a
hin of oil to moisten the fine flour, a
grain offering to the LORD continually[8548]
by a perpetual[5769] [I]ordinance.[2708]
15 "Thus they shall provide the
lamb, the grain offering, and the oil,
morning by morning, for a [a]continual
burnt offering."
16 'Thus says the Lord GOD, "If
the prince gives a [a]gift *out of* his
inheritance[5159] to any of his sons,[1121] it
shall belong to his sons; it is their
possession[272] by inheritance.
17 "But if he gives a gift from his
inheritance to one of his servants,[5650]
it shall be his until the [a]year of liberty;
then it shall return to the prince. His
inheritance *shall be* only his sons'; it shall
belong to them.
18 "And the prince shall [a]not take
from the people's[5971] inheritance,[5159]
[I][b]thrusting them out of[3238] their possession; he shall give his sons inheritance
from his own possession so that My
people shall not be scattered, anyone[376]
from his possession." ' "

The Boiling Places

19 Then he brought me through the
[a]entrance, which *was* at the side of the
gate, into the holy[6944] chambers for
the priests, which faced north; and behold, there *was* a place at the extreme
rear toward the west.
20 And he said[559] to me, "This is
the place where the priests shall boil
the [a]guilt offering[817] and the sin offering,[2403] *and* where they shall [b]bake the
grain offering, in order that they may
not bring *them* out into the outer court
to transmit holiness[6942] to the people."
21 Then he brought me out into the
outer court and led me across to the
four corners of the court; and behold,

3 [b]Ezek. 46:1
4 [a]Ezek. 45:17 [b]Num. 28:9
5 [I]Lit., *for* [II]Lit., *a gift of his hand* [a]Num. 28:12; Ezek. 45:24; 46:7, 11 [b]Ezek. 46:7
6 [a]Ezek. 46:1
7 [I]Lit., *for* [II]Lit., *his hand can reach* [a]Ezek. 46:5 [b]Lev. 14:21; Deut. 16:17; Ezek. 46:5
8 [I]Lit., *by its way* [a]Ezek. 44:3; 46:2
9 [I]Lit., *He shall not* [a]Ex. 34:23; Ps. 84:7; Mic. 6:6
10 [I]So with many mss. and the ancient versions; M.T., *they* [a]2Sam. 6:14, 15; 1Chr. 29:20, 22; 2Chr. 6:3; 7:4; Ps. 42:4
11 [I]Lit., *for* [II]Lit., *a gift of his hand* [a]Ezek. 45:17 [b]Ezek. 46:5, 7
12 [a]Lev. 23:38; 2Chr. 29:31 [b]Ezek. 44:3; 46:1, 2, 8 [c]Ezek. 45:17
13 [a]Num. 28:3-5 [b]Is. 50:4
14 [I]Lit., *statute* [a]Num. 28:5
15 [a]Ex. 29:42; Num. 28:6
16 [a]2Chr. 21:3
17 [a]Lev. 25:10
18 [I]Lit., *oppressing* [a]Ezek. 45:8 [b]1Kin. 21:19; Ezek. 22:27; Mic. 2:1,2
19 [a]Ezek. 42:9; 44:5
20 [a]2Chr. 35:13; Ezek. 44:29 [b]Lev. 2:4-7

in every corner of the court *there was*
a *small* court.
22 In the four corners of the court
there were enclosed courts, forty *cubits*
long[753] and thirty wide; these four in
the corners *were* [I]the same size.
23 And *there was* a row *of masonry*
round about in them, around the four
of them, and boiling places were
made[6213] under the rows round about.
24 Then he said to me, "These are
the boiling [I]places[1004] where the ministers[8334] of the house[1004] shall boil the
sacrifices of the people."

Water from the Temple

47 Then he brought me back to the
[a]door of the house;[1004] and behold, [b]water was flowing from under the
threshold of the house toward the east,
for the house faced east. And the water
was flowing down from under, from the
right side of the house, from south of
the altar.[4196]
2 And he brought me out by way[1870]
of the north gate and led me around
[I]on the outside to the outer gate by way
of *the gate* that faces east. And behold,
water was trickling from the south side.
3 When the man went out toward
the east with a line in his hand,[3027] he
measured a thousand cubits, and he led
me through the water, water *reaching*
the ankles.
4 Again he measured a thousand and
led me through the water, water *reaching* the knees. Again he measured a
thousand and led me through *the water,*
water *reaching* the loins.
5 Again he measured a thousand;
and it was a river that I could not
ford,[5674] for the water had risen,[1342]
enough water to swim in, a [a]river that
could not be forded.[5674]
6 And he said[559] to me, "Son[1121] of
man,[120] have you [a]seen[7200] *this?*" Then
he brought me [I]back[7725] to the bank[8193]
of the river.
7 Now when I had returned,[7725] behold, on the bank[8193] of the river there
were very many [a]trees on the one side
and on the other.
8 Then he said to me, "These waters go out toward the eastern region
and go down into the [a]Arabah;[6160] then
they go toward the sea, being made to
flow into the [b]sea, and the waters *of
the sea* become [I]fresh.
9 "And it will come about that every
living[2416] creature which swarms in
every place where the [I]river goes, will
live.[2421] And there will be very many
fish,[1710] for these waters go there, and
the others [II]become fresh; so [a]everything
will live[2425] where the river goes.
10 "And it will come about that
[a]fishermen will stand beside it; from
[b]Engedi to Eneglaim there will be a place
for the [c]spreading of nets.[2764] Their fish
will be according to their kinds, like the
fish of the [d]Great Sea, [e]very many.
11 "But its swamps[1207] and marshes
will not become [I]fresh; they will be
[II]left for [a]salt.
12 "And [a]by the river on its bank,
on one side and on the other, will grow
all *kinds of* [b]trees for food. Their
[c]leaves will not wither, and their fruit
will not fail.[8552] They will bear every
month because their water flows from
the sanctuary,[4720] and their fruit will be
for food and their [d]leaves for healing."

Boundaries and Division of the Land

13 Thus says[559] the Lord[136]
[I]GOD, "This *shall be* the [a]boundary by
which you shall divide[5157] the land[776] for
an inheritance among the twelve
tribes[7626] of Israel; Joseph *shall have*
two [b]portions.[2256]
14 "And you shall divide it for
an inheritance,[3423] each one[376] [I]equally
with the other; for I [IIa]swore[5375] to give
it to your forefathers,[1] and this land shall
fall to you [III]as an inheritance.[5159]
15 "And this *shall be* the boundary
of the land: on the [a]north side, from
the Great Sea *by* the way of Hethlon,
to the entrance of [Ib]Zedad;
16 [Ia]Hamath, Berothah, Sibraim,

22 [I]Lit., *one measure*
24 [I]Lit., *houses*
1 [a]Ezek. 41:2, 23-25 [b]Ps. 46:4; Is. 30:25; 55:1; Jer. 2:13; Joel 3:18; Zech. 13:1; 14:8; Rev. 22:1, 17
2 [I]Lit., *by way of*
5 [a]Is. 11:9; Hab. 2:14
6 [I]Lit., *and caused me to return* [a]Ezek. 8:6; 40:4; 44:5
7 [a]Is. 60:13, 21; 61:3; Ezek. 47:12
8 [I]Lit., *healed* [a]Deut. 3:17; Is. 35:6, 7; 41:17-19; 44:3 [b]Josh. 3:16
9 [I]Lit., *two rivers* [II]Lit., *are healed* [a]Is. 12:3; 55:1; John 4:14; 7:37, 38
10 [a]Matt. 4:19; 13:47; Luke 5:10 [b]Gen. 14:7; Josh. 15:62; 1Sam. 23:29; 24:1; 2Chr. 20:2 [c]Ezek. 26:5, 14 [d]Num. 34:6; Ps. 104:25; Ezek. 47:15; 48:28 [e]Luke 5:5-9; John 21:6
11 [I]Lit., *healed* [II]Lit., *given* [a]Deut. 29:23
12 [a]Ezek. 47:7; Rev. 22:2 [b]Gen. 2:9 [c]Ps. 1:3; Jer. 17:8 [d]Rev. 22:2
13 [I]Heb., *YHWH,* usually rendered LORD, and so throughout the ch. [a]Num. 34:2-12 [b]Gen. 48:5; Ezek. 48:4, 5
14 [I]Lit., *like his brother* [II]Lit., *lifted up My hand* [III]Lit., *in* [a]Deut. 1:8; Ezek. 20:6
15 [I]Or, *Hamath* [a]Num. 34:7-9 [b]Num. 34:8
16 [I]Or, *Zedad* [a]Num. 13:21; Is. 10:9; Ezek. 47:17, 20; 48:1; Zech. 9:2

which is between the border of [b]Damas-
cus and the border of Hamath; Hazer-
hatticon, which is by the border of Hauran.
17 "And the boundary shall [I]extend
from the sea *to* [a]Hazar-enan *at* the border of Damascus, and on the north toward the north is the border of Hamath.
This is the north side.
18 "And the [a]east side, from between Hauran, Damascus, [b]Gilead, and
the land of Israel, *shall be* the [c]Jordan;
from the *north* border to the eastern
sea you shall measure. This is the east
side.
19 "And the [a]south side toward the
south *shall extend* from [b]Tamar as far
as the waters of [c]Meribath-kadesh, to
the [d]brook *of Egypt, and* to the [e]Great
Sea. This is the south side toward the
south.
20 "And the [a]west side *shall be* the
Great Sea, from the *south* border to a
point opposite [I][b]Lebo-hamath. This is
the west side.
21 "So you shall divide this land
among yourselves according to the
tribes of Israel.
22 "And it will come about that you
shall divide it by [a]lot for an inheritance
among yourselves and among the
[b]aliens[1616] who stay[1481] in your midst,
who bring forth sons[1121] in your midst.
And they shall be to you as the native-
born among the sons of Israel; they shall
be allotted an [c]inheritance with you
among the tribes of Israel.
23 "And it will come about that in
the tribe with which the alien[1616]
stays,[1481] there you shall give *him* his
inheritance," declares[5001] the Lord GOD.

Division of the Land

48 "Now [a]these are the names of
the tribes:[7626] from the northern
extremity, [I]beside the way[1870] of Hethlon to [II]Lebo-hamath, *as far as* Hazar-
enan *at* the border of Damascus, toward
the north [I]beside Hamath, [III]running
from east to west, [b]Dan, one *portion.*
2 "And beside the border of Dan,
from the east side to the west side,
[a]Asher, one *portion.*
3 "And beside the border of Asher,
from the east side to the west side,
[a]Naphtali, one *portion.*
4 "And beside the border of Naphtali, from the east side to the west side,
[a]Manasseh, one *portion.*
5 "And beside the border of Manasseh, from the east side to the west side,
[a]Ephraim, one *portion.*
6 "And beside the border of
Ephraim, from the east side to the west
side, [a]Reuben, one *portion.*
7 "And beside the border of Reuben, from the east side to the west side,
[a]Judah, one *portion.*
8 "And beside the border of Judah,
from the east side to the west side,
shall be the [I]allotment[8641] which you shall
[II]set apart, 25,000 [III]*cubits* in width, and
in length like one of the portions, from
the east side to the west side; and the
[a]sanctuary[4720] shall be in the middle of
it.
9 "The allotment[8641] that you shall
set apart to the LORD *shall be* 25,000
cubits in length, and 10,000 in width.

Portion for the Priests

10 "And the holy[6944] allotment shall
be for these, *namely* for the [a]priests,[3548]
toward the north 25,000 *cubits in length,*
toward the west 10,000 in width, toward
the east 10,000 in width, and toward
the south 25,000 in length; and the
sanctuary of the LORD shall be in its
midst.
11 "*It shall be* for the priests who
are sanctified[6942] of the [a]sons[1121] of Zadok, who have kept[8104] My charge,[4931]
who did not go astray when the sons[1121]
of Israel went astray, as the [b]Levites
went astray.
12 "And it shall be an allotment to
them from the allotment[8642] of the
land,[776] a most holy place,[6944] by the
border of the Levites.
13 "And alongside the border of the

16 [b]Gen. 14:15; Ezek. 47:17, 18; 48:1
17 [I]Lit., *be* [a]Num. 34:9
18 [a]Num. 34:10-12 [b]Gen. 37:25; Jer. 50:19 [c]Gen. 13:10, 11
19 [a]Num. 34:3-5 [b]Ezek. 48:28 [c]Deut. 32:51 [d]Num. 34:5; 1Kin. 8:65; Is. 27:12 [e]Ezek. 47:10, 15
20 [I]Or, *entrance of Hamath* [a]Num. 34:6 [b]Judg. 3:3; 2Chr. 7:8; Ezek. 48:1; Amos 6:14
22 [a]Num. 26:55, 56 [b]Is. 14:1; 56:6, 7 [c]Acts 11:18; 15:9; Eph. 2:12-14; 3:6; Col. 3:11
1 [I]Lit., *at the hand of* [II]Or, *the entrance of Hamath* [III]Lit., *and there shall be to it an east and west side* [a]Ex. 1:1 [b]Josh. 19:40-48
2 [a]Josh. 19:24-31
3 [a]Josh. 19:32-39
4 [a]Josh. 13:29-31; 17:1-11
5 [a]Josh. 16:5-9; 17:8-10, 14-18
6 [a]Josh. 13:15-21
7 [a]Josh. 15:1-63; 19:9
8 [I]Or, *contribution,* and so throughout the ch. [II]Lit., *offer* [III]Or possibly, *reeds,* and so throughout the ch. [a]Is. 12:6; 33:20-22; Ezek. 45:3, 4
10 [a]Ezek. 44:28; 45:4
11 [a]Ezek. 40:46; 44:15 [b]Ezek. 44:10, 12

priests the Levites *shall have* 25,000 *cubits* in length and 10,000 in width. The whole length *shall be* 25,000 *cubits* and the width 10,000.

14 "Moreover, they [a]shall not sell or exchange any of it, or alienate[5674] this [I]choice *portion*[7225] of land; for it is holy to the LORD.

15 "And the remainder,[3498] 5,000 *cubits* in width and 25,000 [I]in length, shall be for [a]common[2455] use for the city, for dwellings[4186] and for [II]open spaces; and the city shall be in its midst.

16 "And these *shall be* its measurements: the north side 4,500 *cubits,* the south side [a]4,500 *cubits,* the east side 4,500 *cubits,* and the west side 4,500 *cubits.*

17 "And the city shall have [I]open spaces: on the north 250 *cubits,* on the south 250 *cubits,* on the east 250 *cubits,* and on the west 250 *cubits.*

18 "And the remainder[3498] of the length alongside the holy[6944] allotment shall be 10,000 *cubits* toward the east, and 10,000 toward the west; and it shall be [I]alongside the holy allotment. And its produce shall be food for the workers[5647] of the city.

19 "And the workers of the city, out of all the tribes of Israel, shall cultivate it.

20 "The whole allotment *shall be* 25,000 by 25,000 *cubits;* you shall [I]set apart the holy allotment, a [II]square, with the [III]property[272] of the city.

Portion for the Prince

21 "And the [a]remainder *shall be* for the prince,[5387] on the one side and on the other of the holy allotment and of the [I]property of the city; in front of the 25,000 *cubits* of the allotment toward the east border and westward in front of the 25,000 toward the west border, alongside the portions, *it shall be* for the prince. And the holy allotment and the sanctuary of the house[1004] shall be in the middle of it.

22 "And exclusive of the [I]property of the Levites and the [I]property of the city, *which* are in the middle of that which belongs to the prince, *everything* between the border of Judah and the border of Benjamin shall be for the prince.

Portion for Other Tribes

23 "As for the rest[3499] of the tribes: from the east side to the west side, [a]Benjamin, one *portion.*

24 "And beside the border of Benjamin, from the east side to the west side, [a]Simeon, one *portion.*

25 "And beside the border of Simeon, from the east side to the west side, [a]Issachar, one *portion.*

26 "And beside the border of Issachar, from the east side to the west side, [a]Zebulun, one *portion.*

27 "And beside the border of Zebulun, from the east side to the west side, [a]Gad, one *portion.*

28 "And beside the border of Gad, at the south side toward the south, the border shall be from [a]Tamar to the waters of Meribath-kadesh, to the brook *of Egypt,* to the [b]Great Sea.

29 "This is the [a]land which you shall divide by lot[5307] to the tribes of Israel for an inheritance,[5159] and these are their *several* portions," declares[5001] the Lord[136] [I]GOD.

The City Gates

30 "And these are the exits of the city: on the [a]north side, 4,500 *cubits* by measurement,

31 [I]shall be the gates of the city, [IIa]named for the tribes of Israel, three gates toward the north: the gate of Reuben, one; the gate of Judah, one; the gate of Levi, one.

32 "And on the east side, 4,500 *cubits,* [I]shall be three gates: the gate of Joseph, one; the gate of Benjamin, one; the gate of Dan, one.

33 "And on the south side, 4,500 *cubits* by measurement, [I]shall be three gates: the gate of Simeon, one; the gate

14 [I]Lit., *first* or *first fruits* [a]Lev. 25:32-34; 27:10, 28, 33
15 [I]Lit., *in front* [II]Or, *pasture land* [a]Ezek. 42:20; 45:6
16 [a]Rev. 21:16
17 [I]Or, *pasture land*
18 [I]Or, *exactly as*
20 [I]Lit., *offer* [II]Lit., *fourth* [III]Or, *possession*
21 [I]Or, *possession* [a]Ezek. 34:24; 45:7; 48:22
22 [I]Or, *possession*
23 [a]Josh. 18:21-28
24 [a]Josh. 19:1-9
25 [a]Josh. 19:17-23
26 [a]Josh. 19:10-16
27 [a]Josh. 13:24-28
28 [a]Gen. 14:7; 2Chr. 20:2; Ezek. 47:19 [b]Ezek. 47:10, 15, 19, 20
29 [I]Heb., *YHWH,* usually rendered *LORD* [a]Ezek. 47:13-20
30 [a]Ezek. 48:32-34
31 [I]Lit., *and* [II]Lit., *according to the names of* [a]Rev. 21:12, 13
32 [I]Lit., *and*
33 [I]Lit., *and*

of Issachar, one; the gate of Zebulun,
one.
34 "On the west side, 4,500 *cubits,*
shall be three gates: the gate of Gad,
one; the gate of Asher, one; the gate
of Naphtali, one.
35 "*The city shall be* 18,000 *cubits*
round about; and the [a]name of the city
from *that* day[3117] *shall be,* '[1]The [b]LORD
is there.'"

35 [1]Heb., *YHWH-shammah* [a]Jer. 23:6; 33:16 [b]Is. 12:6; 14:32; 24:23; Jer. 3:17; 8:19; 14:9; Ezek. 35:10; Joel 3:21; Zech. 2:10; Rev. 21:3; 22:3

The Book of

DANIEL

Daniel went to Babylon during the first deportation in 606 B.C. He and other members of the Judean royal and noble families were given special training to serve in the Babylonian court. He quickly gained a reputation as an interpreter of dreams and riddles, which led to his appointment to high government posts. As an old man, Daniel served in the Medo-Persian administration after Babylon fell in 539 B.C. He was unlike the other prophets in that he did not go around saying, "Thus says the Lord." Instead, he was primarily an interpreter of dreams and riddles and a recipient of visions himself. The book falls naturally into two parts. In the first six chapters, Daniel spoke in the third person about activities involving himself and his three Jewish companions, and he interpreted dreams and riddles received by others. In chapters 7-12, he spoke in the first person about visions which he himself received. Some of the most well-known stories in the Old Testament are found in Daniel, especially those about Daniel's three friends in the fiery furnace (Dan. 3) and Daniel in the lion's den (Dan. 6). The book has become a modern battleground on two counts. Liberal scholarship places the writing of the book in the middle of the second century B.C., whereas conservatives generally believe it was written by Daniel in the sixth century B.C. Secondly, scholars have been divided on the precise historical identification of features of the visions. The book has many important passages, but Dan. 12:2 stands out as the clearest Old Testament reference to the resurrection of the dead. The key Old Testament passage behind Jesus' application of the term "Son of Man" to himself is Dan. 7:13. Material from every chapter in Daniel is either quoted or alluded to in Revelation, and only two chapters are without some background in Daniel.

The Choice Young Men

1 In the third year of the reign[4438] of [a]Jehoiakim king[4428] of Judah, [b]Nebuchadnezzar king of Babylon came to Jerusalem and besieged it.

2 And the [a]Lord[136] gave Jehoiakim king of Judah into his hand,[3027] along with some of the [b]vessels of the house[1004] of God;[430] and he brought them to the land[776] of [c]Shinar, to the house of his [I]god, and he brought the vessels into the treasury of his [I][d]god.

3 Then the king [I]ordered Ashpenaz, the chief of his [II]officials,[5631] to bring in some of the sons[1121] of Israel, including some of the [III]royal [a]family[2233] and of the nobles,[6579]

4 youths in whom was [a]no defect,[3971] who were good-looking, showing [b]intelligence[7919] in every *branch of* wisdom,[2451] endowed with understanding,[1847] and discerning[995] knowledge,[4093] and who had ability for [I]serving in the king's[4428] [II]court;[1964] and *he ordered him* to teach[3925] them the [III]literature[5612] and [c]language of the [d]Chaldeans.

5 And the king appointed for them a daily[3117] ration from the [a]king's choice food and from the wine which he drank,[4960] and *appointed* that they should be [I]educated three years, at the end of which they were to [II][b]enter the king's personal service.

6 Now among them from the sons of Judah were [a]Daniel, Hananiah, Mishael and Azariah.

7 Then the commander[8269] of the officials assigned *new* names to them; and to Daniel he assigned *the name* [a]Belteshazzar, to Hananiah [b]Shadrach, to Mishael [b]Meshach, and to Azariah [b]Abed-nego.

Daniel's Resolve

8 But Daniel [I]made up[7760] his mind[3820] that he would not [a]defile himself

1 [a]2Kin. 24:1; 2Chr. 36:5, 6 [b]Jer. 25:1; 52:12, 28-30
2 [I]Or, *gods* [a]Is. 42:24; Dan. 2:37, 38 [b]2Chr. 36:7; Jer. 27:19, 20; Dan. 5:2 [c]Gen. 10:10; 11:2; Is. 11:11; Zech. 5:11 [d]Jer. 50:2; 51:44
3 [I]Or, *said to* [II]Or, *eunuchs,* and so throughout the ch. [III]Lit., *seed of the* [a]2Kin. 24:15; Is. 39:7
4 [I]Lit., *standing* [II]Lit., *palace* [III]Or, *writing* [a]2Sam. 14:25 [b]Dan. 1:17 [c]Is. 36:11; Jer. 5:15; Dan. 2:4 [d]Dan. 2:2, 4, 5, 10; 3:8; 4:7; 5:7, 11, 30; 9:1
5 [I]Or, *reared* [II]Lit., *stand before the king* [a]Dan. 1:8 [b]1Sam. 16:22; Dan. 1:19
6 [a]Ezek. 14:14, 20; 28:3; Matt. 24:15 **7** [a]Dan. 2:26; 4:8; 5:12 [b]Dan. 2:49; 3:12 **8** [I]Lit., *set upon his heart* [a]Lev. 11:47; Ezek. 4:13, 14; Hos. 9:3, 4

with the [b]king's choice food or with the
[c]wine which he drank; so he sought *permission* from the commander of the officials that he might not defile himself.
9 Now God granted Daniel [I][a]fa-
vor[2617] and compassion in the sight of
the commander of the officials,
10 and the commander of the officials said[559] to Daniel, "I am afraid[3373]
of my lord[113] the king, who has appointed
your food and your drink;[4960] for why
should he see your faces looking more
haggard[2196] than the youths who are
your own age? Then you would [I]make
me forfeit my head[7218] to the king."
11 But Daniel said to the overseer
whom the commander of the officials
had appointed over Daniel, Hananiah,
Mishael and Azariah,
12 "Please[4994] test[5254] your servants[5650] for ten days,[3117] and let us be
[a]given some vegetables to eat and water
to drink.
13 "Then let our appearance[4758] be
[I]observed[7200] in your presence, and the
appearance of the youths who are eating
the king's choice food; and deal[6213] with
your servants according to what you
see."
14 So he listened to them in this
matter[1697] and tested[5254] them for ten
days.
15 And at the end of ten days their
appearance seemed[7200] [a]better[2896] and
[I]they were fatter than all the youths who
had been eating the king's choice food.
16 So the overseer continued to
[I]withhold[5375] their choice food and the
wine they were to drink, and kept
[a]giving them vegetables.
17 And as for these four youths,
[a]God gave them knowledge and intelligence[7919] in every *branch of* [I]litera-
ture and wisdom; Daniel even understood all *kinds of* [b]visions[2377] and
dreams.
18 Then at the end of the days which
the king had [I]specified [II]for presenting
them, the commander of the officials
[III]presented them before Nebuchadnezzar.
19 And the king talked with them,
and out of them all not one was found
like [a]Daniel, Hananiah, Mishael and Azariah; so they [I][b]entered the king's personal service.
20 And as for every matter of
[a]wisdom [I]and understanding[998] about
which the king consulted them, he found
them [b]ten times [c]better than all the
[II][d]magicians[2748] *and* conjurers[825] who
were in all his realm.
21 And Daniel [I]continued until the
[a]first year of Cyrus the king.

The King's Forgotten Dream

2 Now in the second year of the
reign[4438] of Nebuchadnezzar, Nebuchadnezzar [I][a]had dreams; and his spirit
was troubled and his [b]sleep [II]left[1961] him.
2 Then the king[4428] [I]gave orders[559]
to call[7121] in the [II][a]magicians,[2748] the conjurers,[825] the sorcerers[3784] and the
[III]Chaldeans, to tell[5046] the king his
dreams. So they came in and stood before the king.
3 And the king said[559] to them, "I
[I][a]had a dream, and my spirit [II]is anxious
to [III]understand[3045] the dream."
🗝 4 Then the Chaldeans spoke[1696] to
the king[4430] in [I][a]Aramaic: "[b]O king,
live[2418] forever![5957] [c]Tell[560] the dream

8 [b]Ps. 141:4; Dan. 1:5 [c]Deut. 32:38; Dan. 5:4
9 [I]Lit., *lovingkindness* [a]Gen. 39:21; 1Kin. 8:50; Job 5:15, 16; Ps. 106:46; Prov. 16:7
10 [I]Lit., *make my head guilty*
12 [a]Dan. 1:16
13 [I]Lit., *seen*
15 [I]Lit., *fat of flesh* [a]Ex. 23:25; Prov. 10:22
16 [I]Lit., *take away* [a]Dan. 1:12
17 [I]Or, *writing* [a]1Kin. 3:12, 28; Job 32:8; Dan. 1:20; 2:21, 23; Acts 7:22 [b]Dan. 2:19; 7:1; 8:1
18 [I]Lit., *said* [II]Lit., *to bring them in* [III]Lit., *brought in*
19 [I]Lit., *stood before the king* [a]Dan. 1:6, 7 [b]Gen. 41:46; Dan. 1:5
20 [I]Lit., *of* [II]Or, *soothsayer priests* [a]1Kin. 4:30, 31; Dan. 1:17 [b]Gen. 31:7; Num. 14:22; Neh. 4:12; Job 19:3 [c]Dan. 2:27, 28, 46, 48 [d]Is. 19:3; Dan. 2:2; 4:18; 5:7
21 [I]Lit., *was until* [a]Dan. 6:28; 10:1

1 [I]Lit., *dreamed dreams* [II]Lit., *was gone upon him* [a]Gen. 40:5-8; 41:1, 8; Job 33:15-17; Dan. 2:3; 4:5 [b]Esth. 6:1; Dan. 6:18
2 [I]Lit., *said to call* [II]Or, *soothsayer priests* [III]Or, *master astrologers*, and so throughout the ch. [a]Gen. 41:8; Ex. 7:11; Is. 47:12, 13; Dan. 1:20; 2:10, 27; 4:6; 5:7

3 [I]Lit., *dreamed* [II]Lit., *was troubled* [III]Lit., *know* [a]Gen. 40:8; 41:15; Dan. 4:5 **4** [I]The text is in Aramaic from here through 7:28 [a]Ezra 4:7; Is. 36:11 [b]Dan. 3:9; 5:10 [c]Dan. 2:7

🗝 **2:4b—7:28** This middle section of the book was written in Aramaic, rather than in Hebrew, the language of most of the O.T. The post-exilic Book of Ezra also has two sections which are in Aramaic (4:8—6:18; 7:12-26). There is some Aramaic in Jer. 10:11 and in Gen. 31:47. Aramaic was the accepted diplomatic language in the time of Sennacherib (II Kgs. 18:26). From non-biblical evidence the language can be traced as early as the ninth century B.C., and centuries before the birth of Jesus it had already replaced Hebrew as the local vernacular of Palestine. When N.T. writers refer to "Hebrew" it is usually Aramaic (see Acts 22:2).

to your servants,[5649] and we will declare the interpretation."

5 The king answered and said[560] to the Chaldeans, "[I]The command[4406] from me is firm: if you do not make known[3046] to me the dream and its interpretation, you will be [II][a]torn limb from limb, and your houses will be made a rubbish heap.

6 "But if you declare the dream and its interpretation, you will receive from me [a]gifts and a reward and great honor; therefore declare to me the dream and its interpretation."

7 They answered a second time and said, "Let the king [a]tell the dream to his servants, and we will declare the interpretation."

8 The king answered and said, "I know[3046] for certain that you are [I]bargaining for time, inasmuch as you have seen[2370] that [II]the command from me is firm,

9 that if you do not make the dream known to me, there is only [a]one [I]decree[1882] for you. For you have agreed[2164] together to speak[560] lying and corrupt[7844] [II]words[4406] before me until the [III]situation is changed; therefore tell me the dream, that I may [b]know that you can declare to me its interpretation."

10 The Chaldeans answered [I]the king and said, "There is not a man[606] on earth[3007] who could declare the matter[4406] [II]for the king,[4430] inasmuch as no great king or ruler[7990] has *ever* asked[7593] anything like this of any [III][a]magician,[2749] conjurer[826] or Chaldean.

11 "Moreover, the thing which the king demands[7593] is [I]difficult, and there is no one else who could declare it [II]to the king except [a]gods,[426] whose [b]dwelling place is not with *mortal* flesh."[1321]

12 Because of this the king became [a]indignant[1149] and very furious,[7108] and gave orders to destroy[7] all the wise men of Babylon.

13 So the [I]decree went forth that the wise men should be slain; and they looked for [a]Daniel and his friends to [II]kill *them*.

14 Then Daniel replied with discretion and discernment[2942] to [a]Arioch, the captain of the king's [I]bodyguard, who had gone forth to slay the wise men of Babylon;

15 he answered and said to Arioch, the king's commander,[7990] "For what reason is the [I]decree from the king *so* [II]urgent?" Then Arioch informed Daniel about the matter.

16 So Daniel went in and requested[1156] of the king that he would [I]give him time,[2166] in order that he might declare the interpretation to the king.

17 Then Daniel went to his house and informed his friends, [a]Hananiah, Mishael and Azariah, about the matter,

18 in order that they might [a]request[1156] compassion from the God[426] of heaven[8065] concerning this mystery, so that Daniel and his friends might not be [b]destroyed[7] with the rest[7606] of the wise men of Babylon.

The Secret Is Revealed to Daniel

19 Then the mystery was revealed to Daniel in a night[3916] [a]vision.[2376] Then Daniel blessed the God of heaven;

20 Daniel answered and said,
"Let the name of God be
[a]blessed forever and ever,
For [b]wisdom[2452] and power
belong to Him.
21 "And it is He who [a]changes the
times and the epochs;[2166]
He [b]removes kings[4430] and
[I]establishes kings;
He gives [c]wisdom to wise men,
And knowledge[4486] to [II]men of
understanding.[999]
22 "It is He who [a]reveals[1541] the
profound and hidden
things;[5642]
[b]He knows what is in the
darkness,
And the [c]light[5094] dwells with
Him.
23 "To Thee, O [a]God of my fathers,[2]
I give thanks[3029] and
praise,[7624]

5 [I]Another reading is *The word has gone from me* [II]Lit., *made into limbs* [a]Ezra 6:11; Dan. 2:12; 3:29
6 [a]Dan. 2:48; 5:7, 16, 29
7 [a]Dan. 2:4
8 [I]Lit., *buying* [II]V. 5, note 1
9 [I]Or, *law* [II]Lit., *word* [III]Lit., *time* [a]Esth. 4:11; Dan. 3:15 [b]Is. 41:23
10 [I]Lit., *before the* [II]Lit., *of* [III]Or, *soothsayer priest* [a]Dan. 2:2, 27
11 [I]Or, *rare* [II]Lit., *before* [a]Gen. 41:39; Dan. 5:11 [b]Ex. 29:45; Is. 57:15
12 [a]Ps. 76:10; Dan. 2:5; 3:13, 19
13 [I]Or, *law* [II]Lit., *be killed* [a]Dan. 1:19, 20
14 [I]Or, *executioners* [a]Dan. 2:24
15 [I]Or, *law* [II]Or, *harsh*
16 [I]Or, *appoint a time for him*
17 [a]Dan. 1:6
18 [a]Esth. 4:15, 16; Is. 37:4; Jer. 33:3; Ezek. 36:37; Dan. 2:23 [b]Gen. 18:28; Mal. 3:18
19 [a]Num. 12:6; Job 33:15, 16; Dan. 1:17; 7:2, 7, 13
20 [a]Ps. 103:1, 2; 113:1, 2; 115:18; 145:1, 2, 21 [b]1Chr. 29:11, 12; Job 12:13, 16-22; Dan. 2:21-23
21 [I]Or, *sets up* [II]Lit., *knowers* [a]Ps. 31:15; Dan. 2:9; 7:25 [b]Job 12:18; Ps. 75:6, 7; Dan. 4:17, 32 [c]1Kin. 3:9, 10; 4:29; James 1:5
22 [a]Job 12:22; Ps. 25:14; Dan. 2:19, 28 [b]Job 26:6; Ps. 139:12; Is. 45:7; Jer. 23:24; Heb. 4:13 [c]Ps. 36:9; Dan. 5:11, 14; James 1:17; 1John 1:5
23 [a]Gen. 31:42; Ex. 3:15

For Thou hast given me
[b]wisdom and power;
Even now Thou hast made known[3046] to me what we
[c]requested of Thee,
For Thou hast made known to
us the king's matter."

24 Therefore, Daniel went in to Arioch, whom the king had appointed to destroy the wise men of Babylon; he went and spoke to him as follows: "[a]Do not destroy the wise men of Babylon! Take me [I]into the king's presence, and I will declare the interpretation to the king."

🗝 **25** Then Arioch hurriedly[927] [a]brought Daniel [I]into the king's presence and spoke to him as follows: "I have found a man[1400] among the [II] [b]exiles from Judah who can make the interpretation known to the king!"

26 The king answered and said to Daniel, whose name was [a]Belteshazzar, "Are you able to make known to me the dream which I have seen[2370] and its interpretation?"

27 Daniel answered before the king and said, "As for the mystery about which the king has inquired,[7593] neither [a]wise men, conjurers,[826] [I]magicians,[2749] *nor* diviners[1505] are able to declare *it* to the king.

28 "However, there is a [a]God in heaven who reveals mysteries, and He has made known to King Nebuchadnezzar what will take place in the [I][b]latter days.[3118] This was your dream and the [c]visions[2376] [II]in your mind[7217] *while* on your bed.

29 "As for you, O king, *while* on your bed your thoughts [I]turned to what would take place [II]in the future; and [a]He who reveals mysteries has made known to you what will take place.

30 "But as for me, this mystery has not been revealed to me for any [a]wisdom [I]residing in me more than *in* any *other* living[2417] man, but for the purpose[1701] of making the interpretation known to the king, and that you may [II]understand the [b]thoughts of your [III]mind.[3825]

The King's Dream

31 "You, O king, were looking[2370] and behold, there was a single great statue;[6755] that statue, which was large and [I]of extraordinary splendor, was standing in front of you, and its appearance was [a]awesome.[1763]

32 "The [a]head of that statue[6755] *was made* of fine[2869] gold, its breast and its arms of silver, its belly and its thighs of bronze,

33 its legs of iron, its feet partly of iron and partly of clay.

34 "You [I]continued looking until a [a]stone was cut out[1505] [b]without hands,[3028] and it struck[4223] the statue on its feet of iron and clay, and [c]crushed them.

35 "Then the iron, the clay, the bronze, the silver and the gold were crushed [I]all at the same time, and became [a]like chaff from the summer threshing floors; and the wind[7308] carried them away so that [b]not a trace of them was found. But the stone that struck the statue became a great [c]mountain and filled the whole earth.[772]

The Interpretation—Babylon the First Kingdom

36 "This *was* the dream; now we shall tell [a]its interpretation before the king.

37 "You, O king, are the [a]king of kings, to whom the God of heaven has given the [I]kingdom,[4437] the [b]power, the strength, and the glory;

23 [b]Dan. 1:17; 2:21 [c]Ps. 21:2, 4; Dan. 2:18, 29, 30
24 [I]Lit., *in before the king* [a]Dan. 2:12, 13; Acts 27:24
25 [I]Lit., *in before the king* [II]Lit., *sons of the exile of* [a]Gen. 41:14 [b]Dan. 1:6; 5:13; 6:13
26 [a]Dan. 1:7; 4:8; 5:12
27 [I]Or, *soothsayer priests* [a]Dan. 2:2, 10, 11; 5:7,8
28 [I]Lit., *end of the days* [II]Lit., *of your head* [a]Gen. 40:8; 41:16; Dan. 2:22, 45 [b]Gen. 49:1; Is. 2:2; Dan. 10:14; Mic. 4:1 [c]Dan. 4:5
29 [I]Lit., *came up* [II]Lit., *after this* [a]Dan. 2:23, 47
30 [I]Lit., *which is* [II]Lit., *know* [III]Lit., *heart* [a]Gen. 41:16; Dan. 1:17 [b]Ps. 139:2; Amos 4:13
31 [I]Lit., *its splendor was surpassing* [a]Hab. 1:7
32 [a]Dan. 2:38
34 [I]Lit., *were* [a]Dan. 2:45 [b]Dan. 8:25; Zech. 4:6 [c]Ps. 2:9; Is. 60:12
35 [I]Lit., *like one* [a]Ps. 1:4; Is. 17:13; 41:15, 16; Hos. 13:3 [b]Ps. 37:10, 36 [c]Is. 2:2; Mic. 4:1
36 [a]Dan. 2:24
37 [I]Or, *sovereignty* [a]Is. 47:5; Jer. 27:6, 7; Ezek. 26:7 [b]Ps. 62:11

🗝 **2:25-30** This is the first of the dreams which Daniel interpreted and the one which secured for him both his reputation as a dream interpreter and a high government post. Daniel refused to take credit for any of his knowledge, giving it entirely to God. This had a profound effect on Nebuchadnezzar, because, after Daniel gave him the interpretation, he himself attributed the gift to Daniel's God, whom he praised in glowing terms (v. 47).

38 and wherever the sons[1123] of men[606] dwell, *or* the [a]beasts of the field, or the birds of the sky, He has given *them* into your hand[3028] and has caused you to rule[7981] over them all. You are the head of gold.

Medo-Persia and Greece

39 "And after you there will arise another kingdom inferior[772] to you, then another third kingdom of bronze, which will rule[7981] over all the earth.

Rome

40 "Then there will be a [a]fourth kingdom as strong as iron; inasmuch as iron crushes and shatters all things, so, like iron that breaks[7940] in pieces, it will crush[7490] and break all these in pieces.

41 "And in that you saw the feet and toes, partly of potter's clay and partly of iron, it will be a divided[6386] kingdom; but it will have in it the toughness of iron, inasmuch as you saw the iron mixed[6151] with [I]common[2917] clay.

42 "And *as* the toes of the feet *were* partly of iron and partly of pottery, *so* some of the kingdom will be strong and part of it will be brittle.

43 "And in that you saw the iron mixed with [I]common clay, they will combine[6151] with one another [II]in the seed[2234] of men; but they will not adhere to one another, even as iron does not combine with pottery.

The Divine Kingdom

44 "And in the days of those kings the [a]God of heaven will [b]set up a [c]kingdom which will never be destroyed,[2255] and *that* kingdom will not be [I]left for another people;[5972] it will [d]crush and put an end to[5487] all these kingdoms,[4437] but it will itself endure forever.

45 "Inasmuch as you saw that a [a]stone was cut out of the mountain without hands and that it crushed the iron, the bronze, the clay, the silver, and the gold, the [b]great God has made known to the king what [c]will take place [I]in the future; so the dream is true, and its interpretation is trustworthy."[540]

Daniel Promoted

46 Then King Nebuchadnezzar fell[5308] on his face and did [a]homage[5457] to Daniel, and gave orders to present to him an offering[4504] and [I][b]fragrant incense.

🔑 47 The king answered Daniel and said, "Surely[7187] [a]your God is a [b]God of gods and a Lord[4756] of kings and a [c]revealer[1541] of mysteries, since you have been able to reveal[1541] this mystery."

48 Then the king [I][a]promoted Daniel and gave him many great gifts, and he made him ruler over the whole [b]province of Babylon and chief [II]prefect over all the wise men of Babylon.

49 And Daniel made request[1156] of the king, and he [a]appointed [b]Shadrach, Meshach and Abed-nego over the administration of the province of Babylon, while Daniel *was* at the king's [I][c]court.

The King's Golden Image

3 Nebuchadnezzar the king[4430] made an [a]image[6755] of gold, the height of which *was* sixty [I]cubits *and* its width six [I]cubits; he set it up on the plain of Dura in the [b]province of Babylon.

2 Then Nebuchadnezzar the king sent *word* to assemble[3673] the [a]satraps,[324] the prefects and the governors,[6347] the counselors,[148] the treasurers, the judges, the magistrates and all the rulers[7984] of the provinces to come to the dedication[2597] of the image that Nebuchadnezzar the king had set up.

3 Then the satraps, the prefects and the governors, the counselors, the treasurers, the judges, the magistrates and all the rulers of the provinces were

38 [a]Ps. 50:10, 11; Dan. 4:21, 22
40 [a]Dan. 7:23
41 [I]Lit., *clay of mud*
43 [I]Lit., *clay of mud* [II]Or, *with*
44 [I]Or, *passed on to* [a]Dan. 2:28, 37 [b]Is. 9:6, 7 [c]Ps. 145:13; Ezek. 37:25; Dan. 4:3, 34; 6:26; 7:14, 27; Mic. 4:7; Luke 1:32, 33 [d]Ps. 2:9; Is. 60:12; Dan. 2:34, 35
45 [I]Lit., *after this* [a]Dan. 2:34 [b]Deut. 10:17; 2Sam. 7:22; Ps. 48:1; Jer. 32:18, 19; Dan. 2:29; Mal. 1:11 [c]Gen. 41:28, 32
46 [I]Lit., *sweet odors* [a]Dan. 3:5, 7; Acts 10:25; 14:13; Rev. 19:10; 22:8 [b]Lev. 26:31; Ezra 6:10
47 [a]Dan. 3:15; 4:25 [b]Deut. 10:17; Ps. 136:2, 3; Dan. 11:36 [c]Dan. 2:22, 30; Amos 3:7
48 [I]Lit., *made great* [II]Lit., *of the prefects* [a]Gen. 41:39-43; Dan. 2:6; 5:16, 29 [b]Dan. 3:1, 12, 30
49 [I]Lit., *gate* [a]Dan. 3:12 [b]Dan. 1:7 [c]Esth. 2:19, 21; Amos 5:15
1 [I]I.e., One cubit equals approx. 18 in. [a]1Kin. 12:28; Is. 46:6; Jer. 16:20; Dan. 2:31; Hos. 2:8; 8:4; Hab. 2:19 [b]Dan. 2:48; 3:30
2 [a]Dan. 3:3, 27; 6:1-7

🔑 **2:47** See note on Dan. 2:25-30.

assembled[3673] for the dedication of the image that Nebuchadnezzar the king had set up; and they stood before the image that Nebuchadnezzar had set up.

4 Then the herald loudly[2429] proclaimed: "To you [I]the command[560] is given, [a]O peoples,[5972] nations[524] and *men of every* [II]language,

5 that at the moment you [a]hear[8086] the sound of the horn, flute, [I]lyre, [II]trigon, [III]psaltery, bagpipe, and all kinds of music, you are to fall down[5308] and worship[5457] the golden image that Nebuchadnezzar the king has set up.

6 "But whoever does not fall down and worship[5457] shall [I]immediately be [a]cast into the midst of a [b]furnace of blazing fire."

7 Therefore at that time,[2166] when all the peoples heard[8086] the sound of the horn, flute, [I]lyre, trigon, psaltery, bagpipe, and all kinds of music, all the peoples, nations and *men of every* [II]language fell down[5308] *and* worshiped[5457] the golden image that Nebuchadnezzar the king had set up.

Worship of the Image Refused

8 For this reason at that time certain[1400] [a]Chaldeans came forward and [I][b]brought charges against[7170] the Jews.

9 They responded and said[560] to Nebuchadnezzar the king: "[a]O king, live[2418] forever![5957]

10 "You yourself, O king, have [a]made a decree[2942] that every man[606] who hears the sound of the horn, flute, [I]lyre, trigon, psaltery, and bagpipe, and all kinds of music, is to [b]fall down and worship the golden image.

11 "But whoever does not fall down and worship shall be cast into the midst of a furnace of blazing fire.

12 "There are certain Jews whom you have [a]appointed over the administration of the province of Babylon, *namely* Shadrach, Meshach and Abed-nego. These men,[1400] O king, have disregarded you; they do not serve[6399] your gods[426] or worship the golden image which you have set up."

13 Then Nebuchadnezzar in [a]rage[7266] and anger gave orders to bring Shadrach, Meshach and Abed-nego; then these men were brought before the king.

14 Nebuchadnezzar responded and said to them, "Is it true,[6656] Shadrach, Meshach and Abed-nego, that you do not serve [a]my gods or worship the golden image that I have set up?

15 "Now if you are ready, [a]at the moment you hear the sound of the horn, flute, [I]lyre, trigon, psaltery, and bagpipe, and all kinds of music, to fall down and worship the image that I have made, *very well.* But if you will not worship, you will [II]immediately be [b]cast into the midst of a furnace of blazing fire; and [c]what god[426] is there who can deliver you out of my hands?"[3028]

16 [a]Shadrach, Meshach and Abed-nego answered and said to the king, "O Nebuchadnezzar, we do not need to give you an answer concerning this matter.

17 "[I]If it be *so,* our [a]God whom we serve is able to deliver us from the furnace of blazing fire; [II]and [b]He will deliver us out of your hand,[3028] O king.

18 "[a]But *even* if *He does* not, [b]let it be known[3046] to you, O king, that we are not going to serve your gods or worship the golden image that you have set up."

Daniel's Friends Protected

19 Then Nebuchadnezzar was filled with [a]wrath, and his facial[600] expression[6755] was altered toward Shadrach, Meshach and Abed-nego. He answered [I]by giving orders to heat the furnace seven times more than it was usually[2370] heated.

20 And he commanded certain[2429] valiant[1401] warriors who *were* in his army[2429] to tie up Shadrach, Meshach and Abed-nego, in order to cast *them* into the furnace of blazing fire.

21 Then these men were tied up in their [I][a]trousers, their [II]coats, their caps and their *other* clothes, and were

4 [I]Lit., *they command* [II]Lit., *tongue* [a]Dan. 3:7; 4:1; 6:25

5 [I]Or, *zither* [II]I.e., triangular lyre [III]Or, *a type of harp* [a]Dan. 3:7, 10, 15

6 [I]Or, *in the same hour* [a]Dan. 3:11, 15, 21; 6:7 [b]Jer. 29:22; Ezek. 22:18-22; Matt. 13:42, 50; Rev. 9:2; 14:11

7 [I]V. 5, notes 1, 2, 3 [II]Lit., *tongue*

8 [I]Lit., *ate the pieces of* [a]Dan. 2:2, 10; 4:7 [b]Ezra 4:12-16; Esth. 3:8, 9; Dan. 6:12, 13

9 [a]Dan. 2:4; 5:10; 6:6, 21

10 [I]V. 5, notes 1, 2, 3 [a]Esth. 3:12-14; Dan. 3:4-6; 6:12 [b]Dan. 3:5, 7, 15

12 [a]Dan. 2:49

13 [a]Dan. 2:12; 3:19

14 [a]Is. 46:1; Jer. 50:2; Dan. 3:1; 4:8

15 [I]V. 5, notes 1, 2, 3 [II]Or, *in the same hour* [a]Dan. 3:5 [b]Dan. 3:6 [c]Ex. 5:2; Is. 36:18-20; Dan. 2:47

16 [a]Dan. 1:7; 3:12

17 [I]Or, *If our God. . .is able* [II]Or, *then* [a]Job 5:19; Ps. 27:1, 2; Is. 26:3, 4; Jer. 1:8; 15:20, 21 [b]1Sam. 17:37; Mic. 7:7; 2Cor. 1:10

18 [a]Josh. 24:15; 1Kin. 19:14, 18; Is. 51:12, 13; Dan. 3:28 [b]Heb. 11:25

19 [I]Lit., *and ordered to* [a]Esth. 7:7; Dan. 3:13

21 [I]Or, *leggings* [II]Or, *cloaks* [a]Dan. 3:27

cast into the midst of the furnace of blazing fire.

22 For this reason, because the king's[4430] [I]command[4406] *was* [IIa]urgent and the furnace had been made extremely hot, the flame of the fire slew those men who carried up Shadrach, Meshach and Abed-nego.

23 But these three men, Shadrach, Meshach and Abed-nego, [a]fell into the midst of the furnace of blazing fire *still* tied up.

24 Then Nebuchadnezzar the king was astounded[8429] and stood up in haste;[927] he responded and said to his high officials, "Was it not three men we cast bound into the midst of the fire?" They answered and said to the king, "Certainly, O king."

🔑 25 He answered and said, "Look! I see[2370] four men loosed *and* [a]walking *about* in the midst of the fire [I]without harm, and the appearance of the fourth is like a son of *the* [b]gods!"

26 Then Nebuchadnezzar came near to the door of the furnace of blazing fire; he responded and said, "Shadrach, Meshach and Abed-nego, come out, you servants[5649] of the [a]Most High[5943] God, and come here!" Then Shadrach, Meshach and Abed-nego [b]came out of the midst of the fire.

27 And the [a]satraps, the prefects, the governors and the king's high officials gathered around *and* saw in regard to these men that the [b]fire had no [I]effect[7981] on [II]the bodies[1655] of these men nor was the hair of their head[7217] singed, nor were their [IIIc]trousers [IV]damaged, nor had the smell of fire *even* come upon them.

28 Nebuchadnezzar responded and said, "Blessed be the [a]God of Shadrach, Meshach and Abed-nego, who has [b]sent His angel[4398] and delivered His servants who put their [c]trust in Him, [I]violating the king's command,[4406] and yielded up their bodies so as [d]not to serve or worship any god except their own God.

29 "Therefore, I [a]make a decree that any people, nation[524] or tongue that speaks[560] anything offensive[7955] against the God of [b]Shadrach, Meshach and Abed-nego shall be torn limb from limb and their [c]houses reduced to a rubbish heap, inasmuch as there is [d]no other god who is able to deliver[5338] in this way."

30 Then the king [a]caused Shadrach, Meshach and Abed-nego to prosper in the province of Babylon.

The King Acknowledges God

4 [I]Nebuchadnezzar the king[4430] to all the peoples,[5972] nations,[524] and *men of every* [II]language that live in all the earth:[772] "May your [IIIa]peace[8001] abound!

2 "It has seemed good to me to declare the signs and wonders[8540] which the [a]Most High[5943] God[426] has done for me.

3 "How great are His [a]signs,
And how mighty are His
wonders!
His [b]kingdom[4437] is an
everlasting kingdom,
And His dominion[7985] is from
generation[1859] to generation.

The Vision of a Great Tree

4 "[I]I, Nebuchadnezzar, was at ease in my house and [a]flourishing in my palace.[1965]

5 "I saw a [a]dream and it made me fearful;[1763] and *these* fantasies *as I lay* on my bed and the [b]visions[2376] [I]in my mind[7217] kept alarming[927] me.

6 "So I gave orders[2942] to [a]bring into my presence all the wise men of Babylon, that they might make known[3046] to me the interpretation of the dream.

7 "Then the [Ia]magicians,[2749] the conjurers,[826] the [II]Chaldeans, and the

22 [I]Lit., *word* [II]Or, *harsh* [a]Ex. 12:33; Dan. 2:15
23 [a]Is. 43:2
25 [I]Lit., *there is no injury in them* [a]Ps. 91:3-9; Is. 43:2 [b]Jer. 1:8, 19; 15:21
26 [a]Dan. 3:17; 4:2 [b]Deut. 4:20; 1Kin. 8:51; Jer. 11:4
27 [I]Lit., *power over* [II]Lit., *their* [III]Or, *cloaks* [IV]Lit., *changed* [a]Dan. 3:2, 3 [b]Is. 43:2; Heb.11:34 [c]Dan. 3:21
28 [I]Lit., *and changed the king's word* [a]Dan. 2:47; 3:15-17 [b]Ps. 34:7, 8; Is. 37:36; Dan. 3:25; 6:22; Acts 5:19; 12:7 [c]Ps. 22:4, 5; 40:4; 84:12; Is. 12:2; 26:3, 4; 50:10; Jer. 17:7 [d]Dan. 3:16-18
29 [a]Dan. 6:26 [b]Dan. 1:7, 19; 2:17, 49; 3:12 [c]Ezra 6:11; Dan. 2:5 [d]Dan. 2:47; 3:15
30 [a]Dan. 2:49; 3:12

1 [I]Ch. 3:31 in Aram. [II]Lit., *tongue* [III]Or, *welfare or prosperity* [a]Ezra 4:17; Dan. 6:25
2 [a]Dan. 3:26; 4:17, 24, 25, 32, 34
3 [a]Ps. 77:19; 105:27; Is. 25:1; Dan. 6:27 [b]Dan. 2:44; 4:34; 6:26
4 [I]Ch. 4:1 in Aram. [a]Ps. 30:6; Is. 47:7, 8
5 [I]Lit., *of my head* [a]Dan. 2:3 [b]Dan. 2:1, 28; 4:10, 13
6 [a]Gen. 41:8; Dan. 2:2
7 [I]Or, *soothsayer priests*, and so throughout the ch. [II]Or, *master astrologers* [a]Gen. 41:8; Dan. 2:10, 27; 5:7

🔑 **3:25** The identity of this fourth individual has long been a source of speculation. Although the text does not provide enough information to make a determination, some have even thought that it was Jesus in a pre-incarnation manifestation.

diviners[1505] came in, and I related[560] the
dream [III]to them; but they could not
make its [b]interpretation known to me.
8 "But finally Daniel came in before
me, whose name is [a]Belteshazzar according to the name of my god, and in
whom is [I][b]a spirit[7308] of the holy[6922]
gods;[426] and I related the dream [II]to
him, *saying,*
9 'O Belteshazzar, [a]chief of the magicians, since I know[3046] that [b]a spirit
of the holy gods is in you and [c]no mystery
baffles you, [d]tell[560] *me* the visions of my
dream which I have seen,[2370] along with
its interpretation.
10 'Now *these were* the [a]visions
[I]in my mind *as I lay* on my bed: I was
looking, and behold, *there was* a [b]tree
in the midst of the [II]earth, and its height
was great.
11 'The tree grew large and became
strong,[8631]
And its height [a]reached to the
sky,[8065]
And it *was visible*[2379] to the end
of the whole earth.
12 'Its foliage *was* [a]beautiful and its
fruit abundant,
And in it *was* food for all.
The [b]beasts of the field found
[c]shade under it,
And the [d]birds of the sky dwelt
in its branches,
And all [I]living creatures[1321] fed
themselves from it.
13 'I was looking in the [a]visions
[I]in my mind *as I lay* on my bed, and
behold, [b]an *angelic* watcher, a [c]holy
one,[6922] descended from heaven.
14 'He shouted out[2429][7123] and spoke[560]
as follows:
"[a]Chop[1414] down the tree and cut
off its branches,
Strip off its foliage and scatter
its fruit;
Let the [b]beasts flee from under
it,
And the birds from its branches.
15 "Yet [a]leave the stump [I]with its
roots in the ground,
But with a band of iron and
bronze *around it*
In the new grass of the field;
And let him be drenched with
the dew of heaven,
And let [II]him share with the
beasts in the grass of the
earth.
16 "Let his [I]mind[3825] be changed
from *that of* a man,[606]
And let a beast's [I]mind be given
to him,
And let [a]seven [II]periods of time
pass over him.
17 "This sentence[6600] is by the
decree of the *angelic*
watchers,
And the decision[7595] is a
command[3983] of the holy
ones,[6922]
In order[1701] that the living[2417]
may [a]know
That the Most High[5943] is
ruler[7990] over the realm of
mankind,[606]
And [b]bestows it on whom He
wishes,
And sets over it the [c]lowliest
of men."
18 'This is the dream *which* I, King
Nebuchadnezzar, have seen. Now you,
Belteshazzar, tell[560] *me* its interpretation, inasmuch as none of the [a]wise men
of my kingdom is able to make known[3046]
to me the interpretation; but you are
able, for a [b]spirit of the holy gods is in
you.'

Daniel Interprets the Vision

19 "Then Daniel, whose name is
Belteshazzar, was appalled for a while
as his [a]thoughts alarmed[927] him. The
king responded and said, 'Belteshazzar,
do not [b]let the dream or its interpretation
alarm you.' Belteshazzar answered and
said, '[c]My lord,[4756] *if only* the dream
applied to those who hate[8131] you, and
its interpretation to [d]your adversaries!
20 'The [a]tree that you saw,[2370]
which became large and grew strong,
whose height reached to the sky and
was visible to all the earth,
21 and whose foliage *was* beautiful
and its fruit abundant, and in which *was*

7 [III]Lit., before [b]Is. 44:25; Jer. 27:9, 10; Dan. 2:7
8 [I]Or possibly, *the Spirit of the holy God,* and so throughout the ch. [II]Lit., *before* [a]Dan. 1:7; 2:26; 5:12 [b]Dan. 4:9, 18; 5:11, 14
9 [a]Dan. 1:20; 2:48; 5:11 [b]Gen. 41:38; Dan. 4:8 [c]Ezek. 28:3; Dan. 2:47 [d]Gen. 41:15; Dan. 2:4, 5
10 [I]Lit., *of my head* [II]Or, *land,* and so throughout the ch. [a]Dan. 4:5 [b]Ezek. 31:3, 6
11 [a]Deut. 9:1; Dan. 4:21, 22
12 [I]Lit., *flesh* [a]Ezek. 31:7 [b]Jer. 27:6; Ezek. 31:6 [c]Lam. 4:20 [d]Ezek. 17:23; Matt. 13:32; Luke 13:19
13 [I]Lit., *of my head* [a]Dan. 7:1 [b]Dan. 4:17, 23 [c]Deut. 33:2; Ps. 89:7; Dan. 8:13
14 [a]Ezek. 31:10-14; Dan. 4:23; Matt. 3:10; 7:19; Luke 13:7-9 [b]Ezek. 31:12, 13; Dan. 4:12
15 [I]Lit., *of* [II]Lit., *his portion be with* [a]Job 14:7-9
16 [I]Lit., *heart* [II]I.e., years [a]Dan. 4:23, 25, 32
17 [a]Ps. 9:16; 83:18; Dan. 2:21; 5:21 [b]Jer. 27:5-7; Dan. 4:25; 5:18, 19 [c]1Sam. 2:8; Dan. 11:21
18 [a]Gen. 41:8, 15; Dan. 4:7; 5:8, 15 [b]Dan. 4:8, 9
19 [a]Jer. 4:19; Dan. 7:15, 28; 8:27; 10:16, 17 [b]1Sam. 3:17; Dan. 4:4, 5 [c]2Sam. 18:31; Dan. 4:24; 10:16 [d]2Sam. 18:32
20 [a]Dan. 4:10-12

food for all, under which the beasts of the field dwelt and in whose branches the birds of the sky lodged—

22 it is [a]you, O king; for you have become great and grown strong, and your [I]majesty has become great and reached to the sky and your [b]dominion to the end of the earth.

23 'And in that the king saw an *angelic* watcher, a holy one, descending from heaven and saying, "[a]Chop down the tree and destroy[2255] it; yet leave the stump [I]with its roots in the ground, but with a band of iron and bronze *around it* in the new grass of the field, and let him be drenched with the dew of heaven, and let [II]him share with the beasts of the field until [b]seven [III]periods of time pass over him";

24 this is the interpretation, O king, and this is the decree of the Most High, which has [a]come upon my lord the king:

25 that you be [a]driven away from mankind, and your dwelling place be with the beasts of the field, and you be given grass to eat like cattle and be drenched with the dew of heaven; and seven [I]periods of time will pass over you, until you recognize that the [b]Most High is ruler over the realm of mankind, and [c]bestows it on whomever He wishes.

26 'And in that it was commanded[560] to [a]leave the stump [I]with the roots of the tree, your kingdom will be [II]assured to you after you recognize that *it is* [b]Heaven[8065] *that* rules.

27 'Therefore, O king, may my [a]advice be pleasing[8232] to you: [Ib]break away now from your sins[2408] by *doing* righteousness,[6665] and from your iniquities[5758] by [c]showing mercy[2604] to *the* poor, in case there may be a [d]prolonging[754] of your prosperity.'

The Vision Fulfilled

28 "All *this* [a]happened to Nebuchadnezzar the king.

29 "[a]Twelve months later he was walking on the *roof of* the royal palace of Babylon.

30 "The king [I]reflected and said, 'Is this not Babylon the [a]great, which I myself have built as a royal [II]residence by the might of my power and for the glory of my majesty?'[1923]

31 "While the word *was* in the king's[4430] mouth, a voice [I]came[5308] from heaven, *saying,* 'King Nebuchadnezzar, to you it is declared: [II]sovereignty has been removed from you,

32 and [a]you will be driven away from mankind, and your dwelling place *will be* with the beasts of the field. You will be given grass to eat like cattle, and [b]seven [I]periods of time will pass over you, until you recognize that the [c]Most High is ruler over the realm of mankind, and bestows it on whomever He wishes.'

33 "Immediately the word[4406] concerning Nebuchadnezzar was fulfilled;[5487] and he was [a]driven away from mankind and began eating grass like cattle, and his body[1655] was drenched with the dew of heaven, until his hair had grown like eagles' *feathers* and his nails like birds' *claws.*

34 "But at the end of [I]that period[3118] I, Nebuchadnezzar, raised my eyes toward heaven, and my [II]reason[4486] returned[7725] to me, and I blessed the [a]Most High and praised[7624] and honored[1922] [b]Him who lives[2416] forever;[5957]

For His dominion is an
[c]everlasting dominion,
And His kingdom *endures* from
generation to generation.

35 "And [a]all the inhabitants of the earth are accounted as
nothing,
But [b]He does according to His
will in the host[2429] of heaven
And *among* the inhabitants of
earth;
And [c]no one can [I]ward off[4223] His
hand[3028]
Or say[560] to Him, '[d]What hast
Thou done?'

36 "At that time[2166] my [Ia]reason[4486] returned to me. And my majesty[1923] and [b]splendor were [II]restored to me for the glory of my kingdom, and my counselors and my nobles[7261] began seeking me out;

22 [I]Lit., *greatness* [a]2Sam. 12:7; Dan. 2:37, 38 [b]Jer. 27:6, 7

23 [I]Lit., *of* [II]Lit., *his portion be with* [III]I.e., years [a]Dan. 4:14, 15 [b]Dan. 4:16

24 [a]Job 40:11, 12; Ps. 107:40

25 [I]I.e., years [a]Dan. 4:33; 5:21 [b]Ps. 83:18; Jer. 27:5; Dan. 4:2, 17 [c]Dan. 2:37; 4:17; 5:21

26 [I]Lit., *of* [II]Lit., *enduring* [a]Dan. 4:15, 23 [b]Dan. 2:18, 19, 28, 37, 44; 4:31

27 [I]Or, *redeem now your sins* [a]Gen. 41:33-37 [b]Prov. 28:13; Is. 55:6, 7; Ezek. 18:7, 21, 22; Acts 8:22 [c]Ps. 41:1-3; Is. 58:6, 7, 10 [d]1Kin. 21:29; Jon. 3:9

28 [a]Num. 23:19; Zech. 1:6

29 [a]2Pet. 3:9

30 [I]Lit., *answered* [II]Lit., *house* [a]Hab. 2:4

31 [I]Lit., *fell* [II]Or, *kingdom*

32 [I]I.e., years [a]Dan. 4:25 [b]Dan. 4:16 [c]Dan. 4:17

33 [a]Dan. 4:25; 5:21

34 [I]Lit., *the days* [II]Lit., *knowledge* [a]Dan. 4:2; 5:18, 21 [b]Ps. 102:24-27; Dan. 6:26; 12:7; Rev. 4:10 [c]Ps. 145:13; Jer. 10:10; Dan. 4:3; Mic. 4:7; Luke 1:33

35 [I]Lit., *strike against* [a]Ps. 39:5; Is. 40:15, 17 [b]Ps. 33:11; 115:3; 135:6; Dan. 6:27 [c]Job 42:2; Is. 43:13 [d]Job 9:12; Is. 45:9; Rom. 9:20

36 [I]Lit., *knowledge* [II]Lit., *returning* [a]2Chr. 33:12, 13; Dan. 4:34 [b]Dan. 2:31

so I was reestablished in my [III]sover-
eignty, and surpassing [c]greatness was
added to me.
37 "Now I Nebuchadnezzar
praise,[7624] exalt, and honor[1922] the King
of [a]heaven, for [b]all His works are
[I]true[7187] and His ways [II]just,[1780] and He
is able to humble[8214] those who [c]walk
in pride."

Belshazzar's Feast

5 🗝 Belshazzar the king[4430] [I]held a
great [a]feast for a thousand of his
nobles,[7261] and he was drinking wine in
the presence of the thousand.
2 When Belshazzar tasted the wine,
he gave orders[560] to bring the gold and
silver [a]vessels which Nebuchadnezzar
his [I]father[2] had taken out of the
temple[1965] which *was* in Jerusalem, in
order that the king and his nobles,[7261]
his wives, and his concubines might
drink from them.
3 Then they brought the gold vessels that had been taken out of the temple, the house of God[426] which *was* in
Jerusalem; and the king and his nobles,
his wives, and his concubines drank from
them.
4 They [a]drank the wine and
praised[7624] the gods[426] of [b]gold and silver, of bronze, iron, wood, and stone.
5 Suddenly the fingers of a man's[606]
hand[3028] emerged and began writing opposite the lampstand on the plaster of
the wall of the king's[4430] palace,[1965] and
the king saw the [I]back of the hand that
did the writing.
6 Then the king's [Ia]face grew pale,
and his thoughts alarmed[927] him; and
his [b]hip joints went slack, and his
[c]knees began knocking[5368] together.
7 The king called aloud[2429] to bring
in the [a]conjurers,[826] the [I]Chaldeans and
the diviners.[1505] The king spoke and
said[560] to the wise men of Babylon, "Any
man who can read this inscription and
explain its interpretation to me will be
[b]clothed with purple, and *have* a [c]neck-
lace of gold around his neck, and have
authority[7981] as [IId]third *ruler* in the
kingdom."[4437]
8 Then all the king's wise men came
in, but [a]they could not read the inscription or make known[3046] its interpretation
to the king.
9 Then King Belshazzar was greatly
[a]alarmed, his [Ib]face grew *even* paler, and
his nobles were perplexed.
10 The queen[4433] entered the banquet [I]hall because of the words[4406] of
the king and his nobles; the queen spoke
and said, "[a]O king, live forever![5957] Do
not let your thoughts alarm[927] you or
your [II]face be pale.
11 "There is a [a]man[1400] in your kingdom in whom is [I]a [b]spirit[7308] of the
holy[6922] gods; and in the days[3118] of your
father, illumination,[5094] insight,[7924] and
wisdom[2452] like the wisdom of the gods
were found in him. And King Nebuchadnezzar, your father, your father [IIc]the
king, appointed him chief of the [III]magi-
cians,[2749] conjurers, [IV]Chaldeans, *and*
diviners.
12 "*This was* because an [a]extraordi-
nary spirit, knowledge[4486] and insight,
interpretation of dreams, explanation of
enigmas, and solving of difficult problems were found in this Daniel, whom
the king named [b]Belteshazzar. Let Daniel now be summoned, and he will declare the interpretation."

Daniel Interprets Handwriting on the Wall

13 Then Daniel was brought in before the king. The king spoke and said
to Daniel, "Are you that Daniel who is
one of the [Ia]exiles[1547] from Judah, whom

36 [III]Or, *kingdom* [c]Prov. 22:4; Dan. 4:22
37 [I]Lit., *truth* [II]Lit., *justice* [a]Dan. 4:26; 5:23 [b]Deut. 32:4; Ps. 33:4, 5; Is. 5:16 [c]Ex. 18:11; Job 40:11, 12; Dan. 5:20

1 [I]Lit., *made* [a]Esth. 1:3; Is. 22:12-14
2 [I]Or, *forefather,* and so throughout the ch. [a]2Kin. 24:13; 25:15; Ezra 1:7-11; Dan. 1:2
4 [a]Is. 42:8; Dan. 5:23; Rev. 9:20 [b]Ps. 115:4; 135:15; Is. 40:19, 20; Dan. 3:1; Hab. 2:19
5 [I]Or, *palm*
6 [I]Lit., *brightness changed for him* [a]Dan. 5:9, 10; 7:28 [b]Ps. 69:23 [c]Ezek. 7:17; 21:7; Nah. 2:10
7 [I]Or, *master astrologers* [II]Or, *a triumvir* [a]Is. 44:25; 47:13; Dan. 4:6, 7; 5:11, 15 [b]Gen. 41:42-44; Dan. 5:16, 29 [c]Ezek. 16:11 [d]Dan. 2:48; 5:16, 29; 6:2, 3
8 [a]Gen. 41:8; Dan. 2:27; 4:7; 5:15
9 [I]Lit., *brightness was changing upon him* [a]Job 18:11; Is. 21:2-4; Jer. 6:24; Dan. 2:1; 5:6 [b]Is. 13:6-8
10 [I]Lit., *house* [II]Lit., *brightness be changed* [a]Dan. 3:9; 6:6
11 [I]Or possibly, *the Spirit of the holy God* [II]Or, *O king* [III]Or, *soothsayer priests* [IV]Or, *master astrologers* [a]Gen. 41:11-15; Dan. 2:47 [b]Dan. 4:8, 9, 18; 5:14 [c]Dan. 2:48
12 [a]Dan. 5:14; 6:3 [b]Dan. 1:7; 4:8

13 [I]Lit., *sons of the exile* [a]Ezra 4:1; 6:16, 19, 20; Dan. 2:25; 6:13

🗝 **5:1-2** Belshazzar was king in function but not fact. He was regent and crown prince while Nabonidus, his father, was living outside of Babylon. Nebuchadnezzar, who is identified as his father, was actually his forefather or ancestor, in the common biblical sense of "father."

my father the king [b]brought from
Judah?
14 "Now I have heard[8086] about you
that [I]a spirit of the gods is in you, and
that illumination, insight, and extraordinary wisdom have been found in
you.
15 "Just now the [a]wise men *and* the
conjurers were brought in before me
that they might read this inscription and
make its interpretation known to me,
but they [b]could not declare the interpretation of the [I]message.[4406]
16 "But I personally have heard
about you, that you are able to give
interpretations and solve difficult problems. Now if you are able to read the
inscription and make its [a]interpretation
known to me, you will be [b]clothed with
purple and *wear* a necklace of gold
around your neck, and you will have
authority as the [I]third *ruler* in the kingdom."
17 Then Daniel answered and said
before the king, "[I]Keep your [a]gifts for
yourself, or give your rewards to someone else; however, I will read the inscription to the king and make the
interpretation known to him.
18 "[I]O king, the [a]Most High[5943] God
[b]granted [II]sovereignty, [c]grandeur,
glory, and majesty[1923] to Nebuchadnezzar your father.
19 "And because of the grandeur
which He bestowed on him, all the peoples,[5972] nations,[524] and *men of every*
[I]language feared[1763] and trembled before
him; [a]whomever he wished he killed,
and whomever he wished he spared
alive;[2418] and whomever he wished he
elevated, and whomever he wished he
humbled.
20 "But when his heart[3825] was
[a]lifted up and his spirit[7308] became so
[I][b]proud[8631] that he behaved arrogantly,
he was [c]deposed from his royal[4437]
throne,[3764] and *his* glory was taken away
from him.
21 "He was also [a]driven away from
[I]mankind,[606] and his heart was made like
that of beasts, and his dwelling place
was with the [b]wild donkeys. He was
given grass to eat like cattle, and his
body[1655] was drenched with the dew of
heaven,[8065] until he recognized[3046] that
the [c]Most High God is ruler[7990] over
the realm of mankind, and *that* He sets
over it whomever He wishes.
22 "Yet you, his [I]son, Belshazzar,
have [a]not humbled your heart, [II]even
though you knew[3046] all this,
23 but you have [a]exalted yourself
against the [b]Lord[4756] of heaven; and they
have brought the vessels of His house
before you, and you and your nobles,
your wives and your concubines have
been drinking wine from them; and
you have praised the [c]gods of silver
and gold, of bronze, iron, wood and
stone, which do not see,[2370] hear[8086]
or understand.[3046] But the God
[d]in whose hand are your life-breath
and your [e]ways, you have not glorified.[1922]
24 "Then the [I][a]hand was sent from
Him, and this inscription was written
out.
25 "Now this is the inscription that
was written out: '[I]MENĒ, [I]MENĒ,
[II]TEKĒL, [III]UPHARSIN.'
26 "This is the interpretation of the
[I]message: 'MENĒ'—God has numbered your kingdom and [a]put an end
to[8000] it.
27 " 'TEKĒL'—you have been
[a]weighed on the scales and found deficient.
28 " 'PERĒS'—your kingdom has
been divided and given over to the
[a]Medes and [I]Persians."
🗝 **29** Then Belshazzar gave orders,
and they [a]clothed Daniel with purple and
put a necklace of gold around his neck,

13 [b]Dan. 1:1, 2
14 [I]Or possibly, *the Spirit of God*
15 [I]Lit., *word* [a]Dan. 5:7 [b]Is. 47:12f.; Dan. 5:8
16 [I]Or, *triumvir* [a]Gen. 40:8 [b]Dan. 5:7, 29
17 [I]Lit., *Let . . . be for* [a]2Kin. 5:16
18 [I]Lit., *You, O king* [II]Or, *the kingdom* [a]Dan. 4:2; 5:21 [b]Dan. 2:37, 38; 4:17 [c]Jer. 25:9; 27:5-7
19 [I]Lit., *tongue* [a]Dan. 2:12, 13; 3:6; 11:3, 16, 36
20 [I]Lit., *strong* [a]Ex. 9:17; Job 15:25; Is. 14:13-15; Dan. 4:30, 31 [b]2Kin. 17:14; 2Chr. 36:13 [c]Job 40:11, 12; Jer. 13:18
21 [I]Lit., *the sons of man* [a]Job 30:3-7; Dan. 4:32, 33 [b]Job 39:5-8 [c]Ex. 9:14-16; Ps. 83:17, 18; Ezek. 17:24; Dan. 4:17, 34, 35
22 [I]Or, *descendant* [II]Lit., *inasmuch as you* [a]Ex. 10:3; 2Chr. 33:23; 36:12
23 [a]2Kin. 14:10; Is. 2:12; 37:23; Jer. 50:29; Dan. 5:3, 4 [b]Dan. 4:37 [c]Ps. 115:4-8; Is. 37:19; Hab. 2:18, 19 [d]Job 12:10 [e]Job 31:4; Ps. 139:3; Prov. 20:24; Jer. 10:23
24 [I]Lit., *palm of the hand* [a]Dan. 5:5
25 [I]Or, *a mina* (50 shekels) from verb "to number" [II]Or, *a shekel* from verb "to weigh" [III]Or, *and half-shekels* (sing.: *perēs*) from verb "to divide"
26 [I]Lit., *word* [a]Is. 13:6, 17-19; Jer. 50:41-43
27 [a]Job 31:6; Ps. 62:9
28 [I]Aram.: *Pāras* [a]Is. 13:17; 21:2; 45:1, 2; Dan. 5:31; 6:8, 28; Acts 2:9
29 [a]Dan. 5:7, 16

🗝 **5:29-31** Daniel's position as third in the kingdom was short-lived, because that very night Babylon fell to the Medo-Persian Empire. This meant that shortly the Jews would be allowed to return to their land.

and issued a proclamation concerning him that he *now* had authority[7990] as the [I]third *ruler* in the kingdom.

30 That same night[3916] [a]Belshazzar the Chaldean king was [b]slain.

31 [I]So [a]Darius the Mede received the kingdom at about the age of sixty-two.

Daniel Serves Darius

6

[I]It seemed good to Darius to appoint 120 satraps[324] over the kingdom,[4437] that they should be in charge of the whole kingdom,

2 and over them three commissioners[5632] (of whom [a]Daniel was one), that these satraps might be accountable[2941] to them, and that the king[4430] might not suffer [b]loss.

3 Then this Daniel began distinguishing himself [I]among the commissioners and satraps because [II]he possessed an [a]extraordinary spirit,[7308] and the king planned to appoint him over the [b]entire kingdom.[4437]

4 Then the commissioners and satraps began [a]trying to find a ground of accusation against Daniel in regard to [I]government affairs; but they could find [b]no ground of accusation or *evidence of* corruption,[7844] inasmuch as he was faithful,[540] and no negligence[7960] or corruption was *to be* found in him.

5 Then these men[1400] said,[560] "We shall not find any ground of accusation against this Daniel unless we find *it* against him with regard to the [a]law[1882] of his God."[426]

6 Then these commissioners and satraps came [I]by agreement[7284] to the king and spoke to him as follows: "King Darius, [a]live forever![5957]

7 "All the [a]commissioners of the kingdom, the prefects and the satraps, the high officials and the governors[6347] have [b]consulted together that the king should establish a statute[7010] and enforce[8631] an injunction that anyone who makes[1156] a petition[1159] to any god or man[606] besides you, O king, for thirty days,[3118] shall [c]be cast into the lions' [I]den.

8 "Now, O king, [a]establish the injunction and sign the document so that it may not be changed, according to the [b]law of the Medes and Persians, which [I]may not be revoked."

9 Therefore King Darius [a]signed the document, that is, the injunction.

10 Now when Daniel knew[3046] that the document was signed, he entered his house (now in his roof chamber he had windows open [a]toward Jerusalem); and he continued [b]kneeling on his knees three times[2166] a day,[3118] [c]praying[6739] and [d]giving thanks[3029] before his God, [I]as he had been doing previously.

11 Then these men came [I][a]by agreement and found Daniel making petition[1156] and supplication[2604] before his God.

12 Then they approached and [a]spoke[560] before the king about the king's[4430] injunction, "Did you not sign an injunction that any man who makes a petition to any god or man besides you, O king, for thirty days, is to be cast into the lions' den?" The king answered and said, "The statement is true, according to the [b]law of the Medes and Persians, which [I]may not be revoked."

13 Then they answered and spoke before the king, "[a]Daniel, who is one of the [I]exiles[1547] from Judah, pays [b]no attention[2942] to you, O king, or to the injunction which you signed, but keeps making his petition three times a day."

14 Then, as soon as the king heard[8086] this statement,[4406] he was deeply [a]distressed and set *his* mind[1079] on delivering Daniel; and even until sunset he kept exerting himself to rescue[5338] him.

15 Then these men came [I]by agreement to the king and said to the king, "Recognize,[3046] O king, that it is a [a]law of the Medes and Persians that no injunction or statute which the king establishes[6966] may be changed."

29 [I]Or, *triumvir*
30 [a]Dan. 5:1, 2 [b]Is. 21:4-9; 47:9; Jer. 51:11, 31, 39, 57
31 [I]Ch. 6:1 in Aram. [a]Dan. 6:1; 9:1

1 [I]Ch. 6:2 in Aram.
2 [a]Dan. 2:48, 49; 5:16, 29 [b]Ezra 4:22; Esth. 7:4
3 [I]Lit., *above* [II]Lit., *there was in him* [a]Dan. 5:12, 14; 9:23 [b]Gen. 41:40; Esth. 10:3
4 [I]Lit., *the kingdom* [a]Gen. 43:18; Judg. 14:4; Jer. 20:10; Dan. 3:8; Luke 20:20 [b]Dan. 6:22; Luke 20:26; 23:14, 15; Phil. 2:15; 1Pet. 2:12; 3:16
5 [a]Acts 24:13-16, 20, 21
6 [I]Or, *thronging* [a]Neh. 2:3; Dan. 2:4; 5:10; 6:21
7 [I]Or, *pit*, and so throughout the ch. [a]Dan. 3:2, 27 [b]Ps. 59:3; 62:4; 64:2-6; 83:1-3 [c]Ps. 10:9; Dan. 3:6; 6:16
8 [I]Lit., *does not pass away* [a]Esth. 3:12; 8:10; Is. 10:1 [b]Esth. 1:19; 8:8; Dan. 6:12, 15
9 [a]Ps. 118:9; 146:3
10 [I]Or, *because* [a]1Kin. 8:44, 48, 49; Ps. 5:7; Jon. 2:4 [b]Ps. 55:17; 95:6 [c]Dan. 9:4-19 [d]Ps. 34:1; Phil. 4:6; 1Thess. 5:17, 18
11 [I]Or, *thronging* [a]Ps. 37:32, 33; Dan. 6:6
12 [I]Lit., *does not pass away* [a]Dan. 3:8-12; Acts 16:19-21 [b]Esth. 1:19; Dan. 6:8, 15
13 [I]Lit., *sons of the exile* [a]Dan. 2:25; 5:13 [b]Esth. 3:8; Dan. 3:12; Acts 5:29
14 [a]Mark 6:26
15 [I]Or, *thronging* [a]Esth. 8:8; Ps. 94:20, 21; Dan. 6:8, 12

Daniel in the Lions' Den

16 Then the king gave orders,[560] and Daniel was brought in and [a]cast into the lions' den. The king spoke and said to Daniel, "[Ib]Your God whom you constantly serve[6399] will Himself deliver you."

17 And a [a]stone was brought and laid[7760] over the mouth of the den; and the king sealed it with his own signet ring and with the signet rings of his nobles,[7261] so that nothing might be changed in regard to Daniel.

18 Then the king went off to his palace[1965] and spent the night [a]fasting, and no entertainment was brought before him; and his [b]sleep fled from him.

19 Then the king arose with the dawn, at the break of day, and went in haste[927] to the lions' den.

20 And when he had come near the den to Daniel, he cried out with a troubled[6088] voice. The king spoke and said to Daniel, "Daniel, servant[5649] of the living[2417] God, has [a]your God, whom you constantly serve, been [b]able to deliver you from the lions?"

21 Then Daniel spoke [I]to the king, "[a]O king, live forever!

22 "My God [a]sent His angel[4398] and [b]shut the lions' mouths, and they have not harmed[2255] me, inasmuch as [I]I was found innocent before Him; and also [II]toward you, O king, I have committed no crime."

23 Then the king was very pleased and gave orders for Daniel to be taken up out of the den. So Daniel was taken up out of the den, and [a]no injury whatever was found on him, because he had [b]trusted[540] in his God.

24 The king then gave orders, and they brought those men who had [I]maliciously accused[7170] Daniel, and they [a]cast them, their [b]children, and their wives into the lions' den; and they had not reached the bottom of the den before the lions overpowered[7981] them and crushed all their bones.

25 Then Darius the king wrote to all the [a]peoples,[5972] nations,[524] and *men of every* [I]language who were living in all the land:[772] "[b]May your [II]peace[8001] abound!

26 "I [a]make a decree[2942] that in all the dominion[7985] of my kingdom men are to fear[1763] and tremble before the God of Daniel;

For He is the [b]living God and
[c]enduring forever,
And [d]His kingdom is one which
will not be destroyed,[2255]
And His dominion *will be*
[II]forever.

27 "He delivers and rescues[5338] and
performs [a]signs and
wonders[8540]
In heaven[8065] and on earth,
Who has *also* delivered Daniel
from the [I]power[3028] of the
lions."

28 So this [a]Daniel enjoyed success in the reign[4437] of Darius and in the reign of [b]Cyrus the Persian.

Vision of the Four Beasts

7 In the first year of Belshazzar king[4430] of Babylon Daniel saw[2370] a [a]dream and visions[2376] [I]in his mind[7217] *as he lay* on his bed; then he [b]wrote the dream down *and* related[560] the [II]*following* summary[7217] of [III]it.

2 Daniel [I]said, "I was [a]looking in my vision[2376] by night,[3916] and behold, the [b]four winds[7308] of heaven[8065] were stirring up the great sea.

3 "And four great [a]beasts were coming up from the sea, different from one another.

16 [I]Or, *May your God. . . Himself deliver you* [a]2Sam. 3:39; Jer. 38:5; Dan. 6:7 [b]Job 5:19; Ps. 37:39, 40; Is. 41:10; Dan. 3:17, 28; 6:20; 2Cor. 1:10 **17** [a]Lam. 3:53; Matt. 27:66 **18** [a]2Sam. 12:16, 17 [b]Esth. 6:1; Ps. 77:4; Dan. 2:1 **20** [a]Dan. 6:16, 27 [b]Gen. 18:14; Num. 11:23; Jer. 32:17; Dan. 3:17 **21** [I]Lit., *with* [a]Dan. 2:4; 6:6 **22** [I]Lit., *innocence was found for me* [II]Lit., *before* [a]Num. 20:16; Is. 63:9; Dan. 3:28; Acts 12:11; Heb. 1:14 [b]Ps. 91:11-13; 2Tim. 4:17; Heb. 11:33 **23** [a]Dan. 3:25, 27 [b]1Chr. 5:20; 2Chr. 20:20; Ps. 118:8, 9; Is. 26:3; Dan. 3:17, 28 **24** [I]Lit., *eaten the pieces of Daniel* [a]Deut. 19:18, 19; Esth. 7:10 [b]Deut. 24:16; 2Kin. 14:6; Esth. 9:10 **25** [I]Lit., *tongue* [II]Or, *welfare* or *prosperity* [a]Ezra 1:1, 2; Esth. 3:12; 8:9; Dan. 4:1 [b]Ezra 4:17; 1Pet. 1:2 **26** [I]Lit., *From me a decree is made* [II]Lit., *to the end* [a]Ezra 6:8-12; 7:13, 21; Dan. 3:29 [b]Dan. 4:34; 6:20; Hos. 1:10; Rom. 9:26 [c]Ps. 93:1, 2; Mal. 3:6 [d]Dan. 2:44; 4:3; 7:14, 27; Luke 1:33 **27** [I]Lit., *hand* [a]Dan. 4:2, 3 **28** [a]Dan. 1:21 [b]2Chr. 36:22, 23; Dan. 10:1

1 [I]Lit., *of his head* [II]Or, *beginning* [III]Lit., *words* [a]Job 33:14-16; Dan. 1:17; 2:1, 26-28; 4:5-9; Joel 2:28 [b]Jer. 36:4, 32 **2** [I]Lit., *spoke and said* [a]Dan. 7:7, 13 [b]Rev. 7:1 **3** [a]Dan. 7:17; Rev. 13:1; 17:8

6:16-24 This famous event took place when Daniel was an old man, contrary to the representation of it in much Christian art. Daniel was brought to Babylon in 606 B.C., probably as a teenager, and the incident in the lions den could not have been before 539 B.C. Therefore, Daniel was probably in his eighties when this happened.

4 "The first *was* [a]like a lion and had *the* wings of an eagle. I kept looking[2370] until its wings were plucked, and it was lifted up from the ground[772] and made to stand on two feet like a man;[606] a human[606] [I]mind[3825] also was given to it.

5 "And behold, another beast, a second one, resembling a bear. And it was raised up on one side, and three ribs *were* in its mouth between its teeth; and thus they said to it, 'Arise, devour much meat!'[1321]

6 "After this I kept looking, and behold, another one, [a]like a leopard, which had on its [I]back four wings of a bird; the beast also had [b]four heads,[7217] and dominion[7985] was given to it.

7 "After this I kept looking in the night visions, and behold, a [a]fourth beast, dreadful[1763] and terrifying and extremely strong; and it had large iron teeth. It devoured and crushed, and trampled down the remainder[7606] with its feet; and it was different from all the beasts that were before it, and it had [b]ten horns.

8 "While I was contemplating[7920] the horns, behold, [a]another horn, a little one, came up among them, and three of the first horns were pulled out by the roots before it; and behold, [I]this horn possessed eyes like the eyes of a man, and [b]a mouth uttering[4449] great *boasts*.

The Ancient of Days Reigns

9 "I kept looking
Until [a]thrones[3764] were set up,
And the Ancient of Days[3118] took
His seat;
His [b]vesture *was* like white
snow,
And the [c]hair of His head like
pure wool.
His [d]throne[3764] *was* [I]ablaze with
flames,
Its [e]wheels[1535] *were* a burning
fire.
10 "A river of [a]fire was flowing
And coming out from before
Him;
[b]Thousands upon thousands
were attending[8120] Him,
And myriads upon myriads were
standing before Him;
The [c]court[1760] sat,
And [d]the books were opened.

11 "Then I kept looking because of the sound of the [I]boastful words[4406] which the horn was speaking;[4449] I kept looking until the beast was slain, and its body[1655] was destroyed[7] and given to the [a]burning [II]fire.

12 "As for the rest[7606] of the beasts, their dominion was taken away, but an extension of life was granted to them for an appointed period[2166] of time.

The Son of Man Presented

🔑 13 "I kept looking in the night visions,
And behold, with the clouds[6050]
of heaven
One like a [a]Son of Man was
coming,
And He came up to the Ancient
of Days
And was presented before Him.
14 "And to Him was given
[a]dominion,
Glory and [I][b]a kingdom,[4437]
[c]That all the peoples,[5972]
nations,[524] and *men of every*
[II]language
Might serve[6399] Him.
[d]His dominion is an everlasting
dominion
Which will not pass away;

4 [I]Lit., *heart* [a]Jer. 4:7
6 [I]Or, *sides* [a]Rev. 13:2 [b]Dan. 8:22
7 [a]Dan. 7:19, 20, 23 [b]Rev. 12:3; 13:1
8 [I]Lit., *in this horn were eyes* [a]Dan. 8:9 [b]Rev. 13:5, 6
9 [I]Lit., *flames of fire* [a]Rev. 20:4 [b]Mark 9:3 [c]Rev. 1:14 [d]Ezek. 1:13, 26 [e]Ezek. 10:2, 6
10 [a]Ps. 18:8; 50:3; 97:3; Is. 30:27, 33 [b]Deut. 33:2; 1Kin. 22:19; Rev. 5:11 [c]Ps. 96:11-13; Dan. 7:22, 26 [d]Dan. 12:1; Rev. 20:11-15
11 [I]Lit., *great* [II]Lit., *of the fire* [a]Rev. 19:20; 20:10
13 [a]Matt. 24:30; 26:64; Mark 13:26; 14:62; Luke 21:27; Rev. 1:7, 13; 14:14
14 [I]Or, *sovereignty* [II]Lit., *tongue* [a]Dan. 7:27; John 3:35; 1Cor. 15:27; Eph. 1:20-22; Phil. 2:9-11; Rev. 1:6; 11:15 [b]Dan. 2:37 [c]Ps. 72:11; 102:22 [d]Mic. 4:7; Luke 1:33

🔑 **7:13** This verse serves as the clearest O.T. background of Jesus' application of the phrase "Son of Man" to Himself. In His discussion of the destruction of Jerusalem and the end of the world, He used it of the Second Coming of the Son of Man (Mt. 24:30; Mk. 13:26; Lk. 21:27), as He did in His trial before the high priest (Mt. 26:64; Mk. 14:62). John began his Apocalypse with a reference to Christ's Second Coming, as it was foreseen in Dan. 7:13 (Rev. 1:7; see also Rev. 1:13; 14:14).

[e]And His kingdom is one
Which will not be destroyed.

The Vision Interpreted

15 "As for me, Daniel, my spirit[7308]
was distressed [I]within me,[5085] and the
[a]visions [II]in my mind kept [b]alarming[927]
me.
16 "I approached one of those who
were [a]standing by and began asking him
the [I]exact meaning of all this. So he
[b]told me and made known[3046] to me the
interpretation of these things:
17 'These great beasts, which are
four *in number,* are four kings[4430] *who*
will arise from the earth.
18 'But the [Ia]saints[6922] of the
Highest One[5946] will [b]receive the kingdom and possess the kingdom forever,[5957] [II]for all ages to come.'
19 "Then I desired to know the
[I]exact meaning[3321] of the [a] fourth beast,
which was different from all [II]the others,
exceedingly dreadful, with its teeth of
iron and its claws of bronze, *and which*
devoured, crushed, and trampled down
the remainder with its feet,
20 and *the meaning* of the ten horns
that *were* on its head, and the other *horn*
which came up, and before which three
of them fell,[5308] namely, that horn which
had eyes and a mouth uttering great
boasts, and [I]which was larger in appearance[2376] than its associates.
21 "I kept looking, and that horn
was [a]waging war with the [I]saints and
overpowering them
22 until the Ancient of Days came,
and [a]judgment was [I]passed in favor of
the [II]saints of the Highest One, and the
time[2166] arrived when the [II]saints took
possession of the kingdom.
23 "Thus he said: 'The fourth beast
will be a fourth kingdom on the earth,
which will be different from all the *other*
kingdoms,[4437] and it will devour the
whole earth and tread it down and crush
it.
24 'As for the [a]ten horns, out of this
kingdom ten kings will arise; and another
will arise after them, and he will be different from the previous ones and will
subdue three kings.
25 'And he will [a]speak[4449] [I]out
against the [b]Most High[5943] and [c]wear
down the [II]saints of the Highest One,[5946]
and he will intend to make [d]alterations
in times and in law;[1882] and [III]they will
be given into his hand[3028] for a [IVe]time,
[IV]times, and half[6387] a [IV]time.
26 'But the court will sit *for judgment,* and his dominion will be [a]taken
away, [I]annihilated[8046] and destroyed[7]
[II]forever.
27 'Then the [Ia]sovereignty, the dominion, and the greatness of *all* the kingdoms under the whole heaven will be
given to the people of the [II]saints of
the Highest One;[5945] His kingdom *will
be* an [b]everlasting kingdom, and all the
dominions[7985] will [c]serve and obey[8086]
Him.'
28 "[I]At this point the revelation[4406]
ended. As for me, Daniel, my thoughts
were [a]greatly alarming me and my
[II]face grew pale, but I [b]kept the matter
[III]to myself."[3821]

Vision of the Ram and Goat

8 In the third year of the reign[4438]
of Belshazzar the king[4428] a
vision[2377] appeared[7200] to me, [I]Daniel,
subsequent to the one which appeared
to me [II]previously.
2 And I [a]looked[7200] in the vision, and
it came about while I was looking, that
I was in the citadel of [b]Susa, which is
in the province of [c]Elam; and I looked
in the vision, and I myself was beside
the Ulai [I]Canal.
3 Then I lifted[5375] my gaze and
looked, and behold, a [a]ram which had
two horns was standing in front of the
[I]canal. Now the two horns *were* [II]long,
but one *was* [II]longer than the other, with
the [II]longer one coming up[5927] last.
4 I saw the ram [a]butting westward,

14 [e]Heb. 12:28
15 [I]Lit., *in the midst of its sheath* [II]Lit., *of my head* [a]Dan. 7:1 [b]Dan. 4:19; 7:28
16 [I]Lit., *truth concerning* [a]Zech. 1:9, 19; Rev. 5:5; 7:13, 14 [b]Dan. 8:16, 17; 9:22
18 [I]Lit., *holy ones* [II]Lit., *and unto the age of the ages* [a]Dan. 7:22, 25, 27 [b]Ps. 149:5-9; Is. 60:12-14; Dan. 7:14; Rev. 2:26, 27; 20:4; 22:5
19 [I]Lit., *truth concerning* [II]Lit., *of them* [a]Dan. 7:7, 8
20 [I]Lit., *its appearance was larger*
21 [I]Lit., *holy ones* [a]Rev. 11:7; 13:7
22 [I]Lit., *given for* [II]Lit., *holy ones* [a]Dan. 7:10; 1Cor. 6:2, 3
24 [a]Dan. 7:7; Rev. 17:12
25 [I]Lit., *words* [II]Lit., *holy ones* [III]I.e., the saints [IV]I.e., year(s) [a]Dan. 11:36; Rev. 13:6 [b]Dan. 3:26; 4:2, 17, 34 [c]Rev. 13:7; 18:24 [d]Dan. 2:21 [e]Dan. 12:7; Rev. 12:14
26 [I]Lit., *to annihilate and to destroy* [II]Lit., *to the end* [a]Rev. 17:14; 19:2
27 [I]Or, *kingdom* [II]Lit., *holy ones* [a]Is. 54:3; Dan. 7:14, 18, 22; Rev. 20:4 [b]Ps. 145:13; Is. 9:7; Dan. 2:44; 4:34; 7:14; Luke 1:33; Rev. 11:15; 22:5 [c]Ps. 2:6-12; 22:27; 72:11; 86:9; Is. 60:12; Rev. 11:1
28 [I]Lit., *To here the end of the word* [II]Lit., *brightness was changing upon me* [III]Lit., *in my heart* [a]Dan. 4:19 [b]Luke 2:19, 51
1 [I]Lit., *I, Daniel* [II]Lit., *at the beginning*

2 [I]Or, *river* [a]Num. 12:6; Dan. 7:2, 15; 8:3 [b]Neh. 1:1; Esth. 1:2; 2:8 [c]Gen. 10:22; 14:1; Is. 11:11; Jer. 25:25; Ezek. 32:24 **3** [I]Or, *river* [II]Lit., *high(er)* [a]Dan. 8:20
4 [a]Deut. 33:17; 1Kin. 22:11; Ezek. 34:21

northward, and southward, and no *other* beasts[2416] could stand before him, nor was there anyone to rescue[5337] from his [I]power;[3027] but [b]he did[6213] as he pleased[7522] and magnified *himself.*

5 While I was observing,[995] behold, a male goat was coming from the west over the surface of the whole earth[776] without touching[5060] the ground;[776] and the [I]goat *had* a [a]conspicuous[2380] horn between his eyes.

6 And he came up to the ram that had the two horns, which I had seen[7200] standing in front of the [I]canal, and rushed at him in his mighty wrath.

7 And I saw him come[5060] beside the ram, and he was enraged[4843] at him; and he struck[5221] the ram and shattered[7665] his two horns, and the ram had no strength to withstand him. So he hurled him to the ground and trampled on him, and there was none to rescue the ram from his [I]power.

8 Then the male goat magnified *himself* exceedingly. But as soon as [a]he was mighty, the [b]large horn was broken;[7665] and in its place there came up four conspicuous *horns* toward the [c]four winds[7307] of heaven.

The Little Horn

9 And out of one of them came forth a rather [a]small horn which grew exceedingly great toward the south, toward the east, and toward the [Ib]Beautiful[6643] *Land.*

10 And it grew up to the host[6635] of heaven and caused some of the host and some of the [a]stars to fall[5307] to the earth, and it [b]trampled them down.

11 It even [a]magnified *itself* [I]to be equal with the [II]Commander[8269] of the host; and it removed the [b]regular[8548] sacrifice from Him, and the place of His sanctuary[4720] was thrown down.

12 And on account of transgression[6588] the host will be given over *to the horn* along with the regular sacrifice; and it will [a]fling truth[571] to the ground and perform[6213] *its will* and prosper.

13 Then I heard[8085] a [a]holy one speaking,[1696] and another holy one said[559] to that particular one who was speaking,[1696] "[b]How long will the vision *about* the regular sacrifice apply, [I]while the transgression causes horror, so as to allow both the holy place[6944] and the host [II]to be [c]trampled?"

14 And he said to me, "For [a]2,300 evenings *and* mornings; then the holy place will be [I]properly restored."[6663]

Interpretation of the Vision

15 And it came about when [a]I, Daniel, had seen the vision, that I sought [I]to understand[998] it; and behold, standing before me was one [II]who looked like a [b]man.[1397]

16 And I heard the voice of a man[120] between *the banks of* Ulai, and he called out[7121] and said, "[a]Gabriel, give this *man* an understanding[995] of the vision."

17 So he came near to where I was standing, and when he came I was frightened[1204] and [a]fell[5307] on my face; but he said to me, "Son[1121] of man,[120] understand that the vision pertains to the [b]time[6256] of the end."

18 Now while he was talking with me, I [a]sank into a deep sleep with my face to the ground; but he [b]touched me and made me stand [I]upright.

19 And he said, "Behold, I am going to [a]let you know[3045] what will occur at the final period of the indignation,[2195] for *it* pertains to the appointed time[4150] of the end.

The Ram's Identity

20 "The [a]ram which you saw[7200] with the two horns represents the kings[4428] of Media and Persia.

4 [I]Lit., *hand* [b]Dan. 11:3
5 [I]Lit., *buck* [a]Dan. 8:8, 21; 11:3
6 [I]Or, *river*
7 [I]Lit., *hand*
8 [a]2Chr. 26:16; Dan. 5:20 [b]Dan. 8:22 [c]Dan. 7:2; Rev. 7:1
9 [I]I.e., Palestine [a]Dan. 8:23 [b]Ps. 48:2; Dan. 11:16, 41
10 [a]Is. 14:13; Jer. 48:26; Rev. 12:4 [b]Dan. 7:7; 8:7
11 [I]Lit., *up to the* [II]Or, *Prince* [a]2Kin. 19:22, 23; 2Chr. 32:15-17; Is. 37:23; Dan. 8:25; 11:36, 37 [b]Ezek. 46:14; Dan. 11:31; 12:11
12 [a]Is. 59:14
13 [I]Or possibly, *and the transgression that horrifies* [II]Lit., *as a trampling* [a]Dan. 4:13, 23; 1Pet. 1:12 [b]Ps. 74:10; 79:5; Is. 6:11; Dan. 12:6, 8; Rev. 6:10 [c]Is. 63:18; Jer. 12:10; Luke 21:24; Heb. 10:29; Rev. 11:2
14 [I]Lit., *vindicated* [a]Dan. 7:25; 12:7, 11; Rev. 11:2, 3; 12:14; 13:5
15 [I]Lit., *understanding* [II]Lit., *like the appearance of a man* [a]Dan. 8:1 [b]Dan. 7:13; 10:16, 18
16 [a]Dan. 9:21; Luke 1:19, 26
17 [a]Ezek. 1:28; 44:4; Dan. 2:46; Rev. 1:17 [b]Dan. 8:19; 11:35, 40
18 [I]Lit., *on my standing* [a]Dan. 10:9; Luke 9:32 [b]Ezek. 2:2; Dan. 10:10, 16, 18
19 [a]Dan. 8:15-17
20 [a]Dan. 8:3

The Goat

21 "And the shaggy[8163] [I]goat *represents* the [II]kingdom of Greece, and the large horn that is between his eyes is the first[7223] king.

22 "And the [a]broken *horn* and the four *horns that* arose in its place *represent* four kingdoms *which* will arise from *his* nation,[1471] although not with his power.

23 "And in the latter[319] period of their [I]rule,[4438]
When the transgressors have [II]run *their course*,[8552]
A king will arise
[III]Insolent and skilled[995] in [IV]intrigue.[2420]

24 "And his power will be mighty, but not by his *own* power,
And he will [I][a]destroy[7843] to an extraordinary degree[6381]
And prosper and perform *his will*;
He will [I]destroy mighty men and [II]the holy[6918] people.[5971]

25 "And through his shrewdness[7922]
He will cause deceit[4820] to succeed by his [I]influence;
And he will magnify *himself* in his heart,[3824]
And he will [II]destroy many while *they are* [III]at ease.
He will even [IV][a]oppose the Prince of princes,[8269]
But he will be broken [b]without [I]human agency.

26 "And the vision of the evenings and mornings
Which has been told[560] is [a]true;
But [b]keep the vision secret,
For *it* pertains to many [c]days[3117] *in the future*."

27 Then I, Daniel, was [I][a]exhausted[1961] and sick for days. Then I got up *again* and [b]carried on the king's[4428] business;[4399] but I was astounded[8074] at the vision, and there was none to [II]explain[995] *it*.

21 [I]Lit., *buck* [II]Lit., *king*
22 [a]Dan. 8:8
23 [I]Or, *kingdom* [II]Lit., *finished* [III]Lit., *Strong of face* [IV]Or, *ambiguous speech*
24 [I]Or, *corrupt* [II]Lit., *people of the saints* [a]Dan. 8:11-13; 11:36; 12:7
25 [I]Lit., *hand* [II]Or, *corrupt* [III]Or, *secure* [IV]Lit., *stand against* [a]Dan. 8:11 [b]Job 34:20; Dan. 2:34, 45
26 [a]Dan. 10:1 [b]Ezek. 12:27; Dan. 12:4, 9; Rev. 22:10 [c]Dan. 10:14
27 [I]Or, *done in* [II]Lit., *make me understand* [a]Dan. 7:28; 8:17; Hab. 3:16 [b]Dan. 2:48
1 [a]Dan. 5:31; 11:1
2 [a]2Chr. 36:21; Ezra 1:1; Jer. 25:11, 12; 29:10; Zech. 7:5
3 [I]Lit., *set my face*
4 [a]Deut. 7:21; Neh. 9:32 [b]Deut. 7:9
5 [a]1Kin. 8:48; Neh. 9:33; Ps. 106:6; Is. 64:5-7; Jer. 14:7 [b]Lam. 1:18, 20 [c]Ps. 119:176; Is. 53:6; Dan. 9:11
6 [a]2Chr. 36:16; Jer. 44:4, 5
7 [I]Lit., *the shame of face* [a]Jer. 23:6; 33:16; Dan. 9:18 [b]Ps. 44:15; Jer. 2:26, 27; 3:25 [c]Deut. 4:27
8 [I]Lit., *The shame of face*

Daniel's Prayer for His People

9 In the first year of [a]Darius the son[1121] of Ahasuerus, of Median descent,[2233] who was made king[4427] over the kingdom of the Chaldeans—

2 in the first year of his reign[4427] I, Daniel, observed[995] in the books the number of the years which was *revealed as* the word[1697] of the LORD to [a]Jeremiah the prophet[5030] for the completion[4390] of the desolations[2723] of Jerusalem, *namely*, [a]seventy years.

3 So I [I]gave my attention to the Lord[136] God[430] to seek *Him by* prayer[8605] and supplications,[8469] with fasting, sackcloth, and ashes.

4 And I prayed[6419] to the LORD my God and confessed[3034] and said,[559] "Alas, O Lord, the [a]great and awesome[3372] God,[410] who [b]keeps[8104] His covenant[1285] and lovingkindness[2617] for those who love[157] Him and keep[8104] His commandments,[1697]

5 [a]we have sinned,[2398] committed iniquity,[5753] acted wickedly,[7561] and [b]rebelled,[4775] even [c]turning aside from Thy commandments[4687] and ordinances.[4941]

6 "Moreover, we have not [a]listened[8085] to Thy servants[5650] the prophets,[5030] who spoke[8269] in Thy name to our kings,[4428] our princes,[8269] our fathers,[1] and all the people[5971] of the land.[776]

7 "[a]Righteousness[6666] belongs to Thee, O Lord, but to us [I][b]open shame, as it is this day—[3117] to the men[376] of Judah, the inhabitants of Jerusalem, and all Israel, those who are nearby and those who are far away in [c]all the countries[776] to which Thou hast driven them, because of their unfaithful deeds[4604] which they have committed[4603] against Thee.

8 "[I]Open shame belongs to us, O Lord, to our kings, our princes, and our fathers, because we have sinned against Thee.

8:26 The sealing of a vision was a common feature of apocalyptic literature, of which the Book of Daniel is an early example (see also Dan. 12:4). In Isa. 8:16 Isaiah sealed a prophecy for purposes of later validation.

9 "To the Lord our God belong [a]compassion[7356] and forgiveness,[5547] [I]for we have [b]rebelled against Him;

10 nor have we obeyed[8085] the voice of the LORD our God, to walk in His [I]teachings[8451] which He [a]set before us through His servants the prophets.

11 "Indeed [a]all Israel has transgressed[5674] Thy law[8451] and turned aside, not obeying[8085] Thy voice; so the [b]curse[423] has been poured out on us, along with the oath[7621] which is written in the law of Moses the servant[5650] of God, for we have sinned against Him.

12 "Thus He has [a]confirmed His words[1697] which He had spoken against us and against our [Ib]rulers[8199] who ruled[8199] us, to bring on us great calamity;[7451] for under the whole heaven there has [c]not been done[6213] *anything* like what was done to Jerusalem.

13 "As it is written in the [a]law of Moses, all this calamity has come on us; yet we have [b]not [I]sought the favor of the LORD our God by [c]turning[7725] from our iniquity[5771] and [II]giving attention[7919] to Thy truth.[571]

14 "Therefore, the LORD has [Ia]kept the calamity in store and brought it on us; for the LORD our God is [b]righteous[6662] with respect to all His deeds which He has done,[6213] but we have not obeyed His voice.

15 "And now, O Lord our God, who hast [a]brought Thy people out of the land of Egypt with a mighty[2389] hand[3027] and hast [b]made[6213] a name for Thyself, as it is this day—we have sinned, we have been wicked.

16 "O Lord, in accordance with all Thy [I]righteous acts, let now Thine [a]anger[639] and Thy wrath turn away from Thy city Jerusalem, Thy [b]holy[6944] mountain; for because of our sins[2399] and the iniquities of our fathers, Jerusalem and Thy people *have become* a [c]reproach[2781] to all those around us.

17 "So now, our God, listen[8085] to the prayer of Thy servant and to his supplications, and for [I]Thy sake, O Lord, [a]let Thy face shine on Thy [b]desolate[8074] sanctuary.[4720]

18 "O my God, [a]incline Thine ear[241] and hear! Open Thine eyes and [b]see[7200] our desolations[8074] and the city which is [c]called[7121] by Thy name; for we are not [Id]presenting[5307] our supplications before Thee on account of [II]any merits of our own, but on account of Thy great compassion.

19 "O Lord, hear! O Lord, forgive![5545] O Lord, listen[7181] and take action![6213] For Thine own sake, O my God, [a]do not delay, because Thy city and Thy people are called by Thy name."

Gabriel Brings an Answer

20 Now while I was [a]speaking[1696] and praying, and [b]confessing[3034] my sin[2403] and the sin of my people Israel, and [I]presenting my supplication[8467] before the LORD my God in behalf of the holy mountain of my God,

21 while I was still speaking in prayer, then the man[376] [a]Gabriel, whom I had seen[7200] in the vision[2377] [I]previously, [II]came[5060] to me [III]in *my* extreme weariness about the time[6256] of the [b]evening offering.[4503]

22 And he gave *me* instruction[995] and talked[1696] with me, and said, "O Daniel, I have now come forth to give you insight[7919] with [a]understanding.[998]

23 "At the [a]beginning of your supplications the [I]command[1697] was issued, and I have come to tell[5046] *you,* for you are [IIb]highly esteemed; so give heed[995] to the message[1697] and gain [c]understanding[995] of the vision.

Seventy Weeks and the Messiah

24 "Seventy [Ia]weeks have been decreed for your people and your holy city, to [II]finish the transgression,[6588] to [III]make an end of sin, to [b]make atonement[3722] for iniquity,[5771] to bring in [c]everlasting[5769] righteousness,[6664] to

9 [I]Or, *though* [a]Neh. 9:17; Ps. 130:4 [b]Ps. 106:43; Jer. 14:7; Dan. 9:5, 6
10 [I]Or, *laws* [a]2Kin. 17:13-15; 18:12
11 [a]Is. 1:3, 4; Jer. 8:5-10 [b]Deut. 27:15-26
12 [I]Lit., *judges who judged us* [a]Is. 44:26; Jer. 44:2-6; Lam. 2:17; Zech. 1:6 [b]Job 12:17; Ps. 82:2-7; 148:11 [c]Lam. 1:12; 2:13; Ezek. 5:9
13 [I]Lit., *softened the face of* [II]Or, *having insight into* [a]Lev. 26:14-45; Deut. 28:15-68; Dan. 9:11 [b]Job 36:13; Is. 9:13; Jer. 2:30; 5:3 [c]Jer. 31:18
14 [I]Lit., *watched over the evil* [a]Jer. 31:28; 44:27 [b]Ps. 51:14; Dan. 9:7
15 [a]Deut. 5:15 [b]Neh. 9:10; Jer. 32:20
16 [I]Lit., *righteousnesses* [a]Jer. 32:31, 32 [b]Ps. 87:1-3; Dan. 9:20; Joel 3:17; Zech. 8:3 [c]Ezek. 5:14
17 [I]Lit., *the sake of the Lord* [a]Num. 6:24-26; Ps. 80:3, 7, 19 [b]Lam. 5:18
18 [I]Lit., *causing to fall* [II]Lit., *our righteousnesses* [a]Is. 37:17 [b]Ps. 80:14 [c]Jer. 7:10-12 [d]Jer. 36:7
19 [a]Ps. 44:23; 74:10, 11
20 [I]Lit., *causing to fall* [a]Ps. 145:18; Is. 58:9; Dan. 9:3; 10:12 [b]Is. 6:5
21 [I]Lit., *at the beginning* [II]Lit., *was reaching;* or, *touching* [III]Lit., *wearied with weariness* [a]Dan. 8:16; Luke 1:19, 26 [b]Ex. 29:39; 1Kin. 18:36; Ezra 9:4
22 [a]Dan. 8:16; 10:21; Zech. 1:9
23 [I]Lit., *word went out* [II]Lit., *desirable;* or, *precious* [a]Dan. 10:12 [b]Dan. 10:11, 19 [c]Matt. 24:15
24 [I]Or, *units of seven,* and so throughout the ch. [II]Or, *restrain* [III]Another reading is *seal up sins* [a]Lev. 25:8; Num. 14:34; Ezek. 4:5, 6 [b]2Chr. 29:24; Is. 53:10; Rom. 5:10 [c]Is. 51:6, 8; 56:1; Jer. 23:5, 6; Rom. 3:21, 22

seal up vision and [IV]prophecy, and to
anoint[4886] the most holy *place*.[6944]
25 "So you are to know[3045] and discern *that* from the issuing of a [I][a]decree
to restore[7725] and rebuild Jerusalem until
[II][b]Messiah[4899] the [c]Prince[5057] *there will*
be seven weeks and sixty-two weeks;
it will be built again, with [III]plaza and
moat, even in times[6256] of distress.
26 "Then after the sixty-two weeks
the [I]Messiah will be [a]cut off[3772] and have
[II]nothing, and the people of the prince
who is to come will [b]destroy[7843] the city
and the sanctuary.[6944] And [III]its end *will*
come with a [c]flood;[7858] even to the end
[IV]there will be war; desolations are determined.
27 "And he will make a firm covenant with the many for one week, but
in the middle of the week he will put a
stop to[7673] sacrifice[2077] and grain offering; and on the wing[3671] of [I][a]abomi-
nations[8251] *will come* one who [II]makes
desolate,[8076] even until a [b]complete destruction,[3617] one that is decreed, is
poured out on the one who [II]makes desolate."

Daniel Is Terrified by a Vision

10 In the third year of [a]Cyrus
king[4428] of Persia a [I]message
was revealed[1540] to [b]Daniel, who was
named[7121] Belteshazzar; and the [I][c]mes-
sage was true and *one of* great
[II]conflict,[6635] but he understood[995] the
[I]message and had an [d]understanding[998]
of the vision.
2 In those days[3117] I, Daniel, had
been [a]mourning for three entire[3117]
weeks.
3 I [a]did not eat any [I]tasty[2530] food,
nor did meat[1320] or wine enter my
mouth,[6310] nor did I use any ointment[5480]
at all, until the entire[3117] three weeks
were completed.
4 And on the twenty-fourth day[3117]
of the first[7223] month, while I was by
the bank[3027] of the great [a]river, that is,
the [I]Tigris,

24 [IV]Lit., *prophet*
25 [I]Lit., *word* [II]Or, *an anointed one* [III]Or, *streets* [a]Ezra 4:24; 6:1-15; Neh. 2:1-8; 3:1 [b]John 1:41; 4:25 [c]Is. 9:6; Dan. 8:11, 25
26 [I]Or, *anointed one* [II]Or, *no one* [III]Or, *his* [IV]Or, *war will be decreed for desolations* [a]Is. 53:8; Mark 9:12; Luke 24:26 [b]Matt. 24:2; Mark 13:2; Luke 19:43, 44 [c]Nah. 1:8
27 [I]Or, *detestable things* [II]Or, *causes horror* [a]Dan. 11:31; Matt. 24:15; Mark 13:14; Luke 21:20 [b]Is. 10:23; 28:22

1 [I]Lit., *word* [II]Or, *warfare* [a]Dan. 1:21; 6:28 [b]Dan. 1:7 [c]Dan. 8:26 [d]Dan. 1:17; 2:21
2 [a]Ezra 9:4, 5; Neh. 1:4
3 [I]Lit., *bread of desirability* [a]Dan. 6:18
4 [I]Heb., *Hiddekel* [a]Ezek. 1:3; Dan. 8:2
5 [a]Ezek. 9:2; Dan. 12:6, 7 [b]Rev. 1:13; 15:6 [c]Jer. 10:9
6 [I]Or, *yellow serpentine* [II]Lit., *like* [III]Or, *roaring* [a]Rev. 1:14; 2:18; 19:12
7 [a]2Kin. 6:17-20 [b]Acts 9:7 [c]Ezek. 12:18
8 [I]Lit., *splendor* [II]Lit., *corruption* [a]Gen. 32:24 [b]Dan. 7:28; 8:27; Hab. 3:16
9 [a]Gen. 15:12; Job 4:13; Dan. 8:18
10 [I]Lit., *knees and the palms of my hands* [a]Jer. 1:9; Dan. 8:18
11 [I]Lit., *desirability; or, preciousness* [II]Lit., *upon your standing* [a]Dan. 10:19 [b]Dan. 8:16, 17 [c]Ezek. 2:1 [d]Job 4:14, 15

5 I lifted[5375] my eyes and looked,[7200]
and behold, there was a certain man[376]
[a]dressed in linen, whose waist was
[b]girded with *a belt of* pure [c]gold of Uphaz.
6 His body[1472] also was like [I]beryl,
his face [II]had the appearance of lightning,
[a]his eyes were like flaming torches, his
arms and feet like the gleam of polished
bronze, and the sound of his words[1697]
like the sound of a [III]tumult.
7 Now I, Daniel, [a]alone saw[7200] the
vision,[4759] while the [b]men[582] who were
with me did not see the vision; nevertheless, a great [c]dread[2731] fell[5307] on them,
and they ran away to hide themselves.
8 So I was [a]left[7604] alone and saw
this great vision; yet [b]no strength was
left[7604] in me, for my [I]natural color[1935]
turned[2015] to [II]a deathly pallor,[4889] and
I retained no strength.
9 But I heard[8085] the sound of his
words; and as soon as I heard the sound
of his words, I [a]fell into a deep sleep
on my face, with my face to the
ground.[776]

Daniel Comforted

10 Then behold, a hand[3027]
[a]touched[5060] me and set me trembling
on my [I]hands[3027] and knees.
11 And he said[559] to me, "O
[a]Daniel, man of [I]high esteem, [b]un-
derstand[995] the words that I am about
to tell[1696] you and [c]stand [II]upright, for
I have now been sent to you." And when
he had spoken[1696] this word[1697] to me,
I stood up [d]trembling.[7460]
🗝 12 Then he said to me, "[a]Do not
be afraid,[3372] Daniel, for from the first
day that you set your heart[3820] on understanding *this* and on [b]humbling yourself
before your God,[430] your words were
heard, and I have come in response
[c]to your words.
13 "But the prince[8269] of the
kingdom[4438] of Persia was [I]withstanding

12 [a]Is. 41:10, 14; Dan. 10:19 [b]Dan. 9:20-23; 10:2, 3 [c]Acts 10:30, 31 **13** [I]Lit., *standing opposite*

🗝 **10:12-14** See note on Dan. 10:21.

me for twenty-one days; then behold, [a]Michael, one of the chief[7223] princes,[8269] came to help me, for I had been left[3498] there with the kings[4428] of Persia.

14 "Now I have come to [a]give you an understanding of what will happen to your people[5971] in the [I][b]latter[319] days, for the vision[2377] pertains to [c]the days yet *future*."

15 And when he had spoken to me according to these words, I [I]turned my face toward the ground and became [a]speechless.

16 And behold, [I][a]one who resembled[1823] a human[1121] being[120] was [b]touching my lips;[8193] then I opened my mouth and spoke,[1696] and said to him who was standing before me, "O my lord,[113] as a result of the vision [II][c]anguish has come upon me, and I have retained no strength.

17 "For [a]how can such a servant[5650] of my lord talk[1696] with such as my lord? As for me, there remains just now[6258] [b]no strength in me, nor has any breath[5397] been left in me."

18 Then *this* one with human[120] appearance touched me again and [a]strengthened[2388] me.

19 And he said, "O man of [I]high esteem, [a]do not be afraid. Peace [II]be with you; take [b]courage[2388] and be courageous!" Now as soon as he spoke to me, I received strength and said, "May my lord speak, for you have [c]strengthened me."

20 Then he said, "Do you [I]understand[3045] why I came to you? But I shall now return[7725] to fight against the [II]prince of Persia; so I am going forth, and behold, the [II][a]prince of [III]Greece is about to come.

🔑 21 "However, I will tell[5046] you what is inscribed in the writing of [a]truth.[571] Yet there is no one who [I]stands firmly with me against these *forces* except [b]Michael your prince.

Conflicts to Come

11 "And in the [a]first year of Darius the Mede, [I]I arose to be [II]an encouragement[2388] and a protection for him.

2 "And now I will tell[5046] you the [a]truth.[571] Behold, three more kings[4428] are going to arise [I]in Persia. Then a fourth will gain far more riches than all *of them;* as soon as he becomes strong[2393] through his riches, [II]he will arouse the whole *empire* against the realm of [III][b]Greece.

3 "And a [a]mighty king[4428] will arise, and he will rule[4910] with great authority[4474] and [b]do[6213] as he pleases.[7522]

4 "But as soon as he has arisen, his kingdom[4438] will be broken up[7665] and parceled out [a]toward the [b]four [I]points[7307] of the compass, though not to his *own* descendants,[319] nor according to his authority[4915] which he wielded;[4910] for his sovereignty will be [c]uprooted and *given* to others besides [II]them.

5 "Then the [a]king of the South will grow strong,[2388] [I]along with *one* of his princes[8269] [II]who will gain ascendancy over him and obtain dominion;[4910] his domain *will be* a great dominion[4475] *indeed.*

6 "And after some years they will form an alliance, and the daughter of the king[4428] of the South will come to the [a]king of the North to carry out[6213] [I]a peaceful arrangement.[4339] But she will not retain her [II]position of power, nor

13 [a]Dan. 10:21; 12:1; Jude 9; Rev. 12:7
14 [I]Lit., *end of the days* [a]Dan. 8:16; 9:22 [b]Deut. 31:29; Dan. 2:28 [c]Dan. 8:26; 12:4, 9
15 [I]Lit., *set* [a]Ezek. 3:26; 24:27; Luke 1:20
16 [I]Lit., *as a likeness of sons of man* [II]Lit., *my pains have* [a]Dan. 8:15 [b]Is. 6:7; Jer. 1:9 [c]Dan. 7:15, 28; 8:17, 27; 10:8,9
17 [a]Ex. 24:10, 11; Is. 6:1-5 [b]Dan. 10:8
18 [a]Is. 35:3, 4
19 [I]Lit., *desirability; or, preciousness* [II]Lit., *to you* [a]Judg. 6:23; Is. 43:1; Dan. 10:12 [b]Josh. 1:6, 7, 9; Is. 35:4 [c]Ps. 138:3; 2Cor. 12:9
20 [I]Lit., *know* [II]I.e., Satanic angel [III]Heb., *Javan* [a]Dan. 8:21; 11:2
21 [I]Lit., *shows himself strong* [a]Dan. 12:4 [b]Dan. 10:13; Rev. 12:7

1 [I]Lit., *my standing up was* [II]Lit., *for a strengthener* [a]Dan. 5:31; 9:1
2 [I]Lit., *for* [II]Or, *they all will stir up the realm of Greece* [III]Heb., *Javan* [a]Dan. 8:26; 10:1, 21 [b]Dan. 8:21; 10:20
3 [a]Dan. 8:5, 21 [b]Dan. 5:19; 8:4; 11:16, 36
4 [I]Lit., *winds of the heaven* [II]I.e., his descendants [a]Dan. 8:8, 22 [b]Jer. 49:36; Ezek. 37:9; Dan. 7:2; 8:8; Zech. 2:6; Rev. 7:1 [c]Jer. 12:15, 17; 18:7
5 [I]Lit., *and* [II]Lit., *and he* [a]Dan. 11:9, 11, 14, 25, 40
6 [I]Or, *an equitable agreement* [II]Lit., *strength of arm* [a]Dan. 11:7, 13, 15, 40

🔑 **10:21** The angel, Michael, is seen here as the heavenly prince of Israel, as he is in Dan. 12:1. Persia, too, had its own prince, as did Greece (10:13,20). These princes or angels engaged in heavenly combat, and the implication is that what was happening to these nations on the earth was affected by this heavenly struggle (10:12-14,20). During the intertestamental period the Jews greatly expanded the O.T. teaching on angels into a full-blown hierarchy of both good and evil angels. In the N.T., Paul, using different terminology, taught that the Christian's real struggle was with these spiritual beings, rather than with physical ones (Eph. 6:12).

will he remain with his [III]power, but she will be given up, along with those who brought her in, and the one who sired her, as well as he who supported[2388] her in *those* times.[6256]

7 "But one of the [I]descendants of her line will arise in his place, and he will come against *their* army[2428] and enter the [a]fortress of the king of the North, and he will deal[6213] with them and display *great* strength.[2388]

8 "And also their [a]gods[430] with their [I]metal images[5257] *and* their precious vessels of silver and gold he will take into captivity[7628] to Egypt, and he on his part will [II]refrain from *attacking* the king of the North for *some* years.

9 "Then [I]the latter will enter the realm of the king of the South, but will return[7725] to his *own* land.[127]

10 "And his sons[1121] will [I]mobilize and assemble[622] a multitude of great forces;[2428] and one of them will keep on coming and [a]overflow[7857] and pass through,[5674] that he may [II]again wage war up to his *very* fortress.

11 "And the [a]king of the South will be enraged[4843] and go forth and fight [I]with the king of the North. Then the latter will raise a great multitude, but *that* multitude will be given into [II]the hand[3027] of the *former*.

12 "When the multitude is carried[5375] away, his heart[3824] will be lifted up, and he will cause[5307] tens of thousands[506] to fall;[5307] yet he will not prevail.

13 "For the king of the North will again raise a greater multitude than the former,[7223] and [I]after an [a]interval of some years he will [II]press on with a great army and much equipment.

14 "Now in those times many will rise up against the king of the South; the violent ones[6530] among your people[5971] will also lift themselves up in order to fulfill the vision,[2377] but they will [I]fall[3782] down.

15 "Then the king of the North will come, cast up[8210] a [a]siege mound, and capture a well-fortified city; and the forces of the South will not stand *their* *ground*, not even [I]their choicest troops, for there will be no strength to make a stand.

16 "But he who comes against him will [a]do as he pleases, and [b]no one will *be able to* withstand him; he will also stay *for a time* in the [I][c]Beautiful[6643] Land,[776] with destruction[3615] in his hand.

17 "And he will [a]set[7760] his face to come with the power of his whole kingdom, [I]bringing with him [II]a proposal of peace[3477] which he will put into effect; he will also give him the daughter of women to ruin[7843] it. But she will not take a stand *for him* or be [III]on his side.

18 "Then he will turn[7725] his face to the [a]coastlands and capture many. But a commander[7101] will put a stop[7673] to his scorn[2781] against him; moreover, he will [b]repay him for his scorn.[2781]

19 "So he will turn his face toward the fortresses of his own land, but he will [a]stumble[3782] and fall and be [b]found no more.

20 "Then in his place one will arise who will [a]send an [I]oppressor through the [II]Jewel[1925] of *his* kingdom; yet within a few days[3117] he will be shattered,[7665] though neither in anger[639] nor in battle.

21 "And in his place a despicable[959] person will arise, on whom the honor[1935] of kingship has not been conferred, but he will come in a time of tranquility and [a]seize[2388] the kingdom by intrigue.

22 "And the overflowing[7858] [a]forces will be flooded[7857] away before him and shattered, and also the prince[5057] of the covenant.[1285]

23 "And after an alliance is made with him he will practice[6213] deception,[4820] and he will go up[5927] and gain power with a small *force of* people.[1471]

24 "[I]In a time of tranquility he will enter the [a]richest *parts* of the [II]realm, and he will accomplish what his fathers[1] never did,[6213] nor his [III]ancestors; he will distribute plunder, booty, and possessions among them, and he will

6 [III]Lit., *arm*
7 [I]Lit., *branch of her roots* [a]Dan. 11:19, 38, 39
8 [I]Lit., *cast images* [II]Or, *stand against the king* [a]Is. 37:19; 46:1, 2; Jer. 43:12,13
9 [I]Lit., *he will*, and so throughout the ch.
10 [I]Or, *wage war* [II]Or, *return and wage* [a]Is. 8:8; Jer. 46:7, 8; 51:42; Dan. 11:26, 40
11 [I]Lit., *with him, with* [II]Lit., *his hand* [a]Dan. 11:5
13 [I]Lit., *at the end of the times, years* [II]Or, *keep on coming* [a]Dan. 4:16; 12:7
14 [I]Lit., *stumble*, and so throughout the ch.
15 [I]Lit., *the people of its choice ones* [a]Jer. 6:6; Ezek. 4:2; 17:17
16 [I]I.e., Palestine [a]Dan. 5:19; 11:3, 36 [b]Josh. 1:5 [c]Dan. 8:9; 11:41
17 [I]Lit., *and* [II]Lit., *equitable things* [III]Lit., *for him;* i.e., for her father [a]2Kin. 12:17; Ezek. 4:3, 7
18 [a]Gen. 10:5; Is. 66:19; Jer. 2:10; 31:10; Zeph. 2:11 [b]Hos. 12:14
19 [a]Ps. 27:2; Jer. 46:6 [b]Job 20:8; Ps. 37:36; Ezek. 26:21
20 [I]Or, *exactor* of tribute [II]Lit., *adornment;* i.e., probably Jerusalem and its temple [a]Is. 60:17
21 [a]2Sam. 15:6
22 [a]Dan. 9:26; 11:10
24 [I]Lit., *Into tranquility and the richest... he will enter* [II]Or, *province* [III]Lit., *fathers' fathers* [a]Num. 13:20; Neh. 9:25; Ezek. 34:14

devise[2803] his schemes against strongholds, but *only* for a time.[6256]

25 "And he will stir up his strength and [I]courage against the [a]king of the South with a large army; so the king of the South will mobilize an extremely large and mighty army for war; but he will not stand, for schemes will be devised against him.

26 "And those who eat his choice food will [I]destroy[7665] him, and his army will [IIa]overflow, but many will fall down slain.[2491]

27 "As for both kings, their hearts[3824] will be *intent* on [a]evil, and they will [b]speak[1696] lies[3577] *to each other* at the same table; but it will not succeed, for the [c]end is still *to come* at the appointed time.[4150]

28 "Then he will return to his land with much [I]plunder; but his heart will be *set* against the holy[6944] covenant, and he will take action and *then* return to his *own* land.

29 "At the appointed time he will return and come into the South, but [I]this last time it will not turn out the way it did before.

30 "For ships of [Ia]Kittim will come against him; therefore he will be disheartened, and will return and become enraged[2194] at the holy covenant and take action; so he will come back and show regard[995] for those who forsake[5800] the holy covenant.

🗝 31 "And forces from him will arise, [a]desecrate the sanctuary[7420] fortress, and do away with the regular[8548] sacrifice. And they will set up the [b]abomination[8251] [I]of desolation.[8074]

32 "And by [a]smooth *words* he will [I]turn to godlessness[2610] those who act wickedly[7561] toward the covenant, but the people who know[3045] their God[430] will display [b]strength and take action.

33 "And [Ia]those who have insight[7919] among the people will give understanding[995] to the many; yet they will [b]fall by sword[2719] and by flame, by captivity[7628] and by plunder, for *many* days.

34 "Now when they fall they will be granted[5826] a little help, and many will [a]join with them in [b]hypocrisy.

35 "And some of [I]those who have insight will fall, in order to [a]refine,[6884] [b]purge,[1305] and make them [IIc]pure, until the [d]end time; because *it is* still *to come* at the appointed time.

36 "Then the king will [a]do as he pleases, and he will exalt and [b]magnify himself above every god,[410] and will [c]speak [I]monstrous[6381] things against the [d]God of gods;[410] and he will prosper until the [e]indignation[2195] is finished,[3615] for that which is [f]decreed will be done.

37 "And he will show no regard[995] for the [I]gods of his fathers or for the desire of women,[802] nor will he show regard for any *other* god; for he will magnify himself above *them* all.

38 "But [I]instead he will honor[3513] a god of fortresses, a god whom his fathers did not know;[3045] he will honor *him* with gold, silver, costly stones, and treasures.[2530]

39 "And he will take action against the strongest of fortresses with *the help of* a foreign[5236] god; he will give great honor[3519] to [I]those who acknowledge[5234] *him,* and he will cause them to rule over the many, and will parcel out land for a price.

40 "And at the [a]end time the [b]king of the South will collide with him, and the [c]king of the North will [d]storm[8175] against him with chariots, with horsemen, and with many ships; and he will

25 [I]Lit., *heart* [a]Dan. 11:5
26 [I]Lit., *break* [II]Or, *be swept away, and many* [a]Dan. 11:10, 40
27 [a]Ps. 52:1; 64:6 [b]Ps. 12:2; Jer. 9:3-5; 41:1-3 [c]Dan. 8:19; 11:35, 40; Hab. 2:3
28 [I]Lit., *possessions*
29 [I]Lit., *it will not happen as the first and as the last*
30 [I]I.e., Cyprus [a]Gen. 10:4; Num. 24:24; Is. 23:1, 12; Jer. 2:10
31 [I]Lit., *that makes desolate;* or, *that causes horror* [a]Dan. 8:11-13; 12:11 [b]Dan. 9:27; Matt. 24:15; Mark 13:14
32 [I]Or, *pollute those* [a]Dan. 11:21, 34 [b]Mic. 5:7-9; Zech. 9:13-16; 10:3-6
33 [I]Or, *instructors of the people* [a]Mal. 2:7 [b]Matt. 24:9; John 16:2; Heb. 11:36-38
34 [a]Matt. 7:15; Acts 20:29, 30 [b]Dan. 11:21, 32; Rom. 16:18
35 [I]Or, *the instructors* [II]Lit., *white* [a]Deut. 8:16; Prov. 17:3; Dan. 12:10; Zech. 13:9; Mal. 3:2, 3 [b]John 15:2 [c]Rev. 7:14 [d]Dan. 11:27
36 [I]Lit., *extraordinary* [a]Dan. 5:19; 11:3, 16 [b]Is. 14:13; Dan. 5:20; 8:11, 25; 2Thess. 2:4 [c]Rev. 13:5, 6 [d]Deut. 10:17; Ps. 136:2; Dan. 2:47 [e]Is. 10:25; 26:20; Dan. 8:19 [f]Dan. 9:27
37 [I]Or, *God*
38 [I]Lit., *in his place*

39 [I]Lit., *the one who acknowledges* **40** [a]Dan. 11:27, 35; 12:4, 9 [b]Dan. 11:11, 25 [c]Dan. 11:7, 13, 15 [d]Is. 5:28; Jer. 4:13

🗝 **11:31** Jesus saw "the abomination of desolation" mentioned here and in Dan. 12:11 as referring to something in the temple at the time the Romans were about to destroy Jerusalem in A.D. 70. This was the second time that this phrase applied to a profaning of the temple, because the context in Dan. 11 shows that it referred initially to what Antiochus Epiphanes did in the second century B.C. A future fulfillment will occur during the tribulation (Mt. 24:15; Mk. 13:14).

enter countries,[776] [e]overflow *them,* and pass through.[5674]

41 "He will also enter the [I][a]Beautiful Land, and many *countries* will fall;[3782] but these will be rescued[4422] out of his hand: Edom, [b]Moab and the foremost[7225] of the sons[1121] of [c]Ammon.

42 "Then he will stretch out his hand against *other* countries, and the land of Egypt will not escape.[6413]

43 "But he will [I]gain control[4910] over the hidden treasures of gold and silver, and over all the precious things of Egypt; and [a]Libyans and [b]Ethiopians *will follow* at his [II]heels.

44 "But rumors from the East and from the North will disturb him, and he will go forth with great wrath to destroy[8045] and [I]annihilate many.

45 "And he will pitch the tents[168] of his royal pavilion between the seas and the beautiful [a]Holy Mountain; yet he will come to his end, and no one will help him.

The Time of the End

12 🔑 "Now at that time [a]Michael, the great prince[8269] who stands *guard* over the sons[1121] of your people,[5971] will arise. And there will be a [b]time of distress [c]such as never occurred since there was a nation[1471] until that time; and at that time your people, everyone who is found written in the [d]book,[5612] will be rescued.[4422]

🔑 2 "And [a]many of those who sleep in the dust[6083] of the ground[127] will awake, [b]these to everlasting[5769] life, but the others to disgrace[2781] *and* everlasting [I]contempt.

3 "And [I]those who have [a]insight[7919] will [b]shine[2094] brightly like the brightness of the [II]expanse of heaven,[7549] and those who [c]lead the many to righteousness, like the stars forever[5769] and ever.[5703]

🔑 4 "But as for you, Daniel, [a]conceal these words[1697] and [b]seal up the book until the [c]end of time; [d]many will go back and forth, and knowledge will increase."

5 Then I, Daniel, looked[7200] and behold, two others were standing, one on this bank[8193] of the river, and the other on that bank of the river.

6 And [a]one said[559] to the man[376] [b]dressed in linen, who was above the waters of the river, "[c]How long *will it be* until the end of *these* wonders?"[6382]

7 And I heard[8085] the man dressed in linen, who was above the waters of the river, [I]as he [a]raised his right hand and his left toward heaven, and swore[7650] by [b]Him who lives[2416] forever that it would be for a [II][c]time,[4150] [II]times, and half *a* [II]*time;* and as soon as [III]they finish[3615] [d]shattering the [IV]power[3027] of the holy[6944] people, all these *events* will be completed.[3615]

8 As for me, I heard but could not understand;[995] so I said, "My lord, what *will be* the [I]outcome[319] of these *events?*"

9 And he said, "Go *your way,* Daniel, for *these* words are concealed and [a]sealed up until the end time.

10 "[a]Many will be purged,[1305] [I]purified and refined;[6884] but the [b]wicked[7563] will act wickedly,[7561] and none of the wicked will understand,[995] but [II]those who [c]have insight will understand.

🔑 11 "And from the time that the regular[8548] sacrifice is abolished,[5493] and the [I][a]abomination[8251] of desolation[8074] is

40 [e]Dan. 11:10, 26
41 [I]I.e., Palestine [a]Dan. 8:9; 11:16 [b]Jer. 48:47 [c]Jer. 49:6
43 [I]Or, *rule over* [II]Lit., *footsteps* [a]2Chr. 12:3; Nah. 3:9 [b]2Chr. 12:3; Ezek. 30:4, 5; Nah. 3:9
44 [I]Lit., *devote to destruction*
45 [a]Is. 11:9; 27:13; 65:25; 66:20; Dan. 9:16, 20

1 [a]Dan. 10:13, 21; Rev. 12:7 [b]Rev. 7:14; 16:18 [c]Jer. 30:7; Ezek. 5:9; Dan. 9:12; Matt. 24:21; Mark 13:19 [d]Dan. 7:10; 10:21
2 [I]Lit., *abhorrence* [a]Is. 26:19; Ezek. 37:12-14 [b]Matt. 25:46; John 5:28, 29
3 [I]Or, *the instructors will* [II]Or, *firmament* [a]Dan. 11:33, 35; 12:10 [b]John 5:35 [c]Is. 53:11; Dan. 11:33
4 [a]Dan. 8:26; 12:9 [b]Is. 8:16; Dan. 12:9; Rev. 22:10 [c]Dan. 8:17; 12:9, 13 [d]Is. 11:9; 29:18, 19; Dan. 11:33
6 [a]Dan. 8:16; Zech. 1:12, 13 [b]Ezek. 9:2; Dan. 10:5 [c]Dan. 8:13; 12:8; Matt. 24:3; Mark 13:4
7 [I]Lit., *and* [II]I.e., year(s) [III]Lit., *to finish* [IV]Lit., *hand* [a]Ezek. 20:5; Rev. 10:5, 6 [b]Dan. 4:34 [c]Dan. 7:25; Rev. 12:14 [d]Dan. 8:24; Luke 21:24
8 [I]Or, *final end*
9 [a]Dan. 12:4
10 [I]Lit., *made* white [II]Or, *the instructors will* [a]Zech. 13:9 [b]Is. 32:6, 7; Rev. 22:11 [c]Dan. 12:3; Hos. 14:9; John 7:17; 8:47
11 [I]Or, *horrible abomination* [a]Dan. 9:27; 11:31; Matt. 24:15; Mark 13:14

🔑 **12:1** See note on Dan 10:21.

🔑 **12:2** This is perhaps the clearest reference to the resurrection of the dead to be found in the O.T. See also Isa. 26:19. The distinction between the righteous and the wicked at the resurrection was also made by Jesus (Jn. 5:28,29).

🔑 **12:4** See note on Dan 8:26.

🔑 **12:11** See note on Dan. 11:31.

set up, *there will be* 1,290 days.[3117]
12 "How [a]blessed[835] is he who
keeps waiting and attains[5060] to the
[b]1,335 days!
13 "But as for you, go *your way* to
the [I]end; then you will enter into
[a]rest and rise *again* for your [b]allotted
portion at the end of the [II]age."

12 [a]Is. 30:18 [b]Dan. 8:14; Rev. 11:2; 12:6; 13:5
13 [I]I.e., end of your life [II]Lit., *days* [a]Is. 57:2; Rev. 14:13 [b]Ps. 16:5

The Book of
HOSEA

Hosea is the first book in the Book of the Twelve Prophets in the Hebrew Bible. The prophet preached in Israel in the second half of the eighth century B.C., beginning during the reign of Jeroboam II. He was a contemporary of Isaiah and Micah in Judah and began his career shortly after Amos' brief one in Israel. Hosea foresaw Israel's exile to Assyria and actually witnessed some of it happen. He was the last prophet God raised up in Israel to try to get the people to repent. Hosea's task was doubly sad, because, at God's direction, he took a wife who was just as unfaithful to him as Israel was to her God. The first three chapters relate the sordid details of their stormy marriage. Of three children born while they were living together, only one was Hosea's. Gomer left Hosea for other lovers but got herself into such trouble that she wanted to return home. In loving forgiveness, Hosea bought her back. All of this was an object lesson to Israel, who had been just as faithless to God. The remainder of the book records Hosea's portrayal of their sins and the disastrous consequences. Through it all, God's love and compassion stand out to a remarkable extent. The picture of God in Hosea is that of a loving husband who yearns desperately to have a faithful wife. Israel, however, will have none of it, and the consequences of her sins must play themselves out, although hope for the future is never lost.

Hosea's Wife and Children

1 The word[1697] of the LORD which
came to [a]Hosea the son of Beeri,
during the days[3117] of [b]Uzziah, [c]Jotham,
[d]Ahaz, *and* [e]Hezekiah, kings of Judah,
and during the days of [f]Jeroboam the
son of Joash, king of Israel.
2 When the LORD first spoke
through Hosea, the LORD said[559] to Hosea, "[a]Go, take to yourself a wife[802] of
harlotry,[2183] and *have* children of harlotry; for [b]the land[776] commits flagrant
harlotry,[2184] [I]forsaking the LORD."
3 So he went and took Gomer the
daughter of Diblaim, and she conceived
and [a]bore him a son.[1121]
4 And the LORD said to him,
"Name[7121] him [a]Jezreel; for yet a little
while, and [b]I will [I]punish[6485] the
house[1004] of Jehu for the bloodshed[1818]
of Jezreel, and [c]I will put an end[7673] to
the kingdom[4468] of the house of Israel.
5 "And it will come about on that
day,[3117] that I will [a]break[7665] the bow
of Israel in the [b]valley of Jezreel."
6 Then she conceived again and
gave birth to a daughter. And [I]the LORD
said to him, "Name her [II]Lo-ruha-
mah,[7355,3808] for I will no longer [a]have
compassion[7355] on the house of
Israel, that I should ever forgive[5375]
them.
7 "But I will have [a]compassion on
the house of Judah and [b]deliver[3467] them
by the LORD their God,[430] and will not
deliver them by [c]bow, sword,[2719] battle,
horses, or horsemen."
8 When she had weaned Lo-
ruhamah, she conceived and gave birth
to a son.
9 And [I]the LORD said, "Name him

1 [a]Rom. 9:25 [b]2Chr. 26:1-23; Is. 1:1; Amos 1:1 [c]2Kin. 15:5, 7, 32-38; 2Chr. 27:1-9 [d]2Kin. 16:1-20; 2Chr. 28:1-27; Is. 1:1; 7:1-17; Mic. 1:1 [e]2Kin. 18:1-20:21; 2Chr. 29:1-32:33; Mic. 1:1 [f]2Kin. 13:13; 14:23-29; Amos 1:1
2 [I]Lit., *from not following after* [a]Hos. 3:1 [b]Deut. 31:16; Jer. 3:1; Ezek. 23:3-21; Hos. 2:5; 5:3
3 [a]Ezek. 23:4
4 [I]Lit., *visit the bloodshed of Jezreel on the house of Jehu* [a]Hos. 2:22 [b]2Kin. 10:11 [c]2Kin. 15:8-10
5 [a]Jer. 49:35; Ezek. 39:3 [b]Josh. 17:16; Judg. 6:33
6 [I]Lit., *He* [II]I.e., she has not obtained compassion [a]Hos. 2:4
7 [a]2Kin. 19:29-35; Is. 30:18 [b]Jer. 25:5, 6; Zech. 9:9, 10 [c]Ps. 44:3-7; Zech. 4:6
9 [I]Lit., *He*

1:2-4 Gomer's first child, Jezreel, seems to have been legitimate, because she bore *him* a son (1:3). The next two children, however, are not said to be Hosea's (1:6,8), and they are later identified as "children of harlotry" (2:1,4). This harlotry motif is very strong in Hosea. Not only did it apply to Hosea's marriage, but Israel herself was a harlot in her infidelity to the Lord, her husband (Hos. 4:12,18; 5:4; 6:10; 9:1). There was even cultic prostitution (Hos. 4:14). See note on Ezek. 24:15-24.

1:4 See note on Ezek. 24:15-24.

[II]Lo-ammi,[5971][3808] for you are not My people[5971] and I am not [III]your God."
10 [I]Yet the number of the sons of Israel
Will be like the [a]sand of the sea,
Which cannot be measured or numbered;[5608]
And [b]it will come about that, in the place
Where it is said[559] to them,
"You are [c]not My people,"
It will be said to them,
"*You are* the [d]sons of the living[2416] God."[410]
11 And the [a]sons of Judah and the sons of Israel will be
[b]gathered[6908] together,
And they will appoint for themselves [c]one leader,[7218]
And they will go up[5927] from the land,
For great will be the day of Jezreel.

Israel's Unfaithfulness Condemned

2 [I]Say[559] to your brothers,[251] "[II]Ammi,"[5971] and to your sisters,[269] "[III]Ruhamah."[7355]
2 "Contend[7378] with your mother,[517] [a]contend,
For she is [b]not my wife,[802] and I am not her husband;[376]
And let her put away[5493] her [c]harlotry[2183] from her face,
And her adultery[5005] from between her breasts,
3 Lest I strip her [a]naked[6174]
And expose her as on the [b]day[3117] when she was born.
I will also [c]make her like a wilderness,
Make her like desert land,[776]
And slay[4191] her with [d]thirst.
4 "Also, I will have no compassion[7355] on her children,[1121]
Because they are [a]children of harlotry.
5 "For their mother has [a]played the harlot;[2181]
She who conceived them has acted shamefully.
For she said, '[a]I will go after my lovers,[157]
Who [b]give *me* my bread and my water,
My wool and my flax, my [c]oil[8081] and my drink.'
6 "Therefore, behold, I will [a]hedge up [I]her way[1870] with [b]thorns,
And I will build [II]a wall against her so that she cannot find her [c]paths.
7 "And she will [a]pursue her lovers, but she will not overtake them;
And she will seek them, but will not find *them*.
Then she will say, '[b]I will go back[7725] to my [c]first husband,
For it was [d]better[2896] for me then than now!'
8 "For she does [a]not know that it was [b]I who gave her the grain, the new wine, and the oil,[3323]
And lavished on her silver and gold,
Which they [I]used[6213] for Baal.
9 "Therefore, I will [a]take back My grain at [I]harvest time[6256]
And My new wine in its season.[4150]
I will also take away[5337] My wool and My flax
Given to cover[3680] her nakedness.[6172]
10 "And then I will [a]uncover[1540] her lewdness

9 [II]I.e., not my people [III]Lit., *yours*
10 [I]Ch. 2:1 in Heb. [a]Gen. 22:17; 32:12; Jer. 33:22 [b]Rom. 9:26 [c]Is. 65:1; Hos. 1:9 [d]Is. 63:16; 64:8; John 1:12; 1Pet. 2:10
11 [a]Is. 11:12 [b]Jer. 23:5, 6; 50:4, 5; Ezek. 37:21-24 [c]Jer. 30:21; Hos. 3:5
1 [I]Ch. 2:3 in Heb. [II]I.e., my people [III]I.e., she has obtained compassion
2 [a]Ezek. 23:45; Hos. 2:5; 4:5 [b]Is. 50:1 [c]Jer. 3:1, 9, 13
3 [a]Jer. 13:22; Ezek. 16:7, 22, 39 [b]Ezek. 16:4 [c]Is. 32:13, 14; Hos. 13:15 [d]Jer. 14:3; Amos 8:11-13
4 [a]Jer. 13:14
5 [a]Is. 1:21; Jer. 2:25; 3:1, 2; Hos. 3:1 [b]Jer. 44:17, 18; Hos. 2:12 [c]Hos. 2:8
6 [I]So with some ancient versions; Heb., *your* [II]Lit., *her wall so that* [a]Job 19:8; Lam. 3:7, 9 [b]Hos. 9:6; 10:8 [c]Jer. 18:15
7 [a]Hos. 5:13 [b]Luke 15:17, 18 [c]Jer. 2:2; 3:1; Ezek. 16:8; 23:4 [d]Jer. 14:22; Hos. 13:6
8 [I]Or, *made into the* [a]Is. 1:3 [b]Ezek. 16:19
9 [I]Lit., *its time* [a]Hos. 8:7; 9:2
10 [a]Ezek. 16:37

2:5 The Canaanite people believed that they owed all the products of the soil to the Baals, the pagan gods of the land. All fertilization was a result of the power of the Baals. Having intercourse with sacred prostitutes was thought to contribute to the agricultural prosperity of the land. The harlot's pay came from the harvest (v. 12).

In the sight of her lovers,
And no one[376] will rescue[5337] her out of My hand.[3027]

11 "I will also [a]put an end[7673] to all her gaiety,
Her [b]feasts,[2282] her [c]new moons, her sabbaths,[7676]
And all her festal assemblies.[4150]

12 "And I will [a]destroy[8074] her vines and fig trees,
Of which she said, 'These are my wages
Which my lovers have given me.'
And I will [b]make[7760] them a forest,
And the [c]beasts[2416] of the field[7704] will devour them.

13 "And I will punish[6485] her for the [a]days of the Baals
When she used to [I][b]offer[6999] sacrifices to them
And [c]adorn herself with her [II]earrings and jewelry,
And follow her lovers, so that she [d]forgot Me," declares[5001] the LORD.

Restoration of Israel

14 "Therefore, behold, I will allure her,
[a]Bring her into the wilderness,
And speak[1696] [I]kindly[3820] to her.

15 "Then I will give her her [a]vineyards from there,
And [b]the valley of Achor as a door of hope.
And she will [I][c]sing there as in the days of her youth,
As in the [d]day when she came up[5927] from the land of Egypt.

16 "And it will come about in that day," declares the LORD,
"That you will call Me [I][a]Ishi
And will no longer call Me [II]Baali.[1167]

17 "For [a]I will remove[5493] the names of the Baals from her mouth,
So that they will be [I]mentioned[2142] by their names no more.

18 "In that day I will also make[3772] a covenant[1285] for them
With the [a]beasts of the field,
The birds of the sky,[8064]
And the creeping things of the ground.[127]
And I will [I][b]abolish[7665] the bow, the sword, and war from the land,[776]
And will make them [c]lie down in safety.[983]

19 "And I will [a]betroth[781] you to Me forever;[5769]
Yes, I will betroth you to Me in [b]righteousness and in justice,[4941]
In lovingkindness[2617] and in compassion,[7356]

20 And I will betroth you to Me in faithfulness.[530]
Then you will [a]know[3045] the LORD.

21 "And it will come about in that day that [a]I will respond," declares the LORD.
"I will respond to the heavens,[8064] and they will respond to the earth,

22 And the [a]earth will respond to the grain, to the new wine, and to the oil,
And they will respond to [I]Jezreel.

23 "And I will [a]sow her for Myself in the land.
[b]I will also have compassion[7355] on [I]her who had not obtained compassion,[7355]
And [c]I will say[559] to [II]those who were [d]not My people,
'You are My people!'
And [III]they will say, '*Thou art* my God!' "[430]

11 [a]Jer. 7:34; 16:9 [b]Hos. 3:4; Amos 5:21; 8:10 [c]Is. 1:13, 14

12 [a]Jer. 5:17; 8:13 [b]Is. 5:5; 7:23 [c]Hos. 13:8

13 [I]Or, *burn incense* [II]Or, *nose rings* [a]Hos. 4:13; 11:2 [b]Jer. 7:9 [c]Ezek. 16:12, 17; 23:40 [d]Hos. 4:6; 8:14; 13:6

14 [I]Lit., *upon her heart* [a]Ezek. 20:33-38

15 [I]Or, *give answer* [a]Ezek. 28:25, 26 [b]Josh. 7:26 [c]Jer. 2:1-3; Ezek. 16:8-14 [d]Hos. 11:1; 12:9, 13; 13:4

16 [I]I.e., my husband [II]I.e., my master, or my Baal [a]Is. 54:5; Hos. 2:7

17 [I]Or, *remembered* [a]Ex. 23:13; Josh. 23:7; Ps. 16:4

18 [I]Lit., *break* [a]Job 5:23; Is. 11:6-9; Ezek. 34:25 [b]Is. 2:4; Ezek. 39:1-10 [c]Lev. 26:5; Jer. 23:6; Ezek. 34:25

19 [a]Is. 62:4, 5 [b]Is. 1:27; 54:6-8

20 [a]Jer. 31:33, 34; Hos. 6:6; 13:4

21 [a]Is. 55:10; Zech. 8:12; Mal. 3:10, 11

22 [I]I.e., God sows [a]Jer. 31:12; Joel 2:19

23 [I]Heb., *Lo-ruhamah* [II]Heb., *Lo-ammi* [III]Lit., *he* [a]Jer. 31:27 [b]Hos. 1:6 [c]Rom. 9:25; 1Pet. 2:10 [d]Hos. 1:9

2:15 See note on Jer. 2:2.
2:23 See Rom. 9:23-26.

Hosea's Second Symbolic Marriage

3 Then the LORD said[559] to me, "Go
again, love[157] a [I]woman[802] *who* is
loved[157] by *her* [II]husband,[7453] yet an adulteress,[5003] even [a]as the LORD loves[160]
the sons[1121] of Israel, though they turn
to other gods[430] and love[157] raisin
[b]cakes."[809]
2 So I [a]bought her for myself for
fifteen *shekels* of silver and a homer[2563]
and a [I]half[3963] of barley.
3 Then I said to her, "You shall
[a]stay with me for many days. You shall
not play the harlot, nor shall you have[1961]
a [I]man;[376] so I will also be toward you."
4 For the sons of Israel will remain for many days [a]without king or
prince,[8269] [b]without sacrifice[2077] or *sa-*
cred [c]pillar,[4676] and without [d]ephod or
[I][e]household idols.[8655]
5 Afterward the sons of Israel will
[a]return[7725] and seek the LORD their
God[430] and [b]David their king; and
[c]they will come trembling[6342] to the
LORD and to His goodness[2898] in the
last[319] days.

God's Controversy with Israel

4 [a]Listen to the word[1697] of the
LORD, O sons[1121] of Israel,
For the LORD has a [b]case[7379]
against the inhabitants of the
land,[776]
Because there is [c]no
[I]faithfulness[571] or
[II]kindness[2617]
Or [d]knowledge[1847] of God[430] in
the land.
2 *There is* [a]swearing,[422]
[b]deception, [c]murder,
[d]stealing, and [e]adultery.
They employ violence, so that
[f]bloodshed[1818] [I]follows[5060]
bloodshed.
3 Therefore the land [a]mourns,
And everyone who lives in it
languishes
Along with the beasts[2416] of the
field[7704] and the birds of the
sky;[8064]
And also the fish of the sea
[I]disappear.[622]
4 Yet let no one[376] [I][a]find fault,[7378]
and let none offer reproof;[3198]
For your people[5971] are like
those who [b]contend with the
priest.[3548]
5 So you will [a]stumble[3782] by
day,[3117]
And the prophet[5030] also will
stumble with you by
night;[3915]
And I will destroy[1820] your
[b]mother.[517]
6 [a]My people are destroyed for
lack of knowledge.[1847]
Because you have [b]rejected[3988]
knowledge,
I also will [c]reject you from being
My priest.[3547]
Since you have [d]forgotten the
[e]law[8451] of your God,
I also will forget your children.
7 The more they [a]multiplied, the
more they sinned[2398] against
Me;
I will [b]change their glory[3519] into
shame.
8 They [a]feed on the [I]sin[2403] of My
people,
And [b]direct[5375] their desire[5315]
toward their iniquity.[5771]
9 And it will be, like people,
[a]like priest;
So I will [b]punish[6485] them for
their ways,[1870]
And repay[7725] them for their
deeds.
10 And [a]they will eat, but not have
enough;
They will [b]play the harlot,[2181] but
not increase,
Because they have [I][c]stopped[5800]
giving heed[8104] to the LORD.

1 [I]I.e., Gomer [II]Lit., *companion* [a]Jer. 3:20 [b]2Sam. 6:19; 1Chr. 16:3; Song 2:5
2 [I]Heb., *lethech* [a]Ruth 4:10
3 [I]Or, *husband* [a]Deut. 21:13
4 [I]Heb., *teraphim* [a]Hos. 10:3; 13:10, 11 [b]Dan. 9:27; 11:31; 12:11; Hos. 2:11 [c]Hos. 10:1, 2 [d]Ex. 28:4-12; 1Sam. 23:9-12 [e]Gen. 31:19, 34; Judg. 17:5; 18:14, 17; 1Sam. 15:23
5 [a]Jer. 50:4, 5 [b]Jer. 30:9; Ezek. 34:24 [c]Is. 2:2, 3; Jer. 31:9

1 [I]Or, *truth* [II]Or, *loyalty* [a]Hos. 5:1 [b]Hos. 12:2; Mic. 6:2 [c]Is. 59:4; Jer. 7:28 [d]Jer. 4:22
2 [I]Lit., *touches* [a]Deut. 5:11; Hos. 10:4 [b]Hos. 7:3; 10:13; 11:12 [c]Gen. 4:8; Hos. 6:9 [d]Deut. 5:19; Hos. 7:1 [e]Deut. 5:18; Hos. 7:4 [f]Hos. 6:8; 12:14
3 [I]Lit., *are taken away* [a]Is. 24:4; 33:9; Amos 5:16; Zeph. 1:3
4 [I]Lit., *contend* [a]Ezek. 3:26; Amos 5:10, 13 [b]Deut. 17:12
5 [a]Ezek. 14:3, 7; Hos. 5:5 [b]Jer. 15:8; Hos. 2:2, 5
6 [a]Is. 5:13 [b]Hos. 4:14; Mal. 2:7, 8 [c]Zech. 11:8, 9, 15-17 [d]Hos. 2:13; 8:14; 13:6 [e]Hos. 8:1, 12
7 [a]Hos. 10:1; 13:6 [b]Hab. 2:16
8 [I]Or, *sin offering* [a]Hos. 10:13 [b]Is. 56:11; Mic. 3:11
9 [a]Is. 24:2; Jer. 5:31 [b]Hos. 8:13; 9:9
10 [I]Lit., *forsaken giving heed;* or, *forsaken the* LORD *to practice* (v. 11) *harlotry.* [a]Lev. 26:26; Is. 65:13; Mic. 6:14 [b]Hos. 7:4 [c]Hos. 9:17

4:4 The leadership was bad; this caused the people to stray away from God.
4:6 See note on Deut. 6:4-9.

11 Harlotry,[2184] [a]wine, and new
wine take away the
[I]understanding.[3820]
12 My people [a]consult[7592] their
wooden idol, and their
diviner's wand informs[5046]
them;
For a spirit[7307] of harlotry[2183] has
led *them* astray,[8582]
And they have played the harlot,
departing [I]from their God.[430]
13 They offer sacrifices on the
[a]tops[7218] of the mountains
And [Ib]burn incense[6999] on the
hills,
[c]Under oak, poplar, and
terebinth,
Because their shade is
pleasant.[2896]
Therefore your daughters play
the harlot,
And your [II]brides commit
adultery.
14 I will not punish[6485] your
daughters when they play the
harlot
Or your [I]brides when they
commit adultery,
For *the men* themselves go apart
with harlots[2181]
And offer sacrifices with
[a]temple prostitutes;[6948]
So the people without
understanding[995] are [II]ruined.
15 Though you, Israel, play the
harlot,[2181]
Do not let Judah become guilty;
Also do not go to [a]Gilgal,
Or go up[5927] to Beth-aven,
[b]And take the oath:[7650]
"As the LORD lives!"[2416]
16 Since Israel is [a]stubborn[5637]
Like a stubborn heifer,
[I]Can the LORD now [b]pasture
them
Like a lamb in a large field?
17 Ephraim is joined to [a]idols;[6091]
[b]Let him alone.
18 Their liquor gone,[5493]
They play the harlot continually;
[a]Their [I]rulers dearly love[157]
shame.
🔑 19 [a]The wind[7307] wraps them in its
wings,
And they will be ashamed[954]
because of their
sacrifices.[2077]

The People's Apostasy Rebuked

5 Hear this, O priests![3548]
Give heed,[7161] O house[1004] of
Israel!
Listen,[238] O house of the king!
For the judgment[4941] applies to
you,
For you have been a [a]snare[6341]
at Mizpah,
And a net spread out on Tabor.
2 And the [a]revolters have
[Ib]gone deep in depravity,[7819]
But I will chastise[4148] all of
them.
3 I [a]know[3045] Ephraim, and Israel
is not hidden from Me;
For now, O Ephraim, you have
played the harlot,[2181]
Israel has defiled[2930] itself.
4 Their deeds will not allow them
To return[7725] to their God.[430]
For a [a]spirit[7307] of harlotry[2183]
is within them,
And they [b]do not know[3045] the
LORD.
5 Moreover, the [a]pride of Israel
testifies against him,
And Israel and Ephraim
stumble[3782] in their
iniquity;[5771]
[b]Judah also has stumbled with
them.
6 They will [a]go with their flocks
and herds
To seek the LORD, but they will
[b]not find *Him*;
He has [c]withdrawn from them.
7 They have [a]dealt
treacherously[898] against
the LORD,

11 [I]Lit., *heart* [a]Prov. 20:1; Is. 5:12; 28:7
12 [I]Lit., *from under* [a]Is. 44:19; Jer. 2:27
13 [I]Or, *offer sacrifices* [II]Or, *daughters-in-law* [a]Jer. 3:6 [b]Hos. 2:13; 11:2 [c]Is. 1:29; Jer. 2:20
14 [I]Or, *daughters-in-law* [II]Lit., *thrust down* [a]Deut. 23:17
15 [a]Hos. 9:15; 12:11 [b]Jer. 5:2; 44:26; Amos 8:14
16 [I]Or, *Now the LORD will pasture. . . field.* [a]Ps. 78:8 [b]Is. 5:17; 7:25
17 [a]Hos. 13:2 [b]Ps. 81:12; Hos. 4:4
18 [I]Lit., *shields* [a]Mic. 3:11
19 [a]Hos. 12:1; 13:15

1 [a]Hos. 9:8
2 [I]Or, *waded deep in slaughter* [a]Hos. 9:15 [b]Is. 29:15; Hos. 4:2; 6:9
3 [a]Amos 3:2; 5:12
4 [a]Hos. 4:12 [b]Hos. 4:6, 14
5 [a]Hos. 7:10 [b]Ezek. 23:31-35
6 [a]Hos. 8:13; Mic. 6:6, 7 [b]Prov. 1:28; Is. 1:15; Jer. 14:12 [c]Ezek. 8:6
7 [a]Is. 48:8; Jer. 3:20; Hos. 6:7

🔑 **4:19** The "wind" here is the Assyrian invasion just over the horizon.

For they have borne[3205]
[Ib]illegitimate[2114] children.[1121]
Now the [c]new moon will devour
them with their [II]land.
8 [a]Blow[8628] the horn in [b]Gibeah,
The trumpet in Ramah.
Sound an alarm[7321] at Beth-aven:
"[c]Behind you, Benjamin!"
9 Ephraim will become a
[a]desolation[8047] in the [b]day[3117]
of rebuke;[8433]
Among the tribes[7626] of Israel I
[c]declare[3045] what is sure.[539]
🗝 10 The princes[8269] of Judah have become like those who [a]move
a boundary;
On them I will [b]pour out[8210] My
wrath[5678] [c]like water.
11 Ephraim is [a]oppressed, crushed
in judgment,
[b]Because he was determined[2974]
to [I]follow *man's* command.
12 Therefore I am like a [a]moth to
Ephraim,
And like rottenness to the house
of Judah.
13 When Ephraim saw[7200] his
sickness,
And Judah his [I]wound,
Then Ephraim went to
[a]Assyria
And sent to [IIb]King Jareb.[7378]
But he is [c]unable to heal you,
Or to cure[1455] you of your
[I]wound.
14 For I *will be* [a]like a lion to
Ephraim,
And like a young lion to the
house of Judah.
[b]I, even I, will tear to pieces
and go away,
I will carry away, and there will
be [c]none to deliver.[5337]
15 I will go away *and* return[7725] to
My place

7 [I]Lit., *strange* [II]Lit., *portions* [b]Hos. 2:4 [c]Is. 1:14; Hos. 2:11
8 [a]Joel 2:1 [b]Hos. 9:9; 10:9 [c]Judg. 5:14
9 [a]Is. 28:1-4; Hos. 9:11-17 [b]Is. 37:3 [c]Is. 46:10; Zech. 1:6
10 [a]Deut. 19:14; 27:17 [b]Ezek. 7:8 [c]Ps. 32:6; 93:3, 4
11 [I]Or, with some ancient versions, *follow nothingness* [a]Deut. 28:33 [b]Mic. 6:16
12 [a]Ps. 39:11; Is. 51:8
13 [I]Or, *ulcer* [II]Or, *the avenging king* or *the great king* [a]Hos. 7:11; 8:9; 12:1 [b]Hos. 10:6 [c]Jer. 30:12-15
14 [a]Ps. 7:2; Hos. 13:7, 8; Amos 3:4 [b]Ps. 50:22 [c]Mic. 5:8
15 [I]Or, *bear their punishment* [a]Is. 64:7-9; Jer. 3:13, 14 [b]Ps. 50:15; 78:34; Jer. 2:27; Hos. 3:5

1 [I]Lit., *struck* [a]Jer. 50:4, 5 [b]Deut. 32:39; Hos. 5:14 [c]Jer. 30:17; Hos. 14:4 [d]Is. 30:26
2 [a]Ps. 30:5 [b]1Cor. 15:4
3 [a]Is. 2:3; Mic. 4:2 [b]Ps. 19:6; Mic. 5:2 [c]Job 29:23; Ps. 72:6; Joel 2:23
4 [I]Or, *lovingkindness* [a]Hos. 7:1; 11:8 [b]Ps. 78:34-37; Hos. 13:3
5 [a]1Sam. 15:32, 33; Jer. 1:10; 5:14 [b]Jer. 23:29
6 [a]Matt. 9:13; 12:7 [b]Is. 1:11

Until they [Ia]acknowledge[5234]
their guilt and seek My face;
In their affliction they will
earnestly [b]seek Me.

The Response to God's Rebuke

6 "[a]Come, let us return[7725] to the LORD.
For [b]He has torn *us,* but
[c]He will heal us;
He has [I]wounded[5221] *us,* but He
will [d]bandage[2280] us.
2 "He will [a]revive[2421] us after two
days;
He will [b]raise us up on the third
day
That we may live[2421] before
Him.
3 "So let us [a]know, let us press
on to know[3045] the LORD.
His [b]going forth is as certain[3559]
as the dawn;
And He will come to us like the
[c]rain,
Like the spring rain watering the
earth."[776]
4 What shall I do[6213] with you, O
[a]Ephraim?
What shall I do with you, O
Judah?
For your [I]loyalty[2617] is like a
[b]morning cloud,[6051]
And like the dew which goes
away early.
5 Therefore I have [a]hewn[2672] *them*
in pieces by the prophets;[5030]
I have slain[2026] them by the
[b]words of My mouth;[6310]
And the judgments[4941] on you
are *like* the light[216] that goes
forth.
🗝 6 For [a]I delight[2654] in loyalty
[b]rather than sacrifice,[2077]
And in the knowledge[1847] of

🗝 **5:10** See Deut. 19:14; 27:17.
🗝 **6:6** This verse marks the high point of the theology of the Book of Hosea. Its importance was recognized by Jesus, who used it to explain both His association with sinners (Mt. 9:11-13) and why His disciples could pick grain on the sabbath (Mt. 12:1-7). See also God's reaction to insincere offerings in Isa. 1:11-17.

God[430] rather than burnt
offerings.[5930]
7 But [a]like [I]Adam[120] they have
[b]transgressed[5674] the
covenant;[1285]
There they have [c]dealt
treacherously[898] against Me.
8 [a]Gilead is a city of
wrongdoers,[205]
Tracked[6121] with [b]bloody[1818]
footprints.
9 And as [a]raiders[1416] wait for a
man,[376]
So a band of priests[3548]
[b]murder[7523] on the way[1870] to
Shechem;
Surely they have committed[6213]
[I][c]crime.[2154]
10 In the house[1004] of Israel I have
seen[7200] a [a]horrible thing;[8186]
Ephraim's [b]harlotry[2184] is there,
Israel has defiled[2930] itself.
11 Also, O Judah, there is a
[a]harvest appointed for you,
When I [b]restore[7725] the
fortunes[7622] of My people.[5971]

Ephraim's Iniquity

7 When I [a]would heal Israel,
The iniquity[5771] of Ephraim is
uncovered,[1540]
And the evil deeds[7451] of
Samaria,
For they deal [b]falsely;[8267]
The thief enters in,
[c]Bandits[1416] raid outside,
2 And they do not [I]consider[559] in
their hearts[3824]
That I [a]remember[2142] all their
wickedness.
Now their [b]deeds are all around
them;
They are before My face.
3 [a]With their wickedness they
make the [b]king glad,
And the princes[8269] with their
[c]lies.
4 They are [a]all adulterers[5003]
Like an oven heated by the
baker,
Who ceases[7673] to stir up *the fire*
From the kneading of the dough
until it is leavened.
5 On the [I]day[3117] of our king, the
princes [a]became sick with the
heat[2534] of wine;
He stretched out his hand[3027]
with [b]scoffers,
6 For their hearts[3820] are like an
[a]oven
As they approach[7126] their
[I]plotting;
Their [II]anger [III]smolders all
night,
In the morning it burns like a
flaming fire.
7 All of them are hot like an oven,
And they consume their
[a]rulers;[8199]
All their kings have fallen.[5307]
[b]None of them calls[7121] on
Me.
8 Ephraim [a]mixes[1101] himself with
the [I]nations;[5971]
Ephraim has become a cake not
turned.[2015]
9 [a]Strangers[2114] devour his
strength,
Yet he [b]does not know *it;*
Gray hairs also are sprinkled[2236]
on him,
Yet he does not know *it.*
10 Though the [a]pride of Israel
testifies against him,
Yet [b]they have neither
returned[7725] to the LORD their
God,[430]
Nor have they sought Him, for
all this.
11 So [a]Ephraim has become like a
silly dove, [b]without [I]sense;
They call[7121] to [c]Egypt, they go
to [d]Assyria.
12 When they go, I will [a]spread My
net over them;
I will bring them down like the
birds of the sky.[8064]
I will [b]chastise[3256] them in
accordance with the
[I]proclamation to their
assembly.[5712]
13 [a]Woe to them, for they have
[b]strayed from Me!

7 [I]Or, *men* [a]Job 31:33 [b]Hos. 8:1 [c]Hos. 5:7
8 [a]Hos. 12:11 [b]Hos. 4:2
9 [I]Or, *lewdness* [a]Hos. 7:1 [b]Jer. 7:9, 10; Hos. 4:2 [c]Ezek. 22:9; 23:27; Hos. 2:10
10 [a]Jer. 5:30, 31; 23:14 [b]Hos. 5:3
11 [a]Jer. 51:33; Joel 3:13 [b]Zeph. 2:7

1 [a]Ezek. 24:13; Hos. 6:4; 7:13; 11:8 [b]Hos. 4:2 [c]Hos. 6:9
2 [I]Lit., *say to their heart* [a]Ps. 25:7; Jer. 14:10; 17:1; Hos. 8:13; 9:9; Amos 8:7 [b]Jer. 2:19; 4:18; Hos. 4:9
3 [a]Rom. 1:32 [b]Jer. 28:1-4; Hos. 7:5; Mic. 7:3 [c]Hos. 4:2; 11:12
4 [a]Jer. 9:2; 23:10
5 [I]I.e., a festive occasion [a]Is. 28:1, 7 [b]Is. 28:14
6 [I]Lit., *ambush* [II]So with some ancient versions; M.T., *baker* [III]Lit., *sleeps* [a]Ps. 21:9
7 [a]Hos. 13:10 [b]Is. 64:7
8 [I]Lit., *peoples* [a]Ps. 106:35
9 [a]Is. 1:7; Hos. 8:7 [b]Hos. 4:6
10 [a]Hos. 5:5 [b]Is. 9:13
11 [I]Lit., *heart* [a]Hos. 11:11 [b]Hos. 4:6, 11, 14; 5:4 [c]Hos. 8:13; 9:3, 6 [d]Hos. 5:13; 8:9; 12:1
12 [I]Lit., *report* [a]Ezek. 12:13 [b]Lev. 26:14-39; Deut. 28:15
13 [a]Hos. 9:12 [b]Jer. 14:10; Ezek. 34:6; Hos. 9:17

Destruction7701 is theirs, for
they have rebelled6586 against
Me!
I [c]would redeem6299 them, but
they speak1696 lies3577 against
Me.
14 And [a]they do not cry2199 to Me
from their heart
When they wail on their beds;
For the sake of grain and new
wine they [Ib]assemble
themselves,1481
They [c]turn away5493 from Me.
15 Although I trained3256 *and*
strengthened2388 their
arms,
Yet they [a]devise2803 evil7451
against Me.
16 They turn,7725 *but* not [I]upward,
They are like a [a]deceitful bow;
Their princes will fall by the
sword2719
Because of the [IIb]insolence2195
of their tongue.
This *will be* their [c]derision in the
land776 of Egypt.

Israel Reaps the Whirlwind

8 [a]*Put* the trumpet to your [I]lips!
[b]Like an eagle *the enemy comes*
[c]against the house1004 of the
LORD,
Because they have
[d]transgressed5674
My covenant,1285
And rebelled6586 against My
[e]law.8451
2 [a]They cry out to Me,
"My God,430 [b]we of Israel
know3045 Thee!"
3 Israel has rejected the good;2896
The enemy will pursue him.
4 [a]They have set up kings,4427 but
not by Me;
They have appointed6213
princes,7786 but I did not
know *it*.
With their [b]silver and gold they
have made idols6091 for
themselves,
That [I]they might be cut off.3772
5 [I]He has rejected your [a]calf, O
Samaria, saying,
"My anger639 burns2734 against
them!"
How long will they be
incapable3808,3201 of
[b]innocence?5536
6 For from Israel is even this!
A [a]craftsman made it, so it is
not God;
Surely the calf of Samaria will
be broken to [I]pieces.
7 For [a]they sow the wind,7307
And they reap the [b]whirlwind.
The standing grain has no
[I]heads;
It yields6213 [c]no [II]grain.
Should it yield, strangers2114
would swallow it up.1104
8 Israel is [a]swallowed up;
They are now among the
nations1471
Like a [b]vessel in which no one
delights.2656
9 For they have gone up5927 to
[a]Assyria,
Like [b]a wild donkey all alone;
Ephraim has [c]hired [I]lovers.158
10 Even though they hire *allies*
among the nations,1471
Now I will [a]gather6908 them up;
And they will begin [b]to
[I]diminish2490
Because of the burden4853 of the
[c]king of princes.8269
11 Since Ephraim has [a]multiplied
altars4196 for sin,2398
They have become altars of
sinning for him.
12 Though [a]I wrote for him ten
thousand *precepts* of My
[b]law,
They are regarded2803 as a
strange thing.2114

13 [c]Jer. 51:9; Hos. 7:1; Matt. 23:37
14 [I]Or, with Gr. and many ancient mss., *gash themselves* [a]Job 35:9-11; Hos. 8:2; Zech. 7:5 [b]Judg. 9:27; Amos 2:8; Mic. 2:11 [c]Hos. 13:16
15 [a]Nah. 1:9
16 [I]Or possibly, *to the Most High* [II]Lit., *indignation;* or, *cursing* [a]Ps. 78:57 [b]Ps. 12:3, 4; 17:10; 73:9; Dan. 7:25; Mal. 3:13, 14 [c]Ezek. 23:32; Hos. 9:3, 6
1 [I]Lit., *palate* [a]Jer 4:13; Hos. 5:8 [b]Hab. 1:8 [c]Deut. 28:49 [d]Hos. 6:7 [e]Hos. 4:6
2 [a]Ps. 78:34; Hos. 7:14 [b]Titus 1:16
4 [I]Lit., *he* [a]2Kin. 15:13, 17, 25; Hos. 13:10, 11 [b]Hos. 2:8; 13:1, 2
5 [I]Or, *Your calf has rejected you* [a]Hos. 10:5; 13:2 [b]Ps. 19:13; Jer. 13:27
6 [I]Or, *splinters* [a]Hos. 13:2
7 [I]Lit., *growth* [II]Or, *meal* [a]Prov. 22:8 [b]Is. 66:15; Nah. 1:3 [c]Hos. 2:9
8 [a]2Kin. 17:6; Jer. 51:34 [b]Jer. 22:28; 25:34
9 [I]Lit., *loves* [a]Hos. 7:11 [b]Jer. 2:24 [c]Ezek. 16:33, 34
10 [I]Or, *suffer for awhile* [a]Ezek. 16:37; 22:20 [b]Jer. 42:2 [c]Is. 10:8
11 [a]Hos. 10:1
12 [a]Deut. 4:6, 8 [b]Hos. 4:6

8:8,9 Although Israel's full exile did not take place until 722 B.C., some of the northern part of the nation was captured and deported by the Assyrian emperor, Tiglath-pileser III, in 732 B.C. (II Kgs. 15:29). That deportation is reflected in these verses as an event which had already happened.

13 As for My [a]sacrificial[2077]
gifts,[1890]
They [b]sacrifice[2076] the flesh[1319]
and eat *it,*
But the LORD has taken no
delight[7521] in them.
Now He will [c]remember[2142] their
iniquity,[5771]
And [d]punish[6485] *them* for their
sins;[2403]
They will return[7725] to [e]Egypt.
14 For Israel has [a]forgotten his
Maker[6213] and [b]built
palaces;[1964]
And Judah has multiplied fortified
cities,
But I will send a [c]fire on its cities
that it may consume its
palatial dwellings.[759]

Ephraim Punished

9 [a]Do not rejoice, O Israel,
[I]with exultation like the
[II]nations![5971]
For you have [b]played the
harlot,[2181] [III]forsaking your
God.[430]
You have loved[157] *harlots'*
earnings on [IV]every threshing
floor.
2 Threshing floor and wine press
will [a]not feed them,
And the new wine will fail
[I]them.
🔑 3 They will not remain in
[a]the LORD's land,[776]
But Ephraim will return[7725] to
[b]Egypt,
And in [c]Assyria they will eat
[d]unclean[2931] *food.*
4 They will not pour out[5258]
libations of [a]wine to the
LORD,
[b]Their sacrifices[2077] will not
please[6148] Him.
Their bread will [I]*be* like
[II]mourners'[205] bread;
All who eat of it will be
[c]defiled,[2930]
For their bread will be for
[III]themselves[5315] *alone;*
It will not enter the house[1004]
of the LORD.
5 [a]What will you do[6213] on the day
of the appointed[4150] festival
And on the day of the
[b]feast[2282] of the LORD?
6 For behold, they will go because
of destruction;[7701]
Egypt will gather[6908] them up,
[a]Memphis will bury[6912]
them.
Weeds will take over[3423] their
treasures of silver;
[b]Thorns *will be* in their tents.[168]
7 The days[3117] of [a]punishment[6486]
have come,
The days of [b]retribution[7966] have
come;
[I]Let Israel know[3045] *this!*
The prophet[5030] is a [c]fool,
The [II]inspired[7307] man[376] is
[d]demented,
Because of the grossness of
your [e]iniquity,[5771]
And *because* your hostility is *so*
great.
8 Ephraim *was* a watchman with
my God, a prophet;
Yet the snare[6341] of a bird catcher
is in all his ways,[1870]
And there is *only* hostility in the
house of his God.
9 They have gone [a]deep
[I]in depravity
As in the days of [b]Gibeah;
He will [c]remember[2142] their
iniquity,
He will punish[6485] their sins.[2403]
10 I found Israel like [a]grapes in the
wilderness;
I saw[7200] your forefathers[1] as the
[b]earliest fruit on the fig tree
in its first *season.*[7225]
But they came to [c]Baal-peor and

13 [a]Hos. 5:6 [b]Jer. 6:20; 7:21 [c]Jer. 14:10; Hos. 7:2; Luke 12:2; 1Cor. 4:5 [d]Hos. 4:9; 9:7 [e]Hos. 9:3, 6

14 [a]Deut. 32:18; Hos. 2:13; 4:6; 13:6 [b]Is. 9:9, 10 [c]Jer. 17:27

1 [I]Lit., *to* [II]Lit., *peoples* [III]Lit., *away from your God* [IV]Lit., *all threshing floors of grain* [a]Is. 22:12, 13; Hos. 10:5 [b]Hos. 4:12

2 [I]Lit., *her* [a]Hos. 2:9

3 [a]Lev. 25:23; Jer. 2:7 [b]Hos. 7:16; 8:13 [c]Hos. 7:11 [d]Ezek. 4:13

4 [I]Lit., *be to them* [II]Or, *bread of misfortune* [III]Lit., *their appetite* [a]Ex. 29:40 [b]Jer. 6:20; Hos. 8:13 [c]Hag. 2:13, 14

5 [a]Is. 10:3; Jer. 5:31 [b]Hos. 2:11; Joel 1:13

6 [a]Is. 19:13; Jer. 2:16; 44:1; 46:14, 19; Ezek. 30:13, 16 [b]Is. 5:6; 7:23; Hos. 10:8

7 [I]Or, *Israel will know it* [II]Lit., *man of the spirit* [a]Is. 10:3; Jer. 10:15; Mic. 7:4; Luke 21:22 [b]Is. 34:8; Jer. 16:18; 25:14 [c]Lam. 2:14; Ezek. 13:3, 10 [d]Is. 44:25 [e]Ezek. 14:9, 10

9 [I]Lit., *they have corrupted* [a]Is. 31:6 [b]Judg. 19:12, 16-30; Hos. 10:9 [c]Hos. 7:2; 8:13

10 [a]Mic. 7:1 [b]Jer. 24:2 [c]Num. 25:1-5; Ps. 106:28, 29

🔑 **9:3** Israel's return to Egypt and sojourn in a distant land like Assyria are a direct fulfillment of part of the curses which Moses laid down for not living up to the terms of the covenant (Deut. 28:58,63-68). See also Amos 3:9.

devoted[5144] themselves to
[Id]shame,
And they became as
[e]detestable[8251] as that which
they loved.[157]
11 As for Ephraim, their [a]glory[3519]
will fly away like a bird—
No birth, no pregnancy,[990] and
no conception!
12 Though they bring up their
children,[1121]
Yet I will bereave them
[I]until not a man[120] is left.
Yes, [a]woe to them indeed when
I depart from them!
13 Ephraim, as I have seen,
Is planted in a pleasant meadow
like [a]Tyre;
But Ephraim will bring out his
children for slaughter.[2026]
14 Give them, O LORD—what wilt
Thou give?
Give them a [a]miscarrying womb
and dry breasts.
15 All their evil[7451] is at [a]Gilgal;
Indeed, I came to hate[8130] them
there!
Because of the [b]wickedness[7455]
of their deeds
I will drive them out of My
house!
I will love[160] them no more;
All their princes[8269] are
[c]rebels.[5637]
16 [a]Ephraim is stricken,[5221] their
root is dried up,[3001]
They will bear[6213] [b]no fruit.
Even though they bear children,
I will slay[4191] the [c]precious ones
of their womb.
17 My God[430] will cast them
away[3988]
Because they have [a]not
listened[8085] to Him;
And they will be [b]wanderers
among the nations.[1471]

Retribution for Israel's Sin

10 Israel is a [I]luxuriant [a]vine;
He produces fruit for himself.
The more his fruit,
The more altars[4196] he
[b]made;
The [II]richer[2896] his land,[776]
The better[2895] [III]he made the
sacred [c]pillars[4676].
2 Their heart[3820] is [Ia]faithless;
Now they must bear their
[b]guilt.
[II]The LORD will [c]break down
their altars
And destroy[7703] their *sacred*
pillars.
3 Surely now they will say,[559] "We
have [a]no king,
For we do not revere[3372] the
LORD.
As for the king, what can he
do[6213] for us?"
4 They speak[1696] *mere* words,[1697]
[I]With [a]worthless[7723] oaths[422]
they make[3772] covenants;[1285]
And [b]judgment[4941] sprouts like
poisonous weeds in the
furrows[8525] of the field.[7704]
5 The inhabitants[7934] of Samaria
will fear[1481]
For the [Ia]calf of [b]Beth-aven.
Indeed, its people[5971] will mourn
for it,
And its [c]idolatrous priests[3649]
[II]will cry out over it,
Over its [d]glory,[3519] since it has
departed[1540] from it.
6 The thing itself will be carried
to [a]Assyria
As tribute[4503] to [Ib]King
Jareb;
Ephraim will [II]be [c]seized with
shame,
And Israel will be ashamed[954] of
its [d]own counsel.[6098]
7 Samaria will be [a]cut off[1820] *with*
her king,
Like a stick[7110] on the surface
of the water.
8 Also the [a]high places[1116] of
Aven,[205] the [b]sin[2403] of Israel,
will be destroyed;[8045]
[c]Thorn and thistle will grow[5927]
on their altars,
Then they will [d]say to the
mountains,

10 [I]I.e., Baal [d]Jer. 11:13; Hos. 4:18 [e]Ps. 115:8; Ezek. 20:8
11 [a]Hos. 4:7; 10:5
12 [I]Lit., *without a man* [a]Deut. 31:17; Hos. 7:13
13 [a]Ezek. 26:1-21
14 [a]Hos. 9:11
15 [a]Hos. 4:15; 12:11 [b]Hos. 4:9; 7:2; 12:2 [c]Is. 1:23; Hos. 5:2
16 [a]Hos. 5:11 [b]Hos. 8:7 [c]Ezek. 24:21
17 [a]Hos. 4:10 [b]Hos. 7:13

1 [I]Or, *degenerate* [II]Or, *better* [III]Lit., *they* [a]Is. 5:1-7; Ezek. 15:1-6 [b]Jer. 2:28; Hos. 8:11; 12:11 [c]1Kin. 14:23; Hos. 3:4
2 [I]Lit., *smooth* [II]Lit., *He* [a]1Kin. 18:21; Zeph. 1:5 [b]Hos. 13:16 [c]Hos. 10:8; Mic. 5:13
3 [a]Ps. 12:4; Is. 5:19
4 [I]Or, *Swearing falsely in making a covenant* [a]Ezek. 17:13-19; Hos. 4:2 [b]Deut. 31:16, 17; 2Kin. 17:3,4; Amos 5:7
5 [I]So with some ancient versions; Heb., *calves* [II]Or, *who used to rejoice over* [a]Hos. 8:5, 6 [b]Hos. 4:15; 5:8 [c]2Kin. 23:5 [d]Hos. 9:11
6 [I]Or, *the avenging king* or *the great king* [II]Lit., *receive shame* [a]Hos. 11:5 [b]Hos. 5:13 [c]Hos. 4:7 [d]Is. 30:3; Jer. 7:24
7 [a]Hos. 13:11
8 [a]Hos. 4:13 [b]1Kin. 12:28-30; 13:34 [c]Is. 32:13; Hos. 9:6; 10:2 [d]Is. 2:19; Luke 23:30; Rev. 6:16

"Cover[3680] us!" And to the hills,
"Fall[5307] on us!"
9 From the days of Gibeah you
have sinned,[2398] O Israel;
There they stand!
Will not the battle against the
sons[1121] of iniquity[5932]
overtake them in Gibeah?
10 When it is My [a]desire, I will
[I][b]chastise[3256] them;
And [c]the peoples will be
gathered[622] against them
When they are bound for their
double guilt.[5771]
11 And Ephraim is a trained[3925]
[a]heifer that loves[157] to
thresh,
But I will [b]come over[5674] her
fair[2898] neck *with a yoke*;
I will harness Ephraim,
Judah will plow, Jacob will
harrow for himself.
12 [a]Sow with a view to
righteousness,
Reap in accordance with[6310]
[I]kindness;[2617]
[b]Break up your fallow ground,
For it is time[6256] to [c]seek the
LORD
Until He [d]comes to [II][e]rain
righteousness on you.
13 You have [a]plowed
wickedness,[7562] you have
reaped injustice,[5771]
You have eaten the fruit of
[b]lies.
Because you have trusted[982] in
your way,[1870] in your
[c]numerous warriors,
14 Therefore, a tumult[7588] will arise
among your people,
And all your [a]fortresses will be
destroyed,
As Shalman destroyed[7701] Beth-
arbel on the day[3117] of
battle,

10 [I]Or, *bind* [a]Ezek. 5:13 [b]Hos. 4:9 [c]Jer. 16:16
11 [a]Jer. 50:11; Hos. 4:16; Mic. 4:13 [b]Jer. 28:14
12 [I]Or, *loyalty* [II]Or, *teach* [a]Prov. 11:18 [b]Jer. 4:3 [c]Hos. 12:6 [d]Hos. 6:3 [e]Is. 44:3; 45:8
13 [a]Job 4:8; Prov. 22:8; Gal. 6:7, 8 [b]Hos. 4:2; 7:3; 11:12 [c]Ps. 33:16
14 [a]Is. 17:3 [b]Hos. 13:16
1 [a]Hos. 2:15; 12:9, 13; 13:4 [b]Ex. 4:22, 23; Matt. 2:15
2 [I]I.e., God's prophets [a]2Kin. 17:13-15 [b]Hos. 2:13; 4:13 [c]Is. 65:7; Jer. 18:15
3 [I]So ancient versions; Heb., *He . . . His* [a]Deut. 1:31; 32:10, 11 [b]Ps. 107:20; Jer. 30:17
4 [a]Jer. 31:2, 3 [b]Lev. 26:13 [c]Ex. 16:32; Ps. 78:25
5 [I]Lit., *He* [II]Lit., *his* [a]Hos. 7:16
6 [I]Lit., *his* [a]Hos. 13:16 [b]Lam. 2:9 [c]Hos. 4:16, 17
7 [a]Jer. 3:6, 7; 8:5

When [b]mothers[517] were dashed
in pieces with *their* children.
15 Thus it will be done[6213] to you
at Bethel because of your
great wickedness.[7451]
At dawn the king of Israel will
be completely cut off.[1820]

God Yearns over His People

11 🔑 When Israel *was* a youth I
loved[157] him,
And [a]out of Egypt I [b]called[7121]
My son.[1121]
2 The more [I][a]they called them,
The more they went from
[I]them;
They kept [b]sacrificing to the
Baals
And [c]burning incense[6999] to
idols.[6456]
3 Yet it is I who taught Ephraim
to walk,
[I]I [a]took them in My arms;
But they did not know[3045] that
I [b]healed them.
4 I [a]led them with cords[2256] of a
man,[120] with bonds of love,[160]
And [b]I became to them as one
who lifts the yoke from their
jaws;
And I bent down *and* [c]fed them.
5 [I]They will not return[7725] to the
land[776] of Egypt;
But Assyria—he will be [II]their
king,
Because they [a]refused[3985] to
return *to Me*.
6 And the [a]sword[2719] will whirl
against [I]their cities,
And will demolish[3615] [I]their gate
bars
And [b]consume *them* because of
their [c]counsels.
7 So My people[5971] are bent on
[a]turning[4878] from Me.

🔑 **11:1** Mt. (2:15) cited the second half of this verse as having been fulfilled when Joseph took Jesus to Egypt to protect him from Herod the Great. The obvious historical reference is to the Exodus of Israel centuries earlier (see Ex. 4:22), but the Holy Spirit applied this verse to the Lord Jesus Christ (see II Pet. 1:21). Hence, from a Christian perspective, Hos. 11:1 has two vastly different, but equally God-given, meanings.

Though [I]they call [II]them to *the One* on high,
None at all exalts *Him.*
8 [a]How can I give you up, O Ephraim?
How can I surrender you, O Israel?
How can I [I]make you like [b]Admah?
How can I treat[7760] you like [b]Zeboiim?
My heart[3820] is turned[2015] over within Me,
[II]All My compassions are kindled.
9 I will [a]not execute[6213] My fierce anger;[639]
I will not destroy[7843] Ephraim [b]again.
For [c]I am God[410] and not man,[376] the [d]Holy One[6918] in your midst,[7130]
And I will not come in [I]wrath.
10 They will [a]walk after the LORD,
He will [b]roar like a lion;
Indeed He will roar,
And *His* sons will come [c]trembling[2729] from the west.
11 They will come trembling like birds from [a]Egypt,
And like [b]doves from the land of [a]Assyria;
And I will [c]settle them in their houses,[1004] declares the LORD.
12 [I]Ephraim surrounds Me with [a]lies,
And the house[1004] of Israel with deceit;[4820]
Judah is also unruly[7300] against God,[410]
Even against the Holy One who is faithful.[539]

Ephraim Reminded

12 [I]Ephraim feeds on [a]wind,[7307]
And pursues the [b]east wind continually;[3117]
He multiplies lies[3577] and violence.[7701]
Moreover, [II]he makes[3772] a covenant[1285] with Assyria,
And oil[8281] is carried to Egypt.
2 The LORD also has a [a]dispute[7379] with Judah,
And will punish[6485] Jacob [b]according to his ways;[1870]
He will repay[7725] him according to his deeds.
3 In the womb[990] he [a]took[6117] his brother[251] by the heel,[6117]
And in his maturity he [b]contended[8280] with God.[430]
4 Yes, he wrestled with the angel[4397] and prevailed;[7786]
He wept and [a]sought His favor.[2603]
He found Him at [b]Bethel,
And there He spoke[1696] with us,
5 Even the LORD, the God of hosts;[6635]
The LORD is His [I][a]name.[2143]
6 Therefore, [a]return[7725] to your God,
[b]Observe[8104] [I]kindness[2617] and justice,[4941]
And [c]wait[6960] for your God continually.[8548]
7 A [I]merchant, in whose hands[3027] are false[4820] [a]balances,
He loves[157] to oppress.
8 And Ephraim said,[559] "Surely I have become [a]rich,
I have found wealth for myself;
In all my labors they will find in me
[b]No iniquity,[5771] which *would be* sin."[2399]
9 But I *have been* the LORD your God since the land[776] of Egypt;
I will make you [a]live in tents[168] again,
As in the days of the appointed festival.[4150]
10 I have also spoken[1696] to the [a]prophets,[5030]
And I [I]gave numerous visions;[2377]
And through[3027] the prophets I gave [b]parables.[1820]
11 Is there iniquity *in* Gilead?

---

7 [I]I.e., God's prophets [II]Lit., *him;* i.e., Israel

8 [I]Lit., *give* [II]Lit., *Together* [a]Hos. 6:4; 7:1 [b]Gen. 14:8; Deut. 29:23

9 [I]Lit., *excitement* [a]Deut. 13:17 [b]Jer. 26:3; 30:11 [c]Num. 23:19 [d]Is. 5:24; 12:6; 41:14, 16

10 [a]Hos. 3:5; 6:1-3 [b]Is. 31:4; Joel 3:16; Amos 1:2 [c]Is. 66:2,5

11 [a]Is. 11:11 [b]Is. 60:8; Hos. 7:11 [c]Ezek. 28:25, 26; 34:27, 28

12 [I]Ch. 12:1 in Heb. [a]Hos. 4:2; 7:3

1 [I]Ch. 12:2 in Heb. [II]Lit., *they make* [a]Jer. 22:22 [b]Gen. 41:6; Ezek. 17:10

2 [a]Hos. 4:1; Mic. 6:2 [b]Hos. 4:9; 7:2

3 [a]Gen. 25:26 [b]Gen. 32:28

4 [a]Gen. 32:26 [b]Gen. 28:13-19; 35:10-15

5 [I]Lit., *memorial* [a]Ex. 3:15

6 [I]Or, *loyalty* [a]Hos. 6:1-3; 10:12 [b]Mic. 6:8 [c]Mic. 7:7

7 [I]Or, *Canaanite* [a]Prov. 11:1; Amos 8:5; Mic. 6:11

8 [a]Ps. 62:10; Hos. 13:6; Rev. 3:17 [b]Hos. 4:8; 14:1

9 [a]Lev. 23:42

10 [I]Lit., *multiplied the vision* [a]2Kin. 17:13; Jer. 7:25 [b]Ezek. 17:2; 20:49

Surely they are worthless.[7723]
In Gilgal they sacrifice[2076] bulls,
Yes, [a]their altars[4196] are like the
stone heaps
Beside the furrows[8525] of the
field.[7704]
12 Now [a]Jacob fled to the
[I]land[7704] of Aram,
And [b]Israel worked[5647] for a
wife,[802]
And for a wife he kept[8104] *sheep.*
13 But by a [a]prophet the LORD
brought[5927] Israel from
Egypt,
And by a prophet he was
kept.[8104]
14 [a]Ephraim has provoked[3707] to
bitter anger;[3707]
So his Lord[113] will leave[5203] his
[b]bloodguilt[1818] on him,
And bring back[7725] his
[c]reproach[2781] to him.

Ephraim's Idolatry

13 [a]When Ephraim [I]spoke, *there was*
trembling.
He [b]exalted[5375] himself in Israel,
But through [c]Baal he [II]did wrong
and died.[4191]
2 And now they sin[2398] more and
more,
And make[6213] for themselves
[a]molten images,[4541]
Idols[6091] [I][b]skillfully[8394] made
from their silver,
All of them the [c]work of
craftsmen.
They say of them, "Let the
[II]men[120] who sacrifice kiss[5401]
the [d]calves!"
3 Therefore, they will be like the
[a]morning cloud,[6051]
And like dew which [I]soon
disappears,
Like [b]chaff which is blown away
from the threshing floor,
And like [c]smoke from a
[II]chimney.

4 Yet I *have been* the [a]LORD your
God[430]
Since the land[776] of Egypt;
And you were not to know[3045]
[b]any god[430] except Me,
For there is no savior[3467]
[c]besides Me.
5 I [I][a]cared[3045] for you in the
wilderness,
[b]In the land of drought.
6 As *they had* their pasture, they
became [a]satisfied,
And being satisfied, their
[b]heart[3820] became proud;
Therefore, they [c]forgot Me.
7 So I will be [a]like a lion to them;
Like a [b]leopard I will [I]lie in wait
by the wayside.[1870]
8 I will encounter them [a]like a bear
robbed of her cubs,[7909]
And I will tear[7167] open
[I]their chests;
There I will also [b]devour them
like a lioness,
As a wild[7704] beast would tear
them.
9 *It is* your destruction, O Israel,
[I]That *you are* [a]against Me,
against your [b]help.
10 Where now is your [a]king
That he may save[3467] you in all
your cities,
And your [b]judges[8199] of whom
you [I]requested,
"Give me a king and princes"?[8269]
11 I [a]gave you a king in My anger,[639]
And [b]took him away in My
wrath.[5678]
12 The iniquity[5771] of Ephraim is
bound up;
His sin[2403] is [a]stored up.
🔑 13 The pains[2256] of [a]childbirth come
upon him;
He is [b]not a wise son,[1121]
For [I]it is not the time[6256] that

11 [a]Hos. 8:11; 10:1, 2
12 [I]Lit., *field* [a]Gen. 28:5 [b]Gen. 29:20
13 [a]Ex. 14:19-22; Is. 63:11-14
14 [a]2Kin. 17:7-18 [b]Ezek. 18:10-13 [c]Dan. 11:18; Mic. 6:16

1 [I]Or, *spoke with trembling* [II]Or, *became guilty* [a]Job 29:21, 22 [b]Judg. 8:1; 12:1 [c]Hos. 2:8-17; 11:2
2 [I]Or, *according to their own understanding* [II]Lit., *sacrificers of (or, among) mankind* [a]Is. 46:6; Jer. 10:4; Hos. 2:8 [b]Is. 44:17-20 [c]Hos. 8:6 [d]Hos. 8:5, 6; 10:5
3 [I]Lit., *goes away early* [II]Lit., *window* [a]Hos. 6:4 [b]Ps. 1:4; Is. 17:13; Dan. 2:35 [c]Ps. 68:2
4 [a]Hos. 12:9 [b]Ex. 20:3; 2Kin. 18:35 [c]Is. 43:11; 45:21, 22
5 [I]Or, *knew* [a]Deut. 2:7; 32:10 [b]Deut. 8:15
6 [a]Deut. 8:12, 14; 32:13-15; Jer. 5:7 [b]Hos. 7:14 [c]Hos. 2:13; 4:6; 8:14
7 [I]Or, *watch* [a]Lam. 3:10; Hos. 5:14 [b]Jer. 5:6
8 [I]Lit., *the enclosure of their heart* [a]2Sam. 17:8 [b]Ps. 50:22
9 [I]Or, *But in Me is your help* [a]Jer. 2:17, 19; Mal. 1:12, 13 [b]Deut. 33:26, 29
10 [I]Lit., *said* [a]2Kin. 17:4; Hos. 8:4 [b]1Sam. 8:5, 6
11 [a]1Sam. 8:7; 10:17-24 [b]1Sam. 15:26; 1Kin. 14:7-10; Hos. 10:7
12 [a]Deut. 32:34, 35; Job 14:17; Rom. 2:5

13 [I]Lit., *it is the time that he should not tarry at the breaking forth of children* [a]Is. 13:8; Mic. 4:9, 10 [b]Deut. 32:6; Hos. 5:4

🔑 **13:13** This verse is saying that the northern kingdom, from the very beginning, was like a stillborn baby; there had been no life and no growth since its inception.

he should [c]delay at the
opening of the womb.
14 Shall I [a]ransom[6299] them from the
[I]power[3027] of Sheol?[7585]
Shall I redeem[1350] them from
death?
[b]O Death, where are your
thorns?[1698]
O Sheol, where is your sting?[6987]
[c]Compassion[5164] will be hidden
from My sight.
15 Though he [a]flourishes among the
[I]reeds,[251]
An [b]east wind[7307] will come,
The wind of the LORD coming
up[5927] from the wilderness;
And his fountain will [c]become
dry,[954]
And his spring will be dried
up;[2717]
It will [d]plunder[8154] *his* treasury
of every precious article.
16 [I]Samaria will be held [a]guilty,
For she has [b]rebelled[4784] against
her God.[430]
[c]They will fall[5307] by the
[d]sword,[2719]
Their little ones will be
[e]dashed in pieces,
And their pregnant [f]women will
be ripped open.

Israel's Future Blessing

14 [Ia]Return,[7725] O Israel, to the LORD
your God,[430]
For you have stumbled[3782]
[II]because of your [b]iniquity.[5771]
2 Take words[1697] with you and
return[7725] to the LORD.
Say[559] to Him, "[a]Take away all
iniquity,
And [I]receive *us* graciously,[2896]
That we may [b]present
[II]the fruit of our lips.[8193]
3 "Assyria will not save[3467] us,
We will [a]not ride on horses;
Nor will we say again, '[b]Our
god,'[430]
To the [c]work of our hands;[3027]
For in [d]Thee the [I]orphan finds
mercy."[7355]
4 I will [a]heal their apostasy,[4878]
I will [b]love[157] them freely,[5071]
For My anger[639] has [c]turned
away[7725] from them.
5 I will be like the [a]dew to Israel;
He will blossom like the
[b]lily,
And he will [I]take root like *the
cedars of* [c]Lebanon.
6 His shoots will [I]sprout,
And his [II]beauty[1935] will be like
the [a]olive tree,
And his fragrance like *the cedars
of* [b]Lebanon.
7 Those who [a]live in his shadow
Will [I]again raise[2421] [b]grain,
And they will blossom like the
vine.
His renown[2143] *will be* like the
wine of Lebanon.
8 O Ephraim, what more have I
to do with [a]idols?[6091]
It is I who answer and look after
[I]you.
I am like a luxuriant [b]cypress;
From [c]Me comes your fruit.
9 [a]Whoever is wise,[2450] let him
understand[995] these things;
Whoever is discerning,[995] let him
know[3045] them.
For the [b]ways[1870] of the LORD
are right,[3477]
And the [c]righteous[6662] will walk
in them,
But [d]transgressors[6586] will
stumble in them.

13 [c]Is. 37:3; 66:9
14 [I]Lit., *hand* [a]Ps. 49:15; Ezek. 37:12, 13 [b]1Cor. 15:55 [c]Jer. 20:16; 31:35-37
15 [I]Or, *brothers* [a]Gen. 49:22; Hos. 10:1 [b]Gen. 41:6; Jer. 4:11, 12; Ezek. 17:10; 19:12 [c]Jer. 51:36 [d]Jer. 20:5
16 [I]Ch. 14:1 in Heb. [a]Hos. 10:2 [b]Hos. 7:14 [c]2Kin. 8:12 [d]Hos. 11:6 [e]Hos. 10:14 [f]2Kin. 15:16

1 [I]Ch. 14:2 in Heb. [II]Or, *in* [a]Hos. 6:1; 10:12; 12:6; Joel 2:13 [b]Hos. 4:8; 5:5; 9:7
2 [I]Or, *accept that which is good* [II]So with ancient versions; M.T., *our lips as bulls* [a]Mic. 7:18, 19 [b]Ps. 51:16, 17; Hos. 6:6; Heb. 13:15
3 [I]Or, *fatherless* [a]Ps. 33:17; Is. 31:1 [b]Hos. 8:6; 13:2 [c]Hos. 4:12 [d]Ps. 10:14; 68:5
4 [a]Is. 57:18; Hos. 6:1 [b]Zeph. 3:17 [c]Is. 12:1
5 [I]Lit., *strike his roots* [a]Prov. 19:12; Is. 26:19 [b]Song 2:1; Matt. 6:28 [c]Is. 35:2
6 [I]Lit., *go* [II]Or, *splendor* [a]Jer. 11:16 [b]Song 4:11
7 [I]Or, *return, they will raise grain* [a]Ezek. 17:23 [b]Hos. 2:21, 22
8 [I]Lit., *him* [a]Job 34:32; Hos. 14:3 [b]Is. 41:19 [c]Ezek. 17:23
9 [a]Ps. 107:43; Jer. 9:12 [b]Ps. 111:7, 8; Prov. 10:29; Zeph. 3:5 [c]Is. 26:7 [d]Is. 1:28

The Book of
JOEL

Joel, which means "Yahweh is God," is named as the author of these prophecies. The name is found several times elsewhere in the Old Testament, but none of these men can be identified with this prophet who is called the son of Pethuel. Therefore, we know nothing of Joel beyond this writing. It is almost impossible to assign a date for its origin. Scholars have tended to date it either among the earliest or latest of the prophetic writings but more or less agree that his ministry was carried out in Judah. Conservative scholars generally place it during the reign of Joash (ninth century B.C.), before the exile. It is noted that the enemies mentioned in Joel are the Philistines, Phoenicians, Egyptians, and Edomites of their earlier history rather than Assyria and Babylonia of later historical importance. Other scholars place it after the exile, pointing out that no mention is made of the northern kingdom and that elders and priests seem to be in authority rather than the king. Neither of these lines of reasoning is conclusive for dating nor is the fact that it is the second book in order among the minor prophets. The prophecy is clearly divided into two parts. In 1:1—2:17 Joel uses the description of a plague of locusts and a drought to call the people to repentance with fear, fasting and prayer. In 2:18—3:21 God's mercy drives out the locusts and gives a plentiful harvest, bringing blessings to His people and punishment to their enemies. "The day of the Lord" which is coming is a major theme in Joel. On the day of Pentecost Peter quoted Joel 2:28-32 about the outpouring of the Spirit, stating that it was fulfilled on that day (Acts 2:14-21).

The Devastation of Locusts

1 The [a]word[1697] of the LORD that came to [b]Joel, the son[1121] of Pethuel.
2 [a]Hear this, O [b]elders,[2205]
And listen,[238] all inhabitants of the land.[776]
[c]Has *anything like* this happened in your days[3117]
Or in your fathers'[1] days?
3 [a]Tell[5608] your sons[1121] about it,
And *let* your sons *tell* their sons,
And their sons the next generation.[1755]
🗝 4 What the [a]gnawing locust has left,[3499] the swarming locust has eaten;
And what the [b]swarming locust has left, the creeping locust has eaten;
And what the creeping locust has left, the [c]stripping locust has eaten.
5 Awake, [a]drunkards, and weep;
And wail, all you wine drinkers,
On account of the sweet wine
That is [b]cut off[3772] from your mouth.[6310]
6 For a [a]nation[1471] has [I]invaded[5927] my land,
Mighty and without number;
[b]Its teeth are the teeth of a lion,
And it has the fangs of a lioness.
7 It has [a]made[7760] my vine a waste,[8047]
And my fig tree [I]splinters.
It has stripped them bare and cast *them* away;
Their branches have become white.

1 [a]Jer. 1:2; Ezek. 1:3; Hos. 1:1 [b]Acts 2:16
2 [a]Hos. 4:1; 5:1 [b]Job 8:8; Joel 1:14 [c]Jer. 30:7; Joel 2:2
3 [a]Ex. 10:2; Ps. 78:4
4 [a]Deut. 28:38; Joel 2:25; Amos 4:9 [b]Nah. 3:15, 16 [c]Is. 33:4
5 [a]Joel 3:3 [b]Is. 32:10
6 [I]Lit., *come up against* [a]Joel 2:2, 11, 25 [b]Rev. 9:8
7 [I]Or, *a stump* [a]Is. 5:6; Amos 4:9

🗝 **1:4** The four names of the locust possibly represent four different stages of its growth. This verse portrays an event where they would come swarm after swarm and totally consume everything. It would be a plague to end all plagues. It is a fitting representation of the completeness of the Lord's judgment. Absolutely nothing would be able to escape from it.

8 [a]Wail like a virgin[1330] [b]girded with
sackcloth
For the bridegroom[1167] of her
youth.
9 The [a]grain offering[4503] and the
libation[5262] are cut off
From the house[1004] of the LORD.
The [b]priests[3548] mourn,
The ministers[8334] of the LORD.
10 The field[7704] is [a]ruined,[7703]
[b]The land[127] mourns,
For the grain is ruined,
The new wine dries up,[3001]
Fresh oil[3323] [I]fails.
11 [Ia]Be ashamed, O farmers,[406]
Wail, O vinedressers,
For the wheat and the barley;
Because the [b]harvest of the field
is destroyed.[6]
12 The [a]vine dries up,
And the fig tree [I]fails;
The [b]pomegranate, the
[c]palm also, and the [IId]apple
tree,
All the trees of the field dry
up.[3001]
Indeed, [e]rejoicing dries up[3001]
From the sons of men.[120]
13 [a]Gird yourselves *with sackcloth*,
And lament, O priests;
[b]Wail, O ministers of the
altar![4196]
Come, [c]spend the night in
sackcloth,
O ministers of my God,[430]
For the grain offering and the
libation
Are withheld[4513] from the house
of your God.

Starvation and Drought

14 [a]Consecrate[6942] a fast,
Proclaim[7121] a [b]solemn
assembly;[6116]
Gather[622] the elders[2205]
And all the inhabitants of the land
To the house of the LORD your
God,
And [c]cry out[2199] to the LORD.
15 [a]Alas for the day![3117]
For the [b]day of the LORD is near,
And it will come as
[c]destruction[7701]
from the [I]Almighty.[7706]
16 Has not [a]food been cut off before
our eyes,
Gladness and [b]joy from the
house of our God?
17 The [Ia]seeds shrivel under their
[II]clods;
The storehouses[214] are
desolate,[8074]
The barns are torn down,[2040]
For the grain is dried up.
18 How [a]the beasts groan!
The herds of cattle wander
aimlessly
Because there is no pasture for
them;
Even the flocks of sheep
[I]suffer.[816]
19 [a]To Thee, O LORD, I cry;[7121]
For [b]fire has devoured the
pastures[4999] of the
wilderness,
And the flame has burned up all
the trees of the field.
20 Even the beasts of the field
[Ia]pant for Thee;
For the [b]water brooks are dried
up,[3001]
And fire has devoured the
pastures of the wilderness.

The Terrible Visitation

2 [a]Blow[8628] a trumpet in Zion,
And sound an alarm[7321] on My
holy[6944] mountain!
Let all the inhabitants of the land
tremble,[7264]
For the [b]day[3117] of the LORD is
coming;
Surely it is near,

8 [a]Is. 22:12 [b]Joel 1:13; Amos 8:10
9 [a]Hos. 9:4; Joel 1:13; 2:14 [b]Joel 2:17
10 [I]Lit., *wastes away* [a]Is. 24:4, 7 [b]Jer. 12:11
11 [I]Or, *The farmers are ashamed, The vinedressers wail* [a]Jer. 14:4; Amos 5:16 [b]Is. 17:11; Jer. 9:12
12 [I]Lit., *wastes away* [II]Or, *apricot* [a]Joel 1:10; Hab. 3:17 [b]Hag. 2:19 [c]Song 7:8 [d]Song 2:3 [e]Is. 16:10; 24:11; Jer. 48:33
13 [a]Jer. 4:8; Ezek. 7:18 [b]Jer. 9:10 [c]1Kin. 21:27
14 [a]Joel 2:15, 16 [b]Lev. 23:36 [c]Jon. 3:8
15 [I]Heb., *Shaddai* [a]Is. 13:9; Jer. 30:7; Amos 5:16 [b]Joel 2:1, 11, 31 [c]Is. 13:6; Ezek. 7:2-12
16 [a]Is. 3:7; Amos 4:6 [b]Deut. 12:7; Ps. 43:4
17 [I]Or, *dried figs* [II]Or, *shovels* [a]Is. 17:10, 11
18 [I]Lit., *bear punishment* [a]1Kin. 8:5; Jer. 12:4; 14:5, 6; Hos. 4:3
19 [a]Ps. 50:15; Mic. 7:7 [b]Jer. 9:10; Amos 7:4
20 [I]Lit., *long for* [a]Ps. 104:21; 147:9; Joel 1:18 [b]1Kin. 17:7; 18:5
1 [a]Jer. 4:5; Joel 2:15; Zeph. 1:16 [b]Joel 1:15; 2:11, 31; 3:14; Obad. 15; Zeph. 1:14

1:15 "The day of the Lord" is found four other times in Joel (2:1,11,31; 3:14). It is also mentioned by the prophets Amos (5:18,20), Obadiah (v. 15), Zephaniah (1:7,14,18; 2:2) and Malachi (4:5). See note on Zeph. 1:7.

2 A day of [a]darkness[2822] and
gloom,[653]
A day of clouds[6051] and thick
darkness.[6205]
As the dawn is spread over the
mountains,
So there is a [b]great and mighty
people;[5971]
There has [c]never[5769] been[1961]
anything like it,
Nor will there be again after it
To the years of many
generations.[1755]
3 A [a]fire consumes before them,
And behind them a flame
burns.
The land[776] is [b]like the garden
of Eden before them,
But a [c]desolate[8077] wilderness
behind them,
And nothing at all escapes[6413]
them.
4 Their [a]appearance is like the
appearance of horses;
And like war horses, so they
run.
5 [I]With a [a]noise as of chariots
They leap on the tops[7218] of the
mountains,
Like the [II]crackling of a
[b]flame of fire consuming the
stubble,
Like a mighty people arranged
for battle.
6 Before them the people are in
[a]anguish;[2342]
All [b]faces [I]turn[6908] pale.[6289]
7 They run like mighty men;[582]
They climb[5927] the wall like
soldiers;
And they each[376] [a]march
[I]in line,[1870]
Nor do they deviate from their
paths.[734]
8 They do not crowd each
other;[251]
They march everyone[1397] in his
path.
When they [I]burst[5307] through the
[II]defenses,
They do not break ranks.
9 They rush on the city,
They run on the wall;
They climb into the [a]houses,[1004]
They [b]enter through the
windows like a thief.
10 Before them the earth[776]
[a]quakes,[7264]
The heavens[8064] tremble,[7493]
The [b]sun and the moon grow
dark,[6937]
And the stars lose[622] their
brightness.
11 And the LORD [a]utters His voice
before [b]His army;[2428]
Surely His camp[4264] is very
great,
For [c]strong is he who carries
out[6213] His word.[1697]
The [d]day[3117] of the LORD is
indeed great and very
awesome,[3372]
And [e]who can endure it?
12 "Yet even now," declares[5001] the
LORD,
"[a]Return[7725] to Me with all your
heart,[3824]
And with [b]fasting, weeping, and
mourning;
13 And [a]rend[7167] your heart and not
[b]your garments."
Now return to the LORD your
God,[430]
For He is [c]gracious[2587] and
compassionate,
Slow[750] to anger,[639] abounding
in lovingkindness,[2617]
And [d]relenting of evil.[7451]

2 [a]Joel 2:10, 31; Amos 5:18; Zeph. 1:15 [b]Joel 1:6; 2:11, 25 [c]Lam. 1:12; Dan. 9:12; 12:1; Joel 1:2
3 [a]Ps. 97:3; Is. 9:18, 19 [b]Is. 51:3; Ezek. 36:35 [c]Ex. 10:5, 15; Ps. 105:34, 35; Zech. 7:14
4 [a]Rev. 9:7
5 [I]Lit., *Like the noise of chariots* [II]Lit., *noise* [a]Rev. 9:9 [b]Is. 5:24; 30:30
6 [I]Or, *become flushed* [a]Is. 13:8; Nah. 2:10 [b]Jer. 30:6
7 [I]Lit., *in his ways* [a]Prov. 30:27
8 [I]Lit., *fall* [II]Lit., *weapon,* probably *javelin*
9 [a]Ex. 10:6 [b]Jer. 9:21; John 10:1
10 [a]Ps. 18:7; Joel 3:16; Nah. 1:5 [b]Is. 13:10; 34:4; Jer. 4:23; Ezek. 32:7, 8; Joel 2:31; 3:15; Matt. 24:29; Rev. 8:12
11 [a]Ps. 46:6; Is. 13:4; Jer. 25:30; Joel 3:16 [b]Joel 2:25 [c]Jer. 50:34; Rev. 18:8 [d]Jer. 30:7; Joel 1:15; 2:1, 31; 3:14; Zeph. 1:14, 15; Rev. 6:17 [e]Ezek. 22:14; Mal. 3:2
12 [a]Deut. 4:29; Jer. 4:1, 2; Ezek. 33:11; Hos. 12:6 [b]Dan. 9:3
13 [a]Ps. 34:18; 51:17; Is. 57:15 [b]Gen. 37:34; 2Sam. 1:11; Job 1:20; Jer. 41:5 [c]Ex. 34:6 [d]Jer. 18:8; 42:10; Amos 7:3, 6

2:12-14 After painting a picture of a land which will be completely destroyed, without sustenance for man or beast, the Lord called upon Israel to repent. Though the calamity was so serious that it seemed to be the forerunner of the Day of the Lord, He begged the people to return to Him with sincere repentance. Though they certainly deserved the punishment He was reluctant to inflict it upon them. Even at that late moment He would remove the locusts and restore the land to full productivity. Everything depended upon their willingness to humble themselves before Him and "rend your heart and not your garments. Now return to the LORD your God."

14 Who knows[3045] [a]whether He will *not* turn[7725] and relent,[5162]
And leave[7604] a [b]blessing[1293] behind Him,
Even [c]a grain offering[4503] and a libation[5262]
For the LORD your God?
15 [a]Blow a trumpet in Zion,
[b]Consecrate[6942] a fast, proclaim a solemn assembly,[6116]
16 Gather[622] the people, [a]sanctify the congregation,[6951]
Assemble[6908] the elders,[2205]
Gather the children and the nursing infants.
Let the [b]bridegroom come out of his room
And the bride out of her *bridal* chamber.
17 Let the priests,[3548] the LORD's ministers,[8334]
Weep [a]between the porch and the altar,[4196]
And let them say,[559] "[b]Spare Thy people, O LORD,
And do not make Thine inheritance[5159] a [c]reproach,[2781]
A byword[4910] among the nations.[1471]
Why should they among the peoples say,
'[d]Where is their God?' "

Deliverance Promised

18 Then the LORD [I]will be [a]zealous[7065] for His land,
And [II]will have [b]pity on His people.
19 And the LORD [I]will answer and say to His people,
"Behold, I am going to [a]send you grain, new wine, and oil,[3323]
And you will be satisfied *in full* with [II]them;
And I will [b]never again make you a reproach among the nations.
20 "But I will remove the [a]northern *army* far from you,
And I will drive it into a parched[6723] and desolate land,
And its vanguard into the [b]eastern sea,
And its rear guard into the [c]western sea.
And its [d]stench will arise[5927] and its foul smell will come up,[5927]
For it has done[6213] great things."
21 [a]Do not fear, O land,[127] rejoice and be glad,
For the LORD has done[6213] [b]great things.
22 Do not fear, beasts of the field,[7704]
For the [a]pastures of the wilderness have turned green,
For the tree has borne its fruit,
The fig tree and the vine have yielded [I]in full.[2428]
23 So rejoice, O [a]sons[1121] of Zion,
And [b]be glad in the LORD your God;
For He has [c]given you [I]the early rain for *your* vindication.
And He has poured down for you the rain,
The [II]early and [III][d]latter rain [IV]as before.
24 And the threshing floors will be full of grain,
And the vats will [a]overflow with the new wine and oil.
25 "Then I will make up[7999] to you for the years
That the swarming [a]locust has eaten,
The creeping locust, the stripping locust, and the gnawing locust,
My great army which I sent among you.
26 "And you shall have plenty to [a]eat and be satisfied,
And [b]praise[1984] the name of the LORD your God,
Who has [c]dealt[6213] wondrously[6381] with you;

14 [a]Jer. 26:3; Jon. 3:9 [b]Hag. 2:19 [c]Joel 1:9, 13

15 [a]Num. 10:3; 2Kin. 10:20 [b]Joel 1:14

16 [a]1Sam. 16:5; 2Chr. 29:5 [b]Ps. 19:5

17 [a]2Chr. 8:12; Ezek. 8:16 [b]Ex. 32:11, 12; Is. 37:20; Amos 7:2, 5 [c]Ps. 44:13; 74:10 [d]Ps. 42:10; 79:10; 115:2

18 [I]Or, *was zealous* [II]Or, *had pity* [a]Zech. 1:14; 8:2 [b]Is. 60:10; 63:9, 15

19 [I]Or, *answered and said* [II]Lit., *it* [a]Jer. 31:12; Hos. 2:21, 22; Joel 1:10; Mal. 3:10 [b]Ezek. 34:29; 36:15

20 [a]Jer. 1:14, 15 [b]Zech. 14:8 [c]Deut. 11:24 [d]Is. 34:3; Amos 4:10

21 [a]Is. 54:4; Jer. 30:10; Zeph. 3:16, 17 [b]Ps. 126:3; Joel 2:26

22 [I]Lit., *their wealth* [a]Ps. 65:12, 13

23 [I]I.e., autumn; or possibly, *the teacher for righteousness* [II]I.e., autumn [III]I.e., spring [IV]So with ancient versions; Heb., *in the first* [a]Ps. 149:2 [b]Is. 12:2-6 [c]Deut. 11:14; Is. 41:16; Jer. 5:24; Hab. 3:18; Zech. 10:7 [d]Lev. 26:4; Hos. 6:3; Zech. 10:1

24 [a]Lev. 26:10; Amos 9:13; Mal. 3:10

25 [a]Joel 1:4-7; 2:2-11

26 [a]Lev. 26:5; Deut. 11:15; Is. 62:9 [b]Deut. 12:7; Ps. 67:5-7 [c]Ps. 126:2, 3; Is. 25:1

Then My people will [d]never[5769]
be put to shame.[954]
27 "Thus you will [a]know[3045] that I
am in the midst[7130] of Israel,
And that I am the LORD your
God
And there is [b]no other;
And My people will never be
[c]put to shame.

The Promise of the Spirit

28 "[I][a]And it will come about after this
That I will [b]pour out[8210] My
Spirit[7307] on all [II][c]mankind;[1320]
And your sons[1121] and daughters
will prophesy,[5012]
Your old men[2205] will dream
dreams,
Your young men will see[7200]
visions.[2384]
29 "And even on the [a]male and
female servants[5650]
I will pour out My Spirit in those
days.

The Day of the LORD

30 "And I will [a]display wonders[4159]
in the sky and on the earth,
Blood,[1818] fire, and columns of
smoke.
31 "The [a]sun will be turned[2015] into
darkness,[2822]
And the moon into blood,
Before the [b]great and awesome
day of the LORD comes.
32 "And it will come about that
[a]whoever calls[7121] on the
name of the LORD
Will be delivered;[4422]
For [b]on Mount Zion and in
Jerusalem
There will be those who
[c]escape,[6413]
As the LORD has said,
Even among the [d]survivors[8300]
whom the LORD calls.

26 [d]Is. 45:17
27 [a]Lev. 26:11, 12; Joel 3:17, 21 [b]Is. 45:5, 6 [c]Is. 49:23
28 [I]Ch. 3:1 in Heb. [II]Lit., *flesh* [a]Acts 2:17-21 [b]Is. 32:15; 44:3; Ezek. 39:29; Zech. 12:10 [c]Is. 40:5; 49:26
29 [a]1Cor. 12:13; Gal. 3:28
30 [a]Matt. 24:29; Mark 13:24, 25; Luke 21:11, 25, 26; Acts 2:19
31 [a]Is. 13:10; 34:4; Joel 2:10; 3:15; Matt. 24:29; Mark 13:24; Luke 21:25; Acts 2:20; Rev. 6:12, 13 [b]Is. 13:9; Zeph. 1:14-16; Mal. 4:1, 5
32 [a]Jer. 33:3; Acts 2:21; Rom. 10:13 [b]Is. 46:13; Rom. 11:26 [c]Is. 4:2; Obad.17 [d]Is. 11:11; Jer. 31:7; Mic. 4:7; Rom. 9:27

1 [I]Ch. 4:1 in Heb. [a]Jer. 30:3; Ezek. 38:14 [b]Jer. 16:15
2 [I]I.e., YHWH judges [a]Is. 66:18; Mic. 4:12; Zech. 14:2 [b]Joel 3:12, 14 [c]Is. 66:16; Jer. 25:31; Ezek. 38:22 [d]Jer. 50:17; Ezek. 34:6 [e]Ezek. 35:10; 36:1-5
3 [I]Lit., *Given* [a]Obad. 11; Nah. 3:10 [b]Amos 2:6
4 [a]Is. 23:1-18; Amos 1:9, 10; Zech. 9:2-4; Matt. 11:21, 22; Luke 10:13, 14 [b]Is. 14:29-31; Jer. 47:1-7; Ezek. 25:15-17; Amos 1:6-8; Zech. 9:5-7 [c]Is. 34:8; 59:18
5 [I]Lit., *goodly things* [a]2Kin. 12:18; 2Chr. 21:16,17

The Nations Will Be Judged

3 "[I]For behold, [a]in those days[3117] and
at that time,[6256]
When I [b]restore[7725] the
fortunes[7622] of Judah and
Jerusalem,
2 I will [a]gather[6908] all the
nations,[1471]
And bring them down to the
[b]valley of [I]Jehoshaphat.
Then I will [c]enter into judgment
with them there
On behalf of My people[5971] and
My inheritance,[5159] Israel,
Whom they have [d]scattered
among the nations;
And they have [e]divided up My
land.[776]
3 "They have also [a]cast lots for My
people,
[I][b]Traded a boy for a harlot,[2181]
And sold a girl for wine that they
may drink.
4 "Moreover, what are you to Me,
O [a]Tyre, Sidon, and all the regions of
[b]Philistia? Are you rendering Me a
recompense? But if you do recompense[1580] Me, swiftly and speedily I will
[c]return[7725] your recompense on your
head.[7218]
5 "Since you have [a]taken My silver
and My gold, brought My precious[2896]
[I]treasures to your temples,[1964]
6 and sold the [a]sons[1121] of Judah and
Jerusalem to the [I]Greeks in order to
remove them far from their territory,
7 behold, I am going to [a]arouse them
from the place where you have sold
them, and return your recompense on
your head.
8 "Also I will [a]sell your sons[1121] and
your daughters into the hand[3027] of the
sons[1121] of Judah, and they will sell them
to the [b]Sabeans, to a distant nation,"[1471]
for the LORD has spoken.[1696]

6 [I]Lit., *sons of Javan* [a]Ezek. 27:13 7 [a]Is. 43:5, 6; Jer. 23:8; Zech. 9:13 8 [a]Is. 14:2; 60:14 [b]Job 1:15; Ps. 72:10; Ezek. 38:13

2:28-32 When he was confronted with the need to explain the extraordinary miraculous events of the day of Pentecost, Peter quoted this passage as being fulfilled on that day (Acts 2:17-21).

9 [a]Proclaim[7121] this among the
nations:[1471]
[b]Prepare[6942] a war; [c]rouse the
mighty men![582]
Let all the soldiers draw
near,[5066] let them come
up![5927]
10 [a]Beat[3807] your plowshares into
swords,[2719]
And your pruning hooks into
spears;
[b]Let the weak say,[559] "I am a
mighty man."
11 [I][a]Hasten[5789] and come, all you
surrounding nations,[1471]
And gather yourselves there.
Bring down, O LORD, Thy
[b]mighty ones.
12 Let the nations be aroused
And come up to the [a]valley of
[I]Jehoshaphat,
For there I will sit to [b]judge[8199]
All the surrounding nations.
13 [a]Put in the sickle, for the
[b]harvest is ripe.
Come, [c]tread, for the [d]wine
press is full;
The vats overflow, for their
[e]wickedness[7451] is great.
14 [a]Multitudes, multitudes in the
[b]valley of [I]decision!
For the [c]day[3117] of the LORD
is near in the valley of
[I]decision.
15 The [a]sun and moon grow
dark,[6937]
And the stars lose[622] their
brightness.
16 And the LORD [a]roars from Zion
And [b]utters His voice from
Jerusalem,
And the [c]heavens[8064] and the
earth tremble.[7493]
But the LORD is a [d]refuge for
His people
And a [e]stronghold to the sons
of Israel.
17 Then you will [a]know[3045] that I
am the LORD your God,
Dwelling[7931] in Zion My
[b]holy[6944] mountain.
So Jerusalem will be [c]holy,
And [d]strangers[2114] will pass[5674]
through it no more.

Judah Will Be Blessed

18 And it will come about in that
day
That the [a]mountains will drip[5197]
with [I]sweet wine,
And the hills will [b]flow with milk,
And all the [c]brooks of Judah will
flow with water;
And a [d]spring will go out from
the house[1004] of the LORD,
To water the valley of
[II]Shittim.
19 Egypt will become a waste,[8077]
And Edom will become a
desolate wilderness,
Because of the [a]violence[2555]
[I]done to the sons of Judah,
In whose land they have shed[8210]
innocent blood.
20 But Judah will be [a]inhabited
forever,
And Jerusalem for all
generations.[1755]
21 And I will [a]avenge[5352] their blood
which I have not avenged,
For the LORD dwells in Zion.

---

9 [a]Jer. 51:27 [b]Jer. 6:4; Ezek. 38:7; Mic. 3:5 [c]Is. 8:9, 10; Jer. 46:3, 4; Zech. 14:2, 3
10 [a]Is. 2:4; Mic. 4:3 [b]Zech. 12:8
11 [I]Or, *Lend aid* [a]Ezek. 38:15, 16 [b]Is. 13:3
12 [I]I.e., YHWH judges [a]Joel 3:2, 14 [b]Ps. 7:6; 96:13; 98:9; Is. 2:4; 3:13
13 [a]Rev. 14:14-19 [b]Jer. 51:33; Hos. 6:11 [c]Rev. 14:19, 20; 19:15 [d]Is. 63:3; Lam. 1:15 [e]Gen. 18:20
14 [I]I.e., God's verdict [a]Is. 34:2-8 [b]Joel 3:2, 12 [c]Joel 1:15; 2:1, 11, 31
15 [a]Joel 2:10, 31
16 [a]Hos. 11:10; Amos 1:2 [b]Joel 2:11 [c]Ezek. 38:19; Joel 2:10; Hag. 2:6 [d]Ps. 61:3; Is. 33:16; Jer. 17:17 [e]Jer. 16:19; Nah. 1:7
17 [a]Joel 2:27 [b]Is. 11:9; 56:7; Ezek. 20:40 [c]Is. 4:3; Obad. 17 [d]Is. 52:1; Nah. 1:15
18 [I]Lit., *freshly pressed out grape juice* [II]Or, *acacias* [a]Amos 9:13 [b]Ex. 3:8 [c]Is. 30:25; 35:6 [d]Ezek. 47:1-12
19 [I]Lit., *of the sons* [a]Obad. 10
20 [a]Ezek. 37:25; Amos 9:15
21 [a]Is. 4:4

The Book of

AMOS

Amos was a shepherd from a rural area in Judah whom God called to preach at Israel's royal sanctuary at Bethel. His prophesying took place in about 750 B.C. during the reign of Jeroboam II and lasted only a few days. Amos found in Israel great social extremes of comfortable prosperity and abject poverty. His message was against the wealthy. The poor were being exploited and cheated. Merchants were greedy and dishonest. The judicial system was corrupt. There was religious arrogance, as well, and even the attempt to corrupt some of the religious leaders. Affluence had lulled the upper class into such apathy that they refused to recognize the sickness of their society. Amos' warning to the worshipers at Bethel was that, because of their sins, destruction was coming upon them from both Egypt and Assyria, a prophecy made all the more bold because the international scene was relatively quiet, and Assyria was still in a period of decline. Amaziah, the priest at Bethel, made it clear to Amos that he was not welcome and that he should go home to his own country. Amos refused to back down, explaining that he was not a professional prophet, but he was there solely because God had sent him. The book is one of the most outstanding among the prophets, both because of its timeless message and because it contains some of the finest examples of literary artistry in the entire Old Testament.

Judgment on Neighbor Nations

1 🔑 The words[1697] of Amos, who
was among the [a]sheepherders from
[b]Tekoa, which he [I]envisioned in
visions[2372] concerning Israel in the
days[3117] of [c]Uzziah king of Judah, and
in the days of [d]Jeroboam son[1121] of
Joash, king of Israel, two years before
the [e]earthquake.[7494]

2 And he said,[559]
"The [a]LORD roars from Zion,
And from Jerusalem He utters
His voice;
And the shepherds' [b]pasture
grounds[4999] mourn,
And the [Ic]summit[7218] of Carmel
dries up."[3001]

3 Thus says the LORD,
"For [a]three transgressions[6588] of
[b]Damascus and for four
I will not [I]revoke[7725] its
punishment,
Because they threshed Gilead
with *implements* of sharp
iron.

4 "So I will send fire upon the
house[1004] of Hazael,
And it will consume the
citadels[759] of [a]Ben-hadad.

5 "I will also [a]break[7665] the *gate* bar
of Damascus,
And cut off[3772] the inhabitant
from the [I]valley of Aven,[205]
And him who holds the
scepter,[7626] from Beth-eden;
So the people[5971] of Aram will
go exiled[1540] to [b]Kir,"
Says the LORD.

6 Thus says the LORD,
"For three transgressions of
[a]Gaza and for four
I will not revoke its *punishment*,
Because they deported[1540] an
entire[8003] population[1546]
To [b]deliver *it* up to Edom.

1 [I]Lit., *saw concerning* [a]Amos 7:14 [b]2Sam. 14:2; Jer. 6:1 [c]2Chr. 26:1-23; Is. 1:1 [d]2Kin. 14:23-29; Hos. 1:1; Amos 7:10, 11 [e]Zech. 14:5
2 [I]Lit., *head* [a]Is. 42:13; Jer. 25:30; Joel 3:16 [b]Jer. 12:4; Joel 1:18, 19 [c]Amos 9:3
3 [I]Lit., *cause it to turn back*, and so throughout the ch. [a]Amos 2:1, 4, 6 [b]Is. 8:4; 17:1-3; Jer. 49:23-27; Zech. 9:1
4 [a]1Kin. 20:1; 2Kin. 6:24
5 [I]Possibly, *Baalbek* [a]Jer. 51:30; Lam. 2:9 [b]2Kin. 16:9; Amos 9:7
6 [a]1Sam. 6:17; Jer. 47:1, 5; Zeph. 2:4 [b]Ezek. 35:5; Obad. 11

🔑 **1:1** Tekoa was in a desolate area about twelve miles south of Jerusalem. Amos was both a shepherd and a dresser of fig-sycamore trees (Amos 7:14), which was a seasonal job during fruit-bearing time. His call (about 750 B.C.) illustrates the fact that all God's prophets were not professionals, in the sense that it was their total work. Here God's purposes called for a certain shepherd-farmer, and the total ministry reflected in the book covered only a few days.

7 "So I will send fire upon the wall of Gaza,
And it will consume her citadels.
8 "I will also cut off the inhabitant from [a]Ashdod,
And him who holds the scepter, from [b]Ashkelon;
I will even [I]unleash[7725] My [II]power[3027] upon Ekron,
And the remnant[7611] of the [c]Philistines will perish,"[6]
Says the Lord[136] [III]GOD.
9 Thus says the LORD,
"For three transgressions of [a]Tyre and for four
I will not revoke its *punishment*,
Because they delivered[4422] up an entire population to Edom
And did not remember[2142] *the* covenant[1285] of [Ib]brotherhood.[251]
10 "So I will [a]send fire upon the wall of Tyre,
And it will consume her citadels."
11 Thus says the LORD,
"For three transgressions of [a]Edom and for four
I will not revoke its *punishment*,
Because he [b]pursued his brother with the sword,[2719]
While he [I]stifled his compassion;[7356]
His anger[639] also [c]tore continually,[5703]
And he maintained[8104] his fury[5678] forever.[5331]
12 "So I will send fire upon [a]Teman,
And it will consume the citadels of Bozrah."
13 Thus says the LORD,
"For three transgressions of the sons[1121] of [a]Ammon and for four
I will not revoke its *punishment*,
Because they [b]ripped open the pregnant women of Gilead
In order to [c]enlarge their borders.
14 "So I will kindle a fire on the wall of [a]Rabbah,
And it will consume her citadels
Amid [Ib]war cries on the day of battle
And a [c]storm on the day of tempest.
15 "Their [a]king will go into exile,[1473]
He and his princes[8269] together,"
says the LORD.

Judgment on Judah and Israel

2 Thus says the LORD,
"For three transgressions[6588] of [a]Moab and for four
I will not [I]revoke[7725] its *punishment*,
Because he [b]burned[8313] the bones[6106] of the king of Edom to lime.
2 "So I will send fire upon Moab,
And it will consume the citadels[759] of [a]Kerioth;
And Moab will die amid [b]tumult,[7588]
With [I]war cries and the sound of a trumpet.
3 "I will also cut off[3772] the [Ia]judge[8199] from her midst,
And slay[2026] all her [b]princes[8269] with him," says the LORD.
4 Thus says the LORD,
"For three transgressions of [a]Judah and for four
I will not revoke its *punishment*,
Because they [b]rejected[3988] the law[8451] of the LORD
And have not kept[8104] His statutes;[2706]
Their [Ic]lies[3577] also have led them astray,[8582]
Those after which their [d]fathers[1] walked.
5 "So I will [a]send fire upon Judah,
And it will consume the citadels of Jerusalem."
6 Thus says the LORD,
"For three transgressions of [a]Israel and for four
I will not revoke its *punishment*,

8 [I]Lit., *cause to return* [II]Lit., *hand* [III]Heb., *YHWH*, usually rendered LORD [a]2Chr. 26:6; Amos 3:9; Zech. 9:6 [b]Jer. 47:5; Zeph. 2:4 [c]Is. 14:29-31; Jer. 47:1-7; Ezek. 25:16; Joel 3:4-8; Zeph. 2:4-7; Zech. 9:5-7
9 [I]Lit., *brothers* [a]Is. 23:1-18; Jer. 25:22; Ezek. 26:2-4; Joel 3:4-8; Zech. 9:1-4; Matt. 11:21, 22; Luke 10:13, 14 [b]1Kin. 9:11-14
10 [a]Zech. 9:4
11 [I]Lit., *corrupted* [a]Is. 34:5, 6; 63:1-6; Jer. 49:7-22; Ezek. 25:12-14; 35:1-15; Obad. 1-14; Mal. 1:2-5 [b]Num. 20:14-21; 2Chr. 28:17; Obad. 10-12 [c]Is. 57:16; Mic. 7:18
12 [a]Jer. 49:7, 20; Obad. 9
13 [a]Jer. 49:1-6; Ezek. 21:28-32; 25:2-7; Zeph. 2:8, 9 [b]2Kin. 15:16; Hos. 13:16 [c]Is. 5:8; Ezek. 35:10
14 [I]Or, *shouts* [a]Deut. 3:11; 1Chr. 20:1; Jer. 49:2 [b]Ezek. 21:22; Amos 2:2 [c]Is. 29:6; 30:30
15 [a]Jer. 49:3

1 [I]Lit., *cause it to turn back*, and so throughout the ch. [a]Is. 15:1-16:14; 25:10-12; Jer. 48:1-47; Ezek. 25:8-11; Zeph. 2:8, 9 [b]2Kin. 3:26, 27
2 [I]Or, *shouts* [a]Jer. 48:24, 41 [b]Jer. 48:45
3 [I]Or, *executive officer* [a]Ps. 2:10; 141:6; Amos 5:7, 12; 6:12 [b]Job 12:21; Is. 40:23
4 [I]Or, *false gods* [a]2Kin. 17:19; Hos. 12:2; Amos 3:2 [b]Judg. 2:17-20; 2Kin. 22:11-17; Jer. 6:19; 8:9 [c]Is. 9:15, 16; 28:15; Jer. 16:19; Hab. 2:18 [d]Jer. 9:14; 16:11, 12; Ezek. 20:18, 24, 30 Hos. 8:14
5 [a]Jer. 17:27; 21:10;
6 [a]2Kin. 18:11, 12

Because they [b]sell the righteous[6662] for money
And the needy for a pair of sandals.
7 "These who [I]pant after the *very* dust[6083] of the earth[776] on the head[7218] of the [a]helpless
Also [b]turn aside the way[1870] of the humble;
And a [c]man[376] and his father[1] [II]resort to the same [III]girl
In order to profane[2490] My holy[6944] name.
8 "And on garments [a]taken as pledges[2254] they stretch out beside [b]every altar,[4196]
And in the house[1004] of their God[430] they [c]drink the wine of those who have been fined.[6064]
9 "Yet it was I who destroyed[8045] the [a]Amorite before them,
[I]Though his [b]height *was* like the height of cedars
And he *was* strong as the oaks;
I even destroyed his [c]fruit above and his root below.
10 "And it was I who [a]brought you up[5927] from the land[776] of Egypt,
And I led you in the wilderness [b]forty years
[I]That you might take possession[2433] of the land of the [c]Amorite.
11 "Then I [a]raised up some of your sons[1121] to be prophets[5030]
And some of your young men to be [b]Nazirites.[5139]
Is this not so, O sons[1121] of Israel?" declares[5001] the LORD.
12 "But you made the Nazirites drink wine,
And you commanded[6680] the prophets saying,[559] 'You [a]shall not prophesy!'[5012]
13 "Behold, I am [Ia]weighted down beneath you
As a wagon [II]is weighted down when filled with sheaves.
14 "[Ia]Flight will perish[6] from the swift,
And the stalwart[2389] will not strengthen his power,
Nor the [b]mighty man save[4422] his [II]life.[5315]
15 "He who [a]grasps the bow will not stand *his ground,*
The swift of foot will not escape,
Nor will he who rides the [b]horse save his [I]life.
16 "Even the [I]bravest[3820] among the warriors will [a]flee naked[6174] in that day,"[3117] declares the LORD.

All the Tribes Are Guilty

3 Hear this word[1697] which the LORD has spoken[1696] against you, sons[1121] of Israel, against the entire [Ia]family[4940] which [II]He brought up[5927] from the land[776] of Egypt,
2 "[a]You only have I [I]chosen[3045] among all the families of the earth;[127]
Therefore, I will [IIb]punish[6485] you for all your iniquities."[5771]
3 Do two men walk together unless they have made an [I]appointment?[3259]
4 Does a [a]lion roar in the forest when he has no prey?
Does a young lion [I]growl from his den unless he has captured *something?*
5 Does a bird fall[5307] into a trap[6341] on the ground[776] when there is no [I]bait[4170] in it?
Does a trap spring up[5927] from the earth when it captures nothing at all?
6 If a [a]trumpet is blown[8628] in a

2:6 [b]Joel 3:3; Amos 5:11, 12; 8:6
7 [I]Or, *trample* or, *snap at the head of the helpless on the dust* [II]Lit., *go* [III]Possibly a harlot, or a temple prostitute [a]Amos 8:4; Mic. 2:2, 9 [b]Amos 5:12 [c]Hos. 4:14
8 [a]Ex. 22:26 [b]Amos 3:14 [c]Amos 4:1; 6:6
9 [I]Lit., *Whose height* [a]Num. 21:23-25; Josh. 10:12 [b]Num. 13:32 [c]Ezek. 17:9; Mal. 4:1
10 [I]Lit., *To possess* [a]Ex. 12:51; 20:2; Amos 3:1; 9:7 [b]Deut. 2:7 [c]Ex. 3:8
11 [a]Deut. 18:18; Jer. 7:25 [b]Num. 6:2, 3; Judg. 13:5
12 [a]Is. 30:10; Jer. 11:21; Amos 7:13, 16; Mic. 2:6
13 [I]Or, *tottering* [II]Or, *totters* [a]Is. 1:14
14 [I]Or, *A place of refuge* [II]Lit., *soul* [a]Is. 30:16, 17 [b]Ps. 33:16; Jer. 9:23
15 [I]Lit., *soul* [a]Jer. 51:56; Ezek. 39:3 [b]Is. 31:3
16 [I]Lit., *stout of heart* [a]Judg. 4:17

3:1 [I]I.e., nation [II]Lit., *I* [a]Jer. 8:3; 13:11
2 [I]Lit., *known* [II]Lit., *visit* [a]Gen. 18:19; Ex. 19:5, 6; Deut. 4:32-37; 7:6 [b]Jer. 14:10; Ezek. 20:36; Dan. 9:12; Rom. 2:9
3 [I]Or, *agreement*
4 [I]Lit., *give his voice* [a]Ps. 104:21; Hos. 5:14; 11:10
5 [I]Or, *striker-bar set*
6 [a]Jer. 4:5, 19, 21; 6:1; Hos. 5:8; Zeph. 1:16

2:12 The denunciation of efforts to silence the prophets is one of the frequently heard burdens of the prophets (Isa. 30:10; Jer. 11:21; Mic. 2:6). Amaziah, the high priest at Bethel, tried to force Amos to stop preaching and to return home (Amos 7:12,13).

city will not the people[5971] tremble?[2729]
If a [b]calamity[7451] occurs in a city
has not the LORD done[6213] it?
7 [I]Surely the Lord[136] [II]GOD
does[6213] nothing[1697]
Unless He [a]reveals[1540] His
secret[5475] counsel
To His servants[5650] the
prophets.[5030]
8 A [a]lion has roared! Who will not
fear?[3372]
The [b]Lord [I]GOD has spoken!
[c]Who can but prophesy?[5012]

🗝 9 Proclaim[8085] on the citadels[759] in
[a]Ashdod and on the citadels in the land
of Egypt and say,[559] "Assemble[622] yourselves on the [b]mountains of Samaria and
see[7200] *the* great tumults[4103] within her
and *the* [c]oppressions in her midst.

10 "But they [a]do not know[3045] how
to do[6213] what is right,"[5228] declares
the LORD, "these who [b]hoard up [I]vio-
lence[2555] and devastation[7701] in their citadels."

11 Therefore, thus says the Lord
GOD,
"An [a]enemy, even one
surrounding the land,
Will pull down your [I]strength
from you
And your [b]citadels will be
looted."
12 Thus says the LORD,
"Just as the shepherd [Ia]snatches
from[5337] the lion's mouth[6310]
a couple of legs or a piece
of an ear,[241]
So will the sons of Israel dwelling
in Samaria be [II]snatched
away—
With *the* [b]corner of a bed and
the [IIIc]cover of a couch!
13 "Hear and [a]testify[5749] against the
house[1004] of Jacob,"
Declares[5001] the Lord GOD,[430]
the God of hosts.[6635]
14 "For on the day[3117] that I
punish[6485] Israel's
transgressions,[6588]
I will also punish the altars[4196]
of [a]Bethel;
The horns of the altar will be
cut off,
And they will fall to the
ground.[776]
15 "I will also smite[5221] the [Ia]winter
house together with the
[b]summer house;
The houses of [IIc]ivory will also
perish[6]
And the [d]great houses will come
to an end,"[5486]
Declares the LORD.

"Yet You Have Not Returned to Me"

4 🗝 Hear this word,[1697] you cows[6510]
of [a]Bashan who are on the
[b]mountain of Samaria,
Who [c]oppress the poor, who
crush the needy,
Who say to [I]your husbands,[113]
"Bring now, that we may
[d]drink!"
2 The Lord[136] [I]GOD has [a]sworn[7650]
by His [b]holiness,[6944]
"Behold, the days are coming
upon you
When [II]they will take you
away[5375] with [c]meat hooks,
And the last of you[319] with
[d]fish hooks.
3 "You will [a]go out *through*
breaches *in the walls*,
Each one straight before her,
And you [I]will be cast to
Harmon," declares the
LORD.

---

6 [b]Is. 14:24-27; 45:7
7 [I]Or, *For* [II]Heb., *YHWH* [a]Gen. 6:13; 18:17; Jer. 23:22; Dan. 9:22; John 15:15
8 [I]Heb., *YHWH*, usually rendered *LORD*, and so throughout the ch. [a]Amos 1:2 [b]Jon. 1:1-3; 3:1-3 [c]Jer. 20:9; Acts 4:20
9 [a]1Sam. 5:1 [b]Amos 4:1; 6:1 [c]Amos 5:11; 8:6
10 [I]I.e., the booty from violence [a]Ps. 14:4; Jer. 4:22; Amos 5:7; 6:12 [b]Hab. 2:8-10; Zeph. 1:9; Zech. 5:3, 4
11 [I]Or, *stronghold* [a]Amos 6:14 [b]Amos 2:5
12 [I]Or, *delivers* [II]Or, *delivered* [III]Lit., *damask* [a]1Sam. 17:34-37 [b]Ps. 132:3 [c]Esth. 1:6; 7:8; Amos 6:4
13 [a]Ezek. 2:7
14 [a]2Kin. 23:15; Hos. 10:5-8, 14, 15; Amos 4:4; 5:5, 6; 7:10, 13
15 [I]Or, *autumn* [II]I.e., ivory inlay [a]Jer. 36:22 [b]Judg. 3:20 [c]1Kin. 22:39; Ps. 45:8 [d]Amos 2:5; 6:11

1 [I]Lit., *their lords* [a]Ps. 22:12; Ezek. 39:18 [b]Amos 3:9; 6:1 [c]Amos 5:11; 8:6 [d]Amos 2:8; 6:6
2 [I]Heb., *YHWH*, usually rendered *LORD*, and so throughout the ch. [II]Lit., *he* [a]Amos 6:8; 8:7 [b]Ps. 89:35 [c]Is. 37:29; Ezek. 38:4 [d]Jer. 16:16; Ezek. 29:4; Hab. 1:15
3 [I]So Gr.; M.T. reads *will cast* [a]Jer. 52:7

🗝 **3:9** See note on Hos. 9:3.

🗝 **4:1-3** The cows of Bashan, east of the Sea of Galilee, were known for their fine quality. Here this metaphor refers to the well-to-do women of Samaria. The basis of this denunciation seems to have been their complicity with their husbands who were dishonest businessmen, because they urged them to bring home the finer things of life, something which was accomplished at the expense of the poor.

4 "Enter Bethel and transgress;[6586]
In Gilgal multiply
transgression![6586]
[a]Bring your sacrifices[2077] every
morning,
Your tithes[4643] every three days.
5 "[1]Offer[6999] a [a]thank offering[8426]
also from that which is
leavened,[2557]
And proclaim[7121] [b]freewill
offerings,[5071] make them
known.
For so you [c]love[157] *to do,* you
sons[1121] of Israel,"
Declares[5001] the Lord GOD.
6 "But I gave you also
[a]cleanness[5356] of teeth in
all your cities
And lack of bread in all your
places,
Yet you have [b]not returned[7725]
to Me," declares the LORD.
7 "And furthermore, I [a]withheld[4513]
the rain from you
While *there were* still three
months until harvest.
Then I would send rain on one
city
And on [b]another city I would not
send rain;
One part would be rained on,
While the part not rained on
would dry up.[3001]
8 "So two or three cities would
stagger to another city to
drink [a]water,
But would [b]not be satisfied;
Yet you have [c]not returned to
Me," declares the LORD.
9 "I [a]smote[5221] you with scorching
wind and mildew;
And the [b]caterpillar was
devouring
Your many gardens and
vineyards, fig trees and olive
trees;
Yet you have [c]not returned to
Me," declares the LORD.
10 "I sent a [a]plague[1698] among you
after the manner[1870] of
Egypt;
I [b]slew[2026] your young men by
the sword[2719] along with your
[c]captured[7628] horses,
And I made the [d]stench of your
camp[4264] rise up[5927] in your
nostrils;[639]
Yet you have [e]not returned to
Me," declares the LORD.
11 "I overthrew[2015] you as
[a]God[430] overthrew Sodom
and Gomorrah,
And you were like a [b]firebrand
snatched[5337] from a blaze;[8316]
Yet you have [c]not returned to
Me," declares the LORD.
12 "Therefore, thus I will do[6213] to
you, O Israel;
Because I shall do this to you,
Prepare[3559] to [a]meet your God,
O Israel."
13 For behold, He who [a]forms[3333]
mountains and [b]creates[1254]
the wind[7307]
And [c]declares[5046] to man[120] what
are His thoughts,
He who [d]makes[6213] dawn into
darkness[5890]
And [e]treads on the high
places[1116] of the earth,[776]
[f]The LORD God of hosts[6635] is
His name.

"Seek Me that You May Live"

5 Hear this word[1697] which I take
up[5375] for you as a [a]dirge,
O house[1004] of Israel.
2 She has fallen,[5307] she will
[a]not rise again—
The [b]virgin[1330] Israel.
She *lies* neglected[5203] on her
land;[127]
There is [c]none to raise her up.
3 For thus says the Lord[136]
[1]GOD,
"The city which goes forth a
thousand *strong*
Will have a [a]hundred left,[7604]
And the one which goes forth
a hundred *strong*
Will have [b]ten left to the house
of Israel."

4 [a]Num. 28:3; Amos 5:21, 22
5 [1]Lit., *Offer up in smoke* [a]Lev. 7:13 [b]Lev. 22:18-21 [c]Jer. 7:9, 10; Hos. 9:1, 10
6 [a]Is. 3:1; Jer. 14:18 [b]Is. 9:13; Jer. 5:3; Hag. 2:17
7 [a]Deut. 11:17; 2Chr. 7:13; Is. 5:6 [b]Ex. 9:4, 26; 10:22, 23
8 [a]1Kin. 18:5; Jer. 14:4 [b]Ezek. 4:16, 17; Hag. 1:6 [c]Jer. 3:7
9 [a]Deut. 28:22; Hag. 2:17 [b]Joel 1:4, 7; Amos 7:1,2 [c]Jer. 3:10
10 [a]Ex. 9:3; Lev. 26:25; Deut. 28:27, 60; Ps. 78:50 [b]Jer. 11:22; 18:21; 48:15 [c]2Kin. 13:3, 7 [d]Joel 2:20 [e]Is. 9:13
11 [a]Gen. 19:24, 25; Deut. 29:23; Is. 13:19 [b]Zech. 3:2 [c]Jer. 23:14
12 [a]Is. 32:11; 64:2; Jer. 5:22
13 [a]Job 38:4-7; Ps. 65:6; Is. 40:12 [b]Ps. 135:7; Jer. 10:13 [c]Dan. 2:28, 30 [d]Jer. 13:16; Joel 2:2; Amos 5:8 [e]Mic. 1:3 [f]Is. 47:4; Jer. 10:16; Amos 5:8, 27; 9:6

1 [a]Jer. 7:29; 9:10, 17; Ezek. 19:1
2 [a]Amos 8:14 [b]Jer. 14:17 [c]Is. 51:18; Jer. 50:32
3 [1]Heb., *YHWH,* usually rendered LORD, and so throughout the ch. [a]Is. 6:13 [b]Amos 6:9

4 For thus says the LORD to the
house of Israel,
"[a]Seek Me [b]that you may live.[2421]
5 "But do not [I]resort to [a]Bethel,
And do not come to [b]Gilgal,
Nor cross[5674] over to
[c]Beersheba;
For Gilgal will certainly go into
captivity,[1540]
And Bethel will [II]come to
trouble.[205]
6 "[a]Seek the LORD that you may
live,
Lest He break forth like a
[b]fire, [I]O house of Joseph,
And it consume with none to
quench *it* for Bethel,
7 *For* those who turn[2015]
[a]justice[4941] into
wormwood[3939]
And [I]cast righteousness down to
the earth."[776]
8 He who made[6213] the [a]Pleiades
and Orion
And [b]changes deep darkness[6757]
into morning,
[I]Who also [c]darkens[2821] day *into*
night,[3915]
Who [d]calls[7121] for the waters of
the sea
And pours them out[8210] on the
surface of the earth,
The [e]LORD is His name.
9 It is He who [a]flashes forth *with*
destruction[7701] upon the
strong,
So that [b]destruction comes upon
the fortress.
10 They hate[8130] him who
[a]reproves[3198] in the [I]gate,
And they [b]abhor[8581] him who
speaks *with* integrity.[8549]
11 Therefore, because you
[I]impose heavy rent on the
poor
And exact a tribute of grain from
them,
Though you have built
[a]houses of well-hewn[1496]
stone,
Yet you will not live in them;
You have planted pleasant
vineyards, yet you will
[b]not drink their wine.
12 For I know[3045] your
transgressions[6588] are many
and your sins[2403] are great,
You who [a]distress the
righteous[6662] *and* accept
bribes,[3724]
And [I]turn aside the poor in the
[II]gate.
13 Therefore, at [I]such a time[6256]
the prudent person [a]keeps
silent, for it is an evil[7451] time.
14 Seek good[2896] and not evil, that
you may live;[2421]
And thus may the LORD God[430]
of hosts[6635] be with you,
[a]Just as you have said!
15 [a]Hate evil, love[157] good,
And establish justice in the
[I]gate!
Perhaps the LORD God of hosts
[b]May be gracious[2603] to the
[c]remnant[7611] of Joseph.
16 Therefore, thus says the LORD
God of hosts, the Lord,
"There is [a]wailing in all the
plazas,
And in all the streets they say,[559]
'Alas! Alas!'
They also call[7121] the [b]farmer[406]
to mourning
And [I][c]professional[3045] mourners
to lamentation.
17 "And in all the [a]vineyards *there*
is wailing,
Because I shall pass through[7130]
the midst of you," says the
LORD.
🔑 **18** Alas, you who are longing[183] for
the [a]day of the LORD,
For what purpose *will* the
day[3117] of the LORD *be* to you?
It *will be* [b]darkness[2822] and not
light;[216]
19 As when a man[376] [a]flees from a
lion,
And a bear meets[6293] him,

4 [a]Deut. 4:29; 32:46, 47; Jer. 29:13 [b]Is. 55:3
5 [I]Lit., *seek* [II]Or, *become iniquity* [a]1Kin. 12:28, 29; Amos 3:14; 4:4; 7:10, 13 [b]1Sam. 7:16; 11:14 [c]Gen. 21:31-33; Amos 8:14
6 [I]Or, *in the house* [a]Is. 55:3, 6, 7; Amos 5:14 [b]Deut. 4:24
7 [I]Lit., *they have put down* [a]Amos 2:3; 5:12; 6:12
8 [I]Lit., *And He darkened* [a]Job 9:9; 38:31 [b]Job 12:22; 38:12; Is. 42:16 [c]Ps. 104:20 [d]Ps. 104:6-9; Amos 9:6 [e]Amos 4:13
9 [a]Is. 29:5; Amos 2:14 [b]Mic. 5:11
10 [I]I.e., the place where court was held [a]Is. 29:21; Amos 5:15 [b]1Kin. 22:8; Is. 59:15; Jer. 17:16-18
11 [I]Another reading is *trample upon* [a]Amos 3:15; 6:11 [b]Mic. 6:15
12 [I]Lit., *they turn* [II]I.e., the place where court was held [a]Is. 1:23; 5:23; Amos 2:6
13 [I]Lit., *that time* [a]Eccl. 3:7; Hos. 4:4
14 [a]Mic. 3:11
15 [I]I.e., the place where court was held [a]Ps. 97:10; Rom. 12:9 [b]Joel 2:14 [c]Mic. 5:3, 7,8
16 [I]Lit., *those who know lamentation* [a]Jer. 9:10, 18-20; Amos 8:3 [b]Joel 1:11 [c]2Chr. 35:25; Jer. 9:17
17 [a]Is. 16:10; Jer. 48:33
18 [a]Is. 5:19; Jer. 30:7; Joel 1:15; 2:1; 11, 31 [b]Is. 5:30; Joel 2:2
19 [a]Job 20:24; Is. 24:17, 18; Jer. 15:2, 3; 48:44

🔑 **5:18-20** See note on Zeph. 1:7.

ᴵOr goes home, leans his
hand[3027] against the wall,
And a snake[5175] bites him.
20 *Will* not the day of the LORD
be [a]darkness instead of light,
Even gloom[651] with no
brightness in it?
21"I hate, I [a]reject[3988] your
festivals,[2282]
Nor do I [Ib]delight[7306] in your
solemn assemblies.[6116]
22 "Even though you [a]offer[5927] up
to Me burnt offerings[5930] and
your grain offerings,[4503]
I will not accept[7521] *them*;
And I will not *even* look at the
[b]peace offerings[8002] of your
fatlings.
23 "Take away[5493] from Me the
noise of your songs;[7892]
I will not even listen[8085] to the
sound of your harps.5035
24 "But let [a]justice roll down[1556] like
waters
And righteousness like an ever-
flowing stream.
25 "[Ia]Did you present[5066] Me with
sacrifices[2077] and grain offerings[4503] in
the wilderness for forty years, O house
of Israel?
26 "[a]You also carried along[5375]
ᴵSikkuth[5522] your king and ᴵᴵKiyyun,
your images,[6754] ᴵᴵᴵthe star of your
gods[430] which you made[6213] for yourselves.
27 "Therefore, I will make you
go into exile[1540] beyond Damascus,"
says the LORD, whose name is the God
of hosts.

"Those at Ease in Zion"

6 [a]Woe to those who are at ease in
Zion,
And to those who *feel* secure[982]
in the mountain of Samaria,
The [b]distinguished[5344] men[7225] of
the foremost of nations,[1471]
To whom the house[1004] of Israel
comes.
2 Go over[5674] to [a]Calneh and
look,[7200]
And go from there to [b]Hamath
the great,
Then go down to [c]Gath of the
Philistines.
Are ᴵthey better[2896] than these
kingdoms,[4467]
Or is their territory greater than
yours?
3 Do you [a]put off the day[3117] of
calamity,[7451]
And would you [b]bring near[5066]
the seat of violence?[2555]
4 Those who recline on beds of
ivory
And sprawl on their [a]couches,
And [b]eat lambs[3733] from the flock
And calves from the midst of the
stall,
5 Who improvise to the sound[6310]
of the harp,
And like David have
ᴵcomposed[2803] [a]songs[7892] for
themselves,
6 Who [a]drink wine from
ᴵsacrificial bowls
While they anoint[4886]
themselves with the finest of
oils,[8081]
Yet they have not [b]grieved over
the ruin[7667] of Joseph.
7 Therefore, they will now [a]go
into exile[1540] at the head[7218]
of the exiles,
And the [b]sprawlers' ᴵbanqueting
will ᴵᴵpass away.[5493]
8 The Lord[136] ᴵGOD has [a]sworn[7650]
by Himself,[5315] the LORD
God[430] of hosts[6635] has
declared:

19 ᴵOr, *Then*
20 [a]Is. 13:10; Zeph. 1:15
21 ᴵLit., *like to smell* [a]Is. 1:11-16; 66:3; Amos 4:4, 5; 8:10 [b]Lev. 26:31; Jer. 14:12; Hos. 5:6
22 [a]Is. 66:3; Mic. 6:6, 7 [b]Lev. 7:11-15; Amos 4:5
24 [a]Jer. 22:3; Ezek. 45:9; Mic. 6:8
25 ᴵOr, *You presented Me with the sacrifices and a grain offering* [a]Deut. 32:17; Josh. 24:14; Neh. 9:18-21; Acts 7:42, 43
26 ᴵOr, *Sakkuth (Saturn) or shrine of your Moloch* ᴵᴵOr, *Kaiwan (Saturn)* or *stands of* ᴵᴵᴵOr, *your star gods* [a]Acts 7:43

1 [a]Is. 32:9-11; Zeph. 1:12; Luke 6:24 [b]Ex. 19:5; Amos 3:2
2 ᴵOr, *you* [a]Gen. 10:10; Is. 10:9 [b]1Kin. 8:65; 2Kin. 18:34; Is. 10:9 [c]1Sam. 5:8; 2Chr. 26:6
3 [a]Is. 56:12; Amos 9:10 [b]Amos 3:10
4 [a]Amos 3:12 [b]Ezek. 34:2, 3
5 ᴵOr, *invented musical instruments* [a]1Chr. 15:16; 23:5; Is. 5:12
6 ᴵLit., *sprinkling basins* [a]Amos 2:8; 4:1 [b]Ezek. 9:4
7 ᴵOr, *cultic feasts* ᴵᴵLit., *turn aside* [a]Amos 7:11, 17 [b]1Kin. 20:16-21; Dan. 5:4-6, 30
8 ᴵHeb., *YHWH*, usually rendered LORD [a]Gen. 22:16; Jer. 22:5; 51:14; Amos 4:2; 8:7

5:24 This is the most famous verse in the Book of Amos, and it is ethical statements such as this one which stand out so prominently in the prophets. During the period when Amos preached in Israel, justice was a scarce commodity. No prophet exhibited a greater concern for the fair treatment of one's neighbor than Amos.

"I [b]loathe[8374] the arrogance of
Jacob,
And I [II]detest[8130] his
[c]citadels;[759]
Therefore, I will [d]deliver up *the*
city and [III]all it contains."
9 And it will be, if [a]ten men[582] are
left[3498] in one house, they will die.
10 Then one's [I]uncle, or his [IIa]under-
taker, will lift him up to carry out *his*
bones[6106] from the house, and he will
say to the one who is in the innermost
part of the house, "Is anyone else with
you?" And that one will say, "No one."
Then he will [III]answer, "[b]Keep quiet.
For [IV]the name of the LORD is [c]not to
be mentioned."[2142]
11 For behold, the LORD is going
to [a]command[6680] that the [b]great house
be smashed[5221] to pieces and the small
house to fragments.
12 Do horses run on rocks?
Or does one plow [I]them with
oxen?
Yet you have turned[2015]
[a]justice[4941] into poison,[7219]
And the fruit of righteousness
into [II]wormwood,
13 You who rejoice in
[Ia]Lo-debar,[1697,3808]
[II]And say, "Have we not
[b]by our *own* strength[2392]
taken [III]Karnaim for
ourselves?"
14 "For behold, [a]I am going to raise
up a nation against you,
O house of Israel," declares the
LORD God of hosts,
"And they will afflict you from the
[b]entrance of Hamath
To the [c]brook of the
Arabah."[6160]

Warning Through Visions

7 Thus the Lord[136] [I]GOD showed[7200]
me, and behold, He was forming[3335]
a [a]locust-swarm [II]when the spring crop
began to sprout.[5927] And behold, the
spring crop *was* after the king's [III]mow-
ing.
2 And it came about, [I]when it had
[a]finished[3615] eating the vegetation of the
land,[776] that I said,[559]
"[b]Lord GOD, please pardon![5545]
[II]How can Jacob stand,
For he is [c]small?"
3 The LORD [Ia]changed His mind[5162]
about this.
"It shall not be," said the
LORD.
4 Thus the Lord GOD showed me,
and behold, the Lord GOD was calling[7121]
to contend[7378] *with them* by [a]fire, and
it consumed the great deep and began
to consume the [I]farm land.
5 Then I said,
"[a]Lord GOD, please stop!
[b]How can Jacob stand, for he
is small?"
6 The LORD [Ia]changed His mind
about this.
"This too shall not be," said the
Lord GOD.
7 Thus He showed me, and behold, the Lord was standing[5324] [I]by a
[II]vertical wall, with a plumb line[594] in
His hand.[3027]
🔑 8 And the LORD said to me, "[a]What
do you see,[7200] Amos?" And I said, "A
plumb line." Then the Lord said,
"Behold I am about to put a
[b]plumb line
In the midst of My people[5971]
Israel.
I will [Ic]spare[5674] them no
longer.
9 "The [a]high places[1116] of Isaac will
be desolated[8074]
And the [b]sanctuaries of Israel
laid waste.[2717]
Then shall I [c]rise up against the
house[1004] of Jeroboam with
the sword."[2719]

8 [II]Lit., *hate* [III]Lit., *its fulness* [b]Lev. 26:30; Deut. 32:19; Ps. 106:40; Amos 5:21 [c]Amos 3:10, 11 [d]Hos. 11:6
9 [a]Amos 5:3
10 [I]Or, *beloved one* [II]Lit., *one who burns him* [III]Lit., *say* [IV]Lit., *not to make mention of the name of* [a]1Sam. 31:12 [b]Amos 5:13; 8:3 [c]Jer. 44:26; Ezek. 20:39
11 [a]Is. 55:11 [b]2Kin. 25:9; Amos 3:15; 5:11
12 [I]Another reading is *the sea with oxen* [II]I.e., bitterness [a]1Kin. 21:7-13; Is. 59:13, 14; Hos. 10:4; Amos 5:7, 11, 12
13 [I]Lit., *a thing of nothing* [II]Lit., *Who* [III]Lit., *a pair of horns* [a]Job 8:14, 15; Ps. 2:2-4; Luke 12:19, 20 [b]Ps. 75:4, 5; Is. 28:14, 15
14 [a]Jer. 5:15 [b]Num. 34:7, 8; 1Kin. 8:65; 2Kin. 14:25

1 [I]Heb., *YHWH*, usually rendered *LORD*, and so throughout the ch. [II]Lit., *at the beginning of the coming up of* [III]Or, *shearings* [a]Joel 1:4; Amos 4:9; Nah. 3:15
2 [I]Lit., *if* [II]Lit., *As who* [a]Ex. 10:15 [b]Jer. 14:7, 20, 21; Ezek. 9:8; 11:13 [c]Is. 37:4; Jer. 42:2
3 [I]Or, *relented* [a]Deut. 32:36; Jer. 26:19; Hos. 11:8; Amos 5:15; Jon. 3:10
4 [I]Lit., *portion* [a]Deut. 32:22; Is. 66:15, 16; Amos 2:5
5 [a]Ps. 85:4; Joel 2:17 [b]Amos 7:2
6 [I]Or, *relented* [a]Ps. 106:45; Amos 7:3; Jon. 3:10

7 [I]Or, *upon* [II]Lit., *wall of a plumb line* 8 [I]Lit., *pass him by* [a]Jer. 1:11; Amos 8:2 [b]2Kin. 21:13; Is. 28:17; 34:11; Lam. 2:8 [c]Jer. 15:6; Ezek. 7:4-9; Amos 8:2 9 [a]Gen. 46:1; Hos. 10:8; Mic. 1:5 [b]Lev. 26:31; Is. 63:18; Jer. 51:51; Amos 7:13 [c]2Kin. 15:8-10; Amos 7:11

🔑 **7:8** It takes God's straight edge to show us how crooked we really are.

Amos Accused, Answers

🔑 **10** Then Amaziah, the [a]priest[3548] of
Bethel, sent *word* to [b]Jeroboam, king
of Israel, saying,[559] "Amos has [c]con-
spired against you in the midst[7130] of
the house of Israel; the land is unable
to endure all his words.[1697]
11 "For thus Amos says, 'Jeroboam
will die[4191] by the sword and Israel will
certainly go[1540] from its land[127] into
exile.' "[1540]
🔑 12 Then Amaziah said to Amos,
"[a]Go, you seer,[2374] flee away to the land
of Judah, and there eat bread and there
do your prophesying![5012]
13 "But [a]no longer prophesy at
Bethel, for it is a [b]sanctuary of the king
and a royal [I]residence."
🔑 **14** Then Amos answered and said
to Amaziah, "I am not a prophet,[5030]
nor am I the [a]son[1121] of a prophet; for
I am a herdsman and a [I]grower of sycamore figs.
15 "But the LORD took me from
[I]following the flock and the LORD said
to me, 'Go [a]prophesy to My people Israel.'
16 "And now hear the word of
the LORD: you are saying, 'You [a]shall
not prophesy against Israel [b]nor shall
you [I]speak[5197] against the house of
Isaac.'
17 "Therefore, thus says the LORD,
'Your [a]wife[802] will become a harlot[2181]
in the city, your [b]sons and your daughters will fall[5307] by the sword, your land
will be parceled up by a *measuring*
line,[2256] and you yourself will die
[I]upon [c]unclean[2931] soil. Moreover, Israel
will certainly go from its land into exile.' "

Basket of Fruit and Israel's Captivity

8 Thus the Lord[136] [I]GOD showed[7200]
me, and behold, *there was* a basket
of summer fruit.
2 And He said,[559] "What do you
see,[7200] Amos?" And [a]I said, "A basket
of summer fruit." Then the LORD said
to me, "The [b]end has come for My
people[5971] Israel. I will [I][c]spare[5674] them
no longer.
3 "[I]The [a]songs[7892] of the palace[1964]
will turn to [b]wailing in that day,"[3117]
declares[5001] the Lord GOD. "Many *will
be* the [c]corpses;[6297] in every place
[II]they will cast them forth [III]in silence."
4 Hear this, you who [I][a]trample the
needy, to do away with the humble of
the land,[776]
🔑 5 saying,[559]
"When will the [a]new moon
[I]be over,[5674]
So that we may sell grain,[7668]
And the [b]sabbath,[7676] that we
may open the wheat *market*,
To make the [II]bushel smaller and
the shekel bigger,
And to [c]cheat[5791] with
[III]dishonest[4820] scales,
6 So as to [a]buy the helpless for
[I]money
And the needy for a pair of
sandals,

10 [a]1Kin. 12:31, 32; 13:33 [b]2Kin. 14:23, 24 [c]Jer. 26:8-11; 38:4
12 [a]Matt. 8:34
13 [I]Lit., *house* [a]Amos 2:12; Acts 4:18 [b]1Kin. 12:29, 32; Amos 7:9
14 [I]Or, *nipper* [a]1Kin. 20:35; 2Kin. 2:3, 5; 4:38; 2Chr. 19:2
15 [I]Lit., *behind* [a]Jer. 1:7; Ezek. 2:3, 4
16 [I]Lit., *flow* [a]Amos 2:12; 7:13 [b]Deut. 32:2; Ezek. 20:46; 21:2
17 [I]Or, *in an unclean land* [a]Hos. 4:13, 14 [b]Jer. 14:16 [c]2Kin. 17:6; Ezek. 4:13; Hos. 9:3

1 [I]Heb., *YHWH*, usually rendered *LORD*, and so throughout the ch.
2 [I]Lit., *pass him by* [a]Jer. 24:3 [b]Ezek. 7:2, 3, 6 [c]Amos 7:8
3 [I]Or, *They will howl the palace songs* [II]Lit., *he has thrown* [III]Or, *hush!* [a]Amos 5:23; 6:4, 5; 8:10 [b]Amos 5:16 [c]Amos 6:8-10
4 [I]Or, *snap at* [a]Ps. 14:4; Prov. 30:14; Amos 2:7; 5:11, 12
5 [I]Lit., *pass by* [II]Lit., *ephah* [III]Lit., *balances of deception* [a]Num. 28:11; 2Kin. 4:23 [b]Ex. 31:13-17; Neh. 13:15 [c]Hos. 12:7; Mic. 6:11
6 [I]Lit., *silver* [a]Amos 2:6

🔑 **7:10** Bethel was the king's shrine in Israel. When Jeroboam assumed leadership over the ten northern tribes at the beginning of the divided monarchy, he set up golden calves and alternate places of worship in Bethel and Dan, the southern and northern extremities of his kingdom, so that his citizens would not be drawn back to unify with Judah through their frequent contact with the original temple in Jerusalem (I Kgs. 12:26-29). God regarded this as a very serious sin, which Israel never corrected.

🔑 **7:12,13** See note on Amos 2:12.

🔑 **7:14** Amos' response to Amaziah is without verbs in Hebrew. So, he could have been saying either "I *am* no prophet . . ." or "I *was* no prophet . . ."

🔑 **8:5,6** The depths of dishonesty and irreligion to which some merchants had sunk are graphically depicted in these verses. Their greed was so great that they could not wait for religious holidays to end, so that they could start making money again. To compound their guilt, they were selling adulterated wheat, shortchanging the amounts, and increasing the price.

And *that* we may sell the refuse
of the wheat?"
7 The LORD has [a]sworn[7650] by the
[b]pride of Jacob,
"Indeed, I will [c]never[5331] forget
any of their deeds.
8 "Because of this will not the land
[a]quake[7264]
And everyone who dwells in it
[b]mourn?
Indeed, all of it will [c]rise up[5927]
like the Nile,[216]
And it will be tossed about,
And subside like the Nile of
Egypt.
9 "And it will come about in that
day," declares the Lord GOD,
"That I shall make the [a]sun go
down at noon
And [b]make the earth[776] dark[2821]
in [I]broad daylight.[3117,216]
10 "Then I shall [a]turn[2015] your
festivals[2282] into mourning
And all your songs into
[I]lamentation;
And I will bring[5927] [b]sackcloth on
everyone's loins
And baldness on every head.[7218]
And I will make[7760] it [c]like *a time*
of mourning for an only[3173]
son,
And the end[319] of it will be like
a bitter[4751] day.
11 "Behold, days are coming,"
declares the Lord GOD,
"When I will send a famine on
the land,
Not a famine for bread or a thirst
for water,
But rather [a]for hearing[8085] the
words[1697] of the LORD.
12 "And people will stagger from sea
to sea,
And from the north even to the
east;
They will go to and fro to
[a]seek the word of the LORD,
But they will not find *it*.
13 "In that day the beautiful
[a]virgins[1330]
And the young men will
[b]faint from thirst.
14 "*As for* those who swear[7650] by
the [Ia]guilt[819] of Samaria,
Who say, 'As your god[430] lives,
O [b]Dan,'
And, 'As the way[1870] of
[c]Beersheba lives,'[2416]
They will fall[5307] and [d]not rise
again."

God's Judgment Unavoidable

9 I saw[7200] the Lord[136] standing[5324]
beside the [a]altar,[4196] and He said,[559]
"Smite[5221] the capitals[3730] so
that the [b]thresholds will
shake,[7493]
And [c]break them on the
heads[7218] of them all!
Then I will [d]slay[2026] the rest[319]
of them with the sword;[2719]
They will [e]not have a fugitive
who will flee,
Or a refugee who will escape.
2 "Though they dig into [a]Sheol,[7585]
From there shall My hand[3027]
take them;
And though they [b]ascend[5927] to
heaven,[8064]
From there will I bring them
down.
3 "And though they hide on the
summit[7218] of Carmel,
I will [a]search them out and take
them from there;
And though they [b]conceal
themselves from My sight on
the floor of the sea,
From there I will command[6680]
the [c]serpent[5175] and it will bite
them.
4 "And though they go into
[a]captivity[7628] before their
enemies,
From there I will command the
sword that it slay[2026] them,
And I will [b]set[7760] My eyes
against them for evil[7451] and
not for good."[2896]
5 And the Lord [I]GOD of hosts,[6635]
The One who [a]touches[5060] the
land[776] so that it melts,

7 [a]Amos 4:2 [b]Deut. 33:26, 29; Ps. 68:34; Amos 6:8 [c]Ps. 10:11; Hos. 7:2; 8:13

8 [a]Ps. 18:7; 60:2; Is. 5:25 [b]Hos. 4:3 [c]Jer. 46:7, 8; Amos 9:5

9 [I]Lit., *a day of light* [a]Job 5:14; Is. 13:10; Jer. 15:9; Mic. 3:6 [b]Is. 59:9, 10; Amos 4:13; 5:8

10 [I]Or, *a dirge* [a]Job 20:23; Amos 5:21 [b]Is. 15:2, 3; Jer. 48:37; Ezek. 7:18; 27:31 [c]Jer. 6:26; Zech. 12:10

11 [a]1Sam. 3:1; 2Chr. 15:3; Ps. 74:9; Ezek. 7:26; Mic. 3:6

12 [a]Ezek. 20:3, 31

13 [a]Lam. 1:18; 2:21 [b]Is. 41:17; Hos. 2:3

14 [I]Or, *Ashimah* [a]Hos. 8:5 [b]1Kin. 12:28, 29 [c]Amos 5:5 [d]Amos 5:2

1 [a]Amos 3:14 [b]Zeph. 2:14 [c]Ps. 68:21; Hab. 3:13 [d]Amos 7:17 [e]Jer. 11:11

2 [a]Ps. 139:8 [b]Jer. 51:53; Obad.4

3 [a]Jer. 16:16 [b]Job 34:22; Ps. 139:9, 10 [c]Is. 27:1

4 [a]Lev. 26:33 [b]Lev. 17:10; Jer. 21:10; 39:16; 44:11

5 [I]Heb., *YHWH*, usually rendered LORD, and so throughout the ch. [a]Ps. 104:32; 144:5; Is. 64:1; Mic. 1:4

And [b]all those who dwell in it
mourn,
And all of it rises up[5927] like the
Nile
And subsides like the Nile of
Egypt;
6 The One who builds His
[I][a]upper chambers in the
heavens,
And has founded[3245] His vaulted
dome over the earth,[776]
He who [b]calls[7121] for the waters
of the sea
And [c]pours them out[8210] on the
face of the earth,
[d]The LORD is His name.
7 "Are you not as the sons[1121] of
[a]Ethiopia to Me,
O sons of Israel?" declares[5001]
the LORD.
"Have I not brought up[5927] Israel
from the land of Egypt,
And the [b]Philistines from
Caphtor and the [c]Arameans
from [d]Kir?
8 "Behold, the [a]eyes of the Lord
GOD are on the sinful[2403]
kingdom,[4467]
And I will [b]destroy[8045] it from
the face of the earth;[127]
Nevertheless, I will [c]not totally
destroy the house[1004] of
Jacob,"
Declares the LORD.
9 "For behold, I am commanding,
And I will [a]shake the house of
Israel among all nations[1471]
As *grain* is shaken in a sieve,
But not a [I]kernel will fall[5307] to
the ground.
10 "All the [a]sinners[2400] of My
people[5971] will die[4191] by the
sword,
Those who say, '[b]The calamity
will not overtake[5066] or
confront us.'

The Restoration of Israel

11 "In that day[3117] I will [a]raise up
the fallen [I][b]booth[5521] of David,
And wall up its [c]breaches;
I will also raise up its ruins,
And rebuild it as in the
[d]days of old;[5769]
12 [a]That they may possess[3423] the
remnant[7611] of [b]Edom
And all the [I]nations[1471] who are
[c]called by My name,"
Declares the LORD who does[6213]
this.
13 "Behold, days are coming,"
declares the LORD,
"When the [a]plowman will
overtake the reaper
And the treader of grapes him
who sows seed;[2233]
When the [b]mountains will
drip[5197] sweet [c]wine,
And all the hills will be dissolved.
14 "Also I will [a]restore[7725] the
[I]captivity[7622] of My people
Israel,
And they will [b]rebuild the
ruined[8074] cities and live *in
them*,
They will also [c]plant vineyards
and drink their wine,
And make[6213] gardens and eat
their fruit.
15 "I will also plant them on their
land,[127]
And [a]they will not again be
rooted out from their land
Which I have given them,"
Says the LORD your God.[430]

5 [b]Amos 8:8
6 [I]Or, *stairs* [a]Ps. 104:3, 13 [b]Amos 5:8 [c]Ps. 104:6 [d]Amos 4:13
7 [a]2Chr. 14:9, 12; Is. 20:4; 43:3 [b]Deut. 2:23; Jer. 47:4 [c]Amos 1:5 [d]2Kin. 16:9; Is. 22:6
8 [a]Jer. 44:27; Amos 9:4 [b]Amos 7:17; 9:10 [c]Jer. 5:10; 30:11; 31:35, 36; Joel 2:32; Amos 3:12; Obad. 17
9 [I]Or, *pebble* [a]Is. 30:28; Luke 22:31
10 [a]Is. 33:14; Zech. 13:8 [b]Amos 6:3
11 [I]Or, *shelter* or *tabernacle* [a]Acts 15:16-18 [b]Is. 16:5 [c]Ps. 80:12 [d]Is. 63:11; Jer. 46:26
12 [I]Or, *Gentiles* [a]Obad. 19 [b]Num. 24:18; Is. 11:14 [c]Is. 43:7
13 [a]Lev. 26:5 [b]Joel 3:18 [c]Gen. 49:11
14 [I]Or, *fortunes* [a]Ps. 53:6; Is. 60:4; Jer. 30:3, 18 [b]Is. 61:4; 65:21 [c]Jer. 24:6; 31:28
15 [a]Is. 60:21; Ezek. 34:28; 37:25

The Book of

OBADIAH

Obadiah is the shortest book in the Old Testament. Though there are thirteen different men with this name mentioned in the Old Testament, none of them can be identified as this prophet with certainty. Obadiah means "servant of Yahweh". No definite conclusions can be drawn as to the date, though prophecies regarding the destruction of Edom and references to the captivity of Jerusalem within the book have caused many scholars to date it after 586 B.C. Obadiah's prophecy predicts the fall and utter destruction of Edom (compare Isa. 34:5-15; Jer. 49:7-22; Ezek. 25:12-14; Amos 1:11-12). It seems to have been written for the encouragement of the Israelites, rather than to bring Edom to repentance. Edom, the sons of Esau, was the perennial enemy of Judah, the sons of Jacob, and repeatedly displayed their bitter hatred by attacking Judah. Edom openly rejoiced at the defeat of Judah (Psa. 137:7) and filtered into the vacuum created by Babylon's victory. Though they were proud of their mountain strongholds, which seemed to be invincible, they would not be able to stand against the day of the Lord. When Malachi (1:2-5) was written, Edom had been severely defeated. Nabatean Arabs defeated Edom and occupied their territory, which was later called Idumea. The Herods of New Testament times were from the Edomite remnant in Idumea. After the fall of Jerusalem in A.D. 70 the Edomites passed finally from the pages of history.

Edom Will Be Humbled

1 🗝 The vision[2377] of Obadiah.
Thus says the Lord[136] [I]GOD concerning [a]Edom—
[b]We have heard[8085] a report from the LORD,
And an [c]envoy[6735] has been sent among the nations[1471] saying,
"[d]Arise and let us go against her for battle"—
2 "Behold, I will make you [a]small among the nations;
You are greatly despised.
3 "The [a]arrogance[2087] of your heart[3820] has deceived you,
You who live[7931] in the clefts of [I]the [b]rock,
In the loftiness of your dwelling place,
Who say in your heart,
'[c]Who will bring me down to earth?'[776]
4 "Though you [a]build high like the eagle,
Though you set[7760] your nest among the [b]stars,
From there I will bring you down," declares[5001] the LORD.
5 "If [a]thieves came to you,
If [I]robbers[7703] by night—
O how you will be ruined!—[1820]
Would they not steal *only* [II]until they had enough?
If grape gatherers came to you,
[b]Would they not leave[7604] *some* gleanings?
6 "O how Esau will be [a]ransacked,
And his hidden treasures searched out![1158]
7 "All the [a]men[582] [I]allied with you[1285]
Will send you forth to the border,
And the men at peace[7965] with you
Will deceive you and overpower you.
They who eat your [b]bread
Will set[7760] an ambush for you.
(There is [c]no understanding [II]in him.)

1 [I]Heb., *YHWH*, usually rendered *LORD* [a]Ps. 137:7; Is. 21:11, 12; 34:1-17; 63:1-6; Jer. 49:7-22; Ezek. 25:12-14; 35:15; Joel 3:19; Amos 1:11, 12; Mal. 1:4 [b]Jer. 49:14-16; Obad. 1-4 [c]Is. 18:2; 30:4 [d]Jer. 6:4, 5
2 [a]Num. 24:18; Is. 23:9
3 [I]Or, *Sela* [a]Is. 16:6; Jer. 49:16 [b]2Kin. 14:7; 2Chr. 25:11f. [c]Is. 14:13-15; Rev. 18:7
4 [a]Job 20:6, 7; Hab. 2:9 [b]Is. 14:12-15
5 [I]Lit., *devastators of the night* [II]Lit., *their sufficiency* [a]Jer. 49:9 [b]Deut. 24:21
6 [a]Jer. 49:10
7 [I]Lit., *of your covenant* [II]I.e., in Esau; or, *of it* [a]Jer. 30:14 [b]Ps. 41:9 [c]Is. 19:11; Jer. 49:7

🗝 **v. 1** Concerning the Edomites see note on Gen. 27:39,40.

8 "Will I not on that day,"3117
declares the LORD,
"[a]Destroy6 wise2450 men from
Edom
And understanding from the
mountain of Esau?
9 "Then your [a]mighty men will be
dismayed,2865 O [b]Teman,
In order that everyone376 may
be [c]cut off3772 from the
mountain of Esau by
slaughter.
10 "Because of [a]violence2555 to your
brother251 Jacob,
[I]You will be covered3680 *with*
shame,955
[b]And you will be cut off
forever.5769
11 "On the day that you [a]stood
aloof,
On the day that strangers2114
carried off7617 his wealth,2428
And foreigners5237 entered his
gate
And [b]cast lots for Jerusalem—
[c]You too were as one of them.
12 "[a]Do not [I]gloat7200 over your
brother's day,
The day of his misfortune.5235
And [b]do not rejoice over the
sons1121 of Judah
In the day of their destruction;6
Yes, [c]do not [II]boast1230,6310
In the day of *their* distress.
13 "Do not enter the gate of My
people5971
In the [a]day of their disaster.343
Yes, you, do not [I]gloat over their
calamity7451
In the day of their disaster.
And do not [b]loot their
wealth2428
In the day of their disaster.
14 "And do not [a]stand at the fork
of the road
To cut down their fugitives;

8 [a]Job 5:12-14; Is. 29:14

9 [a]Jer. 49:22 [b]Gen. 36:11; 1Chr. 1:45; Job 2:11; Jer. 49:7; Ezek. 25:13; Amos 1:12; Hab. 3:3 [c]Is. 34:5-8; 63:1-3; Obad. 5

10 [I]Lit., *Shame will cover you* [a]Gen. 27:41; Ezek. 25:12; Joel 3:19; Amos 1:11 [b]Ezek. 35:9

11 [a]Ps. 83:5, 6; 137:7; Amos 1:6, 9 [b]Joel 3:3; Nah. 3:10 [c]Ezek. 35:10

12 [I]Lit., *look on* [II]Lit., *make your mouth large* [a]Mic. 4:11; 7:10 [b]Prov. 17:5; Ezek. 35:15; 36:5 [c]Ps. 31:18; Ezek. 35:12

13 [I]Lit., *look on* [a]Ezek. 35:5 [b]Ezek. 35:10; 36:2, 3

14 [a]Is. 16:3, 4

15 [a]Ezek. 30:3; Joel 1:15; 2:1, 11, 31; Amos 5:18, 20 [b]Jer. 50:29; 51:56; Hab. 2:8 [c]Ezek. 35:11

16 [I]Or, *stagger* [a]Jer. 49:12 [b]Joel 3:17 [c]Is. 51:22, 23; Jer. 25:15, 16

17 [a]Is. 4:2, 3 [b]Is. 14:1, 2; Amos 9:11-15

18 [I]I.e., the people of Esau [a]Is. 5:24; 9:18, 19; Zech. 12:6 [b]Jer. 11:23; Amos 1:8

19 [I]I.e., South country [II]I.e., the foothills [a]Is. 11:14; Amos 9:12 [b]Is. 11:14 [c]Jer. 31:5; 32:44

And do not imprison their
survivors8300
In the day of their distress.

The Day of the LORD and the Future

15 "For the [a]day3117 of the LORD
draws near on all the
nations.
[b]As you have done, it will be
done6213 to you.
Your [c]dealings will return7725 on
your own head.7218
16 "Because just as you [a]drank on
[b]My holy6944 mountain,
All the nations [c]will drink
continually.8548
They will drink and [I]swallow,
And become as if they had never
existed.
17 "But on Mount [a]Zion there will
be those who escape,6413
And it will be holy.6944
And the house1004 of Jacob will
[b]possess3423 their
possessions.
18 "Then the house of Jacob will be
a [a]fire
And the house of Joseph a flame;
But the house of Esau *will be*
as stubble.
And they will set [I]them on fire
and consume [I]them,
So that there will be [b]no survivor
of the house of Esau,"
For the LORD has spoken.1696
19 Then *those of* the [I]Negev will
[a]possess the mountain of
Esau,
And *those of* the [II]Shephelah the
[b]Philistine *plain*;
Also, they will [c]possess the
territory7704 of Ephraim and
the territory of Samaria,

v.19 "Those of the Negev" refers to the southernmost part of Canaan (see note on Num. 13:17), which was a dry country of rolling hills in which the patriarchs and many of the tribe of Judah preferred to make their homes. After Judah's defeat it was possessed for a while by the Edomites who were later annihilated by the Nabatean Arabs (see the introduction). "Plain" refers to the foothill region between the coastal plain and the central mountain range of Palestine which was possessed by the Philistines.

And Benjamin *will possess*
Gilead.
20 And the exiles1546 of this host2426
of the sons of Israel,
Who are *among* the Canaanites
as far as [a]Zarephath,
And the exiles of Jerusalem who
are in Sepharad
Will possess the [b]cities of the
Negev.
21 The [a]deliverers3467 will
ascend5927 Mount Zion
To judge8199 the mountain of
Esau,
And the [b]kingdom will be the
LORD'S.

20 [a]1Kin. 17:9; Luke 4:26 [b]Jer. 32:44; 33:13

21 [a]Neh. 9:27 [b]Ps. 22:28; 47:7-9; 67:4; Zech. 14:9; Rev. 11:15

The Book of

JONAH

The Book of Jonah is unique among the prophets in that, instead of containing a group of oracles or visions, it relates an extended episode in the life of the prophet. From II Kgs. 14:25 we learn that Jonah was from Gath-hepher, a town in Galilee, and that he prophesied during the time of Jeroboam II, which means that his book is probably to be dated in the first half of the eighth century B.C. The story line is simple. God called Jonah to go to Nineveh and denounce her wickedness, but he fled by boat in the opposite direction, because he feared that the success of his preaching would cause God to show mercy. He was thrown overboard to save those on his ship from a fierce storm, and God arranged for him to be swallowed by a large fish. After three days the fish spit him out on dry land, and God again called Jonah to preach against Nineveh. This time he went. His message that Nineveh would be overthrown in forty days was as powerful as it was brief. The entire city repented, and God revoked his judgment against them. Jonah became angry and went out of the city to see what would happen to it. God caused a plant to grow up to shade Jonah, and then He caused it to die. Jonah was again angry, because he needed the shade, but God used the incident to teach him a lesson about forgiveness and mercy. God pointed out that Jonah was more concerned about a plant than he was about a city with more than 120,000 inhabitants. The Book of Jonah occupies an important position in the O.T. canon, because it so clearly shows that, although God had a special relationship with Israel, He did not abandon his compassion for other nations. In Jonah's experience with the fish, Jesus saw a sign pointing to His own burial, and He used Nineveh's repentance to chide His unrepentant contemporaries (Mt. 12:39-41).

Jonah's Disobedience

1 The word[1697] of the LORD came to [a]Jonah the son[1121] of Amittai saying,[559]

2 "Arise, go to [a]Nineveh the great city, and [b]cry[7121] against it, for their [c]wickedness[7451] has come up[5927] before Me."

3 But Jonah rose up to flee to [a]Tarshish [b]from the presence of the LORD. So he went down to [c]Joppa, found a ship which was going to Tarshish, paid the fare, and went down into it to go with them to Tarshish from the presence of the LORD.

4 And the [a]LORD hurled a great wind[7307] on the sea and there was a great storm on the sea so that the ship was about[2803] to [I]break up.[7665]

5 Then the sailors became afraid,[3372] and every man[376] cried[2199] to [a]his god,[430] and they [b]threw the [I]cargo[3627] which was in the ship into the sea to lighten[7043] *it* [II]for them. But Jonah had gone below into the hold of the ship, lain down, and fallen sound asleep.

6 So the captain approached[7126] him and said,[559] "How is it that you are sleeping? Get up, [a]call[7121] on your god.[430]

1 [a]2Kin. 14:25; Matt. 12:39-41; 16:4; Luke 11:29, 30, 32
2 [a]Gen. 10:11; 2Kin. 19:36; Is. 37:37; Nah. 1:1; Zeph. 2:13 [b]Is. 58:1 [c]Gen. 18:20; Hos. 7:2
3 [a]Is. 23:1, 6, 10; Jer. 10:9 [b]Gen. 4:16; Ps. 139:7, 9, 10 [c]Josh. 19:46; 2Chr. 2:16; Ezra 3:7; Acts 9:36, 43
4 [I]Lit., *be broken* [a]Ps. 107:23-28; 135:6, 7
5 [I]Lit., *vessels* [II]Lit., *from upon them* [a]1Kin. 18:26 [b]Acts 27:18, 19, 38
6 [a]Ps. 107:28

1:2 In various periods of Assyria's history, Nineveh was the capital, and apparently it was such when Jonah visited there in the eighth century B.C. Within a few decades Assyria became the dominant power in the region and carried Israel into exile. Nineveh's fall finally came in 612 B.C., about a century and a half after Jonah was there. When Haran, the last major Assyrian city, fell in 609 B.C., Babylon became the next undisputed power. The prophets Zephaniah (Zeph. 2:13) and Nahum (Nah. 3:5-7) correctly prophesied that Nineveh would be destroyed.

1:3 Many Bible scholars locate Tarshish (which means "refinery") in the area now known as Spain. It had a copper-smelting station from which Phoenicion traders brought the refined metal to the Middle East to exchange for other commodities.

Perhaps *your* [b]god will be concerned
about us so that we will not perish."[6]
7 And each man said to his mate,[7453]
"Come, let us [a]cast[5307] lots so we may
[I]learn[3045] on whose account this
calamity[7451] *has struck* us." So they cast
lots and the [b]lot fell[5307] on Jonah.
8 Then they said to him, "[a]Tell[5046]
us, now! On whose account *has* this
calamity *struck* us? What is your
[b]occupation?[4399] And where do you come
from? What is your country?[776] From
what people[5971] are you?"
9 And he said to them, "I am a
[a]Hebrew, and I [b]fear[3373] the LORD
[c]God[430] of heaven[8064] who [d]made[6213] the
sea and the dry[3004] land."
10 Then the men[582] became extremely frightened and they said to him,
"[I]How could you do[6213] this?" For the
men knew[3045] that he was [a]fleeing from
the presence of the LORD, because he
had told them.
11 So they said to him, "What should
we do[6213] to you that the sea may become calm [I]for us?"—for the sea was
becoming increasingly stormy.
12 And he said to them, "Pick me
up[5375] and throw me into the sea. Then
the sea will become calm [I]for you, for
I know[3045] that [a]on account of me this
great storm *has come* upon you."
13 However, the men [I]rowed *desperately* to return[7725] to land[3004] but they
could not, for the sea was becoming
even stormier against them.
14 Then they called[7121] on the
[a]LORD and said, "We earnestly pray,[577]
O LORD, do not let us perish[6] on account
of this man's[376] life[5315] and do not put
innocent[5355] blood[1818] on us; for [b]Thou,
O LORD, hast done as Thou hast
pleased."[2654]
15 So they picked up Jonah, threw
him into the sea, and the sea [a]stopped
its raging.[2197]
16 Then the men feared[3372] the
LORD greatly, and they offered[2076] a
sacrifice[2077] to the LORD and made[5087]
[a]vows.[5088]
17 [I]And the LORD appointed a great
fish[1709] to swallow[1104] Jonah, and Jonah
was in the [a]stomach[4578] of the fish three
days[3117] and three nights.

6 [b]2Sam. 12:22; Amos 5:15; Jon. 3:9
7 [I]Lit., *know* [a]Josh. 7:14-18; 1Sam. 10:20, 21; 14:41, 42; Acts 1:23-26 [b]Num. 32:23; Prov. 16:33
8 [a]Josh. 7:19; 1Sam. 14:43 [b]Gen. 47:3; 1Sam. 30:13
9 [a]Gen. 14:13; Ex. 1:15; 2:13 [b]2Kin. 17:25, 28, 32, 33 [c]Ezra 1:2; Neh. 1:4; Ps. 136:26; Dan. 2:18 [d]Neh. 9:6; Ps. 95:5; 146:6
10 [I]Lit., *What is this you have done* [a]Job 27:22; Jon. 1:3
11 [I]Lit., *from upon us*
12 [I]Lit., *from upon you* [a]2Sam. 24:17; 1Chr. 21:17
13 [I]Lit., *dug their oars into the water*
14 [a]Ps. 107:28; Jon. 1:16 [b]Ps. 115:3; 135:6; Dan. 4:34, 35
15 [a]Ps. 65:7; 93:3, 4; 107:29
16 [a]Ps. 50:14; 66:13, 14
17 [I]Ch. 2:1 in Heb. [a]Matt. 12:40; 16:4

Jonah's Prayer

2 [I]Then Jonah prayed[6419] to the LORD
his God[430] [a]from the stomach[4578] of
the fish,[1709]
2 and he said,[559]
"I [a]called[7121] out of my distress
to the LORD,
And He answered me.
I cried for help from the
[I]depth[990] of [b]Sheol;[7585]
Thou didst hear[8085] my voice.
3 "For Thou hadst [a]cast me into
the deep,
Into the heart[3824] of the seas,
And the current [I]engulfed me.
All Thy [b]breakers and billows
passed over[5674] me.
4 "So I said, 'I have been
[a]expelled from [I]Thy sight.
Nevertheless I will look again
[b]toward Thy holy[6944]
temple.'[1964]
5 "[a]Water encompassed me to the
[I]point of death.[5315]
The great [b]deep [II]engulfed me,
Weeds were wrapped[2280] around
my head.[7218]
6 "I [a]descended to the roots of the
mountains.
The earth[776] with its [b]bars *was*
around me forever,[5769]
But Thou hast [c]brought up[5927]
my life[2416] from [I]the pit,[7845]
O LORD my God.
7 "While [I]I was [a]fainting away,
I [b]remembered[2142] the LORD;

1 [I]Ch. 2:2 in Heb. [a]Job 13:15; Ps. 130:1, 2; Lam. 3:53-56
2 [I]Lit., *belly* [a]1Sam. 30:6; Ps. 18:4-6; 22:24; 120:1 [b]Ps. 18:5, 6; 86:13; 88:17
3 [I]Lit., *surrounded* [a]Ps. 69:1, 2, 14, 15; Lam. 3:54 [b]Ps. 42:7
4 [I]Lit., *before Thine eyes* [a]Ps. 31:22; Jer. 7:15 [b]1Kin. 8:38; 2Chr. 6:38; Ps. 5:7
5 [I]Lit., *soul* [II]Lit., *surrounded* [a]Lam. 3:54 [b]Ps. 69:1, 2
6 [I]Or, *corruption* [a]Ps. 18:5; 116:3 [b]Is. 38:10; Matt. 16:18 [c]Job 33:28; Ps. 16:10; 30:3; Is. 38:17
7 [I]Lit., *my soul. . .within me* [a]Ps. 142:3 [b]Ps. :10, 11; 143:5

1:17 See note on Jon. 3:6-9.
2:6 "The pit" here refers to the grave, the dwelling place for the dead.

And my [c]prayer[8605] came to
Thee,
Into [d]Thy holy temple.
8 "Those who [a]regard[8104]
[I]vain[7723] idols
Forsake[5800] their
faithfulness,[2617]
9 But I will [a]sacrifice to Thee
With the voice of
thanksgiving.[8426]
That which I have vowed[5087] I
will [b]pay.
[c]Salvation[3444] is from the LORD."
10 Then the LORD commanded[559]
the [a]fish,[1709] and it vomited Jonah up
onto the dry[3004] land.

Nineveh Repents

3 Now the word of the LORD came
to Jonah the second time, saying,[559]
2 "Arise, go to [a]Nineveh the great
city and [b]proclaim[7121] to it the proclamation which I am going to tell you."
3 So Jonah arose and went to Nineveh according to the word[1697] of the
LORD. Now Nineveh was [I]an [a]exceed-
ingly[430] great city, a three days'[3117] walk.
4 Then Jonah began to go through
the city one day's walk; and he [a]cried
out[7121] and said,[559] "Yet forty days and
Nineveh will be overthrown."[2015]
5 Then the people[582] of Nineveh
believed[539] in God;[430] and they called[7121]
a [a]fast and put on sackcloth from the
greatest to the least of them.
6 When the word[1697] reached[5060] the
king of Nineveh, he arose from his
throne,[3678] laid aside[5674] his robe from
him, [a]covered[3680] *himself* with sackcloth,
and sat on the [I]ashes.
7 And he issued a [a]proclamation[2199]
and it said,[559] "In Nineveh by the
decree[2940] of the king and his nobles:
Do not let man,[120] beast, herd, or flock
taste a thing. Do not let them eat or
drink water.
8 "But both man and beast must be
covered[3680] with sackcloth; and let
[I]men [a]call[7121] on God earnestly[2394] that
each[376] may [b]turn[7725] from his wicked[7451]
way[1870] and from the violence[2555] which
is in [II]his hands.[3709]
9 "[a]Who knows,[3045] God may turn
and relent,[5162] and withdraw[7725] His
burning anger[639] so that we shall not
perish?"[6]
10 When God saw their deeds, that
they [a]turned from their wicked way,
then [b]God relented concerning the calamity which He had declared[1696] He
would [I]bring[6213] upon them. And He
did[6213] not do *it.*

Jonah's Displeasure Rebuked

4 But it greatly displeased[3415] Jonah,
and he became [a]angry.[2734]
2 And he [a]prayed[6419] to the LORD
and said,[559] "Please[577] LORD, was not
this [I]what I said[1697] while I was still in
my *own* country?[127] Therefore, [II]in order
to forestall this I [b]fled to Tarshish, for
I knew[3045] that Thou art a [c]gracious[2587]
and compassionate God,[410] slow[750] to
anger[639] and abundant in lovingkindness,[2617] and one who relents[5162] concerning calamity.[7451]

7 [c]2Chr. 30:27; Ps. 18:6 [d]Ps. 11:4; 65:4; Jon. 2:4; Mic. 1:2; Hab. 2:20
8 [I]Lit., *empty vanities* [a]2Kin. 17:15; Ps. 31:6; Jer. 10:8
9 [a]Ps. 50:14, 23; Jer. 33:11; Hos. 14:2 [b]Job 22:27; Eccl. 5:4, 5 [c]Ps. 3:8; Is. 45:17
10 [a]Jon. 1:17

2 [a]Zeph. 2:13 [b]Jer. 1:17; Ezek. 2:7
3 [I]Lit., *a great city to God* [a]Jon. 1:2; 4:11
4 [a]Matt. 12:41; Luke 11:32
5 [a]Dan. 9:3; Joel 1:14
6 [I]Or, *dust* [a]Esth. 4:1-4; Jer. 6:26; Ezek. 27:30, 31
7 [a]2Chr. 20:3; Ezra 8:21; Jon. 3:5
8 [I]Lit., *them* [II]Lit., *their* [a]Ps. 130:1; Jon. 1:6, 14 [b]Is. 1:16-19; 55:6, 7; Jer. 18:11
9 [a]2Sam. 12:22; Joel 2:14
10 [I]Lit., *do* [a]1Kin. 21:27-29; Jer. 31:18 [b]Ex. 32:14; Jer. 18:8; Amos 7:3, 6

1 [a]Jon. 4:4, 9; Matt. 20:15; Luke 15:28
2 [I]Lit., *my word* [II]Lit., *I was beforehand in fleeing* [a]Jer. 20:7 [b]Jon. 1:3 [c]Ex. 34:6; Num. 14:18; Ps. 86:5, 15; Joel 2:13

3:3 This means that it would require three days for Jonah to travel a circuitous route throughout the entire city, up and down every street, in order to preach his message of repentance.

3:5 This was a very coarse cloth of goats' hair worn by those in mourning. The scratchy properties caused them to feel some pain. They wanted to be reminded of their sins in order to renounce them fully.

3:6-9 Nineveh's wholesale repentance at the message of a Hebrew prophet was remarkable, and Jesus took special note of it (Mt. 12:41). The rabbis thought that it was brought about so quickly because the people of Nineveh had already heard of Jonah's miraculous deliverance. So, his encounter with the fish may have had a positive effect after all. Jesus' statement in Lk. 11:30 that Jonah was a sign to the men of Nineveh as the Son of Man would be to His contemporaries renders this interpretation probable, since Jesus' sign was His three days in the grave (Mt. 12:39,40; see Jon. 1:17). See the note on Jer. 18:7-10.

3 "Therefore now, O LORD, please
[a]take my [I]life[5315] from me, for death[4194]
is [b]better[2896] to me than life."[2416]
4 And the LORD said, "Do you have
good reason[3190] to be angry?"[2734]
5 Then Jonah went out from the city
and sat east of [I]it. There he made[6213]
a shelter[5521] for himself and [a]sat under
it in the shade until he could see what
would happen in the city.
6 So the LORD God[430] appointed a
[I]plant and it grew up[5927] over Jonah to
be a shade over his head[7218] to
deliver[5337] him from his discomfort.[7451]
And Jonah was [II]extremely happy about
the [I]plant.
7 But God appointed a worm when
dawn came[5927] the next day, and it
attacked[5221] the plant and it [a]with-
ered.[3001]
8 And it came about when the
sun came up that God appointed a
scorching[2759] [a]east wind,[7307] and the
[b]sun beat[5221] down on Jonah's head so
that he became faint and begged[7592] with
all his soul[5315] to die,[4191] saying, "[c]Death
is better to me than life."
9 Then God said to Jonah, "Do you
have good reason to be angry about the
plant?" And he said, "I have good reason
to be angry, even to death."[4194]
10 Then the LORD said, "You had
compassion on the plant for which you
did not work, and *which* you did not
cause to grow, which [I]came up overnight
and perished[6] [II]overnight.
11 "And should I not [a]have compassion on Nineveh, the great city in which
there are more than 120,000 persons[120]
who do not [b]know *the difference*[3045] between their right and left hand, as well
as many [c]animals?"

3 [I]Lit., *soul* [a]1Kin. 19:4; Job 6:8, 9 [b]Job 7:15, 16; Eccl. 7:1
5 [I]Lit., *the city* [a]1Kin. 19:9, 13
6 [I]Probably a castor oil plant, and so in vv. 7, 9 and 10 [II]Lit., *greatly*
7 [a]Joel 1:12
8 [a]Ezek. 19:12; Hos. 13:15 [b]Ps. 121:6; Is. 49:10 [c]Jon. 4:3
10 [I]Lit., *was a son of a night* [II]Lit., *a son of a night*
11 [a]Jon. 3:10 [b]Deut. 1:39; Is. 7:16 [c]Ps. 36:6

4:11 The phrase, "persons who do not know the difference between their right hand and left hand," was an idiomatic expression signifying very young children who had not reached the age of accountability, of making moral decisions (cf. Heb. 5:13,14). This verse justifies inclusion of the Book of Jonah in the canon, because it shows so clearly that the Lord is God of all the nations, not just Israel, and that He is concerned with the welfare of all mankind. Jonah represents so many others in Israel who forgot this lesson. Later, prophets like Isaiah tried to expand the people's vision by looking forward to the day when God's message would reach out to all nations, and Jesus' great commission assured that this would indeed take place (Mt. 28:19,20; Mk. 16:15; Lk. 24:46,47).

The Book of

MICAH

The southern prophet, Micah, was a contemporary of Isaiah in Judah and Hosea in Israel, prophesying in the last third of the eighth century B.C. Although his message related to both Israel and Judah, he focused on the latter. He denounced ethical sins primarily, and the social situation which he addressed is markedly similar to that encountered by Amos in Israel a few years earlier. The rich were oppressing the poor. Merchants cheated their customers. The religious and judicial leaders were corrupt, and the true prophets were told to keep quiet. Many people were so insensitive to the problem that they believed God would still defend them. Micah's message reminded them of the consequences of national sin. He foretold the fall of both Samaria and Jerusalem and even the Babylonian exile later. Two passages stand out above the rest: Micah 5:2 prophesied the Messiah's birth in Bethlehem, and this was fulfilled by the birth of Jesus. Micah 6:8 is one of the classical statements of the prophets, and some regard it as the high-water mark of Old Testament religion.

Destruction in Israel and Judah

1 The [a]word[1697] of the LORD which came *to* [b]Micah of Moresheth in the days[3117] of [c]Jotham, [d]Ahaz, *and* [e]Hezekiah, kings of Judah, which he saw[2372] concerning Samaria and Jerusalem.

2 Hear, O peoples,[5971] all of [I]you;
[a]Listen,[7181] O earth[776] and [II]all it contains,
And let the Lord[136] [III]GOD be a [b]witness against you,
The Lord from His holy[6944] temple.[1964]
3 For behold, the LORD is [a]coming forth from His place.
He will come down and [b]tread on the high places[1116] of the [I]earth.
4 [a]The mountains will melt under Him,
And the valleys will be split,
Like wax before the fire,
Like water poured down a steep place.
5 All this is for the rebellion[6588] of Jacob
And for the sins[2403] of the house[1004] of Israel.
What is the [a]rebellion of Jacob?
Is it not [b]Samaria?
What is the [c]high [I]place of Judah?
Is it not Jerusalem?
6 For I will make[7760] Samaria a [a]heap of ruins [I]in the open country,[7704]
[b]Planting places for a vineyard.
I will [c]pour her stones down into the valley,
And will [d]lay bare[1540] her foundations.[3247]
7 All of her [a]idols[6456] will be smashed,[3807]
All of her earnings will be burned[8313] with fire,
And all of her images[6091] I will make[7760] desolate,[8077]
For she collected[6908] *them* from a [b]harlot's[2181] earnings,
And to the earnings of a harlot they will return.[7725]
8 Because of this I must lament and wail,
I must go [a]barefoot and naked;[6174]

1 [a]2Pet. 1:21 [b]Jer. 26:18 [c]2Kin. 15:5, 32-38; 2Chr. 27:1-9; Is. 1:1; Hos. 1:1 [d]2Kin. 16:1-20; 2Chr. 28:1-27; Is. 7:1-12 [e]2Kin. 18:1-20; 2Chr. 29:1-31
2 [I]Lit., *them* [II]Lit., *its fulness* [III]Heb., *YHWH,* usually rendered LORD [a]Jer. 6:19; 22:29 [b]Is. 50:7
3 [I]Or, *land* [a]Is. 26:21 [b]Amos 4:13
4 [a]Ps. 97:5; Is. 64:1, 2; Nah. 1:5
5 [I]Lit., *places* [a]Jer. 2:19 [b]Is. 7:9; Amos 8:14 [c]2Chr. 34:3, 4
6 [I]Lit., *of the field* [a]2Kin. 19:25; Mic. 3:12 [b]Jer. 31:5; Amos 5:11 [c]Lam. 4:1 [d]Ezek. 13:14
7 [a]Deut. 9:21; 2Chr. 34:7 [b]Deut. 23:18; Is. 23:17
8 [a]Is. 32:11

1:1 Micah was from Moresheth, which he also called Moresheth-gath (1:14), probably because it was near the Philistine city of Gath. Moresheth was about twenty miles southwest of Jerusalem and seventeen miles west of Tekoa, where Amos, another eighth century prophet, lived.

1:8 If Micah literally did what he said he would do, he was not the only prophet to go naked to reinforce his message. See Isa. 20:2,3.

I must make[6213] a lament like
the [b]jackals[8577]
And a mourning like the
ostriches.
🗝 9 For her [I][a]wound[4347] is incurable,
For [b]it has come[5060] to Judah;
It has reached the [c]gate of my
people,
Even to Jerusalem.
10 [a]Tell[5046] it not in Gath,
Weep not at all.
At [I]Beth-le-aphrah roll yourself
in the dust.[6083]
11 [I]Go[5674] on your way, inhabitant
of [II]Shaphir, in [a]shameful
nakedness.[6181]
The inhabitant of [III][b]Zaanan does
not [IV]escape.
The lamentation of [V]Bethezel:
"He will take from you its
[VI]support."
12 For the inhabitant of [I]Maroth
Becomes weak [a]waiting[2342] for
good,[2896]
Because a calamity[7451] has come
down from the LORD
To the [b]gate of Jerusalem.
13 Harness the chariot to the team
of horses,
O inhabitant of [a]Lachish—
She was the beginning[7225] of sin
To the daughter of Zion—
Because in you were found
The [b]rebellious acts of Israel.
14 Therefore, you will give parting
[a]gifts
On behalf of Moresheth-gath;
The houses of [b]Achzib *will*
become a [c]deception
To the kings of Israel.
15 Moreover, I will bring on you
The one who takes
possession,[2423]
O inhabitant of [I][a]Mareshah.
The glory[3519] of Israel will enter
[b]Adullam.
16 Make yourself [a]bald and cut off
your hair,
Because of the children[1121] of
your delight;
Extend your baldness like the
eagle,
For they will [b]go from you into
exile.[1540]

Woe to Oppressors

2 Woe to those who [a]scheme
iniquity,[205]
Who work out evil[7451] on their
beds!
[I][b]When morning comes,[216] they
do[6213] it,
For it is in the [c]power[410] of their
hands.[3027]
2 They [a]covet[2530] fields[7704] and
then [b]seize *them,*
And houses,[1004] and take *them*
away.[5375]
They [I][c]rob a man[1397] and his
house,
A man[376] and his inheritance.[5159]
3 Therefore, thus says the LORD,
"Behold, I am [a]planning against
this [b]family[4940] a calamity
From which you [c]cannot remove
your necks;
And you will not walk [d]haughtily,
For it will be an [e]evil time.[6256]
4 "On that day[3117] they will
[a]take up[5375] against you a
[I]taunt
And [II][b]utter a bitter[5093]
lamentation *and* say,
'We are completely
[c]destroyed![7703]
He exchanges the portion of my
people;[5971]
How He removes it from me!
To the apostate[7725] He
[d]apportions our fields.'
5 "Therefore, you will have no one
[I][a]stretching a measuring
line[2256]
For you by lot in the
assembly[6951] of the LORD.

8 [b]Is. 13:21, 22
9 [I]Lit., *wounds* [a]Is. 3:26; Jer. 30:12, 15 [b]2Kin. 18:13; Is. 8:7, 8 [c]Mic. 1:12
10 [I]I.e., house of dust [a]2Sam. 1:20
11 [I]I.e., Go into captivity [II]I.e., pleasantness [III]I.e., going out [IV]Lit., *go out* [V]I.e., house of removal [VI]Lit., *standing place* [a]Ezek. 23:29 [b]Josh. 15:37
12 [I]I.e., bitterness [a]Is. 59:9-11; Jer. 14:19 [b]Mic. 1:9
13 [a]Josh. 10:3; 2Kin. 14:19; Is. 36:2 [b]Mic. 1:5
14 [a]2Kin. 16:8 [b]Josh. 15:44 [c]Jer. 15:18
15 [I]I.e., possession [a]Josh. 15:44 [b]Josh. 12:15; 15:35; 2Sam. 23:13
16 [a]Is. 22:12 [b]2Kin. 17:6; Amos 7:11, 17

1 [I]Lit., *In the light of the morning* [a]Ps. 36:4; Is. 32:7; Nah. 1:11 [b]Hos. 7:6, 7 [c]Gen. 31:29; Deut. 28:32; Prov. 3:27
2 [I]Lit., *oppress* [a]Jer. 22:17; Amos 8:4 [b]Is. 5:8 [c]1Kin. 21:1-15
3 [a]Deut. 28:48; Jer. 18:11 [b]Jer. 8:3; Amos 3:1, 2 [c]Lam. 1:14; 5:5 [d]Is. 2:11, 12 [e]Amos 5:13
4 [I]Or, *proverb* [II]Lit., *lament* [a]Hab. 2:6 [b]Jer. 9:10, 17-21; Mic. 1:8 [c]Is. 6:11; 24:3; Jer. 4:13 [d]Jer. 6:12; 8:10
5 [I]Lit., *casting* [a]Num. 34:13, 16-29; Deut. 32:8; Josh. 18:4, 10

🗝 **1:9** This verse probably refers to the devastation of Judah by the Assyrian king, Sennacherib in 701 B.C. Although many other Judean cities were ravaged, Jerusalem, itself, did not fall; hence, Micah's words, "reached the gate," graphically depict the unsuccessful siege. See the note on Isa. 8:8.

6 "[a]Do not [I]speak5197 out,' *so* they
[I]speak out.
But if [II]they do [b]not [I]speak out
concerning these things,
[c]Reproaches will not be turned
back.
7 "Is it being said, O house1004 of
Jacob:
'Is the Spirit7307 of the LORD
[a]impatient?7114
Are these His doings?'
Do not My words1697 [b]do
good3190
To the one [c]walking
uprightly?3477
8 "[I]Recently My people have
arisen as an [a]enemy—
You [b]strip the [II]robe off the
garment,
From [c]unsuspecting983 passers-
by,5674
From those returned7725 from
war.
9 "The women of My people you
[a]evict,
Each *one* from her pleasant
house.
From her children you take My
[b]splendor1926 forever.5769
10 "Arise and go,
For this is no place [a]of rest
Because of the [b]uncleanness2930
that brings on
destruction,2254
A painful destruction.2256
11 "If a man walking after wind and
[a]falsehood8267
Had told lies3576 *and said,*
'I will [I]speak out to you
concerning [b]wine and liquor,'
He would be [II]spokesman5197 to
[c]this people.
12 "I will surely [a]assemble622 all of
you, Jacob,
I will surely gather6908 the
[b]remnant7611 of Israel.
I will put7760 them together like
sheep in the fold;
Like a flock in the midst of its
pasture
They will be noisy1949 with
men.120
13 "The breaker goes up5927 before
them;
They break out, pass through
the gate, and go out by it.
So their king goes on before
them,
And the LORD at their head."7218

6 [I]Lit., *flow* [II]I.e., God's prophets [a]Is. 30:10; Amos 2:12; 7:16 [b]Is. 29:10; Mic. 3:6 [c]Mic. 6:16

7 [a]Is. 50:2; 59:1 [b]Ps. 119:65, 68, 116; Jer. 15:16 [c]Ps. 15:2; 84:11

8 [I]Lit., *And yesterday* [II]Or, *ornaments* [a]Jer. 12:8 [b]Mic. 3:2, 3; 7:2, 3 [c]Ps. 120:6, 7

9 [a]Jer. 10:20 [b]Ezek. 39:21; Hab. 2:14

10 [a]Deut. 12:9 [b]Ps. 106:38

11 [I]Lit., *flow* [II]Lit., *one who flows* oracles [a]Jer. 5:31 [b]Is. 28:7 [c]Is. 30:10, 11

12 [a]Mic. 4:6, 7 [b]Mic. 5:7, 8; 7:18

1 [a]Is. 1:10; Mic. 3:9 [b]Ps. 82:1-5; Jer. 5:5

2 [a]Ps. 53:4; Ezek. 22:27; Mic. 2:8; 7:2, 3

3 [a]Ps. 14:4; 27:2; Zeph. 3:3 [b]Ezek. 11:3, 6, 7

4 [a]Ps. 18:41; Prov. 1:28; Is. 1:15; Jer. 11:11 [b]Deut. 31:17; Is. 59:2 [c]Is. 3:11; Mic. 7:13

5 [a]Is. 3:12; 9:15, 16; Jer. 14:14, 15 [b]Jer. 6:14

6 [a]Is. 8:20-22; 29:10-12

Rulers Denounced

3 And I said,559
"[a]Hear now, heads7218 of Jacob
And rulers7101 of the house1004
of Israel.
Is it not for you to [b]know3045
justice?4941
2 "You who hate8130 good2896 and
love157 evil,7451
Who [a]tear off their skin5785 from
them
And their flesh7607 from their
bones,6106
3 And who [a]eat the flesh1319 of my
people,5971
Strip off6584 their skin from
them,
Break their bones,
And [b]chop *them* up as for the
pot
And as meat in a kettle."
4 Then they will [a]cry out2199 to the
LORD,
But He will not answer them.
Instead, He will [b]hide His face
from them at that time,6256
Because they have [c]practiced
evil7489 deeds.
5 Thus says the LORD concerning
the prophets5030
Who [a]lead my people astray;8582
When they have *something* to
bite with their teeth,
They [b]cry,7121 "Peace,"7956
But against him who puts
nothing in their mouths,6310
They declare6942 holy war.
6 Therefore *it will be* [a]night for
you—without vision,2377

2:6 See note on Amos 2:12.

And darkness[6937] for you—
without divination.[7080]
The [b]sun will go down on the
prophets,
And the day[3117] will become
dark[2821] over them.
7 The seers[2374] will be
[a]ashamed[954]
And the [b]diviners[7080] will be
embarrassed.
Indeed, they will all [c]cover *their*
[I]mouths[8222]
Because there is [d]no answer
from God.[430]
8 On the other hand [a]I am filled
with power—
With the Spirit[7307] of the LORD—
And with justice and courage
To [b]make known[5046] to Jacob his
rebellious act,[6588]
Even to Israel his sin.[2403]
9 Now hear this, [a]heads of the
house of Jacob
And rulers of the house of Israel,
Who [b]abhor[8581] justice
And twist everything that is
straight,[3477]
10 Who [a]build Zion with
bloodshed[1818]
And Jerusalem with violent
injustice.[5766]
11 Her leaders pronounce
[a]judgment[8199] for a bribe,
Her [b]priests[3548] instruct[3384] for
a price,
And her prophets divine for
money.
Yet they lean[8172] on the LORD
saying,[559]
"[c]Is not the LORD in our midst?[7130]
Calamity will not come upon us."
🗝 12 Therefore, on account of you,
[a]Zion will be plowed as a field,[7704]
[b]Jerusalem will become a heap
of ruins,
And the [c]mountain of the
[I]temple *will become* high
places[1116] of a forest.

6 [b]Is. 59:10

7 [I]Lit., *mustache* [a]Zech. 13:4 [b]Is. 44:25; 47:12-14 [c]Mic. 7:16 [d]1Sam. 28:6; Mic. 3:4

8 [a]Is. 61:1, 2; Jer. 1:18 [b]Is. 58:1

9 [a]Mic. 1:1 [b]Ps. 58:1, 2; Is. 1:23

10 [a]Jer. 22:13, 17; Hab. 2:12

11 [a]Is. 1:23; Mic. 7:3 [b]Jer. 6:13 [c]Is. 48:2

12 [I]Lit., *house* [a]Jer. 26:18 [b]Ps. 79:1; Jer. 9:11 [c]Mic. 4:1

1 [I]Lit., *on* [a]Is. 2:24; Dan. 2:28; 10:14; Hos. 3:5 [b]Ezek. 43:12; Mic. 3:12; Zech. 8:3 [c]Ps. 22:27; 86:9; Jer. 3:17

2 [a]Zech. 2:11; 14:16 [b]Is. 2:3; Jer. 31:6 [c]Ps. 25:8, 9, 12; Is. 54:13 [d]Is. 42:1-4; Zech. 14:8, 9

3 [I]Lit., *at a distance* [II]Lit., *learn* [a]Is. 2:4; 11:3-5 [b]Joel 3:10

4 [a]1Kin. 4:25; Zech. 3:10 [b]Lev. 26:6; Jer. 30:10 [c]Is. 1:20; 40:5

Peaceful Latter Days

4 🗝 And it will come about in the
[a]last[319] days[3117]
That the [b]mountain of the
house[1004] of the LORD
Will be established[3559]
[I]as the chief[7218] of the
mountains.
It will be raised[5385] above the
hills,
And the [c]peoples[5971] will stream
to it.
2 And [a]many nations[1471] will come
and say,
"[b]Come and let us go up[5927] to
the mountain of the LORD
And to the house of the God[430]
of Jacob,
That [c]He may teach[3384] us about
His ways[1870]
And that we may walk in His
paths."[734]
For [d]from Zion will go forth the
law,[8451]
Even the word[1697] of the LORD
from Jerusalem.
3 And He will [a]judge[8199] between
many peoples
And render decisions[3198] for
mighty, [I]distant nations.
Then they will hammer[3807] their
swords[2719] [b]into plowshares
And their spears into pruning
hooks;
Nation will not lift up[5375] sword
against nation,
And never again will they
[II]train[3925] for war.
4 And each of them[376] will
[a]sit under his vine
And under his fig tree,
With [b]no one to make *them*
afraid,[2729]
For the [c]mouth[6310] of the
LORD of hosts[6635] has
spoken.[1696]
5 Though all the peoples walk

🗝 **3:12** Some of the elders of Judah quoted this verse in defense of Jeremiah when his life was in danger because of strong reaction to his temple sermon (Jer. 26:16-19).
🗝 **4:1-3** See note on Isa. 2:2-4.

Each[376] in the [a]name of his
god,[430]
As for us, [b]we will walk
In the name of the [c]LORD our
God[430] forever[5769] and
ever.[5703]
6 "In that day," declares[5001] the
LORD,
"I will assemble[622] the [a]lame,
And [b]gather[6908] the outcasts,
Even those whom I have
afflicted.[7489]
7 "I will make[7760] the lame a
[a]remnant,[7611]
And the outcasts a strong nation,
And the [b]LORD will reign over
them in Mount Zion
From now on and forever.
8 "And as for you, [I][a]tower of the
flock,
[II]Hill of the daughter of Zion,
To you it will come—
Even the [b]former dominion[4475]
will come,
The kingdom[4467] of the daughter
of Jerusalem.
9 "Now, why do you [a]cry out[7321]
loudly?
Is there no king among you,
Or has your [b]counselor[3289]
perished,[6]
That agony has gripped[2388] you
like a woman in childbirth?
🔑 10 "[a]Writhe[2342] and labor to give
birth,
Daughter of Zion,
Like a woman in childbirth,
For now you will [b]go out of the
city,
Dwell[7931] in the field,[7704]
And go to Babylon.
[c]There you will be rescued;[5337]
[d]There the LORD will redeem[1350]
you
From the hand[3709] of your
enemies.
11 "And now [a]many nations have
been assembled against you
Who say, 'Let her be
polluted,[2610]
And let our eyes [I]gloat[2372] over
Zion.'
12 "But they do not [a]know[3045] the
thoughts[4284] of the LORD,
And they do not understand[995]
His purpose;[6098]
For He has gathered them like
sheaves to the threshing
floor.
13 "Arise and [a]thresh, daughter of
Zion,
For your horn I will make[7760]
iron
And your hoofs I will make
bronze,
That you may [b]pulverize many
peoples,
That you may [c]devote[2763] to the
LORD their unjust gain
And their wealth[2428] to the
Lord[113] of all the earth.[776]

Birth of the King in Bethlehem

5 "[I]Now muster yourselves in
troops,[1413] daughter of
troops;[1416]
[II]They have laid[7760] siege against
us;
With a rod[7626] they will
[a]smite[5221] the judge[8199] of
Israel on the cheek.
🔑 2 "[I]But as for [a]you, Bethlehem
Ephrathah,

5 [a]2Kin. 17:29 [b]Zech. 10:12 [c]Josh. 24:15; Is. 26:8, 13
6 [a]Zeph. 3:19 [b]Ps. 147:2; Ezek. 34:13, 16; 37:21
7 [a]Mic. 5:7, 8; 7:18 [b]Is. 24:23
8 [I]Heb., *Migdal-eder* [II]Heb., *Ophel of* [a]Ps. 48:3, 12; 61:3; Mic. 2:12 [b]Is. 1:26; Zech. 9:10
9 [a]Jer. 8:19 [b]Is. 3:1-3
10 [a]Mic. 5:3 [b]2Kin. 20:18; Hos. 2:14 [c]Is. 43:14; 45:13; Mic. 7:8-12 [d]Is. 48:20; 52:9-12
11 [I]Lit., *look on* [a]Is. 5:25-30; 17:12-14
12 [a]Ps. 147:19, 20
13 [a]Is. 41:15 [b]Jer. 51:20-23 [c]Is. 60:9
1 [I]Ch. 4:14 in Heb. [II]Lit., *He has* [a]1Kin. 22:24; Job 16:10; Lam. 3:30
2 [I]Ch. 5:1 in Heb. [a]Gen. 35:19; 48:7; Ruth 4:11; Matt. 2:6

🔑 **4:10** Here, about a century before Babylon even became the dominant empire in the region, Micah predicted both the reality of the Babylonian exile and the return. What was an isolated verse in Micah became an ever growing body of prophetic material, as the date of the exile approached.

🔑 **5:2** The Jews of Jesus' day were not in total agreement about where the Messiah would originate. Some thought that His source would be unknown (Jn. 7:27), but those who believed His place of birth was foretold turned to Mic. 5:2 for the answer. Hence, when Herod was approached by the wise men from the East and he asked his religious experts where the Messiah was to be born, their response was "in Bethlehem," and they quoted Mic. 5:2 (Mt. 2:1-6). This caused some confusion during Jesus' ministry, because He was known to be from Nazareth, but, based on Mic. 5:2, many expected the Messiah to come from Bethlehem, David's town (Jn. 7:41,42).

Too little to be among the clans[505] of Judah,
From [b]you One will go forth for Me to be [c]ruler[4910] in Israel.
[II]His goings forth are [d]from long ago,[6924]
From the days[3117] of eternity."[5769]
3 Therefore, He will [a]give them *up* until the time[6256]
When she [b]who is in labor[3205] has borne a child.
Then the [c]remainder[3499] of His brethren[251]
Will return[7725] to the sons[1121] of Israel.
4 And He will arise and [a]shepherd *His flock*
In the strength of the LORD,
In the majesty of the name of the LORD His God.[430]
And they will [I]remain,
Because [II]at that time He will be great
To the [b]ends of the earth.[776]
5 And this One [a]will be *our* peace.[7965]
When the [b]Assyrian invades our land,[776]
When he tramples on our [I]citadels,[759]
Then we will raise against him
Seven shepherds and eight leaders[5257] of men.[120]
6 And they will [a]shepherd the land of Assyria with the sword,[2719]
The land of [b]Nimrod at its entrances;
And He will [c]deliver[5337] *us* from the Assyrian
When he attacks our land
And when he tramples our territory.
7 Then the [a]remnant[7611] of Jacob
Will be among many peoples[5971]
Like [b]dew from the LORD,
Like [c]showers on vegetation
Which do not wait[6960] for man[376]
Or delay[3176] for the sons[1121] of men.
8 And the remnant of Jacob
Will be among the nations,[1471]

2 [II]Or, *His appearances are from long ago, from days of old* [b]Is. 11:1; Luke 2:4; John 7:42 [c]Jer. 30:21; Zech. 9:9 [d]Ps. 102:25; Prov. 8:22, 23

3 [a]Hos. 11:8; Mic. 4:10; 7:13 [b]Mic. 4:9, 10 [c]Is. 10:20-22; Mic. 5:7, 8

4 [I]Or, *live* in safety [II]Lit., *now* [a]Is. 40:11; 49:9; Ezek. 34:13-15, 23, 24; Mic. 7:14 [b]Is. 45:22; 52:10

5 [I]Or, *palaces* [a]Is. 9:6; Luke 2:14; Eph. 2:14; Col. 1:20 [b]Is. 8:7, 8; 10:24-27

6 [a]Nah. 2:11-13; Zeph. 2:13 [b]Gen. 10:8-11 [c]Is. 14:25; 37:36, 37

7 [a]Mic. 2:12; 4:7; 5:3; 7:18 [b]Deut. 32:2; Ps. 110:3; Hos. 14:5 [c]Ps. 72:6; Is. 44:3

8 [a]Gen. 49:9; Num. 24:9 [b]Ps. 44:5; Is. 41:15, 16; Mic. 4:13; Zech. 10:5 [c]Hos. 5:14 [d]Ps. 50:22

9 [a]Ps. 10:12; 21:8; Is. 26:11

10 [a]Zech. 9:10 [b]Deut. 17:16; Is. 2:7; Hos. 14:3

11 [a]Is. 1:7; 6:11 [b]Is. 2:12-17; Hos. 10:14; Amos 5:9

12 [a]Deut. 18:10-12; Is. 2:6; 8:19

13 [a]Is. 2:18; 17:8; Ezek. 6:9

14 [I]I.e., wooden symbols of a female deity [a]Ex. 34:13; Is. 17:8; 27:9

15 [a]Is. 1:24; 65:12

1 [I]Lit., *with*

2 [a]2Sam. 22:16; Ps. 104:5

Among many peoples
[a]Like a lion among the beasts of the forest,
Like a young lion among flocks of sheep,
Which, if he passes through,[5674]
[b]Tramples down and [c]tears,
And there is [d]none to rescue.
9 Your hand[3027] will be [a]lifted up against your adversaries,
And all your enemies will be cut off.[3772]
10 "And it will be in that day," declares the LORD,
"[a]That I will cut off your [b]horses from among you
And destroy[6] your chariots.
11 "I will also cut off the [a]cities of your land
And tear down[2040] all your [b]fortifications.
12 "I will cut off [a]sorceries[3785] from your hand,
And you will have fortunetellers[6049] no more.
13 "[a]I will cut off your carved images[6456]
And your *sacred* pillars[4676] from among[7130] you,
So that you will no longer bow down[7812]
To the work of your hands.
14 "I will root out your [Ia]Asherim[842] from among you
And destroy[8045] your cities.
15 "And I will [a]execute[6213] vengeance[5359] in anger[622] and wrath[2534]
On the nations[1471] which have not obeyed."[8085]

God's Indictment of His People

6 Hear[8085] now what the LORD is saying,
"Arise, plead[7378] your case [I]before the mountains,
And let the hills hear your voice.
2 "Listen, you mountains, to the indictment[7379] of the LORD,
And you enduring [a]foundations[4146] of the earth,[776]

Because the [b]LORD has a case against His people;[5971]
Even with Israel He will dispute.[3198]
3 "[a]My people, [b]what have I done[6213] to you,
And [c]how have I wearied you? Answer Me.
4 "Indeed, I [a]brought you up[5927] from the land[776] of Egypt
And [b]ransomed[6299] you from the house[1004] of slavery,[5650]
And I sent before you [c]Moses, Aaron, and [d]Miriam.
5 "My people, remember[2142] now
What [a]Balak king of Moab counseled[3289]
And what Balaam son[1121] of Beor answered him,
And from [b]Shittim to [c]Gilgal,
In order [I]that you might know[3045] the [d]righteous acts of the LORD."

What God Requires of Man

6 [a]With what shall I come to the LORD
And bow myself before the God[430] on high?
Shall I come to Him with [b]burnt offerings,[5930]
With yearling[1121] calves?
7 Does the LORD take delight[7521] in [a]thousands of rams,
In ten thousand[505] rivers of oil?[8081]
Shall I present my [b]first-born *for* my rebellious acts,[6588]
The fruit of my body[990] for the sin[2403] of my soul?[5315]
🔑 8 He has [a]told[5046] you, O man,[120] what is good;[2896]
And [b]what does the LORD require of you
But to [c]do[6213] justice,[4941] to [d]love[160] [I]kindness,[2617]
And to walk [II][e]humbly with your God?
9 The voice of the LORD will call[7121] to the city—
And it is sound wisdom[8454] to fear[7200] Thy name:
"Hear, O tribe.[4294] Who has appointed[3259] [I]its time?
10 "Is there yet a man in the wicked[7563] house,
Along with treasures of [a]wickedness,[7562]
And a [I][b]short measure *that is* cursed?[2194]
11 "Can I justify[2135] wicked [a]scales
And a bag of deceptive[4820] weights?
12 "For the rich men of *the* [I]city are full of [a]violence,[2555]
Her residents speak[1696] [b]lies,[8267]
And their [c]tongue is deceitful in their mouth.[6310]
13 "So also I will make *you* [a]sick, striking[5221] you down,
[b]Desolating[8074] *you* because of your sins.
14 "You will eat, but you will [a]not be satisfied,
And your [I]vileness will be in your midst.
You will *try to* remove *for safekeeping*,
But you will [b]not preserve *anything*,
And what you do preserve[6403] I will give to the sword.[2719]
15 "You will sow but you will [a]not reap.
You will tread the olive but will not anoint[5480] yourself with oil;

2 [b]Is. 1:18; Hos. 4:1; 12:2
3 [a]Ps. 50:7 [b]Jer. 2:5 [c]Is. 43:22, 23
4 [a]Ex. 12:51; 20:2 [b]Deut. 7:8 [c]Ex. 4:10-16; Ps. 77:20 [d]Ex. 15:20
5 [I]Lit., *to know* [a]Num. 22:5, 6 [b]Num. 25:1; Josh. 2:1; 3:1 [c]Josh. 4:19; 5:9, 10 [d]1Sam. 12:7; Is. 1:27
6 [a]Ps. 40:6-8 [b]Ps. 51:16, 17
7 [a]Ps. 50:9; Is. 1:1; 40:16 [b]Lev. 18:21; 20:1-5; 2Kin. 16:3; Jer. 7:31
8 [I]Or, *loyalty* [II]Or, *circumspectly* [a]Deut. 30:15 [b]Deut. 10:12 [c]Is. 56:1; Jer. 22:3 [d]Hos. 6:6 [e]Is. 57:15; 66:2
9 [I]Lit., *it*
10 [I]Lit., *shrunken ephah* [a]Jer. 5:26, 27; Amos 3:10 [b]Ezek. 45:9, 10; Amos 8:5
11 [a]Lev. 19:36; Hos. 12:7
12 [I]Lit., *her* [a]Is. 1:23; 5:7; Amos 6:3, 4; Mic. 2:1, 2 [b]Jer. 9:2-6, 8; Hos. 7:13; Amos 2:4 [c]Is. 3:8
13 [a]Mic. 1:9 [b]Is. 1:7; 6:11
14 [I]Or possibly, *garbage* or *excreta* [a]Is. 9:20 [b]Is. 30:6
15 [a]Deut. 28:38-40; Jer. 12:13

🔑 **6:8** Nowhere in the rest of the O.T. is the type of religious devotion that God wants described in a more succinct and elevated manner. Love of God and man are inextricably connected in what can be described as the high-water mark of religious thoughts of the O.T. The message of the prophets concerning the desired conduct of Israel, which was preached over several centuries, can be boiled down to this verse. See Mt. 22:37-40.

And the grapes, but you will
[b]not drink wine.
16 "The statutes[2708] of [a]Omri
And all the works of the house
of [b]Ahab are observed;[8104]
And in their devices you
[c]walk.
Therefore, I will give you up for
[d]destruction[8047]
And [I]your inhabitants for
[e]derision,
And you will bear[5375] the
[f]reproach[2781] of My people."

The Prophet Acknowledges

7 Woe is me! For I am
Like the fruit pickers[625] and the
[a]grape gatherers.
There is not a cluster of grapes
to eat,
Or a [b]first-ripe fig *which*
[I]I[5315] crave.[183]
2 The [I]godly[2623] person has
[a]perished[6] from the land,[776]
And there is no upright *person*
among men.[120]
All of them lie in wait for
[b]bloodshed;[1818]
Each[376] of them hunts the
other[251] with a [c]net.
3 Concerning evil,[7451] both
hands[3709] do it [a]well.[3190]
The prince[8269] asks,[7592] also the
judge,[8199] for a [b]bribe,[7966]
And a great man speaks the
desire of his soul;[5315]
So they weave it together.
4 The best[2896] of them is like a
[a]briar,
The most upright like a
[b]thorn hedge.
The day[3117] when you post a
watchman,
Your [c]punishment[6486] will come.
Then their [d]confusion will
occur.
5 Do not [a]trust[539] in a neighbor;[7453]
Do not have confidence[982] in a
friend.[441]
From her who lies in your bosom
Guard[8104] [I]your lips.[6310]
6 For [a]son[1121] treats father[1]
contemptuously,
Daughter rises up against her
mother,[517]
Daughter-in-law against her
mother-in-law;
[b]A man's[376] enemies are the
men[582] of his own
household.[1004]

God Is the Source of Salvation and Light

7 But as for me, I will [a]watch
expectantly for the LORD;
I will [b]wait[3176] for the God[430] of
my salvation.[3468]
My [c]God will hear[8085] me.
8 [a]Do not rejoice over me, O
[b]my enemy.
Though I fall[5307] I will [c]rise;
Though I dwell in darkness,[2822]
the LORD is a [d]light[216] for me.
9 I will bear[5375] the indignation[2197]
of the LORD
Because I have sinned[2398]
against Him,
Until He [a]pleads[7378] my case[7379]
and executes[6213] justice[4941]
for me.
He will bring me out to the
[b]light,
And I will see[7200] His
[I][c]righteousness.
10 Then my enemy will see,
And shame[955] will cover[3680] her
who [a]said to me,
"Where is the LORD your God?"
My eyes will look on her;
[I]At that time she will [II]be
[b]trampled down,
Like mire of the streets.
11 *It will be* a day for [a]building your
walls.
On that day will your
boundary[2706] be extended.
12 It *will be* a day when [I]they will
[a]come to you
From Assyria and the cities of
Egypt,
From Egypt even to the
[II]Euphrates,

15 [b]Amos 5:11; Zeph. 1:13

16 [I]Lit., *her* [a]1Kin. 16:25, 26 [b]1Kin. 16:29-33 [c]Jer. 7:24 [d]Jer. 18:16; Mic. 6:13 [e]Jer. 19:8; 25:9, 18; 29:18 [f]Ps. 44:13; Jer. 51:51; Hos. 12:14

1 [I]Lit., *my soul* [a]Is. 24:13 [b]Is. 28:4; Hos. 9:10

2 [I]Or, *loyal* [a]Is. 57:1 [b]Is. 59:7; Mic. 3:10 [c]Jer. 5:26; Hos. 5:1

3 [a]Prov. 4:16, 17 [b]Amos 5:12; Mic. 3:11

4 [a]Ezek. 2:6; 28:24 [b]Nah. 1:10 [c]Is. 10:3; Hos. 9:7 [d]Is. 22:5

5 [I]Lit., *openings of your mouth* [a]Jer. 9:4

6 [a]Matt. 10:21, 35; Luke 12:53 [b]Matt. 10:36

7 [a]Hab. 2:1 [b]Ps. 130:5; Is. 25:9 [c]Ps. 4:3

8 [a]Prov. 24:17; Obad. 12 [b]Mic. 7:10 [c]Amos 9:11 [d]Is. 9:2

9 [I]I.e., right dealing [a]Jer. 50:34 [b]Ps. 37:6; Is. 42:7, 16 [c]Is. 46:13; 56:1

10 [I]Lit., *Now* [II]Lit., *become a trampled* place [a]Joel 2:17 [b]Is. 51:23; Zech. 10:5

11 [a]Is. 54:11; Amos 9:11

12 [I]Lit., *he* [II]Lit., *River* [a]Is. 19:23-25; 60:4, 9

Even from sea to sea and
mountain to mountain.
13 And the earth[776] will become
[a]desolate[8077] because of her
inhabitants,
On account of the [b]fruit of their
deeds.
14 [a]Shepherd Thy people[5971] with
Thy [b]scepter,[7626]
The flock of Thy [I]possession[5159]
Which dwells[7931] by itself in the
woodland,
In the midst of [II]a fruitful field.
Let them feed in [c]Bashan and
Gilead
[d]As in the days of old.[5769]
15 "As in the days when you came
out from the land of Egypt,
I will show[7200] [I][a]you
miracles."[6381]
16 Nations[1471] [a]will see and be
ashamed[954]
Of all their might.
They will [b]put[7760] *their* hand[3027]
on *their* mouth,
Their ears[241] will be deaf.
17 They will [a]lick the dust[6083] like
a serpent,[5175]
Like [b]reptiles of the earth.
They will come[7264] [c]trembling
out of their [I]fortresses;
To the LORD our God they will
come in [d]dread,[6342]
And they will be afraid[3372] before
Thee.
18 Who is a God[410] like Thee, who
[a]pardons[5375] iniquity[5771]
And passes[5674] over the
rebellious act[6588] of the
[b]remnant[7611] of His
[I]possession?
He does not [c]retain[2388] His
anger[639] forever,[5703]
Because He [d]delights[2654] in
[II]unchanging love.[2617]
19 He will again[7725] have
compassion[7355] on us;
[a]He will tread our iniquities
under foot.
Yes, Thou wilt [b]cast all
[I]their sins[2403]
Into the depths of the sea.
20 Thou wilt give [I][a]truth[571] to Jacob
And [II]unchanging love to
Abraham,
Which Thou didst [b]swear[7650] to
our forefathers[1]
From the days of old.[6924]

13 [a]Jer. 25:11; Mic. 6:13 [b]Is. 3:10, 11; Mic. 3:4
14 [I]Or, *inheritance* [II]Or, *Carmel* [a]Ps. 95:7; Is. 40:11; 49:10; Mic. 5:4 [b]Lev. 27:32; Ps. 23:4 [c]Jer. 50:19 [d]Amos 9:11
15 [I]Lit., *him* [a]Ex. 3:20; 34:10; Ps. 78:12
16 [a]Is. 26:11 [b]Mic. 3:7
17 [I]Lit., *fastnesses* [a]Ps. 72:9; Is. 49:23 [b]Deut. 32:24 [c]Ps. 18:45 [d]Is. 25:3; 59:19
18 [I]Or, *inheritance* [II]Or, *lovingkindness* [a]Ex. 34:7, 9; Is. 43:25 [b]Mic. 2:12; 4:7; 5:7, 8 [c]Ps. 103:8, 9, 13 [d]Jer. 32:41
19 [I]Several ancient versions read *our* [a]Jer. 50:20 [b]Is. 38:17; 43:25; Jer. 31:34
20 [I]Or, *faithfulness* [II]Or, *lovingkindness* [a]Gen. 24:27; 32:10 [b]Deut. 7:8, 12

The Book of

NAHUM

Nahum was from Elkosh, probably in Judah. His name means "consolation" or "full of comfort." It is mentioned nowhere else in Scripture, with the possible exception of Lk. 3:25. He was a contemporary of Jeremiah, Habakkuk, and Zephaniah. We know nothing of the prophet other than this. Two bits of historical information within the book itself help fix the date. Nahum 3:8-10 refers to the capture of Thebes (No-Amon), which fell to the Assyrians in 661 B.C., as accomplished fact. Throughout the book the fall of Nineveh is still future. It was subsequently taken in 612 B.C. Considering these two events, most scholars place the date about 620 B.C.

Judah was crying out, "Has God forsaken Judah? Why do the Assyrians, so full of evil, prosper, while we are suffering? Are God's promises empty?" The powerful military state of Assyria, with its great wealth, continually oppressed Judah, almost enslaving her. National life was very precarious, spiritual life was diminishing, and the nation was continually endangered by marauding bands from Nineveh. She was desperately needing answers to these questions when Nahum thundered on the scene, proclaiming, "Nineveh will fall! God will save His people!" In light of Assyria's great might, the message seemed incredible. Jonah, a century and a half earlier, had denounced Nineveh if it did not repent. The time of repentance was past. The voice of Nahum is harsh and vengeful. Nineveh will pay for ignoring God and oppressing the weak. The message is timeless: Those who arrogantly ignore and resist God will taste His wrath, but those who trust Him will be saved by His love.

God Is Awesome

1 The [1a]oracle[4853] of [b]Nineveh. The book[5612] of the vision[2377] of Nahum the Elkoshite.

2 A [a]jealous and avenging[5358]
God[410] is the LORD;
The LORD is [b]avenging and
[1]wrathful.[2534]
The LORD takes [c]vengeance[5358]
on His adversaries,
And He reserves wrath for His
enemies.

3 The LORD is [a]slow[750] to anger[639]
and great in power,
And the LORD will by no
means leave *the guilty*
unpunished.[5352]
In [b]whirlwind and storm is His
way,[1870]
And [c]clouds[6051] are the dust[80]
beneath His feet.

4 He [a]rebukes[1605] the sea and
makes it dry;[3001]
He dries up[2717] all the rivers.
[b]Bashan and Carmel wither;
The blossoms of Lebanon
wither.

5 Mountains [a]quake[7493] because of
Him,
And the hills [b]dissolve;
Indeed the earth[776] is [c]upheaved
by His presence,
The [d]world and all the
inhabitants in it.

6 [a]Who can stand before His
indignation?[2195]
Who can endure the [b]burning of
His anger?
His [c]wrath[2534] is poured out like
fire,
And the [d]rocks are broken up[5422]
by Him.

7 The LORD is [a]good,[2896]
A stronghold in the day[3117] of
trouble,
And [b]He knows[3045] those who
take refuge[2620] in Him.

8 But with an [a]overflowing[5674]
flood[7858]
He will make[6213] a complete
end[3617] of [1]its site,

1 [1]Or, *burden* [a]Is. 13:1; 19:1; Jer. 23:33, 34; Hab. 1:1; Zech. 9:1; Mal. 1:1 [b]2Kin. 19:36; Jon. 1:2; Nah. 2:8; Zeph. 2:13
2 [1]Lit., *a possessor of wrath* [a]Ex. 20:5; Josh. 24:19 [b]Deut. 32:35, 41 [c]Ps. 94:1
3 [a]Ex. 34:6, 7; Neh. 9:17; Ps. 103:8 [b]Ex. 19:16; Is. 29:6 [c]Ps. 104:3; Is. 19:1
4 [a]Josh. 3:15, 16; Ps. 106:9; Is. 50:2; Matt. 8:26 [b]Is. 33:9
5 [a]Ex. 19:18; 2Sam. 22:8; Ps. 18:7 [b]Mic. 1:4 [c]Is. 24:1, 20 [d]Ps. 98:7
6 [a]Jer. 10:10; Mal. 3:2 [b]Is. 13:13 [c]Is. 66:15 [d]1Kin. 19:11
7 [a]Ps. 25:8; 37:39, 40; Jer. 33:11 [b]Ps. 1:6; John 10:14; 2Tim. 2:19
8 [1]I.e., Nineveh's [a]Is. 28:2, 17f.; Amos 8:8

And will pursue His enemies into
[b]darkness.[2822]
9 Whatever you [a]devise[2803]
against the LORD,
He will make a [b]complete end
of it.
Distress will not rise up
twice.
10 Like tangled [a]thorns,
And like those who are
[b]drunken with their drink,
They are [c]consumed
As stubble completely
withered.[3002]
11 From you has gone forth
One who [a]plotted evil[7451] against
the LORD,
A [I][b]wicked[1100] counselor.[3289]
12 Thus says the LORD,
"Though they are at full
strength[8003] and likewise
many,
Even so, they will be [a]cut off
and pass away.[5674]
Though I have afflicted you,
I will afflict you [b]no longer.
13 "So now, I will [a]break[7665] his yoke
bar from upon you,
And I will tear off your shackles."
14 The LORD has issued a
command[6680] concerning
[I]you:
"[II]Your name will [a]no longer be
perpetuated.
I will cut off[3772] [III][b]idol[6459] and
[IV]image[4541]
From the house[1004] of your
gods.[430]
I will prepare[7760] your
[c]grave,[6913]
For you are contemptible."[7043]
15 [I]Behold, [a]on the mountains the
feet of him who brings good
news,[1319]
Who announces[8085] peace![7965]
[b]Celebrate your feasts,[2282] O
Judah;
Pay your vows.[5088]
For [c]never again will the
[II]wicked one pass[5674] through
you;
He is [d]cut off completely.

The Overthrow of Nineveh

2 [I]The one who [a]scatters has come
up[5927] against [II]you.
Man[5341] the fortress, watch the
road;[1870]
[III]Strengthen[2388] your back,
[IV]summon all *your* strength.
2 For the LORD will restore[7725] the
[a]splendor of Jacob
[b]Like the splendor of Israel,
Even though devastators have
devastated them
And [c]destroyed their vine
branches.
3 The shields of [I]his mighty men[582]
are *colored* red,
The warriors[2428] are dressed in
[a]scarlet,
The chariots are *enveloped* in
[II]flashing steel
[III]When[3117] he is prepared *to*
march,[3559]
And the cypress [b]*spears* are
brandished.
4 The [a]chariots race madly[1984] in
the streets,
They rush wildly[8264] in the
[I]squares,
Their appearance is like torches,
They dash to and fro like
lightning flashes.
5 He remembers[2142] his
[a]nobles;[117]
They [b]stumble[3782] in their
march,
They hurry to her wall,
And the [I]mantelet is set up.[3559]
6 The gates of the rivers are
opened,
And the palace[1964] is
dissolved.[4127]
7 And it is fixed:[5324]
She is stripped, she is carried
away,[1540]
And her handmaids are
[a]moaning like the sound of
doves,
[b]Beating[8608] on their
[I]breasts.[3824]
8 Though Nineveh *was* like a pool
of water throughout her days,

8 [b]Is. 13:9, 10

9 [a]Ps. 2:1; Nah. 1:11 [b]Is. 28:22

10 [a]2Sam. 23:6; Mic. 7:4 [b]Is. 56:12; Nah. 3:11 [c]Is. 5:24; 10:17; Mal. 4:1

11 [I]Or, *worthless;* Heb., *Belial* [a]Is. 10:7-11; Nah. 1:9 [b]Ezek. 11:2

12 [a]Is. 10:16-19, 33, 34 [b]Lam. 3:31, 32

13 [a]Is. 9:4; 10:27; Jer. 2:20

14 [I]I.e., the king of Nineveh [II]Lit., *No more of your name will be sown* [III]Or, *a graven image* [IV]Lit., *cast metal image* [a]Job 18:17; Ps. 109:13; Is. 14:22 [b]Is. 46:1, 2; Mic. 5:13, 14 [c]Ezek. 32:22, 23

15 [I]Ch. 2:1 in Heb. [II]Or, *worthless one;* Heb., *Belial* [a]Is. 40:9; 52:7; Rom. 10:15 [b]Lev. 23:2, 4 [c]Is. 52:1; Joel 3:17 [d]Is. 29:7, 8

1 [I]Ch. 2:2 in Heb. [II]Lit., *your face* [III]Lit., *Make strong your loins* [IV]Lit., *strengthen power greatly* [a]Jer. 51:20-23

2 [a]Is. 60:15 [b]Ezek. 37:21-23 [c]Ps. 80:12, 13

3 [I]I.e., those attacking Nineveh [II]Lit., *fire of steel* [III]Lit., *On the day of his preparation* [a]Ezek. 23:14, 15 [b]Job 39:23

4 [I]Lit., *broad places* [a]Is. 66:15; Jer. 4:13; Ezek. 26:10; Nah. 3:2, 3

5 [I]Lit., *covering used in a siege* [a]Nah. 3:18 [b]Jer. 46:12

7 [I]Lit., *hearts* [a]Is. 38:14; 59:11 [b]Is. 32:12

Now they are fleeing; "Stop,
stop,"
But [a]no one turns back.
9 Plunder the silver!
Plunder the [a]gold!
For there is no limit to the
treasure—
Wealth[3519] from every kind of
desirable object.
10 She is [a]emptied! Yes, she is
desolate and waste!
[b]Hearts[3820] are melting and
knees knocking![6375]
Also anguish is in [I]the whole
body,
And all their [c]faces are grown[6908]
pale![6289]
11 Where is the den of the lions
And the feeding place of the
[a]young lions,
Where the lion, lioness, and
lion's cub[1482] prowled,
With nothing to disturb[2729] *them?*
12 The lion tore enough for his
cubs,[1484]
[I]Killed *enough* for his lionesses,
And filled his lairs with prey
And his dens with torn flesh.2966
13 "Behold, [a]I am against you,"
declares[5001] the LORD of hosts.[6635] "I
will [b]burn up her chariots in smoke, a
sword[2719] will devour your young lions,
I will [c]cut off[3772] your prey from the
land,[776] and no longer will the voice of
your messengers[4397] be heard."[8085]

Nineveh's Complete Ruin

3 [a]Woe to the bloody[1818] city,
completely full of lies *and*
pillage;
Her prey never departs.
2 The [a]noise of the whip,
The noise of the rattling of the
wheel,[212]
Galloping horses,
And [I]bounding chariots!
3 Horsemen charging,[5927]
Swords[2719] flashing, [a]spears
gleaming,
[b]Many slain,[2491] a mass of
corpses,[6297]
And [I][c]countless dead
bodies—[1472]
They stumble[3782] over
[II]the dead bodies!
4 *All* because of the [a]many
harlotries[2183] of the
harlot,[2181]
The charming[2580] one, the
[b]mistress[1172] of sorceries,[3785]
Who [c]sells nations[1471] by her
harlotries
And families[4940] by her
sorceries.
5 "Behold, [a]I am against you,"
declares[5001] the LORD of
hosts;[6635]
"And I will [I][b]lift up[1540] your skirts
over your face,
And [c]show[7200] to the nations
your nakedness
And to the kingdoms[4467] your
disgrace.
6 "I will [a]throw [I]filth[8251] on you
And [b]make you vile,5034
And set[7760] you up as a
[c]spectacle.[7210]
7 "And it will come about that all
who see[7200] you
Will [I]shrink from you and say,
'Nineveh is devastated![7703]
[a]Who will grieve for her?'
Where will I seek comforters[5162]
for you?"
8 Are you better[3190] than
[I][a]No-amon,[527] 4996
Which was situated by the
[b]waters of the Nile,
With water surrounding her,
Whose rampart[2426] *was*
[II]the sea,
Whose wall *consisted* of
[II]the sea?
9 [a]Ethiopia was *her* might,
And Egypt too, without
limits.
[b]Put and [c]Lubim were among
[I]her helpers.

8 [a]Jer. 46:5; 47:3
9 [a]Rev. 18:12, 16
10 [I]Lit., *all the loin* [a]Is. 24:1; 34:10-13; Nah. 2:2 [b]Ps. 22:14; Is. 13:7, 8; Ezek. 21:7 [c]Joel 2:6
11 [a]Is. 5:29
12 [I]Lit., *Strangled*
13 [a]Jer. 21:13; Ezek. 5:8; Nah. 3:5 [b]Josh. 11:6, 9; Ps. 46:9 [c]Is. 49:24, 25; Nah. 3:1
1 [a]Ezek. 24:6, 9
2 [I]Lit., *skipping* [a]Job 39:22-25; Jer. 47:3; Nah. 2:3, 4
3 [I]Lit., *there is no end to* [II]Lit., *their* [a]Hab. 3:11 [b]Is. 34:3; 66:16 [c]Is. 37:36; Ezek. 39:4
4 [a]Is. 23:17; Ezek. 16:25-29; Rev. 17:1, 2 [b]Is. 47:9, 12, 13 [c]Rev. 18:3
5 [I]Lit., *uncover your* [a]Jer. 50:31; Ezek. 26:3; Nah. 2:13 [b]Is. 47:2, 3; Jer. 13:26 [c]Ezek. 16:37
6 [I]Lit., *detestable things* [a]Job 9:31 [b]Job 30:8; Mal. 2:9 [c]Is. 14:16; Jer. 51:37
7 [I]Lit., *flee* [a]Is. 51:19; Jer. 15:5
8 [I]I.e., the city of Amon: Thebes [II]I.e., the Nile [a]Jer. 46:25; Ezek. 30:14-16 [b]Is. 19:6-8
9 [I]Lit., *your* [a]Is. 20:5 [b]Jer. 46:9; Ezek. 27:10; 30:5; 38:5 [c]2Chr. 12:3; 16:8

3:8-10 Thebes, the Egyptian capital, fell to the Assyrians in 661 B.C. Now, Nineveh, the Assyrian capital, must fall in similar horror.

10 Yet she [a]became an exile,[1473]
She went into captivity;[7628]
Also her [b]small children were
dashed to pieces
[c]At the head[7218] of every
street;
They [d]cast lots for her honorable
men,[3513]
And all her great men were
bound with fetters.
11 You too will become [a]drunk,
You will be [b]hidden.
You too will search for a refuge
from the enemy.
12 All your fortifications are
[a]fig trees with [1][b]ripe fruit—
When shaken, they fall[5307] into
the eater's mouth.[6310]
13 Behold, your people[5971] are
[a]women in your midst!
The gates of your land[776] are
[b]opened wide to your
enemies;
Fire consumes your gate bars.
14 [a]Draw for yourself water for the
siege!
[b]Strengthen[2388] your
fortifications!
Go into the clay and tread the
mortar!
Take hold[2388] of the brick
mold!
15 There [a]fire will consume you,
The sword will cut you
down;[3772]
It will [b]consume you as the locust
does.
Multiply yourself like the
creeping locust,
Multiply yourself like the
swarming locust.
16 You have increased your
[a]traders more than the stars
of heaven—[8064]
The creeping locust [1]strips and
flies away.
17 Your [1][a]guardsmen are like the
swarming locust.
Your [b]marshals[2951] are like
hordes of grasshoppers
Settling in the stone walls on a
cold day.
The sun rises and they flee,
And the place where they are
is not known.[3045]
18 Your shepherds are [a]sleeping,
O [b]king of Assyria;
Your [c]nobles[117] are lying
down.[7931]
Your people are [d]scattered on
the mountains,
And there is no one to
regather[6908] *them.*
19 There is [a]no relief for your
breakdown,
Your [b]wound is incurable.
All who hear [1]about you
Will [c]clap *their* hands over you,
For on whom has not your evil
passed continually?

10 [a]Is. 19:4; 20:4 [b]Ps. 137:9; Is. 13:16; Hos. 13:16 [c]Lam. 2:19 [d]Joel 3:3; Obad. 11
11 [a]Is. 49:26; Jer. 25:27; Nah. 1:10 [b]Is. 2:10, 19; Hos. 10:8
12 [1]Lit., *first fruits* [a]Rev. 6:13 [b]Is. 28:4
13 [a]Is. 19:16; Jer. 50:37; 51:30 [b]Is. 45:1, 2; Nah. 2:6
14 [a]2Chr. 32:3, 4 [b]Nah. 2:1
15 [a]Is. 66:15, 16; Nah. 2:13; 3:13 [b]Joel 1:4
16 [1]I.e., strips vegetation; or, *molts* [a]Is. 23:8
17 [1]Or, *officials* [a]Rev. 9:7 [b]Jer. 51:27
18 [a]Ps. 76:5, 6; Is. 56:10; Jer. 51:57 [b]Jer. 50:18 [c]Nah. 2:5 [d]1Kin. 22:17; Is. 13:14
19 [1]Lit., *your report* [a]Jer. 46:11; Mic. 1:9 [b]Jer. 30:12 [c]Job 27:23; Lam. 2:15

The Book of
HABAKKUK

The prophet, Habakkuk, is a rather obscure figure, but his book is one of the gems of the Old Testament. It seems to have been written shortly before the Battle of Carchemish in 605 B.C., when the Babylonians became the undisputed power in the area. Habakkuk's problem was theodicy or divine justice. Internally, he saw violence, lawbreaking, and injustice go unpunished, so he questioned God about it. God's answer only troubled him more, so he raised the question of God's justice again. God reassured Habakkuk by telling him that if he could only wait, it would all be clear to him. This satisfied Habakkuk, and with renewed faith, he seemed to conclude that, given God's holiness, his own questions were unjustified (Hab. 2:20). Chapter three is a prayer psalm which ends with another strong statement of faith. For a book of such small size, Habakkuk has wielded remarkable influence. The Habakkuk Commentary is the most well-preserved Old Testament commentary of those found among the Dead Sea Scrolls and reflects a type of Old Testament exegesis which helps us understand better much of the New Testament use of the Old Testament. More significantly, Hab. 2:4 was used by Paul in Rom. 1:17 to introduce the principle of justification by faith rather than by works, and it was Martin Luther's interpretation of this verse which totally reoriented his thinking and contributed to the beginning of the Protestant Reformation.

Chaldeans Used to Punish Judah

1 The [I][a]oracle[4853] which Habakkuk the
prophet[5030] saw.[2372]
🔑 2 [a]How long, O LORD, will I call
for help,
And Thou wilt not hear?[8085]
I cry out[2199] to Thee,
"Violence!"[2555]
Yet Thou dost [b]not save.[3467]
3 Why dost Thou make me
[a]see[7200] iniquity,[205]
And cause *me* to look on
wickedness?[5999]
Yes, [b]destruction[7701] and
violence are before
me;
[c]Strife[7379] exists[5375] and
contention arises.
4 Therefore, the [a]law[8451] is
[I]ignored[6313]
And justice[4941] [II]is never[5331]
upheld.
For the wicked[7563] [b]surround the
righteous;[6662]
Therefore, justice comes out
[c]perverted.
🔑 5 "[a]Look[7200] among the nations![1471]
Observe!
Be astonished! [b]Wonder!
Because *I* am doing [c]something
in your days—[3117]
You would not believe[539] if
[I]you were told.[5608]

1 [I]Or, *burden* [a]Is. 13:1; Nah. 1:1

2 [a]Ps. 13:1, 2; 22:1, 2 [b]Jer. 14:9

3 [a]Ps. 55:9-11; Jer. 20:18 [b]Jer. 20:8 [c]Jer. 15:10

4 [I]Or, *ineffective;* lit., *numbed* [II]Lit., *never goes forth* [a]Ps. 58:1, 2; 119:126; Is. 59:12-14 [b]Ps. 22:12; Is. 1:21-23 [c]Is. 5:20; Ezek. 9:9

5 [I]Lit., *it* [a]Acts 13:41 [b]Is. 29:9 [c]Is. 29:14; Ezek. 12:22-28

🔑 **1:2** Here begins a round of two exchanges between Habakkuk and God. First, Habakkuk, in response to the unpunished wickedness of people in Judah, wanted to know why such injustice was occurring without redress (1:2-4). God answered that He was on the verge of responding by raising up that violent nation, the Chaldeans (Babylonians) (1:5-11). Habakkuk was appalled, because he knew about the cruelty and wickedness of the Chaldeans. How could a holy God use such an unholy nation whose actions would be so indiscriminate that men more righteous than they would be swallowed up (1:12-17)? Convinced of the rightness of his complaint, he stationed himself and waited for God's reply (2:1). God did not respond directly, but He assured Habakkuk that the answer would come soon. In the meantime, the righteous man lives by his faith or faithfulness (2:2-4). This seemed to have satisfied Habakkuk, because he asked no more questions. In fact, his conclusion in 2:20 may be as much of a self-criticism as it is a statement of faith. Given the holiness of God, man's best response is silence, not questioning.

🔑 **1:5** Paul quoted this verse in his sermon in the synagogue at Antioch of Pisidia (Acts 13:41).

6 "For behold, I am [a]raising up the
Chaldeans,
That [I]fierce[4751] and impetuous
people[1471]
Who march [II]throughout the
earth[776]
To [III][b]seize[3423] dwelling
places[4908] which are not
theirs.
7 "They are dreaded and
[a]feared.[3372]
Their [b]justice and [I]authority
[II]originate with themselves.
8 "Their [a]horses are swifter[7043]
than leopards
And [I]keener than [b]wolves in the
evening.
Their [II]horsemen come
galloping,
Their horsemen come from
afar;
They fly like an [c]eagle swooping
down to devour.
9 "All of them come for violence.
[I]Their horde of [a]faces *moves*
forward.
They collect[622] captives[7628] like
sand.
10 "They [a]mock at kings,
And rulers[7336] are a laughing
matter to them.
They [b]laugh at every
fortress,
And [c]heap up rubble[6083] to
capture it.
11 "Then they will sweep through
like the [a]wind[7307] and pass
on.[5674]
But they will be held
[b]guilty,[816]
They whose [c]strength is their
god."[433]
12 Art Thou not from
[a]everlasting,[6924]
O LORD, my God,[430] my Holy
One?[6918]
We will not die.[4191]
Thou, O LORD, hast
[b]appointed[7760] them to
judge;
And Thou, O [c]Rock, hast
established[3245] them to
correct.[3198]
13 *Thine* eyes are too [a]pure[2889] to
[I]approve[7200] evil,[7451]
And Thou canst not look on
wickedness[6001] *with favor.*
Why dost Thou [b]look with favor
On those who deal
[c]treacherously?[898]
Why art Thou [d]silent when the
wicked [e]swallow up[1104]
Those more righteous than
they?
14 *Why* hast Thou made[6213] men[120]
like the fish of the sea,
Like creeping things without a
ruler[4910] over them?
15 *The Chaldeans* [a]bring all of them
up[5927] with a hook,
[b]Drag them away with their net,
And gather them together in
their fishing net.[4365]
Therefore, they rejoice and are
glad.
16 Therefore, they offer a sacrifice
to their net.
And [I]burn incense[6999] to their
fishing net;
Because through [a]these things
their [II]catch is [III]large,
And their food is [IV]plentiful.
17 Will they therefore empty their
[a]net
And continually[8548] [b]slay[2026]
nations without sparing?

God Answers the Prophet

2 I will [a]stand on my guard post[4931]
And station myself on the
rampart;
And I will [b]keep watch to see[7200]
[c]what He will speak[1696] to me,
And how I may reply[7725]
[I]when I am reproved.[8433]
2 Then the LORD answered me and
said,[559]
"[a]Record the vision[2377]

6 [I]Lit., *bitter* [II]Lit., *the breadth of* [III]Lit., *take possession of* [a]2Kin. 24:2; Jer. 4:11-13 [b]Jer. 8:10
7 [I]Lit., *eminence* [II]Lit., *proceeds from* [a]Is. 18:2, 7 [b]Jer. 39:5-9
8 [I]Or, *more eager to attack* [II]Or, *steeds paw the ground* [a]Jer. 4:13 [b]Zeph. 3:3 [c]Ezek. 17:3; Hos. 8:1
9 [I]Or, *The eagerness of their faces* [a]2Kin. 12:17; Dan. 11:17
10 [a]2Chr. 36:6, 10; Is. 37:13 [b]Is. 10:9; 14:16 [c]Jer. 32:24; Ezek. 26:8
11 [a]Jer. 4:11, 12 [b]Jer. 2:3 [c]Dan. 4:30; Hab. 1:16
12 [a]Deut. 33:27; Ps. 90:2; Mal. 3:6 [b]Is. 10:5, 6; Mal. 3:5 [c]Deut. 32:4
13 [I]Lit., *look at* [a]Ps. 11:4-6; 34:15, 16 [b]Jer. 12:1, 2 [c]Is. 24:16 [d]Ps. 50:21 [e]Ps. 35:25
15 [a]Jer. 16:16; Amos 4:2 [b]Ps. 10:9
16 [I]Or, *sacrifice* [II]Lit., *portion* [III]Lit., *fat;* or, *plentiful* [IV]Lit., *the fat portion* [a]Jer. 44:17
17 [a]Is. 19:8 [b]Is. 14:5, 6
1 [I]Lit., *upon my reproof* [a]Is. 21:8 [b]Ps. 5:3 [c]Ps. 85:8
2 [a]Deut. 27:8; Rom. 15:4; Rev. 1:19

2:2 See note on Jer. 36:2.

And inscribe *it* on tablets,
That [I]the one who [II]reads[7121] it
may run.
3 "For the vision is yet for the
[a]appointed time;[4150]
It [I]hastens[6315] toward the goal,
and it will not [II]fail.[3576]
Though it tarries, [b]wait for
it;
For it will certainly come, it
[c]will not delay.
4 "Behold, as for the [a]proud one,
His soul[5315] is not right within
him;
But the [b]righteous[6662] will
live[2421] by his [I]faith.[530]
5 "Furthermore, [a]wine betrays[898]
the [b]haughty man,[1397]
So that he does not [c]stay at
home.
He [d]enlarges his appetite[5315] like
Sheol,[7585]
And he is like death,[4194] never
satisfied.
He also gathers[622] to himself all
nations[1471]
And collects[6908] to himself all
peoples.[5971]
6 "Will not all of these [a]take up[5375]
a taunt-song against him,
Even mockery *and*
insinuations[2420] against him,
And say, '[b]Woe to him who
increases what is not his—
For how long—
And makes himself [I]rich[3513] with
loans?'
7 "Will not [I]your creditors
[a]rise up suddenly,
And those who [II]collect[2111] from
you awaken?
Indeed, you will become
plunder[4933] for them.
8 "Because you have [a]looted many
nations,
All the remainder[3499] of the
peoples will loot you—

2 [I]Or, *one may read it fluently* [II]Or, *is to proclaim it*
3 [I]Lit., *pants* [II]Or, *lie* [a]Dan. 8:17, 19; 10:14 [b]Ps. 27:14 [c]Ezek. 12:25; Heb. 10:37
4 [I]Or, *faithfulness* [a]Ps. 49:18; Is. 13:11 [b]Rom. 1:17; Gal. 3:11; Heb. 10:38
5 [a]Prov. 20:1 [b]Prov. 21:24 [c]2Kin. 14:10 [d]Prov. 27:20; 30:16; Is. 5:11-15
6 [I]Lit., *heavy* [a]Is. 14:4-10; Jer. 50:13 [b]Job 20:15-29; Hab. 2:12
7 [I]Lit., *those who bite you* [II]Lit., *violently shake you* [a]Prov. 29:1
8 [I]Lit., *of the land* [a]Is. 33:1; Jer. 27:7; Zech. 2:8
9 [a]Jer. 22:13; Ezek. 22:27 [b]Jer. 49:16
10 [a]2Kin. 9:26; Nah. 1:14; Hab. 2:16 [b]Jer. 26:19
11 [I]Lit., *wood* [a]Josh. 24:27; Luke 19:40
12 [I]Or, *injustice* [a]Mic. 3:10; Nah. 3:1
13 [a]Is. 50:11; Jer. 51:58
14 [a]Ps. 22:27; Is. 11:9; Zech. 14:9
15 [I]Lit., *his neighbor*
16 [I]Lit., *show yourself uncircumcised;* or, *stagger;* so DSS and ancient versions [a]Lam. 4:21 [b]Jer. 25:15, 17

Because of human[120]
bloodshed[1818] and
violence[2555] [I]done to the
land,[776]
To the town and all its
inhabitants.
9 "Woe to him who gets[1214]
[a]evil gain[1215] for his house[1004]
To [b]put[7760] his nest on high
To be delivered[5337] from the
hand[3709] of calamity!
10 "You have devised[3289] a
[a]shameful thing for your
house
By cutting off many peoples;
So you are [b]sinning[2398] against
yourself.
11 "Surely the [a]stone will cry out[2199]
from the wall,
And the rafter will answer it from
the [I]framework.
12 "Woe to him who [a]builds a city
with bloodshed
And founds[3559] a town with
[I]violence![5766]
13 "Is it not indeed from the LORD
of hosts[6635]
That peoples [a]toil for fire,
And nations grow weary for
nothing?
14 "For the earth[776] will be
[a]filled
With the knowledge[3045] of the
glory[3519] of the LORD,
As the waters cover the sea.
15 "Woe to you who make
[I]your neighbors[7453] drink,
Who mix in your venom even
to make *them* drunk
So as to look on their nakedness!
16 "You will be filled with disgrace
rather than honor.
Now you yourself [a]drink and
[I]expose your *own*
nakedness.[6188]
The [b]cup in the LORD's right hand
will come around to you,

2:4 Paul used this famous verse to lay down the principle of justification by faith, not by works of the law (Rom. 1:17; Gal. 3:11). The Hebrew writer employed Hab. 2:3,4 to underscore his point about the need for faithfulness (Heb. 10:37,38). His readers needed to endure to the end, so the writer followed up the Habakkuk quotation with a long list of heroes of persistent faith (Heb. 11).

And [c]utter disgrace *will come*
upon your glory.
17 "For the [a]violence [I]done to
Lebanon will [II]overwhelm
you,
And the devastation[7701] of *its*
beasts [III]by which you
terrified[2865] them,
[b]Because of human bloodshed
and [c]violence [IV]done to the
land,
To the town and all its
inhabitants.
18 "What [a]profit is the [I]idol[6459] when
its maker[3335] has carved[6456]
it,
Or [II]an image,[4541] a [b]teacher[3384]
of falsehood?[8267]
For *its* maker [c]trusts[982] in his
own handiwork[3336]
When he fashions[6213] speechless
idols.[457]
19 "Woe to him who [a]says to a *piece*
of wood, '[b]Awake!'
To a dumb stone, 'Arise!'
And that is *your* teacher?[3384]
Behold, it is overlaid with
[c]gold and silver,
And there is [d]no breath at all
inside it.
20 "But the [a]LORD is in His holy[6944]
temple.[1964]
[I]Let all the earth [b]be silent before
Him."

God's Deliverance of His People

3 A prayer[8605] of Habakkuk the
prophet, according to [I]Shigionoth.
2 LORD, I have [a]heard[8085] [I]the
report about Thee *and* [II]I
[b]fear.[3372]
O LORD, [c]revive[2421] [d]Thy work
in the midst of the years,
In the midst of the years make
it known;
In wrath[7367] remember[2142]
[III][e]mercy.[7355]
3 God[433] comes from [a]Teman,
And the Holy One[6918] from
Mount [b]Paran. Selah.
His [c]splendor[1935] covers[3680] the
heavens,[8064]
And the [d]earth[776] is full of His
praise.[8416]
4 *His* [a]radiance is like the
sunlight;[216]
He has rays *flashing* from His
hand,[3027]
And there is the hiding of His
[b]power.
5 Before Him goes [a]pestilence,[1698]
And [b]plague comes [I]after
Him.
6 He stood and surveyed the
earth;
He looked[7200] and [a]startled the
nations.[1471]
Yes, the perpetual[5703] mountains
were shattered,
The ancient[5769] hills [I]collapsed.
His ways are [b]everlasting.[5769]
7 I saw[7200] the tents[168] of Cushan
under [a]distress,[205]
The tent curtains of the land of
[b]Midian were trembling.[7264]
8 Did the LORD rage[2734] against the
[a]rivers,
Or *was* Thine anger[639] against
the rivers,
Or *was* Thy wrath[5678] against the
[b]sea,
That Thou didst [c]ride on Thy
horses,
On Thy [d]chariots of
salvation?[3444]
9 Thy [a]bow was made bare,[6181]
The rods[4294] of [I]chastisement
were sworn.[7621] Selah.

16 [c]Nah. 3:6 **17** [I]Lit., *of Lebanon* [II]Lit., *cover* [III]Lit., which *terrified them* [IV]Lit., *of the land* [a]Joel 3:19; Zech. 11:1 [b]Ps. 55:23; Hab. 2:8 [c]Jer. 51:35; Hab. 2:8 **18** [I]Or, *a graven image* [II]Lit., a *cast* metal *image* [a]Is. 42:17; 44:9; Jer. 2:27, 28 [b]Jer. 10:8, 14; Zech. 10:2 [c]Ps. 115:4, 8 **19** [a]Jer. 2:27, 28; 10:3 [b]1Kin. 18:26-29 [c]Ps. 135:15-18; Jer. 10:4, 9, 14 [d]Ps. 135:17 **20** [I]Lit., *Hush before Him, all the earth.* [a]Mic. 1:2 [b]Zeph. 1:7; Zech. 2:13

1 [I]I.e., a highly emotional poetic form **2** [I]Or, *Thy report* [II]Or, *I stand in awe of Thy work, O LORD; In the midst of the years revive it,* [III]Or, *compassion* [a]Job 42:5 [b]Ps. 119:120; Jer. 10:7 [c]Ps. 71:20; 85:6 [d]Ps. 44:1-8; Hab. 1:5 [e]Num. 14:19; 2Sam. 24:15-17; Is. 54:8 **3** [a]Jer. 49:7; Amos 1:12; Obad. 9 [b]Gen. 21:21; Deut. 33:2 [c]Ps. 113:4; 148:13 [d]Ps. 48:10 **4** [a]Ps. 18:12 [b]Job 26:14 **5** [I]Lit., *at His feet* [a]Ex. 12:29, 30; Num. 16:46-49 [b]Num. 11:1-3; Ps. 18:12, 13 **6** [I]Lit., *bowed;* or, *sank down* [a]Job 21:18; Ps. 35:5 [b]Hab. 1:12 **7** [a]Ex. 15:14-16 [b]Num. 31:7, 8; Judg. 7:24, 25; 8:12

8 [a]Ex. 7:19, 20; Josh. 3:16; Is. 50:2 [b]Ex. 14:16, 21; Ps. 114:3, 5 [c]Deut. 33:26; Ps. 18:10; Hab. 3:15 [d]Ps. 68:17 **9** [I]Lit., *word* [a]Ps. 7:12, 13; Hab. 3:11

2:20 See note on Hab. 1:2.

3:1-19 Chapter 3 is a self-contained prayer psalm, intended to be sung with stringed accompaniment, so it is not a part of the interaction between Habakkuk and God, as the first two chapters are. Nevertheless, it fits in with the theme of those chapters, as can be seen by the strong expression of faith in spite of all circumstances, which is found in these verses.

Thou didst [b]cleave the earth with rivers.
10 The mountains saw Thee *and* quaked;[2342]
The downpour of waters swept by.[5674]
The deep [a]uttered forth its voice,
It lifted[5375] high its hands.
11 [a]Sun *and* moon stood in their places;
They went away at the [b]light of Thine arrows,
At the radiance of Thy gleaming spear.
12 In indignation[2195] Thou didst [a]march through the earth;
In anger Thou didst [Ib]trample the nations.[1471]
13 Thou didst go forth for the [a]salvation[3468] of Thy people,[5971]
For the salvation of Thine [b]anointed.[4899]
Thou didst strike the [c]head[7218] of the house of the evil[7563]
To lay him open from [I]thigh[3247] to neck. Selah.
14 Thou didst pierce[5344] with his [a]own [I]spears
The head of his [II]throngs.
They [b]stormed in to scatter [III]us;
Their exultation *was* like those
Who [c]devour the oppressed in secret.

15 Thou didst [a]tread on the sea with Thy horses,
On the [b]surge of many waters.
16 I heard and my [I]inward parts[990] [a]trembled,
At the sound my lips[8193] quivered.
Decay enters my [b]bones,[6106]
And in my place I tremble.
Because I must [c]wait quietly for the day[3117] of distress,
[II]For the [d]people to arise[5927] *who* will invade us.
17 Though the [a]fig tree should not blossom,
And there be no [I]fruit on the vines,
Though the yield of the [b]olive should fail,
And the fields produce[6213] no food,
Though the [c]flock should be cut off from the fold,
And there be [d]no cattle in the stalls,
18 Yet I will [a]exult in the LORD,
I will [b]rejoice in the [c]God[430] of my salvation.
19 The Lord[136] [I]GOD is my [a]strength,[2428]
And [b]He has made[7760] my feet like hinds'[355] *feet,*
And makes me walk on my [c]high places.[1116]

For the choir director, on my stringed instruments.

9 [b]Ps. 78:16; 105:41
10 [a]Ps. 93:3; 98:7, 8
11 [a]Josh. 10:12-14 [b]Ps. 18:14
12 [I]Or, *thresh* [a]Ps. 68:7 [b]Is. 41:15; Jer. 51:33; Mic. 4:13
13 [I]Lit., *foundation* [a]Ex. 15:2; 2Sam. 5:20; Ps. 68:19, 20 [b]Ps. 20:6; 28:8 [c]Ps. 68:21; 110:6
14 [I]Lit., *shafts* [II]Or, *warriors* or *villagers* [III]Lit., *me* [a]Judg. 7:22 [b]Dan. 11:40; Zech. 9:14 [c]Ps. 10:8; 64:2-5
15 [a]Ps. 77:19; Hab. 3:8 [b]Ex. 15:8
16 [I]Lit., *belly* [II]Or, *To come upon the people* who *will* [a]Dan. 10:8; Hab. 3:2 [b]Job 30:17, 30; Jer. 23:9 [c]Luke 21:19 [d]Jer. 5:15
17 [I]Lit., *produce* [a]Joel 1:10-12; Amos 4:9; 2Cor. 4:8, 9 [b]Mic. 6:15 [c]Joel 1:18 [d]Jer. 5:17
18 [a]Ex. 15:1, 2; Job 13:15; Is. 61:10; Rom. 5:2, 3 [b]Ps. 46:1-5; Phil. 4:4 [c]Ps. 25:5; 27:1; Is. 12:2
19 [I]Heb., *YHWH,* usually rendered LORD [a]Ps. 18:32, 33; 27:1; 46:1; Is. 45:24 [b]2Sam. 22:34 [c]Deut. 33:29

The Book of

ZEPHANIAH

Zephaniah had a brief but powerful message for a people locked in religious apostasy. His four-generation genealogy, going back to an unidentified Hezekiah, may indicate that he was of royal descent. The conditions which he addressed reflect Judah in the decade before Josiah's reforms in 621 B.C. If he was a member of the royal family, he may have been one of the dominant influences on the young king to reverse the apostasy of his father and grandfather. Zephaniah was an urban prophet whose message to Judah focused on Jerusalem. The description of God searching Jerusalem with lamps (Zeph. 1:12) formed the basis of the way that Zephaniah was represented in Medieval art. Zephaniah addressed a people who had misplaced their religious loyalties. The gods of Canaan, Assyria, and Ammon were being worshiped, but the Lord was being neglected. Some concluded that the Lord was no longer active in their history. To this Zephaniah responded with the strongest development of the theme of "the Day of the Lord" to be found in the prophets. Terrible punishment was coming, but after the return of the faithful, Jerusalem would have a glorious future.

Day of Judgment on Judah

1 The word[1697] of the LORD which came to Zephaniah son[1121] of Cushi,
son of Gedaliah, son of Amariah, son
of Hezekiah, in the days[3117] of [a]Josiah
son of [b]Amon, king of Judah,

2 "I will completely [a]remove[622] all
things
From the face of the [I]earth,"[127]
declares[5001] the LORD.

3 "I will remove [a]man[120] and beast;
I will remove the [b]birds of the
sky[8064]
And the fish of the sea,
And the [Ic]ruins[4384] along with the
wicked;[7563]
And I will cut off[3772] man from
the face of the [II]earth,"
declares the LORD.

4 "So I will [a]stretch out My hand[3027]
against Judah
And against all the inhabitants
of Jerusalem.
And I will [b]cut off the remnant[7605]
of Baal from this place,
And the names of the
[c]idolatrous priests[3649] along
with the priests.[3548]

5 "And those who bow down[7812] on
the [a]housetops to the host[6635]
of heaven,
And those who bow down *and*
[b]swear to the LORD and *yet*
swear[7650] by [Ic]Milcom,[4428]

6 And those who have [a]turned
back from following the
LORD,

1 [a]2Kin. 22:1, 2; 2Chr. 34:1-33; Jer. 1:2; 22:11 [b]2Kin. 21:18-26; 2Chr. 33:20-25
2 [I]Lit., *ground* [a]Gen. 6:7; Jer. 7:20; Ezek. 33:27, 28
3 [I]Or, *stumbling blocks* [II]Lit., *ground* [a]Is. 6:11, 12 [b]Jer. 4:25; 9:10 [c]Ezek. 7:19; 14:3, 4, 8
4 [a]Jer. 6:12; Ezek. 6:14 [b]Mic. 5:13 [c]2Kin. 23:5; Hos. 10:5 [c]1Kin. 11:5, 33; Jer. 49:1
5 [I]Or, *their king;* M.T., *Malcam,* probably a variant spelling of Milcom [a]2Kin. 23:12; Jer. 19:13 [b]Jer. 5:2, 7; 7:9, 10
6 [a]Is. 1:4; Hos. 7:10

1:1 Zephaniah's four-generation genealogy is unprecedented in the prophets. Since it ends with a person named Hezekiah, it seems probable that this was King Hezekiah of Judah, who was so well known that he could simply be referred to by his name alone. Zephaniah prophesied during the reign of the righteous king, Josiah, but the conditions which he addressed point to a period before Josiah's reforms in 621 B.C.

1:4,5 These verses reflect a Jerusalem with deeply divided religious loyalties. Some worshiped the Canaanite god, Baal. Others were involved in the Assyrian worship of the heavenly bodies. Those devoted to Milcom were serving the national god of the Ammonites. Not long after Zephaniah uttered these words, Josiah ordered the destruction of all vestiges of these and all other idolatrous religions throughout Judah (II Kgs. 23:4-20).

And those who have [b]not sought
the LORD or inquired of
Him."
7 [I][a]Be silent before the Lord[136]
[II]GOD!
For the [b]day[3117] of the LORD is
near,
For the LORD has prepared[3559]
a [c]sacrifice,[2077]
He has [d]consecrated[6942] His
guests.
8 "Then it will come about on the
day of the LORD's sacrifice,
That I will [a]punish[6485] the
princes,[8269] the king's
sons,[1121]
And all who clothe themselves
with [b]foreign[5237] garments.
9 "And I will punish on that day
all who leap on the *temple*
threshold,
Who fill the house[1004] of their
[I]lord[113] with [a]violence[2555] and
deceit.[4820]
10 "And on that day," declares the
LORD,
"There will be the sound of a cry
from the [a]Fish Gate,
A wail from the [I][b]Second
Quarter,
And a loud crash[7667] from the
[c]hills.
11 "Wail, O inhabitants of the
[I]Mortar,
For all the [II]people[5971] of
[a]Canaan will be silenced;[1820]
All who weigh out [b]silver will
be cut off.[3772]
12 "And it will come about at that
time[6256]
That I will [a]search Jerusalem
with lamps,[5216]
And I will punish the men[582]
Who are [I][b]stagnant in spirit,
Who say in their hearts,[3824]
'The LORD will [c]not do good[3190]
or evil!'[7489]
13 "Moreover, their wealth[2428] will
become [a]plunder,[4933]
And their houses desolate;[8077]
Yes, [b]they will build houses but
not inhabit *them*,
And plant vineyards but not
drink their wine."
14 Near is the [a]great [b]day[3117] of the
LORD,
Near and coming very quickly;
Listen, the day of the LORD!
[I]In it the warrior [c]cries out
bitterly.[4751]
15 A day[3117] of wrath[5678] is that day,
A day of [a]trouble and distress,
A day of destruction[7722] and
desolation,
A day of [b]darkness[2822] and
gloom,[653]
A day of clouds[6051] and thick
darkness,[6205]
16 A day of [a]trumpet and battle cry,
Against the [b]fortified cities
And the high corner towers.
17 And I will bring [a]distress on
men,[120]
So that they will walk [b]like the
blind,
Because they have sinned[2398]
against the LORD;
And their [c]blood[1818] will be
poured out[8210] like dust,[6083]
And their [d]flesh[3894] like dung.
18 Neither their [a]silver nor their
gold
Will be able to deliver[5337] them
On the day[3117] of the LORD's
wrath;
And [b]all the earth[776] will be
devoured
In the fire of His jealousy,[7068]
For He will [c]make[6213] a complete
end,

6 [b]Is. 9:13
7 [I]Lit., *Hush* [II]Heb., *YHWH*, usually rendered LORD [a]Hab. 2:20; Zech. 2:13 [b]Zeph. 1:14 [c]Is. 34:6; Jer. 46:10 [d]1Sam. 16:5; Is. 13:3
8 [a]Is. 24:21; Hab. 1:10 [b]Is. 2:6
9 [I]Or, *Lord* [a]Jer. 5:27; Amos 3:10
10 [I]I.e., a district of Jerusalem [a]2Chr. 33:14; Neh. 3:3; 12:39 [b]2Chr. 34:22 [c]Ezek. 6:13
11 [I]I.e., a district of Jerusalem [II]Or, *merchant people will* [a]Zeph. 2:5; Zech. 14:21 [b]Job 27:16, 17; Hos. 9:6
12 [I]Lit., *thickening on their lees* [a]Jer. 16:16, 17; Ezek. 9:4-11; Amos 9:1-3 [b]Jer. 48:11; Amos 6:1 [c]Ezek. 8:12; 9:9
13 [a]Jer. 15:13; 17:3 [b]Amos 5:11; Mic. 6:15
14 [I]Lit., *There* [a]Jer. 30:7; Joel 2:11; Mal. 4:5 [b]Ezek. 7:7, 12; 30:3; Joel 1:15; 3:14; Zeph. 1:7 [c]Ezek. 7:16-18
15 [a]Is. 22:5 [b]Joel 2:2, 31; Amos 5:18-20
16 [a]Is. 27:13; Jer. 4:19 [b]Is. 2:12-15
17 [a]Jer. 10:18 [b]Deut. 28:29 [c]Ezek. 24:7, 8 [d]Jer. 8:2; 9:22
18 [a]Ezek. 7:19 [b]Zeph. 3:8 [c]Gen. 6:7; Ezek. 7:5-7

1:7 More than any prophet, Zephaniah is known for the emphasis which he laid upon "the day of the Lord." Earlier, some in Israel had an idealized view of the Day of the Lord, and Amos had to show them that, for those living in sin, that day was to be dreaded in horror (Amos 5:18-20). Zephaniah's message was the same but much more highly developed. The only hope at all was that the righteous might be hidden on that day (2:3).

1:12 See the introduction to Zephaniah and the note on Ezek. 8:7-12.

Indeed a terrifying one,
Of all the inhabitants of the
earth.

Judgments on Judah's Enemies

2 Gather yourselves together,
yes, [a]gather,
O nation[1471] [b]without [I]shame,
2 Before the decree[2706] [I]takes
effect—
The day passes[5674] [a]like the
chaff—
Before the [b]burning anger[639] of
the LORD comes upon you,
Before the [c]day[3117] of the LORD'S
anger comes upon you.
🔑3 [a]Seek the LORD,
All you [b]humble of the [I]earth[776]
Who have carried out His
[II]ordinances;[4941]
[c]Seek righteousness, seek
humility.
Perhaps you will be [d]hidden
In the day of the LORD's anger.
4 For [a]Gaza will be abandoned,[5800]
And Ashkelon a desolation;[8077]
[a]Ashdod will be driven out at
noon,
And [a]Ekron will be uprooted.
5 Woe to the inhabitants of the
seacoast,[2256]
The nation of the [Ia]Cherethites!
The word[1697] of the LORD is
[b]against you,
O [c]Canaan, land of the
Philistines;
And I will [d]destroy[6] you,
So that there will be [e]no
inhabitant.
6 So the seacoast will be
[a]pastures,
With [I]caves for shepherds and
folds for flocks.
7 And the coast will be
For the [a]remnant[7611] of the
house[1004] of Judah,
They will [b]pasture on it.
In the houses of Ashkelon they
will lie down at evening;
For the LORD their God[430] will
[c]care[6485] for them
And [d]restore[7725] their
fortune.[7622]
8 "I have heard[8085] the [Ia]taunting[2781]
of Moab
And the [b]revilings of the sons[1121]
of Ammon,
With which they have [II]taunted
My people[5971]
And [IIIc]become arrogant against
their territory.
9 "Therefore, as I live,"[2416]
declares[5001] the LORD of
hosts,[6635]
The God of Israel,
"Surely [a]Moab will be like
[b]Sodom,
And the sons of [c]Ammon like
[d]Gomorrah—
A place possessed by nettles and
salt pits,
And a perpetual[5769] desolation.
The remnant[7611] of My
people[1471] will [e]plunder them,
And the remainder[3499] of My
nation will inherit[5157] them."
10 This they will have in return for
their [a]pride, because they have [Ib]taunted
and [II]become arrogant against the people
of the LORD of hosts.
11 The LORD will be [a]terrifying[3372]
to them, for He will [I]starve [b]all the
gods[430] of the earth; and all the [c]coast-
lands of the nations[1471] will [d]bow
down[7812] to Him, everyone[376] from his
own place.
12 "You also, O [a]Ethiopians, will be
slain[2491] by My sword."[2719]
🔑13 And He will [a]stretch out His
hand[3027] against the north
And destroy[6] [b]Assyria,
And He will make[7760] [c]Nineveh
a desolation,
Parched like the wilderness.

1 [I]Or, *longing* [a]2Chr. 20:4; Joel 1:14 [b]Jer. 3:3; 6:15
2 [I]Lit., *is born* [a]Is. 17:13; Hos. 13:3 [b]Lam. 4:11; Nah. 1:6 [c]Zeph. 1:18
3 [I]Or, *land* [II]Or, *justice* [a]Ps. 105:4; Amos 5:6 [b]Ps. 22:26; Is. 11:4 [c]Amos 5:14, 15 [d]Ps. 57:1; Is. 26:20
4 [a]Amos 1:7, 8; Zech. 9:5-7
5 [I]I.e., a segment of the Philistines with roots in Crete [a]Ezek. 25:16 [b]Amos 3:1 [c]Zeph. 1:11 [d]Is. 14:29, 30 [e]Zeph. 3:6
6 [I]Or, *meadows* or *wells* [a]Is. 5:17; 7:25
7 [a]Is. 11:16 [b]Is. 32:14 [c]Ex. 4:31; Ps. 80:14 [d]Jer. 32:44; Zeph. 3:20
8 [I]Lit., *reproach* [II]Lit., *reproached* [III]Lit., *made themselves great* [a]Ezek. 25:8 [b]Ezek. 25:3 [c]Amos 1:13
9 [a]Is. 15:1-9; Jer. 48:1-47; Amos 2:1-3 [b]Gen. 19:24 [c]Jer. 49:1-6; Ezek. 25:1-10 [d]Deut. 29:23 [e]Is. 11:14
10 [I]Lit., *reproached* [II]Lit., *made themselves great* [a]Is. 16:6 [b]Zeph. 2:8
11 [I]Lit., *make lean* [a]Joel 2:11 [b]Zeph. 1:4 [c]Is. 24:15 [d]Ps. 72:8-11; Zeph. 3:9
12 [a]Is. 18:1-7; 20:4, 5; Ezek. 30:4-9
13 [a]Is. 14:26; Zeph. 1:4 [b]Is. 10:16; Mic. 5:6 [c]Nah. 3:7

🔑 **2:3** See note on Zeph. 1:7.
🔑 **2:13** Nineveh fell in 612 B.C., two decades or less from when Zephaniah uttered this prophecy. Assyria's destruction was complete by 609 B.C. See the note on Jon. 1:2.

14 And flocks will lie down in her
midst,
[I]All beasts[2416] which range in
herds;
Both the [II][a]pelican and the
hedgehog
Will lodge in [III]the tops of her
pillars;[3730]
[IV]Birds will sing in the window,
Desolation *will be* on the
threshold;
For He has laid bare the cedar
work.
15 This is the [a]exultant city
Which [b]dwells securely,[983]
Who says in her heart,
"[c]I am, and there is no one
besides me."
How she has become a
[d]desolation,[8047]
A resting place for beasts!
[e]Everyone who passes[5674] by
her will hiss
And wave[5128] his hand *in
contempt.*

Woe to Jerusalem and the Nations

3 Woe to her who is [a]rebellious
and [b]defiled,
The [c]tyrannical[3238] city!
2 She [a]heeded[8085] no voice;
She [b]accepted no instruction.[4148]
She did not [c]trust[982] in the LORD;
She did not [d]draw near[7126] to her
God.[430]
3 Her [a]princes[8269] within[7130] her
are roaring lions,
Her judges[8199] are [b]wolves at
evening;
They leave nothing for the
morning.
4 Her prophets[5030] are [a]reckless,
treacherous men;[582]
Her [b]priests[3548] have
profaned[2490] the
sanctuary.[6944]
They have done violence[2554] to
the law.[8451]
5 The LORD is [a]righteous[6662]
[b]within[7130] her;
He will [c]do[6213] no injustice.[5766]
[d]Every morning He brings His
justice[4941] to light;[216]
He does not fail.
But the unjust[5767] [e]knows[3045] no
shame.
6 "I have cut off[3772] nations;[1471]
Their corner towers are in
ruins.[8074]
I have made their streets
[a]desolate,[2717]
With no one passing by;[5674]
Their [b]cities are laid waste,[6658]
Without a man,[376] [c]without an
inhabitant.
7 "I said, 'Surely you will revere[3372]
Me,
[a]Accept instruction.'[4148]
So her dwelling will [b]not be cut
off
According to all that I have
appointed[6485] concerning
her.
But they were eager to
[c]corrupt[7843] all their deeds.
8 "Therefore, [a]wait for Me,"
declares[5001] the LORD,
"For the day[3117] when I rise up
to the prey.
Indeed, My decision is to
[b]gather[622] nations,
To assemble[6908] kingdoms,[4467]
To pour out[8210] on them My
indignation,[2195]
All My burning anger;[639]
For [c]all the earth[776] will be
devoured
By the fire of My zeal.[7068]
9 "For then I will [I]give[2015] to the
peoples[5971] [a]purified[1305]
lips,[8193]
That all of them may [b]call on
the name of the LORD,
To serve[5647] Him [II]shoulder to
shoulder.
10 "From beyond the rivers of
[a]Ethiopia
My [I]worshipers, [II]My dispersed
ones,
Will [b]bring My offerings.[4503]
11 "In that day you will [a]feel no
shame[954]
Because of all your deeds

14 [I]Or, *All* kinds of *beasts in crowds;* lit., *Every* kind of *beast of a nation* [II]Or, *owl or jackdaw* [III]Lit., *her capitals* [IV]Lit., *A voice* [a]Is. 14:23; 34:11

15 [a]Is. 22:2 [b]Is. 32:9, 11; 47:8 [c]Is. 47:8; Ezek. 28:2, 9 [d]Is. 32:14 [e]Jer. 18:16; 19:8

1 [a]Jer. 5:23 [b]Ezek. 23:30 [c]Jer. 6:6

2 [a]Jer. 7:23-28 [b]Jer. 2:30; 5:3; 2Tim. 3:16 [c]Ps. 78:22; Jer. 13:25 [d]Ps. 73:28

3 [a]Ezek. 22:27 [b]Jer. 5:6; Hab. 1:8

4 [a]Judg. 9:4 [b]Ezek. 22:26; Mal. 2:7, 8

5 [a]Deut. 32:4 [b]Zeph. 3:15, 17 [c]Ps. 92:15 [d]Job 7:18 [e]Zeph. 2:1

6 [a]Jer. 9:12; Zech. 7:14; Matt. 23:38 [b]Lev. 26:31; Is. 6:11 [c]Zeph. 2:5

7 [a]Job 36:10; Ps. 32:8; 1Tim. 1:5 [b]Jer. 7:7 [c]Hos. 9:9

8 [a]Ps. 27:14; Is. 30:18; Hab. 2:3 [b]Ezek. 38:14-23; Joel 3:2 [c]Zeph. 1:18

9 [I]Lit., *change* [II]Lit., *with one shoulder* [a]Is. 19:18; 57:19 [b]Ps. 22:27; 86:9; Hab. 2:14; Zeph. 2:11

10 [I]Or, *suppliants* [II]Lit., *the daughter of My dispersed ones* [a]Ps. 68:31; Is. 18:1 [b]Is. 60:6, 7

11 [a]Is. 45:17; 54:4; Joel 2:26, 27

By which you have rebelled[6586]
against Me;
For then I will remove[5493] from
your midst
Your [b]proud, exulting ones,
And you will never again be
haughty
On My [c]holy[6944] mountain.

A Remnant of Israel

12 "But I will leave[7604] among you
A [a]humble and lowly people,
And they will [b]take refuge[2620] in
the name of the LORD.
13 "The [a]remnant[7611] of Israel will
[b]do no wrong
And [c]tell[1696] no lies,[3577]
Nor will a deceitful tongue
Be found in their mouths;[6310]
For they shall [d]feed and lie
down
With no one to make them
tremble."[2729]
14 Shout[7321] for joy, O daughter of
Zion!
[a]Shout *in triumph,* O Israel!
Rejoice and exult with all *your*
heart,[3820]
O daughter of Jerusalem!
15 The LORD has taken away[5493]
[a]*His* judgments against you,
He has cleared away your
enemies.
The King[4428] of Israel, the LORD,
is [b]in your midst;
You will [c]fear disaster[7451] no
more.
16 [a]In that day it will be said[559] to
Jerusalem:
"[b]Do not be afraid, O Zion;
[c]Do not let your hands[3027] fall
limp.[7503]
17 "The LORD your God is
[a]in your midst,
A [I][b]victorious[3467] warrior.
He will [c]exult over you with joy,
He will [II]be quiet in His love,[160]
He will rejoice over you with
shouts of joy.
18 "I will gather[622] those who
[a]grieve about the appointed
feasts—[4150]
They [I]came from you, *O Zion;*
The reproach[2781] *of exile* is a
burden[4864] on [II]them.
19 "Behold, I am going to deal[6213]
at that time[6256]
With[6213] all your [a]oppressors,
I will save[3467] the [b]lame
And gather[6908] the outcast,
And I will turn[7760] their
[c]shame into [d]praise[8416] and
renown
In all the earth.[776]
20 "At that time I will [a]bring you in,
Even at the time when I gather
you together;
Indeed, I will give you
[b]renown and praise
Among all the peoples of the
earth,
When I [c]restore[7725] your
fortunes[7622] before your
eyes,"
Says the LORD.

11 [b]Is. 2:12; 5:15 [c]Is. 11:9; 56:7; Ezek. 20:40
12 [a]Is. 14:30 [b]Is. 14:32; 50:10; Nah. 1:7; Zech. 13:8, 9
13 [a]Is. 10:20-22; Mic. 4:7; Zeph. 2:7 [b]Ps. 119:3; Jer. 31:33; Zeph. 3:5 [c]Zech. 8:3, 16; Rev. 14:5 [d]Ezek. 34:13-15
14 [a]Zech. 9:9
15 [a]Ps. 19:9; John 5:30; Rev. 18:20 [b]Ezek. 37:26-28; Zeph. 3:5 [c]Is. 54:14
16 [a]Is. 25:9 [b]Is. 35:3, 4 [c]Job 4:3; Heb. 12:12
17 [I]Lit., *A warrior who saves* [II]Or, with some ancient versions, *renew you in* [a]Zeph. 3:5, 15 [b]Is. 63:1 [c]Is. 62:5
18 [I]Lit., *were* [II]Lit., *her* [a]Ps. 42:2-4; Ezek. 9:4
19 [a]Is. 60:14 [b]Ezek. 34:16; Mic. 4:6 [c]Ezek. 16:27, 57 [d]Is. 60:18; 62:7; Zech. 8:23
20 [a]Ezek. 37:12, 21 [b]Deut. 26:18, 19; Is. 56:5; 66:22 [c]Jer. 29:14; Joel 3:1; Zeph. 2:7

The Book of

HAGGAI

In 539 B.C. Babylon fell to the Medo-Persian Empire, and a year later Cyrus issued a decree allowing the Jews to return. By 536 B.C. the first group had arrived and laid the foundation of the temple. Because of opposition from neighboring peoples, work on the temple stopped (see Ezra 4:4-5) and was not resumed until God raised up Haggai and Zechariah sixteen years later to preach the need to complete the reconstruction project. Over a four month period in 520 B.C., Haggai delivered four messages concerning this effort. The first and third messages explained that the land's lack of productivity was because the temple lay in ruins and the land was still unclean. The other two were words of reassurance that God was supporting the project and would prosper them. The people quickly responded to the challenge, and the rebuilding of the temple was completed in 515 B.C.

Haggai Begins Temple Building

1 ⊶ In the [a]second year of Darius the king,[4428] on the first day of the sixth month, the word[1697] of the LORD came by the prophet[5030] [b]Haggai to [c]Zerubbabel the son[1121] of Shealtiel, [d]governor[6346] of Judah, and to [e]Joshua the son of Jehozadak, the high priest[3548] saying,[559]

2 "Thus says the LORD of [I]hosts,[6635] 'This people[5971] says, "The time[6256] has not come, *even* the time for the house[1004] of the LORD to be rebuilt." ' "

3 Then the word of the LORD came by Haggai the prophet saying,

4 "Is it time for you yourselves to dwell in your paneled[5603] houses while this house [a]*lies* desolate?"[2720]

5 Now therefore, thus says the LORD of hosts, "[I]Consider your ways![1870]

6 "You have [a]sown much, but [I]harvest little; *you* eat, but *there is* not *enough* to be satisfied; *you* drink, but *there is* [II]not *enough* to become drunk; *you* put on clothing, but no one is warm *enough*; and he who earns, earns wages *to put* into a purse with holes."[5344]

7 Thus says the LORD of hosts, "[I]Consider your ways!

8 "Go up[5927] to the [I]mountains, bring wood and [a]rebuild the [II]temple, that I may be [b]pleased[7521] with it and be [c]glorified,"[3618] says the LORD.

9 "[a]*You* look for much, but behold, *it comes* to little; when you bring *it* home,[1004] I [b]blow it *away*. Why?" declares[5001] the LORD of hosts, "Because of My house which [c]*lies* desolate, while each[376] of you runs to his own house.

10 "Therefore, because of you the [a]sky[8064] has withheld [I]its dew, and the earth[776] has withheld its produce.

11 "And I called[7121] for a [a]drought on the land,[776] on the mountains, on the grain, on the new wine, on the oil,[3323] on what the ground[127] produces, on [b]men,[120] on cattle, and on [c]all the labor of [I]your hands."[3709]

12 Then [a]Zerubbabel the son of Shealtiel, and [b]Joshua the son of Jehozadak, the high priest, with all the remnant[7611] of the people, [c]obeyed[8085] the voice of the LORD their God[430] and the words of Haggai the prophet, as the LORD their God had sent him. And the people [I][d]showed reverence[3372] for the LORD.

13 Then Haggai, the [a]messenger[4397] of the LORD, spoke[559] [I]by the commis-

1 [a]Ezra 4:24 [b]Ezra 5:1; 6:14; Hag. 1:3, 12, 13; 2:1, 10, 20 [c]Ezra 2:2; Neh. 7:7; Hag. 1:12, 14; Zech. 4:6; Matt. 1:12, 13 [d]1Kin. 10:15; Ezra 5:3 [e]Zech. 6:11
2 [I]Lit., *hosts, saying*
4 [a]Jer. 33:10, 12; Hag. 1:9
5 [I]Lit., *Set your heart on*
6 [I]Lit., *bring in* [II]Lit., *not becoming drunk* [a]Deut. 28:38-40; Hos. 8:7; Hag. 1:9, 10; 2:16, 17
7 [I]Lit., *Set your heart on*
8 [I]Lit., *mountain* [II]Lit., *house* [a]1Kin. 6:1 [b]Ps. 132:13, 14 [c]Hag. 2:7, 9
9 [a]Prov. 27:20; Eccl. 1:8 [b]Is. 40:7 [c]Hag. 1:4
10 [I]Lit., *from dew* [a]Deut. 28:23, 24; 1Kin. 17:1; Joel 1:18-20
11 [I]Lit., *the palms* [a]Jer. 14:2-6; Mal. 3:9, 11 [b]Deut. 28:22 [c]Hag. 2:17
12 [I]Lit., *feared before* [a]Hag. 1:1 [b]Hag. 1:14; 2:2 [c]Is. 1:19; 1Thess. 2:13 [d]Deut. 31:12, 13; Ps. 112:1; Is. 50:10
13 [I]Or, *the message* [a]Is. 44:26; Ezek. 3:17; Mal. 2:7; 3:1

⊶ **1:1** The second year of the reign of Darius I was 520 B.C. All four of Haggai's oracles were delivered during that year.

sion of the LORD to the people saying, " '[b]I am with you,' declares the LORD."

14 So the LORD stirred up the spirit of [a]Zerubbabel the son of Shealtiel, [a]governor of Judah, and the spirit of Joshua the son of Jehozadak, the high priest, and the spirit of all the [b]remnant of the people; and they came and [c]worked[4399] on the house of the LORD of hosts, their God,

15 on the twenty-fourth day of the sixth month in the second year of Darius the king.

The Builders Encouraged

2 On the twenty-first of the seventh month, the word[1697] of the LORD came by [a]Haggai the prophet[5030] saying,[559]

2 "Speak[559] now to [a]Zerubbabel the son of Shealtiel, [a]governor[6346] of Judah, and to [a]Joshua the son of Jehozadak, the high priest, and to the [b]remnant[7611] of the people[5971] saying,

3 'Who is [a]left[7604] among you who saw[7200] this [I]temple[1004] in its [b]former glory?[3519] And how do you see it now? Does it not [II]seem to you like nothing [III]in comparison?

4 'But now [Ia]take courage,[2388] Zerubbabel,' declares[5001] the LORD, 'take courage also, Joshua son of Jehozadak, the high priest,[3548] and all you people of the land[776] take courage,' declares the LORD, 'and work;[6213] for [b]I am with you,' says the LORD of hosts.[6635]

5 'As for the [Ia]promise[3772] which I [II]made you when you came out of Egypt, [III]My [b]Spirit[7307] is abiding in your midst; [c]do not fear!'[3372]

6 "For thus says the LORD of hosts, '[a]Once more [I]in a [b]little while, I am going to [c]shake[7493] the heavens[8064] and the earth,[776] the sea also and the dry land.[2724]

7 'And I will shake [a]all the nations;[1471] and [I]they will come with the [b]wealth of all nations; and I will [c]fill this house with glory,' says the LORD of hosts.

8 'The [a]silver is Mine, and the gold is Mine,' declares the LORD of hosts.

9 'The latter [a]glory of this house will be greater than the [b]former,' says the LORD of hosts, 'and in this place I shall give [c]peace,'[7965] declares the LORD of hosts."

10 On the [a]twenty-fourth of the ninth *month,* in the second year of Darius, the word of the LORD came to Haggai the prophet saying,

11 "Thus says the LORD of hosts, '[a]Ask[7592] now the priests *for* a [I]ruling:[8451]

12 'If a man[376] carries[5375] [a]holy[6942] meat[1319] in the [I]fold of his garment, and touches bread with [II]this fold, or cooked food,[5138] wine, oil,[8081] or any *other* food, will it become holy?' "[6942] And the priests answered and said,[559] "No."

13 Then Haggai said, "[a]If one who is unclean[2931] from a [I]corpse[5315] touches[5060] any of these, will *the latter* become unclean?" And the priests answered and said, "It will become unclean."

14 Then Haggai answered and said, " '[a]So is this people. And so is this nation before Me,' declares the LORD, 'and so is every work of their hands;[3027] and what they offer[7126] there is unclean.

15 'But now, do [Ia]consider from this day[3117] [II]onward: before one [b]stone was placed[7760] on another in the temple[1964] of the LORD,

16 [I]from that time *when* one came to a *grain* heap of twenty *measures,* there would be only ten; and *when* one came to the wine vat[3342] to draw fifty [II]measures, there would be *only* twenty.

17 'I smote[5221] you *and* every work of your hands with [a]blasting wind, mildew, and hail; [I]yet you *did* not *come back* to Me,' declares the LORD.

18 'Do [Ia]consider from this day [II]onward, from the [b]twenty-fourth day of the ninth *month*; from the day when the temple of the LORD was [c]founded,[3245] [I]consider:

19 'Is the seed[2233] still in the barn?

13 [b]Ps. 46:11; Is. 41:10; 43:2
14 [a]Hag. 1:1; 2:2, 21 [b]Hag. 1:12 [c]Ezra 5:2; Neh. 4:6

1 [a]Hag. 1:1
2 [a]Hag. 1:1 [b]Hag. 1:12
3 [I]Lit., *house* [II]Lit., *in your eyes* [III]Lit., *like it* [a]Ezra 3:12 [b]Hag. 2:9
4 [I]Lit., *be strong* [a]Deut. 31:23; 1Chr. 22:13; 28:20; Zech. 8:9; Eph. 6:10 [b]2Sam. 5:10; Acts 7:9
5 [I]Lit., *word* [II]Lit., *cut with* [III]Or, *while. . . was standing* [a]Ex. 19:4-6; 29:45, 46; 33:12-14; 34:8-10 [b]Neh. 9:20; Is. 63:11, 14 [c]Is. 41:10, 13; Zech. 8:13
6 [I]Lit., *it is a little* [a]Heb. 12:26 [b]Is. 10:25; 29:17 [c]Hag. 2:21
7 [I]Or, *the desire of all nations will come* [a]Dan. 2:44; Joel 3:9, 16 [b]Is. 60:4-9 [c]1Kin. 8:11; Is. 60:7
8 [a]1Chr. 29:14, 16; Is. 60:17
9 [a]Zech. 2:5 [b]Hag. 2:3 [c]Is. 9:6, 7; 66:12
10 [a]Hag. 2:20
11 [I]Lit., *law* [a]Deut. 17:8-11; Mal. 2:7
12 [I]Lit., *wing* [II]Lit., *his wing* [a]Ex. 29:37; Lev. 6:27, 29; 7:6; Ezek. 44:19; Matt. 23:19
13 [I]Lit., *soul* [a]Lev. 22:4-6; Num. 19:22
14 [a]Prov. 15:8; Is. 1:11-15
15 [I]Lit., *set your heart* [II]Or, *backward* [a]Hag. 1:5, 7; 2:18 [b]Ezra 3:10; 4:24
16 [I]Lit., *since they were* [II]Or, *troughs full*
17 [I]Or, *but what did we have in common?* [a]Deut. 28:22; 1Kin. 8:37; Amos 4:9

18 [I]Lit., *set your heart* [II]Or, *backward* [a]Deut. 32:29; Hag. 2:15 [b]Hag. 2:10 [c]Ezra 5:1, 2; Zech. 8:9, 12

Even including the vine, the fig tree,
the pomegranate, and the olive tree, it
has not borne *fruit.* Yet from this day
on I will [a]bless[1288] *you.*' "
20 Then the word of the LORD came
a second time to Haggai on the [a]twenty-
fourth *day* of the month saying,
21 "Speak to [a]Zerubbabel governor
of Judah saying, 'I am going to [b]shake
the heavens and the earth.
22 'And I will [a]overthrow[2015] the
thrones[3678] of kingdoms[4467] and destroy[8045] the [b]power[2392] of the kingdoms of the [1]nations;[1471] and I will
[c]overthrow the chariots and their riders,
and the [d]horses and their riders will go
down, [e]everyone[376] by the sword[2719] of
another.'[251]
23 'On that day,'[3117] declares the
LORD of hosts, 'I will take you, Zerubbabel, son of Shealtiel, My servant,'[5650]
declares the LORD, 'and I will make[7760]
you like a [1a]signet *ring,* for [b]I have
chosen[977] you,' " declares the LORD of
hosts.

19 [a]Ps. 128:1-6; Jer. 31:12, 14; Mal. 3:10

20 [a]Hag. 2:10

21 [a]Ezra 5:2; Hag. 1:1; Zech. 4:6-10 [b]Hag. 2:6; Heb. 12:26, 27

22 [1]Or, *Gentiles* [a]Ezek. 26:16; Zeph. 3:8 [b]Mic. 7:16 [c]Ps. 46:9; Ezek. 39:20; Mic. 5:10 [d]Amos 2:15 [e]Judg. 7:22; 2Chr. 20:23

23 [1]Or, *seal* [a]Song 8:6; Jer. 22:24 [b]Is. 42:1; 43:10

The Book of

ZECHARIAH

Zechariah and Haggai both preached to the first generation after the return to Judah from the Babylonian exile. In 536 B.C. the temple foundation was laid, but due to local opposition, the work was discontinued for sixteen years. In 520 B.C. God raised up these two prophets to stir up the nation to complete the rebuilding of the temple. Many of the economic hardships which the people had experienced since they returned were caused by the fact that, with no temple in operation, the land was still polluted from their former sins and would not produce well. Response to Zechariah and Haggai's preaching was immediate and complete. By 515 B.C. the temple was finished and in operation again. Chapters 1—8 of Zechariah relate to the years 520–518 B.C. The oracles supported the leadership of Zerubbabel, the civil leader, and Joshua, the high priest, especially in connection with the temple project. The glorious future of Jerusalem and the remnant who returned to it is also vividly depicted. Some of Zechariah's visions are filled with rich apocalyptic-type imagery. Both Zerubabbel and Joshua were anointed leaders, and in certain passages it is difficult to determine whether they are being referred to or whether it is the future Messiah. At any rate, Jesus' dual Messianic role as both king and priest finds its closest O.T. basis here. Chapters 9—14 are very different from the earlier chapters in that they deal exclusively with the future beyond Zechariah's day. The time frame for the fulfillment of individual prophecies is a disputed point among scholars, but several passages were seen by N.T. writers as being fulfilled by Jesus. These include such events as Jesus' triumphal entry into Jerusalem, His arrest, His crucifixion and His Second Coming.

A Call to Repentance

1 🔑 In the eighth month of the second year of [a]Darius, the word[1697]
of the LORD came to [b]Zechariah the
prophet,[5030] the son[1121] of Berechiah,
the son of [c]Iddo saying,[559]
2 "The LORD was very [a]an-
gry[7107,7110] with your fathers.[1]
3 "Therefore say to them, 'Thus
says[5001] the LORD of hosts,[6635] "[a]Re-
turn[7725] to Me," declares the LORD of
hosts, "that I may return to you," says
the LORD of hosts.
4 "Do not be [a]like your fathers, to
whom the [b]former prophets proclaimed,[7121] saying, 'Thus says the LORD
of hosts, "[c]Return now from your evil[7451]
ways[1870] and from your evil deeds." '
But they did [d]not listen[8085] or give
heed[7181] to Me," declares the LORD.

1 [a]Ezra 4:24; 6:15; Hag. 1:15; 2:10; Zech. 1:7; 7:1 [b]Ezra 5:1; 6:14; Zech. 7:1; Matt. 23:35; Luke 11:51 [c]Neh. 12:4, 16
2 [a]2Chr. 36:16; Jer. 44:6; Ezek. 8:18; Zech. 1:15
3 [a]Is. 31:6; 44:22; Mal. 3:7
4 [a]Ps. 78:8; 106:6, 7 [b]2Chr. 24:19; 36:15 [c]Is. 1:16-19; Jer. 4:1; Ezek. 33:11 [d]Jer. 6:17; 11:7, 8
5 [a]Lam. 5:7 [b]John 8:52
6 [a]Jer. 12:16, 17; 44:28, 29; Amos 9:10 [b]Lam. 2:17

5 "Your [a]fathers, where are they?
And the [b]prophets, do they live[2421]
forever?[5769]
6 "But did not My words[1697] and
My statutes,[2706] which I commanded[6680]
My servants[5650] the prophets, [a]overtake
your fathers? Then they repented[7725]
and said,[559] '[b]As the LORD of hosts
purposed[2161] to do[6213] to us in accordance with our ways and our deeds,
so He has dealt[6213] with us.' " ' "

Patrol of the Earth

7 On the twenty-fourth day of the
eleventh month, which is the month Shebat, in the second year of Darius, the
word of the LORD came to Zechariah
the prophet, the son of Berechiah, the
son of Iddo, as follows:
🔑 8 I saw[7200] at night, and behold, a

🔑 **1:1** See note on Hag. 1:1.

🔑 **1:8-17** The eight visions which begin here (1:8—6:8) were all intended to encourage Zerubbabel, Joshua, and the other inhabitants of Judea, as they rebuilt the temple and continued to reestablish

(continued on next page)

man[376] was riding on a [a]red[122] horse,
and he was standing among the [b]myrtle
trees which were in the ravine, with
red, sorrel, and [c]white horses behind
him.
9 Then I said, "My [a]lord,[113] what
are these?" And the [b]angel[4397] who was
speaking with me said to me, "I will
show[7200] you what these are."
10 And the man who was standing
among the myrtle trees answered and
said, "These are those whom the LORD
has sent to [Ia]patrol the earth."[776]
11 So they answered the angel of
the LORD who was [a]standing among the
myrtle trees, and said, "We have
[I]patrolled the earth, and behold, [b]all the
earth is [II]peaceful and quiet."[8252]
12 Then the angel of the LORD answered and said, "O LORD of hosts,
[a]how long wilt Thou [b]have no compassion[7355] for Jerusalem and the cities
of Judah, with which Thou hast been
[c]indignant[2194] these [d]seventy years?"
13 And the LORD answered the
[a]angel who was speaking with me with
[I]gracious[2896] words, [b]comforting words.
14 So the angel who was speaking
with me said to me, "'[a]Proclaim,[7121] saying, 'Thus says the LORD of hosts, "I
am [b]exceedingly jealous[7065,7068,1419] for
Jerusalem and Zion.
15 "But I am very [a]angry with the
nations[1471] who are [b]at ease; for while
I was only a little angry, they [Ic]furthered
the disaster."[7451]
16 'Therefore, thus says the LORD,
"I will [a]return[7725] to Jerusalem with
compassion;[7356] My [b]house[1004] will be
built in it," declares the LORD of hosts,
"and a measuring [c]line will be stretched
over Jerusalem." '
17 "Again, proclaim, saying, 'Thus
says the LORD of hosts, "My [a]cities will

8 [a]Zech. 6:2; Rev. 6:4 [b]Neh. 8:15; Is. 41:19; 55:13; Zech. 1:10, 11 [c]Zech. 6:3; Rev. 6:2
9 [a]Zech. 1:19; 4:4, 5, 13; 6:4 [b]Zech. 2:3; 5:5
10 [I]Lit., *walk about through* [a]Job 1:7; Zech. 1:11; 4:10; 6:5-8
11 [I]Lit., *walked about through* [II]Lit., *sitting* [a]Zech. 1:8, 10 [b]Is. 14:7
12 [a]Ps. 74:10; Jer. 12:4; Hab. 1:2 [b]Ps. 102:13; Jer. 30:18 [c]Ps. 102:10; Jer. 15:17 [d]Jer. 25:11; 29:10; Dan. 9:2; Zech. 7:5
13 [I]Lit., *good* [a]Zech. 1:9; 4:1 [b]Is. 40:1, 2; 57:18
14 [a]Is. 40:2, 6; Zech. 1:17 [b]Zech. 8:2
15 [I]Lit., *helped for evil* [a]Zech. 1:2 [b]Ps. 123:4; Jer. 48:11 [c]Amos 1:11
16 [a]Is. 54:8-10; Zech. 2:10, 11 [b]Ezra 6:14, 15; Zech. 4:9 [c]Jer. 31:39; Zech. 2:2, 4
17 [a]Is. 44:26; 61:4 [b]Is. 51:3 [c]Zech. 2:12
18 [I]Ch. 2:1 in Heb.
19 [a]1Kin. 22:11; Ps. 75:4, 5; Amos 6:13 mg.
20 [a]Is. 44:12; 54:16
21 [a]Zech. 1:19 [b]Ps. 75:10

1 [I]Ch. 2:5 in Heb. [a]Jer. 31:39; Ezek. 40:3; 47:3; Zech. 1:16
2 [a]Jer. 31:39; Ezek. 40:3; Rev. 21:15-17
3 [a]Zech. 1:9

again overflow with prosperity,[2896] and
the LORD will again [b]comfort[5162] Zion and
again [c]choose[977] Jerusalem." ' "
18 [I]Then I lifted up[5375] my eyes and
looked, and behold, *there were* four
horns.
19 So I said to the angel who was
speaking with me, "What are these?"
And he answered me, "These are the
[a]horns which have scattered Judah, Israel, and Jerusalem."
20 Then the LORD showed me four
[a]craftsmen.
21 And I said, "What are these coming to do?" And he said, "These are
the [a]horns which have scattered Judah,
so that no man lifts up[5375] his head;[7218]
but these *craftsmen* have come to
terrify[2729] them, to [b]throw down the
horns of the nations[1471] who have lifted
up *their* horns against the land[776] of
Judah in order to scatter it."

God's Favor to Zion

2 [I]Then I lifted up[5375] my eyes and
looked,[7200] and behold, *there was* a
man[376] with a [a]measuring line[2256] in his
hand.[3027]
2 So I said,[559] "Where are you going?" And he said to me, "To [a]measure
Jerusalem, to see[7200] how wide it is and
how long it is."
3 And behold, the [a]angel[4397] who
was speaking with me was going out,
and another angel was coming out to
meet him,
4 and said to him, "Run, speak[1696]
to that [a]young man, saying,[559] '[b]Jerusa-
lem will be inhabited [Ic]without walls, be-

4 [I]Lit., like *unwalled villages;* or, like *open country* [a]Jer. 1:6; Dan. 1:4; 1Tim. 4:12 [b]Zech. 1:17; 8:4 [c]Ezek. 38:11

(continued from previous page)
their national life. This first vision and the last (6:1-8) make the same point and, thus, frame the whole series of visions. The riders patrolled the earth and found it to be at rest. After a decade and a half of opposition from their enemies and hard times economically, the fact that the earth was at peace meant that the temple project could now proceed and that prosperity would return (1:16,17). These two visions also appear to be faintly in the background of Rev. 6:2-8, but there the point is war and famine, not peace and prosperity.

cause of the [d]multitude of men[120] and
cattle within it.
5 'For I,' declares[5001] the LORD, 'will
be a [a]wall of fire [I]around her, and I will
be the [b]glory[3519] in her midst.' "
6 "[I]Ho there! [a]Flee from the land[776]
of the north," declares the LORD, "for
I have [b]dispersed you as the four
winds[7307] of the heavens,"[8064] declares
the LORD.
7 "Ho, Zion! [a]Escape, you who are
living with the daughter of Babylon."
8 For thus says the LORD of
hosts,[6635] "After [Ia]glory He has sent me
against the nations[1471] which plunder
you, for he who touches[5060] you, touches
the [IIb]apple of His eye.
9 "For behold, I will [a]wave[5130] My
hand over them, so that they will be
[b]plunder for their slaves.[5647] Then you
will know[3045] that the LORD of hosts has
sent Me.
10 "[a]Sing for joy and be glad, O
daughter of Zion; for behold I am coming
and I will [b]dwell[7931] in your midst," declares the LORD.
11 "And [a]many nations will join
themselves to the LORD in that day and
will become My people.[5971] Then I will
[b]dwell in your midst, and you will
[c]know that the LORD of hosts has sent
Me to you.
12 "And the LORD will [Ia]possess[5157]
Judah as His portion in the holy[6944]
land,[127] and will again [b]choose[977] Jerusalem.
13 "[Ia]Be silent, all flesh,[1319] before
the LORD; for He is [b]aroused from His
holy habitation."

Joshua, the High Priest

3 Then he showed[7200] me [a]Joshua the
high priest[3548] standing before the
angel[4397] of the LORD, and [Ib]Satan[7854]
standing at his right hand to accuse him.
2 And the LORD said[559] to Satan,
"[a]The LORD rebuke[1605] you, Satan! Indeed, the LORD who has [b]chosen[977] Jerusalem rebuke you! Is this not a [c]brand
plucked[5337] from the fire?"
3 Now Joshua was clothed with
[a]filthy garments and standing before the
angel.
4 And he spoke and said[559] to those
who were standing before him saying,[559]
"[a]Remove[5493] the filthy garments from
him." Again he said to him, "See,[7200]
I have [b]taken[5674] your iniquity[5771]
away[5674] from you and [I]will [c]clothe you
with festal robes."
5 Then I said, "Let them put[7760] a
clean[2889] [a]turban[6797] on his head."[7218] So
they put a clean turban on his head and
clothed him with garments, while the
angel of the LORD was standing by.
6 And the angel of the LORD
admonished[5749] Joshua saying,
7 "Thus says the LORD of hosts,[6635]
'If you will [a]walk in My ways,[1870] and
if you will perform[8104] My service,[4931]
then you will also [b]govern[1777] My
house[1004] and also have charge of My
[c]courts, and I will grant you [I]free access
among these who are standing *here*.

The Branch

8 'Now listen, Joshua the high
priest, you and your friends[7453] who are
sitting in front of you—indeed they are
men[582] who are a [a]symbol,[4159] for
behold, I am going to bring in My
servant[5650] the [Ib]Branch.
9 'For behold, the stone that I have
set before Joshua; on one stone are
[a]seven eyes. Behold, I will engrave an
inscription[6603] on it,' declares[5001] the
LORD of hosts, 'and I will [b]remove the
iniquity of that land[776] in one day.[3117]
10 'In that day,' declares the LORD
of hosts, 'every one[376] of you will
invite[7121] his neighbor[7453] to *sit* under
his [a]vine and under *his* fig tree.' "

The Golden Lampstand and Olive Trees

4 Then [a]the angel[4397] who was speaking with me returned,[7725] and
[b]roused me as a man[376] who is awakened
from his sleep.

---

4 [d]Is. 49:20; Jer. 30:19; 33:22
5 [I]Lit., *to her* [a]Is. 4:5; 26:1; 60:18 [b]Hag. 2:9; Zech. 2:10, 11
6 [I]Lit., *Ho! ho!* [a]Jer. 3:18 [b]Jer. 31:10; Ezek. 11:16
7 [a]Is. 48:20; Jer. 51:6
8 [I]Or, *the glory* [II]Lit., *pupil* [a]Is. 60:7-9 [b]Deut. 32:10; Ps. 17:8
9 [a]Is. 19:16 [b]Is. 14:2
10 [a]Is. 65:18, 19; Zech. 9:9 [b]Zech. 2:5; 8:3
11 [a]Mic. 4:2 [b]Zech. 2:5, 10 [c]Zech. 2:9
12 [I]Or, *inherit* [a]Deut. 32:9; Ps. 33:12; Jer. 10:16 [b]2Chr. 6:6; Ps. 132:13, 14; Zech. 1:17
13 [I]Lit., *Hush* [a]Hab. 2:20; Zeph. 1:7 [b]Ps. 78:65; Is. 51:9

1 [I]Or, the *Adversary* or *Accuser* [a]Ezra 5:2; Hag. 1:1; Zech. 6:11 [b]1Chr. 21:1; Job 1:6; Ps. 109:6; Rev. 12:10
2 [a]Mark 9:25; Jude 9 [b]Zech. 2:12 [c]Amos 4:11; Jude 23
3 [a]Ezra 9:15; Is. 4:4; 64:6
4 [I]Lit., *to clothe* [a]Is. 43:25; Ezek. 36:25 [b]Mic. 7:18, 19; Zech. 3:9 [c]Is. 52:1; 61:10
5 [a]Job 29:14; Is. 3:23
7 [I]Lit., *goings* [a]1Kin. 3:14 [b]Deut. 17:9, 12 [c]Is. 62:9
8 [I]Lit., *Sprout* [a]Is. 8:18; 20:3; Ezek. 12:11 [b]Is. 11:1; 53:2; Jer. 23:5; 33:15; Zech. 6:12
9 [a]Zech. 4:10 [b]Jer. 31:34; 50:20; Zech. 3:4
10 [a]1Kin. 4:25; Is. 36:16; Mic. 4:4

1 [a]Zech. 1:9 [b]1Kin. 19:5-7; Jer. 31:26

2 And he said[559] to me, "[a]What do
you see?"[7200] And I said, "I see,[7200] and
behold, a [b]lampstand all of gold with its
bowl on the top[7218] of it, and its [c]seven
lamps[5216] on it with seven spouts belonging to each of the lamps which are on
the top of it;
3 also [a]two olive trees by it, one
on the right side of the bowl and the
other on its left side."
4 Then I answered and said[559] to
the angel who was speaking with me
saying,[559] "What are these, [a]my
lord?"[113]
5 So [a]the angel who was speaking
with me answered and said to me, "[b]Do
you not know[3045] what these are?" And
I said, "No, my lord."
6 Then he answered and [I]said to me,
"This is the word[1697] of the LORD to
[a]Zerubbabel saying, '[b]Not by might[2428]
nor by power, but by My [c]Spirit,'[7307]
says the LORD of hosts.[6635]
7 'What are you, O great [a]mountain?
Before Zerubbabel *you will become* a
plain; and he will bring forth the top
stone[7222] with [b]shouts of "Grace,[2580]
grace to it!"'"
8 Also the word of the LORD came
to me saying,
9 "The hands[3027] of Zerubbabel have
[a]laid the foundation of this house,[1004]
and his hands will [b]finish[1214] *it.* Then
you will know that the LORD of hosts
has sent me to [I]you.
10 "For who has despised the
day[3117] of [a]small things? [I]But these
[b]seven will be glad when they see[7200]
the [IIc]plumb line[68] in the hand of Zerubbabel—*these are* the [d]eyes of the LORD
which [e]range to and fro throughout the
earth."[776]
11 Then I answered and said to him,
"What are these [a]two olive trees on the
right of the lampstand and on its left?"
12 And I answered the second time
and said to him, "What are the two olive
[I]branches which are beside the two
golden pipes, which empty the golden
oil from themselves?"
13 So he answered me saying,[559]
"[a]Do you not know what these are?"
And I said, "No, [b]my lord."
14 Then he said, "These are the
two [Ia]anointed[3323] ones,[1121] who are
[b]standing by the [c]Lord[113] of the whole
earth."

The Flying Scroll

5 Then I lifted up[5375] my eyes again
and looked,[7200] and behold, *there
was* a flying [a]scroll.[4039]
2 And he said[559] to me, "[a]What do
you see?"[7200] And I answered,[559] "I see
a flying scroll; its length is twenty
[I]cubits and its width ten cubits."
3 Then he said to me, "This is the
[a]curse[423] that is going forth over the
face of the whole [I]land;[776] surely everyone who [b]steals will be purged away
according to [II]the writing on one side,
and everyone who [c]swears[7650] will be
purged away according to [II]the writing
on the other side.
4 "I will [a]make it go forth,"
declares[5001] the LORD of hosts,[6635] "and
it will [b]enter the house[1004] of the
[c]thief and the house of the one who
swears falsely[8267] by My name; and it
will spend the night within that house
and [d]consume[3615] it with its timber and
stones."
5 Then [a]the angel[4397] who was
speaking with me went out, and said
to me, "Lift up[5375] now your eyes, and
see[7200] what this is, going forth."
6 And I said, "What is it?" And he
said, "This is the [Ia]ephah going forth."
Again he said, "This is their [II]appearance
in all the [III]land
7 (and behold, a lead cover was lifted
up); and this is a woman[802] sitting inside
the ephah."
8 Then he said, "This is [a]Wicked-
ness!"[7564] And he threw her down into

2 [a]Jer. 1:13; Zech. 5:2 [b]Ex. 25:31, 37; Jer. 52:19 [c]Rev. 4:5
3 [a]Zech. 4:11; Rev. 11:4
4 [a]Zech. 1:9; 4:5, 13; 6:4
5 [a]Zech. 1:9; 4:1 [b]Zech. 4:13
6 [I]Lit., *said to me, saying* [a]Ezra 5:2; Hag. 2:4, 5 [b]Is. 11:2-4; 30:1; Hos. 1:7 [c]2Chr. 32:7, 8; Eph. 6:17
7 [a]Ps. 114:4, 6; Is. 40:4; Jer. 51:25; Nah. 1:5; Zech. 14:4, 5 [b]Ezra 3:10, 11; Ps. 84:11
9 [I]Lit., *you* (plural) [a]Ezra 3:8-10; 5:16; Hag. 2:18 [b]Ezra 6:14, 15; Zech. 6:12, 13
10 [I]Or, *But they will rejoice when they see . . . Zerubbabel. These seven are the eyes of the Lord* [II]Lit., *plummet stone* [a]Neh. 4:2-4; Amos 7:2, 5; Hag. 2:3 [b]Zech. 3:9; Rev. 8:2 [c]Amos 7:7, 8 [d]2Chr. 16:9; Prov. 15:3; Jer. 16:17 [e]Zech. 1:10; Rev. 5:6
11 [a]Zech. 4:3; Rev. 11:4
12 [I]Or, *clusters*
13 [a]Zech. 4:5 [b]Zech. 4:4, 5
14 [I]Lit., *sons of fresh oil* [a]Ex. 29:7; 40:15; 1Sam. 16:1, 12, 13; Is. 61:1-3; Dan. 9:24-26 [b]Zech. 3:1-7 [c]Mic. 4:13

1 [a]Jer. 36:2; Ezek. 2:9; Rev. 5:1
2 [I]I.e., One cubit equals approx. 18 in. [a]Zech. 4:2
3 [I]Or, *earth* [II]Lit., *it* [a]Is. 24:6; 43:28; Jer. 26:6 [b]Ex. 20:15; Lev. 19:11; Mal. 3:8, 9 [c]Lev. 19:12; Is. 48:1; Jer. 5:2; Zech. 5:4
4 [a]Mal. 3:5 [b]Hos. 4:2, 3 [c]Jer. 2:26 [d]Lev. 14:34, 35; Job 18:15
5 [a]Zech. 1:9
6 [I]I.e., Approx. one bu. [II]Lit., *eye;* some ancient versions read *iniquity* [III]Or, *earth* [a]Lev. 19:36; Amos 8:5
8 [a]Hos. 12:7; Amos 8:5; Mic. 6:11

4:14 See note on Zech. 6:9-15.

the middle of the ephah and cast the lead weight on its [I]opening.[6310]

9 Then I lifted up my eyes and looked, and there two women were coming out with the wind[7307] in their wings; and they had wings like the wings of a [a]stork, and they lifted up the ephah between the earth and the heavens.[8064]

10 And I said to the angel who was speaking with me, "Where are they taking the ephah?"

11 Then he said to me, "To build a [I]temple for her in the land of [a]Shinar; and when it is prepared,[3559] she will be set there on her own pedestal."

The Four Chariots

6 🔑 Now I lifted up[5375] my eyes again and looked,[7200] and behold, [a]four chariots were coming forth from between the two mountains; and the mountains *were* bronze mountains.

2 With the first chariot *were* [a]red[122] horses, with the second chariot [b]black horses,

3 with the third chariot [a]white horses, and with the fourth chariot strong [b]dappled horses.

4 Then I spoke and said[559] to the angel[4397] who was speaking with me, "[a]What are these, my lord?"[113]

5 And the angel answered and said to me, "These are the [a]four spirits[7307] of heaven,[8064] going forth after standing before the Lord[113] of all the earth,[776]

6 with one of which the black horses are going forth to the [a]north country;[776] and the white ones go forth after them, while the dappled ones go forth to the [b]south country.

7 "When the strong ones went out, they [I]were eager to go to [IIa]patrol the earth." And He said, "Go, [II]patrol the earth." So they [III]patrolled the earth.

8 Then He cried[2199] out to me and spoke[1696] to me saying,[559] "See,[7200] those who are going to the land of the north have [Ia]appeased My wrath in the land of the north."

🔑 9 The [a]word of the LORD also came to me saying,

10 "[a]Take *an offering* from the exiles,[1473] from Heldai, Tobijah, and Jedaiah; and you go the same day[3117] and enter the house[1004] of Josiah the son of Zephaniah, where they have arrived from Babylon.

The Symbolic Crowns

11 "And take silver and gold, make[6213] an *ornate* [a]crown, and set[7760] *it* on the head[7218] of [b]Joshua the son of Jehozadak, the high priest.[3548]

12 "Then say to him, 'Thus says the LORD of hosts,[6635] "Behold, a man[376] whose name is [Ia]Branch, for He will [IIb]branch out from where He is; and He will [c]build the temple[1964] of the LORD.

13 "Yes, it is He who will build the temple of the LORD, and He who will [a]bear[5375] the honor[1935] and sit and [b]rule[4910] on His throne.[3678] Thus, He will be a [c]priest on His throne, and the

8 [I]Lit., *mouth*
9 [a]Lev. 11:13, 19; Ps. 104:17; Jer. 8:7
11 [I]Lit., *house* [a]Gen. 10:10; 11:2; 14:1; Is. 11:11; Dan. 1:2
1 [a]Dan. 7:3; 8:22; Zech. 1:18; 6:5
2 [a]Zech. 1:8; Rev. 6:4 [b]Rev. 6:5
3 [a]Rev. 6:2 [b]Rev. 6:8
4 [a]Zech. 1:9
5 [a]Jer. 49:36; Ezek. 37:9; Dan. 7:2; 11:4; Matt. 24:31; Rev. 7:1
6 [a]Jer. 1:14, 15; 4:6; 6:1; 25:9; 46:10; Ezek. 1:4 [b]Is. 43:6; Dan. 11:5
7 [I]Lit., *sought to go* [II]Lit., *walk about through* [III]Lit., *walked about through* [a]Zech. 1:10
8 [I]Lit., *caused My spirit to rest in* [a]Ezek. 5:13; 24:13; Zech. 1:15
9 [a]Zech. 1:1; 7:1; 8:1
10 [a]Ezra 7:14-16; 8:26-30; Jer. 28:6
11 [a]2Sam. 12:30; Ps. 21:3; Song 3:11 [b]Ezra 3:2; Hag. 1:1; Zech. 3:1
12 [I]Lit., *Sprout* [II]Lit., *sprout up* [a]Is. 4:2; 11:1; Jer. 23:5; 33:15; Zech. 3:8 [b]Is. 53:2 [c]Ezra 3:8, 10; Amos 9:11; Zech. 4:6-9
13 [a]Is. 9:6; 11:10; 22:24; 49:5, 6 [b]Is. 9:7 [c]Ps. 110:1, 4

🔑 **6:1-8** See note on Zech. 1:8-17.

🔑 **6:9-15** This passage seems to merge a discussion of Joshua, the high priest, with that about the future Messiah. It begins by referring to Joshua but then talks of one who sits on a throne with a priest beside him. Joshua and Zerubbabel were both anointed leaders (Zech. 4:14), so it is not out of the question that Joshua could sit on a throne. Whatever the precise meaning for the late sixth century B.C., the Qumran community, which produced the Dead Sea Scrolls, anticipated two messiahs, one a royal figure and the other a priest. When these passages in Zechariah are combined with the N.T. interpretation of Ps. 110:1,4, an O.T. basis for the dual Messiahship of Jesus is also established. Outside the Book of Hebrews, N.T. writers interpret Ps. 110:1 as looking forward to Jesus' sitting on the throne as a royal leader (Mt. 22:44; Mk. 12:36; Lk. 20:42,43; Acts 2:34,35). Hebrews brings Ps. 110:4 into the picture to show that the person on the throne was also to be a priest (Heb. 8:1; 10:12). The closest O.T. parallel to this dual Messianic function is found in Zechariah, where the two roles were assumed by two different persons—Zerubbabel, the governor, and Joshua, the priest.

counsel[6098] of peace[7965] will be between the two [I]offices." '

14 "Now the [a]crown will become a reminder[2146] in the temple of the LORD to Helem, Tobijah, Jedaiah, and [I]Hen the son of Zephaniah.

15 "And [a]those who are far off will come and [I]build the temple of the LORD." Then you will [b]know[3045] that the LORD of hosts has sent me to you. And it will take place, if you completely [c]obey[8085] the LORD your God.[430]

Hearts like Flint

7 Then it came about in the fourth year of King[4428] Darius, that the word[1697] of the LORD came to Zechariah on the fourth *day* of the ninth month, *which is* [a]Chislev.

2 Now *the town of* Bethel[1004,410] had sent Sharezer and Regemmelech and [I]their men[582] to [IIa]seek the favor of the LORD,

3 speaking[559] to the [a]priests[3548] who belong to the house of the LORD of hosts,[6635] and to the prophets[5030] saying,[559] "Shall I weep in the [b]fifth month [I]and abstain,[5144] as I have done[6213] these many years?"

4 Then the word of the LORD of hosts came to me saying,

5 "Say[559] to all the people[5971] of the land[776] and to the priests, 'When you fasted and mourned in the fifth and seventh months [I]these [a]seventy years, was it actually for [b]Me that you fasted?

6 'And when you eat and drink, [I]do you not eat for yourselves and do you not drink for yourselves?

7 'Are not *these* the words which the LORD [a]proclaimed[7121] by the former prophets, when Jerusalem was inhabited and [Ib]prosperous with its cities around it, and the [IIc]Negev and the [III]foothills were inhabited?' "

8 Then the word of the LORD came to Zechariah saying,

9 "Thus has the LORD of hosts said, '[a]Dispense[8199] true[571] justice,[4941] and practice[6213] [b]kindness[2617] and compassion[7356] each[376] to his brother;[251]

10 and [a]do not oppress the widow or the [I]orphan, the [II]stranger[1616] or the poor; and do [b]not devise[2803] evil[7451] in your hearts[3824] against one another.'

11 "But they [a]refused[3985] to pay attention,[7181] and [Ib]turned a stubborn[5637] shoulder and [IIc]stopped[3513] their ears[241] from hearing.[8085]

12 "And they made[7760] their [a]hearts[3820] *like* [Ib]flint[8068] [II]so that they could not hear the law[8451] and the [c]words which the LORD of hosts had sent by His Spirit[7307] through the [d]former prophets; therefore great [e]wrath[7110] came from the LORD of hosts.

13 "And it came about that just as [a]He called[7121] and they would not listen,[8085] so [b]they called and I would not listen,"[8085] says the LORD of hosts;

14 "but I [Ia]scattered them with a [b]storm wind among all the nations[1471] whom they have not known.[3045] Thus the land is [c]desolated[8074] behind them, [II]so that [d]no one went back[7725] and forth,[5674] for they [e]made[7760] the pleasant land desolate."[8047]

The Coming Peace and Prosperity of Zion

8 Then the word[1697] of the LORD of hosts[6635] came saying,[559]

2 "Thus says the LORD of hosts, 'I am [a]exceedingly[7065] jealous[7068] for Zion, yes, with great wrath[2534] I am jealous for her.'

3 "Thus says the LORD, 'I will return[7725] to Zion and will [a]dwell[7931] in the midst of Jerusalem. Then Jerusalem will be called[7121] the City of [b]Truth,[571] and the mountain of the LORD of hosts *will be called* the Holy[6944] Mountain.'

4 "Thus says the LORD of hosts, '[a]Old men[2205] and old women will again sit in the [I]streets of Jerusalem, each man[376] with his staff in his hand[3027] because of [II]age.[3117]

5 'And the [I]streets of the city will

13 [I]Lit., *of them*
14 [I]I.e., Josiah [a]Zech. 6:11
15 [I]Lit., *build in* [a]Is. 56:6-8; 60:10 [b]Zech. 2:9-11; 4:9 [c]Is. 58:10-14; Jer. 7:23; Zech. 3:7

1 [a]Neh. 1:1
2 [I]Lit., *his* [II]Lit., *soften the face of* [a]1Kin. 13:6; Jer. 26:19; Zech. 8:21
3 [I]Lit., *abstaining; or, dedicating myself* [a]Ezra 3:10-12 [b]Zech. 8:19
5 [I]Lit., *and these* [a]Zech. 1:12 [b]Is. 1:11, 12; 58:5
6 [I]Lit., *is it not you who eat and you who drink*
7 [I]Or, *at ease* [II]I.e., South country [III]Heb., *Shephelah* [a]Is. 1:16-20; Jer. 7:5, 23; Zech. 1:4 [b]Jer. 22:21 [c]Jer. 13:19; 32:44
9 [a]Ezek. 18:8; 45:9; Zech. 8:16 [b]2Sam. 9:7; Job 6:14; Mic. 6:8
10 [I]Or, *fatherless* [II]Or, *resident alien* [a]Ex. 22:22; Ps. 72:4; Jer. 7:6 [b]Ps. 21:11; Mic. 2:1; Zech. 8:17
11 [I]Lit., *gave* [II]Lit., *made heavy* [a]Jer. 5:3; 8:5; 11:10 [b]Jer. 7:26; 17:23 [c]Ps. 58:4; Jer. 5:21
12 [I]Lit., *corundum* [II]Lit., *from hearing* [a]2Chr. 36:13; Ezek. 2:4; 3:7-9 [b]Jer. 17:1; Ezek. 3:9 [c]Zech. 7:7 [d]Neh. 9:30 [e]2Chr. 36:16; Dan. 9:11, 12
13 [a]Jer. 11:10, 14; 14:12 [b]Prov. 1:24-28; Is. 1:15
14 [I]Lit., *stormed them away upon all* [II]Lit., *from passing and from returning* [a]Deut. 4:27; 28:64 [b]Jer. 23:19 [c]Jer. 44:6 [d]Is. 60:15 [e]Jer. 12:10

2 [a]Zech. 1:14
3 [a]Zech. 2:10, 11 [b]Zech. 8:16, 19
4 [I]Or, *squares* [II]Lit., *the multitude of days* [a]Is. 65:20
5 [I]Or, *squares*

be filled with [a]boys and girls playing in
its [I]streets.'
6 "Thus says[5001] the LORD of hosts,
'If it is [Ia]too difficult[6381] in the sight of
the remnant[7611] of this people[5971] in
those days,[3117] will it also be [Ib]too difficult in My sight?' declares the LORD of
hosts.
7 "Thus says the LORD of hosts,
'Behold, I am going to save[3467] My people from the land[776] of the [Ia]east and
from the land of the [II]west;
8 and I will [a]bring them *back,* and
they will [b]live in the midst of Jerusalem,
and they will be [c]My people and I will
be their God[430] in [I]truth and righteousness.'
9 "Thus says the LORD of hosts,
'Let your hands[3027] be [a]strong,[2388] you
who are listening[8085] in these days to
these words from the mouth of the
[b]prophets,[5030] *those* who *spoke* in
the day that the foundation[3245] of the
house[1004] of the LORD of hosts was laid,
to the end that the temple[1964] might be
built.
10 'For before those days there
was[1961] [a]no wage for man[120] or any wage
for animal; and for him who went out
or came in there was no [Ib]peace[7965] because of [II]his enemies, and I [c]set all men
one[376] against another.[7453]
11 'But now I will [a]not [I]treat the
remnant[7611] of this people as in the former days,' declares the LORD of hosts.
12 'For *there will be* [a]peace[7965] for
the seed:[2233] the vine will yield its
fruit, the land[776] will yield its produce,
and the heavens[8064] will give their
[b]dew; and I will cause the remnant of
this people to inherit[5157] [c]all these *things.*
13 'And it will come about that just
as you were a [a]curse[7045] among the nations,[1471] O house of Judah and house
of Israel, so I will save[3467] you that you
may become a [b]blessing.[1293] Do not
fear;[3372] let your [c]hands be strong.'
14 "For thus says the LORD of
hosts, 'Just as I [a]purposed[2161] to do
harm[7489] to you when your fathers[1] provoked Me to wrath,' says the LORD of
hosts, 'and I have not [b]relented,[5162]
15 so I have again purposed in these
days to [a]do good[3190] to Jerusalem and
to the house of Judah. [b]Do not fear!
16 'These are the things which you
should do:[6213] speak[1696] the [a]truth to one
another; [b]judge[8199] with truth and judgment[4941] for peace in your [I]gates.
17 'Also let none of you [a]devise[2903]
evil[7451] in your heart[3824] against another,
and do not love[157] [Ib]perjury;[8267,7621] for
all these are what I [c]hate,'[8130] declares
the LORD."
18 Then the word of the LORD of
hosts came to me saying,
19 "Thus says the LORD of hosts,
'The fast of the [a]fourth, the fast of the
[b]fifth, the fast of the [c]seventh, and
the fast of the [d]tenth *months* will become [e]joy, gladness, and [I]cheerful[2896]
feasts[4150] for the house of Judah; so
[f]love[157] truth and peace.'
20 "Thus says the LORD of hosts,
'*It will* yet *be* that [a]peoples will come,
even the inhabitants of many cities.
21 'And the inhabitants of one will
go to another saying, "Let us go at once
to [a]entreat the favor of the LORD, and
to seek the LORD of hosts; [I]I will also
go."
22 'So [a]many peoples and mighty
nations[1471] will come to seek the LORD
of hosts in Jerusalem and to [b]entreat
the favor of the LORD.'
23 "Thus says the LORD of hosts,
'In those days[3117] ten men[582] from all
the [I]nations will [IIa]grasp[2388] the [III]gar-
ment of a Jew[376] saying, "Let us go with
you, for we have heard[8085] that God is
with you." ' "

Prophecies against Neighboring Nations

9 The [I]burden[4853] of the word[1697] of
the LORD is against the land[776] of
Hadrach, with [a]Damascus as its resting
place (for the eyes of men,[120] especially

5 [I]Or, *squares* [a]Jer. 30:19, 20; 31:12, 13
6 [I]Or, *wonderful* [a]Ps. 118:23; 126:1-3 [b]Jer. 32:17, 27
7 [I]Lit., *rising* [II]Lit., *setting sun* [a]Ps. 107:3; Is. 11:11; 27:12, 13; 43:5
8 [I]Or, *faithfulness* [a]Zeph. 3:20; Zech. 10:10 [b]Jer. 3:17; Ezek. 37:25 [c]Ezek. 11:20; 36:28; Zech. 2:11
9 [a]1Chr. 22:13; Is. 35:4; Hag. 2:4 [b]Ezra 5:1; 6:14
10 [I]Or, *safety* [II]Lit., *the adversary* [a]Hag. 2:15-19 [b]2Chr. 15:5 [c]Is. 19:2; Amos 3:6; 9:4
11 [I]Lit., *be to the* [a]Ps. 103:9; Is. 12:1; Hag. 2:19
12 [a]Lev. 26:3-6 [b]Gen. 27:28; Deut. 33:13, 28; Hos. 13:3 [c]Is. 61:7; Obad. 17
13 [a]Jer. 29:18; Dan. 9:11 [b]Ps. 72:17; Is. 19:24, 25; Ezek. 34:26; Zech. 14:11 [c]Zech. 8:9
14 [a]Jer. 31:28 [b]Jer. 4:28; Ezek. 24:14
15 [a]Jer. 29:11; Mic. 7:18-20 [b]Zech. 8:13
16 [I]I.e., the place where court was held [a]Ps. 15:2; Prov. 12:17-19; Zech. 8:3; Eph. 4:25 [b]Is. 9:7; 11:4, 5; Zech. 7:9
17 [I]Lit., *false oath* [a]Prov. 3:29; Jer. 4:14; Zech. 7:10 [b]Zech. 5:4; Mal. 3:5 [c]Prov. 6:16-19; Hab. 1:13
19 [I]Or, *goodly* [a]2Kin. 25:3, 4; Jer. 39:2 [b]Zech. 7:3, 5 [c]2Kin. 25:25; Zech. 7:5 [d]Jer. 52:4 [e]Ps. 30:11; Is. 12:1 [f]Zech. 8:16; Luke 1:74, 75
20 [a]Ps. 117:1; Jer. 16:19; Mic. 4:2, 3; Zech. 2:11; 14:16

21 [I]Or, *let me go too* [a]Zech. 7:2 **22** [a]Is. 2:2, 3; 25:7; 49:6, 22, 23; 60:3-12 [b]Zech. 8:21 **23** [I]Lit., *languages of the nations* [II]Lit., *grasp, and they will grasp* [III]Or, *corner of the garment* [a]Is. 45:14, 24; 60:14 **1** [I]Or, *oracle* [a]Is. 17:1; Jer. 49:23-27; Amos 1:3-5

of all the tribes[7626] of Israel, are toward the LORD),
2 And [a]Hamath also, which
borders on it;
[b]Tyre and [c]Sidon, [I]though
[II]they are [b]very wise.
3 For Tyre built herself a
[a]fortress
And [b]piled up silver like dust,[6083]
And [c]gold like the mire of the
streets.
4 Behold, the Lord[136] will
[a]dispossess[3423] her
And cast[5221] her wealth[2428] into
the sea;
And she will be [b]consumed with
fire.
5 Ashkelon will see[7200] *it* and be
afraid.[3372]
Gaza too will writhe in great
pain;[2342]
Also Ekron, for her expectation
has been confounded.
Moreover, the king will perish[6]
from Gaza,
And Ashkelon will not be
inhabited.
6 And a [I]mongrel race will dwell
in [a]Ashdod,
And I will cut off[3772] the pride
of the Philistines.
7 And I will remove[5493] their
blood[1818] from their
mouth,[6310]
And their detestable things[8251]
from between their teeth.
Then they also will be a
remnant[7604] for our God,[430]
And be like a [I]clan[441] in Judah,
And Ekron like a Jebusite.
8 But I will camp around My
house[1004] [I]because of an
army,
Because of [a]him who passes
by[5674] and returns;[7725]
And [b]no oppressor will pass[5674]
over them anymore,
For now I have seen[7200] with
My eyes.

9 [a]Rejoice greatly, O daughter of
Zion!
Shout[7321] *in triumph,* O daughter
of Jerusalem!
Behold, your [b]king[4428] is coming
to you;
He is [Ic]just[6662] and [d]endowed
with salvation,
[e]Humble, and mounted on a
donkey,
Even on a [f]colt, the [II]foal[1121] of
a donkey.
10 And I will [a]cut off[3772] the chariot
from Ephraim,
And the [b]horse from Jerusalem;
And the [c]bow of war will be cut
off.
And He will speak[1696] [d]peace[7965]
to the nations;[1471]
And His [e]dominion[4915] will be
from sea to sea,
And from the [I]River to the ends
of the earth.[776]

Deliverance of Judah and Ephraim

11 As for you also, because of the
[a]blood of *My* covenant[1285]
with you,
I have set your [b]prisoners free
from the [I]waterless pit.[963]
12 Return[7725] to the [Ia]stronghold,
O prisoners [II]who have the
[b]hope;
This very day I am declaring[5046]
that I will restore[7725] [c]double
to you.
13 For I will [a]bend Judah [I]as My
bow,
I will fill the bow with Ephraim.
And I will stir up your sons,[1121]
O Zion, against your sons,
O [b]Greece;
And I will make[7760] you like a
[c]warrior's sword.[2719]
14 Then the LORD will appear[7200]
[a]over them,
And His [b]arrow will go forth like
lightning;

2 [I]Or, *because* [II]I.e., they think they are [a]Jer. 49:23 [b]Ezek. 28:2-5, 12 [c]Ezek. 28:21
3 [a]Josh. 19:29; 2Sam. 24:7 [b]Job 27:16; Ezek. 27:33; 28:4, 5 [c]1Kin. 10:21, 27
4 [a]Ezek. 26:3-5 [b]Ezek. 28:18
6 [I]Lit., *bastard will* [a]Amos 1:8; Zeph. 2:4
7 [I]Or, *chief*
8 [I]Or, *as a guard, so that none will go back and forth* [a]Is. 52:1 [b]Is. 54:14; 60:18
9 [I]Or, *vindicated and victorious* [II]Lit., *son of a female donkey* [a]Zeph. 3:14, 15; Zech. 2:10 [b]Ps. 110:1; Is. 9:6, 7; Jer. 23:5, 6; Matt. 21:5; John 12:15 [c]Zeph. 3:5 [d]Is. 43:3, 11 [e]Is. 57:15 [f]Judg. 10:4; Is. 30:6
10 [I]I.e., Euphrates [a]Hos. 1:7 [b]Mic. 5:10 [c]Hos. 2:18 [d]Is. 57:19; Mic. 4:2-4 [e]Ps. 72:8; Is. 60:12
11 [I]Lit., *cistern in which there is no water* [a]Ex. 24:8; Heb. 10:2 [b]Is. 24:22; 51:14
12 [I]Or, *Stronghold* [II]Lit., *of the hope* [a]Jer. 16:19; Joel 3:16 [b]Jer. 14:8; 17:13; Heb. 6:18, 19 [c]Is. 61:7
13 [I]Lit., *for Me* [a]Jer. 51:20 [b]Joel 3:6 [c]Ps. 45:3
14 [a]Is. 31:5; Zech. 2:5 [b]Ps. 18:14; Hab. 3:11

9:9 This passage was quoted in the N.T. as having been fulfilled at Jesus' triumphal entry to Jerusalem (Mt. 21:5; Jn. 12:15).

And the Lord [I]GOD will blow the
[c]trumpet,
And will march in the [d]storm
winds of the south.
15 [a]The LORD of hosts[6635] will
defend them.
And they will [b]devour, and
trample on the [c]sling stones;
And they will drink, *and* be
[d]boisterous as with wine;
And they will be filled like a
sacrificial basin,
Drenched like the [e]corners of the
altar.[4196]
16 And the LORD their God will
[a]save[3467] them in that day[3117]
As the flock of His people;[5971]
For *they are as* the stones of a
[b]crown,[5145]
[I]Sparkling in His land.[136]
17 For what [Ia]comeliness[2898] and
[b]beauty *will be* [II]theirs!
Grain will make the young men
flourish, and new wine the
virgins.[1330]

God Will Bless Judah and Ephraim

10 Ask[7592] [a]rain from the LORD at
the time[6256] of the spring
rain—
The LORD who [b]makes[6213] the
[I]storm clouds;
And He will give them
[c]showers of rain, vegetation
in the field[7704] to *each* man.[376]
2 For the [a]teraphim[8655] speak[1696]
[I]iniquity,[205]
And the [b]diviners[7080] see[2372]
[II]lying visions,[8267]
And tell[1696] [c]false[7723] dreams;
They comfort[5162] in vain.
Therefore *the people* [III]wander
like [d]sheep,
They are afflicted, because there
is no shepherd.
3 "My [a]anger[639] is kindled[2734]
against the shepherds,
And I will punish[6485] the
[I]male goats;
For the LORD of hosts[6635] has
[b]visited[6485] His flock, the
house[1004] of Judah,
And will make[7760] them like His
majestic[1935] horse in battle.
4 "From [I]them will come the
[a]cornerstone,
From [I]them the tent peg,
From [I]them the bow of [b]battle,
From [I]them every [II]ruler, *all* of
them together.
5 "And they will be as mighty
men,
[a]Treading down *the enemy* in the
mire of the streets in battle;
And they will fight, for the LORD
will be with them;
And the [b]riders on horses will
be put to shame.
6 "And I shall [a]strengthen the house
of Judah,
And I shall [b]save[3467] the house
of Joseph,
And I shall [Ic]bring them back,
Because I have had
[d]compassion[7355] on them;
And they will be as though I had
[e]not rejected them,
For I am the LORD their God,[430]
and I will [f]answer them.
7 "And Ephraim will be like a
mighty man,
And their heart[3820] will be glad
as if *from* wine;
Indeed, their [a]children[1121] will
see[7200] *it* and be glad,
[I]Their heart will rejoice in the
LORD.
8 "I will [a]whistle for them to
gather[6908] them together,
For I have redeemed[6299] them;
And they will be as [b]numerous
as they [Ic]were before.
9 "When I [I]scatter them among the
peoples,[5971]
They will [a]remember[2142] Me in
far countries,
And they with their children will
live[2421] and come back.[7725]
10 "I will [a]bring them back[7725] from
the land[776] of Egypt,
And gather them from Assyria;
And I will bring them into the
land of [b]Gilead and Lebanon,

14 [I]Heb., *YHWH,* usually rendered LORD [c]Is. 27:13 [d]Is. 21:1; 66:15
15 [a]Is. 37:35; Zech. 12:8 [b]Zech. 12:6 [c]Job 41:28 [d]Ps. 78:65 [e]Ex. 27:2
16 [I]Or, *Displayed over* [a]Jer. 31:10, 11 [b]Is. 62:3
17 [I]Lit., *goodness* [II]Lit., *his* [a]Jer. 31:12, 14 [b]Ps. 27:4; Is. 33:17
1 [I]Or, *thunderbolts* [a]Joel 2:23 [b]Jer. 10:13 [c]Is. 30:23
2 [I]Or, *futility* [II]Lit., *a lie* [III]Lit., *journey* [a]Ezek. 21:21; Hos. 3:4 [b]Jer. 27:9 [c]Jer. 23:32 [d]Ezek. 34:5, 8; Matt. 9:36; Mark 6:34
3 [I]I.e., leaders [a]Jer. 25:34-36 [b]Ezek. 34:12
4 [I]Lit., *him* [II]Or, *oppressor* [a]Luke 20:17; Eph. 2:20; 1Pet. 2:6 [b]Jer. 51:20; Zech. 9:10
5 [a]2Sam. 22:43 [b]Amos 2:15; Hag. 2:22
6 [I]Or, *make them dwell* [a]Zech. 10:12 [b]Zech. 8:7; 9:16 [c]Zech. 8:8 [d]Is. 54:8; Zech. 1:16 [e]Is. 54:4 [f]Zech. 13:9
7 [I]Or, *Let their heart rejoice* [a]Is. 54:13; Ezek. 37:25
8 [I]Lit., *were numerous* [a]Is. 5:26; 7:18, 19 [b]Jer. 33:22; Rev. 7:9 [c]Jer. 30:20; Ezek. 36:11
9 [I]Lit., *sow* [a]1Kin. 8:47, 48; Ezek. 6:9
10 [a]Is. 11:11 [b]Jer. 50:19

[I]Until [c]no *room* can be found for
them.
11 "And He will pass through[5674] the
[a]sea *of* distress,
And strike[5221] the waves in the
sea,
So that all the depths of the
[b]Nile will dry up;[3001]
And the pride of [c]Assyria will
be brought down,
And the scepter[7626] of [d]Egypt
will depart.[5493]
12 "And I shall [a]strengthen them in
the LORD,
And in His name [b]they will walk,"
declares[5001] the LORD.

The Doomed Flock

11 Open your doors, O Lebanon,
That a [a]fire may feed on your
[b]cedars.
2 Wail, O [I]cypress, for the cedar
has fallen,[5307]
Because the glorious *trees*[117]
have been destroyed;[7703]
Wail, O oaks of Bashan,
For the [II]impenetrable forest has
come down.
3 There is a sound of the
shepherds' [a]wail,
For their glory is ruined;
There is a [b]sound of the young
lions' roar,
For the [I]pride of the Jordan is
ruined.
4 Thus says the LORD my God,[430]
"Pasture the flock *doomed* to [a]slaugh-
ter.[2028]
5 "Those who buy them slay[2026]
them and [I]go [a]unpunished,[816][3808] and *each*
of those who sell them says,[559]
'Blessed[1288] be the LORD, for [b]I have
become rich!' And their [c]own shepherds
have no pity on them.
6 "For I shall [a]no longer have pity
on the inhabitants of the land,"[776]
declares[5001] the LORD; "but behold, I
shall [b]cause[5337] the men[120] to [I]fall,[5337]
each[376] into another's[7453] [II]power[3027] and
into the [II]power of his king; and they
will strike[3807] the land, and I shall
[c]not deliver *them* from their [II]power."
7 So I [a]pastured the flock *doomed*
to slaughter, [I]hence the [b]afflicted of the
flock. And I took for myself two [c]staffs:
the one I called[7121] [II][d]Favor, and the
other I called [III][e]Union;[2254] so I pastured
the flock.
8 Then I annihilated the three shepherds in [a]one month, for my soul[5315]
was impatient with them, and their soul
also [I]was weary[973] of me.
9 Then I said, "I will not pasture
you. What is to [a]die,[4191] [I]let it die, and
what is to be annihilated, [II]let it be annihilated; and [III]let those who are left[7604]
eat one[802] another's[7468] flesh."[1319]
10 And I took my staff, [I][a]Favor, and
cut it in pieces, to [II][b]break[6565] my
covenant[1285] which I had made[3772] with
all the peoples.[5971]
11 So it was [I]broken on that day,[3117]
and [II]thus the [a]afflicted of the flock who
were watching me realized that it was
the word[1697] of the LORD.
12 And I said to them, "If it is
good[2896] in your sight, give *me* my
[a]wages; but if not, [I]never mind!" So they
weighed out [b]thirty *shekels* of silver as
my wages.
13 Then the LORD said to me,
"Throw it to the [a]potter,[3335] *that* magnificent price at which I was valued[3365] by
them." So I took the thirty *shekels* of
silver and threw them to the potter in
the house[1004] of the LORD.
14 Then I cut my second staff,
[I][a]Union, in pieces, to [b]break the
brotherhood[264] between Judah and Israel.
15 And the LORD said to me, "Take
again for yourself the equipment of a
[I][a]foolish shepherd.
16 "For behold, I am going to raise
up a shepherd in the land who will
[a]not care for[6485] the perishing, seek the
scattered, heal the broken,[7665] or sustain the one standing,[5324] but will
[b]devour the flesh of the fat *sheep* and
tear off their hoofs.

10 [I]Lit., *And* [c]Is. 49:19, 20
11 [a]Is. 51:9, 10 [b]Is. 19:5-7 [c]Zeph. 2:13 [d]Ezek. 30:13
12 [a]Zech. 10:6 [b]Mic. 4:5

1 [a]Jer. 22:6, 7 [b]Ezek. 31:3
2 [I]Or, *juniper* [II]Another reading is *forest of the vintage*
3 [I]Or, *jungle* [a]Jer. 25:34-36 [b]Jer. 2:15; 50:44
4 [a]Ps. 44:22; Zech. 11:7
5 [I]Lit., *are not held guilty* [a]Jer. 50:7 [b]Hos. 12:8; 1Tim. 6:9 [c]Ezek. 34:2, 3
6 [I]Lit., *find* [II]Lit., *hand* [a]Jer. 13:14 [b]Is. 9:19-21; Mic. 7:2-6; Zech. 14:13 [c]Ps. 50:22; Mic. 5:8
7 [I]Another reading is *for the sheep dealers* [II]Or, *Pleasantness* [III]Or, *Cords* [a]Zech. 11:4 [b]Jer. 39:10; Zeph. 3:12 [c]Ezek. 37:16 [d]Ps. 27:4; 90:17; Zech. 11:10 [e]Ps. 133:1; Ezek. 37:16-23; Zech. 11:14
8 [I]Or, *detested* [a]Hos. 5:7
9 [I]Or, *will die* [II]Or, *will be annihilated* [III]Or, *those . . . will eat* [a]Jer. 15:2
10 [I]Or, *Pleasantness* [II]Or, *annul* [a]Zech. 11:7 [b]Ps. 89:39; Jer. 14:21
11 [I]Or, *annulled* [II]Another reading is *the sheep dealers who* [a]Zeph. 3:12
12 [I]Lit., *cease* [a]1Kin. 5:6; Mal. 3:5 [b]Gen. 37:28; Ex. 21:32; Matt. 26:15; 27:9, 10
13 [a]Matt. 27:3-10; Acts 1:18, 19
14 [I]Or, *Cords* [a]Zech. 11:7 [b]Is. 9:21; Zech. 11:6
15 [I]Or, *useless* [a]Is. 6:10-12; Zech. 11:17
16 [a]Jer. 23:2 [b]Ezek. 34:2-6

17 "[a]Woe to the worthless[457]
shepherd
Who leaves[5800] the flock!
A [b]sword[2719] will be on his arm
And on his right eye!
His [c]arm will be totally
withered,[3001]
And his right eye will be
[I]blind."

Jerusalem to Be Attacked

12 The [I]burden[4853] of the word[1697] of the LORD concerning Israel. *Thus* declares[5001] the LORD who [a]stretches out the heavens,[8064] [b]lays the foundation of the earth,[776] and [c]forms[3335] the spirit[7307] of man[120] within[7130] him,

2 "Behold, I am going to make[7760] Jerusalem a [a]cup [I]that causes reeling to all the peoples[5971] around; and when the siege is against Jerusalem, it will also be against [b]Judah.

3 "And it will come about in that day[3117] that I will make Jerusalem a heavy [a]stone for all the peoples;[1471] all who lift it will be [b]severely [I]injured. And all the [c]nations of the earth will be gathered[622] against it.

4 "In that day," declares the LORD, "I will strike[5221] every horse with bewilderment, and his rider with madness. But I will [I]watch over the house[1004] of Judah, while I strike every horse of the peoples with blindness.

5 "Then the clans[441] of Judah will say in their hearts,[3820] '[I]A strong support for us are the inhabitants of Jerusalem through the LORD of hosts,[6635] their God.'[430]

6 "In that day I will make the clans of Judah like a [a]firepot among pieces of wood and a flaming torch among sheaves, so they will consume on the right hand and on the left all the surrounding peoples, while the [b]inhabitants of Jerusalem again dwell on their own sites in Jerusalem.

7 "The LORD also will [a]save[3467] the tents[168] of Judah first in order that the glory[8597] of the house of [b]David and the glory of the inhabitants of Jerusalem may not be magnified above Judah.

8 "In that day the LORD will [a]defend the inhabitants of Jerusalem, and the one who [I][b]is feeble among them in that day will be like David, and the house of David *will be* like [c]God, like the [d]angel[4397] of the LORD before them.

9 "And it will come about in that day that I will [I][a]set about to destroy all the nations[1471] that come against Jerusalem.

🗝 10 "And I will [a]pour out[8210] on the house of David and on the inhabitants of Jerusalem, [I]the Spirit of grace[2580] and of supplication,[8469] so that they will look on Me whom they have [b]pierced; and they will mourn for Him, as one [c]mourns for an only[3173] son, and they will weep bitterly over Him, like the bitter weeping over a first-born.

11 "In that day there will be great [a]mourning in Jerusalem, like the mourning of Hadadrimmon in the [I]plain of [II]Megiddo.

12 "And the land[776] will mourn, every family[4940] by itself; the family of the house of David by itself,[905] and their wives by themselves; the family of the house of Nathan by itself, and their wives by themselves;

13 the family of the house of Levi by itself, and their wives by themselves; the family of the Shimeites by itself, and their wives by themselves;

14 all the families that remain,[7604] every family by itself, and their wives by themselves.

False Prophets Ashamed

13 "In that day[3117] a [a]fountain will be opened for the house[1004] of David and for the inhabitants of Jerusalem, for [b]sin[2403] and for [c]impurity.

2 "And it will come about[5674] in that day," declares[5001] the LORD of hosts,[6635]

---

17 [I]Lit., *completely dimmed* [a]Jer. 23:1; Zech. 10:2; 11:15 [b]Jer. 50:35-37 [c]Ezek. 30:21, 22

1 [I]Or, *oracle* [a]Is. 42:5; 44:24; Jer. 51:15 [b]Job 26:7; Ps. 102:25, 26; Heb. 1:10-12 [c]Is. 57:16; Heb. 12:9

2 [I]Lit., *of reeling* [a]Ps. 75:8; Is. 51:22, 23 [b]Zech. 14:14

3 [I]Lit., *scratched* [a]Dan. 2:34, 35, 44, 45 [b]Matt. 21:44 [c]Zech. 14:2

4 [I]Lit., *open My eyes*

5 [I]Lit., *My strength is*

6 [a]Is. 10:17, 18; Obad. 18; Zech. 11:1 [b]Zech. 2:4; 8:3-5

7 [a]Jer. 30:18 [b]Amos 9:11

8 [I]Or, *stumbles* [a]Joel 3:16; Zech. 9:14, 15 [b]Lev. 26:8; Josh. 23:10; Mic. 7:8 [c]Ps. 8:5; 82:6 [d]Ex. 14:19; 33:2

9 [I]Lit., *seek to* [a]Zech. 14:2, 3

10 [I]Or, *a spirit* [a]Is. 44:3; Ezek. 39:29; Joel 2:28, 29 [b]John 19:37; Rev. 1:7 [c]Jer. 6:26; Amos 8:10

11 [I]I.e., broad valley [II]Heb., *Megiddon* [a]Matt. 24:30; Rev. 1:7

1 [a]Jer. 2:13; 17:13 [b]Ps. 51:2, 7; Is. 1:16-18; John 1:29 [c]Num. 19:17; Is. 4:4; Ezek. 36:25

🗝 **12:10** John saw this passage as looking forward both to Jesus' death on the cross (Jn. 19:37) and to His second coming (Rev. 1:7; see Mt. 24:30).

"that I will [a]cut off[3772] the names of the idols[6091] from the land,[776] and they will no longer be remembered;[2142] and I will also remove the [b]prophets[5030] and the [c]unclean[2932] spirit[7307] from the land.

3 "And it will come about that if anyone[376] still [a]prophesies, then his father[1] and mother[517] who gave birth to him will say to him, 'You shall [b]not live,[2421] for you have spoken[1696] [c]falsely[8267] in the name of the LORD'; and his [d]father and mother who gave birth to him will pierce him through when he prophesies.[5012]

4 "Also it will come about in that day that the prophets will each[376] be [a]ashamed[954] of his vision[2384] when he prophesies, and they will not put on a [b]hairy robe in order to deceive;

5 but he will say, 'I am [a]not a prophet; I am a tiller of the ground, for a man[120] [I]sold me as a slave in my youth.'

6 "And one will say to him, 'What are these wounds[4347] [a]between your [I]arms?'[3027] Then he will say, '*Those* with which I was wounded[5221] in the house of [II]my friends.'[157]

7 "Awake, O [a]sword,[2719] against
My [b]Shepherd,
And against the man,[1397] My
[c]Associate,"
Declares the LORD of hosts.
"[d]Strike[5221] the Shepherd
that the sheep may be
scattered;
And I will [e]turn[7725] My hand
[I]against the little ones.

8 "And it will come about in all the
land,"
Declares the LORD,
"That [a]two parts[6310] in it will be
cut off *and* perish;[1478]
But the third will be left[3498] in
it.

9 "And I will bring the third part
through the [a]fire,
Refine[6884] them as silver is
refined,
And test them as gold is
tested.[974]
They will [b]call[7121] on My name,
And I will [c]answer them;
I will say, 'They are [d]My
people,'[5971]
And they will say,[559] 'The LORD
is my God.' "[430]

2 [a]Ex. 23:13; Hos. 2:17 [b]Jer. 23:14, 15 [c]1Kin. 22:22; Ezek. 36:25, 29
3 [a]Jer. 23:34 [b]Deut. 18:20; Ezek. 14:9 [c]Jer. 23:25 [d]Deut. 13:6-11; Matt. 10:37
4 [a]Jer. 6:15; 8:9; Mic. 3:7 [b]2Kin. 1:8; Is. 20:2; Matt. 3:4
5 [I]Lit., *caused another to buy me* [a]Amos 7:14
6 [I]Lit., *hands* [II]Lit., *those who love me* [a]2Kin. 9:24
7 [I]Or, *upon* [a]Jer. 47:6; Ezek. 21:3-5 [b]Is. 40:11; Ezek. 34:23, 24; 37:24; Mic. 5:2, 4 [c]Ps. 2:2; Jer. 23:5, 6 [d]Is. 53:4, 5, 10; Matt. 26:31; Mark 14:27 [e]Is. 1:25
8 [a]Is. 6:13; Ezek. 5:2-4, 12
9 [a]Is. 48:10; Mal. 3:3 [b]Ps. 34:15-17; 50:15; Zech. 12:10 [c]Is. 58:9; 65:24; Jer. 29:11-13; Zech. 10:6 [d]Hos. 2:23

God Will Battle Jerusalem's Foes

14 Behold, a [a]day[3117] is coming for the LORD when [b]the spoil taken from you will be divided among[7130] you.

2 For I will [a]gather[622] all the nations[1471] against Jerusalem to battle, and the city will be captured, the [b]houses[1004] plundered, the women ravished, and half of the city exiled,[1473] but the rest[3499] of the people[5971] will not be cut off[3772] from the city.

3 Then the LORD will go forth and [a]fight against those nations, as [I]when He fights on a day of battle.

4 And in that day His feet will [a]stand on the Mount of Olives, which is in front of Jerusalem on the east; and the Mount of Olives will be [b]split in its middle from east to west by a very large valley, so that half of the mountain will move toward the north and the other half toward the south.

5 And you will flee by the valley of My mountains, for the valley of the mountains will reach to Azel; yes, you will flee just as you fled before the [a]earthquake[7494] in the days of Uzziah king of Judah. [b]Then the LORD, my God,[430] will come, *and* all the holy ones[6918] with [I]Him!

6 And it will come about in that day that there will be [a]no light;[216] the [I]luminaries will dwindle.

7 For it will be [a]a unique day which is [b]known[3045] to the LORD, neither day nor night, but it will come about that

1 [a]Is. 13:6, 9; Joel 2:1; Mal. 4:1 [b]Zech. 14:14
2 [a]Zech. 12:2, 3 [b]Is. 13:16
3 [I]Lit., *His day of fighting* [a]Zech. 9:14, 15
4 [a]Ezek. 11:23 [b]Is. 64:1, 2; Ezek. 47:1-10; Mic. 1:3, 4; Hab. 3:6; Zech. 4:7; 14:8
5 [I]So the versions; Heb., *Thee* [a]Is. 29:6; Amos 1:1 [b]Ps. 96:13; Is. 66:15, 16; Matt. 16:27; 25:31
6 [I]Lit., *glorious ones will congeal* [a]Is. 13:10; Jer. 4:23; Ezek. 32:7, 8; Joel 2:30, 31; Acts 2:16, 19
7 [a]Jer. 30:7; Amos 8:9 [b]Is. 45:21; Acts 15:18

13:7 On the Mount of Olives, shortly before His arrest, Jesus applied this passage to what was about to happen to Him and His disciples (Mt. 26:31; Mk. 14:27).

at [c]evening time[6256] there will be light.
8 And it will come about in that day
that [a]living[2416] waters will flow out of
Jerusalem, half of them toward the eastern sea and the other half toward the
western sea; it will be in summer as
well as in winter.

God Will Be King over All

9 And the LORD will be [a]king[4428]
over all the earth;[776] in that day[3117] the
LORD will be *the only* [b]one, and His name
the only one.
10 All the land[776] will be changed
into a plain[6160] from [a]Geba to [b]Rimmon
south of Jerusalem; but [I]Jerusalem will
[c]rise and [d]remain on its site from
[e]Benjamin's Gate as far as the place of
the First Gate to the [f]Corner Gate, and
from the [g]Tower of Hananel to the king's
wine presses.
11 And [I]people will live in it, and
there will be [a]no more curse,[2734] for
Jerusalem will [b]dwell in security.[983]
12 Now this will be the plague with
which the LORD will strike[5062] all the
peoples who have gone to war[6633]
against Jerusalem; their flesh[1319] will
[a]rot while they stand on their feet, and
their eyes will rot in their sockets, and
their tongue will rot in their mouth.[6310]
13 And it will come about in that
day that a great panic[4103] from the LORD
will [I]fall on them; and they will [a]seize[2388]
one[376] another's[7453] hand,[3027] and the
hand of one will [II]be lifted[5927] against
the hand of another.
14 And [a]Judah also will fight at Jerusalem; and the [b]wealth[2428] of all the
surrounding nations[1471] will be gathered,[622] gold and silver and garments
in great abundance.
15 So also like this [a]plague, will be
the plague on the horse, the mule, the
camel, the donkey, and all the cattle
that will be in those camps.[4264]
16 Then it will come about that any
who are left[3498] of all the nations that
went against Jerusalem will [a]go up[5927]
from year to year to worship the King,
the LORD of hosts,[6635] and to celebrate
the [b]Feast[2282] of Booths.[5521]
17 And it will be that whichever of
the families[4940] of the earth does not
go up[5927] to Jerusalem to worship the
[a]King, the LORD of hosts, there will be
[b]no rain on them.
18 And if the family of Egypt does
not go up or enter, then no *rain will*
fall on them; it will be the [a]plague with
which the LORD smites the nations who
do not go up to celebrate the Feast of
Booths.
19 This will be the [I]punishment[2403]
of Egypt, and the [I]punishment of all the
nations who do not go up to celebrate
the Feast of Booths.
20 In that day there will *be inscribed*
on the bells of the horses, "[a]HOLY[6944]
TO THE LORD." And the [b]cooking pots
in the LORD's house will be like the bowls
before the altar.[4196]
21 And every cooking pot in Jerusalem and in Judah will be [a]holy to the
LORD of hosts; and all who sacrifice[2076]
will come and take of them and boil in
them. And there will no longer be a
[I][b]Canaanite in the house of the LORD
of hosts in that day.

7 [c]Is. 58:10; Rev. 22:5
8 [a]Ezek. 47:1-12; Joel 3:18; John 7:38; Rev. 22:1, 2
9 [a]Is. 2:2-4; 45:23; Zech. 9:9; 14:16, 17 [b]Deut. 6:4; Is. 45:21-24
10 [I]Lit., *it* [a]1Kin. 15:22 [b]Josh. 15:32; Judg. 20:45, 47 [c]Is. 2:2; Amos 9:11 [d]Jer. 30:18; Zech. 12:6 [e]Jer. 37:13; 38:7 [f]2Kin. 14:13 [g]Jer. 31:38
11 [I]Lit., *they* [a]Zech. 8:13; Rev. 22:3 [b]Jer. 23:5, 6; Ezek. 34:25-28
12 [a]Lev. 26:16; Deut. 28:21, 22
13 [I]Lit., *be among* [II]Lit., *rise up against* [a]Zech. 11:6
14 [a]Zech. 12:2, 5 [b]Is. 23:18; Zech. 14:1
15 [a]Zech. 14:12
16 [a]Is. 60:6-9; 66:18-21, 23 [b]Lev. 23:34-44
17 [a]Zech. 14:9, 16 [b]Jer. 14:3-6; Amos 4:7
18 [a]Zech. 14:12, 15
19 [I]Lit., *sin*
20 [a]Ex. 28:36-38 [b]Ezek. 46:20
21 [I]Or, *merchant* [a]Neh. 8:10; Rom. 14:6, 7; 1Cor. 10:31 [b]Zeph. 1:11

The Book of
MALACHI

Malachi means "my messenger." Because nothing else is mentioned of him in the Old Testament and because of the meaning of the word, some scholars have thought that Malachi may have been a pen name used by the prophet. This possibility is mentioned in an ancient Jewish tradition. The prophecy was probably written in the period between 450 and 425 B.C. This was the time of Nehemiah, about 100 years after the first exiles had returned from Babylon. The book reflects that era. The temple had been completed and sacrifices were being offered, but the priests were careless. The people doubted God and were intermarrying outside Israel. Judah was under a governor and Edom had been destroyed.

The prophet's style is unique in the Old Testament. He makes a statement and then asks a question growing out of that statement. In the answers to these questions Malachi sets forth the greater portion of his message.

The enthusiasm that marked the Jews' return to Jerusalem 100 years ealier was gone. They were discouraged. There was a drought and the crops were bad. They expected a golden age of prosperity but it had not dawned. Did not God care? Malachi answered these doubts: God is still on His throne! Look what He did to Edom. God deals with sin. Pay your tithes, obey Him, and see how He will bless you. The Messiah is coming! He will destroy the wicked and give victory to the righteous. But before that day the prophet, Elijah, must come.

God's Love for Jacob

1 The [Ia]oracle[4853] of the word[1697] of the LORD to [b]Israel through[3027] [II]Malachi.

2 "I have [a]loved[157] you," says[5001] the LORD. But you say, "How hast Thou loved us?" "*Was* not Esau Jacob's brother?"[251] declares the LORD. "Yet I [b]have loved[157] Jacob;

3 but I have hated[8130] Esau, and I have [a]made[7760] his mountains a desolation,[8077] and *appointed* his inheritance[5159] for the jackals[8568] of the wilderness."

4 Though Edom says, "We have been [a]beaten down, but we will [Ib]return[7725] and build up the ruins";[2723] thus says[559] the LORD of hosts,[6635] "They may [c]build, but I will tear down;[2040] and *men* will call[7121] them the [II]wicked[7564] territory, and the people[5971] [III]toward whom the LORD is indignant[2194] [d]forever."[5769, 5704]

5 And your eyes will see[7200] this and you will say, "[a]The LORD [I]be magnified beyond the [II]border of Israel!"

Sin of the Priests

6 " 'A son[1121] [a]honors[3513] *his* father,[1] and a servant[5650] his master.[113] Then if I am a [b]father, where is My honor?[3519] And if I am a master, where is My [I]respect?'[4172] says the LORD of hosts to you, O [c]priests[3548] who despise My name. But you say, 'How have we despised Thy name?'

7 "*You* are presenting [a]defiled [Ib]food upon My altar.[4196] But you say,[559] 'How have we defiled Thee?' In that you say, 'The [c]table of the LORD is to be despised.'

8 "But when you present[5066] the [a]blind for sacrifice,[2076] is it not evil?[7451] And when you present the lame and sick, is it not evil? [I]Why not offer[7126] it to your [b]governor?[6346] Would he be pleased[7521] with you? Or would he receive[5375] you kindly?" says the LORD of hosts.

1 [I]Lit., *burden* [II]Or, *My messenger* [a]Is. 13:1; Nah. 1:1; Hab. 1:1; Zech. 9:1 [b]Mal. 2:11

2 [a]Deut. 4:37; 7:8; 23:5; Is. 41:8, 9; Jer. 31:3; John 15:12 [b]Rom. 9:13

3 [a]Jer. 49:10, 16-18; Ezek. 35:3, 4, 7, 8, 15

4 [I]Or, *rebuild the ruins* [II]Lit., *border of wickedness* [III]Or, *whom the LORD has cursed* [a]Jer. 5:17 [b]Is. 9:9, 10 [c]Amos 3:15; 5:11; 6:11 [d]Ezek. 35:9; Obad. 10

5 [I]Or, *will be great* [II]Or, *territory* [a]Ps. 35:27; Mic. 5:4

6 [I]Lit., *fear* [a]Ex. 20:12; Prov. 30:11, 17 [b]Deut. 1:31; Is. 1:2; Jer. 3:4; Mal. 2:10 [c]Zeph. 3:4; Mal. 2:1-9

7 [I]Lit., *bread* [a]Mal. 1:8, 13 [b]Lev. 3:11; 21:6, 8 [c]Mal. 1:12

8 [I]Lit., *Offer it, please* [a]Lev. 22:22; Deut. 15:21 [b]Hag. 1:1

9 "But now [I]will you not [a]entreat God's[410] favor, that He may be gracious[2603] to us? [II]With such an offering[3027] on your part, will He [b]receive[5375] any of you kindly?" says the LORD of hosts.

10 "Oh that there were one among you who would [a]shut the [I]gates, that you might not uselessly[2600] kindle *fire on* My altar! I am not pleased[2656] with you," says the LORD of hosts, "[b]nor will I accept an offering[4503] from [II]you.[3027]

11 "For from the [a]rising of the sun, even to its setting, [b]My name *will be* [c]great among the nations,[1471] and in every place [d]incense[6999] is going to be offered to My name, and a grain offering *that is* pure;[2889] for My name *will be* [e]great among the nations,"[1471] says the LORD of hosts.

12 "But you are [a]profaning[2490] it, in that you say, 'The table of the Lord is defiled, and as for its fruit, its food is to be despised.'

13 "You also say, '[I]My, how [a]tiresome it is!' And you disdainfully sniff at it," says the LORD of hosts, "and you bring what was taken by [b]robbery, and *what is* [c]lame or sick; so you bring the offering! Should I [d]receive that from your hand?" says the LORD.

14 "But cursed[779] be the [a]swindler who has a male[2145] in his flock, and vows[5087] it, but sacrifices[2076] a [b]blemished animal[7843] to the Lord,[136] for I am a great [c]King,"[4428] says the LORD of hosts, "and My name is [I][d]feared[3372] among the [II]nations."

Priests to Be Disciplined

2 "And now, this commandment[4687] is for you, O priests.[3548]

2 "If you do [a]not listen,[8085] and if you do not take[7760] it to heart[3820] to give honor[3519] to My name," says the LORD of hosts,[6635] "then I will send the [b]curse[779] upon you, and I will curse your blessings;[1293] and indeed, I have [c]cursed them *already*, because you are not taking *it* to heart.

3 "Behold, I am going to [a]rebuke[1605] your [I]offspring,[2233] and I will [b]spread [II]refuse on your faces, the [II]refuse of your [c]feasts;[2282] and you will be taken away[5375] [III]with it.

4 "Then you will know[3045] that I have sent this commandment to you, [I]that My [a]covenant[1285] may [II]continue with Levi," says the LORD of hosts.

5 "My covenant with him was *one of* life[2416] and [a]peace,[7965] and I gave them to him *as an object of* [I]reverence;[4172] so he [II][b]revered[3373] Me, and stood in awe[2865] of My name.

6 "[I][a]True[571] instruction[8451] was in his mouth,[6310] and unrighteousness[5766] was not found on his lips;[8193] he walked [b]with Me in peace and uprightness,[4334] and he [c]turned many back[7725] from iniquity.[5771]

7 "For the lips of a priest should preserve[8104] [a]knowledge,[1847] and [I]men should [b]seek [II]instruction from his mouth; for he is the [c]messenger[4397] of the LORD of hosts.

8 "But as for you, you have turned aside[5493] from the way;[1870] you have caused many to [a]stumble[3782] [I]by the instruction; you have [II][b] corrupted the covenant of Levi," says the LORD of hosts.

9 "So [a]I also have made you despised and [b]abased [I]before all the people,[5971] just as you are not keeping My ways, but are showing [c]partiality[6440] in the [II]instruction.

Sin in the Family

10 "Do we not all have [a]one father? [b]Has not one God[410] created[1254] us? Why do we deal [c]treacherously[898] each[376] against his brother so as to profane[2490] the [d]covenant of our fathers?[1]

11 "Judah has dealt [a]treacherously, and an abomination[8441] has been committed[6213] in Israel and in Jerusalem; for Judah has [b]profaned the sanctuary[6944] of the LORD [I]which He loves,[157] and has married[1166] the daughter of a foreign[5236] god.[410]

9 [I]Lit., *entreat, please* [II]Lit., *This has been from your hand* [a]Jer. 27:18; Joel 2:12-14 [b]Amos 5:22
10 [I]Or, *doors* [II]Lit., *your hand* [a]Is. 1:13 [b]Jer. 14:10, 12; Hos. 5:6
11 [a]Is. 45:6 [b]Ps. 111:9 [c]Is. 66:18, 19 [d]Is. 60:6 [e]Is. 12:4, 5; 54:5; Jer. 10:6, 7
12 [a]Mal. 1:7
13 [I]Lit., *Behold it is weariness* [a]Is. 43:22 [b]Lev. 6:4; Is. 61:8 [c]Mal. 1:8 [d]Mal. 1:10
14 [I]Or, *revered* [II]Or, *Gentiles* [a]Acts 5:1-4 [b]Lev. 22:18-20 [c]Zech. 14:9 [d]Zeph. 2:11

2 [a]Lev. 26:14, 15; Deut. 28:15 [b]Deut. 28:16-20 [c]Mal. 3:9
3 [I]Lit., *seed* [II]Or, *vomit* [III]Lit., *to* [a]Lev. 26:16; Deut. 28:38 [b]Nah. 3:6 [c]Ex. 29:14
4 [I]Or, *to be My covenant with* [II]Lit., *be* [a]Num. 3:11-13, 45; 18:21; Neh. 13:29; Mal. 3:1
5 [I]Or, *fear* [II]Or, *feared* [a]Num. 25:12 [b]Num. 25:7, 8, 13
6 [I]Or, *Law of truth* [a]Ps. 119:142, 151, 160 [b]Deut. 33:8, 9; Ps. 37:37 [c]Jer. 23:22
7 [I]Lit., *they* [II]Or, *law* [a]Lev. 10:11; Neh. 8:7 [b]Num. 27:21; Deut. 17:8-11; Jer. 18:18; Ezek. 7:26 [c]Hag. 1:13
8 [I]Or, *in the law* [II]Or, *violated* [a]Jer. 18:15 [b]Num. 25:12, 13; Neh. 13:29; Ezek. 44:10
9 [I]Lit., *to* [II]Or, *law* [a]Nah. 3:6 [b]Ezek. 7:26 [c]Deut. 1:17; Mic. 3:11
10 [a]Is. 63:16; 64:8; Jer. 31:9; 1Cor. 8:6; Eph. 4:6 [b]Acts 17:24f. [c]Jer. 9:4, 5 [d]Ex. 19:4-6; 24:3, 7, 8
11 [I]Or, *in that he has loved and married* [a]Jer. 3:7-9 [b]Ezra 9:1, 2

12 "*As* for the man[376] who does[6213] this, may the [a]LORD cut off[3772] from the tents[168] of Jacob *everyone* who awakes and answers, or who [b]presents [I]an offering[4503] to the LORD of hosts.

13 "And this is [I]another thing you do: you cover[3680] the altar[4196] of the LORD with tears, with weeping and with groaning, because He [a]no longer regards the [II]offering or accepts *it with* favor[7522] from your hand.[3027]

14 "Yet you say, 'For what reason?' Because the LORD has been a witness[5749] between you and the [a]wife[802] of your youth, against whom you have dealt [b]treacherously, though she is your companion and your wife by covenant.[1285]

15 "[I]But not one has [a]done[6213] *so* who has a remnant[7605] of the Spirit.[7307] And [II]what did *that* one *do* while he was seeking a [b]godly[430] [III]offspring?[2233] Take heed[8104] then, to your spirit, and let no one deal [c]treacherously against the wife of your youth.

16 "For [I]I hate [II][a]divorce," says the LORD, the God[430] of Israel, "and [III]him who covers[3680] his garment with [IV][b]wrong,"[2555] says the LORD of hosts. "So take heed to your spirit, that you do not deal treacherously."

17 You have [a]wearied the LORD with your words.[1697] Yet you say,[559] "How have we wearied *Him*?" In that you say, "[b]Everyone who does[6213] evil[7451] is good[2396] in the sight of the LORD, and He [c]delights[2654] in them," or, "[d]Where is the God of [e]justice?"[4941]

The Purifier

3 🔑 "[a]Behold, I am going to send [b]My [I]messenger,[4397] and he will [II][c]clear the way[1870] before Me. And the Lord,[113] whom you seek, will suddenly come to His temple;[1964] [III]and the [I][d]messenger of the covenant,[1285] in whom you delight,[2655] behold, He is coming," says the LORD of hosts.[6635]

2 "But who can [a]endure the day[3117] of His coming? And who can stand when He appears?[7200] For He is like a [b]refiner's[6884] fire and like [I]fullers'[3526] soap.

3 "And He will sit as a smelter and purifier[2891] of silver, and He will [a]purify[2891] the sons[1121] of Levi and refine[2212] them like gold and silver, so that they may [b]present to the LORD [I]offerings[4503] in righteousness.

4 "Then the [I]offering of Judah and Jerusalem will be [a]pleasing[6148] to the LORD, as in the [b]days of old[5769] and as in former years.

5 "Then I will draw near[7126] to you for judgment;[4941] and I will be a swift witness against the [a]sorcerers[3784] and against the [b]adulterers[5003] and against those who [c]swear[7650] falsely,[8267] and against those who oppress the [d]wage earner in his wages, the [e]widow and the [I]orphan, and those who turn aside the [II][f]alien,[1616] and do not [III]fear[3372] Me," says the LORD of hosts.

6 "For [I]I, the LORD, [a]do not change; therefore you, O sons of Jacob, [II]are not consumed.[3615]

7 "From the [a]days of your fathers[1] you have turned aside[5493] from My statutes,[2706] and have not kept[8104] *them.* [b]Return[7725] to Me, and I will return to you," says the LORD of hosts. "But you say, 'How shall we return?'

You Have Robbed God

8 "Will a man[120] [I]rob God?[430] Yet you are robbing Me! But you say, 'How have we robbed Thee?' In [a]tithes[4463] and [II]offerings.

9 "You are [a]cursed[779] with a curse, for you are [I]robbing Me, the whole nation[1471] *of you*!

12 [I]Or, *a grain offering* [a]Ezek. 24:21; Hos. 9:12 [b]Mal. 1:10, 13
13 [I]Lit., *second* [II]Or, *grain offering* [a]Jer. 11:14; 14:12
14 [a]Is. 54:6 [b]Jer. 9:2; Mal. 3:5
15 [I]Or, *Did He not make one, although He had the remnant* [II]Or, *why one? He sought a godly offspring* [III]Lit., *seed* [a]Gen. 2:24; Matt. 19:4, 5 [b]Ruth 4:12; 1Sam. 2:20 [c]Ex. 20:14; Lev. 20:10
16 [I]Lit., *He hates* [II]Lit., *sending away* [III]Lit., *he covers* [IV]Or, *violence* [a]Deut. 24:1; Matt. 5:31; 19:6-8 [b]Ps. 73:6; Is. 59:6
17 [a]Is. 43:22, 24 [b]Is. 5:20; Zeph. 1:12 [c]Job 9:24 [d]2Pet. 3:4 [e]Is. 5:19; Jer. 17:15

1 [I]Or, *angel* [II]Or, *prepare* [III]Or, *even* [a]Matt. 11:10, 14; Mark 1:2; Luke 1:76; 7:27 [b]Hag. 1:13; John 1:6, 7 [c]Is. 40:3 [d]Is. 63:9
2 [I]Lit., *laundrymen's* [a]Is. 33:14; Ezek. 22:14; Rev. 6:17 [b]Zech. 13:9; Matt. 3:10-12; 1Cor. 3:13-15
3 [I]Or, *grain offerings* [a]Is. 1:25; Dan. 12:10 [b]Ps. 4:5; 51:19
4 [I]Or, *grain offering* [a]Ps. 51:17-19 [b]2Chr. 7:1-3, 12
5 [I]Or, *fatherless* [II]Or, *sojourner* [III]Or, *revere* [a]Deut. 18:10; Jer. 27:9, 10 [b]Ezek. 22:9-11 [c]Jer. 5:2; 7:9; Zech. 5:4 [d]Lev. 19:13 [e]Ex. 22:22-24 [f]Deut. 27:19
6 [I]Or, *I am the LORD; I do not* [II]Or, *have not come to an end* [a]Num. 23:19; James 1:17
7 [a]Jer. 7:25, 26; 16:11, 12 [b]Zech. 1:3
8 [I]Or, *defraud* [II]Or, *heave offerings* [a]Neh. 13:11, 12
9 [I]Or, *defrauding* [a]Mal. 2:2

🔑 **3:1** Jesus applied this verse to John the Baptist (Mt. 11:10; Lk. 7:27), as did Mark (Mk. 1:2). The allusion to the passage by Zechariah, John's father, in Lk. 1:76 indicates that John's special role was known from the very beginning of his life. See the note on Mal. 4:5-6.

10 "[a]Bring the whole tithe into the storehouse, so that there may be [I]food in My house,[1004] and test[974] Me now in this," says the LORD of hosts, "if I will not [b]open for you the windows of heaven,[8064] and [c]pour out for you a blessing[1293] until [II][d]it overflows.

11 "Then I will rebuke[1605] the [a]devourer for you, so that it may not [I]destroy[7843] the fruits of the ground;[127] nor will your vine in the field[7704] cast *its grapes,*" says the LORD of hosts.

12 "And [a]all the nations will call you blessed,[833] for you shall be a [b]delightful[2656] land,"[776] says the LORD of hosts.

13 "Your words[1697] have been [I]arrogant[2388] against Me," says the LORD. "Yet you say, 'What have we spoken against Thee?'

14 "You have said, 'It is [a]vain[7723] to serve[5647] God; and what [b]profit is it that we have kept His charge,[4931] and that we have walked in mourning[6941] before the LORD of hosts?

15 'So now we [a]call the arrogant[2086] blessed;[833] not only are the doers[6213] of wickedness[7564] built up, but they also test[974] God and [b]escape.' "[4422]

The Book of Remembrance

16 Then those who [I]feared[3373] the LORD spoke to one[376] another,[7453] and the LORD [a]gave attention[7121] and heard *it,* and a [b]book[5612] of remembrance[2146] was written before Him for those who [I]fear the LORD and who esteem His name.

17 "And they will be [a]Mine," says the LORD of hosts, "on the [b]day that I [I]prepare[6213] *My* [II][c]own possession,[5459] and I will [III]spare them as a man[376] [III][d]spares his own son who serves[5647] him."

18 So you will again [a]distinguish[7200] between the righteous[6662] and the wicked,[7563] between one who serves God and one who does not serve Him.

Final Admonition

4 "[I]For behold, the day[3117] is coming, [a]burning like a furnace; and all the arrogant and every evildoer[6213,7564] will be [b]chaff; and the day that is coming will [c]set them ablaze," says the LORD of hosts,[6635] "so that it will leave[5800] them neither root nor branch."

2 "But for you who [I]fear[3373] My name the [a]sun of righteousness will rise with [b]healing in its wings; and you will go forth and [c]skip about like calves from the stall.

3 "And you will [a]tread down the wicked,[7563] for they shall be [b]ashes under the soles[3709] of your feet [c]on the day [I]which I am preparing," says the LORD of hosts.

4 "[I][a]Remember[2142] the law[8451] of Moses My servant,[5650] *even the* statutes[2706] and ordinances[4941] which I commanded[6680] him in Horeb for all Israel.

🔑 5 "Behold, I am going to send you [a]Elijah the prophet[5030] before the coming of the great and terrible[3372] day of the LORD.

6 "And he will [I][a]restore[7725] the hearts[3820] of the fathers[1] to *their* children,[1121] and the hearts of the children to their fathers, lest I come and [b]smite[5521] the land[776] with a [II]curse."[2764]

10 [I]Lit., *prey* [II]Or, *there is not room enough* [a]Lev. 27:30; Num. 18:21-24; Deut. 12:6; 14:22-29; Neh. 13:12 [b]Ps. 78:23-29 [c]Ezek. 34:26 [d]Lev. 26:3-5
11 [I]Lit., *ruin* [a]Joel 1:4; 2:25
12 [a]Is. 61:9 [b]Is. 62:4
13 [I]Lit., *strong*
14 [a]Jer. 2:25; 18:12 [b]Is. 58:3
15 [a]Is. 2:22; Mal. 4:1 [b]Jer. 7:10
16 [I]Or, *revere(d)* [a]Ps. 34:15; Jer. 31:18-20 [b]Is. 4:3; Dan. 12:1
17 [I]Lit., *make* [II]Or, *special treasure* [III]Or, *have (has) compassion on* [a]Is. 43:1 [b]Is. 4:2 [c]Ex. 19:5; Deut. 7:6; Is. 43:21; 1Pet. 2:9 [d]Ps. 103:13
18 [a]Gen. 18:25; Amos 5:15

1 [I]Ch. 3:19 in Heb. [a]Ps. 21:9; Nah. 1:5, 6; Mal. 3:2, 3; 2Pet. 3:7 [b]Is. 5:24; Obad. 18 [c]Is. 9:18, 19
2 [I]Or, *revere* [a]2Sam. 23:4; Is. 30:26; 60:1 [b]Jer. 30:17; 33:6 [c]Is. 35:6
3 [I]Or, *when I act* [a]Job 40:12; Is. 26:6; Mic. 5:8 [b]Ezek. 28:18 [c]Mal. 3:17
4 [I]Ch. 3:22 in Heb. [a]Deut. 4:23; 8:11, 19
5 [a]Matt. 11:14; 17:10-13; Mark 9:11-13; Luke 1:17; John 1:21
6 [I]Or, *turn* [II]Or, *ban of destruction* [a]Luke 1:17 [b]Is. 11:4; Rev. 19:15

🔑 **4:5-6** These last two verses of the O.T., as it is arranged in our English Bibles, point ahead to the coming of Elijah, one of the most unique figures of the O.T. The rabbis taught that Elijah would return to prepare for and announce the coming of the Messiah (see Mt. 17:10; Mk. 9:11). Even in the intertestamental period, Elijah was seen as one of the great O.T. personalities (Sirach 48:1-12a). When asked who he was by Jewish religious leaders from Jerusalem, John the Baptist denied that he was Elijah (Jn. 1:21), but perhaps he meant simply that he was not the actual Elijah reincarnated. This may also have been the point being made by the angel when, in speaking to Zechariah in the temple, he said that John would go "in the *spirit and power* of Elijah" (Lk. 1:17). Jesus publicly identified John as the one whom the Jews were expecting to come as Elijah (Mt. 11:11-14). After meeting with Elijah at His transfiguration, Jesus alluded to Mal. 4:5,6 as He explained to Peter, James and John that John fulfilled the prophecy about Elijah's return (Mt. 17:10-13; Mk. 9:11-13).

The
NEW TESTAMENT
of Our Lord and Saviour
Jesus Christ

The Gospel According to

MATTHEW

Although this account does not say that Matthew (Levi) was the author, it was known from a very early time that Matthew did write this Gospel. The name Matthew means "gift of God" in Hebrew. Matthew was an eyewitness of Jesus' entire ministry. Matthew was one of the original Twelve Apostles (see Mt. 10:3). Jesus called him to leave his occupation of gathering taxes for the Romans (see Mt. 9:9-13). Luke 5:27-32 mentions that Matthew gave a banquet for Jesus and that he forsook everything to follow the Lord, but Matthew's own account modestly omits this. He was present on the day of Pentecost (Acts 1:12—2:47). No one knows precisely *when* Matthew wrote this book, but it is clear that he aimed it at a Jewish audience. There are many quotations from the Old Testament. He stressed the passages which show that Jesus is the Messiah (Christ). For the most part, the narrative is chronological, but some of the material is grouped according to subject matter (e.g., the Sermon on the Mount in Mt. 5—7 and the parables in Mt. 13). The central theme of Matthew's presentation of the life of Jeus is: Jesus is Savior and King of the long-awaited kingdom of God.

Genealogy of Jesus Christ

1 The book[976] of the genealogy[1078] of Jesus Christ,[5547] [a]the son of David, [b]the son of Abraham.

2 To Abraham was born[1080] Isaac; and to Isaac, Jacob; and to Jacob, [I]Judah and his brothers;

3 and to Judah were born Perez and Zerah by Tamar; and to [a]Perez was born Hezron; and to Hezron, [I]Ram;

4 and to Ram was born Amminadab; and to Amminadab, Nahshon; and to Nahshon, Salmon;

5 and to Salmon was born Boaz by Rahab; and to Boaz was born Obed by Ruth; and to Obed, Jesse;

6 and to Jesse was born David the king.[935]

And to David [a]was born Solomon by her *who had been the wife* of Uriah;

7 and to Solomon [a]was born Rehoboam; and to Rehoboam, Abijah; and to Abijah, [I]Asa;

8 and to Asa was born Jehoshaphat; and to Jehoshaphat, [I]Joram; and to Joram, Uzziah;

9 and to Uzziah was born [I]Jotham; and to Jotham, Ahaz; and to Ahaz, Hezekiah;

10 and to Hezekiah was born Manasseh; and to Manasseh, [I]Amon; and to Amon, Josiah;

11 and to Josiah were born [I]Jeconiah and his brothers,[80] at the time of the [a]deportation to Babylon.

12 And after the [a]deportation to Babylon, to Jeconiah was born [I]Shealtiel; and to Shealtiel, Zerubbabel;

13 and to Zerubbabel was born [I]Abihud; and to Abihud, Eliakim; and to Eliakim, Azor;

14 and to Azor was born Zadok; and to Zadok, Achim; and to Achim, Eliud;

15 and to Eliud was born Eleazar; and to Eleazar, Matthan; and to Matthan, Jacob;

16 and to Jacob was born Joseph the husband[435] of Mary, by [f-gc]whom was born Jesus, [a]who is called [I]Christ.[5547]

17 Therefore all the generations from Abraham to David are fourteen generations;[1074] and from David to the [a]deportation to Babylon fourteen generations; and from the [a]deportation to Babylon to *the time of* [I]Christ fourteen generations.

1 [a]2Sam. 7:12-16; Ps. 89:3f.; 132:11; Is. 9:6f.; 11:1; Matt. 9:27; Luke 1:32, 69; John 7:42; Acts 13:23; Rom. 1:3; Rev. 22:16 [b]Matt. 1:1-6; *Luke 3:32-34;* Gen. 22:18; Gal. 3:16
2 [I]Gr., *Judas.* Names of Old Testament characters will be given in their Old Testament form.
3 [I]Gr., *Aram* [a]Ruth 4:18-22; 1Chr. 2:1-15; Matt. 1:3-6
6 [a]2Sam. 11:27; 12:24
7 [I]Gr., *Asaph* [a]1Chr. 3:10ff.
8 [I]Gr., *Jehoram*
9 [I]Gr., *Joatham*
10 [I]Gr., *Amos*
11 [I]Or, *Jehoiachin* [a]2Kin. 24:14f.; Jer. 27:20; Matt. 1:17
12 [I]Gr., *Salathiel* [a]2Kin. 24:14f.; Jer. 27:20; Matt. 1:17
13 [I]Gr., *Abiud*
16 [I]I.e., the Messiah [a]Matt. 27:17, 22; Luke 2:11; John 4:25
17 [I]I.e., the Messiah [a]2Kin. 24:14f.; Jer. 27:20; Matt. 1:11, 12

Conception and Birth of Jesus

18 Now the birth1083 of Jesus Christ
was as follows. When His [a]mother
Mary had been betrothed[3423] to Joseph,
before they came together she was
[b]found to be with child by the Holy
Spirit.[4151]
19 And Joseph her husband, being
a righteous[1342] man, and not wanting[2309]
to disgrace her, desired [I][a]to put[630] her
away secretly.2977
20 But when he had considered this,
behold, an angel[32] of the Lord appeared[5316] to him in a dream, saying,
"[a]Joseph, son of David, do not be
afraid[5399] to take3880 Mary as your wife;
for that which [aptp]has been [I]conceived[1080]
in her is of the Holy Spirit.
21 "And she will bear a Son;[5207] and
[a]you shall call His name[3686] Jesus, for
it is He who [b]will save[4982] His people[2992]
from their sins."[266]
22 Now all this [pfi] [I]took place[1096] that
what was [a]spoken by the Lord through
the prophet might be fulfilled,[4137] saying,
23 "[a]BEHOLD, THE VIRGIN3933 SHALL
BE WITH [b]CHILD, AND SHALL BEAR A SON,
AND THEY SHALL CALL HIS NAME [I]IMMAN-
UEL," which translated means, "[c]GOD[2316]
WITH US."
24 And Joseph arose from his sleep,
and did as the angel of the Lord
commanded4367 him, and took3830 *her* as
his wife,
🔑 25 and [ipf] [I]kept her a virgin until she
[a]gave birth to a Son; and [b]he called His
name Jesus.

Visit of the Wise Men

2 Now after Jesus was [a]born in Bethlehem of Judea in[1722] the days[2250]
of [b]Herod the king,[935] behold, [I]magi
from the east arrived in Jerusalem, saying,
2 "Where is He who [aptp]has been
born[5088] [a]King[935] of the Jews? For we
[ao]saw[1492] [b]His star in the east, and
[ao]have come[2064] to worship Him."
3 And when Herod the king heard[191]
it, he was troubled, and all Jerusalem
with[3326] him.
4 And gathering together[4863] all the
chief priests[749] and scribes[1122] of the
people, he *began* to inquire of them
where [I]the Christ [pin]was to be born.
5 And they said to him, "[a]In Bethlehem of Judea, for so it [pfip]has been written [I]by the prophet,[4396]
6 '[a]AND YOU, BETHLEHEM,
LAND[1093] OF JUDAH,
ARE BY NO MEANS LEAST
AMONG[1722] THE LEADERS OF
JUDAH;
FOR OUT OF YOU SHALL COME
FORTH A RULER,[2233]
WHO WILL [b]SHEPHERD MY
PEOPLE ISRAEL.' "
7 Then Herod secretly2977 called
the magi, and ascertained from them
[I]the time[5550] [a]the star [ppt]appeared.[5316]
8 And he [apt]sent them to Bethle-
hem, and said, [apt]"Go and [aim]make careful search for the Child; and when you
have found *Him,* report[518] to me, that
I too may [apt]come and[2064] [aosb]worship
Him."
9 And having heard the king, they
went their way; and lo, the star, which
they had seen[1492] in the east, [ipf]went
on before them, until it [apt]came and stood
over where the Child was.
10 And when they saw the star, they
rejoiced[5463] exceedingly with great
joy.[5479]
11 And they [apt]came into the
house[3614] and saw the Child with
[a]Mary His mother; and they [apt]fell
down[4098] and [ao] [b]worshiped Him; and
[apt]opening their treasures they presented to Him gifts[1435] of gold and
frankincense3030 and myrrh.4666
12 And having [aptp]been [a]warned *by*
God[5537] [b]in a dream not to return to
Herod, they departed for their own
country by another[243] way.[3598]

18 [a]Matt. 12:46; Luke 1:27 [b]Luke 1:35
19 [I]Or, *to divorce her* [a]Deut. 22:20-24; 24:1-4; John 8:4, 5
20 [I]Lit., *begotten* [a]Luke 2:4
21 [a]Luke 1:31; 2:21 [b]Luke 2:11; John 1:29; Acts 4:12; 5:31; 13:23, 38, 39; Col. 1:20-23
22 [I]Or, *has taken place* [a]Luke 24:44; Rom. 1:2-4
23 [I]Or, *Emmanuel* [a]Is. 7:14 [b]Is. 9:6, 7 [c]Is. 8:10
25 [I]Lit., *was not knowing her* [a]Luke 2:7 [b]Matt. 1:21; Luke 2:21

1 [I]Pronounced may-ji, a caste of wise men specializing in astrology, medicine and natural science [a]Mic. 5:2; Luke 2:4-7 [b]Luke 1:5
2 [a]Jer. 23:5; 30:9; Zech. 9:9; Matt. 27:11; Luke 19:38; 23:38; John 1:49 [b]Num. 24:17
4 [I]I.e., the Messiah
5 [I]Lit., *through* [a]John 7:42
6 [a]Mic. 5:2; John 7:42 [b]John 21:16
7 [I]Lit., *the time of the appearing star* [a]Num. 24:17
11 [a]Matt. 1:18; 12:46 [b]Matt. 14:33
12 [a]Matt. 2:13, 19, 22; Luke 2:26; Acts 10:22; Heb. 8:5; 11:7 [b]Job 33:15, 16; Matt. 1:20

🔑 **1:25** See note on Col. 1:15.

The Flight to Egypt

13 Now when they [apt]had departed,
behold, an [a]angel of the Lord *[b]ap-
peared5316 to Joseph in a dream,
saying, [apt]"Arise and take3880 the Child
and His mother, and flee to Egypt, and
remain there until I tell you; for Herod
is going to search for the Child to
destroy622 Him."
14 And he [apt]arose and took3880 the
Child and His mother by night, and departed for Egypt;
15 and was there until the death5054
of Herod, that what was spoken by the
Lord through the prophet might be fulfilled, saying, "[a]OUT OF EGYPT DID I
[ao]CALL [b]MY SON."

Herod Slaughters Babies

16 Then when Herod [apt]saw that
he had been tricked by [a]the magi, he
became very enraged,2373 and [apt]sent649
and [b]slew all the male children who were
in Bethlehem and in all its environs, from
two years old and under,2736 according
to the time5550 which he had ascertained
from the magi.
17 Then that which was spoken
through Jeremiah the prophet was fulfilled, saying,
18 "[a]A VOICE5456 WAS HEARD191 IN
RAMAH,
WEEPING AND GREAT
MOURNING,
RACHEL WEEPING FOR HER
CHILDREN;
AND SHE REFUSED TO BE
COMFORTED,
BECAUSE THEY WERE NO
MORE."
19 But when Herod [apt]was dead,5053
behold, an angel of the Lord *[a]appeared
in a dream to Joseph in Egypt, saying,
20 [apt]"Arise and take3880 the Child
and His mother, and go into the land1093
of Israel; for those who [ppt]sought the
Child's life [pfi]are dead."2343
21 And he [apt]arose and took3880 the
Child and His mother, and came into
the land of Israel.
22 But when he [apt]heard that Archelaus [pin]was reigning936 over Judea in
place of his father3962 Herod, he was
afraid5399 to go there. And [aptp]being
[a]warned by God5537 in a dream, he departed for the regions of Galilee,
23 and [apt]came and resided2730 in
a city called [a]Nazareth, that what was
spoken through the prophets might
be fulfilled, "He shall be called a [b]Naza-
rene."

John the Baptist Preaches

3 Now [a]in1722 those days [b]John the
Baptist910 [pin] *[I]came, [II]preaching2784
in the [c]wilderness of Judea, saying,
2 [pim]"[a]Repent,3340 for [b]the king-
dom932 of [I]heaven [II]is [pfi]at hand."1448
3 For this is the [a]one referred to
[I]by Isaiah the prophet, saying,
"[b]THE VOICE5456 OF ONE CRYING
IN THE WILDERNESS,
'[aim] [c]MAKE READY THE WAY3598
OF [an]THE LORD,
[pim]MAKE4160 HIS PATHS
STRAIGHT!'"
4 Now John himself [ipf]had2192 [I][a]a
garment of camel's hair, and a leather
belt2223 about his waist; and his food
was [b]locusts and wild honey.
5 Then Jerusalem [ipf] [a]was going out
to him, and all Judea, and all [b]the district
around the Jordan;
6 and they [ipf]were being [a]baptized907
by him in the Jordan River, as they
confessed1843 their sins.266
7 But when he [apt]saw many of the
[a]Pharisees and [b]Sadducees [pin]coming
for baptism,908 he said to them, "You
[c]brood of vipers, who [ao]warned you to
flee from [d]the wrath3709 to come?3195
8 "[a]Therefore [aim]bring forth fruit
[b]in keeping with514 [art]repentance;3341
9 and do not [aim]suppose that you
can say to yourselves, '[a]We have Abraham for our father'; for I say to you,
that God is able1410 from these stones
to raise up children to Abraham.
10 "And [a]the axe is already
[pin]laid2749 at the root of the trees;
[b]every tree therefore that does not
[ppt]bear good fruit is cut1581 down and
thrown906 into the fire.

13 [a]Acts 5:19; 10:7; 12:7-11 [b]Matt. 2:12, 19
15 [a]Hos. 11:1; Num. 24:8 [b]Ex. 4:22f.
16 [a]Matt. 2:1 [b]Is. 59:7
18 [a]Jer. 31:15
19 [a]Matt. 1:20; 2:12, 13, 22
22 [a]Matt. 2:12, 13, 19
23 [a]Luke 1:26; 2:39; John 1:45, 46 [b]Mark 1:24; John 18:5, 7; 19:19

1 [I]Or, *arrived* [II]Or, *proclaiming as a herald* [a]Matt. 3:1-12; *Mark 1:3-8; Luke 3:2-17;* John 1:6-8, 19-28 [b]Matt. 11:11-14; 16:14 [c]Josh. 15:61; Judg. 1:16
2 [I]Lit., *the heavens* [II]Lit., *has come near* [a]Matt. 4:17 [b]Dan. 2:44; Matt. 4:17, 23; 6:10; 10:7; Mark 1:15; Luke 10:9f.; 11:20; 21:31
3 [I]Lit., *through* [a]Luke 1:17, 76 [b]Is. 40:3 [c]John 1:23
4 [I]Lit., *his garment* [a]2Kin. 1:8; Zech. 13:4; Matt. 11:8; Mark 1:6 [b]Lev. 11:22
5 [a]Mark 1:5 [b]Luke 3:3
6 [a]Matt. 3:11, 13-16; Mark 1:5; John 1:25, 26; 3:23; Acts 1:5; 2:38-41; 10:37
7 [a]Matt. 16:1ff.; 23:13, 15 [b]Matt. 22:23; Acts 4:1; 5:17; 23:6ff. [c]Matt. 12:34; 23:33 [d]1Thess. 1:10
8 [a]Luke 3:8; Eph. 5:8, 9 [b]Acts 26:20
9 [a]Luke 3:8; 16:24; John 8:33, 39, 53; Acts 13:26; Rom. 4:1; 9:7, 8; Gal. 3:29
10 [a]Luke 3:9 [b]Ps. 92:12-14; Matt. 7:19; John 15:2

🗝 11 "As for me, [a]I baptize[907] you [I]with water for repentance,[3341] but He who is [ppt]coming after me is mightier than I, and I am[1510] not fit[2425] to remove His sandals;5266 [b]He will [ft]baptize you [I]with the [an]Holy Spirit[4151] and fire.

12 "And His [a]winnowing fork is in His hand, and He will thoroughly [ft]clear His threshing floor; and He will [ft] [b]gather His wheat into the barn,596 but He will [ft]burn up the [c]chaff with [d]unquenchable fire."

The Baptism of Jesus

13 [a]Then Jesus *arrived [b]from Galilee at the Jordan *coming* to John, to be baptized by him.

14 But John tried to [ipf]prevent Him, saying, "I have need to be baptized by You, and do You come to me?"

15 But Jesus answering[611] said to him, "Permit *it* at this time; for in this way it is fitting for us [a]to fulfill[4137] all righteousness."[1343] Then he *permitted Him.

16 And after being baptized, Jesus went up[305] immediately2117 from the water; and behold, the heavens were opened, and [I][a]he saw the Spirit of God descending[2597] as a dove, *and* coming upon Him,

17 and behold, a voice[5456] out of the heavens, saying, "[a]This is [I]My beloved[27] Son,[5207] in whom I am well-[ao]pleased."[2106]

Temptation of Jesus

4 🗝 [a]Then Jesus was led up by the Spirit[4151] into the wilderness [aifp] [b]to be tempted[3985] by the devil.[1228]

2 And after He had [a]fasted3522 forty days and forty nights, He [I]then became hungry.[3983]

3 And [a]the tempter[3985] came and said to Him, "If You are [an]the [b]Son of God, command that these stones become[1096] [I]bread."

4 But He answered[611] and said, "It [pfip]is written,[1125] '[a]MAN[444] SHALL NOT [ft]LIVE[2198] ON BREAD ALONE, BUT ON EVERY WORD[4487] THAT [ppt]PROCEEDS OUT OF THE MOUTH OF GOD.' "

5 Then the devil *took3880 Him into [a]the holy city; and he had Him [pin]stand[2476] on [art]the pinnacle of the temple,[2411]

6 and *said to Him, "If You are the [an]Son of God throw[906] Yourself down;[2736] for it is [pfip]written,[1125]

'[a]HE WILL GIVE HIS ANGELS
CHARGE[1781] CONCERNING
YOU';
and
'ON *their* HANDS THEY WILL
BEAR[142] YOU UP,
LEST YOU [asba]STRIKE[4350] YOUR
FOOT AGAINST A STONE.' "

7 Jesus said to him, "[I]On the other hand, it is written,[1125] '[a]YOU SHALL NOT [II]PUT THE LORD YOUR GOD TO THE [ft]TEST.' "[1598]

8 [a]Again, the devil [pin]*took3880 Him to a very high mountain, and [pin]*showed Him all the kingdoms[932] of the world, and their glory;[1391]

9 and he [ao]said to Him, "[a]All these things will I give You, if You [apt]fall down[4098] and [asba]worship me."

10 Then Jesus *said to him, "Begone, Satan![4567] For it [pfip]is written,[1125] '[a]YOU SHALL WORSHIP THE LORD YOUR GOD, AND [I]SERVE[3000] HIM ONLY.' "

11 Then the devil *left Him; and behold, [a]angels came and *began* to [ipf]minister[1247] to Him.

Jesus Begins His Ministry

12 Now when He heard that [a]John had [I]been taken into custody, [b]He withdrew into Galilee;

13 and leaving Nazareth, He came and [ao] [a]settled[2730] in Capernaum, which

11 [I]The Gr. here can be translated *in, with* or *by* [a]Mark 1:4, 8; Luke 3:16; John 1:26f.; Acts 1:5; 8:36, 38; 11:16 [b]John 1:33; Acts 2:3, 4; Titus 3:5
12 [a]Is. 30:24; 41:16; Jer. 15:7; 51:2; Luke 3:17 [b]Matt. 13:30 [c]Ps. 1:4 [d]Is. 66:24; Jer. 7:20; Matt. 13:41, 42; Mark 9:43, 48
13 [a]Matt. 3:13-17; *Mark 1:9-11; Luke 3:21, 22;* John 1:31-34 [b]Matt. 2:22
15 [a]Ps. 40:7, 8; John 4:34; 8:29
16 [I]Or, *He* [a]Mark 1:10; Luke 3:22; John 1:32; Acts 7:56
17 [I]Lit., *My Son, the Beloved* [a]Ps. 2:7; Is. 42:1; Matt. 12:18; 17:5; Mark 9:7; Luke 9:35; John 12:28

1 [a]Matt. 4:1-11; *Mark 1:12, 13; Luke 4:1-13* [b]Heb. 4:15; James 1:14
2 [I]Lit., *later, afterward* [a]Ex. 34:28; 1Kin. 19:8
3 [I]Lit., *loaves* [a]1Thess. 3:5 [b]Matt. 14:33; 26:63; Mark 3:11; 5:7; Luke 1:35; 4:41; John 1:34, 49; Acts 9:20
4 [a]Deut. 8:3
5 [a]Neh. 11:1, 18; Dan. 9:24; Matt. 27:53
6 [a]Ps. 91:11, 12
7 [I]Lit., *Again* [II]Or, *tempt . . . God* [a]Deut. 6:16
8 [a]Matt. 16:26; 1John 2:15-17
9 [a]1Cor. 10:20f.
10 [I]Or, *fulfill religious duty to Him* [a]Deut. 6:13; 10:20
11 [a]Matt. 26:53; Luke 22:43; Heb. 1:14
12 [I]Lit., *been delivered up*

[a]Matt. 14:3; Mark 1:14; Luke 3:20; John 3:24 [b]Mark 1:14; Luke 4:14; John 1:43; 2:11 **13** [a]Matt. 11:23; Mark 1:21; 2:1; Luke 4:23, 31; John 2:12; 4:46f.

🗝 **3:11** See notes on Acts 1:5; 2:1-13; 11:15-18; 19:1-7.
🗝 **4:1-11** See note on Js. 1:13-15.

is by the sea, in the region of Zebulun
and Naphtali.
14 *This was* to fulfill what was spo-
ken through Isaiah the prophet, saying,
15 "[a]THE LAND[1093] OF ZEBULUN AND
THE LAND OF NAPHTALI,
[I]BY THE WAY[3598] OF THE SEA,
BEYOND THE JORDAN,
GALILEE OF THE
[II]GENTILES—
16 "[a]THE PEOPLE WHO [ppt]WERE
SITTING IN DARKNESS[4655]
SAW A GREAT LIGHT,[5457]
AND TO THOSE WHO [ppt]WERE
SITTING IN THE LAND AND
SHADOW OF DEATH,[2288]
UPON THEM A LIGHT
[ao]DAWNED."
17 [a]From that time Jesus [ao]began[756]
to [I]preach[2784] and say, [pim]"[b]Repent,[3340]
for the kingdom[932] of heaven [pfi]is at
hand."[1448]

The First Disciples

18 [a]And walking by [b]the Sea of Galilee, He saw two brothers, [c]Simon who
was [ppp]called Peter, and Andrew his
brother, casting[906] a net[293] into the sea;
for they were fishermen.
19 And He *said to them, "[I]Follow
Me, and I will make[4160] you fishers of
men."[444]
20 And they immediately[2112]
[apt]left[863] the nets,[1350] and followed[190]
Him.
21 And going on from there He saw
two other[243] brothers, [Ia]James the *son*

15 [I]Or, *Toward the sea* [II]Or, *nations* [a]Is. 9:1
16 [a]Is. 9:2; 60:1-3; Luke 2:32
17 [I]Or, *proclaim* [a]Mark 1:14, 15 [b]Matt. 3:2
18 [a]Matt. 4:18-22; *Mark 1:16-20;* Luke 5:2-11; John 1:40-42 [b]Matt. 15:29; Mark 7:31; Luke 5:1; John 6:1 [c]Matt. 10:2; 16:18; John 1:40-42
19 [I]Lit., *Come here after Me*
21 [I]Or, *Jacob* [II]Gr., *Joannes*, Heb., *Johanan* [a]Matt. 10:2; 20:20
23 [I]Or, *good news* [a]Mark 1:39; Luke 4:14, 44 [b]Matt. 9:35; 13:54; Mark 1:21; 6:2; 10:1; Luke 4:15; 6:6; 13:10; John 6:59; 18:20 [c]Matt. 3:2; 9:35; 24:14; Mark 1:14; Luke 4:43; 8:1; 16:16; Acts 20:25; 28:31 [d]Matt. 8:16; 9:35; 14:14; 15:30; 19:2; 21:14; Mark 1:34; 3:10; Luke 4:40; 7:21; Acts 10:38
24 [I]Lit., *moonsmitten* [a]Mark 7:26; Luke 2:2; Acts 15:23; 18:18; 20:3; 21:3; Gal. 1:21 [b]Matt. 8:16, 28, 33; 9:32; 12:22; 15:22; Mark 1:32; 5:15, 16,

of Zebedee, and [II]John his brother, in
the boat with Zebedee their father,[3962]
mending[2675] their nets;[1350] and He called
them.
22 And they immediately left[863] the
boat and their father, and followed Him.

Ministry in Galilee

23 And *Jesus* was [ipf]going about
[a]in all Galilee, [b]teaching[1321] in their synagogues, and [c]proclaiming[2784] the [I]gos-
pel[2098] of the kingdom, and [d]healing[2323]
every kind of disease[3119] and every kind
of sickness[3554] among the people.
24 And the news[189] about Him went
out [a]into all Syria; and they brought to[4374]
Him all who were ill, [ppt]taken with[4912]
various[4164] diseases[3554] and pains,
[ppt] [b]demoniacs,[1139] [Ic]epileptics, [d]para-
lytics;[3885] and He [ao]healed[2323] them.
25 And great multitudes [a]fol-
lowed[190] Him from Galilee and [b]Decapo-
lis and Jerusalem and Judea and *from*
[c]beyond the Jordan.

The Sermon on the Mount
The Beatitudes

5 🔑 [a]And when He saw the multitudes, He went up[305] on [b]the
[I]mountain; and after He [apt]sat down, His
disciples[3101] came[4334] to Him.

18; Luke 8:36; John 10:21 [c]Matt. 17:15 [d]Matt. 8:6; 9:2, 6; Mark 2:3-5, 9; Luke 5:24
25 [a]Mark 3:7, 8; Luke 6:17 [b]Mark 5:20; 7:31 [c]Matt. 4:15
1 [I]Or, *hill* [a]Matt. 5:1-7:29; Luke 6:20-49 [b]Mark 3:13; Luke 6:17; 9:28; John 6:3, 15

🔑 **5:1-12** The Beatitudes must be taken as a whole having as the basis the last phrase, v. 11, "on account of Me." The Lord said to his disciples, "blessed are you . . . on account of Me." The word for "blessed" is *makarioi,* which means to be characterized by the quality of God, "blessedness," *makariotēs.* When one is indwelt by God, and God's nature is in him, he has the kingdom of God within him (Lk. 17:21). "Blessed" also means to be fully satisfied. This satisfaction, however, is not due to the circumstances of life nor the fulfillment of the conditions prescribed in these Beatitudes, but due to Christ's indwelling. Therefore, it is wrong to translate *makarioi* as "happy" because happy is connected with luck, *hap* from the verb "happen." People can be happy because of favorable circumstances, but they can only be blessed because of Christ. Blessedness is that basic condition created by Christ's indwelling in man's heart which brings a fundamental satisfaction in the life of a believer.

Blessedness, however, is not static, but progressive. This progressiveness of blessedness depends upon the fulfillment of the conditions set down in these Beatitudes: (1) "The poor in spirit . . ." (*ptōchos,* 4434), here indicates the helpless person contrasted to *penēs* (3993), which means "poor but able to help oneself." The first step to blessedness is the realization of one's spiritual helplessness.

(continued on next page)

2 And [apt] [a]opening His mouth He *began* to [ipf]teach them, saying,

3 [ajn]“[a]Blessed[3107] are the poor[4434] in [art]spirit,[4151] for [b]theirs is the kingdom[932] of heaven.[3772]

4 “Blessed are [a]those who [ppt]mourn,[3996] for they [fp]shall be comforted.

5 “Blessed are [a]the [1]gentle,[4239] for they shall inherit[2816] the earth.

6 “Blessed are [a]those who [ppt]hunger and [ppt]thirst for [art]righteousness,[1343] for they [fp]shall be satisfied.

🔑 7 “Blessed are [a]the merciful,[1655] for they [fp]shall receive mercy.

8 “Blessed are [a]the pure[2513] in heart,[2588] for [b]they shall see God.[2316]

9 “Blessed are the peacemakers,[1518] for [a]they shall be called [an]sons[5207] of God.

🔑 10 “Blessed are those who have been [pfpp] [a]persecuted for the sake of righteousness, for [b]theirs is the kingdom of heaven.

11 “Blessed are you when *men* [a]cast [aosb]insults at you, and [aosb]persecute you, and [aosb]say all kinds of evil[4190] against you falsely, on account of Me.

12 [pim]“Rejoice,[5463] and [pim]be glad,[21] for your reward[3408] in heaven[3772] is great, for [a]so they persecuted the prophets[4396] who were before you.

Disciples and the World

13 “You are the salt of the earth; but [a]if the salt has become [asbp]tasteless,[3471] how will it be made [fp]salty *again*? It is good[2480] for nothing anymore, except to be [aptp]thrown[906] out and [pip]trampled under foot by men.

14 “You are [a]the light[5457] of the

2 [a]Matt. 13:35; Acts 8:35; 10:34; 18:14
3 [a]Matt. 5:3-12; Luke 6:20-23 [b]Matt. 5:10; 19:14; 25:34; Mark 10:14; Luke 6:20; 22:29f.
4 [a]Is. 61:2; John 16:20; Rev. 7:17
5 [1]Or, *humble, meek* [a]Ps. 37:11
6 [a]Is. 55:1, 2; John 4:14; 6:48ff.; 7:37
7 [a]Prov. 11:17; Matt. 6:14, 15; 18:33-35
8 [a]Ps. 24:4 [b]Heb. 12:14; 1John 3:2; Rev. 22:4
9 [a]Matt. 5:45; Luke 6:35; Rom. 8:14
10 [a]1Pet. 3:14 [b]Matt. 5:3; 19:14; 25:34; Mark 10:14; Luke 6:20; 22:29f.
11 [a]1Pet. 4:14
12 [a]2Chr. 36:16; Matt. 23:37; Acts 7:52; 1Thess. 2:15; Heb. 11:33ff.; James 5:10
13 [a]Mark 9:50; Luke 14:34f.
14 [a]Prov. 4:18; John 8:12; 9:5; 12:36

(continued from previous page)

(2) “Those who mourn . . .” *hoi penthountes* (3996), sorrow for one’s sins and the sins of others. It is the passive attitude. (3) “Humbleness,” (*prautēs,* 4240, and *praos,* 4235, or *praus,* 4239) which in this context means to become angry at sin. It is the active attitude of the Christian toward sin in combating it instead of a passive, indifferent attitude. (4) When one exercises active combativeness against sin, he hungers for a new filling of God’s righteousness (*dikaiosunē,* 1343) which is the realization of God’s rightful expectation of the beliver. “Those who hunger . . .” in Greek is the present participle *hoi peinōntes,* which is better rendered “the hungering ones,” indicating constant and iterative satisfaction with God’s righteousness, expending the received energy and hungering anew over and over as with physical hunger. (5) The outward demonstration of the Christian character is shown in “mercifulness” (*eleos,* 1656). This is the missionary and altruistic attitude of the Christian in empathizing with the unbeliever and suffering with him the consequences of his sin and doing everything possible to relieve the tragic results. The difference between “grace” *charis* (5485) and *eleos,* is that the first affects the character of a person and changes it. Only God can effect grace but we are admonished to show mercy and be *eleēmones* (1655), “merciful,” to alleviate the consequences of sin. (6) Purity of heart is not something that is achieved once and for all, but it is a continuous cleansing that the believer experiences as a result of the fulfillment of the previous conditions of blessedness. The more pure a person is, the more clear his sight of God becomes. (7) “Peacemaking,” is not simply trying to stop the feuding between nations and people, but bringing the peace of God that the believer has experienced to his fellow human beings. (8) Being “persecuted for the sake of righteousness” causes a person to reach the highest rung of the satisfaction of blessedness.

When does this state of blessedness begin with the believer? It is not something to be experienced in the afterlife as the Greeks believed, but it is something that begins the very moment that a person believes on Jesus Christ. This is demonstrated by the fact that the promise concerning the kingdom of the heavens as in v. 3 and v. 10 is in the present tense while all the other promises are in the future. The fruits of one’s obedience to the conditions for blessedness begin here, but they are not all given here. They will be given in their totality in the future, in heaven (v. 12). For a complete study of the Beatitudes in Matthew and Luke, see the Editor’s book, *The Pursuit of Happiness.*

🔑 **5:7** See note on Js. 2:12-13.

🔑 **5:10** See note on II Tim. 2:12.

world.[2889] A city [ppt]set[2749] on a [I]hill cannot be [aifp]hidden.

15 "[a]Nor do *men* [pin]light a lamp, and put[5087] it under the peck-measure, but on the lampstand; and it gives light to all who are in the house.

16 "Let your light [aim]shine before men in such a way that they may [aosb] [a]see your good works, and [aosb] [b]glorify[1392] your Father who is in heaven.

17 "Do not think that I [am]came to [ainf]abolish the [a]Law[3551] or the Prophets;[4396] I did not come to abolish,[2647] but to [ainf]fulfill.[4137]

18 "For truly281 I say to you, [a]until heaven[3772] and earth[1093] pass away, not [I]the smallest letter2503 or stroke2762 shall pass away from the Law,[3551] until all is accomplished.[1096]

19 "Whoever then annuls[3089] one of the least of these commandments, and so [aosb]teaches[1321] [I]others, shall be called least [a]in the kingdom of heaven; but whoever [aosb] [II]keeps and [aosb]teaches *them,* he shall be [fp]called great in the kingdom of heaven.

20 "For I say to you, that unless your [a]righteousness surpasses *that* of the scribes and Pharisees, you shall [efn]not enter the kingdom of heaven.

Personal Relationships

21 "[a]You have [ao]heard that [I]the ancients[744] were told, '[b]You shall not commit murder' and 'Whoever commits murder shall be [II]liable to [c]the court.'[2920]

🔑 22 "But [epn]I say to you that everyone who is [ppp]angry with his brother[I] [80] shall be [II]guilty before [a]the court;[2920] and whoever shall say to his brother, '[III]Raca,'4469 shall be [II]guilty before [IV][b]the supreme court; and whoever shall say, 'You fool,'[3474] shall be [II]guilty *enough to go* into the [V][c]fiery hell.[1067]

23 "If therefore you are [aosb] [a]presenting4374 your [I]offering[1435] at the altar, and there [asbp]remember that your brother[80] has something against you,

24 leave863 your [I]offering[1435] there before the altar, and go your way; first[4412] be [a]reconciled[1259] to your brother,[80] and then come and present4374 your [I]offering.

25 [ppt]"[a]Make friends[2132] quickly with your opponent[476] at law while you are with him on the way, in order that your opponent may not [aosb]deliver you to the judge, and the judge[2923] to the officer, and you be thrown[906] into prison.

26 "Truly I say to you, [a]you shall [efn]not come out of there, until you have paid up the last[2078] [I]cent.2835

🔑 **27** "[a]You have [ao]heard that it was said, '[b]You shall not [ft]commit adultery';

🔑 28 but [epn]I say to you, that everyone who [ppt]looks on a woman [a]to [aipr]lust[1937] for her has [ao]committed adultery3431 with her already in his heart.[2588]

🔑 29 "And [a]if your right[1188] eye makes you [pin] [I]stumble,[4624] [aim]tear it out, and [aim]throw it from you; for it is better[4851] for you that one of the parts of your body perish, [II]than for your whole body to be thrown into [III][b]hell.[1067]

30 "And [a]if your right[1188] hand makes you [pin] [I]stumble, [aim]cut it off, and [aim]throw[906] it from you; for it is better for you that one of the parts of your

14 [I]Or, *mountain*
15 [a]Mark 4:21; Luke 8:16; 11:33; Phil. 2:15
16 [a]1Pet. 2:12 [b]Matt. 9:8
17 [a]Matt. 7:12
18 [I]Lit., *one iota* (yodh) or *one projection of a letter* (serif) [a]Matt. 24:35; Luke 16:17
19 [I]Lit., *the men* [II]Lit., *does* [a]Matt. 11:11
20 [a]Luke 18:11, 12
21 [I]Lit., *it was said to the ancients* [II]Or, *guilty before* [a]Matt. 5:27, 33, 38, 43 [b]Ex. 20:13; Deut. 5:17 [c]Deut. 16:18; 2Chr. 19:5f.
22 [I]Some mss. insert *without cause* [II]Or, *liable to* [III]Aram. for *empty-head* or *good for nothing* [IV]Lit., *the Sanhedrin* [V]Lit., *Gehenna of fire* [a]Deut. 16:18; 2Chr. 19:5f. [b]Matt. 10:17; 26:59; Mark 13:9; 14:55; 15:1; Luke 22:66; John 11:47; Acts 4:15; 5:21; 6:12; 22:30; 23:1; 24:20 [c]Matt. 5:29f.; 10:28; 18:9; 23:15, 33; Mark 9:43ff.; Luke 12:5; James 3:6
23 [I]Or, *gift* [a]Matt. 5:24
24 [I]Or, *gift* [a]Rom. 12:17, 18
25 [a]Prov. 25:8f.; Luke 12:58
26 [I]Lit., *quadrans* (equaling two lepta or mites); i.e., 1/64 of a denarius [a]Luke 12:59
27 [a]Matt. 5:21, 33, 38, 43 [b]Ex. 20:14; Deut. 5:18
28 [a]2Sam. 11:2-5; Job 31:1; Matt. 15:19; James 1:14, 15
29 [I]I.e., cause to sin [II]Lit., *not your whole body* [III]Gr., *Gehenna* [a]Matt. 18:9; Mark 9:47 [b]Matt. 5:22
30 [I]I.e., cause to sin [a]Matt. 18:8; Mark 9:43

🔑 **5:22,29,30** See note on Mt. 8:11-12.

🔑 **5:27-32** These verses on adultery, divorce, and remarriage ought to be taken together as a whole. It is the person who "keeps on looking" (*ho blepōn,* 991) and caressing with his hands (v. 30) who is trapped (*skandalizō,* 4624, translated as "make you stumble") and desires to dismiss his wife although she is innocent of any moral infidelity.

🔑 **5:28-30** See note on Mt. 19:3-9.

body perish, [II]than for your whole body
to go into [IIIb]hell.[1067]
31 "And it was [aop]said, '[a]WHOEVER
[asba]SENDS HIS WIFE AWAY,[630] [aim]LET
HIM GIVE HER A CERTIFICATE OF DI-
VORCE';[647]
32 [a]but [epn]I say to you that everyone
who [I]divorces[630] his wife, except for
the cause of unchastity,[4202] makes her
[pin]commit adultery;[3431] and whoever
marries a [pfpp II]divorced[630] woman
[pin]commits adultery.
33 "Again, [a]you have [ao]heard that
[I]the ancients[744] [aop]were told, '[IIb]YOU
SHALL NOT [III]MAKE FALSE VOWS, BUT
SHALL FULFILL YOUR [IV]VOWS TO THE
LORD.'
34 "But [epn]I say to you, [a]make no
oath at all, either by heaven,[3772] for it
is [b]the throne of God,[2316]
35 or by the earth,[1093] for it is the
[a]footstool of His feet, or [I]by Jerusalem,
for it is [b]THE CITY OF THE GREAT
KING.[935]
36 "Nor shall you make an oath by
your head, for you cannot make[4160] one
hair white or black.
37 "But [pim]let your statement be,
'Yes, yes' *or* 'No, no'; and anything
beyond[4053] these is [I]of [a]evil.
38 "[a]You have [ao]heard that it was
[aop]said, '[b]AN EYE FOR AN EYE, AND A
TOOTH FOR A TOOTH.'
39 "But [epn]I say to you, do not resist
him who is evil;[4190] but [a]whoever
slaps[4474] you on your right[1188] cheek,
turn to him the other[243] also.
40 "And if anyone wants to sue[2919]
you, and take your [I]shirt,[5509] let him
have[863] your [II]coat also.
41 "And whoever shall force you
to go[29] one mile, go with[3326] him
two.[1417]
42 "[a]Give to him who [ppt]asks of you,
and do not turn[654] away from him who
wants to[2309] [ainf]borrow from you.
43 "[a]You have [ao]heard that it was
[ao]said, '[b]YOU SHALL [ft]LOVE[25] YOUR
NEIGHBOR,[4139] [c]and [ft]hate your enemy.'
44 "But [epn]I say to you, [pim a]love
your enemies, and [pim]pray for those who
[ppt]persecute you
45 in order that you may [aosb I]be[1096]
[a]sons[5207] of your Father who is in
heaven;[3772] for He causes His sun to
[pin]rise on *the* evil and *the* good,[18] and
[pin]sends rain on *the* righteous[1342] and *the*
unrighteous.[94]
46 "For [a]if you [aosb]love those who
[ppt]love you, what reward[3408] have you?
Do not even the [I]tax-gatherers[5057] do
the same?
47 "And if you [aosb]greet your
brothers[80] only, what [pin]do you do
more[4053] *than others?* [pin]Do not even the
Gentiles do the same?
48 "Therefore [a]you are to [ft]be perfect,[5046] as your heavenly[3772] Father is
perfect.

Concerning Alms and Prayer

6 [pim]"Beware of [pinf]practicing your
righteousness before men [a]to be noticed by them; otherwise you have no
reward[3408] with your Father who is in
heaven.[3772]
2 "When therefore you [psa I]give
alms, do not [aosi]sound a trumpet before
you, as the hypocrites[5273] do in the synagogues and in the streets, that they
[asbp a]may be honored[1392] by men.
[b]Truly[281] I say to you, they have[568]
their reward[3408] in full.

30 [II]Lit., *not your whole body* [III]Gr., *Gehenna* [b]Matt. 5:22
31 [a]Deut. 24:1, 3; Jer. 3:1; Matt. 19:7; Mark 10:4
32 [I]Or, *sends away* [II]Or, *sent away* [a]Matt. 19:9; Mark 10:11f.; Luke 16:18; 1Cor. 7:11f.
33 [I]Lit., *it was said to the ancients* [II]*you* and *your* are singular here [III]Or, *break your vows* [IV]Lit., *oaths* [a]Matt. 5:21, 27, 38, 43; 23:16ff. [b]Lev. 19:12; Num. 30:2; Deut. 23:21, 23
34 [a]James 5:12 [b]Is. 66:1; Matt. 23:22
35 [I]Or, *toward* [a]Is. 66:1; Acts 7:49 [b]Ps. 48:2
37 [I]Or, *from the evil one* [a]Matt. 6:13; 13:19, 38; John 17:15; 2Thess. 3:3; 1John 2:13f.; 3:12; 5:18f.
38 [a]Matt. 5:21, 27, 33, 43 [b]Ex. 21:24; Lev. 24:20; Deut. 19:21
39 [a]Matt. 5:39-42; *Luke 6:29, 30;* 1Cor. 6:7
40 [I]Or, *tunic*; i.e., garment worn next to the body [II]Or, *cloak*; i.e., outer garment
42 [a]Deut. 15:7-11; Luke 6:34f.; 1Tim. 6:18
43 [a]Matt. 5:21, 27, 33, 38 [b]Lev. 19:18 [c]Deut. 23:3-6
44 [a]Luke 6:27f.; 23:34; Acts 7:60; Rom. 12:20
45 [I]Or, *show yourselves to be* [a]Matt. 5:9; Luke 6:35; Acts 14:17
46 [I]I.e., Collectors of Roman taxes for profit [a]Luke 6:32
48 [a]Lev. 19:2; Deut. 18:13; 2Cor. 7:1; Phil. 3:12-15
1 [a]Matt. 6:5, 16; 23:5
2 [I]Or, *do an act of charity* [a]Matt. 6:5, 16; 23:5 [b]Matt. 6:5, 16; Luke 6:24

5:31-32 An exegetical paraphrase of these two very difficult verses would be "And it was said, 'Whosoever dismisses his wife, let him give her a bill of divorcement' (see Deut. 24:1-4). But I say unto you that whosoever dismisses his wife except for reason of fornication (while she is his wife) makes her to be considered as having adultery committed against her, and whosoever marries one who is unjustifiably dismissed is considered as committing adultery." See note on Mt. 19:3-9. For a complete examination of this passage and other pertinent passages on marriage, divorce and remarriage from the Old and New Testaments, see the Editor's book, *What About Divorce?*

3 "But when you [ppt]give alms, do
not let your left hand [aim]know what your
right hand[1188] is doing
4 that your [I]alms may be in secret;
and [a]your Father who [ppt]sees in secret
will repay you.
5 "And when you [psa]pray, you [ft]are
not to be as the hypocrites;[5273] for they
love[5368] to [pinf] [a]stand and pray in[1722] the
synagogues and on the street corners,
[I][b]in order to [aosb]be seen[5316] by men.
[c]Truly I say[3004] to you, they have[568] their
reward[3408] in full.
6 "But you when you [psa]pray,[4336]
[a]go into your inner room, and when you
have shut your door, [aim]pray to your
Father [ppt]who is in secret, and [b]your
Father who sees in secret will repay
you.
7 "And when you are [ppt]praying,
[aosi]do not [aosi]use meaningless repetition,[945] as the Gentiles[1482] do, for they
suppose[1380] that they will be heard for
their [a]many words.
8 "Therefore do not be like them;
for [a]your Father knows what you need,
before you [aip]ask Him.
9 "[pim] [a]Pray,[4336] then, in this way:
'Our Father[3962] who art in
[I]heaven,
[aop-opt]Hallowed be[37] Thy
name.[3868]
10 '[a]Thy kingdom[932] [aosi]come.
[b]Thy will be [ao-opt]done,[1096]
On earth[1093] as it is in
heaven.
11 '[aim] [a]Give us this day [I]our
daily[1967] bread.[740]
🔑 12 'And [aim] [a]forgive[863] us our
debts,[3783] as we also have
forgiven our debtors.[3781]
13 'And do not [aosi]lead us into
temptation,[3986] but
[ainf] [a]deliver[4506] us from
[art] [I][b]evil.[4190] [II][For Thine is the
kingdom, and the power, and
the glory, forever.
Amen.]'[281]
14 "[a]For if you [aosb]forgive[863] men
for their transgressions,[3900] your heavenly[3770] Father will also forgive you.
15 "But [a]if you do not [aosb]forgive[863]
men, then your Father will not forgive
your transgressions.

Concerning Fasting
True Treasure
Mammon

16 "And [a]whenever you [psa]fast,[3522]
do[1096] not put on a gloomy face as the
hypocrites[5273] *do,* for they [I]neglect their
[aosb]appearance[4383] in order [ppt]to be
seen[5316] fasting by men. [b]Truly I say
to you, they have[568] their reward[3408]
in full.
17 "But you, when you [ppt]fast,
[aim] [a]anoint your head,[2776] and [aim]wash[3538]
your face[4383]
18 so that you may not be [aosb]seen
fasting by men, but by your Father who
is in secret; and your [a]Father who
[ppt]sees in secret will repay you.

4 [I]Or, *deeds of charity* [a]Jer. 17:10; Matt. 6:6, 18; Heb. 4:13
5 [I]Lit., *to be apparent to men* [a]Mark 11:25; Luke 18:11, 13 [b]Matt. 6:1, 16 [c]Matt. 6:2, 16; Luke 6:24
6 [a]Is. 26:20; Matt. 26:36-39; Acts 9:40 [b]Matt. 6:4, 18
7 [a]1Kin. 18:26f.
8 [a]Ps. 38:9; 69:17-19; Matt. 6:32; Luke 12:30
9 [I]Lit., *the heavens* [a]Matt. 6:9-13; *Luke 11:2-4*
10 [a]Matt. 3:2; 4:17 [b]Matt. 26:42; Luke 22:42; Acts 21:14
11 [I]Or, *our bread for the coming day* or *our needful bread* [a]Prov. 30:8; Is. 33:16; Luke 11:3
12 [a]Ex. 34:7; Ps. 32:1; 130:4; Matt. 9:2; 26:28; Eph. 1:7; 1John 1:7-9
13 [I]Or, *the evil one* [II]This clause omitted in the earliest mss. [a]John 17:15; 1Cor. 10:13; 2Thess. 3:3; 2Tim. 4:18; 2Pet. 2:9; 1John 5:18 [b]Matt. 5:37
14 [a]Matt. 7:2; Mark 11:25f.; Eph. 4:32; Col. 3:13
15 [a]Matt. 18:35
16 [I]Lit., *render their faces unrecognizable* [a]Is. 58:5 [b]Matt. 6:2
17 [a]Ruth 3:3; 2Sam. 12:20
18 [a]Matt. 6:4, 6

🔑 **6:12-15** "Sins" are designated by two words: *opheilēmata* (3783), debts in v. 12, and *paraptōmata* (3900), transgressions in v. 14. Why did the Lord teach His disciples to pray, "Do not lead us into temptation"? Does this necessarily imply that God actually does tempt people? The noun *peirasmos* (3986), temptation, as well as the verb *peirazō* (3985), is made up of the basic word *peira,* experience. When God is the One who leads His people into temptation even as the Spirit led Jesus to be tempted (Mt. 4:1-11), it is for the purpose of proving to His child that when God leads to temptation, He does not abandon him, but He is with him to give him the victory and to make him more experienced in warfare against the devil. The Lord never leads to temptation for the purpose of causing anyone to fall, but for the purpose of proving the sufficiency of His presence. When, however, one allows Satan or his own lusts to tempt him, he should never say that he is tempted of God (Js. 1:13,14). See the Editor's first volume, *The Work of Faith,* in the three-volume set of an exegetical exposition on James. For the particular meaning of these two designations of sin in the N.T., see the Editor's book, *The Lord's Prayer.*

19 "[a]Do not [pim]lay up for yourselves treasures upon earth,[1093] where moth and rust destroy, and where thieves break in and steal.

20 "But [pim]lay up for yourselves [a]treasures in heaven,[3772] where neither moth nor rust destroys, and where thieves do not break in or steal;

21 for [a]where your treasure is, there will your heart[2588] be also.

22 "[a]The lamp of the body is the eye; if therefore your eye is [I]clear,[573] your whole body will be full of light.

23 "But if [a]your eye is bad, your whole body will be full of darkness. If therefore the light[5457] that is in you is darkness,[4655] how great is the darkness!

24 "[a]No one can [pinf]serve two masters;[2962] for either he will hate the one and love[25] the other,[2087] or he will hold[472] to one and despise the other.[2087] You cannot [pinf]serve[1398] God and [I][b]mammon.

The Cure for Anxiety

25 "[a]For this reason I say to you, [pim] [I]do not be [b]anxious for your life, *as to* what you shall [aosb]eat, or what you shall [aosb]drink; nor for your body,[4983] *as to* what you shall [aosb]put on. Is not life more than food, and the body than clothing?

26 [aim]"[a]Look[1689] at the birds of the [I]air, that they do not sow, neither do they reap, nor gather into barns, and *yet* your heavenly[3770] Father feeds them. Are you not worth much more[1308] than they?

27 "And which of you by [ppt]being [a]anxious can [ainf] [b]add a *single* [I]cubit to his [II]life's span?

28 "And why are you [a]anxious about clothing? [aim]Observe how the lilies of the field grow; they do not toil[2872] nor do they spin,

29 yet I say to you that even [a]Solomon in all his glory did not [aom]clothe himself like one of these.

30 "But if God so arrays the [a]grass of the field, which [ppt]is *alive* today and tomorrow [ppp]is thrown into the furnace, *will He* not much more *do so for* you, [b]O men of little faith?[3640]

31 "Do [aosi]not be [a]anxious then, saying, 'What shall we eat?' or 'What shall we drink?' or 'With what shall we clothe ourselves?'

32 "For all these things the Gentiles[1484] eagerly seek; for [a]your heavenly[3770] Father knows that you need[5535] all these things.

33 "But [pim] [I]seek first[4412] [II]His kingdom and His righteousness;[1343] and [a]all these things shall be [III]added to you.

34 "Therefore do [aosi]not be [a]anxious for tomorrow; for tomorrow will [I]care for itself. *Each* day has enough trouble[2549] of its own.

Concerning Judging Others

7 "[a]Do not [pim]judge[2919] lest you be [asbp]judged.[2919]

2 "For in the way[2917] you judge, you will be judged; and [I][a]by your standard[3354] of measure, it will be measured to you.

3 "And why do you [a]look at the speck that is in your brother's eye, but do not notice[2657] the log[1385] that is in your own eye?

4 "[a]Or how [I]can you say to your brother,[80] [apt]'Let me[863] [aosb]take the speck[2595] out of your eye,' and behold, the log is in your own eye?

5 "You hypocrite,[5273] first[4412] [aim]take the log out of your own eye, and then you will see clearly to [ainf]take the speck out of your brother's eye.

6 "[a]Do not [aosi]give what is holy[40] to dogs, and do not [aosi]throw your pearls before swine, lest they trample them under their feet, and turn and tear[4486] you to pieces.

19 [a]Prov. 23:4; Matt. 19:21; Luke 12:21, 33; 18:22; 1Tim. 6:9, 10; Heb. 13:5; James 5:2
20 [a]Matt. 19:21; Luke 12:33; 1Tim. 6:19
21 [a]Luke 12:34
22 [I]Or, *healthy* [a]Matt. 6:22, 23; *Luke 11:34, 35*
23 [a]Matt. 20:15; Mark 7:22
24 [I]Or, *riches* [a]1Kin. 18:21; Luke 16:13; Gal. 1:10; James 4:4 [b]Luke 16:9, 11, 13
25 [I]Or, *stop being anxious* [a]Matt. 6:25-33; *Luke 12:22-31* [b]Matt. 6:27, 28, 31, 34; Luke 10:41; 12:11, 22; Phil. 4:6; 1Pet. 5:7
26 [I]Lit., *heaven* [a]Job 35:11; 38:41; Ps. 104:27, 28; Matt. 10:29ff.; Luke 12:24
27 [I]I.e., One cubit equals approx. 18 in. [II]Or, *height* [a]Matt. 6:25, 28, 31, 34; Luke 10:41; 12:11, 22; Phil. 4:6; 1Pet. 5:7 [b]Ps. 39:5
28 [a]Matt. 6:25, 27, 31, 34; Luke 10:41; 12:11, 22; Phil. 4:6; 1Pet. 5:7
29 [a]1Kin. 10:4-7; 2Chr. 9:4-6, 20-22
30 [a]James 1:10, 11; 1Pet. 1:24 [b]Matt. 8:26; 14:31; 16:8
31 [a]Matt. 6:25, 27, 28, 34; Luke 10:41; 12:11, 22; Phil. 4:6; 1Pet. 5:7
32 [a]Matt. 6:8; Phil. 4:19
33 [I]Or, *continually seek* [II]Or, *the kingdom* [III]Or, *provided* [a]Matt. 19:28; Mark 10:29f.; Luke 18:29f.; 1Tim. 4:8
34 [I]Or, *will worry about itself* [a]Matt. 6:25, 27, 28, 31; Luke 10:41; 12:11, 22; Phil. 4:6; 1Pet. 5:7

1 [a]Matt. 7:1-5; *Luke 6:37f., 41f.*; Rom. 14:10, 13
2 [I]Lit., *by what measure you measure* [a]Mark 4:24; Luke 6:38 **3** [a]Rom. 2:1 **4** [I]Lit., *will* [a]Luke 6:42
6 [a]Matt. 15:26

Encouragement to Pray

7 [pim]"[Ia]Ask,[154] and [b]it shall be given to you; [pim] [II]seek, and you shall find;[2147] [pim] [III]knock, and it shall be opened to you.

8 "For everyone who [ppt]asks [pin]receives, and he who [ppt]seeks [pin]finds,[2147] and to him who [ppt]knocks it shall be [fp]opened.

9 "Or what man[444] is there among you, [I]when his son shall ask[154] him for a loaf, [II]will give him a stone?

10 "Or [I]if he shall [aosb]ask for a fish, he will not give him a snake, will he?

11 "If you then, being evil,[4190] know[1492] how to [pinf]give good[18] gifts[1390] to your children, [a]how much more shall your Father[3962] who is in heaven give what is good to those who [ppt]ask Him!

12 "[a]Therefore, however you [psa]want people to [psa]treat you, [I]so [pim]treat them, for [b]this is the Law[3551] and the Prophets.[4396]

Ways Contrasted
Fruits Contrasted

13 [aim]"[a]Enter by the narrow[4728] gate; for the gate is wide, and the way is broad that leads[520] to destruction,[684] and many are those who [ppt]enter by it.

14 "For the gate is small, and the way is narrow that [ppt]leads[520] to life,[2222] and few are those who [ppt]find it.

15 [pim]"Beware of the [a]false prophets,[5578] who come to you in sheep's clothing, but inwardly are [b]ravenous wolves.

16 "You will [fm] [Ia]know them by their fruits. [II]Grapes are not gathered from thorn *bushes,* nor figs from thistles, are they?

17 "Even so, [a]every[3956] good[18] tree bears good[2570] fruit; but the bad tree bears bad fruit.

18 "A good[18] tree cannot [pinf]produce bad[4190] fruit, nor can a bad tree [ainf]produce good fruit.

19 "[a]Every tree that does not [ppt]bear good[2570] fruit is cut down[1581] and thrown into the fire.

20 "So then, you will [I]know them [a]by their fruits.

🔑 21 "[a]Not everyone who [ppt]says to Me, 'Lord, Lord,' will enter the kingdom[932] of heaven; but he who does the will of My Father who is in heaven.

22 "[a]Many will say to Me on [b]that day,[2250] 'Lord, Lord, did we not [ao]prophesy in Your name,[3686] and in Your name [ao]cast out demons,[1140] and in Your name [ao]perform many [I]miracles?'

23 "And then I will declare[3670] to them, 'I never knew you; [pim] [a]DEPART FROM ME, YOU WHO [ppt]PRACTICE[2038] LAWLESSNESS.'[458]

The Two Foundations

24 "Therefore [a]everyone[3956] who hears these words of Mine, and [I]acts upon them, [II]may be compared to a wise[5429] man, who [ao]built[3618] his house[3614] upon the rock.

25 "And the rain descended,[2597] and the [I]floods came, and the winds blew,[4154] and burst against that house; and *yet* it did not fall,[4098] for it [pipf]had been founded upon the rock.

26 "And everyone who [ppt]hears these words of Mine, and [ppt]does not [I]act upon them, will be like a foolish man, who built[3618] his house[3614] upon the sand.

27 "And the rain descended, and the [I]floods came, and the winds blew,[4154] and burst against[4350] that house; and it fell,[4098] and great was its fall."

28 [Ia]The result was that when Jesus had finished[5048] these words, [b]the multitudes [ipf]were amazed at His teaching;[1322]

29 for He was teaching them as *one* having authority, and not as their scribes.[1122]

7 [I]Or, *Keep asking* [II]Or, *keep seeking* [III]Or, *keep knocking* [a]Matt. 7:7-11; *Luke 11:9-13* [b]Matt. 18:19; 21:22; Mark 11:24; John 14:13; 15:7, 16; 16:23f.; James 1:5f.; 1John 3:22; 5:14f.
9 [I]Lit., *whom* [II]Lit., *he will not give him a stone, will he?*
10 [I]Lit., *also*
11 [a]Ps. 84:11; Is. 63:7; Rom. 8:32; James 1:17
12 [I]Or, *you, too, do so for* [a]Luke 6:31 [b]Matt. 22:40; Rom. 13:8ff.; Gal. 5:14
13 [a]Luke 13:24
15 [a]Matt. 24:11, 24; Mark 13:22; Luke 6:26; Acts 13:6; 2Pet. 2:1; 1John 4:1; Rev. 16:13; 19:20; 20:10 [b]Ezek. 22:27; John 10:12; Acts 20:29
16 [I]Or, *recognize* [II]Lit., *They do not gather* [a]Matt. 7:20; 12:33; Luke 6:44; James 3:12
17 [a]Matt. 12:33, 35
19 [a]Matt. 3:10; Luke 3:9; 13:7; John 15:2, 6
20 [I]Or, *recognize* [a]Matt. 7:16; 12:33; Luke 6:44; James 3:12
21 [a]Luke 6:46
22 [I]Or, *works of power* [a]Matt. 25:11f.; Luke 13:25ff. [b]Matt. 10:15
23 [a]Ps. 6:8; Matt. 25:41; Luke 13:27
24 [I]Lit., *does* [II]Lit., *will be compared to* [a]Matt. 7:24-27; *Luke 6:47-49;* Matt. 16:18; James 1:22-25
25 [I]Lit., *rivers*
26 [I]Lit., *do*
27 [I]Lit., *rivers*
28 [I]Lit., *And it came to pass* [a]Matt. 11:1; 13:53; 19:1; 26:1 [b]Matt. 13:54; 22:33; Mark 1:22; 6:2; 11:18; Luke 4:32; John 7:46

🔑 **7:21-23** See note on Mt. 8:11,12.

Jesus Cleanses a Leper
The Centurion's Faith

8 And when He had come down from
the mountain, great multitudes
followed[190] Him.
2 And behold, [a]a leper [apt]came[2064]
to Him, and [ipf] [Ib]bowed down to Him,
saying, "Lord, if You are willing,[2309] You
can make me clean."[2511]
3 And He [apt]stretched out[1614] His
hand and touched him, saying, "I am
willing; be cleansed."[2511] And immediately his [a]leprosy was cleansed.
4 And Jesus *said to him, "[a]See[3708]
that you tell no one; but [b]go, [c]show yourself to the priest, and present[4374] the
[I]offering[1435] that Moses commanded,[4367]
for a testimony to them."
5 And [a]when He had entered Capernaum, a centurion[1543] came to Him,
entreating Him,
6 and saying, "[I]Lord, my [II]ser-
vant[3816] is [pfip] [III]lying[906] [a]paralyzed[3885]
at home, [IV]suffering great pain."

2 [I]Or, *worshiped* [a]Matt. 8:2-4; *Mark 1:40-44; Luke 5:12-14* [b]Matt. 9:18; 15:25; 18:26; 20:20; John 9:38; Acts 10:25
3 [a]Matt. 11:5; Luke 4:27
4 [I]Or, *gift* [a]Matt. 9:30; 12:16; 17:9; Mark 1:44; 3:12; 5:43; 7:36; 8:30; 9:9; Luke 4:41; 8:56; 9:21 [b]Mark 1:44; Luke 5:14; 17:14 [c]Lev. 13:49; 14:2ff.
5 [a]Matt. 8:5-13; *Luke 7:1-10*
6 [I]Or, *Sir* [II]Lit., *boy* [III]Lit., *throwing* [IV]Lit., *fearfully tormented* [a]Matt. 4:24
8 [I]Or, *Sir* [II]Lit., *say with a word* [III]Lit., *boy*
9 [a]Mark 1:27; Luke 9:1
10 [I]Some mss. read *not even in Israel*

7 And He *said to him, "I will
[apt]come and [ft]heal him."
8 But the centurion [apt]answered and
said, "[I]Lord, I am not worthy for You
to come under my roof, but just [II]say
the word,[3056] and my [III]servant will be
healed.[2390]
9 "For I, too, am a man under
[a]authority, with soldiers under me; and
I say to this one, 'Go!' and he goes,
and to another, 'Come!' and he comes,
and to my slave, 'Do this!' and he does
it."
10 Now when Jesus heard *this,* He
marveled, and said to those who were
[ppt]following, "Truly[281] I say to you, I
have not [ao]found such great faith[4102]
[I]with anyone in Israel.
🗝 11 "And I say to you, that many
[a]shall come from east and west, and
[I]recline *at the table* with Abraham, and
Isaac, and Jacob, in the kingdom[932] of
heaven;

11 [I]Or, *dine* [a]Is. 49:12; 59:19; Mal. 1:11; Luke 13:29

🗝 **8:11,12** The Lord here stresses the element of exclusion awaiting the unrepentant. The background is the demonstration of great faith by a Roman centurion, a Gentile, who came seeking healing for his servant. "Sons of the kingdom," in this instance, refers to the unrepentant Jews who thought that because of their ancestry, they had automatic entrance into the kingdom of God (see Jn. 8:31-59). These false children of the kingdom are not to be confused with the true children of the kingdom referred to in Mt. 13:38 who are the believing witnesses on earth sent forth by the sower. Those who came "from the East and West" are Gentiles who exercised personal faith in Jesus Christ even as this centurion. In Lk. 13:28, we have the expression "yourselves" referring to the unbelieving Jews. In its larger context, Lk. 13:22-30 combines what Matthew tells here and in Mt. 7:23. The whole context is Jesus' teaching concerning the final exclusion from entrance into heaven of anybody who proves to be a hypocrite. Matthew refers to the false disciples reporting their miracles (Mt. 7:22), whereas Luke mentions the ones who reminded Jesus that they once ate with Him in the streets of their city (Lk. 13:26). The Jews thought that they were first, but the Lord reminds them that they could be last and those who thought themselves last, such as sinners, publicans and prostitutes, would be first if they exercised faith in Him (Mt. 21:31). "Shall be cast out" is the Greek *ekblēthēsontai* which is the punctiliar future passive of *ekballō* (1544) from *ek,* "out," and *ballō* (906), "to cast." It refers to a particular time when this is going to happen and it is an action done by someone else other than themselves. It is not a capricious throwing out of the hypocrites, but it is something that they brought upon themselves through their hypocritical pretense that they were the children and followers of Abraham when they really were not. Abraham was the father of the faithful, but they themselves were not faithful. The expression "into outer darkness" occurs three times: Mt. 8:12; 22:13; 25:30. In Greek, the expression is preceded by the definite article. It was an area outside a well-illuminated banquet hall where there was darkness (see the parable of the wedding feast in Mt. 22:1-14). The person who managed to sneak into the banquet hall without the proper dress was cast out into outer darkness. That meant an area farther away than the immediate darkness next to the banquet hall where the darkness was not as dense as in the area that lay farther away. See note on I Pet. 3:18-20. In the first two instances, "outer darkness" refers to the place of suffering for the unbelievers contrasted to the light where the believers dwell (see I Jn. 1:5-7). Unbelievers

(continued on next page)

12 but [a]the sons[5207] of the kingdom
shall be [fp]cast out into [b]the [apt]outer[1857]
darkness;[4655] in that place [c]there shall
be weeping and gnashing[1030] of teeth."
13 And Jesus said to the centurion,
"Go your way; let it be [aipp]done to you
[a]as you [ao]have believed."[4100] And the
[I]servant was healed[2390] that *very* hour.

Peter's Mother-in-law Healed
Many Healed

14 [a]And when Jesus had come to
Peter's [I]home, He saw his mother-in-
law [pfp]lying[906] [ppt]sick in bed with a fever.
15 And He touched her hand, and
the fever left her; and she arose,[1453]
and [ipf] [I]waited on[1247] Him.
16 And when evening had come,
they brought to Him many [a]who were
demon-[ppt]possessed; and He cast out
the spirits[4151] with a word,[3056] and
[b]healed all who were ill
🔑 17 in order that what was spoken
through Isaiah the prophet might be fulfilled, saying, "[a]HE HIMSELF TOOK OUR
INFIRMITIES, AND [I]CARRIED AWAY OUR
DISEASES."

12 [a]Matt. 13:38 [b]Matt. 22:13; 25:30 [c]Matt. 13:42, 50; 22:13; 24:51; 25:30; Luke 13:28

13 [I]Lit., *boy* [a]Matt. 9:22, 29

14 [I]Or, *house* [a]Matt. 8:14-16; *Mark 1:29-34; Luke 4:38-41*

15 [I]Or, *served*

16 [a]Matt. 4:24 [b]Matt. 4:23; 8:33

17 [I]Or, *removed* [a]Is. 53:4

(continued from previous page)
will be thrown into the furnace of fire, whereas believers will shine as the sun in the kingdom of the Father (Mt. 13:42,43). "The outer darkness" in Mt. 8:12 and Mt. 22:13 is *Gehenna,* the place of burning (Mt. 5:22,29,30; 10:28; 18:9). But the "outer darkness" of Mt. 25:30 does not mean *Gehenna.* It is applied not to unbelievers or hypocrites but to the believers who neglected to exercise their God-given talents. In v. 26 the Lord calls such a servant *ponēre* (4190), wicked, and in v. 41 *katēramenoi,* cursed, but these terms may be applied to believers who have failed the Lord in their service. The Lord called Peter, "Satan," in Mt. 16:23. The words of Paul in I Cor. 3:10-15 are in full support of our exegesis that our works of faith as servants will be tried as by fire.

The expression "outer darkness" in Mt. 25:30 occurs at the end of the parable of the talents, a parable to show the necessity of serving Christ faithfully according to His investment in us. Therefore, in this instance, "the outer darkness" must mean a place of far less rewards for the servants who proved themselves less diligent than those who used and exercised their talents to the fullest. The expression must refer to the degrees of the enjoyment of heaven rather than referring to hell. This teaching of varied rewards is part and parcel of the inherent doctrine in the N.T. that neither heaven nor hell is going to be of equal degree for all because this would annul the justice of God. Entrance into heaven is through the acceptance of Christ's sacrifice for our justification. But our rewards in heaven will depend on what we have done for Christ (Mt. 5:3-12; 7:21-23; 10:15; Lk. 6:20-26; 12:47,48; Acts 10:4,31; Rom. 2:1-16; 14:10-23; I Cor. 3:13; 4:5; II Cor. 5:10; I Jn. 4:17; Rev. 20:11-15). The neglect of the Christian's responsibilities and faithfulness to his task as a Christian in the world is considered of such paramount importance that the same simile is used by the Lord, "the outer darkness," to indicate the punishment for the unbeliever for his rejection of God's salvation. In the case of the non-believer, it will be positive punishment, fire and burning (Mt. 13:30; Jn. 15:6); in the case of the believer, it will be weeping which is the expression of sorrow over not having used his God-given opportunities. The gnashing of teeth indicates anger at oneself for missing such marvelous opportunities that the believer had on earth. The same emotional attitude will be expressed by the unbeliever, but in his case, it will be weeping for the lost opportunity of genuine and true repentance followed by the works of repentance. Gnashing of teeth, in the case of the unbeliever, refers to being angry at oneself because he did not decide to go through the narrow gate and live in the straight way when he had the opportunity. The Lord wanted to teach that, after death, we cannot go back and do it over—either repent of our sins or serve Him according to our God-given opportunities. See also note on Lk. 11:33-36.

🔑 **8:17** Isa. 53, from which this quotation is taken, deals with three truths: (1) Jesus Christ is prophetically presented as dying for us which involved His becoming flesh for us (Jn. 1:1,14). (2) In order to die, He had to take upon Himself the infirmities of mankind, and in so doing, He experienced suffering and sickness unto death (Phil. 2:6-8). In his body on the cross He took our transgressions upon Himself, dying on our behalf. "He was crushed for our iniquities." (3) His death on the cross was also the payment of our ultimate and complete liberation from the weakness and mortality of our present body. His death was necessary for His resurrection. As such, His death, along with His resurrection, became the firstfruits of our own resurrection. This however, will not be realized until this mortal body shall be clothed in

(continued on next page)

Discipleship Tested

18 Now when Jesus saw a crowd around Him, [a]He gave orders to depart to the other side.

19 [a]And a certain scribe came and said to Him, "Teacher, I will follow[190] You wherever You go."

20 And Jesus *said to him, "The foxes have holes, and the birds of the [I]air[3772] *have* [II]nests; but [a]the Son of Man[444] has nowhere to lay His head."[2776]

21 And another[2087] of the disciples[3101] said to Him, "Lord, permit[2010] me first[4412] to go and bury my father."

22 But Jesus *said to him, "[a]Follow Me; and allow[863] the dead[3498] to bury their own dead."[3498]

23 [a]And when He got into the [art]boat, His disciples[3101] followed Him.

24 And behold, there arose [I]a great storm[4578] in the sea, so that the boat was covered[2572] with the waves; but He Himself was [ipf]asleep.

25 And they came to *Him,* and awoke[1453] Him, saying, "[a]Save[4982] *us,* Lord; we are perishing!"

26 And He *said to them, "Why are you timid, [a]you men of little faith?"[3640] Then He arose, and rebuked the winds and the sea; and [I]it became[1096] perfectly calm.

27 And the men marveled,[2296] saying, "What kind of a man is this, that even the winds and the sea obey[5219] Him?"

Jesus Casts Out Demons

28 [a]And when He had [apt]come to the other side into the country of the Gadarenes, two men who were [b]demon-possessed[1139] met Him as they were coming out of the tombs; *they were* so exceedingly violent that no one could[2480] pass by that road.[3598]

29 And behold, they cried out, saying, "[a]What do we have to do with You, Son of God? Have You come here to [ainf]torment us before [I]the time?"

30 Now there was at a distance from them a herd of many swine feeding.

31 And the demons[1142] *began* to [ipf]entreat Him, saying, "If You are *going to* [pin]cast us out, send[649] us into the herd of swine."

32 And He said to them, "Begone!" And they came out, and went into the swine, and behold, the whole herd rushed down[2596] the steep bank into the sea and perished[599] in the waters.

33 And the [ppt]herdsmen ran away, and [apt]went to the city, and reported everything, [I]including the *incident* of the [a]demoniacs.[1139]

34 And behold, the whole city came out to meet Jesus; and when they saw Him, [a]they entreated *Him* to depart[3327] from their region.

A Paralytic Cured

9 And [apt]getting into a boat, He crossed over, and came to [a]His own city.

2 [a]And behold, they were [ipf]bringing to Him a [b]paralytic,[3885] [pfpp]lying[906] on a bed; and Jesus [apt]seeing their faith[4102] said to the paralytic, "[c]Take courage, My [I]son, [d]your sins[266] [pfip] [II]are forgiven."[863]

3 And behold, some of the scribes said [I]to themselves, "This *fellow* [a]blasphemes."[987]

4 And Jesus [ppt] [a]knowing their

18 [a]Mark 4:35; Luke 8:22
19 [a]Matt. 8:19-22; *Luke 9:57-60*
20 [I]Or, *sky* [II]Or, *roosting places* [a]Dan. 7:13; Matt. 9:6; 12:8, 32, 40; 13:41; 16:13, 27f.; 17:9; 19:28; 26:64; Mark 8:38; Luke 12:8; 18:8; 21:36; John 1:51; 3:13f.; 6:27; 12:34; Acts 7:56
22 [a]Matt. 9:9; Mark 2:14; Luke 9:59, 60; John 1:43; 21:19
23 [a]Matt. 8:23-27; *Mark 4:36-41; Luke 8:22-25*
24 [I]Lit., *a shaking*
25 [a]Matt. 8:2; 9:18
26 [I]Lit., *a great calm occurred* [a]Matt. 6:30; 14:31; 16:8; 17:20
28 [a]Matt. 8:28-34; *Mark 5:1-17; Luke 8:26-37* [b]Matt. 4:24
29 [I]I.e., the appointed time of judgment [a]Judg. 11:12; 2Sam. 16:10; 19:22; 1Kin. 17:18; 2Kin. 3:13; 2Chr. 35:21; Mark 1:24; 5:7; Luke 4:34; 8:28; John 2:4
33 [I]Lit., *and* [a]Matt. 4:24
34 [a]Amos 7:12; Acts 16:39

1 [a]Matt. 4:13; Mark 5:21
2 [I]Lit., *child* [II]Lit., *are being forgiven* [a]Matt. 9:2-8; *Mark 2:3-12; Luke 5:18-26* [b]Matt. 4:24; 9:6 [c]Matt. 9:22; 14:27; Mark 6:50; 10:49; John 16:33; Acts 23:11 [d]Mark 2:5, 9; Luke 5:20, 23; 7:48
3 [I]Lit., *among* [a]Mark 3:28, 29
4 [a]Matt. 12:25; Luke 6:8; 9:47

(continued from previous page)
immortality (Rom. 8:23; I Cor. 15:53,54; II Cor. 5:4). God has His own timetable for the complete fulfillment of all that He accomplished on the cross: present spiritual salvation that is progressive in its realization; the indwelling of the Spirit of God in our present mortal body; and ultimately the exchange of our present mortal and corruptible body for the resurrection body which will be immortal and incorruptible. For a complete study on the subject, see the Editor's exegetical study on I Cor. 15, *Conquering the Fear of Death* and *Life After Death.* See the note on Js. 5:14-17.

thoughts said, "Why are you thinking evil***4190*** in your hearts?

5 "For which is easier, to say, '[a]Your sins [I]are [pinp]forgiven,'***863*** or to say, [pim]'Rise,***1453*** and [pim]walk'?

6 "But in order that you may know that [a]the Son of Man has authority***1849*** on earth***1093*** to [pinf]forgive sins"—then He *said to the [b]paralytic—[pim]"Rise, take up your bed, and go home."***3624***

7 And he [apt]rose,***1453*** and [I]went home.***3624***

8 But when the multitudes saw *this,* they were [I]filled with awe,***5399*** and [a]glorified***1392*** God, who had given such authority***1849*** to men.

Matthew Called

9 [a]And as Jesus passed on from there, He saw a man, called [b]Matthew, sitting [I]in the tax office;5058 and He *said to him, [pim]"[c]Follow***190*** Me!" And he [apt]rose,***450*** and followed Him.

10 And it happened that as He was reclining *at the table* in the house, behold many [I]tax-gatherers***5057*** and [II]sinners***268*** [apt]came and [III]were dining with Jesus and His disciples.***3101***

11 And when the Pharisees saw *this,* they said to His disciples, "[a]Why is your Teacher eating with the tax-gatherers and sinners?"

12 But when He heard this, He said, "*It is* not [a]those who are healthy***2480*** who need a physician,2395 but those who are sick.

13 "But [apt]go and [aim]learn***3129*** [a]what *this* means, '[b]I DESIRE***2309*** [I]COMPASSION,***1656*** [II]AND NOT SACRIFICE,' for [c]I did not come to call the [an]righteous,***1342*** but sinners."***268***

14 Then the disciples***3101*** of John [pin]*came***4334*** to Him, saying, "Why do we and [a]the Pharisees fast,3522 but Your disciples do not fast?"

15 And Jesus said to them, "The [I]attendants***5207*** of the bridegroom cannot mourn as long as the bridegroom is with them, can they? But the days will come when the bridegroom is taken away from them, and then they will fast.

5 [I]Lit., *are being forgiven* [a]Matt. 9:2, 6; Mark 2:5, 9; Luke 5:20, 23; 7:48
6 [a]Matt. 8:20; John 5:27 [b]Matt. 4:24; 9:2
7 [I]Or, *departed*
8 [I]Or, *afraid* [a]Matt. 5:16; 15:31; Mark 2:12; Luke 2:20; 5:25, 26; 7:16; 13:13; 17:15; 23:47; John 15:8; Acts 4:21; 11:18; 21:20; 2Cor. 9:13; Gal. 1:24
9 [I]Lit., *at the tax booth* [a]Matt. 9:9-17; *Mark 2:14-22; Luke 5:27-38* [b]Matt. 10:3; Mark 2:14; 3:18; Luke 6:15; Acts 1:13 [c]Matt. 8:22
10 [I]I.e., Collectors of Roman taxes for profit [II]I.e., irreligious Jews [III]Lit., *reclined with*
11 [a]Matt. 11:19; Mark 2:16; Luke 5:30; 15:2
12 [a]Mark 2:17; Luke 5:31
13 [I]Or, *mercy* [II]I.e., more than [a]Matt. 12:7 [b]Hos. 6:6 [c]Mark 2:17; Luke 5:32; 1Tim. 1:15
14 [a]Luke 18:12
15 [I]Lit., *sons of the bridalchamber*
16 [I]Lit., *that which is put on* [II]Lit., *that which fills up*
17 [I]I.e., skins used as bottles
18 [I]Or, *one* [II]Lit., *ruler* [III]Or, *worshiped* [a]Matt. 9:18-26; *Mark 5:22-43; Luke 8:41-56* [b]Matt. 8:2
20 [I]Or, *outer garment* [a]Num. 15:38; Deut. 22:12; Matt. 14:36; 23:5
21 [I]Lit., *in herself* [II]Lit., *be saved* [a]Matt. 14:36; Mark 3:10; Luke 6:19
22 [I]Lit., *saved you* [II]Lit., *from that hour* [a]Matt. 9:2 [b]Matt. 9:29; 15:28; Mark 5:34; 10:52; Luke 7:50; 8:48; 17:19; 18:42

16 "But no one puts [I]a patch of unshrunk cloth on an old garment; for [II]the patch***4138*** pulls away from the garment, and a worse tear results.

17 "Nor do *men* put***906*** new***3501*** wine***3631*** into old [I]wineskins; otherwise the wineskins burst, and the wine pours out, and the wineskins are [pin]ruined;***622*** but they put new wine into fresh wineskins, and both are preserved."***4933***

Miracles of Healing

18 [a]While He was saying these things to them, behold, there [apt]came [I]a *synagogue* [II]official,***758*** and [ipf III b]bowed down before Him, saying, "My daughter [ao]has just died;***5053*** but [apt]come and lay Your hand on her, and she will live."***2198***

19 And Jesus rose and *began* to follow him, and *so did* His disciples.***3101***

20 And behold, a woman who had been suffering from a hemorrhage for twelve years, [apt]came***4334*** up behind Him and touched [a]the fringe of His [I]cloak;

21 for she was [ipf]saying [I]to herself, "If I only [asbm a]touch His garment, I shall [II]get well."***4982***

22 But Jesus turning***4762*** and seeing her said, "Daughter, [a]take courage; [b]your faith [pfi]has [I]made you well."***4982*** And [II]at once the woman was [I]made well.

23 And when Jesus came into the [I]official's***758*** house, and [apt]saw [a]the flute-players, and the crowd in noisy disorder,

24 He *began* to say, "Depart; for the girl [a]has not [ao]died, but is [pin]asleep." And they *began* laughing at Him.

25 But [a]when the crowd had been put out, He [apt]entered and [b]took her by the hand; and the girl [I]arose.

26 And [a]this news went out into all that land.***1093***

23 [I]Lit., *ruler's* [a]2Chr. 35:25; Jer. 9:17; 16:6; Ezek. 24:17
24 [a]John 11:13; Acts 20:10
25 [I]Or, *was raised up* [a]Acts 9:40 [b]Mark 9:27
26 [a]Matt. 4:24; 9:31; 14:1; Mark 1:28, 45; Luke 4:14, 37; 5:15; 7:17

27 And as Jesus [ppt]passed on from there, two blind men followed Him, crying out, and saying, "Have [aim]mercy on us, [a]Son of David!"

28 And after He had come into the house, the blind men came*4334* up to Him, and Jesus *said to them, "Do you believe*4100* that I am able to do this?" They [pin]*said to Him, "Yes, Lord."

29 Then He touched their eyes, saying, [aipp]"Be it done to you [a]according*2596* to your faith."

30 And their eyes were opened. And Jesus [a]sternly warned1690 them, saying, "See *here,* let no one know *about this!"*

31 But they went out, and [a]spread the news about Him in all that land.

32 And as they [ppt]were going out, behold, [a]a dumb man, [b]demon-possessed, [I]was brought to Him.

33 And after the demon1140 was cast out, the dumb man spoke;*2980* and the multitudes marveled,2296 saying, "[a]Nothing like this [I]was ever seen in Israel."

34 But the Pharisees were saying, "He [a]casts out the demons1140 by the ruler*758* of the demons."

35 And Jesus was [ipf]going about all the cities and the villages, [a]teaching*1321* in their synagogues, and proclaiming*2784* the gospel*2098* of the kingdom,*932* and healing every kind of disease*3554* and every kind of sickness.*3119*

36 And [a]seeing the multitudes, He felt compassion for them, [b]because they were [pfpp][I]distressed and [pfpp][II]downcast like sheep [III]without a shepherd.*4166*

37 Then He *said to His disciples, "[a]The harvest is plentiful, but the workers are few.

38 "Therefore [aim]beseech*1189* the Lord of the harvest to [aosb]send out workers into His harvest."

27 [a]Matt. 1:1; 12:23; 15:22; 20:30, 31; 21:9, 15; 22:42; Mark 10:47, 48; 12:35; Luke 18:38, 39; 20:41f.
29 [a]Matt. 8:13; 9:22
30 [a]Matt. 8:4
31 [a]Matt. 4:24; 9:26; 14:1; Mark 1:28, 45; Luke 4:14, 37; 5:15; 7:17
32 [I]Lit., *they brought* [a]Matt. 12:22, 24 [b]Matt. 4:24
33 [I]Lit., *ever appeared* [a]Mark 2:12
34 [a]Matt. 12:24; Mark 3:22; Luke 11:15; John 7:20f.
35 [a]Matt. 4:23; Mark 1:14
36 [I]Or, *harassed* [II]Lit., *thrown down* [III]Lit., *not having* [a]Matt. 14:14; 15:32; Mark 6:34; 8:2 [b]Num. 27:17; Ezek. 34:5; Zech. 10:2; Mark 6:34
37 [a]Luke 10:2

1 [a]Mark 3:13-15; 6:7 [b]Matt. 9:35; Luke 9:1
2 [I]Or, *Jacob* [II]Gr., *Joannes,* Heb., *Johanan* [a]Matt. 10:2-4; *Mark 3:16-19; Luke 6:14-16; Acts 1:13* [b]Matt. 4:18 [c]Matt. 4:18 [d]Matt. 4:21
3 [I]I.e., son of Talmai (Aram.) [II]Or, *Jacob* [a]John 1:43ff. [b]John 11:16; 14:5; 20:24ff.; 21:2 [c]Matt. 9:9 [d]Mark 15:40 [e]Mark 3:18; Luke 6:16; Acts 1:13
4 [I]Or, *Cananaean* [a]Matt. 26:14; Luke 22:3; John 6:71; 13:2, 26
5 [I]Or, *go off to* [a]Mark 6:7; Luke

The Twelve Disciples Instructions for Service

10 🔑 And [a]having [apt]summoned*4341* His twelve disciples,*3101* He gave them authority*1849* over unclean spirits, to [pinf]cast them out, and [pinf]to [b]heal*2323* every kind of disease and every kind of sickness.*3119*

2 [a]Now the names*3686* of the twelve apostles*652* are these: The first, [b]Simon, who is called Peter, and [c]Andrew his brother; and [I][d]James the *son* of Zebedee, and [II]John his brother;

3 [a]Philip and [I]Bartholomew; [b]Thomas and [c]Matthew the tax-gatherer;*5057* [II][d]James the *son* of Alphaeus, and [e]Thaddaeus;

4 Simon the [I]Zealot, and [a]Judas Iscariot, the one who [apt]betrayed Him.

5 [a]These twelve Jesus [ao]sent out*649* after [apt]instructing them, saying, "Do not [aosi][I]go in *the* way*3598* of *the* Gentiles,*1484* and do not [aosi]enter *any* city of the [b]Samaritans;

6 but rather [I]go to [a]the lost*622* sheep of the house of Israel.

7 "And as you [I]go, [pim][II]preach,*2784* saying, '[a]The kingdom*932* of heaven [pf][III]is at hand.'*1448*

8 [pim]"Heal*2323* *the* sick,*770* raise*1453* *the* dead,*3498* [pim]cleanse*2511* *the* lepers, [pim]cast out demons;1140 freely you [ao]received, freely [aim]give.

9 "[a]Do not [aosi]acquire gold, or silver, or copper [I]for your money belts,

10 or a [I]bag4082 for *your* journey, or even two [II]tunics, or sandals, or a staff;4464 for [a]the worker is worthy of his [III]support.

9:2 [b]2Kin. 17:24ff.; Luke 9:52; 10:33; 17:16; John 4:9, 39f.; 8:48; Acts 8:25 **6** [I]Or, *proceed* [a]Matt. 15:24
7 [I]Or, *proceed* [II]Or, *proclaim* [III]Lit., *has come near* [a]Matt. 3:2 **9** [I]Lit., *into* [a]Matt. 10:9-15; *Mark 6:8-11; Luke 9:3-5; 10:4-12;* Luke 22:35 **10** [I]Or, *knapsack or beggar's bag* [II]Or, *inner garments* [III]Lit., *nourishment* [a]1Cor. 9:14; 1Tim. 5:18

🔑 **10:1-42** This concerns the special commission of the Twelve Apostles with special instructions and the delineation of the expectations of this ministry, since they were to witness to the Jews first. What is said to them cannot be assumed as being applicable to anyone else, except by general inference in principle. For instance, what the Lord said to them in vv. 9,10 was reversed by what He said to His disciples in Lk. 22:36 as they extended their mission to the Gentiles.

11 "And into whatever city or village
you enter, [aim]inquire who is worthy in
it; and abide there until you [aosb]go
away.
12 "And as you enter the [I]house,
[aim] [a]give it your greeting.
13 "And if the house is worthy, [aim]let
your *greeting of* peace come upon it;
but if it is not worthy, let[2064] your *greeting of* peace return[1994] to you.
14 "And whoever does not receive
you, nor heed your words, as you go
out of that house or that city, [a]shake
off the dust of your feet.
🔑15 "Truly[281] I say to you, [a]it will
be more tolerable[414] for *the* land of
[b]Sodom and Gomorrah in [c]the day of
judgment,[2920] than for that city.

A Hard Road before Them

16 "[a]Behold, I send you out as
sheep in the midst of wolves; therefore
[I]be [b]shrewd[5429] as serpents, and [c]in-
nocent[185] as doves.
17 "But [pim]beware of men; for
they will deliver you up to *the* [a]courts,
and scourge[3146] you [b]in their synagogues;
18 and you shall even be brought
before governors and kings[935] for My
sake, as a testimony[3142] to them and
to the Gentiles.[1484]
19 "[a]But when they [aosb]deliver you
up, [aosi] [b]do not become anxious about
how or what you will speak; for it shall
be given you in that hour what you are
to speak.
20 "For [a]it is not you who [ppt]speak,
but *it is* the Spirit of your Father who
[ppt]speaks in you.
21 "[a]And brother will deliver up
brother to death,[2288] and a father *his*
child; and [b]children will rise up against
parents, and [I]cause them to be put to
death.
22 "And [a]you will be hated by all
on account of My name,[3686] but [b]it is
the one who has [apt]endured[5278] to the
end[5056] who will be saved.[4982]
23 "But whenever they [psa] [a]perse-
cute you in this city, [pim]flee to [I]the
next;[2087] for truly I say to you, you
[efn]shall not finish[5055] *going through* the
cities of Israel, [b]until the Son of Man
[aosb]comes.

The Meaning of Discipleship

24 "[a]A [I]disciple[3101] is not above his
teacher,[1320] nor a slave above his master.
25 "It is enough for the disciple that
he become as his teacher,[1320] and the
slave as his master. [a]If they have
called[1941] the head of the house[3617]
[I][b]Beelzebul, how much more the members of his household![3615]
26 "Therefore do not [aosi] [a]fear[5399]
them, [b]for there is nothing [pfpp]cov-
ered[2572] that will not be revealed,[601]
and hidden that will not be known.
27 "[a]What I tell you in the darkness,[4653] [aim]speak in the light; and what
you hear *whispered* in *your* ear, [aim]pro-
claim[2784] [b]upon the housetops.
🔑28 "And do not [aosi]fear those who
kill the body,[4983] but are [ppt]unable to
kill the soul;[5590] but rather [aim] [a]fear Him
who is able to destroy[622] both soul and
body in [I][b]hell.[1067]
29 "[a]Are not two sparrows sold for
a [I]cent?[787] And *yet* not one of them will
fall[4098] to the ground[1093] apart from your
Father.[3962]
30 "But [a]the very hairs of your
head[2776] are all numbered.
31 "Therefore do not [aosi]fear; [a]you
are of more value[1308] than many sparrows.
32 "[a]Everyone therefore who shall
confess[3670] [I]Me before men,[444] I will also
confess[3670] [II]him before My Father who
is in heaven.

12 [I]Or, *household* [a]1Sam. 25:6; Ps. 122:7, 8
14 [a]Acts 13:51
15 [a]Matt. 11:22, 24 [b]Matt. 11:24; 2Pet. 2:6; Jude 7 [c]Matt. 7:22; 11:22, 24; 12:36; Acts 17:31; 1Thess. 5:4; Heb. 10:25; 2Pet. 2:9; 3:7; 1John 4:17; Jude 6
16 [I]Or, *show yourselves to be* [a]Luke 10:3 [b]Gen. 3:1; Matt. 24:25; Rom. 16:19 [c]Hos. 7:11
17 [a]Matt. 5:22 [b]Matt. 23:34; Mark 13:9; Luke 12:11; Acts 5:40; 22:19; 26:11
19 [a]Matt. 10:19-22; *Mark 13:11-13; Luke 21:12-17* [b]Matt. 6:25; Luke 12:11, 12
20 [a]Luke 12:12; Acts 4:8; 13:9; 2Cor. 13:3
21 [I]Or, *put them to death* [a]Matt. 10:35, 36; Mark 13:12 [b]Mic. 7:6
22 [a]Matt. 24:9; Luke 21:17; John 15:18ff. [b]Matt. 24:13; Mark 13:13
23 [I]Lit., *the other* [a]Matt. 23:34 [b]Matt. 16:27f.
24 [I]Or, *pupil* [a]Luke 6:40; John 13:16; 15:20
25 [I]Or, *Beezebul*; others read *Beelzebub* [a]Matt. 9:34 [b]2Kin. 1:2; Matt. 12:24, 27; Mark 3:22; Luke 11:15, 18, 19
26 [a]Matt. 10:26-33; *Luke 12:2-9* [b]Mark 4:22; Luke 8:17; 12:2; 1Cor. 4:5
27 [a]Luke 12:3 [b]Matt. 24:17; Acts 5:20
28 [I]Gr., *Gehenna* [a]Heb. 10:31 [b]Matt. 5:22; Luke 12:5
29 [I]Gr., *assarion*, the smallest copper coin [a]Luke 12:6
30 [a]1Sam. 14:45; 2Sam. 14:11; 1Kin. 1:52; Luke 21:18; Acts 27:34
31 [a]Matt. 12:12
32 [I]Lit., *in Me* [II]Lit., *in him* [a]Luke 12:8; Rev. 3:5

🔑 **10:15,28** See note on Mt. 8:11,12.

33 "But [a]whoever [aosb]shall deny[720] Me before men, I will also deny him before My Father who is in heaven.

34 "[a]Do not [aosi]think that I came to [ainf] [I]bring peace[1515] on the earth; I did not come to [ainf]bring peace, but a sword.

35 "For I [ao]came to [ainf] [a]SET A MAN AGAINST HIS FATHER, AND A DAUGHTER AGAINST HER MOTHER, AND A DAUGHTER-IN-LAW AGAINST HER MOTHER-IN-LAW;

36 and [a]A MAN'S ENEMIES WILL BE THE MEMBERS OF HIS HOUSEHOLD.[3615]

🔑 37 "[a]He who [ppt]loves[5368] father or mother more than Me is not worthy of Me; and he who loves son or daughter more than Me is not worthy of Me.

38 "And [a]he who does not take his cross[4716] and follow[190] after Me is not worthy of Me.

39 "[a]He who has [apt]found[2147] his [I]life shall lose[622] it, and he who has [apt]lost his [I]life[5590] for My sake shall find it.

40 "[a]He who [ppt]receives you receives Me, and [b]he who [ppt]receives Me receives Him who [apt]sent Me.

41 "[a]He who [ppt]receives a prophet[4396] in *the* name[3686] of a prophet shall receive a prophet's reward;[3408] and he who [ppt]receives a righteous[1342] man in the name of a righteous man shall receive a righteous man's reward.

42 "And [a]whoever in the name of a disciple[3101] [aosb]gives to one of these [I]little ones even a cup of cold water to drink, truly I say to you he shall [efn]not lose his reward."

John's Questions

11 [a]And it came about that when Jesus had finished[5055] [I]giving instructions[1299] to His twelve disciples,[3101] He departed from there [b]to [infg]teach[1321] and [infg] [II]preach[2784] in their cities.

2 [a]Now when [b]John in prison heard of the works[2041] of Christ, he sent *word* by his disciples,

3 and said to Him, "Are You [a]the [ppt] [I]Expected One,[2064] or shall we [pin]look for someone else?"[2087]

4 And Jesus answered[611] and said to them, [apt]"Go and [aim]report to John what you hear and see:[991]

5 [a]*the* BLIND RECEIVE SIGHT[308] and *the* lame walk, *the* lepers are cleansed and *the* deaf hear,[191] and *the* dead[3498] are raised up,[1453] and *the* [b]POOR have THE [I]GOSPEL PREACHED[2097] TO THEM.

6 "And blessed[3107] is he [I]who [a]keeps from [asbp] [II]stumbling over Me."

Jesus' Tribute to John

7 And as these were [ppt]going *away,* Jesus began to [pinf]speak to the multitudes about John, "What did you go out into [a]the wilderness to look at? A reed [ppt]shaken by the wind?

8 "[I]But what did you go out to see? A man dressed in soft *clothing*? Behold, those who [ppt]wear[5409] soft *clothing* are in kings' [II]palaces.[3624]

9 "[I]But why did you go out? To see [a]a prophet?[4396] Yes, I say to you, and one who is more[4055] than a prophet.

10 "This is the one about whom it [I]is [pfip]written,[1125]

'[a]BEHOLD, I SEND MY
MESSENGER[32] BEFORE YOUR
FACE,[4383]
WHO WILL PREPARE YOUR WAY
BEFORE YOU.'

11 "Truly,[281] I say to you, among[1722] those born of women there has not [pfip]arisen *anyone* greater than John the Baptist;[910] yet he who is [I]least in[1722] the kingdom[932] of heaven is greater than he.

🔑 12 "And [a]from the days of John the Baptist until now the kingdom of heaven

---

33 [a]Mark 8:38; Luke 9:26; 2Tim. 2:12
34 [I]Lit., *cast* [a]Matt. 10:34, 35; *Luke 12:51-53*
35 [a]Mic. 7:6; Matt. 10:21; Luke 12:53
36 [a]Mic. 7:6; Matt. 10:21
37 [a]Deut. 33:9; Luke 14:26
38 [a]Matt. 16:24; Mark 8:34; Luke 9:23; 14:27
39 [I]Or, *soul* [a]Matt. 16:25; Mark 8:35; Luke 9:24; 17:33; John 12:25
40 [a]Matt. 18:5; Luke 10:16; John 13:20; Gal. 4:14 [b]Mark 9:37; Luke 9:48; John 12:44
41 [a]Matt. 25:44, 45
42 [I]I.e., humble [a]Matt. 25:40; Mark 9:41

1 [I]Or, *commanding* [II]Or, *proclaim* [a]Matt. 7:28 [b]Matt. 9:35; Luke 23:5
2 [a]Matt. 11:2-19; *Luke 7:18-35;* Matt. 4:12 [b]Matt. 14:3; Mark 6:17; Luke 9:7ff.
3 [I]Lit., *Coming One* [a]Ps. 118:26; Matt. 11:10; John 6:14; 11:27; Heb. 10:37
5 [I]Or, *good news* [a]Is. 35:5f.; Matt. 8:3; 12:13 [b]Is. 61:1; Luke 4:18
6 [I]Lit., *whoever* [II]Or, *taking offense at* [a]Matt. 5:29; 13:57; 24:10; 26:31; Mark 6:3; John 6:61; 16:1
7 [a]Matt. 3:1
8 [I]Or, *Well then,* [II]Lit., *houses*
9 [I]Or, *Well then,* [a]Matt. 14:5; 21:26; Luke 1:76; 20:6
10 [I]Lit., *has been written* [a]Mal. 3:1; Mark 1:2
11 [I]Or, *less*
12 [a]Luke 16:16

🔑 **10:37** See note on Lk. 14:25-33.
🔑 **11:12** See note on I Thess. 4:17.

[I]suffers violence,[971] and violent men [II]take it by force.[726]

13 "For all the prophets and the Law prophesied[4395] until John.

14 "And if you care to [ainf]accept *it,* he himself is [a]Elijah, who [I]was[3195] to [pinf]come.

15 "[a]He who [ppt]has ears to hear,[191] [pim]let him hear.[191]

16 "But to what shall I compare this generation? It is like children3813 sitting in the market places,[58] who call out to the other *children,*

17 and say, 'We [ao]played the flute for you, and you did not [ao]dance; we [ao]sang a dirge,[2354] and you did not [ao] [I]mourn.'

18 "For John came neither [a]eating nor [b]drinking, and they say, '[c]He has a demon!'1140

19 "The Son of Man came eating and drinking, and they say, 'Behold, a gluttonous man and a [I]drunkard,3630 [a]a friend of [II]tax-gatherers[5057] and sinners!'[268] [III]Yet wisdom is [aop]vindicated[1344] by her deeds."

The Unrepenting Cities

20 Then He began to [pinf]reproach3679 the cities in which most of His [I][a]miracles were done, because they did not repent.[3340]

21 "[a]Woe to you, Chorazin! Woe to you, [b]Bethsaida! For if the [I]miracles had occurred in [c]Tyre and [c]Sidon which occurred in[1722] you, they would have repented long ago[3819] in [d]sackcloth4526 and ashes.

22 "Nevertheless I say to you, [a]it shall be more tolerable414 for Tyre and Sidon in [b]*the* day of judgment,[2920] than for you.

23 "And you, [a]Capernaum, will not be [fp]exalted to heaven, will you? You shall [I][b]descend to [c]Hades;[86] for if the [II]miracles had occurred in [d]Sodom which occurred in you, it would have remained[3306] to this day.

24 "Nevertheless I say to you that [a]it shall be more tolerable414 for the land of [b]Sodom in *the* day of judgment, than for you."

Come to Me

25 [a]At that [I]time Jesus answered and said, "I [II]praise[1843] Thee, O [b]Father, Lord of heaven and earth,[1093] that [c]Thou didst hide these things from *the* wise[4680] and intelligent and didst [ao]reveal[601] them to babes.[3516]

26 "Yes, [a]Father, for thus it was well-pleasing[2107] in Thy sight.

27 "[a]All things [I]have been handed over to Me by My Father; and no one [II]knows the Son, except the Father; nor does anyone [II]know the Father, [b]except the Son, and anyone to whom the Son wills to reveal[601] *Him.*

28 "[a]Come to Me, all [I]who are [ppt]weary and [pfpp]heavy-laden,5412 and I will give you rest.373

29 [aim]"Take[142] My yoke upon you, and [aim] [a]learn[3129] from Me, for I am gentle4235 and humble in heart;[2588] and [b]YOU SHALL FIND[2147] REST[372] FOR YOUR SOULS.[5590]

30 "For [a]My yoke is [I]easy,[5543] and My load[5413] is light."

Sabbath Questions

12 [a]At that [I]time Jesus went on the Sabbath4521 through the grainfields, and His disciples[3101] became hungry[3983] and began756 to [b]pick the heads *of grain* and eat.

2 But when the Pharisees saw it, they said to Him, "Behold, Your disciples do what [a]is not lawful to [pinf]do on a Sabbath."

3 But He said to them, "Have you not read[314] what David did, when he

12 [I]Or, *is forcibly entered* [II]Or, *seize it for themselves*
14 [I]Or, *is to come* [a]Mal. 4:5; Matt. 17:10-13; Mark 9:11-13; Luke 1:17; John 1:21
15 [a]Matt. 13:9, 43; Mark 4:9, 23; Luke 8:8; 14:35; Rev. 2:7, 11, 17, 29; 3:6, 13, 22; 13:9
17 [I]Lit., *beat the breast*
18 [a]Matt. 3:4 [b]Luke 1:15 [c]Matt. 9:34; John 7:20; 8:48f., 52; 10:20
19 [I]Or, *wine-drinker* [II]I.e., Collectors of Roman taxes for profit [III]Lit., *And* [a]Matt. 9:11; Luke 5:29-32; 15:2
20 [I]Or, *works of power* [a]Luke 10:13-15
21 [I]Or, *works of power* [a]Matt. 11:21-23; *Luke 10:13-15* [b]Mark 6:45; 8:22; Luke 9:10; John 1:44; 12:21 [c]Matt. 11:22; 15:21; Mark 3:8; 7:24, 31; Luke 4:26; 6:17; Acts 12:20; 27:3 [d]Rev. 11:3
22 [a]Matt. 10:15; 11:24 [b]Matt. 10:15; 12:36; Rev. 20:11, 12
23 [I]Some mss. read *be brought down* [II]Or, *works of power* [a]Matt. 4:13 [b]Is. 14:13, 15; Ezek. 26:20; 31:14; 32:18, 24 [c]Matt. 16:18; Luke 10:15; 16:23; Acts 2:27, 31; Rev. 1:18; 6:8; 20:13f. [d]Matt. 10:15
24 [a]Matt. 10:15; 11:22 [b]Matt. 10:15
25 [I]Or, *occasion* [II]Or, *acknowledge to Thy praise* [a]Matt. 11:25-27; *Luke 10:21, 22* [b]Luke 22:42; 23:34; John 11:41; 12:27, 28 [c]Ps. 8:2; 1Cor. 1:26ff.

26 [a]Luke 22:42; 23:34; John 11:41; 12:27, 28
27 [I]Lit., *were given over* [II]Or, *perfectly know(s)* [a]Matt. 28:18; John 3:35; 13:3; 17:2 [b]John 7:29; 10:15; 17:25
28 [I]Or, *who work to exhaustion* [a]Jer. 31:25; John 7:37
29 [a]John 13:15; Eph. 4:20; Phil. 2:5; 1Pet. 2:21; 1John 2:6 [b]Jer. 6:16 **30** [I]Or, *kindly* or *pleasant* [a]1John 5:3
1 [I]Or, *occasion* [a]Matt. 12:1-8; *Mark 2:23-28; Luke 6:1-5* [b]Deut. 23:25 **2** [a]Matt. 12:10; Luke 13:14; 14:3; John 5:10; 7:23; 9:16

became hungry,[3983] he and his companions;
4 how he entered the house of God,
and [a]they ate the [I]consecrated
bread,[4286,740] which was not lawful for
him to eat, nor for those with him, but
for the priests alone?
5 "Or have you not [ao]read in the
Law, that on the Sabbath the priests
in the temple[2411] [I]break[953] the Sabbath,
and are innocent?
6 "But I say to you, that something
[a]greater than the temple[2411] is here.
7 "But if you had known what this
[I]means, '[a]I DESIRE[2309] [II]COMPASSION,[1656]
AND NOT A SACRIFICE,' you would not
have condemned[2613] the innocent.

Lord of the Sabbath

8 "For [a]the Son of Man is Lord of
the Sabbath."
9 [a]And departing from there, He
went[2064] into their synagogue.
10 And behold, *there was* a man
with a withered hand. And they
questioned[1905] Him, saying, "[a]Is it lawful
to heal on the Sabbath?"—in order that
they might accuse[2723] Him.
11 And He said to them, "[a]What man
shall there be [I]among you, who shall
have one sheep, and if it falls into a pit
on the Sabbath, will he not take hold
of it, and lift it out?[1453]
12 "Of [a]how much more value[1308]
then is a man than a sheep! So then,
it is lawful to do [I]good on the Sabbath."
13 Then He *said to the man,
"Stretch out[1614] your hand!" And
[a]he stretched it out, and it was
restored[600] to [I]normal,[5199] like the
other.[243]
14 But the Pharisees [apt]went out,
and [a]counseled together against Him,
as to how they might destroy Him.
15 But Jesus, [I]aware of *this,* withdrew from there. And many followed
Him, and [a]He healed them all,
16 and [a]warned them not to [I]make
Him known,[5318]
17 in order that what was spoken
through Isaiah the prophet, might be
fulfilled, saying,

18 "[a]BEHOLD, MY [I]SERVANT[3816]
WHOM I [II]HAVE [ao]CHOSEN;[140]
[b]MY BELOVED IN WHOM
MY SOUL [ao] [III]IS WELL-PLEASED;[2106]
[c]I WILL PUT MY SPIRIT UPON
HIM,
[a]AND HE SHALL PROCLAIM[518]
[IV]JUSTICE[2920] TO THE
[V]GENTILES.
19 "[a]HE WILL NOT QUARREL, NOR
CRY OUT;
NOR WILL ANYONE HEAR[191] HIS
VOICE IN THE STREETS.
20 "[a]A BATTERED REED HE WILL
NOT BREAK OFF,[2608]
AND A SMOLDERING WICK HE
WILL NOT PUT OUT,
UNTIL HE [I]LEADS [II]JUSTICE[2920]
TO VICTORY.
21 "[a]AND IN HIS NAME THE
[I]GENTILES WILL HOPE."[1679]

The Pharisees Rebuked

22 [a]Then there was brought to Him
a [b]demon-possessed man *who was* blind
and dumb, and He healed him, so that
the dumb man spoke and saw.
23 And all the multitudes [ipf]were
amazed,[1839] and *began* to say, "This
man cannot be the [a]Son of David, can
he?"
24 But when the Pharisees heard
it, they said, "This man [a]casts out
demons[1140] only by [I]Beelzebul the ruler
of the demons."
25 [a]And [b]knowing their thoughts He
said to them, "[I]Any kingdom[932] divided
against itself is laid waste; and [I]any city
or house divided against itself shall not
stand.[2476]
26 "And if [a]Satan casts out Sa-
tan,[4567] he [I]is [aop]divided against himself;
how then shall his kingdom stand?
27 "And if I [a]by [I]Beelzebul cast out
demons,[1140] [b]by whom do your sons cast
them out? Consequently they shall be
your judges.[2923]
28 "But [a]if I cast out demons by
the Spirit of God, then the kingdom of
God has [ao]come upon you.

4 [I]Or, *showbread;* lit., *loaves of presentation* [a]1Sam. 21:6
5 [I]Or, *profane*
6 [a]2Chr. 6:18; Is. 66:1, 2; Matt. 12:41, 42
7 [I]Lit., *is* [II]Or, *mercy* [a]Hos. 6:6; Matt. 9:13
8 [a]Matt. 8:20; 12:32, 40
9 [a]Matt. 12:9-14; *Mark 3:1-6; Luke 6:6-11*
10 [a]Matt. 12:2; Luke 13:14; 14:3; John 5:10; 7:23; 9:16
11 [I]Lit., *of* [a]Luke 14:5
12 [I]Lit., *well* [a]Matt. 10:31; Luke 14:1-6
13 [I]Lit., *health* [a]Matt. 8:3; Acts 28:8
14 [a]Matt. 26:4; Mark 14:1; Luke 22:2; John 7:30, 44; 8:59; 10:31, 39; 11:53
15 [I]Lit., *knowing* [a]Matt. 4:23
16 [I]Or, *reveal who He was* [a]Matt. 8:4; 9:30; 17:9
18 [I]Lit., *Child* [II]Lit., *chose* [III]Or, *took pleasure* [IV]Or, *judgment* [V]Or, *nations* [a]Is. 42:1 [b]Matt. 3:17; 17:5 [c]Luke 4:18; John 3:34
19 [a]Is. 42:2
20 [I]Or, *puts forth* [II]Or, *judgment* [a]Is. 42:3
21 [I]Or, *nations* [a]Rom. 15:12
22 [a]Matt. 12:22, 24; *Luke 11:14, 15;* Matt. 9:32, 34 [b]Matt. 4:24; 2Thess. 2:9
23 [a]Matt. 9:27
24 [I]Or, *Beezebul;* others read *Beelzebub* [a]Matt. 9:34
25 [I]Lit., *Every* [a]Matt. 12:25-29; *Mark 3:23-27; Luke 11:17-22* [b]Matt. 9:4
26 [I]Lit., *was* [a]Matt. 4:10; 13:19
27 [I]V. 24, note 1 [a]Matt. 9:34 [b]Acts 19:13
28 [a]1John 3:8

29 "Or how can anyone [ainf]enter the strong man's house and [ainf]carry off his property, unless he first binds the strong *man*? And then he will plunder his house.

The Unpardonable Sin

30 "[a]He who is not with Me is against Me; and he who does not [ppt]gather with Me scatters.

🔑 31 "[a]Therefore I say to you, any sin[266] and blasphemy[988] shall be forgiven men, but blasphemy against the Spirit[4151] shall not be forgiven.

32 "[a]And whoever shall [aosb]speak a word against the Son of Man, it shall be forgiven him; but whoever shall [aosb]speak against the Holy Spirit, it shall not be forgiven him, either in [b]this age, or in the *age* to come.

Words Reveal Character

33 "Either [aim]make the tree good, and its fruit good; or [aim]make the tree bad, and its fruit bad; for [a]the tree is known by its fruit.

34 "[a]You brood of vipers, how can you, being evil,[4190] [pinf]speak [I]what is good?[18] [b]For the mouth speaks out of that which fills[4051] the heart.[2588]

35 "[a]The good [art]man out of *his* good treasure brings forth [I]what is good; and the evil man out of *his* evil treasure brings forth [II]what is evil.

36 "And I say to you, that every [I]careless[692] word[4487] that men shall speak, they shall render account[3056] for it in [a]the day of judgment.[2920]

37 "For [I]by your words you shall be justified,[1344] and [I]by your words you shall be condemned."[2613]

The Desire for Signs

38 Then some of the scribes[1122] and Pharisees answered[611] Him, saying, "Teacher, [a]we want[2309] to [ainf]see a [I]sign from You."

39 But He answered and said to them, "[a]An evil and adulterous generation craves for a [I]sign; and *yet* no [I]sign shall be given to it but the [I]sign of Jonah the prophet;

40 for just as [a]JONAH WAS THREE DAYS AND THREE NIGHTS IN THE BELLY OF THE SEA MONSTER,[2785] so shall [b]the Son of Man be [c]three days and three nights in the heart[2588] of the earth.

41 "[a]The [an]men of Nineveh shall stand up with this generation at the judgment,[2920] and shall condemn[2632] it because [b]they repented[3340] at the preaching[2782] of Jonah; and behold, [c]something greater than Jonah is here.

42 "[a]*The* Queen of *the* South shall rise up with this generation at the judgment[2920] and shall condemn[2632] it, because she came from the ends of the earth to hear the wisdom of Solomon; and behold, [b]something greater than Solomon is here.

43 "[a]Now when the unclean spirit [aosb]goes out of a man, it passes through waterless places, seeking rest,[372] and does not find *it*.

44 "Then it says, 'I will return[1994] to my house from which I came'; and when it comes, it finds it unoccupied, [pfpp]swept, and [pfpp]put in order.

45 "Then it goes, and takes along with it seven other[2087] spirits more wicked[4191] than itself, and they go in and live[2730] there; and [a]the last[2078] state of that man becomes worse than the first. That is the way it will also be with this evil generation."

Changed Relationships

46 [a]While He was still [ppt]speaking to the multitudes, behold, His [b]mother and [c]brothers[80] were [pipf]standing[2476] outside,[1854] seeking to speak to Him.

47 And someone said to Him, "Behold, Your mother and Your brothers

30 [a]Mark 9:40; Luke 9:50; 11:23
31 [a]Matt. 12:31, 32; Mark 3:28-30; Luke 12:10
32 [a]Luke 12:10 [b]Matt. 13:22, 39; Mark 10:30; Luke 16:8; 18:30; 20:34, 35; Eph. 1:21; 1Tim. 6:17; 2Tim. 4:10; Titus 2:12; Heb. 6:5
33 [a]Matt. 7:16-18; Luke 6:43, 44; John 15:4-7
34 [I]Lit., *good things* [a]Matt. 3:7; 23:33; Luke 3:7 [b]1Sam. 24:13; Is. 32:6; Matt. 12:34, 35; 15:18; Luke 6:45; Eph. 4:29; James 3:2-12
35 [I]Lit., *good things* [II]Lit., *evil things* [a]Prov. 10:20, 21; 25:11, 12; Matt. 13:52; Col. 4:6
36 [I]Or, *useless* [a]Matt. 10:15
37 [I]Or, *in accordance with*
38 [I]Or, *attesting miracle* [a]Matt. 16:1; Mark 8:11, 12; Luke 11:16; John 2:18; 6:30; 1Cor. 1:22
39 [I]Or, *attesting miracle* [a]Matt. 12:39-42; *Luke 11:29-32;* Matt. 16:4
40 [a]Jon. 1:17 [b]Matt. 8:20 [c]Matt. 16:21
41 [a]Jon. 1:2 [b]Jon. 3:5 [c]Matt. 12:6, 42
42 [a]1Kin. 10:1; 2Chr. 9:1 [b]Matt. 12:6, 41
43 [a]Matt. 12:43-45; *Luke 11:24-26*
45 [a]Mark 5:9; Luke 11:26; Heb. 6:4-8; 2Pet. 2:20
46 [a]Matt. 12:46-50; *Mark 3:31-35; Luke 8:19-21* [b]Matt. 1:18; 2:11ff.; 13:55; Luke 1:43; 2:33f., 48, 51; John 2:1, 5, 12; 19:25f.; Acts 1:14 [c]Matt. 13:55; Mark 6:3; John 2:12; 7:3, 5, 10; Acts 1:14; 1Cor. 9:5; Gal. 1:19

🔑 **12:31,32** See notes on Mk. 3:28,29; Heb. 6:1-6.

are standing outside seeking to speak to You."

48 But He answered the one who was telling Him and said, "Who is My mother and who are My brothers?"

49 And [apt]stretching out His hand toward His disciples,[3101] He said, "Behold, My mother and My brothers!

50 "For whoever does the will of My Father[3962] who is in heaven,[3772] he is My brother and sister and mother."

1 [a]Matt. 9:28; 13:36 [b]Matt. 13:1-15: *Mark 4:1-12; Luke 8:4-10;* Mark 2:13

2 [a]Luke 5:3

3 [a]Matt. 13:10ff.; Mark 4:2ff.

Jesus Teaches in Parables

13 On that day Jesus [apt]went out of [a]the house, and was [ipf]sitting [b]by the sea.

2 And great multitudes gathered to Him, so that [a]He [apt]got into a boat and [pinf]sat down, and the whole multitude was [pipf]standing[2476] on the beach.

3 And He spoke many things to them in [a]parables,[3850] saying, "Behold, the sower went out to sow;

13:1-58 Eight parables are found here. In the first instance of the parable of the sower (v. 18ff.), the sowing of the seed refers to the Word of God (Lk. 8:11). The seed, having grown in the good soil (v. 8), becomes not only one but many believing witnesses cast into the world. Jesus explained that "as for the good seed, these are the sons of the kingdom" (v. 38). See note on Mt. 8:11,12. These parables are given so that we as the children of the kingdom in the world may know that we must expect opposition from the devil (v. 39) and his children (v. 25). In these parables, we are given the negative reaction to Christian action. We must not try to uproot the weeds, representative of the evil ones in the world, because of our inability to judge rightly without the possibility of making a mistake. The ultimate disposition of the evil ones in the world will be accomplished by the angels who are going to be sent by the Lord (v. 41) at the consummation of the age. Actually, the angels are designated as the final reapers of the harvest of our labor (v. 39). Parable no. 2 (vv. 24-30 the wheat and the tares) and parable no. 7 (the net which catches both good and bad fish) are illustrative of the fact that, as a result of the witnessing of the children of the kingdom in this dispensation, there will be both genuine wheat and good fish, as well as tares and bad fish. Not all who are caught in the net of evangelism are genuinely saved. The unsaved will be made manifest in the Day of Judgment at the consummation of the age. See note on Jude 9. In parable no. 3 (vv. 31,32), we have a mustard seed which is the smallest of the seeds taking upon itself an unnatural growth. It represents the secularization of the Christian Church. Christ never meant His Church to wield organizational power. Bigness is unnatural in the kingdom of God but Christ told us what to expect. In these parables we have the history of the witness of the children of the kingdom foretold, just as in Rev. 2—3 the history of the church is foretold. The birds of the air generally represent evil. See also Rev. 18 where a false church is called Babylon. God's genuine people are admonished to separate themselves from his church (Rev. 18:4). Parable no. 4 (v. 33) about the hidden yeast represents the subtle influence of evil (the yeast) in the bread. In spite of the influence of the yeast, the bread is still useful for feeding and nourishment. It represents the Church influenced by evil and yet being the food and strength of Christ in the world. Parable no. 5 (v. 44) about the hidden treasure found in the field are the people in the world in whom He establishes His kingdom. In order to possess them, He gave His own life. He hides this treasure, God's redeemed saints, in the world until He redeems or purchases the whole world when He will come again to liberate not only the believer within the world but the world itself (Rom. 8:19-26; Rev. 21). Parable no. 6 (vv. 45-46) is similar in its message to the fifth parable, with the pearl symbolizing the sinner. The pearl at its heart is a grain of hard and lifeless sand, even as the sinner is dead in his sins and trespasses. But when the sand comes in touch with the living organism, the oyster, the sand becomes transformed into a pearl. As a result of this contact, it becomes a thing of exquisite beauty and precious indeed. Thus, the precious pearls in the world are the sinners who, because of having become absorbed into Jesus Christ, have become His kingdom (Rev. 1:6). For this to be accomplished, Jesus Christ had to sacrifice His own life, but He arose from the dead to be forever the living organism in whom we dwell. Parable no. 7 (vv. 47-50) about the net represents the fishermen or the sons of the kingdom in the sea of humanity. They catch fish which prove to be both good and bad, edible and inedible. This is similar to parable no. 2 about the wheat and the tares. The separation ultimately will be done by the angels and not by the believers down here. In this dispensation, the genuine and the hypocrite, the true believer and the fraud, will jointly inhabit the world until God's appointed time. In parable no. 8 (v. 52), we have the execution of the responsibility of the sons of the kingdom to accomplish their work through sacrifice. The believers' treasures have to be spent so that the Gospel can be preached in this generation.

4 and as he [aie]sowed, some *seeds*
fell[4098] beside the road, and the birds
came and ate them up.
🗝 5 "And others fell upon the rocky
places, where they [I]did not have much
soil;[1093] and immediately[2112] they sprang
up, because they [aid]had no depth of
soil.
6 "But when the sun had risen, they
were scorched; and because they had
no root, they withered away.
7 "And others fell [I]among the
thorns, and the thorns came up[305] and
choked them out.
8 "And others fell on the good
soil,[1093] and *yielded a crop, some a
[a]hundredfold, some sixty, and some
thirty.
9 "[a]He who has ears, let him hear."

An Explanation

🗝 10 And the disciples came and said
to Him, "Why do You speak to them
in parables?"
11 And He answered and said to
them, "[a]To you it has been granted to
[ainf]know the mysteries[3466] of the kingdom[932] of heaven, but to them it has
not been [pfip]granted.
12 "[a]For whoever has, to him shall
more be given, and he shall have an
abundance;[4052] but whoever does not
have, even what he has shall be taken
away from him.
13 "Therefore I speak to them in
parables; because while [a]seeing[991] they
do not see,[991] and while hearing they
do not hear, nor do they understand.
14 "And [I]in their case the
prophecy[4394] of Isaiah is being fulfilled,[378] which [ppt]says,
'[II][a]YOU WILL KEEP ON
[nn]HEARING,[189] [III]BUT WILL
NOT [aosb]UNDERSTAND;
AND [IV]YOU WILL KEEP ON
[ppf]SEEING,[991] BUT [efn]WILL
not [aosb]PERCEIVE;
15 [a]FOR THE HEART OF THIS
PEOPLE HAS BECOME
DULL,[3975]
AND WITH THEIR EARS THEY
SCARCELY [ao]HEAR,
AND THEY HAVE [ao]CLOSED
THEIR EYES
LEST THEY SHOULD [aosb]SEE
WITH THEIR EYES,
AND [aosb]HEAR WITH THEIR
EARS,
AND [aosb]UNDERSTAND WITH
THEIR HEART AND
[aosb]RETURN,[1994]
AND I SHOULD [ft]HEAL[2390]
THEM.'
16 "[a]But blessed[3107] are your eyes,

5 [I]Lit., *were not having*
7 [I]Lit., *upon*
8 [a]Gen. 26:12; Matt. 13:23
9 [a]Matt. 11:15; Rev. 2:7, 11, 17, 29; 3:6, 13, 22
11 [a]Matt. 19:11; 20:23; John 6:65; 1Cor. 2:10; Col. 1:27; 1John 2:20, 27
12 [a]Matt. 25:29; Mark 4:25; Luke 8:18; 19:26
13 [a]Deut. 29:4; Is. 42:19, 20; Jer. 5:21; Ezek. 12:2
14 [I]Lit., *for them* [II]Lit., *With a hearing you will hear* [III]Lit., *and* [IV]Lit., *seeing you will see* [a]Is. 6:9; Mark 4:12; Luke 8:10; John 12:40; Acts 28:26, 27; Rom. 10:16; 11:8
15 [a]Is. 6:10; Ps. 119:70; Zech. 7:11; Luke 19:42; John 8:43,44; 2Tim. 4:4; Heb. 5:11
16 [a]Matt. 13:16, 17; *Luke 10:23, 24;* Matt. 16:17; John 20:29

🗝 **13:5-7** See note on Gal. 3:22.

🗝 **13:10-17,34f.** These passages, along with Mk. 4:10-12 are some of the most difficult sayings of the Lord Jesus. The clue to understanding is found in the correct translation of a Greek word, *mēpote* (Mt. 13:15; Mk. 4:12), usually translated "lest." However, it should be translated as a suppositional particle, "if perhaps." Christ's reasoning was this, "If I speak plainly to these people knowing they are going to reject what I say to them, their understanding of it will increase their guilt. They would be rejecting not what they do not understand, but what they do understand. If I speak to them in parables and they do not understand what I am saying, then their rejection is based on their lack of understanding and it will diminish their guilt. Their guilt is not based upon whether they understand or not, but on their rejection of God and Me, not because of what I say, but because of what I am, which should have been clear enough to them." It is inherent in the entire teaching of the Bible that God will not hold us responsible for what we do not know or understand, but for what we do know and understand (Rom. 2:12-20; 4:15). The nonunderstanding of some of the words of Christ in reality never alleviates unbelievers of their guilt for the rejection of Jesus Christ. Every human being on earth has an inner consciousness of God's requirement of him (Jn. 1:9; Rom. 2:15). As one knows and understands more, his responsibility increases proportionately. This applies to both unbelievers and believers, the former for the degree of their punishment in hell, and the latter for the degree of their heavenly reward. Hiding the meaning of the depths of God by Jesus Christ to unbelievers is an act of mercifulness toward them in reducing their comprehension of His words.

because they see; and your ears, because they hear.

17 “For truly[281] I say to you, that [a]many prophets and righteous[1342] men [ao]desired[1937] to [ainf]see what you see, and did not see *it*; and to [ainf]hear what you hear, and did not [ao]hear *it*.

The Sower Explained

18 [aim]“[a]Hear then the parable of the sower.

19 “When anyone [ppt]hears [a]the word[3056] of the kingdom, and does not [ppt]understand it, [b]the evil[4190] *one* comes and snatches away[726] what has been [pfpp]sown in his heart. This is the one on whom seed [aptp]was sown beside the road.

20 “And the one on whom seed was [aptp]sown[4687] on the rocky places, this is the man who [ppt]hears the word,[3056] and immediately[2117] [ppt]receives it with joy;[5479]

21 yet he has no *firm* root in himself, but is *only* temporary,[4340] and when affliction[2347] or persecution arises because of the word,[3056] immediately he [pinp][1][a]falls away.

22 “And the one on whom seed [aptp]was sown among the thorns, this is the man who [ppt]hears the word, and the worry of [a]the [1]world, and the [b]deceitfulness of riches choke the word,[3056] and it becomes unfruitful.

23 “And the one on whom seed [aptp]was sown on the good soil,[1093] this is the man who [ppt]hears the word[3056] and [ppt]understands it; who indeed bears fruit, and brings forth, some [a]a hundredfold, some sixty, and some thirty.”

Tares among Wheat

🔑 24 He presented another parable to them, saying, “[a]The kingdom of heaven [1]may be [aop]compared to a man who [apt]sowed good seed[4690] in his field.

25 “But while men were [aie]sleeping, his enemy came and sowed [1]tares[2215] also among[3319] the wheat, and went away.

26 “But when the [1]wheat sprang up and bore grain, then the tares became evident[5316] also.

27 “And the slaves[1401] of the landowner came and said to him, ‘Sir,[2962] did you not sow good seed[4690] in your field? [1]How then does it have tares?’

28 “And he said to them, ‘An [1]enemy has [ao]done this!’ And the slaves *said to him, ‘Do you want us, then, to [apt]go and [aosb]gather them up?’

29 “But he *said, ‘No; lest while you are [ppt]gathering up the tares, you may [aosb]root up the wheat with them.

30 ‘Allow[863] both to [pinf]grow together until the harvest; and in the time[2540] of the harvest I will say to the reapers, “First gather up the tares and bind them in bundles to burn them up; but [aim] [a]gather[4863] the wheat into my barn.” ’ ”

The Mustard Seed

31 He presented another parable to them, saying, “[a]The kingdom of heaven is like [b]a mustard seed, which a man [apt]took and sowed in his field;

32 and this is smaller than all *other* seeds;[4690] but when it is full grown, it is larger than the garden plants, and becomes a tree, so that [a]THE BIRDS OF THE [1]AIR[3772] [ainf]come and [pinf]NEST IN ITS BRANCHES.”

The Leaven

33 He spoke another parable to them, “[a]The kingdom[932] of heaven[3772] is like leaven, which a woman took, and hid in [b]three [1]pecks of meal, until it was all leavened.”

🔑 34 All these things Jesus [ao]spoke to the multitudes in parables,[3850] and He did not [ipf]speak to them [a]without a parable,

35 so that what was spoken through the prophet[4396] might be fulfilled, saying,

17 [a]John 8:56; Heb. 11:13; 1Pet. 1:10-12

18 [a]Matt. 13:18-23; *Mark 4:13-20; Luke 8:11-15*

19 [a]Matt. 4:23 [b]Matt. 5:37

21 [1]Lit., *is caused to stumble* [a]Matt. 11:6

22 [1]Or, *age* [a]Matt. 12:32; 13:39; Mark 4:19; Rom. 12:2; 1Cor. 1:20; 2:6, 8; 3:18; 2Cor. 4:4; Gal. 1:4; Eph. 2:2 [b]Matt. 19:23; 1Tim. 6:9, 10, 17

23 [a]Matt. 13:8

24 [1]Lit., *was compared to* [a]Matt. 13:31, 33, 45, 47; 18:23; 20:1; 22:2; 25:1; Mark 4:26-30; Luke 13:18, 20

25 [1]Or, *darnel*, a weed resembling wheat

26 [1]Lit., *grass*

27 [1]Lit., *From where*

28 [1]Lit., *enemy man*

30 [a]Matt. 3:12

31 [a]Matt. 13:31, 32; *Mark 4:30-32; Luke 13:18, 19;* Matt. 13:24 [b]Matt. 17:20; Luke 17:6

32 [1]Or, *sky* [a]Ezek. 17:23; Ps. 104:12; Ezek. 31:6; Dan. 4:12

33 [1]Gr., *sata* [a]Matt. 13:33; *Luke 13:21;* Matt. 13:24 [b]Gen. 18:6; Judg. 6:19; 1Sam. 1:24

34 [a]Mark 4:34; John 10:6; 16:25

🔑 **13:24-30** See note on Jude 9.

"[a]I WILL OPEN MY MOUTH IN
PARABLES;
I WILL UTTER THINGS
[pfpp]HIDDEN SINCE THE
FOUNDATION[2602] OF THE
WORLD."[2889]

The Tares Explained

36 Then He [apt]left[863] the multitudes, and went into [a]the house. And
His disciples[3101] came to Him, saying,
"[b]Explain to us the parable of the
[I]tares$_{2215}$ of the field."
37 And He answered and said, "The
one who [ppt]sows the good seed[4690] is
[a]the Son of Man,
38 and the field is the world;[2889] and
as for the good seed, these are [a]the
sons[5207] of the kingdom;[932] and the tares
are [b]the sons of [c]the evil *one;*
39 and the enemy who [apt]sowed
them is the devil,[1228] and the harvest
is [a]the [I]end[4930] of the age; and the reapers are angels.
40 "Therefore just as the tares are
gathered up and burned with fire, so
shall it be at [a]the [I]end of the age.
41 "[a]The Son of Man [b]will send forth
His angels, and they will gather out of
His kingdom[932] [I]all [c]stumbling blocks,
and those who [ppt]commit lawlessness,[458]
42 and [a]will cast them into the furnace of fire; in that place [b]there shall
be weeping and gnashing$_{1030}$ of teeth.
43 "[a]Then THE RIGHTEOUS[1342] WILL
SHINE FORTH AS THE SUN in the kingdom
of their Father. [b]He who has ears, let
him [pim]hear.

Hidden Treasure

44 "[a]The kingdom of heaven is like
a treasure [pfpp]hidden in the field, which
a man [apt]found and [ao]hid; and from joy
over it he goes and [b]sells all that he
has, and buys[59] that field.

A Costly Pearl

45 "Again, [a]the kingdom[932] of
heaven is like a merchant$_{1713}$ seeking
fine pearls,
46 and upon finding one pearl of
great value, he went and sold all that
he had, and bought[59] it.

A Dragnet

47 "Again, [a]the kingdom[932] of heav-
en[3772] is like a dragnet[4522] cast into the
sea, and [apt]gathering *fish* of every kind;
48 and when it was filled,[4137] they
[apt]drew it up on the beach; and they
[apt]sat down, and gathered the good *fish*
into containers, but the bad they threw
away.
49 "So it will be at [a]the [I]end[4930] of
the age; the angels shall come forth,
and [II]take out[873] the wicked from
among[3319] the righteous,[1342]
50 and [a]will cast them into the furnace of fire; [b]there shall be weeping and
gnashing$_{1030}$ of teeth.
51 "Have you understood all these
things?" They *said to Him, "Yes."
52 And He said to them, "Therefore
every scribe[1122] who has become a
disciple[3100] of the kingdom[932] of
heaven[3772] is like a head of a household,
who brings forth out of his treasure
things new[2537] and old."[3820]

Jesus Revisits Nazareth

53 [a]And it came about that when
Jesus had finished[5055] these parables,
He departed from there.
54 [a]And coming to [I]His home town
He [IIb]*began* [ipf]teaching them in their synagogue, so that [c]they became [pinf]aston-
ished, and [pinf]said, "Where *did* this man
get this wisdom, and *these* [III]miraculous
powers?
55 "Is not this the carpenter's son?
Is not [a]His mother called Mary, and His

35 [a]Ps. 78:2
36 [I]Or, *darnel,* a weed resembling wheat [a]Matt. 13:1 [b]Matt. 15:15
37 [a]Matt. 8:20
38 [a]Matt. 8:12 [b]John 8:44; Acts 13:10; 1John 3:10 [c]Matt. 5:37
39 [I]Or, *consummation* [a]Matt. 12:32; 13:22, 40, 49; 24:3; 28:20; 1Cor. 10:11; Heb. 9:26
40 [I]Or, *consummation* [a]Matt. 12:32; 13:22, 39, 49; 24:3; 28:20; 1Cor. 10:11; Heb. 9:26
41 [I]Or, *everything that is offensive* [a]Matt. 8:20 [b]Matt. 24:31 [c]Zeph. 1:3
42 [a]Matt. 13:50 [b]Matt. 8:12
43 [a]Dan. 12:3 [b]Matt. 11:15
44 [a]Matt. 13:24 [b]Matt. 13:46
45 [a]Matt. 13:24
47 [a]Matt. 13:44
49 [I]Or, *consummation* [II]Or, *separate* [a]Matt. 13:39, 40
50 [a]Matt. 13:42 [b]Matt. 8:12
53 [a]Matt. 7:28
54 [I]Or, *His own part of the country* [II]Or, *was teaching* [III]Or, *miracles* [a]Matt. 13:54-58; *Mark 6:1-6* [b]Matt. 4:23 [c]Matt. 7:28
55 [a]Matt. 12:46

13:38,42,43 See note on Mt. 8:11,12.
13:55 See general remarks on Jude.

[a]brothers,[80] James and Joseph and Simon and Judas?

56 "And [a]His sisters, are they not all with us? Where then *did* this man *get* all these things?"

57 And they [I]took [ipf] [a]offense at Him. But Jesus said to them, "[b]A prophet[4396] is not without honor except in his [II]home town, and in his *own* household."

58 And He [ao]did not do many [I]miracles there because of their unbelief.[570]

John the Baptist Beheaded

14 [a]At that [I]time [b]Herod the tetrarch[5076] heard the news[189] about Jesus,

2 and said to his servants,[3816] "[a]This is John the Baptist;[910] [I]he has [aop]risen[1453] from the dead; and that is why miraculous powers are at work[1754] in him."

3 For when [a]Herod had John [apt]arrested, he bound him, and put[5087] him [b]in prison[5438] on account of [c]Herodias, the wife of his brother Philip.

4 For John had been saying to him, "[a]It is not lawful for you to [pinf]have her."

5 And although he [ppt]wanted[2309] to [ainf]put him to death, he feared[5399] the multitude, because [I]they regarded him as [a]a prophet.[4396]

6 But when Herod's birthday [I]came,[1096] the daughter of [a]Herodias danced [II]before *them* and pleased [b]Herod.

7 Thereupon he promised[3670] with[3326] an oath[3727] to give her whatever she asked.

8 And having been prompted by her mother, she *said, "Give me here on a platter the head of John the Baptist."

9 And although he was grieved,[3076] the king[935] commanded *it* to be given because of his oaths, and because of [I]his dinner guests.

10 And he sent and had John beheaded in the prison.[5438]

11 And his head was brought on a platter and given to the girl; and she brought *it* to her mother.

12 And his disciples [apt]came and took away the body[4430] and buried [I]it; and they [apt]went and reported to Jesus.

Five Thousand Fed

13 [a]Now when Jesus heard *it,* He withdrew from there in a boat, to a lonely place by Himself;[2398] and when the multitudes heard *of this,* they followed Him on foot from the cities.

14 And when He [apt]went [I]ashore, He [a]saw a great multitude, and felt compassion for them, and [b]healed their sick.[732]

15 And when it was evening, the disciples came to Him, saying, "The place is desolate, and the time[5610] is already past; so send[630] the multitudes away, that they may [apt]go into the villages and buy[59] food[1033] for themselves."

16 But Jesus said to them, "They do not need to go away; you [aim]give them *something* to eat!"

17 And they *said to Him, "We have here only [a]five loaves and two fish."

18 And He said, "Bring[5342] them here to Me."

19 And [apt]ordering the multitudes to recline on the grass, He [apt]took the five loaves and the two fish, and [apt]looking up[308] toward heaven, He [a]blessed[2127] *the food,* and [apt]breaking[2806] the loaves He gave them to the disciples, and the disciples[3101] *gave* to the multitudes,

20 and they all ate, and were satisfied. And they picked up what was left over of the broken pieces,[2801] twelve full[4134] [a]baskets.

21 And there were about[5616] five thousand men[435] who [ppt]ate, aside from women and children.

Jesus Walks on the Water

22 [a]And immediately[2112] He [I]made[315] the disciples[3101] get into the boat, and go ahead[4254] of Him to the

55 [a]Matt. 12:46
56 [a]Mark 6:3
57 [I]Lit., *were being made to stumble* [II]Or, *own part of the country* [a]Matt. 11:6 [b]Mark 6:4; Luke 4:24; John 4:44
58 [I]Or, *works of power*

1 [I]Or, *occasion* [a]Matt. 14:1-12; *Mark 6:14-29;* Matt. 14:1, 2; *Luke 9:7-9* [b]Mark 8:15; Luke 3:1, 19; 8:3; 13:31; 23:7f., 11f., 15; Acts 4:27; 12:1
2 [I]Or, *he, himself* [a]Matt. 16:14; Mark 6:14; Luke 9:7
3 [a]Matt. 14:1-12; *Mark 6:14-29;* Mark 8:15; Luke 3:1, 19; 8:3; 13:31; 23:7f., 11f., 15; Acts 4:27; 12:1 [b]Matt. 4:12; 11:2 [c]Matt. 14:6; Mark 6:17, 19, 22; Luke 3:19f.
4 [a]Lev. 18:16; 20:21
5 [I]Lit., *they were holding* [a]Matt. 11:9
6 [I]Lit., *occurred* [II]Lit., *in the midst* [a]Matt. 14:3; Mark 6:17, 19, 22; Luke 3:19 [b]Matt. 14:1-12; *Mark 6:14-29;* Mark 8:15; Luke 3:1, 19; 8:3; 13:31; 23:7f., 11f., 15; Acts 4:27; 12:1
9 [I]Lit., *those who reclined* at the table *with him*
12 [I]Lit., *him*
13 [a]Matt. 14:13-21; *Mark 6:32-44; Luke 9:10-17; John 6:1-13;* Matt. 15:32-38
14 [I]Lit., *out* [a]Matt. 9:36 [b]Matt. 4:23
17 [a]Matt. 16:9
19 [a]1Sam. 9:13; Matt. 15:36; 26:26; Mark 6:41; 8:7; 14:22; Luke 24:30; Acts 27:35; Rom. 14:6
20 [a]Matt. 16:9; Mark 6:43; 8:19; Luke 9:17; John 6:13
22 [I]Lit., *compelled* [a]Matt. 14:22-33; *Mark 6:45-51; John 6:15-21*

other side, while He sent the multitudes
away.
23 And after He had sent the multitudes away, [a]He went up to the mountain
by Himself[2398] to [ainf]pray; and when it
was evening, He was there alone.
24 But the boat was already many
[I]stadia away from the land, [II]battered
by the waves; for the wind was contrary.
25 And in [a]the [I]fourth watch of the
night He came to them, walking on the
sea.
26 And when the disciples saw Him
walking on the sea, they were [I]fright-
ened, saying, "It is [a]a ghost!" And they
cried out for fear.[5401]
27 But immediately Jesus spoke to
them, saying, "[a]Take courage, it is I;
[b]do not be afraid."[5399]
28 And Peter answered Him and
said, "Lord, if it is You, command me
to come to You on the water."
29 And He said, "Come!" And Peter
got out of the boat, and walked on the
water and came toward Jesus.
30 But [ppt]seeing the wind, he became afraid,[5399] and [apt]beginning to sink,
he cried out, saying, "Lord, save me!"
31 And immediately Jesus
[apt]stretched out His hand and [ao]took
hold[1949] of him, and *said to him, "[a]O
you of little faith,[3640] why did you
doubt?"
32 And when they got into the boat,
the wind stopped.[2869]
33 And those who were in the boat
worshiped Him, saying, "You are certainly [an] [a]God's Son!"
34 [a]And when they had crossed
over, they came to [I]land at [b]Gennesaret.
35 And when the men of that place
[I]recognized Him, they sent into all that
surrounding district and brought to Him
all who were sick;[2560]
🔑 36 and they *began* to [ipf]entreat Him
that they might just [aosb]touch [a]the fringe
of His cloak; and as many as [b]touched
it were cured.[1295]

23 [a]Mark 6:46; Luke 6:12; 9:28; John 6:15
24 [I]A stadion was about 600 feet [II]Lit., *tormented*
25 [I]I.e., 3-6 a.m. [a]Matt. 24:43; Mark 13:35
26 [I]Or, *troubled* [a]Luke 24:37
27 [a]Matt. 9:2 [b]Matt. 17:7; 28:5, 10; Mark 6:50; Luke 1:13, 30; 2:10; 5:10; 12:32; John 6:20; Rev. 1:17
31 [a]Matt. 6:30; 8:26; 16:8
33 [a]Matt. 4:3
34 [I]Lit., *the land* [a]Matt. 14:34-36; *Mark 6:53-56;* John 6:24, 25 [b]Mark 6:53; Luke 5:1
35 [I]Or, *knew*
36 [a]Matt. 9:20 [b]Matt. 9:21; Mark 3:10; 6:56; 8:22; Luke 6:19
1 [a]Matt. 15:1-20; *Mark 7:1-23* [b]Mark 3:22; 7:1; John 1:19; Acts 25:7
2 [a]Luke 11:38
3 [I]Or, *you also*
4 [I]Lit., *die the death* [a]Ex. 20:12; Deut. 5:16 [b]Ex. 21:17; Lev. 20:9
5 [I]Or, *a gift, an offering*
6 [I]Many mss. do not contain *or his mother* [II]I.e., by supporting them with it [III]Some mss. read *law*
8 [a]Is. 29:13
9 [a]Col. 2:22
11 [a]Matt. 15:18; Acts 10:14, 15; 1Tim. 4:3
12 [I]Lit., *caused to stumble*

Tradition and Commandment

15 [a]Then some Pharisees and
scribes[1122] *came to Jesus
[b]from Jerusalem, saying,
2 "Why do Your disciples[3101]
transgress[3845] the tradition[3862] of the
elders?[4245] For they [a]do not wash their
hands when they eat bread."
3 And He answered and said to
them, "And why do [I]you yourselves
transgress[3845] the commandment of God
for the sake of your tradition?
4 "For God said, '[a]HONOR YOUR
[art]FATHER AND [art]MOTHER,' and, '[b]HE
WHO [ppt]SPEAKS EVIL OF FATHER OR
MOTHER, LET HIM [pim] [I]BE PUT TO
DEATH.'
5 "But you say, 'Whoever shall say
to *his* [art]father or [art]mother, "Anything
of mine you might have been helped
by has been [I]given[1435] *to God,*"
6 he is not to honor his father
[I]or his mother[II].' And *thus* you invali-
dated the [III]word of God for the sake
of your tradition.
7 "You hypocrites, rightly did Isaiah
prophesy[4395] of you, saying,
8 '[a]THIS PEOPLE HONORS ME WITH
THEIR LIPS,
BUT THEIR HEART[2588] IS FAR
AWAY[568] FROM ME.
9 'BUT IN VAIN[3155] DO THEY
WORSHIP[4576] ME,
TEACHING AS [a]DOCTRINES[1319]
THE PRECEPTS[1778] OF
MEN.' "[444]
10 And after He [apt]called the multitude to Him, He said to them, [pim]"Hear,
and [pim]understand.
11 "[a]Not what [ppt]enters into the
mouth defiles[2840] the man, but what
[ppt]proceeds out of the mouth, this defiles
the man."
12 Then the disciples [apt]*came and
*said to Him, "Do You know that the
Pharisees were [I]offended when they
heard this statement?"[3056]
13 But He answered and said,

🔑 **14:36** See note on Phil. 2:6-8.

"[a]Every plant which My heavenly[3770] Father did not [ao]plant shall be rooted up.

14 "Let them alone; [a]they are blind guides [I]of the blind. And [b]if a blind man guides a blind man, both will fall[4098] into a pit."

The Heart of Man

15 And Peter answered and said to Him, "[a]Explain the parable[3850] to us."

16 And He said, "Are you still lacking in understanding[801] also?

17 "Do you not understand[3539] that everything that goes [ppt]into the mouth passes into the [I]stomach, and is [II]eliminated?856

18 "But [a]the things that proceed out of the mouth come from the heart, and those defile the man.

19 "[a]For out of the heart come evil[4190] thoughts,[1261] murders, adulteries, [I]fornications,4202 thefts, false witness, slanders.[988]

20 "These are the things which [ppt]defile the [art]man; but to eat with unwashed hands does not defile the [art]man."

The Syrophoenician Woman

21 [a]And Jesus [apt]went away from there, and withdrew into the district of [b]Tyre and [c]Sidon.

22 And behold, a Canaanite woman [apt]came out from that region, and *began* to [ao]cry out, saying, "Have mercy on me, O Lord, [a]Son of David; my daughter is cruelly [b]demon-possessed."[1139]

23 But He did not answer her a word. And His disciples [apt]came to *Him* and kept [ipf]asking Him, saying, "Send[630] her away, for she is shouting out after us."

24 But He answered and said, "I was [aop]sent only to [a]the lost[622] sheep of the house of Israel."

25 But she [apt]came and [a]*began* [I]to [ipf]bow down before Him, saying, "Lord, help me!"

26 And He answered and said, "It is not [I]good[2570] to take the children's bread and throw it to the [art]dogs."

27 But she said, "Yes, Lord;[2962] [I]but even the dogs feed on the crumbs which [ppt]fall[4098] from their masters'[2962] table."

28 Then Jesus answered and said to her, "O woman, [a]your faith[4102] is great; be it done for you as you wish."[2309] And her daughter was healed[2390] [I]at once.

Healing Multitudes

29 [a]And [apt]departing from there, Jesus went along[3844] by [b]the Sea of Galilee, and [apt]having gone up to the mountain, He was sitting there.

30 And great multitudes came to Him, bringing with them *those who were* lame, crippled, blind, dumb, and many others, and they laid them down at His feet; and [a]He healed them,

31 so that the multitude marveled2296 as they [ppt]saw the dumb [ppt]speaking, the crippled [I]restored,[5199] and the lame [ppt]walking, and the blind [ppt]seeing; and they [a]glorified[1392] the God of Israel.

Four Thousand Fed

32 [a]And Jesus [apt]called His disciples[3101] to Him, and said, "[b]I feel compassion for the multitude, because they [I]have remained with[4357] Me now three days[2250] and have nothing to eat; and I do not wish to send them away hungry,3523 lest they faint on the way."

33 And the disciples *said to Him, "Where would we get so many loaves in a desolate place to satisfy such a great multitude?"

34 And Jesus *said to them, "How many loaves do you have?" And they said, "Seven, and a few small fish."

35 And He directed the multitude to [I]sit down on the ground;

36 and He took the seven loaves and the fish; and [apt] [a]giving thanks, He broke[2806] them and started [ipf]giving them

13 [a]Is. 60:21; 61:3; John 15:2; 1Cor. 3:9
14 [I]Some mss. do not contain *of the blind* [a]Matt. 23:16, 24 [b]Luke 6:39
15 [a]Matt. 13:36
17 [I]Lit., *belly* [II]Lit., *cast out into the latrine*
18 [a]Matt. 12:34; Mark 7:20
19 [I]I.e., sexual immorality [a]Gal. 5:19ff.
21 [a]Matt. 15:21-28; *Mark 7:24-30* [b]Matt. 11:21
22 [a]Matt. 9:27 [b]Matt. 4:24
24 [a]Matt. 10:6
25 [I]Or, *to worship* [a]Matt. 8:2
26 [I]Or, *proper*
27 [I]Lit., *for*
28 [I]Lit., *from that hour* [a]Matt. 9:22
29 [a]Matt. 15:29-31; Mark 7:31-37 [b]Matt. 4:18
30 [a]Matt. 4:23
31 [I]Or, *healthy* [a]Matt. 9:8
32 [I]Lit., *are remaining* [a]Matt. 15:32-39; *Mark 8:1-10;* Matt. 14:13-21 [b]Matt. 9:36
35 [I]Lit., *recline*
36 [a]Matt. 14:19; 26:27; Luke 22:17, 19; John 6:11, 23; Acts 27:35; Rom. 14:6

to the disciples, and the disciples *in turn,*
to the multitudes.
37 And they all ate, and were satisfied, and they picked up what was left
over of the broken[2801] pieces, seven
large [a]baskets full.[4134]
38 And those who ate were four
thousand men,[435] besides women and
children.
39 And [apt]sending away[630] the multitudes, He got into [a]the boat, and came
to the region of [b]Magadan.

Pharisees Test Jesus

16 [a]And the [b]Pharisees and Sadducees came up, and testing[3985]
Him [c]asked Him to show them a
[I]sign from heaven.
2 But He answered and said to
them, [I]“[a]When it is evening, you say,
'*It will be* fair weather, for the sky is
red.'
3 “And in the morning, '*There will
be* a storm today, for the sky is red
and threatening.' [a]Do you know how to
[pinf]discern[1252] the [I]appearance[4383] of the
sky, but cannot *discern* the signs of the
times?[2540]
4 “[a]An evil[4190] and adulterous generation seeks after a [I]sign; and a [I]sign
will not be [fp]given it, except the sign
of Jonah.” And He left them, and went
away.
5 And the disciples[3101] came to the
other side and had forgotten to take
bread.
6 And Jesus said to them, “Watch
out and [a]beware of the [I]leaven[2219] of
the [b]Pharisees and Sadducees.”
7 And they began to [ipf]discuss[1260]
among themselves, saying, “*It is* because we [ao]took no bread.”
8 But Jesus, aware of this, said,
“[a]You men of little faith,[3640] why do you
discuss among yourselves that you have no
bread?
9 “Do you not yet understand[3539] or
remember [a]the five loaves of the five
thousand, and how many baskets you took
up?
10 “Or [a]the seven loaves of the four
thousand, and how many large baskets you
took up?
11 “How is it that you do not understand that I did not speak to you concerning bread? But [pim][a]beware of the
[I]leaven of the [b]Pharisees and Sadducees.”
12 Then they understood that He
did not say to beware of the leaven of
bread, but of the teaching of the
[a]Pharisees and Sadducees.

Peter's Confession of Christ

13 [a]Now when Jesus came into the
district of [b]Caesarea Philippi, He *began*
[ipf]asking[2065] His disciples,[3101] saying,
“Who do people say that [c]the Son of
Man is?”
14 And they said, “Some *say*
[a]John the Baptist;[910] and others,
[Ib]Elijah; but still others, [II]Jeremiah, or
one of the prophets.”[4396]
15 He *said to them, “But who do
you say that I am?”
16 And Simon Peter answered and
said, “Thou art [Ia]the Christ,[5547] [b]the Son
of [c]the living[2198] God.”[2316]
17 And Jesus answered and said to
him, “Blessed[3107] are you, [a]Simon
[I]Barjona, because [b]flesh[4561] and blood[129]
did not [ao]reveal[601] *this* to you, but My
Father[3962] who is in heaven.[3772]
🔑18 “And I also say to you that you

37 [a]Matt. 16:10; Mark 8:8, 20; Acts 9:25
39 [a]Mark 3:9 [b]Mark 8:10

1 [I]Or, *attesting miracle* [a]Matt. 16:1-12; *Mark 8:11-21* [b]Matt. 3:7; 16:6, 11, 12 [c]Matt. 12:38; Luke 11:16
2 [I]The earliest mss. do not contain the rest of v. 2 and v. 3 [a]Luke 12:54f.
3 [I]Lit., *face* [a]Luke 12:56
4 [I]Or, *attesting miracle* [a]Matt. 12:39; Luke 11:29
6 [I]Or, *yeast* [a]Mark 8:15; Luke 12:1 [b]Matt. 3:7
8 [a]Matt. 6:30; 8:26; 14:31
9 [a]Matt. 14:17-21
10 [a]Matt. 15:34-38
11 [I]Or, *yeast* [a]Matt. 16:6; Mark 8:15; Luke 12:1 [b]Matt. 3:7; 16:6, 12
12 [a]Matt. 3:7; 5:20
13 [a]Matt. 16:13-16; *Mark 8:27-29; Luke 9:18-20* [b]Mark 8:27 [c]Matt. 8:20; 16:27, 28
14 [I]Gr., *Elias* [II]Gr., *Jeremias* [a]Matt. 14:2 [b]Matt. 17:10; Mark 6:15; Luke 9:8; John 1:21
16 [I]I.e., the Messiah [a]Matt. 1:16; 16:20; John 11:27 [b]Matt. 4:3 [c]Ps. 42:2; Matt. 26:63; Acts 14:15; Rom. 9:26; 2Cor. 3:3; 6:16; 1Thess. 1:9; 1Tim. 3:15; 4:10; Heb. 3:12; 9:14; 10:31; 12:22; Rev. 7:2
17 [I]I.e., son of Jonah [a]John 1:42; 21:15-17 [b]1Cor. 15:50; Gal. 1:16; Eph. 6:12; Heb. 2:14

🔑 **16:18,19** A more accurate translation of v. 19 from the Greek is “And I will give thee the keys of the kingdom of the heavens. And whatever thou shalt bind on the earth shall be as having been bound in the heavens; and whatever thou shalt loose on the earth shall be as having been loosed in the heavens.” This is the first time the *ekklēsia,* frequently translated “church” is mentioned in the entire

(continued on next page)

are [Ia]Peter, and upon this [II]rock I will build[3618] My church;[1577] and the [an]gates of [b]Hades[86] shall not overpower[2729] it.

19 "I will give you [a]the keys of the kingdom[932] of heaven;[3772] and [n b]whatever you [aosb]shall bind[1210] on earth [ft I]shall be [pfpp]bound[1210] in heaven, and whatever you [aosb]shall loose on earth[1093] [ft I]shall be [pfpp]loosed[3089] in heaven."

20 [a]Then He [I]warned the disciples that they should [aosb]tell no one that He was [IIb]the Christ.

Jesus Foretells His Death

21 [a]From that time Jesus Christ began to [ppt]show His disciples that He must go to Jerusalem, and [b]suffer[3958] many things from the elders[4245] and chief priests and scribes, and be killed, and be raised up on the third day.

22 And Peter [apt]took Him aside[4355] and began to [pinf]rebuke[2008] Him, saying, "[I]God forbid[2436] *it,* Lord! This [efn]shall never [II]happen to You."

23 But He turned and said to Peter, "Get behind Me, [a]Satan![4567] You are a stumbling block to Me; for you are not setting your mind[5426] on [I]God's interests, but man's."

18 [I]Gr., *Petros,* a stone [II]Gr., *petra,* large rock, bed-rock [a]Matt. 4:18 [b]Matt. 11:23
19 [I]Or, *shall have been* [a]Is. 22:22; Rev. 1:18; 3:7 [b]Matt. 18:18; John 20:23
20 [I]Or, *strictly admonished* [II]I.e., the Messiah [a]Matt. 8:4; Mark 8:30; Luke 9:21 [b]Matt. 1:16; 16:16; John 11:27
21 [a]Matt. 16:21-28; *Mark 8:31-9:1; Luke 9:22-27* [b]Matt. 12:40; 17:9, 12, 22f.; 20:18f.; 27:63; Mark 9:12, 31; Luke 17:25; 18:32; 24:7; John 2:19
22 [I]Lit., (God be) *merciful to You* [II]Lit., *be*
23 [I]Lit., *the things of God* [a]Matt. 4:10
24 [a]Matt. 10:38; Luke 14:27
25 [I]Or, *soul* [a]Matt. 10:39
27 [I]Lit., *doing* [a]Matt. 8:20 [b]Matt. 10:23; 24:3, 27, 37, 39; 26:64; Mark 8:38; 13:26; Luke 21:27; John 21:22; Acts 1:11; 1Cor. 15:23; 1Thess. 1:10; 4:16; 2Thess. 1:7,10; 2:1,8; James 5:7f.; 2Pet. 1:16; 3:4,12; 1John 2:28; Rev. 1:7 [c]Ps. 62:12; Prov. 24:12; Rom. 2:6; 14:12; 1Cor. 3:13; 2Cor. 5:10; Eph. 6:8; Col. 3:25; Rev. 2:23; 20:12; 22:12 **28** [a]Matt. 8:20 [b]Matt. 10:23; 24:3, 27, 37, 39; 26:64; Mark 8:38; 13:26; Luke 21:27; John 21:22; Acts 1:11; 1Cor. 15:23; 1Thess. 1:10; 4:16; 2Thess. 1:7,10; 2:1,8; James 5:7f.; 2Pet. 1:16; 3:4, 12; 1John 2:28; Rev. 1:7

Discipleship Is Costly

24 Then Jesus said to His disciples, "If anyone wishes to come after Me, let him [aim]deny[533] himself, and [aim a]take up[142] his cross,[4716] and [pim]follow[190] Me.

25 "For [a]whoever wishes to [ainf]save[4982] his [I]life[5590] shall lose[622] it; but whoever [aosb]loses[622] his [I]life for My sake shall find it.

26 "For what will a man be profited, if he gains the whole world, and forfeits his soul?[5590] Or what will a man give in exchange[465] for his soul?

27 "For the [a]Son of Man [b]is going to [pinf]come in[1722] the glory[1391] of His Father with His angels; and [c]WILL THEN RECOMPENSE EVERY MAN ACCORDING TO HIS [sg I]DEEDS.[4234]

28 "Truly[281] I say to you, there are some of those who are standing[2476] here who [efn]shall not taste[1089] death[2288] until they see the [a]Son of Man [b]coming in His kingdom."

(continued from previous page)

N.T. A distinction must first be made between the Church referred to in v. 18, being the earthly side of God's kingdom and the kingdom of the heavens in v. 19 which refers to both the Church on earth, the kingdom of God within the believers (Lk. 17:21). The kingdom of heaven has a far larger implication than the Church on earth. The teaching here is that those things which are conclusively decided by the King in the kingdom of heaven, having been so decided upon, are emulated by the Church on earth, the Church being the true believers whose testimony is the Rock, even like Peter's testimony concerning the deity of Jesus Christ upon whom the Church is built (I Cor. 3:11). No reference is made here to the binding or loosing of persons, but of things, *ho* (3739), "whatever" (neuter) and not "whoever," and *hosa* (neuter plural) in Mt. 18:18, "whatever." Reference is made to the acts of persons and not to the decisions concerning persons by the church as an ecclesiastical or organizational body. The Church here is the body of believers themselves. We as believers can never make conclusive decisions about things, but can only confirm those decisions which have already been made by the King Himself as conclusive in the general context of His kingdom both on earth and in heaven. See Mt. 18:18 where the same two verbs, "bind" and "loose," are said to be possessed by all the disciples. See also Jn. 20:23. The two verbs *dedemenon* (*deō,* 1210) and *lelumenon* (*luō,* 3089), are both perfect passive participles which should have been translated respectively as "having been bound" and as "having been loosed" already in the heavens. Believers on earth can only confirm what has already taken place in heaven.

The Transfiguration

17 [a]And six days[2250] later Jesus
*took with Him [b]Peter and
[I]James and John his brother, and
*brought[399] them up[399] to a high moun-
tain by themselves.[2398]
2 And He was transfigured[3339] before them; and His face[4383] shone like
the sun, and His garments [ao]became as
white as light.
3 And behold, Moses and Elijah appeared to them, talking with Him.
4 And Peter answered[611] and said
to Jesus, "Lord, it is good for us to be
here; if You [pin]wish, [a]I will make three
[I]tabernacles[4633] here, one for You, and
one for Moses, and one for Elijah."
5 While he was still [ppt]speaking, behold, a bright cloud overshadowed them;
and behold, [a]a voice out of the cloud,
[ppt]saying, "[b]This is My beloved[27] Son,
with whom I am well-pleased;[2106] [pim]lis-
ten to Him!"
6 And when the disciples[3101] heard
this, they fell on their faces[4383] and were
much[4970] afraid.[5399]
7 And Jesus [ao]came to *them* and
touched them and said, "Arise, and
[a]do not be afraid."
8 And lifting up[1869] their eyes, they
saw no one, except Jesus Himself
alone.
9 [a]And as they were [ppt]coming down
from the mountain, Jesus commanded
them, saying, "[b]Tell the vision[3705] to no
one until [c]the Son of Man [aosb]has
[d]risen[1453] from the dead."
10 And His disciples asked[1905] Him,
saying, "Why then do the scribes[1122]
say that [a]Elijah must [ainf]come first?"
11 And He answered and said, "Elijah is [pin]coming and will restore[600] all
things;
12 but I say to you, that Elijah already [ao]came, and they did not [ao]recog-
nize him, but [ao]did [I]to him whatever they
[ao]wished.[2309] So also [a]the Son of Man
is going to suffer [II]at their hands."
13 Then the disciples understood
that He had spoken to them about John
the Baptist.[910]

The Demoniac

14 [a]And when they came to the multitude, a man came up to Him, falling
on his knees before Him, and saying,
15 "[I]Lord, have mercy on my son,
for he is a [a]lunatic, and is very ill;[2560]
for he often falls into the fire, and often
into the water.
16 "And I brought him to Your disciples, and they [ao]could not [ainf]cure him."
17 And Jesus answered and said, "O
unbelieving[571] and perverted generation, how long shall I be with you? How
long shall I put up with you? Bring[5342]
him here to Me."
18 And Jesus rebuked him, and the
demon came out of him, and the boy
was cured [I]at once.
19 Then the disciples came to Jesus
privately[2398] and said, "Why [ao]could we
not [ainf]cast it out?"
20 And He *said to them, "Because
of the littleness of your faith;[3640] for
truly[281] I say to you, [a]if you have faith[4102]
as [b]a mustard seed, you shall say to
[c]this mountain, 'Move[3327] from here to
there,' and it shall move; and [d]nothing
shall be impossible[101] to you.
21 ["[I][a]But[1161] this kind does not go
out except by prayer and fasting."][3521]
22 [a]And while they were gathering
together[4962] in Galilee, Jesus said to
them, "The Son of Man is going to be
[I]delivered into the hands of men;
23 and [a]they will kill Him, and He
will be raised on the third day." And
they were[3076] deeply grieved.[3076]

The Tribute Money

24 And when they had come to Capernaum, those who collected [a]the
[I]two-drachma *tax* came to Peter, and
said, "Does your teacher not pay[5055]
[a]the [I]two-drachma *tax*?"
25 He *said, "Yes." And when he
came into the house, Jesus [I]spoke to
him first, saying, "What do you think,
Simon? From whom do the kings of the
earth collect [a]customs[5056] or [b]poll-tax,
from their sons or from strangers?"

1 [I]Or, *Jacob* [a]Matt. 17:1-8; *Mark 9:2-8; Luke 9:28-36* [b]Matt. 26:37; Mark 5:37; 13:3
4 [I]Or, *sacred tents* [a]Mark 9:5; Luke 9:33
5 [a]Mark 1:11; Luke 3:22; 2Pet. 1:17f. [b]Is. 42:1; Matt. 3:17; 12:18
7 [a]Matt. 14:27
9 [a]Matt. 17:9-13; *Mark 9:9-13* [b]Matt. 8:4 [c]Matt. 8:20; 17:12, 22 [d]Matt. 16:21
10 [a]Mal. 4:5; Matt. 11:14; 16:14
12 [I]Lit., *in him;* or, *in his case* [II]Lit., *by them* [a]Matt. 8:20; 17:9, 22
14 [a]Matt. 17:14-19; *Mark 9:14-28;* Matt. 17:14-18; *Luke 9:37-42*
15 [I]Or, *Sir* [a]Matt. 4:24
18 [I]Lit., *from that hour*
20 [a]Matt. 21:21f.; Mark 11:23f.; Luke 17:6 [b]Matt. 13:31; Luke 17:6 [c]Matt. 17:9; 1Cor. 13:2 [d]Mark 9:23; John 11:40
21 [I]Many mss. do not contain this v. [a]Mark 9:29
22 [I]Or, *betrayed* [a]Matt. 17:22, 23; *Mark 9:30-32; Luke 9:44, 45*
23 [a]Matt. 16:21; 17:9
24 [I]Equivalent to two denarii or two days' wages paid as a temple tax [a]Ex. 30:13; 38:26
25 [I]Or, *anticipated what he was going to say,* [a]Rom. 13:7 [b]Matt. 22:17, 19

26 And upon his saying, "From strangers," Jesus said to him, "Consequently the sons are [I]exempt.

27 "But, lest we [Ia]give them [aosb]offense,[4624] [apt]go to the sea, and throw in a hook, and take[142] the first fish that comes up; and when you open its mouth, you will find a [II]stater. [apt]Take that and give it to them for you and Me."

Rank in the Kingdom

18 [a]At that [I]time the disciples came to Jesus, saying, "[b]Who then is [II]greatest in the kingdom[932] of heaven?"

2 And He [apt]called a child to Himself and set[2476] him [I]before them,

3 and said, "Truly[281] I say to you, unless you [I]are converted[4762] and [a]become like children, you [efn]shall not enter the kingdom of heaven.

4 "Whoever then humbles himself as this child, he is the greatest in the kingdom of heaven.

5 "And whoever receives one such child in My name[3686] receives Me;

6 but [a]whoever [b]causes one of these little ones who [ppt]believe[4100] in Me to stumble,[4624] it is better for him that a [I]heavy millstone be hung around his neck, and that he be drowned in the depth[3989] of the sea.[2281]

Stumbling Blocks

7 "Woe to the world because of *its* stumbling blocks! For [a]it is inevitable[318] that stumbling blocks[4625] [ainf]come; but woe to that man through whom the stumbling block comes!

8 "And [a]if your hand or your foot causes you to [pin]stumble,[4625] cut it off and throw it from you; it is better for you to enter life[2222] crippled or lame, than having two hands or two feet, to be cast into the [art]eternal fire.

🔑 9 "And [a]if your eye causes you to [pin]stumble, pluck it out, and throw it from you. It is better for you to enter life with one eye, than having two eyes, to be cast into the [art] [Ib]fiery hell.[1067]

10 "See that you do not [aosb]despise one of these little ones, for I say to you, that [a]their angels in heaven continually behold the face of My Father who is in heaven.[3772]

11 ["[Ia]For the Son of Man has [ao]come [ainf]to save[4982] that which was lost.][622]

Ninety-nine Plus One

🔑 12 "What do you think? [a]If any man [I]has a hundred sheep, and one of them has gone astray, does he not [apt]leave the ninety-nine on the mountains and [apt]go and [pin]search for the one that is [ppp]straying?

13 "And if it turns out that he finds it, truly I say to you, he rejoices[5463] over it more than over the ninety-nine which [pfpp]have not gone astray.

14 "Thus it is not *the* will[2307] [I]of your Father who is in heaven that one of these little ones [aosb]perish.[622]

Discipline and Prayer

🔑 15 "And [a]if your brother [aosb]sins[I],[264] go and reprove him [II]in private; if he [aosb]listens to you, you have [ao]won your brother.

16 "But if he does not [aosb]listen[191] *to you,* take one or two more with you, so that [a]BY THE MOUTH OF TWO OR THREE WITNESSES[3144] EVERY [I]FACT[4487] MAY BE CONFIRMED.[2476]

17 "And if he refuses to listen to them, [a]tell it to the church; and if he refuses to listen even to the church,[1577] [b]let him be to you as [I]a Gentile[1482] and [I]a [II]tax-gatherer.[5057]

18 "Truly I say to you, [n][a]whatever you shall [aosb] [I]bind[1210] on earth[1093] [II]shall [ft]be [ftpp]bound[1210] in heaven; and

26 [I]Or, *free*
27 [I]Lit., *cause them to stumble* [II]Or, *shekel,* worth four drachmas [a]Matt. 5:29, 30; 18:6, 8, 9; Mark 9:42, 43, 45, 47; Luke 17:2; John 6:61; 1Cor. 8:13

1 [I]Lit., *hour* [II]Lit., *greater* [a]Matt. 18:1-5; *Mark 9:33-37; Luke 9:46-48* [b]Luke 22:24
2 [I]Lit., *in their midst*
3 [I]Lit., *are turned* [a]Matt. 19:14; Mark 10:15; Luke 18:17; 1Cor. 14:20; 1Pet. 2:2
6 [I]Lit., *millstone turned by a donkey* [a]Mark 9:42; Luke 17:2; 1Cor. 8:12 [b]Matt. 17:27
7 [a]Luke 17:1; 1Cor. 11:19; 1Tim. 4:1
8 [a]Matt. 5:30; Mark 9:43
9 [I]Lit., *Gehenna of fire* [a]Matt. 5:29; Mark 9:47 [b]Matt. 5:22
10 [a]Luke 1:19; Acts 12:15; Rev. 8:2
11 [I]Most ancient mss. do not contain this v. [a]Luke 19:10
12 [I]Or, *comes to have* [a]Matt. 18:12-14; *Luke 15:4-7*
14 [I]Lit., *before*
15 [I]Many mss. add *against you* [II]Lit., *between you and him alone* [a]Lev. 19:17; Luke 17:3; Gal. 6:1; 2Thess. 3:15; James 5:19
16 [I]Lit., *word* [a]Deut. 19:15; John 8:17; 2Cor. 13:1; 1Tim. 5:19; Heb. 10:28
17 [I]Lit., *the* [II]I.e., Collector of Roman taxes for profit [a]1Cor. 6:1ff. [b]2Thess. 3:6, 14f.
18 [I]Or, *forbid* [II]Or, *shall have been* [a]Matt. 16:19; John 20:23

🔑 **18:9,12** See note on Mt. 8:11,12.
🔑 **18:15-18** See notes on Mt. 16:18,19; I Tim. 1:20.

[n]whatever you [aosb][III]loose on earth [II]shall [ft]be [ftp]loosed[3089] in heaven.

19 "Again I say to you, that if two of you agree on earth[1093] about anything that they may [aosb]ask, [a]it shall be [ft]done for them [I]by My Father who is in heaven.

20 "For where two or three have gathered together in My name, [a]there I am in their midst."[3319]

Forgiveness

21 Then Peter [apt]came and said to Him, "Lord,[2962] [a]how often shall my brother sin against me and I forgive him? Up to [b]seven times?"

22 Jesus *said to him, "I do not say to you, up to seven times, but up to [a]seventy times seven.

23 "For this reason [a]the kingdom of heaven may be [aop]compared to a certain king who wished to [ainf] [b]settle accounts with his slaves.

24 "And when he had begun to settle *them,* there was brought to him one who owed[3781] him [I]ten thousand talents.

25 "But since he [I][a]did not have *the means* to repay, his lord[2962] commanded him [b]to be sold, along with his wife and children and all that he had, and repayment to be made.

26 "The slave therefore [apt]falling down, [ipf] [a]prostrated himself before him, saying, [aim]'Have patience[3114] with me, and I will repay you everything.'

27 "And the lord of that slave [aptp]felt compassion and released[630] him and [a]forgave him the [I]debt.

28 "But that slave [apt]went out and found one of his fellow slaves[4889] who [ipf]owed[3784] him a hundred [I]denarii;[1220] and he [apt]seized him and *began* to [ipf]choke *him,* saying, 'Pay back what you owe.'

29 "So his fellow slave [apt]fell down and *began* to [ipf]entreat him, saying, [aim]'Have patience[3114] with me and I will repay you.'

30 "He [ipf]was unwilling[2309] however, but went and [ao]threw him in prison until he should pay back what was owed.[3784]

31 "So when his fellow slaves saw what had happened, they were deeply grieved and [apt]came and reported to their lord all that had happened.

32 "Then summoning him, his lord [pin]*said to him, 'You wicked[4190] slave, I forgave you all that debt[3782] because you entreated me.

33 '[a]Should you not also have had mercy on your fellow slave, even as I had mercy on you?'

34 "And his lord, [aptp]moved with anger,[3710] handed him over to the torturers until he should repay all that was owed[3784] him.

35 "[a]So shall My heavenly[2032] Father also do to you, if each of you[1538] does not [aosb]forgive his brother from [I]your heart."[2588]

Concerning Divorce

19 [a]And it came about that when Jesus had finished these words, He departed from Galilee, and [b]came into the region of Judea beyond the Jordan;

2 and great multitudes followed Him, and [a]He healed them there.

🔑 **3** And *some* Pharisees came to Him,

18 [III]Or, *permit*
19 [I]Lit., *from* [a]Matt. 7:7
20 [a]Matt. 28:20
21 [a]Matt. 18:15 [b]Luke 17:4
22 [a]Gen. 4:24
23 [a]Matt. 13:24 [b]Matt. 25:19
24 [I]About $10,000,000 in silver content but worth much more in buying power
25 [I]Or, *was unable to* [a]Luke 7:42 [b]Ex. 21:2; Lev. 25:39; 2Kin. 4:1; Neh. 5:5
26 [a]Matt. 8:2
27 [I]Or, *loan* [a]Luke 7:42
28 [I]The denarius was equivalent to one day's wage
33 [a]Matt. 6:12; Eph. 4:32
35 [I]Lit., *your hearts* [a]Matt. 6:14
1 [a]Matt. 7:28 [b]Matt. 19:1-9; *Mark 10:1-12*
2 [a]Matt. 4:23

🔑 **19:3-9** One remark, however, is necessary to clearly understand the meaning of the word *apolelumenēn,* "a divorced woman," occuring in v. 9 and also in Mt. 5:32b. It means the innocent dismissed wife of the licentious person described in Mt. 5:28-30 who, lusting after another woman, dismisses his own wife in order to marry the other woman. Such a thing, dismissing one's wife for any reason other than her infidelity, Christ definitely forbids; but people were and are doing it, nevertheless. He expresses His concern about the dismissed, *apolelumenēn,* wife or husband (Mk. 10:12), who is innocent. To clear such a dismissed spouse, the Lord insists that the O.T. provision (Deut. 24:1-4) be adhered to, i.e., the guilty party in dismissing an innocent spouse ought to clear her or him of guilt by giving a bill of divorcement. If the dismissed spouse was guilty, the punishment was death by stoning (Deut. 22:21). Thus there was no reason to give such a bill of divorcement. Divorce papers issued by a judge today

(continued on next page)

testing[3985] Him, and saying, "[a]Is it lawful *for a man* to [I]divorce[630] his wife for[2596] any cause[156] at all?"

4 And He answered and said, "Have you not read, [a]that He who [apt]created *them* from the beginning [ao]MADE THEM MALE AND FEMALE,[2338]

5 and said, '[a]FOR THIS CAUSE A MAN SHALL LEAVE HIS FATHER AND MOTHER, AND SHALL CLEAVE TO HIS WIFE; AND [b]THE TWO[1417] SHALL BECOME ONE FLESH'?

6 "Consequently they are no longer two, but one flesh. What therefore God has joined together, let no man separate."

7 They *said to Him, "[a]Why then did Moses command to GIVE HER A CERTIFICATE[647] OF DIVORCE[630] AND SEND HER AWAY?"

8 He *said to them, "[I]Because[4314] of your hardness of heart,[4641] Moses permitted you to [II]divorce[630] your wives; but from the beginning it [pfi]has not been this way.

9 "And I say to you, [a]whoever [I]divorces[630] his wife, except for [II]immorality,[4202] and marries another woman [pin] [III]commits adultery[IV]."

10 The disciples *said to Him, "If the relationship of the man with his wife is like this, it is better[4851] not to marry."

11 But He said to them, "[a]Not all men *can* accept this statement, but [b]*only* those to whom it has been given.

12 "For there are eunuchs who were born that way from their mother's womb; and there are eunuchs who were made eunuchs by men; and there are *also* eunuchs who made themselves eunuchs for the sake of the kingdom[932] of heaven. He who is [ppt]able to [pinf]accept *this,* let him accept *it.*"

Jesus Blesses Little Children

13 [a]Then *some* children were brought to Him so that He might lay His hands on them and pray; and the disciples rebuked[2008] them.

14 But Jesus said, "[Ia]Let[863] the children alone, and do not hinder[2967] them from coming to Me; for [b]the kingdom[932] of heaven belongs to such as these."

15 And after [apt]laying His hands on them, He departed from there.

The Rich Young Ruler

16 [a]And behold, one came to Him and said, "Teacher, what good thing

3 [I]Or, *send away* [a]Matt. 5:31
4 [a]Gen. 1:27; 5:2
5 [a]Gen. 2:24; Eph. 5:31 [b]1Cor. 6:16
7 [a]Deut. 24:1-4; Matt. 5:31
8 [I]Or, *With reference to* [II]Or, *send away*
9 [I]Or, *sends away* [II]I.e., sexual immorality [III]Some early mss. read *makes her commit adultery* [IV]Some early mss. add *and he who marries a divorced woman commits adultery* [a]Matt. 5:32
11 [a]1Cor. 7:7ff. [b]Matt. 13:11
13 [a]Matt. 19:13-15; *Mark 10:13-16; Luke 18:15-17*
14 [I]Or, *Permit the children* [a]Matt. 18:3; Mark 10:15; Luke 18:17; 1Cor. 14:20; 1Pet. 2:2 [b]Matt. 5:3
16 [a]Matt. 19:16-29; *Mark 10:17-30; Luke 18:18-30;* Luke 10:25-28

(continued from previous page)
should not be equated with this bill of divorcement. God knows who is innocent and who is guilty and the individuals concerned know. The Lord in His pronouncements concerns Himself with the truly innocent and not with the one who may have been able to secure a legal divorce. A legal divorce today does not mean that a person is necessarily innocent. He or she may or may not be. Only the truly innocent, according to the Word of God, has the moral, Scriptural right to remarry. If the guilty dismissing husband gives his innocent wife a bill of divorcement as prescribed by Deut. 24:1-4, then that wife is cleared of the stigma of being considered as an adulteress. If she is not thus cleared of the stigma of guilt, then she herself is considered by the ignorant public as an adulteress and also whosoever should marry her. Sexual infidelity is the only permitted reason for dismissing one's spouse. Both in the O.T. and in the N.T. there were those who wanted to dismiss their innocent wives for reasons other than sexual infidelity. It is to such that reference is made as "the dismissed wife." It is the wife who had been dismissed inequitably who was not an adulteress but who, because she was dismissed without a bill of divorcement, was stigmatized as an adulteress. Naturally, if anyone married such a woman, he would appear to be an adulterer also. However, this should not be considered as true adultery but only the unjust consequence of the first husband's action in allowing his wife to be considered as an adulteress. The word *apolelumenēn* has the meaning of "unjustifiably dismissed" wife who was not given a bill of divorcement by her husband to clear her of any guilt. The only exception is Lk. 16:18 where the *apolelumenēn* does not refer to the innocent wife dismissed by her guilty husband, but the guilty wife who separates herself from her husband. For a complete exegesis of this passage, see the Editor's book, *What About Divorce?*

shall I do that I may obtain [b]eternal life?"[2222]

17 And He said to him, "Why are you asking Me about what is good? There is *only* One who is good; but [a]if you wish[2309] to enter into life, [aim]keep[5083] the commandments."

18 He *said to Him, "Which ones?" And Jesus said, "[a]YOU SHALL NOT COMMIT MURDER; YOU SHALL NOT COMMIT ADULTERY; YOU SHALL NOT STEAL; YOU SHALL NOT BEAR FALSE WITNESS;

19 [pim] [a]HONOR YOUR FATHER AND MOTHER; and [b]YOU SHALL LOVE[25] YOUR NEIGHBOR[4139] AS YOURSELF."

20 The young man *said to Him, "All these things I have kept;[5442] what am I still lacking?"

21 Jesus said to him, "If you wish to be [I]complete,[5046] go *and* [a]sell your possessions[5224] and give to *the* poor, and you shall have [b]treasure in heaven; and come, follow[190] Me."

22 But when the young man heard this statement,[3056] he went away grieved; for he was one who owned much property.

23 And Jesus said to His disciples, "Truly[281] I say to you, [a]it is hard for a rich man to enter the kingdom[932] of heaven.[3772]

24 "And again I say to you, [a]it is easier for a camel to go through the eye of a needle, than for a rich man to [ainf]enter the kingdom of God."

16 [b]Matt. 25:46
17 [a]Lev. 18:5; Neh. 9:29; Ezek. 20:21
18 [a]Ex. 20:13-16; Deut. 5:17-20
19 [a]Ex. 20:12; Deut. 5:16 [b]Lev. 19:18
21 [I]Or, *perfect* [a]Luke 12:33; 16:9; Acts 2:45; 4:34f. [b]Matt. 6:20
23 [a]Matt. 13:22; Mark 10:23f.; Luke 18:24
24 [a]Mark 10:25; Luke 18:25
26 [a]Gen. 18:14; Job 42:2; Jer. 32:17; Zech. 8:6; Mark 10:27; Luke 1:37; 18:27
28 [I]Lit., *the throne of His glory* [a]Matt. 25:31 [b]Luke 22:30; Rev. 3:21; 4:4; 11:16; 20:4
29 [I]Many mss. add *or wife* [II]Many mss. read *a hundredfold* [a]Matt. 6:33; Mark 10:29f.; Luke 18:29f.
30 [a]Matt. 20:16; Mark 10:31; Luke 13:30
1 [I]Lit., *a man, a landowner* [a]Matt. 13:24

25 And when the disciples heard *this,* they were very astonished and said, "Then who can be saved?"

26 And [apt]looking upon[1689] *them* Jesus said to them, "[a]With men this is impossible, but with God all things are possible."

The Disciples' Reward

27 Then Peter answered and said to Him, "Behold, we have left everything and followed You; what then will there be for us?"

28 And Jesus said to them, "Truly I say to you, that you who have [apt]followed Me, in the regeneration[3824] when [a]the Son of Man will sit on [I]His glorious[1391] throne, [b]you also shall sit upon twelve thrones, judging[2919] the twelve tribes of Israel.

29 "And [a]everyone who has [ao]left houses or brothers[80] or sisters or father or mother[I] or children or farms for My name's[3686] sake, shall receive [II]many times as much, and shall inherit[2816] eternal life.

30 "[a]But many *who are* first will be last;[2078] and *the* last, first.

Laborers in the Vineyard

20

"For [a]the kingdom[932] of heaven is like [I]a landowner[3617]

19:27 See note on Mt. 20:1-16.

20:1-16 The understanding of this parable is related to Peter's question in Mt. 19:27. The distinction is between those laborers who were hired (v. 1) for a specific sum of money to do twelve hours of work (6 a.m. and ending at 6 p.m.) and those who were not hired (vv. 2-7), but called with a mere promise by the house despot (*oikodespotēs,* 3617) that he was going to reward justly according to his own estimation. The translation which causes the total misunderstanding of this parable is v. 9 where the word "hired" is inserted. Those who came on the eleventh hour (5 p.m., just one hour before quitting time) and those who came at 9 a.m., at noon, and at 3 p.m. were not hired at all—they were called. Thus v. 9 should be translated: "And those of the eleventh hour having come, each received one dinar." What is translated as "a denarius" was the currency of that day, even as it is today in Jordan. A dinar was the regularly accepted pay for a normal twelve-hour day of work. The Lord rewarded those who did one hour of work equally with those who did twelve hours of work. Those, however, who worked one hour had not agreed to a specific sum with the one who called them, but had left it to his judgment. Those who signed a contract to earn one dinar for twelve hours of work set their own price for their own work and that is what they received. Those who

(continued on next page)

who went out early in the morning to
[ainf]hire laborers [II]for his [b]vineyard.
2 "And when he had agreed with
the laborers for a [I]denarius[1220] for the
day, he sent[649] them into his vineyard.
3 "And he [apt]went out about the
[I]third hour[5610] and saw others [pfp]standing
idle[692] in the market place;[58]
4 and to those he said, 'You too go
into the vineyard, and whatever is
right[1342] I will give you.' And *so* they
went.
5 "Again he [apt]went out about the
[I]sixth and the ninth hour, and did
[II]the same thing.
6 "And about the [I]eleventh *hour* he
[apt]went out, and found others [pfp]stand-
ing; and he *said to them, 'Why have
you been [pfi]standing here idle all day[2250]
long?'
7 "They *said to him, 'Because no
one [ao]hired us.' He *said to them, 'You
too go into the vineyard.'
8 "And when [a]evening had come,
the [I]owner of the vineyard *said to his
[b]foreman, 'Call[2564] the laborers and pay
them their wages,[3408] beginning with the
last *group* to the first.'
9 "And when those *hired* about the
eleventh hour [apt]came, each one received a [I]denarius.
10 "And when those *hired* first
came, they thought that they would receive more; and they also received each
one a denarius.
11 "And when they received it, they
grumbled at the landowner,[3617]
12 saying, 'These last men have
[ao]worked *only* one hour, and you have
[ao]made them equal to us who have
[apt]borne the burden and the [a]scorching
heat of the day.'
13 "But he answered and said to
one of them, '[a]Friend, I am doing[91] you
no wrong;[91] did you not agree with me
for a denarius?
14 'Take[142] what is yours and go
your way, but I wish to give to this
last man the same as to you.
15 'Is it not lawful for me to do what
I wish with what is my [pl]own? Or is
your [a]eye [I]envious[4190] because I am
[II]generous?'[18]
16 "Thus [a]the last[2078] shall be first,
and the first last."

Death, Resurrection Foretold

17 [a]And as Jesus was about to go
up to Jerusalem, He took the twelve
disciples aside by themselves, and on
the way He said to them,
18 "Behold, we are going up to Jerusalem; and the Son of Man [a]will be
[I]delivered to the chief priests and
scribes,[1122] and they will condemn[2632]
Him to death,
19 and [a]will deliver Him to the Gentiles[1484] to [ainf]mock and [ainf]scourge[3146]
and [ainf]crucify[4717] *Him,* and on [b]the
third day He will be raised up."[450]

Preferment Asked

20 [a]Then the mother of [b]the sons
of Zebedee came to Him with her sons,
[c]bowing down, and making a request
of Him.
21 And He said to her, "What do
you wish?" She *said to Him, "Command that in Your kingdom these two
sons of mine [a]may [aosb]sit, one on Your
right[1188] and one on Your left."
22 But Jesus answered and said,
"You do not know what you are asking
for. Are you able [a]to [pinf]drink the cup
that I am about to drink?" They *said
to Him, "We are able."

1 [II]Lit., *into* [b]Matt. 21:28, 33
2 [I]The denarius was equivalent to one day's wage
3 [I]I.e., 9 a.m.
5 [I]I.e., Noon and 3 p.m. [II]Lit., *similarly*
6 [I]I.e., 5 p.m.
8 [I]Or, *lord* [a]Lev. 19:13; Deut. 24:15 [b]Luke 8:3
9 [I]The denarius was equivalent to one day's wage
12 [a]Jon. 4:8; Luke 12:55; James 1:11
13 [a]Matt. 22:12; 26:50
15 [I]Lit., *evil* [II]Lit., *good* [a]Deut. 15:9; Matt. 6:23; Mark 7:22
16 [a]Matt. 19:30; Mark 10:31; Luke 13:30
17 [a]Matt. 20:17-19; *Mark 10:32-34; Luke 18:31-33*
18 [I]Or, *betrayed* [a]Matt. 16:21
19 [a]Matt. 27:2; Acts 2:23; 3:13; 4:27; 21:11 [b]Matt. 16:21; 17:23; Luke 18:32f.
20 [a]Matt. 20:20-28; *Mark 10:35-45* [b]Matt. 4:21; 10:2 [c]Matt. 8:2
21 [a]Matt. 19:28
22 [a]Is. 51:17, 22; Jer. 49:12; Matt. 26:39, 42; Luke 22:42; John 18:11

(continued from previous page)
do what they are called upon by the Lord to do and leave the reward to Him will always be rewarded far more than if they set the worth of their own labor. This is the principal lesson in this parable. It is unfortunate that the word *hetaire* in v. 13 is translated as "friend." The true friend is designated by the Greek word *philos* (5384). The word here, *hetairos* (2083), means a false friend, a deceiver parading as a friend. *Hetairos* is what the Lord Jesus called Judas when he came to arrest Him in Gethsemane (Mt. 26:50).

23 He *said to them, "[a]My cup you shall drink; but to sit on My right[1188] and on *My* left, this is not Mine to give, [b]but it is for those for whom it has been [pfpp] [c]prepared by My Father."

24 And hearing *this,* the ten became indignant with the two brothers.

25 [a]But Jesus called them to Himself, and said, "You know that the rulers[758] of the Gentiles[1484] lord it over them, and *their* great men exercise authority over them.

26 "It is not so among you, [a]but whoever [psa]wishes[2309] to become great among you shall [fi]be your servant,[1249]

27 and whoever [psa]wishes[2309] to be first among you shall be your slave;

28 just as [a]the Son of Man [b]did not come to be [aifp]served, but to [ainf]serve, and to [ainf]give His [1]life[5590] a ransom[3083] for[473] many."

Sight for the Blind

29 [a]And as they [ppt]were going out from Jericho, a great multitude followed Him.

30 And behold, two blind men sitting by the road, hearing that Jesus was passing by, cried out, saying, "Lord, [a]have mercy on us, [b]Son of David!"

31 And the multitude sternly told them to [aosb]be quiet; but they [ipf]cried out all the more, saying, "Lord, have mercy on us, [a]Son of David!"

32 And Jesus [apt]stopped and called them, and said, "What do you want Me to do for you?"

33 They *said to Him, "Lord, *we want* our eyes to be [aosb]opened."

34 And moved with [apt]compassion, Jesus touched their eyes; and immediately they regained their sight[308] and followed Him.

The Triumphal Entry

21 [a]And when they had approached Jerusalem and had come to Bethphage, to [b]the Mount of Olives, then Jesus sent two disciples,

2 saying to them, "Go into the village opposite you, and immediately[2117] you will find a donkey tied *there* and a colt with[3326] her; [apt]untie[3089] *them,* and bring *them* to Me.

3 "And if anyone says something to you, you shall say, 'The Lord has need of them,' and immediately he will send them."

4 [a]Now this [pfi]took place[1096] that what was spoken through the prophet might be fulfilled,[4137] saying,

5 "[a]SAY TO THE DAUGHTER OF ZION,
'BEHOLD YOUR KING[935] IS COMING TO YOU,
GENTLE,[4239] AND [pfp]MOUNTED[1910] ON A DONKEY,
EVEN ON A COLT, THE FOAL OF A BEAST OF BURDEN.' "

6 And the disciples [apt]went and [apt]did just as Jesus had directed[4929] them,

7 and brought the donkey and the colt, and laid on them their garments, [1]on which He sat.

8 And most of the multitude[3793] [a]spread their garments in the road, and others were [ipf]cutting[2875] branches from the trees, and [ipf]spreading[4766] them in the road.

9 And the multitudes [ppt]going before[4254] Him, and those who [ppt]followed[190] after were [ipf]crying out, saying,

"Hosanna to the [a]Son of David;
[b]BLESSED[2127] IS HE WHO [ppt]COMES IN THE NAME OF THE LORD;[2962]
Hosanna [c]in the highest!"

10 And when He had entered Jerusalem, all the city was stirred, saying, "Who is this?"

11 And the multitudes were [ipf]saying, "This is [a]the prophet[4396] Jesus, from [b]Nazareth in Galilee."

Cleansing the Temple

12 [a]And Jesus entered the temple and cast out all those who were [ppt]buying and [ppt]selling in the temple,[2411] and

---

23 [a]Acts 12:2; Rev. 1:9 [b]Matt. 13:11 [c]Matt. 25:34

25 [a]Matt. 20:25-28; Luke 22:25-27

26 [a]Matt. 23:11; Mark 9:35; 10:43; Luke 22:26

28 [1]Or, *soul* [a]Matt. 8:20 [b]Matt. 26:28; John 13:13ff.; 2Cor. 8:9; Phil. 2:7; 1Tim. 2:6; Titus 2:14; Heb. 9:28; Rev. 1:5

29 [a]Matt. 20:29-34; *Mark 10:46-52; Luke 18:35-43;* Matt. 9:27-31

30 [a]Matt. 20:31 [b]Matt. 9:27

31 [a]Matt. 9:27

1 [a]Matt. 21:1-9; *Mark 11:1-10; Luke 19:29-38* [b]Matt. 24:3; 26:30; Mark 11:1; 13:3; 14:26; Luke 19:29, 37; 21:37; 22:39; John 8:1; Acts 1:12

4 [a]Matt. 21:4-9; *Mark 11:7-10; Luke 19:35-38; John 12:12-15*

5 [a]Is. 62:11; Zech. 9:9

7 [1]Lit., *on them*

8 [a]2Kin. 9:13

9 [a]Matt. 9:27 [b]Ps. 118:26 [c]Luke 2:14

11 [a]Matt. 21:26; Mark 6:15; Luke 7:16, 39; 13:33; 24:19; John 1:21, 25; 4:19; 6:14; 7:40; 9:17; Acts 3:22f.; 7:37 [b]Matt. 2:23

12 [a]Matt. 21:12-16; *Mark 11:15-18; Luke 19:45-47;* Matt. 21:12, 13; *John 2:13-16*

overturned the tables of the [b]money-changers and the seats of those who were [ppt]selling [I][c]doves.

13 And He *said to them, "It [pfip]is written, '[a]MY HOUSE SHALL BE CALLED A HOUSE[3624] OF PRAYER'; but you are [pin]making it a [b]ROBBERS' [I]DEN."

14 And *the* blind and *the* lame came to Him in the temple, and [a]He healed them.

15 But when the chief priests and the scribes saw the wonderful[2297] things that He had done, and the children who were crying out in the temple and saying, "Hosanna to the [a]Son of David," they became indignant,[23]

16 and said to Him, "Do You hear what these are saying?" And Jesus *said to them, "Yes; have you never [ao]read, '[a]OUT OF THE MOUTH OF INFANTS[3516] AND NURSING BABES THOU HAST [ao]PREPARED[2675] PRAISE[136] FOR THYSELF'?"

17 And He [apt]left them and went out of the city to [a]Bethany, and lodged there.

The Barren Fig Tree

18 [a]Now in the morning, when He [apt]returned to the city, He became hungry.[3983]

19 And seeing a lone [a]fig tree by the road, He came to it, and found nothing on it except leaves only; and He [pin]*said to it, "No longer shall there ever be *any* fruit from you." And at once the fig tree withered.

20 And seeing *this,* the disciples marveled, saying, "How did the fig tree [ao]wither at once?"

21 And Jesus answered and said to them, "Truly[281] I say to you, [a]if you have faith,[4102] and do not [aosb]doubt,[1252] you shall not only do what was done to the fig tree, but even if you say to this mountain, 'Be taken up and cast into the sea,' it shall happen.

22 "And [a]all things you [aosb]ask in prayer, believing,[4100] you shall receive."

Authority Challenged

23 [a]And when He had come into the temple, the chief priests and the elders of the people came to Him [b]as He was [ppt]teaching, and said, "By what authority are You doing these things, and who gave You this authority?"

24 And Jesus answered and said to them, "I will ask[2065] you one [I]thing too, which if you [aosb]tell Me, I will also tell you by what authority I do these things.

25 "The baptism[908] of John was from what *source,* from heaven[3772] or from men?"[444] And they *began* [ipf]reasoning among themselves, saying, "If we say, 'From heaven,' He will say to us, 'Then why did you not believe[4100] him?'

26 "But if we say, 'From men,' we fear[5399] the multitude; for they all hold John to be [a]a prophet."

27 And answering Jesus, they said, "We do not know." He also said to them, "Neither will I tell you by what authority I do these things.

Parable of Two Sons

28 "But what do you think? A man had two [I]sons, and he [apt]came to the

12 [I]Lit., *the doves* [b]Ex. 30:13 [c]Lev. 1:14; 5:7; 12:8
13 [I]Lit., *cave* [a]Is. 56:7 [b]Jer. 7:11
14 [a]Matt. 4:23
15 [a]Matt. 9:27
16 [a]Ps. 8:2; Matt. 11:25
17 [a]Matt. 26:6; Mark 11:1, 11, 12; 14:3; Luke 19:29; 24:50; John 11:1, 18; 12:1
18 [a]Matt. 21:18-22; *Mark 11:12-14, 20-24*
19 [a]Luke 13:6-9
21 [a]Matt. 17:20; Mark 11:23; Luke 17:6; James 1:6
22 [a]Matt. 7:7
23 [a]Matt. 21:23-27; *Mark 11:27-33; Luke 20:1-8* [b]Matt. 26:55
24 [I]Lit., *word*
26 [a]Matt. 11:9; Mark 6:20
28 [I]Lit., *children*

21:18-22 The Lord did not curse the barren tree in this parable because it did not provide food for His hunger, but because it had leaves and no fruit. This was an exceptional fig tree that produced leaves early but no fruit. Three crops of figs usually follow each other: the early ones come in June, the second in August, and the third in December. These latter figs sometimes hang on the tree until spring. The fig tree is symbolic of Israel who had the privilege of early leaves, but bare no fruit (Isa. 63:7; 64:12; 65:3-7). The Lord was entering Jerusalem for His final overt rejection by Israel. This rejection was due not to the lack of adequate demonstration by Him that He was indeed God incarnate, but to the lack of faith on their part; hence His words in vv. 21,22. This narrative applies particulary to the Jews as a people who were given early opportunities to accept Christ as their Messiah but rejected Him.

21:28-32 The parable of the two sons was given in order to demonstrate that the important thing is

(continued on next page)

first and said, '[II]Son, [pim]go [pim]work[2038]
today in the [a]vineyard.'
29 "And he answered and said, '[I]I
will, sir';[2962] and he did not go.
30 "And he [apt]came to the second
and said [I]the same thing. But he answered and said, '[II]I will[2309] not'; *yet* he
afterward [apt]regretted[3338] *it* and went.
31 "Which of the two[1417] did the will
of his father?" They *said, "The latter."
Jesus *said to them, "Truly I say to
you that [a]the [I]tax-gatherers[5057] and harlots [II]will get into[4254] the kingdom[932] of
God before[4254] you.
32 "For John came to you in the
way[3598] of righteousness[1343] and you did
not believe[4100] him; but [a]the tax-gatherers and harlots did believe him; and
you, [apt]seeing this, did not even feel remorse[3338] afterward so as to [ainf]believe
him.

Parable of the Landowner

33 [aim]"Listen to another parable.
[a]There was a [I]landowner who [b]PLANTED
A [c]VINEYARD AND PUT A WALL AROUND IT
AND DUG A WINE PRESS IN IT, AND BUILT
A TOWER, and rented it out to [II]vine-
growers,[1092] and [d]went on a journey.
34 "And when the [I]harvest time[2540]
approached, he [a]sent his slaves to the
vine-growers to [ainf]receive his produce.
35 "And the vine-growers [apt]took
his slaves and beat one, and killed another, and stoned a third.
36 "Again he [a]sent another group
of slaves larger than the first; and they
did [I]the same thing to them.
37 "But afterward he sent his son
to them, saying, 'They will respect[1788]
my son.'
38 "But when the vine-growers saw
the son, they said among themselves,

28 [I]Lit., *Child* [a]Matt. 20:1; 21:33
29 [I]Some mss. read *'I will not'; yet he afterward regretted and went*
30 [I]Lit., *likewise* [II]Some mss. read *'I will'; and he did not go*
31 [I]I.e., Collectors of Roman taxes for profit [II]Or, *are getting into* [a]Luke 7:29, 37-50
32 [a]Luke 3:12; 7:29f.
33 [I]Lit., *a man, a householder* [II]Or, *tenant farmers*, also vv. 34, 35, 38, 40 [a]Matt. 21:33-46; *Mark 12:1-12; Luke 20:9-19* [b]Is. 5:1, 2 [c]Matt. 20:1; 21:28 [d]Matt. 25:14
34 [I]Lit., *the season of the fruits* [a]Matt. 22:3
36 [I]Lit., *likewise* [a]Matt. 22:4
40 [I]Lit., *lord*
41 [a]Matt. 8:11f.; Acts 13:46; 18:6; 28:28
42 [a]Ps. 118:22f.; Acts 4:11; Rom. 9:33; 1Pet. 2:7
44 [a]Is. 8:14, 15
46 [a]Matt. 21:26 [b]Matt. 21:11
2 [a]Matt. 13:24; 22:2-14; Luke 14:16-24

'This is the heir; come, let us kill him,
and seize[2192] his inheritance.'[2817]
39 "And they [apt]took him, and threw
him out of the vineyard, and killed him.
40 "Therefore when the [I]owner[2962]
of the vineyard [aosb]comes, what will he
do to those vine-growers?"
41 They *said to Him, "He will bring
those wretches to a wretched end, and
[a]will rent out the vineyard to other vine-
growers, who will pay him the proceeds
at the *proper* seasons."[2540]
42 Jesus *said to them, "Did you
never read in the Scriptures,[1124]
'[a]THE STONE WHICH THE
BUILDERS REJECTED,[593]
THIS [ao]BECAME THE CHIEF[2776]
CORNER *stone;*
THIS [ao]CAME ABOUT FROM THE
LORD,
AND IT IS MARVELOUS IN OUR
EYES'?
43 "Therefore I say to you, the kingdom of God will be taken away from
you, and be given to a nation producing
the fruit of it.
44 "And [a]he who [apt]falls on this stone
will be [fp]broken to pieces; but on
whomever it [aosb]falls, it will [ft]scatter him
like dust."
45 And when the chief priests and
the Pharisees [apt]heard His parables,
they understood that He was [pin]speaking
about them.
46 And when they [ppt]sought to
[ainf]seize Him, they [a]feared[5399] the multitudes, because they [ipf]held Him to be
a [b]prophet.

Parable of the Marriage Feast

22 🔑 And Jesus answered[611] and
spoke to them again in parables,[3850] saying,
2 "[a]The kingdom[932] of heaven may

(continued from previous page)
not to say an emotional "yes" and not do anything about it, but to consider the cost of an affirmative answer and then say it and mean it. What is translated in v. 30 and v. 32 as "regretted" and "did not even feel remorse" is from the Greek word *metamellomai* (3338) which means to change one's mind as one considers the consequences of the act as being detrimental to self and not the wrongness of the act itself. The verb that indicates regret for the action itself is *metanoeō* (3340).
🔑 **22:1-14** See note on Mt. 8:11,12.

be compared to [I]a king, who [II]gave a
[b]wedding feast[1062] for his son.
3 "And he [a]sent out his slaves to
call those who had [pfpp]been invited[2564]
to the wedding feast,[1062] and they were
[ipf]unwilling to [ainf]come.
4 "Again he [a]sent out other slaves
saying, 'Tell those who have been [pfpp]in-
vited, "Behold, I have [pfi]prepared my
dinner; my oxen and my fattened livestock are *all* [pfpp]butchered[2380] and
everything is ready; come to the
wedding feast."'[1062]
5 "But they [apt]paid no attention and
went their way, one to his own [I]farm,
another to his business,
6 and the rest [apt]seized his slaves
and mistreated[5195] them and killed them.
7 "But the king was enraged[3710] and
[apt]sent his armies, and destroyed those
murderers,[5406] and set their city on fire.
8 "Then he *said to his slaves, 'The
wedding is ready, but those who were
[pfpp]invited were not worthy.
9 'Go therefore to [a]the main highways, and as many as you find *there,*
invite to the wedding feast.'[1062]
10 "And those slaves [apt]went out
into the streets, and gathered together
all they found, both evil[4190] and good;[18]
and the wedding hall was filled with
[I]dinner [ppt]guests.
11 "But when the king came in to
look over the dinner guests, he saw
there [a]a man not [pfpp]dressed in wedding
clothes,
12 and he *said to him, '[a]Friend,
how did you come in here [I]without[2192 3361]
wedding clothes?' And he was speechless.
13 "Then the king said to the servants, 'Bind[1210] him hand and foot, and
cast him into [a]the outer darkness;[4655]
in that place there shall [ft]be weeping
and gnashing[1030] of teeth.'
14 "For many are [Ia]called,[2822] but
few *are* [a]chosen."

Tribute to Caesar

15 [a]Then the Pharisees [apt]went and
counseled together how they might trap
Him [I]in what He said.[3056]
16 And they [pin]*sent their disciples
to Him, along with the [a]Herodians, saying, "Teacher, we know that You are
truthful and teach the way[3598] of God
in truth,[225] and [I]defer to no one; for
You are not partial to any.
17 "Tell us therefore, what do You
think? Is it [I]lawful to give a [a]poll-tax to
[b]Caesar, or not?"
18 But Jesus [apt]perceived their [I]mal-
ice,[4189] and said, "Why are you testing[3985] Me, you hypocrites?
19 "Show Me the [a]coin *used* for the
poll-tax." And they brought Him a [I]de-
narius.
20 And He *said to them, "Whose
likeness[1504] and inscription is this?"
21 They *said to Him, "Caesar's."
Then He *said to them, "[a]Then render
to Caesar the things that are Caesar's;
and to God the things that are God's."
22 And hearing *this,* they marveled,
and [apt] [a]leaving Him, they went away.

Jesus Answers the Sadducees

23 [a]On that day *some* [b]Sadducees
(who [ppt]say [c]there is no resurrection)[386]
came to Him and questioned[1905] Him,
24 saying, "Teacher, Moses said,
'[a]IF A MAN DIES,[599] HAVING NO CHILDREN,
HIS BROTHER AS NEXT OF KIN SHALL
MARRY HIS WIFE, AND RAISE UP[450] AN
OFFSPRING[4690] TO HIS BROTHER.'
25 "Now there were seven brothers
with us; and the first married and died,
and having no offspring[4690] left his wife
to his brother;
26 so also the second, and the third,
down to the seventh.
27 "And last of all, the woman
died.[599]
28 "In the resurrection therefore
whose wife of the seven shall she be?
For they all had her."
29 But Jesus answered and said to
them, "You are mistaken, [a]not [I]under-
standing the Scriptures,[1124] or the
power of God.
30 "For in the resurrection they neither [a]marry, nor are given in marriage,
but are like angels[32] [I]in heaven.[3772]

2 [I]Lit., *a man, a king* [II]Lit., *made* [b]Luke 12:36; John 2:2
3 [a]Matt. 21:34
4 [a]Matt. 21:36
5 [I]Or, *field*
9 [a]Ezek. 21:21; Obad. 14
10 [I]Lit., *those reclining* at the table
11 [a]2Kin. 10:22; Zech. 3:3, 4
12 [I]Lit., *not having* [a]Matt. 20:13; 26:50
13 [a]Matt. 8:12; 25:30; Luke 13:28
14 [I]Or, *invited* [a]Matt. 24:22; 2Pet. 1:10; Rev. 17:14
15 [I]Lit., *in word* [a]Matt. 22:15-22; *Mark 12:13-17; Luke 20:20-26*
16 [I]I.e., you court no man's favor [a]Mark 3:6; 8:15; 12:13
17 [I]Or, *permissible* [a]Matt. 17:25 [b]Luke 2:1; 3:1
18 [I]Or, *wickedness*
19 [I]The denarius was equivalent to one day's wage [a]Matt. 17:25
21 [a]Mark 12:17; Luke 20:25; Rom. 13:7
22 [a]Mark 12:12
23 [a]Matt. 22:23-33; *Mark 12:18-27; Luke 20:27-40* [b]Matt. 3:7 [c]Acts 23:8
24 [a]Deut. 25:5
29 [I]Or, *knowing* [a]John 20:9
30 [I]Other mss. add *of God* [a]Matt. 24:38; Luke 17:27

31 "But regarding the resurrection of the dead, have you not [ao]read that which was spoken to you by God, saying,

32 '[a]I AM THE GOD OF ABRAHAM, AND THE GOD OF ISAAC, AND THE GOD OF JACOB'? [art]He is not the [an]God of the [an]dead but of the [an]living."

33 And when the multitudes heard *this*, [a]they were astonished at His teaching.

34 [a]But when the Pharisees heard that He had [ao]put [b]the Sadducees to silence, they [ao]gathered themselves together.

35 And one of them, [1a]a lawyer,[3544] asked Him *a question*, testing[3985] Him,

36 "Teacher, which is the great commandment in the Law?"

37 And He said to him, " '[a]YOU SHALL [ft]LOVE THE LORD YOUR GOD WITH ALL YOUR HEART, AND WITH ALL YOUR SOUL,[5590] AND WITH ALL YOUR MIND.'[1271]

38 "This is the great and [1]foremost commandment.

39 "The second is like[3664] it, '[a]YOU SHALL [ft]LOVE YOUR NEIGHBOR[4139] AS YOURSELF.'

40 "[a]On these two commandments depend the whole Law and the Prophets."

41 [a]Now while the Pharisees were gathered together, Jesus asked[1905] them a question,

42 saying, "What do you think about [1]the Christ, whose son is He?" They *said to Him, "[a]*The son* of David."

43 He *said to them, "Then how does David [1a]in the Spirit call Him 'Lord,' saying,

44 '[a]THE LORD SAID TO MY LORD,
"SIT AT MY RIGHT HAND,[1188]
UNTIL I [aosb]PUT THINE
ENEMIES BENEATH THY
FEET" '?

45 "If David then [pin]calls Him 'Lord,' how is He his son?"

46 And [a]no one was able to answer Him a word, nor did anyone dare from that day on to [ainf]ask[905] Him another question.

32 [a]Ex. 3:6
33 [a]Matt. 7:28
34 [a]Matt. 22:34-40; *Mark 12:28-31;* Luke 10:25-37 [b]Matt. 3:7
35 [1]I.e., an expert in the Mosaic Law [a]Luke 7:30; 10:25; 11:45, 46, 52; 14:3; Titus 3:13
37 [a]Deut. 6:5
38 [1]Or, *first*
39 [a]Lev. 19:18; Matt. 19:19; Gal. 5:14
40 [a]Matt. 7:12
41 [a]Matt. 22:41-46; *Mark 12:35-37; Luke 20:41-44*
42 [1]I.e., the Messiah [a]Matt. 9:27
43 [1]Or, *by inspiration* [a]2Sam. 23:2; Rev. 1:10; 4:2
44 [a]Ps. 110:1; Matt. 26:64; Mark 16:19; Acts 2:34f.; 1Cor. 15:25; Heb. 1:13; 10:13
46 [a]Mark 12:34; Luke 14:6; 20:40

1 [a]Matt. 23:1-7; *Mark 12:38, 39; Luke 20:45, 46*
2 [a]Deut. 33:3f.; Ezra 7:6, 25; Neh. 8:4
4 [a]Luke 11:46; Acts 15:10
5 [1]I.e., small boxes containing Scripture texts worn for religious purposes [a]Matt. 6:1, 5, 16 [b]Ex. 13:9; Deut. 6:8; 11:18 [c]Matt. 9:20
6 [a]Luke 11:43; 14:7; 20:46
7 [a]Matt. 23:8; 26:25, 49; Mark 9:5; 10:51; 11:21; John 1:38, 49; 3:2, 26; 4:31; 6:25; 9:2; 11:8; 20:16
8 [a]James 3:1 [b]Matt. 23:7; 26:25, 49; Mark 9:5; 10:51; 11:21; 14:45; John 1:38, 49; 3:2, 26; 4:31; 6:25; 9:2; 11:8; 20:16
9 [a]Matt. 6:9; 7:11
10 [1]Or, *teachers*
11 [a]Matt. 20:26
12 [a]Luke 14:11; 18:14
13 [1]Lit., *in front of* [a]Matt. 23:15, 16, 23, 25, 27, 29 [b]Luke 11:52

Pharisaism Exposed

23 [a]Then Jesus spoke to the multitudes and to His disciples,

2 saying, "[a]The scribes[1122] and the Pharisees have [ao]seated themselves in the chair of Moses;

3 therefore all that they [aosb]tell you, [aim]do and [pim]observe,[5083] but[1161] [pim]do not do according to their deeds; for they say *things*, and do not do *them*.

4 "And [a]they tie up heavy loads,[5413] and lay them on men's shoulders; but they themselves are unwilling to [ainf]move them with *so much as* a finger.

5 "But they do all their deeds [a]to be [ainf]noticed by men; for they [b]broaden their [1]phylacteries,[5440] and lengthen [c]the tassels *of their garments*.

6 "And they [a]love[5368] the place of honor at banquets, and the chief seats in the synagogues,

7 and respectful greetings in the market places,[58] and being [pinf]called by men, [a]Rabbi.

8 "But [a]do not be [aosi]called [b]Rabbi; for One is your Teacher,[1320] and you are all brothers.[80]

9 "And do not call *anyone* on earth[1093] your father;[3962] for [a]One is your Father, He who is in heaven.

10 "And do not be [aosi]called [1]leaders;[2519] for One is your Leader,[2519] *that is*, Christ.

11 "[a]But the greatest among you shall be your servant.

12 "And [a]whoever exalts himself shall be humbled;[5013] and whoever humbles himself shall be exalted.

Seven Woes

13 "[a]But woe to you, scribes[1122] and Pharisees, hypocrites, [b]because you shut off the kingdom[932] of heaven [1]from men; for you do not enter in yourselves, nor do you allow[863] those who are entering to go in.

14 ["[1]Woe to you, scribes and Pharisees, hypocrites, because [a]you devour widows' houses,[3614] even while for a

14 [1]This v. not found in the earliest mss. [a]Mark 12:40; Luke 20:47

pretense you [ppt]make long prayers; therefore you shall receive greater[4055] condemnation.[2917]]

15 "Woe to you, scribes and Pharisees, hypocrites, because you travel about on sea[2281] and land to [ainf]make[4160] one [Ia]proselyte;[4339] and when he becomes one, you make him twice as much a son[5207] of [IIb]hell[1067] as yourselves.

16 "Woe to you, [a]blind guides, who say, '[b]Whoever swears by the [I]temple, that is nothing; but whoever swears by the gold of the [I]temple, he is obligated.'

17 "You fools and blind men; [a]which is [I]more important, the gold, or the [II]temple that [ppt]sanctified the gold?

18 "And, 'Whoever [aosb]swears by the altar, *that* is nothing, but whoever [aosb]swears by the [I]offering[1435] upon it, he is obligated.'

19 "You blind men, [a]which is [I]more important, the [II]offering or the altar that sanctifies the [II]offering?

20 "Therefore he who [apt]swears by the altar, swears *both* by the altar and by everything on it.

21 "And he who [apt]swears by the [I]temple, swears *both* by [II]the temple and by Him who [ppt a]dwells[2730] within it.

22 "And he who [apt]swears by heaven, [a]swears *both* by the throne of God and by Him who [ppt]sits upon it.

23 "[a]Woe to you, scribes and Pharisees, hypocrites! For you tithe the mint and dill[432] and [I]cummin, and have [ao]neglected the weightier provisions of the law:[3551] justice[2920] and mercy[1656] and faithfulness;[4102] but these are the things you should have [ainf]done without [ainf]neglecting[863][3361] the others.

24 "You [a]blind guides, who [ppt]strain out a gnat and [ppt]swallow a camel!

🗝 **25** "Woe to you, scribes and Pharisees, hypocrites! For [a]you clean[2511] the outside of the cup and of the dish, but inside they are full [I]of robbery[724] and self-indulgence.

26 "You blind Pharisee, first [aim a]clean the inside of the cup and of the dish, so that the outside of it [aosb]may become clean also.

27 "[a]Woe to you, scribes and Pharisees, hypocrites! For you are like whitewashed tombs[5028] which on the outside appear beautiful,[5611] but inside they are full of dead men's bones and all uncleanness.[167]

28 "Even so you too outwardly appear[5316] righteous[1342] to men, but inwardly you are full of hypocrisy and lawlessness.[458]

29 "[a]Woe to you, scribes and Pharisees, hypocrites! For you build the tombs of the prophets and adorn[2885] the monuments[3419] of the righteous,

30 and say, 'If we had been *living* in the days[2250] of our fathers,[3962] we would not have been partners[2844] with them in *shedding* the blood[129] of the prophets.'

31 "Consequently you bear witness[3140] against yourselves, that you [a]are [I]sons[5207] of those who [apt]murdered the prophets.

32 [aim]"[I]Fill up[4137] then the measure *of the guilt* of your fathers.[3962]

33 "You serpents, [a]you brood of vipers, how shall you [aosb]escape the [I]sentence[2920] of [IIb]hell?[1067]

34 "[a]Therefore, behold, [b]I am sending you prophets and wise[4680] men and scribes;[1122] some of them you will kill and crucify,[4717] and some of them you will [c]scourge[3146] in your synagogues, and [d]persecute from city to city,

35 that upon you may fall *the guilt of* all the righteous blood[129] [ppt]shed on earth, from the blood of righteous [a]Abel to the blood of Zechariah, the [b]son of Berechiah, whom [c]you murdered between the [I]temple and the altar.

36 "Truly[281] I say to you, all these things shall come upon [a]this generation.

Lament Over Jerusalem

37 "[a]O Jerusalem, Jerusalem, who [ppt b]kills the prophets and [ppt]stones those

---

15 [I]Or, *convert* [II]Gr., *Gehenna* [a]Acts 2:10; 6:5; 13:43 [b]Matt. 5:22
16 [I]Or, *sanctuary* [a]Matt. 15:14; 23:24 [b]Matt. 5:33-35
17 [I]Lit., *greater* [II]Or, *sanctuary* [a]Ex. 30:29
18 [I]Or, *gift*
19 [I]Lit., *greater* [II]Or, *gift* [a]Ex. 29:37
21 [I]Or, *sanctuary* [II]Lit., *it* [a]1Kin. 8:13; Ps. 26:8; 132:14
22 [a]Is. 66:1; Matt. 5:34
23 [I]Similar to caraway seeds [a]Matt. 23:13; Luke 11:42
24 [a]Matt. 23:16
25 [I]Or, *as a result of* [a]Mark 7:4; Luke 11:39f.
26 [a]Mark 7:4; Luke 11:39f.
27 [a]Luke 11:44; Acts 23:3
29 [a]Luke 11:47f.
31 [I]Or, *descendants* [a]Matt. 23:34, 37; Acts 7:51f.
32 [I]Lit., *And fill up*
33 [I]Or, *judgment* [II]Gr., *Gehenna* [a]Matt. 3:7; Luke 3:7 [b]Matt. 5:22
34 [a]Matt. 23:34-36; Luke 11:49-51 [b]2Chr. 36:15, 16 [c]Matt. 10:17 [d]Matt. 10:23
35 [I]Or, *sanctuary* [a]Gen. 4:8ff.; Heb. 11:4 [b]Zech. 1:1 [c]2Chr. 24:21
36 [a]Matt. 10:23; 24:34
37 [a]Matt. 23:37-39; *Luke 13:34, 35* [b]Matt. 5:12

🗝 **23:25** See notes on I Thess. 4:17; Rev. 4 and also the words: *harpagē* (724), robbery, catching up; the verb *harpazō* (726), to catch up or away, and *harpagmos* (725), robbery.

who are [pfp]sent to her! How often I [ao]wanted[2309] to [ainf]gather[1996] your children together, [c]the way a hen gathers[1996] her chicks under her wings, and you were [ao]unwilling.

38 "Behold, [a]your house is being left to you [1]desolate!

39 "For I say to you, from now on you shall not [efn]see Me until you say, '[a]BLESSED[2127] IS HE WHO COMES IN THE [an]NAME OF THE LORD!' "

Signs of Christ's Return

24 🔑 [a]AND Jesus [b]came out from the temple[2411] and was going away [1]when His disciples came up to point out the temple buildings[3619] to Him.

2 And He answered and said to them, "Do you not see all these things? Truly[281] I say to you, [a]not one stone here shall [efn]be left[863] upon another, which will not be torn down."[2647]

🔑 3 And as He was sitting on [a]the Mount of Olives, the disciples came to Him privately, saying, "Tell us, when will these things be, and what *will be* the sign of [b]Your coming, and of the [1]end[4930] of the age?"

4 And Jesus answered and said to them, [pim]"[a]See to it[991] that no one [aosb]misleads you.

5 "For [a]many will come in My name,[3686] saying, 'I am the [1]Christ,' and will mislead many.

6 "And you will be hearing of [a]wars and rumors of wars;[4171] [pim]see that you are not frightened, for *those things* must take place,[1096] but *that* is not yet the end.

7 "For [a]nation[1484] will rise[1453] against nation, and kingdom against kingdom, and in various[2596] places[5117] there will be [b]famines[3042] and earthquakes.

8 "[a]But all these things are *merely* the beginning of birth pangs.[5604]

9 "[a]Then they will deliver you to [nn]tribulation, and will kill you, and [b]you will be hated by all nations on account of My name.

10 "And at that time many will [1a]fall away and will deliver up one another and hate one another.

11 "And many [a]false prophets will arise, and will mislead many.

12 "And because lawlessness[458] is increased, [1]most people's love will grow cold.[5594]

13 "[a]But the one who [apt]endures[5278] to the end,[5056] he shall be saved.[4982]

14 "And this [a]gospel[2098] of the kingdom[932] [b]shall be preached[2784] in the whole [1c]world[3625] for a witness to all the nations, and then the end shall come.

Perilous Times

🔑 15 "Therefore when you see the [a]ABOMINATION[946] OF DESOLATION which was spoken of through Daniel the prophet, standing in [b]the holy[40] place ([c]let the [ppt]reader understand),[3539]

16 then let those who are in Judea [pim]flee to the mountains;

17 let him who is on [a]the housetop not [aim]go down to get the things out that are in his house;

18 and let him who is in the field not [aim]turn[1994] back to [ainf]get his cloak.

19 "But [a]woe to those who [ppt]are with child and to those who [ppt]nurse babes in those days!

20 "But [pim]pray[4336] that your flight may not be in the winter, or on a Sabbath;[4521]

21 for then there will be a [a]great tribulation,[2347] such as [pfi]has not

37 [c]Ruth 2:12
38 [1]Some mss. do not contain *desolate* [a]1Kin. 9:7f.; Jer. 22:5
39 [a]Ps. 118:26; Matt. 21:9

1 [1]Lit., *and* [a]Matt. 24:1-51; *Mark 13; Luke 21:5-36* [b]Matt. 21:23
2 [a]Luke 19:44
3 [1]Or, *consummation* [a]Matt. 21:1 [b]Matt. 16:27f.; 24:27, 37, 39
4 [a]Jer. 29:8
5 [1]I.e., Messiah [a]Matt. 24:11, 24; Acts 5:36f.; 1John 2:18; 4:3
6 [a]Rev. 6:4
7 [a]2Chr. 15:6; Is. 19:2; Rev. 6:8, 12 [b]Acts 11:28; Rev. 6:5, 6
8 [a]Matt. 24:8-20; Luke 21:12-24
9 [a]Matt. 10:17; John 16:2 [b]Matt. 10:22; John 15:18ff.
10 [1]Lit., *be caused to stumble* [a]Matt. 11:6
11 [a]Matt. 7:15; 24:24
12 [1]Lit., *the love of many*
13 [a]Matt. 10:22
14 [1]Lit., *inhabited earth* [a]Matt. 4:23 [b]Rom. 10:18; Col. 1:6, 23 [c]Luke 2:1; 4:5; Acts 11:28; 17:6, 31; 19:27; Rom. 10:18; Heb. 1:6; 2:5; Rev. 3:10; 16:14
15 [a]Dan. 9:27; 11:31; 12:11 [b]Mark 13:14; Luke 21:20; John 11:48; Acts 6:13f.; 21:28 [c]Mark 13:14; Rev. 1:3
17 [a]1Sam. 9:25; 2Sam. 11:2; Matt. 10:27; Luke 5:19; 12:3; 17:31; Acts 10:9
19 [a]Luke 23:29
21 [a]Dan. 12:1; Joel 2:2; Matt. 24:29

🔑 **24—25** Our Lord delivered the Olivet Discourse on the Mount of Olives just prior to His passion. It is in regard to the future. Corresponding chapters are Mk. 13 and Lk. 21. See note on Rev. 6:1-17.

🔑 **24:3** See note on I Thess. 2:19 and the word *parousia* (3952), presence, as it pertains to Christ's Second Coming.

🔑 **24:15** See notes on II Thess. 2:3-8; Rev. 13 and *bdelugma* (946), abomination, and *apostasia* (646), apostasy, staying away.

occurred since the beginning of the world until now, nor ever [efn]shall.

🔑22 "And unless those days had been cut short, no [I]life[4561] would have been [aop]saved; but for [a]the sake of the [II]elect[1588] those days shall be cut short.

23 "[a]Then if anyone says to you, 'Behold, here is the [I]Christ,' or '[II]There *He is,*' do not [aosi]believe *him.*

24 "For false Christs[5580] and [a]false prophets will arise[1453] and will show great [Ib]signs and wonders, so as to [ainf]mislead, if possible, even [c]the [II]elect.

25 "Behold, I have told you in advance.

26 "If therefore they [aosb]say to you, 'Behold, He is in the wilderness,' do not go forth, *or,* 'Behold, He is in the inner rooms,' do not [aosi]believe *them.*

🔑27 "[a]For just as the lightning comes from the east, and flashes[5316] even to the west, so shall the [b]coming[3952] of the [c]Son of Man be.

28 "[a]Wherever the corpse is, there the [I]vultures will gather.

The Glorious Return

29 "But immediately after the [a]tribulation of those days [b]THE SUN WILL BE DARKENED, AND THE MOON WILL NOT GIVE ITS LIGHT,[5338] AND [c]THE STARS WILL FALL from [I]the sky, and the powers of [I]the heavens will be shaken,

30 and then [a]the sign of the Son of Man will appear in the sky,[3772] and then all the tribes of the earth will mourn, and they will see [b]the SON OF MAN COMING ON THE CLOUDS OF THE SKY with[3326] power and great glory.[1391]

🔑31 "And [a]He will send forth His angels WITH[3326] [b]A GREAT TRUMPET and THEY WILL GATHER TOGETHER[1996] His [I][c]elect from [d]the four winds, from one [pl]end of the sky to the [pl]other.

Parable of the Fig Tree

32 "Now [aim]learn the parable[3850] from the fig tree: when its branch has [aosb]already become tender, and [aosb]puts forth its leaves, you know that summer is near;[1451]

33 even so you too, when you see all these things, [I]recognize that [II]He is near,[1451] *right* [a]at the [III]door.

34 "Truly I say to you, [a]this [I]generation[1074] will not [efn]pass away until all these things take place.

35 [art]"[a]Heaven and [art]earth[1093] will [ft]pass away, but My words shall not [efn]pass away.

🔑36 "But [a]of that day and hour no one knows, not even the angels[32] of heaven, nor the Son, but the Father[3962] alone.

37 "For [I]the [a]coming[3952] of the Son of Man will be [b]just like the days of Noah.

38 "For as in those days which were before the flood they were [ppt]eating and [ppt]drinking, they were [ppt] [a]marrying and [ppt]giving in marriage, until the day that [b]Noah entered the ark,

39 and they did not [I]understand until the flood came and took them all away; so shall the [a]coming[3952] of the Son of Man be.

40 "Then there shall be two men in the field; one [I]will be [pin]taken,3880 and one [I]will be [pin]left.

41 "[a]Two women *will be* [ppt]grinding at the [Ib]mill; one [II]will be [pin]taken,3880 and one [II]will be [pin]left.

22 [I]Lit., *flesh* [II]Or, *chosen ones* [a]Matt. 22:14; 24:24, 31; Luke 18:7
23 [I]I.e., Messiah [II]Lit., *here* [a]Luke 17:23f.
24 [I]Or, *attesting miracles* [II]Or, *chosen ones* [a]Matt. 7:15; 24:11 [b]John 4:48; 2Thess. 2:9 [c]Matt. 22:14; 24:22, 31; Luke 18:7
27 [a]Luke 17:24 [b]Matt. 24:3, 37, 39 [c]Matt. 8:20
28 [I]Or, *eagles* [a]Job 39:30; Ezek. 39:17; Hab. 1:8; Luke 17:37
29 [I]Or, *heaven* [a]Matt. 24:21 [b]Is. 13:10; 24:23; Ezek. 32:7; Joel 2:10, 31; 3:15f.; Amos 5:20; 8:9; Zeph. 1:15; Matt. 24:29-35; Acts 2:20; Rev. 6:12-17; 8:12 [c]Is. 34:4; Rev. 6:13
30 [a]Matt. 24:3; Rev. 1:7 [b]Dan. 7:13; Matt. 16:27; 24:3, 37, 39
31 [I]Or, *chosen ones* [a]Matt. 13:41 [b]Ex. 19:16; Deut. 30:4; Is. 27:13; Zech. 9:14; 1Cor. 15:52; 1Thess. 4:16; Heb. 12:19; Rev. 8:2; 11:15 [c]Matt. 24:22 [d]Dan. 7:2; Zech. 2:6; Rev. 7:1
33 [I]Lit., *know* [II]Or, *it* [III]Lit., *doors* [a]James 5:9; Rev. 3:20
34 [I]Or, *race* [a]Matt. 10:23; 16:28; 23:36
35 [a]Matt. 5:18; Mark 13:31; Luke 21:33
36 [a]Mark 13:32; Acts 1:7
37 [I]Lit., *just as. . .were the days* [a]Matt. 16:27; 24:3, 30, 39 [b]Gen. 6:5; 7:6-23; Luke 17:26f.
38 [a]Matt. 22:30 [b]Gen. 7:7
39 [I]Lit., *know* [a]Matt. 16:27; 24:3, 30, 37
40 [I]Lit., *is*
41 [I]I.e., handmill [II]Lit., *is* [a]Luke 17:35 [b]Ex. 11:5; Deut. 24:6; Is. 47:2

🔑**24:22,31** See note on Eph. 1:4,5 and *eklektos* (1588), elect.
🔑**24:27** See note on I Thess. 2:19 and the word *parousia* (3952), presence, as it pertains to Christ's Second Coming.
🔑**24:31** See notes on Eph. 1:4,5; I Thess. 2:19 and also *eklektos* (1588), elect, and *parousia* (3952), presence.
🔑**24:36** See note on Phil. 2:6-8.

Be Ready for His Coming

42 "Therefore [pin] [a]be on the alert, for you do not know which day your Lord is coming.

43 "But [I]be sure of this, that [a]if the head of the house[3617] had known [b]at what time of the night the thief[2812] was [pin]coming, he would have been on the alert and would not have [ao]allowed his house to be [aifp] [II]broken into.

44 "For this reason [a]you [pim]be ready too; for [b]the Son of Man is coming at an hour when you do not think *He will.*

45 "[a]Who then is the [b]faithful and [c]sensible[5429] slave[1401] whom his [I]master [ao] [d]put in charge[2525] of his household[3610] to give them their food at the proper time?[2540]

46 "Blessed[3107] is that slave whom his [I]master finds so doing when he [apt]comes.

47 "Truly I say to you, that [a]he will put him[2525] in charge of all his possessions.[5224]

48 "But if that evil slave says in his heart, 'My [I]master [II]is not [ainf]coming for a long time,'

49 and shall begin [pinf]to beat[5180] his fellow slaves[4889] and [psa]eat and [psa]drink with [ppt] [I]drunkards;

50 the [I]master of that slave will come on a day when he does not expect[4328] *him* and at an hour which he does not know,

51 and shall [I]cut him in pieces and [II]assign[5087] him a place with the hypocrites; [a]weeping shall be there and the gnashing[1030] of teeth.

Parable of Ten Virgins

25 "Then [a]the kingdom[932] of heaven will be comparable to ten virgins,[3933] who [apt]took their [b]lamps, and went out to meet the bridegroom.

2 "And five of them were foolish, and five were [a]prudent.[5429]

3 "For when the foolish [apt]took their lamps, they took no oil with them,

4 but the [a]prudent took oil in flasks along with their lamps.

5 "Now while the bridegroom was [ppt]delaying, they all got drowsy and *began* to [ipf]sleep.

6 "But at midnight[3319] [3571] there [pfi]was a shout, 'Behold, the bridegroom! Come out to meet *him.*'

7 "Then all those virgins rose, and trimmed their lamps.

8 "And the foolish said to the prudent, 'Give us some of your oil, for our lamps are [pin]going out.'

9 "But the [a]prudent answered, saying, 'No, there will not be enough for us and you *too;* [pim]go instead to the [pim]dealers and [aim]buy *some* for yourselves.'

10 "And while they were going away to make the purchase, the bridegroom came, and those who were [a]ready went in with him to [b]the wedding feast;[1062] and [c]the door was shut.

11 "And later the other virgins also [pin]came, saying, '[a]Lord, lord, open up for us.'

12 "But he answered and said, 'Truly[281] I say to you, I do not know[1492] you.'

13 [pim]"[a]Be on the alert then, for you do not know the day nor the hour.

Parable of the Talents

🗝 **14** "[a]For *it is* just like a man [b]*about* to go on a journey, who called[2564] his own slaves, and entrusted his possessions to them.

15 "And to one he gave five [Ia]talents, to another, two, and to another, one, each according to his own ability; and he [b]went on his journey.

16 "Immediately the one who had received the five [a]talents [apt]went and traded[2038] with them, and gained five more talents.

17 "In the same manner the one who *had received* the two *talents* gained two more.

18 "But he who received the one

42 [a]Matt. 24:43, 44; 25:10, 13; Luke 12:39f.; 21:36
43 [I]Lit., *know this* [II]Lit., *dug through* [a]Matt. 24:42, 44; 25:10, 13; Luke 12:39f.; 21:36 [b]Matt. 14:25; Mark 6:48; 13:35; Luke 12:38
44 [a]Matt. 24:42, 43; 25:10, 13; Luke 12:39f.; 21:36 [b]Matt. 24:27
45 [I]Or, *lord* [a]Matt. 24:45-51; *Luke 12:42-46* [b]Matt. 25:21, 23; Luke 16:10 [c]Matt. 7:24; 10:16; 25:2ff. [d]Matt. 25:21, 23
46 [I]Or, *lord*
47 [a]Matt. 25:21, 23
48 [I]Or, *lord* [II]Lit., *lingers*
49 [I]Lit., *those who get drunk*
50 [I]Or, *lord*
51 [I]Or, *severely scourge him* [II]Lit., *appoint his portion* [a]Matt. 8:12

1 [a]Matt. 13:24 [b]John 18:3; Acts 20:8; Rev. 4:5; 8:10
2 [a]Matt. 7:24; 10:16; 25:2ff.
4 [a]Matt. 7:24; 10:16; 25:2ff.
9 [a]Matt. 7:24; 10:16; 25:2ff.
10 [a]Matt. 24:42ff. [b]Luke 12:35f. [c]Matt. 7:21ff.; Luke 13:25
11 [a]Matt. 7:21ff.; Luke 13:25
13 [a]Matt. 24:42ff.
14 [a]Matt. 25:14-30; Luke 19:12-27 [b]Matt. 21:33
15 [I]A talent was $1,000 in silver content, much more in buying power. [a]Matt. 18:24; Luke 19:13 [b]Matt. 21:33
16 [a]Matt. 18:24; Luke 19:13

🗝 **25:14-30** See notes on Mt. 8:11,12; Lk. 19:11-27.

talent went away and dug in the ground,[1093] and his [I]master's money.

19 "Now after a long time[5550] the master of those slaves *came and *[a]settled accounts with them.

20 "And the one who had received the five [a]talents [apt]came up and brought five more talents, saying, 'Master, you entrusted five talents to me; see, I have gained five more talents.'

21 "His master said to him, 'Well done,[2095] good[18] and [a]faithful[4103] slave; you were faithful[4103] with a few things, I will [b]put[2525] you in charge of many things, enter into the joy[5479] of your [I]master.'

22 "The one also who *had received* the two [a]talents [apt]came up and said, 'Master, you entrusted to me two talents; see, I have gained two more talents.'

23 "His master said to him, 'Well done,[2095] good and [a]faithful[4103] slave; you were faithful with a few things, I will put[2525] you in charge of many things; enter into the joy[5479] of your master.'

24 "And the one also who had received the one [a]talent [apt]came up and said, 'Master, I knew you to be a hard[4642] man, reaping where you did not [ao]sow, and gathering where you [ao]scattered no *seed*.[1287]

25 'And I was [apt]afraid, and [apt]went away and hid your talent in the ground; see, you have what is yours.'

26 "But his master answered and said to him, 'You wicked,[4190] lazy slave, you knew that I reap where I did not sow, and gather where I [ao]scattered no *seed*.

27 'Then you [ipf]ought[1163] to have put my money [I]in the bank, and on my [apt]arrival I would have received my *money* back with interest.

28 'Therefore take away the talent from him, and give it to the one who [ppt]has the ten talents.'

29 "[a]For to everyone who has shall *more* be given, and he shall have an abundance; but from the one who does not [ppt]have, even what he does have shall be taken away.

30 "And [aim]cast out the worthless[888] slave into [a]the outer darkness;[4655] in that place there shall be weeping and gnashing[1030] of teeth.

The Judgment

31 "But when [a]the Son of Man comes in His glory,[1391] and all the angels with Him, then [b]He will sit on His glorious throne.

32 "And all the nations[1484] will be [a]gathered before Him; and He will separate[873] them from one another, [b]as the shepherd[4166] separates the sheep from the goats;

33 and He will put the sheep [a]on His right,[1188] and the goats [b]on the left.

34 "Then the King[935] will say to those on His right, 'Come, you who are blessed[2127] of My Father, [aim] [a]inherit[2816] the kingdom prepared for you [b]from the foundation[2602] of the world.

35 'For [a]I was hungry,[3983] and you gave Me *something* to eat; I was thirsty, and you gave Me drink; [b]I was a stranger, and you invited[4863] Me in;

36 [a]naked,[1131] and you clothed Me; I was sick,[770] and you [b]visited[1980] Me; [c]I was in prison, and you came to Me.'

37 "Then the righteous[1342] will answer Him, saying, 'Lord, when did we see You [ppt]hungry,[3983] and feed You, or [ppt]thirsty, and give You drink?

38 'And when did we see You a stranger, and invite You in, or naked, and clothe You?

39 'And when did we see You sick,[770] or in prison, and come to You?'

40 "And [a]the King[935] will [apt]answer and say to them, 'Truly I say to you, [b]to the extent that you did it to one of these brothers[80] of Mine, *even* the least *of them,* you did it to Me.'

41 "Then He will also say to those on His left, [pim]'[a]Depart from Me, accursed ones,[2672] into the [art] [b]eternal fire which has been prepared for [c]the devil and his angels;[32]

42 for I [ao]was hungry,[3983] and you gave Me *nothing* [ainf]to eat; I was

18 [I]Or, *lord's*
19 [a]Matt. 18:23
20 [a]Matt. 18:24; Luke 19:13
21 [I]Or, *lord* [a]Matt. 24:45, 47; 25:23 [b]Luke 12:44; 22:29; Rev. 3:21; 21:7
22 [a]Matt. 18:24; Luke 19:13
23 [a]Matt. 24:45, 47; 25:21
24 [a]Matt. 18:24; Luke 19:13
27 [I]Lit., *to the bankers*
29 [a]Matt. 13:12; Mark 4:25; Luke 8:18; John 15:2
30 [a]Matt. 8:12; 22:13; Luke 13:28
31 [a]Matt. 16:27f.; 1Thess. 4:16; 2Thess. 1:7; Heb. 9:28; Jude 14; Rev. 1:7 [b]Matt. 19:28
32 [a]Matt. 13:49; 2Cor. 5:10 [b]Ezek. 34:17, 20
33 [a]1Kin. 2:19; Ps. 45:9 [b]Eccl. 10:2
34 [a]Matt. 5:3; 19:29; Luke 12:32; 1Cor. 6:9; 15:50; Gal. 5:21; James 2:5 [b]Matt. 13:35; Luke 11:50; John 17:24; Eph. 1:4; Heb. 4:3; 9:26; 1Pet. 1:20; Rev. 13:8; 17:8
35 [a]Is. 58:7; Ezek. 18:7, 16; James 2:15, 16 [b]Job 31:32; Heb. 13:2
36 [a]Is. 58:7; Ezek. 18:7, 16; James 2:15, 16 [b]James 1:27 [c]2Tim. 1:16f.
40 [a]Matt. 25:34; Luke 19:38; Rev. 17:14; 19:16 [b]Prov. 19:17; Matt. 10:42; Heb. 6:10
41 [a]Matt. 7:23 [b]Mark 9:48; Luke 16:24; Jude 7 [c]Matt. 4:10; Rev. 12:9

[ao]thirsty, and you gave Me nothing to drink;

43 I was a stranger, and you did not invite[4863] Me in; naked,[1131] and you did not clothe Me; sick, and in prison, and you did not visit[1980] Me.’

44 “Then they themselves also will answer, saying, ‘Lord, when did we see You [ppt]hungry,[3983] or [ppt]thirsty, or a stranger, or naked, or sick, or in prison, and did not [I]take care[1247] of You?’

45 “Then He will answer them, saying, ‘Truly I say to you, to the extent that you did not do it to one of the least of these, you did not do it to Me.’

46 “And these will go away into [a]eternal punishment,[2851] but the righteous[1342] into [b]eternal life.”[2222]

The Plot to Kill Jesus

26 [a]And it came about that when Jesus had finished all these words,[3056] He said to His disciples,

2 “[a]You know that after two days [b]the Passover[3957] is coming, and the Son of Man is *to be* [c]delivered up for crucifixion.”[4717]

3 [a]Then the chief priests and the elders[4245] of the people were gathered together[4863] in [b]the court of the high priest, named [c]Caiaphas;

4 and they [a]plotted together to seize Jesus by stealth, and kill *Him.*

5 But they were saying, “Not during the festival, [a]lest a riot occur among the people.”[2992]

The Precious Ointment

6 [a]Now when Jesus was[1096] in [b]Bethany, at the home of Simon the leper,

7 [a]a woman came to Him with an alabaster vial of very costly perfume, and she poured it upon His head as He [ppt]reclined *at the table.*

8 But the disciples were indignant when they saw *this,* and said, “Why this waste?[684]

9 “For this *perfume* might have been sold for a high price and *the money* given to the poor.”

44 [I]Or, *serve*
46 [a]Dan. 12:2; John 5:29; Acts 24:15 [b]Matt. 19:29; John 3:15f., 36; 5:24; 6:27, 40, 47, 54; 17:2f.; Acts 13:46, 48; Rom. 2:7; 5:21; 6:23; Gal. 6:8; 1John 5:11

1 [a]Matt. 7:28
2 [a]Matt. 26:2-5; *Mark 14:1, 2; Luke 22:1, 2* [b]John 11:55; 13:1 [c]Matt. 10:4
3 [a]John 11:47 [b]Matt. 26:58, 69; 27:27; Mark 14:54, 66; 15:16; Luke 22:55; John 18:15 [c]Matt. 26:57; Luke 3:2; John 11:49; 18:13, 14, 24, 28; Acts 4:6
4 [a]Matt. 12:14
5 [a]Matt. 27:24
6 [a]Matt. 26:6-13; *Mark 14:3-9;* Luke 7:37-39; John 12:1-8 [b]Matt. 21:17
7 [a]Luke 7:37f.
11 [a]Deut. 15:11; Mark 14:7; John 12:8
12 [a]John 19:40
13 [a]Mark 14:9
14 [a]Matt. 26:14-16; *Mark 14:10, 11; Luke 22:3-6* [b]Matt. 10:4; 26:25, 47; 27:3; John 6:71; 12:4; 13:26; Acts 1:16
15 [I]Lit., *and I will* [II]Or, *betray* [III]Or, *silver shekels* [a]Matt. 10:4 [b]Ex. 21:32; Zech. 11:12
16 [I]Or, *deliver Him up*
17 [a]Matt. 26:17-19; *Mark 14:12-16; Luke 22:7-13* [b]Ex. 12:18-20
18 [a]Mark 14:13; Luke 22:10 [b]John 7:6, 8
20 [a]Matt. 26:20-24; *Mark 14:17-21*
21 [a]Luke 22:21-23; John 13:21f.
22 [I]Or, *one after another*

10 But Jesus, aware of this, said to them, “Why do you bother[2873] the woman? For she [ao]has done[2038] a good deed[2041] to Me.

11 “For [a]the poor you have with you always; but you do not always have Me.

12 “For when she [apt]poured this perfume upon My body, she did it [a]to prepare Me for burial.

13 “Truly[281] I say to you, [a]wherever this gospel[2098] is preached[2784] in the whole world,[2889] what this woman has [ao]done shall also be spoken of in memory of her.”

Judas’ Bargain

14 [a]Then one of the twelve, named [b]Judas Iscariot, [apt]went to the chief priests,

15 and said, “What are you willing[2309] to [ainf]give me [I]to [IIa]deliver Him up to you?” And [b]they weighed out[2476] to him thirty [III]pieces of silver.

16 And from then on he *began* [ipf]looking for a good opportunity[2120] to [I]betray Him.

17 [a]Now on the first *day* of [b]Unleavened Bread[106] the disciples came to Jesus, saying, “Where do You want us to prepare for You to eat the Passover?”

18 And He said, “Go into the city to [a]a certain man, and say to him, ‘The Teacher says, “[b]My time[2540] is at hand;[1451] I *am to* [pin]keep the Passover at your house with My disciples.” ’ ”

19 And the disciples did as Jesus had directed them; and they prepared the Passover.

The Last Passover

20 [a]Now when evening had come, He was reclining *at the table* with the twelve disciples.

21 And as they were [ppt]eating, He said, “[a]Truly I say to you that one of you will betray Me.”

22 And being deeply [ppt]grieved, they [I]each one began to [pinf]say to Him, “Surely not [epn]I, Lord?”

23 And He answered[611] and said,

"[a]He who [apt]dipped[1686] his hand with Me
in the bowl is the one who will betray
Me.
24 "The Son of Man *is to* go,
[a]just as it is [pfip]written of Him; but woe
to that man by whom the Son of Man
is betrayed! [b]It would have been good
[I]for that man if he had not been born."
25 And [a]Judas, who was betraying
Him, answered[611] and said, "Surely it
is not [epn]I, [b]Rabbi?" He [pin]*said to him,
"[c]You have [ao]said *it* yourself."

The Lord's Supper Instituted

26 [a]And while they were [ppt]eating,
Jesus [apt]took *some* bread, and [Ib]after a
[apt]blessing,[2127] He broke *it* and [apt]gave
it to the disciples, and said, "Take, eat;
this is My body."[4983]
27 And when He had [apt]taken a cup
and [apt]given thanks,[2168] He gave *it* to
them, saying, [aim]"Drink from it, all of
you;
28 for [a]this is My blood[129] of the
covenant,[1242] which is [ppt]poured out for
[b]many for forgiveness of sins.[266]
29 "But I say to you, I will not
[efn]drink of this fruit of the vine from
now on until that day when I [psa]drink
it new with you in My Father's
kingdom."[932]
30 [a]And after singing a hymn, they
went out to [b]the Mount of Olives.
31 Then Jesus *said to them, "You
will all [Ia]fall away because of Me this
night, for it is [pfip]written, '[b]I WILL
STRIKE[3960] DOWN THE SHEPHERD,[4166] AND
THE SHEEP OF THE FLOCK[4167] SHALL BE
[c]SCATTERED.'
32 "But after I have been raised,
[a]I will go before[4254] you to Galilee."
33 But Peter answered and said to
Him, "*Even* though all may [I]fall away
because of You, I will never fall away."
34 Jesus said to him, "[a]Truly I say
to you that [b]this *very* night, before a
cock [ainf]crows,[455] you shall [ft]deny[533] Me
three times."
35 Peter *said to Him, "[a]Even if I
have to die[599] with You, I will not
[efn]deny[533] You." All the disciples said
the same thing too.

23 [a]Ps. 41:9; John 13:18, 26
24 [I]Lit., *for him if that man had not been born* [a]Matt. 26:31, 54, 56; Mark 9:12; Luke 24:25-27, 46; Acts 17:2f.; 26:22f.; 1Cor. 15:3; 1Pet. 1:10f. [b]Matt. 18:7; Mark 14:21
25 [a]Matt. 26:14 [b]Matt. 23:7; 26:49 [c]Matt. 26:64; 27:11; Luke 22:70
26 [I]Lit., *having blessed* [a]Matt. 26:26-29; *Mark 14:22-25; Luke 22:17-20; 1Cor. 11:23-25;* 1Cor. 10:16 [b]Matt. 14:19
28 [a]Ex. 24:8; Heb. 9:20 [b]Matt. 20:28
30 [a]Matt. 26:30-35; *Mark 14:26-31; Luke 22:31-34* [b]Matt. 21:1
31 [I]Or, *stumble* [a]Matt. 11:6 [b]Zech. 13:7 [c]John 16:32
32 [a]Matt. 28:7, 10, 16; Mark 16:7
33 [I]Or, *stumble*
34 [a]Matt. 26:75; John 13:38 [b]Mark 14:30
35 [a]John 13:37
36 [a]Matt. 26:36-46; *Mark 14:32-42; Luke 22:40-46* [b]Mark 14:32; Luke 22:39; John 18:1
37 [a]Matt. 4:21; 17:1; Mark 5:37
38 [a]John 12:27 [b]Matt. 26:40, 41
39 [a]Matt. 20:22 [b]Matt. 26:42; Mark 14:36; Luke 22:42; John 6:38
40 [a]Matt. 26:38
41 [a]Matt. 26:38 [b]Mark 14:38
42 [a]Matt. 20:22 [b]Matt. 26:39; Mark 14:36; Luke 22:42; John 6:38
45 [I]Or, *Keep on sleeping therefore* [a]Mark 14:41; John 12:27; 13:1
47 [a]Matt. 26:47-56; *Mark 14:43-50; Luke 22:47-53; John 18:3-11* [b]Matt. 26:14

The Garden of Gethsemane

36 [a]Then Jesus *came with them
to a place called [b]Gethsemane, and *said
to His disciples, "Sit here while [apt]I go
over there and pray."[4336]
37 And He [apt]took with Him [a]Peter
and the two sons of Zebedee, and began
to be grieved[3076] and distressed.
38 Then He *said to them, "[a]My
soul[5590] is deeply grieved, to the point
of death; remain here and [b]keep watch
with Me."
39 And He [apt]went[4281] a little beyond *them,* and fell[4098] on His face and
[ppt]prayed,[4336] saying, "My Father,[3962]
if it is possible, [aim]let [a]this cup pass from
Me; [b]yet not as [epn]I will, but as [epn]Thou
wilt."
40 And He *came to the disciples
and *found them [ppt]sleeping, and *said
to Peter, "So, you *men* [ao]could[2480] not
[a]keep [ainf]watch with Me for one hour?
41 "[a]Keep [pim]watching and [pim]pray-
ing, that you may not [aosb]enter into
temptation;[3986] [b]the spirit[4151] is willing,
but the flesh[4561] is weak."[772]
42 He went away again a second
time and prayed, saying, "My Fa-
ther,[3962] if this [a]cannot [ainf]pass away
unless I drink it, [b]Thy will[2307] be
done."
43 And again He came[apt] and [ao]found
them [ppt]sleeping, for their eyes were
[pfpp]heavy.
44 And He [apt]left them again, and
[apt]went away and prayed[4336] a third
time, [apt]saying the same thing once
more.
45 Then He *came to the disciples,
and *said to them, "[I]Are you still sleeping and [pim]taking your rest? Behold,
[a]the hour[5610] [pfi]is at hand and the Son
of Man is being [pp]betrayed into the hands
of sinners.[268]
46 "Arise, let us be going;[71] behold,
the one who [ppt]betrays Me is at hand!"

Jesus' Betrayal and Arrest

47 [a]And while He was still speaking,
behold, [b]Judas, one of the twelve, came

up, [I]accompanied by a great multitude with swords and clubs, from the chief priests and elders of the people.

48 Now he who was [ppt]betraying Him gave them a sign, saying, "Whomever I shall kiss,[5368] He is the one; [aim]seize Him."

49 And immediately[2112] he [apt]went to Jesus and said, "Hail,[5463] [a]Rabbi!" and kissed Him.

🔑 50 And Jesus said to him, "[a]Friend, *do* what you have come for." Then they came and laid hands on Jesus and seized Him.

51 And behold, [a]one of those who were with Jesus [apt] [I]reached and drew out his [b]sword, and [apt]struck the [c]slave of the high priest, and [II]cut off[851] his ear.

52 Then Jesus *said to him, "Put your sword back[654] into its place; for [a]all those who [apt]take up the sword shall perish[622] by the sword.

53 "Or do you think that I cannot [ainf]appeal to My Father,[3962] and He will at once put at My disposal more than twelve [Ia]legions of [b]angels?

54 "How then shall [a]the Scriptures be fulfilled, that it must happen this way?"

55 At that time Jesus said to the multitudes, "Have you [ao]come out with swords and clubs to arrest Me as against a robber?[3027] [a]Every day I used to sit in the temple[2411] teaching and you did not seize Me.

56 "But all this has taken place that [a]the Scriptures[1124] of the prophets may be fulfilled." Then all the disciples [apt]left[863] Him and fled.

Jesus before Caiaphas

57 [a]And those who had seized Jesus led Him away[520] to [b]Caiaphas, the high priest,[749] where the scribes[1122] and the elders were gathered together.

58 But [a]Peter also was [ipf]following Him at a distance as far as the [b]courtyard of the high priest,[749] and [apt]entered in, and sat down with[3326] the [Ic]officers[5257] to see the outcome.[5056]

59 Now the chief priests and the whole [Ia]Council kept [ipf]trying to obtain false testimony against Jesus, in order that they might put Him to death;

60 and they did not find *any,* even though many false witnesses [apt]came forward. But later on [a]two [apt]came forward,

61 and said, "This man stated, '[a]I am able to destroy[2647] the [I]temple[3485] of God and to rebuild it [II]in three days.' "

62 And the high priest[749] [apt]stood up and said to Him, "Do You make no answer? What is it that these men are testifying against You?"

63 But [a]Jesus [ipf]kept silent. [b]And the high priest [apt]said to Him, "I [Ic]adjure[1844] You by[2596] [d]the living[2198] God, that You tell us whether You are [II]the Christ,[5547] [e]the Son of God."

64 Jesus *said to him, "[a]You have [ao]said it *yourself*; nevertheless I tell you, [I]hereafter you shall see [b]THE SON OF MAN SITTING AT THE RIGHT HAND[1188] OF POWER, and [c]COMING ON THE CLOUDS OF HEAVEN."[3772]

65 Then the high priest [a]tore[1284] his [I]robes,[2440] saying, "He has [ao]blasphemed![987] What further need do we have of witnesses?[3144] Behold, you have now [ao]heard the blasphemy;[988]

🔑 66 what do you think?" They [apt]answered and said, "[a]He is deserving[1777] of death!"

67 [a]Then they [b]spat in His face and beat Him with their fists; and others [I]slapped[4474] Him,

68 and said, "[a]Prophesy to us, You [I]Christ; who is the one who hit[3817] You?"

47 [I]Lit., *and with him*
49 [a]Matt. 23:7; 26:25
50 [a]Matt. 20:13; 22:12
51 [I]Lit., *extended the hand* [II]Lit., *took off* [a]Mark 14:47; Luke 22:50; John 18:10 [b]Luke 22:38 [c]Mark 14:47; Luke 22:50; John 18:10
52 [a]Gen. 9:6; Rev. 13:10
53 [I]A legion equaled 6,000 troops [a]Mark 5:9, 15; Luke 8:30 [b]Matt. 4:11
54 [a]Matt. 26:24
55 [a]Mark 12:35; 14:49; Luke 4:20; 19:47; 20:1; 21:37; John 7:14, 28; 8:2, 20; 18:20
56 [a]Matt. 26:24
57 [a]Matt. 26:57-68; *Mark 14:53-65; John 18:12f., 19-24* [b]Matt. 26:3
58 [I]Or, *servants* [a]John 18:15 [b]Matt. 26:3 [c]Matt. 5:25; John 7:32, 45f.; 19:6; Acts 5:22, 26
59 [I]Or, *Sanhedrin* [a]Matt. 5:22
60 [a]Deut. 19:15
61 [I]Or, *sanctuary* [II]Or, *after* [a]Matt. 27:40; Mark 14:58; 15:29; John 2:19; Acts 6:14
63 [I]Or, *charge You under oath* [II]I.e., the Messiah [a]Matt. 27:12, 14; John 19:9 [b]Matt. 26:63-66; Luke 22:67-71 [c]Lev. 5:1 [d]Matt. 16:16 [e]Matt. 4:3
64 [I]Or, *from now on* [a]Matt. 26:25 [b]Ps. 110:1; Mark 14:62 [c]Dan. 7:13; Matt. 16:27f.
65 [I]Or, *outer garments* [a]Num. 14:6; Mark 14:63; Acts 14:14
66 [a]Lev. 24:16; John 19:7

67 [I]Or possibly, *beat Him with rods* [a]Is. 50:6; Matt. 26:67, 68; Luke 22:63-65; John 18:22 [b]Matt. 27:30; Mark 10:34 **68** [I]I.e., the Messiah [a]Mark 14:65; Luke 22:64

🔑 **26:50** See note on Mt. 20:1-16, *hetairos* (2083), a comrade who attaches himself to someone for selfish purposes.
🔑 **26:66** See note on Mk. 3:28,29.

Peter's Denials

69 [a]Now Peter was [ipf]sitting outside[1854] in the [b]courtyard, and a certain servant-girl came to him and said, "You too were[2258] with Jesus the Galilean."

70 But he denied[720] *it* before them all, saying, "I do not know what you are talking about."

71 And when he had gone out to the gateway, another *servant-girl* saw him and [pin]*said to those who were there, "This man was with Jesus of Nazareth."

72 And again he denied *it* with an oath,[3727] "I do not know[1492] the man."

73 And a little later the bystanders came up and said to Peter, "Surely you too are *one* of them; [a]for the way you talk[2981] [I]gives you away."

74 Then he began to curse and swear, "I do not know[1492] the man!" And immediately a cock crowed.

75 And Peter remembered the word[4487] which Jesus had [pfp]said, "[a]Before a cock [ainf]crows, you will deny[533] Me three times." And he [apt]went out and wept bitterly.

Judas' Remorse

27 [a]Now when morning had come, all the chief priests[749] and the elders of the people took counsel against Jesus to put Him to death;

2 and they [apt]bound[1210] Him, and led Him away, and [a]delivered Him up to [b]Pilate the governor.

3 Then when [a]Judas, who had [apt]betrayed Him, saw that He had been condemned,[2632] he felt [aptp]remorse[3338] and returned[4762] [b]the thirty [I]pieces of silver to the chief priests[749] and elders,

4 saying, "I have [ao]sinned[264] by [apt]betraying innocent [an]blood."[129] But they said, "What is that to us? [a]See *to that* yourself!"

5 And he [apt]threw the pieces of silver into [a]the sanctuary[3485] and departed; and [b]he [apt]went away and hanged himself.

6 And the chief priests [apt]took the pieces of silver and said, "It is not lawful to [ainf]put them into the temple treasury, since it is the price of blood."

7 And they [apt]counseled together and with [I]the money bought the Potter's Field as a burial place for strangers.

8 [a]For this reason that field has been called the Field of Blood to this day.

9 Then that which was spoken through Jeremiah the prophet was fulfilled, saying, "[a]AND [I]THEY TOOK THE THIRTY PIECES OF SILVER, THE PRICE OF THE ONE WHOSE [pfpp]PRICE HAD BEEN SET by the sons of Israel;

10 [a]AND [I]THEY GAVE THEM FOR THE POTTER'S FIELD, AS THE LORD[2962] DIRECTED ME."

Jesus before Pilate

11 [a]Now Jesus stood before the governor, and the governor questioned[1905] Him, saying, "Are You the [b]King of the Jews?" And Jesus said to him, "[c]*It is as* you say."

12 And while He was being [aie]accused by the chief priests and elders, [a]He made no answer.[611]

13 Then Pilate [pin]*said to Him, "Do You not hear how many things they testify against You?"

14 And [a]He did not answer him with regard to even a *single* [I]charge, so that the governor was quite [pinf]amazed.

15 [a]Now at *the* feast the governor was [plpf]accustomed[1486] to [pinf]release[630] for the multitude *any* one prisoner whom they [ipf]wanted.

16 And they were holding at that time a notorious prisoner, called Barabbas.

17 When therefore they were gathered together, Pilate said to them, "Whom do you want me to release for you? Barabbas, or Jesus [a]who is called Christ?"[5547]

18 For he knew that because of envy they had [ao]delivered Him up.

19 And [a]while he was sitting on the judgment seat, his wife sent to him, saying, "Have nothing to do with that [b]righteous[1342] Man; for [I]last night I [ao]suf-

69 [a]Matt. 26:69-75; *Mark 14:66-72; Luke 22:55-62; John 18:16-18, 25-27* [b]Matt. 26:3

73 [I]Lit., *makes you evident* [a]Mark 14:70; Luke 22:59; John 18:26

75 [a]Matt. 26:34

1 [a]Mark 15:1; Luke 22:66; John 18:28

2 [a]Matt. 20:19 [b]Luke 3:1; 13:1; 23:12; Acts 3:13; 4:27; 1Tim. 6:13

3 [I]Or, *silver shekels* [a]Matt. 26:14 [b]Matt. 26:15

4 [a]Matt. 27:24

5 [a]Matt. 26:61; Luke 1:9, 21 [b]Acts 1:18

7 [I]Lit., *them*

8 [a]Acts 1:19

9 [I]Some mss. read *I took* [a]Zech. 11:12

10 [I]Some mss. read *I gave* [a]Zech. 11:13

11 [a]Matt. 27:11-14; *Mark 15:2-5; Luke 23:2, 3; John 18:29-38* [b]Matt. 2:2 [c]Matt. 26:25

12 [a]Matt. 26:63; John 19:9

14 [I]Lit., *word* [a]Matt. 27:12; Mark 15:5; Luke 23:9; John 19:9

15 [a]Matt. 27:15-26; *Mark 15:6-15; Luke 23:[17]-25;* John 18:39-19:16

17 [a]Matt. 1:16; 27:22

19 [I]Lit., *today* [a]John 19:13; Acts 12:21; 18:12, 16f.; 25:6, 10, 17 [b]Matt. 27:24

fered greatly [c]in a dream because of
Him."
20 But the chief priests and the elders persuaded[3982] the multitudes to
[a]ask for Barabbas, and to put Jesus to
death.[622]
21 But the governor answered and
said to them, "Which of the two[1417] do
you want me to release for you?" And
they said, "Barabbas."
22 Pilate *said to them, "Then what
shall I do with Jesus [a]who is called
Christ?" They all *said, "Let Him be
[aipp]crucified!"
23 And he said, "Why, what evil has
He [ao]done?" But they kept [ipf]shouting
all the more,[4057] saying, "Let Him be
crucified!"
24 And when Pilate saw that he was
accomplishing nothing, but rather that
[a]a riot was starting, he [apt]took water
and [ao] [b]washed his hands in front of the
multitude, saying, "I am innocent of
[1c]this Man's blood; [d]see *to that* yourselves."
25 And all the people answered and
said, "[a]His blood[129] *be* on us and on our
children!"
26 Then he released[630] Barabbas
[1]for them; but after having Jesus
[a]scourged,[5417] he delivered Him to be
crucified.

Jesus Is Mocked

27 [a]Then the soldiers of the governor [apt]took[3880] Jesus into [b]the Praetorium and gathered the whole *Roman*
[1c]cohort around Him.
28 And they [apt]stripped Him, and
[a]put a scarlet robe[5511] on Him.
29 [a]And after weaving[4120] a crown
of[1537] thorns, they put it on His head,
and a [1]reed in His right hand; and they
[apt]kneeled down before Him and
[ipf]mocked Him, saying, "[b]Hail,[5463] King
of the Jews!"
30 And [a]they [apt]spat on Him, and
took the reed and *began* to [ipf]beat[5180]
Him on the head.
31 [a]And after they had mocked Him,
they took His robe[5511] off and put His
garments on Him, and led Him away[520]
to crucify *Him.*
32 [a]And as they were coming out,
they found[2147] a man of [b]Cyrene named
Simon, [1]whom they pressed into service[29] to bear[142] His cross.[4716]

The Crucifixion

33 [a]And when they had come to a
place called [b]Golgotha, which means
Place of a Skull,
34 [a]they gave Him [b]wine to drink
[pfpp]mingled with gall; and after tasting[1089] *it,* He was unwilling to drink.
35 And when they had [apt]crucified
Him, [a]they divided up His garments
among themselves, [ppt]casting [1]lots;[2819]
36 and sitting down, they *began* to
[ipf] [a]keep watch[5083] over Him there.
37 And they put up above His head
the charge[156] against Him [1]which read,
"[a]THIS IS JESUS THE KING[935] OF
THE JEWS."
38 At that time two robbers[3027]
*were [pinp]crucified with Him, one on the
right[1188] and one on the left.
39 And those [ppt]passing by were
[ipf] [1]hurling abuse[987] at Him, [a]wagging[2795]
their heads,
40 and saying, "[a]You who *are going*
to [ppt]destroy[2647] the temple and [ppt]re-
build it in[1722] three days, save[4982] Yourself! [b]If You are the Son of God, come
down from the cross."[4716]
41 In the same way the chief
priests[749] also, along with the scribes
and elders,[4245] were [ppt]mocking *Him,*
and saying,
42 "[a]He saved others; [1]He cannot
[ainf]save Himself. [b]He is the King of Israel; let Him now [aim]come down from
the cross,[4716] and we shall believe[4100]
in Him.
43 "[a]HE [pfi]TRUSTS[3982] IN GOD; LET
HIM [aim]DELIVER *Him* now, IF HE TAKES
PLEASURE[2309] IN HIM; for He said, 'I am
the Son of God.'"
44 [a]And the robbers also who had
been crucified[4957] with Him were [ipf]cast-
ing the same insult at Him.

19 [c]Gen. 20:6; 31:11; Num. 12:6; Job 33:15; Matt. 1:20; 2:12f., 19, 22
20 [a]Acts 3:14
22 [a]Matt. 1:16
24 [1]Many mss. read *the blood of this righteous Man* [a]Matt. 26:5 [b]Deut. 21:6-8 [c]Matt. 27:19 [d]Matt. 27:4
25 [a]Josh. 2:19; Acts 5:28
26 [1]Or, *to them* [a]Mark 15:15; Luke 23:16; John 19:1
27 [1]Or, *battalion* [a]Matt. 27:27-31; *Mark 15:16-20* [b]Matt. 26:3; John 18:28, 33; 19:9 [c]Acts 10:1
28 [a]Mark 15:17; John 19:2
29 [1]Or, *staff (made of a reed)* [a]Mark 15:17; John 19:2 [b]Mark 15:18; John 19:3
30 [a]Matt. 26:67; Mark 10:34; 14:65; 15:19
31 [a]Mark 15:20
32 [1]Lit., *this one* [a]Matt. 27:32; *Mark 15:21; Luke 23:26;* John 19:17 [b]Acts 2:10; 6:9; 11:20; 13:1
33 [a]Matt. 27:34-44; *Mark 15:22-32; Luke 23:33-43; John 19:17-24* [b]Luke 23:33; John 19:17
34 [a]Ps. 69:21 [b]Mark 15:23
35 [1]Lit., *a lot* [a]Ps. 22:18
36 [a]Matt. 27:54
37 [1]Lit., *written* [a]Mark 15:26; Luke 23:38; John 19:19
39 [1]Or, *blaspheming* [a]Job 16:4; Ps. 22:7; 109:25; Lam. 2:15; Mark 15:29
40 [a]Matt. 26:61; John 2:19 [b]Matt. 27:42
42 [1]Or, *can He not save Himself* [a]Mark 15:31; Luke 23:35 [b]Matt. 27:37; Luke 23:37; John 1:49; 12:13
43 [a]Ps. 22:8
44 [a]Luke 23:39-43

45 [a]Now from the [I]sixth hour darkness[4655] [II]fell upon all the land until the [III]ninth hour.

46 And about the ninth hour Jesus cried out with a loud voice, saying, "[a]ELI, ELI, LAMA SABACHTHANI?" that is, "MY GOD, MY GOD, WHY HAST THOU FORSAKEN ME?"

47 And some of those who were standing there, when they heard it, *began* saying, "This man is calling for Elijah."

48 And [a]immediately[2112] one of them [apt]ran, and [apt]taking a sponge, he [apt]filled it with sour wine, and [apt]put it on a reed, and [ipf]gave Him a drink.

49 But the rest *of them* said, "[I]Let us see whether Elijah will come to save Him."[II]

50 And Jesus [a]cried out again with a loud voice, and yielded up[863] *His* spirit.[4151]

51 [a]And behold, [b]the veil of the temple[3485] was torn[4977] in two[1417] from top[509] to bottom, and [c]the earth shook; and the rocks were split,

52 and the tombs were opened; and many bodies of the [I]saints[40] who had [a]fallen [pfpp]asleep were raised;

53 and [apt]coming out of the tombs after His resurrection[1454] they entered [a]the holy[40] city and appeared to many.

54 [a]Now the centurion, and those who were with him [b]keeping guard[5083] over Jesus, when they [apt]saw [c]the earthquake and the things that were [apt]happening, became very frightened and said, "Truly this was [I][d]the Son of God!"

55 [a]And many women were there looking on from a distance, who had followed[190] Jesus from Galilee, [I][b]ministering to Him,

56 among whom was [a]Mary Magdalene, *along with* Mary the mother of James and Joseph, and [b]the mother of the sons of Zebedee.

Jesus Is Buried

57 [a]And when it [apt]was evening, there came a rich man from Arimathea, named Joseph, who himself [ao]had also become[3100] a disciple of Jesus.

58 This man [apt]went to Pilate and asked for the body[4983] of Jesus. Then Pilate ordered *it* to be given over *to him.*

59 And Joseph took the body and wrapped it in a clean[2513] linen cloth,

60 and laid it in his own new tomb, which he [ao]had hewn[2998] out in the rock; and he [apt]rolled [a]a large stone against the entrance of the tomb[3419] and went away.

61 And [a]Mary Magdalene was there, and the other Mary, sitting opposite the grave.[5028]

62 Now on the next day, which is *the one* after [a]the preparation, the chief priests and the Pharisees gathered together with Pilate,

63 and said, "Sir,[2962] we [ao]remember that when He was still [ppt]alive[2198] that deceiver said, '[a]After three days I *am to* [pin]rise again.'

64 "Therefore, give orders for the grave to be made secure until the third day, lest the disciples [apt]come and steal Him away and say to the people,[2992] 'He has [ao]risen from the dead,' and the last deception will be worse than the first."

65 Pilate said to them, "You have a [a]guard; go, [aim]make it *as* secure[805] as you know how."[1492]

66 And they [apt]went and [ao]made the grave secure,[805] and along with [a]the guard they set a [b]seal on [c]the stone.

Jesus Is Risen!

28 [a]Now after the Sabbath,[4521] as it began to dawn toward the first *day* of the week, [b]Mary Magdalene and the other Mary came to look at the grave.[5028]

2 And behold, a severe earthquake had [ao]occurred, for [a]an angel of the Lord [apt]descended from heaven[3772] and

45 [I]I.e., noon [II]Or, *occurred* [III]I.e., 3 p.m. [a]Matt. 27:45-56; *Mark 15:33-41; Luke 23:44-49*
46 [a]Ps. 22:1
48 [a]Ps. 69:21; Mark 15:36; Luke 23:36; John 19:29
49 [I]Lit., *Permit that we see* [II]Some early mss. add *And another took a spear and pierced His side, and there came out water and blood.* (cf. John 19:34)
50 [a]Mark 15:37; Luke 23:46; John 19:30
51 [a]Matt. 27:51-56; *Mark 15:38-41;* Luke 23:47-49 [b]Ex. 26:31ff.; Mark 15:38; Luke 23:45; Heb. 9:3 [c]Matt. 27:54
52 [I]Or, *holy ones* [a]Acts 7:60
53 [a]Matt. 4:5
54 [I]Or possibly, *a son of God* or *a son of a god* [a]Mark 15:39; Luke 23:47 [b]Matt. 27:36 [c]Matt. 27:51 [d]Matt. 4:3; 27:43
55 [I]Or, *waiting on* [a]Mark 15:40f.; Luke 23:49; John 19:25 [b]Mark 15:41; Luke 8:2, 3
56 [a]Matt. 28:1; Mark 15:40, 47; 16:9; Luke 8:2; John 19:25; 20:1, 18 [b]Matt. 20:20
57 [a]Matt. 27:57-61; *Mark 15:42-47; Luke 23:50-56; John 19:38-42*
60 [a]Matt. 27:66; 28:2; Mark 16:4
61 [a]Matt. 27:56; 28:1
62 [a]Mark 15:42; Luke 23:54; John 19:14, 31, 42
63 [a]Matt. 16:21; 17:23; 20:19; Mark 8:31; 9:31; 10:34; Luke 9:22; 18:31-33
65 [a]Matt. 27:66; 28:11
66 [a]Matt. 27:65; 28:11 [b]Dan. 6:17 [c]Matt. 27:60; 28:2; Mark 16:4

1 [a]Matt. 28:1-8; *Mark 16:1-8; Luke 24:1-10;* John 20:1-8 [b]Matt. 27:56, 61 **2** [a]Luke 24:4; John 20:12

[apt]came and rolled away [b]the stone and
sat upon it.
3 And [a]his appearance[2397] was like
lightning, and his garment as white as
snow;
4 and the guards[5083] shook for
fear[5401] of him, and became like dead
men.
5 And the angel answered and said
to the women, "[1a]Do not be afraid;[5399]
for I know that you are looking for Jesus
who has been [pfpp]crucified.
6 "He is not here, for He has [ao]risen,
[a]just as He said. Come, see the place
where He was [ipf]lying.
7 "And [apt]go quickly and tell His disciples that He has risen from the dead;
and behold, He is going before[4254] you
[a]into Galilee, there you will see Him;
behold, I have [ao]told you."
8 And they [apt]departed quickly from
the tomb3419 with[3326] fear and great joy
and ran to report it to His disciples.
9 And behold, Jesus met them
[1]and greeted them. And they [apt]came
up and took hold of His feet and worshiped Him.
10 Then Jesus [pin]*said to them,
"[1a]Do not [pim]be afraid;[5399] go and take
word to [b]My brethren[80] to leave
[c]for Galilee, and there they shall see
Me."
11 Now while they were on their
way, behold, some of [a]the guard [apt]came
into the city and reported to the chief
priests all that had happened.
12 And when they had assembled
with the elders and counseled together,
they gave a large sum of money to the
soldiers,
13 and said, "You are to [aim]say, 'His
disciples [apt]came by night and stole Him
away while we were asleep.'
14 "And if this should come to
[a]the governor's ears, we will win[3982] him
over and [1]keep you out of trouble."
15 And they [apt]took the money and
did as they had been instructed;[1321] and
this story[3056] was widely [aop] [a]spread
among the Jews, *and is* [b]to this day.

The Great Commission

16 But the eleven disciples[3101] proceeded [a]to Galilee, to the mountain
which Jesus had designated.[5021]
17 And when they saw Him, they
worshiped *Him*; but [a]some were doubtful.
18 And Jesus [apt]came up and spoke
to them, saying, "[a]All authority[1849] has
been [aop]given to Me in heaven and on
earth.[1093]
🔑 19 [apt]"[a]Go therefore and [aim] [b]make
disciples[3100] of [c]all the nations, [d]bap-
tizing[907] them in the name[3686] of the
Father[3962] and the Son and the Holy[40]
Spirit,[4151]
20 teaching[1321] them to observe all
that I [ao]commanded you; and lo, [a]I am
with you [1]always, even to [b]the end[4930]
of the age."

2 [b]Matt. 27:66; Mark 16:4
3 [a]Dan. 7:9; 10:6; Mark 9:3; John 20:12; Acts 1:10
5 [1]Or, *Stop being afraid* [a]Matt. 14:27; 28:10; Rev. 1:17
6 [a]Matt. 12:40; 16:21; 27:63
7 [a]Matt. 26:32; 28:10, 16; Mark 16:7
9 [1]Lit., *saying hello*
10 [1]Or, *Stop being afraid* [a]Matt. 14:27; 28:5 [b]John 20:17; Rom. 8:29; Heb. 2:11f., 17 [c]Matt. 26:32; 28:7, 16
11 [a]Matt. 27:65, 66
14 [1]Lit., *make you free from care* [a]Matt. 27:2
15 [a]Matt. 9:31; Mark 1:45 [b]Matt. 27:8
16 [a]Matt. 26:32; 28:7, 10; Mark 15:41; 16:7
17 [a]Mark 16:11
18 [a]Dan. 7:13f.; Matt. 11:27; 26:64; Rom. 14:9; Eph. 1:20-22; Phil. 2:9f.; Col. 2:10; 1Pet. 3:22
19 [a]Mark 16:15f. [b]Matt. 13:52; Acts 1:8; 14:21 [c]Matt. 25:32; Luke 24:47 [d]Acts 2:38; 8:16; Rom. 6:3; 1Cor. 1:13, 15ff.; Gal. 3:27
20 [1]Lit., *all the days* [a]Matt. 18:20; Acts 18:10 [b]Matt. 13:39

🔑 **28:19** See notes on I Cor. 10:2; I Pet. 3:20,21 and also *baptisma* (908), baptism, and *baptizō* (907), to baptize.

The Gospel According to

MARK

The book of Mark is the shortest of the four Gospels. About 93% of the material in Mark is covered by Matthew and Luke, but Mark does give more vivid details in his brief account. The Gospel of Mark emphasizes the superhuman power of Jesus. Christ is presented as God's Son in action, demonstrating His divinity by His miracles. Mark tells more of what Jesus did and less of what Jesus said. Like a motion picture camera, the author rushes from one dynamic scene to the next. He uses "immediately" about 40 times to make the transitions. Judging from only a few references to the Old Testament, his translations of Aramaic expressions, and the themes of power, it is safe to say that Mark's Gospel was aimed at those who lived outside Palestine.

Very early tradition states that Mark, the son of Mary of Jerusalem (Acts 12:12), wrote this Gospel. We know that since John Mark was a cousin of Barnabas (Col. 4:10) he may have been a Levite (Acts 4:36). Many scholars believe that Mark was the young man described in Mark 14:51,52. Mark traveled with the Apostle Paul and Barnabas on their first missionary journey (Acts 12:25), but Mark turned back (Acts 13:13). For this reason, Paul refused to consider taking him along on the second missionary journey (Acts 15:36-39). Since both Paul and Barnabas had strong opposite feelings about the matter, they decided to go different directions, Paul with Silas and Barnabas with Mark. However, much later, Paul felt differently about Mark (II Tim. 4:11).

Preaching of John the Baptist

1 The beginning of the gospel[2098] of Jesus Christ,[5547] [1a]the Son of God.[2316]

2 [a]As it is [pfpp]written in Isaiah the prophet,[4396]

"[b]BEHOLD, I SEND MY MESSENGER[32] BEFORE YOUR FACE,
WHO WILL PREPARE YOUR WAY;[3598]

3 [a]THE VOICE OF ONE CRYING IN THE WILDERNESS,
'[aim]MAKE READY THE WAY OF THE LORD,
[pim]MAKE HIS PATHS STRAIGHT.' "

4 John the Baptist[907] [ao]appeared in the wilderness [ppt 1a]preaching[2784] a baptism[908] of repentance[3341] for[1519] the [an b]forgiveness[859] of sins.

5 And all the country of Judea [ipf]was going out to him, and all the people of Jerusalem; and they were being [ipf]baptized by him in the Jordan River, confessing[1843] their sins.

6 And John was clothed with camel's hair and *wore* [a]a leather belt[2223] around his waist, and [1]his diet was locusts and wild honey.

7 And he was [ipf 1]preaching,[2784] and saying, "After me One is coming who is mightier than I, and I am not fit to [apt]stoop down[2955] and [ainf]untie[3089] the thong[2438] of His sandals.

🔑 8 "I [ao]baptized you [1]with water; but He will [ft]baptize you [1]with the Holy Spirit."

The Baptism of Jesus

9 [a]And it came about in those days that Jesus [b]came from Nazareth in Galilee, and was baptized[907] by John in the Jordan.

10 And immediately[2117] coming up out of the water, He saw the heavens [1]opening, and the Spirit like a dove descending upon Him;

11 and a voice came out of the heavens: "[a]Thou art My beloved[27] Son, in Thee I am [ao]well-pleased."

1 [1]Many mss. do not contain *the Son of God* [a]Matt. 4:3
2 [a]Mark 1:2-8: *Matt. 3:1-11; Luke 3:2-16* [b]Mal. 3:1; Matt. 11:10; Luke 7:27
3 [a]Is. 40:3; Matt. 3:3; Luke 3:4; John 1:23
4 [1]Or, *proclaiming* [a]Acts 13:24 [b]Luke 1:
6 [1]Lit., *he was eating* [a]2Kin. 1:8
7 [1]Or, *proclaiming*
8 [1]The Gr. here can be translated *in, with* or *by*
9 [a]Mark 1:9-11: *Matt. 3:13-17; Luke 3:21, 22* [b]Matt. 2:23; Luke 2:51
10 [1]Or, *being parted*
11 [a]Ps. 2:7; Is. 42:1; Matt. 3:17; 12:18; Mark 9:7; Luke 3:22

🔑 **1:8** See notes on Acts 1:5; 2:1-13; 11:14-18; 19:1-7.

12 [a]And immediately the Spirit *impelled Him *to go* out into the wilderness.
13 And He was in the wilderness
forty days being [ppt]tempted[3985] by
[a]Satan;[4567] and He was with the wild
beasts,[2342] and the angels were [ipf]minis-
tering to Him.

Jesus Preaches in Galilee

14 [a]And after John had been
[I]taken into custody, Jesus came into Galilee, [IIb]preaching[2784] the gospel[2098] of
God,
15 and saying, "[a]The time[2540] [pfip]is
fulfilled,[4137] and the kingdom[932] of God
[pfi]is at hand;[1448] [pim] [b]repent[3340] and
[pim] [I]believe[4100] in the gospel."
16 [a]And as He was [ppt]going along
by the Sea of Galilee, He saw Simon
and Andrew, the brother of Simon, casting a net[293] in the sea; for they were
fishermen.
17 And Jesus said to them, "Follow
Me, and I will make you become fishers
of men."[444]
18 And they immediately [apt]left the
nets[1350] and followed Him.
19 And going on a little farther, He
saw [I]James the *son* of Zebedee, and John
his brother, who were also in the boat
mending[2675] the nets.
20 And immediately He called them;
and they [apt]left their father Zebedee in
the boat with the hired servants,[3411] and
went away [I]to follow Him.
21 [a]And they [pin]*went into Capernaum; and immediately on the Sabbath[4521] [b]He [apt]entered the synagogue
and *began* to [ipf]teach.
22 And [a]they were [ipf]amazed at His
teaching; for He was teaching them as
one [ppf]having authority, and not as the
scribes.[1122]
23 And just then there was in their
synagogue a man with an unclean spirit;
and he cried out,
24 saying, "[a]What do we have to
do with You, Jesus [I]of [b]Nazareth? Have
You come to destroy us? I know who
You are—[c]the Holy One of God!"
25 And Jesus rebuked him, saying,
"Be quiet, and come out of him!"
26 And throwing him into convulsions, the unclean spirit [apt]cried out with
a loud voice, and came out of him.
27 And they were all [a]amazed, so
that they [pinf]debated among themselves,
saying, "What is this? A new[2537] teaching
with authority! He commands[2004] even
the unclean spirits, and they obey[5219]
Him."
28 And immediately the news about
Him went out everywhere into all the
surrounding district of Galilee.

Multitudes Healed

29 [a]And immediately [I]after they had
come [b]out of the synagogue, they came
into the house of Simon and Andrew,
with [II]James and John.
30 Now Simon's mother-in-law was
lying [ppt]sick with a fever; and immediately[2117] they *spoke to Him about
her.
31 And He came to her and raised
her up,[1453] taking her by the hand, and
the fever left her, and she [ipf] [I]waited
on[1247] them.
32 [a]And [b]when evening had come,
[b]after the sun had set, they *began*
bringing[5342] to Him all who [ppt]were ill[2560]
and those who were [ppt] [c]demon-
possessed.[1139]
33 And the whole [a]city had gathered[1996] at the door.
34 And He [a]healed many who were
[ppt]ill with various[4164] diseases, and cast
out many demons;[1140] and He was not
permitting the demons[1140] to speak, because they [I]knew who He was.
35 [a]And in the early morning, while
it was still dark, He arose[450] and went
out and departed to a lonely place, and
[b]was [ipf]praying there.
36 And Simon and his companions
hunted for Him;
37 and they found Him, and [pin]*said
to Him, "Everyone is looking for You."
38 And He [pin]*said to them, "Let
us go[71] somewhere else to the towns
nearby, in order that I may [I]preach[2784]

12 [a]Mark 1:12, 13: *Matt. 4:1-11; Luke 4:1-13*

13 [a]Matt. 4:10

14 [I]Lit., *delivered up* [II]Or, *proclaiming* [a]Matt. 4:12 [b]Matt. 4:23

15 [I]Or, *put your trust in* [a]Gal. 4:4; Eph. 1:10; 1Tim. 2:6; Titus 1:3 [b]Matt. 3:2; Acts 20:21

16 [a]Mark 1:16-20: *Matt. 4:18-22;* Luke 5:2-11; John 1:40-42

19 [I]Or, *Jacob*

20 [I]Lit., *after Him*

21 [a]Mark 1:21-28: *Luke 4:31-37* [b]Matt. 4:23; Mark 1:39; 10:1

22 [a]Matt. 7:28

24 [I]Lit., *the Nazarene* [a]Matt. 8:29 [b]Matt. 2:23; Mark 10:47; 14:67; 16:6; Luke 4:34; 24:19; Acts 24:5 [c]Luke 1:35; 4:34; John 6:69; Acts 3:14

27 [a]Mark 10:24, 32; 16:5, 6

29 [I]Some mss. read *after He had come out, He came* [II]Or, *Jacob* [a]Mark 1:29-31: *Matt. 8:14, 15; Luke 4:38, 39* [b]Mark 1:21, 23

31 [I]Or, *served*

32 [a]Mark 1:32-34: *Matt. 8:16, 17; Luke 4:40, 41* [b]Matt. 8:16; Luke 4:40 [c]Matt. 4:24

33 [a]Mark 1:21

34 [I]Some mss. read *knew Him to be Christ* [a]Matt. 4:23

35 [a]Mark 1:35-38: *Luke 4:42, 43* [b]Matt. 14:23; Luke 5:16

38 [I]Or, *proclaim*

there also; for that is what I came out for."

39 [a]And He went into their synagogues throughout all Galilee, [I]preaching and [ppt]casting out the demons.[1140]

40 [a]And a leper *came to Him, beseeching Him and [b]falling on his knees before Him, and saying to Him, "If You are willing, You can make me clean."

41 And moved with compassion, He stretched out His hand, and touched him, and *said to him, "I am willing; be cleansed."

42 And immediately the leprosy left him and he was cleansed.

43 And He sternly [apt]warned[1690] him and immediately sent him away,

44 and He *said to him, "[a]See that you say nothing to anyone; but [b]go, show yourself to the priest and [c]offer for your cleansing what Moses commanded,[4367] for a testimony to them."

🗝 45 But he went out and began to [a]proclaim[2784] it freely and to [a]spread[1310] the news about, to such an extent that [I]Jesus could no longer publicly enter a city, but [II]stayed out[1854] in unpopulated areas; and [b]they were [ipf]coming to Him from everywhere.

The Paralytic Healed

2 And when He had come back to Capernaum several days afterward, it was heard[191] that He was at home.

2 And [a]many were gathered together, so that there was no longer room, even near the door; and He was speaking[2980] the word[3056] to them.

3 [a]And they *came, bringing to Him a [b]paralytic,[3885] [ppt]carried by four men.

4 And being [ppt]unable to [I]get to[4331] Him because of the crowd, they [a]removed the roof [II]above Him; and when they had dug an opening, they let down the pallet on which the [b]paralytic was lying.

5 And Jesus seeing their faith[4102] [pin]*said to the paralytic, "My [I]son, [a]your sins are [pinf]forgiven."

6 But there were some of the scribes sitting there and reasoning[1260] in their hearts,

7 "Why does this man speak that way? He is blaspheming; [a]who can forgive sins [I]but God alone?"

8 And immediately Jesus, aware [I]in His spirit[4151] that they were [pin]reasoning that way within themselves, *said to them, "Why are you reasoning about these things in your hearts?

9 "Which is easier, to say to the [a]paralytic, 'Your sins are [pinp]forgiven'; or to say, 'Arise, and take up your pallet and [pim]walk'?

10 "But in order that you may [pl-aosb]know that the Son of Man has authority[1849] on earth[1093] to forgive sins"—[863] He *said to the paralytic—

11 "I say to you, rise, take up your pallet and go home."

12 And he rose and immediately [apt]took up the pallet and went out in the sight of all; so that they were all [pinf]amazed[1839] and [a]were [pinf]glorifying[1392] God, saying, "[b]We have never seen anything like this."

13 And He went out again by the seashore; and [a]all the multitude were [ipf]coming to Him, and He was [ipf]teaching them.

Levi (Matthew) Called

14 [a]And as He [ppt]passed by, He saw [b]Levi the *son* of Alphaeus sitting in the tax office,[5058] and He *said to him, "[c]Follow Me!" And he rose[450] and followed Him.

15 And it [I]came about that He was reclining *at the table* in his house, and many [II]tax-gatherers[5057] and sinners[268] [III]were [ipf]dining with Jesus and His disciples; for there were many of them, and they were following Him.

16 And when [a]the scribes of the Pharisees saw that He was [ppt]eating with the sinners[268] and tax-gatherers, they

39 [I]Or, *proclaiming* [a]Matt. 4:23; 9:35; Mark 1:23; 3:1

40 [a]Mark 1:40-44: *Matt. 8:2-4; Luke 5:12-14* [b]Matt. 8:2; Mark 10:17; Luke 5:12

44 [a]Matt. 8:4 [b]Matt. 8:4 [c]Lev. 14:1-32

45 [I]Lit., *He* [II]Lit., *was* [a]Matt. 28:15; Luke 5:15 [b]Mark 2:2, 13; 3:7; Luke 5:17; John 6:2

2 [a]Mark 1:45; 2:13

3 [a]Mark 2:3-12: *Matt. 9:2-8; Luke 5:18-26* [b]Matt. 4:24

4 [I]Lit., *bring to* [II]Lit., *where He was* [a]Luke 5:19 [b]Matt. 4:24

5 [I]Lit., *child* [a]Matt. 9:2

7 [I]Lit., *if not one, God* [a]Is. 43:25

8 [I]Lit., *by*

9 [a]Matt. 4:24

12 [a]Matt. 9:8 [b]Matt. 9:33

13 [a]Mark 1:45

14 [a]Mark 2:14-17: *Matt. 9:9-13; Luke 5:27-32* [b]Matt. 9:9 [c]Matt. 8:22

15 [I]Lit., *comes* [II]I.e., Collectors of Roman taxes for profit [III]Lit., *were reclining with*

16 [a]Luke 5:30; Acts 23:9

🗝 **1:45** See note on I Pet. 3:18-20 and also *kērussō* (2784), to preach, proclaim.

began saying to His disciples, "[b]Why is
He eating and drinking with tax-gatherers and sinners?"[268]
17 And hearing this, Jesus *said
to them, "[a]*it is* not those who are
healthy[2480] who need a physician,2395 but
those who are sick; I did not come to
call the righteous,[1342] but sinners."[268]
18 [a]And John's disciples[3101] and the
Pharisees were [ppt]fasting;3522 and they
*came and *said to Him, "Why do John's
disciples and the disciples of the Pharisees fast, but Your disciples do not
fast?"
19 And Jesus said to them, "While
the bridegroom is with them, [I]the
attendants[5207] of the bridegroom do not
[pinf]fast, do they? So long as they have
the bridegroom with them, they cannot
[pinf]fast.
20 "But the [a]days will come when
the bridegroom is taken away from
them, and then they will fast in that
day.
21 "No one sews [I]a patch of unshrunk cloth on an old garment; otherwise [II]the patch[4138] pulls away from it,
the new from the old, and a worse5501
tear[4978] results.
22 "And no one puts[906] new[3501]
wine[3631] into old [I]wineskins; otherwise
the wine will burst the skins, and the
wine is lost, and the skins *as well;* but
one puts new wine into fresh wineskins."

Question of the Sabbath

23 [a]And it came about that He was
[pinf]passing through the grainfields on the
Sabbath,4521 and His disciples began to
make their way along[3598,4160] 756 while
[b]picking the heads *of grain.*
24 And the Pharisees were saying
to Him, "See here, [a]why are they doing
what is not lawful on the Sabbath?"
25 And He *said to them, "Have
you never read what David did when
he was in need and became hungry,[3983]
he and his companions:
26 how he entered the house of God
in the time of [a]Abiathar *the* high priest,
and ate the [I]consecrated bread,[4286]
which [b]is not lawful for *anyone* to eat
except the priests, and he gave *it* also
to those who were with him?"
27 And He was saying to them,
"[a]The Sabbath [I]was made [II]for man,[444]
and [b]not man [II]for the Sabbath.
28 "Consequently, the Son of Man
is Lord even of the Sabbath."

Jesus Heals on the Sabbath

3 [a]And He [b]entered again into a synagogue; and a man was there with
a withered hand.
2 And [a]they were [ipf]watching Him
to see if He would [ft]heal him on the Sabbath,4521 [b]in order that they might accuse
Him.
3 And He *said to the man with the
withered hand, "[I]Rise and *come* forward!"
4 And He *said to them, "Is it lawful
on the Sabbath [ainf]to do[4160] good[18] or
[ainf]to do harm,[2554] to save[4982] a life or
to kill?" But they [ipf]kept silent.
5 And after [a]looking around4017 at
them with anger,[3709] grieved at their
hardness[4457] of heart, He *said to the
man, "Stretch out your hand." And he
stretched it out, and his hand was
restored.[600]
6 And the Pharisees [apt]went out and
immediately[2112] *began* [ipf] [I]taking counsel
with the [a]Herodians against Him, *as to*
how they might destroy Him.
7 [a]And Jesus withdrew to the sea
with His disciples; and [b]a great multitude
from Galilee followed; and *also* from Judea,
8 and from Jerusalem, and from
[a]Idumea, and beyond the Jordan, and
the vicinity of [b]Tyre and Sidon, a great
multitude heard of all that He was doing
and came to Him.
9 [a]And He told His disciples that a
boat should stand ready[4342] for Him because of the multitude, in order that
they might not crowd Him;
10 for He had [a]healed many, with
the result that all those who had
[b]afflictions [pinf]pressed about Him in order
to [aosb] [c]touch Him.

---

16 [b]Matt. 9:11
17 [a]Matt. 9:12, 13; Luke 5:31, 32
18 [a]Mark 2:18-22: *Matt. 9:14-17; Luke 5:33-38*
19 [I]Lit., *sons of the bridalchamber*
20 [a]Matt. 9:15; Luke 17:22
21 [I]Lit., *that which is put on* [II]Lit., *that which fills up*
22 [I]I.e., skins used as bottles
23 [a]Mark 2:23-28: *Matt. 12:1-8; Luke 6:1-5* [b]Deut. 23:25
24 [a]Matt. 12:2
26 [I]Or, *showbread;* lit., *loaves of presentation* [a]1Sam. 21:1; 2Sam. 8:17; 1Chr. 24:6 [b]Lev. 24:9
27 [I]Or, *came into being* [II]Lit., *for the sake of* [a]Ex. 23:12; Deut. 5:14 [b]Col. 2:16

1 [a]Mark 3:1-6: *Matt. 12:9-14; Luke 6:6-11* [b]Mark 1:21, 39
2 [a]Luke 6:7; 14:1; 20:20 [b]Matt. 12:10; Luke 6:7; 11:54
3 [I]Lit., *Arise into the midst*
5 [a]Luke 6:10
6 [I]Lit., *giving* [a]Matt. 22:16; Mark 12:13
7 [a]Mark 3:7-12: *Matt. 12:15, 16; Luke 6:17-19* [b]Matt. 4:25; Luke 6:17
8 [a]Josh. 15:1, 21; Ezek. 35:15; 36:5 [b]Matt. 11:21
9 [a]Mark 4:1; Luke 5:1-3
10 [a]Matt. 4:23 [b]Mark 5:29, 34; Luke 7:21 [c]Matt. 9:21; 14:36; Mark 6:56; 8:22

11 And whenever the unclean spirits
[ipf]beheld Him, they would [ipf]fall down
before Him and [ipf]cry out, saying, "You
are [a]the Son of God!"
12 And He [a]earnestly4183 [ipf]warned
them not to [aosb] [I]make Him known.5318

The Twelve Are Chosen

13 And He *went up to [a]the mountain and *[b]summoned those whom He
Himself [ipf]wanted, and they came to
Him.
14 And He appointed***4160*** twelve[I],
that they might be with Him, and that
He [psa]might send***649*** them out***649*** [pinf]to
preach,***2784***
15 and to [pinf]have authority***1849*** to
cast out the [art]demons.1140
16 And He appointed the twelve:
[a]Simon (to whom He gave the name Peter),
17 and [I]James, the *son* of Zebedee,
and John the brother of [I]James (to them
He gave the name Boanerges, which
means, "Sons***5207*** of Thunder");
18 and Andrew, and Philip, and Bartholomew, and Matthew, and Thomas,
and [I]James the *son* of Alphaeus, and
Thaddaeus, and Simon the [II]Zealot;
19 and Judas Iscariot, who also betrayed Him.

20 And He *came [Ia]home, and the
[b]multitude *gathered again, [c]to such an
extent that they could not even eat
[II]a meal.
21 And when [a]His own [I]people heard
of this, they went out to take custody
of Him; for they were saying, "[b]He [ao]has
lost His senses."***1839***
22 And the scribes who [apt]came
down [a]from Jerusalem were [ipf]saying,
"He is possessed by [Ib]Beelzebul," and
"[c]He casts out the demons1140 by the
ruler of the demons."1140
23 [a]And He [apt]called them to Himself
and began [ipf]speaking to them in [b]para-
bles, "How can [c]Satan [pinf]cast out Satan?***4567***
24 "And if a kingdom is divided
against itself, that kingdom cannot
stand.
25 "And if a house is divided against
itself, that house will not be able to
stand.***2476***
26 "And if [a]Satan [ao]has risen up***450***
against himself and is divided, he cannot
stand, but [I]he is finished!
27 "[a]But no one can enter the strong
man's house and [ainf]plunder his property
unless he first binds the strong man,
and then he will plunder his house.
🗝 28 "[a]Truly281 I say to you, all sins***265***
shall be forgiven the sons of men, and

11 [a]Matt. 4:3
12 [I]Or, *reveal who He was* [a]Matt. 8:4
13 [a]Matt. 5:1; Luke 6:12 [b]Matt. 10:1; Mark 6:7; Luke 9:1
14 [I]Some early mss. add *whom He named apostles*
16 [a]Mark 3:16-19: *Matt. 10:2-4; Luke 6:14-16;* Acts 1:13
17 [I]Or, *Jacob*
18 [I]Or, *Jacob* [II]Or, *Cananaean*
20 [I]Lit., *into a house* [II]Lit., *bread* [a]Mark 2:1; 7:17; 9:28 [b]Mark 1:45; 3:7 [c]Mark 6:31
21 [I]Or, *kinsmen* [a]Mark 3:31f. [b]John 10:20; Acts 26:24
22 [I]Or, *Beezebul; others read Beelzebub* [a]Matt. 15:1 [b]Matt. 10:25; 11:18 [c]Matt. 9:34
23 [a]Mark 3:23-27: *Matt. 12:25-29; Luke 11:17-22* [b]Matt. 13:3ff.; Mark 4:2ff. [c]Matt. 4:10
26 [I]Lit., *he has an end* [a]Matt. 4:10
27 [a]Is. 49:24, 25
28 [a]Matt. 12:31, 32; Mark 3:28-30; Luke 12:10

🗝 **3:28-29** This important saying of our Lord referring to the blasphemy against the Holy Spirit occurs also in Mt. 12:31,32 and Lk. 12:10. It speaks of God's willingness and ability to forgive anyone of any sin and of all their sins put together. It is to be noted that these words of the Lord were spoken immediately after the accusation was made against Him that the works He was doing were done by the power of Beelzebul, the chief of the demons (see Mt. 12:22-30; Mk. 3:20-27). In Lk. 12:10 the Lord's saying about the blasphemy against the Holy Spirit is separated from the context of the discussion concerning Jesus and Beelzebul which is given in Lk. 11:14-23. The words of Christ become far more understandable if we examine what occasioned them. What the Lord wanted to teach after this discussion regarding the activity of the devil among men was this: The devil is really not the countertype of the Lord Jesus in the plan of man's salvation, but he is the countertype of the Holy Spirit whose function is to convict unto repentance or reprove the world of sin, of righteousness, and of judgment (Jn. 16:8-15). The devil counteracts this conviction. The verb that is translated as "convict" in Jn. 16:8 is *elegxei* which means "to bring under conviction." The Holy Spirit here is presented as the one who brings judgment upon the devil. The two are counteracting each other. The first statement that is made by Christ is that each sin (*hamartia,* 266), all sins together (*pasa,* 3956) and blasphemy (*blasphēmia,* 988) shall be forgiven. Mark 3:28, instead of saying every sin and blasphemy, says *panta, "all sins," the neuter plural of pas* (3956). The word "blasphemies" means to say something which hurts a person. *Hamartia* is the inclusive name of all kinds of sins, missing the mark of any kind which God has set for man's goal. What is stated in this first word is that God is both ready and able to forgive anything. In

(continued on next page)

whatever blasphemies[988] they utter;
29 but [a]whoever blasphemes[987]
against the Holy Spirit[4151] never has forgiveness, but is guilty of[1777] an eternal
sin"—[265]
30 because they were saying, "He
has an unclean spirit."
31 [a]And His mother and His
brothers[80] *arrived, and standing outside[1854] they sent *word* to Him, and
called Him.
32 And a multitude [ipf]was sitting
around Him, and they *said to Him, "Behold, Your mother and Your brothers[I]
are outside looking for You."
33 And answering them, He *said,

29 [a]Luke 12:10

31 [a]Mark 3:31-35: *Matt. 12:46-50; Luke 8:19-21*

32 [I]Later mss. add *and Your sisters*

(continued from previous page)

order to comprehend this, we must first understand the meaning of the word "forgiven," (*aphiēmi*, 863). It means to send away, to remove the sin from the sinner, so that he is free from it in order that the sin can never be found and charged against him before the judgment seat of God. It is not overlooking the sin, *paresis* (3929), but removing the sin from the sinner, *aphesis* (859). In this connection see note on Rom. 3:25. Secondly, observe that this verb is in the passive voice, which means any and all sins will be removed by God. God must be understood as the agent who removes the sin from the sinner. This is particularly the function of Jesus Christ who took upon Himself man's sin. We must remember however, that no personality of the triune God acts independently, but always in complete and united agreement and cooperation with the other personalities of the Trinity. Thus the agent of "shall be forgiven," (*aphethēsetai*), must be understood to be God in general and Christ is particular. Thirdly, this verb "shall be forgiven" is in the punctiliar future which means that it will be taken away each time that it is necessary to do so, and it will be done repetitively. It indicates that the forgiveness which man experiences from God is available whenever man asks for it in true repentance. The objects of this forgiveness are "the sons of men" (Mk. 3:28), "men" (Mt. 12:31) and "him" (Lk. 12:10). For a complete examination of the context that gave rise to this saying of Jesus, see the Editor's book entitled, *The Demon World and Jesus*.

In Mk. 3:28 we have *panta ta hamartēmata,* "all the sins." The word for "sins" here is *hamartēmatā* (265) and not *hamartia* as in Mt. 12:31. *Hamartēma* (singular), as all nouns ending in *ma,* indicates the result of an action. In this instance, *hamartēmata* (plural) indicates sins as individual acts or the bad reputation resulting from them. The comprehensiveness of the forgiveness which God can give to the sinner is made very clear here. Not only all sin (*hamartia)* or sinfulness in itself, but also the individual acts of sin, as well as their ill repute brought upon the sinner, are removed. This forgiveness, however, we know from other Scriptures is not automatic, but depends on our true repentance. Every sin is forgiven by God consequent to man's repentance, and man's repentance is consequent to the activity of the Holy Spirit in a man's life. If man resists that activity of the Holy Spirit, he will be unconvicted of either his sinfulness in general or his sin in particular and its ill repute; if man is unconvicted by the Holy Spirit, he will not repent. Consequently, God will not remove that sin or its effects. (For the meaning of the true repentance and following Christ see the Editor's book, *Who Is Worth Following* on the first two commandments of Christ—"Repent and follow after me.")

Mark adds something which the other two evangelists do not in this first statement about God's readiness and ability to forgive all sin and blasphemy: "Whatever blasphemies they utter." More literally this should be translated: "and blasphemies, (the reports that men will give which will hurt God's reputation among men) whatever these blasphemies may be if they shall blaspheme." The verb *blasphēmesōsin,* "will blaspheme," is in the punctiliar future which means at one time and not continuously as a perpetual and uninterrupted mode of life. The Lord is here declaring that no matter how careful we are, we can never live in such a perfect way as to always cause others to believe all that they should about our God whom we represent among them. Our actions portray a different God than what our mouths proclaim. Many times we give the wrong impression to others about our Lord whom we profess to follow. These wrong reputations of God, *blasphēmiai,* will be forgiven. We who love Him allow His Holy Spirit to convict us of our shortcomings in adequately representing God among others. As a result of that conviction, there is the removal of the harm which we have done to the testimony of God.

For a more complete understanding of what these blasphemies are which are generally spoken of by Mark, we must go to Mt. 12:32. Jesus said, "And whoever shall speak a word against the Son of Man, it shall be forgiven him." The Son of Man here is Jesus Christ. In order for a sinner to appropriate Christ he must repent of his sin (Rom. 10:9; Jn. 1:12). But, in order that we may be convicted of our sin, it is necessary for us to allow the Holy Spirit to work in us. In other words, any sin that we confess

(continued on next page)

"Who are My mother and My brothers?"

34 And [apt]looking[4017] about on those who were sitting around Him, He *said, "[a]Behold, My mother and My brothers!

35 "For whoever [a]does the will of God, he is My brother and sister and mother."

34 [a]Matt. 12:49

35 [a]Eph. 6:6; Heb. 10:36; 1Pet. 4:2; 1John 2:17

Parable of the Sower and Soils

4 [a]And He began to [pinf]teach again [b]by the sea. And such a very great multitude [1]gathered to Him that [c]He [apt]got into a boat in the sea and [pinf]sat down; and the whole multitude was by the sea on the land.

2 And He was [ipf]teaching them many things in [a]parables,[3850] and was [ipf]saying to them in His teaching,[1322]

3 "Listen *to this*! [pim]Behold, the sower went out to [infg]sow;

4 and it came about that as he was [aie]sowing, [n]some *seed* fell beside the road, and the birds came and ate it up.

5 "And [n]other *seed* fell on the rocky *ground* where it did not [ipf]have much

1 [1]Lit., *is gathered* [a]Mark 4:1-12: *Matt. 13:1-15; Luke 8:4-10* [b]Mark 2:13; 3:7 [c]Luke 5:1-3

2 [a]Matt. 13:3ff.; Mark 3:23; 4:2ff.

(continued from previous page)

to the Lord Jesus Christ He will forgive, being able and ready to remove it from us. But, if an individual has not been convicted of sin, how can he confess Christ? And this is what makes the next statement of our Lord in Mt. 12:32 understandable: "But whoever shall speak against the Holy Spirit, it shall not be forgiven him." In Mk. 3:29 it says, "But whoever blasphemes against the Holy Spirit never has forgiveness." And in Lk. 12:10 we read, "But he who blasphemes against the Holy Spirit, it shall not be forgiven him." The verb in Mt. 12:32 is *eipē,* the subjunctive aorist of *legō* (3004), which is, "to say at one particular time with full understanding of what one says." In Mk. 3:29 it is *blasphēmēsē,* the aorist subjunctive of *blasphēmeō.* In Lk. 12:10 it is *blasphēmēsanti.* This is a participial noun in the aorist, meaning the one having blasphemed in the past at one particular time or repetitively. It is used as a supposition, meaning that if at any time in the past he did blaspheme. Both words *eipē,* "say," and *blasphemēsanti* (being an aorist participle), "having blasphemed," are indicative of the fact that this saying or blasphemy is a one-time blasphemy either once or on different occasions, and not a continuous life of blasphemy, i.e., constantly attacking the person and work of the Holy Spirit and His reputation among men. This refers first to the resistance against the Holy spirit for His conviction unto salvation, the initial repentance of man. The declaration is that no one who resists the convicting power of the Holy Spirit can be saved. The secondary meaning is that no one, not even the believer, will be able to escape the consequence of his willful sin (*hamartēma*) if he does not allow the Holy Spirit to convict him of these specific sins, or sinfulness in general, which has hurt God's reputation among men (Heb. 10:26,27).

As to the relationship of the sin of blasphemy to the Holy spirit in Mt. 12:32, we have it thus, "But whoever shall speak against (Kata, 2596) the Holy Spirit." In Mk. 3:29 we have, "But whoever blasphemes against the Holy Spirit." In Greek it does not say "against" but "unto" (*eis,* 1519), which means "unto or in the face of." In Lk. 12:10 the same preposition is used. Actually the use of this preposition, *eis,* makes the blasphemy worse. With *kata,* "against," we may understand that the blasphemy is spoken against the Holy Spirit to others, but with the preposition *eis* we may understand that the blasphemy is hurled directly in the face of the Holy Spirit. It is as if man is defying the Holy Spirit and saying, "There is nothing you can do to divert me from my present sinful course. I am going to have my own way regardless of the shame brought upon the name of Christ." The remarks of all three evangelists differ in the last statement concerning the impossibility of forgiveness here and in the hereafter in the absence of man's acknowledgement of his sin, and the consequent convicting of the Holy Spirit. Mt. 12:32 says, "It shall not be forgiven him, either in this age, or in the age to come." The verb *ouk aphethēsetai,* translated "shall not be forgiven," is in the passive punctiliar future, which means it shall not be forgiven by God, and in particular by Jesus Christ, at any specific time in the future. Matthew says, "shall not be forgiven him," (*autō*), meaning, "will not be removed from him." Put positively, it means it will be counted against him, either in hindering him from entrance into heaven if he only had a false repentance. Mark 3:29 says, "never has forgiveness." A more literal translation of the Greek text is, "does not have remission unto the aeon." Luke simply says, "shall not be forgiven" (*ouk aphethēsetai*). Matthew, however,

(continued on next page)

soil; and immediately it sprang up because it [aid]had no depth of soil.

6 "And after the sun had [apt]risen, it was scorched; and because it had no root, it withered away.

7 "And [n]other *seed* fell among the thorns, and the thorns came up and choked it, and it yielded no crop.

8 "And [n]other *seeds* fell into the good [art]soil and as they [ppt]grew up[305] and [ppt]increased, they [ipf]yielded a crop and [ipf]produced[5342] thirty, sixty, and a hundredfold."

9 And He was saying, "[a]He who has ears to hear, let him [pim]hear."

10 And as soon as He was alone, [I]His followers, along with the twelve, *began* asking[2065] Him *about* the parables.[3850]

11 And He was saying to them, "To you has been [pfip]given the mystery[3466] of the kingdom[932] of God; but [a]those who are outside[1854] get everything [b]in parables,

12 in order that [a]WHILE [ppt]SEEING, THEY MAY [psa]SEE AND NOT [aosb]PERCEIVE;

9 [a]Matt. 11:15; Mark 4:23; Rev. 2:7, 11, 17, 29

10 [I]Lit., *those about Him*

11 [a]1Cor. 5:12f.; Col. 4:5; 1Thess. 4:12; 1Tim. 3:7 [b]Mark 3:23; 4:2

12 [a]Is. 6:9f.; 43:8; Jer. 5:21; Ezek. 12:2; Matt. 13:14; Luke 8:10; John 12:40; Rom. 11:8

(continued from previous page)

is the most explicit in saying, "either in this age, or in the age to come." This is proof that the fate of man as it is determined in this age cannot be altered in the next age. If one does not submit to the convicting power of the Holy Spirit and repent, in the future God is not going to grant that person exemption from the consequences of his failure to repent during his earthly life. The bed that one makes in his life will be the one he must lie in for eternity!

Only Mark 3:29 has the concluding phrase, "But is guilty of an eternal sin." The Greek text says, "But guilty is he of eternal judgment." "Guilty" in Greek is *enochos* (1777), from the verb *enechō* and *enechomai* (1758), "to be held fast, bound, obliged."

Therefore, *enochos* means guilty and deserving of the punishment to which he is subject, as also in Mt. 26:66; Mk. 3:29; 14:64. Observe that the verb *estin* (*eimi,* 1510) is in the present tense. He is guilty right now, not will be guilty. This guilt is always upon the man who does not recognize the Holy Spirit's conviction. There is no chance of repenting in the hereafter. If he would recognize it and seek forgiveness here, then he would not be liable at the eternal judgment.

There is, of course, the question of the sins we commit willfully on this earth, for which, if we repent and desist, there is forgiveness, but what about the irreversible consequences of our sins? For those sins there is the doctrine of counteracting mercifulness (Mt. 5:7; Js. 2:13). (See Editor's book, *Faith, Love, Hope;* a three-volume study on James, and *The Pursuit of Happiness,* an in-depth study on the Beatitudes.)

Eternal judgment is based upon the judgment of sin on this earth. In eternity God is going to respect our will which we have exercised in the here and now. If we chose to defy God here and the convicting power of the Holy Spirit, then God is going to defy us in eternity and let us reap the results of the choice which we made. The last phrase of Mk. 3:29 in the Textus Receptus is *aiōnibu kriseōs,* "eternal judgment or condemnation." In other manuscripts, instead of *kriseōs,* "judgment," we have *hamartematos,* "individual sin or the result of sin," which agrees with *hamartēmata* in v. 28 in the phrase "all sins . . . whatever blasphemies." Both words, *krisis* and *hamartēma,* would fit perfectly. If it is *krisis* (2920), it refers to the ultimate judgment of God which means separating or sifting the good from the evil (Mt. 13:41-43; 49-50), but it also includes the punishment for the evil. If we take it as *hamartēmatos,* it would refer to the consequence or the result of our unconfessed and unredeemed sin on earth. The adjective *aiōniou* (166) refers to the eternal judgment, that judgment that will have an effect upon us in the future aeon, "generation" or "age." Since Matthew speaks of both the present generation and the future generation, this must refer to the future generation when we will be judged as to whether we believed on the Lord unto salvation and also for our walk of the life of faith. The phrase *aiōnios krisis,* "eternal judgment," never occurs anywhere else in the N.T. The closest to it we have is in II Thess. 1:9 where it speaks of "everlasting destruction" (*olethron,* 3639, *aiōniou*); and in Jude 7, "the vengeance of eternal fire," which in Greek is "of fire," *puros* (4442), "eternal," *aiōniou* in the genitive, "vengeance or judgment," *dikēn* (1349), as a synonym of *krisis.*

As far as *aiōnion hamartēma,* "eternal result of sin," we find it nowhere else in the N.T. See note on Heb. 6:1-6.

4:10-12 See notes on Mt. 13:10-17,34,35.

AND WHILE [ppt]HEARING, THEY MAY [psa]HEAR AND NOT [psa]UNDERSTAND LEST THEY [aosb]RETURN[1994] AND BE [asbp]FORGIVEN."

Explanation

13 [a]And He *said to them, "Do you not understand this parable? And how will you understand all the parables?

14 "The sower sows the word.[3056]

15 "And these are the ones who are beside the road where the word is sown; and when they [aosb]hear, immediately [a]Satan comes and takes away the word which has been [pfpp]sown in them.

16 "And in a similar way these are the ones on whom seed was [ppp]sown on the rocky *places,* who, when they [aosb]hear the word, immediately receive it with joy;

17 and they have no *firm* root in themselves, but are *only* temporary; then, when affliction or persecution [apt]arises because of the word,[3056] immediately they [I]fall away.

18 "And others are the ones on whom seed was [ppp]sown among the thorns; these are the ones who have [ppt]heard the word,

19 and the worries of [a]the [I]world, and the [b]deceitfulness of riches, and the desires for other things enter in and choke the word, and it becomes unfruitful.

20 "And those are the ones on whom seed was [aptp]sown on the good soil; and they hear the word and accept[3858] it, and [a]bear fruit, thirty, sixty, and a hundredfold."

21 And He was saying to them, "[a]A lamp is not brought[2064] to be put under a peck-measure, is it, or under a bed? Is it not *brought* to be put on the lampstand?

22 "[a]For nothing is hidden, except to be revealed;[5319] nor has *anything* been secret, but that it should [aosb]come[2064] to light.

23 "[a]If any man has ears to hear, let him [pim]hear."

24 And He was saying to them, [pim]"Take care what you listen to. [Ia]By your standard of measure[3358,3354] it shall be measured to you; and more shall be given you besides.

25 "[a]For whoever has, to him shall *more* be given; and whoever does not have, even what he has shall be taken away from him."

Parable of the Seed

26 And He was saying, "The kingdom[932] of God is like a man who [aosb]casts seed upon the soil;

27 and goes to bed at night and [psmp]gets up by day, and the seed sprouts up and grows—how, he himself does not know.

28 "The soil[1093] produces crops by itself; first the blade, then the head, then the mature[4134] grain in the head.

29 "But when the crop permits, he immediately [Ia]puts in[649] the sickle, because the harvest has [pfi]come."

Parable of the Mustard Seed

30 [a]And He said, "How shall we [Ib]picture the kingdom of God, or by what parable[3850] shall we present[5087] it?

31 "*It is* like a mustard seed, which, when sown upon the soil, though it is smaller than all the seeds that are upon the soil,

32 yet when it is sown, grows up[305] and becomes larger than all the garden plants and forms large branches; so that [a]THE BIRDS OF THE [I]AIR can [pinf]NEST UNDER ITS SHADE."

33 And with many such parables[3850] He was [ipf]speaking the word to them as they were able to [pinf]hear it;

34 and He did not speak to them [a]without a parable; but He was [ipf] [b]ex-

13 [a]Mark 4:13-20: *Matt. 13:18-23; Luke 8:11-15*

15 [a]Matt. 4:10f.; 1Pet. 5:8; Rev. 20:2, 3, 7-10

17 [I]Lit., *are caused to stumble*

19 [I]Or, *age* [a]Matt. 13:22; Rom. 12:2; Eph. 2:2; 6:12 [b]Prov. 23:4; 1Tim. 6:9, 10, 17

20 [a]John 15:2ff.; Rom. 7:4

21 [a]Matt. 5:15; Luke 8:16; 11:33

22 [a]Matt. 10:26; Luke 8:17; 12:2

23 [a]Matt. 11:15; 13:9, 43; Mark 4:9; Luke 8:8; 14:35; Rev. 3:6, 13, 22; 13:9

24 [I]Lit., *By what measure you measure* [a]Matt. 7:2; Luke 6:38

25 [a]Matt. 13:12; 25:29; Luke 8:18; 19:26

29 [I]Lit., *sends forth* [a]Joel 3:13

30 [I]Lit., *compare* [a]Mark 4:30-32: *Matt. 13:31, 32; Luke 13:18, 19* [b]Matt. 13:24

32 [I]Or, *sky* [a]Ezek. 17:23; Ps. 104:12; Ezek. 31:6; Dan. 4:12

34 [a]Matt. 13:34; John 10:6; 16:25 [b]Luke 24:27

plaining everything <u>privately</u>[2398] to His own disciples.

Jesus Stills the Sea

35 [a]And on that day, when evening had come, He *said to them, "Let us go over to the other side."

36 And [I]<u>leaving</u>[863] the multitude, they *took Him along with them, just as He was, [a]in the boat; and other boats were with Him.

37 And there *arose a fierce <u>gale</u>[2978] of wind, and the waves were [ipf]breaking over the boat so much that the boat [pinf]was already filling up.

38 And He Himself was in the stern, [ppt]asleep on the cushion; and they *awoke Him and *said to Him, "Teacher, do You not care that we <u>are perishing</u>?"[622]

39 And being aroused, [a]He rebuked the wind and said to the sea, "Hush, be still." And the wind <u>died down</u>[2869] and [I]it became perfectly calm.

40 And He said to them, "Why are you so timid? [a]How is it that you have no <u>faith</u>?"[4102]

41 And they became very much afraid and said to one another, "Who then is this, that even the wind and the sea <u>obey</u>[5219] Him?"

The Gerasene Demoniac

5 [a]And they came to the other side of the sea, into the country of the Gerasenes.

2 And when He had come out of [a]the boat, immediately a man from the tombs [b]with an <u>unclean</u>[169] spirit met Him,

3 and he had his <u>dwelling</u>[2731] among the tombs. And no one was able to <u>bind</u>[1210] him anymore, even with a chain;

4 because he had often been bound with shackles and chains, and the chains had been torn apart by him, and the shackles broken in pieces, and no one [ipf]<u>was strong enough</u>[2480] to [ainf]subdue him.

5 And constantly night and day, among the tombs and in the mountains, he was crying out and gashing himself with stones.

6 And seeing Jesus from a distance, he ran up and bowed down before Him;

7 and [apt]crying out with a loud voice, he *said, "[a]What do I have to do with You, Jesus, [b]Son of [c]the Most High God? I <u>implore</u>[3726] You by God, do not [aosi]torment me!"

8 For He had been saying to him, "Come out of the man, you <u>unclean</u>[169] spirit!"

9 And He was asking him, "What is your name?" And he *said to Him, "My name is [a]Legion; for we are many."

10 And he *began* to [ipf]entreat Him earnestly not to [aosb]send them out of the country.

11 Now there was a big herd of swine feeding there <u>on</u>[4314] the mountain.

12 And *the demons* entreated Him, saying, "Send us into the swine so that we may enter them."

13 And He gave them permission. And [apt]coming out, the <u>unclean</u>[169] spirits entered the swine; and the herd rushed <u>down</u>[2596] the steep bank into the sea, <u>about</u>[5613] two thousand *of them*; and they [I]were [ipf]drowned in the sea.

14 And their [ppt]herdsmen ran away and <u>reported</u>[518] it in the city and *out* in the country. And *the people* came to see what it was that had happened.

15 And they *came to Jesus and *observed the man who had been [ppp] [a]demon-possessed sitting down, [b]clothed and [c]<u>in his right mind</u>,[4993] the very man who had had the "[d]legion"; and they became frightened.

16 And those who had seen it <u>described</u>[1334] to them how it had happened to the [a]demon-possessed man, and *all* about the swine.

17 And they began to [a]entreat Him to depart from their region.

18 [a]And as He was [apt]getting into the boat, the man who had been

---

35 [a]Mark 4:35-41: *Matt. 8:18, 23-27; Luke 8:22, 25*

36 [I]Or, *sending away* [a]Mark 3:9; 4:1; 5:2, 21

39 [I]Lit., *a great calm occurred* [a]Ps. 65:7; 89:9; 107:29; Matt. 8:26; Luke 8:24

40 [a]Matt. 14:31; Luke 8:25

1 [a]Mark 5:1-17: *Matt. 8:28-34; Luke 8:26-37*

2 [a]Mark 3:9; 4:1, 36; 5:21 [b]Mark 1:23

7 [a]Matt. 8:29 [b]Matt. 4:3 [c]Luke 8:28; Acts 16:17; Heb. 7:1

9 [a]Matt. 26:53; Mark 5:15; Luke 8:30

13 [I]Lit., *were drowning*

15 [a]Matt. 4:24; Mark 5:16, 18 [b]Luke 8:27 [c]Luke 8:35 [d]Mark 5:9

16 [a]Matt. 4:24; Mark 5:15

17 [a]Matt. 8:34; Acts 16:39

18 [a]Mark 5:18-20: *Luke 8:38, 39*

[b]demon-possessed was entreating Him that he might [I]accompany Him.

19 And He did not let him, but He *said to him, "[a]Go home to your people and report[518] to them [I]what great things the Lord has done for you, and *how* He [ao]had mercy on you."

20 And he went away and began to [a]proclaim[2784] in [b]Decapolis [I]what great things Jesus had [ao]done for him; and everyone [ipf]marveled.2296

Miracles and Healing

21 [a]And when Jesus had crossed over again in [b]the boat to the other side, a great multitude gathered about Him; and He [I]stayed [c]by the seashore.

22 [a]And one of [b]the synagogue [I]officials756 named Jairus *came up, and upon seeing Him, [pin]*fell at His feet,

23 and [pim]*entreated Him earnestly, saying, "My little daughter is at the point of death; *please* [apt]come and [aosb] [a]lay Your hands on her, that she may [I]get well[4982] and live."[2198]

24 And He went off with him; and a great multitude was [ipf]following Him and [ipf]pressing in on Him.

25 And a woman who had had a hemorrhage[129]4511 for twelve years,

26 and had endured much at the hands of many physicians,2395 and had spent all that she had and was not helped at all, but rather had [apt]grown worse,

27 after hearing about Jesus, [apt]came up in the crowd behind *Him,* and touched His [I]cloak.

28 For she [I]thought, "If I just touch His garments, I shall [II]get well."[4982]

29 And immediately[2112] the flow[4077] of her blood[129] was dried up; and she felt in her body that she was healed[2390] of her [a]affliction.

30 And immediately Jesus, [apt]perceiving in Himself that [a]the power *proceeding* from Him had gone forth, [apt]turned around[1994] in the crowd and said, "Who touched My garments?"

31 And His disciples said to Him, "You see the multitude pressing in on You, and You say, 'Who touched Me?' "

32 And He [ipf]looked around4017 to see the woman who had done this.

33 But the woman [apt]fearing and [ppt]trembling, aware of what had happened to her, came and fell down before Him, and told Him the whole truth.[225]

34 And He said to her, "Daughter, [a]your faith[4102] has [I]made[4982] you well;[4982] [b]go in peace,[1515] and be healed[5199] of your [c]affliction."

35 While He was still [ppt]speaking, they [pin]*came from the *house of* the [a]synagogue official, saying, "Your daughter has [ao]died; why trouble the Teacher anymore?"

36 But Jesus, overhearing what was being spoken, *said to the [a]synagogue official, "[b]Do not be [pim]afraid[5399] *any longer,* only [pim] [I]believe."[4100]

37 And He allowed no one to follow with Him, except [a]Peter and [I]James and John the brother of [I]James.

38 And they *came to the house of the [a]synagogue official; and He *beheld a commotion, and *people* loudly [ppt]weeping and [ppt]wailing.

39 And entering in, He *said to them, "Why make a commotion and weep? The child has not [ao]died, but is asleep."

40 And they *began* [ipf]laughing at Him. But putting them all out, He *took along the child's father and mother and His own companions, and *entered *the room* where the child was.

41 And [apt]taking the child by the hand, He *said to her, "Talitha kum!" (which translated means, "Little girl, [a]I say to you, arise!").

42 And immediately the girl rose and *began* to [ipf]walk; for she was twelve years old. And immediately they were completely astounded.[1839,1611,3173]

43 And He [a]gave them strict orders4183 that no one should know about this; and He said that *something* should be given her to eat.

18 [I]Lit., *be with Him* [b]Matt. 4:24; Mark 5:15, 16

19 [I]Or, *everything that* [a]Luke 8:39

20 [I]Or, *everything that* [a]Ps. 66:16 [b]Matt. 4:25; Mark 7:31

21 [I]Lit., *was* [a]Matt. 9:1; Luke 8:40 [b]Mark 4:36 [c]Mark 4:1

22 [I]Or, *rulers* [a]Mark 5:22-43: *Matt. 9:18-26; Luke 8:41-56* [b]Matt. 9:18; Mark 5:35, 36, 38; Luke 8:49; 13:14; Acts 13:15; 18:8, 17

23 [I]Lit., *be saved* [a]Mark 6:5; 7:32; 8:23; 16:18; Luke 4:40; 13:13; Acts 6:6; 9:17; 28:8

27 [I]Or, *outer garment*

28 [I]Lit., *was saying* [II]Lit., *be saved*

29 [a]Mark 3:10; 5:34

30 [a]Luke 5:17

34 [I]Lit., *saved you* [a]Matt. 9:22 [b]Luke 7:50; 8:48; Acts 16:36; James 2:16 [c]Mark 3:10; 5:29

35 [a]Mark 5:22

36 [I]Or, *keep on believing* [a]Mark 5:22 [b]Luke 8:50

37 [I]Or, *Jacob* [a]Matt. 17:1; 26:37

38 [a]Mark 5:22

41 [a]Luke 7:14; Acts 9:40

43 [a]Matt. 8:4

5:20 See note on I Pet. 3:18-20 and also *kērussō* (2784), to preach.

Teaching at Nazareth

6 [a]And He went out from there, and He *came into [Ib]His home town; and His disciples[3101] *followed Him.

2 And when the Sabbath[4521] had come, He began [a]to [pinf]teach in the synagogue; and the [b]many listeners were [ipf]astonished, saying, "Where did this man *get* these things, and what is *this* wisdom [aptp]given to Him, and such [I]miracles as these performed by His hands?

3 "Is not this [a]the carpenter, [b]the son of Mary, and [an]brother[80] of [I]James, and Joses, and Judas, and Simon? Are not [c]His sisters here with us?" And they [ipf] [II]took [d]offense at Him.

4 And Jesus said to them, "[a]A prophet[4396] is not without honor except in [Ib]his home town and among his *own* relatives and in his *own* household."

5 And He [ipf]could [ainf]do no [I]miracle there except that He [apt] [a]laid His hands upon a few sick people[732] and healed them.

6 And He [ao]wondered at their unbelief.[570]

[a]And He was [ipf]going around the villages teaching.

The Twelve Sent Out

7 [a]And [b]He *summoned the twelve and began to [pinf]send them out [c]in pairs; and He was [ipf]giving them authority[1849] over the unclean spirits;

8 [a]and He instructed[3853] them that they should take[142] nothing for *their* journey, except a mere staff; no bread, no [I]bag,[4082] no money in their belt;

9 but [I]*to* wear[5265] sandals; and *He added,* "Do not put on two [II]tunics."

10 And He said to them, "Wherever you [aosb]enter a house, stay there until you [aosb] [I]leave town.

11 "And any place that does not receive you or listen to you, as you [ppt]go out from there, [aim] [a]shake off the dust [I]from the soles of your feet for a testimony against them."

12 [a]And they [apt]went out and [I]preached[2784] that *men* should [psa]repent.[3340]

13 And they were [ipf]casting out many demons and [a]were [ipf]anointing with oil many sick people[732] and [ipf]healing them.

John's Fate Recalled

14 [a]And King Herod heard *of it,* for His name[3686] had become well known;[5318] and *people* were saying, "[b]John the Baptist[907] has risen from the dead, and that is why these miraculous powers are at work[1754] in Him."

15 But others[243] were saying, "He is [a]Elijah." And others were saying, "*He is* [b]a prophet,[4396] like one of the prophets *of old.*"

16 But when Herod heard *of it,* he kept saying, "John, whom I beheaded, has [aop]risen!"

17 For Herod himself had [apt]sent and had John arrested and bound in prison on account of [a]Herodias, the wife of his brother Philip, because he had married her.

18 For John had been saying to Herod, "[a]It is not lawful for you to have your brother's wife."

19 And [a]Herodias had a grudge[1758] against him and [ipf]wanted to put him to death and could not *do so;*

20 for [a]Herod was [ipf]afraid[5399] of John, knowing that he was a righteous[1342] and holy[40] man, and [ipf]kept him safe.[4933] And when he heard him, he was very perplexed; [I]but he [II]used to [ipf]enjoy listening to him.

21 And a strategic day came when Herod on his birthday [ao] [a]gave a banquet for his lords and [I]military commanders and the leading men [b]of Galilee;

22 and when the daughter of [a]Herodias herself came in and [apt]danced, she [apt]pleased Herod and [I]his dinner

---

1 [I]Or, *His own part of the country* [a]Mark 6:1-6: *Matt. 13:54-58* [b]Matt. 13:54, 57; Luke 4:16, 23
2 [I]Or, *works of power* [a]Matt. 4:23; Mark 10:1 [b]Matt. 7:28
3 [I]Or, *Jacob* [II]Lit., *were being made to stumble* [a]Matt. 13:55 [b]Matt. 12:46 [c]Matt. 13:56 [d]Matt. 11:6
4 [I]Or, *his own part of the country* [a]Matt. 13:57; John 4:44 [b]Mark 6:1
5 [I]Or, *work of power* [a]Mark 5:23
6 [a]Matt. 9:35; Mark 1:39; 10:1; Luke 13:22
7 [a]Mark 6:7-11: *Matt. 10:1, 9-14; Luke 9:1, 3-5;* Luke 10:4-11 [b]Matt. 10:1, 5; Mark 3:13; Luke 9:1 [c]Luke 10:1
8 [I]Or, *knapsack or beggar's bag* [a]Matt. 10:10
9 [I]Lit., *being shod with* [II]Or, *inner garments*
10 [I]Lit., *go out from there*
11 [I]Lit., *under your feet* [a]Matt. 10:14; Acts 13:51
12 [I]Or, *proclaimed as a herald* [a]Matt. 11:1; Luke 9:6
13 [a]James 5:14
14 [a]Mark 6:14-29: *Matt. 14:1-12;* Mark 6:14-16: *Luke 9:7-9* [b]Matt. 14:2; Luke 9:19
15 [a]Matt. 16:14; Mark 8:28 [b]Matt. 21:11
17 [a]Matt. 14:3; Luke 3:19
18 [a]Matt. 14:4
19 [a]Matt. 14:3
20 [I]Lit., *and* [II]Lit., *was hearing him gladly* [a]Matt. 21:26
21 [I]I.e., chiliarchs, in command of a thousand troops [a]Esth. 1:3; 2:18 [b]Luke 3:1
22 [I]Lit., *those who reclined at the table with him* [a]Matt. 14:3

6:3 See general remarks on Jude.

guests; and the king said to the girl, “[aim]Ask me for whatever you want and I will give it to you.”

23 And he swore to her, “Whatever you ask of me, I will give it to you; up to [a]half of my kingdom.”[932]

24 And she [apt]went out and said to her mother, “What shall I ask for?” And she said, “The head of John the Baptist.”[910]

25 And immediately she [apt]came in haste before the king and asked, saying, “I want you to give me right away the head of John the Baptist on a platter.”[4094]

26 And although the king was very sorry, *yet* because of his oaths and because of [I]his dinner guests, he was unwilling to refuse her.

27 And immediately the king [apt]sent an executioner and commanded[2004] *him* to bring *back* his head. And he [apt]went and had him beheaded in the prison,

28 and brought his head on a platter, and gave it to the girl; and the girl gave it to her mother.

29 And when his disciples heard *about this,* they came and took away[142] his body and laid[5087] it in a tomb.

30 [a]And the [b]apostles[652] [pin]*gathered together with Jesus; and they reported to Him all that they had [ao]done and [ao]taught.

31 And He *said to them, “Come away by yourselves to a lonely place and [aim]rest a while.” (For there were many *people* coming and going, and [a]they did not even have time to eat.)

32 [a]And they went away in [b]the boat to a lonely place by themselves.

Five Thousand Fed

33 And *the people* saw them going, and many recognized *them,* and they ran there together on foot from all the cities, and got there ahead of them.

34 And when He went [I]ashore, He [a]saw a great multitude, and He felt compassion for them because [b]they were like sheep without a shepherd;[4166] and He began to teach them many things.

35 And when it was already quite late,[5610][4183] His disciples [apt]came up to Him and *began* [ipf]saying, “The place is desolate and it is already quite late;[5610][4183]

36 send them away so that they may [apt]go into the surrounding countryside and villages and buy[59] themselves [I]something to eat.”

37 But He [apt]answered and said to them, “You give them *something* to eat!” [a]And they *said to Him, “Shall we [apt]go and spend two hundred [Ib]denarii[1220] on bread and give them *something* to eat?”

38 And He *said to them, “How many loaves do you have? Go look!” And when they found out, they *said, “Five and two fish.”

39 And He commanded[2004] them all to recline by groups on the green grass.

40 And they reclined in companies of[2596] hundreds and of[2596] fifties.

41 And He took the five loaves and the two fish, and [apt]looking up toward heaven, He [ao][a]blessed[2127] *the food* and broke the loaves and He kept [ipf]giving *them* to the disciples to set before them; and He divided up the two fish among them all.

42 And they all ate and were satisfied.

43 And they picked up[142] twelve full [a]baskets of the broken pieces,[2801] and also of the fish.

44 And there were [a]five thousand men who ate the loaves.

Jesus Walks on the Water

45 [a]And immediately[2117] He made[315] His disciples[3101] get into [b]the boat and go ahead of *Him* to the other side to [c]Bethsaida, while He Himself was sending the multitude away.

46 And after [a]bidding[657] them farewell,[657] He departed [b]to the mountain to [ainf]pray.

47 And when it was evening, the boat was in the midst of the sea, and He *was* alone on the land.

48 And [apt]seeing them [I]straining at the oars, for the wind was against them, at about the [IIa]fourth watch of the night,

---

23 [a]Esth. 5:3, 6; 7:2

26 [I]Lit., *those reclining at the table*

30 [a]Luke 9:10 [b]Matt. 10:2; Mark 3:14; Luke 6:13; 9:10; 17:5; 22:14; 24:10; Acts 1:2, 26

31 [a]Mark 3:20

32 [a]Mark 6:32-44: *Matt. 14:13-21; Luke 9:10-17; John 6:5-13;* Mark 8:2-9 [b]Mark 3:9; 4:36; 6:45

34 [I]Lit., *out* [a]Matt. 9:36 [b]Num. 27:17; 1Kin. 22:17; 2Chr. 18:16; Zech. 10:2

36 [I]Lit., *what they may eat*

37 [I]The denarius was equivalent to one day's wage [a]John 6:7 [b]Matt. 18:28; Luke 7:41

41 [a]Matt. 14:19

43 [a]Matt. 14:20

44 [a]Matt. 14:21

45 [a]Mark 6:45-51: *Matt. 14:22-32; John 6:15-21* [b]Mark 6:32 [c]Matt. 11:21; Mark 8:22

46 [a]Acts 18:18, 21; 2Cor. 2:13 [b]Matt. 14:23

48 [I]Lit., *harassed in rowing* [II]I.e., 3-6 a.m. [a]Matt. 24:43; Mark 13:35

He *came to them, walking on the sea;
and He intended to pass by them.
49 But when they saw Him walking
on the sea, they supposed[1380] that it
was a ghost,5326 and cried out;
50 for they all saw Him and were
[I]frightened. But immediately He spoke
with them and *said to them, "[a]Take
courage; it is [epn]I, [b]do not be afraid."[5399]
51 And He got into [a]the boat with
them, and the wind stopped;[2869] and
they were greatly[3029,1537,4053] astonished,
52 for [a]they [I]had not gained any
insight[4920] from the *incident of* the
loaves, but [II]their heart [b]was hardened.[4456]

Healing at Gennesaret

53 [a]And when they had crossed
over they came to land at Gennesaret,
and moored to the shore.
54 And when they had come out of
the boat, immediately2117 *the people*
[apt]recognized Him,
55 and ran about that whole country
and began to carry about on their pallets
those who were sick, to [I]the place they
heard He was.
56 And wherever He [ipf]entered villages, or cities, or countryside, they
were laying[5087] the sick in the market
places, and entreating[3870] Him that they
might just [aosb] [a]touch [b]the fringe of His
cloak; and as many as [aom]touched it
[ipf]were being cured.

Followers of Tradition

7 [a]And the Pharisees and some of
the scribes[1122] gathered together
around Him when they had [apt]come
[b]from Jerusalem,
2 and had seen that some of His
disciples[3101] were [pin]eating their bread
with [a]impure[2839] hands, that is, unwashed.
3 (For the Pharisees and all the Jews
do not eat unless they [I]carefully wash[3538]
their hands, *thus* observing the [a]tra-
ditions3862 of the elders;[4245]
4 and *when they come* from the market place,[58] they do not eat unless they
[aosb] [I]cleanse[907] themselves; and there
are many other things[243] which they
have [ao]received in order to [pinf]observe,
such as the [pl] [II]washing[909] of [a]cups and
pitchers and copper pots.)
5 And the Pharisees and the scribes
[pin]*asked Him, "Why do Your disciples
not walk according to[2596] the [a]tradition
of the elders, but eat their bread with
[b]impure hands?"
6 And He said to them, "Rightly did
Isaiah prophesy[4395] of you hypocrites,
as it is written,

'[a]THIS PEOPLE HONORS ME WITH
THEIR LIPS,
BUT THEIR HEART[2588] IS[568] FAR
AWAY FROM ME.
7 '[a]But1161 in vain[3155] do they
worship[4576] Me,
Teaching as doctrines[1319] the
precepts[1778] of men.'

8 [apt]"Neglecting the commandment
of God, you hold to the [a]tradition of
men."
9 He was also saying to them, "You
nicely set aside the commandment of
God in order [aosb]to keep your [a]tradition.
10 "For Moses said, [a][pim]'HONOR
YOUR FATHER AND YOUR MOTHER'; and,
'[b]HE WHO [ppt]SPEAKS EVIL OF FATHER OR
MOTHER, LET HIM [I]BE PUT TO DEATH';
11 but you say, 'If a man says to
his [art]father or *his* [art]mother, anything
of mine you might have been helped
by is [a]Corban[2878] (that is to say, [I]given
to God),'
12 you no longer permit him to
do[4160] anything[3762] for *his* father or *his*
mother;
13 *thus* invalidating the word[3056] of
God by your [a]tradition which you have
handed down; and you do many things
such as that."

The Heart of Man

14 And after He called the multitude
to Him again, He *began* saying to them,
[aim]"Listen to Me, all of you, and [aim]un-
derstand:
15 there is nothing outside1855 the

50 [I]Or, *troubled* [a]Matt. 9:2 [b]Matt. 14:27
51 [a]Mark 6:32
52 [I]Lit., *had not understood on the basis of* [II]Or, *their mind was closed, made dull,* or *insensible* [a]Mark 8:17ff. [b]Rom. 11:7
53 [a]Mark 6:53-56: *Matt. 14:34-36;* John 6:24, 25
55 [I]Or, *where they were hearing that He was*
56 [a]Mark 3:10 [b]Matt. 9:20
1 [a]Mark 7:1-23: *Matt. 15:1-20* [b]Matt. 15:1
2 [a]Matt. 15:2; Mark 7:5; Luke 11:38; Acts 10:14, 28; 11:8; Rom. 14:14; Heb. 10:29; Rev. 21:27
3 [I]Lit., *with the fist* [a]Mark 7:5, 8, 9, 13; Gal. 1:14
4 [I]Or, *sprinkle* [II]Lit., *baptizing* [a]Matt. 23:25
5 [a]Mark 7:3, 8, 9, 13; Gal. 1:14 [b]Mark 7:2
6 [a]Is. 29:13
7 [a]Is. 29:13
8 [a]Mark 7:3, 5, 9, 13; Gal. 1:14
9 [a]Mark 7:3, 5, 8, 13; Gal. 1:14
10 [I]Lit., *die the death* [a]Ex. 20:12; Deut. 5:16 [b]Ex. 21:17; Lev. 20:9
11 [I]Or, *a gift, an offering* [a]Lev. 1:2; Matt. 27:6
13 [a]Mark 7:3, 5, 8, 9; Gal. 1:14

man which going into him can defile him; but the things which [ppt]proceed out of the man are what [ppt]defile the man.

16 [“If any man has ears to [pinf]hear, let him [pim]hear.”]

17 And when leaving the multitude, He had entered [a]the house, [b]His disciples [ipf]questioned Him about the parable.[3850]

18 And He *said to them, “Are you so lacking in understanding[801] also? Do you not understand[3539] that whatever [ppt]goes into the man from outside[1855] cannot [ainf]defile him;

19 because it does not go into his heart, but into his stomach, and [I]is eliminated?”[856] (*Thus He* declared [a]all foods [b]clean.)[2511]

20 And He was saying, “[a]That which [ppt]proceeds out of the man, that is what defiles the man.

21 “For from within, out of the heart of men, proceed the evil thoughts,[1261] [I]fornications,[4202] thefts, murders, adulteries,

22 deeds of coveting[4124] *and* wickedness,[4189] *as well as* deceit, sensuality,[766] [I][a]envy,[4190] slander,[988] [II]pride *and* foolishness.

23 “All these evil things proceed from within and defile the man.”

The Syrophoenician Woman

24 [a]And from there He [apt]arose and went away to the region of [b]Tyre[I]. And when He had entered a house, He [ipf]wanted no one to know *of it;* [II]yet He could not escape notice.

25 But after [apt]hearing of Him, a woman whose little daughter had an unclean spirit,[4151] immediately [apt]came and fell at His feet.

26 Now the woman was a [I]Gentile, of the Syrophoenician race. And she kept [ipf]asking Him to [aosb]cast the demon[1140] out of her daughter.

27 And He was saying to her, “Let the children be [aifp]satisfied first, for it is not [I]good[2570] to take the children’s bread and [ainf]throw it to the dogs.”

28 But she answered and *said to Him, “Yes, Lord, *but* even the dogs under the table feed on the children’s crumbs.”

29 And He said to her, “Because of this [I]answer go your way; the demon has [pfi]gone out of your daughter.”

30 And going back to her home, she found the child [I]lying on the bed, the demon having departed.

31 [a]And again He went out from the region of [b]Tyre, and came through Sidon to [c]the Sea of Galilee, within[303] the region[3319] of [d]Decapolis.

32 And they *brought[5342] to Him one who was deaf and spoke with difficulty, and they *entreated Him to [a]lay His hand upon him.

33 And [a]He [apt]took him aside[618] from the multitude by himself, and put[906] His fingers into his ears, and after [apt] [a]spitting, He touched his tongue[1100] *with the saliva;*

34 and [apt]looking up to heaven with a deep [a]sigh, He *said to him, “Ephphatha!” that is, “Be opened!”

35 And his ears[189] were opened, and the [I]impediment of his tongue [II]was removed, and he *began* [ipf]speaking plainly.

🔑 36 And [a]He gave them orders not to tell anyone; but the more He [ipf]ordered them, the more widely they [b]continued to [ipf]proclaim[2784] it.

37 And they were utterly[5249] [ipf]astonished, saying, “He has done all things well; He makes even the deaf to hear, and the dumb[216] to speak.”[2980]

Four Thousand Fed

8

In those days again, when there was a great multitude and they had nothing to eat, [a]He [apt]called His disciples[3101] and *said to them,

2 “[a]I feel compassion for the multitude because they [pin]have remained

---

16 [I]Many mss. do not contain this verse
17 [a]Mark 2:1; 3:20; 9:28 [b]Matt. 15:15
19 [I]Lit., *goes out into the latrine* [a]Rom. 14:1-12; Col. 2:16 [b]Luke 11:41; Acts 10:15; 11:9
20 [a]Matt. 15:18; Mark 7:23
21 [I]I.e., acts of sexual immorality
22 [I]Lit., *an evil eye* [II]Or, *arrogance* [a]Matt. 6:23; 20:15
24 [I]Some early mss. add *and Sidon* [II]Lit., *and* [a]Mark 7:24-30: *Matt. 15:21-28* [b]Matt. 11:21; Mark 7:31
26 [I]Lit., *Greek*
27 [I]Or, *proper*
29 [I]Lit., *word*
30 [I]Lit., *thrown*
31 [a]Mark 7:31-37; *Matt. 15:29-31* [b]Matt. 11:21; Mark 7:24 [c]Matt. 4:18 [d]Matt. 4:25; Mark 5:20
32 [a]Mark 5:23
33 [a]Mark 8:23
34 [a]Mark 8:12
35 [I]Or, *bond* [II]Lit., *was loosed*
36 [a]Matt. 8:4 [b]Mark 1:45
1 [a]Mark 8:1-9: *Matt. 15:32-39;* Mark 6:34-44
2 [a]Matt. 9:36; Mark 6:34

🔑 **7:36** See note on I Pet. 3:18-20 and also *kērussō* (2784), to preach.

with[4357] Me now three days, and have nothing to eat;

3 and if I send them away hungry[3523] to their home, they will faint on the way; and some[5100] of them have come from a distance."

4 And His disciples answered Him, "Where will anyone be able to *find enough to* satisfy these men with [I]bread here in a desolate place?"

5 And He was [ipf]asking them, "How many loaves do you have?" And they said, "Seven."

6 And He *directed the multitude to [I]sit down on the ground; and [apt]taking the seven loaves, He [apt]gave thanks[2168] and broke them, and started [ipf]giving them to His disciples to [II]serve to them, and they served them to the multitude.

7 They also had a few small fish; and [a]after He had [apt]blessed[2127] them, He ordered these to be [I]served as well.

8 And they ate and were satisfied; and they picked up seven large [a]baskets full of what was left over[4051] of the broken pieces.[2801]

9 And about[5613] four thousand were *there;* and He sent them away.

10 And immediately[2117] He [apt]entered the boat with His disciples, and came to the district of [a]Dalmanutha.

11 [a]And the Pharisees came out and began to argue with Him, [b]seeking from Him a [I]sign from heaven, [II]to test[3985] Him.

12 And [apt] [a]sighing deeply [I]in His spirit, He *said, "Why does this generation seek for a [II]sign? Truly[281] I say to you, [III][b]no [II]sign shall be given to this generation."

13 And [apt]leaving them, He again embarked and went away to the other side.

14 And they had [ao]forgotten to take bread; and [I]did not have more than one loaf in the boat with them.

15 And He was [ipf]giving orders to them, saying, "[a]Watch out![3708] Beware[991] of the leaven[2219] of the Pharisees and the leaven of [b]Herod."

16 And they *began* to discuss with one another *the fact* that they had no bread.

17 And Jesus, aware of this, *said to them, "Why do you discuss *the fact* that you have no bread? [a]Do you not yet see[3539] or understand?[4920] Do you have a [I]hardened heart?

18 "[a]HAVING EYES, DO YOU NOT SEE? AND HAVING EARS, DO YOU NOT HEAR? And do you not remember,

19 when I broke [a]the five loaves for the five thousand, how many [b]baskets full of broken pieces[2801] you picked up?" They *said to Him, "Twelve."

20 "And when *I broke* [a]the seven for the four thousand, how many large [b]baskets full[4138] of broken pieces[2801] did you pick up?" And they *said to Him, "Seven."

21 And He was saying to them, "[a]Do you not yet understand?"

22 And they *came to [a]Bethsaida. And they *brought a blind man to Him, and [pin]*entreated Him to [b]touch him.

23 And [apt]taking the blind man by[1949] the hand, He [a]brought[1627] him out of the village; and after [a]spitting on his eyes, and [apt] [b]laying His hands upon him, He asked him, "Do you see anything?"

24 And he [apt] [I]looked up[308] and [ipf]said, "I see men, for [II]I am seeing *them* like trees, walking about."

25 Then again He laid His hands upon his eyes; and he looked intently and was restored,[600] and *began* to see[1689] everything clearly.

26 And He sent him to his home, saying, "Do not even enter [a]the village."

Peter's Confession of Christ

27 [a]And Jesus went out, along with His disciples, to the villages of [b]Caesarea Philippi; and on the way He questioned His disciples, saying to them, "Who do people say that I am?"

28 [a]And they told Him, saying, "John the Baptist;[910] and others *say* Elijah; but others, one of the prophets."

29 And He *continued* by questioning them, "But who do you say that I am?"

4 [I]Lit., *loaves*
6 [I]Lit., *recline* [II]Lit., *set before*
7 [I]Lit., *set before them* [a]Matt. 14:19
8 [a]Matt. 15:37; Mark 8:20
10 [a]Matt. 15:39
11 [I]Or, *attesting miracle* [II]Lit., *testing Him* [a]Mark 8:11-21: *Matt. 16:1-12* [b]Matt. 12:38
12 [I]Or, *to Himself* [II]Or, *attesting miracle* [III]Lit., *if a sign shall be given* [a]Mark 7:34 [b]Matt. 12:39
14 [I]Lit., *were not having*
15 [a]Matt. 16:6; Luke 12:1 [b]Matt. 14:1; 22:16
17 [I]Or, *dull, insensible* [a]Mark 6:52
18 [a]Jer. 5:21; Ezek. 12:2; Mark 4:12
19 [a]Mark 6:41-44 [b]Matt. 14:20
20 [a]Mark 8:6-9 [b]Mark 8:8
21 [a]Mark 6:52
22 [a]Matt. 11:21; Mark 6:45 [b]Mark 3:10
23 [a]Mark 7:33 [b]Mark 5:23
24 [I]Or, *gained sight* [II]Or, *they look to me*
26 [a]Mark 8:23
27 [a]Mark 8:27-29: *Matt. 16:13-16; Luke 9:18-20* [b]Matt. 16:13
28 [a]Mark 6:14; Luke 9:7, 8

[a]Peter *answered and *said to Him, “Thou art [I]the Christ.”[5547]

30 And [a]He [I]warned them to tell no one about Him.

31 [a]And He began to teach them that [b]the Son of Man must suffer many things and be rejected[593] by the elders[4245] and the chief priests and the scribes, and be killed, and after three days rise again.

32 And He was [ipf]stating the matter [a]plainly. And Peter [apt]took Him aside[4355] and began to rebuke Him.

33 But turning around[1994] and [apt]seeing His disciples, He rebuked Peter, and *said, “Get behind Me, [a]Satan;[4567] for you are not setting your mind on [I]God’s interests, but man’s.”

34 And He summoned the multitude with His disciples,[3101] and said to them, “If anyone [pin]wishes to [pinf]come after Me, let him [aim]deny[533] himself, and [aim][a]take up his cross,[4716] and [pim]follow[190] Me.

35 “For [a]whoever [psa]wishes to [ainf]save[4982] his [I]life[5590] [ft]shall lose it; but whoever [ft]loses his [I]life for My sake and the gospel’s[2098] shall [ft]save it.

36 “For what does it [pin]profit a man to [ainf]gain the whole world, and [aifp]forfeit his soul?[5590]

37 “For what shall a man [ft]give in exchange[465] for his soul?

38 “For [a]whoever is [asbp]ashamed of Me and My words in[1722] this adulterous and sinful[268] generation, [b]the Son of Man will also be ashamed of him when He [aosb] [c]comes in[1722] the glory[1391] of His Father with the holy angels.”

The Transfiguration

9 And He was saying to them, “[a]Truly[281] I say to you, there are some of those who are [pfp]standing here who shall not taste[1089] death[2288] until they see the kingdom[932] of God after it has [pfp]come with power.”

2 [a]And six days later, Jesus *took with Him [b]Peter and [I]James and John, and *brought them up[399] to a high mountain by themselves. And He was transfigured[3339] before them;

3 and [a]His garments became radiant and exceedingly white, as no launderer[1102] on earth[1093] can whiten them.

4 And Elijah appeared to them along with Moses; and they were talking with Jesus.

5 And Peter answered[611] and *said to Jesus, “[a]Rabbi, it is good for us to be here; and [b]let us make three [I]tabernacles,[4633] one for You, and one for Moses, and one for Elijah.”

6 For he did not know what to answer; for they became terrified.[1630]

7 Then a cloud [I]formed, [ppt]overshadowing them, and [a]a voice [I]came out of the cloud, “[b]This is My beloved[27] Son,[5207] [pim] [II]listen to Him!”

8 And all at once they looked around[4017] and saw no one with them anymore, except Jesus alone.

9 [a]And as they were [ppt]coming down from the mountain, He [b]gave them orders not to relate[1334] to anyone what they had seen, [I]until the Son of Man should [aosb]rise from the dead.

10 And they [I]seized upon [II]that statement, discussing with one another [III]what [ainf]rising from the dead might mean.

11 And they asked Him, saying, “*Why is it* that the scribes say that [a]Elijah must[1163] [ainf]come first?”

12 And He said to them, “Elijah does first [apt]come and restore[600] all things. And *yet* how is it written of [a]the Son of Man that [b]He should suffer many things and be treated with contempt?[1847]

13 “But I say to you, that Elijah has [I]indeed [pfi]come, and they did to him whatever they wished, just as it is written of him.”

All Things Possible

14 [a]And when they came *back* to the disciples,[3101] they saw a large crowd around them, and *some* scribes[1122] arguing with them.

15 And immediately,[2117] when the entire crowd saw Him, they were

29 [I]I.e., the Messiah [a]John 6:68, 69
30 [I]Or, *strictly admonished* [a]Matt. 8:4; 16:20; Luke 9:21
31 [a]Mark 8:31-9:1: *Matt. 16:21-28; Luke 9:22-27* [b]Matt. 16:21
32 [a]John 10:24; 11:14; 16:25, 29; 18:20
33 [I]Lit., *the things of God* [a]Matt. 4:10
34 [a]Matt. 10:38; Luke 14:27
35 [I]Or, *soul* [a]Matt. 10:39; Luke 17:33; John 12:25
38 [a]Matt. 10:33; Luke 9:26; Heb. 11:16 [b]Matt. 8:20 [c]Matt. 16:27; Mark 13:26; Luke 9:26

1 [a]Matt. 16:28; Mark 13:26; Luke 9:27
2 [I]Or, *Jacob* [a]Mark 9:2-8: *Matt. 17:1-8; Luke 9:28-36* [b]Mark 5:37
3 [a]Matt. 28:3
5 [I]Or, *sacred tents* [a]Matt. 23:7 [b]Matt. 17:4; Luke 9:33
7 [I]Or, *occurred* [II]Or, *give constant heed* [a]2Pet. 1:17f. [b]Matt. 3:17; Mark 1:11; Luke 3:22
9 [I]Lit., *except when* [a]Mark 9:9-13: *Matt. 17:9-13* [b]Matt. 8:4; Mark 5:43; 7:36; 8:30
10 [I]Or, *kept to themselves* [II]Lit., *the statement* [III]Lit., *what was the rising from the dead*
11 [a]Mal. 4:5; Matt. 11:14
12 [a]Mark 9:31 [b]Matt. 16:21; 26:24
13 [I]Lit., *also*
14 [a]Mark 9:14-28: *Matt. 17:14-19; Luke 9:37-42*

[a]amazed, and *began* running up to [ipf]greet Him.

16 And He asked them, "What are you discussing with them?"

17 And one of the crowd answered[611] Him, "Teacher, I [ao]brought You my son, possessed with a spirit which [ppt]makes him mute;[216]

18 and [I]whenever it [aosb]seizes[2638] him, it [II]dashes him *to the ground* and he foams *at the mouth,* and grinds[5149] his teeth, and [III]stiffens out.[3583] And I told Your disciples to cast it out, and they could[2480] not *do it.*"

19 And He *answered them and *said, "O unbelieving[571] generation, how long shall I be with you? How long shall I put up with[430] you? Bring him to Me!"

20 And they brought [I]the boy to Him. And when he saw Him, immediately[2117] the spirit[4151] threw him into a convulsion, and [apt]falling[4098] to the ground, he *began* [ipf]rolling about and foaming *at the mouth.*

21 And He asked his father, "How long has this been happening to him?" And he said, "From childhood.

22 "And it has often [ao]thrown him both into the fire and into the water to [aosb]destroy[622] him. But if You can do anything, take [apt]pity on us and help us!"

23 And Jesus said to him, " 'If You can!' [a]All things are possible to him who [ppt]believes."

24 Immediately the boy's father cried out and *began* saying, "I do believe; [pim]help my unbelief."[570]

25 And when Jesus saw that [a]a crowd was [I]rapidly gathering, He rebuked[2008] the unclean spirit, saying to it, "You deaf and dumb[216] spirit, [epn]I [II]command you, [aim]come out of him and do not [aosi]enter him [III]again."

26 And after crying out and [apt]throwing him into terrible[4183] convulsions, it came out; and *the boy* became so much like a corpse that most *of them* said, "He is [ao]dead!"

27 But Jesus [apt]took him by the hand and raised[1453] him; and he got up.

28 And when He had come [a]into *the* house, His disciples[3101] *began* [ipf]questioning Him privately, "Why [ao]could we not [ainf]cast it out?"

29 And He said to them, "This kind cannot [ainf]come out by anything but [I]prayer."

Death and Resurrection Foretold

30 [a]And from there they went out and *began* to [ipf]go through Galilee, and He was [ipf]unwilling for anyone to know *about it.*

31 For He was [ipf]teaching[1321] His disciples[3101] and telling them, "[a]The Son of Man is to be [pp][I]delivered into the hands of men, and they will kill Him; and when He has been killed, He will rise three days later."

32 But [a]they [ipf][I]did not understand[50] *this* statement,[4487] and they were [ipf]afraid to [ainf]ask Him.

33 [a]And they came to Capernaum; and when He [apt][I]was[1096] in [b]the house, He *began* to question them, "What were you [ipf]discussing[1260] on the way?"

34 But they [ipf]kept silent, for on the way [a]they had [ao]discussed with one another which *of them was* the greatest.

35 And sitting down, He called the twelve and *said to them, "[a]If anyone wants to be first, [I]he shall be last[2078] of all, and servant of all."

36 And [apt]taking a child, He set[2476] him [I]before them, and taking him in His arms, He said to them,

37 "[a]Whoever receives [I]one child like this in My name[3686] receives Me; and whoever [aosb]receives Me does not receive Me, but Him who sent Me."

Dire Warnings

38 [a]John said to Him, "Teacher, we saw someone casting out demons[1140] in Your name, and [b]we tried to hinder him because he was not following us."

39 But Jesus said, "Do not [pim]hinder him, for there is no one who shall perform a miracle in My name, and be able soon afterward to [ainf]speak evil of Me.

15 [a]Mark 14:33; 16:5, 6

18 [I]Or, *wherever* [II]Or, *tears him* [III]Or, *withers away*

20 [I]Lit., *him*

23 [a]Matt. 17:20; John 11:40

25 [I]Or, *running together* [II]Or, *I Myself command* [III]Or, *from now on* [a]Mark 9:15

28 [a]Mark 2:1; 7:17

29 [I]Many mss. add *and fasting*

30 [a]Mark 9:30-32: *Matt. 17:22, 23; Luke 9:43-45*

31 [I]Or, *betrayed* [a]Matt. 16:21; Mark 8:31; 9:12

32 [I]Lit., *were not knowing* [a]Luke 2:50; 9:45; 18:34; John 12:16

33 [I]Lit., *had come* [a]Mark 9:33-37: *Matt. 18:1-5; Luke 9:46-48* [b]Mark 3:19

34 [a]Matt. 18:4; Mark 9:50; Luke 22:24

35 [I]Or, *let him be* [a]Matt. 20:26; 23:11; Mark 10:43, 44; Luke 22:26

36 [I]Lit., *in their midst*

37 [I]Lit., *one of such children* [a]Matt. 10:40; Luke 10:16; John 13:20

38 [a]Mark 9:38-40: *Luke 9:49, 50* [b]Num. 11:27-29

40 "[a]For he who is not against us is [I]for us.

41 "For [a]whoever [aosb]gives you a cup of water to drink [I]because of your name as *followers* of Christ,[5547] truly I say to you, he shall not lose[622] his reward.[3408]

42 "And [a]whoever causes one of these [I]little ones who [ppt]believe to [aosb]stumble,[4624] it [II]would be better for him if, with a heavy millstone hung around his neck, he [III]had been cast into the sea.[2281]

43 "And [a]if your hand [aosb]causes you to stumble, [aim]cut it off; it is better for you to [ainf]enter life[2222] crippled, than having your two hands, to [ainf]go into [art I][b]hell,[1067] into the [c]unquenchable fire,

44 [[I]where THEIR WORM DOES NOT DIE, AND THE FIRE IS NOT [pin]QUENCHED.]

45 "And if your foot causes you to [psa]stumble, [aim]cut it off; it is better for you to [ainf]enter life lame, than having your two feet, to be cast into [I][a]hell,[1067]

46 [[I]where THEIR WORM DOES NOT DIE, AND THE FIRE IS NOT [pin]QUENCHED.]

47 "And [a]if your eye causes you to [psa]stumble, cast it out; it is better for you to [ainf]enter the kingdom[932] of God with one eye, than having two eyes, to be cast into [art I][b]hell,[1067]

48 [a]where THEIR [art]WORM DOES NOT DIE, AND [b]THE FIRE IS NOT [pin]QUENCHED.

49 "For everyone will be salted with fire.

50 "Salt is good;[2570] but [a]if the salt [aosb]becomes unsalty, with what will you [I]make it salty *again?* [pim] [b]Have salt in yourselves, and [pim] [c]be at peace[1514] with one another."

Jesus' Teaching about Divorce

10 [a]And rising up, He *went from there to the region of Judea, and beyond the Jordan; and crowds *gathered around Him again, and, [b]according to His custom,[5613][1486] He once more *began* [ipf]to teach[1321] them.

2 And *some* Pharisees came up to Him, testing Him, and *began* to question[3985] Him whether it was lawful for a man[435] to [I]divorce[630] a wife.

3 And He answered and said to them, "What did Moses command you?"

4 And they said, "[a]Moses permitted *a man* TO WRITE[1125] A CERTIFICATE[975] OF divorce[647] AND [I]SEND *her* AWAY."[630]

5 But Jesus said to them, "[I][a]Because of your hardness of heart[4641] he wrote you this commandment.

6 "But [a]from the beginning of creation,[2937] *God* [b]MADE THEM MALE AND FEMALE.[2338]

7 "[a]FOR THIS CAUSE A MAN SHALL LEAVE HIS FATHER AND MOTHER,[I]

8 [a]AND THE TWO[1417] SHALL BECOME ONE FLESH; consequently they are no longer two, but one flesh.

9 "What therefore God has [ao]joined together, let no man[444] [pim]separate."

10 And in the house the disciples[3101] *began* questioning Him about this again.

11 And He *said to them, "[a]Whoever [aosb] [I]divorces[630] his wife and [aosb]marries another woman [pin]commits adultery against her;

12 and [a]if she herself [apt] [I]divorces[630] her husband and [asba]marries another man, she is [pin]committing adultery."

Jesus Blesses Little Children

13 [a]And they were bringing children to Him so that He [aosb]might touch them; and the disciples[3101] [ipf]rebuked them.

14 But when Jesus saw this, He was indignant and said to them, "Permit the children to come to Me; do not hinder them; [a]for the kingdom[932] of God belongs to such as these.

15 "Truly[281] I say to you, [a]whoever does not receive the kingdom[932] of God like a child shall not enter it *at all.*"

16 And He [apt] [a]took them in His arms and *began* blessing[2721a] them, [ppt]laying[5087] His hands upon them.

The Rich Young Ruler

17 [a]And as He was setting out on a journey, a man [apt]ran up to Him and

40 [I]Or, *on our side* [a]Matt. 12:30; Luke 11:23
41 [I]Lit., *in a name that you are Christ's* [a]Matt. 10:42
42 [I]I.e., humble [II]Lit., *is better for him if a millstone turned by a donkey is hung* [III]Lit., *has been cast* [a]Matt. 18:6; Luke 17:2; 1Cor. 8:12
43 [I]Gr., *Gehenna* [a]Matt. 5:30; 18:8 [b]Matt. 5:22 [c]Matt. 3:12; 25:41
44 [I]Vv. 44 and 46, which are identical with v. 48, are not found in the best ancient mss.
45 [I]Gr., *Gehenna* [a]Matt. 5:22
46 [I]V. 44, note 1
47 [I]Gr., *Gehenna* [a]Matt. 5:29; 18:9 [b]Matt. 5:22
48 [a]Is. 66:24 [b]Matt. 3:12; 25:41
50 [I]Lit., *season it* [a]Matt. 5:13; Luke 14:34f. [b]Col. 4:6 [c]Mark 9:34; Rom. 12:18; 2Cor. 13:11; 1Thess. 5:13

1 [a]Mark 10:1-12: *Matt. 19:1-9* [b]Matt. 4:23; 26:55; Mark 1:21; 2:13; 4:2; 6:2, 6, 34; 12:35; 14:49
2 [I]Or, *send away*
4 [I]Or, *divorce her* [a]Deut. 24:1, 3; Matt. 5:31
5 [I]Or, *With reference to* [a]Matt. 19:8
6 [a]Mark 13:19; 2Pet. 3:4 [b]Gen. 1:27; 5:2
7 [I]Some mss. add *and shall cleave to his wife* [a]Gen. 2:24
8 [a]Gen. 2:24
11 [I]Or, *sends away* [a]Matt. 5:32
12 [I]Or, *sends away* [a]1Cor. 7:11, 13
13 [a]Mark 10:13-16: *Matt. 19:13-15; Luke 18:15-17*
14 [a]Matt. 5:3
15 [a]Matt. 18:3; 19:14; Luke 18:17; 1Cor. 14:20; 1Pet. 2:2
16 [a]Mark 9:36
17 [a]Mark 10:17-31: *Matt. 19:16-30; Luke 18:18-30*

[apt] [b]knelt before Him, and *began* asking Him, "Good[18] Teacher, what shall I do to [c]inherit[2816] eternal life?"[2222]

18 And Jesus said to him, "Why do you call Me good? No one is good except God alone.

19 "You know the commandments, '[a]DO NOT MURDER, DO NOT COMMIT ADULTERY, DO NOT STEAL, DO NOT BEAR FALSE WITNESS, Do not defraud,[650] HONOR YOUR FATHER AND MOTHER.' "

20 And he said to Him, "Teacher, I have kept [a]all these things from my youth[3503] up."

21 And [apt]looking[1689] at him, Jesus felt a love[25] for him, and said to him, "One thing you lack: go and sell all you possess, and give to the poor, and you shall have [a]treasure in heaven;[3772] and come, [pim]follow Me."

22 But at these words [I]his face [apt]fell, and he went away [ppt]grieved, for he was one who owned much property.

23 And Jesus, [apt]looking around,[4017] *said to His disciples, "[a]How hard it will be for those who [ppt]are wealthy[5536] to [ft]enter the kingdom[932] of God!"

24 And the disciples [a]were [ipf]amazed at His words. But Jesus *answered again and *said to them, "Children, how hard it is [I]to [ainf]enter the kingdom of God!

25 "[a]It is easier for a camel to [ainf]go through the eye of [I]a needle than for a rich man to [ainf]enter the kingdom of God."

26 And they were even more[4057] [ipf]astonished and said [I]to Him, "[II]Then who can be saved?"[4982]

27 Looking upon[1689] them, Jesus *said, "[a]With men it is impossible, but not with God; for all things are possible with God."

28 [a]Peter began to say to Him, "Behold, we have [ao]left everything and [pfi]followed You."

29 Jesus said, "Truly I say to you, [a]there is no one who has [ao]left house or brothers[80] or sisters or mother or father or children or farms, for My sake and for the gospel's[2098] sake,

30 but that he shall receive a hundred times as much now in [I]the present age, houses and brothers and sisters and mothers and children and farms, along with persecutions; and in [a]the age[165] to come,[2064] eternal life.[2222]

31 "But [a]many *who are* first, will be last;[2078] and the last, first."

Jesus' Sufferings Foretold

32 [a]And they were on the road, going up to Jerusalem, and Jesus was walking on ahead of them; and they [b]were [ipf]amazed, and those who followed were [ipf]fearful. And again He [apt]took the twelve aside and began to tell them what was going to [pinf]happen to Him,

33 *saying,* "Behold, we are going up to Jerusalem, and [a]the Son of Man will be [I]delivered to the chief priests and the scribes;[1122] and they will condemn Him to death, and will [II]deliver Him to the Gentiles.

34 "And they will mock Him and [a]spit upon Him, and scourge[3146] Him, and kill *Him,* and three days later He will rise again."

35 [a]And [I]James and John, the two sons of Zebedee, *came up to Him, saying to Him, "Teacher, we want You to [aosb]do for us whatever we ask of You."

36 And He said to them, "What do you want Me to [aosb]do for you?"

37 And they said to Him, "[I]Grant that we [a]may sit in Your glory,[1391] one on Your right,[1188] and one on *Your* left."

38 But Jesus said to them, "You do not know what you are asking for. Are you able [a]to drink the cup that I drink, or [b]to be baptized[907] with the baptism[908] with which I am baptized?"[907]

39 And they said to Him, "We are able." And Jesus said to them, "The cup that I drink [a]you shall drink; and you shall be baptized[907] with the baptism with which I am baptized.[907]

40 "But to [ainf]sit on My right[1188] or on *My* left, this is not Mine to give; [a]but it is for those for whom it has been prepared."

41 [a]And hearing this, the ten began to feel [pinf]indignant with [I]James and John.

42 And calling them to Himself,

17 [b]Mark 1:40 [c]Matt. 25:34; Luke 10:25; 18:18; Acts 20:32; Eph. 1:18; 1Pet. 1:4
19 [a]Ex. 20:12-16; Deut. 5:16-20
20 [a]Matt. 19:20
21 [a]Matt. 6:20
22 [I]Or, *he became gloomy*
23 [a]Matt. 19:23
24 [I]Later mss. insert *for those who trust in wealth* [a]Mark 1:27
25 [I]Lit., *the* [a]Matt. 19:24
26 [I]Later mss. read *to one another* [II]Lit., *And*
27 [a]Matt. 19:26
28 [a]Matt. 4:20-22
29 [a]Matt. 6:33; 19:29; Luke 18:29f.
30 [I]Lit., *this time* [a]Matt. 12:32
31 [a]Matt. 19:30; 20:16; Luke 13:30
32 [a]Mark 10:32-34: *Matt. 20:17-19; Luke 18:31-33* [b]Mark 1:27
33 [I]Or, *betrayed* [II]Or, *betray* [a]Mark 8:31; 9:12
34 [a]Matt. 16:21; 26:67; 27:30; Mark 9:31; 14:65
35 [I]Or, *Jacob* [a]Mark 10:35-45: *Matt. 20:20-28*
37 [I]Lit., *Give to us* [a]Matt. 19:28
38 [a]Matt. 20:22 [b]Luke 12:50
39 [a]Acts 12:2; Rev. 1:9
40 [a]Matt. 13:11
41 [I]Or, *Jacob* [a]Mark 10:42-45; Luke 22:25-27

Jesus *said to them, "You know that
those who are [ppt]recognized as [pinf]rul-
ers[757] of the Gentiles lord it over them;
and their great men exercise authority
over them.
43 "But it is not so among you,
[a]but whoever wishes to become great
among you shall be your servant;[1249]
44 and whoever wishes to be first
among you shall be slave of all.
45 "For even the Son of Man
[a]did not come [ainf]to be served,[1247] but
to [ainf]serve, and to give His [1]life[5590] a
ransom[3083] for many."

Bartimaeus Receives His Sight

46 [a]And they *came to Jericho. And
[b]as He was [ppt]going out from Jericho
with His disciples[3101] and a great[2425] multitude, a blind beggar[4319b] *named* Bartimaeus, the son of Timaeus, was [ipf]sitting
by the road.
47 And when he heard that it was
Jesus the [a]Nazarene, he began to cry
out and say, "Jesus, [b]Son of David, have
mercy on me!"
48 And many were sternly [ipf]telling
him to be quiet, but he kept [ipf]crying
out all the more, "[a]Son of David, have
mercy on me!"
49 And Jesus stopped and said,
[aim]"Call him *here.*" And they *called the
blind man, saying to him, "[a]Take courage, arise! He is calling for you."
50 And casting aside his cloak, he
[apt]jumped up, and came to Jesus.
51 And answering him, Jesus said,
"What do you want Me to do for you?"
And the blind man said to Him, "[1][a]Rab-
boni, *I want* to regain my sight!"
52 And Jesus said to him, "Go your
way; [a]your faith[4102] has [pfi][1]made you
well."[4982] And immediately he regained
his sight and *began* [ipf]following Him on
the road.

The Triumphal Entry

11 [a]And as they [pin]*approached Jerusalem, at Bethphage and
[b]Bethany, near [c]the Mount of Olives,
He *sent two of His disciples,[3101]
2 and *said to them, "Go into the
village opposite you, and immediately
as you [ppp]enter it, you will find a colt
tied *there,* on which no one yet has ever
sat; [aim]untie[3089] it and bring[5342] it *here.*
3 "And if anyone [aosb]says to you,
'Why are you doing this?' you say, 'The
Lord has need of it'; and immediately[2117]
he [1]will send it back here."
4 And they [ao]went away and found
a colt tied at[4314] the door outside[1854] in
the street; and they *untied[3089] it.
5 And some of the [pfp]bystanders
were saying to them, "What are you
doing, untying the colt?"
6 And they spoke to them just as
Jesus [ao]had told *them,* and they gave
them permission.
7 [a]And they *brought the colt to
Jesus and put their garments on it; and
He sat upon it.
8 And many spread their garments
in the road, and others *spread* leafy
branches which they [apt]had cut[2875] from
the fields.
9 And those who went before,[4254]
and those who followed after, were crying out,

"Hosanna![5614]
[a]BLESSED[2127] IS HE WHO
[ppp]COMES IN THE NAME OF
THE LORD;
10 Blessed *is* the coming
kingdom[932] of our father
David;
Hosanna [a]in the highest!"

11 And [a]He entered Jerusalem *and
came* into the temple;[2411] and after
[aptp]looking all around,[4017] [b]He departed
for Bethany with the twelve, since it
was already late.
12 [a]And on the next day, when they
had departed from Bethany, He became
hungry.
13 And seeing at a distance a fig
tree in leaf, He went *to see* if perhaps[686]
He would find anything on[1722] it; and
when He [apt]came to it, He found nothing
but leaves, for it was not the season[2540]
for figs.
14 And He answered and said to it,
"May no one ever eat fruit from you

43 [a]Matt. 20:26; 23:11; Mark 9:35; Luke 22:26
45 [1]Or, *soul* [a]Matt. 20:28
46 [a]Mark 10:46-52: *Matt. 20:29-34; Luke 18:35-43* [b]Luke 18:35; 19:1
47 [a]Mark 1:24 [b]Matt. 9:27
48 [a]Matt. 9:27
49 [a]Matt. 9:2
51 [1]I.e., My Master [a]Matt. 23:7; John 20:16
52 [1]Lit., *saved you* [a]Matt. 9:22
1 [a]Mark 11:1-10: *Matt. 21:1-9; Luke 19:29-38* [b]Matt. 21:17 [c]Matt. 21:1
3 [1]Lit., *sends*
7 [a]Mark 11:7-10: *Matt. 21:4-9; Luke 19:35-38; John 12:12-15*
9 [a]Ps. 118:26; Matt. 21:9
10 [a]Matt. 21:9
11 [a]Matt. 21:12 [b]Matt. 21:17
12 [a]Mark 11:12-14, 20-24: *Matt. 21:18-22*

again!" And His disciples[3101] were listening.

Jesus Drives Moneychangers from the Temple

15 [a]And they *came to Jerusalem.
And He entered the temple[2411] and [ao]be-
gan to cast out those who were buying
and selling in the temple, and overturned
the tables of the moneychangers and
the seats of those who were selling
[I]doves;
16 and He would not [ipf]permit[863]
anyone to carry [I]goods through the temple.
17 And He *began* to teach and say
to them, "Is it not [pfip]written, '[a]MY HOUSE
SHALL BE CALLED A HOUSE OF PRAYER FOR
ALL THE NATIONS'? [b]But [epn]you have
made it a ROBBERS' [I]DEN."
18 And the chief priests[749] and the
scribes[1122] heard *this*, and [a]*began* seeking how to destroy[622] Him; for they were
afraid of Him, for [b]all the multitude was
astonished at His teaching.[1322]
19 And [a]whenever evening came,
[I]they would go out of the city.
20 [a]And as they [ppp]were passing by
in the morning, they saw the fig tree
withered from the roots *up*.
21 And [aptp]being reminded,[363] Peter
*said to Him, "[a]Rabbi, behold, the fig
tree which You cursed[2672] has withered."
22 And Jesus *answered saying to
them, "[a]Have faith[4102] in God.
23 "[a]Truly[281] I say to you, whoever
says to this mountain, 'Be [aipp]taken up
and [aipp]cast into the sea,' and does not
doubt[1252] in his heart, but believes[4100]
that what he says is going to happen,
it shall be *granted* him.
24 "Therefore I say to you, [a]all
things for which you [pim]pray[4336] and ask,
believe that you have received them,
and they shall be *granted* you.
25 "And whenever you [a]stand pray-
ing, [b]forgive,[863] if you have anything[5100]
against anyone; so that your Father also
who is in heaven[3772] may forgive you
your transgressions.[3900]
26 ["[I][a]But if [epn]you do not forgive,
neither will your Father who is in heaven
forgive your transgressions."]

Jesus' Authority Questioned

27 And they [pinp]*came[2064] again[3825]
to Jerusalem. [a]And as He was walking
in the temple,[2411] the chief priests,[749]
and scribes, and elders[4245] *came to
Him,
28 and *began* saying to Him, "By
what authority[1849] are You doing these
things, or who gave You this authority
to do these things?"
29 And Jesus said to them, [epn]"I will
ask you one question, and you answer
Me, and *then* I will tell you by what
authority I do these things.
30 "Was the baptism[908] of John from
heaven,[3772] or from men? Answer Me."
31 And they [ipf]*began reasoning*[1260]
among themselves, saying, "If we say,
'From heaven,' He will say, 'Then why
did you not believe him?'
32 "But [I]shall we say, 'From
men'?"—they were afraid of the multitude, for all considered John to have
been a prophet[4396] indeed.
33 And answering Jesus, they *said,
"We do not know." And Jesus *said to
them, "Neither [I]will [epn]I tell you by what
authority I do these things."

Parable of the Vine-growers

12 [a]And He began to speak to them
in parables:[3850] "[b]A man
[c]PLANTED A VINEYARD, AND PUT A
[I]WALL AROUND IT, AND DUG A VAT UNDER
the wine press, and built a TOWER, and
rented it out to [II]vine-growers[1092] and
went on a journey.
2 "And at the *harvest time*[2540] he
sent a slave[1401] to the vine-growers, in
order to receive *some* of the produce
of the vineyard from the vine-growers.
3 "And they [apt]took him, and beat
him, and sent him away[649] empty-
handed.
4 "And again he sent[649] them another slave, and they [ao]wounded him

15 [I]Lit., *the doves* [a]Mark 11:15-18: *Matt. 21:12-16; Luke 19:45-47;* John 2:13-16
16 [I]Lit., *a vessel;* i.e., a receptacle or implement of any kind
17 [I]Lit., *cave* [a]Is. 56:7 [b]Jer. 7:11
18 [a]Matt. 21:46; Mark 12:12; Luke 20:19; John 7:1 [b]Matt. 7:28
19 [I]I.e., Jesus and His disciples [a]Matt. 21:17; Mark 11:11; Luke 21:37
20 [a]Mark 11:12-14, 20-24: *Matt. 21:19-22*
21 [a]Matt. 23:7
22 [a]Matt. 17:20; 21:21f.
23 [a]Matt. 17:20; 1Cor. 13:2
24 [a]Matt. 7:7f.
25 [a]Matt. 6:5 [b]Matt. 6:14
26 [I]Many mss. do not contain this v. [a]Matt. 6:15; 18:35
27 [a]Mark 11:27-33: *Matt. 21:23-27; Luke 20:1-8*
32 [I]Or, *if we say*
33 [I]Lit., *do I tell*
1 [I]Or, *fence* [II]Or, *tenant farmers,* also vv. 2, 7, 9 [a]Mark 3:23; 4:2ff. [b]Mark 12:1-12: *Matt. 21:33-46; Luke 20:9-19* [c]Is. 5:1, 2

in the head,[2775] and treated him shamefully.
5 “And he sent another, and that
one they killed; and *so with* many others,
[ppt]beating some, and [ppt]killing others.
6 “He had one more *to send,* a
beloved[27] son;[5207] he sent him last *of*
all to them, saying, ‘They will respect[1788] my son.’
7 “But those vine-growers said to
one another, ‘This is the heir;[2818] come,
let us kill him, and the inheritance[2817]
will be ours!’
8 “And they took him, and killed
him, and threw him out of the vineyard.
9 “What will the [I]owner[2962] of the
vineyard do? He will [ft]come and [ft]destroy
the vine-growers, and will give the vineyard to others.
10 “Have you not even read this
Scripture:[1124]
‘[a]THE STONE WHICH THE
BUILDERS REJECTED,[593]
THIS BECAME THE CHIEF
CORNER *stone;*
11 [a]THIS CAME ABOUT FROM THE
LORD,[2962]
AND IT IS MARVELOUS IN OUR
EYES’?”
12 And [a]they were seeking to seize
Him; and *yet* they feared the multitude;
for they understood that He spoke the
parable against[4314] them. And *so*
[b]they left Him, and went away.

Jesus Answers the Pharisees, Sadducees and Scribes

13 [a]And they *sent some of the
Pharisees and [b]Herodians to Him, in order to [aosb] [c]trap Him in a statement.
14 And they *came and *said to
Him, “Teacher, we know that You are
truthful, and [I]defer to no one; for You
are not partial to any,[4383] but teach the
way[3598] of God in truth.[225] Is it [II]lawful
to pay a poll-tax to Caesar, or not?
15 “Shall we [aosi]pay, or shall we not
pay?” But He, knowing their hypocrisy,
said to them, “Why are you testing[3985]
Me? Bring Me a [I]denarius[1220] to
look at.”
16 And they brought *one.* And He
*said to them, “Whose likeness[1504] and
inscription is this?” And they said to
Him, “Caesar’s.”
17 And Jesus said to them, “[a]Render
to Caesar the things that are Caesar’s,
and to God the things that are God’s.”
And they [I]were amazed at Him.
18 [a]And *some* Sadducees (who say
that there is no resurrection)[386] *came
to Him, and *began* questioning Him, saying,
19 “Teacher, Moses wrote[1125] for
us that [a]IF A MAN’S BROTHER[80] DIES, and
leaves behind a wife, AND LEAVES[863] NO
CHILD, HIS BROTHER SHOULD TAKE THE
WIFE, AND RAISE UP[1817] OFFSPRING[4690] TO
HIS BROTHER.
20 “There were seven brothers;[80]
and the first took a wife, and died,
leaving[863] no offspring.[4690]
21 “And the second one took her,
and died, leaving behind no offspring;
and the third likewise;
22 and *so* [I]all seven left no offspring.
Last of all the woman died also.
23 “In the resurrection, [I]when they
rise again,[450] which one’s wife will she
be? For [II]all seven had her as wife.”
24 Jesus said to them, “Is this not
the reason you are mistaken, that you
do not [pfp] [I]understand the Scriptures,
or the power of God?
25 “For when they rise[450] from the
dead, they neither marry, nor are given
in marriage, but are like angels[32] in
heaven.[3772]
26 “But [I]regarding the fact that the
dead rise again, have you not read in
the book of Moses, [a]in the *passage about*
the burning bush, how God spoke to
him, saying, [epn]‘[b]I AM THE GOD OF ABRA-
HAM, AND THE GOD OF ISAAC, AND THE
GOD OF JACOB’?
27 “[a]He is not the God [I]of the dead,
but of the living;[2198] [epn]you are greatly
mistaken.”
28 [a]And one of the scribes[1122] came
and heard them arguing, and [pfp] [b]recog-
nizing that He had answered them well,
asked Him, “What commandment is the
[I]foremost of all?”

9 [I]Lit., *lord*
10 [a]Ps. 118:22
11 [a]Ps. 118:23
12 [a]Mark 11:18 [b]Matt. 22:22
13 [a]Mark 12:13-17: *Matt. 22:15-22; Luke 20:20-26* [b]Matt. 22:16 [c]Luke 11:54
14 [I]Lit., *it is not a concern to You about anyone;* i.e., You court no man's favor [II]Or, *permissible*
15 [I]The denarius was equivalent to one day's wage
17 [I]Or, *were greatly marveling* [a]Matt. 22:21
18 [a]Mark 12:18-27: *Matt. 22:23-33; Luke 20:27-38;* Acts 23:8
19 [a]Deut. 25:5
22 [I]Lit., *the seven*
23 [I]Most ancient mss. do not contain *when they rise again* [II]Lit., *the seven*
24 [I]Or, *know*
26 [I]Lit., *concerning the dead, that they rise* [a]Luke 20:37; Rom. 11:2 [b]Ex. 3:6
27 [I]Or, *of corpses* [a]Matt. 22:32; Luke 20:38
28 [I]Or, *first* [a]Mark 12:28-34: *Matt. 22:34-40;* Luke 10:25-28; 20:39f. [b]Matt. 22:34; Luke 20:39

29 Jesus answered, "The foremost is, '[a]HEAR, O ISRAEL! THE LORD OUR GOD IS ONE LORD;

30 [a]AND YOU SHALL LOVE[25] THE LORD YOUR GOD WITH ALL YOUR HEART, AND WITH ALL YOUR SOUL,[5590] AND WITH ALL YOUR MIND,[1271] AND WITH ALL YOUR STRENGTH.'[2479]

31 "The second is this, '[a]YOU SHALL [ft]LOVE[25] YOUR NEIGHBOR[4139] AS YOURSELF.' There is no other commandment greater than these."

32 And the scribe said to Him, "Right, Teacher, You have truly[225] stated that [a]HE IS ONE; AND THERE IS NO ONE ELSE BESIDES HIM;

33 [a]AND [pinf]TO LOVE HIM WITH ALL THE HEART AND WITH ALL THE UNDERSTANDING AND WITH ALL THE STRENGTH, AND TO LOVE ONE'S NEIGHBOR AS HIMSELF, [b]is much more than all burnt offerings and sacrifices."

34 And when Jesus saw that he had answered intelligently,[3562] He said to him, "You are not far from the kingdom[932] of God." [a]And after that, no one would venture[5111] to ask Him any more questions.

35 [a]And Jesus answering *began* to say, as He [ppt] [b]taught in the temple,[2411] "How *is it that* the scribes[1122] say that [I]the Christ is the [c]son of David?

36 "David himself said [I]in the Holy Spirit,[4151]

'[a]THE LORD SAID TO MY LORD,
"SIT AT MY RIGHT HAND,
UNTIL I [aosb]PUT[5087] THINE
ENEMIES BENEATH THY
FEET."'

37 "David himself calls Him 'Lord'; and *so* in what sense is He his son?" And [a]the great crowd [I]enjoyed listening[191] to Him.

38 [a]And in His teaching[1322] He was saying: "Beware[991] of the scribes[1122] who [ppt]like[2309] to walk around in long robes, and *like* [b]respectful greetings in the market places,

39 and chief seats in the synagogues,[4864] and places of honor at banquets,

40 [a]who [ppt]devour[2719] widows' houses,[3614] and for appearance's sake [ppp]offer long prayers; these will receive greater condemnation."[2917]

The Widow's Mite

41 [a]And He sat down opposite [b]the treasury, and *began* observing how the multitude were [c]putting [I]money into the treasury; and many rich people were putting in large sums.

42 And a poor widow [apt]came and put in two [I]small copper coins,[3016] which amount to a [II]cent.[2835]

43 And calling His disciples to Him, He said to them, "Truly[281] I say to you, this poor widow put in more than all [I]the contributors to the treasury;

44 for they all put in out of their [ppt] [I]surplus, but she, out of her poverty,[5304] put in all she owned, [II]all she had [a]to live on."

Things to Come

13 🔑 [a]And as He was [ppp]going out of the temple,[2411] one of His disciples[3101] *said to Him, "Teacher, behold [I]what wonderful stones and [I]what wonderful buildings!"[3619]

2 And Jesus said to him, "Do you see these great buildings? [efn] [a]Not one stone shall be left[863] upon another which will [efn]not be torn down."[2647]

3 And as He was sitting on [a]the Mount of Olives opposite the temple, [b]Peter and [I]James and John and Andrew were questioning Him privately,

4 "Tell us, when will these things be, and what *will be* the [I]sign when all these things are going to be [pip]fulfilled?"[4931]

5 And Jesus began to say to them, "See to it that no one misleads you.

6 "Many will come in My name,[3686] saying, [epn]'[a]I am *He!*' and will mislead many.

---

29 [a]Deut. 6:4
30 [a]Deut. 6:5
31 [a]Lev. 19:18
32 [a]Deut. 4:35
33 [a]Deut. 6:5 [b]1Sam. 15:22; Hos. 6:6; Mic. 6:6-8; Matt. 9:13; 12:7
34 [a]Matt. 22:46
35 [I]I.e., the Messiah [a]Mark 12:35-37: *Matt. 22:41-46; Luke 20:41-44* [b]Matt. 26:55; Mark 10:1 [c]Matt. 9:27
36 [I]Or, *by* [a]Ps. 110:1
37 [I]Lit., *was gladly hearing Him* [a]John 12:9
38 [a]Mark 12:38-40: *Matt. 23:1-7; Luke 20:45-47* [b]Matt. 23:7; Luke 11:43
40 [a]Luke 20:47
41 [I]I.e., copper coins [a]Mark 12:41-44: *Luke 21:1-4* [b]John 8:20 [c]2Kin. 12:9
42 [I]Gr., *lepta* [II]Gr., *quadrans;* i.e., 1/64 of a denarius
43 [I]Lit., *those who were putting in*
44 [I]Or, *abundance* [II]Lit., *her whole livelihood* [a]Luke 8:43; 15:12, 30; 21:4
1 [I]Lit., *how great* [a]Mark 13:1-37: *Matt. 24; Luke 21:5-36*
2 [a]Luke 19:44
3 [I]Or, *Jacob* [a]Matt. 21:1 [b]Matt. 17:1
4 [I]Or, *attesting miracle*
6 [a]John 8:24

🔑 **13:1-37** See note on Mt. 24-25.

7 "And when you hear of wars[4171] and rumors of wars, do not be frightened; *those things* must take place; but *that is* not yet the end.[5056]

8 "For nation will [fp]arise[1453] against nation, and kingdom against kingdom; there will be earthquakes in various[2596] places; there will *also* be famines. These things are *merely* the beginning of birth pangs.[5604]

9 "But [I]be on your guard; for they will [a]deliver you to *the* [II]courts, and you will be flogged [b]in *the* synagogues,[4864] and you will stand before governors and kings for My sake, as a testimony to them.

10 "[a]And the gospel[2098] must first be [aifp]preached[2784] to all the nations.

11 "[a]And when they [I]arrest[71] you and deliver you up, do not be anxious beforehand about what you are to say, but say whatever is given you in that hour; for it is not [epn]you who speak, but *it is* the Holy Spirit.[4151]

12 "And brother[80] will deliver brother to death,[2288] and a father *his* child; and children will rise up against parents and [I]have them put to death.

13 "And [a]you will be hated by all on account of My name, but the one who [apt]endures to the end,[5056] he shall be saved.[4982]

14 "But [a]when you see the [b]ABOMINATION[946] OF DESOLATION [pfp]standing where it should not be (let the reader understand), then let those who are in Judea flee to the mountains.

15 "[a]And let him who is on the housetop not go down, or enter in, to get anything out of his house;

16 and let him who is in the field not turn back to get his cloak.

17 "But woe to those who [ppt]are[2192] with child and to those who [ppt]nurse[2337] babes in those days!

18 "But pray that it may not happen in the winter.

19 "For those days will be a *time of* tribulation such as has not [pfi]occurred[1096] [a]since the beginning of the creation[2937] which God created,[2936] until now, and [efn]never shall.

20 "And unless the Lord[2962] had shortened *those* days, no [I]life[4561] would have been saved;[4982] but for the sake of the [II]elect[1588] whom He chose, He shortened the days.

21 "And then if anyone says to you, 'Behold, here is [I]the Christ';[5547] or, 'Behold, *He is* there'; do not believe *him;*

🔑 22 for false Christs[5580] and [a]false prophets will arise,[1453] and will show [Ib]signs and [c]wonders, in order, if possible, to [pinf]lead the elect astray.[635]

23 "But take heed;[991] behold, I have told you everything in advance.

The Return of Christ

24 "But in those days, after that tribulation, [a]THE SUN WILL BE DARKENED, AND THE MOON WILL NOT GIVE ITS LIGHT,[5338]

25 [a]AND THE STARS WILL BE FALLING from heaven,[3772] and the powers that are in [I]the heavens will be shaken.

26 "And then they will see [a]THE SON OF MAN [b]COMING IN CLOUDS with great power and glory.[1391]

27 "And then He will send forth the angels, and [a]will gather together[1996] His [I]elect from the four winds, [b]from the farthest end of the earth, to the farthest end of heaven.

28 "Now learn the parable from the fig tree: when its branch has already become tender, and puts forth its leaves, you know that summer is near.

29 "Even so, you too, when you see these things [ppp]happening,[1096] [I]recognize that [II]He is near, *right* at the [III]door.

30 "Truly[281] I say to you, this [I]generation [efn]will not pass away until all these things take place.

31 "Heaven[3772] and earth[1093] will pass away, but My words will not pass away.

🔑 32 "[a]But of that day or hour no one [pin]knows, not even the angels[32] in

9 [I]Lit., *look to yourselves* [II]Or, *Sanhedrin or council* [a]Matt. 10:17 [b]Matt. 10:17
10 [a]Matt. 24:14
11 [I]Lit., *lead* [a]Mark 13:11-13: *Matt. 10:19-22; Luke 21:12-17*
12 [I]Lit., *put them to death*
13 [a]Matt. 10:22; John 15:21
14 [a]Matt. 24:15f. [b]Dan. 9:27; 11:31; 12:11
15 [a]Luke 17:31
19 [a]Dan. 12:1; Mark 10:6
20 [I]Lit., *flesh* [II]Or, *chosen ones*
21 [I]I.e., the Messiah
22 [I]Or, *attesting miracles* [a]Matt. 7:15 [b]Matt. 24:24; John 4:48
24 [a]Is. 13:10; Ezek. 32:7; Joel 2:10, 31; 3:15; Rev. 6:12
25 [I]Or, *heaven* [a]Is. 34:4; Rev. 6:13
26 [a]Dan. 7:13; Rev. 1:7 [b]Matt. 16:27; Mark 8:38
27 [I]Or, *chosen ones* [a]Deut. 30:4 [b]Zech. 2:6
29 [I]Lit., *know* [II]Or, *it* [III]Lit., *doors*
30 [I]Or, *race*
32 [a]Matt. 24:36; Acts 1:7

🔑 **13:22,32** See note on Phil. 2:6-8.

heaven,[3772] nor the Son,[5207] but the Father[3962] *alone.*

33 "Take heed,[991] [a]keep on the alert; for you do not know when the *appointed* time[2540] is.

34 "[a]*It is* like a man, away on a journey, *who* upon leaving his house and [I]putting his slaves[1401] in charge, *assigning* to each one his task, also commanded[1781] the doorkeeper[2377] to stay on the alert.

35 "Therefore, [a]be on the alert—for you do not know when the [I]master[2962] of the house is coming, whether in the evening, at midnight, at [b]cockcrowing, or [c]in the morning—4404

36 lest he [apt]come suddenly and find you [a]asleep.

37 "And what I say to you I say to all, '[a]Be on the alert!' "

Death Plot and Anointing

14 [a]Now [b]the Passover3957 and Unleavened Bread[106] was two days off; and the chief priests[749] and the scribes[1122] [c]were seeking how to seize Him by stealth, and kill *Him;*

2 for they were saying, "Not during the festival, lest there be a riot of the people."

3 [a]And while He was in [b]Bethany at the home of Simon the leper, and [ppp]reclining *at the table,* there came a woman with an alabaster vial211 of very [c]costly perfume of pure nard;3487,4101 *and* she broke the vial and poured it over[2708] His head.

4 But some were indignantly *remarking* to one another, "Why has this perfume been wasted?[684]

5 "For this perfume might have been sold for over1883 three hundred [I]denarii,1220 and *the money* given to the poor." And they [ipf]were scolding1690 her.

6 But Jesus said, "Let her alone;[863] why do you bother her? She has done[2038] a good[2570] deed[2041] to Me.

7 "For [a]the poor you always have with you, and whenever you wish, you can do them good; but you do not always have Me.

8 "She has done what she could; [a]she has anointed3462 My body beforehand4301 for the burial.

9 "And truly281 I say to you, [a]wherever the gospel[2098] is [pp]preached[2784] in the whole world,[2889] that also which this woman has done shall be spoken of in memory3422 of her."

10 [a]And Judas Iscariot, [b]who was one of the twelve, went off to the chief priests,[749] in order to [aosb] [I]betray3860 Him to them.

11 And they were glad[5463] when they heard *this,* and promised[1861] to give him money. And he *began* seeking how to betray Him at an opportune time.

The Last Passover

12 [a]And on the first day of [b]Unleavened Bread,[106] when [I]the Passover3957 *lamb* [ipf]was being [c]sacrificed,[2380] His disciples[3101] *said to Him, "Where do You want us to go and prepare for You to eat the Passover?"

13 And He *sent two of His disciples, and *said to them, "Go into the city, and a man[444] will meet you carrying a pitcher of water; follow him;

14 and wherever he enters, say to the owner of the house,[3617] 'The Teacher says, "Where is My [a]guest room in which I may eat the Passover with My disciples?" '

15 "And [epn]he himself will show you a large upper room [pfpp]furnished *and* ready; and prepare for us there."

16 And the disciples went out, and came to the city, and found *it* just as He had told them; and they prepared the Passover.

17 [a]And when it was evening He *came with the twelve.

18 And as they were reclining *at the table* and eating, Jesus said, "Truly281 I say to you that one of you will [I]betray Me—[II]one who is eating with Me."

19 They began to be grieved and to [pinf]say to Him one by one, "Surely not [epn]I?"

33 [a]Eph. 6:18; Col. 4:2

34 [I]Lit., *giving the authority to* [a]Luke 12:36-38

35 [I]Lit., *lord* [a]Matt. 24:42; Mark 13:37 [b]Mark 14:30 [c]Matt. 14:25; Mark 6:48

36 [a]Rom. 13:11

37 [a]Matt. 24:42; Mark 13:35

1 [a]Mark 14:1, 2: *Matt. 26:2-5; Luke 22:1, 2* [b]Ex. 12:1-27; Mark 14:12; John 11:55; 13:1 [c]Matt. 12:14

3 [a]Mark 14:3-9: *Matt. 26:6-13;* Luke 7:37-39; John 12:1-8 [b]Matt. 21:17 [c]Matt. 26:6f.; John 12:3

5 [I]The denarius was equivalent to one day's wage

7 [a]Deut. 15:11; Matt. 26:11; John 12:8

8 [a]John 19:40

9 [a]Matt. 26:13

10 [I]Or, *deliver Him up* [a]Mark 14:10, 11: *Matt. 26:14-16; Luke 22:3-6* [b]John 6:71

12 [I]Lit., *they were sacrificing* [a]Mark 14:12-16: *Matt. 26:17-19; Luke 22:7-13* [b]Matt. 26:17 [c]Deut. 16:5; Mark 14:1; Luke 22:7; 1Cor. 5:7

14 [a]Luke 22:11

17 [a]Mark 14:17-21: *Matt. 26:20-24; Luke 22:14, 21-23;* John 13:18ff.

18 [I]Or, *deliver Me up* [II]Or, *the one*

20 And He said to them, "*It is* one of the twelve, [I]one who dips[1686] with Me in the bowl.

21 "For the Son of Man *is to* go, just as it is written of Him; but woe to that man [I]by whom the Son of Man is betrayed! *It would have been* good[2570] [II]for that man if he had not been born."

The Lord's Supper

22 [a]And while they were eating, He [apt]took[2983] *some* bread, and [I]after a [apt][b]blessing[2127] He broke *it;* and gave *it* to them, and said, "Take *it;* this is My body."[4983]

23 And when He had [apt]taken a cup, *and* given thanks, He gave *it* to them; and they all drank from it.

24 And He said to them, "This is My [a]blood[129] of the [b]covenant,[1242] which is [ppp]poured out[1632] for many.

25 "Truly[281] I say to you, I shall never again drink of the fruit[1079b] of the vine until that day when I drink it new in the kingdom[932] of God."

26 [a]And after [apt]singing[5214] a hymn, they went out to [b]the Mount of Olives.

27 [a]And Jesus *said to them, "You will all [I]fall away, because it is written, '[b]I WILL STRIKE DOWN THE SHEPHERD, AND THE SHEEP SHALL BE SCATTERED.'

28 "But after I [aime]have been raised,[1453] [a]I will go before you to Galilee."

29 But Peter said to Him, "*Even* though all may [I]fall away, yet I will not."

30 And Jesus *said to him, "Truly[281] I say to you, that you yourself [I][a]this very night, before [b]a cock crows twice, shall three times deny[533] Me."

31 But *Peter* kept saying insistently, "*Even* if I have to[1163] die with You, I will [efn]not deny[533] You!" And they all were saying the same thing, too.

Jesus in Gethsemane

32 [a]And they *came to a place named[3686] Gethsemane; and He *said to His disciples,[3101] "Sit here until I have prayed."

33 And He *took with Him Peter and [I]James and John, and began to be very [pip][a]distressed[1568] and troubled.

34 And He *said to them, "[a]My soul[5590] is deeply grieved to the point of death; remain[3306] here and keep watch."

35 And He went a little [apt]beyond[4281] *them,* and [I]fell to the ground, and *began* to pray that if it were possible, [a]the hour[5610] might [II]pass Him by.

36 And He was saying, "[a]Abba![5] Father! All things are possible for Thee; remove this cup from Me; [b]yet not what [epn]I will, but what [epn]Thou wilt."

37 And He *came and *found them sleeping, and *said to Peter, "Simon, are you [pin]asleep?[2518] Could you not keep watch for one hour?

38 "[a]Keep watching and praying, that you may not come into temptation;[3986] the spirit[4151] is willing, but the flesh[4561] is weak."[772]

39 And again He went away and prayed, [apt]saying the same [I]words.

40 And again He came and found them sleeping, for their eyes were very heavy; and they did not know[1492] what to answer Him.

41 And He *came the third time, and *said to them, "[I]Are you still sleeping and taking your rest? [pin]It is enough;[566] [a]the hour has come; behold, the Son of Man is being [II]betrayed into the hands of sinners.[268]

42 "Arise, let us be [psa]going;[71] behold, the one who betrays Me is at hand!"

Betrayal and Arrest

43 [a]And immediately while He was still speaking, Judas, one of the twelve, *came up, [I]accompanied[3226] by a multitude with[3326] swords and clubs,[3586] from the chief priests and the scribes and the elders.[4245]

44 Now he who [ppt]was betraying[3860] Him had given them a signal,[4953] saying, "Whomever I shall kiss,[5368] He is the

20 [I]Or, *the one*

21 [I]Or, *through* [II]Lit., *for him if that man had not been born*

22 [I]Lit., *having blessed* [a]Mark 14:22-25: *Matt. 26:26-29; Luke 22:17-20; 1Cor. 11:23-25;* Mark 10:16 [b]Matt. 14:19

24 [a]Ex. 24:8 [b]Jer. 31:31-34

26 [a]Matt. 26:30 [b]Matt. 21:1

27 [I]Or, *stumble* [a]Mark 14:27-31: *Matt. 26:31-35* [b]Zech. 13:7

28 [a]Matt. 28:16

29 [I]Or, *stumble*

30 [I]Lit., *today, on this night* [a]Matt. 26:34 [b]Mark 14:68, 72; John 13:38

32 [a]Mark 14:32-42: *Matt. 26:36-46; Luke 22:40-46*

33 [I]Or, *Jacob* [a]Mark 9:15; 16:5, 6

34 [a]Matt. 26:38; John 12:27

35 [I]Lit., *was falling* [II]Lit., *pass from Him* [a]Matt. 26:45; Mark 14:41

36 [a]Rom. 8:15; Gal. 4:6 [b]Matt. 26:39

38 [a]Matt. 26:41

39 [I]Lit., *word*

41 [I]Or, *Keep on sleeping therefore* [II]Or, *delivered up* [a]Mark 14:35

43 [I]Lit., *and with him* [a]Mark 14:43-50: *Matt. 26:47-56; Luke 22:47-53; John 18:3-11*

one; seize Him, and lead Him away
[I]under guard."
45 And after coming, he immedi-
ately[2117] went to Him, saying, "[a]Rabbi!"
and kissed Him.
46 And they laid hands on Him, and
seized Him.
47 But a certain one of those who
stood by [apt]drew[4685] his sword, and
struck the slave[1401] of the high priest,
and [I]cut off his ear.
48 And Jesus answered and said to
them, "Have you come out with swords
and clubs to arrest Me, as against a
robber?[3027]
49 "Every day I was with you
[a]in the temple[2411] teaching, and you did
not seize Me; but [I]*this has happened*
that the Scriptures might be [asbp]ful-
filled."[4137]
50 And they all [apt]left[863] Him and
fled.
51 And a certain young man was
following Him, wearing *nothing but* a
linen sheet over *his* naked[1131] *body;* and
they [pin]*seized[2902] him.
52 But he left the linen sheet behind,
and escaped naked.[1131]

Jesus before His Accusers

53 [a]And they led Jesus away to the
high priest; and all the chief priests and
the elders[4245] and the scribes[1122] *gathered together.
54 And Peter had followed Him at
a distance, [a]right into [b]the courtyard of
the high priest; and he was sitting with
the [I]officers,[5257] and [c]warming himself
at the [II]fire.
55 Now the chief priests and the
whole [Ia]Council kept trying to obtain
testimony[3141] against Jesus to put Him
to [aies]death;[2289] and they were not finding any.
56 For many were giving false testimony against Him, and *yet* their testimony was not consistent.
57 And some stood up and *began*
to give false testimony against Him, saying,
58 "We heard Him say, '[a]I will destroy this [I]temple[3485] made with hands,
and in three days I will build another
made without hands.'"
59 And not even in this respect was
their testimony consistent.
60 And the high priest stood up[450]
and came forward[3319] and questioned
Jesus, saying, "Do You make no answer? [I]What is it that these men are
[pin]testifying[2649] against You?"
61 [a]But He kept silent, and made
no answer. [b]Again the high priest was
questioning Him, and [I]saying to Him,
"Are [epn]You [II]the Christ,[5547] the Son[5207]
of the Blessed *One?*"[2128]
62 And Jesus said, [epn]"I am; and
you shall see [a]THE SON OF MAN SITTING
AT THE RIGHT HAND[1188] OF Power,[1411]
and [b]COMING WITH THE CLOUDS OF
HEAVEN."[3772]
63 And [a]tearing[1284] his clothes,[5509]
the high priest *said, "What further need
do we have of witnesses?[3144]
64 "You have heard[191] the [a]blas-
phemy;[988] how does it seem[5316] to you?"
And they all condemned Him to be
deserving[1777] of death.
65 And some began to [pinf][a]spit[1716]
at Him, and [Ib]to [pinf]blindfold[4028,4383] Him,
and to [pinf]beat[2852] Him with their fists,
and to [pinf]say to Him, "Prophesy!" And
the officers[5257] [II]received Him with
[III]slaps[4475] *in the face.*

Peter's Denials

66 [a]And as Peter was below[2736] in
[b]the courtyard, one of the servant-girls
of the high priest *came,
67 and seeing Peter [a]warming himself, she [apt]looked at[1689] him, and *said,
"You, too, were[2258] with Jesus the
[b]Nazarene."
68 But he denied[720] *it,* saying, "I
neither know nor understand what you

44 [I]Lit., *safely*
45 [a]Matt. 23:7
47 [I]Lit., *took off*
49 [I]Or possibly, *let the Scriptures be fulfilled* [a]Mark 12:35; Luke 19:47; 21:37
53 [a]Mark 14:53-65: *Matt. 26:57-68; John 18:12f., 19-24*
54 [I]Or, *servants* [II]Lit., *light* [a]Mark 14:68 [b]Matt. 26:3 [c]Mark 14:67; John 18:18
55 [I]Or, *Sanhedrin* [a]Matt. 5:22
58 [I]Or, *sanctuary* [a]Matt. 26:61; Mark 15:29; John 2:19
60 [I]Or, *what do these testify?*
61 [I]Lit., *says* [II]I.e., the Messiah [a]Matt. 26:63 [b]Mark 14:61-63: *Matt. 26:63ff.; Luke 22:67-71*
62 [a]Ps. 110:1; Mark 13:26 [b]Dan. 7:13
63 [a]Num. 14:6; Matt. 26:65; Acts 14:14
64 [a]Lev. 24:16
65 [I]Or, *cover over His face* [II]Or, *treated* [III]Or possibly, *blows with rods* [a]Matt. 26:67; Mark 10:34 [b]Esth. 7:8 [c]Matt. 26:68; Luke 22:64
66 [a]Mark 14:66-72: *Matt. 26:69-75; Luke 22:56-62; John 18:16-18, 25-27* [b]Mark 14:54
67 [a]Mark 14:54 [b]Mark 1:24

14:58 See note on II Cor. 5:1.
14:64 See note on Mk. 3:28,29.

are talking about." And he [a]went out onto the [I]porch.[II]

69 And the maid saw him, and began once more to [pinf]say to the bystanders, "This is *one* of them!"

70 But again [a]he was denying[720] it. And after a little while the bystanders were again saying to Peter, "Surely you are *one* of [epn]them, [b]for you are a Galilean too."

71 But he began to [I]curse[332] and swear, "I do not know[1492] this man you are talking about!"

72 And immediately a cock crowed a second time. And Peter [aop]remembered[363] how Jesus had made the remark[4487] to him, "Before [a]a cock crows twice, you will deny[533] Me three times." [I]And he began to weep.

Jesus before Pilate

15 [a]And early[2112] in the morning the chief priests[749] with the elders[4245] and scribes,[1122] and the whole [I][b]Council, immediately held a consultation; and binding Jesus, they led Him away,[667] and delivered Him up to Pilate.

2 [a]And Pilate questioned Him, "Are [epn]You the King of the Jews?" And answering He *said to him, "*It is as* [epn]you say."

3 And the chief priests *began* to accuse Him [I]harshly.

4 And Pilate was questioning Him again, saying, "Do You make no answer? See how many charges they [pin]bring against[2649] You!"

5 But Jesus [a]made no further answer; so that Pilate was amazed.

6 [a]Now at *the* feast he [ipf]used to release[630] for them *any* one prisoner whom they requested.

7 And the man named Barabbas had been imprisoned with the insurrectionists who had [plpf]committed[4160] murder in the insurrection.[4714]

8 And the multitude went up and began [pinf]asking[154] him *to do* as he had been accustomed to do for them.

9 And Pilate answered them, saying, "Do you want me to release for you the King of the Jews?"

10 For he was aware that the chief priests[749] had delivered Him up because of envy.

11 But the chief priests stirred up the multitude [a]*to ask* him to release Barabbas for them instead.

12 And answering again, Pilate was saying to them, "Then what shall I do with Him whom you [pin]call[3004] the King[935] of the Jews?"

13 And they shouted [I]back, "Crucify[4717] Him!"

14 But Pilate was saying to them, "Why, what evil has He done?" But they shouted all the more, "Crucify Him!"

15 And wishing to satisfy the multitude, Pilate released Barabbas for them, and after having Jesus [a]scourged,[5417] he delivered *Him* to be crucified.

Jesus Is Mocked

16 [a]And the soldiers took Him away into [b]the [I]palace (that is, the Praetorium), and they *called together[4779] the whole *Roman* [II][c]cohort.

17 And they *dressed Him up in [I]purple, and after [apt]weaving[4120] a crown of thorns, they put it on Him;

18 and they began to acclaim Him, "Hail,[5463] King of the Jews!"

19 And they kept beating[5180] His head with a [I]reed, and spitting at Him, and kneeling and bowing[5087] before Him.

20 And after they had mocked Him, they took the purple off Him, and put His[846] garments on Him. And they *led[1806] Him out to [aosb]crucify[4717] Him.

21 [a]And they *pressed into service[29] a passer-by coming from the country,[68] Simon of Cyrene (the father of Alexander and [b]Rufus), to bear[142] His cross.

The Crucifixion

22 [a]And they *brought Him to the place [b]Golgotha, which is translated, Place of a Skull.

68 [I]Or, *forecourt, gateway* [II]Later mss. add *and a cock crowed* [a]Mark 14:54

70 [a]Mark 14:68 [b]Matt. 26:73; Luke 22:59

71 [I]Or, *put himself under a curse*

72 [I]Or, *Thinking of this, he began weeping* or *Rushing out, he began weeping* [a]Mark 14:30, 68

1 [I]Or, *Sanhedrin* [a]Matt. 27:1 [b]Matt. 5:22

2 [a]Mark 15:2-5: *Matt. 27:11-14; Luke 23:2, 3; John 18:29-38*

3 [I]Or, *of many things*

5 [a]Matt. 27:12

6 [a]Mark 15:6-15: *Matt. 27:15-26; Luke 23:18-25; John 18:39-19:16*

11 [a]Acts 3:14

13 [I]Or, *again*

15 [a]Matt. 27:26

16 [I]Or, *court* [II]Or, *battalion* [a]Mark 15:16-20: *Matt. 27:27-31* [b]Matt. 26:3; 27:27 [c]Acts 10:1

17 [I]A term for shades varying from rose to purple

19 [I]Or, *staff* (made of a reed)

21 [a]Mark 15:21: *Matt. 27:32; Luke 23:26* [b]Rom. 16:13

22 [a]Mark 15:22-32: *Matt. 27:33-44; Luke 23:33-43; John 19:17-24* [b]Luke 23:33; John 19:17

23 And they tried to give Him [a]wine [pfpp]mixed with myrrh;4669 but He did not take it.

24 And they *crucified Him, and *[a]divided up His garments among themselves, casting [I]lots for them, *to decide* [II]what each should take.

25 And it was the [Ia]third hour [II]when they crucified Him.

26 And the inscription of the charge against Him [pfpp] [I]read, "[a]THE KING935 OF THE JEWS."

27 And they *crucified4717 two robbers3027 with Him, one on His right and one on His left.

28 [[I]And the Scripture1124 was fulfilled which says, "And He was numbered3049 with transgressors."459]

29 And those [ppp]passing by3899 were [I]hurling abuse987 at Him, [a]wagging2795 their heads, and saying, "Ha! You who *are going to* [b]destroy the temple3485 and rebuild it in three days,

30 save4982 Yourself, and come down from the cross!"

31 In the same way the chief priests also, along with the scribes, were mocking *Him* among themselves and saying, "[a]He saved others; [I]He cannot save Himself.

32 "Let *this* Christ,5547 [a]the King of Israel, now come down from the cross,4716 so that we may see and believe!" And [b]those who were [pfpp]crucified with4957 Him were casting the same insult at Him.

33 [a]And when the [Ib]sixth hour had come, darkness4655 [II]fell over the whole land until the [IIIb]ninth hour.

34 And at the [a]ninth hour Jesus cried out with a loud voice, "[ab]ELOI, ELOI, LAMA SABACHTHANI?" which is translated, "MY GOD, MY GOD, WHY HAST THOU FORSAKEN ME?"

35 And when some of the bystanders heard it, they *began* saying, "Behold, He is calling for Elijah."

36 And someone ran and filled a sponge with sour wine, put it on a reed, and gave Him a drink, saying, "[I]Let us see whether Elijah will come to take Him down."

37 [a]And Jesus [apt]uttered a loud cry,863 and breathed His last.1606

38 [a]And the veil of the temple3485 was torn4977 in two1417 from top509 to bottom.

39 [a]And when the centurion, who was standing [I]right in front of Him, saw [II]the way He breathed His last, he said, "Truly this man was [III]the Son of God!"

40 [a]And there were also *some* women looking on from a distance, among whom *were* Mary Magdalene, and Mary the mother of [I]James [b]the [II]Less and Joses, and [c]Salome.

41 And when He was in Galilee, they [ipf]used to follow190 Him and [ipf] [Ia]minister to1247 Him; and *there were* many other women who had come up with Him to Jerusalem.

Jesus Is Buried

42 [a]And when evening had already come, because it was [b]the preparation day, that is, the day before the Sabbath,4315

43 Joseph of Arimathea came, a [a]prominent member of the Council, who himself was [ppp] [b]waiting for4327 the kingdom932 of God; and he [c]gathered up courage and went in before Pilate, and asked for the body of Jesus.

44 And Pilate wondered if He was dead2348 by this time, and summoning the centurion, he questioned him as to whether He was already3819 dead.

45 And ascertaining this from [a]the centurion, he granted the body to Joseph.

46 And *Joseph* bought a linen cloth, took Him down, wrapped Him in the linen cloth, and laid Him in a tomb3418 which had been hewn2998 out in the rock; and he rolled a stone against the entrance of the tomb.

47 And [a]Mary Magdalene and Mary the *mother* of Joses were [ipf]looking on2334 *to see* where He was laid.

23 [a]Matt. 27:34
24 [I]Lit., *a lot upon* [II]Lit., *who should take what* [a]Ps. 22:18; John 19:24
25 [I]I.e., 9 a.m. [II]Lit., *and* [a]Mark 15:33
26 [I]Lit., *had been inscribed* [a]Matt. 27:37
28 [I]Many mss. do not contain this v.
29 [I]Or, *blaspheming* [a]Ps. 22:7; 109:25; Matt. 27:39 [b]Mark 14:58; John 2:19
31 [I]Or, *can He not save Himself?* [a]Matt. 27:42; Luke 23:35
32 [a]Matt. 27:42; Mark 15:26 [b]Matt. 27:44; Mark 15:27; Luke 23:39-43
33 [I]I.e., noon [II]Or, *occurred* [III]I.e., 3 p.m. [a]Mark 15:33-41: *Matt. 27:45-56; Luke 23:44-49* [b]Matt. 27:45f.; Mark 15:25; Luke 23:44
34 [a]Matt. 27:45f.; Mark 15:25; Luke 23:44 [b]Ps. 22:1; Matt. 27:46
36 [I]Lit., *Permit that we see;* or, *Hold off, let us see*
37 [a]Matt. 27:50; Luke 23:46; John 19:30
38 [a]Ex. 26:31-33; Matt. 27:51; Luke 23:45
39 [I]Or, *opposite Him* [II]Lit., *that He thus* [III]Or possibly, *a son of God* or *son of a god* [a]Matt. 27:54; Mark 15:45; Luke 23:47
40 [I]Or, *Jacob* [II]Lit., *little* (either in stature or age) [a]Mark 15:40, 41: *Matt. 27:55f.;* Luke 23:49; John 19:25 [b]Luke 19:3 [c]Mark 16:1
41 [I]Or, *wait on* [a]Matt. 27:55f.
42 [a]Mark 15:42-47: *Matt. 27:57-61; Luke 23:50-56; John 19:38-42* [b]Matt. 27:62
43 [a]Matt. 27:57; Luke 23:50, 51; Acts 13:50; 17:12 [b]Matt. 27:57; Luke 2:25, 38; 23:51; John 19:38 [c]John 19:38
45 [a]Mark 15:39
47 [a]Matt. 27:56; Mark 15:40; 16:1

The Resurrection

16 [a]And when the Sabbath[4521] [apt]was over,[1230] [b]Mary Magdalene, and Mary the *mother* of [I]James, and Salome, [c]bought spices, that they might come and anoint[218] Him.

2 And very early on the first day of the week, they *came to the tomb[3418] when the sun had risen.

3 And they were saying to one another, "Who will roll away [a]the stone for us from the entrance of the tomb?"

4 And looking up, they *saw that the stone [pfip]had been rolled away,[617] [I]although it was extremely large.

5 And [a]entering the tomb, they saw a young man sitting at the right, wearing a white robe; and they [b]were amazed.[1568]

6 And he *said to them, "[a]Do not be amazed; you are looking for Jesus the [b]Nazarene, who has been crucified.[4717] [c]He has [aop]risen;[1453] He is not here; behold, *here is* the place where they laid Him.

7 "But go, tell His disciples[3101] and Peter, '[a]He is going before you into Galilee; there you will see Him, just as He said to you.' "

8 And they went out and fled from the tomb, for trembling and astonishment[1611] had gripped them; and they said nothing to anyone, for they were [ipf]afraid.[5399]

9 [[I]Now after He had risen early on the first[4412] day of the week, He first appeared to [a]Mary Magdalene, from whom He had cast out seven demons.[1140]

10 [a]She went and reported to those who had been with Him, while they were [ppt]mourning[3996] and [ppt]weeping.[2799]

11 And when they [apt]heard[191] that He was alive,[2198] and had been seen by her, [a]they refused to believe[569] it.

12 And after that, [a]He appeared[5319] in a different[2087] form[3444] [b]to two of them, while they [ppt]were walking[4043] along on their way to the country.

13 And they went away and reported it to the others, but they [a]did not believe them either.

The Disciples Commissioned

14 And afterward [a]He appeared[5319] [b]to the eleven themselves as they were reclining *at the table;* and He reproached[3679] them for their [c]unbelief[570] and hardness of heart,[4641] because they had not believed those who had seen Him after He had risen.[1453]

15 And He said to them, [aptp]"[a]Go[4198] into all the world[2887] and preach[2784] the gospel[2098] to all creation.[2937]

16 "[a]He who has [apt]believed[4100] and has been baptized[907] shall be saved;[4982] but he who has disbelieved[569] shall be condemned.[2632]

17 "And these [I]signs[4592] will accompany those who have [apt]believed:[4100] [a]in My name[3686] they will cast out demons,[1140] they will [b]speak[2980] with new[2537] tongues;[1100]

18 they will [a]pick up serpents, and if they drink any deadly *poison,* it shall [efn]not hurt them; they will [b]lay hands on the sick,[732] and they will recover."

19 So then, when the Lord Jesus had [a]spoken to them, He [b]was received up[353] into heaven,[3772] and [c]sat down at the right hand[1188] of God.

20 And they [apt]went out[1831] and preached[2784] everywhere, while the Lord worked with them, and confirmed[950] the word[3056] by the [I]signs[4592] that followed.[II]] [[III]*And they promptly reported all these instructions to Peter and his companions. And after that, Jesus Himself sent out through them from east to west the sacred and imperishable proclamation of eternal salvation.*]

1 [I]Or, *Jacob* [a]Mark 16:1-8: *Matt. 28:1-8; Luke 24:1-10;* John 20:1-8 [b]Mark 15:47 [c]Luke 23:56; John 19:39f.
3 [a]Matt. 27:60; Mark 15:46; 16:4
4 [I]Lit., *for*
5 [a]John 20:11, 12 [b]Mark 9:15
6 [a]Mark 9:15 [b]Mark 1:24 [c]Matt. 28:6; Luke 24:6
7 [a]Matt. 26:32; Mark 14:28
9 [I]Some of the oldest mss. do not contain vv. 9-20 [a]Matt. 27:56; John 20:14
10 [a]John 20:18
11 [a]Matt. 28:17; Mark 16:13, 14; Luke 24:11, 41; John 20:25
12 [a]Mark 16:14; John 21:1, 14 [b]Luke 24:13-35
13 [a]Matt. 28:17; Mark 16:11, 14; Luke 24:11, 41; John 20:25
14 [a]Mark 16:12; John 21:1, 14 [b]Luke 24:36; John 20:19, 26; 1Cor. 15:5 [c]Matt. 28:17; Mark 16:11, 13; Luke 24:11, 41; John 20:25
15 [a]Matt. 28:19; Acts 1:8
16 [a]John 3:18, 36; Acts 16:31
17 [I]Or, *attesting miracles* [a]Mark 9:38; Luke 10:17; Acts 5:16; 8:7; 16:18; 19:12 [b]Acts 2:4; 10:46; 19:6; 1Cor. 12:10, 28, 30; 13:1; 14:2
18 [a]Luke 10:19; Acts 28:3-5 [b]Mark 5:23
19 [a]Acts 1:3 [b]Luke 9:51; 24:51; John 6:62; 20:17; Acts 1:2, 9-11; 1Tim. 3:16 [c]Ps. 110:1; Luke 22:69; Acts 7:55f.; Rom. 8:34; Eph. 1:20; Col. 3:1; Heb. 1:3; 8:1; 10:12; 12:2; 1Pet. 3:22
20 [I]Or, *attesting miracles* [II]Many mss. add *Amen* [III]A few later mss. and versions contain this paragraph, usually after v. 8; a few have it at the end of ch.

16:16 See note on I Pet. 3:20,21.
16:17 See note on I Cor. 14:1-3. The verb "believe" in Greek is in the aorist tense *pisteusasi* (4100) which refers to those who did believe, not those who would believe at that time or in the future.

The Gospel According to

LUKE

The Gospel of Luke portrays Jesus as the long-awaited Messiah of the Jews and also the Savior of all mankind. Special emphasis is placed upon the kindness of Jesus toward women, the poor, the outcasts, the weak, and those who were suffering in different ways. In addition, the book is filled with expressions of praise and prayer. Luke's account had a universal appeal, especially to the Gentiles. Jesus is presented as the perfect Man who is truly interested in every person on earth, no matter what his station in life. Luke was aimed at the Greek mind and, therefore, had to be written in a comprehensive, logical, and orderly manner. There are portions of the book which approach Classical Greek literature. Luke has been called "the most beautiful book ever written."

There is little doubt that the author was Luke, the "beloved physician" (Col. 4:14). From the context of this passage we learn that Luke was not of the circumcision and, consequently, he may have been the only Gentile writer of the New Testament. Paul refers to him as his "fellow-worker" in Philemon 24. Several passages indicate that he was a close companion to the Apostle during the missionary journeys of the book of Acts. He was with Paul until the very end (II Tim. 4:11). Judging from the style of his Greek, we can surmise that he was the most cultured of all the writers of the Gospel.

Introduction

1 Inasmuch as many have undertaken to [ainf]compile[392] an account of the things [pfpp] [Ia]accomplished[4135] among us,

2 just as those who [a]from the beginning [I]were [b]eyewitnesses and [IIc]servants[5257] of [d]the [III]word[3056] have handed them down to us,

3 it seemed fitting for me as well, [a]having [pfp] [I]investigated everything carefully from the beginning,[509] to write *it* out for you [b]in consecutive order, [c]most excellent [d]Theophilus;

4 so that you might know the exact truth about the things you have been [aop] [Ia]taught.

Birth of John the Baptist Foretold

5 [a]In the days[2250] of Herod, king of Judea, there [I]was a certain priest named [II]Zacharias, of the [b]division of [III]Abijah; and he had a wife [IV]from the daughters of Aaron, and her name was Elizabeth.

6 And they were both [a]righteous[1342] in the sight of God,[2316] walking [b]blamelessly[273] in all the commandments and requirements[1345] of the Lord.

7 And they had no child, because Elizabeth was barren, and they were both advanced[4260] in [I]years.

8 Now it came about, while [a]he was [aie]performing his priestly service before God in the *appointed* order[5010] of his division,

9 according to the custom of the priestly office, he was chosen by lot [a]to enter the temple[3485] of the Lord and burn incense.

10 And the whole multitude of the people[2992] were in prayer[4336] [a]outside at[1854] the hour[5610] of the incense offering.

11 And [a]an angel[32] of the Lord appeared to him, standing to the right of the altar of incense.

12 And Zacharias was troubled when he saw *him,* and [a]fear[5401] [I]gripped him.

13 But the angel said to him, "[a]Do not be afraid,[5399] Zacharias, for your petition has been [aop]heard, and your wife Elizabeth will bear[1080] you a son,[5207] and [b]you will [I]give him the name John.

1 [I]Or, *on which there is full conviction* [a]Rom. 4:21; 14:5; Col. 2:2; 4:12; 1Thess. 1:5; 2Tim. 4:17; Heb. 6:11; 10:22
2 [I]Lit., *became* [II]Or, *ministers* [III]I.e., gospel [a]John 15:27; Acts 1:21f. [b]2Pet. 1:16; 1John 1:1 [c]Acts 26:16; 1Cor. 4:1; Heb. 2:3 [d]Mark 4:14; 16:20; Acts 8:4; 14:25; 16:6; 17:11
3 [I]Or, *followed* [a]1Tim. 4:6 [b]Acts 11:4; 18:23 [c]Acts 23:26; 24:3; 26:25 [d]Acts 1:1
4 [I]Or, *orally instructed in* [a]Acts 18:25; Rom. 2:18; 1Cor. 14:19; Gal. 6:6
5 [I]Lit., *came into being* [II]I.e., Zechariah [III]Gr., *Abia* [IV]I.e., of priestly descent [a]Matt. 2:1 [b]1Chr. 24:10
6 [a]Gen. 7:1; Acts 2:25; 8:21 [b]Phil. 2:15; 3:6; 1Thess. 3:13

7 [I]Lit., *days* **8** [a]1Chr. 24:19; 2Chr. 8:14; 31:2
9 [a]Ex. 30:7f. **10** [a]Lev. 16:17 **11** [a]Luke 2:9; Acts 5:19 **12** [I]Or, *fell upon* [a]Luke 2:9 **13** [I]Lit., *call his name* [a]Matt. 14:27; Luke 1:30 [b]Luke 1:60, 63

14 “And you will have joy and gladness,[20] and many will rejoice[5463] at his birth.[1078]

15 “For he will be great in the sight of the Lord, and he will [a]drink no wine or liquor;[4608] and he will be filled with the Holy Spirit,[4151] [I]while yet in his mother’s womb.

16 “And he will [a]turn back[1994] many of the sons[5207] of Israel to the Lord their God.

17 “And it is he who will [a]go *as a forerunner* before Him in the spirit[4151] and power of [b]Elijah, [c]TO TURN THE HEARTS[2588] OF THE FATHERS BACK TO THE CHILDREN, and the disobedient[545] to the attitude of the righteous; so as to [a]make ready a people prepared for the Lord.”

18 And Zacharias said to the angel, “How shall I know this *for certain*? For [a]I am an old man, and my wife is advanced in [I]years.”

19 And the angel answered and said to him, “I am [a]Gabriel, who [pfp] [I][b]stands in the presence of God; and I have been [aop]sent[649] to speak to you, and to [ainf]bring you this good news.[2097]

20 “And behold, you shall be silent and [ppt]unable to [ainf]speak until the day when these things take place, because you did not [ao]believe[4100] my words,[3056] which shall be fulfilled in their proper time.”[2540]

21 And the people were waiting for Zacharias, and were [ipf]wondering at his [aie]delay in the temple.

22 But when he came out, he was unable to speak[2980] to them; and they realized that he had seen a vision in the temple; and he [a]kept [I]making signs to them, and [ipf]remained mute.

23 And it came about, when the days of his priestly service[3009] were ended, that he went back home.

24 And after these days Elizabeth his wife became pregnant; and she [ipf] [I]kept herself in seclusion for five months, saying,

25 “This is the way the Lord has dealt with me in the days when He looked *with favor* upon[1896] *me,* to [a]take away my disgrace among men.”

Jesus’ Birth Foretold

26 Now in the sixth month the angel[32] [a]Gabriel was sent from God to a city in Galilee, called[3686] [b]Nazareth,

27 to [a]a virgin[3933] engaged[3423] to a man whose name was Joseph, [b]of the [I]descendants[3624] of David; and the virgin’s name was Mary.

28 And coming in, he said to her, “Hail,[5463] [pfpp] [I]favored one![5487] The Lord [II]*is* with you.”[III]

29 But she [a]was greatly [aop]troubled at *this* statement, and kept pondering[1260] what kind of salutation this might be.

30 And the angel said to her, “[a]Do not be [pim]afraid,[5399] Mary; for you have [ao]found[2147] favor[5485] with God.

31 “And behold, you will conceive in your womb, and bear a son,[5207] and you [a]shall name Him Jesus.

32 “He will be great, and will be called the Son of [a]the Most High; and the Lord God will give Him [b]the throne of His father[3962] David;

33 [a]and He will reign[936] over the house[3624] of Jacob forever; [b]and His kingdom[932] will have no end.”[5056]

34 And Mary said to the angel, “How [I]can this be, since I [II]am a virgin?”[1097,435][3756]

35 And the angel answered and said to her, “[a]The [an]Holy [an]Spirit will come upon you, and the power of [b]the Most High will overshadow you; and for that reason [c]the [I]holy offspring[40,1080] shall be called [d]the [an]Son of God.

36 “And behold, even your relative Elizabeth has also [pfi]conceived a son in her old age; and [I]she who was [ppp]called barren is now in her sixth month.

37 “For [I][a]nothing[3956,4487][3756] will be [ft]impossible[101] with God.”

38 And [I]Mary said, “Behold, the [II]bondslave of the Lord; be it done to me according to your word.”[4487] And the angel departed from her.

15 [I]Lit., *even from* [a]Num. 6:3; Judg. 13:4; Matt. 11:18; Luke 7:33
16 [a]Matt. 3:2, 6; Luke 3:3
17 [a]Luke 1:76 [b]Matt. 11:14 [c]Mal. 4:6
18 [I]Lit., *days* [a]Gen. 17:17
19 [I]Lit., *stand beside* [a]Dan. 8:16; 9:21; Luke 1:26 [b]Matt. 18:10
22 [I]Or, *beckoning to* or *nodding to* [a]Luke 1:62
24 [I]Lit., *was hidden*
25 [a]Gen. 30:23; Is. 4:1; 25:8
26 [a]Luke 1:19 [b]Matt. 2:23
27 [I]Lit., *house* [a]Matt. 1:18 [b]Matt. 1:16, 20; Luke 2:4
28 [I]Or, *O woman richly blessed* [II]Or, be [III]Later mss. add *you are blessed among women*
29 [a]Luke 1:12
30 [a]Matt. 14:27; Luke 1:13
31 [a]Is. 7:14; Matt. 1:21, 25; Luke 2:21
32 [a]Mark 5:7; Luke 1:35, 76; 6:35; Acts 7:48 [b]2Sam. 7:12, 13, 16; Is. 9:7
33 [a]Matt. 1:1 [b]2Sam. 7:13, 16; Ps. 89:36, 37; Dan. 2:44; 7:14, 18, 27; Matt. 28:18
34 [I]Lit., *shall* [II]Lit., *know no man*
35 [I]Lit., *the holy thing begotten* [a]Matt. 1:18 [b]Luke 1:32 [c]Mark 1:24 [d]Matt. 4:3; John 1:34, 49; 20:31
36 [I]Lit., *this is the sixth month to her who*
37 [I]Lit., *not any word* [a]Gen. 18:14; Jer. 32:17; Matt. 19:26
38 [I]Gr., *Mariam;* i.e., Miriam; so throughout Luke [II]I.e., female slave

Mary Visits Elizabeth

39 Now [I]at this time Mary arose
and went with haste to [a]the hill country,
to a city of Judah,
40 and entered the house of Zacharias and greeted Elizabeth.
41 And it came about that when
Elizabeth heard Mary's greeting, the
baby[1025] leaped in her womb; and Elizabeth was [a]filled with the Holy Spirit.
42 And she cried out with a loud
voice, and said, pfpp"Blessed[2127] among
women *are* you, and pfppblessed *is* the
fruit of your womb!
43 "And [I]how has it *happened* to me,
that the mother of [a]my Lord should come
to me?
44 "For behold, when the sound of
your greeting reached my ears, the baby
leaped in my womb for joy.[20]
45 "And [a]blessed[3107] *is* she who believed [I]that there would be a fulfillment[5050] of what had been pfppspoken
to her [II]by the Lord."

The Magnificat

🔑46 And Mary said:
"[a]My soul[5590] pin [I][b]exalts the Lord,
47 And [a]my spirit has aorejoiced[21]
in [b]God my Savior.[4990]
🔑48 "For [a]He has had regard[1914] for
the humble state[5014] of His
[I]bondslave;
For behold, from this time on
all generations will count me
[b]blessed.[3106]
49 "For the Mighty One has aodone
great things[3173] for me;
And holy[40] is His name.
50 "[a]AND HIS MERCY[1656] IS [I]UPON
GENERATION AFTER
GENERATION

39 [I]Lit., *in these days* [a]Josh. 20:7; 21:11; Luke 1:65
41 [a]Luke 1:67; Acts 2:4; 4:8; 9:17
43 [I]Lit., *whence this to me* [a]Luke 2:11
45 [I]Or possibly, *because there will be* [II]Lit., *from* [a]Luke 1:20, 48
46 [I]Lit., *makes great* [a]Luke 1:46-53: *1Sam. 2:1-10* [b]Ps. 34:2f.
47 [a]Ps. 35:9; Hab. 3:18 [b]1Tim. 1:1; 2:3; Titus 1:3; 2:10; 3:4; Jude 25
48 [I]I.e., female slave [a]Ps. 138:6 [b]Luke 1:45
50 [I]Lit., *unto generations and generations* [a]Ps. 103:17

🔑 **1:46-55** Mary's song of praise, often called the "Magnificat" after the first word of the song in the Vulgate version, is a humble response to God for His display of grace in her life. Twice the angel Gabriel addresses Mary as the recipient of God's grace. In v. 28 Mary is called "favored one" (*kecharitōmenē,* 5487). This word comes from *charis* (5485), grace or undeserved favor. Then in v. 30 Gabriel comforts Mary by saying, you have found favor (*charis*) with God." For a complete exegetical analysis of the Magnificat see the Editor's book entitled *The Song of the Virgin.*

🔑 **1:48** This verse contains one of the most misunderstood words of the N.T. It is the word *makarios,* used repeatedly in the Beatitudes. The verb of the adjective noun *makarios,* "blessed," (*makarizō,* 3106), is used here. The translation says "all generations will count me blessed," but the Greek says *makariousi,* the Attic future of *makarizō,* which in reality means "they shall bless me." But since the meaning of *makarios* is to be indwelt by God and thereby to be fully satisfied, the Virgin Mary was declaring that because she was indwelt by God, this fact was going to be recognized and declared by generations to come. In connection with the meaning of the word *makarios,* note that in v. 45 it states, "And blessed is she who believed." *Makaria* (feminine) is what Elizabeth called her cousin Mary when she saw her and realized that she was indwelt by God. If you go, however, to v. 42, you will find that the word translated "blessed" there is not *makaria,* but is a totally different word, *eulogēmenē,* which in its literal meaning is "eulogized, well spoken of." The verb *eulogeō* (2127) is the more commonly used verb in the N.T. of the two verbs: *makarizō,* "to be declared as indwelt by God and therefore fully satisfied," and *eulogeō,* "to speak well of." When we bless (*eulogeō*) God we are speaking well of Him which is equal to praising or thanking Him. When, however, we ask God to bless us or speak well of us, we are asking Him not merely to approve our plans but to interfere in our lives. God's words are God's actions. Therefore, there is a very definite distinction between these two words. The verb *makarizō* occurs only in Lk. 1:48 and Js. 5:11 in which it is totally mistranslated as "we count those happy who endure." Happiness has absolutely nothing to do with *makariotēs,* "blessedness," an inner quality granted by God. The word "happiness" in its equivalent in Greek and as used in the Classics, *eudaimōn* and *eutuchēs,* "lucky," never occurs in the N.T. The Lord never promised happiness, good luck, or favorable circumstances to the believer, but *makariotēs,* "blessedness." This means His indwelling and the consequent peace and satisfaction to the believer no matter what the circumstances may be. Js. 5:11 should be translated: "Behold, we recognize those who endured as blessed," that is to say, having been indwelt by God and in Him finding their full satisfaction in spite of their suffering. See note on Mt. 5:1-12 and the Editor's book, *The Pursuit of Happiness* concerning the Beatitudes in both Mt. 5:1-12 and Lk. 6:20-24.

TOWARD THOSE WHO FEAR[5399]
HIM.
51 "[a]He has [ao]done [I]mighty deeds
with His arm;
He has [ao]scattered *those who*
were proud[5244] in the
[II]thoughts[1271] of their heart.
52 "He has [ao]brought down[2507]
rulers[1413] from *their* thrones,
And has [a]exalted those who
were humble.
53 "[a]HE HAS [ao]FILLED THE HUNGRY
WITH GOOD THINGS;[18]
AND [ao]sent away the rich empty-
handed.
54 "He has given [ao]help[482] to Israel
His servant,[3816]
[I]In [ainf]remembrance of His
mercy,
55 [a]As He spoke to our fathers,
[b]To Abraham and his
[I]offspring[4690] forever."[1519,165] [3588]
56 And Mary stayed[306] with her
about three months, and *then* returned
to her home.

John Is Born

57 Now the time[5550] [I]had [aop]come
for Elizabeth to [ainf] give birth,[5088] and she
brought forth[1080] a son.
58 And her neighbors and her relatives heard that the Lord had [ipf] [I][a]dis-
played His great mercy toward her; and
they were [ipf]rejoicing with her.
59 And it came about that on [a]the
eighth day they came to circumcise[4059]
the child, and they were going to call
him Zacharias, [I]after his father.
60 And his mother answered and
said, "No indeed; but [a]he shall be called
John."
61 And they said to her, "There is
no one among your relatives who is
called by that name."
62 And they [ipf][a]made signs to his
father, as to what he wanted him called.
63 And he asked for a tablet, and
wrote[1125] as follows, "[a]His name is
John." And they were all astonished.
64 [a]And at once his mouth was
opened and his tongue *loosed,* and he
began to [ipf]speak in [ppf]praise[2127] of God.
65 And fear[5401] came on all those
living around them; and all these
matters[4487] were being [ipf]talked about[255]
in all [a]the hill country of Judea.
66 And all who [apt]heard them kept
them in mind,[2588] saying, "What then
will this child[3813] *turn out to* be?" For
[a]the hand of the Lord was certainly with
him.

Zacharias' Prophecy

67 And his father Zacharias [a]was
filled with the [an]Holy [an]Spirit, and
[b]prophesied,[4395] saying:
68 "[a]Blessed[2128] *be* the Lord God of
Israel,
For He has [ao]visited[1980] us and
accomplished
[b]redemption[3085] for His
people,
69 And has [ao]raised up a [a]horn of
salvation[4991] for us
In the house of David [b]His
servant—[3816]
70 [a]As He spoke by the mouth of
His holy prophets [b]from of
old—
71 [nn] [I][a]SALVATION[4991] [b]FROM OUR
ENEMIES,
And FROM THE HAND OF ALL
WHO [ppt]HATE US;
72 [a]To [ainf]show mercy[1656] toward
our fathers,
[b]And to [ainf]remember His holy[40]
covenant,[1242]
73 [a]The oath[3727] which He swore
to Abraham our father,
74 To grant us that we, being
[aptp]delivered[4506] from the
hand of our enemies,
Might serve[3000] Him without
fear,
75 [a]In holiness[3742] and
righteousness[1343] before Him
all our days.
76 "And you, child, will be called the
[a]prophet of [b]the Most High;
For you will go on [c]BEFORE THE
LORD TO [d]PREPARE HIS
WAYS;[5398]

51 [I]Lit., *might* [II]Lit., *thought, attitude* [a]Ps. 98:1; 118:15

52 [a]Job 5:11

53 [a]Ps. 107:9

54 [I]Lit., *So as to remember*

55 [I]Lit., *seed* [a]Gen. 17:19; Ps. 132:11; Gal. 3:16 [b]Gen. 17:7

57 [I]Lit., *was fulfilled*

58 [I]Lit., *magnified* [a]Gen. 19:19

59 [I]Lit., *after the name of* [a]Gen. 17:12; Lev. 12:3; Luke 2:21; Phil. 3:5

60 [a]Luke 1:13, 63

62 [a]Luke 1:22

63 [a]Luke 1:13, 60

64 [a]Luke 1:20

65 [a]Luke 1:39

66 [a]Acts 11:21

67 [a]Luke 1:41; Acts 2:4, 8; 9:17 [b]Joel 2:28

68 [a]1Kin. 1:48; Ps. 41:13; 72:18; 106:48 [b]Luke 1:71; 2:38; Heb. 9:12

69 [a]1Sam. 2:1, 10; Ps. 18:2; 89:17; 132:17; Ezek. 29:21 [b]Matt. 1:1

70 [a]Rom. 1:2 [b]Acts 3:21

71 [I]Or, *Deliverance* [a]Luke 1:68 [b]Ps. 106:10

72 [a]Mic. 7:20 [b]Ps. 105:8f., 42; 106:45

73 [a]Gen. 22:16ff.; Heb. 6:13

75 [a]Eph. 4:24

76 [a]Matt. 11:9 [b]Luke 1:32 [c]Mal. 3:1; Matt. 11:10; Mark 1:2; Luke 7:27 [d]Luke 1:17

77 To give to His people *the*
knowledge[1108] of
salvation[4991]
[I]By [a]the forgiveness[859] of their
sins,
78 Because of the tender mercy[1656]
of our God,
With which [a]the Sunrise from on
high shall [ao]visit[1980] us,
79 [a]To [ainf]SHINE UPON[2014] THOSE
WHO [ppt]SIT IN DARKNESS[4655]
AND THE SHADOW OF DEATH,
To [ainf]guide our feet into the
[b]way of peace."
80 [a]And the child continued to
[ipf]grow, and to become strong[2901] in
spirit,[4151] and he lived in the deserts
until the day of his public appearance
to Israel.

Jesus' Birth in Bethlehem

2 Now it came about in those days
that a decree[1378] went out from
[a]Caesar Augustus, that a census be
[pip]taken of [b]all [I]the inhabited earth.[3625]
2 [I]This was the first[4413] census
taken while [II]Quirinius was governor of
[a]Syria.
3 And all were [ipf]proceeding to
[pip]register for the census, everyone to
his own[1438] city.
4 And Joseph also went up from Galilee, from the city of Nazareth, to Judea,
to the city of David, which is called Bethlehem, because [a]he was of the house[3624]
and family[3965] of David,
5 in order to [ainf]register, along with
Mary, who was engaged[3423] to him, and
was with child.
6 And it came about that while they
were there, the days were completed
for her to give birth.
7 And she [a]gave birth to her first-
born[4416] son;[5207] and she wrapped Him
in cloths,[4683] and laid Him in a [I]man-
ger,[5336] because there was no room for
them in the inn.
8 And in the same region there were
some shepherds[4166] staying out in the
fields, and keeping[5442] watch[5438] over
their flock[4267] by night.
9 And [a]an angel[32] of the Lord suddenly [b]stood before them, and the
glory[1391] of the Lord shone around them;
and they were terribly[3173] frightened.[5399]
10 And the angel said to them, "[a]Do
not [pim]be afraid;[5399] for behold, I bring
you good news of a great joy[5479] which
shall be for all the people;[2992]
11 for today in the city of David
there has [aop]been born[5088] for you a
[a]Savior,[4990] who is [Ib]Christ[5547] [c]the Lord.
12 "And [a]this *will be* a [art]sign for you:
you will find a baby[1025] wrapped in cloths,
and lying[2749] in a [I]manger."
13 And suddenly there appeared
with the angel a multitude of the
heavenly[3770] host[4756] praising[134]
God,[2316] and saying,
14 "[a]Glory[1391] to God in the highest,
And on earth peace[1515] among
men[444] [Ib]with whom He is
pleased."[2107]
15 And it came about when the angels had gone [ao]away from them into
heaven, that the shepherds[4166] *began*
saying to one another, "Let us go
straight to Bethlehem then, and see this
thing[4487] that has happened which the
Lord has made known to us."
16 And they came in [apt]haste and
found[429] their way to Mary and Joseph,
and the baby[1025] as He lay[2749] in the
[I]manger.
17 And when they had seen this,
they made known[1107] the statement[4487]
which had been told them about this
Child.
18 And all who heard it wondered
at the things which were told them by
the shepherds.[4166]
19 But Mary [ipf a]treasured up all
these things, [ppt]pondering them in her
heart.
20 And the shepherds went
back,[5290] [a]glorifying[1392] and praising[134]
God for all that they had [ao]heard and
[ao]seen, just as had been told them.

77 [I]Or, *Consisting in* [a]Jer. 31:34; Mark 1:4
78 [a]Mal. 4:2; Eph. 5:14; 2Pet. 1:19
79 [a]Is. 9:2 [b]Is. 59:8; Matt. 4:16
80 [a]Luke 2:40
1 [I]I.e., the Roman empire [a]Matt. 22:17; Luke 3:1 [b]Matt. 24:14
2 [I]Or, *This took place as a first census* [II]Gr., *Kyrenios* [a]Matt. 4:24
4 [a]Luke 1:27
7 [I]Or, *feeding trough* [a]Matt. 1:25
9 [a]Luke 1:11; Acts 5:19 [b]Luke 24:4; Acts 12:7
10 [a]Matt. 14:27
11 [I]I.e., Messiah [a]Matt. 1:21; John 4:42; Acts 5:31 [b]Matt. 1:16; 16:16, 20; John 11:27 [c]Luke 1:43; Acts 2:36; 10:36
12 [I]Or, *feeding trough* [a]1Sam. 2:34; 2Kin. 19:29; 20:8f.; Is. 7:11, 14
14 [I]Lit., *of good pleasure;* or possibly, *of good will* [a]Matt. 21:9; Luke 19:38 [b]Luke 3:22; Eph. 1:9; Phil. 2:13
16 [I]Or, *feeding trough*
19 [a]Luke 2:51
20 [a]Matt. 9:8

2:7 See note on Col. 1:15.

Jesus Presented at the Temple

21 And when [a]eight days were completed[4130] [I]before His [ainf]circumcision,[4059] [b]His name was *then* called Jesus, the name given by the angel[32] before He was [aifp]conceived in the womb.

22 [a]And when the days for their purification[2512] according to[2596] the law[3551] of Moses were completed, they [ao]brought Him up to Jerusalem to present Him to the Lord

23 (as it is written[1125] in the Law of the Lord, "[a]EVERY *first-born* MALE THAT [ppt]OPENS THE WOMB SHALL BE CALLED HOLY[40] TO THE LORD"[2962]),

24 and to offer a sacrifice[2378] according to what was said in the Law of the Lord, "[a]A PAIR OF TURTLEDOVES, OR TWO YOUNG PIGEONS."

25 And behold, there was a man in Jerusalem whose name was Simeon; and this man was [a]righteous[1342] and devout,[2126] [b]looking for[4327] the consolation[3874] of Israel; and the [an]Holy [an]Spirit was upon him.

26 And [a]it had been revealed[5537] to him by the Holy Spirit that he would not [b]see[1492] death[2288] before he had seen[1492] the Lord's [I]Christ.

27 And he came in the Spirit into the temple;[2411] and when the parents brought in[1521] the child Jesus, [Ia]to carry out for Him the custom of the Law,

28 then he took[1209] Him into his arms, and blessed[2127] God, and said,

29 "Now Lord,[1203] Thou dost [pin]let
Thy bond-servant depart[630]
In peace, [a]according to Thy word;[4487]

30 For my eyes have [ao][a]seen Thy salvation,[4992]

31 Which Thou hast [ao]prepared in the presence[4383] of all peoples,[2992]

32 [a]A LIGHT[5457] [I]OF REVELATION[602] TO THE GENTILES,
And the glory of Thy people Israel."

33 And His father and [a]mother were amazed at the things which were being [ppp]said about Him.

34 And Simeon blessed them, and said to Mary [a]His mother, "Behold, this *Child* is [pin]appointed[2749] for [b]the fall and [I]rise[386] of many in Israel, and for a sign to be [ppp]opposed—

35 and a sword will pierce even your own soul—[5590] to the end that thoughts[1261] from many hearts may be [asbp]revealed."[601]

36 And there was a [a]prophetess,[4398] [I]Anna the daughter of Phanuel, of [b]the tribe of Asher. She was advanced in [II]years, [c]having [apt]lived[2198] with a husband seven years after her [III]marriage,

37 and then as a widow to the age of eighty-four. And she never [ipf]left[868] the temple,[2411] [ppt]serving[3000] night and day with [a]fastings[3521] and prayers.

38 And at that very [I]moment[5610] she came up and *began* [ipf]giving thanks to God, and continued to [ipf]speak of Him to all those who were [ppt] [a]looking for[4327] the redemption[3085] of Jerusalem.

Return to Nazareth

39 And when they had performed[5055] everything according to the Law of the Lord, they returned to Galilee, to [a]their own city of Nazareth.

40 [a]And the Child continued to [ipf]grow and [ipf]become strong,[2901] [ppp] [I]increasing in wisdom;[4678] and the grace[5485] of God was upon Him.

Visit to Jerusalem

41 And His parents used to [ipf]go to Jerusalem every year at [a]the Feast of the Passover.[3957]

42 And when He became twelve, they went up *there* according to the custom of the Feast;

43 and as they were [aie]returning, after [apt]spending the [a]full number[5048] of days, the boy Jesus stayed behind[5278] in Jerusalem. And His parents were unaware of it,

44 but [apt]supposed Him to be in the caravan, and went[2064] a day's journey;[2250,3598] and they *began* [ipf]looking

---

21 [I]Lit., *so as to circumcise Him* [a]Gen. 17:12; Lev. 12:3; Luke 1:59 [b]Matt. 1:21, 25; Luke 1:31

22 [a]Lev. 12:6-8

23 [a]Ex. 13:2, 12; Num. 3:13; 8:17

24 [a]Lev. 5:11; 12:8

25 [a]Luke 1:6 [b]Mark 15:43; Luke 2:38; 23:51

26 [I]I.e., Messiah [a]Matt. 2:12 [b]Ps. 89:48; John 8:51; Heb. 11:5

27 [I]Lit., *to do for Him according to* [a]Luke 2:22

29 [a]Luke 2:26

30 [a]Ps. 119:166, 174; Is. 52:10; Luke 3:6

32 [I]Or, *for* [a]Is. 9:2; 42:6; 49:6, 9; 51:4; 60:1-3; Matt. 4:16; Acts 13:47; 26:23

33 [a]Matt. 12:46

34 [I]Or, *resurrection* [a]Matt. 12:46 [b]Matt. 21:44; 1Cor. 1:23; 2Cor. 2:16; 1Pet. 2:8

36 [I]Or, *Hannah* [II]Lit., *days* [III]Lit., *virginity* [a]Luke 2:38; Acts 21:9 [b]Josh. 19:24 [c]1Tim. 5:9

37 [a]Luke 5:33; Acts 13:3; 14:23; 1Tim. 5:5

38 [I]Lit., *hour* [a]Luke 1:68; 2:25

39 [a]Matt. 2:23; Luke 1:26; 2:51; 4:16

40 [I]Lit., *becoming full of* [a]Luke 1:80; 2:52

41 [a]Ex. 12:11; 23:15; Deut. 16:1-6

43 [a]Ex. 12:15

for Him among their relatives and [pl]acquaintances.[1110]

45 And when they did not find Him, they returned to Jerusalem, looking for Him.

46 And it came about that after three days they found Him in the temple,[2411] sitting in the midst[3319] of the teachers,[1320] both listening to them, and asking them questions.

47 And all who [ppt]heard Him [a]were amazed at His understanding and His answers.[612]

48 And when they saw Him, they were astonished; and [a]His mother said to Him, "[I]Son,[5043] why have You [ao]treated us this way? Behold, [b]Your father[3962] and I [II]have been anxiously [ipf]looking for You."

49 And He said to them, "Why is it that you were [ipf]looking for Me? Did you not know[1492] that [a]I had to be in My Father's[3962] [I]*house?*"

50 And [a]they did not understand the statement[4487] which He [I]had made to them.

51 And He went down with them, and came to [a]Nazareth; and He continued in subjection[5293] to them; and [b]His mother [ipf] [Ic]treasured[1301] all *these* [II]things in her heart.[2588]

52 And Jesus kept [ipf]increasing in wisdom[4678] and [I]stature, and in [a]favor[5485] with God[2316] and men.[444]

John the Baptist Preaches

3 Now in the fifteenth year of the reign of Tiberius Caesar, when [a]Pontius Pilate was governor5075 of Judea, and [b]Herod was tetrarch of Galilee, and his brother Philip was tetrarch of the region of Ituraea and Trachonitis, and Lysanias was tetrarch of Abilene,

2 in the high priesthood of [a]Annas and [b]Caiaphas, [c]the word[4487] of God came to John, the son of Zacharias, in the wilderness.

3 And he came into all [a]the district around the Jordan, preaching[2784] a [an]baptism[908] of repentance[3341] for the forgiveness[859] of sins;

47 [a]Matt. 7:28; 13:54; 22:33; Mark 1:22; 6:2; 11:18; Luke 4:32; John 7:15

48 [I]Lit., *Child* [II]Lit., *are looking* [a]Matt. 12:46 [b]Luke 2:49; 3:23; 4:22

49 [I]Or, *affairs;* lit., *in the things of My Father* [a]John 4:34; 5:36

50 [I]Lit., *had spoken* [a]Mark 9:32; Luke 9:45; 18:34

51 [I]Lit., *was treasuring* [II]Lit., *words* [a]Luke 2:39 [b]Matt. 12:46 [c]Luke 2:19

52 [I]Or, *age* [a]Luke 2:40

1 [a]Matt. 27:2 [b]Matt. 14:1

2 [a]John 18:13, 24; Acts 4:6 [b]Matt. 26:3 [c]Luke 3:3-10: *Matt. 3:1-10; Mark 1:3-5*

3 [a]Matt. 3:5

4 [a]Is. 40:3

5 [I]Or, *leveled* [a]Is. 40:4

6 [I]Or, *mankind* [a]Is. 40:5 [b]Luke 2:30

7 [a]Matt. 12:34; 23:33

8 [I]Or, *in* [a]Luke 5:21; 13:25, 26; 14:9 [b]John 8:33

9 [a]Matt. 7:19; Luke 13:6-9

10 [a]Luke 3:12, 14; Acts 2:37, 38

11 [a]Is. 58:7; 1Tim. 6:17, 18; James 2:14-20

12 [I]I.e., Collectors of Roman taxes for profit [a]Luke 7:29

13 [I]Or, *Exact*

14 [I]I.e., men in active military service

4 as it is written[1125] in the book[976] of the words of Isaiah the prophet,

"[a]THE VOICE OF ONE CRYING IN
THE WILDERNESS,
'MAKE READY THE WAY[3598] OF
THE LORD,
[pim]MAKE HIS PATHS STRAIGHT.
5 '[a]EVERY RAVINE SHALL BE
FILLED UP,
AND EVERY MOUNTAIN AND
HILL SHALL BE [I]BROUGHT
LOW;
AND THE CROOKED SHALL
BECOME STRAIGHT,
AND THE ROUGH ROADS
SMOOTH;
6 [a]AND ALL [I]FLESH[4561] SHALL
[b]SEE THE SALVATION[4992] OF
GOD.' "[2316]

7 He therefore *began* saying to the multitudes who were [ppt]going out to be [aifp]baptized[907] by him, "[a]You brood of vipers, who warned you to [ainf]flee from the wrath[3709] to come?

8 "Therefore [aim]bring forth fruits in keeping with repentance,[3341] and [a]do not [aosi]begin to [pinf]say [I]to yourselves, '[b]We have Abraham for our father,'[3962] for I say to you that God is able from these stones to raise up children[5043] to Abraham.

9 "And also the axe is already [pin]laid[2749] at the root of the trees; [a]every tree therefore that does not [ppt]bear good fruit is cut down1581 and thrown into the fire."

10 And the multitudes were questioning him, saying, "[a]Then what shall we do?"

11 And he would answer and say to them, "Let the man who has two tunics [a]share with him who [ppt]has none; and let him who has food1033 [pim]do likewise."

12 And *some* [Ia]tax-gatherers[5057] also came to be baptized, and they said to him, "Teacher, what shall we do?"

13 And he said to them, [pim]"[I]Collect no more than what you have been ordered[1299] to."

14 And *some* [I]soldiers were [ipf]questioning him, saying, "And *what about*

us, what shall we do?" And he said to
them, "Do not [aosi]take money from anyone by force, or [aosi] [a]accuse *anyone*
falsely, and [b]be [pim]content with your
wages."[3800]
15 Now while the people were in
a state of expectation and all were
[ppt] [I]wondering[1260] in their hearts[2588]
about John, [a]as to whether he might be
[II]the Christ,[5547]
🔑 16 [a]John answered and said to them
all, "As for me, I baptize[907] you with
water; but One is coming who is mightier
than I, and I am not fit to untie the
thong[2438] of His sandals; He will [ft]baptize
you [I]with the [an]Holy Spirit[4151] and fire.
17 "And His [a]winnowing fork is in
His hand to thoroughly clear His threshing floor, and to gather the wheat into
His barn;[596] but He will burn up the
chaff with [b]unquenchable fire."
18 So with many other [ppt]exhorta-
tions also he [ipf]preached[2097] the gospel
to the people.
19 But when [a]Herod the tetrarch
was reproved by him on account of
[a]Herodias, his brother's wife, and on
account of all the wicked things[4190]
which [b]Herod had [ao]done,
20 he added this also to them all,
that [a]he locked John up in prison.

Jesus Is Baptized

21 [a]Now it came about when all the
people were [aie]baptized[907], that Jesus
also was [aptp]baptized, and while He was
[b]praying, heaven[3772] was [aifp]opened,
22 and the Holy Spirit [ainf]descended
upon Him in bodily[4984] form[1491] like a
dove, and a voice [ainf]came out of heav-
en,[3772] "[a]Thou art My beloved[27] Son,[5207]
in Thee I am [ao]well-pleased."

Genealogy of Jesus

23 And [a]when He began His ministry, Jesus Himself was about[5616] thirty
years of age, [I]being [ipf]supposedly
the [an]son[5207] of [b]Joseph, the *son* of
[II]Eli,
24 the son of Matthat, the *son* of
Levi, the *son* of Melchi, the *son* of Jannai,
the *son* of Joseph,
25 the *son* of Mattathias, the *son*
of Amos, the *son* of Nahum, the *son*
of [I]Hesli, the *son* of Naggai,
26 the *son* of Maath, the *son* of Mattathias, the *son* of Semein, the *son* of
Josech, the *son* of Joda,
27 the *son* of Joanan, the *son*
of Rhesa, [a]the *son* of Zerubbabel, the
son of [I]Shealtiel, the *son* of Neri,
28 the *son* of Melchi, the *son* of
Addi, the *son* of Cosam, the *son* of Elma-
dam, the *son* of Er,
29 the *son* of [I]Joshua, the *son* of
Eliezer, the *son* of Jorim, the *son* of
Matthat, the *son* of Levi,
30 the *son* of Simeon, the *son* of
[I]Judah, the *son* of Joseph, the *son*
of Jonam, the *son* of Eliakim,
31 the *son* of Melea, the *son*
of Menna, the *son* of Mattatha, the *son*
of Nathan, the *son* of David,
32 [a]the *son* of Jesse, the *son* of
Obed, the *son* of Boaz, the *son*
of [I]Salmon, the *son* of [II]Nahshon,
33 the *son* of Amminadab, the *son*
of Admin, the *son* of [I]Ram, the *son* of
Hezron, the *son* of Perez, the *son* of
Judah,
34 the *son* of Jacob, the *son* of Isaac,
[a]the *son* of Abraham, the *son* of Terah,
the *son* of Nahor,
35 the *son* of Serug, the *son* of
[I]Reu, the *son* of Peleg, the *son* of
[II]Heber, the *son* of Shelah,
36 the *son* of Cainan, the *son* of Arphaxad, the *son* of Shem, [a]the *son* of
Noah, the *son* of Lamech,
37 the *son* of Methuselah, the *son*
of Enoch, the *son* of Jared, the *son* of
Mahalaleel, the *son* of Cainan,
38 the *son* of Enosh, the *son* of
Seth, the *son* of Adam, the *son* of
God.[2316]

14 [a]Ex. 20:16; 23:1 [b]Phil. 4:11
15 [I]Or, *reasoning or debating* [II]I.e., the Messiah [a]John 1:19f.
16 [I]The Gr. here can be translated *in, with* or *by* [a]Luke 3:16, 17: *Matt. 3:11, 12; Mark 1:7, 8*
17 [a]Is. 30:24 [b]Mark 9:43, 48
19 [a]Matt. 14:3; Mark 6:17 [b]Matt. 14:1; Luke 3:1
20 [a]John 3:24
21 [a]Luke 3:21, 22: *Matt. 3:13-17; Mark 1:9-11* [b]Matt. 14:23; Luke 5:16; 9:18, 28f.
22 [a]Ps. 2:7; Is. 42:1; Matt. 3:17; 17:5; Mark 1:11; Luke 9:35; 2Pet. 1:17
23 [I]Lit., *as it was being thought* [II]Also spelled *Heli* [a]Matt. 4:17; Acts 1:1 [b]Matt. 1:16; Luke 3:23-27
25 [I]Also spelled *Esli*
27 [I]Gr., *Salathiel* [a]Matt. 1:12
29 [I]Gr., *Jesus*
30 [I]Gr., *Judas*
32 [I]Gr., *Sala* [II]Gr., *Naasson* [a]Luke 3:32-34: *Matt. 1:1-6*
33 [I]Gr., *Arni*
34 [a]Luke 3:34-36: *Gen. 11:26-30; 1Chr. 1:24-27*
35 [I]Gr., *Ragau* [II]Gr., *Eber*
36 [a]Luke 3:36-38: *Gen. 5:3-32; 1Chr. 1:1-4*

🔑 **3:16** See notes on Acts 1:5; 2:1-13; 11:14-18; 19:1-7.

The Temptation of Jesus

4 🔑[a]And Jesus, full of the Holy[40] Spirit,[4151] [b]returned from the Jordan and was [ipf]led about [I]by the Spirit[4151] in the wilderness

2 for [a]forty days, being [ppp]tempted[3985] by the devil.[1228] And He ate nothing during those days; and when they had ended,[4931] He became hungry.[3983]

3 And the devil said to Him, "If You are the Son[5207] of God,[2316] tell this stone to become bread."

4 And Jesus answered him, "It is written, '[a]Man[444] shall not live[2198] on bread alone.' "

5 [a]And he [apt]led Him up and showed Him all the kingdoms of [Ib]the world in a moment of time.[5550]

6 And the devil said to Him, "I will give You all this domain[1849] and [I]its glory;[1391] [a]for it has been [pfip]handed over to me, and I give it to whomever I wish.

7 "Therefore if You [aosb] [I]worship before me, it shall all be Yours."

8 And Jesus answered and said to him, "It is written, '[a]You shall worship the Lord your God and serve Him only.' "

9 [a]And he led Him to Jerusalem and had Him stand on the pinnacle of the temple,[2411] and said to Him, "If You are the Son of God, throw Yourself down[2736] from here;

10 for it is written,

'[a]He will give His angels
charge concerning You
to [infg]guard You,'

11 and,

'[a]On *their* hands they will
bear You up,
Lest You [aosb]strike[4350] Your
foot against a stone.' "

12 And Jesus answered and said to him, "It is said, '[a]You shall not [I]put the [an]Lord your God to the test.' "[1598]

🔑13 And when the devil had finished[4931] every [an]temptation,[3986] he departed[868] from Him until an opportune time.[2540]

Jesus' Public Ministry

14 And [a]Jesus returned to Galilee in the power of the Spirit; and [b]news about Him spread through[2596] all the surrounding district.

15 And He *began* [ipf] [a]teaching in their synagogues and was praised[1392] by all.

16 And He came to [a]Nazareth, where He had been brought up; and as was His custom, [b]He entered the synagogue on the Sabbath,[4521] and [c]stood up to read.

17 And the [I]book[975] of the prophet Isaiah was handed to Him. And He opened the [I]book, and found the place where it was written,

18 "[a]The Spirit[4151] of the Lord is
upon Me,
Because He anointed Me to
[ainf]preach the gospel[2097]
to the poor.
He has [pfi]sent Me to
[ainf]proclaim[2784]
release[859] to the captives,
And recovery of sight[309] to
the blind,
To set free those who are
downtrodden,

19 [a]To [ainf]proclaim the
favorable[1184]
year[1763] of the Lord."

20 And He [apt] [a]closed the [I]book,[975] and [apt]gave it back to the attendant,[5257] and [b]sat down; and the eyes of all in the synagogue were fixed upon Him.

21 And He began to [pinf]say to them, "Today this Scripture[1124] has been fulfilled in your [I]hearing."

22 And all were [ipf] [I]speaking well[3140] of Him, and [ipf]wondering at the gracious[5485] words which [II]were [ppt]falling from His lips; and they were saying, "[a]Is this not Joseph's son?"

23 And He said to them, "No doubt you will quote this proverb[3850] to Me,

1 [I]Or, *under the influence of;* lit., *in* [a]Luke 4:1-13: *Matt. 4:1-11; Mark 1:12, 13* [b]Luke 3:3

2 [a]Ex. 34:28; 1Kin. 19:8

4 [a]Deut. 8:3

5 [I]Lit., *the inhabited earth* [a]Matt. 4:8-10 [b]Matt. 24:14

6 [I]Lit., *their* (referring to the kingdoms) [a]1John 5:19

7 [I]Or, *bow down*

8 [a]Deut. 6:13; 10:20; Matt. 4:10

9 [a]Matt. 4:5-7

10 [a]Ps. 91:11

11 [a]Ps. 91:12

12 [I]Or, *tempt . . . God* [a]Deut. 6:16

14 [a]Matt. 4:12 [b]Matt. 9:26; Luke 4:37

15 [a]Matt. 4:23

16 [a]Luke 2:39, 51 [b]Matt. 13:54; Mark 6:1f. [c]Acts 13:14-16

17 [I]Or, *scroll*

18 [a]Is. 61:1; Matt. 11:5; 12:18; John 3:34

19 [a]Is. 61:2; Lev. 25:10

20 [I]Or, *scroll* [a]Luke 4:17 [b]Matt. 26:55

21 [I]Lit., *ears*

22 [I]Or, *testifying* [II]Lit., *were proceeding out of His mouth* [a]Matt. 13:55; Mark 6:3; John 6:42

🔑 **4:1-13** See note on Js. 1:13-15 and also *peirazō* (3985), to tempt.
🔑 **4:13** See note on II Thess. 2:3.

‘Physician,[2395] [aim]heal yourself! Whatever we heard was [apt]done[1096] [a]at Capernaum, [aim]do[4160] here in [b]your home town as well.’ ”

24 And He said, “Truly[281] I say to you, [a]no prophet[4396] is welcome[1184] in his home town.

25 “But I say to you in truth, there were many widows in Israel [a]in the days[2250] of Elijah, when the sky was shut up for three years and six months, when a great famine came over all the land;

26 and yet Elijah was sent to none of them, but [a]only to [I]Zarephath, *in the land* of [b]Sidon, to a woman who was a widow.

27 “And there were many lepers in Israel in the time of Elisha the prophet; and none of them was cleansed, but [a]only Naaman the Syrian.”

28 And all in the synagogue were filled with rage[2372] as they heard these things;

29 and they rose up and [a]cast Him out of the city, and led[71] Him to the brow of the hill on which their city had been built, in order to throw Him down the cliff.

30 But [apt] [a]passing through their midst,[3319] He [ipf]went His way.

31 And [a]He came down to [b]Capernaum, a city of Galilee. And He was teaching[1321] them on the Sabbath;

32 and [a]they were [ipf]amazed at His teaching, for [b]His [I]message[3056] was with authority.[1849]

33 And there was a man in the synagogue [I]possessed by the spirit[4151] of an unclean demon,[1140] and he cried out with a loud voice,

34 “[I]Ha! [a]What do we have to do with You, Jesus [II]of [b]Nazareth? Have You [ao]come to [ainf]destroy us? I know who You are—[b]the Holy One[40] of God!”[2316]

35 And Jesus [a]rebuked him, saying, “Be quiet and come out of him!” And when the demon had thrown him down in *their* midst, he came out of him without doing him any[3367] harm.

36 And amazement came upon them all, and they *began* [ipf]discussing with one another saying, “What is [I]this message? For [a]with authority[1849] and power[1411] He commands[2004] the unclean spirits, and they come out.”

37 And [a]the report about Him was [ipf]getting out into every locality in the surrounding district.

Many Are Healed

38 [a]And He arose and *left* the synagogue, and entered Simon's home. Now Simon's mother-in-law was [b]suffering[4912] from a high fever; and they [ao]made request of Him on her behalf.

39 And standing over her, He [a]rebuked the fever, and it left her; and she immediately arose and [I]waited[1247] on them.

40 [a]And while [b]the sun was setting, all who had any sick[770] with various[4164] diseases brought them to Him; and [ppt] [c]laying His hands on every one of them, He was [d]healing them.

41 And demons also were coming out of many, crying out and saying, “You are [a]the Son of God!” And [b]rebuking them, He would [c]not allow them to [pinf]speak, because they knew Him to be [I]the Christ.

42 [a]And when day came, He [apt]departed and went to a lonely place; and the multitudes were [ipf]searching for Him, and came to Him, and tried to keep[2722] Him from [pinf]going away from them.

43 But He said to them, “I must [ainf]preach[2097] the kingdom[932] of God[2316] to the other cities also, [a]for I was sent for this purpose.”

44 And He kept on preaching[2784] in the synagogues[4864] [a]of [I]Judea.

The First Disciples

5 [a]Now it came about that while the multitude were pressing around Him and [infg]listening[191] to the word[3056] of God, He was standing by [b]the lake of Gennesaret;

2 and He saw two boats lying at the

23 [a]Matt. 4:13; Mark 1:21ff.; 2:1ff.; Luke 4:35ff.; John 4:46ff. [b]Mark 6:1; Luke 2:39, 51; 4:16
24 [a]Matt. 13:57; Mark 6:4; John 4:44
25 [a]1Kin. 17:1; 18:1; James 5:17
26 [I]Gr., *Sarepta* [a]1Kin. 17:9 [b]Matt. 11:21
27 [a]2Kin. 5:1-14
29 [a]Num. 15:35; Acts 7:58; Heb. 13:12
30 [a]John 10:39
31 [a]Luke 4:31-37: *Mark 1:21-28* [b]Matt. 4:13; Luke 4:23
32 [I]Lit., *word* [a]Matt. 7:28 [b]Luke 4:36; John 7:46
33 [I]Lit., *having a spirit*
34 [I]Or possibly, *Let us alone* [II]Lit., *the Nazarene* [a]Matt. 8:29 [b]Mark 1:24
35 [a]Matt. 8:26; Mark 4:39; Luke 4:39, 41; 8:24
36 [I]Or, *this word, that with authority. . .come out?* [a]Luke 4:32
37 [a]Luke 4:14
38 [a]Luke 4:38, 39: *Matt. 8:14, 15; Mark 1:29-31* [b]Matt. 4:24
39 [I]Or, *served* [a]Luke 4:35, 41
40 [a]Luke 4:40, 41: *Matt. 8:16, 17; Mark 1:32-34* [b]Mark 1:32 [c]Mark 5:23 [d]Matt. 4:23
41 [I]I.e., the Messiah [a]Matt. 4:3 [b]Luke 4:35 [c]Matt. 8:16; Mark 1:34
42 [a]Luke 4:42, 43: *Mark 1:35-38*
43 [a]Mark 1:38
44 [I]I.e., the country of the Jews (including Galilee); some mss. read *Galilee* [a]Matt. 4:23

1 [a]Matt. 4:18-22; Mark 1:16-20; Luke 5:1-11; John 1:40-42 [b]Num. 34:11; Deut. 3:17; Josh. 12:3; 13:27; Matt. 4:18

edge of the lake; but the fishermen had
[apt]gotten out of them, and were washing[4150] their nets.[1350]
3 And [a]He [apt]got into one of the
boats, which was Simon's, and asked
him to put out a little way from the land.
And He sat down and *began* [ipf]teach-
ing[1321] the multitudes from the boat.
4 And when He had finished[3973]
speaking, He said to Simon, "Put out
into the deep water and [a]let down your
nets for a catch."[61]
5 And Simon answered and said,
"[a]Master, [b]we [apt]worked[3872] hard all
night and [ao]caught nothing, but at Your
[I]bidding[4487] I will let down the nets."
6 And when they had done this,
[a]they enclosed a great quantity of fish;
and their nets *began* to [ipf]break;
7 and they signaled to their partners[3353] in the other boat, for them to
come and help them. And they came,
and filled both of the boats, so that they
began to sink.
8 But when Simon Peter saw *that*,
he fell down at Jesus' [I]feet, saying, "Depart from me, for I am a sinful[268] man,
O Lord!"
9 For amazement had seized him
and all his companions because of the
catch of fish which they had taken;
10 and so also [I]James and John, sons
of Zebedee, who were partners[2844] with
Simon. And Jesus said to Simon, "[a]Do
not [pim]fear,[5399] from now on you will
be [b]catching men."
11 And when they had brought their
boats to land,[1093] [a]they [apt]left everything
and followed Him.

The Leper and the Paralytic

12 [a]And it came about that while
He was in one of the cities, behold, *there
was* a man full of leprosy; and when
he saw Jesus, he [apt]fell on his face and
implored[1189] Him, saying, "Lord, if You
are willing, You can make me clean."
13 And He [apt]stretched out His
hand, and touched him, saying, "I am
willing; be cleansed." And immediately
the leprosy left him.
14 And He ordered him to tell no
one, "But go and [a]show yourself to the
priest, and make an offering for your
cleansing,[2512] just as Moses commanded,[4367] for a testimony to
them."
15 But [a]the news[3056] about Him was
[ipf]spreading even farther, and great multitudes were [ipf]gathering to [pinf]hear *Him*
and to be [pip]healed of their sicknesses.[769]
16 But He Himself would *often* slip
away [I]to the [II]wilderness and [ppt] [a]pray.
17 And it came about [I]one day that
He was teaching; and [a]there were *some*
Pharisees and [b]teachers of the law[3547]
sitting *there*, who had [c]come from every
village of Galilee and Judea and *from*
Jerusalem; and [d]the power of the Lord
was *present* for Him to [pinf]perform
healing.[2390]
18 [a]And behold, *some* men *were*
[ppt]carrying on a [I]bed a man[444] who was
paralyzed;[3886] and they were [ipf]trying to
bring him in, and to set him down in
front of Him.
19 And not finding any *way* to bring
him in because of the crowd, they went
up on [a]the roof and let him down
[b]through the tiles with his stretcher,
right in the center,[3319] in front of Jesus.
20 And seeing their faith,[4102] He
said, "[I]Friend, [a]your sins are [pfip]for-
given[863] you."
21 And the scribes and the Pharisees [a]began to reason, saying, "[b]Who
is this *man* who speaks blasphemies?[988]
[c]Who can [pinf]forgive sins, but God[2316]
alone?"
22 But Jesus, [I]aware of their reasonings, answered and said to them, "Why
are you reasoning[1260] in your hearts?
23 "Which is easier, to say, 'Your
sins have been [pfip]forgiven you,' or to
say, 'Rise and [pim]walk'?
24 "But in order that you may know
that the Son of Man[444] has authority[1849]
on earth[1093] to [pinf]forgive[863] sins,"—He
said to the [a]paralytic—"I say to you,
rise, and [apt]take up your stretcher and
[pim]go home."
25 And at once he [apt]rose up before
them, and [apt]took up what he had been

3 [a]Matt. 13:2; Mark 3:9, 10; 4:1
4 [a]John 21:6
5 [I]Or, *word* [a]Luke 8:24; 9:33, 49; 17:13 [b]John 21:3
6 [a]John 21:6
8 [I]Lit., *knees*
10 [I]Or, *Jacob* [a]Matt. 14:27 [b]2Tim. 2:26
11 [a]Matt. 4:20, 22; 19:29; Mark 1:18, 20; Luke 5:28
12 [a]Luke 5:12-14: *Matt. 8:2-4; Mark 1:40-44*
14 [a]Lev. 13:49; 14:2ff.
15 [a]Matt. 9:26
16 [I]Lit., *in* [II]Or, *lonely places* [a]Matt. 14:23; Mark 1:35; Luke 6:12
17 [I]Lit., *on one of the days* [a]Matt. 15:1 [b]Luke 2:46 [c]Mark 1:45 [d]Mark 5:30; Luke 6:19; 8:46
18 [I]Or, *stretcher* [a]Luke 5:18-26: *Matt. 9:2-8; Mark 2:3-12*
19 [a]Matt. 24:17 [b]Mark 2:4
20 [I]Lit., *Man* [a]Matt. 9:2
21 [a]Luke 3:8 [b]Luke 7:49 [c]Is. 43:25
22 [I]Or, *perceiving*
24 [a]Matt. 4:24

lying on, and [ao]went home, [a]glorifying[1392] God.

26 And they were all seized with astonishment[1611] and *began* [ipf] [a]glorifying God; and they were filled [b]with fear,[5401] saying, "We have [ao]seen remarkable things[3861] today."

Call of Levi (Matthew)

27 [a]And after that He went out, and noticed a [I]tax-gatherer[5057] named [b]Levi, sitting in the tax office, and He said to him, [pim]"Follow Me."

28 And he [apt] [a]left everything [apt]behind, and [apt]rose and *began* to follow Him.

29 And [a]Levi gave a big [I]reception[1403] for Him in his house; and there was a great crowd of [b]tax-gatherers[5057] and other *people* who were reclining *at the table* with them.

30 And [a]the Pharisees and their scribes *began* [ipf]grumbling at His disciples,[3101] saying, "Why do you eat and drink with the tax-gatherers and sinners?"[268]

31 And Jesus answered and said to them, "[a]*It is* not those who are well who need a physician,[2395] but those who are sick.

32 "I have not come to call the righteous[1342] but sinners[268] to repentance."[3341]

33 And they said to Him, "[a]The disciples of John often fast[3522] and offer prayers; the *disciples* of the Pharisees also do [I]the same; but Yours eat and drink."

34 And Jesus said to them, "You cannot make the [I]attendants[5207] of the bridegroom [ainf]fast while the bridegroom is with them, can you?

35 "[a]But *the* days[2250] will come; and when the bridegroom is taken away from them, then they will fast in those days."

36 And He was also [ipf]telling them a parable: "No one tears a piece from a new[2537] [I]garment and puts it on an old [I]garment; otherwise he will both [ft]tear[4977] the new, and the piece from the new will not match the old.

37 "And no one puts new wine[3631] into old [I]wineskins; otherwise the new wine will burst the [I]skins, and it will be spilled out, and the [I]skins will be ruined.

38 "But new wine must be put into fresh wineskins.

39 "And no one, after drinking old *wine* wishes for new; for he says, 'The old[3820] is good[5543] *enough.*'"

Jesus Is Lord of the Sabbath

6 [a]Now it came about that on a *certain* [I]Sabbath[4521] He was [pinf]passing through *some* grainfields; and His disciples[3101] [b]were [ipf]picking and [ipf]eating the heads *of grain,* rubbing them in their hands.

2 But some of the Pharisees said, "Why do you do what [a]is not lawful[1832] on the Sabbath?"

3 And Jesus answering them said, "Have you not even read [a]what David did when he was [ao]hungry,[3983] he and those who were with him,

4 how he entered the house[3624] of God,[2316] and took and ate the [I]consecrated bread[4286] which [a]is not lawful for any to eat except the priests alone, and gave it to his companions?"

5 And He was saying to them, "The Son of Man is Lord[2962] of the Sabbath."

6 [a]And it came about [b]on another Sabbath, that He entered [c]the synagogue[4864] and was [pinf]teaching;[1321] and there was a man there [I]whose right[1188] hand was withered.

7 And the scribes[1122] and the Pharisees [a]were [ipf]watching Him closely,[3906] *to see* if He healed on the Sabbath, in order that they might [aosb]find *reason* to accuse[2723] Him.

8 But He [a]knew [I]what they were thinking, and He said to the man with the withered hand, "Rise and [II]come forward!" And he rose and [III]came forward.

9 And Jesus said to them, "I ask you, is it lawful on the Sabbath to [ainf]do good,[15] or to [ainf]do harm,[2554] to [ainf]save[4982] a life, or to [ainf]destroy it?"

10 And after [a]looking around at[4017]

---

25 [a]Matt. 9:8

26 [a]Matt. 9:8 [b]Luke 1:65; 7:16

27 [I]I.e., Collector of Roman taxes for profit [a]Luke 5:27-39: *Matt. 9:9-17; Mark 2:14-22* [b]Matt. 9:9

28 [a]Luke 5:11

29 [I]Or, *banquet* [a]Matt. 9:9 [b]Luke 15:1

30 [a]Mark 2:16; Luke 15:2; Acts 23:9

31 [a]Matt. 9:12, 13; Mark 2:17

33 [I]Or, *likewise* [a]Matt. 9:14; Mark 2:18

34 [I]Lit., *sons of the bridalchamber*

35 [a]Matt. 9:15; Mark 2:20; Luke 17:22

36 [I]Or, *cloak*

37 [I]I.e., skins used as bottles

1 [I]Many mss. read *the second-first Sabbath;* i.e., the second Sabbath after the first [a]Luke 6:1-5: *Matt. 12:1-8; Mark 2:23-28* [b]Deut. 23:25

2 [a]Matt. 12:2

3 [a]1Sam. 21:6

4 [I]Or, *showbread;* lit., *loaves of presentation* [a]Lev. 24:9

6 [I]Lit., *and his* [a]Luke 6:6-11: *Matt. 12:9-14; Mark 3:1-6* [b]Luke 6:1 [c]Matt. 4:23

7 [a]Mark 3:2

8 [I]Lit., *their thoughts* [II]Lit., *stand; or, stood into the midst* [III]Lit., *stood* [a]Matt. 9:4

10 [a]Mark 3:5

them all, He said to him, "Stretch out
your hand!" And he did *so;* and his hand
was restored.[600]
11 But they themselves were filled
with [I]rage,[454] and [ipf]discussed[1255] together what they might do to Jesus.

Choosing the Twelve

12 And it was [I]at this time that He
went off to [a]the mountain to [ainf] [b]pray,
and He spent the whole night in prayer
to God.
13 And when day came, [a]He called
His disciples[3101] to Him; and [apt]chose
twelve of them, whom He also named
as [b]apostles:[652]
14 Simon, whom He also named
Peter, and Andrew his brother; and
[I]James and John; and Philip and Bartholomew;
15 and [a]Matthew and Thomas;
James *the son* of Alphaeus, and Simon
who was called the Zealot;
16 Judas *the son* of James, and Judas
Iscariot, who became a traitor.
17 And He [a]descended with them,
and stood on a level place; and *there*
was [b]a great multitude of His disciples,[3101] and a great throng of people
from all Judea and Jerusalem and the
coastal region of [c]Tyre and Sidon,
18 [I]who had come to hear Him, and
to be healed of their diseases; and those
who were [ppp]troubled[3791] with unclean
spirits were being [ipf]cured.
19 And all the multitude were [ipf]try-
ing to [pinf] [a]touch Him, for [b]power was
[ipf]coming from[3844] Him and [ipf]healing[2390]
them all.

The Beatitudes

20 And [apt]turning His gaze on His
disciples, He *began* to say, "[a]Blessed[3107]
are you *who are* poor,[4434] for [b]yours is
the kingdom[932] of God.
21 "Blessed *are* you who [ppt]hunger
now, for you shall be satisfied. Blessed
are you who [ppt]weep now, for you shall
laugh.
22 "[a]Blessed are you when men
[aosb]hate you, and [aosb] [b]ostracize[893] you,
and [aosb]cast insults at you, and [aosb]spurn
your name as evil,[4190] for the sake of
the Son of Man.
23 [aipp]"Be glad in that day, and
[aim] [a]leap *for joy,* for behold, your
reward[3408] is great in heaven;[3772] for
[b]in the same way their fathers used to
[ipf] [I]treat the prophets.[4396]
24 "But woe to [a]you who are rich,
for [b]you are receiving[568] your comfort[3874] in full.[568]
25 "Woe to you who [I]are [pfpp]well-
fed now, for you shall be hungry. Woe
to you who [ppt]laugh now, for you shall
mourn and weep.
26 "Woe *to you* when all men[444]
speak well of you, for in the same way
their fathers used to [ipf] [I]treat the
[a]false prophets.
27 "But I say to you who [ppt]hear,
[pim] [a]love[25] your enemies, [pim]do good to
those who [ppt]hate you,
28 [pim]bless those who [ppt]curse[2672]
you, [a]pray for those who [ppt] [I]mistreat
you.
29 "[a]Whoever [ppt]hits[5180] you on the
cheek, offer him the other also; and
whoever [ppt]takes away your [I]coat, do
not [aosi]withhold your [II]shirt[5509] from him
either.
30 [pim]"Give to everyone who [ppt]asks
of you, and whoever [ppt]takes away
what is yours, do not [pim]demand it
back.[523]
31 "[a]And just as you want people
to [psa] [I]treat you, [pim] [I]treat them in the
same way.
32 "And [a]if you love those who
[ppt]love you, what credit is *that* to you?
For even sinners[268] love those who
[ppt]love them.
33 "And if you [psa]do good[15] to those
who [ppt]do good[15] to you, what credit
is *that* to you? For even sinners[268] do
the same.

11 [I]Lit., *folly*
12 [I]Lit., *in these days* [a]Matt. 5:1 [b]Matt. 14:23; Luke 5:16; 9:18, 28
13 [a]Luke 6:13-16: *Matt. 10:2-4; Mark 3:16-19; Acts 1:13* [b]Mark 6:30
14 [I]Or, *Jacob,* also vv. 15 and 16
15 [a]Matt. 9:9
17 [a]Luke 6:12 [b]Matt. 4:25; Mark 3:7, 8 [c]Matt. 11:21
18 [I]Most English versions begin v. 18 with *and those who*
19 [a]Matt. 9:21; 14:36; Mark 3:10 [b]Luke 5:17
20 [a]Matt. 5:3-12; Luke 6:20-23 [b]Matt. 5:3
22 [a]1Pet. 4:14 [b]John 9:22; 16:2
23 [I]Lit., *do to* [a]Mal. 4:1-6 [b]2Chr. 36:16; Acts 7:52
24 [a]Luke 16:25; James 5:1 [b]Matt. 6:2
25 [I]Lit., *having been filled*
26 [I]Lit., *do to* [a]Matt. 7:15
27 [a]Matt. 5:44; Luke 6:35
28 [I]Or, *revile* [a]Matt. 5:44; Luke 6:35
29 [I]Or, *cloak;* i.e., outer garment [II]Or, *tunic;* i.e., garment worn next to body [a]Luke 6:29, 30: *Matt. 5:39-42*
31 [I]Lit., *do to* [a]Matt. 7:12
32 [a]Matt. 5:46

6:20-26 See note on Mt. 5:1-12. The woes of vv. 24-26 are not pronounced upon unbelievers but upon selfish believers in contrast to the sacrificial believers described in vv. 20-23.

34 “[a]And if you [asba]lend to those from whom you expect[1679] to [ainf]receive,[2983] what credit is *that* to you? Even sinners lend to sinners, in order to [aosb]receive back the same *amount.*

35 “But [a]love your enemies, and [pim]do good, and [pim]lend, [ppt I]expecting[560] nothing in return;[3367] and your reward[3408] will be great, and you will be [b]sons[5207] of [c]the [an]Most High; for He Himself is kind[5543] to ungrateful and evil *men.*

36 [pim]“[I]Be merciful, just as your Father[3962] is merciful.

37 “[a]And do not [pim]judge[2919] and you will not be judged; and do not [pim]condemn,[2613] and you will not be condemned; [pim I b]pardon,[630] and you will be pardoned.

38 [pim]“Give, and it will be given to you; [a]good measure, [pfpp]pressed down, [ppp]shaken together, [ppp]running over, they will pour [b]into your lap. For by your standard of measure[3354] it will be measured to you in return.”

39 And He also spoke a parable to them: “[a]A [sg]blind man cannot [pinf]guide a [sg]blind man, can he? Will they not both fall into a pit?

40 “[a]A [I]pupil[3101] is not above his teacher;[1320] but everyone, after he has been [pfpp]fully trained,[2675] will [II]be like his teacher.[1320]

41 “And why do you look at the speck that is in your brother’s eye, but do not notice the log that is in your own[2398] eye?

42 “Or how can you say to your brother, ‘Brother, let me take out the speck[2595] that is in your eye,’ when you yourself do not [ppt]see the log that is in your own eye? You hypocrite, first take the log[1385] out of your own eye, and then you will see clearly to [ainf]take out the speck that is in your brother’s eye.

43 “[a]For there is no good tree which [ppt]produces bad fruit; nor, [I]on the other hand, a bad tree which produces good fruit.

44 “[a]For each tree is [pinp]known by its own[2398] fruit. For men do not gather figs from thorns, nor do they pick grapes from a briar bush.

45 “[a]The good[18] man out of the good [I]treasure of his heart brings forth what is good; and the evil *man* out of the evil *treasure* brings forth[4393] what is evil; [b]for his mouth speaks from [II]that which fills[4051] his heart.

Builders and Foundations

46 “And [a]why do you call Me, ‘Lord, Lord,’ and do not do what I say?

47 “[a]Everyone who [ppt]comes to Me, and [ppt]hears My words, and [ppt I]acts upon them, I will show you whom he is like:

48 he is like a man [ppt]building a house, who [I]dug deep and laid[5087] a foundation upon the rock; and when a flood [apt]rose, the [II]torrent burst against[4366] that house and could[2480] not shake it, because it had been well built.

49 “But the one who has [apt]heard, and has not [apt]acted *accordingly,* is like a man who [apt]built a house upon the ground without any foundation; and the [I]torrent burst against it and immediately it collapsed, and the ruin of that house was great.”

Jesus Heals a Centurion’s Servant

7 [a]When He had completed[4137] all His discourse in the hearing of the people, [b]He went to Capernaum.

2 And a certain centurion’s[1543] slave,[1401] [I]who was highly regarded by him, was sick[2560] and about to die.

3 And when he heard about Jesus, [a]he sent some [I]Jewish elders[4245] asking Him to [apt]come and [aosb II]save the life[1295] of his slave.

4 And when they had come to Jesus, they earnestly [ipf]entreated Him, saying, “He is worthy for You to grant this to him;

5 for he loves[25] our nation,[1484] and it was he who [ao]built us our synagogue.”

34 [a]Matt. 5:42

35 [I]Or, *not despairing at all* [a]Luke 6:27 [b]Matt. 5:9 [c]Luke 1:32

36 [I]Or, *Become*

37 [I]Lit., *release* [a]Luke 6:37-42: *Matt. 7:1-5* [b]Matt. 6:14; Luke 23:16; Acts 3:13

38 [a]Mark 4:24 [b]Ps. 79:12; Is. 65:6, 7; Jer. 32:18

39 [a]Matt. 15:14

40 [I]Or, *disciple* [II]Or, *reach his teacher's level* [a]Matt. 10:24; John 13:16; 15:20

43 [I]Lit., *again* [a]Luke 6:43, 44: *Matt. 7:16, 18, 20*

44 [a]Matt. 7:16; 12:33

45 [I]Or, *treasury, storehouse* [II]Lit., *the abundance of* [a]Matt. 12:35 [b]Matt. 12:34

46 [a]Mal. 1:6; Matt. 7:21

47 [I]Lit., *does* [a]Luke 6:47-49: *Matt. 7:24-27;* James 1:22ff.

48 [I]Lit., *dug and went deep* [II]Lit., *river*

49 [I]Lit., *river*

1 [a]Matt. 7:28 [b]Luke 7:1-10: *Matt. 8:5-13*

2 [I]Lit., *to whom he was honorable*

3 [I]Lit., *elders of the Jews* [II]Lit., *bring safely through, rescue* [a]Matt. 8:5

6 Now Jesus *started* on His way with them; and when He was[568] already not far from the house, the centurion sent friends, saying to Him, "[I]Lord, do not [pim]trouble Yourself further, for I am not worthy for You to [aosb]come under my roof;

7 for this reason I did not even consider myself worthy to [ainf]come to You, but *just* [aim] [I]say the word,[3056] and my [II]servant[3816] will be healed.

8 "For I, too, am a man under authority,[1849] with soldiers under me; and I say to this one, [aim]'Go!' and he goes; and to another, [aim]'Come!' and he comes; and to my slave, [aim]'Do this!' and he does it."

9 Now when Jesus heard this, He marveled at him, and turned and said to the multitude that was [ppt]following Him, "I say to you, [a]not even in Israel have I found such great faith."[4102]

10 And when those who had been sent [apt]returned to the house, they found the slave in [ppt]good health.

11 And it came about [I]soon afterwards, that He [aop]went to a city called Nain; and His disciples[3101] were [ipf]going along with Him, [II]accompanied by a large multitude.

12 Now as He approached[1448] the gate of the city, behold, [I]a dead man was being carried out, the [II]only[3439] son[5207] of his mother, and she was a widow; and a sizeable crowd from the city was with her.

13 And when [a]the Lord saw her, He felt compassion for her, and said to her, "[I]Do not [pim]weep."

14 And He came up and touched the coffin; and the [ppt]bearers came to a halt. And He said, "Young man, I say to you, arise!"

15 And the [I]dead man sat up, and began to speak. And *Jesus* gave him back to his mother.

16 And [a]fear[5401] gripped them all, and they *began* [ipf] [b]glorifying[1392] God, saying, "A great [c]prophet[4396] has [aop]arisen among us!" and, "God has [I]visited[1980] His people!"

17 [a]And this report[3056] concerning Him went out all over Judea, and in all the surrounding district.

A Deputation from John

18 [a]And the disciples[3101] of John reported to him about all these things.

19 And summoning [I]two of his disciples, John sent them to [a]the Lord, saying, "Are You the [ppt] [II]Expected One,[2064] or do we look for [III]someone else?"[243]

20 And when the men had come to Him, they said, "John the Baptist[910] has sent us to You, saying, 'Are You the [I]Expected One, or do we look for someone else?' "

21 At that [I]very time He [a]cured many *people* of diseases and [b]afflictions and evil[4190] spirits; and He granted[5483] sight to many *who were* blind.

22 And He answered and said to them, [apt]"Go and [aim]report[518] to John what you have [ao]seen and [ao]heard: *the* [a]BLIND RECEIVE SIGHT, *the* lame walk, *the* lepers are cleansed, and *the* deaf hear, *the* dead are raised up, *the* [b]POOR HAVE THE GOSPEL PREACHED[2097] TO THEM.

23 "And blessed[3107] is he [I]who keeps from [asbp]stumbling over Me."

24 And when the messengers[32] of John had left, He began to [pinf]speak to the multitudes about John, "What did you go out into the wilderness to look at? A reed shaken by the wind?

25 "[I]But what did you go out to see? A man dressed in soft [II]clothing?[2440] Behold, those who are splendidly[1741] clothed[2441] and live[5225] in luxury[5172] are *found* in royal palaces.

26 "But what did you go out to see? A prophet?[4396] Yes, I say to you, and one who is more[4055] than a prophet.

27 "This is the one about whom it [I]is written,

'[a]BEHOLD, I SEND MY
MESSENGER BEFORE YOUR
FACE,
WHO WILL PREPARE YOUR
WAY[3598] BEFORE YOU.'

28 "I say to you, among those born of women, there is no one greater than

6 [I]Or, *Sir*
7 [I]Lit., *say with a word* [II]Or, *boy*
9 [a]Matt. 8:10; Luke 7:50
11 [I]Some mss. read *on the next day* [II]Lit., *and*
12 [I]Lit., *one who had died* [II]Or, *only begotten*
13 [I]Or, *Stop weeping* [a]Luke 7:19; 10:1; 11:1, 39; 12:42; 13:15; 17:5, 6; 18:6; 19:8; 22:61; 24:34; John 4:1; 6:23; 11:2
15 [I]Or, *corpse*
16 [I]Or, *cared for* [a]Luke 5:26 [b]Matt. 9:8 [c]Matt. 21:11; Luke 7:39
17 [a]Matt. 9:26
18 [a]Luke 7:18-35: *Matt. 11:2-19*
19 [I]Lit., *a certain two* [II]Lit., *Coming One* [III]Some early mss. read *one who is different* [a]Luke 7:13; 10:1; 11:1, 39; 12:42; 13:15; 17:5, 6; 18:6; 19:8; 22:61; 24:34; John 4:1; 6:23; 11:2
20 [I]Lit., *Coming One*
21 [I]Lit., *hour* [a]Matt. 4:23 [b]Mark 3:10
22 [a]Is. 35:5 [b]Is. 61:1
23 [I]Lit., *whoever*
25 [I]Or, *Well then, what* [II]Or, *garments*
27 [I]Lit., *has been written* [a]Mal. 3:1; Matt. 11:10; Mark 1:2

John; yet he who is [I]least in the kingdom[932] of God is greater than he."

29 And when all the people and the [I]tax-gatherers[5057] heard *this,* they [II]acknowledged [a]God's justice,[1344] [b]having been [aptp]baptized[907] with [c]the baptism[908] of John.

30 But the Pharisees and the [Ia]lawyers[3544] rejected God's purpose[1012] for themselves, not having been baptized by [II]John.

31 "To what then shall I compare the men of this generation,[1074] and what are they like?

32 "They are like children who sit in the market place and call to one another; and they say, 'We [ao]played the flute for you, and you did not dance; we [ao]sang a dirge,[2354] and you did not [ao]weep.'

33 "For John the Baptist has come [a]eating no bread and drinking no wine; and you say, 'He has a demon!'[1140]

34 "The Son of Man has come eating and drinking; and you say, 'Behold, a gluttonous man, and a [I]drunkard,[3630] a friend of [II]tax-gatherers[5057] and sinners!'[268]

35 "[I]Yet wisdom[4678] [a]is [aop]vindicated[1344] by all her children."

36 Now one of the Pharisees was [ipf]requesting Him to [I]dine with him. And He entered the Pharisee's house, and reclined *at the table.*

37 [a]And behold, there was a woman in the city who was a [I]sinner;[268] and when she learned that He was reclining *at the table* in the Pharisee's house, she [apt]brought an alabaster vial[211] of perfume,

38 and [apt]standing behind *Him* at His feet, weeping, she began to [pinf]wet His feet with her tears, and kept [ipf]wiping them with the hair of her head, and [ipf]kissing His feet, and [ipf]anointing[218] them with the perfume.

39 Now when the Pharisee who had invited[2564] Him saw this, he said [I]to himself, "If this man were [IIa]a prophet[4396] He would know who and what sort of person this woman is who is touching Him, that she is a [III]sinner."

28 [I]Or, *less*

29 [I]I.e., Collectors of Roman taxes for profit [II]Or, *justified God* [a]Luke 7:35 [b]Matt. 21:32; Luke 3:12 [c]Acts 18:25; 19:3

30 [I]I.e., experts in the Mosaic Law [II]Lit., *him* [a]Matt. 22:35

33 [a]Luke 1:15

34 [I]Or, *wine-drinker* [II]I.e., Collectors of Roman taxes for profit

35 [I]Lit., *And* [a]Luke 7:29

36 [I]Lit., *eat*

37 [I]I.e., an immoral woman [a]Matt. 26:6-13; Mark 14:3-9; Luke 7:37-39; John 12:1-8

39 [I]Lit., *to himself, saying* [II]Some mss. read *the prophet* [III]I.e., an immoral woman [a]Luke 7:16; John 4:19

40 [I]Lit., *says*

41 [I]The denarius was equivalent to one day's wage [a]Matt. 18:28; Mark 6:37

42 [a]Matt. 18:25

44 [a]Gen. 18:4; 19:2; 43:24; Judg. 19:21; 1Tim. 5:10

45 [I]Lit., *was not ceasing* [a]2Sam. 15:5

46 [a]2Sam. 12:20; Ps. 23:5; Eccl. 9:8; Dan. 10:3

48 [a]Matt. 9:2; Mark 2:5, 9; Luke 5:20, 23

49 [I]Or, *among* [a]Luke 5:21

50 [a]Matt. 9:22; Luke 17:19; 18:42 [b]Mark 5:34; Luke 8:48

1 [a]Matt. 4:23

2 [a]Matt. 27:55; Mark 15:40, 41; Luke 23:49, 55

Parable of Two Debtors

40 And Jesus answered[611] and said to him, "Simon, I have something to say to you." And he [I]replied, "Say it, Teacher."

41 "A certain moneylender had two debtors: one [ipf]owed five hundred [Ia]denarii,[1220] and the other[2087] fifty.

42 "When they [ppt a]were unable to [ainf]repay, he graciously forgave[5483] them both. Which of them therefore will love[25] him more?"

43 Simon answered and said, "I suppose[5274] the one whom he forgave[5483] more." And He said to him, "You have judged correctly."

44 And turning toward the woman, He said to Simon, "Do you see this woman? I entered your house; you [a]gave Me no water for My feet, but she has [ao]wet My feet with her tears, and wiped them with her hair.

45 "You [a]gave Me no kiss; but she, since the time I came in, [I]has not ceased[1257] to [ppt]kiss My feet.

46 "[a]You did not anoint My head with oil,[1637] but she anointed My feet with perfume.[3464]

47 "For this reason I say to you, her sins, which are many, have been [pfip]forgiven, for she loved[25] much; but he who is forgiven little, loves little."

48 And He said to her, "[a]Your sins have been forgiven."

49 And those who were reclining *at the table* with Him began to [pinf]say [I]to themselves, "[a]Who is this *man* who even forgives sins?"

50 And He said to the woman, "[a]Your faith has saved[4982] you; [pim b]go in peace."

Ministering Women

8 And it came about soon afterwards, that He *began* [ipf]going about from one city and village to another, [a]proclaiming[2784] and preaching[2097] the kingdom[932] of God; and the twelve were with Him,

2 and *also* [a]some women who had

been healed of evil[4190] spirits and sicknesses: [b]Mary who was called Magdalene, from whom seven demons[1140] had [plpf]gone out,

3 and Joanna the wife of Chuza, [a]Herod's [b]steward, and Susanna, and many others who were [ipf]contributing to their support[1247] out of their private means.[5224]

Parable of the Sower

4 [a]And when a great multitude were [ppt]coming together, and those from the various cities were [ppt]journeying to Him, He spoke by way of a parable:[3850]

5 "The sower went out to [infg]sow his seed; and as he [aie]sowed, some fell beside the road; and it was trampled under foot, and the birds of the [l]air[3772] ate it up.

6 "And other *seed* fell on [apt]rocky *soil,* and as soon as it [aptp]grew up,[5453] it withered away, because it [aid]had no moisture.

7 "And other *seed* fell among[3319] the thorns; and the thorns grew up with it, and choked it out.

🗝 8 "And other *seed* fell into the good[18] soil, and grew up, and produced a crop a hundred times as great." As He said these things, He would call out, "[a]He who [ppt]has ears to hear, let him [pim]hear."

9 [a]And His disciples *began* [ipf]questioning Him as to what this parable might be.

10 And He said, "[a]To you it has been [pfip]granted to know the mysteries[3466] of the kingdom[932] of God, but to the rest *it is* in parables, in order that [ppt] [b]SEEING[991] THEY MAY NOT [psa]SEE, AND [ppt]HEARING[191] THEY MAY NOT [psa]UNDERSTAND.[4920]

🗝 11 "Now the parable is this: [a]the seed is the word[3056] of God.[2316]

🗝 12 "And those beside the road are those who have [apt]heard; then the devil[1228] comes and takes away the word from their heart,[2588] so that they may not [apt]believe[4100] and be [asbp]saved.[4982]

13 "And those on the rocky *soil are* those who, when they [aosb]hear,[191] receive the word with joy;[5479] and these have no *firm* root; [l]they believe for a while,[2540] and in time[2540] of temptation[3986] fall away.[868]

🗝 14 "And the *seed* which [apt]fell among the thorns, these are the ones who have [apt]heard, and as they [apt]go on their way they are [pinp]choked with worries and riches and pleasures of *this* life,[979] and [pin]bring no fruit to maturity.[5052]

15 "And the *seed* in the good[2570] soil, these are the ones who have heard the word in an honest and good[18] heart,[2588] and hold it fast,[2722] and bear fruit with [l]perseverance.[5281]

Parable of the Lamp

16 "Now [a]no one after [apl]lighting a lamp[3088] covers it over with a container, or puts it under a bed; but he puts it on a lampstand, in order that those who come in may [psa]see[991] the light.

17 "[a]For nothing is hidden[2927] that shall not become evident, nor *anything* secret[614] that shall not be known and come to light.

18 "Therefore take care how you [pin]listen; [a]for whoever has, to him shall *more* be given; and whoever does not have, even what he [l]thinks[1380] he has shall be taken away from him."

19 [a]And His mother and brothers [ao]came[3854] to Him, and they were [ipf]unable to get to[4940] Him because of the crowd.[3793]

20 And it was reported to Him, "Your mother and Your brothers are [pfi]standing outside, wishing to see[1492] You."

21 But He [apt]answered and said to them, "My mother and My brothers are

2 [b]Matt. 27:56; Mark 16:9
3 [a]Matt. 14:1 [b]Matt. 20:8
4 [a]Luke 8:4-8: *Matt. 13:2-9; Mark 4:1-9*
5 [l]Lit., *heaven*
8 [a]Matt. 11:15; Mark 7:16; Luke 14:35; Rev. 2:7, 11, 17, 29; 3:6, 13, 22; 13:9
9 [a]Luke 8:9-15: *Matt. 13:10-23; Mark 4:10-20*
10 [a]Matt. 13:11 [b]Is. 6:9; Matt. 13:14; Acts 28:26
11 [a]1Pet. 1:23
13 [l]Lit., *who believe*
15 [l]Or, *steadfastness*
16 [a]Matt. 5:15; Mark 4:21; Luke 11:33
17 [a]Matt. 10:26; Mark 4:22; Luke 12:2
18 [l]Or, *seems to have* [a]Matt. 13:12; 25:29; Luke 19:26
19 [a]Luke 8:19-21: *Matt. 12:46-50; Mark 3:31-35*

🗝 **8:8,11** See note on Mt. 13.
🗝 **8:12-14** See note on Gal. 3:22.
🗝 **8:14** See note on II Thess. 2:3. See also *apostasia* (646), apostasy, and *aphistēmi* (868), to stand away from.

these [a]who [ppt]hear the word of God and
[ppt]do[4160] it."

Jesus Stills the Sea

22 [a]Now it came about on one
of *those* days, that He and His disciples got into a boat, and He said to
them, "Let us go over to the other
side of [b]the lake." And they launched
out.[321]
23 But as they were sailing along
He fell asleep; and a fierce gale[2978] of
wind descended upon [a]the lake, and they
began to be [ipf]swamped[4845] and to be
in [ipf]danger.[2973]
24 And they [apt]came[4334] to Him and
woke Him up, saying, "[a]Master,[1988]
Master, we are perishing!" And being
[aptp]aroused, He [b]rebuked the wind and
the surging[2830] waves, and they
stopped, and [I]it became calm.
25 And He said to them, "Where
is your faith?" And they were fearful
and amazed, saying to one another,[240]
"Who then is this, that He commands[2004]
even the winds and the water, and they
[pin]obey Him?"

The Demoniac Cured

26 [a]And they sailed to the country
of the [I]Gerasenes, which is opposite Galilee.
27 And when He had come out onto
the land, He was met by a certain man
from the city who was [ipf]possessed with
demons; and who had not [ipf]put on[1746]
any clothing[2440] for a long time,[5550] and
was not [ipf]living in a house, but in the
tombs.
28 And seeing Jesus, he [apt]cried out
and fell before Him, and said in a loud
voice, "[a]What do I have to do with You,
Jesus, Son of [b]the Most High God? I
beg[1189] You, do not [asba]torment[928] me."
29 For He [I]had been [ao]commanding
the unclean spirit to come out of the
man. For it had [plpf]seized him many
times;[5550] and he was [ipf]bound with
chains and shackles and kept under
guard; and *yet* he would [ppt]burst his fetters and be [ipf]driven[1643] by the demon[1140]
into the desert.
30 And Jesus asked him, "What is
your name?" And he said, "[a]Legion";
for many demons had [ao]entered
him.
31 And they were [ipf]entreating Him
not to [aosb]command[2004] them to depart
into [a]the abyss.[12]
32 Now there was a herd of many
swine feeding there on the mountain;
and *the demons* [ao]entreated Him to
permit[2010] them to enter [I]the swine. And
He gave them permission.
33 And the demons[1140] [apt]came out
from the man and entered the swine;
and the herd rushed down the steep
bank into [a]the lake, and were
drowned.[638]
34 And when the [ppt]herdsmen
[apt]saw what had happened, they ran
away and reported it in the city and *out*
in the country.
35 And *the people* went out to see
what had happened; and they came to
Jesus, and found the man from whom
the demons had gone out, sitting down
[a]at the feet of Jesus, clothed and [ppt]in
his right mind;[4993] and they became
frightened.
36 And those who had seen it reported to them how the man who was
[a]demon-possessed had been [I]made
well.[4982]
37 And all the people of the country
of the [I]Gerasenes and the surrounding
district [ao]asked Him to depart from
them; for they were [ipf]gripped[4912] with
great fear;[5401] and He [apt]got into a boat,
and returned.
38 [a]But the man from whom the demons had [plpf]gone out was [ipf]begging[1189]
Him that he might [I]accompany Him; but
He sent him away, saying,
39 "Return to your house and
[pim]describe[1334] what great things God
has [ao]done for you." And he went away,
[ppt]proclaiming[2784] throughout[2596] the
whole city what great things Jesus had
done for him.

21 [a]Luke 11:28
22 [a]Luke 8:22-25: *Matt. 8:23-27; Mark 4:36-41* [b]Luke 5:1f.; 8:23
23 [a]Luke 5:1f.; 8:22
24 [I]Lit., *a calm occurred* [a]Luke 5:5 [b]Luke 4:39
26 [I]Other mss. read *Gergesenes* or *Gadarenes* [a]Luke 8:26-37: *Matt. 8:28-34; Mark 5:1-17*
28 [a]Matt. 8:29 [b]Mark 5:7
29 [I]Or, *was commanding*
30 [a]Matt. 26:53
31 [a]Rom. 10:7; Rev. 9:1f., 11; 11:7; 17:8; 20:1, 3
32 [I]Lit., *them*
33 [a]Luke 5:1f.; 8:22
35 [a]Luke 10:39
36 [I]Or, *saved* [a]Matt. 4:24
37 [I]Other mss. read *Gergesenes* or *Gadarenes*
38 [I]Lit., *be with* [a]Luke 8:38, 39: *Mark 5:18-20*

Miracles of Healing

40 [a]And as Jesus returned, the multitude welcomed[588] Him, for they had
all been waiting for Him.
41 [a]And behold, there came a man
named Jairus, and he was[5225] an
[I][b]official[758] of the synagogue;[4864] and he
fell at Jesus' feet, and *began* to [ipf]entreat
Him to [ainf]come to his house;
42 for he had an [I]only[3439] daughter,
about twelve years old, and she was
[ipf]dying. But as He [aie]went, the multitudes were [ipf]pressing against Him.
43 And a woman who had a hemorrhage for twelve years, [I]and could not
be [aifp]healed[2323] by anyone,
44 came up behind Him, and
touched the fringe of His [I]cloak; and
immediately her hemorrhage[129, 4511]
stopped.[2476]
45 And Jesus said, "Who is the
one who [apt]touched Me?" And while
they were all [ppt]denying[720] it, Peter
said,[I] "[a]Master, the multitudes are
crowding[4912] and pressing upon
You."
46 But Jesus said, "Someone did
[ao]touch Me, for I was aware that
[a]power[1411] had [pfp]gone out of Me."
47 And when the woman saw that
she had not escaped notice, she came
trembling and [apt]fell down before Him,
and declared[518] in the presence of all
the people the reason[156] why she had
touched Him, and how she had been
immediately healed.
48 And He said to her, "Daughter,
[a]your faith has [I]made you well;[4982]
[pim] [b]go in peace."[1515]
49 While He was still [ppt]speaking,
someone *came from *the house of*
[a]the synagogue official, saying, "Your
daughter [pfi]has died;[2348] do not [pim]trouble
the Teacher anymore."
50 But when Jesus heard *this,* He
answered him, "[a]Do not [pim]be afraid[5399]
any longer; only [pim]believe, and she shall
be [ft] [I]made well."
51 And when He had come to the
house, He did not allow anyone to enter
with Him, except Peter and John and
James, and the girl's[3816] father and
mother.
52 Now they were all [ipf]weeping and
[ipf] [a]lamenting[2875] for her; but He said,
"Stop [pim]weeping, for she has not [ao]died,
but [b]is asleep."
53 And they *began* [ipf]laughing at
Him, knowing that she had died.
54 He, however, [apt]took her by the
hand and called, saying, "Child,[3816]
[pim]arise!"
55 And her spirit[4151] returned, and
she rose immediately;[3916] and He gave
orders[1299] for *something* to be given her
to eat.
56 And her parents were amazed;
but He [a]instructed them to tell no one
what had happened.

Ministry of the Twelve

9 [a]And He [apt]called the twelve together,[4779] and gave them power
and authority over all the demons, and
to [pinf]heal diseases.
2 And He sent them out[649] to
[pinf] [a]proclaim[2784] the kingdom[932] of
God,[2316] and [I]to perform healing.
3 And He said to them, [pim]"[a]Take
nothing for *your* journey, [b]neither a
staff,[4464] nor a [I]bag,[4082] nor bread, nor
money; and do not *even* have [II]two tunics
apiece.
4 "And whatever house you [aosb]en-
ter, [pim]stay there, and [pim]take your leave
from there.
5 "And as for those who do not receive you, as you [ppt]go out from that
city, [pim] [a]shake off the dust from your
feet as a testimony[3142] against them."
6 And departing, they *began* [ipf]going
about [I]among the villages, [a]preaching the
gospel,[2097] and healing everywhere.
7 [a]Now [b]Herod the tetrarch heard
of all that was [ppt]happening; and he was
[ipf]greatly perplexed, because it was
[aid]said by some that [c]John had [aop]risen
from the dead,
8 and by some that [a]Elijah had [aop]ap-
peared, and by others, that one of the
prophets[4396] of old had [ao]risen again.
9 And Herod said, "I myself had

---

40 [a]Matt. 9:1; Mark 5:21
41 [I]Lit., *ruler* [a]Luke 8:41-56: *Matt. 9:18-26; Mark 5:22-43* [b]Mark 5:22; Luke 8:49
42 [I]Or, *only begotten*
43 [I]Some mss. add *who had spent all her living upon physicians*
44 [I]Or, *outer garment*
45 [I]Some early mss. add *and those with him* [a]Luke 5:5
46 [a]Luke 5:17
48 [I]Or, *saved you* [a]Matt. 9:22 [b]Mark 5:34; Luke 7:50
49 [a]Luke 8:41
50 [I]Or, *saved* [a]Mark 5:36
52 [a]Matt. 11:17; Luke 23:27 [b]John 11:13
56 [a]Matt. 8:4
1 [a]Matt. 10:5; Mark 6:7
2 [I]Some mss. read *to heal the sick* [a]Matt. 10:7
3 [I]Or, *knapsack or beggar's bag* [II]Or, *inner garment* [a]Luke 9:3-5: *Matt. 10:9-15; Mark 6:8-11;* Luke 10:4-12; 22:35 [b]Matt. 10:10; Mark 6:8; Luke 22:35f.
5 [a]Luke 10:11; Acts 13:51
6 [I]Or, *from village to village* [a]Mark 6:12; Luke 8:1
7 [a]Luke 9:7-9: *Matt. 14:1, 2;* Mark 6:14f. [b]Matt. 14:1; Luke 3:1; 13:31; 23:7 [c]Matt. 14:2
8 [a]Matt. 16:14

John [ao]beheaded; but who is this man about whom I hear such things?" And [a]he kept [ipf]trying to [ainf]see Him.

10 [a]And when the apostles[652] returned, they gave an account[1334] to Him of all that they had [ao]done. [b]And taking them with Him, He withdrew by Himself to a city called [c]Bethsaida.

11 But the multitudes were aware of this and followed Him; and [apt]welcoming[1209] them, He *began* [ipf]speaking to them about the kingdom[932] of God and [ipf]curing those who had need of healing.[2322]

Five Thousand Fed

12 And the day began to decline, and the twelve [apt]came and said to Him, "Send the multitude away, that they may [aptp]go into the surrounding villages and countryside and [aosb]find lodging[2647] and [aosb]get [I]something to eat;[1979] for here we are in a desolate place."

13 But He said to them, "You give them *something* to eat!" And they said, "We have no more than five loaves and two fish, unless perhaps we go and [aosb]buy food for all these people."

14 (For there were about five thousand men.) And He said to His disciples,[3101] "Have them recline *to eat* [a]in groups of about fifty each."[303]

15 And they did so, and had them all recline.

16 And He [apt]took the five loaves and the two fish, and [apt]looking up to heaven, He blessed[2127] them, and broke *them,* and kept [ipf]giving *them* to the disciples to set before the multitude.

17 And they all ate and were satisfied; and [I]the broken pieces[2801] which they had left over were picked up, twelve [a]baskets *full.*

18 [a]And it came about that while He was [b]praying alone, the disciples[3101] were with Him, and He questioned them, saying, "Who do the multitudes say that I am?"

19 And they answered and said, "John the Baptist,[910] and others *say* Elijah; but others, that one of the prophets[4396] of old has [ao]risen again."

20 And He said to them, "But who do you say that I am?" And Peter answered and said, "[a]The [I]Christ[5547] of God."[2316]

21 But He [apt] [Ia]warned[2008] them, and instructed[3853] *them* not to [pinf]tell this to anyone,

22 [a]saying, "[b]The Son of Man must suffer many things, and be rejected[593] by the elders[4245] and chief priests[749] and scribes,[1122] and be killed, and be raised up on the third day."

23 And He was [ipf]saying to *them* all, "[a]If anyone wishes to [pinf]come after Me, let him [aim]deny[533] himself, and [aim]take up his cross[4716] daily, and [pim]follow Me.

24 "For [a]whoever [psa]wishes to [ainf]save[4982] his [I]life[5590] shall lose[622] it, but whoever [aosb]loses[622] his [I]life for My sake, he is the one who will save it.

🗝 25 "For what is a man profited if he [apt]gains the whole world, and [apt] [a]loses or [aptp]forfeits himself?

26 "[a]For whoever is [aosb]ashamed of Me and My words, of him will the Son of Man be ashamed when He comes in His glory, and *the glory*[1391] of the Father and of the holy angels.[32]

27 "But I say to you truthfully, [a]there are some of those [pfp]standing here who shall not taste[1089] death[2288] until they [aosb]see the kingdom[932] of God."[2316]

The Transfiguration

28 [a]And some eight days after these sayings, it came about that He [apt]took along [b]Peter and John and James, and [c]went up to the mountain [d]to [ainf]pray.

29 And while He was [a]praying, the appearance[1491] of His face[4383] [b]became different,[2087] and His clothing[2441] *became* white *and* [I]gleaming.[1823]

30 And behold, two men were [ipf]talking with Him; and they were Moses and Elijah,

9 [a]Luke 23:8

10 [a]Mark 6:30 [b]Luke 9:10-17: *Matt. 14:13-21; Mark 6:32-44; John 6:5-13* [c]Matt. 11:21

12 [I]Lit., *provisions*

14 [a]Mark 6:39

17 [I]Lit., *that which was left over to them of the broken pieces was* [a]Matt. 14:20

18 [a]Luke 9:18-20: *Matt. 16:13-16; Mark 8:27-29* [b]Matt. 14:23; Luke 6:12; 9:28

20 [I]I.e., Messiah [a]John 6:68f.

21 [I]Or, *strictly admonished* [a]Matt. 8:4; 16:20; Mark 8:30

22 [a]Luke 9:22-27: *Matt. 16:21-28; Mark 8:31-9:1* [b]Matt. 16:21; Luke 9:44

23 [a]Matt. 10:38; Luke 14:27

24 [I]Or, *soul* [a]Matt. 10:39; Luke 17:33; John 12:25

25 [a]Heb. 10:34

26 [a]Matt. 10:33; Luke 12:9

27 [a]Matt. 16:28

28 [a]Luke 9:28-36: *Matt. 17:1-8; Mark 9:2-8* [b]Matt. 17:1 [c]Matt. 5:1 [d]Luke 3:21; 5:16; 6:12; 9:18

29 [I]Lit., *flashing like lightning* [a]Luke 3:21; 5:16; 6:12; 9:18 [b]Mark 16:12

🗝 **9:25** See note on Heb. 6:1-6.

31 who, [apt]appearing in [I]glory,[1391]
were [ipf]speaking of His [a]departure1841
which He was about to accomplish[4137]
at Jerusalem.
32 Now Peter and his companions
[a]had been overcome with sleep; but
when they were fully [apt]awake, they saw
His glory[1391] and the two men
[pfp]standing[4921] with Him.
33 And it came about, as [I]these
were parting from Him, Peter said to
Jesus, "[a]Master, it is good for us to
be here; and [b]let us make three
[II]tabernacles:4633 one for You, and one
for Moses, and one for Elijah"—[c]not
realizing what he was saying.
34 And while he was [ppt]saying this,
a cloud [I]formed and *began* to overshadow
them; and they were afraid as they
[ainf]entered the cloud.
35 And [a]a voice came out of the
cloud, saying, "[b]This is My Son,[5207] *My*
Chosen One;[1586] [pim]listen[191] to Him!"
36 And when the voice [I]had spoken,
Jesus was found alone. And [a]they [ao]kept
silent, and reported to no one in those
days any of the things which they had
seen.[3708]
37 [a]And it came about on the next
day, that when they had [apt]come down
from the mountain, a great multitude
met Him.
38 And behold, a man from the
multitude[3793] shouted out, saying,
"Teacher, I beg[1189] You to look1914 at
my son, for he is my [I]only *boy,*[3439]
39 and behold, a spirit[4151] seizes
him, and he suddenly screams, and it
throws him into a convulsion with foaming *at the mouth,* and as it mauls him,
it scarcely leaves him.
40 "And I begged[1189] Your disciples
to cast it out, and they could not."
41 And Jesus answered and said, "O
unbelieving[571] and perverted generation, how long shall I be with you, and
put up with[430] you? Bring[4317] your son
here."
42 And while he was still approaching, the demon [I]dashed him *to the*
ground, and threw him into a convulsion.
But Jesus rebuked the unclean[169]
spirit,[4151] and healed the boy, and gave
him back to his father.
43 And they were all [ipf]amazed at
the [Ia]greatness of God.
[b]But while everyone was [ppt]marvel-
ing at all that He was doing, He said
to His disciples,
44 "Let these words sink into your
ears; [a]for the Son of Man is going to
be [I]delivered into the hands of men."
45 But [a]they [I]did not [ipf]understand[50]
this statement, and it was concealed
from them so that they might not
[aosb]perceive[143] it; and they [ipf]were afraid
to ask[2065] Him about this statement.

The Test of Greatness

46 [a]And an argument[1261] [I]arose
among them as to which of them might
be the greatest.
47 But Jesus, [a]knowing [I]what they
were thinking[1261] in their heart,[2588]
[apt]took[1949] a child and stood[2476] him by
His side,
48 and said to them, "[a]Whoever
[aosb]receives[1209] this child in My name
receives Me; and whoever [aosb]receives
Me receives Him who [apt]sent Me;
[b]for he who is [I]least among you, this
is the one who is great."
49 [a]And John answered and said,
"[b]Master, we saw someone casting out
demons1140 in Your name; and we tried
to hinder him because he does not follow
along with us."
50 But Jesus said to him, "Do not
[pim]hinder *him;* [a]for he who is not against
you is [I]for you."
51 And it came about, when the
days were [aie]approaching[4845] for [a]His
[I]ascension,354 that He resolutely set4741
His face [b]to go to Jerusalem;
52 and He sent messengers on
ahead[4383]4253 of Him. And they went, and
entered a village of the [a]Samaritans, to
[I]make arrangements for Him.
53 And they did not receive Him,
[a]because [I]He was journeying with His
face toward Jerusalem.
54 And when His disciples[3101]
[a]James and John saw *this,* they said,

31 [I]Or, *splendor* [a]2Pet. 1:15
32 [a]Matt. 26:43; Mark 14:40
33 [I]Lit., *they* [II]Or, *sacred tents* [a]Luke 5:5; 9:49 [b]Matt. 17:4; Mark 9:5 [c]Mark 9:6
34 [I]Or, *occurred*
35 [a]2Pet. 1:17f. [b]Is. 42:1; Matt. 3:17; 12:18; Mark 1:11; Luke 3:22
36 [I]Lit., *occurred* [a]Matt. 17:9; Mark 9:9f.
37 [a]Luke 9:37-42: *Matt. 17:14-18; Mark 9:14-27*
38 [I]Or, *only begotten*
42 [I]Or, *tore him*
43 [I]Or, *majesty* [a]2Pet. 1:16 [b]Luke 9:43-45: *Matt. 17:22f.; Mark 9:30-32*
44 [I]Or, *betrayed* [a]Luke 9:22
45 [I]Lit., *were not knowing* [a]Mark 9:32
46 [I]Lit., *entered in* [a]Luke 9:46-48: *Matt. 18:1-5; Mark 9:33-37;* Luke 22:24
47 [I]Lit., *the reasoning;* or, *argument* [a]Matt. 9:4
48 [I]Or, *lowliest* [a]Matt. 10:40; Luke 10:16; John 13:20 [b]Luke 22:26
49 [a]Luke 9:49, 50: *Mark 9:38-40* [b]Luke 5:5; 9:33
50 [I]Or, *on your side* [a]Matt. 12:30; Luke 11:23
51 [I]Lit., *taking up* [a]Mark 16:19 [b]Luke 13:22; 17:11; 18:31; 19:11, 28
52 [I]Or, *prepare* [a]Matt. 10:5; Luke 10:33; 17:16; John 4:4
53 [I]Lit., *His face was proceeding toward* [a]John 4:9
54 [a]Mark 3:17

"Lord, do You want us to [b]command fire to come down from heaven and consume them[I]?"

55 But He turned and rebuked them, [[I]and said, "You do not know what kind of spirit you are of;

56 for the Son of Man did not [ao]come to [ainf]<u>destroy</u>[622] men's <u>lives</u>,[5590] but to [ainf]save them."] And they went on to <u>another</u>[2087] village.

Exacting Discipleship

57 And [a]as they were [ppt]going along the road, [b]someone said to Him, "I will <u>follow</u>[190] You wherever You go."

58 And Jesus said to him, "The foxes have holes, and the birds of the [I]air *have* [II]nests, but [a]the Son of Man has nowhere to [psa]lay His head."

59 And He said to another, [pim]"[a]Follow Me." But he said, "[I]<u>Permit</u>2010 me first to go and [ainf]bury my father."

60 But He said to him, "Allow the dead to bury their own dead; but as for you, [apt]go and [pim] [a]<u>proclaim everywhere</u>[1229] the <u>kingdom</u>[932] of <u>God</u>."[2316]

61 And another also said, "I will <u>follow</u>[190] You, Lord; but [a]first permit me to [ainf]<u>say good-bye</u>[657] to those at home."

62 But Jesus said to him, "[a]No one, after putting his hand to the plow and looking back, is fit for the kingdom of God."

The Seventy Sent Out

10 Now after this [a]the Lord appointed [I]seventy [b]others, and sent them [c]<u>two and two</u>[303]1417 ahead of Him to every city and place where He Himself was [ipf]going to [pinf]come.

2 And He was saying to them, "[a]The harvest is plentiful, but the laborers are few; therefore [aim]<u>beseech</u>[1189] the Lord of the harvest to [aosb]send out laborers into His harvest.

3 "Go your ways; [a]behold, I send you out as lambs in the midst of wolves.

4 [pim]"[a]Carry no <u>purse</u>,905 no [I]<u>bag</u>,4082 no shoes; and [aosi]greet no one on the way.

5 "And whatever house you [psa]enter, first [pim]say, 'Peace *be* to this house.'

6 "And if a [I]<u>man</u>[5207] of peace is there, your peace will <u>rest</u>[1879] upon him; but if not, it will return to you.

7 "And [pim]stay in [I]that house, [ppt]eating and [ppt]drinking [II]what they give you; for [a]the laborer is worthy of his <u>wages</u>.[3408] Do not [pim]<u>keep moving</u>[3327] from house to house.

8 "And whatever city you [psa]enter, and they [psa]receive you, [pim] [a]eat what is set before you;

9 and [pim]heal those in it who are sick, and say to them, '[a]The <u>kingdom</u>[932] of God has [pf]<u>come near</u>[1448] to you.'

10 "But whatever city you [aosb]enter and they do not [psa]receive you, [apt]go out into its streets and [aim]say,

11 '[a]Even the dust of your city which <u>clings</u>2853 to our feet, we wipe off *in protest* against you; yet [pim] [I]be sure of this, that [b]the kingdom of God has come near.'

12 "I say to you, [a]it will be more <u>tolerable</u>414 in that <u>day</u>[2250] for [b]Sodom, than for that city.

13 "[a]Woe to you, [b]Chorazin! Woe to you, [b]Bethsaida! For if the [I]<u>miracles</u>[1411] had been [aop]performed in [b]Tyre and Sidon which [apt]occurred in you, they would have [ao]<u>repented</u>[3340] <u>long ago</u>,[3819] sitting in [c]<u>sackcloth</u>4526 and ashes.

14 "But it will be more <u>tolerable</u>414 for [a]Tyre and Sidon in the <u>judgment</u>,[2920] than for you.

15 "And you, [a]Capernaum, will not be [fp]exalted to <u>heaven</u>,[3772] will you? You will be [ft]brought down to <u>Hades</u>![86]

16 "[a]The one who [ppt]<u>listens</u>[191] to you <u>listens</u>[191] to Me, and [b]the one who [ppt]rejects you rejects Me; and he who [ppt]rejects Me rejects the One who sent Me."

The Happy Results

17 And the [I]seventy returned with <u>joy</u>,[5479] saying, "Lord, even [a]the

54 [I]Some mss. add *as Elijah did* [b]2Kin. 1:9-16
55 [I]Many mss. do not contain bracketed portion
57 [a]Luke 9:51 [b]Luke 9:57-60: *Matt. 8:19-22*
58 [I]Or, *sky* [II]Or, *roosting-places* [a]Matt. 8:20
59 [I]Some mss. add *Lord* [a]Matt. 8:22
60 [a]Matt. 4:23
61 [a]1Kin. 19:20
62 [a]Phil. 3:13

1 [I]Some mss. read *seventy-two* [a]Luke 7:13 [b]Luke 9:1f., 52 [c]Mark 6:7
2 [a]Matt. 9:37, 38; John 4:35
3 [a]Matt. 10:16
4 [I]Or, *knapsack or beggar's bag* [a]Matt. 10:9-14; Mark 6:8-11; Luke 9:3-5; 10:4-12
6 [I]Lit., *son*
7 [I]Or, *the house itself* [II]Lit., *the things from them* [a]Matt. 10:10; 1Cor. 9:14; 1Tim. 5:18
8 [a]1Cor. 10:27
9 [a]Matt. 3:2; 10:7; Luke 10:11
11 [I]Lit., *know* [a]Matt. 10:14; Mark 6:11; Luke 9:5; Acts 13:51 [b]Matt. 3:2; 10:7; Luke 10:9
12 [a]Gen. 19:24-28; Matt. 10:15; 11:24 [b]Matt. 10:15
13 [I]Or, *works of power* [a]Luke 10:13-15: *Matt. 11:21-23* [b]Is. 23:1-18; Ezek. 26:1-28:26; Joel 3:4-8; Matt. 11:21 [c]Rev. 11:3
14 [a]Matt. 11:21
15 [a]Is. 14:13-15; Matt. 4:13; 11:23
16 [a]Matt. 10:40; Mark 9:37; Luke 9:48; John 13:20; Gal. 4:14 [b]John 12:48; 1Thess. 4:8
17 [I]Some mss. read *seventy-two* [a]Mark 16:17

demons[1140] are subject to[5293] us in Your name."[3686]

18 And He said to them, "I was [ipf]watching[2334] [a]Satan [apt]fall from heaven[3772] like lightning.

19 "Behold, I have given you [art]authority to [pinf] [a]tread[3961] upon serpents and scorpions, and over all the power[1411] of the enemy, and nothing shall injure[91] you.

20 "Nevertheless do not rejoice in this, that the spirits are subject to[5293] you, but rejoice that [a]your names are [pfip]recorded in heaven."[3772]

21 [a]At that very [I]time He rejoiced[21] greatly in the Holy Spirit, and said, "I [II]praise[1843] Thee, O Father,[3962] Lord[2962] of heaven and earth, that Thou didst [ao]hide these things from *the* wise[4680] and intelligent[4908] and didst [ao]reveal[601] them to babes.[3516] Yes, Father, for thus it was well-pleasing[2107] in Thy sight.

22 "[a]All things have been [aop]handed over to Me by My Father, and [b]no one knows who the Son[5207] is except the Father, and who the Father is except the Son, and anyone to whom the Son wills to [ainf]reveal *Him*."

23 [a]And turning to the disciples,[3101] He said privately, "Blessed[3107] *are* the eyes which [ppt]see the things you see,

24 for I say to you, that many prophets[4396] and kings [ao]wished to [ainf]see the things which you see, and did not [ao]see *them*, and to [ainf]hear the things which you hear, and did not [ao]hear *them*."

25 [a]And behold, a certain [Ib]lawyer[3544] stood up and [ppt]put Him to the test,[1598] saying, "Teacher,[1320] what shall I [apt]do to [ft]inherit[2816] eternal[166] life?"[2222]

26 And He said to him, "What is written[1125] in the Law?[3551] How [I]does it read to you?"

27 And he answered and said, "[a]YOU SHALL [ft]LOVE[25] THE LORD[2962] YOUR GOD[2316] WITH ALL YOUR HEART,[2588] AND WITH ALL YOUR SOUL,[5590] AND WITH ALL YOUR STRENGTH,[2479] AND WITH ALL YOUR MIND;[1271] AND YOUR NEIGHBOR[4139] AS YOURSELF."

28 And He said to him, "You have answered correctly; [a]DO THIS, AND YOU WILL LIVE."[2198]

29 But wishing [a]to justify[1344] himself, he said to Jesus, "And who is my neighbor?"[4139]

The Good Samaritan

30 Jesus replied[5274] and said, "A certain man was [ipf] [a]going down from Jerusalem to Jericho; and he fell among robbers,[3027] and they [apt]stripped him and [apt] [I]beat him, and went off [apt]leaving[863] him half dead.

31 "And by chance a certain priest[2409] was [ipf]going down on that road, and when he [apt]saw him, he passed by on the other side.

32 "And likewise a Levite[3019] also, when he [apt]came to[2596] the place and [apt]saw him, passed by on the other side.

33 "But a certain [a]Samaritan,[4541] who [ppt]was on a journey, came upon him; and when he saw him, he felt compassion,[4697]

34 and [apt]came to him, and bandaged up his wounds, pouring oil[1637] and wine on *them;* and he [apt]put him on his own beast, and brought him to an inn, and took care of him.

35 "And on the next day he [apt]took out[1544] two [I]denarii[1220] and gave them to the innkeeper and said, 'Take care of him; and whatever more you [aosb]spend, when I [aie]return, I will repay you.'

36 "Which of these three do you think proved to [pfin]be a neighbor to the man who fell into the robbers' *hands?*"

37 And he said, "The one who [apt]showed mercy[1656] toward him." And Jesus said to him, [pim]"Go and [pim]do [I]the same."

18 [a]Matt. 4:10

19 [a]Ps. 91:13; Mark 16:18

20 [a]Ex. 32:32; Ps. 69:28; Is. 4:3; Ezek. 13:9; Dan. 12:1; Phil. 4:3; Heb. 12:23; Rev. 3:5; 13:8; 17:8; 20:12, 15; 21:27

21 [I]Lit., *hour* [II]Or, *acknowledge to Thy praise* [a]Luke 10:21, 22: *Matt. 11:25-27*

22 [a]John 3:35 [b]John 10:15

23 [a]Luke 10:23, 24: *Matt. 13:16, 17*

25 [I]I.e., an expert in the Mosaic Law [a]Luke 10:25-28: *Matt. 22:34-40; Mark 12:28-31;* Matt. 19:16-19 [b]Matt. 22:35

26 [I]Lit., *do you read?*

27 [a]Deut. 6:5; Lev. 19:18

28 [a]Lev. 18:5; Ezek. 20:11; Matt. 19:17

29 [a]Luke 16:15

30 [I]Lit., *laid blows upon* [a]Luke 18:31; 19:28

33 [a]Matt. 10:5; Luke 9:52

35 [I]The denarius was equivalent to one day's wage

37 [I]Or, *likewise*

10:29 See note on justification in General Remarks on Romans.

Martha and Mary

38 Now as they were [aie]traveling
along, He entered a certain village; and
a [I]woman named [a]Martha welcomed[5264]
Him into her home.
39 And she had a sister called
[a]Mary, who moreover was [ipf]listening[191]
to the Lord's word,[3056] [aptp] [b]seated at
His feet.
40 But [a]Martha [ipf]was distracted[4049]
with [I]all her preparations;[1248] and she
came up *to Him,* and said, "Lord, do
You not care that my sister has [ao]left
me to do all the [pinf]serving[1247] alone?
Then tell her to [aosb]help me."
41 But the Lord answered and said
to her, "[a]Martha, Martha, you are
[b]worried and bothered about so many
things;
42 [I][a]but *only* a few things are necessary, [II]really *only* one, for [b]Mary has
[ao]chosen the good[18] part, which shall
not be taken away from her."

Instruction about Prayer

11 And it came about that while He
was praying in a certain place,
after He had finished, one of His
disciples[3101] said to Him, "Lord, teach
us to [pinf]pray just as John also taught[1321]
his disciples."

🔑 2 And He said to them, "[a]When you
pray, say:
'[I]Father,[3962] [aipp]hallowed be[37]
Thy name.
Thy kingdom[932] [aim]come.
3 '[pim]Give us [a]each day our
[I]daily[1967] bread.
4 'And [aim]forgive[863] us our sins,
For we ourselves also forgive
everyone who [a]is
[ppt]indebted[3784] to us.
And [aosi]lead us not into
temptation.' "[3986]
🔑 5 And He said to them, "[I]Suppose
one of you shall have a friend, and shall
go to him at midnight, and say to him,
'Friend, lend[5531] me three loaves;
6 for a friend of mine has [ao]come
to me from a journey, and I have nothing
to set before him';
7 and from inside he shall answer
and say, 'Do not [pim]bother me; the door
has already been [pfip]shut and my children
[I]and I are in bed; I cannot [apt]get up and
[ainf]give you *anything.*'
8 "I tell you, even though he will
not [apt]get up[450] and give him *anything*
because he is his friend, yet [a]because
of his [I]persistence[335] he will [aptp]get up[1453]
and give him as much as he needs.
🔑 9 "And [epn]I say to you, [pim] [I][a]ask,[154]
and it shall be given to you; [pim] [II]seek,
and you shall find; [pim] [III]knock, and it
shall be opened to you.

38 [I]Lit., *certain woman* [a]Luke 10:40f.; John 11:1, 5, 19ff., 30, 39; 12:2
39 [a]Luke 10:42; John 11:1f., 19f., 28, 31f., 45; 12:3 [b]Luke 8:35; Acts 22:3
40 [I]Lit., *much service* [a]Luke 10:38, 41; John 11:1, 5, 19ff., 30, 39; 12:2
41 [a]Luke 10:38, 40; John 11:1, 5, 19ff., 30, 39; 12 [b]Matt. 6:25
42 [I]Some mss. read *but one thing is necessary* [II]Lit., *or* [a]Ps. 27:4; John 6:27 [b]Luke 10:39; John 11:1f., 19f., 28, 31f., 45; 12:3

2 [I]Some mss. insert phrases from Matt. 6:9-13 to make the two passages closely similar [a]Luke 11:2-4: *Matt. 6:9-13*
3 [I]Or, *bread for the coming day* or *needful bread* [a]Acts 17:11
4 [a]Luke 13:4 mg.
5 [I]Lit., *Which one of you*
7 [I]Lit., *with me*
8 [I]Or, *shamelessness* [a]Luke 18:1-5
9 [I]Or, *keep asking* [II]Or, *keep seeking* [III]Or, *keep knocking* [a]Luke 11:9-13: *Matt. 7:7-11*

🔑 **11:2-4** For the meaning of "temptation," see the notes on Mt. 6:9-14 and also *peirazō* (3985), to tempt.

🔑 **11:5-13** Here we have a parable on the responsibility of the Christian. When someone comes to him at midnight and asks for bread, he cannot remain indifferent. The traveler symbolizes the sinner. The one to whom he goes is the believer. The believer may not have what it takes to satisfy the need of his visitor, but he can always go to others who, being motivated by God, may meet the need. The Lord spoke this parable to teach us that we should earnestly pray on behalf of others and their needs. God wants to satisfy those prayers through us and give us the joy of being intercessors for others. See the Editor's book entitled, *Why Pray?*

🔑 **11:9** The word that is here translated as "ask" is *aiteite* from *aiteō* (154), from which the compound verb *epaiteō* (1871), "to beg," is derived. Asking in this instance and in prayer means coming to the Lord as a beggar to a generous giver. We cannot, however, demand, but only make our needs known to others and to God, and God will give us according to His discernment of what our real needs are. The verb *aiteō* should be distinguished from the Greek word *erōtaō* (2065), when used in the same context. This is the word that our Lord uses when He asks for something from His Father as in Jn. 14:16. In the same context, when it comes to the disciples asking something from the Father, the verb *aiteō* is used in vv. 13,14. These verses do not give blanket authorization for the believer to demand

(continued on next page)

10 "For everyone who [ppt]asks, receives;[2983] and he who [ppt]seeks,[2212] finds;[2147] and to him who [ppt]knocks, it shall be opened.

11 "Now [I]suppose one of you fathers is [ft]asked by his son for a [II]fish; he will not give him a snake instead of a fish, will he?

12 "Or *if* he is [ft]asked for an egg, he will not give him a scorpion, will he?

13 "[a]If you then, being evil,[4190] know[1492] how to give good[18] gifts[1390] to your children,[5043] how much more shall *your* [I]heavenly [art]Father[3962] give the [an]Holy Spirit to those who [ppt]ask Him?"

Pharisees' Blasphemy

🗝 14 [a]And He was casting out a demon,[1140] and it was dumb; and it came about that when the demon had [apt]gone out, the dumb man spoke;[2980] and the multitudes marveled.

15 But some of them said, "He casts out demons[1140] [a]by [I][b]Beelzebul, the ruler of the demons."

16 And others,[2087] [I]to test[3985] *Him,* [a]were [ipf]demanding of Him a [II]sign from heaven.

17 [a]But He knew their thoughts,[1270] and said to them, "[I]Any kingdom[932] [aptp]divided against itself is laid waste; and a house[3624] *divided* against [II]itself falls.

18 "And if [a]Satan[4567] also is [aop]divided against himself, how shall his kingdom stand? For you say that I [pinf]cast out demons[1140] by [b]Beelzebul.

19 "And if I by [a]Beelzebul cast out demons, by whom do your sons cast them out? Consequently they shall be your judges.

20 "But if I cast out demons by the [a]finger of God,[2316] then [b]the kingdom of God has [ao]come upon you.

21 "When [I]a strong *man,* fully armed, [psa]guards[5442] his own homestead, his possessions are [II]undisturbed;[1515]

22 but when someone stronger than he [apt]attacks him and [aosb]overpowers him, he takes away from him all his armor on which he had relied,[3982] and distributes his plunder.

23 "[a]He who is not with Me is against Me; and he who does not [ppt]gather with Me, scatters.

24 "[a]When the unclean[169] spirit[4151] [aosb]goes out of [I]a man, it passes through waterless places seeking rest,[372] and not finding any, it says, 'I will return to my house from which I came.'

25 "And when it [apt]comes, it finds it swept and put in order.

26 "Then it goes and takes *along* seven other[2087] spirits more evil[4191] than itself, and they [apt]go in and live[2730] there; and the last[2078] state of that man[444] becomes worse than the first."

27 And it came about while He [aie]said these things, one of the women in the crowd [apt]raised her voice, and said to Him, "[a]Blessed[3107] is the womb that [apt]bore You, and the breasts[3149] at which You [ao]nursed."

28 But He said, "On the contrary, blessed[3107] are [a]those who [ppt]hear the word[3056] of God, and [ppt]observe[5442] it."

The Sign of Jonah

29 And as the crowds were increasing, He began to [pinf]say, "[a]This generation is a wicked[4190] generation;[1074] it [b]seeks for a [I]sign,[4592] and *yet* no [I]sign shall be [fp]given to it but the [I]sign of Jonah.

11 [I]Lit., *which of you, a son, shall ask the father* [II]Some early mss. insert *loaf, he will not give him a stone, will he, or for a*

13 [I]Lit., *Father from heaven* [a]Matt. 7:11; Luke 18:7f.

14 [a]Luke 11:14, 15: *Matt. 12:22, 24;* Matt. 9:32-34

15 [I]Here and in vv. 18 and 19 some mss. read *Beezebul* [a]Matt. 9:34 [b]Matt. 10:25

16 [I]Lit., *were testing* [II]Or, *attesting miracle* [a]Matt. 12:38; 16:1; Mark 8:11

17 [I]Lit., *every* [II]Lit., *a house* [a]Luke 11:17-22: *Matt. 12:25-29; Mark 3:23-27*

18 [a]Matt. 4:10 [b]Matt. 10:25

19 [a]Matt. 10:25

20 [a]Ex. 8:19 [b]Matt. 3:2

21 [I]Lit., *the* [II]Lit., *in peace*

23 [a]Matt. 12:30; Mark 9:40

24 [I]Lit., *the* [a]Luke 11:24-26: *Matt. 12:43-45*

27 [a]Luke 23:29

28 [a]Luke 8:21

29 [I]Or, *attesting miracle* [a]Luke 11:29-32: *Matt. 12:39-42;* Matt. 16:4; Mark 8:12 [b]Matt. 12:38; Luke 11:16

(continued from previous page)

anything from God, but only to ask in full dependence upon God's discernment of particular needs and action according to His wisdom. Many times what we ask for from God is not in His will. He will give us only what is for our eternal good, (*agathon,* 18) and for the execution of His plan and timetable for the whole world. "Good" for the believer is not what he desires, but what God discerns as the thing which will execute His plan and bring the believer into a closer relationship with Him. For a full discussion of Lk. 11:5-13, see the Editor's book entitled, *Why Pray?*. See note on Js. 5:14-17.

🗝 **11:14-32** See note on Mk. 3:28,29.

30 "For just as [a]Jonah became a [I]sign to the Ninevites, so shall the Son of Man be to this generation.

31 "The [a]Queen of the South shall rise up with the men of this generation[1074] at the judgment[2920] and condemn[2632] them, because she came from the ends of the earth to [ainf]hear[191] the wisdom of Solomon; and behold, something greater than Solomon is here.

32 "The men of Nineveh shall stand up with this generation at the judgment and condemn[2632] it, because [a]they repented[3340] at the preaching[2782] of Jonah; and behold, something greater than Jonah is here.

🔑 33 "[a]No one, after [apt]lighting a lamp, puts it away in a cellar, nor under a peck-measure, but on the lampstand, in order that those who [ppt]enter may [psa]see the light.[5338]

34 "[a]The lamp of your body is your eye; when your eye is [I]clear,[573] your whole body also is full of light; but when it is bad,[4190] your body also is full of darkness.

35 "Then [pim]watch out[4648] that the light[5457] in you may not be darkness.[4655]

36 "If therefore your whole body is full of light, with no dark part in it, it shall be wholly illumined, as when the lamp [psa]illumines[5461] you with its rays."

Woes upon the Pharisees

37 Now when He had spoken, a Pharisee *asked Him to have lunch with him; and He went in, and reclined *at the table.*

38 And when the Pharisee [apt]saw it, he was surprised that He had not first [Ia]ceremonially washed[907] before the [II]meal.

🔑 39 But [a]the Lord said to him, "Now [b]you Pharisees clean[2511] the outside of the cup and of the platter; but [I]inside of you, you are full of robbery[724] and wickedness.[4189]

40 "[a]You foolish ones, did not He who [apt]made the outside[1855] [ao]make the inside also?

41 "But [a]give that which is within as charity,[1654] and [I]then all things are [b]clean[2513] for you.

42 "[a]But woe to you Pharisees! For you [b]pay tithe[586] of mint[2238] and rue[4076] and every *kind of* garden herb, and *yet* disregard justice[2920] and the love[26] of God; but these are the things you should have [ainf]done without [ainf]neglecting[3935] the others.

43 "Woe to you Pharisees! For you [a]love[25] the front seats in the synagogues,[5273] and the respectful [art]greetings in the market places.

44 "[a]Woe to you! For you are like [I]concealed [art]tombs, and the people who [ppt]walk over *them* are unaware *of it.*"

45 And one of the [Ia]lawyers[3544] *said to Him in reply, "Teacher, when You say this, You insult[5195] us too."

46 But He said, "Woe to you [a]lawyers as well! For [b]you [pin]weigh[5412] men down with burdens[5413] hard to bear, [I]while you yourselves will not even touch the burdens with one of your fingers.

47 "[a]Woe to you! For you build the [I]tombs[3419] of the prophets,[4396] and *it was* your fathers[3962] *who* killed them.

48 "Consequently, you are witnesses[3144] and approve the deeds[2041] of your fathers; because it was they who killed them, and you build *their tombs.*

30 [I]Or, *attesting miracle* [a]Jon. 3:4
31 [a]1Kin. 10:1-10; 2Chr. 9:1-12
32 [a]Jon. 3:5
33 [a]Matt. 5:15; Mark 4:21; Luke 8:16
34 [I]Or, *healthy* [a]Luke 11:34, 35: *Matt. 6:22, 23*
38 [I]Lit., *baptized* [II]Or, *lunch* [a]Matt. 15:2; Mark 7:3f.
39 [I]Lit., *your inside is full* [a]Luke 7:13 [b]Matt. 23:25f.
40 [a]Luke 12:20; 1Cor. 15:36
41 [I]Lit., *behold* [a]Luke 12:33; 16:9 [b]Mark 7:19; Titus 1:15
42 [a]Matt. 23:23 [b]Lev. 27:30; Luke 18:12
43 [a]Matt. 23:6f.; Mark 12:38f.; Luke 14:7; 20:46
44 [I]Or, *indistinct, unseen* [a]Matt. 23:27
45 [I]I.e., experts in the Mosaic Law [a]Matt. 22:35; Luke 11:46, 52
46 [I]Lit., *and* [a]Matt. 22:35; Luke 11:45, 52 [b]Matt. 23:4
47 [I]Or, *monuments to* [a]Matt. 23:29ff.

🔑 **11:33-36** In the parable of the talents (Mt. 25:14-30) the expression "outer darkness" (v. 30) refers to a state of less rewards in heaven. Therefore, we find the possibility of degrees of light expressed in this parable of the lamp in Lk. 11:33-36. In coming out of a very bright light into a rather darkened room, we are temporarily blinded. In contrast to the existing brightness, this is darkness; not really total darkness, but only in contrast. The further one is cast out into the periphery of the Light of God, the darker it is. Anything less than basking in the center of God's approval is outer darkness! See note on Mt. 8:11,12. For a complete analysis and exegesis of this passage, see Editor's book entitled, *Conscience.*

🔑 **11:39** See notes on Rev. 4; I Thess. 4:17 and also *harpagē* (724), extortion, catching up or away, and *harpazō* (726), to catch up or away.

49 "For this reason also [a]the wisdom[4678] of God said, '[b]I will send to them prophets and apostles,[652] and *some* of them they will kill and *some* they will [I]persecute,

50 in order that the blood[129] of all the prophets, [ppt]shed [a]since the foundation[2602] of the world,[2889] may be [I]charged against this generation,

51 from [a]the blood[129] of Abel to [b]the blood of Zechariah, who [apt]perished between the altar and the house[3624] *of God;* yes,[3483] I tell you, it shall be [I]charged against this generation.'

52 "Woe to you [Ia]lawyers! For you have [ao]taken away the key of knowledge;[1108] [b]you did not enter in yourselves, and those who were [ppt]entering in you [ao]hindered."

53 And when He left there, the scribes and the Pharisees began to be very hostile[1758][1171] and to [pinf]question Him closely[653] on many subjects,

54 [a]plotting against Him, [b]to catch [I]*Him* in something He might say.

God Knows and Cares

12 Under these circumstances, after [I]so many thousands of the multitude had gathered together that they were [pinf]stepping on[2662] one another, He began saying to His disciples first *of all,* "[a]Beware of the leaven[2219] of the Pharisees, which is hypocrisy.[5272]

2 "[a]But there is nothing covered up that will not be revealed,[601] and hidden that will not be known.

3 "Accordingly, whatever you have said in the dark[4653] shall be heard in the light, and what you have [I]whispered in the inner rooms shall be proclaimed[2784] upon [a]the housetops.

4 "And I say to you, [a]My friends, do not [aosi]be afraid[5399] of those who [pp]kill the body,[4983] and after that [ppt]have no more[4053] that they [ainf]can do.

5 "But I will [I]warn you whom to [aosb]fear: [aim][a]fear[5399] the One who after He has [aime]killed [ppt]has authority[1849] to [ainf]cast into [IIb]hell;[1067] yes, I tell you, fear Him!

6 "Are not [a]five sparrows sold for two [I]cents?[787] And *yet* not one of them is forgotten before God.

7 "[a]Indeed, the very hairs of your head are all [pfip]numbered.[705] Do not [pim]fear; you are of more value[1308] than many sparrows.

8 "And I say to you, everyone who [aosb][a]confesses[3670] Me before men, the Son of Man shall confess him also before the angels[32] of God;

9 but [a]he who [apt]denies[720] Me before men shall be denied[533] [b]before the angels of God.

🔑 10 "[a]And everyone who will speak a word against the Son of Man, it shall be forgiven[863] him; but he who [apt]blasphemes[987] against the Holy Spirit,[4151] it shall not be forgiven him.

11 "And when they bring you before [a]the synagogues[4864] and the rulers[746] and the authorities,[1849] do not become [b]anxious about how or what you should [aosb]speak in your defense, or what you should [aosb]say;

12 for [a]the Holy Spirit will teach[1321] you in that very hour what you ought to say."

Covetousness Denounced

13 And someone [I]in the crowd said to Him, "Teacher,[1320] tell my brother[80] to divide the *family* inheritance[2817] with me."

14 But He said to him, "[a]Man, who appointed[2525] Me a judge[2923] or arbiter over you?"

15 And He said to them, [pim]"[a]Beware, and [pim]be on your guard against every form of greed; for not *even* when one has an abundance does his life consist of his possessions."

16 And He told them a parable,[3850] saying, "The land of a certain rich man [ao]was very productive.[2164]

49 [I]Or, *drive out* [a]1Cor. 1:24, 30; Col. 2:3 [b]Matt. 23:34-36
50 [I]Or, *required of* [a]Matt. 25:34
51 [I]Or, *required of* [a]Gen. 4:8 [b]2Chr. 24:20, 21
52 [I]I.e., experts in the Mosaic Law [a]Matt. 22:35; Luke 11:45, 46 [b]Matt. 23:13
54 [I]Lit., *something out of His mouth* [a]Mark 3:2; Luke 20:20; Acts 23:21 [b]Mark 12:13
1 [I]Lit., *myriads* [a]Matt. 16:6, 11f.; Mark 8:15
2 [a]Luke 12:2-9; *Matt. 10:26-33;* Matt. 10:26; Mark 4:22; Luke 8:17
3 [I]Lit., *spoken in the ear* [a]Matt. 10:27; 24:17
4 [a]John 15:13-15
5 [I]Or, *show* [II]Gr., *Gehenna* [a]Heb. 10:31 [b]Matt. 5:22
6 [I]Gr., *assaria,* the smallest of copper coins [a]Matt. 10:29
7 [a]Matt. 10:30
8 [a]Matt. 10:32; Luke 15:10; Rom. 10:9
9 [a]Matt. 10:33; Luke 9:26 [b]Luke 15:10
10 [a]Matt. 12:31, 32; Mark 3:28-30
11 [a]Matt. 10:17 [b]Matt. 6:25; 10:19; Mark 13:11; Luke 12:22; 21:14
12 [a]Matt. 10:20; Luke 21:15
13 [I]Lit., *out of*
14 [a]Mic. 6:8; Rom. 2:1, 3; 9:20
15 [a]1Tim. 6:6-10

🔑 **12:10** See notes on Mk. 3:28,29; Heb. 6:1-6.

17 "And he began [ipf]reasoning[1260] to himself, saying, 'What shall I do, since I have no place to store my crops?'

18 "And he said, 'This is what I will do: I will tear down my barns and build larger ones, and there I will store all my grain and my goods.[18]

19 'And I will say to my soul,[5590] "Soul, [a]you have many goods [ppt]laid up[2749] for many years *to come;* [pim]take your ease,[373] [aim]eat, [aim]drink *and* [pim]be merry." '[2165]

20 "But God said to him, '[a]You fool! This *very* night [Ib]your soul[5590] is required[523] of you; and [c]*now* who will own what you have [ao]prepared?'

21 "So is the man who [ppt][a]lays up treasure[2343] for himself, and is not [ppt]rich toward God."

22 And He said to His disciples,[3101] "[a]For this reason I say to you, do not [pim]be anxious[3309] for *your* [I]life,[5590] *as to* what you shall eat; nor for your body, *as to* what you shall put on.

23 "For life is more than food, and the body than clothing.[1742]

24 [aim]"Consider[2657] the [a]ravens, for they neither sow nor reap; and they have no storeroom nor [b]barn; and *yet* God[2316] feeds them; how much more valuable[1308] you are than the birds!

25 "And which of you by being anxious can [ainf]add a *single* [Ia]cubit[4083] to his [II]life's span?

26 "If then you cannot do even a very little thing, why are you anxious about other matters?

27 [aim]"Consider the lilies, how [I]they grow; they neither toil nor spin;[3514] but I tell you, even [a]Solomon in all his glory did not [aom]clothe himself like one of these.

28 "But if God so arrays the grass in the field, which is *alive* today and tomorrow is [ppp]thrown into the furnace, how much more *will He clothe* you, [a]O men of little faith![3640]

29 "And do not seek what you shall eat, and what you shall drink, and do not [a]keep worrying.

30 "For [I]all these things the nations of the world[2889] eagerly seek; but your Father[3962] knows that you need these things.

31 "But [pim]seek for His kingdom,[932] and [a]these things shall be added to you.

32 "[a]Do not [pim]be afraid,[5399] [b]little flock,[4168] for [c]your Father has chosen gladly[2106] to give you the kingdom.

33 [aim]"[a]Sell your possessions and give to charity;[1654] [aim]make yourselves purses which do not [ppp]wear out,[3822] [b]an unfailing treasure in heaven,[3772] where no thief comes near, nor moth destroys.

34 "For [a]where your treasure[2344] is, there will your heart[2588] be also.

Be in Readiness

35 "[Ia]Be [pfpp]dressed in [b]readiness, and *keep* your lamps alight.

36 "And be like men who are [ppt]waiting for[4327] their master[2962] when he returns from the wedding feast,[1062] so that they may immediately [aosb]open *the door* to him when he [apt]comes and [apt]knocks.

37 "Blessed[3107] are those slaves[1401] whom the master shall find [a]on the alert when he comes; truly[281] I say to you, that [b]he will gird[4024] himself *to serve,* and have them recline *at the table,* and will [apt]come up and wait[1247] on them.

38 "[a]Whether he comes in the [I]second watch, or even in the [II]third, and finds *them* so, blessed[3107] are those *slaves.*

39 "[a]And [I]be [pim]sure of this, that if the head of the house[3617] had known at what hour the thief [pinp]was coming, he would not have allowed[863] his house to be [IIb]broken into.

40 "[a]You too, be[1096] ready; for the Son of Man is coming at an hour that you do not [I]expect."

41 And Peter said, "Lord,[2962] are You addressing this parable to us, or [a]to everyone *else* as well?"

42 And [a]the Lord said, "[b]Who then is the faithful[4103] and sensible[5429] [c]steward, whom his master will put in charge[2525] of his [I]servants,[2322] to [infg]give them their rations at the proper time?[2540]

19 [a]Eccl. 11:9
20 [I]Lit., *they are demanding your soul from you* [a]Jer. 17:11; Luke 11:40 [b]Job 27:8 [c]Ps. 39:6
21 [a]Luke 12:33
22 [I]Or, *soul* [a]Luke 12:22-31: *Matt. 6:25-33*
24 [a]Job 38:41 [b]Luke 12:18
25 [I]I.e., One cubit equals approx. 18 in. [II]Or, *height* [a]Ps. 39:5
27 [I]Some mss. omit *they grow* [a]1Kin. 10:4-7; 2Chr. 9:3-6
28 [a]Matt. 6:30
29 [a]Matt. 6:31
30 [I]Or, *these things all the nations of the world*
31 [a]Matt. 6:33
32 [a]Matt. 14:27 [b]John 21:15-17 [c]Eph. 1:5, 9
33 [a]Matt. 19:21; Luke 11:41; 18:22 [b]Matt. 6:20; Luke 12:21
34 [a]Matt. 6:21
35 [I]Lit., *Let your loins be girded* [a]Matt. 25:1ff. [b]Eph. 6:14; 1Pet. 1:13
37 [a]Matt. 24:42 [b]Luke 17:8; John 13:4
38 [I]I.e., 9 p.m. to midnight [II]I.e., midnight to 3 a.m. [a]Matt. 24:43
39 [I]Lit., *know* [II]Lit., *dug through* [a]Luke 12:39, 40: *Matt. 24:43, 44* [b]Matt. 6:19
40 [I]Lit., *think, suppose* [a]Mark 13:33; Luke 21:36
41 [a]Luke 12:47, 48
42 [I]Lit., *service* [a]Luke 7:13 [b]Luke 12:42-46: *Matt. 24:45-51* [c]Matt. 24:45; Luke 16:1ff.

43 "Blessed is that [a]slave whom his
[I]master finds so doing when he comes.
44 "Truly I say to you, that he will
put him in charge of all his possessions.
45 "But if that slave [aosb]says in his
heart, 'My master [I]will be a long time
in [pinf]coming,' and begins to beat[5180] the
slaves, *both* men and women, and to
[pinf]eat and [pinf]drink and [pip]get drunk;
46 the master of that slave will come
on a day when he does not expect *him,*
and at an hour he does not know, and
will cut him in pieces,[1371] and assign[5087]
him a place with the unbelievers.[571]
🔑 47 "And that slave who [apt]knew his
master's will and did not [apt]get ready
or [apt]act in accord with his will, shall
[a]receive many lashes,
48 but the one who did not [a]know
it, and committed deeds worthy of
[I]a flogging, will receive but few. [b]And
from everyone who has been [aop]given
much shall much be required; and to
whom they [aom]entrusted much, of him
they will ask all the more.[4053]

Christ Divides Men

49 "I [I]have come to cast fire upon
the earth; and [II]how I wish it were already [aop]kindled!
50 "But I have a [a]baptism[908] to
[I]undergo,[907] and how distressed[4912] I am
until it is accomplished![5055]
51 "[a]Do you suppose that I [aop]came
to [ainf]grant peace[1515] on earth?[1093] I tell
you, no, but rather division;[1267]
52 for from now on five *members*
in one household will be divided, three
against two, and two against three.
53 "They will be divided, [a]father
against son, and son against father;
mother against daughter, and daughter
against mother; mother-in-law against
daughter-in-law, and daughter-in-law
against mother-in-law."
54 And He was also [ipf]saying to the
multitudes, "[a]When you see a cloud
[ppt]rising in the west, immediately[2112] you
say, 'A shower is coming,' and so it
turns out.
55 "And when *you see* a south wind
[ppt]blowing,[4154] you say, 'It will be a
[a]hot day,' and it turns out *that way.*
56 "You hypocrites![5273] [a]You know
how to [pinf]analyze[1381] the appearance[4383]
of the earth[1093] and the sky,[3772] but
[I]why do you not analyze this present
time?[2540]
57 "And [a]why do you not even on
your own initiative judge[2919] what is
right?[1342]
58 "For [a]while you are going with
your opponent[476] to appear before the
magistrate,[758] on *your* way *there* make
an effort to [I]settle with him, in order
that he may not drag[2694] you before the
judge, and the judge [ft]turn you over to
the constable, and the constable [ft]throw
you into prison.
59 "I say to you, you shall not get
out of there until you have paid the very
last [Ia]cent."[3016]

Call to Repent

13 🔑 Now on the same occasion
there were some present who
[ppt]reported[518] to Him about the Galileans, whose blood[129] [a]Pilate had [ao] [I]min-
gled with their sacrifices.[2378]
2 And He answered and said to
them, "[a]Do you suppose that these Galileans were *greater* sinners[268] than all
other Galileans, because they [pfi]suffered
this *fate?*
3 "I tell you, no, but unless you

43 [I]Or, *lord* [a]Luke 12:42
45 [I]Lit., *is delaying to come*
47 [a]Deut. 25:2; James 4:17
48 [I]Lit., *blows* [a]Lev. 5:17; Num. 15:29f. [b]Matt. 13:12
49 [I]Or, *came* [II]Lit., *what do I wish if. . .?*
50 [I]Lit., *be baptized with* [a]Mark 10:38
51 [a]Luke 12:51-53: *Matt. 10:34-36*
53 [a]Mic. 7:6; Matt. 10:21
54 [a]Matt. 16:2f.
55 [a]Matt. 20:12
56 [I]Lit., *how* [a]Matt. 16:3
57 [a]Luke 21:30
58 [I]Lit., *be released from him* [a]Luke 12:58, 59: *Matt. 5:25, 26*
59 [I]Gr., *lepton;* i.e., 1/128 of a denarius [a]Mark 12:42
1 [I]Or, *shed along with* [a]Matt. 27:1-66
2 [a]John 9:2f.

🔑 **12:47,48** See note on Mt. 8:11,12.

🔑 **13:1-5** The Jews of the first century believed that all suffering was due to God's judgment on sin. This concept is shared by some Christians today when they ask, "Then why do the righteous suffer?" The Scripture teaches that God allows temporal disasters to happen for various reasons—one of which is to lead people to repentance. Thus, some suffering may indeed be due to sin, while in other cases it is a testing or learning process. For a complete analysis and exegesis of this passage, see the Editor's book, *Why God Permits Accidents.*

[psa] [I]repent,[3340] you will all likewise perish.[622]

4 "Or do you suppose that those eighteen on whom the tower in [a]Siloam fell[4098] and killed them, were *worse* [Ib]culprits[3781] than all the men who live[2730] in Jerusalem?

5 "I tell you, no, but unless you [psa]repent, you will all likewise perish."

6 And He *began* [ipf]telling this parable:[3850] "A certain man had [a]a fig tree which had been planted in his vineyard; and he came [ppt]looking for fruit on it, and did not find any.

7 "And he said to the vineyard-keeper, 'Behold, for three years I have come looking for fruit on this fig tree [I]without finding any. [a]Cut it down! Why does it even use up[2673] the ground?'

8 "And he answered and said to him, 'Let it alone,[863] sir, for this year too, until I dig around it and put in fertilizer;[2874]

9 and if it [aosb]bears fruit next year, *fine;* but if not, cut it down.'"

Healing on the Sabbath

10 And He was [a]teaching[1321] in one of the synagogues[4864] on the Sabbath.[4521]

11 And behold, there was a woman who for eighteen years had [ppt]had [a]a sickness[769] caused by a spirit;[4151] and she was bent double, and [ppt]could not straighten up[352] at all.

12 And when Jesus saw her, He called her over and said to her, "Woman, you are [pfip]freed[630] from your sickness."

13 And He [a]laid His hands upon her; and immediately she was made erect[461] again, and *began* [ifp] [b]glorifying[1392] God.

14 And [a]the synagogue official,[752] [ppt]indignant because Jesus [b]had [ao]healed on the Sabbath, *began* saying to the multitude in response, "[c]There are six days in which [pinf]work[2038] should be done; therefore [ppt]come during them and get [pim]healed, and not on the Sabbath day."

15 But [a]the Lord answered him and said, "You hypocrites,[5273] [b]does not each of you on the Sabbath untie[3089] his ox or his donkey from the stall, and [apt]lead him away to [pin]water *him?*

16 "And this woman, [a]a daughter of Abraham as she is, whom [b]Satan[4567] has [ao]bound for eighteen long years, should she not have been [aifp]released[3089] from this bond on the Sabbath day?"

17 And as He [ppt]said this, all His opponents were being [ipf]humiliated; and [a]the entire multitude was [ipf]rejoicing over all the glorious things being [ppt]done by Him.

Parables of Mustard Seed and Leaven

18 Therefore [a]He was saying, "[b]What is the kingdom[932] of God[2316] like, and to what shall I compare it?

19 "It is like a mustard seed, which a man [apt]took and [ao]threw into his own garden; and it [ao]grew and [ao]became[1096] a tree; and [a]THE BIRDS OF THE [I]AIR[3772] NESTED IN ITS BRANCHES."

20 And again He said, "[a]To what shall I compare the kingdom[932] of God?[2316]

21 "[a]It is like leaven,[2219] which a woman [apt]took and hid in [b]three [I]pecks[4568] of meal, until it was all leavened."[2220]

Teaching in the Villages

22 And He was [ipf]passing through from one city and village to another, teaching, and [a]proceeding on His way to Jerusalem.

23 And someone said to Him, "Lord, are there *just* a few who are being [ppp]saved?"[4982] And He said to them,

24 [pim]"[a]Strive[75] to [ainf]enter by the narrow[4728] door; for many, I tell you, will seek to enter and will not be [I]able.

25 "Once the head of the house [asbp]gets up and [aosb] [a]shuts the door, and you [asbm]begin to [pfin]stand outside[1854] and knock on the door, saying, '[b]Lord, open up to us!' [I]then He will answer and say

3 [I]Or, *are repentant*

4 [I]Lit., *debtors* [a]Neh. 3:15; Is. 8:6; John 9:7, 11 [b]Matt. 6:12; Luke 11:4

6 [a]Matt. 21:19

7 [I]Lit., *and I do not find* [a]Matt. 3:10; 7:19; Luke 3:9

10 [a]Matt. 4:23

11 [a]Luke 13:16

13 [a]Mark 5:23 [b]Matt. 9:8

14 [a]Mark 5:22 [b]Matt. 12:2; Luke 14:3 [c]Ex. 20:9; Deut. 5:13

15 [a]Luke 7:13 [b]Luke 14:5

16 [a]Luke 19:9 [b]Matt. 4:10; Luke 13:11

17 [a]Luke 18:43

18 [a]Luke 13:18, 19: *Matt. 13:31, 32; Mark 4:30-32* [b]Matt. 13:24; Luke 13:20

19 [I]Or, *sky* [a]Ezek. 17:23

20 [a]Matt. 13:24; Luke 13:18

21 [I]Gr., *sata* [a]Luke 13:20, 21: *Matt. 13:33* [b]Matt. 13:33

22 [a]Luke 9:51

24 [I]Or, *able, once* [a]Matt. 7:13

25 [I]Lit., *and* [a]Matt. 25:10 [b]Matt. 7:22; 25:11

to you, "[c]I do not know where you are
from.'
🔑 26 "Then you will [a]begin to [pinf]say,
'We [ao]ate and [ao]drank in Your presence,
and You [ao]taught in our streets';
🔑 27 and He will say, 'I tell you,
[a]I do not know where you are from;
[aim] [b]DEPART[868] FROM ME, ALL YOU
EVILDOERS.'[93]
🔑 28 "[a]There will be weeping and
gnashing1030 of teeth there when you
see Abraham and Isaac and Jacob and
all the prophets[4396] in the kingdom[932]
of God,[2316] but yourselves being [ppp]cast
out.
29 "And they [a]will come from east
and west, and from north and south,
and will recline *at the table* in the kingdom
of God.
🔑 30 "And behold, [a]*some* are last[2078]
who will be first and *some* are first who
will be last."
31 Just at that time some Pharisees
came up, saying to Him, [aim]"Go away
and [pim]depart from here, for [a]Herod
wants to kill You."
32 And He said to them, [art]"Go and
tell that fox, 'Behold, I cast out
demons1140 and perform[658] cures[2392] today and tomorrow, and the third *day* I
[1a]reach My goal.'[5048]
33 "Nevertheless [a]I must [pinf]journey
on today and tomorrow and the next
day; for it cannot be[1735] that a
[b]prophet[4396] should [ainf]perish outside of
Jerusalem.
34 "[a]O Jerusalem, Jerusalem, *the
city* that [ppt]kills the prophets and
[ppt]stones those [ppt]sent to her! How often
I [ao]wanted to [ainf]gather your children together, [b]just as a hen *gathers* her brood
under her wings, and you [ao]would not
have it!
35 "Behold, your house is [pinp]left to
you [1]*desolate;* and I say to you, you shall
not see Me until *the time* comes when

25 [c]Matt. 7:23; 25:12; Luke 13:27
26 [a]Luke 3:8
27 [a]Luke 13:25 [b]Ps. 6:8; Matt. 25:41
28 [a]Matt. 8:12; 22:13; 25:30
29 [a]Matt. 8:11
30 [a]Matt. 19:30; 20:16; Mark 10:31
31 [a]Matt. 14:1; Luke 3:1; 9:7; 23:7
32 [1]Or possibly, *am perfected* [a]Heb. 2:10; 5:9; 7:28
33 [a]John 11:9 [b]Matt. 21:11
34 [a]Luke 13:34, 35: *Matt. 23:37-39;* Luke 19:41 [b]Matt. 23:37
35 [1]Later mss. add *desolate* [a]Ps. 118:26; Matt. 21:9; Luke 19:38

1 [1]I.e., members of the Sanhedrin [a]Mark 3:2
2 [1]Lit., *behold*
3 [1]I.e., experts in Mosaic Law [a]Matt. 22:35 [b]Matt. 12:2; Luke 13:14
5 [1]Some ancient mss. read *donkey* [a]Matt. 12:11; Luke 13:15
6 [a]Matt. 22:46; Luke 20:40
7 [a]Matt. 23:6
8 [1]Lit., *recline at* [a]Prov. 25:6, 7
9 [1]Lit., *begin* [a]Luke 3:8

you say, "[a]BLESSED[2127] IS HE WHO
[ppt]COMES IN THE NAME OF THE
LORD!' "[2962]

Jesus Heals on the Sabbath

14 And it came about when He
[aie]went into the house of one
of the [1]leaders of the Pharisees on *the*
Sabbath4521 to eat bread, that [a]they were
watching Him closely.[3906]
2 And [1]there, in front of Him was
a certain man suffering from dropsy.[5203]
3 And Jesus answered and spoke to
the [1a]lawyers[3544] and Pharisees, saying,
"[b]Is it lawful to [ainf]heal on the Sabbath,
or not?"
🔑 4 But they kept silent.[2270] And He
took hold of him, and healed him, and
sent him away.
5 And He said to them, "[a]Which one
of you shall have a [1]son or an ox [ft]fall
into a well,[5421] and will not immediately[2112] pull him out on a Sabbath
day?"
6 [a]And they could [ainf]make no reply[470] to this.

Parable of the Guests

7 And He *began* speaking a
parable[3850] to the [pfpp]invited guests[2564]
when He [ppt]noticed how [a]they had been
[ipf]picking out the places of honor *at the
table;* saying to them,
8 "When you are [asbp]invited by
someone to a wedding feast,[1062] [a]do not
[1]take the place of honor, lest someone
more distinguished than you may have
been [pfpp]invited by him,
9 and he who invited[2564] you both
shall [apt]come and say to you, 'Give place
to this man,' and then [a]in disgrace[152]
you [1]proceed to [pinf]occupy[2722] the last[2078]
place.
10 "But when you are invited, [apt]go

🔑 **13:26** See note on Mt. 8:11,12.
🔑 **13:27** See note on II Thess. 2:3 and also *aphistēmi* (868), to stand away from, and *apostasia* (646), apostasy.
🔑 **13:28,30** See note on Mt. 8:11,12.
🔑 **14:4** See note on I Tim. 2:9-15.

and recline at the last place, so that
when the one who has [pfp]invited you
[aosb]comes, he may say to you, 'Friend,
[a]move up higher';[511] then you will have
honor in the sight of all who [ppt] [I]are at
the table with you.
11 "[a]For everyone who [ppt]exalts
himself shall be humbled, and he who
[ppt]humbles himself shall be exalted."
12 And He also went on to [ipf]say
to the one who had [pfp]invited Him,
"When you give a luncheon or a dinner,
do not [pim]invite your friends or your
brothers or your relatives or rich neighbors, lest they also invite you in return,
and repayment come to you.
13 "But when you give a [I]recep-
tion,[1403] [pim]invite *the* poor, *the* crippled,
the lame, *the* blind,
14 and you will be [I]blessed,[3107] since
they [II]do not have *the means* to repay
you; for you will be repaid at [a]the
resurrection[386] of the righteous."[1342]
15 And when one of those who
were reclining *at the table* with Him
heard this, he said to Him, "[a]Blessed[3107]
is everyone who shall eat bread in the
kingdom[932] of God!"[2316]

Parable of the Dinner

16 But He said to him, "[a]A certain
man was giving a big dinner, and he
invited many;
17 and at the dinner hour he sent
his slave[1401] to say to those who had
been invited, [pim]'Come; for everything
is ready now.'
18 "But they all alike began to make
[pinf]excuses.[3868] The first one said to him,
'I have bought a [I]piece of land and I
need to [apt]go out and [ainf]look at it;
[II]please consider me [pinf]excused.'[3868]
19 "And another one said, 'I have
bought five yoke of oxen, and I am going
to [ainf]try them [ainf]out; [I]please consider
me excused.'
20 "And another one said, "[a]I have
[ao]married a wife, and for that reason I
cannot [ainf]come.'
21 "And the slave [apt]came *back* and
[ao]reported this to his master.[2962] Then
the head of the household [aptp]became
angry and said to his slave, 'Go out at
once into the streets and lanes of the
city and bring in here the poor and crippled and blind and lame.'
22 "And the slave said, 'Master,
what you [ao]commanded[2004] has been
done, and still there is room.'
23 "And the master said to the
slave, 'Go out into the highways and
along the hedges,[5418] and compel[315] *them*
to come in, that my house may be filled.
24 'For I tell you, none of those men
who were [pfpp]invited shall taste[1089] of
my dinner.' "[1173]

Discipleship Tested

🗝 **25** Now great multitudes were going along with Him; and He turned and
said to them,
26 "[a]If anyone comes to Me, and
does not [I]hate[3404] his own father and
mother and wife and children and broth-

10 [I]Lit., *recline* at the table [a]Prov. 25:6, 7
11 [a]2Sam. 22:28; Prov. 29:23; Matt. 23:12; Luke 1:52; 18:14; James 4:10
13 [I]Or, *banquet*
14 [I]Or, *happy* [II]Or, *are unable to* [a]John 5:29; Acts 24:15; Rev. 20:4, 5
15 [a]Rev. 19:9
16 [a]Matt. 22:2-14; Luke 14:16-24
18 [I]Or, *field* [II]Lit., *I request you*
19 [I]Lit., *I request you*
20 [a]Deut. 24:5; 1Cor. 7:33
26 [I]I.e., by comparison of his love for Me [a]Matt. 10:37

🗝 **14:25-33** Here we have some of the most problematic sayings of the Lord. The word "hate" ought to be understood in the light of Mt. 10:37 as loving one's relatives less than the Lord. Jesus Christ should never be placed on the same level as human relatives. The word translated "life" in v. 26 is *psuchē* (5590), which, when distinguished from spirit, means animalistic instincts. See in I Cor. 2:1 the word *psuchikos* (5591), as contrasted to *pneumatikos* (4152), "soulish and spiritual." The meaning of the phrase "does not give up" in v. 33 does not mean reckless abandonment of one's belongings, but the proper categorization of them to accomplish their intended purpose. The Greek word is *apotassomai* (657), the middle voice from *apotassō,* from *apo* (575), "from," and *tassō* (5021) which means "to properly categorize." It means that the believer who is worthy of Christ must know how to properly categorize and place material things away from himself, to keep things in their right perspective. When these two proper categorizations are accomplished, our relatives will be positioned where they should be—below Jesus Christ, and our belongings are separated from us. Then the tower will be completed (vv. 28-30) and the war against the enemy king will be won (vv. 31,32). Relative to this, see Editor's study on Lk. 16:10-13 as part of the total study on Lk. 16:1-13 in *How to Manage Money*.

ers and sisters, yes, and even his own life,[5590] he cannot be My disciple.[3101]

27 "Whoever does not [a]carry his own cross[4716] and come after Me cannot be My disciple.

28 "For which one of you, when he wants to build a tower, does not first [apt]sit down and calculate the cost, to see if he has enough to complete it?

29 "Otherwise,[2443,3379] when he has [apt]laid a foundation, and is not [ppt]able to [ainf]finish, all who [ppt]observe it [aosb]begin to [pinf]ridicule him,

30 saying, 'This man began to build and was not [ao]able to [ainf]finish.'

31 "Or what king, when he sets out to [ainf]meet another king in battle, will not first [apt]sit down and take [a]counsel whether he is strong enough with ten thousand *men* to [ainf]encounter the one coming against him with twenty thousand?

32 "Or else, while the other is still far away, he [apt]sends [I]a delegation[4242] and asks[2065] terms of peace.[1515]

33 "So therefore, no one of you can be My disciple who [a]does not [pin]give up[657] all his own possessions.

34 "Therefore, salt is good;[2570] but [a]if even salt has become tasteless,[3471] with what will it be seasoned?

35 "It is useless either for the soil or for the manure pile;[2874] [I]it is thrown out. [a]He who [ppt]has ears to hear, let him [pim]hear."

The Lost Sheep

15 Now all the [Ia]tax-gatherers[5057] and the [II]sinners[268] were coming near[1448] Him to listen to Him.

2 And both the Pharisees and the scribes[1122] *began* to [I]grumble, saying, "This man receives[4327] sinners and [a]eats with them."

3 And He told them this parable,[3850] saying,

4 "[a]What man among you, if he has a hundred sheep and has [apt]lost[622] one of them, does not leave the ninety-nine in the [I]open pasture, and go after the one which is [pfp]lost, until he finds it?

5 "And when he has found it, he lays it on his shoulders, rejoicing.[5463]

6 "And when he comes home, he calls together[4779] his friends and his neighbors, saying to them, [aim]'Rejoice with[4796] me, for I have [ao]found my sheep which was lost!'[622]

7 "I tell you that in the same way, there will be *more* joy[5479] in heaven[3772] over one sinner who [ppt]repents,[3340] than over ninety-nine righteous[1342] persons who need no repentance.[3341]

The Lost Coin

8 "Or what woman, if she has ten [I]silver coins and [aosb]loses one coin, does not light a lamp and sweep the house and search carefully until she [aosb]finds it?

9 "And when she has found it, she calls together[4779] her [I]friends and neighbors, saying, [aim]'Rejoice with[4796] me, for I have [ao]found the coin which I had [ao]lost!'[622]

10 "In the same way, I tell you, there is joy[5479] [a]in the presence of the angels[32] of God[2316] over one sinner[268] who repents."[3340]

The Prodigal Son

11 And He said, "A certain man had two sons;[5207]

12 and the younger of them said to his father,[3962] 'Father, [aim]give me [a]the share of the estate that [ppt]falls to me.' And he divided[1244] his [Ib]wealth[979] between them.

13 "And not many days later, the younger son [apt]gathered everything

27 [a]Matt. 10:38; 16:24; Mark 8:34; Luke 9:23

31 [a]Prov. 20:18

32 [I]Or, *an embassy*

33 [a]Phil. 3:7; Heb. 11:26

34 [a]Matt. 5:13; Mark 9:50

35 [I]Lit., *they throw it out* [a]Matt. 11:15

1 [I]I.e., Collectors of Roman taxes for profit [II]I.e., irreligious or non-practicing Jews [a]Luke 5:29

2 [I]Lit., *grumble among themselves* [a]Matt. 9:11

4 [I]Lit., *wilderness* [a]Matt. 18:12-14; Luke 15:4-7

8 [I]Gr., *drachmas*, one drachma was equivalent to a day's wages

9 [I]Lit., *women friends and neighbors*

10 [a]Matt. 10:32; Luke 15:7

12 [I]Lit., *living* [a]Deut. 21:17 [b]Mark 12:44; Luke 15:30

15:1-32 In these three parables, one basic element is fundamental: the father who loses his son, the woman who loses her coin, and the shepherd who loses his sheep, do not give up the right of ownership. In the same manner, God is presented as still claiming His right of ownership even of those who are lost. When they are reclaimed, it is not He who becomes their Father or their rightful owner, but they become His again. This is in full agreement with Jn. 1:12, "But as many as received Him, to them He gave the right to become children of God."

together[4863] and went on a journey into
a distant country, and there he squandered his estate3776 with loose811
living.[2198]
14 "Now when he had spent everything, a severe famine occurred in that
country, and he began to be in need.5302
15 "And he went and [I]attached himself to one of the citizens of that country,
and he sent him into his fields to [pinf]feed
swine.
16 "And he was [ipf]longing[1937] [I]to
[ainf]fill1072 his [II]stomach with the [III]pods
that the swine were eating, and no
one was [ipf]giving *anything* to him.
17 "But when he came[2064] to
[I]his senses, he said, 'How many of my
father's hired men[3407] have more than
enough4052 bread, but I am dying[622] here
with hunger!
18 'I will get up and go to my father,
and will say to him, "Father, I have
sinned[264] against heaven,[3772] and [I]in
your sight;
19 I am no longer worthy to be
[aifp]called your son; [aim]make[4160] me as
one of your hired men." '[3407]
20 "And he got up and came to
[I]his father. But while he was[568] still a
long way off, his father saw him, and
felt compassion4697 *for him,* and [apt]ran
and [IIa]embraced him, and [ao] [III]kissed him.
21 "And the son said to him, 'Fa-
ther, I have [ao]sinned against heaven and
in your sight; I am no longer worthy
to be called your son.[I]'
22 "But the father said to his
slaves,[1401] 'Quickly [aim]bring out [a]the best
robe and put it on him, and [b]put a ring
on his hand and sandals on his feet;
23 and [pim]bring the fattened calf,
[aim]kill[2380] it, and let us [apt]eat and [asbp]be
merry;[2165]
24 for this son of mine was
[a]dead,[3498] and has [ao]come to life again;326
he was lost,[622] and has been
[aop]found.'[2147] And they began to [pip]be
merry.[2165]
25 "Now his older[4245] son was in
the field, and when he [ppt]came and
approached[1448] the house, he heard music and dancing.
26 "And he [apt]summoned one of the
servants[3816] and *began* [ipf]inquiring what
these things might be.
27 "And he said to him, 'Your
brother[80] has come, and your father has
killed[2380] the fattened calf, because he
has received618 him back safe and
sound.'
28 "But he became angry, and was
not willing to go in; and his father [apt]came
out and *began* [ipf]entreating[3870] him.
29 "But he answered and said to
his father, 'Look! For so many years I
have been serving[1398] you, and I have
never [I]neglected[3928] a command[1785] of
yours; and *yet* you have never given me
a [II]kid, that I might [asbp]be merry[2165] with
my friends;
🔑30 but when this son of yours
[ao]came, who has [apt]devoured your
[Ia]wealth with harlots, you [ao]killed[2380] the
fattened calf for him.'
31 "And he said to him, '*My* child,
you [I]have always been with me, and
all that is mine is yours.
32 'But [I]we had to[1163] be
[aifp]merry[2165] and [aifp]rejoice,[5463] for this
brother of yours was [a]dead[3498] and *has
begun to live,*[2198] and *was* lost[622] and
has been [aop]found.' "[2147]

The Unrighteous Steward

16 🔑Now He was also saying to
the disciples,[3101] "There was a

15 [I]Lit., *was joined to*
16 [I]Some mss. read *to be satisfied with* [II]Lit., *belly* [III]I.e., of the carob tree
17 [I]Lit., *himself*
18 [I]Lit., *before you*
20 [I]Lit., *his own* [II]Lit., *fell on his neck* [III]Lit., *kissed him again and again* [a]Gen. 45:14; 46:29; Acts 20:37
21 [I]Some ancient mss. add *make me as one of your hired men*
22 [a]Zech. 3:4; Rev. 6:11 [b]Gen. 41:42
24 [a]Matt. 8:22; Luke 9:60; 15:32; Rom. 11:15; Eph. 2:1, 5; 5:14; Col. 2:13; 1Tim. 5:6
29 [I]Or, *disobeyed* [II]Or, *young goat*
30 [I]Lit., *living* [a]Prov. 29:3; Luke 15:12
31 [I]Lit., *are always with me*
32 [I]Lit., *it was necessary* [a]Luke 15:24

🔑**15:30** The elder son would not accept his younger brother because he had associated himself with harlots although he repented of the sin and abandoned it. We, as Christians, sometimes, act like the "older son" and not like "fathers" in the case of such prodigal sons and daughters whose sins of such associations are categorized as unforgiveable.

🔑**16:1-13** To understand this parable, two words must be comprehended. The word *dieblēthē* in v. 1, translated as "reported," should actually be translated "falsely accused." It is derived from *diaballō* (1225), from which the word *diabolos* (1228), "devil," is derived. The devil's accusations are always

(continued on next page)

certain rich man who had a steward,[3623]
and this *steward* was [aop] [I]reported[1225] to
him as [ppt] [a]squandering his possessions.
2 "And he called him and said to
him, 'What is this I hear about you?
[aim]Give an [art]account of your stewardship,[3622] for you can no longer [pinf]be
steward.'
3 "And the steward said to himself,
'What shall I do, since my [I]master[2962]
is taking the stewardship away from me?
I am not strong enough to [pinf]dig; I am
ashamed to [pinf]beg.[1871]
4 'I [I]know what I shall do, so that
when I am [asbp]removed from[3179] the
stewardship, they will receive me into
their homes.'
5 "And he [apt]summoned each one
of his [I]master's debtors, and he *began*
[ipf]saying to the first, 'How much do you
owe my master?'
6 "And he said, 'A hundred [I]mea-
sures[943] of oil.' And he said to him, 'Take
your bill,[1121] and sit down quickly and
write[1125] fifty.'
7 "Then he said to another, 'And
how much do you owe?' And he said,
'A hundred [I]measures[2884] of wheat.' He
*said to him, 'Take your bill, and
write[1125] eighty.'
8 "And his [I]master[2962] praised the
unrighteous[93] steward because he had
[ao]acted shrewdly; for the sons[5207] of
[a]this age[165] are more shrewd[5429] in relation to their own [II]kind than the [b]sons
of light.[5457]

1 [I]Or, *accused* [a]Luke 15:13

3 [I]Or, *lord*

4 [I]Lit., *have come to the knowledge of*

5 [I]Or, *lord's*

6 [I]Gr., *baths,* one bath equals between 8 and 9 gal.

7 [I]Gr., *kors,* one kor equals between 10 and 12 bu.

8 [I]Or, *lord* [II]Lit., *generation* [a]Matt. 12:32; Luke 20:34 [b]John 12:36; Eph. 5:8; 1Thess. 5:5

(continued from previous page)
false. The unjust person in this parable is not the business manager, but the rich employer who dismissed his business manager on hearsay or false accusation. The next important word is the one found in v. 4 and translated "when I am removed." The Greek word is *metastathō,* from *methistēmi* (3179), which was a word used by the Greeks to denote one's removal from this world to the next (see Acts 13:22 where the word "removed" is the same as "taken away from this world"). The basic lesson of this parable is that when the business manager was given a termination notice form his job and was required to collect the bad debts due his lord before his final removal, as he engaged in the forgiveness of part of the debts due his lord; so the believer must act from the moment he is saved. In view of his *metastasis,* his removal from this earth, he must engage in the declaration of the forgiveness of debts (sins). This declaration of forgiveness of sins is the most important thing that any believer can engage in during his life of faith before his departure from earth (death). Verse 9 declares what will happen when this believer, here presented as the business manager (see I Cor. 4:1), is finally removed from his job on this earth as the steward of God. The business manager collected at least part of the debts due to his master, thus pleasing his master, who would have otherwise received nothing. It pleased the debtors who were unable to pay the full debt due, and they became friends of the business manager. When this business manager was going to be found in need himself after his removal from his job became effective, they would take him into their homes to give him hospitality. In this same way the Lord says to us in v. 9 that the friends, the people whom we win to Christ by using the mammon of unrighteousness (money) to make the Gospel available, will constitute our welcoming committee in heaven when we die (*hotan,* "when," *eklipēte,* "you are eclipsed, you die").

One more basic thing needs to be made clear in the translation of v. 8. The word "master" is actually *kurios,* Lord, indicating that it is not the servant's master commending him. The literal translation is "And the Lord (Jesus) commended the economist (or business manager) of unrighteousness (or injustice, *adikia,* 93)." It is very unfortunate that the "economist of unrighteousness" has been translated as the "unrighteous steward." The Lord would never commend an unjust steward. In this story, it was not the steward who was unjust, but his employer who dismissed him on a false accusation. The word *adikia,* "unrighteousness," in many instances in the N.T. stands for money, because money is used for unrighteous purposes much of the time (see v. 9). For instance, in Acts 1:18, the money which Judas received for betraying the Lord Jesus is called *misthos* (3408), the reward or pay of *adikias,* "iniquity or unrighteousness," exactly the same word as in Lk. 16:8. The word translated "shrewd" and "more shrewd" in v. 8 is "prudent," *phronimos* (5429), as contrasted to *sophos* (4680) and *sophia* (4678). *Phronimos* means "he who knows how to regulate his affairs with his fellow humans," while *sophos* means "the one who knows how to regulate his relationship with God." The one is a horizontal relationship and the other is a perpendicular one. He who is managed by God manages people best. See a very detailed study in the Editor's book, *How To Manage Money.*

9 "And [epn]I say to you, [aim] [a]make friends for yourselves by means of[1537] the [I][b]mammon[3126] of unrighteousness;[93] that when it fails, [c]they may [aosb]receive you into the eternal[166] dwellings.[4633]

10 "[a]He who is faithful[4103] in a very little thing is faithful also in much; and he who is unrighteous[94] in a very little thing is unrighteous[94] also in much.

11 "If therefore you have not [ao]been faithful in the *use of* unrighteous[94] [I][a]mammon,[3126] who will entrust[4100] the true[228] *riches* to you?

12 "And if you have not been faithful in *the use of* that which is another's,[245] who will give you that which is [I]your own?

13 "[a]No [I]servant[3610] can [pinf]serve[1398] two masters;[2962] for either he will hate the one, and love[25] the other, or else he will hold[472] to one, and despise the other.[2087] You cannot serve[1398] God[2316] and [II][b]mammon."[3126]

14 Now the Pharisees, who were [a]lovers of money, were [ipf]listening to all these things, and they [b]were [ipf]scoffing at Him.

15 And He said to them, "You are those who [ppt] [a]justify[1344] yourselves [I]in the sight of men, but [b]God knows your hearts;[2588] for that which is [II]highly esteemed among men is detestable[946] [III]in the sight of God.

16 "[a]The Law[3551] and the Prophets[4396] *were proclaimed* until John; since then [b]the gospel of the kingdom[932] of God[2316] is [pinp]preached,[2097] and everyone is forcing his way[971] into it.

17 "[a]But it is easier for heaven[3772] and earth[1093] to [ainf]pass away than for one [I]stroke of a letter[2762] of the Law to fail.[4098]

🔑 18 "[a]Everyone who [ppt] [I]divorces[630] his wife and [ppf]marries another[2087] [pin]commits adultery; and he who [ppt]marries one who is [pfpp] [II]divorced from a husband [pin]commits adultery.

The Rich Man and Lazarus

🔑 **19** "Now there was a certain rich man, and he habitually [ipf]dressed in purple and fine linen, [ppt]gaily living[2165] in splendor[2988] every day.

🔑 20 "And a certain poor man[4434] named Lazarus [a]was laid[906] at his gate, [pfpp]covered with sores,

9 [I]Or, *riches* [a]Matt. 19:21; Luke 11:41; 12:33 [b]Matt. 6:24; Luke 16:11, 13 [c]Luke 16:4
10 [a]Matt. 25:21, 23
11 [I]Or, *riches* [a]Luke 16:9
12 [I]Some mss. read *our own*
13 [I]Or, *house-servant* [II]Or, *riches* [a]Matt. 6:24 [b]Luke 16:9
14 [a]2Tim. 3:2 [b]Luke 23:35
15 [I]Lit., *before men* [II]Lit., *high* [III]Lit., *before God* [a]Luke 10:29; 18:9, 14 [b]1Sam. 16:7; Prov. 21:2; Acts 1:24; Rom. 8:27
16 [a]Matt. 11:12f. [b]Matt. 4:23
17 [I]I.e., projection of a letter (serif) [a]Matt. 5:18
18 [I]Or, *sends away* [II]Or, *sent away* [a]Matt. 5:32; 1Cor. 7:10, 11
20 [a]Acts 3:2

🔑 **16:18** This is the only verse on divorce in Luke, the Gospel for the Gentiles. Exegetically rendered, this verse says, "He who dismisses unjustifiably his wife and marries another commits adultery; and whosoever marries a woman (guilty one) who dismissed herself from her innocent husband, commits adultery." This *apolelumenē,* dismissed woman, was justifiably dismissed by her husband. Although this same word is used in Mt. 5:32; 19:9, in these two instances the dismissed wife is not guilty. She simply bears the presumed stigma of adultery because her licentious husband who dismissed her did not give her a bill of divorcement as prescribed by the law in Deut. 24:1-4 and affirmed by Jesus. A guilty dismissed wife was to be stoned to death (Lev. 20:10; Deut. 22:22). A careful reading of Num. 5 and Deut. 22 shows how careful the Lord was in determining who was the guilty party and who should be declared free. The innocent party was to be given a bill of divorcement enabling her or him to remarry (Deut. 24:1-4; Mk. 10:12). However, guilty husbands did not give their wives such certificates of innocence and, therefore, the innocent dismissed wives were bearing the stigma of adultery. Naturally if one married such, he unjustifiably was considered as committing adultery. A full discussion of this and Mt. 5:27-32; Mt. 19:1-12; Mk. 10:2-12 is found in the Editor's book, *What About Divorce?*

🔑 **16:19-31** See note on II Cor. 12:2-10.

🔑 **16:20** From all evidence, Lazarus was suffering from leprosy and had wounds which were open and visible, licked by the dogs. The idea was the Lord wanted to convey is that no person, who on seeing dogs showing a greater compassion toward a helpless creature than he himself and remains indifferent, deserves heaven or is by any stretch of the imagination a believer. The word translated "poor man" in v. 20, *ptōchos* (4434), means "totally helpless." Lazarus is assumed to have been a believer having demonstrated such patience in his great suffering and being found in the bosom of Abraham in his afterlife. See Editor's study, *The Pursuit of Happiness,* on the first Beatitude, "poor in spirit," or being totally helpless spiritually.

21 and longing[1937] to be [aifp]fed with
the *crumbs* which were [ppt]falling from
the rich man's table; besides, even the
dogs[2965] were [ppt]coming and [ipf]licking his
sores.
22 "Now it came about that the poor
man [ainf]died and he was [aifp]carried
away[667] by the angels to [a]Abraham's bosom; and the rich man also died and
was buried.
🗝 23 "And in [a]Hades[86] [I]he [apt]lifted up
his eyes, being[5225] in torment, and *saw
Abraham far away, and Lazarus in his
bosom.[2859]
24 "And he [apt]cried out and said,
'[a]Father Abraham, [aim]have mercy on me,
and [aim]send Lazarus, that he may
[aosb]dip[911] the tip of his finger in water
and [aosb]cool[2711] off my tongue;[1100] for I
am in agony[3600] in [b]this flame.'
25 "But Abraham said, 'Child, remember that [a]during your life[2222] you
[ao]received[618] your good things,[18] and
likewise Lazarus bad things; but now
he is being comforted[3870] here, and you
are in agony.
26 'And [I]besides all this, between
us and you there is a great chasm[5490]
[pfip]fixed, in order that those who [ppt]wish
to [ainf]come over from here to you may
not [psa]be able, and *that* none may
[psa]cross over from there to us.'
27 "And he said, 'Then I beg you,
Father, that you [aosb]send him to my father's house—
28 for I have five brothers—[80] that
he may [psa] [a]warn[1263] them, lest they also
come to this place of torment.'
29 "But Abraham *said, 'They have
[a]Moses and the Prophets;[4396] let them
[aim]hear[191] them.'
30 "But he said, 'No, [a]Father Abraham, but if someone [aosb]goes to them
from the dead,[3498] they will repent!'[3340]
31 "But he said to him, 'If they do
not [pin]listen to Moses and the Prophets,

22 [a]John 1:18; 13:23

23 [I]Lit., *having lifted up* [a]Matt. 11:23

24 [a]Luke 3:8; 16:30; 19:9 [b]Matt. 25:41

25 [a]Luke 6:24

26 [I]Lit., *in all these things*

28 [a]Acts 2:40; 8:25; 10:42; 18:5; 20:21ff.; 23:11; 28:23; Gal. 5:3; Eph. 4:17; 1Thess. 2:11; 4:6

29 [a]Luke 4:17; John 5:45-47; Acts 15:21

30 [a]Luke 3:8; 16:24; 19:9

1 [I]Or, *temptations to sin* [a]Matt. 18:7; 1Cor. 11:19; 1Tim. 4:1

2 [I]I.e., humble [a]Matt. 18:6; Mark 9:42; 1Cor. 8:12

3 [I]Lit., *Take heed to yourselves* [a]Matt. 18:15

4 [I]Lit., *you shall forgive* [a]Matt. 18:21f.

5 [a]Mark 6:30 [b]Luke 7:13

6 [I]Or, *have obeyed* [a]Luke 7:13 [b]Matt. 13:31; 17:20; Mark 4:31; Luke 13:19 [c]Luke 19:4

7 [I]Lit., *recline*

8 [I]Lit., *gird* [II]Lit., *after these things* [a]Luke 12:37

neither will they be persuaded[3982] if
someone [aosb]rises[450] from the dead.'"

Instructions

17 And He said to His disciples,[3101]
"[a]It is inevitable that [I]stumbling
blocks[4625] should [ainf]come, but woe to
him through whom they come!
2 "[a]It would be better for him if a
millstone were hung around his neck
and he were [pfip]thrown into the sea, than
that he should [aosb]cause one of these
[I]little ones to stumble.[4624]
3 [pim]"[I]Be on your guard![4337] [a]If your
brother [aosb]sins,[264] [aim]rebuke him; and
if he [aosb]repents,[3340] [aim]forgive[863] him.
4 "And if he [aosb]sins[264] against you
[a]seven times a day, and [aosb]returns to
you seven times, saying, 'I repent,'
[I]forgive him."
5 And [a]the apostles[652] said to [b]the
Lord,[2962] [aim]"Increase our faith!"[4102]
6 And [a]the Lord said, "If you [pin]had
faith[4102] like [b]a mustard seed, you would
[ipf]say to this [c]mulberry tree, 'Be
[aipp]uprooted and be [aipp]planted in the
sea'; and it would [ao] [I]obey[5219] you.
7 "But which of you, having a
slave[1401] [ppt]plowing or [ppt]tending sheep,
will say to him when he has [apt]come in
from the field, [apt]'Come immediately and
[aim] [I]sit down to eat'?
8 "But will he not say to him,
[aim]'[a]Prepare something for me to eat,
and *properly* [apt] [I]clothe yourself and
[pim]serve[1247] me until I have [aosb]eaten
and [aosb]drunk; and [II]afterward you will
eat and drink'?
9 "He does not thank the slave because he did the things which were commanded,[1299] does he?
10 "So you too, when you [aosb]do
all the things which are [aptp]command-
ed[1299] you, [pim]say, 'We are unworthy[888]
slaves; we have done *only* that which
we ought to have done.'"

🗝 **16:23** Hades (86) was the place for the disembodied spirits of the unrighteous and the righteous separated from the body at death up to the time of Christ's resurrection. Even the Lord's "soul" went there (Acts 2:27,31). Consequent to Christ's resurrection, believers go to be with Christ (II Cor. 5:8; Phil. 1:23). See Mt. 11:23; 16:18; Lk. 10:15; 16:23; I Cor. 15:15; Rev. 1:18; 6:8; 20:13,14 and also the Editor's book, *Life After Death*.

Ten Lepers Cleansed

11 And it came about while He
[aie]was [a]on the way to Jerusalem, that
[b]He was [ipf]passing [I]between[3319] 1223 Samaria
and Galilee.
12 And as He [ppt]entered a certain
village, ten leprous men who [a]stood at
a distance met Him;
13 and they raised their voices,
[ppt]saying, "Jesus, [a]Master, [aim]have
mercy on us!"
14 And when He saw them, He said
to them, [apt]"[a]Go and [aim]show yourselves
to the priests."[2409] And it came about
that as they were [aie]going, they were
cleansed.[2511]
15 Now one of them, when he saw
that he had been healed, turned back,
[ppt] [a]glorifying[1392] God with a loud voice,
16 and he fell on his face at His feet,
giving thanks[2168] to Him. And he was
a [a]Samaritan.
17 And Jesus answered and said,
"Were there not ten [aop]cleansed? But
the nine—where are they?
18 "[I]Was no one found who turned
back to [ainf] [a]give glory[1391] to God, except
this foreigner?"[241]
19 And He said to him, [apt]"Rise, and
[pim]go your way; [a]your faith [I]has [pfi]made
you well."[4982]
20 Now having been questioned by
the Pharisees [a]as to when the kingdom[932] of God was coming, He answered them and said, "The kingdom[932]
of God[2316] is not coming with [Ib]signs
to be observed;[3907]
🔑 21 nor will [a]they say, 'Look, here
it is!' or, 'There *it is!*' For behold, the
kingdom of God is [I]in your midst."

Second Coming Foretold

22 And He said to the disciples,[3101]
"[a]The days[2250] shall come when you will
long[1937] to see one of the days of the
Son of Man, and you will not see it.
23 "[a]And they will say to you, 'Look
there! Look here!' Do not [aosi]go away,
and do not [aosi]run after *them.*
24 "[a]For just as the lightning, when
it [ppt]flashes out of one part [I]of the sky,
shines to the other part [I]of the sky, so
will the Son of Man be in His day.
25 "[a]But first He must [ainf]suffer
many things and be [aifp]rejected[593] by this
generation.[1074]
26 "[a]And just as it happened [b]in
the days of Noah, so it shall be also in
the days of the Son of Man:
27 they were [ipf]eating, they were
[ipf]drinking, they were [ipf]marrying, they
were being [ipf]given in marriage, until
the day that Noah [ao]entered the ark,
and the flood came and destroyed[622]
them all.
28 "[I]It was the same as happened
in [a]the days[2250] of Lot: they were [ipf]eat-
ing, they were [ipf]drinking, they were
[ipf]buying, they were [ipf]selling, they were
[ipf]planting, they were [ipf]building;
29 but on the day that Lot went out
from Sodom it [ao]rained fire and
[I]brimstone 2303 from heaven[3772] and destroyed them all.
30 "It will be [I]just the same on the
day that the Son of Man [a]is revealed.[601]
31 "On that day, let not the one who
is [a]on the housetop and whose goods
are in the house [ao]go down to [ainf]take
them away;[142] and likewise let not the
one who is in the field [aim]turn back.
32 [pim]"[a]Remember Lot's wife.
33 "[a]Whoever [aosb]seeks to
[ainf]keep 4046 his [I]life[5590] shall lose[622] it,
and whoever [aosb]loses *his life* shall preserve it.
34 "I tell you, on that night there
will be two men in one bed; one will
be taken, 3880 and the other[2087] will be
left.
35 "[a]There will be two women
grinding at the same place; [f]one will be
taken, 3880 and the [f]other will be left.
36 ["[I][a]Two men will be in the field;
[m]one will be taken and the [m]other will
be left."]

11 [I]Lit., *through the midst of;* or, *along the borders of* [a]Luke 9:51 [b]Luke 9:52ff.; John 4:3f.
12 [a]Lev. 13:45f.
13 [a]Luke 5:5
14 [a]Lev. 14:1-32; Matt. 8:4; Luke 5:14
15 [a]Matt. 9:8
16 [a]Matt. 10:5
18 [I]Lit., *Were there not found those who* [a]Matt. 9:8
19 [I]Or, *has saved you* [a]Matt. 9:22; Luke 18:42
20 [I]Lit., *observation* [a]Luke 19:11; Acts 1:6 [b]Luke 14:1
21 [I]Or, *within you* [a]Luke 17:23
22 [a]Matt. 9:15; Mark 2:20; Luke 5:35
23 [a]Matt. 24:23; Mark 13:21; Luke 21:8
24 [I]Lit., *under heaven* [a]Matt. 24:27
25 [a]Matt. 16:21; Luke 9:22
26 [a]Luke 17:26, 27: *Matt. 24:37-39* [b]Gen. 6:5-8; 7
28 [I]Lit., *In the same way as* [a]Gen. 19:1-38
29 [I]Or, *sulphur*
30 [I]Lit., *according to the same things* [a]Matt. 16:27; 1Cor. 1:7; Col. 3:4; 2Thess. 1:7; 1Pet. 1:7; 4:13; 1John 2:28
31 [a]Matt. 24:17, 18; Mark 13:15f.; Luke 21:21
32 [a]Gen. 19:26
33 [I]Or, *soul* [a]Matt. 10:39
35 [a]Matt. 24:41
36 [I]Many mss. do not contain this v. [a]Matt. 24:40

🔑 **17:21** See notes on Mt. 5:1-12; Mt. 16:18,19.

37 And answering they *said to Him, "Where, Lord?" And He said to them, "[a]Where the body *is,* there also will the [I]vultures[105] be gathered."

Parables on Prayer

18 Now He was telling them a parable[3850] to show that at all times they [a]ought to [pinf]pray and not to [b]lose heart,

2 saying, "There was in a certain city a judge[2923] who did not [ppt]fear[5399] God,[2316] and did not [ppp] [a]respect[1788] man.[444]

3 "And there was a widow in that city, and she kept [ipf]coming to him, saying, [aim]'[I]Give me legal protection[1551] from my opponent.'[476]

4 "And for a while[5550] he was [ipf]unwilling; but afterward he said to himself, 'Even though I do not fear God nor [a]respect[1788] man,

5 yet [a]because this widow [pinf]bothers[3930,2873] me, I will [I]give her legal protection, lest by continually[5056] [ppt]coming she [psa] [II][b]wear me out.' "

6 And [a]the Lord[2962] said, [aim]"Hear what the unrighteous[93] judge *said;

🔑 7 now shall not God [aosb][a]bring about justice[1557] for His [b]elect,[1588] who [ppt]cry to Him day and night, [I]and will He [pin] [c]delay long[3114] over them?

8 "I tell you that He will bring about justice for them speedily. However, when the Son of Man [apt]comes, [a]will He find [I]faith[4102] on the earth?"[1093]

The Pharisee and the Publican

9 And He also told this parable[3850] to certain ones who [a]trusted[3982] in themselves that they were righteous,[1342] and [ppt] [b]viewed others with contempt:

10 "Two men [a]went up into the temple[2411] to [ainf]pray, one a Pharisee, and the other a [I]tax-gatherer.[5057]

11 "The Pharisee [a]stood and was praying thus to himself, 'God, I thank[2168] Thee that I am not like other people: swindlers,[727] unjust,[94] adulterers, or even like this [I]tax-gatherer.

12 'I [a]fast[3522] twice a week; I [b]pay tithes[586] of all that I get.'

🔑 13 "But the [I]tax-gatherer, [pfp] [a]standing some distance away, [b]was even [ipf]unwilling to [ainf]lift up his eyes to heaven,[3772] but [c]was [ipf]beating[5180] his breast, saying, 'God, [aipp]be [II]merciful[2433] to me, the sinner!'[268]

14 "I tell you, this man went down to his house [pfpp]justified[1344] rather than the other; [a]for everyone who [ppt]exalts himself shall be humbled,[5013] but he who [ppt]humbles himself shall be exalted."

15 [a]And they were [ipf]bringing even their babies[1025] to Him so that He might [psa]touch them, but when the disciples[3101] saw it, they *began* [ipf]rebuking them.

16 But Jesus called for them, saying, [aim]"Permit[863] the children to [pinf]come to Me, and do not [pim]hinder them, for the kingdom[932] of God[2316] belongs to such as these.

17 "Truly[281] I say to you, [a]whoever does not [aosb]receive the kingdom of God like a child shall [efn]not enter it *at all.*"

The Rich Young Ruler

18 [a]And a certain ruler questioned Him, saying, "Good[18] Teacher, what shall I do to inherit[2816] eternal[166] life?"[2222]

19 And Jesus said to him, "Why do you call Me good? No one is good except God[2316] alone.

20 "You know the commandments,[1785] '[a]DO NOT [aosb]COMMIT ADULTERY,[3431] DO NOT [aosb]MURDER, DO NOT [aosb]STEAL, DO NOT [aosb]BEAR FALSE WITNESS,[5576] [pim]HONOR YOUR FATHER AND MOTHER.' "

21 And he said, "All these things I have kept from *my* youth."[3503]

22 And when Jesus heard *this,* He said to him, "One thing you still lack; [aim] [a]sell all that you possess, and

37 [I]Or, *eagles* [a]Matt. 24:28
1 [a]Luke 11:5-10 [b]2Cor. 4:1
2 [a]Luke 18:4; 20:13; Heb. 12:9
3 [I]Lit., *Do me justice*
4 [a]Luke 18:2; 20:13; Heb. 12:9
5 [I]Lit., *do her justice* [II]Lit., *hit me under the eye* [a]Luke 11:8 [b]1Cor. 9:27
6 [a]Luke 7:13
7 [I]Or, *and yet He is long-suffering over them* [a]Rev. 6:10 [b]Matt. 24:22; Rom. 8:33; Col. 3:12; 2Tim. 2:10; Titus 1:1 [c]2Pet. 3:9
8 [I]Lit., *the faith* [a]Luke 17:26ff.
9 [a]Luke 16:15 [b]Rom. 14:3, 10
10 [I]I.e., Collector of Roman taxes for profit [a]1Kin. 10:5; 2Kin. 20:5, 8; Acts 3:1
11 [I]V. 10, note 1 [a]Matt. 6:5; Mark 11:25; Luke 22:41
12 [a]Matt. 9:14 [b]Luke 11:42
13 [I]V. 10, note 1 [II]Or, *propitious* [a]Matt. 6:5; Mark 11:25; Luke 22:41 [b]Ezra 9:6 [c]Luke 23:48
14 [a]Matt. 23:12; Luke 14:11
15 [a]Luke 18:15-17: *Matt. 19:13-15; Mark 10:13-16*
17 [a]Matt. 18:3; 19:14; Mark 10:15; 1Cor. 14:20; 1Pet. 2:2
18 [a]Luke 18:18-30: *Matt. 19:16-29; Mark 10:17-30;* Luke 10:25-28
20 [a]Ex. 20:12-16; Deut. 5:16-20
22 [a]Matt. 19:21; Luke 12:33

🔑 **18:7** See note on Eph. 1:4,5 and also *eklektos* (1588), elect.
🔑 **18:13** See note on Gal. 3:22.

[aim]distribute it to the poor, and you shall have [b]treasure in heaven;[3772] and come, [pim]follow Me."

23 But when he had heard these things, he became very sad; for he was extremely rich.

24 And Jesus looked at him and said, "[a]How hard it is for those who [ppt]are wealthy[5536] to enter the kingdom[932] of God![2316]

25 "For [a]it is easier for a camel to [ainf] [I]go through the eye of a needle, than for a rich man to [ainf]enter the kingdom of God."

26 And they who heard it said, "[I]Then who can be [aifp]saved?"[4982]

27 But He said, "[a]The things impossible with men are possible with God."

28 And Peter said, "Behold, [a]we have [apt]left [I]our own *homes,* and [ao]followed You."

29 And He said to them, "Truly[281] I say to you, [a]there is no one who has [ao]left house or wife or brothers[80] or parents or children, for the sake of the kingdom of God,

30 who shall not [aosb]receive[2983] many times as much at this time and in [a]the age to [ppt]come,[2064] eternal life."

31 [a]And He took the twelve aside and said to them, "Behold, [b]we are going up to Jerusalem, and [c]all things which are written through the prophets[4396] about the Son of Man will be accomplished.

32 "[a]For He will be [I]delivered to the Gentiles, and will be mocked and mistreated[5195] and spit upon,

33 and after they have [apt]scourged[3146] Him, they will kill Him; and the third day He will rise again."

34 And [a]they understood[4920] none of these things, and this saying was hidden from them, and they did not [ipf]comprehend the things that were [ppp]said.

Bartimaeus Receives Sight

35 [a]And it came about that [b]as He was [aie]approaching[1448] Jericho, a certain blind man was sitting by the road, begging.[1871]

36 Now hearing a multitude [ppt]going by, he *began* to inquire what this might be.

37 And they told him that Jesus of Nazareth was passing by.

38 And he called out, saying, "Jesus, [a]Son[5207] of David, [aim]have mercy on me!"

39 And those who [ppt]led the way were [ipf]sternly telling[2008] him to [aosb]be quiet;[4601] but he kept [ipf]crying out all the more, "[a]Son of David, have mercy on me!"

40 And Jesus [I]stopped and commanded that he be [aifp]brought to Him; and when he had [apt]come near, He questioned him,

41 "What do you want Me to do for you?" And he said, "Lord, *I want* to regain my sight!"

42 And Jesus said to him, "[I]Receive your sight; [a]your faith[4102] has [pfi] [II]made you well."

43 And immediately he regained his sight, and *began* [ipf]following Him, [a]glorifying[1392] God; and when [b]all the people saw it, they gave praise[136] to God.

Zaccheus Converted

19 And He [apt] [a]entered and was [ipf]passing through Jericho.

2 And behold, there was a man called by the name of Zaccheus; and he was a chief [I]tax-gatherer,[754] and he was rich.

3 And he was [ipf]trying to [ainf]see who Jesus was, and he was unable because of the crowd,[3793] for he was small in stature.

4 And he [apt]ran on ahead and climbed up into a [Ia]sycamore tree in order to see Him, for He was about to [pinf]pass through that way.

5 And when Jesus came to the place, He [apt]looked up and said to him, "Zaccheus, [apt]hurry and come down, for today I must [ainf]stay at your house."

6 And he hurried and came down, and received[5264] Him [I]gladly.

7 And when they saw it, they all *began* to [ipf] [I]grumble, saying, "He has

22 [b]Matt. 6:20
24 [a]Matt. 19:23; Mark 10:23f.
25 [I]Lit., *enter* [a]Matt. 19:24; Mark 10:25
26 [I]Lit., *And*
27 [a]Matt. 19:26
28 [I]Lit., *our own things* [a]Luke 5:11
29 [a]Matt. 6:33; 19:29; Mark 10:29f.
30 [a]Matt. 12:32
31 [a]Luke 18:31-33: *Matt. 20:17-19; Mark 10:32-34* [b]Luke 9:51 [c]Ps. 22:1-31; Is. 53:1-12
32 [I]Or, *betrayed* [a]Matt. 16:21
34 [a]Mark 9:32; Luke 9:45
35 [a]Luke 18:35-43: *Matt. 20:29-34; Mark 10:46-52* [b]Matt. 20:29; Mark 10:46; Luke 19:1
38 [a]Matt. 9:27; Luke 18:39
39 [a]Luke 18:38
40 [I]Lit., *stood*
42 [I]Or, *Regain* [II]Or, *saved you* [a]Matt. 9:22
43 [a]Matt. 9:8 [b]Luke 9:43; 13:17; 19:37
1 [a]Luke 18:35
2 [I]I.e., Collector of Roman taxes for profit
4 [I]I.e., fig-mulberry [a]1Kin. 10:27; 1Chr. 27:28; 2Chr. 1:15; 9:27; Ps. 78:47; Is. 9:10; Luke 17:6
6 [I]Lit., *rejoicing*
7 [I]Lit., *grumble among themselves*

gone [II]to [ainf]be the guest[2647] of a man
who is a sinner."[268]
8 And Zaccheus [I]stopped and said
to [a]the Lord, "Behold, Lord, half of my
possessions I will give to the poor, and
if I have [ao] [b]defrauded anyone of anything, I will give back [c]four times as
much."
9 And Jesus said to him, "Today
salvation[4991] has [ao]come to this
house,[3624] because he, too, is [a]a son
of Abraham.
10 "For [a]the Son of Man has [ao]come
to [ainf]seek and to [ainf]save[4982] that which
was [pfp]lost."[622]

Parable of Money Usage

11 And while they were [ppt]listening
to these things, He [apt]went on to tell a
parable,[3850] because [a]He [aid]was near Jerusalem, and they supposed that [b]the
kingdom[932] of God[2316] was [pip]going to
appear immediately.
12 He said therefore, "[a]A certain
nobleman went to a distant country to
[ainf]receive a kingdom for himself, and
then [ainf]return.
13 "And he [apt]called ten of his
slaves, and gave them ten [I]minas, and
said to them, [aim]'Do business *with this*
[II]until I come *back*.'
14 "But his citizens [ipf]hated him,
and sent [I]a delegation after him, saying,
'We do not want this man to [ainf]reign
over us.'
15 "And it came about that when
he [aie]returned, after receiving the kingdom, he ordered that these slaves, to
whom he had [plpf]given the money, be
called to him in order that he might know
what business they had done.
16 "And the first appeared, saying,
'[I]Master,[2962] your [II]mina has [ao]made ten
minas more.'
17 "And he said to him, 'Well done,
good[18] slave,[1401] because you have
[ao]been [a]faithful in a very little thing, be
in authority over ten cities.'
18 "And the second came,[2064] saying, 'Your [I]mina, [II]master, has [ao]made
five minas.'
19 "And he said to him also, 'And
you are to be over five cities.'
20 "And another came, saying,
'Master, behold your mina, which I kept
put away in a handkerchief;
21 for I [ipf]was afraid of you, because
you are an exacting[840] man; you take
up what you did not [ao]lay down,[5087] and
reap what you did not [ao]sow.'
22 "He *said to him, '[I]By your own
words I will judge[2919] you, you worthless[4190] slave. Did you know that I am
an exacting man, [ppt]taking up what I did
not lay down, and reaping what I did
not sow?
23 '[I]Then why did you not put the
money in the bank, and having come,
I would have collected it with interest?'[5110]
24 "And he said to the bystanders,
'Take the mina away from him, and give
it to the one who has the ten minas.'
25 "And they said to him, 'Master,
he has ten minas *already*.'
26 "[a]I tell you, that to everyone who
has shall *more* be given, but from the
one who does not have, even what he
does [pin]have shall be taken away.

7 [II]Or, *to find lodging*
8 [I]Lit., *stood* [a]Luke 7:13 [b]Luke 3:14 [c]Ex. 22:1; Lev. 6:5; Num. 5:7; 2Sam. 12:6
9 [a]Luke 3:8; 13:16; Rom. 4:16; Gal. 3:7
10 [a]Matt. 18:11
11 [a]Luke 9:51 [b]Luke 17:20
12 [a]Matt. 25:14-30; Luke 19:12-27
13 [I]A mina is equal to about 100 days' wages [II]Lit., *while I am coming*
14 [I]Or, *an embassy*
16 [I]Lit., *Lord* [II]V. 13, note 1
17 [a]Luke 16:10
18 [I]V. 13, note 1 [II]Lit., *lord*
22 [I]Lit., *Out of your own mouth*
23 [I]Lit., *And*
26 [a]Matt. 13:12; Mark 4:25; Luke 8:18

19:11-27 The contrast between this parable and the parable of the talents in Mt. 25:14-30 is that in this parable the Lord gives equally one pound to each person. But in the parable of the talents in Matthew, He bestows unequal endowments. The lesson is that there is no one who can claim that God has given him nothing for which he must give account. But the parable of the talents also tells us that God distributes His gifts unequally (see I Cor. 12:4-11); to one He gives five, to another two, and to another one. He expects the proper yield proportionate to His endowment in us. This is in confirmation of Paul's statement in I Cor. 4:7: "And what do you have that you did not receive? But if you did receive it, why do you boast as if you had not received it?" All that we have has been received from God and we are responsible for it. None of us can say that we have received nothing. No matter how much or how little we have, we must always recognize that it has come from God, and we are proportionately responsible to Him for all that He has given. For a complete exegesis on the parable of the pounds, see Editor's book entitled, *Did Jesus Teach Capitalism?*

27 "But [a]these enemies of mine, who did not want me to reign over them, bring them here[5602] and [b]slay them in my presence."

Triumphal Entry

28 And after He had said these things, He [a]was [ipf]going on ahead, [b]ascending to Jerusalem.

29 And it came about that [a]when He [ao]approached Bethphage and [b]Bethany, near the [I]mount that is called [IIc]Olivet, He sent two of the disciples,[3101]

30 saying, "Go into the village opposite *you,* in which as you enter you will find a colt[4454] tied, on which no one yet has ever sat; untie it, and bring it *here.*

31 "And if anyone asks[2065] you, 'Why are you untying it?' thus shall you speak, 'The Lord[2962] has need of it.'"

32 And those who were sent went away and found it just as He had told them.

33 And as they were [ppt]untying the colt, its [I]owners[2962] said to them, "Why are you untying the colt?"

34 And they said, "The Lord has need of it."

35 And they brought it to Jesus, [a]and they threw their garments on the colt, and put Jesus *on it.*

36 And as He was going, they were [ipf]spreading their garments in the road.

37 And as He was now approaching, near[4314] the descent of [a]the Mount of Olives, the whole multitude of the disciples began to [pinf] [b]praise[134] God [ppt] [I]joyfully with a loud voice for all the [II]miracles[1411] which they had seen,

38 saying,

"[a]BLESSED[2127] IS THE [b]KING[935]
WHO COMES IN THE NAME OF THE LORD;
Peace[1515] in heaven and
[c]glory[1391] in the highest!"

39 [a]And some of the Pharisees [I]in the multitude said to Him, "Teacher,[1320] rebuke Your disciples."[3101]

40 And He answered and said, "I tell you, if these become silent, [a]the stones will cry out!"

41 And when He approached, He saw the city and [a]wept over it,

42 saying, "If you had known in this day, even you, the things which make for peace! But now they have been [aop]hidden from your eyes.

43 "For the days shall come upon you [I]when your enemies will [a]throw up a [II]bank before you, and [b]surround you, and [ft]hem you in[4912] on every side,

44 and will level you to the ground and your children within you, and [a]they will not leave[863] in you one stone upon another, because you did not recognize [b]the time[2540] of your visitation."[1984]

Traders Driven from the Temple

45 [a]And He entered the temple[2411] and began to [pinf]cast out those who were [ppt]selling,

46 saying to them, "It is written, '[a]AND MY HOUSE SHALL BE A HOUSE OF PRAYER,' [b]but you have made it a ROBBERS' [I]DEN."

47 And [a]He was teaching[1321] daily in the temple; but the chief priests[749] and the scribes[1122] and the leading men among the people [b]were [ipf]trying to [ainf]destroy[622] Him,

48 and they could not [ipf]find[2147] [I]anything that they might do, for all the people were [ipf-ppt]hanging upon [II]His words.

Jesus' Authority Questioned

20 [a]And it came about on one of the days while [b]He was [ppt]teaching[1321] the people in the temple[2411] and [ppt] [c]preaching the gospel,[2097] that the chief priests[749] and the scribes[1122] with the elders[4245] [d]confronted *Him,*

2 and they spoke, saying to Him, "Tell us by what authority[1849] You are doing these things, or who is the one who [apt]gave You this authority?"

3 And He answered and said to them, "I shall also ask[2065] you a [I]question, and you tell Me:

---

27 [a]Luke 19:14 [b]Matt. 22:7; Luke 20:16
28 [a]Mark 10:32 [b]Luke 9:51
29 [I]Or, *hill* [II]Or, *Olive Grove* [a]Luke 19:29-38: *Matt. 21:1-9; Mark 11:1-10* [b]Matt. 21:17 [c]Luke 21:37; Acts 1:12
33 [I]Lit., *lords*
35 [a]Luke 19:35-38: *Matt. 21:4-9; Mark 11:7-10; John 12:12-15*
37 [I]Lit., *as they were rejoicing* [II]Or, *works of power* [a]Matt. 21:1; Luke 19:29 [b]Luke 18:43
38 [a]Ps. 118:26 [b]Matt. 2:2; 25:34 [c]Matt. 21:9; Luke 2:14
39 [I]Lit., *from* [a]Matt. 21:15f.
40 [a]Hab. 2:11
41 [a]Luke 13:34, 35
43 [I]Lit., *and* [II]I.e., a dirt wall or mound for siege purposes [a]Eccl. 9:14; Is. 29:3; 37:33; Jer. 6:6; Ezek. 4:2; 26:8 [b]Luke 21:20
44 [a]Matt. 24:2; Mark 13:2; Luke 21:6 [b]1Pet. 2:12
45 [a]Luke 19:45, 46: *Matt. 21:12, 13; Mark 11:15-17;* John 2:13-16
46 [I]Lit., *cave* [a]Is. 56:7; Jer. 7:11; Matt. 21:13; Mark 11:17 [b]Jer. 7:11
47 [a]Matt. 26:55; Luke 21:37 [b]Luke 20:19
48 [I]Lit., *what they might do* [II]Lit., *Him, listening*
1 [a]Luke 20:1-8: *Matt. 21:23-27; Mark 11:27-33* [b]Matt. 26:55 [c]Luke 8:1 [d]Acts 4:1; 6:12
3 [I]Lit., *word*

4 "Was the baptism[908] of John from heaven[3772] or from men?"

5 And they reasoned among themselves, saying, "If we say, 'From heaven,' He will say, 'Why did you not believe him?'

6 "But if we say, 'From men,' all the people will stone us to death, for they are convinced[3982] that John was a [a]prophet."[4396]

7 And they answered that they did not know where *it came* from.

8 And Jesus said to them, "Neither [I]will I tell you by what authority I do these things."

Parable of the Vine-growers

9 [a]And He began to tell the people this parable:[3850] "A man planted a vineyard and rented it out to [I]vine-growers,[1092] and went on a journey for a long time.[5550]

10 "And at the *harvest* time[2540] he sent a slave[1401] to the vine-growers, in order that they might give him *some* of the produce of the vineyard; but the vine-growers [ao]beat him and sent him away empty-handed.

11 "And he proceeded to send another slave; and they beat him also and [apt]treated him shamefully,[818] and sent him away empty-handed.

12 "And he proceeded to send a third; and this one also they [apt]wounded and [ao]cast out.[1544]

13 "And the [I]owner of the vineyard said, 'What shall I do? I will send my beloved son; perhaps they will [a]respect[1788] him.'

14 "But when the vine-growers saw him, they [ipf]reasoned[1260] with one another, saying, 'This is the heir; let us kill him that the inheritance may be ours.'

15 "And they threw him out of the vineyard and killed him. What, therefore, will the [I]owner[2962] of the vineyard do to them?

16 "He will come and [a]destroy these vine-growers and will give the vineyard to others." And when they heard it, they said, "[b]May it never be!"[1096][3361]

17 But He [apt]looked at[1689] them and said, "What then is this that is written,

'[a]THE [an]STONE WHICH THE
BUILDERS REJECTED,[593]
THIS [ao]BECAME [b]THE CHIEF[2776]
CORNER *stone*'?

18 "[a]Everyone who [apt]falls on that stone will be broken to pieces; but on whomever it falls, it will scatter him like dust."

Tribute to Caesar

19 And the scribes[1122] and the chief priests[749] [a]tried to lay hands on Him that very hour, and they feared the people; for they understood that He spoke this parable against them.

20 [a]And they [apt]watched[3906] Him, and sent spies who [ppt][I]pretended[5271] to be righteous,[1342] in order [b]that they might [II]catch[1949] Him in some [sg]statement,[3056] so as to deliver Him up to the rule[746] and the authority[1849] of [c]the governor.

21 And they questioned Him, saying, "Teacher,[1320] we know that You speak and teach[1321] correctly, and You [I]are not partial to any, but teach the way[3598] of God[2316] in truth.

22 "Is it [I]lawful for us [a]to pay taxes[5411] to Caesar, or not?"

23 But He [apt]detected[2657] their trickery and said to them,

24 "Show Me a [I]denarius.[1220] Whose [II]likeness[1504] and inscription does it have?" And they said, "Caesar's."

25 And He said to them, "Then [a]render to Caesar the things that are Caesar's, and to God the things that are God's."

26 And they were unable to [I][a]catch[1949] Him in a saying in the presence of the people; and [apt]marveling at His answer,[612] they became silent.

Is There a Resurrection?

27 [a]Now there came to Him some of the [b]Sadducees (who [ppt-pinf]say that there is no resurrection),[386]

6 [a]Matt. 11:9; Luke 7:29, 30
8 [I]Lit., *do I tell*
9 [I]Or, *tenant farmers*, also vv. 10, 14, 16 [a]Luke 20:9-19: *Matt. 21:33-46; Mark 12:1-12*
13 [I]Lit., *lord* [a]Luke 18:2
15 [I]Lit., *lord*
16 [a]Matt. 21:41; Mark 12:9; Luke 19:27 [b]Rom. 3:4, 6, 31; 6:2, 15; 7:7, 13; 9:14; 11:1, 11; 1Cor. 6:15; Gal. 2:17; 3:21; 6:14
17 [a]Ps. 118:22 [b]Eph. 2:20; 1Pet. 2:6
18 [a]Matt. 21:44
19 [a]Luke 19:47
20 [I]Lit., *feigned themselves* [II]Lit., *take hold of His word* [a]Luke 20:20-26: *Matt. 22:15-22; Mark 12:13-17;* Mark 3:2 [b]Luke 11:54; 20:26 [c]Matt. 27:2
21 [I]Lit., *do not receive a face*
22 [I]Or, *permissible* [a]Matt. 17:25; Luke 23:2
24 [I]The denarius was equivalent to one day's wage [II]Lit., *image*
25 [a]Matt. 22:21; Mark 12:17
26 [I]Lit., *take hold of His saying* [a]Luke 11:54
27 [a]Luke 20:27-40: *Matt. 22:23-33; Mark 12:18-27* [b]Acts 23:8

28 and they questioned Him, saying,
"Teacher,[1320] Moses wrote for us that
[a]IF A MAN'S BROTHER DIES, having a wife,
AND HE IS CHILDLESS, HIS BROTHER
SHOULD TAKE THE WIFE AND RAISE UP[1817]
OFFSPRING[4690] TO HIS BROTHER.
29 "Now there were seven broth-
ers;[80] and the first [apt]took a wife, and
died[599] childless;
30 and the second
31 and the third took her; and in
the same way [I]all seven [II]died, leaving
no children.
32 "Finally the woman died also.
33 "In the resurrection[386] therefore, which one's wife will she be? For
[I]all seven had her as wife."
34 And Jesus said to them, "The
sons of [a]this age marry and are given
in marriage,
35 but those who are [aptp]considered
worthy2661 to attain5177 to [a]that age and
the resurrection from the dead, neither
marry, nor are given in marriage;
36 for neither can they die anymore,
for they are like angels,[2465] and are
[a]sons of God, being sons[5207] of the resurrection.
37 "But that the dead[3498] are
raised,[1453] even Moses showed, in
[a]the *passage about the burning* bush,
where he calls the LORD[2962] [b]THE GOD
OF ABRAHAM, AND THE GOD OF ISAAC,
AND THE GOD OF JACOB.
38 "[a]Now He is not the God of the
dead,[3498] but of the living;[2198] for
[b]all live[2198] to Him."
39 And some of the scribes[1122] answered and said, "Teacher, You have
[ao]spoken well."
40 For [a]they did not [ipf]have cour-
age5111 to [pinf]question Him any longer
about anything.
41 [a]And He said to them, "How *is
it that* they say [I]the Christ[5547] is [b]David's
son?
42 "For David himself says in the
book of Psalms,
'[a]THE LORD[2962] SAID TO MY
LORD,[2962]
"SIT AT MY RIGHT HAND,[1188]
43 [a]UNTIL I MAKE THINE ENEMIES
A FOOTSTOOL FOR THY
FEET." '
44 "David therefore calls Him
'Lord,' and how is He his son?"[5207]
45 [a]And while all the people were
listening, He said to the disciples,[3101]
46 "Beware of the scribes,[1122]
[a]who [ppt]like to [pinf]walk around in long
robes, and [ppt]love[5368] respectful greetings in the market places, and chief seats
in the synagogues,[4864] and places of
honor at banquets,
47 who devour widows' houses,[3614]
and for appearance's sake offer long
prayers; these will receive greater
condemnation."[2917]

The Widow's Gift

21 [a]And He [apt]looked up and saw
the rich putting their gifts[1435] into
the treasury.
2 And He saw a certain poor widow
putting [I]in [a]two [II]small copper coins.[3067]
3 And He said, "Truly I say to you,
this poor widow put in more than all *of
them;*
4 for they all out of their [I]surplus4052
put into the [II]offering;[1435] but she out
of her poverty[5303] put in all [III]that she
had [a]to live on."[979]
5 [a]And while some were [ppt]talking
about the temple,[2411] that it was
[pfip]adorned with beautiful stones and votive gifts,[334] He said,
6 "*As for* these things which you are
looking at, the days will come in which
[a]there will not be left one stone upon
another which will not be torn down."
7 And they questioned Him, saying,
"Teacher,[1320] when therefore will these
things be? And what *will be* the [I]sign
when these things are about to take
place?"
8 And He said, "See to it[991] that
you be not misled; for many will come
in My name,[3686] saying, '[a]I am *He,*' and,

28 [a]Deut. 25:5
31 [I]Lit., *the seven also* [II]Lit., *left no children, and died*
33 [I]Lit., *the*
34 [a]Matt. 12:32; Luke 16:8
35 [a]Matt. 12:32; Luke 16:8
36 [a]Rom. 8:16f.; 1John 3:1, 2
37 [a]Mark 12:26 [b]Ex. 3:6
38 [a]Matt. 22:32; Mark 12:27 [b]Rom. 14:8
40 [a]Matt. 22:46; Luke 14:6
41 [I]I.e., the Messiah [a]Luke 20:41-44: *Matt. 22:41-46; Mark 12:35-37* [b]Matt. 9:27
42 [a]Ps. 110:1
43 [a]Ps. 110:1
45 [a]Luke 20:45-47: *Matt. 23:1-7; Mark 12:38-40*
46 [a]Luke 11:43; 14:7

1 [a]Luke 21:1-4: *Mark 12:41-44*
2 [I]Or, *therein* [II]Gr., *lepta* [a]Mark 12:42
4 [I]Or, *abundance* [II]Lit., *gifts* [III]Lit., *the living that she had* [a]Mark 12:44
5 [a]Luke 21:5-36: *Matt. 24; Mark 13*
6 [a]Luke 19:44
7 [I]Or, *attesting miracle*
8 [a]John 8:24

21:1-38 See note on Mt. 24-25.

'The time [pfi]is at hand'; [b]do not [aosi]go
after them.
9 "And when you hear of wars and
disturbances,[181] do not be terrified;[4422]
for these things must take place first,
but the end[5056] *does* not *follow* immediately."

Things to Come

10 Then He continued by saying to
them, "Nation[1484] will rise against nation, and kingdom[932] against kingdom,
11 and there will be great earthquakes, and in various[2596] places
plagues[3061] and famines; and there will
be terrors and great [I]signs from heaven.
12 "But before all these things,
[a]they will lay their hands on you and
will persecute you, delivering you to the
synagogues[4864] and prisons, [I]bringing
you before kings[935] and governors for
My name's sake.
13 "[a]It will lead to [I]an opportunity
for your testimony.[3142]
14 "[a]So make up your minds[2588] not
to prepare beforehand to defend yourselves;
15 for [a]I will give you [I]utterance and
wisdom which none of your opponents
will be able to resist or refute.[471]
16 "But you will be delivered up
even by parents and brothers and relatives and friends, and they will put *some*
of you to death,
17 and you will be hated by all on
account of My name.
18 "Yet [a]not a hair of your head will
perish.
19 "[a]By your endurance[5281] you will
[aim]gain your [I]lives.[5590]
20 "But when you see Jerusalem
[ppp] [a]surrounded by armies, then [aim] [I]rec-
ognize that her desolation [pfi]is at hand.
21 "Then let those who are in Judea
[pim]flee to the mountains, and let those
who are in the midst of [I]the city [pim]de-
part, and [a]let not those who are in the
country [pim]enter [I]the city;
22 because these are [a]days of vengeance,[1557] in order that all things which
are written may be fulfilled.
23 "Woe to those who are with child
and to those who nurse babes in those
days; for [a]there will be great distress[318]
upon the [I]land, and wrath[3709] to this people,
24 and they will fall[4098] by [a]the edge
of the sword, and will be led captive
into all the nations;[1484] and [b]Jerusalem
will be [c]trampled underfoot[3961] by the
Gentiles until [d]the times[2540] of the Gentiles be fulfilled.[4137]

The Return of Christ

25 "And there will be [I]signs[4592] in
sun and moon and stars, and upon the
earth[1093] dismay among nations, in
perplexity[640] at the roaring of the sea
and the waves,
26 men fainting[674] from fear[5401] and
the expectation[4329] of the things which
are coming upon the [I]world;[3625] for the
powers[1411] of [II]the heavens[3772] will be
shaken.
27 "And [a]then they will see [b]THE SON
OF MAN COMING IN A CLOUD with power
and great glory.[1391]
28 "But when these things begin to
take place, straighten up[352] and lift up[1869]
your heads, because [a]your redemp-
tion[629] is drawing near."[1448]
29 And He told them a parable:[3850]
"Behold the fig tree and all the trees;
30 as soon as they [aosb]put forth
leaves, you [ppt]see it and [a]know for yourselves that summer is now near.[1451]
31 "Even so you, too, when you
[aosb]see these things [ppt]happening, [I]rec-
ognize that [a]the kingdom[932] of God[2316]
is near.
32 "Truly[281] I say to you, this
[I]generation[1074] will [efn]not pass away until
all things [aosb]take place.
33 "[a]Heaven and earth[1093] will pass
away, but My words[3056] will not pass
away.
34 "[a]Be on guard, that your hearts
may not be weighted down with dissipation[2897] and drunkenness[3178] and the
worries of life, and that day come on
you suddenly like a trap;[160]

8 [b]Luke 17:23
11 [I]Or, *attesting miracles*
12 [I]Lit., *being brought* [a]Luke 21:12-17: *Matt. 10:19-22; Mark 13:11-13*
13 [I]Lit., *a testimony for you* [a]Phil. 1:12
14 [a]Luke 12:11
15 [I]Lit., *a mouth* [a]Luke 12:12
18 [a]Matt. 10:30; Luke 12:7
19 [I]Or, *soul* [a]Matt. 10:22; 24:13; Rom. 2:7; 5:3f.; Heb. 10:36; James 1:3; 2Pet. 1:6
20 [I]Lit., *know* [a]Luke 19:43
21 [I]Lit., *her* [a]Luke 17:31
22 [a]Is. 63:4; Dan. 9:24-27; Hos. 9:7
23 [I]Or, *earth* [a]Dan. 8:19; 1Cor. 7:26
24 [a]Gen. 34:26; Ex. 17:13; Heb. 11:34 [b]Is. 63:18; Dan. 8:13 [c]Rev. 11:2 [d]Rom. 11:25
25 [I]Or, *attesting miracles*
26 [I]Lit., *inhabited earth* [II]Or, *heaven*
27 [a]Matt. 16:27; 24:30; 26:64; Mark 13:26 [b]Dan. 7:13; Rev. 1:7
28 [a]Luke 18:7
30 [a]Luke 12:57
31 [I]Lit., *know* [a]Matt. 3:2
32 [I]Or, *race*
33 [a]Matt. 5:18; Luke 16:17
34 [a]Matt. 24:42-44; Mark 4:19; Luke 12:40, 45; 1Thess. 5:2ff.

35 for it will come upon all those who [ppt]dwell on the face*4383* of all the earth.

36 "But [a]keep on the alert at all times,*2540* [ppt]praying*1189* in order that you may have strength to escape all these things that are about to take place, and to [b]stand before the Son of Man."

37 Now [I]during the day He was [a]teaching*1321* in the temple,*2411* but [IIb]at evening He would [ppt]go out and spend the night on [IIIc]the mount that is called [IV]Olivet.

38 And all the people would [ipf]get up [a]early in the morning3719 *to come* to Him in the temple to [pinf]listen to Him.

Preparing the Passover

22 [a]Now the Feast of Unleavened Bread,*106* which is called the [b]Passover,3957 was [ipf]approaching.

2 And the chief priests*749* and the scribes*1122* [a]were [ipf]seeking how they might [aosb]put Him to death;337 for they [ipf]were afraid*5399* of the people.

3 [a]And [b]Satan*4567* entered into Judas who was called Iscariot, [I]belonging to the number of the twelve.

4 And he went away and discussed with the chief priests and [a]officers how he might betray Him to them.

5 And they were glad, and agreed to give him money.

6 And he consented,*1843* and *began* [ipf]seeking a good opportunity*2120* to betray Him to them [I]apart from the multitude.

7 [a]Then came*2064* the *first* day of Unleavened Bread*106* on which [b]the Passover *lamb*3957 had to be sacrificed.

8 And He sent [a]Peter and John, saying, [apt]"Go and [aim]prepare the Passover for us, that we may eat it."

9 And they said to Him, "Where do You want us to prepare it?"

10 And He said to them, "Behold, when you have entered the city, a man will meet you carrying a pitcher of water; follow him into the house that he enters.

36 [a]Mark 13:33; Luke 12:40 [b]Luke 1:19; Rev. 7:9; 8:2; 11:4
37 [I]Lit., *days* [II]Lit., *nights* [III]Or, *the hill* [IV]Or, *Olive Grove* [a]Matt. 26:55; Luke 19:47 [b]Mark 11:19 [c]Matt. 21:1
38 [a]John 8:2

1 [a]Luke 22:1, 2: *Matt. 26:2-5; Mark 14:1, 2;* Ex. 12:1-27 [b]John 11:55; 13:1
2 [a]Matt. 12:14
3 [I]Lit., *being of* [a]Luke 22:3-6: *Matt. 26:14-16; Mark 14:10, 11* [b]Matt. 4:10; John 13:2, 27
4 [a]1Chr. 9:11; Neh. 11:11; Luke 22:52; Acts 4:1; 5:24, 26
6 [I]Or, *without a disturbance*
7 [a]Luke 22:7-13: *Matt. 26:17-19; Mark 14:12-16* [b]Mark 14:12
8 [a]Acts 3:1, 11; 4:13, 19; 8:14; Gal. 2:9
14 [a]Matt. 26:20; Mark 14:17 [b]Mark 6:30
16 [a]Luke 14:15; 22:18, 30; Rev. 19:9
17 [a]Luke 22:17-20: *Matt. 26:26-29; Mark 14:22-25; 1Cor. 11:23-25;* 1Cor. 10:16 [b]Matt. 14:19
18 [a]Matt. 26:29; Mark 14:25
19 [I]Some ancient mss. do not contain the remainder of v. 19 nor any of v. 20 [a]Matt. 14:19
20 [a]Matt. 26:28; Mark 14:24 [b]Ex. 24:8; Jer. 31:31; 1Cor. 11:25; 2Cor. 3:6; Heb. 8:8, 13; 9:15
21 [a]Luke 22:21-23: *Matt. 26:21-24; Mark 14:18-21;* Ps. 41:9; John 13:18, 21, 22, 26
22 [a]Acts 2:23; 4:28; 10:42; 17:31

11 "And you shall say to the owner*3617* of the house, 'The Teacher*1320* says to you, "Where is the guest room in which I may eat the Passover with My disciples?" '*3101*

12 "And he will show you a large, furnished, upper room; prepare it there."

13 And they departed and found *everything* just as He had told them; and they prepared the Passover.

The Lord's Supper

14 [a]And when the hour had come He reclined *at the table,* and [b]the apostles*652* with Him.

15 And He said to them, "I have earnestly desired*1937* to eat this Passover with you before I suffer;

16 for I say to you, I shall [efn]never again eat it [a]until it is fulfilled in the kingdom*932* of God."*2316*

17 [a]And when He had [apt]taken a cup *and* [apt b]given thanks, He said, "Take this and share it among yourselves;

18 for [a]I say to you, I will [efn]not drink of the fruit of the vine from now on until the kingdom of God comes."

19 And when He had [apt]taken *some* bread *and* [apt a]given thanks, He broke *it,* and gave *it* to them, saying, "This is My body*4983* [I]which is [ppp]given for you; [pim]do this in remembrance*364* of Me."

20 And in the same way *He took* the cup after they had eaten, saying, "This cup which is [ppp a]poured out1632 for you is the [b]new covenant*1242* in My blood.*129*

21 "[a]But behold, the hand of the one [ppt]betraying Me is with Me on the table.

22 "For indeed, the Son of Man is going [a]as it has been determined;*3724* but woe to that man by whom He is betrayed!"

23 And they began to discuss among themselves which one of them it might be who was going to [pinf]do*4238* this thing.

Who Is Greatest

🗝 **24** And there arose also [a]a dispute among them *as to* which one of them was regarded to be greatest.

25 [a]And He said to them, "The kings of the Gentiles lord it over them; and those who [ppt]have authority over[1850] them are called 'Benefactors.'

26 "But not so with you, [a]but let him who is the greatest among you become as [b]the youngest, and the [ppt]leader[2233] as the [ppt]servant.[1247]

27 "For [a]who is greater, the one who [ppt]reclines *at the table,*[345] or the one who [ppt]serves? Is it not the one who reclines *at the table*? But [b]I am among you as the one who serves.

28 "And you are those who have [pfp]stood by[3326] Me in My [a]trials;[3986]

29 and just as My Father has granted Me a [a]kingdom,[932] I grant[1303] you

30 that you may [psa] [a]eat and [psa]drink at My table in My [b]kingdom, and [c]you will sit on thrones judging the twelve tribes of Israel.

31 "Simon, Simon, behold, [a]Satan[4567] has [ao] [1]demanded[1809] *permission* to [ainf] [b]sift you like wheat;

32 but I [a]have [ao]prayed[1189] for you, that your faith[4102] may not [aosb]fail;[1587] and you, when once you have [apt]turned again,[1994] [b]strengthen your brothers."

33 [a]And he said to Him, "Lord,[2932] with You I am ready to [pinf]go both to prison[5438] and to death!"[2288]

34 And He said, "I say to you, Peter, the cock will not crow today until you have denied three times that you know Me."

35 And He said to them, "[a]When I sent you out without purse and bag[4082] and sandals, you did not lack anything, did you?" And they said, "*No,* nothing."

🗝 36 And He said to them, "But now, let him who has a purse take it along, likewise also a bag, and let him who has no sword sell his [1]robe and buy one.

37 "For I tell you, that this which is written must be fulfilled[5055] in Me, '[a]And He was [aop]numbered[3049] with Transgressors';[459] for [b]that which refers to Me has *its* fulfillment."[5056]

38 And they said, "Lord, look, here are two [a]swords." And He said to them, "It is enough."[2425]

The Garden of Gethsemane

39 [a]And He came out and proceeded [b]as was His custom[1485] to [c]the Mount of Olives; and the disciples also followed Him.

40 [a]And when He arrived at the place, He said to them, [pim]"[b]Pray that you may not [ainf]enter into temptation."[3986]

41 And He withdrew from them about a stone's throw, and He [a]knelt down and *began* to [ipf]pray,

42 saying, "Father,[3962] if Thou art willing, [aim]remove this [a]cup from Me; [b]yet not My will,[2307] but Thine be done."

43 [1]Now an [a]angel[32] from heaven[3772] appeared to Him, strengthening Him.

44 And [a]being in agony[74] He was [ipf]praying very fervently;[1617] and His sweat became like drops of blood, falling down upon the ground.

45 And when He rose from prayer, He came to the disciples[3101] and found them sleeping from sorrow,

46 and said to them, "Why are you sleeping? [apt]Rise and [pim] [a]pray that you may not [aosb]enter into temptation."[3986]

Jesus Betrayed by Judas

47 [a]While He was still speaking, behold, a multitude *came,* and the one called Judas, one of the twelve, was preceding them; and he approached[1448] Jesus to kiss[5368] Him.

48 But Jesus said to him, "Judas, are you betraying the Son of Man with a kiss?"

49 And when those who were

24 [a]Mark 9:34; Luke 9:46
25 [a]Luke 22:25-27: *Matt. 20:25-28; Mark 10:42-45*
26 [a]Matt. 23:11; Mark 9:35; Luke 9:48 [b]1Pet. 5:5
27 [a]Luke 12:37 [b]Matt. 20:28; John 13:12-15
28 [a]Heb. 2:18; 4:15
29 [a]Matt. 5:3; 2Tim. 2:12
30 [a]Luke 22:16 [b]Matt. 5:3; 2Tim. 2:12 [c]Matt. 19:28
31 [1]Or, *obtained by asking* [a]Job 1:6-12; 2:1-6; Matt. 4:10 [b]Amos 9:9
32 [a]John 17:9, 15 [b]John 21:15-17
33 [a]Luke 22:33, 34: *Matt. 26:33-35; Mark 14:29-31; John 13:37, 38*
35 [a]Matt. 10:9f.; Mark 6:8; Luke 9:3ff.; 10:4
36 [1]Or, *outer garment*
37 [a]Is. 53:12 [b]John 17:4; 19:30
38 [a]Luke 22:36, 49
39 [a]Matt. 26:30; Mark 14:26; John 18:1 [b]Luke 21:37 [c]Matt. 21:1
40 [a]Luke 22:40-46: *Matt. 26:36-46; Mark 14:32-42* [b]Matt. 6:13; Luke 22:46
41 [a]Matt. 26:39; Mark 14:35; Luke 18:11
42 [a]Matt. 20:22 [b]Matt. 26:39
43 [1]Some ancient mss. do not contain vv. 43 and 44 [a]Matt. 4:11
44 [a]Heb. 5:7
46 [a]Luke 22:40
47 [a]Luke 22:47-53: *Matt. 26:47-56; Mark 14:43-50; John 18:3-11*

🗝 **22:24-34** See note on I Pet. 2:17.
🗝 **22:36** See note on Mt. 10:1-42.

around Him saw what was going to happen, they said, "Lord, shall we strike with the [a]sword?"

50 And a certain one of them struck the slave of the high priest and cut off his right ear.

51 But Jesus answered and said, "[I]Stop! No more of this." And He [apt]touched his ear and [ao]healed[2390] him.

52 And Jesus said to the chief priests[749] and [a]officers of the temple[2411] and elders[4245] who had come against Him, "Have you [ao]come out with swords and clubs[3586] [b]as against a robber?[3027]

53 "While I was with you daily in the temple, you did not lay hands on Me; but [I]this hour and the power[1849] of darkness[4655] are yours."

Jesus' Arrest

54 [a]And having arrested Him, they led Him *away,* and brought Him to the house of the high priest;[749] but [b]Peter was [ipf]following at a distance.

55 [a]And after they had kindled a fire in the middle of [b]the courtyard and had sat down together, Peter was sitting among them.

56 And a certain servant-girl, seeing him as he [ppt]sat in the firelight, and [apt]looking intently[816] at him, said, "This man was with Him too."

57 But he denied[720] *it,* saying, "Woman, I do not know[1492] Him."

58 And a little later, [a]another saw him and said, "You are *one* of them too!" But Peter said, "Man, I am not!"

59 And after about an hour had passed, another man *began* to [ipf]insist, saying, "Certainly this man also was with Him, [a]for he is a Galilean too."

60 But Peter said, "Man, I do not know[1492] what you are talking about." And immediately, while he was still [ppt]speaking, a cock crowed.

61 And [a]the Lord turned and looked at[1689] Peter. And Peter remembered the word[3056] of the Lord, how He had told him, "[b]Before a cock [ainf]crows today, you will deny[533] Me three times."

62 And he went out and wept bitterly.

63 [a]And the men who were [ppt]holding [I]Jesus in custody[4912] were [ipf]mocking Him, and [ppt]beating Him,

64 and they blindfolded Him and were asking Him, saying, "[a]Prophesy,[4395] who is the one who [apt]hit You?"

65 And they were saying many other things against Him, [ppt] [a]blaspheming.[987]

Jesus before the Sanhedrin

66 [a]And when it was day, [b]the [I]Council of elders[4244] of the people assembled, both chief priests[749] and scribes,[1122] and they led Him away to their [c]council *chamber,* saying,

67 "[a]If You are the [I]Christ,[5547] tell us." But He said to them, "If I tell you, you will [efn]not believe;[4100]

68 and if I ask a question, you will not answer.

69 "[a]But from now on [b]THE SON OF MAN WILL BE [ppt]SEATED AT THE RIGHT HAND[1188] of the power[1411] OF God."[2316]

70 And they all said, "Are You [a]the Son[5207] of God,[2316] then?" And He said to them, "[Ib]Yes, I am."

71 And they said, "What further need do we have of testimony?[3141] For we have [ao]heard[191] it ourselves from His own mouth."

Jesus before Pilate

23 Then the whole body of them [apt]arose and [ao] [a]brought Him before Pilate.

2 [a]And they began to [pinf]accuse Him, saying, "We found this man [b]misleading our nation and [c]forbidding to [pinf]pay taxes[5411] to Caesar, and saying that He Himself is [I]Christ,[5547] a King."[935]

3 And Pilate asked Him, saying, "Are You the King of the Jews?" And He answered him and said, "[a]*It is as* you say."

4 And Pilate said to the chief priests and the multitudes, "[a]I find no guilt in this man."

---

49 [a]Luke 22:38
51 [I]Or, *"Let Me at least do this," and He touched*
52 [a]Luke 22:4 [b]Luke 22:37
53 [I]Lit., *this is your hour and power of darkness*
54 [a]Matt. 26:57; Mark 14:53 [b]Matt. 26:58; Mark 14:54; John 18:15
55 [a]Luke 22:55-62: *Matt. 26:69-75; Mark 14:66-72; John 18:16-18, 25-27* [b]Matt. 26:3
58 [a]John 18:26
59 [a]Matt. 26:73; Mark 14:70
61 [a]Luke 7:13 [b]Luke 22:34
63 [I]Lit., *Him* [a]Matt. 26:67f.; Mark 14:65; John 18:22f.
64 [a]Matt. 26:68; Mark 14:65
65 [a]Matt. 27:39
66 [I]Or, *Sanhedrin* [a]Matt. 27:1f.; Mark 15:1; John 18:28 [b]Acts 22:5 [c]Matt. 5:22
67 [I]I.e., Messiah [a]Matt. 26:63-66; Mark 14:61-63; Luke 22:67-71; John 18:19-21
69 [a]Matt. 26:64; Mark 14:62; 16:19 [b]Ps. 110:1
70 [I]Lit., *You say that I am* [a]Matt. 4:3 [b]Matt. 26:64; 27:11; Luke 23:3
1 [a]Matt. 27:2; Mark 15:1; John 18:28
2 [I]I.e., Messiah [a]Luke 23:2, 3: *Matt. 27:11-14; Mark 15:2-5; John 18:29-37* [b]Luke 23:14 [c]Luke 20:22; John 18:33ff.; 19:12; Acts 17:7
3 [a]Luke 22:70
4 [a]Matt. 27:23; Mark 15:14; Luke 23:14, 22; John 18:38; 19:4, 6

5 But they [ipf]kept on insisting,2001 saying, "He stirs up the people, teaching all over[2596] Judea, [a]starting from Galilee, even as far as this place."

6 But when Pilate heard it, he asked whether the man was a Galilean.

7 And when he learned that He belonged to Herod's jurisdiction,[1849] he sent Him to [a]Herod, who himself also was in Jerusalem [I]at that time.

Jesus before Herod

8 Now Herod was very glad when he saw Jesus; for [a]he had wanted[2309] to see Him for a long time, because he had been [aid]hearing about Him and was [ipf]hoping[1679] to see some [I]sign[4592] [ppt]performed by Him.

9 And he [ipf]questioned Him [I]at some length; but [a]He answered him nothing.

10 And the chief priests[749] and the scribes[1122] were standing there, accusing Him vehemently.2159

11 And Herod with his soldiers, after treating Him with contempt1848 and mocking Him, [a]dressed Him in a gorgeous robe and sent Him back to Pilate.

12 Now [a]Herod and Pilate became friends with one another that very day; for before they had been at enmity2189 with each other.

Pilate Seeks Jesus' Release

13 And Pilate summoned[4779] the chief priests and the [a]rulers[758] and the people,

14 and said to them, "You [ao]brought this man to4374 me as one who [ppt] [a]incites[654] the people to rebellion, and behold, having [apt]examined Him before you, I [b]have found no guilt in this man regarding the charges which you make against Him.

15 "No, nor has [a]Herod, for he sent Him back to us; and behold, nothing deserving death[2288] has been done by Him.

16 "I will therefore [apt] [a]punish[3811] Him and release Him."

17 [[I]Now he was [ipf]obliged[2192,318] to [pinf]release to them at the feast one prisoner.]

18 But they cried out all together, saying, "[a]Away with this man, and release[630] for us Barabbas!"

19 (He was one who had been [aptp]thrown into prison for a certain insurrection[4714] [apt]made in the city, and for murder.)

20 And Pilate, wanting to release Jesus, addressed them again,

21 but they kept on [ipf]calling out, saying, "Crucify,[4717] crucify Him!"

22 And he said to them the third time, "Why, what evil has this man [ao]done? I have found in Him no guilt *demanding* death; I will therefore [a]punish Him and release Him."

23 But they were [ipf]insistent, with loud voices asking that He be [aifp]crucified. And their voices *began* to [ipf]prevail.[2729]

24 And Pilate pronounced sentence that their demand[155] should be granted.

25 And he released the man they were [ipf]asking for who had been [pfpp]thrown into prison for insurrection and murder, but he delivered Jesus to their will.[2307]

Simon Bears the Cross

26 [a]And when they led Him away, they laid hold of[1949] one Simon of [b]Cyrene, coming in from the country, and placed on him the cross[4716] to carry behind Jesus.

27 And there were [ipf]following Him a great multitude of the people, and of women who were [ipf] [I][a]mourning[2875] and [ipf]lamenting[2354] Him.

28 But Jesus turning to them said, "Daughters of Jerusalem, stop [pim]weeping for Me, but [pim]weep for yourselves and for your children.[5043]

29 "For behold, the days[2250] are coming when they will say, '[a]Blessed[3107] are the barren, and the wombs that never bore,[1080] and the breasts3149 that never nursed.'

30 "Then they will begin TO [a]SAY TO

---

5 [a]Matt. 4:12
7 [I]Lit., *in these days* [a]Matt. 14:1; Mark 6:14; Luke 3:1; 9:7; 13:31
8 [I]Or, *attesting miracle* [a]Luke 9:9
9 [I]Lit., *in many words* [a]Matt. 27:12, 14; Mark 15:5; John 19:9
11 [a]Matt. 27:28
12 [a]Acts 4:27
13 [a]Luke 23:35; John 7:26, 48; 12:42; Acts 3:17; 4:5, 8; 13:27
14 [a]Luke 23:2 [b]Luke 23:4
15 [a]Luke 9:9
16 [a]Matt. 27:26; Mark 15:15; Luke 23:22; John 19:1; Acts 16:37
17 [I]Many mss. do not contain this v.
18 [a]Luke 23:18-25: *Matt. 27:15-26; Mark 15:6-15;* John 18:39-19:16
22 [a]Luke 23:16
26 [a]Luke 23:26: *Matt. 27:32; Mark 15:21;* John 19:17 [b]Matt. 27:32
27 [I]Lit., *beating the breast* [a]Luke 8:52
29 [a]Matt. 24:19; Luke 11:27; 21:23
30 [a]Hos. 10:8; Is. 2:19, 20; Rev. 6:16

THE MOUNTAINS, [aim]'FALL[4098] ON US,' AND TO THE HILLS, [aim]'COVER[2572] US.'

31 "For if they do these things in the green tree, what will happen in the dry?"

32 [a]And two others also, who were criminals,[2557] were being [ipf]led away to be [aifp]put to death with Him.

The Crucifixion

33 [a]And when they came to the place called [I]The Skull, there they crucified[4717] Him and the criminals, one on the right and the other on the left.

34 [I]But Jesus was [ipf]saying, "[a]Father,[3962] forgive[863] them; for they do not know[1492] what they are doing."[4160] [b]And they [ao]cast lots, [ppt]dividing up His garments[2440] among themselves.

35 And the people stood by, looking on.[2334] And even the [a]rulers were [ipf]sneering at Him, saying, "He saved[4982] others; [b]let Him [aim]save[4982] Himself if this is the [I]Christ[5547] of God,[2316] His Chosen One."

36 And the soldiers also [ao]mocked Him, coming up to Him, [a]offering Him sour wine,

37 and saying, "[a]If You are the King[935] of the Jews, save[4982] Yourself!"

38 Now there was also an inscription above Him, "[a]THIS IS THE KING[935] OF THE JEWS."

39 [a]And one of the criminals who were [aptp]hanged *there* was [ipf] [I]hurling abuse at Him, saying, "Are You not the [II]Christ?[5547] [b]Save[4982] Yourself and us!"

40 But the other answered, and [ipf]rebuking[2008] him said, "Do you not even fear God, since you are under the same sentence of condemnation?[2917]

41 "And we indeed justly,[1346] for we are receiving[618] [I]what we deserve for our deeds;[4238] but this man has [ao]done[4238] nothing wrong."[824]

42 And he was saying, "Jesus, [aim]remember me when You [aosb]come [I]in Your kingdom!"[932]

43 And He said to him, "Truly[281] I say to you, today you shall be with Me in [a]Paradise."[3857]

44 [a]And it was now about [Ib]the sixth hour, and darkness[4655] [II]fell over the whole land[1093] until [III]the ninth hour,

45 the sun [I]being obscured; and [a]the veil of the temple[3485] was torn[4977] [II]in two.

46 And Jesus, [a]crying out with a loud voice, said, "Father, [b]INTO THY HANDS I COMMIT[3908] MY SPIRIT."[4151] And having said this, He breathed His last.[1606]

47 [a]Now when the centurion[1543] saw what had [apt]happened, he *began* [b]praising[1392] God, saying, "Certainly this man was [I]innocent."[1342]

48 And all the multitudes who [apt]came together for this spectacle,[2335] when they observed[2334] what had happened, *began* to [ipf]return, [ppt] [a]beating[5180] their breasts.[4738]

49 [a]And all His acquaintances[1110] and [a]the women who accompanied Him from Galilee, were standing at a distance, seeing these things.

Jesus Is Buried

50 [a]And behold, a man named Joseph, who was a [b]member of the Council,[1010] a good[18] and righteous[1342] man

51 (he had not consented to their plan[1012] and action),[4234] *a man* from Arimathea, a city of the Jews, who was [a]waiting for[4327] the kingdom[932] of God;[2316]

52 this man went to Pilate and asked for the body of Jesus.

53 And he took it down and wrapped it in a linen cloth, and laid Him in a tomb[3418] cut into the rock,[2991] where no one had ever lain.

54 And it was [a]the preparation day, and the Sabbath[4521] was [ipf]about to [I]begin.

55 Now [a]the women who had come with Him out of Galilee [apt]followed after,

32 [a]Matt. 27:38; Mark 15:27; John 19:18
33 [I]In Lat., *Calvarius;* or, *Calvary* [a]Luke 23:33-43: *Matt. 27:33-44; Mark 15:22-32; John 19:17-24*
34 [I]Some mss. do not contain *But Jesus was saying. . .doing.* [a]Matt. 11:25; Luke 22:42 [b]Ps. 22:18; John 19:24
35 [I]I.e., Messiah [a]Luke 23:13 [b]Matt. 27:43
36 [a]Matt. 27:48
37 [a]Matt. 27:43
38 [a]Matt. 27:37; Mark 15:26; John 19:19
39 [I]Or, *blaspheming* [II]I.e., Messiah [a]Matt. 27:44; Mark 15:32; Luke 23:39-43 [b]Luke 23:35, 37
41 [I]Lit., *things worthy of what we have done*
42 [I]Or, *into*
43 [a]2Cor. 12:4; Rev. 2:7
44 [I]I.e., 12 noon [II]Or, *occurred* [III]I.e., 3 p.m. [a]Luke 23:44-49: *Matt. 27:45-56; Mark 15:33-41* [b]John 19:14
45 [I]Lit., *failing* [II]Lit., *in the middle* [a]Ex. 26:31-33; Matt. 27:51
46 [a]Matt. 27:50; Mark 15:37; John 19:30 [b]Ps. 31:5
47 [I]Lit., *righteous* [a]Matt. 27:54; Mark 15:39 [b]Matt. 9:8
48 [a]Luke 8:52; 18:13
49 [a]Matt. 27:55f.; Mark 15:40f.; Luke 8:2; John 19:25
50 [a]Luke 23:50-56: *Matt. 27:57-61; Mark 15:42-47; John 19:38-42* [b]Mark 15:43
51 [a]Mark 15:43; Luke 2:25
54 [I]Lit., *dawn* [a]Matt. 27:62; Mark 15:42
55 [a]Luke 23:49

23:43 See note on II Cor. 12:1-10.

and saw the tomb[3419] and how His body
was laid.
🔑 56 And they returned and [a]prepared
spices and perfumes.
And [b]on the Sabbath[4521] they
rested[2270] according to the commandment.[1785]

The Resurrection

24 [a]But on the first day of the week,
at early dawn, they came to the
tomb,[3418] bringing the spices which they
had [ao]prepared.
2 And they found the stone [pfpp]rolled
away from the tomb,[3419]
3 but when they entered, they did
not find the body of [a]the Lord Jesus.
4 And it happened that while they
were [aie]perplexed about this, behold,
[a]two men suddenly [b]stood near them
in dazzling apparel;
5 and as *the women* were [apt]terrified
and [ppt]bowed their faces to the ground,
the men said to them, "Why do you
seek the living One[2198] among the
dead?[3498]
6 "[I]He is not here, but He [a]has
[aop] [II]risen.[453] [aim]Remember how He
spoke to you [b]while He was still in Galilee,
7 saying that [a]the Son of Man must
be [aifp]delivered into the hands of sinful[268]
men,[444] and be [aifp]crucified,[4717] and the
third day [ainf]rise again."[450]
8 And [a]they remembered His
words,[4487]
9 and returned from the tomb[3419]
and reported all these things to the
eleven and to all the rest.
10 Now they were [a]Mary Magdalene and Joanna and Mary the *mother*
of James; also the other women with
them were [ipf]telling these things to
[b]the apostles.[652]
11 And these words appeared[5316]
[I]to them as nonsense, and they [a]would
[ipf]not believe[569] them.
12 [[I]But Peter arose and [a]ran to the
tomb; [apt]stooping[3879] and looking in, he
*saw the linen wrappings [II]only; and he
went away [b]to his home, marveling at
that which had happened.[1096]]

The Road to Emmaus

13 And behold, [a]two of them were
going that very day to a village named
Emmaus, which was [I]about seven
miles[4712] from Jerusalem.
14 And they were [ipf]conversing with
each other about all these things which
had [pfp]taken place.
15 And it came about that while they
were [aie]conversing and [aie]discussing,
Jesus Himself [apt]approached, and *began*
traveling with them.
16 But [a]their eyes [I]were [ipf]pre-
vented[2902] from [infg]recognizing[1921] Him.
17 And He said to them, "What are
these words[3056] that you are exchanging
with one another as you are [ppt]walking?"
And they stood still, looking sad.
18 And one of them, named Cleopas, answered and said to Him, "Are
You [I]the only one visiting[3939] Jerusalem
and [ao]unaware of the things which have
[apt]happened here in these days?"
19 And He said to them, "What
things?" And they said to Him, "The
things about [a]Jesus the Nazarene, who
was a [b]prophet[4396] mighty in deed[2041]
and word[3056] in the sight of God and
all the people,
20 and how the chief priests and our
[a]rulers delivered Him up to the sentence[2917] of death,[2288] and crucified[4717]
Him.
21 "But we were [ipf]hoping[1679] that
it was He who was going to [pinf] [a]re-
deem[3084] Israel. Indeed, besides[4862] all
this, it is[71] the third day since these
things happened.
22 "But also some women among
us amazed[1839] us. [a]When they were at
the tomb[3419] early in the morning,

56 [a]Mark 16:1; Luke 24:1 [b]Ex. 20:10f.; Deut. 5:14
1 [a]Luke 24:1-10: *Matt. 28:1-8; Mark 16:1-8;* John 20:1-8
3 [a]Luke 7:13; Acts 1:21
4 [a]John 20:12 [b]Luke 2:9; Acts 12:7
6 [I]Some ancient mss. do not contain *He is not here, but He has risen* [II]Or, *been raised* [a]Mark 16:6 [b]Matt. 17:22f.; Mark 9:30f.; Luke 9:44; 24:44
7 [a]Matt. 16:21; Luke 24:46
8 [a]John 2:22
10 [a]Matt. 27:56 [b]Mark 6:30
11 [I]Lit., *in their sight* [a]Mark 16:11
12 [I]Some ancient mss. do not contain v. 12 [II]Or, *by themselves* [a]John 20:3-6 [b]John 20:10
13 [I]I.e., 60 stadia, one stadion was about 600 ft. [a]Mark 16:12
16 [I]Lit., *were being prevented* [a]Luke 24:31; John 20:14; 21:4
18 [I]Or, *visiting Jerusalem alone*
19 [a]Mark 1:24 [b]Matt. 21:11
20 [a]Luke 23:13
21 [a]Luke 1:68
22 [a]Luke 24:1ff.

🔑 **23:56** See note on I Tim. 2:9-15.

23 and did not find His body, they came, saying that they had also [pfin]seen a vision of angels,[32] who said that He [pinf]was alive.[2198]

24 "And some of those who were with us went to the tomb and found it just exactly as the women also had said; but Him they did not see."[1492]

25 And He said to them, "O foolish[453] men and slow[1021] of heart to believe[4100] in all that [a]the prophets[4396] have [ao]spoken!

26 "[a]Was it not necessary for the [I]Christ[5547] to [ainf]suffer these things and to [ainf]enter into His glory?"[1391]

27 And beginning [I]with [a]Moses and [I]with all the [b]prophets, He [ao]explained1329 to them the things concerning Himself in all the Scriptures.[1124]

28 And they approached the village where they were [ipf]going, and [a]He [aom]acted as though He would [pinf]go farther.

29 And they urged Him, saying, "Stay with[3326] us, for it is *getting* toward[4314] evening, and the day [I]is [pfi]now nearly over." And He went in to [infg]stay with them.

30 And it came about that when He had reclined2625 *at the table* with them, He [apt]took the bread and [a]blessed *it,* and [apt]breaking *it,* He *began* [ipf]giving *it* to them.

31 And their [a]eyes were opened and they recognized Him; and He vanished from [I]their sight.

32 And they said to one another, "[I]Were not our hearts[2588] burning within us while He was [ipf]speaking to us on the road, while He [a]was [ipf] [II]explaining the Scriptures to us?"

33 And they arose that very hour and returned to Jerusalem, and [a]found gathered together the eleven and [b]those who were with them,

34 saying, "[a]The Lord[2962] has really [aop]risen,[1453] and [b]has [aop]appeared to Simon."

35 And they [ipf]*began* to relate[1834] [I]their experiences on the road and how [a]He was recognized[1097] by them in the breaking[2800] of the bread.

25 [a]Matt. 26:24
26 [I]I.e., Messiah [a]Luke 24:7, 44ff.; Heb. 2:10; 1Pet. 1:11
27 [I]Lit., *from* [a]Gen. 3:15; 12:3; Num. 21:9 [John 3:4]; Deut. 18:15 [John 1:45]; John 5:46 [b]2Sam. 7:12-16; Is. 7:14 [Matt. 1:23]; Is. 9:1f. [Matt. 4:15f.]; Is. 42:1 [Matt. 12:18ff.]; Is. 53:4 [Matt. 8:17; Luke 22:37]; Dan. 7:13 [Matt. 24:30]; Mic. 5:2 [Matt. 2:6]; Zech. 9:9 [Matt. 21:5]; Acts 13:27
28 [a]Mark 6:48
29 [I]Lit., *has now declined*
30 [a]Matt. 14:19
31 [I]Lit., *them* [a]Luke 24:16
32 [I]Lit., *Was not our heart* [II]Lit., *opening* [a]Luke 24:45
33 [a]Mark 16:13 [b]Acts 1:14
34 [a]Luke 24:6 [b]1Cor. 15:5
35 [I]Lit., *the things* [a]Luke 24:30f.
36 [I]Some ancient mss. insert *And He says to them, "Peace be to you."* [a]Mark 16:14
37 [a]Matt. 14:26; Mark 6:49
38 [I]Lit., *heart*
39 [a]John 20:20, 27 [b]John 20:27; 1John 1:1
40 [I]Many mss. do not contain this v.
41 [I]Lit., *were disbelieving* [a]Luke 24:11 [b]John 21:5
43 [a]Acts 10:41
44 [a]Luke 9:22, 44f.; 18:31-34; 22:37 [b]Luke 24:27 [c]Ps. 2:7ff. [Acts 13:33]; Ps. 16:10 [Acts 2:27]; Ps. 22:1-18 [Matt. 27:34-46]; Ps. 69:1-21 [John 19:28ff.]; Ps. 72; 110:1 [Matt. 22:43f.]; Ps. 118:22f. [Matt. 21:42]
45 [I]Lit., *mind* [a]Luke 24:32; Acts 16:14; 1John 5:20
46 [I]I.e., Messiah [a]Luke 24:26, 44

Other Appearances

36 And while they were [ppt]telling these things, [a]He Himself stood in their midst.[I]

37 But they were [aptp]startled and frightened1719 and [ipf]thought that they were [pinf]seeing [a]a spirit.[4151]

38 And He said to them, "Why are you troubled, and why do doubts[1261] arise in your [I]hearts?[2588]

39 "[a]See My hands and My feet, that it is I Myself; [b]touch[5584] Me and see, for a spirit[4151] does not have flesh[4561] and bones as you see that I have."

40 [[I]And when He had said this, He showed them His hands and His feet.]

41 And while[569] they still [Ia]could [ppt]not believe[569] *it* for joy and were [ppt]marveling, He said to them, "[b]Have you anything here to eat?"

42 And they gave Him a piece of a broiled fish;

43 and He took it and [a]ate *it* before them.

44 Now He said to them, "[a]These are My words[3056] which I spoke to you while I was still with you, that all things which are [pfpp]written about Me in the [b]Law[3551] of Moses and the Prophets[4396] and [c]the Psalms[5568] must be [aifp]fulfilled."[4137]

45 Then He [a]opened their [I]minds[3563] to [infg]understand[4920] the Scriptures,[1124]

46 and He said to them, "[a]Thus it is [pfip]written,[1125] that the [I]Christ[5547] should suffer[3958] and [b]rise again[450] from the dead[3498] the third day;

47 and that [a]repentance[3341] [I]for forgiveness869 of sins should be [aifp]proclaimed[2784] [II]in His name to [b]all the nations, beginning from Jerusalem.

48 "You are [a]witnesses of these things.

49 "And behold, [a]I am sending forth the promise[1860] of My Father upon you; but [b]you are to [aim]stay in the city until

[b]Luke 24:7 **47** [I]Some mss. read *and forgiveness* [II]Or, *on the basis of* [a]Acts 5:31; 10:43; 13:38; 26:18 [b]Matt. 28:19 **48** [a]Acts 1:8, 22; 2:32; 3:15; 4:33; 5:32; 10:39, 41; 13:31; 1Pet. 5:1 **49** [a]John 14:26 [b]Acts 1:4

you are [asbm]clothed with power from on
high."

The Ascension

50 And He [ao]led them out[1806] as far
as [a]Bethany, and He [apt]lifted up[1869] His
hands and blessed them.

51 And it came about that while He
was [aie]blessing them, He [ao]parted from
them.[I]

52 And they[I] [ao]returned to Jerusalem with great joy,

53 and were continually in the temple,[2411] [I]praising[2127] God.

50 [a]Matt. 21:17; Acts 1:12
51 [I]Some mss. add *and was carried up into heaven*
52 [I]Some mss. insert *worshiped Him, and*
53 [I]Lit., *blessing*

The Gospel According to

JOHN

The Gospel of John stresses the deity of Jesus. It begins with: "In the beginning was the Word, and the Word was with God, and the Word was God," and "the Word became flesh, and dwelt among us" (John 1:1,14). And the Gospel concludes with the author's purpose expressed: "Many other signs therefore Jesus also performed in the presence of the disciples, which are not written in this book; but these have been written that you may believe that Jesus is the Christ, the Son of God; and that believing you may have life in his name." (John 20:30,31). This account of Jesus' life is very different from the Synoptic Gospels (Matthew, Mark, and Luke). It offers the things which Jesus said more than the things which He did. Step by step, this Gospel unfolds its proofs until the reader must reach the inescapable conclusion that Jesus is indeed the Son of God. The literary style is unique: the sentence structure is uncomplicated and easy to understand. Every step in a given narrative is presented as though it is an isolated event or statement, rather than attempting to merge it into an overall framework. The same majestic truths are repeated in intricate parallelisms. It is a book of striking contrasts: light and darkness; truth and falsehood; good and evil; life and death; God and Satan. Only in John's Gospel do we learn that the length of Jesus' public ministry was about 3½ years, by counting the Passover feasts. John is saturated with symbolic representations from ordinary life. Jesus used common things (such as water, bread, light, a vine and its branches, a loving shepherd and his pet sheep) to teach spiritual truths. The Gospel of John was written not so much to retell the historical facts of Jesus' brief stay on earth, but to ask us the question: "What does His coming mean?"

The author merely identifies himself as the disciple "whom Jesus loved" (John 13:23; 20:2). The writer was John the Apostle, one of the "sons of thunder" (Mark 3:17). John was very close to Jesus (Matthew 17:1; Mark 5:37; Luke 8:51). It was young John who leaned against the bosom of Jesus (John 13:23), with whom Jesus entrusted His aged mother (John 19:26,27). John was the first male to believe that Jesus rose from death (John 20:1-10), the first to recognize Him on the shore of Lake Galilee (John 21:1-7).

The Deity of Jesus Christ

1 🔑 [a]In the beginning[746] [ipf]was
[b]the Word,[3056] and the Word
[ipf]was [c]with God,[2316] and [d]the Word
[ipf]was [pred]God.
2 [I]He [ipf]was in the beginning[746] with
God.
3 [a]All things[3956] [ao]came into
being[1096] [I]by Him, and apart from Him
nothing [ao]came into being[1096] that has
[pfi]come into being.[1096]
4 [a]In Him [ipf]was life,[2222] and the life
[ipf]was [b]the light[5457] of men.
🔑 5 And [a]the light [pin]shines[5316] in the
darkness,[4653] and the darkness did not
[ao] [I]comprehend[2638] it.

The Witness of John

6 There [ao] [I]came a man, [pfpp]sent
from God, whose name was [a]John.
7 [I]He [ao]came [a]for a witness,[3141] that
he might [aosb]bear witness[3140] of the light,
[b]that all might [aosb]believe through him.
8 [I][a]He [ipf]was not the light, but *came*
that he might [aosb]bear witness of the
light.

1 [a]Gen. 1:1; Col. 1:17; 1John 1:1 [b]John 1:14; Rev. 19:13 [c]John 17:5; 1John 1:2 [d]Phil. 2:6
2 [I]Lit., *This one*
3 [I]Or, *through* [a]John 1:10; 1Cor. 8:6; Col. 1:16; Heb. 1:2
4 [a]John 5:26; 11:25; 14:6 [b]John 8:12; 9:5; 12:46
5 [I]Or, *overpower* [a]John 3:19
6 [I]Or, *came into being* [a]Matt. 3:1
7 [I]Lit., *This one* [a]John 1:15, 19, 32; 3:26; 5:33 [b]John 1:12; Acts 19:4; Gal. 3:26
8 [I]Lit., *That one* [a]John 1:20

🔑 **1:1b** See note on I Cor. 12:1-11.
🔑 **1:1c** See note on Phil. 2:6-8.
🔑 **1:5** See notes on Lk. 11:33-36; and general remarks on I John.

🔑 9 There [ipf]was [a]the true light
[I]which, coming into the world,
[pin]enlightens[5461] every man.
10 He [ipf]was in the world,[2889] and
[a]the world was [ao]made[1096] through Him,
and the [ao]world[1097] did not know Him.
11 He came to His [art-n] [I]own,3588,2398
and those who were His own did not
[ao]receive3880 Him.
🔑 12 But as many as received Him,
to them He [ao]gave the right[1849] to
[ainf]become[1096] [a]children[5043] of God,[2316]
even [b]to those who [ppt]believe[4100] in His
name,[3686]
13 [a]who were [I]born not of
[pl] [II]blood,[129] nor of the [an]will[2307] of the
[an]flesh,[4561] nor of the [an]will of man,[435]
but of God.

The Word Made Flesh

14 And [a]the Word[3056] [ao] [b]be-
came[1096] flesh,[4561] and [I][c]dwelt among
us, and [d]we [ao]beheld His glory,[1391] glory
as of [II]the only begotten[3439] from the
[an]Father, full[4134] of [e]grace[5485] and
[f]truth.[225]
15 John [pin*][a]bore witness of Him,
and cried out, saying, "This was He of
whom I said, '[b]He who [ppt]comes after
me [pfi] [I]has[1096] a higher rank than I,
[c]for He [ipf]existed before me.' "

9 [I]Or, *which enlightens every man coming into the world* [a]1John 2:8
10 [a]1Cor. 8:6; Col. 1:16; Heb. 1:2
11 [I]Or, *own things, possessions, domain*
12 [a]John 11:52; Gal. 3:26 [b]John 1:7; 3:18; 1John 3:23; 5:13
13 [I]Or, *begotten* [II]Lit., *bloods* [a]John 3:5f.; James 1:18; 1Pet. 1:23; 1John 2:29; 3:9
14 [I]Or, *tabernacled* [II]Or, *unique, only one of His kind* [a]Rev. 19:13 [b]Rom. 1:3; Gal. 4:4; Phil. 2:7f.; 1Tim. 3:16; Heb. 2:14; 1John 1:1f.; 4:2; 2John 7 [c]Rev. 21:3 [d]Luke 9:32; John 2:11; 17:22, 24; 2Pet. 1:16f.; 1John 1:1 [e]John 1:17; Rom. 5:21; 6:14 [f]John 8:32; 14:6; 18:37
15 [I]Lit., *is become before me* [a]John 1:7 [b]Matt. 3:11; John 1:27, 30 [c]John 1:30

🔑 **1:9** See notes on Mt. 13; Heb. 6:1-6.

🔑 **1:1-18** These are the axiomatic, authoritative statements which John gives concerning the person of Jesus Christ. The rest of the Gospel gives illustrations to confirm these statements found here.

It is the only Gospel which begins with the story of Jesus Christ, not from the time He appeared on earth, but before there was any beginning whatsoever. He had existed as the Logos, the intelligence, which gave birth to everything that is and who also became the expression, the Word, explaining that intelligence which is undiscoverable except through His word and works (Rom. 1:20).

There are two main verbs throughout this passage. There is *ēn,* the imperfect of *eimi* (1510), "to be," which in this context could have been best translated as "had been" for an indefinite time in the past. Thus, an exegetical paraphrase of the first verse would be: "Before there was any beginning, the Word had been, and the Word has been toward the God, and God had been the Word." This verb *ēn* is to be found in every instance in this context where the person of Jesus Christ is referred to in His eternal self-existent state (vv. 1,2,4,8,9,10,15). The other verb to be contrasted with *ēn* is *egeneto,* the aorist of *ginomai* (1096), "to become" something that one was not before. Thus, in v. 14 we find, "And the Word became flesh. . . ." The Lord Jesus at a particular time in the past became that which He was not before, a physical being. Before that He was essentially Spirit (Jn. 4:24). This verb is in the aorist, *egeneto* (vv. 3,6,10,14,17) or in the perfect, *gegone* (vv. 3,15), which means becoming something that one was not before. This refers to some historical time in the past, as the beginning of this new state. It also implies continuing to be that.

In Jn. 1:18 the verse begins with the word "God," *Theon,* without the definite article which refers to God in His general, total, infinite, eternal, as well as special essence as Spirit. John is declaring that no created being has ever seen God in His totality, eternity, infinity, in His special essence as Spirit. This first statement is to be connected with the first verse which speaks of Jesus Christ also in His eternal self-existence as eternal, infinite Spirit. And then to show the very special relationship of the Son to the Father, he calls Him *monogenēs* (3439). The word is unfortunately translated as "the only begotten" thus giving the idea that, in His eternal state, He was generated by the Father. The meaning in this context is as follows: "the unique Son who being (*ōn,* the present participle of *eimi,* 1510), in the bosom of the Father, He Himself brought Him (God) out (*exēgēsato,* 'exegeted' Him at a particular time in the past)." The second part of v. 18 declares that this unique Son or unique God, as some manuscripts have it, who has always been in the bosom of the Father, He is the One who brought Him out to visibility and made Him understood (that is, where our word exegesis comes from). This second declaration of v. 18 agrees with v. 14 which speaks of the incarnation of the Logos. For a complete exegesis of these eighteen verses, see the Editor's book entitled, *Was Christ God?.*

🔑 **1:12** See notes on Lk. 15; Heb. 6:1-6.

16 For of His [a]fulness[4138] [I]we have all [ao]received,[2983] and [II]grace upon[473] grace.

17 For [a]the Law[3551] was given through Moses; [b]grace and [c]truth[225] were realized through Jesus Christ.[5547]

🔑 18 [a]No man has [pfi]seen[3708] God at any time; [b]the only begotten[3439] [I]God,[2316] who [ppf]is [c]in the bosom of the Father,[3962] [d]He has [ao]explained[1834] *Him.*

The Testimony of John

19 And this is [a]the witness[3141] of John, when [b]the Jews sent to him priests[2409] and Levites [c]from Jerusalem to ask[2065] him, "Who are you?"

20 And he confessed,[3670] and did not deny,[720] and he confessed, "[a]I am not [I]the Christ."

21 And they asked[2065] him, "What then? Are you [a]Elijah?" And he *said, "I am not." "Are you [b]the Prophet?"[4396] And he answered, "No."

22 They said then to him, "Who are you, so that we may give an answer[612] to those who sent us? What do you say about yourself?"

23 He said, "I am [a]A VOICE OF ONE CRYING IN THE WILDERNESS, [aim]'MAKE STRAIGHT THE WAY[3598] OF THE LORD,' as Isaiah the prophet said."

24 Now they had been [pfpp]sent from the Pharisees.

25 And they asked[2065] him, and said to him, "Why then are you baptizing,[907] if you are not the [I]Christ, nor Elijah, nor [a]the Prophet?"

26 John answered them saying, "[a]I baptize [I]in water, *but* among you [pin]stands One whom you do not know.

27 "*It is* [a]He who comes after me, the [b]thong[2438] of whose sandal I am not worthy to [aosb]untie."

28 These things took place in Bethany [a]beyond the Jordan, where John was baptizing.

29 The next day he *saw Jesus coming to him, and *said, "Behold, [a]the Lamb[286] of God who [ppt][b]takes away[142] the sin[266] of the world!

30 "This is He on behalf of whom I said, '[a]After me comes a Man who [I]has a higher rank than I, [b]for He existed before[4413] me.'

31 "And I did not recognize [I]Him, but in order that He might be [asbp]manifested[5319] to Israel, I came baptizing [II]in water."

32 And John [a]bore witness saying, "[b]I have [pfi]beheld the Spirit descending as a dove out of heaven, and He [ao]remained upon Him.

🔑 33 "And I did not recognize [I]Him, but He who [apt]sent me to [pinf]baptize[907] [II]in water said to me, 'He upon whom you [aosb]see the Spirit descending and remaining upon Him, [a]this is the one who [ppt]baptizes [II]in the [an]Holy Spirit.'

34 "And I have seen, and have [pfi]borne witness that this is [a]the Son[5207] of God."[2316]

Jesus' Public Ministry, First Converts

35 Again [a]the next day John was [plpf]standing [I]with two of his disciples,[3101]

36 and he looked upon[1689] Jesus as He walked, and *said, "Behold, [a]the Lamb[286] of God!"

37 And the two disciples heard him [ppt]speak, and they followed Jesus.

38 And Jesus turned, and beheld them following, and *said to them, "What do you seek?" And they said to Him, "[a]Rabbi (which translated means Teacher),[1320] where are You staying?"

39 He *said to them, [pim]"Come, and you will [pin]see." They came therefore

16 [I]Lit., *we all received* [II]Lit., *grace for grace* [a]Eph. 1:23; 3:19; 4:13; Col. 1:19; 2:9
17 [a]John 7:19 [b]John 1:14; Rom. 5:21; 6:14 [c]John 8:32; 14:6; 18:37
18 [I]Some later mss. read *Son* [a]Ex. 33:20; John 6:46; Col. 1:15; 1Tim. 6:16; 1John 4:12 [b]John 3:16, 18; 1John 4:9 [c]Luke 16:22; John 13:23 [d]John 3:11
19 [a]John 1:7 [b]John 2:18, 20; 5:10, 15f., 18; 6:41, 52; 7:1, 11, 13, 15, 35; 8:22, 48, 52, 57; 9:18, 22; 10:24, 31, 33 [c]Matt. 15:1
20 [I]I.e., the Messiah [a]Luke 3:15f.; John 3:28
21 [a]Matt. 11:14; 16:14 [b]Deut. 18:15, 18; Matt. 21:11; John 1:25
23 [a]Is. 40:3; Matt. 3:3; Mark 1:3; Luke 3:4
25 [I]I.e., Messiah [a]Deut. 18:15, 18; Matt. 21:11; John 1:21
26 [I]The Gr. here can be translated *in, with* or *by* [a]Matt. 3:11; Mark 1:8; Luke 3:16; Acts 1:5
27 [a]Matt. 3:11; John 1:30 [b]Matt. 3:11; Mark 1:7; Luke 3:16
28 [a]John 3:26; 10:40
29 [a]Is. 53:7; John 1:36; Acts 8:32; 1Pet. 1:19; Rev. 5:6, 8, 12f.; 6:1 [b]Matt. 1:21; 1John 3:5
30 [I]Lit., *has become before me* [a]Matt. 3:11; John 1:27 [b]John 1:15
31 [I]I.e., as the Messiah [II]The Gr. here can be translated *in, with* or *by* **32** [a]John 1:7 [b]Matt. 3:16; Mark 1:10; Luke 3:22 **33** [I]I.e., as the Messiah [II]The Gr. here can be translated *in, with,* or *by* [a]Matt. 3:11; Mark 1:8; Luke 3:16; Acts 1:5 **34** [a]Matt. 4:3; John 1:49 **35** [I]Lit., *and* [a]John 1:29 **36** [a]John 1:29
38 [a]Matt. 23:7f.; John 1:49

🔑 **1:18** See note on Col. 1:15.
🔑 **1:33** See notes on Acts 1:5; 2:1-13; 11:14-18; 19:1-7; Col. 1:15.

and saw where He was staying;[3306] and
they stayed[3306] with Him that day, for
it was about[5613] the [I]tenth hour.
40 [a]One of the two who [apt]heard
John *speak,* and [apt]followed Him, was
Andrew, Simon Peter's brother.[80]
41 He *found first[4413] his own[2398]
brother Simon, and *said to him, "We
have found the [a]Messiah"[3323] (which
translated means [I]Christ).[5547]
42 He brought him to Jesus. Jesus
looked at[1689] him, and said, "You are
Simon the son of [Ia]John; you shall be
called [b]Cephas" (which is translated[2059]
[IIc]Peter).
43 [a]The next day He purposed
to [ainf]go forth into [b]Galilee, and He
[pfi] *found [c]Philip. And Jesus *said to him,
"[d]Follow Me."
44 Now [a]Philip was from [b]Beth-
saida, of the city of Andrew and Peter.
45 [a]Philip *found [b]Nathanael and
*said to him, "We have found Him of
whom [c]Moses in the Law[3551] and *also*
[c]the Prophets[4396] wrote,[1125] Jesus of
[d]Nazareth, [e]the son of Joseph."
46 And Nathanael *said to him,
"[a]Can any good thing[18] come out of
Nazareth?" [b]Philip *said to him,
[pim]"Come and [aim]see."[1492]
47 Jesus saw Nathanael coming to
Him, and *said of him, "Behold, an
[a]Israelite indeed, in whom is no
guile!"[1388]
48 Nathanael *said to Him, "How
do You know me?" Jesus answered and
said to him, "Before [a]Philip [aip]called you,
when you were[5607] under the fig tree,
I saw you."
49 Nathanael answered Him,
"[a]Rabbi, You are [b]the Son[5207] of God;[2316]
You are the [c]King[935] of Israel."
50 Jesus answered and said to him,
"Because I said to you that I saw you
under the fig tree, do you believe?[4100]
You shall see greater things than
these."
51 And He *said to him, "Truly,[281]
truly, I say to you, you shall see [a]the
heavens [pfp]opened, and [b]the angels[32]
of God ascending and descending on
[c]the Son[5207] of Man."[444]

39 [I]Perhaps 10 a.m. (Roman time)
40 [a]Matt. 4:18-22; Mark 1:16-20; Luke 5:2-11; John 1:40-42
41 [I]Gr., *Anointed One* [a]Dan. 9:25; John 4:25
42 [I]Gr., *Joannes* [II]I.e., Rock or Stone [a]Matt. 16:17; John 21:15-17 [b]1Cor. 1:12; 3:22; 9:5; 15:5; Gal. 1:18; 2:9, 11, 14 [c]Matt. 16:18
43 [a]John 1:29, 35 [b]Matt. 4:12; John 1:28; 2:11 [c]Matt. 10:3; John 1:44-48; 6:5, 7; 12:21f.; 14:8f. [d]Matt. 8:22
44 [a]Matt. 10:3; John 1:44-48; 6:5, 7; 12:21f.; 14:8f. [b]Matt. 11:21
45 [a]Matt. 10:3; John 1:44-48; 6:5, 7; 12:21f.; 14:8f. [b]John 1:46-49; 21:2 [c]Luke 24:27 [d]Matt. 2:23 [e]Luke 2:48; 3:23; 4:22; John 6:42
46 [a]John 7:41, 52 [b]Matt. 10:3; John 1:44-48; 6:5, 7; 12:21f.; 14:8f.
47 [a]Rom. 9:4
48 [a]Matt. 10:3; John 1:44-48; 6:5, 7; 12:21f.; 14:8f.
49 [a]John 1:38 [b]John 1:34 [c]Matt. 2:2; 27:42; Mark 15:32; John 12:13
51 [a]Ezek. 1:1; Matt. 3:16; Luke 3:21; Acts 7:56; 10:11; Rev. 19:11 [b]Gen. 28:12 [c]Matt. 8:20

1 [a]John 1:29, 35, 43 [b]John 2:11; 4:46; 21:2 [c]Matt. 12:46
2 [a]John 1:40-49; 2:12, 17, 22; 3:22; 4:2, 8, 27; 6:8, 12, 16, 22, 24, 60f., 66; 7:3; 8:31
4 [I]Lit., *what to Me and to you* (a Hebrew idiom) [a]John 19:26

Miracle at Cana

2 And on [a]the third day there was a
wedding[1062] in [b]Cana of Galilee, and
the [c]mother of Jesus was there;
2 and Jesus also was invited, and
His [a]disciples,[3101] to the wedding.
3 And when the wine [apt]gave out,
the mother of Jesus *said to Him, "They
have no wine."
4 And Jesus *said to her, "[a]Woman,
[Ib]what do I have to do with you?
[c]My hour has not yet come."
5 His [a]mother *said to the servants,[1249] "Whatever He says to you,
do it."
6 Now there were six stone waterpots set[2749] there [a]for the Jewish custom
of purification,[2512] containing [I]twenty or
thirty gallons[3355] each.[303]
7 Jesus *said to them, "Fill the waterpots with water." And they filled
them up to the brim.[507]
8 And He *said to them, [aim]"Draw
some out now, and [pim]take it to the
[I]headwaiter." And they [ao]took it *to him.*
9 And when the headwaiter
[ao]tasted[1089] the water [a]which [pfpp]had
become[1096] wine,[3631] and did not know
where it came from (but the servants
who had [pfp]drawn the water knew), the
headwaiter *called the bridegroom,
10 and *said to him, "Every man
serves[5087] the good wine first, and when
men [a]have [asbp] [I]drunk freely, *then* that
which is poorer; you have [pfi]kept the
good wine until now."
11 This beginning of *His* [Ia]signs
Jesus did in Cana of [b]Galilee, and
manifested[5319] His [c]glory,[1391] and His
disciples believed[4100] in Him.
12 After this He went down to
[a]Capernaum, He and His [b]mother, and

[b]Matt. 8:29 [c]John 7:6, 8, 30; 8:20 5 [a]Matt. 12:46
6 [I]Two or three metretai [a]Mark 7:3f.; John 3:25
8 [I]Or, *steward* 9 [a]John 4:46 10 [I]Or, *have become drunk* [a]Matt. 24:49; Luke 12:45; Acts 2:15; 1Cor. 11:21; Eph. 5:18; 1Thess. 5:7; Rev. 17:2, 6
11 [I]Or, *attesting miracles*; i.e., one which points to the supernatural power of God in redeeming grace [a]John 2:23; 3:2; 4:54; 6:2, 14, 26, 30; 7:31; 9:16; 10:41; 11:47; 12:18, 37; 20:30 [b]John 1:43 [c]John 1:14 12 [a]Matt. 4:13 [b]Matt. 12:46

His [c]brothers,[80] and His [d]disciples; and there they stayed[3306] a few days.

First Passover—Cleansing the Temple

13 And [a]the Passover[3957] of the Jews was at hand, and Jesus [b]went up to Jerusalem.

14 [a]And He found in the temple[2411] those who were [ppt]selling oxen and sheep and doves, and the money-changers seated.

15 And He made a scourge[5416] of cords, and drove *them* all out of the temple, with the sheep and the oxen; and He poured out the coins of the money-changers, and overturned their tables;

16 and to those who were selling [a]the doves He said, "Take these things away; stop [pim]making [b]My Father's[3962] house a house of merchandise."

17 His [a]disciples[3101] remembered that it was written, "[b]ZEAL[2205] FOR THY HOUSE[3624] WILL [ft]CONSUME ME."

18 [a]The Jews therefore answered and said to Him, "[b]What sign[4592] do You show to us, seeing that You do these things?"

19 Jesus answered and said to them, "[a]Destroy[3089] this [1]temple,[3485] and in three days I will raise[1453] it up."

20 [a]The Jews therefore said, "It took [b]forty-six years to [aop]build this [1]temple, and will You raise it up in three days?"

21 But He was [ipf]speaking of [a]the [1]temple of His body.[4983]

🗝 22 When therefore He was [aop]raised[1453] from the dead, His [a]disciples [b]remembered that He [ipf]said this; and they believed[4100] [c]the Scripture,[1124] and the word[3056] which Jesus had spoken.

23 Now when He was in Jerusalem at [a]the Passover,[3957] during the feast, many believed[4100] in His name,[3686] [ppt] [b]beholding His signs[4592] which He was [ipf]doing.

24 But Jesus, on His part, was not [ipf]entrusting[4100] Himself to them, for [a]He [aid]knew[1097] all men,

25 and because He did not need anyone to [aosb]bear witness concerning man [a]for He Himself [ipf]knew what was in man.

12 [c]Matt. 12:46 [d]John 2:2
13 [a]Deut. 16:1-6; John 5:1; 6:4; 11:55 [b]Luke 2:41; John 2:23
14 [a]John 2:14-16: *Matt. 21:12ff.; Mark 11:15, 17; Luke 19:45f.;* Mal. 3:1ff.
16 [a]Matt. 21:12 [b]Luke 2:49
17 [a]John 2:2 [b]Ps. 69:9
18 [a]John 1:19 [b]Matt. 12:38
19 [1]Or, *sanctuary* [a]Matt. 26:61; 27:40; Mark 14:58; 15:29; Acts 6:14
20 [1]Or, *sanctuary* [a]John 1:19 [b]Ezra 5:16
21 [1]Or, *sanctuary* [a]1Cor. 6:19
22 [a]John 2:2 [b]Luke 24:8; John 2:17; 12:16; 14:26 [c]Ps. 16:10; Luke 24:26f.; John 20:9; Acts 13:33
23 [a]John 2:13 [b]John 2:11
24 [a]Acts 1:24; 15:8
25 [a]Matt. 9:4; John 1:42, 47; 6:61, 64; 13:11

1 [a]John 7:50; 19:39 [b]Luke 23:13; John 7:26, 48
2 [1]Or, *attesting miracles* [a]Matt. 23:7; John 3:26 [b]John 2:11 [c]John 9:33; 10:38; 14:10f.; Acts 2:22; 10:38
3 [1]Or, *from above* [a]2Cor. 5:17; 1Pet. 1:23 [b]Matt. 19:24; 21:31; Mark 9:47; 10:14f.; John 3:5
5 [a]Ezek. 36:25-27; Eph. 5:26; Titus 3:5 [b]Matt. 19:24; 21:31; Mark 9:47; 10:14f.; John 3:3
6 [a]John 1:13; 1Cor. 15:50
7 [1]Or, *from above*
8 [a]Ps. 135:7; Eccl. 11:5; Ezek. 37:9
10 [a]Luke 2:46; 5:17; Acts 5:34
11 [a]John 1:18; 7:16f.; 8:26, 28; 12:49; 14:24 [b]John 3:32

The New Birth

3 Now there was a man of the Pharisees, named [a]Nicodemus, a [b]ruler[758] of the Jews;

2 this man came to Him by night, and said to Him, "[a]Rabbi, we know that You have [pf]come from God[2316] *as* a teacher; for no one can do these [1][b]signs[4592] that You do unless [c]God is with him."

3 Jesus answered and said to him, "Truly,[281] truly, I say to you, unless one [a]is [aspb]born[1080] [1]again,[509] he cannot [ainf]see[1492] [b]the kingdom[932] of God."

4 Nicodemus *said to Him, "How can a man be born when he is old? He cannot [ainf]enter a second time into his mother's womb and be born, can he?"

5 Jesus answered, "Truly, truly, I say to you, unless one is born[1080] of [a]water and the [an]Spirit,[4151] he cannot enter into [b]the kingdom of God.

6 "[a]That which is [pfpp]born of the flesh[4561] is flesh, and that which is born of the Spirit[4151] is spirit.[4151]

7 "Do not [aosi]marvel that I said to you, 'You must be born[1080] [1]again.'[509]

8 "[a]The wind[4151] blows[4154] where it wishes[2309] and you hear the sound[5456] of it, but do not know where it comes from and where it is going; so is everyone who is [pfpp]born of the Spirit."[4151]

9 Nicodemus answered and said to Him, "How can these things [ainf]be?"

10 Jesus answered and said to him, "Are you [a]the teacher[1320] of Israel, and do not understand these things?

11 "Truly, truly, I say to you, [a]we speak that which we know, and [b]bear witness[3140] of that which we have

🗝 **2:22-24** See note on Gal. 3:22.

seen; and [b]you do not receive our
witness.[3141]
12 "If I [ao]told you earthly[1919] things
and you do not believe,[4100] how shall
you believe if I [aosb]tell you heavenly
things?
13 "And [a]no one has [pfi]ascended into
heaven,[3772] but [b]He who [apt]descended
from heaven, *even* [c]the Son[5207] of
[I]Man.[444]
14 "And as [a]Moses lifted up the serpent in the wilderness, even so must
[b]the Son of Man [c]be [aifp]lifted up;
🗝 15 that whoever [ppt I]believes[4100]
may [a]in Him have eternal[166] life.[2222]
16 "For God[2316] so [ao a]loved[25] the
world,[2889] that He [b]gave His [Ic]only
begotten[3439] Son,[5207] that whoever
[ppt d]believes[4100] in Him should not
[asbm]perish,[622] but [psa]have eternal[166]
life.[2222]
17 "For God [a]did not send[649] the
Son into the world [b]to judge[2919] the
world, but that the world should be
[asbp]saved[4982] through Him.
18 "[a]He who [ppt]believes[4100] in Him
is not [pinp]judged;[2919] he who does not
[ppt]believe has been [pfip]judged already,
because he has not [pfi]believed[4100] in the
name[3686] of [b]the [I]only begotten Son of
God.
🗝 19 "And this is the judgment,[2920]
that [a]the light[5457] is [pfi]come[2064] into the
world, and men[444] [ao]loved[25] the darkness[4655] rather than the light; for [b]their
deeds[2041] were evil.[4190]
20 "[a]For everyone who [ppt]does[4238]
evil[5337] hates the light, and does not
come to the light, lest his deeds should
be exposed.
21 "But he who [ppt a]practices the
truth[225] comes to the light, that his
deeds may be [asbp]manifested[5319] as having been wrought[2038] in God."

John's Last Testimony

22 After these things Jesus and His
[a]disciples[3101] came into the land of Judea,
and there He was [ipf]spending time with
them and [ipf b]baptizing.[907]
23 And John also was baptizing in
Aenon near Salim, because there was
[I]much water there; and they were
[ipf]coming and were being [ipf]baptized.
24 For [a]John had not yet been
thrown into prison.
25 There arose therefore a discussion on the part of John's disciples with
a Jew about [a]purification.[2512]
26 And they came to John and said
to him, "[a]Rabbi, He who was with you
[b]beyond the Jordan, to whom you
[c]have [pfi]borne witness,[3140] behold, He
is baptizing, and all are coming to
Him."
27 John answered and said, "[a]A man
can [pinf]receive nothing, unless it [b]has
been given him from heaven.[3772]
28 "You yourselves bear me witness, that I said, '[a]I am not the
[I]Christ,'[5547] but, 'I have been sent before Him.'
29 "He who [ppt]has the bride is
[a]the bridegroom; but the friend of the
bridegroom, who [pfp]stands and [ppt]hears
him, rejoices greatly because of the
bridegroom's voice. And so this [b]joy of
mine has been [pfip]made full.
30 "He must [pinf]increase, but I must
[pinf]decrease.
31 "[a]He who comes from above[509]
is above all, [b]he who is of the earth[1093]
is from the earth[1093] and speaks of the
earth.[1093] [a]He who comes from
heaven[3772] is above all.
32 "What He has seen and heard,
of that He [a]bears witness;[3140] and
[a]no man receives His witness.[3141]
33 "He who has received His wit-
ness [a]has set his seal to *this,* that God
is true.
34 "For He whom God has [a]sent[649]

11 [b]John 3:32
13 [I]Later mss. add *who is in heaven* [a]Deut. 30:12; Prov. 30:4; Acts 2:34; Rom. 10:6; Eph. 4:9 [b]John 3:31; 6:38, 42 [c]Matt. 8:20
14 [a]Num. 21:9 [b]Matt. 8:20 [c]John 8:28; 12:34
15 [I]Some mss. read *believes in Him may have eternal life* [a]John 20:31; 1John 5:11-13
16 [I]Or, *unique, only one of His kind* [a]Rom. 5:8; Eph. 2:4; 2Thess. 2:16; 1John 4:10; Rev. 1:5 [b]Rom. 8:32; 1John 4:9 [c]John 1:18; 3:18; 1John 4:9 [d]John 3:36; 6:40; 11:25f.
17 [a]John 3:34; 5:36, 38; 6:29, 38, 57; 7:29; 8:42; 10:36; 11:42; 17:3, 8, 18, 21, 23, 25; 20:21 [b]Luke 19:10; John 8:15; 12:47; 1John 4:14
18 [I]Or, *unique, only one of His kind* [a]Mark 16:16; John 5:24 [b]John 1:18; 1John 4:9
19 [a]John 1:4; 8:12; 9:5; 12:46 [b]John 7:7
20 [a]John 3:20, 21; Eph. 5:11, 13
21 [a]1John 1:6
22 [a]John 2:2 [b]John 4:1, 2
23 [I]Lit., *many waters*
24 [a]Matt. 4:12; 14:3; Mark 6:17; Luke 3:20
25 [a]John 2:6
26 [a]Matt. 23:7; John 3:2 [b]John 1:28 [c]John 1:7
27 [a]1Cor. 4:7; Heb. 5:4 [b]James 1:17
28 [I]I.e., Messiah [a]John 1:20, 23
29 [a]Matt. 9:15; 25:1 [b]John 15:11; 16:24; 17:13; Phil. 2:2; 1John 1:4; 2John 12

31 [a]Matt. 28:18; John 3:13; 8:23 [b]1Cor. 15:47; 1John 4:5 **32** [a]John 3:11 **33** [a]John 6:27; Rom. 4:11; 15:28; 1Cor. 9:2; 2Cor. 1:22; Eph. 1:13; 4:30; 2Tim. 2:19; Rev. 7:3-8 **34** [a]John 3:17

🗝 **3:15,16** See notes on Gal. 3:22; Eph. 1:4,5; Heb. 6:1-6.
🗝 **3:19** See general remarks on I John.

speaks the words[4487] of God; [Ib]for He
gives the Spirit without measure.
35 "[a]The Father loves[25] the Son,
and [b]has given all things into His hand.
36 "He who [a]believes[4100] in the Son
has eternal life;[2222] but he who [b]does
not [I]obey[544] the Son shall not see life,
but the wrath[3709] of God abides on him."

Jesus Goes to Galilee

4 When therefore [a]the Lord[2962] knew
that the Pharisees had heard that
Jesus was making and [b]baptizing[907] more
disciples[3101] than John
2 (although [a]Jesus Himself was not
[ipf]baptizing, but His [b]disciples were),
3 He left [a]Judea, and departed
[b]again into Galilee.
4 And He had to [pinf]pass through
[a]Samaria.
5 So He *came to a city of [a]Samaria,
called Sychar, near[4139] [b]the parcel of
ground that [c]Jacob gave to his son Joseph;
6 and Jacob's well was there. Jesus
therefore, being [pfp]wearied from His
journey, was sitting thus by the well.
It was about [I]the sixth hour.

The Woman of Samaria

7 There *came a woman of Samaria
to [ainf]draw water. Jesus *said to her,
"Give Me a drink."
8 For His [a]disciples had [plpf]gone
away into [b]the city to buy food.
9 The [a]Samaritan woman therefore
*said to Him, "How is it that You, being
a Jew, ask me for a drink since I am a
Samaritan woman?" (For [b]Jews have no
dealings with Samaritans.)
10 Jesus answered and said to her,
"If you knew the gift of God, and who
it is who says to you, 'Give Me a drink,'
you would have asked Him, and He
would have given you [a]living[2198] water."
11 She *said to Him, "[I]Sir,[2962] You
have nothing to draw with and the
well[5421] is deep; where then do You get
that [art][a]living water?
12 "You are not greater than our
father Jacob, are You, who [a]gave us the
well, and [ao]drank of it himself, and his
sons, and his cattle?"
13 Jesus answered and said to her,
"Everyone who [ppt]drinks of this water
shall thirst again;
14 but whoever [aosb]drinks of the water that I shall give him [a]shall never
[efn]thirst; but the water that I shall give
him shall become in him a well[4077] of
water springing up to [b]eternal[166]
life."[2222]
15 The woman *said to Him, "[I]Sir,
[a]give me this water, so I will not be
thirsty, nor [psa]come all the way here
to [pinf]draw."
16 He *said to her, "Go, call your
husband,[435] and come here."
17 The woman answered and said,
"I have no husband." Jesus *said to her,
"You have well said, 'I have no husband';
18 for you have had five husbands,
and the one whom you now have is
not your husband; this you have said
truly."
19 The woman *said to Him, "[I]Sir,
I perceive that You are [a]a prophet.[4396]
20 "[a]Our fathers [ao]worshiped[4352] in
[b]this mountain, and you *people* say that
[c]in Jerusalem is the place where men
ought to [pinf]worship."
21 Jesus *said to her, "Woman,
[aim]believe Me, [a]an hour[5610] is coming
when [b]neither in this mountain, nor in
Jerusalem, shall you worship the Father.
22 "[a]You worship that which you do
not know; we worship that which we
know, for [art] [b]salvation[4991] is from the
Jews.
23 "But [a]an hour is coming, and now
is, when the true worshipers shall worship the Father[3962] [b]in spirit[4151] and
truth;[225] for such people the Father
seeks to [pinf]be His worshipers.
24 "God is [an-pred] [I]spirit,[4151] and
those who [ppt]worship Him must [pinf]wor-
ship [a]in spirit and truth."[225]
25 The woman *said to Him, "I
know that [a]Messiah[3323] is coming ([b]He
who is called Christ);[5547] when that One

34 [I]Lit., *for He does not give the Spirit by measure* [b]Matt. 12:18; Luke 4:18; Acts 1:2; 10:38
35 [a]Matt. 28:18; John 5:20; 17:2 [b]Matt. 11:27; Luke 10:22
36 [I]Or, *believe* [a]John 3:16 [b]Acts 14:2; Heb. 3:18
1 [a]Luke 7:13 [b]John 3:22, 26; 1Cor. 1:17
2 [a]John 3:22, 26; 1Cor. 1:17 [b]John 2:2
3 [a]John 3:22 [b]John 2:11f.
4 [a]Luke 9:52
5 [a]Luke 9:52 [b]Gen. 33:19; Josh. 24:32 [c]Gen. 48:22; John 4:12
6 [I]Perhaps 6 p.m. (Roman time)
8 [a]John 2:2 [b]John 4:5, 39
9 [a]Luke 9:52 [b]Ezra 4:3-6, 11ff.; Matt. 10:5; John 8:48; Acts 10:28
10 [a]Jer. 2:13; John 4:14; 7:37f.; Rev. 7:17; 21:6; 22:1, 17
11 [I]Or, *Lord* [a]Jer. 2:13; John 4:14; 7:37f.; Rev. 7:17; 21:6; 22:1, 17
12 [a]John 4:6
14 [a]John 6:35; 7:38 [b]Matt. 25:46; John 6:27
15 [I]Or, *Lord* [a]John 6:35
19 [I]Or, *Lord* [a]Matt. 21:11; Luke 7:16, 39; 24:19; John 6:14; 7:40; 9:17
20 [a]Gen. 33:20; John 4:12 [b]Deut. 11:29; Josh. 8:33 [c]Luke 9:53
21 [a]John 4:23; 5:25, 28; 16:2, 32 [b]Mal. 1:11; 1Tim. 2:8
22 [a]2Kin. 17:28-41 [b]Is. 2:3; Rom. 3:1f.; 9:4f.
23 [a]John 4:21; 5:25, 28; 16:2, 32 [b]Phil. 3:3
24 [I]Or, *a Spirit* [a]Phil. 3:3
25 [a]Dan. 9:25; John 1:41 [b]Matt. 1:16; 27:17, 22; Luke 2:11

[aosb]comes, He will declare[312] all things to us."

26 Jesus *said to her, "[a]I who [ppt]speak to you am *He.*"

27 And at this point His [a]disciples came, and they marveled that He had been [ipf]speaking with a woman; yet no one said, "What do You seek?" or, "Why do You speak with her?"

28 So the woman left her waterpot, and went into the city, and *said to the men,

29 "Come, see a man [a]who told me all the things that I *have* done; [b]this is not [1]the Christ, is it?"

30 They went out of the city, and were coming to Him.

31 In the meanwhile the disciples[3101] were [ipf]requesting Him, saying, "[a]Rabbi, eat."

32 But He said to them, "I have food to eat that you do not know about."

33 The [a]disciples therefore were [ipf]saying to one another, "No one brought Him *anything* to eat, did he?"

34 Jesus *said to them, "My food is to [psa] [a]do the will[2307] of Him who [apt]sent Me, and to [b]accomplish[5048] His work.

35 "Do you not say, 'There are yet four months, and *then* comes the harvest'? Behold, I say to you, lift up your eyes, and look on the fields, that they are white [a]for harvest.

36 "Already he who [ppt]reaps is receiving [a]wages,[3408] and is gathering [b]fruit for [c]life[2222] eternal;[166] that he who [ppt]sows and he who [ppt]reaps may [psa]rejoice together.

37 "For in this *case* the saying[3056] is true, '[a]One [ppt]sows, and another[243] [ppt]reaps.'

38 "I sent you to [pinf]reap that for which you have not [pfi]labored; others have [pfi]labored, and you have [pfi]entered into their labor."

The Samaritans

39 And from [a]that city many of the Samaritans believed[4100] in Him because of the word of the woman who testified, "[b]He told me all the things that I *have* done."

40 So when the Samaritans came to Him, they were [ipf]asking Him to [ainf]stay with them; and He [ao]stayed there two days.

41 And many more believed because of His word;

42 and they were saying[2981] to the woman, "It is no longer because of what you said that we believe, for we have heard for ourselves and know that this One is indeed [a]the Savior[4990] of the world."[2889]

43 And after [a]the two days He went forth from there into Galilee.

44 For Jesus Himself testified that [a]a prophet[4396] has no honor in his own country.

45 So when He came to Galilee, the Galileans received Him, [a]having seen all the things that He did in Jerusalem at the feast; for they themselves also went to the feast.

Healing a Nobleman's Son

46 He came therefore again to [a]Cana of Galilee [b]where He had made the water wine. And there was a certain royal official,[937] whose son[5207] was [ipf]sick at [c]Capernaum.

47 When he heard that Jesus had come [a]out of Judea into Galilee, he went to Him, and was [ipf]requesting *Him* to come down and heal his son; for he was at the point of death.

48 Jesus therefore said to him, "Unless you *people* [aosb]see[492] [1a]signs[4592] and [a]wonders,[5059] you *simply* will not believe."[4100]

49 The royal official *said to Him, "[1]Sir, come down before[4250] my child [ainf]dies."

50 Jesus *said to him, [pim]"[a]Go your way; your son lives."[2198] The man believed the word[3056] that Jesus spoke to him, and he started off.

51 And as he was now going down, *his* slaves[1401] met him, saying that his [1]son[3816] was living.[2198]

52 So he inquired of them the hour

26 [a]John 8:24, 28, 58; 9:37; 13:19
27 [a]John 4:8
29 [1]I.e., the Messiah [a]John 4:17f. [b]Matt. 12:23; John 7:26, 31
31 [a]Matt. 23:7; 26:25, 49; Mark 9:5; 11:21; 14:45; John 1:38, 49; 3:2, 26; 6:25; 9:2; 11:8
33 [a]Luke 6:13-16; John 1:40-49; 2:2
34 [a]John 5:30; 6:38 [b]John 5:36; 17:4; 19:28, 30
35 [a]Matt. 9:37, 38; Luke 10:2
36 [a]Prov. 11:18; 1Cor. 9:17f. [b]Rom. 1:13 [c]Matt. 19:29; John 3:36; 4:14; 5:24; Rom. 2:7; 6:23
37 [a]Job 31:8; Mic. 6:15
39 [a]John 4:5, 30 [b]John 4:29
42 [a]Matt. 1:21; Luke 2:11; John 1:29; Acts 5:31; 13:23; 1Tim. 4:10; 1John 4:14
43 [a]John 4:40
44 [a]Matt. 13:57; Mark 6:4; Luke 4:24
45 [a]John 2:23
46 [a]John 2:1 [b]John 2:9 [c]Luke 4:23; John 2:12
47 [a]John 4:3, 54
48 [1]Or, *attesting miracles* [a]Dan. 4:2f.; 6:27; Matt. 24:24; Mark 13:22; Acts 2:19, 22, 43; 4:30; 5:12; 6:8; 7:36; 14:3; 15:12; Rom. 15:19; 1Cor. 1:22; 2Cor. 12:12; 2Thess. 2:9; Heb. 2:4
49 [1]Or, *Lord*
50 [a]Matt. 8:13
51 [1]Or, *boy*

when he began to get better.[2866] They said therefore to him, "Yesterday at the [I]seventh hour the fever left[863] him."

53 So the father knew that *it was* at that hour in which Jesus said to him, "Your son lives"; and he himself believed, and [a]his whole household.[3614]

54 This is again a [a]second [I]sign that Jesus performed, when He had [b]come out of Judea into Galilee.

The Healing at Bethesda

5 After these things there was [Ia]a feast of the Jews, and Jesus went up to Jerusalem.

2 Now there is in Jerusalem by [a]the sheep *gate* a pool, which is called [b]in [I]Hebrew [II]Bethesda, having five porticoes.

3 In these [ipf]lay a multitude of those who were sick,[770] blind, lame, and withered, [[I]waiting for[1551] the moving of the waters;

4 for an angel[32] of the Lord went down at certain seasons[2540] into the pool, and stirred up the water; whoever then first,[4413] after the stirring up of the water, stepped in was made well[5199] from whatever disease[3553] with which he was afflicted.[2772]]

5 And a certain man was there, who [ppt]had been thirty-eight years in his sickness.

6 When Jesus saw him [ppt]lying there, and knew that he [pin]had already been a long time[5550] *in that condition,* He *said to him, "Do you wish to get well?"[5199]

7 The sick man answered Him, "Sir, I have no man to [aosb]put[906] me into the pool when [a]the water is [asbp]stirred up, but while I am coming, another steps down before me."

8 Jesus *said to him, "[a]Arise, take up[142] your pallet,[2895] and [pim]walk."

9 And immediately the man became well,[5199] and took up[142] his pallet and [ipf]*began* to walk.

[a]Now it was the Sabbath[4521] on that day.

10 Therefore [a]the Jews were saying to him who was [pfpp]cured, "It is the Sabbath, and [b]it is not permissible for you to carry your pallet."

11 But he answered them, "He who [apt]made[4160] me well was the one who said to me, [aim]'Take up your pallet and [pim]walk.'"

12 They asked[2065] him, "Who is the man who said to you, 'Take up *your pallet,* and walk'?"

13 But he who was healed did not know[1492] who it was; for Jesus had slipped away while there was a crowd in *that* place.

14 Afterward Jesus *found him in the temple,[2411] and said to him, "Behold, you have [pf]become well;[5199] do not [pim] [a]sin[264] anymore, [b]so that nothing worse may [aosb]befall you."

15 The man went away, and told[312] [a]the Jews that it was Jesus who had made[4160] him well.

16 And for this reason [a]the Jews were [ipf]persecuting Jesus, because He was [ipf]doing these things on the Sabbath.

17 But He answered them, "My Father[3962] is [pin]working until now, and I Myself am [pin]working."

Jesus' Equality with God

18 For this cause therefore [a]the Jews [b]were [ipf]seeking all the more to [pinf]kill Him, because He not only was [ipf]breaking[3089] the Sabbath, but also was calling God His[2398] own Father, [c]making Himself equal with God.

19 Jesus therefore answered and was saying to them, "Truly,[281] truly, I say to you, [a]the Son[5207] can [pinf]do nothing of Himself, unless *it is* something He [psa]sees the Father [ppt]doing; for whatever *the Father* [psa]does, these things the Son also does in like manner.

20 "[a]For the Father loves[5368] the Son, and shows Him all things that He Himself is doing; and [b]greater works[2041] than these will He show Him, that you may [psa]marvel.

21 "For just as the Father raises[1453] the dead and [a]gives them life,[2227] even so [b]the Son also gives life to whom He wishes.

---

52 [I]Perhaps 7 p.m. (Roman time)

53 [a]Acts 11:14

54 [I]Or, *attesting miracle* [a]John 2:11 [b]John 4:45f.

1 [I]Many mss. read *the feast*; i.e., the Passover [a]Deut. 16:1; John 2:13

2 [I]I.e., Jewish Aramaic [II]Many mss. read *Bethsaida* or *Bethzatha* [a]Neh. 3:1, 32; 12:39 [b]John 19:13, 17, 20; 20:16; Acts 21:40; Rev. 9:11; 16:16

3 [I]Many mss. do not contain the remainder of v. 3, nor v. 4

7 [a]John 5:4

8 [a]Matt. 9:6; Mark 2:11; Luke 5:24

9 [a]John 9:14

10 [a]John 1:19; 5:15, 16, 18 [b]Neh. 13:19; Jer. 17:21f.; Matt. 12:2; Luke 6:2; John 7:23; 9:16

14 [a]Mark 2:5; John 8:11 [b]Ezra 9:14

15 [a]John 1:19; 5:16, 18

16 [a]John 1:19; 5:10, 15, 18

18 [a]John 1:19; 5:15, 16 [b]John 5:16; 7:1 [c]John 10:33; 19:7

19 [a]Matt. 26:39; John 5:30; 6:38; 8:28; 12:49; 14:10

20 [a]Matt. 3:17; John 3:35; 2Pet. 1:17 [b]John 14:12

21 [a]Rom. 4:17; 8:11 [b]John 11:25

22 "For not even the Father judges[2919] anyone, but [a]He has [pfi]given all judgment[2920] to the Son,

23 in order that all may [psa]honor the Son, even as they honor the Father. [a]He who does not [ppt]honor the Son does not honor the Father who [apt]sent Him.

24 "Truly, truly, I say to you, he who [ppt]hears My word, and [ppt] [a]believes[4100] Him who [apt]sent Me, has eternal[166] life,[2222] and [b]does not come into judgment,[2920] but has [pfi] [c]passed[3327] out of death[2288] into life.

Two Resurrections

25 "Truly, truly, I say to you, [a]an hour is coming and now is, when [b]the dead shall hear the voice of the Son[5207] of God; and those who [apt] [c]hear shall live.[2198]

26 "For just as the Father has life in Himself, even so He [ao] [a]gave to the Son also to [pinf]have life in Himself;

27 and He [ao]gave Him authority[1849] to [pinf] [a]execute[4160] judgment,[2920] because He is [1]*the* [an]Son of Man.

28 "Do not [pim]marvel at this; for [a]an hour[5610] is coming, in which [b]all who are in the tombs shall hear His voice,

29 and shall come forth; [a]those who [apt]did the good[18] *deeds* to a resurrection[386] of life, those who [apt]committed[4238] the evil[5337] *deeds* to a resurrection of judgment.[2920]

30 [epn]"[a]I can [pinf]do nothing on My own initiative. As I hear, I judge; and [b]My judgment[2920] is just,[1342] because I do not seek My own will,[2307] but [c]the will of Him who [apt]sent Me.

31 "[a]If I *alone* bear witness of Myself, My testimony[3141] is not [1]true.

32 "There is [a]another who [pfi]bears witness[3140] of Me, and I know that the testimony which He bears of Me is true.

Witness of John

33 "You have sent to John, and he [a]has borne witness to the truth.[225]

22 [a]John 5:27; 9:39; Acts 10:42; 17:31
23 [a]Luke 10:16; 1John 2:23
24 [a]John 3:18; 12:44; 20:31; 1John 5:13 [b]John 3:18 [c]1John 3:14
25 [a]John 4:21, 23; 5:28 [b]Luke 15:24 [c]John 6:60; 8:43, 47; 9:27
26 [a]John 1:4; 6:57
27 [1]Or, *a son of man* [a]John 9:39; Acts 10:42; 17:31
28 [a]John 4:21 [b]John 11:24; 1Cor. 15:52
29 [a]Dan. 12:2; Matt. 25:46; Acts 24:15
30 [a]John 5:19 [b]John 8:16 [c]John 4:34; 6:38
31 [1]I.e., admissible as legal evidence [a]John 8:14
32 [a]John 5:37
33 [a]John 1:7, 15, 19, 32; 3:26-30
34 [a]John 5:32; 1John 5:9
35 [a]2Sam. 21:17; 2Pet. 1:19 [b]Mark 1:5
36 [a]Matt. 11:4; John 2:23; 10:25, 38; 14:11; 15:24 [b]John 4:34 [c]John 3:17
37 [a]Matt. 3:17; Mark 1:11; Luke 3:22; 24:27; John 8:18; 1John 5:9
38 [a]1John 2:14 [b]John 3:17
39 [1]Or, (a command) *Search the Scriptures!* [a]John 7:52; Rom. 2:17ff. [b]Luke 24:25, 27; Acts 13:27
41 [a]John 5:44; 7:18; 1Thess. 2:6
43 [a]Matt. 24:5
44 [1]Or, *honor* or *fame* [a]John 5:41 [b]Rom. 2:29 [c]John 17:3; 1Tim. 1:17

34 "But [a]the witness[3141] which I receive is not from man, but I say these things that you may be [asbp]saved.[4982]

35 "He was [a]the lamp that was burning and was shining[5316] and you [b]were [ao]willing to [ainf]rejoice[21] for a while[5610] in his light.[5457]

Witness of Works

36 "But the witness[3141] which I have is greater than *that of* John; for [a]the works[2041] which the Father has given Me [b]to [aosb]accomplish,[5048] the very works that I do, bear witness of Me, that the Father [c]has [pfi]sent Me.

Witness of the Father

37 "And the Father who [apt]sent Me, [a]He has [pfi]borne witness of Me. You have neither [pfi]heard[191] His voice at any time, nor [pfi]seen[3708] His form.[1491]

38 "And you do not have [a]His word[3056] abiding[3306] in you, for you do not believe Him whom He [ao] [b]sent.

Witness of the Scripture

39 "[1][a]You search the Scriptures, because you think that in them you have eternal life; and it is [b]these that bear [ppt]witness of Me;

40 and you are unwilling to [ainf]come to Me, that you may [psa]have life.[2222]

41 "[a]I do not receive glory from men;

42 but I [pfi]know you, that you do not have the love[26] of God[2316] in yourselves.

🔑 43 "I have [pfi]come in My Father's name, and you do not receive Me; [a]if another shall come in his own[2398] name, you will [fi]receive him.

44 "How can you [ainf]believe, when you [ppt] [a]receive [1]glory[1391] from one another, and you do not seek [b]the [1]glory that is from [c]the one and only God?

45 "Do not [pim]think that I will accuse[2723] you before the Father; the

🔑 **5:43** See note on Rev. 13.

one who [ppt]accuses you is [a]Moses, in
whom you have set your [pf]hope.[1679]
46 "For if you [ipf]believed[4100] Moses,
you would [ipf]believe Me; for [a]he wrote
of Me.
47 "But [a]if you do not believe his
writings,[1121] how will you believe My
words?"[4487]

Five Thousand Fed

6 After these things [a]Jesus went away
to the other side of [b]the Sea of Galilee (or [c]Tiberias).
2 And a great multitude was [pif]fol-
lowing Him, because they were [ipf]seeing
the [I][a]signs[4592] which He was performing
on those who were sick.
3 And [a]Jesus went up on the mountain, and there He [ipf]sat with His
disciples.[3101]
4 Now [a]the Passover,3957 the feast
of the Jews, was at hand.
5 Jesus therefore [apt]lifting up His
eyes, and [apt]seeing that a great multitude
was coming to Him, *said to [a]Philip,
"Where are we to buy bread, that these
may [psa]eat?"
6 And this He was saying to
[ppt] [a]test[3985] him; for He Himself knew
what He was [ipf]intending to [pinf]do.
7 [a]Philip answered Him, "[b]Two hundred [I]denarii1220 worth of bread is not
sufficient for them, for everyone to receive a little."
8 One of His [a]disciples, [b]Andrew,
Simon Peter's brother, *said to Him,
9 "There is a lad here who has five
barley loaves and two [a]fish, but what
are these for so many people?"
10 Jesus said, [aim]"Have the people
[ainf] [I]sit down." Now there was [a]much
grass in the place. So the men [I]sat down,
in number about [b]five thousand.
11 Jesus therefore took the loaves;
and [a]having given thanks, He distributed
to those who were [ppt]seated; likewise
also of the [b]fish as much as they wanted.
12 And when they were filled, He
*said to His [a]disciples, "Gather up the
leftover fragments[2801] that nothing may
be lost."
13 And so they gathered them up,
and filled twelve [a]baskets with fragments
from the five barley loaves, which were
left over by those who had eaten.
14 When therefore the people saw
the [I]sign which He had performed, they
said, "This is of a truth the [a]Prophet[4396]
who is to [ppt]come into the world."

Jesus Walks on the Water

🔑 15 Jesus therefore [apt]perceiving
that they were [pin] [I]intending to [pinf]come
and [pinf]take Him by force,[726] [a]to [aosb]make
Him king,[935] [b]withdrew again to [c]the
mountain by Himself alone.
16 Now when evening came, His
[a]disciples went down to the sea,
🔑 17 and after [apt]getting into a boat,
they *started to* [ipf]cross the sea [a]to Capernaum. And it had already [plpf]be-
come dark,[4653] and Jesus had not yet
[plpf]come[2064] to them.
18 And the sea *began* to be [ipf]stirred
up because a strong wind was
[ppt]blowing.[4154]
19 When therefore they had
[pfpp]rowed about[5613] [I]three or four
miles,4712 they *beheld Jesus [ppt]walking
on the sea and drawing near[1451] to the
boat; and they were frightened.[5399]
20 But He *said to them, "It is I;
[I][a]do not be [pim]afraid."
21 They were [ipf]willing therefore to
[ainf]receive Him into the boat; and immediately the boat [ao]was at the land to
which they were going.
22 The next day [a]the multitude that
[pfpp]stood on the other side of the sea
[ao]saw that there was no other small boat
there, except one, and that Jesus
[b]had not [ao]entered with His disciples[3101]
into the boat, but *that* His disciples had
[ao]gone away alone.
23 There came other small boats
from [a]Tiberias near[1451] to the place

45 [a]John 9:28; Rom. 2:17ff.
46 [a]Luke 24:27
47 [a]Luke 16:29, 31
1 [a]John 6:1-13: *Matt. 14:13-21; Mark 6:32-44; Luke 9:10-17* [b]Matt. 4:18; Luke 5:1 [c]John 6:23; 21:1
2 [I]Or, *attesting miracles* [a]John 2:11, 23; 3:2; 6:14, 30; 11:47; 12:18, 37; 20:30
3 [a]Matt. 5:1; Mark 3:13; Luke 6:12; 9:28; John 6:15
4 [a]Deut. 16:1; John 2:13
5 [a]John 1:43
6 [a]2Cor. 13:5; Rev. 2:2
7 [I]The denarius was equivalent to one day's wage [a]John 1:43 [b]Mark 6:37
8 [a]John 2:2 [b]John 1:40
9 [a]John 6:11; 21:9, 10, 13
10 [I]Lit., *recline(d)* [a]Mark 6:39 [b]Matt. 14:21
11 [a]Matt. 15:36; John 6:23 [b]John 6:9; 21:9, 10, 13
12 [a]John 2:2
13 [a]Matt. 14:20
14 [I]Or, *attesting miracle* [a]Matt. 11:3; 21:11; John 1:21
15 [I]Or, *about* [a]John 18:36f. [b]John 6:15-21: *Matt. 14:22-33; Mark 6:45-51* [c]John 6:3
16 [a]John 2:2
17 [a]Mark 6:45; John 6:24, 59
19 [I]I.e., 25 or 30 stadia
20 [I]Or, *stop fearing* [a]Matt. 14:27
22 [a]John 6:2 [b]John 6:15ff.
23 [a]John 6:1

🔑 **6:15** See note on I Thess. 4:17.
🔑 **6:17** See general remarks on I John.

where they [ao]ate the bread after the [b]Lord [c]had [apt]given thanks.

24 When the multitude therefore saw that Jesus was not there, nor His disciples, they themselves got into the small boats, and [a]came to Capernaum, seeking Jesus.

25 And when they [apt]found Him on the other side of the sea, they said to Him, "[a]Rabbi, when did You [pfi]get here?"[5602]

Words to the People

26 Jesus answered them and said, "Truly,[281] truly, I say to you, you [a]seek Me, not because you saw [b]signs, but because you ate of the loaves, and were filled.

27 "Do not [pim] [a]work[2038] for the food which [ppt]perishes, but for the food which [ppt]endures to [b]eternal life,[2222] which [c]the Son of Man shall give to you, for on Him the Father,[3962] *even* God, [d]has set His seal."

28 They said therefore to Him, "What shall we [psa]do, that we may [psa]work[2038] the works[2041] of God?"

29 Jesus answered and said to them, "This is [a]the work of God, that you [aosb]believe[4100] in Him whom He [b]has [ao]sent."

30 They said therefore to Him, "[a]What then do You do for a [b]sign,[4592] that we may [aosb]see, and believe You? What work do You perform?

31 "[a]Our fathers ate the manna[3131] in the wilderness; as it is written, '[b]HE GAVE THEM BREAD[740] OUT OF HEAVEN[3772] TO [ainf]EAT.'"

32 Jesus therefore said to them, "Truly, truly, I say to you, it is not Moses who has [pfi]given you the bread out of heaven,[3772] but it is My Father who gives you the true[228] bread out of heaven.

33 "For the bread of God[2316] is [1]that which [ppt] [a]comes down out of heaven, and [ppt]gives life[2222] to the world."[2889]

34 They said therefore to Him, "Lord, evermore [aim] [a]give us this bread."

35 Jesus said to them, [epn]"[a]I am the bread of life; he who [ppt]comes[2064] to Me shall not [efn]hunger, and he who [ppt]believes in Me [b]shall never [ft]thirst.

36 "But [a]I said to you, that you have [pfi]seen Me, and yet do not believe.

37 "[a]All that the Father[3962] gives Me shall come to Me, and the one who [ppt]comes to Me I will certainly not [efn]cast out.

38 "For [a]I have come down from heaven,[3772] [b]not to [pso]do My own will,[2307] but [c]the will of Him who [apt] [d]sent Me.

39 "And this is the will of Him who [apt]sent Me, that of [a]all that He has [pfi]given Me I [aosb] [b]lose nothing, but [c]raise[450] it up on the last[2078] day.

40 "For this is the will of My Father, that everyone who [ppt] [a]beholds the Son and [ppt] [b]believes[4100] in Him, may [psa]have eternal[166] life;[2222] and I Myself will [c]raise[450] him up on the last day."

Words to the Jews

41 [a]The Jews therefore were [ipf]grumbling about Him, because He said, "I am the bread that [apt] [b]came down out of heaven."

42 And they were saying, "[a]Is not this Jesus, the son of Joseph, whose father and mother [b]we know? How does He now say, '[c]I have [pfi]come down out of heaven'?"

43 Jesus answered and said to them, "Do not [pim]grumble among yourselves.

44 "No one can [ainf]come to Me, unless the Father who [apt]sent Me [aosb] [a]draws[1670] him; and I will [b]raise him up on the last day.

45 "It is written[1125] [a]in the prophets,[4396] '[b]AND THEY SHALL ALL BE [c]TAUGHT OF GOD.' Everyone who has [apt]heard[191] and [apt]learned[3129] from the Father, comes to Me.

46 "[a]Not that any man has [pfi]seen[3708] the Father,[3962] except[1508] the One who is from[3844] God; He has [pfi]seen the Father.

---

23 [b]Luke 7:13 [c]John 6:11
24 [a]Matt. 14:34; Mark 6:53; John 6:17, 59
25 [a]Matt. 23:7
26 [a]John 6:24 [b]John 6:2, 14, 30
27 [a]Is. 55:2 [b]John 3:15f.; 4:14; 6:40, 47, 54; 10:28; 17:2f. [c]Matt. 8:20; John 6:53, 62 [d]John 3:33
29 [a]1 Thess. 1:3; James 2:22; 1 John 3:23; Rev. 2:26 [b]John 3:17
30 [a]Matt. 12:38 [b]John 6:2, 14, 26
31 [a]Ex. 16:4, 15, 21; Num. 11:8; John 6:49, 58 [b]Ps. 78:24; Ex. 16:4, 15; Neh. 9:15; Ps. 105:40
33 [1]Or, *He who comes* [a]John 6:41, 50
34 [a]John 4:15
35 [a]John 6:48, 51 [b]John 4:14
36 [a]John 6:26
37 [a]John 6:39; 17:2, 24
38 [a]John 3:13 [b]Matt. 26:39 [c]John 4:34; 5:30 [d]John 6:29
39 [a]John 6:37; 17:2, 24 [b]John 17:12; 18:9 [c]Matt. 10:15; John 6:40, 44, 54; 11:24
40 [a]John 12:45; 14:17, 19 [b]John 3:16 [c]Matt. 10:15; John 6:39, 44, 54; 11:24
41 [a]John 1:19; 6:52 [b]John 6:33, 51, 58
42 [a]Luke 4:22 [b]John 7:27f. [c]John 6:38, 62
44 [a]Jer. 31:3; Hos. 11:4; John 6:65; 12:32 [b]John 6:39
45 [a]Acts 7:42; 13:40; Heb. 8:11 [b]Is. 54:13; Jer. 31:34 [c]Phil. 3:15; 1 Thess. 4:9; 1 John 2:27
46 [a]John 1:18

47 "Truly,281 truly, I say to you, he who [ppt]believes [a]has eternal life.

48 "[a]I am the bread of life.2222

49 "[a]Your fathers ate the manna3131 in the wilderness, and they [ao]died.599

50 "This is the bread which [ppt] [a]comes down out of heaven, so that one may [aosb]eat of it and [b]not [aosb]die.

51 "[a]I am the living2198 bread that [apt] [b]came down out of heaven; if anyone [aosb]eats of this bread, [c]he shall live2198 forever;165 and the bread also which I shall give [d]for the life of the world2889 is [e]My flesh."4561

52 [a]The Jews therefore [b]*began* to [ipf]argue with one another, saying, "How can this man [ainf]give us *His* flesh to [pinf]eat?"

53 Jesus therefore said to them, "Truly, truly, I say to you, unless you [aosb]eat the flesh of [a]the Son of Man and [aosb]drink His blood,129 you have no life in yourselves.

54 "He who [ppt]eats My flesh and [ppt]drinks My blood has eternal life, and I will [a]raise him up on the last day.

55 "For My flesh is true food, and My blood is true drink.

56 "He who eats My flesh and drinks My blood [a]abides3306 in Me, and I in him.

57 "As the [a]living2198 Father [ao] [b]sent Me, and I live because of the Father, so he who [ppt]eats Me, he also shall live because of Me.

58 "This is the bread which [apt] [a]came down out of heaven; not as [b]the fathers ate, and [ao]died, he who [ppt]eats this bread [c]shall live2198 forever."

Words to the Disciples

59 These things He said [a]in the synagogue,4864 as He [ppt]taught1321 [b]in Capernaum.

60 Many therefore of His [a]disciples,3101 when they heard *this* said, "[b]This is a difficult4642 statement;3056 who can [pinf]listen191 to it?"

61 But Jesus, [a]conscious that His disciples grumbled at this, said to them, "Does this [b]cause you to stumble?4624

62 "*What* then if you should [psa]behold [a]the Son of Man [ppt] [b]ascending where He was before?

63 "[a]It is the Spirit4151 who [ppt]gives life;2227 the flesh4561 profits nothing; [b]the words that I have spoken to you are spirit4151 and are life.2222

64 "But there are [a]some of you who do not believe." For Jesus [b]knew from the beginning who they were who did not [ppt]believe, and [c]who it was that would [1]betray Him.

65 And He was saying, "For this reason I have [a]said to you, that no one can come to Me, unless [b]it has been granted him from the Father."

Peter's Confession of Faith

66 As a result of this many of His [a]disciples3101 [b]withdrew, and were not [ipf]walking with3326 Him anymore.

67 Jesus said therefore to [a]the twelve, "You do not [pin]want to [ainf]go away also, do you?"

68 [a]Simon Peter answered Him, "Lord, to whom shall we go? You have [b]words4487 of eternal166 life.2222

69 "And we have [pfi]believed4100 and have come to [pfi]know that You are [a]the Holy One5547 of God."2316

70 Jesus answered them, "[a]Did I Myself not [ao]choose you, [b]the twelve, and *yet* one of you is [c]a devil?"1228

71 Now He meant Judas [a]*the son* of Simon Iscariot, for he, [b]one of [c]the twelve, [ipf] [1]was going3195 to [pinf]betray Him.

Jesus Teaches at the Feast

7 And after these things Jesus [a]was [ipf]walking in Galilee; for He was unwilling to walk in Judea,2449 because [b]the Jews [c]were [ipf]seeking to kill Him.

2 Now the feast of the Jews, [a]the Feast of Booths,4634 was at hand.

---

47 [a]John 3:36; 5:24; 6:51, 58; 11:26
48 [a]John 6:35, 51
49 [a]John 6:31, 58
50 [a]John 6:33 [b]John 3:36; 5:24; 6:47, 51, 58; 11:26
51 [a]John 6:35, 48 [b]John 6:41, 58 [c]John 3:36; 5:24; 6:47, 58; 11:26 [d]John 1:29; 3:14f.; Heb. 10:10; 1John 4:10 [e]John 6:53-56
52 [a]John 1:19; 6:41 [b]John 9:16; 10:19
53 [a]Matt. 8:20; John 6:27, 62
54 [a]John 6:39
56 [a]John 15:4f.; 17:23; 1John 2:24; 3:24; 4:15f.
57 [a]Matt. 16:16; John 5:26 [b]John 3:17; 6:29, 38
58 [a]John 6:33, 41, 51 [b]John 6:31, 49 [c]John 3:36; 5:24; 6:47, 51; 11:26
59 [a]Matt. 4:23 [b]John 6:24
60 [a]John 2:2; 6:66; 7:3 [b]John 6:52
61 [a]John 6:64 [b]Matt. 11:6
62 [a]Matt. 8:20; John 6:27, 53 [b]Mark 16:19; John 3:13
63 [a]2Cor. 3:6 [b]John 6:68
64 [1]Or, *deliver Him up* [a]John 6:60, 66 [b]John 2:25 [c]Matt. 10:4; John 6:71; 13:11
65 [a]John 6:37, 44 [b]Matt. 13:11; John 3:27
66 [a]John 2:2; 7:3 [b]John 6:60, 64
67 [a]Matt. 10:2; John 2:2; 6:70f.; 20:24
68 [a]Matt. 16:16 [b]John 6:63; 12:49f.; 17:8
69 [a]Mark 1:24; 8:29; Luke 9:20
70 [a]John 15:16, 19 [b]Matt. 10:2; John 2:2; 6:71; 20:24 [c]John 8:44; 13:2, 27; 17:12
71 [1]Or, *was intending to* [a]John 12:4; 13:2, 26 [b]Mark 14:10 [c]Matt. 10:2; John 2:2; 6:70; 20:24

1 [a]John 4:3; 6:1; 11:54 [b]John 1:19; 7:11, 13, 15, 35 [c]John 5:18; 7:19; 8:37, 40; 11:53
2 [a]Lev. 23:34; Deut. 16:13, 16; Zech. 14:16-19

3 His [a]brothers[80] therefore said to Him, "Depart from here, and go into Judea, that Your [b]disciples[3101] also may behold Your works[2041] which You are doing.

4 "For no one does anything in secret, [I]when he himself seeks to be *known* publicly. If You do these things, [aim]show[5319] Yourself to the world."

5 For not even His [a]brothers were [ipf]believing[4100] in Him.

6 Jesus therefore *said to them, "[a]My time[2540] is not yet at hand, but your time is always opportune.

7 "[a]The world[2889] cannot [pinf]hate you; but it hates Me because I testify[3140] of it, that [b]its deeds are evil.[4190]

8 "Go up to the feast yourselves; I do not go up[I] to this feast because [a]My time has not yet [pfip]fully come."[4137]

9 And having said these things to them, He stayed[3306] in Galilee.

10 But when His [a]brothers had gone up to the feast, then He Himself also went up, not publicly, but as it were, in secret.

11 [a]The Jews therefore [b]were [ipf]seeking Him at the feast, and were saying, "Where is He?"

12 And there was much grumbling among the multitudes concerning Him; [a]some were saying, "He is a good[18] man"; others were saying, "No, on the contrary, He leads the multitude astray."

13 Yet[3305] no one was [ipf]speaking openly of Him for [a]fear[5401] of the Jews.

14 But when it was now the midst of the feast Jesus went up into the temple,[2411] and *began to* [ipf] [a]teach.[1321]

15 [a]The Jews therefore were [ipf]marveling, saying, "How has this man [b]become learned, having never been [pfp]educated?"[3129]

16 Jesus therefore answered them, and said, "[a]My teaching[1322] is not Mine, but His who sent Me.

17 "[a]If any man is [psa]willing to [pinf]do His will,[2307] he shall know[1097] of the teaching, whether it is of God, or *whether* I speak from Myself.

🗝 18 "He who [ppt]speaks from himself [pin] [a]seeks his own glory;[1391] but He who is seeking the glory of the One who sent Him, He is true, and there is no unrighteousness[93] in Him.

19 "[a]Did not Moses [ao]give you the Law,[3551] and *yet* none of you carries out the Law? Why do you [b]seek to [ainf]kill Me?"

20 The multitude answered, "[a]You [I]have a demon![1140] Who seeks to kill You?"

21 Jesus answered and said to them, "I did [a]one [I]deed,[2041] and you all marvel.

22 "On this account [a]Moses has [pf]given you circumcision[4061] (not because it is from Moses, but from [b]the fathers), and on *the* Sabbath[4521] you circumcise[4059] a man.

23 "[a]If a man receives circumcision[4061] on *the* Sabbath that the Law of Moses may not be broken,[3089] are you angry with Me because I [ao]made an entire[3650] man well[5199] on *the* Sabbath?

24 "Do not [pim] [a]judge[2919] according to appearance, but [I]judge with [art]righteous[1342] judgment."[2920]

25 Therefore some of the people of Jerusalem were saying, "Is this not the man whom they are seeking to kill?

26 "And look, He is speaking publicly, and they are saying nothing to Him. [a]The rulers[758] do not really [ao]know[1097] that this is [I]the Christ,[5547] do they?

27 "However,[235] [a]we know where this man is from; but whenever the Christ may [psa]come, no one knows where He is from."

28 Jesus therefore cried out in the temple,[2411] [ppt] [a]teaching[1321] and saying, "[b]You both know[1492] Me and know where I am from; and [c]I have not [pf]come of Myself, but He who sent Me is true,[228] whom you do not know.

29 "[a]I know Him; because [b]I am from Him, and [c]He [ao]sent Me."

30 They [a]were [ipf]seeking therefore

3 [a]Matt. 12:46; Mark 3:21; John 7:5, 10 [b]John 6:60
4 [I]Lit., *and*
5 [a]Matt. 12:46; Mark 3:21; John 7:3, 10
6 [a]Matt. 26:18; John 2:4; 7:8, 30
7 [a]John 15:18f. [b]John 3:19f.
8 [I]Some authorities add *yet* [a]John 7:6
10 [a]Matt. 12:46; Mark 3:21; John 7:3, 5
11 [a]John 7:13, 15, 35 [b]John 11:56
12 [a]John 7:40-43
13 [a]John 9:22; 12:42; 19:38; 20:19
14 [a]Matt. 26:55; John 7:28
15 [a]John 1:19; 7:11, 13, 35 [b]Acts 26:24
16 [a]John 3:11
17 [a]Ps. 25:9, 14; Prov. 3:32; Dan. 12:10; John 3:21; 8:43f.
18 [a]John 5:41; 8:50, 54; 12:43
19 [a]John 1:17 [b]Mark 11:18; John 7:1
20 [I]Or, *are demented* [a]Matt. 11:18; John 8:48f., 52; 10:20
21 [I]Or, *work* [a]John 5:2-9, 16; 7:23
22 [a]Lev. 12:3 [b]Gen. 17:10ff.; 21:4; Acts 7:8
23 [a]Matt. 12:2; John 5:9, 10
24 [I]Lit., *judge the righteous judgment* [a]Lev. 19:15; Is. 11:3; Zech. 7:9; John 8:15
26 [I]I.e., the Messiah [a]Luke 23:13; John 3:1
27 [a]John 6:42; 7:41f.; 9:29
28 [a]John 7:14 [b]John 6:42; 7:14f.; 9:29 [c]John 8:42
29 [a]Matt. 11:27; John 8:55; 17:25 [b]John 6:46 [c]John 3:17
30 [a]Matt. 21:46; John 7:32, 44; 10:39

🗝 **7:18** See note on justification on Romans.

to [ainf]seize Him; and no man laid his hand
on Him, because His [b]hour[5610] had not
yet [plpf]come.
31 But [a]many of the multitude
believed[4100] in Him; and they were saying, "[b]When [I]the Christ shall [aosb]come,
He will not perform more [IIc]signs[4592]
than those which this man [ao]has, will
He?"
32 The Pharisees heard the multitude [ppt]muttering these things about
Him; and the chief priests and the Pharisees sent [a]officers to [b]seize Him.
33 Jesus therefore said, "[a]For a little
while[5550] longer I am with you, then
[b]I go to Him who sent Me.
34 "[a]You shall seek Me, and shall
not find Me; and where I am, you cannot
[ainf]come."
35 [a]The Jews therefore said to one
another, "[b]Where does this man intend
to go that we shall not find Him? He is
not intending to go to [c]the Dispersion
among [d]the Greeks, and [pinf]teach[1321] the
Greeks, is He?
36 "What is this statement that He
said, '[a]You will seek Me, and will not
find Me; and where I am, you cannot
come'?"
37 Now on [a]the last day, the great
day of the feast, Jesus stood and cried
out, saying, "[b]If any man is thirsty,
[I]let him come[2064] to Me and [pim]drink.
38 "He who [ppt]believes[4100] in Me,
[a]as the Scripture[1124] said, 'From [I]his innermost being shall flow rivers of
[b]living[2198] water.' "
39 But this He spoke [a]of the Spirit,
whom those who [ppt]believed in Him
[ipf]were to [pinf]receive; [I]for [b]the [an]Spirit[4151]
was not yet *given,* because Jesus was
not yet [aop] [c]glorified.[1392]

Division of People over Jesus

40 *Some* of the multitude therefore,
when they heard these wórds, were saying, "This certainly is [a]the Prophet."[4396]
41 Others were saying, "This is
[I]the Christ." Still others were saying,
"[a]Surely [I]the Christ[5547] is not going to
come from Galilee, is He?
42 "Has not the Scripture[1124] said
that the Christ comes from [a]the offspring[4690] of David, and from Bethlehem, the village where David was?"
43 So [a]there arose a division[4978] in
the multitude because of Him.
44 And [a]some of them [ipf]wanted to
[ainf]seize Him, but no one [ao]laid hands
on Him.
45 The [a]officers therefore came to
the chief priests and Pharisees, and they
said to them, "Why did you not bring
Him?"
46 The [a]officers answered, "[b]Never
did a man[444] speak the way this man
speaks."
47 The Pharisees therefore answered them, "[a]You have not also been
[pfip]led astray, have you?
48 "[a]No one of [b]the rulers or Pharisees has believed[4100] in Him, has he?
49 "But this multitude which does
not [ppt]know[1097] the Law[3551] is accursed."
50 [a]Nicodemus *said to them (he
who [apt]came to Him before, being one
of them),
51 "[a]Our Law[3551] does not judge[2919]
a man, unless it first [aosb]hears from him
and [aosb]knows what he is doing, does
it?"
52 They answered and said to him,
"[a]You are not also from Galilee, are
you? Search, and see that no prophet
[pfip]arises out of Galilee."
53 [[I]And everyone went to his
home.

The Adulterous Woman

8 But Jesus went to [a]the Mount of
Olives.
2 And early in the morning He came
again into the temple,[2411] and all the people were [ipf]coming to Him; and [a]He sat
down and *began* to [ipf]teach[1321] them.
3 And the scribes[1122] and the Pharisees *brought a woman [pfpp]caught[2638]

30 [b]John 7:6; 8:20
31 [I]I.e., the Messiah [II]Or, *attesting miracles* [a]John 2:23; 8:30; 10:42; 11:45; 12:11, 42 [b]John 7:26 [c]John 2:11
32 [a]Matt. 26:58; John 7:45f. [b]Matt. 12:14
33 [a]John 12:35; 13:33; 14:19; 16:16-19 [b]John 14:12, 28; 16:5, 10, 17, 28; 20:17
34 [a]John 7:36; 8:21; 13:33
35 [a]John 7:1 [b]John 8:22 [c]Ps. 147:2; Is. 11:12; 56:8; Zeph. 3:10; James 1:1; 1Pet. 1:1 [d]John 12:20; Acts 14:1; 17:4; 18:4; Rom. 1:16
36 [a]John 7:34; 8:21; 13:33
37 [I]I.e., let him keep coming to Me and let him keep drinking [a]Lev. 23:36; Num. 29:35; Neh. 8:18 [b]John 4:10, 14; 6:35
38 [I]Lit., *out of his belly* [a]Is. 44:3; 55:1; 58:11 [b]John 4:10
39 [I]Other mss. read *for the Holy Spirit was not yet given* [a]Joel 2:28; John 1:33 [b]John 20:22; Acts 1:4f.; 2:4, 33; 19:2 [c]John 12:16, 23; 13:31f.; 16:14; 17:1
40 [a]Matt. 21:11; John 1:21
41 [I]I.e., the Messiah [a]John 1:46; 7:52
42 [a]Ps. 89:4; Mic. 5:2; Matt. 1:1; 2:5f.; Luke 2:4ff.
43 [a]John 9:16; 10:19
44 [a]John 7:30
45 [a]John 7:32
46 [a]John 7:32 [b]Matt. 7:28
47 [a]John 7:12
48 [a]John 12:42 [b]Luke 23:13; John 7:26
50 [a]John 3:1; 19:39
51 [a]Ex. 23:1; Deut. 17:6; 19:15; Prov. 18:13; Acts 23:3 **52** [a]John 1:46; 7:41 **53** [I]John 7:53-8:11 is not found in most of the old mss. **1** [a]Matt. 21:1 **2** [a]Matt. 26:55; John 8:20

in adultery, and having [apt]set her in the
midst,
4 they *said to Him, "Teacher, this
woman has been [ppp]caught in adultery,
in the very act.
5 "Now in the Law[3551] [a]Moses commanded us to [pinf]stone such women;
what then do You say?"
6 And they were saying this,
[a]testing[3985] Him, [b]in order that they
might [aosb]have grounds for [pinf]accusing
Him. But Jesus [apt]stooped[2955] down, and
with His finger [ipf]wrote[1125] on the
ground.
7 But when they persisted in asking
Him, [a]He straightened up, and said to
them, "[b]He who is without sin[361] among
you, let him *be the* [c]first to [aim]throw[906]
a stone at her."
8 And again He stooped down, and
[ipf]wrote on the ground.
9 And when they [ppt]heard it, they
began to go out one by one, beginning
with the older[4245] ones, and He was left
alone, and the woman, where she was,
in the midst.
10 And [a]straightening up, Jesus said
to her, "Woman, where are they? Did
no one condemn[2632] you?"
11 And she said, "No one, [I]Lord."
And Jesus said, "[a]Neither do I condemn[2632] you; [pim]go your way. From now
on [pim] [b]sin[264] no more."]

Jesus Is the Light of the World

🔑 **12** Again therefore Jesus spoke to
them, saying, "[a]I am the light[5457] of the
world;[2889] [b]he who [ppt]follows[190] Me shall
not [efn]walk in the darkness,[4653] but shall
have the light of life."[2222]
13 The Pharisees therefore said to
Him, "[a]You are bearing witness of Yourself; Your witness[3141] is not [I]true."
14 Jesus answered and said to them,
"[a]Even if I bear witness of Myself, My
witness is true; for I know [b]where I
came from, and where I am going; but
[c]you do not know where I come from,
or where I am going.
15 "[a]You people judge[2919] [I]according
to the flesh;[4561] [b]I am not judging anyone.
16 "But even [a]if I do judge,[2919] My
judgment[2920] is true; for I am not alone
in it, but I and [I]He[3962] who [apt]sent Me.
17 "Even in [a]your law[3551] it has been
written, that the testimony[3141] of [b]two
men is [I]true.
18 "I am He who [ppt]bears witness
of Myself, and [a]the Father who [apt]sent
Me bears witness of Me."
19 And so they were saying to Him,
"Where is Your Father?" Jesus answered, "You know neither Me, nor My
Father; [a]if you knew Me, you would
know My Father also."
20 These words He spoke in
[a]the treasury, as [b]He taught in the temple; and no one seized Him, because
[c]His hour[5610] had not yet [plpf]come.
21 He said therefore again to them,
"I go away, and [a]you shall seek Me,
and [b]shall die[599] in your sin;[266] where I
am going, you cannot come."
22 Therefore [a]the Jews were saying, "Surely He will not kill Himself,
will He, since He says, '[b]Where I am
going, you cannot come'?"
23 And He was saying to them,
"[a]You are from below, I am from
above;[507] [b]you are of this world,[2889]
[c]I am not of this world.
24 "I said therefore to you, that you
[a]shall die in your sins; for unless
you [aosb]believe[4100] that [Ib]I am *He,* [c]you
shall die in your sins."
25 And so they were saying to Him,
"Who are You?" Jesus said to them,
"[I]What have I been saying to you *from*
the beginning?
26 "I have many things to [pinf]speak
and to [pinf]judge[2919] concerning you, but
[a]He who [apt]sent Me is true;[227] and
[b]the things which I [ao]heard from Him,
these I speak to the world."
27 They did not realize that He had
been speaking to them about the Father.
28 Jesus therefore said, "When you
[aosb] [a]lift up the Son of Man, then you

5 [a]Lev. 20:10; Deut. 22:22f.
6 [a]Matt. 16:1; 19:3; 22:18, 35; Mark 8:11; 10:2; 12:15; Luke 10:25; 11:16 [b]Mark 3:2
7 [a]John 8:10 [b]Matt. 7:1; Rom. 2:1 [c]Deut. 17:7
10 [a]John 8:7
11 [I]Or, *Sir* [a]John 3:17 [b]John 5:14
12 [a]John 1:4; 9:5; 12:35 [b]Matt. 5:14
13 [I]Or, *valid* [a]John 5:31
14 [a]John 18:37; Rev. 1:5; 3:14 [b]John 8:42; 13:3; 16:28 [c]John 7:28; 9:29
15 [I]I.e., a carnal standard [a]1Sam. 16:7; John 7:24 [b]John 3:17
16 [I]Many ancient mss. read *the Father who sent Me* [a]John 5:30
17 [I]I.e., valid or admissible [a]Deut. 17:6; 19:15 [b]Matt. 18:16
18 [a]John 5:37; 1John 5:9
19 [a]John 7:28; 8:55; 14:7, 9; 16:3
20 [a]Mark 12:41, 43; Luke 21:1 [b]John 7:14; 8:2 [c]John 7:30
21 [a]John 7:34 [b]John 8:24
22 [a]John 1:19; 8:48, 52, 57 [b]John 7:35
23 [a]John 3:31 [b]1John 4:5 [c]John 17:14, 16
24 [I]Most authorities associate this with Ex. 3:14, *I AM WHO I AM* [a]John 8:21 [b]Matt. 24:5; Mark 13:6; Luke 21:8; John 4:26; 8:28, 58; 13:19
25 [I]Or, *That which I have been saying to you from the beginning.*
26 [a]John 3:33; 7:28 [b]John 8:40; 12:49; 15:15
28 [a]John 3:14; 12:32

🔑 **8:12** See general remarks on I Jn.

will know that [I][b]I am *He,* and [c]I do nothing on My own initiative, but I speak
these things as the Father [ao]taught[1321]
Me.
29 "And He who sent Me is with
Me; [a]He [I]has not [ao]left Me alone, for
[b]I always do the things that are
pleasing[701] to Him."
30 As He [ppt]spoke these things,
[a]many came to believe[4100] in Him.

The Truth Shall Make You Free

31 Jesus therefore was saying to
those Jews who had [pfp]believed Him,
"[a]If you [aosb]abide in My word,[3056] *then*
you are truly [b]disciples[3101] of Mine;
32 and [a]you shall know the truth,[225]
and [b]the truth shall make you free."[1659]
33 They answered Him, "[a]We are
Abraham's offspring,[4690] and have never
yet been [pfi]enslaved[1398] to anyone; how
is it that You say, 'You shall become
free'?"[1658]
34 Jesus answered them, "Truly,281
truly, I say to you, [a]everyone who
[ppt]commits[4160] sin[266] is the [an]slave[1401]
of sin.
35 "And [a]the slave[1401] does not remain[3306] in the house forever;[165] [b]the
son[5207] does remain forever.
36 "If therefore the Son [a]shall make
you free, you shall be free indeed.
37 "I know that you are [a]Abraham's
offspring;[4690] yet [b]you seek to kill Me,
because My word [I]has no place in you.
38 "I speak the things which I have
seen [I]with *My* Father; therefore you also
do the things which you heard from
[a]*your* father."
39 They answered and said to Him,
"Abraham is [a]our father." Jesus *said
to them, "[b]If you are Abraham's children,[5043] [ipf]do the deeds of Abraham.
40 "But as it is, [a]you are seeking
to [ainf]kill Me, a man who has [pfi] [b]told
you the truth,[225] which I heard from
God; this Abraham did not do.
41 "You are doing the deeds of
[a]your father."[3962] They said to Him, "We
were not [pfip]born of fornication;4202
[b]we have one Father, *even* God."
42 Jesus said to them, "If God were
your Father, [a]you would [ipf]love[25] Me;
[b]for I [ao]proceeded forth and have come
from God, for I have [c]not even come
on My own initiative, but [I][d]He sent Me.
43 "Why do you not understand
[I][a]what I am saying?2981 *It is* because you
cannot [pinf] [b]hear[191] My word.[3056]
44 "[a]You are of [b]*your* father[3962] the
devil,[1228] and [c]you want[2309] to [pinf]do the
desires of your father. [d]He was a
murderer[443] from the beginning, and
does not stand[2476] in the truth,[225] because [e]there is no truth[225] in him. Whenever he speaks [I]a lie,5579 he [f]speaks from
his own *nature;* for he is a liar,5583 and
the father of [II]lies.
45 "But because [a]I speak the truth,
you do not believe Me.
46 "Which one of you convicts[1651]
Me of sin?[266] If [a]I speak truth, why do
you not believe Me?
47 "[a]He who is of God hears[191] the
words[4487] of God; for this reason you
do not hear[191] *them,* because you are
not of God."
48 [a]The Jews answered and said to
Him, "Do we not say rightly that You
are a [b]Samaritan and [c]have a demon?"1140
49 Jesus answered, "I do not
[a]have a demon;1140 but I honor My Father, and you dishonor Me.
50 "But [a]I do not seek My glory;[1391]
there is One who [ppt]seeks and [ppt]judges.
51 "Truly,281 truly, I say to you, if
anyone [aosb] [a]keeps My word he shall
never [b]see[2334] death."[2288]
52 [a]The Jews said to Him, "Now
we [pfi]know that You [b]have a demon.1140
Abraham [ao]died,[599] and the prophets[4396]
also; and You say, 'If anyone [c]keeps
My word, he shall never [d]taste[1089] of
death.'
53 "Surely You [a]are not greater than
our father Abraham, who [ao]died? The

28 [I]Lit., *I AM* (v. 24 note) [b]Matt. 24:5; Mark 13:6; Luke 21:8; John 4:26; 8:24, 58; 13:19 [c]John 3:11; 5:19
29 [I]Or, *did not leave* [a]John 8:16; 16:32 [b]John 4:34
30 [a]John 7:31
31 [a]John 15:7; 2John 9 [b]John 2:2
32 [a]John 1:14, 17 [b]John 8:36; Rom. 8:2; 2Cor. 3:17; Gal. 5:1, 13; James 2:12; 1Pet. 2:16
33 [a]Matt. 3:9; Luke 3:8; John 8:37, 39
34 [a]Rom. 6:16; 2Pet. 2:19
35 [a]Gen. 21:10; Gal. 4:30 [b]Luke 15:31
36 [a]John 8:32
37 [I]Or, *makes no progress* [a]Matt. 3:9; John 8:39 [b]John 7:1; 8:40
38 [I]Or, *in the presence of* [a]John 8:41, 44
39 [a]Matt. 3:9; John 8:37 [b]Rom. 9:7; Gal. 3:7
40 [a]John 7:1; 8:37 [b]John 8:26
41 [a]John 8:38, 44 [b]Deut. 32:6; Is. 63:16; 64:8
42 [I]Lit., *that One* [a]1John 5:1 [b]John 13:3; 16:28, 30; 17:8 [c]John 7:28 [d]John 3:17
43 [I]Or, *My mode of speaking* [a]John 8:33, 39, 41 [b]John 5:25
44 [I]Lit., *the lie* [II]Lit., *it* [a]1John 3:8 [b]John 8:38, 41 [c]John 7:17 [d]Gen. 3:4; 1John 3:8, 15 [e]1John 2:4 [f]Matt. 12:34
45 [a]John 18:37
46 [a]John 18:37
47 [a]1John 4:6
48 [a]John 1:19 [b]Matt. 10:5; John 4:9 [c]John 7:20
49 [a]John 7:20
50 [a]John 5:41; 8:54
51 [a]John 8:55; 14:23; 15:20; 17:6 [b]Matt. 16:28; Luke 2:26; John 8:52; Heb. 2:9; 11:5
52 [a]John 1:19 [b]John 7:20 [c]John 8:55; 14:23; 15:20; 17:6 [d]John 8:51
53 [a]John 4:12

8:31,32 See note on Gal. 3:22.

prophets [ao]died too; whom do You make Yourself out *to be*?"

54 Jesus answered, "[a]If I [ft]glorify[1392] Myself, My glory[1391] is nothing; [b]it is My Father who [ppt]glorifies Me, of whom you say, 'He is our God';

55 and [a]you have not come to know[1097] Him, [b]but I know[1492] Him; and if I say that I do not know Him, I shall be [c]a liar like you, [d]but I do know Him, and [d]keep His word.

56 "[a]Your father Abraham [b]rejoiced[21] [I]to see My day, and he saw *it* and was glad."

57 [a]The Jews therefore said to Him, "You are not yet fifty years old, and have You seen Abraham?"

58 Jesus said to them, "Truly, truly, I say to you, before Abraham [ainf I]was born, [a]I am."[1510]

59 Therefore they [a]picked up stones to throw[906] at Him; but Jesus [Ib]hid Himself, and [ao]went out of the temple[II].[2411]

Healing the Man Born Blind

9 And as He passed by, He saw a man blind from birth.

2 And His disciples asked[2065] Him, saying, "[a]Rabbi, who sinned,[264] [b]this man or his [c]parents, that he should be born blind?"

🔑 3 Jesus answered, "*It was* neither *that* this man [ao]sinned, nor his parents; but *it was* in order [a]that the works of God might be [asbp]displayed[5319] in him.

4 "We must [pinf]work[2038] the works of Him who sent Me, [a]as long as it is day;[2250] night is coming, when no man can work.

5 "While I am in the world, I am [a]the light[5457] of the world."

6 When He had said this, He [a]spat on the ground, and made clay of the spittle,[4427] and applied[2007] the clay to his eyes,

7 and said to him, "Go, wash[3538] in [a]the pool of Siloam" (which is translated,[2059] Sent). And so he went away and [b]washed, and [c]came *back* seeing.

8 The neighbors therefore, and those who previously saw him as a beggar, were saying, "Is not this the one who used to [ppt a]sit and [ppt]beg?"[4319]

9 Others were saying, "This is he," *still* others[243] were saying, "No, but he is like him." He kept saying, "I am the one."

10 Therefore they were saying to him, "How then were your eyes opened?"

11 He answered, "The man who is called Jesus made clay, and anointed my eyes, and said to me, 'Go to [a]Siloam, and wash'; so I went away and washed, and I [ao]received sight."[308]

12 And they said to him, "Where is He?" He *said, "I do not know."[1492]

Controversy over the Man

13 They *brought to the Pharisees him who was formerly blind.

14 [a]Now it was a Sabbath[4521] on the day when Jesus made the clay, and opened his eyes.

15 [a]Again, therefore, the Pharisees also were asking[2065] him how he [ao]received his sight. And he said to them, "He applied clay to my eyes, and I washed, and I see."

16 Therefore some of the Pharisees were saying, "This man is not from God, because He [a]does not keep[5083] the Sabbath." But others were saying, "How can a man who is a sinner[268] perform such [Ib]signs?"[4592] And [c]there was a division[4978] among them.

17 They *said therefore to the blind man [a]again, "What do you say about Him, since He [ao]opened your eyes?" And he said, "He is a [b]prophet."[4396]

18 [a]The Jews therefore did not believe[4100] *it* of him, that he had been blind, and had [ao]received sight, until they called the parents of the very one who had received his sight,

19 and questioned[2065] them, saying,

---

54 [a]John 8:50 [b]John 7:39
55 [a]John 8:19; 15:21 [b]John 7:29 [c]John 8:44 [d]John 8:51; 15:10
56 [I]Lit., *in order that he might see* [a]John 8:37, 39 [b]Matt. 13:17; Heb. 11:13
57 [a]John 1:19
58 [I]Lit., *came into being* [a]Ex. 3:14; John 1:1; 17:5, 24
59 [I]Lit., *was hidden* [II]Some mss. add *and going through the midst of them went His way and so passed by* [a]Matt. 12:14; John 10:31; 11:8 [b]John 12:36

2 [a]Matt. 23:7 [b]Luke 13:2; John 9:34; Acts 28:4 [c]Ex. 20:5
3 [a]John 11:4
4 [a]John 7:33; 11:9; 12:35; Gal. 6:10
5 [a]Matt. 5:14; John 1:4; 8:12; 12:46
6 [a]Mark 7:33; 8:23
7 [a]Neh. 3:15; Is. 8:6; Luke 13:4; John 9:11 [b]2Kin. 5:13f. [c]Is. 29:18; 35:5; 42:7; Matt. 11:5; John 11:37
8 [a]Acts 3:2, 10
11 [a]John 9:7
14 [a]John 5:9
15 [a]John 9:10
16 [I]Or, *attesting miracles* [a]Matt. 12:2; Luke 13:14; John 5:10; 7:23 [b]John 2:11 [c]John 6:52; 7:12, 43; 10:19
17 [a]John 9:15 [b]Deut. 18:15; Matt. 21:11
18 [a]John 1:19; 9:22

🔑 **9:3** See note on Js. 5:14,15.

"Is this your son,[5207] who you say was born blind? Then how does he now see?"[991]

20 His parents answered them and said, "We know that this is our son, and that he was born blind;

21 but how he now sees, we do not know; or who [ao]opened his eyes, we do not know. Ask[2065] him; he is of age, he shall speak for himself."

22 His parents said this because they [a]were afraid of the Jews; for the Jews [b]had already agreed, that if anyone should [aosb]confess[3670] Him to be [1]Christ,[5547] [c]he should be put out of the synagogue.[656]

23 For this reason his parents said, "[a]He is of age; ask him."

24 So a second time they called the man who had been blind, and said to him, "[a]Give glory[1391] to God; we know that [b]this man is a sinner."[268]

25 He therefore answered, "Whether He is a sinner, I do not know;[1492] one thing I do know, that, whereas I was [ppt]blind, now I see."

26 They said therefore to him, "What did He do to you? How did He open your eyes?"

27 He answered them, "[a]I told you already, and you did not [b]listen; why do you want to [pinf]hear *it* again? You do not want to [ainf]become His disciples[3101] too, do you?"

28 And they reviled[3058] him, and said, "You are His disciple, but [a]we are disciples[3101] of Moses.

29 "We know that God has spoken to Moses; but as for this man, [a]we do not know where He is from."

30 The man answered and said to them, "Well, here is an amazing thing, that you do not know where He is from, and *yet* He [ao]opened my eyes.

31 "We know that [a]God does not hear[191] sinners; but if anyone is God-fearing,[2318] and [psa]does His will,[2307] He hears[191] him.

32 "[1]Since the beginning of time it has never been heard that anyone opened the eyes of a person born blind.

33 "[a]If this man were not from God, He could [pinf]do nothing."

34 They answered and said to him, "[a]You were [aop]born[1080] entirely in sins,[266] and are you teaching[1321] us?" And they [b]put him out.

Jesus Affirms His Deity

35 Jesus heard that they had [a]put him out; and [apt]finding him, He said, "Do you believe[4100] in the [b]Son of Man?"

36 He answered and said, "And [a]who is He, [1]Lord, that I may [aosb]believe in Him?"

37 Jesus said to him, "You have both [pfi]seen[3706] Him, and [a]He is the one who is [ppt]talking with you."

38 And he said, "Lord, I believe." And he [a]worshiped[4352] Him.

39 And Jesus said, "[a]For judgment[2917] I [ao]came into this world,[2889] that [b]those who do not [ppt]see may [psa]see; and that [c]those who [ppt]see may [aosb]become blind."

40 Those of the Pharisees who were with Him heard these things, and said to Him, "[a]We are not blind too, are we?"

41 Jesus said to them, "[a]If you were blind, you would have no sin;[266] but since you say, '[b]We see,' your sin remains.[3306]

Parable of the Good Shepherd

10 "Truly,[281] truly, I say to you, he who does not [ppt]enter by the door into the fold of the sheep, but [ppt]climbs up some other way, he is [a]a thief[2812] and a robber.[3027]

2 "But he who enters by the door is [a]a shepherd of the sheep.

3 "To him the doorkeeper[2377] opens, and the sheep hear[191] [a]his voice, and he calls his own sheep by name, and [b]leads them out.[1806]

4 "When he [aosb]puts forth all his own, he goes before them, and the sheep follow[190] him because they know[1492] [a]his voice.

22 [1]I.e., the Messiah [a]John 7:13 [b]John 7:45-52 [c]Luke 6:22; John 12:42; 16:2
23 [a]John 9:21
24 [a]Josh. 7:19; Ezra 10:11; Rev. 11:13 [b]John 9:16
27 [a]John 9:15 [b]John 5:25
28 [a]John 5:45; Rom. 2:17
29 [a]John 8:14
31 [a]Job 27:8f.; 35:13; Ps. 34:15f.; 66:18; 145:19; Prov. 15:29; 28:9; Is. 1:15; James 5:16ff.
32 [1]Lit., *From antiquity it was not heard*
33 [a]John 3:2; 9:16
34 [a]John 9:2 [b]John 9:22, 35; 3 John 10
35 [a]John 9:22, 34; 3 John 10 [b]Matt. 4:3
36 [1]Or, *Sir* [a]Rom. 10:14
37 [a]John 4:26
38 [a]Matt. 8:2
39 [a]John 3:19; 5:22, 27 [b]Luke 4:18 [c]Matt. 13:13; 15:14
40 [a]Rom. 2:19
41 [a]John 15:22, 24 [b]Prov. 26:12
1 [a]John 10:8
2 [a]John 10:11f.
3 [a]John 10:4f., 16, 27 [b]John 10:9
4 [a]John 10:5, 16, 27

10:1-21 See notes on Gal. 3:22; II Pet. 2:19-22.

5 "And a stranger they simply will
not follow, but will flee from him, because they do not know [a]the voice of
strangers."
6 This [a]figure of speech[3942] Jesus
[ipf]spoke to them, but they did not understand what those things were which He
had been saying to them.
7 Jesus therefore said to them
again, "Truly, truly, I say to you, I am
[a]the door of the sheep.
8 "All who came before Me are
[a]thieves[2812] and robbers,[3027] but the
sheep did not hear[191] them.
9 "[a]I am the door; if anyone [aosb]en-
ters through Me, he shall be saved,[4982]
and shall go in and out, and find pasture.
10 "The thief comes only to steal,
and kill,[2380] and destroy;[622] I [ao]came that
they [a]might [psa]have life,[2222] and might
[psa] [I]have *it* abundantly.[4053]
11 "[a]I am the good shepherd; the
good shepherd [b]lays down His life[5590]
for the sheep.
🔑 12 "He who is a hireling, and not a
[a]shepherd, who is not the owner of the
sheep, beholds[2334] the wolf coming, and
leaves the sheep, and flees, and the wolf
snatches[726] them, and scatters *them.*
13 "*He flees* because he is a hireling,
and is not concerned[3199] about the
sheep.
14 "[a]I am the good shepherd; and
[b]I know[1097] My own, and My own
know[1097] Me,
15 even as [a]the Father [pin]knows[1097]
Me and I know[1097] the Father; and
[b]I lay down My life[5590] for the sheep.
16 "And I have [a]other[243] sheep,
which are not of this fold;[833] I must bring
them also, and they shall [ft]hear My voice;
and they shall become [b]one flock *with*
[c]one shepherd.
17 "For this reason the Father loves
Me, because I [a]lay down My life[5590] that
I may [asba]take it again.
18 "[a]No one [I]has [pin]taken it away
from Me, but I [b]lay it down on My own
initiative. I have authority[1849] to lay it
down, and I have authority[1849] to take
it up again. [c]This commandment I [ao]re-
ceived from My Father."
19 [a]There [ao]arose a division[4978]
again among the Jews because of these
words.
20 And many of them were [ipf]saying,
"He [a]has a demon[1140] and [b]is insane.[3105]
Why do you listen[191] to Him?"
21 Others[243] were [ipf]saying, "These
are not the sayings of one [ppt] [a]demon-
possessed. [b]A demon[1140] cannot [pinf]open
the eyes of the blind, can he?"

Jesus Asserts His Deity

22 At that time the Feast of the
Dedication[1456] took place at Jerusalem;
23 it was winter, and Jesus was
[ipf]walking in the temple[2441] in the portico
of [a]Solomon.
24 [a]The Jews therefore gathered
around Him, and were saying to Him,
"How long will You keep us in suspense?[142] If You are [I]the Christ,[5547]
tell us [b]plainly."
25 Jesus answered them, "[a]I told
you, and you do not [pin]believe;[4100]
[b]the works[2041] that I do in My Father's
name, these bear witness[3140] of Me.
26 "But you do not believe, because
[a]you are not of My sheep.
27 "My sheep [a]hear[191] My voice,
and [b]I know[1097] them, and they follow[190]
Me;
🔑 28 and I give [a]eternal[166] life[2222] to
them, and they shall never [efn]perish;[622]
and [b]no one shall [ft]snatch[726] them out
of My hand.
🔑 29 "[I]My Father, who has given *them*
to Me, is greater than all; and no one
is able to [pinf]snatch[726] *them* out of the
Father's hand.
30 "[a]I and the Father[3962] are
[n] [I]one."[1520]

5 [a]John 10:4, 16, 27
6 [a]John 16:25, 29; 2Pet. 2:22
7 [a]John 10:1f., 9
8 [a]Jer. 23:1f.; Ezek. 34:2ff.; John 10:1
9 [a]John 10:1f., 9
10 [I]Or, *have abundance* [a]John 5:40
11 [a]Is. 40:11; Ezek. 34:11-16, 23; John 10:14; Heb. 13:20; 1Pet. 5:4; Rev. 7:17 [b]John 10:15, 17, 18; 15:13; 1John 3:16
12 [a]John 10:2
14 [a]John 10:11 [b]John 10:27
15 [a]Matt. 11:27; Luke 10:22 [b]John 10:11, 17, 18
16 [a]Is. 56:8 [b]John 11:52; 17:20f.; Eph. 2:13-18; 1Pet. 2:25 [c]Ezek. 34:23; 37:24
17 [a]John 10:11, 15, 18
18 [I]Many Gr. mss. read *takes* [a]Matt. 26:53; John 2:19; 5:26 [b]John 10:11, 15, 17 [c]John 14:31; 15:10; Phil. 2:8; Heb. 5:8
19 [a]John 7:43; 9:16
20 [a]John 7:20 [b]Mark 3:21
21 [a]Matt. 4:24 [b]Ex. 4:11; John 9:32f.
23 [a]Acts 3:11; 5:12
24 [I]I.e., the Messiah [a]John 1:19; 10:31, 33 [b]Luke 22:67; John 16:25
25 [a]John 8:56, 58 [b]John 5:36; 10:38
26 [a]John 8:47
27 [a]John 10:4, 16 [b]John 10:14
28 [a]John 17:2f.; 1John 2:25; 5:11 [b]John 6:37, 39
29 [I]Some early mss. read *What My Father has given Me is greater than all*
30 [I]Lit., (neuter) *a unity;* or, *one essence* [a]John 17:21ff.

🔑 **10:12,28,29** See notes on Gal. 3:22; I Thess. 4:17; II Thess. 2:3 and also *harpazō* (726), to catch up or away.
🔑 **10:29-39** See note on Phil. 2:6-8.

31 The Jews [a]took up stones again to stone Him.

32 Jesus answered them, "I [ao]showed you many good works[2041] from the Father; for which of them are you stoning Me?"

33 The Jews answered Him, "For a good work we do not stone You, but for [a]blasphemy;[988] and because You, being a man, [b]make Yourself out *to be* God."[2316]

34 Jesus answered them, "Has it not been written in [a]your [b]Law,[3551] '[c]I SAID, YOU ARE GODS'?[2316]

35 "If he called them gods, to whom the word[3056] of God came (and the Scripture[1124] cannot be broken),[3289]

36 do you say of Him, whom the Father [ao] [a]sanctified[37] and [b]sent into the world, 'You are blaspheming,' because[3754] I said, '[c]I am the Son[5207] of God'?

37 "[a]If I do not do the works of My Father, do not believe Me;

38 but if I do them, though you do not [psa]believe Me, [pim]believe [a]the works, that you may [I]know and [psa]understand that [b]the Father is in Me, and I in the Father."

39 Therefore [a]they were [ipf]seeking again to [ainf]seize Him, and [b]He eluded their grasp.

40 And He went away [a]again beyond the Jordan to the place where John was first baptizing,[907] and He was staying[3306] there.

41 And many came to Him and were saying, "While John performed no [a]sign,[4592] yet [b]everything John said about this man was true."[227]

42 And [a]many believed in Him there.

The Death and Resurrection of Lazarus

11 Now a certain man was sick, Lazarus of [a]Bethany, the village of Mary and her sister [b]Martha.

2 And it was the Mary who [apt] [a]anointed[218] [b]the Lord with ointment, and wiped His feet with her hair, whose brother Lazarus was sick.

3 The sisters therefore sent to Him, saying, "[a]Lord, behold, [b]he whom You love[5368] is sick."

4 But when Jesus heard it, He said, "This sickness is not unto death,[2288] but for [a]the glory[1391] of God, that the Son[5207] of God may be [asbp]glorified[1392] by it."

5 Now Jesus [ipf]loved[25] [a]Martha, and her sister, and Lazarus.

6 When therefore He heard that he was sick, He stayed then two days *longer* in the place where He was.

7 Then after this He *said to the disciples,[3101] "[a]Let us go to Judea again."

8 The disciples *said to Him, "[a]Rabbi, the Jews were just now [ipf]seeking [b]to stone You, and are You going there[1563] again?"

9 Jesus answered, "[a]Are there not twelve hours in the day? If anyone [psa]walks in the day,[2250] he does not stumble,[4350] because he sees the light[5457] of this world.[2889]

10 "But if anyone walks in the night, he stumbles,[4350] because the light is not in him."

11 This He said, and after that He *said to them, "Our [a]friend Lazarus [b]has [pfip]fallen asleep; but I go, that I may awaken him out of sleep."

12 The disciples therefore said to Him, "Lord, if he has [pfip]fallen asleep, he will [I]recover."[4982]

13 Now[1161] [a]Jesus had [plpf]spoken of his death, but they thought that He was speaking of [I]literal sleep.

14 Then Jesus therefore said to them plainly, "Lazarus is [ao]dead,[599]

15 and I am glad for your sakes that I was not there, so that you may [aosb]believe;[4100] but let us go[71] to him."

16 [a]Thomas therefore, who is called [I][b]Didymus, said to *his* fellow disciples, "Let us also go, that we may die with Him."

17 So when Jesus came, He found that he had already [ppt]been in the tomb [a]four days.

18 Now [a]Bethany was near[1451] Jerusalem, about[5613] [I]two miles[4712] off;

---

31 [a]John 8:59
33 [a]Lev. 24:16 [b]John 5:18
34 [a]John 8:17 [b]John 12:34; 15:25; Rom. 3:19; 1Cor. 14:21 [c]Ps. 82:6
36 [a]Jer. 1:5; John 6:69 [b]John 3:17 [c]John 5:17f.; 10:30
37 [a]John 10:25; 15:24
38 [I]Lit., *know and continue knowing* [a]John 10:25; 14:11 [b]John 14:10f., 20; 17:21, 23
39 [a]John 7:30 [b]Luke 4:30; John 8:59
40 [a]John 1:28
41 [a]John 2:11 [b]John 1:27, 30, 34; 3:27-30
42 [a]John 7:31

1 [a]Matt. 21:17; John 11:18 [b]Luke 10:38; John 11:5, 19ff.
2 [a]Luke 7:38; John 12:3 [b]Luke 7:13; John 11:3, 21, 32; 13:13f.
3 [a]Luke 7:13; John 11:2, 21, 32; 13:13f. [b]John 11:5, 11, 36
4 [a]John 9:3; 10:38; 11:40
5 [a]John 11:1
7 [a]John 10:40
8 [a]Matt. 23:7 [b]John 8:59; 10:31
9 [a]Luke 13:33; John 9:4; 12:35
11 [a]John 11:3 [b]Matt. 27:52; Mark 5:39; John 11:13; Acts 7:60
12 [I]Lit., *be saved*
13 [I]Lit., *the slumber of sleep* [a]Matt. 9:24; Luke 8:52
16 [I]I.e., the Twin [a]Matt. 10:3; Mark 3:18; Luke 6:15; John 14:5; 20:26-28; Acts 1:13 [b]John 20:24; 21:2
17 [a]John 11:39
18 [I]I.e., 15 stadia (9,090 ft.) [a]John 11:1

19 and many of [a]the Jews had [plpf]come to [b]Martha and Mary, [c]to console them concerning *their* brother.

20 [a]Martha therefore, when she heard that Jesus was coming, went to meet Him; but [b]Mary still [ipf]sat in the house.

21 Martha therefore said to Jesus, "[a]Lord, [b]if You had [ipf]been here, my brother[80] would not have [plpf]died.[2348]

22 "Even now I know[1492] that [a]whatever You [aosb]ask[159] of God, God will give You."

23 Jesus *said to her, "Your brother shall rise again."[450]

24 Martha *said to Him, "[a]I know that he will rise again in the resurrection on the last[2078] day."

25 Jesus said to her, "[a]I am the resurrection[386] and the life;[2222] he who [ppt]believes[4100] in Me shall live[2198] even if he [aosb]dies,

26 and everyone who [ppt]lives[2198] and [ppt]believes in Me [a]shall never [efn]die.[599] Do you believe this?"

27 She *said to Him, "Yes, Lord; I have [pf]believed that You are [I][a]the Christ,[5547] the Son[5207] of God,[2316] *even* [II][b]He who [ppt]comes into the world."[2889]

28 And when she had said this, she [a]went away, and called Mary her sister, saying secretly, "[b]The Teacher is here, and is calling for you."

29 And when she heard it, she *arose quickly, and was coming to Him.

30 Now Jesus had not yet [plpf]come into the village, but [a]was still in the place where Martha met Him.

31 [a]The Jews then who were with her in the house, and [ppt] [b]consoling her, when they [apt]saw that Mary rose up quickly and went out, followed her, supposing that she was going to the tomb to [aosb] [I]weep there.

32 Therefore, when Mary came where Jesus was, she [apt]saw Him, and fell at His feet, saying to Him, "[a]Lord, [b]if You had [ipf]been here, my brother would not have died."[599]

33 When Jesus therefore saw her [I]weeping, and [a]the Jews who came with her, *also* [I]weeping, He [b]was deeply moved in spirit,[4151] and [II][c]was troubled,

34 and said, "Where have you [pf]laid him?" They *said to Him, "Lord, come and see."

35 Jesus [a]wept.

36 And so [a]the Jews were saying, "Behold how He [ipf] [I][b]loved[5368] him!"

37 But some of them said, "Could not this man, who [apt] [a]opened the eyes of him who was blind, [I]have [pinf]kept this man also from [aosb]dying?"

38 Jesus therefore again being deeply moved within, *came to the tomb. Now it was a [a]cave, and a stone was [ipf]lying against it.

39 Jesus *said, "Remove[142] the stone." Martha, the sister of the deceased, *said to Him, "Lord, by this time [I]there will be a stench, for he has been *dead* [a]four days."

40 Jesus *said to her, "[a]Did I not say to you, if you [aosb]believe,[4100] you will [ft]see the glory[1391] of God?"

41 And so they removed the [a]stone. And Jesus [b]raised His eyes, and said, "[c]Father, I thank[2168] Thee that Thou heardest[191] Me.

42 "And I knew that Thou hearest Me always; but [a]because of the people [pfp]standing around I said it, that they may [aosb]believe[4100] that [b]Thou didst [ao]send Me."

43 And when He had said these things, He cried out with a loud voice, "Lazarus, come forth."

44 He who had died came forth, [plpf] [a]bound hand and foot with wrappings; and [b]his face was wrapped around with a cloth. Jesus *said to them, "Unbind him, and let him go."

45 [a]Many therefore of the Jews, [b]who had [apt]come to Mary and [apt] [c]beheld what He had done, believed[4100] in Him.

46 But some of them went away to the [a]Pharisees, and told them the things which Jesus had [ao]done.

Conspiracy to Kill Jesus

47 Therefore [a]the chief priests[749] and the Pharisees [b]convened a [c]council, and were [ipf]saying, "What are we doing?

19 [a]John 1:19; 11:8 [b]John 11:1 [c]1Sam. 31:13; 1Chr. 10:12; Job 2:11; John 11:31
20 [a]Luke 10:38-42
21 [a]John 11:2 [b]John 11:32, 37
22 [a]John 9:31; 11:41f.
24 [a]Dan. 12:2; John 5:28f.; Acts 24:15
25 [a]John 1:4; 5:26; 6:39f.; Rev. 1:18
26 [a]John 6:47, 50, 51; 8:51
27 [I]I.e., the Messiah [II]The Coming One was the Messianic title [a]Matt. 16:16; Luke 2:11 [b]John 6:14
28 [a]John 11:30 [b]Matt. 26:18; Mark 14:14; Luke 22:11; John 13:13
30 [a]John 11:20
31 [I]Lit., *wail* [a]John 11:19, 33 [b]John 11:19
32 [a]John 11:2 [b]John 11:21
33 [I]Lit., *wailing* [II]Lit., *troubled Himself* [a]John 11:19 [b]John 11:38 [c]John 12:27; 13:21
35 [a]Luke 19:41; John 11:33
36 [I]Lit., *was loving* [a]John 11:19 [b]John 11:3
37 [I]Lit., *have caused that this man also not die* [a]John 9:7
38 [a]Matt. 27:60; Mark 15:46; Luke 24:2; John 20:1
39 [I]Lit., *he stinks* [a]John 11:17
40 [a]John 11:4, 23ff.
41 [a]Matt. 27:60; Mark 15:46; Luke 24:2; John 20:1 [b]John 17:1; Acts 7:55 [c]Matt. 11:25
42 [a]John 12:30; 17:21 [b]John 3:17
44 [a]John 19:40 [b]John 20:7
45 [a]John 7:31 [b]John 11:19; 12:17f. [c]John 2:23
46 [a]John 7:32, 45; 11:57
47 [a]John 7:32, 45; 11:57 [b]Matt. 26:3 [c]Matt. 5:22

For this man is performing many [Id]signs.[4592]

48 "If we [aosb]let Him *go on* like this, all men will believe in Him, and the Romans will come and take away both our [a]place and our nation."[1484]

49 But a certain one of them, [a]Caiaphas, [b]who was high priest[749] that year, said to them, "You know nothing at all,

50 nor do you take into account[3049] that [a]it is expedient[4851] for you that one man should [aosb]die[599] for the people, and that the whole nation should not [asbm]perish."[622]

51 Now this he did not say [I]on his own initiative; but [a]being high priest that year, he prophesied[4395] that Jesus was going to [pinf]die[599] for the nation,

52 and not for the nation only, but that He might also [a]gather together into one the children[5043] of God[2316] who are [pfpp]scattered abroad.

53 So from that day on they [a]planned together to [psa]kill Him.

54 Jesus therefore [a]no longer continued [ipf]to walk publicly among the Jews, but went away from there to the country near the wilderness, into a city called [b]Ephraim; and there He stayed with the disciples.[3101]

55 Now [a]the Passover[3957] of the Jews was at hand,[1451] and many went up to Jerusalem out of the country before the Passover, [b]to purify[48] themselves.

56 Therefore they [a]were [ipf]seeking for Jesus, and were [ipf]saying to one another, as they [pfp]stood in the temple,[2411] "What do you think; that He will not come to the feast at all?"

57 Now [a]the chief priests[749] and the Pharisees had given orders that if anyone knew where He was, he should report it, that they might seize Him.

Mary Anoints Jesus

12 [a]Jesus, therefore, six days before [b]the Passover,[3957] came to [c]Bethany where Lazarus was, whom Jesus had raised from the dead.[3498]

2 So they made Him a supper there, and [a]Martha was [ipf]serving;[1247] but Lazarus was one of those [ppp]reclining *at the table* with Him.

3 [a]Mary therefore [apt]took a pound of very costly [b]perfume of pure nard,[3487] and anointed[218] the feet of Jesus, and wiped His feet with her hair; and the house was filled[4137] with the fragrance of the perfume.

4 But [a]Judas Iscariot, one of His disciples,[3101] who was [ppt]intending to [pinf] [I]betray Him, *said,

5 "Why was this perfume not sold for [I]three hundred denarii,[1220] and [aop]given to poor *people*?"

6 Now he said this, not because he was [ipf]concerned about the poor, but because he was a thief,[2812] and as he [a]had the money box, he used to pilfer [b]what was [ppt]put into it.

7 Jesus therefore said, "Let her alone, in order that she may [asba]keep [I]it for [a]the day of My burial.

8 "[a]For the poor you always have with you, but you do not always have Me."

9 The [a]great multitude therefore of the Jews learned that He was there; and they came, not for Jesus' sake only, but that they might also see[1492] Lazarus, [b]whom He [ao]raised[1453] from the dead.

10 But the chief priests[749] took counsel that they might put Lazarus to death also;

11 because [a]on account of him [b]many of the Jews were [ipf]going away, and were [ipf]believing[4100] in Jesus.

Jesus Enters Jerusalem

12 On the next day [Ia]the great multitude who had [apt]come to [b]the feast, when they heard that Jesus was coming to Jerusalem,

13 took the branches of the palm trees, and went out to meet Him, and *began* to [ipf]cry out, "[a]Hosanna![5614] BLESSED[2127] IS HE WHO [ppt]COMES IN THE NAME OF THE LORD,[2962] even the [b]King[935] of Israel."

14 And Jesus, finding a young donkey, sat on it; as it is written,

---

47 [I]Or, *attesting miracles* [d]John 2:11
48 [a]Matt. 24:15
49 [a]Matt. 26:3 [b]John 11:51; 18:13
50 [a]John 18:14
51 [I]Lit., *from himself* [a]John 18:13
52 [a]John 10:16
53 [a]Matt. 26:4
54 [a]John 7:1 [b]2Chr. 13:19 mg.
55 [a]Matt. 26:1f.; Mark 14:1; Luke 22:1; John 2:13; 12:1; 13:1 [b]Num. 9:10; 2Chr. 30:17f.; John 18:28
56 [a]John 7:11
57 [a]John 11:47

1 [a]John 12:1-8: *Matt. 26:6-13; Mark 14:3-9; Luke 7:37-39* [b]John 11:55; 12:20 [c]Matt. 21:17; John 11:43f.
2 [a]Luke 10:38
3 [a]Luke 7:37f.; John 11:2 [b]Mark 14:3
4 [I]Or, *deliver Him up* [a]John 6:71
5 [I]Equivalent to 11 months' wages
6 [a]John 13:29 [b]Luke 8:3
7 [I]I.e., The custom of anointing for burial [a]John 19:40
8 [a]Deut. 15:11; Matt. 26:11; Mark 14:7
9 [a]Mark 12:37; John 12:12 mg. [b]John 11:43f.; 12:1, 17f.
11 [a]John 11:45f.; 12:18 [b]John 7:31; 11:42
12 [I]Or, *the common people* [a]John 12:12-15: *Matt. 21:4-9; Mark 11:7-10; Luke 19:35-38* [b]John 12:1
13 [a]Ps. 118:26 [b]John 1:49

15 "[a]FEAR[5399] NOT, DAUGHTER OF ZION; BEHOLD, YOUR KING IS COMING, SEATED ON A DONKEY'S COLT."

16 [a]These things His disciples did not understand at the first; but when Jesus [b]was glorified,[1392] then they remembered that these things were written of Him, and that they had done these things to Him.

17 And so [a]the multitude who were with Him when He called Lazarus out of the tomb, and raised him from the dead, were [ipf]bearing Him witness.[3140]

18 [a]For this cause also the multitude went and met Him, [b]because they heard that He had performed this [I]sign.[4592]

19 The Pharisees therefore said to one another, "You see that you are not doing any good; look, the world[2889] has gone after Him."

Greeks Seek Jesus

20 Now there were certain [a]Greeks among those who were [ppt]going up to [aosb]worship[4352] at [b]the feast;

21 these therefore came to [a]Philip, who was from [b]Bethsaida of Galilee, and *began to* [ipf]ask him, saying, "Sir,[2962] we [pin]wish to [ainf]see[1492] Jesus."

22 Philip *came and *told [a]Andrew; Andrew and Philip *came, and they *told Jesus.

23 And Jesus *answered them, saying, "[a]The hour[5610] has come for the Son of Man to [b]be [asbp]glorified.[1392]

24 "Truly,[281] truly, I say to you, [a]unless a [art]grain of [art]wheat[2848] [apt]falls into the earth and [aosb]dies,[599] it remains[3306] by itself alone; but if it [aosb]dies,[599] it bears[5342] much fruit.

25 "[a]He who [apt]loves[5368] his [I]life[5590] loses[622] it; and he who [b]hates his [I]life in this world shall keep[5442] it to life[2222] eternal.[166]

26 "If anyone [psa]serves[1247] Me, let him [pim]follow[190] Me; and [a]where I am, there shall My servant[1249] also be; if anyone serves Me, the Father[3962] will [b]honor[5091] him.

15 [a]Zech. 9:9 **16** [a]Mark 9:32; John 2:22; 14:26 [b]John 7:39; 12:23 **17** [a]John 11:42 **18** [I]Or, *attesting miracle* [a]Luke 19:37; John 12:12 [b]John 12:11 **20** [a]John 7:35 [b]John 12:1 **21** [a]John 1:44 [b]Matt. 11:21 **22** [a]John 1:44 **23** [a]Matt. 26:45; Mark 14:35, 41; John 13:1; 17:1 [b]John 7:39; 12:16; 13:32 **24** [a]Rom. 14:9; 1Cor. 15:36 **25** [I]Or, *soul* [a]Matt. 10:39; 16:25; Mark 8:35; Luke 9:24; 17:33 [b]Luke 14:26 **26** [a]John 14:3; 17:24; 2Cor. 5:8; Phil. 1:23; 1Thess. 4:17 [b]1Sam. 2:30; Ps. 91:15; Luke 12:37 **27** [a]Matt. 26:38; Mark 14:34; John 11:33 [b]Matt. 11:25 [c]John 12:23 **28** [a]Matt. 11:25 [b]Matt. 3:17; 17:5; Mark 1:11; 9:7; Luke 3:22; 9:35 **29** [a]Acts 23:9 **30** [a]John 11:42 **31** [a]John 3:19; 9:39; 16:11 [b]John 14:30; 16:11; 2Cor. 4:4; Eph. 2:2; 6:12; 1John 4:4; 5:19 **32** [a]John 3:14; 8:28; 12:34 [b]John 6:44 **33** [a]John 18:32; 21:19 **34** [I]I.e., the Messiah [a]John 10:34 [b]Ps. 110:4; Is. 9:7; Ezek. 37:25; Dan. 7:14 [c]Matt. 8:20 [d]John 3:14; 8:28; 12:32 **35** [a]John 7:33; 9:4 [b]John 12:46; 1John 2:10 [c]Gal. 6:10; Eph. 5:8 [d]1John 1:6; 2:11 **36** [I]Lit., *was hidden* [a]John 12:46 [b]Luke 16:8; John 8:12 [c]John 8:59 **37** [I]Or, *attesting miracles*

Jesus Foretells His Death

27 "[a]Now My soul[5590] has become [pfip]troubled; and what shall I say, '[b]Father, save[4982] Me from [c]this hour'?[5610] But for this purpose I came to this hour.

28 "[a]Father, glorify[1392] Thy name." There came therefore a [b]voice out of heaven:[3772] "I have both glorified it, and will glorify it again."

29 The multitude therefore, who stood by and [apt]heard[191] it, were [ipf]saying that it had [pfin]thundered; others[243] were saying, "[a]An angel[32] has [pfi]spoken to Him."

30 Jesus answered and said, "[a]This voice has not [pfi]come for My sake, but for your sakes.

31 "[a]Now judgment[2920] is upon this world;[2889] now [b]the ruler[758] of this world shall be [fp]cast out.

32 "And I, if I [a]be lifted up from the earth, will [b]draw[1670] all men to Myself."

33 But He was saying this [a]to indicate the kind of death[2288] by which He was to die.[599]

34 The multitude therefore answered Him, "We have heard[191] out of [a]the Law[3551] that [I][b]the Christ is to remain[3306] forever;[165] and how can You say, 'The [c]Son of Man must be [aifp] [d]lifted up'? Who is this [c]Son of Man?"

🔑 35 Jesus therefore said to them, "[a]For a little while[5550] longer [b]the light[5457] is among you. [pim] [c]Walk while you have the light, that darkness[4653] may not [aosb]overtake[2638] you; he who [ppt] [d]walks in the darkness[4653] does not know where he goes.

36 "While you have the light, [pim] [a]believe in the light, in order that you may [aosb]become [b]sons[5207] of light."

These things Jesus spoke, and He departed and [I][c]hid Himself from them.

37 But though He had [pfp]performed so many [I]signs[4592] before them, *yet* they were not [ipf]believing in Him;

🔑 **12:35** See general remarks on I Jn.

38 that the word of Isaiah the prophet might be [asbp]fulfilled, which he spoke, "[a]LORD, WHO HAS [ao]BELIEVED[4100] OUR REPORT?[189] AND TO WHOM HAS THE ARM OF THE LORD BEEN [aop]REVEALED?"

39 For this cause they [ipf]could not [pinf]believe, for Isaiah said again,

40 "[a]HE HAS [pfi]BLINDED THEIR EYES, AND HE [ao] [b]HARDENED[4456] THEIR HEART[2588]; LEST THEY [aosb]SEE[492] WITH THEIR EYES, AND [aosb]PERCEIVE[3539] WITH THEIR HEART, AND [I]BE CONVERTED,[1994] AND I HEAL[2390] THEM."

41 These things Isaiah said, because [a]he saw His glory,[1391] and [b]he spoke of Him.

42 Nevertheless [a]many even of [b]the rulers[758] believed[4100] in Him, but [c]because of the Pharisees they were not [ipf]confessing[3670] *Him,* lest they should be [aosb] [I][d]put out of the synagogue;[656]

43 [a]for they loved[25] the approval[1391] of men[444] rather than the approval[1391] of God.[2316]

44 And Jesus cried out and said, "[a]He who [ppt]believes[4100] in Me does not believe in Me, but in Him who [apt]sent Me.

45 "And [a]he who [ppt]beholds Me beholds the One who [apt]sent Me.

46 "[a]I have [pfi]come *as* light[5457] into the world,[2889] that everyone who [ppt]believes in Me may not [aosb]remain[3306] in [art]darkness.[4653]

47 "And if anyone [aosb]hears[191] My sayings,[4487] and does not [aosb]keep them, I do not judge[2919] him; for [a]I did not come to judge the world, but to save[4982] the world.

48 "[a]He who [ppt]rejects Me, and does not [ppt]receive My sayings,[4487] has one who [ppt]judges him; [b]the word I spoke is what will judge him at [c]the last[2078] day.

49 "[a]For I did not speak [I]on My own initiative, but the Father Himself who [apt]sent Me [b]has given Me commandment, what to [aosb]say, and what to speak.

50 "And I know that [a]His commandment is eternal[166] life;[2222] therefore the things I speak, I speak [b]just as the Father has told Me."

The Lord's Supper

13 Now before the Feast of [a]the Passover,[3957] Jesus knowing that [b]His hour[5610] had [ao]come that He should [aosb]depart[3327] out of this world[2889] [c]to the Father, having loved[25] His [m]own who were in the world, He loved them [I]to the end.[5056]

2 And during supper, [a]the devil[1228] having already [pfp]put[906] into the heart[2588] of [b]Judas Iscariot, *the son* of Simon, to betray Him,

3 *Jesus,* [a]knowing[1492] that the Father had [ao]given all things into His hands, and that [b]He had [ao]come forth from God, and was going back to God,

4 *rose from supper, and *laid aside[5087] His garments; and taking a towel, He [a]girded Himself about.

Jesus Washes the Disciples' Feet

5 Then He *poured water into the basin, and began to [pinf] [a]wash[3538] the disciples' feet, and to [pinf]wipe them with the towel with which He was girded.

6 And so He *came to Simon Peter. He *said to Him, "Lord, do You wash my feet?"

7 Jesus answered and said to him, "What [epn]I do you do not realize[1492] now, but you shall understand[1097] [a]hereafter."

8 Peter *said to Him, "Never shall You [efn]wash my feet!" Jesus answered him, "[a]If I do not wash you, [b]you have no part with Me."

9 Simon Peter *said to Him, "Lord, not my feet only, but also my hands and my head."

10 Jesus *said to him, "He who has bathed needs only to wash[3538] his feet, but is completely[3650] clean;[2513] and [a]you are clean, but not all *of you.*"

11 For [a]He knew the one who was [ppt]betraying Him; for this reason He said, "Not all of you are clean."

12 And so when He had washed their feet, and [a]taken His garments, and

38 [a]Is. 53:1; Rom. 10:16
40 [I]Lit., *should be turned*; i.e., turn about [a]Is. 6:10; Matt. 13:14f. [b]Mark 6:52
41 [a]Is. 6:1ff. [b]Luke 24:27
42 [I]I.e., excommunicated [a]John 7:48; 12:11 [b]Luke 23:13 [c]John 7:13 [d]John 9:22
43 [a]John 5:41, 44
44 [a]Matt. 10:40; John 5:24
45 [a]John 14:9
46 [a]John 1:4; 3:19; 8:12; 9:5; 12:35f.
47 [a]John 3:17; 8:15f.
48 [a]Luke 10:16 [b]Deut. 18:18f.; John 5:45ff.; 8:47 [c]Matt. 10:15; John 6:39; Acts 17:31; 1Pet. 1:5; 2Pet. 3:3, 7; Heb. 10:25
49 [I]Lit., *of Myself* [a]John 3:11; 7:16; 8:26, 28, 38; 14:10, 24 [b]John 14:31; 17:8
50 [a]John 6:68 [b]John 5:19; 8:28

1 [I]Lit., *to the uttermost*; or, *eternally* [a]John 2:13; 11:55 [b]John 12:23 [c]John 13:3; 16:28
2 [a]John 6:70; 13:27 [b]John 6:71
3 [a]John 3:35 [b]John 8:42
4 [a]Luke 12:37; 17:8
5 [a]Gen. 18:4; 19:2; 43:24; Judg. 19:21; Luke 7:44; 1Tim. 5:10
7 [a]John 13:12ff.
8 [a]Ps. 51:2, 7; Ezek. 36:25; Acts 22:16; 1Cor. 6:11; Heb. 10:22 [b]Deut. 12:12; 2Sam. 20:1; 1Kin. 12:16
10 [a]John 15:3; Eph. 5:26
11 [a]John 6:64; 13:2
12 [a]John 13:4

reclined *at the table* again, He said to them, "Do you know what I have done to you?

13 "You call Me [a]Teacher[1320] and [b]Lord;[2962] and [l]you are right, for *so* I am.

14 "If I then, [a]the Lord and the Teacher, [ao]washed your feet, you also ought to [pinf]wash one another's feet.

15 "For I gave you [a]an example that you also should [psa]do as I did to you.

16 "Truly,[281] truly, I say to you, [a]a slave[1401] is not greater than his master;[2962] neither *is* [b]one who is sent greater than the one who sent[652] him.

17 "If you know these things, you are [a]blessed[3107] if you do them.

18 "[a]I do not speak of all of you. I know the ones I have [ao] [b]chosen; but *it is* [c]that the Scripture may be [asbp]fulfilled, '[d]HE WHO EATS MY BREAD HAS LIFTED UP[1869] HIS HEEL AGAINST ME.'

19 "From now on [a]I am telling you before *it* [aosb]comes to pass, so that when it does occur, you may [aosb]believe[4100] that [b]I am *He.*

20 "Truly, truly, I say to you, [a]he who [ppt]receives whomever I send receives Me; and he who receives Me receives Him who [apt]sent Me."

Jesus Predicts His Betrayal

21 When Jesus had said this, He [a]became troubled in spirit,[4151] and testified,[3140] and said, "Truly, truly, I say to you, that [b]one of you will [l]betray Me."

22 The disciples *began* [ipf]looking at one another, [a]at a loss *to know* of which one He was speaking.

23 There was reclining on [a]Jesus' breast[2859] one of His disciples, [b]whom Jesus [ipf]loved.[25]

24 Simon Peter therefore *gestured to him, and *said to him, "Tell *us* who it is of whom He is speaking."

25 He, [apt] [a]leaning back thus on Jesus' breast,[4738] *said to Him, "Lord, who is it?"

26 Jesus therefore *answered, "That is the one for whom I shall [ft]dip[911] the morsel[5596] and give it to him." So when He had [apt]dipped the morsel, He *took and *gave it to Judas, [a]*the son* of Simon Iscariot.

27 And after the morsel, [a]Satan then [b]entered into him. Jesus therefore *said to him, "What you do, [aim]do quickly."

28 Now no one of those reclining *at the table* knew for what purpose[4314,5100] He had said this to him.

29 For some were [ipf]supposing, because Judas [a]had the money box,[1101] that Jesus was saying to him, "Buy the things we have need of [b]for the feast"; or else, that he should [c]give something to the poor.

30 And so after receiving the morsel he went out immediately; and [a]it was night.

31 When therefore he had gone out, Jesus *said, "Now [l]is [a]the Son of Man [aop] [b]glorified,[1392] and [c]God [l]is [aop]glorified in Him;

32 [l]if God is glorified in Him, [a]God will also glorify Him in Himself, and will glorify Him immediately.[2117]

33 "[a]Little children, I am with you [b]a little while longer. [c]You shall seek Me; and as I said to the Jews, I now say to you also, 'Where I am going, you cannot come.'

34 "A [a]new[2537] commandment I give to you, [b]that you love[25] one another, [c]even as I have [ao]loved you, that you also love one another.

35 "[a]By this all men will know that you are My disciples,[3101] if you have [psa]love[26] for one another."

36 Simon Peter *said to Him, "Lord, where are You going?" Jesus answered, "[a]Where I go, you cannot [ainf]follow Me now; but [b]you shall follow later."

37 Peter *said to Him, "Lord, why can I not [ainf]follow You right now? [a]I will lay down my life[5590] for You."

38 Jesus *answered, "Will you lay down your life for Me? Truly, truly, I say to you, [a]a cock shall not [efn]crow, until you [aosb]deny[533] Me three times.

13 [l]Lit., *you say well* [a]John 11:28 [b]John 11:2; 1Cor. 12:3; Phil. 2:11
14 [a]John 11:2; 1Cor. 12:3; Phil. 2:11
15 [a]1Pet. 5:3
16 [a]Matt. 10:24; Luke 6:40; John 15:20 [b]2Cor. 8:23; Phil. 2:25
17 [a]Matt. 7:24ff.; Luke 11:28; James 1:25
18 [a]John 13:10f. [b]John 6:70; 15:16, 19 [c]John 15:25; 17:12; 18:32; 19:24, 36 [d]Ps. 41:9; Matt. 26:21ff.; Mark 14:18f.; Luke 22:21ff.; John 13:21, 22, 26
19 [a]John 14:29; 16:4 [b]John 8:24
20 [a]Matt. 10:40; Mark 9:37; Luke 9:48; 10:16; Gal. 4:14
21 [l]Or, *deliver Me up* [a]John 11:33 [b]Matt. 26:21f.; Mark 14:18ff.; Luke 22:21ff.; John 13:18, 22, 26
22 [a]Matt. 26:21ff.; Mark 14:18ff.; Luke 22:21ff.; John 13:18, 21, 26
23 [a]John 1:18 [b]John 19:26; 20:2; 21:7, 20
25 [a]John 21:20
26 [a]John 6:71
27 [a]Matt. 4:10 [b]Luke 22:3; John 13:2
29 [a]John 12:6 [b]John 13:1 [c]John 12:5
30 [a]Luke 22:53
31 [l]Or, *was* [a]Matt. 8:20 [b]John 7:39 [c]John 14:13; 17:4; 1Pet. 4:11
32 [l]Some ancient mss. do not contain this phrase [a]John 17:1
33 [a]1John 2:1 [b]John 7:33 [c]John 7:34
34 [a]John 15:12, 17; 1John 2:7f.; 3:11, 23; 2John 5 [b]Lev. 19:18; Matt. 5:44; Gal. 5:14; 1Thess. 4:9; Heb. 13:1; 1Pet. 1:22; 1John 4:7 [c]Eph. 5:2; 1John 4:10f.
35 [a]1John 3:14; 4:20

36 [a]John 13:33; 14:2; 16:5 [b]John 21:18f.; 2Pet. 1:14
37 [a]John 13:37, 38: *Matt. 26:33-35; Mark 14:29-31; Luke 22:33-34*
38 [a]Mark 14:30; John 18:27

Jesus Comforts His Disciples

14 "[a]Let not your heart[2588] be [pim]troubled; [1]believe[4100] in God, believe[4100] also in Me.

2 "In My Father's house[3614] are many dwelling places;[3438] if it were not so, I would have told you; for [a]I go to [ainf]prepare a place for you.

3 "And if I [aosb]go and prepare a place for you, [a]I will come again, and receive you to Myself; that [b]where I am, *there* you may be also.

4 "[1]And you know[1492] the way where I am going."

5 [a]Thomas *said to Him, "Lord, we do not know where You are going, how do we know the way?"

6 Jesus *said to him, "I am [a]the way,[3598] and [b]the truth,[225] and [c]the life;[2222] no one comes to the Father,[3962] but through Me.

Oneness with the Father

7 "[a]If you had known[1097] Me, you would have known My Father also; from now on you [b]know Him, and have [c]seen[3708] Him."

8 [a]Philip *said to Him, "Lord, show us the Father, and it is enough for us."

9 Jesus *said to him, "Have I been so long with you, and *yet* you have not come to know Me, Philip? [a]He who has seen Me has seen the Father; how do you say, 'Show us the Father'?

10 "Do you not believe that [a]I am in the Father, and the Father is in Me? [b]The words[4487] that I say to you I do not speak on My own initiative, but the Father [ppt]abiding[3306] in Me does His works.

11 [pim]"Believe Me that [a]I am in the Father, and the Father in Me; otherwise [pim] [b]believe on account of the works themselves.

12 "Truly,[281] truly, I say to you, he who [ppt]believes in Me, the works that I do shall he do also; and [a]greater *works* than these shall he do; because [b]I go to the Father.

13 "And [a]whatever you [aosb]ask[154] in My name,[3686] that will I do, that [b]the Father may be [asbp]glorified[1392] in the Son.

14 "If you [aosb]ask[154] Me anything [a]in My name, I will do *it.*

15 "[a]If you [psa]love[25] Me, you will [1]keep My commandments.

Role of the Spirit

16 "And I will ask[2065] the Father,[3962] and He will give you another [1a]Helper,[3875] that He may [psa]be[1510] with you forever;[165]

17 *that is* [a]the Spirit[4151] of truth, [b]whom the world[2889] cannot receive, because it does not behold Him or know Him, *but* you know[1097] Him because He abides with you, and will be in you.

18 "I will not leave[863] you as orphans;[3737] [a]I will come[2064] to you.

19 "[1a]After a little while [b]the world will behold[2334] Me no more; but you *will* behold Me; [c]because I live,[2198] you shall live also.

20 "[a]In that day you shall know that [b]I am in My Father, and you in Me, and I in you.

21 "[a]He who [ppt]has My commandments and [ppt]keeps[5083] them, he it is who [ppt]loves[25] Me; and [b]he who loves Me shall be loved by My Father, and I will love him, and will [c]disclose Myself to him."

22 [a]Judas (not Iscariot) *said to Him, "Lord, what then has happened [b]that You are going to [pinf]disclose Yourself to us, and not to the world?"

23 Jesus answered and said to him, "[a]If anyone [psa]loves Me, he will [b]keep My word; and [c]My Father will love him,

---

1 [1]Or, *you believe in God* [a]John 14:27; 16:22, 24
2 [a]John 13:33, 36
3 [a]John 14:18, 28 [b]John 12:26
4 [1]Many ancient authorities read *And where I go you know, and the way you know*
5 [a]John 11:16
6 [a]John 10:9; Rom. 5:2; Eph. 2:18; Heb. 10:20 [b]John 1:14 [c]John 1:4; 11:25; 1John 5:20
7 [a]John 8:19 [b]1John 2:13 [c]John 6:46
8 [a]John 1:43
9 [a]John 1:14; 12:45; Col. 1:15; Heb. 1:3
10 [a]John 10:38; 14:11, 20 [b]John 5:19; 14:24
11 [a]John 10:38; 14:10, 20 [b]John 5:36
12 [a]John 4:37f.; 5:20 [b]John 7:33; 14:28
13 [a]Matt. 7:7 [b]John 13:31
14 [a]John 15:16; 16:23f.
15 [a]John 14:21, 23; 15:10; 1John 5:3; 2John 6
16 [1]Gr., *Paracletos,* one called alongside to help; or, *Intercessor* [a]John 7:39; 14:26; 15:26; 16:7; Rom. 8:26; 1John 2:1
17 [a]John 15:26; 16:13; 1John 4:6; 5:7 [b]1Cor. 2:14
18 [a]John 14:3, 28
19 [1]Lit., *Yet a little and the world* [a]John 7:33 [b]John 16:16, 22 [c]John 6:57
20 [a]John 16:23, 26 [b]John 10:38; 14:11
21 [a]John 14:15, 23; 15:10; 1John 5:3; 2John 6 [b]John 14:23; 16:27 [c]Ex. 33:18f.; Prov. 8:17
22 [a]Luke 6:16; Acts 1:13 [b]Acts 10:40, 41
23 [a]John 14:15, 21; 15:10; 1John 5:3; 2John 6 [b]John 8:51; 1John 2:5 [c]John 14:21

14:13-16 See note on Lk. 11:9; Js. 5:14,15 and also *aiteō* (154), to request, and *erōtaō* (2065), to ask between equals.

and We [d]will come to him, and make Our abode[3438] with him.

24 "He who does not [ppt]love Me [a]does not keep My words; and [b]the word which you hear is not Mine, but the Father's who sent Me.

25 "These things I have [pfi]spoken to you, while abiding with you.

26 "But the [a]Helper,[3875] the Holy Spirit,[4151] [b]whom the Father[3962] will send in My name, [c]He will teach[1321] you all things, and [d]bring to your remembrance all that I said to you.

27 "[a]Peace[1515] I leave with you; My peace I give to you; not as the world[2889] gives, do I give to you. [b]Let not your heart be troubled, nor let it be fearful.[1168]

28 "[a]You heard that I said to you, 'I go away, and [b]I will come[2064] to you.' If you [ipf]loved Me, you would have [ao]rejoiced, because [c]I go to the Father; for [d]the Father is greater than I.

29 "And now [a]I have [pfi]told you before it [ainf]comes to pass, that when it [aosb]comes to pass, you may [aosb]believe.[4100]

30 "I will not speak much more with you, for [a]the ruler[758] of the world is coming, and he has nothing in Me;

31 but that the world may [aosb]know that I love[25] the Father,[3962] and as [a]the Father gave Me commandment, even so I do. Arise,[1453] [b]let us go from here.

Jesus Is the Vine—Followers Are Branches

15 "[a]I am the true[228] vine, and My Father[3962] is the [b]vinedresser.[1092]

2 "Every branch in Me that does not [ppt]bear fruit, He takes away; and every *branch* that bears fruit, He [1]prunes[2508] it, that it may [psa]bear more fruit.

3 "[a]You are already clean[2513] because of the word[3056] which I have [pfi]spoken to you.

4 "[a][aim]Abide[3306] in Me, and I in you. As the branch cannot bear fruit of itself, unless it [psa]abides[3306] in the vine, so neither *can* you, unless you [psa]abide in Me.

5 "I am the vine, you are the branches;[2814] he who [ppt]abides in Me, and I in him, he [a]bears much fruit; for apart from Me you can [pinf]do nothing.

6 "If anyone does not [psa]abide in Me, he is [aop] [a]thrown away as a branch, and [aop]dries up; and they gather them, and cast them into the fire, and they are burned.

7 "If you [aosb]abide in Me, and My words[4487] [aosb]abide in you, [aim] [a]ask whatever you [psa]wish, and it shall be done for you.

8 "[a]By this is My Father [aop]glorified,[1392] [1]that you [psa]bear much fruit, and *so* [b]prove to be My disciples.[3101]

9 "Just as [a]the Father has [ao]loved[25] Me, I have also [ao]loved you; [aim]abide[3306] in My love.[26]

10 "[a]If you [aosb]keep[5083] My commandments, you will abide[3306] in My love; just as [b]I have [pfi]kept My Father's commandments, and abide in His love.

11 "[a]These things I have [pfi]spoken to you, that My joy may [psa]be in you, and *that* your [b]joy may be made [asbp]full.[4137]

Disciples' Relation to Each Other

12 "This is [a]My commandment, that you love[25] one another, just as I have loved you.

13 "[a]Greater love[26] has no one than this, that one [b]lay down his life[5590] for his friends.[5384]

14 "You are My [a]friends, if [b]you [psa]do what I command you.

15 "No longer do I call you slaves,[1401] for the slave does not know what his master[2962] is doing; but I have [pfi]called you friends, for [a]all things that I have heard from My Father I have [ao]made known[1107] to you.

16 "[a]You did not [ao]choose Me, but

23 [d]2Cor. 6:16; Eph. 3:17; 1John 2:24; Rev. 3:20; 21:3
24 [a]John 14:23 [b]John 7:16; 14:10
26 [a]John 14:16 [b]Luke 24:49; John 1:33; 15:26; 16:7; Acts 2:33 [c]John 16:13f.; 1John 2:20, 27 [d]John 2:22
27 [a]John 16:33; 20:19; Phil. 4:7; Col. 3:15 [b]John 14:1
28 [a]John 14:2-4 [b]John 14:3, 18 [c]John 14:12 [d]John 10:29; Phil. 2:6
29 [a]John 13:19
30 [a]John 12:31
31 [a]John 10:18; 12:49 [b]John 13:1; 18:1

1 [a]Ps. 80:8ff.; Is. 5:1ff.; Ezek. 19:10ff.; Matt. 21:33ff. [b]Matt. 15:13; Rom. 11:17; 1Cor. 3:9
2 [1]Lit., *cleanses*
3 [a]John 13:10; 17:17; Eph. 5:26
4 [a]John 6:56; 15:4-7; 1John 2:6
5 [a]John 15:16
6 [a]John 15:2
7 [a]Matt. 7:7; John 15:16
8 [1]Another reading is *that you bear much fruit, and become My disciples* [a]Matt. 5:16 [b]John 8:31
9 [a]John 3:35; 17:23, 24, 26
10 [a]John 14:15 [b]John 8:29
11 [a]John 17:13 [b]John 3:29
12 [a]John 13:34; 15:17; 1John 3:23; 2John 5
13 [a]Rom. 5:7f. [b]John 10:11
14 [a]Luke 12:4 [b]Matt. 12:50
15 [a]John 8:26; 16:12
16 [a]John 6:70; 13:18; 15:19

14:28 See note on Phil. 2:6-8.

I chose you, and [ao]appointed[5087] you,
that you should [psa]go and [psa] [b]bear fruit,
and *that* your fruit should [psa]remain,[3306]
that [c]whatever you [aosb]ask of the Father
in My name, He may [aosb]give to you.
17 "This [a]I command[1781] you, that
you love[25] one another.

Disciples' Relation to the World

18 "[a]If the world[2889] hates you,
[I]you know that it has [pfi]hated Me
before[4412] *it hated* you.
19 "If you were of the world, the
world would [ipf]love[5368] its own; but because you are not of the world, but
[a]I [ao]chose you out of the world, [b]there-
fore the world hates you.
20 [pim]"Remember the word that I
said to you, '[a]A slave[1401] is not greater
than his master.'[2962] If they [ao]persecuted
Me, [b]they will also persecute you; if
they [ao] [c]kept[5083] My word,[3056] they will
keep yours also.
21 "But all these things they will
do to you [a]for My name's sake, [b]because
they do not know the One who sent
Me.
22 "[a]If I had not come and spoken
to them, they would not [ipf]have [I]sin,[266]
but now they have no excuse for their
sin.
23 "He who [ppt]hates Me hates My
Father also.
24 "[a]If I had not done among them
[b]the works which no one else did, [pfi]they
would not [ipf]have [I]sin; but now they have
both [pfi]seen and [pfi]hated Me and My Father as well.
25 "But *they have done this* in order
that the word may be fulfilled that is
written in their [a]Law,[3551] '[b]THEY HATED
ME WITHOUT A CAUSE.'
26 "When the [Ia]Helper[3875]
[aosb]comes, [b]whom I will send to you from
the Father,[3962] *that is* [c]the Spirit[4151] of
truth,[225] who proceeds from the Father,
[d]He will bear witness[3140] of Me,
27 [I]and [a]you *will* bear witness[3140]

16 [b]John 15:5 [c]John 14:13; 15:7; 16:23
17 [a]John 15:12
18 [I]Or, (imperative) *know that* [a]John 7:7; 1John 3:13
19 [a]John 15:16 [b]Matt. 10:22; 24:9; John 17:14
20 [a]Matt. 10:24; John 13:16 [b]1Cor. 4:12; 2Cor. 4:9; 2Tim. 3:12 [c]John 8:51
21 [a]Matt. 10:22; 24:9; Mark 13:13; Luke 21:12, 17; Acts 4:17; 5:41; 9:14; 26:9; 1Pet. 4:14; Rev. 2:3 [b]John 8:19, 55; 16:3; 17:25; Acts 3:17; 1John 3:1
22 [I]I.e., guilt [a]John 9:41; 15:24
24 [I]I.e., guilt [a]John 9:41; 15:21 [b]John 5:36; 10:37
25 [a]John 10:34 [b]Ps. 35:19; 69:4
26 [I]Gr., *Paracletos*, one called alongside to help; or, *Intercessor* [a]John 14:16 [b]John 14:26 [c]John 14:17 [d]1John 5:7
27 [I]Or, (imperative) *and bear witness* [a]Luke 24:48; John 19:35; 21:24; 1John 1:2; 4:14 [b]Luke 1:2

1 [a]John 15:18-27 [b]Matt. 11:6
2 [I]Or, *They will make you excommunicated* [a]John 9:22 [b]John 4:21; 16:25 [c]Is. 66:5; Acts 26:9-11; Rev. 6:9
3 [a]John 8:19, 55; 15:21; 17:25; Acts 3:17; 1John 3:1
4 [I]Lit., *may remember them, that I told you* [a]John 13:19 [b]Luke 1:2
5 [a]John 7:33; 16:10, 17, 28

also, because you have been with Me
[b]from the beginning.

Jesus' Warning

16 "[a]These things I have spoken to
you, that you may be [asbp]kept
from [b]stumbling.[4624]
2 "[I]They will [a]make you outcasts
from the synagogue,[656] but [b]an hour[5610]
is coming for everyone [c]who [apt]kills you
to [aosb]think[1380] that he is [pinf]offering
service[2999] to God.
3 "And these things they will do,
[a]because they have not known[1097] the
Father, or Me.
4 "But these things I have spoken
to you, [a]that when their hour[5610] comes,
you [I]may [psa]remember that I told you
of them. And these things I did not say
to you [b]at the beginning, because I was
with you.

The Holy Spirit Promised

5 "But now [a]I am going to Him who
sent Me; and none of you asks[2065] Me,
'[b]Where are You going?'
6 "But because I have [pfi]said these
things to you, [a]sorrow has [pfi]filled your
heart.
🗝 7 "But I tell you the truth,[225] it is
to your advantage[4851] that I [aosb]go away;
for if I do not [aosb]go away, the
[Ia]Helper[3875] shall not come to you; but
if I [aosb]go, [b]I will send Him to you.
8 "And He, when He comes, will
convict[1651] the world[2889] concerning
sin,[266] and righteousness,[1343] and
judgment;[2920]
9 concerning sin, [a]because they do
not believe[4100] in Me;
10 and concerning [a]righteousness,
because [b]I go to the Father,[3962] and you
no longer behold[2334] Me;

[b]John 13:36; 14:5 **6** [a]John 14:1; 16:22 **7** [I]Gr., *Paracletos*, one called alongside to help; or, *Intercessor* [a]John 14:16 [b]John 14:26 **9** [a]John 15:22, 24 **10** [a]Acts 3:14; 7:52; 17:31; 1Pet. 3:18 [b]John 16:5

🗝 **16:7-15** See notes on Mk. 3:28,29; Acts 2:1-13.

11 [a]and concerning judgment,[2920] because the ruler[758] of this world has been [pfip]judged.[2919]

12 "I have many more things to say to you, but you cannot [pinf]bear *them* now.

13 "But[1161] when He, [a]the Spirit[4151] of truth,[225] comes, He will [b]guide[3594] you into all the truth; for He will not speak on His own initiative, but whatever He [pin]hears,[191] He will speak;[2980] and He will[312] disclose to you what is to come.[2064]

14 "He shall [a]glorify[1392] [epn]Me; for He shall take of Mine, and shall disclose[312] *it* to you.

15 "[a]All things that the Father has are Mine; therefore I said, that He takes of Mine, and will disclose[312] *it* to you.

Jesus' Death and Resurrection Foretold

16 "[a]A little while, and [b]you will no longer behold Me; and again a little while, and [c]you will see Me."

17 *Some* of His disciples[3101] therefore said to one another, "What is this thing He is telling us, '[a]A little while, and you will not behold Me; and again a little while, and you will see Me'; and, 'because [b]I go to the Father'?"

18 And so they were saying, "What is this that He says, 'A little while'? We do not know what He is talking about."

19 [a]Jesus knew that they [ipf]wished [pinf]to question Him, and He said to them, "Are you deliberating together about this, that I said, 'A little while, and you will not behold Me, and again a little while, and you will see Me'?

20 "Truly,[281] truly, I say to you, that [a]you will weep and lament,[2354] but the world[2889] will rejoice;[5463] you will be sorrowful, but [b]your sorrow will be turned to joy.

21 "[a]Whenever a woman is in travail[5088] she has sorrow, because her hour[5610] has come; but when she gives birth[1080] to the child, she remembers the anguish[2347] no more, for joy that a [I]child[444] has [aop]been born[1080] into the world.

22 "Therefore [a]you too now have sorrow; but [b]I will see you again, and your heart will rejoice, and no one takes your joy away from you.

Prayer Promises

23 "And [a]in that day [b]you will [I]ask[2065] Me no question. Truly, truly, I say to you, [c]if you shall [aosb]ask the Father for anything, He will give it to you in My name.

24 "[a]Until now[2193,737] you have [ao]asked for nothing in My name; [pim]ask, and you will receive, that your [b]joy may be made full.[4137]

25 "These things I have spoken to you in [Ia]figurative language; [b]an hour[5610] is coming when I will speak no more to you in [I]figurative language, but will tell you plainly of the Father.

26 "[a]In that day [b]you will ask[154] in My name, and I do not say to you that I will request[2065] the Father on your behalf;

27 for [a]the Father Himself loves[5368] you, because you have [pfi]loved Me, and [b]have [pfi]believed[4100] that [c]I came forth from the Father.

28 "[a]I came forth from the Father,[3962] and have [pfi]come into the world; I am leaving[863] the world again, and [b]going to the Father."[3962]

29 His disciples *said, "Lo, now You are speaking[2980] plainly, and are not using [a]a [I]figure of speech.

30 "Now we know[1492] that You know[1492] all things, and have no need for anyone to question[2065] You; by this we [a]believe[4100] that You [b]came from God."

31 Jesus answered them, "Do you now believe?[4100]

32 "Behold, [a]an hour[5610] is coming, and has *already* [pfi]come, for [b]you to be [asbp]scattered, each to [c]his own *home*,[2398] and to [aosb]leave[863] Me alone; and *yet* [d]I am not alone, because the Father is with Me.

11 [a]John 12:31
13 [a]John 14:17 [b]John 14:26
14 [a]John 7:39
15 [a]John 17:10
16 [a]John 7:33 [b]John 14:18-24; 16:16-24 [c]John 16:22
17 [a]John 16:16 [b]John 16:5
19 [a]Mark 9:32; John 6:61
20 [a]Mark 16:10; Luke 23:27 [b]John 20:20
21 [I]Lit., *human being* [a]Is. 13:8; 21:3; 26:17; 66:7; Hos. 13:13; Mic. 4:9; 1Thess. 5:3
22 [a]John 16:6 [b]John 16:16
23 [I]Lit., *question Me nothing* [a]John 14:20; 16:26 [b]John 16:19, 30 [c]John 15:16
24 [a]John 14:14 [b]John 3:29; 15:11
25 [I]Lit., *proverbs;* or, *figures of speech* [a]Matt. 13:34; John 10:6; 16:29 [b]John 16:2
26 [a]John 14:20; 16:23 [b]John 16:19, 30
27 [a]John 14:21, 23 [b]John 2:11; 16:30 [c]John 8:42
28 [a]John 8:42; 16:30 [b]John 13:1, 3; 16:5, 10, 17
29 [I]Lit., *proverb* [a]Matt. 13:34; John 10:6; 16:25
30 [a]John 2:11; 16:27 [b]John 8:42; 16:28
32 [a]John 4:23; 16:2, 25 [b]Zech. 13:7; Matt. 26:31 [c]John 19:27 [d]John 8:29

🔑 33 "These things I have spoken to
you, that [a]in Me you may [aosb]have
peace.[1515] [b]In the world you have tribulation,[2347] but [pim] [c]take courage; [d]I have
[pfi]overcome the world."[2889]

The High Priestly Prayer

17 These things Jesus spoke; and
[a]lifting up His eyes to heaven,[3772]
He said, "Father, the hour[5610] has come;
[aim] [b]glorify[1392] Thy Son, that the Son may
[aosb]glorify Thee,
2 even as [a]Thou gavest Him
authority[1849] over all [I]mankind,[4561] that
[b]to [II]all whom Thou hast [pfi]given Him,
[c]He [aosb]may give eternal life.[2222]
3 "And this is [art]eternal life, that they
may know Thee, [a]the only true[228] God,
and Jesus Christ[5547] whom [b]Thou hast
[ao]sent.[649]
4 "[a]I [ao]glorified Thee on the earth,
[b]having [apt]accomplished[5048] the work
which Thou hast given Me to do.
🔑 5 "And now, [aim] [a]glorify Thou Me
together with Thyself, Father, with the
glory[1391] which I had [b]with Thee before
the world[2889] was.
6 "[a]I [ao]manifested[5319] Thy name to
the men[444] whom [b]Thou [ao]gavest Me
out of the world; [c]Thine they were, and
Thou gavest them to Me, and they have
[pfi] [d]kept Thy word.[3056]
7 "Now they have come to know
that everything Thou hast given Me is
from Thee;
8 for [a]the words[4487] which Thou
gavest Me [b]I have [pfi]given to them; and
they [ao]received *them,* and truly [ao]under-
stood that [c]I came forth from Thee, and
they [ao]believed[4100] that [d]Thou didst
send[649] Me.
9 "[a]I ask[2065] on their behalf; [b]I do
not ask on behalf of the world, but of
those whom [c]Thou hast given Me; for
[d]they are Thine;
10 and [a]all things that are Mine are
Thine, and Thine are Mine; and I have
been [pfip]glorified[1392] in them.
🔑 11 "And I am no more in the
world;[2889] and *yet* [a]they themselves are
in the world, and [b]I come to Thee.
[c]Holy[40] Father,[3962] [aim]keep[5083] them in
Thy name, *the name* [d]which Thou hast
given Me, that [e]they may be one, even
as We *are.*
🔑 12 "While I was with them, I was
[ipf]keeping them in Thy name [a]which
Thou hast given Me; and I [ao]guarded[5442]
them, and [b]not one of them [aom]perished
but [c]the son[5207] of perdition,[684] that the
[d]Scripture might be fulfilled.

The Disciples in the World

13 "But now [a]I come to Thee; and
[b]these things I speak in the world, that
they may [psa]have My [c]joy made full in
themselves.
14 "I have given them Thy word;
and [a]the world has hated them, because
[b]they are not of the world, even as I
am not of the world.
15 "I do not ask[2065] Thee to [aosb]take
them out of the world, but to [aosb]keep
them [I]from [II][a]the evil *one.*[4190]
16 "[a]They are not of the world, even
as I am not of the world.
17 "[a]Sanctify[37] them in the truth;
Thy word[3056] is truth.[225]
18 "As [a]Thou didst send[649] Me into
the world, [b]I also have sent them into
the world.
19 "And for their sakes I [a]sanctify[37]
Myself, that they themselves also may
be [b]sanctified [c]in truth.
20 "I do not ask[2065] in behalf of these
alone, but for those also who [ppt]be-
lieve[4100] in Me through their word;[3056]
🔑 21 that they may all [psa]be [a]one;

33 [a]John 14:27 [b]John 15:18ff. [c]Matt. 9:2 [d]Rom. 8:37; 2Cor. 2:14; 4:7ff.; 6:4ff.; Rev. 3:21; 12:11

1 [a]John 11:41 [b]John 7:39; 13:31f.
2 [I]Lit., *flesh* [II]Lit., *all that which Thou hast given Him, to them He* [a]John 3:35 [b]John 6:37, 39; 17:6, 9, 24 [c]John 10:28
3 [a]John 5:44 [b]John 3:17; 17:8, 21, 23, 25
4 [a]John 13:31 [b]Luke 22:37; John 4:34
5 [a]John 17:1 [b]John 1:1; 8:58; 17:24; Phil. 2:6
6 [a]John 17:26 [b]John 6:37, 39; 17:2, 9, 24 [c]John 17:9 [d]John 8:51
8 [a]John 6:68; 12:49 [b]John 15:15; 17:14, 26 [c]John 8:42; 16:27, 30 [d]John 3:17; 17:18, 21, 23, 25
9 [a]Luke 22:32; John 14:16 [b]Luke 23:34; John 17:20f. [c]John 6:37, 39; 17:2, 6, 24 [d]John 17:6
10 [a]John 16:15
11 [a]John 13:1 [b]John 7:33; 17:13 [c]John 17:25 [d]John 17:6; Phil. 2:9; Rev. 19:12 [e]John 17:21f.; Rom. 12:5; Gal. 3:28
12 [a]John 17:6; Phil. 2:9; Rev. 19:12 [b]John 6:39; 18:9 [c]John 6:70 [d]Ps. 41:9; John 13:18
13 [a]John 7:33; 17:11 [b]John 15:11 [c]John 3:29
14 [a]John 15:19 [b]John 8:23;
17:16 **15** [I]Or, *out of* the power of [II]Or, *evil* [a]Matt. 5:37
16 [a]John 17:14 **17** [a]John 15:3 **18** [a]John 3:17; 17:3, 8, 21, 23, 25 [b]Matt. 10:5; John 4:38; 20:21
19 [a]John 15:13 [b]John 15:3 [c]2Cor. 7:14; Col. 1:6; 1John 3:18

🔑 **16:33** See note on II Tim. 1:12.
🔑 **17:5,11,21,22** See note on Phil. 2:6-8.
🔑 **17:12** See note on II Thess. 2:3.

[a]even as Thou, Father, *art* in Me, and
I in Thee, that they also may be in Us;
[b]that the world may [psa] [I]believe that
[c]Thou didst send Me.

Their Future Glory

22 "And the [a]glory[1391] which Thou
hast given Me I have given to them;
that they may be one, just as We are
one;
23 [a]I in them, and Thou in Me,
that they may be perfected[5048] [I]in unity,
that the world may [psa] [II]know[1097] that
[b]Thou didst send Me, and didst [ao] [c]love[25]
them, even as Thou didst love[25] Me.
24 "Father, [I]I desire that [a]they also,
whom Thou hast given Me, [b]be with
Me where I am, in order that they may
[psa]behold[2334] My [c]glory, which Thou hast
given Me; for Thou didst love Me before
[d]the foundation[2602] of the world.[2889]
25 "O [a]righteous[1342] Father, [I]al-
though [b]the world has not [ao]known[1097]
Thee, [I]yet I have [ao]known Thee; and
these have [ao]known that [c]Thou didst
send Me;
26 and [a]I have made Thy name
[ao]known[1107] to them, and will make it
known; that [b]the love wherewith Thou
didst love[26] Me may be in them, and I
in them."

Judas Betrays Jesus

18 When Jesus had spoken these
words, [a]He went forth with His
disciples[3101] over [b]the [I]ravine of the
Kidron, where there was [c]a garden, into
which He Himself entered, and His disciples.
2 Now Judas also, who was [I]betray-
ing Him, knew the place; for Jesus had
[a]often met there[1563] with His disciples.
3 [a]Judas then, having received
[b]the *Roman* [I]cohort, and [c]officers from
the chief priests[749] and the Pharisees,
*came there with lanterns and [d]torches
and weapons.
4 Jesus therefore, [a]knowing all the
things that were coming[2064] upon Him,
went forth, and *said to them, "[b]Whom
do you seek?"
5 They answered Him, "Jesus the
Nazarene." He *said to them, "I am
He." And Judas also who was [ppt]betray-
ing Him, was standing with them.
6 When therefore He said to them,
"I am *He*," they drew back, and fell[4098]
to the ground.
7 Again therefore He asked them,
"[a]Whom do you seek?" And they said,
"Jesus the Nazarene."
8 Jesus answered, "I told you that
I am *He*; if therefore you seek Me, let
these [pinf]go their way,"
9 that the word might be fulfilled[4137]
which He spoke, "[a]Of those whom Thou
hast given Me I [ao]lost[622] not one."
10 Simon Peter therefore [a]hav-
ing[2192] a sword, drew it, and struck[3817]
the high priest's slave,[1401] and cut off
his right ear; and the slave's name was
Malchus.
11 Jesus therefore said to Peter,
"Put[906] the sword into the sheath;
[a]the cup which the Father has given Me,
shall I not [efn]drink it?"

Jesus before the Priests

12 [a]So [b]the *Roman* [I]cohort and the
[II]commander, and the [c]officers of the
Jews, arrested Jesus and bound Him,
13 and led Him to [a]Annas first; for
he was father-in-law of [b]Caiaphas, who
was high priest[749] that year.
14 Now Caiaphas was the one who
had advised the Jews that [a]it was
expedient[4851] for one man[444] to [ainf]die[599]
on behalf of the people.
15 And [a]Simon Peter was [ipf]follow-
ing Jesus, and *so was* another[243]
disciple.[3101] Now that disciple was
known[1110] to the high priest, and entered
with Jesus into [b]the court of the high
priest,
16 [a]but Peter was standing at[4314] the

---

21 [I]Gr. tense indicates *continually believe* [a]John 10:38; 17:11, 23 [b]John 17:8 [c]John 3:17; 17:3, 8, 18, 23, 25
22 [a]John 1:14; 17:24
23 [I]Lit., *into a unit* [II]Gr. tense indicates *continually know* [a]John 10:38; 17:11, 21 [b]John 3:17; 17:3, 8, 18, 21, 25 [c]John 16:27
24 [I]Some mss. read *that which Thou hast given Me, I desire that where I am, they also may be with Me, that* [a]John 17:2 [b]John 12:26 [c]John 1:14; 17:22 [d]Matt. 25:34; John 17:5
25 [I]Lit., *and* [a]John 17:11; 1John 1:9 [b]John 7:29; 15:21 [c]John 3:17; 17:3, 8, 18, 21, 23
26 [a]John 17:6 [b]John 15:9

1 [I]Lit., *winter-torrent* [a]Matt. 26:30, 36; Mark 14:26, 32; Luke 22:39 [b]2Sam. 15:23; 1Kin. 2:37; 15:13; 2Kin. 23:4, 6, 12; 2Chr. 15:16; 29:16; 30:14; Jer. 31:40 [c]Matt. 26:36; Mark 14:32; John 18:26
2 [I]Or, *delivering Him up* [a]Luke 21:37; 22:39
3 [I]Normally 600 men; *a battalion* [a]John 18:3-11: *Matt. 26:47-56; Mark 14:43-50; Luke 22:47-53* [b]John 18:12; Acts 10:1 [c]John 7:32; 18:12, 18 [d]Matt. 25:1
4 [a]John 6:64; 13:1, 11 [b]John 18:7
7 [a]John 18:4
9 [a]John 17:12
10 [a]Matt. 26:51; Mark 14:47
11 [a]Matt. 20:22; 26:39; Mark 14:36; Luke 22:42
12 [I]Or, *battalion* [II]I.e., chiliarch, in command of a thousand troops [a]John 18:12f.: *Matt. 26:57ff.* [b]John 18:3
13 [a]Luke 3:2; John 18:24 [b]Matt. 26:3; John 11:49, 51
14 [a]John 11:50
15 [a]Matt. 26:58; Mark 14:54; Luke 22:54 [b]Matt. 26:3; John 18:24, 28
16 [a]John 18:16-18: *Matt. 26:69f.; Mark 14:66-68; Luke 22:55-57*

door outside.[1854] So the other disciple, who was known to the high priest, went out and spoke to the doorkeeper, and brought in Peter.

17 [a]The slave-girl[3814] therefore who kept the door *said to Peter, "[b]You are not also *one* of this man's disciples, are you?" He *said, "I am not."

18 Now the slaves[1401] and the [a]officers[5257] were [plpf]standing *there,* having [pfp]made [b]a charcoal fire, for it was cold and they were [ipf] [c]warming themselves; and Peter also was with them, [pfp]standing and [ppt]warming himself.

19 [a]The high priest therefore questioned[2065] Jesus about His disciples,[3101] and about His teaching.[1322]

20 Jesus answered him, "I [a]have spoken openly to the world; [epn]I always [ao] [b]taught[1321] in [I]synagogues,[4864] and [c]in the temple,[2411] where[3699] all the Jews come together;[4905] and I [ao]spoke nothing in secret.

21 "Why do you [pin]question[1905] Me? Question those who have [pfp]heard what I spoke to them; behold, these know[1492] what I said."

22 And when He had [apt]said this, one of the [a]officers[5257] standing by [b]gave Jesus a blow, saying, "Is that the way You answer the high priest?"

23 [a]Jesus answered him, "If I have spoken wrongly,[2560] bear witness of the wrong; but if rightly, why do you strike[1194] Me?"

24 [a]Annas therefore [ao]sent Him bound to [a]Caiaphas the high priest.

Peter's Denial of Jesus

25 [a]Now [b]Simon Peter was standing and warming himself. They said therefore to him, "[c]You are not also *one* of His disciples,[3101] are you?" He denied[720] *it,* and said, "I am not."

26 One of the slaves[1401] of the high priest, being a relative of the one [a]whose ear Peter cut off, *said, "Did I not see you in [b]the garden with Him?"

27 Peter therefore denied *it* again; and immediately [a]a cock crowed.

Jesus before Pilate

28 [a]They *led Jesus therefore from [b]Caiaphas into [c]the [I]Praetorium, and it was early; and they themselves did not enter into [c]the [I]Praetorium in order that [d]they might not be [asbp]defiled, but might [aosb]eat the Passover.[3957]

29 [a]Pilate therefore went out to them, and *said, "What accusation[2724] do you bring[5342] against this Man?"

30 They answered and said to him, "If this Man were not an evildoer,[2556,4160] we would not have delivered Him up to you."

31 Pilate therefore said to them, "Take Him yourselves, and [aim]judge[2919] Him according to your law." The Jews said to him, "We are not permitted to put anyone to [ainf]death,"

32 that [a]the word of Jesus might be fulfilled, which He spoke, signifying by what kind of death[2288] He [ipf]was about [pinf]to die.

33 Pilate therefore [a]entered again into the Praetorium, and summoned Jesus, and said to Him, "[b]Are You the King[935] of the Jews?"

34 Jesus answered, "Are you saying this [I]on your own initiative, or did others tell you about Me?"

35 Pilate answered, "I am not a Jew, am I? Your own nation and the chief priests[749] [ao]delivered You up to me; what have You [ao]done?"

36 Jesus answered, "[a]My kingdom[932] [I]is not of this world.[2889] If My kingdom were of this world, then My servants[5257] would be [ipf]fighting,[75] that I might not be [asbp]delivered up to the Jews; but as it is, My kingdom is not [II]of this realm."

37 Pilate therefore said to Him, "So You are a king?" Jesus answered, "[a]You say *correctly* that I am a king.[935] For this I have been [pfip]born, and for this I have [pfi]come into the world, [b]to [aosb]bear witness to the truth.[225] [c]Everyone who is of the truth hears My voice."

38 Pilate *said to Him, "What is truth?"

And when he had said this, he

17 [a]Acts 12:13 [b]John 18:25
18 [a]John 18:3 [b]John 21:9 [c]Mark 14:54, 67
19 [a]John 18:19-24; *Matt. 26:59-68; Mark 14:55-65; Luke 22:63-71*
20 [I]Lit., *the synagogue* [a]John 7:26; 8:26 [b]Matt. 4:23; John 6:59 [c]Matt. 26:55
22 [a]John 18:3 [b]John 19:3
23 [a]Matt. 5:39; Acts 23:2-5
24 [a]John 18:13
25 [a]John 18:25-27: *Matt. 26:71-75; Mark 14:69-72; Luke 22:58-62* [b]John 18:18 [c]John 18:17
26 [a]John 18:10 [b]John 18:1
27 [a]John 13:38
28 [I]I.e., governor's official residence [a]Matt. 27:2; Mark 15:1; Luke 23:1 [b]John 18:13 [c]Matt. 27:27; John 18:33; 19:9 [d]John 11:55; Acts 11:3
29 [a]John 18:29-38: *Matt. 27:11-14; Mark 15:2-5; Luke 23:2, 3*
32 [a]Matt. 20:19; 26:2; Mark 10:33f.; Luke 18:32f.; John 3:14; 8:28; 12:32f.
33 [a]John 18:28, 29; 19:9 [b]Luke 23:3; John 19:12
34 [I]Lit., *from yourself*
36 [I]Or, *is not derived from* [II]Lit., *from here* [a]Matt. 26:53; Luke 17:21; John 6:15
37 [a]Matt. 27:11; Mark 15:2; Luke 22:70; 23:3 [b]John 1:14; 3:32; 8:14 [c]John 8:47; 1John 4:6

[a]went out again to the Jews,2453 and *said to them, "[b]I find2147 no guilt156 in Him.

39 "[a]But you have a custom, that I should release someone [I]for you at the Passover; do you wish then that I [aosb]release [I]for you the King of the Jews?"

40 Therefore they cried out again, saying, "[a]Not this Man, but Barabbas." Now Barabbas was a robber.3027

The Crown of Thorns

19 Then Pilate therefore took Jesus, and [Ia]scourged3146 Him.

2 [a]And the soldiers [apt]wove4120 a crown of thorns and [ao]put it on His head, and arrayed Him in a purple robe;

3 and they *began* to come up to Him, and [ipf]say, "[a]Hail,5463 King of the Jews!" and to [ipfb]give Him blows *in the face.*

4 And Pilate [a]came out again, and *said to them, "Behold, I am bringing Him out to you, that you [aosb]may know that [b]I find2147 no guilt in Him."

5 Jesus therefore came out, [a]wearing5409 the crown of thorns and the purple robe. And *Pilate* *said to them, "Behold, the Man!"

6 When therefore the chief priests749 and the [a]officers5257 saw Him, they cried out, saying, "Crucify,4717 crucify!" Pilate *said to them, [aim]"Take Him yourselves, and [aim]crucify Him, for [b]I find no guilt in Him."

7 The Jews answered him, "[a]We have a law, and by that law He ought to [ainf]die599 because He [b]made Himself out *to be* the [an]Son5207 of God."2316

8 When Pilate therefore heard this statement, he was the more afraid;5399

9 and he [a]entered into the [I]Praetorium again, and *said to Jesus, "Where are You from?" But [b]Jesus gave him no answer.612

10 Pilate therefore *said to Him, "You do not speak to me? Do You not know that I have authority to [ainf]release You, and I have authority1849 to [ainf]crucify You?"

11 Jesus answered, "[a]You would have no authority [I]over Me, unless it had been [pfpp]given you from above;509 for this reason [b]he who [apt]delivered Me up to you has *the* greater sin."266

12 As a result of this Pilate [I]made efforts to [ainf]release Him, but the Jews [ipf]cried out, saying, "[a]If you [aosb]release this Man, you are no friend5384 of Caesar; everyone who [ppt]makes himself out *to be* a king [II]opposes Caesar."

13 When Pilate therefore heard these words, he brought Jesus out, and [a]sat down on the judgment seat at a place called [I]The Pavement, but [b]in [II]Hebrew, Gabbatha.1042

14 Now it was [a]the day of preparation for the Passover;3957 it was about the [Ib]sixth hour. And he *said to the Jews, "Behold, [c]your King!"

15 They therefore cried out, "[a]Away with *Him,* away with *Him,* crucify4717 Him!" Pilate *said to them, "Shall I crucify your King?" The chief priests answered, "We have no king but Caesar."

The Crucifixion

16 So he then [a]delivered Him to them to be [asbp]crucified.

17 [a]They took3880 Jesus therefore, and He went out, [Ib]bearing His own cross,4716 to the place called [c]the Place of a Skull, which is called [d]in [II]Hebrew, Golgotha.1115

18 There they crucified Him, and with Him [a]two other men, one on either side, and Jesus in between.

19 And Pilate wrote1125 an inscription5102 also, and put it on the cross.4716 And it was written, "[a]JESUS THE NAZARENE, [b]THE KING935 OF THE JEWS."

20 Therefore this inscription many of the Jews read,314 for the place where Jesus was crucified was near1451 the city; and it was written [a]in [I]Hebrew, Latin, *and* in Greek.

21 And so the chief priests of the Jews were saying to Pilate, "Do not

38 [a]John 18:33; 19:4 [b]Luke 23:4; John 19:4, 6
39 [I]Or, *to you* [a]John 18:39-19:16: *Matt. 27:15-26; Mark 15:6-15; Luke 23:18-25*
40 [a]Acts 3:14

1 [I]Or, *had Him scourged* [a]Matt. 27:26
2 [a]Matt. 27:27-30: *Mark 15:16-19*
3 [a]Matt. 27:29; Mark 15:18 [b]John 18:22
4 [a]John 18:33, 38 [b]Luke 23:4; John 18:38; 19:6
5 [a]John 19:2
6 [a]Matt. 26:58; John 18:3 [b]Luke 23:4; John 18:38; 19:4
7 [a]Lev. 24:16; Matt. 26:63-66 [b]John 5:18; 10:33
9 [I]I.e., governor's official residence [a]John 18:33 [b]Matt. 26:63; 27:12, 14; John 18:34-37
11 [I]Lit., *against* [a]Rom. 13:1 [b]John 18:13f., 28ff.; Acts 3:13
12 [I]Lit., *was seeking to* [II]Or, *speaks against* [a]Luke 23:2; John 18:33ff.
13 [I]Gr., *The Lithostrotos* [II]I.e., Jewish Aramaic [a]Matt. 27:19 [b]John 5:2; 19:17, 20
14 [I]Perhaps 6 a.m. (Roman time) [a]Matt. 27:62; John 19:31, 42 [b]Matt. 27:45; Mark 15:25 [c]John 19:19, 21
15 [a]Luke 23:18
16 [a]Matt. 27:26; Mark 15:15; Luke 23:25
17 [I]Lit., *bearing the cross for Himself* [II]I.e., Jewish Aramaic [a]John 19:17-24: *Matt. 27:33-44; Mark 15:22-32; Luke 23:33-43* [b]Matt. 27:32; Mark 15:21; Luke 14:27; 23:26 [c]Luke 23:33 [d]John 19:13

18 [a]Luke 23:32 **19** [a]Matt. 27:37; Mark 15:26; Luke 23:38 [b]John 19:14, 21 **20** [I]I.e., Jewish Aramaic [a]John 19:13

[pim]write, "[a]The King of the Jews'; but
that He said, 'I am [a]King of the Jews.'"
22 Pilate answered, "[a]What I have
written I have written."
23 [a]The soldiers therefore, when
they had [ao]crucified Jesus, took His
outer garments and made [b]four parts,
a part to every soldier and *also* the
[I]tunic; now the tunic was seamless,
woven [II]in one piece.
24 They said therefore to one another, "[a]Let us not [aosb]tear4927 it, but
[aosb]cast lots for it, *to decide* whose it
shall be"; [b]that the Scripture might be
fulfilled,[4137] "THEY [c]DIVIDED MY OUTER
GARMENTS[2440] AMONG THEM, AND FOR
MY CLOTHING[2441] THEY CAST [I]LOTS."
25 Therefore the soldiers did these
things. [a]But there were [plpf]standing by
the cross[4716] of Jesus [b]His mother, and
His mother's sister, Mary the *wife* of
Clopas, and [c]Mary Magdalene.
26 When Jesus therefore saw His
mother, and [a]the disciple[3101] whom He
[ipf]loved[25] standing nearby, He *said to
His mother, "[b]Woman, behold, your
son!"
27 Then He *said to the disciple,
"Behold, your mother!" And from that
hour the disciple took her into [a]his
own[2398] *household.*
28 After this, Jesus, [a]knowing that
all things had already been [pfip]accom-
plished,[5055] [b]in order that the Scripture[1124] might be [asbp]fulfilled,[5048] *said,
"[c]I am thirsty."
29 A jar full of sour wine was
standing[2749] there; so [a]they put a sponge
full of the sour wine upon *a branch of*
hyssop,5301 and [apt]brought it up to His
mouth.
30 When Jesus therefore had received the sour wine, He said, "[a]It is
[pfip]finished!"[5055] And He [apt]bowed His
head, and [b]gave up3860 His spirit.[4151]

Care of the Body of Jesus

31 The Jews therefore, because it
was [a]the day of preparation, so that
[b]the bodies should not remain on the
cross on the Sabbath4521 ([I]for that Sabbath was a [c]high *day*), asked Pilate that
their legs might be [asbp]broken,2608 and
that they might be [asbp]taken away.
32 The soldiers therefore came, and
broke2608 the legs of the first man, and
of the other[243] man who was
[aptp] [a]crucified[4957] with Him;
33 but coming to Jesus, when they
saw that He was already [pfp]dead,[2348]
they did not break His legs;
34 but one of the soldiers pierced
His side with a spear, and immediately
there came out [a]blood[129] and water.
35 And he who has [pfp]seen has
[pfi] [a]borne witness, and his witness[3141]
is true;[228] and he knows that he is telling
the truth, so that you also may
[psa]believe.[4100]
36 For these things came to pass,
[a]that the Scripture might be fulfilled,[4137]
"[b]NOT A BONE OF HIM SHALL BE [I]BRO-
KEN."
37 And again another[2087] Scripture[1124] says, "[a]THEY SHALL LOOK ON
HIM WHOM THEY PIERCED."
38 [a]And after these things Joseph
of Arimathea, being a disciple[3101] of
Jesus, but a [b]secret *one,* for [c]fear[5401]
of the Jews, asked Pilate that he might
[aosb]take away the body of Jesus; and
Pilate granted permission. He came
therefore, and took away His body.
39 And [a]Nicodemus came also, who
had first [apt]come to Him by night;
[ppt] [b]bringing a [I]mixture of [c]myrrh4666 and
aloes,250 about a [d]hundred [II]pounds
weight.
40 And so they took the body of
Jesus, and [a]bound[1210] it in [b]linen wrappings with the spices, as is the burial
custom of the Jews.
41 Now in the place where He was
crucified[4717] there was a garden; and
in the garden a [a]new tomb,3419 [b]in which
no one had yet been [aop]laid.
42 Therefore on account of the Jewish day of [a]preparation, because the
tomb was [b]nearby,[1451] they laid Jesus
there.

21 [a]John 19:14, 19
22 [a]Gen. 43:14; Esth. 4:16
23 [I]Gr., *khiton,* the garment worn next to the skin [II]Lit., *woven from the upper part through the whole* [a]Matt. 27:35; Mark 15:24; Luke 23:34 [b]Acts 12:4
24 [I]Lit., *a lot* [a]Ex. 28:32; Matt. 27:35; Mark 15:24; Luke 23:34 [b]John 19:28, 36f. [c]Ps. 22:18
25 [a]Matt. 27:55f.; Mark 15:40f.; Luke 23:49 [b]Matt. 12:46 [c]Luke 8:2; John 20:1, 18
26 [a]John 13:23 [b]John 2:4
27 [a]Luke 18:28; John 1:11; 16:32; Acts 21:6
28 [a]John 13:1; 17:4 [b]John 19:24, 36f. [c]Ps. 69:21
29 [a]John 19:29, 30: *Matt. 27:48, 50; Mark 15:36f.; Luke 23:36*
30 [a]John 17:4 [b]Matt. 27:50; Mark 15:37; Luke 23:46
31 [I]Lit., *for the day of that Sabbath was great* [a]John 19:14, 42 [b]Deut. 21:23; Josh. 8:29; 10:26f. [c]Ex. 12:16
32 [a]John 19:18
34 [a]1John 5:6, 8
35 [a]John 15:27; 21:24
36 [I]Or, *crushed* or *shattered* [a]John 19:24, 28 [b]Ex. 12:46; Num. 9:12; Ps. 34:20
37 [a]Zech. 12:10; Rev. 1:7
38 [a]John 19:38-42: *Matt. 27:57-61; Mark 15:42-47; Luke 23:50-56* [b]Mark 15:43 [c]John 7:13
39 [I]Another reading is *package of* [II]I.e., 100 litras (12 oz. each) [a]John 3:1 [b]Mark 16:1 [c]Ps. 45:8; Prov. 7:17; Song 4:14; Matt. 2:11 [d]John 12:3
40 [a]Matt. 26:12; Mark 14:8; John 11:44 [b]Luke 24:12; John 20:5, 7
41 [a]Matt. 27:60 [b]Luke 23:53
42 [a]John 19:14, 31 [b]John 19:20, 41

The Empty Tomb

20 [a]Now on the first *day* of the week [b]Mary Magdalene *came early to the tomb,[3419] while it *was still dark,[4653] and *saw[991] [c]the stone *already* [pfpp]taken away from the tomb.

2 And so she *ran and *came to Simon Peter, and to the other[243] [a]disciple[3101] whom Jesus [ipf] [1]loved,[5368] and *said to them, "[b]They have [ao]taken away the Lord[2962] out of the tomb, and we do not know where they have [ao]laid Him."

3 [a]Peter therefore went forth, and the other disciple, and they were going to the tomb.

4 And the two were [ipf]running together; and the other disciple ran ahead faster than Peter, and came to the tomb first;[4413]

5 and [apt] [a]stooping[3879] and looking in, he *saw the [b]linen wrappings lying *there;* but he did not go in.

6 Simon Peter therefore also *came,[2064] following him, and entered the tomb; and he *beheld[2334] the linen wrappings [apt]lying *there,*

7 and [a]the face-cloth,[4676] which had been on His head, not lying with the [b]linen wrappings, but rolled up in a place by itself.

8 So the other disciple who [a]had first[4413] [apt]come to the tomb entered then also, and he saw and believed.[4100]

9 For as yet [a]they did not [plpf]understand the Scripture, [b]that He must [ainf]rise again from the dead.[3498]

10 So the disciples went away again [a]to their own homes.

11 [a]But Mary was [plpf]standing outside[1854] the tomb weeping; and so, as she [ipf]wept, she [b]stooped[3879] and looked into the tomb;

12 and she *beheld [a]two angels in white sitting, one at[4314] the head, and one at the feet, where the body of Jesus had been [ipf]lying.

13 And they *said to her, "[a]Woman, why are you weeping?" She *said to them, "Because [b]they have taken away my Lord,[2962] and I do not know where they have [ao]laid Him."

14 When she had said this, she turned around, and *[a]beheld[2334] Jesus standing *there,* and [b]did not know[1492] that it was Jesus.

15 Jesus *said to her, "[a]Woman, why are you weeping? Whom are you seeking?" Supposing Him to be the gardener, she *said to Him, "Sir,[2962] if you have [ao]carried[941] Him away, tell me where you have [ao]laid Him, and I will take Him away."

16 Jesus *said to her, "Mary!" She *turned and *said to Him [a]in [1]Hebrew, "[b]Rabboni!"[4462] (which means, Teacher).

17 Jesus *said to her, "Stop [pim]clinging[680] to Me, for I have not yet [pfi]ascended to the Father; but [pim]go to [a]My brethren,[80] and [aim]say to them, 'I [pin] [b]ascend to My Father[3962] and your Father, and My God[2316] and your God.' "

18 [a]Mary Magdalene *came, [ppt] [b]announcing[518] to the disciples,[3101] "I have [pfi]seen the Lord," and *that* He had said these things to her.

Jesus among His Disciples

19 When therefore it was evening, on that day, the first *day* of the week, and when the doors were [pfpp]shut where the disciples[3101] were, for [a]fear[5401] of the Jews, Jesus came and stood in their midst, and *said to them, "[1][b]Peace[1515] *be* with you."

20 And when He had said this, [a]He showed them both His hands and His side. The disciples therefore [b]rejoiced when they saw the Lord.

1 [a]John 20:1-8; *Matt. 28:1-8; Mark 16:1-8; Luke 24:1-10* [b]John 19:25; 20:18 [c]Matt. 27:60, 66; 28:2; Mark 15:46; 16:3f.; Luke 24:2; John 11:38
2 [1]Lit., *was loving* [a]John 13:23 [b]John 20:13
3 [a]Luke 24:12; John 20:3-10
5 [a]John 20:11 [b]John 19:40
7 [a]John 11:44 [b]John 19:40
8 [a]John 20:4
9 [a]Matt. 22:29; John 2:22 [b]Luke 24:26ff., 46
10 [a]Luke 24:12
11 [a]Mark 16:5 [b]John 20:5
12 [a]Matt. 28:2f.; Mark 16:5; Luke 24:4
13 [a]John 20:15 [b]John 20:2
14 [a]Matt. 28:9; Mark 16:9 [b]John 21:4
15 [a]John 20:13
16 [1]I.e., Jewish Aramaic [a]John 5:2 [b]Matt. 23:7; Mark 10:51
17 [a]Matt. 28:10 [b]Mark 12:26; 16:19; John 7:33
18 [a]John 20:1 [b]Mark 16:10; Luke 24:10, 23
19 [1]Lit., *Peace to you* [a]John 7:13 [b]Luke 24:36; John 14:27; 20:21, 26
20 [a]Luke 24:39, 40; John 19:34 [b]John 16:20, 22

20:1 See general remarks on I Jn.
20:17 The verb *haptou,* the present imperative of *haptō* (681), should be translated "do not continue touching me." It is not "do not touch me" as is commonly translated and should have been translated if this verb had been in the aorist imperative, *hapsou.*

21 Jesus therefore said to them again, "[a]Peace *be* with you; [b]as the Father has [pfi]sent[649] Me, I also send you."

🔑 22 And when He had said this, He breathed on them, and *said to them, [aim]"Receive the [an]Holy Spirit.[4151]

23 "[a]If you [asba]forgive[863] the sins[266] of any, *their sins* [I]have been [pinp]forgiven[863] them; if you [psa]retain[2902] the *sins* of any, they have been [pfip]retained."[2902]

24 But [a]Thomas, one of [b]the twelve, called [Ia]Didymus,[1324] was not with them when Jesus came.

25 The other[243] disciples[3101] therefore were [ipf]saying to him, "We have seen the Lord!"[2962] But he said to them, "Unless I shall see[1492] in [a]His hands the imprint[5179] of the nails, and put my finger into the place of the nails, and put my hand into His side, [b]I will not believe."[4100]

26 And [I]after eight days again His disciples were inside, and Thomas with them. Jesus *came, the doors having been [pfpp] [II]shut, and stood in their midst, and said, "[a]Peace[1515] *be* with you."

27 Then He *said to Thomas, "[a]Reach here your finger, and see My hands; and reach here your hand, and put it into My side; and be not unbelieving,[571] but [ajn]believing."[4103]

28 Thomas answered and said to Him, "My Lord and my God!"[2316]

29 Jesus *said to him, "Because you have seen Me, have you believed? [a]Blessed[3107] *are* they who did not [apt]see, and *yet* [apt]believed."

Why This Gospel Was Written

30 [a]Many other [Ib]signs[4592] therefore Jesus also performed in the presence of the disciples, which are not written in this book;[975]

31 but these have been [pfip]written [a]that you may [psa]believe[4100] that Jesus is [I]the Christ,[5547] [b]the Son[5207] of God;[2316] and that [c]believing you may [psa]have life[2222] in His name.[3686]

Jesus Appears at the Sea of Galilee

21 After these things Jesus [Ia]manifested[5319] Himself [b]again to the disciples[3101] at the [c]Sea of Tiberias, and He manifested *Himself* in this way.

2 There were together Simon Peter, and [a]Thomas called [I]Didymus, and [b]Nathanael of [c]Cana in Galilee, and [d]the *sons* of Zebedee, and two others[243] of His disciples.

3 Simon Peter *said to them, "I am going [pinf]fishing." They *said to him, "We will also come with you." They went out, and got into the boat; and [a]that night they caught nothing.

4 But when the day was now breaking, Jesus stood on the beach; yet the disciples did not [a]know[1492] that it was Jesus.

5 Jesus therefore *said to them, "Children, [a]you do not have [I]any fish,[4371] do you?" They answered Him, "No."

6 And He said to them, "[a]Cast the net[1350] on the right-hand side of the boat, and you will find *a catch*." They cast therefore, and then they were not able to haul[1670] it in because of the great number of fish.

7 [a]That disciple therefore whom Jesus [ipf] [I]loved *said to Peter, "It is the Lord."[2962] And so when Simon Peter heard that it was the Lord, he put his outer garment on[1241] (for he was stripped[1131] *for work*), and threw[906] himself into the sea.

8 But the other[243] disciples came in the little boat, for they were not far from the land,[1093] but about [I]one hundred

21 [a]Luke 24:36; John 14:27; 20:19, 26 [b]John 17:18
23 [I]I.e., have previously been forgiven [a]Matt. 16:19; 18:18
24 [I]I.e., the Twin [a]John 11:16 [b]John 6:67
25 [a]John 20:20 [b]Mark 16:11
26 [I]Or, *a week later* [II]Or, *locked* [a]Luke 24:36; John 14:27; 20:19, 21
27 [a]Luke 24:40; John 20:25
29 [a]1Pet. 1:8
30 [I]Or, *attesting miracles* [a]John 21:25 [b]John 2:11
31 [I]I.e., the Messiah [a]John 19:35 [b]Matt. 4:3 [c]John 3:15

1 [I]Or, *made Himself visible* [a]Mark 16:12; John 21:14 [b]John 20:19, 26 [c]John 6:1
2 [I]I.e., the Twin [a]John 11:16 [b]John 1:45ff. [c]John 2:1 [d]Matt. 4:21; Mark 1:19; Luke 5:10
3 [a]Luke 5:5
4 [a]Luke 24:16; John 20:14
5 [I]Lit., *something eaten with bread* [a]Luke 24:41
6 [a]Luke 5:4ff.
7 [I]Lit., *was loving* [a]John 13:23; 21:20
8 [I]Lit., *200 cubits*

🔑 **20:22,23** This was one of the many times that God "breathed," gave, or filled His people with the Holy Spirit. This giving or filling of the Holy Spirit is not to be confused with the baptism in the Holy Spirit (see note on Acts 1:5) and the special advent of the Holy Spirit, the fulfillment of the baptism in the Holy Spirit at Penecost, Caesarea and Ephesus (Acts 2:1-13; 11:15-18; 19:1-7). See Editor's book on I Cor. 12:13 and related passages entitled, *The Holy Spirit's Baptism and Infilling.*

🔑 **20:23** See note on Mt. 16:18,19.

yards[4083] away, dragging[4951] the net *full* of fish.

9 And so when they [ao]got out upon the land,[1093] they *saw a charcoal [a]fire *already* laid, and [b]fish placed on it, and bread.

10 Jesus *said to them, "Bring some of the [a]fish which you have now [ao]caught."

11 Simon Peter went up, and drew[1670] the net to land,[1093] full of large fish, a hundred and fifty-three; and although there were so many, the net was not torn.

Jesus Provides

12 Jesus *said to them, "Come *and* have [a]breakfast." None of the disciples [ipf]ventured[5111] to [ainf]question Him, "Who are You?" knowing[1492] that it was the Lord.

13 Jesus *came and *took [a]the bread, and *gave them, and the [b]fish likewise.

14 This is now the [a]third time that Jesus [I]was manifested[5319] to the disciples, after He was raised[1453] from the dead.[3498]

The Love Motivation

🔑 15 So when they had [a]finished breakfast, Jesus *said to Simon Peter, "Simon, [I]*son* of John, do you [IIb]love[25] Me more than these?" He *said to Him, "Yes, Lord; You know[1492] that I [III]love[5368] You." He *said to him, "Tend [c]My lambs."[721]

16 He *said to him again a second time, "Simon, *son* of John, do you [I]love[25] Me?" He *said to Him, "Yes, Lord; You know[1492] that I [II]love[5368] You." He *said to him, "[a pim]Shepherd[4165] My sheep."

17 He *said to him the third time, "Simon, *son* of John, do you [I]love[5368] Me?" Peter was grieved because He said to him [a]the third time, "Do you [I]love[5368] Me?" And he said to Him, "Lord, [b]You know[1097] all things; You know that I [I]love[5368] You." Jesus *said to him, "[c]Tend My sheep.

Our Times Are in His Hand

18 "Truly,[281] truly, I say to you, when you were[2258] younger, you used to [ipf]gird yourself, and [ipf]walk wherever you [ipf]wished; but when you [aosb]grow old, you will stretch out your hands, and someone else will gird you, and bring you where you do not wish to *go.*"

19 Now this He said, [a]signifying by [b]what kind of death[2288] he would glorify[1392] God. And when He had spoken this, He *said to him, "[c]Follow[190] Me!"

20 Peter, [apt]turning around, *saw the [a]disciple[3181] whom Jesus loved[25] following *them;* the one who also had [b]leaned back on His breast at the supper, and said, "Lord, who is the one who [ppt]betrays You?"

21 Peter therefore seeing him *said to Jesus, "Lord,[2962] and what about this man?"

22 Jesus *said to him, "If I [psa]want him to [pinf]remain[3306] [a]until I come, what *is that* to you? You [pim b]follow[190] Me!"

23 This saying therefore went out among [a]the brethren[80] that that disciple would not die;[599] yet Jesus did not say to him that he would not die, but *only,* "If I want him to remain [b]until I come, what *is that* to you?"

24 This is the disciple who [ppt a]bears witness[3140] of these things, and [apt]wrote these things; and we know[1492] that his witness[3141] is true.

25 And there are also [a]many other things which Jesus did, which if they *were [psmp]written[1125] in detail, I suppose that even the world itself *would not contain the books which *were written.[1125]

9 [a]John 18:18 [b]John 6:9, 11; 21:10, 13

10 [a]John 6:9, 11; 21:9, 13

12 [a]John 21:15

13 [a]John 21:9 [b]John 6:9, 11; 21:9, 10

14 [I]Or, *made Himself visible* [a]John 20:19, 26

15 [I]Here and in vv. 16 and 17 some mss. read *son of Jonas* [II]Gr., *agapao* [III]Gr., *phileo* [a]John 21:12 [b]Matt. 26:33; Mark 14:29; John 13:37 [c]Luke 12:32

16 [I]Gr., *agapao* [II]Gr., *phileo* [a]Matt. 2:6; Acts 20:28; 1Pet. 5:2; Rev. 7:17

17 [I]Gr., *phileo* [a]John 13:38 [b]John 16:30 [c]John 21:15, 16

19 [a]John 12:33; 18:32 [b]2Pet. 1:14 [c]Matt. 8:22; 16:24; John 21:22

20 [a]John 21:7 [b]John 13:25

22 [a]Matt. 16:27f.; 1Cor. 4:5; 11:26; James 5:7; Rev. 2:25 [b]Matt. 8:22; 16:24; John 21:19

23 [a]Acts 1:15 [b]Matt. 16:27f.; 1Cor. 4:5; 11:26; James 5:7; Rev. 2:25

24 [a]John 15:27

25 [a]John 20:30

🔑 **21:15-23** Two words, *agapaō* (25) and *phileō* (5368), are used here but they are both translated as "love." The word *agapaō* is to love unselfishly to the point that you would be willing to sacrifice. This is the word that we find in Jn. 3:16. The word *phileō* or *philō* actually means to be a friend or to have the same interests with another person.

THE ACTS

of the Apostles

The Book of Acts is the second volume of a two-volume set written by Luke, the physician. The "first account" of Acts 1:1 refers to the Gospel of Luke. Both books were written to Theophilus (Luke 1:3; Acts 1:1). The Acts of the Apostles tells how the early followers of Jesus, led by the Holy Spirit, spread the Gospel far beyond the confines of Jewish life to the whole world. Jesus said: "And you shall be my witnessses both in Jerusalem, and in all Judea and Samaria, and even to the remotest part of the earth" (Acts 1:8). This is the three-fold outline for the Book of Acts. Acts reveals the sometimes painful implications of the Gospel to the Gentiles. The Lord had never intended for the message of Jesus to remain "bottled up" in one little culture. New wine requires new winebags which can stretch. Everything before Acts was focused upon God's untiring love for Israel, His chosen people. But, from Acts onward, the second part of God's promise to Abraham (Gen. 12:1–3), "in you all the families of the earth shall be blessed," is being fulfilled.

From within the Book of Acts itself, one can learn that the writer was with the Apostle Paul on several occasions. Compare the "we" passages in Acts 16:10–17; 20:5–21:18; 27:1–28:16. Many believe that Luke was "the brother" who was praised by all the congregations (II Cor. 8:18). Luke was especially careful to reassure Theophilus that Christians were not a subversive political threat to the Roman Empire. The Book of Acts ends with Paul imprisoned in Rome.

Introduction

1 The first <u>account</u>[3056] I [aom] [I]com-
posed, [a]Theophilus, about all that
Jesus [b]began to [pinf]<u>do</u>[4160] and
[pinf]<u>teach,</u>[1321]
2 until the day when He [a]was <u>taken
up,</u>353 after He [b]had [I]by the [an]Holy
<u>Spirit</u>[4151] [apt]given orders to [c]the
<u>apostles</u>[652] whom He had [ao] [d]<u>chosen.</u>[1586]
3 To [I]these [a]He also presented Him-
self <u>alive,</u>[2198] after His [aime]<u>suffering,</u>[3958]
by many <u>convincing proofs,</u>5039 [ppt]ap-
pearing to them over *a period of* forty
days, and speaking of [b]the things concerning the <u>kingdom</u>[932] of <u>God.</u>[2316]
4 And [I]gathering them together, He
commanded them [a]not to leave Jerusa-
lem, but to [pinf]<u>wait for</u>[4037] [II][b]what the
<u>Father</u>[3962] had <u>promised,</u>[1860] "Which,"
He said, "you [ao]heard of from Me;
🔑 5 for [a]John [ao]<u>baptized</u>[907] with water,

1 [I]Lit., *made* [a]Luke 1:3 [b]Luke 3:23
2 [I]Or, *through* [a]Mark 16:19; Acts 1:9, 11, 22 [b]Matt. 28:19f.; Mark 16:15; John 20:21f.; Acts 10:42 [c]Mark 6:30 [d]John 13:18; Acts 10:41
3 [I]Lit., *whom* [a]Matt. 28:17; Mark 16:12, 14; Luke 24:34, 36; John 20:19, 26; 21:1, 14; 1Cor. 15:5-7 [b]Acts 8:12; 19:8; 28:23, 31
4 [I]Or, *eating with;* or possibly, *lodging with* [II]Lit., *the promise of the Father* [a]Luke 24:49 [b]John 14:16, 26; 15:26; Acts 2:33
5 [a]Matt. 3:11; Mark 1:8; Luke 3:16; John 1:33; Acts 11:16 [b]Acts 2:1-4

🔑 **1:5** This is the fifth time that the phrase "baptized with the Holy Spirit" occurs. The other four times are in the Gospels, and they all refer to the baptism in or with the Holy Spirit in distinction from the baptism in water. The distinction is very clear between the physical water baptism and the spiritual baptism, "in the Spirit." (See Mt. 3:11; Mk. 1:8; Lk. 3:16 and Jn. 1:33.) In each of these four instances, as well as here in Acts 1:5, the Greek preposition *en* or the dative (*hudati,* "in water," or *pneumati,* "in or with Spirit") is used. This should not at any time be translated "by the Spirit" as it would not be translated "by water" as if water or the Spirit were the agent of baptism. It is the element of baptism: water and the Holy Spirit. The agent of baptism in each instance is John the Baptist baptizing in water and Jesus Christ baptizing in the Spirit. Neither the water nor the Spirit is the baptizer.

Whereas in the Gospels the promise is given in the punctiliar future, *baptisei* (Mt. 3:11, Mk. 1:8; Lk. 3:16), in Jn. 1:33, the element of time, the punctiliar future, is missing. Instead we have, "He who sent me to baptize (*baptizein,* present infinitive) in water . . . this is the one who baptizes (*ho baptizōn,* the present participle, the baptizing one) in the Holy Spirit." Here the participle, *ho baptizōn,* characterizes

(continued on next page)

but you shall be [ipf]baptized [I]with the
[an]Holy Spirit [IIb]not many days from
now."
6 And so when they had [apt]come
together, they were [ipf]asking Him, saying, "Lord, [a]is it at this time[5550] You
are restoring[600] the kingdom[932] to Israel?"
7 He said to them, "It is not for
you to [ainf]know times[5550] or epochs[2540]
which [a]the Father has [ao]fixed by His
own authority;[1849]
8 but you shall receive power[1411]
[a]when the Holy Spirit has [apt]come upon
you; and you shall be [b]My witnesses[3144]
both in Jerusalem, and in all Judea and
[c]Samaria, and even to [d]the remotest[2078]
part of the earth."

The Ascension

9 And after He had said these
things, [a]He was lifted up[1869] while they
were [ppt]looking on, and a cloud
received[5274] Him out of their sight.
10 And as they were gazing intently
into [I]the sky[3772] while He was [ppt]depart-
ing, [II]behold, [a]two men[435] in white clothing stood beside them;
⚿ 11 and they also said, "[a]Men of Galilee, why do you stand looking[1689] into
[I]the sky?[3772] This Jesus, who [b]has been
taken up from you into heaven, will
[c]come in just the same way as you have
[ao]watched Him [apt]go into heaven."

The Upper Room

12 Then they [a]returned to Jerusalem from the [Ib]mount called [II]Olivet,
which is near Jerusalem, a Sabbath
day's[4521] journey[3598] away.

13 And when they had entered, they
went up to [a]the upper room, where they
were staying; [b]that is, Peter and John
and [I]James and Andrew, Philip and
Thomas, Bartholomew and Matthew,
[I]James *the son* of Alphaeus, and Simon
the Zealot, and [c]Judas *the* [II]*son* of
[I]James.
14 These all with one mind [a]were
continually[4342] devoting themselves to
prayer,[4335] along with [Ib]*the* women, and
Mary the [c]mother of Jesus, and with
His [d]brothers.[80]
15 And [I]at this time Peter stood
up in the midst of [a]the brethren[80] (a
gathering of about[5613] one hundred and
twenty [II]persons[3676] was there together), and said,
16 "Brethren, [a]the Scripture[1124] had
to be fulfilled,[4137] which the Holy
Spirit[4151] foretold by the mouth of David
concerning Judas, [b]who became a guide
to those who arrested Jesus.
17 "For he was [a]counted among us,
and received his portion[2819] in [b]this ministry."
18 (Now this man [a]acquired a field
with [b]the price[3408] of his wickedness;[93]
and falling headlong, he burst open[2997]
in the middle[3319] and all his bowels[4698]
gushed out.
19 And it became known[1110] to all
who were living[2730] in Jerusalem; so that
in [a]their own[2398] language that field was
called [I]Hakeldama, that is, Field of
Blood.)[129]

5 [I]Or, *in* [II]Lit., *not long after these many days*
6 [a]Matt. 17:11; Mark 9:12; Luke 17:20; 19:11
7 [a]Matt. 24:36; Mark 13:32
8 [a]Acts 2:1-4 [b]Luke 24:48; John 15:27 [c]Acts 8:1, 5, 14 [d]Matt. 28:19; Mark 16:15; Rom. 10:18; Col. 1:23
9 [a]Luke 24:50, 51; Acts 1:2
10 [I]Or, *heaven* [II]Lit., *and behold* [a]Luke 24:4; John 20:12
11 [I]Or, *heaven* [a]Acts 2:7; 13:31 [b]Mark 16:19; Acts 1:9, 22 [c]Matt. 16:27f.; Acts 3:21
12 [I]Or, *hill* [II]Or, *Olive Grove* [a]Luke 24:52 [b]Matt. 21:1
13 [I]Or, *Jacob* [II]Or possibly, *brother* [a]Mark 14:15; Luke 22:12; Acts 9:37, 39; 20:8 [b]Acts 1:13: *Matt. 10:2-4; Mark 3:16-19; Luke 6:14-16* [c]John 14:22
14 [I]Or, *certain women* [a]Acts 2:42; 6:4; Rom. 12:12; Eph. 6:18; Col. 4:2 [b]Luke 8:2f. [c]Matt. 12:46
15 [I]Lit., *in these days* [II]Lit., *names* [a]John 21:23; Acts 6:3; 9:30; 10:23; 11:1, 12, 26, 29; 12:17; 14:2; 15:1, 3, 22, 23, 32f., 40; 16:2, 40; 17:6, 10, 14; 18:18, 27; 21:7, 17; 22:5; 28:14f.; Rom. 1:13

16 [a]John 13:18; 17:12; Acts 1:20 [b]Matt. 26:47; Mark 14:43; Luke 22:47; John 18:3 **17** [a]John 6:70f. [b]Acts 1:25; 20:24; 21:19 **18** [a]Matt. 27:3-10 [b]Matt. 26:14f. **19** [I]Some early mss. read *Hakeldamach* [a]Matt. 27:8; Acts 21:40

(continued from previous page)
the person, that He was going to be the One to baptize, and not so much the act; therefore, it was not necessary to place it in the punctiliar future as a once-and-for-all action.

In Acts 1:5 the expression "You shall be baptized with the Holy Spirit" in Greek is *baptisthēsesthe,* which is in the punctiliar passive future which means that this action was to take place at one particular time, once and for all. The element that is added in Acts 1:5 which is missing in the Gospel promises is an intimation of the time when this was going to take place, "Not many days from now." When did this then materialize? At Pentecost, at Caesarea and at Ephesus. See notes on Acts 2:1-13; 11:14-18; 19:1-7; I Cor. 12:13.

⚿ **1:11** See notes on I Thess. 2:19; 4:13-18.

20 "For it is written in the book of Psalms,

"[a]LET HIS HOMESTEAD[1886] BE MADE DESOLATE,[2048]
AND LET NO MAN DWELL IN IT';

and,

"[b]HIS [I]OFFICE[1984] LET ANOTHER MAN TAKE.'

21 "It is therefore necessary that of the men who have accompanied us all the time[5550] that [a]the Lord Jesus went in and out [I]among us—

22 [a]beginning [I]with the baptism[908] of John, until the day that He [b]was taken up from us—one of these should become a [c]witness[3144] with us of His resurrection."[386]

23 And they put forward[2476] two men, Joseph called Barsabbas (who was also called Justus), and [a]Matthias.

24 And they [a]prayed, and said, "Thou, Lord, [b]who knowest the hearts[2589] of all men, show which one of these two Thou hast chosen

25 to [I]occupy[2819] [a]this ministry[1248] and [b]apostleship[651] from which Judas turned aside[3845] to go to his own place."

26 And they [I][a]drew lots[2819] for them, and the lot fell[4098] [II]to [b]Matthias; and he was [III]numbered with [c]the eleven apostles.[652]

20 [I]Lit., *position as overseer* [a]Ps. 69:25 [b]Ps. 109:8
21 [I]Lit., *to us* [a]Luke 24:3
22 [I]Lit., *from* [a]Matt. 3:16; Mark 1:1-4, 9; Luke 3:21 [b]Mark 16:19; Acts 1:2 [c]Acts 1:8; 2:32
23 [a]Acts 1:26
24 [a]Acts 6:6; 13:3; 14:23 [b]1Sam. 16:7; Jer. 17:10; Acts 15:8; Rom. 8:27
25 [I]Lit., *take the place of* [a]Acts 1:17 [b]Rom. 1:5; 1Cor. 9:2; Gal. 2:8
26 [I]Lit., *gave* [II]Or, *upon* [III]Lit., *chosen* [a]Lev. 16:8; Josh. 14:2; 1Sam. 14:41f.; Neh. 10:34; 11:1; Prov. 16:33 [b]Acts 1:23 [c]Acts 2:14

1 [I]Lit., *was being fulfilled* [a]Lev. 23:15f.; Acts 20:16; 1Cor. 16:8
2 [a]Acts 4:31
3 [I]Or, *being distributed* [II]Lit., *it* [III]Or, *sat*
4 [I]Or, *ability to speak out* [a]Matt. 10:20; Acts 1:5, 8; 4:8, 31; 6:3, 5; 7:55; 8:17; 9:17; 11:15; 13:9, 52

The Day of Pentecost

2 🔑 And when [a]the day of Pentecost[4005] [I]had come,[4845] they were all together in one place.

2 And suddenly there came from heaven[3772] a noise like a violent, rushing[5342] wind,[4157] and it filled [a]the whole house where they were sitting.

3 And there [aop]appeared to them tongues[1100] as of fire [ppt][I]distributing themselves, and [II]they [III]rested on each one of them.

🔑 4 And they were all [a]filled with the [an]Holy Spirit[4151] and began to [b]speak[2980] with other[2087] tongues,[1100] as the Spirit [ipf]was giving them [pinf][I]utterance.

5 Now there were Jews living[2730] in Jerusalem, [a]devout[2126] men, from every nation[1484] under heaven.[3772]

🔑 6 And when [a]this sound occurred, the multitude came together, and were bewildered, because they were each one [ipf]hearing them [ppt]speak in his own [I]language.[1258]

7 And [a]they were [ipf]amazed and [ipf]marveled, saying, "[I]Why, are not all these who are [ppt]speaking [b]Galileans?

🔑 8 "And how is it that we each hear

[b]Mark 16:17; 1Cor. 12:10f.; 14:21 **5** [a]Luke 2:25; Acts 8:2 **6** [I]Or, *dialect* [a]Acts 2:2 **7** [I]Lit., *Behold* [a]Acts 2:12 [b]Matt. 26:73; Acts 1:11

🔑 **2:1-13** See notes on Jn. 20:22,23; Acts 1:5; 11:14-18; 19:1-7, I Cor. 12:13. This constituted the fulfillment of the promise of the baptism in the Holy Spirit. It was Jesus Christ who sent the Spirit in this special manner after His departure from earth as promised in Jn. 16:7-14. The purpose of the coming of the Holy Spirit in this special manner was to glorify Jesus Christ (Jn. 16:14).

The coming of the Holy Spirit at Penecost filled every believer gathered together there (Acts 2:4). It was not sought and it did not come selectively only upon some, but upon all the believers assembled. The result of this baptism in the Holy Spirit promised by Jesus resulted in the speaking in dialects by the people who were baptized in the Holy Spirit. Acts 2:6,8 uses the Greek word for dialects (1258), known and understood ethnic languages. Note that others, v. 13, (*heteroi,* 2087, qualitatively different) mocked. The dialects were immediately understood by others and they needed no interpreter. The people assembled were a homogeneous group of Jews. The word "dialect" is repeated in v. 8, and it is designated as the language of their birth. This speaking in other (*heterais,* 2087), "qualitatively other" or different than theirs, "tongues," *glōssais* (1100), could not by any stretch of the imagination be the same as "the unknown tongue" spoken by the Corinthians in I Cor. 14:2,4,13,19,27 where "unknown tongue" is always designated in the singular with a singular personal pronoun. It was demanded by the Apostle Paul that the unknown tongue should always be interpreted. Not so with the dialects (*dialektoi,* Acts 2:6,8), or *heterai glōssai,* different, other languages spoken of in Acts 2:4 or simply *glōssais,* in tongues or languages as in Acts 10:46; 19:6. These were ethnic languages miraculously spoken as a result of the baptism in the Holy Spirit by those whose mother tongue was different.

🔑 **2:4,6,8** See note on I Cor. 14:1-3.

them in our own [I]language1258 [II]to which
we were born?
9 "Parthians and Medes and Elamites, and residents of Mesopotamia, Judea and [a]Cappadocia, [b]Pontus and
[Ic]Asia,
10 [a]Phrygia and [b]Pamphylia, Egypt
and the districts of Libya around
[c]Cyrene, and [Id]visitors from Rome, both
Jews and [IIe]proselytes,[4339]
11 Cretans and Arabs—we hear[191]
them in our *own* tongues[1100] [ppt]speaking
of the mighty deeds[3167] of God."
12 And [a]they all continued in amazement and great perplexity, saying to one
another, "What does this mean?"
13 But others were [ppt]mocking and
[ipf]saying, "[a]They are full of [I]sweet
wine."[1098]

Peter's Sermon

14 But Peter, [I]taking his stand with
[a]the eleven, raised his voice and declared to them: "Men of Judea, and all
you who live in Jerusalem, let this be
known[1110] to you, and give heed to my
words.[4487]
15 "For these men are not
[pin]drunk, as you suppose,5274 [a]for it is
only the [I]third hour of the day;
16 but this is what was spoken[2046]
of through the prophet Joel:

17 '[a]AND IT SHALL BE IN THE
LAST[2078] DAYS,' God says,
'THAT I WILL POUR FORTH OF
MY SPIRIT[4151] UPON ALL
[I]MANKIND;[4561]
AND YOUR SONS AND YOUR
DAUGHTERS SHALL
PROPHESY,[4395]
AND YOUR YOUNG MEN SHALL
SEE VISIONS,3706
AND YOUR OLD[4245] MEN SHALL
DREAM DREAMS;
18 EVEN UPON MY
BONDSLAVES,[1401] BOTH MEN
AND WOMEN,[1399]
I WILL IN THOSE DAYS POUR
FORTH OF MY SPIRIT
And they shall prophesy.[4395]
19 'AND I WILL GRANT
WONDERS[5059] IN THE SKY
ABOVE,[507]
AND SIGNS[4592] ON THE EARTH
BENEATH,[2736]
BLOOD, AND FIRE, AND VAPOR
OF SMOKE.
20 'THE SUN SHALL BE TURNED
INTO DARKNESS,
AND THE MOON INTO BLOOD,
BEFORE THE GREAT AND
GLORIOUS DAY OF THE LORD
SHALL [ainf]COME.
21 'AND IT SHALL BE, THAT
[a]EVERYONE WHO [aosb]CALLS
ON[1941] THE NAME[3686] OF THE
LORD SHALL BE saved.'[4982]

22 "Men of Israel, [aim]listen[191] to
these words:[3056] [a]Jesus the Nazarene,
[b]a man [pfpp] [I]attested to you by
God with [II]miracles[1411] and [c]wonders[5059]
and [III]signs which God performed
through Him in your midst, just as you
yourselves know—
23 this *Man*, delivered up by the
[pfpp] [a]predetermined[3724] plan[1012] and
foreknowledge[4268] of God, [b]you [apt]nailed
to a cross4362 by the hands of [I]godless[459]
men and [ao]put *Him* to death.
24 "[I]And [a]God [ao]raised Him up[450]
again, putting an end to the [II]agony[5604]
of death,[2288] since it [b]was impossible for
Him to be [pip]held in its power.
25 "For David says of Him,
'[a]I WAS [ipf]ALWAYS BEHOLDING4308
THE LORD[2962] IN MY
PRESENCE;
FOR HE IS AT MY RIGHT
HAND,1118 THAT I MAY NOT
BE SHAKEN.
26 'THEREFORE MY HEART[2588] WAS
GLAD[2165] AND MY TONGUE[1100]
[aop]EXULTED;

8 [I]Or, *dialect* [II]Lit., *in*
9 [I]I.e., west coast province of Asia Minor [a]1Pet. 1:1 [b]Acts 18:2; 1Pet. 1:1 [c]Acts 6:9; 16:6; 19:10; 20:4; 21:27; 24:18; 27:2; Rom. 16:5; 1Cor. 16:19; 2Cor. 1:8; 2Tim. 1:15; Rev. 1:4
10 [I]Lit., *the sojourning Romans* [II]I.e., Gentile converts to Judaism [a]Acts 16:6; 18:23 [b]Acts 13:13; 14:24; 15:38; 27:5 [c]Matt. 27:32 [d]Acts 17:21 [e]Matt. 23:15
12 [a]Acts 2:7
13 [I]Or, *new wine* [a]1Cor. 14:23
14 [I]Or, *being put forward* as spokesman [a]Acts 1:26
15 [I]I.e., 9 a.m. [a]1Thess. 5:7
17 [I]Lit., *flesh* [a]Joel 2:28-32
21 [a]Rom. 10:13
22 [I]Or, *exhibited* or *accredited* [II]Or, *works of power* [III]Or, *attesting miracles* [a]Acts 3:6; 4:10; 10:38 [b]John 3:2 [c]John 4:48; Acts 2:19, 43
23 [I]Or, *men without the Law;* i.e., heathen [a]Luke 22:22; Acts 3:18; 4:28; 1Pet. 1:20 [b]Matt. 27:35; Mark 15:24; Luke 23:33; 24:20; John 19:18; Acts 3:13
24 [I]Lit., *Whom God raised up* [II]Lit., *birth pangs* [a]Matt. 28:5, 6; Mark 16:6; Luke 24:5, 6; Acts 2:32; 3:15, 26; 4:10; 5:30; 10:40; 13:30,33,34,37; 17:31; Rom. 4:24; 6:4; 8:11; 10:9; 1Cor. 6:14; 15:15; 2Cor.4:14; Gal. 1:1; Eph. 1:20; Col. 2:12; 1Thess. 1:10; Heb. 13:20; 1Pet. 1:21 [b]John 20:9
25 [a]Ps. 16:8-11

2:23 See notes on Eph. 1:4,5; II Tim. 1:9 and also *prognōsis* (4268), foreknowledge; *prothesis* (4286), purpose; *eklogē* (1589), election; *proorizō* (4309), foreordain, predestinate.

MOREOVER MY FLESH[4561] ALSO
WILL ABIDE IN HOPE;[1680]
27 BECAUSE THOU WILT NOT
ABANDON MY SOUL[5590] TO
[a]HADES,[86]
[b]NOR [I]ALLOW THY [II]HOLY
ONE[3741] TO [III]UNDERGO[1492]
DECAY.[1312]
28 'THOU HAST MADE [ao]KNOWN TO
ME THE WAYS[3598] OF
LIFE;[2222]
THOU WILT MAKE ME FULL OF
GLADNESS[2167]
WITH THY PRESENCE.'[4383]
29 "[I]Brethren, I may confidently
say[2036] to you regarding the [a]patri-
arch[3966] David that he both [b]died[5053] and
[c]was buried, and [d]his tomb[3418] is
[II]with us to this day.
30 "And so, because he was
[a]a prophet,[4396] and knew that [b]GOD HAD
[ao]SWORN TO HIM WITH AN OATH[3727] TO
SEAT *one* [I]OF HIS DESCENDANTS UPON HIS
THRONE,
31 he looked ahead and spoke of the
resurrection[386] of [I]the Christ, that [a]HE
WAS NEITHER ABANDONED TO HADES,[86]
nor did His flesh[4561] [II]SUFFER DECAY.
32 "This Jesus [a]God raised up[450]
again, to which we are all [b]witnesses.[3144]
33 "Therefore having been [aptp]ex-
alted [I][a]to the right hand[1188] of God,[2316]
and [b]having [apt]received from the
Father[3962] [c]the promise[1860] of the Holy
Spirit,[4151] He has [ao] [d]poured forth this
which you both see and hear.
34 "For it was not David who [ao]as-
cended into [I]heaven,[3772] but he himself
says:

'[a]THE LORD[2962] SAID TO MY
LORD
"SIT AT MY RIGHT HAND,
35 UNTIL I [aosb]MAKE THINE
ENEMIES A FOOTSTOOL FOR
THY FEET." '
36 "Therefore let all the [a]house[3624]
of Israel [pim]know[1097] for certain that
God has [ao]made[4160] Him both [b]Lord[2962]
and [I]Christ—[5547] this Jesus [c]whom you
[ao]crucified."[4717]

The Ingathering

37 Now when they heard *this*, they
were [I]pierced[2660] to the heart,[2588] and
said to Peter and the rest of the apostles,[652] "[II]Brethren,[80] [a]what shall we
do?"
🔑 38 And Peter *said* to them,
"[aim] [a]Repent,[3340] and let each of you
be [aipp] [b]baptized[907] in the name[3686] of
Jesus Christ for the [an]forgiveness[859] of
your sins;[266] and you shall receive the
gift[1431] of the Holy Spirit.[4151]
39 "For [a]the promise[1860] is for you
and your children, and for all who are
[b]far off, as many as the Lord our God
shall [aosb]call[4341] to Himself."
40 And with many other words he
solemnly [ao] [a]testified and kept on [ipf]ex-
horting[3870] them, saying, "[I]Be [aipp]saved
from this [b]perverse generation!"
41 So then, those who had

27 [I]Lit., *give* [II]Or, *devout* or *pious* [III]Lit., *see corruption* [a]Matt. 11:23; Acts 2:31 [b]Acts 13:35
29 [I]Lit., *Men brothers* [II]Lit., *among* [a]Acts 7:8f.; Heb. 7:4 [b]Acts 13:36 [c]1Kin. 2:10 [d]Neh. 3:16
30 [I]Lit., *of the fruit of his loins* [a]Matt. 22:43 [b]Ps. 132:11; 2Sam. 7:12f.; Ps. 89:3f.
31 [I]I.e., the Messiah [II]Lit., *see corruption* [a]Matt. 11:23; Acts 2:27
32 [a]Acts 2:24; 3:15, 26; 4:10; 5:30; 10:40; 13:30, 33, 34, 37; 17:31; Rom. 4:24; 6:4; 8:11; 10:9; 1Cor. 6:14; 15:15; 2Cor. 4:14; Gal. 1:1; Eph. 1:20; Col. 2:12; 1Thess. 1:10; Heb. 13:20; 1Pet. 1:21 [b]Acts 1:8
33 [I]Or, *by* [a]Mark 16:19; Acts 5:31 [b]Acts 1:4 [c]John 7:39; Gal. 3:14 [d]Acts 2:17; 10:45
34 [I]Lit., *the heavens* [a]Ps. 110:1; Matt. 22:44f.
36 [I]I.e., Messiah [a]Ezek. 36:22, 32, 37; 45:6 [b]Luke 2:11 [c]Acts 2:23
37 [I]Or, *smitten in conscience* [II]Lit., *Men brothers* [a]Luke 3:10, 12, 14

38 [a]Mark 1:15; Luke 24:47; Acts 3:19; 5:31; 20:21 [b]Mark 16:16; Acts 8:12, 16; 22:16 **39** [a]Is. 44:3; 54:13; 57:19; Joel 2:32; Rom. 9:4; Eph. 2:12 [b]Eph. 2:13, 17 **40** [I]Or, *Escape* [a]Luke 16:28 [b]Deut. 32:5; Matt. 17:17; Phil. 2:15

🔑 **2:38** See note on I Pet. 3:20,21. Here the main verb is *metanoēsate* (3340), the aorist direct imperative of *metanoeō,* repent. This refers to that initial repentance of the sinner unto salvation. The verb translated "be baptized" is in the indirect passive imperative of *baptizō* (907) which does not give it the same direct command implied in "repent." The preposition "for" in the phrase "for the forgiveness of your sins" in Greek is *eis* (1519), unto. It means "for the purpose of identifying you with the remission of sins." It is the same preposition we find in I Cor. 10:2 in the phrase "and were baptized into (*eis*) Moses." These people were baptized or spiritually identifying themselves with the purposes and vision of Moses. Repentance, therefore, is presented as identifying an individual with the remission of his sins, even as baptism following repentance provides an external identification visible by others. Repentance is something that concerns an individual and God while baptism involves others. That is why *baptisthētō* is in the passive indicating that one does not baptize himself, but is baptized by another usually in the presence of others. Repentance, however, is an act taking place within man's heart as the Holy spirit energizes the sinner.

[apt]received[588] his word were baptized; and there were added that day about three thousand [Ia]souls.[5590]

42 And they were [a]continually devoting[4342] themselves to the apostles'[652] teaching[1322] and to fellowship,[2842] to [b]the breaking[2800] of bread and [Ia]to prayer.[4335]

43 And [I]everyone kept feeling a sense of awe;[5401] and many [a]wonders[5059] and [II]signs[4592] were [ipf]taking place through the apostles[III].

44 And all those who had [apt]believed[4100] [I]were together, and [ipf] [a]had all things in common;[2839]

45 and they [a]*began* [ipf]selling their property and possessions, and were [ipf]sharing them with all, as anyone might have need.

46 [a]And day by day continuing[4342] with one mind in the temple,[2411] and [b]breaking[2806] bread [I]from house to house, they were taking their [II]meals together with gladness[20] and [III]sincerity of heart,[2588]

47 praising[134] God,[2316] and [a]having favor with all the people. And the Lord[2962] [b]was [ipf]adding [I]to their number[1577] day by day [c]those who were being [ppp]saved.[4982]

Healing the Lame Beggar

3 Now [a]Peter and John [ipf]were going up to the temple[2411] at the [I]ninth *hour,* [b]the hour of prayer.[4335]

2 And [a]a certain man who had been lame from his mother's womb was being carried along, whom they [b]used to [ipf]set down every day at the gate of the temple which is called Beautiful,[5611] [c]in order to [infg]beg[154] [I]alms[1654] of those who were [ppt]entering the temple.

3 And when he [apt]saw [a]Peter and John about[3195] to go into the temple, he *began* [ipf]asking to receive alms.

4 And Peter, along with John, [a]fixed his gaze upon him and said, "Look at us!"

5 And he *began* to give them his attention, expecting[4328] to [ainf]receive something from them.

6 But Peter said, "I do not possess silver and gold, but what I do have[5225] I give to you: [a]In the name[3686] of Jesus Christ[5547] the Nazarene—walk!"

7 And seizing him by the right[1188] hand, he raised him up; and immediately his feet and his ankles were strengthened.

8 [a]And [I]with a leap, he stood upright and *began* to [ipf]walk; and he entered the temple with them, walking and leaping and praising[134] God.

9 And [a]all the people saw him walking and praising God;

10 and they were [ipf]taking note of him as being the one who used to [ppt] [a]sit at the Beautiful[5611] Gate of the temple to *beg* alms, and they were filled with wonder[2285] and amazement[1611] at what had [pfp]happened to him.

Peter's Second Sermon

11 And while he was [ppt]clinging to [a]Peter and John, all the people ran together to them at the so-called [Ib]portico of Solomon, full of amazement.

12 But when Peter saw *this,* he replied to the people, "Men of Israel, why do you marvel[2296] at this, or why do you gaze at us, as if by our own power[1411] or piety[2150] we had [pfp]made him [pinf]walk?

13 "[a]The God of Abraham, Isaac, and Jacob, [b]the God of our fathers,[3962] has [ao]glorified[1392] His [Ic]servant[3816] Jesus, *the one* whom [d]you delivered up, and disowned[720] in the presence[4383] of [e]Pilate, when he had [apt] [f]decided[2919] to [pinf]release Him.

14 "But you disowned[720] [a]the Holy[40] and Righteous[1342] One, and [b]asked for a murderer[5406] to be granted[5483] to you,

15 but put to death the [Ia]Prince[747] of life,[2222] *the one* whom [b]God raised[1453] from the dead,[3498] *a fact* to which we are [c]witnesses.[3144]

41 [I]I.e., persons [a]Acts 3:23; 7:14; 27:37; Rom. 13:1; 1Pet. 3:20; Rev. 16:3
42 [I]Lit., *the prayers* [a]Acts 1:14 [b]Luke 24:30; Acts 2:46; 20:7; 1Cor. 10:16
43 [I]Lit., *fear was occurring to every soul* [II]Or, *attesting miracles* [III]Some ancient mss. add *in Jerusalem; and great fear was upon all* [a]Acts 2:22
44 [I]Some ancient mss. do not contain *were* [a]Acts 4:32, 37; 5:2
45 [a]Matt. 19:21; Acts 4:34
46 [I]Or, *in the various private homes* [II]Lit., *food* [III]Or, *simplicity* [a]Acts 5:42 [b]Luke 24:30; Acts 2:42; 20:7; 1Cor. 10:16
47 [I]Lit., *together* [a]Acts 5:13 [b]Acts 2:41; 4:4; 5:14; 6:1, 7; 9:31, 35, 42; 11:21, 24; 14:1, 21; 16:5; 17:12 [c]1Cor. 1:18
1 [I]I.e., 3 p.m. [a]Luke 22:8; Acts 3:3, 4, 11 [b]Ps. 55:17; Matt. 27:45; Acts 10:30
2 [I]Or, *a gift of charity* [a]Acts 14:8 [b]Luke 16:20 [c]John 9:8; Acts 3:10
3 [a]Luke 22:8; Acts 3:1, 4, 11
4 [a]Acts 10:4
6 [a]Acts 2:22; 3:16; 4:10
8 [I]Lit., *leaping up* [a]Acts 14:10
9 [a]Acts 4:16, 21
10 [a]John 9:8; Acts 3:2
11 [I]Or, *colonnade* [a]Luke 22:8; Acts 3:3, 4 [b]John 10:23; Acts 5:12
13 [I]Or, *Child* [a]Matt. 22:32 [b]Ex. 3:13, 15; Acts 5:30; 7:32; 22:14 [c]Acts 3:26; 4:27, 30 [d]Matt. 20:19; John 19:11; Acts 2:23 [e]Matt. 27:2 [f]Luke 23:4
14 [a]Mark 1:24; Acts 4:27; 7:52; 2Cor. 5:21 [b]Matt. 27:20; Mark 15:11; Luke 23:18, 25
15 [I]Or, *Author* [a]Acts 5:31; Heb. 2:10; 12:2 [b]Acts 2:24 [c]Luke 24:48

16 "And on the basis of faith[4102] [a]in His name,[3686] *it is* the name[3686] of [I]Jesus which has strengthened this man whom you see and know; and the faith which *comes* through Him has [ao]given him this perfect health[3647] in the presence of you all.

17 "And now, brethren, I know[1492] that you acted [a]in[2596] ignorance,[52] just as your [b]rulers did[4238] also.

18 "But the things which [a]God [ao]announced beforehand[4293] by the mouth of all the prophets,[4396] [b]that His [I]Christ should [ainf]suffer, He has thus [ao]fulfilled.

19 "[aim] [a]Repent[3340] therefore and [aim]return,[1994] that your sins[266] may be wiped away,[1813] in order that [b]times[2540] of refreshing[430] may [aosb]come from the presence[4383] of the Lord;[2962]

20 and that He may send Jesus, the [I]Christ[5547] [pfpp]appointed[4400] for you,

21 [a]whom heaven[3772] must [ainf]receive until *the* [I]period[5550] of [b]restoration[605] of all things about which [c]God [ao]spoke by the mouth of His holy[40] prophets[4396] from ancient time.[165]

22 "Moses said, '[a]THE LORD[2962] GOD[2316] SHALL RAISE UP[450] FOR YOU A PROPHET[4396] [I]LIKE ME FROM YOUR BRETHREN;[80] TO HIM YOU SHALL GIVE HEED[191] in everything He says to you.

23 '[a]And it shall be that every [b]soul[5590] that does not heed that prophet [c]shall be utterly destroyed from among the people.'

24 "And likewise, [a]all the prophets who have spoken, from Samuel and *his* successors onward, also announced[4293] these days.

25 "It is you who are [a]the sons[5207] of the prophets, and of the [b]covenant[1242] which God [I]made[1303] with your fathers, saying to Abraham, '[c]AND IN YOUR SEED[4690] ALL THE FAMILIES[3965] OF THE EARTH SHALL BE BLESSED.'[1757]

26 "For you [a]first, God [b]raised up His [I]Servant,[3816] and sent[649] Him to [ppt]bless[2127] you by [aie]turning[654] every one *of you* from your wicked ways."[4189]

Peter and John Arrested

4 And as they [ppt]were speaking to the people, the priests and [a]the captain of the temple *guard,* and [b]the Sadducees, [c]came upon them,

2 being greatly disturbed because they [aid]were teaching[1321] the people and [aid]proclaiming[2605] [Ia]in Jesus the resurrection[386] from the dead.[3498]

3 And they laid hands on them, and [a]put them in[1519] jail[5084] until[1519] the next day, for it was already evening.

4 But[1161] many of those who had [apt]heard the [I]message[3056] believed;[4100] and [a]the number of the men came to be about five thousand.

5 And it came about on the next day, that their [a]rulers[758] and elders[4245] and scribes[1122] were gathered together in Jerusalem;

6 and [a]Annas the high priest *was there,* and [b]Caiaphas and John and Alexander, and all who were of high-priestly[748] descent.

7 And when they had placed them in the center, they *began to* [ipf]inquire, "By what power,[1411] or in what name,[3686] have you done this?"

8 Then Peter, [Ia]filled with the [an]Holy Spirit,[4151] said to them, "[IIb]Rulers[758] and elders[4245] of the people,[2992]

9 if we are on trial today for [a]a benefit done to a sick[772] man,[444] [I]as to how this man has been made [pfip]well,[4982]

10 let it be known to all of you, and to all the people of Israel, that [Ia]by the name of Jesus Christ[5547] the Nazarene, whom you crucified,[4717] whom [b]God raised[1453] from the dead—[3498] [I]by [II]this *name* this man stands here before you in good health.[5199]

11 "[Ia]He is the [b]STONE WHICH WAS [aptp] [c]REJECTED by you, THE BUILDERS, *but* WHICH BECAME THE VERY CORNER *stone.*

12 "And there is salvation[4991] in [a]no one else; for there is no other name under heaven[3772] that has been [pfpp]given among men,[444] by which we must be [aifp]saved."[4980]

16 [I]Lit., *His* [a]Acts 3:6
17 [a]Luke 23:34; John 15:21; Acts 13:27; 26:9; Eph. 4:18 [b]Luke 23:13
18 [I]Or, *Anointed One;* i.e., Messiah [a]Acts 2:23 [b]Luke 24:27; Acts 17:3; 26:23
19 [a]Acts 2:38; 26:20 [b]2Thess. 1:7; Heb. 4:1ff.
20 [I]Or, *Anointed One;* i.e., Messiah
21 [I]Lit., *periods, times* [a]Acts 1:11 [b]Matt. 17:11; Rom. 8:21 [c]Luke 1:70
22 [I]Or, *as He raised up me* [a]Deut. 18:15, 18; Acts 7:37
23 [a]Deut. 18:19 [b]Acts 2:41 [c]Lev. 23:29
24 [a]Luke 24:27; Acts 17:3; 26:23
25 [I]Lit., *covenanted* [a]Acts 2:39 [b]Rom. 9:4f. [c]Gen. 22:18
26 [I]Or, *Child* [a]Matt. 15:24; John 4:22; Acts 13:46; Rom. 1:16; 2:9f. [b]Acts 2:24

1 [a]Luke 22:4 [b]Matt. 3:7 [c]Luke 20:1; Acts 6:12
2 [I]Or, *in the case of* [a]Acts 3:15; 17:18
3 [a]Acts 5:18
4 [I]Or, *word* [a]Acts 2:41
5 [a]Luke 23:13; Acts 4:8
6 [a]Luke 3:2 [b]Matt. 26:3
8 [I]Or, *having* just *been filled* [II]Or, *Rulers of the people and elders* [a]Acts 2:4; 13:9 [b]Luke 23:13; Acts 4:5
9 [I]Or, *by whom* [a]Acts 3:7f.
10 [I]Or, *in* [II]Or, *him* [a]Acts 2:22; 3:6 [b]Acts 2:24
11 [I]Lit., *This One* [a]Matt. 21:42 [b]Ps. 118:22 [c]Mark 9:12
12 [a]Matt. 1:21; Acts 10:43; 1Tim. 2:5

Threat and Release

13 Now as they [ppt]observed the [a]confidence of [b]Peter and John, and [apt]understood[2638] that they were uneducated and untrained[2399] men, they were [ipf]marveling, and [c]*began* to [ipf]recognize them [I]as having been with Jesus.

14 And seeing the man who had been healed[2323] standing with them, they had nothing to say in reply.

15 But when they had ordered them to go aside out of the [Ia]Council,[4892] they *began* to [ipf]confer with one another,

16 saying, "[a]What shall we do with these men? For the fact that a [b]noteworthy [I]miracle[4592] has [pfi]taken place[1096] through them is apparent[5318] to all who live in Jerusalem, and we cannot [pinf]deny[720] it.

17 "But in order that it may not spread any further among the people, let us warn[546] them to [pinf]speak no more to any man [a]in this name."

18 And when they had summoned them, they [a]commanded[3853] them not to [pinf]speak[5350] or [pinf]teach[1321] at all [I]in the name[3686] of Jesus.

19 But [a]Peter and John answered and said to them, "[b]Whether it is right[1342] in the sight of God[2316] to [pinf]give heed[191] to you rather than to God, you be the judge;[2919]

20 for [a]we cannot stop speaking[2980] what we have [ao]seen[1492] and [ao]heard."[191]

21 And when they had [apt]threatened them further, they let them go (finding[2147] no basis on which they might punish them) [a]on account of the people, because they were all [ipf] [b]glorifying[1392] God[2316] for what had happened;

22 for the man was more than forty years old on whom this [I]miracle[4592] of healing[2392] had been [pipf]performed.

23 And when they had been released, they went to their own *companions,* and reported all that the chief priests[749] and the elders[4245] had said to them.

24 And when they heard *this,* they lifted[142] their voices to God with one accord and said, "O [I]Lord,[1203] it is Thou who [a]DIDST MAKE THE HEAVEN[3772] AND THE EARTH[1093] AND THE SEA,[2281] and all that is in them,

25 who [a]by the Holy Spirit, *through* the mouth of our father David Thy servant,[3816] didst say,

'[b]WHY DID THE [I]GENTILES[1484]
RAGE,[5433]
AND THE PEOPLES[2992]
DEVISE[3191] FUTILE[3191]
THINGS?

26 '[a]THE KINGS[935] OF THE EARTH
[I]TOOK THEIR STAND,
AND THE RULERS[758] WERE
GATHERED TOGETHER
AGAINST THE Lord,[2962] AND
AGAINST HIS [IIb]CHRIST.'[5547]

27 "For truly[225] in this city there were gathered together against Thy holy[40] [Ia]servant[3816] Jesus, whom Thou didst [ao]anoint,[5548] both [b]Herod and [c]Pontius Pilate, along with [d]the [II]Gentiles[1484] and the peoples[2992] of Israel,

28 to do whatever Thy hand and [a]Thy purpose[1012] predestined[4309] to occur.

29 "And [I]now, Lord, take note of[1896] their threats, and grant that Thy bond-servants[1401] may [pinf] [a]speak[2980] Thy word[3056] with all [b]confidence,

30 while Thou dost extend Thy hand to heal,[2392] and [Ia]signs[4592] and wonders[5059] take place through the name[3686] of Thy holy[40] [IIb]servant[3816] Jesus."

31 And when they had prayed,[1189] the [a]place where they had gathered together was shaken, and they were all [b]filled with the Holy Spirit,[4151] and *began* to [ipf] [c]speak the word of God with [d]boldness.

Sharing among Believers

32 And the [I]congregation of those who believed[4100] were of one heart[2588] and soul;[5590] and not one *of them*

---

13 [I]Lit., *that they had been* [a]Acts 4:31 [b]Luke 22:8; Acts 4:19 [c]John 7:15
15 [I]Or, *Sanhedrin* [a]Matt. 5:22
16 [I]Or, *sign* [a]John 11:47 [b]Acts 3:7-10
17 [a]John 15:21
18 [I]Or, *on the basis of* [a]Acts 5:28f.
19 [a]Acts 4:13 [b]Acts 5:28f.
20 [a]1Cor. 9:16
21 [a]Acts 5:26 [b]Matt. 9:8
22 [I]Or, *sign*
24 [I]Or, *Master* [a]Ex. 20:11; Neh. 9:6; Ps. 146:6
25 [I]Or, *nations* [a]Acts 1:16 [b]Ps. 2:1
26 [I]Or, *approached* [II]Or, *Anointed One;* i.e., Messiah [a]Ps. 2:2 [b]Dan. 9:24f.; Luke 4:18; Acts 10:38; Heb. 1:9
27 [I]Or, *Child* [II]Or, *nations* [a]Acts 3:13; 4:30 [b]Matt. 14:1; Luke 23:7-11 [c]Matt. 27:2; Mark 15:1; Luke 23:1, 12; John 18:28, 29 [d]Matt. 20:19
28 [a]Acts 2:23
29 [I]Or, *as for the present situation* [a]Phil. 1:14 [b]Acts 4:13, 31; 14:3
30 [I]Or, *attesting miracles* [II]Or, *Child* [a]John 4:48 [b]Acts 3:13; 4:27
31 [a]Acts 2:1 [b]Acts 2:4 [c]Phil. 1:14 [d]Acts 4:13; 14:3
32 [I]Or, *multitude*

4:28 See note on Eph. 1:4,5 and also *proorizō* (4309), predestinate.

[II]claimed that anything[5100] belonging to
him was his own;[2398] but [a]all things were
common[2839] property to them.
33 And [a]with great power[1411] the
apostles[652] were [ipf]giving [b]witness[3142] to
the resurrection[386] of the Lord Jesus[I],
and abundant grace[5485] was upon them
all.
34 For there was not a needy person
among them, for all who were[5225] owners of land or houses [a]would [ppt]sell them
and [ipf]bring the [I]proceeds of the sales,
35 and [ipf] [a]lay them at the apostles'
feet; and they [ipf]would be [b]distributed
to each, as any had need.
36 And Joseph, a Levite of [a]Cyprian
birth, who was also called [b]Barnabas by
the apostles (which translated means,
Son[5207] of [I][c]Encouragement),[3874]
37 and who owned a tract of land,
sold it and brought the money[5536] and
[a]laid it at the apostles' feet.

Fate of Ananias and Sapphira

5 🔑 But a certain man named Ananias, with his wife Sapphira, sold a
piece of property,
2 and [a]kept back[3557] *some* of the
price for himself, with his wife's [I]full
knowledge,[4894] and [apt]bringing a portion
of it, he [b]laid it at the apostles'[652] feet.
3 But Peter said, "Ananias, why has
[a]Satan [ao]filled your heart to [ainf]lie
[b]to the Holy[40] Spirit,[4151] and to [ainf] [c]keep
back *some* of the price of the land?
4 "While it remained *unsold,* did it
not remain your own? And after it was
sold, was it not [I]under your control?[1849]
Why is it that you have [II]conceived this
deed in your heart?[2588] You have not
[ao]lied to men,[444] but [a]to God."[2316]
5 And as he heard these words,
Ananias [apt] [a]fell down and breathed his
last;[1634] and [b]great fear[5401] came upon
all who [ppt]heard of it.
6 And the [I]young men arose and
[a]covered him up, and after carrying him
out, they buried him.
7 Now there elapsed an interval of
about three hours, and his wife came
in, not knowing what had happened.
8 And Peter responded to her, "Tell
me whether you sold the land [I][a]for such
and such a price?" And she said, "Yes,
[I]that was the price."
9 Then Peter *said* to her, "Why is
it that you have agreed together to
[a]put [b]the Spirit[4151] of the Lord[2962] to
the test?[3985] Behold, the feet of those
who have buried your husband[435] are
at the door, and they shall carry you
out[1627] *as well.*"
10 And she [a]fell[4098] immediately[3916]
at his feet, and breathed her last;[1634]
and the young men came in and found
her dead,[3498] and they carried her out[1627]
and buried her beside her husband.
11 And [a]great fear came upon the
whole church,[1577] and upon all who
[ppt]heard of these things.
12 And [I]at the hands of the
apostles[652] many [a]signs[4592] and wonders[5059] [ipf]were taking place among the
people;[2992] and they were all with one
accord in [b]Solomon's portico.
13 But none of the rest [ipf]dared[5111]
to associate with them; however,
[a]the people [I]held them in high esteem.
14 And all the more [ppt] [a]believers[4100]
in the Lord,[2962] multitudes of men[435] and
women, were constantly [ipf] [b]added[4369] to
their number;
15 to such an extent that they even
[pinf]carried the sick[772] out into the
streets, and [pinf]laid them on cots and
pallets, so that when Peter came by,
[a]at least his shadow might fall on any
one of them.
16 And also the [I]people from the
cities in the vicinity of Jerusalem [ipf]were
coming together, bringing people who
were sick[7772] [II]or [ppp]afflicted[3791] with
unclean[169] spirits;[4151] and they were all
being [ipf]healed.[2323]

Imprisonment and Release

17 But the high priest[749] rose up,
along with all his associates (that is

32 [II]Lit., *was saying* [a]Acts 2:44
33 [I]Some mss. add *Christ* [a]Acts 1:8 [b]Luke 24:48
34 [I]Lit., *the prices of the things being sold* [a]Matt. 19:21; Acts 2:45
35 [a]Acts 4:37; 5:2 [b]Acts 2:45; 6:1
36 [I]Or, *Exhortation* or *Consolation* [a]Acts 11:19f.; 13:4; 15:39; 21:3, 16; 27:4 [b]Acts 9:27; 11:22, 30; 12:25; 13:1, 2, 7; 1Cor. 9:6; Gal. 2:1, 9, 13; Col. 4:10 [c]Acts 2:40; 11:23; 13:15; 1Cor. 14:3; 1Thess. 2:3
37 [a]Acts 4:35; 5:2

2 [I]Or, *collusion* [a]Acts 5:3 [b]Acts 4:35, 37
3 [a]Matt. 4:10; Luke 22:3; John 13:2, 27 [b]Acts 5:4, 9 [c]Acts 5:2
4 [I]Or, *in your authority* [II]Or, *placed* [a]Acts 5:3, 9
5 [a]Ezek. 11:13; Acts 5:10 [b]Acts 2:43; 5:11
6 [I]Lit., *younger* [a]John 19:40
8 [I]Lit., *for so much* [a]Acts 5:2
9 [a]Acts 15:10 [b]Acts 5:3, 4
10 [a]Ezek. 11:13; Acts 5:5
11 [a]Acts 2:43; 5:5
12 [I]Lit., *through* [a]John 4:48 [b]John 10:23; Acts 3:11
13 [I]Lit., *were holding* [a]Acts 2:47; 4:21
14 [a]2Cor. 6:15 [b]Acts 2:47; 11:24
15 [a]Acts 19:12
16 [I]Lit., *multitude* [II]Lit., *and*

🔑 **5:1-16** See notes on Gal. 3:22; I Tim. 1:20.

[a]the sect[139] of [b]the Sadducees), and they were filled with jealousy;[2205]

18 and they laid hands on the apostles,[652] and [a]put them in a public[1219] jail.[5084]

19 But [a]an angel[32] of the Lord[2962] during the night opened the gates of the prison, and taking them out he said,

20 "[pim]Go your way, [aptp]stand and [pim] [I]speak to the people in the temple[2411] [II][a]the whole message[4487] of this Life."[2222]

21 And upon hearing *this,* they entered into the temple [a]about daybreak, and *began* to [ipf]teach.[1321] Now when [b]the high priest and his associates had come, they called[4779] [c]the [I]Council[4892] together, even all the Senate[1087] of the sons[5207] of Israel, and sent *orders* to the prison house for them to be brought.

22 But [a]the officers who came did not find them in the prison; and they returned, and reported back,

23 saying, "We found the prison house locked quite securely and the guards[5441] standing at the doors; but when we had opened up, we found no one inside."

24 Now when [a]the captain of the temple *guard* and the chief priests heard these words,[3056] they were greatly [ipf]perplexed[1280] about them as to what [I]would come of this.

25 But someone came and reported to them, "Behold, the men whom you put in prison are standing in the temple and teaching the people!"

26 Then [a]the captain went along with [b]the officers and *proceeded* to bring[71] them *back* without violence (for [c]they were [ipf]afraid of the people, lest they should be [asbp]stoned).

27 And when they had brought them, they stood them [I]before [a]the Council. And the high priest questioned them,

28 saying, "We gave you [a]strict orders[3853] not to continue [ppt]teaching[1321] in this name, and behold, you have [pfi]filled Jerusalem with your teaching,[1322] and [b]intend to bring[1863] this man's[444] blood[129] upon[1863] us."

29 But Peter and the apostles[652] answered and said, "[a]We must [pinf]obey[3980] God[2316] rather than men.[444]

30 "[a]The God of our fathers[3962] [b]raised up[1453] Jesus, [I]whom you had [c]put to death by [apt]hanging Him on a [II]cross.

31 "[a]He is the one whom God exalted [I]to His right hand[1188] as a [II][b]Prince[747] and a [c]Savior,[4990] to [ainf]grant [d]repentance[3341] to Israel, and forgiveness[859] of sins.[266]

32 "And we are [a]witnesses[I] [3144] of these things;[4487] and [b]*so is* the Holy[40] Spirit,[4151] whom God has [ao]given to those who [ppt]obey Him."

Gamaliel's Counsel

33 But when they [apt]heard this, they were [ipf] [a]cut[1282] [I]to the quick and [ipf]were intending to slay them.

34 But a certain Pharisee named [a]Gamaliel, a [b]teacher of the Law,[3547] respected by all the people, stood up in [c]the Council[4892] and gave orders to put the men[652] outside for a short time.

35 And he said to them, "Men of Israel, take care what you propose[3195] to do with these men.

36 "For some time ago Theudas rose up,[450] [a]claiming to be somebody; and a group of about four hundred men joined up with him. [I]And he was slain; and all who [ipf] [II]followed[3982] him were dispersed and came to nothing.[1096]

🔑 37 "After this man Judas of Galilee rose up in the days of [a]the census, and drew away[868] *some* people after him, he too perished, and all those who [I]followed him were scattered.

38 "And so in the present case, I say to you, stay away[868] from these men and let them alone, for if this plan[4012]

17 [a]Acts 15:5 [b]Matt. 3:7; Acts 4:1
18 [a]Acts 4:3
19 [a]Matt. 1:20, 24; 2:13, 19; 28:2; Luke 1:11; 2:9; Acts 8:26; 10:3; 12:7, 23; 27:23
20 [I]Or, *continue to speak* [II]Lit., *all the words* [a]John 6:63, 68
21 [I]Or, *Sanhedrin* [a]John 8:2 [b]Acts 4:6 [c]Matt. 5:22; Acts 5:27, 34, 41
22 [a]Matt. 26:58; Acts 5:26
24 [I]Lit., *this would become* [a]Acts 4:1; 5:26
26 [a]Acts 5:24 [b]Acts 5:22 [c]Acts 4:21; 5:13
27 [I]Lit., *in* [a]Matt. 5:22; Acts 5:21, 34, 41
28 [a]Acts 4:18 [b]Matt. 23:35; 27:25; Acts 2:23, 36; 3:14f.; 7:52
29 [a]Acts 4:19
30 [I]Or, *on whom you had laid violent hands* [II]Lit., *wood* [a]Acts 3:13 [b]Acts 2:24 [c]Acts 10:39; 13:29; Gal. 3:13; 1Pet. 2:24
31 [I]Or, *by* [II]Or, *Leader* [a]Acts 2:33 [b]Acts 3:15 [c]Luke 2:11 [d]Luke 24:47; Acts 2:38
32 [I]Some mss. add *in Him, or of Him* [a]Luke 24:48 [b]John 15:26; Acts 15:28; Rom. 8:16; Heb. 2:4
33 [I]Lit., *in their hearts* [a]Acts 2:37; 7:54
34 [a]Acts 22:3 [b]Luke 2:46; 5:17 [c]Acts 5:21
36 [I]Lit., *Who was slain* [II]Lit., *were obeying* [a]Acts 8:9; Gal. 2:6; 6:3
37 [I]Lit., *were obeying* [a]Luke 2:2

🔑 **5:37,38** See note on II Thess. 2:3 and also *aphistēmi* (868), to stand away from, and *apostasia* (646), apostasy.

or [I]action should [a]be of men, it will be overthrown;[2647]

39 but if it is of God,[2316] you will not be able to [ainf]overthrow[2647] them; or else you may even be found [a]fighting against God."

40 And they [I]took his advice;[3982] and after calling[4341] the apostles[652] in, they [a]flogged them and ordered them to [II]speak[2980] no more in the name[3686] of Jesus, and *then* released them.

41 So they went on their way from the presence[4383] of the [Ia]Council,4892 [b]rejoicing that they had been considered worthy to suffer [aifp]shame [c]for [II]*His* name.

42 [a]And every day, in the temple[2411] and [I]from house[3624] to house, they [II]kept right on teaching[1321] and [IIIb]preaching[2097] Jesus *as* the [IV]Christ.[5457]

Choosing of the Seven

6 Now [I]at this time while the [a]disciples[3101] were [ppt] [b]increasing *in number,* a complaint arose on the part of the [IIc]Hellenistic *Jews* against the *native* [d]Hebrews, because their [e]widows were being [ipf]overlooked in [f]the daily serving[1248] *of food.*

2 And the twelve summoned the [I]congregation of the disciples and said, "It is not desirable[701] for us to [apt]neglect the word[3056] of God[2316] in order to [pinf]serve tables.

3 "But [aim]select[1980] from among you, [a]brethren,[80] seven men of good [ppp]reputation,[3140] [b]full of the Spirit[4151] and of wisdom,[4678] whom we may put in charge[2525] of this task.[5532]

4 "But we will [a]devote[4342] ourselves to prayer,7335 and to the [I]ministry[1248] of the word."[3056]

5 And the statement found approval with the whole [I]congregation; and they chose [a]Stephen, a man [b]full of faith[4102] and of the [an]Holy Spirit, and [c]Philip, Prochorus, Nicanor, Timon, Parmenas and [II]Nicolas, a [IIId]proselyte[4339] from [e]Antioch.

6 And these they brought before the apostles;[652] and after [a]praying, they [b]laid their hands on them.

7 And [a]the word of God kept on [ipf]spreading;[837] and [b]the number of the disciples continued to [ipf]increase greatly in Jerusalem, and a great many of the priests were becoming [ipf]obedient[5219] to [c]the faith.[4102]

8 And Stephen, full of grace[5485] and power,[1411] [ipf]was performing great [a]wonders[5059] and [I]signs[4592] among the people.

9 But some men from what was called the Synagogue[4864] of the Freedmen, *including* both [a]Cyrenians and [b]Alexandrians, and some from [c]Cilicia and [Id]Asia, rose up[450] and argued with Stephen.

10 And *yet* they were unable to cope with the wisdom and the Spirit[4151] with which he was speaking.

11 Then they secretly induced5260 men [I]to [ppt]say, "We have [pfi]heard him [ppt]speak blasphemous[989] words against Moses and *against* God."

12 And they stirred up the people,[2992] the elders[4245] and the scribes,[1122] and they [a]came upon him and dragged him away, and brought[71] him [I]before [b]the [II]Council.

13 And they put forward [a]false witnesses[3144] who said, "This man incessantly speaks against this [b]holy[40] place, and the Law;[3551]

14 for we have heard him say that [a]this Nazarene, Jesus, will destroy this place and alter[236] [b]the customs which Moses handed down to us."

15 And fixing their gaze on him, all who were sitting in the [Ia]Council4892 saw his face like the face of an angel.[32]

Stephen's Defense

7 And the high priest[749] said, "Are these things so?"

38 [I]Or, *work* [a]Mark 11:30
39 [a]Prov. 21:30; Acts 11:17
40 [I]Lit., *were persuaded by him* [II]Lit., *not be speaking* [a]Matt. 10:17
41 [I]Or, *Sanhedrin* [II]Lit., the *name* (par excellence) [a]Acts 5:21 [b]1Pet. 4:14, 16 [c]John 15:21
42 [I]Or, *in the various private homes* [II]Lit., *were not ceasing to* [III]Or, *telling the good news of* [IV]I.e., Messiah [a]Acts 2:46 [b]Acts 8:35; 11:20; 17:18; Gal. 1:16

1 [I]Lit., *in these days* [II]I.e., non-Palestinian Jews who normally spoke Greek [a]Acts 11:26 [b]Acts 2:47; 6:7 [c]Acts 9:29; 11:20 [d]2Cor. 11:22; Phil. 3:5 [e]Acts 9:39, 41; 1Tim. 5:3 [f]Acts 4:35; 11:29
2 [I]Or, *multitude*
3 [a]John 21:23; Acts 1:15 [b]Acts 2:4
4 [I]Or, *service* [a]Acts 1:14
5 [I]Lit., *multitude* [II]Gr., *Nikolaos* [III]I.e., a Gentile convert to Judaism [a]Acts 6:8ff.; 11:19; 22:20 [b]Acts 6:3; 11:24 [c]Acts 8:5ff.; 21:8 [d]Matt. 23:15 [e]Acts 11:19
6 [a]Acts 1:24 [b]Num. 8:10; 27:18; Deut. 34:9; Mark 5:23; Acts 8:17ff.; 9:17; 13:3; 19:6; 1Tim. 4:14; 2Tim. 1:6; Heb. 6:2
7 [a]Acts 12:24; 19:20 [b]Acts 6:1 [c]Acts 13:8; 14:22; Gal. 1:23; 6:10; Jude 3, 20
8 [I]Or, *attesting miracles* [a]John 4:48
9 [I]I.e., west coast province of Asia Minor [a]Matt. 27:32; Acts 2:10 [b]Acts 18:24 [c]Acts 15:23, 41; 21:39; 22:3; 23:34; 27:5; Gal. 1:21 [d]Acts 16:6; 19:10; 21:27; 24:18
11 [I]Lit., *saying*
12 [I]Lit., *into* [II]Or, *Sanhedrin* [a]Luke 20:1; Acts 4:1 [b]Matt. 5:22
13 [a]Matt. 26:59-61; Acts 7:58 [b]Matt. 24:15; Acts 21:28; 25:8
14 [a]Matt. 26:61 [b]Acts 15:1; 21:21; 26:3; 28:17
15 [I]Or, *Sanhedrin* [a]Matt. 5:22

2 And he said, "<u>Hear me,</u>[191] [a]<u>brethren</u>[80] and <u>fathers</u>![3962] [b]The God of <u>glory</u>[1391] [aop] [c]appeared to our father Abraham when he was in Mesopotamia, before he [ainf]lived in [I]Haran,

3 and said to him, '[a]DEPART FROM YOUR COUNTRY AND YOUR RELATIVES, AND COME INTO THE LAND THAT I WILL SHOW YOU.'

4 "[a]Then he departed from the land of the Chaldeans, and settled in [I]Haran. And [b]from there, after his father died, *God* removed him into this country in which you are now living.

5 "And He gave him no <u>inheritance</u>[2817] in it, not even a foot of ground; and *yet,* even when he had no child, [a]He [ao]<u>promised</u>[1861] that HE WOULD [ainf]GIVE IT TO HIM AS A POSSESSION, AND TO HIS <u>OFFSPRING</u>[4690] AFTER HIM.

🗝 6 "But [a]God spoke to this effect, that his OFFSPRING WOULD BE <u>ALIENS</u>[3941] IN A <u>FOREIGN</u>[245] LAND, AND THAT THEY WOULD [I]BE [ft]ENSLAVED AND [ft]<u>MISTREATED</u>[2559] FOR FOUR HUNDRED YEARS.

7 " 'AND WHATEVER <u>NATION</u>[1484] TO WHICH THEY SHALL [ft]<u>BE IN BONDAGE</u>[1398] I MYSELF WILL JUDGE,' said God, 'AND [a]AFTER THAT THEY WILL COME OUT AND [I]SERVE ME IN THIS PLACE.'

8 "And He [a]gave him [I]the <u>covenant</u>[1242] of <u>circumcision</u>;[4061] and so [b]*Abraham* became the father of Isaac, and <u>circumcised</u>[4059] him on the eighth day; and [c]Isaac *became the father of* Jacob, and [d]Jacob *of* the twelve [e]<u>patriarchs</u>.[3966]

9 "And the patriarchs [a]became [apt]jealous of Joseph and sold him into Egypt. And *yet* God was with him,

10 and rescued him from all his <u>afflictions</u>,[2347] and [a]granted him favor and wisdom in the sight of Pharaoh, king of Egypt; and he <u>made</u>[2525] him <u>governor</u>[2233] over Egypt and all his household.

11 "Now [a]a <u>famine</u>[3042] came over all Egypt and Canaan, and great affliction *with it;* and our fathers [I]could [ipf]find no [II]food.

12 "But [a]when Jacob heard that there was <u>grain</u>[4621] in Egypt, he sent our fathers *there* the first time.

13 "And on the second *visit* [a]Joseph [aop] [I]<u>made himself known</u>[319] to his brothers, and [b]Joseph's family was [ao]<u>disclosed</u>[5318] to Pharaoh.

14 "And [a]Joseph sent *word* and <u>invited</u>[3333] Jacob his father and all his relatives to come to him, [b]seventy-five [c]<u>persons</u>[5590] *in all.*

15 "And [a]Jacob went down to Egypt and *there* passed away, he and our fathers.

16 "And *from there* they were removed to [I][a]Shechem, and laid in the <u>tomb</u>[3418] which Abraham had purchased for a sum of money from the sons of [II]Hamor in [I]Shechem.

17 "But as the [a]<u>time</u>[5550] of the <u>promise</u>[1860] [ipf]was approaching which God had [ao]assured to Abraham, [b]the people increased and multiplied in Egypt,

18 until [a]THERE <u>AROSE</u>[450] <u>ANOTHER</u>[2087] KING OVER EGYPT WHO KNEW NOTHING ABOUT JOSEPH.

19 "It was he who [apt]<u>took [a]shrewd advantage of</u>[2686] our race, and <u>mistreated</u>[2559] our fathers so that they would [pinf] [I][b]expose their <u>infants</u>[1025] and they would not [aies]survive.

20 "And it was at this <u>time</u>[2540] that [a]Moses was born; and he was <u>lovely</u>[791] [I]in the sight of God; and he was nurtured three months in his father's home.

21 "And after he had been [I]exposed, [a]Pharaoh's daughter [II]took him away, and nurtured him as her own son.

22 "And Moses <u>was [aop]educated</u>[3811] in all [a]the learning of the Egyptians, and he was a man of power in words and deeds.

23 "But when he was approaching the age of forty, [a]it <u>entered</u>[305] his [I]mind to [ainf]<u>visit</u>[1980] his brethren, the sons of Israel.

24 "And when he saw one *of them* being [ppp]<u>treated unjustly</u>,[91] he [ao]defended him and took vengeance for the

2 [I]Gr., *Kharran* [a]Acts 22:1 [b]Ps. 29:3; 1Cor. 2:8 [c]Gen. 11:31; 15:7
3 [a]Gen. 12:1
4 [I]Gr., *Kharran* [a]Gen. 11:31; 15:7 [b]Gen. 12:4, 5
5 [a]Gen. 12:7; 13:15; 15:18; 17:8
6 [I]Lit., *enslave them and mistreat them* [a]Gen. 15:13f.
7 [I]Or, *worship* [a]Ex. 3:12
8 [I]Or, *a* [a]Gen. 17:10ff. [b]Gen. 21:2-4 [c]Gen. 25:26 [d]Gen. 29:31ff.; 30:5ff.; 35:23ff. [e]Acts 2:29
9 [a]Gen. 37:11, 28; 39:2, 21f.; 45:4
10 [a]Gen. 39:21; 41:40-46; Ps. 105:21
11 [I]Lit., *were not finding* [II]Or, *fodder* [a]Gen. 41:54f.; 42:5
12 [a]Gen. 42:2
13 [I]Or, *was made known* [a]Gen. 45:1-4 [b]Gen. 45:16
14 [a]Gen. 45:9, 10, 17, 18 [b]Gen. 46:26f.; Ex. 1:5; Deut. 10:22 [c]Acts 2:41
15 [a]Gen. 46:1-7; 49:33; Ex. 1:6
16 [I]Gr., *Sychem* [II]Gr., *Emmor* [a]Gen. 23:16; 33:19; 50:13; Josh. 24:32
17 [a]Gen. 15:13 [b]Ex. 1:7f.
18 [a]Ex. 1:8
19 [I]Or, *put out to die* [a]Ex. 1:10f., 16ff. [b]Ex. 1:22
20 [I]Lit., *to God* [a]Ex. 2:2; Heb. 11:23
21 [I]Or, *put out to die* [II]Or, *adopted him* [a]Ex. 2:5f., 10
22 [a]1Kin. 4:30; Is. 19:11
23 [I]Lit., *heart* [a]Ex. 2:11f.; Heb. 11:24-26

🗝 **7:6** See general remarks on justification on Romans.

[ppp]oppressed by [apt]striking down the Egyptian.

25 "And he [I]supposed that his brethren [pinf]understood that God was granting them [II]deliverance[4991] [III]through him; but they did not understand.

26 "[a]And on the following day he [aop]appeared to them as they were [ppt]fighting together, and he tried to [ipf]reconcile them in peace, saying, 'Men, you are brethren, why do you injure[91] one another?'

27 "But the one who was [ppt]injuring his neighbor [aom]pushed him away, saying, '[a]WHO MADE[2525] YOU A RULER[758] AND JUDGE[1348] OVER US?

28 '[a]YOU DO NOT MEAN TO [ainf]KILL ME AS YOU [ao]KILLED THE EGYPTIAN YESTERDAY, DO YOU?'

29 "And at this remark [a]MOSES FLED, AND BECAME AN ALIEN[3941] IN THE LAND OF [I]MIDIAN, where he [b]became the father of two sons.

30 "And after forty years had [aptp]passed, [a]AN ANGEL [aop]APPEARED TO HIM IN THE WILDERNESS OF MOUNT Sinai, IN THE FLAME OF A BURNING THORN BUSH.

31 "And when Moses [apt]saw it, he *began* to marvel at the sight;[3705] and as he [ppt]approached to [ainf]look *more* closely,[2657] there came the voice of the Lord:[2962]

32 '[a]I AM THE God[2316] OF YOUR FATHERS, THE GOD OF ABRAHAM AND ISAAC AND JACOB.' And Moses shook with fear and [ipf]would not venture to [ainf]look.

33 "[a]BUT THE LORD SAID TO HIM, '[b]TAKE OFF THE SANDALS FROM YOUR FEET, FOR THE PLACE ON WHICH YOU ARE STANDING IS HOLY[40] GROUND.

34 '[a]I HAVE CERTAINLY [apt]SEEN THE OPPRESSION[2561] OF MY PEOPLE IN EGYPT, AND HAVE [ao]HEARD THEIR GROANS, AND I HAVE [ao]COME DOWN TO [ainf]DELIVER THEM; [I][b]COME NOW, AND I WILL SEND YOU TO EGYPT.'

35 "This Moses whom they [a]disowned,[720] saying, 'WHO [ao]MADE[2525] YOU A RULER AND A JUDGE?'[1348] is the one whom God [pfi] [I]sent[649] *to be* both a ruler and a deliverer[3086] with the [II]help of the [an]angel[32] who [aptp]appeared to him in the thorn bush.

36 "[a]This man led them out, performing [b]wonders[5059] and [I]signs[4592] in the land of Egypt and in the Red Sea and in the [c]wilderness for forty years.

37 "This is the Moses who said to the sons of Israel, '[a]GOD SHALL RAISE UP FOR YOU A PROPHET[4396] [I]LIKE ME FROM YOUR BRETHREN.'

38 "This is the one who [apt]was in [a]the [I]congregation[1577] in the wilderness together with [b]the angel who was [ppt]speaking to him on Mount Sinai, and *who was* with our fathers; and he received [ppt] [c]living[2198] [d]oracles[3051] to [ainf]pass on to you.

39 "And our fathers were [ao]unwilling to be [ainf]obedient[5255] to him, but [a]repudiated him and in their hearts turned back to Egypt,

40 [a]SAYING TO AARON, 'MAKE FOR US GODS[2316] WHO WILL GO BEFORE US; FOR THIS MOSES WHO LED US OUT OF THE LAND OF EGYPT—WE DO NOT KNOW[1492] WHAT [ao]HAPPENED TO HIM.'

41 "And [I]at that time [a]they made a [II]calf and brought a sacrifice[2378] to the idol,[1497] and were [ipf]rejoicing[2165] in [b]the works of their hands.

42 "But God [a]turned[4762] away and delivered them up to [pinf] [I]serve[3000] the [II]host[4756] of heaven; as it is written in the book of the prophets, '[b]IT WAS NOT TO ME THAT YOU [ao]OFFERED VICTIMS AND SACRIFICES [c]FORTY YEARS IN THE WILDERNESS, WAS IT, O HOUSE OF ISRAEL?

43 '[a]YOU ALSO TOOK ALONG THE TABERNACLE[4633] OF MOLOCH AND THE STAR OF THE GOD [I]ROMPHA, THE IMAGES[5179] WHICH YOU MADE TO WORSHIP[4352] THEM. I ALSO WILL REMOVE YOU BEYOND BABYLON.'

44 "Our fathers had [a]the tabernacle of testimony[3142] in the wilderness, just as He who spoke to Moses [ao]directed[1299] *him* to [ainf]make it [b]according to the pattern[5179] which he had [pipf]seen.

45 "And having received[1237] it in their turn, our fathers [a]brought it in with [I]Joshua upon dispossessing the [II]nations

25 [I]Lit., *was thinking* [II]Or, *salvation* [III]Lit., *through his hand*
26 [a]Ex. 2:13f.
27 [a]Ex. 2:14; Acts 7:35
28 [a]Ex. 2:14
29 [I]Gr., *Madiam* [a]Ex. 2:15, 22 [b]Ex. 18:3, 4
30 [a]Ex. 3:1f.; Is. 63:9
32 [a]Ex. 3:6; Matt. 22:32
33 [a]Ex. 3:5 [b]Josh. 5:15
34 [I]Lit., *and now hither!* [a]Ex. 3:7f. [b]Ex. 3:10
35 [I]Lit., *has sent* [II]Lit., *hand* [a]Ex. 2:14; Acts 7:27
36 [I]Or, *attesting miracles* [a]Ex. 12:41; 33:1; Heb. 8:9 [b]Ex. 7:3; 14:21; John 4:48 [c]Ex. 16:35; Num. 14:33; Ps. 95:8-10; Acts 7:42; 13:18; Heb. 3:8f.
37 [I]Or, *as He raised up me* [a]Deut. 18:15, 18; Acts 3:22
38 [I]Or, *church;* Gr., *ekklesia* [a]Ex. 19:17 [b]Acts 7:53 [c]Deut. 32:47; Heb. 4:12 [d]Rom. 3:2; Heb. 5:12; 1Pet. 4:11
39 [a]Num. 14:3f.
40 [a]Ex. 32:1, 23
41 [I]Lit., *in those days* [II]Or, *young bull* [a]Ex. 32:4, 6 [b]Rev. 9:20
42 [I]Or, *worship* [II]I.e., heavenly bodies [a]Josh. 24:20; Is. 63:10; Jer. 19:13; Ezek. 20:39 [b]Amos 5:25 [c]Acts 7:36
43 [I]Other mss. spell it: *Romphan,* or *Rempham,* or *Raiphan,* or *Rephan* [a]Amos 5:26, 27
44 [a]Ex. 25:8, 9; 38:21 [b]Ex. 25:40
45 [I]Gr., *Jesus* [II]Or, *Gentiles* [a]Deut. 32:49; Josh. 3:14ff.; 18:1; 23:9; 24:18; Ps. 44:2f.

whom God drove out before our fathers, until the time of David.

46 "And [a]*David* found[2147] favor in God's sight, and [ao] [b]asked that he might [ainf]find a dwelling place for the [I]God of Jacob.

47 "But it was [a]Solomon who built a house for Him.

48 "However,235 [a]the Most High does not dwell in *houses* made by *human* hands;[3485] as the prophet says:

49 '[a]HEAVEN[3772] IS MY THRONE,
AND EARTH[1093] IS THE FOOT-
STOOL OF MY FEET;
WHAT KIND OF HOUSE[3624] WILL
YOU BUILD FOR ME?' says
the Lord;
'OR WHAT PLACE IS THERE FOR
MY REPOSE?[2663]

50 '[a]WAS IT NOT MY HAND WHICH
[ao]MADE ALL THESE THINGS?'

51 "You men who are [a]stiff-necked and uncircumcised[564] in heart and ears are always resisting the Holy Spirit; you are doing just as your fathers did.

52 "[a]Which one of the prophets[4396] did your fathers not [ao]persecute? And they [ao]killed those who had previously [apt]announced[4293] the coming of [b]the Righteous[1342] One, whose betrayers and murderers [c]you have now [aom]become;

53 you who [ao]received the law as [a]ordained[1296] by angels, and *yet* did not [ao]keep it."

Stephen Put to Death

54 Now when they [ppt]heard this, they were [ipf] [a]cut [I]to the quick, and they *began* [ipf]gnashing1031 their teeth at him.

55 But being [a]full of the [an]Holy Spirit,[4151] he [b]gazed intently into heaven and saw the glory of God, and Jesus standing [c]at the right hand1181 of God;

56 and he said, "Behold, I see the [a]heavens [pfpp]opened up and [b]the Son of Man standing at the right hand of God."

57 But they [apt]cried out with a loud voice, and covered[4912] their ears, and they rushed upon him with one impulse.

58 And when they had [apt] [a]driven him out of the city, they *began* [ipf]stoning *him,* and [b]the witnesses[3144] [aom] [c]laid aside their robes at the feet of [d]a young man named Saul.

59 And they went on [ipf]stoning Stephen as he [a]called upon *the Lord* and said, "Lord Jesus, receive my spirit!"[4151]

60 And [apt] [a]falling on his knees, he cried out with a loud voice, "Lord, [b]do not [aosi]hold[2476] this sin[266] against them!" And having said this, he [I][c]fell asleep.

Saul Persecutes the Church

8 And [a]Saul was in hearty agreement with putting him to death.

And on that day a great persecution arose against [b]the church[1577] in Jerusalem; and they were all [c]scattered throughout the regions of Judea and [d]Samaria, except the apostles.[652]

2 And *some* devout[2126] men buried Stephen, and made loud lamentation over him.

3 But [a]Saul *began* [ipf]ravaging3075 the church, entering house after house; and [b]dragging[4951] off men and women, he would [ipf]put them in prison.

Philip in Samaria

4 Therefore, those [a]who had been scattered went about [I][b]preaching[2097] the word.[3056]

5 And [a]Philip went down to the city of Samaria and *began* [ipf]proclaiming[2784] [I]Christ[5547] to them.

6 And the multitudes with one accord were [ipf]giving attention to what was [ppt]said by Philip, as they [aie]heard and saw the [I]signs[4592] which he was [ipf]performing.

7 For *in the case of* many who had [a]unclean[169] spirits,[4151] they were [ipf]coming out *of them* shouting with a loud voice; and many who had been [b]paralyzed3886 and lame were healed.

8 And there [ao]was [a]much rejoicing in that city.

46 [I]The earliest mss. read *house* instead of *God;* the Septuagint reads *God* [a]2Sam. 7:8ff.; Ps. 132:1-5; Acts 13:22 [b]2Sam. 7:1-16; 1Chr. 17:1-14
47 [a]1Kin. 6:1-38; 8:20; 2Chr. 3:1-17
48 [a]Luke 1:32
49 [a]Is. 66:1; Matt. 5:34f.
50 [a]Is. 66:2
51 [a]Ex. 32:9; 33:3, 5; Lev. 26:41; Num. 27:14; Is. 63:10; Jer. 6:10; 9:26
52 [a]2Chr. 36:15f.; Matt. 5:12; 23:31, 37 [b]Acts 3:14; 22:14; 1John 2:1 [c]Acts 3:14; 5:28
53 [a]Deut. 33:2; Acts 7:38; Gal. 3:19; Heb. 2:2
54 [I]Lit., *in their hearts* [a]Acts 5:33
55 [a]Acts 2:4 [b]John 11:41 [c]Mark 16:19
56 [a]John 1:51 [b]Matt. 8:20
58 [a]Lev. 24:14, 16; Luke 4:29 [b]Deut. 13:9f.; 17:7; Acts 6:13 [c]Acts 22:20 [d]Acts 8:1; 22:20; 26:10
59 [a]Acts 9:14, 21; 22:16; Rom. 10:12-14; 1Cor. 1:2; 2Tim. 2:22
60 [I]Or, *expired* [a]Luke 22:41 [b]Matt. 5:44; Luke 23:34 [c]Dan. 12:2; Matt. 27:52; John 11:11f.; Acts 13:36; 1Cor. 15:6, 18, 20; 1Thess. 4:13ff.; 2Pet. 3:4

1 [a]Acts 7:58; 22:20; 26:10 [b]Acts 9:31 [c]Acts 8:4; 11:19 [d]Acts 1:8; 8:5, 14; 9:31
3 [a]Acts 9:1, 13, 21; 22:4, 19; 26:10f.; 1Cor. 15:9; Gal. 1:13; Phil. 3:6; 1Tim. 1:13 [b]James 2:6
4 [I]Or, *bringing the good tidings of* [a]Acts 8:1 [b]Acts 8:12; 15:35
5 [I]I.e., the Messiah [a]Acts 6:5; 8:26, 30
6 [I]Or, *attesting miracles*
7 [a]Mark 16:17 [b]Matt. 4:24
8 [a]John 4:40-42; Acts 8:39

9 Now there was a certain man
named Simon, who formerly was [ppt]prac-
ticing [a]magic3096 in the city, and
[ppt]astonishing1839 the people1484 of Samaria, [b]claiming to be someone great;
10 and they all, from smallest to
greatest, were giving [ipf]attention to him,
saying, "[a]This man is what is called the
Great Power of God."2316
11 And they were giving him [ipf]at-
tention because he had for a long time5550
[aid]astonished them with his [a]magic
arts.3095
12 But when they believed4100 Philip
[a]preaching2097 the good news about the
kingdom932 of God and the name of Jesus
Christ, they were being [ipf] [b]baptized,907
men and women alike.
13 And even Simon himself believed; and after being baptized, he continued on4342 with Philip; and as he observed [a]signs4592 and [b]great miracles1411
taking place, he was constantly
[ppt]amazed.1839
14 Now when [a]the apostles652 in Jerusalem [apt]heard that Samaria had [pf]re-
ceived the word3056 of God, they sent
them [b]Peter and John,
15 who came down and [ao]prayed for
them, [a]that they might [aosb]receive the
[an]Holy Spirit.4151
🔑16 For He had [a]not yet fallen upon
any of them; they had simply been
[b]baptized [1]in the name3686 of the Lord
Jesus.
17 Then they [a]*began* [ipf]laying their
hands on them, and they were [ipf] [b]receiv-
ing the [an]Holy Spirit.
18 Now when Simon saw that the
Spirit was [pinp]bestowed through the laying on of the apostles' hands, he offered
them money,5536
19 saying, "Give this authority1849
to me as well, so that everyone on whom
I [aosb]lay my hands may [psa]receive the
[an]Holy Spirit."
20 But Peter said to him, "May your
silver694 [apt]perish with you, because you
[ao]thought you could [pinf] [a]obtain the gift
of God with money!

21 "You have [a]no part or portion2819
in this [1]matter, for your heart2588 is not
[b]right before God.
22 "Therefore [aim]repent3340 of this
wickedness2549 of yours, and [aim]pray the
Lord that [a]if possible, the intention1963
of your heart may be [fp]forgiven863 you.
23 "For I see that you are in the
gall5521 of bitterness and in [a]the [1]bondage
of iniquity."93
24 But Simon answered and said,
"[aim] [a]Pray1189 to the Lord for me yourselves, so that nothing of what you have
[pf]said may [aosb]come upon me."

An Ethiopian Receives Christ

25 And so, when they had solemnly
[apt] [a]testified1263 and [apt]spoken [b]the word
of the Lord, they started back to Jerusalem, and were [c]preaching the gospel2097
to many villages of the [d]Samaritans.
26 But [a]an angel32 of the Lord spoke
to [b]Philip saying, "Arise and [pim]go south
to2596 the road that descends from Jerusalem to [c]Gaza." ([1]This is a desert
road.)
27 And he arose and went; and
behold, [a]there was an Ethiopian eunuch,2135 a court official1413 of Candace,
queen of the Ethiopians, who was in
charge of all her treasure; and he
[b]had [plpf]come to Jerusalem to [finf]wor-
ship.4352
28 And he was returning and sitting
in his [1]chariot, and was [ipf]reading the
prophet4396 Isaiah.
29 And [a]the Spirit said to Philip, "Go
up and [aipp]join this [1]chariot."
30 And when Philip had [apt]run up,
he heard him [ppt]reading Isaiah the
prophet, and said, "Do you understand
what you are reading?"
31 And he said, "Well, how [apt]could
I, unless someone [ft]guides me?" And
he invited3870 Philip to [apt]come up and
[inf]sit with him.
32 Now the passage of Scripture
which he was [ipf]reading was this:

9 [a]Acts 8:11; 13:6 [b]Acts 5:36
10 [a]Acts 14:11; 28:6
11 [a]Acts 8:9; 13:6
12 [a]Acts 1:3; 8:4 [b]Acts 2:38
13 [a]Acts 8:6 [b]Acts 19:11
14 [a]Acts 8:1 [b]Luke 22:8
15 [a]Acts 2:38; 19:2
16 [1]Lit., *into* [a]Matt. 28:19; Acts 19:2 [b]Acts 2:38; 10:48
17 [a]Mark 5:23; Acts 6:6 [b]Acts 2:4
20 [a]2Kin. 5:16; Is. 55:1; Dan. 5:17; Matt. 10:8; Acts 2:38
21 [1]Or, *teaching;* lit., *word* [a]Deut. 10:9; 12:12; Eph. 5:5 [b]Ps. 78:37
22 [a]Is. 55:7
23 [1]Or, *fetter* [a]Is. 58:6
24 [a]Gen. 20:7; Ex. 8:8; Num. 21:7; James 5:16
25 [a]Luke 16:28 [b]Acts 13:12 [c]Acts 8:40 [d]Matt. 10:5
26 [1]Or, *This city is deserted* [a]Acts 5:19; 8:29 [b]Acts 8:5 [c]Gen. 10:19
27 [a]Ps. 68:31; 87:4; Is. 56:3ff. [b]1Kin. 8:41f.; John 12:20
28 [1]Or, *carriage*
29 [1]Or, *carriage* [a]Acts 8:39; 10:19; 11:12; 13:2; 16:6, 7; 20:23; 21:11; 28:25; Heb. 3:7

🔑**8:16** See note on I Cor. 10:2.

"[a]He was led as a sheep to
slaughter;
And as a lamb[286] before its
shearer is silent,
So He does not open His
mouth.
33 "[a]In humiliation[5014] His
judgment[2920] was taken
away;
Who shall [I]relate[1334] His
[II]generation?[1074]
For His life is removed
from the earth."
34 And the eunuch answered Philip
and said, "Please *tell me*, of whom does
the prophet say this? Of himself, or of
someone else?"
35 And Philip [a]opened his mouth,
and [b]beginning from this Scripture[1124]
he [c]preached[2097] Jesus to him.
36 And as they [ipf]went along the
road they came to some water; and the
eunuch *said, "Look! Water! [a]What prevents me from being [aifp]baptized?"[907]
37 [[I]And Philip said, "If you believe[4100] with all your heart, you may."
And he answered and said, "I believe
that Jesus Christ[5547] is the Son[5207] of
God."][2316]
38 And he ordered the [I]chariot to
stop;[2476] and they both went down into
the water, Philip as well as the eunuch;
and he baptized him.
🗝 39 And when they came up out of
the water, [a]the Spirit[4151] of the Lord
snatched[726] Philip away; and the eunuch
saw him no more, but [ipf]went on his
way rejoicing.
40 But Philip [I]found himself at
[II][a]Azotus; and as he passed through he
[b]kept [ipf]preaching[2097] the gospel to all
the cities, until he came to [c]Caesarea.

The Conversion of Saul

9 [a]Now Saul, still [b]breathing [I]threats
and murder against the disciples[3101]
of the Lord, [apt]went to the high priest,
2 and asked for [a]letters from him
to [b]the synagogues at [c]Damascus, so
that if he [aosb]found any belonging to
[d]the Way,[3598] both men and women, he
might [aosb]bring them bound to Jerusalem.
3 And it came about that as he journeyed, he was approaching Damascus,
and [a]suddenly a light from heaven flashed
around him;
4 and [a]he [apt]fell to the ground, and
heard a voice saying to him, "Saul, Saul,
why are you persecuting Me?"
5 And he said, "Who art Thou,
Lord?"[2962] And He *said*, "I am Jesus
whom you are persecuting,
6 but rise, and enter the city, and
[a]it shall be told you what you must do."
7 And the men who [ppt]traveled with
him [a]stood speechless, [b]hearing the
[I]voice, but seeing no one.
8 And Saul got up from the ground,
and [a]though his eyes were [pfpp]open, he
[I]could [ipf]see nothing; and [ppt]leading him
by the hand, they brought him into
[b]Damascus.
9 And he was three days without
[ppt]sight, and neither ate nor drank.
10 Now there was a certain disciple
at [a]Damascus, named [b]Ananias; and the
Lord said to him in [c]a vision,[3705] "Ananias." And he said, "Behold, *here am*
I, Lord."
11 And the Lord *said* to him, "Arise
and go to the street called Straight, and
inquire at the house of Judas for a man
from [a]Tarsus named Saul, for behold,
he is praying,
12 and he has [ao]seen [I]in a vision[3705]
a man named Ananias [apt]come in and
[apt] [a]lay his hands on him, so that he might
regain his sight."
13 But Ananias answered, "Lord,
I have [ao]heard from many about this
man, [a]how much harm[2556] he [ao]did to
[b]Thy [I]saints[40] at Jerusalem;
14 and here he [a]has authority[1849]
from the chief priests to bind all who
[ppt] [b]call upon Thy name."

32 [a]Is. 53:7
33 [I]Or, *describe* [II]Or, *family or origin* [a]Is. 53:8
35 [a]Matt. 5:2 [b]Luke 24:27; Acts 17:2; 18:28; 28:23 [c]Acts 5:42
36 [a]Acts 10:47
37 [I]Many mss. do not contain this v.
38 [I]Or, *carriage*
39 [a]1Kin. 18:12; 2Kin. 2:16; Ezek. 3:12, 14; 8:3; 11:1, 24; 43:5; 2Cor. 12:2
40 [I]Or, *was found* [II]O.T.: Ashdod [a]Josh. 11:22; 1Sam. 5:1 [b]Acts 8:25 [c]Acts 9:30; 10:1, 24; 11:11; 12:19; 18:22; 21:8, 16; 23:23, 33; 25:1, 4, 6, 13
1 [I]Lit., *threat* [a]Acts 9:1-22; 22:3-16; 26:9-18 [b]Acts 8:3; 9:13-21
2 [a]Acts 9:14, 21; 22:5; 26:10 [b]Matt. 10:17 [c]Gen. 14:15; 2Cor. 11:32; Gal. 1:17 [d]John 14:6; Acts 18:25f.; 19:9, 23; 22:4; 24:14, 22
3 [a]1Cor. 15:8
4 [a]Acts 22:7; 26:14
6 [a]Acts 9:16
7 [I]Or, *sound* [a]Acts 26:14 [b]John 12:29f.; Acts 22:9
8 [I]Lit., *was seeing* [a]Acts 9:18; 22:11 [b]Gen. 14:15; 2Cor. 11:32; Gal. 1:17
10 [a]Gen. 14:15; 2Cor. 11:32; Gal. 1:17 [b]Acts 22:12 [c]Acts 10:3, 17, 19; 11:5; 12:9; 16:9f.; 18:9
11 [a]Acts 9:30; 11:25; 21:39; 22:3
12 [I]Some mss. do not contain *in a vision* [a]Mark 5:23; Acts 6:6; 9:17
13 [I]Or, *holy ones* [a]Acts 8:3 [b]Acts 9:32, 41; 26:10; Rom. 1:7; 15:25, 26, 31; 16:2, 15; 1Cor. 1:2
14 [a]Acts 9:2, 21 [b]Acts 7:59

🗝 **8:39** See note on I Thess. 4:17 and also *harpazō* (726), to catch up or away.

15 But the Lord said to him, "[pim]Go, for [a]he is a chosen [I]instrument of Mine, to [infg]bear My name before [b]the Gentiles[1484] and [c]kings and the sons of Israel;

16 for [a]I will show him how much he must [ainf]suffer[3958] for My name's sake."

17 And Ananias departed and entered the house, and after [apt] [a]laying his hands on him said, "[b]Brother Saul, the Lord Jesus, who [aptp]appeared to you on the road by which you were [ipf]coming, has [pfi]sent me so that you may regain your [aisb]sight, and be [asbp] [c]filled with the [an]Holy Spirit."

18 And immediately there fell from his eyes something like scales, and he regained his sight, and he arose and was baptized;[907]

19 and he took food and was strengthened.[1765]

Saul Begins to Preach Christ

Now [a]for several days he was with [b]the disciples[3101] who were at Damascus,

20 and immediately[2112] he *began to* [ipf]proclaim[2784] Jesus[5547] [a]in the synagogues, [I]saying, "He is [b]the Son[5207] of God."[2316]

21 And all those [ppt]hearing him continued to be [ipf]amazed, and were [ipf]saying, "Is this not he who in Jerusalem [apt][a]destroyed those who [ppt] [b]called on this name, and *who* had [plpf]come here for the purpose of bringing them bound before the chief priests?"

22 But Saul kept increasing in strength and [ipf]confounding the Jews who [ppt]lived at Damascus by [ppt]proving that this *Jesus* is the [I]Christ.[5547]

23 And when [a]many days had [ipf]elapsed, [b]the Jews plotted together to [ainf]do away with him,

24 but [a]their plot became known to Saul. And [b]they were also [ipf]watching[3906] the gates day and night so that they might [aosb]put him to death;

25 but his disciples took him by night, and let him down through *an opening in* the wall, lowering him in a large basket.

26 And [a]when he had [apt]come to Jerusalem, he was [ipf]trying[3987] to [pip]associate with the disciples; and they were all [ipf]afraid of him, not [ppt]believing[4100] that he was a disciple.[3101]

27 But [a]Barnabas [apt]took[1949] hold of him and brought[71] him to the apostles[652] and described[1334] to them how he had [ao] [b]seen the Lord on the road, and that He had [ao]talked to him, and how [c]at Damascus he had [ao] [d]spoken out boldly[3955] in the name[3686] of Jesus.

28 And he was with them [I]moving about freely in Jerusalem, [a]speaking out boldly in the name of the Lord.

29 And he was [ppt]talking and [ipf]arguing with the [a]Hellenistic *Jews;* but they were [ipf]attempting to [ainf]put him to death.

30 But when [a]the brethren learned *of it,* they brought him down to [b]Caesarea and [c]sent him away to [d]Tarsus.

31 So [a]the church[1577] throughout all Judea and Galilee and Samaria [ipf] [I]enjoyed peace,[1515] being [ppp]built up; and, [ppt]going on in the fear[5401] of the Lord and in the comfort[3874] of the Holy Spirit, it continued to [ipf]increase.

Peter's Ministry

32 Now it came about that as Peter was [ppt]traveling through all *those parts,* he [ainf]came down also to [a]the [I]saints[40] who [ppt]lived at [IIb]Lydda.

33 And there he found a certain man named Aeneas, who had been bedridden eight years, for he was paralyzed.[3886]

34 And Peter said to him, "Aeneas, Jesus Christ heals you; arise, and make your bed." And immediately he arose.

35 And all who lived at [Ia]Lydda and [b]Sharon saw him, and they [c]turned[1994] to the Lord.

36 Now in [a]Joppa there was a certain disciple[3102] named Tabitha (which translated[1329] *in Greek* is called [I]Dorcas); this woman was abounding[4134] with

15 [I]Or, *vessel* [a]Acts 13:2; Rom. 1:1; 9:23; Gal. 1:15; Eph. 3:7 [b]Acts 22:21; 26:17; Rom. 1:5; 11:13; 15:16; Gal. 1:16; 2:7ff.; Eph. 3:1, 8; 1Tim. 2:7; 2Tim. 4:17 [c]Acts 25:22f.; 26:1, 32; 2Tim. 4:17
16 [a]Acts 20:23; 21:4, 11, 13; 2Cor. 6:4f.; 11:23-27; 1Thess. 3:3
17 [a]Mark 5:23; Acts 6:6; 9:12 [b]Acts 22:13 [c]Acts 2:4
19 [a]Acts 26:20 [b]Acts 9:26, 38; 11:26
20 [I]Lit., *that* [a]Acts 13:5, 14; 14:1; 16:13; 17:2, 10; 18:4, 19; 19:8 [b]Matt. 4:3; Acts 9:22; 13:33
21 [a]Acts 8:3; 9:13; Gal. 1:13, 23 [b]Acts 9:14
22 [I]I.e., Messiah
23 [a]Gal. 1:17, 18 [b]1Thess. 2:16
24 [a]Acts 20:3, 19; 23:12, 30; 25:3 [b]2Cor. 11:32f.
26 [a]Acts 22:17-20; 26:20
27 [a]Acts 4:36 [b]Acts 9:3-6 [c]Acts 9:20, 22 [d]Acts 4:13, 29; 9:29
28 [I]Lit., *going in and going out* [a]Acts 4:13, 29; 9:29
29 [a]Acts 6:1
30 [a]Acts 1:15 [b]Acts 8:40 [c]Gal. 1:21 [d]Acts 9:11
31 [I]Lit., *was having* [a]Acts 5:11; 8:1; 16:5
32 [I]Or, *holy ones* [II]I.e., Lod [a]Acts 9:13 [b]1Chr. 8:12; Ezra 2:33; Neh. 7:37; 11:35
35 [I]I.e., Lod [a]1Chr. 8:12; Ezra 2:33; Neh. 7:37; 11:35 [b]1Chr. 5:16; 27:29; Is. 33:9; 35:2; 65:10 [c]Acts 2:47; 9:42; 11:21
36 [I]Or, *Gazelle* [a]Josh. 19:46; 2Chr. 2:16; Ezra 3:7; Jon. 1:3; Acts 9:38, 42f.; 10:5, 8, 23, 32; 11:5, 13

deeds of kindness[18] and charity,[1654]
which she continually [ipf]did.
37 And it came about [I]at that time
that she fell [apt]sick and [ainf]died; and when
they had washed her body, they laid it
in an [a]upper room.
38 And since Lydda was near
[a]Joppa, [b]the disciples,[3101] having heard
that Peter was there, sent two men to
him, entreating[3870] him, "Do not [ainf]delay
to [ainf]come to us."
39 And Peter arose and went with
them. And when he had come, they
brought him into the [a]upper room; and
all the [b]widows stood beside him weeping, and showing all the [I]tunics and garments that Dorcas used to [ipf]make while
she was with them.
40 But Peter [apt] [a]sent them all out
and [apt] [b]knelt down and prayed, and
[apt]turning to the body, he said, "[c]Tabi-
tha, arise." And she opened her eyes,
and when she [apt]saw Peter, she sat up.
41 And he gave her his hand and
raised her up; and calling [a]the [I]saints
and [b]widows, he presented her alive.[2198]
42 And it became known all over
[a]Joppa, and [b]many believed[4100] in the
Lord.
43 And it came about that he
[ainf]stayed many days in [a]Joppa with
[b]a certain tanner, Simon.

Cornelius' Vision

10 Now *there was* a certain man at
[a]Caesarea named Cornelius, a
centurion of what was [b]called the Italian
[I]cohort,
2 a devout[2152] man, and [a]one who
[ppt]feared[5399] God with all his household,[3624] and [ppt] [b]gave many [I]alms to the
Jewish people, and [ppt]prayed to God continually.
3 About [a]the [I]ninth hour of the day
he clearly saw [b]in a vision[3705] [c]an angel[32]
of God who had *just* [apt]come in to him,
and [apt]said to him, "Cornelius!"
4 And [a]fixing his gaze upon him and
being much alarmed, he said, "What is
it, Lord?" And he said to him, "Your
prayers[4335] and [I]alms[1654] [b]have [ao]as-
cended [c]as a memorial before God.
5 "And now dispatch *some* men to
[a]Joppa, and send for a man *named* Simon,
who is also called Peter;
6 he [I]is staying with a certain tanner
named [a]Simon, whose house is by the
sea."
7 And when the angel who was
speaking to him had departed, he summoned two of his [I]servants and a devout
soldier of those who were in constant
attendance[4342] upon him,
8 and after he had explained[1834]
everything to them, he sent them to
[a]Joppa.
9 And on the next day, as they were
on their way, and [ppt]approaching[1448] the
city, [a]Peter went up on [b]the housetop
about [c]the [I]sixth hour to pray.
10 And he became hungry, and was
[ipf]desiring to eat;[1089] but while they were
making [ainf]preparations, he [a]fell into a
trance;[1611]
11 and he *beheld [a]the [I]sky opened
up, and a certain [II]object like a great
sheet coming down, [ppp]lowered by four
corners to the ground,
12 and there were in it all *kinds of*
four-footed animals and [I]crawling creatures of the earth and birds of the
[II]air.
13 And a voice came to him,
[apt]"Arise, Peter, [aim] [I]kill[2380] and [aim]eat!"
14 But Peter said, "By no means,
[a]Lord,[2962] for [b]I have never eaten anything [I]unholy[2839] and unclean."[169]
15 And again a voice *came* to him
a second time, "[a]What God has
[ao]cleansed,[2511] no *longer* consider [I]un-
holy."[2840]
16 And this happened three times;

37 [I]Lit., *in those days* [a]Acts 1:13; 9:39
38 [a]Josh. 19:46; 2Chr. 2:16; Ezra 3:7; Jon. 1:3; Acts 9:36, 42f.; 10:5, 8, 23, 32; 11:5, 13 [b]Acts 11:26
39 [I]Or, *inner garments* [a]Acts 1:13; 9:37 [b]Acts 6:1
40 [a]Matt. 9:25 [b]Luke 22:41; Acts 7:60 [c]Mark 5:41
41 [I]Or, *holy ones* [a]Acts 9:13, 32 [b]Acts 6:1
42 [a]Josh. 19:46; 2Chr. 2:16; Jon. 1:3; Acts 9:38, 42f.; 10:5, 8, 23, 32; 11:5, 13 [b]Acts 9:35
43 [a]Josh. 19:46; 2Chr. 2:16; Ezra 3:7; Jon. 1:3; Acts 9:38, 42f.; 10:5, 8, 23, 32; 11:13, 15 [b]Acts 10:6

1 [I]Or, *battalion* [a]Acts 8:40; 10:24 [b]Matt. 27:27; Mark 15:16; John 18:3, 12; Acts 21:31; 27:1
2 [I]Or, *gifts of charity* [a]Acts 10:22, 35; 13:16, 26 [b]Luke 7:4f.
3 [I]I.e., 3 p.m. [a]Acts 3:1 [b]Acts 9:10; 10:17, 19 [c]Acts 5:19
4 [I]Or, *deeds of charity* [a]Acts 3:4 [b]Rev. 8:4 [c]Matt. 26:13; Phil. 4:18; Heb. 6:10
5 [a]Acts 9:36
6 [I]Or, *is lodging* [a]Acts 9:43
7 [I]Or, *household slaves*
8 [a]Acts 9:36
9 [I]I.e., noon [a]Acts 10:9-32; 11:5-14 [b]Jer. 19:13; 32:29; Zeph. 1:5; Matt. 24:17 [c]Ps. 55:17; Acts 10:3
10 [a]Acts 11:5; 22:17
11 [I]Or, *heaven* [II]Or, *vessel* [a]John 1:51

12 [I]Or possibly, *reptiles* [II]Or, *heaven* 13 [I]Or, *sacrifice*
14 [I]Or, *profane;* lit., *common* [a]Matt. 8:2ff.; John 4:11ff.; Acts 9:5; 22:8 [b]Lev. 11:20-25; Deut. 14:4-20; Ezek. 4:14; Dan. 1:8; Acts 10:28 15 [I]Lit., common [a]Matt. 15:11; Mark 7:19; Rom. 14:14; 1Cor. 10:25ff.; 1Tim. 4:4f.; Titus 1:15

10:4,31 See note on Mt. 8:11,12.

and immediately the [I]object was taken
up into the [II]sky.
17 Now while Peter was greatly
[ipf]perplexed [I]in mind as to what [a]the
vision[3705] which he had [ao]seen might
[opt]be, behold, [b]the men who had been
[pfpp]sent by Cornelius, having asked directions for Simon's house, appeared at
the gate;
18 and calling out, they were asking
whether Simon, who was also called Peter, was [I]staying there.
19 And while Peter was [ppt]reflecting
on [a]the vision, [b]the Spirit[4151] said to him,
"Behold, [I]three men are looking for you.
20 "But [apt]arise, go downstairs, and
[pim] [a]accompany them [I]without [ppt]misgiv-
ings;[1252] for I have [pfi]sent them Myself."
21 And Peter went down to the men
and said, "Behold, I am the one you
are looking for; what is the reason[156]
for which you have come?"
22 And they said, "Cornelius, a centurion, a righteous[1342] and [ppt] [a]God-
fearing[5399] man well [ppp]spoken[3140] of by
the entire nation of the Jews, [b]was divinely directed[5337] by a [c]holy angel to
[ainf]send for you *to come* to his house
and [ainf]hear [I][d]a message[4487] from you."
23 And so he invited them in[1528] and
gave them lodging.

Peter at Caesarea

And on the next day he arose and
went away with them, and [a]some of
[b]the brethren[80] from [c]Joppa accompanied him.
24 And on the following day he entered [a]Caesarea. Now Cornelius was
waiting for them, and had [apt]called
together[4779] his relatives and close[316]
friends.
25 And when it came about that Peter entered, Cornelius [apt]met him, and
[apt]fell at his feet and [I][a]worshiped *him.*
26 But Peter raised him up, saying,
"[a]Stand up; I too am *just* a man."[444]
27 And as he [ppt]talked with him, he
entered, and [I]found [a]many people
[pfp]assembled.
28 And he said to them, "You your-

16 [I]Or, *vessel* [II]Or, *heaven*
17 [I]Lit., *himself* [a]Acts 10:3 [b]Acts 10:8
18 [I]Or, *lodging*
19 [I]One early ms. reads *two* [a]Acts 10:3 [b]Acts 8:29
20 [I]Lit., *doubting nothing* [a]Acts 15:7-9
22 [I]Lit., *words* [a]Acts 10:2 [b]Matt. 2:12 [c]Mark 8:38; Luke 9:26; Rev. 14:10 [d]Acts 11:14
23 [a]Acts 10:45; 11:12 [b]Acts 1:15 [c]Acts 9:36
24 [a]Acts 8:40; 10:1
25 [I]Or, *prostrated himself in reverence* [a]Matt. 8:2
26 [a]Acts 14:15; Rev. 19:10; 22:8f.
27 [I]Lit., *finds* [a]Acts 10:24
28 [I]Or, *profane;* lit., *common* [a]John 4:9; 18:28; Acts 11:3 [b]Acts 10:14f., 35; 15:9
30 [I]I.e., 3 to 4 p.m. [a]Acts 10:9, 22f. [b]Acts 3:1; 10:3 [c]Acts 10:3-6, 30-32
31 [I]Or, *deeds of charity*
32 [I]Or, *lodging* [a]John 4:9; 18:28; Acts 11:3
33 [I]Lit., *done well in coming*
34 [a]Matt. 5:2 [b]Deut. 10:17; 2Chr. 19:7; Rom. 2:11; Gal. 2:6; Eph. 6:9; Col. 3:25; 1Pet. 1:17
35 [I]Or, *reverences* [II]Lit., *works righteousness* [a]Acts 10:28 [b]Acts 10:2
36 [I]Some mss. read *He sent the word to* [II]Or, *the gospel of peace* [a]Acts 13:32 [b]Luke 1:79; 2:14; Rom. 5:1; Eph. 2:17 [c]Matt. 28:18; Acts 2:36; Rom. 10:12
38 [I]Or possibly, *How God anointed Jesus of Nazareth*

selves know how [a]unlawful[111] it is for
a man who is a Jew to [pinf]associate with
a foreigner[246] or to [pip]visit him; and *yet*
[b]God has shown me that I should not
call any man [I]unholy[2839] or unclean.[169]
29 "That is why I came without even
raising any objection[369] when I was
[aptp]sent for. And so I ask for what
reason[3056] you have [ainf]sent for me."
30 And Cornelius said, "[a]Four days
ago to this hour, I was [ipf]praying in my
house during [b]the [I]ninth hour; and behold, [c]a man stood before me in shining
garments,
31 and he *said, 'Cornelius, your
prayer has been [aop]heard and your
[I]alms[1654] have been [aop]remembered before God.
32 'Send therefore to [a]Joppa and
invite[3333] Simon, who is also called Peter, to come to you; he is [I]staying at
the house of Simon *the* tanner by the
sea.'
33 "And so I sent to you immediately, and you have [I]been kind enough
to [apt]come. Now then, we are all here
present before God[2316] to [ainf]hear all that
you have been [pfpp]commanded[4367] by the
Lord."

Gentiles Hear Good News

34 And [a]opening his mouth, Peter
said:
"**I** most certainly understand[2638] *now*
that [b]God[2316] is not one to show partiality,
35 but [a]in every nation the man who
[ppt] [I][b]fears[5399] Him and [ppt] [II]does[2038] what
is right,[1343] is welcome[1184] to Him.
36 "[I]The word[3056] which He sent to
the sons[5207] of Israel, [a]preaching[2097]
[II][b]peace[1515] through Jesus Christ (He is
[c]Lord of all)—
37 you yourselves know the thing
which took place throughout all Judea,
starting from Galilee, after the baptism[908] which John proclaimed.[2784]
38 "[I]*You know of* [a]Jesus of Nazareth, how God [b]anointed[5548] Him with

[a]Acts 2:22 [b]Acts 4:26

the [an]Holy Spirit and with power,
[IIc]and *how* He went about doing good,
and healing all who were [ppp]oppressed
by the devil;[1228] for [d]God was with
Him.
39 "And we are [a]witnesses[3144] of all
the things He did both in the [I]land of
the Jews and in Jerusalem. And they
also [b]put Him to death by hanging Him
on a [II]cross.
40 "[a]God raised Him up on the third
day, and granted that He should become
visible,
41 [a]not to all the people, but to
[b]witnesses[3144] who were [pfpp]chosen beforehand by God, *that is,* to us, [c]who
[ao]ate and [ao]drank with Him after He
[ainf]arose from the dead.
42 "And He [a]ordered us to
[I]preach[2784] to the people, and solemnly
to [b]testify[1263] that this is the One who
has been [pfpp] [c]appointed[3724] by God
as [d]Judge[2923] of the living[2198] and the
dead.
🔑 43 "Of Him [a]all the prophets[4396] bear
witness that through [b]His name[3686]
everyone who [ppt]believes[4100] in Him
[ainf]receives forgiveness[859] of sins."[266]
🔑 **44** While Peter was still speaking
these words, [a]the Holy Spirit fell upon
all those who were [ppt]listening to the
[I]message.[3056]
45 And [a]all the [I]circumcised[4061]
believers[4103] who had come with Peter
were amazed, because the gift[1431] of the
Holy Spirit had been [pfip] [b]poured out
upon the Gentiles also.
🔑 46 For they were [ipf]hearing them
[ppt] [a]speaking[2980] with tongues[1100] and
[ppt]exalting God. Then Peter answered,
47 "[a]Surely no one can [ainf]refuse the
water for these to be [aifp]baptized[907] who
[b]have [ao]received the Holy Spirit just as
we *did,* can he?"
🔑 48 And he [a]ordered[4367] them to be
baptized [b]in the name[3686] of Jesus Christ.
Then they asked him to [ainf]stay on for
a few days.

38 [II]Lit., *who went* [c]Matt. 4:23 [d]John 3:2
39 [I]Or, *country-side* [II]Lit., *wood* [a]Luke 24:48; Acts 10:41 [b]Acts 5:30
40 [a]Acts 2:24
41 [a]John 14:19, 22; 15:27 [b]Luke 24:48; Acts 10:39 [c]Luke 24:43; Acts 1:4 mg.
42 [I]Or, *proclaim* [a]Acts 1:2 [b]Luke 16:28 [c]Luke 22:22 [d]John 5:22, 27; Acts 17:31; 2Tim. 4:1; 1Pet. 4:5
43 [a]Acts 3:18 [b]Luke 24:47; Acts 2:38; 4:12
44 [I]Lit., *word* [a]Acts 11:15; 15:8
45 [I]Lit., *believers from among the circumcision;* i.e., Jewish Christians [a]Acts 10:23 [b]Acts 2:33, 38
46 [a]Mark 16:17; Acts 2:4; 19:6
47 [a]Acts 8:36 [b]Acts 2:4; 10:44f.; 11:17; 15:8
48 [a]1Cor. 1:14-17 [b]Acts 2:38; 8:16; 19:5

1 [a]Acts 1:15
2 [I]Lit., *those of the circumcision;* i.e., Jewish Christians [a]Acts 10:45
3 [I]Or, *entered the house of* [a]Matt. 9:11; Acts 10:28; Gal. 2:12
4 [a]Luke 1:3
5 [I]Or, *vessel* [II]Or, *heaven* [a]Acts 10:9-32; 11:5-14 [b]Acts 9:10
6 [I]Lit., *and I saw* [II]Or possibly, *reptiles* [III]Or, *heaven*
7 [I]Or, *sacrifice*
8 [I]Or, *profane;* lit., *common*
9 [I]Lit., *make common* [a]Acts 10:15
10 [I]Or, *heaven*
11 [a]Acts 8:40

Peter Reports at Jerusalem

11 Now the apostles and [a]the brethren who were throughout Judea
heard that the Gentiles[1484] also had received the word[3056] of God.
2 And when Peter came up to Jerusalem, [Ia]those who were circumcised[4061]
[ipf]took issue[1252] with him,
3 saying, "[a]You [I]went to uncircumcised[203] men and ate with them."
4 But Peter began *speaking* and *pro-*
ceeded to [ipf]explain to them [a]in orderly
sequence, saying,
5 "[a]I was in the city of Joppa praying;
and in a trance[1611] I saw [b]a vision,[3705]
a certain [I]object [ppt]coming down like a
great sheet [pptp]lowered by four corners[746] from [II]the sky;[3772] and it came
right down to me,
6 and when I had [apt]fixed my gaze
upon it and was [ipf]observing[2657] it
[I]I [ao]saw the four-footed animals of the
earth and the wild beasts[2342] and the
[II]crawling creatures and the birds of
the [III]air.[3772]
7 "And I also heard a voice saying
to me, 'Arise, Peter; [I]kill[2380] and eat.'
8 "But I said, 'By no means, Lord,
for nothing [I]unholy[2839] or unclean[169] has
ever entered my mouth.'
9 "But a voice from heaven answered a second time, '[a]What God has
[ao]cleansed,[2511] no longer [pim] [I]consider
unholy.'[2840]
10 "And this happened three times,
and everything was drawn back up into
[I]the sky.
11 "And behold, at that moment
three men [ao]appeared before the house
in which we were *staying,* having been
[pfpp]sent to me from [a]Caesarea.
12 "And [a]the Spirit[4151] told me to
go with them [Ib]without misgivings. And
[c]these six brethren[80] also went with me,
and we entered the man's house.

12 [I]Or, *without making any distinction* [a]Acts 8:29 [b]Acts 15:9; Rom. 3:22 [c]Acts 10:23

🔑 **10:43** See note on Eph. 1:4,5 and also *eklogē* (1589), election.
🔑 **10:44,46,47** See notes on Acts 2:1-13; 11:14-18; 1 Cor. 12:13; 14:1-3.
🔑 **10:48** See note on 1 Pet. 3:20,21.

13 "And he reported to us how he had seen the angel[32] [I]standing in his house, and saying, 'Send to Joppa, and have Simon, who is also called Peter, brought here;

🔑 14 and he shall speak [a]words[4487] to you by which you will be saved,[4982] you and [b]all your household.'

15 "And as I [aie]began to speak,[2980] [a]the Holy Spirit[4151] fell upon them, just [b]as *He did* upon us at the beginning.

16 "And I remembered the word of the Lord, how He used to [ipf]say, '[a]John baptized[907] with water, but you shall be baptized [I]with the [an]Holy Spirit.'

17 "If [a]God therefore gave to them the same gift[1431] as *He gave* to us also after believing[4100] in the Lord Jesus Christ, [b]who was I that I could [ainf] [I]stand in God's way?"

🔑 18 And when they heard this, they [I]quieted down,[2270] and [a]glorified[1392] God, saying, "Well then, God has granted to the Gentiles also the [b]repentance[3341] *that leads* to life."[2222]

The Church at Antioch

19 [a]So then those who were scattered because of the [I]persecution[2347] that arose in connection with Stephen made their way [II]to [b]Phoenicia and [c]Cyprus and [d]Antioch, speaking[2980] the word[3056] to no one except to Jews alone.

20 But there were some of them, men of [a]Cyprus and [b]Cyrene, who came to [c]Antioch and *began* speaking to the [Id]Greeks also, [IIe]preaching[2097] the Lord Jesus.

21 And [a]the hand of the Lord was with them, and [b]a large number who [apt]believed[4100] turned[1994] to the Lord.

22 And the [I]news[3058] about them [II]reached the ears of the church[1577] at Jerusalem, and they sent [a]Barnabas off [III]to [b]Antioch.

23 Then when he had come and [I]witnessed [a]the grace[5485] of God, he rejoiced and *began* to encourage[3870] them all with [II]resolute[4286] heart[2588] to [pinf]remain *true*[4357] to the Lord;

24 for he was a good[18] man, and [a]full of the [an]Holy Spirit and of faith.[4102] And [b]considerable [I]numbers were [II]brought to the Lord.

25 And he left for [a]Tarsus to look for Saul;

26 and when he had found him, he brought him to [a]Antioch. And it came about that for an entire year they [aifp] [I]met with the church,[1577] and [ainf]taught[1321] considerable [II]numbers; and [b]the disciples[3101] were first [ainf]called[5537] [c]Christians[5546] in [a]Antioch.

27 Now [I]at this time [a]some prophets[4396] came down from Jerusalem to [b]Antioch.

13 [I]Or, *after he had stood in his house and said*
14 [a]Acts 10:22 [b]John 4:53; Acts 10:2; 16:15, 31-34; 18:8; 1Cor. 1:16
15 [a]Acts 10:44 [b]Acts 2:4
16 [I]Or, *in* [a]Acts 1:5
17 [I]Or, *prevent God* [a]Acts 10:45, 47 [b]Acts 5:39
18 [I]Lit., *became silent* [a]Matt. 9:8 [b]2Cor. 7:10
19 [I]Or, *tribulation* [II]Lit., *as far as* [a]Acts 8:1, 4 [b]Acts 15:3; 21:2 [c]Acts 4:36 [d]Acts 6:5; 11:20, 22, 27; 13:1; 14:26; 15:22f., 30, 35; 18:22; Gal. 2:11
20 [I]Some mss. read *Greek-speaking Jews* [II]Or, *bringing the good news of* [a]Acts 4:36 [b]Matt. 27:32; Acts 2:10; 6:9; 13:1 [c]Acts 6:5; 11:19, 22, 27; 13:1; 14:26; 15:22f., 30, 35; 18:22; Gal. 2:11 [d]John 7:35 [e]Acts 5:42
21 [a]Luke 1:66 [b]Acts 2:47
22 [I]Lit., *word* [II]Lit., *was heard in* [III]Lit., *as far as* [a]Acts 4:36 [b]Acts 6:5; 11:19, 20, 27; 13:1 18:22; Gal. 2:11
23 [I]Lit., *seen* [II]Lit., *purpose of heart* [a]Acts 13:43; 14:26; 15:40; 20:24, 32
24 [I]Lit., *multitudes* [II]Lit., *added* [a]Acts 2:4 [b]Acts 2:47; 5:14; 11:21
25 [a]Acts 9:11
26 [I]Or, *were gathered together* [II]Lit., *multitude* [a]Acts 6:5; 11:20, 22, 27 [b]John 2:2; Acts 1:15 [c]Acts 26:28; 1Pet. 4:16
27 [I]Lit., *in these days* [a]Luke 11:49; Acts 2:17; 13:1; 1Cor. 12:10, 28f. [b]Acts 6:5; 11:20, 22, 26; 13:1; 14:26; 15:22f., 30, 35; 18:22; Gal. 2:11

🔑 **11:14-18** See notes on Jn. 20:22,23; Acts 1:5; 2:1-13; 19:1-7; I Cor. 12:13. This is the second group baptism in the Holy Spirit, falling upon Cornelius and other Gentiles. As in the case of the baptism at Pentecost, it took place in the presence of at least some of the Twelve Apostles, here in the presence of Peter. This special manifestation of the Holy Spirit was to prove that God was giving the Gentiles an equal gift (v. 17), the same as the Jews. The circumstances by which salvation came unto Cornelius and the Gentiles is detailed in Acts 10-11. As in the case at Pentecost, so here in Acts 10:44, the Holy Spirit fell upon all present. Those on whom the Holy Spirit fell were heard speaking in tongues or languages, *glōssais* (1100). The people who spoke in these languages which were different than their own mother tongue were praising and glorifying God, and so they were understood and needed no interpreter. This baptism in the Holy Spirit (Acts 10;45,46; 11:15,16) was prior to the baptism in water (Acts 10:47) in the case of the Gentiles. Their spiritual baptism preceded their baptism in water. Spiritual baptism as a historical event is what attaches every genuinely repentant believer to the body of Christ (I Cor. 12:13).

🔑 **11:18** See note on I Tim. 2:9-15.

28 And one of them named [a]Agabus
stood up and *began* to indicate [I]by the
Spirit that there would certainly be a
great famine[3042] [b]all over the [II]world.[3625]
And this took place in the *reign* of
[c]Claudius.
29 And in the proportion that any
of [a]the disciples had [ipf]means,[2141] each
of them determined[3724] to [ainf]send *a contribution* for the [I]relief of [b]the brethren[80]
[ppt]living in Judea.
30 [a]And this they did, sending it
[I]in charge of [b]Barnabas and Saul to the
[c]elders.[4245]

Peter's Arrest and Deliverance

12 Now about that time[2540] [I]Herod
the king laid hands on some who
belonged to the church,[1577] in order to
mistreat[2559] them.
2 And he [a]had James the brother
of John [b]put to death with a sword.
3 And when he saw that it
[a]pleased[701] the Jews, he proceeded to
arrest Peter also. Now [I]it was during
[b]the days of Unleavened Bread.[106]
4 And when he had [apt]seized him,
he put him in prison, [apt]delivering him
to four [Ia]squads[5069] of soldiers to
[pinf]guard him, intending after [b]the
Passover[3957] to bring him out before the
people.
5 So Peter was [ipf]kept in the prison,
but prayer[4335] for him was being made
fervently[1618] by the church to God.
6 And on the very night when Herod
was about to bring him forward, Peter
was [ppt]sleeping between two soldiers,
[a]bound with two chains; and guards in
front of the door were [ipf]watching[5083]
over the prison.
7 And behold, [a]an angel[32] of the Lord
suddenly [b]appeared, and a light shone
in the cell;[3612] and he struck Peter's side
and roused[1453] him, saying, "Get up[450]
quickly." And [c]his chains fell off his
hands.
8 And the angel said to him, "Gird
yourself and [I]put on your sandals." And
he did so. And he *said to him, "Wrap
your cloak around you and [pim]follow
me."
9 And he [apt]went out and continued
to [ipf]follow, and he did not know[1492]
that what was being done by the angel
was real, but [ipf]thought he was [pinf]seeing
[a]a vision.[3705]
10 And when they had passed the
first and second guard,[5438] they came
to the iron gate that leads[5342] into the
city, which [aop] [a]opened for them by itself; and they went out and went along
one street; and immediately the angel
departed[868] from him.
11 And when Peter [a]came[1096] to
himself, he said, "Now I know for sure
that [b]the Lord has sent forth His angel
and [aom]rescued me from the hand of
Herod and from all [I]that the Jewish people were expecting."[4329]
12 And when he realized *this,* he
went to the house of Mary, the mother
of [a]John who was also called Mark,
where many were gathered together
and [b]were praying.
13 And when he [apt]knocked at the
door of the gate, [a]a servant-girl[3814]
named Rhoda came to answer.[5219]
14 And when she recognized Pe-
ter's voice, [a]because of her joy she did
not open the gate, but [apt]ran in and announced that Peter was standing in front
of the gate.
15 And they said to her, "You are
out of your mind!" But she kept [ipf]insist-
ing that it [pinf]was so. And they kept
[ipf]saying, "It is [a]his angel."[32]
16 But Peter [ipf]continued [ppt]knock-
ing; and when they had opened *the door,*
they saw him and were amazed.
17 But [a]motioning to them with his
hand to be silent, he described[1334] to
them how the Lord had led him out of
the prison. And he said, "Report these
things to [Ib]James and [c]the brethren."[80]
And he departed and went to another
place.
18 Now when day[2250] came, there
was no small disturbance among the

28 [I]Or, *through* [II]Lit., *inhabited earth* [a]Acts 21:10 [b]Matt. 24:14 [c]Acts 18:2
29 [I]Lit., *service* [a]John 2:2; Acts 1:15; 6:1f.; 9:19, 25, 26, 38; 11:26; 13:52; 14:20, 22, 28 [b]Acts 11:1
30 [I]Lit., *through the hand of* [a]Acts 12:25 [b]Acts 4:36 [c]Acts 14:23; 15:2, 4, 6, 22f.; 16:4; 20:17; 21:18; 1Tim. 5:17, 19; Titus 1:5; James 5:14; 1Pet. 5:1; 2John 1; 3John 1

1 [I]I.e., Herod Agrippa I
2 [a]Matt. 4:21; 20:23 [b]Mark 10:39
3 [I]Lit., *they were the days* [a]Acts 24:27; 25:9 [b]Ex. 12:15; 23:15; Acts 20:6
4 [I]Lit., *quaternions;* one quaternion is composed of four soldiers [a]John 19:23 [b]Ex. 12:1-27; Mark 14:1; Acts 12:3
6 [a]Acts 21:33
7 [a]Acts 5:19 [b]Luke 2:9; 24:4 [c]Acts 16:26
8 [I]Lit., *bind*
9 [a]Acts 9:10
10 [a]Acts 5:19; 16:26
11 [I]Lit., *the expectation of the people of the Jews* [a]Luke 15:17 [b]Dan. 3:28; 6:22
12 [a]Acts 12:25; 13:5, 13; 15:37, 39; Col. 4:10; 2Tim. 4:11; Philem. 24; 1Pet. 5:13 [b]Acts 12:5
13 [a]John 18:16f.
14 [a]Luke 24:41
15 [a]Matt. 18:10
17 [I]Or, *Jacob* [a]Acts 13:16; 19:33; 21:40 [b]Mark 6:3; Acts 15:13; 21:18; 1Cor. 15:7; Gal. 1:19; 2:9, 12 [c]Acts 1:15

12:10 See note on II Thess. 2:3 and also *aphistēmi* (868), to stand away from.

soldiers *as to* [I]what could have [ao]become of Peter.

19 And when Herod had [apt]searched for him and had not [apt]found him, he [apt]examined the guards and ordered that they [a]be led away *to execution.* And he went down from Judea to [b]Caesarea and was spending time there.

Death of Herod

20 Now he was very angry with the people of [a]Tyre and Sidon; and with one accord they came to him, and having won over Blastus the king's chamberlain,2846 they were [ipf]asking[154] for peace, because [b]their country was [aid]fed by the king's[937] country.

21 And on an appointed5002 day Herod, having [apt]put on his royal[937] apparel, took his seat on the [I]rostrum and *began* [ipf]delivering an address to them.

22 And the people[1218] kept [ipf]crying out, "The voice of a god[2316] and not of a man!"

23 And immediately [a]an angel of the Lord struck him because he did not give God[2316] the glory,[1391] and he was eaten by worms and [I]died.[1634]

24 But [a]the word[3056] of the Lord continued to [ipf]grow and to be [ipf]multiplied.

25 And [a]Barnabas and [a]Saul returned [I]from Jerusalem [b]when they had fulfilled[4137] their [II]mission, taking along with *them* [c]John, who was also called Mark.

First Missionary Journey

13 Now there were at [a]Antioch, in the [b]church[1577] that was *there,* [c]prophets[4396] and [d]teachers:[1320] [e]Barnabas, and Simeon who was called Niger, and Lucius of [f]Cyrene, and Manaen who had been brought up with [g]Herod the tetrarch,5076 and Saul.

2 And while they were [ppt]ministering[3008] to the Lord and [ppt]fasting,3522 [a]the Holy Spirit said, "[aim]Set apart[873] for Me [b]Barnabas and Saul for [c]the work[2041] to which I have [pfi]called[4341] them."

3 Then, when they had fasted and [a]prayed and [b]laid their hands on them, [c]they sent them away.

4 So, being [a]sent out by the Holy Spirit, they went down to Seleucia and from there they sailed to [b]Cyprus.

5 And when they reached Salamis, they *began to* [ipf]proclaim[2605] the word[3056] of God in [a]the synagogues of the Jews; and they also had [b]John as their helper.[5257]

6 And when they had gone through the whole island as far as Paphos, they found a certain [a]magician,3097 a Jewish [b]false prophet whose name was Bar-Jesus,

7 who was with the [a]proconsul, Sergius Paulus, a man of intelligence. This man [apt]summoned Barnabas and Saul and sought to [ainf]hear the word[3056] of God.

8 But Elymas the [a]magician (for thus his name is translated)3177 was [ipf]opposing them, seeking to [ainf]turn the [b]proconsul away from [c]the faith.[4102]

9 But Saul, who was also *known as* Paul, [aptp] [I][a]filled with the [an]Holy Spirit, [apt]fixed his gaze upon him,

10 and said, "You who are full of all deceit1388 and fraud, you [a]son[5207] of the devil,[1228] you enemy of all righteousness,[1343] will you not [aosb][b]cease to [ppt]make crooked [b]the straight ways[3598] of the Lord?

11 "And now, behold, [a]the hand of the Lord is upon you, and you will be blind and not see the sun for a time."[2540] And immediately a mist[887] and a darkness[4655] fell upon him, and he [ppt]went about [ipf]seeking those who would lead him by the hand.

12 Then the [a]proconsul believed[4100] when he saw what had happened, being amazed at [b]the teaching[1322] of the Lord.

13 Now Paul and his companions put out to sea321 from [a]Paphos and came to [b]Perga in [c]Pamphylia; and [d]John left them and returned to Jerusalem.

18 [I]Lit., *what therefore had become*
19 [a]Acts 16:27; 27:42 [b]Acts 8:40
20 [a]Matt. 11:21 [b]1Kin. 5:11; Ezra 3:7; Ezek. 27:17
21 [I]Or, *judgment seat*
23 [I]Lit., *breathed his last* [a]2Sam. 24:16; 2Kin. 19:35; Acts 5:19
24 [a]Acts 6:7; 19:20
25 [I]Some ancient mss. read *to Jerusalem* [II]Lit., *ministry* [a]Acts 4:36; 13:1ff. [b]Acts 11:30 [c]Acts 12:12

1 [a]Acts 11:19 [b]Acts 11:26 [c]Acts 11:27; 15:32; 19:6; 21:9; 1Cor. 11:4f.; 13:2, 8f.; 14:29, 32, 37 [d]Rom. 12:6f.; 1Cor. 12:28f.; Eph. 4:11; James 3:1 [e]Acts 4:36 [f]Matt. 27:32; Acts 11:20 [g]Matt. 14:1
2 [a]Acts 8:29; 13:4 [b]Acts 4:36 [c]Acts 9:15
3 [a]Acts 1:24 [b]Acts 6:6 [c]Acts 13:4; 14:26
4 [a]Acts 13:2f. [b]Acts 4:36
5 [a]Acts 9:20; 13:14 [b]Acts 12:12
6 [a]Acts 8:9 [b]Matt. 7:15
7 [a]Acts 13:8, 12; 18:12; 19:38
8 [a]Acts 8:9 [b]Acts 13:7, 12; 18:12; 19:38 [c]Acts 6:7
9 [I]Or, *having* just *been filled* [a]Acts 2:4; 4:8
10 [a]Matt. 13:38; John 8:44 [b]Hos. 14:9; 2Pet. 2:15
11 [a]Ex. 9:3; 1Sam. 5:6f.; Job 19:21; Ps. 32:4; Heb. 10:31
12 [a]Acts 13:7, 8; 18:12; 19:38 [b]Acts 8:25; 13:49; 15:35f.; 19:10, 20

13 [a]Acts 13:6 [b]Acts 14:25 [c]Acts 2:10; 14:24; 15:38; 27:5 [d]Acts 12:12

14 But going on from Perga, they arrived at [a]Pisidian [b]Antioch, and on [c]the Sabbath[4521] day they went into [d]the synagogue[4864] and sat down.

15 And after [a]the reading[320] of the Law[3551] and [b]the Prophets[4396] [c]the synagogue officials[752] sent to them, saying, "Brethren, if you have any word of exhortation[3874] for the people, say it."

16 And Paul [apt]stood up, and [apt] [a]motioning with his hand, he said,

"Men of Israel, and [b]you who fear God,[2316] listen:

17 "The God of this people Israel [a]chose our fathers, and [I][b]made the people great during their stay in the land of Egypt, and with an uplifted[5308] arm [c]He led them out from it.

18 "And for [a]a period[5550] of about forty years [b]He [I]put up with them in the wilderness.

19 "And [a]when He had destroyed [b]seven nations in the land of Canaan, He [c]distributed their land as an inheritance[2624]—*all of which took* [d]about four hundred and fifty years.

20 "And after these things He [a]gave *them* judges[2923] until [b]Samuel the prophet.

21 "And then they [a]asked for a king,[935] and God gave them [b]Saul the son of Kish, a man of the tribe of Benjamin, for forty years.

22 "And after He had [a]removed[3179] him, He raised up[1453] David to be their king, concerning whom He also [apt]testified and said, '[b]I HAVE FOUND DAVID the son of Jesse, A MAN AFTER MY HEART,[2588] who will do all My [I]will.'[2307]

23 "[a]From the offspring of this man,[4690] [b]according to promise,[1860] God has brought to Israel [c]a Savior,[4990] Jesus,

24 after [a]John had proclaimed before[4383] [I]His coming a [b]baptism[908] of repentance[3341] to all the people of Israel.

25 "And while John [a]was [ipf]completing his course, [b]he kept saying, 'What do you suppose[5282] that I am? I am not *He.* But behold, one is coming after me the sandals of whose feet I am not worthy to untie.'

26 "Brethren, sons of Abraham's family, and those among you who [ppt]fear God, to us the word of [a]this salvation[4991] is sent out.

27 "For those who live in Jerusalem, and their [a]rulers, [apt] [b]recognizing neither[50] Him nor the [I]utterances of [c]the prophets which are [d]read every Sabbath, fulfilled *these* by [apt]condemning[2919] *Him.*

28 "And though they [apt]found[2147] no ground for *putting Him to* death, they [a]asked Pilate that He be [I]executed.

29 "And when they had [ao] [a]carried out[5055] all that was written concerning Him, [b]they [apt]took Him down from [c]the [I]cross and [d]laid Him in a tomb.[3419]

30 "But God [a]raised Him from the dead;[3498]

31 and for many days [a]He [aop]appeared to those who came up with Him from Galilee to Jerusalem, the very ones who are now [b]His witnesses[3144] to the people.

32 "And we [a]preach to you the good news[2097] of [b]the promise made to the fathers,

33 that God has [pfi]fulfilled[1603] this *promise* [I]to our children in that He [apt] [a]raised up Jesus, as it is also written in the second Psalm, '[b]THOU ART MY SON;[5207] TODAY I HAVE [pfi]BEGOTTEN[1080] THEE.'

34 "*And as for the fact* that He [a]raised Him up from the dead, no more to [pinf]return to decay, He has spoken in this way: '[b]I WILL GIVE YOU THE HOLY *and* SURE[4103] *blessings* OF DAVID.'

35 "Therefore He also says in another[2087] *Psalm,* '[a]THOU WILT NOT [I]ALLOW THY [II]HOLY[3741] ONE TO [III]UNDERGO DECAY.'

36 "For [a]David, after he had [I]served [b]the purpose[1012] of God in his

14 [a]Acts 14:24 [b]Acts 14:19, 21; 2Tim. 3:11 [c]Acts 13:42, 44; 16:13; 17:2; 18:4 [d]Acts 9:20; 13:5
15 [a]Acts 15:21; 2Cor. 3:14f. [b]Acts 13:27 [c]Mark 5:22
16 [a]Acts 12:17 [b]Acts 10:2; 13:26
17 [I]Or, *exalted* [a]Ex. 6:1, 6; 13:14, 16; Deut. 7:6-8; Acts 7:17ff. [b]Ex. 1:7 [c]Ex. 12:51
18 [I]Some ancient mss. read *bore them up in His arms as a nurse in the wilderness* [a]Num. 14:34; Acts 7:36 [b]Deut. 1:31
19 [a]Acts 7:45 [b]Deut. 7:1 [c]Josh. 14:1; 19:51; Ps. 78:55 [d]Judg. 11:26; 1Kin. 6:1
20 [a]Judg. 2:16 [b]1Sam. 3:20; Acts 3:24
21 [a]1Sam. 8:5 [b]1Sam. 9:1f.; 10:1, 21
22 [I]Lit., *wills* [a]1Sam. 15:23, 26, 28; 16:1, 13 [b]1Sam. 13:14; Ps. 89:20; Acts 7:46
23 [a]Matt. 1:1 [b]Acts 13:32f. [c]Luke 2:11; John 4:42
24 [I]Lit., *the face of His entering* [a]Mark 1:1-4; Acts 1:22; 19:4 [b]Luke 3:3
25 [a]Acts 20:24 [b]Matt. 3:11; Mark 1:7; Luke 3:16; John 1:20, 27
26 [a]John 6:68; Acts 4:12; 5:20; 13:46; 28:28
27 [I]Lit., *voices* [a]Luke 23:13 [b]Acts 3:17 [c]Luke 24:27 [d]Acts 13:15
28 [I]Lit., *destroyed* [a]Matt. 27:22, 23; Mark 15:13, 14; Luke 23:21-23; John 19:15; Acts 3:14
29 [I]Lit., *wood* [a]Acts 26:22 [b]Luke 23:53 [c]Acts 5:30 [d]Matt. 27:57-61; Mark 15:42-47; Luke 23:50-56; John 19:38-42
30 [a]Acts 2:24; 13:33, 34, 37
31 [a]Acts 1:3 [b]Luke 24:48
32 [a]Acts 5:42; 14:15 [b]Acts 13:23; 26:6; Rom. 1:2; 4:13; 9:4
33 [I]Some mss. read *to us their children* [a]Acts 2:24; 13:30, 34, 37 [b]Ps. 2:7
34 [a]Acts 2:24; 13:30, 33, 37 [b]Is. 55:3
35 [I]Lit., *give* [II]Or, *Devout* or *Pious* [III]Lit., *see corruption* [a]Ps. 16:10; Acts 2:27
36 [I]Or, *served his own generation by the purpose of God* [a]Acts 2:29 [b]Acts 13:22; 20:27

own generation,[1074] [c]fell asleep, and was
laid among his fathers, and [II]underwent
decay;
37 but He whom God [a]raised did
not [I]undergo decay.
🔑38 "Therefore let it be known to
you, brethren, that [a]through [I]Him forgiveness[859] of sins[266] is proclaimed[2605]
to you,
39 and through Him [a]everyone who
[ppt]believes is [I]freed[1344] [II]from all things,
from which you could not be [I]freed
through the Law[3551] of Moses.
40 "Take heed[991] therefore, so that
the thing spoken of [a]in the Prophets[4396]
may not [aosb]come upon *you*:
41 '[a]BEHOLD, YOU SCOFFERS, AND
MARVEL, AND [I]PERISH;
FOR I AM ACCOMPLISHING A
WORK IN YOUR DAYS,
A WORK WHICH YOU WILL
NEVER BELIEVE, THOUGH
SOMEONE SHOULD DESCRIBE
IT TO YOU.' "
42 And as [I]Paul and Barnabas were
going out, [II]the people kept [ipf]begging[3870]
that these [III]things[4487] might be spoken
to them the next [a]Sabbath.
43 Now when *the meeting of* the
synagogue[4864] had broken up, many of
the Jews and of the [a]God-fearing[4576]
[Ib]proselytes[4339] followed Paul and Barnabas, who, speaking to them, were
urging[3982] them to continue in [c]the
grace[5485] of God.

Paul Turns to the Gentiles

44 And the next[2064] [a]Sabbath nearly
the whole city assembled to hear the
word[3056] of [I]God.
45 But when [a]the Jews saw the
crowds, they were filled with jealousy,
and *began* [ipf]contradicting the things
[ppp]spoken by Paul, and were [I]blaspheming.[987]
46 And Paul and Barnabas [apt]spoke
out boldly[3955] and said, "It was necessary[316] that the word of God should be
[aifp]spoken to you [a]first; since you repudiate it, and judge[2919] yourselves unworthy of eternal life,[2222] behold, [b]we
are turning[4762] to the Gentiles.[1484]
47 "For thus the Lord has [pfi]commanded[1781] us,
'[a]I HAVE [pfi]PLACED[5087] YOU AS A
[b]LIGHT[5457] FOR THE
Gentiles,
THAT YOU SHOULD [I]BRING
SALVATION TO THE END[2078]
OF THE EARTH.' "
48 And when the Gentiles [ppt]heard
this, they *began* [ipf]rejoicing and
[ipf]glorifying[1392] [a]the word of [I]the Lord;
and as many as [b]had been appointed[5021]
to eternal life [ao]believed.
49 And [a]the word[3056] of the Lord
was being [ipf]spread[1308] through the
whole region.
50 But [a]the Jews aroused the
[Ib]devout[4576] women [c]of prominence and
the leading men of the city, and instigated a persecution against Paul and
Barnabas, and drove them out of their
[II]district.
51 But [a]they [apt]shook off the dust
of their feet *in protest* against them and
went[2064] to [b]Iconium.
52 And the disciples[3101] were continually [ipf] [a]filled with joy and with the
[an]Holy Spirit.

Acceptance and Opposition

14 And it came about that in
[a]Iconium [b]they [ainf]entered the
synagogue of the Jews together,[2956,846]
and [ainf]spoke in such a manner [c]that a
great multitude [ainf]believed,[4100] both of
Jews and of [d]Greeks.
2 But [a]the Jews who [Ib]disbelieved[544]
stirred up the [II]minds[5590] of the Gentiles,
and embittered[2559] them against [c]the
brethren.
🔑3 Therefore they spent a long

36 [II]Lit., *saw corruption* [c]1Kin. 2:10; Acts 8:1 **37** [I]Lit., *see corruption* [a]Acts 2:24; 13:30, 33, 34 **38** [I]Lit., *this One* [a]Luke 24:47; Acts 2:38 **39** [I]Lit., *justified* [II]In the Gr. text the remainder of this v. is part of v. 38 [a]Acts 10:43; Rom. 3:28; 10:4 **40** [a]Luke 24:44; John 6:45; Acts 7:42 **41** [I]Lit., *disappear* [a]Hab. 1:5 **42** [I]Lit., *they were* [II]Lit., *they* [III]Lit., *words* [a]Acts 13:14 **43** [I]I.e., Gentile converts to Judaism [a]Acts 13:50; 16:14; 17:4, 17; 18:7 [b]Matt. 23:15 [c]Acts 11:23 **44** [I]Some ancient mss. read *the Lord* [a]Acts 13:14 **45** [I]Or, *reviling* [a]Acts 13:50; 14:2, 4, 5, 19; 1Thess. 2:16 **46** [a]Acts 3:26; 9:20; 13:5, 14 [b]Acts 18:6; 19:9; 22:21; 26:20; 28:28 **47** [I]Lit., *be for salvation* [a]Is. 42:6; 49:6 [b]Luke 2:32 **48** [I]Some ancient mss. read *God* [a]Acts 13:12 [b]Rom. 8:28ff.; Eph. 1:4f., 11 **49** [a]Acts 13:12 **50** [I]Or, *worshiping* [II]Lit., *boundaries* [a]Acts 13:45; 14:2, 4, 5, 19; 1Thess. 2:14ff. [b]Acts 13:43; 16:14; 17:4, 17; 18:7 [c]Mark 15:43 **51** [a]Matt. 10:14; Mark 6:11; Luke 9:5; 10:11; Acts 18:6 [b]Acts 14:1, 19, 21; 16:2; 2Tim. 3:11 **52** [a]Acts 2:4

1 [a]Acts 13:51; 14:19, 21; 16:2; 2Tim. 3:11 [b]Acts 13:5 [c]Acts 2:47 [d]John 7:35; Acts 18:4 **2** [I]Or, *disobeyed* [II]Lit., *souls* [a]Acts 13:45, 50; 14:4, 5, 19; 1Thess. 2:14ff. [b]John 3:36 [c]Acts 1:15

🔑**13:38,39** See general remarks on justification in Romans, Eph. 1:4,5 and also *eklogē* (1589), election.
🔑**14:3,10** See note on II Tim. 4:20.

time[5550] *there* [a]speaking boldly *with reli-*
ance upon the Lord, who was [ppt]bearing
witness[3140] to the word[3056] of His
grace,[5485] [ppt]granting that [I][b]signs[4592] and
wonders[5059] be [pinf]done by their hands.
4 [a]But the multitude of the city was
divided; and some [I]sided with [b]the Jews,
and some with [c]the apostles.[652]
5 And when an attempt[3730] was
made by both the Gentiles and [a]the Jews
with their rulers, to [ainf]mistreat[5195] and
to [b]stone them,
6 they became aware[4894] of it and
fled to the cities of [a]Lycaonia, [b]Lystra
and [c]Derbe, and the surrounding region;
7 and there they continued to
[a]preach the gospel.[2097]
8 And at [a]Lystra there was sitting
[b]a certain man, without strength[102] in
his feet, lame from his mother's womb,
who had never walked.
9 This man was listening to Paul as
he spoke, who, [a]when he had [apt]fixed
his gaze upon him, and had [apt]seen that
he had [b]faith[4102] to be [aifp] [I]made well,[4982]
10 said with a loud voice, "Stand
upright[3717] on your feet." [a]And he leaped
up and *began* to [ipf]walk.
11 And when the multitudes saw
what Paul had done, they raised their
voice, saying in the [a]Lycaonian language,
"[b]The gods[2316] have [aptp]become like men
and have [ao]come down to us."
12 And they *began* calling Barnabas,
[I]Zeus, and Paul, [II]Hermes, because he
was [III]the chief[2233] speaker.
13 And the priest of Zeus, whose
temple was [I]just outside the city,
[apt]brought oxen and garlands to the
gates, and [ipf] [a]wanted to offer [pinf]sacrifice
with the crowds.
14 But when [a]the apostles,[652] Barnabas and Paul, heard of it, they
[apt] [b]tore[1284] their [I]robes and rushed out
into the crowd,[3793] crying out
15 and saying, "Men, why are you
doing these things? We are also [a]men
of the same nature as you, and
[ppt] [b]preach[2097] the gospel to you in order
that you should [pinf]turn[1994] from these
[I][c]vain things to a [d]living[2198] God,[2316]
[e]WHO MADE THE HEAVEN[3772] AND THE
EARTH[1093] AND THE SEA, AND ALL THAT
IS IN THEM.
16 "[I]And in the generations gone by
He [a]permitted all the [II]nations to [b]go
their own ways;[3598]
17 and yet [a]He did not leave Himself
without witness, in that He [ppt]did good[15]
and [ppt] [b]gave you rains from heaven and
fruitful seasons,[2540] [I]satisfying your
hearts with food and gladness."[2167]
18 And *even* saying these things,
they with difficulty restrained[2664] the
crowds from offering [pinf]sacrifice to
them.
19 But [a]Jews came from [b]Antioch
and [c]Iconium, and having [apt]won over[3982]
the multitudes, they [apt] [d]stoned Paul and
[I]dragged[4951] him out of the city, [ppt]sup-
posing him to be [pfin]dead.
20 But[1161] while [a]the disciples stood
around him, he arose and entered the
city. And the next day he went away
with Barnabas to [b]Derbe.
21 And after they had [a]preached the
gospel[2097] to that city and had [b]made
many disciples,[3100] they returned to
[c]Lystra and to [d]Iconium and to [e]Anti-
och,
22 strengthening the souls[5590] of
[a]the disciples, encouraging[3870] them to
continue[1696] in [b]the faith, and *saying,*
"[c]Through many tribulations[2347] we
must [ainf]enter the kingdom[932] of God."
23 And when [a]they had ap-
pointed[5500] [b]elders[4245] for them in every
church,[1577] having [c]prayed with fasting,[3521] they [d]commended them to the
Lord in whom they had believed.
24 And they passed through [a]Pisidia
and came into [b]Pamphylia.
25 And when they had spoken the
word[3056] in [a]Perga, they went down to
Attalia;
26 and from there they sailed to

3 [I]Or, *attesting miracles* [a]Acts 4:29f.; 20:32; Heb. 2:4 [b]John 4:48
4 [I]Lit., *were* [a]Acts 17:4f.; 19:9; 28:24 [b]Acts 13:45, 50; 14:2, 5, 19; 1Thess. 2:14ff. [c]Acts 14:14
5 [a]Acts 13:45, 50; 14:2, 4, 19; 1Thess. 2:14ff. [b]Acts 14:19
6 [a]Acts 14:11 [b]Acts 14:8, 21; 16:1f.; 2Tim. 3:11 [c]Acts 14:20; 16:1; 20:4
7 [a]Acts 14:15, 21; 16:10
8 [a]Acts 14:6, 21; 16:1f.; 2Tim. 3:11 [b]Acts 3:2
9 [I]Lit., *saved* [a]Acts 3:4; 10:4 [b]Matt. 9:28
10 [a]Acts 3:8
11 [a]Acts 14:6 [b]Acts 8:10; 28:6
12 [I]Lat., *Jupiter* [II]Lat., *Mercurius* [III]Lit., *the leader of the speaking*
13 [I]Lit., *in front of* [a]Dan. 2:46
14 [I]Or, *outer garments* [a]Acts 14:4 [b]Num. 14:6; Matt. 26:65; Mark 14:63
15 [I]I.e., idols [a]Acts 10:26; James 5:17 [b]Acts 13:32; 14:7, 21 [c]Deut. 32:21; 1Sam. 12:21; Jer. 8:19; 14:22; 1Cor. 8:4 [d]Matt. 16:16 [e]Ex. 20:11; Ps. 146:6; Acts 4:24; 17:24; Rev. 14:7
16 [I]Lit., *Who in the generations gone by permitted* [II]Or, *Gentiles* [a]Acts 17:30 [b]Ps. 81:12; Mic. 4:5
17 [I]Lit., *filling* [a]Acts 17:26f.; Rom. 1:19f. [b]Deut. 11:14; Job 5:10; Ps. 65:10f.; Ezek. 34:26f.; Joel 2:23
19 [I]Lit., *were dragging* [a]Acts 13:45, 50; 14:2, 4, 5; 1Thess. 2:14ff. [b]Acts 13:14; 14:21, 26 [c]Acts 13:51; 14:1, 21 [d]Acts 14:5; 2Cor. 11:25; 2Tim. 3:11
20 [a]Acts 11:26; 14:22, 28 [b]Acts 14:6 **21** [a]Acts 14:7 [b]Acts 2:47 [c]Acts 14:6 [d]Acts 13:51; 14:1, 19 [e]Acts 13:14; 14:19, 26 **22** [a]Acts 11:26; 14:28 [b]Acts 6:7 [c]Mark 10:30; John 15:18, 20; 16:33; Acts 9:16; 1Thess. 3:3; 2Tim. 3:12; 1Pet. 2:21; Rev. 1:9
23 [a]2Cor. 8:19; Titus 1:5 [b]Acts 11:30 [c]Acts 1:24; 13:3 [d]Acts 20:32 **24** [a]Acts 13:14 [b]Acts 13:13
25 [a]Acts 13:13

[a]Antioch, from [b]which they had been [c]commended to the grace[5485] of God for the work[2041] that they had [I]accomplished.

27 And when they had arrived and gathered the church[1577] together, they *began* to [a]report[312] all things that God had [ao]done with them and [I]how He had opened a [b]door of faith[4102] to the Gentiles.

28 And they [ipf]spent [I]a long time with [a]the disciples.[3101]

The Council at Jerusalem

15 And [a]some men came down from Judea and *began* [ipf]teaching[1321] [b]the brethren,[80] "Unless you are [asbp] [c]circumcised[4059] according to [d]the custom of Moses, you cannot be saved."[4982]

2 And when Paul and Barnabas had [I]great dissension[4714] and [a]debate[4803] with them, [IIb]*the brethren* determined that Paul and Barnabas and certain others of them should [pinf]go up to Jerusalem to the [c]apostles[652] and elders[4245] concerning this issue.

3 Therefore, being [a]sent on their way by the church,[1577] they were [ipf]passing through both [b]Phoenicia and Samaria, [c]describing[1555] in detail the conversion[1995] of the Gentiles, and were bringing great joy to all [d]the brethren.

4 And when they arrived at Jerusalem, they were received[588] by the church[1577] and [a]the apostles and the elders,[4245] and they [b]reported all that God had [ao]done with them.

5 But certain ones of [a]the sect[139] of the [b]Pharisees who had [pfp]believed,[4100] stood up,[1817] saying, "It is necessary to [pinf] [c]circumcise[4059] them, and to [pinf]direct them to [pinf]observe the Law of Moses."

6 And [a]the apostles and the elders[4245] came together to [I]look into[1492] this [II]matter.[3056]

7 And after there had been much [a]debate, Peter stood up and said to them, "Brethren, you know that [I]in the early days [b]God [ao]made a choice among you, that by my mouth the Gentiles should [ainf]hear the word[3056] of [c]the gospel[2098] and [ainf]believe.

8 "And God, [a]who knows the heart,[2589] bore witness to them, [apt] [b]giving them the Holy Spirit, just as He also did to us;

9 and [a]He made no distinction[1252] between us and them, [apt] [b]cleansing[2511] their hearts[2588] by faith.[4102]

10 "Now therefore why do you [a]put God to the test[3985] by placing upon the neck of the disciples a yoke which [b]neither our fathers[3962] nor we have been able to [ainf]bear?

11 "But we believe that we are [aifp]saved[4982] through [a]the grace of the Lord Jesus, in the same way as they also are."

12 And all the multitude kept silent, and they were listening[191] to Barnabas and Paul as they were [a]relating[1834] what [b]signs and wonders God had done through them among the Gentiles.[1484]

James' Judgment

13 And after they had [aime]stopped speaking, [Ia]James answered, saying, "Brethren,[80] listen to me.

14 "[a]Simeon has related[1834] how God first concerned[1980] Himself about taking from among the Gentiles a people for His name.

15 "And with this the words of [a]the Prophets[4396] agree, just as it is written,

16 '[a]AFTER THESE THINGS [b]I WILL RETURN,
AND I WILL REBUILD THE [I]TABERNACLE[4633] OF DAVID WHICH HAS FALLEN,
AND I WILL REBUILD ITS RUINS,
AND I WILL RESTORE[461] IT,
17 [a]IN ORDER THAT THE REST[2645] OF [I]MANKIND MAY SEEK THE LORD,
AND ALL THE GENTILES

26 [I]Lit., *fulfilled* [a]Acts 11:19 [b]Acts 13:3 [c]Acts 11:23; 15:40
27 [I]Lit., *that* [a]Acts 15:3, 4, 12; 21:19 [b]1Cor. 16:9; 2Cor. 2:12; Col. 4:3; Rev. 3:8
28 [I]Lit., *not a little* [a]Acts 11:26; 14:22

1 [a]Acts 15:24 [b]Acts 1:15; 15:3, 22, 32 [c]Lev. 12:3; Acts 15:5; 1Cor. 7:18; Gal. 2:11, 14; 5:2f. [d]Acts 6:14
2 [I]Lit., *not a little* [II]Or, *it was determined* [a]Acts 15:7 [b]Gal. 2:2 [c]Acts 11:30; 15:4, 6, 22, 23; 16:4
3 [a]Acts 20:38; 21:5; Rom. 15:24; 1Cor. 16:6, 11; 2Cor. 1:16; Titus 3:13; 3John 6 [b]Acts 11:19 [c]Acts 14:27; 15:4, 12 [d]Acts 1:15; 15:22, 32
4 [a]Acts 11:30; 15:6, 22, 23; 16:4 [b]Acts 14:27; 15:12
5 [a]Acts 5:17; 24:5, 14; 26:5; 28:22 [b]Matt. 3:7; Acts 26:5 [c]1Cor. 7:18; Gal. 2:11, 14; 5:2f.
6 [I]Lit., *see about* [II]Lit., *word* [a]Acts 11:30; 15:4, 22, 23; 16:4
7 [I]Lit., *from days of old* [a]Acts 15:2 [b]Acts 10:19f. [c]Acts 20:24
8 [a]Acts 1:24 [b]Acts 2:4; 10:44, 47
9 [a]Acts 10:28, 34; 11:12 [b]Acts 10:43
10 [a]Acts 5:9 [b]Matt. 23:4; Gal. 5:1
11 [a]Rom. 3:24; 5:15; 2Cor. 13:14; Eph. 2:5-8
12 [a]Acts 14:27; 15:3, 4 [b]John 4:48
13 [I]Or, *Jacob* [a]Acts 12:17
14 [a]Acts 15:7; 2Pet. 1:1
15 [a]Acts 13:40

16 [I]Or, *tent* [a]Amos 9:11 [b]Jer. 12:15 **17** [I]Lit., *men* [a]Amos 9:12

[IIb]WHO ARE [pfp]CALLED1945 BY
MY NAME,'
18 [a]SAYS THE LORD, WHO
[ppt I b]MAKES THESE THINGS
KNOWN*1110* FROM OF OLD.
19 "Therefore it is [a]my judgment*2919*
that we do not trouble those who are
turning to God from among the Gentiles,
20 but that we [ainf]write to them that
they abstain*567* from [Ia]things contaminated by idols*1497* and from [b]fornica-
tion4202 and from [c]what is strangled and
from blood.
21 "For [a]Moses from ancient generations has in every city those who
[ppt]preach*2784* him, since he is read in
the synagogues every Sabbath."4521
22 Then it seemed good to [a]the
apostles and the elders,*4245* with the
whole church, to choose men from
among them to send to [b]Antioch with
Paul and Barnabas—Judas called Barsabbas, and [c]Silas, leading men among
[d]the brethren,
23 and they [apt I]sent this letter by
them,

"[a]The apostles and the brethren who are elders, to [b]the
brethren in [c]Antioch and [d]Sy-
ria and [e]Cilicia who are from
the Gentiles, [f]greetings.*5463*
24 "Since we have heard that
[a]some [I]of our number to
whom we gave no instruc-
tion have [b]disturbed you with
their words, unsettling your
souls,*5590*
25 [a]it seemed good to us, having [I]become of one mind, to
select men to send to you with
our beloved Barnabas and
Paul,
26 men who have [pfp Ia]risked
their lives*5590* for the name of
our Lord Jesus Christ.
27 "Therefore we have sent [a]Ju-
das and [b]Silas, who themselves will also [ppt]report
the same things by word *of
mouth*.
28 "For [a]it seemed good*1380* to
[b]the Holy Spirit and to [c]us to
[pip]lay upon you no greater burden than these essentials:*1876*
29 that you abstain*567* from
[a]things sacrificed to idols*1494*
and from [a]blood and from
[a]things strangled and from
[a]fornication; [I]if you [ppt]keep*1301*
yourselves free from such
things, you will do well. Farewell."

30 So, when they were sent away,
[a]they went down to Antioch; and having
gathered the [I]congregation together,
they delivered the letter.1992
31 And when they had read it,
they rejoiced because of its [I]encour-
agement.*3874*
32 And [a]Judas and [b]Silas, also being [c]prophets*4396* themselves, [I]encour-
aged*3870* and strengthened [d]the brethren
with a lengthy message.
33 And after they had spent time*5550*
there, they were sent away from the
brethren [a]in peace*1515* to those who had
[b]sent them out.
34 [[I]But it seemed good to Silas to
[ainf]remain there.]
35 But [a]Paul and Barnabas [ipf]stayed
in Antioch, teaching*1321* and [b]preach-
ing,*2097* with many others also, [c]the
word*3056* of the Lord.

Second Missionary Journey

🔑 **36** And after some days Paul said
to Barnabas, "Let us [apt]return and
[aosb]visit*1980* the brethren in [a]every city
in which we [ao]proclaimed*2605* [b]the word
of the Lord, *and see* how they are."

17 [IILit.], *upon whom My name is called* [b]Deut. 28:10; Is. 63:19; Jer. 14:9; Dan. 9:19; James 2:7
18 [I]Or, *does these things which were known* [a]Amos 9:12 [b]Is. 45:21
19 [a]Acts 15:28; 21:25
20 [I]Lit., *the pollutions of* [a]Ex. 34:15-17; Dan. 1:8; Acts 15:29; 1Cor. 8:7, 13; 10:7f., 14-28; Rev. 2:14, 20 [b]Lev. 18:6-23 [c]Gen. 9:4; Lev. 3:17; 7:26; 17:10, 14; 19:26; Deut. 12:16, 23; 15:23; 1Sam. 14:33
21 [a]Acts 13:15; 2Cor. 3:14f.
22 [a]Acts 15:2 [b]Acts 11:20 [c]Acts 15:27, 32, 40; 16:19, 25, 29; 17:4, 10, 14f.; 18:5; 2Cor. 1:19; 1Thess. 1:1; 2Thess. 1:1; 1Pet. 5:12 [d]Acts 15:1
23 [I]Lit., *wrote by their hand* [a]Acts 15:2 [b]Acts 15:1 [c]Acts 11:20 [d]Matt. 4:24; Acts 15:41; Gal. 1:21 [e]Acts 6:9 [f]Acts 23:26; James 1:1; 2John 10f.
24 [I]Lit., *from us* [a]Acts 15:1 [b]Gal. 1:7; 5:10
25 [I]Or, *met together* [a]Acts 15:28
26 [I]Lit., *given over* [a]Acts 9:23ff.; 14:19
27 [a]Acts 15:22, 32 [b]Acts 15:22
28 [a]Acts 15:25 [b]Acts 5:32; 15:8 [c]Acts 15:19, 25
29 [I]Lit., *from which keeping yourselves free* [a]Acts 15:20
30 [I]Or, *multitude* [a]Acts 15:22f.
31 [I]Or, *exhortation*

32 [I]Or, *exhorted* [a]Acts 15:22, 27 [b]Acts 15:22 [c]Acts 13:1 [d]Acts 15:1 **33** [a]Mark 5:34; Acts 16:36; 1Cor. 16:11; Heb. 11:31 [b]Acts 15:22 **34** [I]Many mss. do not contain this v. **35** [a]Acts 12:25 [b]Acts 8:4 [c]Acts 13:12 **36** [a]Acts 13:4, 13, 14, 51; 14:6, 24f. [b]Acts 13:12

🔑 **15:36; 16:12** See general remarks on I Tim.

37 And Barnabas was desirous of taking [a]John, called Mark, along with them also.

38 But Paul kept insisting that they should not [ainf]take him along who had [apt] [a]deserted[868] them [I]in Pamphylia and had not [apt]gone with them to the work.[2041]

39 And there [ao]arose such a sharp disagreement that they [ainf]separated from one another, and Barnabas [apt]took [a]Mark with him and [ainf]sailed away to [b]Cyprus.

40 But Paul chose [a]Silas and departed, being [b]committed by the brethren to the grace of the Lord.

41 And he was [ipf]traveling through [a]Syria and [b]Cilicia, strengthening the churches.[1577]

The Macedonian Vision

16 And he came also to [a]Derbe and to [a]Lystra. And behold, a certain disciple was there, named [b]Timothy, the son of a [c]Jewish woman who was a believer,[4103] but his father was a Greek,

2 and he was well [ipf]spoken of by [a]the brethren[80] who were in [b]Lystra and [c]Iconium.

3 Paul wanted this man to [ainf] [I]go with him; and he [a]took him and circumcised[4059] him because of the Jews who were in those parts, for they all knew that his father was a Greek.

4 Now while they were [ipf]passing through the cities, they were delivering [a]the decrees,[1378] which had been [pfpp]decided upon[2919] by [b]the apostles[652] and [c]elders[4245] who were in Jerusalem, for them to [ainf]observe.

5 So [a]the churches[1577] were being [ipf]strengthened [I]in the faith,[4102] and were [ipf] [b]increasing in number daily.

6 And they passed through the [Ia]Phrygian and [b]Galatian region, having been [aptp]forbidden by the Holy Spirit[4151] to [ainf]speak[2980] the word[3056] in [IIc]Asia;

7 and when they had come to [a]Mysia, they were [ipf]trying[3985] to [ainf]go into [b]Bithynia, and the [c]Spirit[4151] of Jesus did not permit them;

8 and passing [I]by [a]Mysia, they came down to [b]Troas.

9 And [a]a vision[3705] [aop]appeared to Paul in the night: [I]a certain man of [b]Macedonia was standing and [ppt]appealing[3870] to him, and saying, "[apt]Come over to Macedonia and [aim]help us."

10 And when he had seen [a]the vision, immediately [b]we sought to [I]go into Macedonia, concluding that God had [pfi]called[4341] us to [ainf] [c]preach the gospel[2097] to them.

11 [I]Therefore putting out to sea from [a]Troas, we ran [b]a straight course to Samothrace, and on the day following to Neapolis;

🗝 12 and from there to [a]Philippi, which is a leading[4413] city of the district of [b]Macedonia, [c]a *Roman* colony; and we were staying in this city for some days.

13 And on [a]the Sabbath[4521] day we went outside the gate to a riverside, where we were [ipf]supposing[3543] that there would be a place of prayer; and we [apt]sat down and began [ipf]speaking to the women who had [apt]assembled.

First Convert in Europe

14 And a certain woman named Lydia, from the city of [a]Thyatira, a seller of purple fabrics, [b]a worshiper[4576] of God, was [ipf]listening; [I]and the Lord [c]opened her heart[2588] to [pinf]respond to the things [ppp]spoken by Paul.

15 And when she and [a]her household had been baptized,[907] she urged[3870] us, saying, "If you have [pfi]judged[2919] me to be faithful to the Lord,[2962] [apt]come into my house and [pim]stay." And she prevailed upon us.

16 And it happened that as we were going to [a]the place of prayer, a certain slave-girl[3814] having [b]a spirit[4151] of divi-

37 [a]Acts 12:12
38 [I]Lit., *from* [a]Acts 13:13
39 [a]Acts 12:12; 15:37; Col. 4:10 [b]Acts 4:36
40 [a]Acts 15:22 [b]Acts 11:23; 14:26
41 [a]Matt. 4:24; Acts 15:23 [b]Acts 6:9

1 [a]Acts 14:6 [b]Acts 17:14f.; 18:5; 19:22; 20:4; Rom. 16:21; 1Cor. 4:17; 16:10; 2Cor. 1:1, 19; Phil. 1:1; 2:19; Col. 1:1; 1Thess. 1:1; 3:2, 6; 2Thess. 1:1; 1Tim. 1:2, 18; 6:20; 2Tim. 1:2; Philem. 1:1-25; Heb. 13:23 [c]2Tim. 1:5; 3:15
2 [a]Acts 16:40 [b]Acts 14:6 [c]Acts 13:51
3 [I]Lit., *go out* [a]Gal. 2:3
4 [a]Acts 15:28f. [b]Acts 15:2 [c]Acts 11:30
5 [I]Or, *in faith* [a]Acts 9:31 [b]Acts 2:47
6 [I]Or, *Phrygia and the Galatian region* [II]I.e., west coast province of Asia Minor [a]Acts 2:10; 18:23 [b]Acts 18:23; 1Cor. 16:1; Gal. 1:2; 3:1; 2Tim. 4:10; 1Pet. 1:1 [c]Acts 2:9
7 [a]Acts 16:8 [b]1Pet. 1:1 [c]Luke 24:49; Acts 8:29; Rom. 8:9; Gal. 4:6; Phil. 1:19; 1Pet. 1:11
8 [I]Or, *through* [a]Acts 16:7 [b]Acts 16:11; 20:5f.; 2Cor. 2:12; 2Tim. 4:13
9 [I]Or, *A man* [a]Acts 9:10 [b]Acts 16:10, 12; 18:5; 19:21f., 29; 20:1, 3; 27:2; Rom. 15:26
10 [I]Lit., *go out* [a]Acts 9:10 [b]Acts 16:10-17; 20:5-15; 21:1-18; 27:1-28:16 [c]Acts 14:7
11 [I]Some ancient mss. read *And* [a]Acts 16:8; 20:5f.; 2Cor. 2:12; 2Tim. 4:13 [b]Acts 21:1
12 [a]Acts 20:6; Phil. 1:1; 1Thess. 2:2 [b]Acts 16:9, 10; 18:5; 19:21f., 29; 20:1, 3; 27:2; Rom. 15:26 [c]Acts 16:21
13 [a]Acts 13:14
14 [I]Lit., *whose heart the Lord opened* [a]Rev. 1:11; 2:18, 24 [b]Acts 13:43; 18:7 [c]Luke 24:45
15 [a]Acts 11:14
16 [a]Acts 16:13 [b]Lev. 19:31; 20:6, 27; Deut. 18:11; 1Sam. 28:3, 7; 2Kin. 21:6; 1Chr. 10:13; Is. 8:19

nation met us, who was [ipf]bringing her masters[2962] much profit by fortune-telling.[3132]

17 [ppt]Following after Paul and us, she kept [ipf]crying out, saying, "These men are bond-servants[1401] of [a]the Most High God,[2316] who are proclaiming[2605] to you [I]the way[3598] of salvation."[4991]

🔑 18 And she continued [ipf]doing this for many days. But Paul was greatly annoyed, and turned[1994] and said to the spirit, "I command you [a]in the name[3686] of Jesus Christ to [ainf]come out of her!" And it came out at that very [I]moment.

19 But when her masters saw that their hope[1680] of [a]profit was [I]gone, they seized[1949] [b]Paul and Silas and [c]dragged[1670] them into the market place[58] before the authorities,

20 and when they had brought[4317] them to the chief magistrates, they said, "These men are throwing our city into confusion, being Jews,

21 and [a]are proclaiming[2605] customs which it is not lawful for us to [pinf]accept[3858] or to [pinf]observe, being [b]Romans."

Paul and Silas Imprisoned

22 And the crowd rose up together against them, and the chief magistrates [apt]tore their [I]robes off[4048] them, and proceeded to [ipf]order [II]*them* to be [pinf] [a]beaten with rods.

23 And when they had [apt]inflicted many blows upon them, they threw them into prison, commanding [a]the jailer to guard[5083] them securely;

24 [I]and he, having received such a command,[3852] threw them into the inner prison, and fastened their feet in [a]the stocks.

25 But about midnight [a]Paul and Silas were [ppt]praying and [ipf] [b]singing hymns of praise[5214] to God, and the prisoners were [ipf]listening to them;

26 and suddenly [a]there came a great earthquake, so that the foundations of the prison house were [aifp]shaken; and

17 [I]Lit., *a way* [a]Mark 5:7

18 [I]Lit., *hour* [a]Mark 16:17

19 [I]Lit., *gone out* [a]Acts 16:16; 19:25f. [b]Acts 15:22, 40; 16:25, 29 [c]Acts 8:3; 17:6f.; 21:30; James 2:6

21 [a]Esth. 3:8 [b]Acts 16:12

22 [I]Or, *outer garments* [II]Lit., *to beat with rods* [a]2Cor. 11:25; 1Thess. 2:2

23 [a]Acts 16:27, 36

24 [I]Lit., *who, having received* [a]Job 13:27; 33:11; Jer. 20:2f.; 29:26

25 [a]Acts 16:19 [b]Eph. 5:19

26 [a]Acts 4:31 [b]Acts 12:10 [c]Acts 12:7

27 [a]Acts 16:23, 36 [b]Acts 12:19

29 [a]Acts 16:19

30 [a]Acts 2:37; 22:10

31 [a]Mark 16:16 [b]Acts 11:14; 16:15

32 [I]Some ancient mss. read *God*

33 [a]Acts 16:25

34 [I]Lit., *a table* [II]Or, *greatly with his whole household, having believed in God* [a]Acts 11:14; 16:15

36 [a]Acts 16:27 [b]Acts 15:33

37 [a]Acts 22:25-29

immediately [b]all the doors were opened, and everyone's [c]chains were unfastened.

27 And when [a]the jailer had been roused out of sleep and had seen the prison doors [pfpp]opened, he [apt]drew his sword and was about [b]to kill himself, supposing that the prisoners had [pfip]escaped.

28 But Paul cried out with a loud voice, saying, "Do yourself no harm, for we are all here!"

29 And he called for lights and rushed in and, trembling with fear, he fell down before [a]Paul and Silas,

30 and after he brought[4254] them out, he said, "Sirs,[2962] [a]what must I do to be saved?"

The Jailer Converted

31 And they said, "[aim] [a]Believe[4100] in the Lord Jesus, and you shall be saved,[4982] you and [b]your household."

32 And they spoke the word of [I]the Lord to him together with all who were in his house.

33 And he took them [a]that *very* hour of the night and washed their wounds, and immediately[3916] he was baptized,[907] he and all his *household.*

34 And he brought them into his house and set [I]food before them, and rejoiced[21] [II]greatly, having [pfp]believed[4100] in God with [a]his whole household.[3832]

35 Now when day came, the chief magistrates sent their policemen, saying, "Release those men."

36 And [a]the jailer reported these words to Paul, *saying,* "The chief magistrates have sent to [asbp]release you. Now therefore, come out and [pim]go [b]in peace."[1515]

37 But Paul said to them, "They have [apt]beaten us in public without trial, [a]men who are Romans, and have [ao]thrown us into prison; and now are they sending us away secretly?[2977] No indeed![1063] But let them come themselves and bring us out."

🔑 **16:18** See note on II Tim. 4:20.

38 And the policemen reported[312] these words to the chief magistrates. And [a]they were afraid when they heard that they were Romans,

39 and they came and appealed to them, and when they had [apt]brought them out, they kept [ipf]begging them [a]to [ainf]leave the city.

40 And they went out of the prison and entered *the house of* [a]Lydia, and when they saw [b]the brethren, they [I]encouraged[3870] them and departed.

Paul at Thessalonica

17 [key] Now when they had traveled through Amphipolis and Apollonia, they came to [a]Thessalonica, where there was a synagogue[4864] of the Jews.

2 And [a]according to Paul's custom, he went to them, and for three [b]Sabbaths[4521] [ao]reasoned with them from [c]the Scriptures,[1124]

3 [I]explaining and [II]giving evidence that the [III]Christ[5547] [a]had to [ainf]suffer and [ainf] [b]rise again from the dead, and *saying,* "[c]This Jesus whom I am proclaiming[2605] to you is the [III]Christ."

4 [a]And some of them were persuaded[3982] and joined [b]Paul and Silas, [I]along with a great multitude of the [c]God-fearing[4576] [d]Greeks and [II]a number of the [e]leading women.

5 But [a]the Jews, [apt]becoming jealous and [apt]taking[4335] along some wicked[4190] men from the market place,[60] [apt]formed a mob and set the city in an uproar; and [apt]coming upon the house of [b]Jason, they were [ipf]seeking to [ainf]bring[71] them out to the people.[1218]

6 And when they did not find them, they *began* [a]dragging[4951] Jason and some brethren before the city authorities, shouting, "These men who have [apt]upset[387] [I][b]the world have come here also;

7 [I]and Jason [a]has welcomed[5264] them, and they all act [b]contrary to the decrees of Caesar, saying that there is another[2087] king,[935] Jesus."

38 [a]Acts 22:29
39 [a]Matt. 8:34
40 [I]Or, *exhorted* [a]Acts 16:14 [b]Acts 1:15; 16:2

1 [a]Acts 17:11, 13; 20:4; 27:2; Phil. 4:16; 1Thess. 1:1; 2Thess. 1:1; 2Tim. 4:10
2 [a]Acts 9:20; 17:10, 17 [b]Acts 13:14 [c]Acts 8:35
3 [I]Lit., *opening* [II]Lit., *placing before* [III]I.e., Messiah [a]Acts 3:18 [b]John 20:9 [c]Acts 9:22; 18:5, 28
4 [I]Lit., *and a great* [II]Lit., *not a few* [a]Acts 14:4 [b]Acts 15:22, 40; 17:10, 14f. [c]Acts 13:43; 17:17 [d]John 7:35 [e]Acts 13:50
5 [a]Acts 17:13; 1Thess. 2:14ff. [b]Acts 17:6, 7, 9; Rom. 16:21
6 [I]Lit., *the inhabited earth* [a]Acts 16:19f. [b]Matt. 24:14; Acts 17:31
7 [I]Lit., *whom Jason has welcomed* [a]Luke 10:38; James 2:25 [b]Luke 23:2
9 [I]Or, *bond* [a]Acts 17:5
10 [I]Lit., *who when. . .arrived went* [a]Acts 1:15; 17:6, 14f. [b]Acts 17:4 [c]Acts 17:13; 20:4 [d]Acts 17:1f.
11 [I]Lit., *who received* [II]Lit., *all* [a]Acts 17:1
12 [I]Lit., *and not a few* [a]Acts 2:47 [b]Mark 15:43 [c]Acts 13:50
13 [a]Acts 17:1 [b]Acts 17:10; 20:4
14 [a]Acts 1:15; 17:6, 10 [b]Acts 15:22; 17:4, 10 [c]Acts 16:1
15 [a]Acts 15:3 [b]Acts 17:16, 21f.; 18:1; 1Thess. 3:1 [c]Acts 17:14 [d]Acts 18:5

8 And they stirred up the crowd and the city authorities who heard these things.

9 And when they had [apt]received a [I]pledge from [a]Jason and the others, they released them.

Paul at Berea

10 And [a]the brethren[80] immediately sent [b]Paul and Silas away by night to [c]Berea; [I]and when they arrived, they went into [d]the synagogue[4864] of the Jews.

11 Now these were more noble-minded than those in [a]Thessalonica, [I]for they received the word[3056] with [II]great eagerness, [ppt]examining the Scriptures[1124] daily, *to see* whether these things were so.

12 [a]Many of them therefore believed,[4100] [I]along with a number of [b]prominent Greek [c]women and men.

13 But when the Jews of [a]Thessalonica found out that the word of God had been proclaimed[2605] by Paul in [b]Berea also, they came there likewise, agitating and [ppt]stirring up the crowds.

14 And then immediately [a]the brethren sent Paul out to go as far as the sea; and [b]Silas and [c]Timothy remained[5278] there.

15 Now [a]those who conducted[2525] Paul brought him as far as [b]Athens; and receiving a command for [c]Silas and Timothy to [d]come to him as soon as possible, they departed.

Paul at Athens

16 Now while Paul was waiting for[1551] them at [a]Athens, his spirit was being [ipf]provoked within him as he was [ppt]beholding the city full of idols.[2712]

17 So he was [ipf]reasoning [a]in the synagogue with the Jews and [b]the God-fearing[4576] *Gentiles,* and in the market[58]

16 [a]Acts 17:15, 21f.; 18:1; 1Thess. 3:1 17 [a]Acts 9:20; 17:2 [b]Acts 17:4

[key] **17:1-10** See general remarks on I Thess.

place every day with those who [ppt]happened to be present.

18 And also some of the Epicurean and Stoic philosophers were [ipf] [I]conversing with him. And some were [ipf]saying, "What would [a]this [II]idle babbler[4691] wish to say?" Others, "He seems to be a proclaimer[2604] of strange [III]deities,"—[1140] because he was [ipf]preaching[2097] [b]Jesus and the resurrection.[386]

19 And they [a]took him and brought[71] him [I]to the [II][b]Areopagus, saying, "May we know what [c]this new[2537] teaching[1322] is [III]which you are [ppp]proclaiming?[2980]

20 "For you are bringing some strange things to our ears;[189] we want to know therefore what these things mean."

21 (Now all the Athenians and the strangers [a]visiting there used to [ipf]spend their time in nothing other than [pinf]telling or [pinf]hearing something new.)

Sermon on Mars Hill

22 And Paul stood in the midst of the [I]Areopagus and said, "Men of [a]Athens, I observe that you are very [b]religious[1174] in all respects.

23 "For while I was passing through and [ppt]examining[333] the [a]objects of your worship,[4574] I also found an altar with this inscription, 'TO AN UNKNOWN[57] GOD.'[2316] What therefore [b]you worship[2151] in ignorance,[50] this I proclaim[2605] to you.

24 "[a]The God who [apt]made the world[2889] and all things in it, since He is [b]Lord[2962] of heaven[3772] and earth,[1093] does not [c]dwell in temples[3485] made with hands;

25 neither is He served by human[444] hands, [a]as though He [ppt]needed[4326] anything, since He Himself [ppt]gives to all life[222] and breath[4157] and all things;

26 and [a]He made from [I]one, every nation[1484] of mankind to live[2730] on all the face[4383] of the earth, having [apt] [b]determined[3724] *their* appointed[4384] times,[2540] and the boundaries of their habitation,[2733]

27 that they should seek God, if perhaps[686] they might [opt]grope for Him and [opt]find Him, [a]though He is not far from each one of us;

28 for [a]in Him we live[2198] and move and [I]exist, as even some of your own poets have said, 'For we also are His offspring.'

29 "Being then the offspring of God, we [a]ought not to think that the Divine Nature is like gold or silver or stone, an image formed[5480] by the art and thought of man.

30 "Therefore having [apt] [a]overlooked[5237] [b]the times[5550] of ignorance,[52] God is [c]now declaring[3853] to men[444] that all everywhere should repent,[3340]

31 because He has fixed[2476] [a]a day in which [b]He will [pinf]judge[2919] [I][c]the world[3625] in righteousness[1348] through a Man[435] whom He has [d]appointed,[3724] having furnished proof[4102] to all men [II]by [apt] [e]raising[450] Him from the dead."[3498]

32 Now when they heard of [a]the resurrection[386] of the dead, some *began* to sneer, but others said, "We shall hear you [I]again concerning this."

33 So Paul went out of their midst.

34 But[1161] some men [aptp]joined[2853] him and believed, among whom also were Dionysius the [a]Areopagite and a woman named Damaris and others[2087] with them.

Paul at Corinth

18 After these things he left [a]Athens and went to [b]Corinth.

2 And he found a certain Jew named [a]Aquila, a native of [b]Pontus, having recently come from [c]Italy with his wife [a]Priscilla, because [d]Claudius had commanded[1299] all the Jews to leave Rome. He came to them,

3 and because he was of the same trade, he [ipf]stayed with them and [a]they were [ipf]working;[2038] for by trade they were tent-makers.

18 [I]Or, *disputing* [II]I.e., one who makes his living by picking up scraps [III]Lit., *demons* [a]1Cor. 1:20; 4:10 [b]Acts 4:2; 17:31f.
19 [I]Or, *before* [II]Or, *Hill of Ares, god of war* [III]Lit., *which is being spoken by you* [a]Acts 23:19 [b]Acts 17:22 [c]Mark 1:27
21 [a]Acts 2:10
22 [I]Or possibly, the Council of the Areopagus [a]Acts 17:15 [b]Acts 25:19
23 [a]2Thess. 2:4 [b]John 4:22
24 [a]Is. 42:5; Acts 14:15 [b]Deut. 10:14; Ps. 115:16; Matt. 11:25 [c]1Kin. 8:27; Acts 7:48
25 [a]Job 22:2; Ps. 50:10-12
26 [I]Some later mss. read *one blood* [a]Mal. 2:10 [b]Deut. 32:8; Job 12:23
27 [a]Deut. 4:7; Jer. 23:23f.; Acts 14:17
28 [I]Lit., *are* [a]Job 12:10; Dan. 5:23
29 [a]Is. 40:18ff.; Rom. 1:23
30 [a]Acts 14:16; Rom. 3:25 [b]Acts 17:23 [c]Luke 24:47; Acts 26:20; Titus 2:11f.
31 [I]Lit., *the inhabited earth* [II]Or, *when He raised* [a]Matt. 10:15 [b]Ps. 9:8; 96:13; 98:9; John 5:22, 27; Acts 10:42 [c]Matt. 24:14; Acts 17:6 [d]Luke 22:22 [e]Acts 2:24
32 [I]Lit., *also again* [a]Acts 17:18, 31
34 [a]Acts 17:19, 22

1 [a]Acts 17:15 [b]Acts 18:8; 19:1; 1Cor. 1:2; 2Cor. 1:1, 23; 6:11; 2Tim. 4:20
2 [a]Acts 18:18, 26; Rom. 16:3; 1Cor. 16:19; 2Tim. 4:19 [b]Acts 2:9 [c]Acts 27:1, 6; Heb. 13:24 [d]Acts 11:28
3 [a]Acts 20:34; 1Cor. 4:12; 9:14f.; 2Cor. 11:7; 12:13; 1Thess. 2:9; 4:11; 2Thess. 3:8

4 And he was [ipf]reasoning [a]in the synagogue[4864] every [b]Sabbath[4521] and trying to persuade [c]Jews and Greeks.

🔑 **5** But when [a]Silas and Timothy [b]came down from [c]Macedonia, Paul *began* [ipf]devoting[4912] himself completely to the word, solemnly [ppt] [d]testifying[1263] to the Jews that [e]Jesus was the [I]Christ.

6 And when they [ppt]resisted and [ppt]blasphemed, he [apt] [a]shook out his garments and said to them, "Your [b]blood[129] *be* upon your own heads! I am clean.[2513] From now on I shall go [c]to the Gentiles."[1484]

7 And he departed[3327] from there and went to the house of a certain man named [I]Titius Justus, [a]a worshiper[4576] of God, whose house was next to the synagogue.

8 And [a]Crispus, [b]the leader of the synagogue,[752] believed[4100] in the Lord [c]with all his household, and many of the [d]Corinthians when they heard were [ipf]believing and being [ipf]baptized.[907]

9 And the Lord said to Paul in the night by [a]a vision,[3705] "Do not be afraid[5399] *any longer*, but go on [pim]speaking[2980] and [aosi]do not be silent;

10 for I am with you, and no man will attack you in order to harm[2559] you, for I have many people in this city."

11 And he settled *there* a year and six months, teaching[1321] the word[3056] of God among them.

12 But while Gallio was [a]proconsul of [b]Achaia, [c]the Jews with one accord rose up against Paul and brought him before [d]the judgment seat,

13 saying, "This man persuades men to worship[4576] God contrary[3844] to [a]the law."[3551]

14 But when Paul was about to [a]open his mouth, Gallio said to the Jews, "If it were a matter of wrong[92] or of vicious[4190] crime, O Jews, it would be reasonable[2596,3056] for me to put up with[430] you;

15 but if there are [a]questions about words and names and your own law, look after it yourselves; I am unwilling to be a judge of these matters."

16 And he drove them away from [a]the judgment seat.

17 And they all [apt]took hold of [a]Sosthenes, [b]the leader of the synagogue, and *began* [ipf]beating[5180] him in front of [c]the judgment seat. And Gallio was not concerned about any of these things.

18 And Paul, having [apt]remained[4357] many days longer, [apt] [a]took leave[657] of [b]the brethren and put out to sea for [c]Syria, and with him were [d]Priscilla and [d]Aquila. In [e]Cenchrea [I]he [f]had his hair cut, for he was keeping a vow.

19 And they came to [a]Ephesus, and he left them there. Now he himself [apt]entered [b]the synagogue and reasoned with the Jews.

20 And when they [ppt]asked him to stay for a longer time,[5550] he did not consent,

21 but [a]taking leave[657] of them and saying, "I will return to you again [b]if God wills," he set sail[321] from [c]Ephesus.

22 And when he had landed at [a]Caesarea, he went up and greeted[782] the church,[1577] and went down to [b]Antioch.

Third Missionary Journey

23 And having spent some time *there,* he departed and passed successively through the [a]Galatian region and Phrygia, strengthening all the disciples.[3101]

🔑 **24** Now a certain Jew named [a]Apollos, an [b]Alexandrian by birth, [I]an eloquent man, came to [c]Ephesus; and he was mighty in the Scriptures.

4 [a]Acts 9:20; 18:19 [b]Acts 13:14 [c]Acts 14:1
5 [I]I.e., Messiah [a]Acts 15:22; 16:1; 17:14 [b]Acts 17:15 [c]Acts 16:9 [d]Luke 16:28; Acts 20:21 [e]Acts 17:3; 18:28
6 [a]Neh. 5:13; Acts 13:51 [b]2Sam. 1:16; 1Kin. 2:33; Ezek. 18:13; 33:4, 6, 8; Matt. 27:25; Acts 20:26 [c]Acts 13:46
7 [I]Some ancient mss. read *Titus*, others omit it altogether [a]Acts 13:43; 16:14
8 [a]1Cor. 1:14 [b]Mark 5:22 [c]Acts 11:14 [d]Acts 18:1; 19:1; 1Cor. 1:2; 2Cor. 1:1, 23; 6:11; 2Tim. 4:20
9 [a]Acts 9:10
12 [a]Acts 13:7 [b]Acts 18:27; 19:21; Rom. 15:26; 1Cor. 16:15; 2Cor. 1:1; 9:2; 11:10; 1Thess. 1:7f. [c]1Thess. 2:14ff. [d]Matt. 27:19
13 [a]John 19:7; Acts 18:15
14 [a]Matt. 5:2
15 [a]Acts 23:29; 25:19
16 [a]Matt. 27:19
17 [a]1Cor. 1:1 [b]Acts 18:8 [c]Matt. 27:19
18 [I]Lit., *having his hair cut* [a]Mark 6:46 [b]Acts 1:15; 18:27 [c]Matt. 4:24 [d]Acts 18:2, 26 [e]Rom. 16:1 [f]Num. 6:2, 5, 9, 18; Acts 21:24
19 [a]Acts 18:21, 24; 19:1, 17, 26, 28, 34f.; 20:16f.; 21:29; 1Cor. 15:32; 16:8; Eph. 1:1; 1Tim. 1:3; 2Tim. 1:18; 4:12; Rev. 1:11; 2:1 [b]Acts 18:4
21 [a]Mark 6:46 [b]Rom. 1:10; 15:32; 1Cor. 4:19; 16:7; Heb. 6:3; James 4:15; 1Pet. 3:17 [c]Acts 18:19,24; 19:1, 17, 26, 28, 34f.; 20:16f.; 21:29; 1Cor. 15:32; 16:8; Eph. 1:1; 1Tim. 1:3; 2Tim. 1:18; 4:12; Rev. 1:11; 2:1
22 [a]Acts 8:40 [b]Acts 11:19 **23** [a]Acts 16:6
24 [I]Or, *a learned man* [a]Acts 19:1; 1Cor. 1:12; 3:5, 6, 22; 4:6; 16:12; Titus 3:13 [b]Acts 6:9 [c]Acts 18:19

🔑 **18:5** See general remarks on I Thess.
🔑 **18:24-28** See general remarks on Hebrews.

25 This man had been instructed in [a]the way[3598] of the Lord; and being fervent in spirit, he was [ipf]speaking and [ipf]teaching[1321] accurately the things concerning Jesus, being acquainted only with [b]the baptism[908] of John;

26 and he began to speak out boldly in the synagogue.[4844] But when [a]Priscilla and Aquila heard him, they took him aside and explained to him [b]the way of God more accurately.

27 And when he wanted to go across to [a]Achaia, [b]the brethren [apt]encouraged him and wrote to [c]the disciples to [ainf]welcome[588] him; and when he had arrived, he [1]helped greatly those who had [pfp]believed[4100] through grace;[5485]

28 for he powerfully [ipf]refuted the Jews in public, [ppt]demonstrating [a]by the Scriptures that [b]Jesus was the [1]Christ.[5547]

Paul at Ephesus

19 And it came about that while [a]Apollos was at [b]Corinth, Paul having passed through the [c]upper country came to [d]Ephesus, and found some disciples,[3101]

2 and he said to them, "[a]Did you receive the Holy Spirit[4151] when you [apt]believed?"[4100] And they *said* to him, "No, [b]we have not even heard whether [1]there is a Holy Spirit."

3 And he said, "Into what then were you baptized?"[907] And they said, "[a]Into John's baptism."

4 And Paul said, "[a]John baptized with the baptism of repentance,[3341] telling the people [b]to [aosb]believe in Him who was coming after him, that is, in Jesus."

5 And when they heard this, they were [a]baptized [1]in the name of the Lord Jesus.

6 And when Paul had [a]laid his hands upon them, the Holy Spirit came[2064] on them, and they *began* [ipf] [b]speaking with tongues[1100] and [ipf] [c]prophesying.[4395]

7 And there were in all about twelve men.

25 [a]Acts 9:2; 18:26 [b]Luke 7:29; Acts 19:3 **26** [a]Acts 18:2, 18 [b]Acts 18:25 **27** [1]Or, *helped greatly through grace those who had believed* [a]Acts 18:12; 19:1 [b]Acts 18:18 [c]Acts 11:26 **28** [1]I.e., Messiah [a]Acts 8:35 [b]Acts 18:5

1 [a]Acts 18:24; 1Cor. 1:12; 3:5, 6, 22; 4:6; 16:12; Titus 3:13 [b]Acts 18:1 [c]Acts 18:23 [d]Acts 18:21, 24; 19:17, 26, 28, 34f.; 20:16f.; 21:29; 1Cor. 15:32; 16:8; Eph. 1:1; 1Tim. 1:3; 2Tim. 1:18; 4:12; Rev. 1:11; 2:1 **2** [1]Or, *the Holy Spirit has been given* [a]Acts 8:15f.; 11:16f. [b]John 7:39 **3** [a]Luke 7:29; Acts 18:25 **4** [a]Matt. 3:11; Mark 1:4, 7, 8; Luke 3:16; John 1:26, 27; Acts 13:24 [b]John 1:7 **5** [1]Lit., *into* [a]Acts 8:12, 16; 10:48 **6** [a]Acts 6:6; 8:17 [b]Mark 16:17; Acts 2:4; 10:46 [c]Acts 13:1

19:1-7 See notes on Jn. 20:22,23; Acts 1:5; 2:1-13; 11:14-18; I Cor. 12:13. This event took place in Ephesus and it concerned another group of believers, the third in the series: first were the Jews at Pentecost, then the Gentiles at Caesarea, and now the disciples of John the Baptist in Ephesus. These had already been baptized in water. They had received the baptism of John but not the baptism of Jesus Christ, in His name, which would be consequent to their exercise of faith in the Lord. Again, this event took place in the presence of one of the Apostles, Paul. He was not one of the Twelve but he became one with them in power and designation (I Cor. 9:1). In this instance, the water baptism preceded the Spirit baptism (vv. 5,6) which was different than the previous occasions in regard to the Gentiles (Acts 10:44-48). In this instance, Paul put his hands upon them for they were few, only twelve. This indicates that there is no uniformity in the manner in which this baptism in the Holy Spirit comes. It can come directly without human intermediary, or as in the case when Paul prayed with his hands upon them. The consequence of this spiritual baptism was that these twelve spoke in languages (v. 6) and prophesied. In this instance, it does not say other different languages, but simply languages. In Acts 19:2,6 we do not have the phrase "*baptize* in the Spirit," but we conclude that this must have been one of the three instances of the Spirit baptism from the unique manifestation of speaking in tongues. Historically, this speaking in other understandable languages occurred only consequent to the "baptism in the Spirit." Therefore, the verbs in "Did you receive (v. 2, *elabete,* 2983) the Holy Spirit" and "the Holy Spirit came" (v. 6, *ēlthe,* 2064) must be taken as equivalent to "baptize in the Spirit." In Acts 2:4,6,8 the Scripture says "different other languages and dialects"; in Acts 10:46 it says "in languages," as also in 19:6. Here, as in the previous two instances, there were no interpreters, which indicates that these were spoken, ethnic languages understood by those who heard them.

The exact term "baptize with the Holy Spirit" occurs for the sixth time in Acts 11:16 (the previous occurrences being Mt. 3:11; Mk. 1:8; Lk. 3:16; Jn. 1:33; Acts 1:5).

The last time that the term occurs in the N.T. is I Cor. 12:13. See related note.

19:3,5 See note on I Cor. 10:2.

19:6 See notes on Acts 2:1-13; I Cor. 14:1-3.

8 And he entered [a]the synagogue[4864] and continued [ipf]speaking out boldly for three months, reasoning and [I]persuading *them* [b]about the kingdom[932] of God.

🔑9 But when [a]some[5100] were becoming [ipf]hardened[4645] and [ipf]disobedient,[544] [ppt]speaking evil of [b]the Way[3598] before the multitude, he withdrew[868] from them and took away[873] [c]the disciples,[3101] reasoning daily in the school of Tyrannus.

10 And this took place for [a]two years, so that all who lived in [I][b]Asia heard [c]the word[3056] of the Lord, both Jews and Greeks.

Miracles at Ephesus

🔑11 And God was [ipf]performing [a]extraordinary [I]miracles[1411] by the hands of Paul,

12 [a]so that handkerchiefs or aprons were even [pip]carried from his body to the sick, and the diseases [pip]left[525] them and [b]the evil[4190] spirits [pinf]went out.

13 But also some of the Jewish [a]exorcists,[1845] who went from place to place, attempted to name over those who had the evil spirits the name of the Lord Jesus, saying, "I adjure[3726] you by Jesus whom Paul preaches."[2784]

14 And seven sons of one Sceva, a Jewish chief priest,[749] were [ppt]doing this.

15 And the evil spirit answered and said to them, "I recognize Jesus, and I know about Paul, but who are you?"

16 And the man, in whom was the evil spirit, leaped on them and [apt]subdued all of them and overpowered[2480] them, so that they [ainf]fled out of that house naked[1131] and wounded.

17 And this became known to all, both Jews and Greeks, who lived in [a]Ephesus; and fear[5401] fell upon them all and the name of the Lord Jesus was being [ipf]magnified.

18 Many also of those who had [pfp]believed[4100] kept [ipf]coming, [ppt]confessing[1843] and [ppt]disclosing their practices.

19 And many of those who practiced[4238] magic[4021] [apt]brought[4851] their books together and *began* [ipf]burning them in the sight of all; and they counted up the price of them and found it [I]fifty thousand [a]pieces of silver.

20 So [I][a]the word[3056] of the Lord [b]was [ipf]growing mightily and [ipf]prevailing.[2480]

21 Now after these things were finished, Paul purposed[5087] in the [I]spirit[4151] to [a]go to Jerusalem [b]after he had [apt]passed through [c]Macedonia and [d]Achaia, saying, "After I have been there, [e]I must also see Rome."

22 And having sent into [a]Macedonia two of [b]those who [ppt]ministered[1247] to him, [c]Timothy and [d]Erastus, he himself stayed in [I][e]Asia for a while.[5550]

23 And about that time there arose no small disturbance concerning [a]the Way.[3598]

24 For a certain man named Demetrius, a silversmith, who made silver shrines[3485] of [I]Artemis, [a]was [ipf]bringing no little [II]business to the craftsmen;[5079]

25 these he gathered together with the workmen of similar *trades,* and said, "Men, you know that our prosperity [I]depends upon this business.

26 "And you see and hear that not only in [a]Ephesus, but in almost all of [I][b]Asia, this Paul has persuaded and turned away[3179] a considerable number of people, saying that [II][c]gods[2316] made with hands are no gods *at all.*

27 "And not only is there danger that this trade of ours fall into disrepute,[557] but also that the temple[2411] of the great goddess [I]Artemis be regarded as worthless[3049] and that she whom all of [II][a]Asia and [b]the [III]world worship should

8 [I]Some ancient mss. read *persuading as to the things about* [a]Acts 9:20; 18:26 [b]Acts 1:3
9 [a]Acts 14:4 [b]Acts 9:2; 19:23 [c]Acts 11:26; 19:30
10 [I]I.e., west coast province of Asia Minor [a]Acts 19:8; 20:31 [b]Acts 16:6; 19:22, 26, 27 [c]Acts 13:12; 19:20
11 [I]Or, *works of power* [a]Acts 8:13
12 [a]Acts 5:15 [b]Mark 16:17
13 [a]Matt. 12:27; Luke 11:19
17 [a]Acts 18:19
19 [I]Or probably, fifty thousand Greek drachmas. A drachma approximated a day's wage. [a]Luke 15:8
20 [I]Or, *according to the power of the Lord the word was growing* [a]Acts 19:10 [b]Acts 6:7; 12:24
21 [I]Or, *Spirit* [a]Acts 20:16, 22; 21:15; Rom. 15:25; 2Cor. 1:16 [b]Acts 20:1; 1Cor. 16:5 [c]Acts 16:9; 19:22, 29; Rom. 15:26; 1Thess. 1:7f. [d]Acts 18:12 [e]Acts 23:11; Rom. 15:24, 28
22 [I]I.e., west coast province of Asia Minor [a]Acts 16:9; 19:21, 29 [b]Acts 13:5; 19:29; 20:34; 2Cor. 8:19 [c]Acts 16:1 [d]Rom. 16:23; 2Tim. 4:20 [e]Acts 19:10
23 [a]Acts 19:9
24 [I]Lat., *Diana* [II]Or, *profit* [a]Acts 16:16, 19f.
25 [I]Lit., *is from*
26 [I]V. 22, note 1 [II]Lit., *those* [a]Acts 18:19 [b]Acts 19:10 [c]Deut. 4:28; Ps. 115:4; Is. 44:10-20; Jer. 10:3ff.; Acts 17:29; 1Cor. 8:4; 10:19; Rev. 9:20
27 [I]Lat., *Diana* [II]V. 22, note 1 [III]Lit., *the inhabited earth* [a]Acts 19:10 [b]Matt. 24:14

🔑 **19:9** See note on II Thess. 2:3.
🔑 **19:11** See note on II Tim. 4:20.

even be dethroned from her magnificence."

28 And when they heard *this* and were filled with rage,[2372] they *began* crying out, saying, "Great is [I]Artemis of the [a]Ephesians!"

🔑 29 And the city was filled with the confusion, and they rushed with one accord into the theater, [I]dragging along [a]Gaius and [b]Aristarchus, Paul's traveling [c]companions from [d]Macedonia.

30 And when Paul wanted to go into the [I]assembly,[1218] [a]the disciples would not let him.

31 And also some of the [I]Asiarchs who were friends of his [apt]sent to him and repeatedly urged him not to [II]venture into the theater.

32 [a]So then, some were shouting one thing and some another, for the [I]assembly[1577] was in confusion, and the majority did not know [II]for what cause they had come together.

33 And some of the crowd [I]concluded *it was* Alexander, since the Jews had put him forward; and having [a]motioned with his hand, Alexander was intending to make a defense to the [II]assembly.

34 But when they recognized that he was a Jew, a *single* outcry arose from them all as they shouted for about two hours, "Great is [I]Artemis of the Ephesians!"

35 And after quieting the multitude, the town clerk[1122] *said, "Men of [a]Ephesus, what man is there after all who does not know that the city of the Ephesians is guardian of the temple of the great [I]Artemis, and of the *image* which fell down from [II]heaven?

36 "Since then these are undeniable facts, you ought to keep calm and to do nothing rash.

37 "For you have brought these men *here* who are neither [a]robbers of temples[2417] nor [ppt]blasphemers of our goddess.

38 "So then, if Demetrius and the craftsmen[5079] who are with him have a complaint against any man, the courts are in session[71] and [Ia]proconsuls are *available*; let them bring charges against[1458] one another.

39 "But if you want anything beyond this, it shall be settled in the [I]lawful[1772] [II]assembly.[1577]

40 "For indeed we are in danger of being accused[1458] of a riot[4714] in connection with today's affair, since there is no *real* cause *for it*; and in this connection we shall be unable to account for this disorderly gathering."[4963]

41 And after saying this he dismissed the [I]assembly.[1577]

Paul in Macedonia and Greece

20 🔑 And after the uproar had ceased, Paul [apt]sent for [a]the disciples[3101] and when he had [apt]exhorted them and taken his leave of them, he departed [b]to go to [c]Macedonia.

2 And when he had gone through those districts and had given[3870] them much exhortation, he came to Greece.

3 And *there* he spent three months, and when [a]a plot was formed against him by the Jews as he was about to set sail for [b]Syria, he determined[1106] to return through [c]Macedonia.

🔑 4 And [I]he was accompanied by Sopater of [a]Berea, *the son* of Pyrrhus; and by [b]Aristarchus and Secundus of the [c]Thessalonians; and [d]Gaius of [e]Derbe, and [f]Timothy; and [g]Tychicus and [h]Trophimus of [IIi]Asia.

5 But these had gone on ahead and [ipf]were waiting[3306] for [a]us at [b]Troas.

6 And [a]we sailed from [b]Philippi after [c]the days of Unleavened Bread,[106] and came to them at [d]Troas within five days; and there we stayed seven days.

28 [I]Lat., *Diana* [a]Acts 18:19
29 [I]Lit., *having dragged* [a]Acts 20:4 [b]Acts 20:4; 27:2; Col. 4:10; Philem. 24 [c]Acts 13:5; 19:22; 20:34; 2Cor. 8:19 [d]Acts 16:9; 19:22
30 [I]Lit., *people* [a]Acts 19:9
31 [I]I.e., political or religious officials of the province of Asia [II]Lit., *give himself*
32 [I]Gr., *ekklesia* [II]Or, *on whose account* [a]Acts 21:34
33 [I]Or, *instructed Alexander* [II]Lit., *people* [a]Acts 12:17
34 [I]Lat., *Diana*
35 [I]Lat., *Diana* [II]Lit., *Zeus;* or, *Jupiter* [a]Acts 18:19
37 [a]Rom. 2:22
38 [I]Or, *provincial governors* [a]Acts 13:7
39 [I]Or, *regular* [II]Gr., *ekklesia*
41 [I]Gr., *ekklesia*

1 [a]Acts 11:26 [b]Acts 19:21 [c]Acts 16:9; 20:3
3 [a]Acts 9:23f.; 20:19 [b]Matt. 4:24 [c]Acts 16:9; 20:1
4 [I]Lit., *there accompanied him* [II]I.e., west coast province of Asia Minor [a]Acts 17:10 [b]Acts 19:29 [c]Acts 17:1 [d]Acts 19:29 [e]Acts 14:6 [f]Acts 16:1 [g]Eph. 6:21; Col. 4:7; 2Tim. 4:12; Titus 3:12 [h]Acts 21:29; 2Tim. 4:20 [i]Acts 16:6; 20:16, 18
5 [a]Acts 16:10; 20:5-15 [b]Acts 16:8
6 [a]Acts 16:10; 20:5-15 [b]Acts 16:12 [c]Acts 12:3 [d]Acts 16:8

🔑 **19:29** See note on III Jn. 1.
🔑 **20:1-5** See notes on II Tim. 4:20; III Jn. 1.
🔑 **20:4,5** See general remarks on I Timothy and also notes on Col. 4:7,10; III Jn. 1.

7 And on [a]the first day of the week,
when [b]we were gathered together to
[c]break**2806** bread, Paul *began* [ipf]talking1256
to them, intending**3195** to depart the next
day, and he prolonged his [I]message until
midnight.
8 And there were many [a]lamps in
the [b]upper room where we were gathered together.
9 And there was a certain young
man named Eutychus sitting [I]on the window sill, sinking into a deep sleep; and
as Paul kept on talking, he was [apt]over-
come by sleep and fell down from the
third floor, and was picked up**142** dead.
10 But Paul went down and [a]fell
upon him and after embracing him, he
[b]said, "[I]Do not be troubled, for his life**5590**
is in him."
11 And when he had gone *back* up,
and had [a]broken the bread and [I]eaten,
he talked with them a long while, until
daybreak,**827** and so departed.
12 And they took away the boy**3816**
alive,**2198** and were [I]greatly comforted.**3870**

Troas to Miletus

13 But [a]we, going ahead to the ship,
set sail for Assos, intending**3195** from
there to take Paul on board;353 for thus
he had arranged**1299** it, intending**3195** himself to go [I]by land.
14 And when he met us at Assos,
we took him on board353 and came to
Mitylene.
15 And sailing from there, we arrived the following day opposite Chios;
and the next day we crossed over**3846**
to Samos; and [I]the day following we
came to [a]Miletus.
16 For Paul had decided**2919** to sail
past [a]Ephesus in order that he might
not have to spend time in [Ib]Asia; for
he was hurrying [c]to be in Jerusalem, if
possible, [d]on the day of Pentecost.4005

Farewell to Ephesus

17 And from Miletus he [apt]sent to
[a]Ephesus and called**3333** to him [b]the
elders**4245** of the church.**1577**
18 And when they had come to him,
he said to them,
"You yourselves know, [a]from the
first day that I set foot**1910** in [I]Asia, how
I was with you the whole time,**5550**
19 serving**1398** the Lord with all humility and with tears and with trials**3986**
which came upon me through [a]the plots
of the Jews;
20 how I [a]did not shrink from declaring to you anything that was profitable,
and teaching you publicly and [I]from
house to house,
21 solemnly [a]testifying**1263** to both
Jews and Greeks of [b]repentance**3341** toward God and [c]faith**4102** in our Lord Jesus
Christ.
22 "And now, behold, bound in
[I]spirit, [a]I am on my way to Jerusalem,
not knowing what will happen to me
there,
23 except that [a]the Holy Spirit solemnly [b]testifies**1263** to me in every city,
saying that [c]bonds and afflictions await
me.
24 "But [a]I do not consider my life
of any account as dear to myself, in order
that I may [b]finish**5048** my course, and
[c]the ministry**1248** which I received from
the Lord Jesus, to [d]testify**1263** solemnly
of the gospel**2098** of [e]the grace**5485** of God.
25 "And now, behold, I know that
all of you, among whom I went about
[a]preaching**2784** the kingdom,**932** will see
my face no more.
26 "Therefore I [I]testify**3143** to you
this day, that [a]I am [II]innocent**2513** of the
blood of all men.
27 "For I [a]did not shrink5288 from
declaring**312** to you the whole [b]pur-
pose**1012** of God.
28 "Be on guard for yourselves and
for all [a]the flock,**4168** among which the
Holy Spirit has made**5087** you [I]over-
seers,**1985** to shepherd**4165** [b]the church
of [II]God which [c]He [ao] [III]purchased with
His own blood.**129**

7 [I]Lit., *word, speech* [a]1Cor. 16:2; Rev. 1:10 [b]Acts 16:10; 20:5-15 [c]Acts 2:42; 20:11
8 [a]Matt. 25:1 [b]Acts 1:13
9 [I]Or, *at the window*
10 [I]Or, *Stop being troubled* [a]1Kin. 17:21; 2Kin. 4:34 [b]Matt. 9:23f.; Mark 5:39
11 [I]Lit., *tasted* [a]Acts 2:42; 20:7
12 [I]Lit., *not moderately*
13 [I]Or, *on foot* [a]Acts 16:10; 20:5-15
15 [I]Later mss. add *after staying at Trogyllium, the day following* [a]Acts 20:17; 2Tim. 4:20
16 [I]I.e., west coast province of Asia Minor [a]Acts 18:19 [b]Acts 16:6; 20:4, 18 [c]Acts 19:21; 20:6, 22; 1Cor. 16:8 [d]Acts 2:1
17 [a]Acts 18:19 [b]Acts 11:30
18 [I]V. 16, note 1 [a]Acts 18:19; 19:1, 10; 20:4, 16
19 [a]Acts 20:3
20 [I]Or, *in the various private homes* [a]Acts 20:27
21 [a]Luke 16:28; Acts 18:5; 20:23, 24 [b]Acts 2:38; 11:18; 26:20 [c]Acts 24:24; 26:18; Eph. 1:15; Col. 2:5; Philem. 5
22 [I]Or, *the Spirit* [a]Acts 17:16; 20:16
23 [a]Acts 8:29 [b]Luke 16:28; Acts 18:5; 20:21, 24 [c]Acts 9:16; 21:33
24 [a]Acts 21:13 [b]Acts 13:25; 2 Tim. 4:7 [c]Acts 1:17 [d]Luke 16:28; Acts 18:5; 20:21 [e]Acts 11:23; 20:32
25 [a]Matt. 4:23; Acts 28:31
26 [I]Or, *call you to witness* [II]Lit., *pure from* [a]Acts 18:6

27 [a]Acts 20:20 [b]Acts 13:36 **28** [I]Or, *bishops* [II]Some ancient mss. read *the Lord* [III]Lit., *acquired* [a]Luke 12:32; John 21:15-17; Acts 20:29; 1Pet. 5:2f. [b]Matt. 16:18; Rom. 16:16; 1Cor. 10:32 [c]Eph. 1:7, 14; Titus 2:14; 1Pet. 1:19; 2:9; Rev. 5:9

29 "I know that after my departure [a]savage wolves will come in among you, not sparing [b]the flock;[4168]

30 and from among your own selves men will arise, speaking perverse things, to draw away [a]the disciples after them.

31 "Therefore be on the alert, [ppt]remembering that night and day for a period of [a]three years I did not cease to admonish[3560] each one [b]with tears.

32 "And now I [a]commend you to [I]God and to [b]the word of His grace, which is able to [c]build *you* up[2026] and to give *you* [d]the inheritance[2817] among all those who are sanctified.[37]

33 "[a]I have coveted no one's silver or gold or clothes.[2441]

34 "You yourselves know that [a]these hands ministered to my *own* needs[5532] and to the [b]men who were with me.

35 "In everything I showed you that by working hard in this manner you must help[482] the weak[770] and remember the words of the Lord Jesus, that He Himself said, 'It is more blessed[3107] to give than to receive.' "

36 And when he had said these things, he [a]knelt down and prayed with them all.

37 And [I]they *began* to weep aloud[2425] and [apt II][a]embraced Paul, and repeatedly [ipf]kissed him,

38 [I]grieving especially over [a]the word which he had spoken, that they should see his face no more. And they were [ipf b]accompanying him to the ship.

Paul Sails from Miletus

21 And when it came about that [a]we had parted from them and had set sail, we ran [b]a straight course to Cos and the next day to Rhodes and from there to Patara;

2 and having found a ship crossing over to [a]Phoenicia, we went aboard[1910] and set sail.[321]

3 And when we had come in sight of [a]Cyprus, leaving it on the left, we kept [ipf]sailing to [b]Syria and landed[2609] at [c]Tyre; for [d]there the ship was to unload its cargo.

4 And after looking up[429] [a]the disciples, we stayed there seven days; and they kept [ipf]telling Paul [I b]through the Spirit not to set foot in Jerusalem.

5 And when it came about that [I]our days there were ended,[1822] we departed and started on our journey, while they all, with wives and children, [a]escorted us until *we were* out of the city. And after [b]kneeling down on the beach and praying, we said farewell to one another.

6 Then we went on board[1910] the ship, and they returned [a]home again.

7 And when we had finished the voyage from [a]Tyre, we arrived at Ptolemais; and after greeting [b]the brethren, we stayed with them for a day.

8 And on the next day we departed and came to [a]Caesarea; and entering the house of [b]Philip the [c]evangelist,[2099] who was [b]one of the seven, we stayed with him.

9 Now this man had four virgin[3933] daughters who were [a]prophetesses.[4395]

10 And as we were staying there for some days, a certain prophet[4396] named [a]Agabus came down from Judea.

11 And coming to us, he [apt a]took Paul's belt and [apt]bound his own feet and hands, and said, "This [b]is what the Holy Spirit says: 'In this way the Jews at Jerusalem will [c]bind the man who owns this belt[2223] and [d]deliver him into the hands of the Gentiles.' "

12 And when we had heard this, we as well as the local residents *began* [ipf]begging[3870] him [a]not to go up to Jerusalem.

13 Then Paul answered, "What are you doing, weeping and breaking my heart? For [a]I am ready not only to be bound, but even to die at Jerusalem for [b]the name of the Lord Jesus."

29 [a]Ezek. 22:27; Matt. 7:15 [b]Luke 12:32; John 21:15-17; Acts 20:28; 1Pet. 5:2f.
30 [a]Acts 11:26
31 [a]Acts 19:8, 10; 24:17 [b]Acts 20:19
32 [I]One ancient mss. reads *the Lord* [a]Acts 14:23 [b]Acts 14:3; 20:24 [c]Acts 9:31 [d]Acts 26:18; Eph. 1:14; 5:5; Col. 1:12; 3:24; Heb. 9:15; 1Pet. 1:4
33 [a]1Cor. 9:4-18; 2Cor. 11:7-12; 12:14-18; 1Thess. 2:5f.
34 [a]Acts 18:3 [b]Acts 19:22
36 [a]Acts 9:40; 21:5; Luke 22:41
37 [I]Lit., *a considerable weeping of all occurred* [II]Lit., *fell on Paul's neck* [a]Luke 15:20
38 [I]Lit., *suffering pain* [a]Acts 20:25 [b]Acts 15:3

1 [a]Acts 16:10; 21:1-18 [b]Acts 16:11
2 [a]Acts 11:19; 21:3
3 [a]Acts 4:36; 21:16 [b]Matt. 4:24 [c]Acts 12:20; 21:7 [d]Acts 21:2
4 [I]I.e., because of impressions made by the Spirit [a]Acts 11:26; 21:16 [b]Acts 20:23; 21:11
5 [I]Lit., *we had completed the days* [a]Acts 15:3 [b]Luke 22:41; Acts 9:40; 20:36
6 [a]John 19:27
7 [a]Acts 12:20; 21:3 [b]Acts 1:15; 21:17
8 [a]Acts 8:40; 21:16 [b]Acts 6:5; 8:5 [c]Eph. 4:11; 2Tim. 4:5
9 [a]Luke 2:36; Acts 13:1; 1Cor. 11:5
10 [a]Acts 11:28
11 [a]1Kin. 22:11; Is. 20:2; Jer. 13:1-11; 19:1, 11; John 18 [b]Acts 8:29 [c]Acts 9:16; 21:33 [d]Matt. 20:19
12 [a]Acts 21:15 **13** [a]Acts 20:24 [b]Acts 5:41; 9:16

14 And since he would not be persuaded,[3982] we fell silent,[2270] remarking, "[a]The will[2307] of the Lord[2962] be done!"

Paul at Jerusalem

15 And after these days we got ready and [ipf] [a]started on our way up to Jerusalem.

16 And *some* of [a]the disciples[3101] from [b]Caesarea also came with us, [ppt]taking[71] us to Mnason of [c]Cyprus, a [d]disciple of long standing[744] with whom we were to lodge.

17 And when we had come to Jerusalem, [a]the brethren received us gladly.

18 And now the following day Paul went in with us to [I][a]James, and all [b]the elders[4245] were present.

19 And after he had greeted them, he [a]*began to relate*[1834] one by one the things which God had done among the Gentiles[1484] through his [b]ministry.

20 And when they heard it they *began* [ipf] [a]glorifying[1392] God; and they said to him, "You see, brother, how many [I]thousands there are among the Jews of those who have [pfp]believed,[4100] and they are[5225] all [b]zealous for the Law;

21 and they have been told about you, that you are [a]teaching[1321] all the Jews who are among the Gentiles to forsake[646] Moses, telling them [b]not to circumcise[4059] their children nor to walk according to [c]the customs.

22 "What, then, is *to be done*? They will certainly hear that you have [pf]come.

23 "Therefore do this that we tell you. We have four men who [I][a]are under a vow;

24 take them and [a]purify[48] yourself along with them, and [I]pay their expenses in order that they may [b]shave their [II]heads; and all will know that there is nothing to the things which they have been told about you, but that you yourself also walk orderly, [ppt]keeping the Law.

25 "But concerning the Gentiles who have [pfp]believed, we wrote, [a]having [apt]decided[2919] that they should [pinf]abstain from [I]meat sacrificed to idols and from blood and from what is strangled and from fornication."[4202]

26 Then Paul [apt] [I]took the men, and the next day, [aptp] [a]purifying himself along with them, [b]went into the temple,[2411] [ppt]giving notice[1229] of the completion[1604] of the days of purification,[49] until the sacrifice[4376] was offered for each one of them.

Paul Seized in the Temple

27 And when [a]the seven days were almost[3195] over,[4931] [b]the Jews from [I][c]Asia, upon seeing him in the temple, *began* to [ipf]stir up all the multitude and [ao]laid hands on him,

28 crying out, "Men of Israel, come to our aid! [a]This is the man[444] who [ppt]preaches[1321] to all men everywhere against our people, and the Law,[3551] and this place; and besides he has even brought Greeks into the temple and has [b]defiled[2840] this holy[40] place."

29 For they had previously seen [a]Trophimus the [b]Ephesian in the city with him, and they supposed that Paul had brought him into the temple.

30 And all the city was aroused, and [I]the people rushed together; and taking hold of Paul, they [a]dragged[1670] him out of the temple; and immediately the doors were shut.

31 And while they were seeking to kill him, a report came up to the [I]commander of the [a]*Roman* [II]cohort that all Jerusalem was in confusion.

32 And at once he [a]took along *some* soldiers and centurions, and ran down to them; and when they saw the [I]commander and the soldiers, they stopped beating[5180] Paul.

33 Then the [I]commander came up and took hold of him, and ordered him to be [a]bound with [b]two chains; and he *began* asking who he was and what he had done.

14 [a]Luke 22:42
15 [a]Acts 21:12
16 [a]Acts 21:4 [b]Acts 8:40 [c]Acts 4:36; 21:3 [d]Acts 15:7
17 [a]Acts 1:15; 21:7
18 [I]Or, *Jacob* [a]Acts 12:17 [b]Acts 11:30
19 [a]Acts 14:27 [b]Acts 1:17
20 [I]Lit., *ten thousands* [a]Matt. 9:8 [b]Acts 15:1; 22:3; Rom. 10:2; Gal. 1:14
21 [a]Acts 21:28 [b]Acts 15:19ff.; 1Cor. 7:18f. [c]Acts 6:14
23 [I]Lit., *have a vow on them* [a]Num. 6:13-21; Acts 18:18
24 [I]Lit., *spend on them* [II]Lit., *head* [a]John 11:55; Acts 21:26; 24:18 [b]Acts 18:18
25 [I]Lit., *the thing* [a]Acts 15:19f., 29
26 [I]Or, *took the men the next day, and purifying himself* [a]John 11:55; Acts 21:24; 24:18 [b]Num. 6:13; Acts 24:18
27 [I]I.e., west coast province of Asia Minor [a]Num. 6:9, 13-20 [b]Acts 20:19; 24:18 [c]Acts 16:6
28 [a]Acts 6:13 [b]Matt. 24:15; Acts 6:13f.; 24:6
29 [a]Acts 20:4 [b]Acts 18:19
30 [I]Lit., *a running together of the people occurred* [a]2Kin. 11:15; Acts 16:19; 26:21
31 [I]I.e., chiliarch, in command of one thousand troops [II]Or, *battalion* [a]Acts 10:1
32 [I]V. 31, note 1 [a]Acts 23:27
33 [I]V. 31, note 1 [a]Acts 20:23; 21:11; 22:29; 26:29; 28:20; Eph. 6:20; 2Tim. 1:16; 2:9 [b]Acts 12:6

21:14 See note on I Tim. 2:9-15 and also *hēsuchazō* (2270), to hold peace, calm.
21:27ff See note on II Tim. 4:20.

34 But among the crowd [a]some were [ipf]shouting one thing *and* some another, and when he could not find out the [I]facts on account of the uproar, he ordered him to be brought into [b]the barracks.

35 And when he got to [a]the stairs, it so happened that he was carried by the soldiers because of the violence of the [I]mob;

36 for the multitude of the people kept following behind, crying out, "[a]Away with him!"

37 And as Paul was about to be brought into [a]the barracks, he said to the [I]commander, "May I say something to you?" And he *said, "Do you know Greek?

38 "Then you are not [a]the Egyptian who some [I]time ago stirred up a [apt]revolt[387] and [apt]led the four thousand men of the Assassins[4607] out [b]into the wilderness?"

39 But Paul said, "[a]I am a Jew of Tarsus in [b]Cilicia, a citizen of no insignificant city; and I beg[1189] you, allow me to speak to the people."

40 And when he had given him permission, Paul, standing on [a]the stairs, [b]motioned to the people with his hand; and when there [I]was a great hush, he spoke to them in the [II][c]Hebrew dialect, saying,

Paul's Defense before the Jews

22 "[a]Brethren[80] and fathers,[3962] hear my defense[627] which I now *offer* to you."

🔑 2 And when they heard that he was addressing them in the [I][a]Hebrew dialect, they became even more quiet; and he *said,

3 "[a]I am [b]a Jew, born in [c]Tarsus of [d]Cilicia, but brought up in this city, educated[3811] [I]under [e]Gamaliel, [II][f]strictly according to the law of our fathers, being zealous for God, just as [g]you all are today.

4 "And [a]I persecuted this [b]Way[3598] to the death, binding and putting both men and women into prisons,

5 as also [a]the high priest and all [b]the Council[4244] of the elders [I]can testify.[3140] From them I also [c]received letters to [d]the brethren, and started off for [e]Damascus in order to bring even those who were there to Jerusalem [II]as prisoners to be punished.[5097]

6 "[a]And it came about that as I was on my way, approaching Damascus about noontime, a very bright light suddenly flashed from heaven all around me,

7 and I fell to the ground and heard a voice saying to me, 'Saul, Saul, why are you persecuting Me?'

8 "And I answered, 'Who art Thou, Lord?'[2962] And He said to me, 'I am [a]Jesus the Nazarene, whom you are persecuting.'

9 "And those who were with me [a]beheld the light, to be sure, but [b]did not [I]understand the voice of the One who was [ppt]speaking to me.

10 "And I said, '[a]What shall I do, Lord?' And the Lord said to me, 'Arise and go on into Damascus; and there you will be told of all that has been appointed[5021] for you to do.'

11 "But since I [ipf] [a]could not see[1689] because of the [I]brightness[1391] of that light, I was led by the hand by those who were with me, and came into Damascus.

12 "And a certain [a]Ananias, a man who was devout[2126] by the standard of the Law, *and* [b]well spoken[3140] of by all the Jews who lived there,

13 came to me, and standing near said to me, '[a]Brother Saul, receive your sight!' And [I][b]at that very time I looked up at him.

14 "And he said, '[a]The God of our fathers has [b]appointed you to know His will, and to [c]see the [d]Righteous[1342] One,

34 [I]Lit., *certainty* [a]Acts 19:32 [b]Acts 21:37; 22:24; 23:10, 16, 32
35 [I]Or, *multitude* [a]Acts 21:40
36 [a]Luke 23:18; John 19:15; Acts 22:22
37 [I]V. 31, note 1 [a]Acts 21:34; 22:24; 23:10, 16, 32
38 [I]Lit., *days* [a]Acts 5:36 [b]Matt. 24:26
39 [a]Acts 9:11; 22:3 [b]Acts 6:9
40 [I]Lit., *occurred* [II]I.e., Jewish Aramaic [a]Acts 21:35 [b]Acts 12:17 [c]John 5:2; Acts 1:19; 22:2; 26:14

1 [a]Acts 7:2
2 [I]I.e., Jewish Aramaic [a]Acts 21:40
3 [I]Lit., *at the feet of* [II]Lit., *according to the strictness of the ancestral law* [a]Acts 9:1-22; 22:3-16; 26:9-18 [b]Acts 21:39 [c]Acts 9:11 [d]Acts 6:9 [e]Acts 5:34 [f]Acts 23:6; 26:5; Phil. 3:6 [g]Acts 21:20
4 [a]Acts 8:3; 22:19f.; 26:9-11 [b]Acts 9:2
5 [I]Lit., *testifies for me* [II]Lit., *having been bound* [a]Acts 9:1 [b]Luke 22:66; Acts 5:21; 1Tim. 4:14 [c]Acts 9:2 [d]Acts 2:29; 3:17; 13:26; 23:1; 28:17, 21; Rom. 9:3 [e]Acts 9:2
6 [a]Acts 22:6-11: *Acts 9:3-8; 26:12-18*
8 [a]Acts 26:9
9 [I]Or, *hear* (with comprehension) [a]Acts 26:13 [b]Acts 9:7
10 [a]Acts 16:30
11 [I]Or, *glory* [a]Acts 9:8
12 [a]Acts 9:10 [b]Acts 6:3; 10:22
13 [I]Or, *instantly;* lit., *at that very hour* [a]Acts 9:17 [b]Acts 9:18
14 [a]Acts 3:13 [b]Acts 9:15; 26:16 [c]Acts 9:17; 26:16; 1Cor. 9:1; 15:8 [d]Acts 7:52

🔑 **22:2** See note on I Tim. 2:9-15.

and to hear an [I]utterance from His mouth.

15 'For you will be [a]a witness for Him to all men of [b]what you have seen and heard.

16 'And now why do you delay? [a]Arise, and be baptized,[907] and [b]wash away[628] your sins,[266] [apt] [c]calling on His name.'

17 "And it came about when I [a]returned to Jerusalem and was [ppt]praying in the temple,[2411] that I [b]fell into a trance,[1611]

18 and I saw Him saying to me, '[a]Make haste, and get out of Jerusalem quickly, because they will not accept[3858] your testimony[3141] about Me.'

19 "And I said, 'Lord, they themselves understand that in one synagogue after another [a]I used to imprison 5439 and [b]beat those who [ppt]believed[4100] in Thee.

20 'And [a]when the blood[129] of Thy witness[3144] Stephen was being [ipf]shed, I also was standing by approving, and [ppt]watching out for the cloaks of those who were [ppt]slaying him.'

21 "And He said to me, 'Go! For I will send you far away [a]to the Gentiles.' "[1484]

22 And they [ipf]listened to him up to this statement, and *then* they raised their voices and said, "[a]Away with such a fellow from the earth, for [b]he should not be allowed to live!"[2198]

23 And as they were [ppt]crying out and [ppt] [a]throwing off their cloaks and [ppt] [b]tossing dust into the air,

24 the [I]commander ordered him to be brought into [a]the barracks,[3925] stating that he should be [b]examined by scourging 3148 so that he might find out the reason why they were [ipf]shouting against him that way.

25 And when they stretched him out [I]with thongs, Paul said to the centurion who was standing by, "Is it lawful for you to [pinf]scourge 3147 [a]a man who is a Roman and uncondemned?"

26 And when the centurion heard *this,* he went to the [I]commander and told him, saying, "What are you about to do? For this man is a Roman."

27 And the [I]commander came and said to him, "Tell me, are you a Roman?" And he said, "Yes."

28 And the [I]commander answered, "I acquired this citizenship with a large sum of money." And Paul said, "But I was actually born *a citizen.*"

29 Therefore those who were about to [a]examine him immediately[2112] [I]let go[868] of him; and the [II]commander also [b]was afraid when he found out that he was a Roman, and because he had [III][c]put him in chains.

30 But on the next day, [a]wishing to know for certain why he had been accused by the Jews, he [b]released him and ordered the chief priests and all [c]the [I]Council to assemble, and brought Paul down 2609 and set him before them.

Paul before the Council

23 And Paul, looking intently at [a]the [I]Council, 4892 said, "[b]Brethren,[80] [c]I have [II]lived my life with a perfectly good[18] conscience[4893] before God up to this day."

2 And the high priest[749] [a]Ananias commanded[2004] those standing beside him [b]to strike[5180] him on the mouth.

3 Then Paul said to him, "God is going to strike you, [a]you whitewashed wall! And do you [b]sit to [ppt]try[2919] me according to the Law,[3551] and in violation of the Law 3891 order me to be struck?"

4 But the bystanders said, "Do you revile[3058] God's high priest?"

5 And Paul said, "I was not aware, brethren, that he was high priest; for it is written, '[a]YOU SHALL NOT SPEAK EVIL OF A RULER OF YOUR PEOPLE.' "

6 But perceiving that one part were [a]Sadducees and the other Pharisees, Paul *began* crying out in [b]the [I]Council,

14 [I]Or, *message;* lit., *voice*
15 [a]Acts 23:11; 26:16 [b]Acts 22:14
16 [a]Acts 9:18 [b]Acts 2:38; 1Cor. 6:11; Eph. 5:26; Heb. 10:22 [c]Acts 7:59
17 [a]Acts 9:26; 26:20 [b]Acts 10:10
18 [a]Acts 9:29
19 [a]Acts 8:3; 22:4 [b]Matt. 10:17; Acts 26:11
20 [a]Acts 7:58f.; 8:1; 26:10
21 [a]Acts 9:15
22 [a]Acts 21:36; 1Thess. 2:16 [b]Acts 25:24
23 [a]Acts 7:58 [b]2Sam. 16:13
24 [I]I.e., chiliarch, in command of one thousand troops [a]Acts 21:34 [b]Acts 22:29
25 [I]Lit., *for the thongs* [a]Acts 16:37
26 [I]V. 24, note 1
27 [I]V. 24, note 1
28 [I]V. 24, note 1
29 [I]Or, *withdrew from* [II]V. 24, note 1 [III]Lit., *bound him* [a]Acts 22:24 [b]Acts 16:38 [c]Acts 21:33
30 [I]Or, *Sanhedrin* [a]Acts 23:28 [b]Acts 21:33 [c]Matt. 5:22

1 [I]Or, *Sanhedrin* [II]Or, *conducted myself as a citizen* [a]Acts 22:30; 23:6, 15, 20, 28 [b]Acts 22:5 [c]Acts 24:16; 2Cor. 1:12; 2Tim. 1:3
2 [a]Acts 24:1 [b]John 18:22
3 [a]Matt. 23:27 [b]Lev. 19:15; Deut. 25:2; John 7:51
5 [a]Ex. 22:28
6 [I]Or, *Sanhedrin* [a]Matt. 3:7; 22:23 [b]Acts 22:30; 23:1, 15, 20, 28

22:16 See note on I Pet. 3:20,21.
22:29 See notes on II Thess. 2:3; Col. 4:10.

"[c]Brethren, [d]I am a Pharisee, a son of Pharisees; I am on trial[2919] for [e]the hope[1680] and resurrection[386] of the dead!"

7 And as he said this, there arose a dissension[4714] between the Pharisees and Sadducees; and the assembly was divided.

8 For [a]the Sadducees say that there is no resurrection, nor an angel,[32] nor a spirit;[4151] but the Pharisees acknowledge[3760] them all.

9 And there arose a great uproar; and some of [a]the scribes[1122] of the Pharisaic party [apt]stood up and *began* to [ipf]argue heatedly, saying, "[b]We find nothing wrong with this man; [c]suppose a spirit or an angel has spoken to him?"

🗝 10 And as a great dissension[4714] was developing, the [I]commander was afraid[2125] Paul would be torn to pieces by them and ordered the troops to go down and take him away from them by force,[726] and bring him into [a]the barracks.

11 But on [a]the night *immediately* following, the Lord[2962] stood at his side and said, "[b]Take courage; for [c]as you have [d]solemnly witnessed[1263] to My cause at Jerusalem, so you must witness[3140] at Rome also."

A Conspiracy to Kill Paul

12 And when it was day, [a]the Jews formed a [I]conspiracy and [b]bound themselves under an oath,[332] saying that they would neither eat nor drink until they had killed Paul.

13 And there were more than forty who formed this plot.

14 And they came to the chief priests and the elders, and said, "We have [a]bound ourselves under a solemn oath[331] to taste[1089] nothing until we have killed Paul.

15 "Now, therefore, you [I]and [a]the [II]Council notify the [III]commander to bring him down to you, as though you were going to determine his case by a more thorough investigation;[1231] and we for our part are ready to slay him before he comes near *the place.*"

16 But the son of Paul's sister heard of their ambush, [I]and he came and entered [a]the barracks and told Paul.

17 And Paul called one of the centurions to him and said, "Lead this young man to the [I]commander, for he has something to report to him."

18 So he took him and led him to the [I]commander and *said, "Paul [a]the prisoner [apt]called me to him and asked me to lead this young man to you since he has something to tell you."

19 And the [I]commander took him by the hand and stepping aside, *began* to inquire of him privately, "What is it that you have to report to me?"

20 And he said, "[a]The Jews have agreed to ask you to bring Paul down tomorrow to [b]the [I]Council, as though they were going to inquire somewhat more thoroughly about him.

21 "So do not [I]listen[3982] to them, for more than forty of them are [a]lying in wait for him who have [b]bound themselves under a curse[332] not to eat or drink until they slay him; and now they are ready and waiting for[4327] the promise[1860] from you."

22 Therefore the [I]commander let the young man go, instructing him, "Tell no one that you have notified me of these things."

Paul Moved to Caesarea

23 And he called to him two of the centurions, and said, "Get two hundred soldiers ready by [I]the third hour of the night to proceed to [a]Caesarea, [II]with seventy horsemen and two hundred [III]spearmen."

24 *They were* also to provide mounts to put Paul on and bring him safely[1295] to [a]Felix the governor.

25 And he [apt]wrote[1125] a letter having this form:[5179]

---

6 [c]Acts 22:5 [d]Acts 26:5; Phil. 3:5 [e]Acts 24:15, 21; 26:8

8 [a]Matt. 22:23; Mark 12:18; Luke 20:27

9 [a]Mark 2:16; Luke 5:30 [b]Acts 23:29 [c]John 12:29; Acts 22:6ff.

10 [I]I.e., chiliarch, in command of one thousand troops [a]Acts 21:34; 23:16, 32

11 [a]Acts 18:9 [b]Matt. 9:2 [c]Acts 19:21 [d]Luke 16:28; Acts 28:23

12 [I]Or, *mob* [a]Acts 9:23; 23:30; 1Thess. 2:16 [b]Acts 23:14, 21

14 [a]Acts 23:12, 21

15 [I]Lit., *with* [II]Or, *Sanhedrin* [III]V. 10, note 1 [a]Acts 22:30; 23:1, 6, 20, 28

16 [I]Or, *having been present* with them, *and he entered* [a]Acts 21:34; 23:10, 32

17 [I]V. 10, note 1

18 [I]V. 10, note 1 [a]Eph. 3:1

19 [I]V. 10, note 1

20 [I]Or, *Sanhedrin* [a]Acts 23:14f. [b]Acts 22:30; 23:1, 6, 15, 28

21 [I]Lit., *be persuaded by them* [a]Luke 11:54 [b]Acts 23:12, 14

22 [I]V. 10, note 1

23 [I]I.e., 9 p.m. [II]Lit., *and* [III]Or, *slingers* or *bowmen* [a]Acts 8:40; 23:33

24 [a]Acts 23:26, 33; 24:1, 3, 10; 25:14

🗝 **23:10** See note on I Thess. 4:17.

26 "Claudius Lysias, to the [a]most
excellent governor Felix,
[b]greetings.[5463]
27 "When this man was [aptp]ar-
rested by the Jews and was
about to be slain by them,
[a]I came upon them with the
troops and rescued him,
[b]having learned[3129] that he
was a Roman.
28 "And [a]wanting to ascertain
the charge for which they
were [ipf]accusing[1458] him, I
[b]brought him down[2609] to their
[Ic]Council;
29 and I found him to be [ppp]ac-
cused over [a]questions about
their Law,[3551] but [I]under
[b]no accusation[1462] deserving
death or [II]imprisonment.
30 "And when I was [a]informed
that there would be [b]a plot
against the man, I sent him
to you at once,[1824] also instructing [c]his accusers[2725] to
[I]bring charges against him before you.[II]"
31 So the soldiers, in accordance
with their orders,[1299] took Paul and
brought him by night to Antipatris.
32 But the next day, leaving [a]the
horsemen to go on with him, they returned to [b]the barracks.
33 And when these had come to
[a]Caesarea and delivered the letter[1992]
to [b]the governor, they also presented
Paul to him.
34 And when he had read it, he
asked from what [a]province he was; and
when he learned that [b]he was from Cilicia,
35 he said, "I will give you a hearing
after your [a]accusers arrive also," giving
orders for him to be [b]kept in Herod's
[I]Praetorium.

Paul before Felix

24 And after [a]five days the high
priest[749] [b]Ananias came down
with some elders,[4245] [I]with a certain
[II]attorney *named* Tertullus; and they
[III]brought charges to [c]the governor
against Paul.
2 And after *Paul* had been summoned, Tertullus began to accuse him,
saying *to the governor*,
"Since[1492] we have through you attained much peace,[1515] and since by your
providence[4307] reforms are being carried
out for this nation,
3 we acknowledge[588] *this* in every
way and everywhere, [a]most excellent
Felix, with all thankfulness.
4 "But, that I may not weary you
any further, I beg[3870] you [I]to grant us,
by your kindness,[1932] a brief hearing.
5 "For we have [apt]found this man
a real pest[3061] and a fellow who stirs
up dissension[4714] among all the Jews
throughout [I]the world, and a ringleader
of the [a]sect of the Nazarenes.
6 "And he even tried[3985] to [a]dese-
crate[953] the temple;[2411] and [I]then we
arrested him. [[II]And we wanted to judge
him according to our own Law.
7 "But Lysias the commander came
along, and with much violence took him
out of our hands,
8 [apt]ordering his accusers[2725] to
come before you.] And by examining
him yourself concerning all these matters, you will be able to[1410] ascertain
the things of which we accuse him."
9 And [a]the Jews also joined in the
attack, asserting that these things were
so.
10 And when [a]the governor had
nodded for him to speak, Paul responded:
"**K**nowing that for many years you
have been a judge to this nation, I cheerfully make my defense,
11 since you can take note of the
fact that no more than [a]twelve days ago
I went up to Jerusalem to worship.
12 "And [a]neither in the temple, nor
in the synagogues,[4864] nor in the city
itself did they find me carrying on a
discussion with anyone or [b]causing [I]a
riot.
13 "[a]Nor can they prove to you *the
charges* of which they now accuse me.
14 "But this I admit[3670] to you, that

26 [a]Luke 1:3; Acts 24:3; 26:25 [b]Acts 15:23
27 [a]Acts 21:32f. [b]Acts 22:25-29
28 [I]Or, *Sanhedrin* [a]Acts 22:30 [b]Acts 23:10 [c]Acts 23:1
29 [I]Lit., *having* [II]Lit., *bonds* [a]Acts 18:15; 25:19 [b]Acts 23:9; 25:25; 26:31; 28:18
30 [I]Lit., *speak against him* [II]Some mss. add *Farewell* [a]Acts 23:20f. [b]Acts 9:24; 23:12 [c]Acts 23:35; 24:19; 25:16
32 [a]Acts 23:23 [b]Acts 23:10
33 [a]Acts 8:40; 23:23 [b]Acts 23:24, 26; 24:1, 3, 10; 25:14
34 [a]Acts 25:1 [b]Acts 6:9; 21:39
35 [I]I.e., governor's official residence [a]Acts 23:30; 24:19; 25:16 [b]Acts 24:27

1 [I]Lit., *and* [II]Lit., *orator* [III]Or, *presented their evidence* or *case* [a]Acts 24:11 [b]Acts 23:2 [c]Acts 23:24
3 [a]Acts 23:26; 26:25
4 [I]Lit., *to hear . . . briefly*
5 [I]Lit., *the inhabited earth* [a]Acts 15:5; 24:14
6 [I]Lit., *also* [II]Many mss. do not contain the remainder of v. 6, v. 7, nor the first part of v. 8 [a]Acts 21:28
9 [a]1 Thess. 2:16
10 [a]Acts 23:24
11 [a]Acts 21:18, 27; 24:1
12 [I]Lit., *an attack of a mob* [a]Acts 25:8 [b]Acts 24:18
13 [a]Acts 25:7

according to [a]the Way[3598] which they
call a [b]sect[139] I do serve[3000] [Ic]the God[2316]
of our fathers, [d]believing[4100] everything
that is in accordance with the Law,[3551]
and that is written in the Prophets;[4396]
15 having a hope[1680] in God, which
[a]these men cherish[4327] themselves, that
there shall certainly be a resurrection[386]
of both the righteous[1342] and the
wicked.[94]
16 "In view of this, [a]I also [I]do my
best to maintain always a blameless[677]
conscience[4893] *both* before[4314] God and
before men.[444]
17 "Now [a]after several years I
[b]came to bring [I]alms to my nation and
to present offerings;[4376]
18 in which they found me *occupied*
in the temple,[2411] having been [a]puri-
fied,[48] without *any* [b]crowd or uproar.
But *there were* certain [c]Jews from
[I]Asia—
19 who ought to have been present
before you, and to [a]make accusation, if
they should have anything against me.
20 "Or else let these men themselves tell what misdeed[92] they found
when I stood before [a]the [I]Council,
21 other than for this one statement
which [a]I shouted out while standing
among them, 'For the resurrection of
the dead I am on trial[2919] before you
today.' "
22 But Felix, having a more exact
knowledge about [a]the Way,[3598] put them
off, saying, "When Lysias the [I]comman-
der comes down, I will decide[1231] your
case."
23 And he [apt]gave orders[1299] to the
centurion for him to be [a]kept[5083] in custody and *yet* [b]have *some* freedom,[425] and
not to prevent any of [c]his friends from
ministering to him.
24 But some days later, Felix arrived with Drusilla, his [I]wife who was
a Jewess, and sent for Paul, and heard
him *speak* about [a]faith[4102] in Christ[5547]
Jesus.
25 And as he was discussing [a]righ-
teousness,[1343] [b]self-control[1466] and [c]the
judgment[2917] to come, Felix became
frightened and said, "Go away for the
present, and when I find time,[2540] I will
summon[3333] you."
26 At the same time too, he was
hoping that [a]money[5536] would be given
him by Paul; therefore he also used to
send for him quite often and converse
with him.
27 But after[4137] two years had
passed, Felix [I]was succeeded[1240] by
Porcius [a]Festus; and [b]wishing to do the
Jews a favor, Felix left Paul [c]imprisoned.

Paul before Festus

25 Festus therefore, having arrived
in [a]the province, three days later
went up to Jerusalem from [b]Caesarea.
2 And the chief priests and the leading men of the Jews [a]brought charges
against Paul; and they were [ipf]urging[3870]
him,
3 [ppt]requesting a [I]concession[5485]
against [II]Paul, that he might [III]have him
brought to Jerusalem (*at the same time,*
[a]setting an ambush to kill him on the
way).
4 Festus then [a]answered that Paul
[b]was being kept[5083] in custody at
[c]Caesarea and that he himself was about
to leave shortly.
5 "Therefore," he *said, "let the influential men among you [I]go there with
me, and if there is anything wrong
[II]about the man, let them [III]prosecute
him."
6 And after he had spent not more
than eight or ten days among them, he
went down to [a]Caesarea; and on the
next day he took his seat on [b]the tribunal
and ordered Paul to be brought.
7 And after he had arrived, the Jews
who had come down from Jerusalem
stood around him, bringing[5342] [a]many
and serious charges[157] against him
[b]which they could not prove;
8 while Paul said in his own defense,
"[a]I have committed no offense either
against the Law[3551] of the Jews or
against the temple[2411] or against Caesar."

14 [I]Lit., *the ancestral god* [a]Acts 9:2; 24:22 [b]Acts 15:5; 24:5 [c]Acts 3:13 [d]Acts 25:8; 26:4ff., 22f.; 28:23
15 [a]Dan. 12:2; John 5:28f.; 11:24; Acts 23:6
16 [I]Lit., *practice myself* [a]Acts 23:1
17 [I]Or, *gifts to charity* [a]Acts 20:31 [b]Acts 11:29f.; Rom. 15:25-28; 1Cor. 16:1-4; 2Cor. 8:1-4; 9:1, 2, 12; Gal. 2:10
18 [I]I.e., west coast province of Asia Minor [a]Acts 21:26 [b]Acts 24:12 [c]Acts 21:27
19 [a]Acts 23:30
20 [I]Or, *Sanhedrin* [a]Matt. 5:22
21 [a]Acts 23:6; 24:15
22 [I]I.e., chiliarch, in command of one thousand troops [a]Acts 24:14
23 [a]Acts 23:35 [b]Acts 28:16 [c]Acts 23:16; 27:3
24 [I]Lit., *own wife* [a]Acts 20:21
25 [a]Titus 2:12 [b]Gal. 5:23; Titus 1:8; 2Pet. 1:6 [c]Acts 10:42
26 [a]Acts 24:17
27 [I]Lit., *received a successor, Porcius Festus* [a]Acts 25:1, 4, 9, 12; 26:24f., 32 [b]Acts 12:3; 25:9 [c]Acts 23:35; 25:14

1 [a]Acts 23:34 [b]Acts 8:40; 25:4, 6, 13
2 [a]Acts 24:1; 25:15
3 [I]Or, *favor* [II]Lit., *him* [III]Lit., *send for him to Jerusalem* [a]Acts 9:24
4 [a]Acts 25:16 [b]Acts 24:23 [c]Acts 8:40; 25:1, 6, 13
5 [I]Lit., *go down* [II]Lit., *in* [III]Or, *accuse*
6 [a]Acts 8:40; 25:1, 4, 13 [b]Matt. 27:19; Acts 25:10, 17
7 [a]Acts 24:5f. [b]Acts 24:13
8 [a]Acts 6:13; 24:12; 28:17

9 But Festus, [a]wishing to do the Jews a favor,[5485] answered Paul and said, "[b]Are you willing to go up to Jerusalem and [I]stand trial[2919] before me on these *charges*?"

10 But Paul said, "I am standing before Caesar's [a]tribunal, where I ought to be tried. I have done no wrong[91] to *the* Jews, as you also very well know.

11 "If then I am a wrongdoer,[91] and have committed anything worthy of death, I do not refuse[3868] to die; but if none of those things is *true* of which these men accuse me, no one can hand me over[5483] to them. I [a]appeal to Caesar."

12 Then when Festus had conferred with [I]his council, he answered, "You have appealed to Caesar, to Caesar you shall go."

13 Now when several days had elapsed, King Agrippa and Bernice arrived at [a]Caesarea, [I]and paid their respects to Festus.

14 And while they were spending many days there, Festus laid Paul's case before the king, saying, "There is a certain man [a]left a prisoner by Felix;

15 and when I was at Jerusalem, the chief priests[749] and the elders[4245] of the Jews [a]brought charges against him, asking for a sentence of condemnation[1349] upon him.

16 "And I [a]answered them that it is not the custom of the Romans to hand over[5483] any man before [b]the accused meets his accusers[2725] face to face,[4383] and has an opportunity to make his defense against the charges.[1462]

17 "And so after they had assembled here, I made no delay, but on the next day took my seat on [a]the tribunal, and ordered the man to be brought.

18 "And when the accusers[2725] stood up, they *began* bringing charges against him not of such crimes as I was expecting;[5282]

19 but they *simply* had some [a]points of disagreement with him about their own [Ib]religion[1175] and about a certain dead man, Jesus, whom Paul asserted to be alive.[2198]

20 "And [a]being at a loss how to investigate [I]such matters, I [ipf]asked whether he was willing to go to Jerusalem and there stand trial on these matters.

21 "But when Paul [a]appealed to be held in custody[5083] for [I]the Emperor's[4575] decision,[1233] I ordered him to be kept[5083] in custody until I send him to Caesar."

22 And [a]Agrippa *said* to Festus, "I also would like to hear the man myself." "Tomorrow," he *said, "you shall hear him."

Paul before Agrippa

23 And so, on the next day when [a]Agrippa had come [I]together with [a]Bernice, amid great pomp,[5325] and had entered the auditorium [II]accompanied by the [III]commanders and the prominent men of the city, at the command of Festus, Paul was brought in.

24 And Festus *said, "King Agrippa, and all you gentlemen here present with us, you behold this man about whom [a]all the people of the Jews appealed to me, both at Jerusalem and here, loudly declaring that [b]he ought not to live any longer.

25 "But I found that he had committed [a]nothing worthy of death; and since he himself [b]appealed[1941] to [I]the Emperor,[4575] I decided[2919] to send him.

26 "[I]Yet I have nothing definite about him to write to my lord. Therefore I have brought him before[4254] you *all* and especially before you, King Agrippa, so that after the investigation has taken place, I may have something to write.[1125]

27 "For it seems absurd to me in sending a prisoner, not to indicate also[2532] the charges against him."

Paul's Defense before Agrippa

26 And [a]Agrippa said to Paul, "You are permitted to speak for yourself." Then Paul stretched out his hand and *proceeded* to make his defense:

2 "In regard[4012] to all the things of

9 [I]Lit., *be judged* [a]Acts 12:3; 24:27 [b]Acts 25:20
10 [a]Matt. 27:19; Acts 25:6, 17
11 [a]Acts 25:21, 25; 26:32; 28:19
12 [I]A different body from that mentioned in Acts 4:15 and 24:20
13 [I]Lit., *greeting Festus* [a]Acts 8:40; 25:1, 4, 6
14 [a]Acts 24:27
15 [a]Acts 24:1; 25:2
16 [a]Acts 25:4f. [b]Acts 23:30
17 [a]Matt. 27:19; Acts 25:6, 10
19 [I]Or, *superstition* [a]Acts 18:15; 23:29 [b]Acts 17:22
20 [I]Lit., *these* [a]Acts 25:9
21 [I]Lit., *the Augustus'* (in this case Nero) [a]Acts 25:11f.
22 [a]Acts 9:15
23 [I]Lit., *and Bernice* [II]Lit., *and with* [III]I.e., chiliarchs, in command of one thousand troops [a]Acts 25:13; 26:30
24 [a]Acts 25:2, 7 [b]Acts 22:22
25 [I]V. 21, note 1 [a]Luke 23:4; Acts 23:29 [b]Acts 25:11f.
26 [I]Lit., *About whom I have nothing definite*
1 [a]Acts 9:15

which I am accused[1458] by the Jews, I consider[2233] myself fortunate,[3107] King[935] Agrippa, that I am about to make my defense before you today;

3 [I]especially because you are an expert[1109] in all [a]customs and [II]questions among *the* Jews; therefore I beg[1189] you to listen to me patiently.

4 "So then, all Jews know [a]my manner of life from my youth[3503] up, which from the beginning was spent among my *own* nation[1484] and at Jerusalem;

5 since they have known[4267] about me for a long time previously,[509] if they are willing[2309] to testify, that I [ao]lived *as* a [a]Pharisee [b]according to the strictest[296] [c]sect[139] of our religion.[2356]

6 "And now I am [I]standing trial[2919] [a]for the hope of [b]the promise[1860] made by God[2316] to our fathers;

7 *the promise* [a]to which our twelve tribes hope to attain, as they earnestly serve *God* night and day. And for this [b]hope, O King, I am being [c]accused by Jews.

8 "Why is it considered[2919] incredible[571] among you *people* [a]if God does [pin]raise[1453] the dead?[3498]

9 "So[3303] then, [a]I thought to myself that I had to [ainf]do many things hostile to [b]the name[3686] of Jesus of Nazareth.

10 "And this is [I]just what I [a]did in Jerusalem; not only did I lock up many of the [II]saints[40] in prisons, having [b]received authority[1849] from the chief priests, but also when they were being put to death I [c]cast my vote against them.

11 "And [a]as I punished[5097] them often in all the synagogues, I tried to [ipf]force[315] them to blaspheme;[987] and being [b]furiously[4057] [ppt]enraged at them, I kept pursuing them [c]even to [I]foreign cities.

12 "[I]While thus engaged [a]as I was [ppt]journeying to Damascus with the authority[1849] and commission of the chief priests,

13 at midday,[2250] O King, I saw on the way a light from heaven, [I]brighter than the sun, [apt]shining all around me and those who were [ppt]journeying with me.

14 "And when we had [a]all fallen to the ground, I heard a voice saying to me in the [I][b]Hebrew dialect, 'Saul, Saul, why are you persecuting Me? It is hard for you to kick against the goads.'

15 "And I said, 'Who art Thou, Lord?'[2962] And the Lord said, 'I am Jesus whom you are persecuting.

16 'But arise, and [a]stand on your feet; for this purpose I have [aop]appeared to you, to [b]appoint you a [c]minister[5257] and [d]a witness[3144] not only to the things which you have [I]seen, but also to the things in which I will appear to you;

17 [a]delivering you [b]from the *Jewish* people and from the Gentiles,[1484] to whom I am sending you,

18 to [a]open their eyes so that they may turn[1994] from [b]darkness[4655] to light[5457] and from the dominion[1849] of [c]Satan[4567] to God,[2316] in order that they may receive[2983] [d]forgiveness[859] of sins[266] and an [e]inheritance[2819] among those who have been sanctified[37] by [f]faith[4102] in Me.'

19 "Consequently, King Agrippa, I did not prove disobedient[545] to the heavenly[3770] vision,[3701]

20 but *kept* [ipf]declaring both [a]to those of Damascus first, and *also* [b]at Jerusalem and *then* throughout all the region of Judea, and *even* [c]to the Gentiles, that they should [pinf] [d]repent[3340] and [pinf]turn[1994] to God, [ppt]performing deeds [e]appropriate[514] to repentance.[3341]

21 "For this reason *some* Jews [apt] [a]seized me in the temple[2411] and [ipf]tried[3987] [b]to put me to death.

22 "And so, having obtained[5177] help from God, I stand to this day [a]testifying[3140] both to small and great, stating nothing but what [b]the Prophets[4396] and Moses said was going to take place;

23 [I][a]that [II]the Christ[5547] was [III]to suffer,[3805] *and* [I]that [b]by reason of *His* resurrection[386] from the dead[3498] He

[a]Matt. 26:24; Acts 3:18 [b]1Cor. 15:20, 23; Col. 1:18; Rev. 1:5

3 [I]Or, *because you are especially expert* [II]Or, *controversial issues* [a]Acts 6:14; 25:19; 26:7
4 [a]Gal. 1:13f.; Phil. 3:5
5 [a]Acts 23:6; Phil. 3:5 [b]Acts 22:3 [c]Acts 15:5
6 [I]Lit., *being tried* [a]Acts 24:15; 28:20 [b]Acts 13:32
7 [a]James 1:1 [b]Acts 24:15; 28:20 [c]Acts 26:2
8 [a]Acts 23:6
9 [a]John 16:2; 1Tim. 1:13 [b]John 15:21
10 [I]Lit., *also* [II]Or, *holy ones* [a]Acts 8:3; 9:13 [b]Acts 9:1f. [c]Acts 22:20
11 [I]Or, *outlying* [a]Matt. 10:17; Acts 22:19 [b]Acts 9:1 [c]Acts 22:5
12 [I]Lit., *In which things* [a]Acts 26:12-18: *9:3-8; 22:6-11*
13 [I]Lit., *above the brightness of*
14 [I]I.e., Jewish Aramaic [a]Acts 9:7 [b]Acts 21:40
16 [I]Some early mss. read *seen Me* [a]Ezek. 2:1; Dan. 10:11 [b]Acts 22:14 [c]Luke 1:2 [d]Acts 22:15
17 [a]Jer. 1:8, 19 [b]1Chr. 16:35; Acts 9:15
18 [a]Is. 35:5; 42:7, 16; Eph. 5:8; Col. 1:13; 1Pet. 2:9 [b]John 1:5; Eph. 5:8; Col. 1:12f.; 1Thess. 5:5; 1Pet. 2:9 [c]Matt. 4:10 [d]Luke 24:47; Acts 2:38 [e]Acts 20:32 [f]Acts 20:21
20 [a]Acts 9:19ff. [b]Acts 9:26-29; 22:17-20 [c]Acts 9:15; 13:46 [d]Acts 3:19 [e]Matt. 3:8; Luke 3:8
21 [a]Acts 21:27, 30 [b]Acts 21:31
22 [a]Luke 16:28 [b]Acts 10:43; 24:14
23 [I]Lit., *whether* [II]I.e., the Messiah [III]Lit., *subject to suffering*

should be the first to [pinf]proclaim[2605] [c]light[5457] both to the *Jewish* people[2992] and to the Gentiles."[1484]

24 And while *Paul* was saying this in his defense, Festus *said in a loud voice, "Paul, you are out of your mind! [I]*Your* great [a]learning[1121] is [II]driving you mad."[3130]

25 But Paul *said, "I am not out of my mind, [a]most excellent Festus, but I utter words[4487] [I]of sober[4997] truth.[225]

26 "For the king[935] [Ia]knows about these matters, and I speak to him also with confidence, [II]since I am persuaded that none of these things escape his notice; for this has not been done in a corner.

27 "King Agrippa, do you believe[4100] the Prophets?[4396] I know that you [I]do."

28 And Agrippa *replied* to Paul, "[I]In a short time you [II]will persuade me to [ainf] [III]become[4160] a [a]Christian."[5546]

29 And Paul *said,* "I would to God, that whether [II]in a short or long time, not only you, but also all who hear me this day, might become such as I am, except for these [a]chains."

30 And [a]the king arose and the governor and Bernice, and those who were sitting with them,

31 and when they had drawn aside, they *began* [ipf]talking to one another, saying, "[a]This man is not doing anything worthy of death or [I]imprisonment."

32 And Agrippa said to Festus, "This man might have been [a]set free if he had not [b]appealed to[1941] Caesar."

Paul Is Sent to Rome

27 And when it was decided[2919] that [a]we [b]should sail for [c]Italy, they proceeded to deliver Paul and some other prisoners to a centurion of the Augustan[4575] [Id]cohort named Julius.

2 And embarking in[1910] an Adramyttian ship, which was about to sail to the regions along the coast of [Ia]Asia, we put out to sea, accompanied by [b]Aristarchus, a [c]Macedonian of [d]Thessalonica.

3 And the next day we put in[2609] at [a]Sidon; and Julius [b]treated[5530] Paul with consideration[5364] and [c]allowed him to go to his friends and receive care.[5177]

4 And from there we put out to sea and sailed under the shelter of [a]Cyprus because [b]the winds were contrary.

5 And when we had sailed through the sea[3989] along the coast of [a]Cilicia and [b]Pamphylia, we landed at Myra in Lycia.

6 And there the centurion found an [a]Alexandrian ship sailing for [b]Italy, and he put us aboard it.

7 And when we had sailed slowly for a good many days, and with difficulty had arrived off Cnidus, [a]since the wind did not permit us *to go* farther, we sailed under the shelter of [b]Crete, off Salmone;

8 and with difficulty [a]sailing past it we came to a certain place called Fair Havens, near which was the city of Lasea.

9 And when considerable time[5550] had passed and the voyage was now dangerous, since even [a]the [I]fast[3521] was already over, Paul *began* to admonish them,

10 and said to them, "Men,[435] I perceive that the voyage will certainly be *attended* with [a]damage[5196] and great loss, not only of the cargo[5414] and the ship, but also of our lives."[5590]

11 But the centurion was more [ipf]persuaded[3982] by the [a]pilot[2942] and the [I]captain of the ship, than by what was being said by Paul.

12 And because the harbor was not suitable for wintering, the majority reached a decision[1012] to put out to sea from there, if somehow they could reach Phoenix, a harbor of [a]Crete, facing [I]southwest and northwest, and spend the winter *there.*

13 And [I]when a moderate south wind came up, supposing[1380] that they

23 [c]Is. 42:6; 49:6; Luke 2:32; 2Cor. 4:4
24 [I]Lit., *The many letters* [II]Lit., *turning you to madness* [a]John 7:15; 2Tim. 3:15
25 [I]Lit., *of truth and rationality* [a]Acts 23:26; 24:3
26 [I]Or, *understands* [II]Or, *for* [a]Acts 26:3
27 [I]Lit., *believe*
28 [I]Or, *With a little* [II]Or, *try to convince* [III]Lit., *make* [a]Acts 11:26
29 [I]Lit., *I would pray to* [II]Or, *with a little or with much* [a]Acts 21:33
30 [a]Acts 25:23
31 [I]Lit., *bonds* [a]Acts 23:29
32 [a]Acts 28:18 [b]Acts 25:11

1 [I]Or, *battalion* [a]Acts 16:10; 27:1-28 [b]Acts 25:12, 25 [c]Acts 18:2; 27:6 [d]Acts 10:1
2 [I]I.e., west coast province of Asia Minor [a]Acts 2:9 [b]Acts 19:29 [c]Acts 16:9 [d]Acts 17:1
3 [a]Matt. 11:21 [b]Acts 27:43 [c]Acts 24:23
4 [a]Acts 4:36 [b]Acts 27:7
5 [a]Acts 6:9 [b]Acts 13:13
6 [a]Acts 28:11 [b]Acts 18:2; 27:1
7 [a]Acts 27:4 [b]Acts 2:11; 27:12f., 21; Titus 1:5, 12
8 [a]Acts 27:13
9 [I]I.e., Day of Atonement in September or October [a]Lev. 16:29-31; 23:27-29; Num. 29:7
10 [a]Acts 27:21
11 [I]Or, *owner* [a]Rev. 18:17
12 [I]Or possibly, *northeast and southeast* [a]Acts 2:11; 27:13, 21; Titus 1:5, 12

13 [I]Lit., *a south wind having gently blown*

27:2 See note on Col. 4:10.

had gained their purpose,[4286] they weighed anchor[142] and *began* [ipf] [a]sailing along [b]Crete, close *inshore.*

Shipwreck

14 But before very long there [a]rushed[906] down[2596] from [I]the land a violent wind, called [II]Euraquilo;

15 and when the ship was caught *in it,* and could not face the wind, we gave way *to it,* and let ourselves be driven along.

16 And running under the shelter of a small island called [I]Clauda, we were scarcely able to get the *ship's* boat under control.

17 And after they had hoisted it up, they used[5530] [I]supporting cables in undergirding the ship; and fearing that they might [a]run aground on *the shallows* of Syrtis, they let down the [II]sea anchor, and so let themselves be [ipf]driven[5342] along.

18 The next day as we were being violently [ppt]storm-tossed, [I]they began to [ipf] [a]jettison the cargo;

19 and on the third day they threw the ship's tackle[4631] overboard with their own hands.

20 And since neither sun nor stars appeared[2014] for many days, and no small storm was assailing *us,* from then on all hope[1680] of our being saved[4982] was gradually abandoned.

21 And [I]when they had gone a long time without food, then Paul stood up in their midst and said, "[a]Men,[435] you ought to have [II]followed my advice and not to have set sail from [b]Crete, and [III]incurred this [a]damage[5196] and loss.

22 "And *yet* now I urge you to [a]keep up your courage, for there shall be no loss of life among you, but *only* of the ship.

23 "For this very night [a]an angel of the God to whom I belong and [b]whom I serve [c]stood before me,

24 saying, 'Do not be afraid,[5399] Paul; [a]you must stand before Caesar; and behold, God has granted[5483] you [b]all those who are sailing with you.'

25 "Therefore, [a]keep up your courage, men, for I believe[4100] God, that [I]it will turn out exactly as I have been told.

26 "But[1161] we must [a]run aground on a certain [b]island."

27 But when the fourteenth night had come, as we were being driven about[1308] in the Adriatic Sea, about midnight[3319] the sailors *began* to [ipf]surmise[5282] that [I]they were [pinf]approaching[4317] some land.

28 And they took soundings, and found *it to be* twenty fathoms; and a little farther on they took another sounding and found *it to be* fifteen fathoms.[3712]

29 And fearing that we might [a]run aground somewhere on the [I]rocks, they cast four anchors from the stern and [II]wished for daybreak.[2250]

30 And as the sailors were trying to escape from the ship, and had let down [a]the *ship's* boat into the sea, on the pretense of intending to lay out[1614] anchors from the bow,

31 Paul said to the centurion and to the soldiers, "Unless these men [aosb]remain in the ship, you yourselves cannot be saved."

32 Then the soldiers cut away the [a]ropes of the *ship's* boat, and let it fall away.

33 And until the day[2250] was about to dawn, Paul was [ipf]encouraging[3870] them all to take some food, saying, "Today is the fourteenth day[2250] that you have been constantly watching and going without eating,[777] having taken[4355] nothing.

34 "Therefore I encourage[3870] you to take[4355] some food, for this is[5225] for[4314] your preservation;[4991] for [a]not a hair from the head of any of you shall perish."

35 And having said this, he [apt]took[2983] bread and [a]gave thanks[2168] to God in the presence of all; and he broke it and began to eat.

36 And all [a]of them [I]were encouraged, and they themselves also took[4335] food.

13 [a]Acts 27:8 [b]Acts 2:11; 27:12f., 21; Titus 1:5, 12

14 [I]Lit., *it* [II]I.e., a northeaster [a]Mark 4:37

16 [I]Some ancient mss. read *Cauda*

17 [I]Lit., *helps* [II]Or possibly, *sail* [a]Acts 27:26, 29

18 [I]Lit., *they were doing a throwing out* [a]Jon. 1:5; Acts 27:38

21 [I]Lit., *there being much abstinence from food* [II]Lit., *obeyed me* [III]Lit., *gained* [a]Acts 27:10 [b]Acts 27:7

22 [a]Acts 27:25, 36

23 [a]Acts 5:19 [b]Rom. 1:9 [c]Acts 18:9; 23:11; 2Tim. 4:17

24 [a]Acts 23:11 [b]Acts 27:31, 42, 44

25 [I]Lit., *it will be* [a]Acts 27:22, 36

26 [a]Acts 27:17, 29 [b]Acts 28:1

27 [I]Lit., *some land was approaching them*

29 [I]Lit., *rough places* [II]Lit., *they were praying for it to become day* [a]Acts 27:17, 26

30 [a]Acts 27:16

32 [a]John 2:15

34 [a]Matt. 10:30

35 [a]Matt. 14:19

36 [I]Lit., *became cheerful* [a]Acts 27:22, 25

37 And all of us in the ship were two hundred and seventy-six [I][a]persons.[5590]

38 And when they had eaten enough,[2880] they *began* to lighten the ship by [ppt] [a]throwing out the wheat into the sea.

39 And when day[2250] came, [a]they [I]could not recognize the land; but they [II]did [ipf]observe[2657] a certain bay with a beach, and they [imp] [III]resolved to [IV]drive the ship onto it if they could.

40 And casting off [a]the anchors, they [I]left them in the sea while at the same time they were loosening the ropes of the rudders, and hoisting[1869] the foresail to the wind,[4154] they were heading[2722] for the beach.

41 But striking a [I]reef where two seas met, they ran the vessel aground; and the prow stuck fast and remained immovable, but the stern *began* to be broken[3089] up by the force *of the waves.*

42 And the soldiers' plan[1012] was to [a]kill the prisoners, that none *of them* should swim away and escape;

43 but the centurion, [a]wanting to bring Paul safely[1295] through, kept them from their intention, and commanded that those who could swim should [I]jump overboard first and get to land,

44 and the rest *should follow,* some on planks, and others on various things from the ship. And thus it happened that [a]they all were brought safely[1295] to land.

Safe at Malta

28 And when [a]they had been brought safely[1295] through, [b]then we found out that [c]the island was called [I]Malta.

2 And [a]the [I]natives[915] showed us extraordinary[5177] kindness;[5363] for because of the rain that had set in and because of the cold, they kindled a fire and [b]received us all.

3 But when Paul had gathered a bundle of sticks and laid them on the fire, a viper came out [I]because of the heat, and fastened on his hand.

4 And when [a]the [I]natives[915] saw the creature[2342] hanging from his hand, they *began* [ipf]saying to one another, "[b]Undoubtedly this man is a murderer, and though he has been saved[1295] from the sea, [II]justice[1349] has not allowed him to live."

🔑 5 However [a]he shook the creature[2342] off into the fire and suffered[3958] no harm.

6 But[1161] they were [ipf]expecting that he was about to swell up or suddenly fall down dead. But after they had [ppt]waited a long time and had [ppt]seen nothing unusual [ppt]happen to him, they changed their minds and [a]*began* to say that he was a god.[2316]

7 Now in the neighborhood of that place were[5225] lands belonging to the leading man of the island, named Publius, who welcomed[324] us and entertained us courteously three days.[2250]

🔑 8 And it came about that the father of Publius was lying *in bed* afflicted[4912] with *recurrent* fever and dysentery;[1420] and Paul went in *to see* him and after he had [a]prayed, he [b]laid his hands on him and healed him.

9 And after this had happened, the rest of the people on the island who had diseases were [ipf]coming to him and [ipf]getting cured.

10 And they also honored us with many [I]marks of respect; and when we were setting sail, they [II]supplied *us* with [III]all we needed.

Paul Arrives at Rome

11 And at the end of three months we set sail on [a]an Alexandrian ship which had wintered at the island, and which had [I]the Twin Brothers for its figurehead.

12 And after we put in at Syracuse, we stayed there for three days.[2250]

13 And from there we [I]sailed around and arrived at Rhegium, and a day later

---

37 [I]Lit., *souls* [a]Acts 2:41

38 [a]Jon. 1:5; Acts 27:18

39 [I]Or, *were not recognizing* [II]Or, *were observing* [III]Or, *were resolving* [IV]Some ancient mss. read *bring the ship safely ashore* [a]Acts 28:1

40 [I]Or, *were leaving* [a]Acts 27:29

41 [I]Lit., *place*

42 [a]Acts 12:19

43 [I]Lit., *cast themselves* [a]Acts 27:3

44 [a]Acts 27:22, 31

1 [I]Or, *Melita.* Some mss. read *Melitene* [a]Acts 16:10; 27:1 [b]Acts 27:39 [c]Acts 27:26

2 [I]Lit., *barbarians* [a]Acts 28:4; Rom. 1:14; 1Cor. 14:11; Col. 3:11 [b]Rom. 14:1

3 [I]Or, *from the heat*

4 [I]Lit., *barbarians* [II]I.e., personification of a goddess [a]Acts 28:2 [b]Luke 13:2, 4

5 [a]Mark 16:18

6 [a]Acts 14:11

8 [a]Acts 9:40; James 5:14f. [b]Matt. 9:18; Mark 5:23; 6:5

10 [I]Lit., *honors* [II]Or, *put on board* [III]Lit., *the things pertaining to the needs*

11 [I]Gr., the Dioscuri; i.e., Castor and Pollux, twin sons of Zeus [a]Acts 27:6

13 [I]Some early mss. read *weighed anchor*

🔑 **28:5,8** See note on II Tim. 4:20.

a south wind sprang up, and on the second day we came to Puteoli.
14 [I]There we found *some* [a]brethren,
and were invited[3870] to stay with them
for seven days; and thus we came[2064]
to Rome.
15 And the [a]brethren, when they
heard about us, came from there as far
as the [I]Market of Appius and [II]Three
Inns to meet us; and when Paul saw
them, he thanked[2168] God[2316] and took
courage.
16 And when we entered Rome,
Paul was [a]allowed to stay by himself,
with the soldier who was [ppt]guarding
him.
17 And it happened that after three
days he called[4779] together those who
were [a]the leading men of the Jews, and
when they had come together, he *began*
saying to them, "[b]Brethren, [c]though I
had done nothing against our people,
or [d]the customs of our [I]fathers, yet I
was delivered prisoner from Jerusalem
into the hands of the Romans.
18 "And when they had [a]examined
me, they [b]were willing to release me
because there was [c]no ground [I]for putting me to death.
19 "But when the Jews [I]objected,
I was forced[315] to [a]appeal to[1941] Caesar;
not that I had any accusation against
my nation.
20 "For this reason therefore, I
[I]requested to see[3870] you and to speak
with you, for I am wearing [a]this chain
for [b]the sake of the hope[1680] of Israel."
21 And they said to him, "We have
neither received letters[1121] from Judea
concerning you, nor have any of [a]the
brethren[80] come here and reported or
spoken anything bad[4190] about you.
22 "But we desire to hear from you
what [I]your views[5426] are; for concerning
this [a]sect,[139] it is known to us that
[b]it is spoken against everywhere."
23 And when they had set[5021] a day
for him, they came to him at [a]his lodging
in large numbers; and he was explaining
to them by solemnly [b]testifying[1263] about
the kingdom[932] of God, and trying to
persuade[3982] them concerning Jesus,
[c]from both the Law[3551] of Moses and
from the Prophets, from morning until
evening.
24 And [a]some were being [ipf]per-
suaded[3982] by the things spoken, but
others would not [ipf]believe.[569]
25 And when they did not agree with
one another, they *began* [ipf]leaving[630] after Paul had spoken one *parting*
word,[4487] "The Holy Spirit[4151] rightly
spoke through Isaiah the prophet to your
fathers,
26 saying,

"[a]GO TO THIS PEOPLE AND SAY,
"[I][b]YOU WILL KEEP ON
HEARING,[189] [II]BUT WILL NOT
UNDERSTAND;
AND [III]YOU WILL KEEP ON
SEEING, BUT WILL NOT
PERCEIVE;
27 [a]FOR THE HEART[2588] OF THIS
PEOPLE[2992]
HAS BECOME DULL,[3975]
AND WITH THEIR EARS THEY
SCARCELY HEAR,
AND THEY HAVE CLOSED THEIR
EYES;
LEST THEY SHOULD SEE WITH
THEIR EYES,
AND HEAR WITH THEIR EARS,
AND UNDERSTAND[4920] WITH
THEIR HEART AND
RETURN,[1994]
AND I SHOULD HEAL THEM." '

28 "Let it be known to you therefore, that [a]this salvation[4992] of God has
been sent [b]to the Gentiles;[1484] they will
also listen."
29 [[I]And when he had spoken these
words, the Jews departed, having a
great dispute among themselves.]
30 And he stayed two full years
[I]in his own rented quarters, and was
welcoming[588] all who came to him,
31 [I][a]preaching[2784] the kingdom of
God, and teaching[1321] concerning the
Lord Jesus Christ [b]with all openness,
unhindered.

14 [I]Lit., *where* [a]John 21:23; Acts 1:15; 6:3; 9:30; Rom. 1:13; 28:15

15 [I]Lat., *Appii Forum*, a station about 43 miles from Rome [II]Lat., *Tres Tabernae*, a station about 33 miles from Rome [a]Acts 1:15; 10:23; 11:1, 12, 29; 12:17

16 [a]Acts 24:23

17 [I]Or, *forefathers* [a]Acts 13:50; 25:2 [b]Acts 22:5 [c]Acts 25:8 [d]Acts 6:14

18 [I]Lit., *of death in me* [a]Acts 22:24 [b]Acts 26:32 [c]Acts 23:29; 25:25; 26:31

19 [I]Lit., *spoke against it* [a]Acts 25:11, 21, 25; 26:32

20 [I]Or, *invited you to see me and speak with me* [a]Acts 21:33 [b]Acts 26:6f.

21 [a]Acts 3:17; 22:5; 28:14; Rom. 9:3

22 [I]Lit., *you think* [a]Acts 24:14 [b]1Pet. 2:12; 3:16; 4:14, 16

23 [a]Philem. 1:22 [b]Luke 16:28; Acts 1:3; 23:11 [c]Acts 8:35

24 [a]Acts 14:4

26 [I]Lit., *with a hearing* [II]Lit., *and* [III]Lit., *seeing you will see* [a]Is. 6:9 [b]Matt. 13:14f.

27 [a]Is. 6:10

28 [a]Ps. 98:3; Luke 2:30; Acts 13:26 [b]Acts 9:15; 13:46

29 [I]Many mss. do not contain this v.

30 [I]Or, *at his own expense*

31 [I]Or, *proclaiming* [a]Matt. 4:23; Acts 20:25; 28:23 [b]2Tim. 2:9

The Epistle of Paul to the

ROMANS

Coleridge called Paul's letter to the Romans the "most profound work in existence." By far the Book of Romans contains Paul's most comprehensive statement of the full meaning of the cross of Christ. Paul says: "For I am not ashamed of the gospel, for it is the power of God for salvation to every one who believes, to the Jew first, and also to the Greek." (Rom. 1:16). From the very start, Paul develops the theme that all people, whether Jewish or Gentile, are sinners and, therefore, need God's salvation. But how can this be done? Paul writes meticulously that the only way is through a personal relationship with Jesus Christ through faith and complete obedience to Him. Salvation cannot come through frail human attempts to obey any law perfectly. Then Paul explains what a new life in Christ entails. No longer does an individual need to live under the constant domination of sin, guilt, and death. A believer is liberated by the Spirit of God and has inner peace, as well as peace with God. All hostilities have ceased. Paul goes to great lengths to expound God's original purpose in giving the Law of Moses and how the Jews were a part of God's master plan to bring all nations home through the grace provided by the cross of Jesus Christ. Paul concluded with many practical things about how Christians should live in this world. We must serve one another. We must be good citizens. We must be tolerant and sensitive to the consciences of others.

Paul wrote this letter to the Christians in Rome from Corinth, knowing that he would soon come their way. He had always wanted to visit Spain (Rom. 15:28) to the west. However, he also knew that he would visit Jerusalem first (Rom. 15:31), and that was a foreboding thought! Paul was summarily arrested in Jerusalem, and after a long, involved process, was forced to appeal his case to be heard in Rome by Caesar himself. After all, it was only fitting that the Apostle to the Gentiles should appear in the capital of the world.

The Epistle to the Romans above everything else is an explanation of how God justifies the sinner. The verb in Greek for "justify" is *dikaioō* (1344). In Romans it is used fourteen times and in Galatians eight times. There is a great theological affinity between Romans and Galatians as to how God justifies the sinner. In the rest of the New Testament, the verb is used only fourteen times.

The verb is a legal term meaning to declare someone as just or righteous and to recognize him as such. It refers to one who is not subject to condemnation. A just person in the New Testament is one who meets God's standard for his life. In the New Testament the word for "to justify" never means what the word meant in Classical Greek, i.e., to make anyone righteous by doing away with his violation of law through his own condemnation. The New Testament never speaks of anybody justifying himself because he has paid the penalty for his sin.

It must be pointed out that verbs ending in *oō* such as *dikaioō,* "justify" or *douloō* (1402), "to make a servant, to subject someone, to subjugate" (Acts 7:6; I Cor. 9:19), refer only to the act or activity which is directed toward achieving the desired result without any reference whatsoever to the mode or way whereby this takes place. So when the word *dikaioō,* "to justify," is used in Greek, it has no reference whatsoever to the way that this is accomplished, but only to the act itself, that a person is declared just or righteous.

The important matter is who declares or considers a person just. The Pharisees considered themselves just and righteous. They had their own standard of righteousness. The young lawyer who came to Jesus in Lk. 10:29 wanted to justify himself. One can be just in his own eyes by setting his own standard.

Another can justify himself when he meets his legal obligations toward specific laws. This is "being justified by the law." The law cannot bring this man before the court and charge him with specific violations of the law.

But for one to justify himself before God, he must, first of all, acknowledge what are God's rights upon him. In order to do this, man must know God. This knowing of God is the same as the appropriation of the righteousness of God. It is not the mere proclamation by God that a person is free from the charge that others or the law can bring against him, but that God Himself considers him as having legally and morally fulfilled all that He demands to declare him justified. God could not find such a *dikaios* (1342), or just person, on earth. But when it came to His Son Jesus Christ, there was no unrighteousness in Him (Jn. 7:18).

In Rom. 1:18,19 we find how God considers fallen man, "For the wrath of God is revealed from heaven against all ungodliness and unrighteousness (*adikian,* the opposite of righteousness) of men, who suppress the truth in unrighteousness (*adikia,* 93)." In other words, they do not do what is right because they have not recognized God Himself which is expressed in the word *asebeia* (763), "ungodliness." The person who does not recognize God for what He is, "just," *dikaios,* cannot recognize God's rights upon his life. This, however, leaves man without excuse because God has given him the ability innately to know, at least in part God's rights, but man willfully disregards even that partial knowledge. Observe v. 19, "Because that which is known about God is evident within them; for God made it evident to them." Because, therefore, man has not properly responded to God's rights toward him generally manifested to mankind, he is filled with unrighteousness expressing itself in fornication, wickedness, covetousness, maliciousness, envy, murder, debate, deceit, malignity, whispering, etc. (Rom. 1:29).

The verb *dikaioō,* "to justify," sometimes must be understood as meaning to appear as righteous as in Rom. 2:13, "For not the hearers of the law are just before God, but the doers of the law shall be justified." We cannot take this latter statement to mean truly justified unto salvation, but as appearing justified. The doers of the law are justified by the law but not by God. Therefore, the word "justify" here has a limited application. Otherwise this statement would stand in contradiction to Rom. 3:20: "Therefore by the deeds of the law there shall no flesh be justified in His sight: for by the law is the knowledge of sin." And again in Rom. 4:2 we read, "For if Abraham was justified by works, he has something to boast about; but not before God."

But how can man be justified before God? The answer is given: of Christ in the Spirit (I Tim. 3:16); by His grace (Titus 3:7); not by works of the law (Gal. 2:16); not with the law (Gal. 3:11; 5:4); not by works (Eph. 2:8); but by faith which is followed by works as a demonstration of its genuineness (Js. 2:21-25). In Rom. 4:5 we find that it is God who justifies the ungodly through Jesus Christ (Rom. 3:26; Gal. 2:16).

Above everything else, this must be understood: God does not only declare us justified, but makes us just (Rom. 5:19). The verb "makes us" is *kathistēmi* (2525), meaning "to constitute." He clears us of the guilt of sin and gives us power against sin. For general remarks on election, see note on Eph. 1:4,5.

The Gospel Exalted

1 Paul, a bond-servant[1401] of Christ[5547] Jesus, [Ia]called[2822] *as* an apostle,[652] [b]set apart[873] for [c]the gospel[2098] of God,

2 which He [a]promised beforehand[4279] through His [b]prophets[4396] in the holy Scriptures,[1124]

3 concerning His Son,[5207] who was born [a]of a [I]descendant[4690] of David [b]according to[2596] the flesh,[4561]

4 who was declared [a]the [an]Son of God[2316] with power [I]by the resurrection[386] from the dead,[3498] according to the [II]Spirit[4151] of holiness,[42] Jesus Christ our Lord,

5 through whom we have [ao]received grace[5485] and [a]apostleship[651] [I]to bring about *the* [b]obedience[5218] of faith[4102] among [c]all the Gentiles, for His name's[3686] sake,

6 among whom you also are the [a]called[2822] of Jesus Christ;

7 to all who are [a]beloved of God in Rome, called *as* [Ib]saints:[40] [c]Grace to you and peace[1515] from God our Father[3962] and the Lord Jesus Christ.

8 First, [a]I thank[2168] my God through Jesus Christ for you all, because

1 [I]Lit., *a called apostle* [a]1Cor. 1:1; 9:1; 2Cor. 1:1 [b]Acts 9:15; 13:2; Gal. 1:15 [c]Mark 1:14; Rom. 15:16
2 [a]Titus 1:2 [b]Luke 1:70; Rom. 3:21; 16:26
3 [I]Lit., *seed* [a]Matt. 1:1 [b]John 1:14; Rom. 4:1; 9:3, 5; 1Cor. 10:18
4 [I]Or, *as a result of* [II]Or, *spirit* [a]Matt. 4:3
5 [I]Lit., *for obedience* [a]Acts 1:25; Gal. 1:16 [b]Acts 6:7; Rom. 16:26 [c]Acts 9:15
6 [a]Jude 1:1; Rev. 17:14

7 [I]Or, *holy ones* [a]Rom. 5:5ff.; 8:39 [b]Acts 9:13; Rom. 8:28ff.; 1Cor. 1:2, 24 [c]Num. 6:25f.; 1Cor. 1:3; 2Cor. 1:2; Gal. 1:3; Eph. 1:2; Phil. 1:2; Col. 1:2; 1Thess. 1:1; 2Thess. 1:2 **8** [a]1Cor. 1:4; Eph. 1:15f.; Phil. 1:3f.; Col. 1:3f.; 1Thess. 1:2; 2:13

[b]your faith is being proclaimed[2605] throughout the whole world.[2889]

9 For [a]God, whom I [b]serve in my spirit[4151] in the *preaching of the* gospel of His Son, is my witness[3144] *as to* how unceasingly [c]I make mention of you,

🔑 10 always in my prayers making request, if perhaps now at last by [a]the will of God I may succeed in coming to you.

11 For [a]I long to see you in order that I may impart some spiritual gift to you, that you may be established;

12 that is, that I may be encouraged together[4837] with you *while* among you, each of us by the other's faith, both yours and mine.

13 And [a]I do not want you to be unaware, [b]brethren,[80] that often I [c]have planned[4388] to come to you (and have been prevented thus far) in order that I might obtain some [d]fruit among you also, even as among the rest of the Gentiles.[1484]

14 [a]I am [I]under obligation[3781] both to Greeks and to [b]barbarians,[915] both to the wise[4680] and to the foolish.[453]

15 Thus, for my part, I am eager to [a]preach the gospel[2097] to you also who are in Rome.

16 For I am not [a]ashamed of the gospel,[2098] for [b]it is the power[1411] of God for salvation[4991] to everyone who [ppt]believes,[4100] to the [c]Jew first and also to [d]the Greek.

17 For in it [a]*the* righteousness[1343] of God is [pinp]revealed[601] [I]from faith[4102] to faith; as it is written, "[II][b]BUT THE [sg]RIGHTEOUS[1342] *man* SHALL LIVE[2198] BY FAITH."

8 [b]Acts 28:22; Rom. 16:19
9 [a]Rom. 9:1 [b]Acts 24:14; 2Tim. 1:3 [c]Eph. 1:16; Phil. 1:3f
10 [a]Acts 18:21; Rom. 15:32
11 [a]Acts 19:21; Rom. 15:23
13 [a]Rom. 11:25; 1Cor. 10:1; 12:1; 2Cor. 1:8; 1Thess. 4:13 [b]Acts 1:15; Rom. 7:1; 1Cor. 1:10; 14:20, 26; Gal. 3:15 [c]Acts 19:21; Rom. 15:22f. [d]John 4:36; 15:16; Phil. 1:22; Col. 1:6
14 [I]Lit., *debtor* [a]1Cor. 9:16 [b]Acts 28:2
15 [a]Rom. 15:20
16 [a]Mark 8:38; 2Tim. 1:8, 12, 16 [b]1Cor. 1:18, 24 [c]Acts 3:26; Rom. 2:9 [d]John 7:35
17 [I]Or, *by* [II]Or, *But he who is righteous by faith shall live.* [a]Rom. 3:21; 9:30; Phil. 3:9 [b]Hab. 2:4; Gal. 3:11; Heb. 10:38
18 [I]Or, *by* [a]Rom. 5:9; Eph. 5:6; Col. 3:6 [b]2Thess. 2:6f.
19 [I]Or, *among* [a]Acts 14:17; 17:24ff.
20 [a]Mark 10:6 [b]Job 12:7-9; Ps. 19:1-6; Jer. 5:21f.
21 [I]Lit., *glorify* [a]2Kin. 17:15; Jer. 2:5; Eph. 4:17f.
22 [a]Jer. 10:14; 1Cor. 1:20
23 [I]Or possibly, *reptiles* [a]Deut. 4:16-18; Ps. 106:20; Jer. 2:11; Acts 17:29

Unbelief and Its Consequences

18 For [a]the wrath[3709] of God[2316] is [pinp]revealed from heaven[3772] against all ungodliness[63] and unrighteousness[93] of men,[444] who [ppt] [b]suppress[2722] the truth[225] [I]in unrighteousness,[93]

19 because [a]that which is known[1110] about God is evident[5318] [I]within them; for God [ao]made it evident[5319] to them.

🔑 20 For [a]since the creation[2937] of the world[2889] His invisible attributes, His eternal[126] power and divine nature,[2305] have been clearly seen, [b]being understood[3539] through what has been made, so that they are without excuse.

21 For even though they knew God, they did not [I]honor[1392] Him as God, or give thanks;[2168] but they became [a]futile[3154] in their speculations, and their foolish heart[2588] was darkened.

22 [a]Professing to be wise,[4680] they became fools,[3471]

🔑 23 and [a]exchanged[236] the glory[1391] of the incorruptible[862] God for an image[1504] in the form of[3667] corruptible man and of birds and four-footed animals and [I]crawling creatures.

24 Therefore [a]God gave them over in the lusts of their hearts to impurity,[167] that their bodies might be [b]dishonored among them.

25 For they exchanged[3337] the truth[225] of God[2316] for [I]a [a]lie, and worshiped[4573] and served[3000] the creature[2935] rather than the Creator,[2936] [b]who is blessed[2128] [II]forever. Amen.[281]

26 For this reason [a]God gave them

24 [a]Rom. 1:26, 28; Eph. 4:19 [b]Eph. 2:3 **25** [I]Lit., *the lie* [II]Lit., *unto the ages* [a]Is. 44:20; Jer. 10:14; 13:25; 16:19 [b]Rom. 9:5; 2Cor. 11:31 **26** [a]Rom. 1:24

🔑 **1:10** See note on III Jn. 2 and also *euodoō* (2137), to fare well.

🔑 **1:20** The word translated "divine nature" is theiotēs (2305), which means merely divinity, . . . the demonstrated power of the Godhead and not the essence and the character of the Godhead. By looking at nature one can conclude that indeed God is all-powerful, but not necessarily that He is an all-loving God of righteousness and justice. There is only so much of God that one can know from God's creation (v. 19), but to know the essence of God as a triune Deity, one needs to receive His revelation by faith. The rejection of what knowledge a person does have of God is what brings condemnation to him.

🔑 **1:23** See note on II Tim. 1:12 and also *paschō* (3958), suffer; *aphthartos* (862), incorruptible; *phthartos* (5349), corruptible.

over to [b]degrading[819] passions;[3806] for
their women[2338] exchanged[3337] the natural function[5540] for that which is [I]un-
natural,
27 and in the same way also the men
[apt]abandoned the natural function of the
woman and burned in their desire[3715]
toward one another, [a]men with men
committing [I]indecent acts and receiving[618] in [II]their own persons the due
penalty[1163] of their error.
28 And just as they did not see
fit[1381] [I]to acknowledge[1922] God any
longer, [a]God gave them over to a
depraved[96] mind,[3563] to [pinf]do those
things which are not proper,[2520]
29 being filled with all unrighteousness, wickedness,[4189] greed, evil;[2549]
full of envy, murder, strife,[2054] deceit,
malice;[2550] *they are* [a]gossips,[5558]
30 slanderers,[2637] [Ia]haters of God,
insolent,[5197] arrogant,[5244] boastful,[213] in-
ventors of evil, [b]disobedient[545] to parents,
31 without understanding, untrustworthy,[802] [a]unloving,[794] unmerciful;[415]
32 and, although they [apt]know the
ordinance[1345] of God, that those who
[ppt]practice[4238] such things are worthy
of [a]death, they not only do the same,
but also [b]give hearty approval to those
who [ppt]practice them.

The Impartiality of God

2 Therefore you are [a]without excuse, [b]every man *of you* who
[ppt]passes judgment,[2919] for in that
[c]you judge another, you condemn[2632]
yourself; for you who [ppt]judge practice[4238] the same things.
2 And we know that the judg-
ment[2917] of God[2316] [I]rightly falls[225,2596]
upon those who [ppt]practice such things.
3 And do you suppose this, [a]O man,
[I]when you pass judgment upon those
who practice such things and [ppt]do the
same *yourself,* that you will [fm]escape the
judgment of God?

26 [I]Lit., *against nature* [b]1Thess. 4:5
27 [I]Lit., *the shameless deed* [II]Lit., *themselves* [a]Lev. 18:22; 20:13; 1Cor. 6:9
28 [I]Lit., *to have God in knowledge* [a]Rom. 1:24
29 [a]2Cor. 12:20
30 [I]Or, *hateful to God* [a]Ps. 5:5 [b]2Tim. 3:2
31 [a]2Tim. 3:3
32 [a]Rom. 6:21 [b]Luke 11:48; Acts 8:1; 22:20

1 [a]Rom. 1:20 [b]Luke 12:14; Rom. 2:3; 9:20 [c]2Sam. 12:5-7; Matt. 7:1; Luke 6:37; Rom. 14:22
2 [I]Lit., *is according to truth against*
3 [I]Lit., *who pass judgment* [a]Luke 12:14; Rom. 2:1; 9:20
4 [a]Rom. 9:23; 11:33; 2Cor. 8:2; Eph. 1:7, 18; 2:7; Phil. 4:19; Col. 1:27; 2:2; Titus 3:6 [b]Rom. 11:22 [c]Rom. 3:25 [d]Ex. 34:6; Rom. 9:22; 1Tim. 1:16; 1Pet. 3:20; 2Pet. 3:9, 15
5 [I]Or, *in accordance with* [a]Deut. 32:34f.; Prov. 1:18 [b]Ps. 110:5; 2Cor. 5:10; 2Thess. 1:5; Jude 6
6 [a]Ps. 62:12; Prov. 24:12; Matt. 16:27
7 [a]Luke 8:15; Heb. 10:36 [b]Rom. 2:10; Heb. 2:7; 1Pet. 1:7 [c]1Cor. 15:42, 50, 53f.; Eph. 6:24; 2Tim. 1:10 [d]Matt. 25:46
8 [a]2Cor. 12:20; Gal. 5:20; Phil. 1:17; 2:3; James 3:14, 16 [b]2Thess. 2:12
9 [I]Lit., *upon* [a]Rom. 8:35 [b]Acts 3:26; Rom. 1:16;

4 Or do you think lightly of [a]the
riches of His [b]kindness[5544] and [c]for-
bearance[463] and [d]patience,[3115] not
knowing[50] that the kindness[5543] of God
leads[71] you to repentance?[3341]
5 But [I]because of your stubbornness[4643] and unrepentant[279] heart[2588]
[a]you are storing up wrath[3709] for yourself
[b]in the day of wrath and revelation[602]
of the righteous judgment[1341] of God,
6 [a]who WILL RENDER TO EVERY MAN
ACCORDING TO HIS DEEDS:[2041]
7 to those who by [a]perseverance in
doing[2041] good[18] seek for [b]glory and
honor and [c]immortality, [d]eternal[166]
life;[2222]
8 but to those who are [a]selfishly ambitious and [b]do not obey[544] the truth,[225]
but obey[3982] unrighteousness,[93]
wrath[3709] and indignation.[2372]
9 *There will be* [a]tribulation[2347] and
distress[4730] [I]for every soul[5590] of man
who [ppt]does evil,[2556] of the Jew [b]first
and also of the Greek,
10 but [a]glory[1391] and honor[5092] and
peace[1515] to every man who [ppt]does[2038]
good,[18] to the Jew [b]first and also to the
Greek.
11 For [a]there is no partiality[4382] with
God.
12 For all who have [ao]sinned[264]
[Ia]without the Law will also perish[622]
[I]without the Law;[460] and all who have
sinned [II]under the Law[3551] will be judged
[III]by the Law;
13 for [a]not the hearers [I]of the Law
are [II]just[1342] before God, but the doers
[I]of the Law will be justified.[1344]
14 For when Gentiles[1484] who do
not [ppt]have [I]the Law [psa]do [IIa]instinctively
the things of the Law, these, not having
[I]the Law, are a law to themselves,

1Pet. 4:17 **10** [a]Rom. 2:7; Heb. 2:7; 1Pet. 1:7 [b]Rom. 2:9 **11** [a]Deut. 10:17; Acts 10:34 **12** [I]Or, *without law* [II]Or, *under law* [III]Or, *by law* [a]Acts 2:23; 1Cor. 9:21 **13** [I]Or, *of law* [II]Or, *righteous* [a]Matt. 7:21, 24ff.; John 13:17; James 1:22f., 25 **14** [I]Or, *law* [II]Lit., *by nature* [a]Acts 10:35; Rom. 1:19; 2:15

2:1-16 See notes on Mt. 8:11,12; Gal. 2:16.
2:12-20 See note on Mt. 13.
2:13,20,26 See general remarks on justification on Romans and also *dikaioō* (1344), to justify.

15 in that they show [a]the work[2041] of the Law written in their hearts,[2588] their conscience[4893] bearing witness, and their thoughts[3053] alternately accusing[2723] or else defending them,

16 on the day when, [a]according to my gospel,[2098] [b]God will judge[2919] the secrets of men through Christ Jesus.

The Jew Is Condemned by the Law

17 But if you bear the name "Jew," and [a]rely[1878] [I]upon the Law, and boast in God,

18 and know *His* [art]will,[2307] and [Ia]approve the things that are essential, being instructed out of the Law,

19 and are confident[3982] that you yourself are a guide to the blind, a light[5457] to those who are in darkness,[4655]

🗝 20 a [I]corrector[3810] of the foolish, a teacher[1320] of [II]the immature,[3516] having in the Law [a]the embodiment[3446] of knowledge and of the truth,

21 you, therefore, [a]who [ppt]teach another, do you not teach[1321] yourself? You who [I]preach[2784] that one should not steal, do you steal?

22 You who say that one should not commit adultery, do you commit adultery? You who abhor[948] idols, do you [a]rob temples?

23 You who [a]boast [I]in the Law, through your breaking[3847] the Law, do you dishonor God?

24 For "[a]THE NAME OF GOD IS BLASPHEMED[987] AMONG THE GENTILES [b]BECAUSE OF YOU," just as it is written.

25 For indeed[3303] circumcision[4061] is of value, if you [a]practice[4238] [I]the Law; but if you are a transgressor[3848] [II]of the Law, [b]your circumcision has become uncircumcision.[203]

🗝 26 [a]If therefore [b]the [I]uncircumcised[203] man [c]keeps the requirements[1345] of the Law, will not his uncircumcision be regarded[3049] as circumcision?

27 And will not [a]he who is physically uncircumcised, if he keeps[5055] the Law, will he not [b]judge[2919] you who[3848] [I]though having the letter[1121] *of the Law* and circumcision are a transgressor[3848] [II]of the Law?

28 For [a]he is not a Jew who is one outwardly;[5318] neither is circumcision that which is outward[5318] in the flesh.[4561]

29 But [a]he is a Jew who is one inwardly; and [b]circumcision[4061] is that which is of the heart, by the [c]Spirit, not by the letter;[1121] [d]and his praise is not from men,[4444] but from God.[2316]

All the World Guilty

3 Then what [I]advantage[4053] has the Jew? Or what is the benefit of circumcision?[4061]

2 Great in every respect. First[4412] of all, that [a]they were entrusted[4100] with the [b]oracles[3051] of God.

3 What then? If [a]some [I]did not believe,[569] their [II]unbelief[570] will not nullify the faithfulness[4102] of God, will it?

4 [a]May it never be![1096][3361] Rather, let God be[1096] found true, though every man *be found* [b]a liar, as it is written,

"[c]THAT THOU MIGHTEST BE
JUSTIFIED[1344]
IN THY WORDS,
AND MIGHTEST PREVAIL WHEN
THOU [I]ART JUDGED."[2919]

5 But if our unrighteousness[93] [Ia]demonstrates[4921] the righteousness[1343] of God, [b]what shall we say? The God who inflicts[2018] wrath[3709] is not unrighteous,[94] is He? ([c]I am speaking in human terms.)

6 [a]May it never be! For otherwise how will [b]God judge[2919] the world?

7 But if through my lie [a]the truth[225] of God abounded to His glory,[1398] [b]why am I also still being judged as a sinner?[268]

8 And why not *say* (as we are [pinp]slanderously reported[987] and as some affirm that we say), "[a]Let us do evil that good[18] may come"? [I]Their condemnation[2917] is just.[1738]

---

15 [a]Rom. 2:14, 27
16 [a]Rom. 16:25; 1Cor. 15:1; Gal. 1:11; 1Tim. 1:11; 2Tim. 2:8 [b]Acts 10:42; 17:31; Rom. 3:6; 14:10
17 [I]Or, *upon law* [a]Mic. 3:11; John 5:45; Rom. 2:23; 9:4
18 [I]Or, *distinguish between the things which differ* [a]Phil. 1:10
20 [I]Or, *instructor* [II]Lit., *infants* [a]Rom. 3:31; 2Tim. 1:13
21 [I]Or, *proclaim* [a]Matt. 23:3ff.
22 [a]Acts 19:37
23 [I]Or, *in law* [a]Mic. 3:11; John 5:45; Rom. 2:17; 9:4
24 [a]Is. 52:5; Ezek. 36:20ff. [b]2Pet. 2:2
25 [I]Or, *law* [II]Or, *of law* [a]Rom. 2:13f., 27 [b]Jer. 4:4; 9:25f.
26 [I]Lit., *uncircumcision* [a]1Cor. 7:19 [b]Rom. 3:30; Eph. 2:11 [c]Rom. 2:25, 27; 8:4
27 [I]Lit., *through the letter* [II]Or, *of law* [a]Rom. 3:30; Eph. 2:11 [b]Matt. 12:41
28 [a]John 8:39; Rom. 2:17; 9:6; Gal. 6:15
29 [a]Phil. 3:3; Col. 2:11 [b]Deut. 30:6 [c]Rom. 2:27; 7:6; 2Cor. 3:6 [d]John 5:44; 12:43; 1Cor. 4:5; 2Cor. 10:18

1 [I]Lit., *is the advantage of the Jew*
2 [a]Deut. 4:8; Ps. 147:19; Rom. 9:4 [b]Acts 7:38
3 [I]Or, *were unfaithful* [II]Or, *unfaithfulness* [a]Rom. 10:16; Heb. 4:2
4 [I]Or, *dost enter into judgment* [a]Luke 20:16; Rom. 3:6, 31 [b]Ps. 116:11; Rom. 3:7 [c]Ps. 51:4
5 [I]Or, *commends* [a]Rom. 5:8; 2Cor. 6:4; 7:11 [b]Rom. 4:1; 7:7; 8:31; 9:14, 30 [c]Rom. 6:19; 1Cor. 9:8; 15:32; Gal. 3:15
6 [a]Luke 20:16; Rom. 3:4, 31 [b]Rom. 2:16 **7** [a]Rom. 3:4 [b]Rom. 9:19 **8** [I]Lit., *Whose* [a]Rom. 6:1

9 What then? [Ia]Are we better than
they? Not at all; for we have already
charged that both [b]Jews and [c]Greeks
are [d]all under sin;[266]
10 as it is written,
"[a]THERE IS NONE RIGHTEOUS,[1342]
NOT EVEN ONE;
11 THERE IS NONE WHO
[ppt]UNDERSTANDS,
THERE IS NONE WHO [ppt]SEEKS
FOR GOD;
12 ALL HAVE [ao]TURNED ASIDE,
TOGETHER THEY HAVE
BECOME [aop]USELESS;
THERE IS NONE WHO [ppt]DOES
GOOD,[5544]
THERE IS NOT EVEN ONE."
13 "[a]THEIR THROAT IS AN OPEN
GRAVE,5028
WITH THEIR TONGUES THEY
KEEP [ipf]DECEIVING,"
"[b]THE POISON OF ASPS785 IS
UNDER THEIR LIPS";
14 "[a]WHOSE MOUTH IS FULL OF
CURSING[685] AND
BITTERNESS";
15 "[a]THEIR FEET ARE SWIFT TO
SHED BLOOD,
16 DESTRUCTION AND MISERY ARE
IN THEIR PATHS,[3598]

9 [I]Or possibly, *Are we worse* [a]Rom. 3:1 [b]Rom. 2:1-29 [c]Rom. 1:18-32 [d]Rom. 3:19; 23; 11:32; Gal. 3:22
10 [a]Ps. 14:1-3; 53:1-3
13 [a]Ps. 5:9 [b]Ps. 140:3
14 [a]Ps. 10:7
15 [a]Is. 59:7f.
18 [a]Ps. 36:1
19 [I]Lit., *in* [a]John 10:34 [b]Rom. 2:12 [c]Rom. 3:9
20 [I]Or, *of law* [II]Or, *through law* [a]Ps. 143:2; Acts 13:39; Gal. 2:16 [b]Rom. 4:15; 5:13, 20; 7:7
21 [I]Or, *from law* [a]Rom. 1:17; 9:30 [b]Acts 10:43; Rom. 1:2
22 [a]Rom. 1:17; 9:30 [b]Rom. 4:5 [c]Acts 3:16; Gal. 2:16, 20; 3:22; Eph. 3:12 [d]Rom. 4:11, 16; 10:4 [e]Rom. 10:12; Gal. 3:28; Col. 3:11
23 [I]Or, *all sinned* [a]Rom. 3:9
24 [a]Rom. 4:4f., 16; Eph. 2:8 [b]1Cor. 1:30; Eph. 1:7; Col. 1:14; Heb. 9:15

17 AND THE PATH OF PEACE HAVE
THEY NOT KNOWN."
18 "[a]THERE IS NO FEAR[5401] OF GOD
BEFORE THEIR EYES."
19 Now we know that whatever the
[a]Law[3551] says, it speaks to [b]those who
are [I]under the Law, that every mouth
may be closed, and [c]all the world may
become accountable[5267] to God;
🗝20 because [a]by the works [I]of the
Law no flesh4651 will be justified[1344] in
His sight; for [IIb]through the Law *comes*
the knowledge of sin.[266]

Justification by Faith

21 But now apart [I]from the Law
[a]*the* righteousness[1343] of God has been
[pfip]manifested,[5319] being [b]witnessed by
the Law and the Prophets,
22 even *the* [a]righteousness of God
through [b]faith[4102] [c]in Jesus Christ for
[d]all those who [ppt]believe;[4100] for [e]there
is no distinction;
🗝23 for [I]all [a]have [ao]sinned[264] and fall
short of the glory[1391] of God,
24 being justified as a gift1432 [a]by
His grace[5485] through [b]the redemption[629] which is in Christ Jesus;
🗝25 whom God [ao]displayed[4388]

🗝**3:20,23** See note on Gal. 2:16 and also *dikaioō* (1344), to justify.

🗝**3:25** The word translated "passed over" in this verse is not the word *aphesis* (859), "forgiveness," from *aphiēmi* (863), which means "to remove one's sins from someone," but it is the word *paresis* (3929), occurring only here. Whereas *aphesis* indeed means remission, made up of the preposition *apo* (575), "from," and *hiēmi,* "to send away, to lay aside," the word *paresis* is from the verb *pariēmi* (3935), which means "to place on the side, to disregard, to bypass." It is made up of the preposition *para* (3844) meaning "beside" and the basic verb *hiēmi,* "send." Here the Apostle Paul speaks about the past sins (*hamartēmata,* 265), the results of sin or the acts of sin that were past, which is not the same as *hamartiai* (266), "sins." These past sins God only permitted to be winked at, to be bypassed, to be placed on the side and not be considered as forever removed as a result of man's sacrifices of animals. See Heb. 10:11 where the verb *periaireō* (4014) is used. This verb means to take away on all sides (*peri,* 4012, and *aireō* or *airō,* 142), to lift up and take, to take entirely away (Acts 27:27,40; II Cor. 3:16). The animal sacrifices did not really reveal the righteousness of God, His character or the rights that He has upon man. The best that such sacrifices could accomplish was to set aside the consequences of former acts of sin. They could not remove the sinfulness of man or change his character. But now, through the blood of the Lord Jesus Christ, we are experiencing not *paresin,* the bypassing of the consequences of sin, but the remission, the removal, *aphesin,* of sin itself, i.e., its guilt and power. There is a transformation which occurs in the sinner. It is not only his sins that are dealt with, but he, himself. He becomes sanctified (Heb. 10:10) through the sacrifice of the Lord Jesus once and for all (Heb. 9:26,28; I Pet. 3:18). What Jesus Christ did through His blood was to lift our sins away from us. He did not just wink at them. He changed our character in making us just, people who inherently recognize

(continued on next page)

publicly as [a]a [I]propitiation[2435] [II][b]in His blood[129] through faith. *This was* to demonstrate His righteousness, [III]because in the [c]forbearance[463] of God He [d]passed over[3929] the sins[265] previously [pfp]committed;

26 for the demonstration, *I say,* of His righteousness at the present time,[2540] that He might be just[1342] and the justifier[1344] of the one who [I]has faith[4102] in Jesus.

27 Where then is [a]boasting? It is excluded. By [b]what kind of law?[3551] Of works?[2041] No, but by a law of faith.[4102]

28 [I]For [a]we maintain[3049] that a man[444] is justified[1344] by faith[4102] apart from works[2041] [II]of the Law.

29 Or [a]is God *the God* of Jews only? Is He not *the God* of Gentiles[1484] also? Yes, of Gentiles also,

30 since indeed [a]God [b]who will justify the [I]circumcised[4061] [II]by faith and the [III]uncircumcised[203] through faith [c]is one.

31 Do we then nullify [I]the Law through faith? [a]May it never be![1096 3361] On the contrary, we [b]establish the Law.

Justification by Faith Evidenced in Old Testament

4 What then shall we say that Abraham, [I]our forefather[3962] [a]according to the flesh,[4561] has found?

2 For if Abraham was justified[1344] by works,[2041] he has something to boast about; but [a]not [I]before God.

3 For what does the Scripture[1124] say? "[a]AND ABRAHAM BELIEVED[4100] GOD, and it was reckoned to him as righteousness."[1343]

4 Now to the one who [ppt][a]works, his wage[3408] is not reckoned[3049] as a favor,[5485] but as what is due.[3783]

5 But to the one who does not work, but [ppt][a]believes[4100] in Him who [ppt]justifies[1344] the ungodly,[765] his faith[4102] is reckoned[3049] as righteousness,

6 just as David also speaks of the blessing upon the man to whom God reckons[3049] righteousness apart from works:[2041]

7 "[a]BLESSED[3107] ARE THOSE WHOSE LAWLESS DEEDS[458] HAVE BEEN FORGIVEN,
AND WHOSE SINS[266] HAVE BEEN COVERED.

8 "[a]BLESSED IS THE MAN WHOSE SIN THE LORD WILL NOT [I][b]TAKE INTO ACCOUNT."[3049]

9 Is this blessing then upon [I][a]the circumcised,[4061] or upon [II]the uncircumcised[203] also? For [b]we say, "[c]FAITH[4102] WAS RECKONED TO ABRAHAM AS RIGHTEOUSNESS."

10 How then was it reckoned?[3049] While he was [I]circumcised, or [II]uncircumcised? Not while [I]circumcised, but while [II]uncircumcised;

11 and he [a]received the [an]sign[4592] of circumcision, [b]a seal of the righteousness[1343] of the faith which [I]he had while uncircumcised, that he might be [c]the father of [d]all who [ppt]believe without being circumcised,[203] that righteousness[1343] might be reckoned[3049] to them,

12 and the father of circumcision[4061] to those who not only are of the circumcision, but who also follow in the steps of the faith[4102] of our father Abraham which [I]he had while uncircumcised.

25 [I]Or, *a propitiatory sacrifice* [II]Or, *by* [III]Lit., *because of the passing over of the sins previously committed in the forbearance of God* [a]1John 2:2; 4:10 [b]1Cor. 5:7; Heb. 9:14, 28; 1Pet. 1:19; Rev. 1:5 [c]Rom. 2:4 [d]Acts 14:16; 17:30
26 [I]Lit., *is of the faith of Jesus.*
27 [a]Rom. 2:17, 23; 4:2; 1Cor. 1:29ff. [b]Rom. 9:31
28 [I]Some ancient mss. read *Therefore* [II]Or, *of law* [a]Acts 13:39; Rom. 3:20, 21; Eph. 2:9; James 2:20, 24, 26
29 [a]Acts 10:34f.; Rom. 9:24; 10:12; 15:9; Gal. 3:28
30 [I]Lit., *circumcision* [II]Lit., *out of* [III]Lit., *uncircumcision* [a]Rom. 10:12; Gal. 3:20 [b]Rom. 3:22; 4:11f., 16; Gal. 3:8 [c]Deut. 6:4
31 [I]Or, *law* [a]Luke 20:16; Rom. 3:4 [b]Matt. 5:17; Rom. 3:4, 6; 8:4

1 [I]Or, *our forefather, has found according to the flesh* [a]Rom. 1:3
2 [I]Lit., *toward* [a]1Cor. 1:31
3 [a]Gen. 15:6; Rom. 4:9, 22; Gal. 3:6; James 2:23
4 [a]Rom. 11:6
5 [a]John 6:29; Rom. 3:22
7 [a]Ps. 32:1
8 [I]Or, *reckon* [a]Ps. 32:2 [b]2Cor. 5:19
9 [I]Lit., *circumcision* [II]Lit., *uncircumcision* [a]Rom. 3:30 [b]Rom. 4:3 [c]Gen. 15:6
10 [I]Lit., *in circumcision* [II]Lit., *in uncircumcision*
11 [I]Lit., *was in uncircumcision* [a]Gen. 17:10f. [b]John 3:33 [c]Luke 19:9; Rom. 4:16f. [d]Rom. 3:22; 4:16
12 [I]Lit., *was in uncircumcision*

(continued from previous page)
God's rights upon them (Rom. 5:19). A person who is *dikaios* (1342), "righteous," not only recognizes God's rights over his life, but also, as a child of God, exercises his special rights before God which the unrighteous cannot do. Through justification in Christ, man regains the image he formerly had with God before his fall (Gen. 3) as a result of disobedience.

4:2,5 See general remarks on justification on Romans and also note on Rom. 3:25; Gal. 2:16.

4:8 See general remarks on justification on Romans; also note on Gal. 3:22, and *dikaioō* (1344), to justify.

13 For [a]the promise[1860] to Abraham or to his [I]descendants[4690] [b]that he would be heir[2818] of the world[2889] was not [II]through the Law,[3551] but through the righteousness[1343] of faith.[4102]

14 For [a]if those who are [I]of the Law are heirs, faith is made void[2758] and the promise is nullified;

🔑 15 for [a]the Law[3551] brings about wrath,[3709] but [b]where there is no law, neither is there violation.[3807]

16 For this reason *it is* [I]by faith,[4102] that *it might be* in accordance with [a]grace,[5485] in order that the promise may be certain[949] to [b]all the [II]descendants,[4690] not only to [III]those who are of the Law,[3551] but also to [III][c]those who are of the faith of Abraham, who is [d]the father[3962] of us all,

17 (as it is written, "[a]A FATHER OF MANY NATIONS HAVE I MADE[5087] YOU") in the sight of Him whom he believed, *even* God, [b]who [ppt]gives life[2227] to the dead[3498] and [ppt] [I][c]calls into being [d]that which does not exist.

18 In hope against hope[1680] he believed,[4100] in order that he might become [a]a father of many nations, according to that which had been spoken, "[b]SO SHALL YOUR [I]DESCENDANTS[4690] BE."

19 And without becoming [apt]weak[770] in faith he contemplated his own body, now [a]as good as dead since [b]he was about a hundred years old, and [c]the deadness[3500] of Sarah's womb;

20 yet, with respect to the promise of God, he did not waver[1252] in unbelief,[570] but grew strong in faith, [a]giving glory[1390] to God,

21 and [a]being fully assured[4135] that [b]what He had promised,[1861] He was able also to [ainf]perform.

22 Therefore also [a]IT WAS RECKONED[3049] TO HIM AS RIGHTEOUSNESS.[1343]

23 Now [a]not for his sake only was it written, that it was reckoned to him,

24 but for our sake also, to whom it will be reckoned, as those [a]who believe[4100] in Him who [apt] [b]raised[1453] Jesus our Lord from the dead,

25 *He* who was [a]delivered up because of our transgressions,[3900] and was [b]raised because of our justification.[1347]

Results of Justification

5 [a]Therefore having been [aptp]justified[1344] by faith,[4102] [I][b]we have peace[1515] with God through our Lord Jesus Christ,

2 through whom also we have [pfi] [a]obtained our introduction[4318] by faith into this grace[5485] [b]in which we stand; and [I]we exult in hope[1680] of the glory[1391] of God.

3 [a]And not only this, but [I]we also [b]exult in our tribulations, knowing that tribulation brings about [c]perseverance;

4 and [a]perseverance, [b]proven character;[1382] and proven character, hope;[1680]

5 and hope [a]does not disappoint, because the love[26] of God has been [pfip] [b]poured out within our hearts[2588] through the [an]Holy Spirit[4151] who was [aptp]given to us.

6 For while we were still [a]helpless,[772] [b]at the right time[2540] [c]Christ died[599] for the ungodly.[765]

7 For one will hardly die for a righteous[1342] man; though perhaps[5029] for the good[18] man someone would dare even to die.

8 But God [a]demonstrates[4291] [b]His own love toward us, in that while we were yet sinners,[268] [c]Christ[5547] died for us.

9 Much more then, having now been [aptp]justified[1344] [I][a]by His blood,[129] we shall be saved[4982] [b]from the wrath[3709] *of God* through Him.

13 [I]Lit., *seed* [II]Or, *through law* [a]Rom. 9:8; Gal. 3:16, 29 [b]Gen. 17:4-6; 22:17f.
14 [I]Or, *of law* [a]Gal. 3:18
15 [a]Rom. 7:7, 10-25; 1Cor. 15:56; Gal. 3:10 [b]Rom. 3:20
16 [I]Or, *of* [II]Lit., *seed* [III]Lit., *that which is* [a]Rom. 3:24 [b]Rom. 4:11; 9:8; 15:8 [c]Gal. 3:7 [d]Luke 19:9; Rom. 4:11
17 [I]Lit., *calls the things which do not exist as existing* [a]Gen. 17:5 [b]John 5:21 [c]Is. 48:13; 51:2 [d]1Cor. 1:28
18 [I]Lit., *seed* [a]Rom. 4:17 [b]Gen. 15:5
19 [a]Heb. 11:12 [b]Gen. 17:17 [c]Gen. 18:11
20 [a]Matt. 9:8
21 [a]Rom. 14:5 [b]Gen. 18:14; Heb. 11:19
22 [a]Gen. 15:6; Rom. 4:3
23 [a]Rom. 15:4; 1Cor. 9:9f.; 10:11; 2Tim. 3:16f.
24 [a]Rom. 10:9; 1Pet. 1:21 [b]Acts 2:24
25 [a]Is. 53:4, 5; Rom. 5:6, 8; 8:32; Gal. 2:20; Eph. 5:2 [b]Rom. 5:18; 1Cor. 15:17; 2Cor. 5:15

1 [I]Some ancient mss. read *let us have* [a]Rom. 3:28 [b]Rom. 5:11
2 [I]Or, *let us exult* [a]Eph. 2:18; 3:12; Heb. 10:19f.; 1Pet. 3:18 [b]1Cor. 15:1
3 [I]Or, *let us also exult* [a]Rom. 5:11; 8:23; 9:10; 2Cor. 8:19 [b]Matt. 5:12; James 1:2f. [c]Luke 21:19
4 [a]Luke 21:19 [b]Phil. 2:22; James 1:12
5 [a]Ps. 119:116; Rom. 9:33; Heb. 6:18f. [b]Acts 2:33; 10:45; Gal. 4:6; Titus 3:6 **6** [a]Rom. 5:8, 10 [b]Gal. 4:4 [c]Rom. 4:25; 5:8; 8:32; Gal. 2:20; Eph. 5:2 **8** [a]Rom. 3:5 [b]John 3:16; 15:13; Rom. 8:39 [c]Rom. 4:25; 5:6; 8:32; Gal. 2:20; Eph. 5:2 **9** [I]Or, *in* [a]Rom. 3:25 [b]Rom. 1:18; 1Thess. 1:10

🔑 **4:15** See general remarks on justification in introduction on Romans and also note on Rom. 3:25.

10 For if while we were [a]enemies, we were [aptp]reconciled[2644] to God through the death[2288] of His Son,[5207] much more, having been reconciled, we shall be saved [I][b]by His life.[2222]

11 [a]And not only this, [I]but we also [ppt]exult in God through our Lord Jesus Christ, through whom we have now received [b]the reconciliation.[2643]

12 Therefore, just as through [a]one man[444] sin[266] entered into the world,[2889] and [b]death through sin, and [c]so death[2288] spread to all men, because all sinned—[264]

13 for [I]until the Law[3551] sin[266] was in the world; but [a]sin[266] is not imputed[1677] when there is no law.

14 Nevertheless death reigned[936] from Adam until Moses, even over those who had not sinned [a]in the likeness[3667] of the offense[3847] of Adam, who is a [I][b]type[5179] of Him who was to come.

15 But [I]the free gift[5486] is not like the transgression.[3900] For if by the transgression of [a]the one [b]the many [ao]died, much more did the grace[5485] of God and the gift by [c]the grace of the one Man, Jesus Christ, [ao]abound[4052] to the many.

16 And the gift[1434] is not like *that which came* through the one who sinned; for on the one hand [a]the judgment[2917] *arose* from one *transgression* [I]resulting in condemnation,[2631] but on the other hand the free gift *arose* from many transgressions [II]resulting in justification.[1345]

17 For if by the transgression of the one, death[2288] reigned[936] [a]through the one, much more those who receive the abundance[4050] of grace and of the gift[1431] of righteousness[1343] will [b]reign in life through the One, Jesus Christ.

18 So then as through [a]one transgression [I]there resulted condemnation[2631] to all men, even so through one [b]act of righteousness [II]there resulted [c]justification[1347] of life[2222] to all men.

🔑 19 For as through the one man's disobedience[3876] [a]the many [b]were made[2525] sinners, even so through [c]the obedience[5218] of the One [d]the many will be made righteous.[1342]

20 And [I][a]the Law[3551] came in that the transgression might increase; but where sin increased, [b]grace[5485] abounded all the more,[5248]

21 that, as [a]sin reigned[936] in death, even so [b]grace might [aosb]reign through righteousness[1343] to eternal life through Jesus Christ our Lord.

Believers Are Dead to Sin, Alive to God

6 [a]What shall we say then? Are we to [b]continue in sin[266] that grace[5485] might [aosb]increase?

2 [a]May it never be![1096][3361] How shall we who [b]died[599] to sin still live[2198] in it?

🔑 3 Or do you not know[50] that all of us who have been [a]baptized[907] into [b]Christ Jesus have been baptized into His death?[2288]

4 Therefore we have been [aop][a]buried with Him through baptism[908] into death, in order that as Christ[5547] was [aop][b]raised[1453] from the dead through the [c]glory[1391] of the Father, so we too might [aosb]walk in [d]newness[2538] of life.[2222]

5 For [a]if we have become [I]united[4854] with *Him* in the likeness[3667] of His death, certainly we shall be also [II]*in the likeness* of His resurrection,[386]

🔑 6 knowing this, that our [a]old[3820] [I]self[444] was [aop][b]crucified[4957] with *Him,*

10 [I]Or, *in* [a]Rom. 11:28; 2Cor. 5:18f.; Eph. 2:3; Col. 1:21f. [b]Rom. 8:34; Heb. 7:25; 1John 2:1
11 [I]Lit., *but also exulting* [a]Rom. 5:3; 8:23; 9:10; 2Cor. 8:19 [b]Rom. 5:10; 11:15; 2Cor. 5:18f.
12 [a]Gen. 2:17; 3:6, 19; Rom. 5:15-17; 1Cor. 15:21f. [b]Rom. 6:23; 1Cor. 15:56; James 1:15 [c]Rom. 5:14, 19, 21; 1Cor. 15:22
13 [I]Or, *until law* [a]Rom. 4:15
14 [I]Or, *foreshadowing* [a]Hos. 6:7 [b]1Cor. 15:45
15 [I]Lit., *not as the trespass, so also is the free gift* [a]Rom. 5:12, 18, 19 [b]Rom. 5:19 [c]Acts 15:11
16 [I]Lit., *to condemnation* [II]Lit., *to an act of righteousness* [a]1Cor. 11:32
17 [a]Gen. 2:17; 3:6, 19; Rom. 5:12, 15, 16; 1Cor. 15:21f. [b]2Tim. 2:12; Rev. 22:5
18 [I]Lit., *to condemnation* [II]Lit., *to justification* [a]Rom. 5:12, 15 [b]Rom. 3:25 [c]Rom. 4:25
19 [a]Rom. 5:15, 18 [b]Rom. 5:12; 11:32 [c]Phil. 2:8
20 [I]Or, *law* [a]Rom. 3:20; 7:7f.; Gal. 3:19 [b]Rom. 6:1; 1Tim. 1:14
21 [a]Rom. 5:12, 14 [b]John 1:17; Rom. 6:23

1 [a]Rom. 3:5 [b]Rom. 3:8; 6:15
2 [a]Luke 20:16; Rom. 6:15 [b]Rom. 6:11; 7:4, 6; Gal. 2:19; Col. 2:20; 3:3; 1Pet. 2:24
3 [a]Matt. 28:19 [b]Acts 2:38; 8:16; 19:5; Gal. 3:27
4 [a]Col. 2:12 [b]Acts 2:24; Rom. 6:9 [c]John 11:40; 2Cor. 13:4 [d]Rom. 7:6; 2Cor. 5:17; Gal. 6:15; Eph. 4:23f.; Col. 3:10
5 [I]Or, *united with the likeness* [II]Or, *with* [a]2Cor. 4:10; Phil. 3:10f.; Col. 2:12; 3:1
6 [I]Lit., *man* [a]Eph. 4:22; Col. 3:9 [b]Gal. 2:20; 5:24; 6:14

🔑 **5:19** See general remarks on justification in Romans; also note on Rom. 3:25, and *dikaioō* (1344), to justify.

🔑 **6:3** See note on I Cor. 10:2; 12:13.

🔑 **6:6,7** See note on Gal. 3:22 and also *phthartos* (5349), corruptible; *thnētos* (2349), mortal.

that our [c]body[4983] of sin[266] might be [II]done away with, that we should no longer be [infg]slaves[1398] to sin;

7 for [a]he who has [apt]died[599] is [pfip] [I]freed[1344] from sin.

8 Now [a]if we have [ao]died with Christ, we believe[4100] that we shall also live with[4800] Him,

9 knowing that Christ, having been [a]raised from the dead,[3498] is never to die again; [b]death no longer is master[2961] over Him.

10 For the death[599] that He died, He died to sin, once for all; but the life that He lives,[2198] He lives to God.

🗝 11 Even so consider[3049] yourselves to be [a]dead[3498] to sin, but [ppt]alive[2198] to God in Christ Jesus.

🗝 **12** Therefore do not let sin [a]reign[936] in your mortal body that you should obey[5219] its lusts,

13 and do not go on [aim] [a]presenting [I]the members of your body to sin *as* [II]instruments of unrighteousness;[93] but [b]present yourselves to God as those [ppt]alive from the dead, and your members *as* [II]instruments of righteousness[1343] to God.

14 For [a]sin shall not [b]be master over you, for [c]you are not under law,[3551] but [d]under grace.[5485]

15 What then? [a]Shall we sin[264] because we are not under law but under grace? [b]May it never be![1096][3361]

16 Do you not [a]know that when you present yourselves to someone *as* [b]slaves for obedience,[5218] you are slaves[1401] of the one whom you obey, either of [c]sin[266] [I]resulting in death,[2288] or of obedience[5218] [II]resulting in righteousness?[1343]

17 But [a]thanks be to God that [I]though you were slaves of sin, you became obedient[5219] from the heart[2588] to that [b]form[5179] of teaching[1322] to which you were committed,

18 and having been [a]freed from sin, you became slaves of righteousness.

6 [II]Or, *made powerless* [c]Rom. 7:24
7 [I]Or, *acquitted* [a]1Pet. 4:1
8 [a]Rom. 6:4; 2Cor. 4:10; 2Tim. 2:11
9 [a]Acts 2:24; Rom. 6:4 [b]Rev. 1:18
11 [a]Rom. 6:2; 7:4, 6; Gal. 2:19; Col. 2:20; 3:3; 1Pet. 2:24
12 [a]Rom. 6:14
13 [I]Lit., *your members to sin* [II]Or, *weapons* [a]Rom. 6:16, 19; 7:5; Col. 3:5 [b]Rom. 12:1; 2Cor. 5:14f.; 1Pet. 2:24
14 [a]Rom. 8:2, 12 [b]Rom. 6:12 [c]Rom. 5:18; 7:4, 6; Gal. 4:21 [d]Rom. 5:17, 21
15 [a]Rom. 6:1 [b]Luke 20:16; Rom. 6:2
16 [I]Lit., *to death* [II]Lit., *to righteousness* [a]Rom. 11:2; 1Cor. 3:16; 5:6; 6:2, 3, 9, 15, 16, 19; 9:13, 24 [b]John 8:34; 2Pet. 2:19 [c]Rom. 6:21, 23
17 [I]Lit., *you were slaves. . .but you became* [a]Rom. 1:8; 2Cor. 2:14 [b]2Tim. 1:13
18 [a]John 8:32; Rom. 6:22; 8:2
19 [I]Lit., *to lawlessness* [II]Lit., *to sanctification* [a]Rom. 3:5 [b]Rom. 6:13
20 [a]Matt. 6:24; Rom. 6:16
21 [I]Lit., *fruit* [II]Lit., *having* [III]Lit., *in* [a]Jer. 12:13; Ezek. 16:63; Rom. 7:5 [b]Rom. 1:32; 5:12; 6:16, 23; 8:6, 13; Gal. 6:8
22 [I]Lit., *have* [II]Lit., *fruit* [III]Lit., *to sanctification* [a]John 8:32; Rom. 6:18; 8:2 [b]1Cor. 7:22; 1Pet. 2:16 [c]Rom. 7:4 [d]1Pet. 1:9

19 [a]I am speaking in human terms because of the weakness of your flesh.[4561] For just [b]as you [ao]presented your members *as* slaves to impurity[167] and to lawlessness,[458] [I]resulting in *further* lawlessness, so now [aim]present your members *as* slaves to righteousness, [II]resulting in sanctification.[38]

20 For [a]when you were [an]slaves of sin, you were free in regard to righteousness.

21 Therefore what [I][a]benefit were you then [II]deriving [III]from the things of which you are now ashamed? For the outcome[5056] of those things is [b]death.[2288]

22 But now having been [a]freed from sin and [b]enslaved to God, you [I]derive your [II][c]benefit, [III]resulting in sanctification, and [d]the outcome, eternal[166] life.[2222]

23 For the wages[3800] of [a]sin[266] is death,[2288] but the free gift[5486] of God is [b]eternal[166] life[2222] in Christ Jesus our Lord.

Believers United to Christ

7 Or do you not know,[50] [a]brethren[80] (for I am speaking to those who know the law), that the law[3551] has jurisdiction[2961] over a person as long as he lives?[2198]

2 For [a]the married woman is bound[1210] by law to her husband while he is living; but if her husband [aosb]dies, she is [pfip]released from the law concerning the husband.

3 So then if, while her husband is living, she is joined to another[2087] man, she shall be called[5537] an adulteress; but if her husband [aosb]dies, she is free[1658] from the law, so that she is not an adulteress, though she is joined to another man.

23 [a]Rom. 1:32; 5:12; 6:16, 21; 8:6, 13; Gal. 6:8 [b]Matt. 25:46; Rom. 5:21; 8:38, 39 1 [a]Rom. 1:13
2 [a]1Cor. 7:39

🗝 **6:11** See general remarks on justification on Romans; also note on Rom. 3:25; Gal. 3:22, and *dikaioō* (1344), to justify.

🗝 **6:12** See note on II Tim. 1:12 and also *thnētos* (2349), mortal; *paschō* (3958), to suffer.

4 Therefore, my brethren, you also were [a]made to [aop]die [b]to the Law [c]through the body of Christ, that you might be joined to another, to Him who was raised**1453** from the dead,**3498** that we might bear fruit for God.

5 For while we were [a]in the flesh,**4561** the sinful passions,**3804** which were [b]*aroused* by the Law, were at work**1754** [c]in [I]the members of our body to bear fruit for death.

6 But now we have been [a]released from the Law, having [apt] [b]died to that by which we were bound,**2722** so that we [pinf]serve in [c]newness**2538** of [d]the [I]Spirit**4151** and not in oldness**3821** of the letter.**1121**

7 [a]What shall we say then? Is the Law**3551** sin?**266** [b]May it never be!**1096** **3361** On the contrary, [c]I would not have come to know**1097** sin except [I]through the Law; for I would not have known about [II]coveting**1939** if the Law had not said, "[d]YOU SHALL NOT [III]COVET."**1937**

8 But sin, [apt] [a]taking opportunity [b]through the commandment,**1785** produced in me [I]coveting**1939** of every kind; for [c]apart [II]from the Law sin *is* dead.**3498**

9 And I was once [ipf]alive**2198** apart [I]from the Law; but when the commandment [apt]came, sin became alive, and I died;**599**

10 and this commandment, which was [Ia]to result in life,**2222** proved**2147** [II]to result in death**2288** for me;

11 for sin, [apt] [a]taking opportunity [b]through the commandment, [c]deceived me, and through it killed me.

12 [a]So then, the Law is holy,**40** and the commandment is holy and righteous**1342** and good.**18**

13 Therefore did that which is good become *a cause of* death for me? [a]May it never be! Rather it was sin, in order that it might be shown to be sin by effecting**2716** my death through that which is good, that through the commandment sin might become utterly sinful.**268**

The Conflict of Two Natures

14 For we know that the Law is [a]spiritual;**4152** but I am [a]of flesh,**4559** [b]sold [Ic]into bondage to sin.**266**

15 For that which I am doing, [a]I do not understand; for I am not practicing**4238** [b]what I *would* like to *do,* but I am doing the very thing I hate.

16 But if I do the very thing I do not wish *to do,* I agree with [a]the Law, *confessing* that it is good.

17 So now, [a]no longer am I the one doing it, but sin which [ppt]indwells**3611,1722** me.

18 For I know that nothing good dwells in me, that is, in my [a]flesh;**4561** for the wishing is present in me, but the doing of the good *is* not.

19 For [a]the good**18** that I wish, I do not do; but I practice the very evil**2556** that I do not wish.

20 But if I am doing the very thing I do not wish, [a]I am no longer the one doing it, but sin which [ppt]dwells in me.

21 I find then [a]the [I]principle**3551** that evil is [pin]present in me, the one who [ppt]wishes**2309** to [pinf]do good.

22 For I joyfully concur with the law of God**2316** [I]in [a]the inner man,**444**

23 but I see [a]a different**2087** law in [I]the members of my body, waging war against the [b]law of my mind, and making me a prisoner [II]of [c]the law of sin which is in my members.

24 Wretched man that I am! Who will set me free**4506** from [Ia]the body of this [b]death?**2288**

25 [a]Thanks be to God through Jesus Christ**5547** our Lord!**2962** So then, on the one hand I myself with my mind**3563** am serving**1398** the law of God, but on the other, with my flesh [b]the law of sin.

Deliverance from Bondage

8

🔑 There is therefore now no [a]condemnation**2631** for those who are [b]in [c]Christ**5547** Jesus.

4 [a]Rom. 6:2; 7:6 [b]Rom. 8:2; Gal. 2:19; 5:18 [c]Col. 1:22
5 [I]Lit., *our members to bear* [a]Rom. 8:8f.; 2Cor. 10:3 [b]Rom. 7:7f. [c]Rom. 6:13, 21, 23
6 [I]Or, *spirit* [a]Rom. 7:2 [b]Rom. 6:2 [c]Rom. 6:4 [d]Rom. 2:29
7 [I]Or, *through law* [II]Or, *lust* [III]Or, *lust* [a]Rom. 3:5 [b]Luke 20:16 [c]Rom. 3:20; 4:15; 5:20 [d]Ex. 20:17; Deut. 5:21
8 [I]Or, *lust* [II]Or, *from law* [a]Rom. 7:11 [b]Rom. 3:20; 7:11 [c]1Cor. 15:56
9 [I]Or, *from law*
10 [I]Lit., *to life* [II]Lit., *to death* [a]Lev. 18:5; Luke 10:28; Rom. 10:5; Gal. 3:12
11 [a]Rom. 7:8 [b]Rom. 3:20; 7:8 [c]Gen. 3:13
12 [a]Rom. 7:16; 1Tim. 1:8
13 [a]Luke 20:16
14 [I]Lit., *under sin* [a]1Cor. 3:1 [b]1Kin. 21:20, 25; 2Kin. 17:17; Rom. 6:6; Gal. 4:3 [c]Rom. 3:9
15 [a]John 15:15 [b]Rom. 7:19; Gal. 5:17
16 [a]Rom. 7:12; 1Tim. 1:8
17 [a]Rom. 7:20
18 [a]John 3:6; Rom. 7:25; 8:3
19 [a]Rom. 7:15
20 [a]Rom. 7:17
21 [I]Lit., *law* [a]Rom. 7:23, 25; 8:2
22 [I]Or, *concerning* [a]2Cor. 4:16; Eph. 3:16; 1Pet. 3:4
23 [I]Lit., *my members* [II]Lit., *in* [a]Rom. 6:19; Gal. 5:17; James 4:1; 1Pet. 2:11 [b]Rom. 7:25 [c]Rom. 7:21, 25; 8:2
24 [I]Or, *this body of death* [a]Rom. 6:6; Col. 2:11 [b]Rom. 8:2
25 [a]1Cor. 15:57 [b]Rom. 7:21, 23; 8:2 **1** [a]Rom. 5:16; 8:34 [b]Rom. 8:9f. [c]Rom. 8:2, 11, 39; 16:3

🔑 **8:1-17** See note on Eph. 1:4,5 and also *dikaioō* (1344), to justify.

2 For [a]the law[3551] of the Spirit of life[2222] [I]in [b]Christ Jesus [c]has set [II]you free[1659] from the law of sin[266] and of death.[2288]

3 For [a]what the Law could not do, [ipf][I][b]weak[770] as it was through the flesh,[4561] God *did:* [apt]sending His own Son[5207] in [c]the likeness[3667] of [II]sinful[266] flesh and *as an offering* for sin, He condemned[2632] sin in the flesh,

4 in order that the [a]requirement[1345] of the Law might be fulfilled in us, who [b]do not [ppt]walk according to the flesh, but according to the Spirit.[4151]

5 For those who are according to the flesh set their minds[5426] on [a]the things of the flesh,[4561] but those who are according to the Spirit,[4151] [b]the things of the Spirit.

6 [a]For the mind set on the flesh[4561] is [b]death,[2288] but the mind set on the Spirit is life[2222] and peace,[1515]

7 because the mind set on the flesh is [a]hostile[2189] toward God; for it does not subject[5293] itself to the law[3551] of God, for it is not even able *to do so;*

8 and those who are [a]in the flesh cannot [ainf]please God.

9 However, you are not [a]in the flesh but in the Spirit, if indeed the [an]Spirit[4151] of God [b]dwells[3611] in you. But [c]if anyone does not have the [an]Spirit of Christ, he does not belong to Him.

10 And [a]if Christ[5547] is in you, though the body[4983] is dead because of sin, yet the spirit[4151] is [I]alive because of righteousness.[1343]

11 But if the Spirit of Him who [a]raised[1453] Jesus from the dead dwells[3611] in you, [b]He who raised [c]Christ Jesus from the dead will also give life[2227] to your mortal[2349] bodies [I]through His Spirit who [ppt]indwells you.

12 So then, brethren, we are under obligation,[3781] not to the flesh, to live[2198] according to the flesh—

13 for [a]if you are living according to the flesh, you [I]must die; but if by the Spirit you are [b]putting to death the deeds[4234] of the body, you will live.

14 For all who are [a]being led[71] by the [an]Spirit of God, these are [an] [b]sons[5207] of God.[2316]

15 For you [a]have not [ao]received a [an]spirit[4151] of slavery[1397] [I]leading to fear[5401] again, but you [b]have received [II]a [an]spirit of adoption[5206] as sons by which we cry out, "[c]Abba![5] Father!"[3962]

16 The Spirit Himself [a]bears witness with our spirit[4151] that we are [an] [b]children[5043] of God,

17 and if children, [a]heirs[2818] also, heirs of God and fellow heirs[4789] with Christ, [b]if indeed we suffer with[4841] *Him* in order that we may also be glorified with *Him.*[4888]

18 For I consider that the sufferings[3804] of this present time[2540] [a]are not worthy to be compared with the [b]glory[1391] that is to be revealed to us.

19 For the [a]anxious longing[603] of the creation waits eagerly for[553] [b]the revealing[602] of the [c]sons[5207] of God.

20 For the creation [a]was subjected[5293] to [b]futility,[3153] not of its own will, but [c]because of Him who subjected it, [I]in hope[1680]

21 that [a]the creation itself also will be set free from its slavery[1397] to corruption into the freedom of the glory[1391] of the children of God.

2 [I]Or, *has set you free in Christ Jesus* [II]Some ancient mss. read *me* [a]1Cor. 15:45 [b]Rom. 8:1, 11, 39; 16:3 [c]John 8:32, 36; Rom. 6:14, 18; 7:4 **3** [I]Lit., *wherein it was weak* [II]Lit., *flesh of sin* [a]Acts 13:39; Heb. 10:1ff. [b]Rom. 7:18f.; Heb. 7:18 [c]Phil. 2:7; Heb. 2:14, 17; 4:15 **4** [a]Luke 1:6; Rom. 2:26 [b]Gal. 5:16, 25 **5** [a]Gal. 5:19-21 [b]Gal. 5:22-25 **6** [a]Gal. 6:8 [b]Rom. 6:21; 8:13 **7** [a]James 4:4 **8** [a]Rom. 7:5 **9** [a]Rom. 7:5 [b]John 14:23; Rom. 8:11; 1Cor. 3:16; 6:19; 2Cor. 6:16; Gal. 4:6; Phil. 1:19; 2Tim. 1:14; 1John 4:13 [c]John 14:17 **10** [I]Lit., *life* [a]John 17:23; Gal. 2:20; Eph. 3:17; Col. 1:27 **11** [I]Some ancient mss. read *because of* [a]Acts 2:24; Rom. 6:4 [b]John 5:21 [c]Rom. 8:1, 2, 39; 16:3 **13** [I]Or, *are about to* [a]Rom. 8:6 [b]Col. 3:5 **14** [a]Gal. 5:18 [b]Hos. 1:10; Matt. 5:9; John 1:12; Rom. 8:16, 19; 9:8, 26; 2Cor. 6:18; Gal. 3:26; 1John 3:1; Rev. 21:7 **15** [I]Lit., *for fear again* [II]Or, *the Spirit* [a]2Tim. 1:7; Heb. 2:15 [b]Rom. 8:23; Gal. 4:5f. [c]Mark 14:36; Gal. 4:6 **16** [a]Acts 5:32 [b]Hos. 1:10; Matt. 5:9; John 1:12; Rom. 8:14, 19; 9:8, 26; 2Cor. 6:18; Gal. 3:26; 1John 3:1; Rev. 21:7 **17** [a]Acts 20:32; Gal. 3:29; 4:7; Eph. 3:6; Titus 3:7; Heb. 1:14; Rev. 21:7 [b]2Cor. 1:5, 7; Phil. 3:10; Col. 1:24; 2Tim. 2:12; 1Pet. 4:13 **18** [a]2Cor. 4:17; 1Pet. 4:13 [b]Col. 3:4; Titus 2:13; 1Pet. 1:5; 5:1 **19** [a]Phil. 1:20 [b]Rom. 8:18; 1Cor. 1:7f.; Col. 3:4; 1Pet. 1:7, 13; 1John 3:2 [c]Hos. 1:10; Matt. 5:9; John 1:12; Rom. 8:14, 16; 9:8, 26; 2Cor. 6:18; Gal. 3:26; 1John 3:1; Rev. 21:7 **20** [I]Some ancient mss. read *in hope; because the creation* [a]Gen. 3:17-19 [b]Ps. 39:5f.; Eccl. 1:2 [c]Gen. 3:17; 5:29 **21** [a]Acts 3:21; 2Pet. 3:13; Rev. 21:1

8:7 See note on Gal. 3:22.

8:11 See note on II Tim. 1:12 and also *thnētos* (2349), mortal; *paschō* (3958), to suffer.

8:16 See note on Eph. 1:4,5 and also *eklogē* (1589), election.

8:19-26 See note on Mt. 13 and also *phthora* (5356), corruption; *phtheirō* (5351), to corrupt.

22 For we know that the whole creation [a]groans and suffers the pains of childbirth together[4944] until now.

🔑 23 [a]And not only this, but also we ourselves, having [b]the first fruits of the Spirit, even we ourselves [c]groan within ourselves, [d]waiting eagerly for[533] *our* adoption[5206] as sons, [e]the redemption[629] of our body.[4983]

24 For [a]in hope[1680] we have been [aop]saved,[4982] but [b]hope that is [ppp]seen is not hope; for [I]why does one also hope for[1679] what he sees?

25 But [a]if we hope for what we do not see, with perseverance we wait eagerly for[553] it.

Our Victory in Christ

26 And in the same way the Spirit[4151] also helps our weakness; for [a]we do not know how to [aosb]pray as we should, but [b]the Spirit Himself intercedes[5241] for *us* with groanings too deep for words;

27 and [a]He who [ppt]searches the hearts[2588] knows what [b]the mind[5427] of the Spirit is, because He [c]intercedes[1793] for the [I]saints[40] according to *the will of* God.[2316]

🔑 28 And we know[1492] that [I]God causes [a]all things to work together[4903] for good[18] to those who [ppt]love[25] God, to those who are [b]called[2822] according to *His* purpose.[4286]

29 For whom He [a]foreknew,[4267] He also [b]predestined[4309] *to become* [c]conformed[4833] to the image[1504] of His Son,[5207] that He might be the [d]firstborn[4416] among many brethren;[80]

30 and whom He [a]predestined, these He also [b]called;[2564] and whom He called, these He also [c]justified;[1344] and whom He justified, these He also [d]glorified.[1392]

31 [a]What then shall we say to these things? [b]If God[2316] *is* for us, who *is* against us?

32 He who [a]did not spare His own[2398] Son, but [b]delivered Him up for us all, how will He not also with Him freely give[5438] us all things?

🔑 33 Who will bring a charge against[1488] [a]God's elect?[1588] [b]God is the one who justifies;

34 who is the one who [ppt][a]condemns? Christ Jesus[5547] is He who [b]died,[599] yes, rather who was [apt][I][c]raised,[1453] who [pin]is [d]at the right hand[1188] of God, who also [e]intercedes[1793] for us.

35 Who shall separate us from [a]the love[26] of [I]Christ?[5547] Shall [b]tribulation,[2347] or distress,[4730] or [c]persecution, or [c]famine, or [c]nakedness,[1132] or [c]peril, or sword?

36 Just as it is written,

"[a]FOR THY SAKE WE ARE BEING
PUT TO DEATH ALL DAY
LONG;
WE WERE CONSIDERED[3049] AS
SHEEP TO BE
SLAUGHTERED."

37 But in all these things we overwhelmingly [a]conquer through [b]Him who loved[25] us.

🔑 38 For I am convinced that neither [a]death,[2288] nor life, nor [b]angels, nor principalities,[446] nor [c]things present,[1764] nor things to come, nor powers,

39 nor height, nor depth, nor any other created thing,[2937] shall be able to separate us from [a]the love of God, which is [b]in Christ Jesus our Lord.

Solicitude for Israel

9 [a]I am telling the truth[225] in Christ,[5547] I am not lying, my

22 [a]Jer. 12:4, 11 **23** [a]Rom. 5:3 [b]Rom. 8:16; 2Cor. 1:22 [c]2Cor. 5:2, 4 [d]Rom. 8:15, 19, 25; Gal. 5:5 [e]Rom. 7:24 **24** [I]Some ancient mss. read *who hopes for what he sees?* [a]Rom. 8:20; 1Thess. 5:8; Titus 3:7 [b]Rom. 4:18; 2Cor. 5:7; Heb. 11:1 **25** [a]1Thess. 1:3 **26** [a]Matt. 20:22; 2Cor. 12:8 [b]John 14:16; Rom. 8:15f.; Eph. 6:18 **27** [I]Or, *holy ones* [a]Ps. 139:1f.; Luke 16:15; Acts 1:24; Rev. 2:23 [b]Rom. 8:6 [c]Rom. 8:34 **28** [I]Some ancient mss. read *all things work together for good* [a]Rom. 8:32 [b]Rom. 8:30; 9:24; 11:29; 1Cor. 1:9; Gal. 1:6, 15; 5:8; Eph. 1:11; 3:11; 2Thess. 2:14; Heb. 9:15; 1Pet. 2:9; 3:9 **29** [a]Rom. 11:2; 1Cor. 8:3; 2Tim. 1:9; 1Pet. 1:2, 20 [b]Rom. 9:23; 1Cor. 2:7; Eph. 1:5, 11 [c]1Cor. 15:49; Phil. 3:21 [d]Col. 1:18; Heb. 1:6 **30** [a]Rom. 9:23; 11:29; 1Cor. 2:7; Eph. 1:5, 11 [b]Rom. 8:28; 9:24; 1Cor. 1:9; Gal. 1:6, 15; 5:8; Eph. 1:11; 3:11; 2Thess. 2:14; Heb. 9:15; 1Pet. 2:9; 3:9 [c]1Cor. 6:11 [d]John 17:22; Rom. 8:21; 9:23 **31** [a]Rom. 3:5; 4:1 [b]Ps. 118:6; Matt. 1:23 **32** [a]John 3:16; Rom. 5:8 [b]Rom. 4:25 **33** [a]Luke 18:7 [b]Is. 50:8f. **34** [I]Some ancient mss. read *raised from the dead* [a]Rom. 8:1 [b]Rom. 5:6f. [c]Acts 2:24 [d]Mark 16:19 [e]Rom. 8:27; Heb. 7:25 **35** [I]Some ancient mss. read *God* [a]Rom. 8:37f. [b]Rom. 2:9; 2Cor. 4:8 [c]1Cor. 4:11; 2Cor. 11:26f. **36** [a]Ps. 44:22; Acts 20:24; 1Cor. 4:9; 15:30f.; 2Cor. 1:9; 4:10f.; 6:9; 11:23 **37** [a]John 16:33; 1Cor. 15:57 [b]Gal. 2:20; Eph. 5:2; Rev. 1:5 **38** [a]1Cor. 3:22 [b]1Cor. 15:24; Eph. 1:21; 1Pet. 3:22 [c]1Cor. 3:22 **39** [a]Rom. 5:8 [b]Rom. 8:1 **1** [a]2Cor. 11:10; Gal. 1:20; 1Tim. 2:7

🔑 **8:23** See notes on Mt. 8:17; I Cor. 15; I Pet. 1:5; Js. 5:14,17; and general remarks on I John.
🔑 **8:28,29,33** See notes on Eph. 1:4,5; II Tim. 1:9; Col. 1:15; Js. 5:14,15.
🔑 **8:38,39** See II Thess. 2:3.

conscience[4893] bearing me witness in the [an]Holy Spirit,[4151]

2 that I have great sorrow[3077] and unceasing[88] grief in my heart.

3 For [a]I could [ipf] [I]wish that I myself were [b]accursed,[331] *separated* from Christ for the sake of my brethren,[80] my kinsmen [c]according to the flesh,[4561]

4 who are [a]Israelites, to whom belongs [b]the adoption as sons[5206] and [c]the glory[1391] and [d]the covenants[1242] and [e]the giving of the Law and [f]the *temple* service[2999] and [g]the promises,

5 whose are [a]the fathers,[3962] and [b]from whom is [I]the Christ according to[2596] the flesh,[4561] [c]who is over all, [d]God [e]blessed[2128] [II]forever. Amen.[281]

6 But *it is* not as though [a]the word[3056] of God has [pfi]failed. [b]For they are not all Israel who are *descended* from Israel;

7 neither are they all children[5043] [a]because they are Abraham's [I]descendants,[4690] but: "[b]THROUGH ISAAC YOUR [I]DESCENDANTS WILL BE NAMED."

8 That is, it is not the children of the flesh who are [a]children of God, but the [b]children of the promise[1860] are regarded[3049] as [I]descendants.

9 For this is a word of promise: "[a]AT THIS TIME[2540] I WILL COME, AND SARAH SHALL HAVE A SON."[5207]

10 [a]And not only this, but there was [b]Rebekah also, when she had[2192] conceived *twins* by one man, our father Isaac;

🗝 11 for though *the twins* were not yet born, and had not done[4238] anything good[18] or bad, in order that [a]God's purpose[4286] according to *His* choice[1589] might [psa]stand,[3306] not because of works,[2041] but because of Him who [ppt]calls,

12 it was said to her, "[a]THE OLDER WILL SERVE[1398] THE YOUNGER."

13 Just as it is written, "[a]JACOB I LOVED,[25] BUT ESAU I HATED."

14 [a]What shall we say then? [b]There is no injustice[93] with God, is there? [c]May it never be!

15 For He says to Moses, "[a]I WILL HAVE MERCY ON WHOM I HAVE MERCY, AND I WILL HAVE COMPASSION ON WHOM I HAVE COMPASSION."

16 So then it *does* not *depend* on the man who [ppt]wills or the man who [ppt] [a]runs, but on [b]God who [ppt]has mercy.

17 For the Scripture says to Pharaoh, "[a]FOR THIS VERY PURPOSE I [ao]RAISED YOU UP,[1825] TO [asbm]DEMONSTRATE MY POWER IN YOU, AND THAT MY NAME MIGHT BE PROCLAIMED[1229] [I]THROUGHOUT THE WHOLE EARTH."[1093]

18 So then He has mercy on whom He desires, and He [a]hardens[4645] whom He desires.

19 [a]You will say to me then, "[b]Why does He still find fault? For [c]who [pfi]resists His will?"[1013]

20 On the contrary, who are you, [a]O man, who [ppt] [b]answers back[470] to God? [c]The thing molded will not say to the molder, "Why did you [ao]make me like this," will it?

21 Or does not the potter have a right[1849] over the clay, to make from the same lump one vessel [I]for honorable use, and another [II]for common use?

22 What if God, although willing to demonstrate His wrath[3709] and to make His power known,[1107] endured[5342] with much [a]patience vessels of wrath [pfpp] [b]prepared[2675] for destruction?[684]

23 And *He did so* in order that He might make known[1107] [a]the riches of His glory upon [b]vessels of mercy,[1656] which He [ao] [c]prepared beforehand for glory,

24 *even* us, whom He also [ao] [a]called, [b]not from among Jews only, but also from among Gentiles.[1484]

25 As He says also in Hosea,

"[a]I WILL CALL THOSE WHO WERE NOT MY PEOPLE,[2992] 'MY PEOPLE,'

3 [I]Lit., *pray* [a]Ex. 32:32 [b]1Cor. 12:3; 16:22; Gal. 1:8f. [c]Rom. 1:3; 11:14; Eph. 6:5 **4** [a]Deut. 7:6; 14:1f.; Rom. 9:6 [b]Ex. 4:22; Rom. 8:15 [c]Ex. 40:34; 1Kin. 8:11; Ezek. 1:28; Heb. 9:5 [d]Gen. 17:2; Deut. 29:14; Luke 1:72; Acts 3:25; Eph. 2:12 [e]Deut. 4:13f.; Ps. 147:19 [f]Heb. 9:1,6 [g]Acts 2:39; 13:32; Eph. 2:12 **5** [I]I.e., the Messiah [II]Lit., *unto the ages* [a]Acts 3:13; Rom. 11:28 [b]Matt. 1:1-16; Rom. 1:3 [c]Col. 1:16-19 [d]John 1:1 [e]Rom. 1:25 **6** [a]Num. 23:19 [b]John 1:47; Rom. 2:28f.; Gal. 6:16 **7** [I]Lit., *seed* [a]John 8:33, 39; Gal. 4:23 [b]Gen. 21:12; Heb. 11:18 **8** [I]Lit., *seed* [a]Rom. 8:14 [b]Rom. 4:13, 16; Gal. 3:29; 4:28; Heb. 11:11 **9** [a]Gen. 18:10 **10** [a]Rom. 5:3 [b]Gen. 25:21 **11** [a]Rom. 4:17; 8:28 **12** [a]Gen. 25:23 **13** [a]Mal. 1:2f. **14** [a]Rom. 3:5 [b]2Chr. 19:7; Rom. 2:11 [c]Luke 20:16 **15** [a]Ex. 33:19 **16** [a]Gal. 2:2 [b]Eph. 2:8 **17** [I]Lit., *in* [a]Ex. 9:16 **18** [a]Ex. 4:21; 7:3; 9:12; 10:20, 27; 11:10; 14:4, 17; Deut. 2:30; Josh. 11:20; John 12:40; Rom. 11:7, 25 **19** [a]Rom. 11:19; 1Cor. 15:35; James 2:18 [b]Rom. 3:7 [c]2Chr. 20:6; Job 9:12; Dan. 4:35 **20** [a]Rom. 2:1 [b]Job 33:13 [c]Is. 29:16; 45:9; 64:8; Jer. 18:6; Rom. 9:22f.; 2Tim. 2:20 **21** [I]Lit., *for honor* [II]Lit., *for dishonor* **22** [a]Rom. 2:4 [b]Prov. 16:4; 1Pet. 2:8 **23** [a]Rom. 2:4; Eph. 3:16 [b]Acts 9:15 [c]Rom. 8:29f. **24** [a]Rom. 8:28 [b]Rom. 3:29 **25** [a]Hos. 2:23; 1Pet. 2:10

🗝 **9:11** See notes on Eph. 1:4,5; II Tim. 1:9.

AND HER WHO WAS NOT
BELOVED, 'BELOVED.'"[25]
26 "[a]AND IT SHALL BE THAT IN THE
PLACE WHERE IT WAS SAID
TO THEM, 'YOU ARE NOT MY
PEOPLE,'
THERE THEY SHALL BE CALLED
SONS OF [b]THE LIVING[2198]
GOD."
27 And Isaiah cries out concerning
Israel, "[a]THOUGH THE NUMBER OF THE
SONS[5207] of Israel be [b]AS THE SAND OF
THE SEA, IT IS [c]THE REMNANT THAT WILL
BE SAVED;[498]
28 [a]FOR THE LORD WILL [ppt]EXECUTE[4931] HIS WORD UPON THE EARTH,
[I]THOROUGHLY AND [ppt] [II]QUICKLY."
29 And just as Isaiah foretold,
"[a]EXCEPT [b]THE LORD[2962] OF
[I]SABAOTH[4519] HAD [ao]LEFT TO
US A [II]POSTERITY,
[c]WE WOULD HAVE [aop]BECOME
AS SODOM, AND WOULD
HAVE [aop] [III]RESEMBLED
GOMORRAH."
30 [a]What shall we say then? That
Gentiles, who did not [ppt]pursue righteousness,[1343] [ao]attained[2638] righteousness, even [b]the righteousness which is
[I]by faith;[4102]
31 but Israel, [ppt] [a]pursuing a law[3551]
of righteousness, did not [ao] [b]arrive at
that law.
32 Why? Because *they did* not *pursue it* [I]by faith, but as though *it were*
[I]by [an]works. They stumbled over[4350]
[a]the stumbling stone,
33 just as it is written,
"[a]BEHOLD, I LAY IN ZION
[b]A STONE OF STUMBLING
AND A ROCK OF OFFENSE,[4625]
[c]AND HE WHO [ppt]BELIEVES[4100]
IN HIM [d]WILL NOT BE
[I]DISAPPOINTED."

The Word of Faith Brings Salvation

10 Brethren,[80] my heart's[2588] desire and my prayer to God for
them is for *their* salvation.[4991]
2 For I bear them witness that they
have [a]a zeal[2205] for God, but not in accordance with knowledge.[1922]
3 For not [ppt]knowing[50] about [a]God's
righteousness,[1343] and [ppt] [b]seeking to
[ainf]establish their own, they did not
[aop]subject themselves to[5293] the righteousness of God.
4 For [a]Christ[5547] is the [I]end[5056] of
the law[3551] for righteousness to [b]everyone who [ppt]believes.[4100]
5 For Moses writes that the man
who [apt]practices the righteousness
which is [I]based on law [a]shall live[2198]
[II]by that righteousness.
6 But [a]the righteousness[1343] [I]based
on faith[4102] speaks thus, "[b]DO NOT SAY
IN YOUR HEART,[2588] 'WHO WILL ASCEND
INTO HEAVEN?'[3772] (that is, to bring Christ
down),[2609]
7 or 'WHO WILL DESCEND INTO THE
[a]ABYSS?' (that is, to [b]bring Christ up[321]
from the dead)."
8 But what does it say? "[a]THE WORD
IS NEAR YOU, IN YOUR MOUTH AND IN
YOUR HEART"—[2588] that is, the word[4487]
of faith which we are preaching,[2784]
🔑 9 [I]that [a]if you confess[3670] with your
mouth Jesus *as* Lord,[2962] and [b]believe[4100]
in your heart that [c]God [ao]raised[1453]
Him from the dead, you shall be
saved;[4982]
10 for with the heart man believes,
[I]resulting in righteousness,[1343] and with
the mouth he confesses,[3670] [II]resulting
in salvation.[4991]
11 For the Scripture says, "[a]WHOEVER [ppt]BELIEVES IN HIM WILL NOT BE
[I]DISAPPOINTED."
12 For [a]there is no distinction between Jew and Greek; for the same *Lord*
is [b]Lord of [c]all, abounding in [ppt]riches
for all who [ppt]call upon[1941] Him;
13 for "[a]WHOEVER WILL CALL UPON
THE NAME OF THE LORD WILL BE SAVED."
14 How then shall they call upon
Him in whom they have not [ao]believed?[4100] And how shall they believe

26 [a]Hos. 1:10 [b]Matt. 16:16
27 [a]Is. 10:22 [b]Gen. 22:17; Hos. 1:10 [c]Rom. 11:5
28 [I]Lit., *finishing it* [II]Lit., *cutting it short* [a]Is. 10:23
29 [I]I.e., Hosts [II]Lit., *seed* [III]Lit., *been made like* [a]Is. 1:9 [b]James 5:4 [c]Deut. 29:23; Is. 13:19; Jer. 49:18; 50:40; Amos 4:11
30 [I]Lit., *out of* [a]Rom. 9:14 [b]Rom. 1:17; 3:21f.; 10:6; Gal. 2:16; 3:24; Phil. 3:9; Heb. 11:7
31 [a]Is. 51:1; Rom. 9:30; 10:2f., 20; 11:7 [b]Gal. 5:4
32 [I]Lit., *out of* [a]Is. 8:14; 1Pet. 2:6, 8
33 [I]Lit., *put to shame* [a]Is. 28:16 [b]Is. 8:14 [c]Rom. 10:11 [d]Rom. 5:5

2 [a]Acts 21:20
3 [a]Rom. 1:17 [b]Is. 51:1; Rom. 10:2f., 20; 11:7
4 [I]Or, *goal* [a]Rom. 7:1-4; Gal. 3:24; 4:5 [b]Rom. 3:22
5 [I]Lit., *out of, from* [II]Lit., *by it* [a]Lev. 18:5; Neh. 9:29; Ezek. 20:11, 13, 21; Rom. 7:10
6 [I]Lit., *out of, from* [a]Rom. 9:30 [b]Deut. 30:12
7 [a]Luke 8:31 [b]Heb. 13:20
8 [a]Deut. 30:14
9 [I]Or, *because* [a]Matt. 10:32; Luke 12:8; Rom. 14:9; 1Cor. 12:3; Phil. 2:11 [b]Acts 16:31; Rom. 4:24 [c]Acts 2:24
10 [I]Lit., *to righteousness* [II]Lit., *to salvation*
11 [I]Lit., *put to shame* [a]Is. 28:16; Rom. 9:33
12 [a]Rom. 3:22, 29 [b]Acts 10:36 [c]Rom. 3:29
13 [a]Joel 2:32; Acts 2:21

🔑 **10:9** See note on Mk. 3:28,29.

in Him [a]whom they have not [ao]heard?[191] And how shall they hear without [b]a [ppt]preacher?[2784]

15 And how shall they preach[2784] unless they are [asbp]sent?[679] Just as it is written, "[a]HOW BEAUTIFUL[5611] ARE THE FEET OF THOSE WHO [ppt] [1b]BRING GLAD TIDINGS OF GOOD THINGS!"[18]

16 However, they [a]did not all [ao]heed[5219] the [1]glad tidings;[2098] for Isaiah says, "[b]LORD, WHO HAS [ao]BELIEVED OUR REPORT?"[189]

17 So faith *comes* from [a]hearing,[189] and hearing by [b]the word[4487] [1]of Christ.[2316]

18 But I say, surely they have never [ao]heard, have they? Indeed they have;[3304]

"[a]THEIR VOICE HAS GONE OUT
INTO ALL THE EARTH,[1093]
AND THEIR WORDS[4487] TO THE
ENDS OF THE [1]WORLD."[3625]

19 But I say, surely Israel did not know,[1097] did they? At the first Moses says,

"[a]I WILL [b]MAKE YOU
JEALOUS[3863] BY THAT WHICH
IS NOT A NATION,
BY A NATION WITHOUT
UNDERSTANDING[801] WILL I
ANGER YOU."

20 And Isaiah is very bold and says,

"[a]I WAS FOUND BY THOSE WHO
[ppt]SOUGHT ME NOT,
I BECAME MANIFEST TO THOSE
WHO DID NOT [ppt]ASK FOR
ME."

21 But as for Israel He says, "[a]ALL THE DAY LONG I HAVE [ao]STRETCHED OUT MY HANDS TO A [ppt]DISOBEDIENT[544] AND [ppt]OBSTINATE[483] PEOPLE."[2992]

Israel Is Not Cast Away

11 I say then, God has not [aom] [a]rejected His people, has He? [b]May it never be![1096] [3361] For [c]I too am an Israelite, [1]a descendant of Abraham, of the tribe of Benjamin.

2 God [a]has not rejected His people[2992] whom He [b]foreknew.[4267]

14 [a]Eph. 2:17; 4:21 [b]Acts 8:31; Titus 1:3

15 [1]Or, *preach the gospel* [a]Is. 52:7 [b]Rom. 1:15; 15:20

16 [1]Lit., *gospel* [a]Rom. 3:3 [b]Is. 53:1; John 12:38

17 [1]Or, *concerning Christ* [a]Gal. 3:2, 5 [b]Col. 3:16

18 [1]Or, *inhabited earth* [a]Ps. 19:4; Rom. 1:8; Col. 1:6, 23; 1Thess. 1:8

19 [a]Deut. 32:21 [b]Rom. 11:11, 14

20 [a]Is. 65:1; Rom. 9:30

21 [a]Is. 65:2

1 [1]Lit., *of the seed of Abraham* [a]1Sam. 12:22; Jer. 31:37; 33:24-26 [b]Luke 20:16 [c]2Cor. 11:22; Phil. 3:5

2 [a]Ps. 94:14 [b]Rom. 8:29 [c]Rom. 6:16

3 [a]1Kin. 19:10, 14

4 [1]Lit., *says* [a]1Kin. 19:18

5 [1]Lit., *choice of grace* [a]2Kin. 19:4; Rom. 9:27

6 [a]Rom. 4:4

7 [1]Lit., *the election* [a]Rom. 9:31 [b]Mark 6:52; Rom. 9:18; 11:25; 2Cor. 3:14

8 [a]Deut. 29:4; Is. 29:10; Matt. 13:13f.

9 [a]Ps. 69:22

10 [a]Ps. 69:23

11 [a]Rom. 11:1 [b]Luke 20:16 [c]Acts 28:28 [d]Rom. 11:14

12 [1]Or, *fulness* [a]Rom. 11:25

13 [a]Acts 9:15

[c]Or do you not know[1492] what the Scripture says in *the passage about* Elijah, how he pleads[1793] with God against Israel?

3 "Lord, [a]THEY HAVE KILLED THY PROPHETS,[4396] THEY HAVE TORN DOWN THINE ALTARS, AND I ALONE AM [aop]LEFT, AND THEY ARE SEEKING MY LIFE."[5590]

4 But what [1]is the divine response[5538] to him? "[a]I HAVE KEPT for Myself SEVEN THOUSAND MEN WHO HAVE NOT BOWED THE KNEE TO BAAL."

5 In the same way then, there has also come to [pfi]be at the present time[2540] [a]a remnant[3005] according to *God's* [1]gracious[5485] choice.[1589]

6 But [a]if it is by grace, it is no longer on the basis of works,[2041] otherwise grace[5485] is no longer grace.

7 What then? That which [a]Israel is seeking for, it has not [ao]obtained, but [1]those who were chosen[1589] obtained it, and the rest were [b]hardened;[4456]

8 just as it is written,

"[a]GOD[2316] [ao]GAVE THEM A
SPIRIT[4151] OF STUPOR,
EYES TO [infg]SEE NOT AND EARS
TO [infg]HEAR NOT,
DOWN TO THIS VERY DAY."

9 And David says,

"[a]LET THEIR TABLE BECOME A
SNARE AND A TRAP,
AND A STUMBLING BLOCK[4625]
AND A RETRIBUTION TO THEM.

10 "[a]LET THEIR EYES BE
[aipp]DARKENED TO [infg]SEE NOT,
AND [aim]BEND THEIR BACKS
FOREVER."

11 [a]I say then, they did not [ao]stumble so as to [aosb]fall, did they? [b]May it never be![1096] [3361] But by their transgression[3900] [c]salvation[4991] *has come* to the Gentiles,[1484] to [ainf] [d]make them jealous.[3863]

12 Now if their transgression be riches for the world[2889] and their failure be riches[4149] for the Gentiles, how much more will their [1a]fulfillment[4138] be!

13 But I am speaking to you who are Gentiles. Inasmuch then as [a]I am an apostle[652] of Gentiles, I magnify[1392] my ministry,[1248]

14 if somehow I might [a]move to jealousy [b]my [I]fellow countrymen[4561] and
[c]save[4982] some of them.
15 For if their rejection be the
[a]reconciliation[2643] of the world, what will
their acceptance4356 be but [b]life[2222] from
the dead?[3498]
16 And if the [a]first piece *of dough*[536]
be holy,[40] the lump5445 is also; and if
the root be holy, the branches are too.
17 But if some of the [a]branches
were [aop]broken off, and [b]you, being a
wild olive, were grafted in1461 among
them and became partaker with them
of the [I]rich root of the olive tree,
18 do not be [pim]arrogant toward the
branches; but if you are arrogant, *remember that* [a]it is not you who supports
the root, but the root *supports* you.
19 [a]You will say then, "Branches
were [aop]broken off so that I might be
grafted in."
20 Quite right, they were broken
off for their unbelief,[570] but you [pfi] [a]stand
by your faith.[4102] [b]Do not be conceited,
but fear;[5399]
21 for if God did not spare the natural branches,2798 neither will He spare
you.
22 Behold then the kindness and
severity663 of God; to those who
[apt]fell,[4098] severity,663 but to you, God's
[a]kindness,[5544] [b]if you [aosb]continue in His
kindness; otherwise you also [c]will be
cut off.
23 And they also, [a]if they do not
continue in their unbelief, will be grafted
in; for God is able to [ainf]graft them in1461
again.
24 For if you were cut off1581 from
what is by nature a wild olive tree, and
were grafted contrary to nature into a
cultivated olive tree, how much more
shall these who are the natural *branches*
be grafted into their own olive tree?
25 For [a]I do not want you, brethren,[80] to be uninformed[50] of this
[b]mystery,[3466] lest you be [c]wise[5429] in
your own estimation, that a partial
[d]hardening[4457] has happened to Israel
until the [e]fulness[4138] of the Gentiles has
[aosb]come in;
26 and thus all Israel will be
saved;[4982] just as it is written,
"[a]THE [ppt]DELIVERER[4506] WILL
COME FROM ZION,
HE WILL REMOVE
UNGODLINESS[763] FROM
JACOB."
27 "[a]AND THIS IS [I]MY COVENANT[1242]
WITH THEM,
[b]WHEN I TAKE AWAY THEIR
SINS."[266]
28 [I]From the standpoint[2596] of the
gospel[2098] they are [a]enemies for your
sake, but [II]from the standpoint[2596] of
God's choice[1589] they are beloved[27] for
[b]the sake of the fathers;
29 for the gifts and the [a]calling[2821]
of God [b]are irrevocable.
30 For just as you once were
disobedient[544] to God, but now have
been shown [aop]mercy because of their
disobedience,[543]
31 so these also now have been
[ao]disobedient, in order that because of
the mercy[1658] shown to you they also
may now be shown [asbp]mercy.
32 For [a]God has [ao]shut up all in disobedience that He might show [aosb]mercy
to all.
33 Oh, the depth of [a]the riches
[I]both of the [b]wisdom and knowledge of
God![2316] [c]How unsearchable are His
judgments[2917] and unfathomable His
ways!
34 For [a]WHO HAS KNOWN THE MIND
OF THE LORD,[2962] OR WHO BECAME HIS
COUNSELOR?
35 Or [a]WHO HAS FIRST GIVEN TO HIM
[I]THAT IT MIGHT BE PAID BACK TO HIM
AGAIN?
36 For [a]from Him and through Him
and to Him are all things. [b]To Him *be*
the glory[1391] [I]forever. Amen.281

Dedicated Service

12 [a]I urge[3870] you therefore, brethren,[80] by the mercies3628 of God,

14 [I]Lit., *flesh* [a]Rom. 11:11 [b]Gen. 29:14; 2Sam. 19:12f.; Rom. 9:3 [c]1Cor. 1:21; 7:16; 9:22; 1Tim. 1:15; 2:4; 2Tim. 1:9; Titus 3:5
15 [a]Rom. 5:11 [b]Luke 15:24, 32
16 [a]Num. 15:18ff.; Neh. 10:37; Ezek. 44:30
17 [I]Lit., *root of the fatness* [a]Jer. 11:16; John 15:2 [b]Eph. 2:11ff.
18 [a]John 4:22
19 [a]Rom. 9:19
20 [a]Rom. 5:2; 1Cor. 10:12; 2Cor. 1:24 [b]Rom. 12:16; 1Tim. 6:17; 1Pet. 1:17
22 [a]Rom. 2:4 [b]1Cor. 15:2; Heb. 3:6, 14 [c]John 15:2
23 [a]2Cor. 3:16
25 [a]Rom. 1:13 [b]Matt. 13:11; Rom. 16:25; 1Cor. 2:7-10; Eph. 3:3-5, 9 [c]Rom. 12:16 [d]Rom. 11:7 [e]Luke 21:24; John 10:16; Rom. 11:12
26 [a]Is. 59:20
27 [I]Lit., *the covenant from Me* [a]Is. 59:21; Jer. 31:33, 34; Heb. 8:10 [b]Is. 27:9; Heb. 8:12
28 [I]Lit., *According to the gospel* [II]Lit., *according to the election* [a]Rom. 5:10 [b]Deut. 7:8; 10:15; Rom. 9:5
29 [a]Rom. 8:28; 1Cor. 1:26; Eph. 1:18; 4:1, 4; Phil. 3:14; 2Thess. 1:11; 2Tim. 1:9; Heb. 3:1; 2Pet. 1:10 [b]Heb. 7:21
32 [a]Rom. 3:9; Gal. 3:22f.
33 [I]Or, *and the wisdom* [a]Rom. 2:4; Eph. 3:8 [b]Eph. 3:10; Col. 2:3 [c]Job 5:9; 11:7; 15:8
34 [a]Is. 40:13f.; 1Cor. 2:16
35 [I]Lit., *and it will be paid back* [a]Job 35:7; 41:11
36 [I]Lit., *to the ages* [a]1Cor. 8:6; 11:12; Col. 1:16; Heb. 2:10 [b]Rom. 16:27; Eph. 3:21; Phil. 4:20; 1Tim. 1:17; 2Tim. 4:18; 1Pet. 4:11; 5:11; 2Pet. 3:18; Jude 25; Rev. 1:6; 5:13; 7:12
1 [a]1Cor. 1:10; 2Cor. 10:1-4; Eph. 4:1; 1Pet. 2:11

to [ainf] [b]present your bodies a living[2198]
and holy[40] sacrifice,[2378] [I]acceptable[2101]
to God, *which is* your [II]spiritual[3050]
service[2999] of worship.
2 And do not [a]be [pim]conformed[4964]
to [b]this [I]world, but be [pim]transformed[3339]
by the [c]renewing[342] of your mind,[3563]
that you may [aies] [d]prove what the will[2307]
of God is, that which is good[18] and
[II]acceptable[2101] and perfect.[5046]
3 For through [a]the grace[5485] given
to me I say to every man among you
[b]not to [pinf]think more highly of himself
than he ought to think;[5426] but to think
so as to have sound judgment,[4993] as
God has [ao]allotted to [c]each a measure
of faith.[4102]
4 For [a]just as we have many members in one body[4983] and all the members
do not have the same function,[4234]
5 so we, [a]who are many, are
[b]one body[4983] in Christ,[5547] and individually members one of another.
🔑6 And since we have gifts that
[a]differ[1313] according to the grace[5485]
[aptp]given to us, *let each exercise them*
accordingly: if [b]prophecy,[4394] according
to the proportion[356] of his faith;
7 if [I][a]service,[1248] in his serving;[1248]
or he who [ppt] [b]teaches,[1321] in his
teaching;[1319]
8 or he who [a]exhorts,[3870] in his
exhortation;[3874] he who gives, with
[I][b]liberality;[572] [c]he who [II]leads, with diligence; he who shows mercy, with
[d]cheerfulness.
9 Let [a]love[26] be without hypocrisy.[505] [ppt] [b]Abhor[655] what is evil;[4190]
[ppp]cling[2853] to what is good.[18]
10 Be [a]devoted to one another in
brotherly love;[5360] [I]give preference[4285]
to one another [b]in honor;
11 not lagging behind in diligence,
[ppt] [a]fervent in spirit, [b]serving[1398] the
Lord;
12 [a]rejoicing in hope,[680] [ppt] [b]per-
severing[5278] in tribulation, [c]devoted[4342]
to prayer,
13 [a]contributing[2841] to the needs[5532]
of the [I]saints,[40] [ppt] [II][b]practicing hospitality.
14 [a]Bless[2127] those who [ppt]perse-
cute [I]you; bless and curse[2672] not.
15 [a]Rejoice with those who [ppt]re-
joice, and weep with those who
[ppt]weep.
16 [a]Be of the same [ppt]mind[5426] toward one another; [b]do not be haughty
in mind, but [ppp] [I]associate with the lowly.
[c]Do not [pim]be wise[5429] in your own estimation.
17 [a]Never [ppt]pay back evil for evil
to anyone. [ppt] [I][b]Respect[4306] what is right
in the sight of all men.[444]
18 If possible, [a]so far as it depends
on you, [b]be at [ppt]peace with all men.
19 [a]Never take your own [ppt]re-
venge,[1556] beloved,[27] but [aim] [I]leave room
for the wrath[3709] *of God,* for it is written,
"[b]VENGEANCE[1557] IS MINE, I WILL RE-
PAY," says the Lord.
20 "[a]BUT IF YOUR ENEMY IS [psa]HUN-
GRY, [pim]FEED HIM, AND IF HE IS THIRSTY,
GIVE HIM A [pim]DRINK; FOR IN SO DOING
YOU WILL HEAP BURNING COALS UPON HIS
HEAD."
21 Do not be [pim]overcome by
evil,[2556] but [pim]overcome evil with
good.[18]

Be Subject to Government

13 🔑Let every [I][a]person[5590] [pim]be
in [b]subjection to[5293] the governing authorities.[1849] For [c]there is no
authority except [II]from God,[2316] and
those which exist are established[5021] by
God.

1 [I]Or, *well-pleasing* [II]Or, *rational* [b]Rom. 6:13, 16, 19; 1Cor. 6:20; Heb. 13:15; 1Pet. 2:5
2 [I]Or, *age* [II]Or, *well-pleasing* [a]1Pet. 1:14 [b]Matt. 13:22; Gal. 1:4; 1John 2:15 [c]Eph. 4:23; Titus 3:5 [d]Eph. 5:10, 17; Col. 1:9
3 [a]Rom. 1:5; 15:15; 1Cor. 3:10; 15:10; Gal. 2:9; Eph. 3:7f. [b]Rom. 11:20; 12:16 [c]1Cor. 7:17; 2Cor. 10:13; Eph. 4:7; 1Pet. 4:11
4 [a]1Cor. 12:12-14; Eph. 4:4, 16
5 [a]1Cor. 10:17, 33 [b]1Cor. 12:20, 27; Eph. 4:12, 25
6 [a]Rom. 12:3; 1Cor. 7:7; 12:4; 1Pet. 4:10 [b]Acts 13:1; 1Cor. 12:10
7 [I]Or, *office of service* [a]Acts 6:1; 1Cor. 12:5, 28 [b]Acts 13:1; 1Cor. 12:28; 14:26
8 [I]Or, *simplicity* [II]Or, *gives aid* [a]Acts 4:36; 11:23; 13:15 [b]2Cor. 8:2; 9:11, 13 [c]1Cor. 12:28; 1Tim. 5:17 [d]2Cor. 9:7
9 [a]2Cor. 6:6; 1Tim. 1:5 [b]1Thess. 5:21f.
10 [I]Or, *outdo one another in showing honor* [a]John 13:34; 1Thess. 4:9; Heb. 13:1; 2Pet. 1:7 [b]Rom. 13:7; Phil. 2:3; 1Pet. 2:17
11 [a]Acts 18:25 [b]Acts 20:19
12 [a]Rom. 5:2 [b]Heb. 10:32, 36 [c]Acts 1:14
13 [I]Or, *holy ones* [II]Lit., *pursuing* [a]Rom. 15:25; 1Cor. 16:15; 2Cor. 9:1; Heb. 6:10 [b]Matt. 25:35; 1Tim. 3:2

14 [I]Some ancient mss. do not contain *you* [a]Matt. 5:44; Luke 6:28; 1Cor. 4:12 **15** [a]Job 30:25; Heb. 13:3 **16** [I]Or, *accommodate yourself to lowly things* [a]Rom. 15:5; 2Cor. 13:11; Phil. 2:2; 4:2; 1Pet. 3:8 [b]Rom. 11:20; 12:3 [c]Prov. 3:7; Rom. 11:25 **17** [I]Lit., *Take thought for* [a]Prov. 20:22; 24:29; Rom. 12:19 [b]2Cor. 8:21 **18** [a]Rom. 1:15 [b]Mark 9:50; Rom. 14:19 **19** [I]Lit., *give a place* [a]Prov. 20:22; 24:29; Rom. 12:17 [b]Deut. 32:35; Ps. 94:1; 1Thess. 4:6; Heb. 10:30 **20** [a]2Kin. 6:22; Prov. 25:21f.; Matt. 5:44; Luke 6:27 **1** [I]Or, *soul* [II]Lit., *by* [a]Acts 2:41 [b]Titus 3:1; 1Pet. 2:13f. [c]Dan. 2:21; 4:17; John 19:11

🔑 **12:6-8** See note on I Cor. 12:1-11.
🔑 **13:1** See note on I Pet. 2:17.

2 Therefore he who [ppt]resists
authority has opposed the ordinance[1296]
of God; and they who have opposed will
receive condemnation[2917] upon themselves.
3 For [a]rulers are not a cause of fear
for [I]good[18] behavior, but for evil.[2556] Do
you want to have no [pinf]fear[5399] of authority? [pim]Do what is good, and you will
have praise from the same;
4 for it is a minister[1249] of God to
you for good. But if you [psa]do what is
evil, be [pim]afraid; for it does not bear
the sword for nothing; for it is a minister
of God, an [a]avenger[1558] who brings
wrath[3709] upon the one who [ppt]prac-
tices[4238] evil.
5 Wherefore it is necessary[318] to
be in [pinf]subjection, not only because
of wrath, but also [a]for conscience'[4893]
sake.
6 For because of this you also
pay[5055] taxes,[5411] for *rulers* are servants[3011] of God, [ppt]devoting[4342] themselves to this very thing.
7 [a]Render to all what is due[3782]
them: [b]tax to whom tax *is due;* [c]cus-
tom[5056] to whom custom; fear to whom
fear; honor to whom honor.
8 Owe nothing to anyone except to
[pinf]love one another; for [a]he who [ppt]loves
[I]his neighbor[2087] has [pfi]fulfilled[4137] *the*
law.[3551]
9 For this, "[a]YOU SHALL NOT COMMIT
ADULTERY, YOU SHALL NOT MURDER, YOU
SHALL NOT STEAL, YOU SHALL NOT COV-
ET,"[1937] and if there is any other commandment, it is summed up[346] in this
saying, "[b]YOU SHALL LOVE[25] YOUR
NEIGHBOR[4139] AS YOURSELF."
10 Love[26] [I]does[2038] no wrong[2556] to
a neighbor; [a]love therefore is the
fulfillment[4138] of *the* law.
🔑 **11** And this *do,* knowing the
time,[2540] that it is [a]already the hour for
you to [b]awaken[1453] from sleep; for now
[I]salvation[4991] is nearer to us than when
we believed.[4100]
12 [a]The night is almost [ao]gone, and
[b]the day[2250] is at [pfi]hand. Let us therefore

3 [I]Lit., *good work* [a]1Pet. 2:14
4 [a]1Thess. 4:6
5 [a]Eccl. 8:1-17; 1Pet. 2:13, 19
7 [a]Matt. 22:21; Mark 12:17; Luke 20:25 [b]Luke 20:22; 23:2 [c]Matt. 17:25
8 [I]Lit., *the other* [a]Matt. 7:12; 22:39f.; John 13:34; Rom. 13:10; Gal. 5:14; James 2:8
9 [a]Ex. 20:13ff.; Deut. 5:17ff. [b]Lev. 19:18; Matt. 19:19
10 [I]Lit., *works no evil* [a]Matt. 7:12; 22:39f.; John 13:34; Rom. 13:8; Gal. 5:14; James 2:8
11 [I]Or, *our salvation is nearer than when* [a]1Cor. 7:29f.; 10:11; James 5:8; 1Pet. 4:7; 2Pet. 3:9, 11; 1John 2:18; Rev. 1:3; 22:10 [b]Mark 13:37; 1Cor. 15:34; Eph. 5:14; 1Thess. 5:6
12 [a]1Cor. 7:29f.; 10:11; James 5:8; 1Pet. 4:7; 2Pet. 3:9, 11; 1John 2:18; Rev. 1:3; 22:10 [b]Heb. 10:25; 1John 2:8; Rev. 1:3; 22:10 [c]Eph. 5:11 [d]2Cor. 6:7; 10:4; Eph. 6:11, 13; 1Thess. 5:8
13 [I]Lit., *walk* [a]1Thess. 4:12 [b]Luke 21:34; Gal. 5:21; Eph. 5:18; 1Pet. 4:3
14 [a]Job 29:14; Gal. 3:27; Eph. 4:24; Col. 3:10, 12 [b]Gal. 5:16; 1Pet. 2:11

1 [a]Acts 28:2; Rom. 11:15; 14:3; 15:7 [b]Rom. 14:2; 15:1; 1Cor. 8:9ff.; 9:22
2 [a]Rom. 14:14 [b]Rom. 14:1; 15:1; 1Cor. 8:9ff.; 9:22
3 [a]Luke 18:9; Rom. 14:10 [b]Rom. 14:10, 13; Col. 2:16

[aosb]lay aside [c]the deeds of darkness[4655]
and [aosb]put on [d]the armor of light.
13 Let us [Ia]behave properly as in
the day, [b]not in carousing[2970] and drunkenness,[3178] not in sexual promiscuity and
sensuality,[766] not in strife[2054] and
jealousy.[2205]
14 But [aim] [a]put on the Lord Jesus
Christ, and [pim]make no provision[4307] for
the flesh[4561] [b]in regard to *its* lusts.[1939]

Principles of Conscience

14 Now [pim] [a]accept the one who is
[b]weak[770] in faith,[4102] *but* not for
the purpose of passing judgment[1253] on
his opinions.[1261]
2 [a]One man has faith[4100] that he may
[ainf]eat all things, but he who is [b]weak[770]
eats vegetables *only.*
3 Let not him who [ppt]eats [pim] [a]regard
with contempt him who does not [ppt]eat,
and let not him who does not eat
[b]judge[2919] him who eats, for God has
[ao] [c]accepted him.
4 [a]Who are you to [ppt]judge the
[I]servant[3610] of another?[245] To his
own[2398] [II]master[2962] he stands or
falls;[4098] and stand[2476] he will, for the
Lord is able to make him [ainf]stand.[2476]
5 [a]One man [I]regards[2919] one day
above another, another regards[2919] every day *alike.* Let each man be [b]fully
[pim]convinced[4135] in his own mind.[3563]
6 He who [ppt]observes the day, observes it for the Lord,[2962] and he who
eats, [I]does so for the Lord, for he
[a]gives thanks[2168] to God; and he who
eats not, for the Lord he does not eat,
and gives thanks to God.
7 For not one of us [a]lives[2198] for
himself, and not one dies[599] for himself;
8 for if we live, we live for the Lord,
or if we die, we die for the Lord; there-

[c]Acts 28:2; Rom. 11:15; 14:1; 15:7 **4** [I]Or, *house-servant* [II]Lit., *lord* [a]Rom. 9:20; James 4:12 **5** [I]Lit., *judges* [a]Gal. 4:10 [b]Luke 1:1; Rom. 4:21; 14:23 **6** [I]Lit., *eats* [a]Matt. 14:19; 15:36; 1Cor. 10:30; 1Tim. 4:3f. **7** [a]Rom. 8:38f.; 2Cor. 5:15; Gal. 2:20; Phil. 1:20f.

🔑 **13:11** See note on I Pet. 1:5.

fore [a]whether we live or die, we are the Lord's.

9 For to this end [a]Christ[5547] died and lived[450] *again*, that He might [aosb]be [b]Lord both of the dead[3498] and of the living.

🔑 10 But you, why do you judge your brother? Or you again, why do you [a]regard your brother with contempt?[1848] For [b]we shall all stand before the judgment seat of God.

11 For it is written,

"[a]As I LIVE, SAYS THE LORD, [b]EVERY KNEE SHALL BOW TO ME,
AND EVERY TONGUE SHALL [I]GIVE PRAISE[1843] TO GOD."

12 So then [a]each one of us shall give account[3056] of himself to God.

13 Therefore let us not [a]judge[2919] one another anymore, but rather determine this—[b]not to [pinf]put an obstacle or a stumbling block[4625] in a brother's[80] way.

14 I know and am convinced in the Lord Jesus that [a]nothing is unclean[2839] in itself; but to him who [ppt] [b]thinks[3049] anything to be unclean, to him it is unclean.

15 For if because of food your brother is hurt,[3076] you are no longer [a]walking according to love.[26] [b]Do not [pim]destroy with your food him for whom Christ died.

16 Therefore [a]do not let what is for you a good thing[18] be [pim] [I]spoken of as evil;[987]

17 for the kingdom[932] of God [a]is not eating and drinking, but righteousness[1343] and [b]peace[1515] and [b]joy[5479] in the [an]Holy Spirit.[4151]

18 For he who in this *way* [ppt] [a]serves[1398] Christ is [b]acceptable[2101] to God and approved[1284] by men.

19 So then [I]let us [psa] [a]pursue the things which make for peace and the [b]building up[3619] of one another.

20 [a]Do not [pim]tear down[2647] the work[2041] of God for the sake of food. [b]All things indeed are clean,[2513] but [c]they are evil[2556] for the man who [ppt]eats [I]and gives offense.

21 [a]It is good not to [ainf]eat meat or to [ainf]drink wine,[3631] or *to do anything* by which your brother stumbles.[4350]

22 The faith[4102] which you have, have [I]as your own conviction before God. Happy[3107] is he who [a]does not [ppt]condemn[2919] himself in what he approves.

23 But [a]he who [ppt]doubts[1252] is condemned[2632] if he [aosb]eats, because *his eating is* not from faith; and whatever is not from faith is sin.[266]

Self-denial on Behalf of Others

15 Now we who are strong ought to bear the weaknesses[771] of [a]those without strength and not *just* [pinf]please ourselves.

2 Let each of us [pim] [a]please his neighbor [I]for his good,[18] to his [b]edification.[3619]

3 For even [a]Christ[5547] did not please Himself; but as it is written, "[b]THE REPROACHES OF THOSE WHO [ppt]REPROACHED THEE FELL UPON ME."

4 For [a]whatever was written in earlier times was written for our instruction,[1319] that through perseverance and the encouragement[3874] of the Scriptures[1124] we might have hope.[1680]

5 Now may the [a]God [I]who gives perseverance and encouragement grant you [b]to be of the same mind with one another according to Christ Jesus;

6 that with one accord you may with one [I]voice glorify[1392] [a]the God and Father of our Lord Jesus Christ.

7 Wherefore, [a]accept one another, just as Christ also accepted [I]us to the glory[1391] of God.

8 For I say that Christ [pfin]has become a servant[1249] to [a]the

8 [a]Luke 20:38; Phil. 1:20; 1Thess. 5:10; Rev. 14:13
9 [a]Rev. 1:18; 2:8 [b]Matt. 28:18; John 12:24; Phil. 2:11; 1Thess. 5:10
10 [a]Luke 18:9; Rom. 14:3 [b]Rom. 2:16; 2Cor. 5:10
11 [I]Or, *confess* [a]Is. 45:23 [b]Phil. 2:10f.
12 [a]Matt. 12:36; 16:27; 1Pet. 4:5
13 [a]Matt. 7:1; Rom. 14:3 [b]1Cor. 8:13
14 [a]Acts 10:15; Rom. 14:2, 20 [b]1Cor. 8:7
15 [a]Eph. 5:2 [b]Rom. 14:20; 1Cor. 8:11
16 [I]Lit., *blasphemed* [a]1Cor. 10:30; Titus 2:5
17 [a]1Cor. 8:8 [b]Rom. 15:13; Gal. 5:22
18 [a]Rom. 16:18 [b]2Cor. 8:21; Phil. 4:8; 1Pet. 2:12
19 [I]Many ancient mss. read *we pursue* [a]Ps. 34:14; Rom. 12:18; 1Cor. 7:15; 2Tim. 2:22; Heb. 12:14 [b]Rom. 15:2; 1Cor. 10:23; 14:3f., 26; 2Cor. 12:19; Eph. 4:12, 29
20 [I]Lit., *with offense* [a]Rom. 14:15 [b]Acts 10:15; Rom. 14:2, 14 [c]1Cor. 8:9-12
21 [a]1Cor. 8:13
22 [I]Lit., *according to yourself* [a]1John 3:21
23 [a]Rom. 14:5

1 [a]Rom. 14:1; Gal. 6:2; 1Thess. 5:14
2 [I]Lit., *for what is good to edification* [a]1Cor. 9:22; 10:24, 33; 2Cor. 13:9 [b]Rom. 14:19; 1Cor. 10:23; 14:3f., 26; 2Cor. 12:19; Eph. 4:12, 29
3 [a]2Cor. 8:9 [b]Ps. 69:9
4 [a]Rom. 4:23f.; 2Tim. 3:16
5 [I]Lit., *of perseverance* [a]2Cor. 1:3 [b]Rom. 12:16
6 [I]Lit., *mouth* [a]Rev. 1:6
7 [I]Some mss. read *you* [a]Rom. 14:1
8 [a]Matt. 15:24; Acts 3:26

🔑 **14:10-23** See note on Mt. 8:11,12.

circumcision[4061] on behalf of the
truth[225] of God to [ainf]confirm[950] [b]the
promises[1860] *given* to the fathers,
9 and for [a]the Gentiles[1484] to [ainf] [b]glo-
rify God for His mercy;[1656] as it is written,
"[c]THEREFORE I WILL [I]GIVE
PRAISE[1843] TO THEE AMONG
THE GENTILES,
AND I WILL SING TO THY
NAME."[3686]
10 And again he says,
"[aim] [a]REJOICE,[2165] O GENTILES,
WITH HIS PEOPLE."
11 And again,
"[pim] [a]PRAISE[134] THE LORD ALL
YOU GENTILES,
AND LET ALL THE PEOPLES
[aim]PRAISE HIM."
12 And again Isaiah says,
"[a]THERE SHALL COME [b]THE
ROOT OF JESSE,
AND HE WHO ARISES[450] TO
[pinf]RULE OVER[757] THE
GENTILES,
[c]IN HIM SHALL THE GENTILES
HOPE."[1679]
13 Now may the God of hope[1680]
[opt]fill you with all [a]joy and peace in [pinf]be-
lieving,[4100] that you may [aies]abound in
hope [b]by the power[1411] of the [an]Holy
Spirit.[4151]
14 And concerning you, my brethren, I myself also am [pfip]convinced that
you yourselves are [pfpp]full of [a]good-
ness,[19] filled with [b]all knowledge, and
able[1410] also to [pinf]admonish[3560] one another.
15 But I have written very boldly
to you on some points, so as to remind
you again, because of [a]the grace[5485] that
was [aptp]given me [I]from God,
16 to [aies]be [a]a minister[3011] of Christ
Jesus to the Gentiles,[1484] ministering as
a priest the [b]gospel[2098] of God, that *my*
[c]offering of the Gentiles might become
acceptable,[2144] [pfpp]sanctified[37] by the
Holy Spirit.
17 Therefore in Christ Jesus I have
found [a]reason for boasting in [b]things pertaining to God.
18 For I will not presume to [pinf]speak
of anything [I]except what [a]Christ has
[ao]accomplished through me, [II]resulting
in the obedience[5218] of the Gentiles
by word and deed,[2041]
19 in the power[1411] of [Ia]signs[4592] and
wonders,[5059] [b]in the power[1411] of the
Spirit;[4151] so that [c]from Jerusalem and
round about as [d]far as Illyricum I have
[II]fully [pfin]preached[4137] the gospel of
Christ.
20 And thus I [ppt]aspired to
[pinf] [a]preach the gospel,[2097] not where
Christ was *already* [aop]named, [b]that I
might not [psa]build upon another man's
foundation;
21 but as it is written,
"[a]THEY WHO HAD NO NEWS OF
HIM SHALL SEE,
AND THEY WHO HAVE NOT
HEARD SHALL UNDERSTAND."
22 For this reason [a]I have often
been [ipf]hindered from coming to you;
23 but now, with no further place
for me in these regions, and since I
[a]have had for many years a longing to
come to you
24 whenever I [a]go to Spain—for I
hope to see you in passing, and to be
[b]helped on my way there[1563] by you,
when I have first [c]enjoyed your company
[I]for a while—
25 but now, [a]I am going to Jerusalem
[ppt] [b]serving[1247] the [I]saints.[40]
26 For [a]Macedonia and [b]Achaia have
been pleased[2106] to make a contribution[2842] for the poor among the
[I]saints in Jerusalem.
27 Yes,[1063] they were pleased *to do
so,* and they are indebted to them. For
[a]if the Gentiles have [ao]shared[2841] in their
spiritual things, they are indebted to
minister[3008] to them also in material
things.[4559]
28 Therefore, when I have
[apt]finished[2005] this, and [a]have [I]put my
[apt]seal on this fruit of theirs, I will
[b]go on by way of you to Spain.
29 And I know that when [a]I come
to you, I will come in the fulness[4138] of
the blessing[2129] of Christ.

8 [b]Rom. 4:16; 2Cor. 1:20
9 [I]Or, *confess* [a]Rom. 3:29; 11:30f. [b]Matt. 9:8 [c]2Sam. 22:50; Ps. 18:49
10 [a]Deut. 32:43
11 [a]Ps. 117:1
12 [a]Is. 11:10 [b]Rev. 5:5; 22:16 [c]Matt. 12:21
13 [a]Rom. 14:17 [b]Rom. 15:19; 1Cor. 2:4; 1Thess. 1:5
14 [a]Eph. 5:9; 2Thess. 1:11 [b]1Cor. 1:5; 8:1, 7, 10; 12:8; 13:2
15 [I]Some mss. read *by God* [a]Rom. 12:3
16 [a]Acts 9:15; Rom. 11:13 [b]Rom. 1:1; 15:19, 20 [c]Rom. 12:1; Eph. 5:2; Phil. 2:17
17 [a]Phil. 3:3 [b]Heb. 2:17; 5:1
18 [I]Or, *which Christ has not accomplished* [II]Lit., *to the obedience* [a]Acts 15:12; 21:19; Rom. 1:5; 2Cor. 3:5
19 [I]Or, *attesting miracles* [II]Lit., *fulfilled* [a]John 4:48 [b]Rom. 15:13; 1Cor. 2:4; 1Thess. 1:5 [c]Acts 22:17-21 [d]Acts 20:1f.
20 [a]Rom. 1:15; 10:15; 15:16 [b]1Cor. 3:10; 2Cor. 10:15f.
21 [a]Is. 52:15
22 [a]Rom. 1:13; 1Thess. 2:18
23 [a]Acts 19:21; Rom. 1:10f.; 15:29, 32
24 [I]Lit., *in part* [a]Rom. 15:28 [b]Acts 15:3 [c]Rom. 1:12
25 [I]Or, *holy ones* [a]Acts 19:21 [b]Acts 24:17
26 [I]V. 25, note 1 [a]Acts 16:9; 1Cor. 16:5; 2Cor. 1:16; 2:13; 7:5; 8:1; 9:2, 4; 11:9; Phil. 4:15; 1Thess. 1:7f.; 4:10; 1Tim. 1:3 [b]Acts 18:12; 19:21
27 [a]1Cor. 9:11
28 [I]Lit., *sealed to them this fruit* [a]John 3:33 [b]Rom. 15:24
29 [a]Acts 19:21; Rom. 1:10f.; 15:23, 32

30 Now I urge you, brethren, by our Lord Jesus Christ and by [a]the love[26] of the Spirit,[4151] to [ainf][b]strive together with[4865] me in your prayers to God for me,

31 that I may be [a]delivered[4506] from those who are [ppt]disobedient[544] in Judea, and *that* my [b]service for Jerusalem may prove acceptable[2144] to the [Ic]saints;

32 so that [a]I may come to you in joy by [b]the will of God and find *refreshing* rest in your company.

33 Now [a]the God of peace[1515] be with you all. Amen.[281]

Greetings and Love Expressed

16 🗝 I [a]commend[4921] to you our sister Phoebe, who is a [I]servant[1249] of the church[1577] which is at [b]Cenchrea;

2 that you [aosb] [a]receive[4327] her in the Lord in a manner worthy of the [Ib]saints,[40] and that you [aosb]help her in whatever matter she may have [psa]need[5535] of you; for she herself has also [ao]been a helper[4368] of many, [II]and of myself as well.

3 Greet [a]Prisca and Aquila, my fellow workers [b]in [c]Christ Jesus,

4 who for my life[5590] risked their own necks, to whom not only do I give thanks,[2168] but also all the churches of the Gentiles;

5 also *greet* [a]the church[1577] that is in their house. Greet[782] Epaenetus, my beloved, who is the [b]first convert[536] to Christ from [Ic]Asia.

6 Greet Mary, who has worked hard for you.

7 Greet Andronicus and [I]Junias, my [a]kinsmen, and my [b]fellow prisoners, who are outstanding among the apostles,[652] who also were [c]in Christ before me.

8 Greet Ampliatus, my beloved in the Lord.

9 Greet Urbanus, our fellow worker [a]in Christ, and Stachys my beloved.

10 Greet Apelles, the approved[1384] [a]in Christ. Greet those who are of the *household* of Aristobulus.

11 Greet Herodion, my [a]kinsman. Greet those of the *household* of Narcissus, who are in the Lord.

12 Greet Tryphaena and Tryphosa, [ppt]workers in the Lord. Greet Persis the beloved, who has worked hard in the Lord.

13 Greet [a]Rufus, a choice man in the Lord, also his mother and mine.

14 Greet Asyncritus, Phlegon, Hermes, Patrobas, Hermas and the brethren[80] with them.

15 Greet Philologus and Julia, Nereus and his sister, and Olympas, and all [a]the [I]saints[40] who are with them.

16 [a]Greet one another with a holy[40] kiss. All the churches[1577] of Christ greet you.

17 Now I urge you, brethren, [pinf]keep your eye on[4648] those who [ppt]cause dissensions[1370] and [I]hindrances [a]contrary to the teaching which you [ao]learned,[3129] and [pim] [b]turn away from them.

18 For such men are [a]slaves,[1398] not of our Lord Christ but of [b]their own [I]appetites; and by their [c]smooth and flattering speech[2129] they deceive the hearts of the unsuspecting.[172]

19 For the report of your obedience[5218] [ao] [a]has reached to all; therefore I am rejoicing over you, but [b]I want you to be wise in what is good,[18] and innocent[185] in what is evil.

20 And [a]the God of peace[1515] will soon crush [b]Satan under your feet.

[c]The grace of our Lord Jesus be with you.

🗝 **21** [a]Timothy my fellow worker greets you, and *so do* [b]Lucius and [c]Jason and [d]Sosipater, my [e]kinsmen.

22 I, Tertius, who [a]write this letter,[1992] greet you in the Lord.

30 [a]Gal. 5:22; Col. 1:8 [b]2Cor. 1:11; Col. 4:12 **31** [I]V. 25, note 1 [a]2Cor. 1:10; 2Thess. 3:2; 2Tim. 3:11; 4:17 [b]Rom. 15:25f.; 2Cor. 8:4; 9:1 [c]Acts 9:13, 15 **32** [a]Rom. 15:23 [b]Acts 18:21; Rom. 1:10 **33** [a]Rom. 16:20; 2Cor. 13:11; Phil. 4:9; 1Thess. 5:23; 2Thess. 3:16; Heb. 13:20

1 [I]Or, *deaconess* [a]2Cor. 3:1 [b]Acts 18:18 **2** [I]Or, *holy ones* [II]Lit., *and of me, myself* [a]Phil. 2:29 [b]Acts 9:13, 15 **3** [a]Acts 18:2 [b]Rom. 8:11ff.; 16:7, 9, 10; 2Cor. 5:17; 12:2; Gal. 1:22 [c]Rom. 8:1 **5** [I]I.e., west coast province of Asia Minor [a]1Cor. 16:19; Col. 4:15; Philem. 2 [b]1Cor. 16:15 [c]Acts 16:6 **7** [I]Or, *Junia* (fem.) [a]Rom. 9:3; 16:11, 21 [b]Col. 4:10; Philem. 23 [c]Rom. 8:11ff.; 16:3, 9, 10; 2Cor. 5:17; 12:2; Gal. 1:22 **9** [a]Rom. 8:11ff.; 16:3, 7, 10; 2Cor. 5:17; 12:2; Gal. 1:22 **10** [a]Rom. 8:11ff.; 16:3, 7, 9; 2Cor. 5:17; 12:2; Gal. 1:22 **11** [a]Rom. 9:3; 16:7, 21 **13** [a]Mark 15:21 **15** [I]V. 2, note 1 [a]Rom. 16:2, 14 **16** [a]1Cor. 16:20; 2Cor. 13:12; 1Thess. 5:26; 1Pet. 5:14 **17** [I]Lit., *occasions of stumbling* [a]1Tim. 1:3; 6:3 [b]Matt. 7:15; Gal. 1:8f.; 2Thess. 3:6, 14; Titus 3:10; 2John 10 **18** [I]Lit., *belly* [a]Rom. 14:18 [b]Phil. 3:19 [c]Col. 2:4; 2Pet. 2:3 **19** [a]Rom. 1:8 [b]Jer. 4:22; Matt. 10:16; 1Cor. 14:20 **20** [a]Rom. 15:33 [b]Matt. 4:10 [c]1Cor. 16:23; 2Cor. 13:14; Gal. 6:18; Phil. 4:23; 1Thess. 5:28; 2Thess. 3:18; Rev. 22:21 **21** [a]Acts 16:1 [b]Acts 13:1 [c]Acts 17:5 [d]Acts 20:4 [e]Rom. 9:3; 16:7, 11 **22** [a]1Cor. 16:21; Gal. 6:11; Col. 4:18; 2Thess. 3:17; Philem. 19

🗝 **16:1-4,21** See note on I Tim. 2:9-15.

23 [a]Gaius, host to me and to the whole church,[1577] greets you. [b]Erastus, the city treasurer[3623] greets you, and Quartus, the brother.

24 [[1]The grace of our Lord Jesus Christ be with you all. Amen.]

25 [a]Now to Him who is [ppt]able to [ainf]establish you [b]according to my gospel[2098] and the preaching[2782] of Jesus Christ, according to the revelation[602] of [c]the mystery[3466] which has been [pfpp]kept secret for [d]long ages past,

26 but now is [aptp]manifested,[5319] and by [a]the Scriptures[1124] of the prophets,[4397] according to the commandment[2003] of the eternal[166] God, has been made [aptp]known[1107] to all the nations, *leading* to [b]obedience[5218] of faith;[4102]

27 to the only wise[4680] God, through Jesus Christ, [a]be the glory[1391] forever. Amen.

23 [a]Acts 19:29; 20:4 ; 1Cor. 1:14 [b]Acts 19:22; 2Tim. 4:20
24 [1]Many mss. do not contain this v.
25 [a]Eph. 3:20; Jude 24 [b]Rom. 2:16 [c]Matt. 13:35; Rom. 11:25; 1Cor. 2:1, 7; 4:1; Eph. 1:9; 3:3, 9; 6:19; Col. 1:26f.; 2:2; 4:3; 1Tim. 3:16 [d]2Tim. 1:9; Titus 1:2
26 [a]Rom. 1:2 [b]Rom. 1:5
27 [a]Rom. 11:36

16:23 See note on III Jn. 1.

The First Epistle of Paul to the

CORINTHIANS

Corinth was an important cosmopolitan Greek city located on a large isthmus about fifty miles west of Athens. It was one of the largest cities in the Roman Empire. Only Rome, Alexandria, and Antioch had more people. Corinth was on a major trade route and had a thriving economy, and the vices of East and West converged there. Greeks, Romans, Jews, and a mixed multitude of sailors and merchants flocked to this crossroads. Corinthian-style architecture was famous. The Isthmian athletic games were held biennially there. By the end of the second century, Corinth had become one of richest cities in the world.

Paul believed that Corinth was a strategic center of influence and there was already a large Jewish presence (see Acts 18:4). But Corinth was full of sin. It was one of the most wicked cities of ancient times. Degradation, immorality, and heathen customs abounded. There were many religions represented, even a temple which offered a thousand sacred prostitutes. Pleasure was worshipped more than principles.

Paul stayed in Corinth for eighteen months (probably A.D. 52—53). The congregation was established by Paul during his second missionary journey (see Acts 18:1-11; I Cor. 2:1,2). Paul, also a tentmaker by trade, worked with a husband and wife team, Aquila and Priscilla (Prisca). Apollos came later. After about three years, Paul was in Ephesus, approximately 200 miles due east, across the Aegean Sea. Both cities were on a busy trade route. Communication flowed freely between them. Paul received unfavorable news about the Corinthian congregation from members of the household of Chloe (I Cor. 1:11) and other friends (I Cor. 16:17). They reported that there were divisions and much sin in the congregation. There was gross immorality (an incestuous relationship), lawsuits between Christians in front of unbelievers, many practical problems in living the Christian life, marriage problems, difficulties concerning meat offered to idols and matters of conscience, abuses in taking the Lord's Supper, disorderly conduct in the formal assemblies for worship, confusion about the role of women in the church, and heresies about the afterlife, which produced a tremendous response from Paul to teach the truth about the resurrection. I Corinthians 13, the famous chapter about love, is one of the most beloved passages in the entire Bible. Judging from I Cor. 7:1, the Christians at Corinth had already written Paul at least one letter. And Paul had written them a letter (now lost) before I Corinthians (I Cor. 5:9). Many of the members were recently converted from pagan practices and they were having difficulty in adjusting, breaking with the past. As long as there are human beings in the church, there will be human failures. Paul did not have enough time to ground them well. Paul planned to spend the following winter in Corinth (I Cor. 16:5-8) and did so (Acts 20:2,3).

Appeal to Unity

1 Paul, [a]<u>called</u>[2822] *as* an <u>apostle</u>[652] of
Jesus <u>Christ</u>[5547] [I]by [b]the <u>will</u>[2307] of
<u>God</u>,[2316] and [c]Sosthenes our [d]<u>brother</u>,[80]
2 to [a]the <u>church</u>[1577] of God which
is at [b]Corinth, to those who have been
[pfpp]<u>sanctified</u>[37] in Christ Jesus, [I]<u>saints</u>[40]
[c]by calling, with all who in every place
[ppt] [d]call upon the <u>name</u>[3686] of our <u>Lord</u>[2962]
Jesus Christ, their *Lord* and ours:
3 [a]Grace to you and <u>peace</u>[1515] from
God our <u>Father</u>[3962] and the Lord Jesus
Christ.
🔑 4 [a]I <u>thank</u>[2168] [I]my God always concerning you, for the <u>grace</u>[5485] of God
which was [aptp]given you in Christ Jesus,
5 that in everything you were
[aop] [a]enriched in Him, in all [b]<u>speech</u>[3056]
and [b]all <u>knowledge</u>,[1108]
6 even as [a]the <u>testimony</u>[3142] concerning Christ was confirmed [I]in you,

1 [I]Lit., *through* [a]Rom. 1:1 [b]Rom. 1:10; 2Tim. 1:1 [c]Acts 18:17 [d]Acts 1:15
2 [I]Or, *holy ones* [a]1Cor. 10:32 [b]Acts 18:1 [c]Rom. 1:7; 8:28 [d]Acts 7:59
3 [a]Rom. 1:7
4 [I]Some ancient mss. do not contain *my* [a]Rom. 1:8
5 [a]2Cor. 9:11 [b]Rom. 15:14; 2Cor. 8:7
6 [I]Or, *among* [a]2Thess. 1:10; 1Tim. 2:6; 2Tim. 1:8; Rev. 1:2

🔑 **1:4-7** See note on I Cor. 12:1-11.

7 so that you are not [pip]lacking in
any gift, [a]awaiting eagerly[553] the revelation[602] of our Lord Jesus Christ,
🔑 8 [a]who shall also confirm[950] you to
the end,[5056] blameless[410] in [b]the day[2250]
of our Lord Jesus Christ.
9 [a]God is faithful,[4103] through whom
you were [b]called[2564] into [c]fellowship[2842]
with His Son,[5207] Jesus Christ our
Lord.
10 Now [a]I exhort[3870] you, [b]breth-
ren, by the name of our Lord Jesus
Christ, that you all [I]agree, and there
be no [IIc]divisions[4978] among you, but
you be [III]made complete[2675] in [d]the
same mind[3563] and in the same judgment.[1106]
11 For I have been [aop]informed concerning you, my brethren, by Chloe's
people, that there are quarrels among
you.
12 Now I mean this, that [a]each one
of you is saying, "I am of Paul," and
"I of [b]Apollos," and "I of [c]Cephas," and
"I of Christ."
🔑 13 [I]Has Christ[5547] been [pfip]divided?
Paul was not crucified for you, was he?
Or were you [a]baptized[907] [II]in the name
of Paul?
🔑 14 [I]I thank[2168] God that I [a]baptized
none of you except [b]Crispus and
[c]Gaius,
15 that no man should say you were
baptized [I]in my name.
16 Now I did baptize also the
[a]household of Stephanas; beyond that,
I do not know whether I baptized any
other.
17 [a]For Christ did not send me to
[pinf]baptize, but to preach the gospel,[2097]
[b]not in [I]cleverness of speech,[3056] that
the cross[4716] of Christ should not be
[asbp]made void.[2758]

The Wisdom of God

18 For the word[3056] of the cross
is to [a]those who [I]are [ppt]perishing[622]
[b]foolishness,[3472] but to us who [II]are being [ppp]saved[4982] it is [c]the power[1411] of
God.
19 For it is written,
"[a]I WILL DESTROY[622] THE
WISDOM[4678] OF THE
WISE,[4680]
AND THE CLEVERNESS OF THE
CLEVER I WILL SET ASIDE."
20 [a]Where is the wise man? Where
is the scribe?[1122] Where is the de-
bater of [b]this age?[165] Has not God
[ao] [c]made foolish[3471] the wisdom of [d]the
world?[2889]
21 For since in the wisdom of God
[a]the world through its wisdom did not
come to know God, [b]God was well-
pleased[2106] through the [c]foolishness[3472]
of the [I]message preached[2782] to [ainf] [d]save
those who [ppt]believe.[4100]
22 For indeed [a]Jews ask for [I]signs,
and Greeks search for wisdom;
23 but we preach[2784] [Ia]Christ
[pfpp]crucified,[4717] [b]to Jews a stumbling
block,[4625] and to Gentiles [c]foolish-
ness,[3472]
24 but to those who are [a]the
called,[2822] both Jews and Greeks, Christ
[b]the power[1411] of God and [c]the wisdom[4678] of God.
25 Because the [a]foolishness of God

7 [a]Luke 17:30; Rom. 8:19, 23; Phil. 3:20; 2Pet. 3:12 **8** [a]Rom. 8:19; Phil. 1:6; Col. 2:7; 1Thess. 3:13; 5:23 [b]Luke 17:24, 30; 1Cor. 5:5; 2Cor. 1:14; Phil. 1:6, 10; 2:16; 1Thess. 5:2; 2Thess. 2:2 **9** [a]Deut. 7:9; Is. 49:7; 1Cor. 10:13; 2Cor. 1:18; 1Thess. 5:24; 2Thess. 3:3 [b]Rom. 8:28 [c]1John 1:3 **10** [I]Lit., *speak the same thing* [II]Lit., *schisms* [III]Or, *united* [a]Rom. 12:1 [b]Rom. 1:13 [c]1Cor. 11:18 [d]Rom. 12:16; Phil. 1:27 **12** [a]Matt. 23:8-10; 1Cor. 3:4 [b]Acts 18:24; 1Cor. 3:22 [c]John 1:42; 1Cor. 3:22; 9:5; 15:5 **13** [I]Or, *Christ has been divided!* or, *Christ is divided!* [II]Lit., *into* [a]Matt. 28:19; Acts 2:38 **14** [I]Some ancient mss. read *I give thanks that* [a]Acts 18:8 [b]Rom. 16:23 **15** [I]Lit., *into* **16** [a]1Cor. 16:15, 17 **17** [I]Lit., *wisdom* [a]John 4:2; Acts 10:48 [b]1Cor. 2:1, 4, 13; 2Cor. 10:10; 11:6 **18** [I]Or, *perish* [II]Or, *are saved* [a]Acts 2:47; 2Cor. 2:15; 4:3; 2Thess. 2:10 [b]1Cor. 1:21, 23, 25; 2:14; 4:10 [c]Rom. 1:16; 1Cor. 1:24 **19** [a]Is. 29:14 **20** [a]Job 12:17; Is. 19:11f.; 33:18 [b]Matt. 13:22; 1Cor. 2:6, 8; 3:18, 19 [c]Rom. 1:20ff. [d]John 12:31; 1Cor. 1:27f.; 6:2; 11:32; James 4:4 **21** [I]Lit., *preaching* [a]John 12:31; 1Cor. 1:27f.; 6:2; 11:32; James 4:4 [b]Luke 12:32; Gal. 1:15; Col. 1:19 [c]1Cor. 1:18, 23, 25; 2:14; 4:10 [d]Rom. 11:14; James 5:20 **22** [I]Or, *attesting miracles* [a]Matt. 12:38 **23** [I]I.e., Messiah [a]1Cor. 2:2; Gal. 3:1; 5:11 [b]Luke 2:34; 1Pet. 2:8 [c]1Cor. 1:18, 21, 25; 2:14; 4:10 **24** [a]Rom. 8:28 [b]Rom. 1:16; 1Cor. 1:18 [c]Luke 11:49; 1Cor. 1:30 **25** [a]1Cor. 1:18, 21, 23; 2:14; 4:10

🔑 **1:8** The phrase "the day of our Lord Jesus Christ" is actually a combination of two other phrases, "the day of the Lord" and "the day of Jesus Christ." The first pertains to a period of time during which the judgments of the Lord will fall on unbelievers. The second pertains to God's program for His Church. Paul here combines these concepts, referring in general to that period of time in which God will consummate His programs for both sinners and believers. See note on I Thess. 5:2 and also the Editor's book, *A Richer Life for You in Christ.*

🔑 **1:13** See note on I Cor. 10:2.

🔑 **1:14** See note on III Jn. 1.

is wiser than men,[444] and [b]the weakness[722] of God is stronger than men.
26 For [I]consider your [a]calling,[2821]
brethren, that there were [b]not many
wise[4680] according to [II]the flesh,[4561] not
many mighty, not many noble;
27 but [a]God has [ao]chosen the foolish
things of [b]the world[2889] to shame the
wise, and God has chosen the weak
things of [b]the world to shame the things
which are strong,
28 and the base things of [a]the world
and the [pfpp]despised, God has chosen,
[b]the things that are not, that He might
[c]nullify[2673] the things that are,
29 that [a]no [I]man[4561] should
[aosb]boast[2744] before God.
30 But [I]by His doing you are in
[a]Christ Jesus, who became to us
[b]wisdom from God, [II]and [c]righteous-
ness[1343] and [d]sanctification,[38] and [e]re-
demption,[629]
31 that, just as it is written, "[a]LET
HIM WHO [ppt]BOASTS, [pim]BOAST IN THE
LORD."

Paul's Reliance upon the Spirit

2 And when I came to you, brethren,
I [a]did not come with superiority of
speech[3056] or of wisdom,[4678] proclaiming[2605] to you [b]the [I]testimony[3142] of God.
2 For I determined[2919] to know
nothing among you except [a]Jesus Christ,
and Him crucified.[4717]
3 And I was with you in [a]weakness
and in [b]fear and in much trembling.
4 And my [I]message[3056] and my
preaching[2782] were [a]not in persuasive
words[3056] of wisdom, but in demonstration of [b]the [an]Spirit[4151] and of
power,[1411]
5 that your faith[4102] should not
[I]rest on the wisdom of men,[444] but on
[a]the power of God.[2316]
6 Yet[1161] we do speak wisdom

25 [b]2Cor. 13:4
26 [I]Lit., *see* [II]Or, *human standards* [a]Rom. 11:29 [b]Matt. 11:25; 1Cor. 1:20; 2:8
27 [a]James 2:5 [b]1Cor. 1:20
28 [a]1Cor. 1:20 [b]Rom. 4:17 [c]Job 34:19; 1Cor. 2:6; 2Thess. 2:8; Heb. 2:14
29 [I]Lit., *flesh* [a]Eph. 2:9
30 [I]Lit., *of Him* [II]Or, *both* [a]Rom. 8:1; 1Cor. 4:15 [b]1Cor. 1:24 [c]Jer. 23:5f.; 33:16; 2Cor. 5:21; Phil. 3:9 [d]1Cor. 1:2; 6:11; 1Thess. 5:23 [e]Rom. 3:24; Eph. 1:7, 14; Col. 1:14
31 [a]Jer. 9:23f.; 2Cor. 10:17

1 [I]Some ancient mss. read *mystery* [a]1Cor. 1:17; 2:4, 13 [b]1Cor. 2:7
2 [a]1Cor. 1:23; Gal. 6:14
3 [a]1Cor. 4:10; 2Cor. 11:30; 12:5, 9f.; 13:9 [b]Is. 19:16; 2Cor. 7:15; Eph. 6:5
4 [I]Lit., *word* [a]1Cor. 1:17; 2:1, 13 [b]Rom. 15:19; 1Cor. 4:20
5 [I]Lit., *be* [a]2Cor. 4:7; 6:7; 12:9
6 [a]Eph. 4:13; Phil. 3:15; Heb. 5:14; 6:1 [b]Matt. 13:22; 1Cor. 1:20 [c]1Cor. 1:28
7 [a]Rom. 11:25; 16:25f.; 1Cor. 2:1 [b]Rom. 8:29f. [c]Heb. 1:2; 11:3
8 [a]1Cor. 1:26; 2:6 [b]Matt. 13:22; 1Cor. 1:20 [c]Acts 7:2; James 2:1
9 [a]Is. 64:4; 65:17
10 [I]Some ancient

among those who are [a]mature;[5046] a wisdom, however, not of [b]this age, nor of
the rulers of [b]this age, who [ppp]are [c]pass-
ing away;[2673]
7 but we speak God's [an]wisdom
in a [a]mystery,[3466] the [pfpp]hidden *wisdom,*
which God [b]predestined[4309] before the
[c]ages[165] to our glory;[1391]
8 *the wisdom* [a]which none of the rulers of [b]this age has [pfi]understood; for
if they had [ao]understood it, they would
not have crucified [c]the Lord of glory;
9 but just as it is written,
"[a]THINGS WHICH EYE HAS NOT
[ao]SEEN AND EAR HAS NOT
HEARD,
AND *which* HAVE NOT
ENTERED[305] THE HEART OF
MAN,
ALL THAT GOD HAS PREPARED
FOR THOSE WHO [ppt]LOVE[25]
HIM."
10 [Ia]For to us God [ao]revealed[601]
them [b]through the Spirit; for the Spirit
searches all things, even the [c]depths
of God.
11 For who among men knows[1492]
the *thoughts* of a man except the
[a]spirit[4151] of the man, which is in him?
Even so the *thoughts* of God no one
knows except the Spirit of God.
12 Now we [a]have [ao]received, not
the spirit of [b]the world, but the Spirit
who is from God, that we might know
the things freely given[5483] to us by God,
13 which things we also speak,
[a]not in words taught by human wisdom,
but in those taught by the Spirit,[4151]
[I]combining[4793] spiritual *thoughts* with
spiritual *words.*
🗝 14 But [I]a [an] [a]natural[5591] man [b]does

mss. use *But* [a]Matt. 11:25; 13:11; 16:17; Gal. 1:12; Eph. 3:3, 5 [b]John 14:26 [c]Rom. 11:33ff. **11** [a]Prov. 20:27 **12** [a]Rom. 8:15 [b]1Cor. 1:27 **13** [I]Or, *interpreting spiritual* things *to spiritual* men [a]1Cor. 1:17; 2:1,4 **14** [I]Or, *an unspiritual* [a]1Cor. 15:44, 46; James 3:15; Jude 19 mg. [b]John 14:17

🗝 **2:14** The Greek word for "natural" is *psuchikos* (5591). It refers to the man who is governed only by his environment, by his natural or animal instincts, by his fallen Adamic nature. It is the man who is "in Adam" and estranged from God because of Adam's sin. This man is unable to understand the things of the Spirit of God because his spirit has not been quickened by the Spirit of God. See Editor's book, *A Revolutionary Mystery*.

not accept the things of the Spirit of God; for they are [c]<u>foolishness</u>[3472] to him, and he cannot [ainf]understand them, because they are <u>spiritually</u>[4153] [II]appraised.

15 But he who is [a]<u>spiritual</u>[4152] appraises all things, yet he himself is appraised by no man.

16 For [a]WHO HAS [ao]KNOWN THE <u>MIND</u>[3563] OF THE <u>LORD</u>,[2962] THAT HE SHOULD INSTRUCT HIM? But [b]we have the [an]mind of <u>Christ</u>.[5547]

Foundations for Living

3 And I, brethren, [ao]could not [ainf]speak to you as to [a]<u>spiritual men</u>,[4152] but as to [b]<u>men of flesh</u>,[4560] as to [c]<u>babes</u>[3516] in Christ.

2 I [ao]gave you [a]<u>milk</u>[1051] to drink, not <u>solid food</u>;[1033] for you [b]were not yet [ipf]able *to receive it.* Indeed, even now you are not yet able,

3 for you are still fleshly. For since there is [a]jealousy and strife among you, are you not fleshly, and are you not walking [Ib]like mere men?

4 For when [a]one says, "I am of Paul," and another, "I am of Apollos," are you not *mere* [b]men?

5 What then is Apollos? And what is Paul? [a]<u>Servants</u>[1249] through whom you <u>believed</u>,[4100] even [b]as the Lord gave *opportunity* to each one.

6 [a]I [ao]planted, [b]Apollos watered, but [c]<u>God</u>[2316] was causing the growth.

7 So then neither the one who [ppt]plants nor the one who [ppt]waters is anything, but God who [ppt]causes the growth.

8 Now he who plants and he who waters are one; but each will [a]receive his own [I]reward according to his own labor.

9 For we are God's [a]fellow workers; you are God's [Ib]<u>field</u>,[1091] God's [c]<u>building</u>.[3619]

10 According to [a]the <u>grace</u>[5485] of God which was [aptp]given to me, as a <u>wise</u>[4680] master builder [b]I [ao]laid a foundation, and [c]another is building upon it. But let each man be careful how he <u>builds upon it</u>.[2026]

11 For no man can lay a [a]<u>foundation</u>[2310] other than the one which is [ppt]<u>laid</u>,[2749] which is Jesus Christ.

12 Now if any man <u>builds upon</u>[2026] the foundation with gold, silver, [I]precious stones, wood, hay, straw,

13 [a]each man's <u>work</u>[2041] will become evident; for [b]the day will show it, because it is *to be* [pinp]<u>revealed</u>[601] with fire; and the fire itself will test [I]the quality of each man's work.

14 If any man's work which he has [ao]built upon it remains, he shall [a]receive a reward.

15 If any man's work is burned up, he shall suffer loss; but he himself shall be <u>saved</u>,[4982] yet [a]so as through fire.

16 [a]Do you not know that [b]you are a [an] [I]<u>temple</u>[3485] of <u>God</u>,[2316] and *that* the <u>Spirit</u>[4151] of God <u>dwells</u>[3611] in you?

17 If any man destroys the [I]temple of God, God will destroy him, for the [I]temple of God is <u>holy</u>,[40] and [II]that is what you are.

18 [a]Let no man [pim]deceive himself. [b]If any man among you thinks that he is wise in [c]this age, let him become foolish that he may become <u>wise</u>.[4680]

19 For [a]the wisdom of this world is <u>foolishness</u>[3472] before God. For it is written, "*He is* [b]THE ONE WHO [ppt]CATCHES THE WISE IN THEIR CRAFTINESS";

20 and again, "[a]THE LORD KNOWS THE <u>REASONINGS</u>[1261] of the wise, THAT THEY ARE USELESS."

14 [II]Or, *examined* [c]1Cor. 1:18 **15** [a]1Cor. 3:1; 14:37; Gal. 6:1 **16** [a]Is. 40:13; Rom. 11:34 [b]John 15:15

1 [a]1Cor. 2:15; 14:37; Gal. 6:1 [b]Rom. 7:14; 1Cor. 2:14 [c]1Cor. 2:6; Eph. 4:14; Heb. 5:13 **2** [a]Heb. 5:12f.; 1Pet. 2:2 [b]John 16:12 **3** [I]Lit., *according to man* [a]Rom. 13:13; 1Cor. 1:10f.; 11:18 [b]1Cor. 3:4 **4** [a]1Cor. 1:12 [b]1Cor. 3:3 **5** [a]Rom. 15:16; 2Cor. 3:3, 6; 4:1; 5:18; 6:4; Eph. 3:7; Col. 1:25; 1Tim. 1:12 [b]Rom. 12:6; 1Cor. 3:10 **6** [a]1Cor. 4:15; 9:1; 15:1; 2Cor. 10:14f. [b]Acts 18:24-27; 1Cor. 1:12 [c]1Cor. 15:10 **8** [I]Or, *wages* [a]1Cor. 3:14; 4:5; 9:17; Gal. 6:4 **9** [I]Or, *cultivated land* [a]Mark 16:20; 2Cor. 6:1 [b]Is. 61:3; Matt. 15:13 [c]1Cor. 3:16; Eph. 2:20-22; Col. 2:7; 1Pet. 2:5 **10** [a]Rom. 12:3; 1Cor. 15:10 [b]Rom. 15:20; 1Cor. 3:11f. [c]1Thess. 3:2 **11** [a]Is. 28:16; Eph. 2:20; 1Pet. 2:4ff. **12** [I]Or, *costly* **13** [I]Lit., *of what sort each man's work is* [a]1Cor. 4:5 [b]Matt. 10:15; 1Cor. 1:8; 2Thess. 1:7-10; 2Tim. 1:12, 18; 4:8 **14** [a]1Cor. 3:8; 4:5; 9:17; Gal. 6:4 **15** [a]Job 23:10; Ps. 66:10, 12; Jude 23 **16** [I]Or, *sanctuary* [a]Rom. 6:16 [b]Rom. 8:9; 1Cor. 6:19; 2Cor. 6:16; Eph. 2:21f. **17** [I]Or, *sanctuary* [II]Lit., *which you are* **18** [a]Is. 5:21 [b]1Cor. 8:2; Gal. 6:3 [c]1Cor. 1:20 **19** [a]1Cor. 1:20 [b]Job 5:13 **20** [a]Ps. 94:11

3:13 See note on Mt. 8:11,12.

3:15 A Christian may suffer the loss of worthless works and character, but not his life. It is like one who escapes from a burning building; he has suffered a loss, but he is still alive. So Paul is teaching that there will be a judgment for Christians, but it is not a judgment that consigns people to hell. See Editor's book, *Getting the Most Out of Life.*

21 So then [a]let no one boast in men.
For [b]all things belong to you,
22 [a]whether Paul or Apollos or Cephas or the world[2889] or [b]life[2222] or
death[2288] or things present or things to
come; all things belong to you,
23 and [a]you belong to Christ;[5547] and
[b]Christ belongs to God.

Servants of Christ

4 Let a man regard[3049] us in this
manner, as [a]servants[5257] of Christ,
and [b]stewards[3623] of [c]the mysteries[3466]
of God.
2 In this case, moreover, it is required [I]of stewards that one be found
trustworthy.[4103]
3 But to me it is a very small thing
that I should be examined by you, or
by *any* human [I]court;[2250] in fact, I do
not even examine myself.
4 For I [a]am conscious of nothing
against myself, yet I am not by this
[pfip] [b]acquitted;[1344] but the one who
[ppt]examines me is the Lord.
5 Therefore [a]do not go on [I]passing
judgment[2919] before [II]the time,[2540] *but*
wait [b]until the Lord comes who will both
[c]bring to light[5461] the things hidden in
the darkness[4655] and disclose[5314] the
motives[1012] of *men's* hearts;[2588] and then
each man's [d]praise will come to him from
God.
6 Now these things, brethren, I
have figuratively [ao]applied[3345] to myself
and Apollos for your sakes, that in us
you might learn not to exceed[5228]
[a]what is written, in order that no one
of you might [b]become [I]arrogant [c]in behalf
of one against the other.
7 For who regards you as su-
perior?[1252] And [a]what do you have that
you did not receive? But if you did receive it, why do you boast as if you
had not received it?
8 You are [a]already filled,[2880] you
have already become [ao]rich, you have
[ao]become kings without us; and *I*
would indeed that you had become
kings so that we also might reign with
you.
9 For, I think,[1380] God has [ao]ex-
hibited us apostles last[2078] of all, as
men [a]condemned to death; because we
[b]have [ao]become a spectacle to the world,
[I]both to angels and to men.
10 We are [a]fools for Christ's sake,
but [b]you are prudent[5429] in Christ;
[c]we are weak,[772] but you are strong;
you are distinguished,[1741] but we are
without honor.
11 To this present hour we are both
[a]hungry and thirsty, and are poorly
clothed, and are roughly treated, and
are homeless;[790]
12 and we toil, [a]working[2038] with our
own hands; when we are [b]reviled,[3058]
we bless; when we are [c]persecuted, we
endure;[430]
13 when we are slandered, we try
to [I]conciliate;[3870] we have [ao] [a]become as
the scum[4027] of the world, the dregs
of all things, *even* until now.
14 I do not write these things to
[a]shame[1788] you, but to admonish[3560] you
as my beloved[27] [b]children.[5043]
15 For if you were to have countless
[a]tutors[3807] in Christ, yet *you would* not

21 [a]1Cor. 4:6 [b]Rom. 8:32 **22** [a]1Cor. 1:12; 3:5, 6 [b]Rom. 8:38 **23** [a]1Cor. 15:23; 2Cor. 10:7; Gal. 3:29 [b]1Cor. 11:3; 15:28

1 [a]Luke 1:2 [b]1Cor. 9:17; Titus 1:7; 1Pet. 4:10 [c]Rom. 11:25; 16:25 **2** [I]Lit., *in* **3** [I]Lit., *day* **4** [a]Acts 23:1; 2Cor. 1:12 [b]Ps. 143:2; Rom. 2:13 **5** [I]Lit., *judging anything* [II]I.e., the appointed time of judgment [a]Matt. 7:1; Rom. 2:1 [b]John 21:22; Rom. 2:16 [c]1Cor. 3:13 [d]Rom. 2:29; 1Cor. 3:8; 2Cor. 10:18 **6** [I]Lit., *puffed up* [a]1Cor. 1:19, 31; 3:19f. [b]1Cor. 4:18f.; 8:1; 13:4 [c]1Cor. 1:12; 3:4 **7** [a]John 3:27; Rom. 12:3,6; 1Pet. 4:10 **8** [a]Rev. 3:17f. **9** [I]Or, *and to angels and to men* [a]Rom. 8:36; 1Cor. 15:31; 2Cor. 11:23 [b]Heb. 10:33 **10** [a]Acts 17:18; 26:24; 1Cor. 1:18 [b]1Cor. 1:19f.; 3:18; 2Cor. 11:19 [c]1Cor. 2:3; 2Cor. 13:9 **11** [a]Rom. 8:35; 2Cor. 11:23-27 **12** [a]Acts 18:3 [b]1Pet. 3:9 [c]John 15:20; Rom. 8:35 **13** [I]Or, *console* [a]Lam. 3:45

14 [a]1Cor. 6:5; 15:34 [b]2Cor. 6:13; 12:14; 1Thess. 2:11; 1John 2:1; 3 John 4 **15** [a]Gal. 3:24f.

4:1 A steward (*oikonomos,* 3623) is one who manages a house (*oikos,* 3624) or dispenses what belongs to the house. Christians are called stewards in that they have been entrusted with the Gospel message. It is a responsibility for which believers will be held accountable. See Editor's book, *You and Public Opinion.*

4:5 See note on Mt. 8:11,12.

4:6 This difficult verse becomes clearer when the Greek word *meteschēmatisa* (3345) is understood. It does not mean "I have in a figure transferred to myself" as the A.V. translates it. That would imply that Paul was transferring the blame for the divisions to himself and Apollos. Rather the word applies to his relations with Apollos. This refashioned relationship is set forth as an example for the Corinthians to follow. See Editor's book, *Formula for Happiness.*

4:7 See notes on Lk. 19:11-27; I Cor. 11:2-16; 1 Tim. 2:9-15.

have many fathers;[3962] for in [b]Christ
Jesus I [c]became your father[1080] through
the [d]gospel.[2098]
16 I exhort you therefore, be [a]imi-
tators of me.
🔑 17 For this reason I [a]have sent to
you [b]Timothy, who is my [c]beloved and
faithful[4103] child in the Lord, and he will
remind you of my ways which are in
Christ, [d]just as I teach[1321] everywhere
in every church.[1577]
18 Now some have become [aop] [I][a]ar-
rogant, as though I were not [b]coming
to you.
19 But I [a]will come to you soon,
[b]if the Lord wills, and I shall find out,
not the [I]words[3056] of those who are
[c]arrogant, but their power.
20 For the kingdom[932] of God does
[a]not consist in [I]words,[3056] but in
power.[1411]
21 What do you desire? [a]Shall I
come to you with a rod or with love[26]
and a spirit[4151] of gentleness?

Immorality Rebuked

5 It is actually reported that there is
immorality4202 among you, and immorality of such a kind as does not exist
even among the Gentiles,[1484] that someone has [a]his father's wife.
2 And [I]you [a]have become [II]arrogant,
and [III]have not [ao] [b]mourned[3996] instead,
in order that the one who had [apt]done
this deed[2041] might be [asbp] [c]removed
from your midst.[3319]
3 For I, on my part,3303 though
[a]absent in body but present in spirit,[4151]
have already [pfi]judged[2919] him who has
so [apt]committed this, as though I were
present.
4 [a]In the name of our Lord Jesus,
when you are assembled, and [I]I with
you in spirit, [b]with[4862] the power[1411] of
our Lord Jesus,
🔑 5 *I have decided* to [ainf] [a]deliver such
a one to [b]Satan[4567] for the destruction[3639]
of his flesh,[4561] that his spirit may be
saved[4982] in [c]the day[2250] of the Lord
[I]Jesus.
6 [a]Your boasting is not good.
[b]Do you not know that [c]a little leaven[2219]
leavens[2220] the whole lump *of dough*?
7 Clean out the old leaven, that you
may be a new lump, just as you are *in
fact* unleavened.[106] For Christ[5547] our
[a]Passover3957 also has been [aop]sacri-
ficed.[2380]
8 Let us therefore [psa]celebrate the
feast, [a]not with old leaven, nor with the
leaven of malice[2549] and wickedness,[4189]
but with the unleavened bread of
sincerity[1505] and truth.[225]
9 I wrote you in my letter1992 [a]not
to [pip]associate with immoral people;4205
10 I *did* not at all *mean* with the
immoral people of this world, or with
the covetous and swindlers, or with
[a]idolaters;[1496] for then you would have
to [ainf]go out of the world.[2889]
11 But [I]actually, I wrote to you not
to associate [II]with any [ppp]so-called
[a]brother[80] if he should be an immoral
person,4205 or covetous, or [b]an idolater,

15 [b]1Cor. 1:30; [c]Num. 11:12; 1Cor. 3:8; Gal. 4:19; Philem. 10 [d]1Cor. 9:12, 14, 18, 23; 15:1
16 [a]1Cor. 11:1; Phil. 3:17; 4:9; 1Thess. 1:6; 2Thess. 3:9
17 [a]1Cor. 16:10 [b]Acts 16:1 [c]1Cor. 4:14; 1Tim. 1:2, 18; 2Tim. 1:2 [d]1Cor. 7:17; 14:33; 16:1; Titus 1:5
18 [I]Lit., *puffed up* [a]1Cor. 4:6 [b]1Cor. 4:21
19 [I]Lit., *word* [a]Acts 19:21; 20:2; 1Cor. 11:34; 16:5f.; 16:7-9; 2Cor. 1:15f. [b]Acts 18:21 [c]1Cor. 4:6
20 [I]Lit., *word* [a]1Cor. 2:4
21 [a]2Cor. 1:23; 2:1, 3; 12:20; 13:2, 10

1 [a]Lev. 18:8; Deut. 22:30; 27:20
2 [I]Or, *have you . . . ?* [II]Lit., *puffed up* [III]Or, *have you . . . ?* [a]1Cor. 4:6 [b]2Cor. 7:7-10 [c]1Cor. 5:13
3 [a]Col. 2:5; 1Thess. 2:17
4 [I]Lit., *my spirit, with the power* [a]2Thess. 3:6 [b]John 20:23; 2Cor. 2:10; 13:3, 10
5 [I]Some ancient mss. do not contain *Jesus* [a]Prov. 23:14; Luke 22:31; 1Tim. 1:20 [b]Matt. 4:10 [c]1Cor. 1:8
6 [a]1Cor. 5:2; James 4:16 [b]Rom. 6:16 [c]Hos. 7:4; Matt. 16:6, 12; Gal. 5:9
7 [a]Mark 14:12; 1Pet. 1:19
8 [a]Ex. 12:19; 13:7; Deut. 16:3
9 [a]2Cor. 6:14; Eph. 5:11; 2Thess. 3:6
10 [a]1Cor. 10:27
11 [I]Or, *now I write* [II]Lit., *together if any man called a brother should be* [a]Acts 1:15; 2Thess. 3:6 [b]1Cor. 10:7, 14, 20f.

🔑 **4:17** See general remarks on Timothy.

🔑 **5:5** The expression "the destruction of his flesh" in Greek is *olethron* (3639) which, as in I Thess. 5:3, refers to the earthly body and its sufferings and ultimate death. The Lord brings physical destruction upon a believer as in the case of Ananias and Sapphira in Acts 5:1-11. He may allow prolonged emotional and physical illness and finally death as in the case of I Cor. 11:30 (*astheneis,* 772) which refers to both types of weaknesses, emotional and physical, and *arrōstoi* (732), which refers more to physical illness. The verb for "sleep" (*koimaō* or *koimaomai,* 2837) always refers to the body and not to the soul. Sin has its effect upon the body of the believer, thus bringing God's punishment upon it so that the spirit may be saved. That the destruction of the flesh means suffering, sickness and ultimate death of the body as a punishment for fornication in this particular instance in I Cor. 5 is a view strengthened by the fact that fornication is a sin particularly of the body (see I Cor. 6:13,19). See notes on I Thess. 5:2; I Tim. 1:20.

or a reviler,3060 or a drunkard, or a swindler—not even to eat with such a one.

12 For what have I to do with judging [a]outsiders?1854 [b]Do you not judge those who are within *the church*?

13 But those who are outside, God [I]judges. [aim] [a]REMOVE THE WICKED MAN4190 FROM AMONG YOURSELVES.

Lawsuits Discouraged

6 Does any one of you, when he has a [I]case against his neighbor,2087 dare to go to law2919 before the unrighteous,94 and [a]not before the [II]saints?40

2 Or [a]do you not know that [b]the [I]saints will judge2919 [c]the world?2889 And if the world is judged by you, are you not competent *to* [II]*constitute* the smallest law courts?2922

3 [a]Do you not know that we shall judge angels?32 How much more, matters of this life?

4 If then you have law courts2922 dealing with matters of this life, [I]do you appoint them as judges who are of no account in the church?1577

5 [a]I say *this* to your shame.1791 *Is it* so, *that* there is not among you one wise man4680 who will be able to decide1252 between3319 his [b]brethren,80

6 but brother goes to law2919 with brother, and that before [an] [a]unbelievers?571

7 Actually, then, it is already a defeat for you, that you have lawsuits with one another. [a]Why not rather be wronged? Why not rather be defrauded?

8 On the contrary, you yourselves wrong and defraud, and that *your* [a]brethren.

9 Or [a]do you not know that the unrighteous94 shall not [b]inherit2816 the kingdom932 of God? [c]Do not be deceived; [d]neither fornicators,4205 nor idolaters,1496 nor adulterers, nor [I]effeminate,3120 nor homosexuals,733

10 nor thieves, nor *the* covetous, nor drunkards, nor revilers, nor swindlers,727 shall [a]inherit2816 the kingdom of God.

11 And [a]such were some of you; but you were [ao] [b]washed,628 but you were [c]sanctified,37 but you were [aop] [d]justified1344 in the name3686 of the Lord Jesus Christ, and in the Spirit4151 of our God.

The Body Is the Lord's

12 [a]All things are lawful for me, but not all things are profitable.4851 All things are lawful for me, but I will not be mastered by anything.

⊶ 13 [a]Food is for the [I]stomach, and the [I]stomach is for food; but God will [b]do away with both [II]of them. Yet the body4983 is not for immorality,4202 but [c]for the Lord;2962 and [d]the Lord is for the body.

14 Now God has not only [a]raised1453 the Lord, but [b]will also raise us up1825 through His power.

⊶ 15 [a]Do you not know that [b]your bodies are members of Christ?5547 Shall I then take away the members of Christ and make them members of a harlot? [c]May it never be!1096 3361

16 Or [a]do you not know that the one who [ppt]joins himself to a harlot is one body *with her*? For He says, "[b]THE TWO WILL BECOME ONE FLESH."

17 But the one who [ppt]joins himself to the Lord is [a]one spirit *with Him*.

18 [a]Flee immorality.265 Every *other* sin that a man commits is outside the body, but the [I]immoral man sins264 against his own body.

⊶ 19 Or [a]do you not know that [b]your body4983 is a [I]temple3485 of the Holy40 Spirit4151 who is in you, whom you have from [II]God, and that [c]you are not your own?

12 [a]Mark 4:11 [b]1Cor. 5:3-5; 6:1-4
13 [I]Or, *will judge* [a]Deut. 13:5; 17:7, 12; 21:21; 22:21; 1Cor. 5:2
1 [I]Lit., *matter* [II]Or, *holy ones* [a]Matt. 18:17
2 [I]V. 1, note 2 [II]Or, *try the trivial cases?* [a]Rom. 6:16 [b]Dan. 7:18, 22, 27; Matt. 19:28 [c]1Cor. 1:20
3 [a]Rom. 6:16
4 [I]Or, *appoint them ... church.*
5 [a]1Cor. 4:14; 15:34 [b]Acts 1:15; 9:13; 1Cor. 6:1
6 [a]2Cor. 6:14f.; 1Tim. 5:8
7 [a]Matt. 5:39f.
8 [a]1Thess. 4:6
9 [I]I.e., effeminate by perversion [a]Rom. 6:16 [b]Acts 20:32; 1Cor. 15:50; Gal. 5:21; Eph. 5:5 [c]Luke 21:8; 1Cor. 15:33; Gal. 6:7; James 1:16; 1John 3:7 [d]Rom. 13:13; 1Cor. 5:11; Gal. 5:19-21; Eph. 5:5; 1Tim. 1:10; Rev. 21:8; 22:15
10 [a]Acts 20:32; 1Cor. 15:50; Gal. 5:21; Eph. 5:5
11 [a]1Cor. 12:2; Eph. 2:2f.; Col. 3:5-7; Titus 3:3-7 [b]Acts 22:16; Eph. 5:26 [c]1Cor. 1:2, 30 [d]Rom. 8:30
12 [a]1Cor. 10:23
13 [I]Lit., *belly* [II]Lit., *it and them* [a]Matt. 15:17 [b]Col. 2:22 [c]1Cor. 6:15, 19 [d]Gal. 5:24; Eph. 5:23
14 [a]Acts 2:24 [b]John 6:39f.; 1Cor. 15:23
15 [a]1Cor. 6:3 [b]Rom. 12:5; 1Cor. 6:13; 12:27; Eph. 5:30 [c]Luke 20:16
16 [a]1Cor. 6:3 [b]Gen. 2:24; Matt. 19:5; Mark 10:8; Eph. 5:31
17 [a]John 17:21-23; Rom. 8:9-11; 1Cor. 6:15; Gal. 2:20
18 [I]Or, *one who practices immorality* [a]1Cor. 6:9; 2Cor. 12:21; Eph. 5:3; Col. 3:5; Heb. 13:4
19 [I]Or, *sanctuary* [II]Or, *God? And you ... own* [a]1Cor. 6:3 [b]John 2:21; 1Cor. 3:16; 2Cor. 6:16 [c]Rom. 14:7f.

⊶ **6:13,19** See note on I Cor. 5:5.
⊶ **6:15,16** See note on I Cor. 7:14.

20 For [a]you have been [aop]bought[59] with a price: therefore [aim]glorify[1392] God in [b]your body.

Advice on Marriage

7 Now concerning the things about which you wrote, it is [a]good for a man[444] not to [pinf]touch[680] a woman.

2 But because of immoralities,[4202] let each man have his own wife, and let each woman have her own husband.

3 Let the husband [pim] [I]fulfill his [ppp]duty[2133] to his wife, and likewise also the wife to her husband.

4 The wife does not have authority[1850] over her own body, but the husband *does*; and likewise also the husband does not have authority over his own body, but the wife *does*.

5 [a]Stop [pim]depriving one another, except by agreement for a time[2540] that you may [aosb]devote yourselves to prayer,[4335] and [psa] [I]come together again lest [b]Satan[4567] [psa]tempt[3985] you because of your lack of self-control.[192]

6 But this I say by way of concession,[4774] [a]not of command.[2003]

7 [I]Yet I wish that all men were [a]even as I myself am. However, [b]each man has his own gift from God, one in this manner, and another in that.

8 But I say to the unmarried and to widows that it is [a]good[2570] for them if they [aosb]remain [b]even as I.

9 But if they do not have self-control, [a]let them [aim]marry; for it is better to [ainf]marry than to [pip] [I]burn.

10 But to the [pfp]married I give instructions, [a]not I, but the Lord, that the wife should not [aifp] [I]leave her husband

11 (but if she does [asbp]leave, let her [pim]remain unmarried, or else be [aipp]reconciled[2644] to her husband), and that the husband should not [pinf] [I]send his wife away.[863]

12 But to the rest [a]I say, not the Lord, that if any brother[80] has a wife who is an unbeliever,[571] and she consents to live with him, let him not [pim] [I]send her away.[863]

13 And a woman who has an unbelieving[571] husband, and he consents to live with her, let her not [pim] [I]send her husband away.[863]

🗝 14 For the unbelieving[571] husband is [pfip]sanctified[37] through his wife, and the unbelieving[571] wife is [pfip]sanctified through [I]her believing husband; for otherwise your children [pin]are unclean,[169] but now they are [a]holy.[40]

15 Yet if the [ajn]unbelieving one[571] leaves, let him [pim]leave; the brother or the sister is not under [pfip]bondage in such *cases*, but God[2316] has [pfi]called [I]us [IIa]to peace.[1515]

16 For how[5101] do you know, O wife, whether you will [a]save[4982] your husband? Or how do you know, O husband, whether you will save your wife?

17 Only, [a]as the Lord has [ao]assigned to each one, as God[2962] has

20 [a]Acts 20:28; 1Cor. 7:23; 1Pet. 1:18f.; 2Pet. 2:1; Rev. 5:9 [b]Rom. 12:1; Phil. 1:20

1 [a]1Cor. 7:8, 26

3 [I]Lit., *render*

5 [I]Lit., *be* [a]Ex. 19:15; 1Sam. 21:5 [b]Matt. 4:10

6 [a]2Cor. 8:8

7 [I]Some ancient mss. read *For* [a]1Cor. 7:8; 9:5 [b]Matt. 19:11f.; Rom. 12:6; 1Cor. 12:4, 11

8 [a]1Cor. 7:1, 26 [b]1Cor. 7:7; 9:5

9 [I]I.e., burn with passion [a]1Tim. 5:14

10 [I]Lit., *depart from* [a]Mal. 2:16; Matt. 5:32; 19:3-9; Mark 10:2-12; Luke 16:18; 1Cor. 7:6

11 [I]Or, *leave his wife*

12 [I]Or, *leave her* [a]1Cor. 7:6; 2Cor. 11:17

13 [I]Or, *leave her husband*

14 [I]Lit., *the brother* [a]Ezra 9:2; Mal. 2:15

15 [I]Some ancient mss. read *you* [II]Lit., *in* [a]Rom. 14:19

16 [a]Rom. 11:14; 1Pet. 3:1

17 [a]Rom. 12:3

🗝 **7:14** The verb "sanctify" here should be taken as delineated in I Thess. 4:3,7 where it has the restricted meaning of abstaining from fornication. The verb *hēgiastai* is translated "is sanctified," but it is in the perfect tense which should have been translated "has been sanctified." It refers to an act that began in the past at a specific time and continues to be in effect. The discussion here is about a husband and wife who were both unbelievers but now one of them has believed. From the moment one became a believer, the other, the unbeliever (the word is used in the sense as being a spiritual unbeliever), by virtue of the declared faith of the marital partner in Jesus Christ, has pledged to abstain from fornication. If a new believer finds himself or herself in the position of having to live with a spouse who persistently engages in fornication, he or she will have to sacrifice personal sanctity by coition with someone who in reality causes the believer to be an adulterer or adulteress. Therefore, the choice is between disrupting the marriage or living with a fornicating marital partner. As to the latter choice, it is wise for us to remember that Christ Himself became sin for us and suffered on our behalf. If the unbelieving husband or wife, however, promises to abstain from fornication, then the believing spouse is required to remain with the unbeliever and not separate. For a complete exegetical study, see Editor's book, *May I Divorce and Remarry?*

[pfi]called each, in this manner let him [pim]walk. And [b]thus I direct[1299] in [c]all the [art]churches.

18 Was any man [aop]called *already* [pfpp]circumcised?[4059] Let him not become [pim]uncircumcised.[1986] Has anyone been called in uncircumcision?[203] [a]Let him not be circumcised.

19 [a]Circumcision[4061] is nothing, and uncircumcision[203] is nothing, but *what matters is* [b]the keeping[5084] of the commandments[1785] of God.[2316]

20 [a]Let each man [pim]remain in that [I]condition[2821] in which he was called.

21 Were you [aop]called while a slave?[1401] [I]Do not [pim]worry about it; but if you are able also to become free,[1658] rather [II]do that.

22 For he who was [aptp]called in the Lord while a slave, is [a]the Lord's freedman; likewise he who was called while free, is [b]Christ's[5547] slave.

23 [a]You were [aop]bought[59] with a price; do not become [an]slaves of men.

24 Brethren, [a]let each man [pim]remain with God in that *condition* in which he was [aop]called.

25 Now concerning virgins 3933 I have [a]no command[2003] of the Lord, but I give an opinion[1106] as one who [I][b]by the [pfpp]mercy of the Lord is trustworthy.[4103]

26 I think then that this is good[2570] in view of the [I]present[1764] [a]distress,[318] that [b]it is good for a man[444] [II]to remain as he is.

27 Are you [pfip]bound[1210] to a wife? Do not seek to be released. Are you [pfip]released[3089] from a wife? Do not seek a wife.

28 But if you should [aosb]marry, you have not [ao]sinned; and if a virgin should marry, she has not sinned. Yet such will have [I]trouble[2347] in this life,[4561] and I am trying to spare you.

29 But this I say, brethren,[80] [a]the time has been [pfpp]shortened, so that from now on those who [ppt]have wives should be as though they had none;

30 and those who [ppt]weep, as though they did not weep; and those who [ppt]rejoice, as though they did not rejoice; and those who [ppt]buy, as though they did not possess;[2722]

31 and those who [ppt]use 5530 the world,[2889] as though they did not [a]make full use[2710] of it; for [b]the form[4976] of this world is passing away.

32 But I want you to be free from concern. One who is [a]unmarried is concerned about the things of the Lord,[2962] how he may please the Lord;

33 but one who is [apt]married is concerned about the things of the world, how he may please his [I]wife,

34 and *his interests* are [pfip]divided. And the woman who is unmarried, and the virgin, is concerned about the things of the Lord, that she may be holy[40] both in body[4983] and spirit;[4151] but one who is [apt]married is concerned about the things of the world, how she may please her husband.

35 And this I say for your own benefit; not to [aosb]put a restraint upon you, but [I]to promote what is seemly, 2158 and *to secure* undistracted devotion to the Lord.

36 But if any man thinks that he is acting [pinf]unbecomingly toward his virgin *daughter,* 3933 if she should be of full age, and if it must be so, let him [pim]do what he wishes, he does not sin; let [I]her [pim]marry.

37 But he who stands firm in his heart,[2588] [I]being under no constraint, but has authority[1849] [II]over his own will,[2307] and has [pfi]decided[2919] this in his own heart, to [infg]keep his own virgin *daughter,* he will do well.

38 So then both he who [ppt]gives his own virgin *daughter* in marriage does well, and he who does not give her in marriage will do better.[2908]

39 [a]A wife is [pfip]bound[1210] as long as her husband lives;[2198] but if her husband [I]is dead,[2837] she is free to be [aifp]married to whom she wishes, only [b]in the Lord.

40 But [a]in my opinion[1106] she is happier[3107] if she [aosb]remains as she is; and I think[1380] that I also have the [an]Spirit[4151] of God.[2316]

17 [b]1Cor. 4:17 [c]1Cor. 11:16; 14:33; 2Cor. 8:18; 11:28; Gal. 1:22; 1Thess. 2:14; 2Thess. 1:4

18 [a]Acts 15:1ff.

19 [a]Rom. 2:27, 29; Gal. 3:28; 5:6; 6:15; Col. 3:11 [b]Rom. 2:25

20 [I]Lit., *calling* [a]1Cor. 7:24

21 [I]Lit., *Let it not be a care to you* [II]Lit., *use*

22 [a]John 8:32, 36; Philem. 16 [b]Eph. 6:6; Col. 3:24; 1Pet. 2:16

23 [a]1Cor. 6:20

24 [a]1Cor. 7:20

25 [I]Lit., *has had mercy shown on him by the Lord to be trustworthy* [a]1Cor. 7:6 [b]2Cor. 4:1; 1Tim. 1:13, 16

26 [I]Or, *impending* [II]Lit., *so to be* [a]Luke 21:23; 2Thess. 2:2 [b]1Cor. 7:1, 8

28 [I]Lit., *tribulation in the flesh*

29 [a]Rom. 13:11f.; 1Cor. 7:31

31 [a]1Cor. 9:18 [b]1Cor. 7:29; 1John 2:17

32 [a]1Tim. 5:5

33 [I]Some mss. read *wife. And there is a difference also between the wife and the virgin. One who is unmarried is concerned. . .*

35 [I]Lit., *for what is seemly*

36 [I]Lit., *them*

37 [I]Lit., *having no necessity* [II]Lit., *pertaining to*

39 [I]Lit., *has fallen asleep* [a]Rom. 7:2 [b]2Cor. 6:14

40 [a]1Cor. 7:6, 25

Take Care with Your Liberty

8 Now concerning [a]things sacrificed to idols,[1494] we know[1492] that we all have [b]knowledge.[1108] Knowledge [Ic]makes arrogant, but love[26] [d]edifies.[3618]

2 [a]If anyone supposes that he knows anything, he has not yet [pfi] [b]known as he ought to [ainf]know;

3 but if anyone loves[25] God, he [a]is [pfip]known by Him.

4 Therefore concerning the eating of [a]things sacrificed to idols,[1494] we know that [I]there is [b]no such thing as an idol[1497] in the world, and that [c]there is no God[2316] but one.

5 For even if [a]there are so-called gods[2316] whether in heaven[3772] or on earth,[1093] as indeed there are many gods and many lords,[2962]

6 yet for us [a]there is *but* one God, [b]the Father,[3962] [c]from whom are all things, and we *exist* for Him; and [d]one Lord,[2962] Jesus Christ, [e]by whom are all things, and we *exist* through Him.

7 However[235] not all men [a]have this knowledge; but [b]some, being accustomed[4914] to the idol until now, eat *food* as if it were sacrificed to an idol; and their conscience being weak is defiled.[3435]

8 But [a]food[1033] will not [I]commend us to God; we are neither [II]the worse if we do not eat, nor [III]the better if we do eat.

9 But [a]take care lest this [I]liberty[1849] of yours somehow become a stumbling block to the [b]weak.[770]

10 For if someone [aosb]sees you, who [ppt]have [a]knowledge, [ppt]dining in an idol's temple, will not his conscience, if he is weak, be strengthened[3618] to eat [b]things sacrificed to idols?

11 For through [a]your knowledge he who is weak [b]is ruined, the brother[80] for whose sake Christ died.[599]

12 [a]And thus, by [ppt]sinning[264] against the brethren and [ppt]wounding[5180] their conscience when it is weak, you sin [b]against Christ.[5547]

13 Therefore, [a]if food causes my brother to stumble,[4624] I will never eat meat[2907] again, that I might not cause my brother to [aosb]stumble.

Paul's Use of Liberty

9 Am I not [a]free?[1658] Am I not an [b]apostle?[652] Have I not [pfi] [c]seen Jesus our Lord?[2962] Are you not [d]my work[2041] in the Lord?

2 If to others I am not an apostle, at least I am to you; for you are the [a]seal of my [b]apostleship[651] in the Lord.

3 My defense to those who examine me is this:

4 [Ia]Do we not have a right[1849] to [ainf]eat and [ainf]drink?

🔑 5 [Ia]Do we not have a right to [pinf]take along[4013] a [II]believing wife, even as the rest of the apostles, and the [b]brothers[80] of the Lord, and [c]Cephas?

6 Or do only [Ia]Barnabas and I not have a right to refrain from [pinf]working?[2038]

7 Who at any time serves [a]as a soldier at his own expense?[3800] Who [b]plants a vineyard, and does not eat the fruit of it? Or who tends[4165] a flock[4167] and does not [I]use the milk[1051] of the flock?

8 I am not speaking these things [a]according to [I]human[444] judgment, am I? Or does not the Law[3551] also say these things?

9 For it is written in the Law[3551] of Moses, "[a]YOU SHALL NOT MUZZLE THE OX WHILE HE IS THRESHING." God is not concerned about[3199] [b]oxen, is He?

10 Or is He speaking altogether for our sake? Yes, [a]for our sake it was writ-

---

1 [I]Lit., *puffs up* [a]Acts 15:20; 1Cor. 8:4, 7, 10 [b]Rom. 15:14; 1Cor. 8:7, 10; 10:15 [c]1Cor. 4:6 [d]Rom. 14:19
2 [a]1Cor. 3:18 [b]1Cor. 13:8-12; 1Tim. 6:4
3 [a]Ps. 1:6; Jer. 1:5; Amos 3:2; Rom. 8:29; 11:2; Gal. 4:9
4 [I]I.e., has no real existence [a]Acts 15:20; 1Cor. 8:1, 7, 10 [b]Acts 14:15; 1Cor. 10:19; Gal. 4:8 [c]Deut. 4:35, 39; 6:4; 1Cor. 8:6
5 [a]2Thess. 2:4
6 [a]Deut. 4:35, 39; 6:4; Is. 46:9; Jer. 10:6, 7; 1Cor. 8:4 [b]Mal. 2:10; Eph. 4:6 [c]Rom. 11:36 [d]John 13:13; 1Cor. 1:2; Eph. 4:5; 1Tim. 2:5 [e]John 1:3; Col. 1:16
7 [a]1Cor. 8:4ff. [b]Rom. 14:14, 22f.
8 [I]Or, *present* [II]Lit., *lacking* [III]Lit., *abounding* [a]Rom. 14:17
9 [I]Lit., *right* [a]Rom. 14:13, 21; 1Cor. 10:28; Gal. 5:13 [b]Rom. 14:1; 1Cor. 8:10f.
10 [a]1Cor. 8:4ff. [b]Acts 15:20; 1Cor. 8:1, 4, 7
11 [a]1Cor. 8:4ff. [b]Rom. 14:15, 20
12 [a]Matt. 18:6; Rom. 14:20 [b]Matt. 25:45
13 [a]Rom. 14:21; 1Cor. 10:32; 2Cor. 6:3; 11:29

1 [a]1Cor. 9:19; 10:29 [b]Acts 14:14; Rom. 1:1; 2Cor. 12:12; 1Thess. 2:6; 1Tim. 2:7; 2Tim. 1:11 [c]Acts 9:3, 17; 18:9; 22:14, 18; 23:11; 1Cor. 15:8 [d]1Cor. 3:6; 4:15
2 [a]John 3:33; 2Cor. 3:2f. [b]Acts 1:25
4 [I]Lit., *It is not that we have no right to eat and drink, is it?* [a]1Cor. 9:14; 1Thess. 2:6, 9; 2Thess. 3:8f.
5 [I]Lit., *It is not that we have no right to take along . . . Cephas, is it?* [II]Lit., *sister, as wife* [a]1Cor. 7:7f. [b]Matt. 12:46 [c]Matt. 8:14; John 1:42
6 [I]Lit., *I and Barnabas* [a]Acts 4:36
7 [I]Lit., *eat of* [a]2Cor. 10:4; 1Tim. 1:18; 2Tim. 2:3f. [b]Deut. 20:6; Prov. 27:18; 1Cor. 3:6, 8
8 [I]Lit., *man* [a]Rom. 3:5
9 [a]Deut. 25:4; 1Tim. 5:18 [b]Deut. 22:1-4; Prov. 12:10
10 [a]Rom. 4:23f.

🔑 **9:5** See note on Tit. 2:1-5.

ten, because [b]the plowman ought to plow in hope, and the thresher *to thresh* in hope[1680] of sharing *the crops.*

11 [a]If we [ao]sowed spiritual things in you, is it too much if we should reap material[4559] things from you?

12 If others share the right over you, do we not more? Nevertheless, we [a]did not [ao]use this right, but we endure all things, [b]that we may [aosb]cause no hindrance to the [c]gospel[2098] of Christ.

13 [a]Do you not know that those who [ppt] [b]perform[2038] sacred[2413] services eat the *food* of the temple,[2411] *and* those who [ppt]attend regularly to the altar have their share with the altar?

14 So also [a]the Lord [ao]directed[1299] those who proclaim[2605] the [b]gospel to [c]get their living[2198] from the gospel.

15 But I have [ao] [a]used none of these things. And I am not writing these things that it may be done so in my case; for it would be better for me to die than have any man make [b]my boast an [aosb]empty[2758] one.

16 For if I preach the gospel,[2097] I have nothing to boast of, for [a]I am [pin]under compulsion;[318] for woe is me if I do not preach [b]the gospel.

17 For if I do this voluntarily, I have a [a]reward;[3048] but if against my will, I have a [b]stewardship[3622] [pfip]entrusted[4100] to me.

18 What then is my [a]reward? That, when I [ppt]preach the gospel, I may [aosb]offer[5087] the gospel [b]without charge, so as [c]not to make full [aies]use[2710] of my right[1849] in the gospel.

19 For though I am [a]free[1658] from all *men,* I have made myself [b]a [ao]slave[1402] to all, that I might [aosb] [c]win the more.

20 And [a]to the Jews I became as a Jew, that I might win Jews; to those who are under [1]the Law,[3551] as under [1]the Law, though [b]not being myself under [1]the Law, that I might win those who are under [1]the Law;

21 to those who are [a]without law,[459] [b]as without law, though not being without the law of God but [c]under the law[1772] of Christ, that I might win those who are without law.

22 To the [a]weak[772] I became weak, that I might win the weak; I have [pfi]become [b]all things to all men, [c]that I may by all means save[4982] some.

23 And I do all things for the sake of the gospel, that I may [aosb]become a fellow partaker of it.

24 [a]Do you not know that those who [ppt]run in a race all run, but *only* one receives [b]the prize? [c]Run in such a way that you may [aosb]win.[2638]

25 And everyone who [ppt] [a]competes[75] in the games exercises self-control in all things. They then *do it* to [aosb]receive a perishable [b]wreath, but we an imperishable.[862]

26 Therefore I [a]run in such a way, as not without aim; I box in such a way, as not [b]beating the air;

27 but I [1]buffet [a]my body and make it my slave,[1396] lest possibly, after I have [apt]preached[2784] to others, I myself should [aosb]be disqualified.[96]

Avoid Israel's Mistakes

10 For [a]I do not want you to be [pinf]unaware,[50] brethren, that our fathers[3962] were all [b]under the cloud, and all [c]passed through the sea;[2281]

🔑 2 and all [1]were [aop] [a]baptized[907] into[1519] Moses in the cloud and in the sea;

10 [b]2Tim. 2:6 **11** [a]Rom. 15:27; 1Cor. 9:14 **12** [a]Acts 18:3; 20:33; 1Cor. 9:15, 18 [b]2Cor. 6:3; 11:12 [c]1Cor. 4:15; 9:14, 16, 18, 23; 2Cor. 2:12 **13** [a]Rom. 6:16 [b]Lev. 6:16, 26; 7:6, 31ff.; Num. 5:9f.; 18:8-20, 31; Deut. 18:1 **14** [a]Matt. 10:10; Luke 10:7; 1Tim. 5:18 [b]1Cor. 4:15; 9:12, 16, 18, 23; 2Cor. 2:12 [c]Luke 10:8; 1Cor. 9:4 **15** [a]Acts 18:3; 20:33; 1Cor. 9:12, 18 [b]2Cor. 11:10 **16** [a]Acts 9:15; Rom. 1:14 [b]1Cor. 4:15; 9:12, 14, 18, 23; 2Cor. 2:12 **17** [a]John 4:36; 1Cor. 3:8; 9:18 [b]1Cor. 4:1; Gal. 2:7; Eph. 3:2; Phil. 1:16; Col. 1:25 **18** [a]John 4:36; 1Cor. 3:8; 9:17 [b]Acts 18:3; 2Cor. 11:7; 12:13 [c]1Cor. 7:31; 9:12 **19** [a]1Cor. 9:1 [b]2Cor. 4:5; Gal. 5:13 [c]Matt. 18:15; 1Pet. 3:1 **20** [1]Or, *law* [a]Acts 16:3; 21:23-26; Rom. 11:14 [b]Gal. 2:19 **21** [a]Rom. 2:12, 14 [b]Gal. 2:3; 3:2 [c]1Cor. 7:22; Gal. 6:2 **22** [a]Rom. 14:1; 15:1; 2Cor. 11:29 [b]1Cor. 10:33 [c]Rom. 11:14 **24** [a]1Cor. 9:13 [b]Phil. 3:14; Col. 2:18 [c]Gal. 2:2; 2Tim. 4:7; Heb. 12:1 **25** [a]Eph. 6:12; 1Tim. 6:12; 2Tim. 2:5; 4:7 [b]2Tim. 4:8; James 1:12; 1Pet. 5:4; Rev. 2:10; 3:11 **26** [a]Gal. 2:2; 2Tim. 4:7; Heb. 12:1 [b]1Cor. 14:9 **27** [1]Lit., *bruise* [a]Rom. 8:13 **1** [a]Rom. 1:13 [b]Ex. 13:21; Ps. 105:39 [c]Ex. 14:22, 29; Neh. 9:11; Ps. 66:6 **2** [1]Some ancient mss. read *received baptism* [a]Rom. 6:3; 1Cor. 1:13; Gal. 3:27

🔑 **10:2** Here the meaning of the word *baptizo* (907) is demonstrated in its more general implications. It means "to be identified with." These were identified with the work and purposes of Moses and they were said to be "baptized into" Moses. When the preposition *eis* (1519), "in, into or unto," comes after the verb "baptize" as in Mt. 28:19, "in the name of the Father and the Son and the Holy Spirit," it means "in identification with" that name and all that it stands for. Other Scriptures where the preposition *eis* is used after the verb "baptized" are Acts 8:16; 19:3,5; Rom. 6:3; I Cor. 1:13; 12:13; Gal. 3:27.

3 and all [a]ate the same spiritual[4152]
food;[1033]
4 and all [a]drank the same spiritual
drink, for they were [ipf]drinking from a
spiritual rock which [ppt]followed them;
and the rock was [I]Christ.[5547]
5 Nevertheless, with most of them
God was not well-pleased;[2106] for
[a]they were laid low in the wilderness.
6 Now these things happened as
[a]examples[5179] for us, that we should
not crave evil things, as [b]they also
craved.[1937]
7 And do not be [a]idolaters,[1496] as
some of them were; as it is written,
"[b]THE PEOPLE SAT DOWN TO EAT AND
DRINK, AND STOOD UP TO [c]PLAY."
8 Nor let us act immorally,[4203] as
[a]some of them [I]did, and [b]twenty-three
thousand fell[4098] in one day.
9 Nor let us [psa]try[1598] the Lord, as
[a]some of them [I]did, and were destroyed
by the serpents.
10 Nor [a]grumble, as some of them
[I]did, and [b]were [II]destroyed by the [c]de-
stroyer.
11 Now these things [ipf]happened to
them as an [a]example, and [b]they were
[aop]written for our instruction,[3559] upon
whom [c]the ends[5056] of the ages have
come.
12 Therefore let him who [a]thinks
he stands [pim]take heed lest he fall.[4098]
13 No temptation[3986] has [pfi]over-
taken you but such as is common to
man; and [a]God is faithful,[4103] who will not
allow you to be [aipf] [b]tempted[3985] beyond
what you are able, but with the temptation will provide the way of escape also,
that you may be able to [ainf]endure it.
14 Therefore, my [a]beloved, flee
from [b]idolatry.[1495]
15 I speak as to wise[5429] men; you
judge[2919] what I say.
16 Is not the [a]cup of blessing[2129]
which we bless[2127] a sharing[2842] in the
blood of Christ? Is not the [Ib]bread which
we break[2806] a sharing in the body[4983]
of Christ?[5547]
17 Since there is one [I]bread, we
[a]who are many are one body; for we
all partake of the one [I]bread.

3 [a]Ex. 16:4, 35; Deut. 8:3; Neh. 9:15, 20; Ps. 78:24f.; John 6:31
4 [I]I.e., the Messiah [a]Ex. 17:6; Num. 20:11; Ps. 78:15
5 [a]Num. 14:29ff., 37; 26:65; Heb. 3:17; Jude 5
6 [a]1Cor. 10:11 [b]Num. 11:4, 34; Ps. 106:14
7 [a]Ex. 32:4; 1Cor. 5:11; 10:14 [b]Ex. 32:6 [c]Ex. 32:19
8 [I]Lit., *acted immorally* [a]Num. 25:1ff. [b]Num. 25:9
9 [I]Lit., *made trial* [a]Num. 21:5f.
10 [I]Lit., *grumbled* [II]Lit., *being destroyed* [a]Num. 16:41; 17:5, 10 [b]Num. 16:49 [c]Ex. 12:23; 2Sam. 24:16; 1Chr. 21:15; Heb. 11:28
11 [a]1Cor. 10:6 [b]Rom. 4:23 [c]Rom. 13:11
12 [a]Rom. 11:20; 2Pet. 3:17
13 [a]1Cor. 1:9 [b]2Pet. 2:9
14 [a]Heb. 6:9 [b]1Cor. 10:7, 19f.; 1John 5:21
16 [I]Lit., *loaf* [a]Matt. 26:27f.; Mark 14:23f.; Luke 22:20; 1Cor. 11:25 [b]Matt. 26:26; Luke 22:19; Acts 2:42; 1Cor. 11:23f.
17 [I]Lit., *loaf* [a]Rom. 12:5; 1Cor. 12:12f., 27; Eph. 4:4, 16; Col. 3:15
18 [I]Lit., *Israel according to the flesh* [a]Rom. 1:3 [b]Lev. 7:6, 14f.; Deut. 12:17f.
19 [a]1Cor. 8:4
20 [a]Deut. 32:17; Ps. 106:37; Gal. 4:8; Rev. 9:20
21 [a]2Cor. 6:16 [b]Is. 65:11
22 [a]Deut. 32:21 [b]Eccl. 6:10; Is. 45:9
23 [a]1Cor. 6:12 [b]Rom. 14:19
24 [I]Or, *the other* [a]Rom. 15:2; 1Cor. 10:33; 13:5; 2Cor. 12:14; Phil. 2:21

18 Look at [I]the nation [a]Israel; are
not those who [ppt] [b]eat the sacrifices
sharers[2844] in the altar?
19 What do I mean then? That a
thing sacrificed to idols[1494] is anything,
or [a]that an idol[1497] is anything?
20 *No,* but *I say* that the things
which the Gentiles sacrifice, they
[a]sacrifice to demons,[1140] and not to
God;[2316] and I do not want you to become sharers[2844] in demons.
21 [a]You cannot [pinf]drink the cup of
the Lord and the cup of demons; you
cannot partake[3348] of the table of the
Lord and [b]the table of demons.
22 Or do we [a]provoke the Lord to
jealousy? We are not [b]stronger than He,
are we?
23 [a]All things are lawful, but not
all things are profitable.[4851] All things
are lawful, but not all things [b]edify.
24 Let no one [pim] [a]seek his own
good, but that of his [I]neighbor.
25 [a]Eat anything that is [ppp]sold in
the meat market,[3111] without asking
questions for conscience'[4893] sake;
26 [a]FOR THE EARTH[1093] IS THE
LORD'S,[2962] AND [I]ALL IT CONTAINS.[4138]
27 If [a]one of the [ajn]unbelievers[571] invites you, and you wish to go, [b]eat anything that is set before you, without
asking questions for conscience' sake.
28 But [a]if anyone should say to you,
"This is meat sacrificed to idols," do
not eat *it,* for the sake of the one who
informed *you,* and for conscience' sake;
29 I mean not your own conscience,
but the other *man's;* for [a]why is my
freedom[1657] judged by another's[243] conscience?
30 If I partake[3348] with thankfulness,
[a]why am I slandered[987] concerning that
for which I [b]give thanks?[2168]
31 Whether, then, you eat or drink
or [a]whatever you do, do all to the glory
of God.
32 [a]Give no offense[677] either to Jews

25 [a]Acts 10:15; 1Cor. 8:7 **26** [I]Lit., *its fulness* [a]Ps. 24:1; 50:12; 1Tim. 4:4 **27** [a]1Cor. 5:10 [b]Luke 10:8 **28** [a]1Cor. 8:7, 10-12 **29** [a]Rom. 14:16; 1Cor. 9:19 **30** [a]1Cor. 9:1 [b]Rom. 14:6 **31** [a]Col. 3:17; 1Pet. 4:11 **32** [a]Acts 24:16; 1Cor. 8:13

or to Greeks or to [b]the church[1577] of
God;
33 just as I also [a]please[700] all men
in all things, [b]not seeking my own
profit,[4851] but the *profit* of the many,
[c]that they may be saved.[4982]

Christian Order

11 [a]Be imitators of me, just as I
also am of Christ.
2 Now [a]I praise you because you
[b]remember me in everything, and
[c]hold firmly[2722] to the traditions, just as
I delivered them to you.
3 But I want you to understand that
[I]Christ[5547] is the [a]head of every man,[435]
and [b]the man is the head[2776] of a woman,
and God[2316] is the [c]head of [I]Christ.
4 Every man who has *something* on
his head while praying[4336] or [a]prophesy-
ing,[4395] disgraces his head.
5 But every [a]woman who has her
head uncovered while [ppt]praying or
[ppt]prophesying, disgraces her head; for
she is one and the same with her
[I]whose head is [b]shaved.
6 For if a woman does not cover
[I]her head, let her also [II]have her
hair cut off; but if it is disgraceful for a
woman to [II]have her hair cut off or [I]her
head shaved, let her [pim]cover [I]her head.
7 For a man ought not to have his
head [pinf]covered, since he is the
[a]image[1504] and glory[1391] of God; but
the woman is the glory of man.

32 [b]Acts 20:28; 1Cor. 1:2; 7:17; 11:22; 15:9; 2Cor. 1:1; Gal. 1:13; Phil. 3:6; 1Tim. 3:5, 15
33 [a]Rom. 15:2; 1Cor. 9:22; Gal. 1:10 [b]Rom. 15:2; 1Cor. 13:5; 2Cor. 12:14; Phil. 2:21 [c]Rom. 11:14; 1Thess. 2:16
1 [a]1Cor. 4:16; Phil. 3:17
2 [a]1Cor. 11:17, 22 [b]1Cor. 4:17; 15:2; 1Thess. 1:6; 3:6 [c]2Thess. 2:15; 3:6
3 [I]I.e., the Messiah [a]Eph. 1:22; 4:15; 5:23; Col. 1:18; 2:19 [b]Gen. 3:16; Eph. 5:23 [c]1Cor. 3:23

4 [a]Acts 13:1; 1Thess. 5:20 5 [I]Lit., *who is shaved* [a]Luke 2:36; Acts 21:9; 1Cor. 14:34 [b]Deut. 21:12
6 [I]Lit., *herself* [II]Lit., *shear herself* 7 [a]Gen. 1:26; 5:1; 9:6; James 3:9

11:2-16 Paul is writing here to the Corinthian Christians who, living in Greece, customarily complied with Greek traditions: men had their heads uncovered and the women covered theirs, which, however, was contrary to the Jewish tradition. Even to this day, Jewish men cover their heads at worship, but not the women. The question which faced the Corinthians was what to do with the existing custom of their day. Paul's advice is to examine the symbolism of the custom. If it has nothing in it that is contrary to God's Word or order in creation, accept it. Do not allow contentions to arise regarding customs which symbolize something that is proper (vv. 13,16). In this case, the Greeks believed that by not covering their heads, the men declared their independence as contrasted to the slaves who had to cover themselves. The women covered themselves, symbolizing the protectiveness that they enjoyed from their husbands. Paul intimated that there is nothing wrong with this, for in creation God created man, and from man there came the woman. That is good as far as it goes, but remember that man also, in spite of the fact that he prays without a covering, still has a Head and that is Christ (v. 3). In v. 11, however, he equates both man and woman in the Lord as is also stressed in Gal. 3:28 and I Pet. 3:7. In spite of this equality in Christ, still in creation and in the present order of things, the husband is the head of the family. God made him physically stronger than the woman in order to protect the woman. He ought to recognize his position as protector and show it overtly, and she ought to recognize her protector and abide under his care. God is responsible for the difference in the make-up of male and female (I Cor. 4:7), and no man should at any time endeavor in any way to diminish the difference between the two either in physical or emotional constitution, appearance, or function of life. Since this custom of head coverings showed beautifully that which is true in creation and also in the order of things, why should the Corinthian Christians living in Greece reject the Greek custom and assume the Jewish one? This decision, however, was left entirely to the Corinthians as we see in v. 13 which would have been far better translated: "Decide in regard to it your own selves." Therefore, these are personal decisions which must be exercised in following a custom as long as the symbol is good and there is no contrary teaching involved in the symbolism. This whole Scripture teaches that existing customs, as long as they are not contrary to morals and Scripture, are to be adhered to for the sake of unity and not to be flaunted. The little phrase at the end of v. 10, "because of the angels," means that when a young woman covers her head or wears her hair like a woman it accomplishes four things: (1) She gives a visible attestation to her womanhood. (2) She shows that she recognizes her husband's protectiveness. (3) She does not disturb a good custom. (4) She knows that heaven is pleased by her action. She does what she does also "on account of angels." The preposition *dia* (1223) is better translated "on account of." Whatever we do on earth we must make sure that it also has the approval of heaven. Angels here are representatives of heaven watching the believers as per I Cor. 11:10. See note on I Cor. 14:33-40.

11:4,5 See note on I Tim. 2:9-15.

8 For [a]man [I]does not originate from woman, but woman from man;

9 for indeed man was not created[2936] for the woman's sake, but [a]woman for the man's sake.

10 Therefore the woman ought to have *a symbol of* authority[1849] on her head, because of the angels.[32]

11 However, in the Lord,[2962] neither is woman [I]independent of man, nor is man [I]independent of woman.

12 For as the woman [I]originates from the man, so also the man *has his birth* through the woman; and [a]all things [II]originate [b]from God.

13 [a]Judge[2919] [I]for yourselves: is it proper[4241] for a woman to [pinf]pray[4336] to God *with head* uncovered?

🔑 14 Does not even nature itself teach1421 you that if a man has long hair, it is a dishonor to him,

15 but if a woman has long hair, it is a glory[1391] to her? For her hair is [pfip]given to her for a covering.

16 But if one is inclined to be contentious, [a]we have no [I]other practice, nor have [b]the churches[1577] of God.

17 But in giving this instruction,[3853] [a]I do not praise1867 you, because you come together not for the better[2909] but for the worse.

18 For, in the first place, when you [ppt]come together [I]as a church, I hear that [IIa]divisions[4978] exist among you; and in part, I believe[4100] it.

19 For there [a]must also be factions[139] among you, [b]in order that those who are approved[1384] may have become [I]evident5318 among you.

20 Therefore when you meet together, it is not to [ainf]eat the Lord's[2960] Supper,

21 for in your eating each one takes his own supper first;4301 and one is hungry and [a]another is drunk.

22 What! Do you not have houses in which to eat and drink? Or do you despise the [a]church[1577] of God, and [b]shame those who [ppt]have nothing? What shall I say to you? Shall [c]I praise you? In this I will not praise you.

The Lord's Supper

23 For [a]I [ao]received from the Lord that which I also delivered to you, that [b]the Lord Jesus in the night in which He was [ipf]betrayed took bread;

24 and when He had given thanks,[2168] He broke[2806] it, and said, "This is My body,[4983] which [I]is for you; do this in remembrance[364] of Me."

25 In the same way *He took* [a]the cup also, after supper,[1172] saying, "This cup is the [b]new[2537] covenant[1242] in My blood;[129] do this, as often as you drink *it*, in remembrance[364] of Me."

26 For as often as you eat this bread and drink the cup, you proclaim[2605] the Lord's[2962] death[2288] [a]until He comes.[2064]

8 [I]Lit., *is not from* [a]Gen. 2:21-23; 1Tim. 2:13
9 [a]Gen. 2:18
11 [I]Lit., *without*
12 [I]Lit., *is* [II]Lit., *are* [a]2Cor. 5:18 [b]Rom. 11:36
13 [I]Lit., *in* [a]Luke 12:57
16 [I]Lit., *such* [a]1Cor. 4:5; 9:1-3, 6 [b]1Cor. 7:17
17 [a]1Cor. 11:2, 22
18 [I]Lit., *in church* [II]Lit., *schisms* [a]1Cor. 1:10; 3:3
19 [I]Or, *manifest* [a]Matt. 18:7; Luke 17:1; 1Tim. 4:1; 2Pet. 2:1 [b]Deut. 13:3; 1John 2:19
21 [a]Jude 1:12
22 [a]1Cor. 10:32 [b]James 2:6 [c]1Cor. 11:2, 17
23 [a]1Cor. 15:3; Gal. 1:12; Col. 3:24 [b]1Cor. 11:23-25: *Matt. 26:26-28; Mark 14:22-24; Luke 22:17-20;* 1Cor. 10:16
24 [I]Some ancient mss. read *is broken*
25 [a]1Cor. 10:16 [b]Ex. 24:6-8; Luke 22:20; 2Cor. 3:6
26 [a]John 21:22; 1Cor. 4:5

🔑 **11:14,15** The verb *komaō* (2863) from *komē* (2864), "hair," means to have long hair or to fix the hair in such a way as to distinguish a woman from a man. It occurs only in these two verses. "If a woman has long hair, it is a glory to her." The noun *doxa* (1391) comes from the verb *dokeō* (1380), which means to recognize something for what it is. A woman's hair ought to be longer than a man's hair to distinguish her from the man and identify her as a woman. Paul brings out the point that at no time should a woman make an attempt to look like a man, and by the same token, a man to look like a woman. God made them different, and even natural propensities show forth their particular nature. And then Paul says, "for her hair is given to her for a covering." Actually it is "for the hair has been given to her (*dedotai,* the perfect tense of *didōmi,* 1325, 'to give,' which means that at some time in the past it was given to her and continues to be hers) in lieu of (*anti,* 473) a covering." This word *peribolaiou* (4018), "covering," occurs only here and in Heb. 1:12 and it is made up of the preposition *peri* (4012), "round about," and the verb *ballō* (906), "to place," something that one places around him, a covering or a mantle. In other words, Paul says here that if a woman has sufficient hair to distinguish her from looking like a man, that is the same as if she wore a covering around her head. The fact that a woman has the capability to care for her hair in a somewhat different manner than a man was a gift given to her at creation and continues to be her distinctive gift (*dedotai*). See note on I Cor. 14:33-40.

27 Therefore whoever psaeats the bread or psadrinks the cup of the Lord in an unworthy manner,371 shall be [a]guilty of1777 the body and the blood of the Lord.
28 But let a man444 pim [a]examine1381 himself, and so let him pimeat of the bread and pimdrink of the cup.
29 For he who ppteats and pptdrinks, eats and drinks judgment2917 to himself, if he does not judge the body1252 rightly.
30 For this reason many among you are weak and sick,732 and a number [a]sleep.
31 But if we ipfjudged1252 ourselves rightly, we should not be ipfjudged.2919
32 But when we are pppjudged, we are [a]disciplined3811 by the Lord in order that we may not be condemned2632 along with [b]the world.2889
33 So then, my brethren, when you pptcome together to eat, wait1551 for one another.
34 If anyone is [a]hungry, let him eat [b]at home, so that you may not come together for judgment.2917 And the remaining matters I shall [c]arrange1299 [d]when I come.

27 [a]Heb. 10:29
28 [a]Matt. 26:22; 2Cor. 13:5; Gal. 6:4
30 [a]Acts 7:60
32 [a]2Sam. 7:14; Ps. 94:12; Heb. 12:7-10; Rev. 3:19 [b]1Cor. 1:20
34 [a]1Cor. 11:21 [b]1Cor. 11:22 [c]1Cor. 4:17; 7:17; 16:1 [d]1Cor. 4:19
1 [a]1Cor. 12:4; 14:1 [b]Rom. 1:13

The Use of Spiritual Gifts

12 Now concerning [a]spiritual *gifts,* brethren,80 [b]I do not want you to be unaware.50

11:28-32 See note on Gal. 3:22.

11:30 See notes on I Cor. 5:5; I Tim. 1:20.

12:1-11 This is not a complete list of the gifts of the Spirit. These are mentioned specifically because they perhaps constituted part of the questioning of the Corinthians to Paul (I Cor. 7:1). The other two lists are in Eph. 4:11,12 and Rom. 12:6-8. The word used for "gifts" is *charismata,* the plural of *charisma.* The word is derived from *charis,* "grace," God's unmerited favor for man. The suffix *-ma* after *charis* makes it the result of grace, thus the result of God's grace in man. In I Cor. 1:4-7 we find Paul telling the Corinthians that the grace of God was given unto them in Christ Jesus, and that as a result, they were not lacking in any *charisma* (v. 7). Consequently, every Christian, irrespective of his spiritual standing and because of the indwelling of Christ's grace within him, has the potential of a demonstration of that grace in any gift, *charisma.* This is the fundamental thing for us to realize. The whole tenor of Paul's Epistle to the Corinthians is that they should not seek the *results* of grace, but *grace itself,* and then that grace can exercise itself as the One who gives it discerns the need for that demonstration. The demonstration of grace is not to be activated by the individual, but by the Giver of grace, God Himself.

In I Cor. 12:4-7 we have very clearly demonstrated the interaction of the triune God in His three personalities in the energizing of the gifts which are spiritual. In v. 4 we have the Holy Spirit, in v. 5 the Lord Jesus and in v. 6 God the Father. In Greek, the word "God" in this verse is preceded by the definite article *ho,* in which case reference is made to the Father even as in Jn. 1:1b: "And the word was toward the God (which means the Father)." Thus, it is better not to call these the gifts of the Holy Spirit. They are spiritual gifts given just as much by Jesus Christ and by God the Father as by the Holy Spirit. In I Cor. 12:1 the word "gifts" is inserted and should really not be there. The translation of the first phrase should be: "Now concerning spiritual matters," i.e., anything pertaining to the spiritual welfare of man. Whatever gifts are discussed, they must be viewed primarily as concerning the spiritual welfare of man and not the physical. Sickness and healing, for instance, should not be viewed only as to their effect upon the body, but also as to their results insofar as the spirit of the sick or the healed person is concerned.

A definition of a spiritual gift as a result of the study of this entire chapter could be stated as an instantaneous enablement by God in the power of the Holy Spirit to do or say something beyond one's natural ability in order to fulfill a specific purpose of God in the time-frame in which God permits it. These *charismata* are not permanent acquisitons or talents. They may be specific enablements of accomplishment within the periphery of the talents which were given by God in the first place. We have, for instance, the talents of the medical profession, the linguist, the prophets, etc. It is significant to note that the gifts pertaining to tongues and healings are in the plural which would indicate different kinds of enablements in the fields of speech and bodily health. Whenever languages are referred to in this entire Epistle, they are always in the plural with a personal pronoun in the singular. Whenever the Corinthian practice of speaking in an "unknown tongue" is referred to, which must indicate something of their own

(continued on next page)

2 [a]You know that when you were
pagans,[1484] *you were* [ppp] [b]led astray to
the [c]dumb880 idols,[1497] however you
were [ipf]led.
3 Therefore I make known[1107] to
you, that no one speaking [I][a]by the
[an]Spirit[4151] of God says, "Jesus is
[II][b]accursed";[331] and no one can say,
"Jesus is [c]Lord,"[2962] except [I][a]by the
[an]Holy Spirit.
4 Now there are [a]varieties[1243] of
gifts,[5486] but the same Spirit.
5 And there are varieties[1243] of ministries,[1248] and the same Lord.
6 And there are varieties[1243] of effects,[1755] but the same [a]God who
[ppt]works[1754] all things in all *persons*.
7 But to each one[1538] is [pinp]given
the manifestation[5321] of the Spirit [a]for
the common good.[4851]
8 For to one is given the word[3056]
of [a]wisdom[4678] through the Spirit, and
to another[243] the word of [b]knowledge[1108]
according to the same Spirit;
9 to another[2087] [a]faith[4102] [I]by the
same Spirit, and to another[243] [an] [b]gifts
of [pl] [II]healing2386 [I]by the one Spirit,
10 and to another[243] the [pl] [I]effecting
of [II][a]miracles,[1411] and to another[243]
[b]prophecy,[4394] and to another[243] the
[pl] [III][c]distinguishing[1253] of spirits, to another[2087] *various* [d]kinds of tongues,[1100]
and to another[243] the [an] [e]interpreta-
tion2058 of tongues.
11 But one and the same Spirit
works all these things, [a]distributing[1244]
to each one individually just as He
wills.
12 For even [a]as the body[4983] is one
and *yet* has many members, and all the
members of the body, though they are
many, are one body, [b]so also is
Christ.[5547]
🔑13 For [I][a]by one Spirit we were all
[aop]baptized[907] into one body, whether
[b]Jews or Greeks, whether slaves[1401]
or free,[1658] and we were all made to
[aop] [c]drink of one Spirit.
14 For [a]the body4943 is not one member, but many.
15 If the foot should say, "Because

2 [a]1Cor. 6:11; Eph. 2:11f.; 1Pet. 4:3 [b]1Thess. 1:9 [c]Ps. 115:5; Is. 46:7; Jer. 10:5; Hab. 2:18f.
3 [I]Or, *in* [II]Gr., *anathema* [a]Matt. 22:43; 1John 4:2f.; Rev. 1:10 [b]Rom. 9:3 [c]John 13:13; Rom. 10:9
4 [a]Rom. 12:6f.; 1Cor. 12:11; Eph. 4:4ff., 11; Heb. 2:4
6 [a]1Cor. 15:28; Eph. 1:23; 4:6
7 [a]1Cor. 12:12-30; 14:26; Eph. 4:12
8 [a]1Cor. 2:6; 2Cor. 1:12 [b]Rom. 15:14; 1Cor. 2:11, 16; 2Cor. 2:14; 4:6; 8:7; 11:6
9 [I]Or, *in* [II]Lit., *healings* [a]1Cor. 13:2; 2Cor. 4:13 [b]1Cor. 12:28, 30
10 [I]Lit., *effects* [II]Or, *works of power* [III]Lit., *distinguishings* [a]1Cor. 12:28f.; Gal. 3:5 [b]1Cor. 11:4; 13:2, 8 [c]1Cor. 14:29; 1John 4:1 [d]Mark 16:17; 1Cor. 12:28, 30; 13:1; 14:2ff. [e]1Cor. 12:30; 14:26
11 [a]1Cor. 12:4
12 [a]Rom. 12:4f.; 1Cor. 10:17 [b]1Cor. 12:27
13 [I]Or, *in* [a]Eph. 2:18 [b]Rom. 3:22; Gal. 3:28; Eph. 2:13-18; Col. 3:11 [c]John 7:37-39
14 [a]1Cor. 12:20

(continued from previous page)
formation, it is always in the singular. See chapter 14. We never read that the gift is that of a glossolaliac or a healer. God has not made anyone a healer with the power to heal anybody at any time he wishes, but He has given *charismata* of healings in each instance in vv. 9,28,30. In I Cor. 12:9 the word "healing" in the singular is the wrong translation of the plural *iamatōn.* God has not given to any man indiscriminate and at-will gifts of healing and made him a healer able to practice divine healing. He has given gifts of healings to believers through the infilling of His grace as He sees that they need to have them demonstrated. See notes on Lk. 19:11-27; I Cor. 11:14,15; 14:1-3; Js. 5:14-15.

🔑 **12:13** See note on Acts 1:5. This is the seventh and last time that the baptism in the Spirit is specifically mentioned (Mt. 3:11; Mk. 1:8; Lk. 3:16; Jn. 1:33; Acts 1:5; 11:15; all refer to the baptism in the Spirit as a future historical event). The sixth time in Acts 11:16, it refers to the baptism in the Spirit as a fulfilled promise. In I Cor. 12:13 the verb *ebaptisthēmen* is in the passive aorist which means that at some time in the past we were baptized. The element of this baptism is the Holy Spirit. The element is indicated by the preposition *en* (1722), "in" or "with" one Spirit. The word "Spirit" is in the dative case here, which when used by itself means also "by means of" as the preposition *en* would imply. This baptism in one Spirit into the body of Christ was for all, *pantes* (3956), "each one and all put together"—Jews, Gentiles, and the disciples of John, including all those of the O.T. who were looking forward to the coming of Jesus Christ, those who now believe, and those who will believe in the future. They all constitute the body of Christ. The baptism in the Spirit by Christ of every believer into His body to form His body is a historical event similar to His incarnation, crucifixion, resurrection, ascension and coming again. Christ did it once and for all when He sent His Holy Spirit as we saw in Acts 2:1-13; 10:44-46; 11:15-17; 19:1-10. It is not something that we experience, but something that Jesus Christ did once and for all in joining all believers into His body. See the Editor's complete exegesis on these and other related verses in his book, *The Holy Spirit's Baptism and Infilling.* See notes on Acts 1:5; 2:1-13; 11:14-18; 19:1-7; I Cor. 10:2, II Thess. 2:6,7.

I am not a hand, I am not *a part* of[1537] the body," it is not for this reason[3844 5124] [I]any the less *a part* of the body.

16 And if the ear should say, "Because I am not an eye, I am not *a part* of the body," it is not for this reason[3844 5124] [I]any the less *a part* of the body.

17 If the whole body were an eye, where would the hearing[189] be? If the whole were hearing, where would the sense of smell be?

18 But now God has [aom] [a]placed the members, each one of them, in the body, [b]just as He desired.

19 And if they were all one member, where would the body be?

20 But now [a]there are many members, but one body.

21 And the eye cannot say to the hand, "I have no need of you"; or again the head to the feet, "I have no need of you."

22 On the contrary, [I]it is much truer that the members of the body which seem to be weaker722 are necessary;[316]

23 and those *members* of the body, which we [I]deem less honorable, [II]on these we bestow more abundant[4053] honor,5092 and our unseemly *members come to* have more abundant seemliness,2157

24 whereas our seemly2158 *members* have no need *of it.* But God has *so* [ao]composed the body, giving more abundant honor to that *member* which [ppp]lacked,

25 that there should be no [I]division[4978] in the body, but *that* the members should have the same care for one another.

26 And if one member suffers, all the members suffer with[4841] it; if *one* member is [I]honored,[1392] all the members rejoice with it.

27 Now you are [a]Christ's[5547] body,[4983] and [b]individually members of it.

🔑 28 And God has [aom] [Ia]appointed in [b]the church,[1577] first[4412] [c]apostles,[652] second [d]prophets,[4396] third [e]teachers,[1320] then [IIf]miracles,[1411] then

15 [I]Lit., *not* a part

16 [I]Lit., *not* a part

18 [a]1Cor. 12:28 [b]Rom. 12:6; 1Cor. 12:11

20 [a]1Cor. 12:12, 14

22 [I]Lit., *to a much greater degree the members*

23 [I]Or, *think to be* [II]Or, *these we clothe with*

25 [I]Lit., *schism*

26 [I]Lit., *glorified*

27 [a]1Cor. 1:2; 12:12; Eph. 1:23; 4:12; Col. 1:18, 24; 2:19 [b]Rom. 12:5; Eph. 5:30

28 [I]Lit., *set some in* [II]Or, *works of power* [a]1Cor. 12:18 [b]1Cor. 10:32 [c]Eph. 4:11 [d]Acts 13:1; Eph. 2:20; 3:5 [e]Acts 13:1 [f]1Cor. 12:10, 29

🔑 **12:28-31** The questioning in vv. 29,30 is extremely important. It is put forth with the negative particle *mē* which expects a negative answer. What we have as a question, "All are not apostles, are they?" actually could be taken as a negative statement: "Not all apostles! Not all prophets!" If it is taken as a question, then the answer from the linguistic point of view must necessarily be a "no." Here the Apostle enumerates the gifts which do not pertain to all believers, but only to some. And since they pertain only to some, they are not and should not be placed by us as belonging to the first category of the gifts that God gives. When one subtracts these gifts mentioned in vv. 29,30 from the gifts mentioned in vv. 8-10, we find which are the better of the two categories of gifts. In this connection, we must understand the word *kreittona* in v. 31, not as "the best gifts," but the "better gifts," since *kreitton* or *kreisson* is the comparative of *agathos* (18), "good." There are good gifts, and these are not for all but for specific people in order to accomplish some special purposes for God at particular times designated by Him. These include Apostles and prophets in their particular function as specific teachers to set forth rules of doctrine and conduct for all believers who were to follow. They also included those given the function of miraculous demonstrations of God's power (*dunameis* 1411), those with gifts of healings, and those speaking in unlearned languages and interpreting those languages. These are restricted gifts since only a few could and did have them. By virtue of their restrictiveness, they are deemed inferior. But the gifts available to all at all times are those Paul calls the better gifts, *ta kreittona.* Which then are the better gifts spoken of in v. 31 which we must seek? They are the balance of the gifts mentioned in vv. 8-10, not restricted to a few as per vv. 29,30 the word of wisdom, the word of knowledge, faith, prophecy, and discernments of spirits. Prophecy as a gift here must be distinguished from the prophets. See *prophēteia* (4394), *prophēteuō* (4395), and *prophētēs* (4396). These are all in I Cor. 12:8-10. But there are two more which should be classified among the better gifts at the end of v. 28: helps and administrations or the gifts of administration. These administrations were most probably the elders appointed in apostolic days to examine whether the profession of faith of the candidates for baptism was genuine or not. Paul says in v. 31 that these better gifts are to be sought after and not the gifts which are available only to a few. See note on I Cor. 14:1-3. For this entire discussion, see the Editor's books on I Corinthians 12, volumes I and II, *The Gifts of the Holy Spirit and the Holy Spirit's Baptism and Infilling,* and *Variety in Christ's Body and the Better Gifts of the Holy Spirit.*

[g]gifts[5486] of healings,[2386] helps,[484]
[h]administrations,[2941] *various* [i]kinds of
tongues.[1100]
29 All are not apostles, are they?
All are not prophets, are they? All are
not teachers, are they? All are not *workers of* [l]miracles, are they?
30 All do not have gifts of healings,
do they? All do not speak[2980] with
tongues, do they? All do not [a]inter-
pret,[1329] do they?
31 But [a]earnestly desire the
greater[3173] gifts.
And I show you a still more excellent
way.

The Excellence of Love

13 If I speak with the
[a]tongues[1100] of men[444] and of
[b]angels,[32] but do not have love,[26] I have
[pfi]become a noisy gong or a [c]clanging
cymbal.
2 And if I have *the gift of* [a]proph-
ecy,[4394] and know[1492] all [b]mysteries[3466]
and all [c]knowledge;[1108] and if I have
[d]all faith,[4102] so as to [pinf] [e]remove[3179]
mountains, but do not have love, I am
nothing.
3 And if I [a]give all my possessions
to feed *the poor,* and if I [b]deliver my
body[4983] [l]to be burned, but do not have
love, it profits me nothing.
4 Love [a]is patient,[3114] love is kind,
and [b]is not jealous; love does not
brag[4068] *and* is not [c]arrogant,
5 does not act unbecomingly; it
[a]does not seek its own, is not provoked,
[b]does not take into account[3049] a
wrong[2556] *suffered,*
6 [a]does not rejoice[5463] in unrighteousness,[93] but [b]rejoices with[4796] the
truth;[225]
7 [la]bears[4722] all things, believes[4100]
all things, hopes[1679] all things, endures[5278] all things.
8 Love[26] never fails;[4098] but if *there
are gifts of* [la]prophecy,[4394] they will be
done away;[2673] if *there are* [b]tongues,[1100]
they will cease; if *there is* knowledge,[1108]
it will be done away.
9 For we [a]know[1097] in part, and we
prophesy[4395] in part;
10 but when the perfect[5046]
[aosb]comes,[2064] the partial will be
done away.
11 When I was a child,[3516] I used
to [ipf]speak as a child, [ipf]think as a child,
[ipf]reason as a child; when I [pfi]became a
man,[435] I [pfi]did away with childish[3516]
things.
12 For now we [a]see in a mirror
[l]dimly, but then [b]face to face; now I
know in part, but then I shall know fully
just as I also [c]have been fully [aop]known.
13 But now abide[3306] faith,[4102]
hope,[1680] love,[26] these three; but the
[l]greatest of these is [a]love.

Prophecy a Superior Gift

14 [a]Pursue love,[26] yet [b]desire
earnestly [c]spiritual[4152] *gifts,* but

28 [g]1Cor. 12:9, 30 [h]Rom. 12:8 [i]1Cor. 12:10
29 [l]Or, *works of power*
30 [a]1Cor. 12:10
31 [a]1Cor. 14:1, 39

1 [a]1Cor. 12:10 [b]2Cor. 12:4; Rev. 14:2 [c]Ps. 150:5
2 [a]Matt. 7:22; Acts 13:1; 1Cor. 11:4; 13:8; 14:1, 39 [b]1Cor. 14:2; 15:51 [c]Rom. 15:14 [d]1Cor. 12:9 [e]Matt. 17:20; 21:21; Mark 11:23
3 [l]Some ancient mss. read *that I may boast* [a]Matt. 6:2 [b]Dan. 3:28
4 [a]Prov. 10:12; 17:9; 1Thess. 5:14; 1Pet. 4:8 [b]Acts 7:9 [c]1Cor. 4:6
5 [a]1Cor. 10:24; Phil. 2:21 [b]2Cor. 5:19
6 [a]2Thess. 2:12 [b]2John 1:4; 3John 1:3f.
7 [l]Or, *covers* [a]1Cor. 9:12
8 [l]Lit., *prophecies* [a]1Cor. 13:2 [b]1Cor. 13:1
9 [a]1Cor. 8:2; 13:12
12 [l]Lit., *in a riddle* [a]2Cor. 5:7; Phil. 3:12; James 1:23 [b]Gen. 32:30; Num. 12:8; 1John 3:2 [c]1Cor. 8:3
13 [l]Lit., *greater* [a]Gal. 5:6

1 [a]1Cor. 16:14 [b]1Cor. 12:31; 14:39 [c]1Cor. 12:1

13:1-3 The tongues of men refer to understandable human languages. The tongues of angels may refer to the medium by which angels communicate in heaven. But even though (*ean,* 1437, if) one was gifted to speak in such languages, it should not be considered the ultimate of the Christian experience. The ultimate is the manifestation of love, not the speaking in tongues. The word charity or love is *agapē* (26), that self-giving divine love which emanates from God and is to be seen reflected in believers. It is the love which is concerned for others rather than self and which should govern the practice of all the spiritual gifts. See note on Gal. 1:8 and also *glossa* (1100), tongue, and the Editor's book, *To Love Is to Live.*

13:1,8 See note on I Cor. 14:1-3.

14:1-3 One observation needs to be made. In the three historical occurrences of speaking in tongues in Acts 2:4,6,8; 10:46 and 19:6, these were dialects as specifically stated in Acts 2:6,8, or languages (*heterai,* 2087) other than the ones known by the speakers. Also in Mk. 16:17; I Cor. 12: 10,28,30; 13:1,8; 14:5,6,18,22, when the word *glōssai* is used in the plural with a singular pronoun,

(continued on next page)

especially that you may [d]prophesy.[4395]
🔑 2 For one who [ppt][a]speaks[2980] in a
tongue[1100] does not speak to men, but
to God;[2316] for no one [I]understands,[191]
but[1161] [II]in *his* [an]spirit[4151] he speaks
[b]mysteries.[3466]
3 But one who [ppt]prophesies speaks
to men for [a]edification[3619] and [b]exhortation[3874]
and consolation.[3889]
🔑 4 One who [a]speaks in a tongue [b]edifies[3618]
himself; but one who [c]prophesies
[b]edifies the church.[1577]
5 Now I wish that you all [pinf][a]spoke
in tongues, but [b]*even* more that you
would [psa]prophesy; and greater is one
who [ppt]prophesies than one who [a]speaks
in tongues, unless he [psa]interprets, so
that the church[1577] may [aosb]receive
[c]edifying.[3619]
6 But now, brethren, if I come to
you speaking[2980] in tongues,[1100] what
shall I profit you, unless I speak to you
either by way of [a]revelation[602] or of
[b]knowledge[1108] or of [c]prophecy[4394] or
of [d]teaching?
7 Yet *even* lifeless[895] things, either
flute or harp, in producing a sound,
if they do not produce a distinction
in the tones, how will it be known
what is played on the flute or on the
harp?
8 For if [a]the [I]bugle produces an indistinct
sound, who will prepare himself
for battle?
9 So also you, unless you utter
by the tongue speech that is clear,
how will it be known what is spoken?
For you will be [a]speaking into the
air.
10 There are, perhaps, a great
many kinds of [I]languages in the
world, and no *kind* is without meaning.
11 If then I do not know the
meaning[1411] of the language, I shall be
to the one who [ppt]speaks a [Ia]barbarian,[915]
and the one who [ppt]speaks will be a
[I]barbarian [II]to me.
12 So also you, since you are zealous
of [I]spiritual *gifts,*[4151] seek to
[psa]abound for the [a]edification of the
church.[1577]
🔑 13 Therefore let one who speaks
in a tongue[1100] [pim]pray that he may interpret.
14 For if I pray in a tongue, my
spirit[4151] prays, but my mind is unfruitful.
15 [a]What is *the outcome* then? I shall
pray with the spirit[4151] and I shall pray
with the mind also; I shall [b]sing[5567] with
the spirit and I shall sing with the mind
also.
16 Otherwise if you bless[2127]
[I]in the spirit *only,* how will the one who
[ppt]fills[378] the place of the [II]ungifted[2399]
say [a]the "Amen"[281] at your [b]giving of
thanks, since he does not know what
you are saying?
17 For you are giving thanks well
enough, but the other man is not
[a]edified.[3618]
🔑 18 I thank[2168] God, I speak[2980] in
tongues[1100] more than you all;
19 however, in the church[1577] I desire
to speak five words with my
mind,[3563] that I may instruct[2727] others
also, rather than ten thousand words
in a tongue.[1100]

1 [d]1Cor. 13:2
2 [I]Lit., *hears* [II]Or, *by the Spirit* [a]Mark 16:17; 1Cor. 12:10, 28, 30; 13:1; 14:18ff. [b]1Cor. 13:2
3 [a]Rom. 14:19; 1Cor. 14:5, 12, 17, 26 [b]Acts 4:36
4 [a]Mark 16:17; 1Cor. 12:10, 28, 30; 13:1; 14:18ff., 26f. [b]Rom. 14:19; 1Cor. 14:5, 12, 17, 26 [c]1Cor. 13:2
5 [a]Mark 16:17; 1Cor. 12:10, 28, 30; 13:1; 14:18ff., 26f. [b]Num. 11:29 [c]Rom. 14:19; 1Cor. 14:4, 12, 17, 26
6 [a]1Cor. 14:26; Eph. 1:17 [b]1Cor. 12:8 [c]1Cor. 13:2 [d]Acts 2:42; Rom. 6:17; 1Cor. 14:26
8 [I]Lit., *trumpet* [a]Num. 10:9; Jer. 4:19; Ezek. 33:3-6; Joel 2:1
9 [a]1Cor. 9:26
10 [I]Lit., *voices*
11 [I]Or, *foreigner* [II]Or, *in my estimation* [a]Acts 28:2
12 [I]Lit., *spirits* [a]Rom. 14:19; 1Cor. 14:4, 5, 17, 26
15 [a]Acts 21:22; 1Cor. 14:26 [b]Eph. 5:19; Col. 3:16
16 [I]Or, *with the* [II]I.e., unversed in spiritual gifts [a]Deut. 27:15-26; 1Chr. 16:36; Neh. 5:13; 8:6; Ps. 106:48; Jer. 11:5; 28:6; Rev. 5:14; 7:12 [b]Matt. 15:36
17 [a]Rom. 14:19; 1Cor. 14:4, 5, 12, 26

(continued from previous page)

reference is made to ethnic languages. When the word "tongue" is used in the singular, *glōssa* as in I Cor. 14:2,4,13,19,26,27, it refers to the Corinthian ecstatic utterance. In I Cor. 14:9 it refers to the physical tongue of man, and in I Cor. 14:23, being in the plural with a plural pronoun, it refers to the Corinthian ecstatic utterances. The whole thesis of the Apostle Paul in I Cor. 14 is that no one should be speaking in the presence of other fellow human beings without being understood. This is an expression of common courtesy today. It is not what language one speaks, whether ethnic or an ecstatic utterance, that is important, but whether or not one is understood. For an entire discussion of the subject of tongues, see the Editor's book *Tongues!?*

🔑 **14:2,4-6,13,18,19,22,23,26,27** See note on Acts 2:1-13; I Cor. 14:1-3.

Instruction for the Church

20 [a]Brethren, [b]do not be children in your thinking;[5424] yet[235] in evil[2549] [c]be babes,[3515] but in your thinking be mature.[5046]

21 In [a]the Law[3551] it is written, "[b]BY MEN OF STRANGE TONGUES[2084] AND BY THE LIPS OF STRANGERS I WILL SPEAK[2980] TO THIS PEOPLE,[2992] AND EVEN SO THEY WILL NOT LISTEN[1522] TO ME," says the Lord.

22 So then tongues[1100] are for a sign,[4592] not to those who [ppt]believe,[4100] but to [ajn]unbelievers;[571] but [a]prophecy[4394] *is for a sign*, not to [ajn]unbelievers, but to those who [ppt]believe.

23 If therefore the whole church[1577] should [aosb]assemble together and all speak in tongues, and [l]ungifted[2399] men or unbelievers[571] enter, will they not say that [a]you are mad?

24 But if all [a]prophesy, and an unbeliever or an [l]ungifted man enters, he is [b]convicted by all, he is called to account[350] by all;

25 [a]the secrets of his heart[2588] are disclosed;[5318] and so he will [apt][b]fall on his face and worship God, [ppt][c]declaring that God is certainly among you.

26 [a]What is *the outcome* then, [b]brethren?[80] When you assemble, [c]each one has a [d]psalm,[5568] has a [e]teaching,[1322] has a [e]revelation,[602] has a [f]tongue,[1100] has an [g]interpretation.[2058] Let [h]all things be done for edification.

27 If anyone speaks in a [a]tongue,[1100] *it should be* by[2596] two or at the most three, and *each* in[303] turn, and let one [b]interpret;[1329]

28 but if there is no interpreter, let him keep silent in the church;[1577] and let him speak[2980] to himself and to God.[2316]

29 And let two or three [a]prophets[4396] speak, and let the others[243] [b]pass judgment.[1252]

30 But if a revelation[601] is made to another who is seated, let the first[4413] keep silent.

31 For you can all prophesy one by[2596] one, so that all may learn[3129] and all may be exhorted;[3870]

32 and the spirits[4151] of prophets[4396] are subject[5293] to prophets;

33 for God is not *a God* of [a]confusion[181] but of [l]peace,[1515] as in [b]all the churches[1577] of the [c]saints.[40]

34 Let the women [a]keep [pim]silent

20 [a]Rom. 1:13 [b]Eph. 4:14; Heb. 5:12f. [c]Ps. 131:2; Matt. 18:3; Rom. 16:19; 1Pet. 2:2
21 [a]John 10:34; 1Cor. 14:34 [b]Is. 28:11f.
22 [a]1Cor. 14:1
23 [l]V. 16, note 2 [a]Acts 2:13
24 [l]V. 16, note 2 [a]1Cor. 14:1 [b]John 16:8
25 [a]John 4:19 [b]Luke 17:16 [c]Is. 45:14; Dan. 2:47; Zech. 8:23; Acts 4:13
26 [a]1Cor. 14:15 [b]Rom. 1:13 [c]1Cor. 12:8-10 [d]Eph. 5:19 [e]1Cor. 14:6 [f]1Cor. 14:2 [g]1Cor. 12:10; 14:5, 13, 27f. [h]Rom. 14:19
27 [a]1Cor. 14:2 [b]1Cor. 12:10; 14:5, 13, 26ff.
29 [a]1Cor. 13:2; 14:32, 37 [b]1Cor. 12:10
33 [l]Or, *peace. As in all. . . saints, let* [a]1Cor. 14:40 [b]1Cor. 4:17; 7:17 [c]Acts 9:13
34 [a]1Cor. 11:5, 13

14:33-40 See the note on I Pet. 3:1-4. The question frequently asked concerning this portion of Scripture is "Does the Apostle Paul forbid women to speak at all or to pray or prophesy in church?" This particular passage must be related to what had gone before in the speaking in an unknown tongue which was the practice in Corinth. Across the bay from Corinth was Delphi, Greece's most famous center of oracles. It is impossible that what was happening in Delphi did not affect the Corinthians since intercommerce was common. As in many other cities, there was also a Corinthian treasury in Delphi. Those who wished to consult the Delphic oracle first sacrificed a sheep, goat, boar or other animal, after which, if the omens were favorable, they went into the room adjoining the Adyton or inner shrine. It is interesting that Paul in I Cor. 8 deals with sacrifices to idols, no doubt influenced by these Delphic sacrifices. At the inner shrine they waited their turn, which was determined by lot unless they had received from the Delphians the *promanteia,* or prior right of consultation. No women were admitted. They handed in questions written on leaden tablets, many of which have been discovered. The *pythia,* or priestess, (note that it was a priestess, not a priest) who delivered the oracle was a peasant woman over fifty years of age. At the height of the oracle's fame, there were three priestesses. After purifying herself in the Castalian fountain (see *baptismoi,* 909, ablutions practiced), drinking of the water of the Kassotis (note the parallelism in I Cor. 12:13, "and we were all made to drink of one spirit"), and eating a laurel leaf, she took her seat upon a tripod which was placed over the chasm in the Adyton. Intoxicated by the fumes from the chasm, she uttered incoherent sounds which were interpreted (observe both speaking in an unknown tongue and the interpretation of it) in hexameter verse by a waiting poet. The interpretation, which was always obscure and frequently equivocal, was handed over to the inquirer who usually returned home more mystified than when he had come (Source: Stuart Rossiter, *Greece;* London: Ernest Benn, Ltd. p. 400).

What Paul wrote in I Cor. 14:33-40, therefore, was undoubtedly influenced by this practice and the

(continued on next page)

in the churches; for they are not permitted to speak, but [b]let them [pim]subject[5293] themselves, just as [c]the Law[3551] also says.

35 And if they desire to learn[3129] anything, let them [pim]ask their own husbands at home; for it is [l]improper for a woman to speak in church.

34 [b]1Tim. 2:11f.; 1Pet. 3:1 [c]1Cor. 14:21

35 [l]Or, *disgraceful*

(continued from previous page)

predominant participation of women at the oracles of Delphi. They were not allowed to go into the inner shrine, but it was a woman who was the priestess. Is it any wonder that Paul reacted to a practice so closely related to such paganism within the Christian Church?

Paul's comments in I Cor. 11:2-16 in regard to the covering of the women's head were in reaction to the existence of a thousand priestesses at the Temple of Aphrodite on Acrocorinth. These priestesses, or temple prostitutes, were commonly seen without any covering on their heads and having short hair, which was unbecoming to a modest woman of those days. Paul's concern, therefore, was that Christian women should never allow themselves to be viewed in any way as resembling those of low moral stature. In I Cor. 11:3,16 his concern is that a woman in worship should very clearly be identified as a moral woman, if by nothing else than the long hair or the covering of her head. After all, if one of the prostitutes became saved, the only way she could enter an assembly of believers was to wear a covering (*peribolaion,* 4018, I Cor. 11:15) instead of long hair which would take a while to grow. This was the practice particulary in Corinth in view of the evil behavior which was so nearby at Acrocorinth. It was a good custom that had local meaning. Why flaunt it and produce quarreling within the Christian Church? This was Paul's argument. This passage becomes clearer if we examine the conclusion in v. 16: "But if one is inclined to be contentious, we have no other practice, nor have the churches of God." Good customs that are meaningful locally ought not to be resisted, but kept for what they symbolize. This was the general principle enunciated in I Cor. 11:2-16 and similarly in 14:33-40, but this time it was not in regard to Acrocorinth, but in regard to Delphi. A priestess who speaks incoherently and leads men astray as in Delphi? Never! That was Paul's point of view.

The main verse that constitutes the foundation of all that Paul says in I Cor. 14 is v. 33, "For God is not a God of confusion but of peace, as in all the churches of the saints." The interpreter of the oracles at Delphi always gave an ambiguous interpretation which would please the recipient and never expose the priestess who gave it, whereas God does not speak to confuse men. The verse applies to all that preceded it and all that follows it concerning the speaking of women in the churches. Paul makes it clear that in all the other churches, there was no confusion such as there was in the Corinthian Church to which he was writing. The peace in the other churches and lack of confusion was due to the fact that there was not the same practice of speaking in an unknown tongue as the Corinthians', perhaps allowing their women to imitate the Delphic priestesses. The prohibition of women speaking in churches may have resulted from such practices.

Another very important instruction of Paul is found in vv. 39,40, closing this total discussion that actually begins with I Cor. 12. Paul's conclusion, "Therefore, my brethren, desire earnestly to prophesy," or be zealous about prophesying. This is in the present infinitive which refers to constantly giving forth the Word of God. Because there was confusion among them, it didn't mean that they should stop teaching or witnessing: "And to speak in tongues, do not prohibit." Again, it is in the present imperative, *kōluete* (2967), meaning "When a person does not speak our own language, do not forbid him to minister in his own language which can be interpreted." In v. 40, Paul closes by saying, "But let all things be done properly and in an orderly manner." Again, the imperative is *ginesthō,* "should be done," the present imperative of *ginomai* (1096), which means "to let it be continuous and repetitive." This as a principle applies to all the churches (v. 34) although it was born out of a practice existing only in Corinth. Therefore, his instructions to the Corinthians from vv. 34-38 are to be applied among all the churches. When Paul says in v. 34, "Your women in the churches, let them be silent," it was not an instruction to the men in general in any church not to permit any women to speak, but to husbands to guide and teach their own wives lest they produce confusion and disturbance in a meeting, particularly with their exercise of a gift that they thought they had and were anxious to externalize; namely, speaking in an unknown tongue as was the manner of the Delphic priestesses. The verb *lalein,* the infinitive of *laleō* (2980), has been exclusively used in this whole discussion in speaking both in foreign languages and also particularly in the speaking of the unknown tongue of Corinth. The reason he uses *laleō* and not *legō* (3004) is because *laleō* refers to the mere utterance of sounds without the speaker necessarily

(continued on next page)

36 [l]Was it from you that the word[3056] of God *first* went forth? Or has it come to you only?

37 [a]If anyone thinks he is a prophet[4396] or [b]spiritual,[4152] let him recognize that the things which I write[1125] to you [c]are the Lord's[2962] commandment.[1785]

38 But if anyone [l]does not recognize *this*,[50] he is not recognized.

36 [l]Lit., *Or was* **37** [a]2Cor. 10:7 [b]1Cor. 2:15 [c]1John 4:6 **38** [l]Some ancient mss. read *is ignorant, let him be ignorant*

(continued from previous page)

knowing what he is saying or others understanding. *Legō* on the other hand is saying something that is a product of one's thought. Naturally no thinking person will speak without others understanding him. Therefore, Paul uses *laleō* because among the Corinthians stress was placed upon the languages themselves and not necessarily the content of the speech involved. Since Paul in I Cor. 11:5 assumes that a woman prays or prophesies, and this cannot refer to only a restricted group, then the word *laleō* in I Cor. 14:34-35, if taken to be speaking generally, would contradict I Cor. 11:5. There can be no contradiction in what Paul says, even as there is no contradiction in what he says about himself speaking in languages more than them all (I Cor. 14:18) and at the same time telling them in v. 23 that if a stranger came and heard them speak all at once in their unknown tongue, he would think they were all mad or maniacs. Paul would not include himself as a maniac! In v. 18 he speaks of his knowledge of various languages. In v. 19 he says that he would rather speak five understandable words than 10,000 which were not understood. Paul would have someone translate his words if it were necessary. This is the orderly procedure of communicating a message. He refers to the same thing exactly in I Cor. 14:34-38. The word *laleō* in I Cor. 14:34 must mean to speak either in many languages together, which brings confusion, instead of speaking in one language which the people understood either directly or by translation, or speaking in an unknown tongue which people could not understand. It cannot mean to speak with understanding and being understood.

One cannot take Paul's indirect imperative in I Cor. 14:34, "Let the women keep silent in the churches," as absolute. It must be taken in conjunction with what follows: "for they are not permitted to speak." The word "speak" as we explained is *lalein* which should be taken to mean "uttering sounds that are incoherent and which are not understood by others." Paul says that instead of having anything like that, it is better to have silence. Paul uses the same word "keep silent" in v. 28 when a man speaks in an unknown tongue without an interpreter. Also the same imperative "let the first keep silent," is used in v. 30, "but if a revelation is made to another who is seated, let the first keep silent." Actually that phrase, "let the first keep silent," is the same word meaning, "let him keep silent." That is a man, not a woman. What Paul is saying is that only one man must speak at a time. If two speak at once, there will be confusion. That "let him keep silent" is, therefore, qualified even as the *sigatōsan* of v. 34 in the case of the woman. The verb *sigaō* (4601) is used by Homer only in the imperative with the meaning of "hush, be still" (Liddell and Scott's Greek Lexicon). The imperatives here indicate linear action, i.e., it is not something that has a continuous effect but the action can be thought of as a line or line of dots. Every time one of these three actions appear on the scene during a worship service, the person should hush, be it a man or a woman. In the first two instances it concerns men and in the last women: (1) if a man speaks in an unknown language without anyone interpreting into a language that others can understand; (2) if a man speaks and somebody else gets up to speak, and (3) if a woman begins to act like Delphic priestesses speaking in an unknown tongue.

Under no circumstances does the injunction of Paul in I Cor. 14:34 indicate that women should not utter a word at any time during the church service. It is not men versus women or women versus men, but it is confusion versus order. It makes no difference who causes the confusion. It is as bad if produced by men as it is when produced by women.

Furthermore, the word *gunaikes* (1135) in v. 34 should not be translated as "women" in its generic sense, but as "wives." It is wives who should submit (*hupotassomai,* 5293) to their own husbands (*andras,* 435, v. 35). The whole argument is not the subjection of women to men in general, but of wives to their own husbands in the family unit as ordained by God. Paul states the principle that it was the duty of the husbands to restrain their own wives from such displays. It does not state that a man should restrain the wife of another. It is a shame for any woman to bring confusion into the local church (v. 35), even as it is for any man to do so. Whenever Paul speaks of submissiveness on the part of the woman, it is always on the part of a wife to her own husband. It does not imply that a woman, simply because she is a woman, must be submissive to any man simply because he is a man. See note on I Tim. 2:9-15; Tit. 2:1-5.

39 Therefore, my brethren, [a]de-
sire earnestly to [b]prophesy,[4395] and
do not forbid to speak[2980] in tongues.[1100]
40 But [a]let all things be done
properly[2156] and in an orderly[5010] manner.

The Fact of Christ's Resurrection

15 Now [a]I make known[1107] to
you, brethren,[80] the [b]gospel[2098]
which I preached[2097] to you, which also
you received, [c]in which also you stand,
2 by which also you are
[pinp]saved,[4982] [a]if you hold fast[2722] [I]the
word which I [ao]preached to you, [b]un-
less you believed[4100] in vain.
3 For [a]I delivered to you [I]as of first
importance what I also received, that
Christ[5547] died [b]for our sins[266] [c]according
to the Scriptures,[1124]
4 and that He was buried, and that
He was [pfip] [a]raised[1453] on the third day
[b]according to the Scriptures,
5 and that [a]He appeared to [b]Cephas,
then [c]to the twelve.
6 After that He appeared to more
than[1883] five hundred brethren at one
time, most of whom remain[3306] until
now, but some [a]have fallen [ao]asleep;
7 then He appeared to [Ia]James, then
to [b]all the apostles;[652]
8 and last of all, as it were [I]to one
untimely born, [a]He appeared to me also.
9 For I am [a]the least of the apostles,
who am not fit[2425] to be called an apostle,
because I [b]persecuted the church[1577] of
God.
10 But by [a]the grace[5485] of God I
am what I am, and His grace toward
me did not prove vain; but I [b]labored
even more than all of them, yet [c]not I,
but the grace of God with[4862] me.

39 [a]1Cor. 12:31 [b]1Cor. 13:2; 14:1
40 [a]1Cor. 14:33
1 [a]Rom. 2:16; Gal. 1:11 [b]Rom. 2:16; 1Cor. 3:6; 4:15 [c]Rom. 5:2; 11:20; 2Cor. 1:24
2 [I]Lit., *to what word I* [a]Rom. 11:22 [b]Gal. 3:4
3 [I]Lit., *among the first* [a]1Cor. 11:23 [b]John 1:29; Gal. 1:4; Heb. 5:1, 3; 1Pet. 2:24 [c]Is. 53:5-12; Matt. 26:24; Luke 24:25-27; Acts 8:32f.; 17:2f.; 26:22
4 [a]Matt. 16:21; John 2:20ff.; Acts 2:24 [b]Ps. 16:8ff.; Acts 2:31; 26:22f.
5 [a]Luke 24:34 [b]1Cor. 1:12 [c]Mark 16:14; Luke 24:36; John 20:19
6 [a]Acts 7:60; 1Cor. 15:18, 20
7 [I]Or, *Jacob* [a]Acts 12:17 [b]Luke 24:33, 36f.; Acts 1:3f.
8 [I]Lit., *to an untimely birth* [a]Acts 9:3-8; 22:6-11; 26:12-18; 1Cor. 9:1
9 [a]2Cor. 12:11; Eph. 3:8; 1Tim. 1:15 [b]Acts 8:3
10 [a]Rom. 12:3 [b]2Cor. 11:23; Col. 1:29; 1Tim. 4:10 [c]1Cor. 3:6; 2Cor. 3:5; Phil. 2:13
12 [a]Acts 17:32; 23:8; 2Tim. 2:18
14 [a]1Thess. 4:14
15 [I]Or, *concerning* [II]I.e., the Messiah [a]Acts 2:24
17 [a]Rom. 4:25
18 [a]1Cor. 15:6; 1Thess. 4:16; Rev. 14:13

11 Whether then *it was* I or they,
so we preach[2784] and so you believed.
12 Now if Christ[5547] is
preached,[2784] that He has been raised
from the dead,[3498] how do some among
you say that there [a]is no resurrection[386]
of the dead?
13 But if there is no resurrection
of the dead, not even Christ has been
[pfip]raised;
14 and [a]if Christ has not been raised,
then our preaching[2782] is vain, your
faith[4102] also is vain.
15 Moreover we are even found *to
be* false witnesses [gc]of[2596] God, because
we witnessed [I]against God that He
[a]raised[1453] [II]Christ, whom He did not
raise, if in fact the dead are not raised.
16 For if the dead are not raised,
not even Christ has been raised;
17 and if Christ has not been raised,
your faith is worthless; [a]you are still in
your sins.[266]
18 Then those also who [a]have fallen
[apt]asleep in Christ have [aom]perished.[622]
19 If we have hoped[1679] in Christ
in this life only, we are [a]of all men most
to be pitied.[1652]

The Order of Resurrection

20 But now Christ [a]has been raised
from the dead, the [b]first fruits[536] of those
who [c]are [pfp]asleep.
21 For since [a]by a man *came*
death,[2288] by a man also *came* the
resurrection[386] of the dead.[3498]
22 For [a]as in Adam all die,[599] so also
in [I]Christ all shall be made alive.[2227]

19 [a]1Cor. 4:9; 2Tim. 3:12
20 [a]Acts 2:24; 1Pet. 1:3 [b]Acts 26:23; 1Cor. 15:23; Rev. 1:5 [c]1Cor. 15:6; 1Thess. 4:16; Rev. 14:13
21 [a]Rom. 5:12
22 [I]I.e., the Messiah [a]Rom. 5:14-18

15:1-58 Our bodies as presently constituted are called "perishable" (*phtharta,* 5349), subject to decay and ultimate death. See I Cor. 15:53,54. In the same verses they are also called "mortal" (*thnēta,* 2349). These present characteristics of our bodies are going to be lost only at our resurrection. The liberation from such a state is not ours now, but will come later on. Thus Paul in Rom. 8:23 calls it "the redemption of our body." See the Editor's book on this chapter entitled, *Conquering the Fear of Death.*

15:13-19 See note on Gal. 1:8.

23 But each in his own order:[5001] Christ [a]the first fruits, after that [b]those who are Christ's at [c]His coming,[3952]

24 then *comes* the end,[5056] when He [aosb]delivers up [a]the kingdom[932] to the [b]God[2316] and Father,[3962] when He has [aosb]abolished [c]all rule[746] and all authority[1849] and power.[1411]

25 For He must [pinf]reign[936] [a]until He has [aosb]put all His enemies under His feet.

26 The last enemy that will be [pinp] [a]abolished is death.

27 For [a]HE HAS [ao]PUT[5293] ALL THINGS IN SUBJECTION UNDER HIS FEET. But when He [aosb]says, "[b]All things are [pfip]put in subjection," it is evident that He is excepted who [apt]put all things in subjection to Him.

28 And when [a]all things are [asbp]subjected to[5293] Him, then the Son[5207] Himself also will be subjected to the One who subjected all things to Him, that [b]God may be all in all.

29 Otherwise, what will those do who are [ppp]baptized[907] for the dead? If the dead are not raised at all, why then are they [pinp]baptized for them?

30 Why are we also [a]in danger every hour?

31 I protest, brethren, by the boasting in you, which I have in Christ Jesus our Lord, [a]I die daily.

32 If [I]from human motives I [ao] [a]fought with wild beasts at [b]Ephesus, what does it profit me? If the dead are not raised, [c]LET US EAT AND DRINK, FOR TOMORROW WE DIE.

33 [a]Do not be deceived: "Bad company[3657] corrupts good[5543] morals."

34 [a]Become sober-minded [I]as you ought, and stop [pim]sinning;[264] for some have [b]no knowledge[56] of God.[2316] [c]I speak *this* to your shame.[1791]

35 But [a]someone will say, "How are [b]the dead raised? And with what kind of body[4983] do they come?"

36 [a]You fool! That which you [b]sow does not come to life[2227] unless it [aosb]dies;[599]

37 and that which you sow, you do not sow the body which is to be, but a bare[1131] grain, [opt]perhaps[5177] of wheat or of [I]something else.

38 But God gives it a body just as He wished, and [a]to each of the seeds[4690] a body of its own.

39 All flesh[4561] is not the same flesh, but there is one *flesh* of men, and another flesh of beasts, and another flesh of birds, and another of fish.

40 There are also heavenly bodies[4983] and earthly[1919] bodies, but the glory[1391] of the heavenly is one,[2087] and the *glory* of the earthly is another.[2087]

41 There is one glory of the sun, and another glory of the moon, and another glory of the stars; for star differs from[1308] star in glory.

42 [a]So also is the resurrection[386] of the dead.[3498] It is [pinp]sown [Ib]a perishable *body*, it is [pinp]raised[1453] [IIc]an imperishable *body*;

43 it is sown in dishonor, it is raised in [a]glory; it is sown in weakness,[769] it is raised in power;[1411]

44 it is sown a [a]natural[5591] body,[4983]

23 [a]Acts 26:23; 1Cor. 15:20; Rev. 1:5 [b]1Cor. 6:14; 15:52; 1Thess. 4:16 [c]1Thess. 2:19
24 [a]Dan. 2:44; 7:14, 27; 2Pet. 1:11 [b]Eph. 5:20 [c]Rom. 8:38
25 [a]Ps. 110:1; Matt. 22:44
26 [a]2Tim. 1:10; Rev. 20:14; 21:4
27 [a]Ps. 8:6 [b]Matt. 11:27; 28:18; Eph. 1:22; Heb. 2:8
28 [a]Phil. 3:21 [b]1Cor. 3:23; 12:6
30 [a]2Cor. 11:26
31 [a]Rom. 8:36
32 [I]Lit., *according to man* [a]2Cor. 1:8 [b]Acts 18:19; 1Cor. 16:8 [c]Is. 22:13; 56:12; Luke 12:19
33 [a]1Cor. 6:9
34 [I]Lit., *righteously* [a]Rom. 13:11 [b]Matt. 22:29; Acts 26:8 [c]1Cor. 6:5
35 [a]Rom. 9:19 [b]Ezek. 37:3
36 [a]Luke 11:40 [b]John 12:24
37 [I]Lit., *some of the rest*
38 [a]Gen. 1:11
42 [I]Lit., *in corruption* [II]Lit., *in incorruption* [a]Dan. 12:3; Matt. 13:43 [b]Rom. 8:21; 1Cor. 15:50; Gal. 6:8 [c]Rom. 2:7
43 [a]Phil. 3:21; Col. 3:4
44 [a]1Cor. 2:14

15:23-28 See note on I Pet. 3:18-20.

15:28 The translation of the verb *hupotagēsetai* as "the Son Himself also will be subjected to the One" is very misleading. It is taken as a passive, whereas the exegesis demands that it should be taken as a middle voice which means that the Lord Jesus Christ at the completion of His mediatorial work subjects Himself to the One who had subjected all things unto Him. It is a voluntary and not a compulsory subjugation of one person of the Trinity to the other. This is not something that took place while the Lord Jesus was the God-Man on earth, but it is something that will take place in the future when all people will be made subject unto Christ, and then He will finally subject Himself with the finished work of redemption before God the Father. One of the greatest difficulties of the translation of the N.T. lies in discerning when the passive form should be taken with the passive meaning or the middle voice meaning, as, for instance, Jesus Christ "is made subject" or He "subjects Himself."

15:44 See notes on Lk. 14:25-33; I Pet. 3:18-20.

it is raised a [b]spiritual body. If there is a natural body, there is also a spiritual *body.*

45 So also it is written, "The first[4413] [a]MAN, Adam, BECAME[1096] A LIVING[2198] SOUL."[5590] The [b]last Adam *became* a [ppt] [c]life-giving[2227] spirit.[4151]

46 However,235 the spiritual[4152] is not first, but the natural;[5591] then the spiritual.

🔑 47 The first man is [a]from the earth,[1093] [I][b]earthy;[5517] the second man is from heaven.[3772]

48 As is the earthy, so also are those who are earthy; and as is the heavenly, [a]so also are those who are heavenly.

49 And just as we have [ao] [a]borne5409 the image[1504] of the earthy, [I]we [b]shall also bear5409 the image of the heavenly.

The Mystery of Resurrection

🔑 **50** Now I say this, brethren, that [a]flesh[4561] and blood[129] cannot [ainf] [b]inherit[2816] the kingdom[932] of God; nor does [I]the perishable5336 inherit [II][c]the imperishable.861

51 Behold, I tell you a [a]mystery;[3466] we shall not all sleep, but we shall all be [b]changed,[236]

52 in a moment, in the twinkling of an eye, at the last trumpet; for [a]the trumpet will sound, and [b]the dead will be raised [I]imperishable,[862] and [c]we shall be changed.

🔑 53 For this [I]perishable must [ainf]put on [II][a]the imperishable, and this [b]mortal[2349] must put on immortality.[110]

54 But when this [I]perishable will have [aosb]put on [II]the imperishable, and this mortal will have [aosb]put on immortality, then will come about the saying that is written, "[a]DEATH[2288] IS [aop]SWALLOWED UP in victory.3534

55 "[a]O DEATH, WHERE IS YOUR VICTORY? O DEATH,[2288] WHERE IS YOUR STING?"

56 The sting of [a]death is sin,[266] and [b]the power of sin is the law;[3551]

57 but [a]thanks[5485] be to God, who [ppt]gives us the [b]victory through our Lord Jesus Christ.

58 [a]Therefore, my beloved[27] brethren,[80] [pim]be steadfast, immovable, always [ppt]abounding in [b]the work[2041] of the Lord, knowing that your toil[2873] is not *in vain*[2756] in the Lord.

Instructions and Greetings

16 🔑 Now concerning [a]the collection for [b]the saints,[40] as [c]I directed[1299] the churches[1577] of [d]Galatia, so do you also.

🔑 2 On [a]the first day of every week let each one of you [I]put aside[5087] and save, as he may prosper, that [b]no collections be made when I come.

3 And when I arrive, [a]whomever you may approve, I shall send them with letters to carry667 your gift[5485] to Jerusalem;

4 and if it is fitting514 for me to go also, they will go with me.

5 But I [a]shall come to you after I go through [b]Macedonia, for I [c]am going through Macedonia;

6 and perhaps I shall stay[3887] with you, or even spend the winter, that you may [a]send me on my way wherever I may go.

7 For I do not wish to see you now [a]*just* in passing; for I hope[1679] to remain with you for some time, [b]if the Lord permits.

8 But I shall remain in [a]Ephesus until [b]Pentecost;4005

9 for a [a]wide door [I]for effective *service* has opened to me, and [b]there are many adversaries.

44 [b]1Cor. 15:50
45 [a]Gen. 2:7 [b]Rom. 5:14 [c]John 5:21; 6:57f.; Rom. 8:2
47 [I]Lit., *made of dust* [a]John 3:31 [b]Gen. 2:7; 3:19
48 [a]Phil. 3:20f.
49 [I]Some ancient mss. read *let us also* [a]Gen. 5:3 [b]Rom. 8:29
50 [I]Lit., *corruption* [II]Lit., *incorruption* [a]Matt. 16:17; John 3:5f. [b]1Cor. 6:9 [c]Rom. 2:7
51 [a]1Cor. 13:2 [b]2Cor. 5:2, 4
52 [I]Lit., *incorruptible* [a]Matt. 24:31 [b]John 5:28 [c]1Thess. 4:15, 17
53 [I]Lit., *corruptible* [II]Lit., *incorruption* [a]Rom. 2:7 [b]2Cor. 5:4
54 [I]V. 53, note 1 [II]V. 53, note 2 [a]Is. 25:8
55 [a]Hos. 13:14
56 [a]Rom. 5:12 [b]Rom. 3:20; 4:15; 7:8
57 [a]Rom. 7:25; 2Cor. 2:14 [b]Rom. 8:37; Heb. 2:14f.; 1John 5:4; Rev. 21:4
58 [a]2Pet. 3:14 [b]1Cor. 16:10

1 [a]Acts 24:17; Rom. 15:25f. [b]Acts 9:13 [c]1Cor. 4:17 [d]Acts 16:6
2 [I]Lit., *put by himself* [a]Acts 20:7 [b]2Cor. 9:4f.
3 [a]2Cor. 3:1; 8:18f.
5 [a]1Cor. 4:19 [b]Rom. 15:26 [c]Acts 19:21
6 [a]Acts 15:3; 1Cor. 16:11
7 [a]2Cor. 1:15f. [b]Acts 18:21
8 [a]Acts 18:19 [b]Acts 2:1
9 [I]Lit., *and* [a]Acts 14:27 [b]Acts 19:9

🔑 **15:47** See note on II Cor. 5:1.
🔑 **15:50-55** See notes on Rev. 4; I Thess. 4:17.
🔑 **15:53,54** See notes on Mt. 8:17; II Tim. 1:12; Js. 5:14-17.
🔑 **16:1-4** See notes on II Tim. 4:20; Col. 4:7.
🔑 **16:2** See note on III Jn. 2.

10 Now if [a]Timothy comes, see that he is with you without [I]cause to be afraid; for he is doing [b]the Lord's work,[2041] as I also am.

11 [a]Let no one therefore despise him. But [b]send him on his way [c]in peace,[1515] so that he may come to me; for I expect[1551] him with the brethren.

12 But concerning [a]Apollos our brother, I encouraged[3870] him greatly to come to you with the brethren; and it was not at all *his* desire to come now, but he will come when he has opportunity.

13 [a]Be on the alert, [b]stand firm in the faith,[4102] [c]act like men,[407] [d]be strong.[2901]

14 Let all that you do be done [a]in love.[26]

15 Now I urge[3870] you, brethren (you know the [a]household[3614] of Stephanas, that [I]they were the [b]first fruits[536] of [c]Achaia, and that they have devoted[5021] themselves for [d]ministry to [e]the saints),

16 that [a]you also be in subjection to[5293] such men and to everyone who helps in the work and labors.

10 [I]Lit., *fear; for* [a]Acts 16:1; 1Cor. 4:17; 2Cor. 1:1 [b]1Cor. 15:58
11 [a]1Tim. 4:12; Titus 2:15 [b]Acts 15:3; 1Cor. 16:6 [c]Acts 15:33
12 [a]Acts 18:24; 1Cor. 1:12; 3:5f.
13 [a]Matt. 24:42 [b]1Cor. 15:1; Gal. 5:1; Phil. 1:27; 4:1; 1Thess. 3:8; 2Thess. 2:15 [c]1Sam. 4:9; 2Sam. 10:12 [d]Ps. 31:24; Eph. 3:16; 6:10; Col. 1:11
14 [a]1Cor. 14:1
15 [I]Lit., *it was* [a]1Cor. 1:16 [b]Rom. 16:5 [c]Acts 18:12 [d]Rom. 15:31 [e]1Cor. 16:1
16 [a]1Thess. 5:12; Heb. 13:17
17 [I]Or, *presence* [II]Or, *made up for your absence* [a]2Cor. 7:6f. [b]2Cor. 11:9; Phil. 2:30
18 [a]2Cor. 7:13; Philem. 7, 20 [b]Phil. 2:29; 1Thess. 5:12

17 And I rejoice over the [I][a]coming of Stephanas and Fortunatus and Achaicus; because they have [II]supplied[378] [b]what was lacking on your part.

18 For they [a]have [ao]refreshed my spirit[4151] and yours. Therefore [b]acknowledge such men.

19 The churches[1577] of [a]Asia greet[782] you. [b]Aquila and Prisca greet you heartily in the Lord, with [c]the church that is in their house.

20 All the brethren greet you. [a]Greet[782] one another with a holy[40] kiss.

21 The greeting[783] is in [a]my own hand—[I]Paul.

22 If anyone does not love[5368] the Lord, let him be [I][a]accursed.[331] [II][b]Maranatha.[3134]

23 [a]The grace[5485] of the Lord Jesus be with you.

24 My love[26] be with you all in Christ Jesus. Amen.[281]

19 [a]Acts 16:6 [b]Acts 18:2 [c]Rom. 16:5 **20** [a]Rom. 16:16 **21** [I]Lit., *Paul's* [a]Rom. 16:22; Gal. 6:11; Col. 4:18; 2Thess. 3:17; Philem. 19 **22** [I]Gr., *anathema* [II]I.e., O Lord come! [a]Rom. 9:3 [b]Phil. 4:5; Rev. 22:20 **23** [a]Rom. 16:20

16:10,11 See general remarks on I Timothy.
16:17 See note on I Thess. 2:19.

The Second Epistle of Paul to the

CORINTHIANS

Soon after Paul wrote I Corinthians from Ephesus, there was a riot in Ephesus (see Acts 19:21-41). He had not been to Corinth for three years. The relationship between Paul and his converts in Corinth was strained during the interim. It was a difficult period for both while separated. Then, during Paul's third missionary journey, while traveling into Macedonia (northern Greece) on his way to Corinth in Achaia (southern Greece), Paul encountered Titus and learned that his letter to the Corinthian brothers had accomplished much good (II Cor. 7:5-7). However, there were still some in Corinth who denied that Paul was a true Apostle of Jesus. So, Paul decided to write them the next letter and send it on ahead with Titus before Paul arrived in Corinth (see II Cor. 2:13; 8:1,6,16,17; 9:2-4). Paul explained why the first letter had to be so severe. He suffered much as he waited for their reaction to that letter. He truly cared for them, but he was not going to allow his Apostolic credentials to be questioned by them. He stood ready to confront his accusers (II Cor. 12:20; 13:1-4). He appealed to the brethren to help the starving Jewish Christians in Judea. Paul did spend the next winter in Corinth (Acts 20:2,3), as he had planned (I Cor. 16:5,6). It was probably at that time that he wrote the Roman letter.

Except for Paul's letter to Philemon, II Corinthians is the least systematic and doctrinal and the most personal letter that he wrote. Paul's intense emotion and fiery personality are revealed more clearly here than in any other Epistle. It is full of digressions and meanderings. He tells of some very personal experiences such as his vision of the third heaven (II Cor. 12:1-4) and of his "thorn in the flesh" (II Cor. 12:7-9). Throughout the letter there is a strong undercurrent of defensiveness. He was being attacked and felt forced to justify his authority against false legalistic teachers who had meddled in his work. He warned the congregation against certain errors, instructed them in matters of duty as Christians, and expressed his happiness that they had heeded what he had to say in I Corinthians. But the real watchword of II Corinthians is that we must all be loyal to Christ, not to human personalities.

Introduction

1 Paul, [a]an apostle[652] of [b]Christ[5547]
Jesus [c]by the will[2307] of God,[2316] and
[d]Timothy *our* brother,[80] to [e]the
church[1577] of God which is at [f]Corinth
with all the [I]saints[40] who are throughout
[g]Achaia:
2 [a]Grace[5485] to you and peace[1515]
from God our Father[3962] and the Lord[2962]
Jesus Christ.
3 [a]Blessed[2128] *be* the God and Father of our Lord Jesus Christ, the Father of mercies and [b]God of all comfort;[3874]
4 who [ppt] [a]comforts[3870] us in all our
affliction so that we may be able to
[pinf]comfort those who are in any affliction[2347] with the comfort[3874] with which
we ourselves are comforted by God.
5 For just [a]as the sufferings[3804] of
Christ are [I]ours in abundance,[4052] so also
our comfort[3874] is abundant through
Christ.
6 But if we are afflicted, it is
[a]for your comfort and salvation;[4991] or
if we are comforted, it is for your comfort, which is [ppt]effective[1754] in the patient enduring of the same sufferings
which we also suffer;[3958]
7 and our hope for you is firmly
grounded,[949] knowing that [a]as you are
sharers[2844] of our sufferings, so also you
are *sharers* of our comfort.
8 For [a]we do not want you to be
unaware,[50] brethren, of our [b]affliction
which came *to us* in [Ic]Asia, that we were
burdened excessively, beyond our

1 [I]Or, *holy ones* [a]Rom. 1:1; Gal. 1:1; Eph. 1:1; Col. 1:1; 2Tim. 1:1; Titus 1:1 [b]Gal. 3:26 [c]1Cor. 1:1 [d]Acts 16:1; 1Cor. 16:10; 2Cor. 1:19 [e]1Cor. 10:32 [f]Acts 18:1 [g]Acts 18:12
2 [a]Rom. 1:7
3 [a]Eph. 1:3; 1Pet. 1:3 [b]Rom. 15:5
4 [a]Is. 51:12; 66:13; 2Cor. 7:6, 7, 13
5 [I]Lit., *to us* [a]2Cor. 4:10; Phil. 3:10; Col. 1:24
6 [a]2Cor. 4:15; 12:15; Eph. 3:1, 13; 2Tim. 2:10
7 [a]Rom. 8:17
8 [I]I.e., west coast province of Asia Minor [a]Rom. 1:13 [b]Acts 19:23; 1Cor. 15:32 [c]Acts 16:6

strength, so that we [ainf]despaired even of life;[2198]

9 [I]indeed, we [pfi]had the sentence[610] of death[2288] within ourselves in order that we should not trust[3982] in ourselves, but in God who [ppt]raises[1453] the dead;[3498]

10 who [ao] [a]delivered[4506] us from so great a *peril of* death, and will deliver *us,* [I]He [b]on whom we have set our hope.[1679] And He will yet deliver us,

11 you also [ppt]joining in [a]helping[4943] us through your prayers, that [asbp]thanks may be given[2168] by [b]many persons[4383] on our behalf for the favor[5486] bestowed upon us through *the prayers of* many.

Paul's Integrity

12 For our [I]proud confidence is this, the testimony[3142] of [a]our conscience,[4893] that in holiness and [b]godly sincerity,[1505] [c]not in fleshly[4559] wisdom but in the grace[5485] of God, we have [aop]conducted ourselves in the world, and especially[4056] toward you.[5209]

13 For we write nothing else to you than what you read and understand, and I hope you will understand [a]until the end;[5056]

🔑14 just as you also partially did understand us, that we are your reason to be proud as you also are ours, in [a]the day[2250] of our Lord Jesus.

15 And in this confidence[4006] I [ipf]intended at first to [ainf] [a]come to you, that you might [I]twice receive a [II][b]blessing;[5485]

16 [I]that is, to [a]pass [II]your way into [b]Macedonia, and again from Macedonia to come to you, and by you to be [c]helped on my journey to Judea.

17 Therefore, I was not vacillating when I [ppt]intended to do this, was I? Or that which I purpose, do I purpose [a]according to[2596] the flesh, that with me there should be yes, yes and no, no *at the same time?*

18 But as [a]God is faithful,[4103] [b]our word[3056] to you is not yes and no.

🔑19 For [a]the Son[5207] of God, Christ[5547] Jesus, who was [aptp]preached[2784] among you by us—by me and [b]Silvanus and [c]Timothy—[ao]was not yes and no, but [pfi]is yes [d]in Him.

20 For [a]as many as may be the promises[1860] of God, [b]in Him they are yes; wherefore also by Him is [c]our Amen[281] to the glory[1391] of God through us.

21 Now He who [ppt] [a]establishes[950] us with you in Christ and [apt] [b]anointed[5548] us is God,

22 who also [apt] [a]sealed us and [apt] [b]gave *us* the Spirit[4151] in our hearts[2588] as a [I]pledge.[728]

23 But [a]I call[1941] God as witness[3144] [I]to my soul,[5590] that [b]to spare you I came no more to [c]Corinth.

24 Not that we [a]lord it over your faith,[4102] but are workers with you for your joy;[5479] for in your faith you are [pfi] [b]standing firm.

Reaffirm Your Love

2 But I determined[2919] this [I]for my own sake, that I [a]would not come to you in sorrow again.

2 For if I [a]cause you sorrow,[3076] who then [ppt]makes me glad[2165] but the one whom I [ppp]made sorrowful?[3076]

3 And this is the very thing I [a]wrote[1125] you, lest, [b]when I came, I should have sorrow from those who ought to make me [pinf]rejoice; having [c]confidence[3892] in you all, that my joy[5479] would be *the joy* of you all.

4 For out of much affliction and anguish of heart I [a]wrote to you with many tears; not that you should be made [asbp]sorrowful, but that you might [aosb]know the love[26] which I have especially for you.

9 [I]Lit., *but we ourselves*
10 [I]Or, *on whom we have set our hope that He will also* [a]Rom. 15:31 [b]1Tim. 4:10
11 [a]Rom. 15:30; Phil. 1:19; Philem. 22 [b]2Cor. 4:15; 9:11f.
12 [I]Lit., *boasting* [a]Acts 23:1; 1Thess. 2:10; Heb. 13:18 [b]2Cor. 2:17 [c]1Cor. 1:17; James 3:15
13 [a]1Cor. 1:8
14 [a]1Cor. 1:8
15 [I]Lit., *have a second grace* [II]Some ancient mss. read *joy* [a]1Cor. 4:19 [b]Rom. 1:11; 15:29
16 [I]Lit., *and* [II]Lit., *through you into* [a]Acts 19:21; 1Cor. 16:5-7 [b]Acts 19:21; Rom. 15:26 [c]Acts 15:3; 1Cor. 16:6, 11
17 [a]2Cor. 10:2f.; 11:18
18 [a]1Cor. 1:9 [b]2Cor. 2:17
19 [a]Matt. 4:3; 16:16; 26:63 [b]Acts 15:22; 1Thess. 1:1; 2Thess. 1:1; 1Pet. 5:12 [c]Acts 18:5; 2Cor. 1:1 [d]Heb. 13:8
20 [a]Rom. 15:8 [b]Heb. 13:8 [c]1Cor. 14:16; Rev. 3:14
21 [a]1Cor. 1:8 [b]1John 2:20, 27
22 [I]Or, *down payment* [a]John 3:33 [b]Rom. 8:16; 2Cor. 5:5; Eph. 1:14
23 [I]Lit., *upon* [a]Rom. 1:9; Gal. 1:20 [b]1Cor. 4:21; 2Cor. 2:1, 3 [c]2Cor. 1:1
24 [a]2Cor. 4:5; 11:20; 1Pet. 5:3 [b]Rom. 11:20; 1Cor. 15:1

1 [I]Or, *as far as I am concerned* [a]1Cor. 4:21; 2Cor. 12:21

2 [a]2Cor. 7:8 **3** [a]2Cor. 2:9; 7:8, 12 [b]1Cor. 4:21; 2Cor. 12:21 [c]Gal. 5:10; 2Thess. 3:4; Philem. 21
4 [a]2Cor. 2:9; 7:8, 12

🔑**1:14** See note on I Thess. 5:2.
🔑**1:19** See general remarks on I Timothy.

5 But [a]if any has caused pfi sorrow,3076 he has caused pfi sorrow not to
me, but in some degree—[1]in order not
to psa say too much—to all of you.
6 Sufficient2425 for such a one is
[a]this punishment which was *inflicted by*
the majority,
7 so that on the contrary you should
rather ainf [a]forgive5483 and ainf comfort3870
him, lest somehow such a one be
asbp overwhelmed by excessive4055 sorrow.
8 Wherefore I urge3870 you to
ainf reaffirm *your* love26 for him.
9 For to this end also [a]I wrote1125
that I might [1b]put you to the test,1382
whether you are [c]obedient5255 in all
things.
10 But whom you forgive5483 anything, I *forgive* also; for indeed what I
have pfi forgiven, if I have pfi forgiven anything, *I did it* for your sakes [a]in the
presence4383 of Christ,
11 in order that no asbp advantage be
taken of us by [a]Satan;4567 for [b]we are
not ignorant50 of his schemes.3540
12 Now when I came to [a]Troas for
the [b]gospel2098 of Christ and when a
[c]door was pfpp opened for me in the Lord,
🔑 13 I pfi [a]had no rest425 for my
spirit,4151 not ainf finding [b]Titus my
brother; but apt [c]taking my leave657 of
them, I went on to [d]Macedonia.
14 [a]But thanks5485 be to God, who
always [b]leads us in His ppt triumph in
Christ, and ppt manifests5319 through us
the [c]sweet aroma of the [d]knowledge1108
of Him in every place.
15 For we are a [a]fragrance of Christ
to God among [b]those who are ppp being
saved4982 and among those who are
ppp perishing;622
16 [a]to the pl one an aroma from death
to death,2288 to the pl other an aroma
from life2222 to life. And who is
[b]adequate2425 for these things?
17 For we are not like many,
ppt [1a]peddling2585 the word3056 of God, but
[b]as from sincerity,1505 but as from God,
we speak2980 in Christ [c]in the sight of
God.

Ministers of a New Covenant

3 Are we beginning to pinf [a]commend
ourselves again? Or do we need,
as some, [b]letters1992 of commendation
to you or from you?
2 [a]You are our letter, pfpp written in
our hearts,2588 ppp known and ppp read by
all men;
3 being manifested5319 that you are
a letter of Christ, aptp [1a]cared1247 for by
us, pfpp written1449 not with ink, but with
the an Spirit4151 of [b]the an living2198 God,
not on [c]tablets of stone, but on [d]tablets
of [IIe]human4560 hearts.2588
4 And such [a]confidence4006 we have
through Christ toward God.
5 Not that we are adequate2425 in
ourselves to ainf consider anything as
coming from ourselves, but [a]our
adequacy2426 is from God,
6 who also made us ao adequate *as*
[a]servants1249 of a an [b]new2537 covenant,1242 not of [c]the an letter,1121 but of
the an Spirit;4151 for the letter kills, but
[d]the Spirit gives life.
7 But if the [a]ministry of death,2288
[b]in letters1121 engraved on stones, came
[1]with glory,1391 [c]so that the sons5207 of
Israel pinf could not ainf look intently at the
face of Moses because of the glory of
his face,4383 ppp fading *as* it was,
8 how shall the ministry of the Spirit
fail to be even more with glory?
9 For if [a]the ministry of condemna-
tion2633 has glory,1391 much more does
the [b]ministry of righteousness1343
abound in glory.
10 For indeed what had pfpp glory,

5 [1]Lit., *that I be not burdensome* [a]1Cor. 5:1f.
6 [a]1Cor. 5:4f.; 2Cor. 7:11
7 [a]Gal. 6:1; Eph. 4:32
9 [1]Lit., *know the proof of you* [a]2Cor. 2:3f. [b]2Cor. 8:2; Phil. 2:22 [c]2Cor. 7:15; 10:6
10 [a]1Cor. 5:4; 2Cor. 4:6
11 [a]Matt. 4:10 [b]Luke 22:31; 2Cor. 4:4; 1Pet. 5:8
12 [a]Acts 16:8 [b]Rom. 1:1; 2Cor. 4:3, 4; 8:18; 9:13; 10:14; 11:4, 7; 1Thess. 3:2 [c]Acts 14:27
13 [a]2Cor. 7:5 [b]2Cor. 7:6, 13f.; 8:6, 16, 23; 12:18; Gal. 2:1, 3; 2Tim. 4:10; Titus 1:4 [c]Mark 6:46 [d]Rom. 15:26
14 [a]Rom. 1:8; 6:17; 1Cor. 15:57; 2Cor. 8:16; 9:15 [b]Col. 2:15 [c]Song 1:3; Ezek. 20:41; Eph. 5:2; Phil. 4:18 [d]1Cor. 12:8
15 [a]Song 1:3; Ezek. 20:41; Eph. 5:2; Phil. 4:18 [b]1Cor. 1:18
16 [a]Luke 2:34; John 9:39; 1Pet. 2:7f. [b]2Cor. 3:5f.
17 [1]Or, *corrupting* [a]2Cor. 4:2; Gal. 1:6-9 [b]1Cor. 5:8; 2Cor. 1:12; 1Thess. 2:4; 1Pet. 4:11 [c]2Cor. 12:19

1 [a]2Cor. 5:12; 10:12, 18; 12:11 [b]Acts 18:27; 1Cor. 16:3
2 [a]1Cor. 9:2
3 [1]Lit., *served* [II]Lit., *hearts of flesh* [a]2Cor. 3:6 [b]Matt. 16:16 [c]Ex. 24:12; 31:18; 32:15f.; 2Cor. 3:7 [d]Prov. 3:3; 7:3; Jer. 17:1 [e]Jer. 31:33; Ezek. 11:19; 36:26
4 [a]Eph. 3:12
5 [a]1Cor. 15:10
6 [a]1Cor. 3:5 [b]Jer. 31:31; Luke 22:20 [c]Rom. 2:29 [d]John 6:63; Rom. 7:6
7 [1]Or, *in glory* [a]Rom. 4:15; 5:20; 7:5f.; 2Cor. 3:9; Gal. 3:10, 21f. [b]Ex. 24:12; 31:18; 32:15f.; 2Cor. 3:3 [c]Ex. 34:29-35; 2Cor. 3:13
9 [a]Deut. 27:26; 2Cor. 3:7; Heb. 12:18-21 [b]Rom. 1:17; 3:21f.

🔑 **2:13** See general remarks on Titus.

in this case has no glory on account of
the glory that [ppt]surpasses *it.*
11 For if that which [ppp]fades away
was [I]with glory, much more that which
[ppt]remains *is* in glory.
12 [ppt] [a]Having therefore such a
hope,[1680] [b]we use great boldness in *our*
speech,
13 and *are* not as Moses, [a]*who* used
to [ipf]put a veil over his face that the
sons of Israel [aipr]might not look intently
at the end[5056] of what was [ppp]fading
away.
14 But their minds[3540] were
[aop] [a]hardened;[4456] for until this very day
at the [b]reading[320] of [c]the old[3820]
covenant[1242] the same veil [I]remains
[ppp]unlifted, because it is removed in
Christ.[5547]
15 But to this day whenever Moses
is read, a veil lies over their heart;[2588]
16 [a]but whenever a man [aosb]turns
to the Lord,[2962] the veil is [pinp]taken
away.[4014]
17 Now the Lord is the Spirit; and
where [a]the Spirit[4151] of the Lord is,
[b]*there* is liberty.[1657]
18 But we all, with [pfpp]unveiled face
[a]beholding as in a mirror the [b]glory of
the Lord, are being [pin] [c]transformed[3339]
into the same image from glory to glory,
just as from [d]the [an]Lord, the [an]Spirit.

Paul's Apostolic Ministry

4 Therefore, since we have this
[a]ministry,[1248] as we [aop] [b]received
mercy, we [c]do not lose heart,
2 but we have [aom]renounced the
[a]things hidden because of shame,[152] not
walking in craftiness or [b]adulterating[1389]
the word[3056] of God, but by the manifestation[5321] of truth [c]commending[4921]
ourselves to every man's conscience[4893]
in the sight of God.[2316]
3 And even if our [a]gospel[2098] is
[b]veiled, it is veiled[2572] [I]to [c]those who
are [ppp]perishing,[622]
4 in whose case [a]the god[2316] of
[b]this [I]world[165] has [ao] [c]blinded the
minds[3540] of the unbelieving,[571] [II]that
they might not see the [d]light[5462] of the
gospel[2098] of the [e]glory[1391] of Christ, who
is the [an] [f]image[1504] of God.
5 For we [a]do not preach[2784] ourselves but Christ[5547] Jesus as [an]Lord,[2962]
and ourselves as your bond-servants[1401]
[I]for Jesus' sake.
6 For God,[2316] who [apt]said,
"[a]Light[5457] shall shine out of darkness,"[4655] is the One who has [ao] [b]shone
in our hearts[2588] to give the [c]light[5462]
of the knowledge of the glory[1391] of
God in the face of Christ.
7 But we have this treasure in
[a]earthen vessels, that the surpassing
greatness of [b]the power[1411] may be of
God and not from ourselves;
🔑 8 *we are* [ppp] [a]afflicted in every way,
but not [ppp] [b]crushed; [ppt] [c]perplexed, but
not [ppt]despairing;
9 [ppp] [a]persecuted, but not [ppp] [b]for-
saken;[1459] [ppp] [c]struck down, but not
[ppp]destroyed;[622]
10 [a]always [ppt]carrying about in the
body[4983] the dying[3500] of Jesus, that
[b]the life[2222] of Jesus also may be
[asbp]manifested[5319] in our body.
🔑 11 For we who live are constantly
being delivered over to death[2288] for
Jesus' sake, that the life of Jesus also
may be [asbp]manifested in our mortal[2349]
flesh.
12 So death works[1754] in us, but
life[2222] in you.
13 But having the same [a]spirit[4151]
of faith,[4102] according to what is written,
"[b]I BELIEVED,[4100] THEREFORE I SPOKE,"
we also believe, therefore also we
speak;
14 knowing that He who [apt] [a]raised
the Lord Jesus [b]will raise us also with
Jesus and will [c]present us with you.

11 [I]Lit., *through*
12 [a]2Cor. 7:4 [b]Acts 4:13, 29; 2Cor. 7:4; Eph. 6:19; 1Thess. 2:2
13 [a]Ex. 34:33-35; 2Cor. 3:7
14 [I]Or, *remains, it not being revealed that it is done away in Christ.* [a]Rom. 11:7; 2Cor. 4:4 [b]Acts 13:15 [c]2Cor. 3:6
16 [a]Ex. 34:34; Rom. 11:23
17 [a]Is. 61:1f.; Gal. 4:6 [b]John 8:32; Gal. 5:1, 13
18 [a]1Cor. 13:12 [b]John 17:22, 24; 2Cor. 4:4, 6 [c]Rom. 8:29 [d]2Cor. 3:17

1 [a]1Cor. 3:5 [b]1Cor. 7:25 [c]Luke 18:1; 2Cor. 4:16; Gal. 6:9; Eph. 3:13; 2Thess. 3:13
2 [a]Rom. 6:21; 1Cor. 4:5 [b]2Cor. 2:17 [c]2Cor. 5:11f.
3 [I]Lit., *in* [a]2Cor. 2:12 [b]1Cor. 2:6ff.; 2Cor. 3:14 [c]1Cor. 1:18; 2Cor. 2:15
4 [I]Lit., *age* [II]Or, *that the light . . . image of God, should not dawn upon them* [a]John 12:31 [b]Matt. 13:22 [c]2Cor. 3:14 [d]Acts 26:18; 2Cor. 4:6 [e]2Cor. 3:18; 4:6 [f]John 1:18; Phil. 2:6; Col. 1:15; Heb. 1:3
5 [I]Or, *through Jesus* [a]1Cor. 4:15f.; 1Thess. 2:6f.
6 [a]Gen. 1:3 [b]2Pet. 1:19 [c]Acts 26:18; 2Cor. 4:4
7 [a]Job 4:19; 10:9; 33:6; Lam. 4:2; 2Cor. 5:1; 2Tim. 2:20 [b]Judg. 7:2; 1Cor. 2:5
8 [a]2Cor. 1:8; 7:5 [b]2Cor. 6:12 [c]Gal. 4:20

9 [a]John 15:20; Rom. 8:35f. [b]Ps. 129:2; Heb. 13:5 [c]Ps. 37:24; Prov. 24:16; Mic. 7:8 **10** [a]Rom. 6:5; 8:36; Gal. 6:17 [b]Rom. 6:8 **13** [a]1Cor. 12:9 [b]Ps. 116:10
14 [a]Acts 2:24 [b]1Thess. 4:14 [c]Luke 21:36; Eph. 5:27; Col. 1:22; Jude 24

🔑 **4:8** See note on II Cor. 5:1.
🔑 **4:11** See note on II Tim. 1:12.

15 For all things *are* [a]for your sakes, that the grace[5485] which is apt I[b]spreading to more and more people may cause the giving of thanks to aosb abound4052 to the glory of God.

16 Therefore we [a]do not lose heart, but though our outer man[444] is decaying, yet our [b]inner man is [c]being renewed[341] day[2250] by day.

17 For momentary, [a]light affliction is producing for us an eternal[166] weight of glory[1391] far beyond all comparison,

18 while we ppt [a]look[4648] not at the things which are ppp seen, but at the things which are not seen; for the things which are seen are temporal,4340 but the things which are not seen are eternal.[166]

15 ILit., *being multiplied through the many* aRom. 8:28; 2Cor. 1:6 b1Cor. 9:19; 2Cor. 1:11
16 a2Cor. 4:1 bRom. 7:22 cIs. 40:29, 31; Col. 3:10
17 aRom. 8:18
18 aRom. 8:24; 2Cor. 5:7; Heb. 11:1, 13

The Temporal and Eternal

5 For we know that if I the [a]earthly[1919] [b]tent[3614] which is our house4636 is asbp torn down, we have a building[3619] from God, a house [c]not made

1 ILit., *our earthly house of the tent* aJob 4:19; 1Cor. 15:47; 2Cor. 4:7 b2Pet. 1:13f. cMark 14:58; Acts 7:48; Heb. 9:11, 24

5:1-10 This passage tells us very clearly what happens to the believer when he dies. He goes to be with the Lord. The chapter is closely connected with v. 18 of the previous chapter in which we are told to look at the things which cannot be seen with the physical eye. See note on II Cor. 12:1-10.

5:1 "We know" in Greek is *oidamen* (1492), which means to know intuitively as a result of being the children of God. It is part and parcel of the knowledge that comes to us with our new birth in Christ Jesus. "If our earthly house of our tent" is actually what the Greek text says. Our real self is the spirit within us and not the body. The body is presented as *skēnos* from *skēnē* (4633), tent, which stands for the mortal body. This mortal body has a house, *oikia,* (3614). The moment will come when this earthly house will be taken down, and that is expressed with the verb *kataluthē* (2647), which is made up of the intensive *kata* (2596) "down," and *luō* (3089), "to loose." It is as if it were made of different parts, and it is going to be taken apart, loosened. The verb is in the aorist tense which refers to a specific time in the future at which this is going to be done. It is in the passive voice which means that we are not going to do it, but God Himself. At a certain particular time, God is going to loosen all the parts that are being held together by Him. That is what He calls death. It is the "loosing" time. When that happens, we do not become extinct. We continue to live on. "We have a building from God." There is a difference between the word that is translated earlier as "house," *oikia,* and what is translated as "building," *oikodomē,* which means the building as a process, that which is being built, not that which is already built. In other words, while we are still alive, God is building a new house for our spirit which will be disembodied for a while when it leaves the body on earth. This indicates that God is not taking the old constituent parts of our body to build our new one, but He is building it completely new. God is now in the process of building it; it is out, *ek,* of God. The word "God" here is without the definite article, which means all three Persons of the triune God are engaged in building this new house for us. And then Paul reverts to the same word previously used, *oikian,* "dwelling," which means the completed building even as our present building is now constituted. It will be similar, identifiable, but yet not the same because it is not going to be made by human hands, but it will be a product made directly by God. The word translated "not made with hands" is *acheiropoiēton* (886). The Lord used it in Mark 14:58 when He spoke of destroying, *kataluso,* the temple which was made with hands and that in three days He was going to build another not made by hands. This is exactly the same word as we find in II Cor. 5:1. He was evidently speaking of His resurrection body. Although His own body was made of a woman (Gal. 4:4) the first time, no human being was involved with it the second time. So it is with our bodies. The first time we are born into this world, our bodies are physically produced, but the second time they will be produced without human involvement. That is the first characteristic of our resurrection bodies.

The second quality is that they are going to be eternal, *aiōnion* (166), which means that they are going to be characterized by what characterizes God Himself. The life that He gives us on earth which makes us His children is called "eternal life," *aiōnios* (166), *zōē* (2222). In speaking of eternal life, it does not only refer to the duration of the life, but primarily to the quality of it. The life of God becomes our life. Actually, we never lose this life that He gives us from the moment we become His children through the acceptance of Jesus Christ as our Lord and Savior. The word, *aiōnios,* eternal, however, is always related to time *aiōn,* "age, generation," as contrasted to *kosmos* (2889), which refers to the material world. This word, *aiōnios,* must be interpreted here as it is in II Cor. 4:8,18 where it is contrasted

(continued on next page)

with hands, eternal[166] in the heavens.[3772]
🔑 2 For indeed in this *house* we
[a]groan, [ppt]longing to be [ainf] [b]clothed with
our dwelling[3613] from heaven;[3772]
3 inasmuch as we, having [apt]put it
on, shall not be found naked.[1131]
🔑 4 For indeed while we are in this
tent, we [a]groan, being [ppp]burdened, because we do not want to be [ainf]unclothed,
but to be [ainf] [b]clothed, in order that what
is [c]mortal[2349] may be [asbp]swallowed up
by life.[2222]
5 Now He who [apt]prepared us for
this very purpose is God, who [apt] [a]gave
to us the Spirit[4151] as a [1]pledge.[728]
6 Therefore, being always of good
[ppt]courage, and knowing that [a]while we
are at [ppt]home in the body[4983] we are
absent from the Lord—[2962]
7 for [a]we walk by faith,[4102] not by
[1]sight—[1491]
8 we are of good courage, I say,
and [a]prefer rather to be [ainf]absent from
the body and [b]to be at [ainf]home with
the Lord.
9 Therefore also we have as our ambition, whether at home or absent, to
be [a]pleasing[2101] to Him.
🔑 10 For we must all [aifp]appear[5319] before [a]the judgment seat[968] of Christ,[5547]
that each one may be [asbm]recompensed
for [1]his deeds in the body, according
to[4314] what he has [ao]done,[4238] whether
good[18] or bad.[5337]
11 Therefore knowing the [a]fear[5401]
of the Lord,[2962] we persuade men,[444]
but we are made [pfip]manifest[5319] to God;
and I hope that we are [b]made [pfin]manifest
also in your consciences.[4893]
12 We are not [a]again commending
ourselves to you but *are* [ppt]giving you
an [b]occasion to be proud of us, that you
may have *an answer* for those who take
[ppt]pride in appearance, and not in heart.
13 For if we [1]are [a]beside ourselves,[1839] it is for God; if we are of
sound mind,[4993] it is for you.
14 For the love[26] of Christ [a]con-
trols[4912] us, having [apt]concluded[2919] this,
that [b]one died[599] for all, therefore all
[ao]died;
15 and He died for all, that they who
[ppt]live[2198] should no longer [a]live for
themselves, but for Him who [apt]died and
[aptp]rose again[1453] on their behalf.
16 Therefore from now on we
recognize[1492] no man [1a]according to the
flesh; even though we have known
Christ [1]according to the flesh, yet now
we know *Him thus* no longer.
17 Therefore if any man is [a]in
Christ, [1]*he is* [b]a new[2537] creature;[2937]
[c]the old things passed away; behold, new
things have [pfi]come.
18 Now [a]all *these* things are from
God, [b]who [apt]reconciled[2644] us to Himself
through Christ, and [apt]gave us the
[c]ministry[1248] of reconciliation,[2643]
19 namely, that [a]God was in
Christ[5547] reconciling[2644] the world[2889]
to Himself, [b]not counting[3049] their trespasses[3900] against them, and [1]He has

2 [a]Rom. 8:23; 2Cor. 5:4 [b]1Cor. 15:53f.; 2Cor. 5:4
4 [a]2Cor. 5:2 [b]1Cor. 15:53f.; 2Cor. 5:2 [c]1Cor. 15:54
5 [1]Or, *down payment* [a]Rom. 8:23; 2Cor. 1:22
6 [a]Heb. 11:13f.
7 [1]Or, *appearance* [a]1Cor. 13:12; 2Cor. 4:18
8 [a]Phil. 1:23 [b]John 12:26; Phil. 1:23
9 [a]Rom. 14:18; Col. 1:10; 1Thess. 4:1
10 [1]Lit., *the things through the body* [a]Matt. 16:27; Acts 10:42; Rom. 2:16; 14:10, 12; Eph. 6:8
11 [a]Heb. 10:31; 12:29; Jude 23 [b]2Cor. 4:2
12 [a]2Cor. 3:1 [b]2Cor. 1:14; Phil. 1:26
13 [1]Lit., *were* [a]Mark 3:21; 2Cor. 11:1, 16ff.; 12:11
14 [a]Acts 18:5 [b]Rom. 5:15; 6:6f.; Gal. 2:20; Col. 3:3
15 [a]Rom. 14:7-9
16 [1]I.e., by what he is in the flesh [a]John 8:15; 2Cor. 11:18; Phil. 3:4
17 [1]Or, there is a *new creation* [a]Rom. 16:7 [b]John 3:3; Rom. 6:4; Gal. 6:15 [c]Is. 43:18f.; 65:17; Eph. 4:24; Rev. 21:4f. Col. 1:20 [c]1Cor. 3:5
18 [a]1Cor. 11:12 [b]Rom. 5:10;
19 [1]Lit., *having* [a]Col. 2:9 [b]Rom. 4:8; 1Cor. 13:5

(continued from previous page)
to that which is temporal, comparing the temporal affliction to the more exceeding and eternal weight of glory. Therefore, *aiōnios* must mean that which is not temporal and which cannot be lost, broken up or destroyed. And where is this going to be? "In the heavens." Paul uses the word "heaven" or "heavens" in his two long Epistles to the Corinthians only five times. In I Cor. 8:5 he contrasts it with the earth. In I Cor. 15:47 he speaks of the Lord from heaven; therefore, when we go to heaven, we go to be with the Lord, or when we go to be with the Lord, we go to heaven. The third reference to heaven is II Cor. 5:2, speaking of our house which is from heaven. Thus, our resurrection body is not going to be made here on earth; it is already being made in heaven for us, and it is going to come from heaven or out (*ex*) of heaven and meet with our spirit. The only other place in the Corinthian Epistles where heaven is referred to is II Cor. 12:2, speaking of the third heaven. See note on I Cor. 15.

🔑 **5:2** See note on II Cor. 5:1.

🔑 **5:4** See notes on Mt. 8:17; II Tim. 1:12.

🔑 **5:10** See notes on Mt. 8:11,12; Js. 2:12,13.

[apt] [II]committed to us the word[3056] of reconciliation.[2643]
20 Therefore, we are [a]ambassa-
dors[4243] for Christ, [b]as though God were
[ppt]entreating through us; we beg you
on behalf of Christ, be [aipp] [c]reconciled[2644]
to God.
21 He [ao]made Him who [a]knew[1097]
no sin[266] *to be* [b]sin on our behalf, that
we might [aosb]become the [ao] [c]righ-
teousness[1343] of God in Him.

Their Ministry Commended

6 And [a]working together *with Him,*
[b]we also urge you not to [ainf]receive
[c]the grace[5485] of God in vain—[2756]
2 for He says,
"[a]AT THE ACCEPTABLE[1184]
TIME[2540] I [ao]LISTENED TO
YOU,
AND ON THE DAY[2250] OF
SALVATION[4991] I [ao]HELPED[997]
YOU";
behold, now is "THE ACCEPTABLE[2144]
TIME," behold, now is "THE DAY OF SAL-
VATION"—
3 [a]giving no cause for offense in anything, in order that the ministry[1248] be
not discredited,
4 but in everything [a]commending[4921]
ourselves as [I][b]servants[1249] of God,
[c]in much endurance,[5281] in afflictions,[2347]
in hardships, in distresses,[4730]
5 in [a]beatings, in imprisonments, in
[b]tumults,[181] in labors, in sleeplessness,
in [c]hunger,[3521]
6 in purity,[54] in [a]knowledge, in
[b]patience,[3115] in kindness,[5544] in the
[an] [c]Holy Spirit,[4151] in [d]genuine[505] love,[26]
7 in [a]the word[3056] of truth,[225] in
[b]the power[1411] of God; by [c]the weapons
of righteousness[1343] for the right
hand[1188] and the left,
8 by glory[1391] and [a]dishonor, by
[b]evil report and good report; *regarded*
as [c]deceivers and yet [d]true;
9 as [ppp]unknown yet [ppp]well-known,
as [a]dying yet behold, [b]we live;[2198] as
[I]punished[3811] yet not put to death,
10 as [a]sorrowful yet always [b]rejoic-
ing, as [c]poor yet making many rich, as
[d]having nothing yet possessing[2722]
[e]all things.
11 [a]Our mouth [I]has spoken freely
to you, O Corinthians, our [b]heart[2588] is
opened wide.
12 You are not restrained[4729] [I]by
us, but [a]you are restrained in your own
[II]affections.[4698]
13 Now in a like [a]exchange—I speak
as to [b]children—open wide *to us* also.
14 [a]Do not be [ppt] [I]bound together
with [b]unbelievers;[2086] for what [c]part-
nership[3352] have righteousness[1343] and
lawlessness,[458] or what fellowship[2842]
has light[5457] with darkness?[4655]
15 Or what [a]harmony has Christ
with [I]Belial, or [II]what has a [b]believer[4103]
in common with[3326] an [c]unbeliever?[571]
16 Or [a]what agreement has the
temple[3485] of God with[3326] idols?[1497] For
we are [b]the temple of [c]the living[2198] God;
just as God said,
"[d]I WILL [e]DWELL IN THEM AND
[f]WALK AMONG THEM;
AND I WILL BE THEIR GOD,
AND THEY SHALL BE MY
PEOPLE.[2992]
17 "[a]Therefore, [aim] [b]COME OUT
FROM THEIR MIDST[3319] AND
BE [aipp]SEPARATE," [873] says
the Lord.
"AND DO NOT [pim]TOUCH WHAT IS
UNCLEAN;[169]
And I will welcome[1523] you.
18 "[a]And I will be a father[3962] to you,
And you shall be [b]sons[5207] and
daughters to Me,"
Says the Lord Almighty.[3841]

Paul Reveals His Heart

7 Therefore, having these promises,
[a]beloved,[27] [b]let us cleanse[2511] ourselves from all defilement[3436] of flesh[4561]
and spirit,[4151] perfecting[2005] holiness[42]
in the fear[5401] of God.

19 [II]Lit., *placed in us*
20 [a]Mal. 2:7; Eph. 6:20 [b]2Cor. 6:1 [c]Rom. 5:10; Col. 1:20
21 [a]Acts 3:14; Heb. 4:15; 7:26; 1Pet. 2:22; 1John 3:5 [b]Rom. 3:25; 4:25; 8:3; Gal. 3:13 [c]Rom. 1:17; 3:21f.; 1Cor. 1:30

1 [a]1Cor. 3:9 [b]2Cor. 5:20 [c]Acts 11:23
2 [a]Is. 49:8
3 [a]1Cor. 8:9, 13; 9:12
4 [I]Or, *ministers* [a]Rom. 3:5 [b]1Cor. 3:5; 2Tim. 2:24f. [c]Acts 9:16; 2Cor. 4:8-11; 6:4ff.; 11:23-27; 12:10
5 [a]Acts 16:23 [b]Acts 19:23ff. [c]1Cor. 4:11
6 [a]1Cor. 12:8; 2Cor. 11:6 [b]2Cor. 1:23; 2:10; 13:10 [c]1Cor. 2:4; 1Thess. 1:5 [d]Rom. 12:9
7 [a]2Cor. 2:17; 4:2 [b]1Cor. 2:5 [c]Rom. 13:12; 2Cor. 10:4; Eph. 6:11ff.
8 [a]1Cor. 4:10 [b]Rom. 3:8; 1Cor. 4:13; 2Cor. 12:16 [c]Matt. 27:63 [d]2Cor. 1:18; 4:2; 1Thess. 2:3f.
9 [I]Or, *disciplined* [a]Rom. 8:36 [b]2Cor. 1:8, 10; 4:11
10 [a]John 16:22; 2Cor. 7:4; Phil. 2:17; 4:4; Col. 1:24; 1Thess. 1:6 [b]1Cor. 1:5; 2Cor. 8:9 [c]Acts 3:6 [d]Rom. 8:32; 1Cor. 3:21
11 [I]Lit., *is open to you* [a]Ezek. 33:22; Eph. 6:19 [b]Is. 60:5; 2Cor. 7:3
12 [I]Or, *in us* [II]Lit., *inward parts* [a]2Cor. 7:2
13 [a]Gal. 4:12 [b]1Cor. 4:14
14 [I]Lit., *unequally yoked* [a]Deut. 22:10; 1Cor. 5:9f. [b]1Cor. 6:6 [c]Eph. 5:7, 11; 1John 1:6
15 [I]Gr., *Beliar* [II]Lit., *what part has a believer with an unbeliever* [a]1Cor. 10:21 [b]Acts 5:14; 1Pet. 1:21 [c]1Cor. 6:6
16 [a]1Cor. 10:21 [b]1Cor. 3:16; 6:19 [c]Matt. 16:16 [d]Ex. 29:45; Lev. 26:12; Jer. 31:1; Ezek. 37:27 [e]Ex. 25:8; John 14:23 [f]Rev. 2:1
17 [a]Is. 52:11 [b]Rev. 18:4
18 [a]2Sam. 7:14; 1Chr. 17:13; Is. 43:6; Hos. 1:10 [b]Rom. 8:14
1 [a]Heb. 6:9 [b]1Pet. 1:15f.

2 [aim][a]Make room for us *in your
hearts;* we [ao]wronged no one, we [ao]cor-
rupted no one, we [ao]took advantage[4122]
of no one.
3 I do not speak to condemn[2633] you;
for I have said [a]before that you are
[b]in our hearts to [aies]die together and
to [aies]live together.
4 Great is my [a]confidence [I]in you,
great is my [b]boasting on your behalf; I
am [pfip]filled with [c]comfort.[3874] I am overflowing with [d]joy[5479] in all our affliction.
5 For even when we [apt]came into
[a]Macedonia our flesh had no rest,[425] but
we were [ppp] [b]afflicted on every side:
[c]conflicts without,[1855] fears within.
6 But [a]God, who [ppt]comforts[3870] the
[I]depressed, [b]comforted us by the coming of [c]Titus;
🔑7 and not only by his coming, but
also by the comfort[3874] with which he
was comforted in you, as he [ppt]re-
ported[312] to us your longing, your
mourning, your zeal for me; so that I
[ainf]rejoiced even more.
8 For though I [a]caused you sorrow[3076] by my letter, I do not [ipf]re-
gret[3338] it; though I did regret it—*for* I
see that that letter[1992] [ao]caused you sorrow, though only for a while—[5610]
9 I now rejoice, not that you were
made sorrowful, but that you were made
sorrowful[3076] to *the point of* repentance;[3341] for you were made sorrowful
according to *the will of* God,[2316] in order
that you might not [asbp]suffer loss in anything through us.
10 For the sorrow that is according
to *the will of* God produces a [a]repen-
tance[3341] [I]without regret, *leading* to
salvation;[4991] but the sorrow of the
world[2889] produces death.
11 For behold what earnestness this
very thing, this [I]godly[2316] sorrow, has
[ao]produced[2716] in you: what vindication
of yourselves, what indignation, what
fear, what [a]longing,[1972] what zeal, what
[b]avenging[1557] of wrong! In everything
you [ao] [c]demonstrated[4921] yourselves to
be innocent in the matter.
12 So although [a]I wrote to you *it
was* not for the sake of [b]the offender,[91]
nor for the sake of the one offended,
but that your earnestness on our behalf
might be made known[5319] to you in the
sight of God.
13 For this reason we have been
[a]comforted.

And besides our comfort,[3874] we rejoiced even much more for the joy of
[b]Titus, because his [c]spirit has been
[pfip]refreshed by you all.
🔑14 For if in anything I have
[pfi] [a]boasted to him about you, I was
not put to shame; but as we spoke all
things to you in truth, so also our
boasting before [b]Titus proved to be *the*
truth.
15 And his [I]affection abounds all the
more toward you, as he [ppt]remembers
the [a]obedience[5218] of you all, how you
[ao]received him with [b]fear[5401] and trembling.[5156]
16 I rejoice that in everything [a]I
have confidence in you.

Great Generosity

8 Now, brethren, we *wish to* make
known[1107] to you the grace[5485] of
God which has been [pfpp] [a]given in the
churches of [b]Macedonia,
2 that in a great ordeal[1382] of affliction their abundance[4050] of joy[5479] and
their deep poverty overflowed[4052] in the
[a]wealth of their liberality.[572]
3 For I testify that [a]according to
their ability,[1411] and beyond their ability
they gave of their own accord,
4 begging[1189] us with much entreaty[3874] for the [a]favor[5485] of participation[2842] in the [I][b]support[1248] of the
[II]saints,[40]
5 and *this,* not as we had [I]ex-
pected,[1679] but they first [a]gave themselves to the Lord[2962] and to us by
[b]the will of God.[2316]

2 [a]2Cor. 6:12f.; 12:15
3 [a]2Cor. 6:11f. [b]Phil. 1:7
4 [I]Lit., *to* [a]2Cor. 3:12 [b]2Cor. 7:14; 8:24; 9:2f.; 10:8; Phil. 1:26; 2Thess. 1:4 [c]2Cor. 1:4 [d]2Cor. 6:10
5 [a]Rom. 15:26; 2Cor. 2:13 [b]2Cor. 4:8 [c]Deut. 32:25
6 [I]Or, *humble* [a]2Cor. 1:3f. [b]2Cor. 7:13 [c]2Cor. 2:13; 7:13f.
8 [a]2Cor. 2:2
10 [I]Or, leading *to a salvation without regret* [a]Acts 11:18
11 [I]Lit., *sorrow according to God* [a]2Cor. 7:7 [b]2Cor. 2:6 [c]Rom. 3:5
12 [a]2Cor. 2:3, 9; 7:8 [b]1Cor. 5:1f.
13 [a]2Cor. 7:6 [b]2Cor. 2:13; 7:6, 14 [c]1Cor. 16:18
14 [a]2Cor. 7:4; 8:24; 9:2f.; 10:8; Phil. 1:26; 2Thess. 1:4 [b]2Cor. 2:13; 7:6, 13
15 [I]Lit., *inward parts* [a]2Cor. 2:9 [b]1Cor. 2:3; Phil. 2:12
16 [a]2Cor. 2:3

1 [a]2Cor. 8:5 [b]Acts 16:9
2 [a]Rom. 2:4
3 [a]1Cor. 16:2; 2Cor. 8:11
4 [I]Lit., *service to the saints* [II]Or, *holy ones* [a]Acts 24:17; Rom. 15:25f. [b]Rom. 15:31; 2Cor. 8:19f.; 9:1, 12f.
5 [I]Lit., *hoped* [a]2Cor. 8:1 [b]1Cor. 1:1

🔑 **7:7** See note on I Thess. 2:19.
🔑 **7:14,15** See general remarks on Titus.

6 Consequently we [ainf] [a]urged [b]Ti-
tus that as he had previously [c]made
a beginning, so he would also [aosb]com-
plete[2005] in you [d]this gracious work as
well.
7 But just as you [a]abound [b]in everything, in faith[4102] and utterance[3056] and
knowledge[1108] and in all earnestness4710
and in the [I]love[26] we inspired in you,
see that you [psa] [c]abound in this gracious
work also.
8 I [a]am not speaking *this* as a command,[2003] but as [ppt]proving through the
earnestness4710 of others the sincerity
of your love also.
9 For you know [a]the grace[5485] of
our Lord Jesus Christ,[5547] that [b]though
He was rich, yet for your sake He [ao]be-
came poor, that you through His poverty
might [aosb]become rich.
10 And I [a]give *my* opinion[1106] in this
matter, for this is to your advantage,[4851]
who were the first to begin [b]a year ago
not only to do *this,* but also to desire
to do it.
11 But now [aim]finish[2005] [ainf] [I]doing it
also; that just as *there was* the [a]readiness
to desire[2309] it, so *there may be* also the
completion of it by your ability.
12 For if the readiness is present,
it is acceptable[2144] [a]according to what
a man [psa]has, not according to what he
does not have.
13 For *this* is not for the ease[425]
of others *and* for your affliction, but by
way of equality—
14 at this present time[2540] your
abundance[4051] *being a supply* for [a]their
want, that their abundance also may become *a supply* for [b]your want,[5303] that
there may be equality;
15 as it is written, "[a]HE WHO *gathered* MUCH DID NOT [ao]HAVE TOO MUCH,
AND HE WHO *gathered* LITTLE [ao]HAD NO
LACK."
16 But [a]thanks[5485] be to God, who
[ppt] [b]puts the same earnestness on your
behalf in the heart[2588] of [c]Titus.
🔑17 For he not only accepted our
[a]appeal, but being himself very earnest,
he has gone to you of his own accord.
18 And we have [ao]sent along with
him [a]the brother[80] whose fame in *the
things of* the [b]gospel[2098] *has spread*
through [c]all the churches;[1577]
19 [a]and not only *this,* but he has
also been [aptp] [b]appointed[5500] by the
churches to travel with us in [c]this gracious work, which is being [ppp]adminis-
tered by us for the glory[1391] of the Lord
Himself, and *to show* our [d]readiness,
20 [I]taking precaution[4724] that no one
should [aosb]discredit us in our administration of this generous[100] gift;
21 for we [a]have regard[4306] for what
is honorable, not only in [b]the sight of
the Lord,[2962] but also in the sight of
men.[444]
22 And we have [ao]sent with them
our brother, whom we have often
[ao]tested and found diligent in many
things, but now even more diligent, because of *his* great confidence[4006] in you.
🔑23 As for [a]Titus, *he is* my [b]part-
ner[2844] and fellow worker [I]among you;
as for our [c]brethren, *they are* [II][d]mes-
sengers[652] of the churches, [e]a glory to
Christ.
24 Therefore [I]openly before[4383] the
churches [aim] [II]show them the proof of
your love[26] and of our [a]reason for boasting about you.

God Gives Most

9 For [a]it is superfluous[4053] for me to
write[1125] to you about this [b]minis-
try[1248] to the [I]saints;[40]
2 for I know your readiness,[4288] of
which I [a]boast about you to the [b]Mace-
donians, *namely,* that [c]Achaia has been
[pfi]prepared since [d]last year, and your
zeal[2205] has stirred up most of them.
3 But I have sent the brethren,[80]
that our [a]boasting about you may not
be [asbp]made empty[2758] in this case, that,
[b]as I was saying, you may be prepared;
4 lest3381 if any [a]Macedonians come
with me and find you unprepared, we

6 [a]2Cor. 8:17; 12:18 [b]2Cor. 2:13; 8:16, 23 [c]2Cor. 8:10 [d]Acts 24:17; Rom. 15:25f.
7 [I]Lit., *love from us in you;* some ancient mss. read *your love for us* [a]2Cor. 9:8 [b]Rom. 15:14; 1Cor. 1:5; 12:8
8 [a]1Cor. 7:6
9 [a]2Cor. 13:14 [b]Matt. 20:28; 2Cor. 6:10; Phil. 2:6f.
10 [a]1Cor. 7:25, 40 [b]1Cor. 16:2f.; 2Cor. 9:2
11 [I]Lit., *the doing* [a]2Cor. 8:12, 19; 9:2
12 [a]Mark 12:43f.; Luke 21:3, 4; 2Cor. 9:7
14 [a]Acts 4:34; 2Cor. 9:12
15 [a]Ex. 16:18
16 [a]2Cor. 2:14 [b]Rev. 17:17 [c]2Cor. 2:13; 8:6, 23
17 [a]2Cor. 8:6; 12:18
18 [a]1Cor. 16:3; 2Cor. 12:18 [b]2Cor. 2:12 [c]1Cor. 4:17; 7:17
19 [a]Rom. 5:3 [b]Acts 14:23; 1Cor. 16:3f. [c]2Cor. 8:4, 6 [d]2Cor. 8:11, 12; 9:2
20 [I]Lit., *avoiding this*
21 [a]Rom. 12:17 [b]Prov. 3:4; Rom. 14:18
23 [I]Lit., *for you* [II]Lit., *apostles* [a]2Cor. 8:6 [b]Philem. 1:17 [c]2Cor. 8:18, 22 [d]John 13:16; Phil. 2:25 [e]1Cor. 11:7
24 [I]Lit., *in the face of the churches* [II]Or, *show the proof . . . for boasting to them about you* [a]2Cor. 7:4

1 [I]Or, *holy ones* [a]1Thess. 4:9 [b]2Cor. 8:4
2 [a]2Cor. 7:4 [b]Rom. 15:26 [c]Acts 18:12 [d]2Cor. 8:10
3 [a]2Cor. 7:4 [b]1Cor. 16:2 **4** [a]Rom. 15:26

🔑 **8:17,23** See general remarks on Titus.

(not to speak of you) should be put to [asbp]shame by this confidence.[5287]

5 So I thought[2233] it necessary to [ainf]urge[3870] the [a]brethren that they would go on ahead to you and arrange beforehand[4294] your previously promised[4279] [Ib]bountiful gift,[2129] that the same might be ready as a [Ic]bountiful gift, and not [IId]affected by covetousness.

6 Now this *I say,* [a]he who [ppt]sows sparingly shall also reap sparingly; and he who sows [I]bountifully[2129] shall also reap [I]bountifully.

7 Let each one *do* just as he has purposed in his heart; not [a]grudgingly or under compulsion;[318] for [b]God loves[25] a cheerful giver.

8 And [a]God is able to make all grace[5485] [ainf]abound to you, that always having all sufficiency in everything, you may have an [psa]abundance for every good[18] deed;[2041]

9 as it is written,

"[a]HE [ao]SCATTERED ABROAD, HE
[ao]GAVE TO THE POOR,[3993]
HIS RIGHTEOUSNESS[1343]
ABIDES[3306] FOREVER."[165]

10 Now He who supplies [a]seed[4690] to the sower and bread for food, will [ft]supply and [ft]multiply your seed for sowing and [ft b]increase the harvest of your righteousness;

11 you will be [a]enriched in everything for all liberality,[572] which through us is producing [b]thanksgiving to God.

12 For the ministry[1248] of this service[3009] is not only fully supplying [a]the needs[5303] of the [I]saints, but is also overflowing[4052] [b]through many thanksgivings to God.

13 Because of the proof[1382] given by this [a]ministry[1248] they will [ppt b]glorify[1392] God for *your* obedience[5292] to your [c]confession[3671] of the [d]gospel[2098] of Christ, and for the liberality[572] of your [I]contribution[2842] to them and to all,

14 while they also, by prayer on your behalf, [ppt]yearn for you because of the [ppt]surpassing grace of God in you.

15 [a]Thanks[5485] be to God for His indescribable [b]gift!

5 [I]Lit., *blessing* [II]Lit., *as covetousness* [a]2Cor. 9:3 [b]Gen. 33:11; Judg. 1:15; 2Cor. 9:6 [c]Phil. 4:17 [d]2Cor. 12:17f.
6 [I]Lit., *with blessings* [a]Prov. 11:24f.; 22:9; Gal. 6:7, 9
7 [a]Deut. 15:10; 1Chr. 29:17; Rom. 12:8; 2Cor. 8:12 [b]Ex. 25:2
8 [a]Eph. 3:20
9 [a]Ps. 112:9
10 [a]Is. 55:10 [b]Hos. 10:12
11 [a]1Cor. 1:5 [b]2Cor. 1:11
12 [I]Or, *holy ones* [a]2Cor. 8:14 [b]2Cor. 1:11
13 [I]Or, *sharing with them* [a]Rom. 15:31; 2Cor. 8:4 [b]Matt. 9:8 [c]1Tim. 6:12f.; Heb. 3:1; 4:14; 10:23 [d]2Cor. 2:12
15 [a]2Cor. 2:14 [b]Rom. 5:15f.

1 [I]Lit., *lowly* [a]Gal. 5:2; Eph. 3:1; Col. 1:23 [b]Rom. 12:1 [c]Matt. 11:29; 1Cor. 4:21; Phil. 4:5 [d]1Cor. 2:3f.; 2Cor. 10:10
2 [a]1Cor. 4:21; 2Cor. 13:2, 10 [b]1Cor. 4:18f. [c]Rom. 8:4; 2Cor. 1:17
3 [a]Rom. 8:4; 2Cor. 1:17
4 [I]Or, *mighty before God* [a]1Cor. 9:7; 2Cor. 6:7; 1Tim. 1:18 [b]Jer. 1:10; 2Cor. 10:8; 13:10
5 [a]Is. 2:11f. [b]2Cor. 9:13
6 [a]2Cor. 2:9
7 [I]Or, *Look at . . . or Do you look at . . . ?* [II]Lit., *what is before your face* [a]John 7:24; 2Cor. 5:12 [b]1Cor. 1:12; 14:37 [c]1Cor. 9:1; 2Cor. 11:23; Gal. 1:12
8 [I]Or, *more abundantly* [a]2Cor. 7:4 [b]2Cor. 13:10
9 [I]Lit., *that I may not seem*
10 [I]Lit., *bodily presence is weak* [a]1Cor. 2:3; 2Cor. 12:7; Gal. 4:13f. [b]1Cor. 1:17; 2Cor. 11:6
12 [I]Or, *any* [a]2Cor. 3:1; 10:18

Paul Describes Himself

10 Now [a]I, Paul, myself [b]urge[3870] you by the [c]meekness and gentleness[1932] of Christ—I who [d]am [I]meek when face to face with you, but bold toward you when absent![548]

2 I ask[1189] that [a]when I am present I may not be [ainf]bold with the confidence[4006] with which I propose[3049] to be [ainf]courageous against [b]some, who [ppt]regard us as if we [ppt]walked [c]according to the flesh.[4561]

3 For though we walk in the flesh, we do not war [a]according to the flesh,

4 for the [a]weapons of our warfare are not of the flesh,[4559] but [I]divinely powerful [b]for the destruction of fortresses.

5 *We are* destroying speculations[3053] and every [a]lofty thing raised up against the knowledge[1108] of God, and *we are* taking every thought[3540] captive to the [b]obedience[5218] of Christ,

6 and we are ready to [ainf]punish[1556] all disobedience,[3876] whenever [a]your obedience is complete.

7 [Ia]You are looking at [II]things as they are outwardly.[4383] [b]If anyone is confident[3982] in himself that he is Christ's, let him [pim]consider this again within himself, that just as he is Christ's, [c]so also are we.

8 For even if [a]I should [aosb]boast somewhat [I]further about our [b]authority,[1849] which the Lord gave for building you up[3619] and not for destroying[2506] you, I shall not be put to shame,

9 [I]for I do not wish to [aosb]seem as if I would [pinf]terrify you by my letters.

10 For they say, "His letters are weighty and strong, but his [I]personal presence is [a]unimpressive,[772] and [b]his speech[3056] contemptible."

11 Let such a person [pim]consider this, that what we are in word[3056] by letters when absent,[548] such persons *we are* also in deed[2041] when present.

12 For we are not bold to class[1469] or [ainf]compare[4793] ourselves with [I]some of those who [ppt a]commend them-

selves; but when they [ppt]measure themselves by themselves, and [ppt]compare themselves with themselves, they are without understanding.

13 But we will not boast [a]beyond *our* measure, but [I][b]within the measure of the sphere which God [ao]apportioned to us as a measure, to [ainf]reach even as far as you.

14 For we are not [ppt]overextending ourselves, as if we did not reach to you, for [a]we were the first to come even as far as you in the [b]gospel[2098] of Christ;

15 not [ppt]boasting [a]beyond *our* measure, *that is,* in [b]other men's labors, but with the hope[1680] that as [c]your faith[4102] [ppp]grows, we shall be, [I]within our sphere, [aifp] [d]enlarged[4050] even more by you,

16 so as [ainf]to [a]preach the gospel[2097] even to [b]the regions beyond you, *and* not to [ainf]boast [I][c]in what has been accomplished in the sphere of another.

17 But [a]HE WHO BOASTS,[2744] LET HIM [aim]BOAST IN THE LORD.

18 For not he who [ppt] [a]commends[4921] himself is approved,[1384] but [b]whom the Lord commends.

Paul Defends His Apostleship

11 I wish that you would [ipf] [a]bear with[430] me in a little [b]foolishness; but [I]indeed you are bearing with me.

2 For I am jealous for you with a godly[2316] jealousy; for I [aom] [a]betrothed[718] you to one husband, that to Christ I might [ainf] [b]present you *as* a pure[53] virgin.[3933]

3 But I am afraid,[5399] lest as the [a]serpent [ao]deceived Eve by his craftiness,[3834] your minds[3540] should be led [asbp]astray from the simplicity[572] and purity *of devotion* to Christ.

4 For if one comes and preaches[2784] [a]another Jesus whom we have not [ao]preached, or you receive a [b]different[2087] spirit[4151] which you have not [ao]received, or a [c]different[2087] gospel[2098] which you have not [ao]accepted, you [pin] [d]bear *this* [e]beautifully.

🔑 5 For I consider[3049] myself [a]not[3367] in the least[3367] [pfin]inferior to the [I]most eminent apostles.[652]

6 But even if I am [a]unskilled[2399] in speech,[3056] yet I am not *so* in [b]knowledge;[1108] in fact, in every way we have [apt] [c]made *this* evident[5319] to you in all things.

7 Or [a]did I [ao]commit a sin in [ppt]humbling myself that you might be [asbp]exalted, because I [ao]preached[2097] the [b]gospel of God[2316] to you [c]without charge?

8 I [ao]robbed other[243] churches,[1577] [apt] [a]taking wages[3800] *from them* to serve[1248] you;

9 and when I was present with you and was in need, I was [a]not a [ao]burden to anyone; for when [b]the brethren[80] came from [c]Macedonia, they fully [ao]supplied[4322] my need, and in everything I [ao]kept myself from [a]being a burden to you, [I]and will continue to do so.

10 [a]As the truth[225] of Christ is in me, [b]this boasting of mine will not be stopped in the regions of [c]Achaia.

11 Why? [a]Because I do not love[25] you? [b]God knows *I do!*[1492]

12 But what I am doing, I will continue to do, [a]that I may cut off

13 [I]Lit., *according to the measure* [a]2Cor. 10:15 [b]Rom. 12:3; 2Cor. 10:15f.
14 [a]1Cor. 3:6 [b]2Cor. 2:12
15 [I]Lit., *according to our sphere* [a]2Cor. 10:13 [b]Rom. 15:20 [c]2Thess. 1:3 [d]Acts 5:13
16 [I]Lit., *to the things prepared in the* [a]2Cor. 11:7 [b]Acts 19:21 [c]Rom. 15:20
17 [a]Jer. 9:24; 1Cor. 1:31
18 [a]2Cor. 10:12 [b]Rom. 2:29; 1Cor. 4:5

1 [I]Or, *do indeed bear with me* [a]Matt. 17:17; 2Cor. 11:4, 16, 19f. [b]2Cor. 5:13; 11:17, 21
2 [a]Hos. 2:19f.; Eph. 5:26f. [b]2Cor. 4:14
3 [a]Gen. 3:4, 13; John 8:44; 1Thess. 3:5; 1Tim. 2:14; Rev. 12:9, 15
4 [a]1Cor. 3:11 [b]Rom. 8:15 [c]Gal. 1:6 [d]2Cor. 11:1 [e]Mark 7:9
5 [I]Or, *super-apostles* [a]2Cor. 12:11; Gal. 2:6
6 [a]1Cor. 1:17 [b]1Cor. 12:8; Eph. 3:4 [c]2Cor. 4:2
7 [a]2Cor. 12:13 [b]Rom. 1:1; 2Cor. 2:12 [c]Acts 18:3; 1Cor. 9:18
8 [a]1Cor. 4:12; 9:6; Phil. 4:15, 18
9 [I]Lit., *and I will keep* [a]2Cor. 12:13f., 16 [b]Acts 18:5 [c]Rom. 15:26; Phil. 4:15-18

10 [a]Rom. 1:9; 9:1; 2Cor. 1:23; Gal. 2:20 [b]1Cor. 9:15 [c]Acts 18:12 **11** [a]2Cor. 12:15 [b]Rom. 1:9; 2Cor. 2:17; 11:31; 12:2f. **12** [a]1Cor. 9:12

🔑 **11:5** The phrase "most eminent apostles" can be very easily misunderstood as indicating degrees of authority or station among the Apostles. The Greek word is *huperlian* (5244), which is derived from the preposition *huper* (5228), meaning "above," and *lian* (3029), an adverb meaning "very much, exceedingly." Here the word *huperlian* is used as a superlative adjective referring to those people who wanted to be taken as super Apostles, whose words should prevail over and above the words of the Twelve Apostles so ordained by Jesus Christ. The same expression occurs also in II Cor. 12:11. The context indicates that there were in Corinth those who wanted to impose their views over and above Paul's, and it is to these apostles that he makes reference. No one who claims that he is a "super apostle" has any ground to do so, nor were there super apostles among the Twelve Apostles.

opportunity from those who pptdesire an
opportunity to be [I]regarded just as we
are in the matter about which they are
boasting.
13 For such men are [a]false apostles,5570 [b]deceitful workers, disguising themselves3345 as anapostles of Christ.5547
14 And no wonder, for even [a]Satan4567 disguises himself as an [b]angel32 of light.5457
15 Therefore it is not surprising if his servants1249 also disguise themselves as servants1249 of righteousness;1343 [a]whose end5056 shall be according to their deeds.2041
16 [a]Again I say, let no one aosbthink me foolish; but if *you do,* receive me even as foolish, that I also may boast a little.
17 That which I am speaking, I am not speaking [Ia]as the Lord2962 would, but as [b]in foolishness, in this confidence5287 of boasting.
18 Since [a]many boast [b]according to the flesh,4561 I will boast also.
19 For you, [a]being *so* wise,5429 bear430 with the foolish gladly.
20 For you bear with anyone if he [a]enslaves2615 you, if he [b]devours you, if he [c]takes advantage of you, if he [d]exalts himself,1869 if he [e]hits you in the face.
21 To *my* [a]shame I *must* say that we have been pfi [b]weak770 *by comparison.* But1161 in whatever respect anyone *else* [c]is bold (I [d]speak in foolishness), I am just as bold myself.
22 Are they [a]Hebrews? [b]So am I. Are they [c]Israelites? [c]So am I. Are they [Id]descendants4690 of Abraham? [e]So am I.
23 Are they [a]servants1249 of Christ? (I speak as if pptinsane) I more so; in [Ib]far more labors,2873 in [Ic]far more imprisonments, [IId]beaten times without number, often in [e]danger of death.

24 Five times I aoreceived from the Jews [a]thirty-nine *lashes.*
25 Three times I was aop [a]beaten with rods, once I was aop [b]stoned, three times I was aoshipwrecked, a night and a day I have pfispent in the deep.
🔑 26 *I have been* on frequent journeys, in dangers from rivers, dangers from robbers,3027 dangers from *my* [a]countrymen, dangers from the [b]Gentiles, dangers in the [c]city, dangers in the wilderness, dangers on the sea, dangers among [d]false brethren;5569
27 *I have been* in [a]labor2873 and hardship,3449 [I]through many sleepless nights, in [b]hunger and thirst, often [c]without food,3521 in cold and [IId]exposure.1132
28 Apart from *such* [I]external things, there is the daily pressure1999 upon me *of* concern for [a]all the churches.
29 Who is [a]weak770 without my being weak? Who is [I]led into sin [II]without my intense concern?
30 If I have to pinfboast, I will boast of what pertains to my [a]weakness.
31 The God and Father of the Lord Jesus, [a]He who is blessed2128 forever, [b]knows1492 that I am not lying.
32 In [a]Damascus the ethnarch under Aretas the king was ipf [b]guarding5432 the city of the Damascenes in order to ainfseize me,
33 and I was aoplet down in a basket [a]through a window [I]in the wall, and *so* aoescaped his hands.

Paul's Vision

12 🔑 pinf [a]Boasting is necessary, though it is not profitable; but I

12 [I]Lit., *found*
13 [a]Acts 20:30; Gal. 1:7; 2:4; Phil. 1:15; Titus 1:10f.; 2Pet. 2:1; Rev. 2:2 [b]Phil. 3:2
14 [a]Matt. 4:10; Eph. 6:12; Col. 1:13 [b]Col. 1:12
15 [a]Rom. 2:6; 3:8
16 [a]2Cor. 11:1
17 [I]Lit., *in accordance with the Lord* [a]1Cor. 7:12, 25 [b]2Cor. 11:21
18 [a]Phil. 3:3f. [b]2Cor. 5:16
19 [a]1Cor. 4:10
20 [a]2Cor. 1:24; Gal. 2:4; 4:3, 9; 5:1 [b]Mark 12:40 [c]2Cor. 11:3; 12:16 [d]2Cor. 10:5 [e]1Cor. 4:11
21 [a]2Cor. 6:8 [b]2Cor. 10:10 [c]2Cor. 10:2 [d]2Cor. 11:17
22 [I]Lit., *seed* [a]Acts 6:1 [b]Phil. 3:5 [c]Rom. 9:4 [d]Gal. 3:16 [e]Rom. 11:1
23 [I]Lit., *more abundant* [II]Lit., *exceedingly in stripes* [a]1Cor. 3:5; 2Cor. 3:6; 10:7 [b]1Cor. 15:10 [c]2Cor. 6:5 [d]Acts 16:23; 2Cor. 6:5 [e]Rom. 8:36
24 [a]Deut. 25:3
25 [a]Acts 16:22 [b]Acts 14:19
26 [a]Acts 9:23; 13:45, 50; 14:5; 17:5, 13; 18:12; 20:3, 19; 21:27; 23:10, 12; 25:3; 1Thess. 2:15 [b]Acts 14:5, 19; 19:23ff.; 27:42 [c]Acts 21:31 [d]Gal. 2:4
27 [I]Lit., *often in wakefulness* [II]Lit., *nakedness;* i.e., lack of clothing [a]1Thess. 2:9; 2Thess. 3:8 [b]1Cor. 4:11; Phil. 4:12 [c]2Cor. 6:5 [d]1Cor. 4:11
28 [I]Or, *the things unmentioned* [a]1Cor. 7:17 29 [I]Lit., *made to stumble* [II]Lit., *and I do not burn* [a]1Cor. 8:9, 13; 9:22 30 [a]1Cor. 2:3 31 [a]Rom. 1:25 [b]2Cor. 11:11 32 [a]Acts 9:2 [b]Acts 9:24 33 [I]Lit., *through* [a]Acts 9:25 1 [a]2Cor. 11:16, 18, 30; 12:5, 9

🔑 **11:26** See note on Gal. 2:4.
🔑 **12:1-10** See note on I Thess. 4:17. Here the Apostle Paul reveals the unique experience he had of being raptured to the third heaven. Although he does not name himself in v. 2, it becomes obvious in v. 7 that he is speaking about himself.

(continued on next page)

will go on to visions and [b]revelations
[1]of the Lord.
2 I know[1492] a man [a]in Christ who
fourteen years ago—whether in the
body[4983] I do not know,[1492] or out of
the body[4983] I do not know, [b]God
knows—such a man was [aptp] [c]caught
up[726] to the [d]third heaven.[3772]

1 [1]Or possibly, from [b]1Cor. 14:6; 2Cor. 12:7; Gal. 1:12; 2:2; Eph. 3:3

2 [a]Rom. 16:7 [b]2Cor. 11:11

[c]Ezek. 8:3; Acts 8:39; 2Cor. 12:4; 1Thess. 4:17; Rev. 12:5 [d]Deut. 10:14; Ps. 148:4; Eph. 4:10; Heb. 4:14

(continued from previous page)

Why was it that Paul did not mention this experience to every group of believers to whom he wrote, but only to the Corinthians? Perhaps, because the Corinthians were constantly bragging about their spiritual visions and gifts (I Cor. 12), he wanted to demonstrate to them that in spite of his unique experience, he was a mere human with a mortal body who must not boast about his purely spiritual experiences which are not part and parcel of every believer while in this mortal body. Paul wanted to impress the Corinthians with the fact that he knew what he was talking about when he spoke of spiritual matters (II Cor. 12:1). He came as close to the superterrestrial world as anyone had and was given the opportunity to speak about it had he so chosen. Lazarus, the brother of Mary and Martha, had gone to paradise, but we have no record that he ever spoke about it after his resurrection. Paul did go there too, but he hesitated to speak about it. However, in order to bring about a sense of balance between the spiritual and the natural in the lives of the Corinthians, he found it necessary to refer to this experience.

It is interesting to note that this record of his rapture into paradise comes immediatley after II Cor. 11:32,33 in which he refers to an attempt to rescue him while he was in Damascus. He was lowered in a basket through a window in the wall of the city. We may question why the God who could lift Paul's spirit up into paradise did not also liberate his body in a miraculous manner from those who sought to kill him in Damascus. In II Cor. 11:16-33 we have the enumeration of his sufferings in the body and the spirit which indicates that the most spiritual person, one who was raptured into paradise, was not exempt from physical, mental and emotional anguish. Paul was so modest about this experience that he speaks as if it happened to another person (v. 2). What a contrast from those who pretend they have experiences similar to Paul's and constantly want to recount them! One wonders about the genuineness of such experiences when they are so often spoken of in the first person. Paul never said, "I have been in paradise." He said, "I know a man in Christ who fourteen years ago . . . was caught up to the third heaven." The Greek text has the verb *oida* (vv. 2,3), "I know," in the present tense and not in the past. This experience was constantly with him in spite of the fact that he didn't speak about it. Only the pride over false gifts among the Corinthians necessitated the revelation of his experience.

The verb translated "I know," that is used in vv. 2,3 is *oida* (1492) which means "intuitive knowledge." It stands in contrast to *ginōskō* (1097), referring to experiential knowledge. Because Paul was in Christ, he had intuitive knowledge of this experience. It was an experience confirmed by God's Spirit as real and yet not something that could be experientially proven to others.

Another word that is important is the aorist participle *harpagenta* (v. 2) translated "caught up." It is also used in v. 4 *"hērpagē."* Actually this is the verb, *harpazō* (726), from which rapture, *harpagē* (724), is derived. The same verb is used also in I Thess. 4:17 (see note) where Paul speaks about the believers who are going to be raptured or caught up in the clouds at the *parousia* (3952), coming of the Lord. It is as if Paul were given an actual demonstration in his own lifetime of the rapture of the believers who will be alive at the coming of Christ for His saints. Read I Thess. 4:13-18. It was Paul's spirit which must hve been taken up to paradise even as our spirits will be taken up in a disembodied state to be with Christ.

What is this place called paradise? The word *paradeisos* (3857), "paradise," originally comes from the ancient Iranian, *pairidaēza,* and means "a garden with a wall." The Greek word is used for the first time by Xenophon for the gardens of the Persian kings. The Septuagint translation of the Hebrew word for garden in Gen. 2:8 is *paradeisos.* In the N.T. the word occurs only three times: II Cor. 12:4; Lk. 23:43; Rev. 2:7. It was indicated as the place where the spirits or souls of men go immediately after death, which is also the place that Christ was going to go once His spirit was separated from His body. The continuation of the existence of the personality is also clearly intimated in the story of the rich man and Lazarus in Lk. 16:19-31. The paradise of II Cor. 12:4 is the same as that spoken of by Christ in Lk. 23:43. In Rev. 2:7 the word is spoken of in an eschatological sense as being a gift to be given to the one who overcomes. It is evidently the place where the disembodied personalities as spirits or souls of the believers go immediately at death to be with Christ.

(continued on next page)

3 And I know how such a man—whether in the body or apart from the body[4983] I do not know, [a]God knows—

4 was [aop][a]caught up into [b]Paradise,[3857] and [ao]heard inexpressible words,[4487] which a man is not permitted to [ainf]speak.

5 [a]On behalf of such a man will I boast; but on my own behalf I will not boast, except in regard to *my* [b]weaknesses.

6 For if I do wish to [ainf]boast I shall not be [a]foolish, [b]for I shall be speaking the truth; but I refrain *from this,* so that no one may [aosb]credit[3049] me with more than he sees *in* me or hears from me.

A Thorn in the Flesh

7 And because of the surpassing greatness of the [a]revelations, for this reason, to keep me from [psa]exalting myself, there was [aop]given me a [b]thorn in the flesh,[4561] a [c]messenger[32] of Satan[4567] to [psa]buffet me—to keep me from exalting myself!

8 Concerning this I [ao]entreated[3870] the Lord [a]three times that it might [aosb]depart from me.

9 And He has said to me, "My grace[5485] is sufficient for you, for [Ia]power is perfected[5055] in weakness." Most gladly, therefore, I will rather [b]boast about my weaknesses, that the power[1411] of Christ may [aosb]dwell in me.

10 Therefore [a]I am well content[2106] with weaknesses, with [I]insults,[5196] with [b]distresses,[318] with [c]persecutions, with [b]difficulties,[4730] [d]for Christ's sake; for [e]when I am weak, then I am strong.

🔑 **11** I have [pfi]become [a]foolish; you yourselves [ao]compelled me. Actually I [ipf]should have been [pip]commended[4921] by you, for [b]in no respect [ao]was I inferior to the [I]most eminent apostles, even though [c]I [pin]am a nobody.

12 The [Ia]signs[4592] [II]of a [art]true apostle[652] were [ao]performed[2716] among you with all perseverance, by [I]signs and wonders[5059] and [III]miracles.[1411]

13 For in what respect were you [aop]treated as [aop]inferior to the rest of the churches,[1577] except that [a]I myself did not become a burden to you? [aim]Forgive[5483] me [b]this wrong![93]

14 Here [a]for this third time I am ready to come to you, and I [b]will not be a burden to you; for I [c]do not seek what is yours, but [d]you; for [e]children[5043] are not responsible to [pinf]save up for *their* parents, but [f]parents for *their* children.

15 And I will [a]most gladly spend and be expended for your souls. If [b]I [pin]love[25] you the more, am I to be loved the less?

16 But be that as it may, I [a]did not burden you myself; nevertheless, crafty fellow that I am, I [b]took you in by deceit.[1388]

17 [a]*Certainly* I have not [ao]taken advantage of you through any of those whom I have [pfi]sent to you, have I?

🔑 18 I [a]urged[3870] [b]Titus *to go,* and sent [c]the brother with him. Titus did not take any advantage of you, did he? Did we not [ao][I]conduct ourselves [II]in the same [d]spirit[4151] *and walk* [e]in the same steps?

19 All this time [I]you have been thinking that we are defending ourselves to you. *Actually,* [a]it is in the sight of God that we have been speaking in Christ; and [b]all for your upbuilding, [c]beloved.[27]

3 [a]2Cor. 11:11
4 [a]Ezek. 8:3; Acts 8:39; 2Cor. 12:2; 1Thess. 4:17; Rev. 12:5 [b]Luke 23:43
5 [a]2Cor. 12:1 [b]1Cor. 2:3; 2Cor. 12:9f.
6 [a]2Cor. 5:13; 11:16f.; 12:11 [b]2Cor. 7:14
7 [a]2Cor. 12:1 [b]Num. 33:55; Ezek. 28:24; Hos. 2:6 [c]Job 2:6; Matt. 4:10; 1Cor. 5:5
8 [a]Matt. 26:44
9 [I]Later mss. read *My power* [a]1Cor. 2:5; Eph. 3:16; Phil. 4:13 [b]1Cor. 2:3; 2Cor. 12:5
10 [I]Or, *mistreatment* [a]Rom. 5:3; 8:35 [b]2Cor. 6:4 [c]2Thess. 1:4; 2Tim. 3:11 [d]2Cor. 5:15, 20 [e]2Cor. 13:4
11 [I]Or, *super-apostles* [a]2Cor. 5:13; 11:16f.; 12:6 [b]1Cor. 15:10; 2Cor. 11:5 [c]1Cor. 3:7; 13:2; 15:9
12 [I]Or, *attesting miracles* [II]Lit., *of the apostle* [III]Or, *works of power* [a]John 4:48; Rom. 15:19; 1Cor. 9:1
13 [a]1Cor. 9:12, 18; 2Cor. 11:9; 12:14 [b]2Cor. 11:7
14 [a]2Cor. 1:15; 13:1, 2 [b]1Cor. 9:12, 18; 2Cor. 11:9; 12:13 [c]1Cor. 10:24, 33 [d]1Cor. 9:19 [e]1Cor. 4:14f.; Gal. 4:19 [f]Prov. 19:14; Ezek. 34:2
15 [a]Rom. 9:3; 2Cor. 1:6; Phil. 2:17; Col. 1:24; 1Thess. 2:8; 2Tim. 2:10 [b]2Cor. 11:11
16 [a]2Cor. 11:9 [b]2Cor. 11:20
17 [a]2Cor. 9:5
18 [I]Lit., *walk* [II]Or, *by the same Spirit* [a]2Cor. 8:6 [b]2Cor. 2:13 [c]2Cor. 8:18 [d]1Cor. 4:21 [e]Rom. 4:12
19 [I]Or, *have you been thinking . . . ?* [a]Rom. 9:1; 2Cor. 2:17 [b]Rom. 14:19; 2Cor. 10:8; 1Thess. 5:11 [c]Heb. 6:9

(continued from previous page)

In II Cor. 5:1-9 Paul tells us what happens after death. He tells us that we are going to appear before the Lord Jesus to be judged for all our works in the flesh whether good or evil (II Cor. 5:10). To confirm that this was not merely conjecture, he tells us that he has been there and has come back to tell us about it (II Cor. 12:1-6). For a complete study of the subject, see the Editor's book *Life After Death.*

🔑 **12:11** See note on II Cor. 11:5.

🔑 **12:18** See general remarks on Titus.

20 For I am afraid[5399] that perhaps [a]when I come I may find you to be not what I wish and may be [asbp]found by you to be not what you wish; that perhaps *there may be* [b]strife,[2054] jealousy,[2205] [c]angry tempers,[2372] [d]disputes, [e]slanders,[2636] [f]gossip, [g]arrogance, [h]disturbances;[181]

21 I am afraid that when I come again my God may [aosb]humiliate me before you, and I may mourn[3996] over many of those who have [pfp] [a]sinned in the past and not repented[3340] of the [b]impurity,[167] [I]immorality[4202] and sensuality[766] which they have practiced.

Examine Yourselves

13 [a]This is the third time I am coming to you. [b]EVERY [I]FACT[4487] [II]IS TO BE CONFIRMED[2476] BY THE [III]TESTIMONY OF TWO OR THREE WITNESSES.[3144]

2 I have previously [pf]said when present the second time, and though now absent[548] I [pin]say in advance to those who have [pfp] [a]sinned in the past and to all the rest as well, that [b]if I come again, I will not [c]spare *anyone,*

3 since you are [a]seeking for proof[1382] of the [b]Christ who speaks in me, and who is not weak toward you, but [c]mighty[1414] in you.

4 For indeed He was [a]crucified[4717] because of weakness,[769] yet He lives[2198] [b]because of the power[1411] of God.[2316] For we also are [c]weak [I]in Him, yet [d]we shall live with Him because of the power of God *directed* toward you.

5 [pim] [a]Test[3985] yourselves *to see* if you are in the faith;[4102] [pim] [b]examine[1381] yourselves! Or do you not recognize this about yourselves, that Jesus Christ[5547] is in you—unless indeed you [I][c]fail the test?[96]

6 But I trust that you will realize that we ourselves [I]do not fail the test.

7 Now we pray to God that you [ainf]do no wrong;[2556] not that we ourselves may appear approved,[1384] but that you may [psa]do what is right, even though we should [asbp] [I]appear unapproved.

8 For we can do nothing against the truth,[225] but *only* for the truth.

9 For we rejoice when we ourselves are [psa] [a]weak but you are strong; this we also pray for, [I]that you be [b]made complete.[2676]

10 For this reason I am writing these things while absent,[548] in order that when present [a]I may not [aosb]use [b]severity, in accordance with the [c]authority[1849] which the Lord[2962] [ao]gave me, for building up[3619] and not for tearing down.[2506]

11 [a]Finally, brethren, [I]rejoice,[5463] [II][b]be made [pim]complete, be [pim]comforted, [c]be [pim]like-minded,[5426] [d]live in [pim]peace; and [e]the God of love[26] and peace[1515] shall be with you.

12 [aim] [a]Greet[782] one another with a holy[40] kiss.

13 [a]All the [I]saints[40] greet[782] you.

14 [a]The grace[5485] of the Lord Jesus Christ, and the [b]love of God, and the [c]fellowship[2842] of the Holy Spirit, be with you all.

20 [a]1Cor. 4:21; 2Cor. 2:1-4 [b]1Cor. 1:11; 3:3 [c]Gal. 5:20 [d]Rom. 2:8; 1Cor. 11:19 [e]Rom. 1:30; James 4:11; 1Pet. 2:1 [f]Rom. 1:29 [g]1Cor. 4:6, 18; 5:2 [h]1Cor. 14:33
21 [I]I.e., sexual immorality [a]2Cor. 13:2 [b]1Cor. 6:9, 18; Gal. 5:19; Col. 3:5
1 [I]Lit., *word* [II]Lit., *will be* [III]Lit., *mouth* [a]2Cor. 12:14 [b]Deut. 17:6; 19:15; Matt. 18:16
2 [a]2Cor. 12:21 [b]1Cor. 4:21; 2Cor. 13:10 [c]2Cor. 1:23; 10:11
3 [a]2Cor. 10:1, 10 [b]Matt. 10:20; 1Cor. 5:4; 7:40 [c]2Cor. 9:8; 10:4
4 [I]Some early mss. read *with Him* [a]Phil. 2:7f.; 1Pet. 3:18 [b]Rom. 1:4; 6:4; 1Cor. 6:14 [c]1Cor. 2:3; 2Cor. 13:9 [d]Rom. 6:8
5 [I]Lit., *are unapproved* [a]John 6:6 [b]1Cor. 11:28 [c]1Cor. 9:27
6 [I]Lit., *are not unapproved*
7 [I]Lit., *be as*
9 [I]Lit., *your completion* [a]2Cor. 12:10; 13:4 [b]1Cor. 1:10; 2Cor. 13:11; Eph. 4:12; 1Thess. 3:10
10 [a]2Cor. 2:3 [b]Titus 1:13 [c]1Cor. 5:4; 2Cor. 10:8
11 [I]Or possibly, *farewell* [II]Or, *put yourselves in order* [a]1Thess. 4:1; 2Thess. 3:1 [b]1Cor. 1:10; 2Cor. 13:9; Eph. 4:12; 1Thess. 3:10 [c]Rom. 12:16 [d]Mark 9:50 [e]Rom. 15:33; Eph. 6:23
12 [a]Rom. 16:16 **13** [I]Or, *holy ones* [a]Phil. 4:22
14 [a]Rom. 16:20; 2Cor. 8:9 [b]Rom. 5:5; Jude 1:21 [c]Phil. 2:1

The Epistle of Paul to the

GALATIANS

Galatia was a Roman province which included Lycaonia, Isauria, and parts of Phrygia and Pisidia. It is now southern Turkey. The purpose of this Epistle was to eradicate the doctrinal errors which had been recently introduced by hostile Judaizers and to urge the Galatian Christians to hold firmly to what they had been taught by Paul at the beginning. The people were generally impressionable, fickle, and quick-tempered (see Gal. 4:13-16; Acts 14:8-19). Paul had started these congregations on his first missionary journey (Acts 13 and 14) with considerable success, proclaiming "a door of faith" open to them (Acts 14:27). Then he revisited them on his second missionary journey (Acts 16:1-6) and again on his third missionary journey (Acts 18:23). In the meantime, Judaistic teachers had subverted his work by teaching a new type of legalism to these innocent Gentile believers. These Jewish traditionalists refused to accept the Apostolic teaching (Acts 15:1-31). They felt that they had the copyright on Jesus. They zealously undermined and unsettled these new converts who were unstable and not grounded, persuading them to defect from Paul's teaching. They suggested that Paul had learned his ideas second-hand from the Apostles who were pillars in Jerusalem, while they themselves had the inside story.

The Judaizing threat ended at the fall of Jerusalem in A.D. 70. Prior to that time, Jewish Christians (Messianic believers) were considered to be a sect (Acts 24:5), a new branch of Judaism. But, after A.D. 70, all Christians were on their own; they were recognized as separate from Judaism. Judaizers insisted that non-Jewish believers in Christ could not be true Christians *until* they would submit to circumcision, a Jewish rite from the Old Testament, and keep the Law of Moses. The naive Galatian Christians listened to them with the same enthusiastic receptivity that they had given to Paul originally. Paul did not deny the importance of circumcision or any other Jewish custom *to Jews.* In fact, Paul was formerly a high-ranking Jewish leader himself, and he had even participated in religious practices in the Temple late in his ministry (Acts 21:17-26) to prove that he could be "all things to all men" (I Cor. 9:22). However, circumcision had nothing whatever to do with salvation!

Paul contended that his Apostleship was genuine, not from any human authority, but from God. He had proclaimed the true Gospel to them. The Judaizers were tampering with the essential thrust of the very nature of the Gospel. There was much at stake. If the Judaizers were right, then Christ died on the cross for nothing (Gal. 2:21)! Paul taught that a right relationship with God was based on believing in Christ, not by trying to "make points" through obeying law. Christians already had freedom and should not have been made to feel that they were in bondage again. In this brief letter Paul forever settled the question about the relationship which we have with the Law of Moses.

In Galatians there are a series of important contrasts: a different type of "gospel" versus the authentic Gospel; man's reasoning versus God's revelation; law versus grace; works versus faith; the curse of death versus the blessing of life; condemnation versus exoneration; servants in bondage versus sons in freedom; defeat versus victory; the old covenant versus the new convenant; living in the flesh versus walking in the Spirit; the works of the flesh versus the fruit of the Spirit; falling from grace versus standing firm in grace; the world (self) as the object of boasting versus the cross of Christ. Paul recapitulates by saying that the Christian life is the natural fruit which flows from love (Gal. 5:6).

The date of Paul's writing is uncertain, but it is thought that it was before he wrote the more detailed Book of Romans concerning much of the same subject matter.

Introduction

1 Paul, [a]an apostle[652] ([b]not *sent* from
men,[444] nor through the agency
of man, but [c]through Jesus Christ,[5547]
and God[2316] the Father,[3962] who
[apt] [d]raised[1453] Him from the dead),[3498]
🔑 2 and all [a]the brethren[80] who are
with me, to [b]the churches[1577] of Galatia:
3 [a]Grace to you and peace[1515] from
[I]God our Father, and the Lord Jesus
Christ,
4 who [apt] [a]gave Himself for our
sins,[266] that He might [asbm]deliver us out
of [b]this present evil [I]age,[165] according to the will[2307] of [c]our God and
Father,
5 [a]to whom *be* the glory[1391] forevermore.[165] Amen.[281]

1 [a]2Cor. 1:1 [b]Gal. 1:11f. [c]Acts 9:15; Gal. 1:15f. [d]Acts 2:24
2 [a]Phil. 4:21 [b]Acts 16:6; 1Cor. 16:1
3 [I]Some early mss. read *God the Father, and our Lord Jesus Christ* [a]Rom. 1:7
4 [I]Or, *world* [a]Gal. 2:20 [b]Matt. 13:22; Rom. 12:2; 2Cor. 4:4 [c]Phil. 4:20
5 [a]Rom. 11:36
6 [I]Lit., *in* [a]Rom. 8:28; Gal. 1:15; Gal. 5:8 [b]2Cor. 11:4; Gal. 1:7, 11; Gal. 2:2, 7; Gal. 5:14; 1Tim. 1:3
7 [a]Acts 15:24; Gal. 5:10

Perversion of the Gospel

🔑 6 I am amazed that you are so
quickly deserting [a]Him who [apt]called
you [I]by the grace[5485] of Christ, for a
[b]different[2087] gospel;[2098]
🔑 7 which is *really* not another; only
there are some who are [ppt] [a]disturbing
you, and [ppt]want to [ainf]distort[3344] the
gospel[2098] of Christ.
🔑 8 But even though we, or [a]an angel[32]
from heaven,[3772] should [asbm]preach to
you a gospel[2097] [I]contrary to that which
we have [ao]preached[2097] to you, let him
be [II][b]accursed.[331]
9 As we [a]have [pfi]said before, so I
[pin]say again now, [b]if any man is preaching

8 [I]Or, *other than, more than* [II]Gr., *anathema* [a]2Cor. 11:14 [b]Rom. 9:3 9 [a]Acts 18:23 [b]Rom. 16:17

🔑 **1:2** See general remarks on Titus.

🔑 **1:6** The whole Epistle to the Galatians indicates that a gospel which was different from the Gospel which Paul preached had penetrated the church in Galatia. Paul calls this "a different gospel." The word in Greek for "different" is *heteron* (2087), which means not only another numerically, but qualitatively.

🔑 **1:7** In this verse Paul uses an entirely different word translated "another." It is *allo* (243) which means another of the same kind that is only declared by somebody else. The Gospel can be declared in different ways by different people, but it can never be altered in its substance or message.

Evidently, there were cults during the apostolic era even as there are today. Not all who preach from the Bible preach that the Bible is true, but only that it contains truth.

🔑 **1:8** Here Paul does not introduce the possibility of himself or an angel preaching a false gospel. He is simply giving a hypothesis which has no basis or ground of fact. This is what we find in Paul's Epistles as the *reductio ad absurdum,* the reduction to an absurdity, a method frequently employed by Paul in arguing a case. The hypothesis is necessary to show how absurd it really is from the conclusion. In a positive way, he was teaching that it was impossible for him or for an angel, to preach another gospel.

In I Cor. 13:1-3 we have another example of the hypothetical form of argument the Apostle Paul uses where three distinct hypotheses or suppositions are given without regard to fact.

Also Ezek. 18:24 is clearly hypothetical. This will be seen by comparison with the parallel passage, Ezek. 33:18, "When I say to the righteous he shall surely live, and he so trusts in his righteousness. . . ."

The same argument is given by Paul in I Cor. 15:13-19. He describes the absurd results from the false hypotheses. The first erroneous hypothesis is that Jesus did not rise from the dead, which is based upon a false philosophical assumption that it is impossible for the dead to rise (I Cor. 15:13). And then from the false hypothesis, he enumerates the resultant necessary conclusions that his preaching was in vain, faith was of no value, and that he and others who were preaching Christ and the Gospel were false witnesses, etc.

Another example of such a *reductio ad absurdum* is Heb. 6:4-6. The conclusion from the false fact presented here is that the repentance which is based on the death of Christ, who was sacrificed once and for all for our sins, is absolutely no good if it does not have the lasting effect of salvation that will hold to the very end. The supposition is that if we can fall, then the repentance which we have had is in vain. And if the repentance based on the once-and-for-all sacrifice of Jesus Christ is in vain, then in order to have another qualitatively new repentance which will last, it is necessary for Jesus Christ to die afresh. Of course, this is an impossibility because it will make a ridicule of His first sacrifice for us and indicate that it was ineffective. See note on II Thess. 2:3.

to you a gospel [I]contrary to that which
you [ao]received, let him be [II][c]accursed.
10 For am I now [a]seeking the
favor[3982] of men,[444] or of God?[2316] Or
am I striving to [pinf]please men? If I were
still trying to [ipf]please men, I would not
be a [b]bond-servant[1401] of Christ.

Paul Defends His Ministry

11 For [a]I would have you know,[1107]
brethren,[80] that the gospel[2098] which
was [aptp]preached[2097] by me is [b]not according to man.
12 For [a]I neither received it from
man,[444] nor was I taught[1321] it, but *I*
received it through a [b]revelation[602] of
Jesus Christ.
13 For you have heard of [a]my former manner of life[391] in Judaism, how
I [b]used to [ipf]persecute [c]the church[1577]
of God beyond measure, and [d]tried to
[ipf]destroy[4199] it;
14 and I [a]was [ipf]advancing in Judaism[2454] beyond many of my contemporaries among my [I]countrymen,[1085] being more extremely zealous for my
[b]ancestral traditions.[3862]
15 But when He who had [apt]set me
apart,[873] *even* from my mother's womb,
and [aptp] [a]called[2564] me through His
grace,[5485] was pleased[2106]
16 to [ainf]reveal[601] His Son in me, that
I might [psa] [a]preach[2097] Him among the
Gentiles,[1484] [b]I did not immediately consult with [I][c]flesh[5461] and blood,[129]
17 [a]nor did I go up to Jerusalem to
those who were apostles[652] before me;
but I went away to Arabia, and returned
once more to [b]Damascus.
18 Then [a]three years later I went
up [b]to Jerusalem to [I]become acquainted
with [c]Cephas, and stayed with him fifteen days.
19 But I did not see any other[2087]
of the apostles except [I][a]James, the
Lord's[2962] brother.
20 (Now in what I am writing[1125]
to you, [I]I assure you [a]before God that
I am not lying.)
21 Then [a]I went into the regions
of [b]Syria and [c]Cilicia.
22 And I was *still* unknown[50] by
[I]sight to [a]the churches[1577] of Judea which
were [b]in Christ;
23 but only, they kept hearing, "He
who once [ppt]persecuted us is now
preaching[2097] [a]the faith[4102] which he once
[b]tried to [ipf]destroy."
24 And they [a]were [ipf]glorifying[1392]
God [I]because of me.

The Council at Jerusalem

2 Then after an interval of fourteen
years I [a]went up again to Jerusalem
with [b]Barnabas, taking [c]Titus along also.
2 And [I]it was because of a [a]reve-
lation[602] that I went up; and I submitted
to them the [b]gospel[2098] which I
preach[2784] among the Gentiles,[1484] but
I did so in private to those who were
of reputation, for fear that I might be
[psa] [c]running, or had [ao]run, in vain.
3 But not even [a]Titus who was with
me, though he was a Greek, was
[aop] [b]compelled to be [aifp]circumcised.[4059]
4 But *it was* because of the [a]false
brethren[5569] who [b]had sneaked in[3920] to

9 [I]Or, *other than, more than* [II]Gr., *anathema* [c]Rom. 9:3
10 [a]1Cor. 10:33; 1Thess. 2:4 [b]Rom. 1:1; Phil. 1:1
11 [a]Rom. 2:16; 1Cor. 15:1 [b]1Cor. 3:4; 1Cor. 9:8
12 [a]1Cor. 11:23; Gal. 1:1 [b]1Cor. 2:10; 2Cor. 12:1; Gal. 1:16; Gal. 2:2
13 [a]Acts 26:4f. [b]Acts 8:3; Acts 22:4, 5 [c]1Cor. 10:32 [d]Acts 9:21
14 [I]Lit., *race* [a]Acts 22:3 [b]Jer. 9:14; Matt. 15:2; Mark 7:3; Col. 2:8
15 [a]Is. 49:1, 5; Jer. 1:5; Acts 9:15; Rom. 1:1; Gal. 1:6
16 [I]I.e., human beings [a]Acts 9:15; Gal. 2:9 [b]Acts 9:20 [c]Matt. 16:17
17 [a]Acts 9:19-22 [b]Acts 9:2
18 [I]Or, *visit Cephas* [a]Acts 9:22f. [b]Acts 9:26 [c]John 1:42; Gal. 2:9, 11, 14
19 [I]Or, *Jacob* [a]Matt. 12:46; Acts 12:17
20 [I]Lit., *behold before God* [a]Rom. 9:1; 2Cor. 1:23; 2Cor. 11:31
21 [a]Acts 9:30 [b]Acts 15:23, 41 [c]Acts 6:9
22 [I]Lit., *face* [a]1Cor. 7:17; 1Thess. 2:14 [b]Rom. 16:7
23 [a]Acts 6:7; Gal. 6:10 [b]Acts 9:21
24 [I]Lit., *in me* [a]Matt. 9:8

1 [a]Acts 15:2 [b]Acts 4:36; Gal. 2:9, 13 [c]2Cor. 2:13; Gal. 2:3.
2 [I]Lit., *according to revelation I went up* [a]Acts 15:2; Gal. 1:12 [b]Gal. 1:6 [c]Rom. 9:16; 1Cor. 9:24ff.; Gal. 5:7; Phil. 2:16; 2Tim. 4:7; Heb. 12:1 **3** [a]2Cor. 2:13; Gal. 2:1 [b]Acts 16:3; 1Cor. 9:21 **4** [a]Acts 15:1, 24; 2Cor. 11:13, 26; Gal. 1:7 [b]2Pet. 2:1; 2Pet. 65:4

1:19 See general remarks on Jude.

2:3 See general remarks on Titus.

2:4 The whole thesis of Paul is that in the church in Galatia there was an endeavor to bring the Christians under the Law of Moses. Although Paul circumcised Timothy, who was half Jewish and half Gentile (Acts 16:3), he would not yield to pressure to circumcise Titus. This would have been unwise to show weakness toward their Judaistic tendencies. Had he voluntarily chosen to be circumcised, it would have been acceptable.

The conclusion derived from this incident was that Christians were under obligation to keep the law.

(continued on next page)

spy out our [c]liberty[1657] which we have in Christ Jesus, in order to [ft] [d]bring us into bondage.[2615]

5 But we did not yield in subjection[5292] to them for even an hour, so that [a]the truth[225] of the gospel[2098] might [aosb]remain with you.

6 But from those who [I]were of high [a]reputation (what they were makes no difference[1308] to me; [b]God [II]shows no partiality)—[2983] well, those who were of reputation[1380] [aom]contributed nothing to me.

7 But on the contrary, seeing that I had been [pfip] [a]entrusted[4100] with the [b]gospel [I]to the uncircumcised,[203] just as [c]Peter *had been* [II]to the circumcised[4061]

8 (for He who effectually [apt]worked for Peter in *his* [a]apostleship[651] [I]to the circumcised[4061] effectually worked for me also to the Gentiles),

9 and [apt]recognizing [a]the grace[5485] that had been given to me, [Ib]James and [c]Cephas and John, who were [d]reputed to be [e]pillars, gave to me and [f]Barnabas the [g]right [II]hand[1188] of fellowship,[2842] that we *might* [h]*go* to the Gentiles, and they to the circumcised.

10 *They* only *asked* us to [psa]remember the poor—[a]the very thing I also was [ao]eager to [ainf]do.

Peter (Cephas) Opposed by Paul

11 But when [a]Cephas [ao]came to [b]Antioch, I [ao]opposed him to his face,[4383] because he [I]stood condemned.[2607]

12 For prior to the [aip]coming of certain men from [Ia]James, he used to [ipf] [b]eat with the Gentiles;[1484] but when they came, he *began* to [ipf]withdraw and [ipf]hold himself aloof,[873] [c]fearing[5399] [II]the party of the circumcision.[4061]

13 And the rest of the Jews joined him in hypocrisy, with the result that even [a]Barnabas was carried away by their hypocrisy.[5272]

14 But when I saw that they [a]were not [I]straightforward about [b]the truth[225] of the gospel,[2098] I said to [c]Cephas in the presence of all, "If you, being a Jew, [d]live like[1483] the Gentiles and not like the Jews, how *is it that* you compel the Gentiles to live like Jews?[II]

4 [c]Gal. 5:1, 13; James 1:25 [d]Rom. 8:15; 2Cor. 11:20 **5** [a]Gal. 1:6; Gal. 2:14; Col. 1:5 **6** [I]Lit., *seemed to be something* [II]Lit., *does not receive a face* [a]2Cor. 11:5; 2Cor. 12:11; Gal. 2:9; Gal. 6:3 [b]Acts 10:34 **7** [I]Lit., *of the uncircumcision* [II]Lit., *of the circumcision* [a]1Cor. 9:17; 1Thess. 2:4; 1Tim. 1:11 [b]Acts 9:15; Gal. 1:16 [c]Gal. 1:18; Gal. 2:9, 11, 14 **8** [I]Lit., *of the circumcision* [a]Acts 1:25 **9** [I]Or, *Jacob* [II]Lit., *hands* [a]Rom. 12:3 [b]Acts 12:17; Gal. 2:12 [c]Luke 22:8; Gal. 1:18; Gal. 2:7, 11, 14 [d]2Cor. 11:5; 2Cor. 12:11; Gal. 2:2, 6; Gal. 6:3 [e]1Tim. 3:15; Rev. 3:12 [f]Acts 4:36; Gal. 2:1, 13 [g]2Kin. 10:15 [h]Gal. 1:16 **10** [a]Acts 24:17 **11** [I]Or, *was to be condemned;* lit., *was one who was condemned,* or, *was self-condemned* [a]Gal. 1:18; Gal. 2:7, 9, 14 [b]Acts 11:19; Acts 15:1 **12** [I]Or, *Jacob* [II]Or, *converts from the circumcised;* lit., *those from the circumcision* [a]Acts 12:17; Gal. 2:9 [b]Acts 11:3 [c]Acts 11:2 **13** [a]Acts 4:36; Gal. 2:1, 9 **14** [I]Or, *progressing toward;* lit., *walking straightly* [II]Some close the direct quotation here, others extend it through v. 21 [a]Heb. 12:13 [b]Gal. 1:6; Gal. 2:5; Col. 1:5 [c]Gal. 1:18; Gal. 2:7, 9, 11 [d]Acts 10:28; Gal. 2:12

(continued from previous page)

Paul calls the false teachers *pareisaktous* (3920), from *para* (3844), "on the side" and *eisagō* (1521), "to bring in." These false teachers had infiltrated the church secretly, without declaring from the start who they were or what they intended to do. This does not indicate that they were brought in by the church itself, but that they managed to sneak in themselves. This word *pareisaktos* (3920) is never used anywhere else in the N.T. Paul calls these intruders "false brethren," *pseudadelphoi* (5569) a term that is used only here and in II Cor. 11:26 in which Paul speaks of himself as in "dangers among false brethren." In other words, these false brethren became violently opposed to Paul. We are not sure of the spiritual status of the false brethren, but perhaps they could be called misbelievers. They evidently had petty doctrines on which they constantly harped which could harm the Gospel and those who preached it.

That which is translated "who had sneaked in" in Greek is *pareisēlthon* (*pareiserchomai,* 3922), made up of the same preposition, *para* (3844), "on the side," as the word *eiserchomai* (1525), "those who sneaked in." This indicates the deceitfulness of these people who joined the local church in Galatia in order to spread their own false doctrine of Judaizing Christianity. The verb is in the active voice which means that they managed to sneak in without being noticed. How careful each local church ought to be in regard to such false brethren.

Their purpose is easily demonstrated by the infinitive *kataskopēsai* (2684). It is made up of the preposition *kata* (2596), as an intensive, and *skopeō* (4648), "to look at or view attentively." They came in order to spy out the freedom which these believers had in Jesus Christ. Slavery to any one particular doctrinal spiritual tangent which is stressed above all else is something intolerable for a believer who must be guided by Jesus Christ in a balanced doctrinal stand and saintly behavior.

15 “We *are* [a]Jews by nature, and not [b]sinners[268] from among the Gentiles;

🔑 16 nevertheless knowing that [a]a man[444] is not justified[1344] by the works[2041] of [I]the Law[3551] but through faith[4102] in Christ Jesus, even we have [ao]believed[4100] in Christ Jesus, that we may be [asbp]justified[1344] by [b]faith in Christ, and not by the works of [I]the Law; since [c]by the works of [I]the Law shall no [II]flesh[4561] be justified.

17 “But if, while [ppt]seeking to be [aifp]justified in Christ, we ourselves have also been [aop]found[2147] [a]sinners,[268] is Christ then a minister[1249] of sin?[266] [b]May it never be![1096] [3361]

18 “For if I rebuild what I have *once* destroyed, I [a]prove[4921] myself to be a transgressor.[3848]

19 “For through [I]the Law I [ao][a]died[599] to [I]the Law, that I might [psa]live[2198] to God.

20 “I have been [pfip][a]crucified[4957] with Christ;[5547] and it is no longer I who live, but [b]Christ lives in me; and [I]the *life* which I now live in the flesh[4561] I live by faith[4102] in [c]the Son[5207] of God, who [apt][d]loved[25] me, and [apt][e]delivered Himself up for me.

21 “I do not nullify the grace[5485] of God; for [a]if righteousness[1343] *comes* through [I]the Law,[3551] then Christ [ao]died[599] needlessly.”[1432]

15 [a]Phil. 3:4f. [b]1Sam. 15:18; Luke 24:7
16 [I]Or, *law* [II]Or, *mortal man* [a]Acts 13:39; Gal. 3:11 [b]Rom. 3:22; Rom. 9:30 [c]Ps. 143:2; Rom. 3:20
17 [a]Gal. 2:15 [b]Luke 20:16; Gal. 3:21
18 [a]Rom. 3:5
19 [I]Or, *law* [a]Rom. 6:2; Rom. 7:4; 1Cor. 9:20
20 [I]Or, *insofar as I* [a]Rom. 6:6; Gal. 5:24; Gal. 6:14 [b]Rom. 8:10 [c]Matt. 4:3 [d]Rom. 8:37 [e]Gal. 1:4
21 [I]Or, *law* [a]Gal. 3:21

1 [I]Lit., *O* [a]Gal. 1:2 [b]1Cor. 1:23; Gal. 5:11
2 [I]Or, *law* [II]Lit., *the hearing of faith* [a]Rom. 10:17

Faith Brings Righteousness

3 [I]You foolish[453] [a]Galatians, who has [ao]bewitched you, before whose eyes Jesus Christ [b]was publicly [aop]portrayed *as* [pfpp]crucified?[4717]

2 This is the only thing I want to find out[3129] from you: did you receive the Spirit[4151] by the works[2041] of [I]the Law,[3551] or by [IIa]hearing[189] with faith?[4102]

3 Are you so foolish? Having [apt]be-

🔑 **2:16** See general remarks on justification in Romans. The statement here is that man is justified by the faith of Jesus Christ, i.e., the faith which Christ generates in the human heart (see Rom. 4:2; Gal. 3:11,12). Negatively stated, Rom. 3:20 says, “By the works of the law no flesh will be justified.” On the other hand, James 2:21-24 apparently states that man is not justified by faith only but also by works. The difficulty of the seeming contradiction is accentuated by the statement of Paul himself in Rom. 2:13, “The doers of the law will be justified.” How can these two statements be reconciled?

One way to resolve this apparent contradiction is to go back to Js. 2:14 where it does not say, “What doth it profit though a man have faith?” But it says, “What use is it, my brethren, if a man says he has faith (*legē,* which means ‘makes a reasoned statement’).” A mere profession of faith does not mean the possession of faith or the natural accompaniments of faith. Faith that is not accompanied by its inevitable and expectant fruits of faith is no faith at all. It is a mockery. James calls such a faith dead faith. We call a corpse a body, but a living body can breathe. A body that does not breathe is necessarily dead.

Paul speaks of a true, lively faith which purifies the heart and works by love (Gal. 5:6). James in this instance speaks of a profession or presumption of faith, barren and destitute of good fruit. Such a faith is dead (v. 17); it is a faith as the devils may have (v. 19) and consists only of an intellectual belief of God’s being or existence, not consenting to His offer of salvation through repentance and turning from sin nor a reliance on His promises. When Paul speaks of faith, he speaks of it as including the works of faith. When James speaks of faith in this instance, he speaks of false faith that does not result in the works of faith. When any Apostle speaks of works resulting from faith as saving any one, inherent in those works is included the faith that is the only way whereby those works can be produced. When I speak of fruit, the whole process of the development of the fruit is included. When works, however, are spoken about as the works not resulting from faith, they are meant to be false works or fruits, fruits of a nonexistent faith. One cannot have the fruits of faith that are true and real without true and real faith, no more than oranges can come from pine trees.

This sort of reasoning would bring light upon a statement such as that which we find in I Pet. 3:21 concerning baptism which results from the exercise of living faith in Jesus Christ. It is not actually the baptism that saves, because the act of physical baptism without the antecedent living, spiritual faith in Christ is nothing but an empty and ineffective act. Here the baptism mentioned in I Pet. 3:21 as saving a believer presupposes the root which produced it, i.e., living faith in Jesus Christ.

gun [I]by the Spirit, are you now [II]being perfected[2005] by the flesh?[4561]

4 Did you [ao]suffer[3958] so many things in vain—1500 [a]if indeed it was in vain?

5 Does He then, who [ppt] [a]provides you with the Spirit and [ppt] [b]works [I]miracles[1411] among you, do it by the works[2041] of [II]the Law,[3551] or by [III][c]hearing[189] with faith?[4102]

6 [I]Even so [a]Abraham [b]BELIEVED[4100] GOD, AND IT WAS RECKONED TO HIM AS RIGHTEOUSNESS.[1343]

7 Therefore, [I]be sure that [a]it is those who are of faith who are [b]sons[5207] of Abraham.

8 And the Scripture,[1124] [apt]foreseeing4257 that God [I]would justify[1344] the [II]Gentiles[1484] by faith,[4102] [ao]preached the gospel beforehand[4283] to Abraham, *saying*, "[a]ALL THE NATIONS[1484] SHALL BE BLESSED IN YOU."

9 So then [a]those who are of faith are blessed[2127] with [I]Abraham, the believer.[4103]

10 For as many as are of the [an]works[2041] of [I]the [an]Law[3551] are under a curse;[2671] for it is written, "[a]CURSED[1944] IS EVERYONE WHO DOES NOT ABIDE[1696] BY ALL THINGS WRITTEN IN THE BOOK975 OF THE LAW, TO PERFORM THEM."

🔑 11 Now that [a]no one is justified[1344] [I]by [II]the [an]Law before God is evident; for, "[III][b]THE RIGHTEOUS[1342] MAN SHALL LIVE[2198] BY FAITH."[4102]

12 [I]However, the Law is not [II]of faith; on the contrary, "[a]HE[444] WHO [apt]PRACTICES THEM SHALL LIVE[2198] [III]BY THEM."

13 Christ[5547] [a]redeemed[1805] us from the curse[2671] of the Law, having [apt]become a curse for us—for it is written, "[b]CURSED[1944] IS EVERYONE WHO HANGS ON [c]A [I]TREE"—

14 in order that [a]in Christ[5547] Jesus the blessing[2129] of Abraham might [aosb] [I]come to the Gentiles,[1484] so that we [b]might [aosb]receive [c]the promise[1860] of the Spirit[4151] through faith.[4102]

Intent of the Law

15 [a]Brethren, [b]I speak [I]in terms of human relations: [c]even though it is *only* a man's [II]covenant,[1242] yet when it has been [pfpp]ratified, no one sets it aside or adds [III]conditions to it.

16 Now the promises were [aop]spoken [a]to Abraham and to his seed.[4690] He does not say, "And to seeds,"[4690] as *referring* to many, but *rather* to one, "[b]And to your seed," that is, Christ.[5547]

🔑 17 What I am saying is this: the Law, which [pfp]came [a]four hundred and thirty years later, does not invalidate a covenant previously [pfpp]ratified by God, so as to [ainf]nullify the promise.[1860]

18 For [a]if the inheritance[2817] is [I]based on law,[3551] it is no longer [I]based on a promise; but [b]God has [pfi]granted[5483] it to Abraham by means of a promise.

19 [a]Why the Law[3551] then? It was added [I]because of transgressions,[3847] having been [aptp] [b]ordained[1299] through angels[32] [c]by the [II]agency of a mediator,[3316] until [d]the seed[4690] should [aosb]come to whom the [pfip]promise had been made.[1861]

3 [I]Or, *with* [II]Or, *ending with*
4 [a]1Cor. 15:2
5 [I]Or, *works of power* [II]Or, *law* [III]Lit., *the hearing of faith* [a]2Cor. 9:10; Phil. 1:19 [b]1Cor. 12:10 [c]Rom. 10:17
6 [I]Lit., *Just as* [a]Rom. 4:3 [b]Gen. 15:6
7 [I]Lit., *know* [a]Rom. 4:16; Gal. 3:9 [b]Luke 19:9; Gal. 6:16
8 [I]Lit., *justifies* [II]Lit., *nations* [a]Gen. 12:3
9 [I]Lit., *the believing Abraham* [a]Gal. 3:7
10 [I]Or, *law* [a]Deut. 27:26
11 [I]Or, *in* [II]Or, *law* [III]Or, *But he who is righteous by faith shall live.* [a]Gal. 2:16 [b]Hab. 2:4; Rom. 1:17; Heb. 10:38
12 [I]Or, *And* [II]Or, *based on* [III]Or, *in* [a]Lev. 18:5; Rom. 10:5
13 [I]Or, *cross;* lit., *wood* [a]Gal. 4:5 [b]Deut. 21:23 [c]Acts 5:30
14 [I]Or, *occur* [a]Rom. 4:9, 16; Gal. 3:28 [b]Gal. 3:2 [c]Acts 2:33; Eph. 1:13
15 [I]Lit., *according to man* [II]Or, *will or testament* [III]Or, *a codicil* [a]Acts 1:15; Rom. 1:13; Gal. 6:18 [b]Rom. 3:5 [c]Heb. 6:16
16 [a]Luke 1:55; Rom. 4:13, 16; Rom. 9:4 [b]Acts 3:25
17 [a]Gen. 15:13f.; Ex. 12:40; Acts 7:6
18 [I]Lit., *out of, from* [a]Rom. 4:14 [b]Heb. 6:14
19 [I]Or, *for the sake of defining* [II]Lit., *hand* [a]Rom. 5:20 [b]Acts 7:53 [c]Ex. 20:19; Deut. 5:5 [d]Gal. 3:16

🔑 **3:11,12** See general remarks on justification on Romans and also Gal. 2:16.

🔑 **3:17** This verse speaks of the sojourning of the Israelites for 430 years in agreement with Ex. 12:40. Nevertheless, this presents an apparent contradiction with Gen. 15:13 which states that the sojourning of the Israelites was 400 years. Gen. 15:13 distinctly states that the sojourning of the seed of Abraham was to be "in a land that is not theirs . . . four hundred years," which was not necessarily Egypt, but included other lands, too. The Septuagint in Ex. 12:40 states, "the sojourning of the sons of Israel (which took place in the land of Egypt and in the land of Caanan), they and their fathers, were 430 years." In Gen. 17:8 and Ps. 105:11,12 we read that even in Caanan the Israelites were considered as strangers. For although Caanan was theirs by promise to be fulfilled in aftertimes, it was not immediately theirs by actual domination and possession.

20 Now [a]a mediator is not [I]for one *party only*; whereas God is *only* one.
21 Is the Law then contrary to the promises of God? [a]May it never be![1096] [3361] For [b]if a law had been [aop]given which was able[1410] to [ainf]impart life, then[3689] righteousness[1343] [I]would indeed have been [II]based on law.
22 But the Scripture has [ao] [a]shut up all [I]men under sin,[266] that the promise

20 [I]Lit., *of one* [a]1 Tim. 2:5; Heb. 8:6; Heb. 9:15; Heb. 12:24
21 [I]Or, *would indeed be* [II]Lit., *out of, from* [a]Luke 20:16; Gal. 2:17 [b]Gal. 2:21
22 [I]Lit., *things* [a]Rom. 11:32

3:22 Paul here says that "the Scripture has shut up all men under sin." He says the same thing in Rom. 3:23, "All have sinned. . . ." One of the greatest controversial issues in Christendom is the belief that if a believer commits sin, he ceases to be a child of God; then if he is to escape the misery of the lost, he must be saved over again. Gal. 3:22 and Rom. 3:23 state that such a person's former condition was not that of sinlessness but that of being a sinner. A Christian never becomes sinless, for sinlessness would be a complete and perfect accomplishment of all that God would want him to accomplish. To sin means to miss the mark, not the mark which one places for himself, but that which God places for each individual. There is not a single person on the face of this earth that could honestly say that every moment of his life of faith he has truly known what God's purpose in his life has been and that he has met in full God's expectation of him. In this respect, one must remember that even the sin of omission, not doing what one knows he ought to do, is sin according to James 4:17.

When a sinner believes, his sins are forgiven; he is justified, and henceforth, sin is not imputed to him (Rom. 4:8). From the moment he believes, he has two natures—the old as incorrigible as ever (Rom. 8:7), and the new which cannot sin. The old nature as viewed by God is forever set aside in the death of Christ. "Knowing this, that our old self was crucified with Him, that our body of sin might be done away with, that we should no longer be slaves to sin; for he who has died is freed (or justified) from sin" (Rom. 6:6,7). Therefore, the believer is to reckon himself "to be dead to sin, but alive to God in Christ Jesus" (Rom. 6:11). Thus, being made free from sin, sin is no more his master, and the believer becomes the servant of righteousness. But should the believer become unwatchful, i.e., fail to reckon himself dead, the old nature immediately manifests its presence by producing its evil feats—sins (*hamartēmata,* the plural of *hamartēma,* which refers to the act of sin as its product and not sinfulness in itself). See in the lexical aids *hamartēma* (265) as contrasted to *hamartia* (266), "sin, sinful nature," from which *hamartēma* springs. See also the same contrast existing between *skotia* (4653), "the consequence of darkness," and *skotos* (4655), "darkness" itself, or the nature of sin as used constantly in I John. See general remarks on I John.

The difficulty is the presumption by some that once someone is a child of God, he cannot commit sin. Such a presumption in itself is sin since only God is sinless. Truly a child of God ought not to commit sin, and especially willful sin, knowing it to be sin. Paul's constant argument is that although we know what we ought to do, yet we don't do it (Rom. 7:15,16). One fundamental truth, however, which ought to be borne in mind, is that the believer who performs acts displeasing to God, not habitually, but as digressions, has not ceased to be a child of God. Communion is interrupted and joy is lost, but the relationship remains untouched. God is still his Father, and the believer still His child. When the believer occasionally sins, he is like a naughty child, wayward, rebellious, disobedient, and he has done what a child ought not to have done—he has sinned. Morally, for the moment, he has allowed himself to sink to the world's level and the condition he was in when God lifted him up in grace and saved him for Christ's sake. His conduct has not been one that honors God, for he has allowed the flesh to act, which God has judged and set aside forever. There are two kinds of sins: the sins committed by those who have never been born again as part of their sinful nature, and the sins which are committed as transgressions (*paraptōma,* 3900) by those who have been born again. The believer sins as a child of God and not as a person totally unrelated to God. But is it not more grievous to sin as God's child than to sin as a sinner far from God? When the unsaved sins, it is as an enemy who is sinning against God. But when the believer sins as a child of God, he sins against the One who has shown him perfect grace, the One who loves him and has adopted him as His child. Would we treat our own child, who has willfully damaged our property, in the same manner that we would some young vandal who had done the same kind of mischief? No. As the parent, we would correct our child for his good; in the case of the other, as a citizen, we should refer him to justice for his good and the good of the community. The judgment brought upon our own child is the judgment of grace, and the judgment brought upon a stranger by the law is simply the application of the law. Thus, when a believer sins, he still remains a

(continued on next page)

by faith in Jesus Christ might be
[asbp]given to those who [ppt]believe.[4100]
23 But before faith [aip]came, we
were [ipf]kept in custody under the law,
[a]being [ppp]shut up to the faith[4102] which
was later to be [aifp]revealed.
24 Therefore the Law has [pfi]become
our [Ia]tutor[3807] *to lead us* to Christ,[5547]
that [b]we may be [asbp]justified[1344] by faith.
25 But now that faith has [apt]come,
we are no longer under a [Ia]tutor.
26 For you are all [a]sons[5207] of
God[2316] through faith in [b]Christ Jesus.
🔑 27 For all of you who were
[aop] [a]baptized[907] into Christ have
[aom] [b]clothed yourselves with Christ.
🔑 28 [a]There is neither Jew nor Greek,
there is neither slave[1401] nor free
man,[1658] there is [I]neither male[730] nor
female;[2338] for [b]you are all one in
[c]Christ Jesus.
29 And if [a]you [I]belong to Christ,
then you are Abraham's [II]offspring,[4690]
heirs[2818] according to [b]promise.[1860]

Sonship in Christ

4 Now I say, as long as the heir[2818]
is a [I]child,[3516] he does not differ at
all from[1308] a slave[1401] although he is
[II]owner[2962] of everything,
2 but he is under guardians and
[I]managers until the date set[4287] by the
father.[3962]
3 So also we, while we were children,[3516] were held [a]in bondage under
the [Ib]elemental things[4747] of the
world.[2889]
4 But when [a]the fulness[4138] of the

23 [a]Rom. 11:32
24 [I]Lit., *child-conductor* [a]1Cor. 4:15 [b]Gal. 2:16
25 [I]Lit., *child-conductor* [a]1Cor. 4:15
26 [a]Rom. 8:14; Gal. 4:5 [b]Rom. 8:1; Gal. 3:28; Gal. 4:14; Gal. 5:6, 24; Eph. 1:1; Phil. 1:1; Col. 1:4; 54:1:12; 2Tim. 1:1; Titus 1:4
27 [a]Matt. 28:19; Rom. 6:3; 1Cor. 10:2 [b]Rom. 13:14
28 [I]Lit., *not male and female* [a]Rom. 3:22; 1Cor. 12:13; Col. 3:11 [b]John 17:11; Eph. 2:15 [c]Rom. 8:1; Gal. 3:26; Gal. 4:14; Gal. 5:6, 24; Eph. 1:1; Phil. 1:1; Col. 1:4; 54:1:12; 2Tim. 1:1; Titus 1:4
29 [I]Lit., *are Christ's* [II]Lit., *seed* [a]Rom. 4:13; 1Cor. 3:23 [b]Rom. 9:8; Gal. 3:18; Gal. 4:28 **1** [I]Or, *minor* [II]Lit., *lord* **2** [I]Or, *stewards* **3** [I]Or, *rudimentary teachings or principles* [a]Gal. 2:4; Gal. 4:8f., 24f. [b]Gal. 4:9; Col. 2:8, 20; Heb. 5:12 **4** [a]Mark 1:15

(continued from previous page)
child of God but brings himself under the governmental dealings of God as a result. When the sin is confessed and there is true self-judgment, the believer is forgiven and and restored to communion. But even then he is often permitted to suffer the temporal consequences of his wrong-doing in bodily suffering, circumstances, or otherwise. It is true that God forgives us of our sins, but we must bear the consequences of our sins this is the emphasis of I John. John speaks of the believer not being in *skotos,* darkness which characterizes unbelief, but *skotia,* the consequence of his sin brought upon him by God Himself as the inexorable consequence of his willful sin. If self-judgment is lacking, most assuredly the disobedient believer will come under the chastening hand of God (Acts 5:1-16; I Cor. 11:28-32).

There is another category of people, however, which may be confused with the true believers who may sin in spite of the fact that they are the children of God. These are those who seem to have been saved and to have been the children of God but who have reverted to the world and remain there. These simply belong to the class spoken of in Mt. 13:5-7 and Lk. 8:12-14. For instance Lk. 8:13, "who, when they hear, receive the word with joy; and these have no firm root; they believe for a while, and in time of temptation fall away." The word "believe" should not be confused here as the exercise of true faith in Jesus Christ which transforms a person from a confirmed sinner to a sanctified sinner, saved by the grace of God (see Jn. 2:23,24; 8:31,32). The belief of these people is merely an intellectual assent. It is not a repentant belief which justifies them before God and causes them to be made righteous and to hate sin (Rom. 5:19). These who have no deep roots are the ones who profess faith but who do not possess Christ. Peter refers to the same class in II Pet. 2:19-22 when he says, "It has happened to them according to the true proverb, 'A dog returns to its own vomit,' and, 'A sow (pig), after washing, returns to the wallowing in the mire." Those who merely profess faith are compared here to the dog and the pig, but not to the sheep which is used to designate the true Christian (Jn. 10). The dog illustrates one who, through the action of the Word of God, gives up what his evil flesh formerly fed upon, turns from it for a time, only to return and devour the evil again. Scripture bids us to beware of dogs whose portion is without the city (Phil. 3:2; Rev. 22:15). The pig represents one externally washed, who reforms outwardly, but has never been born again. A sheep receives eternal life, and shall never perish (Jn. 3:15,16; 10:28). It is possible that for a time there may appear to be a great change in any particular person, but that change then disappears, an evidence that there has been no change of nature or disposition. A pig may be washed, but its unclean nature still remains.

🔑 **3:27** See note on I Cor. 10:2.

🔑 **3:28** See notes on I Cor. 11:2-16; 14:33-40; I Tim. 2:9-15.

time [ao]came,[2064] God[2316] sent forth His
Son,[5207] [b]born of a woman, born [c]un-
der [I]the Law,[3551]
5 in order that He might [aosb]re-
deem[1805] those who were under [I]the
Law, that we might [aosb]receive[618] the
adoption as [a]sons.[5206]
6 And because you are sons,
[a]God has [ao]sent forth the Spirit[4151] of
His Son into our hearts,[2588] crying,
"[b]Abba![5] Father!"[3962]
7 Therefore you are no longer a
slave, but a son; and [a]if a son, then an
heir[2818] [I]through God.
8 However[235] at that time, [a]when
you did not know God,[2316] you were
[b]slaves to [c]those which by nature are
no gods.[2316]
9 But now that you have come to
know God, or rather to be [apt] [a]known[1097]
by God, [b]how is it that you turn back
again to the weak[772] and worthless
[Ic]elemental things,[4747] to which you
desire to be [ainf]enslaved[1398] all over
again?[3825]
10 You [a]observe[3906] days and
months and seasons[2540] and years.
11 I fear[5399] for you, that perhaps
I have [pfi]labored [I]over you in vain.
12 I beg of you, [a]brethren,[80]
[pim] [b]become as I *am*, for I also *have become* as you *are*. You have [ao]done me
no wrong;
13 but you know[1492] that it was because of a [I]bodily illness that I preached
the gospel[2097] to you the [II]first time;
14 and that which was a [I]trial[3986] to
you in my [II]bodily condition[4561] you did
not despise or [III]loathe, but [a]you received me as an angel[32] of God, as
[b]Christ Jesus *Himself*.
15 Where then is [I]that sense of
blessing you had? For I bear you witness, that if possible, you would have
[apt]plucked out your eyes and [ao]given
them to me.
16 Have I therefore [pfi]become your
enemy [a]by [ppt] [I]telling you the truth?[226]
17 They eagerly seek[2206] you, not
commendably, but they wish to [ainf]shut
you out, in order that you may [psa]seek
them.
18 But it is good always to be eagerly [pip]sought in a commendable manner, and [a]not only when I am present
with you.
19 [a]My children, with whom [b]I am
again in labor[5605] until [c]Christ[5547] is
[asbp]formed[3445] in you—
20 but I could wish to be present
with you now and to change[236] my tone,
for [a]I am perplexed about you.

Bond and Free

21 [pim]Tell me, you who [ppt]want to
be under law,[3551] do you not [a]listen to
the law?
22 For it is written that Abraham
had two sons,[5207] [a]one by the bondwoman and [b]one by the free woman.
23 But [a]the son by the bondwoman
was [pfip]born according to the flesh,[4561]
and [b]the son by the free woman through
the promise.[1860]
24 [Ia]This is allegorically[238] speaking:
for these *women* are two covenants,[1242]
one *proceeding* from [b]Mount Sinai
[ppt]bearing children[1080] [II]who are to be
[c]slaves;[1397] [III]she is Hagar.
25 Now this Hagar is Mount Sinai
in Arabia, and corresponds to the present Jerusalem, for she is in slavery[1398]
with her children.
26 But [a]the Jerusalem above[507] is
free; [I]she is our mother.
27 For it is written,
"[aipp] [a]REJOICE,[2165] BARREN
WOMAN WHO DOES NOT
[ppt]BEAR;
[aim]BREAK FORTH AND [aim]SHOUT,
YOU WHO ARE not IN
LABOR;[5605]
FOR MORE ARE THE CHILDREN
OF THE DESOLATE
THAN OF THE ONE WHO HAS A
HUSBAND."
28 And you brethren, [a]like Isaac,
are [b]children[5043] of promise.[1860]
29 But as at that time [a]he who was
[aptp]born according to the flesh [ipf] [b]perse-

4 [I]Or, *law* [b]John 1:14; Rom. 1:3; Rom. 8:3; Phil. 2:7 [c]Luke 2:21f., 27
5 [I]Or, *law* [a]Rom. 8:14; Gal. 3:26
6 [a]Acts 16:7; Rom. 5:5; Rom. 8:9, 16; 2Cor. 3:17 [b]Mark 14:36; Rom. 8:15
7 [I]I.e., through the gracious act of [a]Rom. 8:17
8 [a]1Cor. 1:21; Eph. 2:12; 1Thess. 4:5; 2Thess. 1:8 [b]Gal. 4:3 [c]2Chr. 13:9; Is. 37:19; Jer. 2:11; 1Cor. 8:4f.; 1Cor. 10:20
9 [I]Or, *rudimentary teachings or principles* [a]1Cor. 8:3 [b]Col. 2:20 [c]Gal. 4:3
10 [a]Rom. 14:5; Col. 2:16
11 [I]Or, *for*
12 [a]Gal. 6:18 [b]2Cor. 6:11, 13
13 [I]Lit., *weakness of the flesh* [II]Or, *former*
14 [I]Or, *temptation* [II]Lit., *flesh* [III]Lit., *spit out at* [a]Matt. 10:40; 1Thess. 2:13 [b]Gal. 3:26
15 [I]Lit., *the congratulation of yourselves*
16 [I]Or, *dealing truthfully with you* [a]Amos 5:10
18 [a]Gal. 4:13f.
19 [a]143:2:1 [b]1Cor. 4:15 [c]Eph. 4:13
20 [a]2Cor. 4:8
21 [a]Luke 16:29
22 [a]Gen. 16:15 [b]Gen. 21:2
23 [a]Rom. 9:7; Gal. 4:29 [b]Gen. 17:16ff.; Gen. 18:10ff.; Gen. 21:1; Gal. 4:28; Heb. 11:11
24 [I]Lit., *Which* [II]Lit., *into slavery* [III]Lit., *which* [a]1Cor. 10:11 [b]Deut. 33:2 [c]Gal. 4:3
26 [I]Lit., *which* [a]Heb. 12:22; Rev. 3:12; Rev. 21:2, 10
27 [a]Is. 54:1
28 [a]Gal. 4:23 [b]Rom. 9:7ff.; Gal. 3:29
29 [a]Gal. 4:23 [b]Gen. 21:9

cuted him *who was born* according to
the Spirit, [c]so it is now also.
30 But what does the Scripture[1124]
say?

"[a]CAST OUT THE BONDWOMAN
AND HER SON,
FOR [b]THE SON OF THE
BONDWOMAN SHALL NOT BE
AN HEIR[2816] WITH THE SON
OF THE FREE WOMAN."

31 So then, brethren, we are not
children[5043] of a bondwoman, [I]but of the
free woman.

Walk by the Spirit

5 [Ia]It was for freedom[1657] that
Christ[5547] [ao]set us free; therefore
[b]keep [pim]standing firm and do not be
[pim]subject again to a [c]yoke of slavery.[1397]
2 Behold I, [a]Paul, say to you that
if you [psmp]receive [b]circumcision,[4059]
Christ will be of no benefit to you.
3 And I [a]testify[3143] again to every
man who [ppp]receives [b]circumcision, that
he is under obligation[3781] to [c]keep the
whole Law.[3551]
🔑 4 You have been [aop]severed from
Christ, you who [I]are seeking to be
justified[1344] by law; you have [ao][a]fallen
from grace.[5485]
5 For we through the Spirit, by
faith,[4102] are [a]waiting for[553] the hope[1680]
of righteousness.[1343]
🔑 6 For in [a]Christ Jesus [b]neither
circumcision[4061] nor uncircumcision[203]
means[2480] anything, but [c]faith[4102]
[ppt]working[1754] through love.[26]
7 You were [ipf][a]running well; who
hindered you from [pip]obeying[3982] the
truth?[225]
8 This persuasion *did* not *come* from
[a]Him who [ppt]calls you.
9 [a]A little leaven[2219] leavens[2220] the
whole lump *of dough.*
10 [a]I have confidence[3982] [I]in you in
the Lord, that you [b]will adopt no other
view; but the one who is [ppt] [c]disturbing
you shall bear his judgment,[2917] whoever
he is.
11 But I, brethren, if I still
preach[2784] circumcision, why am I still
[a]persecuted? Then [b]the stumbling

29 [c]Gal. 5:11
30 [a]Gen. 21:10, 12 [b]John 8:35
31 [I]V. 5:1, note I

1 [I]Some authorities prefer to join with 4:31 and render *but with the freedom of the free woman Christ set us free* [a]John 8:32, 36; Rom. 8:15; 2Cor. 3:17; Gal. 2:4; Gal. 5:13 [b]1Cor. 16:13 [c]Acts 15:10; Gal. 2:4
2 [a]2Cor. 10:1 [b]Acts 15:1; Gal. 5:3, 6, 11
3 [a]Luke 16:28 [b]Acts 15:1; Gal. 5:2, 6, 11 [c]Rom. 2:25
4 [I]Or, *would; be* [a]Heb. 12:15; 2Pet. 3:17
5 [a]Rom. 8:23; 1Cor. 1:7
6 [a]Gal. 3:26 [b]1Cor. 7:19; Gal. 6:15 [c]Col. 1:4f.; 1Thess. 1:3; James 2:18, 20, 22
7 [a]Gal. 2:2
8 [a]Rom. 8:28; Gal. 1:6
9 [a]1Cor. 5:6
10 [I]Lit., *toward*

[a]2Cor. 2:3 [b]Gal. 5:7; Phil. 3:15 [c]Gal. 1:7; Gal. 5:12
11 [a]Gal. 4:29; Gal. 6:12 [b]Rom. 9:33; 1Cor. 1:23

🔑 **5:4** See general remarks on justification in Romans. This text is often misused as teaching that one can fall from God's saving grace. The passage must be read in its total context. In v. 1 Paul is speaking about the freedom that the believer has in Christ Jesus. In v. 2 he says that if a person trusts in the ordinance of circumcision as more important than trusting in Christ, then Christ would be of none effect. In v. 3 he tells the Galatians that if one is forced to keep one part of the law, he must keep all of it, and this is impossible. Then in v. 4 he speaks about those who justify themselves in or by means of the law or through the law. Naturally, if they believe in justification in or through the law, they will have no room for Jesus Christ and His grace. The exact translation of this verse is "You were rendered useless as far as Christ is concerned." In other words, you were cut off from Christ (*katēgēthēte* from *katargeō,* 2673), not that you belonged to Him at any time; you were never His. Believing that the law was enough to justify you, you never allowed yourself to participate in grace.

The second part of the verse says, "You who are seeking to be justified by law." This can refer to the law of Moses or any other law. Your presumed justification depends, Paul says, on keeping a particular law or set of rules, and you are justified by and before that law. But this does not mean that you are justified before God, because His justification requires the standard set by Him, in and through Christ.

And then the third sentence which Paul gives is "you have fallen from grace." The verb translated "have fallen" is *exepesate,* the aorist of *ekpiptō* (1601), from *ek* (1537), "from," and *piptō* (4098), which means "to fall off." It does not mean that you lost the grace of God that was yours at one time, but that you are off the path of grace since you chose justification by law instead of justification by grace. The two steps, justification in and through the law and justification in and through grace, are two parallel lines that never meet. To be justified by both law and grace is impossible. Grace has a law entitled in it, but the law has no grace. This expression actually means that you could not be justified by grace since you sought your justification in or through the law or set of rules.

🔑 **5:6** See note on Gal. 2:16.

block[4625] of the cross[4716] has been [pfip]abolished.

12 Would that [a]those who are [ppt]troubling[387] you would even [Ib]mutilate themselves.

13 For you were [aosb]called to [a]freedom,[1657] brethren; [b]only *do* not *turn* your freedom into an opportunity for the flesh,[4561] but through love [pim c]serve[1398] one another.

14 For [a]the whole Law is [pfip]fulfilled in one word,[3056] in the *statement,* "[b]YOU SHALL LOVE[25] YOUR NEIGHBOR AS YOURSELF."

15 But if you [a]bite and devour one another, [pim]take care lest you be [asbp]consumed by one another.

16 But I say, [pim a]walk[4043] by the Spirit,[4151] and you will not [efn]carry out[5055] [b]the desire[1939] of the flesh.[4561]

17 For [a]the flesh [I]sets its desire[1937] against the Spirit, and the Spirit against the flesh; for these are in opposition to one another, [b]so that you [psa]may not do the things that you [psa II]please.

18 But if you are [pinp a]led[71] by the Spirit, [b]you are not under the Law.

19 Now the deeds[2041] of the flesh are evident,[5318] which are: [Ia]immorality,[4202] impurity,[167] sensuality,[766]

20 idolatry,[1495] [a]sorcery, enmities, [pl b]strife,[2054] jealousy,[2205] outbursts of anger,[2372] [c]disputes, dissensions,[1370] [Id]factions,[139]

21 envying, [pl a]drunkenness,[3178] carousing,[2970] and things like[3664] these, of which I [pin]forewarn you just as I have [ao]forewarned you that those who [ppt]practice[4238] such things shall not [b]inherit[2816] the kingdom[932] of God.

22 But [a]the fruit of the Spirit is [b]love,[26] joy,[5479] peace,[1515] patience, kindness,[5544] goodness,[19] faithfulness,

23 gentleness, [a]self-control; against such things [b]there is no law.

24 Now those who [I]belong to [a]Christ Jesus have [ao b]crucified[4717] the flesh[4561] with its passions[3804] and [c]desires.

25 If we live[2198] by the Spirit, let us also [psa I]walk [a]by the Spirit.

26 Let us not [psa]become [a]boastful, [ppt]challenging one another, [ppt]envying one another.

Bear One Another's Burdens

6 [a]Brethren, even if a man[444] is [asbp]caught[4301] in any trespass,[3900] you who are [b]spiritual, [pim c]restore[2675] such a one [d]in a spirit[4151] of gentleness; *each one* [ppt]looking to[4648] yourself, lest you too be [asbp]tempted.[3985]

2 [a pim]Bear one another's burdens, and thus [ft]fulfill[378] [b]the law[3551] of Christ.

3 For [a]if anyone thinks he is something when he is nothing,[3367] he deceives himself.

4 But let each one [pim a]examine his own work,[2341] and then he will have *reason for* [b]boasting in regard to himself alone, and not in regard to another.[2087]

5 For [a]each one shall bear his own load.[5413]

6 And [a]let the one who is [ppp]taught[2227] [b]the word[3056] [pim]share[2841] all good things[18] with him who [ppt]teaches.[2727]

7 [a]Do not be [pim]deceived, [b]God[2316] is not mocked; for [c]whatever a man[444] [psa]sows, this he will also reap.

8 [a]For the one who [ppt]sows to his own flesh[4561] shall from the flesh reap [b]corruption,[5356] but [c]the one who sows to the Spirit shall from the Spirit reap eternal[166] life.[2222]

9 And [a]let us not [psa]lose heart[1573] in [ppt]doing[4160] good,[2570] for in due[2398] time[2540] we shall reap if we [b]do not [psa]grow weary.[1590]

10 So then, [Ia]while we have opportunity,[2540] let us [psa]do[2038] good[18] to all men, and especially to those who are of the [b]household[3609] of [c]the faith.[4102]

11 See with what large letters[1121] I [I]am writing[1125] to you [a]with my own hand.

---

12 [I]Or, *cut themselves off* [a]Gal. 2:4; Gal. 5:10 [b]Deut. 23:1
13 [a]Gal. 5:1 [b]1Cor. 8:9; 2:16 [c]1Cor. 9:19; Eph. 5:21
14 [a]Matt. 7:12; Matt. 22:40; Rom. 13:8, 10; Gal. 6:2 [b]Lev. 19:18; Matt. 19:19; John 13:34
15 [a]Gal. 5:20; Phil. 3:2
16 [a]Rom. 8:4; Rom. 13:14; Gal. 5:24f. [b]Rom. 13:14; Eph. 2:3
17 [I]Lit., *lusts against* [II]Lit., *wish* [a]Rom. 7:18, 23; Rom. 8:5ff. [b]Rom. 7:15ff.
18 [a]Rom. 8:14 [b]Rom. 6:14; Rom. 7:4; 1Tim. 1:9
19 [I]I.e., sexual immorality [a]1Cor. 6:9, 18; 2Cor. 12:21
20 [I]Or, *heresies* [a]Rev. 21:8 [b]2Cor. 12:20 [c]Rom. 2:8; James 3:14ff. [d]1Cor. 11:19
21 [a]Rom. 13:13 [b]1Cor. 6:9
22 [a]Matt. 7:16ff.; Eph. 5:9 [b]Rom. 5:1-5; 1Cor. 13:4; Col. 3:12-15
23 [a]Acts 24:25 [b]Gal. 5:18
24 [I]Lit. *are of Christ Jesus* [a]Gal. 3:26 [b]Rom. 6:6; Gal. 2:20; Gal. 6:14 [c]Gal. 5:16f.
25 [I]Or, *follow the Spirit* [a]Gal. 5:16
26 [a]Phil. 2:3

1 [a]Gal. 6:18; 1Thess. 4:1 [b]1Cor. 2:15 [c]2Cor. 2:7; 2Thess. 3:15; Heb. 12:13; James 5:19f. [d]1Cor. 4:21
2 [a]Rom. 15:1 [b]Rom. 8:2; 1Cor. 9:21; James 1:25; James 2:12; 2Pet. 3:2
3 [a]Acts 5:36; 1Cor. 3:18; 2Cor. 12:11
4 [a]1Cor. 11:28 [b]Phil. 1:26
5 [a]Prov. 9:12; Rom. 14:12; 1Cor. 3:8
6 [a]1Cor. 9:11, 14 [b]2Tim. 4:2
7 [a]1Cor. 6:9 [b]Job 13:9 [c]2Cor. 9:6
8 [a]Job 4:8; Hos. 8:7; Rom. 6:21 [b]1Cor. 15:42 [c]Rom. 8:11; James 3:18
9 [a]1Cor. 15:58; 2Cor. 4:1 [b]Matt. 10:22; Heb. 12:3, 5; James 5:7f.
10 [I]Or, *as* [a]Prov. 3:27; John 12:35 [b]Eph. 2:19; Heb. 3:6; 2:5; 4:17 [c]Acts 6:7; Gal. 1:23
11 [I]Or, *have written* [a]1Cor. 16:21

12 Those who desire [a]to [ainf]make a
good showing[2146] in the flesh[4561] try to
[b]compel you to be [pip]circumcised,[4059]
simply that they [c]may not be [psmp]perse-
cuted [I]for the cross[4716] of Christ.
13 For those who [I]are [ppp]circum-
cised do not even [a]keep[5442] [II]the Law[3551]
themselves, but they desire to have you
[pip]circumcised, that they may [aosb] [b]boast
in your flesh.
14 But [a]may it never be[1096 3361] that I
should [pinf]boast, [b]except in the cross of
our Lord Jesus Christ, [c]through [I]which
the world[2889] has been [pfip]crucified[4717]
to me, and [d]I to the world.
15 For [a]neither is circumcision[4061]
anything, nor uncircumcision,[203] but a
[b]new[2537] [I]creation.[2937]
16 And those who will [I]walk by this
rule, peace[1515] and mercy[1656] *be* upon
them, and upon the [a]Israel of God.
17 From now on let no one [pim]cause
trouble for me, for I bear on my body[4983]
the [a]brand-marks of Jesus.
18 [a]The grace[5485] of our Lord Jesus
Christ be [b]with your spirit, [c]brethren.
Amen.[281]

12 [I]Or, *because of* [a]Matt. 23:27f. [b]Acts 15:1 [c]Gal. 5:11
13 [I]Some ancient mss. *read have been* [II]Or, *law* [a]Rom. 2:25 [b]Phil. 3:3
14 [I]Or, *whom* [a]Luke 20:16; Gal. 2:17; Gal. 3:21 [b]1Cor. 2:2 [c]Gal. 2:20; Col. 2:20 [d]Rom. 6:2, 6; Gal. 2:19f.; Gal. 5:24
15 [I]Or, *creature* [a]Rom. 2:26, 28; 1Cor. 7:19; Gal. 5:6 [b]2Cor. 5:17; Eph. 2:10, 15; Eph. 4:24; Col. 3:10
16 [I]Or, *follow this rule* [a]Rom. 9:6; Gal. 3:7, 29; Phil. 3:3
17 [a]Is. 44:5; Ezek. 9:4; 2Cor. 4:10; 2Cor. 11:23; Rev. 13:16 **18** [a]Rom. 16:20 [b]2Tim. 4:22 [c]Acts 1:15; Rom. 1:13; Gal. 3:15; Gal. 4:12, 28, 31

6:17 See note on II Tim. 1:12.

The Epistle of Paul to the

EPHESIANS

Ephesus was the capital of pro-consular Asia. It was about one mile inland from the eastern portion of the Aegean Sea. A great theater, seating about 50,000 people, was located there (see Acts 19:31). Also, one of the seven wonders of the world, the temple of Diana (Artemis), was located in Ephesus. Next to Jerusalem and Antioch, Ephesus proved to be a very powerful springboard for influencing the world for Christ.

Paul visited Ephesus during his second missionary journey (Acts 18:18-21). He left Aquila and Priscilla (Prisca) there to help them. He spent three years in Ephesus on his third tour (Acts 19). He exerted so much influence there that the idol-makers became worried and incited a riot against him. He had to leave for Macedonia (Acts 20:1). Upon his return trip, heading for Jerusalem, he asked the elders of the Ephesian congregation to meet with him at Miletus, thirty-five miles to the north, on a quick stopover (Acts 20:16-38).

Ephesians is one of Paul's five "Prison Epistles," probably written while in prison in Rome from about A.D. 60 to A.D. 64. Ephesians, Colossians, and Philemon were written and sent about the same time. Paul's letter to the Laodiceans (Col. 4:16) did not survive. This Ephesian letter was addressed to the congregation in Ephesus (see Acts 19), but was also probably intended as a circulating letter to other area churches. This may account for the absence of specific information in the letter. Also, there is a textual problem in Eph. 1:1. The words "at Ephesus" are absent from several important manuscripts.

Ephesians is quite similar to Colossians. There are seventy-eight verses between them which are almost the same. Each is devoted half to doctrine and half to practical Christian duty. Colossians portrays Christ as the head of the Church, but Ephesians goes further to display Jesus as the ascended, glorified Christ. In Colossians Paul is within the throes of fighting against a serious heresy, but in Ephesians Paul is relishing the grandeur of Christ in quiet meditation.

Paul's letter to the Ephesians is truly profound. The major theme of Ephesians is that the Church (*ekklesia*) is the mystical body of Christ; God's great master plan was to bring everything together (Eph. 1:10) under Christ as head (Eph. 1:22,23); we, as the body of Christ on earth, have a part in this plan and the Holy Spirit is the guarantee of God's promise (Eph. 1:13,14).

"There is one body" (Eph. 4:4), not two. Paul emphasizes the unity of the Church. Jews and Gentiles are now one in Christ. Gentiles could become Christians without first becoming Jewish converts (proselytes). But many Jewish Christians, who had always been prejudiced against the pagan Gentiles, thought that Gentiles should not presume to call themselves followers of the Messiah unless they were first circumcised and obedient to the Law of Moses. In other words, the Jewish believers tended to see themselves at the center of God's plan of salvation instead of seeing the centrality of Christ. However, Paul taught that they should view the Gentiles as their brothers in Christ, on an equal footing. Jesus soars high above all cultural barriers. The large gift from Gentile congregations offered to Jewish brethren in need in Judea (Acts 24:17,18; Rom. 15:25-28; II Cor. 8:1-15; Gal. 2:10) bound the Jews and Gentiles together more closely and promoted a better feeling among them. Christ is sovereign over all races, divergent positions, cultures, problems of humanity (social and family life, see Eph. 5:22—6:9), and even the unseen beings (Eph. 3:10).

Paul used several figures of speech to explain the relationship between Christ and the Church. The Church is like a body with Christ as head (Eph. 1:22,23; 2:15,16); the Church is like a building with Christ as the cornerstone (Eph. 2:20-22); the Church is like a wife with Christ as the husband (Eph. 5:21-33).

God's chosen people have been set free from sin by Jesus, and they must live consistently with the oneness which is in Christ.

The Blessings of Redemption

1 Paul, [a]an apostle[652] of [b]Christ Jesus
[I][c]by the will[2307] of God,[2316] to the
[II][d]saints[40] who are [III]at [e]Ephesus, and
[f]*who are* faithful[4103] in [b]Christ Jesus:
2 [a]Grace[5485] to you and peace[1515]
from God our Father[3962] and the
[an]Lord[2962] Jesus Christ.[5547]

1 [I]Lit., *through* [II]Or, *holy ones* [III]Some ancient mss. do not contain *at Ephesus* [a]2Cor. 1:1 [b]Rom. 8:1 [c]1Cor. 1:1 [d]Acts 9:13 [e]Acts 18:19 [f]Col. 1:2
2 [a]Rom. 1:7

3 [a]Blessed[2128] *be* the God and Father of our Lord Jesus Christ, who has
[apt]blessed us with every spiritual[4152]
blessing[2129] in [b]the heavenly *places* in
Christ,
4 just as [a]He [ao]chose us in Him

3 [a]2Cor. 1:3 [b]Eph. 1:20; 2:6; 3:10; 6:12 4 [a]Eph. 2:10; 2Thess. 2:13f.

1:4,5 There are two verbs in this passage that introduce to us the much debated subject of God's election. One is in v. 4, "He chose us." In Greek it is the aorist of *eklegōmai* (1586) which means "to select or choose out of." From this verb, we have the noun *eklogē* (1589) which means "choice or election." We also have the adjectival noun *eklektos* (1588), "chosen out." The verb *exelexato* is in the aorist which means that at one particular time in the past, God chose us in Him before the foundation of the world, that we should be holy and without blame before Him in love. It is in the middle voice which means this was His own decision.

The second verb that addresses itself to the subject of God's election of the believer is in v. 5, *proorisas,* from *proorizō* (4309) made up of the preposition *pro* (4253), "before," and *horizō* (3724), "to determine." The compound verb means to determine or decree beforehand or to predestinate. This is the same verb used in Rom. 8:29 and translated "predestined." See Mt. 24:22,31: Lk. 18:7; Acts 4:28; Rom. 8:29,33; 9:11; Eph. 3:11; II Tim. 2:10; Js. 2:5; I Pet. 1:2,20.

In the Bible there is set forth on the one hand the sovereignty of God, and on the other, man's free choice and hence responsibility.

Peter, in speaking of Christ on the day of Pentecost, said, "This *Man,* delivered up by the predetermined plan and foreknowledge of God, you nailed to a cross by the hands of godless men and put *Him* to death" (Acts 2:23). Here in one verse we have the two principles brought together: the sovereign purpose of God in the delivering up of Christ so that men might be blessed, and human choice and responsibility in crucifying the "Prince of Life" on the other.

The perplexing question which arises is "Can a man know that he is one of the elect?"

A careful reading of the Epistle to the Romans will throw much light on the subject. There is not a word about election until we are more than halfway through the eighth chapter. The reason is clear because, until we know we are children of God and free from condemnation (Rom. 8:1-17), we are neither in the right position nor condition to receive the truth.

In the early chapters of Romans, we have described man's ruined condition and his standing before God as a guilty sinner. Then follows the sinner's justification by faith without works through the finished work of Christ, the way in which the believer is freed from the mastery of sin and delivered from the law. The result is that there is "no condemnation," the spirit bearing witness that "we are children of God" (Rom. 8:16).

It is then, and not until then, that the believer learns that he has been predestinated and is one of the elect. Then it is stated that, as believers, "we know that God causes all things to work together for good to those who love God, to those who are called according to *His* purpose. For whom He foreknew, He also predestined *to become* conformed to the image of His Son, that he might be the first-born among many brethren; and whom He predestined, these He also called; and whom He called, these He also justified; and whom He justified, these He also glorified" (Rom 8:28-30).

The person who may find himself described in the third chapter of Romans is a sinner under condemnation who stands in need of justification by faith in Christ as his Saviour, "for all have sinned and fall short of the glory of God" (Rom. 3:23). He does not know, nor is it any concern of his, whether he is one of the elect or not. No one who desires the peace of God is refused it. If one, however, finds himself described in the eighth chapter of Romans and is already a believer, he knows that he is an elect child of God and that he has been predestinated unto salvation.

The important point is that no one who is saved can say that he is saved because of his own choice of God. His salvation is in response to God's choice of him. And, on the other hand, no one who is lost can say that he is lost because God willed him to be lost.

A very helpful illustration may be derived from family life: A stranger is denied a share in the little

(continued on next page)

before [b]the foundation of the world,[2889]
that we should be [c]holy[40] and blameless[299] before [I]Him. [d]In love
5 [I]He [apt] [a]predestined[4309] us to
[b]adoption as sons[5206] through Jesus
Christ to Himself, [c]according to the
[II]kind intention of His will,[2307]
🔑 6 [a]to the praise of the glory[1391] of
His grace,[5485] which He freely [ao]be-
stowed on[5487] us in [b]the Beloved.[25]
7 [a]In [I]Him we have [b]redemption[629]
[c]through His blood,[129] the [d]forgive-
ness[859] of our trespasses,[3900] according
to [e]the riches of His grace,[5485]
8 which He [ao] [I]lavished upon [II]us. In
all wisdom[4678] and insight[5428]
9 He [Ia]made [apt]known to us the
mystery[3466] of His will,[2307] [b]according
to His [II]kind intention[2107] which He
[aom] [c]purposed[4388] in Him
10 with a view to an administra-
tion[3622] [I]suitable to [a]the fulness[4138]
of the times,[2540] *that is,* [b]the [ainf]sum-
ming up[346] of all things in Christ,[5547]
things [II]in the heavens[3772] and things
upon the earth.[1093] In Him
🔑 11 [I]also we [IIa]have [aop]obtained an inheritance,[2820] having been [aptp] [b]predes-
tined[4309] [c]according to His purpose[4286]
who [ppt]works[1754] all things [d]after the
counsel[1012] of His will,
12 to the end that we who were
the first to hope in [I]Christ should be
[a]to the praise[1868] of His glory.[1391]

4 [I]Or, *Him, in love.* [b]Matt. 25:34 [c]Eph. 5:27; Col. 1:22 [d]Eph. 4:2, 15, 16; 5:2
5 [I]Lit., *having predestined* [II]Lit., *good pleasure* [a]Acts 13:48; Rom. 8:29f. [b]Rom. 8:14ff. [c]Phil. 2:13; Col. 1:19
6 [a]Eph. 1:12, 14 [b]Matt. 3:17
7 [I]Lit., *whom* [a]Col. 1:14 [b]Rom. 3:24; 1Cor. 1:30; Eph. 1:14 [c]Acts 20:28; Rom. 3:25 [d]Acts 2:38 [e]Rom. 2:4; Eph. 1:8; 2:7; 3:8, 16
8 [I]Lit., *made abundant toward* [II]Or, *us, in all wisdom and insight*
9 [I]Lit., *making known* [II]Lit., *good pleasure* [a]Rom. 11:25; Eph. 3:3 [b]1Cor. 1:21; Gal. 1:15 [c]Rom. 8:28; Eph. 1:11
10 [I]Lit., *of* [II]Lit., *upon* [a]Mark 1:15 [b]Eph. 3:15; Phil. 2:9f.; Col. 1:16, 20
11 [I]Lit., *in whom also* [II]Or, *were made a heritage* [a]Deut. 4:20; Eph. 1:14; Titus 2:14 [b]Eph. 1:5 [c]Rom. 8:28f., Eph. 3:11 [d]Rom. 9:11; Heb. 6:17

13 In [I]Him, you also, after [apt]listen-
ing to [a]the message[3056] of truth,[225]
the gospel[2098] of your salvation—[4991]
having also [apt] [II]believed,[4100] you were
[aop] [b]sealed[4972] in [I]Him with [c]the Holy[40]
Spirit[4151] of promise,[1860]
14 who is [Ia]given as a pledge[728]
of [b]our inheritance,[2817] with a view
to the [c]redemption[629] of [d]*God's own*
possession, [e]to the praise of His
glory.
15 For this reason I too, [a]having
heard of the faith[4102] in the Lord[2962]
Jesus which *exists* among you, and [I]your
love[26] for [b]all the [II]saints,[40]
16 [a]do not cease [ppt]giving thanks[2168]
for you, [b]while [ppt]making mention *of you*
in my prayers;[4335]
17 that the [a]God of our Lord Jesus
Christ, [b]the Father[3962] of glory, may give
to you a spirit[4151] of [c]wisdom[4678] and
of [d]revelation[602] in the [I]knowledge[1922]
of Him.
18 *I pray that* [a]the eyes of your
heart[2588] [I]may be [pfpp]enlightened,[5461] so
that you may know what is the [b]hope[1680]

12 [I]I.e., the Messiah [a]Eph. 1:6, 14 **13** [I]Lit., *whom* [II]Or, *believed in Him, you were sealed* [a]Eph. 4:21; Col. 1:5 [b]Eph. 4:30 [c]Acts 2:33 **14** [I]Or, *a down payment* [a]2Cor. 1:22 [b]Acts 20:32 [c]Eph. 1:7 [d]Eph. 1:11 [e]Eph. 1:6, 12 **15** [I]Many ancient mss. do not contain *your love* [II]V. 1, note 2 [a]Col. 1:4; Philem. 5 [b]Eph. 1:1; 3:18 **16** [a]Rom. 1:8f.; Col. 1:9 [b]Rom. 1:9 **17** [I]Or, *true knowledge* [a]John 20:17; Rom. 15:6 [b]Acts 7:2; 1Cor. 2:8 [c]Col. 1:9 [d]1Cor. 14:6 **18** [I]Lit., *being* [a]Acts 26:18; 2Cor. 4:6; Heb. 6:4 [b]Eph. 4:4

(continued from previous page)
familiarities and secrets of a family. No one in the family is willing to take him into the delightful confidence of its innermost secrets. In the same manner, the unregenerate are excluded from the sweet, inner experiences and knowledge of the secrets of God which He entrusts to the members of His household. Ps. 25:14 declares that "the secret of the Lord is for those who fear Him, and He will make them know His covenant." Truly, therefore, the doctrine of election is a family secret, and only the children of God know it and have the capacity of grasping or understanding the deep things of God. I Cor. 2:14 states, "But a natural man does not accept the things of the Spirit of God; for they are foolishness to him, and he cannot understand them, because they are spiritually appraised."

Christ died for all. It does not mean only some, and while this truth is clearly revealed, nowhere does it say that His sacrifice was a substitute for all. I Jn. 2:2 states, "And he himself is the propitiation for our sins; (i.e., believers) and not for ours only, but also for those of the whole world." It is to be noted that the expression "the sins of" in the translation is not in the Greek text. Therefore, the Gospel is preached to all, and over and over again God says that whosoever believeth in Him (that means anybody) shall receive everlasting life (Jn. 3:16; Acts 10:43; 13:38,39). The Gospel invitation is for all, and therefore all who hear are responsible and without excuse. Thus, if one perishes in his sin, he will be lost, because he himself chose to be condemned (Tit 3:10,11) and not because God willed it so.

🔑 **1;6** See note on Heb. 6:1-6.

🔑 **1:11** See note on II Tim. 1:9.

of His [c]calling,[2821] what are [d]the riches
of the glory[1391] of [e]His inheritance in
[f]the [II]saints,
19 and what is the surpassing greatness of His power[1411] toward us who
[ppt]believe. [a]*These are* in accordance with
the working of the [b]strength[2904] of His
might[2479]
🔑 20 which He [pfi]brought about[1754] in
Christ, when He [a]raised[1453] Him from
the dead,[3498] and [apt] [b]seated Him at His
right hand[1188] in [c]the heavenly *places,*
21 far above [a]all rule and authority[1849] and power[1411] and dominion,[2963] and every [b]name[3686] that is
[ppp]named, not only in [c]this age,[165] but
also in the one to come.[3195]
22 And He [ao] [a]put all things in
subjection[5293] under His feet, and gave
Him as [b]head[2776] over all things to the
church,[1577]
23 which is His [a]body,[4983] the [b]ful-
ness[4138] of Him who [c]fills [d]all in all.

Made Alive in Christ

2 And you [I]were [a]dead[3498] [II]in your
trespasses[3900] and sins,[266]
2 in which you [a]formerly walked
according to the [I]course[165] of [b]this
world,[2889] according to [c]the prince of
the power[1849] of the air, of the spirit[4151]
that is now [ppt]working in[1754] [d]the sons[5207]
of disobedience.[543]
3 Among them we too all [a]formerly
[aop]lived[390] in [b]the lusts[1939] of our
flesh,[4561] [ppt] [I]indulging the desires[2307] of
the flesh and of the [II]mind,[1271] and were
[c]by nature[5449] [d]children[5043] of wrath,[3709]
[e]even as the rest.
4 But God,[2316] being [a]rich in
mercy,[1656] because of [b]His great love[26]
with which He loved[25] us,
5 even when we were [a]dead[3498]
[I]in our transgressions,[3900] [ao]made us
alive together[4806] [II]with Christ ([b]by
grace[5485] you have been saved),[4982]
6 and [a]raised us up with Him, and

18 [II]Or, *holy ones* [c]Rom. 11:29 [d]Eph. 1:7 [e]Eph. 1:11 [f]Col. 1:12
19 [a]Eph. 3:7; Col. 1:29 [b]Eph. 6:10
20 [a]Acts 2:24 [b]Mark 16:19 [c]Eph. 1:3
21 [a]Matt. 28:18; Col. 1:16 [b]Phil. 2:9; Rev. 19:12 [c]Matt. 12:32
22 [a]Ps. 8:6; 1Cor. 15:27 [b]1Cor. 11:3; Eph. 4:15; Col. 1:18
23 [a]1Cor. 12:27; Eph. 4:12; Col. 1:18, 24 [b]John 1:16; Eph. 3:19 [c]Eph. 4:10 [d]Col. 3:11

1 [I]Lit., *being* [II]Or, *by reason of* [a]Eph. 2:5; Col. 2:13
2 [I]Lit., *age* [a]1Cor. 6:11; Eph. 2:3 [b]Eph. 1:21 [c]John 12:31; Eph. 6:12 [d]Eph. 5:6
3 [I]Lit., *doing* [II]Lit., *thoughts* [a]Eph. 2:2 [b]Gal. 5:16f. [c]Rom. 2:14; Gal. 2:15 [d]Rom. 5:9; Col. 1:21; 2Pet. 2:14 [e]Rom. 5:12
4 [a]Eph. 1:7 [b]John 3:16
5 [I]Or, *by reason of* [II]Some ancient mss. read *in Christ* [a]Eph. 2:1 [b]Acts 15:11
6 [a]Col. 2:12 [b]Eph. 1:20 [c]Eph. 1:3 [d]Eph. 1:1; 2:10, 13
7 [a]Rom. 2:4; Eph. 1:7 [b]Titus 3:4
8 [I]I.e., that salvation [a]Acts 15:11; Eph. 2:5 [b]1Pet. 1:5 [c]John 4:10
9 [a]Rom. 3:28; 2Tim. 1:9 [b]1Cor. 1:29
10 [a]Eph. 2:15; 4:24; Col. 3:10 [b]Eph. 1:1; 2:6, 13 [c]Titus 2:14 [d]Eph. 1:4 [e]Eph. 4:1

[ao] [b]seated us with Him in [c]the heavenly
places, in [d]Christ[5547] Jesus,
7 in order that in the ages[165] to come
He might [asbm]show the [ppt]surpassing
[a]riches of His grace in [b]kindness[5544] toward us in Christ Jesus.
🔑 8 For [a]by grace[5485] you have been
saved[4982] [b]through faith;[4102] and [I]that
not of yourselves, *it is* [c]the gift[1435] of
God;
9 [a]not as a result of works,[2041] that
[b]no one should boast.
10 For we are His workmanship,
[aptp] [a]created[2936] in [b]Christ Jesus for
[c]good[18] works, which God [ao] [d]prepared
beforehand, that we should [aosb] [e]walk in
them.
11 Therefore [pim]remember, that
[a]formerly [b]you, the Gentiles[1484] in the
flesh, who are [ppp]called "[c]Uncircum-
cision"[203] by the [ppp]so-called "[c]Circum-
cision,"[4061] *which is* performed in the
flesh by human hands—
12 *remember* that you were at that
time[2540] separate from Christ, [I][a]ex-
cluded[526] from the commonwealth[4174]
of Israel, and strangers to [b]the covenants[1242] of promise,[1860] having [c]no
hope[1680] and [d]without God in the
world.[2889]
13 But now in [a]Christ Jesus you who
[b]formerly were [c]far off [I]have [c]been
[aop]brought near[1451] [II][d]by the blood[129]
of Christ.
14 For He Himself is [a]our peace,[1515]
[b]who [apt]made both *groups into* one, and
[apt]broke down[3089] the [I]barrier of the dividing wall,
15 [I]by [apt] [a]abolishing in His flesh[4561]
the enmity,[2189] *which is* [b]the Law[3551]
of commandments[1785] *contained* in

11 [a]Eph. 2:2 [b]1Cor. 12:2; Eph. 5:8 [c]Rom. 2:28f.; Col. 2:11 **12** [I]Or, *alienated* [a]Rom. 9:4; Col. 1:21 [b]Gal. 3:17; Heb. 8:6 [c]1Thess. 4:13 [d]Gal. 4:8; 1Thess. 4:5 **13** [I]Lit., *became;* or, *were made* [II]Or, *in* [a]Eph. 1:1; 2:6 [b]Eph. 2:2 [c]Is. 57:19; Acts 2:39; Eph. 2:17 [d]Rom. 3:25; Col. 1:20 **14** [I]Lit., *the dividing wall of the barrier* [a]Is. 9:6; Eph. 2:15; Col. 3:15 [b]1Cor. 12:13; Gal. 3:28; Col. 3:11 **15** [I]Or, *the enmity, by abolishing in His flesh the Law* [a]Eph. 2:16; Col. 1:21f. [b]Col. 2:14, 20

🔑 **1:20-23** See note on I Thess. 2:19.
🔑 **2:8** See general remarks on justification on Romans and also note on I Pet. 3:20,21.

ordinances,[1378] that in Himself He might [II][c]make[2936] the two[1417] into [d]one new[2537] man,[444] *thus* establishing [e]peace,[1515]

16 and might [aosb] [a]reconcile them both in [b]one body[4983] to God through the cross,[4716] [I]by it having [apt] [c]put to death the enmity.[2189]

🗝 17 AND [a]HE CAME AND [ao]PREACHED[2097] [b]PEACE[1515] TO YOU WHO WERE [c]FAR AWAY, AND PEACE TO THOSE who were [c]NEAR;[1451]

18 for through Him we both have [a]our access[4318] in [b]one Spirit[4151] to [c]the Father.[3962]

19 So then you are no longer [a]strangers and aliens,[3941] but you are [b]fellow citizens with the [I]saints,[40] and are of [c]God's household,[3609]

20 having been [aptp] [a]built upon[2026] [b]the foundation of [c]the apostles[652] and prophets,[4396] [d]Christ Jesus Himself being the [e]corner *stone*,

21 [a]in whom the whole building,[3619] being [ppp]fitted together is growing into [b]a holy[40] [I]temple[3485] in the Lord;[2962]

22 in whom you also are being [a]built together[4925] into a [b]dwelling[2732] of God in the Spirit.

Paul's Stewardship

3 For this reason I, Paul, [a]the prisoner of [b]Christ Jesus [c]for the sake of you [d]Gentiles—[1484]

2 if indeed you have [ao]heard of the [a]stewardship[3622] of God's grace[5485] which was [aptp]given to me for you;[5209]

3 [a]that [b]by revelation[602] there was [aop] [c]made known[1107] to me [d]the mystery,[3466] [e]as I wrote before in brief.

4 [I]And by referring to this, when you [ppt]read you can [ainf]understand[3539] [a]my insight [II]into the [b]mystery[3466] of Christ,

5 which in other[2087] generations was not [aop]made known[1107] to the sons[5207] of men,[444] as it has now been [aop]revealed[601] to His holy[40] [a]apostles[652] and prophets[4396] [I]in the Spirit;

6 *to be specific,* that the Gentiles[1484] are [a]fellow heirs[4789] and [b]fellow members of the body,[4954] and [c]fellow partakers[4830] of the promise[1860] in [d]Christ Jesus through the gospel,[2098]

7 [a]of which I was made a [b]minister,[1249] according to the gift of [c]God's grace[5485] which was [aptp]given to me [d]according to the working of His power.[1411]

8 To me, [a]the very least of all [I]saints,[40] this grace was [aop]given, to [ainf] [b]preach[2097] to the Gentiles the unfathomable [c]riches of Christ,[5547]

9 and to [ainf] [I]bring to light[5461] what is the administration[2842] of the [a]mystery[3466] which for ages has been [pfpp] [b]hidden in God, [c]who [apt]created[2936] all things;

10 in order that the manifold [a]wisdom[4678] of God might now be [b]made [asbp]known through the church[1577] to the [c]rulers[746] and the authorities[1849] in [d]the heavenly *places.*

🗝 11 *This was* in [a]accordance with the [I]eternal[165] purpose[4286] which He [II]carried out in [b]Christ Jesus our Lord,

12 in whom we have boldness and [I][a]confident[4006] [b]access[4318] through faith[4102] [II]in Him.

13 Therefore I ask [I]you not [a]to [pinf]lose heart[1573] at my tribulations [b]on your behalf, [II]for they are your glory.[1391]

15 [II]Lit., *create* [c]Gal. 3:28; Eph. 2:10; Col. 3:10, 11 [d]Gal. 3:28; Col. 3:10f. [e]Is. 9:6; Eph. 2:14; Col. 3:15
16 [I]Or, *in Himself* [a]2Cor. 5:18; Col. 1:20, 22 [b]1Cor. 10:17; Eph. 4:4 [c]Eph. 2:15
17 [a]Is. 57:19; Rom. 10:14 [b]Acts 10:36; Eph. 2:14 [c]Eph. 2:13
18 [a]Rom. 5:2; Eph. 3:12 [b]1Cor. 12:13; Eph. 4:4 [c]Col. 1:12
19 [I]Or, *holy ones* [a]Eph. 2:12; Heb. 11:13; 1Pet. 2:11 [b]Phil. 3:20; Heb. 12:22f. [c]Gal. 6:10
20 [a]1Cor. 3:9 [b]Matt. 16:18; 1Cor. 3:10; Rev. 21:14 [c]1Cor. 12:28; Eph. 3:5 [d]1Cor. 3:11 [e]Ps. 118:22; Luke 20:17
21 [I]Or, *sanctuary* [a]Eph. 4:15f.; Col. 2:19 [b]1Cor. 3:16f.
22 [a]1Cor. 3:9, 16; 2Cor. 6:16 [b]Eph. 3:17

1 [a]Acts 23:18; Eph. 4:1; 2Tim. 1:8; Philem. 1, 9, 23 [b]Gal. 5:24 [c]2Cor. 1:6; Eph. 3:13 [d]Eph. 3:8
2 [a]Eph. 1:10; 3:9; Col. 1:25; 1Tim. 1:4
3 [a]Acts 22:17, 21; 26:16ff. [b]Gal. 1:12 [c]Eph. 1:9; 3:4, 6, 9 [d]Rom. 11:25; 16:25; Eph. 3:4, 9; 6:19; Col. 1:26f.; 4:3 [e]Eph. 1:9f.; Heb. 13:22; 1Pet. 5:12
4 [I]Lit., *To which, when you read* [II]Lit., *in* [a]2Cor. 11:6 [b]Rom. 11:25; 16:25; Eph. 3:3, 9; 6:19; Col. 1:26f.; 4:3

5 [I]Or, *by* [a]1Cor. 12:28; Eph. 2:20 **6** [a]Gal. 3:29 [b]Eph. 2:16 [c]Eph. 5:7 [d]Gal. 5:24 **7** [a]Col. 1:23, 25 [b]1Cor. 3:5 [c]Acts 9:15; Rom. 12:3; Eph. 3:2 [d]Eph. 1:19; 3:20 **8** [I]Or, *holy ones* [a]1Cor. 15:9 [b]Acts 9:15; Eph. 3:1f. [c]Rom. 2:4; Eph. 1:7; 3:16 **9** [I]Some ancient mss. read *make all know* [a]Rom. 11:25; 16:25; Eph. 3:3, 4; 6:19; Col. 1:26f.; 4:3 [b]Col. 3:3 [c]Rev. 4:11 **10** [a]Rom. 11:33; 1Cor. 2:7 [b]Eph. 1:23; 1Pet. 1:12 [c]Eph. 1:21; 6:12; Col. 2:10, 15 [d]Eph. 1:3 **11** [I]Lit., *purpose of the ages* [II]Or, *formed* [a]Eph. 1:11 [b]Gal. 5:24; Eph. 3:1 **12** [I]Lit., *access in confidence* [II]Lit., *of Him* [a]2Cor. 3:4; Heb. 4:16; 10:19, 35; 1John 2:28; 3:21 [b]Eph. 2:18 **13** [I]Or, *that I may not lose* [II]Lit., *which are* [a]2Cor. 4:1 [b]Eph. 3:1

🗝 **2:17** See note on I Pet. 3:18-20.
🗝 **3:11** See notes on Eph. 1:4-5; II Tim. 1:9.

14 For this reason, I [a]bow my knees before the Father,[3962]

15 from whom [I]every family[3965] in heaven[3772] and on earth[1093] derives its name,

16 that He would grant you, according to [a]the riches of His glory,[1391] to be aifp [b]strengthened2901 with power through His Spirit[4151] in [c]the inner man;[444]

17 so that [a]Christ[5547] may ainfdwell[2730] in your hearts[2588] through faith;[4102] *and* that you, being pfpp [b]rooted and pfpp [c]grounded in love,[26]

18 may be aosbable to ainfcomprehend[2638] with [a]all the [I]saints[40] what is [b]the breadth and length and height and depth,

19 and to ainfknow[1097] [a]the love[26] of Christ which ppt [b]surpasses knowledge,[1108] that you may be [c]filled up to all the [d]fulness[4138] of God.

20 [a]Now to Him who is ppt [b]able to ainfdo exceeding abundantly[4053] beyond all that we ask[154] or think,[3539] [c]according to the power[1411] that pptworks[1754] within us,

21 [a]to Him *be* the glory[1391] in the church[1577] and in Christ Jesus to all generations[1074] [I]forever and ever.[165] Amen.281

Unity of the Spirit

4 I, therefore, [a]the prisoner of the Lord, [b]entreat you to ainf [c]walk4043 in a manner worthy of the [d]calling[2821] with which you have been aop [e]called,[2564]

2 with all [a]humility and gentleness, with patience,[3115] pptshowing forbearance[430] to one another [b]in love,[26]

14 [a]Phil. 2:10
15 [I]Or, *the whole*
16 [a]Eph. 1:18; 3:8 [b]1Cor. 16:13; Phil. 4:13; Col. 1:11 [c]Rom. 7:22
17 [a]John 14:23; Rom. 8:9f.; 2Cor. 13:5; Eph. 2:22 [b]1Cor. 3:6; Col. 2:7 [c]Col. 1:23
18 [I]V. 8, note 1 [a]Eph. 1:15 [b]Job 11:8f.
19 [a]Rom. 8:35, 39 [b]Phil. 4:7 [c]Col. 2:10 [d]Eph. 1:23
20 [a]Rom. 16:25 [b]2Cor. 9:8 [c]Eph. 3:7
21 [I]Lit., *of the age of the ages* [a]Rom. 11:36

1 [a]Eph. 3:1 [b]Rom. 12:1 [c]Eph. 2:10; Col. 1:10; 2:6; 1Thess. 2:12 [d]Rom. 11:29 [e]Rom. 8:28f.
2 [a]Col. 3:12f. [b]Eph. 1:4
3 [a]Col. 3:14f.
4 [a]1Cor. 12:4ff.; Eph. 2:16, 18 [b]Eph. 1:18
5 [a]1Cor. 8:6
6 [a]Rom. 11:36
7 [a]1Cor. 12:7, 11 [b]Eph. 3:2 [c]Rom. 12:3
8 [I]Or, *He* [a]Ps. 68:18 [b]Col. 2:15
9 [I]Lit., *is it except* [II]Some ancient mss. read *had first descended* [a]John 3:13 [b]Is. 44:23
10 [a]Eph. 1:20f.; Heb. 4:14; 7:26 [b]Eph. 1:23
11 [a]Eph. 4:8 [b]Acts 13:1; 1Cor. 12:28 [c]Acts 21:8 [d]Acts 13:1
12 [I]Or, *holy ones* [a]2Cor. 13:9 [b]1Cor. 12:27; Eph. 1:23

3 being diligent to pinfpreserve the unity of the Spirit[4151] in the [a]bond of peace.[1515]

4 *There is* [a]one body[4983] and one Spirit, just as also you were aopcalled in one [b]hope[1680] of your calling;[2821]

5 [a]one Lord,[2962] one faith,[4102] one baptism,[908]

6 one God[2316] and Father[3962] of all [a]who is over all and through all and in all.

7 But [a]to each one of us [b]grace[5485] was aopgiven [c]according to the measure of Christ's[5547] gift.

🔑 8 Therefore [I]it says,

"[a]WHEN HE aptASCENDED[305] ON HIGH,
HE ao [b]LED CAPTIVE A HOST OF CAPTIVES,
AND HE GAVE GIFTS[1390] TO MEN."[444]

9 (Now this *expression,* "He [a]ascended," what [I]does it mean except that He also [II]had aodescended[2597] into [b]the lower[2737] parts of the earth?

10 He who descended is Himself also He who ascended [a]far above all the heavens, that He might aosb [b]fill all things.)

🔑 11 And He [a]gave [b]some *as* apostles,[652] and some *as* prophets,[4396] and some *as* [c]evangelists,[2099] and some *as* pastors[4166] and [d]teachers,[1320]

12 [a]for the equipping of the [I]saints[40] for the work[2041] of service,[1248] to the building up of [b]the body of Christ;

13 until we all aosbattain to [a]the unity of the faith, and of the [I][b]knowledge[1922] of the Son[5207] of God, to a [c]mature[5046] man, to the measure of the stature

13 [I]Or, *true knowledge* [a]Eph. 4:3, 5 [b]John 6:69; Eph. 1:17; Phil. 3:10 [c]1Cor. 14:20; Col. 1:28; Heb. 5:14

🔑 **4:8-10** See note on I Pet. 3:18-20. The descent of the Lord Jesus into the lower parts of the earth is His incarnation which made it possible for Him to taste death. The ascension referred to here is His ascension from earth after He had died. His resurrection and ascension captivated what rendered Him captive unto death. He captivated death to which He previously voluntarily succumbed. Thus, this is His proclamation of victory over death. The gifts that He gave to men were consequent to His victory over death. The gifts He gave to His own were secured consequent to His victory over death to enable them to also be victorious while carrying on His work on earth and hereafter (I Cor. 15:24-28).

🔑 **4:11,12** See note on I Cor. 12:1-11.

[II]which belongs to the [d]fulness[4138] of Christ.

14 [I]As a result, we are [a]no longer to be children,[3516] [ppt] [b]tossed here and there by waves, and [ppt]carried about by every wind of doctrine,[1319] by the trickery[2940] of men, by [c]craftiness [II]in [d]deceitful scheming;

15 but [ppt] [I]speaking the truth[226] [a]in love,[26] we [II]are to [aosb] [b]grow up in all *aspects* into Him, who is the [c]head,[2776] *even* Christ,

16 from whom [a]the whole body,[4983] being [ppp]fitted and [ppp]held together [I]by that which every joint supplies, according to the [II]proper working of each individual part, causes the growth of the body for the building up of itself [b]in love.

The Christian's Walk

17 [a]This I say therefore, and affirm[3143] together with the Lord, [b]that you [pinf]walk[4043] no longer just as the Gentiles[1484] also walk, in the [c]futility[3153] of their mind,[3563]

18 being [pfpp] [a]darkened in their understanding,[1271] [pfpp] [I][b]excluded[526] from the life[2222] of God, because of the [c]ignorance[52] that is in them, because of the [d]hardness[4457] of their heart;[2588]

19 and they, having [a]become [pfp]callous, [b]have [ao]given themselves over to [c]sensuality,[766] [I]for the practice of every kind of impurity[167] with greediness.

20 But you did not [ao] [a]learn[3129] [I]Christ[5547] in this way,

21 if indeed you [a]have [ao]heard Him and have [b]been [aop]taught in Him, just as truth[225] is in Jesus,

22 that, in reference to your former manner of life,[391] you [ainf] [a]lay aside the [b]old[3820] [I]self,[444] which is being corrupted in accordance with the [c]lusts of deceit,

23 and that you be [a]renewed[365] in the spirit[4151] of your mind,[3563]

24 and [ainf] [a]put on the [b]new[2537] [I]self,[444] which [II][c]in *the likeness of* God has been [aptp]created[2936] in righteousness[1343] and holiness[3742] of the truth.[225]

25 Therefore, [apt] [a]laying aside falsehood, [pim] [b]SPEAK[2980] TRUTH,[225] EACH ONE *of you,* WITH HIS NEIGHBOR, for we are [c]members of one another.

26 [pim] [a]BE ANGRY, AND *yet* DO NOT [pim]SIN;[265] do not let the sun [pim]go down on your anger,[3950]

27 and do not [pim] [a]give the devil[1228] [I]an opportunity.

28 Let him who [ppt]steals [pim]steal no longer; but rather [a]let him [pim]labor, [ppt] [b]performing with his own hands what is good,[18] [c]in order that he may [psa]have *something* to [pinf]share with him who has [ppt]need.

29 Let no [I][a]unwholesome[4550] word[3056] [pim]proceed from your mouth, but only such *a word* as is good for [b]edification[3619] [II]according to the need *of the moment,* that it may [aosb]give[1325] grace[5485] to those who hear.

30 And [a]do not [pim]grieve[3076] the Holy[40] Spirit[4151] of God, [I]by whom you were [aop] [b]sealed[4972] for the day of redemption.[629]

31 [a]Let all bitterness and wrath[2372] and anger[3709] and clamor and slander[988] be [aipp] [b]put away from you, along with all [c]malice.[2549]

32 And [pim] [a]be kind[5543] to one another, tender-hearted, forgiving[5483] each other, [b]just as God in Christ also has [ao]forgiven [I]you.

Be Imitators of God

5 [a]Therefore [pim]be imitators of God, as beloved children;[5043]

2 and [pim] [a]walk[4043] in love,[26] just as Christ also [ao] [b]loved[25] [I]you, and [ao] [c]gave Himself up for us, an [d]offering[4376] and a sacrifice[2378] to God [II]as a [e]fragrant aroma.

13 [II]Lit., *of the fulness* [d]John 1:16; Eph. 1:23
14 [I]Lit., *that we may no longer be* [II]Lit., *with regard to the scheming of deceit* [a]1Cor. 14:20 [b]James 1:6; Jude 12 [c]1Cor. 3:19; 2Cor. 4:2; 11:3 [d]Eph. 6:11
15 [I]Or, *holding to or walking in* [II]Lit., *may grow up* [a]Eph. 1:4 [b]Eph. 2:21 [c]Eph. 1:22
16 [I]Lit., *through every joint of the supply* [II]Lit., *working in measure* [a]Rom. 12:4f.; Col. 2:19 [b]Eph. 1:4
17 [a]Col. 2:4 [b]Eph. 2:2; 4:22 [c]Rom. 1:21; Col. 2:18; 1Pet. 1:18; 2Pet. 2:18
18 [I]Or, *alienated* [a]Rom. 1:21 [b]Eph. 2:1, 12 [c]Acts 3:17; 17:30; 1Cor. 2:8; Heb. 5:2; 9:7; 1Pet. 1:14 [d]Mark 3:5; Rom. 11:7, 25; 2Cor. 3:14
19 [I]Or, *greedy for the practice of every kind of impurity* [a]1Tim. 4:2 [b]Rom. 1:24 [c]Col. 3:5
20 [I]I.e., the Messiah [a]Matt. 11:29
21 [a]Rom. 10:14; Eph. 1:13; 2:17; Col. 1:5 [b]Col. 2:7
22 [I]Lit., *man* [a]Eph. 4:25, 31; Col. 3:8; Heb. 12:1; James 1:21; 1Pet. 2:1 [b]Rom. 6:6 [c]2Cor. 11:3; Heb. 3:13
23 [a]Rom. 12:2
24 [I]Lit., *man* [II]Lit., *according to God* [a]Rom. 13:14 [b]Rom. 6:4; 7:6; 12:2; 2Cor. 5:17; Col. 3:10 [c]Eph. 2:10
25 [a]Eph. 4:22, 31; Col. 3:8; Heb. 12:1; James 1:21; 1Pet. 2:1 [b]Zech. 8:16; Eph. 4:15; Col. 3:9 [c]Rom. 12:5
26 [a]Ps. 4:4
27 [I]Lit., *a place* [a]Rom. 12:19; James 4:7
28 [a]Acts 20:35; 1Cor. 4:12; Gal. 6:10 [b]1Thess. 4:11; 2Thess. 3:8, 11f.; Titus 3:8, 14 [c]Luke 3:11; 1Thess. 4:12
29 [I]Lit., *rotten* [II]Lit., *of the need* [a]Matt. 12:34; Eph. 5:4; Col. 3:8 [b]Eccl. 10:12; Rom. 14:19; Col. 4:6
30 [I]Lit., *in* [a]Is. 63:10; 1Thess. 5:19 [b]John 3:33; Eph. 1:13
31 [a]Rom. 3:14; Col. 3:8, 19 [b]Eph. 4:22 [c]1Pet. 2:1
32 [I]Some ancient mss. read *us* [a]1Cor. 13:4; Col. 3:12f.; 1Pet. 3:8 [b]Matt. 6:14f.; 2Cor. 2:10
1 [a]Matt. 5:48; Luke 6:36; Eph. 4:32
2 [I]Some ancient mss. read *us* [II]Lit., *for an odor of fragrance* [a]Rom. 14:15; Col. 3:14 [b]John 13:34; Rom. 8:37 [c]John 6:51; Rom. 4:25; Gal. 2:20; Eph. 5:25 [d]Heb. 7:27; 9:14; 10:10, 12 [e]Ex. 29:18, 25; 2Cor. 2:14

3 But do not let [a]immorality[4202] [I]or any impurity[167] or greed[4124] even be [pim]named among you, as is proper among [II]saints;[40]

4 and *there must be no* [a]filthiness and silly talk,[3473] or coarse jesting,[2160] which [b]are not fitting,[433] but rather [c]giving of thanks.

5 For this you know with certainty, that [a]no [I]immoral[4205] or impure person[169] or covetous man, who is an idolater,[1496] has an inheritance[2817] in the kingdom[932] [b]of Christ and God.

6 [a]Let no one [pim]deceive you with empty[2756] words,[3056] for because of these things [b]the wrath[3709] of God comes upon [c]the sons of disobedience.[543]

7 Therefore do not [pim]be [a]partakers[4830] with them;

8 for [a]you were formerly [b]darkness,[4655] but now you are light[5457] in the Lord; [pim]walk as [c]children of light

9 (for [a]the fruit of the light[5457] *consists* in all [b]goodness[19] and righteousness[1343] and truth),[225]

10 [I][a]trying to [ppt]learn what is pleasing[2101] to the Lord.

11 And [a]do not [pim]participate in[4790] the unfruitful [b]deeds of [c]darkness, but instead even [pim] [I][d]expose them;

12 for it is disgraceful even to [pinf]speak of the things which are [ppt]done by them in secret.

13 But all things [ppt]become visible [a]when they are [I]exposed[5319] by the light, for everything that becomes visible is light.

14 For this reason [I]it says,
"[pim] [a]Awake,[1453] sleeper,
And [aim]rise[450] from [b]the dead,[3498]
And Christ [c]will shine on you."

15 Therefore [I]be careful how you [a]walk, not [b]as unwise men, but as wise,[4680]

16 [I][a]making the most of[1805] your time,[2540] because [b]the days are evil.[4190]

17 So then do not [pim]be foolish, but [a]understand[4920] what the will[2307] of the Lord is.

18 And [a]do not get [pim]drunk with wine,[3631] [I]for that is [b]dissipation,[810] but be [pim] [c]filled with the Spirit,[4151]

19 [ppt] [a]speaking[2980] to [I]one another in [b]psalms[5568] and [c]hymns[5215] and spiritual [d]songs,[5603] [e]singing and making melody with your heart[2588] to the Lord;

20 [a]always giving thanks[2168] for all things in the name of our Lord Jesus Christ to [I][b]God, even the Father;

🗝 21 [I][a]and be subject[5263] to one another in the [II][b]fear[5401] of Christ.

Marriage Like Christ and the Church

22 [a]Wives, [b]*be subject* to your own husbands,[435] [c]as to the Lord.[2962]

23 For [a]the husband is the head of the wife, as Christ[5547] also is the [b]head[2776] of the church,[1577] He Himself [c]*being* the Savior[4990] of the body.[4983]

24 But as the church is subject to[5293] Christ, so also the wives *ought to be* to their husbands in everything.

25 [a]Husbands, [pim]love[25] your wives, just as Christ also loved the church and [b]gave Himself up for her;

26 [a]that He might [aosb]sanctify[37] her, having [apt] [b]cleansed[2511] her by the [c]washing[3067] of water with [d]the word,[4487]

27 that He might [aosb] [a]present to Himself the church[1577] [I]in all her glory,[1741] having no spot[4695] or wrinkle or any such thing; but that she should be [b]holy[40] and blameless.[299]

28 So husbands ought also to [pinf] [a]love their own wives as their own bodies.[4983] He who [ppt]loves his own wife loves himself;

29 for no one ever hated his own flesh,[4561] but nourishes and cherishes

3 [I]Lit., *and all* [II]Or, *holy ones* [a]Col. 3:5
4 [a]Matt. 12:34; Eph. 4:29; Col. 3:8 [b]Rom. 1:28 [c]Eph. 5:20
5 [I]I.e., one who commits sexual immorality [a]1Cor. 6:9; Col. 3:5 [b]Col. 1:13
6 [a]Col. 2:8 [b]Rom. 1:18; Col. 3:6 [c]Eph. 2:2
7 [a]Eph. 3:6
8 [a]Eph. 2:2 [b]Acts 26:18; Col. 1:12f. [c]John 12:36; Rom. 13:12
9 [a]Gal. 5:22 [b]Rom. 15:14
10 [I]Lit., *proving what* [a]Rom. 12:2
11 [I]Or, *reprove* [a]1Cor. 5:9; 2Cor. 6:14 [b]Rom. 13:12 [c]Acts 26:18; Col. 1:12f. [d]1Tim. 5:20
13 [I]Or, *reproved* [a]John 3:20f.
14 [I]Or, *He* [a]Is. 26:19; 51:17; 52:1; 60:1; Rom. 13:11 [b]Eph. 2:1 [c]Luke 1:78f.
15 [I]Lit., *look carefully* [a]Eph. 5:2 [b]Col. 4:5
16 [I]Lit., *redeeming the time* [a]Col. 4:5 [b]Gal. 1:4; Eph. 6:13
17 [a]Rom. 12:2; Col. 1:9; 1Thess. 4:3
18 [I]Lit., *in which is* [a]Prov. 20:1; 23:31f.; Rom. 13:13; 1Cor. 5:11; 1Thess. 5:7 [b]Titus 1:6; 1Pet. 4:4 [c]Luke 1:15
19 [I]Or, *yourselves* [a]Col. 3:16 [b]1Cor. 14:26 [c]Acts 16:25 [d]Rev. 5:9 [e]1Cor. 14:15
20 [I]Lit., *the God and Father* [a]Rom. 1:8; Eph. 5:4; Col. 3:17 [b]1Cor. 15:24
21 [I]Lit., *being subject* [II]Or, *reverence* [a]Gal. 5:13; Phil. 2:3; 1Pet. 5:5 [b]2Cor. 5:11 **22** [a]Eph. 5:22-6:9: *Col. 3:18-4:1* [b]1Cor. 14:34f.; Titus 2:5; 1Pet. 3:1 [c]Eph. 6:5 **23** [a]1Cor. 11:3 [b]Eph. 1:22 [c]1Cor. 6:13 **25** [a]Eph. 5:28, 33; Col. 3:19; 1Pet. 3:7 [b]Eph. 5:2 **26** [a]Titus 2:14; Heb. 10:10, 14, 29; 13:12 [b]2Pet. 1:9 [c]Acts 22:16; 1Cor. 6:11; Titus 3:5 [d]John 15:3; 17:17; Rom. 10:8f.; Eph. 6:17 **27** [I]Lit., *glorious* [a]2Cor. 4:14; 11:2; Col. 1:22 [b]Eph. 1:4 **28** [a]Eph. 5:25, 33; 1Pet. 3:7

🗝 **5:21,22** See notes on I Cor. 14:33-40; I Tim. 2:9-15.

it, just as Christ also *does* the church,

30 because we are [a]members of His [b]body.

31 [a]FOR THIS CAUSE A MAN[444] SHALL LEAVE HIS FATHER AND MOTHER, AND SHALL CLEAVE TO HIS WIFE; AND THE TWO SHALL BECOME ONE FLESH.

32 This mystery[3466] is great; but I am speaking with reference to Christ and the church.[1577]

33 Nevertheless let each individual among you also [pim] [a]love[25] his own wife even as himself; and *let* the wife *see to it* that she [psa] [I][b]respect[5399] her husband.

Family Relationships

6 [a]Children,[5043] obey[5219] your parents in the Lord,[2962] for this is right.[1342]

2 [a]HONOR YOUR FATHER[3962] AND MOTHER[3384] (which is the first commandment with a promise),[1860]

3 THAT IT MAY [aosb]BE WELL WITH YOU , AND THAT YOU MAY LIVE LONG ON THE EARTH.[1093]

4 And, [a]fathers, do not provoke your children to anger;[3949] but [b]bring them up in the discipline and instruction[3559] of the Lord.[2962]

5 [a]Slaves,[1401] be [pim]obedient[5219] to those who are your [I]masters[2962] according to the flesh, with [b]fear and trembling, in the sincerity[572] of your heart,[2588] [c]as to Christ;

6 [a]not [I]by way of eyeservice,[3787] as [b]men-pleasers,[441] but as [c]slaves[1401] of Christ, [d]doing the will[2307] of God from the [II]heart.[5590]

7 With good will[2133] [I]render service,[1398] [a]as to the Lord,[2962] and not to men,[444]

8 [a]knowing that [b]whatever good thing[18] each one [aosb]does, this he will receive back from the Lord, [c]whether slave[1401] or free.[1658]

9 And, masters, [pim]do the same things to them, and [a]give up threatening, knowing that [b]both their Master[2962] and yours is in heaven,[3772] and there is [c]no partiality[4382] with Him.

30 [a]1Cor. 6:15; 12:27 [b]Eph. 1:23
31 [a]Gen. 2:24; Matt. 19:5; Mark 10:7f.
33 [I]Lit., *fear* [a]Eph. 5:25, 28; 1Pet. 3:7 [b]1Pet. 3:2, 5f.

1 [a]Prov. 6:20; 23:22; Col. 3:20
2 [a]Ex. 20:12; Deut. 5:16
4 [a]Col. 3:21 [b]Gen. 18:19; Deut. 6:7; 11:19; Ps. 78:4; Prov. 22:6; 2Tim. 3:15
5 [I]I.e., earthly masters, with fear [a]Col. 3:22; 1Tim. 6:1; Titus 2:9 [b]1Cor. 2:3 [c]Eph. 5:22
6 [I]Lit., *according to* [II]Lit., *soul* [a]Col. 3:22 [b]Gal. 1:10 [c]1Cor. 7:22 [d]Mark 3:35
7 [I]Lit., *rendering* [a]Col. 3:23
8 [a]Col. 3:24 [b]Matt. 16:27; 2Cor. 5:10; Col. 3:24f. [c]1Cor. 12:13; Col. 3:11
9 [a]Lev. 25:43 [b]Job 31:13ff.; John 13:13; Col. 4:1 [c]Deut. 10:17; Acts 10:34; Col. 3:25
10 [a]1Cor. 16:13; 2Tim. 2:1 [b]Eph. 1:19
11 [a]Rom. 13:12; Eph. 6:13 [b]Eph. 4:14
12 [I]Lit., *blood and flesh* [a]1Cor. 9:25 [b]Matt. 16:17 [c]Eph. 1:21; 2:2; 3:10 [d]John 12:31 [e]Acts 26:18; Col. 1:13 [f]Eph. 3:10 [g]Eph. 1:3
13 [a]Eph. 6:11 [b]James 4:7 [c]Eph. 5:16
14 [a]Is. 11:5; Luke 12:35; 1Pet. 1:13 [b]Is. 59:17; Rom. 13:12; Eph. 6:13; 1Thess. 5:8
15 [a]Is. 52:7; Rom. 10:15
16 [I]Lit., *in all* [a]1Thess. 5:8 [b]Ps. 7:13; 120:4 [c]Matt. 5:37
17 [a]Is. 59:17 [b]Is. 49:2; Hos. 6:5; Heb. 4:12

The Armor of God

10 Finally, [a]be [pim]strong[1743] in the Lord, and in [b]the strength[2904] of His might.[2479]

11 [aim] [a]Put on the full armor of God, that you may be able to stand firm against the [b]schemes[3180] of the devil.[1228]

12 For our [a]struggle is not against [I][b]flesh[4561] and blood,[129] but [c]against the rulers,[746] against the powers,[1849] against the [d]world[165] forces[2888] of this [e]darkness,[4655] against the [f]spiritual *forces*[4152] of wickedness[4189] in [g]the heavenly *places.*

13 Therefore, [aim]take up[353] [a]the full armor of God, that you may be [aosb]able to [ainf] [b]resist[436] in [c]the evil[4190] day,[2250] and having done everything, to [ainf]stand firm.[2476]

14 [aim]Stand firm therefore, [a]HAVING GIRDED[4024] YOUR LOINS[3751] WITH TRUTH,[225] and HAVING [b]PUT ON THE BREASTPLATE OF RIGHTEOUSNESS,[1343]

15 and having [a]shod[5265] YOUR FEET WITH THE PREPARATION OF THE GOSPEL[2098] OF PEACE;[1515]

16 [I]in addition to all, [apt]taking up[353] the [a]shield of faith[4102] with which you will be able to [ainf]extinguish all the [b]flaming missiles of [c]the evil *one.*[4190]

17 And [aim]take [a]THE HELMET OF SALVATION,[4992] and the [b]sword of the Spirit,[4151] which is [c]the word[4487] of God.

18 With all[2540] [a]prayer[4336] and petition[1162] [I][b]pray at all times [c]in the Spirit, and with this in view, [II][d]be on the alert with all [e]perseverance[4343] and [f]petition for all the saints,[40]

19 and [a]*pray* on my behalf, that utterance[3056] may be [asbp]given to me [b]in the opening of my mouth, to [ainf]make known[1107] with [c]boldness [d]the mystery[3466] of the gospel,

20 for which I am an [a]ambassador[4243] [b]in [I]chains; that [II]in *proclaiming*

[c]Eph. 5:26; Heb. 6:5 **18** [I]Lit., *praying* [II]Lit., *being* [a]Phil. 4:6 [b]Luke 18:1; Col. 1:3; 4:2; 1Thess. 5:17 [c]Rom. 8:26f. [d]Mark 13:33 [e]Acts 1:14 [f]1Tim. 2:1
19 [a]Col. 4:3; 1Thess. 5:25 [b]2Cor. 6:11 [c]2Cor. 3:12 [d]Eph. 3:3 **20** [I]Lit., *a chain* [II]Some ancient mss. read *I may speak it boldly* [a]2Cor. 5:20; Philem. 9 mg. [b]Acts 21:33; 28:20; Eph. 3:1; Phil. 1:7; Col. 4:3

it I may aosbspeak [c]boldly, [d]as I ought[1163]
to ainfspeak.
🔑21 [a]But that you also may know
about my circumstances, how I am do-
ing, [b]Tychicus, [c]the beloved[27] brother[80]
and faithful[4103] minister[1249] in the
Lord, will make everything known to
you.
22 [I]And [a]I have sent him to you
for this very purpose, so that you
may aosbknow [II]about us, and that he
may aosb [b]comfort your hearts.[2588]
23 [a]Peace be to the brethren, and
[b]love[26] with faith,[4102] from God the Father and the Lord Jesus Christ.
24 Grace be with all those who
pptlove[25] our Lord Jesus Christ [I]with *a
love* incorruptible.

20 [c]2Cor. 3:12 [d]Col. 4:4

21 [a]Eph. 6:21, 22: *Col. 4:7-9* [b]Acts 20:4; 2Tim. 4:12 [c]Col. 4:7

22 [I]Lit., *Whom I have sent to you* [II]Lit., *the things about us* [a]Col. 4:8 [b]Col. 2:2; 4:8

23 [a]Rom. 15:33; Gal. 6:16; 2 Thess. 3:16; 1Pet. 5:14 [b]Gal. 5:6; 1Thess. 5:8 **24** [I]Lit., *in incorruption*

🔑 **6:21,22 See general remarks on Colossians and also Col. 4:7.**

The Epistle of Paul to the

PHILIPPIANS

Philippi had a checkered history. It was named after Philip of Macedon who seized the city in 358 B.C. from the Thracians. He was the father of Alexander the Great. In 42 B.C. Mark Anthony and Octavius defeated Brutus and Cassius nearby and thereby transformed the Roman Republic (Oligarchy) into the Roman Empire. Later Augustus Caesar made Philippi a Roman colony. It was a principal stop on the great highway. Traders going East or West would come there. Therefore, it was a strategic place for the spread of the Gospel.

In the early portion of Paul's second missionary journey, the Lord indicated that He wanted Paul to cross over into Macedonia (Acts 16:9,10), an event which has affected all of our lives in the West. This was the first congregation ever to be established on European soil. Acts 16:6-40 describes Paul's contact with Lydia and the Philippian jailor's household. Paul may have visited them again when he journeyed from Ephesus to Macedonia (Acts 20:1; II Cor. 2:12,13; 7:5,6). We know that he spent time there that spring (Acts 20:6).

It is ironic that Philippians was written in another prison (in Rome) a decade later. Paul, who supported himself, ordinarily refused to receive financial assistance from the churches (I Cor. 9:11,12; Acts 18:3). However, he did accept encouragement and support from the Philippian brethren when he was in Thessalonica (Phil. 4:16,18) and while in Corinth (II Cor. 11:9). Epaphroditus arrived in Rome from Philippi with another offering of love. He nearly died, but recovered (Phil. 2:25-30; 4:18). Paul sent him back to Philippi with this letter and with his heartfelt thanks for their gift. He reassured them that they would be victorious if they had the same attitude of Christ instead of conceited pride. Phil. 2:5-11 is a classic passage.

Although, strictly speaking, there is no development of one theme, the main thought of Philippians is the all-sufficiency of Christ in any circumstance, good or bad. Christ is the very meaning of life and death (Phil. 1:20,21). More than a dozen passages exude Paul's joy and confidence. He loved them very much and urged them to persevere.

Thanksgiving

1 [a]Paul and [b]Timothy, [c]bond-servants[1401] of [d]Christ[5547] Jesus, to [e]all the [I][f]saints[40] in Christ Jesus who are in [g]Philippi, including the [h]overseers[1985] and [i]deacons:[1249]

2 [a]Grace[5485] to you and peace[1515] from God[2316] our Father[3962] and the Lord[2962] Jesus Christ.

3 [a]I thank[2168] my God in all my remembrance of you,

4 always offering prayer[1162] with joy[5479] in [a]my every prayer for you all,

5 in view of your [I][a]participation[2842] in the [b]gospel[2098] [c]from the first day until now.

🔑 6 *For I am* confident[3982] of this very thing, that He who [apt]began a good[18] work in you will perfect[2005] it until [a]the day[2250] of Christ Jesus.

7 [I]For [a]it is only right for me to [pinf]feel this way about you all, because I [b]have you in my heart, since both in my [II][c]imprisonment and in the [d]defense and confirmation[951] of the [e]gospel,[2098] you all are partakers of grace with me.

8 For [a]God is my witness,[3144] how I long for you all with the [I]affection[4698] of [b]Christ Jesus.

9 And this I pray, that [a]your love[26] may [psa]abound still more and more in [b]real knowledge[1922] and all discernment,[144]

🔑 10 so that you may [aies] [I][a]approve the things that are excellent,[1308] in order

1 [I]Or, *holy ones* [a]2Cor. 1:1 [b]Acts 16:1 [c]Rom. 1:1; Gal. 1:10 [d]Gal. 3:26 [e]2Cor. 1:1; Col. 1:2 [f]Acts 9:13 [g]Acts 16:12 [h]Acts 20:28; 1Tim. 3:1f.; Titus 1:7 [i]1Tim. 3:8ff.
2 [a]Rom. 1:7
3 [a]Rom. 1:8
4 [a]Rom. 1:9
5 [I]Or, *sharing in the preaching of the gospel* [a]Acts 2:42; Phil. 4:15 [b]Phil. 1:7; 2:22; 4:3, 15 [c]Acts 16:12-40; Phil. 2:12; 4:15
6 [a]1Cor. 1:8; Phil. 1:10; 2:16
7 [I]Lit., *Just as it is right* [II]Lit., *bonds* [a]2Pet. 1:13 [b]2Cor. 7:3 [c]Acts 21:33; Eph. 6:20; Phil. 1:13f., 17 [d]Phil. 1:16 [e]Phil. 1:5, 12, 16, 27; 2:22; 4:3, 15
8 [I]Lit., *inward parts* [a]Rom. 1:9 [b]Gal. 3:26
9 [a]1Thess. 3:12 [b]Col. 1:9
10 [I]Or, *distinguish between the things which differ* [a]Rom. 2:18

🔑 **1:6,10** See note on I Thess. 5:2.

to be sincere[1506] and blameless[677] [II]until [b]the day of Christ;

11 having been [pfpp]filled with the [a]fruit of righteousness[1343] which *comes* through Jesus Christ, to the glory[1391] and praise[1868] of God.

The Gospel Is Preached

12 Now I want you to [pinf]know,[1097] brethren,[80] that my circumstances [a]have [pfi]turned out[2064] for the greater progress of the [b]gospel,

13 so that my [Ia]imprisonment in *the cause of* Christ has become well known[5318] throughout the whole [II]praetorian guard and to [b]everyone else,

14 and that most of the [I]brethren, trusting[3982] in the Lord because of my [IIa]imprisonment, have [b]far more [pinf]courage to speak the word[3056] of God without fear.

15 [a]Some, to be sure, are preaching[2784] Christ even from envy and strife, but some also from good will;

16 [I]the [pl]latter *do it* out of love, knowing that I am appointed[2749] for the defense of the [a]gospel;

17 the [pl]former proclaim[2605] Christ [a]out of selfish ambition, [I]rather than from pure motives, thinking to [pinf]cause me distress in my [IIb]imprisonment.

18 What then? Only that in every way, whether in pretense or in truth,[225] Christ is proclaimed; and in this I rejoice,[5463] yes, and I will rejoice.

19 For I know that this shall turn out for my [I]deliverance[4991] [a]through your [II]prayers and the provision of [b]the Spirit of Jesus Christ,

20 according to my [a]earnest expectation[603] and [b]hope,[1680] that I shall not be put to shame in anything, but *that* with [c]all boldness, Christ[5547] shall even now, as always, be [d]exalted in my body,[4983] [e]whether by life[2222] or by death.[2288]

To Live Is Christ

21 For to me, [a]to [pinf]live[2198] is Christ, and to [ainf]die[599] is gain.

22 [I]But if *I am* to [pinf]live *on* in the flesh,[4561] this *will mean* [a]fruitful labor[2041] for me; and I do not know[1107] [II]which to choose.[138]

23 But I am hard-pressed[4912] from both *directions,* having the [a]desire to [ainf]depart and [b]be with Christ, for *that* is very much better;

24 yet to [pinf]remain on in the flesh is more necessary for your sake.

25 And [a]convinced[3982] of this, I know that I shall remain and continue with you all for your progress and joy[5479] in the faith,[4102]

26 so that your [a]proud confidence in me may [psa]abound in Christ Jesus through my coming to you again.

27 Only [pim]conduct[4176] yourselves in a manner [a]worthy of the [b]gospel of Christ; so that whether I [apt]come and [apt]see you or remain absent,[548] I may hear of you that you are [c]standing firm in [d]one spirit,[4151] with one [I]mind[5590] [ppt] [e]striving together for the faith of the gospel;

28 in no way [ppt]alarmed by *your* [ppt]opponents—which is a [a]sign of destruction[684] for them, but of salvation for you, and that *too,* from God.

29 For to you [a]it has been [aop]granted[5483] for Christ's sake, not only to [pinf]believe[4100] in Him, but also to [pinf] [b]suffer[3958] for His sake,

30 experiencing the same [a]conflict[73] which [b]you saw in me, and now hear *to be* in me.

Be Like Christ

2 If therefore there is any encouragement[3874] in Christ, if there is any consolation of love,[26] if there is any [a]fellowship[2842] of the [an]Spirit, if any [Ib]affection[4698] and compassion,[3628]

2 [aim] [a]make my joy[5479] complete[4137] [I]by [b]being of the same mind, maintaining the same love, united in spirit,[4861] intent on one purpose.

3 Do nothing from [Ia]selfishness or

10 [II]Lit., *for* [b]1Cor. 1:8; Phil. 1:6; 2:16
11 [a]James 3:18
12 [a]Luke 21:13 [b]Phil. 1:5, 7, 16, 27; 2:22; 4:3, 15
13 [I]Lit., *bonds* [II]Or, *governor's palace* [a]Phil. 1:7; 2Tim. 2:9 [b]Acts 28:30
14 [I]Or, *brethren in the Lord, trusting because of my bonds* [II]Lit., *bonds* [a]Phil. 1:7; 2Tim. 2:9 [b]Acts 4:31; 2Cor. 3:12; 7:4; Phil. 1:20
15 [a]2Cor. 11:13
16 [I]Some later mss. reverse the order of vv. 16 and 17 [a]Phil. 1:5, 7, 12, 27; 2:22; 4:3, 15
17 [I]Lit., *not sincerely* [II]Lit., *bonds* [a]Rom. 2:8; Phil. 2:3 [b]Phil. 1:7; 2Tim. 2:9
19 [I]Or, *salvation* [II]Lit., *supplication* [a]2Cor. 1:11 [b]Acts 16:7
20 [a]Rom. 8:19 [b]Rom. 5:5; 1Pet. 4:16 [c]Acts 4:31; 2Cor. 3:12; 7:4; Phil. 1:14 [d]1Cor. 6:20 [e]Rom. 14:8
21 [a]Gal. 2:20
22 [I]Or, *But if to live in the flesh, this will be fruitful labor for me, then I* [II]Lit., *what I shall choose* [a]Rom. 1:13
23 [a]2Cor. 5:8; 2Tim. 4:6 [b]John 12:26
25 [a]Phil. 2:24
26 [a]2Cor. 5:12; 7:4; Phil. 2:16
27 [I]Lit., *soul* [a]Eph. 4:1 [b]Phil. 1:5 [c]1Cor. 16:13; Phil. 4:1 [d]Acts 4:32 [e]Jude 1:3
28 [a]2Thess. 1:5
29 [a]Matt. 5:11, 12 [b]Acts 14:22
30 [a]Col. 1:29; 2:1; 1Thess. 2:2; 1Tim. 6:12; 2Tim. 4:7; Heb. 10:32; 12:1 [b]Acts 16:19-40; Phil. 1:13

1 [I]Lit., *inward parts* [a]2Cor. 13:14 [b]Col. 3:12

2 [I]Lit., *that you be* [a]John 3:29 [b]Rom. 12:16; Phil. 4:2
3 [I]Or, contentiousness [a]Rom. 2:8; Phil. 1:17

[b]empty conceit, but with humility of mind
let [c]each of you [ppt]regard[2233] one another
as more important than himself;
4 [a]do not *merely* [ppt]look out for[4648]
your own personal interests, but also
for the interests of others.

5 [a]Have this attitude [1]in yourselves
which was also in [b]Christ[5547] Jesus,
6 who, although He [a]existed[5225] in
the [b]form[3444] of God,[2316] [c]did not

3 [b]Gal. 5:26 [c]Rom. 12:10; Eph. 5:21
4 [a]Rom. 15:1f.
5 [1]Or, *among* [a]Matt. 11:29; Rom. 15:3 [b]Phil. 1:1
6 [a]John 1:1 [b]2Cor. 4:4 [c]John 5:18; 10:33; 14:28

2:6-8 This passage concerns the deity of Jesus Christ prior to His incarnation and continuing during His sojourn on earth as the God-Man.

There are two main considerations in the N.T. One is that Christ is equal with God, which is clear from Jn. 10:30, "I and the Father are one," and also Phil. 2:6, "who, although He existed in this form of God, did not regard equality with God a thing to be grasped."

There are, however, some Scriptures that indicate that Christ was not seemingly equal with God, such as Jn. 14:28, "The Father is greater than I," and Mt. 24:36, "Of that day and hour no one knows, not even the angels of heaven, nor the Son, but the Father alone." There appears to be a seeming contradiction in these statements, and yet there is none. Christ, in speaking to His disciples in Jn. 10:29, said, "My Father who has given *them* to me, is greater than all; and no one is able to snatch *them* out of the Father's hand." And then follows v. 30, "I and the Father are one." The word for "one" in Greek is *hen* (*heis,* 1520), which is in the neuter gender and which does not mean one person, but one in essence, power, and quality. The Lord Jesus meant that to snatch His true disciples out of His hand would be to snatch them out of His Father's hand because He and His Father are One—in power, design, action, agreement and essence. They are not one person but two persons, and yet both of them are God.

Christ also prays for His disciples to become *one* (*hen*) in the same sense that He and the Father are one (Jn. 17:11,21,22). No one for a moment imagines that the Lord Jesus intended in that prayer that His disciples should become one person. The Lord Jesus, as the Athanasian Creed states, was equal to the Father as touching His Godhead, and inferior to the Father as touching His manhood.

In Phil. 2:6 we read, "Who, although He existed in the form of God, did not regard equality with God a thing to be grasped;" i.e., Jesus did not regard it as an act of injustice to the Father for Him to exert His miraculous powers demonstrating His deity on proper occasions as deemed by Himself.

The entire passage in Phil. 2:6-8 deals with the humiliation of Christ for the purpose of dying. It is brought forth as an illustration of humility (v. 3). This humility is expressed in thoughtfulness of others (v. 4). And then comes the illustration of how Christ humbled Himself and in His death He thought of nothing else but others. Although He was God incarnate and He could avoid death, He did not do it for the sake of man. He allowed Himself to die in His manhood. A translation more expressive of the true meaning of the Greek text of this passage would be, "Who, Christ, being in the form of God." The word translated "existed" is the Greek *huparchōn,* which means that He was in continuation of what He had been before. It is not the participle *ōn,* from *eimi* (1510), but the verb *huparchōn* from *huparchō* (5225), which in this context means "being what He was before." Being in His essential form as God (Jn. 1:1), He continued to be that when He became and continued to be man. And then the second statement is ". . . did not regard equality with God a thing to be grasped." He did not consider being equal with God as something to be forceably grasped from God. His essence of deity was not something that He took at any time, but it was something that He always had and never lost.

Then in v. 7 we are actually told what He voluntarily did in order to make possible His humiliation unto death: "But emptied Himself." The verb "emptied Himself" in Greek is *ekenōse,* from the verb *kenoō* (2758) in the active form. Nobody took away from Him what He was, but being Himself God, He voluntarily emptied Himself. It does not tell us of what He emptied Himself. Jn. 17:5 provides the meaning in the very words of Christ Himself. Prior to His death, He was asking the Father to glorify Him in a position next to Him (that is the exact meaning of the Greek), with the glory which He had (imperfect tense *eichon,* which means from all the way back in the past, before the world was). The glory (*doxa,* 1391) comes from the verb *dokeō* (1380), which means to think, to recognize. *Doxa,* glory, is the recognition which the Lord Jesus had with the Father before the world was even created and before He came to this world. The Lord Jesus lacked this full recognition by men on earth while He was the incarnate God, but He had never lost this recognition insofar as the Father was concerned and it was His to enjoy again after the resurrection. That is the meaning of Jesus emptying Himself. "Taking upon Him,"

(continued on next page)

[ao]regard equality[2470] with God a thing
to be grasped,[725]
7 but [ao] [1][a]emptied[2758] Himself, [ppt]tak-
ing the form[3444] of a [b]bond-servant,[1401]
and [c]being [apt]made in the likeness[3667]
of men.[444]
8 And being [aptp]found in appearance[4976] as a man, [a]He [ao]humbled[5013]
Himself by [apt]becoming [b]obedient[5255] to
the point of death,[2288] even [c]death
[1]on a cross.[4716]
🔑 9 [a]Therefore also God [b]highly [ao]ex-
alted Him, and [ao]bestowed[5483] on Him
[c]the name[3686] which is above every
name,
10 that at the name of Jesus
[a]EVERY KNEE SHOULD [aosb]BOW, of [b]those
who are in heaven,[2032] and on earth,[1919]
and under the earth,
11 and that every tongue should
[aosb]confess[1843] that Jesus Christ is
[a]Lord,[2962] to the glory[1391] of God the
Father.[3962]
12 So then, my beloved,[27] [a]just as
you have always [ao]obeyed,[5219] not as
in my presence only, but now much
more in my absence, [pim]work out your
[b]salvation[4991] with [c]fear[5401] and trembling;[5156]
13 for it is [a]God who is at work in

7 [1]I.e., laid aside His privileges [a]2Cor. 8:9 [b]Matt. 20:28 [c]John 1:14; Rom. 8:3; Gal. 4:4; Heb. 2:17
8 [1]Lit., *of* [a]2Cor. 8:9 [b]Matt. 26:39; John 10:18; Rom. 5:19; Heb. 5:8 [c]Heb. 12:2
9 [a]Heb. 1:9 [b]Matt. 28:18; Acts 2:33; Heb. 2:9 [c]Eph. 1:21
10 [a]Is. 45:23; Rom. 14:11 [b]Eph. 1:10
11 [a]John 13:13; Rom. 10:9; 14:9
12 [a]Phil. 1:5, 6; 4:15 [b]Heb. 5:9 [c]2Cor. 7:15

13 [a]Rom. 12:3; 1Cor. 12:6; 15:10; Heb. 13:21

(continued from previous page)
or better, "when He took the form of a servant." The aorist participle *labōn,* "when He took,"indicates that this is not the principal verb. There is a principal verb in v. 6 and it is *hēgēsato* (2233), "did not regard." In v. 7 the principal verb is *ekenōse,* He "emptied Himself," and in v. 8 it is *etapeinōsen,* "He humbled Himself." All the other verbs are participles which means that the actions indicated by them are dependent or serve those actions indicated by the principal verbs. To make it clear what a participle is and what a principal verb is, this passage can be literally translated, "Who (Jesus Christ) being—having always been—in the form of God, He did not think it robbery to be equal with God, but Himself He emptied, when He took the form of a servant, when He became in the likeness of men and when He found Himself in shape as a man, He humbled Himself when He became obedient unto death or until death, the death of the cross." See *morphē* (3444), form, which means essence, what one really is and not apears to be, as contrasted to the word *schēma* (4976), shape, in v. 8 translated "appearance" and meaning "external shape," and the word *homoiōma* (3667) in v. 7 translated "likeness." He became like ourselves, taking upon Himself the likeness (*homoiōma,* 3667) of the flesh of sin (see Rom. 1:23; 8:3 and Jn. 1:14). See note on Col. 1:15.

That the Lord Jesus while He was here on earth positively laid claim to deity is clear from the fact that the Jews reproached Him with two accusations: first, that He placed God on par with Himself—and this they called blasphemy; secondly, that He made Himself God—and in this they thought they recognized the false prophet, although both ideas undoubtedly merged into each other (see Jn. 10:30-39).

The Lord Jesus Christ, being the Son of God, could not and did not claim to be the Father, but He could and did claim to be God. A human son cannot claim to be his human father but he is and can claim to be a human being. A claim to a sameness of nature is consistent and intelligible in the case of the divine Sonship of the Son of God, but a claim to sameness of personality would be a contradiction both in the one case and in the other. But undoubtedly there is such a similarity of persons that the one who has seen the Son has seen the Father, but this is a very different thing compared to absolute identical sameness. Identity in essence with the Father and distinction of person from the Father were essential to the person and work of the Son of God as Redeemer of mankind.

Christ was not half man and half God. He was wholly man and wholly God. We meet with incidents in His life which compel us to say categorically, "This is God"; and we also meet with incidents which force us to say as emphatically, "This is a man." Jesus prayed because He was a man. Human nature, even in Him, was a feeble, tender thing. He had to fall back upon the strength found in prayer. It is the uniform teaching of the N.T. that Christ, with regard to the Godhead, is equal to the Father, but with regard to His manhood, is inferior. Hence, when Christ says, "But of that day and hour no one knows, not even the angels of heaven nor the Son" (Mt. 24:36), He meant that He knew it not in the sense of making it known, as it formed no part of that revelation which He was commissioned to disclose to the world. As the Messiah, He was the delegate of the Father and only delivered such doctrines and instructions as were in keeping with that mission. See note on Col. 1:15.

🔑 **2:9** See note on I Thess. 2:19.

you, both to [pinf]will[2309] and to [pinf]work[1754] [b]for *His* good pleasure.

14 [pim]Do all things without [a]grumbling or disputing;[1261]

15 that you may [aosb] [I]prove yourselves to be [a]blameless[273] and innocent,[185] [b]children[5043] of God above reproach in the midst of a [c]crooked and perverse generation,[1074] among whom you [II][d]appear[5316] as [III]lights[5458] in the world,[2889]

🔑 16 holding [I]fast the word[3056] of life,[2222] so that in [a]the day[2250] of Christ I may have [nn]cause to glory because I did not [ao] [b]run in vain nor [ao] [c]toil in vain.

17 But even if I am being [a]poured out as a drink offering upon [b]the sacrifice and service[3009] of your faith,[4102] I rejoice[5463] and share my joy with[4796] you all.

18 And you too, *I urge you,* rejoice in the same way and share your joy with me.

Timothy and Epaphroditus

19 But I hope[1679] [I]in the Lord Jesus to [a]send [b]Timothy to you shortly, so that I also may be [psa]encouraged when I [apt]learn of your condition.

20 For I have no one *else* [a]of kindred spirit[2473] who will genuinely be concerned for your welfare.

21 For they all [a]seek after their own interests, not those of Christ Jesus.

22 But you know [a]of his proven[1382] worth that [b]he [ao]served[1398] with me in the furtherance of the gospel[2098] [c]like a child *serving* his father.

23 [a]Therefore I hope[1679] to send him immediately, as soon as I see[872] how things *go* with me;

24 and [a]I trust[3982] in the Lord that I myself also shall be coming shortly.

🔑 25 But I thought it necessary[316] to send to you [a]Epaphroditus, my brother[80] and [b]fellow worker and [c]fellow soldier, who is also your [I][d]messenger[652] and [e]minister[3011] to my need;[5532]

26 because he was longing [I]for you all and was [ppt]distressed because you had [ao]heard that he was [ao]sick.

27 For indeed he was sick to the point of death,[2288] but God had [ao]mercy on him, and not on him only but also on me, lest I should have [aosb]sorrow upon sorrow.

28 Therefore I have sent him all the more eagerly in order that when you see him again you may [aosb]rejoice and I may be less concerned *about you.*

29 Therefore [a]receive[4327] him in the Lord with all joy, and [pim] [b]hold men like him in high regard;

30 because he came [ao]close to death [a]for the work[2041] of Christ, [apt]risking his life[5590] to [aosb] [b]complete[378] [I]what was deficient in your service[3009] to me.

The Goal of Life

3 Finally, my brethren,[80] [a]rejoice[5463] in the Lord. To [pinf]write the same things *again* is no trouble to me, and it is a safeguard for you.

🔑 2 [pim]Beware[991] of the [a]dogs, beware of the [b]evil workers, beware of the [I]false circumcision;[2699]

3 for [a]we are the *true* [I]circumcision,[4061] who [ppt] [b]worship in the [an]Spirit of God and [ppt] [c]glory in [d]Christ Jesus and put no confidence[3982] in the flesh,[4561]

4 although [a]I myself might [ppt]have confidence[4006] even in the flesh. If anyone else has a mind to put confidence[3982] in the flesh, I far more:

5 [a]circumcised[4061] the eighth day, of the [b]nation of Israel, of the [c]tribe of Benjamin, a [b]Hebrew of Hebrews; as to the Law,[3551] [d]a Pharisee;

6 as to[2596] zeal, [a]a persecutor of the church;[1577] as to[2596] the [b]righteous-

13 [b]Eph. 1:5
14 [a]1Cor. 10:10; 1Pet. 4:9
15 [I]Or, *become* [II]Or, *shine* [III]Or, *luminaries, stars* [a]Luke 1:6; Phil. 3:6 [b]Matt. 5:45; Eph. 5:1 [c]Deut. 32:5; Acts 2:40 [d]Matt. 5:14-16
16 [I]Or, *forth* [a]Phil. 1:6 [b]Gal. 2:2 [c]Is. 49:4; Gal. 4:11; 1Thess. 3:5
17 [a]2Cor. 12:15; 2Tim. 4:6 [b]Num. 28:6, 7; Rom. 15:16
19 [I]Or, *trusting in* [a]Phil. 2:23 [b]Phil. 1:1
20 [a]1Cor. 16:10; 2Tim. 3:10
21 [a]1Cor. 10:24; 13:5; Phil. 2:4
22 [a]Rom. 5:4; Acts 16:2 [b]Acts 16:3; 1Cor. 16:10; 2Tim. 3:10 [c]1Cor. 4:17
23 [a]Phil. 2:19
24 [a]Phil. 1:25
25 [I]Lit., *apostle* [a]Phil. 4:18 [b]Rom. 16:3, 9, 21; Phil. 4:3; Philem. 1, 24 [c]Philem. 1:2 [d]John 13:16; 2Cor. 8:23 [e]Phil. 4:18
26 [I]Some ancient mss. read *to see you all*
29 [a]Rom. 16:2 [b]1Cor. 16:18
30 [I]Lit., *your deficiency of service* [a]Acts 20:24 [b]1Cor. 16:17; Phil. 4:10

1 [a]Phil. 2:18; 4:4
2 [I]Lit., *mutilation;* Gr., *katatome* [a]Ps. 22:16, 20; Gal. 5:15; Rev. 22:15 [b]2Cor. 11:13
3 [I]Gr., *peritome* [a]Rom. 2:29; 9:6; Gal. 6:15 [b]Gal. 5:25 [c]Rom. 15:17; Gal. 6:14 [d]Rom. 8:39; Phil. 1:1; 3:12
4 [a]2Cor. 5:16; 11:18
5 [a]Luke 1:59 [b]Rom. 11:1; 2Cor. 11:22 [c]Rom. 11:1 [d]Acts 22:3; 23:6; 26:5
6 [a]Acts 8:3; 22:4, 5; 26:9-11 [b]Phil. 3:9

🔑 **2:16** See note on I Thess. 5:2.
🔑 **2:25** See note on Col. 1:7.
🔑 **3:2** See note on Gal. 3:22.

ness[1343] which is in the Law, found [c]blameless.[273]

7 But [a]whatever things were gain to me, those things I have [pfip]counted as loss for the sake of Christ.[5547]

8 More than that, I count all things to be loss in view of the surpassing value of [Ia]knowing [b]Christ Jesus my Lord,[2962] for whom I have [aop]suffered the loss of all things, and count them but rubbish4657 in order that I may gain Christ,

9 and may be found in Him, not having [a]a righteousness[1343] of my own derived from *the* Law,[3551] but that which is through faith[4102] in Christ, [b]the righteousness which *comes* from God on the basis of faith,

10 that I may [infg] [a]know[1097] Him, and [b]the power[1411] of His resurrection[386] and [Ic]the fellowship[2842] of His sufferings,[3804] being [ppp] [d]conformed to His death;[2288]

11 [I]in order that I may [a]attain to the resurrection[1815] from the dead.[3498]

12 Not that I have already [ao] [a]obtained *it,* or have already [pfip] [b]become perfect,[5048] but I press on [I]in order that I may [aosb] [c]lay hold of[2638] that [II]for which also I [d]was [aop]laid hold of by [e]Christ Jesus.

13 Brethren, I do not regard[3049] myself as having [pfin]laid hold of *it* yet; but one thing *I do*: [a]forgetting what *lies* behind and reaching forward to what *lies* ahead,

14 I [a]press on toward the goal[4649] for the prize of the [b]upward[507] call[2821] of God in [c]Christ Jesus.

15 Let us therefore, as many as are [Ia]perfect,[5046] [psa]have this attitude;[5426] and if in anything you have[5426] a [b]different[2088] attitude,[5426] [c]God will reveal[601] that also to you;

16 however, let us keep [pinf] [Ia]living by that same *standard* to which we have [ao]attained.

17 Brethren, [a]join in following my example, and [pim]observe[4648] those who [ppt]walk according to the [b]pattern[5179] you have in us.

18 For [a]many walk, of whom I often [ipf]told you, and now tell you even

6 [c]Phil. 2:15 **7** [a]Luke 14:33 **8** [I]Lit., *the knowledge of* [a]Jer. 9:23f.; John 17:3; Eph. 4:13; Phil. 3:10; 2Pet. 1:3 [b]Rom. 8:39; Phil. 1:1; 3:12 **9** [a]Rom. 10:5; Phil. 3:6 [b]Rom. 9:30; 1Cor. 1:30 **10** [I]Or, *participation in* [a]Jer. 9:23f.; John 17:3; Eph. 4:13; Phil. 3:8; 2Pet. 1:13 [b]Rom. 6:5 [c]Rom. 8:17 [d]Rom. 6:5; 8:36; Gal. 6:17 **11** [I]Lit., *if somehow* [a]Acts 26:7; 1Cor. 15:23; Rev. 20:5f. **12** [I]Lit., *if I may even* [II]Or, *because also* [a]1Cor. 9:24f.; 1Tim. 6:12, 19 [b]1Cor. 13:10 [c]1Tim. 6:12, 19 [d]Acts 9:5f. [e]Rom. 8:39; Phil. 1:1; 3:3, 8 **13** [a]Luke 9:62 **14** [a]1Cor. 9:24; Heb. 6:1 [b]Rom. 8:28; 11:29; 2Tim. 1:9 [c]Phil. 3:3 **15** [I]Or, *mature* [a]Matt. 5:48; 1Cor. 2:6 [b]Gal. 5:10 [c]John 6:45; Eph. 1:17; 1Thess. 4:9 **16** [I]Lit., *following in line* [a]Gal. 6:16 **17** [a]1Cor. 4:16; 11:1; Phil. 4:9 [b]1Pet. 5:3 **18** [a]2Cor. 11:13 [b]Acts 20:31 [c]Gal. 6:14 **19** [I]Lit., *belly* [a]Rom. 16:18; Titus 1:12 [b]Rom. 6:21; Jude 13 [c]Rom. 8:5f.; Col. 3:2 **20** [I]Lit., *commonwealth* [a]Eph. 2:19; Phil. 1:27; Col. 3:1; Heb. 12:22 [b]1Cor. 1:7 **21** [I]Or, *our lowly body* [II]Or, *His glorious body* [a]1Cor. 15:43-53 [b]Rom. 8:29; Col. 3:4 [c]1Cor. 15:43, 49 [d]Eph. 1:19 [e]1Cor. 15:28

1 [I]Lit., *and longed for* [a]Phil. 1:8

[b]weeping, *that they are* enemies of [c]the cross[4716] of Christ,

19 whose end[5056] is destruction,[684] whose god is *their* [Ia]appetite, and *whose* [b]glory[1391] is in their shame,[152] who [ppt] [c]set their minds[5426] on earthly things.[1919]

20 For [a]our [I]citizenship is in heaven,[3772] from which also we eagerly [b]wait for[553] a Savior,[4990] the Lord[2962] Jesus Christ;[5547]

21 who will [a]transform[3345] [I]the body[4983] of our humble state[5014] into [b]conformity4833 with [II]the [c]body of His glory,[1391] [d]by the exertion of the power that He has even to [ainf] [e]subject[5293] all things to Himself.

Think of Excellence

4 Therefore, my beloved[27] brethren[80] [I]whom I [a]long *to see,* my joy[5479] and crown, so [b]stand firm in the Lord, my beloved.

2 I urge Euodia and I urge Syntyche to [Ia]live in harmony[5426]846 in the Lord.

3 Indeed, true comrade, I ask you also to [pim]help these women who have shared my struggle in *the cause of* the gospel,[2098] together with Clement also, and the rest of my [a]fellow workers, whose [b]names[3686] are in the book[976] of life.[2222]

4 [a]Rejoice[5463] in the Lord always; again I will say, rejoice!

5 Let your forbearing1933 *spirit* be [aipp]known to all men.[444] [a]The Lord is [I]near.[1451]

6 [a]Be [pim]anxious for nothing,[3367] but in everything by [b]prayer[4335] and supplication[1162] with thanksgiving let your requests[155] be [pim]made known[1107] to God.

7 And [a]the peace[1515] of God, which [ppt]surpasses all [I]comprehension,[3563]

[b]1Cor. 16:13; Phil. 1:27 **2** [I]Or, *be of the same mind* [a]Phil. 2:2 **3** [a]Phil. 2:25 [b]Luke 10:20 **4** [a]Phil. 3:1 **5** [I]Or, *at hand* [a]1Cor. 16:22 mg.; Heb. 10:37; James 5:8f. **6** [a]Matt. 6:25 [b]Eph. 6:18; 1Tim. 2:1; 5:5 **7** [I]Lit., *mind* [a]Is. 26:3; John 14:27; Phil. 4:9; Col. 3:15

shall [b]guard your hearts[2588] and your
[c]minds[3540] in [d]Christ Jesus.
8 Finally, brethren, [a]whatever is
true,[227] whatever is honorable,[4586]
whatever is right,[1342] whatever is
pure,[53] whatever is [I]lovely,4375 whatever is [II]of good repute,[2163] if there is
any excellence[703] and if anything worthy
of praise,1868 [III]let your mind [pim]dwell
on these things.
9 The things you have [ao]learned[3129]
and [ao]received and [ao]heard and [ao]seen
[a]in me, [pim]practice[4238] these things; and
[b]the God of peace[1515] shall be with you.

God's Provisions

10 But I rejoiced in the Lord
greatly, that now at last [a]you have [ao]re-
vived your concern for me; indeed, you
were concerned *before,* but you [ipf]lacked
opportunity.
11 Not that I speak [I]from want;5304
for I have [ao]learned to be [IIa]content in
whatever circumstances I am.
12 I know how to [pip]get along with
humble means,[5013] and I also know how
to [pinf]live in prosperity; in any and every
circumstance I have [pfip]learned the secret of being filled and going [a]hungry,
both of having abundance and [b]suffering
need.
13 I can do all things [I]through Him
who [ppt a]strengthens me.
14 Nevertheless, you have done
well to [apt a]share[4790] *with me* in my affliction.
15 And you yourselves also know,
Philippians, that at the [Ia]first preaching
of the gospel, after I departed from
[b]Macedonia, no church[1577] [c]shared[2841]
with me in the matter of giving[1394] and
receiving[3028] but you alone;
16 for even in [a]Thessalonica you
sent *a gift* more than once for my needs.
17 [a]Not that I seek the gift[1390] itself,
but I seek for the [I]profit which [ppt]in-
creases to your account.[3056]
🗝 18 But I have received everything in full,[568] and have an abundance;
I am [I]amply [pfip]supplied, having [apt]re-
ceived from [a]Epaphroditus [II]what you
have sent, [IIIb]a fragrant aroma, an
acceptable[1184] sacrifice,[2378] well-pleasing[2101] to God.
19 And [a]my God shall supply[4137]
[I]all your needs according to His [b]riches
in glory[1391] in Christ Jesus.
20 Now to [a]our God and Father[3962]
[b]*be* the glory [I]forever[165] and ever.[165]
Amen.281
21 [aim]Greet782 every [I]saint[40] in
Christ Jesus. [a]The brethren who are
with me greet you.
22 [a]All the [Ib]saints greet you, especially those of Caesar's household.
23 [a]The grace of the Lord Jesus
Christ [b]be with your spirit.

7 [b]1Pet. 1:5 [c]2Cor. 10:5 [d]Phil. 1:1; 4:19, 21
8 [I]Or, *lovable and gracious* [II]Or, *attractive* [III]Lit., *ponder these things* [a]Rom. 14:18; 1Pet. 2:12
9 [a]Phil. 3:17 [b]Rom. 15:33
10 [a]2Cor. 11:9; Phil. 2:30
11 [I]Lit., *according to* [II]Or, *self-sufficient* [a]2Cor. 9:8; 1Tim. 6:6, 8; Heb. 13:5
12 [a]1Cor. 4:11 [b]2Cor. 11:9
13 [I]Lit., *in* [a]2Cor. 12:9; Eph. 3:16; Col. 1:11
14 [a]Heb. 10:33; Rev. 1:9
15 [I]Lit., *beginning of* [a]Phil. 1:5 [b]Rom. 15:26 [c]2Cor. 11:9
16 [a]Acts 17:1; 1Thess. 2:9
17 [I]Lit., *fruit* [a]1Cor. 9:11f.; 2Cor. 9:5
18 [I]Lit., *made full* [II]Lit., *the things from you* [III]Lit., *an odor of fragrance* [a]Phil. 2:25 [b]Ex. 29:18; 2Cor. 2:14; Eph. 5:2
19 [I]Or, *every need of yours* [a]2Cor. 9:8 [b]Rom. 2:4
20 [I]Lit., *to the ages of the ages* [a]Gal. 1:4 [b]Rom. 11:36
21 [I]Or, *holy one* [a]Gal. 1:2
22 [I]V. 21, note 1 [a]2Cor. 13:13 [b]Acts 9:13
23 [a]Rom. 16:20 [b]2Tim. 4:22

🗝 **4:18** See note on Col. 1:7.

The Epistle of Paul to the

COLOSSIANS

Colossae was an important city of Phrygia in Asia Minor, situated to the east of Ephesus. It is not definitely known that Paul visited it, but it is quite possible that he did so on his third missionary journey. Most probably this Epistle was written by Paul while he was a prisoner in Rome, about A.D. 62, and delivered by Tychicus (4:7,8).

Colossians is the sister Epistle to Ephesians even as Romans is to Galatians. It was written almost simultaneously and sent by the same messenger, Tychicus (Eph. 6:21,22). The central theme of Colossians is Christ, while that of Ephesians is the Church.

The Colossian heresy combined philosophical speculations, astral powers, reverence to angelic intermediaries, food taboos, and ascetic practices with Judaistic borrowings (Col. 2:8-23).

Paul does not confront the heresies that existed in Colossae point by point but, he presents related truth in a positive manner. From the subjects he touches upon we conclude the following: (1) Inordinate attention was given to the powers of the spirit world to the detriment of the place given to Christ. In 2:18 he speaks of "worship of the angels," and in other references to the relation of the spiritual creation to Christ (1:16,20; 2:15). (2) Undue attention was given to outward observances such as feasts and fasts, new moons and sabbaths (2:16f), and probably also circumcision (2:11). These were presented as the true way of self-discipline and the subjection of the flesh (2:20ff). (3) They were also definitely influenced by Gnosticism, a heresy that plagued the early church in the first 200 years of its existence. The word is derived from the Greek word *gnōsis* (1108) meaning "knowledge." This heresy was repudiated not only by the writers of the N.T. Epistles but also by the church fathers who lived in the period after the early church. It is from them that we acquire a knowledge of Gnosticism's general tenets.

The Gnostics separated matter from thought. They considered matter as evil and thought or knowledge as the ultimate for salvation. This is why they did not want to attribute humanity to Jesus Christ since humanity, being material, to them was evil. From this we have the Docetic heresy which believed that the body of Christ was only something that appeared material, but in reality it was not. Such a belief led to an immoral life for since the spirit was entirely separate they were not responsible for the acts of the body. This is the reason why Paul in 2:9 stressed that in Jesus Christ, as He appeared on earth, dwelt all the fullness of the Godhead bodily. He was truly God in the flesh. As a result of the philosophical concept of the evil of the body, the Gnostics ignored or diminished the significance of the historic facts of the ministry, death, and resurrection of Jesus Christ as not being real but simply apparent. To them, all the secrets of God were in the mind, an immaterial identity. The result developed in two divergent directions, one being a complete denial of sexual and other bodily appetites, i.e., virtual asceticism; and stemming from the same premises, the practice of unrestrained indulgence of the body.

Paul in this Epistle counters the teaching that stresses that the way of holiness is through an asceticism that promotes only spiritual selfishness. He stresses that spirituality is not achieved by self-centered efforts to control the passions, but by putting on Christ, setting one's affections on Him, and so stripping off all that is contrary to His will (2:20ff; 3:1ff).

He stresses furthermore that as far as immaterial knowledge is concerned, true wisdom is not a man-made philosophy (2:8), but the "mystery" (revealed secret) of God in Christ, who indwells all who receive Him (1:27) without distinction of persons (3:10f).

The occasion of the writing and sending of this Epistle was that of Paul sending a messenger to Philemon in Colossae in connection with his runaway, but now converted, slave, Onesimus (4:7-9). Furthermore, Epaphras had brought Paul a report of the church in Colossae which included many encouraging things (1:4-8), but also disturbing news of the false teaching that threatened to lead its members away from the truth of Christ.

Thankfulness for Spiritual Attainments

1 [a]Paul, [b]an apostle[652] of Jesus Christ[5547] [Ic]by the will[2307] of God,[2316] and [d]Timothy [II]our brother,[80]

2 to the [Ia]saints[40] and faithful[4103] brethren in Christ *who are* at Colossae: [b]Grace[5485] to you and peace[1515] from God our Father.[3962]

3 [a]We give thanks[2168] to God, [b]the Father of our Lord Jesus Christ, praying[4336] always for you,

🔑 4 [a]since we heard of your faith[4102] in Christ Jesus and the [b]love[26] which you have [I]for [c]all the [II]saints;

5 because of the [a]hope[1680] [ppt] [b]laid up for you in [I]heaven,[3772] of which you previously [c]heard in the word[3056] of truth,[225] [II]the gospel,[2098]

6 which has come to you, just as [Ia]in all the world[2889] also it is constantly bearing [b]fruit and [II]increasing, even as *it has been doing* in you also since the day you [c]heard *of it* and [III]understood[1921] the grace[5485] of God in truth;

🔑 7 just as you learned[3129] *it* from [a]Epaphras, our [b]beloved fellow bondservant,[4889] who is a faithful[4103] servant[1249] of Christ on [I]our behalf,

8 and he also informed us of your [a]love[26] in the Spirit.[4151]

🔑 9 For this reason also, [a]since the day we heard *of it*, [b]we have not ceased to [ppt]pray[4336] for you and to [ppt]ask that you may be [asbp]filled with the [Ic]knowledge[1922] of His will[2307] in all spiritual[4152] [d]wisdom[4678] and understanding,[4907]

10 so that you may [ainf] [a]walk[4043] in a manner worthy of the Lord, [Ib]to please[699] *Him* in all respects, [c]bearing fruit in every good[18] work and [II]increasing in the [III]knowledge[1922] of God;

11 [a]strengthened[1412] with all power,[1411] according to [I]His glorious[1391] might,[2904] [II]for the attaining of all steadfastness[5281] and [III]patience; [b]joyously[5479]

12 giving thanks[2168] to [a]the Father, who has [apt]qualified us [I]to share[2427] in

1 [I]Lit., *through* [II]Lit., *the* [a]Phil. 1:1 [b]2Cor. 1:1 [c]1Cor. 1:1 [d]2Cor. 1:1; 1Thess. 3:2
2 [I]Or, *holy ones* [a]Acts 9:13 [b]Rom. 1:7
3 [a]Rom. 1:8 [b]Rom. 15:6; 2Cor. 1:3
4 [I]Or, *toward* [II]Or, *holy ones* [a]Eph. 1:15 [b]Gal. 5:6 [c]Eph. 6:18
5 [I]Lit., *the heavens* [II]Or, *of the gospel* [a]Acts 23:6 [b]2Tim. 4:8 [c]Eph. 1:13
6 [I]Or, *it is in the world* [II]Or, *spreading abroad* [III]Or, *came really to know* [a]Rom. 10:18 [b]Rom. 1:13 [c]Eph. 4:21
7 [I]Some later mss. read *your* [a]Col. 4:12 [b]Col. 4:7
8 [a]Rom. 15:30
9 [I]Or, *real knowledge* [a]Col. 1:4 [b]Eph. 1:16 [c]Phil. 1:9 [d]Eph. 1:17
10 [I]Lit., *unto all pleasing* [II]Or, *growing by the knowledge* [III]Or, *real knowledge* [a]Eph. 4:1 [b]Eph. 5:10 [c]Rom. 1:13
11 [I]Lit., *the might of His glory* [II]Lit., *unto all* [III]Or, *patience with joy* [a]1Cor. 16:13 [b]Eph. 4:2
12 [I]Lit., *unto the portion of* [a]Eph. 2:18

🔑 **1:4-8** See Introduction.

🔑 **1:7** Epaphras (also mentioned in 4:12 and Phile. 23) was one of Paul's friends and associates, called by him "fellow bondservant" and "fellow prisoner." Perhaps he may have been imprisoned with Paul. The name is abbreviated from Epaphroditus, but Epaphras is probably not to be identified with Epaphroditis in Phil. 2:25; 4:18. Epaphras evangelized the cities of the Lycus Valley in Phrygia under Paul's direction and founded the churches of Colossae, Hierapolis, and Laodicea. Later he visited Paul during his Roman captivity and it was his news of conditions in the churches of the Lycus Valley that caused Paul to write the Epistle to the Colossians.

🔑 **1:9** The heresy that prevailed in Colossae as well as in other contemporary churches was Gnosticism, the heresy of *gnōsis* (1108), "knowledge." To counter this heresy of knowledge, Paul uses a compound word, *epignōsis* made up of the preposition *epi* which is used as an intensive, "on top of, in addition to," and *gnōsis* (1922). The verb from which *gnōsis* is derived is *ginōskō* (1097), and the verb from which *epignōsis* is derived is *epiginōskō* (1921). The difference between these two verbs is that *ginōskō* sometimes means "to merely take notice or to recognize a thing unintentionally," while *epiginōskō* implies at least a special participation in the thing known. Compare the use of the two words in Jn. 8:32, *ginōskō,* "know" the truth, and I Tim. 4:3, "those who have had full appropriated knowledge" of the truth, *epegnōkosi,* the perfect active of *epiginōskō* which means not only knowing the truth in its initial state, but also having appropriated it.

The verb *epiginōsko* is found in Mt. 7:16,20; 11:27; 14:35; 17:12; Mk. 2:8; 5:30; 6:33,54; Lk. 1:4,22; 5:22; 7:37; 23:7; 24:16,31; Acts 3:10; 4:13; 9:30; 12:14; 19:34; 22:24,29; 24:8; 25:10; 27:39; 28:1; Rom. 1:32; I Cor. 13:12; 14:37; 16:18; II Cor. 1:13,14; 6:9; 13:5; Col. 1;6; I Tim. 4:3; II Pet. 2:21.

The noun *epignōsis* (1922), unfortunately translated merely as "knowledge" as if it were simply *gnōsis* (1108), which it is not, occurs in Rom. 1:28; 3:20; 10:2; Eph. 1:17; 4:13; Phil. 1:9; Col. 1:9,10; 2:2; 3:10; I Tim. 2:4; II Tim. 3:7; Tit. 1:1; Phile. 6; Heb. 10:26; II Pet. 1:2,3,8; 2:20.

[b]the inheritance[2819] of the [II]saints in
[c]light.[5457]

The Incomparable Christ

13 For He [ao]delivered[4506] us from
the [Ia]domain[1849] of darkness,[4655] and
[ao]transferred[3179] us to the kingdom[932]
of [IIb]His beloved[26] Son,[5207]
14 [a]in whom we have redemp-
tion,[629] the forgiveness[859] of sins.[266]
🔑 15 And He is the [a]image[1504] of the
[b]invisible God,[2316] the [c]first-born[4416] of
all creation.
16 For [Ia]by Him all things were
[pfip]created,[2937] [b]*both* in the heavens[3772]
and on earth,[1093] visible and invisible,
whether [c]thrones or dominions[2963] or
rulers[746] or authorities—[1849] [c]all things
have been created[2936] [II]by Him and for
Him.
17 And He [Ia]is before all things, and
in Him all things [pfi] [II]hold together.[4921]
18 He is also [a]head of [b]the body,[4983]
the church;[1577] and He is [c]the beginning,[746] [d]the first-born[4416] from the
dead; so that He Himself might come
to have first place in everything.
19 For [I]it was [a]the *Father's* good
pleasure[2106] for all [b]the [II]fulness[4138] to
[ainf]dwell[2730] in Him,
20 and through Him to [ainf] [a]recon-
cile[604] all things to Himself, having made
[apt] [b]peace through [c]the blood of His
cross;[4716] through Him, *I say,* [d]whether
things on earth[1093] or things in
[I]heaven.[3772]
21 And although you were [a]formerly
[pfpp]alienated[526] and hostile in mind,[1271]
engaged in evil[4190] deeds,
22 yet He has now [ao] [a]reconciled[604]
you in His fleshly[4561] [b]body[4983] through
death,[2288] in order to [ainf] [c]present you
before Him [d]holy[40] and blameless[299] and
beyond reproach—
23 if indeed you continue in [I]the
faith[4102] firmly [pfpp] [a]established and
steadfast, and not [ppt]moved away from
the [b]hope[1680] of the gospel[2098] that you

12 [II]Or, *holy ones* [b] Acts 20:32 [c]Acts 26:18
13 [I]Lit., *authority* [II]Lit., *the Son of His love* [a]Eph. 6:12 [b]Eph. 1:6
14 [a]Rom. 3:24
15 [a]2Cor. 4:4 [b]John 1:18 [c]Rom. 8:29
16 [I]Or, *in* [II]Or, *through* [a]Eph. 1:10 [b]Eph. 1:20f.; Col. 2:15 [c]John 1:3; Rom. 11:36; 1Cor. 8:6
17 [I]Or, *has existed prior to* [II]Or, *endure* [a]John 1:1; 8:58
18 [a]Eph. 1:22 [b]Eph. 1:23; Col. 1:24; 2:19 [c]Rev. 3:14 [d]Acts 26:23
19 [I]Or, *all the fulness was pleased to dwell* [II]I.e., fulness of deity [a]Eph. 1:5 [b]John 1:16
20 [I]Lit., *the heavens* [a]2Cor. 5:18; Eph. 2:16 [b]Rom. 5:1; Eph. 2:14 [c]Eph. 2:13 [d]Col. 1:16

21 [a]Rom. 5:10; Eph. 2:3, 12 **22** [a]2Cor. 5:18; Eph. 2:16 [b]Rom. 7:4 [c]Eph. 5:27; Col. 1:28 [d]Eph. 1:4
23 [I]Or omit, *the* [a]Eph. 3:17; Col. 2:7 [b]Col. 1:5

🔑 **1:15ff.** Here Jesus Christ is presented as the image of God, the invisible One (Jn. 1:18). The order of the Greek text has the word *eikōn* preceding *prōtotokos. Eikōn* (1504), "image," means that which resembles an object, which represents it. This word *eikōn* always assumes a prototype, not merely what it resembles, but from which it is drawn. For instance, the reflection of the sun in the water is called by Plato *eikōn*. Paul was telling the Colossians here that Jesus Christ has a "prototype," God the Father who is invisible. He is real because Jesus is real and not imaginary. The relationship between the Son and the Father, Christ and the Father God, is not coincidental as, for instance, two persons being similar, *homoi* (3664). (See also *homoiōma,* 3667, "resemblance.") Paul's teaching to the Colossians was that there was not a mere coincidental resemblance between Jesus Christ and His Father (*homoiōma*), but they were eternally related One to the Other (*eikōn*). The One was the reflection of the Other who was real and not merely the figment of thought or imagination. And this is so in spite of the fact that God is invisible. That which is invisible, nevertheless, can be and is real. See the notes on Jn. 1:18; Phil. 2:6-8.

The other word to which we must turn our attention and which is used twice in this context is the word *prōtotokos* (4416), translated as "first born" or "first begotten." It is used twice in Col. 1:15,18. Elsewhere, it is used in Mt. 1:25; Lk. 2:7; Rom. 8:29; Heb. 1:6; 11:28; 12:23 and Rev. 1:5. What it means here is that Christ holds the same relation to all creation as God the Father and that He is above all creation. It does not mean that He is part of the creation made by God, but that the relation of the whole creation to Him was determined by the fact that He is the cause of the creation of all things (Jn. 1:1; Rev. 3:14) and that without Him there could be no creation (Jn. 1:3,4; Col. 1:16). It is not said of Christ that He was *ktistheis,* "created," from *ktizō* (2936) "to create," a verb used of the creation of the world by Him in Col. 1:16. We never find this verb *ktizō* as referring to Jesus Christ as having been created. The verb is used in Mt. 19:4; Mk. 13:19; Rom. 1:25; I Cor. 11:9; Eph. 2:10; 3:9; 4:24; Col. 1:16 (twice); 3:10; I Tim. 4:3; Rev. 4:11; 10:6. In Rev. 3:14 the Lord Jesus Christ is called "the Beginning of the creation of God." But the word "beginning," *archē* (746), in this instance is not used as the result of God's creation but the cause of God's creation. See the Editor's book on Jn. 1:1-18, entitled *Was Christ God?.*

have [ao]heard, which was proclaimed[2784]
[c]in all creation[2937] under heaven, [d]and
of which I, Paul, [II]was [ao]made a
[III][e]minister.[1249]
24 [a]Now I rejoice in my sufferings[3804] for your sake, and in my
flesh[4561] [b]I [I]do my share on behalf of
[c]His body[4983] (which is the church)[1577]
in filling up that which is lacking [II]in
Christ's[5547] afflictions.
25 [a]Of *this church* I [I]was made a
minister according to the [b]steward-
ship[3622] from God [aptp]bestowed on me
for your benefit, that I might [ainf] [II]fully
carry out[4137] the *preaching of* the
word[3056] of God,
26 *that is,* [a]the mystery[3466] which
has been [pfpp]hidden from the *past* ages[165]
and generations;[1074] but has now [ao]been
manifested[5319] to His [I]saints,[40]
27 to whom [a]God [ao]willed to make
known[1107] what is [b]the riches of the
glory[1391] of this mystery[3466] among the
Gentiles,[1484] which is [c]Christ[5547] in you,
the [d]hope[1680] of glory.
28 And we proclaim[2605] Him,
[ppt] [a]admonishing[3560] every man[444] and
teaching[1321] every man [I]with all [b]wis-
dom,[4678] that we may [aosb] [c]present every
man [II][d]complete[5046] in Christ.
29 And for this purpose also I
[a]labor, [b]striving[75] [c]according to His
[I]power, which [II]mightily [ppt]works[1754]
within me.

You Are Built Up in Christ

2 For I want you to know how great
a [a]struggle[73] I have on your behalf,
and for those who are at [b]Laodicea, and
for all those who have not [I]personally
seen my face,
2 that their [a]hearts may be encouraged, having been [aptp] [b]knit together in
love,[26] and *attaining* to all [c]the wealth
[I]that comes from the full assurance[4136]
of understanding, *resulting* in a [d]true
knowledge[1922] of [e]God's[2316] mystery,
that is, Christ[5547] *Himself,*
3 in whom are hidden all [a]the treasures of wisdom[4678] and knowledge.[1108]
4 [a]I say this in order that no one
may [psa]delude3884 you with [b]persuasive
argument.
5 For even though I am [a]absent[548]
in body,[4561] nevertheless I am with you
in spirit,[4151] rejoicing [I]to see [II]your
[b]good discipline[5010] and the [c]stability of
your faith[4102] in Christ.
6 As you therefore have [ao]received
[a]Christ Jesus the Lord,[2962] *so* [pim] [I][b]walk
in Him,
7 having been firmly [pfpp][a]rooted *and*
now being [ppp] [b]built up[2026] in Him and
[ppp] [c]established[950] [I]in your faith,[4102] just
as you [d]were [aop]instructed,[1321] *and*
[ppt]overflowing [II]with gratitude.
🔑**8** [a]See to it[991] that no one [ppt]takes
you captive through [b]philosophy and
empty[2756] deception, according to the
tradition3862 of men,[444] according to
the [c]elementary principles[4747] of the
world,[2889] [I]rather than according to
Christ.[5547]
9 For in Him all the [a]fulness[4138] of
Deity[2320] dwells in bodily form,4985
10 and in Him you have been
[a]made [I]complete, and [b]He is the head[2776]
[II]over all [c]rule[746] and authority;[1849]
11 and in Him [a]you were also
[aop]circumcised[4059] with a circumcision[4061] made without hands, in the removal of [b]the body[4983] of the flesh[4561]
by the circumcision of Christ;
12 having been [aptp] [a]buried with Him
in baptism,[908] in which you were also
[aop] [b]raised up with Him through faith[4102]
in the working of God, who [apt] [c]raised[1453]
Him from the dead.[3498]
13 And when you were [a]dead
[I]in your transgressions[3900] and the
uncircumcision[203] of your flesh, He

23 [II]Lit., *became* [III]Or, *servant* [c]Mark 16:15; Acts 2:5; Col. 1:6 [d]Eph. 3:7; Col. 1:25 [e]1Cor. 3:5
24 [I]Or, *representatively . . . fill up* [II]Lit., *of* [a]Rom. 8:17; 2Cor. 1:5; 12:15; Phil. 2:17 [b]2Tim. 1:8; 2:10 [c]Col. 1:18
25 [I]Lit., *became* [II]Lit., *make full the word of God* [a]Col. 1:23 [b]Eph. 3:2
26 [I]Or, *holy ones* [a]Rom. 16:25f.; Eph. 3:3f.; Col. 2:2; 4:3
27 [a]Matt. 13:11 [b]Eph. 1:7, 18; 3:16 [c]Rom. 8:10 [d]1Tim. 1:1
28 [I]Lit., *in* [II]Or, *perfect* [a]Acts 20:31; Col. 3:16 [b]1Cor. 2:6f.; Col. 2:3 [c]Col. 1:22 [d]Matt. 5:48; Eph. 4:13
29 [I]Lit., *working* [II]Lit., *in power* [a]1Cor. 15:10 [b]Col. 2:1; 4:12 [c]Eph. 1:19; Col. 2:12

1 [I]Lit., *in the flesh* [a]Col. 1:29; 4:12 [b]Col. 4:13, 15f.; Rev. 1:11
2 [I]Lit., *of the full assurance* [a]1Cor. 14:31; Eph. 6:22; Col. 4:8 [b]Col. 2:19 [c]Eph. 1:7, 18; 3:16 [d]Matt. 13:11 [e]Rom. 16:25f.; Eph. 3:3f.; Col. 1:26; 4:3
3 [a]Is. 11:2; Rom. 11:33
4 [a]Eph. 4:17 [b]Rom. 16:18
5 [I]Lit., *and seeing* [II]Or, *your ordered array* [a]1Cor. 5:3 [b]1Cor. 14:40 [c]1Pet. 5:9
6 [I]Or, *lead your life* [a]Gal. 3:26 [b]Col. 1:10
7 [I]Or, *by* [II]Some mss. read *in it with* [a]Eph. 3:17 [b]1Cor. 3:9; Eph. 2:20

[c]1Cor. 1:8 [d]Eph. 4:21 **8** [I]Lit., *and not* [a]1Cor. 8:9; 10:12; Gal. 5:15; Heb. 3:12 [b]Eph. 5:6; Col. 2:23; 1Tim. 6:20 [c]Gal. 4:3; Col. 2:20 **9** [a]2Cor. 5:19; Col. 1:19 **10** [I]Or, *full* [II]Lit., *of* [a]Eph. 3:19 [b]Eph. 1:21f. [c]1Cor. 15:24; Eph. 3:10; Col. 2:15 **11** [a]Rom. 2:29; Eph. 2:11 [b]Rom. 6:6; 7:24; Gal. 5:24; Col. 3:5 **12** [a]Rom. 6:4f. [b]Rom. 6:5; Eph. 2:6; Col. 2:13; 3:1 [c]Acts 2:24 **13** [I]Or, *by reason of* [a]Eph. 2:1

🔑 **2:8-23** See general remarks on the Colossian heresy; Col. 1:15-18.

ao [b]made you alive together 4806 with Him, having forgiven ***5483*** us all our transgressions, ***3900***

14 having apt canceled out [a]the certificate of debt consisting of decrees ***1378*** against us *and* which was hostile to us; and [b]He has pfi taken it out of the way, ***3319*** having apt nailed it to the cross. ***4716***

15 When He had apt [Ia]disarmed the [b]rulers ***746*** and authorities, ***1849*** He ao [c]made a public display of them, having apt [d]triumphed over them through [II]Him.

16 Therefore let no one pim [Ia]act as your judge ***2919*** in regard to [b]food or [c]drink or in respect to a [d]festival or a [e]new moon or a [f]Sabbath [II]day— 4521

17 things which are [a]a *mere* shadow of what is to come; but the [I]substance ***4983*** [II]belongs to Christ.

18 Let no one keep pim [Ia]defrauding you of your prize by [b]delighting in [II]self-abasement and the worship 2356 of the angels, ***32*** taking his stand on *visions* he has pfi seen, ***3708*** ppp [c]inflated without cause by his [d]fleshly mind, ***3563***

19 and not holding fast to [a]the head, ***2776*** from whom [b]the entire body, ***4983*** being ppp supplied and ppp held together by the joints and [I]ligaments, grows with a growth [II]which is from God.

20 [a]If you have ao died ***599*** with Christ [I]to the [b]elementary principles ***4747*** of the world, ***2889*** [c]why, as if you were living ***2198*** in the world, do you submit yourself to [d]decrees, ***1379*** such as,

21 "Do not aosi handle, ***680*** do not aosi taste, ***1089*** do not aosi touch!" ***2345***

13 [b]Eph. 2:5; Col. 2:12
14 [a]Eph. 2:15; Col. 2:20 [b]1Pet. 2:24
15 [I]Or, *divested Himself of* [II]Or, *it;* i.e., the cross [a]Eph. 4:8 [b]John 12:31; 1Cor. 15:24; Eph. 3:10; Col. 2:10 [c]Eph. 4:8 [d]2Cor. 2:14
16 [I]Lit., *judge you* [II]Or, *days* [a]Rom. 14:3 [b]Mark 7:19; Rom. 14:17; Heb. 9:10 [c]Lev. 23:2; Rom. 14:5 [d]1Chr. 23:31; 2Chr. 31:3; Neh. 10:33 [e]Mark 2:27f.; Gal. 4:10
17 [I]Lit., *body* [II]Lit., *of Christ* [a]Heb. 8:5; 10:1
18 [I]Or, *giving judgment against you* [II]Or, *humility* [a]1Cor. 9:24; Phil. 3:14 [b]Col. 2:23 [c]1Cor. 4:6 [d]Rom. 8:7
19 [I]Lit., *bonds* [II]Lit., *of God* [a]Eph. 1:22 [b]Eph. 1:23; 4:16
20 [I]Lit., *from* [a]Rom. 6:2 [b]Col. 2:8 [c]Gal. 4:9 [d]Col. 2:14, 16
22 [I]Or, *by being consumed* [a]1Cor. 6:13 [b]Is. 29:13; Matt. 15:9; Titus 1:14
23 [I]Or, *delight in religiousness* [a]Col. 2:18 [b]1Tim. 4:3

22 (which all *refer* [a]*to* things destined to perish [I]with the using)— 671 in accordance with the [b]commandments ***1778*** and teachings ***1319*** of men? ***444***

23 These are matters which have, to be sure, the appearance ***3056*** of wisdom ***4678*** in [Ia]self-made religion and self-abasement and [b]severe treatment of the body, ***4983*** *but are* of no value against [c]fleshly ***4561*** indulgence.

Put On the New Self

3 🗝 If then you have been aop [a]raised up with Christ, keep pim seeking the things above, ***507*** where Christ is, [b]seated at the right hand ***1188*** of God.

2 [Ia]Set your mind ***5426*** on the things above, ***507*** not on the things that are on earth. ***1093***

3 For you have ao [a]died ***599*** and your life ***2222*** is hidden with Christ in God.

4 When Christ, [a]who is our life, is asbp revealed, ***5319*** [b]then you also will be revealed with Him in glory. ***1391***

🗝 **5** [a]Therefore aim [I]consider [b]the members of your earthly body as dead to [IIc]immorality, impurity, ***167*** passion, ***3806*** evil desire, ***1939*** and greed, ***4124*** which [III]amounts to idolatry. ***1495***

[c]Rom. 13:14; 1Tim. 4:8 **1** [a]Col. 2:12 [b]Ps. 110:1; Mark 16:19 **2** [I]Or, *Be intent on* [a]Matt. 16:23; Phil. 3:19, 20 **3** [a]Rom. 6:2; 2Cor. 5:14; Col. 2:20 **4** [a]John 11:25; Gal. 2:20 [b]1Cor. 1:7; Phil. 3:21; 1Pet. 1:13; 1John 2:28; 3:2 **5** [I]Lit., *put to death the members which are upon the earth* [II]Lit., *fornication* [III]Lit., *is* [a]Rom. 8:13 [b]Col. 2:11 [c]Mark 7:21f.; 1Cor. 6:9f., 18; 2Cor. 12:21; Gal. 5:19f.; Eph. 4:19;5:3, 5

🗝 **3:1ff** See general remarks on the Colossian heresy.

🗝 **3:5** This verse again combats Gnosticism (see general remarks) which taught that the body is evil, and since it is evil in itself and cannot be redeemed from its evil ways, it might as well do whatever it wants. This is the reason why Paul says, "Consider the members of your earthly body as dead." Bring them under control. Treat them as if they were dead. Your spirit should have them under subjection because the two, the spirit and the body, are interrelated and the body behaves only as the spirit commands it. The evils of the body which Paul lists result in material expressions: *porneia* (4202), "immorality," including all sexual sins among unmarried or married persons, including adultery, homosexuality, incest, etc.: *akatharsia* (167), uncleanness of all kinds that defile the body; *pathos* (3806), passion; *epithumia* (1939), "desire," which in this instance is similar to "lust" because it is coupled with the adjective *kakē* (2556), "bad" or constitutionally evil (these two words are translated as "evil" which actually means lustful desire; *pleonexia* (4124), "greed," desiring to have more than one has, not because it is insufficient but because others have more. Such desire is called "idolatry."

6 For it is on account of these things
that [a]the wrath[3709] of God will come[I],
7 and [a]in them you also once walked,
when you were [ipf]living[2198] in them.
8 But now you also, [aim a]put them
all aside: [b]anger,[3709] wrath,[2372] malice,[2549] slander,[988] *and* [c]abusive speech
from your mouth.
9 [Ia]Do not [pim]lie to one another,
since you [apt b]laid aside the old [II]self[444]
with its *evil* practices,4234
10 and have [apt a]put on the new[3501]
[I]self who is being [ppp IIb]renewed[341] to a
true knowledge[1922] [c]according to the
image[1504] of the One who [apt d]created
him
🔑 11 —*a renewal* in which [a]there is
no *distinction between* Greek and Jew,
[b]circumcised[4061] and uncircumcised,[203]
[c]barbarian,915 Scythian, [d]slave[1401] and
freeman,[1658] but [e]Christ[5547] is all, and
in all.
12 And so, as those who have been
[a]chosen[1588] of God, holy[40] and beloved,[25]
[aim b]put on a [c]heart4698 of compassion,3628
kindness,[5544] [d]humility, gentleness and
[Ie]patience;
13 [a]bearing with[430] one another, and
[b]forgiving[5483] each other, whoever
[psa]has a complaint against anyone; [b]just
as the Lord forgave you, so also should
you.
14 And beyond all these things *put
on* love,[26] which is [Ia]the perfect bond
of [b]unity.[5047]
15 And let [a]the peace[1515] of Christ
[pim I]rule in your hearts,[2588] to which
[II]indeed you were [aop]called in [b]one
body;[4983] and [III]be thankful.[2170]
🔑 16 Let [a]the word[3056] of [I]Christ richly
[pim]dwell within you, [II]with all wisdom[4678]
[b]teaching[1321] and admonishing[3560] one
another [c]with psalms[5568] *and* hymns[5215]
and spiritual[4152] songs,[5603] [d]singing
[III]with thankfulness[5485] in your hearts[2588]
to God.
17 And [a]whatever you [psa]do in
word[3056] or deed,[2041] *do* all in the
name[3686] of the Lord Jesus, [b]giv-
ing thanks[2168] through Him to God the
Father.

Family Relations

🔑 18 [a]Wives, [pim b]be subject to[5293]
your husbands, as is fitting in the
Lord.
19 [a]Husbands, [pim]love[25] your wives,
and do not be [pim]embittered against
them.
20 [a]Children, [pim]be obedient to[5219]
your parents in all things, for this is
well-pleasing[2101] [I]to the Lord.[2962]
21 [a]Fathers, do not [pim I]exasper-
ate2042 your children, that they may not
[psa]lose heart.
22 [a]Slaves,[1401] in all things obey[5219]
those who are your masters[2962] [I]on
earth, [b]not with [II]external service,[3787]
as those who *merely* please men,[441] but
with sincerity[572] of heart, fearing[5399] the
Lord.
23 Whatever you [psa]do, [pim]do your
work [I]heartily,[1537,5590] [a]as for the Lord
[II]rather than for men;[444]
24 [a]knowing that from the Lord you
will receive618 the reward [I]of [b]the
inheritance.[2817] It is the Lord[2962]
Christ[5547] whom you [c]serve.[1398]
25 For [a]he who [ppt]does wrong[91] will
receive the consequences of the wrong

6 [I]Some early mss. add *upon the sons of disobedience* [a]Rom. 1:18; Eph. 5:6
7 [a]Eph. 2:2
8 [a]Eph. 4:22 [b]Eph. 4:31 [c]Eph. 4:29
9 [I]Or, *Stop lying* [II]Lit., *man* [a]Eph. 4:25 [b]Eph. 4:22
10 [I]Lit., *man* [II]Lit., *renovated* [a]Eph. 4:24 [b]Rom. 12:2; 2Cor. 4:16; Eph. 4:23 [c]Gen. 1:26; Rom. 8:29 [d]Eph. 2:10
11 [a]Rom. 10:12; 1Cor. 12:13; Gal. 3:28 [b]1Cor. 7:19; Gal. 5:6 [c]Acts 28:2 [d]Eph. 6:8 [e]Eph. 1:23
12 [I]I.e., forbearance toward others [a]Luke 18:7 [b]Eph. 4:24 [c]Luke 1:78; Gal. 5:22f.; Phil. 2:1 [d]Eph. 4:2; Phil. 2:3 [e]1Cor. 13:4; 2Cor. 6:6
13 [a]Eph. 4:2 [b]Rom. 15:7; Eph. 4:32
14 [I]Lit., *the uniting bond of perfectness* [a]Eph. 4:3 [b]John 17:23; Heb. 6:1
15 [I]Or, *act as arbiter* [II]Lit., *also* [III]Or, *show yourselves thankful* [a]John 14:27 [b]Eph. 2:16
16 [I]Some mss. read *the Lord;* others read *God* [II]Or, *in* [III]Or, *by;* lit., *in His grace* [a]Rom. 10:17; Eph. 5:26; 1Thess. 1:8 [b]Col. 1:28 [c]Eph. 5:19 [d]1Cor. 14:15
17 [a]1Cor. 10:31 [b]Eph. 5:20; Col. 3:15
18 [a]Col. 3:18-4:1: *Eph. 5:22-*
6:9 [b]Eph. 5:22
19 [a]Eph. 5:25; 1 Pet. 3:7
20 [I]Lit., *in* [a]Eph. 6:1
21 [I]Some early mss. read *provoke to anger* [a]Eph. 6:4
22 [I]Lit., *according to the flesh* [II]Lit., *eyeservice* [a]Eph. 6:5 [b]Eph. 6:6
23 [I]Lit., *from the soul* [II]Lit., *and not* [a]Eph. 6:7
24 [I]I.e., consisting of [a]Eph. 6:8 [b]Acts 20:32; 1Pet. 1:4 [c]1Cor. 7:22
25 [a]Eph. 6:8

🔑 **3:11** The Scythians were a tribe of nomads and warriors from western Siberia inhabiting the Caspian area of the Black Sea from about 2000 B.C. In the late eighth century B.C. they moved into northern Persia. Their initial advances to the southwest were checked by Sargon II of Assyria (727-705 B.C.). Paul is using them here as an example of barbaric people who were constantly at war.

🔑 **3:16** The expression "the word (*logos,* 3056) of Christ" is used only here, and it means the revelation which Jesus Christ brought into the world. See Jn. 1:1,14 and the corresponding notes.

🔑 **3:18,19** See note on I Tim. 2:9-15.

which he has done, and [I][b]that without partiality.[4382]

Fellow Workers

4 Masters,[2962] grant to your slaves[1401] justice[1342] and fairness,[2471] [a]knowing that you too have a Master[2962] in heaven.[3772]

2 [a]Devote[4342] yourselves to prayer,[4335] [ppt]keeping alert in it with *an attitude of* thanksgiving;

3 praying[4336] at the same time[260] [a]for us as well, that God may [aosb]open up to us a [b]door for [c]the word,[3056] so that we may [ainf]speak forth [d]the mystery[3466] of Christ, for which I have also [e]been imprisoned;

4 in order that I may [aosb]make it clear[5319] [a]in the way I ought to speak.

5 [I][a]Conduct yourselves[4043] with wisdom[4678] toward [b]outsiders,[1854] [II][c]making the most of[1805] the opportunity.

6 [a]Let your speech[3056] always be [I]with grace,[5485] seasoned, *as it were,* with [b]salt, so that you may know how you should [pinf] [c]respond to each person.

🔑 7 [a]As to all my affairs, [b]Tychicus, *our* [c]beloved brother and faithful[4103] servant[1249] and fellow bond-servant[4889] in the Lord,[2962] will bring you information.[1107]

8 [a]For I have sent him to you for this very purpose, that you may know *about* our circumstances and that he may [aosb] [b]encourage your hearts;[2588]

9 [I]and with him [a]Onesimus, *our* faithful and [b]beloved[27] brother,[80] [c]who is one of your *number.* They will inform[1107] you about the whole situation here.

🔑 10 [a]Aristarchus, my [b]fellow prisoner, sends you his greetings; and *also* [c]Barnabas' cousin Mark (about whom you received [I]instructions: [d]if he comes to you, welcome him);

11 and *also* Jesus who is called Justus; these are the only [a]fellow workers for the kingdom[932] of God [b]who are from the circumcision;[4061] and they have proved to be an encouragement to me.

🔑 12 [a]Epaphras, [b]who is one of your number, a bondslave[1401] of Jesus Christ, sends you his greetings,[782] always [c]laboring earnestly[75] for you in his prayers, that you may [asbp] [I]stand [II][d]perfect and [III]fully [pfpp]assured in all the will[2307] of God.

13 For I bear him witness that he has [I]a deep concern for you and for those who are in [a]Laodicea and Hierapolis.

14 [a]Luke, the beloved physician,[2395] sends you his greetings, and *also* [b]Demas.

15 Greet the brethren who are in [a]Laodicea and also [I]Nympha and [b]the church[1577] that is in [II]her house.

16 And [a]when [I]this letter[1992] is read[314] among you, have it also read in the church of the Laodiceans; and you, for your part [a]read [I]my letter *that is coming* from [b]Laodicea.

25 [I]Lit., *there is no partiality* [b]Deut. 10:17; Acts 10:34; Eph. 6:9
1 [a]Eph. 6:9
2 [a]Acts 1:14; Eph. 6:18
3 [a]Eph. 6:19 [b]Acts 14:27 [c]2Tim. 4:2 [d]Eph. 3:3, 4; 6:19 [e]Eph. 6:20
4 [a]Eph. 6:20
5 [I]Lit., *Walk* [II]Lit., *redeeming the time* [a]Eph. 5:15 [b]Mark 4:11 [c]Eph. 5:16
6 [I]Or, *gracious* [a]Eph. 4:29 [b]Mark 9:50 [c]1Pet. 3:15
7 [a]Col. 4:7-9: *Eph. 6:21, 22* [b]Acts 20:4; 2Tim. 4:12 [c]Eph. 6:21; Col. 1:7
8 [a]Eph. 6:22 [b]Col. 2:2
9 [I]Lit., *along with Onesimus* [a]Philem. 1:10 [b]Col. 1:7 [c]Col. 4:12
10 [I]Or, *orders* [a]Acts 19:29; 27:2; Philem. 24 [b]Rom. 16:7 [c]Acts 4:36; 12:12, 25; 15:37, 39 [d]2Tim. 4:11
11 [a]Rom. 16:3 [b]Acts 11:2
12 [I]Or, *stand firm* [II]Or, *complete* or *mature* [III]Or, *made complete* [a]Col. 1:7; Philem. 23 [b]Col. 4:9 [c]Rom. 15:30 [d]Col. 1:28
13 [I]Or, *much toil* or *great pain* [a]Col. 2:1; 4:15f.
14 [a]2Tim. 4:11; Philem. 24 [b]2Tim. 4:10; Philem. 24

15 [I]Or, *Nymphas* (masc.) [II]Some ancient mss. read *their* [a]Col. 2:1; 4:13, 16 [b]Rom. 16:5 **16** [I]Lit., *the* [a]1Thess. 5:27; 2Thess. 3:14 [b]Col. 2:1; 4:13, 15

🔑 **4:7** Tychicus was an Asian, most probably an Ephesian who accompanied Paul to Jerusalem, doubtless as a delegate of his church carrying the collection (Acts 20:4; compare I Cor. 16:1-4). He was Paul's personal representative to the Colossians and Ephesians (Eph. 6:21,22). Paul possibly considered him a replacement for Titus in Crete (Tit. 3:12). He would have sent him to Ephesus, but it was discovered that he was needed elsewhere (II Tim. 4:12). He was well trusted by Paul (Eph. 6:21). See general remarks on the Colossian heresy.

🔑 **4:10** The first reference to Aristarchus in Acts 19:29 describes him as being Paul's fellow traveler when seized by the Ephesian mob. In Acts 20:4 he accompanies Paul to Jerusalem, probably as an official Thessalonian delegate with the collection, and in Acts 27:2 he is in a ship with Paul as they sailed from Caesarea. He possibly rejoined Paul and became His fellow prisoner, possibly alternating with Epaphras in voluntary imprisonment (Phile. 23,24).

🔑 **4:12** See note on Col. 1:7.

17 And say to [a]Archippus, "Take heed to the [b]ministry[1248] which you have received in the Lord, that you may [I]fulfill[4137] it."
18 [I]I, Paul, [a]write this greeting with my own hand. [b]Remember my [IIc]imprisonment. [d]Grace be with you.

17 [I]Or, *continually fulfill* [a]Philem. 1:2 [b]2Tim. 4:5

18 [I]Lit., *The greeting by my hand of Paul* [II]Lit., *bonds* [a]1Cor. 16:21 [b]Heb. 13:3 [c]Phil. 1:7; Col. 4:3 [d]1Tim. 6:21; 2Tim. 4:22; Titus 3:15; Heb. 13:25

The First Epistle of Paul to the

THESSALONIANS

Paul and his companions had to leave Thessalonica hastily early in the summer of A.D. 50 after making a number of converts and planting a church in this city which today is the capital of Greek Macedonia (Acts 17:1-10). Thessalonica was the first place where Paul's preaching achieved a numerous and socially prominent following (Acts 17:4). Thessalonica remained a triumphant crown to his efforts (I Thess. 1:8).

The sudden departure of Paul and his companions from Thessalonica left the newly founded church exposed to great persecution for which they were not prepared (see Acts 17:5-9) since Paul did not have time to adequately teach them. At the earliest opportunity, he sent Timothy back to see how the Thessalonian Christians were faring. When Timothy returned to him in Corinth (Acts 18:5), he brought good news of their steadfastness and zeal in propagating the Gospel, but reported that they had certain problems, some ethical (with special reference to sexual relations, see I Thess. 4:4-7) and some eschatological. They were concerned that those who had died would be at a disadvantage not being alive when the *parousia,* the coming of the Lord, would be realized. Consequently, Paul writes about the coming of the Lord as the result of this concern that existed among the Thessalonians. He wanted to assure them that those who had died would not miss any of the glory that those who are alive at the coming of the Lord (I Thess. 4:13-18) would experience.

Thanksgiving for These Believers

1 [a]Paul and [b]Silvanus and [c]Timothy
to the [d]church[1577] of the Thessalonians in God[2316] the Father[3962] and the
Lord[2962] Jesus Christ:[5547] [e]Grace[5485] to
you and peace.[1515]
2 [a]We give thanks[2168] to God always
for all of you, [b]making mention *of you*
in our prayers;[4335]
3 constantly bearing in mind your
[a]work[2041] of faith[4102] and labor[2873] of
[b]love[26] and [I][c]steadfastness[5281] of
hope[1680] [II]in our Lord Jesus Christ in
the presence of [d]our God and Father,
4 knowing, [a]brethren[80] beloved[25] by
God, [b]*His* choice[1589] of you;
5 for our [a]gospel[2098] did not come
to you in word[3056] only, but also
[b]in power[1411] and in the [an]Holy Spirit[4151]
and with [c]full conviction;[4136] just as you
know [d]what kind of men we [I]proved to
be among you for your sake.

1 [a]2Thess. 1:1
[b]2Cor. 1:19
[c]Acts 16:1
[d]Acts 17:1
[e]Rom. 1:7
2 [a]Rom. 1:8; 2Thess. 1:3
[b]Rom. 1:9
3 [I]Or, *perseverance* [II]Lit., *of*
[a]John 6:29
[b]1Cor. 13:13
[c]Rom. 8:25; 15:4 [d]Gal. 1:4
4 [a]Rom. 1:7; 2Thess. 2:13
[b]2Pet. 1:10
5 [I]Lit., *became*
[a]1Cor. 9:14
[b]Rom. 15:19
[c]Luke 1:1; Col. 2:2 [d]1Thess. 2:10
6 [a]1Cor. 4:16; 11:1f. [b]Acts 17:5-10 [c]2Tim. 4:2 [d]Acts 13:52; 2Cor. 6:10; Gal. 5:22
7 [a]Rom. 15:26
[b]Acts 18:12
8 [a]Col. 3:16; 2Thess. 3:1
[b]Rom. 10:18
[c]Rom. 15:26

6 You also became [a]imitators of us
and of the Lord, [b]having [apt]received
[c]the word[3056] in much tribulation with
the [d]joy of the [an]Holy Spirit,
7 so that you [ainf]became an
example[5179] to all the believers[4100] in
[a]Macedonia and in [b]Achaia.
8 For [a]the word of the Lord has
[pfip] [b]sounded forth from you, not only
in [c]Macedonia and [d]Achaia, but also
[e]in every place your faith toward God
has [pfi]gone forth, so that we have no
need to [pinf]say anything.
9 For they themselves report about
us what kind of a [I][a]reception we had
[II]with you, and how you [b]turned to
God[2316] [c]from [III]idols[1497] to serve[1398]
[IV][d]a living[2198] and true[228] God,
10 and to [pinf] [a]wait for His Son[5207]

[d]Acts 18:12 [e]Rom. 1:8; 16:19; 2Cor. 2:14 9 [I]Lit., *entrance* [II]Lit., *to* [III]Or, *the idols* [IV]Or, *the* [a]1Thess. 2:1 [b]Acts 14:15 [c]1Cor. 12:2 [d]Matt. 16:16
10 [a]Matt. 16:27f.; 1Cor. 1:7

1:10 This is the only instance in the entire N.T. that the verb *anamenō* (362) is used. It is composed of the emphatic *ana* (303) and *menō* (3306), "to stay." It means to wait for or await. This word is still used in Modern Greek today to stress a certain eagerness in this waiting. This waiting or looking forward to implies a state of readiness on the part of the Thessalonians who in v. 9 were commended as

(continued on next page)

from [I]heaven,[3772] whom He [b]raised[1453]
from the dead,[3498] *that is* Jesus, who
[ppt] [c]delivers[4506] us from [d]the wrath[3709]
to come.[2064]

Paul's Ministry

2 For you yourselves know, brethren,[80] that our [I][a]coming to you
[pfi] [b]was not in vain,[2756]
🗝 2 but after we had already suffered
and been [a]mistreated[5195] in [b]Philippi, as
you know, we had the boldness in our
God [c]to speak to you the [d]gospel[2098] of
God amid much [I][e]opposition.[73]
3 For our [a]exhortation[3874] does not
come from [b]error or [c]impurity[167] or [I]by
way of [d]deceit;[1388]
4 [a]but just as we have been approved by God to be [b]entrusted with[4100]
the gospel, so we speak, [c]not as pleasing
men[444] but God, who [ppt] [I][d]examines our
hearts.[2588]
5 For we never came [I]with flattering
speech,[3056] as you know, nor with
[a]a pretext for greed—[b]God is witness—[3144]
6 nor did we [ppt] [a]seek glory[1391] from
men, either from you or from others,
even though as [b]apostles[652] of Christ
we might[1410] have [I]asserted our authority.
7 But we [I]proved to be [II][a]gentle[2261]
[III]among you, [b]as a nursing *mother*[5162]
[IV]tenderly cares for her own children.[5043]
8 Having thus a fond affection for
you, we were well-pleased[2106] to
[a]impart to you not only the [b]gospel of
God but also our own [I]lives,[5590] because
you had [aop]become [II]very dear to us.
9 For you recall, brethren, our
[a]labor[2873] and hardship,[3449] *how* [b]work-
ing[2038] night and day so as not to be a
[c]burden to any of you, we proclaimed[2784]
to you the [d]gospel of God.
10 You are witnesses,[3144] and *so
is* [a]God, [b]how devoutly[3743] and uprightly[1346] and blamelessly we [I]be-
haved toward you [II]believers;[4100]
11 just as you know how we *were*
[ppt][a]exhorting and [ppt]encouraging and
[ppt] [I][b]imploring[3140] each one of you as [c]a
father[3962] *would* his own children,[5043]
12 so that you may [aies] [a]walk in a
manner worthy of the God who
[ppt] [b]calls[2564] you into His own kingdom[932]
and [c]glory.[1391]
13 And for this reason we also constantly [a]thank God that when you received from us the [b]word of God's
message, you accepted *it* [c]not *as* the
word of men,[444] but *for* what it really
is, the word[3056] of God,[2316] [d]which also
performs its work[1754] in you who [ppt]be-
lieve.

10 [I]Lit., *the heavens* [b]Acts 2:24 [c]Rom. 5:9 [d]Matt. 3:7; 1Thess. 2:16; 5:9
1 [I]Lit., *entrance* [a]1Thess. 1:9 [b]2Thess. 1:10
2 [I]Or, *struggle, conflict* [a]Acts 14:5; 16:19-24; Phil. 1:30 [b]Acts 16:22-24 [c]Acts 17:1-9 [d]Rom. 1:1 [e]Phil. 1:30
3 [I]Lit., *in deceit* [a]Acts 13:15 [b]2Thess. 2:11 [c]1Thess. 4:7 [d]2Cor. 4:2
4 [I]Or, *approves* [a]2Cor. 2:17 [b]Gal. 2:7 [c]Gal. 1:10 [d]Rom. 8:27
5 [I]Lit., *in a word of flattery* [a]Acts 20:33; 2Pet. 2:3 [b]Rom. 1:9; 1Thess. 2:10
6 [I]Or, *been burdensome* [a]John 5:41, 44; 2Cor. 4:5 [b]1Cor. 9:1f.
7 [I]Lit., *became gentle* [II]Some ancient mss. read *babes* [III]Lit., *in the midst of you* [IV]Or, *cherishes* [a]2Tim. 2:24 [b]Gal. 4:19; 1Thess. 2:11
8 [I]Or, *souls* [II]Lit., *beloved* [a]2Cor. 12:15; 1John 3:16 [b]Rom. 1:1
9 [a]Phil. 4:16; 2Thess. 3:8 [b]Acts 18:3 [c]1Cor. 9:4f.; 2Cor. 11:9
[d]Rom. 1:1 **10** [I]Lit., *became* [II]Or, *who believe* [a]1Thess. 2:5 [b]2Cor. 1:12; 1Thess. 1:5
11 [I]Or, *testifying* [a]1Thess. 5:14 [b]Luke 16:28; 1Thess. 4:6 [c]1Cor. 4:14; 1Thess. 2:7 **12** [a]Eph. 4:1 [b]Rom. 8:28; 1Thess. 5:24; 2Thess. 2:14 [c]2Cor. 4:6; 1Pet. 5:10
13 [a]Rom. 1:8; 1Thess. 1:2 [b]Rom. 10:17; Heb. 4:2 [c]Matt. 10:20; Gal. 4:14 [d]Heb. 4:12

(continued from previous page)
serving the Lord faithfully. Their expectation of God's Son from heaven undoubtedly refers to His Second Coming. This must refer to what the Apostle Paul in I Thess. 4:14-18 calls the rapture (only the verb is used in v. 17, *harpagēsometha* from *harpazō,* 726). If these believers were going to go through the tribulation, how could Paul possibly present the fact of the coming of God's Son out of the heavens as something that they could, at that time, be looking forward to with such great and joyful expectation? Here the Lord Jesus is presented as coming by Himself from heaven for His saints, both dead and alive. In I Thess. 3:13 He is presented as coming with His saints. This is at the end of the tribulation period, so that His saints may reign with Him.

The translation of the last part of this verse "who (Jesus) delivers us from the wrath to come" speaks of present deliverance. The present participle *rhuomenon* means "the one delivering us" from the present persecution is able also to deliver us from the future one. Paul is comforting the Thessalonians, who were then being so greatly persecuted, by the fact that they would be delivered by the Lord from the great future tribulation and that they would not need to go through the coming wrath of God. What could that coming wrath be except the great tribulation? See note on I Thess. 2:19.

🗝 **2:2** See note on I Thess. 5:2.

14 For you, brethren, became [a]imitators of [b]the churches[1577] of God in Christ Jesus that are [c]in Judea, for [d]you also [ao]endured the same sufferings at the hands of your own countrymen, [e]even as they *did* from the Jews,

15 [a]who both [apt]killed the Lord Jesus and [b]the prophets,[4396] and [apt] [I]drove us out. [II]They are not [ppt]pleasing to God, [III]but hostile to all men,

16 [a]hindering us from speaking to the Gentiles[1484] [b]that they might be [asbp]saved;[4982] with the result that they always [aies] [c]fill up[378] the measure of their sins.[266] But [d]wrath[3709] has [ao]come upon them [I]to the utmost.[5056]

17 But we, brethren, having been [aptp]bereft of you for a [I]short[5610] while—[2540] [a]in [II]person, not in [III]spirit—[2588] were all the more eager with great desire [b]to see your face.

18 [I]For [a]we wanted to come to you—I, Paul, [II][b]more than once—and *yet* [c]Satan[4567] [d]thwarted us.

🗝 19 For who is our hope or [a]joy[5479] or crown of exultation? Is it not even you, in the presence of our Lord Jesus at His [I][b]coming?[3952]

20 For you are [a]our glory and joy.

Encouragement of Timothy's Visit

3 Therefore [a]when we could [ppt]endure *it* no longer, we thought it best[2106] to be left behind at [b]Athens alone;

2 and we sent [a]Timothy, our brother[80] and God's fellow worker[1249] in the gospel[2098] of Christ, to strengthen and encourage you as to your faith,[4102]

3 so that no man may be [pip] [I]disturbed by these afflictions; for you yourselves know that [a]we have been [pin]destined[2749] for this.

4 For indeed[2532] when we were with you, we *kept* [ipf]telling you in advance that we were going to [pip]suffer affliction; [I][a]and so it came to pass, [II]as you know.

5 For this reason, [a]when I could [ppt]endure *it* no longer, I also [b]sent to [I]find out about your faith, for fear that [c]the [ppt]tempter[3985] might have [ao]tempted you, and [d]our labor[2873] should be in vain.[2756]

14 [a]1Thess. 1:6 [b]1Cor. 7:17; 10:32 [c]Gal. 1:22 [d]Acts 17:5; 1Thess. 3:4; 2Thess. 1:4f. [e]Heb. 10:33f. **15** [I]Or, *persecuted us* [II]Lit., *and* [III]Lit., *and* [a]Luke 24:20; Acts 2:23 [b]Matt. 5:12; Acts 7:52 **16** [I]Or, *forever* or *altogether* [a]Acts 9:23; 13:45, 50; 14:2, 5, 19; 17:5, 13; 18:12; 21:21f., 27; 25:2, 7 [b]1Cor. 10:33 [c]Gen. 15:16; Dan. 8:23; Matt. 23:32 [d]1Thess. 1:10 **17** [I]Lit., *occasion of an hour* [II]Lit., *face* [III]Lit., *heart* [a]1Cor. 5:3 [b]1Thess. 3:10 **18** [I]Or, *Because* [II]Lit., *both once and twice* [a]Rom. 15:22 [b]Phil. 4:16 [c]Matt. 4:10 [d]Rom. 1:13; 15:22 **19** [I]Or, *presence* [a]Phil. 4:1 [b]Matt. 16:27; Mark 8:38; John 21:22; 1Thess. 3:13; 4:15; 5:23 **20** [a]2Cor. 1:14

1 [a]1Thess. 3:5 [b]Acts 17:15f. **2** [a]2Cor. 1:1; Col. 1:1 **3** [I]Or, *deceived* [a]Acts 9:16; 14:22 **4** [I]Lit., *just as* [II]Lit., *and* [a]1Thess. 2:14 **5** [I]Or, *to know, to ascertain* [a]Phil. 2:19; 1Thess. 3:1 [b]1Thess. 3:2 [c]Matt. 4:3 [d]2Cor. 6:1; Phil. 2:16

🗝 **2:19** The word translated "coming" is *parousia* (3952), which means basically "presence" or "arrival" (I Cor. 16:17; II Cor. 7:7). In Hellenistic Greek it was used to designate the visit of a ruler. The same Jesus who ascended to heaven will again visit the earth in personal presence (Acts 1:11) at the end of the age (Mt. 24:3) in power and glory (Mt. 24:27) to destroy the antichrist and evil (II Thess. 2:8), to raise the righteous dead (I Cor. 15:23), and to gather the redeemed (Mt. 24:31,37,39; Jn. 5:28,29; I Thess. 3:13; 4:15; 5:23; II Thess. 2:1; Js. 5:7,8.

The word *parousia* is used in Mt. 24:3,27,37,39; I Cor. 15:23; 16:17; II Cor. 7:6,7; 10:10; Phil. 1:26; 2:12; I Thess. 2:19; 3:13; 4:15; 5:23; II Thess. 2:1,8,9; Js. 5:7,8; II Pet. 1:16; 3:4,12; I Jn. 2:28. The specific meaning of *parousia* is made clear in I Thess. 4:15 where it is defined as the time when the Lord shall come out of heaven (I Thess. 1:10). At that time the dead who are believers will rise first, and those who are believers and are alive will be changed and be caught up in the air by Jesus Christ.

The return of Christ will also be an *apokalupsis* (602), a revelation or taking the cover off of something that is hidden. It is an unveiling or disclosure when the power and glory which are now His by virtue of His exaltation in heavenly session (Eph. 1:20-23; Phil. 2:9; Heb. 1:3; 2:9) will be disclosed to the world (I Pet. 4:13). Christ is now reigning as Lord at God's right hand (I Cor. 15:25; Heb. 1:3; 12:2) and sharing God's throne (Rev. 3:21). His reign is now invisible to the world. It will, however, be made visible by His *apokalupsis,* "revelation." The word *apokalupsis,* "revelation," occurs in Lk. 2:32; Rom. 2:5; 8:19; 16:25; I Cor. 1:7; 13:6,26; II Cor. 12:1,7; Gal. 1:12; 2:2; Eph. 1:17; 3:3; II Thess. 1:7; I Pet. 1:7,13; 4:13; Rev. 1:1.

There is yet a third word used which is related to the Second Coming of the Lord and that is *epiphaneia* (2015) which means "a manifestation." In Ancient Greek, it was used especially of the appearing of the gods and also of the manifestation of divine power and providence in extraordinary events. In the N.T. it is used of the appearing of the manifestation of Jesus Christ on earth (II Thess. 2:8; I Tim. 6:14; II Tim. 1:10; 4:1,8; Tit. 2:13). These are the only references in the N.T. of the word *epiphaneia.*

6 But now that [a]Timothy has come
to us from you, and has brought us good
news[2097] of [b]your faith and love,[26] and
that you always [c]think kindly[18] of us,
longing to see us just as we also long
to see you,
7 for this reason, brethren, in all
our distress and affliction we were comforted about you through your faith;
8 for now we *really* live,[2198] if you
[a]stand firm in the Lord.
9 For [a]what thanks can we render
to God for you in return for all the joy
with which we rejoice before our God
on your account,
10 as we [a]night and day keep praying
most earnestly[4053] that we may [b]see
your face, and may [c]complete[2675] what
is lacking in your faith?
11 [a]Now may [b]our God and
Father[3962] [c]Himself and Jesus our
Lord[2962] [d]direct our way[3598] to you;
12 and may the Lord[2962] cause you
to [opt]increase and [opt] [a]abound in love[26]
for one another, and for all men, just
as we also *do* for you;
🔑 13 so that He may [aies] [a]establish4741
your hearts [b]unblamable[273] in holiness[42]
before [c]our God and Father at the
[Id]coming[3952] of our Lord Jesus [e]with all
His [II]saints.[40]

Sanctification and Love

4 [a]Finally then, [b]brethren, we request
and exhort3872 you in the Lord
Jesus, that, as you [ao]received from us
instruction as to how you ought to
[pinf] [Ic]walk and [pinf] [d]please God (just as
you actually do [I]walk), that you may
[psa] [e]excel still more.
2 For you know what commandments[3852] we gave you [I]by *the authority of* the Lord Jesus.
🔑 3 For this is the will[2307] of God, your
sanctification; *that is,* that you [pinf] [a]ab-
stain[567] from [I]sexual immorality;4202
🔑 4 that [a]each of you know how to
[pinf] [I]possess his own [IIb]vessel in sanctification and [c]honor,
5 not in [Ia]lustful[3806] passion,[1939] like
the Gentiles who [b]do not know God;
6 *and* that no man [pinf]transgress[5233]
and [pinf] [a]defraud his brother [b]in the matter because [c]the Lord is *the* avenger[1558]
in all these things, just as we also
[d]told you before and solemnly
warned[1263] *you.*
🔑 7 For [a]God has not [ao]called us for
[b]the purpose of impurity,[167] but [I]in sanctification.[38]
8 Consequently, he who [ppt]rejects
this is not rejecting man but the God
who [ppt] [a]gives His Holy[40] Spirit[4151] to
you.
9 Now as to the [a]love of the brethren,[5360] you [b]have no need for *anyone*
to write to you, for you yourselves are
[c]taught by God to [pinf]love[25] one another;
10 for indeed [a]you do practice it toward all the brethren who are in all
Macedonia. But we urge[3870] you, brethren, to [pinf] [b]excel still more,
🔑 11 and to [pinf]make it your ambition
[pinf] [a]to lead a quiet life[2270] and [pinf] [b]at-
tend[4238] to your own business and
[pinf] [c]work with your hands, just as we
commanded you;
12 so that you may [psa] [Ia]behave
properly toward [b]outsiders1854 and [IIc]not
[psa]be in any need.

Those Who Died in Christ

🔑 **13** But [a]we do not want you to be
uninformed,[50] brethren, about those

6 [a]Acts 18:5 [b]1Thess. 1:3 [c]1Cor. 11:2
8 [a]1Cor. 16:13
9 [a]1Thess. 1:2
10 [a]2Tim. 1:3 [b]1Thess. 2:17 [c]2Cor. 13:9
11 [a]2Thess. 2:16 [b]Gal. 1:4; 1Thess. 3:13 [c]1Thess. 4:16; 5:23; 2Thess. 2:16; 3:16; Rev. 21:3 [d]2Thess. 3:5
12 [a]Phil. 1:9; 1Thess. 4:1, 10; 2Thess. 1:3
13 [I]Or, *presence* [II]Or, *holy ones* [a]1Cor. 1:8; 1Thess. 3:2 [b]Luke 1:6 [c]Gal. 1:4; 1Thess. 3:11 [d]1Thess. 2:19 [e]Matt. 25:31; Mark 8:38; 1Thess. 4:17; 2Thess. 1:7

1 [I]Or, *conduct yourselves* [a]2Cor. 13:11; 2Thess. 3:1 [b]Gal. 6:1; 1Thess. 5:12; 2Thess. 1:3; 2:1; 3:1, 13 [c]Eph. 4:1 [d]2Cor. 5:9 [e]Phil. 1:9; 1Thess. 3:12; 4:10; 2Thess. 1:3
2 [I]Lit., *through the Lord*
3 [I]Or, *fornication* [a]1Cor. 6:18
4 [I]Or, *acquire* [II]I.e., body; or possibly, wife [a]1Cor. 7:2, 9 [b]2Cor. 4:7; 1Pet. 3:7 [c]Rom. 1:24
5 [I]Lit., *passion of lust* [a]Rom. 1:26 [b]Gal. 4:8
6 [a]1Cor. 6:8 [b]2Cor. 7:11 [c]Rom. 12:19; 13:4; Heb. 13:4 [d]Luke 16:28; 1Thess. 2:11; Heb. 2:6
7 [I]I.e., in the state or sphere of [a]1Pet. 1:15 [b]1Thess. 2:3
8 [a]Rom. 5:5; 2Cor. 1:22; Gal. 4:6; 1John 3:24
9 [a]John 13:34; Rom. 12:10 [b]2Cor. 9:1; 1Thess. 5:1 [c]Jer. 31:33f.; John 6:45; 1John 2:27
10 [a]1Thess. 1:7 [b]1Thess. 3:12
11 [a]2Thess. 3:12 [b]1Pet. 4:15 [c]Acts 18:3; Eph. 4:28; 2Thess. 3:10-12
12 [I]Lit., *walk* [II]Lit., *have need of nothing* [a]Rom. 13:13; Col. 4:5 [b]Mark 4:11 [c]Eph. 4:28
13 [a]Rom. 1:13

🔑 **3:13** See notes on I Thess. 1:10; 2:19; Rev. 11.
🔑 **4:3,7** See note on I Cor. 7:14.
🔑 **4:4-7** See general remarks on I Thessalonians.
🔑 **4:11** See note on I Tim. 2:9-15.
🔑 **4:13-18** See general remarks on I Thessalonians and see also note on I Thess. 1:10.

who [b]are [ppt]asleep, that you may not
[psa]grieve, as do [c]the rest who have
[d]no hope.[1680]
14 For if we believe[4100] that Jesus
died[599] and rose again,[450] [a]even so God
will bring with Him [b]those who have
[apt]fallen asleep [I]in Jesus.
🔑15 For this we say to you [a]by the
word[3056] of the Lord, that [b]we who
are [ppt]alive,[2198] [I]and [ppp]remain until
[c]the coming[3952] of the Lord, shall not
[efn]precede [d]those who have [apt]fallen
asleep.
16 For the Lord [a]Himself [b]will
descend[2597] from heaven[3772] with a
[Ic]shout, with the voice of [d]*the* archangel,[743] and with the [e]trumpet of God;
and [f]the dead[3498] in Christ shall rise[450]
first.
🔑17 Then [a]we who are [ppt]alive
[I]and [ppp]remain shall be [fp] [b]caught up[726]

13 [b]Acts 7:60 [c]Eph. 2:3; 1Thess. 5:6 [d]Eph. 2:12

14 [I]Lit., *through* [a]Rom. 14:9; 2Cor. 4:14 [b]1Cor. 15:18; 1Thess. 4:13

15 [I]Lit., *who* [a]1Kin. 13:17f.; 20:35; 2Cor. 12:1; Gal. 1:12 [b]1Cor. 15:52; 1Thess. 5:10 [c]1Thess. 2:19 [d]1Cor. 15:18; 1Thess. 4:13

16 [I]Or, *cry of command* [a]1Thess. 3:11 [b]1Thess. 1:10; 2Thess. 1:7 [c]Joel 2:11 [d]Jude 1:9 [e]Matt. 24:31 [f]1Cor. 15:23; 2Thess. 2:1; Rev. 14:13

together with them [c]in the clouds to
meet the Lord in the air, and thus we
shall always [d]be with the Lord.
18 Therefore [pim]comfort[3870] one another with these words.

The Day of the Lord

5 Now as to the [a]times[5550] and the
epochs,[2540] brethren, you [b]have no
need of anything to be written[1125] to
you.
🔑2 For you yourselves know full well
that [a]the day[2250] of the Lord[2962] [I]will
come [b]just like a thief in the night.

17 [I]Lit., *who* [a]1Cor. 15:52; 1Thess. 5:10 [b]2Cor. 12:2 [c]Dan. 7:13; Acts 1:9; Rev. 11:12 [d]John 12:26
1 [a]Acts 1:7 [b]1Thess. 4:9 2 [I]Lit., *is coming* [a]1Cor. 1:8 [b]Luke 21:34; 1Thess. 5:4; 2Pet. 3:10; Rev. 3:3; 16:15

🔑**4:15** See note on I Thess. 2:19. The word that is translated "precede" is the Greek verb *phthanō* (5348) meaning "to anticipate, to be before." Here the dead are called "those who have fallen asleep." The Greek word is *koimaō* (2837) or *koimaomai* in the middle or passive voice. In the N.T. this always refers to the body that is asleep and not to the soul. See note on Rev. 4 and also the Editor's book *Conquering the Fear of Death,* an exegetical exposition of I Cor. 15.

🔑**4:17** See note on II Cor. 12:2-10. There are two important words here. One is *harpagēsometha* which is in the punctiliar future. This means that at a specific moment in the future we shall be caught up by Someone other than ourselves which is, of course, Jesus Christ who will descend from heaven. The noun is not used in the N.T. with eschatological meaning. *Harpagē* (724), "a forceable taking away," is only used in Mt. 23:25; Lk. 11:39 and Heb. 10:34. The verb *harpazō* (726), "to seize upon with force," is also used generally as meaning to forceably seize upon or take to oneself. This verb is used in Mt. 11:12; 13:19; Jn. 6:15; 10:12,28,29; Acts 8:39; 23:10; II Cor. 12:2,4; I Thess. 4:17; Jude 23; Rev. 12:5. See the derivative *harpagmos* (725), which means "a thing robbed." The other important word which is translated, "to meet" in Greek is expressed with a preposition, *eis,* "unto or for," and *apantēsin* (529), "meeting," from the verb *apantaō* (528). This verb is used in Mt. 28:9; Mk. 5:2; 14:13; Lk. 14:31; 17:12; Jn. 4:51; Acts 16:16. It is made up of the preposition *apo,* "from," *antaō,* "to meet," meaning "to come into the presence of, to meet." In Modern Greek it means exactly what it has always meant, to leave a place and go to meet one who is coming toward you. It also means to reply to a question that has been put forth. It involves responding to an action of another. Here Paul is speaking of the reaction of the believers as a result of the initiative that Christ will take when He comes to take His own unto Himself, after the dead have been raised by Him and the living transformed according to this entire passage and also I Cor. 15:51-53. See note on I Thess. 1:10.

🔑**5:2** The expression "the day of the Lord" forms part of the eschatology of the Bible. In the O.T. it meant the day when Jehovah would intervene to put Israel at the head of nations, irrespective of Israel's faithlessness to Him. Amos declares that the day means judgment for Israel (see Isa. 2:12f; Ezek. 13:5; Joel 1:15; 2:1,11; Zeph. 1:7,14; Zech. 13:1).

Other prophets speak of it as God's Day of Judgment upon other individual nations such as Babylon (Isa. 13:6,9); Egypt (Jer. 46:10); Edom (Obad. 8); many nations (Joel 2:31; 3:14; Obad. 15). In the O.T. then, the Day of the Lord represents the occasion when Jehovah will actively intervene to punish sin which will reach its climax.

On the Day of the Lord there are truly repentant believers who are saved (Joel 2:28-32), while those

(continued on next page)

3 While they are [psa]saying, "[a]Peace[1515] and safety!"[803] then [I][b]destruction[3639] [II]will come upon them suddenly like [c]birth pangs[5604] upon a woman with child; and they shall not escape.

4 But you, brethren, are not in [a]darkness,[4655] that the day should [aosb]overtake[2638] you [I][b]like a thief;

5 for you are all [a]sons[5207] of light[5457] and sons of day. We are not of night nor of [b]darkness;

6 so then let us not [psa] [a]sleep as [I][b]others do, but let us be [psa]alert and [psa] [II][c]sober.

7 For those who [ppt]sleep do their sleeping at night, and those who get [ppp]drunk get [a]drunk at night.

8 But since [a]we are of *the* day, let us [b]be [psa] [I]sober, having [apt]put on the [c]breastplate of [d]faith[4102] and love,[26] and as a [e]helmet, the [f]hope[1680] of salvation.[4991]

9 For God has not [aom]destined us for [a]wrath,[3709] but for [b]obtaining salvation through our Lord Jesus Christ,

10 [a]who [apt]died for us, that whether we are [psa]awake or [psa]asleep, we may [aosb]live[2198] together with Him.

11 Therefore [I]encourage[3870] one another, and [a]build up one another, just as you also are doing.

Christian Conduct

12 But we request of you, brethren, that you [I][a]appreciate[1492] those [b]who diligently [ppt]labor among you, and [c]have [ppt]charge over you in the Lord and [ppt]give you [II]instruction,[3560]

13 and that you [pinf]esteem[2233] them very highly[4053] in love because of their work.[2041] [pim] [a]Live in peace with one another.

14 And we urge[3870] you, brethren, [pim]admonish[3560] [a]the [I]unruly,[813] [pim]encourage [b]the fainthearted,[3642] help[472] [c]the weak,[772] be [d]patient[3114] with all men.

15 See[3708] that [a]no one [aosb]repays another with evil[2556] for evil, but always [pim] [b]seek after that which is good[18] for one another and for all men.

16 [pim] [a]Rejoice[5463] always;

3 [I]Or, *sudden destruction* [II]Lit., *is at hand* [a]Jer. 6:14; 8:11; Ezek. 13:10 [b]2Thess. 1:9 [c]John 16:21
4 [I]Some early mss. read *like thieves* [a]Acts 26:18; 1John 2:8 [b]Luke 21:34; 1Thess. 5:2; 2Pet. 3:10; Rev. 3:3; 16:15
5 [a]Luke 16:8 [b]Acts 26:18; 1John 2:8
6 [I]Lit., *the remaining ones* [II]Or, *self-controlled* [a]Rom. 13:11; 1Thess. 5:10 [b]Eph. 2:3; 1Thess. 4:13 [c]1Pet. 1:13
7 [a]Acts 2:15; 2Pet. 2:13
8 [I]Or, *self-controlled* [a]1Thess. 5:5 [b]1Pet. 1:13 [c]Is. 59:17; Eph. 6:14 [d]Eph. 6:23 [e]Eph. 6:17 [f]Rom. 8:24
9 [a]1Thess. 1:10 [b]2Thess. 2:13f.
10 [a]Rom. 14:9
11 [I]Or, *comfort* [a]Eph. 4:29
12 [I]Lit., *know* [II]Or, *admonition* [a]1Cor. 16:18; 1Tim. 5:17 [b]Rom. 16:6, 12; 1Cor. 15:10; 16:16 [c]Heb. 13:17
13 [a]Mark 9:50
14 [I]Or, *undisciplined* [a]2Thess. 3:6, 7, 11 [b]Is. 35:4 [c]Rom. 14:1f.; 1Cor. 8:7ff.; Rom. 15:1 [d]1Cor. 13:4
15 [a]Matt. 5:44; Rom. 12:17; 1Pet. 3:9 [b]Rom. 12:9; Gal. 6:10; 1Thess. 5:21
16 [a]Phil. 4:4

(continued from previous page)

who remain enemies of the Lord, whether Jews or Gentiles, are punished. There are also physical effects on the world of nature (Isa. 2).

In the N.T. the Day of the Lord is related to the Second Coming of Christ. So also is the phrase "the day of our Lord Jesus Christ" or an equivalent which occurs in I Cor. 1:8; 5:5; Phil. 1:6,10; 2:16; II Thess. 2:2. When we read of the Day of the Lord or the Day of Christ, we are not to think of it as a twenty-four hour day, but a period of time during which the judgments of the Lord Jesus Christ will take place. Both expressions mean a time of judgment. The Day of the Lord will include the time of the tribulation described in Revelation. Zech. 14:1-4 makes it clear that the events of the Second Advent are included in the program of the Day of the Lord. II Pet. 3:10 gives authority for including the entire millennial age within this period. If the Day of the Lord did not begin until after the Second Advent, since that advent is preceded by signs, it could not come as a "thief in the night," unexpected and unheralded, as it is said to come in I Thess. 5:2. The only way this day could break unexpectedly upon the world is for it to begin immediately after the rapture of the Church. The Day of the Lord is, therefore, that extended period of time which begins with God's dealing with Israel after the rapture, at the beginning of the tribulation, and which extends through the Second Advent and the millennial age unto the creation of the new heavens and new earth after the millennium.

The expression "the day of the Lord Jesus" or the "day of Christ" occurring in I Cor. 5:5; II Cor. 1:14; Phil. 1:6,10; 2:16, and II Thess. 2:2 relates to the liberation by Jesus Christ of His own, His Church. The Day of the Lord and the Day of Christ occur simultaneously. For the Church, it is the rapture, and for the unbelieving world, it is the beginning of judgment and the tribulation. See the Editor's book *A Richer Life for You in Christ,* an exegetical exposition on I Cor. 1.

17 pim [a]pray**4336** without ceasing;89
18 in everything pim [a]give thanks; for
this is God's will**2307** for you in Christ
Jesus.
19 [a]Do not pimquench the Spirit;**4151**
20 do not pimdespise [a]prophetic [1]ut-
terances.**4394**
21 But pim [a]examine everything
carefully; [b]hold fast**2722** to that which is
good;
22 pimabstain**567** from every [1]form**1491**
of evil.**4190**
23 Now [a]may the God of peace**1515**
[b]Himself optsanctify**37** you entirely;**3651**
and may your [c]spirit and soul**5590** and
body**4983** be optpreserved complete,
[d]without blame274 at [e]the coming**3952** of
our Lord Jesus Christ.
24 [a]Faithful**4103** is He who ppt [b]calls
you, and He also will bring it to pass.
25 Brethren, [a]pray for us[1].
26 aim [a]Greet782 all the brethren**80**
with a holy kiss.
27 I adjure you by the Lord to
[a]have this letter1992 read to all the
[b]brethren.
28 [a]The grace of our Lord Jesus
Christ be with you.

17 [a]Eph. 6:18
18 [a]Eph. 5:20
19 [a]Eph. 4:30
20 [1]Or, *gifts* [a]Acts 13:1; 1Cor. 14:31
21 [a]1Cor. 14:29; 1John 4:1 [b]Rom. 12:9; Gal. 6:10; 1Thess. 5:15
22 [1]Or, *appearance*
23 [a]Rom. 15:33 [b]1Thess. 3:11 [c]Luke 1:46f.; Heb. 4:12 [d]James 1:4; 2Pet. 3:14 [e]1Thess. 2:19
24 [a]1Cor. 1:9; 2Thess. 3:3 [b]1Thess. 2:12

25 [1]Some mss. add *also* [a]Eph. 6:19; 2Thess. 3:1; Heb. 13:18 **26** [a]Rom. 16:16 **27** [a]Col. 4:16 [b]Acts 1:15 **28** [a]Rom. 16:20; 2Thess. 3:18

5:23 See note on I Thess. 2:19.

The Second Epistle of Paul to the

THESSALONIANS

The Second Letter of Paul to the Thessalonians was written soon after his first letter in A.D. 51-52 from Corinth. Some members from the congregation in Thessalonica had inferred that, since the coming of the Lord Jesus was imminent, there was no point in continuing to work. Paul went on in the Second Epistle to explain that certain events must take place before the Lord Jesus' return. In particular, there will be a world-wide rebellion against God, led by one who will be the incarnation of lawlessness and anarchy. These persons are being held in check by a power which he did not need to name in writing, since his readers already knew that he spoke of the Holy Spirit. He told the Thessalonians not to live at the expense of others, to get back to work. The Thessalonians were apparently confusing the suddenness of the Lord's coming with its immediacy.

Thanksgiving for Faith and Perseverance

1 [a]Paul and [b]Silvanus and [c]Timothy
to the [d]church[1577] of the Thessalonians in God[2316] our Father[3962] and the
Lord[2962] Jesus Christ:[5547]
2 [a]Grace[5485] to you and peace[1515]
from God the Father and the Lord Jesus
Christ.
3 We [pin]ought always [a]to [pinf]give
thanks[2168] to God for you, [b]brethren,
as is *only* fitting,[514] because your faith
is greatly enlarged, and the [c]love[26] of
each one of you toward one another
grows *ever* greater;
4 therefore, we ourselves [pinf] [a]speak
proudly of you among [b]the churches of
God for your [I]perseverance and faith
[b]in the midst of all your persecutions
and afflictions which you endure.[430]
5 *This is* a [a]plain indication of God's
righteous[1342] judgment[2920] so that you
may be [aies] [b]considered worthy of the
kingdom[932] of God, for which indeed you
are suffering.[3958]
6 [I]For after all [a]it is *only* just
[II]for God to [ainf]repay with affliction those
who [ppt]afflict you,
🔑 7 and *to give* relief[425] to you who
are [ppp]afflicted [I]and to us as well
[IIa]when the Lord Jesus shall be
revealed[602] [b]from heaven[3772] [c]with
[III]His mighty angels[32] [d]in flaming fire,
8 dealing out retribution to those
who [a]do not know God and to those
who [b]do not [ppt]obey[5219] the gospel[2098]
of our Lord Jesus.
🔑 9 And these will pay the penalty of
[a]eternal[166] destruction,[3639] [b]away from
the presence of the Lord and from the
glory[1391] of His power,
10 when He comes to be
[a]glorified[1740] [I]in His [II]saints[40] on that
[b]day,[2250] and to be marveled[2296] at
among all who have [apt]believed—[4100]
for our [c]testimony[3142] to you was believed.
11 To this end also we [a]pray for
you always that our God may [aosb] [Ib]count
you worthy of your [c]calling, and [aosb]fulfill
every desire[2107] for [d]goodness[19] and the
[e]work[2041] of faith with power;
12 in order that the [a]name of our
Lord Jesus may be glorified[1740] in you,
and you in Him, according to the
grace of our God and [I]the Lord Jesus
Christ.

1 [a]1Thess. 1:1 [b]2Cor. 1:19 [c]Acts 16:1 [d]Acts 17:1; 1Thess. 1:1
2 [a]Rom. 1:7
3 [a]Rom. 1:8; Eph. 5:20; 1Thess. 1:2; 2Thess. 2:13 [b]1Thess. 4:1; 2Thess. 2:1 [c]1Thess. 3:12
4 [I]Or, *steadfastness* [a]2Cor. 7:4; 1Thess. 2:19 [b]1Cor. 7:17; 1Thess. 2:14
5 [a]Phil. 1:28 [b]Luke 20:35; 2Thess. 1:11
6 [I]Lit., *If indeed* [II]Or, *in the sight of* [a]Ex. 23:22; Col. 3:25; Heb. 6:10
7 [I]Lit., *along with us* [II]Lit., *at the revelation of the Lord Jesus* [III]Lit., *the angels of His power* [a]Luke 17:30 [b]1Thess. 4:16 [c]Jude 14 [d]Ex. 3:2; 19:18; Is. 66:15; Ezek. 1:13; Dan. 7:9; Matt. 25:41; 1Cor. 3:13; Heb. 10:27; 12:29; 2Pet. 3:7; Jude 7; Rev. 14:10
8 [a]Gal. 4:8 [b]Rom. 2:8

9 [a]Phil. 3:19; 1Thess. 5:3 [b]Is. 2:10, 19, 21; 2Thess. 2:8 **10** [I]Or, *in the persons of* [II]Or, *holy ones* [a]Is. 49:3; John 17:10; 1Thess. 2:12 [b]Is. 2:11ff.; 1Cor. 3:13 [c]1Cor. 1:6; 1Thess. 2:1 **11** [I]Or, *make* [a]Col. 1:9 [b]2Thess. 1:5 [c]Rom. 11:29 [d]Rom. 15:14 [e]1Thess. 1:3 **12** [I]Or omit, *the* [a]Is. 24:15; 66:5; Mal. 1:11; Phil. 2:9ff.

🔑 **1:7** See note on I Thess. 2:19.
🔑 **1:9** See note on Mk. 3:28,29.

Man of Lawlessness

2 Now we request you, [a]brethren,
with regard to the [Ib]coming[3952] of
our Lord Jesus Christ, and our [c]gather-
ing together[1997] to Him,
2 that you may not be quickly
[aifp]shaken from your [I]composure[3563]
or be disturbed either by a [a]spirit[4151]
or a [IIb]message[3056] or a [c]letter as if
from us, to the effect that [d]the day[2250]
of the Lord [pfi][e]has come.[1764]
3 [a]Let no one in any way [aosb]deceive
you, for *it will not come* unless the
[Ib]apostasy[646] [aosb]comes[2064] first, and
the [c]man[444] of [II]lawlessness[458] is
[asbp]revealed, the [d]son[5207] of destruction,[684]
4 who [ppt]opposes[480] and [ppt]exalts
himself above [Ia]every [ppp]so-called god

1 [I]Or, *presence* [a]2Thess. 1:3 [b]1Thess. 2:19 [c]Mark 13:27; 1Thess. 4:15-17
2 [I]Lit., *mind* [II]Lit., *word* [a]1Cor. 14:32; 1John 4:1 [b]1Thess. 5:2; 2Thess. 2:15 [c]2Thess. 3:17 [d]1Cor. 1:8 [e]1Cor. 7:26
3 [I]Or, *falling away from the faith* [II]Some early mss. read *sin* [a]Eph. 5:6 [b]1Tim. 4:1 [c]Dan. 7:25; 8:25; 11:36; 2Thess. 2:8; Rev. 13:5ff. [d]John 17:12
4 [I]Or, *all that is called God* [a]1Cor. 8:5

2:1 See note on I Thess. 2:19.

2:2 See note on I Thess. 5:2.

2:3 In this verse we have the two signs which precede the *parousia* of the Lord Jesus. One is translated "the apostasy," *hē apostasia,* although it does not exactly mean that. The verb from which this substantive is derived is *aphistēmi,* made up of the preposition *apo* (575), "from," and *histēmi,* "to place or to stand." In its strict sense, it means to place oneself away from or to stand away from someone. It does not necessarily mean to remove oneself from someone or somewhere. The verb occurs in the N.T. in Lk. 2:37; 4:13; 8:14; 13:27; Acts 5:37,38; 12:10; 15:38; 19:9; 22:29; II Cor. 12:8; I Tim. 4:1; 6:5; II Tim. 2:19; Heb. 3:12. This departing from someone does not necessarily imply wholehearted agreement or disagreement, but it is separating oneself for the purpose of not incurring the dangers of that association. This seems to be the meaning here. In those days, there were a great number of people who were associating with the Christians but were not necessarily themselves believers. But when persecution arose against the Christians, these people did not want to maintain the association any longer since they were fearful that they would be considered sympathetic to Christians and would themselves be persecuted. Another passage similar to this one is I Tim. 4:1 which also refers to the end times when we are told that "some will fall away from the faith" or better still "shall stand aloof from the faith." In II Thess. 2:3 we have apostasy mentioned without telling us from whom or from what they stand off. But in I Tim. 4:1 Paul says that there will be some people who will stand off from the faith. These were people who were associating themselves with the faith but who were not in reality faithful. If this referred to the falling away from the true faith, then the words of Christ in Jn. 10:28 would not be true: "And I give eternal life to them, and they shall never perish; and no one shall snatch them out of my hand." If persecution could cause a true believer to lose his faith or to fall from the faith, then how could the Apostle Paul have spoken the truth when he wrote in Rom. 8:38,39, "For I am convinced that neither death, nor life, nor angels, nor principalities, nor things present, nor things to come, nor powers, nor height, nor depth, nor any other created thing, shall be able to separate (*chōrisai,* 5563) us from the love of God, which is in Christ Jesus our Lord." Furthermore, the Lord said in Jn. 17:12, "I was keeping them in thy name which thou hast given me; and I guarded them, and not one of them perished but the son of perdition." The son of perdition was always lost. He was never saved. See also notes on Gal. 1:8; Heb. 6:1-6.

2:3-8 "The man of lawlessness" referred to by the Apostle Paul here is the same person referred to in other Scriptures with other names such as "antichrist" in John's writings (I Jn. 2:18; 4:3; II Jn. 7). The preposition *anti* indicates opposition and not in place of Christ. This personage will be one who is opposed to Christ and not one who tries to take the place of Christ. Such a person is also described in Dan. 7:7,8,21; Mt. 24:15, and Rev. 13. The characteristic of this individual is that he "opposes and exalts himself above every so-called god or object of worship" (v. 4). He claims to be God. He is not Satan, but his coming "is in accord with the activity of Satan" (v. 9). He will be a miracle worker. It is clear that Paul thinks of the supreme effort of Satan as not in the past, but in the future. He does not think of the world as gradually evolving into a perfect state, but of evil continuing right up till the end. At that time, evil will make its greatest challenge to good, and this challenge will be led by the mysterious figure who owes his power to Satan and who is the instrument of Satan's culminating challenge to the things of God. Paul predicts the outcome of Christ consuming the man of sin "with the breath of his mouth" (v. 8). The last supreme challenge of Satan will be defeated.

2:3-12 See note on Rev. 13.

or object of worship,[4574] so that he
[ainf]takes his seat in the temple[3485]
of God, [ppt] [b]displaying himself as being
God.[2316]
5 Do you not remember that
[a]while I was still with you, I was [ipf]telling
you these things?
🔑 6 And you know [a]what [ppt]re-
strains[2722] him now, so that in his
time[2540] he may be [aies]revealed.
7 For [a]the mystery[3466] of lawlessness[458] is already at work;[1754] only
[b]he who now [ppp]restrains[2722] *will do so*
until he is [aosb]taken out of the way.
🔑 8 And then that lawless[459] one
[a]will be revealed[601] whom the Lord[2962]
will slay [b]with the breath[4151] of His
mouth and bring to an end by the
[c]appearance[2015] of His [I]coming;
🔑 9 *that is,* the one whose [I]coming is
in accord with the activity of [a]Satan,[4567]
with all power[1411] and [IIb]signs[4592] and
false wonders,[5059]
🔑 10 and with [I]all the deception of
wickedness for [a]those who [ppt]perish,
because they did not [ao]receive the
love[26] of [b]the truth[225] so as to be
[aies]saved.[4982]
11 And for this reason [a]God [I]will
send upon them [II]a [b]deluding influence
so that they might believe[4100] [III]what is
false,
12 in order that they all may be

4 [b]Is. 14:14; Ezek. 28:2
5 [a]1Thess. 3:4
6 [a]2Thess. 2:7
7 [a]Rev. 17:5, 7 [b]2Thess. 2:6
8 [I]Or, *presence* [a]Dan. 7:25; 8:25; 11:36; 2Thess. 2:3; Rev. 13:5ff. [b]Is. 11:4; Rev. 2:16; 19:15 [c]1Tim. 6:14; 2Tim. 1:10; 4:1, 8; Titus 2:13
9 [I]Or, *presence* [II]Or, *attesting miracles* [a]Matt. 4:10 [b]Matt. 24:24; John 4:48
10 [I]Or, *every deception* [a]1Cor. 1:18 [b]2Thess. 2:12, 13
11 [I]Lit., *sends* [II]Lit., *an activity of error* [III]Or, *the lie* [a]1Kin. 22:22; Rom. 1:28 [b]1Thess. 2:3; 2Tim. 4:4
12 [I]Or, *condemned* [II]Or, *approved* [a]Rom. 2:8 [b]Rom. 1:32; 1Cor. 13:6
13 [I]Some ancient mss. read *first fruits* [II]Lit., *in* [III]Lit., *of* [a]2Thess. 1:3 [b]1Thess. 1:4 [c]Eph. 1:4ff. [d]1Cor. 1:21; 1Thess. 2:12; 5:9; 1Pet. 1:5 [e]1Thess. 4:7; 1Pet. 1:2

[asbp] [I]judged[2919] who [a]did not [apt]believe
the truth, but [IIb]took [apt]pleasure[2106] in
wickedness.[93]
13 [a]But we [pin]should always [pin]give
thanks[2168] to God for you, [b]brethren
beloved[25] by the Lord, because [c]God
has [aom]chosen[138] you [I]from the beginning
[d]for salvation[4991] [IIe]through sanctification[38] [III]by the Spirit and faith in the
truth.
14 And it was for this He [a]called
you through [b]our gospel,[2098] [I]that you
may gain the glory of our Lord Jesus
Christ.
15 So then, brethren, [a]stand firm
and [b]hold to the traditions[3862] which
you were [aop]taught,[1321] whether [c]by
word[3056] *of mouth* or [c]by letter[1992]
[I]from us.
16 [a]Now may our Lord Jesus Christ
[b]Himself and God our Father, who has
[apt] [c]loved[25] us and [apt]given us eternal
comfort[3874] and [d]good[18] hope by
grace,[5485]
17 [opt] [a]comfort[3870] and [opt] [b]strength-
en your hearts[5485] in every good work[2041]
and word.

14 [I]Lit., *to the gaining of* [a]1Thess. 2:12 [b]1Thess. 1:5 **15** [I]Lit., *of* [a]1Cor. 16:13 [b]1Cor. 11:2; 2Thess. 3:6 [c]2Thess. 2:2 **16** [a]1Thess. 3:11 [b]1Thess. 3:11 [c]John 3:16 [d]Titus 3:7; 1Pet. 1:3 **17** [a]1Thess. 3:2, 13 [b]2Thess. 3:3

🔑 **2:6,7** Paul refers here to the Holy Spirit who is the restraining force in this world, curbing the many little antichrists as they exist today and the final antichrist who will appear in connection with the Second Coming of the Lord (I Jn. 2:18). The Holy Spirit in v. 6 is called *to katechon* (2722), in the neuter, even as the Holy Spirit is, for the most part, called *to Hagion Pneuma,* also in the neuter. In v. 7 it is *ho katechōn,* "he who holds fast or retains or restrains." The antichrist cannot now, and will not in the future, be able to do anything without the specific permission of the Holy Spirit who regulates the events of the world to accomplish God's eternal plan. Of course, v. 7 does not refer to a departure of the Holy Spirit from the world. The Holy Spirit has always been accomplishing the will of the triune God from the beginning. There are specific times, however, when the Holy Spirit has come in unique ways even as the Lord Jesus did in His incarnation and will do so in His Second Coming. The same Holy Spirit came at Pentecost, at Caesarea, and at Ephesus as the agent of Christ baptizing the believers into His body. The reference here is not to the departure of the Holy Spirit, but to the removal of His restraining power. This will allow certain things to take place in order to accomplish God's plan according to His own timetable. See note on I Cor. 12:13 and the Editor's book, *The Holy Spirit's Baptism and Infilling.*

🔑 **2:8** See note on I Thess. 2:19.

🔑 **2:9** In this one verse we have the three names by which supernatural manifestations or miracles were called. They are *dunamis* (1411), *sēmeion* (4592), and *teras* (5059). Observe how these miracles are accomplished by the energy of Satan. Miracle working is not necessarily evidence of God's power.

🔑 **2:10-12** See note on Rev. 7.

Exhortation

3 [a]Finally, brethren, [b]pray for us that
[c]the word3056 of the Lord2962 may
psa [I]spread rapidly and be psmpglori-
fied,1392 just as *it did* also with you;
2 and that we may be asbp[a]de-
livered4506 from [I]perverse and evil4190
men;444 for not all have [II]faith.4102
3 But [a]the Lord is faithful,4103 and
[I]He will strengthen and protect you
[II]from [b]the evil4190 *one.*
4 And we have [a]confidence3982 in the
Lord concerning you, that you [b]are doing
and will *continue to* do what we com-
mand.3853
5 And may the Lord opt [a]direct your
hearts2558 into the love26 of God and
into the steadfastness of Christ.5547
6 Now we command you, breth-
ren,80 [a]in the name3686 of our Lord Jesus
Christ, that you pim [I][b]keep aloof4724 from
every brother who ppt [II]leads an
[III][c]unruly814 life and not according to
[d]the tradition3862 which [IV]you received
from us.
7 For you yourselves know how you
ought to pinf [I][a]follow our example, because we did not act in an undisci-
plined812 manner among you,
8 nor did we [a]eat [I]anyone's bread
[II]without paying1432 for it, but with
[b]labor and hardship3449 we *kept*
ppt [c]working2038 night and day so that we
might not be a burden to any of you;
9 not because we do not have [a]the
right1849 *to this,* but in order to aosbof-
fer ourselves [b]as a model5179 for you,
that you might aies [I]follow our example.
10 For even [a]when we were with
you, we used to ipfgive you this order:
[b]if anyone will not pinfwork,2038 neither
let him pimeat.
11 For we hear that some among
you are ppt [a]leading an undisciplined814
life, doing no work at all, but pptacting
like [b]busybodies.
12 Now such persons we com-
mand3853 and [a]exhort3870 in the Lord
Jesus Christ to ppt [b]work in quiet2271 fashion and psaeat their own bread.
13 But as for you, [a]brethren, [b]do
not aosigrow weary1573 of pptdoing good.
14 And if anyone does not obey5219
our [I]instruction3056 [II][a]in this letter,1992
pimtake special note of that man [III][b]and
do not pimassociate with him, so that
he may be [c]put to asbpshame.1788
15 And *yet* [a]do not pimregard him as
an enemy, but pim [I][b]admonish3560 him as
a [c]brother.
16 Now [a]may the Lord of peace1515
[b]Himself continually optgrant1325 you
peace in every [I]circumstance. [c]The Lord
be with you all!
17 [I]I, Paul, write this greeting783
[a]with my own hand, and this is a distinguishing mark4592 in every letter;1992 this
is the way I write.1125
18 [a]The grace of our Lord Jesus
Christ be with you all.

1 [I]Lit., *run* [a]1Thess. 4:1 [b]1Thess. 5:25 [c]1Thess. 1:8
2 [I]Lit., *improper* [II]Or, *the faith* [a]Rom. 15:31
3 [I]Lit., *will* [II]Or, *from evil* [a]1Cor. 1:9; 1Thess. 5:24 [b]Matt. 5:37
4 [a]2Cor. 2:3 [b]1Thess. 4:10
5 [a]1Thess. 3:11
6 [I]Or, *avoid* [II]Lit., *walks disorderly* [III]Or, *undisciplined* [IV]Many ancient mss. read *they* [a]1Cor. 5:4 [b]Rom. 16:17; 1Cor. 5:11; 2Thess. 3:14 [c]1Thess. 5:14; 2Thess. 3:7, 11 [d]1Cor. 11:2; 2Thess. 2:15
7 [I]Lit., *imitate us* [a]1Thess. 1:6; 2Thess. 3:9
8 [I]Lit., *from anyone* [II]Lit., *freely* [a]1Cor. 9:4 [b]1Thess. 2:9 [c]Acts 18:3; Eph. 4:28
9 [I]Lit., *imitate us* [a]1Cor. 9:4ff. [b]2Thess. 3:7
10 [a]1Thess. 3:4 [b]1Thess. 4:11
11 [a]2Thess. 3:6 [b]1Tim. 5:13; 1Pet. 4:15
12 [a]1Thess. 4:1 [b]1Thess. 4:11
13 [a]1Thess. 4:1 [b]2Cor. 4:1; Gal. 6:9
14 [I]Lit., *word* [II]Lit., *through* [III]Lit., *not to associate* [a]Col. 4:16 [b]2Thess. 3:6 [c]1Cor. 4:14
15 [I]Or, *keep admonishing* [a]Gal. 6:1 [b]1Thess. 5:14 [c]2Thess. 3:6, 13
16 [I]Lit., *way* [a]Rom. 15:33 [b]1Thess. 3:11 [c]Ruth 2:4
17 [I]Lit., *The greeting by my hand of Paul* [a]1Cor. 16:21
18 [a]Rom. 16:20; 1Thess. 5:28

The First Epistle of Paul to

TIMOTHY

The two Epistles to Timothy and the one to Titus, commonly known as the Pastoral Epistles, belong to the period at the close of Paul's life and provide valuable information about the great missionary Apostle's thoughts as he prepared to pass on his tasks to others. It is generally believed that I Timothy was written about A.D. 63.

Timothy was the son of a mixed marriage; his mother, who evidently instructed him in the Scriptures, was a Jewess, and his father was a Greek (Acts. 16:1; II Tim. 1:5). He was a native of Lystra (Acts 16:1) and was highly esteemed by his Christian brethren both there and in Iconium (Acts 16:2). He came to know the Lord on Paul's first missionary journey which included Lystra in its itinerary. When Paul took his second missionary journey, Timothy's mother was also a Christian.

Paul added Timothy to his party as he traveled with Silas who had replaced Barnabas. Timothy probably replaced John Mark whom Paul had refused to take (Acts 15:36ff). To avoid criticism from local Jews, Timothy was circumcised before setting out on his journeys.

Timothy was first assigned to minister to the believers in Thessalonica. He was associated with Paul and Silvanus in the greetings of both Epistles directed to the church and was present with Paul during his preaching at Corinth (II Cor. 1:19). He is next heard of during the Apostle's Ephesian ministry when he was sent with Erastus on another important mission to Macedonia. From there he was to proceed to Corinth (I Cor. 4:17). Apparently, Timothy was of a timid nature; hence, the admonition of Paul to encourage him (I Cor. 16:10,11, compare II Tim. 4:17ff).

Timothy also went with Paul on the journey to Jerusalem with the collection (Acts 20:4,5) and is next heard of when Paul, then a prisoner, wrote Collossians, Philemon, and Philippians. When Paul was released from imprisonment and engaged in further activity in the East, as the Pastoral Epistles indicate, it would seem that Paul left Timothy at Ephesus (I Tim. 1:3) and commissioned him to deal with false teachers and supervise public worship and the appointment of church officials. Although Paul evidently hoped to rejoin Timothy, the fear that he might be delayed occasioned the writing of the first letter to him. This was followed by another when Paul was not only re-arrested, but put on trial for his life. We have no indication as to whether Timothy was able to go to Paul as Paul had urged him to do. Later, Timothy himself became a prisoner as Heb. 13:23 shows, but no details are given. No further information about Timothy is given after that.

Misleadings in Doctrine and Living

1 🔑 Paul, [a]an apostle[652] of [b]Christ[5547]
Jesus [c]according to the commandment[2003] of [d]God[2316] our Savior,[4990] and of [e]Christ Jesus, *who is* our [f]hope;[1680]

2 to [a]Timothy, [b]*my* true child[5043] in *the* faith:[4102] [c]Grace,[5485] mercy[1656] *and* peace[1515] from God the Father[3962] and [d]Christ Jesus our Lord.

🔑 3 As I urged you [I]upon my departure for [a]Macedonia, [II]remain[4357] on at [b]Ephesus, in order that you may [aosb]instruct certain men not to [c]teach[2085] strange doctrines,

4 nor to [pinf] [I]pay attention to [a]myths[3454] and endless [b]genealogies,[1076] which give rise[3930] to mere [c]speculation rather than [d]*furthering* [II]the administration[3620] of God which is by faith.[4102]

1 [a]2Cor. 1:1 [b]1Tim. 1:12 [c]Titus 1:3 [d]Titus 1:3 [e]Col. 1:27

2 [a]2Tim. 1:2 [b]2Tim. 1:2 [c]Rom. 1:7; 2Tim. 1:2; Titus 1:4 [d]1Tim. 1:12

3 [I]Lit., *while departing* [II]Lit., *to remain* [a]Rom. 15:26 [b]Acts 18:19 [c]Rom. 16:17; 2Cor. 11:4; Gal. 1:6f.; 1Tim. 6:3

4 [I]Or, *occupy themselves with* [II]Lit., *God's provision* [a]1Tim. 4:7; 2Tim. 4:4; Titus 1:14; 2Pet. 1:16 [b]Titus 3:9 [c]2Tim. 2:23 [d]Eph. 3:2

🔑 **1:1,2** See note on I Pet. 2:17.

🔑 **1:3** See general remarks on I Timothy.

5 But the goal[5056] of our [I][a]instruc-
tion[3852] is love[26] [b]from a pure[2513]
heart[2588] and a [c]good[18] conscience[4893]
and a sincere[505] [d]faith.
6 For some men, [apt]straying from
these things, have [aop]turned aside to
[a]fruitless discussion,[3150]
7 [a]wanting to be [b]teachers of the
Law, even though they do not understand[3539] either what they are saying
or the matters about which they make
confident assertions.[1226]
8 But we know that [a]the Law[3551]
is good,[2570] if one uses it lawfully,
9 realizing the fact that [a]law is not
[pinf]made[2749] for a righteous[1342] man, but
for those who are lawless[459] and
[b]rebellious,[506] for the [c]ungodly[765] and
sinners,[268] for the unholy[462] and [d]pro-
fane,[952] for those who kill their fathers
or mothers, for murderers
10 [I]and [II][a]immoral men[4205] [I]and
[b]homosexuals [I]and [c]kidnappers [I]and
[d]liars [I]and [e]perjurers, and whatever else
is contrary to [f]sound[5198] teaching,[1319]
11 according to [a]the glorious[1391]
gospel[2098] of [b]the blessed[3107] God, with
which I have been [c]entrusted.[4100]
12 I thank[5485] [a]Christ Jesus our
Lord, who has [apt] [b]strengthened me, because He considered me faithful,[4103]
[apt] [c]putting me into service;[1248]
13 even though I was formerly a
blasphemer[989] and a [a]persecutor and a
violent aggressor.[5197] And yet I was
[aop] [b]shown mercy, because [c]I acted
[ppt]ignorantly[50] in unbelief;[570]
14 and the [a]grace[5485] of our Lord
was more than abundant, with the
[b]faith[4102] and love[26] which are *found* in
Christ Jesus.
15 [a]It is a trustworthy[4103] statement,[3056] deserving full acceptance,[594]
that [b]Christ Jesus came into the
world[2889] to [ainf] [c]save[4982] sinners,[268]
among whom [d]I am foremost *of all*.

5 [I]Lit., *commandment* [a]1Tim. 1:18 [b]2Tim. 2:22 [c]1Tim. 1:19; 3:9; 2Tim. 1:3; 1Pet. 3:16, 21 [d]2Tim. 1:5
6 [a]Titus 1:10
7 [a]James 3:1 [b]Luke 2:46
8 [a]Rom. 7:12, 16
9 [a]Gal. 5:23 [b]Titus 1:6, 10 [c]1Pet. 4:18; Jude 15 [d]1Tim. 4:7; 6:20; Heb. 12:16
10 [I]Lit., *for* [II]Or, *fornicators* [a]1Cor. 6:9 [b]Lev. 18:22 [c]Ex. 21:16; Rev. 18:13 [d]Rev. 21:8, 27; 22:15 [e]Matt. 5:33 [f]1Tim. 4:6; 6:3; 2Tim. 4:3; Titus 1:9, 13; 2:1, 2
11 [a]2Cor. 4:4 [b]1Tim. 6:15 [c]Gal. 2:7
12 [a]Gal. 3:26 [b]Acts 9:22; Phil. 4:13; 2Tim. 4:17 [c]Acts 9:15
13 [a]Acts 8:3 [b]1Cor. 7:25 [c]Acts 26:9
14 [a]Rom. 5:20; 1Cor. 3:10; 2Cor. 4:15; Gal. 1:13-16 [b]1Thess. 1:3; 1Tim. 2:15; 4:12; 6:11; 2Tim. 1:13; 2:22; Titus 2:2
15 [a]1Tim. 3:1; 4:9; 2Tim. 2:11; Titus 3:8 [b]Mark 2:17; Luke 15:2ff.; 19:10 [c]Rom. 11:14 [d]1Cor. 15:9; Eph. 3:8
16 [I]Or, *destined to* [a]1Cor. 7:25; 1Tim. 1:13 [b]Eph. 2:7
17 [I]Lit., *of the ages* [II]Lit., *to the ages of the ages* [a]Rev. 15:3 [b]1Tim. 6:16 [c]Col. 1:15 [d]John 5:44; 1Tim. 6:15; Jude 25 [e]Rom. 2:7, 10; 11:36; Heb. 2:7
18 [I]Lit., *child* [a]1Tim. 1:5

16 And yet[235] for this reason I
[a]found mercy, in order that in me as
the foremost, Jesus Christ might
[b]demonstrate His perfect patience, as
an example[5296] for those [I]who would
[pinf]believe[4100] in Him for eternal[166]
life.[2222]
17 Now to the [a]King[935] [I]eternal,[165]
[b]immortal,[862] [c]invisible, the [d]only
God,[2316] [e]*be* honor and glory[1391] [II]for-
ever[165] and ever.[165] Amen.[281]
18 This [a]command[3852] I entrust to
you, Timothy, [b]my [I]son, in accordance
with the [c]prophecies[4394] previously
[ppt]made[4254] concerning you, that by
them you may [psa] [d]fight the good
fight,
19 keeping [a]faith[4102] and a good[18]
conscience,[4893] which some have [apt]re-
jected and [ao]suffered shipwreck in regard to [I][b]their faith.
🔑 20 [I]Among these are [a]Hymenaeus
and [b]Alexander, whom I have [ao] [c]deliv-
ered over to Satan,[4567] so that they
may be [asbp] [d]taught[3811] not to [pinf]blas-
pheme.[987]

A Call to Prayer

2 First[4412] of all, then, I urge that
[a]entreaties[1162] *and* prayers,[4335]
petitions[1783] *and* thanksgivings, be
[pip]made on behalf of all men,[444]
2 [a]for kings[935] and all who are in
[I]authority,[5247] in order that we may
[psa]lead a tranquil and quiet[2272] life[979] in
all godliness[2150] and [II]dignity.[4587]
3 This is good[2570] and acceptable[587]
in the sight of [a]God our Savior,[4990]

[b]1Tim. 1:2 [c]1Tim. 4:14 [d]2Cor. 10:4; 1Tim. 6:12; 2Tim. 2:3f.; 4:7
19 [I]Lit., *the* [a]1Tim. 1:5 [b]1Tim. 6:12, 21; 2Tim. 2:18
20 [I]Lit., *Of* [a]2Tim. 2:17 [b]2Tim. 4:14 [c]1Cor. 5:5 [d]1Cor. 11:32; Heb. 12:5ff.
1 [a]Eph. 6:18
2 [I]Or, *a high position* [II]Or, *seriousness* [a]Ezra 6:10; Rom. 13:1
3 [a]Luke 1:47; 1Tim. 1:1; 4:10

🔑 **1:20** "Delivered over to Satan" means allowing them to be buffeted by Satan so that they may repent from their sin which, in this instance, was blasphemy. Paul believes that people who are openly sinning should be excluded from the local fellowship of believers. Neither Paul nor any other human being is given the right to assign anyone to eternal perdition, but only to punishment in this life even as in the case of Ananias and Sapphira in Acts 5:1-11. See note on I Cor. 5:5; 11:30; Mt. 18:15-18.

4 [a]who desires all men[444] to be
[aifp] [b]saved[4982] and to [ainf] [c]come to the
[I]knowledge[1922] of the truth.[225]
5 For there is [a]one God,[2316] *and*
[b]one mediator[3316] also between God and
men, *the* [an] [c]man Christ Jesus,
6 who [a]gave Himself as a ransom[487]
for all, the [b]testimony[3142] [I]*borne* at [II][c]the
proper[2398] time.[2540]
7 [a]And for this I was [aop]appointed[5087]
a [I]preacher[2783] and [b]an apostle[652] ([c]I am
telling the truth,[225] I am not lying) as
a teacher[1320] of [d]the Gentiles[1484] in
faith[4102] and truth.[225]
8 Therefore [a]I want the men[435]
[b]in every place to [pinf]pray, [c]lifting up[1869]
[d]holy[3741] hands, without wrath[3709] and
dissension.[1261]

Women Instructed

9 Likewise, *I want* [a]women to
[pinf]adorn themselves with proper[2887]
clothing, [I]modestly[127] and discreetly,[4997]
not with braided hair and gold or pearls
or costly garments;[2441]

4 [I]Or, *recognition* [a]Ezek. 18:23, 32; John 3:17; 1Tim. 4:10; Titus 2:11; 2Pet. 3:9 [b]Rom. 11:14 [c]2Tim. 2:25; 3:7; Titus 1:1; Heb. 10:26
5 [a]Rom. 3:30; 10:12; 1Cor. 8:4 [b]1Cor. 8:6; Gal. 3:20 [c]Matt. 1:1; Rom. 1:3
6 [I]Or, to be borne [II]Lit., *its own times* [a]Matt. 20:28; Gal. 1:4 [b]1Cor. 1:6 [c]Mark 1:15; Gal. 4:4; 1Tim. 6:15; Titus 1:3
7 [I]Or, *herald* [a]Eph. 3:8; 1Tim. 1:11; 2Tim. 1:11 [b]1Cor. 9:1 [c]Rom. 9:1 [d]Acts 9:15
8 [a]Phil. 1:12; 1Tim. 5:14; Titus 3:8 [b]John 4:21; 1Cor. 1:2; 2Cor. 2:14; 1Thess. 1:8 [c]Ps. 63:4; Luke 24:50 [d]Ps. 24:4; James 4:8
9 [I]Lit., *with modesty* [a]1Pet. 3:3

2:9-15 This passage indicates that women were full and active members in the early church (I Cor. 11:4-5; 14:33-35; Eph. 5:21,22; Col. 3:18,19; Tit. 2:1-10). Peter also had something to say concerning the witness of women and their conduct at home (I Pet. 3:1-7). In the marital relationships, a woman is not presented as having any fewer rights upon her husband than he has upon his wife.

In Gal. 3:28 Paul very clearly wrote that there are no distinctions between male and female in Christ. He did not indicate that there were no differences between the sexes, but that there are no distinctions in Christ. The whole thesis of the teaching of Paul concerning women is that there must be respect for the differences which exist between men and women as such, and that the external differing aspects of appearance should be maintained. A man should never be mistaken as a woman nor a woman as a man from the way that they maintain their hair or dress or behavior. God has appointed tasks for women and tasks for men. No man can bear a child and no woman can assume the role of a husband. These are the basic teachings on which Paul insists. Throughout his teaching, he emphatically stresses that there are differences between men and women which must be respected because these were differences created by God Himself, but that in spite of the differences, the equality of the sexes before God must be emphasized. In I Pet. 3:7 women are called the fellow heirs of the grace of life. In no way are they inferior to men in the sight of God. On the other hand, it must be observed that God expects of each one the performance of duty according to his or her God-given endowments.

Often in the Scriptures we find Paul recognizing women as friends and co-workers in the Gospel (Rom. 16:1-4). Priscilla is called a fellow worker in Christ Jesus (Rom. 16:3). Paul does not differentiate between Priscilla and her husband Acquila. Rather he calls them both by the same name, *sunergous* (4904), meaning fellow workers. He does not distinguish between the work each can do because one is male and the other female. Later on in Rom. 16:21, he calls Timothy by the same name, *sunergos.* In Phile. 24 he calls all men who were his co-workers, among whom was Luke, by the same name.

However, there are some difficult passages in regard to the position of women in the Christian Church. One of them is I Cor. 14:33-40; see note for the explanation of this passage. For a detailed examination of Paul's attitude toward women in the marital relationship and also in their relationship to God and the Christian Church, see the Editor's book on I Cor. 7 entitled, *May I Divorce and Remarry?*.

See also the note on I Cor. 11:2-16. From the examination of this passage, it is clear that Paul recognized that both wives and husbands could pray and prophesy in the worship service (v. 5).

In all this discussion, Paul's main concern is that no woman would appear as a woman of immoral character by having short hair or a shaven head, because in this manner she dishonored God and her husband's character as well as her own.

The general attitude of Paul is that one should not flaunt customs if such customs are good ones. If the acceptable code of behavior indicates a definite distinction between the mode of dress of a man and a woman, adhere to the mode of dress which characterizes one's sex. And if there is a way whereby women and men are differentiated from the way that they care for their hair, by all means maintain that accepted distinctive demonstration.

In this particular passage in I Timothy we should not begin the discussion about women with v. 11

(continued on next page)

10 but rather by means of good[18] works,[2041] as befits women making a claim[1861] to godliness.[2317]

11 [a]1Cor. 14:34; Titus 2:5

11 [a]Let a woman quietly[2271] [pim]receive instruction[3129] with entire submissiveness.[5292]

(continued from previous page)

but with v. 9. The Apostle Paul is concerned about women dressing themselves modestly. There is one Greek word in v. 9 which provides the clue for the interpretation of this whole difficult passage. It is the Greek word *sōphrosunē* (4997) translated as discreetly. The adjective is *sōphrōn* (4998) and the adverb is *sōphronōs* (4996). The verbs are *sōphroneō* (4993) or *sōphronizō* (4994), and the result is demonstrated by the substantive *sōphronismos* (4995). There is absolutely no English equivalent to this beautiful Greek word. To make its meaning simple we should say that it is the voluntary limitation of one's freedom of thought and behavior. The closest in English would be sober mindedness. The truth of the matter is that in Christianity women became free, equal to their husbands. The danger, however, was always present that they might misuse this new-found freedom and take it beyond the limitations that God had placed in appointing man as head over woman in the marital relationship. There can be absolutely no two people or things exactly the same (I Cor. 4:7). The inherent differences in people and things must be recognized by a *sōphrōn* person. This is a person who recognizes who he is, what he is, what he can and cannot do, and how he must behave in certain given circumstances. The whole thesis of the Apostle Paul is that women should not try to look or act like men and should not attempt to usurp the position of their husbands in the home and in the church, thus maintaining the parallel of the Church as the bride of Christ.

This in no way implied that men are superior to women, but to function properly, everything needs a head, including a family. This is true in all relationships constituting a unit made up of varied personalities. One of the cardinal doctrines of the Godhead is the Trinity. Mt. 28:19 gives us the words of Christ. "Go therefore and make disciples of all the nations, baptizing them in the name (singular). . . ." But in this name—God—there are three distinctive personality names: the Father, the Son, and the Holy Ghost. Jesus said in John 10:30, "I and the Father are one." They are both God. But in I Cor. 11:3 Paul says, "God is the head of Christ." There is no verb in the Greek indicating that this has always been so. This does not mean that Christ was inferior to the Father. His position under the Father is of the nature as a wife's position is to her own husband as stated immediately prior in I Cor. 11:3, "the man is the head of a woman." Again in the Greek there is no verb which indicates that this relationship has always been and was made that way by God who is the creator of the husband-wife relationship (I Cor. 11:8-12).

In marriage, two people constitute a single unit, and yet in that one body there are two personalities. These two, if they are going to be united, must have a headship, and that head is the man according to God's creation and ordinance.

Paul's concern is that a woman should not dress in such a way as to attract and lure men other than her own husband. A Christian woman should not be *a* man's woman, but she should be *her* man's woman (I Tim. 5:9), the same as an exemplary Christian man should not be a lady's man (I Tim. 3:2,12; Tit. 1:6).

The relationship expressed in this passage is not that of women being inferior to men, but of a wife in her proper relationship to her husband. Observe I Tim. 2:11. It does not say women but a woman, and better still, a wife. The word in Greek is *gunē* (1135), which indicates either a woman generically speaking or a wife, depending on the context. In this instance, since it stands in apposition to the word *andros* (the genitive singular of *anēr* here meaning only "husband" and not "man" generically, 435), it must be translated as "a wife." It is because of the mistranslations of these passages that the Christian world has had so much difficulty in understanding the proper position of a woman in the Christian Church. I Timothy 2:11 should be translated "Let the wife learn (the indirect imperative of the present tense which means continuously to learn at any time and at all times) in tranquility in her positioning under." The word translated "quietly" is the noun *hēsuchia* (2271). In the N.T. it occurs in Acts 22:2; II Thess. 3:12 and I Tim. 2:11,12. The adjective of the same word is *hēsuchios,* and it is used in I Tim. 2:2 and is translated with the word "peaceable," and in I Pet. 3:4, it is translated with the word "quiet." In both instances it means "tranquil, not disturbed." The verb is *hēsuchazō* (2270) and in Lk. 14:4 it is translated as "kept silent." In Lk. 23:56 it is translated as "rested." In Acts 11:18 it is translated as "quieted down." In Acts 21:14 it is translated as "fell silent." In I Thess. 4:11, it is translated as "to lead a quiet

(continued on next page)

12 [a]But I do not allow a woman to
[pinf]teach[1321] or exercise authority over[831]
a man,[435] but to remain quiet.[2271]
13 [a]For it was Adam who was first
[aop] [I]created, *and* then Eve.
14 And *it was* not Adam *who* was
deceived, but [a]the woman being quite
[aptp]deceived, [pfi]fell into transgression.[3847]

12 [a]1Cor. 14:34; Titus 2:5
13 [I]Or, *formed* [a]Gen. 2:7, 22; 3:16; 1Cor. 11:8ff.
14 [a]Gen. 3:6, 13; 2Cor. 11:3
15 [I]Lit., *saved* [II]Or, *discretion* [a]1Tim. 1:14
1 [a]1Tim. 1:15

15 But *women* shall be [I]pre-
served[4982] through the bearing of children if they [aosb]continue[3306] in [a]faith[4102]
and love[26] and sanctity[38] with [II]self-
restraint.[4997]

Overseers and Deacons

3 [a]It is a trustworthy[4103] statement:[3056] if any man aspires to the

(continued from previous page)
life." The correct meaning, therefore, of the word *hēsuchia* in this text is not silence, but it is "tranquility, not in a disturbing way."

Another important word in I Tim. 2:11 is the word *hupotagē* (5292), which is translated as "submissiveness." This noun is made up of the preposition *hupo* (5259), "under," and the verb *tassō* (5021) which means "to place in proper order." There are many derivatives of this verb.

What did Paul want to teach in I Tim. 2:11? It was that a wife should display a tranquil spirit in her attempt to learn. We must bear in mind here that during that period usually only men had the privilege of education. If the word *hēsuchia* meant complete silence, how could she ever learn or satisfy her hunger for knowledge if she did not have the opportunity to ask questions. Paul encouraged a wife to ask questions and to learn, but always to realize that her questions should not be of a nature which would disturb the peace that existed between her and her husband or which in any way would embarrass her husband. She should bear in mind the proper positioning of a wife in relationship to her husband, who is her head, and consequently responsible to provide for and protect her. "To be in subjection" means to recognize one's position in relationship to one's husband. The two who constitute one body have one head under Christ, and that is the husband.

Verse 12 is again poorly translated in the K.J.V. It should not be "But I suffer not a woman to teach," but "I suffer not a wife. . . ." As Paul continues the discussion, the word *gunē* is here used in contrast to *anēr,* "husband," and not "man" as the A.V. has it. *Gunē* in this verse must also be translated as "a wife" as in v. 11. Paul says, "I do not permit a wife to teach." The word for "teach" in Greek is the infinitive *didaskein* in the present tense which means to teach continuously. The situation presented is that of the common presence of a wife and husband in the home or the assembly or anywhere else. Paul says, "I do not want a wife to constantly teach." If she did, she would undermine her husband's position, giving the impression that she is the head of her husband, which is contrary to God's ordained order between husband and wife. A wife should place limitations on her own liberty in Christ in both her dress, her adornment and her speech. Paul does not want women to be drab or mute, but to be careful lest they go beyond the bounds of accepted propriety. A wife should be characterized by *sōphrosunē,* sober mindedness, and also *aidō,* modesty, so that her husband may not be embarrassed. In view of vv. 9,10 we are told that she should not dress in such a way as to be the center of attraction, but rather should express her goodness by her good works.

The word translated "exercise authority" is the Greek word *authentein* or *authenteō* (831), and this is the only place in the N.T. that it occurs. Interestingly enough, in Classical Greek an *authentēs* was an autocrat, a person who ruled even to the point of committing murder. In one instance, it referred to a murder of one of the same family. The noun *authentia* means absolute sway or authority. In other words, a wife in her private or public life should not do anything to kill the position that her husband has been given by God. A wife should never be a usurper of the role of a husband or a father.

In v. 13 Paul explains why, "For it was Adam who was first created, and then Eve." It is not because the husband is better or more intelligent or more worthy. It is simply the order originally ordained by God, and as such it must be respected. Two personalities constituting one body, one flesh, can only have one head. This is intrinsic in God's creation. See Editor's book, *How to Manage Money,* and especially the portions on Lk. 16:13.

The word *sōphrosunē,* again translated "self-restraint," is used at the end of v. 15 which indicates, as previously explained, personal limitation of one's freedom. Paul argues in vv. 14,15 that it was the woman who was deceived by Satan, but that in childbearing she has regained her position before God in equality with man. However, she must beware lest she misuse that freedom granted to her by God. See note on Tit. 2:1-5; I Pet.3:1-4.

[b]office of [I]overseer,[1984] it is a fine[2570]
work[2041] he desires[1937] *to do.*
🔑2 [Ia]An overseer,[1985] then, must be
above reproach,[423] [b]the [an]husband[435]
of one wife, [c]temperate, prudent,[4998]
respectable,[2887] [d]hospitable, [e]able to
teach,[1317]
3 [a]not addicted to wine [I]or pugnacious, but gentle,1933 uncontentious,
[b]free from the love of money.146
4 *He must be* one who [ppt] [a]manages
his own household well, keeping his
children[5043] under control5292 with all
dignity[4587]
5 (but if a man does not know how
to [ainf]manage his own household, how
will he take care of [a]the church[1577] of
God?);[2316]
6 *and* not a new convert,[3504] lest
he become [aptp] [a]conceited[5187] and fall into
the [b]condemnation[2917] [I]incurred by the
devil.[1228]
7 And he must [a]have a good[2570]
reputation[3141] with [b]those outside1855 *the
church,* so that he may not [aosb]fall into
reproach and [c]the snare of the devil.
8 [a]Deacons[1249] likewise *must be* men
of dignity,[4586] not [I]double-tongued, [IIb]or
addicted to much wine[3631] [IIc]or fond of
sordid gain,146
9 [a]*but* holding to the mystery[3466]
of the faith[4102] with a clear[2513] conscience.[4893]
10 And [a]let these also first be
[pim]tested; then let them [pim]serve as
deacons[1247] if they are beyond reproach.[410]
11 [I]Women *must* likewise *be* dignified,[4586] [a]not malicious gossips,[1228] but
[b]temperate, faithful in all things.
12 Let [a]deacons be [b]husbands[435] of
only one wife, *and* [Ic]good managers of
their children[5043] and their own households.
13 For those who have served well
as deacons[1247] [a]obtain for themselves
a [I]high[2570] standing and great confidence
in the faith[4102] that is in Christ Jesus.
14 I am writing these things to you,
hoping to come to you before long;
15 but [I]in case I am delayed, *I write*
so that you may know how [II]one ought
to [pinf]conduct himself in [a]the household
of God, which is the [b]church[1577] of
[c]the living[2198] God, the [d]pillar and support of the truth.[225]
🔑16 And by common confession[3672]
great is [a]the mystery[3466] of godliness:[2150]

[I]He who was [b]revealed[5319] in the
flesh,[4561]

1 [I]Or, *bishop* [b]Acts 20:28; Phil. 1:1
2 [I]Lit., *The* [a]1Tim. 3:2-4; Titus 1:6-8 [b]Luke 2:36f.; 1Tim. 5:9; Titus 1:6 [c]1Tim. 3:8, 11; Titus 2:2 [d]Rom. 12:13; Titus 1:8; Heb. 13:2; 1Pet. 4:9 [e]2Tim. 2:24
3 [I]Lit., *not* [a]Titus 1:7 [b]1Tim. 3:8; 6:10; Titus 1:7; Heb. 13:5
4 [a]1Tim. 3:12
5 [a]1Cor. 10:32; 1Tim. 3:15
6 [I]Lit., *of the devil* [a]1Tim. 6:4; 2Tim. 3:4 [b]1Tim. 3:7
7 [a]2Cor. 8:21 [b]Mark 4:11 [c]1Tim. 6:9; 2Tim. 2:26
8 [I]Or, *given to double-talk* [II]Lit., *not* [a]Phil. 1:1; 1Tim. 3:12 [b]1Tim. 5:23; Titus 2:3 [c]1Tim. 3:3; Titus 1:7; 1Pet. 5:2
9 [a]1Tim. 1:5, 19
10 [a]1Tim. 5:22
11 [I]I.e., either deacons' wives or deaconesses [a]2Tim. 3:3; Titus 2:3 [b]1Tim. 3:2
12 [I]Lit., *managing well* [a]Phil. 1:1; 1Tim. 3:8 [b]1Tim. 3:2 [c]1Tim. 3:4

13 [I]Lit., *good* [a]Matt. 25:21 **15** [I]Lit., *if I delay* [II]Or, *you ought to conduct yourself* [a]1Cor. 3:16; 2Cor. 6:16; Eph. 2:21f.; 1Pet. 2:5; 4:17 [b]1Tim. 3:5 [c]Matt. 16:16; 1Tim. 4:10 [d]Gal. 2:9; 2Tim. 2:19 **16** [I]Some later mss. read *God* [a]Rom. 16:25 [b]John 1:14; 1Pet. 1:20; 1John 3:5, 8

🔑 **3:2** "The husband of one wife" does not mean that he, the bishop or the deacon (see v. 12), was never married before. Nor does it mean that in order to be a bishop or a deacon, one must be married. Paul was certainly considered both a bishop and a deacon, and he was never married. If this meant that a bishop or a deacon was never to have been married before, then it would exclude a remarried widower. But the Apostle Paul in Rom. 7:1-3 places no restriction upon a widower to remarry. In the case of divorce, neither the Lord Jesus nor the Apostle Paul places such a restriction on a divorced person who was the innocent party in the unfortunate and God-hated divorce process which is the result of man's sinfulness. See the Editor's two volumes on the subject: vol. I on the teaching of the O.T. pertinent passages as well as the teaching of the Lord Jesus Christ and the Apostle Paul in Rom. 7 entitled, *What About Divorce?* and vol. II containing a complete exegesis of I Cor. 7 entitled, *May I Divorce and Remarry?.*

One of the meanings of this expression, but not the principal one, is that the bishop or the deacon should not be married to more than one woman simultaneously. The expression *mias gunaikos* is known in Greek grammar as an attributive genitive, which is equivalent to an adjective, and would have been better translated as "a one-woman's husband," not a ladies' man, in other words. The total context speaks of the moral conduct of the bishop and the deacon. He should be one totally dedicated to his wife and not be flirtatious. Paul brings out the same thought in the similar passage in Tit. 1:6 where the expression is exactly the same, except as pertaining to a woman that she should be one man's woman, not flirting with other men.

🔑 **3:16** See general remarks on justification on Romans and also I Pet. 3:18-20.

Was aop [II][c]vindicated[1344] [III]in
the Spirit,[4151]
aop [d]Beheld by angels,[32]
aop [e]Proclaimed[2784] among the
nations,[1484]
aop [f]Believed on[4100] in the
world,[2889]
aop [g]Taken up in glory.[1391]

Apostasy

4 🔑 But [a]the Spirit[4151] explicitly says
that [b]in later times[2540] some will fall
away[868] from the faith,[4102] paying attention to [c]deceitful spirits[4151] and [d]doc-
trines[1319] of demons,[1140]
2 by means of the hypocrisy of liars
pfpp [a]seared in their own conscience[4893]
as with a branding iron,
3 *men* who [a]forbid marriage *and ad-*
vocate pinf [b]abstaining[567] from foods,
which [c]God has ao created to be [d]grate-
fully shared in by those who ajn believe[4103] and pfp know the truth.[225]
4 For [a]everything created[2938] by
God is good,[2570] and nothing is to be
rejected, if it is ppp [b]received[2983] with
gratitude;
5 for it is sanctified[32] by means of
[a]the word[3056] of God and prayer.[1783]

A Good Minister's Discipline

6 In ppt pointing out these things to
[a]the brethren,[80] you will be a good[2570]
[b]servant[1249] of Christ Jesus, *constantly*
ppt nourished on the words of the faith[4102]
and of the [I][c]sound doctrine[1319] which you
[d]have been pfi following.
7 But pim have nothing to do with[3868]
[a]worldly[952] [b]fables[3454] fit only for old
women. On the other hand, pim discipline
yourself for the purpose of [c]godli-
ness;[2150]
8 for [a]bodily[4984] discipline is only of
little profit, but [b]godliness is profitable
for all things, since it [c]holds promise
for the [d]present life and *also* for the
life to come.[3195]
9 [a]It is a trustworthy[4103] statement[3056] deserving full acceptance.[594]
10 For it is for this we labor and
strive, because we have pfi fixed [a]our
hope[1679] on [b]the living[2198] God, who is
[c]the Savior[4990] of all men,[444] especially
of believers.
11 pim [I][a]Prescribe[3853] and pim teach[1321]
these things.
🔑 12 [a]Let no one pim look down on
your youthfulness,[3503] but *rather* in
speech,[3056] conduct,[391] [b]love,[26] faith[4102]
and purity,[47] pim show yourself [c]an example [I]of those who believe.[4103]
13 [a]Until I come, give attention to
the *public* [b]*reading of Scripture*,[320] to
exhortation[3874] and teaching.[1319]
🔑 14 Do not pim neglect the spiritual
gift[5486] within you, which was bestowed
upon you through [a]prophetic utterance[4394] with [b]the laying on of hands
by the [I][c]presbytery.[4244]
15 pim Take pains with these things;
be *absorbed* in them, so that your progress may be evident[5318] to all.
16 [a]Pay close attention to yourself
and to your teaching; persevere in these
things; for as you do this you will
[I][b]insure salvation[4982] both for yourself
and for those who ppt hear you.

Honor Widows

5 [a]Do not aosi rebuke an
[b]older man,[4245] but *rather* pim appeal
to *him* as a father,[3962] *to* [c]the younger
men as brothers,[80]
2 the older women as mothers, *and*
the younger women as sisters, in all
purity.[47]

16 [II]Or, *justified* [III]Or, *by* [c]Rom. 3:4 [d]Luke 2:13; 24:4; 1Pet. 1:12 [e]Rom. 16:26; 2Cor. 1:19; Col. 1:23 [f]2Thess. 1:10 [g]Mark 16:19; Acts 1:9

1 [a]John 16:13; Acts 20:23; 21:11; 1Cor. 2:10f. [b]2Thess. 2:3ff.; 2Tim. 3:1; 2Pet. 3:3; Jude 18 [c]1John 4:6 [d]James 3:15
2 [a]Eph. 4:19
3 [a]Heb. 13:4 [b]Col. 2:16, 23 [c]Gen. 1:29; 9:3 [d]Rom. 14:6; 1Cor. 10:30f.; 1Tim. 4:4
4 [a]1Cor. 10:26 [b]Rom. 14:6; 1Cor. 10:30f.; 1Tim. 4:3
5 [a]Gen. 1:25, 31; Heb. 11:3
6 [I]Lit., *good* [a]Acts 1:15 [b]2Cor. 11:23 [c]1Tim. 1:10 [d]Luke 1:3; Phil. 2:20, 22; 2Tim. 3:10
7 [a]1Tim. 1:9 [b]1Tim. 1:4 [c]1Tim. 4:8; 6:3, 5f.; 2Tim. 3:5
8 [a]Col. 2:23 [b]1Tim. 4:7; 6:3, 5f.; 2Tim. 3:5 [c]Ps. 37:9, 11; Prov. 19:23; 22:4; Matt. 6:33 [d]Matt. 6:33; 12:32; Mark 10:30
9 [a]1Tim. 1:15
10 [a]2Cor. 1:10; 1Tim. 6:17 [b]1Tim. 3:15 [c]John 4:42; 1Tim. 2:4
11 [I]Or, *Keep commanding and teaching* [a]1Tim. 5:7; 6:2
12 [I]Or, *to* [a]1Cor. 16:11; Titus 2:15 [b]1Tim. 1:14 [c]Titus 2:7; 1Pet. 5:3
13 [a]1Tim. 3:14 [b]2Tim. 3:15ff.
14 [I]Or, *board of elders* [a]1Tim. 1:18 [b]Acts 6:6; 1Tim. 5:22; 2Tim. 1:6 [c]Acts 11:30

16 [I]Lit., *save both yourself and those* [a]Acts 20:28 [b]1Cor. 1:21 **1** [a]Lev. 19:32 [b]Titus 2:2 [c]Titus 2:6

🔑 **4:1-3** See note on II Thess. 2:3.
🔑 **4:12** See general remarks on Titus.
🔑 **4:14** See note on II Tim. 1:6.

3 [pim]Honor widows who are [a]widows indeed;

4 but if any widow has children or grandchildren, [a]let them first [pim]learn to [pinf]practice piety[2151] in regard to their own family, and to [pinf] [I]make some return to their parents; for this is [b]acceptable[587] in the sight of God.

5 Now she who is a [a]widow indeed, and who has been left alone [b]has [pfi]fixed her hope[1679] on God, and continues[4357] in [c]entreaties[1162] and prayers[4335] night and day.

6 But she who [ppt] [a]gives herself to wanton pleasure[4684] is [pfi] [b]dead[2348] even while she [ppt]lives.[2198]

7 [Ia]Prescribe these things as well, so that they may be above reproach.[423]

8 But if anyone does not provide for[4306] his own, and especially for those of his household,[3609] he has [pfi] [a]denied the faith,[4102] and is worse than an unbeliever.[571]

🔑 9 Let a widow be [pim] [a]put on the list only if she is not less than sixty years old, *having been* [b]the wife of one man,

10 [ppp]having a reputation for [a]good[2570] works;[2041] *and* if she has [ao]brought up children, if she has [ao] [b]shown hospitality to strangers, if she [c]has [ao]washed the [I]saints'[40] feet, if she has [ao] [d]assisted those in distress, *and* if she has [ao]devoted herself to every good[18] work.[2041]

11 But refuse[3868] *to put* younger widows *on the list,* for when they [aosb]feel [a]sensual desires in disregard of[2691] Christ, they want to [pinf]get married,

12 *thus* incurring condemnation,[2917] because they have [ao]set aside their previous [I]pledge.[4102]

13 And at the same time[260] they also learn *to be* idle,[692] as they go around from house to house; and not merely idle, but also [a]gossips and [b]busybodies, talking about [c]things not proper *to mention.*

14 Therefore, I want younger *widows* to [pinf]get [a]married, bear children, [b]keep house,[3616] *and* [c]give the enemy no occasion for reproach;

15 for some [a]have already turned aside to follow [b]Satan.

16 If any woman who is a believer[4103] [a]has *dependent* widows, let her [pim] [b]assist them, and let not the church[1577] be [pim]burdened, so that it may [aosb]assist those who are [c]widows indeed.

Concerning Elders

17 Let [a]the elders[4245] who [pfp] [b]rule well be [pim]considered worthy of double honor,[5092] especially those who [ppt] [c]work hard [I]at preaching[3056] and teaching.[1319]

18 For the Scripture says, "[a]YOU SHALL NOT MUZZLE THE OX WHILE HE IS THRESHING," and "[b]The laborer is worthy of his wages."[3408]

19 Do not [pim]receive[3858] an accusation[2724] against an [a]elder except on the basis of [b]two or three witnesses.[3144]

20 Those who [ppt]continue in sin,[264] [pim] [a]rebuke in the presence of all, [b]so that the rest also may be fearful *of sinning.*[5401]

21 [a]I solemnly charge[1263] you in the presence of God and of Christ Jesus and of *His* chosen[1588] angels,[32] to [aosb]maintain these *principles* without bias,[4299] doing nothing in a *spirit of* partiality.

22 [a]Do not [pim]lay hands upon anyone *too* hastily and [I]thus [pim]share [b]*responsibility for*[2841] the sins[266] of others; [pim]keep yourself [II]free from sin.[53]

3 [a]Acts 6:1; 9:39, 41; 1Tim. 5:5, 16
4 [I]Lit., *give back recompenses* [a]Eph. 6:2 [b]1Tim. 2:3
5 [a]Acts 6:1; 9:39, 41; 1Tim. 5:3, 16 [b]1Cor. 7:34; 1Pet. 3:5 [c]Luke 2:37; 1Tim. 2:1; 2Tim. 1:3
6 [a]James 5:5 [b]Luke 15:24; 2Tim. 3:6; Rev. 3:1
7 [I]Or, *Keep commanding* [a]1Tim. 4:11
8 [a]2Tim. 2:12; Titus 1:16; 2Pet. 2:1; Jude 4
9 [a]1Tim. 5:16 [b]1Tim. 3:2
10 [I]Or, *holy ones* [a]Acts 9:36; 1Tim. 6:18; Titus 2:7; 3:8; 1Pet. 2:12 [b]1Tim. 3:2 [c]Luke 7:44; John 13:14 [d]1Tim. 5:16
11 [a]Rev. 18:7
12 [I]Lit., *faith*
13 [a]3 John 10 [b]2Thess. 3:11 [c]Titus 1:11
14 [a]1Cor. 7:9; 1Tim. 4:3 [b]Titus 2:5 [c]1Tim. 6:1
15 [a]1Tim. 1:20 [b]Matt. 4:10
16 [a]1Tim. 5:4 [b]1Tim. 5:10 [c]1Tim. 5:3
17 [I]Lit., *in word* [a]Acts 11:30; 1Tim. 4:14; 5:19 [b]Rom. 12:8 [c]1Thess. 5:12
18 [a]Deut. 25:4; 1Cor. 9:9 [b]Lev. 19:13; Deut. 24:15; Matt. 10:10; Luke 10:7; 1Cor. 9:14
19 [a]Acts 11:30; 1Tim. 4:14; 5:17 [b]Deut. 17:6; 19:15; Matt. 18:16
20 [a]Gal. 2:14; Eph. 5:11; 2Tim. 4:2 [b]2Cor. 7:11

21 [a]Luke 9:26; 1Tim. 6:13; 2Tim. 2:14; 4:1 **22** [I]Lit., *do not share* [II]Lit., *pure* [a]1Tim. 3:10; 4:14 [b]Eph. 5:11; 1Tim. 3:2-7

🔑 **5:9** Here the Apostle Paul in using the expression "the wife of one man" means that this widow is not a flirt; she is a moral woman. Her behavior when married should be considered; she has not been a flirt. If a woman has become widowed and it was known, however, that she has been living an immoral life, then she should receive no charity from the church. This is made clear by the context and especially the verses that follow. See note on I Tim. 3:2.

23 No longer drink water *exclusively,* but pim [a]use a little wine3631 for the sake of your stomach and your frequent ailments.

24 The sins of some men are quite evident, going before4254 them to judgment;2920 for others, their *sins* [a]follow after.

25 Likewise also, deeds that are good are quite evident, and [a]those which are otherwise247 cannot be concealed.

Instructions to Those Who Minister

6 [a]Let all who are under the yoke as slaves1401 pimregard their own masters1203 as worthy of all honor so [b]that the name3686 of God and *our* doctrine1319 may not be psmpspoken against.987

2 And let those who have believers4103 as their masters not be disrespectful to them because they are [a]brethren, but let them pimserve1398 them all the more, because those who ppt [I]partake482 of the benefit are believers4103 and beloved.27 [b]Teach and [II]preach these *principles.*

3 If anyone [a]advocates a different doctrine,2085 and does not [I]agree4334 with [b]sound words, those of our Lord Jesus Christ, and with the doctrine1319 [c]conforming2596 to godliness,2150

4 he is pfip [a]conceited5187 *and* understands nothing; but he [I]has a morbid interest3552 in [b]controversial questions and [c]disputes about words, out of which arise envy, strife, abusive language,988 evil4190 suspicions,5283

5 and constant friction3859 between [a]men of depraved mind3563 and pfppdeprived of the truth,225 who [b]suppose that [I]godliness2150 is a means of gain.

6 [a]But godliness *actually* is a means of [b]great gain, when accompanied by [c]contentment.

7 For [a]we have aobrought nothing into the world,2889 [I]so we cannot ainftake anything out1627 of it either.

8 And if we [a]have food and covering, with these we shall be content.

9 [a]But those who pptwant to get rich fall into temptation3986 and [b]a snare and many foolish453 and harmful desires1939 which plunge men444 into ruin3639 and destruction.684

10 For [a]the love of money is a root of all [I]sorts of evil,2556 and some by pptlonging for it have aop [b]wandered away from the faith,4102 and aopierced themselves with many a pang.

11 But [a]flee from these things, you [b]man444 of God; and pursue righteousness,1343 godliness,2150 [c]faith,4102 [d]love,26 [I]perseverance5281 *and* gentleness.4236

12 [a]Fight75 the good2570 fight73 of [b]faith; [c]take hold of1949 the eternal166 life2222 [d]to which you were aopcalled,2564 and you aomade3670 the good2570 [e]confession3671 in the presence of [f]many witnesses.3144

13 [a]I charge you in the presence of God, who ppt [I]gives life2227 to all things, and of [b]Christ Jesus, who apttestified the [c]good confession3671 [d]before Pontius Pilate,

14 that you ainfkeep the commandment without stain784 or reproach423 until the [a]appearing2015 of our Lord Jesus Christ,

15 which He will [I]bring about at [a]the proper2398 time—2540 He who is [b]the blessed3107 and [c]only Sovereign,1413 [d]the King935 of ppt [II]kings936 and [e]Lord2962 of ppt [III]lords;2961

16 [a]who alone pptpossesses immortality110 and [b]dwells3611 in unapproachable light;5457 [c]whom no man has aoseen or can see. [d]To Him *be* honor5092 and eternal166 dominion!2904 Amen.281

17 pimInstruct those who are rich in [a]this present world165 [b]not to be pinfconceited or to pfin [c]fix their hope1679

23 [a]1Tim. 3:8
24 [a]Rev. 14:13
25 [a]Prov. 10:9

1 [a]Eph. 6:5; Titus 2:9; 1Pet. 2:18 [b]Titus 2:5
2 [I]Or, *benefit by their service* [II]Lit., *exhort, urge* [a]Acts 1:15; Gal. 3:28; Philem. 16 [b]1Tim. 4:11
3 [I]Lit., *come to;* or, *come with* [a]1Tim. 1:3 [b]1Tim. 1:10 [c]Titus 1:1
4 [I]Lit., *is sick about* [a]1Tim. 3:6 [b]1Tim. 1:4 [c]Acts 18:15; 2Tim. 2:14
5 [I]Or, *religion* [a]2Tim. 3:8; Titus 1:15 [b]Titus 1:11; 2Pet. 2:3
6 [a]Luke 12:15-21; 1Tim. 6:6-10 [b]1Tim. 4:8 [c]Phil. 4:11; Heb. 13:5
7 [I]Later mss. read *it is clear that* [a]Job 1:21; Eccl. 5:15
8 [a]Prov. 30:8
9 [a]Prov. 15:27; 23:4; 28:20; Luke 12:21; 1Tim. 6:17 [b]1Tim. 3:7
10 [I]Lit., *the evils* [a]Col. 3:5; 1Tim. 3:3; 6:9 [b]James 5:19
11 [I]Or, *steadfastness* [a]2Tim. 2:22 [b]2Tim. 3:17 [c]1Tim. 1:14 [d]2Tim. 3:10
12 [a]1Cor. 9:25f.; Phil. 1:30; 1Tim. 1:18 [b]1Tim. 1:19 [c]Phil. 3:12; 1Tim. 6:19 [d]Col. 3:15 [e]2Cor. 9:13; 1Tim. 6:13 [f]1Tim. 4:14; 2Tim. 2:2
13 [I]Or, *preserves alive* [a]1Tim. 5:21 [b]Gal. 3:26; 1Tim. 1:12, 15; 2:5 [c]2Cor. 9:13; 1Tim. 6:12 [d]Matt. 27:2; John 18:37
14 [a]2Thess. 2:8
15 [I]Lit., *show* [II]Lit., *those who reign as kings* [III]Lit., *those who rule as lords* [a]1Tim. 2:6 [b]1Tim. 1:11 [c]1Tim. 1:17 [d]Deut. 10:17; Rev. 17:14; 19:16 [e]Ps. 136:3
16 [a]1Tim. 1:17 [b]Ps. 104:2; James 1:17; 1John 1:5 [c]John 1:18 [d]1Tim. 1:17
17 [a]Matt. 12:32; 2Tim. 4:10; Titus 2:12 [b]Ps. 62:10; Luke 12:20; Rom. 11:20; 1Tim. 6:9 [c]1Tim. 4:10

6:5 See note on II Thess. 2:3.

on the uncertainty of riches, but on
God, [d]who richly [ppt]supplies us with all
things to enjoy.
18 *Instruct them* to [pinf]do good,[14] to
be rich in [a]good [I]works, [b]to be generous
and ready to share,[2843]
19 [ppt] [a]storing up for themselves the
treasure of a good foundation for the
future,[3195] so that they may [aosb] [b]take
hold of that which is life indeed.

17 [d]Acts 14:17
18 [I]Or, *deeds* [a]1Tim. 5:10 [b]Rom. 12:8; Eph. 4:28
19 [a]Matt. 6:20 [b]1Tim. 6:12
20 [a]1Tim. 1:2 [b]2Tim. 1:12, 14 [c]1Tim. 1:9; 2Tim. 2:16
21 [I]Lit., *concerning*

20 O [a]Timothy, [aim]guard [b]what
has been entrusted to you, avoiding
[c]worldly[952] *and* empty chatter[2757] *and*
the opposing arguments[1108] of what is
falsely called "knowledge"—
21 which some have professed[1861]
and thus [ao] [a]gone astray [I]from [b]the faith.
[c]Grace be with you.

[a]2Tim. 2:18 [b]1Tim. 1:19 [c]Col. 4:18

The Second Epistle of Paul to

TIMOTHY

The Apostle Paul wrote this Epistle to Timothy, his "beloved son" (II Tim. 1:1-2). He wanted to prescribe the path which Timothy should follow in troubled times, both inside and outside the church.

Paul was clearly writing from a prison in Rome (II Tim. 1:8). The Book of Acts ends with Paul under house arrest (Acts 28:30-31), but there is abundant evidence that II Timothy describes his second imprisonment (II Tim. 4:16-18). Most scholars believe that Paul was acquitted at the first trial. Then he returned to Greece and Asia Minor for more missionary work. Later he was arrested again, taken back to Rome, and beheaded. Many believe that Paul was made the chief scapegoat for Nero's burning of Rome. Nero set fire to Rome in order to rebuild it to his liking. Since Nero was suspected of starting the blaze, he blamed the Christians for it and ordered them all to be executed. This time Paul was charged as a criminal (II Tim. 2:9), not on a technicality as before. Paul resigned himself to the inevitable, but he was very happy with the life of service that he had lived, confident that the cause of Christ would ultimately triumph (II Tim. 4:6-8). He urged Timothy to arrive in Rome before winter with a warm coat and some of the Scriptures (II Tim. 4:13,21).

Paul's second Epistle to Timothy was written approximately A.D. 66, while Paul was expecting his execution. This is Paul's last letter.

Timothy Charged to Guard His Trust

1 Paul, [a]an apostle[652] of [b]Christ Jesus
[Ic]by the will[2307] of God,[2316] according to the promise[1860] of [d]life[2222] in
Christ[5547] Jesus,
2 to [a]Timothy, my beloved[27]
[Ib]son:[5043] [c]Grace,[5485] mercy[1656] *and*
peace[1515] from God the Father[3962] and
Christ Jesus our Lord.[2962]
3 [a]I thank[5485] God, whom I
[b]serve[3000] with a [c]clear[2513] conscience[4893] [I]the way my forefathers did,
[d]as I constantly[88] remember you in my
[II]prayers night and day,
4 [a]longing to see you, [b]even as I
[pfpp]recall your tears, so that I may be
[asbp]filled with joy.
🔑 5 [I]For I am mindful[5280] of the [a]sin-
cere[505] faith[4102] within you, which first
dwelt in your grandmother Lois, and
[b]your mother Eunice, and I am sure
that *it is* in you as well.
🔑 6 And for this reason I remind you
to [pinf]kindle afresh [a]the gift[5486] of God
which is in you through [b]the laying on
of my hands.
7 For God has not [ao]given us a
[a]spirit[4151] of timidity,[1167] but of power[1411]
and love[26] and [I]discipline.[4995]

1 [I]Lit., *through* [a]2 Cor. 1:1 [b]Gal. 3:26 [c]1 Cor. 1:1 [d]1Tim. 6:19
2 [I]Lit., *child* [a]Acts 16:1; 1Tim. 1:2 [b]1Tim. 1:2; 2Tim. 2:1; Titus 1:4 [c]Rom. 1:7
3 [I]Lit., *from my forefathers* [II]Or, *petitions* [a]Rom. 1:8 [b]Acts 24:14 [c]Acts 23:1; 24:16; 1Tim. 1:5 [d]Rom. 1:9
4 [a]2Tim. 4:9, 21 [b]Acts 20:37
5 [I]Lit., *Receiving remembrance of* [a]1Tim. 1:5 [b]Acts 16:1; 2Tim. 3:15
6 [a]1Tim. 4:14
7 [I]Or, *sound judgment* [a]John 14:27; Rom. 8:15

🔑 **1:5** See general remarks on I Timothy.

🔑 **1:6** Paul speaks here about a gift which Timothy possessed as a result of laying his hands on him. The gift is called *charisma* (5486), the result of grace, *charis* (5485). It is exactly the same word as we find in I Cor. 12 where gifts (*charismata*) are enumerated. This gift referred to in II Tim. 1:6 is not identified and therefore we don't know whether it is included in the list of I Cor. 12. There is no complete list of all the gifts that God grants to His children as a result of His grace. Undoubtedly this was the gift that came upon Timothy as a result of his ordination to the ministry of the Gospel. The same gift is referred to in I Tim. 4:14. Observe that here Paul speaks of "the presbytery" having participated in Timothy's ordination. This is an indication that in a local church in addition to deacons (I Tim. 3:12) and deaconesses (Rom. 16:1) there should be "a presbytery," a body of elders (presbyters), and not only the pastor acting as an elder in a local church body.

8 Therefore [a]do not be [aosi]ashamed
of the [b]testimony[3142] of our Lord, or
of me [c]His prisoner; but [aim]join with *me*
in [d]suffering[4777] for the [e]gospel[2098] according to the power of God,
🔑 9 who has [a]saved[4982] us, and
[apt] [b]called us with a holy[40] [c]calling,[2821]
[d]not according to our works,[2041] but according to His own [b]purpose[4286] and
grace[5486] which was [aptp]granted us in
[e]Christ Jesus from [f]all eternity,
10 but [a]now has been [aptp]re-
vealed[5319] by the [b]appearing[2015] of our
Savior[4990] [c]Christ Jesus, who [apt] [d]abol-
ished death,[2288] and [apt]brought life and
immortality to light[5461] through the gospel,
11 [a]for which I was [aop]appointed[5087]
a preacher[2783] and an apostle[652] and a
teacher.[1320]
🔑 12 For this reason I also suffer these
things, but [a]I am not ashamed; for I
know[1492] [b]whom I have [pfi]believed[4100]
and I am convinced that He is able to
[ainf] [c]guard what I have entrusted to Him
[l]until [d]that day.
13 [l][a]Retain the [b]standard[5296] of
[c]sound[5198] words[3056] [d]which you have
[ao]heard from me, in the [e]faith and love
which are in [f]Christ Jesus.
14 [aim]Guard, through the [an]Holy
Spirit[4151] who [a]dwells in us, the [l][b]trea-
sure which has been [ppt]entrusted to *you.*
15 You are aware of the fact that
all who are in [l][a]Asia [aop] [b]turned away
from[654] me, among whom are Phygelus
and Hermogenes.
16 The Lord [opt]grant mercy[1656] to

8 [a]Mark 8:38; Rom. 1:16; 2Tim. 1:12, 16 [b]1Cor. 1:6 [c]Eph. 3:1; 2Tim. 1:16 [d]2Tim. 2:3, 9; 4:5 [e]2Tim. 1:10; 2:8
9 [a]Rom. 11:14 [b]Rom. 8:28ff. [c]Rom. 11:29 [d]Eph. 2:9 [e]2Tim. 1:1 [f]Rom. 16:25; Eph. 1:4; Titus 1:2
10 [a]Rom. 16:26 [b]2Thess. 2:8; 2Tim. 4:1, 8; Titus 2:11 [c]2Tim. 1:1 [d]1Cor. 15:26; Heb. 2:14f.
11 [a]1Tim. 2:7
12 [l]Or, *for* [a]2Tim. 1:8, 16 [b]Titus 3:8 [c]1Tim. 6:20; 2Tim. 1:14 [d]1Cor. 1:8; 3:13; 2Tim. 1:18; 4:8
13 [l]Or, *Hold the example* [a]2Tim. 3:14; Titus 1:9 [b]Rom. 2:20; 6:17 [c]1Tim. 1:10 [d]2Tim. 2:2 [e]1Tim. 1:14 [f]2Tim. 1:1
14 [l]Lit., *good deposit* [a]Rom. 8:9 [b]1Tim. 6:20; 2Tim. 1:12
15 [l]I.e., the province of Asia [a]Acts 2:9 [b]2Tim. 4:10, 11, 16
16 [l]Lit., *chain* [a]2Tim. 4:19 [b]2Tim. 1:8 [c]Eph. 6:20
18 [a]1Cor. 1:8; 3:13; 2Tim. 1:12; 4:8 [b]Acts 18:19; 1Tim. 1:3

[a]the house of Onesiphorus for he often
refreshed[404] me, and [b]was not ashamed
of my [l][c]chains;
17 but when he was[1096] in Rome,
he eagerly searched for me, and found
me—
18 the Lord [opt]grant to him to
[ainf]find[2147] mercy[1656] from the Lord on
[a]that day—[2250] and you know very well
what services[2250] he rendered[1247] at
[b]Ephesus.

Be Strong

2 You therefore, my [l][a]son,[5043] [b]be
[pim]strong[1743] in the grace that is
in [c]Christ Jesus.
2 And the things [a]which you have
[ao]heard from me in the presence of
[b]many witnesses,[3144] these [aim] [c]entrust
to [d]faithful[4103] men,[444] who will be
[e]able to teach[1321] others[2087] also.
3 [aim] [a]Suffer hardship[2553] with *me,* as
a good [b]soldier of [c]Christ Jesus.
4 No soldier in active service
[a]entangles himself in the affairs of everyday life,[979] so that he may [aosb]please
the one who [apt]enlisted him as a soldier.
5 And also if anyone [psa] [a]competes
as an athlete, he [l]does not win the prize
unless he [aosb]competes according to the
rules.

1 [l]Lit., *child* [a]2Tim. 1:2 [b]Eph. 6:10 [c]2Tim. 1:1
2 [a]2Tim. 1:13 [b]1Tim. 6:12 [c]1Tim. 1:18 [d]1Tim. 1:12 [e]2Cor. 2:14ff.; 3:5 **3** [a]2Tim. 1:8 [b]1Cor. 9:7; 1Tim. 1:18 [c]2Tim. 1:1 **4** [a]2Pet. 2:20 **5** [l]Lit., *is not crowned* [a]1 Cor. 9:25

🔑 **1:9** What is translated here as "purpose" in the phrase "according to his own purpose and grace" is the Greek word *prothesis* (4286) which actually means God's intention beforehand. This is the same word occurring in Rom. 8:28; 9:11; Eph. 1:11; 3:11. See notes on these passages as well as the notes on Eph. 1:4,5 on God's election unto salvation and grace.

🔑 **1:12** Paul, speaking about himself, says that "I . . . suffer." This does not mean that he was suffering because he deserved the suffering due to some sin in his own life, but because suffering is inevitable in the life of the Christian as a result of his sharing the same mortal and corruptible body as unbelievers (Rom. 6:12; 8:11; I Cor. 15:53,54; II Cor. 4:11; 5:4). The word *thnētos* (2349), "mortal," occurs in all the Scriptures quoted and refers to believers. The word "corruptible," *phthartos* (5349) referring to the corruptibility and deterioration of the human body, occurs in Rom. 1:23; I Cor. 15:53,54. These refer to the body of the believer which is called corruptible. It means that upon receiving Christ, the body of the believer does not become exempt from mortality or corruptibility. Suffering may come as a result of persecution because the Christian should not conform to the standards of the world (Jn. 16:33; Gal. 6:17; II Tim. 3:12). Therefore, Paul says, "I suffer, but I'm not ashamed of it."

6 [a]The hard-working[1092] farmer
ought to be the first to [pinf]receive his
share of the crops.
7 [pim]Consider[3539] what I say, for the
Lord will [ft]give you understanding in
everything.
8 [pim]Remember Jesus Christ,
[pfpp] [a]risen[1453] from the dead,[3498] [b]de-
scendant[4690] of David, [c]according to my
gospel,[2098]
9 [I]for which I [a]suffer hardship[2553]
even to [b]imprisonment as a [c]criminal;[2557]
but [d]the word[3056] of God [e]is not [pfip]im-
prisoned.
10 For this reason [a]I endure[5278] all
things for [b]the sake of those who are
chosen,[1588] [c]that they also may [aosb]ob-
tain[5177] the [d]salvation[4991] which is in
[e]Christ Jesus *and* with *it* [f]eternal
glory.[1391]
11 [a]It is a trustworthy[4103] statement:[3056]

For [b]if we [ao]died with Him, we
shall also live with Him;
12 If we endure,[5278] [a]we shall also
reign with Him;
If we [I][b]deny[720] Him, He also will
deny us;
13 If we are faithless,[569] [a]He
remains faithful; for [b]He
cannot [ainf]deny Himself.

An Unashamed Workman

14 [pim]Remind *them* of these things,
and solemnly [a]charge[1263] *them* in the
presence of God not to [pinf] [b]wrangle
about words, which is useless,[5539] *and*
leads to the ruin of the hearers.
15 Be diligent to [ainf] [a]present yourself approved[1384] to God as a workman
who does not need to be ashamed, handling accurately[3718] [b]the word of truth.
16 But [a]avoid [b]worldly[952] *and* empty
chatter,[2757] for [I]it will lead to further
ungodliness,[763]
17 and their [I]talk will spread like
[II]gangrene.[1044] Among them are [a]Hyme-
naeus and Philetus,
18 *men* who have gone [ao]astray from
the truth saying that [a]the resurrection[386]
has already [pfin]taken place, and thus they
upset [b]the faith[4102] of some.
19 Nevertheless, the [a]firm foun-

6 [a]1Cor. 9:10 **8** [a]Acts 2:24 [b]Matt. 1:1 [c]Rom. 2:16 **9** [I]Lit., *in which* [a]2Tim. 1:8; 2:3 [b]Phil. 1:7 [c]Luke 23:32 [d]1Thess. 1:8 [e]Acts 28:31; 2Tim. 4:17 **10** [a]Col. 1:24 [b]Luke 18:7; Titus 1:1 [c]2Cor. 1:6; 1Thess. 5:9 [d]1Cor. 1:21 [e]2Tim. 1:1; 2:1, 3 [f]2Cor. 4:17; 1Pet. 5:10 **11** [a]1Tim. 1:15 [b]Rom. 6:8; 1Thess. 5:10 **12** [I]Lit., *shall deny* [a]Matt. 19:28; Luke 22:29; Rom. 5:17; 8:17 [b]Matt. 10:33; Luke 12:9; 1Tim. 5:8 **13** [a]Rom. 3:3; 1Cor. 1:9 [b]Num. 23:19; Titus 1:2 **14** [a]1Tim. 5:21; 2Tim. 4:1 [b]1Tim. 6:4; 2Tim. 2:23; Titus 3:9 **15** [a]Rom. 6:13; James 1:12 [b]Eph. 1:13; James 1:18 **16** [I]Lit., *they will make further progress in ungodliness* [a]Titus 3:9 [b]1Tim. 1:9; 6:20 **17** [I]Lit., *word* [II]Or, *cancer* [a]1Tim. 1:20 **18** [a]1Cor. 15:12 [b]1Tim. 1:19; Titus 1:11 **19** [a]Is. 28:16f.; 1Tim. 3:15

2:10 See note on Eph. 1:4,5 and also *eklogē* (1589), election.

2:12 In the face of suffering, the Christian may resist or may exercise patience. If he does exercise patience, then he will reign together with Christ. The believer's enjoyment in heaven will be enhanced proportionately to his patient endurance of suffering, sickness, and persecution in this life. He does have, however, the freedom to resist against the circumstances which God brings into his life which are not pleasant. If the believer denies Christ on this earth by claiming that God is unjust in bringing upon him unwanted circumstances, then the Lord will also deny him those rewards in heaven which he would otherwise deserve. This does not refer to a denial of entrance into heaven, even as the believer does not deny his faith, but only the privation of privileges and rewards even as the believer failed his Lord on earth. See note on Mt. 5:7 on mercifulness and the Editor's book on the Beatitudes entitled, *The Pursuit of Happiness.*

2:13 The word for "faithless" in Greek is *apisteō* (569), which here means to fail to exercise the proper faith, confidence, dependence, or trustworthiness. When we do not exercise the proper faith in the Lord, He still remains faithful; He is trustworthy. His trustworthiness does not depend on our trustworthiness. There is a certain faithfulness which God demonstrates toward His children which is not conditional. If we are sinning, missing His mark for our lives, He still demonstrates faithfulness to us in keeping us in His fold. He cannot cut out a part of His body, and that is what we actually are as believers (I Cor. 12:13). But He allows us to suffer in proportion to our unfaithfulness to Him.

He cannot deny Himself because He indwells us. "Denying Himself" would be denying us since we are indwelt by Christ. The Lord is faithful to us in spite of our unfaithfulness to Him, but according to v. 12, we shall be held accountable for our unfaithfulness by the denial of some of our earthly spiritual joy, but particularly our heavenly privileges. God holds us accountable for all that we do or think and rewards or punishes us accordingly. See note on II Thess. 2:3; II Tim. 3:3.

2:19 See note on II Thess. 2:3.

dation of God [pfi]stands, having this [b]seal, "[c]The Lord [ao]knows those who are His," and, "[d]Let everyone who [ppt]names the name[3686] of the Lord [aim]abstain[868] from wickedness."[93]

20 Now in a large house there are not only gold and silver vessels, but also vessels of wood and of earthenware, and [a]some to honor and some to dishonor.

21 Therefore, if a man [aosb]cleanses himself from [a]these *things*, he will be a vessel for honor, sanctified,[37] useful[2173] to the Master,[1203] [pfpp] [b]prepared for every good[18] work.[2041]

22 Now [pim] [a]flee from youthful lusts, and [pim]pursue righteousness,[1343] [b]faith,[4102] love[26] *and* peace,[1515] with those who [ppt] [c]call on[1941] the Lord [d]from a pure[2513] heart.[2588]

23 But [pim]refuse[3868] foolish[3474] and ignorant[521] [a]speculations, knowing that they [b]produce[1080] [1]quarrels.

24 And [a]the Lord's bond-servant[1401] must not be quarrelsome, but be kind[2261] to all, [b]able to teach,[1817] patient[420] when wronged,

25 [a]with gentleness correcting[3811] those who are in opposition, [b]if perhaps God may [opt]grant them repentance[3341] leading to [c]the [an]knowledge[1922] of the [an]truth,

26 and they may [aosb]come to their senses *and escape* from [a]the snare of the devil,[1228] having been [b]held [pfpp]captive [1]by him to do his will.[2307]

"Difficult Times Will Come"

3 But realize this, that [a]in the last[2078] days difficult times[2540] will come.[1764]

2 For men will be [a]lovers of self,[5367] [b]lovers of money, [c]boastful,[213] [c]arrogant,[5244] [d]revilers,[989] [c]disobedient[545] to parents, [e]ungrateful, [f]unholy,[462]

🔑 3 [a]unloving,[794] irreconcilable,[786] [b]malicious gossips,[1228] without self-control,[193] brutal, [1c]haters of good,[865]

4 [a]treacherous, [b]reckless,[4312] [c]conceited,[5187] [d]lovers of pleasure rather than lovers of God;

5 holding to a form[3446] of [1a]godliness,[2150] although they have [pfp] [b]denied[720] its power;[1411] and [c]avoid such men as these.

6 For among them are those who [ppt] [1a]enter into households and [ppt]captivate [b]weak women weighed down with sins,[266] led on[71] by [c]various[4164] impulses,[1939]

7 always learning[3129] and never able to [ainf] [a]come to the [1]knowledge[1922] of the truth.[225]

8 And just as [a]Jannes and Jambres [b]opposed Moses, so these *men* also oppose the truth, [c]men of [pfpp]depraved mind,[3563] rejected[96] as regards the faith.[4102]

9 But they will not make further progress; for their [a]folly[454] will be obvious to all, [b]as also that of those *two* came to be.

10 But you [ao] [a]followed my teaching,[1319] conduct, purpose,[4286] faith,[4102] patience,[3115] [b]love,[26] [1]perseverance,[5281]

11 [a]persecutions, *and* [b]sufferings, such as happened to me at [c]Antioch, at [d]Iconium *and* at [e]Lystra; what [f]persecutions I endured, and out of them all [g]the Lord delivered[4506] me!

🔑 12 And indeed, all who [ppt]desire to [pinf]live[2198] godly[2153] in Christ Jesus [a]will be persecuted.

19 [b]John 3:33 [c]John 10:14; 1Cor. 8:3 [d]Luke 13:27; 1Cor. 1:2
20 [a]Rom. 9:21
21 [a]1Tim. 6:11; 2Tim. 2:16-18 [b]2Cor. 9:8; Eph. 2:10; 2Tim. 3:17
22 [a]1Tim. 6:11 [b]1Tim. 1:14 [c]Acts 7:59 [d]1Tim. 1:5
23 [1]Lit., *fightings* [a]1Tim. 6:4; 2Tim. 2:14; Titus 3:9 [b]Titus 3:9; James 4:1
24 [a]1Tim. 3:3; Titus 1:7 [b]1Tim. 3:2
25 [a]Gal. 6:1; Titus 3:2; 1Pet. 3:15 [b]Acts 8:22 [c]1Tim. 2:4
26 [1]Or possibly, *by him, to do His will* [a]1Tim. 3:7 [b]Luke 5:10

1 [a]1Tim. 4:1
2 [a]Phil. 2:21 [b]Luke 16:14; 1Tim. 3:3; 6:10 [c]Rom. 1:30 [d]2Pet. 2:10-12 [e]Luke 6:35 [f]1Tim. 1:9
3 [1]Lit., *not loving good* [a]Rom. 1:31 [b]1Tim. 3:11 [c]Titus 1:8
4 [a]Acts 7:52 [b]Acts 19:36 [c]1Tim. 3:6 [d]Phil. 3:19
5 [1]Or, *religion* [a]1Tim. 4:7 [b]1Tim. 5:8 [c]Matt. 7:15; 2Thess. 3:6
6 [1]Or, *creep into* [a]Jude 4 [b]1Tim. 5:6; Titus 3:3 [c]Titus 3:3
7 [1]Or, *recognition* [a]2Tim. 2:25
8 [a]Ex. 7:11 [b]Acts 13:8 [c]1Tim. 6:5
9 [a]Luke 6:11 [b]Ex. 7:11, 12; 8:18; 9:11
10 [1]Or, *steadfastness* [a]Phil. 2:20, 22; 1Tim. 4:6 [b]1Tim. 6:11

11 [a]2Cor. 12:10 [b]2Cor. 1:5, 7 [c]Acts 13:14, 45, 50 [d]Acts 14:1-7, 19 [e]Acts 14:8-20 [f]2Cor. 11:23-27 [g]Rom. 15:31 **12** [a]John 15:20; Acts 14:22; 2Cor. 4:9f.

🔑 **3:3** What is translated as "unloving" is the Greek word *astorgoi* (794) occurring only here and in Rom. 1:31. It is made up of the negative *a,* "without," and *storgē,* which means "love within the family members." *Storgē* is one of the four words used in Greek and translated as "love." The other three are *agapē* (26), "benevolent love"; *erōs,* which does not occur in the N.T. and which means "selfish love or lust"; and *philia* (5373), "friendship." For a complete understanding of these four words, see Editor's book on I Cor. 13 entitled, To Love Is to Live.

🔑 **3:12** See note on II Tim. 1:12.

13 But evil[4190] men and impostors [a]will proceed[4298] *from bad* to worse, [b]deceiving and being deceived.

14 You, however, [a]continue in the things you have [ao]learned and become convinced of,[4104] knowing from whom you have learned *them*;

15 and that [a]from childhood[1025] you have known[1492] [b]the sacred writings[2413] which are able[1410] to [c]give you the wisdom[4679] that leads to [d]salvation[4991] through faith[4102] which is in [e]Christ Jesus.

16 [I][a]All Scripture is [II]inspired by God and profitable for teaching,[1319] for reproof,[1650] for correction,[1882] for [III]training[3809] in righteousness;[1343]

17 that [a]the man[444] of God[2316] may be adequate,[739] [pfpp] [b]equipped[1822] for every good[18] work.[2041]

"Preach the Word"

4 [a]I solemnly charge[1263] *you* in the presence of God and of Christ Jesus, who is to [b]judge[2919] the living[2198] and the dead,[3498] and by His [c]appearing[2015] and His kingdom:[932]

2 [aim]preach[2784] [a]the word;[3056] be [aim]ready in season *and* out of season; [aim] [b]reprove, [aim]rebuke, [aim]exhort,[3870] with [I]great [c]patience and instruction.[1322]

3 For [a]the time[2540] will come when they will not endure[430] [b]sound[5198] doctrine;[1319] but *wanting* to have their ears tickled,[1939] they will accumulate for themselves teachers[1320] in accordance to their own desires;

4 and [a]will turn away[654] their ears[189] from the truth,[225] and [b]will turn aside to myths.[3454]

5 But you, [a]be sober in all things, [aim] [b]endure hardship,[2553] do the work[2041] of an [c]evangelist,[2099] fulfill[4135] your [d]ministry.[1248]

6 For I am already being [a]poured out as a drink offering, and the time of [b]my departure [pfi]has come.

7 [a]I have [pfi]fought[75] the good[2570] fight,[73] I have [pfi]finished [b]the course, I have [pfi]kept [c]the faith;[4102]

8 in the future there [a]is laid up for me [b]the crown of righteousness,[1343] which the Lord, the righteous[1342] Judge,[2923] will award to me on [c]that day;[2250] and not only to me, but also to [d]all who have [pfp]loved[25] His [e]appearing.[2015]

Personal Concerns

9 [a]Make every effort to come to me soon;

🔑 10 for [a]Demas, having [apt]loved [b]this present [I]world,[165] has [ao]deserted[1459] me and gone to [c]Thessalonica; Crescens *has gone* to [II][d]Galatia, [e]Titus to Dalmatia.

11 [a]Only [b]Luke is with me. [apt]Pick[353] up [c]Mark and bring[71] him with you, [d]for he is useful[2173] to me for service.[1248]

🔑 12 But [a]Tychicus I have [ao]sent to [b]Ephesus.

13 When you come bring the cloak which I left at [a]Troas with Carpus, and the books, especially the parchments.

14 [a]Alexander the coppersmith [ao]did me much harm; [b]the Lord will [ft]repay him according to his deeds.[2041]

15 Be on guard[5442] against him yourself, for he vigorously [ao]opposed our [I]teaching.

16 At my first[4413] defense no one [ao]supported me, but all [ao]deserted[1459] me; [a]may it not be [opt]counted[3049] against them.

🔑 17 But the Lord stood with me, and [a]strengthened me, in order that through me [b]the proclamation[2782] might [I]be

13 [a]2Tim. 2:16 [b]Titus 3:3
14 [a]2Tim. 1:13; Titus 1:9
15 [a]2Tim. 1:5 [b]John 5:47; Rom. 2:27 [c]Ps. 119:98f. [d]1Cor. 1:21 [e]2Tim. 1:1
16 [I]Or possibly, *Every Scripture inspired by God is also profitable* [II]Lit., *God-breathed* [III]Lit., *training which is in* [a]Rom. 4:23f.; 15:4; 2Pet. 1:20f.
17 [a]1Tim. 6:11 [b]2Tim. 2:21; Heb. 13:21
1 [a]1Tim. 5:21; 2Tim. 2:14 [b]Acts 10:42 [c]2Thess. 2:8; 2Tim. 1:10; 4:8
2 [I]Lit., *all* [a]Gal. 6:6; Col. 4:3; 1Thess. 1:6 [b]1Tim. 5:20; Titus 1:13; 2:15 [c]2Tim. 3:10
3 [a]2Tim. 3:1 [b]1Tim. 1:10; 2Tim. 1:13
4 [a]2Thess. 2:11; Titus 1:14 [b]1Tim. 1:4
5 [a]1Pet. 1:13 [b]2Tim. 1:8 [c]Acts 21:8 [d]Eph. 4:12; Col. 4:17
6 [a]Phil. 2:17 [b]Phil. 1:23; 2Pet. 1:14
7 [a]1Cor. 9:25f.; Phil. 1:30; 1Tim. 1:18; 6:12 [b]Acts 20:24; 1Cor. 9:24 [c]2Tim. 3:10
8 [a]Col. 1:5; 1Pet. 1:4 [b]1Cor. 9:25; 2Tim. 2:5; James 1:12 [c]2Tim. 1:12 [d]Phil. 3:11 [e]2Tim. 4:1
9 [a]2Tim. 1:4; 4:21; Titus 3:12
10 [I]Or, *age* [II]Some ancient mss. read *Gaul* [a]Col. 4:14 [b]1Tim. 6:17 [c]Acts 17:1 [d]Acts 16:6 [e]2Cor. 2:13; 8:23; Gal. 2:3; Titus 1:4
11 [a]2Tim. 1:15 [b]Col. 4:14; Philem. 24 [c]Acts 12:12, 25; 15:37-39; Col. 4:10 [d]2Tim. 2:21
12 [a]Acts 20:4; Eph. 6:21, 22; Col. 4:7f. [b]Acts 18:19
13 [a]Acts 16:8
14 [a]Acts 19:33; 1Tim. 1:20 [b]Ps. 62:12; Rom. 2:6; 12:19
15 [I]Lit., *words*
16 [a]Acts 7:60; 1Cor. 13:5
17 [I]Or, *be fulfilled* [a]1Tim. 1:12; 2Tim. 2:1 [b]Titus 1:3

🔑 **4:10** See general remarks on Titus.
🔑 **4:12** See note on Col. 4:7.
🔑 **4:17ff** See general remarks on I Timothy.

[c]fully accomplished,**4135** and that all
[d]the Gentiles might hear; and I was
[e]delivered**4506** out of [f]the lion's mouth.
18 The Lord will deliver me from
every evil**4190** deed,**2041** and will [I][a]bring
me safely**4982** to His [b]heavenly kingdom;**932** [c]to [II]Him *be* the glory**1391** forever**165** and ever. Amen.281
19 Greet Prisca and [a]Aquila, and
[b]the household of Onesiphorus.
20 [a]Erastus remained at [b]Corinth,
but [c]Trophimus I left sick at [d]Miletus.
21 [a]Make every effort to come before [b]winter. Eubulus greets you, also
Pudens and Linus and Claudia and all
the brethren.
22 [a]The Lord be with your spirit.
[b]Grace be with you.

17 [c]2Tim. 4:5 [d]Acts 9:15; Phil. 1:12ff. [e]Rom. 15:31; 2Tim. 3:11 [f]1Sam. 17:37; Ps. 22:21

18 [I]Or, *save me for* [II]Lit., *Whom* [a]1Cor. 1:21 [b]1Cor. 15:50; 2Tim. 4:1; Heb. 11:16; 12:22 [c]Rom. 11:36; 2Pet. 3:18

19 [a]Acts 18:2 [b]2Tim. 1:16

20 [a]Acts 19:22; Rom. 16:23 [b]Acts 18:1 [c]Acts 20:4; 21:29 [d]Acts 20:15 **21** [a]2Tim. 4:9 [b]Titus 3:12
22 [a]Gal. 6:18; Phil. 4:23; Philem. 25 [b]Col. 4:18

4:20 Who was this Trophimus whom Paul left sick in Miletus? He was an Ephesian Christian who evidently accompanied Paul to Europe after the Ephesian riot, later recrossing and waiting for Paul at Troas for the journey to Jerusalem as one of the delegates of the Asian churches with the collection for the saints (Acts 20:1-5, compare I Cor. 16:1-4). In Jerusalem, however, Jewish pilgrims from Asia recognized him in Paul's company, and afterwards, finding Paul in the Temple with four others, jumped to the false conclusion that he had introduced Trophimus there (Acts 21:27ff). To take Trophimus beyond the court of the Gentiles would be to risk the death penalty. The incident precipitated a riot and Paul's arrest.

Here in II Tim. 4:20 Paul states that he left Trophimus sick at Miletus. This was near Trophimus' own city. But if Timothy was himself also in the area of Ephesus, it may seem strange that he needed this information. Most probably Paul left Trophimus sick when he was heading westward where he would undergo his second Roman imprisonment.

Did not Paul who spoke about the gifts of healings in I Cor. 12 have the gift of healing in regard to Trophimus? Paul healed the lame man (Acts 14:10), the damsel with the spirit of divination (Acts 16:18), he suffered no harm as a result of the viper's bite (Acts 28:5), he healed the father of Publius (Acts 28:8), and he performed other special miracles (Acts 14:3; 19:11). But Paul did not heal this beloved fellow traveler and faithful co-worker called Trophimus. Undoubtedly he must have prayed for him, but it was not the Lord's will to heal him and thus Paul accepts God's will in everything even if it is not healing.

The Epistle of Paul to

TITUS

Titus was probably a Gentile from Antioch (Gal. 2:3) who was brought to Christ by Paul (see Titus 1:4) fourteen years after Paul himself had been converted. At that time, when the dispute arose about the circumcision of Gentiles, Titus accompanied Paul to Jerusalem. While there, some dogmatic Jewish brethren insisted that Titus be circumcised. Paul would not allow it for the sake of principle (Gal. 2:5,16). To do otherwise would imply that all non-Jewish Christians were second-class citizens in the church.

Titus remained as Paul's traveling companion and was probably with Paul when he wrote the letter to the Galatians. Titus is not mentioned again until the events which triggered the writing of I Corinthians and II Corinthians. After Paul's release from his first Roman imprisonment, he traveled with Titus in the East. They landed at Crete and evangelized several towns (Titus 1:5). However, Paul was unable to remain any longer. So, he left Titus behind to appoint others and to complete the organization of congregations in that region. Titus found considerable opposition, especially from the Jews (Titus 1:10), and a strong tendency toward insubordination. Quite possibly, Titus had written to Paul to report this and to ask for his spiritual advice. Consequently, Paul wrote a short letter pressing him to complete the process of organization, to ordain elders, to teach sound doctrine and avoid empty disputations, and to exercise his own authority firmly. The letter was probably delivered by Zenas and Apollos (Titus 3:13). Titus was requested to be ready to leave Crete and join Paul at Nicopolis (Titus 3:12) where he was staying for the winter. It is probable that Paul dispatched Titus from there on a new mission to Dalmatia (II Tim. 4:10). A comparison of I Tim. 4:12 and Titus 2:15 suggests that Titus may have been older than Timothy and that he had been the stronger of the two during the difficulties in Corinth (I Cor. 16:10; II Cor. 7:13-15). Titus volunteered readily for a delicate task (II Cor. 8:17). He was full of affection and enthusiasm for the Corinthian brethren (II Cor. 7:15). He was effective, free from all sordid motives, and shared in Paul's spirit and example (II Cor. 12:18). Paul regarded him as if he were his own son (Titus 1:4), his brother (II Cor. 2:13), and his partner in Christ (II Cor. 8:23). The epistle to Titus was probably written almost simultaneously with I Timothy from Nicopolis in Macedonia (Titus 3:12).

Salutation

1 Paul, [a]a bond-servant[1401] of God,[2316]
and an [b]apostle[652] of Jesus Christ,
[I]for the faith[4102] of those [c]chosen[1588] of
God and [d]the knowledge[1922] of the
truth[225] which is [e]according to godliness,[2150]
2 in [a]the hope[1680] of eternal[166]
life,[2222] which God,[2316] [b]who cannot lie,
[c]promised[1861] [I][d]long ages[166] ago,
3 but [a]at the proper time[2540] manifested,[5319] *even* His word,[3056] in [b]the
proclamation[2782] [c]with which I was [aop]en-
trusted [d]according to the commandment[2003] of [e]God our Savior;[4990]
4 to [a]Titus, [b]my true child[5043] [I]in
a [c]common[2839] faith: [d]Grace and peace
from God the Father[3962] and [e]Christ[5547]
Jesus our Savior.

Qualifications of Elders

5 For this reason I left you in
[a]Crete, that you might [aosb]set in
order[1930] what remains, and [aosb] [b]ap-
point[2525] [c]elders[4245] in every city as I
[aom]directed[1299] you,

1 [I]Or, *according to* [a]Rom. 1:1; James 1:1; Rev. 1:1 [b]2Cor. 1:1 [c]Luke 18:7 [d]1Tim. 2:4 [e]1Tim. 6:3
2 [I]Lit., *before times eternal* [a]2Tim. 1:1; Titus 3:7 [b]2Tim. 2:13; Heb. 6:18 [c]Rom. 1:2 [d]2Tim. 1:9
3 [a]1Tim. 2:6 [b]Rom. 16:25; 2Tim. 4:17 [c]1Tim. 1:11 [d]1Tim. 1:1 [e]Luke 1:47; 1Tim. 1:1; Titus 2:10; 3:4
4 [I]Lit., *according to* [a]2Cor. 2:13; 8:23; Gal. 2:3; 2Tim. 4:10 [b]2Tim. 1:2 [c]2Pet. 1:1 [d]Rom. 1:7 [e]1Tim. 1:12; 2Tim. 1:1
5 [a]Acts 27:7; Titus 1:12 [b]Acts 14:23 [c]Acts 11:30

1:4,5 See general remarks on Titus.

🔑 6 *namely,* [a]if any man be above reproach,[410] the [b]husband[435] of one wife,
having children[5043] who believe,[4103] not
accused[2724] of [c]dissipation[810] or [d]rebel-
lion.[506]
7 For the [1a]overseer[1985] must be
above reproach as [b]God's steward,[3623]
not [c]self-willed, not quick-tempered,3711
not [d]addicted to wine, not pugnacious,
[e]not fond of sordid gain,146
8 but [a]hospitable, [b]loving what is
good,[5358] sensible,[4998] just,[1342] devout,[3741] self-controlled,1468
9 [a]holding fast[472] the faithful
word[3056] which is in accordance with the
teaching,[1322] that he may be able both
to [pinf]exhort[3870] in [b]sound doctrine
and to refute[1651] those who [ppt]contra-
dict.483
🔑 **10** [a]For there are many [b]rebel-
lious[506] men, [c]empty talkers[3151] and deceivers, especially [d]those of the circumcision,[4061]
11 who must be [pinf]silenced because
they are upsetting [a]whole families,
teaching [b]things they should not *teach,*
[c]for the sake of sordid gain.2771
12 One of themselves, a prophet[4396]
of their own, said, "[a]Cretans are always
liars, evil beasts, lazy[692] gluttons."
13 This testimony[3141] is true. For
this cause [pim] [a]reprove them [b]severely
that they may be [psa] [c]sound in the
faith,[4102]
14 not paying attention to Jewish
[a]myths[3454] and [b]commandments of men
who [ppt] [c]turn away from[654] the truth.[225]
15 [a]To the pure,[2513] all things are
pure; but [b]to those who are [pfpp]defiled
and [ajn]unbelieving,[571] nothing is pure,
but both their [c]mind[3563] and their conscience[4893] are [pfip]defiled.
16 [a]They profess[3670] to know God,
but by *their* deeds they [b]deny[720] *Him,*
being [c]detestable[947] and [d]disobedient,[545]
and [e]worthless[96] [f]for any good[18]
deed.[2041]

Duties of the Older and Younger

2 🔑 But as for you, speak[2980] the
things which are fitting for
[a]sound[5198] doctrine.

6 [a]1Tim. 3:2-4; Titus 1:6-8 [b]1Tim. 3:2 [c]Eph. 5:18 [d]Titus 1:10
7 [1]Or, *bishop* [a]1Tim. 3:2 [b]1Cor. 4:1 [c]2Pet. 2:10 [d]1Tim. 3:3 [e]1Tim. 3:3, 8
8 [a]1Tim. 3:2 [b]2Tim. 3:3
9 [a]2Thess. 2:15; 1Tim. 1:19; 2Tim. 1:13 [b]1Tim. 1:10; Titus 2:1
10 [a]2Cor. 11:13 [b]Titus 1:6 [c]1Tim. 1:6 [d]Acts 11:2
11 [a]1Tim. 5:4; 2Tim. 3:6 [b]1Tim. 5:13 [c]1Tim. 6:5
12 [a]Acts 2:11; 27:7
13 [a]1Tim. 5:20; 2Tim. 4:2; Titus 2:15 [b]2Cor. 13:10 [c]Titus 2:2
14 [a]1Tim. 1:4 [b]Col. 2:22 [c]2Tim. 4:4
15 [a]Luke 11:41; Rom. 14:20 [b]Rom. 14:14, 23 [c]1Tim. 6:5
16 [a]1John 2:4 [b]1Tim. 5:8 [c]Rev. 21:8 [d]Titus 3:3 [e]2Tim. 3:8 [f]2Tim. 3:17; Titus 3:1

1 [a]Titus 1:9

🔑 **1:6** "The husband of one wife" means exactly the same as the expression in I Tim. 3:2,12. The context is the same, that of moral conduct. See note on I Tim. 3:2.

🔑 **1:10** See general remarks on Titus.

🔑 **2:1-5** See notes on I Tim. 2:9-15; I Cor. 14:34-40. Titus was probably never married. According to church historians, he became a bishop of Crete and lived a celibate life there to an old age. It is interesting indeed that Paul, a bachelor himself, writes to another bachelor and tells him that the aged women should teach the younger women. In v. 4 the English says, "that they may encourage the young women . . ." In Greek the verb *sōphronizō* (4994) is used. It means to be sober minded or to voluntarily place limitations on their own freedom. And why should the aged women teach the younger women? Because it avoids even the appearance of evil and behooves a preacher not to place himself in the position where he can be tempted while having to deal with young women and their particular problems. So many have stressed erroneously that the same Apostle in the two pertinent passages of I Cor. 14:34-40 and I Tim. 2:11-12 instructs that women should not teach at all in church. But here in Tit. 2:3 Paul instructs the aged women to be good teachers or "teaching what is good." The word *sōphronas* (4998), the adjective of *sōphronizō,* is used in v. 1 and also in v. 5. Paul instructs Titus to teach the older men (v. 2) and also older women (v. 3). But when it comes to younger women, he tells him to have the older women whom Titus instructs to be good teachers among younger women. If the prohibition against teaching by women young and old was absolute in I Cor. 14:32-40 and I Tim. 2:11,12, how could it be that he is instructing Timothy to have older women teach younger women? This surely was in the context of the church. From I Cor. 9:5, we deduce that Paul was circumspect in regard to permitting himself to be found in the company of a sister in the Lord. This was not because he hated women, but because he never wanted to allow himself to give the appearance of evil or to fall into temptation. The translation of I Cor. 9:5 says, "Do we not have a right to take along a believing wife." If we translate *gunaika* (1135) as "wife" we must find contextual justification to do so. The basic generic meaning of

(continued on next page)

2 [a]Older men are to be [b]temperate,3524 dignified,[4586] sensible,[4998] [ppt] [c]sound [d]in faith,[4102] in love,[26] in [1]perseverance.[5281]

3 Older women likewise are to be reverent in their behavior, [a]not malicious gossips,[1228] nor [pfpp] [b]enslaved to much wine,[3631] teaching what is good,

4 that they may [1]encourage the young[3501] women to love their husbands, to love their children,

5 *to be* sensible,[4998] pure,[53] [a]workers at home,[3626] kind,[18] being [b]subject[5293] to their own husbands, [c]that the word[3056] of God may not be [psmp]dishonored.[987]

6 Likewise urge[3870] [a]the young men to be [pinf][1]sensible;4993

7 in all things show yourself to be [a]an example[5179] of good[2570] deeds,[2041] *with* [1]purity in doctrine,[1319] dignified,

8 sound[5199] *in* speech[3056] which is beyond reproach,[176] in order [a]that the opponent [asbp]may be put to shame,1788 having nothing bad[5337] to [pinf]say about us.

9 *Urge* [a]bondslaves[1401] to be subject to their own masters[1203] in everything, to be well-pleasing,[2101] not [1]argumentative,

10 not pilfering,[3557] but [psa]showing all good faith[4103] that they may [psa]adorn the doctrine[1319] of [a]God our Savior[4990] in every respect.

11 For the grace[5485] of God has [aop] [a]appeared,[2014] [1][b]bringing salvation[4992] to all men,[444]

12 [1]instructing[3811] us to [apt]deny[720] ungodliness[763] and [a]worldly[2886] desires[1939] and [b]to [aosb]live[2198] sensibly,4996 righteously[1346] and godly2153 [c]in the present age,[165]

13 [ppt]looking for[4327] the blessed[3107] hope[1680] and the [a]appearing[2015] of the glory[1391] of [1][b]our great God[2316] and Savior,[4990] Christ[5547] Jesus;

14 who [a]gave Himself for us, [b]that He might [asbm]redeem[3084] us from every lawless deed[458] and [aosb] [c]purify[2511] for Himself a [d]people for His own possession,[4041] [e]zealous for good[2570] deeds.[2041]

🔑 15 These things speak and [a]exhort and [a]reprove with all [1]authority. [b]Let no one disregard you.

2 [1]Or, *steadfastness* [a]Philem. 9 [b]1Tim. 3:2 [c]Titus 1:13 [d]1Tim. 1:2, 14
3 [a]1Tim. 3:11 [b]1Tim. 3:8
4 [1]Or, *train*
5 [a]1Tim. 5:14 [b]Eph. 5:22 [c]1Tim. 6:1
6 [1]Or, *sensible in all things; show* [a]1Tim. 5:1
7 [1]Or, *soundness;* lit., *uncorruptness* [a]1Tim. 4:12
8 [a]2Thess. 3:14; 1Pet. 2:12
9 [1]Lit., *contradicting* [a]Eph. 6:5; 1Tim. 6:1
10 [a]Titus 1:3
11 [1]Or, *to all men, bringing* [a]2Tim. 1:10; Titus 3:4 [b]1Tim. 2:4
12 [1]Or, *disciplining* [a]1Tim. 6:9; Titus 3:3 [b]2Tim. 3:12 [c]1Tim. 6:17
13 [1]Or, *the great God and our Savior* [a]2Thess. 2:8 [b]1Tim. 1:1; 2Tim. 1:2; Titus 1:4; 2Pet. 1:1
14 [a]1Tim. 2:6 [b]Ps. 130:8; 1Pet. 1:18f. [c]Ezek. 37:23; Heb. 1:3; 9:14; 1John 1:7 [d]Ex. 19:5; Deut. 4:20; 7:6; 14:2; Eph. 1:11; 1Pet. 2:9 [e]Eph. 2:10; Titus 3:8; 1Pet. 3:13
15 [1]Lit., *command* [a]1Tim. 4:13; 5:20; 2Tim. 4:2 [b]1Tim. 4:12

Godly Living

3 🔑 [a]Remind them [b]to be subject to[5293] rulers,[746] to authorities,[1849] to be obedient, to be [c]ready for every good[18] deed,[2041]

2 to [pinf]malign[987] no one, [a]to be uncontentious, [a]gentle, [b]showing every consideration for all men.

3 [a]For we also once were foolish[453] ourselves, [b]disobedient,[545] [c]deceived, [d]enslaved to[1398] [e]various4164 lusts[1939] and pleasures, spending our life in [f]malice[2549] and [f]envy, hateful, hating one another.

1 [a]2Tim. 2:14 [b]Rom. 13:1 [c]2Tim. 2:21 2 [a]1Tim. 3:3; 1Pet. 2:18 [b]2Tim. 2:25 3 [a]Rom. 11:30; Col. 3:7 [b]Titus 1:16 [c]2Tim. 3:13 [d]Rom. 6:6, 12 [e]2Tim. 3:6; Titus 2:12 [f]Rom. 1:29

(continued from previous page)
gunē is "woman" and when the context indicates it then it means "wife." If this were to be understood as "wife" then Paul's meaning would be that he had authority to take around a sister who is the wife of someone else or to take to himself a sister or a wife as if there were an evil in itself. In our opinion Paul means to take around a woman who is a sister in the Lord. Being a sister does not excuse his taking her around because she is a woman and one should be circumspect in his behavior as a servant of Christ as he deals with women. Some ministers who counsel women have found temptation beyond their ability to resist and have shattered their marriages and the marriages of others, not to mention the shame brought on the name of Christ. No servant of Christ should allow himself to be found in such a vulnerable position by teaching or counseling women in private. Strong emphasis should be placed on the counsel of Paul to Titus concerning safeguarding both the young women and men teachers. While a spiritual leader may have the power to do so, it is best to follow Paul's example and avoid such temptation by appointing older, spiritual women to such tasks.

🔑 **2:15** See general remarks on Titus.

🔑 **3:1** See note on I Pet. 2:17.

4 But when the [a]kindness[5544] of
[b]God our Savior[4990] and *His* love[5363] for
mankind [aop] [c]appeared,[2014]
5 [a]He saved[4982] us, [b]not on the basis
of deeds which we have [ao]done in righteousness,[1343] but [c]according to His
mercy,[1656] by the [d]washing[3067] of regeneration[3824] and [e]renewing[342] by the
[an]Holy[40] Spirit,[4151]
6 [a]whom He poured out upon us
[b]richly through Jesus Christ our Savior,[4990]
🔑7 that being [aptp]justified[1344] by
His grace[5485] we might be [asbp]made
[a]heirs[2818] [1]according to *the* hope[1680] of
eternal[166] life.[2222]
8 [a]This is a trustworthy[4103]
statement;[3056] and concerning these
things I [b]want you to [pinf]speak confidently,[1226] so that those who have
[pfp] [c]believed[4100] God may be [psa]careful
to [pinf] [d]engage in good deeds. These
things are good and profitable for men.
9 But [pim] [a]shun [b]foolish[3474] controversies and [c]genealogies[1076] and strife
and [d]disputes[3163] about the Law; for they
are [e]unprofitable and worthless.

4 [a]Rom. 2:4; Eph. 2:7; 1Pet. 2:3 [b]Titus 2:10 [c]Titus 2:11
5 [a]Rom. 11:14; 2Tim. 1:9 [b]Eph. 2:9 [c]Eph. 2:4; 1Pet. 1:3 [d]John 3:5; Eph. 5:26; 1Pet. 3:21 [e]Rom. 12:2
6 [a]Rom. 5:5 [b]Rom. 2:4; 1Tim. 6:17
7 [1]Or, *of eternal life according to hope* [a]Matt. 25:34; Mark 10:17; Rom. 8:17, 24; Titus 1:2
8 [a]1Tim. 1:15 [b]1Tim. 2:8 [c]2Tim. 1:12 [d]Titus 2:7, 14; 3:14
9 [a]2Tim. 2:16 [b]1Tim. 1:4; 2Tim. 2:23 [c]1Tim. 1:4 [d]James 4:1 [e]2Tim. 2:14
10 [a]2John 10 [b]Rom. 16:17 [c]Matt. 18:15f.
11 [a]Titus 1:14
12 [a]Acts 20:4; Eph. 6:21f.; Col. 4:7f.; 2Tim. 4:12 [b]2Tim. 4:9 [c]2Tim. 4:21

🔑10 [pim] [a]Reject[3868] a [b]factious[141] man
[c]after a first and second warning,[3559]
🔑11 knowing that such a man is
[pfip] [a]perverted and is sinning,[264] being
self-condemned.[843]

Personal Concerns

🔑12 When I send Artemas or
[a]Tychicus to you, [b]make every effort
to [ainf]come to me at Nicopolis, for I
have [pfi]decided[2919] to [c]spend the winter
there.
🔑13 Diligently help Zenas the [a]lawyer
and [b]Apollos on their way so that nothing
is [psa]lacking for them.
14 And let [a]our *people* also [psa]learn
to [pinf] [b]engage in good [1]deeds to meet
[c]pressing[316] needs, that they may not
be [d]unfruitful.
15 [a]All who are with me greet[782]
you. Greet[782] those who [ppt]love[5368] us
[b]in *the* faith.[4102]
[c]Grace be with you all.

13 [a]Matt. 22:35 [b]Acts 18:24; 1Cor. 16:12 14 [1]Or, *occupations* [a]Titus 2:8 [b]Titus 3:8 [c]Rom. 12:13; Phil. 4:16 [d]Matt. 7:19; Phil. 1:11; Col. 1:10 15 [a]Acts 20:34 [b]1Tim. 1:2 [c]Col. 4:18

🔑 **3:7** See general remarks on justification on Romans.
🔑 **3:10,11** See note on Eph. 1:4,5.
🔑 **3:11** What is translated as "self-condemned" in Greek is *autokatakritos* (843). See note on Acts 2:23.
🔑 **3:12** See general remarks on Titus and also note on Col. 4:7.
🔑 **3:13** See general remarks on Titus.

The Epistle of Paul to

PHILEMON

The Epistle to Philemon touches upon servitude among the Jews in the time of Christ and His Apostles. It was written during Paul's first imprisonment in Rome (A.D. 62).

The key to Paul's Epistle to Philemon is the Hebrew fugitive law in Deut. 23:15,16. This Epistle is proof that he acted in strict accordance with its requirements.

Paul gives Onesimus shelter in his own hired house. He does not betray him or deliver him up into the power of his master as a fugitive. He does not send word to Philemon to come to Rome to prove that he was his slave and to take him. Paul kindly protects and instructs Onesimus. He sends Onesimus back with his own consent as a trusted messenger and brother bearing a request to Philemon concerning his freedom. Paul does not accuse Onesimus of running away wrongly, but on the contrary, we have Paul stating that it was by the merciful providence of God that Onesimus had departed from Philemon for a season that he might be received back, no more as a servant, but above a servant, a brother beloved. Paul beseeches Philemon to receive Onesimus as he would Paul himself, as a partner. Whatever wrong Onesimus may have done to Philemon, even though he may have been unprofitable to him, Paul takes upon himself. He does not intimate that this wrong was the running away from Philemon, but whatever wrong Onesimus did during his unprofitable state of bondage, this state should now cease. In order that there might be no shadow of claim remaining by Philemon against Onesimus whereby he may have said, "I will keep you still in bondage till you work out your debt," Paul takes all Onesimus' debts upon himself, whatever they might be, and becomes security for him. The result is that Onesimus is a free man.

Salutation

1 [a]Paul, [b]a prisoner of [c]Christ[5547] Jesus, and [d]Timothy [I]our brother,[80] to Philemon our beloved[27] *brother* and [e]fellow worker,

2 and to Apphia [Ia]our sister, and to [b]Archippus our [c]fellow soldier, and to [d]the church[1557] in your house:[3624]

3 [a]Grace[5485] to you and peace[1515] from God[2316] our Father[3962] and the Lord[2962] Jesus Christ.

Philemon's Love and Faith

4 [a]I thank[2168] my God always, making mention of you in my prayers,[4335]

5 because I [a]hear of your love,[26] and of the faith[4102] which you have toward the Lord Jesus, and toward all the [I]saints;[40]

6 *and I pray* that the fellowship[2842] of your faith may become effective [I]through the [a]knowledge of every good thing[18] which is in [II]you [III]for Christ's sake.

7 For I have come to have much [a]joy[5485] and comfort[3874] in your love, because the [I]hearts[4698] of the [II]saints have been [pfip] [b]refreshed through you, brother.

8 Therefore, [a]though I have [I]enough confidence in Christ to order[2004] you *to do* that which is [b]proper,[433]

9 yet for love's sake I rather [a]appeal[3870] *to you*—since I am such a person as Paul, [I]the [b]aged, and now also [c]a prisoner of [d]Christ Jesus—

Plea for Onesimus, a Free Man

10 I [a]appeal to you for my [b]child,[5043] whom I have [ao]begotten[1080] in my [I]imprisonment, [IIc]Onesimus,

11 who formerly was useless[890] to you, but now is useful[2173] both to you and to me.

12 And I have [ao]sent him back to

1 [I]Lit., *the* [a]Phil. 1:1 [b]Eph. 3:1 [c]Gal. 3:26 [d]2 Cor. 1:1; Col. 1:1 [e]Phil. 2:25; Philem. 24
2 [I]Lit., *the* [a]Rom. 16:1 [b]Col. 4:17 [c]Phil. 2:25; 2Tim. 2:3 [d]Rom. 16:5
3 [a]Rom. 1:7
4 [a]Rom. 1:8f.
5 [I]Or, *holy ones* [a]Eph. 1:15; Col. 1:4; 1Thess. 3:6
6 [I]Or, *in* [II]Some ancient mss. read *us* [III]Lit., *toward Christ* [a]Phil. 1:9; Col. 1:9; 3:10
7 [I]Lit., *inward parts* [II]Or, *holy ones* [a]2Cor. 7:4, 13 [b]1Cor. 16:18 Philem. 20
8 [I]Lit., *much* [a]2Cor. 3:12; 1Thess. 2:6 [b]Eph. 5:4
9 [I]Or, *an ambassador* [a]Rom. 12:1 [b]Titus 2:2 [c]Philem. 1 [d]Gal. 3:26; 1Tim. 1:12; Philem. 23

10 [I]Lit., *bonds* [II]I.e., useful [a]Rom. 12:1 [b]1Cor. 4:14f. [c]Col. 4:9

you in person, that is, *sending* my very
heart,4698
13 whom I [pfi]wished to [pinf]keep[2722]
with me, that in your behalf he might
[psa]minister[1247] to me in my [I][a]imprison-
ment for the gospel;[2098]
14 but without your consent I did
not [ao]want to [ainf]do anything, that your
goodness[18] should [a]not be as it were
by compulsion,[318] but of your own free
will.
15 For perhaps [a]he was for this reason [ao]parted *from you* for a while,[5610]
that you should [psa]have[568] him back forever,
16 [a]no longer as a slave, but more
than a slave,[1401] [b]a beloved brother,[80]
especially to me, but how much more
to you, both [c]in the flesh and in the
Lord.
17 If then you regard me a [a]part-
ner,[2844] accept him as *you would*
me.
18 But if he has [ao]wronged[91] you
in any way, or owes you anything,
[pim]charge that to my account;[1677]
19 [a]I, Paul, am [ao]writing this with
my own hand, I will repay it ([b]lest
I should [I]mention to you that you
owe to me even your own self as
well).
20 Yes, brother, let me [opt]benefit
from you in the Lord; [aim] [a]refresh my
heart in Christ.
21 [a]Having confidence in your obedience,[5218] I write to you, since I know
that you will do even more than what
I say.
22 And at the same time260 also
[pim]prepare me a [a]lodging; for [b]I hope
that through [c]your prayers [d]I shall be
given[5483] to you.
🗝 **23** [a]Epaphras, my [b]fellow prisoner
in Christ Jesus, greets782 you,
24 *as do* [a]Mark, [b]Aristarchus,
[c]Demas, [c]Luke, my [d]fellow workers.
25 [a]The grace of the Lord Jesus
Christ be [b]with your spirit.[I]

13 [I]Lit., *bonds* [a]Phil. 1:7; Philem. 10
14 [a]2Cor. 9:7; 1Pet. 5:2
15 [a]Gen. 45:5, 8
16 [a]1Cor. 7:22 [b]Matt. 23:8; 1Tim. 6:2 [c]Eph. 6:5; Col. 3:22
17 [a]2Cor. 8:23
19 [I]Lit., *say* [a]1Cor. 16:21; 2Cor. 10:1; Gal. 5:2 [b]2Cor. 9:4
20 [a]Philem. 7
21 [a]2Cor. 2:3
22 [a]Acts 28:23 [b]Phil. 1:25; 2:24 [c]2Cor. 1:11 [d]Acts 27:24; Heb. 13:19
23 [a]Col. 1:7; 4:12 [b]Rom. 16:7; Philem. 1
24 [a]Acts 12:12, 25; 15:37-39; Col. 4:10 [b]Acts 19:29; 27:2; Col. 4:10 [c]Col. 4:14; 2Tim. 4:10f. [d]Philem. 1
25 [I]Some ancient mss. add *Amen* [a]Gal. 6:18 [b]2Tim. 4:22

🗝 **23** See note on Col. 1:7; 4:10.

The Epistle to the

HEBREWS

We do not know exactly who wrote the Epistle to the Hebrews. Perhaps it was Apollos. According to Acts 18:24-28, he was a well-read Hellenistic Jew from Alexandria in Egypt. Martin Luther guessed that he wrote it. Tertullian (A.D. 150-230) said that Hebrews was a letter of Barnabas. Adolf Harnack and J. Rendel Harris speculated that it could have been written by Priscilla (Prisca). William Ramsey suggested that it was done by Phillip. However, the traditional position is that the Apostle Paul wrote Hebrews. From the very beginning, the eastern church attributed the letter to him, but the western church did not accept this untill the fourth century. Eusebius (A.D. 263-339?) believed that Paul wrote it, and Origen (A.D. 185?-254?) was not sure. About the end of the second century, Clement of Alexandria thought that Paul originally wrote the letter in the Hebrew language and that it was later translated by Luke or someone else into polished Greek. It certainly is a superb, literary Greek masterpiece which is well-organized, logical, and comprehensive.

Whoever the author was, he wanted to reassure Jewish believers that their faith in Jesus as Messiah was secure and reasonable. He tried to prepare them for the impending disaster. The Temple with its attendant animal sacrifices would soon be destroyed by the Romans, just as Jesus predicted. There was no need for the Temple, because Jesus had cleared the way for direct access to God's throne (Heb. 4:14-16; 10:19-22). Animal blood was no longer necessary, because the blood of the Lamb of God now continually takes away sin (Heb. 9:18-26). His system is vastly superior to the abolished Jewish system.

The date is also a matter of conjecture, but it seems certain that it was prior to the fall of Jerusalem in A.D. 70, because the Temple was still standing (Heb. 10:11; 13:10-11).

God's Final Word in His Son

1 God,[2316] after He [apt] [a]spoke[2980] long
ago[3819] to the fathers[3962] in [b]the
prophets[4396] in many portions[4181] and
[c]in many ways,[4187]
2 [I][a]in these last[2078] days [b]has [ao]spo-
ken to us in [c]*His* Son,[5207] whom He
[ao]appointed[5087] [d]heir[2818] of all things,
[e]through whom also He made[4160] the
[II][f]world.[165]
🔑3 [I]And He is the radiance[541] of
His glory[1391] and the exact [a]rep-
resentation[5481] of His nature,[5287]
and [II][b]upholds[5342] all things by
the word[4487] of His power.[1411]
When He had made [c]purification[2512]
of sins,[266] He [d]sat down at
the right hand[1188] of the [e]Majesty on
high;
4 having [apt]become as much
better[2909] than the angels,[32] as He [pfi]has
inherited[2816] a more excellent[1313]
[a]name[3686] than they.
5 For to which of the angels did He
ever say,

"[a]THOU ART MY SON,[5207]
TODAY I HAVE [pfi]BEGOTTEN[1080]
THEE"?

And again,

"[b]I WILL BE A FATHER TO HIM
AND HE SHALL BE A SON TO
ME"?

🔑6 And [I]when He again
[aosb] [a]brings[1521] the first-born[4416] into
[II][b]the world, He says,

"[c]AND LET ALL THE ANGELS OF
GOD [aim]WORSHIP[4352] HIM."

7 And of the angels He says,

"[a]WHO [ppt]MAKES HIS ANGELS
WINDS,[4151]

1 [a]John 9:29; 16:13; Heb. 2:2f.; 3:5; 4:8; 5:5; 11:18; 12:25 [b]Acts 2:30; 3:21 [c]Num. 12:6, 8; Joel 2:28
2 [I]Or, *at the end of these days* [II]Lit., *ages* [a]Matt. 13:39; 1Pet. 1:20 [b]John 9:29 [c]John 5:26, 27; Heb. 3:6; 5:8; 7:28 [d]Ps. 2:8; Matt. 28:18; Mark 12:7; Rom. 8:17; Heb. 2:8 [e]John 1:3; 1Cor. 8:6; Col. 1:16 [f]1Cor. 2:7; Heb. 11:3
3 [I]Lit., *Who being* [II]Lit., *upholding* [a]2Cor. 4:4 [b]Col. 1:17 [c]Titus 2:14; Heb. 9:14 [d]Mark 16:19; Heb. 8:1; 10:12; 12:2 [e]2Pet. 1:17
4 [a]Eph. 1:21
5 [a]Ps. 2:7; Acts 13:33; Heb. 5:5 [b]2Sam. 7:14
6 [I]Or, *again when He brings* [II]Lit., *the inhabited earth* [a]Heb. 10:5 [b]Matt. 24:14 [c]Ps. 97:7
7 [a]Ps. 104:4

🔑 **1:3** See note on I Thess. 2:19.
🔑 **1:6** See note on Col. 1:15.

AND HIS MINISTERS3011 A
FLAME OF FIRE."
8 But of the Son *He says,*
"[a]THY THRONE, O GOD, IS
FOREVER[165]
AND EVER,
AND THE RIGHTEOUS2118
SCEPTER4464
IS THE SCEPTER
of [I]HIS KINGDOM.[932]
9 "[a]THOU HAST [ao]LOVED[25]
RIGHTEOUSNESS[1343] AND
[ao]HATED LAWLESSNESS;[458]
[b]THEREFORE GOD, THY GOD,
HATH [c][ao]ANOINTED[5548] THEE
WITH THE OIL[1637] OF
GLADNESS[20] ABOVE THY
COMPANIONS."3533
10 And,
"[a]THOU, LORD, IN THE
BEGINNING[746] DIDST [ao]LAY
THE FOUNDATION OF THE
EARTH,
AND THE HEAVENS ARE THE
WORKS OF THY HANDS;
11 [a]THEY WILL PERISH,[622] BUT
THOU REMAINEST;
[b]AND THEY ALL WILL BECOME
OLD3822 AS A GARMENT,
12 [a]AND AS A MANTLE4018 THOU
WILT ROLL THEM UP;
AS A GARMENT THEY WILL ALSO
BE CHANGED.[236]
BUT THOU ART [b]THE SAME,
AND THY YEARS WILL NOT
COME TO AN END."
13 But to which of the angels has
He ever said,
"[a]SIT AT MY RIGHT HAND,[1188]
[b]UNTIL I MAKE THINE ENEMIES
A FOOTSTOOL FOR THY FEET"?
14 Are they not all [a]ministering3010
spirits,[4151] [ppp]sent out to render ser-
vice[1248] for the sake of those who will
[pinf] [b]inherit[2816] [c]salvation?[4991]

Give Heed

2 For this reason we must pay much
closer attention to [I]what we have
[aptp]heard, lest [a]we [aosb]drift away
from it.
2 For if the word[3056] [aptp] [a]spoken
through [b]angels[32] proved [I]unalterable,[949]
and [c]every transgression[3847] and disobedience[3876] received a just[1738] [d]rec-
ompense,[3405]
3 [a]how shall we escape if we [apt]ne-
glect so great a [b]salvation?[4991] [I]After it
was at the first [pip] [c]spoken through the
Lord, it was [d]confirmed[950] to us by those
who [apt]heard,
4 God also bearing witness4901 with
them, both by [a]signs[4592] and wonders[5059]
and by [b]various4164 [I]miracles[1411] and by
[II][c]gifts[3311] of the [an]Holy Spirit [d]according
to His own will.

Earth Subject to Man

5 For He did not [ao]subject[5293] to an-
gels [I][a]the world[3625] to come,[3195] con-
cerning which we are speaking.
6 But one has testified[1263] [a]some-
where, saying,
"[b]WHAT IS MAN,[444] THAT THOU
REMEMBEREST HIM?
OR THE SON OF MAN, THAT
THOU ART CONCERNED[1980]
ABOUT HIM?
7 "[a]THOU HAST MADE HIM [I]FOR A
LITTLE WHILE LOWER THAN
THE ANGELS;
THOU HAST [ao]CROWNED HIM
WITH GLORY[1391] AND HONOR,
[II]AND HAST [ao]APPOINTED HIM
OVER THE WORKS OF THY
HANDS;
8 [a]THOU HAST PUT ALL THINGS IN
SUBJECTION UNDER HIS
FEET."
For [aie]in subjecting[5293] all things to him,
He left nothing that is not subject[506] to
him. But now [b]we do not yet see all
things [pfpp]subjected to him.

Jesus Briefly Humbled

9 But we do see Him who has been
[a]made [I]for a little while lower than the
angels, *namely,* Jesus, [b]because of the

---

8 [I]Some mss. read *Thy* [a]Ps. 45:6
9 [a]Ps. 45:7 [b]John 10:17; Phil. 2:9; Heb. 2:9 [c]Is. 61:1, 3
10 [a]Ps. 102:25
11 [a]Ps. 102:26 [b]Is. 51:6; Heb. 8:13
12 [a]Ps. 102:26, 27 [b]Heb. 13:8
13 [a]Ps. 110:1; Matt. 22:44; Heb. 1:3 [b]Josh. 10:24; Heb. 10:13
14 [a]Ps. 103:20f.; Dan. 7:10 [b]Matt. 25:34; Mark 10:17; Titus 3:7; Heb. 6:12 [c]Rom. 11:14; 1Cor. 1:21; Heb. 2:3; 5:9; 9:28

1 [I]Lit., *the things that have been heard* [a]Prov. 3:21
2 [I]Or, *steadfast* [a]Heb. 1:1 [b]Acts 7:53 [c]Heb. 10:28 [d]Heb. 10:35; 11:26
3 [I]Lit., *Which was* [a]Heb. 10:29; 12:25 [b]Rom. 11:14; 1Cor. 1:21; Heb. 1:14; 5:9; 9:28 [c]Heb. 1:1 [d]Mark 16:20; Luke 1:2; 1John 1:1
4 [I]Or, *works of power* [II]Lit., *distributions* [a]John 4:48 [b]Mark 6:14 [c]1Cor. 12:4, 11; Eph. 4:7 [d]Eph. 1:5
5 [I]Lit., *the inhabited earth* [a]Matt. 24:14; Heb. 6:5
6 [a]Heb. 4:4 [b]Ps. 8:4
7 [I]Or, *a little lower* [II]Some ancient mss. do not contain *And . . . hands* [a]Ps. 8:5, 6
8 [a]Ps. 8:6; 1 Cor. 15:27 [b]1Cor. 15:25
9 [I]Or, *a little lower* [a]Heb. 2:7 [b]Phil. 2:9; Heb. 1:9

2:9 See note on I Thess. 2:19.

suffering[3804] of death[2288] [pfpp] [c]crowned with glory and honor, that [d]by the grace[5485] of God He might [aosb] [e]taste[1089] death [f]for everyone.

10 For [a]it was fitting for Him, [b]for whom are all things, and through whom are all things, in [apt]bringing many sons to glory, to [ainf] [c]perfect[5048] the [I][d]author[747] of their salvation[4991] through sufferings.

11 For both He who [ppt] [a]sanctifies[37] and those who [b]are [ppp] [I]sanctified are all [c]from one *Father*; for which reason He is not ashamed to call them [d]brethren,[80]

12 saying,

"[a]I WILL PROCLAIM[518] THY
NAME[3686] TO MY BRETHREN,
IN THE MIDST OF THE
[I]CONGREGATION[1577] I WILL
SING THY PRAISE."

13 And again,

"[a]I WILL PUT MY TRUST[3982] [2071] IN
HIM."

And again,

"[b]BEHOLD, I AND THE CHILDREN
WHOM GOD HAS [ao]GIVEN
ME."

14 Since then the children [pfi]share[2841] in [I][a]flesh[4561] and blood,[129] [b]He Himself likewise also [ao]partook of the same, that [c]through death He might [aosb]render powerless [d]him who [ppt]had the power of death, that is, the devil;[1228]

15 and might [aosb]deliver[525] those who through [a]fear[5401] of death were subject[1777] to slavery[1397] all their lives.[2198]

16 For assuredly[1222] He does not [I]give help to angels, but He gives help to the [II]descendant[4690] of Abraham.

17 Therefore, He [I]had[3780] [a]to be [aifp]made like His brethren[80] in all things, that He might [b]become a merciful and faithful[4103] [c]high priest[749] in [d]things pertaining to God, to [e][aies]make propitiation for[2433] the sins[266] of the people.[2992]

18 For since He Himself was [a]tempted[3985] in that which He has [pfi]suffered, He is able to [ainf]come to the aid of[977] those who are tempted.

Jesus Our High Priest

3 Therefore, [a]holy[40] brethren,[80] partakers[3353] of a [b]heavenly calling,[2821] [aim]consider[2657] Jesus, [c]the Apostle[652] and [d]High Priest[749] of our [e]confession.[3671]

2 [I]He was faithful[4103] to Him who [apt] [II]appointed Him, as [a]Moses also was in all His house.

3 [a]For He has been [pfip]counted worthy of more glory[1391] than Moses, by just so much as the builder of the house has more honor than the house.

4 For every house is built by someone, but the builder of all things is God.[2316]

5 Now [a]Moses was faithful in all His house as [b]a servant, [c]for a testimony of those things [d]which were to be spoken later;

6 but Christ *was faithful* as [a]a Son[5207] over His house [b]whose house we are, [c]if we [aosb]hold fast[2722] our [d]confidence and the boast of our [e]hope[1680] firm[949] until the end.[5066]

7 Therefore, just as [a]the Holy Spirit says,

"[b]TODAY IF YOU [aosb]HEAR[191] HIS
VOICE,
8 [a]DO NOT [psa]HARDEN[4645] YOUR
HEARTS[2588] AS [I]WHEN THEY
PROVOKED ME,
AS IN THE DAY OF TRIAL[3986] IN
THE WILDERNESS,
9 [a]WHERE YOUR FATHERS
TRIED[3985] *Me* BY TESTING
Me,
AND SAW MY WORKS FOR
[b]FORTY YEARS.
10 "[a]THEREFORE I WAS [ao]ANGRY
WITH THIS GENERATION,[1074]
AND SAID, 'THEY ALWAYS GO
ASTRAY IN THEIR HEART;
AND THEY DID NOT [ao]KNOW MY
WAYS';
11 [a]AS I [ao]SWORE IN MY
WRATH,[3709]

9 [c]Acts 2:33; 3:13; 1Pet. 1:21 [d]John 3:16 [e]Matt. 16:28; John 8:52 [f]Heb. 7:25
10 [I]Or, *leader* [a]Luke 24:26 [b]Rom. 11:36 [c]Heb. 5:9; 7:28 [d]Acts 3:15; 5:31
11 [I]Or, *being sanctified* [a]Heb. 13:12 [b]Heb. 10:10 [c]Acts 17:28 [d]Matt. 25:40; Mark 3:34f.; John 20:17
12 [I]Or, *church* [a]Ps. 22:22
13 [a]Is. 8:17 [b]Is. 8:18
14 [I]Lit., *blood and flesh* [a]Matt. 16:17 [b]John 1:14 [c]1Cor. 15:54-57; 2Tim. 1:10 [d]John 12:31; 1John 3:8
15 [a]Rom. 8:15
16 [I]Lit., *take hold of angels, but He takes hold of* [II]Lit., *seed*
17 [I]Lit., *was obligated to be* [a]Phil. 2:7; Heb. 2:14 [b]Heb. 4:15f.; 5:2 [c]Heb. 3:1; 4:14f.; 5:5, 10; 6:20; 7:26, 28; 8:1, 3; 9:11; 10:21 [d]Rom. 15:17; Heb. 5:1 [e]Dan. 9:24; 1John 2:2; 4:10
18 [a]Heb. 4:15

1 [a]Acts 1:15; Heb. 2:11; 3:12; 10:19; 13:22 [b]Phil. 3:14 [c]John 17:3 [d]Heb. 2:17; 4:14f.; 5:5, 10; 6:20; 7:26, 28; 8:1, 3; 9:11; 10:21 [e]2Cor. 9:13; Heb. 4:14; 10:23
2 [I]Lit., *Being faithful* [II]Or, *made* [a]Ex. 40:16; Num. 12:7; Heb. 3:5
3 [a]2Cor. 3:7-11
5 [a]Ex. 40:16; Num. 12:7; Heb. 3:2 [b]Ex. 14:31; Num. 12:7 [c]Deut. 18:18f. [d]Heb. 1:1
6 [a]Heb. 1:2 [b]1Cor. 3:16; 1Tim. 3:15 [c]Rom. 11:22; Heb. 3:14; 4:14 [d]Eph. 3:12; Heb. 4:16; 10:19, 35 [e]Heb. 6:11; 7:19; 10:23; 11:1; 1Pet. 1:3
7 [a]Acts 28:25; Heb. 9:8; 10:15 [b]Ps. 95:7; Heb. 3:15; 4:7
8 [I]Lit., *in the provocation* [a]Ps. 95:8
9 [a]Ps. 95:9-11 [b]Acts 7:36
10 [a]Ps. 95:10
11 [a]Ps. 95:11; Heb. 4:3, 5

'THEY SHALL NOT ENTER MY
REST.' "[2663]

The Peril of Unbelief

🔑 12 [a]Take care, brethren, lest there
should be in any one of you an evil,[4190]
unbelieving[570] heart,[2588] in [ainf]falling
away[868] from [b]the living[2198] God.
13 But [a]encourage[3870] one another
day after day, as long as it is *still* called
"Today," lest any one of you be
[asbp]hardened[4645] by the [b]deceitfulness of
sin.
14 For we have [pfi]become
partakers3353 of Christ,[5547] [a]if we
[aosb]hold[2722] fast the beginning of our
[b]assurance[5287] firm until the end;[5056]
15 while it is said,
"[a]TODAY IF YOU [aosb]HEAR HIS
VOICE,
DO NOT HARDEN[4645] YOUR
HEARTS, AS [I]WHEN THEY
PROVOKED[3894] ME."
16 For who [a]provoked3893 *Him*
when they had heard? Indeed,235
[b]did not all those who came out of Egypt
led by Moses?
17 And with whom was He [ao]angry
for forty years? Was it not with those
who [apt]sinned,[264] [a]whose bodies fell[4098]
in the wilderness?
18 And to whom did He swear
[a]that they should not enter His rest,[2663]
but to those who were [b]disobedient?[544]
19 And *so* we see that they were
not able to [ainf]enter because of [a]unbe-
lief.[570]

The Believer's Rest

4 Therefore, let us [aosb]fear[5399] lest,
while a promise[1860] remains of
[ainf]entering His rest,[2663] any one of you
should [psa]seem to have [pfin] [a]come short
of it.
2 For indeed we have had good
news preached[2097] to us, just as they
also; but [a]the word[3056] [I]they heard
did not profit them, because [II]it was not
[pfpp]united by faith[4102] in those who
[apt]heard.
3 [I]For we who have [apt]believed[4100]
enter that rest,[2663] just as He has said,
"[a]AS I SWORE IN MY WRATH,[3709]
THEY SHALL NOT ENTER MY
REST,"
although His works[2041] were [aptp]finished
[b]from the foundation of the world.
4 For He has thus said [a]somewhere
concerning the seventh *day*, "[b]AND GOD
[ao] [c]RESTED[2664] ON THE SEVENTH DAY FROM
ALL HIS WORKS";
5 and again in this *passage*, "[a]THEY
SHALL NOT ENTER MY REST."
6 Since therefore it remains for
some to enter it, and those who formerly
had good news [aptp]preached[2097] to them
failed to enter because of [a]disobedi-
ence,[543]
7 He again fixes[3724] a certain day,
"Today," saying [I]through David after so
long a time just [a]as has been said before,
"[b]TODAY IF YOU [aosb]HEAR HIS
VOICE,
DO NOT [psa]HARDEN[4645] YOUR
HEARTS."[2588]
8 For [a]if [I]Joshua had [ao]given them
rest,[2664] He would not have [ipf]spoken
of another day after that.
9 There remains therefore a Sabbath rest for the people of God.
10 For the one who has [apt]entered
His rest[2663] has himself also
[ao] [a]rested[2664] from his works, as [b]God
did from His.
11 Let us therefore be diligent to
[ainf]enter that rest, lest anyone [aosb]fall
through *following* the same [a]example of
[b]disobedience.[543]
12 For [a]the word[3056] of God is
[b]living[2198] and [c]active and sharper than
any two-edged [d]sword, and piercing as
far as the division[3311] of [e]soul[5590] and
[e]spirit,[4151] of both joints and marrow,
and [f]able to judge[2924] the thoughts1761
and intentions[1771] of the heart.[2588]
13 And [a]there is no creature[2937] hidden from His sight, but all things are
[b]open and laid bare[1131] to the eyes of
Him with whom we have to do.

12 [a]Col. 2:8; Heb. 12:25 [b]Matt. 16:16; Heb. 9:14; 10:31; 12:22
13 [a]Heb. 10:24f. [b]Eph. 4:22
14 [a]Heb. 3:6 [b]Heb. 11:1
15 [I]Lit., *in the provocation* [a]Ps. 95:7f.; Heb. 3:7; 4:7
16 [a]Jer. 32:29; 44:3, 8 [b]Num. 14:2, 11, 30; Deut. 1:35, 36, 38
17 [a]Num. 14:29; 1Cor. 10:5
18 [a]Num. 14:23; Deut. 1:34f.; Heb. 4:2 [b]Rom. 11:30-32; Heb. 4:6, 11
19 [a]John 3:18, 36; Rom. 11:23; Heb 3:12

1 [a]2Cor. 6:1; Gal. 5:4; Heb. 12:15
2 [I]Lit., *of hearing* [II]Or, *they were . . . faith with those who heard* [a]Rom. 10:17; Gal. 3:2; 1Thess. 2:13
3 [I]Some ancient mss. read *Therefore* [a]Ps. 95:11; Heb. 3:11 [b]Matt. 25:34
4 [a]Heb. 2:6 [b]Gen. 2:2 [c]Ex. 20:11; 31:17
5 [a]Ps. 95:11; Heb. 3:11
6 [a]Heb. 3:18; 4:11
7 [I]Or, *in* [a]Heb. 3:7f. [b]Ps. 95:7f.
8 [I]Gr., *Jesus* [a]Josh. 22:4
10 [a]Rev. 14:13 [b]Gen. 2:2; Heb. 4:4
11 [a]2Pet. 2:6 [b]Heb. 3:18; 4:6
12 [a]Jer. 23:29; Eph. 5:26; Heb. 6:5; 1Pet. 1:23 [b]Acts 7:38 [c]1Thess. 2:13 [d]Eph. 6:17 [e]1Thess. 5:23 [f]John 12:48; 1Cor. 14:24f.
13 [a]2Chr. 16:9; Ps. 33:13-15 [b]Job 26:6

🔑 **3:12** See note on II Thess. 2:3.

14 Since then we have a great [a]high priest[749] who has [pfp] [b]passed through the heavens,[3772] Jesus [c]the Son[5207] of God,[2316] let us [psa]hold fast our [d]confession.[3671]

15 For we do not have [a]a high priest who cannot [ainf]sympathize[4834] with our weaknesses, but One who has been [pfpp] [b]tempted[3985] in all things as *we are, yet* [c]without sin.[266]

16 Let us therefore [a]draw near[4334] with [b]confidence to the throne of grace,[5485] that we may [aosb]receive mercy[1656] and may [aosb]find grace[5485] to help in time of need.

The Perfect High Priest

5 For every high priest[749] [a]taken from among men is appointed[2525] on behalf of men in [b]things pertaining to God, in order to [psa] [c]offer both gifts[1435] and sacrifices[2378] [d]for sins;[266]

2 [I][a]he can deal gently[3356] with the [b]ignorant[50] and [c]misguided, since he himself also is [II][d]beset with weakness;

3 and because of it he is obligated to [pinf]offer *sacrifices* [a]for sins, [b]as for the people, so also for himself.

4 And [a]no one takes the honor to himself, but *receives it* when he is [ppp]called by God, even [b]as Aaron was.

5 So also Christ [a]did not glorify[1392] Himself so as to [aifp]become a [b]high priest, but He who [apt] [c]said to Him,

"[d]THOU ART MY SON,
TODAY I HAVE BEGOTTEN[1080]
THEE";

6 just as He says also in another *passage,*

"[a]THOU ART A PRIEST FOREVER
ACCORDING[2596] TO [b]THE
ORDER[5010] OF
MELCHIZEDEK."

7 In the days of His flesh,[4561] [I][a]He [apt]offered up both prayers[1162] and supplications[2428] with [b]loud crying and tears to the One [c]able to [pinf]save[4982] Him [II]from death,[2288] and He [III]was [aptp]heard because of His [d]piety.[2124]

8 Although He was [a]a Son,[5207] He learned[3129] [b]obedience[5218] from the things which He suffered.

9 And having [aptp]been made [a]perfect,[5048] He became to all those who [ppt]obey[5219] Him the source[159] of eternal[166] salvation,[4991]

10 being [aptp]designated[4316] by God as [a]a high priest[749] according[2596] to [b]the order[5010] of Melchizedek.

11 Concerning [I]him we have much to say, and *it is* hard to explain, since you have [pfi]become dull of hearing.

12 For though [I]by this time[5550] you [ppt]ought to be teachers,[1320] you have need again for someone to [pinf]teach[1321] you [a]the [II][b]elementary principles[4747] of the [c]oracles[3051] of God, and you have [pfi]come to [ppt]need [d]milk[1051] and not solid food.

13 For everyone who [ppt]partakes[3348] *only* of milk[1051] is not accustomed to the word of righteousness,[1343] for he is a [a]babe.[3516]

14 But solid food is for [a]the mature,[5046] who because of practice have their senses[145] [pfpp] [b]trained to [c]discern[1253] good and evil.

The Peril of Falling Away

6 🔑 Therefore [apt] [a]leaving [b]the [I]elementary teaching about the [II]Christ, let us [psmp]press[5342] on to [III][c]maturity,[5047] not [ppt]laying again a foun-

14 [a]Heb. 2:17 [b]Eph. 4:10; Heb. 6:20; 8:1; 9:24 [c]Matt. 4:3; Heb. 1:2; 6:6; 7:3; 10:29 [d]Heb. 3:1
15 [a]Heb. 2:17 [b]Heb. 2:18 [c]2Cor. 5:21; Heb. 7:26
16 [a]Heb. 7:19 [b]Heb. 3:6

1 [a]Ex. 28:1 [b]Heb. 2:17 [c]Heb. 7:27; 8:3f.; 9:9; 10:11 [d]1Cor. 15:3; Heb. 7:27; 10:12
2 [I]Lit., *being able to* [II]Or, *subject to weakness* [a]Heb. 2:18; 4:15 [b]Eph. 4:18; Heb. 9:7 mg. [c]James 5:19; 1Pet. 2:25 [d]Heb. 7:28
3 [a]1Cor. 15:3; Heb. 7:27; 10:12 [b]Lev. 9:7; 16:6; Heb. 7:27; 9:7
4 [a]Num. 16:40; 18:7; 2Chr. 26:18 [b]Ex. 28:1; 1Chr. 23:13
5 [a]John 8:54 [b]Heb. 2:17; 5:10 [c]Heb. 1:1, 5 [d]Ps. 2:7
6 [a]Ps. 110:4; Heb. 7:17 [b]Heb. 5:10; 6:20; 7:11, 17
7 [I]Lit., *who having offered up* [II]Or, *out of* [III]Lit., *having been heard* [a]Matt. 26:39, 42, 44; Mark 14:36, 39; Luke 22:41, 44 [b]Matt. 27:46, 50; Mark 15:34, 37; Luke 23:46 [c]Mark 14:36 [d]Heb. 11:7; 12:28
8 [a]Heb. 1:2 [b]Phil. 2:8
9 [a]Heb. 2:10
10 [a]Heb. 2:17; 5:5 [b]Heb. 5:6
11 [I]Or, *Him or this*
12 [I]Lit., *because of the time* [II]Lit., *elements of the beginning* [a]Gal. 4:3 [b]Heb. 6:1 [c]Acts 7:38 [d]1Cor. 3:2; 1Pet. 2:2
13 [a]1Cor. 3:1; 14:20; 1Pet. 2:2
14 [a]1Cor. 2:6; Eph. 4:13; Heb. 6:1 [b]1Tim. 4:7 [c]Rom. 14:1ff.
1 [I]Lit., *word of the beginning* [II]I.e., Messiah [III]Or, *perfection* [a]Phil. 3:13f. [b]Heb. 5:12 [c]Heb. 5:14

🔑 **6:1-6** We should move forward to achieve the goal set for us by God (v. 1). That is the meaning of the word "maturity," *teleiotēs* (5047) from *telos* (5056), "goal, purpose."

We should not go back to the initial rudiments of Christianity and our basic faith (v. 2). We should not live in constant fear that we may lose our salvation and that we need to be regenerated again and again, i.e., "laying again a foundation."

The expression "it is impossible" is linked to the verb *anakainizein* (340), "to renew," in the infinitive

(continued on next page)

dation of repentance[3341] from [d]dead[3498] works[2041] and of faith[4102] toward God,
2 of [a]instruction[1322] about washings,[909] and [b]laying on of hands, and the [c]resurrection[386] of the dead, and [c]eternal[166] judgment.[2917]

1 [d]Heb. 9:14
2 [a]John 3:25; Acts 19:3f. [b]Acts 6:6 [c]Acts 17:31f.

(continued from previous page)

in v. 6. In the Greek text this expression is found in v. 4. Hence, the most important fact about his whole argument, the thing that is mentioned first, is that the whole idea is hypothetical. The author of Hebrews introduces his argument with a detailed description of the process of salvation. And having accepted, for the sake of argument, the supposition that one who has undergone this process might actually fall away, he proceeds to prove the impossibility of it.

In v. 3 "those who have once been enlightened" (*phōtisthentas,* 5461), or better still, "having been enlightened," is a participle in the passive voice, referring to those who were once enlightened by God Himself (Jn. 1:9). It was God who took the initiative to throw His light upon them. In the process of salvation, God always takes the initiative.

"And have tasted," (*geusamenous,* 1089) or better, "having tasted," is in the middle voice referring to people who, responding to the initiative of God, exercised their choice to taste the heavenly gift of God. This is the exact process of the Gospel: God offers salvation to us, but we must take the initiative to receive it (Jn. 1:12; 3:16).

In spite of the fact that to be saved we must receive the light which comes from God, nevertheless, we must not forget that salvation is always a gift and not anything to be earned by us. This is made explicitly clear by the fact that the Apostle refers to this offer as a gift (*dōrea,* 1431). Its derivation is from heaven. Other Greek words could have indicated the principle of a gift, but *dōrea* stresses the complimentary aspect of the gift which is offered. He could have used *dōron* (1435), "a gift," or *dōrēma* (1434), "gift, the result of giving." The gift was to be stressed. Lest salvation be thought of as something of earthly derivation, it is called "heavenly."

In vv. 4-6 the third participle, *genēthentas,* "have been made," or better still "having been made," indicates the result of man receiving God's free gift of salvation. "And have been made partakers of the Holy Spirit," the participle is the passive voice of *ginomai* (1096), "to be made," indicating that he who accepts God's free offer of salvation, by virtue of that reception is made a partaker of the Holy Spirit. The Holy Spirit comes to indwell and become a part of the believer, making the believer a possessor of the Holy Spirit. The aorist tense of *genēthentas* stresses the past divine action in making us partakers of the Holy Spirit. The Holy Spirit is mentioned in order to indicate to us that the whole process of revelation and conviction in salvation is based on the activity and energy of the Holy Spirit. (See notes on Mt. 12:31,32; Mk. 3:28,29; Lk. 12:10). "Have tasted the good word of God" (v. 5), the fourth participle *geusamenous,* "having tasted," is exactly like the second participle of v. 4 referring to the tasting of the heavenly gift. As in v. 4 it is also in the middle voice which places man as responding to God's Word. The Holy Spirit energizes man to receive God's Word as something that is good in itself.

It is not only God's Word that a person tastes as he is energized by the Holy Spirit, but also "the powers of the age to come" (v. 5). The word for "powers" is *dunameis* (1411), one of the words that is used in the N.T. to indicate miracles. He who is energized by the Holy Spirit and has received God's salvation comes to understand not only that God's Word (*rhēma,* 4487) is good (*kalon,* 2570), but also that God's future exercise of power is going to be for the benefit of the believer and not for his destruction.

"Have fallen," in v. 6 is translated from the participle *parapesontas* (3895). The word is made up of the preposition *para,* which means "besides, on the side," and the verb *piptō* (4098), "to fall." If a person has been enlightened by God and tasted His free heavenly gift of salvation; if the Holy Spirit has come to indwell him and he was made a possessor of the Holy Spirit; if he has thus understood God's Word and the future demonstration of God's power in the age to come as good—if he falls, what happens?

That the participle can be used to introduce a supposition is indisputable as one compares Mt. 16:25 which has an *apolesē,* "if he lose," and the parallel passage in Lk. 9:25 which has the participle *apolesas,* correctly translated as "if he lose."

We must go back now to the discussion of the phrase, "It is impossible to renew them again to repentance" (v. 6). The key to the understanding of this difficult passage is the meaning of the Greek infinitive *anakainizō* (340), "to renew." It is made up of the preposition *ana* (303), which means "again," and *kainizō* from *kainos* (2537), which means "new but qualitatively different." Therefore, *anakainizō* means to have a qualitatively new, different repentance.

Why is it impossible to have a qualitatively different or a new repentance? Because to have a

(continued on next page)

3 And this we shall do, [a]if God
[psa]permits.
4 For in the case of those who have
once been [aptp] [a]enlightened[5461] and have
[apt]tasted[1089] of [b]the heavenly gift and
have been [aptp]made [c]partakers[3353] of the
[an]Holy Spirit,[4151]
5 and [a]have [apt]tasted the good[2570]
[b]word[4487] of God and the powers[1411] of
[c]the age[165] to come,[3195]
6 and *then* have [apt]fallen away,[3895]
it is [a]impossible to [pinf]renew[340] them
again to repentance, [I][b]since they again
[ppt]crucify[388] to themselves the Son[5207]
of God,[2316] and put Him to open shame.
7 For ground[1093] that [apt]drinks the
rain which often [ppt] [I]falls upon it and
[ppt]brings forth vegetation useful[2111] to
those [a]for whose sake it is also tilled,
receives[3335] a blessing[2129] from God;
8 but if it [ppt]yields[1627] thorns and
thistles, it is worthless[96] and [a]close
[I]to being cursed,[2671] and [II]it ends[5056] up
being burned.

Better Things for You

9 But, [a]beloved, we are convinced
of better things concerning you, and
things that [I]accompany salvation,[4991]
though we are speaking in this way.
10 For [a]God is not unjust so as to
[ainf]forget [b]your work[2041] and the love[26]
which you have [aom]shown toward His
name, in having [apt] [c]ministered and in
still [ppt]ministering to the [I]saints.[40]
11 And we desire[1937] that each one
of you [pinf]show the same diligence
[I]so as to realize the [a]full assurance of
[b]hope[1680] until the end,[5056]
12 that you may not [aosb]be sluggish,[3576] but [a]imitators of those who
through [b]faith and patience [c]inherit[2816]
the promises.[1860]
13 For [a]when God [apt]made the
promise[1861] to Abraham, since He
[ipf]could [ainf]swear by[2596] no one greater,
He [ao] [b]swore by[2596] Himself,
14 saying, "[a]I WILL SURELY BLESS
YOU, AND I WILL SURELY MULTIPLY
YOU."
15 And thus, [a]having [apt]patiently
waited,[3114] he obtained the promise.

3 [a]Acts 18:21 **4** [a]2Cor. 4:4, 6; Heb. 10:32 [b]John 4:10; Eph. 2:8 [c]Gal. 3:2; Heb. 2:4 **5** [a]1Pet. 2:3 [b]Eph. 6:17 [c]Heb. 2:5 **6** [I]Or, *while* [a]Matt. 19:26; Heb. 10:26f.; 2Pet. 2:21; 1John 5:16 [b]Heb. 10:29 **7** [I]Lit., *comes* [a]2Tim. 2:6 **8** [I]Lit., *to a curse* [II]Lit., *its end is for burning* [a]Gen. 3:17f.; Deut. 29:22ff. **9** [I]Or, *belong to* [a]1Cor. 10:14; 2Cor. 7:1; 12:19; 1Pet. 2:11; 2Pet. 3:1; 1John 2:7; Jude 3 **10** [I]Or, *holy ones* [a]Prov. 19:17; Matt. 10:42; 25:40; Acts 10:4 [b]1Thess. 1:3 [c]Rom. 15:25; Heb. 10:32-34 **11** [I]Lit., *to the full* [a]Heb. 10:22 [b]Heb. 3:6 **12** [a]Heb. 13:7 [b]2Thess. 1:4; James 1:3; Rev. 13:10 [c]Heb. 1:14 **13** [a]Gal. 3:15, 18 [b]Gen. 22:16; Luke 1:73 **14** [a]Gen. 22:17 **15** [a]Gen. 12:4; 21:5

(continued from previous page)
different kind of repentance, it would be necessary for Jesus Christ to die again on the cross. According to the entire teaching of Hebrews (Heb. 9:28; 10:11,12), Jesus Christ died once and for all for man's sin. He cannot come back and die again in order to gain for us another redemption which will see us through this time.

Not only is it impossible to have Jesus Christ die again, but having failed to save to the end the ones who trusted in Him, it would cause His crucifixion on the cross to become as something to be ridiculed. It did not work; it was not sufficient.

This is what we call in philosophical language *reductio ad absurdum,* or reduction to an absurdity. From a false assumption we deduce absurd conclusions. It is false to suppose that we could fall, because that would invalidate the crucifixion of Christ on which our repentance was based if we were to be saved to the end. In order to have a lasting salvation it would be necessary for Christ to be recrucified which is an impossibility, for He died only once and for all. But it would also make His crucifixion be declared as ineffective. The great difficulty in this whole question is that we interpret our own "decision to follow Christ" as salvation per se. It is the second step toward salvation, the first having been the offer of that salvation by God through Christ in the convicting energy of the Holy Spirit. (See note on Mk. 3:28,29.) But our acceptance of God's offer of grace is not salvation. We are truly saved when God sees that our repentance of our sin is genuine and accepts us and makes us part of His body. Salvation presupposes truly genuine repentance on our part and such being accepted by God (Eph. 1:6). Therefore we should never speak of salvation as a decision of ours only, but rather as God's acceptance of a truly repentant sinner. If He accepts someone whom He is not able to keep to the very end, then Christ has failed. Only that decision which is man-initiated and constitutes merely man's emotion, and not God's acceptance of that decision, can be ineffective (II Thess. 2:13). See general remarks on I John and also notes on Gal. 1:8; I Tim. 4:1-3. For a thorough exegetical exposition of this passage, see *The Patience of Hope,* vol. III of the Editor's study on James.

16 [a]For men swear by[2596] one greater *than themselves*, and with them [b]an oath[3727] *given* as confirmation[951] is an end of every dispute.

17 [I]In the same way God, desiring even more to [ainf]show to [a]the heirs[2818] of the promise [b]the unchangeableness[276] of His purpose,[1012] [ao] [II]interposed[3315] with an oath,

18 in order that by two unchangeable[276] things, in which [a]it is impossible for God to [ainf]lie, we may [psa]have strong encouragement, we who have [apt]fled for refuge in laying [ainf]hold of [b]the hope[1680] set before us.

19 [I]This [a]hope we have as an anchor of the soul,[5590] a *hope* both sure and steadfast[949] and one which [ppt] [b]enters [II]within the veil,

20 [a]where Jesus has entered as a forerunner[4274] for us, having [apt]become a [b]high priest[749] forever[165] according to the order[5010] of Melchizedek.

Melchizedek's Priesthood Like Christ's

7 For this [a]Melchizedek, king of Salem, priest of the [b]Most High God, who [apt] met Abraham as he was returning from the slaughter of the kings[935] and [apt]blessed him,

2 to whom also Abraham [ao]apportioned a tenth part of all *the spoils*, was first of all, [ppp]by the translation[2059] *of his name*, king of righteousness,[1343] and then also king of Salem, which is king[935] of peace.[1515]

3 Without father, without mother, [a]without genealogy, having neither beginning of days nor end[5056] of life,[2222] but [pfpp]made like [b]the Son of God, he abides[3306] a priest perpetually.

4 Now [pim]observe[2334] how great this man was to whom Abraham, the [a]patriarch,[3966] [b]gave a tenth of the choicest spoils.

5 And those indeed[3303] of [a]the sons of Levi who [ppt]receive the priest's office[2405] have commandment [I]in the Law to collect [II]a tenth from the people, that is, from their brethren, although these [III]are [pfp]descended from Abraham.

6 But the one [a]whose genealogy[1075] is not traced from them [b]collected [I]a tenth from Abraham, and [pfi] [c]blessed the one who [c]had the promises.[1860]

7 But without any dispute the lesser is blessed by the greater.

8 And in this case mortal men receive tithes, but in that case one *receives them*, [a]of whom it is [ppp]witnessed that he lives[2198] on.

9 And, so to speak, through Abraham even Levi, who [ppt]received tithes, [pfip]paid tithes,

10 for he was still in the loins of his father when Melchizedek met him.

11 [a]Now if perfection[5050] was through the Levitical priesthood[2420] (for on the basis of it [b]the people [pfpp]received the Law), what further need *was there* for another priest[2409] to arise[450] [c]according to the order[5010] of Melchizedek, and not be [pip]designated according to the order of Aaron?

12 For when the priesthood is [ppp]changed, of necessity there takes place a change of law also.

13 For [a]the one concerning whom [b]these things are spoken [pfi]belongs[3348] to another tribe, from which no one has [pfi]officiated at the altar.

14 For it is evident that our Lord [I]was [pfi] [a]descended from Judah, a tribe with reference to which Moses [ao]spoke nothing concerning priests.

15 And this is clearer still, if another priest arises[450] according to the likeness[3665] of Melchizedek,

16 who has [pfi]become *such* not on the basis of a law[3551] of [a]physical[4559] requirement,[1785] but according to the power of [b]an indestructible life.[222]

17 For it is witnessed *of Him*,

"[a]THOU ART A PRIEST FOREVER
ACCORDING TO THE ORDER OF
MELCHIZEDEK."

18 For, on the one hand, there is a setting aside of a former commandment [a]because of its weakness[772] and uselessness

19 (for [a]the Law[3551] [ao]made nothing perfect),[5048] and on the other hand there

16 [a]Gal. 3:15 [b]Ex. 22:11
17 [I]Or, *Therefore God* [II]Or, *guaranteed* [a]Heb. 11:9 [b]Ps. 110:4; Prov. 19:21; Heb. 6:18
18 [a]Num. 23:19; Titus 1:2 [b]Heb. 3:6; 7:19
19 [I]Lit., *Which we have* [II]Or, *inside* [a]Ps. 39:7; 62:5; Acts 23:6; Rom. 4:18; 5:4, 5; 1Cor. 13:13; Col. 1:27; 1Pet. 1:3 [b]Lev. 16:2, 15; Heb. 9:3, 7
20 [a]John 14:2; Heb. 4:14 [b]Ps. 110:4; Heb. 2:17; 5:6

1 [a]Gen. 14:18-20; Heb. 7:6 [b]Mark 5:7
3 [a]Heb. 7:6 [b]Matt. 4:3; Heb. 7:1, 28
4 [a]Acts 2:29; 7:8f. [b]Gen. 14:20
5 [I]Lit., *according to* [II]Or, *tithes* [III]Lit., *have come out of the loins of* [a]Num. 18:21, 26; 2Chr. 31:4f.
6 [I]Or, *tithes* [a]Heb. 7:3 [b]Heb. 7:1f. [c]Rom. 4:13
8 [a]Heb. 5:6; 6:20
11 [a]Heb. 7:18f.; 8:7 [b]Heb. 9:6; 10:1 [c]Heb. 5:6; 7:17
13 [a]Heb. 7:14 [b]Heb. 7:11
14 [I]Lit., *rose from* [a]Num. 24:17; Is. 11:1; Mic. 5:2; Matt. 2:6; Rev. 5:5
16 [a]Heb. 9:10 [b]Heb. 9:14
17 [a]Ps. 110:4; Heb. 5:6; 6:20; 7:21
18 [a]Rom. 8:3; Gal. 3:21; Heb. 7:11
19 [a]Acts 13:39; Rom. 3:20; 7:7f.; Gal. 2:16; 3:21; Heb. 9:9; 10:1

is a bringing in of a better[2909] [b]hope,[1680] through which we [c]draw near[1448] to God.

20 And inasmuch as *it was* not without an oath

21 (for they indeed became priests without an oath,[3728] but He with an oath through the One who said to Him,

"[a]THE LORD HAS [ao]SWORN
AND [b]WILL NOT CHANGE HIS
MIND,[3338]
'THOU ART A PRIEST
[c]FOREVER' ");[165]

22 so much the more also Jesus has [pfi]become the [a]guarantee of [b]a better covenant.[1242]

23 And the *former* priests, on the one hand, existed in greater numbers, because they were [aid]prevented by death[2288] from [pinf]continuing,[3887]

24 but He, on the other hand, because He [aid]abides[3306] [a]forever,[165] holds His priesthood permanently.[531]

25 Hence, also, He is able to [pinf] [a]save[4982] [I]forever[3838] those who [ppt] [b]draw near to God through Him, since He always [ppt]lives to [c]make [aies]intercession for them.

26 For it was [ipf]fitting that we should have such a [a]high priest, [b]holy,[3741] [c]innocent,[172] undefiled,[283] [pfpp]separated from [art]sinners[268] and [apt] [d]exalted above the heavens;

27 who does not need daily, like those high priests, to [pinf] [a]offer up sacrifices,[2378] [b]first for His own sins,[266] and then for the *sins* of the people, because this He did [c]once for all when He [apt] [d]offered up[399] Himself.

28 For the Law appoints[2525] men as high priests [a]who are weak, but the word of the oath, which came after the Law, *appoints* [b]a Son, [pfpp] [c]made perfect[5048] forever.[165]

A Better Ministry

8 Now the main point in what has been said *is this*: we have such a [a]high priest, who has [ao]taken His seat at [b]the right hand[1188] of the throne of the [b]Majesty in the heavens,[3772]

2 a [a]minister[3011] [I]in the sanctuary,[39] and [I]in the [b]true[228] [II]tabernacle,[4633] which the Lord[2962] [ao] [c]pitched, not man.[444]

3 For every [a]high priest[749] is appointed[2525] [b]to [pinf]offer both gifts[1435] and sacrifices;[2378] hence it is necessary[316] that this *high priest* also have something to [aosb]offer.

4 Now if He were on earth,[1093] He would not be a priest at all, since there are those who [ppt] [a]offer the gifts according to the Law;[3551]

5 who serve[3000] [a]a copy and [b]shadow of the heavenly things, just as Moses [I]was [pfip] [c]warned[5537] *by God* when he was about to [pinf]erect[2005] the [II]tabernacle; for, "[d]SEE," He says, "THAT YOU MAKE all things ACCORDING TO THE PATTERN[5179] WHICH WAS [aptp]SHOWN YOU ON THE MOUNTAIN."

6 But now He has [pfi]obtained[5177] a more excellent[1313] ministry,[3009] by as much as He is also the [a]mediator[3316] of [b]a better[2909] covenant,[1242] which has been [pfip]enacted on better promises.[1860]

A New Covenant

7 For [a]if that first *covenant* had been faultless,[273] there would have been no occasion [ipf]sought for a second.

8 For finding fault with them, He says,

"[a]BEHOLD, DAYS ARE COMING,
SAYS THE LORD,
[I]WHEN I WILL EFFECT[4931]
[b]A NEW[2537] COVENANT
WITH THE HOUSE OF ISRAEL
AND WITH THE HOUSE OF
JUDAH;
9 [a]NOT LIKE THE COVENANT
WHICH I MADE WITH THEIR
FATHERS
ON THE DAY WHEN I [apt]TOOK
THEM BY THE HAND
TO [ainf]LEAD THEM OUT OF THE
LAND OF EGYPT;
FOR THEY DID NOT
CONTINUE[1696] IN MY
COVENANT,
AND I DID NOT [ao]CARE FOR
THEM, SAYS THE LORD.

19 [b]Heb. 3:6 [c]Lam. 3:57; Heb. 4:16; 7:25; 10:1, 22; James 4:8
21 [a]Ps. 110:4; Heb. 5:6; 7:17 [b]Num. 23:19; 1Sam. 15:29; Rom. 11:29 [c]Heb. 7:23f., 28
22 [a]Ps. 119:122; Is. 38:14 [b]Heb. 8:6
24 [a]Is. 9:7; John 12:34; Rom. 9:5; Heb. 7:23f., 28
25 [I]Or, *completely* [a]1Cor. 1:21 [b]Heb. 7:19 [c]Rom. 8:34; Heb. 9:24
26 [a]Heb. 2:17 [b]2Cor. 5:21; Heb. 4:15 [c]1Pet. 2:22 [d]Heb. 4:14
27 [a]Heb. 5:1 [b]Lev. 9:7; Heb. 5:3 [c]Heb. 9:12, 28; 10:10 [d]Eph. 5:2; Heb. 9:14, 28; 10:10, 12
28 [a]Heb. 5:2 [b]Heb. 1:2 [c]Heb. 2:10

1 [a]Col. 3:1; Heb. 2:17; 3:1 [b]Ps. 110:1; Heb. 1:3
2 [I]Or, *of* [II]Or, *sacred tent* [a]Heb. 10:11 [b]Heb. 9:11, 24 [c]Ex. 33:7
3 [a]Heb. 2:17 [b]Rom. 4:25; 5:6, 8; Gal. 2:20; Eph. 5:2; Heb. 5:1; 8:4
4 [a]Heb. 5:1; 7:27; 8:3; 9:9; 10:11
5 [I]Lit., *is* [II]Or, *sacred tent* [a]Heb. 9:23 [b]Col. 2:17; Heb. 10:1 [c]Matt. 2:12; Heb. 11:7; 12:25 [d]Ex. 25:40
6 [a]1Tim. 2:5 [b]Luke 22:20; Heb. 7:22; 8:8; 9:15; 12:24
7 [a]Heb. 7:11
8 [I]Lit., *And* [a]Jer. 31:31 [b]Luke 22:20; 2Cor. 3:6; Heb. 7:22; 8:6, 13; 9:15; 12:24
9 [a]Ex. 19:5; 24:6-8; Deut. 5:2, 3; Jer. 31:32

10 "[a]FOR THIS IS THE COVENANT
THAT I WILL MAKE[1303] WITH
THE HOUSE OF ISRAEL
AFTER THOSE DAYS, SAYS THE
LORD:
I WILL [ppt]PUT MY LAWS[3551] INTO
THEIR MINDS,[1271]
AND I WILL WRITE[1924] THEM
[b]UPON THEIR HEARTS.[2588]
AND I WILL BE THEIR GOD,[2316]
AND THEY SHALL BE MY
PEOPLE.[2992]

11 "[a]AND THEY SHALL NOT
TEACH[1321] EVERYONE HIS
FELLOW CITIZEN,
AND EVERYONE HIS BROTHER,[80]
SAYING, [aim]'KNOW[1097] THE
LORD,'[2962]
FOR [b]ALL SHALL KNOW[1492] ME,
FROM THE LEAST TO THE
GREATEST OF THEM.

12 "[a]FOR I WILL BE MERCIFUL[2436]
TO THEIR INIQUITIES,[93]
[b]AND I WILL [efn]REMEMBER
THEIR SINS[266] NO MORE."

13 [I]When He said, "[a]A new[2537] *covenant*," He has made the first [pfi]obsolete.[3822] [b]But whatever is [ppp]becoming obsolete[3822] and [ppt]growing old[1095] is [II]ready to disappear.

The Old and the New

9 Now even[3303] the first *covenant* [ipf]had [a]regulations[1345] of divine worship[2999] and [b]the earthly[2886] sanctuary.[39]

2 For there was [a]a [I]tabernacle[4633] [aop]prepared, the [II]outer one, in which *were* [b]the lampstand[3087] and [c]the table and [d]the [III]sacred bread;[4286] this is called the holy place.[39]

3 And behind [a]the second veil, there was a [I]tabernacle which is called the [b]Holy of Holies,[39]

4 having a golden [Ia]altar of incense and [b]the ark of the covenant [pfpp]covered on all sides with gold, in which *was* [c]a golden jar holding the manna,[3131] and [d]Aaron's rod which [apt]budded, and [e]the tables of the covenant.[1242]

5 And above it *were* the [a]cherubim[5502] of glory[1391] [b]overshadowing the mercy seat;[2435] but of these things we cannot now [pinf]speak in detail.[2596]

6 Now when these things have been thus [pfpp]prepared, the priests [a]are continually entering the [I]outer [II]tabernacle, performing[2005] the divine worship,[2999]

7 but into [a]the second only [b]the high priest *enters*, [c]once a year, [d]not without *taking* blood,[129] which he [e]offers for himself and for the [If]sins[51] of the people[2992] committed in ignorance.

8 [a]The Holy Spirit *is* [ppt]signifying this, [b]that the way into the holy place[39] has not yet been [pfin]disclosed,[5319] while the [I]outer tabernacle is still standing,[4714]

9 which *is* a symbol[3850] for the present time. Accordingly [a]both gifts[1435] and sacrifices[2378] are offered which [b]cannot make the worshiper[3000] [ainf]perfect[5048] in conscience,[4893]

10 since they *relate* only to [a]food and [b]drink and various[1313] [c]washings,[909] [d]regulations[1345] for the [I]body[4561] [ppt]imposed until [e]a time[2540] of reformation.[1357]

11 But when Christ[5547] [apt]appeared *as* a [a]high priest[749] of the [b]good things[18] [I]to come, *He entered* through [c]the greater and more perfect[5046] [II]tabernacle,[4633] [d]not made with hands, that is to say, [e]not of this creation;[2937]

12 and not through [a]the blood[129] of goats and calves, but [b]through His own blood, He [c]entered the holy place[39] [d]once for all, [I]having [apt]obtained [e]eternal[166] redemption.[3085]

13 For if [a]the blood[129] of goats and bulls and [b]the ashes of a heifer sprinkling[4472] those who have been defiled,[2840] sanctify[37] for the [I]cleansing[2514] of the flesh,[4561]

14 how much more will [a]the blood[129] of Christ,[5547] who through [Ib]the eternal Spirit[4151] [ao] [c]offered Himself without

10 [a]Jer. 31:33; Rom. 11:27; Heb. 10:16 [b]2Cor. 3:3
11 [a]Jer. 31:34 [b]Is. 54:13; John 6:45; 1John 2:27
12 [a]Is. 43:25; Jer. 31:34; 50:20; Mic. 7:18, 19 [b]Heb. 10:17
13 [I]Or, *In His saying* [II]Or, *near* [a]Luke 22:20; 2Cor. 3:6; Heb. 7:22; 8:6, 8; 9:15; 12:24 [b]2Cor. 5:17; Heb. 1:11

1 [a]Heb. 9:10 [b]Ex. 25:8; Heb. 8:2; 9:11, 24
2 [I]Or, *sacred tent* [II]Lit., *first* [III]Lit., *loaves of presentation* [a]Ex. 25:8, 9; 26:1-30 [b]Ex. 25:31-39 [c]Ex. 25:23-29 [d]Ex. 25:30; Lev. 24:5ff.; Matt. 12:4
3 [I]Or, *sacred tent* [a]Ex. 26:31-33; 40:3 [b]Ex. 26:33
4 [I]Or, *censer* [a]Ex. 30:1-5; 37:25f. [b]Ex. 25:10ff.; 37:1ff. [c]Ex. 16:32f. [d]Num. 17:10 [e]Ex. 25:16; 31:18; 32:15; Deut. 9:9, 11, 15; 10:3-5
5 [a]Ex. 25:18ff. [b]Ex. 25:17, 20; Lev. 16:2; 1Kin. 8:7
6 [I]Lit., *first* [II]Or, *sacred tent* [a]Num. 18:2-6; 28:3
7 [I]Lit., *ignorance of the people* [a]Heb. 9:3 [b]Lev. 16:12ff. [c]Ex. 30:10; Lev. 16:34; Heb. 10:3 [d]Lev. 16:11, 14 [e]Heb. 5:3 [f]Num. 15:25; Heb. 5:2
8 [I]Lit., *first* [a]Heb. 3:7 [b]John 14:6; Heb. 10:20
9 [a]Heb. 5:1 [b]Heb. 7:19
10 [I]Lit., *flesh* [a]Lev. 11:2ff.; Col. 2:16 [b]Num. 6:3 [c]Lev. 11:25; Num. 19:13; Mark 7:4 [d]Heb. 7:16 [e]Heb. 7:12

11 [I]Some ancient mss. read *that have come* [II]Or, *sacred tent* [a]Heb. 2:17 [b]Heb. 10:1 [c]Heb. 8:2; 9:24 [d]Mark 14:58; 2Cor. 5:1 [e]2Cor. 4:18; Heb. 12:27; 13:14
12 [I]Or, *obtaining* [a]Lev. 4:3; 16:6, 15; Heb. 9:19 [b]Heb. 9:14; 13:12 [c]Heb. 9:24 [d]Heb. 7:27 [e]Heb. 5:9; 9:15
13 [I]Lit., *purity* [a]Lev. 16:15; Heb. 9:19; 10:4 [b]Num. 19:9, 17f. **14** [I]Or, His *eternal spirit* [a]Heb. 9:12; 13:12 [b]1Cor. 15:45; 1Pet. 3:18 [c]Eph. 5:2; Heb. 7:27; 10:10, 12

blemish[299] to God, [d]cleanse[2511] [II]your conscience[4893] from [e]dead[3498] works[2041] to [aies]serve[3000] [f]the living[2198] God?[2316]

15 And for this reason [a]He is the [b]mediator[3316] of a [c]new[2537] covenant,[1242] in order that since a death[2288] has taken place for the redemption[629] of the transgressions[3847] that were *committed* under the first covenant, those who have been [d]called[2564] may [aosb] [e]receive the promise[1860] of [f]the eternal[166] inheritance.[2817]

16 For where a [I]covenant is, there must of necessity [II]be[5342] the death of the one who made it.[1303]

17 For a [I]covenant[1242] is valid[949] *only* when [II]men are dead, [III]for it is never in force[2480] while the one who made it lives.[2198]

18 Therefore even the first *covenant* was not [pfip]inaugurated[1457] without blood.[129]

19 For when every commandment had been [a]spoken by Moses to all the people[2992] according to the Law,[3551] [b]he [apt]took the [c]blood[129] of the calves and the goats, with [d]water and scarlet wool and hyssop,[5301] and sprinkled[4472] both [e]the book itself and all the people,

20 saying, "[a]THIS IS THE BLOOD OF THE COVENANT WHICH GOD [ao]COMMANDED YOU."

21 And in the same way he [a]sprinkled[4472] both the [I]tabernacle[4633] and all the vessels of the ministry[3009] with the blood.

22 And according to the [I]Law, *one may* [a]almost *say,* all things are cleansed[2511] with blood, and [b]without shedding of blood[130] there is no forgiveness.[859]

23 Therefore it was necessary for the [a]copies of the things in the heavens[3772] to be [pip]cleansed[2511] with these, but [a]the heavenly things themselves with better sacrifices than these.

🔑 24 For Christ [a]did not [ao]enter a holy place[39] made with hands, a *mere* copy[499] of [b]the true[228] one, but into [c]heaven[3772] itself, now [d]to [aifp]appear in the presence of God for us;

25 nor was it that He should offer Himself often, as [a]the high priest enters [b]the holy place[39] [a]year by year with blood[129] not his own.[245]

🔑 26 Otherwise, He would have needed to [ainf]suffer often since [a]the foundation of the world;[2889] but now [b]once at [c]the consummation[4930] of the ages[165] He has been [pfip] [d]manifested[5319] to put away sin[266] [I][e]by the sacrifice[2378] of Himself.

27 And inasmuch as [a]it is [I]appointed for men[444] to [ainf]die[599] once and after this [b]*comes* judgment,[2920]

🔑 28 so Christ[5547] also, having been [aptp] [a]offered once to [aies] [b]bear[399] the [an]sins of many, shall appear [c]a second time for [d]salvation[4991] [e]without *reference to* sin, to those who [ppt] [f]eagerly await[553] Him.

One Sacrifice of Christ Is Sufficient

10 For the Law,[3551] since it has *only* [a]a shadow of [b]the good things[18] to come[3195] *and* not the very [I]form[1504] of things, [II]can [c]never by the same sacrifices[2378] year by year, which they offer continually, [d]make [ainf]perfect[5048] those who draw near.

2 Otherwise, would they not have [aom]ceased to be [ppp]offered, because the worshipers,[3000] having once been [pfpp]cleansed,[2508] would no longer have had [a]consciousness[4893] of sins?[266]

3 But [a]in [I]those *sacrifices* there is a reminder[364] of sins year by year.

4 For it is [a]impossible for the [b]blood[129] of bulls and goats to [pinf]take away sins.

14 [II]Some ancient mss. read *our* [d]Acts 15:9; Titus 2:14; Heb. 1:3; 10:2, 22 [e]Heb. 6:1 [f]Matt. 16:16; Heb. 3:12
15 [a]Rom. 3:24 [b]1Tim. 2:5; Heb. 8:6; 12:24 [c]Heb. 8:8 [d]Matt. 22:3ff.; Rom. 8:28f.; Heb. 3:1 [e]Heb. 6:15; 10:36; 11:39 [f]Acts 20:32
16 [I]Or, *testament* [II]Lit., *be brought*
17 [I]V. 16, note 1 [II]Lit., *over the dead* [III]Some ancient mss. read *for is it then . . . lives?*
19 [a]Heb. 1:1 [b]Ex. 24:6ff. [c]Heb. 9:12 [d]Lev. 14:4, 7; Num. 19:6, 18 [e]Ex. 24:7
20 [a]Ex. 24:8; Matt. 26:28
21 [I]Or, *sacred tent* [a]Ex. 24:6; 40:9; Lev. 8:15, 19; 16:14-16
22 [I]Or, *Law, almost all things* [a]Lev. 5:11f. [b]Lev. 17:11
23 [a]Heb. 8:5
24 [a]Heb. 4:14; 9:12 [b]Heb. 8:2 [c]Heb. 9:12 [d]Matt. 18:10; Heb. 7:25
25 [a]Heb. 9:7 [b]Heb. 9:2; 10:19
26 [I]Or, *by His sacrifice* [a]Matt. 25:34; Heb. 4:3 [b]Heb. 7:27; 9:12 [c]Matt. 13:39; Heb. 1:2 [d]1John 3:5, 8 [e]Heb. 9:12, 14
27 [I]Lit., *laid up* [a]Gen. 3:19 [b]2Cor. 5:10; 1John 4:17
28 [a]Heb. 7:27 [b]Is. 53:12; 1Pet. 2:24 [c]Acts 1:11 [d]Heb. 5:9 [e]Heb. 4:15 [f]1Cor. 1:7; Titus 2:13

1 [I]Lit., *image* [II]Some ancient mss. read *they can* [a]Heb. 8:5 [b]Heb. 9:11 [c]Rom. 8:3; Heb. 9:9; 10:4, 11 [d]Heb. 7:19
2 [a]1Pet. 2:19
3 [I]Lit., *them there is* [a]Heb. 9:7
4 [a]Heb. 10:1, 11 [b]Heb. 9:12f.

🔑 **9:24** See note on I Pet. 3:20,21.
🔑 **9:26,28** See note on Rom. 3:25.
🔑 **9:28** See note on Heb. 6:1-6.

5 Therefore, [a]when He comes into
the world, He says,
"[b]SACRIFICE AND OFFERING[4376]
THOU HAST NOT
[ao]DESIRED,[2309]
BUT [c]A BODY[4983] THOU HAST
[aom]PREPARED[2675] FOR ME;
6 [a]IN WHOLE BURNT OFFERINGS
AND *sacrifices* FOR SIN THOU
HAST TAKEN NO
[ao]PLEASURE.[2106]
7 "[a]THEN I SAID, 'BEHOLD, I HAVE
COME
(IN [b]THE ROLL OF THE BOOK IT
IS WRITTEN OF ME)
TO [infg]DO THY WILL,[2307] O
GOD.' "
8 After saying above,[511] "[a]SACRI-
FICES AND OFFERINGS AND [b]WHOLE
BURNT OFFERINGS AND *sacrifices* [c]FOR
SIN THOU HAST NOT DESIRED, NOR
HAST THOU TAKEN PLEASURE *in them*"
(which are offered according to the
Law),[3551]
9 then He said, "[a]BEHOLD, I HAVE
COME TO DO THY WILL." He takes away
the first in order to [aosb]establish the second.
🔑 10 By [l]this will we have been
[a]sanctified[37] through [b]the offering of
[c]the body of Jesus Christ[5547] [d]once for
all.
🔑 11 And every priest[2409] stands daily
ministering[3008] and [a]offering time after
time the same sacrifices, which [b]can
never [ainf]take away[4014] sins;
12 but He, having [apt]offered one
sacrifice[2378] [a]for [l]sins[266] [b]for all time,[1336]
[c]SAT DOWN AT THE RIGHT HAND[1188] OF
GOD,
13 [ppt]waiting[1551] from that time onward [a]UNTIL HIS ENEMIES BE [asbp]MADE
A FOOTSTOOL FOR HIS FEET.
14 For by one offering[4376] He has
[pfi] [a]perfected[5048] [b]for all time those who
are [ppp] [l]sanctified.
15 And [a]the Holy Spirit[4151] also
bears witness[3140] to us; for after [aime]say-
ing,

5 [a]Heb. 1:6 [b]Ps. 40:6 [c]Heb. 2:14; 5:7; 1Pet. 2:24
6 [a]Ps. 40:6
7 [a]Ps. 40:7, 8 [b]Ezra 6:2; Jer. 36:2; Ezek. 2:9; 3:1f.
8 [a]Ps. 40:6; Heb. 10:5f. [b]Mark 12:33 [c]Rom. 8:3
9 [a]Ps. 40:7, 8; Heb. 10:7
10 [l]Lit., *which* [a]John 17:19; Eph. 5:26; Heb. 2:11; 10:14, 29; 13:12 [b]John 6:51; Eph. 5:2; Heb. 7:27; 9:14, 28; 10:12 [c]Heb. 2:14; 5:7; 1Pet. 2:24 [d]Heb. 7:27
11 [a]Heb. 5:1 [b]Mic. 6:6-8; Heb. 10:1, 4
12 [l]Or, *sins, forever sat down* [a]Heb. 5:1 [b]Heb. 10:14 [c]Ps. 110:1; Heb. 1:3
13 [a]Ps. 110:1; Heb. 1:13
14 [l]Or, *being sanctified* [a]Heb. 10:1 [b]Heb. 10:12
15 [a]Heb. 3:7
16 [a]Jer. 31:33; Heb. 8:10
17 [a]Jer. 31:34; Heb. 8:12
19 [a]Heb. 3:6; 10:35 [b]Heb. 9:25
20 [a]Heb. 9:8 [b]Heb. 6:19; 9:3
21 [a]Heb. 2:17 [b]1Tim. 3:15; Heb. 3:6
22 [l]Lit., *true* [a]Heb. 7:19; 10:1 [b]Heb. 6:11 [c]Ezek. 36:25; Heb. 9:19; 12:24; 1Pet. 1:2 [d]Acts 22:16; 1Cor. 6:11; Eph. 5:26; Titus 3:5; 1Pet. 3:21
23 [a]Heb. 3:1 [b]Heb. 3:6 [c]1Cor. 1:9; 10:13; Heb. 11:11
24 [a]Heb. 13:1 [b]Titus 3:8
25 [a]Acts 2:42 [b]Heb. 3:13 [c]1Cor. 3:13

16 "[a]THIS IS THE COVENANT[1242]
THAT I WILL MAKE[1303] WITH
THEM
AFTER THOSE DAYS, SAYS THE
LORD:
I WILL [ppt]PUT MY LAWS UPON
THEIR HEART,[2588]
AND UPON THEIR MIND[1271] I
WILL WRITE[1924] THEM,"
He then says,
17 "[a]AND THEIR SINS[266] AND THEIR
LAWLESS DEEDS[458]
I WILL REMEMBER NO
MORE."
18 Now where there is forgive-
ness[859] of these things, there is no
longer *any* offering for sin.

A New and Living Way

19 Since therefore, brethren,[80]
we [a]have confidence to [b]enter the
holy place[39] by the blood[129] of
Jesus,
20 by [a]a new and living[2198] way[3598]
which He inaugurated[1457] for us through
[b]the veil, that is, His flesh,
21 and since *we have* [a]a great priest
[b]over the house of God,
22 let us [psa] [a]draw near[4334] with
a [l]sincere[228] heart[2588] in [b]full assurance of faith,[4102] having our hearts
[pfpp] [c]sprinkled[4472] *clean* from
an evil[4190] conscience[4893] and our
bodies [pfpp] [d]washed with pure[2513] water.
23 Let us [psa]hold fast[2722] the
[a]confession[3671] of our [b]hope[1680] without
wavering, for [c]He who [apt]promised[1861]
is faithful;[4103]
24 and let us [psa]consider[2657] how
[a]to stimulate[2948] one another to love[26]
and [b]good[2570] deeds,[2041]
25 not [ppt]forsaking[1459] our own [a]as-
sembling together,[1997] as is the habit
of some, but [b]encouraging[3870] *one another*; and all the more, as you see
[c]the day drawing near.

🔑 **10:10** See note on Rom. 3:25.
🔑 **10:11,12** See note on Heb. 6:1-6.

Christ or Judgment

🔑 **26** For if we go on [ppt] [a]sinning[264] willfully after [aime]receiving [b]the knowledge[1922] of the truth,[225] there no longer remains a sacrifice for sins,[266]

27 but a certain terrifying expectation[1561] of [a]judgment,[2920] and [b]THE FURY OF A FIRE WHICH WILL [pinf]CONSUME THE ADVERSARIES.

28 [a]Anyone who has [apt]set aside the Law[3551] of Moses dies[599] without mercy3628 on *the testimony of* two or three witnesses.[3144]

29 [a]How much severer5501 punishment[5098] do you think he will deserve [b]who has [apt]trampled under foot the Son[5207] of God,[2316] and has [apt]regarded as unclean[2839] [c]the blood[129] of the covenant[1242] [d]by which he was sanctified, and has [apt] [e]insulted the Spirit[4151] of grace?[5485]

30 For we know[1492] Him who said, "[a]VENGEANCE[1557] IS MINE, I WILL REPAY." And again, "[b]THE LORD[2962] WILL JUDGE[2919] HIS PEOPLE."[2992]

31 It is a [a]terrifying thing to [ainf]fall into the hands of the [b]living[2198] God.

32 But remember [a]the former days, [I]when, after being [aptp] [b]enlightened,[5461] you endured a great [c]conflict of sufferings,

33 partly, by being [ppp] [a]made a public spectacle2301 through reproaches and tribulations, and partly by [aptp]becoming [b]sharers[2844] with those who were so [ppt]treated.

🔑 34 For you [ao] [a]showed sympathy[4834] to the prisoners, and [ao]accepted[4327] [b]joyfully the seizure[724] of your property, knowing that you have for yourselves [c]a better[2909] possession5223 and an abiding[3306] one.

35 Therefore, do not [aosi]throw away your [a]confidence, which has a great [b]reward.[3405]

36 For you have need of [a]endurance, so that when you have [apt] [b]done the will[2307] of God, you may [c]receive [I]what was promised.[1860]

37 [a]FOR YET IN A VERY LITTLE
WHILE,
[b]HE WHO IS [ppt]COMING WILL
COME, AND WILL NOT DELAY.

38 [a]BUT MY RIGHTEOUS[1342] ONE
SHALL LIVE[2198] BY FAITH;[4102]
AND IF HE [asbm]SHRINKS BACK,
MY SOUL[5590] HAS NO
PLEASURE[2106] IN HIM.

39 But [I]we are not of those who shrink back to destruction,[684] but of those who have faith[4102] to the [II]preserving4047 of the soul.[5590]

The Triumphs of Faith

11 Now faith[4102] is the [Ia]assurance[5287] of *things* [ppp] [b]hoped for,[1679] the [II]conviction[1650] of [c]things not [ppp]seen.

2 For by it the [a]men of old[4245] [aop] [Ib]gained approval.[3140]

3 By faith we understand[3539] that the [Ia]worlds[165] were prepared[2675] [b]by the word[4487] of God,[2316] so that what is [ppp]seen [c]was not [pfi]made[1096] out of things which are [ppp]visible.

4 By faith [a]Abel [ao]offered to God a better sacrifice[2378] than Cain, through which he [aop] [b]obtained the testimony that he was righteous,[1342] God testifying [I]about his [c]gifts,[1435] and through [II]faith, though [d]he is [apt]dead,[599] he still speaks.[2980]

5 By faith [a]Enoch was [aop]taken up3346 so that he should not [infg] [b]see[1492] death;[2288] AND HE WAS NOT [ipf]FOUND[2147] BECAUSE GOD [ao]TOOK HIM UP; for he obtained the [pfip]witness[3140] that before his being taken up he was [pfin]pleasing[2100] to God.

6 And without faith it is impossible to [ainf]please *Him,* for he who [ppt] [a]comes to[4334] God must [ainf]believe[4100] that He is, and *that* He is a rewarder[3406] of those who [ppt]seek Him.

26 [a]Num. 15:30; Heb. 6:4-8; 2Pet. 2:20f. [b]1Tim. 2:4
27 [a]John 5:29; Heb. 9:27 [b]Is. 26:11; 2Thess. 1:7
28 [a]Deut. 17:2-6; 19:15; Matt. 18:16; Heb. 2:2
29 [a]Heb. 2:3 [b]Heb. 6:6 [c]Ex. 24:8; Matt. 26:28; Heb. 13:20 [d]Eph. 5:26; Heb. 9:13f.; Rev. 1:5 [e]1Cor. 6:11; Eph. 4:30; Heb. 6:4
30 [a]Deut. 32:35; Rom. 12:19 [b]Deut. 32:36
31 [a]2Cor. 5:11 [b]Matt. 16:16; Heb. 3:12
32 [I]Lit., *in which* [a]Heb. 5:12 [b]Heb. 6:4 [c]Phil. 1:30
33 [a]1Cor. 4:9; Heb. 12:4 [b]Phil. 4:14; 1Thess. 2:14
34 [a]Heb. 13:3 [b]Matt. 5:12 [c]Heb. 9:15; 11:16; 13:14; 1Pet. 1:4f.
35 [a]Heb. 10:19 [b]Heb. 2:2
36 [I]Lit., *the promise* [a]Luke 21:19; Heb. 12:1 [b]Mark 3:35 [c]Heb. 9:15
37 [a]Hab. 2:3; Heb. 10:25; Rev. 22:20 [b]Matt. 11:3
38 [a]Hab. 2:4; Rom. 1:17; Gal. 3:11
39 [I]Lit., *we are not of shrinking back . . . but of faith* [II]Or, *possessing*

1 [I]Or, *substance* [II]Or, *evidence* [a]Heb. 3:14 [b]Heb. 3:6 [c]Rom. 8:24; 2Cor. 4:18; 5:7; Heb. 11:7, 27
2 [I]Lit., *obtained a testimony* [a]Heb. 1:1 [b]Heb. 11:4, 39
3 [I]Lit., *ages* [a]John 1:3; Heb. 1:2 [b]Gen. ch. 1; Ps. 33:6, 9; Heb. 6:5; 2Pet. 3:5 [c]Rom. 4:17

4 [I]I.e., by receiving his gifts [II]Lit., *it* [a]Gen. 4:4; Matt. 23:35; 1John 3:12 [b]Heb. 11:2 [c]Heb. 5:1 [d]Gen. 4:8-10; Heb. 12:24 **5** [a]Gen. 5:21-24 [b]Luke 2:26; John 8:51; Heb. 2:9 **6** [a]Heb. 7:19

🔑 **10:26** See note on Js. 2:12,13.
🔑 **10:34** See notes on Rev. 4; I Thess. 4:17.

7 By faith [a]Noah, [aptp]being [b]warned *by God*[5337] about [c]things not yet [ppp]seen, [I][d]in [apt]reverence[2125] [e]prepared an ark for the salvation[4991] of his household, by which he condemned[2632] the world,[2889] and became an heir[2818] of [f]the righteousness[1243] which is according to faith.

8 By faith [a]Abraham, when he was [ppp]called, [ao]obeyed[5219] by [ainf]going out to a place which he [ipf]was to [pinf][b]receive for an inheritance;[2817] and he [ao]went out, not knowing where he was going.

9 By faith he lived[3939] as an alien in [a]the land of promise, as in a foreign[245] *land,* [apt][b]dwelling in tents[4633] with Isaac and Jacob, [c]fellow heirs[4789] of the same promise;[1860]

10 for he was [ipf]looking for[1551] [a]the city which has [b]foundations, [c]whose architect[5079] and builder[1217] is God.[2316]

11 By faith even [a]Sarah herself received [I]ability to conceive,[2602] even beyond[3844] the proper time of life, since she considered Him [b]faithful[4103] who had [apt]promised;[1861]

12 therefore, also, there was born of one man, and [a]him as good as [pfpp]dead[3499] [I]at that, *as many descendants* [b]AS THE STARS[3772] OF HEAVEN IN NUMBER, AND INNUMERABLE AS THE SAND WHICH IS BY THE SEASHORE.

13 [a]All these died[599] in faith,[4102] [b]without receiving the promises,[1860] but [c]having seen them and having [apt]welcomed them from a distance, and [d]having [apt]confessed[3670] that they were strangers[3581] and exiles[3927] on the earth.[1093]

14 For those who [ppp]say such things make it clear that they are seeking a country of their own.

15 And indeed if they had been [ipf] [I]thinking of that *country* from which they went out, [a]they would have had opportunity to [ainf]return.

16 But as it is, they desire a better[2909] *country,* that is a [a]heavenly one. Therefore [b]God is not [I]ashamed to be [c]called their God;[2316] for [d]He has [ao]prepared a city for them.

17 By faith [a]Abraham, when he was [ppp]tested,[3985] offered up[4374] Isaac; and he who had [apt] [b]received[324] the promises was offering up his only begotten[3439] *son;*

18 *it was he* to whom it was said, "[a]IN ISAAC YOUR [I]DESCENDANTS SHALL BE CALLED."

19 [I]He [apt]considered[3049] that [a]God is able to [pinf]raise[1453] *men* even from the dead;[3498] from which he also [aom]received him back [II]as a [b]type.[3850]

20 By faith [a]Isaac blessed[2127] Jacob and Esau, even regarding things to come.

21 By faith [a]Jacob, as he was [ppt]dying, blessed each of the sons of Joseph, and [b]worshiped, *leaning* on the top of his staff.

22 By faith [a]Joseph, when he was [ppt]dying, made mention of the exodus of the sons of Israel, and gave orders concerning his bones.

23 By faith [a]Moses, when he was born, was hidden for three months by his parents,[3962] because they saw he was a beautiful[791] child; and they were not afraid[5399] of the [b]king's edict.[1297]

24 By faith Moses, [a]when he had grown up, refused[720] to be called the son of Pharaoh's daughter;

25 choosing[138] rather to [a]endure ill-treatment with the people[2992] of God, than to enjoy the passing pleasures of sin;[266]

26 [apt] [a]considering the reproach of [I]Christ[5547] greater riches than the treasures of Egypt; for he was [ipf]looking[578] to the [b]reward.[3405]

27 By faith he [a]left Egypt, not [apt] [b]fearing[5399] the wrath[2372] of the king; for he endured,[2594] as [c]seeing Him who is unseen.

🔑 28 By faith he [a]kept the

7 [I]Lit., *having become reverent* [a]Gen. 6:13-22 [b]Heb. 8:5 [c]Heb. 11:1 [d]Heb. 5:7 [e]1Pet. 3:20 [f]Gen. 6:9; Ezek. 14:14, 20; Rom. 4:13; 9:30
8 [a]Gen. 12:1-4; Acts 7:2-4 [b]Gen. 12:7
9 [a]Acts 7:5 [b]Gen. 12:8; 13:3, 18; 18:1, 9 [c]Heb. 6:17
10 [a]Heb. 12:22; 13:14 [b]Rev. 21:14ff. [c]Heb. 11:16
11 [I]Lit., *power for the laying down of seed* [a]Gen. 17:19; 18:11-14; 21:2 [b]Heb. 10:23
12 [I]Lit., *in these things* [a]Rom. 4:19 [b]Gen. 15:5; 22:17; 32:12
13 [a]Matt. 13:17 [b]Heb. 11:39 [c]John 8:56; Heb. 11:27 [d]Gen. 23:4; 47:9; 1Chr. 29:15; Ps. 39:12; Eph. 2:19; 1Pet. 1:1; 2:11
15 [I]Or, *remembering* [a]Gen. 24:6-8
16 [I]Lit., *ashamed of them, to be* [a]2Tim. 4:18 [b]Mark 8:38; Heb. 2:11 [c]Gen. 26:24; 28:13; Ex. 3:6, 15; 4:5 [d]Heb. 11:10; Rev. 21:2
17 [a]Gen. 22:1-10; James 2:21 [b]Heb. 11:13
18 [I]Lit., *seed* [a]Gen. 21:12; Rom. 9:7
19 [I]Lit., *Considering* [II]Or, *figuratively speaking;* lit., *in a parable* [a]Rom. 4:21 [b]Heb. 9:9
20 [a]Gen. 27:27-29, 39f.
21 [a]Gen. 48:1, 5, 16, 20 [b]Gen. 47:31; 1Kin. 1:47
22 [a]Gen. 50:24f.; Ex. 13:19
23 [a]Ex. 2:2 [b]Ex. 1:16, 22

24 [a]Ex. 2:10, 11ff. **25** [a]Heb. 11:37 **26** [I]I.e., the Messiah [a]Luke 14:33; Phil. 3:7f. [b]Heb. 2:2 **27** [a]Ex. 2:15; 12:50f.; 13:17f. [b]Ex. 2:14; 10:28f. [c]Col. 1:15; Heb. 11:1, 13 **28** [a]Ex. 12:21ff.

🔑 **11:28** See note on Col. 1:15.

Passover[3957] and the sprinkling of the blood, so that [b]he who [ppt]destroyed the firstborn[4416] might not [aosb]touch[2345] them.

29 By faith they [a]passed through the Red Sea as though *they were passing* through dry land; and the Egyptians, when they attempted[3984] it, were [I]drowned.

30 By faith [a]the walls of Jericho fell down,[4098] [b]after they had been encircled for seven days.

31 By faith [a]Rahab the harlot did not perish along with those who were disobedient,[544] after she had [apt]welcomed the spies [I]in peace.[1515]

32 And what more shall I say? For time[5550] will [ft]fail me if I [ppt]tell[1334] of [a]Gideon, [b]Barak, [c]Samson, [d]Jephthah, of [e]David and [f]Samuel and the prophets,[4396]

33 who by faith [a]conquered[2610] kingdoms,[932] [b]performed[2038] *acts of* righteousness,[1343] [c]obtained promises,[1860] [d]shut the mouths of lions,

34 [a]quenched the power of fire, [b]escaped the edge of the sword, from weakness were made strong, [c]became[1096] mighty in war, [c]put foreign[245] armies to flight.

35 [a]Women received *back* their dead[3498] by resurrection;[386] and others were tortured, not accepting[4327] their [I]release,[629] in order that they might [aosb]obtain a better[2909] resurrection;[386]

36 and others [I]experienced[3984] mockings and scourgings,[3148] yes, also [a]chains and imprisonment.

37 They were [a]stoned, they were [b]sawn in two, [I]they were tempted,[3985] they were [c]put to death with the sword; they went about [d]in sheepskins, in goatskins, being [ppp]destitute, [ppp]afflicted, [ppp] [e]ill-treated

38 (*men* of whom the world[2889] was not worthy), [a]wandering in deserts and mountains and caves and holes [I]in the ground.[1093]

39 And all these, having [Ia]gained approval[3140] through their faith, [b]did not receive [II]what was promised,[1860]

40 because God had [I]provided [a]something better for us, so that [b]apart from us they should not be [asbp]made perfect.[5048]

Jesus, the Example

12 Therefore, since we have so great a cloud of witnesses[3144] surrounding us, let us also [apt] [a]lay aside every encumbrance, and the sin[266] which so easily entangles us, and let us [psa] [b]run with [c]endurance[5281] the race[73] that is [ppt]set before us,

🔑 2 [I]fixing our eyes[872] on Jesus, the [IIa]author[747] and perfecter[5051] of faith,[4102] who for the joy[5479] [ppt]set before Him [b]endured[5278] the cross,[4716] [apt] [c]despising the shame,[152] and has [d]sat down at the right hand[1188] of the throne of God.

3 For [aim] [a]consider Him who has [pfp]endured such hostility by sinners[268] against Himself, so that you may not [aosb]grow weary[2577] [Ib]and lose heart.[5590]

A Father's Discipline

4 [a]You have not yet resisted [Ib]to the point of shedding blood in your striving against[464] sin;

5 and you have forgotten the exhortation[3874] which is addressed to you as sons,[5207]

"[a]MY SON,[5207] DO NOT REGARD
LIGHTLY THE DISCIPLINE OF
THE LORD,[2962]
NOR [b]FAINT WHEN YOU ARE
[ppp]REPROVED BY HIM;
6 [a]FOR THOSE [b]WHOM THE LORD
LOVES[25] HE DISCIPLINES,

28 [b]Ex. 12:23, 29f.; 1Cor. 10:10
29 [I]Lit., *swallowed up* [a]Ex. 14:22-29
30 [a]Josh. 6:20 [b]Josh. 6:15f.
31 [I]Lit., *with* [a]Josh. 2:9ff.; 6:23; James 2:25
32 [a]Judg. ch. 6-8 [b]Judg. ch. 4, 5 [c]Judg. ch. 13-16 [d]Judg. ch. 11, 12 [e]1Sam. 16:1, 13 [f]1Sam. 1:20
33 [a]Judg. ch. 4, 7, 11, 14; 2Sam. 5:17-20; 8:1f.; 10:12 [b]1Sam. 12:4; 2Sam. 8:15 [c]2Sam. 7:11f. [d]Judg. 14:6; 1Sam. 17:34ff.; Dan. 6:22
34 [a]Dan. 3:23ff. [b]Ex. 18:4; 1Sam. 18:11; 19:10; 1Kin. ch. 19; 2Kin. ch. 6; Ps. 144:10 [c]Judg. 7:21; 15:8, 15f.; 1Sam. 17:51f.; 2Sam. 8:1-6; 10:15ff.
35 [I]Lit., *redemption* [a]1Kin. 17:23; 2Kin. 4:36f.
36 [I]Lit., *received the trial of* [a]Gen. 39:20; 1Kin. 22:27; 2Chr. 18:26; Jer. 20:2; 37:15
37 [I]Some mss. do not contain *they were tempted* [a]1Kin. 21:13; 2Chr. 24:21 [b]2Sam. 12:31, 1Chr. 20:3 [c]1Kin. 19:10; Jer. 26:23 [d]1Kin. 19:13, 19; 2Kin. 2:8, 13f.; Zech. 13:4 [e]Heb. 11:25; 13:3
38 [I]Lit., *of* [a]1Kin. 18:4, 13; 19:9
39 [I]Lit., *obtained a testimony* [II]Lit., *the promise* [a]Heb. 11:2 [b]Heb. 10:36; 11:13
40 [I]Or, *foreseen* [a]Heb. 11:16 [b]Rev. 6:11

1 [a]Rom. 13:12; Eph. 4:22 [b]1Cor. 9:24; Gal. 2:2 [c]Heb. 10:36 **2** [I]Lit., *looking to* [II]Or, *leader* [a]Heb. 2:10 [b]Phil. 2:8f.; Heb. 2:9 [c]1Cor. 1:18, 23; Heb. 13:13 [d]Heb. 1:3 **3** [I]Lit., *fainting in your souls* [a]Rev. 2:3 [b]Gal. 6:9; Heb. 12:5 **4** [I]Lit., *as far as blood* [a]Heb. 10:32ff.; 13:13 [b]Phil. 2:8 **5** [a]Job 5:17; Prov. 3:11 [b]Heb. 12:3 **6** [a]Prov. 3:12 [b]Ps. 119:75; Rev. 3:19

🔑 **12:2** See note on I Thess. 2:19.

AND HE SCOURGES[3146] EVERY SON WHOM HE RECEIVES."[3858]

7 It is for discipline that you endure; [a]God deals[4374] with you as with sons; for what son is there whom *his* father[3962] does not discipline?

8 But if you are without discipline, [a]of which all have become partakers,[3353] then you are illegitimate children[3541] and not sons.[5207]

9 Furthermore, we had [I]earthly fathers[3962] to discipline[3810] us, and we [a]respected[1788] them; shall we not much rather be subject[5293] to [b]the Father[3962] of [II]spirits,[4151] and [c]live?[2198]

10 For they [I]disciplined us for a short time as seemed best to them, but He *disciplines us* for *our* good,[4851] [a]that we may [aies]share His holiness.[41]

11 All discipline [a]for the moment seems not to be joyful, but sorrowful; yet to those who have been [pfpp]trained by it, afterwards it yields the [b]peaceful fruit of righteousness.[1343]

12 Therefore, [Ia]strengthen[461] the hands that are weak and the knees that are feeble,

13 and [a]make straight[3717] paths for your feet, so that *the limb* which is lame may not be put out of joint, but rather [b]be healed.

14 [a]Pursue peace[1515] with all men, and the [b]sanctification[38] without which no one will [c]see the Lord.

15 See to it[1983] that no one [ppt] [a]comes short[5302] of the grace[5485] of God; that no [b]root of bitterness springing[5453] up[507] causes trouble, and by it many be [c]defiled;

16 that *there be* no [a]immoral[4205] or [b]godless person[952] like Esau, [c]who sold his own birthright for a *single* meal.

17 For you know that even afterwards, [a]when he [ppt]desired to [ainf]inherit[2816] the blessing, he was rejected,[593] for he found no place for repentance,[3341] though he [apt]sought for it with tears.

Contrast of Sinai and Zion

18 [a]For you have not [pfi]come to [b]*a mountain* that may be [ppp]touched and to a [pfpp]blazing fire, and to darkness[1105] and gloom[2217] and whirlwind,[2366]

19 and to the [a]blast of a trumpet and the [b]sound of words[4487] which *sound was such that* those who heard [c]begged[3868] that no further word should be spoken to them.

20 For they could not [ipf]bear[5342] the command, "[a]IF EVEN A BEAST[2342] [aosb]TOUCHES THE MOUNTAIN, IT WILL BE STONED."

21 And so terrible was the sight, *that* Moses said, "[a]I AM FULL OF FEAR and trembling."

22 But [a]you have [pfi]come[4334] to Mount Zion and to [b]the city of [c]the living God, [d]the heavenly Jerusalem, and to [e]myriads of [I]angels,

🗝 23 to the general assembly[3831] and [a]church[1577] of the [pl]first-born[4416] who [pfpp] [b]are enrolled in heaven,[3772] and to God,[2316] [c]the Judge[2923] of all, and to the [d]spirits[4151] of righteous[1342] men [pfpp]made perfect,[5048]

24 and to Jesus, the [a]mediator[3316] of a new[3501] covenant,[1242] and to the [b]sprinkled[4473] blood, which [ppt]speaks[2980] better[2909] than [c]*the blood* of Abel.

The Unshaken Kingdom

25 [a]See to it that you do not [aosb]refuse[3868] Him who is [ppt] [b]speaking. For [c]if those [I]did not escape when they [d]refused him who [ppt] [e]warned[5537] *them* on earth, much [II]less *shall* we *escape* who turn away from[654] Him who [f]*warns* from heaven.

26 And [a]His voice shook the earth[1093] then, but now He has [pfi]promised,[1861] saying, "[b]YET ONCE MORE I WILL

7 [a]Deut. 8:5; 2Sam. 7:14; Prov. 13:24; 19:18; 23:13f.
8 [a]1Pet. 5:9
9 [I]Lit., *fathers of our flesh* [II]Or, *our spirits* [a]Luke 18:2 [b]Num. 16:22; 27:16; Rev. 22:6 [c]Is. 38:16
10 [I]Lit., *were disciplining* [a]2Pet. 1:4
11 [a]1Pet. 1:6 [b]Is. 32:17; 2Tim. 4:8; James 3:17f.
12 [I]Lit., *make straight* [a]Is. 35:3
13 [a]Prov. 4:26; Gal. 2:14 [b]Gal. 6:1; James 5:16
14 [a]Rom. 14:19 [b]Rom. 6:22; Heb. 12:10 [c]Matt. 5:8; Heb. 9:28
15 [a]2Cor. 6:1; Gal. 5:4; Heb. 4:1 [b]Deut. 29:18 [c]Titus 1:15
16 [a]Heb. 13:4 [b]1Tim. 1:9 [c]Gen. 25:33f.
17 [a]Gen. 27:30-40
18 [a]2Cor. 3:7-13; Heb. 12:18ff. [b]Ex. 19:12, 16ff.; 20:18; Deut. 4:11; 5:22
19 [a]Ex. 19:16, 19; 20:18; Matt. 24:31 [b]Ex. 19:19; Deut. 4:12 [c]Ex. 20:19; Deut. 5:25; 18:16
20 [a]Ex. 19:12f.
21 [a]Deut. 9:19
22 [I]Or, *angels in festal assembly, and to the church* [a]Rev. 14:1 [b]Eph. 2:19; Phil. 3:20; Heb. 11:10; Rev. 21:2 [c]Heb. 3:12 [d]Gal. 4:26; Heb. 11:16 [e]Rev. 5:11
23 [a]Ex. 4:22; Heb. 2:12 [b]Luke 10:20 [c]Gen. 18:25; Ps. 50:6; 94:2 [d]Heb. 11:40; Rev. 6:9, 11

24 [a]1Tim. 2:5; Heb. 8:6; 9:15 [b]Heb. 9:19; 10:22; 1Pet. 1:2 [c]Gen. 4:10; Heb. 11:4 **25** [I]Lit., *were not escaping* [II]Lit., *more* [a]Heb. 3:12 [b]Heb. 1:1 [c]Heb. 2:2f.; 10:28f. [d]Heb. 12:19 [e]Ex. 20:22; Heb. 8:5; 11:7
26 [a]Ex. 19:18; Judg. 5:4f. [b]Hag. 2:6

🗝 **12:23** See note on Col. 1:15.

SHAKE NOT ONLY THE EARTH, BUT ALSO THE HEAVEN."

27 And this *expression*, "Yet once more," denotes [a]the removing of those things which can be [ppp]shaken, as of [pfpp]created things, in order that those things which cannot be [ppp]shaken may [aosb]remain.

28 Therefore, since we receive a [a]kingdom[932] which cannot be shaken, let us [I]show gratitude,[5485] by which we may [psa] [b]offer to God an acceptable[2102] service[3000] with reverence[2124] and awe;

29 for [a]our God is a consuming fire.

The Changeless Christ

13 Let [a]love of the brethren[5360] continue.

2 Do not neglect to [apt] [a]show hospitality to strangers,[5381] for by this some have [b]entertained angels[32] without knowing it.[2990]

3 [a]Remember [b]the prisoners, as though in prison with them, and those who are [ppp]ill-treated, since you yourselves also are in the body.

4 [a]*Let* marriage[1062] *be held* in honor among all, and let the *marriage* bed *be* undefiled;[283] [b]for fornicators[4205] and adulterers God will judge.[2919]

5 Let your character be [a]free from the love of money, [b]being content with what you have; for He Himself has [pfi]said, "[c]I WILL NEVER DESERT YOU, NOR WILL I EVER FORSAKE YOU,"

6 so that we confidently say,

"[a]THE LORD IS MY HELPER, I
WILL NOT BE AFRAID.[5399]
WHAT SHALL MAN[444] DO TO
ME?"

7 Remember [a]those who led[2233] you, who [ao]spoke[2980] [b]the word[3056] of God to you; and considering[333] the [I]result of their conduct, [c]imitate their faith.

8 [a]Jesus Christ[5547] *is* the same yesterday and today, *yes* and forever.

9 [a]Do not be carried away by varied[4164] and strange[3581] teachings;[1322] for it is good[2570] for the heart to [b]be [pim]strengthened by grace,[5485] not by [c]foods, [d]through which those who [I]were thus [apt]occupied were not [aop]benefited.

10 We have an altar, [a]from which those [b]who [ppt]serve[3000] the [I]tabernacle[4633] have no right[1849] to eat.

11 For [a]the bodies[4983] of those animals[2226] whose blood[129] is brought into[1533] the holy place[39] by the high priest[749] *as an offering* for sin,[266] are burned outside[1854] the camp.

12 Therefore Jesus also, [a]that He might [aosb]sanctify[37] the people[2992] [b]through His own blood,[129] suffered [c]outside the gate.

13 Hence, let us go out to Him outside the camp, [a]bearing[5342] His reproach.

14 For here [a]we do not have a lasting city, but we are seeking [b]*the city* which is to come.

God-pleasing Sacrifices

15 [a]Through Him then, let us continually offer up a [b]sacrifice[2378] of praise[133] to God, that is, [c]the fruit of lips that [I]give thanks[3670] to His name.[3686]

16 And do not neglect doing good and [a]sharing;[2842] for [b]with such sacrifices God is pleased.[2100]

17 [a]Obey[3982] your leaders,[2233] and submit[5226] *to them*; for [b]they keep watch over your souls,[5590] as those who will give an account.[3056] [I]Let them [psa]do this with joy[5479] and not [II]with [ppt]grief, for this would be unprofitable for you.

18 [pim] [a]Pray for us, for we are sure[3982] that we have a [b]good conscience,[4893] desiring to [pinf]conduct ourselves honorably in all things.

19 And I urge *you* all the more[4056] to [ainf]do this, [a]that I may be restored[600] to you the sooner.

27 [a]Is. 34:4; 54:10; 65:17; Rom. 8:19, 21; 1Cor. 7:31; Heb. 1:10ff.
28 [I]Lit., *have* [a]Dan. 2:44 [b]Heb. 13:15, 21
29 [a]Deut. 4:24; 9:3; Is. 33:14; 2Thess. 1:7; Heb. 10:27, 31

1 [a]Rom. 12:10; 1Thess. 4:9; 1Pet. 1:22
2 [a]Matt. 25:35; Rom. 12:13; 1Pet. 4:9 [b]Gen. 18:1ff.; 19:1f.
3 [a]Col. 4:18 [b]Matt. 25:36; Heb. 10:34
4 [a]1Cor. 7:38; 1Tim. 4:3 [b]1Cor. 6:9; Gal. 5:19, 21; 1Thess. 4:6
5 [a]Eph. 5:3; Col. 3:5; 1Tim. 3:3 [b]Phil. 4:11 [c]Deut. 31:6, 8; Josh. 1:5
6 [a]Ps. 118:6
7 [I]Or, *end of their life* [a]Heb. 13:17, 24 [b]Luke 5:1 [c]Heb. 6:12
8 [a]2Cor. 1:19; Heb. 1:12
9 [I]Lit., *walked* [a]Eph. 4:14; 5:6; Jude 12 [b]2Cor. 1:21; Col. 2:7 [c]Col. 2:16 [d]Heb. 9:10
10 [I]Or, *sacred tent* [a]1Cor. 10:18 [b]Heb. 8:5
11 [a]Ex. 29:14; Lev. 4:12, 21; 9:11; 16:27; Num. 19:3, 7
12 [a]Eph. 5:26; Heb. 2:11 [b]Heb. 9:12 [c]John 19:17
13 [a]Luke 9:23; Heb. 11:26; 12:2
14 [a]Heb. 10:34; 12:27 [b]Eph. 2:19; Heb. 2:5; 11:10, 16; 12:22
15 [I]Lit., *confess* [a]1Pet. 2:5 [b]Lev. 7:12 [c]Is. 57:19; Hos. 14:2
16 [a]Rom. 12:13 [b]Phil. 4:18
17 [I]Lit., *in order that they may do this* [II]Lit., *groaning* [a]1Cor. 16:16; Heb. 13:7, 24 [b]Is. 62:6; Ezek. 3:17; Acts 20:28
18 [a]1Thess. 5:25 [b]Acts 24:16; 1Tim. 1:5
19 [a]Philem. 22

Benediction

20 Now [a]the God of peace,*1515* who
apt [b]brought up from the dead the
[c]great Shepherd*4166* of the sheep
[I]through [d]the blood*129* of the [e]eternal*166*
covenant,*1242* *even* Jesus our Lord,
21 opt [a]equip*2675* you in every good*18*
thing*2041* to aies do His will, ppt [b]working
in us that [c]which is pleasing*2101* in His
sight, through Jesus Christ, [d]to whom
be the glory*1391* forever*165* and ever.
Amen.281
22 But [a]I urge you, [b]brethren,*80*
[I]bear with*430* [II]this [b]word of exhortation,*3874* for [c]I have written to you
briefly.
23 Take notice that [a]our brother
Timothy has been released,*630* with
whom, if he comes soon, I shall see
you.
24 Greet782 [a]all of your leaders*2233*
and all the [Ib]saints.*40* Those from [c]Italy
greet you.
25 [a]Grace be with you all.

20 [I]Or, *in* [a]Rom. 15:33 [b]Acts 2:24; Rom. 10:7 [c]Is. 63:11; John 10:11; 1Pet. 2:25 [d]Zech. 9:11; Heb. 10:29 [e]Is. 55:3; Jer. 32:40; Ezek. 37:26
21 [a]1Pet. 5:10 [b]Phil. 2:13 [c]Heb. 12:28; 1John 3:22 [d]Rom. 11:36
22 [I]Or, *listen to* [II]Lit., *the* [a]Acts 13:15; Heb. 3:13; 10:25; 12:5; 13:19 [b]Heb. 3:1 [c]1Pet. 5:12
23 [a]Acts 16:1; Col. 1:1
24 [I]Or, *holy ones* [a]1Cor. 16:16; Heb. 13:7, 17 [b]Acts 9:13 [c]Acts 18:2
25 [a]Col. 4:18

13:23 See general remarks on I Timothy.

The Epistle of

JAMES

There were two Apostles with the name of James. One was the brother of John, son of Zebedee. The other was the son of Alphaeus (Mt. 10:2,3). However, neither of them is thought to have been the author of this Epistle. The oldest half-brother of Jesus was also named James (Mt. 13:55). Jesus appeared to him after He rose from the grave (I Cor. 15:7). He was present in Acts 1:14. Later he became a great leader in the Jerusalem congregation (see Acts 12:17; Gal. 1:18,19). Most scholars believe that he wrote this general letter. Tradition has it that he spent so much time on his knees in prayer that they became as callous as the knees of camels. Paul listened to his advice in Acts 21:18-26. Though he was a very conservative Jewish believer, he moderated a potentially explosive situation in Jerusalem and helped draft a very tolerant letter to the Gentile Christians in Antioch regarding their status (Acts 15:13,19; Gal. 2:1,9,10,12). Though James certainly recognized Paul's role to the Gentiles, he concentrated on his own mission, that of winning his Jewish brethern to Jesus.

The Book of James is the most Jewish book of the New Testament and fits well within the stream of wisdom literature from the Old Testament. It is closer in the New Testament to the Gospel of Matthew, especially the Sermon on the Mount. The book is representative of Jewish Christianity of the type found in the Jerusalem congregation, where James was the dominant figure from about A.D. 45 until his martyrdom in A.D. 62.

Testing Your Faith

1 [Ia]James, a [b]bond-servant[1401] of God[2316] and [c]of the Lord[2962] Jesus Christ,[5547] to [d]the twelve tribes who are [IIe]dispersed abroad, [f]greetings.[5463]

2 [aim] [a]Consider it all joy,[5479] my brethren,[80] when you [aosb]encounter [b]various[4164] [I]trials,[3986]

3 knowing that [a]the testing[1383] of your [b]faith[4102] produces [Ic]endurance.[5281]

4 And let [Ia]endurance have *its* perfect[5046] [II]result,[2041] that you may be [IIIb]perfect and complete,[3648] lacking in nothing.

5 But if any of you [a]lacks wisdom,[4678] let him ask[154] of God,[2316] who [ppt]gives to all men generously and [I]without reproach,[3679] and [b]it will be given to him.

6 But let him [pim] [a]ask in faith [b]without any doubting,[1252] for the one who doubts is like the surf of the sea [ppp] [c]driven and [ppp]tossed by the wind.

7 For let not that man expect that he will receive anything from the Lord,

8 *being* a [Ia]double-minded[1374] man, [b]unstable[182] in all his ways.[3598]

9 [a]But let the [I]brother of humble circumstances [pim]glory in his high position;

10 and *let* the rich man *glory* in his humiliation,[5014] because [a]like [I]flowering grass he will pass away.

11 For the sun [ao]rises with [Ia]a scorching wind, and [ao] [b]withers the grass; and its flower falls off, and the beauty of its appearance[4383] is [aom]destroyed; so too the rich man in the midst of his pursuits will fade away.[3133]

12 [a]Blessed[3107] is a man who perseveres[5278] under trial;[3986] for once he has [I]been approved,[1384] he will receive [b]the crown of life,[2222] which *the Lord* [c]has [ao]promised[1861] to those who [ppt] [d]love[25] Him.

🔑 13 Let no one say when he is

1 [I]Or, *Jacob* [II]Lit., *in the Dispersion* [a]Acts 12:17 [b]Titus 1:1 [c]Rom. 1:1 [d]Luke 22:30 [e]John 7:35 [f]Acts 15:23
2 [I]Or, *temptations* [a]Matt. 5:12; James 1:12; 5:11 [b]1Pet. 1:6
3 [I]Or, *steadfastness* [a]1Pet. 1:7 [b]Heb. 6:12 [c]Luke 21:19
4 [I]V. 3, note 1 [II]Lit., *work* [III]Or, *mature* [a]Luke 21:19 [b]Matt. 5:48; Col. 4:12
5 [I]Lit., *does not reproach* [a]1Kin. 3:9ff.; James 3:17 [b]Matt. 7:7
6 [a]Matt. 21:21 [b]Mark 11:23; Acts 10:20 [c]Matt. 14:28-31; Eph. 4:14
8 [I]Or, *doubting, hesitating* [a]James 4:8 [b]2Pet. 2:14
9 [I]I.e., church member [a]Luke 14:11
10 [I]Lit., *the flower of the grass* [a]1Cor. 7:31; 1Pet. 1:24
11 [I]Lit., *the* [a]Matt. 20:12 [b]Ps. 102:4, 11; Is. 40:7f.
12 [I]Or, *passed the test* [a]Luke 6:22; James 5:11; 1Pet. 3:14; 4:14 [b]1Cor. 9:25 [c]Ex. 20:6; James 2:5 [d]1Cor. 2:9; 8:3

🔑 **1:13-15** There is an apparent contradiction in the KJV here in that this statement declares that no

(continued on next page)

tempted,[3985] "[a]I am being [ppp]tempted [I]by God"; for God cannot be tempted[2076,551] [II]by evil,[2556] and He Himself does not tempt anyone.

14 But each one is tempted when he is [ppp]carried away and [ppp]enticed by his own lust.[1939]

15 Then [a]when lust has [apt]conceived, it gives birth[5088] to sin;[266] and when [b]sin is [aptp]accomplished, it brings forth[616] death.[2288]

16 [a]Do not be [pim]deceived, [b]my beloved brethren.

17 Every good[18] thing[1394] bestowed and every perfect[5046] gift[1434] is [a]from above,[509] coming down from [b]the Father[3962] of lights,[5457] [c]with whom there is no variation, or [I]shifting shadow.

18 In the exercise of [a]His will He [b]brought us forth[616] by [c]the word[3056] of truth,[225] so that we might be, [I]as it were, the [d]first fruits[536] [II]among His creatures.[2938]

19 [I]*This* [a]you know, [b]my beloved[27] brethren.[80] But let everyone be quick to [aies]hear, [c]slow[1021] to [aies]speak *and* [d]slow to anger;[3709]

20 for [a]the anger[3709] of man[435] does not achieve the righteousness[1343] of God.

21 Therefore [apt] [a]putting aside all filthiness and *all* [I]that remains[4050] of wickedness,[2549] in [II]humility[4240] [aim]receive [b]the word implanted,[1721] which is able to [ainf]save[4982] your souls.[5590]

22 [a]But [pim]prove yourselves doers of the word,[3056] and not merely hearers who delude themselves.

13 [I]Lit., *from* [II]Lit., *of evil things* [a]Gen. 22:1
15 [a]Job 15:35; Ps. 7:14; Is. 59:4 [b]Rom. 5:12; 6:23
16 [a]1Cor. 6:9 [b]Acts 1:15; James 1:2, 19; 2:1, 5, 14; 3:1, 10; 4:11; 5:12, 19
17 [I]Lit., *shadow of turning* [a]John 3:3; James 3:15, 17 [b]Ps. 136:7; 1John 1:5 [c]Mal. 3:6
18 [I]Lit., *a certain first fruits* [II]Lit., *of* [a]John 1:13 [b]James 1:15; 1Pet. 1:3, 23 [c]2Cor. 6:7; Eph. 1:13; 2Tim. 2:15 [d]Jer. 2:3; Rev. 14:4
19 [I]Or, *Know this* [a]1John 2:21 [b]Acts 1:15; James 1:2, 16; 2:1, 5, 14; 3:1, 10; 4:11; 5:12, 19 [c]Prov. 10:19; 17:27 [d]Prov. 16:32; Eccl. 7:9
20 [a]Matt. 5:22; Eph. 4:26
21 [I]Lit., *abundance of malice* [II]Or, *gentleness* [a]Eph. 4:22; 1Pet. 2:1 [b]Eph. 1:13; 1Pet. 1:22f.
22 [a]Matt. 7:24-27; Luke 6:46-49; Rom. 2:13; James 1:22-25; 2:14-20
23 [I]Lit., *the face of his birth;* or, *nature* [a]1Cor. 13:12
24 [I]Lit., *and he*

23 For if anyone is a hearer of the word and not a doer, he is like a man who looks at his [I]natural[1078] face[4383] [a]in a mirror;

24 for *once* he has [ao]looked at himself and [pf]gone away, [I]he has immediately[2112] [ao]forgotten what kind of person he was.

25 But one who [apt]looks[3879] intently at the perfect[5046] law,[3551] [a]the *law* of liberty,[1657] and [apt]abides[3887] by it, not having become a forgetful hearer but [I]an effectual doer, this man shall be [b]blessed[3107] in [II]what he does.

26 If anyone thinks himself to be religious,[2357] and yet does not [ppt] [a]bridle his tongue but [ppt]deceives his *own* heart,[2588] this man's religion[2356] is worthless.

27 This is pure[2513] and undefiled[283] religion [a]in the sight of *our* God[2316] and Father,[3962] to [pinf] [b]visit[1980] [c]orphans and widows in their distress,[2347] *and* to [pinf]keep oneself unstained[784] [I]by [d]the world.[2889]

The Sin of Partiality

2 [a]My brethren,[80] [b]do not hold your faith[4102] in our [c]glorious[1391] Lord

25 [I]Lit., *a doer of a work* [II]Lit., *his doing* [a]John 8:32; Rom. 8:2; Gal. 2:4; 6:2; James 2:12; 1Pet. 2:16 [b]John 13:17
26 [a]Ps. 39:1; 141:3; James 3:2-12 27 [I]Lit., *from* [a]Rom. 2:13; Gal. 3:11 [b]Matt. 25:36 [c]Deut. 14:29; Job 31:16, 17, 21; Ps. 146:9; Is. 1:17, 23 [d]Matt. 12:32; Eph. 2:2; Titus 2:12; James 4:4; 2Pet. 1:4; 2:20; 1John 2:15-17 1 [a]James 1:16 [b]Heb. 12:2 [c]Acts 7:2; 1Cor. 2:8

(continued from previous page)
man may say when he is tempted that he is tempted of God, while Gen. 22:1 says, "And it came to pass after these things, that God did tempt Abraham."

The Hebrew word *nissah,* rendered "tempt," literally means "to try, prove," or "put to the test," as the Greek word *peirazō* (3985) sometimes means. The rendering in Gen. 22:1 is correctly given in the Geneva Bible as "God did prove Abraham." James is saying, "Let no one who is tempted (to sin) say that he is tempted of God." God does not tempt anyone to sin, but He tempts only in the sense of proving somebody to create confidence in the Lord and in himself and to give him experience. The word "experience" (*peira,* 3984), is the noun from which the verb *peirazō* is derived. In each instance when this verb is used, we must distinguish who the one who tempts is and then we shall understand whether the meaning is to endeavor to lead a person to fall, which is always the purpose of Satan as he tempts us, or whether it is God who never tricks us or deceives us or causes us to fall, but rather tests to prove our progress. See Editor's book, *The Work of Faith.*

Jesus Christ with *an attitude of* [d]personal favoritism.

2 For if a man [aosb]comes into your [I]assembly[4864] with a gold ring and dressed in [IIa]fine clothes, and there also [aosb]comes in a poor man in [b]dirty[4508] clothes,

3 and you [aosb] [I]pay special attention to the one who is wearing the [a]fine[2986] clothes, and [aosb]say, "You sit here in a good place," and you [aosb]say to the poor man, "You stand over there, or sit down by my footstool,"

4 have you not [ao]made distinctions[1252] among yourselves, and [ao]become judges [a]with evil[4190] [I]motives?[1261]

5 Listen, [a]my beloved brethren: did not [b]God [ao]choose the poor [I]of this world[2889] *to be* [c]rich in faith[4102] and [d]heirs[2818] of the kingdom[932] which He [ao] [e]promised[1861] to those who [ppt]love[25] Him?

6 But you have [ao]dishonored the poor man. Is it not the rich who oppress you and [I]personally [a]drag[1670] you into [II]court?[2922]

7 [a]Do they not blaspheme[987] the fair name[3686] [I]by which you have been [aptp]called?[1941]

8 If, however, you [a]are [pin]fulfilling[5055] the [I]royal[937] law,[3551] according to the Scripture,[1124] "[b]YOU SHALL LOVE[25] YOUR NEIGHBOR[4139] AS YOURSELF," you are doing well.

9 But if you [pin] [a]show partiality,[4380] you are committing[2038] sin[266] *and* are [ppp]convicted by the [I]law[3551] as transgressors.[3848]

10 For whoever [aosb]keeps the whole [I]law and yet [aosb] [a]stumbles in one *point,* he has [pfi]become [b]guilty[1777] of all.

11 For He who said, "[a]DO NOT [aosi]COMMIT ADULTERY," also said, "[b]DO NOT [aosi]COMMIT MURDER." Now if you do not commit adultery, but do commit murder, you have [pfi]become a transgressor of the [I]law.

12 So speak[2980] and so act, as those who are to be [pip]judged[2919] by [a]*the* law[3551] of liberty.[1657]

13 For [a]judgment[2920] *will be* merciless[448] to one who has [apt]shown no mercy;[1656] mercy [I]triumphs over judgment.

1 [d]Acts 10:34; James 2:9
2 [I]Or, *synagogue* [II]Or, *bright* [a]Luke 23:11; James 2:3 [b]Zech. 3:3f.
3 [I]Lit., *look upon* [a]Luke 23:11
4 [I]Lit., *reasonings* [a]Luke 18:6; John 7:24
5 [I]Lit., *to the* [a]James 1:16 [b]Job 34:19; 1Cor. 1:27f. [c]Luke 12:21; Rev. 2:9 [d]Matt. 5:3; 25:34 [e]James 1:12
6 [I]Lit., *they themselves* [II]Lit., *courts* [a]Acts 8:3; 16:19
7 [I]Lit., *which has been called upon you* [a]Acts 11:26; 1Pet. 4:16
8 [I]Or, *law of our King* [a]Matt. 7:12 [b]Lev. 19:18
9 [I]Or, *Law* [a]Acts 10:34; James 2:1
10 [I]Or, *Law* [a]James 3:2; 2Pet. 1:10; Jude 24 [b]Matt. 5:19; Gal. 5:3
11 [I]Or, *Law* [a]Ex. 20:14; Deut. 5:18 [b]Ex. 20:13; Deut. 5:17
12 [a]James 1:25
13 [I]Lit., *boasts against* [a]Prov. 21:13; Matt. 5:7; 18:32-35; Luke 6:37f.

2:5 See note on Eph. 1:4,5.

2:12,13 The more correct literal translation of these two verses is "Thus speak and thus do, as if you are going to be judged by a law of freedom or liberality." James tells us here that the believer is going to be judged (see note on II Cor. 5:10). The Judge, of course, is Jesus Christ. He is not going to be absolutely rigid. He is going to exercise liberality or generosity in many cases toward those who are judged. Verse 13 explains how His judgment is going to be determined: "For judgment will be merciless to one who has shown no mercy." This explains the fifth Beatitude in Mt. 5:7, "Blessed are the merciful, for they shall receive mercy." The Judge's generosity toward the believer will be proportionate to the amount of mercy that the believer showed while on earth. If he showed no mercy, he will receive no mercy. The entrance into heaven is a result of the work which Christ alone did, yet the enjoyment of heaven and its rewards will be proportionate to what the believer did for Christ in his life of faith on earth. Salvation is undeserved mercy obtained by man because of Christ's work, but the rewards are given in proportion to the believer's mercifulness on earth. There are consequences of our willful or unwillful sins on earth for which we may not have repented, or if we had repented, we may have been unable to provide restoration for the evil that we have caused. For these, according to Heb. 10:26, there can be no future sacrifice on the part of Christ. The consequences of our unrestored sinning on earth are compensated in proportion to the mercifulness we have shown while on earth. And then follows the last part of Js. 2:13 which literally translated says, "Mercy or mercifulness boasts against judgment." This means that the believer whose life has been full of mercifulness will face the Judge unafraid because the Judge in His liberality will take into account the mercy that the believer demonstrated on earth as counteracting the consequences of his sin. See Editor's study on the Beatitudes entitled, *The Pursuit of Happiness.*

Faith and Works

🔑 14 [a]What use is it, [b]my brethren,
if a man [psa]says he has faith,[4102] but
he [psa]has no works?[2041] Can [I]that faith
save[4982] him?
15 [a]If a brother or sister is without
clothing and in need of daily food,
16 and one of you [aosb]says to them,
"[a]Go in peace,[1515] be warmed and be
filled," and yet you do not [aosb]give them
what is necessary for *their* body, what
use is that?
🔑 17 Even so [a]faith, if it [psa]has no
works, is dead,[3498] *being* by itself.
18 [a]But someone [I]may *well* say,
"You have faith, and I have works; show
me your [b]faith without the works, and
I will [c]show you my faith [d]by my
works."
19 You believe[4100] that [Ia]God[2316] is
one. [b]You do well; [c]the demons[1140] also
believe, and shudder.
20 But are you willing to recognize,
[a]you foolish[2756] fellow, that [b]faith without
works is useless?
21 [a]Was not Abraham our father
justified[1344] by works, when he [apt]offered
up Isaac his son on the altar?
22 You see that [a]faith was [ipf]working
with his works, and [I]as a result of the
[b]works, faith [aop]was [II]perfected;[5048]
23 and the Scripture was fulfilled
which says, "[a]AND ABRAHAM
BELIEVED[4100] GOD, AND IT WAS
[aop]RECKONED[3049] TO HIM AS RIGHTEOUS-
NESS,"[1343] and he was called [b]the friend
of God.
24 You see that a man is [pinp]justi-
fied by works,[2041] and not by faith[4102]
alone.
25 And in the same way was not
[a]Rahab the harlot also justified by works,
[b]when she received[5264] the messengers and sent them out by another[2087]
way?
26 For just as the body[4983] without
the spirit[4151] is dead,[3498] so also [a]faith
without works is dead.

The Tongue Is a Fire

3 [a]Let not many *of you* [pim]become
teachers,[1320] [b]my brethren, knowing that as such we shall incur a [I]stricter
judgment.[2917]
2 For we all [a]stumble in many *ways.*
[b]If anyone does not stumble in [I]what
he says,[3056] he is a [c]perfect[5046] man,
able to [ainf] [d]bridle the whole body as well.
3 Now [a]if we put the bits into the
horses' mouths so that they may
obey[3982] us, we direct their entire
body[4983] as well.
4 Behold, the ships also, though
they are so great and are driven by
strong winds, are still directed by a very
small rudder, wherever the inclination
of the pilot [pin]desires.
5 So also the tongue[1100] is a small
part of the body, and *yet* it [a]boasts of
great things. [b]Behold, how great a forest
is set aflame by such a small fire!
6 And [a]the tongue is a fire, the *very*
world of iniquity;[93] the tongue is set[2525]
among our members as that which
[b]defiles[4696] the entire body, and [ppt]sets
on fire the course of *our* [I]life,[1078] and
is [ppp]set on fire by [IIc]hell.[1067]
7 For every [I]species of beasts and
birds, of reptiles and creatures of the
sea, is [pinp]tamed, and has been [pfip]tamed
by the human [I]race.
8 But no one can [ainf]tame the
tongue; *it is* a restless evil *and* full of
[a]deadly poison.
9 With it we bless [a]*our* Lord and
Father; and with it we curse[2672] men,
[b]who have been [pfp]made in the likeness[3669] of God;
10 from the same mouth come *both*
blessing[2129] and cursing.[2671] My brethren, these things ought[5334] not to be
this way.
11 Does a fountain send out from
the same opening *both* [I]fresh and bitter
water?

14 [I]Lit., *the* [a]James 1:22ff. [b]James 1:16
15 [a]Matt. 25:35f.; Luke 3:11
16 [a]1John 3:17f.
17 [a]Gal. 5:6; James 2:20, 26
18 [I]Lit., *will* [a]Rom. 9:19 [b]Rom. 3:28; 4:6; Heb. 11:33 [c]James 3:13 [d]Matt. 7:16f.; Gal. 5:6
19 [I]Or, *there is one God* [a]Deut. 6:4; Mark 12:29 [b]James 2:8 [c]Matt. 8:29; Mark 1:24; 5:7; Luke 4:34; Acts 19:15
20 [a]Rom. 9:20; 1Cor. 15:36 [b]Gal. 5:6; James 2:17, 26
21 [a]Gen. 22:9, 10, 12, 16-18
22 [I]Or, *by the deeds* [II]Or, *completed* [a]John 6:29; Heb. 11:17 [b]1Thess. 1:3
23 [a]Gen. 15:6; Rom. 4:3 [b]2Chr. 20:7; Is. 41:8
25 [a]Heb. 11:31 [b]Josh. 2:4, 6, 15
26 [a]Gal. 5:6; James 2:17, 20

1 [I]Or, *greater condemnation* [a]Matt. 23:8; Rom. 2:20f.; 1Tim. 1:7 [b]James 1:16; 3:10
2 [I]Lit., *word* [a]James 2:10 [b]Matt. 12:34-37; James 3:2-12 [c]James 1:4 [d]James 1:26
3 [a]Ps. 32:9
5 [a]Ps. 12:3f.; 73:8f. [b]Prov. 26:20f.
6 [I]Or, *existence, origin* [II]Gr., *Gehenna* [a]Ps. 120:2, 3; Prov. 16:27 [b]Matt. 12:36f.; 15:11, 18f. [c]Matt. 5:22
7 [I]Lit., *nature*
8 [a]Ps. 140:3; Eccl. 10:11; Rom. 3:13
9 [a]James 1:27 [b]Gen. 1:26; 1Cor. 11:7

11 [I]Lit., *sweet*

🔑 **2:14** See note on Gal. 2:16.
🔑 **2:17-26** See note on Gal. 2:16.

12 [a]Can a fig tree, my brethren, [ainf]produce olives, or a vine produce figs? Neither *can* salt water [ainf]produce [I]fresh.

Wisdom from Above

13 Who among you is wise*4680* and understanding? [a]Let him [aim]show by his [b]good*2570* behavior391 his deeds*2041* in the gentleness*4240* of wisdom.*4678*

14 But if you have bitter [a]jealousy and [I]selfish ambition in your heart,*2588* do not be arrogant and *so* lie against [b]the truth.*225*

15 This wisdom*4678* is not that which [ppt]comes down [a]from above, but is [b]earthly,*1919* [Ic]natural,*5591* [d]demonic.

16 For where [a]jealousy and [I]selfish ambition exist, there is disorder*181* and every evil*5337* thing.

17 But the wisdom [a]from above*509* is first [b]pure,*53* then [c]peaceable, [d]gentle,1933 [I]reasonable, [e]full of mercy*1656* and good*18* fruits, [f]unwavering,*87* without [g]hypocrisy.*505*

18 And the [Ia]seed whose fruit is righteousness*1343* is sown in peace*1515* [II]by those who [ppt]make peace.

Things to Avoid

4 [I]What is the source of quarrels and [a]conflicts among you? [II]Is not the source your pleasures that wage [b]war in your members?

2 You lust*1937* and do not have; *so* you [a]commit murder. And you are envious and cannot obtain; *so* you fight and quarrel. You do not have because you do not [aid]ask.*154*

3 You ask and [a]do not receive,*2983* because you ask [I]with wrong motives,*2560* so that you may spend *it* [II]on your pleasures.2237

4 You [a]adulteresses, do you not know that friendship with [b]the world*2889* is [c]hostility2189 toward God? [d]Therefore whoever wishes to be a friend of the world makes*2525* himself an enemy of God.

🔑 5 Or do you think that the Scripture*1124* [a]speaks to no purpose: "[I]He [II]jealously desires [b]the Spirit*4151* which He has made to dwell in us"?

6 But [a]He gives a greater grace.*5485* Therefore *it* says, "[b]GOD IS OPPOSED TO THE PROUD,*5244* BUT GIVES GRACE*5485* TO THE HUMBLE."*5011*

7 [aipp] [a]Submit*5293* therefore to God. [aim] [b]Resist the devil*1228* and he will flee from you.

8 [aim] [a]Draw near*1448* to God and He will draw near to you. [aim] [b]Cleanse*2511* your hands, you sinners;*268* and [aim] [c]purify*48* your hearts,*2588* you [d]double-minded.*1374*

9 [a]Be [aim]miserable and [aim]mourn*3996* and [aim]weep; let your laughter be turned into mourning, and your joy*5479* to gloom.

10 [aipp] [a]Humble yourselves in the presence of the Lord, and He will exalt you.

11 [a]Do not [pim]speak against*2635* one another, [b]brethren. He who [ppt]speaks against a brother, or [ppt] [c]judges his brother, speaks against [d]the law, and judges*2919* the law; but if you judge*2919* the law, you are not [e]a doer of the law, but a judge *of it.*

12 There is *only* one [a]Lawgiver and Judge, the One who is [b]able*1410* to save*4982* and to destroy;*622* but [c]who are you who judge*2919* your neighbor?

---

12 [I]V. 11, note 1 [a]Matt. 7:16
13 [a]James 2:18 [b]1Pet. 2:12
14 [I]Or, *strife* [a]Rom. 2:8; 2Cor. 12:20; James 3:16 [b]1Tim. 2:4; James 1:18; 5:19
15 [I]Or, *unspiritual* [a]James 1:17 [b]1Cor. 2:6; 3:19 [c]2Cor. 1:12; Jude 19 [d]2Thess. 2:9f.; 1Tim. 4:1; Rev. 2:24
16 [I]V. 14, note 1 [a]Rom. 2:8; 2Cor. 12:20; James 3:14
17 [I]Or, *willing to yield* [a]James 1:17 [b]2Cor. 7:11; James 4:8 [c]Matt. 5:9; Heb. 12:11 [d]Titus 3:2 [e]Luke 6:36; James 2:13 [f]James 2:4 [g]Rom. 12:9; 2Cor. 6:6
18 [I]Lit., *fruit of righteousness* [II]Or, *for* [a]Prov. 11:18; Is. 32:17; Hos. 10:12; Amos 6:12; Gal. 6:8; Phil. 1:11

1 [I]Lit., *Whence wars and whence fightings* [II]Lit., *Are they not hence, from your* [a]Titus 3:9 [b]Rom. 7:23
2 [a]James 5:6; 1John 3:15
3 [I]Lit., *wickedly* [II]Lit., *in* [a]1John 3:22; 5:14
4 [a]Jer. 2:2; Ezek. 16:32 [b]James 1:27 [c]Rom. 8:7; 1John 2:15 [d]Matt. 6:24; John 15:19
5 [I]Or, *The Spirit which He has made to dwell in us jealously desires us* [II]Lit., *desires to jealousy* [a]Num. 23:19 [b]1Cor. 6:19; 2Cor. 6:16
6 [a]Is. 54:7f.; Matt. 13:12 [b]Ps. 138:6; Prov. 3:34; Matt. 23:12; 1Pet. 5:5
7 [a]1Pet. 5:6 [b]Eph. 4:27; 6:11f.; 1Pet. 5:8f.
8 [a]2Chr. 15:2; Zech. 1:3; Mal. 3:7; Heb. 7:19 [b]Job 17:9; Is. 1:16; 1Tim. 2:8 [c]Jer. 4:14; James 3:17; 1Pet. 1:22; 1John 3:3 [d]James 1:8
9 [a]Neh. 8:9; Prov. 14:13; Luke 6:25
10 [a]Job 5:11; Ezek. 21:26; Luke 1:52; James 4:6
11 [a]2Cor. 12:20; James 5:9; 1Pet. 2:1 [b]James 1:16; 5:7, 9, 10 [c]Matt. 7:1; Rom. 14:4 [d]James 2:8 [e]James 1:22
12 [a]Is. 33:22; James 5:9 [b]Matt. 10:28 [c]Rom. 14:4

🔑 **4:5** The most natural interpretation of this difficult verse is not to interpret the word "Spirit" as referring to the Holy Spirit (as is done here), but to the fallen spirit of man, the spirit which is responsible for man's propensity to sin. The fallen spirit in man yearns (*epipothei,* 1971) toward envy. This envy manifests itself in selfishness and malevolence. See Editor's book, *The Labor of Love.*

13 [a]Come now, you who [ppt]say, "[b]Today or tomorrow, we shall go to such and such a city, and spend a year there and engage in business and make a profit."

14 [I]Yet you do not know [II]what your life[2222] will be like tomorrow. [a]You are *just* a vapor that appears for a little while and then vanishes away.

15 [I]Instead, *you ought* to say, "[a]If the Lord wills, we shall live[2198] and also do this or that."

16 But as it is, you boast[212] in your [I]arrogance; [a]all such boasting is evil.[4190]

17 Therefore, [a]to one who knows[1492] *the* [I]right thing[2570] to [pinf]do,[4160] and [ppt]does not do it, to him it is sin.[266]

Misuse of Riches

5 [a]Come now, [b]you rich, [c]weep and howl for your miseries which are coming upon you.

2 [a]Your riches have rotted and your garments have become moth-eaten.

3 Your gold and your silver have rusted; and their rust will be a witness[3142] against you and will consume your flesh like fire. It is [a]in the last[2078] days that you have [ao]stored up your treasure!

4 Behold, [a]the pay[3408] of the laborers who [apt]mowed your fields, *and* which has been withheld by you, cries out *against you*; and [b]the outcry of those who did the harvesting has reached the ears of [c]the Lord[2962] of [I]Sabaoth.[4519]

5 You have [ao] [a]lived luxuriously[5171] on the earth and led a life of wanton pleasure; you have [ao] [I]fattened your hearts in [b]a day of slaughter.

6 You have condemned[2613] and [I][a]put to death [b]the righteous[1342] *man;* he does not resist you.

13 [a]James 5:1 [b]Prov. 27:1; Luke 12:18-20
14 [I]Lit., *Who do not* [II]Some mss. read *the morrow; for what kind of life is yours* [a]Job 7:7; Ps. 39:5; 102:3; 144:4
15 [I]Lit., *Instead of your saying* [a]Acts 18:21
16 [I]Or, *pretensions* [a]1Cor. 5:6
17 [I]Or, *good* [a]Luke 12:47; John 9:41; 2Pet. 2:21

1 [a]James 4:13 [b]Luke 6:24; 1Tim. 6:9 [c]Is. 13:6; 15:3; Ezek. 30:2
2 [a]Job 13:28; Is. 50:9; Matt. 6:19f.
3 [a]James 5:7, 8
4 [I]I.e., Hosts [a]Lev. 19:13; Job 24:10f.; Jer. 22:13; Mal. 3:5 [b]Ex. 2:23; Deut. 24:15; Job 31:38f. [c]Rom. 9:29
5 [I]Lit., *nourished* [a]Ezek. 16:49; Luke 16:19; 1Tim. 5:6; 2Pet. 2:13 [b]Jer. 12:3; 25:34
6 [I]Or, *murdered* [a]James 4:2 [b]Heb. 10:38; 1Pet. 4:18
7 [I]Or, *he* [a]James 4:11; 5:9, 10 [b]John 21:22; 1Thess. 2:19 [c]Gal. 6:9 [d]Deut. 11:14; Jer. 5:24; Joel 2:23
8 [a]Luke 21:19 [b]1Thess. 3:13 [c]John 21:22; 1Thess. 2:19 [d]Rom. 13:11, 12; 1Pet. 4:7
9 [I]Lit., *groan* [II]Lit., *before* [III]Lit., *doors* [a]James 4:11 [b]James 5:7, 10 [c]1Cor. 4:5; James 4:12;

Exhortation

7 Be patient,[3114] therefore, [a]brethren,[80] [b]until the coming of the Lord. [c]Behold, the farmer[1092] waits for[1551] the precious produce of the soil, being patient[3114] about it, until [I]it gets [d]the early and late rains.

8 [a]You too be patient;[3114] [b]strengthen your hearts, for [c]the coming[3952] of the Lord is [d]at hand.

9 [a]Do not [I]complain, [b]brethren, against one another, that you yourselves may not be [asbp]judged; behold, [c]the Judge[2923] is standing [II][d]right at the [III]door.

10 As an example, [a]brethren, of suffering[2552] and patience,[3115] take [b]the prophets[4396] who spoke in the name[3686] of the Lord.

11 Behold, we count those [a]blessed[3106] who [ppt]endured.[5278] You have heard of [b]the [I]endurance of Job and have seen [c]the [II]outcome[5056] of the Lord's dealings, that [d]the Lord is full of compassion and *is* merciful.

12 But above all, [a]my brethren, [b]do not swear, either by heaven[3772] or by earth[1093] or with any other oath;[3727] but [I]let your yes be yes, and your no, no; so that you may not [aosb]fall under judgment.

13 Is anyone among you [a]suffering?[2553] [b]Let him [pim]pray. Is anyone cheerful? Let him [pim] [c]sing praises.

14 Is anyone among you sick? Let him [aim]call for[4341] [a]the elders[4245] of the church,[1577] and let them [aim]pray over

1Pet. 4:5 [d]Matt. 24:33; Mark 13:29 **10** [a]James 4:11; 5:7, 9 [b]Matt. 5:12 **11** [I]Or, *steadfastness* [II]Lit., *end of the Lord* [a]Matt. 5:10; 1Pet. 3:14 [b]Job 1:21f.; 2:10 [c]Job 42:10, 12 [d]Ex. 34:6; Ps. 103:8 **12** [I]Lit., *let yours be the yes, yes, and the no, no* [a]James 1:16 [b]Matt. 5:34-37 **13** [a]James 5:10 [b]Ps. 50:15 [c]1Cor. 14:15; Col. 3:16 **14** [a]Acts 11:30

4:17 See notes on Mt. 8:11,12; Gal. 3:22.

5:7,8 See note on I Thess. 2:19.

5:11 See note on Lk. 1:48.

5:14,15 The question that arises here is whether Christianity prohibits the use of medicine. Verse 14 begins with a statement rather than a question. At the time the Bible was written, there were no punctuation marks. These were added by the editors later as they understood the text. James starts

(continued on next page)

him, [apt] [I][b]anointing[218] him with oil in the
name of the Lord;
15 and the [a]prayer[2171] [I]offered in
faith[4102] will [II][b]restore[4982] the one who
is sick,[2577] and the Lord will [c]raise him
up, and if he has committed sins,[266]
[III]they will be forgiven[863] him.
16 Therefore, [pim] [a]confess[1843] your
sins[266] to one another, and [pim]pray
for one another, so that you may
be [asbp] [b]healed. [c]The effective[1754]
[I]prayer[1162] of a righteous[1342] man
can accomplish[2480] much.
17 Elijah was [a]a man[444] with a nature
like ours, and [b]he [ao]prayed[4336] [I]ear-
nestly[4335] that it might not [infg]rain; and
it did not rain on the earth for [c]three
years and six months.
18 And he [a]prayed again, and [b]the
[I]sky[3772] [II]poured rain, and the earth produced its fruit.

14 [I]Lit., *having anointed* [b]Mark 6:13; 16:18
15 [I]Lit., *of* [II]Or, *save* [III]Lit., *it* [a]James 1:6 [b]1Cor. 1:21; James 5:20 [c]John 6:39; 2Cor. 4:14
16 [I]Lit., *supplication* [a]Matt. 3:6; Mark 1:5; Acts 19:18 [b]Heb. 12:13; 1Pet. 2:24 [c]Gen. 18:23-32; John 9:31

17 [I]Lit., *with prayer* [a]Acts 14:15 [b]1Kin. 17:1; 18:1 [c]Luke 4:25 **18** [I]Lit., *heaven* [II]Lit., *gave* [a]1Kin. 18:42 [b]1Kin. 18:45

(continued from previous page)
this verse with a universal fact that all people get sick. Even the Apostle Paul who wrote about the gifts of healings in I Cor. 12 was sick and eventually died. Death is the ultimate result of the deterioration of our mortal body. Thus the statement is "Someone is sick among you." In other words, James states that the Christian is not exempt from sickness.

The second thing is that the initiative to call the elders of the church must come from the sick believer himself. At the time of the apostolic church, the elders performed many duties, even treating sick people in whatever manner they could. What are these elders supposed to do when they come to the home of the sick brother? "Let them pray on him or over him." But before they pray, they must render whatever medical or physical therapeutic assistance they can. The order of the two things that the elders are supposed to do is not made clear from the translation, but it is absolutely clear from the Greek text. The word translated "anointing him" is in the aorist participle, *aleipsantes,* which makes it an act which precedes the prayer, "having rubbed him with oil." Oil in the Scriptures is used for religious anointing as well as for lighting and medicinal purposes. The word *aleipho* (218), from which comes *aleipsantes,* normally is not used in a religious sacramental sense as the word *chriō* (5548). Usually it means to rub or to apply ointment. Therefore, this refers to the application of medicinal assistance to the sick person first, and then the elders are commanded to pray for the sick. There is a restrictive qualification as to the possible result of the application of medicine and the offering of prayer in regard to a believing, sick person. The prayer is to be made "in the name of the Lord." In this verse there are two verbs. The one is the indirect imperative in the aorist of the verb *proseuchomai* (4336). The aorist tense indicates that this is not repeated prayer but a single prayer. This is the principal verb in the third clause of this verse. The verb *proseuxasthōsan,* "let them pray," is the aorist indirect imperative of *proseuchomai* even as the verb *proskalesasthō,* "let him call," is the aorist indirect imperative of *proskaleomai* (4341). The invitation to come was one single invitation, and so was the prayer one single prayer, not repetitious. "And let them pray over him, anointing him with oil in the name of the Lord." A participle as *aleipsantes,* "when they rubbed him," in the Greek does not denote the main verb or the main action in a clause. "Anointing him" is in the aorist participle and refers to a completed act in the past, "having anointed (rubbed) him, let them pray over him." The main verb is "let them pray," and, therefore, the qualification "in the name of the Lord" refers to the prayer of the elders and not necessarily to the rubbing of his body with oil. Both unbelieving and and believing doctors can apply medicine on anybody, but when it comes to believers, they must seek God's will in the result of both the practice of medicine and the exercise of faith. See note on Lk. 11:9.

But what does "in the name of the Lord" mean? The phrase does not mean that as a matter of habit we must close our prayers in the name of the Lord. It rather indicates our willingness to permit our prayers to be acted upon under the sovereign will and purpose of God. In Jn. 14:13 our Lord said, "And whatever you ask in my name, that will I do, that the Father may be glorified in the Son." We perfectly well know that we, as believers, do not always get from God all that we ask. If we did, none of us would ever die because all of us want to live, and if it were in God's purpose and timetable to keep us alive forever, He could do it. However, this is not the period of time when our bodies are indestructible. That day is coming when our bodies are going to be redeemed (Rom. 8:23), but the redemption of our bodies purchased on the cross of Christ (Mt. 8:17) will be realized only as we are

(continued on next page)

19 My brethren, [a]if any among you
[asbp]strays from [b]the truth,[225] and one
turns him back,[1994]
20 let him know that he who [apt]turns
a sinner[268] from the error of his way
will [a]save his soul[5590] from death,[2288]
and will [b]cover[2572] a multitude of
sins.[266]

19 [a]Matt. 18:15; Gal. 6:1 [b]James 3:14
20 [a]Rom. 11:14; 1Cor. 1:21; James 1:21 [b]Prov. 10:12; 1Pet. 4:8

(continued from previous page)
given our resurrection bodies (I Cor. 15:51-54). The name of the Lord indicates His character and His purpose. If a parent says to a child, "Respect my name," he means, "Do what I want to see done." The Lord certainly gives us the freedom and commands us to pray for all that we wish our Heavenly Father should do for us. But our Heavenly Father, knowing more and better than we do, gives us not that which we ask for, but that which He discerns as the best for us. And the best for God's child is not necessarily health and wealth, but sometimes it may be sickness and privation if these are designed by God to bring the believer into a closer walk with Him. Let us be honest. When do we turn our thought more toward God? When we are healthy and wealthy or when we are sick and dependent on God for our daily bread? The word "good," *agathon* (18), in Rom. 8:28 does not mean more of what we would like to have, but a closer relationship with our God.

It is God who heals all people, unbelievers and believers, with or without medicine. In the case of the believer, however, there must be the realization that after the application of medicine and then prayer, it is God who heals, honoring our prayer. Many times, of course, God heals even when we do not pray. We must understand that He is a sovereign God. But at the same time, God is a prayer-hearing and a prayer-answering God. And whatever benefit we receive, we must consider it as coming from Him. Therefore, we are given the assurance, "And the prayer of faith shall save the one who has it bad, and the Lord shall raise him up." This is the literal translation of the Greek text.

James furthermore projects the possibility that this sickness from which the believer may be suffering may be a result of his own sin (see Jn. 9:3). "And if he has committed sins, they will be forgiven him." The same Lord who heals the body also forgives the sin of the soul. The sin of the soul or spirit of the believer may result in physical or emotional sickness, but the same Lord can remove both sickness and sin. See Editor's book, *The Patience of Hope.*

The First Epistle of

PETER

The imprint of Peter upon the early church was stronger than that of any of the other original Twelve Apostles. He was the most prominent disciple during Jesus' lifetime, and the first twelve chapters of Acts are devoted to his ministry and to that of the church in the East, where he was still the dominant figure. Paul mentioned him in Galatians (1:18; 2:7-9,11,14) and I Cor. (1:12; 3:22; 9:5; 15:5), and two New Testament Epistles bear his name. His first letter is one of the seven general letters and is addressed to the five Roman provinces in Asia Minor north of the Taurus Mountains. The occasion of writing was persecution in the area, and the letter tries to encourage and equip the readers for the difficult times ahead. There were no empire-wide persecutions of Christians until the brutal one under Decius (A.D. 249-51), but local ones could be quite severe. One of the worst persecutions known to have struck the early church took place early in the second century in Bithynia, one of the provinces to which I Peter was written. In a letter sent from Pliny, governor of Bithynia, to the Roman emperor, Trajan, in A.D. 112, the official explained that he had been executing people who confessed that they were Christians. Trajan's reply indicated approval of Pliny's policy but allowed Christians who renounced their faith and worshiped Roman gods to go free. Since I Peter was probably written in the A.D. 60's, persecution of the severest kind for its recipients was only a few decades away. Peter used Jesus' own suffering as the cornerstone of his exhortation. Another key concern was that Christians suffer as Christians, not as lawbreakers. In this connection, he produced one of only three instances of the word "Christian" to be found in the New Testament (Acts 11:26; 26:28; I Pet. 4:16). Peter wrote from Babylon, which was sometimes a code word for Rome (see Rev. 14:8; 17:5), so it was probably actually written from Rome.

A Living Hope, and a Sure Salvation

1 [a]Peter, an apostle[6521] of Jesus
Christ,[5547] to those who reside as
[b]aliens,[3927] [c]scattered throughout [d]Pon-
tus, [e]Galatia, [d]Cappadocia, [d]Asia, and
[f]Bithynia, [g]who are chosen[1588]
🔑 2 according to the [a]foreknowl-
edge[4268] of God[2316] the Father,[3962]
[b]by the sanctifying[38] work of the Spirit,[4151] [I]that you may [c]obey[5218] Jesus
Christ and be [d]sprinkled[4473] with His
blood:[129] [e]May grace[5485] and peace[1515]
[II]be yours in fullest measure.
3 [a]Blessed[2128] be the God and Father of our Lord Jesus Christ, who
[b]according to His great mercy[1656]
[c]has [apt]caused us to be born[313] again
to [d]a [ppt]living[2198] hope[1680] through the
[e]resurrection[386] of Jesus Christ from the
dead,[3498]
4 to *obtain* an [a]inheritance[2817] *which*
is imperishable[862] and undefiled[283] and
[b]will not fade away,[263] [pfpp] [c]reserved[5083]
in heaven[3772] for you,
🔑 5 who are [ppp] [a]protected by the
power[1411] of God[2316] [b]through faith[4102]
for [c]a salvation[4991] ready [d]to be [aifp]re-
vealed[601] in the last time.[2540]

1 [a]2Pet. 1:1 [b]1Pet. 2:11 [c]James 1:1 [d]Acts 2:9 [e]Acts 16:6 [f]Acts 16:7 [g]Matt. 24:22; Luke 18:7
2 [I]Lit., *unto obedience and sprinkling* [II]Lit., *be multiplied for you* [a]Rom. 8:29; 1Pet. 1:20 [b]2Thess. 2:13 [c]1Pet. 1:14, 22 [d]Heb. 10:22; 12:24 [e]2Pet. 1:2
3 [a]2Cor. 1:3 [b]Gal. 6:16; Titus 3:5 [c]James 1:18; 1Pet. 1:23 [d]1Pet. 1:13, 21; 3:5, 15; 1John 3:3 [e]1Cor. 15:20; 1Pet. 3:21
4 [a]Acts 20:32; Rom. 8:17; Col. 3:24 [b]1Pet. 5:4 [c]2Tim. 4:8
5 [a]John 10:28; Phil. 4:7 [b]Eph. 2:8 [c]1Cor. 1:21; 2Thess. 2:13 [d]1Pet. 4:13; 5:1

🔑 **1:2** See notes on Eph. 1:4,5; Gal. 1:8.

🔑 **1:5** Here reference is made to those whom God has regenerated (v. 3). They become the heirs of a resurrection body because the resurrection of Jesus Christ was the firstfruits of their own resurrection (v. 4). This inheritance is kept for them (the verb *tetērēmenēn,* 5083, "reserved," is a perfect participle in the passive voice which means that this inheritance was made possible by Jesus Christ sometime in the past and is now kept by Him until the proper time of delivery). It is not this inheritance of the

(continued on next page)

6 [a]In this you greatly rejoice,[21] even
though now [b]for a little while, [c]if necessary,[1163] you have been [aptp]distressed
by [d]various [I]trials,[3986]
🔑 7 that the [Ia]proof[1383] of your
faith,[4102] *being* more precious than gold
which [II]is perishable, [b]even though
[ppp]tested[1381] by fire, [c]may be found[2147]
to result in praise and glory[1391] and honor
at [d]the revelation[602] of Jesus Christ;
8 and [a]though you have not seen
Him, you [b]love[26] Him, and though you
do not [ppt]see Him now, but believe[4100]
in Him, you greatly rejoice with joy[5479]
inexpressible and [I]full of glory,[1392]
9 obtaining as [a]the outcome[5056] of
your faith the salvation[4991] of [I]your
souls.[5590]
10 [a]As to this salvation, the
prophets[4396] who [b]prophesied[4395] of the
[c]grace[5485] that *would come* to you made
careful search and inquiry,
11 [I]seeking to know what person or
time [a]the Spirit[4151] of Christ[5547] within
them was [ipf]indicating as He [b][ppt]predicted
the sufferings of Christ and the glories
[II]to follow.
12 It was revealed[601] to them that
they were not [ipf]serving[1247] themselves,
but you, in these things which now have
been announced to you through those
who [apt] [a]preached the gospel[2097] to you
by [b]the [an]Holy Spirit[4151] sent from
heaven—[3772] things into which [c]angels[32]
long[1937] to [I]look.[3879]
🔑 **13** Therefore, [apt] [a]gird [I]your
minds[3751] for action, [IIb]keep [ppt]sober *in
spirit,* [aim]fix your [c]hope completely[5049]
on the [d]grace[5485] [III]to be [ppp]brought to
you at [e]the revelation[602] of Jesus Christ.
14 As [Ia]obedient[5218] children,[5043] do
not [IIb]be conformed[4964] to the former
lusts[1939] *which were yours* in your
[c]ignorance,[52]
15 but [Ia]like the Holy[40] One who
[apt]called you, [IIb]be holy yourselves also
[c]in all *your* behavior;[391]
16 because it is written, "[a]You
shall be holy, for I am holy."
17 And if you [a]address as Father[3962] the One who [b]impartially[678]
[ppt] [c]judges[2919] according to each man's
work,[2041] [aipp]conduct yourselves [d]in
fear[5401] during the time[5550] of your
[e]stay[3940] *upon earth;*
18 knowing that you were not
[Ia]redeemed[3084] with perishable things
like silver or gold from your [b]futile way
of life inherited from your forefathers,
19 but with precious [a]blood, as of
a [b]lamb unblemished[299] and spotless,[784]
the blood of Christ.[5547]
🔑 20 For He [pfpp]was [a]foreknown[4267]
before [b]the foundation of the world,[2889]
but has [c]appeared[5319] [I]in these last[2078]
times [d]for the sake of you
21 who through Him are [a]be-
lievers[4100] in God, who [apt]raised[1453] Him
from the dead[3498] and [b]gave Him
glory,[1391] so that your faith[4102] and
[c]hope[1680] are in God.[2316]
22 Since you have [a]in obedience[5218]
to the truth [pfp] [b]purified[48] your souls[5590]
for a [Ic]sincere[505] love of the brethren,[5360]
fervently[1619] [aim]love[25] one another from
[II]the heart,[2588]

6 [I]Or, *temptations* [a]Rom. 5:2 [b]1Pet. 5:10 [c]1Pet. 3:17 [d]James 1:2; 1Pet. 4:12
7 [I]Or, *genuineness* [II]Lit., *perishes* [a]James 1:3 [b]1Cor. 3:13 [c]Rom. 2:7 [d]Luke 17:30; 1Pet. 1:13; 4:13
8 [I]Lit., *glorified* [a]John 20:29 [b]Eph. 3:19
9 [I]Some ancient mss. do not contain *your* [a]Rom. 6:22
10 [a]Matt. 13:17; Luke 10:24 [b]Matt. 26:24 [c]1Pet. 1:13
11 [I]Lit., *inquiring* [II]Lit., *after these* [a]2Pet. 1:21 [b]Matt. 26:24
12 [I]Or, *gain a clear glimpse* [a]1Pet. 1:25; 4:6 [b]Acts 2:2-4 [c]1Tim. 3:16
13 [I]Lit., *the loins of your mind* [II]Lit., *be sober* [III]Or, *which is announced* [a]Eph. 6:14 [b]1Thess. 5:6, 8; 2Tim. 4:5; 1Pet. 4:7; 5:8 [c]1Pet. 1:3 [d]1Pet. 1:10 [e]1Pet. 1:7
14 [I]Lit., *children of obedience* [II]Or, *conform yourselves* [a]1Pet. 1:2 [b]Rom. 12:2; 1Pet. 4:2f. [c]Eph. 4:18
15 [I]Lit., *according to* [II]Or, *become* [a]1Thess. 4:7; 1John 3:3 [b]2Cor. 7:1 [c]James 3:13
16 [a]Lev. 11:44f.; 19:2; 20:7
17 [a]Ps. 89:26; Jer. 3:19; Matt. 6:9 [b]Acts 10:34 [c]Matt. 16:27 [d]2Cor. 7:1; Heb. 12:28; 1Pet. 3:15 [e]1Pet. 2:11
18 [I]Or, *ransomed* [a]Is. 52:3; 1Cor. 6:20; Titus 2:14; Heb. 9:12 [b]Eph. 4:17
19 [a]Acts 20:28; 1Pet. 1:2 [b]John 1:29
20 [I]Lit., *at the end of the times* [a]Acts 2:23; Eph. 1:4; 1Pet. 1:2; Rev. 13:8 [b]Matt. 25:34 [c]Heb. 9:26 [d]Heb. 2:14
21 [a]Rom. 4:24; 10:9 [b]John 17:5, 24; 1Tim. 3:16; Heb. 2:9 [c]1Pet. 1:3
22 [I]Lit., *unhypocritical* [II]Some mss. read *a clean heart* [a]1Pet. 1:2 [b]James 4:8 [c]John 13:34; Rom. 12:10; Heb. 13:1; 1Pet. 2:17; 3:8

(continued from previous page)
believer only that is kept in heaven, but also we who are currently alive on earth are being guarded (*phrouroumenous,* 5432) which is in the present participle, meaning that we are being guarded by God who is in heaven while, through faith, we are awaiting our liberation from earth. This guarding has as its purpose our deliverance at the resurrection. The word translated "salvation" (v. 5) is equivalent to the redemption of Rom. 8:23 which refers to our body. It does not refer to salvation from sin, but to our liberation or salvation from our present mortal and corruptible body. The word "salvation" here is used exactly with the same meaning as in Rom. 13:11.

🔑 **1:7,13** See note on I Thess. 2:19.

🔑 **1:20** See note on Eph. 1:4,5.

23 for you have been [a]born again313 [b]not of seed which is perishable but imperishable, *that is,* through the [ppt]living2198 and [ppt]abiding3306 [c]word3056 of God.

24 For,

"[a]ALL FLESH4561 IS LIKE GRASS,
AND ALL ITS GLORY LIKE THE FLOWER OF GRASS.
THE GRASS [aop]WITHERS,
AND THE FLOWER [ao]FALLS OFF,

25 [a]BUT THE WORD4487 OF THE LORD2962 ABIDES3306 FOREVER."

And this is [b]the word which was [aptp] [I]preached2097 to you.

As Newborn Babes

2 Therefore, [apt] [a]putting aside all [I]malice2549 and all guile1388 and [II]hypocrisy and [II]envy and all [II][b]slander,

2 [a]like newborn738 babes,1025 [aim]long for the [I][b]pure97 [II]milk1051 of the word,3050 that by it you may [asbp] [c]grow [III]in respect to salvation,

3 if you have [ao] [a]tasted1098 [I][b]the kindness5543 of the Lord.

As Living Stones

4 And coming to Him as to a living2198 stone, [pfpp] [a]rejected593 by men, but [I]choice1588 and precious in the sight of God,

5 [a]you also, as [ppt]living2198 stones, [I]are being built up as a [b]spiritual house for a holy40 [c]priesthood,2406 to [d]offer up spiritual sacrifices2378 acceptable2144 to God through Jesus Christ.

6 For *this* is contained in [I]Scripture:1124

"[a]BEHOLD I LAY IN ZION A CHOICE STONE, A [b]PRECIOUS CORNER *stone,*
AND HE WHO [ppt]BELIEVES4100 IN [II]HIM SHALL NOT BE [efn] [III]DISAPPOINTED."

7 [a]This precious value, then, is for you who [ppt]believe. But for those who [ppt]disbelieve,544

"[b]THE STONE WHICH THE BUILDERS [c]REJECTED,593
THIS BECAME THE VERY CORNER *stone,*"

8 and,

"[a]A STONE OF STUMBLING AND A ROCK OF OFFENSE";4625

[b]for they stumble4350 because they are [ppt]disobedient to the word,3056 [c]and to this *doom* they were also appointed.

9 But you are [a]A CHOSEN RACE, A royal [b]PRIESTHOOD, A [c]HOLY NATION,1484 [d]A PEOPLE2992 FOR *God's* OWN POSSESSION,4047 that you may [aosb]proclaim1804 the excellencies of Him who has [apt]called you [e]out of darkness4655 into His marvelous light;5457

10 [a]for you once were NOT A PEOPLE,2992 but now you are THE PEOPLE OF GOD; you had NOT RECEIVED MERCY, but now you have RECEIVED MERCY.

11 [a]Beloved, [b]I urge3870 you as [c]aliens3941 and strangers3927 to [pinf]abstain567 from [d]fleshly lusts,1939 which wage [e]war against the soul.5590

12 [a]Keep your behavior391 excellent among the Gentiles,1484 so that in the thing in which they [b]slander2635 you as evildoers,2555 they may [I]on account of your good deeds, as they [ppt]observe2029 *them,* [aosb] [c]glorify1392 God [d]in the day2250 of [II]visitation.1984

Honor Authority

13 [aipp] [a]Submit yourselves5293 for the Lord's sake to every human institution,2937 whether to a king935 as the one in authority,

14 or to governors as [ppp]sent [I]by him [a]for the punishment1557 of evildoers2555 and the [b]praise of those who do right.

23 [a]John 3:3; 1Pet. 1:3 [b]John 1:13 [c]Heb. 4:12
24 [a]Is. 40:6ff.; James 1:10f.
25 [I]Lit., *preached as good news to you* [a]Is. 40:8 [b]Heb. 6:5

1 [I]Or, *wickedness* [II]plural nouns [a]Eph. 4:22, 25, 31; James 1:21 [b]James 4:11
2 [I]Or, *unadulterated* [II]Or, *spiritual* (Gr., *logikos*) *milk* [III]Or, *up to salvation* [a]Matt. 18:3; 19:14; Mark 10:15; Luke 18:17; 1Cor. 14:20 [b]1Cor. 3:2 [c]Eph. 4:15f.
3 [I]Lit., *that the Lord is kind* [a]Heb. 6:5 [b]Ps. 34:8; Titus 3:4
4 [I]Lit., *chosen;* or, *elect* [a]1Pet. 2:7
5 [I]Or, *allow yourselves to be built up or build yourselves up* [a]1Cor. 3:9 [b]Gal. 6:10; 1Tim. 3:15 [c]Is. 61:6; 66:21; 1Pet. 2:9; Rev. 1:6 [d]Rom. 15:16; Heb. 13:15
6 [I]Or, *a scripture* [II]Or, *it* [III]Or, *put to shame* [a]Is. 28:16; Rom. 9:32, 33; 10:11; 1Pet. 2:8 [b]Eph. 2:20
7 [a]2Cor. 2:16; 1Pet. 2:7, 8 [b]Ps. 118:22; Matt. 21:42; Luke 2:34 [c]1Pet. 2:4
8 [a]Is. 8:14 [b]1Cor. 1:23; Gal. 5:11 [c]Rom. 9:22
9 [a]Is. 43:20f.; Deut. 10:15 [b]Is. 61:6; 66:21; 1Pet. 2:5; Rev. 1:6 [c]Ex. 19:6; Deut. 7:6 [d]Ex. 19:5; Deut. 4:20; 14:2; Titus 2:14 [e]Is. 9:2; 42:16; Acts 26:18; 2Cor. 4:6
10 [a]Hos. 1:10; 2:23; Rom. 9:25; 10:19
11 [a]Heb. 6:9; 1Pet. 4:12 [b]Rom. 12:1 [c]Lev. 25:23; Ps. 39:12; Eph. 2:19; Heb. 11:13; 1Pet. 1:17 [d]Rom. 13:14; Gal. 5:16, 24 [e]James 4:1
12 [I]Or, *as a result of* [II]I.e., Christ's coming again in judgment [a]2Cor. 8:21; Phil. 2:15; Titus 2:8; 1Pet. 2:15; 3:16 [b]Acts 28:22 [c]Matt. 5:16; 9:8; John 13:31; 1Pet. 4:11, 16 [d]Is. 10:3; Luke 19:44
13 [a]Rom. 13:1
14 [I]Lit., *through* [a]Rom. 13:4 [b]Rom. 13:3

15 For [a]such is the will[2307] of God
that by [ppt]doing[15] right you may [b]silence
the ignorance[56] of foolish men.
16 *Act* as [a]free men, and do not use
your freedom[1657] as a covering for
evil,[2549] but *use it* as [b]bondslaves[1401] of
God.
🔑 17 [aim][a]Honor all men; [pim][b]love[25]
the brotherhood,[81] [pim][c]fear[5399] God,
[pim][d]honor the [I]king.[935]
18 [a]Servants,[3610] be submissive to
your masters[1203] with all respect,[5401] not
only to those who are good[18] and
[b]gentle,[1933] but also to those who are
[I]unreasonable.[4646]
19 For this *finds* [I]favor, if for the
sake of [a]conscience[4893] toward God a
man bears up under sorrows when suffering unjustly.
20 For what credit is there if, when
you sin[264] and are harshly [ppp]treated,
you endure it with patience?[5278]
But if [a]when you [ppt]do what is right[15]
and [ppt]suffer *for it* you patiently
endure it, this *finds* [I]favor[5485] with
God.

Christ Is Our Example

21 For [a]you have been [aop]called
for this purpose, [b]since Christ[5547] also
suffered for you, leaving you [c]an
example[5261] for you to follow in His
steps,
22 WHO [a]COMMITTED NO SIN,[266] NOR
WAS ANY DECEIT FOUND IN HIS
MOUTH;
23 [I]and while being [ppp][a]reviled,[3058]
He [II]did not revile in return; while [ppt]suf-
fering, He uttered no threats, but kept
[ipf]entrusting *Himself* to Him who
judges[2919] righteously;[1346]
24 and He Himself [I][a]bore[399] our sins
in His body[4983] on the [II][b]cross, that we
[c]might [apt]die[581] to [III]sin and [aosb]live[2198]
to righteousness;[1343] for [d]by His
[IV]wounds you were [aop][e]healed.[2390]
25 For you were [a]continually straying like sheep, but now you have

15 [a]1Pet. 3:17 [b]1Pet. 2:12
16 [a]John 8:32; James 1:25 [b]Rom. 6:22; 1Cor. 7:22
17 [I]Or, *emperor* [a]Rom. 12:10; 13:7 [b]1Pet. 1:22 [c]Prov. 24:21 [d]Matt. 22:21; 1Pet. 2:13
18 [I]Or, *perverse* [a]Eph. 6:5 [b]James 3:17
19 [I]Or, *grace* [a]Rom. 13:5; 1Pet. 3:14, 16f.
20 [I]V. 19, note 1 [a]1Pet. 3:17
21 [a]Acts 14:22; 1Pet. 3:9 [b]1Pet. 3:18; 4:1, 13 [c]Matt. 11:29; 16:24
22 [a]Is. 53:9; 2Cor. 5:21
23 [I]Lit., *who* [II]Lit., *was not reviling* [a]Is. 53:7; Heb. 12:3; 1Pet. 3:9
24 [I]Or, *carried . . . up to the cross* [II]Lit., *wood* [III]Lit., *sins* [IV]Lit., *wound;* or, *welt* [a]Is. 53:4, 11; 1Cor. 15:3; Heb. 9:28 [b]Acts 5:30 [c]Rom. 6:2, 13 [d]Is. 53:5 [e]Heb. 12:13; James 5:16
25 [a]Is. 53:6

🔑 **2:17** This verse teaches the Christian's submission to higher powers. The same is taught in Rom. 13:1; Tit. 3:1, and I Tim. 2:1,2. The objection arises when those who rule over us are tyrannical, oppressive and ungodly. Political, social, domestic and national evils existed in the days when these words were written. These words cannot be construed as the Bible favoring kingship, tyranny or oppression.

At the time Peter wrote these words, there was not a single king professing Christianity, nor was there one until centuries later. It was a pagan king whom Peter exhorted the Christians "scattered throughout Pontus, Galatia, Cappadocia, Asia, and Bithynia" to honor. No doubt Peter had fully explained to them that Christ had abolished forever, in most emphatic and unmistakable terms, kingship and lordship among His followers. Peter wrote to the church and advised the members that because of the great spiritual freedom and privileges bestowed upon them, they were not to be puffed up and rebellious thus bringing themselves into collision with the governing powers under which they lived. Rather, they were to quietly submit themselves to their heathen rulers, giving them due honor or respect so that as law-abiding subjects they could claim protection if needed and not bring shame on the name of Christ by having the reputation of being rebels.

The same remarks apply to the text in I Tim. 2:1,2 that prayer be made for kings and all in authority. Here again, the kings were unbelievers. The object of the prayer explains itself, "That we may lead a tranquil and quiet life." One doesn't have to approve of what a worldly king does in order to pray for him. Praying for a person does not necessarily involve approving of his personality or acts. In no way do these references imply that kingship is to be practiced among Christians, but simply that Christians should make the best of the situation while living under their own particular governmental circumstance.

It is to be remembered that atheists were the ruling powers at the time that these words were written. "The Roman Senate," says Voltaire, "was composed almost entirely of theoretical or practical atheists, i.e., believing neither in providence nor in a future state." The Roman Senate was an assembly of philosophers, men of pleasure and ambition, men who were all very dangerous and eventually ruined their empire. See notes on Rom. 13:1; Tit. 3:1.

returned to the [b]Shepherd[4166] and [I]Guardian[1985] of your souls.[5590]

Godly Living

3 ⊶ [a]In the same way, you wives, [b]be submissive[5293] to your own husbands so that even if any *of them* are disobedient[544] to the word,[3056] they may be [fp c]won without a word by the behavior[391] of their wives,

2 as they [apt]observe[2029] your chaste[53] and [I]respectful behavior.

3 [a]And let not your adornment[2889] be *merely* external—braiding[1708] the hair, and wearing gold jewelry, or putting on dresses;

4 but *let it be* [a]the hidden person of the heart,[2588] with the imperishable[862] quality of a gentle[4239] and quiet[2272] spirit,[4151] which is precious in the sight of God.

5 For in this way in former times the holy[40] women also, [a]who [ppt]hoped[1679] in God, used to [ipf]adorn themselves, being submissive to their own husbands.

6 Thus Sarah obeyed[5219] Abraham, [a]calling him lord,[2962] and you have [aop]become her children if you [ppt]do what is right[15] [I b]without being [ppt]frightened[5399] by any fear.

⊶ **7** [a]You husbands likewise, [ppt]live with[4924] your wives in an understanding[1108] way, as with a weaker[772] [b]vessel, since she is a woman; and grant her honor as a fellow heir[4789] of the grace[5485] of life,[2222] so that your prayers[4335] may not be [aies]hindered.

8 [I]To sum up,[5056] [a]let all be harmonious, sympathetic,[4835] [b]brotherly,[5361] [c]kindhearted, and [d]humble in spirit;

9 [a]not returning evil[2556] for evil, or [b]insult for insult, but [I]giving a [c]blessing[2127] instead; for [d]you were called[2564] for the very purpose that you might [e]inherit[2816] a blessing.

10 For,

“[a]LET HIM WHO MEANS TO
[pinf]LOVE[25] LIFE[2222] AND
SEE[1492] GOOD[18] DAYS
REFRAIN HIS TONGUE FROM
EVIL AND HIS LIPS FROM
[infg]SPEAKING GUILE.[1388]

11 “[a]AND LET HIM TURN AWAY
FROM[1578] EVIL AND [aim]DO
GOOD;
LET HIM [aim]SEEK PEACE[1515] AND
[aim]PURSUE IT.

12 “[a]FOR THE EYES OF THE
LORD[2962] ARE UPON THE
RIGHTEOUS,[1342]
AND HIS EARS ATTEND TO
THEIR PRAYER,[1162]
BUT THE FACE OF THE LORD IS
AGAINST THOSE WHO [ppt]DO
EVIL.”

13 And [a]who is there to harm[2559] you if you [aosb]prove zealous for what is good?

14 But even if you should [opt a]suffer for the sake of righteousness,[1343] [b]*you are* blessed.[3107] [c]AND DO NOT [aosi]FEAR THEIR [I]INTIMIDATION, AND DO NOT BE [aosi]TROUBLED,

15 but [aim I]sanctify[37] [a]Christ as Lord in your hearts,[2588] always *being* ready [b]to make a defense to everyone who [ppt]asks you to give an account for the [c]hope[1680] that is in you, yet [d]with gentleness[4240] and [II e]reverence;[5401]

16 [I]and keep a [a]good[18] conscience[4893] so that in the thing in which [b]you are slandered,[2635] those who revile[1908] your good behavior[391] in Christ may be put to shame.

17 For [a]it is better,[2909] [b]if [I]God should will[2307] it so, that you [pinf]suffer for [ppt]doing what is right[15] rather than for [ppt]doing what is wrong.[2554]

25 [I]Or, *Bishop, Overseer* [b]John 10:11; 1Pet. 5:4
1 [a]1Pet. 3:7 [b]Eph. 5:22; Col. 3:18 [c]1Cor. 9:19
2 [I]Lit., *with fear*
3 [a]Is. 3:18ff.; 1Tim. 2:9
4 [a]Rom. 7:22
5 [a]1Tim. 5:5; 1Pet. 1:3
6 [I]Lit., *and are not* [a]Gen. 18:12 [b]1Pet. 3:14
7 [a]Eph. 5:25; Col. 3:19 [b]1Thess. 4:4
8 [I]Or, *Finally* [a]Rom. 12:16 [b]1Pet. 1:22 [c]Eph. 4:32 [d]Eph. 4:2; Phil. 2:3; 1Pet. 5:5
9 [I]Lit., *blessing instead* [a]Rom. 12:17; 1Thess. 5:15 [b]1Cor. 4:12; 1Pet. 2:23 [c]Luke 6:28; Rom. 12:14; 1Cor. 4:12 [d]1Pet. 2:21 [e]Gal. 3:14; Heb. 6:14; 12:17
10 [a]Ps. 34:12, 13
11 [a]Ps. 34:14
12 [a]Ps. 34:15, 16
13 [a]Prov. 16:7
14 [I]Lit., *fear* [a]Matt. 5:10; 1Pet. 2:19ff.; 4:15f. [b]James 5:11 [c]Is. 8:12f.; 1Pet. 3:6
15 [I]I.e., set apart [II]Or, *fear* [a]1Pet. 1:3 [b]Col. 4:6 [c]1Pet. 1:3 [d]2Tim. 2:25 [e]1Pet. 1:17
16 [I]Lit., *having a good* [a]1Tim. 1:5; Heb. 13:18; 1Pet. 3:21 [b]1Pet. 2:12, 15
17 [I]Lit., *the will of God* [a]1Pet. 2:20; 4:15f. [b]Acts 18:21; 1Pet. 1:6; 2:15; 4:19

⊶ **3:1-4** See notes on I Cor. 14:33-40 and I Tim. 2:9-15. The word that is used in I Pet. 3:4 translated as “quiet spirit” is the same word in its adjectival form, *hēsuchiou* (2272), which is translated in its substantive form, *hēsuchia* (2271), in I Tim. 2:12 as “quiet.” Peter certainly did not mean by a “quiet spirit” that a woman must be silent. He simply meant a tranquil, gentle spirit.
⊶ **3:7** See note on I Cor. 11:2-16.

🔑 18 For [a]Christ also [aor]died for sins
[b]once for all, *the* just[1342] for *the* unjust,[94]
in order that He might [aosb] [c]bring[4317] us
to God, having been put to death [d]in
the flesh,[4561] but made alive[2227] [e]in the
[1]spirit;[4151]

18 [1]Or, *Spirit*
[a]1Pet. 2:21
[b]Heb. 9:26, 28; 10:10 [c]Rom. 5:2; Eph. 3:12
[d]Col. 1:22; 1Pet. 4:1 [e]1Pet. 4:6

🔑 **3:18-20** See note on Eph. 4:8-10. One common interpretation of this passage is that subsequent to our Lord's death, possibly between His death and resurrection, His disembodied spirit went to the unseen world and there preached to the disobedient dead. We must reject such an interpretation because this passage only speaks of the dead in the days of Noah. There is no justification at all that such a small number of people who lived during the span of about 120 years should be singled out from the great mass of mankind for so singular and great a blessing. Those who hold such a theory of interpretation extend it to include the theory of the doctrine of probation after death, meaning that the impenitent dead have a second chance. Nowhere in Scripture do we find any indication that those who die unrepentant have a second chance.

In I Pet. 3:19 it simply states that Christ preached. It does not say what He preached. We must not take it for granted that every time we read the word *kērussō* (2784) preach, it means "to preach the Gospel." Even the word *euaggelizō* (2097), "to proclaim good news," does not necessarily mean to preach salvation. In Eph. 2:17 we have the same verb used but the object of the verb is peace, "He came and preached (*euēggelisato*) peace to you."

Another popular interpretation is that these words refer to Christ who in His spirit descended especially to preach in the days of Noah to men who were then on earth, but who, when the Apostle wrote, were in the unseen world—"spirits now in prison."

A more correct translation of this passage from the Greek will help in the interpretation. In v. 18 the expression "made alive in the Spirit," referring to Jesus Christ, does not have the definite article in front of the word "spirit," and thus it is not to be understood as God the Holy Spirit, but as the spirit or reasonable soul of Christ, that spirit which He delivered to the Father when He was dying on the cross. The last clause, therefore, of v. 18, should read, "Being put to death in the flesh, but quickened in the spirit." Here the two clauses form what is termed an antithetical or contrasted parallelism. "Quickened in spirit" is set over against "put to death in flesh." The word "flesh," *sarki,* also does not have the definite article in front of it. The law of translation compels us to give the same preposition to both "flesh" and "spirit." Whichever we use in one part of the clause, we must employ the same as an equivalent in the other. Thus, if we translate *thanatōtheis men sarki,* "put to death in the flesh," we must also render *zōopoiētheis de pneumati,* "made alive in the Spirit," and vice versa. It must either be "put to death by the flesh, but made alive by the spirit," or, "put to death in the flesh, but made alive in the spirit." We must also note that here there is no preposition used at all in the Greek which is translated once in regard to the flesh as "in" and in regard to the spirit as "by." The dative case is used. To translate, however, the dative case in regard to the flesh as "put to death by the flesh" has no meaning, and so we conclude that the preposition "by," presumed by the dative, is unacceptable either in the case of the flesh or the spirit. Therefore, the preposition "by" in the English translation cannot be employed, either regarding "flesh" or "spirit."

The next thing to be accomplished is to ascertain the aim of the Apostle in this portion of his Epistle. He is here dwelling upon the issue of the sufferings of God's persecuted people, illustrating the same by the glorious results of the sufferings of Christ. The first of these results is manifested or seen in the difference between the nature of that body that was put to death and that body in which He was brought back to life again. Only in respect to the natural body or fleshly organism was it possible for Christ to be put to death. In order that He might become subject to death we are informed that "the Word became flesh." And only by the withdrawal of the reasonable soul or spirit of Christ from the fleshly organism could death be manifested. By the use of this language, the Apostle distinguishes between the mortal body in which Christ was born and crucified, and the imperishable immortal body in which He was raised from the dead. In other words, Christ suffered death in what the Apostle Paul would have termed a "natural body," but was quickened or made alive again in a "spiritual body" (I Cor. 15:44). This seems to be the only intelligent interpretation of this passage. To speak of Christ as being quickened in His human spirit conveys no adequate sense, for that spirit (or reasonable soul) never died, and to speak of His being quickened in the Holy Spirit is equally vague, but to say that He was quickened in a spiritual body makes the whole passage clear. We see the mortal and immortal here being brought out

(continued on next page)

19 in [I]which also He went and
[a]made proclamation2784 to the spirits4151
now in prison,

19 [I]Or, *whom*
[a]1Pet. 4:6
20 [a]Rom. 2:4
[b]Gen. 6:3, 5, 13f.

20 who once were [apt]disobedient,544
when the [a]patience3115 of God [b]kept
[ipf]waiting1551 in the days of Noah, during

(continued from previous page)

in striking contrast. Just as He was put to death in the flesh (or natural body), so in like manner He was quickened in the spirit (or spiritual) body. Peter was writing to persecuted Christians, and this interpretation would convey the very encouragement and comfort they so much needed. Concerning being put to death "the just for the unjust," Christ had, as it were, changed the frail body of flesh in which He had tabernacled, "endured such hostility by sinners against himself," for a glorious, spiritual, immortal body which was not subject to pain or death any longer. Even so, the believer suffering the martyr's painful death would, by the very blow that crushed the poor, frail tabernacle of flesh, come into possession of a glorious resurrection body, spiritual and immortal.

This view throws a flood of light upon another somewhat obscure passage in I Tim. 3:16, "He who was revealed (manifested or made incarnate) in the flesh, was vindicated (or raised again for our justification) in the Spirit, beheld by angels (at His resurrection), proclaimed among the nations, believed on in the world, taken up in glory." In translating the words "flesh" and "spirit" in this passage as we have done in I Pet. 3:18, the obscurity of "justified in the spirit" disappears.

The glorious result of Christ being put to death, "the just for the unjust," was not merely the attainment of a resurrection body, for the Apostle goes on to say "in which also He went and made proclamation," etc. Whatever the nature of this preaching may have been, it had to take place between His death and resurrection. There is certainly no need to put an arbitrary interpretation on the words "spirits in prison," as referring simply to those who had passed to the unseen world, because the ungodly are constantly spoken of in Scripture as being in a state of imprisonment, bondage or captivity. If, therefore, we do not refer the expression to certain individuals but to the whole lost race, the difficulty vanishes. Christ did not preach to the same persons who were disobedient before the flood; but He preached to all who had disobeyed (v. 20), under the same spiritual conditions.

If, however, this preaching of Christ did not include an offer of salvation, as we have already intimated, what was the nature and import of the proclamation? It is to be noted that what is translated in I Pet. 3:19 is not the word *euaggelizō* (2097), "declare good news," but the verb *ekēruxen,* the aorist of *kēruttō* or *kērussō* (2784). The word *euaggelizō* is usually, but not exclusively (see Eph. 2:17), used to express the offer of salvation. The verb *kērussō,* "to proclaim," simply means to herald forth or make proclamation of something without determining what that proclamation is. There is really no necessity of introducing into the word *ekēruxen* a meaning which it does not have in so many other passages (see Mk. 1:45; 5:20; 7:36, etc. in which it simply means published or proclaimed).

The aim of the Apostle appears to have been to set forth the glorious issue of Christ's sufferings, and thus what He proclaimed was the completion of His mediatorial work in His final victory over death and the grave. It was part of the triumph that awaited the Redeemer. In His resurrection body He would ascend from earth, enter the invisible world, and there, as a mighty Conqueror returning from His successful campaign, make the proclamation that His mission to earth was accomplished, that He had made an end of sin, brought in an everlasting righteousness and had "abolished death and brought life and immortality to light." The Scripture is full of the most glowing allusions to this triumphant ascension of our Lord, "led captive a host of captives" (Eph. 4:8), as if death and hades were bound to His chariot wheels. Thus, the Apostle presents our Lord ascending in His resurrection body, heralding to all worlds tidings of His victory and the completion of His work. So universal and far-sounding is this proclamation that it reaches "even to the spirits in prison," and as such I Pet. 3:18,19 (see note) should certainly be rendered. Evidently the thought in the Apostle's mind is that the heralding was of such a far-reaching character as to extend even to those antediluvian sinners who, both on account of the remoteness of the period of their life on earth, and because of the enormity of their guilt that brought down the judgment of the flood, might be supposed to occupy the extreme limit of that circle of outer darkness (see note on Mt. 8:11,12), penetrated by such proclamation. The relation of this line of interpretation to the Apostle's object—that of fortifying Christians against persecution—is very clear. It is an indication of the glory which awaits every soldier of the cross who is "faithful unto death," (Rev. 2:10) and who stands steadfast in face of the sword, the torch or the lions. He shall one day go up in his resurrection body to share the triumphs of his all-conquering Lord. Therefore, we conclude that this passage allows no hope whatsoever to those who believe that there can be salvation after death. See notes on Rom.

(continued on next page)

the construction of [c]the ark, in which a
few, that is, [d]eight [e]persons,[5590] were
brought safely[1295] through *the* water.
21 [a]And corresponding to[499] that,
baptism[908] now saves[4982] you—[b]not the
removal of dirt from the flesh, but an

20 [c]Heb. 11:7 [d]Gen. 8:18; 2Pet. 2:5 [e]Acts 2:41; 1Pet. 1:9, 22; 2:25; 4:19

21 [a]Acts 16:33; Titus 3:5 [b]Heb. 9:14; 10:22

(continued from previous page)
3:25; Eph. 4:8-10, and the Editor's book entitled, *Conquering the Fear of Death,* an exegetical exposition of I Cor. 15 and related passages, and also see W. R. Bradlaugh, *The Christian's Armory,* London, 1902.

🗝 **3:20,21** Here we have the only place in the entire N.T. where the expression "baptism saves" occurs. In Mk. 16:16 the statement is "He who has believed and been baptized shall be saved; but he who has disbelieved shall be condemned." I Pet. 3:21 is incorrectly interpreted as meaning that baptism in and of itself saves or will save anyone. The verb in Mk. 16:16 that is translated "has believed" is in the aorist, *pisteusas,* which is a participle referring to one who believed at some time in the past. Also, the participle *baptistheis* (907), translated "has been baptized," is an aorist participle but in the passive voice. It refers to an act performed on the one who had already believed and which was exercised by someone else other than himself. Therefore, the correct translation here should be "He who believed and who was baptized shall be saved," *sōthēsetai,* the punctiliar future in the passive voice which means will be saved sometime in the future, and this salvation will not be caused by himself but by someone else. The two acts of the exercise of personal faith and of submitting oneself to baptism are in the past.

However, in order that no one may think that baptism by itself saves or will save anyone, the Lord adds, "But he who has disbelieved shall be condemned." The translation, "He who has disbelieved," in Greek is the aorist participle *apistēsas,* "He who did not believe." The verb translated "shall be condemned" in Greek is *katakrithēsetai,* which is the punctiliar future, passive voice of *katakrinō* (2632), "to condemn." The negative statement does not include baptism. It does not say "he who did not believe and who was not baptized is condemned." Therefore, it is absolutely clear that what saves a person is living faith in Jesus Christ which may be followed by baptism. However, there surely were people who were baptized and whose baptism was not the true outward demonstration of their inner, saving faith (Acts 8:9-25). These people will perish. We never find the expression in the N.T. that he who was not baptized will perish. It is constantly that he who did not believe will not only be condemned, but is already condemned (John 3:18). Therefore, the statement in I Pet. 3:21 that baptism now saves cannot mean baptism in and of itself, without the antecedent saving faith. It must include living faith in Jesus Christ.

That baptism is consequent to salvation is clear by the order of the two words not only in Mark 16:16, but all throughout the Scriptures such as Acts 2:38 and 10:48. In Mt. 28:19, teaching precedes baptism. In Acts 22:16, baptism was enjoined upon ascertaining living faith in Christ. The fact that living faith in Christ is the first and absolutely necessary element unto salvation is made clear by many Scriptures, but particularly by Eph. 2:8, "For by grace you have been saved through faith." The word "saved" in Greek is *sesōsmenoi* which is a perfect participle in the passive voice. It means that this salvation took place sometime in the past and continues in the present and that it is accomplished by someone other than oneself. If baptism were necessary for salvation, this verse and many others should have said that we are saved through faith and baptism.

Thus the word "baptism" in I Pet. 3:21 cannot mean baptism isolated from faith, but only as an evidence of the exercise of faith which preceded the baptism.

Peter had been speaking in v. 20 about the eight souls who believed Noah and entered the ark and were saved through the water as the preposition *dia,* "through," really means. They were not saved by the water but they were saved through the water as a result of having entered the ark. Being in the ark, they were able to pass safely through the waters.

Physical baptism involves water. Therefore, Peter uses the symbolism of baptism, v. 21, which saves us even now as an antitype (499), "corresponding to." The word is made up of the preposition *anti* denoting correspondency, and *tupos,* "a form or figure," thus meaning "a form, a figure correspondent to some other," as the impression on the wax corresponds to the sculpture on the seal, or the sculpture on the seal to the impression on the wax. This word is used in Heb. 9:24 as a figure or type answering to and representing a reality. For instance, the ancient Christians used to call the bread and wine in the

(continued on next page)

appeal to God for a [c]good conscience—through [d]the resurrection[386] of Jesus Christ,
22 [a]who is at the right hand[1188] of God, [b]having [apt]gone into heaven,[3772]
[c]after angels[32] and authorities[1849] and powers[1411] had been [aptp]subjected to[5293] Him.

21 [c]1Tim. 1:5; Heb. 13:18; 1Pet. 3:16 [d]1Pet. 1:3
22 [a]Mark 16:19 [b]Heb. 4:14; 6:20 [c]Rom. 8:38f.; Heb. 1:6

(continued from previous page)
communion the *antitupa* (plural) of Christ's body and blood. In I Pet. 3:21, however, an antitype stands for something answering to and represented by a type.

The relative pronoun *ho* does not refer to the water, but to the baptism which is called antitype.

An antitype is something represented by an earlier type or symbol. Thus baptism is called an antitype because it is a symbol of salvation, an affirmation of living faith in Christ. Romans 6:3-14 speaks of the death, burial and resurrection of Jesus Christ being the real thing symbolized by baptism in or with water. The important thing is not the physical act of baptism but what it represents, the death and resurrection of Christ and our spiritual burial and resurrection. It is a symbolism of our death unto sin and our resurrection unto newness of life.

Thus, v. 21 should read, "which (baptism) being an antitype (symbol) of Christ's death and resurrection saves even us now baptism," or to put it in better English: "which baptism, as an antitype (of Christ's death and resurrection), now saves even us." The word *antitupon,* "antitype," explains the word "baptism," being in apposition to it. "Baptism," being an antitype, means a copy of something that has reality. The basic word *tupos* (5179), "print, type," was used in Jn. 20:25; Acts 7:43,44; 23:25; Rom. 5:14; 6:17; I Cor. 10:6; Phil. 3:17; I Thess. 1:7; II Thess. 3:9; I Tim. 4:12; Tit. 2:7; Heb. 8:5 and I Pet. 5:3. An antitype is something which stands instead of the real thing. In the case of Jesus' pierced hands, the nails left a mark, *tupos* (Jn. 20:25). Those were the prints, the types. The copy of that print would be an antitype. Therefore, baptism in v. 21 is called the antitype of salvation. In this context, baptism does not refer to the water at all, but to the ark in which Noah and his family found their salvation through the water. The water in the case of the flood symbolizes not salvation, but the means of destruction used by God. Therefore, baptism, which is a symbol of our having been rescued by God through our voluntary entrance into the ark of His salvation, is here called the symbol that saves us. But in actuality, it is not the symbol itself which saves us, but that which it symbolizes. When we see a person who is saved, we see a person who has voluntarily entered into the ark of salvation and has been rescued by God Himself. It was He who commanded Noah to build the ark according to His plans and with materials He had provided, even as Jesus Christ came into the world with the full consent and plan of the Father. Therefore, we arrive at the conclusion that it is not the symbol of baptism in itself that saves anyone, but it is what Christ did for us and the acceptance of that work. Peter himself in II Pet. 3:6,7 makes the contrast that as in the days of Noah the world was destroyed in water, so the second time it is going to be destroyed by fire (II Pet. 3:10).

To take away any possible misunderstanding that he is speaking here about an outward ablution, even as ablutions or washings were practiced by the Jews to cleanse their bodies before worship, Peter says, "not the removal of dirt from the flesh." Baptism does not symbolize bodily cleansing without a previous inner cleansing having first taken place. It is the testimony of an already cleansed soul. It is not actually the putting away (*apothesis,* 595) of bodily filth from oneself, but it is the outward expression of a work already done in one's heart through the cleansing blood of the Lord Jesus Christ.

After giving us negatively his view of baptism, that it is not the putting away from oneself of the filth of the body, Peter goes on to tell us positively what it is. In contrast to the *apothesis,* "the putting away from oneself," he presents the Greek word *eperōtēma* (1906), which in our English versions is translated as "appeal." The verb *eperōtaō,* used many times in the N.T., signifies not only to ask, but to make a demand upon oneself. The noun is *eperōtēma* which is a legal term equivalent in meaning to claim or demand. Peter says that baptism as a symbol, referring, of course, to water baptism to which a believer commits himself, is not a cleansing thing; it is a demand or a claim that God legally has upon the person who has believed. It is not the baptism which produces a life conformable to God's will, but the baptism, having been a public declaration of one's inner faith, demands that that person externalize the inner cleansing of the Lord through the actions of his life. A baptized person is one who is under obligation to God to live a holy life. Once the declaration is made to the world that a person has been identified with Christ in baptism, the Lord and the world have every right to expect to see clear evidence of a

(continued on next page)

Keep Fervent in Your Love

4 Therefore, since [a]Christ has [apt] [I]suf-
fered in the flesh,[4561] [aim] [b]arm yourselves also with the same purpose,[1771]
because [c]he who has [I]suffered in the
flesh has ceased from sin,
2 [a]so as to [aies]live [b]the rest of the
time[5550] in the flesh[4561] no longer for
the lusts[1939] of men, but for the [c]will[2307]
of God.
3 For [a]the time already past is sufficient *for you* to have carried out the
desire[1013] of the Gentiles, [b]having pursued a course of sensuality,[766] lusts,[1939]
drunkenness, carousals,[2970] drinking
parties[4224] and [I]abominable[111] idolatries.[1495]
4 And in *all* this, they are surprised
that you do not [ppt]run with *them* into
the same excess of [a]dissipation,[810] and
they [b]malign[987] *you;*
5 but they shall give account to Him
who is ready to [ainf]judge[2919] [a]the living[2198]
and the dead.[3498]
6 For [a]the gospel has for this purpose been preached[2097] even to those
who are dead, that though they are
[asbp]judged in the flesh as men, they
may [psa]live[2198] in the spirit[4151] according
to *the will of* God.
7 [a]The end[5056] of all things [I]is at
hand; therefore, [aim] [b]be of sound judgment[4993] and sober *spirit* for the purpose
of [II]prayer.[4335]
8 Above all, [a]keep fervent[1618] in
your love[26] for one another, because
[b]love covers[2572] a multitude of sins.[266]
9 [a]Be hospitable to one another
without [b]complaint.
10 [a]As each one has [ao]received a
special gift,[5486] [ppt]employ[1247] it in serving[1247] one another, as good [b]stew-
ards[3623] of the manifold grace[5485] of God.
11 [a]Whoever speaks,[2980] *let him*
speak, as it were, the [b]utterances[3051]
of God; whoever serves, *let him do so*
as [Ic]by the strength which God supplies;
so that [d]in all things God may be
[psmp]glorified[1392] through Jesus Christ,
[e]to whom belongs the glory[1391] and
dominion[2904] forever[165] and ever.
Amen.[281]

Share the Sufferings of Christ

12 [a]Beloved, do not be surprised
at the [b]fiery ordeal among you, which
comes upon you for your testing,[3986]
as though some strange thing were
[ppt]happening to you;
🔑 13 but to the degree that you
[a]share[2841] the sufferings[3804] of Christ,
keep on rejoicing;[5463] so that also at the
[b]revelation[602] of His glory,[1391] [c]you may
rejoice[5463] with exultation.[21]

1 [I]I.e., suffered death [a]1Pet. 2:21 [b]Eph. 6:13 [c]Rom. 6:7
2 [a]Rom. 6:2; Col. 3:3 [b]1Pet. 1:14 [c]Mark 3:35
3 [I]Lit., *lawless* [a]1Cor. 12:2 [b]Rom. 13:13; Eph. 2:2; 4:17ff.
4 [a]Eph. 5:18 [b]1Pet. 3:16
5 [a]Acts 10:42; Rom. 14:9; 2Tim. 4:1
6 [a]1Pet. 1:12; 3:19
7 [I]Lit., *has come near* [II]Lit., *prayers* [a]Rom. 13:11; Heb. 9:26; James 5:8; 1John 2:18 [b]1Pet. 1:13
8 [a]1Pet. 1:22 [b]Prov. 10:12; 1Cor. 13:4ff.; James 5:20
9 [a]1Tim. 3:2; Heb. 13:2 [b]Phil. 2:14
10 [a]Rom. 12:6f. [b]1Cor. 4:1
11 [I]Lit., *from* [a]1Thess. 2:4; Titus 2:1, 15; Heb. 13:7 [b]Acts 7:38 [c]Eph. 1:19; 6:10 [d]1Cor. 10:31; 1Pet. 2:12 [e]Rom. 11:36; 1Pet. 5:11; Rev. 1:6; 5:13
12 [a]1Pet. 2:11 [b]1Pet. 1:6f.
13 [a]Rom. 8:17; 2Cor. 1:5; 4:10; Phil. 3:10 [b]1Pet. 1:7; 5:1 [c]2Tim. 2:12

(continued from previous page)
transformed life. *Eperōtēma* refers not to what establishes a good conscience, but it refers rather to a claim which a good conscience has upon God. A person who has believed and been baptized and who bears a clear conscience, not because of his baptism but because of the work of grace in his heart, has a claim upon God. A believer who has accepted and conforms to God's right over his life, in turn has special rights in the presence of God as His child. The closer one lives to God in conformity to His will, the greater the claim he has upon God. Which is the child who has greater freedom to make a request of his father? The child who does not conform to the standard his father has set for his life or the one who does? Baptism, therefore, demands a good conscience. But what is a good conscience? The word for "conscience" in Greek is *suneidēsis* (4893), from the verb *suneideō* or *suneidō* (4894), which is made up of *sun,* "together with," and the verb *eideō* or *eidō* (1492), "to know intuitively." *Suneidēsis,* then, is intuitively knowing together with God, i.e., consciously knowing what God expects. Therefore, a person who has believed and been baptized should know God's expectations upon his life and should make every effort to meet those expectations.

In this connection see *dikaioō* (1344), "to justify," in the lexical aids and the general remarks on justification on Romans. The adjective translated "good" in Greek is *agathēs,* in the feminine because conscience is in the feminine gender in Greek (see *agathos,* 18). The word means not only constitutionally good, but benevolently good. A person who has been baptized, Peter says, must externalize his baptism in benevolent actions that show that he knows what God's will for him is.

🔑 **4:13** See note on I Thess. 2:19.

14 If you are reviled[987] [Ia]for the name[3686] of Christ,[5547] [b]you are blessed,[3107] [c]because the Spirit[4151] of glory and of God[2316] rests upon you.

15 By no means [a]let any of you [pim]suffer as a murderer,[5406] or thief, or evildoer,[2555] or a [Ib]troublesome meddler;[244]

16 but if *anyone suffers* as a [a]Christian,[5546] let him not feel [pim]ashamed, but in that name let him [pim] [b]glorify God.

17 For *it is* time[2540] for judgment[2917] [a]to [ainf]begin [I]with [b]the household[3624] of God; and if *it* [c]*begins* with us first, what *will be* the outcome[5056] for those [d]who do not [ppt]obey[544] the [e]gospel[2098] of God?

18 [a]AND IF IT IS WITH DIFFICULTY THAT THE RIGHTEOUS[1342] IS SAVED,[4982] [I]WHAT WILL BECOME OF THE [b]GODLESS[765] MAN AND THE SINNER?[268]

19 Therefore, let those also who [ppt]suffer according to [a]the will[2307] of God [pim]entrust their souls[5590] to a faithful[4103] Creator[2939] in doing what is right.[16]

Serve God Willingly

5 [a]Therefore, I exhort[3870] the elders[4245] among you, as *your* [b]fellow elder[4850] and [c]witness of the sufferings of Christ, and a [d]partaker[2844] also of the glory[1391] that is to be revealed,

2 shepherd[4165] [a]the flock[4168] of God among you, exercising oversight[1983] [b]not under compulsion, but voluntarily, according to *the will of* God; and [c]not for sordid gain,[147] but with eagerness;

3 nor yet as [a]lording it over [I]those allotted to your charge,[2819] but [II]proving to be [b]examples[5179] to the flock.[4168]

4 And when the Chief [a]Shepherd[750] [aptp]appears,[5319] you will receive the [b]unfading[262] [Ic]crown of glory.

5 [a]You younger men, likewise, [b]be subject to[5293] your elders;[4245] and all of you, [aim]clothe yourselves with [c]humility toward one another, for [d]GOD IS OPPOSED TO THE PROUD,[5244] BUT GIVES GRACE[5485] to the humble.

6 [a]Humble yourselves, therefore, under the mighty[2900] hand of God, that He may exalt you at the proper time,[2540]

7 [apt]casting all your [a]anxiety upon Him, because He cares for you.

8 [a]Be of sober *spirit*, [b]be on the alert. Your adversary,[476] [c]the devil,[1228] prowls about like a roaring [d]lion, [ppt]seeking someone to [ainf]devour.

9 [Ia]But resist him, [b]firm in *your* faith,[4102] knowing that [c]the same experiences of suffering are being accomplished[2005] by your [II]brethren[81] who are in the world.[2889]

10 And after you have [apt]suffered[3958] [a]for a little while, the [b]God[2316] of all grace,[5485] who [c]called you to His [d]eternal[166] glory[1391] in Christ, will Himself [e]perfect,[2675] [f]confirm,[4741] strengthen[4599] *and* establish you.

11 [a]To Him *be* dominion[2904] forever[165] and ever. Amen.[281]

12 Through [a]Silvanus, our faithful[4103] brother[80] [I](for so I regard[3049] *him*), [b]I have written to you briefly, exhorting and testifying[1957] that this is [c]the true grace of God. [d]Stand firm in it!

13 [I]She who is in Babylon, chosen together with[4899] you, sends you greetings,[782] and *so does* my son,[5207] [a]Mark.

14 [a]Greet[782] one another with a kiss of love.[26]

[b]Peace[1515] be to you all who are in Christ.

14 [I]Lit., *in* [a]John 15:21; Heb. 11:26; 1Pet. 4:16 [b]Matt. 5:11; Luke 6:22; Acts 5:41 [c]2Cor. 4:10f., 16
15 [I]Lit., *one who oversees others' affairs* [a]1Pet. 2:19f.; 3:17 [b]1Thess. 4:11; 2Thess. 3:11; 1Tim. 5:13
16 [a]Acts 5:41; 28:22; James 2:7 [b]1Pet. 4:11
17 [I]Lit., *from* [a]Jer. 25:29; Ezek. 9:6; Amos 3:2 [b]1Tim. 3:15; Heb. 3:6; 1Pet. 2:5 [c]Rom. 2:9 [d]2Thess. 1:8 [e]Rom. 1:1
18 [I]Lit., *where will appear* [a]Prov. 11:31; Luke 23:31 [b]1Tim. 1:9
19 [a]1Pet. 3:17

1 [a]Acts 11:30 [b]2John 1; 3John 1 [c]Luke 24:48; Heb. 12:1 [d]1Pet. 1:5, 7; 4:13; Rev. 1:9
2 [a]John 21:16; Acts 20:28 [b]Philem. 14 [c]1Tim. 3:8
3 [I]Lit., *the allotments* [II]Or, *becoming* [a]Ezek. 34:4; Matt. 20:25f. [b]John 13:15; Phil. 3:17; 1Thess. 1:7; 2Thess. 3:9; 1Tim. 4:12; Titus 2:7
4 [I]Lit., *wreath* [a]1Pet. 2:25 [b]1Pet. 1:4 [c]1Cor. 9:25
5 [a]Luke 22:26; 1Tim. 5:1 [b]Eph. 5:21 [c]1Pet. 3:8 [d]Prov. 3:34; James 4:6
6 [a]Matt. 23:12; Luke 14:11; 18:14; James 4:10
7 [a]Ps. 55:22; Matt. 6:25
8 [a]1Pet. 1:13 [b]Matt. 24:42 [c]James 4:7 [d]2Tim. 4:17

9 [I]Lit., *whom resist* [II]Lit., *brotherhood* [a]James 4:7 [b]Col. 2:5 [c]Acts 14:22 **10** [a]1Pet. 1:6 [b]1Pet. 4:10 [c]1Cor. 1:9; 1Thess. 2:12 [d]2Cor. 4:17; 2Tim. 2:10 [e]1Cor. 1:10; Heb. 13:21 [f]Rom. 16:25; 2Thess. 2:17; 3:3 **11** [a]Rom. 11:36; 1Pet. 4:11 **12** [I]Lit., *(as I consider)* [a]2Cor. 1:19 [b]Heb. 13:22 [c]Acts 11:23; 1Pet. 1:13; 4:10 [d]1Cor. 15:1 **13** [I]Some mss. read *The church which* [a]Acts 12:12, 25; 15:37, 39; Col. 4:10; Philem. 24 **14** [a]Rom. 16:16 [b]Eph. 6:23

5:1 See general remarks on II John.

The Second Epistle of

PETER

Although the author claimed to be the Apostle Peter (II Pet. 1:1), no book of the New Testament had a more difficult time establishing its authenticity and place in the canon. This was due in part to the fact that it was not widely known very early, and so many people in the second and third centuries A.D. were writing under the name Peter. Nevertheless, the traditional view has been that the Apostle Peter was the author. There is a literary relationship between II Peter and Jude, because the material in II Pet. 2:1—3:3 is very similar to that in Jude 3-18, in both order and content. The specific application, however, is slightly different. II Peter was occasioned by the presence of a group of false teachers who were about to cause problems for its readers. In chapter 2 we learn about their licentious life style. And in the third chapter, because of their skepticism of Christ's return, Peter gives one of the most detailed Biblical discussions on the end of the world. The seeming delay of Jesus' return is only apparent, because God lives outside the dimension of time. One day, the Day of the Lord will occur, and it will be accompanied by the total destruction of this physical universe. In the meantime, the readers were to be careful, lest they be infected by the false teachers' life style and teachings.

Growth in Christian Virtue

1 [I]Simon Peter, a [a]bond-servant[1401]
and [b]apostle[652] of Jesus Christ,[5547]
to those who have received [c]a faith[4102]
of the same [II]kind as ours, [III]by [d]the
righteousness[1343] of [e]our God[2316] and
Savior,[4990] Jesus Christ:
2 [a]Grace[5485] and peace[1515] be multiplied to you in [b]the knowledge[1922] of
God and of Jesus our Lord;[2962]
3 seeing that His [a]divine[2304]
power[1411] has granted to us everything
pertaining to life[2222] and godliness,[2150]
through the true [b]knowledge[1922] of Him
who [apt] [c]called us [I]by His own glory[1391]
and [II]excellence.[703]
4 [I]For by these He has granted to
us His precious and magnificent [a]prom-
ises,[1862] in order that by them you might
become [b]partakers[2844] of *the* divine nature,5449 having [c]escaped the [d]corruption
that is in [e]the world[2889] by lust.[1939]
5 Now for this very reason also, applying all diligence, in your faith[4102]
[a]supply [b]moral [I]excellence, and in *your*
moral excellence,[703] [c]knowledge;[1108]
6 and in *your* knowledge, [a]self-con-
trol,1466 and in *your* self-control, [b]per-
severance,[5281] and in *your* perseverance, [c]godliness;
7 and in *your* godliness,[2150] [a]broth-
erly kindness, and in *your* brotherly
kindness,[5360] love.[26]
8 For if these *qualities* are[5225] yours
and are [ppt]increasing, they render[2525]
you neither useless[692] nor [a]unfruitful in
the true [b]knowledge[1922] of our Lord
Jesus Christ.
9 For he who lacks these *qualities*
is [a]blind *or* short-sighted, having forgotten *his* [b]purification[2512] from his former[3819] sins.[266]
10 Therefore, brethren, be all the
more diligent to [pinf]make certain[949] about
His [a]calling[2821] and [b]choosing[1589] you;
for as long as you [ppt]practice these
things, you will never [efn] [c]stumble;4417
11 for in this way the entrance into
[a]the eternal[166] kingdom[932] of our
[b]Lord and Savior Jesus Christ will be
[c]abundantly [d]supplied to you.
12 Therefore, [a]I shall always be
ready to [pinf]remind you of these things,
even though you *already* know[1492] *them*,
and have been established in [b]the
truth[225] which is present with *you*.

1 [I]Most early mss. read *Simeon* [II]Or, *value* [III]Or, *in* [a]Rom. 1:1; Phil. 1:1; James 1:1; Jude 1 [b]1Pet. 1:1 [c]Rom. 1:12; 2Cor. 4:13; Titus 1:4 [d]Rom. 3:21-26 [e]Titus 2:13
2 [a]Rom. 1:7; 1Pet. 1:2 [b]John 17:3; Phil. 3:8; 2Pet. 1:3, 8; 2:20; 3:18
3 [I]Or possibly, *to* [II]Or, *virtue* [a]1Pet. 1:5 [b]John 17:3; Phil. 3:8; 2Pet. 1:2, 8; 2:20; 3:18 [c]1Thess. 2:12; 2Thess. 2:14; 1Pet. 5:10
4 [I]Lit., *Through which* (things) [a]2Pet. 3:9, 13 [b]Eph. 4:13, 24; Heb. 12:10; 1John 3:2 [c]2Pet. 2:18, 20 [d]2Pet. 2:19 [e]James 1:27
5 [I]Or, *virtue* [a]2Pet. 1:11 [b]2Pet. 1:3 [c]Col. 2:3; 2Pet. 1:2
6 [a]Acts 24:25 [b]Luke 21:19 [c]2Pet. 1:3
7 [a]Rom. 12:10; 1Pet. 1:22
8 [a]Col. 1:10 [b]John 17:3; Phil. 3:8; 2Pet. 1:2, 3; 2:20; 3:18
9 [a]1John 2:11 [b]Eph. 5:26; Titus 2:14
10 [a]Matt. 22:14; Rom. 11:29; 2Pet. 1:3 [b]1Thess. 1:4 [c]James 2:10; 2Pet. 3:17; Jude 24
11 [a]2Tim. 4:18 [b]2Pet. 2:20; 3:18 [c]Rom. 2:4; 1Tim. 6:17 [d]2Pet. 1:5
12 [a]Phil. 3:1; 1John 2:21; Jude 5 [b]Col. 1:5f.; 2John 2

13 And I consider it [a]right,[1342] as long as I am in [b]this *earthly* dwelling,[4638] to [c]stir you up by way of reminder,[5280]

14 knowing that [a]the laying aside of my *earthly* dwelling is imminent, [b]as also our Lord Jesus Christ has made clear to me.

15 And I will also be diligent that at any time after my [a]departure you may be able to call these things to mind.

Eyewitnesses

16 For we did not follow cleverly devised[4679] [a]tales[3454] when we made known[1107] to you the [b]power[1411] and coming[3952] of our Lord Jesus Christ, but we [aptp]were [c]eyewitnesses[2030] of His majesty.

17 For when He [apt]received honor[5092] and glory[1391] from God the Father,[3962] such an [Ia]utterance as this was [aptp II]made to Him by the [b]Majestic Glory, "This is My beloved[27] Son[5207] with whom I am well-pleased"—[2106]

18 and we ourselves heard this [I]utterance [aptp]made from heaven[3772] when we were with Him on the [a]holy[40] mountain.

19 [I]And *so* we have [a]the prophetic[4397] word[3056] *made* more [b]sure,[949] to which you do well to pay attention as to [c]a lamp [ppt]shining[5316] in a dark place, until the [d]day [aosb]dawns and the [e]morning star [aosb]arises [f]in your hearts.[2588]

20 But [a]know this first[4412] of all, that [b]no prophecy[4394] of Scripture[1124] is *a matter* of one's own[2398] interpretation,[1955]

21 for [a]no prophecy[4394] was ever made by an act of human[444] will,[2307] but men[444] [b]moved[5342] by the [an]Holy Spirit[4151] spoke[2980] from God.

The Rise of False Prophets

2 But [a]false prophets also arose among the people,[2992] just as there will also be [b]false teachers[5527] [c]among you, who will [d]secretly introduce[3919] [e]destructive[684] heresies,[139] even [f]denying[720] the [g]Master[1203] who [h]bought[59] them, bringing swift destruction[684] upon themselves.

2 And many will follow their [a]sensuality,[766] and because of them [b]the way[3598] of the truth[225] will be [c]maligned;[987]

3 and in *their* [a]greed they will [b]exploit you with [c]false[4112] words; [d]their judgment[2917] from long ago is not idle, and their destruction[684] is not asleep.

4 For [a]if God did not spare angels[32] when they [apt]sinned,[264] but cast them into hell[5020] and [b]committed them to pits of darkness,[2217] [ppp]reserved[5083] for judgment;[2920]

5 and did not spare [a]the ancient world,[2889] but preserved [b]Noah, a [I]preacher[2783] of righteousness,[1343] with seven others, when He [apt]brought a [c]flood upon the world of the ungodly;[765]

6 and *if* He [a]condemned[2632] the cities of Sodom and Gomorrah to destruction by reducing *them* to ashes, having [pfp]made them an [b]example to those who would [c]live ungodly[764] thereafter;

7 and *if* He [a]rescued[4506] righteous[1342] Lot, oppressed[2669] by the [b]sensual[766] conduct[391] of [c]unprincipled men

8 (for by what he saw and heard *that* [a]righteous[1342] man, while living among them, felt *his* righteous soul[5590] [ipf]tormented day after day with *their* lawless[459] deeds),

9 [a]*then* the Lord knows[1492] how to rescue the godly[2152] from [I]temptation,[3986] and to [pinf]keep[5083] the unrighteous[94] under punishment for the [b]day of judgment,

10 and especially those who [ppt Ia]indulge

13 [a]Phil. 1:7 [b]2Cor. 5:1, 4; 2Pet. 1:14 [c]2Pet. 3:1
14 [a]2Cor. 5:1; 2Tim. 4:6 [b]John 13:36; 21:19
15 [a]Luke 9:31
16 [a]1Tim. 1:4; 2Pet. 2:3 [b]Mark 13:26; 14:62; 1Thess. 2:19 [c]Matt. 17:1ff.; Mark 9:2ff.; Luke 9:28ff.
17 [I]Lit., *voice* [II]Lit., *borne* [a]Matt. 17:5; Mark 9:7; Luke 9:35 [b]Heb. 1:3
18 [I]Lit., *voice borne* [a]Ex. 3:5; Josh. 5:15
19 [I]Or, *And we have the even surer prophetic word* [a]1Pet. 1:10f. [b]Heb. 2:2 [c]Ps. 119:105 [d]Luke 1:78 [e]Rev. 22:16 [f]2Cor. 4:6
20 [a]2Pet. 3:3 [b]Rom. 12:6
21 [a]Jer. 23:26; 2Tim. 3:16 [b]2Sam. 23:2; Luke 1:70; Acts 1:16; 3:18; 1Pet. 1:11

1 [a]Deut. 13:1ff.; Jer. 6:13 [b]2Cor. 11:13 [c]Matt. 7:15; 1Tim. 4:1 [d]Gal. 2:4; Jude 4 [e]1Cor. 11:19; Gal. 5:20 [f]Jude 4 [g]Rev. 6:10 [h]1Cor. 6:20
2 [a]Gen. 19:5ff.; 2Pet. 2:7, 18; Jude 4 [b]Acts 16:17; 22:4; 24:14 [c]Rom. 2:24
3 [a]1Tim. 6:5; 2Pet. 2:14; Jude 16 [b]2Cor. 2:17; 1Thess. 2:5 [c]Rom. 16:18; 2Pet. 1:16 [d]Deut. 32:35
4 [a]Jude 6 [b]Rev. 20:1f.
5 [I]Or, *herald* [a]Ezek. 26:20; 2Pet. 3:6 [b]Gen. 6:8, 9; 1Pet. 3:20 [c]2Pet. 3:6
6 [a]Gen. 19:24; Jude 7 [b]Is. 1:9; Matt. 10:15; 11:23; Rom. 9:29; Jude 7 [c]Jude 15
7 [a]Gen. 19:16, 29 [b]Gen. 19:5ff.; 2Pet. 2:2, 18; Jude 4 [c]2Pet. 3:17
8 [a]Heb. 11:4
9 [I]Or, *trial* [a]1Cor. 10:13; Rev. 3:10 [b]Matt. 10:15; Jude 6
10 [I]Lit., *go after* [a]2Pet. 3:3; Jude 16, 18

1:16 See note on I Thess. 2:19.

dulge the <u>flesh</u>[4561] in *its* <u>corrupt</u>[3394] <u>desires</u>[1939] and [ppt] [b]despise <u>authority</u>.[2963] Daring, [c]self-willed, they do not tremble when they [ppt] [b]<u>revile</u>[987] <u>angelic</u> [II]<u>majesties</u>,[1391]

11 [a]whereas <u>angels</u>[32] who are greater in <u>might</u>[2479] and <u>power</u>[1411] do not bring a <u>reviling</u>[989] <u>judgment</u>[2920] against them before the <u>Lord</u>.[2962]

12 But [a]these, like unreasoning <u>animals</u>,[2226] [b]<u>born</u>[1080] as creatures of instinct to be captured and killed, <u>reviling</u>[987] where they have <u>no knowledge</u>,[50] will in [I]the destruction of those creatures also be destroyed,

13 suffering wrong as [a]the <u>wages</u>[3408] of <u>doing wrong</u>.[93] They [ppt]count it a pleasure to [b]<u>revel</u>[5172] in the [c]daytime. They are <u>stains</u>[4695] and <u>blemishes</u>,[3470] [d]<u>reveling in their</u>[1792] [I]deceptions, as they [e]carouse with you,

14 having eyes full of adultery and that <u>never cease</u>180 from <u>sin</u>,[266] [a]<u>enticing</u>1185 [b]unstable <u>souls</u>,[5590] having a <u>heart</u>[2588] trained in [c]greed, [d]<u>accursed</u>[2671] <u>children</u>;[5043]

15 forsaking [a]the <u>right</u>2117 way they have gone astray, having [apt]followed [b]the way of Balaam, the *son* of Beor, who <u>loved</u>[25] [c]the <u>wages</u>[3408] of unrighteousness,

16 but he received a rebuke for his own <u>transgression</u>;[3892] [a]*for* a dumb donkey, speaking with a voice of a <u>man</u>,[444] restrained the madness of the <u>prophet</u>.[4396]

17 These are [a]springs without water, and mists driven by a <u>storm</u>,[2978] [b]for whom the [I]<u>black</u>2217 <u>darkness</u>[4655] has been [pfp]<u>reserved</u>.[5083]

18 For [ppt]speaking out [a]arrogant *words* of [b]<u>vanity</u>[3153] they [c]entice by <u>fleshly</u>[4561] <u>desires</u>,[1939] by [d]<u>sensuality</u>,[766] those who barely [apt] [e]escape from the ones who live in error,

🔑 19 [ppt]<u>promising</u>[1861] them <u>freedom</u>[1657] while they themselves are <u>slaves</u>[1401] of corruption; for [a]by what a man is overcome, by this he is enslaved.

20 For if after they have [apt] [a]escaped the <u>defilements</u>[3393] of the <u>world</u>[2889] by [b]the <u>knowledge</u>[1922] of the [c]<u>Lord</u>[2962] and <u>Savior</u>[4990] Jesus <u>Christ</u>,[5547] they are again [aptp] [d]entangled in them and are overcome, [e]the <u>last state</u>[2078] has become worse for them than the first.

21 [a]For it would be <u>better</u>[2909] for them not to have [pfin]known the <u>way</u>[3598] of <u>righteousness</u>,[1343] than having [apt]known it, to [ainf]turn away from [b]the <u>holy</u>[40] <u>commandment</u>[1785] [c]delivered to them.

22 It has happened to them according to the true proverb, "[a]A DOG [apt]RETURNS TO ITS OWN VOMIT," and, "A sow, after washing, *returns* to wallowing in the <u>mire</u>."[1004]

Purpose of This Letter

3 This is now, [a]beloved, the second <u>letter</u>1992 I am <u>writing</u>[1125] to you in which I am [b]stirring up your <u>sincere</u>[1506] <u>mind</u>[1271] by way of <u>reminder</u>,[5280]

2 that you should [a]remember the words spoken beforehand by [b]the holy <u>prophets</u>[4396] and [c]the commandment of the <u>Lord</u>[2962] and <u>Savior</u>[4990] *spoken* by your <u>apostles</u>.[652]

The Coming Day of the Lord

3 [a]<u>Know</u>[1097] this <u>first</u>[4412] of all, that [b]in the <u>last</u>[2078] days [c]mockers will come with *their* mocking, [d]following after their own <u>lusts</u>,[1939]

4 and saying, "[a]Where is the <u>promise</u>[1860] of His [b]<u>coming</u>?3592 For *ever* since the fathers [c]<u>fell asleep</u>,[2837] all continues just as it was [d]from the beginning of <u>creation</u>."[2937]

10 [II]Lit., *glories* [b]Ex. 22:28; Jude 8 [c]Titus 1:7
11 [a]Jude 9
12 [I]Lit., *their destruction also* [a]Jude 10 [b]Jer. 12:3; Col. 2:22
13 [I]Some ancient mss. read *love feasts* [a]2Pet. 2:15 [b]Rom. 13:13 [c]1Thess. 5:7 [d]1Cor. 11:21; Jude 12
14 [a]2Pet. 2:18 [b]James 1:8; 2Pet. 3:16 [c]2Pet. 2:3 [d]Eph. 2:3
15 [a]Acts 13:10 [b]Num. 22:5, 7; Deut. 23:4; Neh. 13:2; Jude 11; Rev. 2:14 [c]2Pet. 2:13
16 [a]Num. 22:21, 23, 28, 30ff.
17 [I]Lit., *blackness of darkness* [a]Jude 12 [b]Jude 13
18 [a]Jude 16 [b]Eph. 4:17 [c]2Pet. 2:14 [d]2Pet. 2:2 [e]2Pet. 1:4; 2:20
19 [a]John 8:34; Rom. 6:16
20 [a]2Pet. 2:18 [b]2Pet. 1:2 [c]2Pet. 1:11; 3:18 [d]2Tim. 2:4 [e]Matt. 12:45; Luke 11:26
21 [a]Ezek. 18:24; Heb. 6:4ff.; 10:26f.; James 4:17 [b]Gal. 6:2; 1Tim. 6:14; 2Pet. 3:2 [c]Jude 3
22 [a]Prov. 26:11

1 [a]1Pet. 2:11; 2Pet. 3:8, 14, 17 [b]2Pet. 1:13
2 [a]Jude 17 [b]Luke 1:70; Acts 3:21; Eph. 3:5 [c]Gal. 6:2; 1Tim. 6:14; 2Pet. 2:21
3 [a]2Pet. 1:20 [b]1Tim. 4:1; Heb. 1:2 [c]Jude 18 [d]2Pet. 2:10
4 [a]Is. 5:19; Jer. 17:15; Ezek. 11:3; 12:22, 27; Mal. 2:17; Matt. 24:48 [b]1Thess. 2:19; 2Pet. 3:12 [c]Acts 7:60 [d]Mark 10:6

🔑 **2:19-22** See note on Gal. 3:22. A dog or pig may symbolize a temporary external change as a result of conformity to a false temporary profession of faith. A sheep, however, is designated as the one representing a true believer with a living faith in Jesus Christ and whose faith is indicated by the fruits of faith. See Jn. 10:1-21 and also note on Gal. 1:8.

5 For [I]when they maintain[2309] this,
it escapes their notice that [a]by the
word[3056] of God *the* heavens[3772] existed
long ago and *the* earth[1093] was
[b]formed[4921] out of water and by water,
🔑6 through which [a]the world[2889] at
that time was [b]destroyed,[622] being
[aptp]flooded with water.
7 But [a]the present heavens and
earth by His word are being [ppp]re-
served[5083] for [b]fire, kept for [c]the day[2250]
of judgment[2920] and destruction[684] of
ungodly[765] men.[444]
8 But do not let this one *fact* escape
your notice, [a]beloved, that with the
Lord[2962] one day[2250] is as a thousand
years, and [b]a thousand years as one day.
9 [a]The Lord is not slow[1019] about
His promise,[1860] as some count slowness,[1022] but [b]is patient[3114] toward you,
[c]not wishing for any to perish but for
all to come to repentance.[3341]

A New Heaven and Earth

🔑10 But [a]the day of the Lord [b]will
come like a thief, in which [c]the heavens
[d]will pass away with a roar and the
[e]elements[4747] will be [fp]destroyed[3089]
with intense heat, and [f]the earth and
[I]its works[2041] will be [II]burned up.
11 Since all these things are to be
[ppp]destroyed[3089] in this way, what sort
of people ought you to be in holy[40]
conduct[391] and godliness,[2150]
12 [a]looking for and hastening the
coming of the day of God, on account
of which [b]the heavens will be destroyed
by burning, and the [c]elements will
[pinp]melt with intense heat!
13 But according to His [a]promise[1862]
we are looking for [b]new[2537] heavens and
a new earth, [c]in which righteousness[1343]
dwells.[2730]
14 [a]Therefore, [b]beloved, since you
[ppt]look for these things, be diligent to
be [aifp] [c]found by Him in peace,[1515]
[d]spotless[784] and blameless,
15 and regard the [a]patience of our
Lord *to be* salvation;[4991] just as also
[b]our beloved brother Paul, [c]according
to the wisdom given him, wrote to you,
16 as also in all *his* letters,[1992]
speaking in them of [a]these things,
[b]in which are some things hard to understand,[1425] which the untaught and
[c]unstable distort, as *they do* also [d]the
rest of the Scriptures,[1124] to their own
destruction.[684]
17 You therefore, [a]beloved,
[ppt]knowing this beforehand,[4267] [b]be on
your guard[5442] lest, being carried away
by [c]the error[4106] of [d]unprincipled men,[113]
you [aosb] [e]fall from your own steadfastness,
18 but grow in the grace[5485] and
[a]knowledge[1108] of our [b]Lord and Savior
Jesus Christ. [c]To Him *be* the glory,[1391]
both now and to the day of eternity.[165]
Amen.[281]

5 [I]Or, *they are willfully ignorant of this fact, that* [a]Gen. 1:6, 9; Heb. 11:3 [b]Ps. 24:2; 136:6
6 [a]2Pet. 2:5 [b]Gen. 7:11, 12, 21f.
7 [a]2Pet. 3:10, 12 [b]Is. 66:15; Dan. 7:9f.; 2Thess. 1:7; Heb. 12:29 [c]Matt. 10:15; 1Cor. 3:13; Jude 7
8 [a]2Pet. 3:1 [b]Ps. 90:4
9 [a]Hab. 2:3; Rom. 13:11; Heb. 10:37 [b]Rom. 2:4; Rev. 2:21 [c]1Tim. 2:4; Rev. 2:21
10 [I]Lit., *the works in it* [II]Some ancient mss. read *discovered* [a]1Cor. 1:8 [b]Matt. 24:43; Luke 12:39; 1Thess. 5:2; Rev. 3:3; 16:15 [c]Is. 34:4; 2Pet. 3:7, 12 [d]Matt. 24:35; Rev. 21:1 [e]Is. 24:19; Mic. 1:4 [f]2Pet. 3:7
12 [a]1Cor. 1:7 [b]2Pet. 3:7, 10 [c]Is. 24:19; 34:4; Mic. 1:4
13 [a]Is. 65:17; 66:22 [b]Rom. 8:21; Rev. 21:1 [c]Is. 60:21; 65:25; Rev. 21:27
14 [a]1Cor. 15:58; 2Pet. 1:10 [b]2Pet. 3:1 [c]1Pet. 1:7 [d]Phil. 2:15; 1Thess. 5:23; 1Tim. 6:14; James 1:27
15 [a]2Pet. 3:9 [b]Acts 9:17; 15:25; 2Pet. 3:2 [c]1Cor. 3:10; Eph. 3:3
16 [a]2Pet. 3:14 [b]Heb. 5:11 [c]2Pet. 2:14 [d]2Pet. 3:2
17 [a]2Pet. 3:1 [b]1Cor. 10:12 [c]2Pet. 2:18 [d]2Pet. 2:7 [e]Rev. 2:5
18 [a]2Pet. 1:2 [b]2Pet. 1:11; 2:20 [c]Rom. 11:36; 2Tim. 4:18; Rev. 1:6

🔑 **3:6,7** See note on I Pet. 3:20,21.
🔑 **3:10** See note on I Thess. 5:2.

The First Epistle of

JOHN

John examines the question of whether the person who is born of God can commit sin. In I Jn. 3:6 we are told that "No one who abides in Him sins," but in v. 8 it says, "The one who practices sin is of the devil." Then in v. 9 we have the emphatic declaration that "No one who is born of God practices sin . . . and he cannot sin." But if it is possible for a Christian to sin, and experience teaches that it is, does there not appear to be a direct contradiction between these portions of Scripture? While, on the one hand, John says that if it is not possible for those who are really born again to sin, must it not be a fact that there can be but very few genuine Christians, if any? One doctrine appears to be prevalent; that those who are Christ's cannot be eternally lost and though they may fall into sin, this does not affect their sonship, or eternal salvation. (See note on Heb. 6:1-6.)

In this Epistle, the Apostle is striking a deadly blow at two erroneous doctrines which from his own time until now have been prevalent: antinomianism and perfectionism. Antinomians (*anti,* "against," and *nomos,* "law") contend that the covenant of grace, even as the Abrahamic Covenant of the O.T., is not established on conditions; therefore, man cannot be held accountable to any moral law. It is only required for him to believe that he is justified. The so-called perfectionists believe that the sin nature is eradicated from them as though surgically removed as a cancer. The life of the believer, in spite of occasionally missing the mark and bearing responsibility for it, is equivalent to the Sinaitic Covenant of God in the O.T.

In I Jn. 2:1 the Apostle strikes a blow at these doctrines in the command, "My little children, I am writing these things to you that you may not sin. And if anyone (of us) sins, we have an Advocate with the Father, Jesus Christ the righteous." This is how this portion should be rendered, but our A.V. conveys the idea of a habit of sinning, and not a mere act of sin. If there was no other portion of Scripture to disprove the doctrine held by some that in this life the sin nature is completely eradicated from them, this passage alone would be sufficient to disprove it. If any mere man since the fall attained to that high standard, then it would be John himself, "the disciple whom Jesus loved." And yet he speaks even of himself, as well as those whom he addresses, as capable of committing sin—sin considered, however, not as a habit, but as an uncharacteristic act. In regard to I Jn. 3:9, it should be rendered, "He cannot continue in sin, because he is born of God." If, however, the Apostle had really said, "He cannot commit an act of sin," the so-called perfectionists would have been justified in using it as a proof text in support of their favorite dogma. These two passages (I Jn. 2:1; 3:9) form then, as it were, a two-edged sword which destroys the doctrines of the antinomians on the one hand and the perfectionists on the other. Whereas, if the present continuous tense had been implied in the former passage, and the aorist in the latter, both doctrines would have been established. The moods of the aorist as in I Jn. 2:1 (a Greek tense expressing time of an indefinite date or character) usually express single definite actions not contemplated as continuing; those of the present tense (as the verb *poiei,* 4160, and the noun *hamartian,* 266, "does or practices sin habitually") contemplate them as continuing.

In the days of the Apostle there were those who taught that a mere intellectual knowledge was enough to recommend men and make them acceptable to God though they lived impure lives. John, therefore, inculcates (3:7) that only those who did righteousness, that is, in a continued course (*ho poiōn,* 4160, "the one habitually doing"), living conformable to the Gospel, were righteous; not only making the righteousness and holy life of Christ the object of their trust, but also the pattern of their walk and practice. See *dikaioō,* (1344).

John's idea of committing sin on a permanent customary basis is further explained by III Jn. 11, "The one who does good is of God; the one who does evil has not seen God."

There are two participial nouns here, *ho agathopoiōn* (215), "the one being a doer of good, a benevolent person," and *ho kakopoiōn* (2554), "the one doing evil, the malevolent person." This is the same as in I Jn. 3:7, "the doer of or the one practicing (*ho poiōn*) righteousness is righteous." He does not imply that an attempt at an act of goodness makes one righteous any more than someone pounding a nail into a piece of wood makes that person a skilled carpenter. We term a man an artisan who has acquired a skill and works at that trade as his calling or occupation. This is really the meaning of the Greek word *poieō* (4160) rendered "practices" (I Jn. 3:4,8,9) and "does" (III Jn. 11), and hence we render I Jn. 3:8. "The one who practices sin," a worker or maker of sin. In other words, he is a habitual or customary sinner; one who sins deliberately and from a prevailing habit, not unwarily. In the same sense the Apostle uses the expression, "practices sin," (*hamartanei,* 264) in v. 6.

The expression, "he cannot sin," (3:9) simply means he cannot sin habitually, deliberately, easily and maliciously as Cain (v. 12) did out of hatred of goodness. The divine nature of man, of course, cannot sin. But while John speaks of the divine nature in this abstract way, he does not, on the other hand, ignore the existence of the sinful nature in the believer, who is still in a mortal and corruptible body and living in a corrupt world. Consequently, in I Jn. 1:8 we find him saying, "If we say that we have no sin (meaning the sin nature occasionally manifesting its ugly head), we are deceiving ourselves, and the truth is not in us."

Dreams of perfection in the flesh would be little entertained if we kept clearly in view the distinction between what we are in Christ and what we are in ourselves. To be in Him is to be saved once and forever from the condemnation of sin, but not immediately from the presence and inworking of sin, as the lives of the saints testify. We are saved from the guilt and power of sin, but not from its presence while in this body and world. That is a state of being that will yet come when our bodies are redeemed when our resurrection takes place (Rom. 8:23). Christ had sin upon Him, though there was no sin in Him. Therefore, he that is in Christ has no sin upon him (in the sense of condemnation), though he still has sin in him in the form of the sin-nature in the mortal body. The believer is unconditionally saved from sin and conditionally saved from the power of sin. Victory is conditioned in proportion to the believer's unequivocal obedience to Christ and His command.

Let us, therefore, not be deceived and claim to have reached a state of practical and completely realized sanctification, merely because the Spirit addresses us as those who are "sanctified in Christ Jesus" (I Cor. 1:2). For while it is perfectly true that we are in Him, and in Him is no sin, yet "if we say that we have no sin, we are deceiving ourselves, and the truth is not in us." While the forgiven soul may and does occasionally sin and come under God's fatherly displeasure and thus needs daily renewal of the joys of salvation at the mercy seat, he can never come again under the divine wrath and curse. His Father in heaven may visit his transgressions with a rod of correction, "but I will not break off My lovingkindness from him, nor deal falsely in My faithfulness." (Ps. 89:33). See note on Gal. 3:22.

Introduction
The Incarnate Word

1 What was [a]from the beginning, what
we have pfi [b]heard, what we have
pfi [c]seen with our eyes, what we ao [d]beheld and our hands ao [e]handled,[5584] concerning the [f]Word[3056] of Life—[2222]
2 and [a]the life was aop manifested,[5319]
and we have pfi [b]seen and [c]bear pin witness
and pin proclaim[518] to you [d]the eternal
life, which was [e]with the Father[3962] and
was aop [a]manifested to us—
3 what we have [a]seen and [b]heard
we proclaim[518] to you also, that you also
may psa have fellowship[2842] with us; and
indeed our [c]fellowship is with the Father,
and with His Son[5207] Jesus Christ.[5547]

1 [a]John 1:1f.; 1John 2:13, 14 [b]Acts 4:20; 1John 1:3 [c]John 19:35; 2Pet. 1:16; 1John 1:2 [d]John 1:14; 1John 4:14 [e]Luke 24:39; John 20:27 [f]John 1:1, 4

2 [a]John 1:4; 1John 3:5, 8; 5:20 [b]John 19:35; 1John 1:1 [c]John 15:27; 1John 4:14 [d]John 10:28; 17:3; 1John 2:25; 5:11, 13, 20 [e]John 1:1 **3** [a]John 19:35; 2Pet. 1:16; 1John 1:1 [b]Acts 4:20; 1John 1:1 [c]John 17:3, 21; 1Cor. 1:9

4 And [a]these things we write,[1125] so that our [b]joy[5479] may be made complete.[4137]

God Is Light

5 And [a]this is the message[31] we have heard from Him and announce[312] to you, that [b]God[2316] is light,[5457] and in Him there is no darkness[4653] at all.

6 [a]If we say that we have fellowship with Him and *yet* walk[4043] in the darkness,[4655] we [b]lie and [c]do not practice the truth;[225]

7 but if we [a]walk in the light as [b]He Himself is in the light, we have fellowship with one another, and [c]the blood[129] of Jesus His Son cleanses[2511] us from all sin.[266]

8 [a]If we say that we have no sin,[266] we are deceiving ourselves, and the [b]truth is not in us.

9 [a]If we [psa]confess[3670] our sins, He is faithful[4103] and righteous[1342] to [aosb]forgive[863] us our sins and [b]to [aosb]cleanse[2511] us from all unrighteousness.[93]

10 [a]If we [aosb]say that we have not [pfi]sinned,[264] we [b]make Him a liar, and [c]His word[3056] is not in us.

Christ Is Our Advocate

2 [a]My little children,[5040] I am [b]writing[1125] these things to you that you may not [aosb]sin.[264] And if anyone [aosb]sins, [c]we have an [1d]Advocate[3875] with the Father,[3962] Jesus Christ[5547] the righteous;[1342]

2 and He Himself is [a]the [1]propitiation[2434] for our sins;[266] and not for ours only, but also [b]for *those of* the whole world.[2889]

3 And [a]by this we [pin]know that we have come to [pfi] [b]know Him, if we [c]keep[5083] His commandments.[1785]

4 The one who says, "[a]I have come to [pfi] [b]know Him," and does not [ppt]keep His commandments, is a [c]liar, and [d]the truth[225] is not in him;

5 but whoever [psa] [a]keeps His word,[3056] in him the [b]love[26] of God has truly[230] been [pfip]perfected. [c]By this we know that we are in Him:

6 the one who says he [pinf] [a]abides in Him [b]ought himself to [pinf]walk in the same manner as He walked.

7 [a]Beloved, I am [b]not writing a new[2537] commandment to you, but an old commandment which you [1]have [ipf]had [c]from the beginning; the old commandment is the word which you have [ao]heard.

8 [1]On the other hand, I am writing [a]a new commandment to you, which is true in Him and in you, because [b]the darkness[4653] is passing away, and [c]the true[228] light[5457] is already shining.[5316]

9 The one who says he is in the light and *yet* [ppt] [a]hates his [b]brother[80] is in the darkness until now.

10 [a]The one who [ppt]loves[25] his brother abides in the light and there is no cause for stumbling in him.

11 But the one who [ppt] [a]hates his brother is in the darkness and [b]walks in the darkness, and does not know

4 [a]1John 2:1 [b]John 3:29 **5** [a]John 1:19; 1John 3:11 [b]1Tim. 6:16; James 1:17 **6** [a]John 8:12; 1John 2:11 [b]John 8:55; 1John 2:4; 4:20 [c]John 3:21 **7** [a]Is. 2:5 [b]1Tim. 6:16 [c]Titus 2:14 **8** [a]Job 15:14; Prov. 20:9; Rom. 3:10ff.; James 3:2 [b]John 8:44; 1John 2:4 **9** [a]Ps. 32:5; Prov. 28:13 [b]Titus 2:14 **10** [a]Job 15:14 [b]John 3:33; 1John 5:10 [c]1John 2:14

1 [1]Gr., *Paracletos,* one called alongside to help [a]John 13:33; Gal. 4:19; 1John 2:12, 28; 3:7, 18; 4:4; 5:21 [b]1John 1:4 [c]Rom. 8:34; 1Tim. 2:5; Heb. 7:25; 9:24 [d]John 14:16 **2** [1]Or, *satisfaction* [a]Rom. 3:25; Heb. 2:17; 1John 4:10 [b]John 4:42; 11:51f.; 1John 4:14 **3** [a]1John 2:5; 3:24; 4:13; 5:2 [b]1John 2:4; 3:6; 4:7f. [c]John 14:15; 15:10; 1John 3:22, 24; 5:3; Rev. 12:17; 14:12 **4** [a]Titus 1:10 [b]1 John 3:6; 4:7f. [c]1 John 1:6 [d]1John 1:8 **5** [a]John 14:23 [b]1John 4:12 [c]1John 2:3; 3:24; 4:13; 5:2 **6** [a]John 15:4 [b]John 13:15; 15:10; 1Pet. 2:21 **7** [1]Lit., *were having* [a]Heb. 6:9; 1John 3:2, 21; 4:1, 7, 11 [b]John 13:34; 1John 3:11, 23; 4:21; 2John 5 [c]1John 2:24; 3:11; 2John 5, 6 **8** [1]Lit., *Again* [a]John 13:34 [b]Rom. 13:12; Eph. 5:8; 1Thess. 5:4f. [c]John 1:9 **9** [a]1John 2:11; 3:15; 4:20 [b]Acts 1:15; 1John 3:10, 16; 4:20f. **10** [a]John 11:9; 1John 2:10, 11 **11** [a]1John 2:9; 3:15; 4:20 [b]John 12:35; 1John 1:6

1:5 What is translated in the N.T. as "darkness" may be one of two Greek words: *skotos,* which symbolizes sin itself (4655), or *skotia* (4653), which symbolizes the consequence of sin. The word *skotos* occurs in Jn. 3:19 and the word *skotia* occurs in Jn. 1:5; 6:17; 8:12; 12:35,46; 20:1. When it comes to John's Epistles, *skotos* occurs only in I Jn. 1:6, but *skotia* occurs in I Jn. 1:5; 2:8,9,11. See Editor's book entitled, *Was Christ God?* on Jn. 1:1-18 for a comparison of the two words.

1:5-7 See note on Mt. 8:11,12.

1:6,8 See general remarks on I John.

1:7-10 See note on Mk. 3:28,29.

2:1 See general remarks on I John.

where he is going because the darkness
has [ao] [c]blinded his eyes.
12 I am writing to you, [a]little children, because [b]your sins[266] are [pfip]for-
given[863] you for His name's[3686] sake.
13 I am writing to you, fathers,[3962]
because you [pfi]know[1097] Him [a]who has
been from the beginning. I am writing
to you, young men, because [b]you have
[pfi]overcome [c]the evil[4190] one. I have
[ao]written to you, children, because
[d]you [pfi]know the Father.
14 I have written to you, fathers,
because you [pfi]know Him [a]who has been
from the beginning. I have written to
you, young men, because you are
[b]strong, and the [c]word[3056] of God abides
in you, and [d]you have [pfi]overcome the
evil one.

Do Not Love the World

15 Do not [pim]love[25] [a]the world,[2889]
nor the things in the world. [b]If anyone
loves the world, the love[26] of the Father
is not in him.
16 For all that is in the world,
[a]the lust of the flesh[4561] and [b]the lust
of the eyes and [c]the boastful pride[212]
of life,[979] is not from the Father, but
is from the world.
17 And [a]the world is passing away,
and *also* its lusts;[1939] but the one who
[ppt] [b]does the will[2307] of God abides[3306]
forever.[165]
18 Children, [a]it is the last[2078]
hour;[5610] and just as you [ao]heard that
[b]antichrist[500] is [pin]coming, [c]even now
many antichrists have [pfi]arisen; from this
we know that it is the last hour.
19 [a]They went out from us, but they
were not *really* of us; for if they had
been of us, they would have [pipf]remained
with us; but *they went out*, [b]in order
that [I]it might be shown[5319] that they all
are not of us.
20 [I]But you have an [a]anointing[5545]
from [b]the Holy One, and [II][c]you all
know.[1492]
21 I have not written to you because
you do not know the truth,[225] but
[a]because you do know it, and [I]because
no lie is [b]of the truth.
22 Who is the liar but [a]the one who
[ppt]denies[720] that Jesus is the [I]Christ?[5547]
This is [b]the antichrist, the one who denies the Father[3962] and the Son.[5207]
23 [a]Whoever denies the Son does
not have the Father; the one who confesses the Son has the Father also.
24 As for you, let that abide in you
which you [ao]heard [a]from the beginning.
If what you heard from the beginning
[aosb]abides in you, you also [b]will abide
in the Son and in the Father.

The Promise Is Eternal Life

25 And [a]this is the promise[1860] which
He Himself [I]made[1861] to us: eternal[166]
life.[2222]
26 These things I have written to
you concerning those who are trying
to [ppt] [a]deceive you.
27 And as for you, the [a]anointing[5545]
which you [ao]received from Him
abides[3306] in you, and you have no need
for anyone to [psa]teach[1321] you; but as
His anointing [b]teaches you about all
things, and is [c]true and is not a lie, and
just as it has [ao]taught you, [I]you abide
in Him.
🔑 28 And now, [a]little children,[5040]
[pim]abide in Him, so that when He
[asbp] [b]appears,[5319] we may [asba]have
[c]confidence and [d]not [asbp] [I]shrink away
from Him in shame [II]at His [e]coming.[3952]
29 If you know that [a]He is righteous,
you know that everyone also who
[ppt]practices righteousness[1343] [b]is
[pfip] [I]born[1080] of Him.

11 [c]2Cor. 4:4; 2Pet. 1:9
12 [a]1John 2:1 [b]Acts 13:38; 1Cor. 6:11
13 [a]1John 1:1 [b]John 16:33; 1John 2:14; 4:4; 5:4f.; Rev. 2:7 [c]Matt. 5:37; 1John 2:14; 3:12; 5:18f. [d]John 14:7; 1John 2:3
14 [a]1John 1:1 [b]Eph. 6:10 [c]John 5:38; 8:37; 1John 1:10 [d]1John 2:13
15 [a]Rom. 12:2; James 1:27 [b]James 4:4
16 [a]Rom. 13:14; Eph. 2:3; 1Pet. 2:11 [b]Prov. 27:20 [c]James 4:16
17 [a]1Cor. 7:31 [b]Mark 3:35
18 [a]Rom. 13:11; 1Tim. 4:1; 1Pet. 4:7 [b]Matt. 24:5, 24; 1John 2:22; 4:3; 2John 7 [c]Mark 13:22; 1John 4:1; 3
19 [I]Lit., *they might be made manifest* [a]Acts 20:30 [b]1Cor. 11:19
20 [I]Lit., *And* [II]Some ancient mss. read *you know all things* [a]2Cor. 1:21; 1John 2:27 [b]Mark 1:24; Acts 10:38 [c]Prov. 28:5; Matt. 13:11; John 14:26; 1Cor. 2:15f.; 1John 2:27
21 [I]Or, know *that* [a]James 1:19; 2Pet. 1:12; Jude 5 [b]John 8:44; 18:37; 1John 3:19
22 [I]I.e., Messiah [a]1John 4:3; 2John 7 [b]Matt. 24:5, 24; 1John 2:18; 4:3; 2John 7
23 [a]John 8:19; 16:3; 17:3; 1John 4:15; 5:1; 2John 9
24 [a]1John 2:7 [b]John 14:23; 1John 1:3; 2John 9
25 [I]Lit., *promised us* [a]John 3:15; 6:40; 1John 1:2

26 [a]1John 3:7; 2John 7 27 [I]Or, *abide in Him* [a]John 14:16; 1John 2:20 [b]John 14:26; 1Cor. 2:12; 1Thess. 4:9 [c]John 14:17 28 [I]Lit., *be put to shame from Him* [II]Or, *in His presence* [a]1John 2:1 [b]Luke 17:30; Col. 3:4; 1John 3:2 [c]Eph. 3:12; 1John 3:21; 4:17; 5:14 [d]Mark 8:38 [e]1Thess. 2:19 29 [I]Or, *begotten* [a]John 7:18; 1John 3:7 [b]John 1:13; 3:3; 1John 3:9; 4:7; 5:1, 4, 18; 3John 11

🔑 **2:28** See note on I Thess. 2:19.

Children of God Love One Another

3 See [Ia]how great a love[26] the Father[3962] has [pfi]bestowed upon us, that we should be [asbp]called [b]children[5043] of God;[2316] and *such* we are. For this reason the world[2889] does not know[1097] us, because [c]it did not know Him.

2 [a]Beloved, now we are [b]children of God, and [c]it has not [aop]appeared[5319] as yet what we shall be. We know that, when He [d]appears, we shall be [e]like Him, because we shall [f]see Him just as He is.

3 And everyone who [ppt]has this [a]hope[1680] *fixed* on Him [b]purifies[48] himself, just as He is pure.

4 Everyone who [ppt]practices sin[266] also practices lawlessness;[458] and [a]sin is lawlessness.[458]

5 And you know[1492] that He [a]appeared[5319] in order to [aosb] [b]take away[142] sins;[266] and [c]in Him there is no sin.

🔑 6 No one who [ppt]abides[3306] in Him [a]sins;[264] no one who [ppt]sins has [pfi]seen Him or [pfi] [Ib]knows Him.

7 [a]Little children,[5040] let no one [pim] [b]deceive you; [c]the one who [ppt]practices righteousness[1343] is righteous, just as He is righteous;[1342]

8 the one who [ppt]practices sin is [a]of the devil; for the devil[1228] [I]has sinned from the beginning. [b]The Son of God [c]appeared[5319] for this purpose, [d]that He might [aosb]destroy[3089] the works[2041] of the devil.

9 No one who is [pfpp] [Ia]born[1080] of God [b]practices sin, because His seed[4690] abides in him; and he cannot [pinf]sin, because he is [pfip] [I]born of God.

10 By this the [a]children[5043] of God[2316] and the [b]children[5043] of the devil are obvious:[5318] anyone who does not [ppt]practice righteousness is not of God, nor the one who [c]does not [ppt]love[25] his [d]brother.[80]

11 [a]For this is the message[31] [b]which you have heard from the beginning, [c]that we [psa]should love one another;

12 not as [a]Cain, *who* was of [b]the evil[4190] one, and slew his brother. And for what reason did he [ao]slay him? Because [c]his deeds were evil,[4190] and his brother's were righteous.

13 Do not marvel, brethren, if [a]the world hates you.

14 We know that we have [pfi] [a]passed out of death[2288] into life,[2222] [b]because we love the brethren. He who does not [ppt]love abides in death.

15 Everyone who [ppt] [a]hates his brother is a murderer; and you know that [b]no murderer has eternal life [ppt]abiding in him.

16 We [pfi]know love[26] by this, that [a]He laid down His life[5590] for us; and [b]we ought to lay down our lives for the [c]brethren.

17 But [a]whoever [psa]has the world's goods,[979] and [psa]beholds his brother in need and [aosb] [b]closes his [I]heart[4698] [II]against him, [c]how does the love of God abide in him?

18 [a]Little children, let us not [psa]love with word[3056] or with tongue,[1100] but in deed[2041] and [b]truth.

19 We shall know[1097] by this that we are [a]of the truth, and shall [I]assure[3982] our heart [II]before Him,

20 in whatever our heart[2588] [psa]condemns[2607] us; for God is greater than our heart, and knows all things.

21 [a]Beloved, if our heart does not condemn us, we have [b]confidence[3954] [I]before God;

22 and [a]whatever we [psa]ask[154] we receive from Him, because we [b]keep[5083] His commandments[1785] and do [c]the things that are pleasing[701] in His sight.

1 [I]Lit., *what kind of love* [a]John 3:16; 1John 4:10 [b]John 1:12; 11:52; Rom. 8:16; 1John 3:2, 10 [c]John 15:18, 21; 16:3
2 [a]1John 2:7 [b]John 1:12; 11:52; Rom. 8:16; 1John 3:1, 10 [c]Rom. 8:19, 23f. [d]Luke 17:30; Col. 3:4; 1John 2:28 [e]Rom. 8:29; 2Pet. 1:4 [f]John 17:24; 2Cor. 3:18
3 [a]Rom. 15:12; 1Pet. 1:3 [b]John 17:19; 2Cor. 7:1; 2Pet. 3:13f.; 1John 2:6
4 [a]Rom. 4:15; 1John 5:17
5 [a]1John 1:2; 3:8 [b]John 1:29; 1Pet. 1:18-20; 1John 2:2 [c]2Cor. 5:21; 1John 2:29
6 [I]Or, *has known* [a]1John 3:9 [b]1John 2:3; 3John 11
7 [a]1John 2:1 [b]1John 2:26 [c]1John 2:29
8 [I]Lit., *sins* [a]Matt. 13:38; John 8:44; 1John 3:10 [b]Matt. 4:3 [c]1John 3:5 [d]John 12:31; 16:11
9 [I]Or, *begotten* [a]John 1:13; 3:3; 1John 2:29; 4:7; 5:1, 4, 18; 3John 11 [b]1Pet. 1:23; 1John 3:6; 5:18
10 [a]John 1:12; 11:52; Rom. 8:16; 1John 3:1, 2 [b]Matt. 13:38; John 8:44; 1John 3:8 [c]Rom. 13:8ff.; Col. 3:14; 1Tim. 1:5; 1John 4:8 [d]1John 2:9
11 [a]1John 1:5 [b]1John 2:7 [c]John 13:34f.; 15:12; 1John 4:7, 11f., 21; 2John 5
12 [a]Gen. 4:8 [b]Matt. 5:37; 1John 2:13f. [c]Ps. 38:20; Prov. 29:10; John 8:40, 41
13 [a]John 15:18; 17:14
14 [a]John 5:24 [b]John 13:35; 1John 2:10
15 [a]Matt. 5:21f.; John 8:44 [b]Gal. 5:20f.; Rev. 21:8
16 [a]John 10:11; 15:13 [b]Phil. 2:17; 1Thess. 2:8 [c]1John 2:9
17 [I]Lit., *inward parts* [II]Lit., *from* [a]James 2:15f. [b]Deut. 15:7 [c]1John 4:20
18 [a]1John 2:1; 3:7 [b]2John 1; 3John 1
19 [I]Or, *persuade* [II]Or, *before Him; because if our heart* [a]1John 2:21
21 [I]Lit., *toward* [a]1John 3:2 [b]1John 2:28; 5:14
22 [a]Job 22:26f.; Matt. 7:7; 21:22; John 9:31 [b]1John 2:3 [c]John 8:29; Heb. 13:21

🔑 **3:6-9** See general remarks on I John.

23 And this is His commandment, that we [aosb] [Ia]believe[4100] in [b]the name[3686] of His Son[5207] Jesus Christ, and [psa]love[25] one another, just as [c]He [II]commanded us.

24 And the one who [ppt] [a]keeps His commandments [b]abides in Him, and He in him. And [c]we know by this that [d]He abides[3306] in us, by the Spirit[4151] whom He has given us.

Testing the Spirits

4 [a]Beloved, do not believe[4100] every [b]spirit,[4151] but test the spirits to see whether they are from God; because [c]many false prophets have [pfi]gone out into the world.[2889]

2 By this you know the Spirit of God: [a]every spirit that [b]confesses[3670] that [c]Jesus Christ[5547] has come in the flesh is from God;

🔑 3 and every spirit that [a]does not confess[3670] Jesus is not from God; and this is the *spirit* of the [b]antichrist,[500] of which you have [pfi]heard that it is coming, and [c]now it is already in the world.

4 You are from God, [a]little children, and [b]have overcome them; because [c]greater is He who is in you than [d]he who is in the world.

5 [a]They are from the world; therefore they speak *as* from the world, and the world listens to them.

6 [a]We are from God; [b]he who [ppt]knows[1097] God listens[191] to us; [c]he who is not from God does not listen to us. By this we know [d]the spirit of truth[225] and [e]the spirit of error.[4106]

God Is Love

7 [a]Beloved, let us [psa] [b]love[25] one another, for love[26] is from God; and [c]everyone who [ppt]loves is [pfip] [Id]born[1080] of God and [e]knows God.

8 The one who does not love does not [ao]know God, for [a]God is love.

9 By this the love of God was manifested[5319] [Ia]in us, that [b]God has [pfi]sent His [II]only begotten[3439] Son[5207] into the world so that we might [aosb]live[2198] through Him.

10 In this is love, [a]not that we [I]loved God, but that [b]He loved us and sent[649] His Son *to be* [c]the propitiation[2434] for our sins.[266]

11 [a]Beloved, if God so loved us, [b]we also ought to [pinf]love one another.

12 [a]No one has [pfi]beheld God at any time; if we [psa]love one another, God abides[3306] in us, and His [b]love is perfected[5048] in us.

13 [a]By this we know that we abide in Him and He in us, because He has [pfi]given us of His Spirit.

14 And we have beheld and [a]bear witness that the Father has [pfi] [b]sent[649] the Son *to be* the Savior[4990] of the world.[2889]

15 [a]Whoever [aosb]confesses[3670] that [b]Jesus is the Son of God, God [c]abides in him, and he in God.

16 And [a]we have come to [pfi]know and have [pfi]believed the love which God has [Ib]for us. [c]God is love,[26] and the one who [ppt] [d]abides in love abides in God, and God abides in him.

17 By this, [a]love is [pfip]perfected[5048] with us, that we may [psa]have [b]confidence in [c]the day[2250] of judgment;[2920] because [d]as He is, so also are we in this world.

18 There is no fear[5401] in love; but [a]perfect[5046] love casts out fear, because fear [I]involves punishment,[2861] and the one who [ppt]fears[5399] is not [pfip] [b]perfected[5048] in love.

19 [a]We love,[25] because He first loved us.

20 [a]If someone says, "I love God," and [b]hates his brother,[80] he is a [c]liar; for [d]the one who does not [ppt]love his

23 [I]Or, *believe the name* [II]Or, *gave us a commandment* [a]John 6:29 [b]John 1:12; 2:23; 3:18 [c]John 13:34; 15:12; 1John 2:8
24 [a]1John 2:3 [b]John 6:56; 10:38; 1John 2:6, 24; 4:15 [c]John 14:17; Rom. 8:9, 14, 16; 1Thess. 4:8; 1John 4:13 [d]1John 2:5

1 [a]3John 11 [b]Jer. 29:8; 1Cor. 12:10; 1Thess. 5:20f.; 2Thess. 2:2 [c]Jer. 14:14; 2Pet. 2:1; 1John 2:18
2 [a]1Cor. 12:3 [b]1John 2:23 [c]John 1:14; 1John 1:2
3 [a]1John 2:22; 2John 7 [b]1John 2:18, 22 [c]2Thess. 2:3-7; 1John 2:18
4 [a]1John 2:1 [b]1John 2:13 [c]Rom. 8:31; 1John 3:20 [d]John 12:31
5 [a]John 15:19; 17:14, 16
6 [a]John 8:23; 1John 4:4 [b]John 8:47; 10:3ff.; 18:37 [c]1Cor. 14:37 [d]John 14:17 [e]1Tim. 4:1
7 [I]Or, *begotten* [a]1John 2:7 [b]1John 3:11 [c]1John 5:1 [d]1John 2:29 [e]1Cor. 8:3; 1John 2:3
8 [a]1John 4:7, 16
9 [I]Or, *in our case* [II]Or, *unique*, only one of His kind [a]John 9:3; 1John 4:16 [b]John 3:16f.; 1John 4:10; 5:11
10 [I]Some mss. read *had loved* [a]Rom. 5:8, 10; 1John 4:19 [b]John 3:16f.; 1John 4:9; 5:11 [c]1John 2:2
11 [a]1John 2:7 [b]1John 4:7
12 [a]John 1:18; 1Tim. 6:16; 1John 4:20 [b]1John 2:5; 4:17f. 13 [a]Rom. 8:9; 1John 3:24 14 [a]John 15:27; 1John 1:2 [b]John 3:17; 4:42; 1John 2:2 15 [a]1John 2:23 [b]Rom. 10:9; 1John 3:23; 4:2; 5:1, 5 [c]1John 2:24; 3:24 16 [I]Lit., *in* [a]John 6:69 [b]John 9:3; 1John 4:9 [c]1John 4:7, 8 [d]1John 4:12f. 17 [a]1John 2:5; 4:12 [b]1John 2:28 [c]Matt. 10:15 [d]John 17:22; 1John 2:6; 3:1, 7, 16 18 [I]Lit., *has* [a]Rom. 8:15 [b]1John 4:12 19 [a]1John 4:10 20 [a]1John 1:6, 8, 10; 2:4 [b]1John 2:9, 11 [c]1John 1:6 [d]1John 3:17

🔑 **4:3** See general remarks on I John and also note on II Thess. 2:3-8.

brother whom he has [pfi]seen, [Ie]cannot love God whom he has not [pfi]seen.

21 And [a]this commandment[1785] we have from Him, that the one who [ppt]loves God [b]should love his brother also.

Overcoming the World

5 [a]Whoever [ppt]believes[4100] that Jesus is the [I]Christ[5547] is [pfip] [IIb]born[1080] of God; and whoever [ppt]loves[25] the [III]Father [c]loves the *child* [pfpp] [II]born[1080] of Him.

2 [a]By this we know that [b]we love the children[5043] of God,[2316] when we love God and [I]observe[5083] His commandments.

3 For [a]this is the love[26] of God, that we [b]keep His commandments; and [c]His commandments are not burdensome.

4 For whatever is [pfpp] [Ia]born[1080] of God [b]overcomes[3528] the world;[2889] and this is the victory that has [apt]overcome the world—[2889] our faith.[4102]

5 And who is the one who [ppt]overcomes the world, but he who [ppt] [a]believes that Jesus is the Son[5207] of God?[2316]

6 This is the one who [apt]came [a]by water and blood, Jesus Christ; not [I]with the water only, but [I]with the water and [I]with the blood.[129]

7 And it is [a]the Spirit who [ppt]bears witness, because the Spirit[4151] is the truth.[225]

8 For there are [a]three that bear witness,[3140] [I]the Spirit and the water and the blood; and the three are [II]in agreement.

9 [a]If we receive the witness[3141] of men,[444] the witness of God is greater; for the witness of God is this, that [b]He has [pfi]borne witness concerning His Son.

10 The one who [ppt]believes in the Son of God [a]has the witness in himself; the one who does not believe God has [pfi] [b]made Him a liar, because he has not [pfi]believed in the witness[3141] that God has [pfi]borne concerning His Son.

11 And the witness is this, that God has [ao]given us [a]eternal[166] life,[2222] and [b]this life is in His Son.

12 [a]He who [ppt]has the Son has the life; he who does not have the Son of God does not have the life.

This Is Written That You May Know

13 [a]These things I have written[1125] to you who [ppt] [b]believe in the name[3686] of the Son of God, in order that you may know that you have [c]eternal life.

14 And this is [a]the confidence[3954] which we have [I]before Him, that, [b]if we [psa]ask anything according to His will, He hears[191] us.

15 And if we know that He hears us *in* whatever we ask,[154] [a]we know that we have the requests[155] which we have asked[154] from Him.

16 If anyone sees his brother [ppt] [I]committing[264] a sin[266] not *leading* to death,[2288] [a]he shall ask and *God* will for him give life to those who commit sin not *leading* to death. [b]There is a sin *leading* to death; [c]I do not say that he should make [aosb]request for this.

17 [a]All unrighteousness[93] is sin, and [b]there is a sin not *leading* to death.

18 [a]We know that [b]no one who is [pfpp] [I]born[1080] of God sins; but He who was [aptp] [I]born[1080] of God [c]keeps him and [d]the evil[4190] one does not [e]touch[680] him.

19 [a]We know that [b]we are of God, and [c]the whole world[2889] lies[2749] in *the power of* the evil[4190] one.

20 And [a]we know that [b]the Son of God has come, and has [pfi] [c]given us understanding,[1271] in order that we might [psa]know[1097] [d]Him who is true,[228] and we [e]are in Him who is true, in His Son Jesus Christ. [f]This is the true God and [g]eternal life.

21 [a]Little children,[5040] guard yourselves from [b]idols.[1497]

20 [I]Some mss. read *how can he love God . . . seen?* [e]1Pet. 1:8; 1John 4:12
21 [a]Lev. 19:18; Matt. 5:43f.; 22:37ff.; John 13:34 [b]1John 3:11

1 [I]I.e., Messiah [II]Or, *begotten* [III]Lit., *one who begets* [a]1John 2:22f.; 4:2, 15 [b]John 1:3; 3:3; 1John 2:29; 5:4, 18 [c]John 8:42
2 [I]Lit., *do* [a]1John 2:5 [b]1John 3:14
3 [a]John 14:15; 2John 6 [b]1John 2:3 [c]Matt. 11:30; 23:4
4 [I]Or, *begotten* [a]John 1:13; 3:3; 1John 2:29; 5:1, 18 [b]1John 2:13; 4:4
5 [a]1John 4:15; 5:1
6 [I]Lit., *in* [a]John 19:34
7 [a]Matt. 3:16f.; John 15:26; 16:13-15
8 [I]A few late mss. read *in heaven, the Father, the Word, and the Holy Spirit, and these three are one. And there are three that bear witness on earth, the Spirit* [II]Lit., *for the one thing* [a]Matt. 18:16
9 [a]John 5:34, 37; 8:18 [b]Matt. 3:17; John 5:32, 37
10 [a]Rom. 8:16; Gal. 4:6; Rev. 12:17 [b]John 3:18, 33; 1John 1:10
11 [a]John 3:36; 1John 1:2; 2:25; 4:9; 5:13, 20 [b]John 1:4
12 [a]John 3:15f., 36
13 [a]John 20:31 [b]1John 3:23 [c]1John 1:2; 2:25; 4:9; 5:11, 20
14 [I]Lit., *toward* [a]1John 2:28; 3:21f. [b]Matt. 7:7; John 14:13; 1John 3:22
15 [a]1John 5:18-20
16 [I]Lit., *sinning* [a]James 5:15 [b]Num. 15:30; Heb. 6:4-6; 10:26 [c]Jer. 7:16; 14:11
17 [a]1John 3:4 [b]1John 2:1f.; 5:16
18 [I]Or, *begotten* [a]1John 5:15, 19, 20 [b]1John 3:9 [c]James 1:27; Jude 21 [d]1John 2:13 [e]John 14:30
19 [a]1John 5:15, 18, 20 [b]1John 4:6 [c]John 12:31; 17:15; Gal. 1:4
20 [a]1John 5:15, 18, 19 [b]John 8:42; 1John 5:5 [c]Luke 24:45 [d]John 17:3; Rev. 3:7 [e]John 1:18; 14:9; 1John 2:23; Rev. 3:7 [f]1John 1:2 [g]1John 5:11
21 [a]1John 2:1 [b]1Cor. 10:7, 14; 1Thess. 1:9

The Second Epistle of
JOHN

The Second Epistle of John is a personal letter. One gets the impression that John wrote other letters which we do not have (I Jn. 2:14; III Jn. 9). II John was just long enough to be accommodated on a standard-sized sheet of papyrus (10″ × 8″), conforming to the pattern of letters in that period. It is addressed from the "elder" to "the chosen lady and her children," which could symbolically mean a congregation. It may have been so stated in order to confuse any enemy who might come to possess the Epistle. The occasion of the letter is similar to that of I John: False teachers were traveling from congregation to congregation denying that the Son of God had really been incarnate. This was the Gnostic heresy. John cautioned his friends not to extend even normal hospitality to such people. To do so would imply endorsement (II Jn. 10-11). Loving people (II Jn. 5-6) must not be construed as the encouragement of false doctrine.

Walk According to His Commandments

1 [a]The elder4525 to the [b]chosen***1588***
[c]lady and her children,***5043*** whom I
[d]love***25*** in truth;***225*** and not only I, but
also all who [pfp] [e]know the truth,
2 for [a]the sake of the truth which
abides [b]in us and will be [c]with us
forever:***165***
3 [a]Grace, mercy***1656*** *and* peace***1515***
will be with us, from God***2316*** the
Father***3962*** and from Jesus Christ,***5547*** the
Son***5207*** of the Father, in truth and love.
4 [a]I was very glad to [pfi]find *some*
of your children***5043*** [ppt]walking4043 in
truth, just as we have [ao]received commandment *to do* from the Father.
5 And now I ask you, lady, [a]not as
[ppt]writing to you a new***2537*** commandment, but the one which we have [ipf]had
[a]from the beginning, that we [psa] [b]love
one another.
6 And [a]this is love,***26*** that we [psa]walk
according to His commandments. This
is the commandment, [b]just as you have
[ao]heard [c]from the beginning, that you
should [psa]walk in it.
🔑 7 For [a]many deceivers have [ao] [b]gone
out into the world, those who [c]do not
[ppt]acknowledge***3670*** Jesus Christ***5547*** *as*
[ppt]coming in the flesh.***4561*** This is [a]the
deceiver and the [d]antichrist.***500***
8 [a]Watch yourselves, [b]that you
might not [aosb]lose what [1]we have accomplished,***2038*** but that you may [aosb]re-
ceive618 a full***4134*** reward.***3408***
9 Anyone who [ppt] [1]goes too far***3845***
and [a]does not [ppt]abide in the teaching***1322***
of Christ, does not have God; the one
who abides***3306*** in the teaching, he has
both the Father and the Son.
10 If anyone comes to you and does
not bring this teaching, [a]do not receive
him into *your* house, and do not give
him a greeting;***5463***
11 for the one who [ppt]gives***3004*** him
a greeting [a]participates***2841*** in his evil***4190***
deeds.***2041***
12 [a]Having many things to write to
you, I do not [ao]want to *do so* with paper
and ink; but I hope to come to you and
speak face to face, that [1]your [b]joy may
be made full.
13 The children of your [a]chosen sister greet you.

1 [a]Acts 11:30; 1Pet. 5:1; 3John 1 [b]Rom. 16:13; 1Pet. 5:13; 2John 13 [c]2John 5 [d]1John 3:18; 2John 3; 3John 1 [e]John 8:32; 1Tim. 2:4
2 [a]2Pet. 1:12 [b]1John 1:8 [c]John 14:16
3 [a]Rom. 1:7; 1Tim. 1:2
4 [a]3John 3f.
5 [a]1John 2:7 [b]John 13:34, 35; 15:12, 17; 1John 3:11; 4:7, 11
6 [a]1John 2:5; 5:3 [b]1John 2:24 [c]1John 2:7
7 [a]1John 2:26 [b]1John 2:19; 4:1 [c]1John 4:2f. [d]1John 2:18
8 [1]Some ancient mss. read *you* [a]Mark 13:9 [b]1Cor. 3:8; Heb. 10:35
9 [1]Lit., *goes on ahead* [a]John 7:16; 8:31; 1John 2:23
10 [a]1Kin. 13:16f.; Rom. 16:17; 2Thess. 3:6, 14; Titus 3:10
11 [a]Eph. 5:11; 1Tim. 5:22; Jude 23
12 [1]Some ancient mss. read *our* [a]3John 13, 14 [b]John 3:29; 1John 1:4
13 [a]2John 1

🔑 **7** See note on II Thess. 2:3-8.

The Third Epistle of

JOHN

Like the Epistle to Philemon, III John is a private letter addressed to the elder's friend, Gaius, who was a leading member in another congregation. There was a Gaius in Corinth (I Cor. 1:14; Rom. 16:23). A group of Christians met in his home. One tradition says that he later became John's scribe. However, we do not know if he is the same Gaius. One thing is certain; John truly loved him (vv. 1, 2, 5, 11). This Gaius is recommended for his attachment to the truth and for showing practical love to traveling preachers who depended on the congregations for their support.

There was another individual in that vicinity whom John did not appreciate. His name was Diotrephes. He was a self-appointed, domineering man who summarily excommunicated anyone who did not agree with his policies. He was so arrogant that he ignored even John's authority. A confrontation was inevitable (III Jn. 9-11).

John's idea of committing sin may be interpreted by his own phrase in III Jn. 11—"a doer of evil." This does not mean the mere commission of a single act of sin, but denotes an habitual sinner, one who sins from deliberation, from his prevailing custom.

You Walk in the Truth

1 🔑 [a]The elder[4245] to the beloved[27]
[b]Gaius, whom I [c]love[25] in truth.[225]
🔑 2 Beloved,[27] I pray that in all respects you may [pinf]prosper and be in
good health, just as your soul[5590] prospers.
3 For I [1a]was very glad[5463] when
[b]brethren[80] came and bore [ppt]witness to
your truth, *that is,* how you [a]are
walking[4043] in truth.
4 I have no greater joy[5479] than
[1]this, to hear of [a]my children[5043] [ppt] [b]walk-
ing in the truth.
5 Beloved, you are [aosb]acting faithfully[4103] in whatever you accomplish[2038]
for the [a]brethren, and especially *when*
they are [b]strangers;
6 and they bear [ao]witness to your
love[26] before the church;[1577] and you
will do well to [a]send them on their way
in a manner [b]worthy of God.[2316]

1 [a]2John 1 [b]Acts 19:29; 20:4; Rom. 16:23; 1Cor. 1:14 [c]1John 3:18; 2John 1 **3** [1]*Or, am very glad when brethren come and bear witness* [a]2John 4 [b]Acts 1:15; Gal. 6:10; 3John 5, 10 **4** [1]*Lit., these things, that I hear* [a]1Cor. 4:14f.; 2Cor. 6:13; Gal. 4:19; 1Thess. 2:11; 1Tim. 1:2; 2Tim. 1:2; Philem. 10; 1John 2:1 [b]2John 4 **5** [a]Acts 1:15; Gal. 6:10; 3John 3, 10 [b]Rom. 12:13; Heb. 13:2 **6** [a]Acts 15:3; Titus 3:13 [b]Col. 1:10; 1Thess. 2:12

🔑 **1** Gaius was a Macedonian caught in the Ephesian riot (Acts 19:29). He was also a companion of Paul's to Jerusalem, a member of the party which awaited the Apostle at Troas (Acts 20:4ff), perhaps an official delegate of his church in Derbe. Some think that Gaius was a Thessalonian. He was baptized by Paul in Corinth (1 Cor. 1:14). A church met in his house, and Paul stayed with him on his third Corinthian visit (Rom. 16:23). In III John, the elder commends his right attitude and his hospitality which he asks for again as he expects to see him shortly.

🔑 **2** This verse is often misapplied as meaning that it is God's will for His children to always prosper and be in health. Actually, it is nothing more than a wish from John, the writer, to Gaius that his letter might find him well and in good health. It is used in the same way that we frequently begin our letters to our friends expressing the wish, "I hope you are well and healthy." This verse is mistranslated in the KJV. The preposition *peri* (4012) is not "above," but "concerning" or "about." John is not saying that prosperity and wealth should be considered as the greatest gifts of life. He is just saying that his hope is that all is well with Gaius. It is a mere wish expressed in the verb *euchomai* (2172) and not a promise that is given by an Apostle to a fellow believer. The verb that is translated "prosper" is *euodousthai,* the present infinitive of *euodoō* (2137). The word is made up of *eu* (2095), "well, good," and *hodos* (3598), "a way, a journey." The word essentially means to have a good journey, a safe journey through life. It is used in this way in Rom. 1:10. In 1 Cor. 16:2 it is used in regard to the giving of benevolence to the church. Although it is translated "as he may prosper," yet we should not get the idea that this prospering necessarily means riches. It means as the Lord has made good provision for the believer, in

(continued on next page)

7 For they went out for the sake
of [a]the Name,[3686] [b]accepting nothing
from the Gentiles.[1484]
8 Therefore we ought to [pinf] [I]support
such men, that we may be fellow workers [II]with the truth.
🗝 9 I wrote[1125] something to the
church; but Diotrephes, who loves to
[a]be first among them, does not accept
[I]what we say.
10 For this reason, [a]if I come, I will
call attention to his deeds[2041] which he
does, unjustly accusing[5396] us with
wicked[4190] words; and not satisfied with
this, neither does he himself [b]receive
the [c]brethren, and he forbids those who
desire *to do so,* and [d]puts *them* out of
the church.

7 [a]John 15:21; Acts 5:41; Phil. 2:9 [b]Acts 20:33, 35
8 [I]Or, *receive such men as guests* [II]Or, *for*
9 [I]Lit., *us* [a]2John 9
10 [a]2John 12 [b]2John 10; 3John 5 [c]Acts 1:15; Gal. 6:10; 3John 3, 5 [d]John 9:34
11 [a]Ps. 34:14; 37:27 [b]1John 2:29; 3:10 [c]1John 3:6
12 [a]Acts 6:3; 1Tim. 3:7 [b]John 19:35; 21:24
13 [a]2John 12
14 [a]John 20:19, 21, 26; Eph. 6:23; 1Pet. 5:14 [b]John 10:3

🗝 11 Beloved,[27] [a]do not imitate what
is evil,[2556] but what is good.[18] [b]The one
who [ppt]does good[15] is of God;[2316] [c]the
one who [ppt]does evil[2554] has not [pfi]seen
God.
12 Demetrius [a]has received a *good*
testimony[3140] from everyone, and from
the truth itself; and we also bear witness, and [b]you know[1492] that our witness[3141] is true.
13 [a]I had many things to write to
you, but I am not willing to write *them*
to you with pen and ink;
14 but I hope to see you shortly,
and we shall speak[2980] face to face.
[a]Peace *be* to you. The friends
greet[782] you. Greet[782] the friends
[b]by name.

(continued from previous page)
the same measure he should also lay aside a corresponding offering. The idea of wealth is really missing from the word "prosper."

The second infinitive is *hugiainein* (5198), "to be healthy." This is not a guarantee from the Apostle to Gaius that he is going to be healthy, but it simply expresses a wish.

The last expression of v. 2 translated "just as your soul prospers," actually means "in the measure that your soul walks in a proper and right manner." In other words, he is saying to Gaius that his wish is that everything about him is doing well and that he is healthy.

🗝 **9** Diotrephes was an over-ambitious person who resisted authority. He attacked the elder publicly, forbade the reception of his adherents, and, whether by formal excommunication or physical violence, excluded those who did receive them.

🗝 **11** See general remarks on I John.

The Epistle of

JUDE

The author of this small letter identifies himself as "Jude (or, Judas), a bond-servant of Jesus Christ, and brother of James" (Jude 1). In the early church, there was only one James who could be referred to in this way without further specification, and that was "James, the Lord's brother," as he is called in Galatians 1:19. This Jude was probably the same one who is numbered among the physical brothers of the Lord Jesus in Mt. 13:55 and Mk. 6:3. A few scholars identify Jude as the Apostle Judas (not Iscariot) in Lk. 6:16 and Acts 1:13, also called Lebbaeus or Thaddaeus (Mt. 10:2-3).

Little is known of the circumstances to which Jude addresses himself, and no one knows the precise time of writing. Jude is quite similar to some of the content of II Peter. Both writers were alarmed at the inroads which false teachers were making. Jude urges the Christians to "contend earnestly for the faith which was once for all delivered to the saints" (Jude 3). The apostasy of which Paul spoke (Acts 20:29-31) was threatening. It was a very serious situation.

The Warnings of History to the Ungodly

1 [I][a]Jude, a [b]bond-servant[1401] of Jesus
Christ,[5547] and brother of [II]James,
to [c]those who are the called,[2822]
beloved[27] in God[2316] the Father,[3962] and
[d]kept[5083] for Jesus Christ:
2 [a]May mercy[1656] and peace[1515] and
love[26] [b]be multiplied to you.
3 [a]Beloved,[27] while I was making
every effort to write you about our
[b]common[2839] salvation,[4991] I felt the
necessity[318] to write to you appealing[3870]
that you [c]contend earnestly[1864] for
[d]the faith[4102] which was once for all
[e]delivered to [f]the [I]saints.[40]
4 For certain persons have [a]crept
in unnoticed,[3921] those who were long
beforehand [I][b]marked out for this condemnation,[2917] ungodly persons[765] who
turn [c]the grace[5485] of our God into
[d]licentiousness[766] and [e]deny[720] our only
Master[1203] and Lord, Jesus Christ.
5 Now I desire to [a]remind you,
though [b]you know all things once for
all, that [I]the Lord, [c]after saving[4982] a
people out of the land of Egypt, [II]subse-
quently destroyed those who did not
believe.[4100]
6 And [a]angels[32] who did not keep
their own domain, but [apt]abandoned their
proper abode,[3613] He has [pfi] [b]kept[5083] in
eternal[126] bonds under darkness[2217] for
the judgment[2920] of the great day.[2250]
7 Just as [a]Sodom and Gomorrah and
the [b]cities around them, since they in
the same way as these [apt]indulged in
gross immorality[1608] and [apt] [c]went after
strange[2087] flesh,[4561] are exhibited as an
[I][d]example, in undergoing the [e]punish-
ment[1349] of eternal[166] fire.
8 Yet in the same manner these
men, also by dreaming, [a]defile the flesh,
and reject authority,[2963] and revile[987]
[I]angelic majesties.[1391]
🔑 9 But [a]Michael [b]the archangel,[743]
when he [ipf]disputed[1252] with the devil[1228]

1 [I]Gr., *Judas* [II]Or, *Jacob* [a]Matt. 13:55; Mark 6:3; 6:16; John 14:22; Acts 1:13? [b]Rom. 1:1 [c]Rom. 1:6f. [d]John 17:11f.; 1Pet. 1:5; Jude 21
2 [a]Gal. 6:16; 1Tim. 1:2 [b]1Pet. 1:2; 2Pet. 1:2
3 [I]Or, *holy ones* [a]Heb. 6:9; Jude 1, 17, 20 [b]Titus 1:4 [c]1Tim. 6:12 [d]Acts 6:7; Jude 20 [e]2Pet. 2:21 [f]Acts 9:13
4 [I]Or, *written about* [a]Gal. 2:4; 2Tim. 3:6 [b]1Pet. 2:8 [c]Acts 11:23 [d]2Pet. 2:7 [e]2Tim. 2:12; Titus 1:16; 2Pet. 2:1; 1John 2:22
5 [I]Some ancient mss. read *Jesus* [II]Lit., *the second time* [a]2Pet. 1:12f.; 3:1f. [b]1John 2:20 [c]Ex. 12:51; 1Cor. 10:5-10; Heb. 3:16f.

6 [a]2Pet. 2:4 [b]2Pet. 2:9 **7** [I]Or, *example of eternal fire, in undergoing punishment* [a]Gen. 19:24f.; 2Pet. 2:6 [b]Deut. 29:23; Hos. 11:8 [c]2Pet. 2:2 [d]2Pet. 2:6 [e]Matt. 25:41; 2Thess. 1:8f.; 2Pet. 3:7 **8** [I]Lit., *glories* [a]2Pet. 2:10 **9** [a]Dan. 10:13, 21; 12:1; Rev. 12:7 [b]1Thess. 4:16; 2Pet. 2:11

🔑 **9** This refers to an otherwise unknown incident in which there was a dispute between the Archangel Michael and the devil concerning the burial of Moses' body. Jude related this incident to tell us that the archangel Michael did not bring a railing accusation against the devil, but said, "The Lord rebuke you." He wanted to show that neither we nor angels, no matter how hard we try, will be able to put the devil out of commission, but that his time is coming one day. It is said of him in Rev. 20:2 that he will be

(continued on next page)

and argued about [c]the body of Moses, did not dare pronounce against[2018] him a railing[988] judgment,[2920] but said, "[d]THE LORD REBUKE YOU."

10 But [a]these men revile the things which they do not understand; and [b]the things which they know by instinct, [a]like unreasoning animals, by these things they are [I]destroyed.

11 Woe to them! For they have [ao]gone [a]the way[3598] of Cain, and for pay [I]they have rushed headlong into [b]the error of Balaam, and [c]perished[622] in the rebellion[485] of Korah.

12 These men are those who are [I]hidden reefs [a]in your love feasts[26] when they [ppt]feast with you [b]without fear, caring for themselves; [c]clouds without water, [d]carried along by winds; autumn trees without fruit, [II]doubly dead,[599] [e]uprooted;

13 [a]wild waves of the sea, casting up [b]their own [I]shame[152] like foam; wandering stars, [c]for whom the [II]black[2217] darkness[4655] has been reserved[5083] forever.

14 And about these also [a]Enoch, *in* the seventh *generation* from Adam, prophesied, saying, "[b]Behold, the Lord [ao]came with [I]many thousands of His holy ones,

15 [a]to execute judgment[2920] upon all, and to convict all the ungodly of all their ungodly[763] deeds[5041] which they have done in an ungodly way,[764] and of all the harsh things which [b]ungodly sinners[268] have spoken against Him."

16 These are [a]grumblers, finding fault, [b]following[4198] after their *own* lusts;[1939] [I]they speak [c]arrogantly, flattering people [d]for the sake of *gaining an* advantage.

9 [c]Deut. 34:6 [d]Zech. 3:2
10 [I]Lit., *corrupted* [a]2Pet. 2:12 [b]Phil. 3:19
11 [I]Lit., *they have poured themselves out* [a]Gen. 4:3-8; Heb. 11:4; 1John 3:12 [b]Num. 31:16; 2Pet. 2:15; Rev. 2:14 [c]Num. 16:1-3, 31-35
12 [I]Or, *stains* [II]Lit., *twice* [a]1Cor. 11:20ff.; 2Pet. 2:13 and mg. [b]Ezek. 34:2, 8, 10 [c]Prov. 25:14; 2Pet. 2:17 [d]Eph. 4:14 [e]Matt. 15:13
13 [I]Or, *shameless deeds* [II]Lit., *blackness of darkness;* or, *nether gloom* [a]Is. 57:20 [b]Phil. 3:19 [c]2Pet. 2:17; Jude 6
14 [I]Lit., *His holy ten thousands* [a]Gen. 5:18, 21ff. [b]Deut. 33:2; Dan. 7:10; Matt. 16:27; Heb. 12:22
15 [a]2Pet. 2:6ff. [b]1Tim. 1:9
16 [I]Lit., *their mouth speaks* [a]Num. 16:11, 41; 1Cor. 10:10 [b]2Pet. 2:10; Jude 18 [c]2Pet. 2:18 [d]2Pet. 2:3
17 [a]Jude 3 [b]2Pet. 3:2 [c]Heb. 2:3
18 [a]Acts 20:29; 1Tim. 4:1; 2Tim. 3:1f.; 4:3; 2Pet. 3:3 [b]Jude 4, 16
19 [I]Or, *merely natural* [II]Lit., *not having* [a]1Cor. 2:14f.; James 3:15
20 [a]Jude 3 [b]Col. 2:7; 1Thess. 5:11

Keep Yourselves in the Love of God

17 But you, [a]beloved, [b]ought to remember the words[4487] that were spoken beforehand by [c]the apostles[652] of our Lord Jesus Christ,

18 that they were [ipf]saying to you, "[a]In the last[2078] time[5550] there shall be mockers, [b]following after their own ungodly[763] lusts."

19 These are the ones who cause divisions,[592] [I][a]worldly-minded,[5591] [II]devoid of the Spirit.

20 But you, [a]beloved, [b]building yourselves up on[2026] your most holy [a]faith; [c]praying in the Holy Spirit;[4151]

21 keep[5083] yourselves in the love[26] of God, [a]waiting anxiously for the mercy[1656] of our Lord Jesus Christ to eternal[166] life.[2222]

22 And [I]have mercy on some, who are doubting;[1252]

🔑 23 save[4982] others, [a]snatching[726] them out of the fire; and on some have mercy with fear,[5401] [b]hating even the garment polluted[4695] by the flesh.[4561]

24 [a]Now to Him who is able to keep[5442] you from stumbling, and to [b]make you stand in the presence of His glory[1391] blameless[299] with [c]great joy,[20]

25 to the [a]only [b]God our Savior,[4990] through Jesus Christ our Lord, [c]*be* glory, majesty, dominion[2904] and authority,[1849] [d]before all time and now and [I]forever.[165] Amen.[281]

[c]Eph. 6:18 **21** [a]Titus 2:13; Heb. 9:28; 2Pet. 3:12
22 [I]Some ancient mss. read *convince* **23** [a]Amos 4:11; Zech. 3:2; 1Cor. 3:15 [b]Zech. 3:3f.; Rev. 3:4
24 [a]Rom. 16:25 [b]2Cor. 4:14 [c]1Pet. 4:13 **25** [I]Lit., *to all the ages* [a]John 5:44; 1Tim. 1:17 [b]Luke 1:47 [c]Rom. 11:36 [d]Heb. 13:8

(continued from previous page)
bound up for a thousand years during Christ's millennial kingdom and that finally he is going to be cast into the lake of fire and brimstone (Rev. 20:10). In this respect we are reminded of the parable of the wheat and the tares (Mt. 13:24-30). The disciples wanted to pull out the tares planted by the devil, but they were told not to do so until harvest time when the tares were going to be uprooted and utterly burned.

🔑 **23** See note on I Thess. 4:17.

THE REVELATION

to John

Revelation means "to take the cover off," or *apokalupsis* (602), from the preposition *apo* (575), from, and *kaluptō* (2572), to cover. It is the uncovering, especially of the glory of Christ and of what the future holds.

This book is full of symbolism and prophecies in regard to the future. What the Book of Daniel is to the Old Testament, Revelation is to the New Testament. The apocalyptic passages in the Gospels are Mt. 24—25; Mk. 13; Lk. 21.

The author is John (Rev. 1:1,9; 21:2; 22:8), the same John who wrote the Gospel and the three Epistles of John.

This book was written at a time when the Church was undergoing persecution and difficulty. The two most important such periods were during the reigns of Nero in A.D. 37-68 and Domitian in A.D. 51-96.

Revelation was addressed to the churches of Asia Minor which are mentioned in chapters 2-3.

There are four views of interpreting Revelation. The first, or preterist view, places the events and visions described as belonging to the past, particularly to the Roman Empire of the first century A.D. The believers of this view explain the highly symbolic character of the book as an endeavor by John to hide the real meaning of what he was saying from the general populace but make it apparent to the believers who lived at that time. People holding to this view believe that the main purpose of this writing was to encourage the believers regarding God's ultimate intervention in the affairs of men. It is very unlikely that this view is correct in light of the prophetic nature of the book (Rev. 1:3). Some of the descriptions of future events cannot possibly be identified as historical ones.

The second view, or the historicist view, maintains that what we have in Revelation is a panoramic view of history from the first century to the Second Coming of Christ. This is the view of most of the Protestant Reformers. In our opinion, this is an untenable position also because historians have been unable to identify precise events in history which would answer to the visions symbolized.

The third view is the symbolic view which holds that Revelation portrays the continuing conflict between the forces of good and evil throughout the entire span of human history. The book according to this view is designed to give encouragement since at the end the good will triumph.

The fourth view is the futuristic view which maintains that from chapter 4 on, Revelation deals with events at the end time. According to this view, Revelation is not concerning events of John's own day as much as later historical events, and particularly those happenings that will take place in connection with the Second Coming of the Lord. This view takes seriously the predictive element in the book (Rev. 1:19; 4:1). Very definitely the final chapters of Revelation deal with the last days and a definitive change in things as they are today. Chapter 1 deals with the past; chapters 2-3 tell us about things that were present at that time and which were to follow; chapters 4-22 tell us the things that are to follow the church age and the Second Coming of Christ.

The Revelation of Jesus Christ

1 🗝 The Revelation[602] of Jesus Christ,[5547] which [a]God[2316] gave Him to [b]show to His bond-servants,[1401] [c]the things which must shortly take place; and He sent and [I]communicated *it* [d]by His angel[32] to His bond-servant [e]John,

1 [I]Or, *signified* [a]John 17:8; Rev. 5:7 [b]Rev. 22:6 [c]Dan. 2:28f.; Rev. 1:19 [d]Rev. 17:1; 19:9f.; 21:9; 22:16 [e]Rev. 1:4, 9; 22:8

🗝 **1:1-20** It has four distinct divisions: introduction (vv. 1-3); salutation (vv. 4-8); Christ in His glory (vv. 9-18); the instruction to write (vv. 19,20).

(continued on next page)

2 who bore witness to [a]the word[3056] of God and to [b]the testimony[3141] of Jesus Christ, *even* to all that he saw.

3 [a]Blessed[3107] is he who [ppt]reads and those who [ppt]hear the words of the prophecy,[4394] and [ppt] [1]heed the things which are written in it; [b]for the time[2540] is near.

Message to the Seven Churches

4 [a]John to [b]the seven churches[1577] that are in [c]Asia: [d]Grace[5485] to you and peace,[1515] from [e]Him who is and who was and who is to come; and from [f]the seven Spirits[4151] who are before His throne;

🗝 5 and from Jesus Christ, [a]the faithful[4103] witness,[3144] the [b]first-born[4416] of the dead,[3498] and the [c]ruler[758] of the kings[935] of the earth.[1093] To Him who [ppt] [d]loves[25] us, and [apt]released us from our sins[266] [1]by His blood,[129]

6 and He has [ao]made us *to be* a [a]kingdom,[932] [a]priests[2409] to [1b]His God and Father; [c]to Him *be* the glory[1391] and the dominion[2907] forever[165] and ever. Amen.[281]

7 [a]BEHOLD, HE IS COMING WITH THE CLOUDS, and [b]every eye will see Him, even those who pierced Him; and all the tribes of the earth will [c]mourn[2875] over Him. Even so. Amen.

8 "I am [a]the Alpha[1] and the Omega,"[5598] says the [b]Lord God, "[c]who is and who was and who is to come, the Almighty."[3841]

The Patmos Vision

9 [a]I, John, your [b]brother[80] and [c]fellow partaker in the tribulation[2347] and [d]kingdom[932] and [1e]perseverance[5281] *which are* in Jesus, [ao]was on the island called Patmos, [f]because of the word[3056] of God and the testimony[3141] of Jesus.

10 I [ao]was [1a]in the Spirit[4151] on [b]the Lord's[2960] day,[2250] and I heard behind me a loud voice [c]like *the sound* of a trumpet,

11 saying, "[a]Write[1125] in a [1]book what you see, and send *it* to the [b]seven churches: to [c]Ephesus and to [d]Smyrna and to [e]Pergamum and to [f]Thyatira and to [g]Sardis and to [h]Philadelphia and to [i]Laodicea."

12 And I turned to see the voice that was [ipf]speaking[2980] with me. And having turned I saw [a]seven golden lampstands;

13 and [a]in the middle of the lampstands one [b]like [1]a son[5207] of man,[444] [c]clothed in a robe reaching to the

2 [a]Rev. 1:9; 6:9; 12:17; 20:4 [b]1Cor. 1:6; Rev. 12:17
3 [1]Or, *keep* [a]Luke 11:28; Rev. 22:7 [b]Rom. 13:11; Rev. 3:11; 22:7, 10, 12
4 [a]Rev. 1:1, 9; 22:8 [b]Rev. 1:11, 20 [c]Acts 2:9 [d]Rom. 1:7 [e]Rev. 1:8, 17; 4:8; 16:5 [f]Is. 11:2; Rev. 3:1; 4:5; 5:6; 8:2
5 [1]Or, *in* [a]Rev. 3:14; 19:11 [b]1Cor. 15:20; Col. 1:18 [c]Rev. 17:14; 19:16 [d]Rom. 8:37
6 [1]Or, *God and His Father* [a]Rev. 5:10; 20:6 [b]Rom. 15:6 [c]Rom. 11:36
7 [a]Dan. 7:13; 1Thess. 4:17 [b]Zech. 12:10-14; John 19:37 [c]Luke 23:28
8 [a]Is. 41:4; Rev. 21:6; 22:13 [b]Rev. 4:8; 11:17 [c]Rev. 1:4
9 [1]Or, *steadfastness* [a]Rev. 1:1 [b]Acts 1:15 [c]Matt. 20:23; Acts 14:22; 2Cor. 1:7; Phil. 4:14 [d]2Tim. 2:12; Rev. 1:6 [e]2Thess. 3:5; Rev. 3:10 [f]Rev. 1:2
10 [1]Or, *in spirit* [a]Matt. 22:43; Rev. 4:2; 17:3; 21:10 [b]Acts 20:7 [c]Rev. 4:1
11 [1]Or, *scroll* [a]Rev. 1:2, 19 [b]Rev. 1:4, 20 [c]Rev. 2:1 [d]Rev. 2:8 [e]Rev. 2:12 [f]Acts 16:14; Rev. 2:18, 24 [g]Rev. 3:1, 4 [h]Rev. 3:7 [i]Col. 2:1; Rev. 3:14
12 [a]Ex. 25:37; 37:23; Zech. 4:2; Rev. 1:20; 2:1
13 [1]Or, *the Son of Man* [a]Rev. 2:1 [b]Ezek. 1:26; Dan. 7:13; 10:16; Rev. 14:14 [c]Dan. 10:5

(continued from previous page)

In the Gospels Christ is presented as the Lamb sacrificed for our sins. Here He is presented as the Roaring Lion. The interesting thing is that in John 1:29,36, Jesus is presented as the *amnos* (286), the Lamb for sacrifice, while throughout Revelation He is never presented as *amnos* but as *arnion* (721), the Lamb which lives and is not distinctly marked for sacrifice (Rev. 5:6,8,12,13; 6:1,16; 7:9,10,14,17; 12:11; 13:8; 14:1,4,10; 15:3; 17:14; 19:7,9; 21:9,14,22,23,27; 22:1,3).

🗝 **1:1** The expression "must shortly take place" is translated from the Greek *en tachei*. The words *tachos* (5034), *tachus* (5036) and *tachu* (5035) essentially do not mean "at once" or "shortly," but mean "with speed, swiftness, or quickness." At least this is the first element of information that John wants to pass on to us. He speaks primarily about God's intervention in history, whether it is past or future history. God allows man to have his day, but God is also going to have His day in which He will intervene suddenly and speedily. This is clear throughout the entire Book of Revelation, and especially toward the end when God suddenly intervenes in the affairs of men. The other possible but secondary meaning is "in a short time." Indeed, the things described in Revelation, especially in the second and third chapters, had begun and were actual current events at the time when John was writing. They began to happen then; they are continuing to happen as God described them. We must not interpret "quickly" or "soon" only in relation to final events. They must take their time in the order that God meant them to take place.

🗝 **1:5** See note on Col. 1:15.

feet,[4158] and [d]girded across[4314] His breast[3149] with a golden girdle.[2223]

14 And His head and His [a]hair were white like white wool, like snow; and [b]His eyes were like a flame of fire;

15 and His [a]feet *were* like burnished bronze, when it has been caused to glow in a furnace, and His [b]voice *was* like the sound of many waters.

16 And in His right[1188] hand He [ppt]held [a]seven stars; and out of His mouth came a [b]sharp two-edged sword; and His [c]face[3799] was like [d]the sun [I]shining[5316] in its strength.[1411]

17 And when I saw Him, I [a]fell at His feet as a dead man. And He [b]laid His right hand upon me, saying, "[c]Do not be afraid;[5399] [d]I am the first[4413] and the last,[2078]

🔑18 and the [a]living[2198] One; and I [I][b]was dead,[3498] and behold, I am alive[2198] forevermore,[165] and I have [c]the keys of death[2288] and of Hades.[86]

19 "[a]Write[1125] therefore [b]the things which you have seen, and the things which are, and the things which shall take place [c]after these things.

20 "As for the [a]mystery[3466] of the [b]seven stars which you saw in My right hand, and the [c]seven golden lampstands: the [b]seven stars are the angels[32] of [d]the seven churches,[1577] and the seven [e]lampstands are the seven churches.

Message to Ephesus

2 🔑"To the angel[32] of the church[1577] in [a]Ephesus write:

The One who [ppt]holds [b]the seven stars in His right hand,[1188] the One who [ppt]walks [I][c]among the seven golden lampstands, says this:

2 '[a]I know your deeds[2041] and your toil and [I]perseverance, and that you cannot endure evil[2556] men, and you [b]put to the test[3985] those who call themselves [c]apostles,[652] and they are not, and you found them *to be* false;

3 and you have [I]perseverance[5281] and have endured [a]for My name's sake, and have not grown weary.[2872]

4 'But I have *this* against you, that you have [a]left your first love.[26]

5 'Remember therefore from where you have [pfi]fallen, and [a]repent[3340] and [b]do the [I]deeds[2041] you did at first; or else I am coming to you, and will remove your [c]lampstand out of its place—unless you [aosb]repent.

🔑6 'Yet this you do have, that you hate the deeds[2041] of the [a]Nicolaitans, which I also hate.

7 '[a]He who has an ear, let him hear what the Spirit[4151] says to the churches. [b]To him who [ppt]overcomes, I will grant to eat of [c]the tree of life,[2222] which is in the [d]Paradise[3857] of God.'

Message to Smyrna

🔑8 "And to the angel[32] of the church[1577] in [a]Smyrna write:

13 [d]Rev. 15:6
14 [a]Dan. 7:9 [b]Dan. 7:9; 10:6; Rev. 2:18; 19:12
15 [a]Ezek. 1:7; Dan. 10:6; Rev. 2:18 [b]Ezek. 1:24; 43:2; Rev. 14:2; 19:6
16 [I]Lit., *shines* [a]Rev. 1:20; 2:1; 3:1 [b]Is. 49:2; Heb. 4:12; Rev. 2:12, 16; 19:15 [c]Matt. 17:2; Rev. 10:1 [d]Judg. 5:31
17 [a]Dan. 8:17; 10:9, 10, 15 [b]Dan. 8:18; 10:10, 12 [c]Matt. 14:27; 17:7 [d]Is. 41:4; 44:6; 48:12; Rev. 2:8; 22:13
18 [I]Lit., *became* [a]Luke 24:5; Rev. 4:9f. [b]Rom. 6:9; Rev. 2:8; 10:6; 15:7 [c]Job 38:17; Matt. 11:23; 16:19; Rev. 9:1; 20:1
19 [a]Rev. 1:11 [b]Rev. 1:12-16 [c]Rev. 4:1
20 [a]Rom. 11:25 [b]Rev. 1:16; 2:1; 3:1 [c]Ex. 25:37; 37:23; Zech. 4:2; Rev. 1:12; 2:1 [d]Rev. 1:4, 11 [e]Matt. 5:14f.

1 [I]Lit., *in the middle of* [a]Rev. 1:11 [b]Rev. 1:16 [c]Rev. 1:12f.
2 [I]Or, *steadfastness* [a]Rev. 2:19; 3:1, 8, 15 [b]John 6:6; 1John 4:1 [c]2Cor. 11:13 **3** [I]V. 2, note 1 [a]John 15:21 **4** [a]Jer. 2:2; Matt. 24:12 **5** [I]Lit., *first deeds* [a]Rev. 2:16, 22; 3:3, 19 [b]Heb. 10:32; Rev. 2:2 [c]Matt. 5:14ff.; Phil. 2:15; Rev. 1:20 **6** [a]Rev. 2:15 **7** [a]Matt. 11:15; Rev. 2:11, 17; 3:6, 13, 22; 13:9 [b]Rev. 2:11, 17, 26; 3:5, 12, 21; 21:7 [c]Gen. 2:9; 3:22; Prov. 3:18; 11:30; 13:12; 15:4; Rev. 22:2, 14 [d]Ezek. 28:13; 31:8f.; Luke 23:43 **8** [a]Rev. 1:11

🔑**1:18** See note on Lk. 16:23.

🔑**2:29—3:22** These chapters contain letters to the seven churches. These were local churches in Asia MInor, but they were each representative of a particular age in church history. Therefore, in a very marvelous way, the Lord takes churches currently existing at that time and compares their behavior and their circumstances with certain epochs which were yet to appear in church history. Throughout the Book of Revelation, the Lord wants to make clear that He is writing the history of the future.

🔑**2:1-7** The church of Ephesus was sixty miles northeast of the Isle of Patmos from where the Apostle John was writing and 35 miles South of modern Izmir. The church of Ephesus corresponds to the apostolic church.

🔑**2:8-11** The church in Smyrna finds its counterpart in the martyr church of the second and third centuries. Smyrna, today Izmir, was thirty-five miles north of Ephesus. It was the most splendid of the Seven Cities and was the pride of Asia. The Caesar cult had emerged and the Christians suffered a great deal because they would not worship Caesar. Polycarp, the bishop of the church, was martyred here in A.D. 156 because he refused to call Caesar "Lord."

[b]The first[4413] and the last,[2078] who [Ic]was dead,[3498] and has come to life,[2198] says this:

9 'I know your [a]tribulation and your [b]poverty (but you are [b]rich), and the blasphemy[988] by those who [c]say they are Jews and are not, but are a synagogue[4864] of [d]Satan.[4567]

10 'Do not fear[5399] what you are about to suffer. Behold, the devil[1228] is about to cast some of you into prison, that you may be [a]tested,[3985] and you will have tribulation[2347] [b]ten days. Be [c]faithful[4103] until death,[2288] and I will give you [d]the crown of life.[2222]

11 '[a]He who [ppt]has an ear, let him hear what the Spirit says to the churches. [b]He who [ppt]overcomes shall not be hurt[91] by the [c]second death.'[2288]

Message to Pergamum

12 "And to the angel[32] of the church[1577] in [a]Pergamum write:

The One who has [b]the sharp two-edged sword says this:

13 'I know where you dwell, where [a]Satan's[4567] throne is; and you hold fast My name, and did not [ao]deny [b]My faith,[4102] even in the days of Antipas, My [c]witness,[3144] My [d]faithful[4103] one, who was killed among you, [e]where Satan dwells.

14 'But [a]I have a few things against you, because you have there some who [ppt]hold the [b]teaching[1322] of Balaam, who kept [ipf]teaching[1321] Balak to [ainf]put a stumbling block[4625] before the sons[5207] of Israel, [c]to eat things sacrificed to idols, and to commit *acts of* immorality.[4203]

15 'Thus you also have some who in the same way [ppt]hold the teaching of the [a]Nicolaitans.

16 '[a]Repent[3340] therefore; or else [b]I am coming to you quickly, and I will make war against them with [c]the sword of My mouth.

17 '[a]He who has an ear, let him hear what the Spirit says to the churches. [a]To him who [ppt]overcomes, to him I will give *some* of the hidden [b]manna,[3131] and I will give him a white stone, and a [c]new[2537] name[3686] written on the stone [d]which no one knows but he who [ppt]receives it.'

Message to Thyatira

18 "And to the angel[32] of the church[1577] in [a]Thyatira write:

[b]The Son[5207] of God,[2316] [c]who [ppt]has [I]eyes like a flame of fire, and His feet are like burnished bronze, says this:

19 '[a]I know your deeds, and your love[26] and faith[4102] and service[1248] and [I]perseverance,[5281] and that your [II]deeds[2041] of late[2078] are greater than [III]at first.[4413]

20 'But [a]I have *this* against you, that you tolerate the woman [b]Jezebel, who calls herself a prophetess,[4398] and she teaches[1321] and leads My bond-servants[1401] astray, so that they [c]commit *acts of* immorality and eat things sacrificed to idols.

21 'And [a]I gave her time[5550] to repent;[3340] and she [b]does not want to repent of her immorality.

22 'Behold, [I]I will cast her [II]upon a bed *of sickness*, and those who [a]commit

8 [I]Lit., *became* [b]Is. 44:6; 48:12; Rev. 1:17; 22:13 [c]Rev. 1:18
9 [a]Rev. 1:9 [b]2Cor. 6:10; 8:9; James 2:5 [c]Rev. 3:9 [d]Matt. 4:10; Rev. 2:13, 24
10 [a]Rev. 3:10; 13:14ff. [b]Dan. 1:12, 14 [c]Rev. 2:13; 12:11; 17:14 [d]1Cor. 9:25; Rev. 3:11
11 [a]Matt. 11:15; Rev. 2:7, 17, 29; 3:6, 13, 22; 13:9 [b]Rev. 2:7, 17, 26; 3:5, 12, 21; 21:7 [c]Rev. 20:6, 14; 21:8
12 [a]Rev. 1:11 [b]Rev. 1:16; 2:16
13 [a]Matt. 4:10; Rev. 2:24 [b]1Tim. 5:8; Rev. 14:12 [c]Acts 22:20; Rev. 1:5; 11:3; 17:6 [d]Rev. 2:10; 12:11; 17:14 [e]Rev. 2:9
14 [a]Rev. 2:20 [b]Num. 31:16; 2Pet. 2:15 [c]Num. 25:1f.; Acts 15:29; 1Cor. 10:20; Rev. 2:20
15 [a]Rev. 2:6
16 [a]Rev. 2:5 [b]Rev. 22:7, 20 [c]2Thess. 2:8; Rev. 1:16
17 [a]Rev. 2:7 [b]Ex. 16:33; John 6:49f. [c]Is. 56:5; 62:2; 65:15 [d]Rev. 14:3; 19:12
18 [I]Lit., *His eyes* [a]Rev. 1:11; 2:24 [b]Matt. 4:3 [c]Rev. 1:14f.
19 [I]Or, *steadfastness* [II]Lit., *last deeds* [III]Lit., *the first* [a]Rev. 2:2
20 [a]Rev. 2:14 [b]1Kin. 16:31; 21:25; 2Kin. 9:7, 22, 30 [c]Acts 15:29; 1Cor. 10:20; Rev. 2:14
21 [a]Rom. 2:4; 2Pet. 3:9 [b]Rom. 2:5; Rev. 9:20f.; 16:9, 11 **22** [I]Lit., *I cast* [II]Lit., *into* [a]Rev. 17:2; 18:9

2:12-17 The church in Pergamum (or Pergamos) represents the state church, beginning with Constantine and continuing to the end. It was fifteen miles from the Aegean Coast and fifty-five miles north of Smyrna. The acropolis (the upper or higher part of the city) crowned a steep hill that rose 1,000 feet above the plain on which there was an immense altar to Zeus, the chief of the Greek mythological gods.

2:18-29 The church in Thyatira has the features of the firmly established church that is not only a church but a state, such as the Vatican which is indeed both. It begins with Gregory the Great and continues to the end. Thyatira was the least important of the Seven Cities and was about halfway between Pergamum and Sardis. It was an important city, commercially more than politically.

adultery with her into great tribulation,[2347] unless they repent of [III]her deeds.[2041]

23 'And I will kill her children with [I]pestilence; and all the churches will know that I am He who [ppt] [a]searches the [II]minds[3510] and hearts;[2588] and [b]I will give to each one of you according to your deeds.[2041]

24 'But I say to you, the rest who are in [a]Thyatira, who do not hold this teaching,[1322] who have not [ao]known the [b]deep things of Satan,[4567] as they call them—I [pin] [c]place no other burden on you.

25 'Nevertheless [a]what you have, hold fast [b]until I come.

26 'And [a]he who overcomes, and he who keeps My deeds [b]until the end,[5056] [c]TO HIM I WILL GIVE AUTHORITY[1849] OVER THE [I]NATIONS;[1487]

27 AND HE SHALL [Ia]RULE[4165] THEM WITH A ROD OF IRON, [b]AS THE VESSELS OF THE POTTER ARE BROKEN TO PIECES,[4937] as I also have received *authority* from My Father;[3962]

28 and I will give him [a]the morning star.

29 '[a]He who has an ear, let him hear what the Spirit says to the churches.'

Message to Sardis

3 "And to the angel[32] of the church[1577] in [a]Sardis write:

He who [ppt]has [b]the seven Spirits[4151] of God, and [c]the seven stars, says this: '[d]I know your deeds,[2041] that you have a name[3686] that you are alive,[2198] but you are [e]dead.[3498]

2 'Wake up, and strengthen the things that remain, which were about to die; for I have not found your deeds completed[4137] in the sight of My God.

3 '[a]Remember therefore [I]what you have [pfi]received and heard; and [pim]keep *it,* and [aim] [b]repent.[3340] If therefore you will not [aosb]wake up, [c]I will come [d]like a thief, and you will not [efn]know at [e]what hour I will come upon you.

4 'But you have a few [Ia]people[3686] in [b]Sardis who have not [ao] [c]soiled[3435] their garments; and they will walk with Me [d]in white; for they are worthy.

5 '[a]He who [ppt]overcomes shall thus be clothed in [b]white garments; and I will not [c]erase his name from the book[976] of life,[2222] and [d]I will confess[3670] his name before My Father,[3962] and before His angels.

6 '[a]He who has an ear, let him [aim]hear what the Spirit says to the churches.'

Message to Philadelphia

7 "And to the angel[32] of the church[1577] in [a]Philadelphia write:

[b]**He** who is holy,[40] [c]who is true,[228] who has [d]the key of David, who [ppt]opens and no one will [ft]shut, and who [ppt]shuts and no one [ft]opens, says this:

8 '[a]I know your [I]deeds.[2041] Behold, I have put before you [b]an open door which no one can [ainf]shut, because you have a little power, and have [ao]kept My word,[3056] and [c]have not denied[720] My name.[3686]

9 'Behold, I [I]will cause *those* of [a]the synagogue[4864] of Satan,[4567] who say that they are Jews, and are not, but lie—behold, I will make them to [b]come and bow down[4352] [II]at your feet, and to know that [c]I have loved[25] you.

22 [III]Some mss. read *their*
23 [I]Lit., *death* [II]Lit., *kidneys,* i.e., inner man [a]Ps. 7:9; 26:2; 139:1; Jer. 11:20; 17:10; Matt. 16:27; Luke 16:15; Acts 1:24; Rom. 8:27 [b]Ps. 62:12
24 [a]Rev. 2:18 [b]1Cor. 2:10 [c]Acts 15:28
25 [a]Rev. 3:11 [b]John 21:22
26 [I]Or, *Gentiles* [a]Rev. 2:7 [b]Matt. 10:22; Heb. 3:6 [c]Ps. 2:8; Rev. 3:21; 20:4
27 [I]Or, *shepherd* [a]Ps. 2:9; Rev. 12:5; 19:15 [b]Is. 30:14; Jer. 19:11
28 [a]1John 3:2; Rev. 22:16
29 [a]Rev. 2:7

1 [a]Rev. 1:11 [b]Rev. 1:4 [c]Rev. 1:16 [d]Rev. 2:2; 3:8, 15 [e]1Tim. 5:6
3 [I]Lit., *how* [a]Rev. 2:5 [b]Rev. 2:5 [c]1Thess. 5:2; 2Pet. 3:10; Rev. 16:15 [d]Matt. 24:43; Luke 12:39f.
4 [I]Lit., *names* [a]Rev. 11:13 [b]Rev. 1:11 [c]Jude 23 [d]Eccl. 9:8; Rev. 3:5; 18; 4:4; 6:11; 7:9, 13f.; 19:8, 14
5 [a]Rev. 2:7 [b]Rev. 3:4 [c]Ex. 32:32f.; Ps. 69:28; Luke 10:20; Rev. 13:8; 17:8; 20:12, 15; 21:27 [d]Matt. 10:32; Luke 12:8
6 [a]Rev. 2:7
7 [a]Rev. 1:11 [b]Rev. 6:10 [c]1John 5:20; Rev. 3:14; 19:11 [d]Job 12:14; Is. 22:22; Matt. 16:19; Rev. 1:18
8 [I]Or, *deeds (behold, . . . shut), that you* [a]Rev. 3:1 [b]Acts 14:27 [c]Rev. 2:13
9 [I]Lit., *give* [II]Lit., *before* [a]Rev. 2:9 [b]Is. 45:14; 49:23; 60:14 [c]Is. 43:4; John 17:23

3:1-6 The church in Sardis pictures the Reformation church, beginning with the sixteenth century. Sardis was thirty miles southeast of Thyatira and fifty miles due east of Smyrna. The richest man living, Croesus, reigned here. The city was devastated by an earthquake in A.D. 17 but was later rebuilt.

3:7-13 The church in Philadelphia sets forth the characteristics of the missionary church, beginning with the rise of modern missions under William Carey. It was built in a dangerous volcanic area located about twenty-eight miles southeast of Sardis. It was completely destroyed by an earthquake in A.D. 17 but was completely rebuilt.

10 'Because you have [a]kept the word[3056] of [b]My [I]perseverance,[5281] [c]I also will keep you from the hour[5610] of [II][d]testing,[3986] that *hour* which is about to come[2064] upon the whole [III][e]world,[3625] to [IV]test[3985] [f]those who dwell upon the earth.[1093]

11 '[a]I am coming quickly; [b]hold fast what you have, in order that no one take your [c]crown.[4735]

12 '[a]He who overcomes, I will make him a [b]pillar in the temple[3485] of My God, and he will not go out from it anymore; and I will write[1125] upon him the [c]name of My God, and [d]the name[3686] of the city of My God, [e]the new[2537] Jerusalem, which comes down out of heaven[3772] from My God, and My [f]new[2537] name.

13 '[a]He who has an ear, let him [aim]hear what the Spirit says to the churches.'

Message to Laodicea

🔑 14 "And to the angel[32] of the church[1577] in [a]Laodicea write:

[b]The Amen,[281] [c]the faithful[4103] and true[228] Witness,[3144] [d]the [I]Beginning[746] of the creation[2937] of God, says this:

15 '[a]I know your deeds,[2041] that you are neither cold nor hot; [b]I would that you were[1510] cold or hot.

16 'So because you are lukewarm, and neither hot nor cold, I will [I]spit[1692] you out of My mouth.

17 'Because you say, "[a]I am rich, and have become wealthy, and have need of nothing," and you do not know that you are wretched and miserable[1652] and poor and blind and naked,[1131]

18 I advise you to [ainf][a]buy from Me [b]gold refined by fire, that you may become rich, and [c]white garments, that you may clothe yourself, and *that* [d]the shame[152] of your nakedness[1132] may not be revealed;[5319] and eye salve to anoint your eyes, that you may see.

19 '[a]Those whom I love,[5386] I reprove[1651] and discipline;[3811] be zealous therefore, and [aim] [b]repent.[3340]

20 'Behold, I stand [a]at the door and [b]knock; if anyone [aosb]hears My voice and [aosb]opens the door, [c]I will come in to him, and will dine[1172] with him, and he with Me.

🔑 21 '[a]He who [ppt]overcomes, I will grant to him [b]to [ainf]sit down with Me on My throne, as [c]I also overcame and [ao]sat down with My Father[3962] on His throne.

22 '[a]He who [ppt]has an ear, let him [aim]hear what the Spirit says to the churches.' "

Scene in Heaven

4 🔑 After [a]these things I looked, and behold, [b]a door *standing* open in

10 [I]Or, *steadfastness* [II]Or, *temptation* [III]Lit., *inhabited earth* [IV]Or, *tempt* [a]John 17:6; Rev. 3:8 [b]Rev. 1:9 [c]2Tim. 2:12; 2Pet. 2:9 [d]Rev. 2:10 [e]Matt. 24:14; Rev. 16:14 [f]Rev. 6:10; 8:13; 11:10; 13:8, 14; 17:8
11 [a]Rev. 1:3; 22:7, 12, 20 [b]Rev. 2:25 [c]Rev. 2:10
12 [a]Rev. 3:5 [b]1Kin. 7:21; Jer. 1:18; Gal. 2:9 [c]Rev. 14:1; 22:4 [d]Ezek. 48:35; Rev. 21:2 [e]Gal. 4:26; Heb. 13:14; Rev. 21:2, 10 [f]Is. 62:2; Rev. 2:17
13 [a]Rev. 3:6
14 [I]I.e., origin or source [a]Rev. 1:11 [b]2Cor. 1:20 [c]Rev. 1:5; 3:7 [d]Gen. 49:3; Deut. 21:17; Prov. 8:22; John 1:3; Col. 1:18; Rev. 21:6; 22:13
15 [a]Rev. 3:1 [b]Rom. 12:11
16 [I]Lit., *vomit*
17 [a]Hos. 12:8; Zech. 11:5; Matt. 5:3; 1Cor. 4:8
18 [a]Is. 55:1; Matt. 13:44 [b]1Pet. 1:7 [c]Rev. 3:4 [d]Rev. 16:15
19 [a]Prov. 3:12; 1Cor. 11:32; Heb. 12:6 [b]Rev. 2:5
20 [a]Matt. 24:33; James 5:9 [b]Luke 12:36; John 10:3 [c]John 14:23 **21** [a]Rev. 2:7 [b]Matt. 19:28; 2Tim. 2:12; Rev. 2:26; 20:4 [c]John 16:33; Rev. 5:5; 6:2; 17:14
22 [a]Rev. 2:7 **1** [a]Rev. 1:12ff., 19 [b]Ezek. 1:1; Rev. 19:11

🔑 **3:14-22** The church in Laodicea portrays the apostate church of the last days. It is about forty miles southeast of Philadelphia and east of Ephesus. It was a banking center and had a famous medical school. The city is in complete ruins today.

🔑 **3:21** See note on I Thess. 2:19.

🔑 **4:1-11** In Rev. 2-3 we see Christ working on earth in His Church. In the fourth chapter, however, we are transferred to the heavenly or spiritual realm. But how is it that the Church is now found in heaven? Something must have intervened, thus bringing about this transfer of the earthly residence of the Church to the heavenly one. This transfer is not mentioned in the Book of Revelation, but it is mentioned elsewhere. The Bible should be viewed as a whole and not in fragments. One prophecy complements another. The event which describes this transfer is called, "the rapture of the Church." The word "rapture," *harpagē* (724), as a substantive is used only in Mt. 23:25; Lk. 11:39 translated as "robbery," and in Heb. 10:34 translated as "seizure." In these three instances, it has nothing to do with this event of the transfer of the earthly Church to its heavenly abode, but the verb *harpazō* (726) is used to describe this event in I Thess. 4:17. It is used in the context of the

(continued on next page)

heaven,[3772] and the first voice which I
had heard, [c]like *the sound* of a trumpet
speaking with me, [I]said, "[d]Come up
here, and I will [e]show you what must
take place after these things."
2 Immediately I [ao]was [Ia]in the
Spirit;[4151] and behold, [b]a throne was
[ipf]standing[2749] in heaven, and [c]One [ppt]sit-
ting on the throne.
3 And He who was sitting *was* like
a [a]jasper stone and a [b]sardius in
appearance;3706 and *there was* a [Ic]rainbow
around the throne, like an [d]emerald in
appearance.3706
4 And [a]around the throne *were*
[b]twenty-four thrones; and upon the
thrones *I saw* [c]twenty-four elders[4245]
[d]sitting, clothed in [e]white garments,[2440]
and [f]golden crowns on their heads.

The Throne and Worship of the Creator

5 And from the throne proceed
[a]flashes of lightning and sounds and peals
of thunder. And *there were* [b]seven lamps
of fire burning before the throne, which
are [c]the seven Spirits of God;
6 and before the throne *there was,*
as it were, a [a]sea of glass like crystal;
and in the [I]center and [b]around the
throne, [c]four living creatures[2226] [d]full of
eyes in front and behind.
7 [a]And the first creature *was* like a
lion, and the second creature like a calf,
and the third creature had a face like
that of a man, and the fourth creature
was like a flying eagle.
8 And the [a]four living creatures,
each[303] one of them [ppt]having [b]six wings,
are [c]full of eyes around and within; and
[d]day and night [I]they do not cease[372] to
say,

"[e]HOLY,[40] HOLY, HOLY, *is* THE
[f]LORD[2962] God,[2316] THE
ALMIGHTY,3841
[g]who was and who is and who
is to come."

9 And when the living creatures
[ft]give glory[1391] and honor and thanks to
Him who [ppt a]sits on the throne, to
[b]Him who [ppt]lives[2198] forever[165] and
ever,
10 the [a]twenty-four elders[4245] will
[ft b]fall down before Him who [c]sits on the
throne, and will [ft]worship [d]Him who lives
forever and ever, and will [ft]cast their
[e]crowns[4735] before the throne, saying,
11 "[a]Worthy art Thou, our Lord and
our God, To [ainf]receive glory
and honor and power;
For Thou [b]didst [ao]create[2936] all
things,
And because of Thy will they
[I]existed, and were created."

The Book with Seven Seals

5 🗝 And I saw [I]in the right hand[1188]
of Him who [ppt a]sat on the throne
a [IIb]book975 written inside and on the
back, [pfpp c]sealed up with seven seals.
2 And I saw a [a]strong angel[32]
proclaiming[2784] with a loud voice, "Who
is worthy514 to [ainf]open[3089] the [I]book and
to [ainf]break its seals?"

1 [I]Lit., *saying* [c]Rev. 1:10 [d]Rev. 11:12 [e]Rev. 1:19; 22:6
2 [I]Or, *in spirit* [a]Rev. 1:10 [b]1Kin. 22:19; Is. 6:1; Ezek. 1:26; Dan. 7:9; Rev. 4:9f. [c]Rev. 4:9
3 [I]Or, *halo* [a]Rev. 21:11 [b]Rev. 21:20 [c]Ezek. 1:28; Rev. 10:1 [d]Rev. 21:19
4 [a]Rev. 4:6; 5:11; 7:11 [b]Rev. 11:16 [c]Rev. 4:10; 5:6, 8, 14; 19:4 [d]Matt. 19:28; Rev. 20:4 [e]Rev. 3:18 [f]Rev. 4:10
5 [a]Ex. 19:16; Rev. 8:5; 11:19; 16:18 [b]Ex. 25:37; Zech. 4:2 [c]Rev. 1:4
6 [I]Lit., *middle of the throne and around* [a]Ezek. 1:22; Rev. 15:2; 21:18, 21 [b]Rev. 4:4 [c]Ezek. 1:5; Rev. 4:8f.; 5:6; 6:1, 6; 7:11; 14:3; 15:7; 19:4 [d]Ezek. 1:18; 10:12
7 [a]Ezek. 1:10; 10:14
8 [I]Lit., *they have no rest, saying,* [a]Ezek. 1:5; Rev. 4:6, 9; 5:6; 6:1, 6; 7:11; 14:3; 15:7; 19:4 [b]Is. 6:2 [c]Ezek. 1:18; 10:12 [d]Rev. 14:11 [e]Is. 6:3 [f]Rev. 1:8 [g]Rev. 1:4
9 [a]Ps. 47:8; Is. 6:1; Rev. 4:2 [b]Deut. 32:40; Dan. 4:34; 12:7; Rev. 10:6; 15:7
10 [a]Rev. 4:4 [b]Rev. 5:8, 14; 7:11; 11:16; 19:4 [c]Ps. 47:8; Is. 6:1; Rev. 4:2 [d]Deut. 32:40; Dan. 4:34; 12:7 [e]Rev. 4:4; 10:6; 15:7
11 [I]Lit., *were* [a]Rev. 1:6; 5:12 [b]Acts 14:15; Rev. 10:6; 14:7
1 [I]Lit., *upon* [II]Or, *scroll* [a]Rev. 4:9; 5:7, 13 [b]Ezek. 2:9, 10 [c]Is. 29:11; Dan. 12:4
2 [I]Or, *scroll* [a]Rev. 10:1; 18:21

(continued from previous page)
parousia (3952), "the coming of the Lord," which undoubtedly means the Second Coming and not the first coming of Jesus (I Thess. 4:15,16). The first thing to take place at that time is the raising of the dead who are in Christ and the transforming of the bodies of the believers who are still alive (see I Thess. 4:13-18; I Cor. 15:50-55).

🗝 **5:1-14** In chapter 5 our attention is drawn to a book (scroll) which is held in the hand of God. It is sealed with seven seals. Seven is the number which is a symbol of perfection. It contains secrets which were completely unknown until that time.

In vv. 5-14 the Lord Jesus is described as both the Lion and the Lamb who opens the seals to reveal the contents of the book.

3 And no one [a]in heaven,[3772] or on the earth, or under the earth,[1093] was able to [ainf]open the [I]book, or to [pinf]look into it.

4 And I *began* to [ipf]weep greatly, because no one was found[2147] worthy to open the [I]book, or to look into it;

5 and one of the elders[4245] *said to me, "Stop [pim]weeping; behold, the [a]Lion that is [b]from the tribe of Judah, the [c]Root of David, has [ao]overcome so as to open the [I]book and its seven seals."

6 And I saw [I]between the throne (with the four living creatures[2226]) and [a]the elders a [b]Lamb[721] standing, as if [pfpp] [c]slain, having seven [d]horns and [e]seven eyes, which are [f]the seven Spirits[4151] of God, sent out into all the earth.[1093]

7 And He came, and He took [a]*it* out of the right hand[1188] of Him who [a]sat on the throne.

8 And when He had [ao]taken the [I]book, the [a]four living creatures and the [b]twenty-four elders [c]fell down before the [d]Lamb, having each one a [e]harp, and [f]golden bowls full of incense, which are the [g]prayers[4335] of the [II]saints.[40]

9 And they [pin]*sang a [a]new[2537] song,[5603] saying,

"[b]Worthy art Thou to [ainf]take the [I]book, and to [ainf]break its seals;
For Thou wast [c]slain,[4969] and didst [d]purchase[59] for God with Thy blood[129]
Men from [e]every tribe[5443] and tongue[1100] and people[2992] and nation.[1484]

10 "And Thou hast [ao]made them *to be* a [a]kingdom[932] and [a]priests[2409] to our God;

3 [I]Or, *scroll* [a]Phil. 2:10; Rev. 5:13
4 [I]Or, *scroll*
5 [I]Or, *scroll* [a]Gen. 49:9 [b]Heb. 7:14 [c]Is. 11:1, 10; Rom. 15:12; Rev. 22:16
6 [I]Lit., *in the middle of the throne and of the four living creatures, and in the middle of the elders* [a]Rev. 4:4; 5:8, 14 [b]John 1:29; Rev. 5:8, 12f.; 13:8 [c]Rev. 5:9, 12; 13:8 [d]Dan. 8:3f. [e]Zech. 3:9; 4:10 [f]Rev. 1:4
7 [a]Rev. 5:1
8 [I]Or, *scroll* [II]Or, *holy ones* [a]Rev. 4:6; 5:6, 11, 14 [b]Rev. 4:4; 5:14 [c]Rev. 4:10 [d]John 1:29; Rev. 5:6, 12f.; 13:8 [e]Rev. 14:2; 15:2 [f]Rev. 15:7 [g]Ps. 141:2; Rev. 8:3f.
9 [I]Or, *scroll* [a]Ps. 33:3; 40:3; 98:1; 149:1; Is. 42:10; Rev. 14:3; 15:3 [b]Rev. 4:11 [c]Rev. 5:6, 12; 13:8 [d]1Cor. 6:20; Rev. 14:3f. [e]Dan. 3:4; 5:19; Rev. 7:9; 10:11; 11:9; 13:7; 14:6; 17:15
10 [a]Rev. 1:6 [b]Rev. 3:21; 20:4
11 [a]Rev. 4:4 [b]Rev. 4:6; 5:6, 8, 14 [c]Rev. 4:4; 5:6, 14 [d]Dan. 7:10; Heb. 12:22; Jude 14; Rev. 9:16
12 [a]Rev. 1:6; 4:11; 5:9 [b]John 1:29; Rev. 5:6, 13;

And they will [b]reign[936] upon the earth."

Angels Exalt the Lamb

11 And I looked, and I heard the voice of many angels[32] [a]around the throne and the [b]living creatures and the [c]elders; and the number of them was [d]myriads of myriads, and thousands of thousands,

12 saying with a loud voice,

"[a]Worthy[514] is the [b]Lamb that was [pfpp] [c]slain
To [ainf]receive power[1411] and riches[4149] and wisdom[4678] and might[2479] and honor[5092] and glory[1391] and blessing."[2129]

13 And [a]every created[2938] thing which is in heaven[3772] and on the earth[1093] and under the earth and on the sea, and all things in them, I heard saying,

"To Him who [ppt] [b]sits on the throne, and to the [c]Lamb,
[d]*Be* blessing and honor and glory and dominion[2904] forever[165] and ever."

14 And the [a]four living creatures kept [ipf]saying, "[b]Amen."[281] And the [c]elders[4245] [d]fell down and worshiped.[4352]

The Book Opened The First Seal—False Christ

6 🔑 And I saw when the [a]Lamb broke one of the [b]seven seals, and I heard

13:8 **13** [a]Phil. 2:10; Rev. 5:3 [b]Rev. 5:1 [c]John 1:29; Rev. 5:6, 12f.; 13:8 [d]Rom. 11:36; Rev. 1:6
14 [a]Rev. 4:6; 5:6, 8, 11 [b]1Cor. 14:16; Rev. 7:12; 19:4 [c]Rev. 4:4; 5:6, 8 [d]Rev. 4:10 **1** [a]John 1:29; Rev. 5:6, 12f.; 13:8 [b]Rev. 5:1

🔑 **6:1-17** This chapter begins with what is commonly known in the Scriptures as the "Day of the Lord," or the day of God's judgment on the earth. This is the beginning also of the Day of Christ, because on the same day the believers are caught up in the air to be with the Lord. The believers are taken from the earth, and God's judgment is then poured upon those who have rejected Christ. Here we have the beginning of the seven years of tribulation or great suffering. These seven years of tribulation form the seventieth week in the prophetical seventy weeks of Daniel. Each week stands for seven years (Dan. 9:24-27). The events that take place during this seventieth week of Daniel, or in this period of seven years, are described in Rev. 6-19. The same events are also covered in Mt. 24-25. There has

(continued on next page)

one of the [c]four living creatures[2226]
saying as with a [d]voice[5456] of thunder,
"Come[I]."
2 And I looked, and behold, a
[a]white horse, and he who [ppt]sat on it
[ppt]had a bow; and [b]a crown was given
to him; and he went out [c]conquering,
and to [aosb]conquer.

The Second Seal—War

3 And when He [ao]broke the second
seal, I heard the [a]second living creature
saying, "Come[I]."
4 And another, [a]a red horse, went
out; and to him who sat on it, it was
granted to [ainf] [b]take peace[1515] from the
earth,[1093] and that *men* should [ft]slay one
another; and a great sword was given
to him.

The Third Seal—Famine

5 And when He [ao]broke the third
seal, I heard the [a]third living creature
saying, "Come[I]." And I looked, and behold, a [b]black horse; and he who [ppt]sat
on it [ppt]had a [c]pair of scales in his hand.
6 And I heard as it were a voice in
the center of the [a]four living creatures
saying, "A [I]quart[5518] of wheat for a
[II]denarius, and three [I]quarts of barley
for a [II]denarius;[1220] and [b]do not harm[91]
the oil and the wine."

The Fourth Seal—Death

7 And when He [ao]broke the fourth
seal, I heard the voice of the [a]fourth
living creature saying, "Come[I]."
8 And I looked, and behold, an
[I][a]ashen horse; and he who sat on it had
the name [b]Death;[2288] and [b]Hades[86] was
[ipf]following with him. And authority[1849]
was given to them over a fourth of the
earth, [c]to [ainf]kill with sword and with
famine and with [II]pestilence and by the
wild beasts[2342] of the earth.

The Fifth Seal—Martyrs

9 And when He [ao]broke the fifth
seal, I saw [a]underneath the [b]altar[2379] the
[c]souls[5590] of those who had been slain
[d]because of the word[3056] of God, and
because of the [e]testimony which they
had [ipf]maintained;
10 and they cried out with a loud
voice, saying, "[a]How long, O [I][b]Lord,[1203]
[c]holy[40] and true,[228] [II]wilt Thou refrain
from [d]judging[2919] and avenging[1556] our
blood[129] on [e]those who [ppt]dwell on the
earth?"
11 And [a]there was given to each of
them a white robe; and they were told
that they should [asbm] [b]rest for a little
while longer,[5550] [c]until *the number of*
their fellow servants[4889] and their

1 [I]Some mss. add *and see* [c]Rev. 4:6; 5:6, 8, 11, 14 [d]Rev. 14:2; 19:6
2 [a]Zech. 1:8; 6:3f.; Rev. 19:11 [b]Zech. 6:11; Rev. 9:7; 14:14; 19:12 [c]Rev. 3:21
3 [I]Some mss. add *and see* [a]Rev. 4:7
4 [a]Zech. 1:8; 6:2 [b]Matt. 10:34
5 [I]Some mss. add *and see* [a]Rev. 4:7 [b]Zech. 6:2, 6 [c]Ezek. 4:16
6 [I]Gr., *choenix;* i.e., a dry measure almost equal to a qt. [II]The denarius was equivalent to one day's wage [a]Rev. 4:6f. [b]Rev. 7:3; 9:4
7 [I]Some mss. add *and see* [a]Rev. 4:7
8 [I]Or, *sickly pale* [II]Or, *death* [a]Zech. 6:3 [b]Prov. 5:5; Hos. 13:14; Matt. 11:23; Rev. 1:18; 20:13f. [c]Jer. 14:12; 15:2f.; 24:10; 29:17f.; Ezek. 5:12, 17; 14:21; 29:5
9 [a]Ex. 29:12; Lev. 4:7; John 16:2 [b]Rev. 14:18; 16:7 [c]Rev. 20:4 [d]Rev. 1:2, 9 [e]Rev. 12:17
10 [I]Or, *Master* [II]Lit., *dost Thou not judge and avenge* [a]Zech. 1:12 [b]Luke 2:29; 2Pet. 2:1 [c]Rev. 3:7 [d]Deut. 32:43; Ps. 79:10; Luke 18:7; Rev. 19:2 [e]Rev. 3:10
11 [a]Rev. 3:4, 5; 7:9 [b]2Thess. 1:7; Heb. 4:10; Rev. 14:13 [c]Heb. 11:40

(continued from previous page)
never been a period in the history of the world with the characteristic events described in this passage of Scripture. The Day of the Lord also includes the thousand year reign of Christ on earth commonly known as the millennium.

References to the Day of the Lord are also found in Isa. 2:12; 13:6,9; Jer. 46:10; Joel 2:1,11; 3:14; Amos 5:20; Zeph. 1:7; Zech. 14:1. It is also called the time of Jacob's distress (Jer. 30:7), a time of distress (Dan. 12:1), the hour of testing (Rev. 3:10), and the great day of their wrath (Rev. 6:17).

The series of these divine judgments are symbolized: first, as the seals; secondly, as the trumpets; and thirdly, as the bowls. Between the sixth and the seventh seals, the sixth and the seventh trumpets, and the sixth and seventh bowls of wrath there is a parenthetical portion. This is meant to give some further explanation or to reveal something new.

As the Lord Jesus takes the book He begins to open the seals of the book and the following is seen: (1) a rider on a white horse representing the false peace which the antichrist will bring; (2) a rider on a red horse representing war; (3) a rider on a black horse representing famine; (4) a rider on a pale horse representing death; (5) the martyred souls under the altar representing persecution; and (6) catastrophic changes on earth bringing about destruction.

brethren[80] who were to be killed even as they had been, should be [aosb] [d]completed[4137] also.

The Sixth Seal—Terror

12 And I looked when He broke the sixth seal, and there [ao]was a great [a]earthquake; and the [b]sun became black as [c]sackcloth[4526] *made* of hair, and the whole moon became like blood;

13 and [a]the stars of the sky fell to the earth, [b]as a fig tree casts its unripe figs when [ppp]shaken by a great wind.

14 And [a]the sky[3772] was split apart like a scroll when it is [ppp]rolled up; and [b]every mountain and island were moved out of their places.

15 And [a]the kings[935] of the earth and the great men and the [I]commanders and the rich and the strong and every slave[1401] and free man, hid themselves in the caves and among the rocks of the mountains;

16 and they *[a]said to the mountains and to the rocks, "Fall[4098] on us and [aim]hide us from the [I]presence of Him [b]who [ppt]sits on the throne, and from the [c]wrath[3709] of the Lamb;

17 for [a]the great day[2250] of their wrath has [ao]come; and [b]who is able to [aifp]stand?"

An Interlude

7 ⚿ After this I saw [a]four angels[32] standing at the [b]four corners of the earth,[1093] holding back [c]the four winds of the earth, [d]so that no wind should [psa]blow[4154] on the earth or on the sea or on any tree.

2 And I saw another angel ascending [a]from the rising of the sun, having the [b]seal of [c]the living God;[2316] and he cried out with a loud voice to the [d]four angels to whom it was granted to [ainf]harm[91] the earth and the sea,

3 saying, "[a]Do not [aosi]harm the earth or the sea or the trees, until we have [aosb] [b]sealed the bond-servants[1401] of our God on their [c]foreheads."

A Remnant of Israel—144,000

4 And I heard the [a]number of those who were [pfpp]sealed, [b]one hundred and forty-four thousand sealed from every tribe of the sons[5207] of Israel:

5 from the tribe of Judah, twelve thousand *were* sealed, from the tribe of Reuben twelve thousand, from the tribe of Gad twelve thousand,

6 from the tribe of Asher twelve thousand, from the tribe of Naphtali twelve thousand, from the tribe of Manasseh twelve thousand,

7 from the tribe of Simeon twelve thousand, from the tribe of Levi twelve thousand, from the tribe of Issachar twelve thousand,

8 from the tribe of Zebulun twelve thousand, from the tribe of Joseph twelve thousand, from the tribe of Benjamin, twelve thousand *were* sealed.

11 [d]Acts 20:24; 2Tim. 4:7
12 [a]Matt. 24:7; Rev. 8:5; 11:13; 16:18 [b]Is. 13:10; Joel 2:10, 31; 3:15; Matt. 24:29; Mark 13:24 [c]Is. 50:3; Matt. 11:21
13 [a]Matt. 24:29; Mark 13:25; Rev. 8:10; 9:1 [b]Is. 34:4
14 [a]Is. 34:4; 2Pet. 3:10; Rev. 20:11; 21:1 [b]Is. 54:10; Jer. 4:24; Ezek. 38:20; Nah. 1:5; Rev. 16:20
15 [I]I.e., chiliarchs, in command of one thousand troops [a]Is. 2:10f., 19, 21; 24:21; Rev. 19:18
16 [I]Lit., *face* [a]Hos. 10:8; Luke 23:30; Rev. 9:6 [b]Rev. 4:9; 5:1 [c]Mark 3:5
17 [a]Is. 63:4; Jer. 30:7; Joel 1:15; 2:1f., 11, 31; Zeph. 1:14f.; Rev. 16:14 [b]Ps. 76:7; Nah. 1:6; Mal. 3:2; Luke 21:36

1 [a]Rev. 9:14 [b]Is. 11:12; Ezek. 7:2; Rev. 20:8 [c]Jer. 49:36; Dan. 7:2; Zech. 6:5; Matt. 24:31 [d]Rev. 7:3; 8:7; 9:4
2 [a]Is. 41:2 [b]Rev. 7:3; 9:4 [c]Matt. 16:16 [d]Rev. 9:14
3 [a]Rev. 6:6 [b]John 3:33; Rev. 7:3-8 [c]Ezek. 9:4, 6; Rev. 13:16; 14:1, 9; 20:4; 22:4
4 [a]Rev. 9:16 [b]Rev. 14:1, 3

⚿ **7:1-17** This contains the parenthetical portion between the sixth and seventh seals mentioning two distinct groups: (1) The 144,000, which are sealed, are from the twelve tribes of the children of Israel. This does not mean that the number of Israelites who will be saved will be limited to 144,000. Rather, it refers to 12,000 out of each tribe who are sealed from the wrath of Satan and the antichrist. These are called "the first fruits to God and to the Lamb" (Rev. 14:4). (2) A great multitude, without naming the exact number from all nations as distinct from the nation of Israel, will also be saved. These are described as "the ones who come out of the great tribulation, and they have washed their robes and made them white in the blood of the Lamb" (Rev. 7:14). These who will be saved will seal their testimony with their own blood. It has been made clear, however, and we learn from II Thess. 2:10-12, that those who have heard the Gospel during the church age, or the age of grace, and have rejected it wil be damned. These will not have a second chance to be saved during the tribulation. The only ones who will be saved during the tribulation will be those who have not heard the Gospel previous to that time.

A Multitude from the Tribulation

9 After these things I looked, and
behold, a great multitude, which no one
[ipf]could count, from [a]every nation[1484]
and *all* tribes[5443] and peoples[2992] and
tongues,[1100] standing [b]before the throne
and [c]before the Lamb,[721] [pfpp]clothed in
[d]white robes, and [e]palm branches *were*
in their hands;
10 and they cry out with a loud
voice, saying,
"[a]Salvation[4991] to our God[2316] [b]who
sits on the throne, and to the Lamb."
11 And all the angels were standing
[a]around the throne and *around* [b]the
elders[4245] and the [c]four living creatures;
and they [d]fell on their faces before the
throne and worshiped[4352] God,
12 saying,
"[a]Amen,[281] [b]blessing[2129] and
glory[1391] and wisdom[4678] and thanksgiving[2169] and honor[5092] and power[1411]
and might,[2419] *be* to our God[2316]
forever[165] and ever. [c]Amen."
13 And one of the elders [a]answered,
saying to me, "These who are
[pfpp]clothed in the [b]white robes, who are
they, and from where have they come?"
14 And I [I]said to him, "My lord,[2962]
you know." And he said to me, "These
are the ones who [ppt]come out of the
[a]great tribulation, and they have
[ao] [b]washed[4150] their robes and made
them [c]white in the [d]blood[129] of the
Lamb.[721]
15 "For this reason, they are
[a]before the throne of God; and they
[b]serve Him day and night in His
[I][c]temple;[3485] and [d]He who sits on the
throne shall spread His [e]tabernacle over
them.
16 "[a]They shall hunger no more,
neither thirst anymore; neither shall the
sun [I]beat down on them, nor any heat;
17 for the Lamb in[303] the center of
the throne shall be their [a]shepherd,[4165]
and shall guide them to springs[4077] of
the [I][b]water of life;[2198] and [c]God shall
wipe every tear from their eyes."

The Seventh Seal—the Trumpets

8 🔑 And when He broke the [a]sev-
enth seal, there [ao]was silence in
heaven[3772] for about[5613] half an hour.
2 And I saw [a]the seven angels[32] who
stand before God;[2316] and seven
[b]trumpets were given to them.
3 And [a]another angel came and
stood at the [b]altar,[2379] holding a [c]golden
censer;[3031] and much [d]incense was given
to him, that he might [ft] [I]add it to the
[d]prayers[4335] of all the [II]saints[40] upon
the [e]golden altar which was before the
throne.
4 And [a]the smoke of the incense,
[I]with the prayers of the [II]saints, went
up before God out of the angel's hand.
5 And the angel took the censer;
and he [a]filled it with the fire of the altar
and [b]threw it to the earth; and there
followed [c]peals of thunder and sounds
and flashes of lightning and an [d]earth-
quake.
6 [a]And the seven angels who had

9 [a]Rev. 5:9 [b]Rev. 7:15 [c]Rev. 22:3 [d]Rev. 6:11; 7:14 [e]Lev. 23:40
10 [a]Ps. 3:8; Rev. 12:10; 19:1 [b]Rev. 22:3
11 [a]Rev. 4:4 [b]Rev. 4:6 [c]Rev. 4:10
12 [a]Rev. 5:14 [b]Rev. 5:12
13 [a]Acts 3:12 [b]Rev. 7:9
14 [I]Lit., *have said* [a]Dan. 12:1; Matt. 24:21; Mark 13:19 [b]Zech. 3:3-5; Rev. 22:14 [c]Rev. 6:11; 7:9 [d]Heb. 9:14; 1 John 1:7
15 [I]Or, *sanctuary* [a]Rev. 7:9 [b]Rev. 4:8f.; 22:3 [c]Rev. 11:19; 21:22 [d]Rev. 4:9 [e]Lev. 26:11; Ezek. 37:27; John 1:14; Rev. 21:3
16 [I]Lit., *fall* [a]Ps. 121:5f.; Is. 49:10
17 [I]Lit., *waters* [a]Ps. 23:1f.; Matt. 2:6; John 10:11 [b]John 4:14; Rev. 21:6; 22:1 [c]Is. 25:8; Matt. 5:4; Rev. 21:4

1 [a]Rev. 5:1; 6:1, 3, 5, 7, 9, 12
2 [a]Rev. 1:4; 8:6-13; 9:1, 13; 11:15 [b]1 Cor. 15:52; 1 Thess. 4:16
3 [I]Lit., *give* [II]Or, *holy ones* [a]Rev. 7:2 [b]Amos 9:1; Rev. 6:9 [c]Heb. 9:4 [d]Ex. 30:1; Rev. 5:8 [e]Ex. 30:3; Num. 4:11; Rev. 8:5; 9:13
4 [I]Or, *for* [II]V. 3, note 2 [a]Ps. 141:2
5 [a]Lev. 16:12 [b]Ezek. 10:2 [c]Ex. 19:16; Rev. 4:5; 11:19; 16:18 [d]Rev. 6:12
6 [a]Rev. 8:2

🔑 **8:1—9:21** Here we have the opening of the seventh seal which is accompanied by silence in heaven. This is in preparation of the sounding of the seven trumpet judgments which are to follow. This silence is said to be for half an hour.

In v. 7 the sounding of the trumpets begins. Whereas the six seals show God's judgments as a result of man's unrestrained wrath, the first six trumpets indicate Satan's unrestrained activity. We must not misunderstand the term "unrestrained activity." It is only as unrestrained as God allows. We find angels standing in heaven and blowing their trumpets. The blowing of the trumpets announces the following events: (1) Hail, fire, and blood are cast upon the earth and a third of the earth is destroyed (one-third of the trees are burned and all grass is burned). (2) A falling meteor destroys one-third of the ships, and one-third of the sea becomes blood which kills the sea life. (3) A falling star poisons one-third of all water on the earth. (4) The third part of the sun, moon, and stars are affected so that they do not shine for a third part of the day and night. (5) A star falls from heaven to the earth. This star

(continued on next page)

the seven trumpets prepared themselves to sound them.

7 And the first sounded, and there came [a]hail and fire, mixed with blood,[129] and they were thrown to the earth; and [b]a third of the earth was burned up, and [b]a third of the [c]trees were burned up, and all the green [c]grass was burned up.

8 And the second angel[32] sounded, and *something* like a great [a]mountain burning with fire was thrown into the sea; and [b]a third of the [c]sea became blood;

9 and [a]a third of the creatures,[2938] which were in the sea [I]and had life,[5590] died; and a third of the [b]ships were destroyed.

10 And the third angel[32] sounded, and a great star [a]fell from heaven, burning like a torch, and it fell on a [b]third of the rivers and on the [c]springs[4077] of waters;

11 and the name of the star is called Wormwood; and a [a]third of the waters became [b]wormwood;[894] and many men died from the waters, because they were made bitter.

12 And the fourth angel[32] sounded, and a [a]third of the [b]sun and a third of the [b]moon and a [a]third of the [b]stars were smitten, so that a [a]third of them might be darkened and the day might not shine[5316] for a [a]third of it, and the night in the same way.

13 And I looked, and I heard [I]an eagle flying in [a]midheaven, saying with a loud voice, "[b]Woe, woe, woe, to [c]those who dwell on the earth,[1093] because of the remaining blasts of the trumpet of the [d]three angels who are about to sound!"

7 [a]Ex. 9:23ff.; Is. 28:2; Ezek. 38:22; Joel 2:30 [b]Zech. 13:8, 9; Rev. 8:7-12; 9:15, 18; 12:4 [c]Rev. 9:4
8 [a]Jer. 51:25 [b]Zech. 13:8, 9; Rev. 8:7-12; 9:15, 18; 12:4 [c]Ex. 7:17ff.; Rev. 11:6; 16:3
9 [I]Lit., *those which had* [a]Zech. 13:8, 9; Rev. 8:7-12; 9:15, 18; 12:4 [b]Is. 2:16
10 [a]Is. 14:12; Rev. 6:13; 9:1 [b]Zech. 13:8, 9; Rev. 8:7-12; 9:15, 18; 12:4 [c]Rev. 14:7; 16:4
11 [a]Zech. 13:8, 9; Rev. 8:7-12; 9:15, 18; 12:4 [b]Jer. 9:15; 23:15
12 [a]Zech. 13:8, 9; Rev. 8:7-12; 9:15, 18; 12:4 [b]Ex. 10:21ff.; Is. 13:10; Ezek. 32:7; Joel 2:10, 31; 3:15; Rev. 6:12f.
13 [I]Lit., *one eagle* [a]Rev. 14:6; 19:17 [b]Rev. 9:12; 11:14; 12:12 [c]Rev. 3:10 [d]Rev. 8:2

1 [I]Lit., *shaft of the abyss* [a]Rev. 8:2 [b]Rev. 8:10 [c]Rev. 1:18 [d]Luke 8:31; Rev. 9:2, 11
2 [I]V. 1, note 1 [a]Gen. 19:28; Ex. 19:18 [b]Joel 2:2, 10
3 [I]Lit., *into* [a]Ex. 10:12-15; Rev. 9:7 [b]2Chr. 10:11, 14; Ezek. 2:6; Rev. 9:5, 10
4 [a]Rev. 6:6 [b]Rev. 8:7 [c]Ezek. 9:4; Rev. 7:2, 3

The Fifth Trumpet—the Bottomless Pit

9 And the [a]fifth angel[32] sounded, and I saw a [b]star from heaven[3772] which had [pip]fallen to the earth;[1093] and the [c]key of the [Id]bottomless pit[5421] was given to him.

2 And he opened the [I]bottomless pit; and [a]smoke went up out of the pit, like the smoke of a great furnace; and [b]the sun and the air were darkened by the smoke of the pit.

3 And out of the smoke came forth [a]locusts [I]upon the earth; and power[1849] was given them, as the [b]scorpions of the earth have power.

4 And they were told that they should not [aosb] [a]hurt[91] the [b]grass of the earth, nor any green thing, nor any tree, but only the men[444] who do not have the [c]seal of God[2316] on their foreheads.

5 And [I]they were not permitted to kill [II]anyone, but to torment for [a]five months; and their [fp]torment was like the torment of a [b]scorpion when it [III]stings a man.[444]

6 And in those days [a]men will seek death[2288] and will not find it; and they will long to die[599] and death flees from them.

7 And the [Ia]appearance[3667] of the locusts was like horses prepared for battle; and on their heads, as it were, crowns like gold, and their faces were like the faces of men.[444]

8 And they had hair like the hair of women, and their [a]teeth were like *the teeth* of lions.

5 [I]Lit., *it was given to them* [II]Lit., *them* [III]Lit., *strikes* [a]Rev. 9:10 [b]2Chr. 10:11, 14; Ezek. 2:6; Rev. 9:3, 10
6 [a]Job 3:21; 7:15; Jer. 8:3; Rev. 6:16 **7** [I]Lit., *appearances* [a]Joel 2:4 **8** [a]Joel 1:6

(continued from previous page)
refers to a person because he is said to receive the key to the bottomless pit. When the bottomless pit is opened, a great swarm of locusts pour forth from the earth as from a great cloud of smoke. We are told that the locusts are like horses having the faces of men, the hair of women, the teeth of lions, breastplates of iron, and that the sound of their wings is like the sound of the chariots of many horses running to battle. They sting men with their tails and the sting lasts for five months. (6) When the sixth angel sounds his trumpet, four angels are loosed which have been bound in the river Euphrates. These four angels have been prepared for an hour, a day, a month, and a year to slay the third part of the men. Here we have 200 million warriors killing one-third of mankind.

9 And they had breastplates like
breastplates of iron; and the [a]sound of
their wings was like the sound of chariots, of many horses rushing to battle.
10 And they have tails like [a]scor-
pions, and stings; and in their [b]tails is
their power[1849] to [ainf]hurt men[444] for
[c]five months.
11 They have as king[935] over them,
the angel[32] of the [a]abyss; his name in
[b]Hebrew is [Ic]Abaddon,[3] and in the Greek
he has the name [II]Apollyon.[623]
12 [a]The first woe is past; behold,
two woes are still coming after these
things.

The Sixth Trumpet—Army from the East

13 And the sixth angel[32] sounded,
and I heard [I]a voice from the [II]four
[a]horns of the [b]golden altar[2379] which is
before God,[2316]
14 one saying to the sixth angel
who[ppt] had the trumpet, "Release the
[a]four angels who are [pfpp]bound at the
[b]great river Euphrates."
15 And the four angels, who had
been [pfpp]prepared for the hour and day
and month and year, were [a]released,
so that they might kill[615] a [b]third of
[I]mankind.
16 And the number of the armies
of the horsemen was [a]two hundred million; [b]I heard the number of them.
17 And [I]this is how I saw [a]in the
vision[3706] the horses and those who
[ppt]sat on them: *the riders* had breastplates *the color* of fire and of hyacinth[5191]
and of [IIb]brimstone;[2306] and the heads
of the horses are like the heads of lions;
and [c]out of their mouths proceed fire
and smoke and [IIb]brimstone.
18 A [a]third of [I]mankind was killed[615]
by these three plagues, by the [b]fire and
the smoke and the [II]brimstone, which
[ppt]proceeded out of their mouths.
19 For the power[1849] of the horses
is in their mouths and in their tails;
for their tails are like serpents and
have heads; and with them they do
harm.[91]
20 And the rest of [I]mankind,[444] who
were not killed by these plagues,
[a]did not repent[3340] of [b]the works[2041] of
their hands, so as not to [aosb] [c]worship[4352]
demons,[1140] and [d]the idols[1497] of gold
and of silver and of brass and of stone
and of wood, which can neither [pinf]see
nor [pinf]hear nor [pinf]walk;
21 and they [a]did not repent of their
murders nor of their [b]sorceries[5331] nor
of their [c]immorality[4202] nor of their
thefts.

The Angel and the Little Book

10 And I saw another [a]strong
angel[32] [ppt] [b]coming down out of
heaven,[3772] clothed with a cloud; and
the [c]rainbow was upon his head, and
[d]his face was like the sun, and his
[e]feet like pillars of fire;
2 and he [ppt]had in his hand a
[a]little book which was open. And he
placed [b]his right[1188] foot on the sea and
his left on the land;
3 and he cried out with a loud voice,
[a]as when a lion roars; and when he had
cried out, the [b]seven peals of thunder
[I]uttered their voices.
4 And when the seven peals of thunder had spoken, [a]I was about to
write;[1125] and I [b]heard a voice from
heaven saying, [aim]"[c]Seal up the things
which the seven peals of thunder have
spoken, and do not write them."
5 And the angel whom I saw

9 [a]Jer. 47:3; Joel 2:5
10 [a]2Chr. 10:11, 14; Ezek. 2:6; Rev. 9:3, 5 [b]Rev. 9:19 [c]Rev. 9:5
11 [I]I.e., destruction [II]I.e., destroyer [a]Luke 8:31; Rev. 9:1, 2 [b]John 5:2; Rev. 16:16 [c]Job 26:6; 28:22; 31:12; Ps. 88:11 mg.; Prov. 15:11
12 [a]Rev. 8:13; 11:14
13 [I]Lit., *one voice* [II]Some ancient mss. do not contain *four* [a]Ex. 30:2f., 10 [b]Rev. 8:3
14 [a]Rev. 7:1 [b]Gen. 15:18; Deut. 1:7; Josh. 1:4; Rev. 16:12
15 [I]Lit., *men* [a]Rev. 20:7 [b]Rev. 8:7; 9:18
16 [a]Rev. 5:11 [b]Rev. 7:4
17 [I]Lit., *thus I saw* [II]Or, *sulphur* [a]Dan. 8:2; 9:21 [b]Rev. 9:18; 14:10; 19:20; 20:10; 21:8 [c]Rev. 11:5
18 [I]Lit., *men* [II]Or, *sulphur* [a]Rev. 8:7; 9:15 [b]Rev. 9:17
20 [I]Lit., *men* [a]Rev. 2:21 [b]Deut. 4:28; Jer. 1:16; Mic. 5:13; Acts 7:41 [c]1Cor. 10:20 [d]Ps. 115:4-7; 135:15-17; Dan. 5:23
21 [a]Rev. 9:20 [b]Is. 47:9, 12; Rev. 18:23 [c]Rev. 17:2, 4, 5

1 [a]Rev. 5:2 [b]Rev. 18:1; 20:1 [c]Rev. 4:3 [d]Matt. 17:2; Rev. 1:16 [e]Rev. 1:15
2 [a]Rev. 5:1; 10:8-10 [b]Rev. 10:5, 8
3 [I]Or, *spoke* [a]Is. 31:4; Hos. 11:10 [b]Ps. 29:3-9; Rev. 4:5
4 [a]Rev. 1:11, 19 [b]Rev. 10:8 [c]Dan. 8:26; 12:4, 9; Rev. 22:10

10:1-11 This is the parenthetical portion between the sixth and the seventh trumpets. Here we have the only thing that remains sealed and is not revealed. When John heard the voice of the seven thunders, he started to write, but he heard a voice from heaven saying to him, "Seal up the things which the seven peals of thunder have spoken, and do not write them" (Rev. 10:4). In the last part of this chapter, we read of a little book which was as sweet as honey in John's mouth, but which became bitter in his stomach.

standing on the sea and on the land [a]lifted up[142] his right hand to heaven,

6 [a]and swore by [b]Him who [ppt]lives[2198] forever[165] and ever, [c]WHO CREATED[2936] HEAVEN AND THE THINGS IN IT, AND THE EARTH AND THE THINGS IN IT, AND THE SEA AND THE THINGS IN IT, that [d]there shall be delay no longer,

7 but in the days of the voice of the [a]seventh angel, when he is about[3195] to [pinf]sound, then [b]the mystery of God is [aop]finished,[5055] as He [ao] [I]preached[2097] to His servants[1401] the prophets.[4396]

8 And [a]the voice which I heard from heaven, *I heard* again [ppt]speaking with me, and [ppt]saying, "Go, take [b]the [I]book which is open in the hand of the angel who [b]stands on the sea and on the land."

9 And I went to the angel, telling him to [ainf]give me the little book. And he *said to me, [aim]"[a]Take it, and [aim]eat it; and it will make your stomach bitter, but in your mouth it will be sweet as honey."

10 And I took the little book out of the angel's hand and ate it, and it was in my mouth sweet as honey; and when I had [ao]eaten it, my stomach was made bitter.

11 And [a]they *said to me, "You must [ainf] [b]prophesy[4395] again concerning [c]many peoples[2992] and nations[1484] and tongues[1100] and [d]kings."[935]

The Two Witnesses

11 And there was given me a [Ia]measuring rod like a staff; [II]and [b]someone said, "Rise[1453] and measure the [III]temple[3485] of God, and the altar,[2379] and those who [ppt]worship[4352] in it.

2 "And [I]leave out the [a]court which is outside[1855] the [II]temple, and do not measure it, for [b]it has been given to the nations;[1484] and they will [c]tread under foot[3961] [d]the holy[40] city for [e]forty-two months.

3 "And I will grant *authority* to my two [a]witnesses,[3144] and they will prophesy for [b]twelve hundred and sixty days, clothed in [c]sackcloth."[4526]

4 These are the [a]two olive trees and the two lampstands that stand before the Lord[2316] of the earth.

5 And if anyone desires to [ainf]harm[91] them, [a]fire proceeds out of their mouth and devours their enemies; and if anyone would desire to [ainf]harm them, [b]in this manner he must be killed.

6 These have the power[1849] to [ainf] [a]shut up the sky,[3772] in order that rain may not fall during [b]the days of their prophesying;[4394] and they have power[1849] over the waters to [pinf] [c]turn them into blood,[129] and [d]to [ainf]smite the earth with every plague, as often as they desire.

7 And when they have finished their testimony,[3141] [a]the beast[2342] that [ppt]comes up out of the [b]abyss will [c]make war with them, and overcome them and kill[615] them.

8 And their dead [I]bodies *will lie* in the street of the [a]great city which [II]mystically[4153] is called [b]Sodom and [c]Egypt, where also their Lord[2962] was crucified.[4717]

9 And those from [a]the peoples[2992] and tribes[5443] and tongues[1100] and nations[1484] *will* look at their dead [I]bodies for three and a half days, and

5 [a]Deut. 32:40; Dan. 12:7
6 [a]Gen. 14:22; Ex. 6:8; Num. 14:30; Ezek. 20:5 [b]Rev. 4:9 [c]Ex. 20:11; Rev. 4:11 [d]Rev. 6:11; 12:12; 16:17; 21:6
7 [I]Lit., *preached the gospel* [a]Rev. 11:15 [b]Amos 3:7; Rom. 16:25
8 [I]Or, *scroll* [a]Rev. 10:4 [b]Rev. 10:2
9 [a]Jer. 15:16; Ezek. 2:8; 3:1-3
11 [a]Rev. 11:1 [b]Ezek. 37:4, 9 [c]Rev. 5:9 [d]Rev. 17:10, 12

1 [I]Lit., *reed* [II]Lit., *saying* [III]Or, *sanctuary* [a]Ezek. 40:3-42:20; Zech. 2:1; Rev. 21:15f. [b]Rev. 10:11
2 [I]Lit., *throw out* [II]Or, *sanctuary* [a]Ezek. 40:17, 20 [b]Luke 21:24 [c]Is. 52:1; Matt. 4:5; 27:53; Rev. 21:2, 10; 22:19 [d]Dan. 7:25; 12:7; Rev. 12:6; 13:5
3 [a]Rev. 1:5; 2:13 [b]Dan. 7:25; 12:7; Rev. 12:6; 13:5 [c]Gen. 37:34; 2Sam. 3:31; 1Kin. 21:27; 2Kin. 19:1f.; Neh. 9:1; Esth. 4:1; Ps. 69:11; Joel 1:13; Jon. 3:5f., 8
4 [a]Ps. 52:8; Jer. 11:16; Zech. 4:3, 11, 14
5 [a]2Kin. 1:10-12; Jer. 5:14; Rev. 9:17f. [b]Num. 16:29, 35
6 [a]1Kin. 17:1; Luke 4:25 [b]Rev. 11:3 [c]Ex. 7:17ff.; Rev. 8:8 [d]1Sam. 4:8

7 [a]Rev. 13:1ff.; 17:8 [b]Rev. 9:1 [c]Dan. 7:21; Rev. 13:7
8 [I]Some ancient mss. read *body* [II]Lit., *spiritually* [a]Rev. 14:8; 16:19; 17:18; 18:2, 10, 16, 18, 19, 21 [b]Is. 1:9, 10; 3:9; Jer. 23:14; Ezek. 16:46, 49 [c]Ezek. 23:3, 8, 19, 27
9 [I]Lit., *body* [a]Rev. 5:9: 10:11

11:1-19 Here we have the activity of two witnesses, Moses and Elijah (Mt. 17:3) or Enoch (Gen. 5:24; Heb. 11:5) and Elijah (II Kgs. 2:11). When the seventh trumpet sounded, there were great voices in heaven saying, "The kingdom of the world has become the kingdom of our Lord, and of His Christ, and He will reign forever and ever" (v. 15). This kingdom, however, is not ushered in gradually, but *en tachei* (Rev. 1:1), "swiftly, suddenly," when the Lord comes back with His saints (I Thess. 3:13). Here we are told that the Lord Jesus will rule and reign upon the earth. We are also clearly taught that this millennial age cannot come by man's efforts.

[IIb]will not permit their dead bodies to be laid in a tomb.

10 And [a]those who [ppt]dwell on the earth *will* rejoice over them and make merry; and they will [b]send gifts[1435] to one another, because these two prophets[4396] tormented [c]those who dwell on the earth.

11 And after the three and a half days [a]the breath[4151] of life[2222] from God came into them, and they stood on their feet; and great fear[5401] fell upon those who were [ppt]beholding them.

12 And they heard a loud voice from heaven saying to them, "[a]Come up here." And they [b]went up into heaven in the cloud, and their enemies beheld them.

13 And in that hour there [ao]was a great [a]earthquake, and a tenth of the city fell; and [I]seven thousand people were killed in the earthquake, and the rest3062 were terrified1719 and [b]gave glory[1391] to the [c]God[2316] of heaven.

14 The second [a]woe is past; behold, the third woe is coming quickly.

The Seventh Trumpet—Christ's Reign Foreseen

15 And the [a]seventh angel sounded; and there [ao]arose [b]loud voices in heaven, saying,

"[c]The kingdom[932] of the world[2889] has become *the kingdom* of our Lord,[2962] and of [d]His [I]Christ;[5547] and [e]He will reign[936] forever[165] and ever."

16 And the twenty-four elders,[4245] who [ppt] [a]sit on their thrones before God, [b]fell on their faces and worshiped4352 God,

17 saying,

"**We** give[2168] Thee thanks, [a]O Lord[2962] God,[2316] the Almighty,3841 who art and who wast,3801 because Thou hast [pf]taken Thy great power[1411] and [I]hast begun to [ao] [b]reign.[936]

18 "And [a]the nations were enraged, and [b]Thy wrath[3709] [aop]came, and [c]the time[2540] *came* for the dead[3498] to be [aifp]judged,[2919] and *the time* to [ainf]give their reward to Thy [d]bond-servants[1401] the prophets[4396] and to the [I]saints[40] and to those who [ppt]fear[5399] Thy name,[3686] [e]the small and the great, and to [ainf]destroy1311 those who [ppt]destroy the earth."[1093]

19 And [a]the [I]temple[3485] of God which is in heaven[3772] was opened; and [b]the ark of His covenant[1242] appeared in His [I]temple, and there [ao]were flashes of [c]lightning and sounds and peals of thunder and an earthquake and a [d]great [II]hailstorm.

The Woman, Israel

12 ⚿ And a great [a]sign [aop]appeared [b]in heaven:[3772] [c]a woman [d]clothed with the sun, and the moon under her feet, and on her head a crown of twelve stars;

2 and she was with child; and she *[a]cried out, being in labor[5605] and in pain to give birth.[5088]

The Red Dragon, Satan

3 And [a]another sign appeared in heaven: and behold, a great red [b]dragon having [c]seven heads and [d]ten horns, and on his heads *were* [e]seven diadems.[1238]

4 And his tail *swept away a [a]third of the stars of heaven, and [b]threw them to the earth. And the

9 [II]Lit., *do not permit* [b]1Kin. 13:22; Ps. 79:2f.
10 [a]Rev. 3:10 [b]Neh. 8:10, 12; Esth. 9:19, 22
11 [a]Ezek. 37:5, 9, 10, 14
12 [a]Rev. 4:1 [b]2Kin. 2:11; Acts 1:9
13 [I]Lit., *names of men, seven thousand* [a]Rev. 6:12; 8:5; 11:19; 16:18 [b]John 9:24; Rev. 14:7; 16:9; 19:7 [c]Rev. 16:11
14 [a]Rev. 8:13; 9:12
15 [I]I.e., Messiah [a]Rev. 8:2; 10:7 [b]Rev. 16:17; 19:1 [c]Rev. 12:10 [d]Ps. 2:2; Acts 4:26 [e]Ex. 15:18; Dan. 2:44; 7:14, 27; Luke 1:33
16 [a]Matt. 19:28; Rev. 4:4 [b]Rev. 4:10
17 [I]Lit., *didst reign* [a]Rev. 1:8 [b]Rev. 19:6
18 [I]Or, *holy ones* [a]Ps. 2:1 [b]Ps. 2:5; 110:5 [c]Dan. 7:10; Rev. 20:12 [d]Rev. 10:7; 16:6 [e]Ps. 115:13; Rev. 13:16; 19:5
19 [I]Or, *sanctuary* [II]Lit., *hail* [a]Rev. 4:1; 15:5 [b]Heb. 9:4 [c]Rev. 4:5; 8:5; 16:18 [d]Rev. 16:21

1 [a]Matt. 24:30; Rev. 12:3 [b]Rev. 11:19 [c]Gal. 4:26 [d]Ps. 104:2; Song 6:10
2 [a]Is. 26:17; 66:6-9; Mic. 4:9f.
3 [a]Rev. 12:1; 15:1 [b]Is. 27:1; Rev. 12:4, 7, 9, 13, 16f.; 13:2, 4, 11; 16:13; 20:2 [c]Rev. 13:1; 17:3, 7, 9ff. [d]Dan. 7:7, 20, 24; Rev. 13:1; 17:12, 16 [e]Rev. 13:1; 19:12
4 [a]Rev. 8:7, 12 [b]Dan. 8:10

⚿ **12:1-17** Here we have five personalities. The first one is a woman clothed with the sun. Some believe that this is the Church and others believe it is Israel from whom Christ came forth (vv. 1,2). The second personality is a great red dragon (vv. 3,4). He is identified as the devil or Satan, but we are not told by what group or person he is represented. The third personality is the manchild (v. 5-6) who is the Lord Jesus Christ. He will rule the nations with a rod of iron. When He came the first time, He died for mankind; He did not rule it, but He will. The fourth personality is Michael, the Archangel (vv. 7-9). The fifth personality (v. 17) is the Jewish remnant.

[c]dragon stood before the woman who
was about to give birth, so that when
she gave birth [d]he might devour her
child.[5043]

The Male Child, Christ

🔑 5 And [a]she gave birth to a son, a
male *child*, who is to [pinf] [Ib]rule[4165] all the
[II]nations[1484] with a rod of iron; and her
child was [c]caught up[726] to God and to
His throne.

6 And the woman fled into the wilderness where she *had a place [pfpp]pre-
pared by God, so that there [I]she might
be [psa]nourished for [a]one thousand two
hundred and sixty days.

The Angel, Michael

7 And there [ao]was war in heaven,
[a]Michael and his angels[32] [ainf]waging war
with the [b]dragon. And the dragon and
[c]his angels waged war,

8 and they were not strong[2480]
enough, and there was no longer a place
found for them in heaven.

9 And the great [a]dragon was thrown
down, the [b]serpent of old who is called
the devil[1228] and [c]Satan,[4567] who [ppt][d]de-
ceives the whole [I]world; he was [e]thrown
down to the earth,[1093] and his angels[32]
were thrown down with him.

10 And I heard [a]a loud voice in
heaven, saying,
"Now the [b]salvation,[4991] and the
power,[1411] and the [a]kingdom[932] of our
God[2316] and the authority[1849] of His
Christ[5547] have [ao]come, for the
[c]accuser[2725] of our brethren[80] has been
thrown down, who [ppt]accuses[2723] them
before our God day and night.

11 "And they [a]overcame him because of [b]the blood[129] of the Lamb[721]
and because of [c]the word[3056] of their
testimony,[3141] and they [d]did not love[25]
their life[5590] even to death.[2288]

12 "For this reason, [a]rejoice,[2165] O
heavens[3772] and [b]you who [ppt] [I]dwell in
them. [c]Woe to the earth and the sea,
because [d]the devil has come down to
you, having great wrath,[2372] knowing
that he has *only* [e]a short time."[2540]

13 And when the [a]dragon saw that
he was thrown down to the earth, he
persecuted [b]the woman who gave birth
to the male *child*.

14 And the [a]two wings of the great
eagle were given to the woman, in order
that she might fly [b]into the wilderness
to her place, where she *was nourished
for [c]a time and times and half a time,
from the [I]presence of the serpent.

15 And the [a]serpent [I]poured water
like a river out of his mouth after the
woman, so that he might cause her to
be swept away with the flood.

16 And the earth[1093] helped the
woman, and the earth opened its mouth
and drank up the river which the dragon
[I]poured out of his mouth.

17 And the dragon was enraged[3710]
with the woman, and went off to
[ainf] [a]make war with the rest[3062] of her
[b]offspring,[4690] who [ppt] [c]keep[5083] the
commandments[1785] of God and [ppt] [d]hold
to the testimony[3141] of Jesus.

The Beast from the Sea

13 🔑 And [I]he stood on the sand
of the [II]seashore.

4 [c]Is. 27:1; Rev. 12:3, 7, 9, 13, 16f.; 13:2, 4, 11; 16:13; 20:2 [d]Matt. 2:16
5 [I]Or, *shepherd* [II]Or, *Gentiles* [a]Is. 66:7 [b]Ps. 2:9; Rev. 2:27 [c]2Cor. 12:2ff.
6 [I]Lit., *they may nourish her for* [a]Rev. 11:3; 13:5
7 [a]Dan. 10:13, 21; 12:1; Jude 9 [b]Rev. 12:3 [c]Matt. 25:41
9 [I]Lit., *inhabited earth* [a]Rev. 12:3 [b]Gen. 3:1; 2Cor. 11:3; Rev. 12:15; 20:2 [c]Matt. 4:10; 25:41 [d]Rev. 13:14; 20:3, 8, 10 [e]Luke 10:18; John 12:31
10 [a]Rev. 11:15 [b]Rev. 7:10 [c]Job 1:11; 2:5; Zech. 3:1; Luke 22:31; 1Pet. 5:8
11 [a]John 16:33; 1John 2:13; Rev. 15:2 [b]Rev. 7:14 [c]Rev. 6:9 [d]Luke 14:26; Rev. 2:10
12 [I]Or, *tabernacle* [a]Ps. 96:11; Is. 44:23; Rev. 18:20 [b]Rev. 13:6 [c]Rev. 8:13 [d]Rev. 12:9 [e]Rev. 10:6
13 [a]Rev. 12:3 [b]Rev. 12:5
14 [I]Lit., *face* [a]Ex. 19:4; Deut. 32:11; Is. 40:31 [b]Rev. 12:6 [c]Dan. 7:25; 12:7
15 [I]Lit., *threw* [a]Gen. 3:1; 2Cor. 11:3; Rev. 12:9; 20:2
16 [I]Lit., *threw*
17 [a]Rev. 11:7; 13:7 [b]Gen. 3:15 [c]1John 2:3; Rev. 14:12 [d]Rev. 1:2; 6:9; 14:12; 19:10

1 [I]Some mss. read *I stood* [II]Lit., *sea*

🔑 **12:5** See note on I Thess. 4:17.

🔑 **13:1-18** The sixth personality is the antichrist (vv. 1-10). In Rev. 13 we have two beasts mentioned: the first, the antichrist, is out of the sea (vv. 1-10), and the second beast is out of the earth. The first beast is a political ruler while the second is a religious leader. The antichrist was already revealed in Rev. 6:2 as the rider of the white horse who brought false peace. We are reminded of the words of Christ in Jn. 5:43, "I have come in My Father's name, and you do not receive Me; if another shall come in his own name, you will receive him." Reference is made by Christ to the future antichrist who

(continued on next page)

And I saw a [a]beast[2342] [ppt]coming up out of the sea, having [b]ten horns and [b]seven heads, and on his horns *were* [c]ten diadems,[1238] and on his heads *were* [d]blasphemous[988] names.

2 And the beast which I saw was [a]like a leopard, and his feet were like *those* of [b]a bear, and his mouth like the mouth of [c]a lion. And the [d]dragon gave him his power[1411] and his [e]throne and great authority.[1849]

3 And *I saw* one of his heads as if it had been [pfpp I]slain, and his [a]fatal wound was healed. And the whole earth[1093] [b]was amazed *and followed* after the beast;

4 and they worshiped[4352] the [a]dragon, because he [pfp b]gave his authority[1849] to the beast; and they worshiped the beast, saying, "[c]Who is like the beast, and who is able to [ainf]wage war with him?"

5 And there was given to him a mouth [a]speaking[2980] [I]arrogant words and blasphemies;[988] and authority to [ainf II]act for [b]forty-two months was given to him.

6 And he opened his mouth in blasphemies[988] against God, to [ainf]blaspheme[987] His name and His tabernacle,[4633] *that is,* [a]those who [ppt I]dwell in heaven.[3772]

7 And it was given to him to [ainf a]make war with the [I]saints[40] and to [ainf]overcome them; and authority[1849] over [b]every tribe[5443] and people and tongue[1100] and nation[1484] was given to him.

8 And all who [ppt a]dwell on the earth will worship him, *everyone* [b]whose name[3686] has not been [pfip I]written [c]from the foundation of the world[2889] in the [d]book[976] of life[2222] of [e]the Lamb[721] who has been slain.

9 [a]If anyone has an ear, let him [aim]hear.

10 [a]If anyone [I]*is destined* for captivity, to captivity he [pin]goes; [b]if anyone kills with the sword, with the sword he must be [aifp]killed. Here is [c]the [II]perseverance[5281] and the faith[4102] of the [III]saints.

The Beast from the Earth

11 And [a]I saw another beast coming up out of the earth; and he [I]had [b]two horns like a lamb, and he [ipf II]spoke as a [c]dragon.

12 And he [a]exercises all the authority of the first beast [I b]in his presence. And he makes [c]the earth and those who [ppt]dwell in it to [aosb d]worship the first beast, whose [e]fatal wound was healed.

13 And he [a]performs great signs, so that he even [psa]makes [b]fire [pinf]come down out of heaven to the earth in the presence of men.

14 And he [a]deceives [b]those who [ppt]dwell on the earth because of [c]the

1 [a]Dan. 7:3; Rev. 11:7; 13:14, 15; 15:2; 16:13; 17:8 [b]Rev. 12:3 [c]Rev. 12:3; 17:12 [d]Dan. 7:8; 11:36; Rev. 17:3
2 [a]Dan. 7:6; Hos. 13:7f. [b]Dan. 7:5 [c]Dan. 7:4 [d]Rev. 12:3; 13:4, 12 [e]Rev. 2:13; 16:10
3 [I]Lit., *smitten to death* [a]Rev. 13:12, 14 [b]Rev. 17:8
4 [a]Rev. 12:3; 13:2, 12 [b]Ex. 15:11; Is. 46:5; Rev. 18:18
5 [I]Lit., *great things* [II]Lit., *do* [a]Dan. 7:8, 11, 20, 25; 11:36; 2Thess. 2:3f. [b]Rev. 11:2
6 [I]Or, *tabernacle* [a]Rev. 7:15; 12:12
7 [I]Or, *holy ones* [a]Dan. 7:21; Rev. 11:7 [b]Rev. 5:9
8 [I]Or, *written in the book . . . slain from the foundation of the world* [a]Rev. 3:10; 13:12, 14 [b]Rev. 3:5 [c]Matt. 25:34; Rev. 17:8 [d]Ps. 69:28 [e]Rev. 5:6
9 [a]Rev. 2:7
10 [I]Or, *leads into captivity* [II]Or, *steadfastness* [III]Or, *holy ones* [a]Is. 33:1; Jer. 15:2; 43:11 [b]Gen. 9:6; Matt. 26:52; Rev. 11:18 [c]Heb. 6:12; Rev. 14:12
11 [I]Lit., *was having* [II]Lit., *was speaking* [a]Rev. 13:1; 16:13 [b]Dan. 8:3 [c]Rev. 13:4
12 [I]Or, *by his authority* [a]Rev. 13:4 [b]Rev. 13:14; 19:20 [c]Rev. 13:8 [d]Rev. 13:15; 14:9, 11; 16:2; 19:20; 20:4 [e]Rev. 13:3
13 [a]Matt. 24:24; Rev. 16:14; 19:20 [b]1Kin. 18:38; Luke 9:54; Rev. 11:5; 20:9
14 [a]Rev. 12:9 [b]Rev. 13:8 [c]2 Thess. 2:9f.

(continued from previous page)
would be welcomed as the producer of great peace among men. In Mt. 24:15 the Lord Jesus calls this antichrist, "THE ABOMINATION OF DESOLATION."

Daniel describes this antichrist as "another horn, a little one" which arises among the ten horns, which are kings (dictators) who will be ruling in the area of the old Roman Empire in the last days. Daniel describes him as having the eyes of a man and a mouth which speaks great things (Dan. 7:8). He calls him a king of fierce countenance who understands dark sentences (Dan. 8:23-25). See also Dan. 9:26,27 which agrees fully with what the Lord said in Mt. 24:25 concerning this antichrist. See also Dan. 11:36-45 and compare all these references in Daniel with Rev. 13:1-10. In II Thess. 2:3-12 Paul identifies this man as "the man of lawlessness . . . the son of destruction," and the "lawless" one. In Rev. 19:19,20 we have the prediction of the final doom of the antichrist. The seventh personality is the beast out of the earth (Rev. 13:11-18). He has the horns of a lamb, but speaks as a dragon. He is worshipped by all. He causes all to receive a mark on their right hand or on their forehead. According to Rev. 14:9-11, all who receive this mark of the beast will be cast into hell to burn forever and ever. See note on II Thess. 2:3-8.

signs which it was given him to [ainf]perform [I][d]in the presence of the beast, telling those who dwell on the earth to make an image[1504] to the beast who *had the [e]wound of the sword and has come to life.[2198]

15 And there was [aop]given to him to [ainf]give breath[4151] to the image of the beast, that the image of the beast might even [aosb] [I]speak and cause [a]as many as do not [aosb] [b]worship the image of the beast to be [asbp]killed.

16 And he causes all, [a]the small and the great, and the rich and the poor, and the free men and the slaves,[1401] [I]to be [aosb]given a [b]mark[5480] on their right hand, or on their forehead,

17 and *he provides* that no one should be [psa]able to [ainf]buy or to [ainf]sell, except the one who has the [a]mark, *either* [b]the name of the beast or [c]the number of his name.

18 [a]Here is wisdom.[4678] Let him who has understanding [aim]calculate the number of the beast, for the number is that [b]of a man; and his number is [I]six hundred and sixty-six.

The Lamb and the 144,000 on Mount Zion

14 ⊶ And I looked, and behold, [a]the Lamb[721] *was* standing on [b]Mount Zion, and with Him [c]one hundred and forty-four thousand, having [d]His name and the [d]name[3686] of His Father[3962] [pfpp]written [e]on their foreheads.

2 And I heard a voice from heaven,[3772] like [a]the sound of many waters and like the [b]sound of loud thunder, and the voice which I heard *was* like *the sound* of [c]harpists playing on their harps.

3 And they [pin] [I]*sang [a]a new[2537] song[5603] before the throne and before the [b]four living creatures and the [c]elders;[4245] and [d]no one [ipf]could [ainf]learn the song except the [e]one hundred and forty-four thousand who had been [pfpp] [a]purchased[59] from the earth.[1093]

4 [a]These are the ones who have not been defiled[3435] with women, for they [I]have kept themselves chaste.[3933] These *are* the ones who [ppt][b]follow[190] the Lamb[721] wherever He [psa]goes. These have been [c]purchased[59] from among men[444] [d]as first fruits[536] to God and to the Lamb.[721]

5 And [a]no lie[1388] was found in their mouth; they are [b]blameless.[299]

Vision of the Angel with the Gospel

6 And I saw another angel[32] [ppt]flying in [a]midheaven, having [b]an eternal[166] gospel[2098] to [ainf]preach[2097] to [c]those who [ppt] [I]live on the earth, and to [d]every nation[1484] and tribe[5443] and tongue[1100] and people;[2992]

7 and he said with a loud voice, [aim]"[a]Fear[5399] God, and [b]give Him glory,[1391] because the hour[5610] of His judgment[2920] has [ao]come; and [aim]worship[4352] Him who [c]made the heaven and the earth and sea and [d]springs[4077] of waters."

8 And another angel, a second one, followed,[190] saying, [ao]"[a]Fallen, fallen is [b]Babylon the great, she who has [c]made all the nations drink of the [d]wine[3631] of the [I]passion[2372] of her immorality."[4202]

14 [I]Or, *by the authority of* [d]Rev. 13:12; 19:20 [e]Rev. 13:3
15 [I]Some ancient mss. read *speak, and he will cause* [a]Dan. 3:3ff. [b]Rev. 13:12; 14:9, 11; 16:2; 19:20; 20:4
16 [I]Lit., *that they give to them a mark* [a]Rev. 11:18; 19:5, 18 [b]Gal. 6:17; Rev. 7:3; 14:9; 20:4
17 [a]Gal. 6:17; Rev. 7:3; 14:9; 20:4 [b]Rev. 14:11 [c]Rev. 15:2
18 [I]Some mss. read 616 [a]Rev. 17:9 [b]Rev. 21:17

1 [a]Rev. 5:6 [b]Ps. 2:6; Heb. 12:22 [c]Rev. 7:4; 14:3 [d]Rev. 3:12 [e]Ezek. 9:4; Rev. 7:3
2 [a]Rev. 1:15 [b]Rev. 6:1 [c]Rev. 5:8
3 [I]Some ancient mss. read *sing, as it were, a new song* [a]Rev. 5:9 [b]Rev. 4:6 [c]Rev. 4:4 [d]Rev. 2:17 [e]Rev. 7:4; 14:1
4 [I]Lit., *are chaste men* [a]Matt. 19:12; 2Cor. 11:2; Eph. 5:27; Rev. 3:4 [b]Rev. 3:4; 7:17; 17:14 [c]Rev. 5:9 [d]Heb. 12:23; James 1:18
5 [a]Ps. 32:2; Zeph. 3:13; Mal. 2:6; John 1:47; 1Pet. 2:22 [b]Heb. 9:14; 1Pet. 1:19; Jude 24
6 [I]Lit., *sit* [a]Rev. 8:13 [b]1Pet. 1:25; Rev. 10:7 [c]Rev. 3:10 [d]Rev. 5:9
7 [a]Rev. 15:4 [b]Rev. 11:13 [c]Rev. 4:11 [d]Rev. 8:10
8 [I]Or, *wrath* [a]Is. 21:9; Jer. 51:8; Rev. 18:2 [b]Dan. 4:30; Rev. 16:19; 17:5; 18:10 [c]Jer. 51:7 [d]Rev. 17:2, 4; 18:3

⊶ **14:1-20** In this chapter, we have the ultimate triumph of the Lord Jesus Christ and a preview of some of the things that are to take place.

The following subjects are covered: the Lamb and the 144,000 on Mount Zion; the angel with the everlasting Gospel; the fall of Babylon; the judgment on the worshipers of the beast; the blessing upon those who die in the Lord; and preview of the last battle of Armageddon.

Although man has desperately tried to abolish war, the Word of God clearly teaches that he will be unsuccessful. The Lord in Mt. 24:6 said that there would be wars and rumors of wars until the Second Coming of Christ. The battle of Armageddon is predicted and described in many O.T. Scriptures (Isa. 34:1-8; 63:1-6; Joel 2:1-11; 3:9-13; Zeph. 1:14-18; 3:8; Zech. 12:9-11; 14:1-3).

Doom for Worshipers of the Beast

9 And another angel, a third one,
followed them, saying with a loud voice,
"If anyone [pin][a]worships the beast and
his [b]image, and receives a [c]mark[5480] on
his forehead or upon his hand,
10 he also will drink of the [a]wine
of the wrath of God, which is [pfpp]mixed
[I]in full strength [b]in the cup of His
anger;[3709] and he will be tormented with
[c]fire and brimstone[2303] in the presence
of the [d]holy[40] angels and in the presence
of the Lamb.
11 "And the [a]smoke of their torment
goes up forever[165] and ever; and
[b]they have no rest[372] day and night,
those who [c]worship the beast and his
[c]image, and whoever receives the
[d]mark[5480] of his name."[3686]
12 Here is [a]the [I]perseverance[5281] of
the [II]saints[40] who [ppt][b]keep[5083] the
commandments[1785] of God and [III][c]their
faith[4102] in Jesus.
13 And I heard a voice from heaven,
saying, [aim]"Write,[1125] '[a]Blessed[3107] are
the dead[3498] who [ppt][b]die[599] in the
Lord[2962] from now on!'" "Yes," [c]says
the Spirit,[4151] "that they may [fm][d]rest
from their labors, for their [e]deeds[2041]
follow[190] with them."

The Reapers

14 And I looked, and behold, a
[a]white cloud, and sitting on the cloud
was one [b]like [I]a son[5207] of man,[444] having
a golden [c]crown on His head, and a sharp
sickle in His hand.
15 And another angel[32] [a]came out
of the [I]temple,[3485] crying out with a loud
voice to Him who sat on the cloud,
"[II][b]Put in your sickle and reap, because the hour[5610] to [ainf]reap has [ao]come,
because the [c]harvest of the earth
[III]is [ao]ripe."
16 And He who [ppt]sat on the cloud
[I]swung[906] His sickle over the earth; and
the earth[1093] was reaped.
17 And another angel [a]came out of
the [I]temple which is in heaven, [II]and
he also had a sharp sickle.
18 And another angel, [a]the one who
[ppt]has power[1849] over fire, came out from
[b]the altar;[2379] and he called with a loud
voice to him who had the sharp sickle,
saying, "[I][c]Put in your sharp sickle, and
gather the clusters [II]from the vine of
the earth, [d]because her grapes are
[ao]ripe."
19 And the angel [I]swung[906] his sickle
to the earth, and gathered *the clusters*
from the vine of the earth, and threw[906]
them into [a]the great wine press of the
wrath[2372] of God.[2316]
20 And [a]the wine press was
trodden[3961] [b]outside[1854] the city, and
[c]blood[129] came out from the wine press,
up to the horses' bridles, [I]for a distance
of [II]two hundred miles.[4712]

A Scene of Heaven

15 And I saw [a]another sign[4592]
in heaven,[3772] great and marvelous, [b]seven angels who had [c]seven
plagues, *which are* [d]the last,[2078] because

9 [a]Rev. 13:12; 14:11 [b]Rev. 13:14f.; 14:11 [c]Rev. 13:16
10 [I]Lit., *unmixed* [a]Is. 51:17; Jer. 25:15f., 27; Rev. 16:19; 19:15 [b]Ps. 75:8; Rev. 18:6 [c]Gen. 19:24; Ezek. 38:22; 2Thess. 1:7; Rev. 19:20; 20:10, 14f.; 21:8 [d]Mark 8:38
11 [a]Is. 34:8-10; Rev. 18:9, 18; 19:3 [b]Rev. 4:8 [c]Rev. 13:12; 14:9 [d]Rev. 13:17
12 [I]Or, *steadfastness* [II]Or, *holy ones* [III]Lit., *the faith of* [a]Rev. 13:10 [b]Rev. 12:17 [c]Rev. 2:13
13 [a]Rev. 20:6 [b]1Cor. 15:18; 1Thess. 4:16 [c]Rev. 2:7; 22:17 [d]Heb. 4:9ff.; Rev. 6:11 [e]1Tim. 5:25
14 [I]Or, *the Son of Man* [a]Matt. 17:5 [b]Dan. 7:13; Rev. 1:13 [c]Ps. 21:3; Rev. 6:2
15 [I]Or, *sanctuary* [II]Lit., *Send forth* [III]Lit., *has become dry* [a]Rev. 11:19; 14:17; 15:6; 16:17 [b]Joel 3:13; Mark 4:29; Rev. 14:18 [c]Jer. 51:33; Matt. 13:39-41
16 [I]Lit., *cast*
17 [I]Or, *sanctuary* [II]Lit., *having himself also* [a]Rev. 11:19; 14:15; 15:6; 16:17
18 [I]Lit., *Send forth* [II]Lit., *of* [a]Rev. 16:8 [b]Rev. 6:9; 8:3 [c]Joel 3:13; Mark 4:29; Rev. 14:15 [d]Joel 3:13
19 [I]Lit., *cast* [a]Is. 63:2f.; Rev. 19:15
20 [I]Lit., *from two hundred miles* [II]Lit., *sixteen hundred stadia;* a stadion was approx. 600 ft. [a]Is. 63:3; Lam. 1:15; Rev. 19:15 [b]Heb. 13:12; Rev. 11:8 [c]Gen. 49:11; Deut. 32:14
1 [a]Rev. 12:1, 3 [b]Rev. 15:6-8; 16:1; 17:1; 21:9 [c]Lev. 26:21 [d]Rev. 9:20

15:1-8 Here we have the preparation for the seven vials which will constitute the expression of the final wrath of the tribulation.

The first expression of wrath is given through the seven seals (6:1-17). Out of the seventh seal came the seven trumpets (8:1-13; 9:1-21; 11:15-19). Then out of the seventh trumpet comes the last seven vials (bowls) of God's wrath (15:1; 16:1-21). Bowls are used because the contents can be poured out of them very suddenly, again leading us to accept the meaning of *en tachei* (Rev. 1:1), not as things that were to come soon, but suddenly. Rev. 15:1 introduces the bowls, and then after an intermission of a few verses, Rev. 16 records how they are poured out in quick succession. The tribulation of seven years is finished when the pouring of the bowls of God's wrath is completed. This period ends with the return of Christ at which time He brings an end to the final battle of Armageddon dealing definitively with the antichrist and the false prophet.

in them the wrath[2372] of God[2316] is [aop]finished.[5055]

2 And I saw, as it were, a [a]sea of glass mixed with fire, and those who had [b]come off victorious from the [c]beast[2342] and from [d]his image and from the [e]number of his name, standing on the [f]sea of glass, holding [g]harps of God.

3 And they *sang the [a]song[5603] of Moses [b]the bond-servant[1401] of God and the [c]song of the Lamb, saying,

"[d]Great and marvelous are Thy works,
[e]O Lord[2962] God,[2316] the Almighty;[3841]
Righteous[1342] and true[228] are Thy ways,
Thou [f]King[935] of the [I]nations.[40]

4 "[a]Who will not [aosb]fear,[5399]
O Lord, and [ft]glorify[1392] Thy name?
For Thou alone art holy;[3741]
For [b]ALL THE NATIONS[1484] WILL COME AND WORSHIP[4352] BEFORE THEE,
For Thy [Ic]righteous acts[1345] have [aop]been revealed."[5319]

5 After these things I looked, and [a]the [I]temple[3485] of the [b]tabernacle[4633] of testimony[3142] in heaven was opened,

6 and the [a]seven angels who had the seven plagues [b]came out of the [I]temple, clothed in [II]linen, clean[2513] *and* bright, and [c]girded around their breasts with golden girdles.[2223]

7 And one of the [a]four living creatures gave to the [b]seven angels seven [c]golden bowls full of the [d]wrath[2372] of God,[2316] who [e]lives[2198] forever[165] and ever.

8 And the [I]temple was filled with [a]smoke from the glory[1391] of God and from His power;[1411] and no one was [ipf]able to [ainf]enter the [I]temple until the seven plagues of the seven angels were [asbp]finished.[5055]

2 [a]Rev. 4:6 [b]Rev. 12:11 [c]Rev. 13:1 [d]Rev. 13:14f. [e]Rev. 13:17 [f]Rev. 5:8
3 [I]Some ancient mss. read *ages* [a]Ex. 15:1ff. [b]Josh. 22:5; Heb. 3:5 [c]Rev. 5:9f., 12f. [d]Deut. 32:3f.; Ps. 111:2; 139:14 [e]Hos. 14:9; Rev. 1:8 [f]1Tim. 1:17
4 [I]Or, *judgments* [a]Jer. 10:7; Rev. 14:7 [b]Ps. 86:9; Is. 66:23 [c]Rev. 19:8
5 [I]Or, *sanctuary* [a]Rev. 11:19 [b]Ex. 38:21; Num. 1:50; Heb. 8:5; Rev. 13:6
6 [I]Or, *sanctuary* [II]Some mss. read *stone* [a]Rev. 15:1 [b]Rev. 14:15 [c]Rev. 1:13
7 [a]Rev. 4:6 [b]Rev. 15:1 [c]Rev. 5:8 [d]Rev. 14:10; 15:1 [e]Rev. 4:9
8 [I]Or, *sanctuary* [a]Ex. 19:18; 40:34f.; Lev. 16:2; 1Kin. 8:10f.; 2Chr. 5:13f.; Is. 6:4

Six Bowls of Wrath

16 And I heard a loud voice from [a]the [I]temple,[3485] saying to the [b]seven angels,[32] "Go and [c]pour out the seven bowls[5357] of the wrath[2372] of God into the earth."[1093]

2 And the first *angel* went and poured out his bowl [a]into the earth; and it became a loathsome[2556] and malignant[4190] [b]sore[1668] upon the men [c]who [ppt]had the mark[5480] of the beast and who [ppt]worshiped[4352] his image.

3 And the second *angel* poured out his bowl [a]into the sea, and it became blood[129] like *that* of a dead[3498] man; and every living[2198] [I]thing[5590] in the sea died.[599]

4 And the third *angel* poured out his bowl into the [a]rivers and the springs[4077] of waters; and [I]they [b]became blood.

5 And I heard the angel of the waters saying, "[a]Righteous[1392] art Thou, [b]who art and who wast,[3801] O [c]Holy One, because Thou didst [ao] [d]judge[2919] these things;

6 for they [ao] poured out [a]the blood[129] of saints[40] and prophets,[4396] and Thou hast [pfi]given them [b]blood to [ainf]drink. They [I]deserve it."[514]

7 And I heard [a]the altar[2379] saying, "Yes, O [b]Lord God, the Almighty,[3841] [c]true[228] and righteous[1342] are Thy judgments."[2920]

1 [I]Or, *sanctuary* [a]Rev. 11:19 [b]Rev. 15:1 [c]Ps. 79:6; Jer. 10:25; Ezek. 22:31; Zeph. 3:8; Rev. 16:2ff.
2 [a]Rev. 8:7 [b]Ex. 9:9-11; Deut. 28:35; Rev. 16:11 [c]Rev. 13:15-17; 14:9
3 [I]Lit., *soul.* Some ancient mss. read *thing; the things in the sea.* [a]Ex. 7:17-21; Rev. 8:8f.; 11:6
4 [I]Some ancient mss. read *it* became [a]Rev. 8:10 [b]Ex. 7:17-20; Ps. 78:44; Rev. 11:6
5 [a]John 17:25 [b]Rev. 11:17 [c]Rev. 15:4 [d]Rev. 6:10
6 [I]Lit., *are worthy* [a]Rev. 17:6; 18:24 [b]Is. 49:26; Luke 11:49-51
7 [a]Rev. 6:9; 14:18 [b]Rev. 1:8 [c]Rev. 15:3; 19:2

16:1-21 Here we have the pouring out of seven vials of God's wrath constituting the fiercest expression of His anger. The seven vial judgments are: (1) The vial of noisome and grievous sores covering the bodies of men who have received the mark of the beast. (2) The sea of blood when everything in the sea dies. (3) The rivers become bloody. (4) Men are scorched with great heat and they blaspheme the name of God. (5) The earth is filled with darkness and men gnaw their tongues in pain, curse, and blaspheme the God of heaven, and yet do not repent of their evil deeds. (6) The river Euphrates dries up, and an army marches on Israel. (7) The air is affected, a great earthquake occurs and huge hailstones fall from heaven.

8 And the fourth *angel* poured out his bowl upon [a]the sun; [b]and it was given to it to [ainf]scorch men with fire.

9 And men[444] were scorched with [I]fierce heat; and they [a]blasphemed[987] the name[3686] of God who has the power[1849] over these plagues; and they [b]did not repent,[3340] so as to [ainf] [c]give Him glory.[1391]

10 And the fifth *angel* poured out his bowl upon the [a]throne of the beast; and his kingdom[932] became [b]darkened; and they [ipf]gnawed their tongues because of pain,[4192]

11 and they [a]blasphemed the [b]God of heaven[3772] because of their pains and their [c]sores; and they [d]did not repent of their deeds.[2041]

12 And the sixth *angel* poured out his bowl upon the [a]great river, the Euphrates; and [b]its water was dried up, that [c]the way might be prepared for the kings[935] [d]from the [I]east.

Armageddon

13 And I saw *coming* out of the mouth of the [a]dragon and out of the mouth of the [b]beast and out of the mouth of the [c]false prophet, three [d]unclean spirits[4151] like [e]frogs;

14 for they are [a]spirits[4151] of demons,[1142] [b]performing signs,[4592] which go out to the kings of the [c]whole [I]world,[3625] to [ainf] [d]gather them together for the war of the [e]great day[2250] of God, the Almighty.3841

🔑 15 ("Behold, [a]I am coming like a thief. [b]Blessed[3107] is the one who [ppt]stays awake and [ppt]keeps his garments, [c]lest he [psa]walk about naked[1131] and [I]men [psa]see his shame.")

16 And they [a]gathered them together to the place which [b]in Hebrew is called [I]Har-[c]Magedon.717

Seventh Bowl of Wrath

17 And the seventh *angel* poured out his bowl upon [a]the air; and a [b]loud voice came out of the [Ic]temple[3485] from the throne, saying, "[d]It is done."

18 And there [ao]were flashes of [a]lightning and sounds and peals of thunder; and there [ao]was [b]a great earthquake, [c]such as there [ao]had not been since man[444] came to be upon the earth,[1093] so great an earthquake *was it, and* so mighty.

19 And [a]the great city [ao]was split into three parts, and the cities of the [I]nations fell. And [b]Babylon the great was [c]remembered before God, to [ainf]give her [d]the cup of the wine[3631] of His fierce[2372] wrath.[3709]

20 And [a]every island fled away, and the mountains were not found.[2147]

21 And [a]huge [I]hailstones, about [II]one hundred pounds each, *came down from heaven upon men; and men[444] [b]blasphemed[987] God[2316] because of the [c]plague of the hail, because its plague *was extremely [III]severe.

The Doom of Babylon

17 🔑 [a]And one of the [b]seven angels[32] had the [c]seven bowls5357 came and spoke with me, saying, "Come

8 [a]Rev. 6:12 [b]Rev. 14:18
9 [I]Lit., *great* [a]Rev. 16:11, 21 [b]Rev. 2:21 [c]Rev. 11:13
10 [a]Rev. 13:2 [b]Ex. 10:21f.; Is. 8:22; Rev. 8:12; 9:2
11 [a]Rev. 16:9, 21 [b]Rev. 11:13 [c]Rev. 16:2 [d]Rev. 2:21
12 [I]Lit., *rising of the sun* [a]Rev. 9:14 [b]Is. 11:15f.; 44:27; Jer. 51:36 [c]Is. 41:2, 25; 46:11 [d]Rev. 7:2
13 [a]Rev. 12:3 [b]Rev. 13:1 [c]Rev. 13:11, 14; 19:20; 20:10 [d]Rev. 18:2 [e]Ex. 8:6
14 [I]Lit., *inhabited earth* [a]1Tim. 4:1 [b]Rev. 13:13 [c]Rev. 3:10 [d]1Kin. 22:21-23; Rev. 17:14; 19:19; 20:8 [e]Rev. 6:17
15 [I]Lit., *they* [a]Matt. 24:43f.; Luke 12:39f.; Rev. 3:3, 11 [b]Luke 12:37 [c]Rev. 3:18
16 [I]Some authorities read *Armageddon* [a]Rev. 19:19 [b]Rev. 9:11 [c]Judg. 5:19; 2Kin. 23:29f.; 2Chr. 35:22; Zech. 12:11
17 [I]Or, *sanctuary* [a]Eph. 2:2 [b]Rev. 11:15 [c]Rev. 14:15 [d]Rev. 10:6; 21:6
18 [a]Rev. 4:5 [b]Rev. 6:12 [c]Dan. 12:1; Matt. 24:21
19 [I]Or, *Gentiles* [a]Rev. 11:8; 17:18; 18:10, 18f., 21 [b]Rev. 14:8 [c]Rev. 18:5 [d]Rev. 14:10
20 [a]Rev. 6:14; 20:11
21 [I]Lit., *hail* [II]Lit., *the weight of a talent* [III]Lit., *great* [a]Rev. 8:7; 11:19 [b]Rev. 16:9, 11 [c]Ex. 9:18-25
1 [a]Rev. 1:1; 21:9 [b]Rev. 15:1 [c]Rev. 15:7

🔑 **16:15,16** Again a parenthetical portion appears between the sixth and seventh vials as in the case of the sixth and seventh seals and the sixth and seventh trumpets.

🔑 **17:1—18:24** These two chapters elaborate on Babylon, called the great whore which sits upon many waters. She is also called, "The Mother of Harlots and Abominations of the Earth." She appears as a great persecutor because she is said to be drunk with the blood of saints and of martyrs. Babylon appears as religious, but it is actually contrasted with the true saints of God as a filthy woman who is clothed in purple, scarlet, gold, precious stones and pearls. The true Church of Christ is not Babylon but the bride of Christ. It is interesting to note that the Babylon in Rev. 18 is both a city and a system.

here, I shall show you [d]the judgment[2917] of the [e]great harlot[4204] who [ppt][f]sits on many waters,

2 with whom [a]the kings[935] of the earth[1093] [ap]committed *acts of* immorality,[4203] and [b]those who dwell on the earth were [c]made [aop]drunk with the wine of her immorality."

3 And [a]he carried me away[667] [Ib]in the Spirit[4151] [c]into a wilderness; and I saw a woman [ppt]sitting on a [d]scarlet beast, full of [e]blasphemous[988] names, having [f]seven heads and ten horns.

4 And the woman [a]was clothed in purple and scarlet, and [I]adorned[5558] with gold and precious [II]stones and pearls, having in her hand [b]a gold cup full of abominations[946] and of the unclean things[168] of her immorality,

5 and upon her forehead a name[3686] *was* written, a [a]mystery,[3466] "[b]BABYLON THE GREAT, THE MOTHER OF HARLOTS[4204] AND OF [c]THE ABOMINATIONS[946] OF THE EARTH."[1093]

6 And I saw the woman [ppt]drunk with [a]the blood[129] of the [I]saints,[40] and with the blood of the witnesses[3144] of Jesus. And when I saw her, I wondered [II]greatly.

7 And the angel said to me, "Why [I]do you wonder? I shall tell you the [a]mystery of the woman and of the beast that [ppt]carries her, which has the [b]seven heads and the ten horns.

8 "[a]The beast that you saw [b]was and is not, and is about to [c]come up out of the [d]abyss and [I]to [pin][e]go to destruction.[684] And [f]those who [ppt]dwell on the earth will [g]wonder, [h]whose name has not been [pfip]written in the book[975] of life[2222] [i]from the foundation of the world, when they [ppt]see the beast, that he was and is not and will come.

9 "[a]Here is the mind which has wisdom.[4678] The [b]seven heads are seven mountains on which the woman sits,

10 and they are seven [a]kings;[935] five have fallen, one is, the other has not yet [ao]come; and when he [aosb]comes, he must [ainf]remain a little while.

11 "And the beast which [a]was and is not, is himself also an eighth, and is *one* of the seven, and he [b]goes to destruction.

12 "And the [a]ten horns which you saw are ten kings, who have not yet [ao]received a kingdom,[932] but they receive authority[1849] as kings with the beast [b]for one hour.

13 "These have [a]one [I]purpose[1106] and they give their power[1411] and authority[1849] to the beast.

Victory for the Lamb

14 "These will wage [a]war against the Lamb,[721] and the Lamb will [b]overcome them, because He is [c]Lord[2962] of lords and [c]King[935] of kings, and [d]those who are with Him *are the* [e]called[2822] and chosen and faithful."[4103]

15 And he *said to me, "The [a]waters which you saw where the harlot sits, are [b]peoples[2992] and multitudes and nations[1484] and tongues.[1100]

16 "And the [a]ten horns which you saw, and the beast, these will hate the harlot and will make her [b]desolate and [c]naked,[1131] and will [d]eat her flesh[4561] and will [e]burn her up with fire.

17 "For [a]God has [ao]put it in their hearts[2588] to [ainf]execute His [I]purpose[1106] [II]by [b]having a common purpose, and by [ainf]giving their kingdom to the beast, until the [c]words[4487] of God should be [fp]fulfilled.[5055]

18 "And the woman whom you saw is [a]the great city, which [I]reigns over the kings[935] of the earth."[1093]

Babylon Is Fallen

18 After these things I saw another [a]angel[32] [ppt][b]coming down from heaven,[3772] having great authority,[1849] and the earth[1093] was [c]illumined[5461] with his glory.[1391]

2 And he cried out with a mighty voice, saying, [ao]"[a]Fallen, fallen is Bab-

1 [d]Rev. 16:19 [e]Is. 1:21; Jer. 2:20; Nah. 3:4; Rev. 17:5, 15f.; 19:2 [f]Jer. 51:13; Rev. 17:15
2 [a]Rev. 2:22; 18:3, 9 [b]Rev. 3:10; 17:8 [c]Rev. 14:8
3 [I]Or, *in spirit* [a]Rev. 21:10 [b]Rev. 1:10 [c]Rev. 12:6, 14; 21:10 [d]Matt. 27:28; Rev. 18:12, 16 [e]Rev. 13:1 [f]Rev. 12:3; 17:7, 9, 12, 16
4 [I]Lit., *gilded* [II]Lit., *stone* [a]Ezek. 28:13; Rev. 18:12, 16 [b]Jer. 51:7; Rev. 18:6
5 [a]2Thess. 2:7; Rev. 1:20; 17:7 [b]Rev. 14:8; 16:19 [c]Rev. 17:2
6 [I]Or, *holy ones* [II]Lit., *with great wonder* [a]Rev. 16:6
7 [I]Lit., *have you wondered* [a]2Thess. 2:7; Rev. 1:20; 17:5 [b]Rev. 17:3
8 [I]Some ancient mss. read *he goes* [a]Dan. 7:7 [b]Rev. 13:3, 12, 14; 17:11 [c]Rev. 11:7; 13:1 [d]Rev. 9:1; 13:1 [e]Rev. 13:10; 17:11 [f]Rev. 3:10 [g]Rev. 13:3 [h]Ps. 69:28; Rev. 3:5 [i]Matt. 25:34; Rev. 13:8
9 [a]Rev. 13:18 [b]Rev. 17:3
10 [a]Rev. 10:11
11 [a]Rev. 13:3, 12, 14; 17:8 [b]Rev. 13:10; 17:8
12 [a]Dan. 7:24; Rev. 12:3; 13:1; 17:16 [b]Rev. 18:10, 17, 19
13 [I]Or, *mind* [a]Rev. 17:17
14 [a]Rev. 16:14 [b]Rev. 3:21 [c]1Tim. 6:15; Rev. 19:16 [d]Rev. 2:10f. [e]Matt. 22:14
15 [a]Is. 8:7; Jer. 47:2; Rev. 17:1 [b]Rev. 5:9
16 [a]Rev. 17:12 [b]Rev. 18:17, 19 [c]Ezek. 16:37, 39 [d]Rev. 19:18 [e]Rev. 18:8
17 [I]Or, *mind* [II]Lit., *even to do one mind and to give* [a]2Cor. 8:16 [b]Rev. 17:13 [c]Rev. 10:7
18 [I]Lit., *has a kingdom* [a]Rev. 11:8; 16:19
1 [a]Rev. 17:1, 7 [b]Rev. 10:1 [c]Ezek. 43:2
2 [a]Is. 21:9; Jer. 51:8 Rev. 14:8

ylon the great! And she [b]has [ao]become a dwelling place[2732] of demons[1142] and a [I]prison[5438] of every [c]unclean spirit,[4151] and a [I]prison[5438] of every unclean and hateful bird.

3 "For all the nations[1484] [I]have [pfi]drunk of the [a]wine of the [II]passion[2372] of her immorality,[4202] and [b]the kings of the earth have committed *acts of* immorality with her, and the [c]merchants[1713] of the earth have become rich[4147] by the [III]wealth of her [IV][d]sensuality."[4764]

4 And I heard another voice from heaven, saying, "[a]Come out of her, my people,[2992] that you may not [aosb]participate[4790] in her sins[266] and that you may not [aosb]receive of her plagues;

5 for her sins have [aop] [I][a]piled up as high as heaven, and God has [ao] [b]remembered her iniquities.[92]

6 "[a]Pay her back even as she has paid, and [I]give back *to her* double according to her deeds;[2041] in the [b]cup which she has [ao]mixed, [aim]mix twice as much for her.

7 "[a]To the degree that she [ao]glorified[1392] herself and [b]lived [I]sensuously,[4763] to the same degree [aim]give her torment and mourning; for she says in her heart,[2588] '[c]I SIT *as* A QUEEN AND I AM NOT A WIDOW, and will never [efn]see mourning.'

8 "For this reason [a]in one day her plagues will come, [I]pestilence[2288] and mourning and famine, and she will be [b]burned up with fire; for the Lord God who [apt]judges[2919] her [c]is strong.[2478]

Lament for Babylon

9 "And [a]the kings[935] of the earth,[1093] who committed *acts of* immorality and [apt] [b]lived [I]sensuously with her, will [c]weep[2799] and lament[2875] over her when they [aosb] [d]see the smoke of her burning,

10 [a]standing at a distance because of the fear[5401] of her torment, saying, '[b]Woe, woe, [c]the great city, Babylon, the strong city! For in [d]one hour your judgment[2920] has [ao]come.'

11 "And the [a]merchants[1713] of the earth [pin] [b]weep and [pin]mourn over her, because no one buys their cargoes any more;

12 cargoes of [a]gold and silver and precious [I]stones and pearls and fine linen and purple and silk and scarlet, and every *kind of* citron wood and every article of ivory and every article *made* from very costly[2367] wood and [II]bronze and iron and marble,

13 and cinnamon and [I]spice and incense and perfume and frankincense[3030] and wine and olive oil and fine flour and wheat and cattle and sheep, and *cargoes* of horses and chariots and [II]slaves[4983] and [III][a]human[444] lives.[5590]

14 "And the fruit [I]you long[1939] for has [aom]gone from you, and all things that were luxurious and splendid have passed away from you and *men* will no longer [efn]find them.

15 "The [a]merchants of [b]these things, who became rich from her, will [c]stand at a distance because of the fear[5401] of her torment, weeping and mourning,

16 saying, '[a]Woe, woe, [b]the great city, she who [c]was clothed in fine linen and purple and scarlet, and [I]adorned[5558] with gold and precious [II]stones and pearls;

17 for in [a]one hour such great wealth has been laid [b]waste!' And [c]every shipmaster and every [I]passenger and sailor, and as many as make their living[2038] by the sea, [a]stood at a distance,

18 and were [ipf] [a]crying out as they [ppt] [b]saw the smoke of her burning, saying, '[c]What *city* is like [d]the great city?'

19 "And they threw [a]dust on their heads and were crying out, weeping and mourning, saying, '[b]Woe, woe, the great city, in which all who had ships at sea [c]became rich by her [I]wealth, for in [b]one hour she has been laid [d]waste!'

2 [I]Or, *haunt* [b]Is. 13:21f.; 34:11, 13-15; Jer. 50:39; 51:37; Zeph. 2:14f. [c]Rev. 16:13
3 [I]Many ancient mss. read *have fallen by* [II]Lit., *wrath* [III]Lit., *power* [IV]Or, *luxury* [a]Jer. 51:7; Rev. 14:8 [b]Rev. 17:2; 18:9 [c]Ezek. 27:9-25; Rev. 18:11, 15, 19, 23 [d]1Tim. 5:11; Rev. 18:7, 9
4 [a]Is. 52:11; Jer. 50:8; 51:6, 9, 45; 2Cor. 6:17
5 [I]Lit., *joined together* [a]Jer. 51:9 [b]Rev. 16:19
6 [I]Lit., *double* to her [a]Ps. 137:8; Jer. 50:15, 29 [b]Rev. 17:4
7 [I]Or, *luxuriously* [a]Ezek. 28:2-8 [b]1Tim. 5:11; Rev. 18:3, 9 [c]Is. 47:7f.; Zeph. 2:15
8 [I]Or, *death* [a]Is. 47:9; Jer. 50:31f.; Rev. 18:10 [b]Rev. 17:16 [c]Jer. 50:34; Rev. 11:17f.
9 [I]Or, *luxuriously* [a]Rev. 17:2; 18:3 [b]1Tim. 5:11; Rev. 18:3, 7 [c]Ezek. 26:16f.; 27:35 [d]Rev. 14:11; 18:18; 19:3
10 [a]Rev. 18:15, 17 [b]Rev. 18:16, 19 [c]Rev. 11:8; 16:19; 18:16, 18, 19, 21 [d]Rev. 17:12; 18:8, 17, 19
11 [a]Ezek. 27:9-25; Rev. 18:3, 15, 19, 23 [b]Ezek. 27:27-34
12 [I]Lit., *stone* [II]Or, *brass* [a]Ezek. 27:12-22; Rev. 17:4
13 [I]Gr., *amomon* [II]Lit., *bodies* [III]Lit., *souls of men* [a]1Chr. 5:21; Ezek. 27:13; 1Tim. 1:10
14 [I]Lit., *of your soul's desire*
15 [a]Rev. 18:3 [b]Rev. 18:12, 13 [c]Rev. 18:10
16 [I]Lit., *gilded* [II]Lit., *stone and* pearl [a]Rev. 18:10, 19 [b]Rev. 18:10, 18, 19, 21 [c]Rev. 17:4
17 [I]Lit., *one who sails anywhere* [a]Rev. 18:10 [b]Rev. 17:16; 18:19 [c]Ezek. 27:28f.
18 [a]Ezek. 27:30 [b]Rev. 18:9 [c]Ezek. 27:32; Rev. 13:4 [d]Rev. 18:10
19 [I]Lit., *costliness* [a]Josh. 7:6; Job 2:12; Lam. 2:10 [b]Rev. 18:10 [c]Rev. 18:3, 15 [d]Rev. 17:16; 18:17

20 [pim]“[a]Rejoice[2165] over her, O heaven,[3772] and you [I]saints[40] and [b]apostles[652] and prophets,[4396] because [c]God has [II]pronounced judgment for you against her.”

21 And [I]a [a]strong angel[32] [b]took up a stone like a great millstone and threw it into the sea, saying, “Thus will Babylon, [c]the great city, be thrown down with violence, and [d]will not be [efn]found[2147] any longer.

22 “And [a]the sound of harpists and musicians and flute-players and trumpeters will not be [efn]heard in you any longer; and no craftsman[5079] of any craft will be [efn]found in you any longer; and the [b]sound of a mill[3458] will not be [efn]heard in you any longer;

23 and the light of a lamp will not [efn]shine in you any longer; and the [a]voice of the bridegroom and bride will not be [efn]heard in you any longer; for your [b]merchants[1713] were the great men of the earth,[1093] because all the nations[1484] were deceived [c]by your sorcery.[5331]

24 “And in her was found the [a]blood[129] of prophets[4396] and of [I]saints[40] and of [b]all who have been slain on the earth.”

The Fourfold Hallelujah

19 🔑 After these things I heard, as it were, a [a]loud voice of a great multitude in heaven,[3772] saying,

“[b]Hallelujah![239] [c]Salvation[4991] and [d]glory[1391] and power[1411] belong to our God;[2316]

2 [a]BECAUSE HIS [b]JUDGMENTS[2920] ARE [c]TRUE[228] AND RIGHTEOUS;[1342] for He has [ao]judged[2919] the [d]great harlot[4204] who was corrupting the earth with her immorality,[4202] and HE HAS [ao] [e]AVENGED[1556] THE BLOOD[129] OF HIS BOND-SERVANTS[1401] [I]ON HER.”

3 And a second time they said, “[a]Hallelujah! [b]HER SMOKE RISES UP FOREVER[165] AND EVER.”

4 And the [a]twenty-four elders[4245] and the [b]four living creatures [c]fell down and worshiped[4352] God who sits on the throne saying, “[d]Amen.[281] [e]Hallelujah!”[239]

5 And a voice came from the throne, saying,

“[a]Give [pim]praise[1314] to our God,[2316] all you His bond-servants,[1401] [b]you who [ppt]fear[5399] Him, the small and the great.”

6 And I heard, as it were, [a]the voice of a great multitude and as [b]the sound of many waters and as the [c]sound of mighty peals of thunder, saying,

“[a]Hallelujah! For the [d]Lord[2962] our God,[2316] the Almighty,[3841] [ao]reigns.[936]

Marriage of the Lamb

7 “Let us [psa]rejoice[5463] and be [psa]glad[21] and [ft] [a]give the glory[1391] to Him, for [b]the marriage[1062] of the Lamb has [ao]come and His [I][c]bride has made herself ready.”

8 And it was given to her to [asbm]clothe herself in [a]fine linen, bright *and* clean;[2513] for the fine linen is the [b]righteous acts[1345] of the [I]saints.[40]

9 And [a]he *said to me, [aim]“[b]Write,[1125] ‘[c]Blessed[3107] are those who are [pfpp]invited to the marriage[1062] supper of the Lamb.’ ”[721] And he *said to me, “[d]These are true[228] words[3056] of God.”

10 And [a]I fell at his feet to [ainf]worship[4352] him. [b]And he *said to me, “Do not do that; I am a [c]fellow servant[4889] of yours and your brethren[80] who [ppt] [d]hold the testimony[3141] of Jesus; [aim]worship God.

20 [I]Or, *holy ones* [II]Lit., *judged your judgment of her* [a]Jer. 51:48; Rev. 12:12 [b]Luke 11:49f. [c]Rev. 6:10; 18:6ff.; 19:2
21 [I]Lit., *one* [a]Rev. 5:2; 10:1 [b]Jer. 51:63f. [c]Rev. 18:10 [d]Ezek. 26:21
22 [a]Is. 24:8; Ezek. 26:13; Matt. 9:23 [b]Eccl. 12:4; Jer. 25:10
23 [a]Jer. 7:34; 16:9 [b]Is. 23:8; Rev. 6:15; 18:3 [c]Nah. 3:4; Rev. 9:21
24 [I]Or, *holy ones* [a]Rev. 16:6; 17:6 [b]Matt. 23:35

1 [a]Jer. 51:48; Rev. 11:15; 19:6 [b]Ps. 104:35; Rev. 19:3, 4, 6 [c]Rev. 7:10 [d]Rev. 4:11
2 [I]Lit., *from her hand* [a]Ps. 19:9 [b]Rev. 6:10 [c]Rev. 16:7 [d]Rev. 17:1 [e]Deut. 32:43; 2Kin. 9:7; Rev. 16:6; 18:20
3 [a]Ps. 104:35; Rev. 19:1, 4, 6 [b]Is. 34:10; Rev. 14:11
4 [a]Rev. 4:4, 10 [b]Rev. 4:6 [c]Rev. 4:10 [d]Ps. 106:48; Rev. 5:14 [e]Ps. 104:35; Rev. 19:3, 6
5 [a]Ps. 22:23; 115:13; 134:1; 135:1 [b]Rev. 11:18
6 [a]Jer. 51:48; Rev. 11:15; 19:1 [b]Ezek. 1:24; Rev. 1:15 [c]Rev. 6:1 [d]Ps. 93:1; 97:1; 99:1; Rev. 1:8
7 [I]Lit., *wife* [a]Rev. 11:13 [b]Matt. 22:2; 25:10; Luke 12:36; John 3:29; Eph. 5:23, 32; Rev. 19:9 [c]Matt. 1:20; Rev. 21:2, 9
8 [I]Or, *holy ones* [a]Rev. 15:6; 19:14 [b]Rev. 15:4
9 [a]Rev. 17:1; 19:10 [b]Rev. 1:19 [c]Matt. 22:2f.; Luke 14:15 [d]Rev. 17:17; 21:5; 22:6
10 [a]Rev. 22:8 [b]Acts 10:26; Rev. 22:9 [c]Rev. 1:1f. [d]Rev. 12:17

🔑 **19:1-21** Here we come to the climax of Revelation which is the Second Coming of the Lord Jesus Christ. Heaven is opened and a white horse with a rider that is called “Faithful and True” appears. This is truly the Lord Jesus Christ who is about to introduce real peace and righteousness in contrast to the false peace brought by the first white horse and its rider which was the antichrist.

For the testimony of Jesus is the spirit[4151] of prophecy."[4394]

The Coming of Christ

11 And I saw [a]heaven [pfpp]opened; and behold, a [b]white horse, and He who [ppt]sat upon it *is* called [c]Faithful[4103] and True; and in [d]righteousness[1343] He judges[2919] and wages war.

12 And His [a]eyes *are* a flame of fire, and upon His head *are* many [b]diadems;[1238] and He has a [c]name written[1125] *upon Him* which no one knows except Himself.

13 And *He is* clothed with a [a]robe[2440] [pfpp]dipped[911] in blood;[129] and His name[3686] is [pfip]called [b]The Word[3056] of God.[2316]

14 And the armies which are in heaven,[3772] clothed in [a]fine linen, [b]white *and* clean,[2513] were [ipf]following[190] Him on white horses.

15 And [a]from His mouth comes a sharp sword, so that [b]with it He may [asba]smite the nations; and He will [Ic]rule[4165] them with a rod of iron; and [d]He treads[3961] the [II]wine press of the fierce[2372] wrath[3709] of God,[2316] the Almighty.[3841]

16 And on His robe and on His thigh He has [a]a name written, "[b]KING[935] OF KINGS, AND LORD[2962] OF LORDS."

17 And I saw [I]an angel[32] standing in the sun; and he cried out with a loud voice, saying to [a]all the birds which [ppt]fly in [b]midheaven, "[c]Come, [aipp]assemble for the great supper of God;[2316]

18 in order that you may [aosb] [a]eat the flesh[4561] of kings[935] and the flesh of [I]commanders and the flesh of mighty men and the flesh of horses and of those who sit on them and the flesh of all men, [b]both free men and slaves,[1401] and [c]small and great."

🔑 **19** And I saw [a]the beast and [b]the kings of the earth[1093] and their armies, assembled to [ainf]make war against Him who [c]sat upon the horse, and against His army.

Doom of the Beast and False Prophet

20 And the beast was seized, and with him the [a]false prophet who [apt] [b]performed the signs[4592] [Ic]in his presence, by which he [d]deceived those who had [apt]received the [e]mark[5480] of the beast and those who [ppt] [f]worshiped[4352] his image; these two were thrown alive[2198] into the [g]lake of [h]fire which burns with brimstone.[2303]

21 And the rest[3062] were killed[615] with the sword which [apt] [a]came from the mouth of Him who [b]sat upon the horse, and [c]all the birds were filled with their flesh.[4561]

Satan Bound

20 🔑 And I saw [a]an angel[32] [ppt]coming down from heaven,[3772] having the [b]key of the abyss and a great chain [I]in his hand.

🔑 2 And he laid hold of the [a]dragon, the serpent of old, who is the devil[1228] and Satan,[4567] and [b]bound[1210] him for a thousand years,

3 and threw[906] him into the [a]abyss, and shut *it* and [b]sealed *it* over him, so that he should [c]not [aosb]deceive the nations[1484] any longer, until the thousand years were [asbp]completed;[5055] after

11 [a]Ezek. 1:1; John 1:51; Rev. 4:1 [b]Rev. 6:2; 19:19, 21 [c]Rev. 3:14 [d]Ps. 96:13; Is. 11:4
12 [a]Dan. 10:6; Rev. 1:14 [b]Rev. 6:2; 12:3 [c]Rev. 2:17; 19:16
13 [a]Is. 63:3 [b]John 1:1
14 [a]Rev. 19:8 [b]Rev. 3:4; 19:8
15 [I]Or, *shepherd* [II]Lit., *wine press of the wine of His fierce wrath* [a]Rev. 1:16; 19:21 [b]Is. 11:4; 2Thess. 2:8 [c]Ps. 2:9; Rev. 2:27 [d]Is. 63:3; Joel 3:13; Rev. 14:19, 20
16 [a]Rev. 2:17; 19:12 [b]Rev. 17:14
17 [I]Lit., *one* [a]Rev. 19:21 [b]Rev. 8:13 [c]1Sam. 17:44; Jer. 12:9; Ezek. 39:17
18 [I]I.e., chiliarchs, in command of one thousand troops [a]Ezek. 39:18-20 [b]Rev. 6:15 [c]Rev. 11:18; 13:16; 19:5
19 [a]Rev. 11:7; 13:1 [b]Rev. 16:14, 16 [c]Rev. 19:11, 21
20 [I]Or, *by his authority* [a]Rev. 16:13 [b]Rev. 13:13 [c]Rev. 13:12 [d]Rev. 13:14 [e]Rev. 13:16f. [f]Rev. 13:12, 15 [g]Rev. 20:10, 14f.; 21:8 [h]Is. 30:33; Dan. 7:11; Rev. 14:10
21 [a]Rev. 19:15 [b]Rev. 19:11, 19 [c]Rev. 19:17

1 [I]Lit., *upon* [a]Rev. 10:1 [b]Rev. 1:18; 9:1
2 [a]Gen. 3:1; Rev. 12:9 [b]Is. 24:22; 2Pet. 2:4; Jude 6
3 [a]Rev. 20:1 [b]Dan. 6:17; Matt. 27:66 [c]Rev. 12:9; 20:8, 10

🔑 **19:19,20** See note on Rev. 13.

🔑 **20:1-15** In this chapter, we find Jesus Christ coming back to rule and reign on the earth for a thousand years. The length of time is specific and definite and cannot be mistaken otherwise. There are a number of O.T. references which describe this particular time of the millennium (II Sam. 7:14-17; Ps. 24:1-10; 72:1-20; Isa. 2:1-4; 11:5-10; 35:1-10; Dan. 2:44). Here we have the judgment for the dead who are now in the afterlife (v. 12). The believers have already been raised, and now the unbelievers are raised so that each group may receive its punishment.

🔑 **20:2-10** See note on Jude 9.

these things he must be [aifp]released for a short time.[5550]

4 And I saw [a]thrones, and [b]they sat upon them, and [c]judgment[2917] was given to them. And I *saw* [d]the souls[5590] of those who had been [pfpp]beheaded because of the [e]testimony[3141] of Jesus and because of the word[3056] of God, and those who had not [ao] [f]worshiped[4352] the beast or his image,[1504] and had not received the [g]mark[5480] upon their forehead and upon their hand; and they [h]came to life[2198] and [i]reigned[936] with Christ[5547] for a thousand years.

5 The rest of the dead[3498] did not come to life until the thousand years were [asbp]completed.[5055] [a]This is the first resurrection.[386]

6 [a]Blessed[3107] and holy[40] is the one who [ppt]has a part in the first resurrection;[386] over these the [b]second death[2288] has no power,[1849] but they will be [c]priests[2409] of God[2316] and of Christ[5547] and will [d]reign[936] with Him for a thousand years.

Satan Freed, Doomed

7 And when the thousand years are [asbp]completed,[5055] Satan[4567] will be [a]released from his prison,

8 and will come out to [ainf] [a]deceive the nations[1484] which are in the [b]four corners of the earth, [c]Gog and Magog, to [ainf] [d]gather them together for the war; the number of them is like the [e]sand of the [I]seashore.

9 And they [a]came up on the [I]broad plain of the earth and surrounded[2944] the [b]camp of the [II]saints[40] and the [c]beloved[25] city, and [d]fire came down from heaven and devoured them.

10 And [a]the devil[1228] who [ppt] [b]deceived them was [aop]thrown into the [c]lake of fire and brimstone,[2303] where the [d]beast and the [c]false prophet are also; and they will be [d]tormented day and night forever[165] and ever.

Judgment at the Throne of God

🔑 11 And I saw a great white [a]throne and Him who sat upon it, from whose [I]presence [b]earth[1093] and heaven[3772] fled away, and [c]no place was found for them.

12 And I saw the dead,[3498] the [a]great and the small, standing before the throne, and [Ib]books[975] were opened; and another [II]book was opened, which is [c]*the book* of life;[2222] and the dead [d]were judged[2919] from the things which were [pfpp]written in the [I]books, [e]according to their deeds.[2041]

13 And the sea gave up the dead which were in it, and [a]death[2288] and Hades[86] [b]gave up the dead which were in them; and they were judged, every one *of them* [c]according to their deeds.[2041]

14 And [a]death and Hades were thrown into [b]the lake of fire. This is the [c]second death, the lake of fire.

15 And if [I]anyone's name was not found [pfpp]written in [a]the book[976] of life, he was thrown into the lake of fire.

The New Heaven and Earth

21 🔑 And I saw [a]a new[2537] heaven[3772] and a new[2537] earth;[1093] for [b]the first heaven and the first earth passed away, and there is no longer *any* sea.

2 And I saw [a]the holy[40] city, [b]new Jerusalem, [c]coming down out of

4 [a]Dan. 7:9 [b]Matt. 19:28; Rev. 3:21 [c]Dan. 7:22; 1Cor. 6:2 [d]Rev. 6:9 [e]Rev. 1:9 [f]Rev. 13:12, 15 [g]Rev. 13:16f. [h]John 14:19 [i]Rev. 3:21; 5:10; 20:6; 22:5
5 [a]Luke 14:14; Phil. 3:11; 1Thess. 4:16
6 [a]Rev. 14:13 [b]Rev. 2:11; 20:14 [c]Rev. 1:6 [d]Rev. 3:21; 5:10; 20:4; 22:5
7 [a]Rev. 20:2f.
8 [I]Lit., *sea* [a]Rev. 12:9; 20:3, 10 [b]Ezek. 7:2; Rev. 7:1 [c]Ezek. 38:2; 39:1, 6 [d]Rev. 16:14 [e]Heb. 11:12
9 [I]Lit., *breadth of the earth* [II]Or, *holy ones* [a]Ezek. 38:9, 16 [b]Deut. 23:14 [c]Ps. 87:2 [d]Ezek. 38:22; 39:6; Rev. 13:13
10 [a]Rev. 20:2f. [b]Rev. 19:20; 20:14, 15 [c]Rev. 16:13 [d]Rev. 14:10f.
11 [I]Lit., *face* [a]Rev. 4:2 [b]Rev. 6:14; 21:1 [c]Dan. 2:35; Rev. 12:8
12 [I]Or, *scrolls* [II]Or, *scroll* [a]Rev. 11:18 [b]Dan. 7:10 [c]Rev. 3:5; 20:15 [d]Rev. 11:18 [e]Matt. 16:27; Rev. 2:23; 20:13
13 [a]1Cor. 15:26; Rev. 1:18; 6:8; 21:4 [b]Is. 26:19 [c]Matt. 16:27; Rev. 2:23; 20:12
14 [a]1Cor. 15:26; Rev. 1:18; 6:8; 21:4 [b]Rev. 19:20; 20:10, 15 [c]Rev. 20:6
15 [I]Lit., *anyone* was [a]Rev. 3:5; 20:12

1 [a]Is. 65:17; 66:22; 2Pet. 3:13 [b]2Pet. 3:10; Rev. 20:11 **2** [a]Is. 52:1; Rev. 11:2; 21:10; 22:19 [b]Rev. 3:12; 21:10 [c]Heb. 11:10, 16; Rev. 21:10

🔑 **20:11-15** See note on Mt. 8:11,12.

🔑 **21:1—22:21** Here we have the description of a new heaven and a new earth. The word "new" in Greek is rendered by the word *kainos* (2537) which means "qualitatively new" and not simply another earth and another heaven. Since our resurrection bodies will be changed, so will the environment in which these new bodies will live.

That the believers are not going through the terrible period of the expression of the wrath of God is made clear from I Thess. 5:9. (See also I Thess. 4:13-18 and the note on Mt. 13.)

heaven3772 from God, [d]made ready as
a bride [pfpp]adorned for her husband.
3 And I heard a loud voice from the
throne, saying, "Behold, [a]the taber-
nacle4633 of God2316 is among men,444
and He shall [I][b]dwell among them, and
they shall be His people,2992 and
God2316 Himself shall be among them,[II]
4 and He shall [a]wipe away every tear
from their eyes; and [b]there shall no
longer be *any* death;2288 [c]there shall no
longer be *any* mourning, or crying, or
pain;4192 [d]the first things have [ao]passed
away."
5 And [a]He who [ppt]sits on the throne
said, "Behold, I am [b]making all things
new."2537 And He *said, "Write,1125 for
[c]these words are faithful4103 and
true."228
6 And He said to me, "[I][a]It is [pfi]done.
I am the [b]Alpha1 and the Omega,5598
the beginning746 and the end.5056
[c]I will give to the one who [ppt]thirsts from
the spring4077 of the [d]water of life2222
without cost.
7 "[a]He who [ppt]overcomes shall
inherit2816 these things, and [b]I will be
his God2316 and he will be My son.5207
8 "[a]But for the cowardly and
[I]unbelieving571 and abominable948 and
murderers5406 and immoral persons4205
and sorcerers5332 and idolaters1496 and
all liars, their part *will be* in [b]the lake
that [ppp]burns with fire and brimstone,2303 which is the [c]second
death."2288
9 [a]And one of the seven angels32
who had the [b]seven bowls5357 [I]full of
the [c]seven last plagues, came and spoke
with me, saying, "[d]Come here, I shall
show you the [e]bride, the wife of the
Lamb."721

The New Jerusalem

10 And [a]he carried me away667
[I][b]in the Spirit4151 to a great and high
mountain, and showed me [c]the holy city,
Jerusalem, coming down out of heaven
from God,
11 having [a]the glory1391 of God. Her
[I]brilliance5458 was like a very costly
stone, as a [b]stone of [c]crystal-clear jasper.
12 [I]It [ppt]had a great and high wall,
[I][a]with twelve [b]gates, and at the gates
twelve angels; and names *were*
[pfpp]written on them, which are *those*
of the twelve tribes of the sons of
Israel.
13 *There were* three gates on the
east and three gates on the north and
three gates on the south and three gates
on the west.
14 And the wall of the city had
[a]twelve foundation stones, and on them
were the twelve names of the [b]twelve
apostles652 of the Lamb.721
15 And the one who [ppt]spoke with
me had a [I]gold measuring [a]rod to
[aosb]measure the city, and its [b]gates and
its wall.
16 And the city is laid out as a
square, and its length is as great as the
width; and he measured the city with
the [I]rod, [II]fifteen hundred miles;4712
its length and width and height are
equal.
17 And he measured its wall,
[I]seventy-two yards,4083 *according to*
[a]human444 [II]measurements, which are
also [b]angelic32 *measurements*.
18 And the material of the wall was
[a]jasper; and the city was [b]pure2513 gold,
like [I]clear2513 [c]glass.
19 [a]The foundation stones of the city
wall were [pfpp]adorned with every kind
of precious stone. The first foundation
stone was [b]jasper; the second, sapphire;
the third, chalcedony; the fourth,
[c]emerald;
20 the fifth, sardonyx; the sixth,
[a]sardius; the seventh, chrysolite; the
eighth, beryl; the ninth, topaz; the
tenth, chrysoprase; the eleventh, jacinth; the twelfth, amethyst.
21 And the twelve [a]gates were
twelve [b]pearls; each one of the gates
was a single pearl. And the street of

2 [d]Is. 61:10; Rev. 19:7; 21:9; 22:17
3 [I]Or, *tabernacle* [II]Some ancient mss. add, and be *their God* [a]Lev. 26:11f.; Ezek. 37:27; 48:35; Heb. 8:2; Rev. 7:15 [b]John 14:23; 2Cor. 6:16
4 [a]Is. 25:8; Rev. 7:17 [b]1Cor. 15:26; Rev. 20:14 [c]Is. 35:10; 51:11; 65:19 [d]2Cor. 5:17; Heb. 12:27
5 [a]Rev. 4:9; 20:11 [b]2Cor. 5:17; Heb. 12:27 [c]Rev. 19:9; 22:6
6 [I]Lit., *They are* [a]Rev. 10:6; 16:17 [b]Rev. 1:8; 22:13 [c]Is. 55:1; John 4:10; Rev. 7:17; 22:17 [d]Rev. 7:17
7 [a]Rev. 2:7 [b]2Sam. 7:14; Ps. 89:26f.; 2Cor. 6:16, 18; Rev. 21:3
8 [I]Or, *untrustworthy* [a]1Cor. 6:9; Gal. 5:19-21; Rev. 9:21; 21:27; 22:15 [b]Rev. 19:20 [c]Rev. 2:11
9 [I]Lit., *who were full* [a]Rev. 17:1 [b]Rev. 15:7 [c]Rev. 15:1 [d]Rev. 17:1 [e]Rev. 19:7; 21:2
10 [I]Or, *in spirit* [a]Ezek. 40:2; Rev. 17:3 [b]Rev. 1:10 [c]Rev. 21:2
11 [I]Lit., *luminary* [a]Is. 60:1f.; Ezek. 43:2; Rev. 15:8; 21:23; 22:5 [b]Rev. 4:3; 21:18, 19 [c]Rev. 4:6
12 [I]Lit., *having* [a]Ezek. 48:31-34 [b]Rev. 21:15, 21, 25; 22:14
14 [a]Heb. 11:10 [b]Acts 1:26
15 [I]Lit., *measure, a gold reed* [a]Ezek. 40:3; Rev. 11:1 [b]Rev. 21:12, 21, 25
16 [I]Lit., *reed* [II]Lit., *twelve thousand stadia;* a stadion was approx. 600 ft.
17 [I]Lit., *one hundred forty-four cubits* [II]Lit., *measure* [a]Deut. 3:11; Rev. 13:18 [b]Rev. 21:9
18 [I]Lit., *pure* [a]Rev. 21:11 [b]Rev. 21:21 [c]Rev. 4:6
19 [a]Ex. 28:17-20; Is. 54:11f.; Ezek. 28:13 [b]Rev. 21:11 [c]Rev. 4:3
20 [a]Rev. 4:3
21 [a]Rev. 21:12, 15, 25 [b]Rev. 17:4

the city was [c]pure gold, like transparent [d]glass.

22 And I saw [a]no [I]temple[3485] in it, for the [b]Lord[2962] God,[2316] the Almighty,[3841] and the [c]Lamb,[721] are its [I]temple.

23 And the city [a]has no need of the sun or of the moon to [psa]shine[5316] upon it, for [b]the glory[1391] of God has illumined it,[5461] and its lamp[3088] *is* the [c]Lamb.

24 And [a]the nations shall walk by its light,[5457] and the [b]kings[935] of the earth[1093] [I]shall bring their glory[1391] into it.

25 And in the daytime (for [a]there shall be no night there) [b]its gates [c]shall never be closed;

26 and [a]they shall bring the glory and the honor of the nations[1484] into it;

27 and [a]nothing unclean[2480] and no one who practices abomination and lying, shall ever [efn]come into it, but only those [I]whose names are [b]written in the Lamb's book[975] of life.[2222]

The River and the Tree of Life

22 And [a]he showed me a [b]river of the [c]water of life,[2222] [I]clear [d]as crystal, coming from the throne of God[2316] and of [II]the Lamb,[721]

2 in the middle of [a]its street. And [b]on either side of the river was [c]the tree of life, [ppt]bearing twelve [I]*kinds of* fruit, [ppt]yielding its fruit every month; and the leaves of the tree were for the healing[2322] of the nations.[1484]

3 And [a]there shall no longer be any curse; and [b]the throne of God and of the Lamb shall be in it, and His bond-servants[1401] shall [c]serve Him;

4 and they shall [a]see His face, and His [b]name *shall be* on their [c]foreheads.

5 And [a]there shall no longer be *any* night; and they [I]shall not have need [b]of the light of a lamp nor the light of the sun, because the Lord God shall illumine[5461] them; and they shall [c]reign[936] forever[165] and ever.

6 And [a]he said to me, "[b]These words[3056] are faithful[4103] and true";[228] and the Lord, the [c]God of the spirits of the prophets,[4396] [d]sent His angel[32] to [ainf]show to His bond-servants the things which must shortly take place.

7 "And behold, [a]I am coming quickly. [b]Blessed[3107] is he who [ppt] [I]heeds [c]the words of the prophecy[4394] of this book."[975]

8 And [a]I, John, am the one who [ppt]heard and [ppt]saw these things. And when I [ao]heard and [ao]saw, [b]I fell down to [ainf]worship[4352] at the feet of the angel who [ppt]showed me these things.

9 And [a]he *said to me, "Do not do that; I am a [b]fellow servant[4889] of yours and of your brethren[80] the prophets[4396] and of those who [I]heed[5083] the words[3056] of [c]this book; worship God."

The Final Message

10 And he *said to me, "[a]Do not [aosi]seal up [b]the words of the prophecy of this book, [c]for the time[2540] is near.[1451]

11 "[a]Let the one who [ppt]does wrong,[91] still do wrong; and let the one who is filthy, still be filthy; and let the one who is righteous, still practice righteousness;[1344] and let the one who is holy,[40] still keep himself holy."

12 "Behold, [a]I am coming quickly, and My [b]reward[3408] *is* with Me, [c]to [ainf]render to every man [I]according to what he has done.[2041]

13 "I am the [a]Alpha[1] and the Omega,[5598] [b]the first[4413] and the last,[2078] [c]the beginning[746] and the end."[5056]

14 Blessed[3107] are those who [a]wash their robes, that they may have the right[1849] to [b]the tree of life,[2222] and may [aosb] [c]enter by the [d]gates into the city.

21 [c]Rev. 21:18 [d]Rev. 4:6
22 [I]Or, *sanctuary* [a]Matt. 24:2; John 4:21 [b]Rev. 1:8 [c]Rev. 5:6; 7:17; 14:4
23 [a]Is. 24:23; 60:19, 20; Rev. 21:25; 22:5 [b]Rev. 21:11 [c]Rev. 5:6; 7:17; 14:4
24 [I]Lit., *bring* [a]Is. 60:3, 5 [b]Ps. 72:10f.; Is. 49:23; 60:16; Rev. 21:26
25 [a]Zech. 14:7; Rev. 21:23; 22:5 [b]Rev. 21:12, 15 [c]Is. 60:11
26 [a]Ps. 72:10f.; Is. 49:23; 60:16
27 [I]Lit., *who are* [a]Is. 52:1; Ezek. 44:9; Zech. 14:21; Rev. 22:14f. [b]Rev. 3:5

1 [I]Lit., *bright* [II]Or, *the Lamb. In the middle of its street, and on either side of the river, was* [a]Rev. 1:1; 21:9; 22:6 [b]Ps. 46:4; Ezek. 47:1 [c]Zech. 14:8; Rev. 7:17; 22:17 [d]Rev. 4:6
2 [I]Or, *crops of fruit* [a]Rev. 21:21 [b]Ezek. 47:12 [c]Gen. 2:9; Rev. 2:7; 22:14, 19
3 [a]Zech. 14:11 [b]Rev. 21:3 [c]Rev. 7:15
4 [a]Ps. 17:15; 42:2; Matt. 5:8 [b]Rev. 14:1 [c]Rev. 7:3
5 [I]Lit., *do not have* [a]Zech. 14:7; Rev. 21:25 [b]Is. 60:19; Rev. 21:23 [c]Dan. 7:18, 27; Matt. 19:28; Rom. 5:17; Rev. 20:4
6 [a]Rev. 1:1; 21:9 [b]Rev. 19:9; 21:5 [c]1Cor. 14:32; Heb. 12:9 [d]Rev. 1:1; 22:16
7 [I]Or, *keeps* [a]Rev. 1:3; 3:3, 11; 16:15; 22:12, 20 [b]Rev. 1:3; 16:15 [c]Rev. 1:11; 22:9, 10, 18f.
8 [a]Rev. 1:1 [b]Rev. 19:10
9 [I]Or, *keep* [a]Rev. 19:10 [b]Rev. 1:1 [c]Rev. 1:11; 22:10, 18f.
10 [a]Dan. 8:26; Rev. 10:4 [b]Rev. 1:11; 22:9, 18f. [c]Rev. 1:3
11 [a]Ezek. 3:27; Dan. 12:10
12 [I]Lit., *as his work is* [a]Rev. 22:7 [b]Is. 40:10; 62:11 [c]Ps. 28:4; Jer. 17:10; Matt. 16:27; Rev. 2:23
13 [a]Rev. 1:8 [b]Is. 44:6; 48:12; Rev. 1:17; 2:8 [c]Rev. 21:6
14 [a]Rev. 7:14 [b]Gen. 2:9; 3:22; Rev. 22:2 [c]Rev. 21:27 [d]Rev. 21:12

🔑 **15** [a]<u>Outside</u>[1854] are the [b]dogs and the <u>sorcerers</u>[5333] and the <u>immoral persons</u>[4205] and the murderers and the <u>idolaters</u>,***[1456]*** and everyone who [ppt]<u>loves</u>***[5368]*** and [ppt]practices lying.

16 "[a]I, Jesus, have sent [b]My <u>angel</u>***[32]*** to [ainf]testify to you these things [I][c]for the <u>churches</u>.***[1577]*** I am [d]the root and the [e]offspring of David, the bright [f]morning star."

17 And the [a]<u>Spirit</u>***[4151]*** and the [b]bride say, "<u>Come</u>."***[2064]*** And let the one who [ppt]hears [aim]say, "Come." And [c]let the one who is [ppt]thirsty [pim]come; let the one who [ppt]<u>wishes</u>***[2309]*** [aim]take the [d]water of life without cost.

18 I testify to everyone who [ppt]hears [a]the <u>words</u>***[3056]*** of the <u>prophecy</u>***[4394]*** of this <u>book</u>:[975] if anyone [aosb] [b]adds to them, God shall add to him [c]the plagues which are [pfpp]written in [d]this book;

19 and if anyone [aosb] [a]takes away from the [b]words of the <u>book</u>***[976]*** of this prophecy, God shall take away his part from [c]the <u>tree</u>***[976]*** of <u>life</u>***[2222]*** and [I]from the <u>holy</u>***[40]*** city, [d]which are [pfpp]written in this book.

20 He who [ppt] [a]testifies to these things says, "Yes, [b]I am coming quickly." <u>Amen</u>.[281] [c]Come, <u>Lord</u>***[2962]*** Jesus.

21 [a]The <u>grace</u>***[5485]*** of the Lord Jesus be with [I]all. Amen.

15 [a]Matt. 8:12; 1Cor. 6:9f.; Gal. 5:19ff.; Rev. 21:8 [b]Deut. 23:18; Matt. 7:6; Phil. 3:2
16 [I]Or, *concerning* [a]Rev. 1:1 [b]Rev. 1:1; 22:6 [c]Rev. 1:4, 11; 3:22 [d]Rev. 5:5 [e]Matt. 1:1 [f]Matt. 2:2; Rev. 2:28
17 [a]Rev. 2:7; 14:13 [b]Rev. 21:2, 9 [c]Is. 55:1; Rev. 21:6 [d]Rev. 7:17; 22:1
18 [a]Rev. 22:7 [b]Deut. 4:2; 12:32; Prov. 30:6 [c]Rev. 15:6-16:21 [d]Rev. 22:7
19 [I]Lit., *out of* [a]Deut. 4:2; 12:32; Prov. 30:6 [b]Rev. 22:7 [c]Rev. 22:2 [d]Rev. 21:10-22:5
20 [a]Rev. 1:2 [b]Rev. 22:7 [c]1Cor. 16:22
21 [I]Some ancient mss. read *the saints* [a]Rom. 16:20

🔑 **22:15** See note on Gal. 3:22.

GRAMMATICAL CODES TO THE GRAMMATICAL NOTATIONS

The grammatical codes, which appear in the New Testament text of this Bible, explain structures in simple terms which, while common in Greek, are difficult or impossible to convey in any English translation. The small codes at the upper left of words in the text refer to the grammatical terms listed alphabetically below. In parenthesis after each term are numbers referring to one or more of the grammatical notations. For example, the aorist tense, *ao,* is explained by notation number 9, while the future middle, *fm,* is explained by notation 21 (future tense) and notation 28 (middle voice).

aid . . . . . .articular infinitive with *dia* **(10)**

aie . . . . . .articular infinitive with *en* **(12)**

aies . . . . .articular infinitive with *eis* **(11)**

aifp . . . . .aorist infinitive passive **(9,25,33)**

aim . . . . .aorist imperative **(7)**

aime . . . .articular infinitive with *meta* **(13)**

ainf . . . . .aorist infinitive **(5,25)**

aip . . . . . .articular infinitive with *pro* **(14)**

aipp . . . . .aorist imperative passive **(4,33)**

aipr . . . . .articular infinitive with *pros* **(15)**

ajn . . . . . .adjectival noun **(2)**

an . . . . . .anarthrous **(3)**

ao . . . . . .aorist **(9)**

aom . . . . .aorist middle **(9,28)**

aop . . . . .aorist passive **(9,33)**

aosb . . . .aorist subjunctive **(7,43)**

aosi . . . . .aorist subjunctive used as an imperative **(8)**

apt . . . . . .aorist participle **(6,32)**

aptp . . . .aorist participle passive **(6,32,33)**

art . . . . . .article (definite) **(17)**

asba . . . .aorist subjunctive active **(7,43,1)**

asbm . . .aorist subjunctive middle **(7,-43,28)**

asbp . . . .aorist subjunctive passive **(7,-43,33)**

cd . . . . . .comparative degree **(16)**

efn . . . . . .emphatic future negative **(18)**

epn . . . . .emphatic personal pronoun **(19)**

f . . . . .feminine gender **(20)**

finf . . . . . .future infinitive **(21,25)**

fm . . . . . .future middle **(21,28)**

fp . . . . . . .future passive **(21,33)**

ft . . . . . . .future tense **(21)**

gc . . . . . .genitive case **(22)**

infg . . . . .infinitive with genitive article **(26)**

ipf . . . . . .imperfect **(23)**

m . . . . . . .masculine gender **(27)**

n . . . . . . .neuter gender **(29)**

nn . . . . . .noun **(30)**

opt . . . . . .optative mood **(31)**

pf . . . . . . .perfect tense **(34)**

pfi . . . . . .perfect indicative **(34,24)**

pfin . . . . .perfect infinitive **(34,25)**

pfip . . . . .perfect indicative passive **(34,-24,33)**

pfp . . . . . .perfect participle **(34,32)**

pfpp . . . .perfect passive participle **(34,-33,32)**

pim . . . . .present imperative **(37)**

pin . . . . . .present indicative **(41,24)**

pinf . . . . .present infinitive **(38,25)**

pinp . . . .present indicative passive **(41,24,33)**

pip . . . . . .present infinitive passive **(38,-25,33)**

pl . . . . . . .plural **(36)**

plpf . . . . .pluperfect **(35)**

pp . . . . . .present passive **(41,33)**

ppp . . . . .present passive participle **(39,33,32)**

ppt . . . . . .present participle **(39)**

pred . . . .predicate **(44)**

psa . . . . .present subjunctive active **(40,1)**

psmp . . .present subjunctive middle passive **(40,28,33)**

sg . . . . . .singular **(42)**

GRAMMATICAL NOTATIONS

DEFINITIONS OF THE GRAMMATICAL CATEGORIES

1. The *Active Voice* represents the action as accomplished by the subject of the verb. In Greek it is to be distinguished from the *Middle* **(28)** and *Passive* **(33)** voices. Examples: he came, they see, you have believed.

2. An *Adjectival Noun* **(ajn)** is an adjective used as a noun. Example: *makarioi,* "blessed," in the Beatitudes.

3. *Anarthrous* **(an)** refers to a word or group of words which appear without the definite article, "the." Greek has no indefinite article, "a" or "an," as in English. Sometimes it is best to translate an anarthrous word by supplying "a" or "an" before it, and for reasons of English style, "the" is even appropriate in some cases. At other times, supplying an article would be incorrect. Example: It is the difference between "God is *a* Spirit" and "God is Spirit" (Jn. 4:24). See also Definite *Article* **(17)**.

4. The *Aorist Imperative* **(aim)** means a command for doing something in the future that is a simple action. This is contrasted with the present imperative, which involves a command for a continuous or repetitive action.

5. The *Aorist Infinitive* **(ainf)** refers to simple action and not the linear action represented by the present infinitive. Examples: *elpizō,* "I hope," *grapsai* (aorist infinitive of *graphō*) *epistolēn humin* would be translated, "I hope to write a letter to you." It does not signify the time of action. See also *Infinitive* **(25)**.

6. The *Aorist Participle* **(apt)** expresses simple action, as opposed to the continuous action of the *Present Participle* **(39)**. It does not in itself indicate the time of the action. However, when its relationship to the main verb is temporal, it usually signifies action prior to that of the main verb. Example: "He took some bread, and after a blessing (aorist participle) He broke it" (Mk. 14:22). See also *Participle* **(32)**.

7. The *Aorist Subjunctive* **(aosb)** is to be distinguished from the *Present Subjunctive* **(40)** in that it refers to simple, undefined action, while the latter refers to continuous or repeated action. It does not signify the time of the action. See also *Subjunctive Mood* **(43)**.

8. The *Aorist Subjunctive used as an imperative* **(aosi)** usually forbids an action which is not in progress and thus commands that it not be started. Example: *mē,* "not," *eisenegkēs,* "lead," in the aorist subjunctive (Mt. 6:13), indicates that when the Lord taught us to pray that God would not lead us into temptation, God was not already leading us into temptation. For the opposite of this, see *Present Imperative* **(37)**.

9. The *Aorist Tense* **(ao)** is used for simple, undefined action. In the indicative mood the aorist tense usually denotes a simple act occurring in past time. It should be distinguished from the imperfect tense which signifies continuous action in past time. With few exceptions, whenever the aorist tense is used in any mood other than the indicative, the verb does not have any temporal significance. In other words, it refers only to the reality of an event or action.

10. The *Articular Infinitive with the preposition dia,* "because of" **(aid),** is used with the accusative article and denotes cause. Example: *dia,* "for," *to,* neuter accusative of the article, *einai,* the infinitive of *eimi,* "to be," *philos,* "friend" (Lk. 11:8). The expression *dia to einai* is best translated "because he is." The whole construction, therefore, would be rendered "because he is a friend."

11. The *Articular Infinitive with the preposition eis,* "unto" **(aies),** is used with the accusative article and most commonly denotes purpose. Example: *eis,* "unto," *to,* the definite article in the neuter accusative, *thanatōsai,* "to kill," *auton,* "him" (Mk. 14:55) would be translated, "in order to put him (Jesus) to death."

12. The *Articular Infinitive with the preposition en,* "in" **(aie),** is used with the dative article and usually expresses the time at which something occurs. It is usually translated "while" or "when." Example: *en,* "in," *tō,* "the," *hupagein,* "to go," *auton,* "him" (Lk. 8:42). This is best translated, "while he was going" or "when he was going."

13. The *Articular Infinitive with the preposition meta,* "after" **(aime),** is used with the accusative article. Example: *meta,* "after," *to,* the neuter accusative article, *paradothēnai,* "to be delivered," *ton,* "the," *Ioannēn,* "John" (Mk. 1:14) is best translated, "after John was arrested."

14. The *Articular Infinitive with the preposition pro,* "before" **(aip),** is used with the genitive article. Example: *eichon,* "I was having," *pro,* "before," *tou,* the genitive of the neuter *to,* "the," *ton,* "the" in the accusative, *kosmon,* "world" in the accusative, *einai,* the infinitive of *eimi,* "to be," *para,* "with," *soi,* "you" (Jn. 17:5) would be translated, "(the glory which) I was having with you before (*pro*) the world was."

15. The *Articular Infinitive with the preposition pros,* "toward" **(aipr),** is used with the accusative article and usually denotes purpose. Example: *pros,* "toward," *to,* neuter definite article in the accusative, *dunasthai,* "to be able," *humas,* "you" (Eph. 6:11) would be translated, "in order that you may be able."

16. The *Comparative Degree* **(cd)** is used when two items are being compared, as opposed to three or more, when the superlative is used. In New Testament Greek, however, there is a tendency for the degree to move up one step. Hence, the positive degree can be used with the comparative meaning, the comparative with superlative meaning, and the superlative with elative meaning ("very"). Example: *meizōn,* "greater" (comparative degree), *toutōn,* "these," *hē,* "the," *agapē,* "love" (I Cor. 13:13) should be translated "the greatest of these is love," since three items are being compared.

17. The *Definite Article* "the" **(art)** is found in Greek, but there is no indefinite article, "a" or "an," as in English. There are many reasons in Greek why a definite article may or may not be used. And these uses of the article often do not parallel English usage. In Greek its presence or absence is often critical to the understanding of a passage. See also *Anarthrous* **(3).**

18. The *Emphatic Future Negative* **(efn)** is indicated by the negative particles *ou,* "not," and *mē,* "not," as if it were "not, not," a double negative. It is usually used with the aorist subjunctive, but sometimes with the future indicative and indicates strong future negation. Example: *ou,* "not," *mē,* "not," *parelthē,* "will pass away," *hē,* "the," *genea,* "generation," *autē,* "this" (Mt. 24:34) would be translated, "This generation will definitely not pass away."

19. The *Emphatic Personal Pronoun* **(epn)** is used when emphasis is being placed on a person. This is especially useful when the subject of a verb is being emphasized. Since the verb ending in Greek indicates the person and number of the subject, a personal pronoun subject is not usually expressed as a separate word. Hence, when the pronoun is used, it calls special attention to the subject. Example: It is the difference between *legō,* "I say," *humin,* "to you," "I say to you," and the way the passage actually reads, *egō,* emphatic personal pronoun, *legō,* "I say," *humin,* "to you;" i.e., "I say to you" (Mt. 5:22).

20. *Feminine Gender* **(f)** may refer to a female or to a noun which has no relation to gender. Examples: *hē gunē,* "the woman," *hē heortē,* "the feast."

21. The *Future Tense* **(ft)** is concerned with the time of action, not the kind of action, although the future by itself almost always refers to a punctiliar action.

22. The *Genitive case* **(gc)** is used primarily to indicate possession, although it has several other functions. Example of the possessive use: my *mother's* sister, the sister of my mother.

23. The *Imperfect Tense* **(Ipf)** is only used in the indicative mood and refers to continuous or linear action in past time. It is to be distinguished from the aorist indicative, which conceives of an action in past time as simply having taken place. Example: The aorist *eschon* would be translated "I had," but the imperfect *eichon,* "I was having."

24. The *Indicative Mood* makes an assertion of fact and is used with all six Greek tenses.

It is the only mood in which distinctions can regularly be made about the time when an action occurs. Examples: he will go, they had said, she saw.

25. The *Infinitive* is a verbal noun, which has many more uses in Greek than it does in English. However, its most common use is best translated by the English infinitive. Examples: to see, to go, to throw. See also *Articular Infinitive* for some other uses.

26. The *Infinitive with a genitive article* **(infg)** frequently denotes purpose. It has the same meaning as the articular infinitive with *eis* and *pros,* to denote purpose, but it does not have a preposition before it. Example: *zētein,* "seeking," *to,* "the," *paidion,* "child," *tou,* genitive article, *apolesai,* "to destroy," *auto,* "it" (Mt. 2:13) would be translated, "seeking the child to (in order to) destroy him."

27. *Masculine Gender* **(m)** may refer to a male or to a noun which has no relation to gender. Example: *huios,* "son," or *naos,* "temple."

28. The *Middle Voice* represents the subject as acting in some way upon himself or concerning himself. Since English does not have a middle voice, it is usually difficult to render the middle voice into smooth English.

29. *Neuter Gender* **(n)** may refer to a thing or to a noun which, though neuter, refers to a person. Examples: *hieron,* "temple" or *teknon,* "child." Hence, for example, the fact that *pneuma,* "spirit" or "Spirit" is neuter has no bearing on whether or not the Holy Spirit is a person.

30. A *Noun* **(nn)** is the name of anything. Examples: Peter, sister, justice.

31. The *Optative Mood* **(opt)** is rare in New Testament Greek. It is a weaker mood than the subjunctive and usually expresses a wish.

32. The *Participle* is a verbal adjective. It has a wide range of possible meanings, some of which can only be inferred from the context. It is often best translated by the English participle. Examples: having gone, seeing the multitude, receiving the gift.

33. The *Passive Voice* represents the subject as receiving the action of the verb and English usually uses a form of the verb "to be" to express the passive. A passive form may sometimes be translated by an intransitive verb in English. Example: The verb "to burn" in I Cor. 7:9 could either be translated "be burned" or "burn," in the sense of "being inflamed."

34. The *Perfect Tense* **(pf)** represents an action that was completed in the past but has continuing results. It has no exact equivalent in English, but it is usually best translated by using the auxiliary "has" or "have." Example: "It has been written, i.e. It *stands* written."

35. The *Pluperfect Tense* **(plpf)** is like the *Perfect Tense,* except that the existing result of the action is also in past time. Usually the English auxiliary "had" is used when translating a pluperfect. However, it may also be used when translating an aorist.

36. The *Plural* **(pl)** number in New Testament Greek, as in English, refers to two or more items. Example: twelve apostles, two brothers, forty years.

37. The *Present Imperative* **(pim)** is a command to do something in the future and involves continuous or repeated action. When it is negative and prohibits an action, it usually carries with it the implication of stopping an action which has been taking place. For the opposite of this, see *Aorist Subjunctive used as an imperative* **(8).**

38. The *Present Infinitive* **(pinf)** refers to continuous or repeated action, without implying anything about the time of the action. See also *Infinitive* **(25).**

39. The *Present Participle* **(ppt)** expresses continuous or repeated action. It does not in itself indicate the time of the action, but when its relationship to the main verb is temporal, it usually signifies action contemporary with that of the main verb. Example: "While they were eating (present participle), . . . he broke (the bread)" (Mk. 14:22). See also *Participle* **(32).**

40. The *Present Subjunctive Mood* refers to continuous or repeated action, without implying anything about the time of the action. See also *Subjunctive Mood* **(43).**

41. The *Present Tense* in the *Indicative Mood* **(24)** represents contemporaneous action, as opposed to action in the past or the future. It refers only to continuous or repeated action, except in the indicative mood where it may also represent punctiliar action.

42. The *Singular Number* **(sg)** in Greek, as in English, refers to one of something. Examples: one woman, a house, the seventh commandment.

43. The *Subjunctive Mood* makes an assertion about which there is some doubt, uncertainty, or indefiniteness. It is closely related to the future tense, which helps point up the fact that often the uncertainty only arises because the action has not yet occurred. An example of this is the *Emphatic Future Negative* **(18).** A Greek subjunctive cannot always be rendered precisely into good English. Examples: I would have come, had you been here, let us go.

44. The *Predicate* **(pred).** Every sentence has two parts: the subject which names the person or thing uppermost in mind and the predicate which makes an assertion about the subject. The predicate may be a noun: He is *the teacher;* a pronoun: I am *yours;* a predicate adjective: *Theos ēn ho logos,* "God was the word" (Jn. 1:1c), "the word" with the definite article is the subject and "God" is the predicate.

WORD STUDIES

LEXICON TO THE OLD AND NEW TESTAMENTS

EDITED BY SPIROS ZODHIATES, TH.D.

The following Lexical Aids provide easy access to more extended definitions than Strong's dictionary. With this extensive treatment of important biblical words, the reader has in the same volume with the Bible text, information normally found only in Hebrew and Greek lexicons, word studies and commentaries.

LEXICAL AIDS TO THE OLD TESTAMENT

1. 'Âb; father, begetter, parent; progenitor, forefather, ancestor (generally used for any senior male relative); an originator, creator, inventor (Gen. 10:21; Job 38:28; Isa. 63:16; 64:8; Jer. 2:27; 3:19; Mal. 2:10); a benefactor or guardian (Job 29:16; Isa. 9:6; 22:21); a head, chief, or ruler (often applied to kings, prophets, and priests); lord, master, teacher; advisor, counsellor (the Messiah is called the Everlasting Father in Isa. 9:6). In Gen. 45:8 Joseph is called a "father" to Pharaoh, i.e., counsellor. The Heb. expression, *'bêth* (house) *'âb* (of father) may be rendered "family." The word occurs about 1,200 times in the Heb. O.T. Most occurrences refer to a literal father, but may denote any man who occupies a similar position, e.g., grandfather, a protector, governor, or one in authority. It is personified as the grave in Job 17:14. By extension the word *'âb* can refer to a more remote ancestor (Ex. 10:6), the founder of a tribal unit (Deut. 26:5) or clan (I Chr. 2:24,42). Metaphorically, *'âb* can refer to the founder of a group or guild (Gen. 4:21). God (Jehovah) is the Father of Israel (Deut. 32:18; Ps. 68:5; Isa. 63:16; Jer. 31:20; Hos. 11:1). David appealed to God as his Father (II Sam. 7:12-14), but this has Messianic implications. Also, see Ps. 2:7 as it relates to Acts 13:33. The names Abram and Abraham both contain a portion of this word. (See Gen. 11:26—12:1; 17:1,3,5). Abraham is the father of the faithful (see Rom. 4:11,13,16; Gal. 3:7,29). *'âb* can be a title of respect (Judg. 17:10; I Sam. 24:11; II Kgs. 2:12; 6:21; Jer. 3:4). The term, *'âb,* occurs in several phrases throughout the O.T. which show a strong bond of continuity between generations. The idea of sleeping with one's fathers (lying down with them, Gen. 47:30; Deut. 31:16; II Sam. 7:12; and 35 times in I Kgs., II Kgs., and II Chr.) usually refers to kings who died a natural death. The phrase "he was gathered to his people," is similar in meaning, but that is found only in the Pentateuch. "He was gathered to his fathers" appears outside the Pentateuch (Judg. 2:10; II Kgs. 22:20; II Chr. 34:28). Individuals were buried at the family grave. Jehovah is referred to as "the God of the fathers" (Gen. 26:24; 28:13; 31:5,-29,42; Ex. 3:6,15). It stresses the link between one generation and earlier generations.

2. 'Âb; this is the Aramaic equivalent to (1). It occurs nine times in the O.T. (in Ezra and Dan.). As Spanish is similar to its sister language, Portuguese, so Aramaic is a cognate language to Heb. Jesus probably spoke Aramaic as His native tongue. However, according to Lk. 4:14-22, Jesus had the ability to read the ancient Heb. Scriptures. In the time of Jesus, Heb. gradually was becoming only a language of literature. In Mk. 14:36 Jesus cried out with the word "Abba," an endearing term (see Rom. 8:15; Gal. 4:6).

6. 'Âbad; there are more than fifty Heb. words which have been rendered by some syn. of "destroy," "destruction," or "perish." *'âbad* is one of the most important. It is also translated as "escape," "fail," "flee," and "lost," in the K.J.V. It is generally used of persons when it is signifying death, but it implies desolation when used of lands. Its Gr. equivalences are: *apollumi* (622) and *apōleia* (684), and *olethros* (3639). See the lexical comments in the N.T. The name Abaddon (Rev. 9:11) comes from this Heb. word, and Apollyon comes from (630). *'âbad* is used to describe the downfall of nations, the withering away of crops, and the fading away of strength, hope, wisdom, knowledge and wealth. It is applied to the destruction of temples, images, and pictures. It suggests utter defeat (Josh. 7:7), overthrowing a nation (Deut. 28:51), and the taking of a life (Ex. 10:7; Lev. 23:30; Deut. 7:10,20; II Kgs. 10:19). *'Âbad* is associated with *sh^e'ôwl* (7585) in Job 26:6; Prov. 15:11 and *qeber* (6913) in Ps. 88:10-12. *'Âbad* can also mean to wander about aimlessly without orientation, to be lost, whether literally or morally (Ps. 119:176; Jer. 50:6; Ezek. 34:4,16).

7. 'Ăbad; this is the Aramaic equivalent of *'âbad* (6). It is found only within the seven chapters of Aramaic of the O.T. (Dan. 2:12,18,24; 7:11,26; Jer. 10:11).

8. 'Ôbêd; see (6) from which this part, derives. It is found only in Num. 24:20,24.

9. 'Ăbêdâh; see (6) which is the root. It appears in Ex. 22:9; Lev. 6:3,4; and Deut. 22:3 to refer to a physical, misplaced object.

10. 'Ăbaddôh; from the root (6). It is found only once in the O.T. as the kethib (text) in Prov. 27:20, "Abaddon."

11. 'Ăbaddôwn; deriving from the root (6). The word is used only six times in the O.T. and means "the place of destruction." Though it certainly refers to the destruction of the grave, it is also quite possible that it denotes eternal destruction. This word is translated in Rev. 9:11 as the Heb. name of the devil. He "Abaddon."

12. 'Abdân; see the root (6). This occurs only once in the O.T. in Esth. 9:5 and is translated "destruction."

13. 'Obdân; coming from the root (6). Esth. 8:6 is the only occurrence where it is translated "killing and destroying."

14. 'Âbâh; to be willing, desirous, consent, obey. Except for Isa. 1:19 and Job 39:9, it is always accompanied by a negation. Therefore, it is the opp. of *nâdab* (5068), volunteering, *râtsôwn* (7522) which implies a compliance which suits what is fitting, and *yâ'al* (2974) which denotes an exertion of a person's will to do something. *'Âvâh* (183), *yâ'ab* (2968), and *tâ'ab* (8373) are similar. The root, *'abâh* (14), occurs 112 times in the Heb. O.T. Generally speaking, it represents the inclination or disposition which leads toward action, rather than the volition which immediately precedes the action.

47. 'Abbîyr; this is a word which marks strength and excellence, from the root *'âbar* (82), to soar, fly, be strong. *'Abbîyr* occurs only in poetical passages in the O.T. and means mighty (and an epithet of God); strong, valiant, noble, a hero, illustrious, chief, noble. The marginal reading of Ps. 78:25, "bread of angels," is "the bread of the mighty." Compare Gen. 31:42,53 where *pâchad* (6342) is used as a substitute word for God. The Mighty One is God (Jehovah). The word is used to show strength or leadership, the hardness of the heart, stubbornness, and the strength of bulls and horses.

80. 'Âbâq; powder, very fine, light dust which was easily driven by the wind or raised by the running of horses. It is distinguished from *'âphar* (6080) which is thick, heavy dust (Deut. 28:24). Also, compare *dâqaq* (1854), to crush into dust, and *shachaq* (7834), a powder which has been beaten like a pestle, a cloud, the sky. *'Âbâq* (80) occurs in Ex. 9:9; Deut. 28:24; Isa. 5:24; 29:5; Ezek. 26:10; and Nah. 1:3. A fem. deriv. is rendered "powders of the merchant" in Song of Sol. 3:6. This probably refers to spices. *'Âbaq* may originate from *'âbag* (79) which is to wrestle, because ancient wrestlers were accustomed to covering their bodies with dust before commencing (see Gen. 32:24,25).

113. 'Âdôwn; proprietor, master, lord, Lord (exclusively applied to Jehovah God), owner, ruler, commander. The Ugaritic and Akkadian cognate words carry the meaning of "lord," "father," and "mighty." When used to refer to men, it was merely a term of respect. For example, Sara called her husband by this title (Gen. 18:12), and the Apostle Peter in I Pet. 3:6 stated that this was virtuous. The Pharaoh was referred to by this title (Gen. 40:1) and Joseph (Gen. 42:10). Ruth called Boaz by this term before they were married (Ruth 2:13). Hannah referred to Eli with this word (I Sam. 1:15). When used exclusively as a divine name, the form *'âdôwn* appears 439 times. The usual inten.

pl. may refer to the plural of majesty of God. Devout Jews began to substitute this word very early for the proper name of Jehovah (YHWH) when reading the Bible aloud (qere). When the Masoretes inserted vowels later into the consonantal Heb. text, they left the original tetragrammaton (four Heb. consonants YHWH), but added the vowels for *'âdôwn* as a signal for the reader to substitute what they considered to be a more reverent word instead of the actual personal name of God. This phenonemon occurs almost 7,000 times in the printed Heb. Bible. With the exception of the A.S.V. (A.D. 1901) and the Jehovah's Witnesses' New World Translation (Rev. A.D. 1961), both of which use the rendering "Jehovah," most English Bibles translate with the traditional LORD and distinguish that from *'âdôwn* (113) by the use of lower case. The Jerusalem Bible renders the personal name of God with "Yahweh." Mk. 14:61,62 is another example of a euphemism for God. Actually, no one knows precisely how the divine name was pronounced. (See the comments on *kurios* (2962), "Lord," in the lexical section for the N.T.

117. 'Addîyr; there are a variety of translations of this word in the K.J.V.: mighty, nobles, lordly, excellent, mightier, gallant, principal, famous, and worthies. This Heb. adj. means great, powerful, glorious, majestic, mighty, splendid, stately, and distinguished. When used as a noun, it parallels "warriors" (Judg. 5:13), "leaders" (Jer. 30:21), "captains" and "rulers" (II Chr. 23:20), and the "Messiah." It even refers to Jehovah (Isa. 33:21). It can mean a luxurious outer garment, a mantle, or a cloak (Gen. 25:25; Mic. 2:8). It occurs about two dozen times in the O.T., the most notable of which is Ps. 8:1.

119. 'Âdam; this root is translated as "ruddy," "dyed red," and "red" in the K.J.V. in its ten occurrences. It means reddish brown, turning red, to be erubescent. There are several deriv. from this root. *'Âdôm* (122), "rosy;" [1]*ôdem* Strong's (124), "redness," "carnelian," "a red gem," "a ruby;" *'ĕdôm* (123), the name of a condiment which looked reddish, Edom, the name of Jacob's twin brother (Gen. 25:25), the Edomites who were Esau's descendants, which later became Idumea in the N.T. times; *'ădamdâm* (125), to be "reddish;" and *'admônîy* (132), "to have a ruddy (complexion)." The Ugaritic root depicts the application of rouge by nobility after they bathed. Akkadian roots indicate the dark red color of a garment, soil, and blood. Lam. 4:7 describes the color of human skin as being like coral. Nah. 2:3 portrays war shields as scarlet-colored. The word is used to describe wine in a fermented condition (Prov. 23:31). The curtains in the tabernacle were this color (Ex. 25:5). Sinfulness in Isa. 1:18 is as red as crimson, the opp. white (purity). In Genesis, Esau, who desired red pottage more than his birthright (Gen. 25:30; 36:1), had a "red" appearance at birth. His descendents were identified either by the name of Edom (Gen. 36:9) or Esau (Jer. 49:8, 10) or by Seir, the mountain where he settled (II Chr. 20:22,23).

120. 'Âdâm; this noun usually refers to mankind in the collective sense. It is also a proper noun, the first man whom God created. It is translated "persons" in Num. 31:28,30,35,40,46. Sometimes in Heb. it means an indefinite "someone." It generally corresponds to *anthrōpos* (444). See the comments in the N.T. lexical section. It is very similar to *homo* in Latin. There is probably some original connection to the ruddiness of men's complexion; see *'âdam* (119). *'Âdâm* (120) refers to generic man as the image of God, the crown of His creation, distinct from the rest of creation. God created human beings by a special, immediate act. God put Adam and Eve in a position of honor (Gen. 1:28), and had great plans for them. However, even after their fall, *'âdâm* (120) is used of mankind. Murder is viewed as an attack upon the image of God (Gen. 9:6), but the Fall did lower man's position before God (Gen. 6:5,6; 8:21). Jesus, who is identified with mankind and a little lower than the angels (Ps. 8:4-6; Heb. 2:5-10), came to fulfill what Adam failed to do. Jesus was the second Adam who came to redeem us (Rom. 5:12-21). A good modern translation might be "people." This Heb. word occurs more than 500 times in all periods of biblical Heb. Sometimes *'âdâm* (120) identifies a specific group of men (Gen. 11:5; Jer. 47:2). It can refer to any given person, whether male or female (Lev. 13:2). The word is generally used in the Heb. Bible to denote the human race and its characteristic nature in contrast to God in heaven. Sometimes the contr. is between the human species and animals. The expression, "Son of Man," (see Dan. 7:13,14; and several passages in the N.T.) certainly has Messianic overtones, but there is a hint of Jesus' identification with humanity in general. Just as Jesus was simultaneously God and the Son of God, He was, in a parallel manner, man (*anthrōpos*) and the Son of Man. Although Jesus was not the son of any particular individual human father, He was a partaker of our human nature in every sense of the word (Heb. 2:8-10), so that He could truly experience all things that we experience (Heb. 4:14-16), yet without sin. The title "Son of Man" occurs fifty-seven times in Ezekiel and once in Dan. 8:17. Jesus became a part of the great family of man by participating in a human body. Another Heb. word, *'îysh* (376), is also translated "man." Essentially *'îysh* signifies maleness in contradistinction to the female gender. The first occurrence is in Gen. 2:24: "For this cause a man shall leave his father and his mother, and shall cleave to his wife." The Gr. word *anēr* (435) usually translates the term in the Septuagint. See the notes in the N.T. lexical section. Another term, *'ĕnâsh* (606), is the usual generic word for "man" in biblical Aramaic. It has the connotation of weakness. In a few places this word has no moral overtones and is exactly parallel to the Heb. *'âdâm*. Another word which is translated "man" is *geber* (1397). It bears the connotation of strength, and sometimes functions as a syn. for *'îysh* (376). Finally, *bâchûwr* (970) is a "young man." This word indicates a vigorous, virile, unmarried man who could be conscripted for the army.

122. 'Âdôm; see note under 119.

125. 'Âdamdâm; see note under 119.

127. 'Âdâmâh; this Heb. word is translated as "earth," "ground," "land," and "country" in the K.J.V. It is clearly derived from an underlying root. See 119 and 120 for further discussion. *'Ădâmâh* (127) refers to the soil, agriculture, fruit, produce, region, and even the entire earth. It is humus, arable land. It is a proper noun, a town in the Valley of Siddim (Josh. 19:36). There are 224 occurrences in the Heb. O.T. *'Ădâmâh* supports water and plants (Gen. 1:25; 2:6). The body of the first man, Adam, was formed from *'ădâmâh* (Gen. 2:7,9), a play on the words in Heb. *'Ădâmâh* is cultivated soil owned by a specific group of people, a land (Deut. 26:15). It can refer to the actual soil itself (II Kgs. 5:17). Moses stood upon holy ground (Ex. 3:5), a generic sense. Sometimes it has the nuance of property or possessed land (Ps. 49:11; Zech. 2:12). *'Adâmâh* is probably not used in a political sense. Another word, *'erets* (776), frequently translated as "earth" and "land," is quite similar but distinguishable. *'Erets* refers more to the whole surface of this planet which we call Earth and the political divisions upon it. Sometimes it is contrasted with the ocean. However, *'erets* comes very close to the meaning of "ground" in Gen. 1:26. *Chelqâh* (2513) denotes more a parcel of ground, a field (II Sam. 23:12). *Chârîysh* (2758) is ground for tillage (I Sam. 8:12). *Nîyr* (5215) is freshly plowed land, fallow ground (Jer. 4:3; Hos. 10:12). *'Âphâr* (6083) is the loose dust which lies at the surface of the soil (Job 14:8). *Sâdeh* (7704) is a field (Josh. 24:32; I Sam. 14:25).

132. 'Admônîy; see notes in 119.

136. 'Ădônây; this pl. noun is a form of 120, which see. Like the pl. form of *'ĕlôhîym* (430), this pl. form is not to be taken literally. When the divine name (YHWH), the tetragrammaton, is adjacent to *'ădônây*, the Jewish scribes usually substituted the vowels for *'ĕlôhîym* instead, i.e., the Lord God.

142. 'Âdar; glorious, honorable, majestic. This verb only occurs in Ex. 15:6,11 and Isa. 42:21. There are twelve other syn. in the Heb. O.T., the most notable of which is *kâbad* (3513), which see. *'Âdar* essentially connotes that which is superior to something else.

148. 'Ădargâzêr; this word occurs only in Dan. 3:2,3, an Aramaic section of Scripture. It is a loanword from Persian meaning "officers of the court at Babylon." The nature of their office is unknown.

157. 'Âhab; love, desire, delight, like, be fond of, covet, be beloved, amiable, be a passionate lover or paramour. It implies an ardent and vehement inclination of the mind and a tenderness of affection at the same time. *'Âhab* has the extensive sense of the English word "love." *'Âhab* is often used to describe the unspeakable love and tender mercies of God in the covenant relationship with His people. This word appears in all periods of Heb., about 250 times in the Heb. Bible. It denotes a strong emotional attachment for and a desire to possess or be in the presence of the object of love. It can be sexual within God's laws of marriage (Gen. 24:67), or illicit eroticism (Gen. 34:3), and pure lust (II Sam. 13:1). Jacob truly loved Rachel before they were sexually one in marriage (Gen. 29:30). Rarely does *'âhab* refer to lovemaking (I Kgs. 11:1; Jer. 2:25; Hos. 3:1). Usually *yâda'* (3045), "to know (sexually)" or *shâkab* (7901), "to lie down with (for copulation)," perform this function. *'Âhab* is used to describe the close attachment between parents and children (Gen. 22:2; 37:3; Ex. 21:5), even relationships by marriage (Ruth 4:15), also represented by the word *râcham* (7355). One special use of *'âhab* is the close ties of friendship (Lev. 19:18,34; Deut. 10:19; I Sam. 18:1). "Hiram had always been a friend of David" in a political sense of loyalty (I Kgs. 5:1). Nowhere in the O.T. are children to "love" their parents. Instead, they are instructed to honor, revere, and obey them! Things were loved in the O.T.: savory meat (Gen. 27:4), oil (Prov. 21:17), silver (Ecc. 5:9), gifts (Isa. 1:23), God's Law (Ps. 119), evil (Ps. 52:3), good (Amos 5:15), truth and peace (Zech. 8:19), salvation (Ps. 40:16), wisdom (Prov. 29:3), vanity (Ps. 4:2), cursing (Ps. 109:17), a false oath (Zech. 8:17) and even death (Prov. 8:36). But, above all else, Jesus instructed us to *'âhab* (love) God more than anything or anyone else (Deut. 6:5), which Jesus indicated was one of the two main pillars upon which the entire O.T. rested (Mt. 22:33-40). God certainly loved His people (Deut. 4:37; Isa. 43:4; Mal. 1:2). The Gr. counterpart is *agapē* (26) and *agapaō* (25) found in Jn. 3:16. See the comments in the N.T. lexical section. When this root is used as a part, it is often translated as "friend." Abraham was the "friend" of God (II Chr. 20:7; see Js. 2:23). The Piel (inten.) part. carries the unfortunate connotation of prostitution (Jer. 22:20,22; 30:14; Lam. 1:19; Ezek. 16:33,36,37; Hos. 2:7,9,12). Other Heb. syn. are: *dôwd* (1730), used only in the pl. from a root meaning "to boil," a lover, friend, uncle; *châbab* (2245), cherish (as in the bosom), protect (Deut. 33:3); *machmâd* (4261), what is the object of desire, lovely, a pleasant thing; *cheçed* (2617), kindness, mercy, lovingkindness; *châshaq* (2836), to connect or join together, a clinging love; *tôwb* (2896), good, loving; *y^edîyd* (3039), beloved; *'âgab* (5689), to love (sensually), usually of impure love; *râcham* (7355), to be tender, to have compassion; and *rêa'* (7453), friend, companion, lover. The Septuagint always uses *agapaō* (25) instead of *phileō* (5368) where God's love is mentioned. See the note on *phileō* in the N.T. lexical section. In fact, *agapē* made its first appearance in the Septuagint and was generally unknown to early Classical Greek authors. It is used in the N.T. to designate the essential nature of God, His regard for mankind, and also the most marked characteristic of the Divine life as manifested in Christ and in Christians. The Gr. word *erōs* is only used in the Septuagint in Prov. 7:18 and 30:16. It is not used in the N.T. at all.

158. 'Ahab; this mas. pl. noun occurs only twice in the Heb. O.T. at Prov. 5:19 and Hos. 8:9. The passage in Proverbs carries a good flavor, "lovely doe," but the one in Hosea is used pejoritively, "hired lovers." The Jerusalem Bible translates Prov. 5:19 as "fair." The Berkeley Version translates Hos. 8:9 as "love-gifts." For more information see 157.

159. 'Ôhab; a mas. pl. noun parallel to "shame" and "Baal." It has illicit overtones in Prov. 7:18. The Jerusalem Bible uses the word "delight" in Prov. 7:18. See its root in 157.

160. 'Ahăbâh; love, beloved. Heb. abstract nouns are typically fem. in gender. Proverbs uses *'ahăbâh* in its most abstract form: "Love covers all transgressions" (Prov. 10:12; cf. Js. 5:20). See also Ecc. 9:1,6. It is a key word in Song of Sol. (2:4,5; 5:8; 8:6,7). The Prophets were fond of the word (Jer. 31:3; Hos. 11:4; Mic. 6:8). This noun appears fifty-five times.

168. 'Ôhel; the K.J.V. translates this word with the following words: "tent," "tabernacle," "covering," and "dwelling place." It is also the name of a man (I Chr. 3:20). It can also be a hut, habitation, or family. This mas. noun occurs 340 times and is used for the animal skin or hair of a goat (Song of Sol. 1:5), a dwelling of nomadic people (Gen. 4:20; 13:5; 18:6; 25:27), shepherds (Jer. 6:3), women (Gen. 31:33; Judg. 4:17 cf. Isa. 54:2), warriors (I Sam. 17:54; Jer. 37:10), and cattle (II Chr. 14:14). It is also used for the bridal tent (II Sam. 16:22). It means a private home in Judg. 19:9; I Kgs. 8:66; 12:16; Ps. 91:10, including the palace of David (Isa. 16:5), long after the Israelites stopped using tents. The word is used figuratively for the people of Edom, Qedar, Judah, Cushan and others. It is a figure for Jerusalem in Lam. 2:4. God's tabernacle was basically a tent, comprised of two layers of cloth and two layers of animal skins which were stretched over a wooden framework (Ex. 26:7,14,15). The expression *'ohel mo'ed* is often translated as "tent of meeting" (Ex. 33:7-11); it refers to the tabernacle. This phrase occurs 139 times, mostly in Exodus, Leviticus, and Numbers. It was the appointed place where God's presence was felt most. God's people were reassured that He was among them. Another phrase, "tent of the testimony" (*'ôhel 'êdûwth*) is used in several places (e.g., Num. 9:15; 17:7,8) to denote the tabernacle also. *Mishkân* (4908) is evidently the tabernacle structure as a whole, and it is regarded as the shekinah, the dwelling-place of God. *'Ôhel* was the awning of goat's hair. Both *'ôhel* and *mishkân* (4908) occur together in Ex. 26:7. *'Ôhel* derives from the verb *'âhal* (167) which means "to pitch a tent" (Gen. 13:12,18; Isa. 13:20). A similar word is *chânah* (2583), "to bend or stoop," as in pitching a tent (Gen. 26:17; 33:18; Num. 1:52; 9:17; Deut. 1:33). It is the root for camp or encampment (Num. 13:19; I Sam. 17:53; II Kgs. 7:16; II Chr. 31:2; Zech. 14:15). In one passage, II Sam. 11:11, the Heb. word *çukkâh* (5521) was used by David to describe the tents in which Israel, Judah, and the ark resided. Normally, this is the word for "booths," as the "Feast of Booths (Tabernacles)." Finally, *qubbâh* (6898) is a pavilion (as a domed cavity). It was probably a vaulted pleasure-tent, devoted to the impure worship of Baal (Num. 25:8).

178. 'Ôwb; there are sixteen occurrences of this word in the K.J.V.; it is translated as "familiar spirit(s)." This is necromancy, a spirit of divination, and a conjuring ghost. A necromancer, or sorcerer, is one who calls up spirits from the abyss to foretell future events, to practice the art of necromancy. It has a secondary meaning of animal skins used to contain wine, flexible bottles, leather bags. Ventriloquists were thought to speak from the hollow in their bellies. Modern translations have: "medium," "ghost," "spirit," "spirit of the dead" and "wizard." The N.E.B. has "bellows" at Job 32:19. The Israelites were commanded by God to stay away from the occult (Lev. 19:31; 20:27; Deut. 18:10,11; Ezek. 21:21). The famous "witch" of Endor was an *'ôwb* (I Sam. 28). This event could have come from God without involving any actual transportation of Samuel from the dead. Note that the woman herself was amazed. There may be no relationship whatever between the two meanings of *'ôwb;* they may merely be homonymous. Other Heb. words for diviners and divination are: *'ittî* (from *'âtam,* 331); *'ânan* (6049); *'ashshâph* (825); *chartôm* (2748); *yidd^e'* *ônîy* (3049); *kashshâph* (3786); *nâchash* (5172) and *qâçam* (7080). A *ba'ălâh* (1172) is a mistress of a familiar spirit (I Sam. 28:7).

183. 'Âvâh; a natural desire for food, eager desire, to covet, long, wait longinaly, wish, sigh, crave, want, be greedy, prefer, lust after. The subject noun of this verb is often *nephesh* (5315), "soul," "self," "appetite." The most notable reference is one of the Ten Commandments (Deut. 5:21). *Châmad* (2530) is the parallel in Ex. 20:17. There are at least sixteen syn. with the basic meaning of "desire."

205. 'Âven; this is a major Heb. word for sin: vanity, breath, vainness, nothingness, falseness, falsehood, idol, idolatry, sin, wickedness, sorrow, distress, hardship, toil. The K.J.V. translates the word with: iniquity, wicked, sorrow, vanity, wickedness, mourning, mourners, affliction, false, unjust. There are two aspects to the primary meaning of the word: (a) emphasis upon trouble which moves onward to wickedness; (b) emptiness which results in idolatry. The word is used eighty-five times. "Misfortune" comes close to encompassing many of the meanings above. It is the hard way of life of those who are living without God (Isa. 32:6). Some sinners enjoy making a difficult life harder (Job 15:35; Ps. 7:14). The word focuses upon the planning and expression of deception, pointing more to the consequences of sin. It is the Heb. word which is most frequently rendered "iniquity," though there are six other Heb. words. The connection of *'âven* with idolatry is patiently obvious; an idol is a vacuous thing. It is a proper name in Ezek. 30:17; Hos. 10:8; and Amos 1:5. The most prominent syn. for sin are: *châtâ'* (2398), to miss the mark; *shâgâh* (7686), to err; *pesha'* (6588), rebellion, transgression; *'âvâh* (5753), to be bent or crooked; *'âmâl* (5999), travail, the burdensome, toilsome aspect of sin; *'âval* (5765), to distort, iniquity; *'âbar* (5674), to cross over, transgress; *ra'* (7451), evil, wickedness, ruin, bad, harm; *râshâ'* (7563), wicked, wrong, bad, condemned, guilty; *mâ'al* (4603), treachery, wrongdoing as a breach of trust, trespass, acting covertly, transgression; *ḇâgad* (898), deal deceitfully, as under a cloak; *'âsham* (817), a mistake, trespass, fault, guilt.

212. 'Ôwphân; wheel. The early wheels were made from wooden planks joined together by pegs. The Egyptians began using much lighter wheels about B.C. 1500. The horses could pull them much faster for military advantage. Prov. 25:11 says, "A word spoken in right circumstances." Literally, it says, "spoken upon his wheels." Potters used two stones in the shape of wheels, *'ôben* (70). A rolling thing, a well apparatus, and the wheel of a chariot is *galgal* (1534), from which Galilee was derived. The regular beat of the revolutions of a wheel is *pa'am* (6471), as in Judg. 5:28.

216. 'Ôwr; except for one instance in Job 36:32, this is a mas. noun meaning light, brightness, lightning, luminary, daylight, sunlight, illumination, enlightenment, happiness, cheerfulness. Light is an important concept in the entire Bible, whether literal or metaphorical. God is closely associated with it; He created it (Gen. 1:3). Light is often used as an indicator of time, particularly dawn (Gen. 44:3; Judg. 16:2; Neh. 8:3), though there is a distinction between daybreak and daylight (Judg. 19:26; Isa. 60:1-3). Light was distinct from the luminaries in space (Gen. 1:3). The sun is the "greater light" and the moon is the "lesser light" (Gen. 1:16; Ps. 136:7). Then there are the "stars of light" (Ps. 148:3). Like a clock they regulate the seasons (Gen. 1:14; Ps. 104:19; Jer. 31:35,36). God's pillar of fire displayed God's glory when the sons of Israel wandered in the wilderness (Ex. 13:21; Job 36:32; Ps. 77:18; 97:4; 105:39). The sacred lampstand was in the tabernacle (Num. 4:9,16; 8:2). The opp. is "walk in darkness" (Isa. 9:2). *'Ôwr* signifies life in contrast to death (Ps. 56:13; 89:15; Prov. 16:15; Mic. 7:8). *'Ôwr* is closely related to life and happiness, not walking in the valley of the shadow of death (Ps. 23:4). Note the famous priestly blessing of Num. 6:24, "The Lord make His face shine upon you." See the formula in Ps. 31:16; 67:1; 80:3,7,19; 119:135. Light can also symbolize prosperity (Job 29:3; Ps. 36:9; Isa. 58:8), being born (Job 3:16), or just being alive (Job 33:30; Ps. 56:13). A prominent metaphorical meaning is instruction (Ps. 19:8; 119:105,130; Prov. 6:23; Ecc. 8:1). Generally speaking, darkness is associated with death, failure, suffering, folly, and sin. Light is associated with life, salvation, prosperity, wisdom, and justice. This noun occurs 120 times in the Heb. O.T.

217. 'Uwr; this mas. noun occurs thirteen times. It is derived from the verb *'ôwr* (215). It means fire, the light of fire, a flame, enlightenment, revelation. It is particularly known for the expression, "Urim and Thummim," a part of the high priest's breastplate (Ex. 28:30; Lev. 8:8; Num. 27:21), "lights and perfections." The Gr. Septuagint translates these words with "illumination" and "truth." No one knows exactly how the Urim and Thummim were consulted. The breastpiece with its Urim must have perished in the Babylonian exile (Ezra 2:63).

219. 'Ôwrâh; deriving from *'ôwr* (216), this fem. noun means "light" in Ps. 139:12, "prosperity" or "joy" in Esth. 8:16, "dew of the dawn" in Isa. 26:19, and "herbs" in II Kgs. 4:39.

226. 'Ôwth; sign, mark, token, badge, standard, monument, memorial, warning, omen, prodigy, symbol, miracle, miraculous sign, proof. There are approximately eighty occurrences of *'ôwth* in the Heb. O.T. Most of them have the flavor of the miraculous. Many of them are used in the same context with *môwphêth* (4159), "wonder" (Ex. 7:3; Deut. 4:34; 6:22; 7:19; 26:8; Neh. 9:10; Isa. 20:3). *'Ôwth* is an indicator or signal of something. It may be marking time (Gen. 1:14), pointing to God's promise in the rainbow (Gen. 9:12,13,17), His covenant as confirmed by circumcision (Gen. 17:11), to remember an event (Num. 16:38; Josh. 4:6; Isa. 19:20), or predict the future (I Sam. 14:10; Isa. 55:13). A prophet may be known by the evidence (Deut. 13:1ff.; Jer. 44:29). The Gr. word *sēmeion* (4592) was the corresponding term. See the comments in the N.T. lexical section. *'Ôwth* showed or confirmed anything in the past, present or future. It excited attention or consideration. It distinguished one thing from another. It was an inducement to believe what was affirmed, professed, or promised. It was the acid test of prophecy. Other syn. are *âbâr* (1697), "word," (Ps. 105:27), *nêc* (5251), "banner, (Num. 26:10), *mas'êth* (4864), "a raising," *tsîyûwn* (6725), "a guiding pillar," and *r^esham* (7560), in Aramaic, "write."

227. 'Âz; then, at that time, therefore, from that time, of old, before, formerly, heretofore, since, whence. This demonstrative adv. occurs (with prefix) about 130 times. As a temporal adv., it can refer to either the past or the present (Ex. 15:1; Num. 21:17; Josh. 10:12; I Kgs. 8:1). It also occurs in future contexts (Isa. 35:5; 60:5). It can express strict logical sequence (Isa. 58:14).

238. 'Âzan; to turn, lend an ear to, listen, attend to, ponder, give ear to, harken, to answer (a prayer), to obey. Closely related to *'ôzen* (241), "ear," *'âzan* means "to pay attention." It occurs mostly in the poetic books of the Heb. O.T. as a parallel to the syn. *shâma'* (8085). Even where it appears in non-poetic books, it occurs in poetic passages within those books (Gen. 4:23; Deut. 32:1; Judg. 5:3). Most of the forty-two occurrences are commands.

241. 'Ôzen; this mas. noun comes from *'âzan* (238). It refers to the ear, the organ of hearing. It occurs almost 200 times and is applied most often to men, though it can refer to the ears of a dog (Prov. 26:17) or sheep (Amos 3:12). God has ears, because He made them (Ps. 94:9). However, idols made by men do not hear (Ps. 115:6; 135:17). In the Heb. O.T. the ear often represents hearing and obedience. Therefore, it is frequently used in a symbolic way. A permanent slave's ear was pierced with an awl (Ex. 21:6; Deut. 15:17; Ps. 40:6). Sacrificial blood was put upon the lobes of the right ears of the priesthood (Lev. 8:23,24; Ex. 29:20). One who was cleansed from leprosy in a purification ceremony had blood and olive oil put upon his right ear. God pleads for Israel to heed His warnings (Prov. 22:17; Jer. 13:15; Hos. 5:1). There are several reactions of the ears: they may ring or tingle from a shocking message (I Sam. 3:11; II Kgs. 21:12; Jer. 19:3). They may be stopped up from heaviness (Zech. 7:11,12) or judicial deafness (Isa. 6:10). People could be informed (Ezek. 24:26), learn to pay attention (Ps. 10:17), and listen closely (Ps. 78:1). God did not want "closed" ears (Jer. 6:10). "To uncover the ear" means to disclose important information (Ruth 4:4; I Sam. 9:15; II Sam. 7:27).

251. 'Âch; this mas. noun means: a brother, near relation, a relative, cousin, a fellow countryman, fellow-man, friend. It does not matter whether the relationship exists from the same father, or mother, or both, it is a general relationship whether by blood or affinity. *'Âch* is any person or thing which is similar to another. It is generally a term of affection. The word occurs 630 times in the Heb. O.T. From the start, every man is expected to be his brother's keeper (Gen. 4:9). David loved Jonathan so much that he was almost like a physical brother to him (II Sam. 1:26). It has the meaning of companion or colleague (II Kgs. 9:2), or ally (Gen. 19:6,7; Num. 20:14; I Kgs. 9:13). Sometimes nations achieve the status of "brother" (Amos 1:11; Obad. 10,12). Finally, it can merely be a polite term of address (Gen. 29:4; Judg. 19:23). Dr. E. A. Speiser explains that the wives of Abraham and Isaac were "sisters" in a legal sense. This was similar to a custom in Nuzi where a high-born wife was also adopted as a sister, thus giving her greater legal status. However, this custom was not recognized in Egypt and Gerar. Syn. are: *'ĕnôwsh* (582), (Gen. 13:8); *dôwd* (1730), (Num. 36:11; II Kgs. 24:17); *yâbâm* (2993), "to marry as the nearest relative," (Deut. 25:5-10; Gen. 38:7-9), levirate marriage, to keep a dead brother's lineage alive; *réa'* (7453), a companion, acquaintance, friend (Deut. 24:10).

252. 'Ach; this is the Aramaic (Chaldean) equivalent to (252). It occurs only in Ezra 7:18.

264. 'Achăvâh; deriving from *'âch* (251), it means brotherhood or fraternity. Its lone occurrence is in Zech. 11:14.

269. 'Achôwth; this word is derived from the same root as "brother" (251) with the same general range of meaning. It means sister (properly a sister of full blood, i.e., both from the same father and mother), half-sister, female relation, kinswoman, countrywoman, ally, friend, or anything with which we are intimately connected (Prov. 7:4; Job 17:14), a spouse (Song of Sol. 4:9). The word occurs 114 times. *Yᵉbêmeth* (2994) is a sister-in-law, a brother's wife or the wife of a husband's brother (Ruth 1:15). *Dôwdâh* (1733) is an aunt, father's sister (Ex. 6:20).

272. 'Ăchuzzâh; this fem. noun comes from the verb *'âchaz* (270). It means possession, property, occupation, tenure. It occurs sixty-six times, mostly in Genesis to Joshua and Ezekiel. It usually refers to the land of Canaan which had been promised to Abraham (Gen. 17:8). Abraham's down payment was his purchase of the Cave of Machpelah (Gen. 23:4,9,20; 49:30; 50:13) for burying Sarah. "The land of the Lord's Possession" is distinguished from the portions of Reuben, Gad, and Manasseh (Josh. 22:9,19). In Lev. 25:45,46 human beings are called "property." So, *'ăchuzzâh* is primarily a legal term, normally referring to land, especially family holdings which were passed down to the heirs. The Lord Himself was the property of the Levites (Ezek. 44:28), not physical land.

319. 'Achărîyth; this fem. noun comes from *'achar* (310). The K.J.V. translates it as: latter, end, posterity, reward, latter end, last end, remnant, residue, uttermost parts. *'Achărîyth* refers to the latter time, the latter days, the latest part, the future. It is used sixty-one times and has importance theologically. The general meaning is: "after," "later," "behind," "following." The Hebrew way of thinking was like a man rowing a boat; he backs into the future. Therefore, what is "behind" and what is "future" come from the same root *'achar*. It is debatable whether the expression "the end of the days" refers to the general future or to a specific segment of time. Also, scholars differ about whether *'achărîyth* refers to the future life.

324. 'Achashdarpan; there are nine occurrences of this Aramaic noun in the Book of Daniel. It refers to the chief satraps, doorkeepers, the officers of the Persian court, Persian governors. It is a loanword from the Persian language. Persian officers had the civil and military jurisdiction over several smaller provinces, each of which had its own governor. There are fourteen other words in the K.J.V. which are translated as "prince."

328. 'at; the meaning is whisper, low speech, noiseless speaking, sorcerers, necromancers. The K.J.V., A.S.V., and N.A.B. have "charmer." The R.S.V. and A.B. have "sorcerer." The Berkeley translation has "magician." The Jerusalem Bible has "wizard." The New English Bible has "oraclemonger," cf. Ex. 8:7. The general context of Isa. 19:3 lists occultists, but the precise meaning of *'at* is sketchy. Perhaps these individuals made strange sounds while practicing their dark art.

342. 'Êybâh; this is a fem. noun which derives from *'âyab* (340), to be an enemy, to be hostile to, to treat as an enemy, to hate. *'Êybâh* only occurs five times in the Heb. O.T. The most notable passage is the Protoevangelium, the first announcement of the Gospel, in Gen. 3:15. The word describes the friction between males and females as a result of the sin in the Garden of Eden. The other instances are Num. 35:21,22; Ezek. 25:15; 35:5. Basically, it is a state of hostility.

343. 'Êyd; this Heb. mas. noun refers to a calamity, destruction, ruin, or disaster. All twenty-two occurrences of this word appear in poetical sections. The expression "day of calamity" constitutes one-third of the references.

367. 'Êymâh; in all of its occurrences, this fem. noun connotes the concept of "fear." It occurs only once in a metaphorical sense in Jer. 50:38, where it means "idol," evidently in the sense of that which is feared.

376. 'Îysh; this mas. Heb. noun may be related to 582. It means a man, a male (Ex. 35:29), a husband (Gen. 3:6; Jer. 29:26), a mate (Gen. 7:2); a possessor of manliness, a soldier (Isa. 21:9); an inhabitant, a citizen; mankind; a person, a human being (Num. 23:19); someone, anyone (Gen. 13:16); each (Gen. 40:5), every (Jer. 23:35). The word is used more than 2,000 times in the O.T. and usually refers to men seen as individuals rather than indicating mankind, although it can be employed in the more general sense (Ex. 21:12). See 120. The basic idea being conveyed by the word is maleness, as opposed to femaleness, and humanity in contrast to God (Num. 23:19) and animals, although in a rare meaning it can refer to animals (Gen. 7:2). Such expressions as "man of blood" or "man of the earth" are a favorite way in Heb. to attribute a quality to someone. For the female counterpart of *'îysh*, see 802.

410. 'Êl; this mas. Heb. noun emphasizes might; hence, it is used of men (Job 41:25; Ezek. 32:21), angels (Ps. 29:1), pagan gods or idols (Ex. 15:11; Isa. 43:10), mighty (natural objects, Ps. 36:6; 80:10); God (Gen. 46:3; Isa. 42:5), especially as modified by such attributes as holy (Isa. 5:16), compassionate (Ex. 34:6), jealous (Ex. 20:5), living (Josh. 3:10), great (Ps. 77:13); strength, power (Gen. 31:29). In the ancient Near East it was the most widespread word for god. For example, El was the name of the chief Canaanite god and father of Baal. It refers to God in many O.T. proper names, such as Immanuel (Isa. 7:14), Ezekiel (Ezek. 1:3), and Elijah (I Kgs. 17:1). See 430.

422. 'Âlâh; to swear, to make a solemn oath. This Heb. verb is used in expressing solemn oaths among men, and between God and man.

423. 'Âlâh; this noun's basic meaning is for a solemn promise between men (Gen. 24:41; 26:28). For that reason it is also applied to solemn statements of testimony given in court (Lev. 5:1; Prov. 29:24) and before God (Num. 5:21ff.). From this, one can see how it was used to express the very solemn covenant between God and His people (Deut. 29:12) and in particular, the curse for the breaking of this covenant should the people prove to be faithless (Deut. 29:14-21; Isa. 24:6).

426. 'Ělâhh; this Aramaic term corresponds to the Heb. (433) for God or god, which see. The total number of occurrences is eighty-nine in the Bible.

430. 'Ělôhîym; this mas. Heb. noun is pl. in form, but it has both sing. and pl. uses. In a pl. sense it refers to rulers or judges with divine connections (Ex. 21:6); gods (pagan) (Ex. 18:11; Ps. 86:8 and many other O.T. passages); and probably angels (Ps. 8:5; 97:7). In both of the passages where angels is the apparent meaning, it is so translated in the Septuagint. On the former see Heb. 2:7. In the sing. sense it is used of a god, a goddess (I Sam. 5:7; II Kgs. 18:34); a man in a position like a god (Ex. 7:1); God (Deut. 7:9; Ezra 1:3; Isa. 45:18 and many other O.T. passages). With the latter meaning it occurs with several modifiers, such as righteous (Ps. 7:10), living (I Sam. 17:26), holy (Josh. 24:19), and true (II Chr. 15:3). It usually takes a sing. verb, so no implication of any plurality in the divine nature can be inferred from the fact that the word is plural. Scholars are divided on whether *'ělôhîym* has an etymological connection with *'el* (410). There is an apparent relationship between *'ělôhy* and *'ělôwahh* (433), a singular word for god, God, but its exact nature is not clear. Some scholars regard 430 as a deriv. of 433, while others reverse the connection. *'elôhîm* is the most common Heb. word translated God in the O.T.

433. 'Ělôwahh or **'ělôahh;** this mas. sing. Heb. noun means god (pagan) (II Chr. 32:15); God (Deut. 32:15; Job 3:4; Isa. 44:8). It is used fifty-five times in the O.T., forty of which are in Job. Most of the occurrences appear in poetry. Since it occurs only in the sing., some scholars have concluded that it is the implied singular of *'ělôhîym* (430), but the exact relationship between the two words is uncertain. On this see the note on 430.

441. 'Allûwph or **'allûph;** used as an adj., this word has reference to an object which is familiar, gentle, or tame as in Jer. 11:19, "But I was like a gentle lamb." As a noun, this word may mean an ox (as being tame and accustomed to the yoke) or a leader of a family or a ruler of a clan (Gen. 36:15ff.; Ex. 15:15; I Chr. 1:51ff.)

457. 'Ělîyl; this probably comes from a root meaning "to be weak, deficient." It is used primarily to describe vain objects of worship (Isa. 2:8), but may describe anything worthless, empty, or vain (I Chr. 16:26).

488. 'Almân; this adj. means one widowed or forsaken and occurs once in Jer. 51:5 in the sense of Israel abandoned by God, as a widow.

490. 'Almânâh; this fem. noun has only one basic meaning, "widow." God's great concern and care for widows is seen throughout the Scriptures. God hears their cry (Ex. 22:22,24) and He executes justice on their behalf (Deut. 10:18). He is their judge in a special way (Ps. 68:5), treating them with the same tenderness that He shows to the orphans (Ps. 146:9).

502. 'Âlaph; to accustom oneself, to be accustomed, to be familiar; to be tame, gentle, to learn; to join together, to associate. This verb comes from the idea of being accustomed to something or having close association with an object; hence the idea of learning from association.

503. 'Âlaph; to produce thousands, to bring forth or make thousands. This verb, deriving from 502, occurs only once (Ps. 144:13).

505. 'Eleph; this numeral, a fem. noun, is the Heb. word for "one thousand." This word is often used in a figurative sense to represent the extreme, i.e., Ecc. 6:6, an extreme number of years. A notable use of the term is in connection with God. In such contexts the basic idea seems to be "indefinite" or "innumerable."

506. 'Alaph or **'eleph;** this Aramaic word corresponds to 505 and means "thousand." There are only four occurrences (Dan. 5:1 [twice]; 7:10 [twice]).

517. 'Êm; this word always (except once) means "mother." In most occurrences it refers literally to the female parent. At times it is used in a figurative sense. This noun is used to describe Eve as mother of all living beings (Gen. 3:20) and to describe Deborah as a mother in Israel (Judg. 5:7) and even of a worm as mother of Job (Job 17:14). Its occurrence in Ezek. 21:21 is unique and evidently means "the parting (fork) of the road" in the sense of origin (mother) of the road.

523. 'Ummâh; this fem. noun means people or tribe and is only found in the plural.

524. 'Ummâ; this Aramaic word is similar in usage to the Heb. (523) and means "nation." There are eight occurrences (Ezra 4:10; Dan. 3:4,7,29; 4:1; 5:19; 6:25; 7:14).

527. 'Âmôwn; this noun, which occurs only twice, seems to have the meaning of an artificer, one true in hand and skill (Prov. 8:30). In Jer. 52:15, it may simply mean "people" or perhaps "the skilled ones."

529. 'Êmûwn; this term, a deriv. of 539, connotes faithfulness or righteousness. It is applied to nations in Deut. 32:20 and to individuals in Prov. 13:17.

530. 'Ěmûwnâh or **'ěmûnâh;** this fem. noun is derived from *'âman* (539). It means firmness, steadiness (Ex. 17:12), steadfastness (Isa. 33:6); faithfulness, trust, honesty (Ps. 37:3; Prov. 12:17; Isa. 25:1). This word, which is used in the Psalms twenty-two of its forty-nine times in the O.T., has as its key idea faithfulness or certainty. It is especially important in expressing God's faithfulness (Deut. 32:4; Ps. 33:4; 89:49), a key divine attribute in the O.T. Synonyms include *cheçed* (2617) (see their use together in Ps. 98:3), *mishpât* (4941) (see their use together in Jer. 5:1), and *tsedeq* (6664) (used together in parallelism in Isa. 11:5). Hos. 2:19,20 (21,22) employs all four nouns to describe God's covenant faithfulness. *'Âmên* (543), amen, truly, and *'emeth* (571), truth, faithfulness, are two of several words also derived from 539.

539. 'Âman; in a transitive sense to make firm; to confirm (I Kgs. 8:26), to support (II Kgs. 10:1); in an intransitive sense to be firm, to stand firm (Job 39:24); to be enduring; to trust, to believe (Ex. 4:31; Ps. 116:10). Sub. uses include foster-father (Num. 11:12); nurse (Ruth 4:16); pillar (II Kgs. 18:16); adj. uses include reliable, faithful (Deut. 7:9; Jer. 42:5). See *'ěmûwnâ* (530) and *'emeth* (571) for important words based on this verb.

540. 'Âman; corresponding to the Heb. 539, this Aramaic word means to trust or to believe in; to be faithful, to be sure, to believe. It is used only in the Haphel stem. The pass. part. means "trustworthy." There are only three occurrences, all in Daniel (2:45; 6:4,23).

541. 'Âman; this word derives from 3225. It means to take the righthand road or to turn to the right. Its lone occurrence is found in Isa. 30:21.

546. 'Omnâh; this adv., which comes from 539, means truly, verily, or actually. In the two contexts in which the word occurs, the speaker is perhaps seeking to excuse his wrong, therefore "actually" may be the best translation (Gen. 20:12; Josh. 7:20).

548. 'Ămânâh; this noun, deriving from 539, is used to mean a covenant, a firm commitment, or a settled provision. It is used in connection with a firm commitment on the part of the people of Jerusalem to God in Neh. 9:38, and is also applied to a fixed provision for the singers of that day (Neh. 11:23).

551. 'Omnâm; this adv., which comes from 539, means in truth, truly, or indeed.

552. 'Umnâm; this word is always found in interrogative sentences and is usually translated verily or indeed. This word always suggests doubt on the part of the asker: Sarah's doubt of having a child (Gen. 18:13); Balaam's doubt of Balak's power to promote him (Num. 22:37); the Psalmist's doubt that pagan gods judge righteously (Ps. 58:1).

559. 'Âmar; to say, to speak, to utter; to tell, to declare (Ps. 40:10); to name, to mention (Gen. 43:27), to designate (Gen. 22:2; Ex. 32:13); to answer (Jer. 5:19); to call (Isa. 61:6; Jer. 7:32); to admonish; to promise (II Kgs. 8:19; Esth. 4:7); to praise; to say in the heart, to think (Gen. 44:28; Deut. 8:17), to intend, to purpose (Ex. 2:14), to expect (II Sam. 21:16); to command (Num. 15:38; II Sam. 16:11); to boast, to act proudly (Isa. 61:6). This is the major word for "saying" in the O.T., being used 5,280 times. The basic idea is the uttering of some type of spoken word. Of special interest are the eight uses in Gen. 1, where God speaks the world into existence. In Ps. 105:31,34; 107:25 the creative character of God's word in other settings is affirmed. The introductory formula, "Thus says the Lord" and concluding formula, "Says the Lord" occur quite often in the Prophets.

560. 'Âmar; this Aramaic word corresponds to 559 and means to declare, to command, to say, to speak, to tell, to relate. It is used like the Heb. *'amar*. The Heb. *dabar* has no parallel in biblical Aramaic. The verb is often used with *'ănâ* in the idiom "answered and said," a common semitism in the N.T. The total number of occurrences is sixty-six.

561. 'Êmer; this mas. Heb. noun means speech, an utterance, a word (Job 32:12; Num. 24:4); a promise (Ps. 77:9); a decree (Job 20:29); a command (Ps. 68:11; 107:11); a plan, a purpose. The word is derived from *'âmar* (559) and is used nearly fifty times in the O.T., most frequently in Job, Psalms, and Proverbs.

562. 'Ômer; this is the same word as *'êmer* (561), which see.

565. 'Imrâh; this fem. Heb. noun is related to *'êmer* (561) in meaning and means an utterance, speech (Isa. 28:23), a word (Ps. 12:6), song. It is derived from *'âmar* (559). Nineteen of the word's thirty-six uses in the O.T. are in Ps. 119, and it occurs only ten times outside of the Psalms. Except for its use for a prayer in Ps. 17:6, it is always employed in the Psalms of the Word of God. The wide range of attributes of *'imrh* in the sense of the Word of God in Ps. 119 paint a multi-colored picture. In this psalm *dâbâr* (1697) is the other noun which is frequently used of the Word of God.

571. 'Emeth; this fem. Heb. noun means firmness, stability (Isa. 39:8; Jer. 33:6), continuance; faithfulness (of man, Neh. 7:2; of God, Ps. 71:22), sureness (Prov. 11:18; Jer. 2:21); truth (Deut. 22:20; Prov. 14:25; Jer. 9:5); as an adv., truly (Ps. 145:18; Jer. 10:10). It is used 127 times in the O.T. and, being derived from *'âman* (539), has firmness or stability as its basic meaning. In the sense of faithfulness it is used frequently of God and expresses one of His key O.T. attributes. It is the principal Heb. word for truth, the term that quite often renders it in our English translations.

577. 'Ânnâ; this interjection is one of entreaty and is translated "ah, now!" or "ah, I pray!"

582. 'Ěnôwsh; this mas. noun is derived from *'ânash* (605). It means an individual man or human being (Job 5:17; Ps. 55:13); man in general, mankind (Deut. 32:26; Ps. 73:5; Isa. 24:6); a mortal; Enosh, son of Seth (Gen. 4:26). The word occurs forty-two times in the Heb. O.T., almost always in poetry. Since one of the meanings of its root (605) is "to be weak," not surprisingly it is frequently used in contexts where man's weakness or frailty is emphasized (Job 4:17; 7:1; Ps. 103:15). *'Ěnôwsh* is also an Aramaic word which is employed twenty-five times in the O.T., usually as a syn. for the Heb. word *'âdâm* (120).

599. 'Ânaph; to breathe, to emit breath through the nostrils, to be angry, to be displeased. This verb is used figuratively to express anger, as expressed by the act of breathing. Perhaps it was observed that the nose dilates in anger. See 639.

606. 'Ěnâsh or **'ěnash;** this Aramaic term corresponds to the Heb. 582, meaning man or mankind. It is used with *bar* (1247) "son" in the expression "Son of man" (Dan. 7:13), the only occurrence. It refers to a heavenly person coming before the Ancient of Days in the judgment scene. Jesus applied this verse to Himself in Mt. 26:64ff., thus filling His often-used self-designation "Son of Man" with the greatest significance. There are twenty-five occurrences, two instances in Ezra and twenty-three instances in Daniel.

611. 'Âçôwn; this mas. Heb. noun means hurt or harm (Gen. 42:4; Ex. 21:22). Its deriv. is unknown, and in all of its five uses in the O.T. it refers to physical harm coming to some person.

622. 'Âcaph; to gather, to remove, to gather in, to collect, to take away, to destroy. This verb, occurring 199 times, is one of the two principal words for "gather." Transitively, this verb denotes "to bring together," or "collect" as in harvest. Intransitively, the word usually means "to come together" or "assemble." The phrase "gathered to his fathers" is frequently used for "to die" or "death" (Gen. 25:8,17). Figuratively, the verb is used to mean a period of God's punishment as in the "time of harvest" mentioned in Jer. 51:33. A derived use of the verb occurs with the meaning of "withdraw" or "remove."

624. 'Âcûph; this part., a form of 622, is used only in the pl. to connote collections or storehouses (I Chr. 26:15,17).

625. 'Ôçeph; this noun, from 622, means a collection, a gathering, or a harvest, especially of fruits (Isa. 32:10).

626. 'Ăcêphâh; this noun is used only in Isa. 24:22 to mean a "collection" or "gathering." The writer literally says "they are gathered in a gathering," i.e., together.

627. 'Ăçuppâh; this fem. noun is found only in the pl. and denotes congregations or assemblies, especially of learned, wise men discussing divine things (Ecc. 12:11).

628. 'Açp^{e}çûph; this mas. coll. noun occurs once in Num. 11:4 in reference to the mixed crowd or potpourri of individuals who followed Israel out of Egypt.

639. 'Aph; this mas. noun, a deriv. of 599, refers to the breathing part of the body, specifically the nose, nostril, or face (II Sam. 25:23). It is considered a vital part of the body. God made man a living being by breathing into his nostrils (Gen. 2:7). By the act of breathing, emotions can be expressed. In anger the nose dilates and breathing becomes more intense. This word, therefore, is normally used to refer to the anger of men and of God. This anger is expressed in the appearance of the nostrils. The word gives specific emphasis to the emotional aspect of anger and wrath, whereas its synonyms relate other aspects.

651. 'Âphêl; this adj. refers to something obscure, gloomy, or dark (as the day, Amos 5:20).

652. 'Ôphel; this mas. noun appears nine times throughout the O.T. and is translated darkness, gloom, calamity, and figuratively, spiritual darkness. Most occurrences of this word are in Job.

653. 'Ăphêlâh; this noun means thick darkness, calamity, or gloominess. The term is used literally when the plague of darkness fall upon Egypt (Ex. 10:21,22). It is also used figuratively of distress, calamity, or wretchedness (Isa. 8:22). The majority of its ten usages occur in the prophetic works.

678. 'Âtsîyl; this noun connotes a side, a corner, or an extremity (Isa. 41:9). The word is also used to mean a chief man or noble (Ex. 24:11).

724. 'Arûwkâh or **'arûkâh;** this fem. pass. part. of 748 means healing or health (Isa. 58:8) with the sense of restoring to soundness.

727. 'Ârôwn or **'ârôn;** this Heb. noun means chest (money, II Chr. 24:8), box; coffin (of Joseph, Gen. 50:26); ark, i.e., the sacred box which was kept in the holy of holies in the tabernacle and later the temple. The word's deriv. is not known. It is used about 200 times in the O.T. and basically means a container. Hence, the ark was used as a receptacle for some of Israel's sacred objects: the tables of stone upon which the Ten Commandments were written (Ex. 25:16; Deut. 10:1-5), a pot of manna (Heb. 9:4), and Aaron's rod that budded (Heb. 9:4). By the time of Solomon, however, only the tables of stone remained (I Kgs. 8:9). When the word is used of the ark, it is often modified by other nouns or phrases, such as "of the covenant" (Num. 10:33; Josh. 3:6), "of the testimony" (Ex. 25:22; Josh. 4:16), "of God" (I Sam. 3:3), "of the God of Israel" (I Sam. 5:7), "of the Lord" (I Chr. 15:12), or "Of Thy might" (II Chr. 6:41). The ark was made of acacia wood and was overlaid completely with gold. The golden mercy seat served as its lid. It was the place where Moses met God to receive messages from Him (Ex. 25:22). Once a year, on the Day of Atonement, the high priest brought the blood of a bull and a goat and sprinkled it on the mercy seat as an atonement for himself and the people (Lev. 16:11-16; Cf. Heb. 9:7).

734. 'Ôrach; this noun is normally translated "way" or "path" and appears fifty-eight times in the O.T. Forty-five of these occurrences are limited to three books: Proverbs, Psalms, and Job. Most often the word is used in a figurative way, describing the way to life or to death (Prov. 4:14).

748. 'Ârak; to make long, to lengthen, to prolong. This verb is found most frequently in Deuteronomy, mainly in the formula, "That you may live long on the land" (Deut. 4:40).

750. 'Ârêk; this adj. is used fifteen times and comes from 748. Its meaning is "long," and is used ten times in connection with God. The word is most frequently used with the word *'appayim* (639) and is translated longsuffering, slow to anger/wrath. Literally, when the Bible says God is "longsuffering" (Ex. 34:6; Num. 14:18), it literally reads, "God is long of nose."

752. 'Ârôk; this adj. stemming from 748 is used only three times, meaning long or protracted.

753. 'Ôrek; this noun, derived from 748, means length and is frequently used as a measurement of some structure such as the ark (Gen. 6:15). The word is used often with "day(s)" to express a protracted period of time (Ps. 21:4).

754. 'Arkâ' or **'arkâh;** a lengthening, prolonged length; from the Aramaic 749. Used similarly to the Heb. root *'arak* (748). There is only one occurrence (Dan. 7:12).

759. 'Armôwn; this noun means a citadel, a fortress, or a fortified palace. It describes a fortified dwelling, usually a part of the royal area. Of the thirty-two uses of the word, twenty-two of them are in the prophetic books. In most instances, God will burn up "the palaces" of a certain individual or nation in divine judgment.

772. 'Ăra'; corresponding to the Heb. 776, it means earth, world, or ground. There are twenty-one occurrences. All but two instances (Ezra 5:11; Jer. 10:11) appear in Daniel.

776. 'Erets; this Heb. noun means the earth (that is, the physical planet, Gen. 18:18; Jer. 25:26); the earth (as opposed to heaven, Gen. 1:2; Ps. 146:6); the earth (i.e., inhabitants, Gen. 6:11; I Kgs. 2:2); land (Gen. 11:31); land (i.e., inhabitants, Lev. 19:29); ground (Gen. 1:26), soil (Gen. 1:11; Lev. 25:19); country, territory (Gen. 10:10; Deut. 34:2). It is used in many phrases, such as "people of the land" (Gen. 23:7), "land of the living" (Ps. 27:13), and "end of the earth" (Isa. 42:10). The word is much more diverse and frequent in its use than *'ădâmâh* (127). It occurs 2,504 times in the Heb. O.T.

778. 'Ăraq; earth. There is only one appearance (Jer. 10:11).

779. 'Ârar; to curse. This verb is one of the six common Heb. words translated "to curse." This word occurs sixty-three times, and has been interpreted as meaning to bind (with a spell), to hem in with obstacles, to render powerless to resist. Thus the first curse in Gen. 3:14,17, "Cursed are you more than all cattle" and "Cursed is the ground because of you" means "You are banned from all the other animals" and "Condemned be the soil (i.e., fertility to men is banned) on your account."

801. 'Ishshâh; this noun means a fire offering, a burnt sacrifice, or an offering made by fire. It can be applied to any offering which was wholly or partially consumed by fire. It is, therefore, applied to the burnt offering (Lev. 1:9,13), the cereal grain offering (Lev. 2:3), peace offering (Lev. 3:3), the guilt offering (Lev. 7:5), and the consecration offering (Lev. 8:28). This word is used over sixty times in the O.T.

802. 'Ishshâh; this fem. Heb. noun means a woman, a wife (Gen. 3:17), a bride (Gen. 29:21; Deut. 20:7), a female (of animals, Gen. 7:2); a concubine (Judg. 19:1); a widow (II Sam. 14:5); each, every (Ex. 3:22; Amos 4:3). The word is used almost 800 times in the O.T. and its basic meaning is a female, as opposed to a male. Although the deriv. of *'ishshâh* is uncertain and no linguistic etymology appears to be involved, Adam makes a beautiful play on words in Gen. 2:23 in the passage where the word is first used. "This is now bone of my bones, . . . She shall be called Woman, (*'ishshâh*), because she was taken out of Man" (*'îysh*, 376). A similar pun occurs in English translation, because the word "woman" has the word "man" in it.

815. 'Êshel; this mas. Heb. noun comes from an uncertain root and means a tamarisk tree. However, by extension, it refers to a grove of any species of tree. There are only three occurrences (Gen. 21:33; I Sam. 22:6; 31:13).

816. 'Âsham or 'âshêm; to be or become guilty (Lev. 4:13; Jer. 50:7); to trespass, to offend, to commit an offense, to do wrong (Lev. 5:19; Ezek. 25:12); to suffer for (Joel 1:18), to be destroyed, to be held guilty (Ps. 34:22,23) (21,22); to declare guilty (Ps. 5:10). This is one of the key verbs for sin in the O.T., and basically means to be guilty.

817. 'Âshâm; this mas. Heb. noun means guilt (Ps. 68:21; Prov. 14:9), fault, trespass, offense; trespass or guilt offering (Lev. 6:17; Ezek. 40:39); restitution for a wrong (Num. 5:8). It is derived from *'âsham* (816) and occurs forty-six times in the O.T. Most of the uses have to do with the actual offering which is made as a restitution or compensation for a wrong. It can be made either to God or man, depending on the offense. In Isa. 53:10 the Lord's servant becomes the compensation for the sin of the people.

818. 'Âshêm; this Heb. adj. means guilty (Gen. 42:21), bound to make a guilt offering (Ezra 10:19). It occurs only three times in the O.T. and is derived from *'âsham* (816).

819. 'Ashmâh; this fem. Heb. noun means fault, trespass (II Chr. 24:18), guilt, guiltiness; trespass offering (Lev. 6:5). It is derived from *'âsham* (816).

825. 'Ashshâph; this noun describes an astrologer, enchanter, magician, conjurer, or necromancer. All occurrences of the word are in the Book of Daniel.

826. 'Ashshâph; this aramaic word corresponds to the Heb. 825 and means enchanter, conjurer; astrologer. There is a total of six occurrences (Dan. 2:10,27; 4:7; 5:7,11,15).

833. 'Âshar; to go (straight), to walk, to be successful, to prosper, to guide, to lead straight, to bless. This verb is used of going in a straight way, and, therefore, the other connotations of prosperity and successful living result. This word is one of the two Heb. verbs meaning "to bless." This word is never used by God, but is reserved for man. This verb is used when a man has done something positive deserving of congratulations and blessing, i.e., one who trusts the Lord without equivocation.

835. 'Esher; this word is used only in the pl. and means blessed (Job 5:17; Ps. 2:12; 119:1). Twenty-five of its forty-four occurrences in the O.T. appear in the Psalms.

837. 'Ôsher; this noun, deriving from 833, occurs only in Gen. 30:13 and is translated as happy in "Happy am I!"

842. 'Ăshêrâh; this word means either Asherah or Asherah's pillar or symbol (Deut. 16:21; I Kgs. 16:33). It is used forty times in the O.T., mostly in I Kings and II Chronicles. Asherah was a major Canaanite goddess associated with passion and the sea. The sacred objects which represented her seem to have been made of wood (see Deut. 12:3; Judg. 6:26). According to the Baal Epic from Ras Shamra, she was the wife of El and the mother of Baal. Although in these tablets she is the deadly enemy of Baal, she appears to have been Baal's consort in the Southern Canaanite version of the religion, because Baal and Asherah were worshiped together. When Elijah confronted the 450 prophets of Baal at Mount Carmel, 400 prophets of Asherah were also there (I Kgs. 18:19).

887. Bâ'ash; to have a bad smell, to stink (Ex. 7:18,21; 8:14; 16:20); to be foul or loathsome; to be hateful (I Sam. 27:12); to act wickedly (Prov. 13:5); defamed, to become odious, abhorrent, abominable. So, the word describes objects which have a bad odor, bad relationships between people, and evil deeds which are rotten to God.

898. Bâgad; to act covertly or fraudulently, secretly, deceptively; to cheat, betray; to oppress, to afflict, to spoil (Isa. 21:2; 24:16; 33:1). In the K.J.V. it is translated as: "transgress," "transgressor," "offend," "be unfaithful," "deal treacherously." Most of these are figurative uses of the literal root, "to cover (with a garment)." It is similar to our expression "cloak and dagger." The verb appears forty-seven times in the context of marriage (Ex. 21:8; Jer. 3:20; Mal. 2:10), Israel's unfaithfulness to the Lord (Jer. 9:2), and interpersonal human relationships (Judg. 9:23; Job 6:15; Jer. 12:6). Wine may cause people to behave this way (Hab. 2:5).

914. Bâdal; to separate, to disjoin (Gen. 1:4,6; Ex. 26:33; Lev. 1:17; Ezek. 42:20); to distinguish diverse things (Lev. 10:9,10; 11:47; 20:25); to select out of a group (Lev. 20:24,26; Num. 8:14; 16:9); to shut out (Neh. 13:3; Isa. 56:3); to separate oneself (Ezra 6:21; 9:1; 10:11); to sever, divide, discern, make a difference. Israel is separate from foreigners (Neh. 10:28) in post-exilic times to preserve their ethnic integrity as a nation. It can mean to discharge an army (II Chr. 25:10), designate cities for a special purpose (Deut. 4:41; 19:2,7) or individuals for service (I Chr. 25:1; Ezek. 39:14). The word is used in the sense of "ban" in Ezra 10:8. It has the sense of consecration (Num. 16:9; Deut. 10:8; I Kgs. 8:53; I Chr. 23:13). Sin separates us from God (Isa. 59:2).

926. Bâhal; to be terrified, frightened, perplexed; to be quick, overhasty; to flee; to frighten, confound, perplex; to accelerate, to do something hastily; to scare away; to terrify, panic, alarm. The verb occurs fifty times, counting eleven instances in the Aramaic section of Daniel. Gentile nations became alarmed at God's power (Ex. 15:15; Ps. 2:5, 6:10; 83:17; Isa. 13:8). Individuals are also sometimes disturbed at the thought of God (Job 23:15; Dan. 4:5; 5:6). Saul was confronted with an unexpected, threatening appearance of Samuel (I Sam. 28:21).

927. B^{e}hal; this is the Aramaic equivalent of 926.

928. Behâlâh; fear, fright, terror (Lev. 26:16); sudden destruction (Isa. 65:23 in K.J.V. is "trouble"). See also Ps. 78:33 and Jer. 15:8. *Behâlâh* is the sudden terror of God brought upon a disobedient Israel.

947. Bûwç; to tread with the feet, to trample on, to tread down, to profane, to crush, to be crushed under foot, to be abandoned to kicking. The general idea of this word has to do with a neglected, despised thing. In the Hebrew culture, the feet were of lesser importance than the head. The verb occurs twelve times in the Heb. O.T., often connected with enemies bent upon total destruction. Sometimes God is the agent (Ps. 44:5; Isa. 14:25; 63:6). There is a latent overtone of anger. In Isa. 63:18 and Jer. 12:10 it has the metaphorical sense of desecrating or polluting the sanctuary.

953. Bôwr; a pit, hole, cistern, well, dungeon, or grave. It comes from the root 952, *bûwr,* "to bore" in the sense of examine. Empty cisterns were used for prisons (Jer. 38:6; Zech. 9:11). The Hebrews conceived of death as a giant pit (Ps. 28:1; 30:3; 88:4; Isa. 38:18).

954. Bûwsh; to be ashamed, to feel ashamed, to be confounded, to be disappointed, to make ashamed, to keep waiting, to deceive, to act shamefully; to disgrace. This is a root meaning "to become pale" or "to blush." When failure of sin occurs, there is a disconcerting feeling, a flushing of the face. The root occurs 155 times. Except for twenty-five occurrences, all instances are in the Psalms or the Prophets. Thirty-eight occurrences are found in Jeremiah and twenty in Isaiah alone. The word often occurs in contexts of humiliation and shattered human emotions. It is the feeling of public disgrace. *Bûwsh* is the confusion, embarrassment, or dismay when things do not turn out as expected. The idea of shame at the hands of an utter defeat pervade the mood. Disillusionment and a broken spirit follow (Ezra 9:6; Isa. 1:29; 30:5; Jer. 2:36; 9:19; Dan. 9:7). The opposite meaning is trusting God (Isa. 29:22; Joel 2:26,27; Zeph. 3:11). There is a strong connotation of guilt (Jer. 6:15; Ezek. 16:63; note the name changes in II Sam. 2:8; 9:6).

955. Bûwshâh; shame, disgrace (Ps. 89:45; Ezek. 7:18; Obad. 10; Mic. 7:10 are the only occurrences in the Heb. O.T.). It comes from the root 954.

973. Bâchal; there are two senses: to feel loathing, to detest, to be nauseated, to reject. This meaning occurs only once in Zech. 11:8 where it describes Israel's reaction as the flock to God, the Good Shepherd. The second meaning occurs only in Prov. 20:21 describing an inheritance which was gotten by greed.

974. Bâchan; to try, prove, test, examine, search out, purify; to look out, to watch. This root and its deriv. occur thirty-two times in the Heb. O.T., primarily in Job, Psalms, and Jeremiah. The word denotes an investigation to determine the essential qualities of the object, especially integrity. It is used almost exclusively in the spiritual sense, attaining knowledge intuitively.

976. Bôchan; trial, proof, testing. This word appears only in Isa. 28:16, which is extremely important because it was quoted in I Pet. 2:4-6; Rom. 9:33. It is a description of the foundation stone of God's Kingdom (Jesus Christ). Jesus is the Rock (Acts 4:11,12; I Cor. 3:11; Eph. 2:20,21), a proven footing which is suitable to build our lives upon. This word probably comes from the root 974.

977. Bâchar; to prove, try, choose, select, distinguish, love, like, to be pleasing, to be especially chosen. Something is acceptable or judged to be excellent after it has been tested. In other words, it is considered to be the best. This root and its deriv. occurs 198 times with this meaning. It is taking a keen look at something (Isa. 48:10). Silver has been assayed (Prov. 10:20). In non-theological terms it involves a careful, well thought-out choice (I Sam. 17:40; I Kgs. 18:25; Isa. 1:29; 40:20). Lot shrewdly chose the better land (Gen. 13:11). Usually the word expresses choices with eternal consequences (Deut. 12:5; I Sam. 10:24; II Sam. 6:21; I Kgs. 8:16; I Chr. 28:5; Ps. 78:68; 135:4). God's purpose and personality are at the helm of the universe, not randomness. God reserves the right to reject one of His previous choices should the situation dictate it (I Sam. 2:27ff.).

981. Bâṭâ'; to talk idly, to babble, to talk rashly and inconsiderately. The K.J.V. of Ps. 106:33 translates it as "unadvisedly."

982. Bâṭach; to attach oneself, to trust, confide in, feel safe, be confident, secure; to be careless. The R.S.V. sometimes renders it "rely on." The basic idea is associated with firmness or solidity. The word expresses the sense of well-being which results from knowing that the "rug won't be pulled out from under you." The Septuagint uses *elpizō* (1679) to translate this word (see the comments in the N.T. lexical section). The folly of relying upon any other type of security is strongly contrasted with depending upon God alone (I Chr. 5:20; Ps. 22:4; 31:14; 33:21; Isa. 26:3; 30:12; Jer. 17:7). Out of a total of 181 instances, Psalms has fifty occurrences. This type of hope is a confident expectation, not a constant anxiety. We can truly relax when we know Who is in control. Note particularly II Kgs. 18 and 19.

983. Beṭach; this mas. noun derives from the root 982. It is a place of refuge, strictly speaking, but usually describes a confident mind (Gen. 34:25), security (Isa. 32:17), safety, confidence. In Judg. 8:11 the word is used of one who is over-confident and shows no caution whatever. Those who are in a proper relationship with God will dwell securely (Lev. 25:18; Ps. 16:9). Only a security rooted in God is permanent (Judg. 18:7; Isa. 47:8; Ezek. 30:9).

985. Biṭchâh; confidence, hope. Isa. 30:15 is the sole occurrence. There it expresses a sense of resignation. In other words, there is nothing more that one can do.

986. Biṭṭâchôwn; confidence (Isa. 36:4); hope (Ecc. 9:4). A mas. counterpart to the fem. 985.

987. Baṭṭûchôwth; "security," from the root 982. Job 12:6 is the only place in the Heb. O.T. where this word appears. Job states sarcastically that those who provoke God are "secure."

990. Beṭen; belly, the womb, the inmost part, the bottom of the heart; the belly-shaped protuberances on pillars. It comes from an unused Heb. root meaning "to be hollow." It may be the bosom or emptiness of anything. The essential meaning is "interior." The phrases "from the womb" and "issue from the body" mean "from birth" and "children." Sometimes *beṭen* is used to express the deepest recesses of an individual (Job 15:35; 20:20; Prov. 18:8,20). It often describes the totality of a human being.

995. Bîyn; to discern, perceive, observe, pay attention to, understand; to be intelligent, knowing; to heed; to make intelligent; to instruct, teach; to attend to; to be sensible. Other K.J.V. renderings are: "regard," "deal wisely," "direct," "prudent," "discreet," "eloquent," "skillful," "cunning," "consider," and "wise." This verb and its derivatives are used 247 times in the Heb. O.T. The primary meaning is "understanding" or "insight." Discernment is a closely-related idea. The word inculcates the concept of distinguishing between good and evil (I Kgs. 3:9). The word does not refer to the mere accumulation of data, but superior knowledge. One must know how to use information wisely. We perceive through our senses (Job 6:30; Ps. 58:9; Prov. 7:7; 29:19). As Jesus noted in Mt. 13:13, it is possible to hear without perceiving (Prov. 29:7; Dan. 12:8). Moral understanding can be a gift from God (Dan. 1:17). We can pray for it (Ps. 119:34), and God can chose to reveal it or not (Isa. 29:14). The seat for this ethical insight is the heart (Prov. 28:5). We must diligently pursue it.

998. Bîynâh; understanding (Isa. 33:19; Dan. 8:15; 9:22; 10:1); insight, prudence, intelligence (Job 28:12,20; 38:4; Prov. 4:5,7; 8:14; 9:6,10; 16:16; Isa. 27:11; 29:24); skill (I Chr. 12:32; II Chr. 2:12). This fem. noun derives from *bîyn* (995). It is used to predict that Israel will never be exposed to another foreign language which is difficult to understand (Isa. 33:19). Daniel had a grasp of any topic which Nebuchadnezzar desired (Dan. 1:20). We are not to lean upon our own understanding (Prov. 3:5).

999. Bînâh; this Aramaic term corresponds to the Heb. word 998.

1004. Bayith; this noun probably comes from *bânâh* (1129), "to build." Tent, hut, house, mansion; palace, temple; dwelling-place, receptacle, place where things are found; interior; toward the inside, within; family, household, race, descendants. The word is used of the temples of idols (I Sam. 5:2,5; Isa. 37:38; 44:13) and of God's temple in Jerusalem (I Kgs. 6:5,37; 7:12; Isa. 66:1). The same word is used for a grave (Ecc. 12:5; Isa. 14:18). It can be where anyone lives, e.g., Hades (Job 17:13), a work house (Ex. 20:2), a barn (Job 39:6; Ps. 84:4; 104:17), the house of a spider (Job 8:14), the house of a moth (Job 27:18). It can be a perfume box (Isa. 3:20), or just about any container. The word is used to describe ordinary houses (Ex. 12:7), dwelling houses (Lev. 25:29), houses made of solid materials with doorposts (Deut. 11:20), walls (Lev. 14:37) of stones, wood, and mortar (Lev. 14:45). Some of the better houses were built upon the walls of a city (Josh. 2:19); or had roofs where people could relax (II Sam. 11:2). When Israel made God's house into a den of robbers, God threatened to destroy it (Jer. 7). *Bayith* can also describe rooms in a large house (Esth. 2:3; 7:8; Jer. 36:22). *Bayith* is applied to a corporate group (Gen. 18:19; 35:2; 46:27; Ex. 16:31; Num. 1:2; Josh. 2:12; 6:22; 7:1-5; 24:15; II Sam. 7:11). The word includes what is inside the house (Ex. 20:17).

1079. Bâl; this is an Aramaic word from *b*[e]*lâ'* (1080). It occurs only once (Dan. 6:14). It means "heart," "mind."

1100. B[e]**lîya'al;** this mas. Heb. noun comes from two words, *blîy* (1097) and *yâ'al* (3276). It means worthlessness, good-for-nothingness, wickedness; perdition, a wicked man; a destroyer. It is possible that it derives from the verb *bâlâh* (1086), "to become old" or "worn out." Some derive it from *bâla'* (1104), "to swallow." The word occurs twenty-seven times in the Heb. O.T. The K.J.V. and the Latin Vulgate treat it as a proper name in many instances. In time it became a proper name, Belial, for Satan, the prince of evil (see II Cor. 6:15; II Thess. 2:3).

1101. Bâlal; this is a primary root which means to pour over (Lev. 2:4,5; 7:10,12; 14:21; Num. 7:13,19), to be anointed (Ps. 92:10); to pour together, to confound (Gen. 11:7), to mix, to stain, to soil, to be moistened; to give fodder to animals (Judg. 19:21). This was often a term for the ritual of mingling oil into flour (Ex. 29:2,40). The word Babel does not mean "confuse" but sounds enough like it for there to be an effective word play (Gen. 11:9).

1104. Bâla'; to swallow, devour, eat up; to be destroyed or overcome. Who can swallow? Men (Isa. 28:4), a great fish (Jon. 1:17), snakes (Ex. 7:12), and other animals (Gen. 41:7,24). God caused the earth (Num. 16:30,32,34; 26:10; Deut. 11:6; Ps. 106:17) and the sea (Ex. 15:12) to swallow groups of men alive as punishment. It is symbolic of destruction and ruin (Isa. 3:12; 49:19; Lam. 2:2,5,8).

1105. Bela'; this mas. noun which comes from *bâla'* (1104) indicates something which is swallowed, a swallowing, destruction. The word occurs only twice in the Heb. O.T. (Ps. 52:4 which refers to Doeg's devouring words, and Jer. 51:44 which describes the idol Bel's voracious appetite).

1116. Bâmâh; height, hill, elevation; stronghold; a high place which was destined for unauthorized worship; grave-mound, a tomb-hill. It was a general word which included mountains and hills, fortresses, and castles, which were usually built on strategically-placed sites at higher elevations. Pagan societies were fond of performing sacred rites on mountains and hills. They believed this was more acceptable to their gods. The Israelites began imitating the practice, not only to idols, but even offering sacrifices to God Himself (I Sam. 9:12ff.; I Kgs. 3:4; I Chr. 16:39ff.; Isa. 36:7). They erected sanctuaries, chapels, and shrines at those places (I Kgs. 13:32; II Kgs. 17:29) and installed priests and ministers to preside (I Kgs. 12:32; II Kgs. 17:32). Even after Solomon's temple was built, the forbidden worship continued in the high places (II Kgs. 12:3; 14:4; 15:4,35). Even Solomon himself offered sacrifices at these locations (I Kgs. 3:2,3; 11:7). The pagan cultic places were usually located on natural heights (I Sam. 9:13ff.; 10:5; I Kgs. 11:7; II Kgs. 17:9,29; 23:5,8). They were supplied with idols (II Chr. 33:19), usually an *'ăshêrâh* (842), a wooden pole which symbolized the goddess of fertility, and a *matstsêbâh* (4676), one or more stone pillars which symbolized the male deity (II Kgs. 3:2). The altar was built of stones and could be either separate from the *bâmâh* or part of it. The *bâmâh* contained a tent or room where the cultic vessels were stored and where the sacrificial meals were eaten (I Kgs. 12:31; 13:32; II Kgs. 17:29; 23:19). They burned incense, sacrificed, ate sacrificial meals, prayed, conducted sacred prostitution, and sacrificed children (Jer. 7:31).

1121. Bên; son, child, boy, young one; grandson, grandchild, descendant, a member of a group; pupil; subject, disciple, favorite. When it occurs with a sub. noun, it functions as an adj., e.g., "a son of five years" means "five years old." "A son of fat" means "stout." It is believed that this word comes from *bânâh* (1129), "to build." This word occurs almost 5,000 times in the Heb. O.T. It is basically a reference to the male offspring of human parents, though not exclusively. In general, it is used idiomatically for "children" and "descendants." In the ancient Near East, a man was thought to achieve social continuity through his son (Deut. 25:6; II Sam. 18:18). The loss of an only son must be understood against this historical background (Gen. 22:2; Zech. 12:10). Isaiah (7:14) predicted the birth of a special *Bên,* Jesus Christ (Isa. 9:6; Mt. 1:23). The adoption procedure was important at the time of Abraham (Gen. 15:2ff.). This was especially common in Nuzi law. Pharaoh's daughter adopted Moses (Ex. 2:10). God declared that the seed of David would be his "son" (II Sam. 7:14). Note the Messianic Psalm, "Thou art My Son, today I have begotten Thee." (Ps. 2:7). *Bên* specifies an intimate relationship (Ps. 103:13). Sons were blessed by their fathers (Gen. 27:28,29; 48:14ff.) or cursed (Ex. 20:5; 34:7). The firstborn male child of the Israelites were dedicated to the Lord (Ex. 13:13; 34:20; Num. 18:16). The phrase "sons of Israel" occurs 630 times and refers to all the people of Israel, not merely the males. "Son of man" simply means "a man" or "an individual" in some instances (Num. 23:19; Job 25:6; 35:8; Ps. 8:4), judging from the parallelism of the poetry, but, in other instances (Dan. 7:13), it has Messianic overtones. The "sons of God" in Gen. 6 probably refers to the godly lineage of Seth. Other occurrences of "sons of God" generally signify heavenly creatures.

1123. Bên; this is the Aramaic equivalent of 1121. There are eleven occurrences in Ezra and Daniel.

1149. Beˣnaç; this is another Aramaic word which occurs only once in the Heb. O.T. (Dan. 2:12). It means "to be enraged," "to be angry," "to be indignant." This word is often found in the Targums.

1156. Beʻâ'; this Aramaic word occurs only in the Book of Daniel. In the K.J.V. it is translated in a variety of ways: "sought," "desired," "requested," "asked," and "praying." In the Targums it often translates the Heb. *bâqash* (1245), "to search out."

1158. Bâʻâh; to cause to bubble up, to boil, to cause water to swell; to desire, covet, demand, ask, to bulge, to project; to be searched. There are five occurrences in the Heb. O.T. It suggests a search for what is covered or sealed. This was their way of expressing absorption.

1159. Bâʻûw; this Aramaic word occurs only twice (Dan. 6:7,13). It was a petitionary type of prayer.

1164. Beʻîy; this word comes from the root *bâʻâh* (1158). The solitary appearance is Job 30:24, "grave." The marginal reading in the K.J.V. is "heap." Instead, it should read, "prayer," or "entreaty."

1166. Bâʻal; to be master, to rule, possess, marry, to be married, to be taken as a wife. The verb, along with its deriv., excluding compounds and proper names, occurs more than 100 times in the Heb. O.T. God is the husband (*bâʻal*) of Israel (Isa. 54:5ff.; Jer. 3:14; 31:32; Mal. 2:11). The land is "married" (*bâʻal*) to Jehovah in the Book of Isaiah. This is similar to the relationship between Christ as "husband" of His people, the *ekklēsia* (Eph. 5:21ff.). There is a covenantal tie of love and loyalty between God and His people. He has dominion over us (Isa. 62:4).

1167. Baʻal; there are several principal meanings. The main idea is "owner." Hence, master, lord, possessor, husband, citizen, burgess, inhabitant, and Baal (a Canaanite god). The word can refer to a partner or ally (Gen. 14:13). It is used as an idiom to indicate mastery (Jer. 37:13) or ownership (Gen. 37:13; Prov. 22:24; 23:2). Because of the pervasive influence of the powerful storm, fertility god, Baal, the names of many people and places contain this word. Baal-zebub (II Kgs. 1:2), "lord of flies," was a parody on his name. Baal, who was also called Haddu or Hadad, allegedly gave the sweet rain and revived vegetation each spring. Droughts indicated that he was either dead or temporarily captive. However, when he came back, the fields, flocks, and families flourished. He was also considered to be a war god who consorted with Anat (Astarte). The people were taught to act out a magical ritual of sacred marriage in order to insure the fertility of the earth. Cultic objects on the scene were exaggerated sexual models. The worship of Baal (the sun god) included sexual orgies, with homosexuality (I Kgs. 14:24), and even child sacrifice (Jer. 19:5). The sons of Israel fell into the sin of this local cult (Judg. 2:11ff.; 6:25). Baal worship became the official state religion of the northern kingdom (I Kgs. 16:31). However, Elijah and Elisha demonstrated that fire, rain, food, children, and resurrection were traceable to God, not Baal. The Book of Hosea describes the tantalizing, titillating character of Baal worship. Unfortunately, it even influenced the southern kingdom (II Kgs. 11:18; 21:2ff.), and, in spite of Josiah's reforms (II Kgs. 23:4ff.), eventually caused Israel to go into exile (II Kgs. 17:16).

1169. Beʻêl; this is the Aramaic equivalent of 1167. It is translated in the K.J.V. as "chancellor" in the only three places that it occurs (Ezra 4:8,9,17). Literally, it reads, "master of council."

1172. Baʻălâh; there are three occurrences (I Sam. 28:7; I Kgs. 17:17; Nah. 3:4), all with occultic nuances with the exception of I Kgs. 17:17. This fem. noun means "female owner," "mistress." Metaphorically, it was one who was possessed of a familiar spirit, a sorceress, and enchantress, one who possessed charms.

1200. Beʻêrâh; this word comes from *bâʻar* (1197). It is a fem. noun signifying burning, especially used of grain in a field (Ex. 22:5, the sole instance). This is a figurative "fire," emphasizing the contagious quality of fire.

1204. Bâʻath; to be frightened, to overtake, to strike with fear, to be afraid, to dread, to be terrified, to be overtaken by a sudden terror. It is the strongest intimidation.

1214. Bâtsaʻ; to cut off, to break; to get unrighteous gain, to overreach; to rob; to complete, to finish. The main thrust of this word is tearing something to pieces, ripping, breaking. To the victor belongs the spoils (Ps. 10:3; Prov. 1:19; 15:27; Jer. 6:13; 8:10; Hab. 2:9). The word and its nominal deriv. occurs thirty-nine times. Dalman says that it was a technical term used by weavers to describe the action of cutting a piece of cloth free from the loom after it had been woven (Isa. 38:12). In a sense, therefore, it is a completion or finishing of the task, e.g., rebuilding the temple (Zech. 4:9).

1249. Bar; this Heb. adj. derives from 1305. It is used only seven times (Job 11:4; Ps. 19:8; 24:4; 73:1; Prov. 14:4; Song of Sol. 6:9,10). It means chosen, pure, clear, sincere; empty.

1252. Bôr; this word also originates from 1305. It is a mas. noun meaning purity, innocence; salt of lye, alkali, lixivium, that which has a cleansing property (Job 9:30). In ancient times they used alkali mixed with oil instead of potash soap for washing, and also in smelting metals so that the metal would melt more quickly (Isa. 1:25).

1254. Bârâ'; to create, form, make, produce; to cut, to cut down; to engrave, to carve. This word occurs in the very first verse of the Bible (Gen. 1:1). *Bârâ'* emphasizes the initiation of the object, not manipulating it after original creation. The word as used in the Qal refers only to an activity which can be performed by God. Entirely new productions are associated with *bârâ'* (Ex. 34:10; Num. 16:30; Ps. 51:10; Isa. 4:5; 41:20; 48:6,7; 65:17,18; Jer. 31:22). The word *bârâ'* also possesses the meaning of "bringing into existence" in Isa. 43:1; Ezek. 21:30; 28:13,15. Therefore, it is not surprising that bârâ' is used in Gen. 1:1,21,27; 2:3, etc. There is every reason to believe that *bârâ'* was *ex nihilo* (out of nothing).

1285. Berîyth; determination, stipulation, covenant. The K.J.V. also translates it as "league" and "confederacy." The fem. noun may come from 1262. See Gen. 15:9 for the ancient custom of ratifying solemn covenants by passing between the divided parts of victims. An agreement was possible between nations (Josh. 9:6ff.), between individuals and friends (I Sam. 18:3; 23:18), or between husband and wife (Mal. 2:14). The most important covenant was the one between God and Abraham (Gen. 15:18), confirmed by Moses (Ex. 24:7,8; 34:27; Deut. 5:2) and renewed and amended after the exile through the intervention of the prophets (Isa. 42:6; 49:8) and the Messiah (Mal. 3:1; cf. Jer. 31:33). It was a treaty, alliance of friendship, a pledge, an obligation between a monarch and his subjects, a constitution. It was a contract which was accompanied by signs, sacrifices, and a solemn oath which sealed the relationship with promises of blessing for obedience and curses for disobedience.

1288. Bârak; to bend the knee, to kneel down; to bless, praise; to be blessed; to pray to, to invoke, to ask a blessing; to greet; to curse. This root and its deriv. occur 415 times in the Heb. O.T. Two hundred and fourteen of them are translated "to bless." The Qal pass. part. "blessed" occurs sixty-one times. The meaning of "to kneel" appears only three times (Gen. 24:11; II Chr. 6:13; Ps. 95:6). There was a close association felt between kneeling and receiving a blessing. It was also considered a kindly or benevolent greeting from one person to another (I Sam. 26:25; II Kgs. 4:29). The rendering "curse" is a Heb. euphemism.

1293. B^{e}râkâh; this fem. noun comes from 1288. It is a blessing, benediction, benefit, favor, peace, invocation of good, a happy, or blessed man. It is used in the sense of a gift or present to gain goodwill (Gen. 33:11; I Sam. 25:27; 30:26; II Kgs. 5:15). Also, it has the sense of *shâlôwm* (7965), "welfare," (II Kgs. 18:31; Isa. 36:16). It occurs sixty-seven times.

1305. Bârar; to separate, secrete, single out, choose; to cleanse, purify, polish; to prove; to keep oneself pure, to show oneself pure. The etymological history of this root in cognate languages is unclear.

1319. Bâsar; the basic meaning is "to be fresh." Deriv.: to announce, to bring good news, to tell glad tidings, to receive good news. Often the recently-received news pertains to military encounters (I Sam. 31:9; II Sam. 1:20; 4:10; 18:19,20). It is normally good news, but not always so (I Sam. 4:17; II Sam. 18:20).

1320. Bâsâr; flesh (of men and animals), body, living creature; man, mankind; blood-relation; skin. This mas. noun occurs 273 times in the Heb. O.T. One hundred and fifty-three of them are found in the Pentateuch. The essential meaning refers to animal musculature, and the meaning extended to the human body, blood relations, the human race, living things, life itself, and created life as opposed to God. Generally speaking, *bâsâr* referred to the external form of a person, while *lêb* (3820), "heart," and *nephesh* (5315), "soul," comprised the internal part of man. "Flesh" is contrasted to the Spirit of God (Gen. 6:3; Ps. 56:4; Isa. 31:3; 40:6; Jer. 17:5). Flesh is weak, temporary and mortal, especially in relationship to God. *Bâsâr* is not used as a symbol of man's rebellion, as *sarx* (4561) is. See the comments in the N.T. lexical section. The problem is not with man's flesh, it is with his heart (Ezek. 11:19; 44:7). The Greeks, not the Hebrews, believed that sin was resident in the flesh.

1321. B^{e}sar; this is the Aramaic equivalent of 1320. It occurs only three times (Dan. 2:11; 4:12; 7:5).

1330. B^{e}thûwlâh; virgin, bride, chaste maiden; a city or state (figuratively). This fem. noun has been thoroughly studied in connection with the word *'almâh* (5959) in Isa. 7:14, which is translated as *parthenos* (3933) in the Septuagint and quoted in Mt. 1:23. The argument has been put forth from some circles that if Isaiah had intended the specific meaning of "virgin," he would have used *b^{e}thûwlâh* as a more precise term than *'almâh*. However, *'almâh* does mean "virgin" in several instances, and *b^{e}thûwlâh* does not always mean "virgin" (Deut. 22:13-21; 32:25; II Chr. 36:17; Ps. 148:12; Isa. 62:5; Jer. 51:22; Lam. 1:18; 2:21; Zech. 9:17). This is certainly not the case for Joel 1:8, a young widow. They spent the night with the king in Esth. 2:17. The two girls in Ezek. 23:3 were not virgins. And, it was not wrong for Job to look on a virgin (Job 31:1). See *'almâh* (5959) for a thorough discussion on Isa. 7:14.

1331. B^{e}thûwlîym; virginity, maidenhood; the period of a young woman's life just before marriage. There are ten occurrences in the Heb. O.T.

1342. Gâ'âh; to rise, grow up; to be high, elevated, majestic, exalted in triumph. This word occurs seven times in the Heb. O.T. The main idea is that of rising, and this is then associated with pride. Pride is not intrinsically wrong unless it becomes independent of God.

1350. Gâ'al; to redeem, to ransom, release, deliver; to fulfill the duties of relationship, to marry a childless widow of an older brother. The Qal part. form means redeemer, avenger, kinsman-helper. The main idea is that of buying back something. It could be a field or a farm (Lev. 25:25; Ruth 4:4,6), something consecrated to God (Lev. 27:13,15,19,20,31), a slave (Lev. 25:48,49) or animals (Lev. 27:11ff.). God is the Redeemer of Israel (Isa. 43:1-3), re-purchasing them from slavery (sin). Of course, the best known instance of redemption of the poor is found in the Book of Ruth. It describes in detail the law of levirate marriage. However, redemption by a kinsman and levirate marriage are to be distinguished. A man who was more closely related to Naomi's son (Ruth's former husband) wanted the land, but he did not want to marry Ruth and raise children. Therefore, Boaz, the next nearest of kin, did both. Also, it is important not to confuse the "avenger of blood" or "revenger" with the above. He was merely a guiltless executioner who repaid a murder in kind. The famous Job 19:25 is now believed to refer to God's work of redeeming Job from the dust of death.

1353. G^{e}ullâh; this is a fem. noun deriving from 1350. It means redemption, release, re-purchase, duty of relationship. It occurs thirteen times in the Heb. O.T.

1397. Geber; coming from the root *gâbar* (1396), "to be strong," this word means man, valiant man, male person, boy, husband, warrior; everyone, each (Lam. 3:1; Joel 2:8). It is also a proper name in I Kgs. 4:19. It has the flavor of prevailing in a virile manner and being arrogant about it (Isa. 42:13). The Heb. verb root was commonly associated with warfare and had to do with the strength and vitality of the successful warrior. Note the feats and exploits of Israel's heroes (II Sam. 23; I Chr. 11:15-19). It may have been a technical term for nobility. God was often depicted as a "mighty man" (Job 12:13; Ps. 106:8; 145:4,11,12; Prov. 8:14; Isa. 9:6; 10:21). The prowess of men was weaker than God (Ps. 33:16; Ecc. 9:11). A *geber* was a male at the very peak of his natural strength. There are sixty-six occurrences.

1399. G^{e}bar; another form of 1397, which occurs only in Ps. 18:25.

1400. G^{e}bar; this is the Aramaic equivalent of 1397. It occurs in Ezra 4:21; 5:4,10; 6:8; Dan. 2:25; 3:8,12, 13,20-27; 5:11; 6:5,11,15,24.

1401. Gibbâr; this is an inten. form of the Aramaic 1400. It means mighty, valiant, warrior or soldier.

1404. G^{e}bereth; this fem. noun derives from 1376, which, in turn, comes from 1396. It means lady, mistress, or queen. There are nine occurrences.

1413. Gâdad; to cut; to break in, to fall upon; to make cuts; to collect in a crowd; invade. This verb root is used eleven times. Seven of them are the causitive, reflexive stem and refer to the act of self-laceration in worshipping or mourning. See I Kgs. 18:28. Moses forbad this (Deut. 14:1). So did Jeremiah (16:6; 41:5; 47:5). The other instances have the usual flavor of gathering (Ps. 94:21; Jer. 5:7; Mic. 5:1). The name of Gad was drawn from this root (Gen. 49:19), because he had military capabilities (Deut. 33:20; I Chr. 5:18; 12:8).

1416. G^{e}dûwd; arising from 1413, this word means cut, furrow; collection of warriors, troop of soldiers, army, band (of men), company, plunderers, scouring party, attack. This noun appears thirty-two times in the Heb. O.T. Generally, it describes a marauding military raid. They could have even been mercenaries or looters.

1460. Gêv; this word derives from 1342. It is translated in the K.J.V. as "back, the back part of the body" in Prov. 10:13; 19:29; 26:3; Isa. 38:17; 50:6 (and as "body" in Isa. 51:23). It connotes the idea of the middle, interior, circle.

1471. Gôwy; it originates from 1465. It means person, inhabitant, populace, people, tribe, nation; the non-Israelitic or heathen peoples. It is a general word used to refer to nations at large, particularly Gentiles (as distinguished from Jews). Scholars now believe that the basic idea of *gôwy* is a defined group of people or a large segment of a given body which is defined by context. The pl. form is often used to refer to the pagan nations which surrounded Israel. They were defined politically, ethnically, and territorially (Gen. 10:5). In its general sense the term could even be applied to the descendants of Abraham (Gen. 12:2; 17:20; 21:18). Moses called Israel by that word (Ex. 33:13; Deut. 4:6,7). Israel was a nation among other nations in the time of Moses, just as she was in Joshua's time (Josh. 3:17; 4:1; 5:6) and in Jeremiah's time (Jer. 31:36). The pejorative sense includes uncircumcised nations (Jer. 9:26). They were wicked (Deut. 9:4,5), abominable (Deut. 18:9; II Chr. 33:2), and idolatrous (II Kgs. 17:29). Moses and the prophets warned the Israelites not to imitate the other nations

(Deut. 32:28; Isa. 1:4; Mal. 3:9). God planned to save them through the Messiah (Isa. 2:2ff.; 11:10; 42:6; 60:10ff.).

1472. G^eviyâh; this fem. noun derives from 1465. It means body, corpse, dead body, carcass. Sometimes the physical body as an object is dead (Judg. 14:8,9; I Sam. 31:10,12) or alive (Gen. 47:18; Ezek. 1:11,23). The Hebrews thought of the physical body as a hollow shell.

1473. Gôwlâh; this is a fem. active part. from 1540, "to denude," "uncover," "remove." It means emigration, evacuation, exile, banishment; exiles, captives. It refers to anyone who has been deported as a slave or to the captivity itself. This word occurs 41 times, mostly referring to the Babylonian exile of Judah, which was the result of rebellion against God.

1475. Gûwmmâts; this mas. noun means "pit." It is found only once (Ecc. 10:8). The root word is used in Heb. and Aramaic to signify digging.

1478. Gâva'; to expire, to breathe out one's life, to be dead, die, give up the ghost, yield up the ghost, perish, to be ready to die. It may not always connote the precise moment of death.

1480. Gûwphâh; this word comes from *gûwph* (1479), "hollow," "to close" or "shut." The word means body or corpse. Perhaps, since the Jews conceived of the physical human body to be hollow, it was also thought to be an enclosure. This word is used only once (I Chr. 10:12).

1481. Gûwr; the basal definition is "to turn aside (from the road)," i.e., for the purpose of lodging for the night, to sojourn (as a guest); to take up one's abode, to dwell (as a stranger); to fear, to be afraid or anxious, to revere; to crowd together, to meet; to stir, to excite; to settle, dwell, sojourn; to assemble, to gather; to remain, inhabit, continue. This root verb essentially means to live among people who are not one's blood relatives. Though enjoying native civil rights, these people were dependent on available hospitality. Because Abraham and his first descendants lived as protected citizens outside the promised land (Gen. 12:10; 26:3; 47:4), God directed the Israelites to practice the Golden Rule with those non-Israelites who wanted to live among them as proselytes. The sons of Israel were outsiders, visitors, in Egypt (Lev. 19:34; Deut. 10:17-19). Because of disobedience, the Jews were exiled in Mesopotamia to sojourn there (Ezra 1:4).

1504. Gâzar; to cut, to fell, to divide; to eat, consume; to decide; to be cut off, to be gone; to be separated, excluded; to be undone or lost; to be decreed. The basic meaning is "to sever."

1505. G^ezar; the Aramaic correlate to 1504. The word is used in the context of quarrying in Dan. 2:34,45. In the K.J.V. it is translated "soothsayers" in Dan. 2:27; 4:7; 5:7,11. These were Aramaic astrologers who attempted to determine the outcome of events through the position of the stars at the time of birth.

1506. Gezer; piece, part. It comes from 1504 and is used only in two places in the O.T. It describes the pl. of the halves of animals (Gen. 15:17) when God made a covenant with Abraham, and the divided portions of the Red Sea (Ps. 136:13).

1534. Galgal; wheel, water-wheel; whirlwind, whirling dust or chaff. It is particularly used of the wheel of a chariot (Isa. 5:28; Ezek. 10:2,6; 23:24; 26:10) and of a well-wheel used to draw water (Ecc. 12:6). The N.I.V. has "tumbleweed" in Ps. 83:13, signifying what the rolling thing was. Ezekiel used another word for the wheels of his vision. The N.T. region, Galilee, is believed to have come from this root.

1535. Galgal; this is the Aramaic word corresponding to 1534. Dan. 7:9 is the only place where it is found.

1536. Gilgâl; wheel. This is a variation of 1534 in Heb. It is only found in Isa. 28:28.

1538. Gulgôleth; this fem. noun comes from 1556. It means head, skull (from the round form). Sometimes it means "person," particularly counting heads for census purposes (Ex. 16:16; 38:26; Num. 1:2,18; 3:47; I Chr. 23:3,24), cf. the Aramaic term, "Golgotha," in the Gospels (Mt. 27:33; Mk. 15:22; Jn. 19:17), where Jesus was crucified.

1539. Geled; the skin (of a man), particularly when naked (Job 16:15). This is the only occurrence.

1540. Gâlâh; to bare, denudate, strip, unveil, disclose, reveal; to evacuate a country, to emigrate, to go into exile; to be uncovered, unveiled, revealed; to appear, to show, reveal or bare oneself; to be led away; to uncover, open, to be removed; to be led into exile, driven into exile. This Heb. word contains the principal idea of stark exposure, to make naked. In many passages it has the connotation of "to shame." It is ironic that God was forced to evict His people from the very land which He had promised them!

1541. G^elâh; this is the Aramaic equivalent of 1540.

1544. Gillûwl; this mas. pl. noun comes from 1556. It means roller, log, trunks, blocks, idols. The biblical writers used the term derisively; the pagans were worshipping silly, dead beams of wood (Lev. 26:30; Deut. 29:17; I Kgs. 21:26; II Kgs. 17:12; 21:21). This is one of ten basic words for an idol in the Heb. O.T. The prophets scorned physical idols by declaring that the material object itself was the god of the pagan sculptor. See Isa. 44:9-20.

1546. Gâlûwth; this fem. noun comes from 1540. It means deportation, captivity, exile; captives, exiles.

1547. Gâlûwth; this is the Aramaic equivalent to 1546. It occurs in Ezra 6:16; Dan. 2:25; 5:13; 6:13.

1556. Gâlal; to whirl, to roll, turn, drive away; to be rolled together, to roll oneself upon; to be rolled (in blood), to be dyed red. The picture is rolling oneself upon the Lord, trusting (Ps. 22:8), to commit one's life to the Lord (Ps. 37:5; Prov. 16:3), or to remove contempt (Ps. 119:22). Amasa wallowed in his own blood (II Sam. 20:12). There is a word play in Joshua 5:9, Gilgal.

1580. Gâmal; to become ripe; to make ripe; to wean; to do, perform, accomplish; to deal with, to repay, to requite, to recompense. The verb can mean either to render good (Isa. 63:7), evil (Gen. 50:15,17; Prov. 3:30), or either (I Sam. 24:17; Prov. 31:12).

1584. Gâmar; to cease, disappear, vanish; to finish, accomplish, come to an end, fail, perfect, perform. All the occurrences are in Psalms (7:9; 12:1; 57:2; 77:8; 138:8). It is an abrupt, permanent termination. Gomer, Hosea's unfaithful wife (Hos. 1:3), had a name which came from this root.

1585. G^emar; this is the Aramaic equivalent of 1584 and is found only in Ezra 7:12. It means perfect or complete, especially in skill or learning.

1602. Gâ'al; to abhor, loathe, detest, reject; to be rejected or thrown away, to be cast away in a vile manner; to waste, to fall. This verbal root expresses a very intense aversion which is often accompanied by strong measures of reaction.

1605. Gâ'ar; to address harshly, to scold, rebuke, reprove, threaten, corrupt. Jacob admonished Joseph (Gen. 37:10). God checked aggressive nations (Isa. 17:13). God rebuked Satan (Zech. 3:2). Ruth was not prevented from gleaning though she was a Moabitess (Ruth 2:16). God held the waters of the Red Sea back for Israel (Ps. 106:9).

1606. G^e'ârâh; this word derives from 1605. This fem. Heb. noun occurs fourteen times. It is a scolding, a threatening, a rebuke.

1616. Gêr; this noun originates from 1481. It is a stranger, foreigner, alien, pilgrim, sojourner, guest, visitor. Though God promised the land of Canaan to Abraham, the iniquity of the Amorites was not yet full (Gen. 15:16), and the patriarchs were considered as sojourners there. The bulk of their descendants were called by this term while in Egypt (Ex. 23:12). In fact, Moses named his son Gershom to commemorate his stay in Midian (Ex. 18:3). He had been exiled from both Egypt and Canaan. The classification of *gêr* meant that one enjoyed certain civil rights but not property rights. Much of the Law of Moses applied to those who preferred to live among the Israelites (Ex. 12:19,48,49; 20:10; 22:21; 23:12; Lev. 16:29; 17:8, 9,10,12,13,15,16; 18:26; 19:10,33,34; 20:2; 23:22; Num. 19:10; 35:15; Deut. 1:16; 10:18,19; 14:21,29; 16:11,14; 24:17,19,20,21; 26:12,13; 27:19). David used them as stonecutters (I Chr. 22:2) and soldiers

(II Sam. 1:13). Solomon forced them to be stonecutters and to carry heavy burdens (II Chr. 2:17,18).

1641. Gârar; scrape, to sweep, to saw, to draw, collect, snatch away; to chew the cud, ruminate; to be sawed in two; to whirl; to drag, to drag away (Prov. 21:7; Hab. 1:15).

1655. Geshem; this is an Aramaic equivalent to 1653. It is translated as "body" or "bodies" in Dan. 3:27,28; 4:33; 7:11. Perhaps it is conveying the figurative idea of a hard rain.

1672. Dâ'ag; to be anxious or troubled, to fear, be afraid, careful. It is often applied to the feeling of melting away in terror, deep anxiety. It can be the inconsolable worry of a parent looking for a lost son (I Sam. 9:5; 10:2). Zedekiah was afraid he would be considered a traitor (Jer. 38:19), if he surrendered to the Babylonians.

1674. D^e'âgâh; this fem. Heb. noun comes from 1672. It is fear, dread, anxious care, sorrow, heaviness.

1680. Dâbab; to go slowly and gently, to creep, to glide, to flow. It occurs only in Song of Sol. 7:9, indicating a type of speech.

1684. D^ebach; this is the Aramaic equivalent to 2076. (Linguistically speaking, the "d" sound and "z" sound are quite similar.) It means to offer a sacrifice and is only found in Ezra 6:3.

1685. D^ebach; this Aramaic word derives from 1684. It is a cognate accus. construction in Ezra 6:3.

1687. D^ebîyr; coming from 1696, it was the western part of the temple (on the back side), the inner sanctuary, the holy of holies, the innermost recess, or adytum of Solomon's Temple. In the K.J.V. it is translated "oracle." The R.S.V. and other modern versions translate the word as "sanctuary," "inner sanctuary," "inner temple," "inner room," etc. This was never used to denote the former holy of holies of the tabernacle in the wilderness.

1696. Dâbar; this is one of the most general words in the entire Heb. O.T. The verb occurs more than 1,100 times. It is one of the basic words for "say" and "speak." About thirty different English words are used to translate it in the K.J.V. Some are synonyms, but many are not. Mental or oral communication is the main idea. Here are a few meanings: to speak, to accost; to say (when used with a direct objective), to promise, command, exhort; to be spoken; to be wooed; to speak to one another, to consult; to converse; to answer. It has the rare meaning of "subdue" in Ps. 18:47; 47:3.

1697. Dâbâr; this Heb. noun, which comes from 1696, essentially means "word" or "matter" or "thing." It occurs more than 1400 times and is translated by no less than eighty-five different English words in the K.J.V.! The Ten Commandments are actually ten declarations or statements, words (Ex. 34:28; Deut. 4:13; 10:4). Sometimes *dâbâr* is what is done, and sometimes it is a report of what is done, an account of the actions (II Chr. 33:18). The essential content of God's revelation is described by the phrase, "the word of God came" (I Chr. 17:3, etc.). "The word of the Lord" was a technical expression for prophetic revelation 225 times in singular form. Sometimes it is personified (Ps. 107:20; 147:15; Isa. 9:8). Some of the major meanings are: word, saying, speech, news, command, promise; thing, incident, occurrence, history, concern, cause, question, and lawsuit.

1698. Deber; destruction, pestilence, plague. It comes from 1696. The K.J.V. translates it with "murrain" in Ex. 9:3. It is a punishment of God which results in death.

1700. Dibrâh; this fem. noun comes from 1696. It means manner, fashion, cause, sake, intent, reason, order, estate, end, regard. The N.E.B. translates the word as "succession" in the famous Ps. 110:4.

1701. Dibrâh; this is the corresponding term in Aramaic for 1700. It occurs only in Dan. 2:30; 4:17.

1703. Dabbârâh; it is an inten. form from 1696. It means "words" or "precepts" and is found only once (Deut. 33:3). It is probably a poetic collective for everything that Moses said.

1709. Dâg; this mas. noun comes from 1711. It is a fish, even a large fish (Jon. 1:17; 2:1,10). The K.J.V. correctly translates the passages in Jonah as "fish." However, the K.J.V. translators incorrectly rendered it as "whale's belly" in Mt. 12:40.

1710. Dâgâh; there is apparently no difference in meaning for this fem. coll. noun than 1709.

1711. Dâgâh; to increase, multiply (as prolifically as fish do). Occurring only once (Gen. 48:16), Jacob blessed Joseph and his sons with this word.

1730. Dôwd; this mas. noun means love; one beloved, friend; relation, cousin, uncle. Thirty-eight of the fifty-eight occurrences in the K.J.V. are translated "beloved," and except for Isa. 5:1 all are in the Song of Sol. Eight times it is translated "love," and seventeen times as "uncle."

1736. Dûwday; this mas. noun occurs only in the pl. form. It derives from 1731 and means basket; mandragora; loveapple. The K.J.V. uses the term "mandrakes," an aphrodisiac herb which had red and white blossoms with a sweet smell (Song of Sol. 7:13) and a yellowish fruit which was ripe from May to July.

1740. Dûwach; to expel, to cast out; to wash off, to cleanse, to purge. There were separate facilities for cleansing offerings in the temple of Solomon, unlike the tabernacle in the wilderness (II Chr. 4:6). The legs and internal organs of the burnt offerings were washed there (Isa. 4:4 depicts a similar image in the future spiritual cleansing of Israel). Jer. 51:34 calls the destruction of Jerusalem and Judah by Nebuchadnezzar a purging. Compare a similar image in Tit. 3:5.

1755. Dôwr; this mas. noun comes from 1752 and seems to refer to a revolution (of time). The period of a man's life, generation, age; race, class of men, contemporaries. The essence of *dûwr* (1752) is "to move in a circle," "to surround." Therefore, it is the cycle of a man's lifetime, beginning with the womb of earth and returning to it (Gen. 3:19). *Dûwr* is the conception and birth of a man until the conception and birth of his offspring. Eventually, *Dûwr* was used to describe extended time periods. See the Gr. *genea* (1074) and the comments in the N.T. lexical section. In the chronological sense, *dûwr* is only one of many Heb. and Gr. words for time. This demonstrates that revelation presents time as linear and measurable.

1763. D^echal; this is an Aramaic word corresponding to 2119. It means to fear in a timid sense. It only occurs in Dan. 2:31; 4:5; 5:19; 6:26; 7:7,19.

1777. Dîyn; to rule, to regulate, to sway; to judge, defend, punish; to litigate, to contend with, strife, controversy, to plead. This word appears twenty-three times. It is almost identical in meaning with *shâphat* (8199), "to judge." Essentially it means to govern, whether legislatively, judicially, in an executive manner, or in any other way.

1778. Dîyn; this is the Aramaic correlate to 1777. It occurs only once (Ezra 7:25).

1779. Dîyn; this mas. Heb. noun means judgment, sentence, lawsuit, cause, quarrel. The K.J.V. also translates it as "plea" and "strife."

1780. Dîyn; this is the Aramaic term corresponding to 1779. It appears in Ezra 7:26; Dan. 4:37; 7:10,22,26.

1781. Dayân; this mas. Heb. noun is judge (I Sam. 24:16) or a defender, an advocate (Ps. 68:5). See its root in 1777 for more information.

1782. Dayân; this is the Aramaic equivalent of 1781. There is only one occurrence (Ezra 7:25).

1792. Dâkâ'; to be cast down, to be humbled; to break, to crush, to oppress, humble, tread down; to be broken in pieces, crushed, humbled, afflicted. This verb is used only in Heb. poetry and is applicable only to people. God is often the agent. Man is a frail creature with a short lifespan (Job 4:19).

1793. Dakkâ'; this Heb. adj. comes from 1792. It means bruised, humbled, discouraged, broken (in spirit), cast down, contrite. When we are in that state, God can mold us (Ps. 34:18; 90:3; Isa. 57:15; Jer. 44:10).

1818. Dâm; this is a very important Heb. mas. noun which means blood, bloodshed, slaughter, the guilt of murder. It is used to describe the juice of grapes (Gen. 49:11; Deut. 32:14), red wine. The K.J.V. uses additional terms: "bloody," "bloodguiltiness," "blood thirsty" (literally "men of blood" in Prov. 29:10). *Dâm* occurs 360 times in the Heb. O.T. Of these it appears most often in Lev. (eighty-eight times), Ezek. (fifty-five times), Ex. (twenty-nine times), Deut. (twenty-three times), and Ps. (twenty-one times). There are two main categories: (1) a violent shedding of blood usually resulting in death, such as during war or in a murder; (2) shedding blood while making a sacrifice to God, which always results in a death. What is the significance of "blood" in the Bible? "The life of the flesh is in the blood" (Gen. 9:4; Lev. 17:11,14; Deut. 12:23). It could be the moment where life is most precious, at the point of death. Blood is the source of life; without it we die. To remove blood is to terminate life. Life is holy. Therefore, it is entirely just for a killer to be killed by a "blood redeemer" (Num. 35:19; Deut. 19:12). The death penalty is described as: "His blood is upon him" (Lev. 20:9,11-13,16,27) or "His blood shall be upon his head" (Josh. 2:19; I Kgs. 2:37). All the blood of a sacrificial animal had to be drained and disposed of (Ex. 12:7; Lev. 1:5; 4:6; Deut. 12:24). Eating blood was forbidden (Lev. 3:17; 17:10-13; I Sam. 14:31-35; Ezek. 33:25). The life blood of the animal sacrifice was a substitute for the worshipper's own life, an atonement for his sins. According to Rom. 5:10, we are reconciled to God by the death of Jesus, and we will be saved by His life.

1820. Dâmâh; to cease, to rest, to be silent, to be quiet; to make an end, to destroy, to lay waste, to desolate; to be destroyed, to be cut off, to perish. This Heb. verb depicts a violent end (Isa. 15:1; Jer. 47:5; Hos. 4:5,6; 10:15). It has a different meaning in Jer. 14:17; Lam. 3:49.

1822. Dummâh; this fem. noun derives from 1820. It means stillness, desolation, that which is laid waste, the result of utter destruction. It occurs only in Ezek. 27:32.

1823. Dᵉmûwth; this fem. Heb. noun comes from 1819. It means likeness, resemblance, similitude; image, model, pattern, shape. It is used as an adv., "like" or "as" in Isa. 13:4; Ps. 58:4. As a noun it occurs twenty-six times in the Heb. O.T. Ezekiel never claims to say that he saw God, only the "appearance" of God (Ezek. 1:5,10,13,16,22,26,28; 10:1,10,21,22; cf. Dan. 10:16 and Rev. 1:13). Isa. 13:4 uses the word for audible and structural similarities. The two most important passages are Gen. 1:26 and Gen. 5:1.

1843. Dêa'; this mas. noun derives from 3045. It is what one knows, knowledge, wisdom, opinion. It occurs only in Job (32:6,10,17; 36:3; 37:16).

1844. Dê'âh; this fem. Heb. noun also comes from 3045 and is the fem. form of 1843. It is knowledge, knowing. The Septuagint uses the Gr. term *gnōsis* (1108). See the comments in the N.T. lexical section. Jehovah is the God of all knowledge (Job 36:4; I Sam. 2:3).

1847. Da'ath; deriving from 3045, this noun means knowledge, insight, intelligence, understanding, wisdom, cunning. It is knowledge which was gained through the senses. The Latin Vulgate uses *scientia* to translate this idea. It occurs ninety-three times in the Heb. O.T. Though it is a general term for knowledge, it can be personal (Prov. 24:5), technical "know-how" (Ex. 31:3; 35:31; I Kgs. 7:14), or discernment (Ps. 119:66). God possesses it (Job 10:7; Ps. 139:6; Prov. 3:20) and nothing can be hidden from Him (Ps. 139:1-18). He teaches *da'ath* to man (Ps. 94:10; 119:66; Prov. 2:6). This kind of wisdom is the opp. of "folly" (Prov. 12:23; 13:16; 14:18; 15:10). It is the contemplative perception of a wise man (Prov. 1:4; 2:6; 5:2; Ecc. 1:18). This word is also used for moral cognition (Gen. 2:9,17). The "knowledge of God" along with the "fear of the Lord" (Isa. 11:2; 58:2; Jer. 22:16) describes the proper relationship between God and a man who truly obeys Him. See also Jer. 22:15,16; Hos. 4:1,2,6; 6:6. During the Messianic age, the knowledge of God would cover the earth like the ocean (Isa. 11:9; Hab. 2:14).

1859. Dâr; this is the Aramaic term corresponding to 1755. It occurs only twice (Dan. 3:33; 4:3,34).

1860. Dᵉrâ'ôwn; this Heb. mas. noun means aversion, the object of aversion, abhorring, abomination. It occurs in Isa. 66:24 and Dan. 12:2. Its root is unknown.

1870. Derek; this noun derives from 1869. It means a going, walk, journey; way, path, road; mode, manner, course, way of life, lot in life; worship. *Derek* can be a physical passageway (Gen. 3:24; 16:7; 38:21; Ex. 4:24; 13:17; Num. 20:17; 21:22; Isa. 9:1). It can also mean "trip" (Gen. 24:21; 45:23; Josh. 9:13; I Kgs. 18:27). More often it refers to the actions and behavior of men, whether wicked (Ps. 1:6) or righteous (Gen. 18:19; I Kgs. 2:3; Prov. 22:6; Isa. 55:7-9). *Derek* is the word chosen for courting (Prov. 30:19), custom (Gen. 19:31), menstruation (Gen. 31:35), sexual favors (Prov. 31:3; Jer. 3:13), and creation (Job 26:14; 40:19; Prov. 8:22).

1878. Dâshên; this Heb. adj. means to be fat, to become fat, juicy, well fed; to be rich, to be mighty. In Prov. 15:30, good news fills one's bones with marrow or imparts strength; cf. anointing in Ps. 23:5. "Pronounce thy burnt offering fat;; (Ps. 20:3) means to accept it. *Dâshên* means "to clear from ashes" in Ex. 27:3; Num. 4:13. This refers to the "fatty ashes" which were left subsequent to the burning of sacrificial animals. Fat animals were considered to be the most healthy. Therefore, the concept of prosperity was associated with fatness. However, Deut. 31:20 warns that this condition could lull us into forsaking God.

1881. Dâth; this fem. noun is of uncertain origin. Perhaps it was borrowed from Persian. It means royal command, prescription, law, decree, edict, regulation. It is found in the Book of Esther twenty times, in Ezra 8:36, and several times with the Aramaic equivalent in Ezra and Daniel (the spelling is the same in Heb. or Aramaic). Whatever the Persian kings said was an immutable law.

1882. Dâth; this is the Aramaic correlate to 1881.

1890. Habhâb; this is a reduplicated mas. noun from 3051. It is an offering, a sacrifice, a gift. It occurs only once (Hos. 8:13).

1897. Hâgâh; to murmur, to mutter, to growl, to coo, to sigh, to moan, to roar; to meditate, to muse, to speak, to praise; to whisper. The word occurs mostly in poetry, especially in Psalms and Isaiah. It describes a low moaning sound like that of a dove (Isa. 38:14; 59:11) or the growling of a lion which has trapped its prey (Isa. 31:4). Sometimes it was used to describe the context of mourning (Isa. 16:7; Jer. 48:31) or the whispering of the enemy after the collapse of Jerusalem (Lam. 3:62). Wizards made strange noises when they practiced the occult (Isa. 8:19). The Psalmist (5:1) cried out to God for help while in distress. Sometimes the term refers to plots (Ps. 2:1; Prov. 24:2; Isa. 59:3,13), or righteous ponderings (Ps. 35:28; 37:30; 71:24; Prov. 15:28), or meditation (Ps. 1:2; 38:12; 63:6; 77:12; 143:5). It is possible that the Scriptures were read somewhat audibly during the process of meditation.

1899. Hegeh; this mas. noun comes from 1897. It means a murmur, sighing, meditation, a thought, growling (used of thunder in Job 37:2, i.e., rumbling). Compare the related term *higgâyôwn* (1902) which was a musical notation which possibly referred to a harp (Ps. 92:3). Or, it may have meant that a period of meditation was to follow (Ps. 9:16).

1900. Hâgûwth; this fem. noun which comes from 1897 means "meditation." It occurs only once (Ps. 49:3).

1921. Hâdar; to be large, swollen, to adorn, to decorate, to honor; to be esteemed, to be honored; to boast, to act proudly (Prov. 25:6). This verb occurs seven times in the Heb. O.T. There is an uncertain reading in Isa. 45:2. It is the idea of showing respect, especially to the elderly from youth. God's appearance is described as "glorious" by this word (Isa. 63:1).

1922. Hădar; this is the Aramaic equivalent of 1921. All the references in Daniel (4:34,37; 5:23) refer to honoring or glorifying God.

1923. Hădar; this Aramaic deriv. is equivalent to the Heb. term (1922). It is to be translated "majesty" or "honor." It appears only in Dan. 4:30,36; 5:18.

1925. Heder; this Heb. mas. noun derives from 1921. It means ornament, splendor, or glory. It occurs only in Dan. 11:20. Palestine was considered to be the most excellent part of the kingdom.

1926. Hâdâr; this noun comes from 1921. It is translated in the K.J.V. as: "goodly," "glory," "beauty," "beauties," "majesty," "excellency," and "comeliness." The word occurs twenty-nine times in the Heb. O.T. Sixteen of the occurrences are in Psalms.

1927. Hădârâh; this Heb. word is only a fem. form of 1926. It occurs in I Chr. 16:29; II Chr. 20:21; Ps. 29:2; 96:9; Prov. 14:28.

1935. Hôwd; splendor, majesty, glory, honor, renown, ornament. This mas. Heb. noun is used twenty-four times in the Heb. O.T. It appears eight times in Psalms. It is unique to Heb. and is not found in other Semitic languages. It describes men (Num. 27:20; Prov. 5:9; Jer. 22:18; Dan. 10:8; Hos. 14:6), animals (Job 39:20; Zech. 10:3), and the olive tree (Hos. 14:6). However, most of the time the term is associated with God (I Chr. 29:25; Ps. 8:1; 21:5; 104:1; 145:5; 148:13; Isa. 30:30; Hab. 3:3) and the Messiah (Zech. 6:13).

1942. Havvâh; this fem. noun comes from 1933. The K.J.V. translates it by: "calamity," "perverse things," "wickedness," "mischievous things," "mischiefs," "noisome (pestilence)," "iniquity," "substance," "naughtiness," and "naughty."

1943. Hôvâh; this is another form of 1942. It occurs only in Isa. 47:11 and Ezek. 7:26.

1949. Hûwm; to perplex, confound; to put into motion, to disturb; to be agitated; to be excited; to sigh, to moan, to be noisy. The R.S.V. has in addition: "throw into confusion," "be distraught," and "be in an uproar." This root connotes a severe disturbance or stirring. The thought of the awesomeness of God was extremely disconcerting.

1961. Hâyâh; probably related to 1933, "to breathe." This major Heb. verb means to exist, to be; to become, to come to pass; to be done, to happen, to be finished. The term occurs 3,540 times in the Heb. O.T. It is notable that this verb was not used as a copulative construction in Heb. Boman maintains that the Hebrews thought only in dynamic categories, not static ones. The key to the meaning of Jehovah/Yahweh is undoubtedly found in this verb. See the exegetical note on Ex. 3:14. Perhaps "I am that I am" should be translated "I am He who is," or "I am He who exists." The Septuagint has *egō eimi ho ōn*. The timelessness of God, as well as His ever-present existence, is something which must be believed (Heb. 1:3).

1962. Hayâh; this is another fem. form for 1943. It occurs only in Job 6:2; 30:13 in the Kethib (written text).

1964. Hêykâl; deriving from 3201, this is a large house, a palace, a citadel; a temple, a nave, a sanctuary, a tabernacle. This term generally denotes a magnificent building (Prov. 30:28; Isa. 39:7; Dan. 1:4). Specifically, it referred to Solomon's temple in Jerusalem (II Kgs. 24:13; II Chr. 3:17; Jer. 50:28; Hag. 2:15; Zech. 6:14,15) and the holy tabernacle (tent) which was used before the permanent structure (temple) was built (I Sam. 1:9; 3:3; Ps. 5:7). The term can even mean "heaven." (II Sam. 22:7; Ps. 11:4; 18:6; 29:9; Mic. 1:2). Finally, it was the holiest part of the temple in Jerusalem (I Kgs. 6:5,17; 7:50). See *naos* (3485) and the comments in the N.T. lexical section. Sometimes it meant the domicile of a king (II Kgs. 20:18; II Chr. 36:7; Ezra 3:6; Hos. 8:14; Amos 8:3).

1965. Hêykal; this is the corresponding Aramaic term to the Heb. 1964. It may have been a loan word from the Sumerian language via Akkadian. It occurs only in Ezra 4:14; 5:14,15; 6:5; Dan. 4:4,29; 5:2,3,5; 6:18.

1984. Hâlal; to be bright, to shine; to be splendid; to boast; to praise, to celebrate, glorify; to be praised, to be famous; to cause to shine, to make bright, to give light; to deserve praise. At the heart of this Heb. root is the idea of radiance. From this came the connotation of the ebullience of rejoicing and praising God. The well-known imperative praise in Heb., "hallelujah," called for giving the glory to God. There are instances where the word is applied to human beings (Gen. 12:15; II Sam. 14:25; I Kgs. 20:11; Ps. 63:11; Prov. 12:8; 31:28,31).

1986. Hâlam; to strike, to hammer, to stamp; to beat to pieces; to be dissolved, to break up, to be scattered, to disperse. It occurs nine times in the Heb. O.T.

1999. Hămullâh; this Heb. noun means noise or sound. It occurs only in Jer. 11:16 and Ezek. 1:24.

2000. Hâmam; to put in motion, to impel, to drive, to agitate, to trouble, to confound, to disturb, to put in commotion, to put to flight, to disperse; to undo, to utterly destroy, to make extinct. The essential idea of this verb is "to give attention to" in the negative sense, i.e., "harass." It occurs thirteen times in the Heb. O.T. God is the subject in ten of those instances, striking panic in the enemies of Israel. This root is related to another similar root, *hûwm* (1949).

2015. Haphak; to turn, to turn over, to turn around, to overturn, to overthrow, to turn back; to convert, to change, to pervert; to destroy. This Heb. root, along with its derivatives, occurs 118 times in the Heb. O.T. Ninety-four of them are this verb. God poured out His anger upon the impenitent Sodom and Gomorrah (Gen. 19:21,25,29; Deut. 29:23; Isa. 13:19; Jer. 20:16; 49:18; 50:40; Lam. 4:6; Amos 4:11). The people were totally annihilated. God promised the same sort of thing to Jerusalem (II Kgs. 21:13), Nineveh (Jon. 3:4), the unbelieving nations (Hag. 2:22) and the wicked (Prov. 12:7). God transformed the Nile into blood (Ex. 7:17,20; Ps. 78:44; 105:29). Pharaoh and his servants changed their minds (Ex. 14:5). God turned the sea into dry land (Ps. 66:6). He used a strong west wind for the plague of locusts (Ex. 10:19). God changed the rod into a serpent (Ex. 7:15) and the rock into a pool of water (Ps. 114:8). And, God made the curse of Balaam into a blessing (Deut. 23:5). The word is used to describe hair in cases of leprosy (Lev. 13). Often it has a neutral meaning of turning, like *shûwb* (7725).

2026. Hârag; to kill a person (homicide), to murder, to kill animals, to slay, to destroy. This verb is used a total of 172 times in the Heb. O.T. The first occurrence is in Gen. 4:8, describing the murder of Abel. However, it can be a formal execution (II Sam. 4:11,12). *Hârag* is seldom used for killing animals (Isa. 22:13; 27:1). It is once applied even to plants (Ps. 78:47). It has the connotation of violence, especially in war or intrigue.

2027. Hereg; a killing, a murder, a slaughter. This mas. noun comes from 2026. It is used five times (Esth. 9:5; Prov. 24:11; Isa. 27:7; 30:25; Ezek. 26:15).

2028. Hărêgâh; this is the fem. form of 2027. It is used in Jer. 7:32; 12:3; 19:6 and Zech. 11:4,7.

2040. Hâraç; to pull down, to tear, to break, to destroy; to break through, to break in; to be pulled down, to be destroyed, to tear down, to overthrow, to pluck down, to be utterly ruined.

2054. Vâzâr; to bear guilt, to be laden with guilt, be guilty. This word occurs only once (Prov. 21:8). The K.J.V. translators incorrectly analyzed this word into two parts: (1) "and"; (2) "strange." This word could be related to an Arabic term which means "to bear a burden."

2076. Zâbach; to slaughter, kill, sacrifice (sometimes repeatedly). This verb is used primarily to describe the killing of animals for sacrifices, even idolatrous sacrifices (II Kgs. 12:3; Hos. 11:2). The inten. form refers to prolific sacrifices (I Kgs. 8:5; II Chr. 5:6; 30:22). It is not used of priests slaying animal victims, but of private individuals who brought sacrifices at their own expense.

2077. Zebach; this mas. noun comes from 2076. It means slaughtering, sacrifice, an offering, a victim; a meal, repast. This can be a generic noun which is often connected with offerings (Ps. 40:6), burnt offerings (Ex. 10:25; I Sam. 6:15), or peace offerings (Lev. 3:1; 17:5). Sometimes it is distinguished from peace offerings (Num. 15:8; Josh. 22:27).

2086. Zêd; this Heb. adj. comes from 2101. It has the meaning of proud, insolent, wanton, wicked. Since its root means "to seethe," it has the flavor of inflated pride, swelling up. In Psalm 19:13, it is correctly translated "presumptuous (sins)." There are thirteen occurrences in the Heb. O.T.

2087. Zâdôwn; this mas. noun also comes from 2102

and means pride, haughtiness, arrogance, insolence, rebelliousness. It occurs eleven times. This kind of pride presumes to have more authority than is warranted. Disobedience is inevitable. This is clearly an intentional sin.

2094. Zâhar; to shine, to be bright, to make to shine; to enlighten, to teach, to warn, admonish, dissuade; to be brilliant (Dan. 12:3). There may be two roots with the same spelling, or a primary and secondary meaning of the same root.

2095. Z^e^har; this is the Aramaic equivalent to 2094. It is used only once (Ezra 4:22). It means "to be admonished."

2111. Zûwâ'; to shake, to agitate; to move oneself, to tremble; to vex, to trouble. There are only three occurrences (Esth. 5:9; Ecc. 12:3; Hab. 2:7). It had the connotation of quivering in terror. The reference in Ecclesiastes depicts the tremors of the jaw in old age.

2112. Zûwa'; this is the Aramaic equivalent of 2111. It occurs only twice (Dan. 5:19; 6:26).

2114. Zûwr; to press together, to press out, to bind up, to crush, to squeeze; to recede, to retreat, to turn away or aside; to be a stranger or foreigner, to be adulterous; to be estranged. Perhaps the root idea is that of deviating, nonacquaintance, or unrelatedness. The fem. form was frequently used in Proverbs to describe "the other woman" (Prov. 2:16; 5:3,20; 7:5; 22:14; 23:33).

2119. Zâchal; to creep, crawl; to be afraid, to steal away in a timid manner. This verb is used only three times. Deut. 32:24 and Mic. 7:17 seem to be describing snakes. Job 32:6 depicts walking cautiously with faltering steps. It is even possible that these are two different roots, homophones.

2134. Zak; transparent, clear, pure, innocent. This Heb. adj. originates from 2141. It is used of olive oil (Ex. 27:20; Lev. 24:2) and of frankincense (Ex. 30:34; Lev. 24:7). The rest of the references in Job and Proverbs are used figuratively of the soul and morality.

2135. Zâkâh; to be transparent, clear, pure, innocent; to cleanse (oneself), to purify. Often appearing with "washing," this verb refers to purity of conduct (Isa. 1:16).

2141. Zâkak; this is probably a by-form of 2135. They often occur together (Job 9:30; 15:14,15; 25:4,5). It means to shine, to be bright, pure; to cleanse.

2142. Zâkar; to pierce; to impress (on the memory), to remember, to recollect, to mention; to be remembered, to be mentioned; to record, to bring to remembrance, to declare, to recite, to proclaim, to commemorate; to be born as a male; to praise, to offer praise, to burn incense; to invoke; to accuse; to confess. There are three basic sets of meanings which range in overlapping mental states and external actions.

2143. Zêker; this mas. noun comes from 2142. It means a remembrance, memory; memorial, commemoration; fame, name, praise; invocation. This verbal noun contains almost the same large range of meanings resident in the verb *zâkar.* It is the permanent notice, the conscious effort to remember.

2146. Zikrôwn; this noun derives from 2142. It is a memorial, remembrance, record, account; memorable saying; celebration. This is an object reminder or token act by which something is brought to mind. The Passover feast was a memorial (Ex. 12:14) of one of the greatest historical events which was very important to the sons of Israel.

2152. Zal'âphâh; hot wind, raging heat. This word comes from 2196. It occurs in Ps. 11:6; 119:53; Lam. 5:10.

2154. Zimmâh; this fem. noun derives from 2161. It is a plan, a counsel; evil deed, lewdness, a wicked deed; incest; apostasy. More often bad advice (Prov. 21:27; 24:9), but sometimes in a good sense (Job 17:11). It is a sin of uncleanness, particularly fornication, rape, or incest (Lev. 18:17; Job 31:11; Ezek. 16:27; 22:9,11).

2161. Zâmam; to muse, to meditate, to think, to devise, to purpose, to resolve, to consider, to plot. This Heb. verb is mostly used to describe either the Lord carrying out His purposes and judgment against the wicked nations, or of wicked men who connive against God and His people. One notable passage is Gen. 11:6. Men were scheming to build the tower of Babel. However, in Prov. 31:16, a good wife is clever to plan what is best for her family.

2162. Zâmâm; this mas. Heb. noun comes from 2161. It means a plan, a plot, a device. It is usually the carrying out, if possible, of an evil scheme. It is a mind-set which stays up nights trying to think of new ways to sin. It occurs only once (Ps. 140:8).

2163. Zâman; to be appointed, to be determined, to be fixed. It appears only in Ezra 10:14; Neh. 10:34; 13:31. It usually refers to time. The Samaritan Pentateuch of Gen. 11:6 has this word instead of the Heb. *zâmam* (2161), which may be related.

2164. Z^e^man; this is the Aramaic correlate to 2163. It occurs only once (Dan. 2:9). It means to agree (on a time and place), i.e., to prepare, make an appointment.

2165. Z^e^mân; this Heb. noun occurs only in Neh. 2:6; Esth. 9:27,31; Ecc. 3:1. It derives from 2163. It means appointed time or times.

2166. Z^e^mân; this is the Aramaic equivalent to 2165. It occurs in Ezra 5:3; Dan. 2:16,21; 3:7,8; 4:36; 6:10,13; 7:12,22,25. It is used to describe time in the sense of seasons, appointed times, and periods of times. It may have come from the Persian language.

2167. Zâmar; this Heb. verb means to play, to make music, to sing, to sing praises, to celebrate. It is used almost exclusively in poetry, namely in songs. There are two passages which refer to songs in a negative sense (Isa. 25:5; Amos 5:23).

2181. Zânâh; to fornicate, to whore, to commit fornication, to be a harlot, to play the harlot, to commit adultery; to apostatize, to have intercourse with false gods or foreigners; to seduce. The verb appears ninety-five times. The main idea is to commit illicit sexual intercourse, particularly women. However, this strong image is used in a figurative sense to describe illegal contact between Israel and other nations and their gods. Only twice does it refer to men (Ex. 34:16; Num. 25:1). Some have tried to protect the honor of Rahab by saying that she was only an "innkeeper," but there is not enough evidence to support this (Josh. 2:1; 6:17,22,25).

2183. Zânûwn; this is a Heb. mas. noun which always occurs in the pl. form. It comes from 2181. It means whoredom, fornication; idolatry (unfaithfulness to the true God); intercourse with foreigners (business).

2184. Z^e^nûwth; this is a fem. Heb. noun which derives from 2181. It can mean adultery, infidelity, idolatry, apostasy, unfaithfulness. The sons of Israel were tempted to worship idols (Jer. 3:2,9; Ezek. 23:27; 43:7,9; Hos. 4:11) as a spouse or another mate.

2194. Zâ'am; to be indignant, express indignation, to be irritated, to be angry; to punish, to curse; to denounce. This Heb. verb describes both the state of mind and the activity which results. It can describe the feelings of either man or God. Notice the contrast with other Heb. verbs in Num. 23:7,8. It approaches rage (Prov. 25:23).

2195. Za'am; this mas. Heb. noun comes from 2194. It means anger, wrath, indignation, rage. It occurs twenty-two times in the Heb. O.T., referring more often to God than to man. Jeremiah says that the earth will tremble at God's fury (Jer. 10:10).

2196. Zâ'aph; from an original root signifying boiling. In a figurative sense it means to be angry, to look sorrowful or sullen, to be sad, to fret. The essential idea is almost "foaming at the mouth." This produced the later idea of being morose (Gen. 40:6,7; Dan. 1:10). Jesus did not want those who fasted to have this appearance (Mt. 6:16). It is like a storm brewing within a person until it gives way to rage. It caused Uzziah to sin (II Chr. 26:19). We need to have peace in our hearts.

2197. Za'aph; deriving from 2196, this mas. noun means anger, rage, raging (ocean). The word was used to describe Asa's state of mind when he was rebuked by the prophet Hanani (II Chr. 16:10). This inner rage caused him to commit atrocities. He pouted for years after that. This feeling in the heart is like the roaring of a lion (Prov. 19:12), and like a raging storm at sea (Jon. 1:15). God felt that way when the Assyrians exulted over the destruction of Israel (Isa. 30:30). However, the indignation of the Lord will subside (Mic. 7:9).

2198. Zâ'êph; this Heb. adj., deriving from 2196, means angry, irritated, out of humor, vexed. There are two occurrences (I Kgs. 20:43; 21:4).

2199. Zâ'aq; to shriek (from anguish or a sense of danger), to cry, to cry out, to call. Basically, it is a distress signal. It is parallel in meaning to the similar verb *tsâ'aq* (6817). No doubt these two roots were variations of the initial alveolar sound. Usually it is directed toward God (Judg. 6:6,7), but can be aimed at a false god (Jer. 11:12). It is a cry for help.

2204. Zâqên; to be old, to grow old, to become old. Here is a case where the verb form may have derived from a noun; *zâqân* (2206), "beard." It refers to either men or women, however. The Psalmist says that seventy years was a normal lifespan and eighty was unusual (Ps. 90:10). The age of sixty separated the senior citizens from the rest of society (Lev. 27:1-8), but the Levites could retire at the age of fifty (Num. 4:3,-23,30).

2205. Zâqên; old, aged, ancient (man), eldest, senator. It derives from 2204. See the Septuagint's rendering of this (*presbuteros,* 4245) in the comment in the N.T. lexical section. It is the phase of life which we call "old age" for men or women. It is contrasted with *na'ar* (5288) in Gen. 19:4; Ps. 37:25. When it is used as a sub. pl. (about 100 times), the context determines whether it is a ruling body of elders or the classification of old men. They often sat at the city gate (Deut. 21:19; 22:15; Prov. 31:23; Lam. 5:14) to settle many questions (Deut. 19:12; 21:1ff.,19; Josh. 20:4; Ruth 4:9,11). They were an important governing body even while Moses was the leader (Ex. 3:16; 17:5,6; 18:12; 24:1,9,14; Lev. 4:15; Num. 11:16,24,25). A quorum of ten men was necessary (Ruth 4:2). They continued to have much influence during the period of the monarchy, the divided kingdom, during the exile, and in the post-exilic community of Israel. The precedent had been set for synagogues and congregations of Christians.

2206. Zâqân; this is a mas. noun which can refer to the whiskers of a man's chin (II Sam. 20:9), or of a lion (I Sam. 17:35). It was long enough to be grabbed. Levites were commanded to shave it (Lev. 14:9) to be declared clean. Israelites and priests were forbidden to cut the corners of their beards (Lev. 19:27; 21:5) to conform to pagan practices in surrounding areas. Plucking the beard (Ezra 9:3) or shaving it (Isa. 15:2; Jer. 41:5; 48:37) was a cultural sign of distress. It was a symbol of the destruction to come upon Jerusalem in Ezek. 5:1. The most famous beard was that of Aaron (Ps. 133:2).

2207. Zôqen; this mas. Heb. noun means "old age." In Gen. 48:10 it refers to age as a quality, senility. Jacob was not like the robust Moses (Deut. 34:7).

2208. Zâqûn; this Heb. noun comes from 2204 and also means "old age." It refers to a state of being (Gen. 21:2,7; 37:3; 44:20). Abraham was past the normal age for starting a family.

2209. Ziqnâh; this fem. Heb. noun comes from 2205. It means old or old age. It was used for the advanced ages of Sarah, Solomon, and Asa (Gen. 24:36; I Kgs. 11:4; 15:23). God cares about the infirmed (Ps. 71:9,18; Isa. 46:4).

2212. Zâqaq; originally, the idea was that of straining or extracting. This gave rise to the meanings of purifying, refining, clarifying, purging. The main idea is that of testing to determine the degree of purity. All but two instances refer to metal refining which was accomplished with fire. It could be applied to wine (Isa. 25:6). Job 36:27 might refer to the natural process of evaporation.

2233. Zera'; this mas. noun derives from 2232. It means seed, grain, sowing, crop; offspring, issue, progeny, posterity, family, race. In Lev. 15:16ff., 18:21, 19:20, and Num. 5:28 it refers to semen. This noun is used 224 times. The term in Gen. 3:15 has enormous implications. It is clearly singular, not plural, indicating that the entire line of descendants from our first parents is being treated as a unit. The word is flexible enough to mean either one person (Christ), who represents the entire human race, or mankind in general. The servants of Satan will always be doing battle with the servants of God. This first announcement of the Gospel was enlarged with the Abrahamic covenant (Gen. 12:7), made more specific in David's lineage (II Sam. 7:12; 22:51; Ps. 18:50; 89:4,29,36) and finally realized in Jesus Christ. Compare Rom. 16:20.

2234. Z^{e}ra'; this is the corresponding Aramaic term to 2233. It is used only once (Dan. 2:43).

2236. Zâraq; to scatter, to strew, to sprinkle (whether fluids or solid particles). It has the idea of being here and there. The word occurs thirty-five times. The Septuagint translates it as "poor," when it refers to the blood of the sacrifices upon the altar. This action symbolized an unbreakable bond between God and men. It was an integral part of the ceremony of purification. It confirmed sanctification (Ex. 29:20; Lev. 1:5).

2245. Châbab; to love, to cherish. It is used only once (Deut. 33:3). The original idea was to hold warmly to the bosom or lap.

2254. Châbal; to bind, to pledge, to be in travail, to labor in childbirth, to bring forth with pain. The Brown, Driver, and Briggs lexicon unites these under one root. The K.J.V. also translates it as "deal corruptly," "offend," "destroy," "spoil," and "bands."

2255. Châbal; this Aramaic word corresponds to the Heb. 2254. It means to ruin, to destroy, to hurt, to injure. It is found only in Ezra 6:12; Dan. 2:44; 4:23; 6:22,26; 7:14. Dan. 2:44 is a very important passage concerning the kingdom of God.

2256. Chebel; this mas. Heb. noun derives from 2254. It is a cord, a rope, a line; something twisted, a snare; a measuring line; a portion of land, a district, a coast; a region; a troop, a band of men, a company. The term is used figuratively in connection with death (Ps. 116:3) or Sheol (II Sam. 22:6). The "silver cord" (Ecc. 12:6) may refer to the spinal cord. It is a term of captivity or subjection (I Kgs. 20:31,32). It is also used in a figurative way for the enslaving nature of sin (Job 18:10; Ps. 119:61; 140:5; Prov. 5:22).

2258. Chăbôl; this mas. noun comes from 2254. It appears only in Ezek. 18:12,16; 33:15. The fem. form is found in Ezek. 18:7. It is a pledge, a pawn (as a security for debt).

2267. Cheber; this mas. noun comes from 2266, which has the additional connotation of "to unite" or "to tie a magic knot." It means a community, a company, a society; a spell, a charm, an enchantment. This has the flavor of casting a spell (except for Prov. 21:9; 25:24). There was an association of priests in Hos. 6:9.

2280. Châbash; to bind on, to wrap around; to bind up (a wound), to bandage; to saddle; to cover, to envelope, to enclose; to govern, to rule. Some scholars in several translations believe that Job 28:11 comes from a different root which means "to search." Therefore, it would not refer to binding (damming).

2282. Chag; this mas. noun comes from 2287. It means festival or feast. The main idea was the celebration of a holiday. This noun occurs sixty-one times and usually refers to the three main festivals of Israel which required a pilgrimage: the Passover with the Feast of Unleavened Bread, the Feast of Weeks, and the Feast of Tabernacles. It was a season of religious joy.

2283. Châgâ'; fear, terror, trembling. This fem. Heb. noun occurs only once (Isa. 19:17). It has the sense of reeling.

2309. Chedel; this mas. Heb. noun comes from 2308. It is the resting place of the dead, the grave, cessation. The only occurrence is Isa. 38:11 which the K.J.V. translates as "world," from an amended reading of *cheled* (2465).

2342. Chûwl; to turn in a circle, to whirl, to twist, to writhe; to be in labor (of childbirth); to be afraid, to tremble, to reel; to wait, to hope; to revolve, to rage, to assault, to be strong or pithy; to dance in a circle; to bear a child, to produce; to cause to bring forth; to hope, to wait; to be born; to cause to tremble; to twist, to shake, to tremble; to wait anxiously; to writhe with pain; to be terrified; to be grieved. There are two main ideas to this verb: (1) spinning; (2) twisting in labor pangs. It is unclear whether there are two different roots that are homophonous or two basic sets of meaning from the same root.

2370. Chăzâ'; this is an Aramaic verb corresponding to the Heb. 2372. The word is used often in the normal sense of "see" and also with reference to seeing visions. Biblical Aramaic does not call a prophet by the name of "seer." It occurs thirty times.

2372. Châzâh; to split, to divide; to see, to look, to behold, to observe, to gaze; to select; to prophesy; provide. This word is used almost entirely in poetry. It occurs about fifty times. The verb is used of the real sight of the divine presence (Ex. 24:11; Job 19:26). It was especially appropriate for the visions presented to the minds of the prophets, oracular revelations (Num. 24:4; Isa. 1:1; 2:1; 13:1; 30:10; Lam. 2:14; Ezek. 13:6; Amos 1:1; Hab. 1:1; Zech. 10:2). The meaning of delight is in Job 36:25; Ps. 27:4; Song of Sol. 6:13; Mic. 4:11. The roots of plants are said to perceive or to feel stones in the earth (Job 8:17).

2374. Chôzeh; this act. part. comes from 2372. It is one who beholds, a seer, a prophet, an astrologer; a covenant. Of the twenty-two occurrences, eleven of them are associated with the name of a particular person, indicating his office as prophet (Gad, II Sam. 24:11; I Chr. 21:9; 29:29; II Chr. 29:25; Heman, I Chr. 25:5; Iddo, II Chr. 9:29; 12:15; Hanai, II Chr. 19:2; Asaph, II Chr. 29:25; Jeduthun, II Chr. 35:15; and the Prophet Amos). See the closely-related noun, *nâbîy'* (5030). They are contrasted in II Kgs. 17:13; Isa. 29:10; Amos 7:12. Another word *rô'eh* (7203), is almost identical in meaning to *chôzeh* (see I Sam. 9:9; I Chr. 29:29). *Nâbîy'* means "a spokesman" (Ex. 7:1,2). *Rô'eh* and *chôzeh* reflect that God sometimes revealed Himself to prophets by visions. Used with the meaning of contemplation in Isa. 47:13.

2376. Chêzev; this is an Aramaic mas. noun which is roughly equivalent to 2370. It occurs only in the Book of Daniel.

2377. Châzôwn; this mas. noun derives from 2372. It is a mental sight, a dream, a vision, a revelation, an oracle, a prophecy. It is used in the titles of Isaiah and Nahum. It is the sort of thing which happened in Acts 12:5; 16:9.

2378. Châzôwth; this fem. noun comes from 2372. It is a vision or revelation. It occurs only in II Chr. 9:29.

2380. Châzûwth; this fem. noun originates from 2372. It is a look, an appearance, a conspicuousness; a vision, a revelation; a covenant. The word occurs five times.

2384. Chizzâyôwn; a revelation (especially delivered via a dream), a vision. This mas. noun comes from 2372. Of the nine times that it occurs in the Heb. O.T., five of them describe a prophetic function.

2388. Châzaq; to be bound fast, to be attached; to make firm, to support, to preserve; to be firm, strong, courageous; to conquer, to hold fast; to bind fast, to gird; to make firm, to encourage; to strengthen, to support; to harden, to be obdurate; to seize, to retain, to keep; to be confirmed; to prove courageous, valiant, helpful. It is a word frequently used to describe battle scenes. Twelve times in the book of Exodus this verb is used to describe the condition of Pharaoh's heart. Pharaoh was an obstinate sinner who reacted negatively to God's decree. Since the Hebrews thought of God as being in control of everything, this included Pharaoh. Pharaoh had the choice of compliance with God's will, but he refused. Compare Acts 4:25-28. The term was also frequently used for construction.

2389. Châzâq; strong, firm, valiant; sound, powerful, violent, hard. It means powerful and able to resist. Usually it has a bad sense of violence. Twenty-three of the fifty-seven occurrences refer to God's strong hand. It can have a connotation of stubbornness, impudence, and being unyielding (Ezek. 2:4; 3:7,8).

2390. Châzêq; this is another adj. which is roughly equivalent to 2389. It occurs only in Ex. 19:19 and II Sam. 3:1.

2391. Chêzeq; this mas. Heb. noun comes from 2388. It means strength, might, help. It occurs only once (Ps. 18:2).

2392. Chôzeq; this mas. noun is equivalent to 2391. It appears in Ex. 13:3,14,16; Amos 6:13; Hag. 2:22. It is describing military prowess.

2393. Chezqâh; this fem. noun derives from 2391. It means prevailing power, strength, overcoming.

2394. Chozqâh; this is the fem. form of 2392. It is a strengthening, a repairing; force, violence, severity.

2398. Châṭâ'; to miss, to miss the way, to fail; to sin, to forfeit; to endanger; to atone for, to expiate, to clear from sin; to cause to sin, to seduce, to incure guilt, to make guilty, to condemn; to free oneself from sin, to purify from uncleanness. The root occurs about 580 times in the Heb. O.T. It is the most important word for sin. It is very similar to the Gr. word, *hamartanō* (264). See the comments in the N.T. lexical section. The idea of being off target is found in Judg. 20:16 (or of getting lost in Prov. 19:2). It is coming up short of the goal (Prov. 8:36). It can be a breach of civil law (Gen. 40:1; II Kgs. 18:14), a fault (Ex. 5:7), a serious breakdown in a personal relationship (Judg. 11:27; I Sam. 19:4; 24:11; 26:21), bearing the blame (Gen. 43:9; 44:32), failure (Lev. 4:2; 5:16), not respecting another's rights (Gen. 20:9; Judg. 11:27; II Chr. 6:22), and sinning against God (Ex. 10:16; I Sam. 2:25). It is falling short of God's standard. See the Gr. word *anomia* (458) in the N.T. lexical section.

2399. Chêṭ'; this mas. Heb. noun comes from 2398. It means sin, transgression, fault, flaw; punishment of sin. It is a turning away from obeying God; therefore, God cannot accept this and we are not whole. It can refer to a breach of civil law (Gen. 41:9; Ecc. 10:4), disobedience to God (Num. 27:3; Deut. 15:9; II Kgs. 10:29; Ps. 103:10; Isa. 38:17; Lam. 1:8; Dan. 9:16), a capital crime (Deut. 21:22; 22:26), or guilt (Lev. 20:20; Num. 9:13; Isa. 53:12; Ezek. 23:49). Lam. 3:39 uses it in the sense of punishment.

2400. Chaṭṭâ'; this mas. noun originates from 2398. It means sinner, offender, criminal, sinful. The word occurs eighteen times in the Heb. O.T. It is a person who sins habitually and is subject to the consequences of his actions.

2401. Chăṭâ'âh; this is a fem. form of 2399. It means sin, offense, guilt, punishment, sin (offering). It occurs eight times. Except for Ps. 40:6, it has an abstract connotation.

2402. Chaṭṭâ'âh; this is the Aramaic equivalent of 2401. It is used only once (Ezra 6:17) and is translated as "a sin offering."

2403. Chaṭṭâ'âh or **chaṭṭâ'th;** this fem. Heb. noun derives from 2398. It means an offense (sometimes habitual sinfulness), sin, a sinful thing. The term is used only three times. In Ex. 34:7 it is linked with *'âvôn* (5771) and *pesha'* (6588). It has a concrete meaning in Isa. 6:7. An Aramaic form appears in Ezra 6:17 with the meaning of sin-offering.

2408. Chăṭîy; this is an Aramaic word corresponding to 2398. It appears only in Dan. 4:27.

2409. Chaṭṭâyâ'; this is an Aramaic fem. noun which is equivalent to 2408. It is the Kethib (written text) in Ezra 6:17, which is its only occurrence. It is an expiatory sin offering.

2416. Chay; this Heb. adj. comes from 2421. Some of its meanings are: living, alive, have life, remain alive, sustain life, live prosperously, live forever, be quickened, revive from sickness, discouragement, or even death; vigorous; raw, fresh, running (water); by the life of, as one lives (as used in oaths and exclamations), livelihood, life, refreshment. The O.T. puts a real premium upon life as being intrinsically good. It came from God (Gen. 2:7), but death ensued because of sin. He was no longer allowed to partake of the tree of life (Gen. 3:22). God is the Source of life (Ps. 36:9; 139:13ff.) and the Lord of life and death (Num. 27:16; Deut. 32:39; Job 12:10). *Chay* is a set of experiences, not an abstract principle of vitality which is separate from the body. The Hebrews viewed man holistically, i.e., body, mind, and spirit were a unified whole. Life was associated with health, prosperity, vitality, etc., while death was the very opposite.

2417. Chay; this is the Aramaic equivalent of 2418. It appears in Ezra 6:10; Dan. 2:30; 4:17,34; 6:20,26; 7:12.

2418. Chăyâ'; this is the verbal correlate to the Heb. 2421. It is used five times in Daniel as a courtly imperative, "O king, live forever." That was similar to the English, "Long live the king!" Dan. 5:19 has the idea of the preservation of life.

2420. Chîydâh; this fem. noun derives from 2330. It is a puzzle, a trick, a dark saying, maxim, riddle, parable, proverb, oracle; song, intrigue. The most famous convolution was the one put forth by Samson (Judg. 14:12-19). It was so complicated that no one could decipher it without inside information from Delilah. It could be any enigmatic sentence or thought.

2421. Châyâh; to live, to exist, to enjoy life; to live anew, to recover, to be well; to make alive, to enliven, to animate, to quicken; to preserve, to refresh, to rebuild; to restore to life. The first few chapters of Genesis clearly establish that life comes from a right relationship with God. The forces of life are not to be seized by incantations. The choice between life and death is ours (Deut. 30:15-20). Life is completely related to the Word of God (Ezek. 3:18ff.; 14:13ff.; 18:1ff.; 20:1ff.; 33:1ff.). As Jesus pointed out, we gain our very life from God's words (Deut. 8:3; Ps. 119:50,93) and not merely from bread. Evil men cannot live in their sins forever (Ps. 49:7-9,18,19).

2422. Châyeh; this Heb. adj., which derives from 2421, means lively, having the vigor of life, vigorous, living. It occurs only once (Ex. 1:19) to explain why the Hebrews survived.

2424. Chayûwth; this fem. noun originates from 2421 and means life or lifetime. It occurs only in II Sam. 20:3, "living as widows." The marginal reading in the K.J.V. is "in widowhood of life."

2425. Châyay; this is another root which is very similar to 2421. It also means "to live." Causitively, it means "to revive."

2426. Chêyl; this is a related form of 2428. It has its origins in the verb 2342. It means power, strength, valor; military force, army; wealth; virtue, honesty.

2428. Chayil; deriving from 2342, and related as another mas. form of 2426, it means might, strength, power; able, valiant, virtuous, valor; army, host, forces; riches, substance, wealth. The main meanings of this noun, which occurs 244 times in the Heb. O.T., are "strength," "army," and "wealth." Note the interesting usage of *chayil* for the entourage of the queen of Sheba (I Kgs. 10:2; II Chr. 9:1).

2429. Chayil; this Aramaic word is equivalent to the Heb. form 2428. There are six occurrences (Ezra 4:23; Dan. 3:4,20; 4:14,35; 5:7).

2449. Châkam; to be wise, to act wisely, to be intelligent, to be prudent; to become wise, to make wise, to teach; to be cunning, clever; to think oneself wise, to show oneself wise. The verb is used twenty-six times in the Heb. O.T. It is an intelligent attitude toward the experiences of life. This includes matters of general interest, basic morality, prudence in secular affairs, skills in the arts, moral sensitivity, and spiritual experience. At times it seems almost philosophical. Hebrew wisdom was very different from other ancient world views. Israel believed that there was a personal God who is holy and just. He expects us to live our lives according to His principles. They did not speculate like the Greeks. They emphasized the human will of the heart, not the intellect (the head). Therefore, Hebrew wisdom was very practical. It was based on what God revealed about right and wrong. This all applied to daily life.

2450. Châkâm; this Heb. adj. comes from 2449. It means wise, intelligent, prudent, experienced, clever. When used substantively, it is a wise man, a philosopher, a magician. This could refer to the skillfulness of artisans (Ex. 35:10; Jer. 10:9), diplomats (I Kgs. 5:7) and the shrewd (II Sam. 14:2). Men from other nations had this quality (Egypt, Gen. 41:8; Babylon, Isa. 44:25; Persia, Esth. 6:13). A wise man gave practical advice based on divine revelation in addition to his own experience and personal observation.

2451. Chokmâh; this fem. noun originates from 2449. It means wisdom, knowledge, experience, intelligence, insight, judgment. It is always used in a positive sense. *Chokmâh* is used to describe an entire range of human experience: embroidering (Ex. 28:3), metal working (Ex. 31:3,6), military strategy (Isa. 10:13), diplomacy (Deut. 34:9; II Sam. 14:20; Ezek. 28:4,5), shrewdness (II Sam. 20:22), prudence (Ps. 37:30; 90:12; Prov. 10:31), and practical spirituality (Isa. 33:6). God is all-powerful and all-knowing. Therefore, all wisdom has its source in Him (Job 11:6; 12:13; 28:20,28; 38:37; Prov. 2:6; 3:19; Jer. 10:12). *Chokmâh* is personified only to a point—it does not have a separate existence (Prov. 1:20; 8:1-31; 9:1,2). The figure of wisdom was never regarded as independent of God. It is only one of His attributes. The noun is not a woman, only feminine in gender. True wisdom leads to reverence for the Lord (Job 28:28; Prov. 2:2). Therefore, skeptics will never find this kind of wisdom (see Js. 3:13-18), and they will never know the true meaning of life (Prov. 14:6,7).

2452. Chokmâh; this is the Aramaic equivalent to 2451. It occurs in Ezra 7:25; Dan. 2:20,21,23,30; 5:11,14).

2454. Chokmôwth; this is a fem. pl. noun form which is equivalent to 2451. It is used only once (Prov. 14:1).

2455. Chôl; profane, unholy, common. This adj. comes from 2490. It is the opp. of holy and consecrated (see Lev. 10:10 and I Sam. 21:4,5). It is used seven times. It describes a non-sacred place in Ezekiel (42:20; 48:15). It was the opp. of what was ceremonially clean (Ezek. 22:26; 44:23).

2465. Cheled; this mas. noun means life, lifetime; world, worldliness. It occurs only five times (Job 11:17; Ps. 17:14; 39:5; 49:1; 89:47). It has the flavor of transitory time, the fleeting nature of our existence.

2490. Châlal; to be profaned, to be defiled; to profane, to defile, to pollute, to prostitute; to make common; to loose, to break. The core meaning of this root and its history in cognate languages is rather uncertain. There are eighty-three uses of this word and its derivatives. Generally speaking, the word refers to doing violence to the established law of God (Ps. 55:20; 89:31; Zeph. 3:4). It is a desecration of something which is holy. Originally, the word was used earlier to refer to sexual defilement (Gen. 49:4) or incest.

2491. Châlâl; though this verb root is homophonous with 2490, it is an independent verb form. It means to be pierced, to be perforated, to wound, to bore through; to play on the flute. There are only eight occurrences of the verb itself, though there are eighty-eight derivative forms. It usually connotes the fatal wounding of a person. See the important Messianic passage of Isa. 53:5. The Jerusalem Bible translates it as "pierced through." This is important in light of Jn. 19:34 (cf. Zech. 12:10).

2502. Châlats; to draw off, to draw out, to withdraw, to take off; to rescue, to be rescued; to be delivered; to be drawn out, to extricate; to rob.

2530. Châmad; to desire, to covet, to long for; to be desirable, costly, precious; to feel delight. This word describes the pleasant trees in Eden (Gen. 2:9). Unfortunately, the forbidden tree became desirable (Gen. 3:6). Stolen waters seem sweeter. It is part of one of the Ten Commandments; we are not to covet (Ex. 20:17). This refers to an inordinate, ungoverned, selfish desire, whether it be the gold of idols (Deut. 7:25), or lusting after prostitutes (Prov. 6:25), or craving fields (Mic. 2:2; cf. Ex. 34:24). Achan's theft started with *châmad* (Josh. 7:21).

2534. Chêmâh; this fem. noun comes from 3179. It means warmth, heat, anger, wrath, rage, indignation; poison (Deut. 32:24; Ps. 58:4).

2551. Chemlâh; this fem. noun derives from 2550. It means pity, mercy, compassion. It is used only twice (Gen. 19:16; Isa. 63:9). It describes God's loving mercy and willingness to deliver His people from danger. It is parallel to *'âhab* (157) in the Isaiah passage.

2553. Chammân; this mas. noun, which only appears in pl. form. comes from 2535. It refers to the idols of

Baal, sun-pillars. These were incense altars. Parallel to *'âshêrâh* (842) in Isa. 17:8. Recent excavations have produced small, stone, cup-shaped objects. The word occurs eight times.

2554. Châmaç; to oppress, to be bold, to be violent, to do violence to someone, to treat violently, to hurt, to overthrow, to tear down; to be disgraced. This was the word for sinful violence, extreme wickedness. It was one of the main causes for the flood in the time of Noah.

2555. Châmâç; this is the noun form of 2554. It is violence, oppression, wickedness, wrong; unrighteous gain. The K.J.V. also has: "wrong," "cruelty," "unrighteous," "false," injustice," "violent dealing," "damage." Gen. 16:5 should be translated "injustice." Sarah wanted Abraham to vindicate it.

2556. Châmêts; to be sharp, sour, salted, to be leavened; to be deep red or purple; to be violent; to be excited, to be bitterly moved. The basic meaning was fermentation.

2557. Châmêtz; this mas. noun derives from 2556. It is anything which is fermented or leavened (even ill-gotten wealth). The normal process of bread-making included some form of yeast to make the bread rise, i.e., the natural fermentation of benign bacteria. During the Passover, no one was allowed to eat leavened bread (Ex. 12:15; 13:3,7). Unleavened bread signified the suddenness of the deliverance of the Israelites by God (Deut. 16:3). Ordinary leavened bread was prohibited on other occasions (Ex. 23:18; 34:25; Lev. 2:11; 6:17), but allowable under certain circumstances (Lev. 7:13; 23:17; Amos 4:5). It later became a symbol of corruption and impurity (see Mt. 16:12; Mk. 8:15; I Cor. 5:8).

2580. Chên; this mas. Heb. noun comes from 2603. It means favor, kindness, grace, loveliness, charm, preciousness. This word occurs sixty-nine times in the Heb. O.T., forty-seven of which were found in the expression, "Find favor in the eyes of." Most of the occurrences are secular and not theological in importance. Its thirteen appearances in Proverbs have to do with aesthetic charm or beauty. It is often found in a superior-inferior relationship. In Deut. 24:1 the word appears concerning divorce, which gave rise to centuries of debate about its meaning. It is possible that Zech. 4:7 has the sense of "Bravo!"

2587. Channûwn; this Heb. adj. derives from 2603. It means gracious, merciful. The term occurs thirteen times. The gracious acts of Jehovah are often revealed together with His righteousness, as He judged evil. All instances refer to God. The most striking passage is Ex. 34:6.

2596. Chânak; to initiate, to teach; to dedicate, to consecrate, to inaugurate. This Heb. verb occurs only five times (Deut. 20:5; twice; I Kgs. 8:63; II Chr. 7:5; Prov. 22:6). It was similar to our "ground-breaking ceremony." Very early training for children is indicated by the word in Prov. 22:6. It was a community action.

2597. Chânukkâ'; this is the Aramaic equivalent to 2598. It occurs in Ezra 6:16,17; Dan. 3:2,3.

2598. Chănukkâh; this fem. noun comes from 2596. It means a dedicatory sacrifice, a dedication, an inauguration. It appears in Num. 7:10,11,84,88; II Chr. 7:9; Neh. 12:27; and in the title of Ps. 30:1. The term is most famous for its use between the O.T. and the N.T. when worship was reestablished in the temple in B.C. 165 after Antiochus Epiphanes desecrated it. Today it is known as the Hanukkah feast, and it occurs in late December. It was mentioned once in the N.T. (Jn. 10:22).

2603. Chânan; to be inclined, to be favorable, to be kind, gracious, to pity, to have mercy, to bestow; to be pitied, to complain; to make lovely; to implore, to seek mercy. The verb is used a total of seventy-eight times. It is often used in the context of the strong and the weak in negotiation. Many times it has the connotation of showing kindness to the poor and needy. Jehovah is the subject of this verb forty-one times in the Qal stem. Fifty-one individuals in the O.T. drew at least part of their name from this verb. Even the Punic name, Hannibal, might be traceable to it. The Heb. name Hannah produced these modern names: Ann, Anna, Nan, Nancy, Anita, and Annette. The Heb. name Johanan gave us the following names in modern times: John, Jean, Giovanni, Juan, Johann, Hans, Jan, and Ivan.

2604. Chănan; this is the Aramaic correlate to 2603. It occurs only in Dan. 4:27 and Dan. 6:11. It has the sense of imploring favor or making supplication.

2610. Chânêph; this Heb. word means profane, wicked, defiled, polluted, profaned, corrupt, hypocritical. The main idea is that of straying away from the right path. Transgressing God's laws, violating His statutes, and breaking His covenant all contribute to "pollution" of the land (Isa. 24:5; Jer. 3:1,2) and Zion (Mic. 4:11). A murder does the same thing (Num. 35:33). The evil actions of religious leaders polluted the temple (Jer. 23:11). Daniel predicted Antiochus Epiphanes' actions in Dan. 11:32 long before the event took place in the time of the Maccabeans. The values of godless people were completely twisted.

2611. Chânêph; this Heb. adj. derives from 2610. It means hypocrite or hypocritical. The A.S.V., R.S.V., and New English Bible usually translate this word as "godless." It appears thirteen times in the Heb. O.T.

2612. Chôneph; this mas. Heb. noun means impiety, godlessness, hypocrisy. It occurs only once (Isa. 32:6). It derives from 2610.

2613. Chănûphâh; this is a fem. Heb. noun which is equivalent to 2612. It appears only once (Jer. 23:15). The worst type of fool is the one who practices the worst type of ungodliness or profaneness.

2616. Châçad; to show oneself kind, merciful. By antithesis it means reproach or disgrace (Prov. 25:10). The other two occurrences are II Sam. 22:26; Ps. 18:25.

2617. Cheçed; this mas. Heb. noun derives from 2616. It is one of the most important words in the Heb. O.T. The opinions of notable scholars differ. Were the tenets of God's covenant with Israel only stipulations of an agreement which was restricted to Israel, to which God remains true and to which He demands loyalty? Or, were they eternal principles which stemmed from God's nature and His creation to which all men are obligated and accountable? The real question is whether the passages ascribe God's *cheçed* to His covenants or to His everlasting love? Love is a covenant word, and God is love (I Jn. 4:8,16). The term is closely related to the forgiveness of sins. God was obviously in a covenant relationship with Israel and expressed this relationship in *cheçed*, which was eternal (Ps. 136). *Cheçed* does not necessarily involve a covenant, nor does it necessarily mean fidelity to a covenant. It is more the attitude of love which contains mercy. The K.J.V.'s "lovingkindness" is archaic, but not far from capturing the full meaning of the word. Other definitions are: love, benevolence, kindness, good will, favor, benefit, grace, mercy, piety, loyalty, unfailing love, beauty.

2620. Châçâh; to flee (for protection), to seek refuge, to take refuge; to trust (in God), to confide in, to hope in (someone). This root is distinguished from *beṭach* (983) because it indicates more precipitate action. Along with its derivatives, the verb is mostly used in psalms and hymns in the Heb. O.T. Though it can mean to take shelter in a literal sense (Job 24:8; Ps. 104:18; Isa. 4:6; 25:4), it is used more often in a figurative sense of seeking spiritual refuge and putting trust in one's deity. There is a strong motif in several passages which expressed a belief that defense positions high in the rocks were secure. However, one could seek solace in the temple of God (Isa. 14:32; cf. I Kgs. 1:50; Ps. 61:4). Even the strongest people must retreat sometimes. God is the only stronghold (Ps. 46:1), which gave rise to Martin Luther's famous hymn, "A Mighty Fortress Is Our God."

2622. Châçûwth; this fem. Heb. noun means refuge, refuge-seeking, shelter. Its only occurrence is found in Isa. 30:3. It derives from 2620.

2623. Châçîyd; this Heb. adj. comes from 2616. It means kind, benevolent, gracious; pious, good. When used as a substantive, it means saint, or holy one. It is not entirely clear that god's people were referred to by *châçîyd*. Does this mean they were characterized by *cheçed* (2617)? Or, were they called this because they were the objects of God's *cheçed* (2617)? The word is used thirty-two times, and twenty-five of them are found in Psalms. Ps. 16:10 is very important because it refers to *the* holy one (Jesus) to come. Peter referred to this passage in Acts 2:27. In Maccabean times, the word came to be used in connection with the Orthodox Jewish party. Compare the term Hasidic today.

2654. Châphêts; to find pleasure in, to take delight in, to be pleased with, to have an affection for, to desire, to choose; to bend, to bow. The main meaning is to feel a strong positive attraction for something. Unlike other synonyms for this emotion, this word connotes subjective involvement. This root is used a total of 123 times in all its derivatives. Either God or men can have this feeling. It means to like someone or something very, very much.

2655. Châphêts; deriving from 2654, this Heb. adj. means taking pleasure in, liking, willing, delighting in. It occurs eleven times in the Heb. O.T.

2656. Chêphets; this mas. Heb. noun originates from 2654. It signifies pleasure, delight, wish, desire; a matter, business, pursuit. The term is used thirty-nine times in many different types of contexts. Isa. 53:10 says that God's delight will prosper in the hand of the Messiah.

2706. Chôq; this mas. Heb. noun comes from 2710. It is a statute, regulation, law, custom; decree; share, task, term, limit, boundary. The R.S.V. also translates it as "ordinance," "due," and "bound." It occurs 128 times in the Heb. O.T. The ancient people often engraved their laws upon slabs of stone or metal and then displayed them in public places. However, the root was not limited to these materials. These are precepts and rules which must be strictly obeyed. Sometimes it designates a legal right (Gen. 47:26). This extended to natural laws (Job 28:26; 38:10; Ps. 148:6; Prov. 8:29; Jer. 5:22). At other times it denotes privilege or due (Gen. 47:22; Ex. 29:28; Lev. 24:9).

2708. Chuqqâh; this is the fem. noun form of 2706. It means law, statute, custom, enactment. It appears 102 times in the Heb. O.T. The fem. form often has the added qualifier of *'owlâm* (5769, perpetual). This was an ordinance from God which was permanently binding (Ex. 12:14,17; 13:10; 27:21; 28:43; 29:9; Lev. 16:29,31,34; 23:41; 24:3; Num. 10:8; 15:15; 19:10,21).

2710. Châqaq; to cut, to engrave, to inscribe, to trace; to establish, to ordain, to prescribe, to decree, to portray; to be a leader, a ruler, a law-giver; sceptre. It occurs nineteen times in the Heb. O.T. The primary meaning is that of writing or drawing, in the sense of etching (Isa. 22:16; Ezek. 4:1; 23:14). It was done in the palm of one's hand (Isa. 49:16), in a book (Job 19:23; Isa. 30:8), or on other objects. The root can mean to enact a decree (Prov. 8:15; Isa. 10:1 cf. Jer. 31:35). The part. form denotes a ruler, law-giver (Gen. 49:10; Isa. 33:22), or a commander (Judg. 5:9,14). It occurs in the important Messianic passage (Gen. 49:10), which promises the kingship to Judah.

2711. Chêqeq; this mas. Heb. noun comes from 2710. It means enactment or resolution. It appears only in Judg. 5:15, where it is translated "thoughts" (i.e., impressions) in the K.J.V., and Isa. 10:1, "decrees."

2715. Chôr or **Chôwr** or **Chûr;** this mas. Heb. noun usually occurs only in the pl. form. Deriving from 2787 (which has to do with "white" or "pure"), it means the free or the noble. It occurs thirteen times. In Ecc. 10:17 the R.S.V. translates it as "free-men." Along with the elders, these leaders governed cities (I Kgs. 21:8; Jer. 39:6). Along with the priests and rulers, they helped in the reconstruction period following Babylonian exile (Neh. 4:14,19; 5:7; 6:17; 13:17). It is possible that the word was originally an Aramaic loanword. Sometimes they seem to be administrators, and sometimes just influential people. There was no aristocracy.

2717. Chârab or **Chârêb;** to dry up, to become dry, to be dry; to be stupified; to parch. See Gen. 8:13; Job 14:11; Ps. 106:9; Isa. 19:6. It denotes the absence of water. In a secondary sense, it means to be desolate or laid waste; to destroy, to lay waste; to fight with one another. Jer. 2:12 may mean to be amazed or astonished. Generally speaking, it is the condition which results following a drought or a battle.

2718. Chărab; this is the Aramaic equivalent of 2717. It means to demolish. Ezra 4:15 is its sole occurrence.

2719. Chereb; this fem. Heb. noun originates from 2717. It appears 407 times in the Heb. O.T. The majority of cases refer to a weapon, whether a sword in general, a short sword, a straight sword, a knife, or a dagger. Rather short, straight swords, which were made of bronze, were popular in the third and early second millenia B.C. Curved, sickle-shaped swords were more common in the second millenium. The Philistines introduced a long, straight sword made of iron at the end of the second millenium (I Sam. 13:19). They were worn in a scabbard (I Sam. 17:51) which was attached to a belt. I Sam. 13:19-22 describes how the Philistines maintained a military advantage by keeping secret their method of forging iron. The short, bronze daggers of the Israelites were no match for the long, iron swords of the Philistines. Compare the short sword of Ehud (Judg. 3:15,16,21,22). Eventually Israelite swords could penetrate armor (I Sam. 17:5,38,51; 21:9). Saul committed suicide on the point of his sword (I Sam. 31:4). Ex. 17:13; Num. 21:24; Josh. 6:21, and other passages literally read "mouth of the sword," which should be translated "edge of the sword." The Heb. text, "a sword of mouths" in Ps. 149:6 and Prov. 5:4 refers to a "two-edged" sword. The sword is said to "devour" its victims (Deut. 32:42; II Sam. 2:26; 11:25). See Ezek. 21 for Jehovah's sword. Sometimes the word stands for war (Lev. 26:25; II Chr. 29:9; Jer. 14:15; 24:10; Ezek. 7:15; 33:2ff.). It means violent end in Ps. 22:20. Harsh words and sharp tongues are similar to swords (Ps. 52:2; 57:4; 64:3; Prov. 12:18). The "flaming sword" of Gen. 3:24 may refer to lightning (cf. Ps. 104:3,4), symbolic of God's holiness and judgment. Early stone altars to Jehovah were not to be built with these tools (Ex. 20:25; Deut. 27:5).

2720. Chârêb; this Heb. adj. comes from 2717. It means dry, parched, ruined, desolate. It occurs in Lev. 7:10; Neh. 2:3,17; Prov. 17:1; Jer. 33:10,12; Ezek. 36:35,38; Hag. 1:4,9.

2723. Chorbâh; this fem. Heb. noun derives from 2721 and indirectly from 2717. It means desert, dry country, desolate places, desolation, in ruins. It usually describes the rubble of cities in the wake of total destruction.

2724. Chârâbâh; this fem. Heb. noun derives from 2720. It means dryness, dry land, a desert. See 2717 also.

2727. Chârag; to tremble, to quake, to run away while in a state of terror. It is like the sudden rush of frightened birds who are flushed from their hiding place.

2729. Chârad; to quake, to move around; to be afraid, to be startled, to be anxious, to tremble; to come with trepidation; to frighten, to terrify. The primary meaning is shaking. Trembling and fear are deriv. meanings. Mount Sinai shook (Ex. 19:18). Earthquakes are similar to the trembling of human beings (Isa. 10:29; 41:5; Ezek. 26:18). See Hos. 11:10,11 for nervous, bird-like characteristics. Most instances refer to deep emotional reactions (Gen. 27:33; Deut. 28:26; Judg. 8:12; Ruth 3:8; I Sam. 13:7; 14:15; II Sam. 17:2; I Kgs. 1:49; Job 11:19; Isa. 17:2; Jer. 7:33; 30:10; Ezek. 34:28).

2730. Chârêd; this Heb. adj. comes from 2729. It occurs only in Judg. 7:3; I Sam. 4:13; Ezra 9:4; 10:3; Isa. 66:2,5. It means afraid, trembling, fearful, anxious, reverent. It could be a technical term for awe for God's reforms in Ezra.

2731. Chărâdâh; this fem. Heb. noun comes from 2730. It means quaking, trembling; terror, fear, consternation; care, careful service. The R.S.V. uses the word "panic" (I Sam. 14:15). Basically, it is the feeling of dread before something terrible which is about to happen, a premonition, an expectation. It occurs nine times in the Heb. O.T.

2734. Chârâh; this root means to burn, to be kindled; to glow with anger, to be incensed; to be zealous, to rival; to act zealously; to grow indignant, to become angry. This verb and its derivatives appear 139 times in the Heb. O.T. Unlike some of its Heb. synonyms, it points to the fire or heat of the anger just after it has been ignited. It can refer to the anger of either men or God. It has the sense of fretting in Ps. 37:1,7,8; Prov. 24:19.

2747. Chereṭ; it is not certain what this mas. Heb. noun derives from. It may be 2790 or 2801. It occurs only in Ex. 32:4 and Isa. 8:1. It is a graving tool (used by sculptors) or pen.

2748. Charṭôm; this Heb. noun originates from 2747. It occurs eleven times in the Heb. O.T. It is always in the pl. form. It means scribes, writers of hieroglyphics, Egyptian or Babylonian sages, magicians. They practiced the occult, sorcery, and incantations.

2749. Charṭôm; this is the Aramaic equivalent of 2748. It appears in Dan. 2:10,27; 4:7,9; 5:11. It is possible that it came from an Egyptian loanword through the Heb. It is interesting that it has a four-consonant structure, rather than the usual three, like most Semitic words.

2750. Chŏrîy; this Heb. noun derives from 2734. It refers to heat or burning (especially of anger). The word is used twice of God and four times of man. It is always followed by *'aph* (639), "nose." For example, King Saul hated David so much (I Sam. 20:34), that Jonathan could not remain in the presence of his father. The fierceness of his anger was too intense.

2763. Charam; to ban, devote, dedicate; to curse, to destroy utterly; to be doomed, exterminated. The basic idea was that of setting something aside strictly for God's use. It was considered most holy by God, and therefore could not be sold or redeemed by any substitutionary measure. All such designated objects were to be given to the priests for the support of the religious ceremonies (Num. 18:14; Josh. 6:19; Ezek. 44:29). Once invoked, it was absolutely compulsory. Canaanite cities were treated like contraband (Num. 21:2,3; Deut. 7:2-6; 13:12-15; 20:17,18; Josh. 6:21; 8:26; 10:28; 11:11). The lure toward idolatry was removed by devastating the sources. If people were included (Lev. 27:28,29; I Sam. 15:3), they were executed. The root, *qâdâsh* (6942), is a setting apart of non-offensive objects from ordinary use, in surrender to God.

2764. Chêrem or **cherem;** this Heb. mas. noun derives from 2763. It occurs twenty-eight times in the Heb. O.T. and means a devoted thing, devotion; a ban, a curse, extermination; a person or thing which has been marked for destruction; a net, an enticement. Our word "harem," the special quarters for Muslim wives, comes from this etymology. The essential meaning is "forbidden" or "prohibited." It was an object which was surrendered to God and to His service, or something declared for utter destruction. The most famous example was the entire city of Jericho and everything in it (Josh. 6:17). Everything flammable was to be burned or reserved for God. However, Achan took some things which were in the city. This caused the whole community of Israel to be affected by the violation. They lost an easy battle at Ai (Josh. 7:12,13). Sin was in the camp, and it had to be removed before God would make them victorious again. Jericho was a pagan city which defiantly opposed God's work. Through Achan, Israel unwittingly became associated with Jericho. *Chêrem* seems to refer to the ban itself in I Kgs. 20:42 and Isa. 34:5; 43:28.

2781. Cherpâh; this fem. Heb. noun comes from 2778. It means reproach, shame, the object of reproach; scorn, contempt. It has the connotation of blaming others, of pointing the finger, a stigma (Isa. 25:8; Jer. 31:19; Ezek. 36:30). In a figurative sense, it is someone or something which is despised (Neh. 2:17; Ps. 22:6; 69:10; Dan. 12:2; Joel 2:17,19). The verbal form *châraph* (2778) seems to indicate defamation (Neh. 6:13), dishonor or disgrace (Prov. 14:31), taunting (Judg. 8:15; Ps. 119:42), or mocking (II Kgs. 19:22).

2787. Chârar; to burn, to glow; to be burned, to be parched, to be charred. The R.S.V. renders Isa. 24:6 with "scorched." The basic meaning is the residue which is left from burning. It is used twelve times in the Heb. O.T. It can refer to the after-effects of fever (Job 30:30) or excessive crying (Ps. 69:3).

2788. Chârêr; this comes from 2787 and means a parched place, a dry country, sun-burned, arid. It only appears in Jer. 17:6, where it refers to the life of godless people in a figurative way.

2789. Cheres; this mas. Heb. noun means clay, pottery, earthenware, potsherd. It occurs seventeen times in the Heb. O.T. It is what the potter produces (Isa. 45:9). Sometimes it is dried and fired (Ps. 22:15) or glazed (Prov. 26:23). Besides ordinary household use, documents were stored in them (Jer. 32:14). That was certainly the case for the Dead Sea Scrolls of the Qumran community.

2803. Châshab; to count, to count for, to impute, to esteem, to reckon; to think, to plan, to make a judgment, to imagine, to combine, to devise, to invent; to meditate, to abound. Its part. form indicates a weaver. The principal idea is that of using the mind in the activity of thinking, creating new ideas. This verb occurs 121 times. It can be done by God or man, for good or evil. It is the key theological word in Gen. 15:6 and Rom. 4:3, where God registered faith as tantamount to exoneration. A man is blessed if the Lord does not condemn him for sin (Ps. 32:2; Rom. 4:8). The word can describe skill in art (Ex. 31:4; 35:32,35) and clever military inventions (II Chr. 26:15). It was an accounting term (Lev. 25:27,50,52; 27:18,23).

2821. Châshak; to be dark, to grow dark, to be obscured, to be surrounded with darkness; to make dark, to darken; to spread darkness; to be dim, to be hidden. This verb comes from the noun *châshak*. Of the eighteen occurrences, only Ex. 10:15 is in prose; the rest are in Heb. poetry and indicate a curse or judgment. Ecc. 12:3 describes impaired vision which is associated with old age, cf. Lam. 5:17 also.

2822. Chôshek; dark, darkness, obscurity, night, dusk; misery, falsehood, ignorance. About half of its eighty occurrences refer to a state which is opposite of light. It accompanied God's appearance on Mount Sinai (Ex. 14:20; Deut. 4:11; 5:23). It can refer to the darkness of the grave (I Sam. 2:9; Job 10:21; 18:18; 34:22; Ps. 88:12; Ecc. 6:4). The term appears much more frequently in Job, Psalms, and Isaiah. It has the figurative meaning of blindness, hiddenness, and judgment. See *skotia* (4653) and *skotos* (4655) in the N.T. lexical section.

2824. Cheshkâh; this fem. Heb. noun comes from 2822. The meaning is also the same. It appears only in Ps. 18:12.

2825. Chăshêkâh; this is another fem. form equivalent to 2824.

2831. Chashmân; appearing only in pl. form, it means noble, distinguished, rich. The K.J.V. translates it as "princes" in its lone appearance (Ps. 68:31). It has the sense of ambassadors. Its deriv. is uncertain.

2836. Châshaq; to be attached to, to love, to have pleasure, to delight in. It has the sense of joining together, adhering, cleaving. This kind of love is already bound to its object. It occurs twelve times. It can be used to describe God's feelings (Isa. 38:17) or a man's devotion toward God (Ps. 91:14). It is a love which will not let go.

2837. Chêsheq; desire, delight, the thing desired. It appears in I Kgs. 9:1, 19; II Chr. 8:6; Isa. 21:4. The K.J.V. also translates it as "pleasure." The temple and palace of Solomon were functional parts of the kingdom, but the king was emotionally attached to them.

2847. Chittâh; this fem. Heb. noun derives from 2865. It means fear or terror. It occurs only in Gen. 35:5 to describe the supernatural shock which the surrounding towns felt after the massacre at Shechem.

2849. Chathchath; this mas. noun occurs only once (Ecc. 12:5) and only in the plural. It comes from 2844. It means fears or terrors. Elderly people have many anxieties according to the Preacher.

2851. Chittîyth; this fem. Heb. noun comes from 2865. It means terror or alarm. It is found in Ezek. 26:17; 32:23-32, describing the terror imposed upon the nations by Tyre and by the military power of the other nations mentioned there.

2865. Châthath; to be broken, abolished, afraid, dismayed, confounded, alarmed, in fear, in despair, crushed; to terrify; to break. The meaning ranges from a literal breaking to abstract destruction, to demoralization, and finally to panic. Even in our times, we speak of someone "cracking" under stress. The K.J.V. also has: "amazed," "broken down," "chapped," "broken in pieces," "discouraged," "affrighted," "beaten down," etc.

2873. Tâbach; to butcher, to slaughter, to slay, to kill ruthlessly; to cook; to be an executioner, to be a guardsman. Although the main sense referred to animals, this idea was often employed for people. *Zâbach* (2076) is very similar, but adds the idea of "slaughter for sacrifice." *Hârag* (2026) has the connotation of killing with violence in war or conflict. *Shâchat* (7819) conveys the sense of beating the animal in order to kill it. This often included skinning or dressing the animal. Compare Nebuchadnezzar's carnage (Jer. 25:34; Lam. 2:21; Ezek. 21:10). Babylon was used as a "sword" to judge Israel. Babylon herself was to be slaughtered like a lamb (Jer. 51:40). The victim was oblivious to his fate (Prov. 7:22; Jer. 11:19). The executioner acts upon a plan (Ps. 37:14). See the contr. of noun and verb in Prov. 9:2.

2874. Tebach; this mas. Heb. noun has 2873 as its origin. It is a killing, a slaughter, a slaughtering, a massacre; an animal that has been killed, a meal of meat, a banquet (Gen. 43:16; Prov. 9:2). Most of the other passages refer to the judgment which God is about to execute upon the nations. One of the most important passages is Isa. 53:7, a clear-cut prediction of the crucifixion of Jesus. The Ethiopian eunuch was reading this passage when Philip came along. Philip explained its true meaning (Acts 8:26-40).

2878. Tibchâh; this is the fem. equivalent of 2874. It means slaughtered meat, flesh, a slaughter-house (Ps. 44:22; Jer. 12:3). There seems to be a textual problem in Ezek. 20:15. This word also occurs at I Sam. 25:11.

2881. Tâbal; to dip, to immerse, to plunge; to be moistened. It occurs sixteen times in the Heb. O.T. It means the submersion of one thing into another; bread in vinegar (Ruth 2:14), feet in water (Josh. 3:15), a coat in blood (Gen. 37:31). The Gr. word *baptō* (911) was the usual rendering of this root in the Septuagint. It was a regular part of a cleansing ceremony (Lev. 4:6,17; 9:9). The animal died, its blood having been shed; the sinner was identified with the life blood of the animal. Heb. 9:19-22 discusses the importance of this for forgiveness. The blood of lambs substituted for the firstborn in the events of the first Passover (Ex. 12:22). Other cleansing rituals included: lepers (Lev. 14:6,16,51; II Kgs. 5:14) and the dead (Num. 19:18).

2889. Tâhôwr; this Heb. adj. derives from 2891. It means pure, clean, purified, unalloyed. It occurs ninety-four times in the Heb. O.T. in a ritualistic sense, an ethical connotation, and metallurgically speaking.

2890. Teh̄ôwr; this word comes from 2891. It means clean, pure, etc. It appears only in Job 17:9 and Prov. 22:11.

2891. Tâhêr; to be clean, pure, innocent, righteous; to make clean, to purify; to be cleansed; to purify oneself. This verb occurs ninety-four times in the Heb. O.T. Except for Job 37:21 and Mal. 3:3, it is used almost exclusively of ritual or moral purity. Those who have contracted impurity, *ṭâmê'* (2931), were not permitted to participate in the rituals until they were purified (Lev. 22:4-7). This disqualification might be due to the afterbirth (Lev. 12:7,8) or some other bodily discharges (Lev. 15:13). The priests were to be the medical examiners to determine when lepers were "cleansed" (Lev. 14). Jesus instructed a leper to go to them (Mt. 8:4; Mk. 1:44; Lk. 5:14; cf. Lk. 17:14). See Num. 19 for instructions for purifying those who were defiled by handling corpses. Soldiers needed to be purified after battle (Num. 31:19; cf. Ezek. 39:12,14,16). Moses was commanded to sprinkle "the water of expiation" (R.S.V.) upon the Levites in order to cleanse them for their duties (Num. 8:5-22). Later they cleansed everything which was considered holy in the temple (I Chr. 23:28). The temple itself was purified in the reform of Hezekiah (II Chr. 29:15). There were similar purifications for the sake of rededication in Ezra 6:20; Neh. 12:30,45; 13:9,22,30. The purpose of ritual purity was to teach the holiness of God and the need to be moral before Him (Ex. 19:10; Lev. 16:30; Num. 8:15). God must forgive us. External ritual does not guarantee it (Isa. 66:17; Mal. 1:7-11). We cannot declare ourselves pure unilaterally (Job 4:17; Prov. 30:12). Only God can cleanse us (Jer. 13:27; 33:8). David craved this (Ps. 51:2,7,10) after his sin with Bath-sheba.

2892. Tôhar; it means splendor, brightness, clearness, purity, purification. In Lev. 12:4,6 it is used in connection with ritual purification. The only other occurrence is Ex. 24:10 where it describes the clearness of the sky. The N.E.B. translates this passage as "clear blue."

2893. Tohŏrâh; this fem. Heb. noun comes from its mas. equivalent 2892, and indirectly from 2891. It occurs thirteen times in the Heb. O.T., always in the context of ritual purity.

2895. Towb; this primary root means to be good, beneficial; well, pleasing, pleasant, favorable, lovely; cheerful, happy, comfortable; right; to make good; to do well; to do good; to adorn, to cheer up, to please. *Towb* refers to "good" or "goodness" in the broadest sense. It ranges from practical, economic, or material good to abstract good (desirability, pleasantness, and beauty). It may refer to moral goodness or what is good philosophically. Finally, it can refer to good quality, i.e., expensive.

2896. Tôwb; this Heb. adj. derives from 2895. It means good, pleasant, beautiful, excellent, lovely, delightful, convenient, joyful, fruitful, precious, sound, cheerful, kind, correct, righteous; the good, the right, virtue, happiness, pleasantness. It may refer to practical or economic benefits, wisdom, esthetic or sensual goodness, happiness, or preference. An important meaning of the term is moral goodness, as contrasted with moral evil (I Kgs. 8:36; II Chr. 14:2; 31:20; Ps. 34:14). It is the *summum bonum* in Ecc. 2:24; 3:22; 8:15. "Good and evil" sometimes is only an idiom of universality (Gen. 2:9; Num. 24:13; II Sam. 13:22).

2898. Tûwb; this mas. Heb. noun originates from 2896. It is goodness, beauty, excellence, cheerfulness, well-being; good things, the best things; goods, wealth, property; beauty; welfare, happiness; prosperity; fairness; graciousness. Except for the philosophical meaning, the meanings of 2895 and 2896 are applicable here.

2930. Tâmê'; to be unclean (in a ritual or moral sense), to become unclean, to be polluted, to defile oneself; to make unclean, to profane, to desecrate, to pronounce unclean. This verb occurs 155 times in the Heb. O.T. There are 125 more occurrences which derive from it. Certain animals and foods were considered clean or unclean by their nature. Persons and objects could become ritually unclean. Birth, menstruation, emissions from the body, leprosy, sexual relations, contact with death could cause personal uncleanness. It was the business of the priests and Levites to be concerned with these matters (see Lev. 11—15). Idolatry was the most serious type of uncleanness. All these regulations were object lessons for Israel about God's holiness (Heb. 8:5; 10:1). Ritual uncleanness was used several times in the Prophets as metaphors for moral uncleanness (Isa. 6:5; 64:6; Jer. 2:23; 13:27; Ezek. 23:7,13,17; 24:13; 43:7; Hos. 5:3; 6:10; MIc. 2:1-10). There was a growing tendency for the Jews to concentrate too much on the details of ritual (the external), and to forget the deeper moral implications. Jesus denounced these exaggerations (Mt. 15:10-20; 23:25-28). He declared all foods to be clean (Mk. 7:19; cf. I Tim. 4:4,5). How ironic it was that the values of the Jewish leaders would not permit them to be defiled (so as to become unfit to eat the Passover meal) if they entered Pilate's judgment hall (Jn. 18:28), but it was perfectly acceptable for them to commit murder!

2931. Tâmê'; this Heb. adj. derives from 2930. It means to be unclean (either ritually or morally). In a Levitical sense, it could apply to persons, animals, or things (see Lev. 5:2; Deut. 14:19). Or it could be used in a moral sense (Job 14:4; Ezek. 22:5).

2932. Tum'âh; this fem. Heb. noun comes from 2930. It means uncleanness, impurity, pollution. Like the verb, it has priestly and moral connotations. See Lev. 5:3; 7:21; 16:19; Judg. 13:7,14; II Chr. 29:16.

2933. Tâmâh; this is a related form to 2930. It means to be impure (in a religious sense), to be defiled, to be unclean, to be considered vile. It occurs only in Lev. 11:43 and Job 18:3.

2940. Ta'am; this mas. Heb. noun derives from 2938. It is taste, flavor; feeling, understanding, judgment; royal decree. The Heb. *bîyn* (995) emphasizes understanding as well as decision-making. It is more comprehensive and includes perception through all the senses, not merely taste. Another Heb. syn., *nâkar* (5234), stresses recognition and acknowledgment. This word has the sense of discretion and discernment through experience. After a judgment has been made and formalized, it is a decree (Jon. 3:7).

2941. Ta'am; this is an Aramaic mas. noun which is found only in Ezra 4:21; 5:5; 6:14; 7:23 and Dan. 6:2. It means commandment, edict, decree, an account. The Assyrian kings may have influenced the earlier Heb. meaning of the word.

2942. Te'êm; this is the Aramaic equivalent of 2939. It means decree, command, wisdom. This meaning is rare in Heb. The usual meaning is expressed in Dan. 5:2 where Belshazzar "tasted" the wine.

2945. Taph; this mas. Heb. noun derives from 2952. It means children, especially little ones. Presumably, the term came from the brisk, tripping gait or short steps of little children. The R.S.V. translates the word with "families" and "dependents" in Gen. 47:12. The age range could be anywhere from toddlers to adolescents.

2951. Tiphçar; an Assyrian dignitary, a commander, a captain. This is not a Heb. word. It probably came from the Sumerian through the Akkadian etymological route. It occurs only in Jer. 51:27 and Nah. 3:17. These were governors or satraps of provinces and soldiers among the Assyrians and Medes.

2974. Yâ'al; to be willing, to show willingness; to be determined; to undertake to do; to begin, to make a beginning, to venture; to be pleased, to be content. It is making up one's mind to commence a given activity. Today we use terms such as "initiative," or "motivation," or "decisiveness." The word has the nuance of determination and resolve. Man does have a free will and can make decisions, but God holds him responsible for his actions.

2976. Yâ'ash; to desist from, to despair; to cause to despair; to abandon. There are only six occurrences in the Heb. O.T. (I Sam. 27:1; Job 6:26; Ecc. 2:20; Isa. 57:10; Jer. 2:25; 18:12). The picture is one who is downcast in spirit, devoid of hope.

3001. Yâbêsh; to be dry, to become dry, to dry up, to be parched, to wither, to be dried up; to make dry; to be drained. *Yâbêsh* is used more often to describe vegetation which has lost necessary moisture. The Heb. syn. *chârab* (2717) is almost equivalent to *yâbêsh,* but it is used to portray bodies of water which are becoming dry. God allowed the sons of Israel to walk upon dry ground when they crossed the Red Sea and the Jordan River (Josh. 2:10; Ps. 74:15). God has the power to cause plants or lands to dry up at His command (Job 12:15; Isa. 40:24; Ezek. 17:24). He can withhold rain as judgment (Isa. 15:6; 19:5-7; 42:15; Jer. 12:4; 50:38; 51:36; Joel 1:20; Zech. 10:11). See the "dry bones" of Ezek. 37:11. Those who forget God will wither like a plant (Job 8:12; 15:30; 18:16). Life and human beings are frail like the grass that withers (Job 14:11; Ps. 22:15; 90:6; 102:4,11; Isa. 40:7,8). A broken spirit "dries up the bones" (Prov. 17:22).

3002. Yâbêsh; this Heb. adj. comes from 3001. It means dry, parched, dried up. It is probably a participial form which became an adj., often acting like a stative verb. This word is used mostly in a figurative sense. It refers to decisions of the Lord (Ezek. 20:47; Nah. 1:10), harrassment (Job 13:25), the captivity of Israel (Ezek. 37:2,4), the sovereignty of Jehovah (Ezek. 17:24), desire for food (Num. 11:6), and the sterility of a eunuch (Isa. 56:3).

3004. Yabbâshâh; this fem. noun derives from 3001. It means dry land or dry ground. Usually, it is contrasting dry land and bodies of water (cf. Jon. 2:10). God separated them at creation (Gen. 1:9,10). And, God provided solid footing in the middle of the Red Sea and the Jordan River (Ex. 14:16-29; Neh. 9:11).

3006. Yabbesheth; this is a fem. variation of 3004. It occurs only in Ex. 4:9 and Ps. 95:5.

3007. Yabbesheth; this is the Aramaic correlate to 3006. Its only occurrence is found in Dan. 2:10. The Aramaic word is less specialized than the Heb. Here it may emphasize the land part of the earth where people live, rather than the total earth.

3025. Yâgôr; to be afraid, to fear, to dread. This is probably very closely related to *gûwr* (1481). It is similar in meaning to *pâchad* (6342) and *yârê'* (3372). There are nuances of "reverence," along with the dominant emotion of dread. It is like a child who knows he has done wrong and expects to be punished soon (Deut. 9:19; 28:60; Job 9:28; Ps. 119:39).

3027. Yâd; hand; power, strength, assistance; axle, tenon; side; part, place; time, times; monument. It is the physical hand (Gen. 5:29) which may do good or evil (Gen. 4:11). *Yâd* is used in a variety of idiomatic ways: "into someone's hand" means authority, responsibility, care, or dominion (Gen. 9:2; 16:6,9; 39:3-8; Num. 33:1; II Sam. 24:14; I Chr. 18:3; Ps. 31:5). Contrariwise, one can be delivered out of another's hands (Gen. 49:8; Ex. 3:8; Josh. 6:2). *Yâd* sometimes symbolizes power or strength (Ex. 10:12-25; 13:3-16; Lev. 14:21-32; Num. 33:3; Deut. 8:17; 32:36; Josh. 4:24; Ps. 8:6; 10:12; 37:24; 89:13; 95-5; 111:7; 139:10; Isa. 59:1). *Yâd* often has the connotation of possession (Gen. 39:1; I Kgs. 11:12,31-35) or submission (I Chr. 29:24). "To stretch out the hand" means either to attack (Josh. 8:19,26) or to yearn for the Lord (Ps. 143:6). "Putting one's hand to" expresses work (Deut. 2:7; 30:9), like our "rolling up the sleeves." "Strengthening the hands" is helping and encouraging someone (I Sam. 23:16). A "high hand" (Num. 15:30) is obstinate rebellion, but it can mean a mighty deliverance from God (Ex. 14:8). "Shaking the hand" symbolized God's warning and destruction of judgment (Isa. 10:32; 19:16). *Yâd* can be symbolic for contempt (Zeph. 2:15). "Laying hands on" someone could mean killing (Gen. 37:22,27), a ritual ceremony of blessing (Gen. 48:17), ordination (when Moses commissioned Joshua; cf. Acts 13:1-3), or a symbolic substitutionary act designed to transfer sins from man to animal (Ex. 29:10-19; Lev. 1:4; Num. 8:12). An "uplifted hand" described prayer toward the sanctuary (Ps. 28:2), a public blessing (Lev. 9:22), or taking an oath. "Fill the hands" refers to consecration (Ex. 29:9-35; 16:29). "Washing the hands" was a ritual cleansing (Lev. 5:11; II Sam. 22:21). It was a symbolic action to absolve one from guilt (Deut. 21:6,7; cf. Mt. 27:24). To "open the hand" (Deut. 15:8,11) was to give to another, but to "shut the hand" (Deut. 15:7) was to withhold gifts. God is benevolent (Ps. 145:16). "Withdrawing the hand" is giving up (Josh. 10:6). A lazy man buries his hand in a dish of food, but will not even bring the morsel to his mouth (Prov. 19:24). Self-restraint (silence) is covering one's mouth with his own hand (Prov. 30:32). *Yâd* can mean an ordinance (Ezra 3:10) or a monument (I Sam. 15:12). Compare phylacteries (Deut. 6:8). *Yâd* was used in constructing axles (I Kgs. 7:32,33) and joints (Ex. 26:17-19; I Kgs. 7:35,36). In Ex. 2:5; Num. 2:17; 34:3 it means edge, coast, or border. "Spreading the hands" (Gen. 34:21) denoted space. Finally, Gen. 43:34; 47:24 refers to "part" or "time."

3028. Yad; this is the Aramaic equivalent of 3027. It occurs in Ezra 5:8,12; 6:12; 7:14,25; Dan. 2:34,38,45; 3:15,17; 4:35; 5:5,23,24; 6:27; 7:25.

3029. Y^{e}dâ'; this is the Aramaic word which corresponds to the Heb. 3034. It means to praise or give thanks (to God). It occurs only in Dan. 2:23; 6:10.

3033. Y^{e}dîdûwth; this fem. Heb. noun originates from 3039. It means darling or the object of one's love. Jer. 12:7 is the only occurrence.

3034. Yâdâh; to throw, to cast; to speak out, to confess; to praise, to sing, to give thanks, to thank. Essentially, it is the acknowledgment of sin, man's character, or the nature and work of God. The Heb. syn. *hâlal* (1984) emphasizes pride in an object. *Yâda'* (3045) stresses recognition and declaration of a fact, whether it is good or bad. David made his sin known to God and did not attempt to hide it (Ps. 32:5). For a national confession on the Day of Atonement see Lev. 16:21; Ezra 10:1; Neh. 1:6; 9:2,3; Dan. 9:4,20. According to the Apostle John, God wants us to be cleansed through confession (I Jn. 1:9). This constant acknowledgment maintains a proper relationship with God. The secondary meaning of this verb is the expression of thanks to God by way of praising. In these contexts, "bless" would be a good translation. Praise leads to thanksgiving. The name, Judah, comes from this root (Gen. 29:35).

3039. Y^{e}dîyd; this Heb. adj. derives from 1730. It means beloved, lovely, pleasant; friend; lovely things. It occurs only in Deut. 33:12; Ps. 60:5; 84:1; 108:6; 127:2; Isa. 5:1; Jer. 11:15. Also, it appears in the title of Ps. 45.

3045. Yâda'; to perceive, to understand, to acquire knowledge, to know, to discern; to be acquainted with; to become acquainted with a woman (in a sexual way, i.e., sexual intercourse); to be known; to make oneself known, to appear; to cause to know; to be familiar, to be aware of; to let know, to inform; to announce; to reveal oneself; to appoint, to order. This is one of the most important Heb. roots in the O.T. It occurs 944 times. It expresses a broad variety of meanings about various types of knowledge which are gained through the senses. The closest Heb. syn. are *bîyn* (995) and *nâkar* (5234). Unfortunately, the K.J.V. uses "wot" and "wist" sometimes to translate this word. *Yâda'* describes God's knowledge of man (Gen. 18:19; Deut. 34:10; Ps. 1:6; 37:18; Isa. 48:8; Jer. 1:5). It is also used for man's knowledge and for that of animals (Isa. 1:3). It can refer to skill in hunting (Gen. 25:27), learning (Isa. 29:11-13), lamentation (Amos 5:16), sailing the sea (II Chr. 8:18), or playing an instrument (I Sam. 16:16). One must be able "to distinguish" (*yâda'*) between right and wrong (Gen. 3:5,22; Deut. 1:39; II Sam. 19:45; Isa. 7:15; Jon. 4:11). This verb ranges from acquaintances (Gen. 29:5; Ex. 1:8; II Sam. 3:25), to relatives (II Kgs. 10:11), to friends (Ruth 2:1; Job 19:14), to God on a personal level (Ex. 33:17; Deut. 34:10; Ps. 139:2). Euphemistically, *yâda'* is used for coitus (Gen. 4:1; 19:8; Num. 31:17,35; Judg. 11:39; 21:11; I Sam. 1:19; I Kgs. 1:4). The word is also used for rape (Judg. 19:25) and homosexuality (Gen. 19:5; Judg. 19:22). It describes a person's relationship to the true God (I Sam. 2:12; 3:7) or false gods (Deut. 13:3,6,13). The pagans do not know God (Jer. 10:25), and sometimes Israel did not know Him (Jer. 4:22). The ten disasters which hit Egypt were to teach the Egyptians to know that Jehovah is God (Ex. 10:2, cf. Isa. 60:16; Ezek. 6:7,10,13,14; 7:4,9,27).

3046. Y^{e}da'; this is the Aramaic equivalent to 3045. Carnal knowledge was not one of the Aramaic usages.

3049. Yidd^{e}'ônîy; this Heb. adj. which is used as a sub. means knowing; sorcerer, magician, wizard, prophesying spirit. The Berkeley Translation and the N.A.B. translate it as "fortune-teller." The N.E.B. has "familiar spirit." It comes from 3045. Therefore, an occultist possessed the esoteric knowledge of his craft which he would not share with commoners. It is possible that this is the mas. counterpart to *'ôwb* (178). It was forbidden by God to consult them (Lev. 19:31; 20:6,27; Deut. 18:11) or other diviners. The good kings did not do so (II Kgs. 21:6; 23:24; II Chr. 33:6). Isaiah denounced them (8:19; 19:3).

3117. Yôwm; day, a number of days, some time, year, life (when in the pl.); today; in the daytime, on the same day; at present, now. A point in time and a sphere of time are both expressed by *yôwm*. It is the period of light which is not darkness. It can be 24 hours, time in general, a specific point in time, or a year. When used in construction with other Heb. parts of speech, it can mean "when," "on some particular day," "in the time of," "as long as," or "continually." The Heb. syn., *'ôwr* (216), "light," and *bôqer* (1242), "morning," are sometimes translated as "day." Daytime was divided by natural phenomena, not regular hourly divisions (Gen. 43:16; 15:12; 18:1; Ex. 18:13). The "day" sometimes begins with evening (Esth. 4:16) and sometimes with morning (Deut. 28:66,67). *Yôwm* is connected with the sovereignty of God. He existed before eternity began (Ps. 90:4; Isa. 43:13; Dan. 7:9). God created time (Gen. 1:1) and it is under His control (Ps. 74:16). Mankind must recognize this sovereignty by conforming (Ex. 20:11; 31:17). God assured the regularity of time (Gen. 8:22), but will suspend it someday (Zech. 14:7). God is interested in time and human events (Gen. 24:55; 26:33). Gen. 1 portrays time as linear and events occur successively within it. History has meaning, and time is not cyclical. Man must prove the worth of his life within that framework. The expression "the day when" introduces events with particular importance in the history of salvation (Num. 15:23; Deut. 4:32). "The Day" is a time of repentance (Ps. 95:7), salvation (Ps. 118:24), an adoption (Ps. 2:7). The "Day of the Lord" can be used eschatologically or non-eschatologically. This word occurs 2,355 times in the Heb. O.T.

3118. Yôwm; this is the Aramaic word which corresponds to 3117. It occurs fifteen times. See the famous passage in Dan. 2:28, "In the latter days."

3119. Yôwmâm; this Heb. adv. derives from 3117. It means by day; day and night; always. It occurs fifty-one times and specifies that an activity happened while it was still light. It means "daily" in Ezek. 30:16.

3173. Yâchîyd; this Heb. adj. comes from 3161. It means only, alone, forsaken; soul, life. It appears twelve times in the Heb. O.T. The basic meaning of the word is "an only child." In view of Jn. 3:16 and other N.T. passages, this word is very important. The preciousness of a unique individual is shown in Gen. 22:2,-12,16; Judg. 11:34; Jer. 6:26; Amos 8:10; Zech. 12:10. It is very interesting that the Septuagint does not render *yâchîyd* in Gen. 22 with the Gr. word *monogenēs* (3439), but *agapētos* (27). Isaac had a half brother (Ishmael). However, Jephthah's daughter was referred to by *monogenēs* (Judg. 11:34). Jesus was especially dear to His Father, just as Isaac was to Abraham (Mt. 3:17; 17:5; Jn. 1:14,18; 3:16,18; I Jn. 4:9). Ps. 22:20 and Ps. 35:17 refer to the uniqueness of the soul. It is quite possible that *monogenēs* does not refer to the derivation of the Son from the Father, but the uniqueness of the love between them. *Yâchîyd* also means solitary or isolated (Prov. 4:3).

3175. Yâchîyl; this Heb. adj. originates from 3176. It occurs only once (Lam. 3:26). It means waiting, hoping, expecting.

3176. Yâchal; to wait, to hope, to expect, to be patient; to tarry. It occurs thirty-six times. It can mean waiting for the passage of time (Gen. 8:12; I Sam. 13:8; Job 14:14). Or it can have the sense of expectation in hope (Ps. 71:14; Ezek. 13:6). It is rooted in God (Ps. 42:5,11; 43:5; 130:7; 131:3). The textual variants of Job 13:15 make interpretation difficult. See Mic. 7:7 for this word and close synonyms.

3190. Yâṭab; to be good, to be well, to be beautiful, to be pleasant, to be lovely, to be glad, to be cheerful. This Heb. verb is used 105 times in the O.T. God is in covenant relationship with His people. Therefore, He blesses them (Gen. 32:9,12; Ex. 1:20; Deut. 4:40; 5:16,29; 6:3,18; 12:25,28; 22:7; I Kgs. 1:47; Jer. 7:23; 38:20; 40:9; 42:6). See especially Ps. 51:18. This vertical bond with God should reflect in horizontal social relationships (Gen. 34:18; Neh. 2:5,6; Prov. 15:13; 17:22; Ecc. 7:3). Jesus "went around doing good" (Acts 10:38). However, *yâṭab* can refer to doing "good" in general (Gen. 34:18; 45:16; Judg. 18:20; II Sam. 18:4; Mic. 7:3). Righteousness is not always implied.

3198. Yâkach; to dispute with someone, to argue; to be convicted, to be reproved; to decide, to judge, to prove, to rebuke, to reprove, to correct; to mediate or to arbitrate; to punish, to chide; to be punished. This word occurs fifty-seven times in the Heb. O.T. The most famous passage is probably Isa. 1:18, which is in the context of a covenant lawsuit. Judah had been practicing religious festivals of their own design in rebellion against Jehovah, the plaintiff (Isa. 1:10-15). Isaiah calls upon them to repent (Isa. 1:16-20). The K.J.V. has: "Let us reason together." The prophet is saying, "Let us debate our case in court." See Mic. 6:2. The connotation of legal confrontation is clearly attached to this term.

3238. Yânâh; to oppress, maltreat, vex, do wrong, overreach, drive away. It is used twenty times in the Heb. O.T. There is a broad range of afflictions expressed in this word. Generally, it means to wrong someone. It is the opposite of loving one's neighbor as yourself (Lev. 19:33). A common syn. is *tsârar* (6887), "to treat someone with hostility" or "to constrict someone." In the vernacular, it means to give someone a hard time. The Law of Moses was concerned about civil rights (Ex. 22:21; Lev. 25:14,17; Deut. 23:16). Jer. 46:16; 50:16 picture Jerusalem as an "oppressing city," because their leaders had turned away from the Lord. See *lâchats* (3905).

3245. Yâçad; to establish, to set, to found, to build up, to lay a foundation; to appoint, to assign; to be settled; to take counsel together; to ordain; to be founded, to be established. It carries the idea of fixing something firmly. It can be literal (Josh. 6:26; I Kgs. 5:17; 6:37; 16:34; Ezra 3:6,10,12; Isa. 14:32; Zech. 4:9) or metaphorical (Job 26:7; Ps. 24:2; 78:69; 89:11; 102:25; 104:5; Isa. 48:13; 51:13; 54:11). The N.T. often uses this motif (Lk. 6:48,49; 14:29; Acts 16:26; Heb. 11:10; Rev. 21—22). The most famous usage occurs in the Messianic prophecy found in Isa. 28:16. The Apostle Peter gave the inspired interpretation of this when he related it to Jesus Christ, "the precious cornerstone" (I Pet. 2:4-8). Paul associated Isa. 28:16 with Isa. 8:14 in Rom. 9:32f. Jesus is also a stumbling stone. Isa. 28:14 is the background for Jesus' statement in Mt. 16:18. See also Eph. 2:20; Rev. 21:14,-19,20. Those who take counsel (Ps. 2:2) have fixed (seated) themselves in a close-knit conclave, as if to plot some terrible deed.

3247. Y^eçôwd; ground, foundation, bottom, repairing; (in the plural) princes. This mas. Heb. noun derives from 3245. Essentially, it means a base. Seven of its eighteen occurrences refer to the bottom of the altar. II Chr. 24:27 employs the word in the sense of maintenance.

3248. Y^eçûwdâh; a foundation. This fem. Heb. noun comes from 3246. It occurs only in Ps. 87:1 with reference to the founding of the city.

3250. Yiççôwr; a reprover, a blamer, one who rebukes. It occurs only once (Job 40:2) and originates from 3256. See the similar Gr. word, *paideutēs* (3810) in the N.T. lexical section.

3256. Yâçar; to chastise, reprove, discipline, chasten, instruct; to be chastised, to learn reproof, to take a warning; to punish, correct, admonish; to be instructed. This Heb. root has the definite connotation of either physical enforcement or verbal reinforcement. One becomes educated when the proper amount of training and correction are imposed. The derivatives occur almost ninety times in the Heb. O.T. Thirty-six of them are in Proverbs alone. The purpose of the discipline from God is reformation (Lev. 26:18,23,24,28). We must learn from God's mighty acts (Deut. 11:2ff.,7; cf. 4:35f.). The Lord's discipline tests us (Deut. 8:2,3,5). Jehovah is like a father (Ex. 4:22; Deut. 1:31; 32:6; Isa. 1:2). Therefore, He disciplines us as a father would discipline his son (Heb. 12:5-11). It is a sign of His love (Prov. 1:7,8; 3:11,12; 8:10; 15:5,32). The prophets developed the theme of discipline (Isa. 8:11; 53:5; Jer. 2:30; 5:3; 7:28; 17:23; 32:33; Hos. 5:2; 7:12). Jesus took our beating (Isa. 53:5).

3259. Yâ'ad; to appoint, to fix (a place or time); to order (punishment); to betroth, to give in marriage; to meet by agreement, to come together, to repair, to gather together; to summon, to cite; to be directed. The basic meaning is "to appoint," but this is closely associated with the idea of a congregation assembling to worship God. In other words, there were designated times and places for that purpose. See Ex. 25:22; 29:43f.; 30:6,36; Num. 10:3; I Kgs. 8:5; II Chr. 5:6. It is a set time for marriage (Ex. 21:8), the betrothal of a woman. It refers to a rebellious gathering against the Lord (Num. 14:35; 16:11; 27:3) or any military swarming (Josh. 11:5). It is a time for meeting (Job 2:11; Ps. 48:4; Amos 3:3) or a call (Job 9:19; Jer. 50:44).

3289. Yâ'ats; to advise, counsel, admonish; to direct, to resolve, to decide, to devise, to plan, to purpose; to consult with one another, to counsel together, to be advised. The first occurrence of the word is in Ex. 18:19, where Jethro suggests that Moses delegate some of his responsibilities to others. Rehoboam rejected the wisdom of his advisers (I Kgs. 12:8,13). So did Absalom (II Sam. 17). II Kgs. 18:20 could refer to military intelligence. Ps. 33:10,11 contrasts God's counsel and that of man. His way overrides all human machinations. God's will is sovereign and eternal (Isa. 46:9-11). Compare Acts 2:23; 4:28; 5:38,39; 20:27; Eph. 1:11; Heb. 6:17. The Messiah is called the "Wonderful Counsellor" (Isa. 9:6; cf. Isa. 11:2).

3321. Y^etsêb; this Aramaic word is a correlate to 3320. It means to be firm, to speak the truth, to be sure. Dan. 7:19 is the only occurrence.

3323. Yitshâr; oil (for producing light); anointing. This mas. Heb. noun comes from *tsâhar* (6671) to make oil.

3335. Yâtsar; this is probably identical with 3334. It means to form, to fashion, to devise, to frame; to produce, to create; to be formed or fashioned; to exist; to be predestined. In its part. form it is a potter or a creator. The narrowness or distressing situation of 3334 is very similar to the squeezing or moulding of 3335. See the somewhat synonymous *bârâ'* (1254) and *'âsâh* (6213). Prophets carried a shaped message (Isa. 29:16; Jer. 18:2,4,6; Zech. 11:13). Idols were sculpted and manipulated (Isa. 44:9,10,12; Hab. 2:18). God is like a Divine Potter (Gen. 2:7,8,19; Isa. 45:18; Jer. 33:2; Amos 4:13, especially note Isa. 64:8). See also Ps. 33:15; 74:17; 94:9; 95:5; Jer. 10: 16; 51:19; Zech. 12:1. The term can also refer to constructed thoughts and purposes, either in advance (II Kgs. 19:25; Isa. 37:26; 46:11; Ps. 139:16) or in present time (Jer. 18:11). God brought Israel into existence gradually (Isa. 43:1,7,21; 44:2,21,24). The word implies initiation as well as structuring.

3336. Yêtser; this mas. Heb. noun means formation, frame, pattern, image; conception, imagination, thought; device. It originates from 3335. The primary meaning is "form." It may refer either to the shape of an object or the object itself (Isa. 29:16; Hab. 2:18). It is what is formed in the mind (i.e., plans and purposes) (Gen. 6:5; 8:21; Deut. 31:21; Isa. 26:3).

3349. Yiqqâhâh; this fem. Heb. noun means obedience. Like 3348, it comes from an unused Heb. root which meant "to obey." It occurs only twice (Gen. 49:10 and Prov. 30:17). In the well-known Shiloh passage, the Septuagint renders it with the Gr. word *prosdokia* (4329), "expectation." See the N.T. lexical section for further information. Obeying one's father and mother seems to be the flavor of the term.

3369. Yâqôsh; to ensnare, lay a snare; to be snared, caught, or ensnared. The part. is a fowler who sets a trap. This root and its derivatives occur forty times in the Heb. O.T. Although it often refers to setting a trap for the purpose of catching prey, it is also used in a metaphorical sense of the entrapment of people (Isa. 28:13; Jer. 50:24). Hebrew synonyms with the same idea include *yaquwsh* (3353) (Jer. 5:26); *moqesh* (4170) (Ex. 10:7; I Sam. 18:21; Ps. 18:5; Prov. 22:25); *pach* (6341) (Hos. 9:8); *qowsh* (6983) (Isa. 29:21), and *resheth* (7568) (Ps. 9:15). See the Gr. words, *skandalizo* (4624) and *skandalon* (4625) in the N.T. lexical section.

3372. Yârê'; to be afraid, to fear, to revere; to be feared, to be dreadful, to be reverenced; to terrify, to make afraid. There are two main types of fear described by *yârê':* (a) the emotion and intellectual anticipation of harm, what one feels may go wrong for him; (b) a very positive feeling of awe or reverence for God, which may be expressed in piety or formal worship. For the emotion of trembling, see the Heb. syn. *pâchad* (6342), *châthath* (2865), and *chârad* (2729). Security is the lack of fear (Ps. 56:4). For "holy respect" see Lev. 19:3; 26:2; Job 6:21; Ps. 86:11; 112:1; Hab. 3:2. "Fearing" God is often the motivation which effects godly living (Ex. 1:17,21; Lev. 19:14; 25:17; Deut. 10:18-20; 17:19; 25:18; 31:11,12; II Kgs. 17:34). However, II Kgs. 17:32-34 should be studied more closely. It shows that God is interested in much more than outward conformity. II Chr. 6:33 and Job 1:9 mean "being a devotee or follower."

3373. Yârê'; this Heb. adj. means fearing, being afraid, anxious, timid, or reverent. It serves as a sub. and as a part. for its root, *yârê'* (3372). The semantic range is almost the same as the verb. Eventually, it became a technical term, a "God-fearer" (Neh. 7:2; Job 1:1; Ps. 22:23,25; 31:19; 33:18,19; 34:9; 103:11; 115:11,13; 118:4; 128:1; 145:19; Ecc. 8:13). See the Gr. word *phobeō* (5399) in the N.T. lexical section and especially the way it is used for "Godfearers" in the N.T. (Acts 10:2,22,35; 13:16,26).

3374. Yir'âh; this fem. Heb. noun means fear, terror, reverence, awe; piety, religion. Except for the meaning of formal worship, this term has the same range of meanings as its source (3372). Abject terror is found in Ex. 20:20; Deut. 2:25; Ps. 55:5; Ezek. 30:13. If one truly recognizes God as all-powerful, this will be reflected in his attitude and daily life in the form of reverence (Job 28:28; Ps. 111:10; Prov. 9:10; 15:33). There are thirteen occurrences of the expression "the fear of the Lord," which refers to a pious posture which performs practical functions in life. It predated the Golden Rule (Neh. 5:9; Job 6:14).

3384. Yârâh or **yârâ';** to cast, to shoot; to pour; to lay (a foundation), to found, to erect, to establish; to shed (water), to irrigate; to wet, to give water. Its part. form means archer, because they sent forth missiles or arrows. The most common uses have to do with shooting arrows, sending rain, or teaching (putting out words). The word definitely has the connotation of aiming or controlling.

3409. Yârêk; thigh; haunch, ham; loin, side; lower end; stem. This fem. Heb. noun derives from an unused Heb. root which presumably meant "to be soft." It is possible that it is used euphemistically for the genitals in some cases. This term stood for man's foundation (Gen. 46:26; Judg. 3:16,21; 8:30); the source of life. The strongest possible oath was ratified by placing one's hand there (Gen. 24:9). Num. 5:21f. may refer to the miscarriage of an illegitimate child. It is the "side" of the tabernacle (Ex. 40:22) and of the altar (Lev. 1:11) and the "base" of the lampstand (Ex. 25:31). The angel was able to break Jacob's grip by striking Jacob in that spot (Gen. 32:25,31f.).

3415. Yâra'; to be afraid, to tremble, to quiver. It means to be in distress or in a state of terror. The noun form, 3407, means "curtain," which hung and sometimes shook.

3423. Yârash or **yârêsh;** to seize, to take possession of, to possess, to inherit; to occupy, to drive away, to expel, to take away; to be an heir, to disinherit, to dispossess; to be dispossessed, to become poor, to be impoverished; to devour; to make poor, to impoverish. This important Heb. root and its deriv. occur more than 250 times. It has the legal sense of becoming an heir (Jer. 32:8) and the military sense of invasion for the purpose of settling in the territory. Both meanings are dominant with regard to God's covenant with Israel. God told Abraham that the land of Canaan would belong to his descendants; but, after leaving Egypt, they had to take possession of the Promised Land. Most of the occurrences appear in Deuteronomy because the people needed to be reminded of their legacy after forty years of wandering in the wilderness and just prior to Joshua's military campaign. This was a new generation; they believed that God would make them victorious if they had the proper faith. Gen. 15:16, coupled with Lev. 18:24-30, teaches that a nation cannot occupy a land for long if they are in rebellion against God. God is righteous to punish them (Deut. 9:1-5; 18:12; Isa. 10:5f.). Like the Amorites before them, the Israelites repeated history. Therefore, God used other nations to drive them out (Neh. 9:26-31; Ezek. 33:24-36). However, since they repented of their sin, God allowed them to return under the Persians (Ezra 9:10-15). The land belongs to those who fear God (Ps. 25:12f.; 37:9,11,22,29). Compare one of Jesus' beatitudes (Mt. 5:5). This concept carries over into the N.T. in several passages. Our inheritance is in heaven, but Satan must be defeated before we obtain it.

3424. Y^e^rêshâh; possession, occupancy, inheritance. This fem. Heb. noun appears only in Num. 24:18. It comes from 3423.

3425. Y^e^rushshâh; this fem. Heb. noun is another form of 3424. It means something occupied, a conquest, a heritage.

3444. Y^e^shûw'âh; help, deliverance, salvation, victory, welfare. This fem. pass. part. derives from 3467. In the abstract sense, it is something saved or delivered. If one is fortunate enough to find himself in that condition, he is in good health and enjoys prosperity. It connotes the idea of being comfortable, having no problems. The act of giving aid to the distressed produces deliverance and safety. The source of this salvation comes from outside the situation of oppression. A saviour may rescue people from national or individual emergencies, enemies, natural catastrophies, plagues, famine or sickness. At first, the term was used in an ordinary sense (e.g., Ex. 2:17). But later, both in the O.T. and N.T., the term acquired a very strong spiritual meaning. Jehovah is the God of our salvation (Ps. 68:19f.). Salvation is associated with the forgiveness of sin (Lk. 1:77). Satan must be defeated and we must be delivered from him and his power.

3451. Y^e^shîymâh; desolation, devastation, destruction. This fem. Heb. noun comes from 3456. There is no place which is more desolate than Sheol (death). See Ps. 55:15 and its marginal reading.

3453. Yâshîysh; a very aged man, an old man, very old, ancient, decrepit. This mas. Heb. noun originates from 3486. Its sole occurrence is found in II Chr. 36:17.

3456. Yâsham; to be desolate, to be waste, to be in ruins, to be deserted. This root and its deriv. occur eighteen times in the Heb. O.T. It describes the desolate condition of an arid land, like the Negeb, the Sinai Peninsula, or the region which surrounds the Dead Sea. The Egyptians did not want their land to be like this (Gen. 47:19). The Prophet Ezekiel warned that Judah's land would become desolate if they did not heed God's warning (Ezek. 6:6; 12:19; 19:7). God will provide even in the starkest of circumstances (Isa. 43:19).

3467. Yâsha'; originally, this root was believed to mean "to be open, wide, or free." It is the opposite of *tsârar* (6887), "to cramp," having the connotation of distress, being in trouble or affliction. In other words, when one has plenty of room in which to move, he feels safe and secure. *Yâsha'* means, therefore, to be delivered, saved, to get help; to deliver, give victory, to help; to take vengeance; to preserve. The A.S.V. has "rescue," "defend cause." The R.S.V. uses the word "saviour." It is noteworthy that the personal name of our Saviour, Jesus, derives from this root (see Mt. 1:21). Also, in the N.T., when the crowds cried out to Jesus at His triumphal entry, they used the word "Hosanna" (Mt. 21:9), which is directly traceable to this verb in the O.T. *Yâsha'* and its deriv. appear 353 times in the Heb. Bible. At first, the word pointed to a physical deliverance from very real enemies or catastrophies. Later, "save" developed a theological meaning. God is concerned about our physical well-being, our emotional status, and the salvation of our souls. God has the ability to save us from anything which would harm us. Salvation is God's love in action. There is none outside of Him. Isaiah (49:6; 52:10) hints at an everlasting salvation which was coming. Some, like Simeon (Lk. 2:29,30) and those who were like Anna (Lk. 2:38), were waiting for it.

3468. Yesha' or **yêsha';** liberty, deliverance, help, salvation, freedom; welfare, prosperity. This mas. Heb. noun has 3467 as its source, which see.

3474. Yâshar; to be level, straight, right, upright, just, lawful; convenient, even, tranquil; to go straight, to make straight; to declare right, to approve; to be made even, to be beaten out flat (e.g., metal); to look straight on. There are two main meanings: (a) literally, straight (I Sam. 6:12; I Kgs. 6:35; II Chr. 32:30; Prov. 4:25); (b) ethically, an upright (moral) life (Ps. 119:128; Prov. 11:5; Ecc. 7:29; Hab. 2:4). This concept is reflected in many of our modern-day expressions: "the straight and narrow"; "standing straight and tall (the good sense of pride)"; "straight from the shoulder (honesty)"; straight shooter"; "go straight" and "straighten out/up."

3476. Yôsher; this mas. Heb. noun is derived from 3474. It means straightness, right, equity, uprightness, truth, duty, honesty. This moral quality of the heart (Deut. 9:5; I Kgs. 9:4; Prov. 2:13; 4:11) directs good people into "right paths" (Job 33:23). See I Kgs. 3:6; Job 6:25; Ecc. 12:10.

3477. Yâshâr; this Heb. adj. comes from 3474 and means straight, even, right, upright, level, just, righteous; pleasing, agreeing. It refers to God (Deut. 32:4; Ps. 111; 119:137; Hos. 14:9) or some of His outstanding people (Job 1:1,8; Ps. 7:10; 11:2; 33:1). The Heb. idiom "to be right in the eyes of (someone)" means to have that person's approval (Num. 23:27; Judg. 14:3,7; I Sam. 18:26; II Sam. 17:4; II Chr. 30:4; Jer. 18:4; 27:5). "To do what is right in the sight of the Lord" meant to obey His commands (Ex. 15:26; Deut. 6:17,18; 12:28; 13:18; I Kgs. 3:3,14; 14:8; 15:5-7,11; II Kgs. 14:3; 15:3; 18:6; 22:2; II Chr. 20:32; 14:2; 25:2).

3483. Yishrâh; this fem. Heb. noun comes from 3477 and appears only once in the O.T. (I Kgs. 3:6). It means uprightness, integrity, straight.

3486. Yâshêsh; old, gray-headed, gray-haired (i.e., an aged or old man). II Chr. 36:17 is the only occurrence of this mas. Heb. noun.

3498. Yâthar; to be left, to remain; to let remain, to leave, to spare; to prefer, to give superiority or abundance. The part. form means remnant or remainder. It is the residue, the excess. This verb and its deriv. are used more than 225 times in the Heb. O.T. After a portion has been divided, this is the smaller part, which is left over. Often it is of lesser quality. There are many contexts and meanings: it can refer to food (Ruth 2:14; II Chr. 31:10), contributions (Ex. 36:7), sacrificial offerings and the leftovers (Ex. 12:10; Lev. 7:16f.; 8:32), the remaining lifetime of a person (Isa. 38:10), or a reign. Hard work produces abundance (Prov. 14:23; 21:5), but some must be kept as an inheritance (Ps. 17:14). Like the Apostle Paul, we need to be content (Phil. 4:11,12), having enough (I Tim. 6:6-10); not too much or too little. The term can mean survivors (Josh. 11:11,22; 12:4; 23:12; Judg. 9:5). Elijah thought he was the only one left (I Kgs. 18:22). Some Israelites survived the destruction of Jerusalem and Babylonian exile (Isa. 1:9; Ezek. 6:8; 12:16; Zeph. 2:9; Zech. 14:2). See Paul's discussion in Rom. 9—11.

3499. Yether; this mas. Heb. noun comes from 3498. It means rope, cord, thread, bowstring, string; remainder, remnant, rest; abundance, preference, excellence. The adverbial form means over and above, besides. The term is used six times in the Heb. O.T. This is what Delilah attempted to use to restrain Samson (Judg. 16:7ff.). Job 4:21 and Job 30:11 are describing broken health.

3513. Kâbad or **kâbêd;** to be heavy, weighty, grievous, severe, numerous, consideration, honored, renowned, honorable, glorious; to be dull; to be honored, to be esteemed; to show oneself great or mighty; to be wealthy, rich; to honor, to make heavy, hard, dull; to oppress; to get renown. This root and its deriv. occur 376 times in the Heb. O.T. One hundred and fourteen of them are the verb form. The main idea is "to be heavy," which then becomes "wealthy" (heavy with goods, property, money)," "sinful (heavy with guilt)," "insensitive (heavy ears)," "severity (heavy hand)," "great (large, heavy)," "noteworthy (impressive, heavy)," "honored (carries a lot of weight)," "glory (heavy, awesome)," etc. A visible manifestation of the glory of God appears forty-five times. See *doxa* (1391) in the N.T. lexical section. That glory was ultimately revealed in Jesus (Jn. 1:14; 17:1-5).

3519. Kâbôwd or **kâbôd;** this mas. Heb. noun comes from 3513. It means weight, honor, esteem, glory, majesty; abundance, wealth. Poetically, it refers to a soul or a person. The term occurs about 200 times.

3526. Kâbaç; to trample, to tread; to wash, to bleach, to cleanse; to be washed, to be purified. This verb occurs fifty-one times. The ancient method of laundering required treading with the feet, kneading, and beating clothes in cold water. This word is not used to refer to washing the body. Except for II Sam. 19:24, all of the instances are associated with ceremonial cleanness. The people and the priests were to appear before God in clean clothes (Ex. 19:10,14; Num. 8:7; 19:7). Defilement required a washing of the clothes (Lev. 16:26,28; Num. 19:7,8,10,19,21). Twenty-eight occurrences relate to washing contaminated clothing. Ps. 51:2; Jer. 2:22; 4:14 and Mal. 3:2 apply this image to sin.

3547. Kâhan; to act as a priest, to be a priest, to minister in a priest's office, to adorn with priestly dress. This root occurs twenty-three times in the Heb. O.T. The R.S.V. translates it as: "minister in a priest's office," "be priest," and "serve as priest." Priests acted as God's ordained mediators to receive the gifts of the people. They officiated over the ceremonies.

3548. Kôhên; this act. part. comes from 3547. It is an acting priest, a chief ruler, priest, or principal officer. Besides the well-known Levitical priests and high priests, there seems to have developed non-Levitical priests (high officials). See II Sam. 8:18; 20:26; I Kgs. 4:5; I Chr. 18:16,17. Perhaps they were confidential advisors to the king. There may be a transcriptional problem with II Sam. 8:18 and I Kgs. 4:5. If so, they may indeed be Levitical priests. Melchizedek (Gen. 14:18) and Jethro (Ex. 18:12) were the first priests to be mentioned in the O.T. At first, men functioned as their own priests (Gen. 4:3; Job 1:5), but later the patriarchal head of the family performed the task (Gen. 8:20; 12:8; Ex. 19:22,24; Job 1:5). In a sense, all Israelites were priests of the Lord (Ex. 19:6; cf. Hos. 4:6). That concept carried over to the N.T. (I Pet. 2:5,9). However, at Mount Sinai, God designated that the prieslthood would be the tribe of Levi, and the family of Aaron in particular (Ex. 28:1; 40:12-15; Num. 16:17; 17:8). The O.T. priests were types of Christ (Heb. 4:14-16; 5:1-10; 7:1-28; 8:1-4). He offered the ultimate propitiation for the sins of the people (Heb. 2:17). O.T. prophecy predicted a future reappearance of the Levites (Jer. 31:34; 33:18; Zech. 12:13). Rev. 5:10 reads: ". . . hast made them to be a kingdom and priests to our God; and they will reign upon the earth."

3550. K^{e}hunnâh; priesthood, the priest's office. This fem. Heb. noun has its origins in 3547. An efficacious priesthood can exist only when it is established by the Lord (Num. 18:7).

3559. Kûwn; to stand firm, to be established; to be firm, steadfast, faithful, sure, reliable, fixed, sure, certain; to be ready, to be prepared, to be determined; to set up, to make firm, to establish, to build, to make ready, to direct; to be formed; to aim, to attend to; to be set in order; to make oneself ready, right. This root, along with all of its deriv., occurs more than 288 times, 217 of which are the verb form. The main idea is to bring something into an incontrovertible existence. This process passes through five phases: (a) formation (Judg. 12:6; Job 31:15; Ps. 119:73; Ezek. 16:7) without firmness. It is the initial preparation (II Chr. 1:4; Job 38:41; Ps. 65:9; 78:20; Prov. 6:8). (b) Actual preparation for a future event, such as meals (Gen. 43:16; Josh. 1:11; Neh. 8:10), a military campaign (Josh. 8:4; Ezek. 7:14; 38:7; Amos 4:12), spiritual preparation (I Chr. 29:18; II Chr. 12:14; Ps. 57:7). God is ready (Job 28:27; Ps. 7:13; 9:7; 147:8; Prov. 8:27; 19:29; Zeph. 1:7). (c) Although Prov. 8:27 says that God "prepared" (K.J.V.) the heavens, Prov. 3:19 shows that He has also "established" (fixed) the heavens. We can be sure that God created the world and has it under control (Ps. 119:90; Jer. 33:2). The heavens have been established as His throne (Ps. 103:19) and the earth as His dominion (I Chr. 16:30; Ps. 93:1; Isa. 45:18). He reigns through wisdom and understanding (Prov. 3:19; Jer. 10:12; 51:15). (d) This word is used twenty-five times to refer to the establishment of a dynasty. Without God, no human line can be perpetuated forever (Ps. 89:37; Isa. 9:7). A king cannot remain on the throne without the principles of righteousness (Prov. 16:12). God guarantees His kingship by establishing His sanctuary among His people (Ex. 15:17; Isa. 2:2). (e) The deep satisfaction and sense of well-being comes from the certainty that our hearts are fixed upon God (Ps. 112:7). We can be confident that He will direct our paths (Ps. 37:23; 90:17; Prov. 16:9; Jer. 10:23).

3576. Kâzab; to lie, to speak falsehood, to be found a liar, to be false, to deceive, to be faithless, to prove untrue; to charge one with a lie; to fail; to be in vain. This root and its deriv. occur forty-nine times in the Heb. O.T. It often appears in the same context with forms of *shâv'* (7723), "vanity, emptiness." *Kâzab* is the act of lying—the words themselves. Jehovah does not lie (Num. 23:19; Ps. 89:35). A false witness has violated a holy trust; he was calling upon the God of Truth to testify to the "truth" of his lie (Prov. 6:19; 19:5)! False prophecy in the name of God (Ezek. 13: 6-9,19; Mic. 2:11) also had no basis in reality. Man's nature has become so corrupt that black is white, and white is black to him (Ps. 4:2; 62:4; Isa. 28:17; 57:11). Everything but God is a lie (Job 41:9; Prov. 30:6; Isa. 28:15,17; Amos 2:4). Satan "is a liar, and the father of lies" (Jn. 8:44).

3577. Kâzâb; this mas. Heb. noun comes from 3576. It is a lie, falsehood, deception; idolatry, an idol. This noun occurs thirty-one times in the Heb. O.T. The prophets used the term as a derogatory substitute for false idols. They were the ultimate untruths.

3586. Kechâsh; appearing in the mas. pl. form, this Heb. noun occurs in Isa. 30:9 and comes from 3584. It means lying ones or false ones. Here Israel, because of her refusal to trust God, proves to be a rebellious nation, false sons.

3589. Kîyd; calamity, destruction. This mas. Heb. noun occurs only once (Job 21:20). Literally, it is a striking, a crushing, which led to the metaphorical usage.

3615. Kâlâh; to be completed, finished, accomplished, ready; to be at an end, to be consumed, destroyed, to vanish; to cease, end; to spend, to destroy; to determine. There are 206 occurrences of this verbal root. Essentially, it means to bring a process to completion. It appears both transitively and intransitively throughout the Heb. Bible. The processes may be either positive or negative, i.e., something may be continually added to until it is full or complete, or something may be taken away from until there is nothing left. The English word "finish" has a similar semantic range in both directions. It is the total task, working until the job is done. Sometimes the idea of exhaustion, being entirely consumed, is included in the word. It is an all-or-nothing sort of word.

3617. Kâlâh; this fem. noun stems from 3615. It is a completion, a consumption, a consummation, an utter end, destruction. The adverbial usage means "totally" or "entirely." It is the final and full end of a thing. It expresses the limits of something. The term appears twenty-two times in the Heb. O.T.

3632. Kâlîyl; this Heb. adj. comes from 3634. It means "complete" or "perfect." When used as a sub., it is the whole, a complete sacrifice, a holocaust. Concerning offerings, it is a sacrifice which has been entirely consumed, a whole burnt offering which has been fully and utterly committed to the flames.

3634. Kâlal; to complete, to perfect, to make perfect. This common Semitic root appears in the Book of Ezekiel (27:4,11). Both of these verbal usages are associated with beauty. The very common particle, *kôl*, "all," derives from it.

3635. K^elal; is the Aramaic word corresponding to 3634. It means to complete, to finish, to perfect; to set up; to make up. It is possibly a loanword from Akkadian. It is used eight times, all in the Book of Ezra.

3649. Kâmâr; this Heb. word occurs only in the pl. form. It means priests, idolatrous priests, ascetics. It derives from 3648. It is found only in II Kgs. 23:5; Hos. 10:5; Zeph. 1:4. All of these passages refer to priests who had led Israel in idolatrous worship, whether bull worship in North Israel, Baalism in Judah, or fertility rites on the "high places." The etymology of this root is uncertain.

3651. Kên; this is a Heb. adv. which originates from 3559, which see. It means so, thus, just so, such, so much; therefore, on account of, nevertheless. In addition, there is a homophone which means right, upright, honest when used adjectivally. However, when used as a sub. it means "the right." This word has come to mean "yes" in Modern Hebrew. The adverb was widely used in discourse structure to couple a main section with a preceding one.

3664. K̂anaç; to collect, to gather (together), to heap up, to wrap oneself in a cover (to enfold, to hide oneself); to assemble. This root occurs eleven times in the Heb. O.T. David gathered (*kânaç*) the people to prepare them to construct the temple of Solomon (I Chr. 22:2). Esther and Mordecai mobilized all the Jews in Shushan (Esth. 4:16). God's mighty power gathers the ocean waters like a heap (Ps. 33:7). Certain men collected offerings, tithes, and portions of the harvests for priests and Levites (Neh. 12:44). Israel was warned that they would be gathered for judgment (Ezek. 22:21). Israel was like a man in the uncomfortable position of trying to cover himself with a very narrow blanket (Isa. 28:20).

3673. Kânash; this Aramaic word, meaning to gather together or to assemble, occurs only three times (Dan. 3:2,3,27). It corresponds to the Heb. 3664. Compare the modern-day Israeli kibbutz.

3678. Kiççê' or **kiççêh;** throne (canopied), high seat, chair, royal throne (II Sam. 3:10; Job 36:7). This Heb. mas. noun occurs 136 times in the Heb. O.T. In every case it is a seat of honor (II Kgs. 4:10 is a possible exception). Only a few of the instances are literal thrones (I Kgs. 10:18; 22:10; II Kgs. 25:28; Esth. 5:1; Jer. 1:15; Ezek. 1:26). The great majority of the passages are figurative, either referring to God, David, or Solomon. Since God is the true King of Israel and the Messiah was to come through the lineage of David, this fact is not surprising. See the striking contrasts between God's kingship and that of man (I Kgs. 22). The Jews yearned to have a righteous king, like the Messiah (Isa. 9:7; 16:5; Jer. 22:11—23:6; Zech. 6:13). Mary was told that Jesus "will be great, and will be called the Son of the Most High; and the Lord God will give Him the throne of His father David; and He will reign over the house of Jacob forever; and His kingdom will have no end." (Lk. 1:32,33). After his successful mission on earth, Jesus proclaimed, "All authority has been given to Me in heaven and on earth" (Mt. 28:18).

3680. Kâçâh; to cover, to conceal, to hide; to clothe, to cover sin, to forgive; to keep secret; to hide oneself, to wrap oneself up. Frogs covered Egypt (Ex. 8:6) and the pillar of cloud covered the tabernacle (Num. 9:16). Sometimes it means hidden from view (Gen. 7:19,20; 37:26; Prov. 10:18) or overwhelm (Prov. 10:6,11). Js. 5:20 says, "Let him know that he who turns a sinner from the error of his way will save his soul from death, and will cover a multitude of sins." This is quite similar to another meaning of *kâçâh*. Covering or hiding sins is forgiveness (Ps. 32:1; 85:2; 103:3,11,12; cf. Prov. 17:9; 28:13; Neh. 4:5). See *kâphar* (3722).

3687. K^eçîylûwth; folly, foolishness, silliness. This fem. Heb. noun occurs only once in the O.T. (Prov. 9:13). It stems from 3684.

3688. Kâçal; to be foolish, to be silly, to be engaged in folly. This root word is scarcely used as a verb. Many nouns originate from it including *k^eçîyl* (3684) and *keçel* (3689). Other meanings include: to be fleshy, to be fat (in the loin or flank); strength (firmness, boldness, confidence); to be languid or inert. It appears only in Jer. 10:8.

3689. Keçel; loin, interior; folly; confidence. It is amazing that this word could have such opposite meanings. However, when one considers the root word, the basic idea of fatness leads to either the connotation of satisfaction in prosperity (trust) or the nuance of sluggishness and inactivity (folly). *Keçel* is to be rendered "flanks" in Lev. 3:4,10,15; Ps. 38:7; "folly" (in an evil sense) in Ecc. 7:25; and "confidence" in Prov. 3:26; Job 8:14.

3690. Kiçlâh; occurs only twice in the Heb. O.T. In Job 4:6 it means confidence or hope (the fear of God) and in Ps. 85:8 it refers to the folly of those who knew God's peace but would turn away from it. It is the fem. form of 3689.

3707. Kâ'aç; to be disturbed, fretful, angry, vexed, indignant, grieved; to provoke to anger, to irritate; to excite, to vex, to grieve. It is the stirring up or provoking of the heart to a heated condition. This in turn leads to some action. God has feelings, too. He becomes very upset when those whom He loves sin against Him, forgetting the covenant (Deut. 4:25; 9:18; II Kgs. 21: 1-26; 23:26). He is a jealous God (Ex. 34:14; Ezek. 16:42). It is the emotion of exasperation (II Chr. 16:10; Neh. 4:1; Ecc. 7:9).

3708. Ka'aç or **ka'as;** this mas. Heb. noun means sorrow, vexation, anger, provocation, fretfulness, wrath, spite, grief. The nominal form shows the trouble which man causes, thus triggering hurt feelings. Various forms of idolatry were provocative (I Kgs. 15:30; Ezek. 20:28). Many tears flow at the human level also (I Sam. 1:7,16; Ps. 6:7; Prov. 17:25).

3709. Kaph; this fem. noun is also the name of the eleventh character in the Heb. alphabet. In its initial and medial forms it looks similar to its meaning: the curved or hollow hand, palm, sole (of the hand or foot), paw, forefoot; pan, dish; handle; twig, branch. It is opened or turned upward in such a way as to expose the inside of the hand. See the more common *yâd* (3027), which means "hand" in general (even a fist). *Kaph* is the flat part of the hand or the sole of the foot (Gen. 8:9; 40:11; Lev. 14:16; II Kgs. 4:34; Josh. 3:13). In I Kgs. 17:12 it means a "handful" (of meal). It is also used of the hands when they are spread out in prayer (Ex. 9:29; Isa. 1:15). It refers to a concave vessel (Ex. 25:29; Num. 4:7) or the hollow pouch of a sling (I Sam. 25:29). It is possible that Judg. 8:6,15 may refer to the amputated hands of the enemy.

3722. Kâphar; the primary meaning of this root word is to cover. In time it came to mean to expiate, to make an atonement, to make reconciliation, to placate, or to cancel. It conveys the sense of appeasing, cleansing, disannulling, forgiving, pacifying, being merciful, purging, and putting off. This verb is used about 150 times in the Heb. O.T. It is one of the most important words in the Bible. The verb probably derives from the noun *kippûr* (3725) (its first usage appears in Gen. 6:14 where Noah is given instructions to cover the ark inside and outside with pitch [bitumen]). Most of the time the verb is used to "cover" (hide) sin with the blood of a sacrifice, implying that the sin is wiped away (atoned for) in this process. Lev. 4:13-21 gives detailed instructions to the priests. When Isaiah received God's call in a vision, his lips were touched with a fiery coal from God's altar. Therefore, his sin was purged (*kâphar*). See Isa. 6:7. The New English Bible sometimes translates this term as "wiped away." It was a technical term in the sacrificial ritual ceremonies of Israel. It denoted a material transaction or "ransoming" procedure, i.e., a compensating, propitiating.

3724. Kôpher; this mas. Heb. noun derives from 3725. It means village; pitch (coating); a cypress flower (used for a dye); a redemption price, ransom, satisfaction, sum of money, bribe. Every Israelite was supposed to give a half a shekel for the sanctuary (Ex. 30:12). Jesus did (Mt. 17:24-27). This word is parallel to the word "redeem" in Ps. 49:7. No *kôpher* can be given in exchange for the life of a man who is guilty of murder (Num. 35:31); he must be killed. It is a bribe in I Sam. 12:3. Most of the time, however, it means to atone by offering of substitute payment. Forty-nine times alone in Leviticus it denotes the priestly ritual of sprinkling sacrificial blood as "making an atonement" for the worshipper. Appeasement is clear in Gen. 32:20; Prov. 16:14; and Isa. 28:18. By constant repetition, the Israelites were made to feel the removal of guilt by this cultural mechanism, i.e., the innocent life-blood of an animal "paid for" the life of the worshipper. This identification was further symbolized when the worshipper put his hands upon the head of the animal sacrifice and confessed his sin over the animal before it was killed or sent away (Lev. 1:4; 4:4; 16:21).

3725. Kippûr; only in the pl., this Heb. noun means expiation or atonement. The English word "atonement" has its roots in Middle English and means "to be 'at one'," i.e., to be reconciled, in concord, etc. Therefore, atonement means the condition which results when one makes amends, a satisfactory reparation. The Jewish holiday (*yom kippur*) is the Day of Atonement. It was the tenth day of the seventh month, Tishri. This was and is the only obligatory day of fasting prescribed for Israel. On that day a special sin offering was made for the entire nation. The high priest, only once per year, went behind the curtain which led to the Holy of Holies carrying the blood of the sin offering which he sprinkled upon the mercy seat itself (Lev. 16). Jesus, our High Priest, offered His own blood for the sins of others (Heb. 9). According to Ps. 50: 7-15 and Mic. 6:6-8, all the sacrifices in the world would not satisfy God's strict requirements for righteousness. Only God could provide the perfect, sinless sacrifice which would atone for our sins. In a way, the Aaronic priest at the altar represented God HImself, bringing the necessary offering, with God initiating the merciful action, not man.

3727. Kappôreth; a cover, the lid of the Ark of the Covenant, the propitiatory, the mercy seat. This Heb. noun derives from 3725. It is used twenty-seven times and always refers to the golden cover of the sacred chest deep inside the tabernacle or Solomon's temple. This was the exact spot where God promised to meet with human beings (Num. 7:89). See the Gr. *hilastērion* (2435), "place (or object) of propitiation." This Gr. word was applied to Christ in Rom. 3:25. The Jewish high priest sprinkled the blood of the sin offering seven times upon the lid of the Ark of the Covenant on the Day of Atonement.

3728. Kâphash; to tread down, to trample down, to press down; to humiliate; to cover over. The only occurrence is in Lam. 3:16 which states: "He has made me cower in the dust." It conveys the idea of being bent or overwhelmed.

3733. Kar; lamb, sheep; battering-ram (from butting). It contains the idea of a blunt head.

3742. K^erûwb; a cherub, a winged figure who stood over the mercy seat of the Ark of the Covenant (Ex. 25:18; 37:7-9), an order of angels, usually ranked below the seraphim, a composite being (Ezek. 1 and 10). The pl. form in Heb. is cherubim. Sometimes English translations add the pl. "-s" also! The Vulgate has *cherubin*. The etymological origins of this word are quite doubtful. The Akkadian cognate verb means "to bless, to praise, to adore." They first appear in Gen. 3:24 to guard against man's unauthorized re-entry into paradise. In Solomon's temple two large cherubim, made of olive wood which was overlaid with gold, were placed in the Most Holy Place. They faced forward, side by side, with a combined wingspan of about fifteen feet (see I Kgs. 6:29,32; 7:29). The original Ark of the Covenant was directly beneath their center. God reigned "above" the place for atonement, from between the cherubim (see Ex. 25:22; Num. 7:89). Cherubim were used for decoration in Ezekiel's symbolic temple (Ezek. 41:18-20,25). Each one of them had two faces, the face of a man and the face of a lion, pointing in opposite directions. However, they were probably not sphinx-like. See also Ezek. 9:3 and 11:22. They had a human body and hands, but the feet went straight down like a calf's. They possessed four wings, two of which covered their bodies in modesty, and two of which extended upward. The seraphim (Isa. 6) were similar beings who had six wings (cf. Rev. 4:6-8). The cherubim of Ezek. 1 had four faces (man, lion, ox, and eagle). They could travel in any direction with lightning speed. They always appear next to the throne of God, worshipping and serving Him.

3746. Kârîy; this mas. coll. noun refers to the royal bodyguards or palace soldiers who had the responsibility of inflicting capital punishment. They were the executioners. The word occurs three times in the O.T. (See II Sam. 20:23 for the Cherethites of King David's guards.) It also refers to captains or leaders (II Kgs. 11:4, 19).

3748. K[e]rîythûwth; implies the cutting off of a marriage by means of a bill of divorcement; a divorce, a separation. This fem. Heb. noun occurs four times in the Heb. O.T. (Deut. 24:1,3; Isa. 50:1; Jer. 3:8).

3764. Korçê'; this Aramaic word appears only in Daniel (Dan. 5:20; 7:9). It is used like the Heb. word *kiççê'* (3678) and means throne or tribunal.

3766. Kâra'; to bend (the knees), to kneel down, to bow down, to sink down, to cower, to writhe in pain, to be prostrate, to afflict, to grieve. The kneeling may be a general bowing down or for rest (e.g., animals) or worship (before God) or obeisance (before a king). Most of Gideon's army got down on their knees to drink (Judg. 7:6) which was a vulnerable position for a soldier. Animals crouched (Num. 24:9) and women doubled over in childbirth (I Sam. 4:19). Bending the knees necessitated bending the back, i.e., bowing like Muslims. It does not mean to fall prostrate (prone) upon the ground. It was a humbled position which belied a humble attitude.

3772. Kârath; to cut, to cut off; to cut off a part of the body (e.g., head, hand, foreskin), to maim, to castrate; to cut down trees, idols; to root out, to cut out, to eliminate, to kill, to destroy; to cut (make) a covenant; to be felled, to be cut off, to be consumed, to be exiled, to be destoryed, to be cut down; to withdraw; to be withdrawn. Besides the literal meaning (Ex. 4:25; I Sam. 5:4; I Kgs. 5:6; Isa. 14:8), there are metaphorical meanings of elimination or removal. It is difficult to determine whether "cut off" means to be killed or only to be excommunicated. "Cutting a covenant" was literal, because animals had to be slaughtered in order to ratify the agreement (Gen. 15). The flame passed through between the two cut pieces (Gen. 15:18). See also Jer. 34:18. It is quite possible that one is pledging death (like the animal) if the pact is broken. The verb occurs about 290 times in the Heb. Bible, in all periods.

3782. Kâshal. to totter, to fail, to stumble, to stagger, to faint, to fall; to become weak; to cause to fall; to seduce, to lead astray; to be overthrown, to be felled. See the very similar Gr. word *skandalizō* (4624) in the N.T. lexical section. It can be either a physical falling or a figurative falling (ruin). It is often used to describe the consequences of God's judgment upon sin (e.g., Jer. 6:21; 50:32). It occurs about sixty times in the Heb. O.T.

3784. Kâshaph; to whisper (a magical spell), to use songs of magic, to mutter magical words or incantations; to enchant; to practice magic, to be a sorcerer, to use witchcraft. Occurring six times, it is always restricted to the worship of idols.

3785. Kesheph; found in the pl., it means witchcrafts (II Kgs. 9:22; Mic. 5:12; Nah. 3:4) and sorceries (Isa. 47:9,12). It originates from 3784.

3786. Kashshâph; this mas. Heb. noun, meaning an enchanter, sorcerer, or magician, stems from 3784. It is found only once (Jer. 27:9).

3787. Kâshêr; to be right or straight, to be proper, to be acceptable; to direct, to give prosperity; to succeed or prosper, to thrive, to grow. It occurs three times in the Heb. O.T. (Esth. 8:5; Ecc. 10:10; 11:6). Medieval Heb. produced the familiar *kosher*, which means that something is according to the Jewish rules of ritual purity.

3788. Kishrôwn; right, good; equity, success, skill, advantage, profit, prosperity. This mas. Heb. noun is a deriv. of 3787.

3807. Kâthath; to crush to pieces, to crush fine; to hammer, to forge; to beat to pieces, to shatter; to castrate; to ruin, destroy; to be dashed together; to scatter, to rout; to be broken; to be destroyed.

3816. L[e]ôm or **l[e]'ôwm;** this mas. Heb. noun is of uncertain ancestry. It means a community, a nation, people. The principal meaning of the word is togetherness, i.e., what a group of people share in common as a cohesive unit. It is an ethnic group that has an internal cultural bond. This word and two other Heb. synonyms, *gôwy* (1471) and *'am* (5971), all appear in Ps. 67. Everyone, no matter what their interrelationships or characteristics are, ought to praise the Lord. Mankind is essentially one piece, even though there are diverse, definable groups and sub-groups.

3820. Lêb; this is a shorter form of 3824 but it derives from 3823. This mas. Heb. noun is the heart, the center; or the middle of somthing. Often this word and its Heb. correlate, *lêbâb* (3824), means the physical heart, the blood-pumping organ. However, of the 850 times in the Heb. O.T., it is more common to interpret the term as the totality of man's inner or immaterial nature. This usage has passed into common English with expressions such as: "heart and soul," "the heart goes out (to someone)," "one's heart is in one's mouth," "his heart is in the right place," "heart of gold," "from the bottom of our hearts," and "a heart to heart talk." These are the deepest, innermost feelings. In the Bible the whole spectrum of human emotions is attributed to the heart. See *kardia* (2588) in the N.T. lexical section. There are many Heb. idioms which are built with *lêb.* Wisdom and understanding reside in the heart (I Kgs. 3:12; Prov. 16:23). It is almost a synonym for "mind" (II Chr. 9:23) or "sense" (Prov. 11:12) or "perceptive nature" (II Kgs. 5:26). However, it can be deceived (Isa. 44:20). The heart is the seat of the will (Num. 16:28; Judg. 9:3; II Chr. 12:14). To refuse to make the proper decision is to harden the heart (Ex. 10:1; Josh. 11:20). The heart is the seat of moral evil (Jer. 17:9). The term may refer to the inner part of a thing (Ex. 15:8; Deut. 4:11; Prov. 23:34).

3821. Lêb; Dan. 7:28 is the only occurrence of this mas. Aramaic word which corresponds to 3820. It also means "heart."

3823. Lâbab; to be deprived, to be void of heart (understanding), to rob the heart, to be hollow, to ravish the heart (Song of Sol. 4:9); to be wise, to be intelligent (Job 11:12); to make cakes (II Sam. 13:6,8). These are the only five appearances.

3824. Lêbâb; this is only another form of *lêb* (3820), which see.

3825. L[e]bab; this is the Aramaic correlate to 3824. It means "heart" in the seven references in Daniel (2:30; 4:16, twice; 5:20-22; 7:4).

3826. Libbâh; this fem. Heb. noun is probably a variant of *lêb* (3820). It also means "heart." In the Heb. O.T. it occurs eight times. In the sing. form it is found in Prov. 24:12 and Ezek. 16:30. It appears in Ps. 7:9; 125:4; Prov. 15:11; 17:3; 21:2; Isa. 44:18 in the pl. form. It is possible that it could mean "rage."

3858. Lahaṭ; this mas. Heb. noun originates from 3857 and occurs only in Ex. 7:11, where it means "secret arts" (in the pl.). It had the meaning of flaming, burning, blaze, and a flashing blade; to hide, i.e., to wrap, to be covert, to practice magic. See Gen. 3:24 for the "flaming sword," which may refer to the blade of the sword.

3887. Lûwts; to mock, deride, scorn; to interpret; to meditate; to act as a mocker. This word is believed to have come from a root which meant to "make mouths at," i.e., to scoff. Therefore, it soon came to mean the effort to pronounce a foreign language (interpret) or to intercede (ambassador, teacher).

3894. Lâchûwm or **lâchûm;** this mas. Heb. noun originates from 3898 and means food, flesh, nourishment, body. It appears twice in the Heb. O.T. (Job 20:23; Zeph. 1:17).

3907. Lâchash; to whisper (II Sam. 12:19; Ps. 41:7), to mutter incantations, to mumble a spell (like a magician); charmers (Ps. 58:5), enchanters, sorcerers. It has the sense of "to hiss like a serpent," in Aramaic and later rabbinical Heb. It may indeed be a dialectal variant of *nâchash* (5172). The initial letters are formed in a similar way, one nasal alveolar and the other lateral alveolar.

3908. Lachash; this mas. Heb. noun stems from 3907. It occurs five times in the Heb. O.T., and each occurrence is translated differently in the K.J.V. Isa. 3:3 refers to the skillful orator who is skillful of speech. Isa. 3:20 uses the word "amulets," which were gems and precious stones inscribed with magical formulae and worn around the necks of the women in the East or in their ears. In Isa. 26:16 the phrase "whisper a prayer" is used. In Ecc. 10:11 and Jer. 8:17 *lachash* refers to the charming or enchantment of serpents through using magical incantations or spells. All these superstitious behaviors show that Israel had sunk very low spiritually (Isa. 26:16 may not be an incantation).

3909. Lâṭ; this mas. Heb. noun derives from 3874. It is a variant form of 3814. It means secrecy; an incantation, enchantments; hidden, privily. The term occurs eight times in the Heb. O.T. In the pl. it refers to the secret arts which were practiced by Pharaoh's magicians (Ex. 7:11,22; 8:7,18). The other instances function as an adv., "secretly" or "softly" (Judg. 4:21; Ruth 3:7; I Sam. 18:22; 24:5).

3915. Layil or **lêyl** or **layᵉlâh;** this mas. Heb. noun comes from 3883 which means a twisting (away of the light), i.e., "night." In other words, when the light "folds back," darkness sets in. In a figurative sense, it can mean ominous. However, since God created both light and darkness (Gen. 1:4,5; Ps. 74:16), both are good. God does not sleep during the night; He provides for the animals in the forest (Ps. 104:20-22) and protects men (Ps. 91:5,6). Each day and night is a regular remainder of His covenant with mankind (Gen. 8:22; Jer. 33:20-26). Night is like day to God (Ps. 139:11,12). The most important night was when God delivered His people from slavery (Ex. 11:4; 12:12,29). In a nonliteral sense, the term appears as a time of trial, weeping, suffering, and communion with God. This word occurs 242 times.

3916. Leylᵉyâ; only occurs five times in the Book of Daniel. It is the Aramaic word for night, corresponding to the Heb. 3915.

3925. Lâmad; to learn, to study, to be accustomed to; to teach, to instruct, to practice, to train; to be taught, to be trained. A derived form, *malmâd* (4451), was a goad for oxen. Through a yoke and a goad, Ephraim was taught like a cow (Hos. 10:11). *Lâmad* has both the idea of training and educating. Greek required two words, *manthanō* (3129), "to learn," and *didaskō* (1321), "to teach," to achieve what the Heb. does in one word, *lâmad*. All knowledge resides in the "fear of the Lord" (Deut. 4:10; 14:23; 17:19; 31:12,13). No one teaches Him or advises Him (Isa. 40:14). He is the Source of all truth.

3928. Limmûwd or **limmûd;** learned, taught, trained, skilled, accumstomed. This Heb. adj. is used six times in the Heb. O.T. and is traceable to 3925. It means "disciple" in some cases.

3937. Lâ'az; to speak in a foreign language or a strange language; to speak unintelligibly, to stammer. It occurs only once (Ps. 114:1).

3948. Leqach; something received or learned, instruction, knowledge, doctrine, learning, fair speech. This mas. Heb. noun is derived from 3947 and occurs nine times in the Heb. O.T. (Deut. 32:2; Job 11:4; Prov. 1:5; 4:2; 7:21; 9:9; 16:21,23; Isa. 29:24). In a sense, the mind "grasps," having the nuance of perception. It has the meaning of persuasiveness in a good sense (Prov. 16:21) or in an evil sense (Prov. 7:21).

3950. Lâqat; to pick up, to collect, to gather, to glean; to be gathered, to assemble. Almost anything can be accumulated: stones, manna, money, grain, fallen grapes, arrows, firewood, food off the ground, a group of troublemakers. Even animals gathered food (Ps. 104:28). The sons of Israel were commanded not to reap the corners of their grain fields or to gather the secondary gleanings of their harvest; they were to be left for the poor and strangers who lived among them (Lev. 19:9,10; 23:22; Ruth 2:15-18).

3953. Lâqash; to gather the late fruit, to glean the residue of the aftercrop; to be ripe, to be late. It occurs only once in the O.T. (Job 24:6).

3971. M'ûwm or **mûwm;** this mas. Heb. noun means defect, spot, blemish, stain. It may be physical (Lev. 21:17ff.; Dan. 1:4ff.) or moral (Deut 32:5; Job. 11:15; 31:7). All animal sacrifices which were offered to God had to be perfect, without spot or blemish (Lev. 22:20,21,25; Num. 19:2; Deut. 15:21; 17:1). God wants the best, not the faulty rejects.

3974. Mâ'ôwr or **mâ'ôr** or **mᵉôwrâh** or **mᵉ'ôrâh;** these words arise from 216. The meaning is: a luminous body, a light, a luminary, a lump.

3982. Ma'ămar; an edict, a commandment, a decree, something which is said (in an authoritative manner). All three occurrences of this word are in Esther (1:15; 2:20; 9:32).

3983. Mê'mar; this Aramaic mas. noun means appointment, word. It corresponds to the Heb. 3982. It occurs only twice in the Heb. O.T. (Ezra 6:9; Dan. 4:17).

3985. Mâ'ên; to be unwilling, to refuse. Pharaoh refused to obey the commands of God (Ex. 4:23; 7:14; 10:3). Later Israel also refused to repent (Ps. 78:10; Jer. 3:3; 8:5; Hos. 11:5) or to receive instruction (Jer. 5:3; 9:6; 11:10; Zech. 7:11). Once God refused to allow Balaam to curse Israel (Num. 22:13).

3986. Mâ'ên; this Heb. verbal adj. was derived from 3985 and means "unwilling" or "refusing." Three times it describes Pharaoh's refusal to release Israel from bondage (Ex. 8:2; 9:2; 10:4). Zedekiah refused to surrender to the Babylonians (Jer. 38:21).

3987. Mê'ên; this pl. Heb. adj. also comes from 3985 and occurs only once in the O.T. (Jer. 13:10). It means refusing, refractory, pertinacious. Israel rebelled against God by continually refusing to listen to Him an by worshipping other gods.

3988. Mâ'aç; to melt, to feel undone; to melt away, to dissolve. It has the sense of flowing or running out. It is similar to our concept of feeling "drained." See Ps. 58:8 for example.

4032. Mâgôwr or **mâgûwr;** fear, terror. See Lam. 2:22. It seems to derive from *gûwr* (1481) in the sense of fearing, i.e., the anxiety of "turning aside" from the road or being in a strange place, where one is not at home.

4033. Mâgûwr or **mâgûr;** a temporary abode, a sojourn; an inn, a dwelling, a pilgrimage, being a stranger or alien. See 4032.

4034. Mᵉgôwrâh; this is the fem, form of 4032. It means fear or terror. It occurs only once in the O.T. (Prov. 10:24).

4035. Mᵉgûwrâh; fright, fear, the object of fear (Ps. 34:4; Isa. 66:4). Granary, a barn, a storehouse (Hag. 2:19). This is the fem. form of 4032 or 4033.

4039. Mᵉgillâh; this fem. Heb. noun derives from 1556. It is a roll, a scroll, a volume, an ancient book. Jehoiakim cut the scroll of Jeremiah and burned it (see Jer. 36). It was probably made of Egyptian papyrus. See also Ezra 6:2; Ps. 40:7; Ezek. 2:9; 3:1-3; Zech. 5:1,2. Something could be written on both sides (Ezek. 2:10). The Dead Sea Scrolls were written on treated animal skins which were stitched together. Later, the precursor to our modern books, the codex form, used "pages" or leather, beginning in the first and second centuries after Christ. The five *Megilloth,* the five Hebrew scrolls from the O.T., were read on annual festivals: the Song of Solomon (at Passover), Ruth (at Pentecost), Lamentations (on the ninth day of Ab), Ecclesiastes (at the Feast of Tabernacles), and Esther (at Purim).

4040. Mᵉgillâh; this is the Aramaic word which corresponds to 4039. It occurs only once (Ezra 6:2).

4048. Mâgar; to give up, to cast before, to deliver over, to throw down, to yield up, to abandon; to be in terror. It occurs only twice in the Heb. O.T. (Ps. 89:44; Ezek. 21:12).

4049. Mᵉgar; this Aramaic word occurs only once in the O.T. (Ezra 6:12). It means to overthrow or to destroy, corresponding to the Heb. 4048.

4103. Mᵉhûwm̂ah; confusion, consternation, disturbance, noise, destruction, discomfiture, trouble, tumult, vexation. This fem. Heb. noun derives from 1949. The R.S.V. also translates it as "panic." The picture is one of severe turmoil which the enemies of the Lord felt (Deut. 7:23) and Israel herself (Deut. 28:20).

4135. Mûwl; to cut off, to circumcise, to let oneself be circumcised; to destroy. Circumcision was and is very important to the Jews, because it is a distinctive token of God's original covenant with Abraham in Gen. 12: 1-3, although Abraham was not actually circumcised until Gen. 17. It is the practice of cutting off the foreskin (prepuce) of the male sex organ. Except for the uncircumcised Philistines, circumcision was not uncommon in ancient times, but non-Jews practiced it as a puberty rite at about the age of 13. God commanded Abraham, however, to circumcise his male offspring on the eighth day after birth. This transformed the operation to have a religious meaning. Infant circumcision was unique to the Jews. Though modern medicine suggests that the practice is indeed hygienic, nothing is mentioned in the O.T. concerning that point. It was like a mark of God's ownership for the male leadership of HIs people. Unfortunately, the sign degenerated in its spiritual significance. The Prophet Jeremiah preached that mere circumcision of the flesh was worthless unless it was coupled with a living faith (Jer. 4:4). By N.T. times it had become a technical term which was synonymous with "Jews," even Jewish Christians (Acts 10:45; 11:2; Rom. 15:8; Gal. 2:7-9, 12; Eph. 2:11; Phil. 3:3; Col. 3:11; 4:11; Tit. 1:10). Deut. 30:6 captures the deep spiritual meaning of circumcision. It is a work of God upon the human heart (Rom. 2:25-29; 3:1,30; 4:9-12; Col. 2:11,12). See also Jn. 7:22,23; Acts 7:8; 10:45; 11:2; I Cor. 7:19; Gal. 2:7-9; 5:6,11; 6:15. The inspired Council of Jerusalem forever defined the truth of the matter (Acts 15:1-35). See *peritemnō* (4059) and peritomē (4061) in the N.T. lexical section.

4139. Mûwlâh; occurring in the pl. form, this fem. Heb. noun comes from 4135. It means "circumcision" and is found only once (Ex. 4:26). God placed great importance on this practice. Even Moses was not allowed to neglect it for his son.

4143. Mûwçâd; means foundation, foundation laying and is derived from 3245, which see.

4145. Mûwçâdâh; this fem. Heb. noun means foundation, grounded; an appointment, a decree. It occurs only twice in the Heb. O.T. (Isa. 30:32; Ezek. 41:8).

4146. Môwçâdâh or **môçâdâh;** this fem. Heb. noun derives from 3245, meaning "foundation," always appearing in the pl. form. There are thirteen occurrences in the Heb. O.T. (Deut. 32:22; IISam. 22:8,16; Ps. 18:7,15; 82:5; Prov. 8:29; Isa. 24:18; 40:21; 58:12; Jer. 31:37; 51:26; Mic. 6:2).

4148. Mûwçâr; chastisement, punishment, correction, discipline, instruction, self-control. This mas. Heb. noun derives from 3256. Essentially, it is a bond, a checking, restraint, i.e., correction which results in education. (See Deut. 11:2ff.; cf. Deut. 4:35f.). The term is very frequent in Proverbs (e.g., Prov. 3:11,12). Often it is oral not corporal discipline. The prophets developed the theme of God's discipline (Isa. 8:11; 53:5; Jer. 2:30; 5:3; 7:28; 17:23; 32:33)

4150. Môw'êd or **mô'êd** or **môw'âdâh;** congregation, festive gathering; appointment, signal. Deriving from 3259, *môw'êd,* the Heb. form, appears 223 times in the O.T. It often designates a determined time or place without any regard for the purpose. Since the Jewish festivals occurred at regular intervals, this word becomes closely identified with them. See *chag* (2282). *Môw'êd* is used in a broad sense for all religious assemblies. It was closely associated with the tabernacle itself (Ex. 29:42; 33:7,11; Num. 7:89; 12:8). God met Israel there at specific times for the purpose of revealing His will. It is a common term for the worshipping assembly of God's people. See also *qâhâl* (6951). The fem. form appears in the pl. and occurs only once in the O.T. (II Chr. 8:13), where it means "solemn feasts."

4151. Môw'âd; this mas. Heb. noun, which is derived from 3252. occurs only once (Isa. 14:31). There it means "ranks."

4159. Môwphêth or **môphêth;** this mas. Heb. noun, occurring in the pl. form, means wonderful deed, wonder, miraculous sign, miracle, prodigy, portent, omen. The etymology is uncertain. No other Heb. verb or noun uses the same triconsonantal letters. However, the meaning is very clear. The Septuagint renders it with the well-known *terata* (the pl. of *teras,* 5059, in the N.T. lexical section). The mighty acts of God included the provision of water, manna, quails, the pillar of fire, etc. The word also has a bad sense: Israel became a spectacular demonstration, an object lesson, of disobeying God (Deut. 28:46; Ps. 71:7; Isa. 8:18; 20:3; Ezek. 12:6,11; 24:24,27; Zech. 3:8). Sometimes it is an authenticating sign (I Kgs. 13:3,5; II Chr. 32:24,31; Ezek. 24:24,27). Peter quoted Joel 2:30 in Acts 2:19.

4167. Mûwq; Ps. 73:8 is the only occurrence of this root verb which means to be corrupt; to mock, to deride, to jeer, to blaspheme.

4170. Môwqêsh or **môqêsh;** this mas. Heb. noun derives from 3369. It is a noose for catching animals, possibly even a hook. Quite possibly it could have been the upper movable part of a jaw-like trap and then later was used to describe the whole trap or snare. The animal would wander into it and be caught suddenly. The word is often used metaphorically to describe the lure and entanglements of sin. See *skandalon* (4625) in the N.T. lexical section.

4172. Môwrâ' or **môrâ'** or **môrâh;** these mas. forms originate from 3372. There are twelve occurrences in the Heb. O.T. It means a fearful thing, fear (Gen. 9:2; Ps. 9:20; Mal. 2:5); dread (Deut. 11:25); terror, a stupendous or wonderful deed (Deut. 4:34; 34:12; Jer. 32:21); terribleness (Deut. 26:8); reverence (Mal. 1:6); and an object of fear or reverence (when referring to God) in Isa. 8:12,13; Ps. 76:11.

4181. Môwrâshâh; possessions, heritage, property, inheritance. This fem. Heb. noun occurs nine times in the O.T. See the discussion under 4180, its source.

4186. Môwshâb or **môshâb;** this mas. Heb. noun means a seat; a session; dwelling place; a stay, a time of abode; the inhabitants of a place; the site of a town. 3427 is its root. It occurs forty-five times in the Heb. O.T. It was the seat of Saul or David at the banquet table (1 Sam. 20:18,25; cf. Job 29:7) or a collective sitting (I Kgs. 10:5; Ps. 1:1; 107:32). Zion was the dwelling place of Jehovah (Ps. 132:13). It refers to houses (Ex. 12:20; Lev. 25:29) and their dwellers (II Sam. 9:12). It can mean site (II Kgs. 2:19) or location (Ezek. 8:3). There is a textual problem at Ezek. 37:23.

4190. Môwshâ'âh; this fem. Heb. noun, which appears in the pl. form, means "salvations" or "deliverances." It occurs only once in the O.T. (Ps. 68:20).

4191. Mûwth; to die, to kill, to slay, to bring to death, to have one executed. Death is a very important concept throughout the entire Bible. The Scriptures present it as unnatural, as something which God did not want to happen, but which is very necessary. God take no pleasure in it (Ezek. 18:32). Death was the result of sin (Gen. 3:3). A holy God must separate Himself from anything which is not in harmony with His character. Therefore, when our first parents sinned, they had to leave Paradise. They were no longer permitted to continue eating from the tree of life, living in sin. Every human being must face physical death (Heb. 9:27), but Jesus Christ came to this earth to "taste death for everyone" (Heb. 2:9), so that we would not have to undergo the "second death" (Rev. 20:11-15), being severed from God eternally. The pagan Canaanites used *mûwth* as the name of their god of death. His name was Mot. He ruled over the netherworld, a place of slime and filth. He fought with Baal, the god of fertility, for which he suffered the displeasure of El, the head of the pantheon. The Canaanites normalized death through these myths. They practice elaborate rituals which included mutilation of their bodies and sacrifices for the dead. These were strictly forbidden to the sons of Israel (Deut. 14:1). They even sacrificed children (Deut. 12:31). The low view of life held by the Canaanites was not shared by the inspired O.T. writers (Ps. 16:11; 21:4; 73:23-26; Prov. 3:2).

4192. Mûwth; see Ps. 48:14 and the title to Ps. 9, Muthlabben, which means "To die for the son." This was probably the title of a popular song at that time. It derives from 4191 and 1121.

4193. Môwth; this Aramaic term occurs only in Ezra 7:26. It corresponds to 4194 and means death.

4194. Mâveth; this mas. Heb. noun means death, realm of the dead, dying, Death (when personified); deadly sickness, pestilence, destruction. It stems from 4191, which see. Also, cf *thanatos* (2288) in the N.T. lexical section.

4196. Mizbêach; this important mas. Heb. noun derives from 2076. It is an altar, a place of sacrifice. The term is used mostly in the Pentateuch and in the other historical books. Altars were made of stone (Josh. 8:31), diret (Ex. 20:24), wood and bronze (Ex. 38:1), and wood with gold (Ex. 30:1-6). Sometimes altars had names (Gen. 33:20; Ex. 17:15; Judg. 6:24). There were unauthorized, forbidden altars to false gods (pillars, Ex. 34:13; high places, II Kgs. 23:15). In the Patriarchal Age, Noah, Abraham, Isaac, and Jacob all built altars. Building an altar ratified agreements (Gen. 31:45,46; Ex. 24:4,5; Ps. 50:5). God told Moses that His only altar would be associated with the tabernacle. See Ex. 29:44; 30:1-6,28; 38:1,2; 39:38; 40:5,10; Lev. 4:7; 8:11,15; 16:20,33; Num. 7:10,11,84. For Solomon's altar of burnt offering see I Kgs. 8:54; II Chr. 4:1; 8:12. It played a prominent part in the post-Solomonic age (II Kgs. 16:14,15; II Chr. 15:8; 26:16; 29:18). For other altars see Josh. 8:31; 22:11,26; I Kgs. 18:30-32; II Sam. 24:25. For the special horns of the altar, compare Ex. 21:14; I Kgs. 1:50,51; 2:28. The inspired authors emphasized that sincerity and true obedience was more important than massive proliferation of animal sacrifices (I Sam. 15:22; Neh. 12:43; Ps. 50:14,23; 51:17; Prov. 21:3; Isa. 1:11; 6:6). The sons of Israel apostatized by becoming deeply involved in pagan sacrifices on Canaanite altars at the high places (Ex. 34:13; Lev. 17:7; Num. 25:2ff; Deut. 7:5; 32:17; Judg. 6:30; I Kgs. 12:32; 16:32; 19:10; 22:43; II Kgs. 10:19;16:4; 23:15; II Chr. 33:15; 28:23; 33:22; Ps. 106:37,38; Ezek. 16:20,21).

4209. M^{e}zimmâh; meditation, thought, prudence; plan, device, plot, purpose, intrigue, mischief. This fem. Heb. noun comes from 2161. A scheming, conniving man is portrayed in Prov. 12:2; 14:17 in the plural. See also Ps. 10:4. The sing. form is consistently positive, meaning "discretion," (Prov. 1:4; 2:11; 3:21; 5:2, 8:12).

4223. M^{e}châ'; this Aramaic verb means to strike (in pieces), to smite, to kill, to slay, to impale, to arrest, to hang, to destroy. It occurs four times (Ezra 6:11; Dan. 2:34,35; 4:35)

4229. Mâchâh; to wipe, to wipe off, to blot out; to adjoin, to touch on; to be wiped out, to be wiped off, to be removed, to be effaced, to be destroyed; to be smeared with fat; to put away. There are thirty-three instances of this verbal root in the Heb. O.T. Every living thing was blotted out by the flood (Gen. 7:22,23). Israel came close to being blotted out of God's book (Ex. 32:32,33; Deut. 9:14; 29:20; Ps. 69:28). Compare Col. 2:14. In ancient leather scrolls erasures were made by washing off the ink, wiping it. The entire tribe of Benjamin was almost wiped out (Judg. 21:17). David prayed that his sins would be removed (Ps. 51:1,9). When God forgives, He forgets (Neh. 4:5; cf. Ps. 109:14; Isa. 43:25; 44:22) When God punished Jerusalem, it was pictured as someone wiping a dish and turning it upside down (II Kgs. 21:13).

4236. Machăzeh; this mas. Heb. noun originates from 2372. It means vision, apparition, sight. It occurs in Gen. 15:1; Num. 24:4,16; and Ezek. 13:7.

4241. Michyâh; preservation of life, sustenance, food supplies, reviving, livelihood; and indication, a sign, a mark, a stroke. The fem. Heb. noun occurs eight times in the O.T. The K.J.V. uses the archaic "victuals" (Judg. 17:10) and "recover" (II Chr. 14:13).

4263. Machmâl; originates from 2550, *châmal*. This mas. Heb. noun occurs only in Ezek. 24:21 and means pity, compassion, sympathy, delight, desire, the object of deep love. The Prophet Ezekiel was describing the temple sanctuary in which the Israelites took great pride and pleasure. They firecely desired to preserve it from any desecration or destruction.

4264. Machăneh; camp, encampment, army, host, troop; band, station of priests. Deriving from 2583 (*chânâh*), meaning to decline, to bend down, to encamp, to lay siege against, this Heb. noun is a temporary and protective enclosure for a tribe or army. It may have been circular in shape. Early American settlers saw the advantage of arranging their wagons in this shape. However, Num. 1:47—2:34; 3:14-16; 10:11-28 show that the Israelite camp in the wilderness was square-shaped around the tabernacle, with three tribes on each side. To set up camp, water was needed (Josh. 11:5; Judg. 7:1) and a natural defense barrier (I Sam. 17:3; 26:6). Cleanliness was mandatory (Num. 5: 1-4; Deut. 23:10-14). The dead were buried outside the camp (Lev. 10:4,5) and lepers were exluded (Lev. 13:46). Criminals were banished (Lev. 24:23; cf. Heb. 13:12). See *parembolē* (3925) in Rev. 20:9 in Strong's Gr. Dictionary.

4272. Mâchats; to split, to cleave, to crush, to wound severely, to strike; to shake, to dip. The term carries the connotation of annihilation. Jael delivered a decisive, lethal blow to Sisera's head (Judg. 5:26). The Lord deals severely with sinful individuals and nations (Deut. 33:11; Ps. 68:21; 110:5,6). No one will escape Him (Deut. 32:29; Job 5:18; Hab. 3:13). Compare the vivid picture in Ps. 68:23.

4273. Machats; contusion, stroke, severe wound. It occurs only in Isa. 30:26 and stems from 4272.

4277. Mâchaq; to smite in pieces, to destroy, to pierce, to crush, to cut through. This root is found only in Judg. 5:26.

4284. Machăshâbâh or **machăshebeth;** this fem. Heb. noun is derived from *châshab* (2803). It means thought, imaginations, intentions, purpose, plan, means, device (as seen in Job 5:12; 21:27; Ps. 94:11; Prov. 20:18); contrivance, curious works, cunning works, artificial work (as seen in Ex. 31:4; 35:32); machine, invention, skillful work, fortification (as seen in Ex. 35:33; II Chr. 26:15).

4285. Machshâk; darkness, dark place, the realm of the dead, obscure. This mas. Heb. noun originates from 2821. It is parallel to "grave" in Ps. 88:6 (it refers to Hades in Ps. 143:3 and Lam. 3:6). It is used on connection with wickedness (Ps. 74:20; Isa. 29:15), terror (Ps. 88:18), and blindness (Isa. 42:16).

4288. M^{e}chittâh; this fem. Heb. noun comes from 2846. It is desolation, ruin, crushing, destruction, terror, consternation, dismay. The three basic meanings are: literal physical ruins (Ps. 89:40); destruction in an abstract sense (Prov. 10:14; 18:7) and an external object of terror (Jer. 17:17; 48:39). It is not entirely clear at all that *m^{e}chittâh* is the internal emotion of terror.

4294. Maṭṭeh or **maṭṭâh;** this mas. Heb. noun derives from 5186. It means a branch (extended), a twig; a rod, staff, stick, sceptre, spear; stem, tribe. A rod signified correction in the sense of chastisement. A sceptre connoted ruling. A staff was used to walk, i.e., to support life, therefore, (figuratively) it meant "bread." Lances were thrown and a tribe was an offshoot of the nation. This word is found about 250 times in the Heb. O.T; a hundred and eighty of those instances are rendered "tribe," usually one of the twelve tribes of Israel. In the beginning each tribal ruler seems to have led his group with a staff (*maṭṭeh*); therefore, it became a symbol of the tribe itself (Num. 17:2-10) and eventually leadership and authority (Ps. 110:2; Jer. 48:17). See *phulē* (5443). Moses misused the rod of God (Num. 20:10-12). It can be the shaft of an arrow (Hab. 3:9,14). Ezekiel uses the word for the branch of a vine (19:11,12,14). Isaiah uses the term as a symbol of oppression and judgment (Isa. 9:4; 10:5,24; 14:5; 30:32).

4297. Muṭṭeh; this word originates from 5186. It is a stretching, an extension, i.e., a distortion of warping of justice, therefore, perverseness, turning aside, or twisting judgment. It occurs only once in the O.T. (Ezek. 9:9), describing the injustice of the city of Jerusalem.

4334. Mîyshôwr or **mîyshôr;** this mas. Heb. noun stems from 3474. It is a plain (sometimes even used as a proper name), level land; (figuratively) concord, straightness, justice, honesty, righteousness, equity, uprightness, justly (with justice), lawfully. It is the lord who declares justice and this was thoroughly understood in a theocratic society (Dan. 11:6; Mal. 2:6). In Mesopotamia the sun-god was Shamash, the principal god of justice.

4347. Makkâh or **makkeh;** has 5221 as its origin. It means a blow, a stroke; a beating; a wound; slaughter; defeat. Two-thirds of the forty-eight occurrences of this word are translated by the Septuagint with *plēgē* (4127). For the English word "plague" there are four basic sets of meaning. One can easily see the progression of severity between them. Whipping was formal punishment limited to forty lashes (Deut. 25:3). However, the Jews eventually reduced this to thirty-nine strokes (cf. II Cor. 11:24), thirteen across the chest and twenty-six across the back. King Ahab was mortally wounded (I Kgs. 22:35). King Joram received battle wounds from the Syrians (II Kgs. 8:29; 9:15; II Chr. 22:6). The prophets used the term in a symbolic way to describe how Israel was wounded by her enemies because of her own sins (Jer. 30:14; cf. Isa. 1:5,6; Jer. 10:19; 14:17; 30:12). However, God would cure them (Isa. 30:26; Jer. 30:17). The affliction of epidemic diseases was often sent by God as punishment for sin (Lev. 26:21; Num. 11:33; Deut. 28:59,61; I Sam. 4:8). The meaning is "defeat" in I Sam. 4:10; 14:30, and "slaughter" in Josh. 10:10,20; Judg. 11:33; 15:8; I Sam. 6:19; 19:8; 23:5; I Kgs. 20:21.

4383. Mikshôwl or **mikshôl;** this mas. Heb. noun derives from 3782. It means stumbling block, either literally or figuratively. It is an obstacle, a cause of falling or sinning, an enticement (especially an idol), an offense, scruple. The occasion for stumbling is found in Lev. 19:14; Isa. 57:14. See the cause for guilt in Ezek. 7:19; 14:4. In I Sam. 25:31 it means a defense of the heart.

4384. Makshêlâh; this is a fem. Heb. noun which is derived from 3782, and occurs only in Isa. 3:6 and Zeph. 1:3. It means ruin, stumbling block, obstacle, the cause of falling or sinning, enticement, offense.

4397. Mal'âk; this is from an unused root meaning to dispatch someone as a deputy, a messenger, a herald. When God is doing the sending, it may be an angel, a prophet, a priest, or a teacher. The general sense is an ambassador representing someone who sent him. Such a person carried a message, or performed some other specific commission, or represented the sender in official negotiations. He could be a simple message bearer (Gen. 32:3) with good news (I Sam. 6:21), threats (I Kgs. 19:2), or requests (Num. 20:14; 22:5; Judg. 7:24). A *mal'âk* could spy (Josh. 6:25) or kill (I Sam. 19:11; II Kgs. 6:32). David sent messengers to summon Bath-sheba (II Sam. 11:4). They were diplomats (Judg. 11:12-14; II Sam. 5:11; I Kgs. 20:2). The prophets represented God by preaching His official message (II Chr. 36:15,16; Hag. 1:13). Angels could also carry simple messages (Zech. 1:9; 5:5). Usually though, they performed some specific commission for God's purpose among His people (Gen. 19:12-17; 24:40; Ex. 23:20; II Sam. 24:17; Ps. 78:49; 91:11). Their very presence betokened God's glory (Gen. 28:12-17; cf. Isa. 6; Ezek. 1; Rev. 4:6-8, and the Cherubim in the Holy of Holies). They actively praise God (Ps. 148:2; cf. Isa. 6:3; Lk. 2:13,14). The Angel of Jehovah was very special. He brought good messages (Gen. 16:10-13) and threatening ones (Judg. 5:23). He performed specific commissions of judgment (II Kgs. 19:35; Ps. 35:5,6) and deliverance (Gen. 22:11; Ps. 34:7). He is also called the "angel of God" (Judg. 13:6,9, cf. v. 3), though that title does not belong exclusively to Him. He alone seems to have had the ministry of intercession with God in behalf of men (Zech. 1:12; 3:1-5). There is little doubt that He is the pre-incarnate Christ. Those who saw Him said that they had seen God (Judg. 13:21,22), and He spoke for God in the first person (Gen. 16:10; Ex. 3:2,6; Judg. 2:1). He interceded for us as a Mediator long before I Tim. 2:5 was written.

4398. Mal'ak; this Aramaic mas. noun corresponds to 4397 and means angel. It occurs only in Dan. 3:28 and Dan. 6:22.

4399. M^elâ'kâh; this fem. Heb. noun is traceable to 4397. The principal meaning is deputyship, i.e., ministry, service, employment (but never servile), work, labor, performance, business, trade, errand; property, the goods gained by labor; cattle. It is a flexible word which may refer to the actual activity of work, the skills in order to work, or the fruits of one's labor. Unlike *âmâl* (5999) or *yâg'* (3021), which emphasized the toilsome, laborious side of work, *m^elâ'kâh* stressed skilled labor, and the benefits which came as a result. All work was taboo on the weekly Sabbaths (Ex. 20:9, 10) and on the festal Sabbaths (Lev. 16:29) because God Himself ceased from working after creation (Gen. 2:1,2). The term could refer to a specific task (Neh. 5:16) or everyday business (Gen. 39:11; Prov. 18:9), or royal transactions (I Sam. 8:16; I Kgs. 9:23). Craftsmanship is the meaning in Ex. 31:3 and I Kgs. 7:14. The finished product of the tabernacle was a "work" (Ex. 39:43).

4400. Mal'ăkûwth; a message. This is a fem. Heb. word which occurs only once in the O.T. (Hag. 1:13).

4405. Millâh or **milleh;** this fem. Heb. noun arises from 4448. A word; (collectively) a discourse, a speech; (figuratively) a topic, a matter, a thing. Though it is possible that *millâh* might relate more to "word" as expression and *dâbâr* (1697) is more associated to the content or meaning, there is little or no discernible difference between the two words. It is anything to say or answer. *Millâh* occurs thirty-four times in Job alone.

4406. Millâh; this Aramaic word corresponds to 4405. It means a word, a command, a discourse, a subject, a matter, a thing. The term occurs twenty-four times in Daniel, referring to the substance or interpretation of dreams, official statements, decress, or verdicts.

4422. Mâlat; this verbal root has the sense of being smooth, i.e., escaping through slipperiness, to deliver oneself; to be delivered, saved, freed; to hasten away; to deliver, to save; to cause to escape; to let slip, to lay (eggs). The Septuagint uses *sōzō* (4982), *rhuomai* (4506), and *exaireō* (1807) to translate a set of Heb. syn. to which *mâlat* belongs: *gâ'al* (1350), *yâsha'* (3467), *nâtsal* (5337), *pâlat* (6403), and *shâlôwm* (7965). *Mâlat* can mean a leave of absence (I Sam. 20:29), the deliverance of the needy from affliction (Job 29:12), escape from the threat of death (I Sam. 19:11; 23:13; II Sam. 19:9), or deliverance from sickness (Ps. 107:20). Jehovah is the Saviour (Job 22:30; Prov. 28:26) of the righteous, but His judgment upon sin cannot be escaped (I Kgs. 19:17; Amos 2:14,15). Only those who call upon God will be delivered (Joel 2:32; cf. Acts 2:21). We must not trust in the strength of horses (Ps. 33:17), political alliances (Isa. 20:6), or wealth (Job 20:20).

4427. Mâlak; to be king, to become king, to rule, to reign; to consult, to determine; to constitute as king, to cause to reign, to induct into royalty, to be made king (or queen). It is quite possible that *mâlak* comes from the noun *melek* (4428). The essential meaning of *mâlak* is the exercise the functions of a monarch, whether as a male or a female. Jewish kings were inaugurated by anointing (II Sam. 2:9; 5:17) or by anointing and crowning (II Chr. 23:11). It can be the act of God or men in exalting a person to the office (I Sam. 15:35; I Kgs. 12:20).

4428. Melek; this mas. noun means a king, a ruler, a prince; god; a false god; an idol-king. Officials of many levels were designated by this title. It was a very common term for virtually any magistrate. There are more than 2,500 occurrences in the Heb. O.T. In that day and time, all civil society was based on common law. They could not function on statutory laws alone. Therefore, their custom was to rely on the decisions of their magistrates who were perceived to be moral men. Rulers were thought to be constituted by divine authority rather than human authority. To come before the judge was equivalent to coming before God (Ex. 22:8,9). *'Ělôhîym* (430) is sometimes translated as "judges." The approximate meaning of this root is the same across many Semitic cognate languages. It was a concept which was shared by many Oriental cultures. It can range in meaning from an emperor of an empire (Jer. 46:2) to the chieftain of a tiny city-state (Gen. 14:2-8; 20:2; 26:1,8). Even joint-kingships were possible (Dan. 5:11,30).

4430. Melek; this is the Aramaic correlate to 4428, having the same general meanings.

4433. Malkâ; this Aramaic fem. noun corresponds to 4436. It occurs twice in Dan. 5:10. It means queen.

4434. Malkôdeth; a net, a snare, a trap. This fem. Heb. noun occurs only once in the O.T. (Job 18:10). It derives from 3920.

4436. Malkâh; this is the fem. form of 4428. A queen, a princess. Except for Song of Sol. 6:8,9, this word is always used of foreigners. Sometimes it is the head of state (I Kgs. 10:1), as with the case of Sheba, but much more frequently as the consort of a king (Esth. 1:9, 2:22). Here are the name of known queens; Athaliah (II Kgs. 11:3; II Chr. 22:12), Esther (Esth. 2:4), Vashti (Esth. 1:9), and the consorts of Nebuchadnezzar (Dan. 5:10). Some had civil power and some did not. There are thirty-three occurrences.

4437. Malkûw; this common Aramaic word corresponds to 4438. It means royalty, reign, or kingdom. There are fifty-four occurrences in the Aramaic portions of the Bible.

4438. Malkûwth or **malkûth** or **malkûyâh;** this fem. Heb. noun is a deriv. of 4427. It is a dominion, an empire, a kingdom, a realm, a reign, royal rule, sovereign power.

4446. M^{e}leketh; a queen. This fem. Heb. noun appears in Jer. 7:18; 44:17-19,25. The "queen of heaven" was a pagan female deity worshipped at Jerusalem. This goddess probably referred to the "moon" or Astarte (which may have been the planet Venus).

4448. Mâlal; to speak, to tell, to utter, to relate. It is mostly used in Heb. poetry and occurs five times in the O.T. (Gen. 21:7; Job 8:2; 33:3; Ps. 106:2; Prov. 6:13). Its major syn. is *dâbar* (1696).

4449. M^{e}lal; to speak, to say. This Aramaic verbal root corresponds to 4448 and occurs only in Dan. (6:21; 7:8,11,20,25).

4467. Mamlâkâh; this fem. Heb. noun has its origin in 4428. It means kingdom, dominion, reign, realm, royal rule, sovereignty.

4468. Mamlâkûwth; kingdom, dominion, realm, reign. This fem. Heb. noun is equivalent to 4467 and occurs only nine times in the Heb. O.T.

4473. Mimshach; expansion, outspread (like outstretched wings); anointed, anointing unction. This mas. Heb. noun occurs only in Ezek. 28:14 (cf. Ex. 25:20). It comes from 4886.

4474. Mimshâl; dominion, rule, a ruler. This mas. Heb. noun stems from 4910 and occurs three times in the O.T. (I Chr. 26:6; Dan. 11:3,5).

4475. Memshâlâh; the fem. Heb. noun is a deriv. of 4474. It means dominion, rule, reign, realm, government, power. It is used of God's sovereignty and scope of His rule in Ps. 103:22; 145:13. It describes man's rule in II Chr. 32:9; Isa. 22:21; Mic. 4:8. Gen. 1:16 and Ps. 136:8,9 describe the sun's prevailing dominance during the day and the moon's strength by night. It appears seventeen times in the Heb. O.T.

4478. Mân; springing from 4100, this Heb. mas. noun literally means "whatness," i.e., manna (the fully formed question: "What is it?"). It is similar to our "What's his name," when we cannot think of a person's name. For about forty years, while wandering in the wilderness, manna was the basic food which God provided to the Israelites. He also gave them water and quail. Except for Ex. 16:31 where the Septuagint reads *man*, our English spelling "manna" derived from the Septuagint. This word appears only fourteen times in the Heb. O.T. It was "bread" from God (Ex. 16:15), "food from heaven" (Ps. 78:24) and "angels' food" (in K.J.V. Ps. 78:25). Only the small portion which Aaron put in the tabernacle remained after that forty-year period. God taught them to depend upon Him and His words for their lives (Deut. 8:3,16). Jesus quoted this passage against Satan in Mt. 4:4 and Lk. 4:4. Jesus Himself is the true manna (Jn. 6). Manna could be ground or milled, baked or boiled (Ex. 16:23; Num. 11:8). It was God's miraculous provision for the nation of Israel, not some natural edible substance which happened to grow in the Sinai Peninsula.

4486. Manda'; widsom; intelligence, knowledge, understanding, reason. This Aramaic noun corresponds to *mad-daw* (4093). It was used as the equivalent to the Gr. *gnōsis* (1108). The Mandaeans, Aramaic Gnostics, took their name from this term. The word occurs four times in the O.T. (Dan. 2:21; 4:34,36; 5:12).

4503. Minchâh; this fem. Heb. noun comes from an uncertain root. Perhaps it meant to apportion, i.e., bestow; a donation. Most scholars postulate that there was a Heb. root M-N-Ch, which meant "to give." The word means present, gift; tribute; sacrifice (mostly an unbloody one), a meat offering, an offering (in general), an oblation, a sacrifice. The R.S.V. uses "cereal-offering" and tribute."

4504. Minchâh; this fem. Aramaic noun is similar to the Heb. (4503). It is a sacrificial offering, an oblation, a meat offering. The term is found in Ezra 7:17 and Dan. 2:46.

4531. Maççâh; this fem. noun derives from 5254. Essentially, it is a testing, whether by men or by God. Other meanings are: trial, temptation, testing by misfortune, proving. This was also used as a place name (Massah) where the "trial" over water occurred in the wilderness (see Ex. 17:1-7). See *peirasmos* (3986).

4541. Maççêkâh; this fem. Heb. noun originates from 5258. It is a pouring over, i.e., fusion of metal (especially a cast image), a founding, a molten idol; covenant, league, covering; a drink offering, a libation. *Maççêkâh* describes images made of molten metal about twenty-five times in the Heb. O.T. They were cast by pouring hot, liquid metal into a mold or over a frame (Isa. 40:18-20). Often they were cast of gold (Isa. 30:22, cf. Ex. 32:4,8; I Kgs. 14:9). Others were made of silver, bronze, or iron. Worshipping such images was forbidden by the Law of Moses (Ex. 34:17; Lev. 19:4; Deut. 27:15) and by the prophets (Isa. 41:29; 42:17; 44:10; Jer. 10:14; 51:17; Hos. 13:2; Hab. 2:18).

4578. Mê'âh; this is a mas. Heb. noun which occurs only in the pl. form. It is from an unused root which probably meant "to be soft." The noun means the intestines, the bowels, the abdomen, the womb, the uterus, the body, the belly, the stomach; the inmost part, the heart; the sands of the sea. The term is used thirty-two times in the Heb. O.T. With the exception of three or four instances it is associated with either male or female human beings. Jon. 2:1,2 uses the word for the "belly" of the great fish. It is associated with God's emotions (Isa. 63:15; Jer. 31:20). If it is literal, it is referring to one's internal organs; sometimes reproductive organs. However, it is also used in the metaphorical sense for the seat of emotions (cf. Col. 3:12; Phil. 2:1). See *splagchnon* (4698). It was common for a Hebrew to use organs of the body to express emotions; the liver showed joy, the kidneys denoted affections, and the heart was used for affections, mind, and the abdominal organs meant compassion.

4603. Mâ'al; this primary root means to cover up, to veil; to act secretly, covertly, faithlessly, treacherously; to transgress, commit a trespass; to steal. This verb occurs thirty-five times the Heb. O.T. It designates the violation of religious law as a conscious act of treachery. In other words, it is directed at God (Lev. 6:2; Num. 5:6; Josh. 22:31; I Chr. 10:13; II Chr. 12:2; 26:16; 28:19,22; 30:7). There are a few occurrences where it has a human object (Num. 5:12,13,27; Job 21:34; Prov. 16:10). An individual is deliberately defecting from the faith. It is often used in parallel phrases with *châtâ'* (2398). See *parapiptō* (3895), "to trespass," and *asunthetos* (802), "treacherous, a covenant-breaker." Our expression "break faith" captures the essence of this word.

4604. Ma'al; this mas. Heb. noun comes from 4603. It is an unfaithful act, faithlessness, treachery, falsehood, transgression. Twenty of the twenty-nine occurrences are cognate accusative constructions: "If a man commit (*mâ'al*) a trespass (*ma'al*). . . ."

4622. Ma'tsôwr; this mas. Heb. noun is a deriv. of 6113 and appears only once in the O.T. (I Sam. 14:6). It means restraint or hindrance.

4623. Ma'tsâr; control, rule, restraint. It occurs only once (Prov. 25:28) and originates from 6113.

4635. Ma'ăreketh; an arrangement, a row, order, a show, showbread, a pile (of loaves), an exhibition, an array, an army, a setting forth. This fem. Heb. noun is traceable to 6186. It appears nine times in the O.T. (Lev. 24:6,7; I Chr. 9:32; 23:29; 28:16; II Chr. 2:4; 13:11; 29:18; Neh. 10:33).

4643. Ma'ăsêr or **ma'ăsar** or **ma'asrâh;** these Heb. nouns come from 6240 and mean a tenth (part) or a tithe. The first mention of one was Abram's offering to Melchizedek (Gen. 14:20). Moses handed down strict rules in Lev. 27, Num. 18, and Deut. 12,14,26. See also II Chr. 31:5ff.; Ezek. 45:11,14; Amos 4:4; Mal. 3:8,10. The word occurs six times in Nehemiah.

4646. Mappâch; this mas. deriv. of 5301 means a giving up, a breathing out (of life), and expiring. The only occurrence is found in Job 11:20.

4653. Miphlaggâh; from the root word *pâlag* (6385) meaning a division, a classification, a class, or a category. This fem. pl. noun occurs only once in the O.T. (II Chr. 35:12).

4656. Miphletseth; a terror, a hideous idol, a monster, a horrid thing. The only occurrences of this fem. Heb. noun are in I Kgs. 15:13 (twice) and in II Chr. 15:16 (twice). It relates to 6426.

4658. Mappeleth; this fem. Heb. noun is derived from *nâphal* (5307). It means a fall, ruin, a fallen trunk, decadence, a carcass, a corpse. It occurs eight times (Judg. 14:8; Prov. 29:16; Ezek. 26:15,18; 27:27; 31:13,16; 32:10).

4660. Mappâts; a bruising, a smashing, a crushing, a breaking (to pieces), slaughter. This mas. Heb. noun comes from 5310. It occurs only once in the O.T. (Ezek. 9:2).

4662. Miphqâd; from the root *pâqad* (6485). This Heb. mas. noun means (1) a census, a numbering people (II Sam. 24:9; I Chr. 21:5); (2) a commandment, a mandate (II Chr. 31:13; Neh. 3:31); (3) an appointment, an arrangement, an appointed place (Ezek. 43:21).

4676. Matstsêbâh; this is the fem. causative part. which has 5324 as its source. Literally, it is something which is stationed, i.e., a column, a pillar, a memorial stone, a monument, a statue (usually of idols); a stump, a trunk. The K.J.V. incorrectly renders Ezek. 26:11 as "garrison," when it should be "pillar." Although Rachel's grave marker (Gen. 35:20) and Absalom's memorial monument (II Sam. 18:18) had no cultic ramifications, archeological discoveries indicate that *matstsêbâh* usually did have a religious significance. See Gen. 31:45; 35:14; Ex. 24:4. This is the only Heb. word which is translated as "pillar" which has any religious importance. The writer of Josh. 24:26,27 intentionally avoided using *matstsêbâh*.

4678. Matstsebeth; something stationary, a monumental stone, a monument, a pillar, a column, a statue (of idols); a stump, a trunk, a stock or stem (of a tree). This fem. Heb. noun is a deriv. of 5324 and appears in the following places in the O.T.: Gen. 35:14,20; II Sam. 18:18; Isa. 6:13.

4682. Matstsâh; this fem. Heb. noun arises from 4711. It means unleavened bread, unleavened cakes, bread-cake. It has the connotation of sweetness (i.e., not soured or bittered with yeast). Specifically, it is an unfermented loaf. Yeast was normally used to make the bread rise during baking, but the Israelites left Egypt so suddently that they had no time to make their bread in the normal way. Therefore, the Passover festival is traditionally celebrated with unleavened bread to commemorate God's sudden deliverance (Ex. 12:8) and during the first stages of their travels (Ex. 12:39). It was called the "bread of affliction" (Deut. 16:3) and was to be eaten with bitter herbs to remind them of their oppression. The Passover feast was celebrated on one night. The Feast of Unleavened Bread followed for the next seven days. In time, both days were referred to as either "the Passover" or the "Days of Unleavened Bread." See *azumos* (106).

4685. Mâtsôwd or **m^etsôwdâh** or **m^etsôdâh;** has the meaning of capture or gain (Prov. 12:12). In Ecc. 7:26 it is used as a snare or net, and in Ecc. 9:14 the meaning is fortress, bulwark, tower, stronghold, or defense. This mas. Heb. noun derives from 6679.

4687. Mitsvâh; this fem. Heb. noun is a deriv. of 6680. It is a command (whether human or divine), a precept, a law, the Law (of Moses when used collectively), an ordinance; the due. It was the terms of the contract in a deed of purchase for a plot of land (Jer. 32:11). Sometimes it was the instruction of a teacher to his pupil (Prov. 2:1; 3:1). Once it was used for the Ten Commandments (Ex. 24:12). *Mitsvâh* was used much more often to describe the particular conditions of God's covenant with Israel. They were clear-cut directives which were revealed by inspiration and in effect until the cross of Christ (Col. 2:14).

4720. Miqdâsh or **miqq^edâsh;** this mas. Heb. noun derives from 6942. It is a consecrated (holy) thing or place, especially a sanctuary or a palace (whether of Jehovah or of idols), a hallowed part, like a chapel; an asylum. The R.S.V. translates it as "holy things" (Num. 10:21; Ezek. 44:8), "sacred area" (Ezek. 43:21), and "temple" (Dan. 11:31). Usually the word refers to the tabernacle and the temple, what was devoted to the sphere of the sacred. This physical area was sacred because it was the place where God dwelled among His people (Ex. 25:8) and its sanctity was not to be profaned (Lev. 12:4; 19:30; 20:3; 21:12,23). The articles of the tabernacle which were devoted to the Levitical worship were called *miqdâsh* (Num. 10:21) and the portions of the sacrifice which were particularly holy were also known by this term (Num. 18:29). Ps. 68:25 may refer to heaven or the temple in Jerusalem. *Miqdâsh* is used metaphorically to refer to a place of refuge in Isa. 8:14 and Ezek. 11:16. Finally, *miqdâsh* even meant sanctuaries which were devoted to false worship in a few instances (Lev. 26:31; Isa. 16:12; Ezek. 21:2; Amos 7:9).

4723. Miqveh or **miqvêh** or **miqvě';** this mas. Heb. noun comes from 6960. Literally, it is something that is waited for, i.e., confidence, hope, trust. Also, it is a collection, i.e., (of water) a pond, a confluence of water, a gathering (of men and horses), a troop, a company, a caravan. For the first basic meaning of expectation see I Chr. 29:15; Ezra 10:2; Jer. 14:8; 17:13; 50:7. For a gathering together of water see Gen. 1:10; Ex. 7:19; Lev. 11:36. For the meaning of a congregation see I Kgs. 10:28 (though there is some difference of scholarly opinon here).

4744. Miqrâ; this mas. Heb. noun originates from 7121. Literally, it is something which has been called out, i.e., a public meeting, a calling together, a convocation, an assembly, a congregation; a place of meeting; a reading, a recital. In the Heb. O.T. there are two basic meanings: (1) a convocation of Israel, i.e., God summons them. (2) The result of reading aloud (Neh. 8:8). See *môw'êd* (4150), "an appointed time" or "an appointed gathering." *Miqrâ'* designated the weekly Sabbaths (Lev. 23:2) and the new moons (Ezek. 46:3; cf. Isa. 66:23). It was also used for the seven special convocation Sabbaths. Such times included a formal call of the people to worship by means of the blast of trumpets (Num. 10:2,10).

4751. Mar or **mârâh;** this Heb. adj. stems from 4843. It means bitter (literally or figuratively), sad, embittered, fierce, violent, wild. As a sub, it means bitterness or sadness. It is also used as an adv. It definitely has a strong connotation in the thirty-seven instances in the Heb. O.T. The "water of bitterness" in Num. 5:18,19,23,24,27 was very unhealthly and certainly not beneficial or hygienic, because the water contained dust and ink. This liquid was used to determine whether a jealous husband's suspicions were founded or not. Today, criminal investigators know that the body emits certain measurable signals when a person is lying. As in this example in the Book of Numbers, an innocent person would have a clear conscience and, therefore, would have nothing to worry about. This was not a trial by ordeal; God was doing the punishing. Other literal examples are: bitter water (Ex. 15:23), bitter grape clusters (Deut. 32:32) and food (Prov. 27:7; Isa. 5:20). Emotionally speaking, the word is used to describe the heart-crushing experience of family turmoil (Gen. 27:34), sterility (I Sam. 1:10), the thought of death (I Sam. 15:32), discontent (I Sam. 22:2), exploitation (Esth. 4:1), and an unfulfilled death-wish (Job 3:20), personal suffering and hardship (Job 7:11; 10:1; Isa. 38:15), a hostile and precarious situation (Ps. 64:3), grief (Jer. 2:19), disillusionment (Ezek. 27:30,31), the Lord's judgment upon unbelievers (Zeph. 1:14).

4756. Mârê'; this mas. Aramaic noun for domineering, Lord, lord, or master corresponds to 4754. It refers to God or the king, appearing only in Dan. 2:47; 4:19,24; 5:23.

4759. Mar'âh; this fem. Heb. noun has its source in 4758. It is a sight, a vision, a revelation; a mirror, looking-glass. The overall source is the verb *râ'âh* (7200), "to see, to look at, to inspect." This noun can mean almost anything connected with outward appearance, i.e., the way things look, a phenomenon, something which is usually seen (Lev. 13:3ff.), something extraordinary (Ex. 3:3), the act of looking (Isa. 11:3), the faculty of seeing (Ecc. 6:9), and superficiality (I Sam. 16:7). The word also can mean face (countenance), the part of a person which is visible to the eye (Song of Sol. 2:14; 5:15). *Mar'âh* is often used with adjectives for fair or ugly and desirable or undesirable. The outward appearance of Jesus was marred beyond our comprehension. Isa. 52:14 predicted this with the word *mar'âh.* Christ was illegally convicted as though He were a common criminal, tortured and abused as though He had no status, and then either made fun of or totally ignored by His executioners. What a sight! The Son of God allowed Himself to be brought this low because He loved us so. From a purely external viewpoint (Isa. 53:2), nothing would have attracted us to Him.

4775. Mârad; this primary root means to be obstinate, to resist, to rebel, to be rebellious, to revolt, to disobey. This verb is used twenty-five times in the Heb. O.T., five of which are in Joshua. About half of the occurrences refer to rebellion against man and the other half denote rebellion against God. The uncertainty of the translation of Josh. 22:19 may be resolved by the Jerusalem Bible's rendering: "Do not rebel . . . or make us accomplices in rebellion." In the human rebellions, it is a technical term for political resistance, an attempt of a vassal to nullify a previous agreement. In international contexts it refers to disloyalty and disunity among nations. Concerning God, the disposition of mankind is such that he always "breaks with" God (Rom. 3:23).

4776. M^e^rad; this Aramaic noun corresponds to 4775 and also means rebellion. It occurs only in Ezra 4:19.

4777. Mered; rebellion, obstinacy, defection. This mas. Heb. noun is traceable to 4775 and occurs only once in the O.T. (Josh. 22:22). There is a parallel to *ma'al* (4604), "transgression, breach of faith."

4779. Mârâd; this Aramaic adj. originates from the root word *m^e^rad* (4776) and means rebellious. It occurs twice in the Bible (Ezra 4:12,15).

4780. Mardûwth; rebellion, obstinacy, refractoriness. This fem. Heb. noun stems from 4775 and occurs only once (I Sam. 20:30). King Saul charged his own son, Jonathan, with subversive activity because Saul thought that he was helping young David, his friend. On the basis of the Septuagint's rendering, most scholars believe the phrase should be translated: "You son of a rebellious woman."

4784. Mârâh; to be rebellious against, to be disobedient toward someone, to be refractory; to rebel, to resist, to despise; to quarrel, to dispute; to offend. Literally, it means to be (or make) bitter or unpleasant. Provocation is an inherent component of this term. This verb occurs forty times in the Heb. O.T., ten of which are in Psalms. The idea of defiance is conveyed in this word rather strongly. Except for five instances, all derivatives of the word refer to the rebellion of the Jews against God, particularly while in the wilderness in route to Canaan. The three exceptions are: Deut. 21:18,20; Job 17:2.

4795. Mârûwq; this mas. Heb. noun in pl. form appears only once in the O.T. (Esth. 2:12). It means purification, rubbing (with perfume), an anointing, a cleansing.

4805. M^e^rîy; rebellion, perverseness, refractoriness. This mas. Heb. noun is a deriv. of 4784. Sixteen of its twenty-three appearances in the O.T. are found in Ezekiel, usually the phrase, "house of rebellion," referring to Judah.

4820. Mirmâh; it means craft, deceit, fraud, falsehood, guile, treachery; ill-gotten wealth. This is actually a part. which occurs almost forty times in the O.T. It describes Jacob's swindling of Esau (Gen. 27:35) and tricky speech (Gen. 34:13; Ps. 10:7; 17:1; 24:4). *Mirmâh* is also used of false, weighted scales (Amos 8:5). Deceitful speech was considered to be a terrible sin (Jer. 9:6).

4853. Massâ; this mas. Heb. noun derives from 5375. It is a carrying, a lifting; a burden, a load; tribute, a present; elevation of the voice, a song, an utterance, an oracle; desire, longing, yearning. The term occurs sixty-six times in the Heb. O.T. In a literal sense, it depicts the packs upon the backs of the donkey (Ex. 23:5), the mule (II Kgs. 5:17), and camel (II Kgs. 8:9). Isaiah pointed out that the false gods of the Babylonians had to be carried (Isa. 46:1,2). Tribute in the form of silver was carried (II Chr. 17:11). Some of the Levites were given the responsibility of carrying various parts of the tabernacle (Num. 4:15,19,24,-27,31,32,47,49). In a figurative sense, Ezek. 24:25 describes the uplifting of souls, i.e., the desire of their hearts. Isaiah 22:25 may refer to the Messiah. *Massâ'* also appears in prophetic contexts twenty-five times. They were "burdens" within the prophets until they expressed them.

4864. Mas'êth; this fem. Heb. noun comes from 5375. It is a raising (of the hands in prayer), a lifting up or a rising (of a flame), a fire signal, a beacon; tribute, a tax, a present, a gift, oblation, reward: a burden; a saying, an utterance, an oracle. There are seventeen occurrences of this word. Literally, it refers to smoke which rises (Judg. 20:38,40) or a signal which is lifted up (Jer. 6:1). Sometimes Jewish worshippers lifted up their hands in prayer (Ps. 141:2). For prophetic speech see Lam. 2:14 and Zeph. 3:18. It means portion (in Gen. 43:34), present (in II Sam. 11:8), and share (in II Sam. 19:43). Amos 5:11 uses *mas'êth* for an unjust taxation. However, the term can be used for sacred payments or contributions to God (II Chr. 24:6,9; Ezek. 20:40).

4876. Mashshûw'âh or **mashshû'âh;** ruins, desolation, destruction. In the pl. form this fem. Heb. noun is found in Ps. 73:18 and 74:3. It has 4875 as its source.

4886. Mâshach; this primary verbal root means to rub with oil, to besmear, to paint, i.e., to anoint, and by implication, to consecrate. The verb with its derivatives occurs about 140 times in the Heb. O.T. Not every instance was religious, e.g., rubbing a shield with oil (Isa. 21:5), painting a house (Jer. 22:14), or the application of oil to the human body (Amos 6:6). However, the word has a very important part in Jewish ceremony. They applied oil to the tabernacle, the altar or laver (Ex. 40:9-11), and the sin offering (Ex. 29:36). It was a formal way of inducting certain leaders into office, similar to coronation (when referring to kings). See II Sam. 12:7; I Kgs. 19:15. The high priest (Ex. 29:7; Num. 35:25) and other priests (Ex. 30:30) were anointed. I Kgs. 19:16 and Isa. 61:1 mentioned that a prophet was anointed. This action signified, in the cultural terms of their theocratic society, that the anointed individual was separated for God's service and chosen by Him. It was a very serious responsibility, and God was the authorizing agent. The Spirit of God accompanied that person (I Sam. 10:6ff.; 16:13ff.). This practice provided the backdrop for the ultimate Anointed One, Jesus Christ, who was predicted in the O.T. (Isa. 9:1-7; 11:1-5; 61:1) and fulfilled in the N.T. (Mt. 3:16,17; 17:5; Acts 13:33; II Pet. 1:17,18, cf. Lk. 23:35).

4887. M^{e}shach; this Aramaic word meant oil and corresponded to 4886. It occurs only twice (Ezra 6:9; 7:22). The Heb. cognate term meant more the compounded anointing oil.

4888. Mishchâh or **moshchâh;** this fem. Heb. noun derives from 4886. It means the act of anointing, an unction, ointment, anointing oil, anointment; a consecratory gift; part, portion. The term is found only in Exodus, Leviticus, and Numbers. It refers to the oil which was used in the anointing ritual. The oil was prepared in a prescribed manner (Ex. 30:22ff.) and was sprinkled upon officials and their clothing (Ex. 29:21), but poured on the head of the high priest (Ex. 29:7; cf. Lev. 8:10-12). By applying this holy substance to the tabernacle and its furnishings, it made them holy. After priests were anointed, they were restricted from certain activities (Lev. 21:12; cf. Lev. 10:7). This fragrant oil was used as a tangible symbol to symbolize the meaning of holiness. A part of the peace offering (Lev. 7:28-35) was reserved as a consecrated portion for the priests.

4889. Mashchîyth; this mas. Heb. noun arises from 7843. It means destruction; corruption; ambush; snare, trap; destroyer. The word is used to describe a lion (Jer. 2:30) and an angel (I Chr. 21:12,15), particularly "the destroyer," the angel of destruction at the Passover (Ex. 12:23).

4899. Mâshîyach; this Heb. adj., often used as a noun, is one of the most important words in the Hebrew Bible. It originates from 4886, which see. It means besmeared or anointed. Patriarchs, priests, or kings were anointed ones. This term underlies the word Messiah and the Gr. deriv., Christ. See *Christos* (5547) and *chriō* (5548) in the N.T. lexical section. The term occurs about forty times in the Heb. O.T., principally in I Samuel, II Samuel, and Psalms. It could designate the office of the high priest (Lev. 4:3), but it was usually reserved as a syn. for "king." The Patriarchs were called "anointed ones" (Ps. 105:15) and some prophets were anointed (I Kgs. 19:16). See the parallelism in I Sam. 2:10; II Sam. 22:51; Ps. 2:2; 18:50. Since Jehovah made the selection, it was a very special title of honor which highlighted a unique relationship between God and that individual. As its verbal root indicates, *mâshîyach* implied an anointing from God for a special function. Even though King Saul proved to be unworthy, David respected him as "the Lord's anointed" (I Sam. 24:6). I Sam. 11 gives an account of how Samuel anointed Saul. However, it was David, the ancestor of Jesus, who became the archetype of the Messiah. Even a non-Israelite was appointed by God Himself as the Lord's anointed one. Cyrus was not a righteous king or even monotheistic, but God chose him for a specific task—delivering Israel from their Babylonian captors and returning them to their homeland (Isa. 45:1). This is not unlike what Paul said about God-ordained secular authorities (Rom. 13:1-14). Paul said, "For it is a minister of God to you for good" (Rom. 13:4). This was probably written during the reign of the infamous Nero! The Persian king was unaware that God was using him as an instrument. The inspired interpretation of Ps. 2 is found in Acts 13:32ff. and Heb. 1:5; 5:5. The coming Messiah (Jesus Christ) would administer true justice, rule all men, and bring salvation. Dan. 9:25 transliterates the term and Jn. 1:41 shows how the translation from Messiah to Christ came about. Ps. 45:6 spoke of the Messianic king as divine, and Ps. 110:1-5 referred to David's Son as being David's Lord. Verse 4 specifically stated: "Thou art a priest forever according to the order of Melchizedek." How could a king of Israel simultaneously be a priest? The author of Hebrews explains that Jesus, the Messiah, was both (Heb. 5:6-10; 7:1-28).

4906. Maskîyth; picture, image, figure (Lev. 26:1; Num. 33:52; Prov. 25:11; Ezek. 8:12); conceit, imagination, opinion (Ps. 73:7; Prov. 18:11). This fem. Heb. noun comes from 7906 and occurs only six times (listed above).

4908. Mishkân; this mas. Heb. noun is traceable to 7931 and has the basic meaning of residence. It could be a shepherd's hut, an animal's lair, or the grave. However, the dwelling place (tent) in the Hebrew Bible usually referred to is the tabernacle in the wilderness (Ex. 25:9) and later the more permanent temple of Solomon. The term is found mostly in Exodus and Numbers, where it designated the sanctuary of God. About 100 out of the 140 occurrences signify the temple as God's dwelling place. It was the "tent of meeting." The tabernacle was a physical and symbolic representation of God's presence among His people (Lev. 15:31; 26:11-13; Num. 19:13). This sacred "building" was portable and fully mobile. It was constructed according to the exact specifications which God gave to Moses in Ex. 25—31 and Ex. 35—40. The term shekinah, which was used widely in later Judaism, referred to the presence of God. The initial meeting at Mount Sinai between God and the nation of Israel was continually reinforced in the tabernacle. God chose this means to show the continuity between His former revelations and ongoing ones. Eventually, *mishkân* included the entire area surrounding the temple in Jerusalem (Ps. 46:4; 87:2). When the city was defiled with sin, God could no longer reside in the temple (Ezek. 10), and He permitted the destruction of it (Ps. 74:7). God planned to restore His people to their land and a new temple along with it (Ezek. 37:27,28). Ultimately, Jesus Christ Himself was the embodiment of God's tabernacle (Jn. 1:14). Jesus viewed His own body as the temple of God (Jn. 2:21).

4910. Mâshal; to rule, to reign, to govern; to rule over, to have dominion, to manage; to cause to rule. This verbal root occurs eight-three times. Gen. 1:18 indicates the prominence of the sun over the daytime and the moon over the nighttime. Part of Eve's punishment was submission to the appropriate leadership of her husband over the family (Gen. 3:16). Cain was urged to master emerging sin (Gen. 4:7). Eliezer managed all of Abraham's material goods (Gen. 24:2). The jealous brothers of Joseph could not entertain the thought of ever submitting themselves to Joseph's rule (Gen. 37:8), but Joseph eventually became the Prime Minister of Pharaoh (Gen. 45:8, 26). See also Ex. 21:8 and Deut. 15:6, which show subservience to a higher jurisdiction. The supremacy of the rich (Prov. 22:7), an oppressive king (Isa. 19:4), cultural domination (Judg. 14:4; 15:11), political leadership (I Kgs. 4:4-21), self-control (Prov. 16:32) and God's providence (Ps. 89:9) all use the word *mâshal.* All types of authority have their source in God Himself (see Rom. 13:1-7).

4915. Môshel; empire, rule, dominion; likeness, similitude. This Heb. mas. noun derives from 4910 in the former definitions, occurring only three times (Job 41:33; Dan. 11:4; Zech. 9:10), and from 4911 in the later meanings. It is unclear whether the word refers to the rule of sovereignty or sphere.

4928. Mishma'ath; audience, access to a prince, admission at court; obedience; subjects, body guards. Occurring four times in the Heb. O.T. (I Sam. 22:14; II Sam. 23:23; I Chr. 11:25; Isa. 11:14), this fem. Heb. noun came from *mish maw* (4926).

4931. Mishmereth; watch (i.e., the act of custody), a guard, a watch-post, a sentry; service, duty; keeping, preservation, safeguard, usage; command, law; fidelity. This fem. Heb. noun has two main senses: (1) an obligation or service to be performed; (2) something which must be preserved, e.g., the Paschal lamb (Ex. 12:6), the manna (Ex. 16:32-34), and the ashes of the red heifer (Num. 19:9).

4940. Mishpâchâh; this fem. Heb. noun derives from

8192. It means species, kind, sort; family, clan, kindred; tribe; race; people. Essentially, it is an ever-burgeoning circle of relatives with strong blood ties. The term is much broader in its scope than our English word "family." It was a subdivision of the larger tribe or nation (Num. 11:10; Josh. 7:16-18). Levirate marriage went along these lines (Num. 27:11). *Mishpâchâh* occurs about 300 times in the Heb. O.T. Besides the consanguinous extended family, the word was used for zoological phyla (Gen. 8:19) and anthropological categories (Gen. 10:5; Ps. 22:27; 96:7). Especially see God's promise to Abraham (Gen. 12:3). Close relatives are indicated by Gen. 24:38 and Lev. 25:48,29.

4941. Mishpât; properly, a verdict (whether favorable or unfavorable) which was pronounced judicially, a judgment, a sentence, a formal decree; justice, right, privilege; place of judgment; cause, suit; crime, guilt; law, rule, ordinance, custom, manner; what is due. This is an extremely important word for the proper understanding of all government (human or divine). There are about 400 occurrences of this word in the Heb. O.T. Unlike our modern democratic tripartite conception (legislative, executive, and judicial), the verbal root, *shâphat* (8199), from which this Heb. noun originates, refers to all functions of government, not merely the judicial process. The concept of "justice" inculcates the full range of meaning in English. This noun was used to describe any aspect of civil or religious government in the O.T. More than 200 cases deal with the act of deciding a case of litigation brought before a civil magistrate (e.g., Deut. 25:1; Josh. 20:6). I Kgs. 7:7 defines it as the place of deciding such cases. Isa. 3:14 was the process of litigation itself. A particular case might be I Kgs. 3:11; cf. I Kgs. 8:59; Job 13:18. Sometimes it is the formal decision from the magistrate (I Kgs. 20:40; Jer. 26:11,16). Ps. 1:5 and Ecc. 12:14 point to a specific time of judgment. In the Heb. Scriptures the ultimate authority (sovereignty) is not found in documents like the United States Constitution or commonly-accepted inalienable rights. All authority belongs to Jehovah God (Deut. 1:17; Ps. 72:1,2; 103:19; Prov. 16:33; Jer. 8:7). Justice is primarily an attribute of God (Isa. 30:18; cf. Gen. 18:25). He loves *mishpâṭ* (Ps. 37:28). It is rooted in His character and ought to be emulated by godly people (Ps. 37:30; Prov. 12:5; 21:15; 29:4; Mic. 3:1, 6:8). The word can designate a separate ordinance of the Law of Moses (Ex. 15:25; Lev. 5:10; 9:16; Deut. 33:10,21; cf. Ps. 119; Isa. 42:4). Other extended meanings are: one's right under law (Deut. 18:3; Jer. 32:7), a plan (Ex. 26:30), custom (II Kgs. 17:33), and a measurement (I Kgs. 4:28).

4960. Mishteh; this mas. Heb. noun stems from 8354. It means a drink, and by implication, (the act of) drinking; the place of drinking; a banquet, a feast. Dan. 1:5,8,16 and Ezra 3:7 refer to what was ingested, namely wine. The term was also used to denote a special meal which was prepared for honored guests (Gen. 19:3; 26:30; II Sam. 3:20). It was a wedding feast for Jacob (Gen. 29:22) and Samson (Judg. 14:10-17). According to Esth. 9:19,22 and Job 1:4,5, it was a yearly holiday. In fact, anything, which called for a celebration could be termed a *mishteh*. Judah forgot God because she spent so much time in such revelry (Isa. 5:12). The positive aspects of this rich imagery are emphasized in Isa. 25:6 and Prov. 15:15.

4994. Nâ'; a particle of entreaty or exhortation. It means pray! Now! O! It was used in submissive and modest requests (Gen. 18:21; Ex. 3:3; II Sam. 14:15; I Chr. 22:5) when speaking to superiors. See Ps. 118:25, a cry at the time of the triumphal entry (cf. Mt. 21:9). Hosanna is a transliteration of the Hebrew phrase, "O save us!" Jesus approved of this enthusiastic outburst (Lk. 19:40). He did not consider it blasphemous at all.

4999. Nâ'âh; this fem. noun derives from 4998. It is a home, a habitation, a dwelling, a pasture, a pleasant place. It is altogether a poetic word.

5001. Nâ'am; to whisper, to murmur. This Heb. verb occurs 361 times and often in the prophetic books. It was used especially of the voice of God by which oracles were revealed to the prophets (utilizing the pass. part. construction). Characteristically, the word ended God's message—"declares the Lord GOD of hosts" (Isa. 3:15). Occasionally it appeared in the middle of the message (Amos 2:11,16), but rarely at the beginning (Ps. 110:1). See II Sam. 23:1 for the oracle of David and Num. 24:3,15 for the oracle of Baalam.

5006. Nâ'ats; to revile, to scorn, to despise, to reject; to condemn, to deride, to reject; to be derided, to be scorned. This primary Heb. verb was often used of God rejecting men (Deut. 32:19; Jer. 14:21; Lam. 2:6). It occurs twenty-nine times. It contains the idea of disdain for one who formerly received favorable attention and then rebelled.

5012. Nâbâ'; to cause to bubble up, to pour forth words abundantly; to be inspired, to prophesy, to speak or sing as a prophet (by divine power), to rave, to play the madman, to act as if one is insane (I Sam. 18:10) through agitated, spasmodic movements often applied to false prophets (see *mainomai*, 3105, in Strong's Gr. Dictionary). Both senses are found in Jer. 29:26, and a true prophet was called a madman in derision (II Kgs. 9:11). The first occurrence of nâbâ' is I Sam. 10:6. The true prophet spoke God's message to the people under the influence of God's Spirit (I Kgs. 22:8; Jer. 29:27; Ezek. 37:10). A prophet had the prophecy (Jer. 20:7; Amos 3:8). "The word of the Lord came" to a prophet. Sometimes it was an ecstatic experience (I Sam. 10:6,11; 19:20). Sometimes false prophets were in a state of frenzy (I Kgs. 22:10), but they did not represent God (Jer. 23:21), nor did they speak an authentic word from the Lord (Ezek. 13:2,3). True prophets preached to the people that they should be faithful to God's covenant. The outcome of their message depended upon the penitent response of the people (Jon. 3:1-10). Sometimes prophets did predict events (Isa. 9:1-6; 11:1-9; 52:13—53:12; Nah. 2:13). See *prophēteuō* (4395) in the N.T. lexical section. The verb occurs 115 times in the Heb. O.T.

5013. Nᵉbâ'; this Aramaic word corresponds to the Heb. 5012 and means to prophesy. It occurs only once (Ezra 5:1).

5016. Nᵉbûw'âh; this fem. Heb. noun comes from 5012. It is a prophecy or prediction (written or spoken). It was used of any book which was written by a prophet (II Chr. 9:29). It has the meaning of prediction in II Chr. 15:8 and Neh. 6:12.

5017. Nᵉbûw'âh; this Aramaic noun is a correlate of 5016. It means inspired teaching or prophesying. It appears only once (Ezra 6:14).

5029. Nᵉbîy'; this mas. Aramaic noun is the corresponding term to 5030, a prophet. It is found only in Ezra 5:1,2; 6:14.

5030. Nâbîy'; prophet, an inspired man, a speaker of oracles, one who was actuated by a divine Spirit; an authorized spokesman (usually for God). Such an individual did not speak his own words, but those which he had received from God (cf. II Pet. 1:20,21). One can more easily see the function in the Book of Exodus where Aaron serves as Moses' prophet to Pharaoh (Ex. 4:10-16; 6:28-30; 7:1,2). Although Moses, as the mediator of the divine revelation to Israel, had direct conversations with God, the Lord chose to communicate with prophets through dreams and visions (Num. 12:1-8; cf. Jer. 23). Even Abraham was called a prophet (Gen. 20:7). In Deut. 18:9-22 Moses spoke of One who would come and would be the Prophet. Jesus Christ was that individual (cf. Acts 22:22; 3:22; 7:37). He was an Israelite who spoke in the name of Jehovah and should not have been killed for preaching the truth. He had supernatural knowledge and divine credentials. He performed miraculous signs (Deut. 13:1-18). His authority superseded even that of Moses (Mt. 17:1-5). In the time of Samuel there were men who followed him, praising God in song and attempting to call the people back to God (I Sam. 10:5,10; 19:20). Elijah and Elisha formed groups of followers who were called "the sons of the prophets" (I Kgs. 20:35). They were companions of the true prophets. They were taught by the prophets, i.e. brought up for the prophetic office (see II Kgs. 2:3,5,7,15; 4:1,38; 5:22; 6:1; 9:1). In the O.T., there were also false prophets who pretended to be divinely inspired and who preached pleasing words to the people (Isa. 28:7-13; Jer. 14:13; 27:9ff.; 28:10ff.). Some soothsayers prophesied in the name of Baal and Ashteroth (I Kgs. 18:19,40; II Kgs. 10:19; Hos. 4:5; 9:7,8; cf. Isa. 3:2). *Nâbîy'* occurs 309 times throughout the Hebrew Bible. There are three key Heb. words for this type of individual found in I Chr. 29:29. Besides *nâbîy'*, there is *rô'eh* (7203) and *chôzeh* (2374). Prophets saw visions.

5031. Nᵉbîy'âh; this fem. Heb. noun comes from 5030. The word occurs six times in the O.T. It meant prophetess (Judg. 4:4; II Kgs. 22:14; II Chr. 34:22; Neh. 6:14). Miriam was called by this term (Ex. 15:20), and so was the wife of Isaiah (Isa. 8:3). In this case, perhaps it means only a companion.

5038. Nᵉbêlâh; this Heb. noun derives from 5034. It means carcass, carrion (animal or human), a corpse; an idol. Deut. 21:23 uses this to describe the dead bodies of men. In a collective sense, it means corpses (Lev. 11:11; Isa. 26:19) and the remains of animals (Lev. 5:2; 7:24). The term is used in a figurative sense of idols in Jer. 16:18; cf. Lev. 26:30.

5046. Nâgad; to bring forward, to be in front; to bring to the light; to declare, to explain an enigma (Judg. 14:19) or a dream (Gen. 41:24); to announce, to confess (Ps. 38:18; Isa. 48:5), to profess openly (Isa. 3:9), to celebrate with praise (Ps. 9:11; 71:17; 92:2), to make known, to betray (Job 17:5); to be announced, to be shown, to be told (Josh. 9:24; Ruth 2:11). The word can be the messenger, the message, or the one to whom the message was told. The receptor was usually separated spatially from the original source of the information. It can mean to reveal something which one would not otherwise know (Gen. 3:11; 41:24). The verb occurs about 350 times in the Heb. O.T.

5057. Nâgîyd or **nâgîd;** a high person, a leader, a commander, a noble one, a prince, an overseer; noble or excellent things (Prov. 8:6). This is a general term which could be equivalent to a king (I Kgs. 9:16) or the ruler of a small region (I Chr. 9:11) or the head of a family (I Chr. 9:20). It could refer to the temple (II Chr. 31:13), the treasury (I Chr. 26:24; II Chr. 31:12), the palace (II Chr. 28:7), or military affairs (I Chr. 13:1; II Chr. 32:21). Generally speaking, it is the man at the top, depending on the field of leadership. Even the Messiah is called a *nâgîyd* in Dan. 9:25. The word occurs forty-four times.

5060. Nâga'; to smite, to beat, to strike; to punish; to touch; to reach, to arrive; to be smitten; to inflict plagues; to cause to touch, to cause to reach; to arrive at, to obtain. The essential meaning is to physically contact something or someone. The first occurrence is Gen. 3:3. She added the phrase about not touching the forbidden fruit. Was she exaggerating or merely reporting? It means sexual contact in Gen. 20:6; cf. Ruth 2:9; Prov. 6:29. Compare 1 Cor. 7:1 and *haptō* (681) in the N.T. lexical section. I Sam. 10:26 describes touching in the sense of emotional involvement. It has the meaning of divine chastisement in Job 19:21. It can mean to be struck down with a disease (II Chr. 26:20). However, sometimes God's touch has been official, enabling someone to serve (Isa. 6:7; Jer. 1:9; Dan. 10:16). God's touch is always authoritative, whether He touches mountains (Ps. 104:32; cf. Amos 9:5), a sacrifice (Judg. 6:21; cf. II Sam. 23:7), or men (I Sam. 10:26; I Kgs. 19:7). This verb occurs 150 times in the Heb. O.T.

5061. Nega'; this mas. Heb. noun has its source in 5060. It means a blow, a stroke (Deut. 17:8; 21:5), a wound (Prov. 6:33), punishment, a plague (Gen. 12:17; Ex. 11:1), leprosy, pestilence, a plague-spot, scurf. The main idea is that of being sticken in some way. God is usually the One who metes out the punishment or the disease (Ps. 38:11; 39:10; 91:10). The chastened individual ought to beg God for forgiveness and relief (I Kgs. 8:38; cf. Js. 5:13ff.). The Messiah bore divine punishment in our stead (Isa. 53:8). This noun occurs more than seventy-five times.

5062. Nâgaph; to smite, to strike, to push, to thrust; to be beaten or routed; to stumble. This word is a blow which is fatal or disastrous. In Ex. 21:22 it was one which was delivered with malice, potentially capable of causing death (Ex. 21:35). Ps. 91:12 which contains this verb is quoted by Satan, while tempting Jesus (Mt. 4:6). The term was used of the Lord striking men with some plague, sickness, or death (Ex. 8:2; Judg. 20:35; I Sam. 4:3; 25:38; II Chr. 13:15; 21:14,18; Ps. 89:23). The word is used in connection with the Messiah, the stone of stumbling.

5063. Negeph; this Heb. noun arises from 5062. It means a trip (of the foot), a stumbling; an affliction, a plague, punishment. It connotes a mortal blow or a plague or a fatal disease sent from God (Ex. 12:13; 30:12; Num. 8:19; 16:46,47; Josh. 22:17; Isa. 8:14).

5066. Nâgash; to come near, to approach, to touch; to draw near; to stand back; to bring near, to present; to be brought near, to be offered. The main idea is that of coming into the near proximity to an object. It does not usually denote actual contact, like *qârab* (7126). However, it is near enough to touch (Gen. 27:21; 29:10), eat (Gen. 27:25), kiss (Gen. 27:27), or embrace (Gen. 48:10). It is the ordinary contact of one person with another (Gen. 27:22; 43:19). Sometimes, it refers to sexual contact (Ex. 19:15). In a military context, when two opposing armies converged in battle, *nâgash* was used (Judg. 20:23; I Chr. 19:14). However, sometimes it is merely being arrayed for battle (Joel 3:9; cf. I Sam. 17:16,40). The root can be used of approaching a person of exalted position with respect (Gen. 43:19; 45:4; II Kgs. 5:13). *Nâgash* was used of the priests who approached the altar in that way (Ex. 30:20; Ezek. 44:13), and Malachi later refers to bringing an offering to the altar (Mal. 1:7). Men approach God through His servants to learn His will (Jer. 42:1; compare the use of the ephod, I Sam. 23:9, and the lot, I Sam. 14:38). It is like coming into a courtroom prepared to argue a case (Gen. 18:23). Isaiah called Israel and the nations into account (Isa. 41:1,21); 45:20,21). Like a powerful attorney, Isaiah had no fear of being proven wrong (Isa. 50:8). Elijah had done the same sort of thing against the prophets of Baal (I Kgs. 18:30). God was displeased that His people were so close to Him with their mouths, but so far removed in their hearts (Isa. 29:13). One gets a good picture of the meaning of this word in Job 41:16 where it describes the close-fitting scales of the crocodile. The word occurs 125 times in the Heb. O.T.

5068. Nâdab; to incite, to impel; to impel oneself, to be willing, to do freely, to give freely. This root has the flavor of an uncompelled, free movement of the will for divine service or sacrifice. It occurs seventeen times in the O.T. It was used especially of volunteer soldiers (Judg. 5:2,9; cf. Ps. 110:3), and volunteers for sacred military service (II Chr. 17:16). This word described the inner state of those who contributed to the construction of the temple, a spontaneous giving (I Chr. 29:9,14,17; Ezra 1:6; 2:68; 3:5). Deborah commended the people (Judg. 5:2) and the leaders (Judg. 5:9) of Israel for giving so liberally and voluntarily to the cause.

5069. Nᵉdab; this Aramaic noun corresponds to 5068. There are only four occurrences (Ezra 7:13,15,16 [twice]).

5071. Nᵉdâbâh; willingness; a free-will gift, a freewill offering; plenty; spontaneously, voluntarily, freely. This Heb. noun, which originates from 5068, appears twenty-six times in the Heb. O.T. It denotes what was offered of one's own free will. In Ex. 36 the people made so many voluntary contributions that Moses had to ask them to stop giving! Such giving came from a willing mind (Num. 15:3; Deut. 23:23; Ps. 54:6; 110:3; Hos. 14:4) and was completely spontaneous (Ex. 35:29; Lev. 22:23; Ezra 1:4,7). God sent rain voluntarily (Ps. 68:9), even though Israel had broken His covenant (Hos. 14:4). God truly desires heart-felt obedience (I Sam. 15:22; Hos. 6:6) more than a multitude of sacrifices (Amos 4:5).

5081. Nâdîyb; this word is used as a noun and as an adj., deriving from 5068. It means willing, prompt, generous (Isa. 32:5,8; Prov. 17:7,26), liberal (Prov. 19:6); a noble, a prince, a tyrant (Job 21:28; Isa. 13:2). This word occurs twenty-seven times in the Heb. O.T. The term can refer either to common people (Ex. 35:5) or to overlords (I Sam. 2:8), as those who voluntarily serve God. They are righteous (Prov. 17:26) and contrasted with the fool (Prov. 17:7).

5085. Nidneh; this mas. Aramaic noun corresponds to 5084. It is the flexible sheath of a sword. The ancients thought of the human body as being like the sheath of a sword, like an envelope (Dan. 7:15). See *skeuos* (4632) in the N.T. lexical section.

5087. Nâdar; to promise, to vow, to make a vow. It is the act of verbally consecrating to God. In other words, vowing to perform something (Gen. 28:20ff.), making an offering (Lev. 27), or abstaining from something out of devotion to God (Ps. 132:2ff.). Contr. *charam* (2763). See Num. 30 for the laws concerning vows. The Septuagint had *euchomai* (2172). The word was used thirty-one times in the Heb. O.T. and later appeared in the Dead Sea Scrolls, Rabbinic Hebrew, Medieval Hebrew, and Modern Hebrew.

5088. Neder or **nêder;** a promise (to God), a vow, a vowed sacrifice, a votive offering, anything vowed (Lev. 7:16; 22:18,21; Deut. 12:6). It is the opp. to *n*ᵉ*dâbâh* (5071), a voluntary, spontaneous gift. This Heb. noun, which derives from 5087, represents either the result of the vow itself or the thing offered to fulfill the vow. It occurs in the lists of sacrifices (e.g., Deut. 12:6,11) as a type of peace offering (Lev. 7:16). Nineteen times the cognate accus. construction with the verb *nâdar* (5087) is used, i.e., to swear to God with an oath, a verbal promise to the Lord (Num. 30:3,4). There were unconditional and conditional vows. The unconditional one was an oath which was absolutely binding (Ps. 116:14; Ecc. 5:4-6). The conditional vow was preceded by "if . . . , then . . ." (Gen. 28:20,21). Rash vows were to be avoided (Prov. 20:25). Jephthah made such a vow before a battle (Judg. 11:30,31; cf. Num. 21: 1-3). Hannah wanted a child very much (I Sam. 1:11), so she made a vow to dedicate that child to God. Even non-Israelites made vows to God (Jon. 1:16). A *neder* was a kind of thank-offering which would even be made by Gentiles (Nah. 1:15). It was entirely voluntary, but once made, it could not be annulled (Lev. 27:1-25). Jesus made a point of opposing the current degenerated practice of flippant vowing (Mt. 5:33-37; 23:16-22; cf. Js. 5:12). God did not need them (Ps. 50:9-13), nor could He be obligated. God desired spiritual devotion (love) from His people (Deut. 6:5). The Septuagint has *euchē* (2171). The two most noteworthy special vows were the Nazarite vow (Num. 6:13ff.) and the *cheram* (2764) vow (Num. 21:2).

5094. Nᵉhîyr or **nehîyrûw;** these mas. and fem. Aramaic nouns are correlates to 5105, meaning illumination, light; wisdom. For the fem. see Dan. 5:11,14, and for the mas. see Dan. 2:22.

5130. Nûwph; to quiver, to vibrate up and down, to rock to and fro; to cause to move, to shake, to swing, to save, to move up and down; to wave (a sacrifice), to dedicate; to sprinkle, to moisten; to be waved; to beckon to someone (Isa. 13:2), to threaten (Job 31:21; Isa. 11:15; 19:16; Zech. 2:9); to wave the hand over any member to heal it (II Kgs. 5:11). When parts of the flesh of a sacrificial victim were offered to God in a ceremony, they were waved back and forth before they were placed upon the altar (Lev. 7:30; 8:27,29; 10:15; 14:12,24; 23:11,12,20; Num. 5:25; 6:20). Living victims and Levites in their initiation were paraded up and down (Ex. 35:22; Num. 8:11-21). It was a threatening gesture in Isa. 10:32. The Hiphil stem was used once for bringing rain (i.e., causing the sprinkle, Ps. 68:9). In Deut. 23:25 it was a sickle.

5137. Nâzâh; to spurt, to gush, to squirt; to sprinkle; to spatter (Lev. 6:27; II Kgs. 9:33; Isa. 63:3); to cause to start; to startle. *Zâraq* (2236) was a heavier sprinkling which was executed with the whole hand (Ex. 9:8; 29:20,21; Lev. 4:6). *Nâzâh* occurs twenty-four times in the O.T. It has to do with cleansing from sin (Isa. 52:15; I Pet. 1:2; Heb. 9:13,14) to obtain ritual purity. The Servant of the Lord, though considered impure, came to expiate the sins of the Gentiles (Isa. 52:15; Acts 8:32-37). Besides blood, sprinkling could also be done with oil (Lev. 8:11), oil and blood (Ex. 29:21), and water (Num. 8:7).

5139. Nâzîyr or **nâzîr;** this mas. Heb. noun is traceable to 5144. It means a separate one, a dedicated one; a Nazarite; a prince; the unpruned vine (like an unshorn Nazarite). Nazarites were Hebrew ascetics (Num. 6:13ff.; Judg. 13:5,7; 16:17; Amos 2:11,12). Nazarites vowed to refrain from certain things for a period for time voluntarily (Num. 6), however, Samson's parents dedicated him for life. Only Samson, Samuel, and John the Baptist were known lifelong Nazarites. The Jewish Mishna stated that the Nazarite vow was in effect for 30 days, sometimes 60 days, or even 100 days. In the N.T. Paul shaved his head because of a vow (Acts 18:18) and paid the expenses of others in the temple area (Acts 21:23,24). Gen. 49:26 is the earliest occurrence out of sixteen appearances, but the translation of the term there is problematic. Deut. 33:16 is a parallel passage concerning the blessing of Joseph. Should it be translated "separate" or "prince"? A similar problem exists in Lam. 4:7. The word is applied to a vine in Lev. 25:5,11 (which was not to be pruned during the Sabbatical year and left to grow on its own). It was a singling out, similar to a Nazarite.

5144. Nâzar; to hold aloof, to separate oneself; to abstain; to devote oneself; to refrain, to restrain; to consecrate; turning aside from the worship of the Lord (Lev. 14:7). The senses of separation and consecration were not distinguished in the Pentateuch (Lev. 15:31; 22:2). Aaron and his sons were commanded to keep away from the holy offerings which were presented to the Lord. They could not use them as long as they were ceremonially unclean. Ironically, Israel abandoned (separated) herself from Jehovah and consecrated herself to Baal (Hos. 9:10). The word occurs ten times in the Heb. O.T. and may be related to *nâdar* (5087).

5145. Nezer or **nêzer;** this mas. Heb. noun stems from 5144. A consecration; consecrated (unshorn) head; a diadem, a crown. It refers to the period of abstention which was part of the Nazarite vow (Num. 6:1-21). Lev. 21:12 mentions the consecration of the anointing oil. The priest was prohibited from being defiled, i.e., he was to be separated from anything secular. *Nezer* is used in the sense of headgear in Ex. 29:6; 39:30; Lev. 8:9. It was an engraved plate which the priest wore over his forehead (Ex. 28:36-38), designating that he was a consecrated person. However, the word was also used of a royal crown or diadem which was the token by which anyone was separated from the people at large and indicated royalty (II Sam. 1:10; II Kgs. 11:12; Ps. 89:39; 132:18) or the high priest (Ex. 29:6; 39:30; Lev. 8:9).

5148. Nâchâh; to guide, to lead (Ex. 32:34; Num. 23:7; I Sam. 22:4; Job 38:32), to lead troops forth (I Kgs. 10:26; II Kgs. 18:11); to transport (into exile), to lead back (Job 12:23). This verb, which occurs thirty-nine times, was often used of God governing men (Ps. 5:8; 27:11; 31:3; 61:2; 73:24; 143:10). It could mean to herd a flock (Ps. 78:53,72). God guided Abraham's servant (Gen. 24:27). The pillars of cloud and fire showed the Israelites which way that God wantd them to go (Ex. 13:21). In the Messianic kingdom, the nations are obligated to worship God because He will judge and govern (Ps. 67:4; cf. 31:3).

5157. Nâchal; to seize, to take into possession; to get, to inherit; to take or have for one's own; to give in possession or inheritance; to distribute, to allot; to be made to possess; to possess for oneself. The verb is found about sixty times and means giving or receiving property which is part of a permanent possession and as a result of succession. Succession may not always be present in the word, but possession carries the flavor of permanence (Ex. 34:9; Prov. 14:18). The sons of Israel acquired Canaan as their possession

(Ex. 32:13). The Lord took Israel as His own, guarding and defending her (Zech. 2:12). It means to inherit in Deut. 21:16.

5159. Nachălâh; this fem. Heb. noun is a deriv. of 5157. It means a possession, property, something inherited, an inheritance, a heirloom, an estate, a portion, occupancy. The term is used of specific territory assigned to one tribe (Josh. 13:23), of the entire holy land given to the Israelites (Deut. 4:21), and of Israel herself, who belonged to Jehovah (Deut. 4:20; 9:26,29; Ps. 28:9; cf. Acts 15:16ff.; Eph. 1:3,4). In Ps. 127:3 it refers to a possession granted by Jehovah, as a gift from Him. It means an inheritance in I Kgs. 21:3,4; Prov. 19:14 and a lot which has been assigned by God in Job 20:29; 27:13; 31:2. This noun occurs 223 times, mostly in the Pentateuch and in Joshua. The basic translation is "inheritance," i.e., a possession to which one has received the legal claim. The Promised Land was divided into shares which were determined by lot (Num. 26:56) shortly before the death of Moses. After the conquest this term was no longer used to refer to new territory gained by warfare. After that time, the legal process among the Jews was simple—the property had to remain within the family which inherited it from their forefathers. This is the reason why Naboth could not sign over his rights to King Ahab (I Kgs. 21:3,4). However, land could be redeemed under certain circumstances (Ruth 4:10). Because Israel rebelled against God. He abandoned them to fall into the hands of their enemies (Isa. 47:6) and later permitted a remnant of them (the "possession") to return (Mic. 7:18). Since the priest and the Levites had no earthly possessions, the Lord was their inheritance (Deut. 10:9; cf. 12:12; Num. 18:23). See the Septuagint's *klēronomia* (2817) and *klēros* (2819).

5162. Nâcham; to draw the breath forcibly, to pant, to breathe strongly, to groan; to be sorry, to pity, to grieve; to feel repentance, to repent; to take revenge or vengeance; to have compassion, to console, to comfort oneself; to be comforted. The idea of breathing deeply was a physical display of one's feeling, usually sorrow, compassion, or comfort. The K.J.V. translates *nâcham* as "repent" thirty-eight times. Most of these refer to God's repentance. Usually, when man repents, the verb *shûwb* (7725) is used, "to turn" (from sin to God). Since God is free from sin, how can He repent (Gen. 6:6,7; Ex. 32:14; Judg. 2:18; I Sam. 15:11)? Essentially, *nâcham* is a change of heart or disposition, a change of mind, a change of purpose, or a change of one's conduct. When man changes his attitude, God makes the corresponding change. God is morally bound not to change His stance if man continues to travel on an evil path. There is a point beyond which God will not go (Jer. 15:6). Jehovah is not whimsical or fickle (I Sam. 15:29). When God did change his mind, it was because of the intercession of man and because of man's true repentance (Ex. 32:12,14; Jer. 31:19,20; Jon. 3:10). God is consistent (Ps. 110:4; Js. 1:17). Though it may appear that God's purpose has changed, according to God's perspective, nothing has changed. Most prophecy is conditional upon the response of men. The second main meaning of *nâcham* is "to comfort" or "to be comforted." This meaning occurs about sixty-five times. See especially Ps. 23:4 and Isa. 40:1. It means being consoled over the death of an infant child (II Sam. 12:24), a teenage son (Gen. 37:35), a mother (Gen. 24:67), and a wife (Gen. 38:12). A mother comforts her child (Isa. 66:13). In a similar way, God comforts His people (Ps. 71:21; 86:17; 119:82; Isa. 12:1; 49:13; 52:9). His compassion for Israel was warm and tender (Hos. 11:8). This root is found in the names of Nehemiah, Nahum, and Menehem. The Septuagint translates *nâcham* by both *metanoeō* (3340) and *metamellomai* (3338). See the discussion on these Gr. words in the N.T. lexical section.

5164. Nôcham; this mas. Heb. noun comes from 5162. It means repentance, ruefulness, desistance. It appears only once (Hos. 13:14).

5165. Nechâmâh; this fem. Heb. noun is a deriv. of 5162, meaning consolation or comfort. It appears only twice in the Heb. O.T. (Job 6:10; Ps. 119:50).

5172. Nâchash; to hiss; to whisper (a magical spell), to practice sorcery or enchantment, to take as an omen (I Kgs. 20:33), to give oracles, to divine, to foretell, to prognosticate; to learn by experience, to diligently observe. Divination was outlawed in Lev. 19:26 and condemned in II Kgs. 17:17; 21:6; cf. II Chr. 33:6. It was on the list of forbidden occult practices (Deut. 18:10).

5173. Nachash; this Heb. noun has its source in 5172. It means an incantation, an omen, enchantment, sorcery, augury. Num. 23:23 is clearly parallel to *qeçem* (7081), indicating some type of occult practice. The only other occurrence of this word is in Num. 24:1. Though this term is related to *nâchâsh* (5175), "a snake," it has nothing to do with snake charming. Enchanters probably made a hissing sound like serpents.

5175. Nâchâsh; a hissing creature, a serpent, a snake (Gen. 3:1ff.; Ex. 4:3; 7:15; II Kgs. 18:4), the constellation of the dragon (Job 26:13). This is the most common word for a snake and is found thirty times in the Heb. O.T. Normally, the serpent was something evil, dating back to the temptation in the Garden of Eden (see Gen. 3; cf. II Cor. 11:3; Rev. 12:9ff.), but one could look at the bronze serpent after being bitten by a venomous snake (Num. 21:6,7,9) and be healed. In a similar way, Jesus would be lifted up from the earth (Jn. 12:32) on the cross like the bronze snake (Jn. 3:14). It is interesting that the bronze serpent eventually became a relic which men wanted to worship (II Kgs. 18:4). Such is the tendency of men to change things into religious fetishes.

5197. Nâṭaph; to ooze, to distill gradually; to drop, to drip, to flow; (figuratively) to trickle speech (Job 29:22), to speak by inspiration, to prophesy (Ezek. 21:2,9; Amos 7:16; Mic. 2:6). This root occurs eighteen times in the Heb. O.T., exclusively in the poetic sections. Many of the occurrences deal with rain or clouds (Judg. 5:4; Ps. 68:8). The prophets predicted a time when "the mountains will drip with sweet wine" (Joel 3:18; cf. Amos 9:13). Prov. 5:3 refers to the seductive speech of an adulterous woman.

5203. Nâṭash; to pound; to stretch, to extend (of warriors in battle, Judg. 15:9; I Sam. 4:2; 30:16; II Sam. 5:18,22), to spread (out), to disperse (I Sam. 4:2; 30:16); to scatter; to reject, to leave, to give up, to remit, to allow (Gen. 31:28); to draw (a sword, Isa. 21:15), to brandish; to be loosened (like a rope, Isa. 33:23); to be left, to be forsaken (Isa. 32:14). There are forty occurrences of this word in the Heb. O.T., half of which connote the idea of forsaking or rejecting. Because of Israel's sin, God cast off His people (Judg. 6:13; I Sam. 12:22; I Kgs. 8:57; II Kgs. 21:14; Ps. 94:14; Isa. 2:6; Jer. 7:29; 12:7; 23:33,39). However, Israel left God first (Deut. 32:15). The temple was forsaken at Shiloh (Ps. 78:60). *Nâṭash* described a fallow field in the Sabbatical year (Ex. 23:11) or forgoing the harvesting of crops (Neh. 10:31). It can mean to drop a dispute, to let trouble lie (Prov. 17:14). It has the sense of ejecting in Ezek. 29:5; 32:4. It refers to the spreading tendrils or shoots of a vine (Isa. 16:8).

5216. Nîyr or **nîr** or **nêyr** or **nêr** or **nêrâh;** a light, a lamp; prosperity, instruction: (figuratively) progeny, e.g., David's lineage would continue forever (I Kgs. 11:36; 15:4; II Kgs. 8:19; II Chr. 21:7). This derives from 5214. It refers to the small bowl-like objects which contained oil and a wick for providing light. This noun occurs forty-nine times with the various spellings.

5221. Nâkâh; to strike (lightly or severely, literally or figuratively); to hit, to hurt, to wound, to pierce; to kill, to slay; to rout, to defeat, to conquer; to be beaten; to be killed, to be slain; to be punished. This root occurs about 500 times in the Heb. O.T. It was often a non-fatal striking of an object, e.g., a donkey (Num. 22:23,25,27), a person's cheek (Ps. 3:7; Lam. 3:30), or the eye (Ex. 21:26). The famous rod of Moses was used to strike the river (Ex. 7:17), the dust (Ex. 8:16,17), and a rock (Ex. 17:6). A stone from a sling

(I Sam. 17:49), an arrow (I Kgs. 22:34), and a spear (I Sam. 19:10; cf. 26:8) found their mark. One can strike (clap) his hands (II Kgs. 11:12). Even the conscience can be "smitten" (I Sam. 24:5). Sometimes it is a repetitive beating (Ex. 2:11,13; Deut. 25:2,3,11; Neh. 13:25; Prov. 19:25; 23:13,14; Song of Sol. 5:7; Isa. 50:6; Jer. 20:2; 37:15). In about ninety places it has the meaning of being struck dead. It is used of murdering another man (Ex. 21:12; Josh. 10:26) whether intentionally (II Sam. 2:23) or unintentionally (Deut. 19:4). A man killed a lion (I Sam. 17:35) and another was killed by a lion (I Kgs. 20:36). A plant was killed by a worm (Jon. 4:7). It has the sense of attack in Gen. 32:8,11; Josh. 8:21; 10:28; and Amos 3:15. Many times God is the subject; He "struck" people with blindness (II Kgs. 6:18) and plagues (Deut. 28:22,27,28,35). He brings judgment upon man for his sin (Lev. 26:24; I Kgs. 14:15), even death (II Sam. 6:7). God, not Baal, controls nature, because it was He who struck down the vines and fig trees of Israel (Ps. 105:33).

5228. Nâkôach; straightforward, equitable, correct, honest, right, righteous; lying ahead, straight on; (as a noun) justice, righteousness. This Heb. adj., which is sometimes used as a noun, originates from 5226. It describes the ethical quality of life in actions, e.g., the righteous man who dies in peace because he walked a straight path through life (Isa. 57:2). It means what is just and proper (Isa. 26:10; 30:10; 59:14; Amos 3:10). A "right" answer in a legal matter is an honest reply (Prov. 24:26). It is a syn. for justice, righteousness, and truth (Isa. 59:14). The word occurs nine times in the O.T.

5234. Nâkar; to scrutinize, to look at something intently; to feign, to make oneself unknown; to find strange, not to know; to disdain, to deny, to reject; to find out, to recognize, to regard, to observe, to perceive, to understand; to honor; to be recognized, to be known. This verbal root occurs about fifty times in the Heb. O.T. The basic meaning is physical apprehension (recognition), whether through sight, touch, or hearing. *Nâkar* is one of the main words for "know." It can be an intellectual awareness (Job 7:10), special recognition (Ruth 2:19), or to distinguish (Ezra 3:13; Job 4:16). It can be a visual inspection with the intention of recognizing it (Gen. 31:32; 37:32; 38:25). *Nâkar* sometimes means recognizing an object which one formerly knew (Gen. 37:33; 38:26; I sam. 26:17; I Kgs. 18:7; 20:41). Recognition is not always possible because of partial blindness (Gen. 27:23), the passage of years (Gen. 42:7), darkness (Ruth 3:14), or the change of one's appearance (Job 2:12). It means to acknowledge in Deut. 21:17; 33:9; Isa. 61:9; Dan. 11:39.

5235. Neker or **nôker;** strangeness; strange or foreign land; something strange (unexpected), a misfortune, a calamity. This Heb. noun comes from 5234. It occurs only twice in the O.T. (Job 31:3 and Obad. 12).

5236. Nêkâr; that which is foreign, a foreigner; strange, a stranger. This Heb. noun is traceable to 5234. It is used of a foreign god (Deut. 32:12; Ps. 81:9; Mal. 2:11), of foreign altars (II Chr. 14:3), a foreign country (Ps. 137:4), and everything foreign (Neh. 13:30). It means foreigners in Gen. 17:12,27; Ex. 12:43, and there was hostility toward them (Ps. 18:44,45).

5237. Nokrîy; this Heb. adj. stems from 5235. It means strange, foreign, alien, unknown; (as a noun) an outsider, a foreigner (Deut. 17:15), a foreign land (Ex. 2:22), from another country and people (Ex. 21:8), one who comes from another family and is not a lawful heir (Ecc. 6:2), or a strange woman, one who is not one's own wife, who initiates illicit sexual intercourse (Prov. 5:20; 6:24; 7:5; 23:27). A *nokrîy,* unlike a *gêr* (1616), was a permanent resident alien who had once been a citizen of another land. The term occurs over forty times in the Heb. O.T. The Septuagint has *allotrios* (245), which see in the N.T. lexical section. In Modern Hebrew, *nokrîy* can mean "Gentile."

5243. Nâmal; to be clipped; specifically, to be circumcised. See Job 14:2; 18:16; 24:24; Ps. 37:2.

5254. Nâçâh; to test, to try, to prove, to tempt, to assay, to put to the test, to put to the proof, to attempt, to venture. In most places this verb carries with it the idea of testing the quality of someone or something through a demonstration of stress. At the time the K.J.V. was translated (1611 A.D.), "tempt" meant "to test," rather than the current meaning of "to entice to do wrong." Since God does not tempt man (Js. 1:13), the rendering of "tempt" for *nâçâh* in Gen. 22:1 (as in the KJV) became a problem in time. However, God was testing (refining) the character of Abraham in this instance. He did the same thing with Hezekiah in II Chr. 32:31. God wants us to walk more closely to His way (Ex. 16:4; Deut. 8:2; Judg. 2:22; Ps. 26:1-3). Massah ("trial") in the wilderness was a pun on this word; we must not put God to the test (Deut. 6:16). Note that the Queen of Sheba tested Solomon with hard questions (I Kgs. 10:1; II Chr. 9:1). The word occurs thirty-six times in the Heb. O.T. See *peirazō* (3985) in the N.T. lexical section.

5255. Nâçach; to tear away, to destroy, to pluck out, to pull out, to root out, to expel, to banish; to pull down; to be driven out. This verb is used four times in the O.T. It means to seize someone from his house (Ps. 52:5) or be driven into exile (Deut. 28:63; Prov. 2:22). Also, it can mean to destroy a house (Prov. 15:25).

5256. N^eçach; this Aramaic noun corresponds to 5255 and appears only in Ezra 6:11.

5257. N^eçîyk; this Heb. noun comes from 5258. It means something poured out, a libation, a drink-offering (Deut. 32:38); a cast (molten) image (Dan. 11:8); an (anointed) prince (Josh. 13:21; Ps. 83:11; Ezek. 32:30; Mic. 5:5).

5258. Nâçak; to pour out (especially a libation); to cast (metals) cf. Isa. 40:19; 44:10; to appoint, to consecrate, to ratify a covenant (Isa. 30:1), to anoint a king (Ps. 2:6). This verb occurs about twenty times in the Heb. O.T. Before Israel settled in the Promised Land, the Canaanites were accustomed to pour out drink offerings to their gods (cf. Ex. 30:9; Hos. 9:4). They thought that their deities needed food and drink like human beings. Eventually, these pagan libations influenced Israelite worship. The prophets strongly opposed the practice (Isa. 57:6; cf. 65:11; Jer. 32:29; cf. 7:18; 19:13; 44:17; cf. 44:18,19,25: Ezek. 20:28). Jacob was the first on record to present a drink-offering (Gen. 35:14). According to the Law of Moses, a drink-offering was to be presented along with the burnt-offerings and cereal-offerings (Ex. 29:40; Lev. 23:13; Num. 15:1-10). It was poured out daily to the Lord (Num. 28:7,8) and at each of the most important feasts. Num. 6:15,17 informs us that it was part of the conclusion of a Nazarite vow. Usually it was wine (Ex. 29:40; Num. 15:5,10) or another fermented drink (Num. 28:7). Sometimes water was poured out to the Lord (II Sam. 23:16; I Chr. 11:18). And, occasionally, olive oil was used (Mic. 6:7). Since the life was in the blood, a libation of blood was forbidden (Ps. 16:4). When Jesus uttered Jn. 7:37. He was probably referring to the daily drink-offering of the Feast of Tabernacles which lasted one week (Num. 29:12ff.). Paul used the same imagery of the drink-offering in Phil. 2:17 and II Tim. 4:6. See *spendō* (4689) in the N.T. lexical section.

5261. N^eçak; this mas. Aramaic noun is a correlate to 5262. It means libation or drink-offering. It occurs only once (Ezra 7:17).

5262. Neçek or **nêçek;** this mas. Heb. noun is a deriv. of 5258. It means a libation, a drink-offering; a molten image (which was cast by pouring hot liquid metal into a mold or over a frame (Isa. 40:18-20). The worship of idols cast out of metal was severely denounced in the Law of Moses (Ex. 34:17; Lev. 19:4; Deut. 27:15) and the Prophets (Isa. 41:29; 42:17; 44:10; Jer. 10:14; 51:17; Hos. 13:2; Hab. 2:18).

5303. N^ephîyl or **n^ephîl;** this mas. Heb. noun has its origin in 5307. It means a bully, a tryant, a giant. It appears three times in the O.T. (Gen. 6:4; Num. 13:33, twice). There was much controversy concerning these individuals. Since the etymology is uncertain, there is much speculation among reputable scholars. The translation "giants" in the KJV came from the Septuagint and may be misleading. Does Gen. 6:4 refer to the fall of angels? Were they apostates? It is possible that the word means "heroes" or "fierce warriors." Until more evidence becomes available, perhaps it is wise to do as the R.S.V. and N.I.V. translations did, to render it "Nephilim."

5307. Nâphal; to fall, to fall down, to be prostrate, to drop; to be born; to fall out, to happen, to turn out; to fall away, to sink; to be overthrown, to decay; to settle down, to abide; to make fall, to cause to fall, to throw down, to fell, to make the face fall; to lay down, to desist; to cast oneself down; to fall upon, to attack. The main idea behind this root is a violent or accidental circumstance or event. The meaning can range from a simple, literal falling, e.g., Ahaziah fell down through the lattice (II Kgs. 1:2), to falling in battle (Judg. 20:44) or into the hands of another (Lam. 1:7) or by the hand of an opponent (I Chr. 20:8). This verb occurs 365 times in the Heb. O.T.

5308. N^ephal; this Aramaic verb corresponds to 5307. It means to fall down (Dan. 4:31; 7:20); to prostrate oneself (Dan. 2:46; 3:6,7,10,11); to be cast down (Dan. 3:23); and to happen (Ezra 7:20). There are eleven occurrences.

5309. Nephel or **nêphel** or **n^ephîl;** this mas. Heb. noun originates from 5307. It is something which has fallen, i.e., an abortion, an untimely or premature birth which "falls" from the womb (Job 3:16; Ps. 58:8; Ecc. 6:3). It has this sense in the Jewish Talmud. The Arabic cognate term means to miscarry.

5315. Nephesh; this Heb. noun arises from 5314. It is a breathing creature (man or animal), breath, respiration, life; soul, spirit, mind; a living being, a creature, person, self. Most of them are closely-related concepts which break down to a few basic meanings. The verb *nâphash* occurs three times in the Niphal stem (Ex. 23:12; 31:17; II Sam. 16:14) and means "to refresh oneself." *Nephesh,* the deriv. noun, appears to denote "breath" in Gen. 1:30; cf. Gen. 2:7; I Kgs. 17:22; Job 41:21. It is the soul by which the body lives, i.e., continues to live by drawing breath. Another important meaning is life, the vital principle which results in death when it leaves the body (Gen. 35:18; I Kgs. 17:21). *Nephesh* can die or stop (Judg. 16:30); it can be killed (Num. 31:19) and poured out with the blood (Isa. 53:12; Lam. 2:12). Animals have *nephesh* (Gen. 1:21,24; 2:7,19; 9:10,12,15; Lev. 11:10; Josh. 10:28,30,32,35,37). *Nephesh* is often used in phrases which relate either to the loss of life or its preservation and sustenance. Sometimes it is synonymous with *chay* (2417). To take one's life (*nephesh*) into one's own hands is to put oneself in danger (Judg. 12:3). Ex. 4:19 means "seeking to kill." See also Josh. 2:13; I Sam. 19:11; II Sam. 19:5; Ps. 6:4; 49:15; 72:13; Isa. 44:20. Elijah ran for his life (*nephesh*) (I Kgs. 19:3). Life (*hephesh*) is most precious (II Kgs. 1:13; Ex. 21:30; 30:12; cf. I Sam. 26:21). The "life for life" principle was in effect in the O.T. (Ex. 21:23; Lev. 24:18; Deut. 19:21; cf. I Kgs. 20:39,42; II Kgs. 10:24). The vitality, the passionate existence of an individual was denoted in Lev. 17:11, "For the life (*nephesh*) of the flesh is in the blood." There are about 775 occurrences of *nephesh* in the Heb. O.T. The Septuagint renders some 600 of these with *psuchē* (5590). See the N.T. lexical section for a thorough discussion there. The Heb. concept of man was not dichotomous like our Greek and Latin traditions. Unlike the West, the Hebrew conception was "the inner self" and the "the outer appearance," i.e., what one is to oneself and what one appears to those who observe him. The inner person was *nephesh* to the Hebrews, while the outer person was reputation, *shêm* (8034), "name." "Soul" makes no sense in historical passages such as Lev. 17:11. In Gen. 1:20,21,24, "living creature" appears, associating man with other creatures as sharing the experience of life and he is not being defined as distinct from them. However, the source of the *nephesh* of animals is the ground, but God is the source of the *nephesh* of Adam. Gen. 2:7 makes it clear that *nephesh* stands for the entire person, cf. a census of persons (Ex. 1:5; 16:16; Deut. 10:22; I Pet. 3:20). Ps. 3:2 and Ps. 6:3 distinguish between the *nephesh* and some aspect of the self. Note that Isa. 26:9 puts *nephesh* and *rûwach* (7308) in synonymous parallelism. Sometimes *nephesh* is best translated as "person" (Lev. 7:20; Jer. 52:29,30), "persons" (Lev. 27:2), "self," or by the personal pronoun (Gen. 19:19; Isa. 3:9). *Nephesh* is used of slaves (Gen. 12:5; Ezek. 27:13; cf. Rev. 18:13). Job 16:4 refers to the feelings of the mind (*nephesh*). The term is translated as "heart" in the K.J.V., connoting the inner man, e.g., Prov. 23:7. *Nephesh* can refer to the appetite (Deut. 23:24; cf. Ps. 78:18; Hos. 9:4). Sometimes it means "desire" or "will" (Gen. 23:8; Ex. 15:9; Deut. 21:14). In about twenty occurrences *nephesh* is what possesses the appetite (e.g., Deut. 12:20; I Sam. 2:16), or even sexual drive (Jer. 2:24). Isa. 26:8,9 suggests that the object for which the soul craves may be a person. See especially Ps. 42:1,2. The soul may also yearn for His courts (Ps. 84:3), for God's Law (Ps. 119:20), or His salvation (Ps. 119:81). In some cases, *nephesh* is the inclination of the soul, even love (Gen. 34:3; Ps. 63:9; Song of Sol. 1:7; 3:1-4; cf. Jer. 12:7). The greatest command in the entire O.T. was to love God with the whole heart and soul (Deut. 6:5). The most interesting meaning of the word *nephesh,* in light of everything said heretofore, is the sense of a dead person (Lev. 21:11; 22:4; Num. 5.2; 6:6; 9:6,7,10; 19:13; Hag. 2:13). It really means, "one who has died," with the emphasis on the personal identify of an individual while alive. Since God cannot die and He does not have the same kinds of human cravings or appetites which we do, it is not surprising that *nephesh* seldom occurs with reference to God. However, there are a few anthropopathic usages (Isa. 42:1; Jer. 6:8; cf. Jer. 5:9,29; 9:9; 15:1). Man is not merely a physical being like the animals. He has a spirit (*rûwach,* 7308, which see), a heart (*lêb,* 3820, which see), was made in the image (*tselem,* 6754, which see) of God, and is the object of God's love.

5324. Nâtsab; to be set up, to be stationed, to station oneself, to stand; to be firm or healthy; to set, to place, to erect, to establish; to be placed; to be planted (Judg. 9:6); to establish boundaries (Deut. 32:8; Ps. 74:17; Prov. 15:25). The main idea of this verb can best be seen in Ex. 7:15 where God ordered Moses to station himself by the edge of the Nile to meet Pharaoh. In another place, Moses was to "present" himself before God on Mount Sinai (Ex. 34:2). God is described as "standing in the congregation" (Ps. 82:1) for administering justice. So, *nâtsab* portrays various types of standing, waiting, postures (Gen. 37:7; Ps. 78:13), etc. In I Kgs. 4:5 it means to be in a position of authority. Transitively, it means to erect in Gen. 33:20; 35:14; Ps. 78:13.

5331. Netsach or **nêtsach;** this mas. Heb. noun is traceable to 5329. It means a goal; splendor, glory (I Sam. 15:29; 1 Chr. 29:11), truth (Prov. 21:28), power, firmness, confidence (Lam. 3:18), duration, perpetuity (Job 34:36; Isa. 34:10), completeness (Job 23:7; Ps. 13:1; 74:3; 79:5), sincerity (Hab. 1:4). The double nuance of this root in Isa. 25:8 is enligtening when one compares it with I Cor. 15:54. As an adv. the term means always, forever, until eternity, everlasting, unceasing, constantly.

5332. Nêtsach; this word comes from 5331. It means the brillant juice of the grape (blood, strength), or liquor. It depicts a scene of grapes being trampled in the winepress. See the only occurrence in Isa. 63:3,6.

5337. Nâtsal; to snatch away (for good or bad), to be snatched out of; to be drawn out, to be delivered, to be saved; to free, to free oneself; to rob, to plunder; to deliver, to save; to tear apart, to pull away; to withdraw, to escape; to strip off, to put off (a garment). II Sam. 14:6 tells about two sons fighting with one another with no one to pull them apart. Physical deliverance is the meaning in Judg. 10:15; I Sam. 12:10; 1 Chr. 16:35; Ps. 7:1 (even spiritual salvation); Ps. 39:8; 51:14; 69:14; 79:9.

5338. N^etsal; this Aramaic word corresponds to 5337 and means to extricate, to deliver, to rescue. It occurs only three times (Dan. 3:29; 6:14,27).

5341. Nâtsar; to guard, to protect, to maintain, to obey; to observe, to behold; to watch, to inspect, to keep, to preserve; to besiege a city (Isa. 1:8; Jer. 4:16); to hide, to conceal. This verbal root appears about sixty times in the Heb. O.T. One can guard a vineyard (Job 27:18; Isa. 27:3), a fig tree (Prov. 27:18), a fortification (Nah. 2:1). Those who performed this function were "watchmen," the Qal act. part. form (Jer. 31:6; II Kgs. 17:9; 18:8). Israel was likened to a vineyard and Jehovah served as a keeper of her (Job 7:20). In an ethical sense, one can keep the mouth (Ps. 141:3; Prov. 13:3), one's path in life (Prov. 16:17), the heart (Prov. 4:23), the lips (Ps. 141:3), and the tongue (Ps. 34:13). The idea of keeping the covenant (with faithfulness) is prominent (Ex. 34:7; Deut. 33:9; Ps. 25:10; 78:7; 105:45; 119:2,22,33,34,56,69,-100,115,129,145). The sons of Israel were urged to observe the commands of parents (Prov. 6:20; 28:7) and the discipline of wisdom (Prov. 3:1,21; 4:13; 5:2). The more common *shâmar* (8104) is a closely-related syn.

5344. Nâqab; to puncture, to bore a hole (II Kgs. 12:9; 18:21; Job 40:24; 41:2; Hab. 3:14; Hag. 1:6), to pierce, to perforate; to excavate, to hollow out; to mark, to distinguish, to fix, to specify, to declare distinctly; to be marked, to be called by name (Gen. 30:28; Isa. 62:2; Amos 6:1); to curse, to blaspheme. Archeologists have discovered an important inscription in the Siloam Tunnel, which, considering the times, was an amazing engineering feat of two groups successfully digging to meet. *Nâqab* was found in that inscription.

5347. Neqêbâh; this fem. Heb. noun has its source *nâqab* in 5344. It means a woman, a female, whether human (Gen. 1:27; 5:2) or animal (Gen. 6:19; Lev. 3:1,6; 4:28,32; 5:6; 12:5), the opp. of male (*zâkar,* 2142). In Jer. 31:22 this word stands in contrast with *geber* (1397), "man," "hero."

5352. Nâqâh; to be clean, to be pure, to be guiltless, to be free from punishment (Ex. 21:19; Num. 5:19; Prov. 6:29); to be free, empty (spoken of a city, Isa. 3:26), vacant, evacuated, destroyed (concerning conquered men, Zech. 5:3); to absolve or declare innocent (Job 9:28; 10:14; Ps. 19:13), to let something or someone go unpunished, to acquit, to pardon (Ex. 20:7; I Kgs. 2:9; Jer. 30:11; 46:28), to be clear from an obligation; to cleanse by punishment. This Heb. verb occurs forty-four times in the O.T. The original sense was probably "to empty out." The derived idea of "clean" eventually took on a judicial flavor. Most of the occurrences have a moral connotation associated with them. Many of the instances are synonymous with *tsâdaq* (6663). One use of this term is freedom (exemption) from military service (Deut. 24:5). It contains the idea of no longer having an obligation to be responsible (Num. 5:31). When Samson spoke to his father-in-law (Judg. 15:3), it was as if he were saying in our modern vernacular, "I can't be responsible for what will happen now! You shouldn't have done that, but you did. Therefore, you can't blame me for the consequences which are about to happen!" See the Gr. term *athōos* (121). The Heb. is decidedly wider in scope than the Gr. counterpart. The meaning extends from being emptied (cleaned out) to the forensic connotation of acquittal.

5355. Nâqîy or **nâqîy';** pure, innocent, guiltless (free from blame, II Sam. 3:28), exempted (from military service, Deut. 24:5; I Kgs. 15:22). This Heb. adj. derives from 5352. "Clean hands" is a figure for innocent behavior (Ex. 23:7; Job 4:7; 9:23; Ps. 24:4). A righteous man does not take a bribe against the innocent (Ps. 15:5). In Gen. 44:10 it denoted freedom from slavery. Like *nâqâh* (5352), this word has the nuances of the courtroom. The word occurs forty-three times in the Heb. O.T.

5356. Niqqâyôwn or **niqqâyôn;** this mas. Heb. noun originates from 5352. It means clearness, cleanness, innocence (Gen. 20:5; Ps. 26:6; 73:13), innocency; bareness. In Hos. 8:5 God taunts the rulers of Samaria about how they will ever manage to claim that they are innocent. The "cleanness of teeth" (Amos 4:6) refers to a lack of food. There are only five occurrences of this word.

5358. Nâqam; to have a grudge; to punish, to avenge, to take vengeance, to get revenge; to avenge oneself; to be avenged, to be punished; to be revengeful, to inflict a penalty. The primary idea of this verbal root is that of breathing forcibly. It may very well be related to *nâcham* (5162). At the very beginning of the Bible, violence is prominent. Lamech's sword song (Gen. 4:23,24) was a taunting challenge to men and a blatant attack upon God's justice. However, vengeance belongs to the Lord (Deut. 32:35,43), and Moses stated that personal vengeance was forbidden (Lev. 19:18), though the "avenger of blood" (Deut. 19:6) was provided for. David, a "man after God's own heart," committed his case to God (I Sam. 24:12). No one ever really "gets even." All wrongs will be righted by the Lord on the Judgment Day. There is perfect balance between God's vengeance and His mercy throughout the Scriptures. In Mt. 5:43ff., about turning the other cheek, Jesus was probably quoting Lev. 19:18. Paul quoted Prov. 25:21,22 in Rom. 12:20. This root and its deriv. occur eighty-seven times in the Heb. O.T.

5359. Nâqâm; this mas. Heb. noun is traceable to 5358. It means revenge, vengeance, the desire for vengeance (Lam. 3:60; Ezek. 25:15), retaliation, punishment, a quarrel. Since vengeance belongs to God, He takes it (Isa. 47:3), returns it (Deut. 32:41,43), executes it (Mic. 5:15), comes with it (Isa. 35:4), and metes it out (Ezek. 25:14). If blood has been shed, then He sheds it also (Ps. 79:10). This word is closely associated with *chêmâh* (2534), "rage," and *qin'âh,* (7068) "jealousy."

5360. Neqâmâh; this fem. Heb. noun is the equivalent of 5359. It means vengeance, retaliation, punishment, vindictiveness.

5362. Nâqaph; to strike, to go around, to move in a circle, to surround, to circulate, to encompass, to enclose; to draw around. It describes the cycle of days (Job 1:5) or taking turns. Job 19:6 describes the encircling technique of hunting nets. Moses commanded the Israelites not to shave or trim around the head, leaving a tuft of hair on top, because this imitated pagan practices (Lev. 19:27). It means "everywhere" in Isa. 15:8.

5367. Nâqash; to entrap (with a noose); to ensnare, to snare; to be snared, to be seduced, to lay a snare, to catch (either literally or figuratively). The term occurs only five times (Deut. 12:30; I Sam. 28:9; Ps. 9:16; 38:12; 109:11).

5368. Neqash; it means to catch in a snare. Its only occurrence is found in Dan. 5:6.

5375. Nâsâ' or **nâçâh;** to raise, to lift up (the face, the eyes, the voice, or the soul); to bear, to carry, to wear, to take, to take away; to accept, to be partial; to be lifted up, to be raised, to be elevated, to be extolled, to be exalted; to be borne, to be carried, to be taken away; to raise, to heighten; to support, to help; to carry off; to cause to bear; to apply to; to raise oneself; to be proud, to be haughty. This verbal root is used more than 650 times in the O.T. Whether literally or figuratively, the word's basic meaning is "to lift up." *Nâsâ'* participates in a number of idiomatic expressions: "lifting up the heads" meant to take a census (Ex. 30:12), but it could also mean to declare independence (Judg. 8:28), to be free (II Kgs. 25:27; cf. Gen. 40:13), or to die (Gen. 40:19). "To lift up one's face" meant to be able to look someone straight in the eye, to have a clear conscience (II Sam. 2:22) or to anticipate that things would go well (Job 22:26). "To lift up one's hand" could be a hostile gesture (II Sam. 20:21), a part of taking an oath (Ex. 6:8), something which was done while praying (Ps. 28:9), or signaling (Isa. 49:22). "To lift up one's eyes" meant to look up (Gen. 13:10), even to lust for someone (Gen. 39:7). "To lift up one's voice" meant to wail or lament (Gen. 21:16), to call out loudly (Judg. 9:7), to speak a proverb (Num. 23:7), to declare an oracle

(II Kgs. 9:25), to slander (Ps. 15:3), to carry a false rumor (Ex. 23:1), or merely to speak a name (Ex. 20:7). "To lift up one's soul" meant to be entirely dependent upon something (Deut. 24:15). The heart is said to "lift one up," inciting action (Ex. 35:21,26; 36:2) or presumption and pride (II Kgs. 14:10). One could begin to bear sin (Gen. 18:24; Ex. 28:30) or contract iniquity by profaning the tabernacle (Ex. 28:43; Num. 18:22), by hating one's neighbors (Lev. 19:17), by touching the carcasses of animals (Lev. 22:9), or by violating the offerings (Num. 18:32). The idea of bearing the guilt or punishment of sin is found in Gen. 4:13; Lev. 5:1,17; 7:18; Num. 5:31; 14:34. Therefore, a substitionary representative is needed to carry the guilt elsewhere (Lev. 10:17; 16:22; Isa. 53:4,12). *Nâsâ'* also signifies the taking away of sin (Ps. 32:1,5). God is a forgiving God (Ex. 34:7; Num. 14:18; Mic. 7:18). Finally, in a physical sense the meaning of the term is clearly seen in Gen. 44:1 where they carried as much as they could carry. The flood waters "lifted up" Noah's ark so that it floated (Gen. 7:17). It means support in Gen. 45:23, and they knew the land could not provide enough sustenance for everyone in Gen. 13:6, i.e., could not support too many animals. *Nâsâ'* means "transport" in II Sam. 5:21. The word refers to taking a wife (Ruth 1:4) or stealing one (Judg. 21:23).

5387. Nâsîy' or **nâsî';** an exalted one, a prince (of families, Num. 3:24,30,35), a sheik, a chief, a governor, a king; rising vapor, a moist, a cloud. This Heb. noun derives from 5375 and appears almost 130 times in the Heb. O.T., mostly in Numbers and Ezekiel. It refers to either Israelite or non-Israelite leaders: e.g., the Ishmaelites (Gen. 17:20), the leaders of particular tribes (Num. 7:11ff.; 34:18ff.); they were pillars of civil and religious matters in the Jewish community. Moses consulted them (Ex. 22:28; 34:31; Josh. 22:30). It was a general name used of kings, which itself is rather broad in meaning (I Kgs. 11:34; Ezek. 12:10; 45:7ff.; 46:2ff.). Abraham was a Phylarch (Gen. 23:6). Literally, *nâsîy'* is one lifted up in a public way, i.e., an elected official. The Septuagint has *archōn* (758). About twenty instances refer to the future Davidic Prince, the Messiah. Although certainly homophonous, *nâsîy'* may have a different etymology, it refers to vapors which ascend from the earth to make clouds (Jer. 10:13; 51:16) or the clouds themselves (Ps. 135:7; Prov. 25:14).

5395. Nâsham; to blow away, to destroy; to breathe, to pant like a woman in childbirth (Isa. 42:14, the sole occurrence).

5397. Neshâmâh; this fem. Heb. noun arises from 5395. It means a puff of air, a breath, breathing, panting (of those who are angry, Ps. 18:15; Isa. 30:33); a breathing being, an animal, a living creature (Deut. 20:16; Josh. 10:40), a living soul; spirit (of man, Gen. 2:7), Spirit of God, imparting life and wisdom (Job 32:8; 33:4; cf. 26:4), divine inspiration; the mind (Prov. 20:27); blast (II Sam. 22:16), anger. *Neshâmâh* seems to be synonymous with *nephesh* (5315), and is often found in combination with *rûwach* (7307). The K.J.V. even translates it twice as "spirit" (Job 26:4; Prov. 20:27). Frailty is shown by man's "breath of life is in his nostrils" (Isa. 2:22).

5401. Nâshaq; to kiss (to join mouth to mouth); to be attached; to put on, to arm oneself; to touch (Ezek. 3:13), to fit one to another. Kissing signified homage (Gen. 27:26; I Sam. 20:41; Ps. 85:10), love (Song of Sol. 1:2), or false love (Prov. 27:6; cf. Judas Iscariot, Mt. 26:48-50). Conquered people kiss to show their submission (Gen. 31:28; Ps. 2:12). This custom was well known from Babylonian and Egyptian documents. Some kissed idols in worship (I Kgs. 19:18; Job 31:27; Hos. 13:2). Kissing was very common in the ancient Near East among relatives (Ruth 1:9), fellow countrymen (II Sam. 15:5), and lovers (Song of Sol. 8:1; Prov. 7:13). A kiss on the lips was like an honest answer (Prov. 24:26). Sometimes it denoted respect (I Sam. 10:1; II Sam. 19:39). There seems to be a homonym from which "armed," "bowmen," "in array," etc., originated.

5402. Nesheq or **nêsheq;** this Heb. mas. noun has its origin in 5401, i.e., the homonym which had to do with weaponry. It means military equipment, arms, armor, armory (Neh. 3:19), arsenal, or weapons (I Kgs. 10:25; Ps. 140:7; Ezek. 39:9,10). The term occurs ten times in the Heb. O.T.

5422. Nâthats; to tear down, to pull down, to break down, to destroy, to overthrow, to throw down; to knock out (the teeth, Ps. 58:6); to be torn down, to be destroyed; to break, to smash; to be broken, to be smashed; to be broken up. The word has the sense of overthrow in Deut. 12:3. Typically, *nâthats* is used for the literal pulling down of a structure such as an altar, a house, a city wall, or a tower in the sense of demolishing. However, it can be figurative, such as the breaking of a nation's power or the destruction of an individual's life (Job 19:10). When Jeremiah was commissioned by the Lord, he was to destroy the nations or kingdoms which opposed him (Jer. 1:10). Nah. 1:6 uses the word for a rock that was torn away.

5456. Çâgad; to prostrate oneself (in homage), to bow down, to fall down; to adore or worship (an idol, Isa. 44:15,17,19; 46:6). These are the only four occurrences in the O.T. This verb may have been borrowed from Aramaic.

5457. Çegîd; this Aramaic equivalent of 5456 refers to worship or paying homage. It was used of God, idols (Dan. 3:6), and men (Dan. 2:46). This term is related to the Arabic word for mosque.

5459. Çegullâh; the source of this fem. Heb. noun is unknown. It has to do with property, possessions, and wealth. It may be a private possession which one has personally acquired and carefully preserves or private property (I Chr. 29:3; Ecc. 2:8). The word is used to refer to the people of Israel as God's possession (Ex. 19:5; Deut. 7:6; 14:2; 26:18), because He chose them, delivered them from Egyptian bongage, and shaped them into what He wanted them to be. See also Ps. 135:4 and Mal. 3:17. There are eight occurrences in the Heb. O.T. No doubt, Tit. 2:14 and I Pet. 2:9 had this concept in mind.

5460. Çegan; this word corresponds to 5461 in Heb., but was probably an Akkadian loanword. It meant prefect or governor. The noun is found only five times in the Bible (Dan. 2:48; 3:2,3,27; 6:7).

5461. Çâgân; like 5460, this word was probably borrowed from Akkadian. It means prefect, governor, nobleman, superintendent, prince, or ruler. In effect, this official was a substitute deputy of a prince, whether a magistrate of the Babylonians (Jer. 51:23,28,57; Ezek. 23:6,12,23; cf. Isa. 41:25) or the rulers of the people of Jerusalem in the time of Ezra and Nehemiah (Ezra 9:2; Neh. 2:16; 4:14,19; 5:7; 7:5; 12:40).

5475. Çôwd; this mas. Heb. noun derives from 3245. It is a couch, a cushion, a pillow; a friendly conversation among friends (Jer. 6:11; 15:17) or a serious consultation among judges (like God, Job 15:8; Ps. 89:7; Jer. 23:18) or of wicked men who are debating evil plans, a session (i.e., a company of persons in close or secret talks), deliberation (Prov. 15:22), a sitting, a consultation, an association, council, a secret (Prov. 11:13; 20:19; 25:9; Amos 3:7), a familiar acquaintance (Job 19:19; Ps. 55:14).

5480. Çûwk; to smear over (with oil), to pour out, to anoint, to anoint oneself. Unlike *mâshach* (4886), *çûwk* was always used of anointing the human body after a bath (II Sam. 12:20), especially for fragrant effect (Ruth 3:3). It was often used for medicinal needs (Ezek. 16:9; cf. Lk. 10:34). The term was used as a symbol for gladness, signifying hospitality and concern (II Chr. 28:15; cf. Lk. 7:46). *Çûwk* also designated pouring out the pure, most fragrant, specially mixed, anointing oils for holy use by Aaron and his sons. Compare II Cor. 2:14-16 and I Pet. 2:5-9.

5486. Çûwph; to snatch away, to terminate, to consume, to be at an end, to cease, to vanish, to perish; to bring to an end, to destroy. This word is used of God's judgment (Ps. 73:19; Jer. 8:13; Amos 3:15), especially concerning the end of things (Isa. 66:17; Zeph. 1:2,3), and of the neverending annual observance of Purim (Esth. 9:28).

5487. Çûwph; this Aramaic correlate to 5486 is a fulfilled prediction. The Heb. is similar in meaning, but does not include the idea of fulfillment. There are only two occurrences (Dan. 2:44; 4:33).

5493. Çûwr or **sûwr;** to turn off (literally or figuratively), to turn aside, to go away, to recede, to depart, to apostatize; to forsake; to pass away, to cease; to turn to, to apply to, to approach, to turn in, to alight; to pervert, to cause to turn away, to depart or disappear, to put away, to take away, to remove, to cause to turn to, to let something come to; to be taken away, to be carried away, to be removed. The primary meaning of this Heb. verb is "to turn aside." It occurs 191 times in the Heb. O.T. Sometimes it is a simple motion (Ex. 3:3,4; Judg. 4:18; Ruth 4:1) or departing (Num. 12:10). Spiritually speaking, Samson was not aware that the Lord had departed from him (Judg. 16:20). The Lord departed from Saul (I Sam. 16:14; 28:16). Israel chose not to depart "from the sins of Jeroboam" (II Kgs. 10:31; 13:2,6,11; 14:24; 15:9,18,24,28; 17:22; cf. 3:3), and instead to depart from God, i.e., to turn away from His worship (I. Sam. 12:20; II Kgs. 10:29; 18:6; II Chr. 25:27; Jer. 17:5; Ezek. 6:9; Hos. 7:14). Being faithful to God meant to veer neither to the right nor to the left (II Kgs. 22:2; cf. Deut. 2:27; 5:32; Josh. 1:7). The meaning of "remove" is very common. Asa deposed Maachah for her habitual idolatry (II Chr. 15:16). Hezekiah took away the places of idolatry and their cultic objects (II Kgs. 18:4; II Chr. 30:14). God's people were urged to "put away" evil things: strange gods (Gen. 35:2), wine (I Sam. 1:14), false ways (Ps. 119:29), all types of evil (Isa. 1:16), and false worship (Amos 5:21-23). The wisdom authors advised to "fear the Lord and turn away from evil" (Prov. 3:7; cf. 16:6,17; Job 28:28; Ps. 34:14; 37:27).

5521. Çukkâh; this fem. Heb. noun comes from 5520. It is a lair (for a lion, Job 38:40), a hut, a booth (during the Feast of Tabernacles, Lev. 23:34: Deut. 16:13), an arbor (made of leaves and branches interwoven, Job 27:18; Isa. 4:6; Jon. 4:5), a tent, a house, a small, ruined house (Amos 9:11), a barn for cattle (Gen. 33:17), a cottage, a pavillion, a tabernacle. Basically, it was a temporary abode (II Sam. 11:11; Job 36:29). Isaiah foresaw that God's people would be reduced to living in temporary shelters (Isa. 1:8). Figuratively, God provides shelter for the believer's temporary afflictions (Ps. 31:20). The most common use of the term had to do with the yearly booth made in conjunction with the Feast of the Tabernacles, using the branches of a tree (Lev. 23:34-41) at the end of the agricultural season to remind the people (Deut. 16:13ff.) of God's care during the wandering in the wilderness of their ancestors (Lev. 23:42,43). Amos 9:11 stated that God would raise up the fallen booth of David. Shelter would be given to God's penitent people (Isa. 4:6).

5522. Çikkûwth; this is a fem. form from 5519, meaning an idolatrous booth which the Israelites constructed for an idol (Amos 5:26), just as they had built the tabernacle for the Lord. This is the sole occurrence. Some scholars believe that its etymology goes back to Saturn, the star god, in the Mesopotamian region. If so, Amos would be saying something different, namely that the Israelites would be destroyed for forsaking their trust in God for a deal with their oppressors. Acts 7:43 may lend some support to the Saturn theory.

5545. Çâlach; to forgive, to pardon, to spare. The first occurrence of this verb is found in Ex. 34:9 where Moses pled on behalf of Israel for the forgiveness of her sins. No other O.T. Heb. verb means "to forgive," strictly speaking, although there are several combinations of words which include the idea of forgiveness. The word is never used on a human level, with people forgiving one another. According to Heb. 9:9 and 10:4, O.T. forgiveness was ineffectual and impossible, although personally efficacious, until the Lamb of God (Jn. 1:29), Jesus Christ, died on the cross, forever blotting out our sins (Col. 2:13,14). Jer. 31:34; 33:8; 50:20 anticipated and celebrated the forgiveness to be provided in the new covenant. *Çâlach* occurs forty-six times in the Heb. O.T. See the N.T. lexical section for the following Gr. terms: *hilaskomai* (2433), *hileōs* (2436), and *aphiēmi* (863).

5546. Çallâch; this Heb. adj. is a deriv. of 5545. It means ready to forgive, forgiving, gracious, merciful, placable. Its only occurrence is found in Ps. 86:5, which describes the character of the Lord.

5547. Çᵉlîychâh; this fem. Heb. noun has its origin in 5545. It signifies forgiveness or pardon. There are only three occurrences in the Heb. O.T. (Ps. 130:4; Neh. 9:17; Dan. 9:9). Only God has the right to forgive.

5566. Çemel or **çêmel;** this Heb. noun comes from an unused root which probably meant "to resemble." The noun means likeness, image, idol, statue. This meaning was found frequently in Phoenician inscriptions. Idolatry was strictly prohibited because it was a deviation from the true God. Physical idols symbolized something real to the worshipper. Idols represented something created, less than the Creator (cf. Rom. 1:23). Compare *tselem* (6754). See Deut. 4:16; II Chr. 33:7,15; Ezek. 8:3,5. These are the only occurrences of *çemel*.

5587. Çâ'îph or **sâ'îph;** divided opinion, division, a party, opposite sides. Elijah asked, 'Why do you hesitate between the worship of Jehovah and the worship of Baal?' (I Kgs. 18:21). This was the fem. form. The only other occurrences of this word (mas. form) are found in Job (4:13; 20:2).

5595. Çâphâh; to scrape, to shave together (accumulate, Deut. 32:23), to scrape away (scatter, remove, ruin), to scrape off (Isa. 7:20); to destroy (Gen. 18:23,24); to perish (Jer. 12:4), to die in battle (I Sam. 12:25; 26:10; 27:1), to take away life (Ps. 40:14); to add, to augment; to be taken away; to be seized; to collect, to heap up. The main picture evoked by *çâphâh* is collecting something into a heap and then sweeping it away. Usually, it has a hostile connotation, frequently found in contexts of judgment (e.g., Gen. 19:15ff.; I Chr. 21:12,13; Isa. 7:20; Jer. 12:4).

5596. Çâphach or **sâphach;** to attach, to associate; to attach oneself, to join oneself; to adhere to; to pour out, to be poured out; to anoint (in the sense of constituting or inaugurating (I Sam. 2:36); to be prostrate.

5606. Çâphaq or **sâphaq;** to clap the hands (to show derision or grief or indignation, Num. 24:10 or punishment), to strike, to slap (the thigh, i.e., a cultural sign of indignation or lamentation, Jer. 31:19; Ezek. 21:17); to thrust; to punish, to chastise (used of God, Job 34:26); to fall into.

5608. Çâphar; to score (with a mark as a tally); to inscribe; to enumerate; to recount, to celebrate, to tell, to narrate, to make known, to praise; to be told; to speak; to polish. When used as a part. it means writer, scribe, secretary, or chancellor. Of the 110 times that it appears in the Heb. O.T., about ninety times occur in an intensive form meaning to recount, i.e., to list in detail orally. God promised to Abraham a posterity which was as countless as the stars in the sky (Gen. 15:5; 32:12; cf. Jer. 33:22; Hos. 1:10; Rom. 4:11-13; 9:7-8,26; Gal. 4:28). Jewish fathers were instructed to teach their children to recount the miracles and mighty deeds of god who delivered them (I Chr. 16:24; cf. Ps. 9:1,14; 26:7; 73:28; 75:1; 107:22; Jer. 51:10). The Lord keeps a record of human actions (Ps. 69:28; 139:16; cf. Ex. 32:32; Ps. 87:6; Isa. 4:3; 34:16; Dan. 7:10; 12:1; Mal. 3:16). The *sopherim* (scribes) held a very important position in the ancient Near East. There were schools in Babylon for training them; their entire society depended upon their functioning. The Pharaohs of Egypt likewise depended heavily upon this professional class. Before the exile in Israel, there were scribes who assisted the king (II Sam. 8:17; 20:25; I Kgs. 4:3: II Kgs. 12:10; 19:2; 22:3-7; Isa. 36:3). They even lived in the palace (II Kgs. 18:18; Jer. 36:12). Baruch was Jeremiah's scribe (Jer. 36). Hezekiah's scribe was Shebna. But the most famous scribe of all was Ezra. Sometimes scribes performed military purposes (Jer. 37:15; 52:25; II Kgs. 25:19; cf. II Chr. 26:11; Isa. 33:18). Besides the literary function, they performed other tasks (Judg. 5:14; II Kgs. 25:19). The English word "secretary" has the same type of semantic range, i.e., Secretary of Defense, one who types letters. Eventually, after the exile, a distinct class of specialists arose among the priests. They were skilled in the sacred writings, both preserving it and interpreting it. See I Chr. 27:32; Neh. 8:13ff.; 12:26,36; Ezra 7:6,11. During the intertestamental period, this group evolved into a very powerful, sociopolitical, religious force which we encounter in the N.T. See *grammateus* (1122) in the N.T. lexical section.

5609. Ç^{e}phar; this mas. Aramaic noun is equivalent to 5612. It means a book, a roll, a scroll. There are only five occurrences: Ezra 4:15 (twice); 6:1,18; Dan. 7:10.

5612. Çêpher or **çiphrâh;** this mas. Heb. noun derives from 5608. It is a writing, a letter, a document, a bill; a register; a book, a scroll. The term occurs 187 times in the Heb. O.T. The first occurrence is found in Gen. 5:1, concerning the "generations of Adam." There are many books which are named in the O.T.: the Book of Remembrance (Mal. 3:16), the Book of Life (Ps. 69:28), the Book of Jasher (Josh. 10:13; II Sam. 1:18), the Book of the Chronicles of the Kings of Israel (eighteen times), the Book of the Chronicles of the Kings of Judah (fifteen times, I Chr. 29:29), the Annotations on the Book of the Kings (II Chr. 24:27). Other source books which were mentioned were: the Book of the Generations of Adam (Gen. 5:1), the Book (concerning Amalek, Ex. 17:14), the Book of the Covenant (Ex. 24:7; II Kgs. 23:2), and the Book of the Law of the Lord (Deut. 31:24). *Çêpher* referred to important legal documents (Deut. 24:1,3; Isa. 50:1; Jer. 3:8) or official letters (I Kgs. 21:8ff.; II Kgs. 19:14; Esth. 1:22; Jer. 29:1ff.). No doubt these were mostly in the form of scrolls (e.g., Num. 5:23; Ps. 40:7; cf. Heb. 10:7; Isa. 34:4; Ezek. 2:9), written in columns (Jer. 36:23) and occasionally on both sides (Ezek. 2:9,10; cf. Rev. 5:1). Nahum's vision was called a *çêpher* (Nah. 1:1). In Strong's Gr. Dictionary, see *biblion* (975), *biblos* (976), and *gramma* (1121).

5613. Çâphêr; this Aramaic noun is equivalent to 5612. It is a scribe (secular or sacred). In the Aramaic portions of the Bible, there are six occurrences, denoting a royal scribe who accompanied a satrap (Ezra 4:8,9,17,23) or one like Ezra who was skilled in the sacred books (Ezra 7:12,21). Like *çêpher* (5612), this word was not limited to mere writing, but was sometimes applicable to governmental and military officials.

5627. Çârâh; this Heb. noun originated from 5493. It is a crime, a turning away, an apostasy, a departure (from Jehovah, Deut. 13:5; Jer. 28:16; 29:32; Isa. 1:5; 31:6; 59:13), a departing, a violation of a law, an offense (Deut. 19:16); a cessation (Isa. 14:6), remission. It carries the notion of defection or rebellion in man's relationship to God (Deut. 19:16). Israel was rebelling against God totally (Isa. 1:22; Jer. 6:28). There are eight occurrences.

5629. Çerach; this mas. Heb. noun comes from 5628. It means a redundancy, an overhang, the superfluous part, a remnant, what remains. Its only occurrence is found in Ex. 26:12.

5631. Çârîyç or **çârîç;** this mas. Heb. noun stems from an unused root which meant "to castrate." Therefore, the noun means castrated one, a eunuch, a valet, a courtier, a minister, a chamberlain, an officer. Eastern kings were accustomed to put castrated males over the care of their royal women and over other offices of the court (Esth. 1:10,12,15; 2:3,14,15; 4:5; cf. Isa. 56:3,4; Dan. 1:3). Not every minister of the court was castrated. Potiphar was a *çârîyç* but he had a wife (Gen. 37:36; 39:1; 40:2,7). The term sometimes means a military leader (II Kgs. 25:19). Whatever their function happened to be, they were renowned for their faithfulness to their masters. See *eunouchos* (2135) in Strong's Gr. Dictionary.

5632. Çârêk; this Aramaic word found in Dan. 6:2ff., may have been a loanword from Persian, or possibly Hittite. It referred to the royal ministers of the Persians, i.e., an emir.

5633. Çeren; this mas. Heb. noun derives from an unused root of uncertain meaning. The term was used for the axles of a chariot (I Kgs. 7:30) or for a lord. Perhaps, a prince was a hinge of the people. This word is only applied to the five princes of Philistines (Josh. 13:3; Judg. 3:3; 16:5ff.; I Sam. 5:8ff.; 6:4ff.; 29:6). It is possible that it is a loanword from the Philistines. The five cities were: Ashdod, Ashkelon, Ekron, Gath, and Gaza. They formed an amphyctionic league. The *çeren* of Gath was called a king in I Sam. 21:10ff.

5637. Çârar; to turn away (morally), to be refractory, to be rebellious, to apostatize, to revolt, to be stubborn, to withdraw. Hos. 4:16 presents the picture of Israel as being like an untamed cow, a stubborn animal shaking the yoke from its shoulders. In Jer. 6:28 there is a paronomasia. Sometimes *çârar* strengthens the verb *mârâh* (4784). See Deut. 21:18,20; Ps. 78:8; Jer. 5:23. Israel chose to go their own way (Isa. 65:2), to be recalcitrant (Neh. 9:29), to turn a deaf ear to God (Zech. 7:11), and to persist with a rebellious heart (Jer. 5:23). A certain restlessness, lack of stability, seems to be present in the woman of the streets (Prov. 7:11).

5642. Ç^{e}thar; this Aramaic word corresponds to 5641. It means to conceal secrets (Dan. 2:22) or to destroy (Ezra 5:12). These are the only two occurrences.

5647. 'Âbad; to work, to labor, to toil; to be worked; to till, to plow; to cause to work, to make weary, fatigued; to serve, to work as a slave; to enslave; to be made to serve; to be served or honored; to worship; to cause to worship. This Heb. verb occurs 290 times in the O.T. The service may be directed toward things, people, or God. Physical objects include: a field (Gen. 2:5), vineyards, flax (Isa. 19:9), or city construction (Ezek. 48:18). Jacob served Laban (Gen. 29:15; 30:26,29). Sometimes a slave is used (Ex. 1:14; Jer. 22:13). Serving as subjects to a king or ruler is found in Judg. 9:28 and I Sam. 11:1. It means to compel someone to labor as a slave in Ex. 1:13, impressing into service. Service to God is an exhilarating experience which does not seem like bondage at all (Ex. 3:12; 4:23; 7:16,26; 10:26; Ps. 22:30; Job 21:15; Jer. 2:20; Mal. 3:14). *'Âbad* is also used with reference to false gods (Deut. 7:16; II Kgs. 10:18,19,21-23). In a specialized sense, *'âbad* means to serve Jehovah in a Levitical context (Num. 3:7,8; 4:23,30,47; 8:11,-19ff.). The Septuagint uses *latreuō* (3000) for the exclusive service provided by the priests. Except for Rom. 15:16, the N.T. does not use *latreuō* in a ritualistic sense for Christian worship.

5649. 'Âbad; this Aramaic noun comes from 5648, the corresponding term to 5647. The word means servant, and appears in seven places (Ezra 4:11; 5:11; Dan. 2:4,7; 3:26,28; 6:20).

5650. 'Ebed; this Heb. noun derives from 5647. It is a laborer, a servant, a slave, a man in bonds, a subject; a worshipper. Slavery in Israel amounted to indentured servitude. A fellow Israelite could not be held indefinitely against his will; his time of service was limited to six years (Ex. 21:2). The master could be punished if evil intent against the salve was proven (Ex. 21:14) or if the salve died (Ex. 21:20). These types of servants held a position of honor (Gen. 24; 41:12; cf. 15:2). A king's subjects were his servants (Gen. 21:25; Ex. 7:20). Vassal kings served him (II Sam. 10:19) and satellite nations (I Chr. 18:2,6,13). Servants included ministers and courtiers of a king (Gen. 40:20; 41:10,37,38; 50:7; Ex. 5:21; 7:10; 10:7), ambassadors (Num. 22:18), officers (I Sam. 19:1), ordinary soldiers (II Sam. 2:12,13,15,30,31; 3:22; 8:7), messengers (II Sam. 10:2-4), officials (II Kgs. 22:12), and military captains (Isa. 36:9). God sent His ambassadors to accomplish a specific mission (Isa. 49:6; Jer. 25:9; 27:6; 43:10). *'Ebed* is applied to the Messiah in this sense (Zech. 3:8). The term is a very important one in the last twenty-seven chapters of Isaiah. It occurs in the sing. twenty times (Isa. 39—53) and eleven times in the pl. (Isa. 54—66). Some of the examples refer to the nation of Israel and some are a very personal, technical term for the Messiah Himself (Isa. 42:1-7; 49:1-9; 50:4-10; 52:13—53:12). The Suffering Servant had a mission to Israel, but He was clearly distinguished from them. Jeremiah (30:10; 46:27,28) and Ezekiel (28:25; 37:25) apply *'ebed* to the covenant people. The two prophets also apply the word to David's lineage (Jer. 33:21,22,26; Ezek. 34:23,24; 37:24,25). Hag. 2:23 uses the term for Zerubbabel, David's descendant. Often the term "servant" was used as a polite and humble reference to oneself (Gen. 33:5), even in extreme self-reference (II Sam. 9:8; II Kgs. 8:13). The term was used frequently when speaking to superiors (Gen. 18:3; 19:19, etc.), functioning much like a pronoun. The expression "Thy servant" was frequently used when addressing God in prayer (Ex. 4:10; Ps. 19:11,13; 109:28). *'Ebed* is a worshipper of God (Ezra 5:11; Neh. 1:10), particularly of godly men: Abraham (Ps. 105:6,42), Job (Job 1:8; 2:3; 42:8), Joshua (Josh. 24:29; Judg. 2:8), David (Ps. 18:1; 36:1; 89:3,20; Jer. 33:21ff.; Ezek. 34:23), Eliakim (Isa. 22:20), and Zerubbabel (Hag. 2:23). On twenty-four occasions, *'ebed* occurs in phrases as a title for God's prophets.

5656. 'Ǎbôdâh or **'ǎbôwdâh;** this fem. Heb. noun derives from 5647. It means work, rustic labor, husbandry, agricultural activity (Ex. 1:14; I Chr. 27:26; Neh. 10:37), service, employment, business, constructing the tabernacle (Ex. 35:24), repairing the temple (II Chr. 34:13), working in fine linen (I Chr. 4:21); worship, sacred or divine service (Ex. 30:16; Num. 4:23,35; I Chr. 9:13); furniture, instruments, implements (Num. 3:26,31,36). This term appears 145 times in the Heb. O.T. The word is used in connection with the sacrifices brought by the people (Josh. 22:27) and the service of the Levites and priests (Num. 4:19; II Chr. 8:14). It had the flavor of bondage, particularly the bondage of Israel in Egypt, in Ex. 1:14; Neh. 5:18; II Chr. 10:4; Isa. 14:3. Sometimes it refers to military service (Ezek. 29:18).

5657. 'Ǎbuddâh; this fem. Heb. noun has its source in 5647. It is something worked, service; servants, a household. There are only two occurrences (Gen. 26:14; Job 1:3).

5659. 'Abdûwth; this Heb. noun is a deriv. of 5647, meaning servitude or bondage. There are only three appearances of this word in the O.T. (Ezra 9:8,9; Neh. 9:17).

5674. 'Âbar; to cross over, to pass over, to go over, to go through; to penetrate, to go beyond, to pass by, to pass along, to travel; to pass away, to disappear; to go forward, to pass on; to transgress; to depart; to be crossed; to bolt, to shut up; to impregnate; to cause to pass, to cause to cross over, to lead over, to transport, to conduct across; to remove, to transfer; to cause to trespass; to let something or someone pass through, to lead along, to lead through, to bring; to be irritated, to be angry, to fall into a passion. The principal meaning of this verb is movement of something in relationship to a stationary object. The 550 occurrences in the O.T. cover a very broad spectrum of meanings and nuances. There are four basic shades of meaning: (1) going beyond a certain physical point, e.g., Abraham wanted to host his heavenly visitors, after which they could pass on (Gen. 18:5). There is no specific relationship between movement and a fixed object in Ex. 38:26; Deut. 2:14; Job 13:13. (2) Sometimes there is movement between two particular places, e.g., Jacob crossed the Euphrates River as he was running away from Laban (Gen. 31:21). Moses asked King Sihon to permit Israel to pass through his land (Num. 21:22). Israel passed over the Jordan River to enter the Promised Land (Deut 27:3). (3) Solomon's wealth was surpassing that of all others. When men die, they pass away (Job 30:15; Prov. 22:3). An army can spread like a flood (Dan. 11:10,40). (4) Spiritually, when men move outside the requirements of the covenant by committing sin, they transgress (Deut. 17:2). *'Âbar* means to violate a law (II Kgs. 18:12; Esth. 3:3; Jer. 34:18; Dan. 9:11). Even Balaam knew where the line was (Num. 22:18). The following uses fit into one of the four categories above: to pass over a stream or the sea (Deut. 3:27; 4:21; Josh. 4:22; 24:11; Amos 6:2). Waters may overflow their banks (Isa. 8:8; 54:9; Nah. 1:8; Hab. 3:10). Winds can pass over (Ps. 103:16). The feelings of the soul may pour out like a torrent of words (Ps. 73:7). Tears flow from the eyes (Song of Sol. 5:5,13). Time passes by (Gen. 50:4). One can vanish like a cloud (Job 30:15) or a shadow (Ps. 144:4) or chaff (Jer. 13:24). It means to forgive in Prov. 19:11; Mic. 7:18; Amos 7:8; 8:2.

5678. 'Ebrâh; this is a Heb. fem. noun which comes from 5674. It is an outburst (of passion), anger, rage, wrath, an overflowing, fury, pride, haughtiness. Judging from the root, it is a type of arrogance or anger which has gone too far. This is a syn. to *getseph;* (7110) and *chêmâh* (2534). When referring to God, the fierceness is overwhelming and complete (Ps. 78:49; Isa. 13:9; Ezek. 22:21,31). Nothing stands before God's burning anger. Man's insolence is described as cruel and merciless (Amos 1:11), probably because it is motivated by a wounded pride. It is no wonder why James said: "For the anger of man does not achieve the righteousness of God" (Js. 1:20).

5689. 'Âgab; to breathe after, to love (in a sensual way), to desire, to be inflamed, to lust after, to dote on. This type of inordinate affection describes the more violent feelings of the mind, especially love between the sexes, licentious and erotic. All seven occurrences are found in Jeremiah (4:30) and Ezekiel (23:5,7,9,-12,16,20).

5703. 'Ad; this mas. noun arises from 5710, meaning *terminus,* duration, advance, perpetuity, eternity. The A.S.V. has "world without end," while the R.S.V. has "to all eternity." Hebrew had no special terms for the past, the present, the future, or eternity. There simply was no general word for time in that language. See *'ôwlâm* (5769) for further information. *'Ad* and *'ôwlâm* appear together nineteen times. Only twice as *'ad* used with regard to the past (Job 20:4; Hab. 3:6). Otherwise, it always denotes the unforeseeable future. Frequently the word *'ad* is applied to God. His existence is eternal (Isa. 57:15). While His righteousness endures forever (Ps. 111:3; 112:3,9), His anger does not (Mic. 7:18). The throne of God (Ps. 10:16) and the Law of God (Ps. 19) will endure forever. The dynasty of David will continue forever (Ps. 89:29; 132:12). And, Zion is God's dwelling place forever (Ps. 48:14; 132:14; I Chr. 28:9). *'Ad* also functions as a prep. and a conj. And, *'ad* can also be used in a comparative or superlative sense.

5712. 'Êdâh; this fem. Heb. noun comes from 5707. It means assembly, meeting, congregation, company; household, family (Job 16:7; 15:34); troop, gang, crowd (of wicked men, Num. 16:5; Ps. 22:16), herd (Ps. 68:30), swarm (of bees, Judg. 14:8). Many scholars believe that the source for *'êdâh* is *yâ'ad* (3259), "to appoint." The noun occurs 140 times in the O.T., of which 127 are rendered as *sunagōgē* (4864) in the Septuagint. The purpose of the gathering is not implied. *'Êdâh* occurs with its very close syn., *qâhâl* (6951), in Prov. 5:14, *'Êdâh* is used for groups of animals, while *qâhâl* is not. *'Êdâh* occurs most frequently in Exodus, Leviticus, and Numbers, but occurs only three times in the Prophets (Jer. 6:18; 30:20; Hos. 7:12). *Qâhâl* is infrequent in Exodus, Leviticus, and Numbers, but appears often in Deuteronomy. The Books of Chronicles used *qâhâl* often, but only employed *'êdâh* once (II Chr. 5:6). Compare Ex. 12:19 and Num. 19:20 for an almost identical meaning. The expression "the congregation" occurs seventy-seven times in Exodus, Leviticus, Numbers, and Joshua. "The congregation of the Lord" appears in Num. 27:17; 31:16; Josh. 22:16,17. Ex. 12:3 has "the congregation of Israel" and Josh. 22:20 has "all the congregation of Israel." Ex. 12:6 reads: "the whole assembly of the congregation of Israel." The text contains "all the assembly of the congregation of the children of Israel" in Num. 14:5. When two silver trumpets were blown (Num. 10:2), the *'êdâh* assembled. The meeting might be for war (Judg. 20:1), to deal with a breach of the convenant of the Lord, concerning tribal matters, for worship (I Kgs. 8:5; Ps. 111:1), for a national calamity, to crown a king (I Kgs. 12:20), or some other political affair.

5713. 'Êdâh; this fem. noun originates from 5707. It means witness, something that testifies (Gen. 31:52), testimony (Gen. 21:30), attestation; prescription, a precept (of God, Ps. 119:22,24,59,79,138,146,168). This noun was used only of things affirming permanence and unequivocal facts such as ownership, a contract, or a covenant with God (Josh. 24:27).

5715. 'Êdûwth; this is a fem. noun deriving from 5707. It means testimony, witness, prescription, precept, law (especially the Ten Commandments) (Ex. 25:21; 16:34; II Kgs. 11:12), revelation (Ps. 60 [Title]; 80 [Title]), a reminder, a warning sign. This word is always used with reference to the testimony of God. It is most frequently connected with the tabernacle (Ex. 38:21; Num. 1:50,53). It was also closely associated with the ark (Ex. 25:22; 26:33,34; 30:6,26). Sometimes it stands alone and yet indicates the ark (Ex. 16:34; 27:21; 30:36; Lev. 16:13). *'Êdûwth* is clearly associated with the Law in Ps. 19 and Ps. 119. Samaria did not heed the warnings of the Lord (II Kgs. 17:15) to obey the Law of the Lord.

5749. 'Uwd; here is a rare case of a verb deriving from a noun, *'êd* (5707). It means to duplicate, to repeat, to say again and again; to protest, to testify (Amos 3:13; Mal. 2:14) against someone (I Kgs. 21:10,13) or in behalf of someone (Job 29:11; cf. Lk. 4:22), to attest, to assure, to exhort (Lam. 2:13); to surround (Ps. 119:61); to affirm solemnly, i.e., calling upon God as witness (Gen. 43:3; Deut. 8:19; 32:46; I Kgs. 2:42; Zech. 3:6); to be a witness, to take as a witness, to call as witness, to invoke (Deut. 4:26; 30:19; 31:28; Isa. 8:2; Jer. 32:10,25,44); to adjure, to admonish (Ex. 19:21; I Sam. 8:9) (see the Gr. *martureō*, 3140, in the N.T. lexical section), to warn (Gen. 43:3), to chide (Neh. 13:15,21), to comfort, to punish, to chastise; to be established, to stand upright, to confirm (Ps. 146:9; 147:6).

5753. 'Âvâh; to crook, to be bent, to writhe; to act perversely, to sin, to do wrong, to commit iniquity, to be perverse; to subvert (to distort, to twist), to turn upside down, to make impassable; to make crooked. This verb occurs seventeen times in the Heb. O.T. Its essential meaning is to deviate from the proper path. See Job 33:27; Ps. 38:6; Prov. 12:8; Isa. 24:1; Lam. 3:9.

5758. 'Ivyâ'; this is an Aramaic word from a root which corresponds to 5753. It means perverseness or iniquity. It occurs only in Dan. 4:27, but often in the Targums.

5760. 'Âvîyl; a Heb. noun which derives from 5765 and means perverse (morally), insolent, wicked, ungodly, evil. It is used only once in the O.T. (Job 16:11), as a label for Job's enemies from whom God had delivered him. There it should be translated "unjust one."

5765. 'Âval or **'ôwl;** to distort (morally), to deal unjustly, to be unrighteous, to do wrong, to act wickedly. There are only two occurrences (Ps. 71:4; Isa. 26:10).

5766. 'Evel or **'âvel** or **'avlâh** or **'ôwlâh** or **'ôlâh;** these nouns stem from 5765. The meaning is perverseness, wickedness, dishonesty, wrong, injustice, unrighteousness, depravity. See *adikia* (93) and *anomia* (458) in the N.T. lexical section.

5767. 'Avvâl; this mas. Heb. noun has its origin in 5765. It means a wicked one, an unrighteous one, a wrongdoer, an unjust one. It refers mostly to oppressive rulers in its five occurrences (Job 18:21; 27:7; 29:17; 31:3; Zeph. 3:5).

5769. 'Ôwlâm or **'ôlâm;** this Heb. noun comes from 5956. It is what is hidden, concealed (i.e., to the vanishing point); time immemorial, time past, antiquity (from the most ancient times, Gen. 6:4; I Sam. 27:8; Isa. 63:16; Jer. 2:20; 5:15; Ps. 25:6); eternity, the distant future (*terminus ad quem*); duration, perpetual, without end, always, everlasting time; lifetime. In the pl. form it means ages or endless times. The K.J.V. translates the word as "beginning of the world" in Isa. 64:4 and as "world" in Ps. 73:12 and Ecc. 3:11. There are 440 occurrences of *'ôwlâm* in the Heb. O.T. More than 300 of these instances indicate an indefinite continuance into the very near future. However, the meaning of the word is not confined to the future. There are at least twenty instances where *'ôwlâm* clearly refers to the past, though rately a limitless past. Deut. 32:7 and Job 22:15 point to the time of one's elders. Prov. 22:28; 23:10; Jer. 6:16; 18:15; 28:8 seem to go back even further. Sometimes the time just prior to the exile is referred to (Isa. 58:12; 61:4; Mic. 7:14; Mal. 3:4; Ezra 4:15,19). At other times it goes back further, to the events of the exodus from Egypt (I Sam. 27:8; Isa. 51:9; 63:9,11). Gen. 6:4 indicates the time shortly before the flood. The basic meaning of *'ôwlâm* is "most distant times," whether the remote past or the future, depending upon the accompanying prepositions. Therefore, *'ôwlâm* is a broad range between the remotest time and perpetuity (from the viewpoint of the speaker). Here are some examples: eternity in the sense of not being limited to the present (Ecc. 3:11); remotest time (I Chr. 16:36); either at the very beginning (Isa. 46:9) or from pre-creation unitl now (Ps. 25:6); from older times (Gen. 6:4), for a long time (Isa. 42:14); long ago (Jer. 2:20); formerly, in ancient times (Josh. 24:2); never (when used with the negative, Isa. 63:19); into the indefinite future (Deut. 23:3); forever (i.e., from the time of the speaker forward, I Sam. 1:22); as long as one lives (i.e., a simple duration extended into the indefinite future, Ex. 21:6); continuity without change (Gen. 3:22); day by day (Ps. 61:7,8); the most distant future (Gen. 9:16); without beginning, without end, and ever-continuing (Isa. 26:4). *'Ôwlâm*, the same Heb. word, can describe a short period of only three days (though it must have seemed like an eternity to Jonah as "forever," Jon. 2:6) or it can be used in conjunction with God—the God of eternity, the everlasting God, God forever. Temporal categories are inadequate to describe the nature of God's existence. The Creator has been "from everlasting to everlasting" (Ps. 90:2). Even then, it still expresses the idea of a continued, measurable existence, rather than a state of being independent of time considerations. *'Êl 'ôwlâm*, "the Everlasting God," was predominantly associated with Beersheba (Gen. 21:33). The God of Abraham was not touched by the vicissitudes of time. Compare Isa. 40:28. *'Ad* (5703, which see) has about the same spectrum of meaning as *'ôwlâm*. The Septuagint generally translates *'ôwlâm* by *aiōn* (165), cf. N.T. lexical section, referring to a long age or period of time, often translated as "world."

5771. 'Âvôn or **'âvôwn;** a depraved action (Gen. 4:13; 44:16), perversity, perverseness, sin, guilt, a crime, a fault, iniquity, mischief; punishment, the penalty of sin (Isa. 5:18); suffering, misery (Ps. 31:10). This Heb. noun derives from 5753. This is the abstract, crooked behavior or infraction of moral law. Note the collective nature of Gen. 15:16. The *'âvôn* (sing.) of the Amorite is not complete. The same is true of the widow of Zarephath (I Kgs. 17:18). The totality is clearly seen in Isa. 53:6. *'Âvôn* denotes both the deed and its consequences, though the focus may be on one or the other. On the misdeed (Isa. 30:13; cf. Ezek. 18:30; 44:12; Hos. 5:5; Job 31:11,28); on the punishment (Jer. 51:6; Ps. 39:11; 106:43; Job 13:26; 19:29; Ezra 9:7); on the guilt (I Sam. 25:24). Sin and the results of sin are much more closely associated in the O.T. than we tend to think of them. *'Âvôn* is often the sum of past misdeeds against God and man (Num. 14:34; I Sam. 25:24; II Sam. 22:24; I Kgs. 17:18; Ezra 9:6; Isa. 1:4; Jer. 11:10). On the other hand, *'âvôn* can refer to specific sins, e.g., adultery (Num. 5:31), idolatry (Hos. 5:5; Jer. 16:10,11), etc. *'Âvôn* results in separation from God, alienation (Lev. 26:40; Isa. 59:2), and uncleanness (Ps. 51:2). Man must be aware of *'âvôn* and confess it (Lev. 16:21: Neh. 9:2; Ps. 32:5; 38:18). He must direct his request to God (Ex. 34:9; Num. 14:19; Job 7:21; Ps. 25:11) and must change his way of life (Ezek. 18:30; 36:31). Provision was made for a substitute in punishment (Lev. 16:22; Isa. 53:5,6,11; Ezek. 4:4-6). God will forgive it (Num. 14:18; Ps. 51:2; 65:3; 78:38; 103:3; Prov. 16:6; Isa. 6:7; Jer. 32:18; 33:8; Ezek. 36:33; Dan. 9:24; Mic. 7:18,19; Zech. 3:4,9).

5785. 'Ôwr; this Heb. noun is a deriv. of 5783. It is skin (as naked, especially of a man. Ex. 34:30,35; Lev. 13:2; Job 7:5); leather (Lev. 4:11; 13:48), hide (of animals, Gen. 3:21; 27:16); body, flesh. On fifty-five occasions the skin of man is indicated by this word. Besides the outer covering of the body, it is used metonymically to indicate the entire body (Ex. 22:27; Job 19:26). The familiar expression, "the skin of the teeth" (Job 19:20) probably refers to the gums. *'Ôwr* is used forty-four times to indicate the skin of an animal, usually after skinning.

5789. 'Ûwsh; to hasten, to hurry up, to accelerate; to lend aid, to come to help. The word occurs only once (Joel 3:11).

5790. 'Ûwth; to hasten (in order to help); to support, to come to the aid. This term appears only one time (Isa. 50:4). The Latin Vulgate has *sustentare*.

5791. 'Âvath; to wrestle, to bend, to make crooked, to pervert (the cause of someone, Job 19:6; Ps. 119:78; Lam. 3:36); and to falsify, to corrupt, to seduce, to lead someone astray (Ps. 146:9), to subvert, to turn upside down; to be crooked, to be curved; to bend oneself, to stoop; to deal perversely; to overthrow. The meaning is shaky and unreliable, like the legs of an elderly man (Ecc. 12:3). The word pertains to dishonest business transactions in Amos 8:5. Bildad (Job 8:3) and Elihu (Job 34:12) argued that if Job is innocent, that would be tantamount to accusing God of perverting justice. Job's answer is found in Job 19:6,7. This world simply contains moral crookedness, and we have to accept that fact (Ecc. 1:15; 7:13). The psalmist appealed to God (Ps. 119:78).

5792. 'Avvâthâh; this Heb. noun has its origin in 5791. It means oppression or wrong. See Lam. 3:36,59, where injustice prevailed.

5800. 'Âzab; to loosen, to relinquish, to permit, to release, to set free; to leave, to forsake, to abandon, to leave behind; to omit, to relax; to be forsaken, to be abandoned. People (Gen. 44:22; Num. 10:31; Ruth 1:16; II Kgs. 4:30), places (II Kgs. 8:6; Jer. 18:14; 25:38), and objects (Gen. 39:12,13; 50:8; Ex. 9:21) can be left behind. To leave can mean to entrust (Gen. 39:6; Job 39:11), to expose (Job 39:14), to permit (Ruth 2:16), to allow to continue as is (Josh. 8:17; II Chr. 24:25; Ezek. 23:29), to neglect (Deut. 12:19; 14:27; Job 20:19), to put aside (Job 9:27), and to release (Job 10:1). Israel apostatized (Deut. 28:20; 31:16; Judg. 10:10; Jer. 1:16). And, in forsaking the Lord and following after idols, she was guilty of breaking the covenant (Deut. 29:25; I Kgs. 19:10,14; Jon. 2:8) and of committing spiritual adultery (Hos. 4:10). However, man may forsake sin (Prov. 28:13; Isa. 55:7). God will never forsake the righteous person by allowing him to fall into the hands of the wicked (Ps. 37:25,33). The Lord does not abandon the poor and the oppressed (Ps. 9:10; Isa. 41:17). God warned the nation of Israel that if they forsook Him, He would forsake them (II Chr. 12:1,5; 15:2). On the cross, when Jesus cried out, "My God, my God, why hast thou forsaken me?" He was quoting Ps. 22:1, probably in Aramaic translation. As far as their personal relationship, God had not forsaken His Son, but Jesus did have to go through the suffering alone.

5890. 'Êyphâh; this fem. Heb. noun comes from 5774. It means darkness or obscurity (as if from a covering). There are only two occurrences in the Heb. O.T. (Job 10:22; Amos 4:13).

5927. 'Âlâh; to ascend, to mount up, to go up, to rise; to grow up; to be lifted up, to be put up; to be led up, to be led away; to rise up; to be high, to be exalted; to cause to go up, to lead up, to bring up, to raise, to impose; to take away, to remove; to overlay (I Kgs. 10:17); to be brought up, to be offered; to be elated, to pride oneself. There are almost 900 occurrences of this verb in the Heb. O.T. The most common meanings are in the sense of going up (over 300 times), coming up (over 160 times) and ascending (seventeen times). The Heb. causative stems have two predominant meanings: (1) "to bring up" (more than 100 times); (2) "to offer" (seventy-seven times). The remaining uses of the term are translated with about eighty-five different words in the K.J.V. Here are some prominent examples: *'âlâh* is often used in traveling from a lower elevation to a higher one, e.g., from Egypt to Judea (Gen. 13:1; 44:24; Ex. 1:10), from Assyria (Isa. 36:1,10), from Babylonia (Ezra 2:1; Neh. 7:6), from all countries (Zech. 14:16,17). The temple sanctuary was located on a mountain, therefore, those who journeyed there "went up" (Ex. 34:24; I Sam. 1:3; 10:3). Most cities were built on hills or tels (Judg. 8:8; 20:18,31; I Sam. 9:11; Hos. 8:9). Princes resided in citadels (Num. 16:12,14; Judg. 4:5; 20:3; Ruth 4:1; Deut. 17:8). Vapor (Gen. 2:6) and smoke (Gen. 19:28) went up. Anger, like smoke, also "came up" (II Sam. 11:20; Ps. 18:8; 78:21,31). *'Âlâh* was sometimes used in conjunction with the morning (Gen. 19:15; 32:24,26) or plants (Gen. 40:10; 41:22; Deut. 29:23). *'Âlâh* was also used to describe a battle becoming heavy (I Kgs. 22:35), increasing wealth (Deut. 28:43), putting on a garment (Lev. 19:19), when a razor is used on the head (Judg. 16:17), and when God is exalted (Ps. 47:9; 97:9).

5928. 'Ălâh; this fem. Aramaic noun corresponds to 5930. It appears only once (Ezra 6:9). It means burnt offering.

5930. 'Ôlâh or **'ôwlâh;** this fem. act. part. has its source in 5927. A burnt offering (which "goes up" in smoke), a sacrifice which is entirely burned (Gen. 22:3,6; Lev. 1:4ff.), a holocaust; an ascent, stairs, ascending steps (Ezek. 40:26). As a nominal form, it occurs 286 times, sixty-three of which appear with the verb *'âlâh* (5927), "presenting a whole burnt offering" to God. The first instance is found in Gen. 8:20 where Noah built an altar. It could be a bull (Lev. 1:3-5), a sheep or a goat (Lev. 1:10), or a bird (Lev. 1:14). The worshipper placed his hands upon the sacrificial victim which symbolized the transmission of his sins to the animal. The killing took place on the north side of the altar. Then the priest took its blood and presented it before the Lord just prior to sprinkling it around the altar. For the poor, the priest received birds, wrung their necks, and allowed their blood to drain beside the altar (Lev. 1:15). The *'ôlâh* was then divided into sections and the purifiable parts were carefully arranged upon the altar (Lev. 1:6-9,12,13). The entire sacrifice was totally consumed by fire after that. The skin of the animal was given to the priest as his share (Lev. 7:8). This was the most frequent offering. Every day one male lamb was sacrificed, morning and evening (Ex. 29:38-42). Two young bulls, one ram, and seven male lambs were consecrated as a whole burnt offering each month. The same sacrifice was offered for each day of the festivals of Passover and Unleavened Bread (Num. 28:19-24) and the Feast of Weeks (Num. 28:26-29). The various purification rites required both whole burnt offerings and sin offerings. *'Ôlâh* signified the total surrender of a worshipper's heart and life to God. He also had the option of offering sin offerings (II Chr. 29:27) or peace offerings (II Chr. 29:31-35). Before the Law of Moses was instituted, *'ôlâh* had an all-inclusive meaning for different kinds of sacrifices.

5932. 'Alvâh; this Heb. noun stems from 5766 and means moral perverseness, iniquity, wrong, wickedness. Its only occurrence is found in Hos. 10:9. Since the first two consonants are transposed in many copies, some scholars believe that this single instance may be a transcriptional problem.

5943. 'Illay or **'Alyâh;** (see 5933). This is the Aramaic correlate to 5942. It refers to the Supreme (God), the Most High, the Highest One. It occurs nine times (Dan. 3:26; 4:2,17,24,25,34; 5:18,21; 7:25).

5945. 'Elyôwn; this Heb. adj. originates from 5927. It means elevated, high, exalted; the Most High, the Supreme Being (the true God). The Phoenicians and Carthagenians used a related word in speaking of their gods. The term occurs less than twenty-five times and is used to refer to Israel (Deut. 26:19; 28:1), the Davidic kings (Ps. 89:27), baskets (Gen. 40:17), rooms (Ezek. 41:7), gates (II Chr. 23:20), the upper pool (Isa. 7:3; II Kgs. 18:17), upper Beth-horon (Josh. 16:5), about one-third of the occurrences are adjectives or in apposition with one of the other divine names. The other two-thirds use it as a proper name for God, signifying the exaltedness, supremacy, and overwhelming majesty of deity. Appearing only in poetry, *'elyôwn* reflects omnipotence (Ps. 18:13; Lam. 3:38), universality (Ps. 83:18), and constancy (Ps. 21:7). The king of Babylon sinned in that he wanted to be like the Highest God (Isa. 14:14). It occurs in several compounds: (1) *'êl 'elyôwn,* which occurs in Gen. 14:18-22, the encounter between Melchizedek and Abraham. He possesses all the earth. See Ps. 78:35; cf. Num. 24:16. (2) *YHWH 'elyôwn* occurs in Ps. 7:17; 47:2; 97:9. (3) *'ĕlôhîym 'elyôwn* appears twice (Ps. 57:2; 78:56).

5946. 'Elyôwn; this is the Aramaic term corresponding to 5945. There are only four occurrences (Dan. 7:18,22,25,27). See *hupsistos* (5310) in Strong's Gr. Dictionary.

5957. 'Âlam; this is the Aramaic equivalent of 5769. It means remote time, antiquity, perpetuity. Its Heb. counterpart shows the tendency to change an accented "ā" to "o." This word can be used either with reference to the past (Ezra 4:15) or the future (Dan. 4:3; 4:34; 7:27). Compare Dan. 2:20.

5958. 'Elem or **'ôlâm;** it is not entirely certain what the source of this Heb. mas. noun is. It could be 'âlam (5956) or another root, *'-L-M,* "to be ripe," "to be mature." The fem. form is *'almâh* (5959), which see. The mas. form appears twice in the O.T. (I Sam. 17:56; 20:22). The term means one kept out of sight, a lad, a youth, a young man, a stripling, a male above the age of puberty. A close syn. is *na'ar* (5288) which occurs nearby (I Sam. 20:21) and in another 250 places. The reference is simply to the approximate age and vigor of the boy.

5959. 'Almâh; this fem. Heb. noun is probably the most controversial word in the entire O.T. because of its use in Isa. 7:14 and its connection with the virgin birth of Jesus Christ. Therefore, special treatment will be given to the meaning of the word, the meanings of other related words, the historical context of Isaiah's statement, the background of Mt. 1:23, and the Septuagint's rendering. First of all, there is no discrepancy whatsoever between Isa. 7:14 and Mt. 1:23! The absolute authority and inspiration of the Bible is quite sufficient to settle the question for the Christian. The Isaiah passage occurred about seven centuries before Jesus was born. Whatever it meant is discernible from the historical context of that time. The inspired, historical record of the virgin birth of our Lord does not depend upon Isa. 7:14. That event was narrated by Matthew and Luke and was an integral part of their accounts. The fact of the virgin birth of Christ is completely independent of the O.T. passage. If Matthew had never quoted the Septuagint's translation of Isa. 7:14, we believe that Jesus would still have been born of the virgin Mary. Secondly, because most people are more familiar with the Gospel accounts, perhaps it would be wise to study this first. The least controversial of the two accounts concerning Joseph and Mary is found in Lk. 2:1-20. Without any reference to Isa. 7:14, Luke refers to Mary as a *parthenos* (3933) in Lk. 1:27 (twice). She was betrothed to Joseph, a direct descendant to King David. However, the text makes it very clear that Mary was pure, i.e., she had no sexual experience with Joseph or any other man (Lk. 1:34). In other words, Mary was definitely a virgin. She called herself a *doulē* (1399), "a bondslave" (Lk. 1:38). Mt. 1:18 states that God's instructions came "before they came together" (sexually). And that this conception was "from the Holy Spirit." (See also Mt. 1:20.) It is interesting to note that the angel of the Lord who appeared in a dream to Joseph convinced him that Mary was still acceptable, because a miraculous conception had already been predicted by Isaiah. Mt. 1:23 was not merely a comment made by Matthew; it was part of the angel's message. Again, Mt. 1:25 reports that Joseph did not "know" (KJV) Mary until after she gave birth to Jesus. (For the meaning of this Gr. word, *ginōskō* (1097), see the Heb. *yâda'* (3045) in the O.T. lexical section; cf. Gen. 4:1.) In quoting Isa. 7:14, Matthew chose not to mention certain aspects of the underlying Heb. word (*'almâh*) or the original historical setting of Isaiah's conversation with King Ahaz. Matthew simply quoted the authoritative Septuagint, the ancient Greek translation of the O.T., which had *parthenos* in Isa. 7:14. Was *parthenos* an accurate translation of the Heb. *'almâh?* Was Matthew wrong to use it? How did Isa. 7:14 apply to Joseph and Mary? Thirdly, concerning the meaning of *parthenos,* its etymology is uncertain. At first, in Classical Greek literature, the word was used in the general sense of "girl" or "young woman." Long before the Septuagint was translated (second century B.C.?), this Gr. word had no specific connotation of virginity. *Parthenos* was a young female individual who was in the process of maturing. However, in time *parthenos* gradually became more specialized to mean a woman with no sexual experience, our English "virgin." The word *parthenos* appears a total of sixty-five times in the Septuagint with the meaning of "virgin." The Heb. *b^{e}thûwlâh* (1330) was translated with *parthenos* forty-five times, the kindred *b^{e}thûwlîym* (1331) was translated with *parthenos* once. *Parthenos* was used to translate *na'ărâh* (5291) five times and *'almâh* twice. The relevant passages are Gen. 24:43; 34:3 and Isa. 7:14. In Gen. 24:43, *parthenos* translates *'almâh* in describing Rebekah. Earlier in Gen. 24:16 Rebekah is called a *na'ărâh* and a *b^{e}thûwlâh* "whom no man had known." The Septuagint translates both of these words with *parthenos*. It is extremely important that one understands the implication of this passage. The key words (both Heb. and Gr.) all converge here to teach us that one can look at the same referent (Rebekah) from several different angles. It also shows that at the time when the Septuagint was translated, *parthenos* had a broader range of meaning. In this context *b^{e}thûwlâh* simply means "young girl" with no particular reference to virginity, while it is used metaphorically in most other places. In Gen. 34:3 the word *parthenos* appears twice as a translation of *na'ărâh.* Concerning the use of *parthenos* in Isa. 7:14, how should we interpret it? Why did the Septuagint translators use *parthenos* here? On four other occasions they used the Gr. word *neanis* to translate *'almâh.* Later Greek translators of the O.T.—Aquila, Symmachus, and Theodotion—all rendered Isa. 7:14 with *neanis.* Since they were post-N.T., they all had a conscious purpose in doing so, namely to avoid further use of *parthenos* which favored the virgin birth of Jesus. The Septuagint had no ulterior motive to translate Isa. 7:14 with any other Gr. word. As we will see, *parthenos* was quite adequte to translate *'almâh.* *Parthenos* was used of both a virgin and a non-virgin in the Septuagint and in earlier Classical Greek. Isa. 7:14 was discussing a mature young woman and was not focusing on sexual experience in that context. The translators of the Septuagint found nothing mysterious in the passage, and *parthenos* was generally used for "girl" or "young woman" (Gen. 24:16,43). If one maintains that *parthenos/almâh* only means "virgin," he would have a definite problem: besides the fulfillment in Mt. 1:23, he would have to take the position that there was another virgin birth (conception) in the time of King Ahaz! Such an individul would have to ignore the specific historic circumstances which were explicitly detailed by the prophet in connection with the child's birth and early life in the time of Isaiah. The truth is probably this: In Isa. 7:14 a young girl of marriageable age who was a virgin *at that time* would soon marry and give birth to a baby in the normal way. The child would not reach the age of moral accountability before the events which Isaiah prophesied would come to pass. The Heb. text is ambiguous and could be translated either "*is* with child" or "*will* be with child." However, the Septuagint makes it explicit with the future tense. They understood that there was a woman who was currently a virgin (at the time Isaiah was speaking to Ahaz), but, later, she would conceive after losing her virginity to her new husband. *Parthenos* was a good choice of words by the Septuagint translators, becaue it was flexible and potentially prophetic of the Messiah. We are committed to this position, because Matthew gives the inspired interpretation of Isa. 7:14. No one understood the far-reaching implications of *parthenos* in Isa. 7:14 until after it was quoted in Mt. 1:23. Fourthly, the Heb. word *'almâh* may not be derived from *'âlam* (5957), as many first thought. Modern lexicographers and Hebraists now believe that the source of *'almâh* was the Heb. root *'-L-M,* "to be ripe" or "to be mature." One can easily see how the noun form came to mean being of marriageable age, the age of puberty, a young woman (who is sexually ripe), a maid or newly married girl, a mature woman who is near marriage. The English word "virgin" applies to such an individual or not, depending on the specific context, e.g., Dinah, Rebekah, the woman in Isa. 7, etc. The cognate word in several other Semitic languages seems to refer to a state of maturity, leaving the status of virginity open. Therefore, the primary meaning of *'almâh* has to do with sexual maturity (the age of a young woman), not with her sexual experience or lack of it. Usually *'almâh* would not be used to define her virginity, but her capacity for marriage. There are only nine occurrences of *'almâh* in the Heb. O.T. Two of these passages (I Chr. 15:20 and the title of Ps. 46) are musical terms, perhaps referring to young female singers, soprano voices, treble, or even falsetto mode. The other seven references are: Gen. 24:43; Ex. 2:8; Ps. 68:25; Prov. 30:19; Song of Sol. 1:3; 6:8; Isa. 7:14. From Gen. 24:16 in the story about Rebekah, *b^ethûwlâh* seems to be used deliberately when her virginity was specified. The fact that Gen. 24:43 uses *'almâh* does not mean that the emphasis of *'almâh* is upon the strict state of virginity, but it does show that *'almâh* does at least include that meaning in this context. Since Miriam, Moses' sister, was still living in her father's house and presumably unmarried, we could probably safely assume that she was a virgin. Ps. 68:25 does not specify whether the girls were married or unmarried. They were old enough to play timbrels in the solemn religious processions to the temple. Prov. 30:19 may refer to sexual love. There is nothing in the context of Song of Sol. 1:3 which informs us about the sexual status of these young women. Song of Sol. 6:8 is ambiguous about the precise status in the king's harem. In none of the passages is there any overt reference to the sexual experience of these girls as such. The word *'almâh* simply indicated a young woman who was sexually mature, capable of having sexual intercourse, but not specifying whether or not she has had it. Whether or not she has had sexual experience must be inferred from the historical context and it is independent of the meaning of the word itself. Virginity is neither included nor excluded per se. Also, the young woman may be married or not married. Many believe that *b^ethûwlâh,* from the presumed root *B-T-L,* "to sever" or "to separate," was the technical term for "virgin" in the Heb. O.T. In other words, she was a young girl who was separated (from men). The word occurs some fifty times in the O.T. The term is often used naturally in passages where the lack of sexual experience is not a significant factor (cf. II Chr. 36:17; Ps. 148:12; Isa. 23:4; Jer. 31:13; 51:22; Lam. 1:4,18; 2:10,21; Ezek. 9:6; Amos 8:13; Zech. 9:17). *B^ethûwlâh* is also used metaphorically (II Kgs. 19:21; Isa. 23:12; 47:1; Jer. 14:17; 18:13; 31:4,21; 46:11; Lam. 1:15; 2:13; Amos 5:2). Usually, *b^ethûwlâh* is the specific, precise Heb. word which was used to refer to the lack of sexual experience on the part of a young woman. However, there is a particular Ugaritic text in which *'almâh* and *b^ethûwlâh* are parallel in meaning: "A virgin (*b^ethûwlâh*) will give birth . . . Lo, a maid (*'almâh*) will bear a son." (See Cyrus H. Gordon, *Journal of Bible and Religion,* XXI, 1953, p. 106). So, *b^ethûwlâh* can be used in the general sense for maidens, young women, or girls, where their lack of sexual experience is not a factor. The fem. Heb. noun *na'ărâh* occurs some sixty-three times in the O.T. It may be used of a virgin (cf. Gen. 24:14,-16a; Deut. 22:25,28; I Kgs. 1:3,4; Esth. 2:7,9,12) or of a non-virgin (cf. Deut. 22:19a,20,21,24,26 [twice]; Judg. 19:3,4,5,6,8,9; Ruth 2:5,6; 4:12; Amos 2:7). Where virginity is a factor, the phrase, *na'ărâh b^ethûwlâh"* is used (Deut. 22:23; Judg. 21:12; I Kgs. 1:2; Esth. 2:2). It also means "maiden," in the sense of "female attendant" or "servant girl" (cf. Gen. 24:61; Ex. 2:5; Ruth 2:8,22,23; 3:2; I Sam. 9:11; 25:42; Esth. 2:9; 4:4,16; Prov. 9:3; 31:15). This word emphasizes youth. *Yaldâh* (3207) occurs three times: in Gen. 34:4 where it is used to describe Dinah, who was of marriageable age but no longer a virgin; in Joel 3:3, "girls" (Septuagint has *korasia,* 2877); and in Zech. 8:5, "boys and girls (*korasia*)." This Heb. word is also neutral in itself, so far as sexual experience is concerned. It is a virtual equivalent of *na'ărâh.* Fifthly, since *'almâh* is a neutral word, so far as virginity is concerned, and can be inferred or not, depending on the historical context of the passage where the word is used, it is imperative that we now examine the context and historical setting of Isa. 7:14 in order to determine the exact meaning of *'almâh* in that particular passage. Why did not Isaiah use the precise, technical term for "virgin," i.e., *b^ethûwlâh* in Isa. 7:14? Was Isaiah proclaiming a parthenogenesis in his own time? Why did Isaiah use a word (*'almâh*) which is in itself somewhat vague concerning virginity? The historical situation was as follows: About B.C. 734, Pekah, the king of Israel, made an alliance with Rezin, the king of Syria, and marched against Ahaz, the king of Judah. When Ahaz heard this news, he lost heart. The Prophet Isaiah went to Ahaz (a man who had indulged in pagan worship, cf. II Kgs. 16:1-4; II Chr. 28:1-4) with a message of redemption (Isa. 7: 3-9). However, this salvation was contingent upon Ahaz' faith. "If you will not believe, you surely shall not last." Isaiah told the king to ask for a sign from Jehovah, of whatever nature he deisred, to validate the message of Isaiah, but the king refused the offer. However, Isaiah gave the sign (*'ôwth*): "Behold, a virgin (*'almâh*) will be with child and bear a son, and she will call His name Immanuel." (Isa. 7:14). In Isa. 7:15-25 the prophet gives further details concerning the historical events which would take place in the early childhood of this boy. What was the purpose of this prophecy and the corroborating proof of divine attestation? Clearly, Isaiah was addressing himself to a contemporary situation in which a Jewish king was facing danger. There is little doubt that the meaning is that this promised child would be fulfilled soon, when he was old enough to exercise moral discrimination. In other words, Isaiah was predicting that the northern kingdom of Israel and Syria would be left desolate (Isa. 7:16). Was Isaiah predicting an immediate virgin birth? No. There was no notion of a virgin birth among the Hebrews until the time of Jesus Christ. If Isaiah had meant to say that, he would have probably used the word *b^ethûslâh,* which does occur elsewhere in the book, cf. 23:4,12; 37:22; 47:1; 62:5. Even then, Ahaz would not have perceived it as a virgin birth, but only that a virgin *at that time* would subsequently marry and give birth to a son in the normal manner. The promised *'ôwth* in the time of Isaiah did not have much to do with an extraordinary conception. The crux of the meaning was the name Immanuel ("God with us"), which reassured King Ahaz that he was not being abandoned despite his unfaithfulness to the Lord. The sign did not refer merely to the birth of the child, but to the whole and sudden sequence of events which were prophesied in Isa. 7:14-17 and expanded in Isa. 7:18-25. In the seven other passages in the O.T. where the Heb. adj. *hârâh* (2029) is used in the predicate position, as in Isa. 7:14, four of them occur in narratives where conception has already taken place (Gen. 38:24,25; I Sam. 4:19; II Sam. 11:5). In the other three passages, the adj. is used in promises which were made to women that they would bear a child in Gen. 16:11 (to Hagar, who was already pregnant) and in Judg. 13:5,7 (to the wife of Manoah, who conceived soon afterward). Therefore, it is quite possible that the *'almâh* to whom Isaiah referred was already pregnant, or, at least, would soon be so. The secondary fulfillment in Mt. 1:23 was of no interest or relevance to King Ahaz. Surely we must assume that a child was conceived and born in the normal way during the lifetime of Ahaz. Otherwise, Isaiah's prophecy was not pertinent at all to the contemporary historical situation. Throughout the entire passage (Isa. 7:13—8:22), the person of the child is inextricably connected with the events which were being forecasted. The identity of the *'almâh* in Isa. 7:14 remains a matter of speculation. It is possible that she was the wife of the prophet himself (Isa. 8:3).

5971. 'Am; a people (as a congregated unit), a nation, a tribe (Lev. 21:1,4; 19:16), a community; the common people, men (human beings in general, i.e., the whole human race, Isa. 40:7; 42:5; 44:7; Job 12:2), mankind, inhabitants, the populace, folk; countrymen (Ruth 1:16); servants (of a private master, I Kgs. 19:21; II Kgs. 4:41); a herd (of animals, Prov. 30:25,26; Ps. 74:14). See the Heb. synonyms *gôwy* (1471) and *l^eôm* (3816). *'Am* is different in that it is the view of an insider of the group or it refers to "people" in general. Usually, it denotes a group of people which is larger than a tribe or a clan, but less numerous than a race (*l^eôm*). An *'am* is a group which has certain unified, sustained relationships within itself. It may be characterized by religious fellowship (Gen. 17:14), a maternal relationship (Gen. 17:16), an ancestral relationship (Gen. 25:8,17; 49:33), family ties (Gen. 36:6), social inter-relationships (Num. 5:27) or adoption (Ruth 1:16). The first time when God referred to the descendants of Abraham as "my people" was Ex. 3:7ff. See also Ps. 78:52-66; 95:7. He sealed this relationship and solidified their relatedness by delivering them as a people from Egypt (Ex. 5:1ff.). Israel was called the people of God (Ex. 15:13; Deut. 32:36), the holy people (Deut. 7:6), and those who particularly belonged to God (Deut. 4:20). Probably the most famous use of the term is found in Hos. 1:9,10; 2:23, where the covenant people were so completely unfaithful to God that He promises to have a new relationship with Gentiles. See the Apostle Paul's comments in Rom. 9:22-26. Although many of the Jews turned away from God and were punished (Jer. 15:7), God promised to maintain a remnant *'am* (Isa. 11:11,16; 46:3; cf. Ex. 8:9,11). Not everyone among God's people would be a biological descendant of Abraham (Isa. 19:25; Ps. 87). See *dēmos* (1218) and *laos* (2992) in the N.T. lexical section.

5972. 'Am; this Aramaic noun corresponds to 5971. It is used in Dan. 3:4,7,29; 4:1; 5:19; 6:25; 7:14 with the general sense of "men" or "folk."

5999. 'Âmâl; this mas. Heb. noun originates from 5998. It means heavy labor (Ecc. 1:3; 2:11), toil; gain by labor, the produce of labor (Ps. 105:44; Ecc. 2:19); trouble, misery, distress, sorrow, suffering; mischief, wrong, oppression, iniquity, perverseness, travail; weariness (Gen. 41:51; Deut. 26:7; Job 3:10; 16:2; Isa. 53:11), effort, worry, and wickedness. This word definitely has a negative connotation. It contains the nuance of drudgery, rather than noble work. In other words, this is the dark side of labor, the unsatisified feeling of being on a treadmill. See the Gr. word *ponos* (4192) in the N.T. lexical section.

6001. 'Âmêl; this Heb. adj. derives from 5998. It means laboring (to the point of exhaustion), toiling (Ecc. 2:18,22; 3:9; 4:8; 9:9); suffering, misery (Job 3:20), wretched (Job 3:20; 20:22); (as a sub.) a workman (Prov. 16:26), a laborer, an artisan (Judg. 5:26). There is a total of nine occurrences in the Heb. O.T.

6012. 'Âmêq; as a deriv. of 6009, this Heb. adj. means deep (literally or figuratively), unintelligible, strange. It appears four times in the Heb. O.T. and only in the pl. construction. The term is used to describe an obscure foreign language which cannot be understood; literally "deep of lip." See Prov. 9:18; Isa. 33:19; Ezek. 3:5,6.

6049. 'Ânan; this root means to cover; to act covertly, to practice magic (Deut. 18:10,14; II Kgs. 21:6; Isa. 2:6; 57:3; Mic. 5:12), to soothsay, to divine; (when used as a part.) a sorcerer, an enchanter; to gather clouds (Gen. 9:14). Some scholars believe that there is no connection between occultism and clouds. Therefore, two homophonous roots may have existed. On the other hand, some may have studied cloud patterns to gain information about the future, much as some examine the entrails of animals, use tarot cards, or read palms or tea leaves. Spiritism was forbidden (Lev. 19:26), and it was among the sins of Manasseh (II Chr. 33:6).

6050. 'Ănan; this is the Aramaic correlate to the Heb. 6051, meaning cloud. Its sole occurrence is found in Dan. 7:13.

6051. 'Ânân; this Heb. noun has its origin in 6049. It is a cloud (covering the sky), a thunder-cloud, clouds; a crowd, a host, a very large army (Ezek. 30:18; 38:9). A morning cloud was used as the timage of something transient (Hos. 6:4; cf. Job 7:9). Of the total of eighty occurrences in the Heb. O.T., about three-fourths of them refer to the pillar of cloud which directed the Israelites through the desert. It represented the presence of God over the tabernacle (Ex. 13,14,16,33,40; Num. 9—12,14,16). In Num. 9:15-22 alone *'ânân* is used eleven times. The cloud was present in or over the temple of Solomon (cf. I Kgs. 8:10,11; II Chr. 5:13,14). Clouds accompanied the presence of God at Mount Sinai (Ex. 19:9,16; 24:15,16,18; Deut. 4:11; 5:22; Ps. 97:2). They have eschatological importance (Ezek. 30:3; 32:7; Joel 2:2; Zeph. 1:15; cf. Dan. 7:13; Mt. 17:5; 24:30; 26:64; Acts 1:9; I Cor. 10:1,2; I Thess. 4:17; Rev. 1:7; 10:1; 11:12; 14:14,15,16).

6064. 'Ânash; this verbal root means to urge, to inflict a penalty, to impose a fine (Deut. 22:19), to enforce a contribution, to exact sums of money in war (II Chr. 36:3); to punish, to be punished (Prov. 22:3; 27:12); to be fined (Ex. 21:22). This is a term of legal redress, a monetary fine which was assessed for a criminal act.

6065. 'Ănash; this is the Aramaic equivalent of 6064. It occurs only once in the O.T. (Ezra 7:26). It means confiscation.

6066. 'Ônesh; this mas. Heb. noun has its origin in 6064. It means contribution, fine, punishment, penalty (Prov. 19:19), tribute (II Kgs. 23:33), money exacted from someone. The word occurs only twice.

6080. 'Âphar; this denominative verb occurs only once (II Sam. 16:13), where Shimei was harassing David and his men along the road, cursing, throwing stones, and showering him with dirt. This pelting with dust showed Shimei's absolute hatred for David.

6083. 'Âphâr; this mas. Heb. noun occurs 109 times in the O.T. It means dust, fine particles of earth, dry earth, fine dust (as blown by the wind, Ps. 18:42), soil, loam, clay (Lev. 14:42,45), lumps (of gold, Job 28:6), clods (of earth, Prov. 8:26); ground, the ground (Job 22:24; Isa. 47:1), earth, mortar, ashes, a heap of rubbish (Hab. 1:10), powder; gold dust; the grave (Job 20:11; 21:26); the world (Job 19:25; 39:14; 41:33). The usual meaning is dust or loose earth (Gen. 2:7; 26:15; Josh. 7:6; Job 2:12). Throwing dust upon one's head was a sign of grief and mourning or distress (Job 2:12; Lam. 2:10; Ezek. 27:30; Mic. 1:10; Mt. 11:21; Acts 22:23). There are several expressions which incorporate the word *'âphâr.* returning to the dust (Gen. 3:19; Ps. 104:29) means to die and to be buried. "Dust and ashes" was a proverbial phrase to express the lowliness and fragility of human nature (Gen. 18:27). "The dust of Jacob" shows the numerous descendants of Jacob (Num. 23:10. Lam. 3:29 has ". . . put his mouth in the dust," i.e., to be silent and wait for God's help. Man must never forget where he came from, or the God who made him (Isa. 29:16; 45:9; 64:8; Jer. 18:1-14; cf. Rom. 9:21).

6087. 'Âtsab; properly, this root means to carve, i.e., to fabricate or fashion (later, an image), form or shape; to worry, to grieve oneself, to be sorrowful; to afflict, to grieve, to pain; to offend; to be angry. It is a term of physical and mental discomfort. It described the feeling of anguish felt by Joseph's brothers when they recognized him for the first time in Egypt (Gen. 45:5) or the emotion of shock when the Israelites heard the Torah after a long hiatus (Neh. 8:10,11). Israel "grieved" the Holy Spirit of God (Isa. 63:10; cf. Eph. 4:30). It depicts a feeling of outrage, e.g., the brothers of Dinah when they learned of how their sister had been raped (Gen. 34:7). Prior to the flood, when God considered the abject wickedness of mankind and their continual patterns of evil thoughts, He felt great sorrow (Gen. 6:6).

6088. 'Ătsab; this Aramaic word corresponds to the Heb. 6087. Its only occurrence is in Dan. 6:20.

6089. 'Etseb; this Heb. mas. noun stems from 6087. It is a thing formed or shaped; an earthen vessel; labor, toil, gain; trouble, grievance; the kind of pain which women experience when they are about to give birth (Gen. 3:16). See also Ps. 127:2; Prov. 5:10; 10:22; 14:23; 15:1; Jer. 22:28. There are seven occurrences in the O.T.

6090. 'Ôtseb; this mas. Heb. noun is a variant of 6089. It means image, idol (Isa. 48:5; Ps. 139:24); pain, labor, affliction, sorrow (I Chr. 4:9; Isa. 14:3). There are four appearances.

6091. 'Âtsâb; this mas. Heb. noun occurs only in the pl. and it derives from 6087. It referred to the false images of idols (I Sam. 31:9; II Sam. 5:21; Hos. 4:17). Even though these idols were made of precious silver and gold, they were poor substitutes for the living God (Ps. 115:3-11).

6092. 'Âtsêb; this Heb. word is a deriv. of 6087. It is a (hired) workman or laborer. Its lone occurrence is found in Isa. 58:3.

6093. 'Itstsâbôwn; this Heb. noun arises from 6087. It means worrisomeness, labor, toil, hard work (Gen. 3:17; 5:29); pain, sorrow, birth pangs (Gen. 3:16), being in labor. These are the only three occurrences in the O.T.

6094. 'Atstsebeth; this mas. Heb. noun originates from 6087. It is an idol; a pain, a wound; sorrow, affliction, grievance. There are only five occurrences in the Heb. O.T. (Job 9:28; Ps. 16:4; 147:3; Prov. 10:10; 15:13).

6098. 'Êtsâh; this fem. Heb. noun comes from 3289. It means counsel, advice; consultation; purpose, project, plan, design; wisdom, deliberation. The noun is translated in the Septuagint by *boulē* (1012), a Gr. word of enormous theological significance in the N.T. (see Acts 2:23; 4:28; 5:38,39; 20:27; Eph. 1:11; Heb. 6:17). Rehoboam rejected the counsel of the older men of Israel (I Kgs. 12:8,13). Similarly, Absalom rejected Ahithophel's good advice (II Sam. 17).

6106. 'Etsem; this Heb. noun is traceable to 6105. It means bone (in the sense of strong and firm, Gen. 2:23; Ex. 12:46; Num. 9:12); body, frame, a bodily frame (Lam. 4:7); substance (Ex. 24:10), essence, self; the same. When followed by a gen., it is used instead of the pron. itself (Gen. 7:13; 17:23,26; Ex. 24:10; Job 21:23). *'Etsem* was often used of the bones of the dead (Ex. 13:19; Josh. 24:32; II Sam. 21:12-14; II Kgs. 23:18,20). The well-known expression "bone and flesh" was descriptive of a close genetic relationship (Gen. 29:14; Judg. 9:2; II Sam. 5:1; II Sam. 19:13; I Chr. 11:1). The pl. was often used to refer to the corpse (Gen. 50:25; II Sam. 21:12-14). Jeremiah spoke of God's message as a burning fire shut up in his bones (Jer. 20:9; cf. 23:9), a parallel to "heart."

6116. 'Ătsârâh or **'ătsereth;** this fem. noun derives from 6113. It is a solemn assembly (especially a festival), a festive gathering, a holiday meeting.

6117. 'Âqab; to swell out, to swell up; to seize by the heel (which curves outward and is therefore last), to come from behind; to circumvent (as if tripping up the heels), to throw someone down; to supplant (Gen. 27:36), to defraud (Jer. 9:4), to deceive; to keep back, to restrain, to retard (Job 37:4). Jacob is a proper name which derives from this denominative verb. See Gen. 25:21-26 for the account of his birth, along with his twin brother, Esau. Jacob was so named because he was grasping Esau's heel at birth. This proved to be prophetic, because Jacob was a very shrewd and crafty person. He talked Esau out of his birthright for just one meal (Gen. 25:31-33; Heb. 12:16). Jacob was deceptive when he deceived his father Isaac to bless him instead of Esau (Gen. 27:18-29). However, he received some of his own medicine later (Gen. 27:42,43). Eventually, he became reverent (Gen. 28:10,20,21), affectionate (Gen. 29:18), industrious (Gen. 31:40), prayerful (Gen. 32:9-12,24-30), disciplined (Gen. 42:36), and a hero of faith (Heb. 11:21).

6119. 'Âqêb or **'iqq^{e}bâh;** this mas. Heb. noun originates from 6117. It is a protuberant, a heel (of men, Gen. 3:15; Job. 18:9; Jer. 13:22; Song of Sol. 1:8; of horses (Gen. 49:17; Judg. 5:22); a step (Ps. 56:6), a footprint (Ps. 77:19; 89:51); the extreme rear of an army (Josh. 8:13; Gen. 49:19); a lier in wait (Ps. 49:5). Ps. 77:19 speaks of when Jehovah led Israel through the Red Sea, which obliterated the tracks of the Israelites when the water came back together again. The metaphorical "lifting up the heel" (Ps. 41:9), was quoted by Jesus in Jn. 13:18 to describe the treachery of Judas Iscariot. Probably the most famous usage is found in Gen. 3:15 where mankind (particulary Jesus) achieves victory over Satan, but at a tremendous cost—the cross. Compare Rom. 16:20.

6121. 'Âaqôb; this Heb. word, arising from 6117, is a knoll, a hill (which swells up), an uneven place; deceitful (Jer. 17:9), fraudulent, crooked, polluted; a lier in wait. They conceived of hills as retarding the progress of those who were going upward (Isa. 40:4). There are only three occurrences.

6148. 'Ârab; this root means to braid, to intermix (Ps. 106:35; Prov. 14:10; 20:19; 24:21), to interweave, to intermingle, to have intercourse; to traffic (as if by barter, Ezek. 27:9,27), to exchange; to mortgage, to pledge (Neh. 5:3), to give security, to be a co-signer (liable for another's debt, Prov. 11:15; 20:16; 27:13), to be a guarantor for the life of another (Gen. 43:9; 44:32; cf. Job 17:3; Isa. 38:14; Ps. 119:22), to warrant, to rival, to undertake; to dare (i.e., risk one's life, Jer. 30:21). In II Kgs. 18:23 and Isa. 36:8 the Hithpael means "to make a wager."

6151. 'Ărab; this Aramaic correlate to 6148 means to commingle or to mix. It occurs only in Dan. 2:41 and Dan. 2:43 (three times).

6154. 'Êreb or **'ereb;** this mas. Heb. noun derives from 6148. It is a web (the transverse threads of cloth); woof (Lev. 13:48-59), weft; a mixture (a mongrel race), a mixed multitude, and promiscuous mass of foreigners, strangers, and wanderers (Ex. 12:38; Neh. 13:3).

6160. 'Ărâbâh; this fem. noun has its origin in 6150. It means dry land, a desert (Job 24:5; Isa. 33:9; 35:1; 51:3; Jer. 50:12; 51:43); a wilderness, a desert plain, steppe. The Arabah was the low region into which the valley of the Jordan River runs near Jericho (Deut. 1:1; 2:8; Josh. 12:1; II Sam. 4:7; II Kgs. 25:5). This word has the distinct flavor of sterility.

6161. 'Ărubbâh; this is a fem. pass. part. which derives from 6048. It means bargain, exchange, pawn, surety; pledge (I Sam. 17:18), something given as security (Prov. 17:18) or a token. These are the only two occurrences in the Heb. O.T.

6162. 'Ărâbôwn; this mas. Heb. noun comes from 6148. It is a pledge, warrant-money, a pawn (given as security). The term appears only three times in the Heb. O.T. (Gen. 38:17,18,20). This word was peculiar to traders. The Greeks and Romans seem to have borrowed it from the Phoenicians. It is an important loanword in the N.T. (Eph. 1:14; cf. II Cor. 5:5), referring to the Holy Spirit as the guarantee of our inheritance in Heaven. See *arrhabōn* (728) in the N.T. lexical section.

6172. 'Ervâh; this fem. Heb. noun has its source in 6166. It means nudity (literal, Hos. 2:9; metaphorical, i.e., unfortified land, easy access, Gen. 42:9,12), nakedness, bareness, the pudenda, the genitals (Gen. 9:22,23; Lev. 20:11; I Sam. 20:30); shame, disgrace, blemish, a defect (in a woman, Deut. 24:1); a shameful thing, a foul thing, ignominy (Isa. 20:4); filthiness, uncleanness, excrement (Deut. 23:4).

6174. 'Ârôwm or **'ârôm;** this Heb. adj. comes from 6191. It means nude, naked (Job 1:21), bared, half-dressed, ragged, badly clad (Job 22:6; 24:7,10; Isa. 58:7). See *gumnos* (1131) in the N.T. lexical section. Js. 2:15 refers to the clothing of extremely poor people. Also, *gumnos* was used to describe Peter's appearance at the Sea of Galilee (Jn. 21:7). *'Ârôwm* was used of one who had taken off his mantle and was dressed only in his tunic (I Sam. 19:24; Isa. 20:2).

6175. 'Ârûwm; this Heb. adj. has its origin in 6191. It means cunning, crafty (Gen. 3:1; Job 5:12; 15:5), sly, subtle; prudent (Prov. 12:16,23). The connotation is determined by the context. See *phronimos* (5429) in the N.T. lexical section.

6181. 'Eryâh; this fem. Heb. noun arises from 6172. It means nudity, nakedness, bareness; want (Ezek. 16:7). Hab. 3:9 is rather emphatic: "Thy bow was made bare," literally, will be made naked with nakedness.

6183. 'Ârîyph; this Heb. mas. noun appears only in the pl. form, deriving from 6201. It means the sky (as though drooping at the horizon), the clouds, the darkness of clouds, heaven. Its lone occurrence is found in Isa. 5:30.

6189. 'Ârêl; this Heb. adj., stemming from 6188, means exposed (projecting loosely, i.e., the foreskin), still having the prepuce uncurtailed, uncircumcised, unclean, unconsecrated, having the foreskin intact. Israel never had a monopoly on circumcision as a surgical operation. However, circumcision was instituted by God in Gen. 17 as a token of His covenant with Abraham and his descendants. Every male, whether free or slave, was commanded to be circumcised at the age of eight days. The uncircumcised were to be cut off from the community. This act of the Patriarchal covenant was reaffirmed in the Law of Moses (Lev. 12:3). In Ex. 4:24-26, scholars differ regarding who was in danger. The "uncircumcised" was a term which was used pejoratively of the Gentiles, particularly the Philistines (Judg. 14:3; 15:18; I Sam. 14:6; 17:26,26; 31:4; II Sam. 1:20; I Chr. 10:4). This term was associated with moral and spiritual uncleanness (Isa. 52:1). Metaphorically, it was used of uncircumcised lips which were closed with the foreskin and too thick to utter speech with ease (Ex. 6:12,30). "Closed ears" could not hear God's message (Jer. 6:10). For an uncircumcised heart, see Lev. 26:41; Ezek. 44:9. Therefore, Israel was commanded to circumcise the foreskin of the heart (Deut. 10:16; Jer. 4:4; cf. Rom. 2:28,29). See *peritomē* (4061) and *akrobustia* (203) in the N.T. lexical section.

6190. 'Orlâh; this fem. Heb. noun is a deriv. of 6189. It is the prepuce, the foreskin; uncleanness, insensibility; unclean fruit. See *mûwl* (4135), "to circumcise."

6191. 'Âram; this root means to be bare, to be smooth; to be cunning, to be crafty (I Sam. 23:22; Ps. 83:3); to act craftily, to form a cunning plan, to deal subtly; to act prudently (Prov. 15:5; 19:25). Since it is a neutral term, the context determines the nuance.

6192. 'Âram; this root is homophonous with 5191. It means to pile up, to gather together; to be heaped up, to be amassed. It appears only once in the Heb. O.T. (Ex. 15:8).

6193. 'Ôrem or **'Êrôm** or **'ârôm;** this mas. Heb. noun is traceable to 6191. It means strategem; cunning, craftiness. Its lone appearance is found in Job 5:13.

6195. 'Ormâh or **'arêmâh;** this fem. Heb. noun is a deriv. of 6193. It means trickery, guile (Ex. 21:14), subtlety, williness (Josh. 9:4), cunning, craft; prudence (Prov. 1:4; 8:5,12), discretion, wisdom. There are only five occurrences.

6201. 'Âraph; this verbal root means to droop, to drip, to drop down. Metaphorically, it was used of speech in Deuteronomy (32:2; 33:28).

6205. 'Ărâphel; this Heb. mas. noun probably derives from 6201. It means gloom (like a frowning sky); thick, dark clouds; darkness. The term probably is the result of a merging of *'ârîyph* (6183), "sky," and *'âphêl* (651), "dark." It is a rare four-consonant Heb. word in the O.T. It was used to describe the thick darkness which enveloped the appearance of Jehovah on Mount Sinai (Ex. 20:21; cf. Deut. 4:11). The glory of Jehovah filled the temple with a cloud and thick darkness when Solomon dedicated it (I Kgs. 8:10-12; II Chr. 5:13—6:1). It was used poetically of darkness (Job 38:9), as well as the ignorance, misery, and sin of mankind (Isa. 60:2). It was symbolic of the Lord's judgment upon sin (Jer. 13:16; Ezek. 34:12; Joel 2:2; Zeph. 1:15).

6206. 'Ârats; to awe; to dread, to be afraid, to fear; to frighten, to terrify; to harass, to oppress; to inspire fear or terror. The term was used to describe the terror of the Lord's judgment (Isa. 2:19,21), but His people have nothing to fear (Deut. 1:29; 7:21; 20:3; 31:6; Josh. 1:9). Some important Heb. synonyms are *yârê'* (3372), *pâchad* (6342), and *châthath* (2865). Though Jehovah is indeed awesome (Ps. 89:7), if we are living by His will, there is no need to fear anyone else.

6213. 'Âsâh; this important Heb. root means to work, to labor, to toil; to make, to create, to construct, to build, to accomplish; to acquire, to earn, to procure; to prepare, to offer, to sacrifice; to appoint, to constitute; to keep, to fulfill; to be made, to be done, to be created, to be prepared; to happen, to be; to handle, to squeeze. The basic meaning of *'âsâh* is "do" or "make" in a general sense. It has the connotation of ethical obligation (obedience) for Israel (Ex. 23:22; Lev. 19:37; Deut. 6:18). It is used almost as an auxiliary verb in certain Heb. constructions: to do folly (Deut. 22:21), to deal kindly (Judg. 1:24), to keep the Passover (Ex. 12:48), to show faithfulness (Gen. 32:10, to execute vengeance (Judg. 11:36), and to make war (Gen. 14:2). In the account of creation in Genesis, *bârâ'* (1254) and *'âsâh* alternate. *Bârâ'* conveys the thought of creation *ex nihilo,* while *'âsâh* is broader in scope and dealt with refinement. In other words, the emphasis was on fashioning the created objects (cf. Gen. 8:6; 33:17; Ex. 25:10,11,13,17). However, the word *'âsâh* is used in Scripture to describe God's creative activity (Ps. 86:9; 95:5; 96:5). See the Gr. word *mochthos* (3449) in the N.T. lexical section.

6225. 'Âshan; this verbal root means to smoke or to burn; to be angry. In Ex. 19:18 it refers to vapor. The term was used metaphorically to describe God's anger (Deut. 29:20; Ps. 74:1; 80:4).

6237. 'Âsar; this Heb. verb may be identified with 6238 in some way. It means to tithe, to take the tenth part (of the produce, I Sam. 8:15,17); to give the tenth part (Neh. 10:37). The concept of tithing is a very important one in the Bible. Even before the Law of Moses was introduced, Abraham paid a tithe to Melchizedek out of his treasures from the battle (Gen. 14:20; cf. Heb. 7:1-4). Also, Jacob vowed to give tithes to God at Bethel (Gen. 28:22). Everything belonged to God, but He knew that they needed enough to live on. Therefore, God introduced the principle of tithing to teach them perspective (Lev. 27:30-34). The Levites and the priests were God's representatives. Since they had no land inheritance, they were completely dependent upon their Jewish brothers for support (Num. 18:21-32). Deut. 12:1-14; 14:22-29 instructed the Israelites where to give their tithes.

6256. 'Êth; this fem. Heb. noun is a deriv. of 5703. It means time, the right time, the proper time (Ecc. 10:17), a season, a short-lived season (Ecc. 3:1,17); prematurely (Job 22:16); a longer time (Hos. 13:13); the vicissitudes of events (I Chr. 29:30; Job 24:1; Ps. 31:15); an unhappy time (Isa. 13:22; Jer. 27:7); at this time, now (Judg. 13:23; 21:22; Job 39:18). In the plural it means circumstances, courses of time, occurrences, events. There are three principal situations which *'êth* describes: (1) regular events; (2) the appropriate time for an unrecurring incident; (3) a set time. See the Gr. equivalent, *kairos* (2540), in the N.T. lexical section.

6279. 'Âthar; this Heb. verbal root means to burn incense in worship; to intercede in prayer, to pray, to entreat, to supplicate; to let oneself be entreated, to listen (to a prayer). There are twenty occurrences in the Heb. O.T., eight of which are found in Ex. 8–10. This word for prayer depicts an imploring, beseeching, spontaneous petition of God who is waiting to listen. See *epakouō* (1873) in Strong's Gr. Dictionary. Other significant Heb. syn. are *chânan* (2603), "to plead for grace," *pâga'* (6293), "to urge strongly," *pâlal* (6419), "to pray," *shâ'al* (7592), "to ask," and *châlâh* (2470), "to appease, entreat."

6286. Pâ'ar; to gleam, to embellish, to adorn, to beautify, to glorify; to glean from a fruit tree; to be glorified, to glorify oneself; to boast, to glory; to declare, to speak plainly. This Heb. verb occurs thirteen times in the O.T. In the six Piel instances of the term, the subject is always God. The secondary meaning of boasting is found in Ex. 8:9; Judg. 7:2; Isa. 10:15, etc.

6289. Pâ'rûwr; this mas. Heb. noun derives from 6286. It means illuminated, a glow, redness, a flash (of anxiety). It is found only in Joel 2:6 and Nah. 2:10.

6292. Piggûwl or **piggûl;** this mas. Heb. noun occurs in the pl. form. It comes from an unused root which meant "to stink." Therefore, it meant filth, what is putrefied, unclean, to abominable. It was used of food (Lev. 7:18; 19:7), of unclean flesh (Ezra 4:14), and of unclean meats (Isa. 65:4). These are the only four occurrences in the O.T.

6293. Pâga'; to impinge, to meet with, to encounter (Gen. 28:11; 32:1; Num. 35:19,21; Ex. 23:4; I Sam. 10:5; Amos 5:19), to push against, to strike, to hit, to attack, to rush at someone with hostile violence (I Sam. 22:17,18; Ruth 2:22), to kill (Judg. 8:21; 15:12; II Sam. 1:15); to entreat; to intercede for help (Isa. 53:12; 59:16; Jer. 15:11; 36:25); to reach to, to reach something (Josh. 16:7; 17:10; 19:11,22,26; 27:34), to border upon; to cause to fall on, to lay upon; to assail (in a good sense, i.e., with petitions to urge a desired request, Ruth 1:16; Jer. 7:16; 27:18; Job 21:15); to make a pact (Isa. 47:3; 64:5), i.e., to make peace, a peace treaty. The term appears forty-four times in the O.T. with a very wide range of meanings.

6297. Peger; this Heb. noun, usually in the pl. form, is traceable to 6296. It means a carcass (of men or animals, with the flavor of limpness), a dead body, a corpse; the ruins of idols (Lev. 26:30). The word occurs twenty-two times in the Heb. O.T. It can refer even to the badly decomposed corpse (Isa. 34:3; cf. Jn. 11:39). This gruesome sight was often the result of divine punishment, not a natural death (I Sam. 17:46; Isa. 14:19; Amos 8:3; Nah. 3:3). There is some new evidence that Lev. 26:30 should be translated as "stelae."

6299. Pâdâh; this Heb. root means to sever; to redeem by paying a price (Ex. 13:13; 34:20), to ransom, to set free (from servitude, Deut. 7:8; 13:5; Jer. 15:21; 31:11), to let go (Num. 18:15,16,17); to dismiss, to rescue, to deliver from danger (II Sam. 4:9; I Kgs. 1:29; Job 6:23; Ps. 34:22); to be redeemed, to be released; to cause to be redeemed. The essential meaning is achieving the transfer of ownership from one to another through payment or by something of equivalent value. This verb and its deriv. occur sixty-nine times in the Heb. O.T. At first it was a commercial term (Lev. 19:20; I Sam. 14:45). The Exodus was accomplished through a tremendous price, namely the firstborn were slaughtered (Ex. 4:23; 12:29). Since the Israelites were spared, their firstborn was consecrated each year thereafter as a memorial (Ex. 13:13,15). The Levites were exempted (Num. 3:44ff.). The rest of the firstborn were redeemed at the price of five shekels a piece. See also Ex. 13:11-16; 34:19,20; Num. 18:8-32. Sacred things were unredeemable (Lev. 27:28,29). See *gâ'al* (1350) and *charam* (2763). Israel itself was the firstborn of God (Ex. 4:22) and had been redeemed by Jehovah (Deut. 15:15; 24:18). The theme of redemption pervades the O.T. (e.g., II Sam. 7:23; Ps. 78:42; 111:9; Isa. 29:22; 35:10; 50:2; 51:11; Mic. 6:4; Zech. 10:8; cf. I Pet. 1:18). Originally, *pâdâh* overlapped with *kâphar* (3722), but they developed divergent paths. *Pâdâh* is an intervening action which effects a release from an undesirable condition, and money is not necessarily an integral part of the word. However, usually it does presuppose some kind of bondage. God is the only true liberator of human beings. (I Kgs. 1:29; Ps. 21:5; 26:11; 71:23). Only once was this term used to describe liberation from sin (Ps. 130:8). The Septuagint uses *lutroō* (3084) forty-three times to translate *pâdâh*.

6302. Pâdûwy; this pass. Heb. part. stems from 6299, and means redeemed. It is used substantively in Num. 3:49; Isa. 35:10; 51:11 with the meaning of "the redeemed" or "the preserved." In Num. 3:46ff. it is the price of redemption.

6304. P^{e}dûwth or **p^{e}dûth;** this fem. Heb. noun comes from 6299. It means distinction (Ex. 8:23); deliverance; redemption, division, separation, interval. See also Ps. 111:9; 130:7; Isa. 50:2. It is difficult to fully understand the significance of this term in Ex. 8:23.

6306. Pidyôwm or **pidyôm** or **pidyôwn** or **pidyôn;** these words originate from 6299. The meaning is redemption-money or a ransom. There are only four occurrences in the Heb. O.T. It is the price of redemption in Ex. 21:30; Num. 3:49; Ps. 49:8. See also Num. 3:51. The equivalent Gr. term is *lutron* (3083), which see in the N.T. lexical section.

6308. Pâda'; this Heb. verbal root means to deliver or to rescue. Its only occurrence in the O.T. is found in Job 33:24, where there is a textual problem. The full meaning is uncertain.

6310. Peh; this Heb. noun derives from 6284. It means the mouth (of men, Ex. 4:16); or an animal (Num. 22:28), the bill or beak (of a bird, Gen. 8:11; Isa. 10:14); an opening (of a bag, Gen. 42:27), an entrance (of a city, Prov. 8:3); a well (Gen. 29:2); a collar of a tunic, (Ex. 28:32); or the collar itself (Job 30:18; Ps. 133:2); an edge (I Sam. 13:21; Prov. 5:4; Isa. 19:7), a border of a garment (Job 30:18); the ocean or sea shore (Prov. 8:29); the mouth (of a brook, Isa. 19:7); a mouthful, i.e., as much food as anyone can take in his mouth (Deut. 21:17; II Kgs. 2:9; Zech. 13:8); the human organ of speech (Ex. 4:11), and orator (Ex. 4:16); commandment (Gen. 45:21); the organ of taste (Gen. 25:28); Hades (Ps. 141:7). There are several idioms which employ this noun: "Mouth to mouth" means person to person, eyeball to eyeball, i.e., direct communication (Num. 12:8; cf. 34:3). A gesture of silence was to place one's hands upon one's mouth (Job 29:9). "To inquire at her mouth" was to ask him personally (Gen. 24:57). "The mouth of two witnesses" means mutually confirming testimony (Num. 35:30). However, in Jer. 36:4 it means dictation. "Two mouths" means a double portion or two parts (Deut. 21:17). However, in Zech. 13:8, it means two-thirds! And, it means "speech" in Ps. 66:17. *Peh* occurs almost 500 times in the Heb. O.T. It is most frequent in Psalms and Proverbs. There are fifty occurrences which speak of God's mouth, divine revelation. There is a prominent phrase: "According to the mouth of the Lord," which occurs twenty-four times. God has the last word. When the prophets spoke, they were only passing on what God said. When referring to man, the mouth is portrayed as the external manifestation of an individual's character and disposition, whether for good or for bad.

6315. Pûwach; to puff, to breathe, to pant (Hab. 2:3), to blow (upon a fire, Ezek. 21:31), to become cool (i.e., the evening, when the heat departs, Song of Sol. 2:17); to breathe through, to blow through; to kindle (a fire); to blow up; to scoff; to speak, to utter (lies, Prov. 6:19; 14:5; 19:5,9; or the truth, Prov. 12:17); to incite sedition (Prov. 29:8); to address in a harsh manner; to bring into a snare. This verb appears seventeen times in the Heb. O.T., seven of which are in Proverbs.

6341. Pach; this Heb. noun is a deriv. of 6351. It means a snare, a trap-net, a net (Job 18:9; Prov. 7:23; Ecc. 9:12; Amos 3:5); to lay snares, i.e., to plot, to devise a trap for someone (Ps. 119:110; 140:5; 141:9; Jer. 18:22); anything which causes someone to fall (Josh. 23:13; Ps. 69:22; Isa. 8:14); danger, calamity, destruction (Isa. 24:17; Jer. 48:43); lightning (Ps. 11:6). In the literal sense, the *pach* was believed to be a metallic sheet which had been pounded very thin into plates (Ex. 39:3; Num. 16:38). The net could also be spread out. See *pagis* (3803) in Strong's Gr. Dictionary.

6342. Pâchad; this Heb. verb means to be startled (by sudden alarm), to tremble, to quake, to be afraid; to palpitate with joy; to be timid, to be cautious; to make to tremble. It emphasizes either the immediacy of the object of fear or the aftermath of trembling. It is a strong, poetic syn. for *yârê'* (3372). Unlike *yârê'*, however, it is not used to refer to reverent worship.

Note the interesting cognate accusative in Job 3:25.

6343. Pachad; this Heb. noun clearly derives from 6342. It means fear, terror, dread, awe; an object of fear. It may refer to the emotion or to the subject which causes the emotion. Often it is the terror which Jehovah causes (Isa. 2:10,19; II Chr. 14:14), the fear of God (Ps. 36:1). This term was elevated to the status of a proper noun, namely the Fear of Isaac (Gen. 31:42,53). There was panic among the Egyptians (Ps. 105:38) and the Persians (Esth. 8:17) and even the Israelites (I Sam. 11:7).

6345. Pachdâh; this fem. Heb. noun is the equivalent of 6343. It means alarm, fear, terror, awe. Its only occurrence is found in Jer. 2:19, where it refers to the fact that the fear of God was no longer in the hearts of the Jews.

6346. Pechâh; this Heb. word was probably borrowed from either Akkadian, Babylonian, or Persian. It means a prefect, a governor, a captain, a deputy, a pasha, one who was less than a satrap (II Kgs. 18:24; Isa. 36:9) in the Assyrian Empire and Babylonian Empire (Ezek. 23:6,23; Jer. 51:23). The word was used of the governor of Judea in the time of Solomon (I Kgs. 10:15) and of the governors of Syria (I Kgs. 20:24). The term was also used during the reign of the Persian kings (Esth. 8:9; 9:3), particularly of the Persian governor of Judea (Neh. 5:14,18; 12:26; Hag. 1:1,14; 2:2,21: Mal. 1:8).

6347. Pechâh; this is the corresponding Aramaic term to 6346. It appears ten times in the Aramaic portions of the Bible (Ezra 5:3,6,14; 6:6,7,13; Dan. 3:2,3,27; 6:7).

6354. Pachath; this Heb. noun probably derives from an unused root. It means a pit (especially for catching animals, II Sam. 17:9; 18:17), a hole, a fissure; a snare; destruction (Isa. 24:17: Lam. 3:47). There is a play on words in Jer. 48:43. This term was never used for the pit of the grave; see *shachath* (7845) and *bôwr* (953).

6365. Pîyd; this mas. Heb. noun derives from an unused root. It means misfortune, destruction, disaster, or ruin. It occurs only three times in the Heb. O.T. (Job 30:24; 31:29; Prov. 24:22).

6375. Pîyq; this mas. Heb. noun is a deriv. of 6329. It is a tottering or a smiting together. Its only occurrence is found in Nah. 2:10.

6381. Pâlâ; to be separate, to be distinguished, to be singular, to be extraordinary, to be wonderful, to be miraculous, to be astonishing; to be hard; (as a fem. pl. part.) wondrous things, miracles; to separate, to consecrate; to make extraordinary; to act miraculously; to act marvelously; to sanctify; to show oneself extraordinary. This Heb. verb occurs seventy times in the O.T. Its basic meaning is "to be wonderful" and "to cause a wonderful thing to happen." Its first occurrence is found in Gen. 18:14: "Is anything too difficult for the Lord?" *Pâlâ'* is used primarily with God as the subject. He does things which are beyond the bounds of human powers or expectations (Ex. 3:20; Deut. 30:11; Ps. 9:1; 118:23; Zech. 8:6). It is not merely the unusual act or even the degree of astonishment, but the clear-cut exhibition of God's capable care of Israel. The term is applied to men about fifteen times, signifying insoluble or inaccessible wonders (Deut. 17:8; 30:11; Prov. 30:18). In the Piel *pâlâ'* means "to fulfill (a vow)" (Lev. 22:21; Num. 15:3,8; cf. Lev. 27:2; Num. 6:2). It means remarkable in II Sam. 1:26 and blasphemous words in Dan. 11:36.

6382. Pele'; this mas. Heb. noun arises from 6381. It is a miracle, a wonder, a wonderful thing, a wonderful deed. Except for Lam. 1:9, *pele'* always appears in a context of God's acts or words. Of the eight-four occurrences of the root and its derivaties, thirty-seven of them are in the Book of Psalms. *Pele'* points to the extraordinary aspects of how God dealt with His people (Ex. 15:11; Ps. 77:11; Isa. 29:14)—His miracles (Ps. 77:11; 78:12; 88:10). Isa. 9:6 reads: "And His name will be called Wonderful Counselor." This is one of several titles for the Messiah, showing that Jesus would continue the work of God.

6383. Pil'îy or **pâlîy';** this Heb. adj. comes from 6381. It means incomprehensible, wonderful, remarkable, something which appears to be supernatural (Judg. 13:18; cf. Ps. 139:6). There are only two occurrences.

6385. Pâlag; this Heb. root means to split, to divide; to make discordant; to be divided. It occurs only in the Niphal and Piel. There are four occurrences (Gen. 10:25; I Chr. 1:19; Job 38:25; Ps. 55:9).

6386. P^elag; this Aramaic word corresponds to 6385. Its single occurrence is found in Dan. 2:41, a pass. part.

6387. P^elag; this Aramaic term is equivalent to another Aramaic word (6386). It means a half, a dividing. It occurs only once in the O.T. (Dan. 7:25).

6390. P^elaggâh; this fem. Heb. noun occurs only in the pl. form. It means a division of a family, kindred, a clan; a gully; a river, a stream, a brook. The only three appearances in the O.T. are Judg. 5:15,16; Job 20:17. It derives from 6385.

6391. P^eluggâh; this fem. Heb. noun is traceable to 6385. It means a division, a class, a section. Its lone occurrence is II Chr. 35:5, referring to a class of priests.

6392. P^eluggâh or **pîlegesh;** this fem. Aramaic term is a correlate to the Heb. 6391. It means division and appears only once (Ezra 6:18).

6399. P^elach; this Aramaic word corresponds to 6398 in Heb. It means to serve, to minister, to worship God. There are ten occurrences (Ezra 7:24; Dan. 3:12,-14,17,18,28; 6:16,20; 7:14,27).

6413. P^elêyṭâh or **p^elêṭâh;** these fem. Heb. nouns are derivatives of 6412. They mean a deliverance, an escape, or a remnant. The word is used twenty-eight times in the Heb. O.T. to refer to the remnant of God's people (II Kgs. 19:30,31 which is equivalent to Isa. 37:31,32). It was especially used for those who had survived a terrible ordeal (Gen. 45:7; II Sam. 15:14; Ezra 9:8). The providence of God watched over Israel to preserve her for His purpose.

6414. Pâlîyl; this mas. Heb. noun comes from 6419 and appears only in the pl. form. It is a magistrate or a judge. There are only three occurrences in the Heb. O.T. (Ex. 21:22; Deut. 32:31; Job 31:11).

6415. P^elîylâh; this fem. Heb. noun derives from 6414. It means justice, judgment, decision; arbitrator, the office of judge, an umpire. Its solitary occurrence is found in Isa. 16:3.

6419. Pâlal; this verbal root means to judge (officially or mentally); to decide, to punish; to adjudge; to think; to act as a mediator; to pray (to God), to entreat, to intervene, to interpose, a intercede, to make supplication. This important root is found eight-four times in the O.T. and is a common word for "pray," also producing the most common word for "prayer" (*t^ephillâh,* 8605). Of the total number of occurrences, eighty instances are reflexive, thus expressing the idea of interceding for or praying on behalf of someone, e.g., Num. 21:7; Deut. 9:20; I Sam. 12:23. In other words, *pâlal* has a reciprocal meaning between its subject and its object. Prayer is essentially a two-way street of communication.

6427. Pallâtsûwth; this fem. Heb. noun is a deriv. of 6426. It means trembling, terror, horror, or fearfulness. There are four occurrences in the O.T. (Job 21:6; Ps. 55:5; Isa. 21:4; Ezek. 7:18).

6452. Pâçach; to hop, to skip over; to pass through, to pass over; to spare (Ex. 12:13,23,27; Isa. 31:5); to hesitate, to waver (in opinion), to fluctuate (I Kgs. 18:21); to be made lame (II Sam. 4:4); to dance in a halting or lame manner, to leap, to hobble, to be wrenched (I Kgs. 18:26). Some scholars believe that there were two homophonous verbs with two distinct sets of meanings. Of course, the name "Passover" is derived from this verb. In the Book of Exodus (12:13,23,27) Jehovah passed over the homes of those who put lamb's blood around their doors in response to His command. There is a similar promise found in Isa. 31:5 later in Israelite history.

6453. Peçach; this mas. Heb. noun originates from 6452. It is a sparing, an exemption, an immunity (from penalty and calamity); the Passover Feast, the Paschal Lamb. For the historical background of the institution and perpetuation of the Passover, see Ex. 12; Lev. 23:5-8; Num. 9:1-14; 28:16-25; Deut. 16:1-8; Josh.

5:10-12; II Kgs. 23:21-23; II Chr. 30:1-27; 35:1-19; Ezra 6:19-22. The Lord selectively protected the houses of the Israelites because of the blood of the lamb. Much is made of this imagery in the N.T. Jesus celebrated this feast (Mt. 26:17-30). In fact, the elements of the Lord's Supper were taken from the Passover meal. Christ is our Passover (I Cor. 5:7). See also Jn. 1:29; I Cor. 10:10; Heb. 11:28; I Pet. 1:19. The Passover festival occurred on the 14th day of Nisan (Lev. 23:5), which was followed by the seven days of the Feast of Unleavened Bread (Lev. 23:6).

6456. Peçîyl; this mas. Heb. noun, arising from 6458, appears only in the pl. form. It is an image or idol which has been cast or molten, carved or graven; a stone quarry (Judg. 3:19,26). Man-made idols were strictly forbidden (Deut. 7:25; Isa. 21:9; Jer. 8:19; 51:52). Sometimes they were made of wood (Deut. 7:5,25).

6458. Pâçal; this Heb. verb means to carve (wood or stone), to cut, to hew, to engrave. Throughout the O.T., objects of adoration were detestible. How can man give his allegiance to something so temporary and material, which he himself manufactured? Sometimes they formed them by cutting stones (Ex. 34:1,4; Deut. 10:1,3; I Kgs. 5:18) or wood (Hab. 2:18). There are only six occurrences in the O.T.

6459. Peçel; this Heb. noun derives from 6458. It refers to an idol which has been carved (Ex. 20:4; Judg. 17:3ff.), or cast (Isa. 40:19; 44:10; Jer. 10:14; 51:17), or made of wood (Isa. 44:15,17; 45:20).

6485. Pâqad; to visit, to inspect, to review; to muster, to number; to care for; to look after (Ex. 3:16ff.); to miss; to chastise (Jer. 9:25; 44:13), to punish (Jer. 9:9); to attack (Job 31:14; 35:15; Isa. 26:14); to cause to inspect, to appoint, to charge with, to entrust; (as a part.) an officer, an overseer; to be visited; to be punished, to be mustered; to be missed; to be set over; to be entrusted with, to be charged with; to deposit, to lay up; to be appointed; to be punished; to be numbered; to be deposited. This important Heb. verb occurs 285 times in the Heb. O.T. Its first occurrence is found in Gen. 21:1 where the Lord intervened on behalf of Sarah in a miraculous way, so that she could conceive at an advanced age. The strong undercurrent meaning is a positive action by a superior in relation to his subordinates. Bible translators have a difficult time translating this verb because there is such a broad spectrum of meanings. The Greek Septuagint and the Latin Vulgate were forced to resort to many terms to attempt to translate this term. See *episkeptomai* (1980). By far, the most prevalent meaning (110 times) was that of drawing up troops for marching or for a battle (e.g., Ex. 30:12; often in Numbers, I Samuel, II Samuel). "Take a census" only captures part of the meaning of *pâqad*. The Septuagint renders it by *arithmeō* (705) in only eight occurrences. It was more than a census; it was organizing troops for battle "by their armies" (Num. 1:3). There was probably much more to David's "census" in II Sam. 24 than a simply head-count. *Pâqad* is translated with "visit" fifty-seven times. This is a misleading term. The true meaning is an action on the part of God which produces a beneficial result for His people (Gen. 50:24,25; Ruth 1:6; I Sam. 2:21; Ps. 8:4; Jer. 15:15; 29:10) or evil (Isa. 24:21). However, *pâqad* can mean to visit in the sense of making a call (I Sam. 15:2). God is in control; He is the Overseer.

6486. Pequddâh; this fem. pass. part. derives from 6485. It is a numbering, an enumeration (I Chr. 23:11), a mustering, a review; visitation, punishment (Isa. 10:3); a charge (Num. 4:16), service, care (Job 10:12), a watch, custody (II Kgs. 11:18); office (II Chr. 23:18), goods in trust, stores, property; oversight; riches (to be guarded, Isa. 15:7); a prison (Jer. 52:11). The basic meaning is intervention by a superior power (usually God or a king) in order to bring about a great change in the situation of one of his subordinates. There is an implied desire to help to injure the object, depending on the context.

6487. Piqqâdôwn; this Heb. mas. noun derives from 6485. It means goods in trust, a deposit, what was delivered (to keep), store. The term occurs only three times in the O.T. (Gen. 41:36; Lev. 6:2,4).

6488. Peqîdûth; this fem. Heb. noun is a deriv. of 6496. It means oversight, office, supervision, or ward. Its single occurrence is found in Jer. 37:13.

6490. Piqqûwd or **piqqûd;** this Heb. noun is used in the pl. form and comes from 6485. It means appointment, allocation, what is mandated (by God); commandment, precept, order, statute.

6493. Piqqêach; this Heb. adj. has its origin in 6491. It means clear-sighted, open-eyed (Ex. 4:11), seeing; intelligent, wise (Ex. 23:8). It is either the opposite of blindness or the epitome of alertness.

6496. Pâqîyd; this mas. Heb. noun arises from 6485. It means a superintendent (civil, military, or religious), an officer, an overseer, a prefect, a magistrate, a commander, a governor, any person who is in charge, i.e., one who looks after things. In II Chr. 24:11 and Jer. 20:1, it was probably the one who drew up the troops. It means military officer (in II Kgs. 25:19) and civil officer (in Gen. 41:34; Neh. 11:22). There are thirteen occurrences in the Heb. O.T.

6530. Perîyts; this Heb. adj. has its source in 6555. It means violent, wild; ravenous; (as a part.) a tyrant, a robber. It refers to ferocious animals (Isa. 35:9) or a violent man (Ps. 17:4; Jer. 7:11; Ezek. 7:22; 18:10; Dan. 11:14). These are the only six occurrences in the O.T.

6544. Pâra'; to loosen, to dismiss (from work, Ex. 5:4), to absolve (to remit a penalty, Ezek. 24:14); to let go, to let loose, to ignore; to expose, to make bare; to reject (counsel, Prov. 1:25; 4:15; 8:33; 13:18; 15:32); to lead, to be at the head, to go ahead (Judg. 5:2), to be unruly, to be unbridled (Ex. 32:25), to become lawless (Prov. 29:18); to make unruly; to liberate (from work). This verb occurs sixteen times in the Heb. O.T. When used of hair, it has the sense of cutting (Lev. 10:6; 13:45; 21:10) or "unbraiding" (Num. 5:18). Moses observed that his people had gotten out of hand; they were running wild (Ex. 32:25). In Proverbs, the sense is to let something slip through the fingers by ignoring an opportunity. It proably means undisciplined in Prov. 29:18.

6546. Par'âh; this is the fem. form of 6545. It means leadership, leaders, princes, i.e., those who go in front. It appears only twice in the Heb. O.T. (Deut. 32:42; Judg. 5:2).

6565. Pârar; to split, to break up, to break in pieces, to crush; to break, to dissolve, to violate, to frustrate, to annihilate, to annul; to be dissolved, to be destroyed; to cleave, to divide; to shatter; to be torn adunder, to be shaken. See Ps. 74:13 and Isa. 24:19.

6579. Partam; this is a loanword from the Old Persian language. It means nobleman among the Persians (Esth. 1:3; 6:9) or princes among the Jews (Dan. 1:3). Etymologically it may be related to the Greek *prōtos* (4413) and the Latin *primus,* because these languages are all members of the Indo-European stock.

6586. Pâsha'; this signigicant Heb. verb means to send, to break away (from a righteous authority), to trespass, to transgress, to rebel, to apostatize, to be refractory; to quarrel; to be offended. The basic idea is an aggressive breach of a civil or religous relationship between two parties. In international political alliances it connoted the deliberate casting off of an allegiance, a conscious revolt. This secular meaning is common in I Kings, II Kings, and II Chronicles. Sometimes the purpose was to achieve the state of independence (II Kgs. 8:20). Edom was successful in their revolution. However, sometimes it is not goal-oriented (e.g., I Kgs. 12:19; II Chr. 21:8,10). In a religious sense, it is a rebellious sin, e.g., Israel, like a headstrong youth, breaking with God's covenant (Isa. 1:28; 48:8; Ezek. 2:3; Hos. 8:1). This seems to be a human trait (Hos. 14:9). Going beyond the limits of God's laws causes people to be deceitful (Isa. 59:13) and too independent (Amos 4:4). Sinners lose the ability to distinguish right and wrong (Ps. 51:13) and refuse to accept correction from God (Jer. 2:8,29; Hos. 7:13; Zeph. 3:11). Even though God wants to provide salvation, He is forced to exert His authority in the form of punishment (Ps. 37:38; Dan. 8:23). He pleads for repentance (Isa.

46:8; 53:12). See *asebeō* (764), *aphistēmi* (868), *anomos* (459), and *hamartia* (266) in the N.T. lexical section. *Pâsha'* occurs forty-one times in the Heb. O.T.

6588. Pesha'; this Heb. mas. noun stems from 6586. It is a revolt (national, moral, or religious), transgression, sin, a trespass, wickedness, rebellion, faithlessness, apostasy, defection (Prov. 28:2); sin-offering (Mic. 6:7); the punishment for transgression (Dan. 8:12,13); the guilt of rebellious sin (Job 33:9). *Pesha'* occurs ninety-three times in the Heb. O.T. It is the technical term for willful deviation from the path of righteousness (see especially Amos 2:4). It is a premeditated crossing of the line of God's law, a rebellious act of rejecting God's authority (Job 34:37; 35:6; 36:9; Ps. 32:1). There are a few secular instances which refer to the violations of personal and property rights of others (Gen. 31:36; 50:17; I Sam. 24:11; 25:28).

6599. Pithgâm; this Heb. word is believed to have been borrowed from Persian. It means word, a (judicial) sentence, a decree, an edict. It occurs only in late Hebrew. There are only two occurrences in the O.T. (Esth. 1:20; Ecc. 8:11).

6600. Pithgâm; this Aramaic word, corresponding to 6599, also came from Persian. It means command, a mandate (Dan. 4:17); a word, something, anything (Ezra 6:11), a letter (Ezra 5:7); an edict (Dan. 3:16; Ezra 4:17; 5:11); affair. These are the only six occurrences in the Aramaic portions of the O.T.

6633. Tsâbâ'; this verbal root means to amass (an army or servants), to assemble, to muster (soldiers, II Kgs. 25:19; Jer. 52:25), to collect; to fight, to perform, to go forth to war, to wage war (Num. 31:7; Isa. 29:7,8; 31:4; Zech. 14:12), to do military service; to do sacred service (the ministry of the priests, Num. 4:23; 8:24; I Sam. 2:22), to wait upon (the Lord); to levy a tax for the military. This verb appears fourteen times in the Heb. O.T. The general sense is that of rendering service.

6635. Tsâbâ' or **tsᵉbâ'âh;** this Heb. mas. noun derives from 6633. It is a mass (of persons or things, especially for war), a campaign, an army, troops, a host; the host of heaven (meaning angels or stars; cf. Lk. 2:13 for the host of angels which surrounds the throne of God); military service, warfare, heavy service, hardship (i.e., like the miserable condition of warfare, Job 7:1; 10:17; 14:14; Isa. 40:2; Dan. 10:1), calamity; temple service. This noun occurs 486 times in the Heb. O.T. The basic meaning is service done for a superior, usually military service. The army of Abimelech (Gen. 21:22), the army of Israel (Num. 31:21,48), and even a non-military host (Ps. 68:11) are mentioned. The "host of heaven," stars, visual indicators, were worshipped as pagan gods (Deut. 4:19; Zeph. 1:5). Man had a tendency to worship those created objects (II Kgs. 17:16), even though to do so was supposed to result in death (Deut. 17:2-7). Unfortunately, both the northern kingdom of Israel and the southern kingdom of Judah yielded to the temptation at different times (II Kgs. 21:3; 23:5). This Heb. word is used of the sun, the moon, and the stars (Isa. 34:4; 40:26; 45:12; Jer. 33:22; Dan. 8:10; cf. Mt. 24:29). Everything in creation is included in the term (Gen. 2:1). God created them by His power (Ps. 33:6) and preserves their existence. "The host of heaven" may mean angels in I Kgs. 22:19; Dan. 8:10. The Lord (Jehovah/Yahweh) of Hosts is a special name for God. Either YHWH or *'ĕlôhîym* (430) appears with the pl. form of this word about 285 times. It occurs sixty-two times in Isaiah, seventy-seven times in Jeremiah, fourteen times in Haggai, fifty-three times in Zechariah, and twenty-four times in Malachi. Interestingly enough, it does not appear in the Pentateuch. This expression depicts Yahweh as the mightiest Warrior or all-powerful King of Israel. The word became a technical term, a proper noun in the Septuagint, see *sabaōth* (4519). Compare Rom. 9:29 and Js. 5:4. Also, see the Gr. word *pantokratōr* (3841). Although the title of *tsâbâ'* had military overtones, it pointed directly to Jehovah's rulership over the entire universe. He stands ready to intervene for His people at any moment (cf. Ps. 80:19; 84:1; Isa. 28:5,6; Amos 4:13; 5:8,9; 9:5,6). See the Gr. word *stratos* (4756) in the N.T. lexical section.

6643. Tsᵉbîy; this mas. Heb. noun has its source in 6688. It means prominence, splendor, an ornament, glory, duty. The superlative of splendor (Isa. 4:2; 24:16; 28:1,4,5) is beautiful or glorious, whether it be the Promised Land (Ezek. 20:6,15; Dan. 11:16,41), the mountain upon which the temple was built (Dan. 11:45), the strategic cities of Moab (Ezek. 25:9), the Babylonian kingdom (Isa. 13:19), or a gazelle (Prov. 6:5). Jehovah will destroy all beauty which has its own source (Isa. 23:9; 28:1-4). He alone will be the crown of beauty to His remnant people (Isa. 28:5).

6656. Tsᵉdâ'; this is an Aramaic word from an unused root, and it corresponds to 6658 in Heb. It has the same evil, sinister purpose or design. Its lone occurrence is found in Dan. 3:14.

6658. Tsâdâh; to chase, to look for; to lie in wait for, to be ready to ambush (Ex. 21:13; I Sam. 24:11); to be laid waste, to be desolated, to be destroyed (Zeph. 3:6). These are the only three occurrences in the O.T.

6662. Tsaddîyq; this Heb. adj. derives from 6663. It means just (i.e., one who has a just forensic cause, Ex. 9:27; 23:8; Prov. 18:17), lawful, righteous, honest, right. "The Lord is righteous in all this ways, and holy in all his works" (Ps. 145:17). God is the standard of ethics and morality; it is part of His very nature and will. Jehovah is the just Judge (II Chr. 12:6; Ps. 11:7; Jer. 12:1; Lam. 1:18). He is the Judge of the entire world (Deut. 32:4; Ps. 119:137; Isa. 5:16). God righteously fulfills His part of the bargain with Israel (Isa. 54:14). Depending on our response, He rewards (Ps. 112:6; 129:4; 145:17; Isa. 24:16) or punishes (II Chr. 12:6; Ezra 9:15; Lam. 1:18; Dan. 9:14). The term also describes a human judge who dispenses true justice (II Sam. 23:3). *Tsaddîyq* portrays an ordinary person who is honest with other men (Prov. 29:7) and obedient to the laws of God (Gen. 6:9; Job 12:4; Ps. 5:12). However, even a just man is not sinless (Ecc. 7:20). We should never become self-righteous (Ecc. 7:16). See these Gr. words in the N.T. lexical section: *dikaios* (1342), *dikaiosunē* (1343), and *eleēmosunē* (1654).

6663. Tsâdaq; this important Heb. verb means to be right (in a moral or forensic sense); to clear oneself; to cleanse; to be straight, to be just, to be true, to be upright, to be righteous; to be in the right; to be justified, to obtain one's cause (in a forensic sense, Isa. 45:25), to be restored, to be exonerated; to justify, to declare to be righteous; to make righteous, to declare someone innocent or righteous (Ezek. 16:52); to be vindicated from wrongs (Dan. 8:14), to be exonerated; to absolve, to acquit, to approve of; to have a just cause (Gen. 38:26; Job 9:15,20; 10:15; 13:18; 34:5); to speak the truth among disputants (Job 33:12); rationalization (Jer. 3:11; Ezek. 16:51). This Heb. verb is used less than forty times in the O.T., seventeen alone of which occur in Job concerning the suffering of the righteous. Essentially, it is a legal term. God is righteous (Ps. 51:4) and so are His laws (Ps. 19:9). When injustice prevails, God is the One who sets things right (Ex. 23:6,7; Ps. 82:3). Man is not righteous at all in comparison with God, but God remains constantly righteous (Job 4:17). When men such as Absalom corrupt justice (II Sam. 15:4), we can still appeal to God for a judicial pronouncement of innocence (Deut. 25:1) or vindication (Job 13:18). The Septuagint uses *dikaioō* (1344), which see in Strong's Gr. Dictionary.

6664. Tsedeq; this Heb. mas. noun is traceable to 6663. It is (the) right thing (whether nationally, morally, or legally); equity (in an abstract sense); prosperity (in a figurative sense), straightness (in a physical sense. Ps. 23:3); rectitude (in an ethical sense, i.e., what ought to be, Job 8:3; 36:3; Ps. 15:2; Isa. 64:5); justice (Lev. 19:15) of a king (Isa. 11:4,5; 16:5; 32:1) or of God (Ps. 9:8, 35:24,28; 50:6; 72:2; 96:13), justness; honesty, integrity (Ps. 17:15; Isa. 1:21; 51:1,7; 59:4; Hos. 2:19); liberation (Isa. 42:6). This noun occurs 118 times. The decisions of a judge are to be made according to the truth and without partiality (Lev.

19:15). The term was applied to weights and measures in a similar way (Lev. 19:36). The essential meaning is not deviating from the standard of fairness. Righteous conduct issues from a new heart (Ezek. 36:25-27). A person who possesses this attribute will live his daily life by the same principle (Hab. 2:4). Noah, Daniel, and Job were righteous (Ezek. 14:14,20). In Isa. 11:5 *tsedeq* is synonymous with *'ĕmûwnâh* (530), "truth." Also, *tsedeq* is also closely associated with peace in Ps. 85:10: "Righteousness and peace have kissed each other."

6665. Tsidqâh; this is the Aramaic equivalent of 6666. It means righteousness or doing right. Daniel 4:27 is the only instance in biblical Aramaic. This fem. noun has the flavor of liberality and beneficence.

6666. Tsᵉdâqâh; this fem. Heb. noun is equivalent to 6664 and ultimately derived from 6663. There is no discernible difference in the meaning of this fem. form and its Heb. counterpart. *Tsᵉdâqâh* is rightness, recititude, justice (divine and human), right, righteousness, a claim, justness, faithfulness; virtue, piety (of ordinary people, Isa. 5:7; 28:17; 46:12; 54:14; 59:14), mercy, mildness, moderation; prosperity. This fem. form occurs 157 times. It is a legal term. Relationships between God and mankind or relationships among people are frequently described by this word, if the parties are faithful to the expectations of one another. Note the business relationship between Laban and Jacob (Gen. 30:33). The New American Standard Bible and the New International Version have "honesty" here. The New American Bible has "fair offer." Fairness is defined as what is good for both parties. No one should expect the other party to do all the compromising. Value is determined by what the buyer regards as an affordable price and by what the seller is willing to relinquish ownership. God is the ultimate Law-giver, but even He is willing to abide by His own standards. Justice is what conforms with the legal corpus (Deut. 16:20), the judicial process (Jer. 22:3), the mind of the king serving as judge (I Kgs. 10:9; Ps. 119:121; Prov. 8:15), and also the Source of Justice, God Himself (Ps. 35:24,28). The Judge (Isa. 59:16,17) rewards the godly (Ps. 24:5; 36:10) and punishes the wicked (Isa. 5:16; 10:22). Being in a proper relationship with God, i.e., being right with God is of paramount importance to all of us. Therefore, one particular usage of *tsᵉdâqâh* is of extreme importance to us—Gen. 15:6. When God told Abraham (then quite elderly) that Eliezer would not be the heir, but that it would be Abraham's own son Abraham believed it. Gen. 15:6 plainly states that God treated that sort of faith as being equivalent to *tsᵉdâqâh,* "righteousness." In other words, in accounting terms, God summarily transferred Abraham and his faith onto the righthand side (*tsᵉdâqâh*) of His ledger book. Such piety pleases God (Ps. 5:8). The Septuagint translated it with *dikaiosunē* (1343) and the Vulgate had *iustitia*. The entire fourth chapter of Romans is where Paul explains how the principle of faith (like Abraham's) justifies. No amount of human effort can obligate God to repay us with salvation or to force Him to grant righteousness to us because we earned it or deserve it. In the O.T. one could be in a state of righteousness only if he were perfect, i.e., had never deviated from God's standard. In the N.T. because of the grace of Christ, it is now possible for a Christian to sin (I Jn. 2:1) and still be considered "innocent" before God! Gen. 15:6 as interpreted by Rom. 4:1-12; Gal. 3:5-8; and James 2:21-24, is the *Magna Charta* for the Christian. Also read Acts 13:38,39; Rom. 5:1,18; 9:30; I Cor. 6:11; and Gal. 3:24. When an individual who was involved in litigation was not guilty of breaking a given law, he was in the state of *tsᵉdâqâh* (Gen. 30:33). One is righteous when one is declared to be right (Ex. 23:7; Deut. 25:1; Job 19:7). However, when the law is God's perfect law, only He can declare when we are in a state of righteousness. He made that affirmation in Gen. 15:6.

6680. Tsâvâh; this Heb. root means to constitute, to make firm, to establish, to appoint anyone over anything (I Sam. 13:14; 25:30; II Sam. 6:21; Neh. 5:14; 7:2), to arrange; to command, to charge (Gen. 2:16; 26:11; 32:4; 50:16; Ex. 1:22; Ex. 5:6; Esth. 2:10,20), to ordain, to commission (I Chr. 22:12; Ezra 8:17; Esth. 4:5; Jer. 14:14; 23:32), to delegate something to someone with orders; to be commanded; to send a messenger, to set in order. This root occurs about 485 times in the Heb. O.T. It is the picture of a superior giving a verbal communication to a subordinate. The word includes the content of what was said (Gen. 12:20). Gen. 2:16 focused upon the action itself, where God set down the rule. God is not to be questioned regarding the work of His creative hands (Isa. 45:11). His commands are unique, requiring an inner commitment, not mere, external, superficial obedience (Isa. 29:13). When God commands, it happens (Ps. 33:9). Sometimes He issues orders through His prophets (Jer. 27:4) who speak for His (Jer. 1:17). No determinative event in the course of history happens unless God ordained it (Lam. 3:37). And, He decrees that His people will be victorious (Ps. 44:4). *Tsâvâh* is also used on a human level for the instruction of a father to his son (I Sam. 17:20), a farmer to his workers (Ruth 2:9), and a king to his subjects (II Sam. 21:14). Jacob gave orders to his sons in considerable detail about burying his bones in Canaan (Gen. 49:29,33).

6736. Tsîyr; this mas. Heb. noun is identical to 6735 which also comes from 6696. It means the hinge of a door; pain, labor in childbirth; a messenger; a form (the Kethib of Ps. 49:14), a shape, an idol (Isa. 45:16). These are the only two occurrences in the O.T.

6739. Tsᵉlâ'; this is an Aramaic word which is not used in the Heb. in this form, but which is related to the Heb. 6760. It means "to pray." There are only two occurrences (Ezra 6:10; Dan. 6:10).

6751. Tsâlal; to shade, to give shadow, to become overshadowed. There are only two occurrences (Neh. 13:19; Ezek. 31:3) in the Heb. O.T. There is a homophonous root meaning to sink or to be submerged which is found only in Ex. 15:10.

6752. Tsêlel or **tsêl;** this Heb. mas. noun comes from 6751. It means shadow or shade. There are two distinctly different connotations of this word. First, a shadow can convey the sense of protection from the heat (Job 7:2; Isa. 4:6), shelter (Gen. 19:8; Isa. 30:2,3; cf. Ps. 17:8; 36:7; 91:1; 121:5,6; Isa. 49:2; Ezek. 17:23; Hos. 14:7). Second, man's life is similar to a temporary, fleeting shadow (I Chr. 29:15). In Job 17:7 the term is used to describe the failing, frail condition of an individual within the throes of sickness.

6754. Tselem; this Heb. mas. noun comes from an unused root which probably meant "to shade." The meaning is image, likeness, resemblance, illusion; a representative figure, an idol; a phantom, nothingness. This word is used sixteen times in the Heb. O.T. Five of them refer to man, who was created in the image (*tselem*) of God. Most of the time it denotes an idol. Twice it refers to the golden copies of the mice and swellings which afflicted the Philistines (I Sam. 6:5,11). These were mere representational images. Note that the golden Cherub, though sculpture, was not forbidden, because it was never intended to symbolize God Himself. However, it was a forbidden, idolatrous statue in Num. 33:52 and II Kgs. 11:18. Since God is Spirit (Jn. 4:24), nothing material can be used to represent Him. To attempt to do so is tantamount to a contradiction of terms. The Creator is non-material (Deut. 4:15-19). God made man in such a way as to reflect some of His own perfections— perfect in knowledge, righteousness, and holiness, with dominion over the creatures (Gen. 1:26). Perhaps even the loving unity within the Godhead is reflected in mankind (Gen. 1:27). *Tselem* is not an exact duplicate. Ps. 39:6 shows that it is only the shadow of a thing, representing the original in an imprecise manner, lacking the essential characteristics (reality) of the original cf. Ps. 73:20 for a dream image. Also, see Ezek. 23:14 for a wall painting. Even though man has been tarnished by sin as a result of the fall, he still maintains the essential nature of God (Gen. 5:3). According to Gen. 5:1, *dᵉmûwth* (1823) is an exact equivalent to *tselem*.

6755. Tselem or **tsᵉlem;** this is the Aramaic equivalent of 6754 in Heb. It is an idolatrous figure, a form, an image, an idol (Dan. 2:31ff., 3:1ff.). However, Dan. 3:19 uses the expression "facial expressions" to mean "attitude," an extension not paralleled in biblical Hebrew.

6757. Tsalmâveth; this fem. Heb. compound noun comes from two parts: *tsêl* (6738) and *mâveth* (4194). It means shade of death, the shadow of death, the grave, deep darkness, terror, calamity. This is one of the few compound Heb. words in the O.T. The final *mem* ("m") consonant in Heb. of the first portion contracted with the initial *mem* of the second portion. It is a poetic term for very thick darkness (e.g., Job 3:5; 10:21; 28:3; 34:22; 38:17). It is most well known for its appearance in Ps. 23:4, where it means that God will lead His people (sheep) safely through a matter how dark a place (the experience of death) is. It is also used to describe the inernal anguish of a person who has rebelled against God (Ps. 107:10-14). God promised to send His Messiah as a light (Isa. 9:2).

6783. Tsᵉmîythûth or **tsᵉmîthûth;** this fem. Heb. noun arises from 6789. It means excision, destruction, extinction (perpetually, forever, Lev. 25:23,30). These are the only two occurrences in the O.T.

6789. Tsâmath; to put an end to, to cut off, to destroy, to wipe out, to extirpate; to be destroyed, to become extinct, to vanish (Job 6:15ff.); to be consumed, to be cut off; to annihilate, to be extinguished (Job 6:17; 23:17); to bring to silence (Lam. 3:53). This verbal root occurs fourteen times in the O.T. It is a very strong word to express obliteration (cf. Ps. 143:12). It is interesting to note that the all-consuming zeal which Jesus felt in clearing the temple court area was mentioned beforehand in Ps. 119:139.

6884. Tsâraph; to fuse metal, to refine (literally or figuratively), to melt a metal, to purge gold or silver by fire (in order to separate it from the impurities, Ps. 12:6; Isa. 1:25), to smelt; (metaphorically) to test, to prove, to purge away, to try, to examine someone (Ps. 17:3; 26:2; 105:19; to be purified (Dan. 12:10); (as a part.) a goldsmith, a smelter. The pass. part. means sincere or pure (Ps. 18:30; 119:140). This Heb. verb was used less than thirty-five times. In order to see who was qualified for battle, Gideon set aobut to test 10,000 men, but only 300 of them were chosen (Judg. 7:4). *Tsâraph* is similar to the English "—smith," e.g., silversmith (Judg. 17:4). Jeremiah described the process of smelting and refining (Jer. 6:29,30) and so did Isaiah (Isa. 40:19; 41:7). Our moral character is forged through suffering (Ps. 66:10-12; 119:140; Isa. 1:25; Zech. 13:9; Mal. 3:2,3; cf. Ps. 18:30; Prov. 30:5). The Apostle Peter referred to the same imagery (I Pet. 1:7). See the Gr. word *dokimazō* (1381).

6895. Qâbab; to arch, to vault; to scoop out (with words); to curse, to blaspheme, to execrate (Num. 23:8ff.). This word occurs fifteen times in the Heb. O.T. It is possible that there is another homophonous root among that number. It seems to connote the act of uttering a magical formula which is designed to utterly undo the target. In Lev. 24:11 it may mean that a man of mixed parentage used the sacred name of the true God in a magical incantation. However, there are other instances which seem to have no magical connotations at all. Job 3:8 is a disputed case.

6898. Qubbâh; this fem. Heb. noun comes from 6895. It is a large, vaulted tent (sleeping compartment or bedchamber, from its arched form); a domed cavity; a pavillion. This word occurs only once (Num. 25:8) in the Heb. O.T.

6900. Qᵉbûwrâh or **qᵉbûrâh;** this Heb. word is the fem. pass. part. which originates from 6912. It means interment, burial (Jer. 22:19), burying place, grave (Gen. 35:20; 47:30).

6908. Qâbats; to grasp (with the hand), to collect (Gen. 41:48) things (Deut. 13:16; Prov. 13:11), grapes (Isa. 62:9), water (Isa. 22:9), food (Gen. 31:35), money (II Chr. 24:5); to gather (persons, i.e., to congregate, Deut. 30:3,4; II Sam. 3:21; I Kgs. 18:19; 20:1; Isa. 40:11; Jer. 23:3; 31:10), to assemble; to be gathered (Ezek. 29:5), to be collected, to be assembled, to gather oneself; to seize, to take, to take up, to gather in. This verb occurs 130 times in the Heb. O.T. Its principal meaning is to gather the objects to a single location, focusing on the process of gathering (Gen. 41:35) and the result (Gen. 41:48). Unlike one of its important Heb. synonyms, *qâhal* (6950), it is not a call to gather. David did not summon his band of men; they were simply attracted to him (I Kgs. 11:24). *Qâbats* emphasized the central spot to which the people converged. There is a variety of social reasons for coming there. God pledged to assemble His people from all places where He had scattered them (Deut. 30:3,4). Isa. 11:12 recalled this promise. After the return from the exile God reminded His people (Ps. 107:3; Neh. 1:9).

6910. Qᵉbûtsâh; this fem. pass. Heb. part. is a deriv. of 6908. It means a collection, a heap, or a hoarding. There is only one occurrence (Ezek. 22:20).

6912. Qâbar; this Heb. verb means to bury someone, i.e., to heap up a mound (Gen. 23:4,19; 25:9; Ezek. 39:12). The term is used almost exclusively of burying human beings. However, Jer. 22:19 prophesied that Jehoiakim would be buried like a donkey, beyond the gates of Jerusalem. *Qâbar* is the act of placing a corpse into a grave. Proper burials were a very important obligation of any responsible survivor. The Law required burial to take place before nightfall (Deut. 21:23). Lying unburied was the sign of divine disapproval (I Kgs. 14:11,13; cf. Jer. 8:2). Job 27:15 seems to denote the entire act of dying. This root occurs about 130 times in the Heb. O.T., seldom in poetry.

6913. Qeber or **qibrâh** or **qᵉbûrâh;** these Heb. nouns are deriv. of 6912. The meaning is a burying place (specifically an open pit, Jer. 26:23), a literal grave (Gen. 23:9,20; Ex. 14:11), a family grave site (Judg. 8:32), the underworld (Ps. 88:11). The term appears sixty-seven times in the Heb. O.T., mostly in prose.

6918. Qâdôwsh or **qâdôsh;** this important Heb. adj. comes from 6942. It means sacred (ceremonially or morally); selected, pure, holy, consecrated, pious; (as a sub.) sanctuary, the Holy One, i.e., God, an angel, a saint. This term occurs 116 times in the Heb. O.T. Its first appearance is found in Ex. 19:6; "And you shall be to Me a kingdom of priests, and a holy nation." All Israel was holy, a nation which was separated for God's service. In other words, God had dedicated Israel to be His special people. They were considered holy by their relationship to the holy God. Therefore, they were urged to keep themselves separated from other nations and unholy things to please the Lord (Lev. 20:26; Num. 16:3). Israel was to abstain from every kind of impurity (Deut. 7:5,6; 14:2,21; 26:19). The priests were holy before God (Lev. 21:6,7). Aaron consecrated them (Ps. 106:16). They officiated at the holy place of the tabernacle or the temple, acting as intermediaries between God and Israel. They were completely dedicated to His service. They wore sacred priestly garments (Ex. 28:2). Some things were to be used only in the sanctuary by the priests (Ex. 28:38). Certain holy things were for the priests and the Levites (Ex. 29:32,33), but some could be given to others (Deut. 26:13). There were holy sacrifices (Ex. 30:25; Lev. 27:10). God designated a place to be His (Ex. 3:5). His sanctuary was a holy place (Ex. 36:1). The outer part was "the holy place" and the inner part was "the holy of holies" (Ex. 26:33). The altar was "a most holy place." All these locations were varying distances away from the holy God (II Sam. 6:10,11). God is separate from all sin, death, and idolatry (Ezek. 39:25). His majestic holiness is without equal and is completely perfect (Ex. 15:11). He is "the Holy One of Israel" (Isa. 1:4), the "holy God" (Isa. 5:16), and "the Holy One" (Isa. 40:25). His name is holy (Isa. 57:15), none is as holy as He (I Sam. 2:2). Isa. 6:3 says: "Holy, Holy, Holy, is the Lord of Hosts." He is the Judge of what is right and pure (Ps. 22:2-4; Isa. 6:3,5ff.). Because God is holy, He is free from the moral imperfections and failures associated with mankind (Hos. 11:9). We can depend on Him to be faithful to His promises (Ps. 22:3-5). He is absolutely separated from evil (Isa. 17:7). He cannot tolerate sin. The angels, who are closely associated with Him, are called the holy ones (Job 5:1; 15:15; Ps. 89:5,7; Dan. 8:13; Zech. 14:5). Pious worshippers of God (saints) were also called holy ones (Deut. 33:3; Ps. 16:3; 34:9). A special category were Nazarites, who were as pure from the defilements of sin as possible, completely set apart for God's purpose (Num. 6:5). Dan. 8:24 uses the term of Jews in general. So, the basic meaning of *qâdôwsh* is what is intrinsically sacred and distinct (even opposed to) what is common. See the Gr. terms, *hagios* (40) and *hagnos* (53), in the N.T. lexical section.

6922. Qaddîysh; this is the Aramaic correlate to 6918, which see. It is used of God or false deities (Dan. 4:8,9; 5:11), of angels (Dan. 4:13,17), and of the Jews (Dan. 7:18,21,22,25).

6924. Qedem or **qêdmâh;** what is in front, what is before (Ps. 139:5); what is positioned to the east, the eastern quarter (Job 23:8), from the east (Gen. 2:8; 12:8), anywhere eastward (Gen. 3:24; Num. 34:11; Josh 7:2; Judg. 8:11); time, antiquity, ancient time (Ps. 44:1; 74:12; 77:5,11; Isa. 23:7), anciently. This Heb. noun, which arises from 6923, is unusual in that it has both a geographical meaning and a temporal notion. The term occurs sixty-one times in the Heb. O.T. It has the definite flavor of an idyllic state. Compare other Heb. synomyms: *'ôwlâm* (5769) and *'ad* (5703) denote perpetuity. *Zâqên* (2205) means agedness and *rî'shôwn* (7223) refers to primacy. The "East" may have either good or bad connotations. On the one hand, it was the location of Eden, but on the other hand, it was the habitat of men who built Babel (Gen. 11:2). "The sons of the east" refers to the inhabitants of the Arabian Desert, which stretches eastward of Palestine to the Euphrates (Gen. 25:6; 29:1; Judg. 6:3ff.; I Kgs. 4:30; Job 1:3; Isa. 11:14; Jer. 49:28; Ezek. 25:4). It refers to the desert itself. Sometimes, however, the word includes Mesopotamia and Babylonia (Num. 23:7; Isa. 2:6). Being "full of the East" means being full of the superstitions and sorceries which were brought from Babylonia. Isa. 11:14 envisions a day when they would be subject to Israel. The Hebrews "backed into" time, i.e., they saw the past as "before" them and the future was "behind"! *Qedem* was also used as an adv., before; of old, the past, in ancient or primitive times.

6927. Qadmâh; this fem. Heb. noun stems from 6923. It is priority (in time), origin (speaking of Tyre, Isa. 23:7), primitive state; (as an adv.) before, before that (Ps. 129:6), a former, pristine state (Ezek. 16:55), old estates (Ezek. 36:11), antiquity. This Heb. noun occurs five times.

6928. Qadmâh or **qêdmâh;** this is the fem. Aramaic equivalent to 6927. It means former time (Dan. 6:10) or formerly (Ezra 5:11). These are the only two occurrences in the Aramaic portions of the O.T.

6937. Qâdar; to be ashy, to be dark-colored, to be black; to wear dark clothes (which show sadness), to mourn (in sackcloth); to be gloomy, to be soiled, to be foul, to be turbid; to darken the sun or the stars (Ezek. 32:7,8), to obscure; to be darkened (Jer. 4:28; Joel 2:10; 3:15; Mic. 3:6); to cause to mourn (Ezek. 31:15); to grow dark. The term occurs nineteen times in the Heb. O.T. with the clear overtone of mourning, even in eschatological contexts. Compare Acts 2:20; Rev. 6:12,17; 8:12. In the Heb. culture, darkness denoted the entire range of what was harmful or evil.

6940. Qadrûwth; this fem. Heb. noun has its origin in 6937. It means darkness, obscurity, gloom, like the dusk. Its sole occurrence is found in Isa. 50:3.

6941. Q^edôranniyth; this Heb. adv. comes from 6937. It means blackish ones (i.e., those who wore sackcloth in mourning). The only appearance of the term is in Mal. 3:14.

6942. Qâdâsh; to be clean, to make clean, to pronounce clean (ceremonially or morally); to hallow, to dedicate, to sanctify, to purify, to make oneself clean (Ex. 19:22; II Sam. 11:4; II Chr. 5:11; 29:15), to consecrate to God (Lev. 27:14ff.; Judg. 17.3; II Sam. 8:11); to be selected, to be pure, to be holy, to be sacred, to be consecrated, to be devoted; to be regarded as holy (Lev. 10:3; 22:32), to show oneself holy (Ezek. 38:23), to be consecrated; to seclude; to declare as holy; to treat as holy, to purify oneself. This Heb. verb captures the element of being pure or devoted to God. The concept of "being separated" is a derived meaning, not the primary one. It signifies an act or a state in which people or things are set aside for use in the worship of God, i.e., they are consecrated or made sacred for that purpose. They must be withheld from ordinary (secular) use and treated with special care as something which belongs to God (Ex. 29:21). Otherwise, defilement makes the sanctified object unusable (cf. Deut. 22:9; Ezek. 44:19; 46:20). Certain things were dedicated solely for God's consecrated use (Ex. 29:36; Lev. 16:19). *Qâdâsh* is used with various objects: the people of Israel (Ex. 19:10,14; Josh. 7:13), the altar in the temple (Ex. 29:36; I Kgs. 8:64), the priests (Ex. 28:41; 29:1; I Sam. 7:1), the mountain (Ex. 19:23), the Sabbath (Gen. 2:3; Ex. 20:8), a new building (Neh. 3:1), and a fast (Joel 1:14; 2:15). Jer. 6:4 uses the term in the sense of making the proper sacred preparations (cf. Mic. 3:5). It was anything which was reserved exclusively for God (Ex. 13:2,-12,13; Num. 18:15,16; I Sam. 1:24). This included certain kinds of war, i.e., a holy war (I Sam. 7:9,10; Ps. 110:3). Soldiers were sometimes consecrated before battle (Isa. 13:3; Jer. 51:27). *Qâdâsh* is the sphere of what is considered sacred.

6944. Qôdesh; this mas. Heb. noun originates from 6942. It means apartness, holiness, sacredness; a holy thing (Lev. 12:4; 21:6; Jer. 2:3), a most holy thing (e.g., the ark, the holy vessels, the sacred oblations, Ex. 29:37; Lev. 21:22; II Chr. 31:14; Ezek. 42:13; 44:13), something consecrated (to God, Lev. 21:22; 22:2,-3,15; I Chr. 26:20), a sacred place or thing, a dedicated thing, a hallowed thing; holiness; sanctity; a sanctuary, the "holy of holies" (the innermost part of the temple, Ex. 26:33,34; II Chr. 3:8,10), a temple (Ps. 20:2; Dan. 8:14), the holy tabernacle (Ex. 28:43; 29:30; 35:19; 39:1). Compare its relationship to the word *hêykâl* (1964) in I Kgs. 8:8; II Chr. 29:7. Once *Qôdesh* is used of the innermost part (Ezek. 41:23). This noun appears 470 times in the O.T. See the Gr. words, *naos* (3485) and *hieron* (2411), in the N.T. lexical section.

6945. Qâdêsh; this Heb. adj. derives from 6942. It means a consecrated one, a devoted one, a sacred person; a devotee to licentious idolatry, a cultic prostitute or priest of Astarte (I Kgs. 22:46). It is ironic that such a "holy" word could be applied to the abominable practices of male homosexuals dedicating themselves to the honor of a false god (Deut. 23:17; I Kgs. 14:24; 15:12; II Kgs. 23:7; Job 36:14)! There are six occurrences in the Heb. O.T.

6948. Q^edêshâh; this is the fem. form of the Heb. 6945, which see. It means harlot, whore, "sacred" temple prostitute. Prostitution received official sanction from the Canaanite religion which made reproductivity part of its *summum bonum.* As in India today at the Holi festival, there were seasons of sexual orgy associated with Astarte. The temple precincts became an inglorious brothel (Prov. 6:24; Hos. 4:13,14; Amos 2:7). This idea of unnatural and wicked abasement of sex, along with the revolt against marriage vows, was used by God's prophets to show how far they had fallen away from God. Even in N.T. times, the tendency to identify religious fervor and sexual excitement was present (cf. Acts 15:20; Rom. 1:24; I Cor. 6:9). There are five occurrences of *Q^edêshâh* in the Heb. O.T.

6950. Qâhal; to convoke or summon an assembly, to call together, to assemble people (Num. 8:9; 10:7; 20:8), to gather a group of people; to be assembled, to be congregated, to be called together. This Heb. verb occurs thirty-nine times and is probably derived from the noun 6951. It contains the idea of assembling without regard to the purpose, though it may be for judgment (Job 11:10), to make war (Josh. 22:12; Judg. 20:1), for rebellion (Num. 16:3; 20:2; II Sam. 20:14), for mutual defense (Esth. 8:11; 9:2), to ask for idols (Ex. 32:1), to anoint Aaron (Lev. 8:4), to erect the tent of meeting (Josh. 18:1), to transport the ark (I Kgs. 8:2; II Chr. 5:3), or to worship (II Chr. 20:26).

6951. Qâhâl; this mas. Heb. noun is one of the most important terms in the entire O.T. It is a convocation, a congregation, an assembly, a crowd, a multitude, an army (Ezek. 17:17), a gathering (for deliberation, Ezek. 23:45-47), the Heb. community, an assembly of nations (Gen. 28:3; 35:11; 48:4). Usually, it refers directly to the congregation of the people of Israel (Ex. 16:3; Lev. 4:13; Num. 16:3; 20:4; Deut. 31:30; Neh. 13:1). This might mean the whole assembly of Israel (I Chr. 13:1,2) or the assembled leaders of Israel (II Chr. 1:3). The elders represented the whole congreation in some respects (Lev. 4:13). At other times, *Qâhâl* is applied to all the males of Israel, i.e., the worshipping, eligible members of the assembly (not those who were living in Israel temporarily or permanent non-Hebrew residents). See Num. 15:15; 16:3,33; 18:4; Deut. 23:1). In I Kgs. 12:3 refers to the assembly of Israel who withdrew from Rehoboam. "The day of the assembly" (Deut. 9:10; 10:4; 18:16) was the time when Israel met God at Mount Sinai to receive God's Law. An assembly of any kind or for any purpose could also be called a *Qâhâl,* not just religious ones. Some were for plotting (Gen. 49:6; Ps. 26:5), civil affairs (Job 30:28; Prov. 5:14; 26:26), war (Num. 22:4; Judg. 20:2), battle (I Sam. 17:47), and exile (Jer. 31:8; Ezra 2:64). Prov. 21:16 mentions a gathering of dead people. Some of the occasions were: feasts, fasts, and worship (II Chr. 20:5; 30:25; Neh. 5:13; Joel 2:16). *'Edâh* (5712) is a syn. for *Qâhâl* (e.g., Ex. 12:3). Both terms occur conjointly in Ex. 12:6, "The whole assembly of the congregation of Israel." However, a slight distinction may exist between them in Lev. 4:13, where *Qâhâl* denotes the judicial representatives of the community. Also, certain Israelite persons cannot enter the *Qâhâl* (Deut. 23:2). In general, the two Heb. terms are almost identical. The Gr. Septuagint usually translates *Qâhâl* with *ekklēsia* (1577), but it uses *sunagōgē* (4864) thirty-six times. *Qâhâl* occurs 123 times in the Heb. O.T.

6952. Qᵉhillâh; this fem. Heb. noun comes from 6950. It is an assembly or congregation. There are only two occurrences in the O.T. (Deut. 33:4; Neh. 5:7).

6953. Qôheleth; this is the fem. form of the act. part., deriving from 6950. It is one who assembles others. The fem. ending denotes an office, i.e., one who addresses a public assembly and discourses on human affairs. See the introduction to the Book of Ecclesiastes, the only place where the term occurs. Sometimes it has the article (Ecc. 12:8) and sometimes it does not have it (Ecc. 1:1,2; 12:9,10). There are seven occurrences. If King Solomon is the author, this is his surname. The full meaning of the Heb. term is not at all clear. The English "Preacher" came from Jerome's *concionatur* ("a speaker before an assembly") in Latin. The Heb. word certainly does not connote formal orations or sermons to which we are accustomed today.

6960. Qâvâh; to bind together (by twisting), to collect (Gen. 1:9; Isa. 60:9; Jer. 3:17); to be gathered together, to be joined, to meet; to lie in wait (for someone, Ps. 56:6; 119:95); to expect, to await, to look for patiently, to wait, to hope, to be confident, to trust; to be enduring (another kind of strength, Ps. 25:3; 37:9; 69:6). Some scholars believe that *qâvâh* should be considered as two homophonous Heb. roots.

6973. Qûwts; to sever oneself; to loathe, to have a disgust, to be abhorred (I Kgs. 11:25), to feel displeasure, horror, or fear; to fear (Ex. 1:12; Num. 22:3; Isa. 7:16); to terrify, to alarm, to put a city in fear, i.e., to besiege it (Isa. 7:6); to be weary (Gen. 27:46; Prov. 3:11). Gesenius thinks that the primary idea of *qûwts* is that of vomiting (cf. Lev. 20:23; Num. 21:5). It is a deep emotional reaction of revulsion.

6983. Qôwsh or **qûwsh;** this Heb. root means to bend (like a bow, i.e., in the shape of a circle); to set a trap, to lay a snare; bait, a lure. Its only appearance is found in Isa. 29:21.

6986. Qeṭeb; this mas. Heb. noun comes from an unused Heb. root which probably meant "to cut off." This word means destruction (Isa. 28:2), ruin, defeat, a plague, pestilence (Deut. 32:24; Ps. 91:6). These are the only three occurrences in the Heb. O.T.

6987. Qôṭeb; this Heb. noun means extermination, destruction, or contagion (Hos. 13:14). This is the lone appearance in the Heb. O.T.

6999. Qâṭar; fumigating in a closed place (thus driving out the occupants); to cause to rise up in smoke (to offer true offerings, i.e., convert them to smoke, the ethereal essence of the offering which ascends to God as a pleasing smell), to offer things up in smoke; to burn incense (in honor of a deity, Jer. 1:16; 7:9; 11:13; 19:4); to kindle (turn into fragrance by fire as an act of worship; almost always used of idolatrous worship); burned incense (Ex. 29:18; Lev. 1:9,17; 2:2,16); (fem. part.) the altar upon which the incense was burned; the incense itself (Song of Sol. 3:6); a sacrifice. After the books of the Pentateuch, *qâṭar* meant false worship (II Chr. 25:14; Isa. 65:7; Jer. 11:12,17; 19:4). Some of the kings of Israel tried to legitimitize their idolatrous offerings in this manner (I Kgs. 12:33; cf. II Kgs. 16:13; II Chr. 28:4). This Heb. verb appears 115 times in the O.T.

7004. Qᵉṭûreth; this fem. Heb. noun is traceable to 6999. It means a fumigation, (sweet) incense (Ex. 30:1ff.; Lev. 4:7; 10:1), an offering of incense; perfume (Prov. 27:9), the fat parts of a sacrifice (Ps. 66:15). It denotes what produces a sweet-smelling odor when it is burned. The word occurs sixty times in the Heb. O.T.

7010. Qᵉyâm; this mas. Aramaic word comes from 6966. It is a statute or edict (Dan. 6:7,15). These are the only two occurrences in the Aramaic portions of the O.T.

7023. Qîyr or **qîr** or **qîyrâh;** this mas. Heb. noun stems from 6979. It is a wall (of a house or a town); a rampart, a fortress, a walled city. Of particular interest is Jer. 4:19: "I am in anguish! Oh, my heart!" Literally, it is "the walls of my heart."

7035. Qâlahh; to assemble, to gather together, to be called together. The only occurrence is found in II Sam. 20:14 (Kethib), which has a textual problem. A metathesis is believed to have occurred in transcription, i.e., the switching of the last two consonants. If this is true, the true reading would be *qâhal* (6950).

7043. Qâlal; to be small, to be light (Jer. 6:14; 8:11); to be swift or fleet (II Sam. 1:23; Job 7:6; 9:25; Hab. 1:8); to be lessened, to be despised (Job 40:4; Nah. 1:14); to be little, to be insignificant, to be of small worth (I Sam. 18:23; Isa. 49:6; Ezek. 8:17); to be easy (II Kgs. 20:10; Prov. 14:6); to esteem lightly, to revile, to curse, to execrate (Gen. 8:21; 12:3; Ex. 21:17; Lev. 19:14; 20:9; II Sam. 16:7); to be lightly esteemed (Gen. 16:4,5; II Sam. 6:22); to be cursed (Job 24:18; Ps. 37:22; Isa. 65:20); to bring a curse upon oneself (I Sam. 3:13); to lift (a weight, Ex. 18:22; I Sam. 6:5; I Kgs. 12:10); to bring into contempt; to shake; to sharpen (Ecc. 10:10); to be moved, to be shaken; to belittle (Ex. 21:17), to make light of; to be trifling; to subside (Gen. 8:8). This root occurs 130 times in the Heb. O.T. The core meaning conveys the quality of slightness, speed, or lowly circumstances.

7045. Qᵉlâlâh; this fem. Heb. noun has its source in 7043. It is a vilification, a reviling, a reproach, a curse or cursing (II Sam. 16:12), malediction, execration or imprecation (Gen. 27:12; I Kgs. 2:8). It was the opposite of blessing (Gen. 27:12; Deut. 27:13; cf. Jer. 24:9). It is the lowering to a lesser state.

7065. Qânâ'; the cognate Arabic root means to become very red. Therefore, from the redness of the face, this Heb. verb means jealous (Gen. 30:1; Num. 5:14; Deut. 32:21; I Kgs. 14:22), to be envious (Gen. 26:14; 30:1, Prov. 3:31); (of someone, Gen. 37:11; Ps. 37:1; 73:3; Prov. 23:17; 24:1,19); to be zealous for, to burn with zeal (Num. 25:11,13; II Sam. 21:2; I Kgs. 19:10), to be filled with righteous zeal (Num. 5:30), to advance God's cause and glory over any rivals; to excite jealousy or envy; to make jealous, to provoke jealousy, to provoke someone to anger (Deut. 32:16). This verb, which may have been derived from the noun *qin'âh* (7068), is a very strong emotion which desires some quality or possession of another. The central meaning is jealousy (in a negative sense) and zeal (in a positive sense). In a very real way, severing the one flesh (Gen. 2:24) was a form of murder, and adultery was punishable by death (Lev. 20:10; Deut. 22:22). Using the marriage motif, God is often depicted in the O.T. as the Husband of Israel. He is a jealous God (Ex. 20:5). Since He is not really capable of being envious like humans, perhaps "jealous" should be translated "zealous" here (cf. Ezek. 39:25; Joel 2:18; Zech. 1:14; 8:2). Idolatry is spiritual adultery and therefore merits death (cf. Num. 25:11). God does not tolerate competitors or those who sin against Him. He will punish His people for their unfaithfulness (Ezek. 5:13; 8:3,5; 16:38). Sometimes His warnings and arduous love effects repentance (Isa. 42:13). The Messiah was consumed by an ardor to exalt God by maintaining purity of worship (Ps. 69:9; Jn. 2:17). The Septuagint has *zēlos* (2205).

7067. Qannâ'; this mas. Heb. adj. and noun is equivalent to 7068. It is a jealous one, usually God (in the Scriptures). The Lord permits no rivals (Ex. 20:5; 34:14; Deut. 4:24; 5:9; 6:15). He is the sole Object of human worship. He does not tolerate the sins of mankind (cf. Josh. 24:19; Nah. 1:2). There are only six occurrences in the O.T.

7068. Qin'âh; this fem. Heb. noun means ardent zeal (II Kgs. 10:16; Isa. 9:7; 26:11), jealousy (of lovers, Prov. 6:34; 27:4; of God, Ezek. 8:3; of rival peoples, Isa. 11:13), envy (excited by the prosperity of others, Job 5:2), ardor, anger, indignation (Deut. 20:20; Ps. 79:5). Song of Sol. 8:6 should be translated: "Ardent zeal is as strong as the grave." There are forty-three occurrences in the Heb. O.T.

7080. Qâçam; to distribute; to cut, to divide; to draw lots; to divine, to prophesy (always used of false prophets among the Hebrews, Deut. 18:10,14; II Kgs. 17:17; Isa. 3:2; Mic. 3:6,7,11; or of the false prophets of foreign nations, I Sam. 6:2); to evoke or conjure up the dead (I Sam. 28:8), to practice soothsaying. The root occurs eleven times as a verb and nine times as a part. Practicing divination was a pagan parallel to biblical prophesying. It was an attempt to learn the will of the gods in order to manipulate the circumstances (Josh. 13:22; cf. I Cor. 10:20, conversing with demons). Diviners offered sacrifices to their god on an altar (Num. 23:1ff.), and spoke to the spirits of the dead through a hole in the ground (I Sam. 28:8), shaking arrows, consulting with household gods, or examining the livers of dead animals (Ezek. 21:21). Since they did not submit to God's sovereignty (Deut. 18:14), it was the opposite of true prophecy. Balaam was a soothsayer. Though Balaam recognized Jehovah as the true God (Num. 22:18), his motive for gain was too strong. The participial and nominal forms are used in connection with him (Num. 22:7; 23:23; Josh. 13:22). Isaiah (3:2; 44:25), Jeremiah (27:9; 29:8), Ezekiel (13:9; 21:21,23,29; 22:28), Micah (3:6,7,11), and Zechariah (10:2) were all true prophets, denouncing these diviners as false prophets.

7081. Qeçem; this Heb. mas. noun derives from 7080. It is a decision, divination (I Sam. 15:23; Ezek. 13:6,23; 21:21); the reward of divination (Num. 22:7) an oracle (in a good sense, Prov. 16:10), a divine sentence, witchcraft. The exact meaning of this variety of occultism is unknown. In Num. 23:23 *qeçem* is parallel to *nachash* (5173) (cf. II Kgs. 17:17). In Jer. 14:14 *qeçem* is parallel to "a false vision," "futility," and "the deception of their own minds" (cf. Ezek. 13:6,23). The Jerusalem Bible uses the term "sorcery" and the Berkeley translation has "fortune-telling."

7089. Qᵉphâdâh; this fem. Heb. noun comes from 7088. It means shrinking terror, horror, a cutting off, destruction. Its only occurrence is found in Ezek. 7:25.

7101. Qâtsîyn; this mas. Heb. noun is traceable to 7096. It is a judge, a magistrate (Isa. 1:10; 3:6,7; Mic. 3:9), a leader, a military leader (Josh. 10:24; Judg. 11:6,11; Dan. 11:18), a commander, a captain, a general, a guide, a prince (Prov. 6:7; 25:15), a ruler (Isa. 1:10; Mic. 3:1). This word appears twelve times in the Heb. O.T.

7107. Qâtsaph; to crack off; to be angry, to break out in anger (Gen. 40:2; 41:10; Ex. 16:20; Josh. 22:18; Isa. 57:16; 64:9), to fly into a rage; to fret; to provoke; to provoke the Lord to be angry (Deut. 9:7,8,22; 29:27; Ps. 106:32; Jer. 21:5). There are thirty-four occurrences of this verb in the Heb. O.T. Twenty-three instances refer to God and eleven refer to men (e.g., Pharaoh, Moses, Naaman, some Philistine princes, etc.). It is a strong emotional outbrust of anger, especially with men (cf. I Sam. 29:4; II Kgs. 5:11; 13:19; Esth. 1:12) and usually of a superior against an inferior (Esth. 2:21 is an exception). One could say that it is the spark in a relationship which ignites into white heat anger.

7108. Qᵉtsaph; this is the Aramaic correlate to 7107 which means to become enraged. Its sole occurrence, Dan. 2:12, describes the wrath of the king. The K.J.V. has "very furious."

7109. Qᵉtsaph; this mas. Aramaic noun comes from 7108 and means anger or rage. There is only one appearance in the Aramaic portions of the O.T. (Ezra 7:23).

7110. Qetseph; this mas. Heb. noun is a deriv. of 7107. It is a fragment of wood, a splinter (as though chipped off), a twig (broken off, Hos. 10:7); an outburst of anger (Ecc. 5:17, especially the anger of Jehovah, Josh. 9:20; 22:20; II Chr. 19:10; Isa. 34:2; 54:8; 60:10; Zech. 1:2), man's wrath (II Kgs. 3:27; Esth. 1:18), strife, altercation, indignation, fury, a quarrel. This noun occurs twenty-eight times in the Heb. O.T., generally referring to God, e.g., II Chr. 29:8. This is the strongest of six main Heb. synonyms for anger.

7121. Qârâ'; to cry out, to call aloud, to roar; to proclaim, to pronounce, to preach; to call, to summon (to court, Deut. 25:8), to invite (Ex. 2:20; I Sam. 9:13); to implore; to call together, to appoint, to praise, to celebrate; to call by name, to name; to call out, to recite; to be called, to be summoned, to be named; to read aloud (Ex. 24:7); to dictate (Jer. 36:18); to muster any army (Judg. 8:1). The basic meaning of *qârâ'* is the enunciation of a specific vocable or message. It is usually addressed to a specific recipient and intended to elicit a specific response. Rarely does it refer to a random outcry (Ps. 147:9; Isa. 34:14). This verb is used to represent the specification of a name. The act of naming is sometimes an assertion of sovereignty over the thing which is being named (e.g., Gen. 1:5; Ps. 147:4; Isa. 40:26). God wanted Adam to assert his own authority in this world (Gen. 2:19). Naming a person may specify an individual's primary characteristic (Gen. 27:36), be an evaluation (Isa. 58:13; 60:14), or recognize an eternal truth (Isa. 7:14). Another important meaning is "to summon" for a specific task (Gen. 12:18; Ex. 2:7; Isa. 55:5; 65:12). Another prominent usage has to do with calling upon the name of God, i.e., to summon His aid (Gen. 4:26; Ps. 145:18; Isa. 55:6). Usually, the context has to do with a critical need (Ps. 34:6; 81:7) or chronic need. The people were urged to pray to God (I Kgs. 8:43) to reverse the curse (Isa. 55:6,13). The prophets predicted that even the Gentiles (Isa. 55:5) would call upon God and serve Him (Zeph. 3:9) and He will answer them (Isa. 65:24). Joel 2:32 uses *qârâ'* in this sense: "And it will come about that whoever calls on the name of the Lord will be delivered." Immediately after Jesus' death, on the day of Pentecost, the Apostle Peter quoted this verse (Acts 2:21). In that same vein, the term means to declare a prophetic message (I Kgs. 13:32) in the sense of proclamation (Gen. 41:43; Ex. 32:5; Judg. 21:13; Esth. 6:9). Also, *qârâ'* means to shout (Deut. 20:10; I Sam. 17:8), to call out loudly in order to get someone's attention so that contact can be initiated (Job 5:1). Sometimes it is sustained calling (Gen. 3:9). This Heb. root occurs 689 times in the O.T. See the Gr. terms *krazō* (2896), *kērussō* (2784), and *kaleō* (2564) in Strong's Gr. Dictionary.

7126. Qârab; to approach, to draw near, to appear (before God), to come near, to advance; to bring near, to admit; to give access; to offer, a present a gift. The basic meaning is being or coming very near, i.e., intimate proximity (Gen. 12:11 means being close), mere spatial proximity, with no sense of intimacy. *Qârab* means close enough to see (Ex. 32:19), to speak to (Num. 9:6), or even to touch (Ex. 36:2). Sometimes the term is coupled with "far" (*râchôwq,* 7350) as a technical phrase for "all" (I Kgs. 8:46; Ezek. 22:5). *Qârab* means to engage in battle (Deut. 2:19,37; Josh. 8.5; cf. Ps. 27:2,3; 91:10; 119:150). It can refer to having sexual relations (Gen. 20:4; cf. Deut. 22:14; Isa. 8:3) or coming for a legal decision (Josh. 7:14; Isa. 41:1; 48:16). It denotes temporal nearness in Gen. 27:41 and Deut. 15:9. *Qârab* is used to express each phase of presenting an offering to God (Ex. 3:5; 16:9; Lev. 1:5,13,14; Deut. 5:23,27). This verb occurs 295 times in Heb. and nine times in Aramaic (see *q^erêb,* 7127).

7130. Qereb; this mas. Heb. noun originates from 7126. It means the nearest part, the center; the interior of a thing (e.g., land, Gen. 45:6; Ex. 8:22; Isa. 7:22; 10:23); the streets (Isa. 5:25), the midst, the bowels (of the human body, Gen. 41:21; Ex. 29:13,22); the heart or the mind as the seat of thought and desire, Ps. 5:9; 49:11; 64:6), the intestines, the cavity of the belly, the insides of animals (Ex. 12:9), all that is within (Ps. 103:1); the approaching, nearness (I Kgs. 18:30); physical proximity (I Kgs. 21:2), the camp (Josh. 1:11), the Canaanites (Judg. 1:32); amid the years (Hab. 3:2). It is also used grammatically as a prep. (e.g., "in the midst of" or "among," Num. 14:13; Hab. 3:2) *Qereb* is predominant in the Pentateuch, especially in Deuteronomy, but it also appears often in Psalms. In Gen. 18:12 it is the inward part of the body which is the seat of laughter. It refers to the thoughts of a person in Jer. 4:14. The basic meaning is the internal, internal organs, groups of people, or social structures. The spirit (inculcating a man's entire inner being) was created by God (Zech. 12:1). This word occurs 222 times in the Heb. O.T. See these Gr. terms: *kardia* (2588), *koilia* (2836), and *mesos* (3319).

7133. Qorbân or **qurbân;** this Heb. mas. noun stems from 7126. It means something which is brought near (the altar), a sacrificial present, an offering, an oblation, a gift in the form of a sacrifice (either bloody or unbloody, Lev. 2:1,4,12,13; 7:13; 9:7,15). It can be an offering which is to be sacrificed or destined to be used in the sanctuary (Num. 7:13ff.). It is called the priest's offering in Lev. 7:16. In Num. 7 alone the word is used twenty-eight times, referring to all kinds of animal and cereal offerings. It has a general sense of offering in Ezek. 20:28, but regular animal sacrifices in Ezek. 40:43. The term occurs eighty times and only in Leviticus, Numbers and Ezekiel. However, Neh. 10:34 and Neh. 13:31 appear to be a late pronunciation of this word. Wood offerings were provided for the burning of the sacrifice in the second temple. Lots were cast among the people, priests, and Levites to determine who would bring the wood offering (fuel) at the scheduled times throughout the year. In general, *Qorbân* was a general term used for all sacrifices, whether animal or vegetable. See Mk. 7:11 ("Corban") for the corrupt practice which developed by the time of Jesus. There it represented a vow whereby one's goods were ideally given to the temple (but in reality retained), and could therefore not be given to others.

7171. Qerets; this mas. Heb. noun arises from 7169. It means extirpation, destruction; a biting gadfly. See Jer. 46:20.

7181. Qâshab; to prick up (the ears, i.e., sharpening them like an alert animal); to listen, to give heed, to pay attention; to attend to something; to make attentive. This verb appears fifty-four times in the O.T., almost exclusively in poetry. It appears in the famous I Sam. 15:22; cf. Deut. 6:4-6.

7186. Qâsheh; this Heb. adj. comes from 7185. It means hard (servitude, Ex. 1:14; 6:9; I Kgs. 12:4), difficult (Ex. 18:26), severe, unfeeling, cruel, harsh (words, Gen. 42:7,30); inflexible, obstinate, hardened, stubborn (Ex. 32:9; 34:9; of heart, Isa. 48:4; Ezek. 3:7); an unhappy lot (Job 30:25), unfortunate, melancholy, heavy or sad in spirit (I Sam. 1:15); strong, violent, vehement (wind, Isa. 27:8), heavy (battle, II Sam. 2:17), powerful (II Sam. 3:39). The general meaning of this term sprang from the farm. They put heavy yokes on oxen to force them to pull plows. These were very hard to bear and sometimes the oxen rebelled (cf. Ex. 32:9). In a similar way, Israel was sometimes not responsive to the guidance of the Lord (Deut. 10:16; Judg. 2:19; II Kgs. 17:14; Neh. 9:16) and intractable. Compare the attitude of Pharaoh (Ex. 13:15) and those who heard Stephen preach (Acts 7:51). Therefore, it has the nuance of a deliberate stiffening. All the derivatives of 7185 number sixty-four in the Heb. O.T.

7187. Q^eshôwṭ or **q^eshôṭ;** this may be an original Aramaic word which produced its Heb. counterpart (7189). It means fidelity or truth. There are only two occurrences of this mas. noun (Dan. 2:47; 4:37).

7188. Qâshach; to harden (the heart, Isa. 63:17); to treat harshly (Job 39:16); to be insensitive. These are the only two occurrences in the Heb. O.T.

7189. Qôsheṭ or **qôshṭ** or **qôshôṭ;** this mas. Heb. noun may have derived from the Aramaic term *q^eshôwṭ* (7187). It means faithfulness; justness; equity; reality, truth. It is similar to our conception of a blindfolded, impartial woman balancing the scales of justice. See Ps. 60:4 and Prov. 22:21.

7200. Rââh'; to see, to see intellectually (Job 3:16; cf. 33:28), to look, to look at, to view, to inspect, to regard, to perceive (Deut. 4:28); to feel, to experience (Jer. 5:12), to understand, to learn; to live to see, to enjoy (Isa. 44:16); to be seen; to show oneself; to appear, to reveal oneself; to be shown; to cause to see, to show, to ascertain (Gen. 16:4), to verify (Gen. 26:28); to make one feel or know, to perceive (in the sense of hearing, Gen. 2:19); to cause to enjoy; to be made to see; to gain understanding (Isa. 52:15); to be fully aware (in life, Job 4:8); having a position of trust (II Kgs. 25:19); to examine, to investigate (Gen. 11:5); to supervise (Gen. 39:23); to attend to (II Sam. 13:5); to select (Gen. 41:33); to observe, to imitate (Judg. 7:17); to discover (Judg. 16:5). This word occurs about 1,300 times in the Heb. O.T. See the Gr. *horaō* (3708) which corresponds to the Latin *video.*

7202. Râ'eh; this Heb. adj., deriving from 7200, means seeing or experiencing. Its lone occurrence is found in Job 10:15 in the construct state.

7203. Rô'eh; this is a mas. act. part. which has its source in 7200. It means seer, prophet; vision, oracle. According to I Sam. 9:9ff., this word had been used from ancient times. It is applied to Samuel (I Chr. 9:22; 26:28; 29:29) and other prophets (II Chr. 16:7,10). The three words for the functional prophet are found in I Chr. 29:29: *rô'eh, nâbîy'* (5030), and *chôzeh* (2374). "Seer" emphasized the means by which the prophet communicated with God, the means by which the revelation was received (I Sam. 9:9) in relationship to vision (Isa. 28:7). *Rô'eh* is the alternate term for *nâbîy'. Nâbîy'* stressed the objective or active work of the messenger of the Lord in speaking God's Word.

7207. Ra'ăvâh; this fem. Heb. noun arises from 7200. It is a (satisfying) sight, a seeing, a spectacle. Ecc. 5:11 is the only appearance in the O.T. This is the Qal inf. form.

7209. R^e'îy; this mas. Heb. noun is traceable to 7200 and means a mirror or a looking glass. There is only one occurrence in the O.T. (Job 37:18).

7210. Rô'îy; this mas. Heb. noun derives from 7200, meaning a sight, an appearance (I Sam. 16:12; Job 33:21), a spectacle (Nah. 3:6), a warning example, a gazing-stock, looking, a vision (Gen. 16:13). There are only six occurrences in the O.T.

7212. R^e'îyth; this fem. Heb. noun originates from 7200. It means a sight, a beholding, a seeing. Its only occurrence is found in Ecc. 5:11.

7217. Rê'sh; this Aramaic mas. noun corresponds to the Heb. 7218. It means the head (Dan. 2:38), the visions presented to the mind (Dan. 4:5,10,13; 7:15), or the sum or the amount of something (Dan. 7:1,6; cf. Ezra 5:10). There are fourteen appearances in the Aramaic portions of the O.T.

7218. Rô'sh; the head, person; chief, leader (whether appointed, elected, or self-appointed, Ex. 18:25; Num. 1:16; Judg. 10:18; II Sam. 23:8; II Kgs. 25:18), prince (of the people, I Sam. 15:17; Isa. 7:8), captain; the head of a family (Ex. 6:14,25; Num. 7:2; 32:28; 36:1);

chief town or city (Josh. 11:10; Isa. 7:8); point, top, first rank (Ex. 12:2), the best, whatever is highest and supreme, the highest place (Job. 29:25), the summit of a mountain (Gen. 8:5); total (amount, Lev. 5:24), the sum (of words, Ps. 119:160), used in numbering men, especially soldiers, i.e., an individual (Judg. 5:30; I Chr. 12:23; even an individual donkey, II Kgs. 6:25); multitude (of soldiers, Judg. 7:16,20; 9:34,-37,43; I Sam. 11:11), a band, a troop; the beginning (in a whole series of acts, I Chr. 16:7); commencement (Gen. 2:10; Ex. 12:2; Prov. 8:26; Isa. 40:21; 41:4,26; 48:16; Lam. 2:19; Ezek. 16:25; Amos 6:7), what is foremost (Deut. 20:9; cf. I Kgs. 21:9); a column (I Kgs. 7:19), a chapiter; principal; an ear of grain (Job 24:24); a tower (Gen. 11:4), the head stone of a corner (Ps. 118:22); (metaphorically) extreme joy (Ps. 137:6), the most excellent spices (Ex. 30:23; Song of Sol. 4:14; Ezek. 27:22). The basic meaning of *rô'sh* is "head." This verb occurs almost 600 times with a large variety of meanings. It can be the head of the human body (Gen. 40:20; II Sam. 4:8) or the head of an animal (Gen. 3:15) or of a statue (Dan. 2:32). In Dan. 7:9 even God is pictured as having a head. In Lev. 14:9 it refers to the hair on one's head. Also, it can be the head of a bed (Gen. 47:31) or the ends of poles (I Kgs. 8:8). It is when a journey begins (Ezek. 16:25), the source (Gen. 2:10). In Job 22:12 it is the zenith of the sky. *Rô'sh* is also used in some idioms: "To bring their conduct upon their head" means to repay him for his evil deeds (Ezek. 9:10; 11:21; 16:43). "Lifting up one's own head" is declaring one's innocence (Job 10:15) or the intention not to begin a war (Judg. 8:28). "Lifting someone else's head" means to restore that person to his previous position (Gen. 40:13). When *rô'sh* is used with the Heb. verb *rûwm* (7311), it can signify the victory and power of an enthroned king (Ps. 3:3; 110:7). Of interest to Christians is the usage of this word for both "top stone" (Zech. 4:7) and "chief corner stone" (Ps. 118:22). They were carried over into the N.T. and quoted by Jesus (Mt. 21:42; Lk. 20:17; Eph. 2:20; I Pet. 2:7). Jesus is the "head of the church" (Eph. 5:23).

7221. Rî'shâh; this fem. Heb. noun comes from 7218. It means top, head; a beginning; a beginning time, and early time. This was a Syriacism. Its only occurrence is found in Ezek. 36:11.

7222. Rô'shâh; this fem. Heb. noun arises from 7218. It is the topmost stone at a corner. The only occurrence is Zech. 4:7.

7223. Rî'shôwn or **rî'shôn;** this Heb. adj. derives from 7221. It means first (in place, time, or rank), foremost, chief, former, earlier, preceding, ancient; (as an adv.) first, before, sooner, formerly. This word occurs 182 times in the O.T. and has a very wide range of connotations. With reference to time, it means first (Gen. 32:17; Num. 10:13,14), previous (Num. 21:26), or formerly (Isa. 43:18; 46:9; Dan. 11:29). "Former things" in prophetic contexts means the past sins of Israel and God's judgment upon them (Isa. 42:9). There were forefathers or patriarchs (Deut. 19:14), former days (Deut. 10:10), former prophets (Zech. 1:4; 7:7,12), and things which were formerly foretold (Isa. 42:9; 43:9; 48:3). Gen. 40:13 means former position. Another basic meaning is "first in a series." It is the opp. of *'achărôwn* (314). It may refer to the first month (Ex. 40:2), the first day (Ex. 12:15), the former temple (Ezra 3:12), or the first born (Gen. 25:25ff.). Sometimes it denotes the most prominent in a series, e.g., God is the First and the Last (Isa. 41:4). The most prominent people sat at a banquet in first place (Esth. 1:14; cf. Lk. 14:7-11). *Rî'shôwn* refers to precedence (Gen. 13:4; 33:2; Ezra 9:2). In Gen. 8:13 it means first in a temporal sequence. The most common usage is the sense of "before" or "formerly" (Gen. 28:19; Deut. 13:9). See these Gr. words: *proteros* (4387), *prōtos* (4413), *emprosthen* (1715), and *archē* (746).

7224. Rî'shônîy; this Heb. adj. originates from 7223, meaning "first." It occurs only once in the Heb. O.T. (Jer. 25:1).

7225. Rê'shîyth; this fem. Heb. noun has its source in 7218. It means the first (in place, time, order, or rank), first (with regard to dignity, e.g., Amos 6:1,6), the first of its kind (e.g., with regard to time, firstfruits (Gen. 49:3; cf., Rev. 3:14 where Jesus Christ is the Source of creation); the beginning of a fixed period of time (Gen. 1:1; Deut. 11:12; Job 42:12), commencement, origin (Gen. 10:10; Jer. 28:1), former state (Job 42:12), former times (Isa. 46:10); the best, the choicest, firstling. This noun appears fifty times in almost all parts of the O.T. In Heb. this is the first word in the Bible. Some modernistic translators have attempted to translate this first phrase as: "When God began to create. . . ." Both the Septuagint translation of Gen. 1:1 and the Gr. construction of Jn. 1:1 properly translate the text. They leave no doubt that Gen. 1:1 was the initial act of creation. *Rê'shîyth* refers to the initiation of a series of historical events (Gen. 10:10; Jer. 26:1) as well as a foundation (Ps. 111:10; Prov. 1:7). It is the start, not the end (Job 8:7; 42:12). Quite often it is used of the firstfruits which were offered in the tabernacle (Lev. 2:12; 23:10; Deut. 18:4; 26:10; Neh. 12:44) and the choicest "fruits" were so distinguished (Num. 18:12). See *archē* (746) in the N.T. lexical section.

7261. Rabr^{e}bân; this Aramaic term comes from 7260. It is a mas. noun which means a magnate, a lord, a prince, or a noble. The word only appears in the Book of Daniel (Dan. 4:36; 5:1-3,9,10,23; 6:17). There are eight instances.

7264. Râgaz; to quiver (with any violent emotion, especially anger or fear), to be afraid, to stand in awe, to be disquieted (I Sam. 28:15; Jer. 50:34), to fret, to be in trouble, to be stirred, to be moved, to be moved with fear, i.e., to tremble (Ps. 4:4; Isa. 32:10,11), to cause to fear, to make tremble (Job 9:6; Isa. 14:16; 13:13; 33:9); to be excited; to be moved for joy (Jer. 33:9); to tremble, to quake; to agitate; to be disturbed (II Sam. 7:10; Isa. 14:9); to be angry (Prov. 29:9; Isa. 28:21; Ezek. 16:43), to be enraged, to act with anger (Isa. 37:28,29), to provoke to anger, to irritate (Job 12:6). The basic meaning is "to shake" resulting from fear, anxiety, and anger. Sometimes it is literal (I Sam. 14:15). See the related Gr. term, *orgē* (3709).

7265. R^{e}gaz; this Aramaic verb corresponds to 7264. It means to provoke to anger. Its sole occurrence is found in Ezra 5:12.

7266. R^{e}gaz; this mas. Aramaic noun derives from 7265. It means violent anger or rage. Dan. 3:13 is the only appearance in the Aramaic portions of the Bible.

7267. Rôgez; this mas. Heb. noun originates from 7264. It means commotion, perturbation (Job 3:17,26; 14:1; Isa. 14:3), restlessness, agitation, excitement, rage (of a horse, Job 39:24), the raging of thunder (Job 37:2), anger (Hab. 3:2), tumult, trouble, turmoil, noise, crash. The term occurs seven times in the Heb. O.T.

7268. Raggâz; this Heb. adj. arises from 7264. It means timid or trembling. There is only one occurrence (Deut. 28:65).

7269. Rogzâh; this fem. Heb. noun is the fem. form of 7267, which comes from 7264. It means trepidation, trembling, or quaking. The single occurrence is found in Ezek. 12:18.

7283. Râgash; to be noisy, to be tumultuous; enrage; to plot, to conspire. Quoted in Acts 4:25, this word was used of the opposing nations in Ps. 2:1, the only occurrence in the Heb. O.T. See *phruassō* (5433) in Strong's Gr. Dictionary.

7284. R^{e}gash; this Aramaic term corresponds to the Heb. 7283. It means to gather in a tumultuous way, to run together with tumult; to assemble noisily (Dan. 6:6,-11,15). These are the only three occurrences in the Aramaic portions of the Bible.

7285. Regesh or **rigshâh;** these Heb. nouns derive from 7283. The meaning is a crowd of people, a noisy crowd, an insurrection. The mas. form (*regesh*) is found in Ps. 55:14 and the fem. form (*rigshâh*) is found in Ps. 64:2. These are the only two appearances.

7287. Râdâh; to tread down as a winepress with the feet, to subjugate, to crumble, to subdue (Gen. 1:28; Lev. 26:17; Num. 24:19; I Kgs. 4:24; Ps. 68:27; Isa. 14:6; Ezek. 34:4), to oppress, to walk on a person (Ps.

49:14); to rule, to sway; to cause to rule; to have dominion; to prevail against, to reign, to take (possession of honey from a hive, Judg. 14:9), to scrape out (Jer. 5:31). The Talmud used the word for taking bread out of an oven.

7297. Râhâh; this is a primary Heb. root which means to fear or to tremble. It may be related to either 3384 or 6342. Its lone occurrence is found in Isa. 44:8.

7300. Rûwd; to tramp around, to ramble freely, to rove around, to be restless, to roam, to wander; to have dominion, to be lord, to rule; to mourn; to neglect (God). This word is used of animals who had broken the yoke and were wandering around freely (they were on the loose). The term is also used to describe God's people in their unbridled moral state (Jer. 2:31; Hos. 11:12).

7304. Râvach; to breathe freely, to revive; to have ample room, to be wide or easy, to be spacious, to be loose (I Sam. 16:23; Job 32:20), to be airy (Jer. 22:14), to be extended, to be large; to be refreshed. These are the only three occurrences in the Heb. O.T.

7305. Revach; a room, an interval, a space (Gen. 32:16); deliverance, relief, enlargement, relaxation, liberation from distress (Esth. 4:14). These are the only two appearances.

7306. Rûwach; to blow, to breathe (especially with the nostrils as in smelling, Gen. 8:21; 27:27), to smell, to presage (as a horse, the scent of battle, Job 39:25), to enjoy the odor, to smell with pleasure (Ex. 30:38; Lev. 26:31); to delight in (Isa. 11:3; Amos 5:21, with the signification of sweet smell); (metaphorically) used with the sense of feeling fire which has been brought near (Judg. 16:9). There are eleven occurrences in the Heb. O.T.

7307. Rûwach; this fem. Heb. noun derives from 7306. It means air for breathing, air that is being breathed (Judg. 15:19; Jer. 14:6), breath (Job 41:16; Jer. 2:24; 10:14; 14:6), breath of the nostrils, sniffing, snorting (Job 4:9; Ps. 18:15), the breath of one's mouth (Ps. 33:6, i.e., the creative Word of God; cf. Isa. 11:4), anything which passes quickly, the air put in motion by divine breath (Ex. 15:8; Job 15:30), the blast of God (I Kgs. 18:12; II Kgs. 2:16; Isa. 40:7; 59:19; Ezek. 3:14; 11:24), to respire (Job 9:18); the cool evening breeze (Gen. 3:8), the wind (Gen. 8:1; Isa. 7:2; 41:16), a gale or tornado (Jer. 4:11; Hos. 8:7), a very strong wind (Ex. 10:19), wind as a quarter of heaven (I Chr. 9:24), a storm (Job 1:19; 30:15; Isa. 27:8; 32:2); air in motion, breeze, blowing; the invisible, intangible, fleeting quality of air (Job 7:7); speaking (Ex. 15:8); the vital spirit (Gen. 6:17; 7:15,22; Job 17:1; 19:17; Ps. 135:17), the element of life in a person, i.e., his natural "spirit," even animals (Gen. 7:22; Ps. 104:29), ghost, soul (Prov. 16:2), life (Ecc. 3:21; 8:8; 12:7); even dead and inanimate things (Ezek. 37:8; Hab. 2:19), the human spirit as breathed by God into man (Gen. 2:7; Job 27:3; cf. Num. 16:22), the divine, miraculous power by which inanimate things begin to move (Ezek. 10:17; Zech. 5:9), the Spirit of God (Gen. 1:2; Ps. 51:12; Isa. 63:10,11), the Holy Spirit (Num. 11:17,25; Neh. 9:20; Job 26:13; 33:4; Ps. 104:30; Isa. 48:16; Ezek. 11:19; 36:26,27), the future empowering of the Messiah (Isa. 11:2; 42:1; 61:1) and His people (Isa. 32:15; Joel 2:28); the rational mind as the seat of the senses, affections, and emotions of various kinds (Gen. 41:8; Josh. 2:11; 5:1; Prov. 25:28; Ecc. 7:8; Dan. 2:1), the mode of thinking and action (Ps. 32:2; Prov. 18:14; 11:13; Isa. 19:14; 28:6; 29:10; Ezek. 11:19; 18:31; 36:26,27; Hos. 4:12), the human will (I Chr. 5:26; II Chr. 21:16; 36:22; Ezra 1:1,5; Hag. 1:14), the intellect (Ex. 28:3; Job 20:3; 32:8,18; Isa. 29:24), disposition (Ezek. 13:3; Josh. 2:11), temper (Ecc. 10:4), the essence of a particular quality (II Kgs. 2:9, Elisha); the Spirit endows a craftsman (Ex. 31:3; 35:31), a prophet (Num. 24:2; I Sam. 10:6,10; 19:20,23; Isa. 42:1; 59:21), an interpreter of dreams (Gen. 41:38), the courage of a military leader (Judg. 3:10; 6:34; 11:29; 13:25); purposelessness, uselessness, emptiness (Job 15:2; 16:3; Ecc. 1:14,17; Jer. 5:13; cf. Ecc. 5:16; Prov. 11:29); (metaphorically) anger (Judg. 8:3; Prov. 16:32; 29:11; Isa. 25:4; 30:28; Zech. 6:8); anything vain (Isa. 26:18; 41:29; Mic. 2:11), vain words (Job 16:3), vain knowledge (Job 15:2). This important Heb. noun occurs 387 times in the Heb. O.T. The basic meaning is "air in motion." Animals or men have breath (Gen. 7:22,23). This air may be inhaled (Jer. 2:24), on the lips (Isa. 11:4), or in the nostrils (Job 27:3). Rushing air through one's nose (a snort) depicts emotions of aggressiveness (Isa. 25:4) or anger. When one is sick, his spirit is consumed (Job 17:1). However, he gets his "second wind" when his spirit returns (Judg. 15:19; I Sam. 30:12; cf. Gen. 45:27). The *rûwach* of all mankind is in God's hands (Job 12:10; Isa. 42:5). It was bestowed by a special creative act of God (Gen. 2:7; cf. 1:24). Man's inner being reflects the image of God (Gen. 1:26). Eventually, *rûwach* came to mean the entire immaterial consciousness of man (Ps. 32:2; Prov. 16:32; Isa. 26:9). Though the O.T. usually treats man as a whole, it also recognizes that he essentially has two parts; flesh and spirit combine to form the "self" (*nephesh*). Man has a *rûwach,* but he is a *nephesh.* The *rûwach* is contained within its bodily "sheath" (Dan. 7:15; cf. Zech. 12:1). When someone dies, the immortal *rûwach* returns to God who gave it (Ecc. 12:7). Sometimes *rûwach* and *nephesh* overlap (Job 7:11; Isa. 26:9; cf. Ex. 6:9 with Num. 21:4). Both *nephesh* and *rûwach* leave the body at death. See Gen. 3:19; 35:18; Ps. 86:13; I Kgs. 17:22. *Rûwach* may designate a supernatural, angelic being from God (I Sam. 16:23). Satan is the accusing spirit (I Kgs. 22:22).

7308. Rûwach; this Aramaic term corresponds to 7307. It means wind (Dan. 7:2); mind (Dan. 5:20); Spirit (of God, Dan. 4:8; 5:12). During the intertestamental period "Holy Spirit" began to replace "Spirit." This is true in the Dead Sea Scrolls.

7309. Revâchâh; this fem. Heb. noun comes from 7305. It means breathing; respite (Ps. 66:12), relief, ease, relaxation (Ex. 8:15; Lam. 3:56).

7321. Rûwa'; to suddenly mar, to become evil, to be made worse (Prov. 13:20); to split the ears (with sound), to sound a trumpet (horn, Num. 10:9; Joel 2:1), to sound a shofar (Josh. 6:5); to shout with joy or for joy (Judg. 15:14; I Sam. 10:24; praising God, Ps. 60:8; 65:14; 108:10); to cry out, to cry out with a loud voice, to vociferate (in a war-like manner, Josh. 6:16; I Sam. 17:20), to raise a cry (exulting out loud over a conquered enemy, Ps. 41:11; for someone's honor, Ps. 47:1; 95:2), a mournful cry (Isa. 15:4; Mic. 4:9), to lament, to be noisy; to sound an alarm (Num. 10: 1-7); to triumph. There are two important Heb. synonyms: *yôwbêl* (3104) was the joyful sound which is applied to the sound of a trumpet signal (e.g., jubilee). *Tâqa'* (8628) was a single blast of a trumpet to summon an assembly. The primary overall meaning is "to raise a noise" by shouting or with an instrument. There are forty-two occurrences of this verb in the Heb. O.T., most of which are in Psalms. It was for encouragement in Ps. 95 and Ps. 98.

7333. Râzôwn; this Heb. mas. noun has its source in 7336. It means a prince or a dignitary. Its only occurrence is found in Prov. 14:28.

7336. Râzan; to be heavy, to be weighty (in the sense of august, Judg. 5:3; Ps. 2:2; Prov. 8:15; 31:4; Isa. 40:23; Hab. 1:10), to be judicious, to be commanding, to be honorable; (part.) a prince, a ruler, a king. These are the only six occurrences in the Heb. O.T.

7355. Râcham; to fondle, to soothe, to cherish; to love deeply (like parents, Isa. 49:15; Ps. 103:13), to be compassionate, to have compassion (as God does toward men, Ps. 116:5), to show pity, to be tender, to have mercy, to demonstrate mercy; to obtain mercy (Prov. 28:13; Hos. 14:3; cf. Hos. 1:6). This verb occurs 125 times in the Heb. O.T. and usually refers to a strong love which is rooted in some kind of natural bond, often from a superior one to an inferior one. It denotes the humane quality which should be innate (Jer. 50:42), because we all share the same struggle for existence. Small babies evoke this feeling (Isa. 13:18), but heartlessness sometimes prevailed (Jer. 6:23). God was compassionate even with the enemies of Isreal (I Kgs. 8:50; Jer. 42:12). God looked upon

His own people as a father looks upon his children; He has pity for them (cf. Mic. 7:19). He is gracious and merciful to whomever He chooses (Ex. 33:19). See especially the suffering Servant-Messiah message (Isa. 54:7,8).

7356. Racham; a womb (Gen. 49:25; Job 10:18; 38:8; Isa. 46:3; Jer. 20:17), a maiden; (in the pl.) the bowels, compassion, mercy, sympathy, tenderness, pity, sensitive love. *Racham* or *rechem* (7358), the mas. equivalent, is distinguished from *beṭen* (990), "belly." *Racham* is most often used of God (e.g., II Sam. 24:14). See the Gr. *eleos* (1656), cf. Mt. 9:27; Lk. 1:50.

7364. Râchats; to wash, to rinse; to wash oneself, to bathe (Ex. 2:5; II Sam. 11:2); to be washed (Prov. 30:12). There are a variety of objects to *râchats:* the human body (Gen. 18:4; 43:31; Lev. 14:9; Deut. 21:6), meats (Lev. 1:9), sacrificial animals parts (Ex. 29:17), etc. Beautiful eyes were figuratively "washed with milk" (Song of Sol. 5:12) and feet were washed for adornment (Song of Sol. 5:3). Compare Ruth 3:3. Washing the hands showed that one was declaring himself to be innocent (Ps. 26:6; 73:13; cf. Pilate's action in Mt. 27:24). Metaphorically, *râchats* was used to describe the defilement of sin which adheres to men (Isa. 4:4). Of the total seventy-five occurrences in the Heb. O.T., twenty-six of them appear in the ritual washings of Leviticus. The concept of cleansing from sin (Isa. 1:16; Ezek. 16:4,9; 23:40) was carried over into the N.T. in purification ceremonies and association with baptism (immersion). See Mt. 15:2; Mk. 7:1-5; Jn. 2:6; 3:5,6,25; Acts 22:16; Eph. 5:26; Tit. 3:5; Heb. 9:10; I Pet. 3:20,21. *kâbaç* (3526), a Heb. syn., was used for washing garments.

7366. Rachats; this mas. Heb. noun originates from 7366. It means a washing or a bath. The only two occurrences in the Heb. O.T. are Ps. 60:8 and Ps. 108:9.

7367. Rachtsâh; this fem. Heb. noun is equivalent to 7366. It is a bathing place, a washing, a watering place. There are only two occurrences in the Heb. O.T. (Song of Sol. 4:2; 6:6).

7374. Reṭeṭ; this mas. Heb. noun comes from an unused root which probably meant "to tremble." The sub. means fear, terror, or panic. There is only one occurrence in the Heb. O.T. (Jer. 49:24).

7378. Rîyb or **rûwb;** to toss, to grapple, to wrangle, to strive, to contend, to quarrel, to hold a controversy, to plead; to conduct a legal case, to make a charge, to defend, to be an adversary, to complain (Judg. 21:22; Job 33:13; Jer. 2:29; 12:1), to debate; to contend forensically, to plead a cause or case (I Sam. 24:15; 25:39; Ps. 43:1; Isa. 1:17; 51:22); (part.) a pleader, a defender (Jer. 19:20); an adversary. This Heb. verb occurs seventy times in the Heb. O.T. It has the idea of seizing another by the hair (cf. the Heb. syn. *nâtsâh,* 5327). It means to strive with words (Gen. 26:20; 31:36; Judg. 8:1; 21:22; Job 9:3; 10:2; 33:13; Ps. 103:9; Isa. 27:8, 45:9). Contentious words sometimes lead to bodily struggle and injury (Ex. 21:18). In Isa. 3:13 Israel herself is on trial with God bringing the indictment (cf. Amos 7:4). A valid legal case could be made against Judah (Mic. 6). In many cases the Septuagint has *machomai* (3164). In other places it renders *rîyb* with *loidoreō* (3058). This sort of thing is severely forbidden in the N.T. (Mt. 5:11; 1 Cor. 6:10; 15:11; I Tim. 5:14). I Sam. 15:5 is the only reference which means "set an ambush." In summary, *rîyb* has to do with either physical, verbal, or legal combat most of the time.

7379. Rîyb or **rîb;** this mas. Heb. noun is a deriv. of 7378. It means quarrel, contest (personal or legal), strife (Gen. 13:7; Deut. 25:1), contention, controversy, feud, dispute (Ex. 17:7), a judicial or forensic cause (Ex. 23:2; Judg. 12:2), a lawsuit, litigation, a plea; an adversary (Job 31:35; cf. Isa. 41:11). In some poetic passages it has the distinct connotation of chastisement or punishment (Ps. 43:1). It is contrasted with *shalvâh* (7962), "quietness," in Prov. 17:1. There are sixty occurrences of this Heb. noun in the O.T. It covers the entire process of adjudication (Ex. 23:3; cf. Deut. 19:17) and various parts of a lawsuit (Job 29:16; 13:6; Jer. 18:19; Isa. 34:8). Even conflicts outside the courtroom employ this term, e.g., a quarrel between individuals (Deut. 25:1; Prov. 17:14) or between groups (Gen. 13:7,8). It is desirable to settle out of court if possible (Prov. 25:8,9; cf. Mt. 5:25,26).

7451. Ra'; this common Heb. adj. arises from 7489. It smeans bad, inferior quality (Gen. 41:3,19; Lev. 27:10,12,14; Num. 13:19; Jer. 24:2), wicked, evil (words, Prov. 15:26; thoughts, Gen. 6:5; actions, Deut. 17:5; Neh. 13:17), mischievous, severe (Ezek. 14:21; cf. Deut. 6:22), malignant, noxious, injurious, hurtful (I Sam. 30:22; Esth. 7:6; Job 35:12), unpleasant (i.e., giving pain or causing unhappiness, Gen. 47:9; Ex. 33:4; cf. Gen. 37:2; Prov. 15:10), hideous fierce, wild (Gen. 37:20; Ps. 78:49; cf. Gen. 37:33; Lev. 26:6); as a sub., an evil, a wickedness (Hos. 10:15), a wrong, a moral deficiency, mischief, misfortune, adversity, a bad thing which someone does (Job 20:12; Ps. 97:10), a calamity which happens to someone (Gen. 19:19; 44:4), unpleasantness (Deut. 7:15; cf. 28:59), deadliness (Ps. 144:10; Ezek. 5:16), sadness (Neh. 2:2). The essential meaning of either the adj. or noun is the inability to come up to good standards which will benefit. It is the opp. of *ṭôwb* (2896), "good." God exhorted His people to turn away from *ra'* (Deut. 13:11; II Kgs. 17:13; II Chr. 7:14; Ezek. 33:11; 36:31; Zech. 1:4). It is unethical, immoral activity against other people, whether by speech (Ps. 41:5; 73:8; 109:20), by practice (Mic. 2:1; 7:3), or by offering improper sacrifices (Mal. 1:8). This depicts a very negative inner attitude toward God or man (Ps. 7:9; Prov. 12:21).

7453. Rêa' or **rêya';** this mas. Heb. noun comes from 7462. It has an extensive range of meanings: a friend, a personal friend (Ex. 33:11), a superficial friend (Prov. 19:4), a companion (Job 2:11; 19:21; Prov. 25:17), a fellow, an associate, a neighbor (Ex. 22:14; Lev. 19:18; Isa. 3:5; Jer. 5:8), another (Judg. 6:29), one another (Gen. 11:3; 31:49; I Sam. 10:11; 20:41), anyone of the human race (Ex. 20:17ff.; 22:26), anyone with whom one has reciprocal relations (Jon. 1:7), one who is like a brother or son, part of the family (Ps. 122:8; cf. Ex. 32:27; Deut. 13:6; I Kgs. 16:11); a marriage partner (Song of Sol. 5:16; Jer. 3:1), a lover (Jer. 3:20; Hos. 3:1); a thought, will (Ps. 139:2); used of inanimate things (Gen. 15:10). This noun occurs 187 times in the Heb. O.T. It refers to a close friend or an occasional one, a chance acquaintance or an intimate companion In Ex. 21:14 a man was murdered by his *rêa'.* It simply means "colleague" in Judg. 7:13. The relationship between David and Jonathan went much deeper. Jesus forever defined this term, which was used in Lev. 19:18, the second greatest Law of the O.T., in His famous story about the Good Samaritan (Lk. 10:25-37). See the Gr. terms *plēsion* (4139) and *philos* (5384).

7455. Rôa'; this mas. Heb. noun derives from 7489. It means badness, wickedness, wretchness, sadness (of heart, Neh. 2:2; or the appearance of the face, Ecc. 7:3), sorrow, an evil condition (Jer. 24:2,3,8), especially in an ethical sense (Jer. 4:4; 21:12; 23:2; 26:3); a deformity (Gen. 41:19); unfit food (Jer. 29:17); a negative attitude (I Sam. 17:28). The word occurs nineteen times in the Heb. O.T., eleven of which refer to an immoral quality of man's activity.

7460. Râ'ad; to shudder violently, to tremble (before a vision, Dan. 10:11; cf. Ezra 10:9), to quake, to shake (i.e., an earthquake, Ps. 104:32). These are the only three appearances in the Heb. O.T.

7461. Ra'ad or **r^{e}âdâh;** this mas. Heb. noun has its source in 7460. It means trembling or terror. The mas. form appears in Ex. 15:15; Ps. 55:5, and the fem. form occurs in Job 4:14; Ps. 2:11; 48:6; Isa. 33:14. These are the only six occurrences in the O.T.

7468. R^{e}'ûwth; this fem. Heb. noun is a deriv. of 7462. It is a female friend, neighbor, or companion; a mate; another (Isa. 34:15,16; Jer. 9:20; Zech. 11:9). There are six instances.

7489. Râ'a'; this Heb. verb means to spoil by breaking to pieces, to break (Job 34:24; Ps. 2:9; Jer. 15:12); to make something good for nothing (bad), to make something evil (Mic. 3:4), to afflict; to dash in pieces, to shatter; to be broken (Jer. 11:16); to destroy; to be shaken violently; to perish; to be bad, to be evil (in the sense of having an evil, raging disposition, Num. 11:10; II Sam. 19:7), to live in a wicked way (I Kgs. 14:9; Ps. 37:9; Prov. 4:16; Isa. 1:16; 11:9), to be angry, to be sorrowful, to be sullen, to be envious (when used with the eye, Deut. 15:9; or sad when used with the face, Ecc. 7:3), to be wicked, to be displeasing; to do evil (Gen. 44:5), to act badly or wickedly; (as a part.) an evil-doer (Ps. 22:16; 37:9; Isa. 1:4). This root can have either a pass. or act. connotation in secular or sacred contexts. The denominative verb occurs seventy-five times in the Heb. O.T. with a broad range of meaning designating painful physical or emotional experiences. In the moral realm, it denotes any activity which is contrary to God's will, i.e., an attitude which rejects God's authority. Those who sin like this lack understanding (Jer. 4:22), deliberately plan to hurt others (Prov. 24:8) in a habitual way (Jer. 13:23) and compulsively (Gen. 19:9; Prov. 4:16; 17:4). The truth is that they injure themselves (I Sam. 12:25; Ps. 44:2; Jer. 13:23). However, God will inflict pain upon such people (Ps. 44:2; Jer. 25:29; 31:28; Mic. 4:6; Zech. 8:14) unless they change their ways (I Sam. 25:34; Ps. 15:4; 37:1,8; Prov. 24:19).

7490. Rᵉ'a'; this Aramaic word is the equivalent of 7489. It means to break in pieces or to bruise. There are only two occurrences, both of which are in Dan. 2:40.

7493. Râ'ash; to undulate, to be agitated, to tremble (of the earth, Judg. 5:4; Isa. 13:13; cf. Job 9:6; of heaven, Joel 2:10; 3:16; of the mountains, Jer. 4:24; Nah. 1:5), to quake, to shake; to wave; to terrify (the nations, Ezek. 31:16); to make (teach) a locust to leap (Job 39:20). This verb appears almost thirty times in the Heb. O.T., never in the Pentateuch. Hag. 2:6,21 is quoted in Mt. 24:29 and Lk. 21:26 to describe the Parousia. Hag. 2:6 is quoted in Heb. 12:26 to show the awesome power of God. *Râ'ash* describes the action of horses shaking the ground and the din of battle (Jer. 8:16). The primary notion of this term is a loud crashing noise. However, it seems to refer to the rustling sound of grain stalks which are moved by the wind in the poetic passage of Ps. 72:16.

7496. Râphâ'; this mas. pl. noun originates from 7495. It describes those flaccid, feeble, weak persons who are living in Hades. They were languid (Isa. 14:9), devoid of blood and animal life, but not lacking the powers of the mind, such as memory (Ps. 88:10; Prov. 2:18; 9:18; 21:16; Isa. 14:9ff.; 26:14,19). They were the dead inhabitants of the netherworld, the ghosts of the dead, shades in Sheol. The term is only a syn. for "the dead" or the "place of the dead."

7497. Râphâ' or **râphâh;** this mas. Heb. noun also derives from 7495. Appearing in the pl. form, Rephaim is a gentilic noun (cf. II Sam. 21:16,18). They were a very ancient, primitive nation of pre-Semitic peoples of Canaan who lived to the east of the Jordan River. They seemed to have been famous for their gigantic stature (Gen. 14:5; 15:20; Isa. 17:5; cf. Deut. 3:11). Some of them lasted until the time of David. This name appears to have been an inclusive term, referring to other tribal nations in Palestine—the Emim, the Zamzummim, and the Anakim (Deut. 2:11,20). At least, that is what the Ammonites called them. The Septuagint was the first to use the equivalent term for "giant." Regarding Og's famous bed, it may have been a sarcophagus.

7503. Râphâh; to be slack, remiss, or idle (Ex. 5:8,17), to be weak, to be feeble; to desist (Judg. 11:37; Deut. 9:14), to sink down, to be despondent, to be disheartened; to be lazy (II Chr. 15:7); to loosen (a belt, Job 12:21), to let fall, to let drop; to withdraw (Ps. 46:11); to let alone, to abandon, to desert (Deut. 4:31; 31:6,8; Josh. 1:5; Ps. 138:8), to leave off, to relax (Ex. 4:26; Judg. 8:3; Neh. 6:9), to quit (Neh. 6:3), to stop (i.e., to let down the hand, II Sam. 24:16); to let someone go (Job 7:19; 27:6; Song of Sol. 3:4); to attempt (I Sam. 15:16; Ps. 46:10). This verb appears forty-three times in the Heb. O.T. with a wide variety of meanings and connotations. The basic idea of relaxing the hands, a letting down, can connote the loss of courage (II Sam. 4:1; Isa. 13:7; Jer. 6:24; 50:43; Ezek. 7:17; 21:7; Zeph. 3:16) or to discourage (Jer. 38:4; Ezra 4:4). The nouns of 7496 and 7497 may be related to this verbal root, but the connection is not entirely clear. See the Gr. *rhiptō* (4496).

7521. Râtsâh; to be pleased with (especially to pay off a debt), to take pleasure in, to delight, to like, to love, to be fond of, to be favorable to, to be kind, to be gracious, to be propitious, to receive graciously; to be pleasing or agreeable; to seek favor or appease; to show oneself pleasing; punishment which was accepted as satisfactory (Isa. 40:2). This verb occurs sixty times throughout all parts of the Heb. O.T. There are six instances in Leviticius which have the special sense of being ritualistically clean or acceptable. The root frequently describes God's pleasure with His servants, particularly the Messiah (Isa. 42:1). Sometimes it is paralleled with *'âhab* (157), e.g., Prov. 3:12.

7522. Râtsôwn or **râtsôn;** this Heb. mas. noun has its orign in 7521. It means delight, goodwill, inclination, pleasure, delight, favor, grace, kindness, willfulness. *Râtsôwn* is what a king can do if he chooses to do so (Prov. 14:35). It is the concrete reaction of a superior to an inferior, particularly God (Deut. 33:16; Isa. 49:8; 58:5; 61:2). This word is used when God felt favorably disposed toward the petitioner (Ex. 28:38). In other words, the high priest was "accepted," (i.e., permissibility). It was a voluntary, arbitrary decision (Ezra 10:11).

7523. Râtsach; to dash in pieces (Ps. 62:3), to kill a human being, to murder, to slay, to commit manslaughter; to destroy, to crush; to be crushed. *Râtsach* is a purely Heb. term, having no clear cognate in any of the ancient languages. It appears about forty times in the Heb. Bible, mostly in the Pentateuch. There are fourteen occurrences alone in Num. 35, which deals with the cites of refuge. Num. 35:11 delineates how those who were guilty of unpremeditated, accidental killings could seek asylum there. The root also describes killing for revenge (Num. 35:27,30) and assassination (II Kgs. 6:32) of many people (Isa. 1:21; Hos. 6:9), i.e., a massacre. In Prov. 22:13 *râtsach* was used for the killing of a man by an animal. This verb occurs in one of the Ten Commandments, referring to an unlawful killing of a human being with malice aforethought, either expressed or implied. The rights of helpless murder victims must not be deprived (Ps. 94:6). Life is sacred and retribution is just. See the Gr. term *phoneus* (5406) in the N.T. lexical section.

7549. Râqîya'; this mas. Heb. noun comes from 7554. It means an expanse, the sky, the vault of heaven (space), the arch above; pavement, floor. Literally, the Heb. term means "an expansion of plates," i.e., broad plates which have been beaten out. It may refer to a limited space, such as that of the canopy over the Cherubim under the throne in the vision of Ezek. 1:22,26. Or, *râqîya'* may refer to the broad expense of heaven (Dan. 12:3). Of the seventeen total occurrences, thirteen of them have this meaning, i.e., God's heavenly expanse. Gen. 1:20 denotes the open expanse of the heavens, where birds fly, i.e., the atmosphere. Gen. 1:14,17 points to an expanse of the sky which is farther from earth, containing the stars, the sun, and the moon. Job 26:7 depicts empty space. From Isa. 5:6, it is clear that the Hebrews knew that rain came from the clouds. Unfortunately, because many ancient people believed that the stars were fixed on the inside of a dome, and that the heavens were like an ocean (Gen. 1:7; 7:11; Ps. 104:3; 148:4; cf. Gen. 2:6), some liberals have affirmed that the Heb. Bible portrays the same world view. Under the influence of Alexandrian theories of a "stone vault" of heaven, the Greek translators of the Septuagint mistranslated *râqîya'* with *stereōma* (4733) and the Latin Vulgate followed suit with *"firmamentum."* Hence, our "firmament" in the K.J.V. Unlike Babylonian accounts, the Heb. Scriptures in a pre-scientific age accuragely insisted that God stretched out the heavens like gauze (Isa. 40:22). The limited *râqîya'* of Ezek. 1:22 means transparent. Was not *râqîya'* an apt, accurate description of what we now know as "space"?

7554. Râqa'; to pound, to expand (by hammering), to overlay (with malleable thin sheets of metal), to stamp (the ground with the feet in indignation, Ezek. 6:11; or in exultation, Ezek. 25:6), to beat, to spread out by beating (as God did with the earth, Ps. 136:6; Isa. 42:5; 44:24; as a thin plate Ex. 39:3; Num. 16:39); to overlay, (Isa. 40:19; with a hammer, Jer. 10:9), to spread out heaven (Job 37:18). In a figurative sense *râqa'* was used to describe crushed enemies (II Sam. 22:43), those who were downtrodden. It meant to stretch a precious metal over a solid object, like gold leaf. In a similar way, God had spread forth the tangible earth, expanding its land above the water and the sky to who knows where. There are eleven occurrences in the Heb. O.T.

7555. Riqqûa'; this mas. noun occurs only in the pl. form. It refers to thin plates, beaten-out metal which has been spread out broadly. Its lone occurrence is found in Num. 16:38.

7561. Râsha'; to be godless, to be wicked, to be lawless, to be fractious, to be guilty (Job 9:29; 10:7,15); to violate; to convict, to declare guilty, to condemn someone (Ex. 22:9; Deut. 25:1; Job 32:3; Isa. 50:9), to overcome (I Sam. 14:47); to act wickedly, to act in an unrighteous manner (II Chr. 20:35; 22:3; Job 34:12; Dan. 12:10), to be unrighteous (I Kgs. 8:47; Dan. 9:15; Ecc. 7:17), to act mischievously, to make trouble, to vex, to depart from God (Ps. 18:21); to have an unrighteous cause; to make a noise (Job 3:17; 34:29; Isa. 57:20). This verb occurs thirty-three times in the Heb. Bible with two basic meanings: to act wickedly and to condemn as guilty. It is the opp. of *tsâdaq* (6663) and *tsedeq* (6664). In summary, *râsha'* is negative behavior from evil thoughts, words, and deeds which is contrary to God's character and hostile to the human family (cf. Isa. 57:20). Because of this inner disharmony and unrest, social relationships of all types will be ruptured (I Sam. 14:47; Ps. 94:21). In short, one who lives like this has a lifestyle which is completely contrary to the laws of God (Prov. 17:15; Dan. 12:10). Only through true repentance, confession, and prayer can it be reversed (II Chr. 6:37; Neh. 9:33; Ps. 106:6; Dan. 9:5), *râsha'* is grouped with two other Heb. synonyms for sin in Ps. 106:6. Scholars believe that this verb was derived from the noun *râshâ'* (7563).

7562. Resha'; this mas. Heb. noun is probably traceable to another Heb. noun, 7563. It is a wrong (especially a moral one), iniquity, wickedness, godlessness, unrighteousness (Ps. 5:4; 45:7), lawlessness, injustice (Ecc. 3:16), dishonesty, fraudulent scales (Mic. 6:11), falsehood (Prov. 8:7), unlawful gain, wealth which was obtained in a wicked way (Mic. 6:10). This noun is found thirty times in the Heb. Bible. It denotes the kind of life which is antithetical to the character of God (Job 34:10) and draws statements of indictment and judgment (Isa. 58:4; Ezek. 3:19). One who pursues *resha'* will be destroyed (Prov. 10:2; 12:3; Ecc. 7:25; 8:8; Hos. 10:13). However, men can be forgiven if they truly repent (Ezek. 33:12).

7563. Râshâ'; this Heb. adj. derives from 7561. It means (morally) wrong, bad, wicked, unrighteous (Gen. 18:23; Job 9:24; 15:20; 20:29; Ps. 1:1,4-6; 3:7; 7:9; 9:17; 11:6, etc.), sinful, godless, lawless, vicious, guilty (Ex. 23:1; Prov. 19:28); 25:5; cf. 20:26), (i.e., liable to punishment, Gen. 18:23,25; Num. 35:31), (as a part.) sinner, oppressor, apostate. The term appears more than 265 times, mostly in Job, Psalms, Proverbs, and Ezekiel. It is rare in the Pentateuch and the historical books of the O.T. *Râshâ'* is used in parallel with practically every Heb. word for sin, evil, and iniquity. It is an objective fact rather than a subjective phenomenon, pointing to the attitudes and intentions of people. God is opposed to these types of people (Ex. 23:7; Job 9:22; Ezek. 38:11; Mic. 6:10). Generally, *râshâ'* connotes turbulence, restlessness, what is disjointed and poorly regulated. Girdlestone suggested that it was the confusion in which the wicked live and the perpetual agitation which they cause others. People with this characteristic are guilty of violating the social rights of others through oppression, greed, exploitation, murder, dishonesty in business, and twisting justice (e.g., Ex. 2:13; Num. 35:31; II Sam. 4:11). They hate the Lord (II Chr. 19:2). They are hostile toward God and His people (Ps. 7:9; 17:13; Isa. 13:11; Hab. 1:13). About forty times *râshâ'* is the opp. of *tsaddîyq* (6662) in Proverbs. Other antonyms are: *yâshâr* (3477), *maskîyl* (4905), *'ânâv* (6035), *'ânîy* (6041), and *tâm* (8535). *Râshâ'* is wrongdoing, being in the wrong. It is a legal term describing the state of one who has broken the law (Prov. 28:4; 29:2; cf. II Chr. 6:23). See the Gr. *anomos* (459), particularly in Acts 2:23. In a forensic sense, it means to have an unrighteous cause (Ex. 23:7; Deut. 25:1). It is an entire category of people who have done wrong, who are still living in sin, and who intend to continue with it. They do not seek God (Ps. 10:4), but challenge Him (Ps. 10:13). They love violence (Ps. 11:5), oppress the righteous (Ps. 17:9), do not repay their debts (Ps. 37:21), and lay snares to trap the righteous (Ps. 119:110). Especially see Ps. 1:6 and Ps. 73. God will judge them during this life in the hope that they will be ashamed of their deeds (Ps. 31:17), be overcome by sorrows (Ps. 32:10), will fall by their devices (Ps. 141:10), and may die a premature death (Prov. 10:27), but there will be no more memory of them (Prov. 10:7). Instead, there will be great rejoicing when they die (Prov. 11:10). In Mal. 3:18 a clearcut distinction between good people and wicked people is predicted in the future. Even though the inner lives of the sinners are haughty, vicious, treacherous, vile, unstable, and polluted, they sometimes come out on top temporarily (Job 9:24; 10:3; 16:11; 21:7; Ecc. 7:15; 8:14; Jer. 12:1). However, God will judge them severely (Job 36:17; Ps. 9:5; Prov. 24:20-24; Jer. 25:31; Zeph. 1:3; Mal. 4:3). If they truly repent, they could be forgiven (Ps. 71:4; 82:4; Isa. 53:9; 55:7). It was strictly up to the individual (see Ezek. 18 and Ezek. 33). The Septuagint has *asebēs* (765), *hamartōlos* (268), and *anomos* (459).

7564. Rish'âh; this is the fem. counterpart of 7562. It is a moral wrong, a fault, wickedness, unrighteousness (Isa. 9:18; Mal. 3:15), a wicked deed (Deut. 25:2), fraud, falsehood (Prov. 13:6), guilt. The term appears fifteen times in the Heb. O.T., mostly in the abstract sense of the act of wickedness. The Canaanites were expelled from Palestine because of it (Deut. 9:4,5). It contrasted with *tsedeq* (Prov. 11:5; 13:6).

7584. Sha'âvâh; this fem. Heb. noun arises from 7582. It refers to a din, a crash, a roaring, a rushing, a tumult, a devastating storm, a tempest, destruction, desolation, ruins. Its lone occurrence is found in Prov. 1:27.

7585. She'ôwl or she'ôl; depth, abyss, the netherworld, the realm of dead people, the world of the dead (like a subterranean retreat), the final resting place of everyone (Job 21:13), the grave, the pit; Hades; hell. There are sixty-six occurrences. The K.J.V. translates *she'ôwl* as "grave" thirty-one times, as "hell" thirty times, and "pit" three times. The A.S.V. and R.S.V. transliterate the word (Sheol). The N.I.V. has "grave," but with a footnote ("Sheol"). Although many like Gesenius believed that this word was derived from the idea of asking (*shâ'al*) (7592), i.e., demanding that everyone, without distinction, be in this hollow place, the actual etymology is uncertain. Except for the Jewish Elephantine Papyri where it means "grave," *she'ôwl* does not appear outside of the Heb. O.T. It simply meant the place of the dead. Though a future life is affirmed in the O.T., the details are sketchy. The Heb. Scriptures do not delineate the intermediate state and destiny of the wicked, but the resurrection of righteous people is clearly assured. Both good men (Gen. 37:35) and evil men (Num. 16:30) go there. In fact, the omnipotent God brings people there (I Sam. 2:6). It is a place of conscious existence after death (Ps. 16:10). *She'ôwl* definitely had negative, foreboding connotations. It was dreaded because it meant the end of physical life on earth and the beginning of an unknown, dark (Job 10:21,22) state. Deliverance from it was considered a blessing (Ps. 30:3). It was the land of no return (Job 16:22; 17:14-16). *Sh^e'ôwl* refers to the destination of human bodies—the grave, which is pictured as a dark, dusty location filled with mangled bones. All people end up there. *Sh^e'ôwl* should not be translated as "hell" in the sense of the Gr. *geenna* (1067). Though all people go to the grave, the souls of some will receive punishment in *sh^e'ôwl* (Num. 16:30; Deut. 32:22; Ps. 9:17; 31:17), but this is not spelled out in the O.T. In Mt. 11:23 Jesus alluded to Isa. 14:13-15, using the Gr. word *haidēs* (86). Also, Ps. 16:10 and Hos. 13:14 are quoted in the N.T. (Acts 2:27; cf. Acts 13:35; I Cor. 15:55). Jesus went to *sh^e'ôwl* (Hades), but rose from the grave. This was the foretaste of the resurrection of all believers. Lk. 16:19-31 shows two compartments. Eph. 4:9,10 and I Pet. 3:19 refer respectively to the descent of Christ from Heaven and His return there, as well as the preaching of Noah by the Spirit of Christ. On the very day of death, Jesus promised paradise to the thief on the cross (Lk. 24:43). The Bible does not favor the view of soulsleeping or annihilation of the wicked. O.T. passages merely assert a well-known fact—that each person's body will be buried. The Heb. Scriptures do not focus too much emphasis on the condition or destiny of the souls of men until the resurrection. The development of that theme is left for the N.T. and the resurrection of Jesus Christ, the Son of God.

7588. Shâ'ôwn; this mas. Heb. noun stems from 7582. It denotes an uproar, a noise, a tumult, a roar, a rumbling (Isa. 17:12), a rushing (of waters, Ps. 65:7; of a great crowd of men, Isa. 5:14; 13:4; 24:8; of war, Hos. 10:14; Amos 2:2; of clamor, Ps, 74:23; Jer. 25:31), devastation, desolation, destruction, horror (Ps. 40:3). The term is used eighteen times in the Heb. O.T., mostly in the Prophets, Isaiah, Jeremiah, Hosea, and Amos. Usually, it depicts the crashing din of a huge crowd. Twice it is a caricature of boisterousness (Jer. 46:17; 48:45). "The sons of noise" (KJV) means tumultuous soldiers (Isa. 13:4). Ps. 40:2 is problematic in interpretation. *Shâ'ôwn* is a syn. in parallel with *hâmôwn* (1995).

7591. Sh^e'îyâh; this fem. Heb. noun comes from 7582. It means destruction or ruins. The only occurrence is found in Isa. 24:12.

7592. Shâ'al or **shâ'êl;** to ask (in the sense of request, Deut. 18:16: Judg. 5:25; I Kgs. 2:20,22; 3:10; Ps. 21:4; Isa. 7:11); to inquire, to require, to request (information, Gen. 24:47; or an object, Judg. 5:25), to demand (Deut. 14:26; I Sam. 8:10; 12:13; I Kgs. 19:4; Job 31:30; Ps. 2:8; 137:3; Isa. 45:11; Jon. 4:8), to entreat, to beg (for aims, Ps. 109:10; Prov. 20:4), to ask for a loan, to borrow (Ex. 3:22; 11:2; 12:35; I Sam. 1:28; 2:20: II Kgs. 6:5), to ask for oneself (i.e., permission, I Sam. 20:6,28; Neh. 13:6), to ask about someone else's health (Gen. 43:27; Ex. 18:7; I Sam. 10:4; 17:22; 30:21); to beg (as a beggar); to question, to interrogate (Gen. 24:47,57; Josh. 9:14; Judg. 4:20ff.; II Sam. 20:18; Job 8:8; 40:7), to consult (God's direction or counsel, Josh. 9:14; I Sam. 30:8; the oracle of Jehovah, Judg. 1:1; 18:5; 20:18; the teraphim, Ezek. 21:21), to grant, to lend (Ex. 12:36; I Sam. 1:28). *Shâ'al* is a request for something. The intensity or the object varies. This verb occurs 176 times in the Heb. O.T.

7593. Sh^e'êl; this is the Aramaic equivalent to 7592. It appears six times in the Aramaic portions of the Bible. It means to ask, to demand (Dan. 2:10,11,27; Ezra 7:21) or to interrogate (Ezra 5:9,10).

7595. Sh^e'êlâ'; this fem. Aramaic noun comes from 7593. Properly, it is a question (at law), i.e., a judicial decision or mandate, a petition or anything which has been asked. Its only occurrence is found in Dan. 4:17.

7596. Sh^e'êlâh or **shêlâh;** this fem. Heb. noun originates from 7592. It is a request, a petition, a prayer (Judg. 8:24; I Kgs. 2:16); granting a petition (Esth. 5:6,8; Job 6:8); a loan (I Sam. 2:20). Something obtained by entreaty. See I Sam. I:27. This term appears fifteen times in the Heb. O.T.

7604. Shâ'ar; to swell up; to be redundant; to be left, to remain (I Sam. 16:11), to be left over (Gen. 7:23; 42:38; 47:18); to survive; to leave, to let remain (Ex. 10:12), to leave behind (Deut. 28:51; Joel 2:14), to have left, to retain (Num. 21:35; Deut. 3:3); (as a part.) a survivor (Ezek. 6:12). This verb is used 130 times in the Heb. O.T. Isaiah (4:3; 24:6) stressed the remnant concept before the Babylonian exile. This motif can be found even as far back as the Pentateuch (Deut. 4:27; 28:62). See Neh. 1:2,3.

7605. Sh^e'âr; this mas. Heb. noun has its source in 7604. It means the rest, the residue, the remainder, the remnant. This Heb. noun is used twenty-six times in the Heb. O.T. It is a syn. of *sh^e'êrîyth* (7611), which see. It refers to what has survived after a judgment, an elimination, or a catastrophe (e.g., I Chr. 11:8; II Chr. 24:14). Though there was a remnant of Syria (Isa. 17:3), *sh^e'âr* usually refers to the remnant of Israel, those who would survive after the punishment of the Babylonian exile (Isa. 10:19,20), and therefore, have hope for the future (Isa. 11:11,16). In order to accentuate that belief, Isaiah named one of his children "Shear-Yashub," "a-remnant shall-return" (Isa. 7:3). See the Gr. word *kataleimma* (2640).

7606. Sh^e'âr; this mas. Aramaic noun corresponds to the Heb. 7605. There are twelve occurrences in the Aramaic portions of the Bible (Ezra 4:9,10 [twice, 17, [twice]; 6:16; 7:18,20; Dan. 2:18; 7:7,12,19).

7607. Sh^e'êr; this mas. Heb. noun comes from 7604. It means flesh (i.e., swelling out, mostly poetic, Ps. 73:26; 78:20,27; Jer. 51:35); any food (Ex. 21:10); a relation by blood (Lev. 12:12,13; 18:6; 25:49), kindred. Some scholars believe that it comes from a second root which is homophonous, having to do with blood revenge.

7611. Sh^e'êrîyth; this fem. Heb. noun is a driv. of 7604. It is a remainder, a remnant, a residue, survivors (especially after a slaughter, Jer. 11:23; 44:14), posterity, the final portion. It is either morally good or bad, depending upon the context. The vast majority of instances use it as a technical term for the remnant of Israel, particularly in the Prophets (e.g., Hag. 1:12,14). Sometimes it is a syn. for *yether* (3499) (see Mic. 5:3 and Zeph. 2:9). It was a key concept for the Israelites who survived such calamities as war, pestilence, and famine (II Kgs. 19:31; cf. Ezra 9:14). The Jews suffered major catastrophies which brought them to the very brink of extinction (Jer. 42:2). Isaiah uses *sh^e'êrîyth* five times to refer to those who would be left after the Syrian invasion (e.g., Isa. 37:32). It also refers to the regathering of the Jews after the Babylonian exile (Mic. 2:12; 4:7; 5:7,8; 7:18). Jeremiah (40:11,15) discussed the plight of the Jews in Egypt. Zephaniah identified the remnant with the poor and the humble (Zeph. 2:3; 3:13) and he said that a remnant would be present when the kingdom of the Messiah appeared (Zech. 12:16—13:1,8,9). The Septuagint has *loipoi* (3062) and *kataloipos* (2645).

7617. Shâbâh; to transport (into captivity); to lead away captive (of persons, Gen. 34:29; I Kgs. 8:48; Ps. 137:3; of wealth, II Chr. 21:17), to carry off, to hold captive, to lead into captivity or exile; to be led away, to be held captive (by the sword, II Kgs. 6:22). The main idea is that of a military force subduing their enemies and taking them as prisoners. However, the male adults who survive are usually executed by the sword (I Sam. 30:2; I Chr. 5:21). Paul quoted Ps. 68:18 in Eph. 4:8. This imagery was emblematic of the ascension of Christ who rose in triumph over a host of opponents now taken captive. Isa. 61:1 predicted that the Messiah would proclaim liberty to those who had been taken captive. This was fulfilled in Lk. 4:18. See the Gr. term *aichmalōtos* (164).

7621. Sh^{e}bûw'âh; grammatically, this is a fem. pass. part. which means something sworn, swearing, an oath (Gen. 6:3; 24:8) by Jehovah (Ex. 22:11) or a convenant confirmed by an oath (II Sam. 21:7); an oath of execration, or imprecation (Num. 5:21; Dan. 9:11; Isa. 65:15), a curse. (Contr. *sh^{e}bûw'âh* with *b^{e}rîyth,* 1285). An oath is a solemn verbal statement or pledge which is affirmed, while a covenant is the substance of the agreement itself. Oaths were made by the Lord to show one's absolute certainty that the promise would be kept. Even God employed this instrument to teach us His reliability (Heb. 6:13-18). It could be a vow to perform some future action (Josh. 2:17,20), to ratify and solemnize a peace treaty (Josh. 9:20), or a simple renewal of devotion to God (II Chr. 15:15). There are twenty occurrences in the Heb. O.T.

7622. Sh^e^bûwth or **sh^e^bîyth;** this fem. Heb. noun has its origin in 7617. It means captivity (Num. 21:29), captives (Deut. 30:3; Ps. 14:7; 53:6; 126:4; Jer. 29:14; 30:3; Ezek. 29:14; 39:25; Amos 9:14; Zeph. 3:20); exile; misery, affliction. There are thirty-five occurrences in the Heb. O.T.

7623. Shâbach; to address in a loud tone, to be loud; to glorify, to praise God (for His mighty acts and deeds, I Chr. 16:35; Ps. 117:1; 145:4; 147:12); to boast (Ps. 106:47), to triumph; to pacify (through words), to calm anger (Prov. 29:11), to still (the waves, Ps. 65:7; 89:9); to praise, i.e., soothe with praises (Ps. 63:3). The idea is Ps. 65:7 is similar to the violent waves which Jesus calmed in Mt. 8:23-27. There are eleven occurrences in the Heb. O.T.

7624. Sh^e^bach; this Aramaic word corresponds to the Heb. 7623. It means to adore, to adulate, to praise. It only occurs five times in Daniel (2:23; 4:34,37; 5:4,23).

7625. Sh^e^baṭ; this is the Aramaic term which corresponds to 7626. It is a clan or a tribe, and is found only in Ezra 6:17.

7626. Shêbeṭ; a branch, a scion, a stick (for punishing, fighting, ruling, or walking), a staff (for striking, Isa. 10:15; 14:5; for chastening, Prov. 10:13; 13:24; 22:8), a rod (of a shepherd, Lev. 27:32; Ps. 23:4), a crook, a thrashing-stick; a ruler's staff, a sceptre (of a king, Gen. 49:10; Num. 24:17; Ps. 45:6; Isa. 14:5; Amos 1:5,8; of a leader, Judg. 5:14); a stem, a tribe of the Israelites (Ex. 28:21; Judg. 20:2), a family (Num. 4:18; Judg. 20:12; I Sam. 9:21), a division; a lance, a spear, the shaft with the spearhead (II Sam. 18:14), a dart; a measuring rod or a portion which has been measured off (Ps. 74:2; Jer. 10:16; 51:19). The rod was a symbol of authority in the hands of a ruler, whether it was a sceptre (Amos 1:5,8) or a weapon of war (Ps. 2:9; cf. Zech. 10:11). A Heb. syn. is *maṭṭeh* (4294), but it does not mean sceptre. The "rod of His mouth" indicates severe sentences (cf. II Thess. 2:8). God sent calamities like a rod of punishment (Job 9:34; 21:9; 37:13; Isa. 10:5). Jacob predicted that the sceptre would not depart from Judah (Gen. 49:10), and the psalmist foretold that the rule of Israel's ideal king would endure forever (Ps. 45:6). *Shêbeṭ* represents in a symbolic way words of authority from the Messiah (Ps. 2:9; Isa. 11:4). The most common meaning of *shêbeṭ* is "tribe," because each of the twelve tribes of Israel had originally been shepherded by a rod or staff. It had the meaning of tribe thirteen times. In fact, Jer. 51:19 even refers to all of Israel as "the tribe." The Septuagint translated *shêbeṭ* with *phulē* (5443), *rhabdos* (4464), *skēptron*.

7628. Sh^e^bîy; this mas. Heb. noun comes from 7618. It means a leading away, captivity (Deut. 21:13; Jer. 22:22; 30:16; Lam. 1:5), captured (animals, Amos 4:10), captives (Num. 21:1; Ps. 68:18), exile. The term is used forty-seven times in the Heb. O.T. with 75 percent of the occurrences indicating "captivity." The Assyrians scattered the northern kingdom of Israel in B.C. 721. The Babylonians took the southern kingdom of Judah into captivity in successive waves of B.C. 606, B.C. 597, and B.C. 586.

7633. Shibyâh; this fem. Heb. noun is a deriv. of 7628. It means exile, captivity (Neh. 4:4), captives (Deut. 21:11; 32:42). There is a total of nine occurrences in the Heb. O.T., all describing those who were captured during and after military engagements.

7637. Sh^e^bîyth; see 7622 for more information.

7650. Shâba'; to complete (seven), to swear, to confirm with an oath, to swear to, to take an oath, to pledge allegiance to God through an oath (Isa. 19:18); to cause to swear, to bind by an oath; to adjure. This verb occurs 184 times in the Heb. O.T. It is apparent that the word is related to *sheba'* or *shib'âh* (7651), "seven." The number seven was sacred. Oaths were confirmed by seven sacrifices (Gen. 21:28ff.) or by seven witnesses or seven pledges. The number was also considered sacred in the Ethiopic language, according to Gesenius. To "seven oneself" meant perhaps to bind oneself with seven things (Judg. 16:7,13). Herodotus (iii:8) and Homer (Iliad, xix:243) seemed to substantiate a septenary confirmation of a contract. According to I Sam. 20:17, *shâba'* refers to a human pact which was confirmed by an oath. Whether in religious or secular contexts, swearing was the giving of one's unbreakable word that he would faithfully perform a promised deed or that he would not harm his partner. God used this human convention on occasion. Since there was no higher authority than Himself, He swore by Himself (Gen. 22:16,17; cf. Isa. 45:23; Jer. 22:5) or by His holiness (Amos 4:2). Especially see Heb. 6:13-18. He did so by His own right hand (Isa. 62:8) and by His great name (Jer. 44:26). Some of the Jews swore by false gods (Jer. 5:7). Zephaniah condemned syncretistic oaths (Zeph. 1:5). Eventually, swearing degenerated to "one-upmanship" or even cursing (see Mt. 5:33-37 and Js. 5:12).

7663. Sâbar or **shâbar;** to look at, to view (Neh. 2:13,15), to expect, to wait for (Ruth 1:13), to hope (Esth. 9:1; Ps. 104:27; 119:166; Isa. 38:18). The primary idea seems to be that of digging out and exploring. It is unclear whether there is one root or two roots here.

7665. Shâbar; to burst, to break in pieces, to break to pieces (Gen. 19:9; Jer. 2:20; 19:10; Isa. 42:3; Amos 1:5), to rend, to tear in pieces (like a wild beast, I Kgs. 13:26,28), to break, to destroy, to perish (such as a kingdom, a city, or a people, Isa. 8:15; 24:10; 28:13; Jer. 48:4; Dan. 8:25; 11:4), to hurt, to quench (thirst, Ps. 104:11); to be broken, to be wrecked (used of ships broken by the wind, Ezek. 27:26) or founded, to be injured (having a broken member, Lev. 22:22; Isa. 8:15; 28:13); to break one's heart (Ezek. 6:9), to be maimed, to be destroyed (Hos. 2:18), to be torn in pieces (Ps. 124:7; used of wounded cattle, Ex. 22:10,14; Ezek. 34:4,16; Zech. 11:16); to be broken by penitence (i.e., to be contrite, Ps. 51:17); to shiver, to wreck, to crush, to smash; to cause to break forth, to open (the womb, i.e., the infant appears, Isa. 66:9; cf. Isa. 37:3; Hos. 13:13). This verb occurs 147 times in the Heb. O.T. with a broad range of violent meanings, for example, homosexual men threatened to "break down" (*shâbar*) Lot's door in order to sexually molest his house guests (Gen. 19:9). In one of the great plagues of Egypt the hail "completely shattered" (*shâbar*) the trees (Ex. 9:25). When Moses saw his people engaged in an orgy, he "shattered" (*shâbar*) the tablets of the Law (Ex. 32:19). The images of idols were "smashed" (*shâbar*) in II Kgs. 11:18. It was a common word for the breaking of earthen vessels (Judg. 7:20; Jer. 19:10), bows (Hos. 1:5), swords (Hos. 2:18), bones (Ex. 12:46), and yokes, i.e., bonds (Jer. 28:10,12,13). Metaphorically, it was a shattered heart (Ps. 69:20). God is the subject of this verb on thirty-three occasions. The altars of false gods were often the target of *shâbar* (e.g., II Kgs. 18:4; 23:14; II Chr. 34:4, etc.).

7667. Sheber or **shêber;** a bruise, a hurt, a fracture, a breaking, a shattering, a breach, an opening in the wall (Isa. 30:13,14), an injury (of a member, Lev. 21:19; 24:20); a wound (of a state, Ps. 60:2); sorrow, (Isa. 65:14), destruction, misfortune, ruin; a solution (to a dream), an interpretation. There are forty-five occurrences of *sheber* in the Heb. O.T. Twenty-eight of them are found in the Prophets, describing impending political disaster.

7668. Sheber; this mas. Heb. noun is identical in form to 7667. No one is certain if the two words emanate from the same root. This word means grain (possibly broken into kernels). There are nine occurrences in the Heb. O.T. (Gen. 42:1,2,19,26; 43:2; 44:2; 47:14; Neh. 10:31; Amos 8:5).

7670. Shibrôwn; this Heb. noun derives from 7665. It means rupture, pang, a breaking (Ezek. 21:6), pain; destruction. The word is used also in Jer. 17:18, "Crush them with twofold destruction."

7673. Shâbath; to repose, (intransitive) to desist (from exertion), to cease, to leave off (Job 32:1; Jer. 31:36; Hos. 7:4), to rest, to come to an end; to keep or celebrate the Sabbath (Lev. 23:32, a cognate accusative construction), to observe the sacred day; to be ended; (transitive) to sever, to put an end to (war, Ps. 46:9; contention, Prov. 18:18), to cause to rest, to let rest, to bring to an end, to cease to exist, to have an end (Gen. 8:22; Isa. 24:8; Lam. 5:15), to abolish, to remove, to take away (Ex. 12:15; Lev. 26:6; Ps. 119:119; Isa. 30:11; Jer. 7:34; Ezek. 34:25; 23:27,48; 30:13), to destroy. This Heb. verb occurs about 200 times in the O.T. The primary idea appears to be to sit down or to sit still. It describes men (Ex. 23:12; 34:21), land which lies fallow (Lev. 26:34,35; cf. 25:2), and the opposite of laboring or toiling (Gen. 2:2,3; Ex. 31:17). The traveler rests (abstains) from traveling (Isa. 33:8). The elders rested from the gate, i.e., did not go to the forum to the Sabbath. The seventh day "put to stop to" the week's work. Other related meanings are: to put away (Ex. 12:15), to put down (II Kgs. 23:5), to be lacking (Lev. 2:13), and to eliminate (Lev. 26:6). The most basic meaning is found in Gen. 8:22. There will be no "interrupting" (cf. II Chr. 16:5). The continuity of the rainbow in God's promise bcame a prophetic sign of the faithfulness of God (Jer. 31:36). Finally, God was not tired in Gen. 2:2,3. *Shâbath* may imply rest, but it does not necessarily do so. God's work was completed, and, therefore, there was no need to continue. He did not need to rest like a weary man; He only "stopped" His creative activity.

7676. Shabbâth; this Heb. noun means intermission, the Sabbath, the day of rest, the holy seventh day; a week (Lev. 23:15; cf. Deut. 16:9; Mt. 28:1), the sacred seventh year, a sabbatical year. The doubling of the middle consonant may indicate that this word is actually a Piel inten. noun, although the verb (7673) is never used that way. The concept of the Sabbath is very important throughout the Bible. It is the fourth commandment of the Decalogue. The Israelites were commanded to rest on the seventh day of the week (Ex. 23:12; 31:15). This meant not to work (Ex. 20:10). It was only on this day that God Himself "rested," i.e., ceased creating the world (Gen. 2:2,3). He sanctified the Sabbath as the climax of creation, as a time to enjoy by reflecting. Deut. 5:15 suggests that the Israelites needed to remember their hard work as slaves in Egypt. The Sabbath also had a humanitarian purpose which allowed dependent laborers to have a day of rest. A man's rest included his servants and animals (Ex. 23:12) even at harvest time (Ex. 34:21). It was a day of quiet worship (Lev. 23:3) as well as one of refreshment for man. The Sabbath was a covenant sign of God's authority. When Israel kept the Sabbath, they made a statement that they were subject to that authority, that they wanted to obey the entire Law of God (Lev. 25). It was a way of showing their trust in God, that He would honor their labors with fruit. We may plant the seeds and water them, but it is God who gives the increase (I Cor. 3:6). The prophets rebuked Israel for their neglect of the Sabbath (Isa. 1:13; Jer. 17:21-27; Ezek. 20:12-24; Amos 8:5). They also proclaimed Sabbath observance as a blessing in the Messianic age and a sign of its fullness (Isa. 56:2-5; 58:13; 66:23; Ezek. 44:24; 45:17; 46:1,3,4,12). The sabbatical year was the year when the land was not tilled (Lev. 25:4ff.). In a very real sense, the land of Palestine needed a rest from the sin of the sons of Israel. The length of the Babylonian captivity was determined by the extent of Israel's abuse of the sabbatical year (II Chr. 36:21; cf. Lev. 26:34,35). After they had learned their lesson, in about 70 years, God allowed some of them to return from exile. For the Christian, God's promises are fulfilled in Jesus Christ. Through Him we enter into God's own rest—heaven itself (Heb. 4:1-11).

7677. Shabbâthôwn; this mas. Heb. noun is a deriv. of 7676. It means a sacred time of rest, a great or solemn Sabbath (Ex. 16:23; 31:15; 35:2). The term applies to the Day of Atonement (Lev. 16:31; 23:32), the Feast of Trumpets (Lev. 23:24), and the first and eighth days of tabernacles (Lev. 23:39). The ending indicates that it is an abstract noun. There are a total of eleven occurrences in the O.T.

7683. Shâgag; to stray, to go astray, to wander; to transgress, to err by ignorance, imprudence, or inadvertently, to sin unwittingly, to commit a fault (Lev. 5:18; Num. 15:28; Ps. 119:67). In Job 12:16 there is a proverbial phrase, "misled and misleader," which denotes men of every type. Also compare similar phrases in Deut. 32:35 and Mal. 2:8.

7684. Sh^{e}gâgâh; this fem. Heb. noun stems from 7683. It is an error, a mistake, an unconscious or unwitting sin, a fault committed through inadvertence (Ecc. 5:6; cf. Lev. 4:2,27; Num. 15:27 in connection with *châtâ'*, 2398). The word appears nineteen times in the Heb. O.T. in connection with a special sin offering in atonement for this type of sin in ignorance. Whether one knowingly or unknowingly breaks the Law (sins), it is a violation. The presence or absence of one's will does not change the situation. Personal responsibility was being taught; negligence or ignorance were not valid excuses. At the other end of the spectrum were sins which were committed with a "high hand" (Num. 15:30), presumption. There was no atonement sacrifice provided for this type of sin.

7686. Shâgâh; to waiver, to wander, to go astray (Ezek. 34:6), to err, to transgress; to cause to wander, to lead astray (Job 12:16), to misdirect (the blind, Deut. 27:18), to seduce, to sin through ignorance, to transgress through inadvertence (I Sam. 26:21); to reel (as if intoxicated after drinking wine, Prov. 20:1; Isa. 28:7; even used of a man intoxicated with love, Prov. 5:19,20). This Heb. verb occurs twenty-one times in the O.T. The primary meaning is an unintentional, ignorant breaking of the Law. Job never denied that he had sinned, but he was not always aware of it (Job 6:24; 19:4). Like grazing sheep (Ezek. 34:6), we can gradually stray away from God's commands (Ps. 119:21,118; Prov. 19:27). What can cause such a thing? Alcoholic beverages (Prov. 20:1; Isa. 28:7), a seductive woman who is not one's wife (Prov. 5:19,-20,23), and the inability to fend off evil talk (Prov. 19:27).

7691. Sh^{e}gîy'âh; this fem. Heb. noun arises from 7686. It is a moral mistake, an error, a transgression, a sin committed through inadvertence. Its single occurrence is found in Ps. 19:12, where it is a parallel to a form which derives from *çâthar* (5641), "to hide" or "to conceal." Therefore, hidden faults are not apparent to the conscience.

7694. Shêgâl; this fem. Heb. noun has its source in 7693. It refers to a queen (who became so through cohabitation), a king's wife, a paramour, the consort of an Oriental king, i.e., his favorite wife. There are only two occurrences in the Heb. O.T. (Neh. 2:6; Ps. 45:9).

7700. Shêd; this mas. Heb. noun comes from 7736. It means an evil or wicked demon, an idol, a lord (cf. Baal). The word appears only twice in the Heb. O.T. (Deut. 32:17; Ps. 106:37) and only in the pl. form. If the Masoretic text is vocalized differently, it could appear in Amos 2:1. The Septuagint has the pl. of *daimonion* (1140). Even today in pagan religions the line between gods and demons is not sharply drawn. They consider that some of these beings are good and some are bad. However, the Jews generally regarded idols to be demons who allowed themselves to be worshipped by men. See the Apostle Paul's comments in I Cor. 8:4-13; 10:19-22.

7701. Shôd or **shôwd;** this mas. Heb. noun originates from 7736. It means violence, severity, oppression (of the week, Ps. 12:5; Prov. 21:7; 24:2), havoc, destruction (Job 5:22; Isa. 51:19; 59:7; Jer. 48:3; Hab. 2:17), desolation, ruin, spoil, wealth obtained by violence (Amos 3:10), ravage, a tempest (Isa. 13:6); an imprecation. Of the twenty-five total occurrences of *shôd* in the Heb. Bible, twenty of them are in the Prophets. A closely-related word is *châmâç* (2555), especially in Gen. 6:11. There it probably refers not so much to deeds of outrage and violence but to social unrighteousness.

7703. Shâdad; to be burly, to be powerful, to ravage, to be violent, to act violently, to use violence, to oppress, to rob (Obad. 5), to destroy (Ps. 17:9; Prov. 11:3;

Isa. 33:1), to plunder; to be laid waste (Isa. 15:1; 23:1; Jer. 4:13; Mic. 2:4); to lay waste (a country or a city, Ps. 137:8; Jer. 25:36; 48:8,18; 51:55,56); to be in ruins, to be destroyed, to be slain (Judg. 5:27), especially by a hostile invasion (Isa. 15:1; 33:1). This verb occurs fifty-seven times in the Heb. O.T. Twenty-six instances alone are found in Jeremiah. Twenty-two more instances are found in the Prophets. Babylon was the "destroyer" of Jerusalem (Jer. 6:26; 12:12) chosen by God to fulfill His purpose. However, Babylon herself would be devastated (Jer. 51:48,53,55,56). *Shâdad* is like the mauling action of a wolf (Jer. 5:6).

7704. Sâdeh or **sâday;** a plain (e.g., the country of Syria, Mesopotamia, Hos. 12:12), a field (the opposite of gardens and vineyards, Ex. 9:25; 22:5; Num. 20:17; Ruth 2:2), an open or cultivated field (a meadow which is plowed and sown, Gen. 3:18; 47:20,24), a piece of land, arable land (land that is either cultivated or could be cultivated. Gen. 23:8,9), a parcel of land (e.g., the field of a city, Neh. 12:29), the fields which surrounded a town (Josh. 21:12; cf. Neh. 11:25), open country (where the animals roam wild, Gen. 2:5; 25:27), territory, the borders (of a people, Gen. 14:7; 32:3; 36:35), district (used of the countries or empires of a king and metonymically of his subjects, Ecc. 5:9). *Sâdeh* could be used of pasture land (Gen. 29:2), unfrequented country which is potentially dangerous because of the isolation (Gen. 4:8; Deut. 21:1; 22:25) because of wild beasts (Ex. 22:31). It was open country outside a walled city (Judg. 9:32,42; I Sam. 19:3) and an expanse of country in contrast to mountains (Judg. 5:18; Jer. 17:3). A definite portion of ground may be cultivated (II Sam. 19:29), private property (Gen. 47:20; Isa. 5:8), city land which is adjacent to the town and subject to its control (Gen. 41:48; Lev. 25:34), the territory of a nation or a tribe (Gen. 41:48; Lev. 25:34), or a personal estate of a king (II Sam. 9:7; 19:29,30). In I Sam. 27:5, David and his men stayed in a city in the open field (*sâdeh*) which was unfortified. He intended to show that he was not hostile or a threat. The prophet Micah (3:12) predicted that Jerusalem would be plowed like a field because of the judgment of God. However, Jeremiah (32:7-44) stated that God would redeem the fields of Israel once again. This Heb. noun occurs 320 times in the O.T.

7706. Shadday; this Heb. word can function as a mas. noun or an adj. It is deriv. of 7703, meaning the Almighty, the Powerful One, or the Mighty One (God). Sometimes this term was used as an epithet of Jehovah, occurring with *'êl* (410), e.g., Gen. 17:1; 28:3; Ex. 6:3, and sometimes by itself (Gen. 49:25; Ruth 1:20,21: Job 5:17; 6:4; 8:3; 13:3). Like the Heb. word for God (*'elôhîym,* 430), *Shadday* is the pl. of majesty. The Septuagint has *pantokratōr* (3841) and the Latin Vulgate has *omnipotens* in the Pentateuch. The earliest appearance of this name was in Gen. 17:1 where God identified Himself to Abraham in this way. Later it appeared in personal names such as Zurishaddai (Num. 1:6) and Ammishaddai (Num. 1:12). The Akkadian word for mountain is *shadū*. Perhaps God was revealing His mighty power as being something like a volcanic eruption or like the "everlasting hills" (Gen. 49:26). In other words, God is strong and unchanged. However, Jehovah was not a mountain god like the Mesopotamian deities who favored mountain-top dwellings or temple-towers (ziggurats). The Tetragrammaton (YHWH), Jehovah (Yahweh), replaced this name (Ex. 3:15; 6:3). El Shaddai was the covenant name for God to the Patriarchs until the time of Moses. His covenant was moral and ethnical in character, not ritualistic or orgiastic. As a divine title, Shaddai is used forty-eight times in the O.T., thirty-one of which occur in Job, a contemporary to Abraham. There are seven occurrences where El precedes the word. Rabbis believed that the term meant the "One who is self-sufficient." It is used synonymously with Jehovah in Ruth 1:21 and Ps. 91:1,2.

7722. Shôw' or **shôw'âh** or **shô'âh;** these nouns come from an unused Heb. root which probably meant "to rush over," like a storm. It means destruction or ruin. The mas. form occurs only in Ps. 35:17. The other twelve occurrences are the fem. form (Job 30:3,14; 38:27; Ps. 35:8 [twice]; 63:9; Prov. 1:27; 3:25; Isa. 10:3; 47:11; Ezek. 38:9; Zeph. 1:15). Some have suggested that it was a poetic term for hell.

7723. Shâv' or **shav;** this mas. Heb. noun probably derives from the same Heb. root as 7722. It means nothingness, emptiness, vanity, anything which disappoints the hope which rests upon it (Job 15:31; Ps. 31:6; Mal. 3:14); falsehood (Job 31:5; Ps. 12:2; 41:6), lying, vainness, "in vain" (Jer. 2:30; 4:30; 6:29), sin, wickedness, iniquity (Job 11:11; Isa. 5:18); calamity, destruction (Job 7:3; Isa. 30:28). This noun appears fifty-three times in the Heb. O.T., mostly in poetry. Taking the name of the Lord "in vain" (Ex. 20:7; Deut. 5:11) is a very serious matter indeed. Not only does it mean profanity or swearing falsely, but it also includes using the Lord's name (reputation) lightly or without thinking (cf. Mt. 12:31,32,36,37). It could even mean habitual, rote, verbal expressions used in prayer (cf. "meaningless repetition," Mt. 6:7). The Septuagint translated it as *epi mataiō* (3154), "thoughtlessly." It is interesting that two meanings are found in the same verse (Job 15:31). The term designates anything which is not substantial, is not real, or is worthless (whether materially or morally).

7725. Shûwb; to turn back, to turn (oneself), to turn around, to return (Judg. 14:8; 19:7; II Sam. 6:20), to come back, to turn around (figuratively), to turn to Jehovah (i.e., a spiritual return to the Lord. Num. 14:43; Deut. 30:2; I Kgs. 8:34; II Chr. 30:9; Ps. 22:27; Isa. 19:22; Hos. 12:6; Joel 2:12; Amos 4:6); to be converted to God (Isa. 49:5), to turn to, to turn from, to cease from (Gen. 27:44), to leave off, e.g., from an evil way. I Kgs. 13:33; Zech. 1:4; from sin, Job 36:10; Ezek. 3:19; 14:6; 33:14; from anger, Ex. 32:12; from justice (Ezek. 18:24), to turn oneself away from Jehovah (Josh. 22:16; I Sam. 15:11) or from the worship of idols (Ezek. 14:6); to be restored; to restore, to repeat; to cause to return, to lead back, to seduce; to refresh; to be turned aside; to turn away, to turn upon; to draw, to bring, to drive, to lead back; to give back; to answer; to recall, to revoke; to render, to offer; to be brought back, to be given back; to and fro (Gen. 8:7), here and there (to recede, i.e., floodwaters, Gen. 8:3, to where they were before). The basic meaning of *shûwb* is movement back to the point of departure (Gen. 3:19; 33:16). A good example of reversal in direction is found in II Kgs. 20:10 concerning the sundial. *Shûwb* is the twelfth most frequently used Heb. verb in the O.T. It occurs 1,060 times, with an additional eight times in biblical Aramaic, where it is spelled *tûwb*. *Shûwb* occurs most often in the Book of Jeremiah (111 times). Man has a responsibility to repent, to return to God, turning away from evil toward good. The word is used for simple physical motion about 270 times. It is used like an auxiliary verb to repeat the action of the second verb more than 120 times (e.g., Gen. 26:18). Holladay claims that there are 164 uses of *shûwb* in a convenantal context, mostly in the Prophets. A number of places (e.g., Ezra. 2:1; Neh. 7:6; Isa. 10:22; Jer. 22:10; Zech. 10:9) refer to the return from exile.

7745. Shûwchâh; this fem. Heb. noun is a deriv. of 7743. It is a chasm, a depression, a pit, a ditch; depth. There are five occurrences in the Heb. O.T. (Prov. 22:14; 23:27; Jer. 2:6; 18:20,22).

7760. Sûwm or **sîym;** to set, to establish, to erect, to plant, to put, to set down, to lay in, to make, to constitute, to appoint; to turn; to be put, to be set. This is one of the most common Heb. verbs in the O.T. It is used 575 times. The basic meaning is to put something somewhere. The various meanings cluster into six sets: (1) to place a location (Gen. 2:8; Lev. 8:8; I Sam. 17:54; II Kgs. 21:4); (2) to appoint people to positions (II Sam. 17:25; I Chr. 11:25); (3) to establish a new relationship (Gen. 21:18; Judg. 1:28); (4) to assign something to someone (II Sam. 23:5; Ps. 19:4); (5) to bring about a change (Ex. 14:21; Isa. 41:15,18; Ezek. 35:4); (6) to set aside for special purposes (Ex. 9:5). See the Gr. equivalent, *tithēmi* (5087).

7786. Sûwr; to vanquish; to saw; to contend (Hos. 12:4), to strive; to rule, to hold dominion (Judg. 9:22), to reign, to have power, to govern; to make or constitute princes (Hos. 8:4). Compare the similar *sârar* (8323). There are only three occurrences of *sûwr* in the Heb. O.T.

7812. Shâchâh; to depress, to prostrate oneself (in homage to royalty or to God, Gen. 23:7; 37:7,9,10; Lev. 26:1), to bow oneself down (Isa. 51:23), to crouch, to fall down, to sink down, to humbly beseech, to do obeisance, to worship (I Sam. 15:25; Jer. 7:2) even before false gods and idols (Isa. 2:20; 44:15,17). This verb occurs 170 times in the Heb. O.T. It was not used in the general sense of worship, but specifically to bow down, to prostrate oneself as an act of respect before a superior being. Joseph saw the sheaves, representing his brothers, bowing down before his sheaf (Gen. 37:5,9,10). Ruth bowed before Boaz (Ruth 2:10). David bowed before Saul (I Sam. 24:8). This honor was shown not only to superiors, such as kings and princes (II Sam. 9:8), but also to equals (Gen. 23:7), but especially in worshipping a deity. Therefore, it meant to honor God with prayers (Gen. 22:5; I Sam. 1:3), even without prostration of the body (Gen. 47:31; I Kgs. 1:47). However, those who used this mode of salutation often fell upon their knees and touched the ground with their foreheads (Gen. 19:1; 48:12). In short, it was a way of showing submission (Ps. 45:11). The Akkadian cognate term meant "to wallow" or "to descend." See the Gr. equivalent, *proskuneō* (4352).

7815. Sh^echôwr or **shîchôwr** or **shâchôwr;** this mas. Heb. noun comes from 7835. It means blackness, and occurs only once (Lam. 4:8).

7816. Sh^echûwth; this fem. Heb. noun arises from 7812. It means pit. Prov. 28:10 is the only verse which contains the word.

7819. Shâchaṭ; to slaughter (in sacrifice or by massacre), to kill people (II Kgs. 25:7; Jer. 39:6), to slaughter animals (Gen. 37:31; Isa. 22:13) and human victims (Gen. 22:10; Isa. 57:5; Ezek. 16:21; 23:39; Hos. 5:2), to butcher animals for food (I Sam. 14:32,34; Isa. 22:13) and people (Judg. 12:6; I Kgs. 18:40; II Kgs. 10:7), to murder; to shoot out; to hammer out, to beat thin, to sharpen; to be killed, to be slaughtered. The Akkadian term meant "to flay" (cf. I Kgs. 10:16,17). This verb appears eighty-four times in the Heb. O.T., fifty-one of which refer to slaying for sacrifice. The word occurs in Lev. alone thirty times. It is translated in the Septuagint with *sphazō* (4969) and *thuō* (2380). Compare Rev. 5:6,9,12; 13:8 for the "slain" Lamb, representing Christ.

7825. Sh^echîyth; this fem. Heb. noun is a deriv. of 7812 and appears only in the pl. form. It means pit or destruction. The only two occurrences in the O.T. are Ps. 107:20 and Lam. 4:20.

7833. Shâchaq; to comminate, to wear down, to rub or beat in pieces (Ex. 30:36), to pulverize; to defeat, to rout; to wear out, to wear away (i.e., erosion of stones by water, Job 14:19), to hollow out. The word is figuratively applied to enemies in Ps. 18:42. The fourth and last occurrence of the word is found in II Sam. 22:43.

7834. Shachaq; this mas. Heb. noun has its source in 7833. It is a powder (which has been beaten fine), dust (Isa. 40:15); vapor, a thin cloud (Job 38:37); the sky (Job 37:18), heaven.

7843. Shâchath; to decay, to destroy, to ruin (Gen. 9:11; 19:13; Josh. 22:33; II Sam. 24:16; Jer. 12:10) by pulling down (Gen. 13:10; Ezek. 26:4), by wounding (Ex. 21:26), or by killing individuals (II Sam. 1:14) or the entire community (Gen. 6:17; 9:15; Num. 32:15; Isa. 14:20), by killing enemies (II Sam. 11:1), by harming in some manner (Prov. 11:9); to violate, to injure, to wound, to devastate; to act wickedly (Ex. 32:7; Deut. 9:12; 32:5), to act perversely, to be wicked, to kill, to mar; the destroying angel (Ex. 12:23; II Sam. 24:16; I Chr. 21:15). Several Psalms (57,58,59,75) have the title "Destroy Not." This may have been the tune to which the psalms were sung. The word is first found in Gen. 6:11,12,17, describing the corruption which prompted the devastating flood. It means to corrupt morally (Isa. 1:4; Ezek. 23:11; Zeph. 3:7). Jer. 2:30 uses the term to describe a lion on the rampage. It was a symbol for a trap in Jer. 5:26. A vineyard (Jer. 12:10), cities (Gen. 13:10), and a temple (Lam. 2:6) could be corrupted. This verb occurs 151 times in the Heb. O.T.

7844. Sh^echath; this Aramaic word corresponds to the Heb. 7843. It means "to destroy" in Dan. 2:9, where it is used as a pass. part. It occurs twice in Dan. 6:4 and means "crime." These are the only appearances in the Aramaic portions of the Bible.

7845. Shachath; this fem. Heb. noun derives from 7843. It is a pit (especially used as a trap), a pitfall; a water pit, a cistern (which has mud, Job 9:31); a grave (Job 17:14; 33:18,24,28,30; Ps. 30:9; 55:23), a ditch; corruption, destruction. The rich imagery of a pit in which snares were laid for wild animals provides the background for a figurative use of the word (Ps. 7:15; 9:15; 35:7; 94:13; Prov. 26:27). *Shachath* appears in the famous Ps. 16:10, where the Septuagint rendered it with *diaphthora* (1312) and Luke understood it in the sense of "corruption" (Acts 2:27; 13:35ff.). There is a total of twenty-three occurrences in the Heb. O.T. A full fourteen of these instances in Psalms and Job clearly point to an afterlife.

7853. Sâṭan; this verb means to attack, to accuse, to be an adversary, to resist; (part.) an accuser, an adversary, a lier in wait (Ps. 71:13; 109:20,29). The verb occurs six times in the Heb. O.T. with the flavor of bearing a grudge or cherishing animosity. David used the word to describe his enemies (Ps. 38:20; 109:4) who returned evil for the good he did.

7854. Sâṭân; this Heb. mas. noun comes from 7853. It is Satan (the arch-enemy of all good), an opponent, an adversary, an accuser, an enemy in war (I Sam. 29:4; I Kgs. 5:4; 11:14,23,25) or in a court of justice (Ps. 109:6; cf. Zech. 3:1,2). David referred to Abishai as a *saṭân* (II Sam. 19:22). Even the Angel of Jehovah stood in Balaam's way to oppose him (Num. 22:32). When the definite art. is attached, it assumes the nature of a proper noun, namely Satan or the devil. He seduces men (I Chr. 21:1; cf. II Sam. 24:1) and then accuses them like a prosecuting attorney in the courtroom of God (Job 1:7; 2:2ff.; Zech. 3:1,2; cf. Rev. 12:10). There is a diversity of opinion concerning the interpretation of Ezek. 28:12-16. Is this Satan? Is the King of Tyre to be identified with Satan? Satan's sin was pride (I Tim. 3:6). Perhaps Satan was addressed through the King of Tyre, as Jesus rebuked Satan through Peter (Mt. 16:23). Satan was the tempting power behind the fall of Adam (Gen. 3:15; cf. Rom. 16:20). However, Jesus was victorious over death and cast him from heaven (Jn. 12:31; Rev. 12:10). He will be completely destroyed (Rev. 20:10). He was not all-powerful (Job 1:10). Job learned that Satan could be defeated by making the right choices and that God could be glorified in every circumstance. See the Gr. word *diabolos* (1228) and *Satanas* (4567).

7855. Siṭnâh; this fem. Heb. noun is a deriv. of 7853. It is an accusation, a letter of accusation; opposition. In Gen. 26:21 it is a proper noun, Sitnah, which was a well so named because of the contention between the Philistines and the men of Isaac. There is only one occurrence of the common noun (Ezra 4:6).

7857. Shâṭaph; to gush out (Ps. 78:20), to inundate, to flow, to rush swiftly (like a horse, Jer. 8:6), to pour out abundantly; to overflow (Ezek. 13:13; 38:22), to overwhelm (used of a river, Isa. 30:28; 66:12; figuratively used of an army, Dan. 11:10,26,40), to swallow up with water (Ps. 69:2,15;124:4; Isa. 43:2), to sweep away (with a flood, Job 14:19; Isa. 28:17; Ezek. 16:9), to wash away, to drown; to wash something (Lev. 15:11; I Kgs. 22:38), to rinse (Lev. 6:28), to erode (Job 14:19), to (figuratively) wash off (Ezek. 16:9), to cleanse; to be overwhelmed (with a hostile force, Dan. 11:22), to be washed, to be rinsed.

7858. Sheṭeph or **shêṭeph;** this Heb. mas. noun arises from 7857. It is an effusion, a deluge, a downpour, an outpouring (e.g., of rain, Job 38:25; of anger, as viewed as a rapid torrent, Prov. 27:4), an inundation, a flood (Ps. 32:6; Nah. 1:8), an outrage; a sudden end (Dan. 9:26). There are six occurrences in the Heb. O.T.

7860. Shôṭêr; this noun is an act. part. form from an unused root which probably meant "to write." Therefore, it means a writer, a scribe, a superintendent, a magistrate, an officer, overseer, a prefect, or a ruler. It was quite general and was often used for many types of officials at different levels of society. The Egyptian taskmasters had Jewish sub-officials who drove their brothers in hard labor (Ex. 5:6,10). There were leaders during the wanderings in the wilderness (Num. 11:16). The term was used of the seventy elders who helped Moses with some of the administrative duties (Deut. 1:15; 20:9; 29:10; 31:28) and continued (Josh. 1:10; 3:2; 8:33; 23:2; 24:1). The word describes magistrates in the towns of Palestine (Deut. 16:18; I Chr. 23:4; 26:29; II Chr. 19:11; 34:13) and of superior civil magistrates (II Chr. 26:11; Prov. 6:7). In Josh. 23:2 it is parallel with elders, *zâqên* (2205).

7867. Sîyb; to become old, to be old (Job 15:10), to become gray, to have gray hair (I Sam. 12:2). These are the only two uses of the term in the Heb. O..T.

7868. Sîyb; this Aramaic word corresponds to 7867, elder. It only occurs in the Book of Ezra (5;5,9; 6:7,8,14).

7869. Sêyb; this Heb. mas. noun stems from 7867. It means old age, gray hair; an old man. There is only one occurrence (I Kgs. 14:4). The K.J.V. translates it as "by reason of his age."

7872. Sêybâh; this fem. Heb. noun arises from 7869. It means old age, gray hair. See Deut. 32:25.

7878. Sîyach; to ponder, to meditate, to muse; to speak, to talk, to converse (aloud, or even with oneself), to utter (with the mouth, Job 12:8; Ps. 69:13; Prov. 6:22); to complain, pray (Ps. 55:17; 77:3), to talk disparagingly (Ps. 69:12); to declare; to pray, to talk with oneself (i.e., to meditate, especially upon divine things, Ps. 77:6,12; 119:15,23,27,48,78,148); to sing (Judg. 5:10; Ps. 145:5), to celebrate something in song (Ps. 105:2); to consider, to think upon something (Isa. 53:8). This verb conveys the idea of going over a matter in one's mind, i.e., rehearsing it, whether inwardly or outwardly.

7879. Sîyach; this Heb. mas. noun derives from 7878. It is a contemplation, an utterance, a meditation (I Kgs. 18:27; Ps. 104:34), a thought; a speech, a discourse (II Kgs. 9:11), communication (II Kgs. 9:11), babbling (Prov. 23:29), talking (I Kgs. 18:27); a complaint (I Sam. 1:16; Job 7:13); prayer (Ps. 64:1).

7880. Sîyach; this Heb. mas. noun has its origin in 7878. It refers to a shoot (like a word which has been put forth); shrubbery, a shrub, a plant, or a bush. There are only four occurrences (Gen. 2:5; 21:15; Job 30:4,7).

7881. Sîychâh; this fem. Heb. noun comes from 7879. It means reflection, devotion, meditation, or prayer. There are only three instances in the O.T. (Job 15:4; Ps. 119:97,99). "It is my meditation (*sîychâh*) all the day!"

7882. Shîychâh; this fem. Heb. noun originates from 7745, and means a pit or a pitfall. It appears in Ps. 119:85 and Jer. 18:22. Also, it is the Kethib of Ps. 57:6.

7891. Shîyr or **shûwr;** to sing (Judg. 5:1; Job 36:24; Ps. 65:13; Zeph. 2:14), to sing (like a strolling minstrel), to celebrate in song (Ps. 13:6; 27:6; 33:3), to sing of someone (Ps. 138:5; Isa. 5:1), to sing to someone (Prov. 25:20), to praise; (part.) a singer (I Chr. 9:33; 15:16; Neh. 12:28ff.; 13:5), a female singer (II Sam. 19:35; II Chr. 35:25; Ecc. 2:8); to resound; to be sung. This noun was found about thirty times in the titles of various psalms. There were different kinds of songs; a joyous song (Gen. 31:27), a triumphant song (Judg. 5:12), a religious song (Neh. 12:46), and a love song (the Song of Solomon). This form seems to be identical with 7788.

7892. Shîyr or **shîyrâh** or **sîys;** these nouns mean singing (II Chr. 29:27,28), a song, a hymn, a poem. Instruments of music were sometimes employed (I Chr. 16:42; II Chr. 7:6; 34:12; Amos 6:5; Neh. 12:27). The song could be sacred (Ps. 33:3; 40:3) or secular (Isa. 23:16; 24:9; Ecc. 7:5; Ezek. 33:32). Amos 8:10 was a joyful song, the opposite of *qîynâh* (7015), a funeral dirge. The word occurs twice in Song of Sol. 1:1 and is to be translated "song of songs," i.e., the most excellent song. The Vulgate has *"canticum canticorum."*

7907. Sekvîy; this Heb. word comes from 7906, meaning observant, the mind, heart, intellect, understanding. Its single occurrence is found in Job 38:36.

7908. Sh[e]kôwl; this mas. Heb. noun is a deriv. of 7921. It means bereavement (Isa. 47:8,9), childlessness, loss of children, abandonment, the condition of one who has been left by everyone (Ps. 35:12). These are the only three appearances in the Heb. O.T.

7909. Shakkuwl or **shakkul;** this Heb. adj. comes from 7921. It means bereaved (robbed) of children (Jer. 18:21), of young bear cubs (II Sam. 17:8; Hos. 13:8) or "whelps" (Prov. 17:12), childless, barren, devoid of young (Song of Sol. 4:2; 6:6).

7919. Sâkal; to be circumspect, to be intelligent (Job 22:2; Prov. 10:5), to have insight, to be prudent (I Sam. 18:30), to act prudently (Ps. 36:3; Amos 5:13); to do purposely; to look at (Gen. 3:6), to behold, to pay attention to (Isa. 41:20), to turn the mind to (Deut. 32:29; Neh. 8:13; Ps. 41:2; 64:10; Prov. 16:20; Dan. 9:13); to have understanding, insight, or intellectual comprehension (Jer. 9:23,24); to have success, to give success, (I Kgs. 2:3), to be successful (i.e., to act in a prosperous manner, Josh. 1:7,8; II Kgs. 18:17; Prov. 17:8; Isa. 52:13; Jer. 10:21); to make prudent, to teach (Ps. 32:8; Prov. 21:11; Dan. 9:22); to have wisdom, skill, or expertise; to be upright, to be pious (Ps. 14:2; Dan. 11:33,35; 12:3,10). This verb is used about seventy-five times in the Heb. O.T. Contr. with *bîyn* (995), which indicates an understanding from distinguishing, *sâkal* relates to an intelligent knowledge of the reason. In other words, success comes through applying common sense.

7920. S[e]kal; this Aramaic word corresponds to 7919 in Heb., meaning to attend to something. There is only one occurrence (Dan. 7:8).

7922. Sekel or **sêkel;** this mas. Heb. noun has its source in 7919. It means intelligence, success, happiness (Prov. 3:4), discretion, knowledge, understanding, prudence (I Chr. 22:12; 26:14; II Chr. 30:22; Ps. 111:10; Prov. 13:15), insight, cunning (Dan. 8:25), good sense, wisdom, policy. A good example of a person with this trait is Abigail who exhibited common sense in a crisis (I Sam. 25:3).

7924. Sokl[e]thânûw; this Aramaic word comes from the Aramaic 7920. It means intelligence or understanding, appearing only in the Book of Daniel (5:11,12,14).

7931. Shâkan; to reside (permanently stay, either figuratively or literally), to settle down (e.g., the pillar of fire and cloud, Ex. 24:16; Num. 9:19,22; 10:12). To lie down for rest (used of the lion, Deut. 33:20; used of a nation encamped in tents. Num. 24:2; used of overcast clouds, Job 3:5), to rest (Judg. 5:17; Prov. 7:11), to abide (Gen. 9:27; 14:13; 26:2; Judg. 8:11; Ps. 68:6; Isa. 33:16), to remain, to dwell (i.e., Jehovah caused His name to be fixed, Deut. 12:11; 14:23; 16:6,11; 26:2), to place a tent (Josh. 18:1), to inhabit, to possess; to cause someone to dwell (Gen. 3:24; Job 11:14); (part.) a dwelling. This verb is used about 130 times in the Heb. O.T. The Israelites lived a nomadic life. Therefore, living in tents (Num. 24:2) was quite normal. In Ps. 102:28 the meaning is temporary camping. They needed more stability (II Sam. 7:10). God is the subject of this verb on forty-three occasions. He dwelled among them. Everlasting life is hinted at in Ps. 37:27. See the Gr. words *katoikeō* (2730, cf. Eph. 3:17), and *skēnoō* (4637, cf. Jn. 1:14; Rev. 21:3). Many scholars believe that *shâkan* is somehow related to 7901.

7934. Shâkên; this Heb. adj. is used as a noun. It means a resident, an inhabitant (Isa. 33:24), one who lives nearby, a neighbor (used of nations, Ps. 44:13; or an individual (Prov. 27:10), a dwelling, an abiding. *Shâkên* may denote those who are friendly (Ex. 3:22; Ruth 4:17) or unfriendly (Ps. 44:13; 79:4,12).

7944. Shal; this Heb. mas. noun is believed to be an abbreviated form of 7952. It means an error, a crime, a transgression, a fault. II Sam. 6:7 is the only occurrence in the O.T.

7952. Shâlâh; to be quiet, to be tranquil, to be at ease; to be secure, to be negligent; to wander; to deceive, to mislead, to seduce; to sin inadvertently from ignorance. There are only two instances of this word in the Heb. O.T. (II Kgs. 4:28; II Chr. 29:11).

7965. Shâlôwm or **shâlôm;** this Heb. mas. noun originates from 7999. It means health, security, tranquility (Job 21:9), welfare (i.e., asking about the welfare of someone in a greeting, Gen. 37:14; I Sam 17:18; II Sam. 11:7; II Kgs. 10:13; Esth. 2:11), good condition, success, comfort; peace (the opp. of war, Lev. 26:6; Judg. 4:17: I Kgs. 2:5), offering terms of peace (Deut. 20:10; Judg. 21:13), accepting terms of peace (Deut. 20:11), to make peace with someone (Josh. 9:15; Isa. 27:5), a peaceful man (Ps. 37:37), words of peace (Deut. 2:26), salvation; salutation (of departure, I Sam. 1:17; 20:42; II Sam. 15:9; cf. Mk. 5:34; Lk. 7:50); (as an adj.) well, peaceful, whole, secure, safe, happy, friendly (cf. Ps. 55:20), healthy, sound (used of the body, Gen. 43:27; I Sam. 25:6; II Sam. 17:3; 20:9; Job 5:24; Ps. 38:3; Isa. 26:3); (as a part.) wholeness (Ps. 69:22), safety, soundness, health (I Kgs. 2:13; II Kgs. 5:21; 9:11,17,22), concord, friendship (Ps. 41:9; Jer. 20:10; 38:22; Obad. 7), those who speak in a friendly way (Ps. 28:3; cf. Esth. 9:30), those who seek peace in full number (when used mathematically, Jer. 13:19); to encourage one who is fearful, to reassure him that everything is O.K. (Gen. 43:23; Judg. 6:23; 19:20; Dan. 10:19). This is a very important word in the Bible. It appears 237 times. In modern Israel the greeting is, *"Mah shlomkha?"* ("What is your peace?" or "How are you doing?"). One hundred and seventy-two occurrences are translated as "peace" in the K.J.V. The remainder is rendered by thirty different terms. *Shâlôwm* is clearly depicted as a satisfied condition, an unconcerned state of peacefulness, on the part of Abraham's ancestors (Gen. 15:15). It is a sense of well being. In Gen. 26:29 it means to be unharmed or unhurt. The "friend of my peace" (KJV) of Ps. 41:9 denoted a very close, trusted, familiar friend. Judas Iscariot, whom Jesus chose to be an apostle, treacherously fulfilled the prophecy. And so, *shâlôwm* is a harmonious state of soul and mind, both externally and internally (Ps. 4:8). Deut. 20:11; Judg. 4:17; and Jer. 9:8 demonstrate that it is a prosperous relationship between two parties or more. The "Prince of Peace" (Isa. 9:6) is the Messiah. He was destined to usher in a government of peace (Isa. 9:7). The new covenant would be one of *shâlôwm* (Ezek. 37:26). The Septuagint used *eirēnē* (1515), *eirēnikos* (1516), sōtēria (4991), and *hugiainō* (5198). Though *shâlôwm* can mean the absence of strife, it usually is much more. It expreses completeness, harmony, and fulfillment. To wish one *shâlôwm* implies a blessing (II Sam. 15:27), but to withhold it implies a curse (I Kgs. 2:6). Jesus said, "Peace I leave with you; My peace I give to you; not as the world gives, do I give to you" (Jn. 14:27). Here Jesus was clearly defining two radically different conceptions of peace. The only true source of peace is God (Ps. 85:8; cf. I Chr. 22:9,10. Christ is our peace (Eph. 2:14).

7966. Shillûwm or **shillûm;** this mas. Heb. noun comes from 7999. It is a requital, retribution, recompense, or a reward. There are only three occurrences in the Heb. O.T. (Isa. 34:8; Hos. 9:7; Mic. 7:3).

7980. Shâlaṭ; to rule, to rule over someone (Neh. 5:15; Ecc. 2:19; 8:9), to have dominion over, to govern; to cause to rule (Ps. 119:133); to permit, to give power, to give power over something (Ecc. 5:19; 6:2), to obtain power, to get the mastery (Esth. 9:1). The main meaning is that of exercising autocratic control, having one's way. A person with this quality would be a self-serving, domineering tyrant. There are eight occurrences in the Heb. O.T.

7981. Shᵉlêṭ; this Aramaic word corresponds to the Heb. counterpart 7980. It means to have dominion, to rule (Dan. 2:39; 5:7,16), to have power over something (Dan. 3:27), to rush upon something (Dan. 6:24), to cause to rule, to make a ruler (Dan. 2:38,48). There are seven occurrences in the Aramaic portions of the Bible.

7982. Sheleṭ; this mas. Heb. noun is a deriv. of 7980, and appears only in the pl. form. It refers to a shield (perhaps from its hardness, II Sam. 8:7; II Kgs. 11:10; II Chr. 23:9; Song of Sol. 4:4; Ezek. 27:11). In Jer. 51:11 it means to cover the body with a shield.

7983. Shilṭôwn; this Heb. adj. stems from 7980, meaning powerful (Ecc. 8:4) or having power over someone (Ecc. 8:8), i.e., a potentate. These are the only two instances in the Heb. O.T.

7984. Shilṭôwn or **shilṭôn;** these Aramaic mas. nouns are the equivalent to the Heb. forms of 7983. The meaning is ruler, lord, or magistrate. There are only two places in the Bible (Dan. 3:2,3).

7985. Sholṭân; this mas. Aramaic noun derives from the Aramaic verb 7981. It means dominion, rule (Dan. 4:3,22,34 [twice]; 6:26 [twice]; 7:6,12,14 [twice], 26,27 [twice]); kingdom (Dan. 7:27).

7989. Shallîyṭ; this Heb. adj. is traceable to 7980. It means potent, having power, imperious; (used as a sub.) a ruler, a magistrate, a master, a tyrant, a prince, a warrior, a governor, a mighty person. There are only four appearances in the Heb. O.T. (Gen. 42:6; Ecc. 7:19; 8:8; 10:5). Pharaoh designated that Joseph would be the ruler with absolute control and authority.

7990. Shallîyṭ; this is the Aramaic correlate to 7989. It means powerful (Dan. 2:10; 4:26), having power over something (Dan. 4:17,25,32; 5:21); (as a sub.) prince (Ezra 4:20; Dan. 2:15; 5:29), the power to do anything (Ezra 7:24).

7991. Shâlîysh or **shâlôwsh** or **shâlôsh;** these nouns arise from 7969. The meaning is: a third part (of an ephah, about a quart, Isa. 40:12), a third, a dry measure of grain; a musical instrument, a triangle (I Sam. 18:6), a three-stringed lute; a hero, a chariot warrior, a prince, a captain (II Sam. 23:8; I Chr. 12:18), a general of the third rank (which is the highest), a tristata, a noble rank of soldiers who fought from chariots (Ex. 14:7), of the bodyguard of kings (Ex. 15:4; I Kgs. 9:22; cf. II Kgs. 9:25; 10:25; I Chr. 11:11; 12:18). According to Origen, there were three soldiers in chariots; one drove the horses and two men fought the enemy. Sometimes *shâlîysh* simply means a close companion of the king (II Kgs. 7:2,17,19; 9:25; 15:25).

7999. Shâlam; to be whole, to be sound, to be safe (Job 9:4; 22:21), to be uninjured, to be safe and sound, to keep safe (Job 8:6), to make secure, to be peaceful, to live in harmony with God (Isa. 42:19), to have peace or friendship (II Sam. 20:19; Ps. 7:4; 41:10), to be friendly, to make someone a friend (Prov. 16:7); to be complete or finished (used of a building, I Kgs. 7:51; 9:25; Neh. 6:15; used of time, Isa. 60:20), to restore (Ex. 21:36; II Kgs. 4:7; Ps. 37:21), to give back, to repay (evil for good, Gen. 44:4), to pay vows (Ps. 50:14), to requite, to recompense (Judg. 1:7; II Kgs. 9:26; Ps. 31:23; 35:12; 62:12; Prov. 13:21; Jer. 50:29), to reward; to be paid, to be repaid, to be requited, to be rewarded; to be at friendship, to be a friend to someone (Job 5:23); to perform, to finish; to make peace with someone (Deut. 20:12; Josh. 10:1,4; I Kgs. 22:44), to submit oneself by a treaty of peace (Josh. 11:19); (figuratively) to impart comfort (Isa. 57:18). The Arabic terms, "Muslim" and "Islam," are derived from the Arabic root which is related to the Heb. *shâlam.* The principal meaning is completion and fulfillment. It is the desirable state of wholeness in which relationships are restored. Meeting one's obligation in full is "making it good" (Ex. 22:9,14; Lev. 24:18; II Sam. 12:6; II Kgs. 4:7; Ps. 37:21; Ezek. 33:15). *Shâlam* can mean simple restitution or repayment, like a good business transaction. It is an attitude of the heart in other cases (e.g., I Kgs. 8:61; I Chr. 28:9)—"perfect." True perfection can only be attributed to God. He needs nothing from us and He is absolutely self-sufficient (Job 21:31; 41:11). It is interesting that the stones for the original altar and Solomon's temple were uncut (*shâlêm*). See Deut. 27:6; Josh. 8:31; I Kgs. 6:7. This verb occurs more than 100 times in the Heb. O.T.

8000. Shᵉlam; this Aramaic word corresponds to 7999. It means to complete, to finish (a work, Ezra 5:16), to make an end (Dan. 5:26), to restore (Ezra 7:19). These are the only three occurrences in the Aramaic portions of Scripture.

8001. Sh^e^lâm; this Aramaic term is equivalent to the Heb. 7965. It means welfare or peace. There are only four occurrences (Ezra 4:17; 5:7; Dan. 4:1; 6:25).

8002. Shelem; this Heb. mas. noun is a deriv. of 7999. It means requital, retribution, remuneration, reward; hence, thanksgiving, a sacrifice offered to give thanks (Lev. 3:1ff.; 7:11ff.; Num. 7:17ff.; Amos 5:22), a voluntary sacrifice in thanks, sacrifices offered in distress (Judg. 20:26; 21:4), a peace-offering. This word appears almost ninety times in the Heb. O.T. According to Lev. 3, a *shelem* offering was similar to an *'ôlâh* (5930) with one exception. The fat which is around the intestines, the kidneys, the liver, and the fat of the sheep's tail was burned on the altar. The priest and the worshipper who brought the sacrifice shared the rest of the meat. For further study see Lev. 7:12-17,28-34; 10:14,15; 22:18-30. Some think that the *shelem* gift typified the worshipper's feeling of peace with God. Others see it as a communal meal of joy in sharing with the priest (Lev. 7:32). Still others believe that it was the concluding sacrifice (cf. Eph. 2:14; Heb. 9:27; 10:12).

8003. Shâlêm; this Heb. adj. comes from 7999. It means complete, whole, perfect (i.e., a full and just measure, weight, or number, Deut. 25:15; cf. Gen. 15:16; Amos 1:6,9), uninjured, unhewn, untouched stones (i.e., rough, uncut stones which have not been "violated" by iron, Deut. 27:6; I Kgs. 6:7); peaceful, friendly, cherishing peace and friendship (Gen. 34:21; I Kgs. 8:61; 11:4; 15:3,14), quiet, made ready, fair (Deut. 25:15), just, full; finished, completed (I Kgs. 9:25; II Chr. 8:16). God demanded total obedience from His people (II Kgs. 20:3). Gen. 15:16 says: "Then in the fourth generation they shall return here, for the iniquity of the Amorite is not yet complete (*shôlêm*)." In other words, God was giving the Amorites every opportunity to repent of their sin. Once national sin reaches a certain level of fullness, God takes action. This Heb. verb occurs 103 times in the O.T.

8005. Shillêm; this mas. Heb. noun emanates from 7999. It means retribution, requital, or recompense. It appears only once in the Heb. O.T. (Deut. 32:35).

8011. Shillumâh; this fem. Heb. noun has its origin in 7966, but ultimately in 7999. It means retribution, recompense, punishment, penalty, or requital. Its lone occurrence is found in Ps. 91:8.

8021. Shalmôn; this Heb. mas. noun is traceable to 7999 and appears only in the pl. form. It means a gift, a reward; a bribe, a pay-off. The only place where it is found is Isa. 1:23.

8045. Shâmad; to be desolate; to lay waste (cities or altars, Lev. 26:30; Num. 33:52), to be laid waste (a field, Jer. 48:8), to be destroyed, to be annihilated; utter destruction (of the high places, Hos. 10:8; of Baal and his images, II Kgs. 10:28); to destroy (persons and people, Deut. 1:27; 2:12,21,22,23; Esth. 3:6), to extirpate, to overthrow; to be cut off (used of groups of people, Deut. 4:26; 28:20; and of individuals, Gen. 34:30; Ps. 37:38); (used as a sub.) destruction (Isa. 14:23), a literal destruction of people (Judg. 21:16). The verb occurs sixty-three times in the Heb. O.T., thirty-eight of which are translated by "destroy" in the K.J.V. Usually it was in the context of a warning of the consequences of forsaking God (Deut. 4:25,26).

8046. Sh^e^mad or **shâmeh;** this Aramaic word corresponds to 8045. It means to consume or to destroy. It is only found in Dan. 7:26.

8047. Shammâh; this fem. Heb. noun arises from 8074. It means waste, ruin; astonishment (Deut. 28:37; Jer. 8:21; 19:8; 25:9,18; 51:37), consternation; horror; desolation (Ps. 73:19; Isa. 5:9; Jer. 2:15). It emphasizes the spectacle of the desolation and the reaction which that causes.

8059. Sh^e^miṭṭâh; this fem. Heb. noun comes from 8058. It means remission (of debt), a release (Deut. 15:1,2), the suspension (of labor), the year of jubilee in which debts were to be remitted (Deut. 15:9; 31:10). The basic meaning is to drop something or throw it down, whether figurative or literal. There are only five appearances in the Heb. O.T.

8064. Shâmayim or **shâmeh;** these nouns arise from an unused Heb. root which presumably meant "to be lofty." Therefore, the meaning is: aloft, the sky, height, heaven(s). *Shâmayim* is a dual form of an unused singular form. This important Heb. word occurs 420 times in the O.T. There are two main categories of meaning: (1) the physical heavens; (2) where God lives. In the first group it can be the realm of the sky where birds fly (Deut. 4:17). It can allude either to the visible arch in which the clouds move or the higher realm where the celestial bodies revolve. II Sam. 18:9 indicates that *shâmayim* is high above the ground but below the stars. David saw a vision in that area (I Chr. 21:16). Sometimes it denotes a location which is far removed from the earth's surface where frost comes from (Job 38:29), and snow (Isa. 55:10), and dust (Deut. 28:24), and hail (Josh. 10:11), and rain (Gen. 8:2), and dew (Deut. 33:13), and thunder (I Sam. 2:10), and even fire (Gen. 19:24). Some passages point to the realm where the sun, the moon, and the stars are located (Gen. 1:14; Ps. 104:2; Isa. 34:4). It can designate the entire creation (Gen. 1:1), constituting the universe outside planet earth. "Heaven and earth" means *mundus universus* (Gen. 14:19,22). According to Deut. 10:14 and I Kgs 8:27, the heaven of heavens is referring to all the spaces of heaven, no matter how vast and infinite. Secondly, *shâmayim* is the dwelling place of God (Ps. 2:4; cf. Deut. 4:39; 10:14; 26:15; I Kgs. 8:30). Jehovah is called "the God of heaven" (Gen. 24:7; II Chr. 36:23; Ezra 1:2; Neh. 1:4,5; 2:4,20; Ps. 136:26; Jon. 1:9). The heavens tell about the glory of God (Ps. 19:1), declare His righteousness (Ps. 50:6), and praise Him (Ps. 69:34). Isaiah (65:17; 66:22) predicted that God would create a new heaven and a new earth.

8065. Shâmayin; this mas., duel, Aramaic noun corresponds to 8064. Sometimes it is used for the inhabitants of heaven, i.e., God, along with His ministering angels (Dan. 4:23; cf. Mt. 21:25). The expression, "The God of heaven," appears in Ezra 5:11,12; 6:9,10; Dan. 2:18,37; cf. Rev. 11:13).

8074. Shâmêm; to stun, to grow numb, to devastate, to stupefy; to be astonished, to be appalled; to be desolate, waste, ravaged, solitary, or depopulated; to destroy, to lay waste; to despair, to ruin oneself, to be destitute; (as a part.) the desolater (which may have specifically predicted Antiochus Epiphanes, Dan. 9:27; cf. Dan. 8:13; 12:11; Mt. 24:15). This Heb. verb appears ninety times in the O.T. Twenty-five instances alone are in Ezekiel. The word was used to describe Tamar after she was raped by Amnon (II Sam. 13:20). It is something so horrible that it can leave a person speechless (Job 21:5).

8076. Shâmêm; this Heb. adj. derives from 8074. It means wasted, ruined, or desolate. There are only two occurrences in the Heb. O.T. (Jer. 12:11; Dan. 9:17).

8077. Sh^e^mâmâh or **shîmămâh;** this fem. Heb. noun derives from 8076, but is also closely related to 8047. *Sh^e^mâmâh* means devastation, desolation, desert (Isa. 1:7; Jer. 12:10; Ezek. 33:28,29; 35:3); astonishment (Ezek. 7:27), horror. *Sh^e^mâmâh* stresses the desolation itself, not the spectacle of it, or the human reaction from it.

8081. Shemen; this Heb. mas. noun originates from 8080. It refers to grease, liquid, (olive) oil (Gen. 28:18; I Kgs. 6:23; Neh. 8:15) which was sometimes perfumed (Song of Sol. 1:3); fat, fatness (Isa. 10:27; 25:6), fat foods, (metaphorically) of a fat bull which had cast off its yoke and broken loose (Deut. 32:15; Hos. 4:16); fertility, fruitfulness of the earth (Isa. 28:1), strength; oil, ointment (Ps. 133:2; Prov. 21:17; Isa. 1:6). This word occurs 190 times in the Heb. O.T. It usually refers to olive oil which was prepared for various purposes. The technical syn. for olive oil is *yitshâr* (3323), but *shemen* is the general word. Jer. 40:10 designates the olive itself. The Cherubim in the inner sanctuary were made of olive wood (I Kgs. 6:23). It was used for shortening in cooking (I Kgs. 17:12-16), mixing the oil with flour in the baking of bread. Also, *shemen* played an important part in sacrifices and worship. Jacob poured oil on top of the stone (Gen. 28:18). It was used to anoint a future office holder (Ex. 25:6; II Kgs. 9:6). It was put on one's earlobe, thumb, and large toe as a ritual cleansing (Lev. 14:17). The oil itself was given as an offering (Lev. 2:15,16; Ezek. 45:14), or it was mixed with flour (Ex. 29:40; Lev. 2:1-3; 8:26). The sin offering (Lev. 5:11) and the grain offering of jealousy (Num. 5:15) were specifically not to have any oil added to them. Kings and priests were anointed with *shemen* (Ex. 30:23-33; Lev. 8:12; I Sam. 16:13; I Kgs. 1:39). The tabernacle and its contents were consecrated with oil (Lev. 8:10). It was put upon a person's head as a sign of mourning (II Sam. 14:2) or a sign of rejoicing (Ps. 23:5). It served as fuel for light (Ex. 25:6) and was a valuable item for trading (Ezek. 27:17). Lavish dishes were mixed with olive oil (Isa. 25:6). *Shemen* was used as medication (Ezek. 16:9; cf. Lk. 10:34; Js. 5:14). The substance was useful as a preservative on the leather covering of shields (II Sam. 1:21).

8085. Shâma'; to hear (Gen. 3:10; 18:10; 24:52; 37:17; 42:2; Ex. 2:15; I Sam. 17:28; II Sam. 11:26; Isa. 6:9), to hear intelligently (with attention or obedience), to give undivided listening attention (Gen. 37:6; I Chr. 28:2), overhear (Gen. 37:17), to eavesdrop (Gen. 18:10), to lend an ear to, to listen (Gen. 23:8,11,15; I Kgs. 12:15; Job 31:35; 37:2; Ecc. 7:5; Isa. 46:3,12); to understand what one has heard (Gen. 11:7; 42:23), an understanding heart (I Kgs. 3:9); to obey, to give heed (Gen. 3:17; 22:18; 27:13; 28:7; 39:10; Ex. 18:19; 24:7; Num. 14:27; Deut. 18:19; 26:14; Josh. 1:17; Judg. 2:20; II Sam. 12:18; Ps. 58:5); to be heard (I Sam. 1:13; Neh. 1:6), to be heard and answered (Dan. 10:12; cf. II Chr. 30:27), to be listened to (I Sam. 15:14; 23:8); to be understood (Ps. 19:3); to call, to cause to hear (i.e., to call); to make heard; to sound, to sing with the voice (Neh. 12:42), to cry, to utter a voice (Ps. 26:7; Ezek. 27:30), to announce, to tell (Isa. 44:8; 45:21; 48:5,6), to summon (I Kgs. 15:22; Jer. 50:29; 51:27); to be cared for (Ecc. 9:16), to have knowledge (Gen. 21:26), to get knowledge (Jer. 37:5), to gain new knowledge (Num. 9:8); to hear (spiritually, Num. 24:4), to hear (cases, i.e., to examine the merits of a case to render a just decision, Deut. 1:16). This is one of the most important verbs in the Heb. O.T. It appears 1,160 times. The main idea is preceiving a message or sensing a sound. Some Heb. synonyms are the Hiphil *qâshab* (7181), "to give attention," *'âzan* (238), "to give ear," (cf. *'ôzen,* 241), and *'ânâh* (6030), "to answer." See the Gr. word *akouō* (191), which has different meanings with the gen. and the accus.

8086. Shᵉma'; this is the Aramaic equivalent to 8085. The term only occurs in the Book of Daniel (3:5,7,-10,15; 5:14,16,23; 6:14; 7:27). There are nine occurrences.

8088. Shêma'; this Heb. mas. noun comes from 8085. It is hearing (as opposed to sight, Job 42:5), a hearing, something heard, sound, fame, a rumor, a report (Gen. 29:13; Ex. 23:1; I Kgs. 10:1; Isa. 23:5; 66:19; Hos. 7:12), an account, an announcement, speech, singing, music (Ps. 150:5). The basic meaning is news in general (e.g., Laban heard the news of Jacob, Gen. 29:13), whether good or bad news. The fame of Solomon had gone as far as Sheba (I Kgs. 10:1). Job admitted that his knowledge of God formerly came from hearsay (Job 42:5). There are seventeen occurrences of this word in the O.T.

8104. Shâmar; to hedge around something (as with thorns), to keep, to guard (a garden, Gen. 2:15; 3:24; a flock, Gen. 30:31; a house, Ecc. 12:3), to watch (as a watchman of cattle or sheep, I Sam. 17:20; as a prophet, Isa. 21:11; 62:6), to keep safe, to preserve (I Sam. 26:15,16; II Sam. 18:12; Job 2:6; Prov. 6:22; 13:3), to protect (Gen. 28:15,20; Ps. 12:7; 16:1; 25:20), to retain (Gen. 37:11; 41:35), to abstain oneself (Deut. 4:9; Josh. 6:18); to observe (I Sam. 1:12; Ps. 17:4), to observe (a covenant, Gen. 17:9,10; 18:19; the commandments of God, I Kgs. 11:10; the Sabbath, Isa. 56:2,6; a promise, I Kgs. 3:6; 8:24,25), to regard, to attend; to be kept, to be guarded; to take heed, to beware; to revere (Ps. 31:6). This important Heb. verb appears 470 times in the O.T. The first occurrence is Gen. 2:15 which has the sense of tending or exercising great care over the garden. In the same way, Harhas kept the priests' garments (II Kgs. 22:14). God was the Keeper of Israel (Ps. 121:4). It has the sense of watching over someone in I Sam. 26:15 and besieging a city in II Sam. 11:16. In a religious vein, *shâmar* expresses the careful attention which was paid to the obligations of a covenant, to laws or to statutes. Abraham gave orders to his childeren to "keep" the way of the Lord (Gen. 18:19; cf. Ex. 20:6; Lev. 18:26; Deut. 26:16; Ezek. 11:20). Also, the word can refer to a narrow watching, i.e., lying in wait for someone to ambush him (Job 13:27; 33:11; Ps. 56:6; 71:10). The Cherubim "guarded" against intruders (Gen. 3:24). Cain asked, "Am I my brother's keeper?" (Gen. 4:9). Satan was warned not to touch Job's life (Job 2:6).

8120. Shᵉmash; this Aramaic word corresponds to the root of 8121. It means to serve or to minister, appearing only once (Dan. 7:10).

8130. Sânê'; to hate (personally), to hate people (Deut. 22:13; II Sam. 13:15,22; Ps. 5:5; 31:6) or things (Ps. 11:5; Prov. 1:22; Isa. 1:14); to hate violently; to be odious, to be hated, to be hateful, to be alienated (Ezek. 23:28), to become unloving (Deut. 22:16); to be untrustworthy (Gen. 26:27); preference (Gen. 29:31; Deut. 21:15; Prov. 30:23; this is the key to the meaning of Lk. 14:26); (used as a part.) a hater, an enemy, a foe. This Heb. verb is used 145 times in the O.T., ranging from intense hatred to simple opposition of persons or things (ideas, words, inanimate objects). Compare the hatred which Joseph's brothers felt for him (Gen. 37). Amnon began to hate Tamar even more intensely than he had lusted for her before the rape (II Sam. 13:15). The cognate accus. is used in Judg. 15:2 when the father of Delilah responded to Samson with this: "I really thought that you hated her intensely; so I gave her to your companion." *Sânê'* expresses the ill-will and aversion between a husband and a wife (Gen. 29:31,33), by a parent for his son (Prov. 13:24), among neighbors (Deut. 19:11), among poor people (Prov. 19:7), and among nations (Isa. 66:5). It is the desire to have no contact or relationship with another, the opposite of love. Love unites and hate separates. God hates idolatry (Deut. 16:22) and hypocrisy (Amos 5:15; Zech. 8:17; cf. Isa. 1:13-15). Sometimes men even hate God (Ex. 20:5; Deut. 5:9; II Chr. 19:2).

8131. Sᵉnê'; this is the Aramaic word which corresponds to the Heb. form 8130. Its only occurrence is found in Dan. 4:19, where it means "enemy."

8135. Sin'âh; this Heb. fem. noun is a deriv. of 8130. It means hate, hatred, or enmity. In Rom. 9:13 Paul quoted from Mal. 1:2,3. Did God hate Esau before he was born? It does not necessarily follow logically, because the statement in Rom. 9:11 that God's choice of Jacob was apart from works may be completely satisfied by the quotation from Gen. 25:23, which was certainly spoken before Esau and Jacob were born. Mal. 1:3 was written long *after* Esau had lived his worldly life (cf. Heb. 12:16).

8136. Shin'ân; this mas. Heb. noun has its origin in 8132. It is a change, a repeating, a repetition, an iteration. It occurs only once in the Heb. O.T. (Ps. 68:17).

8146. Sânîy'; this Heb. adj. comes form 8130, meaning "hated." In the only occurrence of the Heb. Bible (Deut. 21:15), Moses used this word to state plainly that a man is not justified in disinheriting his firstborn son because of his negative feelings toward the first wife. He is not allowed to give preference.

8150. Shânan; to point, to pierce through (as with grief, Ps. 73:21), to sharpen (a sword or arrows. Deut. 32:41; Ps. 45:5; 120:4; Prov. 25:18; Isa. 5:28; the tongue, Ps. 64:3; 140:3); to enforce, to inculcate (Deut. 6:7), to whet; to teach diligently; to be stung; to be wounded; to be vexed. There are nine occurrences in the Heb. O.T.

8154. Shâçâh or **shâsâh;** to plunder, to rob, to spoil (I

Sam. 14:48; Ps. 44:10; Hos. 13:15); to be plundered; (used as a part.) spoilers, plunderers (Judg. 2:14; I Sam. 23:1). See Isa. 10:13 for the variant spelling. This word is often used in parallel with *bâzaz* (962). It is related to *shâlal* (7997).

8163. Sâ'iyr or **sâ'ir;** this Heb. adj. comes from 8175. It means shaggy, hairy, rough (Gen. 27:11,23); (used as a sub.) a buck, a he-goat (Gen. 37:31; Lev. 4:24; 16:5,9) which was worshipped as a false god (lev. 17:7; II Chr. 11:15); a hairy demon, a goat-demon, a goat idol, a satyr which resembled a he-goat and inhabited deserts (Isa. 13:21; 34:14). There are fifty-two usages of this word. Most of them relate to the male goat which was used for the sin offering on the Day of Atonement (Lev. 16). There are four cases where the word is translated by the K.J.V. as "satyr" or "demon" (Lev. 17:7; II Chr. 11:15; Isa. 13:21; 34:14). The N.I.V. translated the first two passages with "goat idol" and the last two with "goat" or "wild goat." The N.A.S.B. uses "satyr" in II Chr. 11:15, where Jeroboam manufactured these idols. However, in the reform of Josiah they were torn down (II Kgs. 23:8).

8172. Shâ'an; to support oneself, to lean against (Num. 21:15; Judg. 16:26), to lean upon a spear (i.e., to commit suicide, II Sam. 1:6), to rest upon, to rely on; to adjoin, to lie near, to recline (i.e., to rest upon the elbow, Gen. 18:4), to stay; to place confidence in someone or something (II Chr. 13:18; 14:11; 16:7; Job 8:15; 24:23; Prov. 3:5; Isa. 10:20; 31:1; 50:10; Mic. 3:11). The idiom "to lean upon someone's hand," often spoke of kings who were accustomed to appear in public leaning on their friends and ministers (II Kgs. 5:18; 7:2,17) as confidants. This verb depicts an attitude of trust. Our ultimate dependence should be upon the Lord, not political alliances (Ezek. 29:6,7). Egypt was likened to a flimsy stick.

8175. Sâ'ar; to bristle with terror, to shiver, to fear, to be horribly afraid, to have a feeling of sacred awe (Deut. 32:17); to be agitated, to be tempestuous, to be firece like a tempest (Ps. 50:3), to rush like a storm (Dan. 11:40; cf. Hab. 3:14), to sweep away (like the commotion of a storm, Job 27:21; Ps. 58:9), to come like a whirlwind; to carry away; to assail. Basically, it is the motion and creeping of human skin when a person is terror-stricken, quivering, or shuddering (Jer. 2:12; Ezek. 27:35; 32:10). We have an expression: "It made my skin crawl!" There are eight occurrences in the Heb. O.T.

8176. Shâ'ar; to split, to open; to act as a gate keeper (see 7778); (figuratively) to think, to estimate, to set a price (i.e., verbs of cleaving often had the sense of judging). Prov. 23:7 is the only occurrence in the Heb. O.T. The city gate was where the people congregated for business and social reasons. The administration of justice was often administered at the gate. It was the place of controlled access to a walled city.

8178. Sa'ar; this Heb. mas. noun arises from 8175. It means horror (Job 18:20; Ezek. 27:35; 32:10) or a storm (Isa. 28:2, with a slightly different spelling). These are the only four occurrences.

8182. Shô'âr; this Heb. adj. occurs only in the pl. form, deriving from 8176. It means harsh, horrid, offensive, bad, vile, disagreeable. Its single occurrence (Jer. 29:17) described disgustingly bad figs.

8186. Sha'ărûwrâh or **sha'ărîyrîyâh** or **sha'ărûrîth;** this Heb. adj. is related to 8175 and 8176. It means horrible, fearful; a horrible thing (Hos. 6:10), something fearful, something horrible (Jer. 5:30; 18:13; 23:14). There are four occurrences.

8193. Sâphâh or **sepheth;** this fem. Heb. noun is traceable either to 5595 or 8192. It means a lip (I Sam. 1:13; Ps. 22:7), mouth, speech, dialect (Gen. 11:1ff.; Isa. 19:18; 33:19), language (talk, words); border (of a garment, Ex. 28;32), boundary (of land, Judg. 7:22), edge (of a vessel, I Kgs. 7:26); brink, brim, shore, bank (Gen. 22:17; 41:3; Ex. 14:30), margin, side. *Sâphâh* is the organ of speech, perceived as gates of honesty or deception (Ps. 31:18; Prov. 10:21). It was natural to be used metonymically for language. With the lips one may flatter (Ps. 12:2), lie (Ps. 31:18), speak mischief (Ps. 140:9), or perversity (Prov. 4:24). But the speech of God's people is not to be sinful (Job 2:10), but rejoicing (Job 8:21) and prayerful (Ps. 17:1). God's Word (Ps. 119:13) is truthful (Prov. 12:19), wise (Prov. 14:7; 15:7), righteous (Prov. 16:13), and excellent (Prov. 17:7). There are several idioms which contain the word: "to open the lips," i.e., to begin to talk (Job 11:5; 32:20); "to open someone's lips," i.e., to enable one to speak (Ps. 51:15); "to restrain the lips" (Prov. 10:19); trying to stop the lips refers to hindering a loquacious, garrulous person (Job 11:2); "futile, foolish words" (II Kgs. 18:20; Prov. 14:23; cf. Lev. 5:4; Ps. 106:33; Prov. 10:8); "fraudulent words" (Ps. 120:2; Prov. 10:18); "burning lips," i.e., words which feigned ardent love (Prov. 26:23); compressing the lips indicated evil thoughts or evil motivation (Prov. 16:30). *Sâphâh* is a close syn. to the Heb. *lâshôwn* (3956), denoting speech or human language (Isa. 19:18; 33:19). The Gr. Septuagint has *cheilos* (5491). *Sâphâh* appears about 175 times in the Heb. O.T.

8199. Shâphaṭ; to decide, to judge (to give justice or equity, Ps. 75:2), to be an arbitrator (Gen. 16:5; 31:53; Isa. 2:4), to administer the right, to vindicate, to litigate (Prov. 29:9; Isa. 43:26; Jer. 25:31; Ezek. 17:20; 20:35,36; Joel 3:2), to condemn, to contend with the notion of punishing (Isa. 66:16; Ezek. 38:22; cf. II Chr. 22:8), to punish the guilty (I Sam. 3:13; Ps. 109:31; Obad. 21); to govern, to rule (Judg. 16:31; I Sam. 8:20; II Chr. 1:10); to be judged (Ps. 37:33), to be condemned; to go to law, to plead, to defend; to execute (judgment); (used as a sub.) judge (Deut. 16:18), magistrate, ruler; (used as a part.) a prince (Ps. 2:10; Amos 2:3). The term was especially used of the heroic leaders of the Israelites who delivered their people from the oppression of neighboring nations between the time of Joshua and Samuel. They governed them in peace as supreme magistrates (Judg. 2:16,18; 4:5; Ruth 1:1; II Kgs. 23:22). The term is used elsewhere in a similar way as defending someone's cause, especially the poor and the oppressed (Ps. 10:18; 26:1; Isa. 1:17; Jer. 5:28; Lam. 3:59). Abraham was functioning as both judge and jury when Sarah invited him to arbitrate (Gen. 16:5). She wanted a definite decision concerning the legal rights of Isaac. *Shâphaṭ* means to hear a case and render a decision in Gen. 18:25, and to deliver the sentence in I Sam. 3:13. This was the process by which law and order were maintained during the period of the judges. However, later, the people clamored for a king to fulfill the same function (I Sam. 8:6-18). They wanted (what they considered) more permanence and stability. They spurned the rather simple, direct method of combining legislative, executive, and judicial decisions in wise, patriarchal seniors. This is the most common word to designate the function of government in any realm and in any form. See a Heb. syn., *dîyn* (1777). Also, see the Gr. word *katakrinō* (2632). *Shâphaṭ* occurs 125 times in the Heb. O.T.

8200. Sh^ephaṭ; this Aramaic word corresponds to 8199. Its only occurrence is found in Ezra 7:25.

8201. Shepheṭ; this Heb. mas. noun derives from 8199 and occurs only in the pl. form. It means a sentence, an affliction, an act of judgment, a punishment. In several cases the punishments are divine judgments (e.g., Ex. 6:6; 7:4; 12:12). Num. 33:4 describes the disasters which God brought upon the Egyptians. However, the punishments which were meted out by civil magistrates to offenders were also designated by this word (Prov. 19:29). The term occurs sixteen times in the Heb. O.T.

8205. Sh^ephîy; this Heb. mas. noun comes from 8192. It is bareness (Job 33:21), baldness, a bare place (Isa. 41:18), a naked hill (i.e., devoid of trees, Num. 23:3; Jer. 3:2,21; 4:11; 7:29; 12:12; 14:6; 41:18; 49:9), a high place, something which sticks out. There are ten occurrences.

8210. Shâphak; to spill forth, to pour out (a drink offering, Isa. 57:6; blood, i.e., to commit slaughter, Gen. 9:6; 37:22; Ezek. 14:19); (metaphorically) to bare one's soul, i.e., in tears and complaints, I Sam. 1:15; Ps. 42:4; 62:8; Lam. 2:19; anger, Lam. 2:4; Ezek. 14:19; 22:22, to heap up a mound (Ezek. 26:8), to shed; to throw out, to cast up; to be poured out (i.e., profusely spent, like money, Ezek. 16:36; used of one's steps, i.e., to slip, the Qere of Ps. 73:2, to be shed; to be lavished. In a literal sense, *shâphak* is often used of pouring out the contents of a vessel, such as water (Ex. 4:9; I Sam. 7:6), plaster or dust (Lev. 14:41), libations of false gods (Isa. 57:6), or blood (murder, Gen. 9:6). In the figurative sense, *shâphak* is "pouring out" God's punishment (Hos. 5:10), contempt (Job 12:21), wickedness (Jer. 14:16), and the Spirit of God (Ezek. 39:29). This word is used to describe the helpless condition of the psalmist (and Jesus on the cross) in Ps. 22:14. This Heb. verb is used more than 100 times in the O.T.

8211. Shephek; this Heb. mas. noun stems from 8210. It is an emptying place, a place where something is poured out, an ash heap. The term is used twice in Lev. 4:12, but appears nowhere else in the O.T.

8222. Sâphâm; this mas. Heb. noun has its source in 8193. It is a mustache (literally, a lip-piece) or a beard. Perhaps it was so called because it covered the chin (II Sam. 19:24). Mourners customarily covered their beards (Lev. 13:45; Ezek. 24:17,22; Mic. 3:7). There are only five occurrences in the O.T.

8251. Shiqqûwts or **shiqqûts;** this Heb. mas. noun comes from 8262. The meaning is a disgusting thing, a filthy thing; an abomination, an idol, a destestable thing. The word is used to refer to idols themselves or anything associated with idolatrous practices (II Chr. 15:8; Jer. 16:18; Ezek. 5:11; 7:20). Because idol worshippers are wholly identified with idols, they, too, are detestable (Hos. 9:10). Dan. 11:31 accurately predicted the actions of Antiochus Epiphanes, who set up an altar and the image of Zeus in the sacred Jewish temple. This desecration of the true altar was the abomination (*shiqqûwts*) which caused desolation (cf. Mt. 24:15; Mk. 13:14; Lk. 21:20; II Thess. 2:3,4). The Antichrist would establish a demonic, counterfeit worship in the temple sanctuary (Dan. 9:27; 12:11). *Shiqqûwts* is a very strong word which shows how God feels. We need to learn His perspective (Deut. 7:26).

8252. Shâqaṭ; to rest, to repose, to have quiet (used of one whom no one harasses, Judg. 3:11; 5:31; 8:28; Jer. 30:10; 46:27; used of one who harasses no one, Judg. 18:7,27; used of a person who does nothing, Isa. 62:1; Jer. 47:6), to lie quietly, to be undisturbed, to be unmolested, to be inactive; to give rest, to quiet, to calm; to cause to be quiet (i.e., to allay strife, Prov. 15:18), to give quiet (Job 34:29; Ps. 94:13), to keep oneself quiet (Isa. 7:4; 57:20), to be still, to settle, to appease, to be idle. Tranquility is the main idea of this verbal root. When used as a sub., it means rest or quiet (Isa. 30:15; 32:17). It overlaps in meaning with the following Heb. synonyms; *beṭach* (983), "security;" *nûwach* (5117), "to settle down;" *chârash* (2790), "to be silent;" *dâmâh* (1820), "to be silent;" *dâmam* (1826), "to be motionless;" and *shâbath* (7673), "cessation from activity."

8253. Sheqeṭ; this Heb. mas. noun originates from 8252. It means tranquility, quietness, rest, quiet. Its only occurrences is found in I Chr. 22:9.

8262. Shâqats; to be filthy, to loathe, to pollute, to make unclean, to be loathsome; to detest, to reject; to be base, to be impure, to be abominable; to contaminate, to pollute (Lev. 11:43; 20:25). What has been forbidden by God should be considered abhorrent.

8263. Sheqets; this mas. Heb. noun is a deriv. of 8262. It means filth, loathing, abomination; an idolatrous object, an unclean thing. In contrast to *shiqqûwts* (8251), *sheqets* is not necessarily related to idolatry but mostly has reference to unclean and forbidden foods in Lev. 11. There are eleven occurrences.

8266. Shâqar; to cheat, to lie, to deceive (Gen. 21:23; Lev. 19:11; I Sam. 15:29) in a covenant, i.e., to break a covenant (Ps. 44:17), to act falsely, to be false to one's faith (Ps. 89:33; Isa. 63:8), to be untrue (usually in words). The cognate Arabic root means "to be read," i.e., to paint a falsehood. In other words, *shâqar* has the nuance of duplicity. See the Heb. synonyms, *kâchash* (3584) in the Piel stem and *râmâh* (7411), also in the Piel stem. This is the picture of one whose word is not good.

8267. Sheqer; this Heb. mas. noun comes from 8266. It is an untruth, a sham, a lie, lying words (Ex. 5:9), a liar (Prov. 17:4), a lying witness (Deut. 19:18), a falsehood, fraud (Ps. 33:17), decit; decitfulness, a vain, unreliable thing, perjury (Lev. 6:5: 19:12); false prophecy (Jer. 5:31; 20:6; 29:9); (when used as an adv.) in vain (I Sam. 25:21; Jer. 3:23); without cause, undeservedly (Ps. 38:19; 69:4; 119:78,86). This Heb. word is used 113 times in the O.T. Psalms contains twenty-four instances. Proverbs has twenty, and Jeremiah thirty-seven. It is a way of life which goes completely contrary to God's Law. It describes groundless words or activities which have no basis in fact or reality—completely worthless. The Gr. Septuagint has *adikia* (93), *adikos* (94), and *pseudēs* (5571).

8269. Sar; this Heb. mas. noun has its origin in 8323. The meaning is a head, a person (of any rank or class), a captain, a master, a chief, a ruler (over cattle, Gen. 47:6), a commander, a prefect, a leader, a nobleman, a countier (Gen. 12:15), a prince (Ex. 2:14; Isa. 23:8), a steward; (poetically) priests (Isa. 43:28), the Messiah (Dan. 8:25), archangels (Dan. 10:13,20; cf. Rev. 8:2). The word is used 381 times in the Heb. O.T. It was often applied to certain non-Israelite officials or representatives of the king (e.g., Gen. 12:15; 21:22; 37:36). However, it could also refer to notable men within Israel (Num. 21:18; Judg. 5:15; 7:25; II Sam. 3:38; 23:19). It could be any government official (Neh. 3:14) or ruler of a city (Judg. 9:30) or religious official (I Chr. 15:16; Ezek. 8:24; 11:1; Jer. 35:4). In Isa. 9:6 the Messiah Himself is called Sar-Shalom, "Prince of Peace."

8275. Sharbîyṭ; this Heb. mas. noun originates from 7626, and means a rod or a sceptre. This seems to be a later Aramaic-influenced form in which the resh ("r") was inserted. It only occurs in the Book of Esther (4:11; 5:2 twice; 8:4). If anyone dared to enter the throne room of the Persian king uninvited and unannounced, just one nod of this golden sceptre would signify that the intruder would be executed.

8280. Sârâh; to prevail, to strive, to contend, to wage war, to have power (as a prince). There are only two occurrences in the Heb. O.T. (Gen. 32:28; Hos. 12:4), both referring to the struggle of Jacob with the angel of Jehovah at Peniel. Because he persisted so, refusing to let the angel go until he received a blessing from him, Jacob's name ("supplanter," see *'âqab,* 6117) was changed to "Israel," meaning "prince of God" (3478).

8281. Shârâh; to loose, to set free, to direct. This verb occurs in Job 37:3 and the Qere of Jer. 15:11, where it meant to desert.

8282. Sârâh; this fem. Heb. noun is a deriv. of 8269. It is a mistress, a princess, a noble lady (Judg. 5:29; Esth. 1:18; Isa. 49:23), especially used of the wives of a king of noble birth (I Kgs. 11:3), not concubines; a queen; used metaphorically in Lam. 1:1; a proper noun (Sarah). When God changed Abram's name to Abraham, He also changed Sarai's name to Sarah. This term was always used of royal women of the court. There are only five occurrences.

8293. Shêrûwth; this fem. Heb. noun derives from 8281. It means freedom, remnant, or beginning. It appears only in the Kethib of Jer. 15:11.

8300. Sârîyd; this Heb mas. noun comes from 8277. It refers to a survivor who escaped from a great slaughter (Num. 21:35; 24:19; Deut. 3:3; Josh. 8:22), a fugitive, a remnant, one who is left, the remaining one; to rest, used collectively in Judg. 5:13, used of things in Job 20:21.

8307. Sh^erîyrûwth; this fem. Heb. noun has its origin in 8324. It is something which is twisted; firmness, strength; obstinancy, obduration, stubbornness of heart (Deut. 29:19; Ps. 81:12); imagination, lust. The word occurs ten times in the Heb. O.T., eight of which are in Jeremiah (3:17; 7:24; 9:14; 11:8; 13:10; 16:12; 18:12; 23:17). The Aramaic counterpart to the Heb. root means "to be hard" or "to be firm." The peopl refused to respond to God's warnings.

8312. Sar'aph; this Heb. mas. noun is probably rel

to 5587. The resh ("r") may have been inserted in later Heb. The word occurs only in the pl. and means cogitation, thought, meditation. There are only two occurrences in the Heb. O.T. (Ps. 94:19; 139:23).

8313. Sâraph; to be on fire, to burn, to absorb with fire, to destroy by fire, to consume (e.g., towns, houses, altars, Lev. 4:21; 8:17; 9:11; Josh. 11:9,11; Judg. 18:27; II Kgs. 23:11; 25:9); to be burnt; to kindle, to set on fire; to cremate (Jer. 34:5); to bake (bricks, Gen. 11:3). The verb, which occurs 120 times, is frequently used for a literal burning. The word is never used for the burning of a sacrifice on the altar, though sometimes it does designate disposal of refuse, unused sacrificial parts, and some diseased parts. Usually, it is employed to describe the complete destruction of objects (e.g., the door of a city tower, Judg. 9:52; various cities, Josh. 6:24; I Sam. 30:1; chariots, Josh. 11:6,9; idols, Ex. 32:20; Deut. 9:21; and the scroll of Jeremiah, Jer. 36:25,27,28). Also, see I Kgs. 13:2; Ezek. 5:4; Amos 2:1. Jer. 7:31 depicts the burning of children in human sacrifice. There are very few cases where fire was used to execute people (Lev. 20:14; 21:9; cf. Gen. 38:24). It is not an ordinary kindling of fire, but destructive burning. There are more than fifteen Heb. synonyms which mean "to burn." Two of the most common are *bâ'ar* (1197), "to consume by fire," and *qâtar* (6999), "to burn incense or sacrifices."

8314. Sârâph; this Heb. mas. noun is a deriv. of 8313. It means burning, a poisonous serpent, a species of venomous snakes (Num. 21:6,8; Deut. 8:15); a seraph or symbolic creature (from their copper color), a flying dragon (Isa. 14:29; 30:6), winged angels; the noble, the high; a fiery snake. Most scholars believe that there are two referents here. God used the natural phenomenon of poisonous snakes to punish Israel for their constant lack of faith. The bite was fatal and was probably preceded with great pain and fever. However, God provided a brass serpent which Moses caused to be prominently displayed for true believers to look upon. Jn. 3:14 refers to the similarity between Jesus' public crucifixion and the incident in the wilderness. Jesus also said, "And I, if I be lifted up from the earth (a euphemism for a crucifixion), will draw all men to Myself" (Jn. 12:32). The "flying serpents" of Isaiah were no doubt a reference to the incredibly swift strike of the darting snakes. The second referent denotes angelic creatures, like the Cherubim of the temple and Ezekiel's vision (Ezek. 1). There are only two instances (Isa. 6:2,6). Also, read the vivid description in Rev. 4. They appeared to be brilliant, with a glowing quality like flaming fire. This was symbolic of the purity and power of the heavenly court. The Sanskrit word for serpent is *sarpa* and it is *sarpin* for reptile. The Gr. verb is *herpō* and the Latin word is *serpere*.

8316. S^e^rêphâh; this fem. Heb. noun has its origin in 8313. It is a burning with fire (Gen. 11:3), a conflagration, a setting on fire (Lev. 10:6; Amos 4:11), the solemn burning of dead bodies (II Chr. 16:14; 21:19), cremation, being consumed (Isa. 9:5; 64:11; Jer. 51:25). There are thirteen occurrences in the Heb. O.T.

8323. Sârar; to have dominion (Esth. 1:22; Isa. 32:1; Prov. 8:16), to exercise dominion, to get dominion, to rule, to reign (Judg. 9:22), to govern; to make oneself a prince (Num. 16:13). These are the only five occurrences. This verb was not used often and seems to have merged with *sârâh* (8280) and *sûwr* (7786).

8334. Shârath; to serve (as a menial person or worshipper), to minister to (Gen. 39:4; 40:4; Num. 3:6; 4:9; I Kgs. 1:15), to attend, to wait on, to do service (as a priest), to worship Jehovah (Deut. 18:5,7); (used as a part.) servant, minister (Josh. 1:1; I Kgs. 1:15; Ezra 8:17), attendant. The term occurs ninety-six times in the Heb. O.T. and is always in the Piel form. Twenty instances are participles. It denotes a higher level of service which was not as menial as *'âbad* (5647). There are two main categories of meaning; (1) personal services rendered to important people. It was the service provided by royal household workers (I Kgs. 10:5) toward officials or public servants (I Chr. 27:1; Esth. 1:10). Elisha ministered (*shârath*) to Elijah (I Kgs. 19:21). Abishag waited upon David (I Kgs. 1:15) and so did some of his officials (I Chr. 28:1). Amnon had a valet who served him (II Sam. 13:17). King Ahazuerus had personal servants who attended to his needs (Esth. 2:2). The word is always used of a servant of higher rank (cf. Joseph managing all of Potiphar's affairs, Gen. 39:4,8,9). (2) The ministry of worship. About sixty of the total occurrences have this meaning (e.g., Ex. 29:30; I Sam. 2:11; 3:1). The Levitical priests conducted special worship services (Num. 16:9; Deut. 10:8). The term is also used with reference to the Levites (Ezek. 44:11-14). The priesthood constituted Israel's access to God; it was a serious responsibility, not merely performing rituals.

8335. Shârêth; this is the inf. form of 8334, meaning service (in the tabernacle or in the temple), the ministry. There are only two occurrences in the Heb. O.T. (Num. 4:12; II Chr. 24:14).

8374. Tâ'ab; to detest, to loathe, to abominate, to abhor. Amos 6:8 is the only occurrence in the Heb. O.T.

8382. Tâ'am; to be complete; to be doubled, to be paired, to be twins, to duplicate, to be jointed; to give birth to twins (Song of Sol. 4:2; 6:6). The part. form is used to describe planks (Ex. 26:24 twice; 36:29 twice). These are the only six occurrences in the Heb. O.T.

8394. Tâbûwn or **t^e^bûwnâh** or **tôwbûnâh;** these nouns originate from 995. The meaning is insight, intelligence (Job 32:11), prudence, understanding (Hos. 13:2), discretion, reason, skillfulness, wisdom. The word is used forty-two times in the Heb. O.T., especially denoting the concept of wisdom. It may be the act of wisdom (Job 26:12), the faculty of wisdom (Ex. 31:3), the object of wisdom (Prov. 2:3), or the personification of wisdom (Prov. 8:1). The fem. form, *t^e^bûwnâh,* is used of God or men (Deut. 32:28; Prov. 2:6; 3:19; 21:30). The pl. form appears in Prov. 11:12; 28:16; Isa. 40:14.

8395. T^e^bûwçâh; this fem. Heb. noun comes from 947. It is a treading down, destruction, or ruin. The only occurrence is found in II Chr. 22:7.

8398. Têbêl; this fem. Heb. noun stems from 2986. It is the earth (moist, inhabited), the globe and its inhabitants (i.e., all the people on earth, Ps. 9:8; 24:1; 33:8; 96:13; 98:9), land, the habitable part of the world (Job 37:12; Ps. 90:2; Prov. 8:31; Isa. 14:17); (hyperbolically) the kingdom of Babylon (Isa. 13:11), Israel (Isa. 24:4). It is a poetic word which is usually considered to be opp. of *midbâr* (4057). The most common Heb. syn. is *'erets* (776). See the Gr. word *oikoumenē* (3625).

8399. Tablîyth; this fem. Heb. noun is a deriv. of 1086, meaning consumption or destruction. Its only occurrence is found in Isa. 10:25, but there is a textual problem there. Also, compare Job 21:13; 36:11.

8400. T^e^ballûl; this Heb. adj. arises from 1101. It means flowing, blemish, stained, spotted, cataract. Lev. 21:20 is the only place where it is found in the Heb. Bible. Origen's Hexapla has the Gr. word *leukōma*.

8403. Tabnîyth; this fem. Heb. noun derives from 1129. It is structure, pattern, an exemplar, a model for building (Ex. 25:9,40; II Kgs. 16:10), resemblance, image, likeness (Deut. 4:16-18; Ezek. 8:10; 10:8), figure, form; manner of building (Ps. 144:12).

8414. Tôhûw; this word comes from an unused Heb. root. It means desolation, desert (Deut. 32:10; Job 6:18; 12:24), a desolated city (Isa. 34:11), a worthless thing, confusion, emptiness, vanity (I Sam. 12:21; Isa. 41:29; 44:9; 49:4; 59:4), wasteness (Gen. 1:2; Job 26:7), unreality, nothing (Isa. 40:17,23); (used as an adv.) in vain (Isa. 45:19). This word has no certain parallels in other languages. Therefore, its meaning must be determined entirely from O.T. contexts. One thing is very clear—*tôhûw* has a very negative connotation. It is amazing that Job 26:7 actually asserted that an omnipotent and sovereign God could easily stretch out the north over *tôhûw* and hang the earth upon nothing, anticipating later discoveries about space! Gen. 1:2 has been translated several ways by different scholars: "without form and void," "unformed and unfilled," "void and vacancy," "absolutely nothing whatever," "a formless waste," "waste and void," "void and vacant," "a desolate waste," and "unformed and void."

8416. Tᵉhillâh; this fem. Heb. noun is traceable to 1984. The meaning is laudation, a hymn (Ps. 22:3; 66:2; 145:1); praise (Ps. 22:25; 48:10; 51:15), a song of praise (a technical musical term for a song which exults God, Ps. 145's title and Neh. 12:46), a psalm (the title to the entire Book of Psalms is in the pl. form), a celebrity (Deut. 26:19; Jer. 13:11; 33:9; Zeph. 3:19,20), glory (Ps. 9:14; Isa. 42:8), praiseworthiness (i.e., a quality describing God, Deut. 10:21; Isa. 62:7; cf. Jer. 13:11), deeds which are worthy of praise (Ex. 15:11). This word occurs fifty-seven times in the Heb. O.T.

8426. Tôwdâh; this fem. Heb. noun has its source in 3034. It means an extension of the hand, a confession (Josh. 7:19; Ezra 10:11), a vow; thanks, thanksgiving (Ps. 26:7; 42:4), a sacrifice of thanksgiving (Ps. 56:12), a type of peace offering (Lev. 7:12); offering praise to God for a sacrifice (Ps. 50:14,23; 107:22; 116:17); a thanksgiving choir or procession who gave thanks in praising God (Neh. 12:31,38,40). This word appears about thirty times in the Heb. O.T.

8431. Tôwcheleth; this fem. Heb. noun comes from 3176. It means expectation or hope. There are six occurrences in the Heb. O.T. (Job 41:9; Ps. 39:7; Prov. 10:28; 11:7; 13:12; Lam. 3:18).

8433. Tôwkêchâh or **tôwkachath;** these fem. Heb. nouns stem from 3198. The meaning is chastisement, justification, pleading, the act of arguing, defense, maintaining the right (Job 23:4); correction, refutation, contradicting (Ps. 38:14; Prov. 29:1), proof, punishment, chastening (Ps. 39:11; 73:14; Ezek. 5:15; 25:17), rebuke, reproof (Prov. 1:23,25,30: 3:11; 5:12; 27:5; 29:15); complaint (Hab. 2:1).

8435. Tôwlᵉdah or **tôlᵉdâh;** this fem. Heb. noun originates from 3205. It means descent, family, race (Gen. 10:32; 25:13; Ex. 6:16; Num. 1:20ff.), history (Gen. 6:9; 37:2), birth, generation, origin (Gen. 2:4), lineage, family register, record of the family, pedigree, genealogy (Gen. 5:1). The word occurs thirty-nine times in the Heb. O.T. It is always used in the pl. form and in the construct state or with a pronominal suffix. It refers to what is produced or brought into being by someone, and sometimes the results. Usually, it does not include the birth of the individual who started the line of descendants. Therefore, Gen. 2:4 does not indicate the process of how heaven and earth came into existence, but the events which followed their establishment. In other words, it is not a summary of the events which preceded Gen. 2:4.

8441. Tôw'êbâh or **tô'êbâh;** this is the fem. act. part. which comes from 8581. It is something which is morally disgusting, an abomination (Prov. 3:32; 11:1,20; 21:27; 28:9), an abominable thing (i.e., for Egyptians to eat with Hebrews, Gen. 43:32; cf. Ex. 8:26), things which belong to the worship of idols (I Kgs. 14:24; II Kgs. 16:3; 21:2; Ezra 9:1; Ezek. 16:2) and of the idols themselves (II Kgs. 23:13; Isa. 44:19). Here are other things which are repugnant to God: homosexuality and other perversions (Lev. 18:22-30; 20:13), idolatry (Deut. 7:25), human sacrifice (Deut. 12:31), eating animals which are ritually unclean (Deut. 14:3-8), sacrificing defective animals (Deut. 17:1), engaging in occult activities (Deut. 18:9-14), dishonest business practices (Deut. 25:13-16), practicing cultic prostitution (I Kgs. 14:23,24), and similar acts of disobedience (list of seven, Prov. 6:16-19). Ps. 88 is a prayer for help written by a man who was on his deathbed. He was physically repulsive (*tôw'êbâh*) in appearance (see v. 8). Basically, it is a clash of basic dispositions between unrighteous people and righteous people (Prov. 29:27). Because of God's warnings, the people of the Lord regard certain actions, characteristics, and behaviors as destructive to the family and society (Prov. 24:9). A close syn. in Heb. is *sheqets* (8263). *Tôw'êbâh* occurs 117 times in the Heb. O.T.

8451. Tôwrâh or **tôrâh;** this Heb. noun comes from 3384. The meaning is instruction, doctrine (Job 22:22), a regulation, direction, a precept, a statute, (human) law (II Sam. 7:19), (divine) law (e.g., the law of sacrifice, Lev. 6:14; 7:7), collective laws (Ex. 18:20; Lev. 26:46; Josh. 1:8; 8:34; II Kgs. 22:8,11; Neh. 8:3). *Tôwrâh* often has the definite art. prefixed to it when referring to the Law of Moses (Deut. 4:44; Neh. 8:18: Ps. 119:1; Mal. 4:4). The A.S.V. always has "law," but the R.S.V. uses "teaching," "instruction," and "decisions." This important Heb. noun occurs about 220 times in the O.T. The essential meaning of *tôwrâh* is "teaching," whether it is the wise man who gently instructs his own son or God patiently teaching Isreal. It can refer to any set of regulations (Lev. 7:37; 14:57; Num. 5:29) or the whole. The Book of Deuteronomy clearly shows that the Law of Moses encompassed history, statutes with their interpretation, and exhortations, not like Hammurabi's code. Eventually, *tôwrâh* became synonymous with the Pentateuch. Covenant precedes law, i.e., after the basic agreement is made, stipulations are spelled out. However, breaking a specific law is equivalent to sinning against God, i.e., breaking with one's covenant relationship. The Levitical priests were to teach precepts of the Law and follow its regulations (Deut. 17:11,18; 33:10). They were called "those who handle the law" (Jer. 2:8). Unfortunately, they became blind and arrogant. They forgot God (Hos. 4:6). They used it to enhance their own power and wealth (Ezek. 22:26; Zeph. 3:4). Therefore, God sent His prophets to call Israel back to true obedience to the Law (II Kgs. 17:13). They showed how the Law was either misapplied or neglected. Ezra and Nehemiah in post-exilic times prodded the people out of complacency (Neh. 8:2-9,13-17) as Moses commanded (Deut. 31:10,11). Moses had predicted an entirely new law (Jer. 31:33; cf. Heb. 8:10). So, *tôwrâh* was much more than a law or set of rules. It was not to be perceived as restrictions, but the very means by which one could reach a spiritual ideal. If Israel would keep the Torah, then Israel would be kept safe. However, the people came to understand it as something which was imposed for its own sake rather than what God intended for them to become. Therefore, the means became the end. And, instead of being seen as a guideline, it became a heavy, external set of rules which were stifling (cf. Acts 15:10). Failure to understand the perfect law of liberty (Js. 1:25) led to severe legalism as taught by the Judaizers in the first century. Paul struggled to define the true place of the Law in Rom. 1—8 and Gal. 1—3. Two Heb. synonyms *mitsvâh* (4687) and *chôq* (2706), both appear with *tôwrah* in Gen. 26:5. See the Gr. word *nomos* (3551) in the N.T. lexical section.

8453. Tôwshâb or **tôshâb;** this mas. Heb. noun originates from 3427. It is a settler, an inhabitant, a foreigner, an alien, an emigrant. A *tôwshâb* was to be distinguished from a temporary visitor (*gêr,* 1616) or a mere lodger (*lûwn,* 3885). Essentially, *tôwshâb* denotes a squatter who could not possess land. He was a sojourner in a foreign country where he was not naturalized (Lev. 22:10; 25:47; 1 Kgs. 17:1; Ps. 39:12). These are the only four occurrences in the O.T.

8454. Tûwshîyâh or **tûshîyâh;** these fem. nouns come from an unknown root. The meaning is help, aid (Job 6:13; 30:22), support (i.e., a poetic word which literally meant to lift up (that which is erect), salvation; insight, wisdom (Job 11:6; 12:16; 26:3; Prov. 2:7; 3:21; 8:14; 18:1; Isa. 28:29; Mic. 6:9), counsel (i.e., the raising of something, Job 5:12), understanding. There are twelve occurrences in the O.T.

8457. Taznûwth or **taznûth;** these fem. nouns arise from 2181. The meaning is whoredom, harlotry, fornication; (metaphorically) idolatry, the worship of idols. This word occurs twenty times and only in the Book of Ezekiel (16:15,20,22,25,26,29,33,34,36; 23:7,8 [twice], 11,14,17,18,19,29,35,43).

8467. Tᵉchinnâh; this fem. Heb. noun derives from 2603. It means graciousness, grace, mercy (Josh. 11:20; Ezra 9:8), favor, compassion; prayer, entreaty, supplication (i.e., a cry for mercy, Ps. 6:9; 55:1; 119:170).

8469. Tachănûwn or **tachănûwnâh;** the original source root is 2603. The mas. form appears only in the p meaning earnest prayer, entreaty, supplication. Th are seventeen occurrences in the Heb. O.T. (II Chr. 6:21; Job 41:3; Ps. 28:2,6; 31:22; 116:1; 130:2; 140:6; 143:1; Prov. 18:23; Jer. 3:21; 31:9; Dan. 9:3,17,18,23; Zech. 12:10).

8535. Tâm; this Heb. adj. comes from 8552. It means complete, whole, upright (always in a moral sense, Job 1:1; 8:20; 9:20-22), perfect (an endearing term for a beloved female, Song of Sol. 6:9), simple, pious, innocent, sincere, undefiled, having integrity (Ps. 37:37), sound, wholesome (Gen. 25:27), plain, mild, placid, harmless, quiet. There are thirteen occurrences in the Heb. O.T.

8537. Tôm; this Heb. mas. noun is a deriv. of 8552. The meaning is completeness, fullness (Job 21:23), wholeness, perfection, integrity (Gen. 20:5), soundness, simplicity, innocence (Ps. 26:1; Prov. 10:9), uprightness, prosperity (Job 21:23; Ps. 41:12), strength (Isa. 47:9). *Tôm* is the opposite of mischief (II Sam. 15:11). When a certain soldier drew his bow randomly and unsuspectingly, he brought down the king of Israel, according to prophecy (I Kgs. 22:34). The pl. form describes the Thummim, the precous stones of Aaron's breastpiece. This word occurs twenty-five times in the O.T.

8538. Tummâh; this is the fem. equivalent of 8537. It means integrity or innocence (Job 2:3,9; 27:5; 31:6; Prov. 11:3). These are the only five occurrences in the Heb. Scriptures.

8540. T^emahh; this Aramaic word corresponds to 8539, meaning something astonishing, a miracle. There are only three occurrences (Dan. 4:2,3; 6:27).

8544. T^emûwnâh or **t^emûnâh;** this fem. Heb. noun comes from 4327. It is something shaped, a fashioning, a form, an appearance, an image, a phantom, an embodiment, a manifestation, a likeness. In Job 4:16 it is a nocturnal apparition of a spirit with an undiscernible form. Moses witnessed a manifestation of God's glory when He passed by (Num. 12:8; cf. Ex. 33:22). The Israelites were warned not to attempt to create an image of God from this world which God created (Ex. 20:4; Deut. 5:8). There are ten occurences of this word in the Heb. Bible.

8545. T^emûwrâh; this fem. Heb. noun has its origin in 4171. It refers to barter, exchange (especially in buying and selling, Lev. 27:10,33; Ruth 4:7; Job 28:17), compensation, retribution, recompense (Job 15:31; 20:18), restitution, wages, pay. These are the only occurrences in the Heb. Bible.

8546. T^emûwrthâh; this fem. Heb. noun arises from 4191. It means execution (doom), death, dying. The term appears only in the phrases, "sons of death (KJV)," i.e., condemned to die (Ps. 79:11; 102:20). These are the only two occurrences.

8548. Tâmîyd; this mas. Heb. noun originates from an unused root. The meaning is duration, extension, continuance (Ezek. 39:14), continuity (Isa. 21:8); (as an adv.) continually (Ps. 16:8; 25:15; 34:1), perpetually, daily (both morning and evening, Ex. 29:38; Num. 28:6,10,15,23,24), at all times (Ex. 25:30), continuously without interruption, regularly (II Sam. 9:7; cf. II Sam. 9:10). This word is used most often in an adjectival genitive construction with *'ôlâh* (5930), "whole burnt offerings." Each morning the *minchâh* (4503) was offered (Lev. 6:13; Num. 4:16; Neh. 10:33). It means "the bread that was always there" in Num. 4:7. *Tâmîyd* was used to emphasize personal devotion in I Chr. 16:11; Ps. 34:1; 40:11; 71:6,14: 72:15; 119:44; Hos. 12:6. It describes God (Num. 9:16) and His care for His people (Isa. 58:11). It was employed of Jerusalem (Isa. 49:16), pehaps as a foretaste of the New Jerusalem (cf. Rev. 21:25), and the gates of Zion would be open continually (Isa. 60:11). If one were to visit a synagogue today, he would notice the *ner tâmîyd,* "the continual light." This word occurs about 100 times in the Heb. O.T.

8549. Tâmîym; this Heb. adj. comes from 8552. It means entire (literally, figuratively, or morally) whole (Josh. 10:13), complete (Lev. 23:15; Job 36:4; 37:16; Ps. 19:7), perfect, sound (i.e., free from blemishes in sacrifical victims, Ex. 12:5; Lev. 1:3), faultless, upright in one's conduct, blameless (Gen. 6:9; 17:1; Ps. 119:1; especially toward God, Deut. 18:13; II Sam. 22:24; Ps. 18:23), innocent, simple, honest, sincere (Judg. 9:16), secure (Prov. 1:12); (used as a sub.) honesty, integrity (Josh. 24:14; Judg. 9:16,19; Ps. 15:2; 84:11). *Tâmîym* is the divine standard which man must attain. He must try to meet all the requirements of God's Law (Ps. 18:23). Noah was not odious in his relationship with God (Gen. 6:9; cf. Gen. 17:1; Rom. 4).

8552. Tâmam; this Heb. verb means to complete (in a good sense or in a bad sense); to be completed (Job 31:40), to be finished (I Kgs. 6:22), to be ended (Gen. 47:18), to be depleted (Gen. 47:15,18; Jer. 37:21), to be ready, to be whole; to be consumed, to be gone, to perish; to completely destroy (Num. 14:35; Ezek. 22:15); to be innocent, to be blameless; to make whole; to make full, to make perfect; to cause to cease; to pay off; to act honestly, to be morally and ethically sound (Ps. 19:13). Lev. 22:21,22 is a type of Jesus Christ, the spotless Lamb of God (I Pet. 1:19; cf. Jn. 1:29). Amos 5:10 describes speech which is complete, i.e., entirely in accord with truth and fact. Job is probably the best example of a well-rounded, balanced, finished spiritual product who pleased God. A number of derivatives of *tâmam* were used to describe him (Job 1:1,8; 2:3,9; 9:21,22; 12:4; 27:5; 31:6). Job admitted his sins (Job 7:20,21; 9:2,15; 10:6; 14:16,17), even from his youth (Job 13:26). He confessed that he was not innocent (Job 9:28). Job retracted his rash statements against God and repented (Job 42:6). He remained totally committed to God. *Tâmam* occurs sixty-four times in the Heb. O.T.

8562. Tamrûwq or **tamrûq** or **tamrîyq;** these nouns derive from 4838, only in the pl. form, referring to a scouring, precious ointments (Esth. 2:3,9), remedies, detergents, soaps for bathing, purifications (when the virgins were received into the women's house of the king of Persia, Esth. 2:12); (metaphorically) a cleansing (the Qere of Prov. 20:30). These are the only four occurrences in the O.T.

8573. T^enûwphâh; this fem. Heb. noun is a deriv. of 5130. It is brandishing (as a threat); moving to and fro, shaking (the hand as a gesture of threatening, Isa. 19:16), waiving (sacrifices before the Lord, Ex. 29:27; 38:24; Lev. 7:34); consecration; movement, shaking; tumult (Isa. 30:32), excitement. The word was used as a general term applied to a variety of gifts and offerings, and employed as a specific term for those parts of the offerings which were dedicated for the officiating priests.

8577. Tannîyn or **tannîym;** a huge fish (Gen. 1:21; Job 7:12; Isa. 27:1), a marine or land monster, a dragon (Jer. 51:34), a sea serpent, a water animal, a whale, a shark, a crocodile (Ezek. 29:3), a snake (Ex. 7:9ff.; Deut. 32:33; Ps. 91:13); used as an image of Egypt (Ps. 74:13,14; Isa. 51:9; Ezek. 32:2). The biblical writers used this sort of imagery to show the Lord's power in history over His political enemies (cf. Rev. 12:3). On two occasions, (Ezek. 29:3; 32:2) the second spelling above is used in the Masoretic text, apparently through confusion with the pl. of *tan* (8565), "jackal." Lam. 4:3 should be "jackal." It is notable that this is not the word used in Jon. 1:17; 2:1,10. The Gr. word is *kētos* (2785).

8581. Tâ'ab; to loathe, to detest, to morally abhor; to be abominable, to be abhorred; to be refused, to reject; to make one abhorred; to do or act abominably, to treat as abhorrent. The R.S.V. translates the verb as "prostitute" in Ezek. 16:25. There are twenty-two occurrences in the Heb. O.T.

8582. Tâ'âh; to vacillate (reel) or to stray, used (literally or figuratively), to err, to wander (Gen. 21:14); to go astray (mentally, morally, or spiritually, e.g., Ps. 58:3; 95:10); to be giddy; to stagger around (because of drunkenness, Isa. 28:7), to reel; to be deceived; to cause to wander, to lead astray, to seduce. Some of Israel's shepherds (leaders) led them astray (Jer. 50:6). The famous Isa. 53:6 describes the condition of every one of us: "All of us like sheep have gone astray (*tâ'âh*), each of us has turned to his own way." However, the Son of David was destined to be the great Shepherd (Ezek. 14:11).

8584. Teʻûwdâh; this fem. Heb. noun is traceable to 5749. It means attestation, a precept, a law, a statute, a custom; an announcement. There are only three occurrences in the Heb. O.T. (Ruth 4:7; Isa. 8:16,20).

8595. Ta'tûa'; this mas. Heb. noun is a deriv. of 8591, appearing only in the pl. form. It means a fraud, an error, works of mockery (Jer. 10:15; 51:18), delusion. Idols delude men and mock God. These are the only two occurrences in the O.T.

8597. Tiph'ârâh or **tiph'ereth;** these nouns come from 6286. The meaning is ornament, splendor (Ex. 28:2,40; Prov. 28:12; Isa. 3:18; 52:1; Ezek. 16:17), beauty, magnificence, honor, glory (Judg. 4:9), glorious name (Isa. 63:14), glorying (Isa. 10:12), a boast, renown (Deut. 26:19), majesty (poetically used of the ark of the covenant as the seat of divine majesty, Ps. 78:61). It has to do with one's rank (Esth. 1:4; Zech. 12:7).

8605. Tephillâh; this fem. Heb. noun derives from 6419. It means intercession for someone (II Kgs. 19:4; Isa. 37:4; Jer. 7:16; 11:14), prayer (Ps. 4:1; 6:9; 109:4), entreaty, supplication, hymn. This is the most general Heb. word for prayer in the O.T. Isa. 56:7 stated that God's house would be a house of prayer. Jesus quoted this verse when He "cleansed" the temple courtyard (Mt. 21:13; Mk. 11:17; Lk. 19:46). *Tephillâh* was used as a title in five Psalms (17,86,90,102,142) and the title for the prayer of Habakkuk (3:1). The word appears in Ps. 72:20 to describe all the psalms of Ps. 1—72, only one of which is truly a "prayer" in the strict sense (Ps. 17:1). The term denotes a prayer which is set to music and sung in formal worship. There is a similar use of the verb in I Sam. 2:1. The word occurs seventy-seven times in the Heb. O.T.

8628. Tâqa'; to clatter, to slap or clap the hands together (in rejoicing, Ps. 47:1; at another's misfortune, Neh. 3:19; in becoming a guarantor, like shaking hands on an agreement, Prov. 6:1; 11:15; 17:18; 22:26), to clang (an instrument); to strike or drive (a nail, a tent peg, a dart), to beat, to fix (I Sam. 31:10; Isa. 22:23,25); to thrust (e.g., a spear or a sword, Judg. 3:21; II Sam. 18:14); to blow (a trumpet or horn one time sharply to give a signal, Num. 10:6,7; Ps. 81:3; Jer. 4:5; 6:1; 51:27); to throw (into the sea, Ex. 10:19); to be struck, to be blown. *Tâqa'* appear almost seventy times in the Heb. O.T. with a broad range of meanings. The basic meaning is sharp movement. A strong wind drove (*tâqa'*) the locusts into the Red Sea (Ex. 10:19). Jael hammered a large tent pin into Sisera's head (Judg. 4:21). Jacob pitched his tent with a similar motion (Gen. 31:25). The Israelites produced blasts on trumpets, causing the walls of Jericho to crumble (Josh. 6:4,8,9,13,16,20). Normally, trumpets were blown to summon people (Num. 10:3) or to sound an alarm (Jer. 6:1).

8631. Teqêph; this Aramaic word corresponds to 8630, meaning to be strong or mighty (Dan. 4:11,22) or to confirm (Dan. 6:7). In Dan. 5:20 it is used in a bad sense, that of an obstinate mind.

8641. Terûwmâh or **terûmâh;** this fem. Heb. noun arises from 7311. It is a present (offering), an oblation (Ezek. 45:1; 48:9,20,21, where it was the portion of land upon which the post-exilic temple was to be built), a gift (usually brought to the tabernacle and the temple and the priests, Ex. 25:2,3; 30:13,14; Lev. 7:32; 22:12; Prov. 29:4), tribute, a contribution; a heave-offering (Ex. 29:27), the heave-shoulder (Lev. 7:34). This word occurs about seventy times in the Heb. O.T. One-third of its appearances are translated as "heave-offering." Perhaps the priests raised such offerings high in some special motion as it was being placed upon the altar (Num. 15:20). It consisted of agricultural produce (Deut. 12:6,11,17). These gifts which were presented to God became the property of the priests (Lev. 7:13,14; Num. 5:9; 18:19). It could also be a portion of an animal sacrifice (Lev. 7:32; cf. Num. 6:20). Since the tribe of Levi was given no land inheritance, they depended on the other tribes for sustenance. The Levites tithed the tithes which they received. Part of that tithe was to be a *terûwmâh* for the priests, the descendants of Aaron (Num. 18:25-32). It consisted of precious metals and stones, wood and skins (Ex. 25:3-9) to construct the tabernacle in the wilderness. It had the sense of an obligatory tax from every Jewish male who was older than twenty years for the upkeep of the tabernacle or the temple (Ex. 30:11-16). Later it became associated with the census (II Sam. 24:1) and heavy taxation (I Kgs. 12). In Modern Hebrew *terûwmâh* is often used in the sense of contribution (similar to Ezek. 45:13,16).

8642. Terûwmîyâh; this Heb. adj. is a deriv. of 8641, belonging to a heave-offering, a sacrificial offering, or an oblation. There is only one occurrence (Ezek. 48:12).

8655. Terâphîym; this Heb. noun appears only in the pl. form. It refers to domestic or household gods, family idols, images, cultic masks, or a deed of ownership. The word appears fourteen times in each period of Israelite history in the O.T. The term probably is a loanword from Hittite-Hurrian (*tarpish*), corresponding to the contemporary *ilānu* (gods) of Nuzi. See Gen. 31:19,30,32; Judg. 18:17,24. In the time of Rachel, Hurrian law recognized these household pagan idols as deeds to the family's goods. Therefore, it was very important for Laban to recover them. Was Rachel completely separated from her polytheistic heritage? See Gen. 35:2 and Josh. 24:2. She may have stolen the gods for the purpoe of divining, because Nuzi law implied that bequeathal (not mere possession) of the *terâphîym* determined family leadership. *Terâphîym* continued to be present among Israel to seek oracles (I Sam. 15:23; II Kgs. 23:24; Ezek. 21:21; Zech. 10:2), often found to be associated with the ephod (Judg. 17:5; 18:14,17,18,20; Hos. 3:4). They probably came from Mesopotamia (Gen. 31:19-21; Ezek. 21:21). The *terâphîym* in I Sam. 19:11-17 is problematic. Archaeologists have found no *terâphîym* which approximate the size of a full-grown man. All known *terâphîym* were small figurines. Therefore, this particular passage may refer to the bust of a human head or a cultic mask. It may have been a symbol of divine presence.

8668. Teshûw'âh or **teshû'âh;** this fem. Heb. noun originates from 7768. It means help, assistance, deliverance (Judg. 15:18), welfare (Ps. 37:39; 40:10; 71:15), salvation (Isa. 45:17), rescue (whether personally, nationally, or spiritually), victory (II Sam. 19:2; II Kgs. 5:1). *Teshûw'âh* refers primarily to God's acts of help which have already occurred and have been experienced. It could also be a human act (I Sam. 14:45; Prov. 11:14) or help effected by things (Isa. 12:3). The Septuagint translates it with *sōtēria* (4991) and *sōtērion* (4992). There are thirty-four occurrences in the Heb. O.T.

8669. Teshûwqâh; this fem. Heb. noun comes from 7783. It means stretching out after, a yearning, a longing, a desire. The word appears only three times in the O.T. Two of them refer to the strong attraction between the sexes. One is in the context of love and joy (Song of Sol. 7:10) and the other is in the context of sin and judgment (Gen. 3:16). The third passage describes personified sin as being like a crouching animal ready to pounce on Cain (Gen. 4:7).

WORD STUDIES

LEXICON TO THE NEW TESTAMENT

BY SPIROS ZODHIATES, TH.D.

LEXICAL AIDS TO THE NEW TESTAMENT

14. Agathoergeō; to do good, from *agathos* (18), benevolent, and *ergeō* from *ergon* (2041), work. To work good, i.e., to act for someone's advantage. Only in I Tim. 6:18. See *agathopoieō* (15).

15. Agathopoieō; from *agathos* (18), benevolent, and *poieō* (4160), to do. To do the good as opp. to *hamartanō* (264), to miss the mark, sin (Js. 4:17; I Pet. 2:20; III Jn. 11). To do good so that someone derives advantage from it; contr. *agathoergeō* (14). Opp.: *kakopoieō* (2554), to do evil (Mk 3:4; Lk. 6:9; I Pet. 3:17; III Jn. 11). The sub.: *agathopoiia* (16), well doing (I Pet. 4:19), the practice of good. See *agathopoios* (17).

18. Agathōs; good and benevolent, profitable, useful; contr. *kalos* (2570), constitutionally good but not necessarily benefiting others. Related words: *agathōsunē* (19), goodness; *agathoergeō* (14), to do good to benefit others (I Tim. 6:18); *agathopoiia* (16), well doing (I Pet. 4:19); *agathopoios* (17), doer of good (I Pet. 4:19); *philagathos* (5358), from *philos* (5384) friend, and *agathos,* friend or lover of good men (Tit. 1:8); *aphilagathos* (865), from the negative *a* (1) and *philagathos,* not a lover or a friend of good men or of goodness (II Tim. 3:3). See *chrēstotēs* (5544) and *agathopoieō* (15).

19. Agathōsunē; active goodness. In Gal. 5:22 referred to as goodness, but the English word is inclusive of particular graces whereas Paul must refer to a particular grace. It is more than *chrēstotēs* (5544), a mellowing of character. It is character energized expressing itself in *agathon* (18), active good. There is more activity in *agathōsunē* than in *chrēstotēs,* which is potential *agathōsunē* which is energizing *chrēstotēs*. A person may display his *agathōsunē,* his zeal for goodness and truth in rebuking, correcting, chastising. Christ's righteous indignation in the temple (Mt. 21:13) showed His *agathōsunē,* but not His *chrēstotēs,* mellowness. *Agathōsunē* does not spare sharpness and rebuke to cause good, *agathon,* in others whereas *chrēstotēs* demonstrates only its softness and benignity.

20. Agalliasis; exultation, exuberant joy. See verb *agalliaō* (21). Syn.: *chara* (5479), joy, delight; *euphrosunē* (2167), good cheer, joy, mirth, gladness of heart.

21. Agalliaō; used in the pass. and mid. voice from *agan,* very much, and *allomai,* to leap. To exult, leap for joy, to show one's joy by leaping and skipping denoting excessive or ecstatic joy and delight (Jn. 5:35; Acts 16:34); hence it is sometimes put after *chairō* (5463), to rejoice, which is of less intense signification (Mt. 5:12; I Pet. 4:13; Rev. 19:7). To be transported with desire, to leap forward with joy, to meet the object of one's wishes (Jn. 8:56). Noun: *agalliasis* (20). Syn.: *euphrainō* (2165), to cheer, gladden.

25. Agapaō; to love, indicates a direction of the will and finding one's joy in anything. Contr. with *phileō* (5368), to be contented with, denoting common interests, hence befriending. *Agapaō* is used of God's love toward man and vice versa, but *phileō* is never used of the love of men toward God. *Agapaō* and never *phileō* is used of love toward our enemies. The range of *phileō* is wider than that of *agapaō* which stands higher above *phileō* because of its moral import; love that expresses compassion.

26. Agapē; love, a word not found in Class. Gr. but only in revealed religion. Translated "charity" meaning benevolent love. Its benevolence, however, is not shown by doing what the person loved desires but what the one who loves deems as needed by the one loved; e.g., "For God so loved (*ēgapēsen*) the world . . . that He gave. . . ." What did He give? Not what man wanted but what man needed as God perceived his need. His Son to bring forgiveness to man. God's love for man is God doing what He thinks best for man and not what he desires. It is God's willful direction toward man. But for man to show love to God, he must first appropriate God's *agapē,* for only God has such an unselfish love. Contr. *philia* (5373), friendship, based on having common interests. Deriv.: *agapaō* (25); *agapētos* (27).

27. Agapētos; beloved, dear. In the N.T it is used with the force of the perfect part. pass., *ēgapēmenos,* beloved, dear. N.T. meanings: (1) as an adj., "My son, the beloved" (Mt. 3:17; 17:5; Mk. 1:11; 9:7; Lk. 3:22; II Pet. 1:17; Mk. 12:6). We must not, however, connect this use with the designation in Mt. 3:17, etc., as the latter is traceable to Lk. 9:35 and expresses the relation of the Son to the Father in the history of redemption (Rom. 11:28) and also the addition "in whom I am well pleased" (Mt. 3:17; 17:5; Mk. 1:11; Lk. 3:22; II Pet. 1:17). (2) As a sub. in Rom. 11:28 it is used also in address as in III Jn. 2,5,11, or in the pl. in Rom. 12:19; II Cor. 7:1; 12:19, etc. The importance of the expression is in agreement with the meaning of the verb *agapaō* (25), to love.

29. Aggareuō; to press into service; to send off an *aggaros* or public courier. This word is of Persian origin, and after being received into the Gr. language, passed also into use among the Jews and Romans. The *aggaroi* couriers had authority to press into their service men, horses, ships or anything which came in their way and which might serve to hasten their journey. Afterwards *aggareuō* came to mean to press into service for a journey in the manner of *aggaros*. In the N.T. used as a trans. verb, to compel, to press, to accompany one (Mt. 5:41; 27:32; Mk. 15:21). Contr. *anagkazō* (315), to constrain.

31. Aggelia; message, related to *aggelos* (32), messenger, occurs only in 1 Jn. 3:11. Some mss. have *epaggelia* (1860) from *epi* (1909), upon, and *aggelia* (31), a promise.

32. Aggelos; messenger, from *aggellō,* to bring a message, announce, proclaim. As a simple verb it does not occur in the N.T. but it does occur in its comp. forms: *apaggellō* (518), to announce (Jn. 20:18); *anaggellō* (312), to report, announce. These two comp. verbs are variously employed to designate the proclamation of salvation. *Aggelos* is a name not of nature but of office, or human messenger (Mt. 11:10; Mk. 1:2, etc.); a bishop or presiding elder of a particular church (Rev. 1:20; 2:1, etc.); or created spiritual angel, whether good (Mt. 24:36; Mk. 13:32, etc.) or evil (Mt. 25:41; I Cor. 6:3, etc.). The angel of the Lord was a human form surrounded with light or glory with or in which Jehovah was present (Lk. 2:9; Acts 10:3,31, etc.). Angels are always spoken of in the mas. gender. Other deriv.: *aggelia* (31), message; *diaggellō* (1229), to divulge (Lk. 9:60; Rom. 9:17) or to declare; *exaggellō* (1804), to declare abroad (I Pet. 2:9); *kataggello* (2605), to proclaim, preach, publish (Acts 4:2; 13:5,38; 16:21; 17:23; Rom. 1:8); *kataggeleus* (2604), a proclaimer, publisher; *prokataggellō* (4293), to declare or speak beforehand (Acts 3:18,24; 7:52; II Cor. 9:5) or signify plainly (Acts 21:26).

35. Agenealogētos; from the neg. *a,* and *genealogeō,* to trace a genealogy. Without a genealogy or pedigree, having no genealogy, i.e., from any sacerdotal family as the Levitical priests had from Aaron (Ex. 40:15; Heb. 7:3) which might prove the right of Melchizedek to the priesthood (Neh. 7:14).

37. Hagiazō; to hallow, sanctify. *Hagios* (40) stands in contr. with *koinos* (2839), defiled or common, thus the verb *hagiazō,* to sanctify, when its object is something that is filthy or common, cannot be accomplished without someone separating himself (*aphorizō,* 873) or withdrawing from fellowship with the world. *Hagiazō* means to withdraw from fellowship with the world and from selfishness by first gaining fellowship with God and toward God. Related words: *hagiasmos* (38), sanctification; *hagion* (39), sacred thing; *hagiotēs* (41) and *hagiōsunē* (42), holiness, from *hagios,* holy, sanctity, the abstract quality of holiness, used of God (Heb. 12:10); of its manifestation in the conduct of the Apostle Paul and his fellow laborers (II Cor. 1:12). In this passage some mss. have *haplotēs* (572), sincerity without duplicity related to *haplous* (573). *Hagiotēs* is to be distinguished from *hosiotēs* (3742), sanctity related to *hosios* (3741) as contr. with *hagios. Hagiotēs* is to be distinguished from *hagiasmos,* sanctification which is active sanctification as effected by God and passed on to the character of man. *Hagiotēs* is syn. with *hagiōsunē* as the attribute of holiness.

38. Hagiasmos; sanctification, translated "holiness" (Rom. 6:19,22; I Thess. 4:7; I Tim. 2:15; Heb. 12:14). Separation unto God (I Cor. 1:30; II Thess. 2:13; I Pet. 1:2). The resultant state, the behavior befitting those so separated (I Thess. 4:3,4,7), this sanctification resulting in the abstaining from fornication. There are two other Gr. words which are translated as "holiness" but they must be distinguished from *hagiasmos,* sanctification. *Hagiasmos* is not like *hagiotēs* and *hagiōsunē,* the attribute of holiness, but is the state of being sanctified, sanctification not as a process, but as the result of a process. Similar to *dikaiōsis* (1347), not only denoting the activity of God's justification in Christ for the sinner, but also the result of that justification upon the sinner in making him just, recognizing the rights of God on his life. Therefore, *hagiasmos* (II Thess. 2:13) means not only the activity of the Holy Spirit to set man apart unto salvation but also enabling him to be holy even as God is holy. It is not only the transfer of a sinner into the ranks of the redeemed but the change in the character of the redeemed sinner to be holy even as God is. See *hagiotēs* (41); *hagiōsunē* (42); and *hagiazō* (37).

39. Hagion; neut. of the adj. *hagios* (40), holy. Used of those structures set apart for God. (1) Of the Tabernacle in the wilderness (Heb. 9:1). In v. 2 *hagia,* pl. without the art. as *hagia hagiōn,* holies of holies. The term *hagia* is probably intended to fix attention on the character of the sanctuary as being holy. The pl. suggests the idea of the sanctuary with all its parts. The *hagia hagiōn,* holies of holies in v. 3 as well as the phrase with the definite art. in the pl., *tōn hagiōn* of v. 8, may very well refer to the inner part, the holy of holies, the holiest of all. In v. 24, *hagia,* pl. without the art.; v. 25, *ta hagia,* the holies with the art. In Mt. 24:15, *en,* in, *topō,* place, dat. without the art., *hagiō,* the dat. holy, "in a holy place." (2) *Hagiōn* (Heb. 8:2) in the pl. gen. *tōn hagiōn* refers to heaven itself, the immediate presence of God and His throne (v. 1). Heb. 9:24,25 refers to heaven as *ta hagia,* the holies, also Heb. 13:11. Heaven is designated as the true Tabernacle (Heb. 8:2; 9:12; 10:19).

40. Hagios; holy, set apart, sanctified, consecrated. It has a common root, *hag-,* with *hagnos* (53), chaste, pure. Its fundamental idea is separation, consecration, devotion to the service of *Deity,* sharing in God's purity and abstaining from earth's defilement. Contr. to *hieros* (2413), *hagios* has moral significance while *hieros* has only ritual significance. Thus *hiereus* (2409), priest, may not be *hagios,* as long as he performs priestly duties or ordinances and is *hosios* (3741). Deriv.: verb, *hagiazō* (37), to render holy, separate from sin in general and in particular as abstaining from fornication (I Thess. 4:3); noun, *hagiasmos* (38), the act of sanctification as completed; *hagiotēs* (41), sanctification, the result of sanctification. *Hagiōsunē* (42), holiness, the quality of sanctification. See *hagnos* (53), *to hagion* (39), sacred thing; *hagios* (40), saint, separated not only ceremonially but also morally. Contr. with *hagnos* (53), pure, sometimes only externally or ceremonially pure.

41. Hagiotēs; holiness. Like all deriv. of *hagios* (40), holy, the word is unknown in Class. Gr. In the N.T. it occurs only in Heb. 12:10. The quality of holiness per se. Syn. *hagiōsunē* (42), a quality that can be perceived by others, while *hagiotēs* speaks of the essence of the character of God.

42. Hagiōsunē; sanctity or holiness. Derived not from *hagiazō* (37), but from *hagios* (40), holy. Denotes sanctity, not sanctification. It does not need to be proved. *Hagiōsunē* with *hagiotēs* (41) are qualities of character for which there need not be any proof; but for *hagiasmos,* the process of sanctification and the result of that process upon the individual, proof has to be at each stage of its progressive achievement. *Hagiōsunē* occurs in only three places in the N.T. (1) Rom. 1:4, of the holiness of God pervading and molding the scheme of redemption and manifested finally in and by Christ. The topic here is not the contrast of natural and moral qualities, but of human and divine relationship or dependence. Here we do not have Holy Spirit (*pneuma hagion*) but *pneuma hagiōsunēs,* spirit of sanctity or holiness which is not what Christ achieved but what Christ was in Himself, holy. In His flesh the Lord Jesus did not achieve holiness, but manifested the holiness that was His forever. (2) II Cor. 7:1, perfecting holiness in the fear of God. (3) I Thess. 3:13 speaks of the holiness of man. Also see Eph. 1:4; 5:27; Col. 1:22.

47. Hagneia; purity, from *hagnos* (53). Refers to chastity. Used only in I Tim. 4:12; 5:2. In 5:2 refers to one's moral attitude toward younger sisters in Christ and denotes the chastity which shuts out whatever impurity of spirit or manner might be mixed up with a Christian benevolent task of comforting. When a male comforts young women, he must be especially careful lest he mix his divine task with any impure thoughts.

48. Hagnizō; to consecrate, to purify, from *hagnos* (53), dedicated or adored by sacrifice. Such purification was required in priests for the divine service (Num. 8:21), and indeed in all who belong to the chosen people (Ex. 19:10,11; Josh. 3:5; II Chron. 30:17, etc.). Opp.: *miainō* (3392), to contaminate, defile. In the N.T. used much in the same sense as in the O.T. on the same ground as the Israelite's relation to God (Jn. 11:55; Acts 21:24,26; 24:18). Used not only with the meaning of purifying or cleansing, but also with the collateral meaning of consecration.

49. Hagnismos; act of consecration, purification, from *hagnos* (53), dedicated or adored by sacrifice. To expiate, referring to the purification and consecration of the Levites (Num. 8:7; 31:23). In the N.T. only in Acts 21:26.

50. Agnoeō; from the neg. *a* and *noeō* (3539), not to recognize, not to know, to be unacquainted with, usually followed by the accus. (Acts 17:23; II Cor. 2:11; Rom. 10:3; 11:25). Followed by the prep. *peri,* concerning, meaning to be in ignorance concerning anything (I Cor. 12:1; I Thess. 4:13). Followed by *hoti,* that (Rom. 1:13; 2:4; 6:3; 7:1; 11:25; I Cor. 10:1; II Cor. 1:8). In the pass. form, to be unknown, unrecognized. In antithesis with *epiginōskō* (1921), to know clearly, it means to be mistaken, misunderstood (I Cor. 14:38; II Cor. 6:9; Gal. 1:22). It came to mean to be ignorant, to have no discernment of, not to understand (Mk. 9:32; Lk. 9:45; Acts 13:27; I Cor. 2:8; 14:38). To err, to commit a fault or faults arising from the want of discernment or knowledge or insight, denoting conduct the result and import of which is unperceived by the agent (Lk. 23:34; Heb. 5:2, cf. Rom. 7:7,8,13) in which case the conduct cannot be regarded as deliberate and intentional opposition, though in consequence of the interposition of the law it has become *parabasis* (3847), transgression, i.e., involving guilt (Rom. 7:7,8). Ignorant ones, *agnoousi,* those who are under the power of sin but not actively pursuing it and yet passively subject to it (Heb. 5:2). Deriv.: *agnoēma* (51), mistake, oversight; *agnoia* (52), want of knowledge, ignorance.

51. Agnoēma; error, only in Heb. 9:7. Derived from *agnoia* (52), ignorance, and designates sin where an excuse is interpolated. Such a sin is considered as mitigated sinfulness. Its forgiveness cannot be demanded due to ignorance although it can be requested (Lk. 23:34; I Tim. 1:13). The *agnoēmata,* errors of the people for which the high priest offered sacrifice on the great day of atonement, were not willful transgressions, presumptuous sins (Ps. 19:13). Verb: *agnoeō* (50), to be ignorant. Deriv.: *noeō* (3539), to think.

52. Agnoia; want of knowledge, ignorance, which leads

to mistaken conduct and forbids unconditional imputation of the guilt of the acts performed (I Pet. 1:14; Acts 3:17, cf. Lk. 23:34; I Cor. 2:8). This *agnoia*, ignorance, according to Paul is the characteristic of heathendom (Acts 17:30; Eph. 4:18, cf. v. 17) and is a state which renders repentance necessary (Acts 17:30) and, therefore, eventually furnishes ground for blame (Eph. 4:18), or otherwise for forbearance. Deriv.: *agnoeō* (50), not to know.

53. Hagnos; chaste, pure. An adj. predominantly used to express freedom from defilements or impurities. In a more restricted sense, not only chastity but also virginity. Deriv.: verb, *hagnizō* (48), to purify (Jn. 11:55; Acts 21:24,26; 24:18; Js. 4:8; I Pet. 1:22; I Jn. 3:3); *hagnismos* (49), purification (Acts 21:26); *hagnotēs* (54), the quality of purity (II Cor. 6:6); adv., *hagnōs* (55), purely (Phil. 1:16). Joseph (Gen. 39:7-12 in the Septuagint) was *hosios* (3741), unpolluted, in that he reverenced the everlasting sanctities of marriage the defilement of which he considered sinning against God, the originator of marriage; he was *hagios* (40), holy, in that he separated himself from any unholy fellowship with his temptress; he proved himself *hagnos*, pure, in that he kept his body pure and undefiled.

54. Hagnotēs; purity, sincerity (II Cor. 6:6). In II Cor. 11:3 the T.R. has *haplotēs* (572), singleness, the opp. of duplicity, instead of *hagnotēs*, the two words coinciding in meaning. Refers to sincerity as part of the character of a person and not necessarily its influence on others.

55. Hagnōs; adv. of *hagnos* (53), chaste. Purely, sincerely. In Phil. 1:16 refers to the simplicity of the spirit with the absence of other motives that could be selfish. Therefore, *hagnōs* can really mean without duplicity.

56. Agnōsia; ignorance, from the neg. *a*, and *gnōsis* (1108), knowledge. In Class. Gr., not being acquainted with anything. In the N.T., corresponds to the use of *ginōskō* (1097), to know, to be influenced by one's knowledge of an object. *Agnōsia* means not merely an intellectual, but a moral defect or fault (I Cor. 15:34; Eph. 2:12). In I Pet. 2:15 we have the demonstration of something that is more than an intellectual defect and the *gnōsis* supposed is that of moral discernment.

57. Agnōstos; from the neg. *a*, and *gnōstos* (1110), known. Unknown. In the Class. Gr., not knowable, withdrawing itself from being known, unrecognizable. In the N.T. used with a pass. meaning (Acts 17:23), to the unknown god, to the god who did not make himself known to man. In the pantheon of Athenian gods there were those who they thought did not reveal themselves to man. Therefore, the altars were to these unknown deities and not to the true God which would have given hint of a monotheistic religion. Their unknown god did not refer to the true God revealed to them by the Apostle Paul.

58. Agora; from the verb *agō* (71), to lead. A place in which the people assemble, assembly. Then the place of meeting, a market place, serving also as a court of justice (Mt. 11:16; 20:3; 23:7; Mk. 7:4; Acts 17:17; 16:19).

59. Agorazō; from *agora* (58), market place. To buy. With the accus., to buy a thing (Mt. 13:44,46; 14:15, etc.). With the gen. it indicates the value (Mk. 6:37). In the pass., see I Cor. 6:20; 7:23. In these passages: "you were bought with a price" or "for a price," the word indicates the opp. of free acquisition, and the consequence is that something or someone having been bought, the one who buys it or him has the right of possession. Transferred to the redemptive work of Christ (I Cor. 6:20; 7:23; II Pet. 2:1; Rev. 5:9; 14:3,4). The idea is that Christ, by offering for us satisfaction due (Gal. 3:13), freed us from our liability in paying it ourselves. He, having paid the price, binds us to Him.

71. Agō; to lead, to lead along, to bring, carry, remove. Trans., to bring, to lead gently and without violence (Acts 5:26; 9:27; 21:16; II Tim. 4:11). To bring, carry, drag, or hurry away by force and violence (Mk. 13:11; Lk. 4:29; Acts 6:12; 17:5,19, etc.); to lead, rule, govern (Rom. 8;14; Gal. 5:18; II Tim. 3:6); to entice (Rom. 2:4); to spend, hold or celebrate a particular day or time (Mt. 14:6; Lk. 24:21; Acts 19:38). Intrans., to carry or convey oneself. To go, go away (Mt. 26:46; Mk. 1:38; 14:42; Jn. 11:15,16, etc.). Deriv.: *agōgē* (72), course of life, manner of leading or spending it (II Tim. 3:10); *anagō* (321) (*ana*, up, again, or away) to bring, lead, carry, or take up (Acts 9:39; Lk. 4:5, etc.); to bring or offer up as a sacrifice (Acts 7:41). In the pass. voice *anagomai* (321), literally to be carried up as a term of navigation, to put out to sea, to set sail (Lk. 8:22; Acts 13:13; 18:21, etc.), to bring back (Rom. 10:7; Heb. 13:20). *Apagō* (520) (*apo*, from) to lead, carry or take away (Mt. 26:57; 27:31; Acts 24:7). In the pass., to be led or carried away to execution or death (Acts 12:19); to lead or tend, as a way (Mt. 7:13,14). *Eisagō* (1521) (*eis*, into, in), to bring in, introduce (Lk. 2:27; Heb. 1:6, figuratively); *exagō* (1806) (*ex*, out), to lead forth or bring out (Mk. 8:23; 15:20; Lk. 24:50; Jn. 10:3; Acts 5:19; 7:36; 16:37); *epagō* (1863) (*epi*, upon), to bring upon (Acts 5:28; II Pet. 2:1,5); *katagnumi* (2608) (*kata*, down, as an inten.), to break in pieces (Mt. 12:20; Jn. 19:31-33); *katagō* (2609), to bring down (Acts 9:30; 22:30; 23:15,20,28; Rom. 10:6); as a term of navigation (Lk. 5:11; Acts 21:3; 27:3; 28:12); *pareisagō* (3919) (*para*, denoting ill, and *eisagō*, to bring in), to introduce craftily or secretly (II Pet. 2:1). Derived from *pareisaktos* (3920) adj. used as a noun, one or something brought in secretly, introduced by craftiness, those that have crept in (Gal. 2:4). *Proagō* (4254) (*pro*, before or forth), of place it means to go before, or lead properly when others follow (Mt. 14:22; 21:9; 26:32; 28:7, etc.), less properly when others do not follow (Mt. 21:31); to go before, to proceed in time (I Tim. 1:18; 5:24; Heb. 7:18); to bring out or forth (Acts 16:30; 25:26) particularly to condemnation or punishment (Acts 12:6); *prosagō* (4317) (*pros*, to, or towards), to bring to, to bring (Lk. 9:41; Acts 16:20; I Pet. 3:18); to come to or towards, to approach (Acts 27:27). The noun of this verb *prosagōgē* (4318), approach, access or introduction (Rom. 5:2; Eph. 2:18; 3:12). *Sunagō* (4863) (*sun*, together), to bring together (Mt. 2:4; 26:3, etc.); to take in or receive with hospitality and kindness (Mt. 25:35,43). From this we have the noun *sunagōgē* (4864), a public or large assembly of men (Mt. 6:2); a synagogue, a building where the Jews met for the purpose of public prayer and hearing the Scriptures read and expounded (Lk. 7:5; Acts 18:7). *Episunagō* (1996) (*epi*, to, and *sunagō*, to gather, collect); to gather together in one place (Mk. 1:33; Lk. 12:1); to gather together as a hen does her chickens under her wings (Mt. 23:37; Lk. 13:34); to assemble the elect into the Christian Church (Mt. 24:31; Mk. 13:27); *episunagōgē* (1997), a being gathered together (II Thess. 2:1); an assembling together at one place (Heb. 10:25); *epeisagōgē* (1898), from *epeisagō*, to superinduce from *epi*, upon, and *eisagō*, to introduce, bring in; a superinduction, a bringing in one thing after or upon another, an introduction of somewhat more (Heb. 7:19).

73. Agōn; from the verb *agō* (71), implying force or violence. N.T. meanings: (1) Strife, contention, contest for victory or mastery such as was used in the Greek games of running, boxing, wrestling, etc. It is not used strictly in this sense, which was very common in the Gr. writers, but Paul plainly alludes to this in I Tim. 6:12; II Tim. 4:7 and applies the word to the evangelical contest against the enemies of man's salvation (cf. I Cor. 9:24, etc.). (2) A race, a place to run (Heb. 12:1). (3) A struggle, contest, contention (Phil. 1:29,30; Col. 2:1; I Thess 2:2). In the N.T. presented as the life task of man or of the Christian.

74. Agōnia; combat, more abstract and eclectic than *agōn* (73), contest, giving prominence to the pain and labor of the conflict. It used to refer to the trembling excitement and anxiety produced by fear or tension before a wrestling match or a fight. In the N.T. it occurs in Lk. 22:44 (cf. Mt. 26:37,38; Jn. 12:27), denoting not the fear which shrinks and would flee, but the fear which trembles in the face of the issue, spurring on to the uttermost.

75. Agōnizomai; to contend for victory in the public games (I Cor. 9:25) and then it generally came to mean fight, to wrestle (Jn. 18:36). The task of faith in persevering amid temptation and opposition (I Tim. 6:12; II Tim. 4:7). It came also to mean to take pains, to wrestle as in a prize contest, straining every nerve to the uttermost towards the goal (Lk. 13:24, cf. I Cor. 9:25; Phil. 3:12ff; Heb. 4:1). Special pains and toil (Col. 1:29; I Tim. 4:10; Col. 4:12). Implies hindrances in the development of the Christian life.

80. Adelphos; a brother, from the coll. *a* and *delphus,* a womb; a brother, and the fem. *adelphē,* a sister. The Heb. word was used of more distant relatives (Gen. 14:16; 29:12,15) and, because of that, some think that this circumstance ought to be taken into consideration where brothers and sisters of the Lord Jesus are referred to (Mt. 12:46,47; 13:55; Mk. 3:31,32; 6:3; Lk. 8:19,20; Jn. 2:12; 7:3,5,10; Acts 1:14). But the conjoined mention of the mother of Jesus (besides Jn. 7:3,5,10) appears to imply that children of the same mother are meant, against which no argument is furnished by Jn. 19:26 which ought rather to be explained by Mt. 19:29 and it parallels. The answer to this question depends on the view taken of the relation between James the son of Alphaeus and James the brother of the Lord (Mk. 15:47; Jn. 19:25, cf. Mt. 13:55). Further, *adelphos* denotes in general a fellowship of life based on identity of origin as, e.g., the members of the same tribe, countrymen, etc. (Acts 3:22; 7:23; Rom. 9:3). A neighbor is regarded as a brother (Mt. 5:22-24,47, etc.). *Adelphos* also came to designate a community of love equivalent to or bringing with it a community of life (Mt. 12:50; Mk. 10:29,30; Acts 12:17). In this manner Jesus speaks of His brethren (Mt. 25:40; 28:10; Jn. 20:17; Rom. 8:29; Heb. 2:11,17). The members of the same Christian community are called brothers (Jn. 21:23; Acts 9:30; Rom. 16:14; I Cor. 7:12).

81. Adelphotēs; brotherhood, a brotherly or sisterly relation. Occurs only in I Pet. 2:17; 5:9. Equivalent to *philadelphia* (5360), brotherly love (Rom. 12:10; 1 Thess. 4:9; Heb. 13:1; I Pet. 1:22; II Pet. 1:7) and *philadelphos* (5361), friend of brethren, the adj. in I Pet. 3:8. While *adelphotēs* is especially used in the N.T. and ecclesiastical Gr., it is not used by Class. Gr. writers who used *philadelphia* to denote only the love of brothers and sisters by birth to each other. In Christianity it is *adelphotēs,* a brotherhood or sisterhood which has been made possible by Jesus Christ, and since all believers are given the new birth, it is truly indeed by spiritual birth that men and women are brothers and sisters.

86. Hadēs; the region of departed spirits of the lost but including the blessed dead in periods preceding the ascension of Christ (Lk. 16:23). Most probable derivation is from *hadō,* all-receding. It corresponds to *sheol* in the O.T. Both the O.T. and N.T. words have been translated in the A.V. unfortunately as hell (Ps. 16:10) or the grave (Gen. 37:35) or the pit (Num. 16:30,33). *Hadēs* never denotes the physical grave nor is it the permanent region of the lost. It is the intermediate state between death and the ultimate hell, Gehenna. *Hadēs* is used four times in the Gospels and always by the Lord (Mt. 11:23; 16:18; Lk. 10:15; 16:23). Used with reference to the soul of Christ (Acts 2:27,31). Christ declares that He has the keys of *hadēs* (Rev. 1:18). In Rev. 6:8 it is personified with the meaning of the temporary destiny of the doomed; it is to give up those who are in it (Rev. 20:13) and is to be cast into the lake of fire (Rev. 20:14). See *geenna* (1067); *tartaroō* and *tartaros* (5020).

87. Adiakritos; from the neg. *a,* without, and *diakrisis* (1253), separation, discrimination. Indistinguishable, making no partial distinctions, free from partial regards, impartial (Js. 3:17).

91. Adikeō; to do wrong, hurt, damage; from the neg. *a,* without, and *dikē* (1349), right, justice. Intrans., to act unjustly, do wrong (Acts 25:11; II Cor. 7:12; Col. 3:25; Rev. 22:11). Trans., to act unjustly, to do wrong to or injure someone (Mt. 20:13; Acts 7:24,26,27; 25:10; Phile. 18, etc.); to hurt, damage, harm (Lk. 10:19; Rev. 2:11; 6:6; 7:2,3, etc.). Deriv.: *adikēma* (92); *adikia* (93); *adikos* (94).

92. Adikēma; from *adikeo* (91), to injure, to act unjustly. That which results from an injustice, a crime, a criminal act (Acts 18:14; 24:20; Rev. 18:5).

93. Adikia; from *a,* neg., *dikē* (1349), justice. What is not conformable with justice, what ought not to be, that which is wrong. Related to *adikos* (94), unjust, hence: injustice, unrighteousness. There is an *adikia* only because there is an *alētheia* (225), truth, which occupies the place of *dikē* (1349), justice. In I Jn. 5:17 "All unrighteousness (*adikia*) is sin (*hamartia*)." Whatever does not meet God's justice is missing God's justice or His goal for us. The result of *adikia,* unrighteousness, is *adikēma* (92), evil doing (Acts 18:14). In the context of Lk. 16:8, *adikia* is used to symbolize money. The steward of unrighteousness or injustice is wrongly translated "the unrighteous steward" as having been commended by the Lord. It should be the "steward of unrighteousness" which stands for money. It is so-called because money is used for unjust purposes. In Acts 1:18 the reward of iniquity is the pay of *adikia,* the pay of unrighteousness, unrighteousness here standing for unrighteous money. See Lk. 16:1-13.

94. Adikos; from *a,* neg., and *dikē* (1349), justice. Unjust, unrighteous, falling short of the righteousness required by divine laws (I Pet. 3:18). Wanting the imputed righteousness of faith and the inherent righteousness wrought by the Spirit of God (Mt. 5:45; Acts 24:15; I Cor. 6:9). Opp. *dikaios* (1342), fair, just (Mt. 5:45; Acts 24:15). Not in conformity with *dikē,* justice, the opp. of *endikos* (1738), not as it should and ought to be; unjust, unrighteous. In Lk. 16:10,11; 18:11 it stands as the opp. of *pistos* (4103), faithful or dependable. In this sense *adikos* is one who does not disappoint expectations nor neglect claims. Used as an adj. in Lk. 16:11 referring to mammon, the god of money who disappoints and deceives. *Adikos* (II Pet. 2:9) may stand in contr. with *eusebēs* (2152), devout, Godly. It could, therefore, be taken as syn. with *asebēs* (765), impious, ungodly.

96. Adokimos; unapproved, unworthy, from the neg. *a,* and *dokimos* (1384), acceptable. Spurious, worthless. In a pass. sense, disapproved, rejected, cast away (I Cor. 9:27; Heb. 6:8, cf. II Cor. 13:5-7; II Tim. 3:8; Tit. 1:16). In the act, sense, undiscerning, not distinguishing, void of judgment (Rom. 1:28); although in this text it may be understood in the pass., a reprobate, abominable mind, a mind to be abhorred by God and man.

97. Adolos; sincere. Only in I Pet. 2:2, from the priv. *a* and *dolos* (1388), guile. Indicates the absence of fraud and deceit as in Nathanael in whom there was no guile (Jn. 1:47). See *haplous* (573), single, without duplicity; *akakos* (172), constitutionally harmless; and *akeraios* (185), without admixture.

100. Hadrotēs; bounty (II Cor. 8:20), derived from *hadros,* thick, fat, full-grown, rich. Bountiful giving or fat offering and not just mere abundance. See *perisseia* (4050), overflowing, and *perisseuma* (4051), abundance in a slightly more concrete form as in II Cor. 8:13,14 where it stands for the gifts in kind supplied by the saints.

106. Azumos; unleavened. In the N.T. used of the Feast of the Passover (Mt. 26:17; Mk. 14:1, 12; Lk. 22:1,7; Acts 12:3; 20:6). Figuratively meaning unpenetrated by evil (I Cor. 5:7,8). Deriv.: see *zumē* (2219).

110. Athanasia; from the priv. *a,* without, and *thanatos* (2288), death. Rendered immortality in I Cor. 15:53,54 of the glorified body of the believer. In I Tim. 6:16 used of the nature of God. In the N.T. it expresses the nature not of life itself, but strictly speaking, only a quality of life such as the quality of the life of God and the resurrection body of the believer. See *thnētos* (2349), mortal, from *thanatos,* death. Our bodies are subject to death, mortal (related to *thnēskō,* 2348, to die). Used in Rom. 6:12 of the body where it is called mortal, not simply because it is liable to death but because it is the organ in and through which death carries on its fatal activities. In Rom. 8:11 the stress is on the liability to death, and the quickening is not reinvigoration, but the impartation of life when Jesus returns (I Cor. 15:53,54; II Cor. 5:4). In II Cor. 4:11 applied to the flesh, which stands not simply for the body, but the body as that which consists of the element of decay and is thereby doomed.

111. Athemitos; from the neg. *a*, and *themitos*, an adj. from *themis*, law. Unlawful (Acts 10:28; I Pet. 4:3). See *athesmos* (113).

112. Atheos; from the neg. *a*, without, and *Theos* (2316), God. In Class. Gr., it primarily and actively meant godless, destitute of God, without God and consequently *alogos* (249), devoid of reason, denoting a person who was forgetful of God and did not care about the existence of the gods and consequently did not honor them. In the N.T. occurs only in Eph. 2:12 in the pass., meaning without divine help, forsaken by God, excluded from communion with God. "Without God" does not really convey the full meaning. It means more than not knowing God. It means neglectful of God. See also I Thess. 4:5.

126. Aidios; from *aei* (104), ever, always. Eternal, absolutely, without beginning or end (Rom. 1:20). Perpetual, without end (Jude 6).

127. Aidōs; modesty, an innate moral repugnance to a dishonorable act, which repugnance scarcely or not at all exists in *aischunē* (152), shame. The grief which a man conceives from his own imperfections considered with relation to the world taking notice of them; grief upon the sense of disesteem. *Aidōs* finds its motive in itself, implies reverence for the good as good, not merely as that to which honor and reputation are attached. Only in I Tim. 2:9; Heb. 12:28.

129. Haima; the blood of the human or animal body (Mk. 5:25,29; Lk. 8:43,44; 13:1, etc.). Meanings: (1) Blood as the substantial basis of the individual life (Jn. 1:13; Acts 17:26). Although the O.T. contains nothing parallel to these two passages, yet the expression corresponds to the idea contained in Lev. 17:11, "For the life of the flesh is in the blood." There is a conjoining of the word "blood" with "flesh" in Heb. 2:14. Flesh and blood designate mankind, insofar as they owe their distinctive character to the material aspect of their being (Eph. 6:12). The expression means the physical origin of man in Mt. 16:17; I Cor. 15:50; Gal. 1:16. The physical and the spiritual natures of man are contr. in Eph. 6:12, cf. Heb. 2:14 (see also Mt. 16:17; I Cor. 15:50; Gal. 1:16). (2) *Haima* by itself serves to denote life passing away in bloodshed, and generally life taken away by force (Mt. 23:30,35; 27:4; Lk. 11:50,51; Acts 1:19, etc.). The expression "to shed blood," *haima ekcheō* (1632), emphasizes not so much the manner of slaying, but rather the fact of the forcible taking away of life, whether produced by or only accompanied with the shedding of blood (Mt. 26:28; Mk. 14:24; Lk. 22:20; Acts 22:20). (3) Related to no. 2, *haima* is used to denote life given up or offered as an atonement since, in the ritual of sacrifice, special emphasis is laid upon it as the material basis of the individual life. The life of the animal offered for propitiation appears in the blood separated from the flesh (Lev. 17:11-14; Heb. 9:13,18,19,21,22,25; 10:4; 13:11) which life is, on the one hand, in the blood, presented to God; on the other by sprinkling, appropriated to man (Heb. 9:7,19,20) by which this blood becomes the blood of the covenant which God commanded to us (Heb. 9:20). The same is true of the blood of Christ (Heb. 10:29); the blood of the covenant (Mt. 26:28; Mk. 14:24; Lk. 22:20; Heb. 13:20), the New Testament in my blood (I Cor. 11:25; I Pet. 1:2). Designates the life of Christ offered for an atonement contr. with the blood of beasts slain in sacrifice (Heb. 9:12, cf. vv. 14,25). The blood of Christ, therefore, represents the life that He gave for our atonement (Mt. 26:28; Heb. 9:12,25; I Jn. 1:7, etc.).

130. Haimatekchusia; shedding of blood, from *haima*, blood, and *ekchuō* or *ekcheō* (1632), to pour out. Strictly speaking, the bringing of the blood to the altar, the application of the blood for objective expiation (Ex. 29:16; Lev. 8:15; 9:9; Deut. 12:27; II Kgs. 16:15) whose correlative is *rhantismos* (4473), sprinkling, the application of the atonement to its object. *Haimatekchusia* does not include the shedding of blood or the slaying of a victim, or the sprinkling of that blood on the object to be expiated. The question dealt with in Heb. 9:22 is not the manner, but the means of atonement, *haima*, blood (see vv. 18,19,22a,23,25) denoting only a part of the act of atonement, and as such would exclude the sprinkling of the people (v. 19); it could not include this, and at the same time the sprinkling of the holy vessels (v. 21). Thus the shedding of blood denotes not only the shedding of the blood as the act of killing, but the ritualistic act of blood outpouring always requires an addition unto the altar or toward the altar (Lev. 8:15; 9:9) or on the altar (II Kgs. 16:15). The verb *proscheō* and the noun *proschusis* (4378) are commonly used and should not be translated as "sprinkling" but as "shedding forth, toward." Therefore, *haimatekchusia* means blood shedding and not the actual pouring out of the blood, the expression employed concerning the blood of Christ (Lk. 22:20) which for our sakes was poured out. The word means only blood shedding, slaying, murder, and not the application of it.

133. Ainesis; from *aineō* (134), the act of praise (Heb. 13:15).

134. Aineō; from *ainos* (136). To sing alternately praises to God (Ex. 15:21; I Sam. 21:11). In the N.T. it only refers to praising God (Lk. 2:13, 20, etc.).

136. Ainos; praise returned for benefits received or expected (Mt. 21:16; Lk. 18:43). See *ainesis* (133) and *aineō* (134).

138. Haireomai; from *hairō* (142), to take up. To lift up, as the hands (Rev. 10:5), the eyes (Jn. 11:41); to lift or take up (Mk. 6:29,43; Acts 20:9); applied to the mind, to hold in suspense (Jn. 10:24); to take up as a yoke (Mt. 11:29), as a burden (Mt. 4:6; 27:32; Mk. 15:21; Jn. 5:8,9); to remove, take away (Mt. 22:13; Jn. 11:39,41); to bear and take away such as sins (Jn. 1:29; I Jn. 3:5); to receive, take (Mt. 20:14; Mk. 6:8); to loose a ship from shore (Acts 27:13); to lift up or raise the voice (Lk. 17:31; Acts 4:24). Cf. *eklegomai* (1586), to choose out, elect; *epilegomai* (1951), to be called or named; *hairetizō* (140), to choose, akin to *hairetos*, a verbal adj. signifying that which may be taken.

139. Hairesis; heresy, from *haireō* or *haireomai* (138), to choose, select (Phil. 1:22; II Thess. 2:13; Heb. 11:25). A form of religious worship, discipline or opinion. In contr. to *schisma* (4978), schism, it is only theoretical. One can hold different views than the majority and remain in the same body but he is a "heretic." But when he tears himself away, *schizō* (4977), then he is schismatic. Heresy is theoretic schism; schism is practical heresy.

140. Hairetizō; choose, only in Mt. 12:18, related to the verbal adj. *hairetos*, that which may be taken. To take with the implication that what is taken is eligible or suitable; to choose by reason of its suitability. Contr. *eklegomai* (1586), meaning to choose because of love and desirability of attaching the object to oneself. See also *epilegomai* (1951); *haireomai* (138).

141. Hairetikos; heretic, pertaining to choice, capable of choice in an act. sense. In ecclesiastical Gr., heretical (Tit. 3:10). The noun *hairesis* used in I Cor. 11:19; Gal. 5:20; II Pet. 2:1. See Rom. 16:17 where clearly one still belongs to the fellowship, but whom the fellowship eventually had to exclude.

142. Airō; to lift, raise, take up; to lift up the hands (Rev. 10:5); the eyes (Jn. 11:41); to lift or take up (Mt. 17:27; Mk. 6:29,43; Acts 20:9); as applied to the mind, keep in suspense (Jn. 10:24); take up as a yoke (Mt. 11:29); a cross (Mt. 16:24); bear or carry as a burden (Mt. 4:6; 27:32; Mk. 15:21; Jn. 5:8,9); remove (Mt. 22:13; Jn. 11:39,41); take away (Jn. 1:29; I Jn. 3:5); receive, take (Mt. 20:14; Mk. 6:8); to loose a ship, namely from shore (Acts 27:13); lift up or raise the voice (Lk. 17:31; Acts 4:24). Deriv.: *epairō* (1869) (with prefix *epi*, upon), to lift up, as the eyes (Mt. 17:8; Lk. 6:20, etc.); the head (Lk. 21:28); the hands (Lk. 24:50; I Tim. 2:8); the heel (Jn. 13:18). In the pass. voice *epair-*

omai, to be lifted up from the ground as our Lord at His ascension (Acts 1:9); to hoist a sail (Acts 27:40); in the middle or pass., to lift up or exalt oneself, to be lifted up or exalted in pride (II Cor. 11:20); lift up, exalt, raise the voice (Lk. 11:27, etc.).

143. Aisthanomai; to perceive, primarily with the senses. Figuratively of spiritual perception: to become conscious of, observe, understand, more of immediate knowledge than that arrived at by reasoning (Lk. 9:45).

144. Aisthēsis; perception, sensational as well as mental. Pass., to become cognizant of, to make oneself observed by anyone. Involves knowledge based upon experience, experimental knowledge. In Phil. 1:9 contr. *epignōsis* (1922), the insight obtained by penetrating knowledge, going down to the foundation. *Aisthēsis,* however, is experimental knowledge which is or becomes naturally manifold, and therefore has the addition of *pasa,* all (Phil. 1:9).

145. Aisthētērion; organ of sense, seldom applied to the spiritual life, and manifestly in a figurative manner (Heb. 5:14).

152. Aischunē; shame, that feeling which leads to shun what is unworthy out of a prospective anticipation of dishonor (Lk. 14:9; II Cor. 4:2; Phil. 3:19; Heb. 12:2; Jude 13; Rev. 3:18).

154. Aiteō; ask, request, beg; from which is derived *epaiteō* (1871), to beg for alms (Lk. 16:3). The seeking by the inferior from the superior (Acts 12:20); by a beggar from the giver (Acts 3:2); by the child from the parent (Mt. 7:9); by man from God (Mt. 7:7; Js. 1:5; I Jn. 3:22). Contr. *erōtaō* (2065), ask, when it is not used as a mere interrogatory which implies that he who asks stands on a certain footing of equality with the giver (Lk. 14:32). The Lord never uses *aiteō,* to beg, but *erōtaō,* to ask as an equal of the Father on behalf of Himself or His disciples (Jn. 14:16; 16:26; 17:9,15,20). Martha reveals her false concept of Christ when she tells Him He should *aitein* of the Father (Jn. 11:22).

155. Aitēma; occurs twice in the N.T. (Phil. 4:6; I Jn. 5:15) in the sense of a petition of men to God, both times in the pl. They are particular requests of which prayer, *proseuchē* (4335), may consist, e.g., in the Lord's Prayer there are seven *aitēmata,* petitions, although some have regarded the first three as *euchai* (2171), wishes. *Aitēma* is used in Lk. 23:24 in the sense of petition by the Jews for releasing Barabbas. Related words: *deēsis* (1162), supplication or prayer for particular benefits; *enteuxis* (1783), intercession; *eucharistia* (2169), thanksgiving; *hiketēria* (2428), entreaty, supplication.

156. Aitia; accusation true or false (Mt. 27:37; Mk. 15:26; Jn. 18:38). Derived from *aiteō* (154), to ask, require, because an accusation or crime is that for which one is required to appear before a judge to be questioned. A cause, reason, incitement (Mt. 19:3; Lk. 8:47; Acts 10:21). Deriv.: *aitiōma,* charge, sometimes *aitiama* (157) (Acts 25:7).

165. Aiōn; age, refers to an age or time in contr. to *kosmos* (2889), referring to people or space. Derived from *aei* (104), always, and *ōn,* being. Denotes duration or continuance of time, but with great variety. (1) Both in the sing. and pl. it signifies eternity whether past or to come (Mt. 6:13; Mk. 3:29; Lk. 1:55; Jn. 4:14; 6:51; Acts 15:18; Eph. 3:11, etc.); for ages, of ages (Rev. 1:6,18; 5:14; 10:6; 14:11; 15:7; 20:10). (2) The duration of this world (Mt. 28:20; Jn. 9:32; Acts 3:21); since the beginning of the world (Mt. 13:39, etc.). (3) Pl., *hoi aiōnes,* the ages of the world (I Cor. 2:7; Eph. 3:9; Col. 1:26). (4) *Ho aiōn houtos,* this age, generation (Lk. 16:8; 20:34, cf. Mt. 13:22; I Cor. 1:20; 2:6; Gal. 1:4; Eph. 2:2; I Tim. 6:17; II Tim. 4:10; Tit. 2:12). (5) *Ho aiōn ho erchomenos,* the age, the coming one meaning the next life (Mk. 10:30; Lk. 18:30, cf. Lk. 20:35). (6) An age or dispensation of providence (Mt. 24:3, cf. Mt. 12:32; I Cor. 10:11; Heb. 1:2; 6:5; 9:26). (7) *Aiōnes,* ages, in Heb. 11:3 refers to the great occurrences which took place in the universe. *Aiōn* primarily has physical meaning (time) but also ethical. Signifies time, short or long in its unbroken duration, all of which exists in the world under conditions of time; ethically, the cause and current of this world's affairs. It has acquired, like *kosmos* (2889), an unfavorable meaning (Lk. 16:8; 20:34; Eph. 2:2; Gal. 1:4).

166. Aiōnios; eternal, belonging to the *aiōn* (165), to time in its duration, constant, abiding, eternal. When referring to eternal life, the life which is God's and hence not affected by the limitations of time. *Aiōnios* is specially predicated of the saving blessings of divine revelation, denoting not belonging to what is transitory. Meanings: (1) Having neither beginning nor end (Rom. 16:26; Heb. 9:14). (2) Without end (Mt. 25:41,46; II Thess. 1:9, etc.). In Phile. 15, forever, not only during the term of one's natural life, but through endless ages of eternal life and blessedness. (3) In Jude 7, eternal fire refers to the miraculous fire from heaven which destroyed the cities of Sodom and Gomorrha, not only because the effect thereof shall be of equal duration with the world, but also because the burning of those cities is a dreadful emblem of that everlasting fire (Mt. 25:41) which awaits the ungodly and unclean (cf. II Pet. 2:6). (4) *Chronoi,* times, *aiōnioi,* eternal, means the ages of the world, the times since the beginning of its existence (Rom. 16:25; II Tim. 1:9; Tit. 1:2, cf. Eph. 1:4; I Pet. 1:20).

167. Akatharsia; from the neg. *a,* and *kathairō* (2508), to cleanse. Uncleanness, filth, in a natural or physical sense (Mt. 23:27); moral uncleanness, lewdness, incontinence in general (Rom. 6:19; Eph. 4:19; I Thess. 2:3; 4:7); any kind of uncleanness different from whoredom (II Cor. 12:21); any unnatural pollution, whether acted out by oneself (Gal. 5:19; Col. 3:5), or with another (Rom. 1:24, cf. vv. 26,27). Deriv.: *katharizō* (2511), to cleanse.

168. Akathartēs; an abbreviation of *akatharotēs,* from the neg. *a,* and *katharotēs,* cleanness; uncleanness, filthiness (Rev. 17:4). Deriv.: *katharizō* (2511), to cleanse.

169. Akathartos; from the neg. *a,* and *kathairō* (2508), to cleanse. Meanings: (1) Unclean by legal or ceremonial uncleanness (Acts 10:14,28; 11:8, cf. Lev. 5:2; 11:25; 13:45) whereas in the Septuagint it compares with II Cor. 6:17 where *akathartos* seems ultimately to refer to all idolatrous worship and heathen impurity. (2) Unclean, unfit to be admitted to the peculiar rights and privileges of the church and particularly to baptism (I Cor. 7:14). (3) Unclean by unnatural pollution (Eph. 5:5). (4) Unclean as applied to the devils who are frequently called unclean spirits in the N.T. because, having lost their original purity, they are become unclean themselves and through their solicitations have filled mankind with all uncleanness and every abomination which the Lord hates (Mk. 5:2,8,13). Deriv.: *katharizō* (2511), to cleanse.

172. Akakos; harmless (Rom. 16:18; Heb. 7:26) from the neg. *a,* without, and *kakos* (2556), constitutionally bad. Contr. *haplous* (573), single or without duplicity; *adolos* (97), without guile; *akeraios* (185), without any foreign matter or without admixture.

176. Akatagnōstos; from the neg. *a,* without, and *katagnōstos,* blamed, from *kataginōskō* (2607), condemn. Irreprehensible, not to be condemned or blamed (Tit. 2:8).

181. Akatastasia; from the neg. *a,* not, and *katastasis,* a setting in its place, from *kathistēmi* (2525), to place, set in its place. Commotion, tumult (Lk. 21:9; I Cor. 14:33; II Cor. 6:5; 12:20; Js. 3:16). Related to *akatastatos* (182), unsettled. See *histēmi* (2476), to hold, to stand, to place.

182. Akatastatos; from the neg. *a,* not, and *kathistēmi* (2525), to settle. Unsettled, unsteady, unstable (Js. 1:8). See *akatastasia* (181); *histēmi* (2476).

185. Akeraios; from the neg. *a,* and *keraō,* to mix (Mt. 10:16; Rom. 16:19; Phil. 2:15). Without any mixture of deceit, without any foreign material in him. Distinguished from *akakos* (172), without being constitutionally bad; *adolos* (97), without any guile; and *haplous* (573), without wrinkles or duplicity, single or simple.

189. Akoē; hearing, from *akouō* (191). The act of hearing (Rom. 10:17, cf. Mt. 13:14; Acts 28:26; Gal. 3:2,5); the sense of hearing (I Cor. 12:17; Heb. 5:11); the organ or instrument of hearing, the ear (Mk. 7:35; Acts 17:20; II Tim. 4:4); something which is or may be heard, a rumor, report (Mt. 4:24; 14:1; Jn. 12:38; Rom. 10:16).

190. Akoloutheō; from the coll. *a*, together, and *keleuthos*, a way; from *kellō*, to move quickly and *euthus*, straight. Related to *akolouthos*, attendant. To be an attendant, to accompany, to go with or follow (Mt. 4:20,22,25; 27:55; Jn. 12:26). Opp. *proagō* (4254), to go before (Mt. 4:20,22,25; 21:9; Mk. 11:9). With reference to time, *akoloutheo* means to follow thereupon (Rev. 14:8,9). Figuratively it refers to spiritual or moral relations. Syn.: *hupakouō* (5219), to obey, to serve the time or to act according to circumstances. Distinguish from the occasional and temporary following of Jesus by the crowds (Mt. 4:25; 8:1) and the following to which Jesus calls individuals (Mt. 9:9; 19:21) or people generally (Mt. 10:38; 16:24; Jn. 8:12; 12:26), or which was undertaken by individuals (Mt. 8:19; Lk. 9:57,61). The individual calling to follow Jesus involved abiding fellowship with Him, not only for the sake of learning as a scholar from his teacher (Mt. 8:19), but also for the sake of the salvation known or looked for, which presented itself in this fellowship (Mt. 19:21; Lk. 9:61, etc.). The first thing involved in following Jesus is a cleaving to Him in believing trust and obedience, those cleaving to Him also following His leading, acting according to His example (Jn. 8:12; 10:4,5,27). Hence the constant stress laid by the Lord Jesus upon the need of self-denial and fellowship in the cross (Mt. 8:19,20; 10:38; Mk. 8:34; Jn. 8:12; 12:26). Thus following Jesus denotes a fellowship of faith as well as a fellowship of life, sharing in His sufferings not only inwardly, but outwardly if necessary (Mt. 9:9,19:21, etc.). Such outward fellowship with Jesus, however, could not continue without inner moral and spiritual fellowship, without a life resembling His and in a self-denying sharing of His cross. The expression "following Jesus" occurs only in Rev. 14:4. In Jn. 8:12; 10:4,5,27; 12:26, to follow Jesus appears as an independent concept apart from any outward act or momentary circumstances of time and place which union with Jesus might involve.

191. Akouō; to hear. It governs a gen. either of the person or thing, to hear someone or something, or more usually an accus. of the thing. To hear in general (Mt. 2:3,18; 11:5; 12:19; Mk. 14:64, etc.); to hear, hearken, or listen to (Mk. 12:37; Lk. 5:1; 10:39; 11:31; Acts 15:12); to understand, hear with the ear of the mind (Mt. 11:15; Jn. 8:43,47; I Cor. 14:2); to hear effectually or so as to perform or grant what is spoken (Mt. 18:16; Jn. 9:31; 11:41; I Jn. 5:14,15); to obey (Lk. 10:16; 16:29,31, cf. Jn. 8:47; I Jn. 4:6).

203. Akrobustia; from *akros*, the extreme, and *buō* or *buzō*, to fill up, plug, stop up, cover. The foreskin (Acts 11:3); uncircumcision (Rom. 4:10; I Cor. 7:18). In the N.T., and especially the Pauline writings, the word is never applied to moral and spiritual things. Col. 2:13; 3:11 only seem to hint of such a figurative application. A state of being uncircumcized means to designate somebody as outside of the promises (Rom. 2:26,27; 3:30; Eph. 2:11).

210. Akōn; unwillingly, against one's will, forced. Occurs only in I Cor. 9:17. Opp. *hekōn* (1635), willing. Syn.: *akousiōs*, unwillingly, often used in the Septuagint, but not in the N.T.

213. Alazōn; boaster in words (Rom. 1:30; II Tim. 3:2). Noun: *alazoneia* (212), vaunting in those things one does not possess (Js. 4:16; I Jn. 2:16). Contr.: *perperos* and the verb *perpereuomai* (4068), boasting about things one has with contempt for others (I Cor. 13:4); *huperēphanos* (5244), proud (Lk. 1:51; Rom. 1:30; II Tim. 3:2; Js. 4:6; I Pet. 5:5), one who shows himself above his fellows, *tuphoō* (5187), from *turphos*, smoke, or *tuphoomai* (I Tim. 3:6; 6:4; II Tim. 3:4), to be drunk with pride with a heart lifted up not only against man but against God; *hubristēs* (5197), insolent wrong doer to others for the pleasure which the affliction imparts (Rom. 1:30; I Tim. 1:13).

218. Aleiphō; to rub, to cover over, from *liparos* (3045), greasy. Contr. *chriō* (5548), anoint, pertaining to the sacred and religious. *Aleiphō* is used indiscriminately in all actual anointings, whether with oil or ointment (*aleiphē* in Mod. Gr.).

225. Alētheia; truth, as the unveiled reality lying at the basis of and agreeing with an appearance; the manifested, the veritable essence of matter. The reality pertaining to an appearance. The adj. *alēthēs* also means the same thing (Rom. 1:18,25). Therefore, *alētheia* denotes the reality clearly lying before our eyes as opp. to a mere appearance, without reality (Mk. 5:33; Jn. 5:33; 16:7; Acts 26:25; Rom. 9:1; II Cor. 12:6; Eph. 4:25; II Tim. 3:7). Used with three distinctive meanings: (1) Truth as opp. to falsehood, error or insincerity (Mt. 22:16; Mk. 5:33; 12:14,32; Eph. 4:25; Col. 1:5; Gal. 2:5,14; Phil. 1:18; I Jn. 3:18, etc.). (2) Truth as opp. to types, emblems or shadows (Jn. 1:14,17, cf. Col. 2:17; Jn. 4:23,24, cf. Jn. 14:6). (3) Integrity, rectitude of nature (Jn. 8:44).

226. Alētheuō; to be *alēthēs*, real, actual, not counterfeit, and to act as such. Answering to the truth, to make it one's study. Thus in Eph. 4:15 the expression "speaking the truth in love" is *alētheuontes* which means to make it one's business to express the reality of love and not to feign it. In Gal. 4:16, not only speaking the truth but presenting an action as the truth and not counterfeit.

227. Alēthēs; true, one who cannot lie. Distinguished from *alēthinos* (228), real, genuine (Jn. 17:3; I Thess. 1:9). The one true God as distinguished from idols and all other false gods.

228. Alēthinos; real, genuine, as distinguished from *alēthēs* (227), true, one who cannot lie.

236. Allassō; or *allattō*, to change (Acts 6:14; Gal. 4:20); transform (I Cor. 15:51,52; Heb. 1:12); exchange (Rom. 1:23). Deriv.: *antallagma* (465); *apallassō* (525); *diallassō* (1259); *katallagē* (2643); *katallassō* (2644); *metallassō* (3337).

238. Allēgoreō; to speak differently from what one thinks or actually means, to speak allegorically where the thing spoken of is the emblem or representative (Gal. 4:24). See *tupos* (5179), type.

240. Allēlōn; genitive of the reciprocal pron. *allēlous*, one another. This pron. has no nominative and no sing. Used only in the accus., gen. and dat.: *allēlous*, one another; *allēlōn*, of one another; *allēlois*, for, in, to one another.

241. Allogenēs; from *allos* (243), other, and *genos* (1085), a nation, race. One of another nation, a stranger, foreigner (Lk. 17:18).

243. Allos; another numerically but of the same kind. Contr. *heteros* (2087), another qualitatively. In the pl. *alloi*, others, in an inclusive sense (Mt. 4:21; Mk. 7:4, etc.) or an exclusive one (Mt. 2:12; 10:23, etc.). With the definite art., *ho, he, to* (3588), the, (mas., fem., neut.) prefixed, the other of two, the two being of the same kind (Mt. 5:39; 12:13; Jn. 19:32). *Hoi alloi*, the others, the rest (Jn. 20:25; 21:8; I Cor. 14:29). *Allos* and *allos* repeated in different members of a sentence, one and another (Mk. 6:15; Jn. 4:37). Belonging to another (I Cor. 10:29). Deriv.: *allotrios* (245), another's; *apallotrioō* (526), to alienate; *allogenēs* (241), one of another nation; *allophulos* (246), one of another race or nation; *allōs* (247), adv. meaning otherwise.

244. Allotriepiskopos; from *allotrios* (245), another's, and *episkopeō* (1983), to inspect, observe. See *allos* (243) for the basic meaning as an adj. A curious inspector and meddler in other people's affairs, a busybody in other people's matters (I Pet. 4:15).

245. Allotrios; from *allos* (243), other, the opp. of *idios* (2398) and *oikeios* (3609), the same, a relative. Meanings: (1) Belonging to another, not one's own. When used in the pl. *ta allotria*, it means others' goods (Lk. 16:12; Rom. 14:4; Heb. 9:25). (2) Spoken of a country, strange, foreign, belonging to other people. Opp. *oikeios*, relative (Acts 7:6; Heb. 11:9). (3) Spoken of men or nations, a stranger, foreigner, alien (Heb. 11:34). Distinguished from *allophulos* (246), one of another race; from *allos*, other, different; *phulē* (5443), a tribe or race; *allogenēs* (241), from *allos*, other and *genos*, a nation, race, one of another nation, not a Jew, a stranger, a foreigner (Lk. 17:18).

246. Allophulos; from *allos* (243), other, and *phulē* (5443), a tribe or race. One of another race or nation (Acts 10:28).

247. Allōs; adv. of *allos* (243), other. Otherwise (I Tim. 5:25).

262. Amarantinos; made of *amaranths,* a fabled flower that did not fade away. Used in I Pet. 5:4 and should not be translated "unfading" which corresponds to *amarantos* (I Pet. 1:4), the quality of the heavenly inheritance whereas the crown of the believer (I Pet. 5:4) is made up of unfading flowers, *amaranths.* See also *amarantos* (263); *aphthartos* (862); *amiantos* (283).

263. Amarantos; unfading, only in I Pet. 1:4. Our heavenly inheritance is exempt from that swift withering *marainomai,* from *marainō* (3133) which is the portion of all the loveliness springing out of an earthly root. The flower is said to fade away, and yet for the time of its life is something of great beauty. It is beautiful, yet short-lived, falls away, fades, and dies quickly (Job 14:2; Ps. 37:2; 103:15; Isa. 40:6,7; Mt. 6:30; Js. 1:11; I Pet. 1:24). Our heavenly inheritance is not something beautiful which lasts only for a while and then fades away. It is of unfailing loveliness, reserved for the faithful in heaven. Another Gr. word *amarantinos* (262) is unfortunately translated "unfading" (I Pet. 5:4) which corresponds more to the meaning of *amarantos,* spoken of the equality of the crown of glory. The suffix in *amarantinos, -inos,* indicates the substance of which something is made and not the quality of it as *amarantos.* The crown of glory will be *amarantinos,* made up of *amaranths,* fabled unfading flowers. The heavenly inheritance of the believer does not decay; corruption cannot touch it or ever wear out its freshness, brightness, and beauty. See also *amiantos* (283), undefiled.

264. Hamartanō; to sin, to miss, not to hit; one who keeps missing the mark in his relationship to God. Opp.: *sophos* (4680), wise, one who knows how to regulate his relationship with God. See *hamartia* (266); *hamartēma* (265).

265. Hamartēma; deed of disobedience to a divine law, nouns ending in *-ma* indicate the result of a certain action, in this case *hamartia* (266), sin. *Hamartēma* is sin as an individual act. See *hamartanō* (264), to sin.

266. Hamartia; sin, missing the true end and scope of our lives, which is God. An offense in relation to God with emphasis on guilt. See *hamartēma* (265), sin as an individual act; a determination of the nature of man as a personal power and also used of individual acts. Used absolutely or relatively. Individual sins do not annul the general character of the actions of the regenerate. There is a sin, *hamartia* (266), unto death (I Jn. 5:16) which refers to the willful and intentional sin (Heb. 10:26,29), death being physical death (Acts 5:1-11; I Cor. 5; 11:30); and sin not unto death. The sins of the regenerate are regrettably unavoidable in view of our present unredeemed body (Rom. 8:23) and the environment in which we live (I Jn. 2:2). The sinfulness of sin depends on the innate or acquired knowledge of God's expectations (Js. 4:17). See *hamartanō,* to sin (264).

268. Hamartōlos; from *hamarteō,* to deviate, sin. A sinner in general (Mt. 9:13; I Tim. 1:15; Heb. 7:26). Frequently denotes a heinous and habitual sinner (Mt. 11:19; Mk. 2:15; Lk. 7:37). Used also as an adj. (Mk. 8:38; Lk. 5:8; Rom. 7:13, etc.). Opp. *dikaios* (1342), just, one who recognizes that God has rights upon his life and has received Christ as Saviour and become the rightful possession of God and, therefore, acquired God's nature and performed his duty to God because of the enablement of the indwelling Christ. One who exercises first his duties and then his rights toward God (Mt. 9:13; Mk. 2:17; Lk. 5:32). Syn.: *asebēs* (765), ungodly (I Tim. 1:9; Jude 15); *apistos* (571), an unbeliever (Rev. 21:8). Often connected with *telōnēs* (5057), publicans or tax collectors (Mt. 9:10,11; 11:19; Mk. 2:15,16; Lk. 7:34; 15:1) who were in bad repute among Jews and Greeks.

273. Amemptos; unblamed, from the neg. *a* and *memptos,* blameable, and the verb *memphomai* (3201), to find fault. Distinguished from *amōmos* (299), unblemished, unspotted (Eph. 1:4; 5:27; Col. 1:22; Heb. 9:14; I Pet. 1:19; Jude 24; Rev. 14:5). Christ was not *amemptos* and is never said to be so. This is because He took upon Himself our sin and consequently became blamed. Believers, however, should strive to be unblamed, i.e., that fault, just or unjust, will not be found in them. The *amōmos,* the unblemished, may be *amemptos,* unblamed (Lk. 1:6; Phil. 2:15), although not always proving themselves so (I Pet. 2:12,15). Related words: *aspilos* (784), without spot (I Tim. 6:14; Js. 1:27; I Pet. 1:19; II Pet. 3:14); *anegkiētos* (410), legally irreproachable (I Cor. 1:8; Col. 1:22; I Tim. 3:10; Tit. 1:6,7); *anepilēptos* (423), irreprehensible, one who cannot be caught and accused (I Tim. 3:2; 5:7; 6:14).

279. Ametanoētos; from the priv. *a* (1) and *metanoeō* (3340), to repent or change one's mind. Unrepenting, impenitent (Rom. 2:5). See *noeō* (3539); *nous* (3563). Contr. *ametamelētos* (278), not to be concerned after an act has been committed (Rom. 11:29; II Cor. 7:10).

283. Amiantos; from the neg. *a,* not or without, and *miainō* (3392), to defile. That which has nothing in it that defiles, unpolluted (Heb. 7:26; 13:4; Js. 1:27; I Pet. 1:4). See also *miasma* (3393), pollution; *amarantinos* (262), not capable of fading; *amarantos* (263), unfading; *apthartos* (862), incorruptible.

286. Amnos; lamb. After Jn. 1:29,36, "Behold the Lamb of God" (*amnos* and not *arnion,* 721), it became usual to designate Christ as *amnos.* In later Gr. the term *arnos* or *arnion* was adopted throughout Revelation where it is never *amnos* but always *arnion.* In fact, *amnos* is found only in Jn. 1:29,36; Acts 8:32; I Pet. 1:19. In Ex. 12:5 in the Septuagint, *arnos* is used for the Paschal Lamb. In the Septuagint in Lev. 14:10ff; Num. 6:12; Ex. 29:38ff, the expression *ho amnos,* the lamb, *tou Theou,* of God, means the lamb provided by God (see Gen. 22:8). The Lord Jesus is called the *amnos* of God because He sacrificed Himself at the time of the Passover (see Jn. 2:13; I Cor. 5:7). His deliverance of sinners would be like the deliverance of Israel out of Egypt. Thus John the Baptist recognized in Jesus Christ the One who was to bring in that day of deliverance. The lamb during the Exodus was the means of sparing the people, and on account of it, destruction passed them by. In like manner Jesus will now be the means of sparing those who are willing to apply His blood in order to bypass the judgment of God. *Amnos* is used to designate more the sacrifice of the Lamb (I Pet. 1:19), referring to the Paschal Lamb or a lamb given up to death in the service of God.

293. Amphiblēstron; a casting net which, when skillfully cast from over the shoulder by one standing on the shore or in a boat, spreads out into a circle (*amphiballetai*) as it falls upon the water, then sinking swiftly by the weight of the leads attached to it, encloses whatever is below it (Mt. 4:18; Mk. 1:16). See *diktuon* (1350); *sagēnē* (4522).

299. Amōmos; inaccurately rendered as "without blame" or "unblameable," from the neg. *a,* without, and *mōmos* (3470), spot, blemish. In Class. Gr. used as a technical word to designate the absence of anything amiss in a sacrifice or anything which would render it unworthy to be offered (Ex. 29:1; Num. 6:14; Ez. 43:22). Occurs in Eph. 1:4; 5:27; Col. 1:22; Heb. 9:14; I Pet. 1:19; Jude 24; Rev. 14:5. Used in conjunction with *aspilos* (784), without spot, unspotted. In this case, *amōmos* would indicate the absence of internal blemish, and *aspilos,* that of external spot. Used in Col. 1:22 with *anegklētos* (410), legally unaccused, and Eph. 1:4; 5:27 with *hagios* (40), holy. Therefore, *amōmos* is the unblemished. Cf. *amemptos* (273), unblamed. Christ was *amōmos* in that there was no spot or blemish in Him, and He could say, "Which of you convinceth me of sin?" But strictly He was not *amemptos,* unblamed. This adjective is never attributed to Him in the N.T. seeing that He endured the contradiction of sinners against Himself who slandered Him and laid to His charge things that He knew not, *anegklētos,* without any legal charge or accusation brought against Him. See also *anepilēptos* (423), irreprehensible.

302. An; a part. used with the optative sub. and indicative moods; sometimes properly rendered by "perhaps"; more commonly not to be expressed in English by any corresponding particle, but only giving to a prep. or sentence a stamp of uncertainty and mere possibility and indicating a dependence on circumstances. In this way it serves to modify or strengthen the intrinsic force of the optative and sub. while it can also, similarly, affect the meaning of the indicative (the present and perf. excepted) and other verbal forms. Uses: (1) A conditional conj., if (Jn. 20:23; I Thess. 2:7). (2) Indefinite, answering to "soever." (Mt. 10:33; Mk. 3:28; Rev. 14:4). (3) Potential. Added to verbs of the indicative and sometimes of the optative moods, giving the meaning of may, might, would, could, or should placed before them (Mt. 11:21,21; 23:30; 25:27; Jn. 11:21; 18:30; Acts 2:12). (4) *Heōs an,* until (Mt. 2:13; 5:18,19; 16:28, etc.). (5) *Hopōs an,* that, to the end that (Mt. 6:5; Rom. 3:4, cf. Acts 3:19). (6) *Hōs an,* even as (I Thess. 2:7).

303. Ana; on, upon, in. With the accus. it forms a periphrase for an adv.; e.g., *ana meros,* by turns, alternatively (I Cor. 14:27); *ana meson* followed by the gen., in the midst of, through the midst of, between; spoken of place (Mt. 13:25; Mk. 7:31; Rev. 7:17); spoken of persons (I Cor. 6:5). With numerical words it marks distribution (Mk. 6:40; Lk. 9:3,14; 10:1; Jn. 2:6; Rev. 4:8). In composition with other words forming a comp., *ana* denotes: up, upward, as *anabainō* (305), I go up; back, again, equal to the English return, implying repetition, increase, intensity, etc., as *anakainizō* (340), to renew.

305. Anabainō; from *ana,* up, and *bainō,* to go. The simple *bainō* verb does not occur in the N.T. To go or come up, to ascend in whatever manner (Mt. 3:16; 5:1, etc.); to spring or grow up, as vegetables (Mt. 13:7; Mk. 4,7,8,32); to arise, of thoughts (Acts 7:23; I Cor. 2:9, etc.).

312. Anaggellō; to announce, from *ana,* back, and *aggellō,* to announce (in its basic form in the UBS Gr. text in Jn. 20:18). Possibly the *ana* carries the significance of upward, i.e., heavenly, as characteristic of the nature of the tidings. To tell in return, bring word back (Jn. 5:15; Acts 14:27; 16:38; II Cor. 7:7); to tell or declare freely, openly or eminently (Mk. 5:14,19; Jn. 4:25; 16:13-15; Acts 20:20,27). See *apaggellō* (518) (*apo,* from, and *aggellō,* announce, declare), to tell from someone; *exaggellō* (1804) (*ex,* out, and *aggellō*), to tell out, abroad (I Pet. 2:9).

313. Anagennaō; to beget again, to regenerate (I Pet. 1:3). In the pass. *anagennaomai,* to be begotten again, to be regenerated (I Pet. 1:23). The sub. *anagennēsis,* new birth, never occurs in the N.T. However, *paliggenesia* (3824), restoration, becoming something new, is the closest to *anagennēsis,* new birth. *Paliggenesia* comes from *palin* (3825), once more, again, and *ginomai,* to become, whereas *anagennaō* comes from *ana,* again, and *gennaō,* to beget.

314. Anaginōskō; from the emph. *ana* and *ginōskō* (1097), to know, take knowledge of. To perceive accurately. Later it came to mean to recognize. In Attic Gr. it usually meant to read and so always in the N.T. and the Septuagint. The consequential meaning is to know by reading (Mt. 12:3; Jn. 19:20; Col. 4:16, etc.).

315. Anagkazō; from *anagkē,* necessity. To force, compel by external violence (Acts 26:11). To force, compel in a moral sense as by authoritative command (Mt. 14:22; Mk. 6:45); by importunate persuasion (Lk. 14:23); by prevalent example (Gal. 2:14); by injustice (Acts 28:19). See also *aggareuō,* to press into service (29). Noun: *anagkē* (318), need. Adj.: *anagkaios* (316), needful.

316. Anagkaios; an adj. from the noun *anagkē* (318), necessity. Necessary by a physical need (I Cor. 12:22, cf. Tit. 3:14); necessary by a moral or spiritual need (II Cor. 9:5; Phil. 2:25; Acts 13:46; Heb. 8:3); near, intimate, closely connected (Acts 10:24). Verb: *anagkazō* (315).

318. Anagkē; from *ana,* an emph., and *agchō,* to constrict, bind hard, compress. Necessity, compelling force, as opp. to willingness (II Cor. 9:7; Phile. 14); moral necessity (Mt. 18:7), which means that as a result of the depravity and wickedness of men, there is a moral necessity that offenses should come (also Lk. 14:18; 23:17, etc.); spiritual or religious necessity (Rom. 13:5; I Cor. 9:16; Jude 3); distress, affliction (Lk. 21:23; I Cor. 7:26; II Cor. 6:4; 12:10; I Thess. 3:7). Deriv.: *anagkazō* (315), to force; the adj. *anagkaios* (316), necessary; syn. *chreia* (5532), a need.

319. Anagnōrizō; from *ana,* again, and *gnōrizō* (1107), to know. To know again. Pass.: *anagnōrizomai,* to be, be made known again (Acts 7:13).

320. Anagnōsis; reading (Acts 13:15; II Cor. 3:14) and especially the public reading of Holy Scriptures (Neh. 8:8). In I Tim. 4:13 it refers to the public reading of the O.T. Scriptures or of the portion of Scripture appointed to be read in public which is called *anagnōsma.* The readers in the church upon whom originally devolved the duty of reading and expounding or application of that portion chosen were called *anagnōstai,* the public readers.

324. Anadechomai; from the emph. *ana,* and *dechomai* (1209), to receive. To undertake, to take up, to take upon oneself. Used in Heb. 11:17, "He who had taken up, undertaken," not merely "received." The verb implies the seizing or laying hold upon that which is presented. In Acts 28:7, to receive hospitably.

331. Anathema; from the same root verb *anatithemai* or *anatithēmi* (394), to separate as *anathema* (331), a consecrated gift. A gift given by vow or in fulfillment of a promise, and given up or devoted to destruction for God's sake (Deut. 13:16-18; Num. 21:1-3); therefore, given up to the curse and destruction, accursed (Gal. 1:8,9; I Cor. 12:3; 16:22). In Rom. 9:3, estrangement from Christ and His salvation. The word does not denote punishment intended as discipline but a being given over, or devotion, to divine condemnation (Ex. 32:32; Gal. 3:13). It denotes an indissoluble vow.

332. Anathematizō; from *anathema* (331), a curse. To bind by a curse (Acts 23:12,14,21) or simply to curse (Mk. 14:71).

334. Anathēma; a consecrated gift hung or laid up in a temple (Lk. 21:5), from *anatithemai* (394) or *anatithēmi,* to separate, lay up. Such a gift was dedicated to God for its own honor as well as for God's glory. Contr. *anathema* (331).

335. Anaideia; recklessness, audacity, shamelessness. Recklessness or disregard of considerations, of the man making the request (Lk. 11:8). The adj. *anaidēs,* one who knows no restraint, no deference, who is reckless, imprudent in his relationship with others.

340. Anakainizō; to renew, from *ana,* again, and *kainizō,* to renew, from *kainos* (2537), qualitatively new. Occurs only in Heb. 6:6 meaning to have a new kind or qualitatively different repentance which would see the person who had it through to the very end. Syn. to *anakainoō* (341), a different form used only in the pass. by the Apostle Paul.

341. Anakainoō; used only in the pass., to be renewed completely by God (II Cor. 4:16; Col. 3:10). Refers to the redemptive activity of God corresponding to the creation of man, which, by putting an end to man's existing corrupt state, establishes a new beginning, qualitatively different than the past in agreement with the meaning of the word *kainos* (2537), qualitatively new as contr. to *neos* (3501), numerically another or a new one. Used in the act. voice in Heb. 6:6 as *anakainizō* (340) which means that man himself must have a new and qualitatively different kind of repentance if the first repentance did not see him through to its desired purpose of eternal redemption. Deriv.: *anakainōsis* (342) qualitative renewal; *kainotēs* (2538), newness; *egkainizō* (1457), to dedicate. Contr.: *ananeoō* (365), to reform, to renew with the same kind of experience as in the past; *neotēs* (3503), youth with reference simply to age and not quality of life.

342. Anakainōsis; from *ana,* again, and *kainōsis,* related to *kainos* (2537), qualitatively new. Therefore, a renewing or a renovation which makes a person different than in the past. Occurs in Rom. 12:2; Tit. 3:5. Deriv.: see *anakainoō* (341), to renew qualitatively.

346. Anakephalaioomai; to be reduced to a *kephalaion,* a head or sum total. In the mid. voice, to gather together again in one, to reunite under one head (Eph. 1:10). In the pass., to be summed up, to be comprised (Rom. 13:9).

356. Analogia; from *ana,* denoting distribution, and *logos,* account, proportion. Analogy, the right relation, the coincidence or agreement existing or demanded according to the standard of the several relations, not agreement as equality. In Aristotle it meant arithmetical or geometric proportion. It is unfortunate that the word is translated as "proportion of faith" in Rom. 12:6. The faith spoken of here is not that of the individual, but that which is made available by God Himself. One should not allow his presumed faith to guide him in what he says, but that faith that is assured in God's revelation to man. What Paul means here is that prophecy is to stand in a right relation to the faith, the established doctrine, and is to correspond thereto. Prophesying is to build itself up upon the foundation of a rightly acting faith, which in turn is to build up and promote (cf. I Cor. 14:1ff). The imminent danger is that a pretended prophecy should affect the faith of the individual and the church. What one preaches ought not to stand in opposition or in disproportion to the doctrine, but in analogy to it. The faith should be preserved and cherished by the exercise of this gift, prophecy.

361. Anamartētos; from the neg. *a* and *hamartanō,* to sin (264). Without sin, sinless, but not absolutely, only in a particular case. Occurs only in Jn. 8:7, referring to one who was not guilty of the particular sin of which they were accusing the woman whom they had brought to Jesus; not to be confused with *teleios* (5046), perfect, reaching one's goal.

364. Anamnēsis; remembrance. A commemoration (Heb. 10:3). A memorial (Lk. 22:19; I Cor. 11:24,25), as applied to the Lord's Supper. "In remembrance of me" means that the participant may remember Christ and the expiatory sacrifice of His death. The memory of the greatness of the sacrifice should cause the believer to abstain from sin. Deriv.: *anamimnēskō* (363), to call to mind.

365. Ananēoō; to renew, to make young. Used in Eph. 4:23, *ananeoomai,* and is to be taken in the pass., made up of *ana* (303), again, and *neos* (3501), new. To be renewed insofar as spiritual vitality is concerned. Contr. *anakainizō* (340); *anakainoō* (341), with *kainos* (2537), qualitatively new.

372. Anapausis; pause or cessation from labor, from *ana* (303), again, and *pauō* (3973), to cease. To give rest (Mt. 11:29; 12:43; Lk. 11:24; Rev. 4:8; 14:11). Verb: *anapauō* (373), act., and *anapauomai,* mid. On the other hand, *anesis* (425) implies the relaxing or letting down of chords or strings which have been strained or drawn tight (Acts 24:23; II Cor. 2:13; 7:5; 8:13; II Thess. 1:7). In Mt. 11:28,29 the Lord promises *anapausin* (cessation from their toils) to the weary and heavy laden who come to Him.

378. Anaplēroō; from *ana* (303), up, or as an emph., and *plēroō* (4137), to fill. To fill, as a seat or place (I Cor. 14:16); to fill up, complete (I Thess. 2:16); to fill up or supply a deficiency (I Cor. 16:17; Phil. 2:30); to fulfill a prophecy (Mt. 13:14), a law (Gal. 6:2); in I Thess. 2:16, to make the measure of sin quite full, distinguishing it from *plēroō* meaning just to make it full. The word is stronger than *plēroō* and means very full, to perfection, to the very end. Thus *plēroō* emphasizes the act while *anaplēroō* emphasizes the measure.

386. Anastasis; from *anistēmi,* to rise (450); a standing on the feet again or rising as opposed to falling; used figuratively in Lk. 2:34. A rising or resurrection of the body from the grave (Jn. 5:29; Acts 1:22; 2:31; 24:15, etc.). See *histēmi* (2476), to stand.

387. Anastatoō; from *anastatos,* disturbed; in turn from *anistēmi* (450), to stand up. To disturb, disquiet, unsettle (Acts 17:6; Gal. 5:12); to excite, stir up to sedition (Acts 21:38). See *histēmi* (2476), to stand.

388. Anastauroō; from *ana* (303), again or up, and *stauroō,* to crucify. To crucify again or afresh (Heb. 6:6).

392. Anatassomai; to compose in an orderly manner, from *ana* (303), an inten., and *tassō* (5021) to place in one's proper category.

404. Anapsuchō; from *ana* (303), again, and *psuchos* (5592), cold. To make cool, to refresh. Cooling again, refrigerating or refreshing with cool air as the body when overheated. Not used in the N.T. in this sense, but used figuratively meaning to refresh, to relieve when under distress (II Tim. 1:16). Deriv.: sub., *anapsuxis* (403), recreation, refreshment, only in Acts 3:20.

410. Anegklētos; from the neg. *a,* without, and *egkaleō* (1458), to accuse in court. Not merely unaccusable but unaccused, free from any legal charge at all. Occurs in I Cor. 1:8; Col. 1:22; I Tim. 3:10; Tit. 1:6,7. Related words: *amemptos* (273), unblamable; *amōmos* (299), unblemished; *anepilēptos* (423), irreproachable; *aspilos* (784), unspotted.

415. Aneleēmōn; from the neg. *a,* without, and *eleēmōn* (1655), merciful. Unmerciful, not compassionate (Rom. 1:31).

417. Anemos; violent wind; from *aēmi,* to blow, or *aneimai,* perf. pass. of *aniēmi* (447), to loose, let loose. Wind (Mt. 7:25; 11:7; Jn. 6:18; Acts 27:14,15, etc., cf. Eph. 4:14). The four winds are used for the four cardinal points, or the East, West, North and South (Mt. 24:31; Mk. 13:27). See *pnoē* (4157), breath.

420. Anexikakos; from *anechomai* (430), to bear, and *kakos* (2556), bad. Occurs only in II Tim. 2:24, translated "patient." One who bears evil, sorrow, ill.

423. Anepilēptos; from the neg. *a,* without, and *epilambanomai* (1949), to seize; one who has nothing which an adversary could seize on which to base a charge. Rendered in I Tim. 3:2; 5:7 as blameless and in I Tim. 6:14 as irreprovable. Irreprehensible is a closer translation giving the true meaning of the word.

425. Anesis; rest, relaxation (II Cor. 8:13) from strain (*entasis*), tribulation or affliction (*thlipsis,* 2347). Paul promises to the troubled, tense Thessalonians that they should find *anesin* in the Day of Christ (II Thess. 1:7) as he anticipates for them not so much cessation from labor (*anapausis,* 372), as relaxation of the chords of affliction, now so tightly drawn, strained, and stretched to the uttermost (Acts 24:23; II Cor. 2:13; 7:5).

430. Anechomai; from *ana,* up, and *echomai,* the mid. voice of *echō* (2192), to have, to hold. Used only in the mid. voice. To hold up against a thing; to bear with (I Cor. 4:12; II Cor. 11:19,20; Heb. 13:22); to bear with, endure (Mt. 17:17; II Cor. 11:1,4; Eph. 4:2; Col. 3:13; II Thess. 1:4; II Tim. 4:3). Related words: *anochē* (463), forbearance, a delay of punishment (Rom. 2:4; 3:26); *anektos,* tolerable, used in the comparative form; *anektoteros* (414) (Mt. 10:15; 11:22,24; Lk. 10:12,14, in some texts also in Mk. 6:11). Contr. *epieikeia* (1932), clemency; *makrothumia* (3115), longsuffering, *hupomonē* (5281), patience. *Anochē* and *makrothumia* used together in Rom. 2:4; Eph. 4:2.

435. Anēr; man, male, as contr. with the generic *anthrōpos* (444) which may refer to either sex. A man as distinguished from a woman or child (Mt. 14:21; 15:38; I Cor. 13:11). A man as related to a woman, a husband (Mt. 1:16; Mk. 10:2; Jn. 1:13; 4:16-18).

441. Anthrōpareskos; from *anthrōpos,* man, and *areskō* (700), to try to please men and not God. Denotes one who endeavors to please all (Eph. 6:6; Col. 3:22).

443. Anthrōpoktonos; man slayer or one who commits homicide (Jn. 8:44; I Jn. 3:15). Contr. with the more general word *phoneus* (5406), murderer, and *sikarios* (4607), used in Acts 21:38 and involving an assassin hired to kill someone.

444. Anthrōpos; man, a generic name in distinction from gods and the animals. In the N.T. used to make the distinction between sinful man, whose conduct or way or nature is opposed to God, and *anēr* (435), male or husband. Derived from *anō* (507), upwards, and *athrein tē ōpi,* looking upwards with the eyes, or from *anō trepein ōpa,* turning one's view upwards. N.T. meanings: A name of the species without respect of sex (Mt. 5:13,16; 6:1, etc.); a man as distinguished from a woman (Mt. 19:3,5,10); every man, every one, any one (I Cor. 4:1; 11:28; Gal. 3:12).

448. Anileō; or *anileōs* unmerciful. The Class. Gr. form would be *anēleēs,* without mercy. Occurs only in Js. 2:13 where it means that in the day of the judgment of the believer's works, he will not be shown mercy if he did not perform works of mercifulness on earth. A leniency of the judge is expressed in proportion to one's mercifulness on earth.

450. Anistēmi; from *ana* (303), again, and *histēmi* (2476), to stand. Meanings: (1) In the second aor. act. intrans., to stand again, to rise from a sitting or reclining posture (Mt. 9:9; Mk. 1:35; 2:14; 14:60). In Acts 12:7, *anasta,* rise up, the second aor. imper., second person act. for *anastēthi* (Eph. 5:14). (2) In the second aor. act. and first fut. mid. used intrans., to rise or arise from the dead. It is applied to Christ in Mt. 17:9; 20:19, etc., referring to the fact that He was going to rise in His own strength and will. It also applies to men in general (Mk. 12:23,25; Lk. 16:31; Jn. 11:23,24; I Thess. 4:16). Yet to show the equality of the Father, He also is presented as raising Jesus from the dead (Acts 2:24,32). In this case, however, the verb is used trans. in the future and aor. act. meaning to raise, cause to rise from the dead. Jesus is also said to be the One who will raise the dead (Jn. 6:39,40). Thus we have both the Lord Jesus raising Himself and being raised by the Father. (3) To rise from the spiritual death of sin (Eph. 5:14, cf. Jn. 5:25; Eph. 2:5,6; Col. 3:1). (4) In the second aor. act. intrans., to rise, arise, appear, begin to act (Acts 5:36,37; 7:18); *anistamai* in the pass. meaning the same (Rom. 15:12; Heb. 7:11,15). In the first fut. act. used trans., to raise up, cause to appear (Mt. 22:24; Acts 2:30; 3:22). (5) In the second aor. act. used intrans. it emphasizes hostility or opposition; to rise up, to begin hostilities or opposition (Mk. 3:26; Acts 6:9). The noun *anastasis* (386), rising up or resurrection.

453. Anoētos; lacking intelligence but demonstrating moral fault; one who does not govern his lusts, one without *nous* (3563), mind, the highest knowing power in man, the organ by which divine things are comprehended and known, being the ultimate seat of the error (Lk. 24:25; Rom. 1:14; Gal. 3:1,3; I Tim. 6:9; Tit. 3:3).

454. Anoia; from *anous,* mad, foolish, from the priv. *a,* without, and *nous* (3563), mind, understanding. Madness, folly, want of understanding (Lk. 6:11; II Tim. 3:9). See *noeō* (3539), to understand.

458. Anomia; transgression of the law, iniquity. Adj.: *anomos* (459), lawless, not having, knowing, or acknowledging the law. Adv.: *anomōs* (460), without having the law.

459. Anomos; from the neg. *a,* without, and *nomos* (3551), law. Without law, lawless. Not having, knowing or acknowledging the law (I Cor. 9:21); lawless in the sense of transgressing the law, a transgressor, wicked (Mk. 15:28; Acts 2:23; II Pet. 2:8, etc.). Syn.: *adikos* (94), unjust, *anosios* (462), wicked, unholy, is the strongest term denoting presumptuous and wicked self-assertion. In the N.T., *anomos* and the sub. *anomia* (458) are predicated of the sinner in order to describe his sin as opposition to or contempt of the will of God.

461. Anorthoō; from *ana* (303), again or up, and *orthoō,* to erect. To make straight or upright again (Lk. 13:13, cf. Heb. 12:12); to erect again (Acts 15:16).

463. Anochē; forbearance, from *anechomai* (430), to bear with, suffer, from *ana* (303), up, and *echō* (2192), to hold, bear. Indulgence, temporary longsuffering as in Rom. 3:26. The temporary character of God's attitude toward sin is demonstrated in Rom. 3:25 where the word *paresis* (3929), bypassing, is used which does not mean remission of sins. *Paresis* was temporary. God winked at the sins of the people because of their animal sacrifices. That was the *paresis* of v. 25, the overlooking, which in this verse is also called *anochē,* forbearance. The sacrifice of Christ provides *aphesis* (859), remission, the forgiveness of sins which is once and for all, taking them away, and is more than *paresis,* bypassing, or skirting their sins. Before Christ's sacrifice for the punishment of sin, God provided *paresis* through His *anochē,* temporary suspension of His wrath. Redemption through Christ's blood, however, provided permanent satisfaction of His justice.

464. Antagōnizomai; from *anti* (473), against, and *agōnizomai* (75), to fight against a person. To be in conflict with someone (Heb. 12:14).

465. Antallagma; that which is given in exchange, from *antallassō,* to exchange barter (Mt. 16:26; Mk. 8:37). In the N.T. equivalent to *lutron* (3083), ransom.

470. Antapokrinomai; from *anti* (473), against, and *apokrinomai* (611), to answer; to answer against (Lk. 14:6). To reply to something, make a declaratory and argumentative reply, dispute (see Rom. 9:20).

472. Antechomai; from *anti* (473), against or to, and *echō* (2192), have; in the mid. voice *antechomai,* to hold firmly, to cleave to (Mt. 6:24; Lk. 16:13); of holding to the faithful word (Tit. 1:9); to support (I Thess. 5:14).

473. Anti; prep. meaning both equivalence and exchange; in our stead. Christ died *anti,* in our stead. He was equal to the need and was accepted in exchange for our dying. Syn.: prep. *huper* (5228), for, also embraces both meanings. He died on behalf of us and for our good. *Anti,* in our stead, is used to provide absolute and definitive proof of the death of Christ being vicarious. Christ died *anti,* on behalf of many (Mt. 20:28) and gave Himself as an *anti-lutron* (487), ransom on behalf (I Tim. 2:6).

476. Antidikos; from *anti* (473), against, and *dikē* (1349), a cause or fault at law. An adversary or opponent in a lawsuit (Mt. 5:25; Lk. 12:58; 18:3) and also applied to the devil, the great adversary of man and the accuser of our brethren (I Pet. 5:8; Rev. 12:10, cf. Job. 1:9; 2:5; Zech. 3:1).

482. Antilambanō; used in the pass. form *antilambanomai,* from *anti* (473), mutually or against, and *lambanō* (2983), to take, to hold. To take hold of another mutually as by the hand, hence figuratively to support, as by the hand, from falling, to support, help assist (Lk. 1:54; Acts 20:35); to take hold, as it were, on the opposite side (I Tim. 6:2) which refers to taking hold of the glorious benefit of Christ's redemption on the other side, properly denoting to support a burden with another person on the other side. In this view, the expression beautifully represents the masters as laying hold of the benefit of the Gospel on one side while their slaves also, who are now the lord's free men, have hold of it in similar manner on the other side. *Antilambanomai,* however, often means in Class. Gr. writings to partake of, receive, enjoy, and would explain I Tim. 6:2 as "but rather let them do service, because they who receive the benefit of their service are believers, and beloved" (cf. Eph. 6:8; Phile. 16).

484. Antilēpsis; literally the receiving of remuneration. It came to mean a laying hold of anything, the hold which one has, perception, apprehension. In N.T. Gr. used like the verb *antilambanomai* (482), to receive in return for, to denote a rendering of assistance, help. It is in this way that we must understand the meaning of the word "helps" as one of the gifts of the Spirit (I Cor. 12:28), implying the duties toward the poor and sick even as the deacons were appointed to attend to. If we take it as manual services or helps associated with the office of the deacon, then the *kubernēsis* (2941), translated "government," must be attributed to the elders.

487. Antilutron; from *anti* (473), in return, or correspondency, and *lutron* (3083), a ransom (I Tim. 2:6). "The ransom for many" used in Mt. 20:28; Mk. 10:45 is here called *antilutron* in order to lay stress upon the fact of Christ's coming and suffering in the place of all and for their advantage (*huper,* 5228). There is a reference to expiation in I Pet. 1:18,19 where giving Himself denotes self-surrender to death (see Tit. 2:14; Gal. 1:4).

499. Antitupon; antitype, from *anti* (473), denoting correspondency; and *tupos* (5179), a form or figure. A form or figure corresponding to some other, as the impression on the wax to the sculpture on the seal, or the sculpture on the seal to the impression on the wax. A figure or type answering to and representing a reality (Heb. 9:24). The ancient Christians used to call the bread and wine in the communion the *antitupa* (pl.) of Christ's body and blood. It is usually used in the neut. An antitype, somewhat answering to and represented by a type (I Pet. 3:21). See also *hupotupōsis* (5296).

500. Antichristos; antichrist, from *anti* (473), instead of or against. It may mean substitution or opposition. The term *antichristos* is peculiar to John's Epistles (I Jn. 2:18,22; 4:3; II Jn. 7). It occurs nowhere else in the N.T. Paul's reference to the same person is called the man of sin, son of perdition, wicked one (*anomos,* 459) as in II Thess. 2:3,8. He is the one opposing (*antikeimenos,* 480) as in II Thess. 2:4, not substituting Christ. He will assert the fulfillment of God's Word in himself and shall seek to establish his own throne. See *pseudochristos* (5580), false Christ.

505. Anupokritos; from the neg. *a,* and *hupokrinomai* (5271), to pretend, simulate. Originally it meant inexperienced in the art of acting. In the N.T. it came to mean unfeigned, genuine (Rom. 12:9; II Cor. 6:6; I Tim. 1:5; II Tim. 1:5; I Pet. 1:22; Js. 3:17).

506. Anupotaktos; from the neg. *a,* and *hupotaktos* from *hupotassō* (5293), to subject. Not subject (Heb. 2:8); disobedient to authority, disorderly (I Tim. 1:9; Tit. 1:6,10).

507. Anō; above, in a higher place (Acts 2:19). Opp. *katō* (2736), below. With the neut. pl. art., *ta,* the things above (Jn. 8:23; Col. 3:1,2); with the sing. neut. art. *to,* that which is above (Gal. 4:26; Phil. 3:14). With *heōs* (2193), as far as, up to the brim (Jn. 2:7); upwards (Jn. 11:41; Heb. 12:15). Deriv.: *anōteros* (511), the comparative degree meaning higher; neut. used of motion to a higher place (Lk. 14:10); of location in a higher place meaning in the preceding part of a passage from above (Heb. 10:8); *epanō* (1883), from *epi,* over, and *anō,* above, used verbally of number (Mk. 14:5; I Cor. 15:6); *anōthen* (509), the suffix *-then* denotes source, i.e., from; used of a place meaning from the top (Mt. 27:51; Mk. 15:38; Jn. 19:23); of things which come from heaven or from God in heaven (Jn. 3:31; 19:11; Js. 1:17; 3:15,17). In Jn. 3:3,7,31 it could be understood as again, anew, since Nicodemus was perplexed not that the person could be born from heaven, but whether a person could be born a second time. Cf. Gal. 4:9. It may also mean from the first as in Lk. 1:3; Acts 26:5.

509. Anōthen; an adv. of place or time, from *ano,* above, and the suffix *-then* denoting from. From above (Jn. 3:31; Js. 1:17, etc.); from the beginning (Lk. 1:3; Acts 26:5); again, anew, as before (Gal. 4:9; Jn. 3:3,7). In these two passages it is plain that it means again, and not the literal from above. Nicodemus understood the Lord to mean again because in v. 4 he mentions being born for the second time. With a prep. as in Mt. 27:51; Mk. 15:38, it is used in the sense of a noun, the top, or upper part. See *anō* (507), up.

518. Apaggellō; from *apo* (575), from, and *aggellō,* to tell, declare; tell from someone else (Mt. 12:18; Heb. 2:12; I Jn. 1:2,3). To bring or carry word back (Mt. 2:8; 11:4; Lk. 7:22); to tell (Lk. 8:34,47; 13:1).

521. Apaideutos; from the neg. *a,* without, and *paideuō* (3811), to instruct, chastise, correct; unlearned. Used only in II Tim. 2:23.

523. Apaiteō; from *apo* (575), again, and *aiteō* (154), to ask. To recall, demand back, legal exaction of a demand or legitimate claim (Deut. 15:2,3). To require, ask again (Lk. 6:30). To require, demand again in Lk. 12:20 is in the third person plural, *apaitousin,* they require thy soul of thee. The "they require" must be understood as the three Persons of the Triune God (Deut. 32:39; I Sam. 2:6; II Kgs. 5:7; Lk. 6:38; 12:48).

525. Apallassō; to transfer from one state to another; a stronger form of *allassō* (236). Strictly to change by separating, therefore, to break up an existing connection and set the one part into a different state, a different relation; set free, make loose. In the mid. voice, *apallassomai,* to escape (Acts 19:12). In the act., to set free (Heb. 2:15). In the pass., to be freed, get loose (Lk. 12:58). *Apallassō* is also a technical term to denote the satisfaction of the plaintiff by the defendant, especially of the creditor by the debtor.

526. Apallotrioō; from *apo* (575), from, *aleotrioō,* to alienate, and from *allotrios* (245), alien, strange, foreign. To estrange, alienate entirely (Eph. 2:12; 4:18; Col. 1:21).

531. Aparabatos; from the neg. *a,* and *parabainō,* to go beyond, transgress. That which does not pass from one to another as the Jewish high priesthood did from father to son and successor (Heb. 7:24). This word speaks of an unchangeable, eternal priesthood.

533. Aparneomai; from the prep. *apo,* from, denoting a putting away on part of the speaker, a recoiling on his part, and *arneomai* (720), to deny. To remove from oneself, refuse, deny, disown. It must be emphasized that where it signifies a denial, in linguistic usage it always expresses a false denial, and thus it differs from the simple verb. In the N.T. usage the back reference to the subj. always gives a very strong sense. Occurs only with a personal obj. which means to decline or withdraw from fellowship with anyone. The N.T. use of this comp. verb is related to the simple verb *arneomai,* to deny something or someone. To deny Christ or to remove oneself from Him (Mt. 26:34,35; Mk. 14:30,31,72; Lk. 22:61; Jn. 13:38). To deny oneself (Mt. 16:24; Mk. 8:34; Lk. 9:23), to refuse oneself, to give up oneself. See also Jn. 12:25; Gal. 5:24. The fut. *aparnēthēsomai,* to deny oneself, occurs once in Lk. 12:9.

536. Aparchē; firstfruits, but in Gr. always sing.; from *apo* (575), from, and *archē* (746), beginning; the first of the ripe fruits. Applied to Christ risen from the dead with believers to follow (I Cor. 15:20,23); to the gifts of the Holy Spirit as a foretaste of their eternal inheritance (Rom. 8:23, cf. Eph. 1:14; Heb. 6:5); to believers first converted in any particular place or country (Rom. 16:5; I Cor. 16:15); to believers in general consecrated to God from among the rest of mankind (Js. 1:18; Rev. 14:4); to the Patriarchs and ancestors of the Jewish people (Rom. 11:16).

541. Apaugasma; from *apaugazō,* to emit light or splendor, in turn from *apo* (575), from, and *augazō* (826), to shine. Occurs only in Heb. 1:3 in reference to the person of Jesus Christ meaning effulgence, light, or splendor emitted or issuing from a luminous body. Jesus as the Son is called the effulgence or shining forth of God's glory, and being the likeness of the Father, there is no time when He was not exactly that. The Lord Jesus being the effulgence of the eternal light, must also be Himself eternal. The Father being eternal, the Son is also eternal being light of light (Jn. 1:4,5). The all-glorious divinity of the Son of God is essentially one, but not personally with the Father. To distinguish the meaning of *apaugasma* with the word *charaktēr* found in the same verse and translated as "the express image," see the discussion under 5481 and *eikōn* (1504), image. Contr. *homoiōma* (3667), similitude; *homoiōsis* (3669), likeness.

543. Apeitheia; from the neg. *a,* without, and *peithō* (3982), to persuade. Disobedience. In the N.T. it corresponds in its use with the verb unbelief which opposes the gracious word and purpose of God; a stronger term than the syn. *apistia* (570), disbelief, unbelief (Heb. 3:18,19); hence we have the sons of *apeitheias,* disobedience (Eph. 2:2; 5:6; Col. 3:6; Heb. 4:6,11; Rom. 11:30,32).

544. Apeitheō; from the neg. *a,* without, and *peithō* (3982), to persuade. Not to believe, to disbelieve implying disobedience also (Jn. 3:36; Acts 14:2; Rom. 10:21; Heb. 3:18); to disobey as through unbelief (Rom. 2:8; I Pet. 3:20). The above two meanings seem almost to coincide, only *apeitheō* sometimes refers more to inward attitude which is, and sometimes outwardly expressed. Opp.: *peithomai,* verb, in the mid. and pass., to allow oneself to be persuaded, to obey; *pisteuō* (4100), to believe (Jn. 3:36; Acts 14:1; I Pet. 2:7).

545. Apeithēs; from the neg. *a,* without, and *peithō* (3982), to persuade. Unbelieving (Lk. 1:17); disobedient (Acts 26:19; Rom. 1:30; II Tim. 3:2; Tit. 1:16); not letting oneself be persuaded, hard, stubborn (Tit. 3:3). Deriv. verb: *apeitheō* (544).

548. Apeimi; to be absent, from *apo* (575), from, and *eimi* (1510), to be (I Cor. 5:3; II Cor. 10:1,11; 13:2,10; Phil. 1:27; Col. 2:5). Deriv.: *apousia* (666), absence (Phil. 2:12). Contr. *parousia* (3952), presence.

551. Apeirastos; a verbal adj. from the neg. *a,* without, and *peirazō* (3985), to tempt or to test. Used only in Js. 1:13, meaning incapable of being tempted to do evil.

553. Apekdechomai; from *apo,* an inten., and *ekdechomai* (1551), to expect, look for. To wait for, used as a suitable expression for Christian hope including the two elements of hope and patience (Rom. 8:25). In Rom. 8:23 the obj. of this fut. expectation is the *huiothesia,* the adoption, as will be realized in the redemption of the body (v. 19; Gal. 5:5; Phil. 3:20; I Cor. 1:7; Heb. 9:28, cf. I Pet. 3:20).

558. Apeleutheros; from *apo,* from, and *eleutheros* (1658), free. Freed from, emancipated. Occurs only in I Cor. 7:22 because the dependence which the earthly relation may involve does not really exist in the new sphere into which the divine calling introduces.

560. Apelpizō; from *apo* (575), from, and *elpizō* (1679), to hope. To cease to hope, renounce or give up a thing or a person, to despair. With the accus., to give up what one does not expect to keep, to give up in despair. Used only in Lk. 6:35 in the phrase *"lend mēden apelpizones,"* hoping for nothing, meaning having no hope to take anything away or for oneself. Such a translation, however, would be contrary to Christ's general teaching. Jesus is not speaking about an outright gift here, nor does He teach irresponsibility on the part of the lender or the borrower, encouraging anyone to borrow without returning what he owes. The obj. of the verb *apelpizo* is *mēden,* nothing, in the neut. But some mss. have *mēdena,* in the mas. which would make the obj. of the verb a person. Do not cause anyone desperation by making an irresponsible loan to him. Do not bring the borrower to despair. Understand his situation.

564. Aperitmētos; from the neg. *a,* without, and *peritmētos,* circumcised, which in turn is derived from *peri,* around, and *temnō,* to cut, circumcise. Uncircumcised (Acts 7:51, cf. Lev. 26:41; Ez. 44:7,9; Jer. 6:10; 9:25).

566. Apechei; used impersonally, it is enough, sufficient (Mk. 14:41), implying that no further directions are needed on the subject. See *apechō* (568).

567. Apechomai; the mid. voice of *apechō* (568), to keep oneself from, to abstain or refrain from (Acts 15:20,29).

568. Apechō; from *apo* (575), from, and *echō* (2192), to have, be. To receive or obtain from another (Mt. 6:2,5; Phil. 4:18; Phile. 15); to be distant or at a distance (Lk. 7:6; 15:20; 24:13). Applied figuratively to the heart (Mt. 15:8; Mk. 7:6). Receiving in full without expectation of any more coming (Mt. 6:2,5,16; Lk. 6:24). See *apechei* (566); *apechomai* (567).

569. Apisteō; from the neg. *a,* without, and *pistis* (4102), faith, belief. To put no confidence in, not to believe or to disbelieve (Mk. 16:11,16; Lk. 24:11,41; Acts 28:24; Rom. 3:3). To be unfaithful as in II Tim. 2:13 where it is opp. to *pistos* (4103), faithful; to doubt or not to acknowledge.

570. Apistia; faithlessness or uncertainty, distrust, unbelief. In the N.T., the lack of acknowledgment or the nonacknowledgment of Christ (Mt. 13:58; Mk. 6:6); want of confidence in Christ's power (Mt. 17:20; Mk. 9:24). In general, a want of trust in the God of promise (Rom. 4:20; Heb. 3:12,19). Deriv.: *pistos* (4103), a believer.

571. Apistos; not worthy of confidence, untrustworthy, unbeliever. In the N.T. in a pass. sense, a thing not to be believed, incredible (Acts 26:8); in an act. sense, not believing (Mt. 17:17; Lk. 12:46; Jn. 20:27). Denotes one who disbelieves the Gospel of Christ, an unbeliever, an infidel (I Cor. 6:6; 7:12-15; II Cor. 6:15). Deriv.: *pistos* (4103), a believer.

572. Haplotēs; simplicity, purity, sincerity, faithfulness, plenitude. In the N.T. used only in a moral sense as the opp. of duplicity meaning sincerity, faithfulness toward others, manifest in helpfulness and giving assistance to others. Equivalent to being faithful and benevolent. Although in some portions (II Cor. 8:2; 9:11,13) translated "liberality or boutifulness," it is not exactly so. It is rather faithful benevolence out of proper motivation.

573. Hapious; occurs only in Mt. 6:22; Lk. 11:34 translated "clear." From the verb *haploō,* to spread out. Singleness, simplicity, absence of folds. This, however, does not involve stupidity on the part of the Christian, but rather *phronēsis* (5428), prudence, knowing how to deal with fellow humans and the circumstances of life. Thus the Christian is supposed to be not only *haplous,* single, without duplicity, but also *phronimos* (5429), prudent (Mt. 10:16; Rom. 16:19). See also *akakos* (172), harmless, without willingness to hurt which willingness is innate in the corrupted nature of man; *akeraios* (185), harmless; *adolos* (97), without guile.

581. Apoginomai; *apogenomenos* (second aor. part.), from *apo* (575), from, and *ginomai* (1096), to become. To be afar off, separated, take no part in, and later it came to mean to cease to be, to die. Used in this sense in I Pet. 2:24 corresponding with Rom. 6:11. Denotes not a legal, but a moral, relation to sin which is here represented according to its individual manifestations (Rom. 6:2; 7:6; Col. 2:20), and indeed a relation of such a kind that the molding of the character of the person by sin ceases.

587. Apodektos; from *apodechomai* (588), to welcome, from the inten. *apo* (575) and *dechomai* (1209), to receive. Acceptable (I Tim. 2:3; 5:4), pleasing, grateful.

588. Apodechomai; from *apo* (575), an inten., and *dechomai* (1209), to receive. Used only by Luke of persons; to receive kindly or hospitably (Lk. 8:40; Acts 15:4; 18:27); of God's Word, to receive or embrace heartily (Acts 2:41); of benefits, to receive or accept gratefully (Acts 24:3).

592. Apodiorizō; from *apo* (575), from, and *diorizō,* to divide, separate, derived from *dia* (1223), denoting separation, and *horizō* (3724), to limit. Occurs only in Jude 19, to separate from other Christians.

593. Apodokimazō; from *apo* (575), from, and *dokimazō* (1381), prove. To reject as the result of examination, answering to the Attic use of *dokimazō* (1381), to denote testing or qualification of one nominated to an office. Later it came to mean to put out of office or place, to reject, to disapprove, to refuse. Used in Mt. 21:42; Mk. 8:31; 12:10; Lk. 9:22; 17:25; 20:17; I Pet. 2:4,7 of the rejection of Christ; in Heb. 12:17 of Esau's being refused.

594. Apodochē; the sub. of *apodechomai* (588), to receive from. Recognition, acknowledgment, approval, or more exactly, ready or willing acknowledgment. Used only in I Tim. 1:15; 4:9.

599. Apothnēskō; from *apo* (575), as an inten., and *thnēskō* (2348), to die. Literally, to die away, but used with the meaning of plainly to die. N.T. meanings: to die a natural death, applied to both men and animals (Mt. 8:32; 22:24,27; 26:35, etc.); to be dead to sin, as the truly regenerate are, by having renounced and abandoned it in consequence of their conformity with Christ in His death (Rom. 6:2, cf. Col. 3:3); when applied to Christ, to die for or on account of sin, i.e., to make an atonement and satisfaction for it (Rom. 6:10, cf. Heb. 9:26-28); to be dead to the law, i.e., to have no more dependence upon mere legal righteousness for justification and salvation than a dead man would have; as being one self-crucified and dead together with Christ (Gal. 2:19, cf. Rom. 6:4; Col. 2:20).

600. Apokathistēmi; or *apokathistanō,* from *apo* (575), back again, and *kathistēmi* or *kathistanō* (2525), to constitute. To restore, as to health or soundness (Mt. 12:13; Mk. 3:5; 8:25; Lk. 6:10). To restore, reform, applied to the reformation brought about by the preaching and ministry of John the Baptist (Mt. 17:11; Mk. 9:12, cf. Lk. 1:16,17; Mal. 4:6). To restore lost dominion or authority (Acts 1:6). In the pass., to be restored, brought or sent back again (Heb. 13:19). The noun, *apokatastasis* (605), restitution of a thing to its former condition.

601. Apokaluptō; from *apo* (575), from, and *kaluptō* (2572), to cover, conceal. Meanings: (1) Literally, to remove a veil or covering exposing to open view what was before hidden. Opp. of *kaluptō* (Mt. 10:26); *sugkaluptō* (4780), from *sun,* an inten., and *kaluptō,* to cover or conceal closely (Lk. 12:2); *kruptō* (2928), to hide (Mt. 11:25); *apokruptō* (613), to hide from someone (Lk. 10:21). (2) To make manifest or reveal a thing previously secret or unknown (Lk. 2:35; I Cor. 3:13). Particularly applied to supernatural revelation (Mt. 11:25,27; 16:17; I Cor. 2:10).

602. Apokalupsis; revelation, uncovering, unveiling, disclosure. One of three words referring to the Second Coming of Christ (I Cor. 1:7; II Thess. 1:7; I Pet. 1:7,13). The other two words are *epiphaneia* (2015) and *parousia* (3952). *Apokalupsis* a grander and more comprehensive word, includes not merely the thing shown and seen but the interpretation, the unveiling of the same. The *epiphaneiai* (pl.), appearings, are contained in the *apokalupsis,* revelation, being separate points or moments therein. Epiphanies must be theophanies also. Thus Christ's first coming was an epiphany and the second, or *apokalupsis,* will be far more glorious.

603. Apokaradokia; from *apo* (575), from, and *kara,* the head, and *dokaō,* to expect. Attentive or earnest expectation or looking for, as with the neck stretched out and the head thrust forward (Rom. 8:19; Phil. 1:20), where it is *karadokia* in some mss.

604. Apokatallassō; the stronger term for reconcile with the prep. *apo* (575), from, indicating the state to be left, and *kata* (2596), an inten. or toward the state to be sought after. It differs from *katallassō* (2644), the setting up of a relationship of peace not existing before, while *apokatallassō* is the restoration of a relationship of peace which has been disturbed (Eph. 2:16; Col. 1:20,21).

605. Apokatastasis; from the verb *apokathistēmi* (600), which in turn is derived from *apo* (575), back again, and *kathistēmi* (2525), or *kathistano,* to constitute. A restitution of a thing to its former condition. Occurs only in Acts 3:21 where the restitution of all things is to be understood as the day of judgment and of the consummation of the age when the Lord will return. It is at that time that life will be restored to the bodies of the dead, and the image of God in man, defaced by Adam's fall, will be perfectly renewed in righteousness. This restoration affects not only man as he has been depraved of the character of God his Creator, but also it affects God's glory. At this time, God is not recognized in nature and among men for all that He rightly is, a wise God who governs the affairs of men. God's power and justice will be recognized once again. He will then render to each person according to his works (II Cor. 5:10). At that time the veracity of God's predictions will be proven which are now being questioned (II Pet. 3:3,4). In Acts 3:21 the relative pron. *hōn,* translated "which" in the phrase "whom heaven must receive until the period of restoration of all things, about which God spoke by the mouth of His holy prophets from ancient time," does not refer to *pantōn,* "of all things," because then it would limit *pantōn,* e.g., this restoration would concern not all things, but only those things spoken by God through the mouth of His saints, etc. The relative pron. *hōn* in the mas. gen. pl. must, therefore, refer to the times of restoration and be taken as its attribute. An understandable translation then would be "Whom (the ascended Christ; see Acts 1:11) the heaven must receive until the period of restoration of all things, of which (period of restoration) God spoke by the mouth of all His holy prophets," etc. See also Col. 4:3; I Cor. 14:2,3; Heb. 2:3. *Apokatastasis* may be taken as syn. with *paliggenesia* (3824) in its application in Mt. 19:28. See also Rev. 21:5; Rom. 8:19ff. Although the believer enjoys Christ's salvation on this earth, it is not complete in view of the fact that man is still in his mortal body and the environment in which he lives has been tainted by sin. Both the body and the environment will one day be changed completely for this restoration to take place (Rom. 8:23; Rev. 21:1) where a qualitatively new heaven and earth are going to be created (*kainē,* 2537, new, and *gē,* earth).

610. Apokrima; answer, not the act of answering (*apokrisis,* 612) but the answer itself. Used in II Cor. 1:9 as syn. with *katakrima* (2631), condemnation, in the sense of those who have been rejected, who have been given a verdict against, sentenced to death in the opinions and minds of others.

611. Apokrinomai; from *apo* (575), from, and *krinō* (2919), to separate, discern, judge. Used only in the pass. meaning to be separated, selected. In the mid. voice, to answer, to return answer which ought to be done with discretion (Mt. 3:15; 4:4; 26:23; 27:12, etc.) and also to take occasion to speak or say, not strictly in answering but in relation or reference to preceding circumstances (Mt. 11:4; 12:38; 17:4; 22:1; 26:25,63; Mk. 9:5,17; Lk. 7:40).

612. Apokrisis; from *apokrinomai* (611), answer. Decision or answer (Lk. 2:47; 20:26; Jn. 1:22; 19:9).

616. Apokueō; from *apo* (575), from, and *kuō,* to be pregnant. To beget (Js. 1:15,18, cf. I Cor. 4:15; I Pet. 1:3,23). To bring forth, as sin brings death (Js. 1:15). Related to *tiktō* (5088) which properly denotes bringing forth as by a female, but is often spoken of the male as Paul applies it to himself as being in labor in Gal. 4:19.

622. Apollumi; or *apolluō,* from the inten. *apo* (575), and *olluō,* to destroy. In the N.T. to kill, destroy, whether temporarily (Mt. 2:13; 27:20; Mk. 11:18; Jn. 10:10) or eternally (Mt. 10:28; 18:14); in the mid. and pass., to be destroyed, perish, whether temporarily (Mt. 26:52, cf. 9:17; Heb. 1:11; Mk. 4:38; Lk. 11:51; 15:17), or eternally (Jn. 3:15,16; 10:28; Rom. 2:12; I Cor. 1:18); to lose (Lk. 15:4; Mt. 10:39; 16:25); in the pass. and mid., to be lost (Mt. 15:24; 18:11; Lk. 15:4,6,24). The part. noun *ho apolluōn,* the destroyer or the destroying one (Rev. 9:11). Deriv.: *ollumi,* to ruin or destroy, lose; *apōleia* (684), lost; *Apolluōn* (623), the Destroyer.

623. Apolluōn; from *apollumi* (622), to destroy, corrupt. The Destroyer (Rev. 9:11). A Gr. name for the angel of the abyss, *abussos* (12). In Hebrew the name is *Abaddōn* (3).

628. Apolouō; from *apo* (575), from, and *louō* (3068), to wash, bathe. The comp. verb means to wash away. In Acts 22:16 it gives prominence to the cleansing from sin connected with baptism. In I Cor. 6:11, a confounding of the outward with the inward cleansing is guarded against by the use of *apelousasthe* instead of *ebaptisthēte,* "you were washed away," instead of "you were baptized." In the mid. voice, to have oneself washed or to wash oneself.

629. Apolutrōsis; redemption from, from the prep. *apo* (575), from, and *lutrōsis* (3085), redemption (Lk. 1:68; 2:38; Heb. 9:12). A *lutron* (3084), ransom, or *antallagma* (465), a price paid (Mt. 16:26; I Pet. 1:18,19). The recalling of captives (sinners) from captivity (sin) through the payment of a ransom for them, i.e., Christ's death. Sin is presented as slavery and sinners as slaves (Jn. 8:34; Rom. 6:17,20; II Pet. 2:19). Deliverance from sin is freedom (Jn. 8:33,36; Rom. 8:21; Gal. 5:1).

630. Apoluō; from *apo,* from, and *luō* (3089), to loose. To loose, set loose, release as from bond; a disease (Lk. 13:12, cf. v. 16); bonds or imprisonment (Mt. 27:15,17,21,26; Heb. 13:23, etc.); obligation to punishment (Mt. 18:27; Lk. 6:37). To dismiss, suffer to depart (Mt. 14:15; 15:23,39; Lk. 2:29), in the mid. and pass. *apoluomai,* to depart (Acts 28:25). To dismiss, suffer to depart from the body or out of this life (Lk. 2:29). To dismiss a wife by loosing her from the bond of marriage (Mt. 1:19; 5:31,32; 19:3, etc.); to put away a husband (Mk. 10:12).

646. Apostasia; from *apo* (575), from, and *histēmi* (2476), to place, stand. Derived from the verb *aphistēmi* (868). Occurs in Acts 21:21 translated "forsake" and in II Thess. 2:3; "apostasy." In the majority of occasions, the verb is intrans. meaning that person does not depart from where he is, to go somewhere else, but stays away, having chosen from the beginning to stay away, not to believe instead of believing, in which case the basic verb *histēmi* (2476) is to be interpreted not as departing, but as standing away, placing oneself away; with the prep. *apo*, to stay away from. In Acts 21:21 the new Christian believers among the Jews decided to stand apart from the Jewish practices of Moses for they were in a new dispensation. They were not Judaizing Christians, but Christians standing apart from Moses. Having departed from Moses and coming to Jesus Christ, they decided that they should stay apart from Moses, that is, his Judaistic practices. In II Thess. 2:3 the word *apostasia* does not refer to the Christians who would depart from the faith, but those who would reject Christ.

649. Apostellō; from *apo* (575), from, and *stellō* (4724), to send. Distinguished from *pempō* (3992), to send, in that *apostellō* is to send forth on a certain mission such as to preach (Mk. 3:14; Lk. 9:2); speak (Lk. 1:19); bless (Acts 3:26; 7:35); rule, redeem, propitiate (I Jn. 4:10); save (I Jn. 4:14). The expression that Jesus was sent by God (Jn. 3:34) denotes the mission which He had to fulfill and the authority which backed Him. The importance of this mission is denoted by the fact that it is His Son whom God sent. In the N.T., to send forth from one place to another, to send upon some business or employment (Mt. 2:16; 10:5; 20:2); to send away, dismiss (Mk. 12:3,4); to send or thrust forth as a sickle among corn (Mk. 4:29). Deriv.: *apostolos* (652), one sent, apostle, ambassador; *apostolē* (651), dispatching or sending forth; *stellō* (4724), literally, to place, arrange, dispatch.

651. Apostolē; dispatching or sending forth; also that which is sent, e.g., a present. In the N.T., apostleship (Acts 1:25; Rom. 1:5; I Cor. 9:2; Gal. 2:8).

652. Apostolos; primarily an adj., sent forth. Used as a sub., one sent, apostle, ambassador. From the verb *apostellō* (649), from the prep. *apo* (575), from, and *stellō* (4724), to send. Sometimes used syn. with *presbus*, ambassador, related to *presbeuō* (4243), to act as an ambassador (II Cor. 5:20; Eph. 6:20). The ambassador can never be greater than the one who sends him (Jn. 13:16). The reason why the Lord chose the term *apostoloi* to indicate the distinctive relation of the Twelve whom He chose to be His witnesses is because in the Class. Gr. the word was seldom used (Lk. 6:13; Acts 1:2,26). Therefore, it designates the office as instituted by Christ to witness of Him before the world (Jn. 17:18). It also designates the authority which those called to this office possess. See the verb *apostellō* in Rom. 10:15. Paul combines both these meanings (Rom. 1:1; I Cor. 1:1; 9:1,2; 15:9; II Cor. 1:1; 12:12; Gal. 1:1, etc.). The distinctive name of the Twelve (or eleven) with whom Paul himself was reckoned, as he says in I Cor. 15:7,9, justifying his being thus counted as an apostle by the fact that he had been called to the office by Christ Himself. And yet the name seems from the very beginning to have been applied, in a much wider sense, to all who bore witness of Christ (Acts 14:4,14; 15:2); and even by Paul (II Cor. 11:13; I Thess. 2:6). This general meaning of the word held its place side by side with its special and distinctive application. There is no continuity of the office of an apostle as in no place were the churches instructed to ordain apostles. The term is applied to Christ once in Heb. 3:1 who was sent by the Father into the world, not to condemn but to save it (Jn. 3:17; 17:3,8,21,23; 20:21).

654. Apostrephō; from *apo* (575), from or back again, and *strephō* (4762), to turn. To turn away from (Acts 3:26; Rom. 11:26; II Tim. 4:4); to return, put back (Mt. 26:52); to return, bring back (Mt. 27:3); in the pass., *apostrephomai* with an accus. following, to turn or be turned away from, to reject (Mt. 5:42; II Tim. 1:15; Tit. 1:14; Heb. 12:25).

655. Apostugeō; to abhor, detest with horror (Rom. 12:9); from *apo* (575), from, or inten. and *stugeō*, to shudder with horror, from stux *stugos* (4767), gen., a shuddering or shivering from intense cold.

656. Aposunagōgos; separated from the synagogue, excommunicated. Only in Jn. 9:22; 12:42; 16:2. There were three degrees of excommunication or banishment among the Jews. The first step was only a temporary exclusion from the congregation and a restriction upon communication with others for thirty days. The second step was an exclusion from the congregation and from all communication with others for an indefinite period or forever. Jn. 16:2, in particular, hardly allows us to suppose a mere temporary exclusion such as the first step involved, which might be proposed and even decreed for the injured person, without consultation with the Sanhedrin. This did not necessarily mean exclusion from attendance on and participation in the synagogue worship, but exclusion from the fellowship of the congregation and their blessings and privileges. Thus *aposunagōgos* denotes one who has been excommunicated from the commonwealth of the people of God and is given over to the curse (Ezra 10:8). See Lk. 6:22 where it uses the term *aphorizō* (873), to put out of bounds or to excommunicate.

657. Apotassomai; from *apo* (575), from, and *tassō* (5021), to place in order. Translated "give up" in Lk. 14:33 but has the meaning of our belongings being placed away from us into their proper category and not being permitted to become part of us. In Lk. 9:61 the man who expressed the desire to follow Jesus wanted first to see that his own family was properly cared for. Jesus knew that by the time he did that he would have forgotten his promise to Him. In other references it means separating oneself from others, places, or things (Mk. 6:46; Acts 18:18,21; II Cor. 2:13).

674. Apopsuchō; from *apo* (575), denoting privation, and *psuchē*, breath, life, soul. To expire, die (Lk. 21:26).

677. Aproskopos; from the neg. *a*, and *proskopē*, an occasion of stumbling. Intrans., not stumbling or falling, figuratively speaking, in the path of duty and religion (Phil. 1:10). Applied to the conscience, not stumbling or impinging against anything for which our heart condemns us (Acts 24:16, cf. Acts 23:1; I Cor. 4:4; II Cor. 1:12; II Tim. 1:3). Trans., causing others to stumble, giving occasion to fall into sin (I Cor. 10:32, cf. II Cor. 6:3).

680. Haptomai; from *haptō* (681), touch. Refers to such handling of an object as to exert a modifying influence upon it or upon oneself. The same effect may be conveyed by the verb *thigganō* (2345). These words sometimes may be exchanged one for the other as they are in the Septuagint (Ex. 19:12). They are used together in Col. 2:21. *Haptomai* is usually stronger than *thigganō* (Ps. 104:15 Septuagint; I Jn. 5:18). *Thigganō* is correctly translated in Col. 2:21 in the KJV as "handle not," but the basic meaning is touching for the purpose of manipulating. Distinguished from *psēlaphaō* (5584), which actually only means to touch the surface of something (Lk. 24:39; I Jn. 1:1).

681. Haltō; handle an object so as to exert a modifying influence upon it. Syn.: *thigganō* (2345), to touch, stronger than *thigōō* (183), to finger. *Haptō* (I Jn. 5:18) involves a self-conscious effort which is sometimes present but such is always absent from *thigō*. Col. 2:21 is properly translated, "Do not handle, do not taste, do not touch"; thus *haptomai* is "handle" and *thigō* is "touch."

684. Apōleia; trans., the losing or loss (Mt. 26:8); intrans., perdition, ruin. In the N.T. *apōleia* refers to the state after death wherein exclusion from salvation is a realized fact, wherein man, instead of becoming what he might have been, is lost and ruined. Destruction, either temporal (Acts 25:16, cf. Acts 8:20), or eternal (Mt. 7:13; Phil. 1:28; 3:19; II Pet. 2:1, etc.). Destruction or waste (Mt. 26:8; Mk. 14:4). Deriv.: *apollumi* (622), to destroy, ruin, lose.

685. Ará; originally it meant prayer, but more often the imprecation of something evil, a curse which the deity is to execute. Opp. *euchē* (2171), wish, vow. *Ará* is the basic word from which *katara* (2671), from *kata*, against, and *ará* curse, is derived. Finally the word came to mean the evil imprecated, the mischief itself, the realized curse. Used only in Rom. 3:14 while the comp. *katara* is used more frequently (Gal. 3:10,13;

Heb. 6:8; Js. 3:10; II Pet. 2:14).

691. Argeō; to be an *argos* (692), idle, to do nothing. Only in II Pet. 2:3, to be inactive, to rest. Deriv.: *katargeō* (2673), to render inactive.

692. Argos; contr. from *aergos,* from *a,* neg., and *ergon* (2041), work. Not at work, idle, not employed, inactive (Mt. 20:3,6; I Tim. 5:13; Tit. 1:12; II Pet. 1:8). Idle, unprofitable (Mt. 12:36, cf. II Pet. 1:9).

699. Areskeia; an endeavor to please, sometimes referring to an excessive desire to please in a bad sense. In a good sense, to please God. Only in Col. 1:10. Derived from *areskeuō,* to act as an *arestos,* one who tries to please. Deriv.: *anthrōpareskos* (441), a pleaser of men.

700. Areskō; to please. The future is *aresō* and the aor. *ēresa;* to make one inclined to, to be content with, soften one's heart towards one. In the N.T. the meaning has evolved from the active "to please" into "to be pleasing," i.e., passing from a relationship to behavior (I Thess. 2:15). The present and imper. tenses denote intentional, deliberate and continuous conduct and have nothing to do with verbs denoting states or relationships; yet the word involves a relationship prior to behavior. It is actually satisfying or behaving properly toward one with whom one is related. Syn.: *dektos* (1184), approved, indicates only relationship. *Arestos* presupposes man's relationship with God, but it also relates God's judgment on man's conduct. In I Cor. 10:33 the expression *panta* (all things), *pasin* (to anyone), *areskō* (I am pleasing to), means to do something to please someone. Deriv.: *arestos* (701), dear, pleasant, well-pleasing; *areskeia* (699), the endeavor to please; *anthrōpareskos* (441), one who endeavors to please men; *euarestos* (2101), pleasing, agreeable; *euarestōs* (2102), well-pleasing as an adverb; *euaresteō* (2100), to be well-pleasing.

701. Arestos; from *areskō* (700), to please one or to be content with. To be dear, pleasant, well-pleasing as in Acts 12:3 but elsewhere used only of God's will (Jn. 8:29); doing that which pleases somebody. It is in this sense that it is used in I Jn. 3:22, distinguishing between claim or requirement and satisfaction, the claim being the commandments and the satisfaction being those things that we do out of the love that we have for God. In Acts 6:2 reference is made to that which is pleasing to God and not to the apostles.

703. Aretē; from the verb *areskō* (700), to please. Superiority or being pleasing to God, or the superiority of God revealed in the work of salvation. *Aretē* denotes in a moral sense what gives man his worth, his efficiency. In the N.T.: virtue, excellency, perfection (I Pet. 2:9); the virtue as a force or energy of the Holy Spirit accompanying the preaching of the glorious Gospel, called "glory" in II Pet. 1:3; human virtue in general (Phil. 4:8); courage, fortitude, resolution (I Cor. 16:13; I Pet. 2:9; II Pet. 1:5); moral excellence.

720. Arneomai; from *airō* (142), to take away. It has a variety of N.T. meanings: (1) To deny, refuse (Heb. 11:24). Related to this meaning is (2) with the accus. of person, meaning to refuse anyone, not to know or recognize him, to reject him either in the face of former relationship or better knowledge. To deny, decline, reject, give up (Mt. 10:33; Lk. 9:23, *aparneomai* (533); II Tim. 2:12,13; I Jn. 2:22,23). It can include the idea of falsehood or of contradiction, not only with reference to the object, but on the part of the subject against himself (Mt. 10:33; Lk. 12:9; 22:57; Jn. 13:38, *aparneomai;* Acts 3:13,14; 7:35; II Pet. 2:1; I Jn. 2:22; Jude 4; Rev. 3:8). (3) Used with something as its object; to reject anything, retract, renounce, deny, disown, depending on the collection (I Tim. 5:8; II Tim. 3:5; Tit. 1:16; 2:12; Rev. 2:13). Used absolutely in II Tim. 2:12. (4) The verb with *hoti* making it a very periphrastic statement following as in I Jn. 2:22, denying Jesus, etc. (5) To gainsay, without further specification of the object (Lk. 8:45; Acts 4:16). Falsely, to deny, disown (Mt. 26:70,72; Mk. 14:68,70; Jn. 18:25,27). Opp. *homologeō* (3670), to confess or say together with (Mt. 10:32; Jn. 1:20; Tit. 1:16).

721. Arnion; the diminutive of *arēn,* later *arnos,* lamb (Jn. 21:15). Designation of the exalted Christ in Rev. 5:6, where the little Lamb is contr. to the Lion of the tribe of Judah in v. 5 (see Acts 8:32). The words *hōs esphagmenon,* as slaughtered, point to His death. *Sphazō* (4969) is the usual expression in the Class. Gr. and the Septuagint for sacrifice to kill. Denotes sacrificial death as demonstrated in Rev. 7;14; 12:11; 14:4. See also Heb. 9:26; I Pet. 1:19,20; I Jn. 1:7; Rev. 13:8. Later the term *arnion* became syn. with *amnos* (286), the sacrificial lamb.

724. Harpagē; in the act. sense, robbery, plundering as in Lk. 11:39, although the reference to the contents of the cup as in Mt. 23:25 may make it pass. In combination with *akrasia* (192), incontinency, denotes an attribute, and the partial explanation of the figure of Luke is in favor of the act. meaning. Deriv.: *harpazō* (726), to seize upon with force.

725. Harpagmos; robbery, occurs only in Phil. 2:6. "Who (Christ), being in the form of God thought it not robbery (*harpagmon*) to be equal with God: but. . . ." (KJV) should be taken with the trans. meaning, not equivalent to *harpagma,* a plundering. The expression "to be equal with God" is to be taken as the subj. of the verb "thought it not robbery" (*harpagmon hēgēsato*), meaning He did not esteem being equal with God as identical with the coming forth or action of a robber (*harpax*). Therefore, the trans. meaning of *harpagmos,* robbery, is necessary here. This is clear from the fact that the expression "to be equal with God" cannot be taken as the obj. of *harpazō* or *hēgēsato harpagmon,* to snatch or consider a snatching affair. If it were the obj. of the verb, then it must be essentially different from *morphē Theou* (a form of God), which it can no more be than "and was made in the likeness of man" can be essentially different from "took upon Him the form of a servant." The "form of a servant" includes "being made in the likeness of man." Similarly, the "form of God" includes the "being equal with God." Certainly the two expressions do not in both cases denote absolutely the same thing; they differ: absolute divine existence is indicated by *huparchōn* (5225), being, in the form of God. The participle *huparchōn* means that Jesus continued to be in the flesh what He was before He became man. He has always been in the form of God. In essence He has always been God. His divine existence in relation to the world is indicated by the phrase, "He did not think being equal with God a robbery" as He was Man among men. In *schēma* (4976), outer appearance, He was man. In essence (*morphē*) He was God. When He became man, He truly took the form (essence, *morphē,* 3444) of a servant. He esteemed not His equality with God as something requiring an act of force against the world or a thing to be forced upon the world. Deriv.: *harpazō* (726).

726. Harpazō; to strip, spoil, snatch. In Class. Gr. the fut. pass. *harpazomai* is used more often than in the N.T. (Jn. 10:28). Literally, to seize upon with force, to rob; differing from *kleptō* (2813), to steal secretly. An open act of violence in contr. to cunning and secret thieving. Though generally *harpazō* denotes robbery of another's property, it is not exclusively used thus, but sometimes generally meaning forcibly to seize upon, to snatch away, or take to oneself (Mt. 13:19; Jn. 6:15; 10:12,28,29; Acts 23:10; Jude 23). Especially used of rapture (Acts 8:39; II Cor. 12:2,4; I Thess. 4:17; Rev. 12:5); to use force against one (Mt. 11:12). Deriv.: *harpagē* (724), robbery, plundering; *harpagmos* (725), robbery, usurpation.

728. Arrabōn; a word adopted by the Greeks, Romans and Egyptians from the Phoenicians meaning earnest money, pledge. Something which stands for part of the price and paid beforehand to confirm the bargain. Used in the N.T. only in a figurative sense and spoken of the Holy Spirit which God has given to believers in this present life to assure them of their future and eternal inheritance (II Cor. 1:22; 5:5; Eph. 1:14). Syn.: *aparchē* (536), translated as "first-fruits."

732. Arrhōstos; from *a,* without, and *rhōstos,* strong, from *rhōnnumi* (4517), *rhōnnuo,* to strengthen. Infirm, sick, invalid (Mt. 14:14; Mk. 6:5,13; 16:18; I Cor. 11:30). Used in ancient Greece to indicate moral weakness or slack. Noun: *arrhōstia,* weakness, sickness, a lingering ailment, bad state of heath; not occurring in the N.T.

738. Artigennētos; from *arti,* now, lately, and *gennētos* (1084), born, which in turn is derived from *gennaō* (1080), to bring forth. Lately born, newborn; occurs only in I Pet. 2:2.

739. Artios; from *arō,* to fit. Complete, sufficient, completely qualified (II Tim. 3:17). More closely syn. with *holoklēros* (3648), one, all the parts of which are complete, whole, what they are supposed to be so that they might serve their destined purpose.

743. Archaggelos; from *archē* (746), first in time or rank, and *aggelos* (32), angel or messenger. Denotes the first or highest angel, archangel, leader of the angels. Denotes a definite rank by virture of which one is qualified for special work and service. The prefix *archi-* always expresses a gradation in the sphere spoken of as in the N.T. *archiereus* (749), chief priest; *archipoimēn* (750), chief shepherd; *architelōnēs* (754), chief tax collector, etc. It always expresses a distinction of rank and not only of the special work and service for which one is sent. The archangel, head or ruler of the angels, sometimes denotes Christ being the God-Man (I Thess. 4:16, cf. Jn. 5:25-27; Jude 9, cf. Zech. 3:2).

744. Archaios; old, but expressing that which was from the beginning, *archē* (746). Contr. to *palaios* (3820), old, as having existed a long period of time (*palai*). Since there may be many later beginnings, it is quite possible to conceive the *palaios* as older than *archaios. Archaios* reaches back to a beginning, whatever that beginning may have been. *Archaios* disciple (Acts 21:16), not necessarily an old disciple but one who had been such from the beginning of the faith, from the day of Pentecost (Acts 2). See also Mt. 5:21; Lk. 9:8,19; Acts 15:7,21; II Cor. 5:17; II Pet. 2:5; Rev. 12:9; 20:2.

746. Archē; beginning. The verb *archō* (757), to be first or to rule (Mk. 10:42; Rom. 15:12). The noun *archōn* (758) denotes a ruler. *Archē* means a pass. beginning or an act. cause as in Col. 1:18; Rev. 3:14, cf. Rev. 1:8; 21:6; 22:13. Christ is called the beginning because He is the efficient cause of the creation; the head because He is before all things and all things were created by Him and for Him (Jn. 1:1-3; Col. 1:16-17; Heb. 1:10). *Archē* also means extremity or outermost point (Acts 10:11; 11:5); rule, authority, dominion, power (Lk. 20:20; I Cor. 15:24). See *archaios* (744), of old time; *archēgos* (747), leader.

747. Archēgos; from *archē* (746), beginning or rule. As a sub. it means originator, founder, leader, chief, first, prince. Syn.: *aitios,* he who is the cause of something and the result. Yet there is a distinction between *archēgos* as beginning from simply being the cause. One may be the cause of something but not the beginning. *Archē,* like *archēgos,* denotes the founder as the first participator, possessor; e.g., Jesus Christ is called the *archēgos* of life (Acts 3:15) because He is *hē archē,* the beginning or the originator of God's creation. This excludes Him from being Himself a product of that beginning. Jesus Christ is called *archēgos,* the originator of faith in Heb. 12:2 and, therefore, He is the originator of those who believe (see Heb. 2:10). He is also called the first fruits, *aparchē,* of them that sleep, the originator of the resurrection of those who are going to be raised from the dead. *Archēgos* occurs also in Acts 5:31. See *aparchē* (536).

749. Archiereus; from *archē* (746), a head or chief, and *hiereus* (2409), a priest. The high or chief priest, applied by way of eminence and according to its spiritual and real import to Christ (Heb. 2:17; 3:1; 5:10; 6:20; 9:11); the Jewish high or chief priest, properly so-called, who was the instituted type of Christ in offering gifts and sacrifices for sins, entering into the Holy of Holies, not without blood, there to appear in the presence of God to make intercession for us (Mt. 26:57-58,62,63,65; Heb. 9:7, 11,25, etc.); in the pl., chief priests means not only the high priest for the time being, and his deputy, with those who had formerly borne the high priest's office, but also the chiefs or heads of the twenty-four Sacerdotal families which David distributed into as many courses (I Chr. 24). These are called chiefs of the priests (II Chr. 36:14; Ezra 8:24; 10:5) and heads of the priests (Neh. 12:7; see Mt. 2:4; 27:1,3,41; Mk. 11:27; Lk. 22:52, etc.). Used in the sing. in this sense for a chief of the priests in Acts 19:14.

750. Archipoimēn; from *archē* (746), chief, and *poimēn* (4166), a shepherd. Used in I Pet. 5:4 with the meaning of a chief shepherd, applying the word spiritually to Christ (cf. Heb. 13:20).

757. Archō; from *archē* (746), rule, beginning. N.T. meaning: to rule, govern (Mk. 10:42; Rom. 15:12). To the Gr. writers, the verb *archō* in the act. voice and *archomai* in the mid. voice meant to begin. But in the N.T., *archomai* (756) is used only in this sense in Mt. 4:17; 11:7; 12:1, etc. Also in Lk. 24:47 where *arxamenon* is an impersonal part, and may be rendered as a beginning being made, in making a beginning, or so that a beginning be made.

758. Archōn; a ruler, chief, prince, magistrate (Mt. 9:34; 20:25; Lk. 12:58; Jn. 14:30; Acts 4:8; 7:27; Rev. 1:5). It should seem from a comparison of Jn. 3:1 with Jn. 7:50 that *archōn* of the Jews in the former passage means a member of the Jewish Sanhedrin, though it is plain from comparing Mt. 9:18,23 with Mk. 3:22 and Lk. 8:41 that *archōn* in those texts of Matthew means only a ruler of a synagogue. Deriv.: *archē* (746), beginning, rule; *archō* (757), to be first, to begin, to rule.

763. Asebela; from the neg. *a* and *sebōmai* (4576), to worship. Impiety towards God, ungodliness, lack of reverence (Rom. 1:18); wickedness in general, neglect or violation of duty towards God, our neighbor or ourselves, joined with and springing from impiety towards God (Rom. 11:26; II Tim. 2:16; Tit. 2:12; Jude 15,18). *Asebeō* (764), verb, to act impiously or wickedly (II Pet. 2:6; Jude 15). *Asebēs* (765), adj., impious, ungodly, not observing the true religion and worship of God (I Tim. 1:9; I Pet. 4:18); wicked (Rom. 4:5; II Pet. 2:5, etc.). See *sebazomai* (4573), to venerate. Sub.: *sebasma* (4574), the object of holy respectful reverence.

764. Asebeō; from the neg. *a,* without, and *sebomai* (4576), to worship, venerate. To act impiously, to sin against anything which we should consider sacred. Without an obj. to trespass, commit an offense. In the N.T. it occurs in a very strong reference to sinfulness in II Pet. 2:6; Jude 15.

765. Asebēs; from the neg. *a,* without, and *sebomai* (4576), to worship, venerate. Basically it means godless, without fear and reverence of God. It does not mean irreligious, but one who actively practices the opposite of what the fear of God demands. Derived from the intrans. *sebomai;* to revere. *Asebēs* is the one characterized by immoral and impious behavior. Often opp. of *dikaios* (1342), just (Rom. 4:5; 5:6). Syn.: *hamartōlos* (268), sinful, sinner (Rom. 5:6,8), and joined with it in I Tim. 1:9; I Pet. 4:18; Jude 15. *Asebēs* also occurs in II Pet. 2:5; 3:7; Jude 4,15.

766. Aselgeia; lasciviousness (Mk. 7:22; II Cor. 12:21; Gal. 5:19; Eph. 4:19; I Pet. 4:3; Jude 4); wantonness (Rom. 13:13; II Pet. 2:18), readiness for all pleasure. *Aselgēs,* adj., is one who acknowledges no restraints, who does whatever his caprice and unmanageable frowardness dictates. Syn.: *asōtia* (810), wastefulness and riotous excess.

769. Astheneia; from *a,* without, and *sthenos,* strength. Weakness, sickness. In the N.T. this word and related words, *asthenēs* (772), weak, sick, and *astheneō* (770), to be of sickness or weakness, are the most common expressions for sickness and are used in the comprehensive sense of the whole man; but it can also refer to a special form of bodily weakness, sickness. Figuratively, *astheneia* can mean impotence (Rom. 8:3; I Cor. 12:22; Gal. 4:9; Heb. 7:18) and also economic weakness or literal poverty (Acts 20:35).

770. Astheneō; from *asthenēs* (772), without strength, powerless, sick. To be weak, in the strict sense does not occur in the N.T.; infirm, sick (Mt. 10:8; 25:36; Lk. 4:40); weak spiritually as in faith (Rom. 4:19; 14:1,2;

I Cor. 8:9); weak in riches, poor, indigent (Acts 20:35); weak, destitute of authority, dignity, or power, contemptible (II Cor. 11:21). Deriv.: *asthenēs* (772), without strength, sick; *astheneia* (769), weakness, sickness; *asthenēma*, the result of weakness.

771. Asthenēma; from *astheneō* (770), to be weak or powerless. The suffix *-ma* indicates the result of being weak (Rom. 15:1, cf. II Cor. 11:29).

772. Asthenēs; from the neg. *a*, and *sthenoō* (4599), to strengthen. Basically it means without strength, powerless. In Class. Gr. never used with the meaning of moral weakness, but only in a physical sense, weak, powerless, without ability; so also in I Cor. 12:22; II Cor. 10:10; in I Pet. 3:7 of the wife as the weaker vessel; in I Cor. 1:25,27; 4:10 with reference to Christ crucified. Infirm, sick, sickly (Mt. 25:39; Acts 4:9; 5:15,16); without strength or weak in a spiritual sense, weak with regard to spiritual things (Mt. 26:41; Mk. 14:38; Rom. 5:6; I Cor. 9:22). Related words: *astheneia* (769), lack of strength, powerlessness, weakness; *astheneō* (770), to be weak or powerless, sick; *asthenēma* (771), infirmity.

784. Aspilos; from the neg. *a*, without, and *spilos*, spot. Without spot, free from spot. In I Pet. 1:19 the *amōmos* (299) indicates the absence of internal blemish, and *aspilos* that of external spot. See I Tim. 6:14; Js. 1:27; II Pet. 3:14. Related words; *amemptos* (273), blameless; *anegklētos* (410), unaccused; *anepilēptos* (423), unindictable.

786. Aspondos; the absolutely irreconcilable who, being at war, refuses to lay aside his enmity or to listen to terms of reconciliation, implacable, in a state of war (Rom. 1:31; II Tim. 3:3). See *asunthetos* (802), covenant breaker (Rom. 1:31).

790. Astateō; from the neg. *a*, not, and *statos*, fixed, settled. Derived from *histēmi* (2476), to stand, be fixed. To be unsettled, have no certain or fixed abode (I Cor. 4:11).

791. Asteios; translated "lovely; beautiful" (Acts 7:20; Heb. 11:23). Derived from *astu*, a city, and came to mean one who dwells in a city and by consequence is well-bred, polite, eloquent, as the inhabitants of cities frequently are in comparison with those of the country. Used only of Moses. The Greeks used to call the opp. of *asteios*, the urban person, the *agroikos*, the one who comes from *agros*, field or countryside. Therefore, *asteios* came to be assumed as one who is fair to look on and comely, a suggestion of beauty but not generally of a high character. Syn.: *hōraios* (5611), beautiful (Mt. 23:27; Acts 3:2,10; Rom. 10:15). Derived from *hōra*, which basically means hour, indicating the turning point of one's existence, the time when one is at its loveliest and best. The first meaning, however, of *hōraios* is timely. Thus, *asteios* and *hōraios* may mean the same thing, fair or beautiful, but they reach that beauty by paths which are entirely different, resting as they do on different images. *Asteios* belongs to art and to it are attributed the notions of neatness, symmetry, and elegance. *Hōraios* receives its hour of beauty by nature which may be brief but which constitutes the season of highest perfection. Syn.: *kalos*, occurring many times in the N.T. and usually translated "good." It may be used, however, to mean beautiful, but its beauty is contemplated from a point of view which is especially dear to the Greek mind, namely, as the harmonious completeness, the balance, proportion and measure of all the parts with one another.

794. Astorgos; from the priv. *a*, without, and the noun *storgē*, family love. Without family love (Rom. 1:31; II Tim. 3:3).

801. Asunetos; without insight, unintelligent (Mt. 15:16; Mk. 7:18; Rom. 1:21,31; 10:19), without *sunesis* (4907), knowledge, understanding. Mk. 12:33; Lk. 2:47; I Cor. 1:19; Eph. 3:4; Col. 1:9; 2:2; II Tim. 2:7). Opp.: *sunetos* (4908), prudent (Mt. 11:25; Lk. 10:21; Acts 13:7; I Cor. 1:19).

802. Asunthetos; the pass. sense of not put together or not made up of several parts (Rom. 1:31), but Paul uses it with an act. sense referring to those who, being in covenant and treaty with others, refuse to abide by these covenants and treaties. Contr. *aspondos* (786), implacable (Rom. 1:31; II Tim. 3:3).

810. Asōtia; extravagant squandering on one extreme (Eph. 5:18; Tit. 1:6; I Pet. 4:4), the other being *aneleutheria*, stinginess. In the middle stands *eleutheria* (1657), freedom to do as one ought to. An *asōtos*, a prodigal (Lk. 15:13), is one who spends too much, who slides easily under the fatal influence of flatterers and the temptations with which he has surrounded himself into spending freely on his own lusts and appetites. *Asōtia* is a dissolute, debauched, profligate manner of living. Contr. *aselgeia* (766), lawless insolence and unmanageable caprice (Mk. 7:22; Rom. 13:13; II Cor. 12:21; Gal. 5:19; Eph. 4:19; I Pet. 4:3; II Pet. 2:7,18; Jude 4).

812. Atakteō; from *ataktos* (813), one out of order. To behave irregularly or disorderly (II Thess. 3:7).

813. Ataktos; from the neg. *a*, and *tetaktai*, perf. pass. of *tassō* (5021), to set in order. Disorderly, irregular (I Thess. 5:14). Verb: *atakteō* (812), to behave irregularly (II Thess. 3:7). *Ataktōs* (814), adv. of *ataktos*, irregularly in a disorderly fashion (II Thess. 3:6,11).

816. Atenizō; to look fixedly, gaze; from *atenēs*, strained, intent. See Lk. 4:20; 22:56; Acts 1:10; 3:4,12; 6:15; 7:55; 10:4; 11:6; 13:9; 23:1; II Cor. 3:7.

826. Augazō; used trans.: to illuminate. Intrans.: to shine, appear, used in II Cor. 4:4 meaning to irradiate, beam, shine forth.

827. Augē; brightness, light, splendor, as used by the Class. Gr. In the N.T., the dayspring, daybreak, first appearance of daylight (Acts 20:11). Verb: *augazō* (826), to shine (II Cor. 4:4).

829. Authadēs; from *autos*, himself, and *hadeō*, to please. One who is pleased with himself and despises others, insolent, surly, the contrary of courteous or affable. A person who obstinately maintains his own opinion or asserts his own rights but is reckless of the rights, feelings, and interests of others. He regulates his life with no respect to others (Tit. 1:7; II Pet. 2:10). See *philautos* (5367), selfish (II Tim. 3:2).

840. Austēros; austere as related to the taste (Lk. 19:21,22). Contr. *sklēros* (4642), related to the touch. Often associated with honor meaning earnest and severe, but not so with *sklēros* which always conveys a harsh, inhuman character (Mt. 25:24; Jn. 6:60; Acts 9:5; Js. 3:4; Jude 15).

843. Autokatakritos; from *autos*, himself, and *katakrinō* (2632), to condemn. Self-condemned, condemned by his own sentence (Tit. 3:11), meaning passing sentence upon himself, either as voluntarily cutting himself off from the church by an open revolt, or as rendering himself incapable of the privileges and blessings that belong to the church by renouncing his faith which is actually judging or declaring himself unworthy of the blessings tendered by the church.

859. Aphesis; forgiveness, remission, from the verb *aphiēmi* (863), to cause to stand away, to release one's sins from the sinner. This required Christ's sacrifice as punishment of sin, hence the putting away of sin and the deliverance of the sinner from the power—although not from the presence of sin which will come later after the resurrection when our very bodies will be redeemed (Rom. 8:23). See Mt. 26:28; Mk. 3:29; Lk. 1:77; 3:3; 4:18; 24:47; Acts 10:43; 13:38; 26:18; Eph. 1:7; Col. 1:14; Heb. 9:22; 10:18. Distinguished from *paresis* (3929), the temporary bypassing of sin (only in Rom. 3:25).

862. Aphthartos; from the priv. *a*, not, and *phthartos* (5349), corruptible. Incorruptible, not capable of corruption. See I Cor. 9:25; 15:52; I Pet. 1:23. The word is not found in the Septuagint. In Rom. 1:23 Paul calls God *aphthartos*, incorruptible, an attribute of deity that even the heathen recognize. I Tim. 1:17 incorrectly renders *aphthartos* as immortal. It should be rendered as incorruptible. Distinguished from *athanatos*, immortal and as the one having *athanasian* (110), immortality (I Tim. 6:16). When predicated of God, *aphthartos* means that He is exempt from the wear, waste, and final perishing which characterize the present body of man. Therefore, *phthora* (5356), corruptibility, is the characteristic of the perishableness of the body of man as presently constituted. This body which is now corruptible will receive God's *aphtharsia* (861), incorruptibility on the day of the resurrection (Isa. 51:6; I Cor. 15:52; Heb. 1:10-12). Therefore, the two words *athanasia* (110), immortality, and *aphtharsia, incorruption, aphthartos*, incorruptible, not like the body that is going to be done away with. It is something that the believer receives in this life and will continue to have after this life is over. It is not subject to the same kind of deterioration as the present body in which the believer suffers. See *amiantos* (283), undefiled, and *amarantos* (263), unfading.

863. Aphiēmi; from *apo,* from, and *hiēmi,* to send. To send away, dismiss (Mt. 13:36; Mk. 4:36); to emit, send forth as a voice (Mk. 15:37); to yield, give up as a ghost or spirit (Mt. 27:50) referring to Christ's voluntarily giving up of His spirit; to dismiss, put away a wife (I Cor. 7:11-13); to forsake, leave, (Mt. 4:20,22; 5:24,40; 26:56; Jn. 14:18; 16:28,32, etc.); to leave behind after one (Mt. 24:2; Mk. 12:19,20; Lk. 19:44); to leave or let alone (Mk. 14:6; Lk. 13:8); to omit or neglect (Mt. 23:23; Lk. 11:42); to permit, suffer, let (Mt. 3:15; 7:4; 8:22; 13:30; 19:14); to remit, forgive debts, sins, or offenses (Mt. 6:12,14,15; 9:2,5). The expression "to forgive sins" means to remove the sins from another. Only God is said to be able to do this (Mk. 2:10). To forgive sins is not to disregard them and do nothing about them, but to liberate a person from them, their guilt, and their power. We are to ask God to forgive us our sins, remove them away from us so that we do not stand guilty of them or under their power. We are never expected to forgive the sins of others because we have no power to do so, but we are expected to forgive others ("Forgive us our debts, as we forgive those who trespass against us" or those who are our debtors Mt. 6:12). This means that we should do everything in our power to see that the sins of others are removed from them through the grace and power of Jesus Christ.

865. Aphilagathos; from the neg. *a,* and *philagathos* (5358), a lover of being beneficently good. A person who may have pity but does not necessarily do anything to relieve the suffering of another through self-denial. Occurs only in II Tim. 3:3 meaning incapable of any self-denial in order to be kind.

868. Aphistēmi; from *apo,* from, and *histēmi* (2476), to stand, to place. Trans.: to put away, remove, as in Acts 5:37 in which the word means to seduce, make disloyal. Intrans.: to withdraw, remove oneself, retire, cease from something (Lk. 4:13; 13:27; Acts 5:38; 12:10; 15:38; 19:9; 22:29; II Cor. 12:8; I Tim. 6:5). In all of the above, the verb is followed with the phrase *apo tinos,* from someone or something; in Lk. 2:37 followed by the simple gen. Transferred to moral conduct in II Tim. 2:19, it is followed by *apo adikias,* from unrighteousness; in Heb. 3:12, from the living God. This latter expression does not mean that they once belonged to God and now they no longer belong to Him, but rather that they stood away from God, never having belonged to Him. The same is true with I Tim. 4:1 in which the word is translated as "fall away." Rather, the word expresses standing alone in contr. to *pisteuō* (4100), to believe. This does not refer to those who had at one time been believers, but to those who refuse to believe, who stand aloof, alone (Heb. 3:12). The word is also used in Lk. 8:13 in connection with the interpretation of the seed that falls on stony ground. The seed finds a little soil on top of the stone, but it is not enough to take root and so the growth is only seasonal. When testing comes, there is no root to hold it down. The word *aphistantai* here does not indicate uprooting because there never was a root; the temporary plant stood by itself. The union with the soil was only an apparent union, never a true foundation with roots capable of holding up the plant.

873. Aphorizō; from *apo,* from, and *horizō* (3724), to define. To separate locally (Mt. 13:49; 25:32, cf. Acts 19:9; II Cor. 6:17; Gal. 2:12); to separate from or cast out of society as wicked and abominable (Lk. 6:22); to separate, select to some office or work (Acts 13:2; Rom. 1:1; Gal. 1:15). The Pharisees, the sect to which Paul belonged before his conversion (Acts 23:6; 26:5; Phil. 3:5), had their names from this word which meant to separate, *aphōrismenoi,* separated ones. This is probably what Paul alludes to in Rom. 1:1 where he who was before separated unto the law, or to the study of it, now says of himself that he was separated to the Gospel.

887. Achlus; a thick mist, found only in Acts 13:11. Denotes a collection of heavy vapors which diverts the rays of light by turning them out of their direct course. Hence a certain disorder of the eye is called *achlus* and those who are afflicted with it seem to see through a thick mist or fog. Elymas the Sorcerer was miraculously punished by Paul with a disorder of this kind, previous to his total blindness. Syn.: *skotos* (4655), darkness; *gnophos* (1105), a thick dark cloud; and *zophos* (2217), thick darkness resulting from foggy weather or smoke.

888. Achreios; from the neg. *a,* and *chreia,* utility, usefulness. One who has been set aside and is no more useful (Mt. 25:30; Lk. 17:10).

890. Achrēstos; from the neg. *a,* and *chrēstos* (5543), profitable. Unprofitable, useless (Phile. 11). See also *chrēstotēs* (5544), profitableness.

895. Apsuchos; from the neg. *a,* without, and *psuchē,* soul or the breathing of life. Lifeless (I Cor. 14:7). In Class. Gr. it means without character, spiritless, cowardly. Ant. *empsuchos,* possessing a soul, does not occur in the N.T.

906. Ballō; to cast off or to bring, to carry. The verb in all its applications retains the idea of impulse. To cast, throw (Mt. 3:10; 4:6,18; 5:13,25,30; Jn. 8:7,59, etc.); to put (Mt. 9:17; Mk. 2:22; 7:33; Jn. 5:7; 13:2); to thrust (Rev. 14:16,19); to strike (Mk. 14:65); in an intrans. sense to rush (Acts 27:14); in the pass. perf., to be cast down, lie as upon a bed or the ground (Mt. 8:6,14; 9:2; Lk. 16:20, etc.).

907. Baptizō; to immerse, submerge for a religious purpose, baptize (Jn. 1:25). Washing or ablution was frequently by immersion, hence the pass. or mid., *baptizomai,* to wash oneself, be washed, wash, i.e., the hands (Mk. 7:4; Lk. 11:38, cf. Mk. 7:3); to baptize or immerse in or wash with water in token of purification from sin and from spiritual pollution (Mt. 3:6,11; Mk. 1:8; Lk. 3:16; Acts 2:38; 22:16). In I Cor. 15:29 the expression *hoi baptizomenoi huper tōn nekrōn,* those who are being baptized for or over the dead. Baptism in those days was a public declaration that the Christian thus giving his testimony for Christ was willing to die for Christ following those who indeed became victims of persecution unto death. Without the resurrection of Christ and the Christian hope being a reality, such a baptism even unto death would be mockery. Therefore, the expression means to succeed into the place of those who are fallen martyrs in the cause of Christ. To baptize in its general signification means to be identified with, as the Israelites were identified with the work and purpose of Moses (I Cor. 10:2). The baptism in or with the Holy Ghost means the work of Christ through the miraculous effusion of the Holy Spirit upon the apostles and other believers at Pentecost (Acts 1:5); at Caesarea (Acts 10:47; 11:15,16); at Ephesus (Acts 19:1-7). The baptism in or with the Holy Spirit was a historical event (I Cor. 12:13) whereby all believers were baptized or identified spiritually into the body of Christ, the Church (Mt. 3:11; Mk. 1:8; Lk. 3:16; Jn. 1:33). Figuratively, it also means to be immersed or plunged into a flood or sea, as it were of grievous afflictions and sufferings (Mt. 20:22,23; Mk. 10:38,39; Lk. 12:50).

908. Baptisma; baptism, derived from *baptō,* to dip. The suffix *-ma* indicates the result of the act of dipping. Contr. to *baptisis,* the suffix *-is* indicates the act of baptism while *baptismos* (909) with the suffix *-os,* indicates the completed act. See Mk. 7:4,8; Heb. 6:2; 9:10.

909. Baptismos; washing, from *baptizō* (907), to baptize. In Heb. 9:10 the word translated "various washings" is not *baptismata,* pl. of *baptisma* (baptism), but the pl. of *baptismos,* i.e., *baptismoi,* washings, as constituents of the rites of O.T. law. *Baptismos* denotes the act as a fact, *baptisma* the result of the act; hence the former word is suitable as a designation of the institution (Mk. 7:4,8; Heb. 6:2).

910. Baptistēs; from *baptizō* (907), a baptizer or baptist (Mt. 3:1; 11:11, etc.). A name given to John, suggested by the function committed to and exercised by him (Mt. 21:25; Mk. 11:30; Lk. 20:4; Jn. 1:33).

911. Baptō; to immerse (Lk. 16:24; Jn. 13:26). Dye by dipping (Rev. 19:13). As a comp. with the prep. *en,* in, *embaptō* (1686), to dip in (Mt. 26:23; Mk. 14:20). Deriv.: *baptizō* (907), to baptize.

932. Basileia; from *basileus* (935), king. Royal dominion, kingdom (Mt. 4:8). The kingdom of heaven or of the heavens, a phrase peculiar to Matthew for which the other evangelists use *basileia tou Theou,* "the kingdom of God" (Mt. 4:17, cf. Mk. 1:15; Mt. 19:14, cf. Mk. 10:14; Mt. 11:11, cf. Mt. 13:11; Mk. 4:11, cf. Lk. 8:10). Essentially the two terms mean the same and are interchangeable (Mt. 19:23f.). Spiritually the kingdom of God is within the human heart (Lk. 17:21). Both expressions also refer to the prophecies of Dan. 2:44; 7:13f. and denote the everlasting kingdom which God would set up and give to Christ, or the spiritual and eternal kingdom which was to subsist first in more imperfect circumstances on earth, but afterwards to appear complete in the world of glory. In some verses the kingdom of heaven more particularly signifies God's rule within us while we are on this earth (Mt. 13:41,47; 20:1); at other times it indicates only the state of glory (I Cor. 6:9,10; 15:50; Gal. 5:21).

934. Basileios; royal, belonging to, appointed, suitable for the king. The neut. pl. (Lk. 7:25) means royal palaces. Royal priesthood, *basileion,* neut. (I Pet. 2:9) suggests a priesthood called to royal dominion or clothed with royal dignity (Rev. 1:6).

935. Basileus; from *basis,* the support, *tou laou,* of the people. A king, monarch. Applies to God and Christ (Mt. 5:35; 25:34,40; Jn. 18:37; I Tim. 1:17); to men (Mt. 1:6; 2:1; 10:18; 14:9; I Pet. 2:13,17).

936. Basileuō; to be king, to rule (Mt. 2:22; Lk. 1:33; I Tim. 6:15). Applies to God (Rev. 11:15,17; 19:6); to Christ (I Cor. 15:25); those who belong to Christ (Rev. 5:10; 20:4,6; 22:5). Paul's usage; to reign or have predominance (Rom. 5:14,17,21; 6:12).

937. Basilikos; from *basileus* (935), king. Kingly, belonging to a king (Acts 12:20; Jn. 4:46,49). Befitting a king, of kingly dignity (Acts 12:21; Js. 2:8).

945. Battologeō; to speak foolishly. Not to be confused with *battarizō,* to stutter. Characterizes *polulogia,* wordiness, much talking (Mt. 6:7) as contr. to succinct, knowledgeable speech, thus foolish speaking or indiscrete vowing in prayer. Much useless speaking without distinct expression of the purpose.

946. Bdelugma; from *bdelussō* or *bdelussomai* (948), to turn away through loathing or disgust, to abhor (Rom. 2:22; Rev. 21:8). An abomination, an abominable thing (Mt. 24:15; Lk. 16:15). By a comparison of Mt. 24:15f.; Mk. 13:14 with Lk. 21:20f., it is plain that the expression "the abomination of desolation" or that which makes desolate, refers to the Roman ensigns, and especially the eagle which was carried at the head of every Roman legion. Desecrating the Jewish places of worship; they later themselves became objects of worship; therefore, they are called an abomination. An abomination is anything that loosens the connection of man with God referring to sinful actions and sinful men.

947. Bdeluktos; abominable (Tit. 1:16). That which is an abomination to God. Does not occur in Class. Gr. and not to be confused with *bdeluros,* shameless, disgusting.

948. Bdelussō; or *bdelussomai,* to render foul, from *bdeō,* to stink. To cause to be abhorred, turn oneself away from a stench, detest (Rom. 2:22; Rev. 21:8). Noun: *bdelugma* (946), an abomination (Mt. 24:15; Mk. 13:14; Lk. 16:15; Rev. 17:4,5; 21:27). Adj.: *bdeluktos* (947), abominable (Tit. 1:16).

949. Bebaios; firm, from *bainō,* to go. Fixed, sure, certain. Syn.: *alēthēs* (227), true; *asphalēs* (804), safe, sure; *pistos* (4103), faithful, trustworthy. Equivalent to *stereos* (4731), fast, firm, hard. Figuratively, that upon which one may build, rely or trust. In the N.T. not used of persons but objects (Heb. 6:19), that which does not fail or waver, immovable, and on which one may rely. See Rom. 4:16; Gal. 3:15; Heb. 2:2; 9:17; II Pet. 1:10,19. Used as a subj. in II Cor. 1:7; Heb. 3:6,14.

950. Bebaioō; to make firm or reliable so as to warrant security and inspire confidence, to strengthen, make true, fulfill (Mk. 16:20; Rom. 15:8; I Cor. 1:6; Heb. 2:3). In the N.T. used with the personal obj. and signifies confirming a person's salvation, preservation in a state of grace. Syn.: *stērizō* (4741), to steadfastly set (I Thess. 3:13; I Pet. 5:10).

951. Bebaiōsis; ratification, confirmation, corroboration (Phil. 1:7; Heb. 6:16). See *bebaioō* (950), to make firm or reliable.

952. Bebēlos; profane, void of religion, piety. Applied to persons (I Tim. 1:9; Heb. 12:16). From *bainō,* to go, and *bēlos,* a threshold. Unhallowed, opp. of *hieros* (2413), sacred. *Bebēlos* lacks all relationship or affinity to God.

953. Bebēloō; to profane, to cross the threshold (Mt. 12:5; Acts 24:6). See *bebēlos* (952), profane.

971. Biazō; or *biazomai,* to overpower, compel. In the N.T. only in Mt. 11:12; Lk. 16:16. In Matthew used in the pass., meaning the kingdom of God is overpowered. In the mid. voice, meaning presses himself in with energy (Lk. 16:16).

976. Biblos; the Egyptian papyrus from which paper was made. A book, roll, volume, as of the prophet Isaiah, of John's Gospel, of the law (Mk. 12:26; Lk. 3:4; 4:17,20; Jn. 20:30; Gal. 3:10); a scroll, a bill as of divorcement, which according to the Talmudists was always to consist of twelve lines, no more, no less (Mt. 5:31; 19:7; Mk. 10:4; cf. Deut. 24:1; Jer. 3:8). A catalog, an account (Mt. 1:1). The Book of Life is designated as the book in which the names of the redeemed are written (Phil. 4:3; Rev. 13:8; 20:15; 22:19). In Rev. 3:5 the blotting out of a name from the Book of Life is presented as an utter impossibility with a double negative *ou* (3756) and *mē* (3361). If it were possible then the Lord Jesus would admit He was wrong in recording the name in the first place. See *biblion* (975), a diminutive of *biblos.*

979. Bios; life, but not as in *zōē* (2222), life, in which is meant the element or principle of the spirit and soul. *Bios,* from which biography is derived, refers to duration, means, and manner of life. See Mk. 12:44; Lk. 8:14,43; 15:12,30; 21:4; I Tim. 2:2; II Tim. 2:4; I Pet. 4:3; I Jn. 2:16; 3:17.

987. Blasphēmeō; to blaspheme, revile; derived either from *blaptō* (984), to hurt, and *phēmē* (5345), reputation, fame; or from *ballō* (906), to cast, and *phēmai,* pl. dat. of *phēmē.* To hurt the reputation or smite with reports or words, speak evil of, rail (Rom. 3:8, I Cor. 4:13; 10:30; Tit. 3:2, etc.). To speak with impious irreverence concerning God Himself, or what stands in some peculiar relation to Him, to blaspheme, a transliteration of the Gr. word (Mt. 9:3; 26:65; 27:39; Mk. 3:29; Lk. 22:65; Acts 13:45; Tit. 2:5). In the N.T. generally syn. with *oneidizō* (3679), revile, and *loidoreō* (3058), to reproach (Mt. 27:39; Mk. 15:29; Lk. 22:65; 23:39; Rom. 3:8; 14:16; I Cor. 4:13; Tit. 3:2; II Pet. 2:10; Jude 8); especially to revile God and divine things (Rev. 13:6). Reviling against the Holy Spirit (Mk. 3:29; Lk. 12:10), means to resist the convicting power of the Holy Spirit unto repentance. Deriv.: *blasphēmia* (988), blasphemy; *blasphēmos* (989), a blasphemer.

988. Blasphēmia; blasphemy, abuse against someone. Denotes the very worst type of slander mentioned in Mt. 15:19 with false witness; wounding one's reputation by evil reports, evil speaking. See Mk. 7:22; Eph. 4:31; Col. 3:8; I Tim. 6:4; II Pet. 2:11; Jude 9, *blasphēmos* (989), a blasphemer. Used especially in a religious sense; blasphemy toward or against God (Rev. 13:6); against the Holy Spirit (Mt. 12:31; Mk. 3:28; and in Lk. 12:10 the verb *blasphēmeō,* 987) including the resistance against the convincing power of the Holy Spirit.

989. Blasphēmos; derived probably from *blax,* sluggish, slow, stupid. To be abusive, reviling, destroying one's good name (II Tim. 3:2); blasphemous, a blasphemer (Acts 6:11,13; I Tim. 1:13). See the sub. *blasphēmia* (988), blaspheming abuse against someone.

991. Blepō; to see, of bodily vision (Mt. 11:4); of mental vision (Mt. 13:13,14). Stresses the perception of the seeing one. To perceive (Mt. 13:13, etc.); to take heed (Mk. 13:23,33 where it indicates greater vividness than *horaō,* 3708, expressing a more intent, earnest contemplation); to beware as a warning (Mk. 8:15; 12:38; Acts 13:40; Phil. 3:2; Col. 2:8); heed implying more an intent, earnest contemplation (Mt. 24:4, etc.). Deriv.: *emblepō* (1689), from *en,* in (inten.), and *blepō,* earnest looking (Mt. 6:26; 19:26; Mk. 8:25; 10:21,27; 14:67; Lk. 20:17; 22:61; Jn. 1:36,42; Acts 1:11; 22:11); *anablepō* (308), with *ana,* up or again, to look up (Mt. 14:19; Mk. 8:24), to recover sight (Mt. 11:5; 20:34; Jn. 9:11); *anablepsis* (309), recovering sight (Lk. 4:18); *periblepō* (4017) with *peri,* around, to look around (Mk. 3:5,34; 5:32; 9:8; 10:23; 11:11; Lk. 6:10); *apoblepō* (578), with *apo,* from, to look away from all else to one object, to look steadfastly (Heb. 11:26); *epiblepō* (1914), with *epi,* upon, used of favorable regard (Lk. 1:48; 9:38; Js. 2:3).

1006. Boskō; feed the sheep (Mt. 8:30,33; Mk. 5:11,14; Lk. 8:32,34; 15:15; Jn. 21:15,17). Contr. *poimainō* (4165), to shepherd, tend; involving much more than feeding (Mt. 2:6; Lk. 17:7; Jn. 21:16; Acts 20:28; I Cor. 9:7; I Pet. 5:2; Jude 12; Rev. 2:27; 7:17; 12:5; 19:15).

1012. Boulē; will, project, intention, as the result of reflections; counsel, decree, aim, or estimation, as it denotes deliberation and reflection; the assembly of the council. In Mod. Gr., parliament is called *boulē.* Distinguished from *thelēma* (2307) which stands also for the commanding and executing will of God. The will (*boulē*) of God refers only to God's own act, His saving purpose. *Thelēma* signifies the will urging on to action, while *boulē,* the counsel preceding the resolve, the decision. Therefore, Eph. 1:11 should be translated "according to the decision or plan of His will." The Apostle not only gives prominence to the absolute freedom of the decision of the divine will, but calls attention to the saving plan lying at the basis of the saving will as it manifests itself. In some instances *boulē* and *thelēma* are perfectly syn. *Boulē* is also used to denote the divine decree lying at the basis of the history of redemption (Lk. 7:30; Acts 2:23; 4:28; 13:36; 20:27; Heb. 6:17). Occurs also in Lk. 23:51; Acts 5:38; 27:12,42; I Cor. 4:5.

1013. Boulēma; the thing willed, the intention. Contr. *thelēma* (2307), which is not only a will or a wish, but also the execution of it or the desire to execute it. *Thelēma* gives prominence to the element of wish or inclination (Acts 27:43; Rom. 9:19; I Pet. 4:3 T.R.).

1014. Boulomai; to will, denotes the unconscious willing, while *thelō* (2309) indicates conscious willing. *Thelō* denotes a more active resolution urging on to action, while *boulomai* designates an inner decision or thinking.

1021. Bradus; slow as opp. to *tachus* (5036), swift or quick. Implies no moral fault or blame. In the three occasions used, it has a good meaning (Lk. 24:25; Js. 1:19 twice). The sub. *bradutēs* (1022), in II Pet. 3:9. Syn.: *nōthros* (3576), sluggish, found only in Heb. 5:11; 6:12; *argos* (692), inactive.

1025. Brephos; babe, an unborn child (Lk. 1:41,44); a newborn child, an older infant (Lk. 2:12,16; 18:15, etc.); from *pherbos* by transposition from *pherbō,* to feed, nourish, for babes are nourished in the womb and when born require frequent nourishment.

1041. Bōmos; an idol altar (Acts 17:23). Contr. *thusiastērion* (2379), an altar of the true God.

1051. Gala; milk (I Cor. 9:7). Figuratively, the sincere and sweet word of Christ by which believers grow in grace and are nourished to life eternal (I Pet. 2:2). The rudiments of Christianity are to nourish the babes in Christ (I Cor. 3:2; Heb. 5:12,13).

1062. Gamos; marriage, marriage feast (Lk. 14:8; Jn. 2:1,2); the actual joining of a husband and wife (Heb. 13:4). Used also in the pl., *gamoi* (Lk. 12:36; Mt. 22:2-4,9, alternatively with the sing., vv. 8,10-12; 25:10). The expression, "The wedding feast of the Lamb" (Rev. 19:7,9), rests like the parables (Mt. 22:2ff; 25:1-10) upon the relation of God to Israel and points back thereto as it is presented in Isa. 54:4ff; Ezek. 16:7ff; Hosea 2:19. This relationship of Jehovah to Israel was accomplished in the Messianic time, to which the expression in Jn. 3:29, and perhaps Mt. 9:15, points. This relationship of God to His people in the N.T. is Christ's relation to His redeemed Church (II Cor. 11:2; Eph. 5:26,27; Rev. 21:2; 22:17). The marriage of the Lamb is the consummation of salvation to be ushered in by the *parousia* (3952), the appearing of the Lord.

1067. Geenna; hell, the place or state of the lost and condemned (Mt. 5:29,30; 10:28, cf. Mt. 23:15; Js. 3:6). Represents the Hebrew *ge, hinnom* (the Valley of Tophet) and a corresponding Aramaic word. Found twelve times in the N.T., eleven of which are in the Synoptic Gospels, in every instance as uttered by the Lord Himself. Many times the word *hadēs* (86) is wrongly translated as hell or grave. Terms descriptive of hell are found in Mt. 13:42; 25:46; Phil. 3:19; II Thess. 1:9; Heb. 10:39; II Pet. 2:17; Jude 13; Rev. 2:11; 19:20; 20:6,10,14; 21:8. See also *tartaroō* and *tartaros* (5020), to cast down to hell.

1074. Genea; a coll. noun whose original meaning is generation, i.e., a multitude of contemporaries. In N.T. Gr. *genea* literally means space of time, circle of time, which only in a derived sense signifies the meaning of a time, a race; then generally in the sense of affinity of communion based upon the sameness of stock. Race or posterity (Acts 8:33). Generation (Mt. 1:17), occurs with special reference to the physical or moral circumstances, just as we speak of an age or time referring to the spiritual state of society at that time (Heb. 3:10, cf. Lk. 7:31; 11:31; Acts 13:36, etc.). The connection alone must decide whether the sense is limited to the state of society at a certain time or whether the word refers simply to race or stock. The word *genea* in Mt. 24:34 meant the type of Jew with whom Jesus was conversing during that particular time (Mt. 21:23; 23:29). He was telling them that this generation or type, such as the Sadducees and Pharisees of that day, would not pass away until all these things occurred and until His coming again in His *parousia* (3952), Second Coming, which has proven to be true. He was prophesying the destruction of their nation (Mt. 24:15-28).

1075. Genealogeō; or *genealogeomai,* to make a genealogical register. To trace one's descent (Heb. 7:6).

1076. Genealogia; genealogy. The expression in I Tim. 1:4 denotes busying oneself about traditions of the past, based upon the slightest historical hints, which diverted the heart from God's truth and which, as appears from Tit. 1:10, was especially the practice of Jewish false teachers though this is not implied in the expression itself (see also Tit. 3:9). These Jews were turning the entire historical substance into mere myth, claiming that whether something occurred or not was unimportant, but what one felt about it was important, thus resorting to a subjectivism without objective reality. The Jews studied genealogies while the Greeks studied mythology (fables). Since Timothy was partly Greek and partly Jewish, he refers to both myths and genealogies. One was the Greek manipulation and the other was the Jewish manipulation of truth in Scripture. Since these did not represent belief based on fact, they were useless.

1078. Genesis; in the act., origin, rise. From the verb *ginomai* (1096), to form. In Mt. 1:18; Lk. 1:14 T.R. Contr. *gennēsis* (1083), birth, the becoming of Christ as a human being with *genesis* which means origination, the beginning of existence. In Jn. 1:14 "And the Word became (*egeneto* from *ginomai,* to become) flesh." He began His life in the body at Bethlehem, but this was not His origination as a personality. He had been as *Logos* (3056), Word, spiritual, immaterial (Jn. 4:24) prior to His becoming flesh (man). In the pass., *genesis* means race, lineage, equivalent to *genea* (Mt. 1:1), meaning genealogy, book of genealogy. It also means generation, kind, species, as well as being, existence, in which latter sense used in Js. 1:23; 3:6, meaning the aspect, the form of His being.

1080. Gennaō; to beget, pass. voice, to be born, mainly used of men begetting children (Mt. 1:2-16); more rarely of women begetting children (Lk. 1:13,57; 23:29; Jn. 16:21). Syn.: *tiktō* (5088), deliver. Used allegorically (Gal. 4:24); of conception (Mt. 1:20); of the act of God in the birth of Jesus (Acts 13:33; Heb. 1:5; 5:5; Ps. 2:7, none of which indicate that Christ became the Son of God at His birth); metaphorically of God's divine nature imparted in the believer (Jn. 3:3,5,7; I Jn. 2:29; 3:9; 4:7; 5:1,4,18); of a Gospel preacher used as a means in the impartation of spiritual life (I Cor. 4:15; Phile. 10); of the animal nature of the unregenerate (II Pet. 2:12); of engendering strife (II Tim. 2:23). Deriv.: *anagennaō* (313), to beget again, and the composite *gennaō anōthen* (509), to beget from above.

1089. Geuō; or *geuomai,* to give or receive a taste. Usually used in the mid. voice, to taste, to try or perceive the taste (Mt. 27:34; Lk. 14:24; Jn. 2:9; Acts 23:14; Col. 2:21). In later writings it meant to get or take food (Acts 10:10; 20:11). Metaphorically, to have or receive a sensation or impression of anything, practically and in fact to experience anything (I Pet. 2:3; Heb. 6:4,5). Used in combination with death, to taste or to experience death (Mt. 16:28; Mk. 9:1; Lk. 9:27; Jn. 8:52; Heb. 2:9). When used in this connection, it gives prominence to what is really involved in dying.

1093. Gē; earth. The part of creation which denotes man's domain and the history transacted between God and man (Mt. 6:10; 11:25; 24:35; 28:18; Mk. 13:31; Lk. 21:33; Acts 4:24; 14:15; 17:24; I Cor. 8:5; Eph. 1:10; 3:15; Col. 1:16,20; Heb. 12:26; II Pet. 3:13; Rev. 20:11; 21:1). The earth, land, or ground considered as fit or unfit for producing fruit (Mt. 13:5,8,23; Mk. 4:28, cf. Heb. 6:7); the dry land or ground, as distinguished from the waters (Lk. 5:11; Jn. 21:8,9,11, etc.); a particular land, tract, or country (Mt. 2:5,20f.; 4:15; 9:26, etc.); the globe of earth and water as distinguished either from the material or from the holy heavens (Mt. 5:18,35; 6:10; 16:19); the earth or ground in general (Mt. 10:29; 25:18, etc.). The earth which is given to man stands in a relation of dependence to heaven which is the dwelling place of God (Ps. 2:4; Mt. 5:35), for which reason the question always is "How will that which occurs on earth be estimated in heaven?" (See Mt. 9:6; 16:19; 18:18f.; 23:9; Mk. 2:10; Lk. 5:24). Since earth stands in antithesis to heaven, it is associated with the idea of emptiness, weakness, sinfulness, and does not correspond with the wisdom and power of God (Mt. 6:10; Mk. 9:3; Jn. 3:31; I Cor. 15:47; Rev. 14:3; 17:5). Thus the earth is the sphere of the *kosmos* (2889), the people dwelling on earth; *aiōn* (165), age, *houtos,* this age, generation or group of people holding on to earthly principles (see Mt. 6:19; Phil. 2:10; I Tim. 6:17,19; Heb. 11:13; Rev. 5:3,13).

1096. Ginomai; or *gignomai,* to become, from *geinō* or *genō,* to form. To be made or formed (Mt. 4:3; Jn. 1:12,14; 2:9; Acts 26:28, etc.); to be made or created from nothing (Jn. 1:3,10; Heb. 11:3); to occur, come to pass (Mt. 1:22; 21:4; 24:6); to be or become in general (Mt. 5:45; 6:16; 8:26; Lk. 12:40); to be done, performed (Mt. 6:10; Acts 4:16, etc.); to be fulfilled, accomplished (Mt. 5:18; 6:10; I Cor. 15:45); of a place followed by *en* or *eis,* in, to be in or at (Mt. 26:6; Mk. 9:33; II Tim. 1:17, etc.); to come to oneself, to have recoverd one's senses or understanding (Acts 12:11). *Mē,* not, *genoito,* to be, may it not be (Lk. 20:16; Rom. 3:4,6,31, etc.).

1097. Ginōskō; or *gignōskō,* usually to know experientially as contr. to *oida* or *eidō* (1492), usually to know intuitively. Formed from the obsolete verb *gnoō,* to know, by adding the reduplication *gi* as a prefix. It means to know (Mk. 7:24; 9:30; Lk. 2:43, etc.); to perceive (Mk. 5:29; Lk. 8:46); to know, be acquainted with a person (Mt. 25:24; Acts 19:15; II Cor. 5:16, cf. Jn. 1:10); to know, understand (Mt. 12:7; 13:11; 16:3; Mk. 4:13; Acts 8:30, etc.); to know, be conscious of (II Cor. 5:21); discern, distinguish (Mt. 12:33; Lk. 6:44; Jn. 13:35); approve, acknowledge with approbation (Mt. 7:23; Rom. 7:15; II Tim. 2:19); to have sexual relations (Mt. 1:25; Lk. 1:34); to think, beware (Mt. 24:50; Lk. 12:46); as a part., *ginōskōn,* thinking, reflecting upon, being mindful of (Rom. 6:6; II Pet. 1:20).

1098. Gleukos; from *glukus* (1099), sweet. Musk, sweet wine (Acts 2:13). Some believe that it is what distills of its own accord from the grapes which is the sweetest and smoothest. It was mentioned at Pentecost (Acts 2:13) indicating that the ancients probably had a method of preserving the sweetness, and by consequence the strongly inebriating quality of the *gleukos,* for a long time. In instituting the Lord's Supper, the Lord speaks of the contents of the cup as neither wine, *oinos* (3631), nor *gleukos,* but as the fruit, *gennēma* (1081), *tēs ampelou* (288), of the vine (Mt. 26:29; Mk. 14:25; Lk. 22:18). The word *gennēma* also means offspring (Mt. 3:7; 12:34, etc.). But in connection with *ampelos,* vine, it means fruit or produce.

1100. Glōssa; tongue. Distinct N.T. meanings: the tongue of a man (Mk. 7:33,35; Lk. 16:24; I Pet. 3:10); used for the fiery tongues appearing upon the apostles on the day of Pentecost (Acts 2:3); a tongue, language (Acts 2:4,11; 10:46); people of different languages (Rev. 5:9; 7:9; 14:6); a foreign or strange language which one has not learned but yet is enabled to speak as a result of the supernatural intervention of the Holy Spirit, particularly in what the N.T. calls the baptism in the Holy Spirit by Jesus Christ. See *baptizō* (907); *baptisma* (908). These were languages foreign to the speaker, which he never learned but which he was enabled to speak at that particular time as a result of the baptism in the Holy Spirit. Promise of this event was given in Mk. 16:17. In connection with this verse it should be noted that these signs were not for future believers but for past ones since the part. *pisteusasi* is in the aor. tense indicating those who at some time in the past had believed. The historic events of speaking in foreign tongues or dialects came with the Jews at Pentecost in Acts 2:4,11, the Gentiles at Caesarea in Acts 10:46, and the disciples of John the Baptist at Ephesus in Acts 19:6. These were all languages unknown to the speakers, spoken at that particular time in demonstration of their being baptized into the body of Jesus Christ (I Cor. 12:13). These are the same languages demonstrated as *charismata* (the results of the grace of God in the human heart) spoken of by Paul in I Cor. 12:10,30; 14:5,6,18,22,39. It is to be observed that whenever the word *glōssa* is used in the pl., *glōssai* with a sing. pron. or subj., it refers to dialects (Acts 2:3f.,8,11) which were not learned by the individual concerned. Such an individual was enabled instantly and temporarily by the Holy Spirit to speak in a language other than his native tongue. In I Cor. 14:6,18 Paul refers to speaking in *glōssais,* languages or tongues. He meant the languages which he already knew or the ones that he was enabled to speak by the Holy Spirit when and if so needed. The pl. *glōssai* with a sing. pron. or subj. refers to known, understandable languages and not to an unknown tongue as practiced in Corinth. But even when utilizing these, one must make sure he is understood by those who hear him otherwise he will be taken as a maniac, *mainomai* (3105), be beside oneself, mad (I Cor. 14:23). Whenever the word *glōssa* in the sing. with a sing. subj. or pron. is used, translated in the K.J.V. as "unknown tongue" (I Cor. 14:2,4,13,14,19,26,27), it refers to the Corinthian practice of speaking in an unknown tongue not comprehended by anyone and, therefore, not an ordinarily spoken language. Such was the unknown language of the priestesses spoken in the oracles at Delphi; e.g., I Cor. 14:26 may refer to a language foreign to the hearers and uninterpreted. See note on I Cor. 14:33-40.

1105. Gnophos; from *nephos* (3509), a cloud. A thick dark cloud, only in Heb. 12:18. Syn.: *skotos* (4655), darkness; *zophos* (2217), darkness, foggy weather, smoke which is used to imply infernal darkness and occurs only in II Pet. 2:4,17; Jude 6,13; *achlus* (887), a thick mist or a fog.

1106. Gnōmē; the sub. of the verb *gnōnai* and *ginōskō* (1097), to discern, to know. Generally meaning capacity of judgment, faculty of discernment as far as conduct is determined. In I Cor. 1:10 used in conj. with *nous;* (3563), mind. These two, although connected, must be distinguished. The distinction cannot be that of the organ being *nous,* mind, and *gnōmē,* its function. *Gnōmē* includes the direction by the subject to a certain object or the determining of the subject by some object. It is discernment which determines conduct. *Nous,* mind, refers only to thinking without direction. *Nous* signifies consciousness, mind, opinion, thought. *Gnōmē* can be syn. with will, as in Rev. 17:13 which must be taken in conj. with v. 17, meaning God's direction, inclination. *Gnōmē,* when referring to pleasure or purpose means decision as in Acts 20:3; judgment, conviction, opinion in the sense of *dokeō* (1380), to think, to recognize, indicating purely subjective opinion in I Cor. 7:25,40; II Cor. 8:10 where Paul gives an entirely subjective view of the matter. By using this word, Paul indicates that he expects the counsel he gives will be recognized without a command on his part.

1107. Gnōrizō; to know, from *ginōskō* (1097), to know or perceive. Except for Col. 4:7,9; Eph. 6:21; II Cor. 8:1, used mainly in the N.T. of the revelation of God's saving purpose; also of apostolic activity (I Cor. 12:3; 15:1; Gal. 1:11; II Pet. 1:16); of divinely communicated things (Rom. 16:26; Eph. 3:3,5,10; 6:19; Col. 1:27); of God making His power known (Rom. 9:22,23); of Christ's work in revealing (Jn. 15:15; 17:26); used in the pass. in Rom. 16:26; Phil. 4:6 of communications made to God.

1108. Gnōsis; knowledge, from *ginōskō* (1097), to know experientially. Present and fragmentary knowledge as contr. with *epignōsis* (1922), from *epi,* inten., and *gnōsis,* clear and exact knowledge which expresses a more thorough participation in the object or knowledge on the part of the knowing subject. Present intuitive knowledge is expressed by the verb *oida* or *eidō* (1492) (Lk. 1:77; 11:52; Rom. 11:33; I Cor. 13:2; Col. 2:3; II Pet. 1:5,6).

1109. Gnōstēs; one who knows (Acts 26:3). Deriv.: *kardiognōstēs* (2589), knower of the heart (Acts 1:24; 15:8).

1110. Gnōstos; from *ginōskō* (1097), to know, perceive, learn, recognize. In post-Class. Gr. used with a pass. meaning, to be known. N.T. meanings: known (Acts 1:19; 2:14; 15:18, etc.); pl., known to one, acquaintances (Lk. 2:44; 23:49, cf. Jn. 18:15,16); knowable, which may be known (Rom. 1:19). The Greeks used it as a syn. of *noētos,* from *noeō* (3539), to know with one's mind, hence that which could be known, capable of being known. The question is whether to take the phrase in Rom. 1:19, *to gnōston,* "that which is known of God and manifest in them" with the same sense. The gen. *tou theou,* of God, is not gen. partitive here, but gen. poss. It is not what is knowable or known of God, but rather God, as He is knowable or known. Thus it refers to the fact that God is knowable or known in His power in creation. God can be known by man because of the demonstration of His power in His creation. Here reference is made not to the knowledge possessed by God, but to our knowledge of God. Ant.: *agnōstos* (57), unknown (Acts 17:23).

1121. Gramma; that which is written, a letter of the alphabet, a book, letter, bond, etc. N.T. meanings: a letter or character of literal writing (Lk. 23:38, cf. II Cor. 3:7; Gal. 6:11); a writing (Jn. 5:47); a bill, an account (Lk. 16:6,7); the letter of the law, i.e., the literal sense and outward ordinances of the law (Rom. 2:27,29; 7:6; II Cor. 3:6,7); a letter, an epistle (Acts 28:21); pl.: *grammata* with the definite art. *ta,* letters, learning, erudition gained from books (Jn. 7:15; Acts 26:24); *hiera* (holy), *grammata,* letters, the Holy Scriptures (II Tim. 3:15, cf. Jn. 5:47). *Ta hiera grammata,* an expression distinct from *hē graphē* (the writing), describing them as the object of study or knowledge; whereas *graphē* (1124) describes them as an authority (II Tim. 3:15). It cannot be proved that *ta grammata,* the writings of the Scriptures, without the qualifying word *hiera,* holy, means Holy Scriptures; at least there is no sufficient reason for taking it thus in the single passage of Jn. 7:15 where it occurs without the article: "How has this man become learned, having never been educated?" The expression means knowledge contained in writings, learning, or usually the elements of knowledge. At a later period it meant science. The Jews simply said, "How has this man attained knowledge or science which he has not acquired by pursuing the usual course of study?" The word in Acts 26:24 means, "Thou hast studied too much." In the letters of Paul we have the antithesis between *gramma,* letter, and *pneuma* (4151), spirit (Rom. 2:29; 7:6; II Cor. 3:6). This antithesis may be explained thus: *gramma* denotes the law in its written form whereby the relation of the law to the man whom it concerns is the more inviolably established (Rom. 2:27; II Cor. 3:7). Thus the antithesis is between the external, fixed, and governing law, and the *pneuma,* the spirit, meaning the inner, effective, energizing, and divine principle of life (Rom. 7:6).

1122. Grammateus; from *gramma* (1121), a writing, letter, a scribe or writer. Such was in public service among the Greeks and acted as the reader of legal and state papers; hence, scholar (Ezra 7:11,12). In the O.T. it meant one well versed in the law, a clever scribe, read in the Scriptures (cf. Ezra 7:6). Scribes were well versed in the law, i.e., in the Holy Scriptures, and expounded them (Mt. 7:29; 17:10; 23:2,13; Mk. 1:22, etc.). They were supposed to be acquainted with and the interpreters of God's saving purpose (Mt. 13:52; 23:34), but in the time of Jesus they opposed His saving purpose. Where they appear clothed with special authority or side by side with those in authority (Mt. 2:4; 20:18; 23:2; 26:57; Mk. 14:1; Lk. 22:2,66; 23:10), they can hardly be regarded as in legal possession of such authority. Their authority seems to have been granted to them in a general way only by virtue of their occupation (Mt. 13:52; Jn. 7:15) and did not have decisive power. Authorities allied themselves with them for the sake of the respect attached to them due to their knowledge of the law. Syn.: *nomikos* (3544), lawyer (Mt. 22:35); *nomodidaskalos* (3547), teacher of the law (Lk. 5:17). In the Septuagint *grammateus* is frequently used for a political officer who assisted kings or magistrates by keeping written accounts of public acts and occurrences or royal revenues (II Kgs. 12:10). Used for one skilled in the Mosaic law (Jer. 36:26; Ezra 7:6,11,12,21), and commonly used in the same sense in the N.T. (Mt. 2:4; 13:52; 23:34; I Cor. 1:20); especially for those who sat in Moses' seat (Mt. 23:2,3) explaining the law in the schools and synagogues. Thus it became syn. with public instructors (Mt. 2:4, cf. Neh. 8:4); hence, *nomodidaskalos,* teacher or doctor of the law or *nomikos,* lawyer. In the N.T., scribes are frequently joined with Pharisees, and probably many were of that sect (Acts 23:9). The civil magistrate of Ephesus, a town clerk, a recorder or chancellor (Acts 19:35).

1124. Graphē; used in the pl. in the N.T. for the Holy Scriptures, or in the sing. for a part of it (Mt. 21:42; 22:29; Mk. 12:10; 15:28; Rom. 1:2); in II Tim. 3:16 called "God-breathed" or "inspired." Rom. 16:26 and Mt. 26:56 have reference to the prophetic Scriptures within the totality of Scriptures. The Holy Scriptures are everywhere termed as *hē,* the, *graphē,* Scripture, giving it authoritativeness. The Scripture may refer to a single text (Mk. 12:10; Lk. 4:21; Jn. 19:37; Acts 1:16; 8:35) or to the whole (Jn. 2:22; 7:38,42; 10:35; Acts 8:32; Rom. 4:3, etc.).

1125. Graphō; primarily to engrave, write (Mk. 10:4; Lk. 1:63; Jn. 21:25; Gal. 6:11; II Thess. 3:17, etc.). The ancient Greeks equated *graphō* with *xeō,* to carve. They carved figures with meaning on wooden tablets and later replaced these when letters were developed. The engraved tablet was covered with another, and being tied together and sealed, constituted the form of an ancient letter. The Septuagint several times applies the word in this sense of engraving, carving, or cutting out (I Kgs. 6:29; Isa. 22:16, cf. Job. 19:23,24). From Ex. 31:18; 32:16; II Cor. 3:7 we deduce that the first literal writing was of this kind. Thus originally the word meant to cut in, make an incision. Later, with the invention of the parchment and paper, it came to mean to write, to delineate literal characters on a tablet, parchment or paper (Lk. 1:63; 16:6,7; Jn. 8:6; 19:19; Acts 23:25; III Jn. 13). It also came to mean to describe in writing (Jn. 1:45; Rom. 10:5); write a law, command in writing, as a legislator (Mk. 12:19). The writing of names in heaven emphasizes that God remembers and will not forget, since by writing, the name of a person is fixed. The use of *gegraptai,* it is written, in the perf. tense refers absolutely to what is found written in Holy Scripture and denotes legislative act or enactment. In the sphere of revelation the written records hold this authoritative position, and *gegraptai* always implies an appeal to the indisputable and legal authority of the passage quoted (Mt. 4:4,6,7,10; 11:10, etc.). It is completed by additions such as "in the law" (Lk. 2:23; 10:26); "in the book of the words of Isaiah" (Lk. 3:4); "in the prophets" (Jn. 6:45, etc.).

1127. Grēgoreō; from *egeirō,* to rouse. To watch, to refrain from sleep. It was finally transferred in meaning from the physical to the moral religious sphere (Mt. 26:38,40,41). It denotes attention (Mt. 13:34) to God's revelation or to the knowledge of salvation (I Thess. 5:6); a mindfulness of threatening dangers which, with conscious earnestness and the mind alert, keeps from it all drowsiness and all slackening in the energy of faith and conduct (Mt. 26:40; Mk. 14:38; I Pet. 5:8; I Thess. 5:6). It denotes the caution needed against the anxiety resulting from the fear of the loss of one's salvation (I Cor. 16:13; Col. 4:2; Rev. 16:15, etc.); the care for the salvation and preservation of others (Acts 20:31; Rev. 3:2,3). In His eschatological discourses, the Lord in His Word demands constant watching and preparation for the decisive day of His appearing, *parousia* (Mt. 24:42,43; 25:13; Mk. 13:34,35,37; Lk. 12:37,39). It is equivalent to "be ready" of Lk. 12:40. It is used only once of life as opp. to sleeping, *katheudō* (2518), to die (I Thess. 5:10). Syn.: *agrupneō* (69), keep awake (Mk. 13:33; Lk. 21:36; Eph. 6:18; Heb. 13:17; II Cor. 6:5; 11:27).

1131. Gumnos; naked, stark naked (Mk. 14:51,52, cf. Rev. 17:16); comparatively naked or ill- dressed (Mt. 25:36,38,43,44; Js. 2:15, cf. II Cor. 5:3); naked or stripped of the upper garment (Jn. 21:7; Acts 19:16); naked, open, uncovered, manifest (Heb. 4:13, cf. Job 26:6); naked, bare, mere (I Cor. 15:37); naked of spiritual clothing, i.e., the imputed righteousness of faith (Rev. 3:17; 16:15).

1132. Gumnotēs; from *gumnos* (1131), naked. Nakedness, destitute of convenient or decent clothing (Rom. 8:35; II Cor. 11:27); spiritual nakedness, being destitute of the spiritual clothing of the righteousness which is by faith (Rev. 3:18).

1139. Daimonizomai; (pass.) from *daimonion* (1140), little demon, and *daimōn* (1142), demon. The Class. Gr. form: *daimonaō,* to be violently possessed by, to be in the power of a demon. N.T. meanings: possessed by a demon or a devil (Mt. 8:28,33, etc.); having a demon (Jn. 7:20). The *daimonizomenoi,* those violently possessed by demons, are distinguished from other sick folk in Mt. 4:24; Mk. 1:32.

1142. Daimōn; demon (Mt. 8:31; Mk. 5:12; Lk. 8:29; Rev. 16:14 T.R.; 18:2 T.R.). Elsewhere in the N.T. instead of *ho daimōn,* we have the diminutive to *daimonion* (1140), in the neut. but with the same sense. The Greeks gave the word *daimōn* the same meaning as "god." What they meant, however, by the word is still a conjecture. They may have related a demon with *daēmon* as knowing, experienced in a thing, or they may have derived the word from *daiomai,* to assign or award one's lot in life (*diaitētai kai dioikētai tōn anthrōpōn*), the arbitrators or umpires and governors of men. They conceived of them as those who rule and direct human affairs, not as a personality but primarily as a destructive power. Thus they called the happy or lucky person *eudaimōn,* one who is favored by this "divine" power. The adj. *daimonios* was used for one who demonstrated power irrespective of whether it was saving or destructive. The Tragic Poets use *daimōn* to denote fortune or fate, frequently bad fortune, but also good fortune if the context represents it so. Thus, *daimōn* is associated with the idea of a destiny independent of man, gloomy and sad, coming upon and prevailing over him. Consequently, *daimōn* and *tuchē,* luck, are often combined and the doctrine of demons developed to become a beneficent or evil power in the lives of people. The diminutive to *daimonion,* being abstract and generally less used than *daimōn,* fell into disuse as a belief in or doctrine of demons became more defined and concrete. In N.T. Gr., on the contrary, the use of *daimonion* prevailed probably for the same reason, that strange gods, on account of their remote relations in dark mysterious essence, were called *daimonia* (not *daimones*) instead of *theoi,* gods, the nature of the evil spirits thus designated being obscure to human knowledge and alien to human life. The Septuagint does not use *daimōn.* In Plutarch and Xenophon, the verb *daimonaō* (in the N.T. *daimonizomai,* 1139) meant to be deranged, a syn. of *paraphroneō* (3912), to act insanely. *Daimōn* or *daimonion* was applied especially to evil spirits (Ps. 78:49; Prov. 16:14). They were considered unclean spirits (Mk. 5:12; 3:22,30 and also Lk. 4:33; 8:2,29; Rev. 16:13,14; 18:2), wicked or evil spirits. They make their appearance in connection with Satan (Mt. 12:24ff; Mk. 3:22ff; Lk. 10:17,18; 11:18, cf. Mt. 12:26; 9:34; 12:24; Mk. 3:22; Lk. 11:15). These are put into opposition with God (I Cor. 10:20,21; as also in Deut. 32:17, cf. I Tim. 4:1; Js. 2:19; Rev. 9:20). While in some parts of the N.T., *daimonia* (1140), demons, are viewed in their morally destructive influence (I Cor. 10:20f.; I Tim. 4:1; Rev. 9:20; 16:14), they appear in the Gospel as special powers of evil, as spirits (Lk. 10:17,20) in the service of Satan (Mt. 12:26-28); influencing the life, both spiritual and physical, of individuals, so that the man is no longer master of himself (Lk. 13:11,16). Demoniacal possession never seems to occur without some outward signs of derangement (Mt. 11:18; Lk. 7:33; Jn. 7:20; 8:48-52; 10:20,21). This demoniacal violent overpowering of the man (Mk. 9:20) essentially differs from satanic influence (Jn. 13:2,27) wherein the man becomes, like the demons, in the range of human activity analogously the instrument of Satan. The kingdom of God, including all divine influences obtained by Christ's mediation, testifies effectually against demoniacal violence as the worst form of human suffering produced by Satan's agency (I Jn. 3:8; see also Mt. 12:28; 7:22; 9:33,34; 10:8; Mk. 1:34,39; 3:15; 6:13; 7:26; 9:38; 16:9,17; Lk. 9:49; 11:14,15,18-20; 13:32).

1162. Deēsis; supplication or prayer for particular benefits. *Proseuchē* (4335), a more general word for prayer to God in particular. *Deēsis* can be a request for specific benefits from God or anyone else. Therefore, *proseuchē* is a more sacred word.

1163. Dei; must, necessary in the nature of things; contr. to *opheilō* (3784), obliged to, morally or by virtue of personal obligation. An unavoidable, urgent compulsory necessity.

1167. Deilia; cowardice, timidity, fearfulness (II Tim. 1:7). Deriv.: *deiliaō* (1168), to shrink for fear (Jn. 14:27); *deilos* (1169), adj., fearful, timid (Mt. 8:26; Mk. 4:40; Rev. 21:8). Used always in a bad sense as contr. with *phobos* (5401), fear, from *pephoba* (perf. mid. of *phebomai*), to flee or run away from, which is also capable of a good interpretation such as reverence (Acts 9:31; Rom. 3:18, etc.). *Phobos* lies in between *deilia,* cowardice, and *eulabela* (2124), religious reverence (Heb. 5:7; 12:28).

1174. Deisidaimonesteros; is the comparative form of *deisidaimōn* in Acts 17:22. The sub. *deisidaimonia,* piety that leads to fear instead of worship (Acts 25:19). It is *deilia* (1167), fear of the demon-gods (*daimonia,* 1140); superstitious but not in a bad sense; the recognition of God or the gods mingled with more fear than trust. Related words: *eusebēs* (2152), godly; *theosebēs* (2318), devout, godly; *eulabēs* (2126), pious; *thrēskos* (2357), religious.

1175. Deisidaimonia; commonly translated "superstition" from *deisidaimōn,* superstitious. Actually the word had a milder meaning than superstition, i.e., reverence towards the deity or fear of God in which sense it may be used in Acts 25:19. Indicates a dread of the gods, usually in a condemnatory or contemptuous sense.

1184. Dektos; a verbal adj. with the meaning of the perf. part. pass. of *dechomai* (1209), to accept, decide favorably. Elected, acceptable, one of whom there is or has been a favorable decision of the will. Particularly used of the sacrifice; not to distinguish it from unacceptable sacrifices, but to specify it as the object of the divine approval (Lev. 1:3,4; Phil. 4:18). Used with elements of time such as *kairos* (2540), season, and *eniautos* (1763), year, meaning a time which God has pleasure in, which He Himself has chosen (Lk. 4:19; II Cor. 6:2). When spoken of men (Lk. 4:24), it means liked or valued men (Acts 10:35).

1188. Dexios; right side, from *dexasthai,* first aor. inf. of the deponent verb *dechomai* (1209), to receive, take on account of the aptitude of the right hand for this purpose. When giving or receiving is spoken of, preference is given to the right hand (Mt. 6:3; Lk. 6:6; Rev. 5:7). In the case of division and apportionment, the right hand is chosen as that which comes first (Mt. 5:29,30,39; Rev. 10:2), both when the division is indifferent (Mt. 20:21,23; Mk. 10:37,40; II Cor. 6:7, cf. I Kgs. 22:19; II Sam. 16:6; II Chr. 18:18), and when preference is clearly given to one side (Mt. 25:33,34). In all-important transactions when definiteness must be given to the action, in full participation of the actor made prominent and when energy and emphasis are intended, the right hand is employed (Rev. 1:16,17,20; 2:1; 5:1,7). Not only in the case of the actor, but also in that of the person acted upon, the right hand or side is preferred (Acts 3:7), hence God is said to be at the right hand of the person whom He helps as the enemy is to the right of him whom he seeks to overcome and the accuser to the right of the accused. By the right hand the whole man is claimed, whether in action or in suffering (Ps. 109:6,31; Acts 2:25; quoted from Ps. 16:8; Ps. 73:23; 110:5; 121:5; Isa. 41:13; Zech. 3:1). A person of high rank who puts anyone on his right hand gives him equal honor with himself and recognizes him as of equal dignity (I Kgs. 2:19; Ps. 45:9; Mt. 20:21,23; 22:44; 26:64; 27:38; Mk. 14:62; Lk. 22:69; Acts 2:33,34; 5:31; 7:55,56; Rom. 8:34; Eph. 1:20; Col. 3:1 where Christ is said to sit on the right hand of God the Father; Heb. 1:13; I Pet. 3:22).

1189. Deomai; act. *deō,* to be deprived of, want, need; used chiefly in the impersonal form *dei* (1163), it is necessary, it ought or must be, for which Homer always uses *chrē* (5534), it needs, ought. *Deomai,* by some construed as pass. and meaning to be reduced to want, is perhaps more correctly to be regarded as mid. voice, meaning to be in want of for oneself, to need. Hence, *deēsis* (1162), prayer for a particular need, supplication. Used with the gen. of the person (Lk. 8:38; 9:40, cf. Acts 26:3; II Cor. 10:2). With the accus. (II Cor. 8:4). Followed with *hopōs* (3704), so that (Mt. 9:38; Lk. 10:2, cf. Acts 8:24). Followed with *hina* (2443), in order (Lk. 9:40, cf. 21:36; 22:32). Followed with *mē* (3378), an interrogative neg. meaning never, not (Lk. 8:28). While *proseuchē* (4335) refers to prayer in general, *deēsis* refers to a particular need for which one prays. Thus *deomai* is related to *aiteō* (154), to make a request, ask as an inferior of a superior.

1203. Despotēs; despot, more commonly as a comp. noun with *oikos* (3624), house, household, *oikodespotēs* (3617), master in respect of his slaves. Contr. *kurios* (2962), lord, master in regard to his wife and children. *Despotēs* wields unlimited authority not always for good, while *kurios* exercises morally restricted authority for good. Jesus is predominantly called *Kurios,* Lord, because of His omnipotent concern.

1209. Dechomai; to accept an offer deliberately and readily. Distinguished from *lambanō* (2983) which sometimes means to receive as merely a self-prompted action without necessarily signifying a favorable reception (Gal. 2:6). Deriv.: *apodechomai* (588), from *apo* (575), from, inten., and *dechomai* meaning to receive heartily, welcome (Lk. 8:40; Acts 2:41; 18:27; 24:3; 28:30). See *prosdokaō* (4328), to anticipate. *Ekdechomai* (1551), from *ek* (1537), from, and *dechomai,* literally to take or receive from, hence to await, expect, suggesting a reaching out eagerly to receive something (I Cor. 16:11; Heb. 10:13; Js. 5:7). *Ekdochē* (1561), the noun of *ekdechomai* (1551), meaning a looking for, expectation (Heb. 10:27) contr. to *prosdokia* (4329), only expectation of evil. *Dochē* (1403), a noun meaning an entertainment, a feast (Lk. 5:29; 14:13). Related words: *apodochē* (594), from *apodechomai* (588), acceptance, reception (I Tim. 1:15; 4:9); *apekdechomai* (553), from *apo,* an inten., and *ekdechomai* (1551), to expect, wait for with earnest expectation and desire (Rom. 8:19,23,25; I Cor. 1:7; Gal. 5:5; Phil. 3:20; Heb. 9:28); *eisdechomai* (1523) from *eis* (1519), in, and *dechomai,* to receive into, namely, favor or communion (II Cor. 6:17); *prosdechomai* (4327) with *pros* (4314), receive, or take, e.g., take as the spoiling of one's goods with joy (Heb. 10:34), accept as deliverance (Heb. 11:35), receive kindly as a friend (Lk. 15:2); entertain (Rom. 16:2; Phil. 2:29); receive, admit as a hope (Acts 24:15); expect, look or wait for (Mk. 15:43; Lk. 2:25,38; 12:36; 23:51; Acts 23:21; Tit. 2:13); *dektos* (1184), accepted, acceptable, agreeable (Lk. 4:19,24; Acts 10:35; II Cor. 6:2; Phil. 4:18); *apodektos* (587), from *apodechomai* (588), acceptable, pleasing, grateful (I Tim. 2:3; 5:4); *euprosdektos* (2144), from *eu* (2095), well, and *prosdektos,* from *pros,* unto, and *dektos,* accepted, acceptable (Rom. 15:16,31; II Cor. 8:12; I Pet. 2:5).

1210. Deō; to fasten or tie. N.T. meanings: to bind, tie, as with a chain or cord (Mt. 22:13; 27:2; Mk. 5:3,4, etc.); bind up, swathe (Jn. 19:40); bind or oblige by a moral or religious obligation (Rom. 7:2; I Cor. 7:27,39); bind, pronounce or determine to be binding or obligatory, i.e., of duties for performance, trangressions for punishment (Mt. 16:19; 18:18). As an impersonal verb *dei* (1163), need, necessity or want (Mt. 25:27; Mk. 9:11; 14:31; Eph. 6:20); in the expression *to deon,* that which is needful, need (I Tim. 5:13; I Pet. 1:6); in the pass. *deomai* (1189), to be in want or need. Not used in this sense by the writers of the N.T. in the simple form, although used in the comp. forms as in *prosdeomai* (4326), to make one's need known to somebody (Acts 17:25). *Deomai* in the mid. form means to pray, beseech, supplicate for special benefits (Mt. 9:38; Lk. 5:12; Acts 4:31; 21:39, etc.). From this verb is derived *deēsis* (1162), supplication, or prayer for a specific need.

1217. Dēmiourgos; from *dēmios,* public, which in turn is from *dēmos,* a people, and *ergon,* work. One who works for the public or performs public works such as an architect. Applied to God, the architect of that continuing and glorious city which Abraham looked for (Heb. 11:10). It brings out the power of the divine creator in contr. to *technitēs* (5079), from *technē,* trade, and *teuchō,* to fabricate, meaning an artificer, craftsman, workman. *Technitēs* expresses rather God's manifold wisdom, the infinite variety and beauty of the works of His hand (Acts 19:24,38; Heb. 11:10; Rev. 18:22).

1218. Dēmos; from *deō,* to bind. A people, so called because they are united by laws and ties of society (Acts 12:22; 17:5; 19:30,33). Deriv.: *dēmosios* (1219), public, common (Acts 5:18); *dēmosia,* adv., publicly (Acts 16:37). From this word is derived democracy where the people, the public rules.

1225. Diaballō or **diaballomai;** (mid. voice) from the prep. *dia* (1223), through, and *ballō* (906), to cast, throw. The verb from which is derived the noun *diabolos* (1228), the devil or false accuser. Used in the pass. voice only in Lk. 16:1 and should be translated "he was falsely accused" if this difficult parable is to be understood.

1226. Diabebaioomai; a deponent verb in the pass. form but used as in the act. voice. Firmly to assure, from *dia,* an intens., and *bebaioō* (950), make firm

(I Tim. 1:7; Tit. 3:8).

1228. Diabolos; the devil, from the prep. *dia,* through, and the verb *ballō* (906), to cast. One who falsely accuses and divides people without any reason. He is an accuser, a slanderer (I Tim. 3:11; II Tim. 3:3; Tit. 2:3) called by that name because originally he accused or slandered God in paradise; averse to the increase of man's knowledge and happiness (Gen. 3:5; Jn. 8:44). The devil still slanders God by false and blasphemous suggestions, and because he is also the accuser of the brethren before God (Rev. 12:9,10, cf. Job. 1:2). Called our adversary, *antidikos* (476), or opponent. *Diabolos* is used either for the prince of devils (Mt. 4:1; Rev. 12:9; 20:2) or for those evil spirits in general (Acts 10:38; Eph. 4:27; 6:11). The Lord Jesus calls Judas *diabolos* (Jn. 6:70), because under the influence of this evil spirit he would be Christ's accuser and betrayer (cf. Mt. 16:23 where the Lord calls Peter *Satanas,* 4567, Satan, and not *diabolos,* devil). This prince of the devils is called *diabolos* thirty-eight times, and *Satanas,* Satan, thirty-four times in the N.T.

1229. Diaggellō; to announce, declare fully or far and wide (Lk. 9:60; Rom. 9:17), to declare plainly (Acts 21:26).

1231. Diaginōskō; from the prep. *dia* (1223), denoting separation or emphasis, and *ginōskō* (1097), to know. To discuss, examine thoroughly (Acts 23:15; 24:22). Generally it means to perceive clearly, discriminatingly, discern, distinguish, decide. Deriv.: *diagnōsis* (1233), discernment, used in English as diagnosis.

1232. Diagnōrizō; from *dia* (1223), denoting separation, and *gnōrizō* (1107), to know. To know by distinguishing. In Lk. 2:17, to make known through a district, spread abroad the tidings.

1233. Diagnōsis; discernment or distinguishing (English, diagnosis) from the verb *diaginōskō,* discriminatingly to discern, only in Acts 25:21.

1237. Diadechomai; from *dia* (1223), denoting transition, and *dechomai* (1209), receive. To receive by succession from another or former possessor (Acts 7:45).

1238. Diadēma; diadem, being not a crown, but a filament of silk, linen or some such thing. Used in Rev. 12:3; 13:1; 19:12. Contr. *stephanos* (4735), crown, used numerous times and always refers to the conqueror's, and not the king's, crown.

1240. Diadochos; from the verb *diadechomai.* A successor (Acts 24:27).

1242. Diathēkē; testament, covenant. In Class. Gr. it always meant the disposition which a person makes of his property in prospect of death, i.e., his testament. This is the meaning when used either in the sing. or pl. The pl. also means the testamentary arrangements of a person. It should be understood that the disposition of God becomes an institution of God. In the N.T. it means a solemn disposition, institution or appointment of God to man (Heb. 9:16-18), to which our word "dispensation" answers adequately; for the religious dispensation or institution which God appointed to Abraham and the patriarchs (Acts 3:25); for the dispensation from Sinai (Heb. 8:9); for the dispensation of faith and free justification of which Christ is the mediator (Heb. 7:22; 8:6) and which is called new (*kainē,* 2537), qualitatively new in that it is a dispensation of faith in respect of the old, the old being the Sinaitical one (II Cor. 3:6; Heb. 8:8,13; 9:15). On the other hand, the old dispensation is called *palaia* (3820) *diathēkē* and should be distinguished from *archaia* (744) which is related to *archē* (746) referring to the beginning. *Palaia,* which relates to the O.T., is not the original testament and dispensation of God but is simply the old contr. to the new and refers to the dispensation contained in the books of Moses (II Cor. 3:14). *Diathēkē* translated "covenant" gives the misleading idea that God came to an agreement with fallen man as if signing a contract. Rather, it involves only the declaration of God's unconditional disposition as given to Abraham in regard to Israel as a nation (Gen. 13:14-17; 15:18; 17:7-8; 17:19-21; 21:12; 22:2,12). God is bringing about His prearranged disposition in regard to Israel in spite of the fact that Israel has not yet believed in the Messiah. The Sinaitic *diathēkē* to Moses, however, was a conditional dispensation or series of promises (Ex. 19:5-8; 20-23; Heb. 12:18-21) which God made for the Jews only if they obeyed. In the N.T. God provided His Son in the execution of His plan and dispensation but not as a result of the obedience to any rule that He preset. However, the giving of eternal life to individuals is presupposed on the acceptance of that sacrifice of the Son of God. It also means a solemn disposition or appointment of man (Gal. 3:15). Deriv.: *tithēmi* (5087), to set, place, lay. The term "the covenant of the new testament" may be understood as personally referring to Christ (Mt. 26:28; Mk. 14:24). The same meaning would pertain to the blood of His covenant which would be the blood of His promise, the blood of His own body (Heb. 9:20; 10:29).

1243. Diairesis; from *dia* (1223), involving separation, and *haireō* or *haireomai* (138), to take, grasp, seize. Dividing, distribution, classification or separation. Used only in I Cor. 12:4-6 in regard to the gifts, services and results of energies or operations. Apportionments or distributions in a pass. sense. Here the Apostle does not merely mean the Spirit bestows different gifts, but bestows certain gifts to certain people, not the same to all. The possessors of these gifts are exhorted to a mutual communication and fellowship.

1244. Diaireō; from *dia* (1223), through or with the meaning of separation, and *haireō* or *haireomai* (138), to take, grasp, seize. To take one from another, divide, part, apportion, assign. In the N.T. it means to take one or something from another (Lk. 15:12; I Cor. 12:11).

1247. Diakoneō; to serve, wait upon, with emphasis on the work to be done and not on the relationship between lord and servant. In *doulos* (1401), slave, the work is involuntary and to a lesser degree in *hupēretēs* (5257), servant, in contr. to the voluntary service of *therapōn* (2324) attendant. In its narrowest sense, *diakoneō* means to wait on a table, serve at dinner (Mt. 8:15; Mk. 1:31; Lk. 4:39; 10:40; 12:37; 17:8; Jn. 12:2). Generally it means to do anyone a service, care for someone's needs (Mt. 4:11; 25:44, etc.). There is an inferred service rendered, bringing advantage to others, to help. One may work, *douleuō,* and not help anybody, but when *diakoneō* is used, then helping someone directly is involved (Jn. 12:26; Acts 19:22; I Tim. 3:10,13).

1248. Diakonia; serviceable labor, service (Lk. 10:40; Heb. 1:14), assistance (II Cor. 11:8; II Tim. 4:11). *Diakonia* involves compassionate love towards the needy within the Christian community (Acts 6:1,4; II Cor. 8:4; 9:12,13; Rev. 2:19, etc.). Every business, every calling, so far as its labor benefits others is a *diakonia.* In this sense Paul and Luke in the Acts use the word to designate the vocation of those who preach the Gospel and have the care of the churches (Acts 20:24; Rom. 11:13; I Cor. 12:5; Col. 4:17; I Tim. 1:12; II Tim. 4:5). Therefore, *diakonia* is an office or ministration in the Christian community viewed with reference to the labor needed for others, both in the case of individuals (I Cor. 12:5, etc.), and generally as a total concept including all branches of service (Rom. 12:7; II Cor. 4:1; 6:3; Eph. 4:12; I Tim. 1:12). See *diakoneō* (1247), to minister; *diakonos* (1249) deacon, minister.

1249. Diakonos; a minister, servant, deacon. The deriv. is uncertain. According to some it comes from *diakonis,* in the dust laboring, or running through dust. Others derive it from *diakō,* the same as *diēkō,* to hasten, related to *diōkō,* to pursue. Verb: *diakoneō* (1247), from the emph. prep. *dia* (1223), and *koneō,* to minister, adjust, regulate, set in order. Not servile as a *doulos* (1401), slave, but voluntary as a *therapōn* (2324), attendant. Those who serve at a feast are *douloi,* but those who execute the king's sentence are *diakonoi* (Mt. 22:2-14). In *doulos* the relation of dependence upon the master is prominent and a state of servitude is the main thought, while in *diakonos* the main reference is to the service or advantage rendered to another (serviceableness). In *hupēretēs* (5257), servant, the predominant reference is to the labor done for a lord. In *therapōn* the idea originally was of voluntary subjection and honorable rendering of service, the opp. of *doulos,* a slave. *Diakonos* thus represents the servant in this activity for the work, not in his relation, either servile as that of the *doulos* or more voluntary as in the case of the *therapōn,* to a person. The emphasis in *diakonos* is the service rendered. It also means the servant of an employer, as is said of the magistrate that he is God's deacon (Rom. 13:4). He acts in the employ of God (I Tim. 4:6) being a good deacon of Jesus Christ (Jn. 12:26; II Cor. 6:4; 11:15,23; Col. 1:7; I Thess. 3:2). Also used in the N.T. as a technical term side by side with *episkopos* (1985), bishop or overseer (I Tim. 3:8,12; Phil. 1:1). The deacons in this sense were helpers or serving the bishops or elders, and this is why they were probably called deacons. Tychicus was called a deacon in his relation to Paul (Eph. 6:21; Col. 4:7, cf. Acts 19:22). The origin of this relationship is found in Acts 6:1–4. Stephen and Philip were deacons and were first chosen as distributors of alms but soon appear side by side with the Apostles and as their helpers as evangelists (Acts 6:8-10; 8:5-8). The care of the churches devolved upon the deacons as the helpers of the elders who held distinct offices. In Rom. 16:1 a woman, Phoebe, is named as a *diakonos,* deacon, of the church (I Tim. 5:10, cf. Rom. 16:2; I Tim. 3:11). Deriv.: *diakoneō* (1247), to serve; *diakonia* (1248), ministry.

1252. Diakrinō; from *dia* (1223), denoting separation, and *krinō* (2919), to distinguish, decide, judge. To discern, distinguish (Mt. 16:3); to make a distinction or difference (Acts 15:9); to distinguish, make to differ (I Cor. 4:7; 11:29); to judge, determine (I Cor. 6:5, cf. I Cor. 14:29); in the pass. *diakrinomai,* to contend, dispute with another, i.e., to be distinguished or divided from him in discourse (Acts 11:2; Jude 9); also in the pass., to doubt, to be distinguished or divided in one's mind (Mt. 21:21; Mk. 11:23; Acts 10:20; Rom. 4:20; Js. 1:6). In the mid. or pass. (Js. 2:4; Jude 22).

1253. Diakrisis; from *diakrinō* (1252), to separate one from another, divide, part. Discerning, distinguishing (I Cor. 12:10; Heb. 5:14); a difference, dispute, controversy (Rom. 14:1).

1257. Dialeipō; from *dia* (1223), between, and *leipō* (3007), to leave. To intermit, desist, cease, leave an interval whether of space or time (Lk. 7:45). Related words: *adialeiptos* (88), from *a,* neg., *dia,* through, and *leipō,* to leave; unceasing, continual (Rom. 9:2; II Tim. 1:3). The meaning is not of unbroken continuity but without the omission of any occasion. *Adialeiptōs* (89), adv. unceasingly, not interruptedly, but that which is constantly reoccurring (Rom. 1:9; I Thess. 1:3; 2:13; 5:17).

1259. Diallassō; in the mid. voice, *diallassomai* or *dialatomai,* to be reconciled, only in Mt. 5:24. Applies to a quarrel in which the fault may be two-sided or one-sided. The context must show on which side is the active enmity. *Katallassō* (2644) is more frequent in later Gr. and differs from *diallassō* (act.) only in that in the same construction the accus. may denote either of the parties.

1260. Dialogizomai; from the emph. *dia* (1223), denoting separation, and *logizomai* (3049), to reckon, reason. To reason, discourse, whether in silence with oneself (Mk. 2:6; Lk. 1:29; 3:15; 5:22; 12:17), or by speech with others (Mt. 16:7,8; Lk. 20:14); to consider (Jn. 11:50); to dispute (Mk. 9:33). Deriv.: *logizomai* (3049).

1261. Dialogismos; from *dialogizomai* (1260). In the N.T. with a negative meaning only and refers to objectionable thoughts and directions in some way or other. Reasoning, rationalization (Mt. 15:19; Mk. 7:21; Lk. 2:35; I Cor. 3:20; Js. 2:4); doubtful reasoning, doubt (Lk. 24:38; I Tim. 2:8); discourse, dispute, disputation (Lk. 9:46,47; Rom. 14:1; Phil. 2:14). Deriv.: *logizomai* (3049), to reckon.

1263. Diamarturomai; from the emph. *dia* (1223) and *marturomai* (3143), to witness, bear witness, or from *dia,* meaning in the presense of, and *martur* or *martus* (3144), a witness. To bear witness, testify earnestly or repeatedly, or to charge as it were before witnesses (Acts 20:23, Heb. 2:6). Attesting to facts and truths of redemption or the Word of the Lord, of Christ, the Gospel, the kingdom of God, etc. (Acts 8:25; 10:42; 18:5; 20:21,24; 23:11; 28:23; I Thess. 4:6). To charge anyone, exhort earnestly (II Tim. 2:14; 4:1), Followed by *hina,* so that (Lk. 16:28; I Tim. 5:21).

1270. Dianoēma; from *dionoeō,* to agitate in mind from the prep. *dia* (1223), denoting separation, and *noeō* (3539), think. A thought, reflection (Lk. 11:17). See *nous* (3563), mind.

1271. Dianoia; understanding, intellect, intellectual faculty, mind (Mt. 22:37; Eph. 1:18; 4:18; Heb. 8:10); an operation of the understanding, thought, imagination (Lk. 1:51). See *noeō* (3539), to think; *nous* (3563), mind.

1295. Diasōzō; from *dia* (1223), through, an emph., and *sōzō* (4982), to save. To save or preserve (Acts 27:43; I Pet. 3:20); carry or convey safely (Acts 23:24). Pass.: *diasōzomai,* to be carried safely, escape safely (Acts 27:44; 28:1,4); heal, save, deliver from some present bodily disorder (Mt. 14:36; Lk. 7:3).

1296. Diatagē; order, from *diatassō* (1299), to appoint, order, a disposition, ordinance, appointment (Rom. 13:2; Acts 7:53). The expression "received the law as ordained by angels," *eis diatagas aggelōn,* means by or through the dispositions of angels. No other angels were present at the giving of the law but the material ones in the form of fire, light, darkness, cloud and thick darkness (Ex. 19:18; Deut. 4:11; 5:22,26; 33:2; Hab. 3:3). Cf. Deut. 5:26 with v. 22, *dietagē,* was placed, or stood by Him as a servant ready to execute His pleasure. Thus these, and particularly the fire, were the immediate instruments of His agency (Deut. 5:25) and, therefore, His angels, agents, or ministers. The Septuagint translates the word "saints" in Deut. 33:2 as "angels" (*aggeloi*). Through the dispositions (*diatagas*) of these terrible agents (Ex. 19:16; Deut. 5:24,25; Heb. 12:21) on the right and left of Jehovah (for He spoke to them out of the midst of the fire, of the cloud and of the thick darkness, Deut. 5:22) the Israelites received the law, which was in a sense only *diatageis,* ordained (Gal. 3:19) or *lalētheis,* spoken (Heb. 2:2) by or with the ministry of angels, for it was Jehovah Himself and no other, though attended by His material agents who ordained or spoke the law (Ex. 20; Deut. 5). Deriv.: *diatagma* (1297), an order, commandment (Heb. 11:23).

1297. Diatagma; the order, commandment, or edict itself. Only in Heb. 11:23.

1299. Diatassō; from *dia* (1223), through, inten., and *tassō* (5021), to appoint, order. To command, used in connection with what was appointed for tax officials to collect (Lk. 3:13); of the tabernacle as appointed by God for Moses to make (Acts 7:44); of arrangements made by Paul (Acts 20:13); of what the Apostle ordained in the churches in regard to marital conditions (I Cor. 7:17); of what the Lord ordained in regard to the support of those who proclaimed the Gospel (I Cor. 9:14); of the law as administered through angels, by Moses (Gal. 3:19). In Tit. 1:5 the meaning is command rather than appoint. *Diatagē* (1296), an ordinance (Rom. 13:2). In Acts 7:53 Stephen mentions the angels to stress the majesty of the law. *Diatagma* (1297), what is imposed by decree or law (Heb. 11:23) stressing the concrete character of the commandment more then *epitagē* (2003), with a stress on the commanding. Deriv.: *anatassomai* (392); *epitassō* (2004); *apotassomai* (657); hupotassō (5293); *prostassō* (4367).

1301. Diatēreō; to keep carefully, from *dia,* inten., and *tēreō* (5083), as the mother of Jesus in keeping His saying in her heart (Lk. 2:51); the command of the Apostles (Acts 15:29).

1303. Diatithemai; from *dia,* an emph., and *tithēmi* (5087), to place. To place separately, distribute, arrange, appoint anyone to a place. In biblical Gr. used usually in the mid. voice, to dispose or arrange for oneself (Acts 3:25; Heb. 8:10; 9:16,17; 10:16). Commonly it means to arrange and dispose of one's effects by will and testament. Followed by the dat. of the person, to bequeath a thing to anyone, (Lk.

22:29), allow or assign. As a verb it is important in its bearing upon the Scriptural use of the sub. *diathēkē* (1242), testament.

1317. Didaktikos; apt to teach. A quality named as a requisite in the bishop (I Tim. 3:2; II Tim. 2:24); cf. with reference to Christian teaching (Acts 18:24,25).

1319. Didaskalia; that which belongs to a *didaskalos* (1320), teacher. That which is taught, teaching, instruction. In the N.T. commonly used obj. and, therefore, in a pass. sense meaning that which is taught, doctrine (Mt. 15:9; Mk. 7:7; Col. 2:22, cf. Eph. 4:14; I Tim. 4:1 in antithesis to Tit. 2:10). Distinguished from *didachē* (1322), the act of teaching, instructing, tutoring. *Didaskalia* refers not only to that which is taught but also to the authority of the teacher, thus not simply the subject taught but also the act of teaching or instructing. Used absolutely as *hē didaskalia,* the teaching (Rom. 12:7; I Tim. 1:10; 4:6,16; 6:1,3; II Tim. 4:3; Tit. 1:9; 2:1,7,10); used with the authority of the teacher behind the teaching (Rom. 15:4; II Tim. 3:10,16).

1320. Didaskalos; a teacher (Rom. 2:20; Heb. 5:12), from *didaskō* (1321), to teach. It correlates with *mathētēs* (3101), a learner, pupil, disciple (Mt. 10:24,25; Lk. 6:40). When used in addressing Jesus (Mt. 22:16; Jn. 1:38), it is meant as a name of respect as given to the Jewish scribes (Lk. 2:46) as was the custom of the time. The Pharisees opposed the title of father, *patēr* (3962), and *kathēgētēs* (2519), a guide, leader, hence a teacher or master or *kurios* (2962), lord (Jn. 13:13,14). Acts 13:1 refers to *didaskaloi,* teachers, with *prophētai* (4396), prophets. From this it is concluded that in the Christian Church the *didaskaloi,* teachers, appear as having a special function (Acts 13:1; I Cor. 12:28,29; Eph. 4:11; Js. 3:1). These *didaskaloi* answer to the Jewish *grammateis,* pl., (1122), scribes and are to be viewed, like them, as in a special sense acquainted with and interpreters of God's salvation (Mt. 13:52). Upon them developed the duty of giving progressive instruction of God's redeeming purposes, a function which, with that of *poimēn* (4166), pastor, seems to have been united in one person (Eph. 4:11). Cf. the *hēgoumenoi,* leaders, from *hēgeomai* (2233), in Heb. 13:7,17; the *poimenes,* pastors or shepherds and the *didaskaloi,* teachers, seem to have been members of the presbytery (Acts 20:28; I Tim. 3:2; II Tim. 2:24). The *didaskalos* was distinct from the *kērux* (2783), preacher, and *euaggelistēs* (2099), the evangelist (Eph. 4:11; I Tim. 2:7). Side by side with them false teachers appear, not only outside, but probably within the presbytery (I Tim. 1:3; II Tim. 4:3) called *pseudodidaskaloi* (5572), false teachers (II Pet. 2:1); *heterodidaskalein* (2085), teaching qualitatively different doctrine (I Tim. 1:3; 6:3). Paul called himself, besides *kērux,* preacher, an *apostolos,* apostle in a restrictive sense as with the same authority as the Twelve and with special emphasis, *didaskalos ethnōn,* teacher of nations or the Gentiles (I Tim. 2:7; II Tim. 1:11; see also Jn. 3:10; Gal. 2:7ff., Eph. 3:8,9).

1321. Didaskō; either from *daiō* or *daō,* to know or teach, and the Ionic *daskō* with the reduplicate syllable *di.* Teach, instruct by word of mouth (Mt. 28:15,20; Lk. 11:1; 12:12; Acts 15:1; I Cor. 11:14; Rev. 2:14). *Didaskō* has inherent in it the calculation to influence the understanding of the person who is taught. Its counterparts are *akouō* (191), to hear for the purpose of understanding and *manthanō* (3129), to learn, from which *mathētēs* (3101), learner, pupil, disciple, is derived. The one teaches, *didaskei,* and the other *mathēteuei* (3100), learns or assimilates as part of himself (Mt. 10:24,25; Lk. 6:40; 19:39). *Kērussō* (2784), preach, proclaim, does not have inherent the same expectation of learning and assimilation as that which is being taught (*didaskō*) (Mt. 4:23; 9:35; 11:1; 13:54; Lk. 20:1; Acts 5:42; 15:35). The thing aimed at when one teaches, *didaskō* is to shape the will of the one taught by the communication of the knowledge (Mt. 5:19; Acts 21:21; Col. 1:28). It is used absolutely of Christ's teaching (Mk. 9:31; 10:1; Jn. 18:20; Col. 1:28, etc.); as instruction in the Christian faith and Christian teaching (Acts 11:26; Rom. 12:7; Col. 1:28; Heb. 5:12, etc.).

1322. Didachē; in an act. sense it means the art of teaching, instructing, tutoring (Mk. 4:2; 12:38; II Tim. 4:2); in a pass. sense, teaching which is given, that which anyone teaches (Mt. 7:28, etc.). In an absolute sense, it denotes the teaching of Jesus (II Jn. 9,10), the Lord (Acts 13:12); the Apostles (Acts 2:42; Tit. 1:9), etc.

1334. Diēgeomai; from *dia* (1223), through, inten., and *hēgeomai* (2233), to lead; to conduct a narration through to the end. To recount, relate in full (Mk. 5:16; 9:9; Lk. 8:39; 9:10; Acts 8:33; 9:27; 12:17; Heb. 11:32). Noun: *diēgēsis* (1335), a narrative and not a declaration. Deriv.: *ekdiēgeomai* (1555), from *ek,* out, and *diēgeomai,* to recount, rehearse or relate particularly (Acts 13:41; 15:3).

1341. Dikaiokrisia; from *dikaios* (1342), just, and *krisis* (2920), judgment. A judgment which renders justice, which produces right. Righteous judgment (Rom. 2:5).

1342. Dikaios; adj. or adj. noun from *dikē* (1349), right, justice. Used in the neut. to *dikaion,* that which is right, conformable to right, pertaining to right, that which is just, which is expected by the one who sets the rules and regulations whereby man must live, whether that be society or God. Therefore, that which is expected as duty and which is claimed as a right because of one's conformity to the rules of God or society. When used in the mas. or fem. as an adj. or an adj. noun and used of persons, it refers to the one who acts conformably to justice and right without any deficiency or failure. Thus it is applied to God (Jn. 17:25; Rom. 3:26); Christ as God-Man (Acts 3:14; 7:52; 22:14; I Pet. 3:18; I Jn. 2:1). Being *dikaios,* just, means that one conforms in his actions to his constitutionally just character. The rules are self-imposed. When this absolute justice is applied to man, it is stated that there is no man who in his behavior can fully meet the expectations of God in his life (Rom. 3:10). *Dikaios* may also apply to the person who establishes his own rules of life. Such were the Pharisees whom the Lord exposed as righteous in themselves (Mt. 9:13; Lk. 18:9). Having set up and kept, or pretended to keep, certain standards, they called themselves righteous or just in the sight of God. Most of these rules and regulations, however, were not those of inner holiness and conformity to God, but mere performance of external ceremonial ordinances (Rom. 10:3). In the N.T. those are called righteous, *dikaioi,* who have conditioned their lives by the standard which is not theirs, but God's. They are the people related to God and who as a result of this relationship walk with God (Rom. 1:17; 3:21-22; Eph. 4:24). A righteous person is one justified by faith and showing forth his faith by his works. The nonbelievers, the heathen, call others righteous or just as they compare them with their own standards, such as social virtues. It has more a social than a divine reference. In the heathen mind a *dikaios* is one who does not selfishly nor self-forgetfully transgress the bounds fixed for him and gives to everyone his own, yet still desires what is his, and does not in the least withdraw an assertion of his own claims. Christianity must continually combat such a view. The heathen say, "My right is my duty," whereas the Christian says, "My duty is my right." Plato designated *dikaiosunē* (1343), righteousness, as inseparably linked with *sōphrosunē* (4997), soberness or sobriety, the expression of a sound mind, the ability to place restrictions on one's freedom in action. *Dikaios* is equivalent to *eusebēs* (2152), pious (Acts 10:2) and fearing God (v. 22). Peter spoke of Cornelius as having fear of God and his righteousness as accepted by God (Acts 10:35). This coincides with the Pauline doctrine of justification. A person is just or righteous with the righteousness which is through the faith of Christ, the righteousness which is of God by faith (Phil. 3:9). He is justified through faith (Rom. 5:19), and brings forth the fruits of righteousness or justification (Phil. 1:11; see also Mt. 13:43; 25:46; Lk. 14:14; Heb. 11:4). The O.T. righteous were those whose conduct was made conformable to God and whose justification was made possible through their faith in the promised Redeemer (Hab. 2:4; Gal. 3:11, cf. Gen. 6:9; Heb. 11:7). The word *dikaios* is also used of things to indicate their just or right or conformable relation to justice or righteousness (Jn. 7:24; Rom. 7:12). Syn.: *agathos* (18), good, whose goodness and works of goodness are transferred to others; yet *dikaios* is a concept of a relation and presupposes a norm, whereas the subject of *agathos*, good and doing good, is its own norm. Therefore, *agathos* includes the pred. of *dikaios*. In the N.T. *dikaios* stands in opp. to *paranomos*, unlawful (related to *paranomia*, 3892), transgression. In I Pet. 3:12 the righteous stand as opp. to those who do evil; in I Pet. 4:18 as contrary to the ungodly and the sinner; in II Pet. 2:7 as opp. to *athesmoi* (113), translated "wicked" (KJV) but actually meaning without an acceptable standard, from the neg. *a*, and *thesmos*, that which is laid down and established, an ordinance; and in v. 8 contr. to *anomos* (459), lawless. See also I Tim. 1:9. In most instances *dikaios* stands in opp. to *adikos* (94), unrighteous. Syn. of *dikaios*: *hagios* (40), holy in the sense of blameless; *hosios* (3741), the performer of the ordinances. Deriv.: *dikē* (1349).

1343. Dikaiosunē; from *dikaios* (1342), righteous, and *dikē* (1349), justice or righteousness. It is the essence of *to dikaion*, that which is just, or *dikaios*, of him who is just or righteous. Righteousness fulfills the claims of *dikē*, which in the case of the believer is God's claims; and in the case of the nonbeliever, the claim of that higher authority which a person adopts as his own standard. *Dikaiosunē*, righteousness, is thus conformity with the claims of higher authority and stands in opp. to *anomia* (458), lawlessness. In both the O.T. and N.T., righteousness is the state commanded by God and standing the test of His judgment (II Cor. 3:9; 6:14; Eph. 4:24). It is conformity to all that He commands or appoints. Since God Himself is the standard of the believers, the righteousness of God means the righteousness which belongs to God or to oneself for God, or God-like righteousness (Mt. 6:33; Js. 1:20). Thus righteousness in general is God's uprightness or standard, without reference to any particular form of its embodiment, to which man is expected to conform. The righteousness of God is the right which God has upon man. In order for man to recognize and fully submit to that right of God upon his life, he must receive God as He offers Himself or His righteousness to him as a gift (Rom. 5:17). The recognition and acceptance of God's right upon man realized through faith stands in opp. to the righteousness which is of the law (Rom. 10:5; Gal. 3:21) which is man's acceptance of the claims of the law upon his life. Man in his natural, fallen condition tends rather to accept his own set of standards, creating his own righteousness (Rom. 10:3; Phil. 3:6). Such, however, is not really righteousness (Rom. 10:5,3; Gal. 3:21) and does not satisfy God. God's righteousness is imputed and imparted as a gift to man and not earned. It results in God's act of justification by faith through Christ. Man can only accept the claims of God upon his life as he repents of his sin and receives Christ as his Saviour by faith, and thus becomes a child of God, realizing God's claims upon him by the miraculous regenerating action of the Holy Spirit. (Jn. 1:12; Rom. 4:11-13; 5:21; 6:16; 8:10; 9:30; 10:6; II Cor. 6:7,14; Eph. 4:24; 6:14; II Pet. 1:1).

1344. Dikaioō; to justify. Verbs which end in *-oō* generally mean to bring out that which a person is or that which is desired. In the case of *dikaioō*, it means either to bring out the fact that a person is righteous, or if he is not, to make him righteous. Usually the verbs ending in *-oō* do not have reference to the mode in which the action takes place. To justify someone, therefore, means to bring out the fact that he is just or to make him just without necessarily referring to how it is accomplished. In Class. Gr. *dikaioō* could also mean to make anyone righteous by permitting such a one to bear for himself his condemnation, judgment, punishment, or chastisement. Such action of guilt upon the one being tried in court would have been better expressed by the verb *dikazō* which does not occur in the N.T. although the sub. *dikastēs* (1348), a judge, does occur (Lk. 12:14; Acts 7:27,35, T.R.). The more common word referring to the condemning of a guilty person examined in court is *katadikazō* (2613), to condemn (Mt. 12:7,37; Lk. 6:37; Js. 5:6). The noun *katadikē* does not occur in the N.T. but it does in Class. Gr. and means a judgment given against one, a sentence. It must be clearly understood that in the N.T. the verb *dikaioō*, to justify, never means to make anyone righteous by doing away with his violation of law by himself bearing the condemnation and the imposed sentence. In the N.T. man in his fallen condition can never do anything in order to pay for his own sinfulness and thus be liberated from the sentence of guilt that is upon him as it happens in the mundane world; i.e., when a guilty person has paid the penalty of a crime, he is free from condemnation. In the N.T. *dikaioō* in the act. mood means to recognize, to set forth as righteous, to justify, first of all as a judicial act. This is clear from Lk. 10:29 in which a lawyer who came to Jesus asked Him how he could inherit eternal life. "Wishing to justify himself" means that he wanted to set himself as righteous. The same was the case with the Pharisees to whom the Lord said in Lk. 16:15, "You are those who justify yourselves in the sight of men"; i.e., you have set yourselves forth as righteous, as if there is nothing wrong with you if you were to stand in a court of justice. The word is used in the same sense in Lk. 7:29 in stating that the people recognized that God acted justly in sending John the Baptist to preach repentance. This was an indirect recognition that indeed man needed to repent. In the O.T. in some instances such as Ps. 73:13, the Septuagint translation of *edikaiōsa*, "I justified my heart," really means I cleansed my heart. Elsewhere the verb used in regard to a thing or a person means to find anything as right, to recognize or acknowledge anyone as just, to set forth as right or just. Noteworthy is Ex. 23:7 in the Septuagint; "Keep thee far from a false matter; and the innocent (*athōon*, 121) and righteous (*dikaion*, 1342) slay thou not: for I will not justify (thou shall not justify) because of receiving gifts." In other words, no man can declare someone righteous because of the gifts he receives from him or from anybody else. *Dikaioō* is one aspect of judicial activity as demonstrated in the Septuagint by the expression *dikaion*, just, and the verb *krinō* (2919), which in the Bible is the main verb referring to judicial activity, deciding whether a person is guilty or not; "He who justifies the wicked, and he who condemns the righteous, both of them alike are an abomination to the Lord" (Prov. 17:15). In this verse *dikaion* is translated "just," and *adikon* (94), "the wicked" which really means unjust. Everywhere in the O.T. the root meaning of *dikaioō* is to set forth as righteous, to justify in a legal sense (Ez. 16:51,52). In the N.T. it means to recognize, set forth as righteous, justify as a judicial act (Lk. 10:29; 16:15). It has the same meaning in the pass., to be recognized, found, set forth as righteous, justified (Mt. 12:37; Rom. 2:13; 3:20). A comment is necessary on Rom. 2:13: "For not the hearers of the Law are just before God, but the doers of the Law will be justified." Here there is a contr. between the hearers *akroatai* (202), and the doers, *poiētai* (4163). The verb used here is *dikaiōthēsontai*, fut. pass. punctiliar, which indicates that at a particular time in the future they will be judicially declared as righteous. The first part of the verse could be better translated: "For the hearers of the law not just by the side or before God." There is no verb at all which makes the statement true without any time limitation. What it declares was, is, and will be true. It declares that the mere hearers of the law have never been and never will be considered by God as just. If, however, they change from mere hearers to doers of the law, then God will pronounce them as just. This verse declares a standard, a norm, that not he who knows the law but he who does the law can be declared just before the Judge. Cf. Rom. 3:20 where seemingly a contradictory statement is given: "because by the works of the Law no flesh will be justified in His sight; for through the Law comes the knowledge of sin." The explanation is that whereas Rom. 2:13 declares the norm that the doer will be declared just, in Rom. 3:20 a matter-of-fact declaration is made that by the deeds of the law no man can be justified. Even if man is able to do the works of the law, he still cannot be justified since a person can be legally correct but morally wrong. He may conform to a certain law in spite of the fact that he may hate it, and if he did not fear the consequences of transgression, he might never obey it. No law can make a person morally right, although he can be proven legally conforming to the law if he does the works that are detailed by it. Therefore, *dikaiōthēsontai,* shall be justified, in Rom. 2:13 must be interpreted as not to be made or found righteous in character, but simply to appear as righteous because of having conformed to the directions of the law. This is made clear in Rom. 4:2: "For if Abraham was justified by works, he has something to boast about; but not before God." Here the verb *edikaiōthē,* was justified, does not have the meaning of being declared righteous in reality but only in appearance. No law could condemn a person who keeps it, but that does not mean that God will declare him morally right before Him as recognizing His (God's) rightful ownership of the individual. Abraham, because he obeyed the law, could not stand before God as righteous and boast about it. His declaration of his righteousness by the law was not equal to God's declaration of righteousness. Paul says in I Tim. 3:16 that Jesus Christ was not declared righteous by the law, but in the Spirit. This means that His high claims of being the Son of God, the Messiah, the Redeemer, were justified or proved true by the descent of the Holy Spirit upon Him at His baptism, by the miracles that He performed, the life that He lived, and finally through His resurrection from the dead (Rom. 1:4; I Pet. 3:18). The N.T. tells how being justified by God and declared just before Him is achieved in the lives of men. We are justified before God by Christ through grace (Gal. 2:16; 3:11; Tit. 3:6,7). When we receive Christ, we recognize God's right over us, and then we become just (Rom. 5:19). Our justification simultaneously performs a miracle in us and changes our character. We do not then obey God because we are afraid of the consequences of our disobedience, but because of His grace in Christ which has changed our character, made us just. When we become the children of God, we exercise rights toward God and act as His children. We are thus liberated from the guilt and power of sin, but not from the presence of it. That will come later (Rom. 8:23). In I Tim. 3:16 it is said of Jesus Christ, God incarnate, that He was justified in, *en* (1722), the Spirit or by means of the Spirit. In the appearance of the Spirit upon Jesus, there was the acknowledgment of the claims of the Son of God that He was the Messiah, the King of Israel, the Redeemer of mankind. This refers to the descent of the Holy Spirit upon Him at His baptism and through the miracles which He performed in full agreement with the Spirit and with God the Father. The justification of His claims, however, were through His resurrection (Rom. 1:4; I Pet. 3:18). The phrase "the righteousness of God," *dikaiosunē Theou,* constantly referred to, especially in Romans, must never be taken as meaning the righteousness which God acquired as if He needed such righteousness, but the righteousness which characterizes Him and which He dispenses. It refers to what God wants to achieve in the lives of men since their recognition of His rights upon them is naturally missing because of man's fall in Adam (Rom. 5:12), and His standard of integrity should characterize the life of man when he acknowledges God's rights upon him and what God in Christ can do in him. *Dikaiosunē* should be clearly distinguished from *dikaiōsis* (1347), the first being the state of having the right to demand duties from people, inherent righteousness, and the other an action which establishes righteousness or which makes a person righteous, *dikaion.* Hence, the first should be translated as "righteousness" and the second as "justification." Deriv.: *dikē* (1349).

1345. Dikaiōma; the product or result of being justified by God. The rights or claims which one has before God when he becomes His child by faith through Christ. In Rev. 19:8 where the translation is "the righteousness of saints," it is actually the legal rights of saints (*dikaiōmata*). In Heb. 9:1 what is translated as "ordinances" of divine service actually are *dikaiōmata,* legal rights. See also Lk. 1:6; Rom. 1:32; 2:26; 5:16,18; 8:4; Heb. 9:10; Rev. 15:4.

1346. Dikaiōs; an adv. from *dikaios* (1342), just. Justly, conformable to justice (I Pet. 2:23); honestly, without injuring anyone (I Thess. 2:10; Tit. 2:12); deservedly (Lk. 23:41); as it is fit, proper, right (I Cor. 15:34). Deriv.: *dikē* (1349).

1347. Dikaiōsis; the act which establishes a right or a just person; justification, but as an act and not as the essence or character of justice which is *dikaiosunē* (1343). Opp.: *katakrima* (2631), condemnation (Rom. 5:18).

1348. Dikastēs; judge (Lk. 12:14; Acts 7:27,35). One who executes *dikē* (1349), justice; one who maintains law and equity. Because he arrives at a conclusion and gives final judgment, the judge is called *kritēs* (2923), a more general term for judge while *dikastēs* is a judge who is nominated or elected to become part of a tribunal and arrive at a conclusion concerning a person or a case.

1349. Dikē; a fem. noun connected with the verb *deiknumi* or *deiknuō* (1166), to show. Originally *dikē* meant manner, tendency. Gradually it became the designation for the right of established custom or usage and was personified as the daughter of the mythological Gr. god Zeus and goddess Themis (see Acts 28:4). The basic meaning of the word involves the assertion by human society of a certain standard expected by its people and, if not kept, can mean the ensuing judgment. Thus it can be said that *dikē* is expected behavior or conformity, not according to one's own standard, but according to an imposed standard with prescribed punishment for non-conformity. It refers to legitimate custom. When *dikē* as expected conformity becomes judgment for violation, it becomes in Gr. *katadikē,* used in the N.T. only in a verbal form, *katadikazō* (2613), to condemn (Mt. 12:7,37; Lk. 6:37; Js. 5:6). In all instances when *dikē* occurs in the N.T. (Acts 25:15; 28:4; II Thess. 1:9; Jude 7) it is used with the sense of *katadikē,* judgment, to render justice, and refers to those who suffer punishment in order that the acceptable behavior or custom violated by them might be reestablished. From the basic word comes *dikaiōma* (1345), legitimate claim. The person adhering to the expectations of his society has certain legitimate claims (*dikaiōmata*) of which a stranger or one violating the standard of expectation is deprived. The enjoyment of one's right in a society presupposes the acceptance of duties by that citizen. In this is the total idea of the use of this whole group of words emanating from *dikē.* In the Scriptures, God is presented as the One who expects a certain conformity of man to His principles. They are man's duties toward God. When they are accepted and conformed to, then God gives man certain rights which do not belong to those who do not recognize His authority or their duties. Other important deriv.: *dikaios* (1342), just; *dikaiōs* (1346), an adv. meaning justly or righteously; *dikaiosunē* (1343), righteousness or justice; *dikaioō* (1344), to declare innocent or just or to justify; *dikaiōsis* (1347), justification; *dikastēs* (1348), judge; *adikos* (94), unjust or unrighteous; *adikia* (93), injustice or unrighteousness; *adikeō* (91), to act unjustly toward or to do wrong; *ekdikos* (1558), a punisher or one who carries out the right of an issue, an avenger; *ekdikeō* (1556), to take revenge or avenge; *ekdikēsis* (1557), the fem. noun, revenge; *endikos* (1738), one who acts within his rights, fair, just, a syn. of *dikaios; hupodikos* (5267), under sentence, guilty, or one who comes under *dikē,* the standard by God or by society.

1350. Diktuon; net, from *dikō,* to cast, cast down. A general name for all nets including the hunting net, the net with which birds are taken and the fishing net (Mt. 4:20,21; Mk. 1:18,19; Lk. 5:2,4-6; Jn. 21:6,8,11). Other names for nets: *amphiblēstron* (293), a casting net which, when skillfully cast from over the shoulder by one standing on the shore or in a boat, spreads out into a circle (*amphibalettai*) as it falls upon the water and then sinks swiftly by the weight of the leads attached to it enclosing whatever is below it (Mt. 4:18; Mk. 1:16, cf. Eccl. 9:12; Ps. 141:10); *sagēnē* (4522), a sweep-net, the ends of which being carried out in boats so as to include a large extent of open sea are then drawn together and all which is enclosed is taken (Mt. 13:47, cf. Isa. 19:8).

1357. Diorthōsis; from *diorthoō,* to correct, amend, which in turn is made up of *dia* (1223), an emph., and *orthoō,* to make right, which is derived from *orthos,* right (3717). Amendment, reformation, only in Heb. 9:10.

1370. Dichostasia; from *dicha,* separately, and *stasis,* faction, sedition. A separate faction, division, separation (Rom. 16:17; I Cor. 3:3; Gal. 5:20). See *histēmi* (2476), to stand.

1374. Dipsuchos; from *dis* (1364), twice, and *psuchē* (5590), soul, mind. Double-minded, which can mean doubting. Only in Js. 1:8 referring to the doubter or waverer which corresponds to *diakrino* (1252) and Js. 4:8 used in a general sense as an unstable person.

1378. Dogma; from the verb *dokeō* (1380), to think. Conclusion, ordinance, opinion, proposition, dogma. With the meaning of conclusion (Acts 16:4); as decree or command (Lk. 2:1; Acts 17:7; Eph. 2:15; Col. 2:14). Used as dogmas of Christianity, it means views, doctrinal statements, principles.

1379. Dogmatizō; to conclude, ordain, establish as a dogma, conclusion or ordinance (1378). In the mid. voice, *dogmatizomai,* to let oneself fall into a certain order, subject oneself to ordinances (Col. 2:20).

1380. Dokeō; to think, imagine, consider, appear. Expresses the subjective mental estimate or opinion about a matter which men form. Noun: *doxa* (1391), glory, estimate recognition of what one or something is. Such recognition may be correct (Acts 15:28; I Cor. 4:9; 7:40), or incorrect, involving error (Mt. 6:7; Mk. 6:49; Jn. 16:2; Acts 27:13). Contr. *phainō* or *phainomai* (5316), to appear, be conspicuous, shine, be seen. Deriv.: *doxazō* (1392), to glorify, make glorious or honorable or cause to appear as one really is (Jn. 11:4; 12:28, etc.), to admit to the eternal state of glory (Rom. 8:30); *sundoxazō* (4888) (*sun,* together), to glorify together (Rom. 8:17); *endoxos* (1741) (*en,* in), glorious, honorable (Lk. 13:17; I Cor. 4:10; Eph. 5:27), splendid of dress (Lk. 7:25). *Endoxazō* or *endoxazomai* (1740) (*en,* in) in the pass., to be glorified or exhibit one's glory (II Thess. 1:10,12).

1381. Dokimazō; to try, prove, discern, distinguish, approve. It has the notion of proving a thing whether it be worthy to be received or not. Deriv.: *dokimion* (1383), test (Js. 1:3; I Pet. 1:7); *dokimos* (1384), that which endures the test, worthy (*axios,* 514) (Rom. 14:18; 16:10; I Cor. 11:19; II Cor. 10:18; 13:7; II Tim. 2:15; Js. 1:12). The opp. of *dokimos* is *adokimos* (96), unapproved, reprobate (Rom. 1:28; I Cor. 9:27; II Cor. 13:5,6,7; II Tim. 3:8; Tit. 1:16; Heb. 6:8). Something good is expected of every *dokimē* (1382), trial, proof. *Dokimazō* is to prove or bring forth the good in us or to make us good as contr. with *peirazō* (3985), to tempt, which purposes to discover what good or evil is in us (Mt. 16:1; 19:3; 22:18). *Dokimazō* could not be used of Satan since he never wants us to experience God's approval. He always tempts us, *peirazei,* with the intent to make us fall.

1382. Dokimē; proof of genuineness, trustworthiness. Distinguish between a present and past, an act. and a pass. meaning for this word which has a reflexive sense; hence, it must be either the experience itself or the fact that one has proved oneself true or the act of proving oneself true; e.g., II Cor. 13:3 has the meaning: You desire that Christ speaking in me shall prove itself true. In II Cor. 2:9 it means: Whether you prove yourselves true (also Rom. 5:4). The meaning in Phil. 2:22 is: How he has proved himself true (also II Cor. 8:2; 9:13).

1383. Dokimion; the means of proving, a criterion, test, by which anything is proved or tried, as faith by afflictions (Js. 1:3; I Pet. 1:7).

1384. Dokimos; from *dokeō* (1380), to appear, form an opinion, to recognize. To be proved, to be tried as metals by fire and thus be purified. Hence to be approved as acceptable men in the furnace of adversity (Js. 1:12, cf. Rom. 16:10); be approved or accepted (Rom. 14:18; II Cor. 10:18; 13:7, II Tim. 2:15, cf. I Cor. 11:19). Ant.: *adokimos* (96), unapproved.

1389. Doloō; to adulterate for the sake of it (II Cor. 4:2) as being part of *kapēleuō* (2585), to adulterate for the sake of unworthy personal gain. Mixing human traditions with the pure word of the Gospel. *Kapēleuō* always includes *dolos* (1388), deceit, but *doloō* never extends to *kapēleuō* which in addition to adulterating has an additional notion of unjust lucre, gain, profit, advantage.

1390. Doma; gift (Mt. 7:11; Lk. 11:13; Eph. 4:8; Phil. 4:17); lends greater emphasis to the character of the gift rather than its beneficent nature.

1391. Doxa; glory. The meanings of this word divide themselves conformably with the use of the verb *dokeō* (1380), to think, recognize for what a person or a thing is. Thus, *doxa* can mean appearance, reputation, glory. Basically, in the Bible, refers to the recognition belonging to a person, honor, renown. Opp. *atimia* (819) (I Cor. 11:14,15; II Cor. 6:8). When we read in Rom. 3:23 that they come short of or lack the glory of God, it means they are not what God intended them to be. They lack His image and character. The predominating meaning of the noun *doxa* in Scripture is recognition. *Doxa* may stand in opp. to *alētheia* (225), truth, denoting seeming appearance, from *dokeō,* to appear, in opp. to *einai* (1511), to be. May denote appearance, form, aspect, that appearance of a person or thing which catches the eye or attracts attention, commanding recognition, looking like something; thus equivalent to splendor, brilliance, glory attracting the gaze which makes it a strong syn. of *eikōn* (1504), image (Rom. 1:23). *Doxa* embraces all which is excellent in the divine nature, coinciding with His self-revelation. It comprises all that God will appear to be in His final revelation to us (Lk. 2:9; Rom. 5:2; 6:4; Rev. 21:23). God's glory made itself manifest in and through Jesus Christ (Jn. 1:14; II Cor. 4:6; Heb. 1:3, etc.). His Second Coming is spoken of as the blessed hope and the appearing of His glory. It is not "the glorious appearing" as the translation has it, but *epiphaneia* (2015), *tēs doxēs,* the appearance of the glory of the great God and our Saviour Jesus Christ (Tit. 2:13). Then, at Christ's Second Coming He will be truly recognized for all that He is. The glory of the Son of Man in Mt. 19:28; 25:31; Mk. 10:37, cf. Lk. 9:32; 24:26 is to be understood in contrast with His earthly manifestation (Jn. 17:22,24; Phil. 3:21) and is brought by Christ Himself into connection with the *doxa,* glory, which He had before His humiliation in the incarnation (Jn. 17:5, cf. 12:41; Phil. 2:11). Heb. 1:3 equates the glory of Jesus to God's glory, being the self-revelation of God in the economy of redemption. In this sense, future glory is the hope of Christians. More specifically, *doxa* means not the outward glorious appearance, attracting attention to the person or thing itself, but that glory shown from within reflecting in the appearance which attracts attention, e.g., splendor, glory, brightness, adornment (Mt. 4:8; Lk. 4:6, etc.).

1392. Doxazō; from *doxa* (1391), glory. To glorify from *dokeō,* esteem, think, be of opinion, suppose which is the opp. of *eidō* (1492), to know intuitively, and *ginōskō* (1097), to know experientially or by learning. The consequential meaning from the opinion which one forms is to recognize, honor, praise, invest with dignity, give anyone esteem or honor by putting him into an honorable position. In the N.T. meaning to recognize, honor, praise (Mt. 6:2; Lk. 4:15; Rom. 11:13, etc.); to bring to honor, (strictly, to give anyone importance), make glorious, glorify (I Cor. 12:26; Heb. 5:5; I Pet. 1:8, etc.). In the writings of John, the *doxa* of God is the revelation and manifestation of all that He has and is. It is His self-revelation in which He manifests all the goodness that He is (Jn. 12:28). Since Christ made this manifest, He is said to glorify the Father (Jn. 17:1,4); or the Father is glorified in Him (Jn. 13:31; 14:13). When Christ is said to be glorified, it means simply that His innate glory is brought to light, made manifest (Jn. 11:4; 7:39; 12:16,23; 13:31; 17:1,5). Christ glorified in His disciples (Jn. 17:10, cf. 14:13). The revelation of the Holy Spirit in the glorification of Christ (Jn. 16:14).

1394. Dosis; the act of giving (Phil. 4:15; Js. 1:17). Contr. *dōrēma* (1434), the result of giving or the thing given.

1396. Doulagōgeō; from *doulos* (1401), servant, and *agō* (71), to lead, bring. To bring into servitude or subjection (I Cor. 9:27).

1397. Douleia; servitude, dependence; the state of a *doulos* (1401), slave. That state of man in which he is prevented from freely possessing and enjoying his life; a state opposed to liberty. In N.T. used only figuratively (Rom. 8:15,21; Gal. 4:24; 5:1; Heb. 2:15).

1398. Douleuō; from *doulos* (1401), servant. To be in the position of a servant and act accordingly; to be subject and serve in subjection, bondage; used of actions which are directed by others. N.T. meanings: subjugated, reduced to bondage under someone (Jn. 8:33; Acts 7:7; Rom. 9:12); used in the absolute sense, it means to be deprived of freedom (Gal. 4:25,26); to be under the law (v. 21); serve in bondage, put one's dependence into effect, i.e., to obey (Mt. 6:24; Lk. 15:29; 16:13; Gal. 5:13; Eph. 5:21; 6:7; I Tim. 6:2); metaphorically, to be a slave to, such as to pleasures (Rom. 7:25; Tit. 3:3, etc.).

1401. Doulos; slave, one who is in a permanent relation of servitude to another, his will altogether consumed in the will of the other (Mt. 8:9; 20:27; 24:45,46, etc.). Verb: *douloō* (1402), reduce to servitude; in the pass., to be enslaved; made a servant, become a servant; derived from *deō* (1210), to bind.

1402. Douloō; from *doulos* (1401), slave. To make a servant, subject, subjugate (Acts 7:6; I Cor. 9:19); in the pass., to be subjugated, subdued (Rom. 6:18,22). In the perf. tense, to be dependent (Gal. 4:3). Denotes not so much a relation of service, as primarily a relation of dependence upon, bondage to anyone; i.e., in the case of subjugated nations, etc. (II Pet. 2:19; Tit. 2:3). In I Cor. 7:15 the verb refers to a brother or sister being bound by law.

1403. Dochē; from *dechomai* (1209), to receive. A reception, entertainment, banquet (only in Lk. 5:29; 14:13).

1410. Dunamai; to be able, have power, whether by virtue of one's own ability and resources (Rom. 15:14); through a state of mind or favorable circumstances (I Thess. 2:6); by permission of law or custom (Acts 24:8,11), or simply to be able, powerful (Mt. 3:9; II Tim. 3:15, etc.).

1411. Dunamis; power, especially inherent power. All the words derived from the stem *duna-* have the basic meaning of being able, capable. Contr. *ischus* (2479) which stresses the factuality of the ability. It may even mean to will. *Dunatos* (1415), the adj. noun means one who has an ability, the opp. of which is *adunatos* (102), not able, incapable or incompetent, impossible. Verbs: *dunamai* (1410), to be able; *dunateō* (1414), to have great ability (II Cor. 13:3); *dunamoō* (1412) and *endunamoō* (1743), to strengthen (Col. 1:11). Nouns: *dunastēs* (1413), one who exercises dominion, authority (Lk. 1:52; Acts 8:27; I Tim. 6:15); *dunameis* (pl.). powers, miracles coming out of that mighty power of God inherent in Christ and which power was lent to His witnesses and ambassadors. See *sēmeia* (4592), signs; *megaleia* (3167), great works; *endoxa* (1741), glorious works; *paradoxa* (3861), strange works; *thaumasia* (2297), marvelous works; *terata* (5059), terrifying works.

1412. Dunamoō; to strengthen. In the N.T. used in the pass., to be strengthened, grow strong (Col. 1:11), of moral strengthening (cf. Eph. 3:16). Related to *dunamis* (1411), power.

1413. Dunastēs; possessor of power or authority, one who occupies high position (Acts 8:27), especially of independent rulers of territories (Lk. 1:52). Referring to the Lord as the absolute ruler (I Tim. 6:15).

1425. Dusnoētos; from *dus-* (1418), hardly, and *noētos*, understood. Hardly understood, hard to be understood (II Pet. 3:16). See *noeō* (3539), to understand; *nous* (3563), mind.

1431. Dōrea; a free gift with emphasis on its gratuitous character. Used in the N.T. of a spiritual or supernatural gift (Jn. 4:10; Acts 2:38; 8:20; 10:45; 11:17; Rom. 5:15,17; II Cor. 9:15; Eph. 3:7; 4:7; Heb. 6:4). Adv.: *dōrean* (1432), freely (Mt. 10:8; Rom. 3:24; II Cor. 11:7, etc.).

1434. Dōrēma; the thing given (Rom. 5:16; Js. 1:17). The suffix *-ma* makes it the result of *dosis* (1394), the act of giving.

1435. Dōron; gift, related to *didōmi* (1325), to give. Used of gifts given as an expression of honor (Mt. 2:11); for support of the temple (Mt. 15:5; Mk. 7:11; Lk. 21:1,4); for God (Mt. 5:23,24; 8:4; 23:18,19; Heb. 5:1; 8:3,4; 9:9; 11:4); as the gift of salvation (Eph. 2:8); for celebrating (Rev. 11:10).

1448. Eggizō; to bring near and come near in a trans. and intrans. sense, as is often the case with verbs of motion such as *agō* (71), lead. Usually in the N.T. used intrans. meaning to come near, approach (Lk. 7:12; 15:1,25; 22:47; Acts 10:9, etc.); in the expression *ēggiken* is near, the kingdom of God or heaven (Mt. 3:2; 4:17; 10:7; Mk. 1:15; Lk. 10:11). The verb has reference to space, meaning that something is here. When used in speaking of approaching God or coming near to God (Heb. 7:19; Js. 4:8), it means communion with God in prayer and the desired and cherished fellowship with Him. Deriv.: *proseggizō* (4331), approaching, coming close to (Mk. 2:4).

1450. Egguos; bail, security. In the N.T. occurs only in Heb. 7:22 which is not to be used in reference to the death of Christ by which He has answered for us, but to His eternal life through which (not with which) He is surety for the better covenant (cf. vv. 21,24,25).

1451. Eggus; close, near. Near as to time and space as well as absolutely (Mt. 24:32,33; 26:18; Phil. 4:5). Figuratively used of spiritual relations (Eph. 2:13,17).

1453. Egeirō; to awaken, wake up. Primarily used of waking those who sleep. In the pass., to wake up (Mt. 1:24; Rom. 13:11). Used figuratively meaning to become attentive to one's own dangerous position and to the salvation of God delivering therefrom (Rom. 13:11; Eph. 5:14); also used of those who are sick and needing help to raise them up (Mk. 1:31; 9:27, cf. Mt. 12:11). In the pass. sense, to recover, rise up from bed (Mt. 8:15; 9:5-7, etc.). Especially, however, used of the dead recalled to life or who rise to new life (Mt. 10:8; Acts 3:15; I Cor. 6:14, etc.). The pass. "to rise again," with or without "from the dead," always refers to the resurrection of the body (Mt. 11:5; 14:2, etc.). To erect, build up (Jn. 2:19). Syn.: *anistēmi* (450), to stand up or arise. With a personal obj., to call forth, cause to appear; in the pass., to appear, come forth (Mt. 24:7,11,24; Mk. 13:8,22; Acts 13:22, etc.). The pass. generally denotes to quit one's previous position, rise, get up (Jn. 14:31; Rev. 11:1, etc.).

1454. Egersis; from *egeirō* (1453), to wake up. Resurrection, resuscitation of the dead (Mt. 27:53).

1456. Egkainia; from *en* (1722), in or at, and *kainos* (2537), qualitatively new. Occurs only in Jn. 10:22 referring to the Feast of Dedication which were festival solemnities in memory of the dedication of the Temple at Jerusalem, or of its purification and making it qualitatively new, as it were, after it had been polluted by heathen idolatries and impurities. Deriv.: *egkainizō* (1457), dedicate (Heb. 9:18; 10:20). For deriv. of *kainos*, qualitatively new, see *anakainoō* (341), to renew.

1457. Egkainizō; from *en* (1722), in or at, and *kainos* (2537), qualitatively new. To dedicate, consecrate (Heb. 9:18; 10:20). Deriv.: *egkainia* (1456), used in the neut. pl. (Jn. 10:22), referring to the Feast of Dedication, *anakainoō* (341), to renew.

1458. Egkaleō; to bring a change against, from *en* (1722), in, and *kaleō* (2564), to call. Call to account, accuse

(Acts 19:38,40; 23:28,29; 26:2,7; Rom. 8:33).

1462. Egklēma; an accusation made in public but not necessarily before a tribunal (Acts 23:29), complaint, charge (Acts 25:16).

1469. Egkrinō; from *en* (1722), in or among, and *krinō* (2919), to judge, to reckon. In II Cor. 10:12 it is joined with *heautous* (1438), ourselves, and the dat. *tisi* (5100), to someone; to adjudge ourselves to the number or rank of. In later Gr. it came to mean to approve, esteem as being up to the standard and therefore admissible.

1482. Ethnikos; from *ethnos* (1484), nation. In the N.T. this word answers to the biblical idea of *ethnē*, nations, and means heathenish, that which pertains to those who are unconnected with the people and the God of salvation (only in Mt. 6:7; 18:17).

1483. Ethnikōs; an adv. from *ethnikos* (1482), a heathen, Gentile. Heathenishly, after the manner of the heathen of the Gentiles. Used only in Gal. 2:14 meaning to live in a non-Israelitish manner, not bound to the Israelitish mode of life.

1484. Ethnos; a nation, people (Mt. 24:7; 25:32; Lk. 7:5; Jn. 11:48; Acts 7:7; 8:9). Used by Paul for the whole race of mankind considered in a noble or enlarged view as one nation (Acts 17:26). *Ethnē*, pl., frequently signifies the heathen or Gentiles as distinguished from the Jews or believers. The Jews usually are called *laos* (2992), the people of God or the Israel of God. Syn.: *dēmos* (1218), a popular assembly or organized crowd from which is derived the English word "democracy," the rule of organized people; *ochlos* (3793), unorganized multitude.

1491. Eidos; the act of seeing, from *eidō* (1492), to see. Sight (II Cor. 5:7); the object of sight, form, appearance (Lk. 3:22; 9:29; Jn. 5:37; I Thess. 5:22). In II Cor. 5:7 it refers to the visible appearance of things which are set, in contr. to that which directs faith, meaning that the believer is guided not only by what he beholds; but by what he knows to be true though invisible. In I Thess. 5:22, the appearance of evil.

1492. Eidō; or *eideō, oida* (1492); to perceive with the outward senses, particularly with physical sight (Mt. 2:2,9,10, etc.); perceive with the mind, understand (Jn. 21:15,16; Rom. 8:28; I Cor. 2:11; II Cor. 11:31; Heb. 10:30, etc.); to experience, such as death, corruption, grief (Lk. 2:26; Acts 2:27; Heb. 11:5, etc.); be acquainted with, as a person (Mt. 26:72,74; Mk. 14:71); esteem, regard (II Cor. 5:16; I Thess. 5:12); acknowledge, own (Mt. 25:12); to know how, implying both knowledge and inclination (Mt. 7:11; Lk. 11:13; II Pet. 2:9, cf. Mt. 27:65); consider (Acts 15:6); converse with (Lk. 8:20).

1492a. Oida; or *eidō, eideō* (1492), to perceive, know intuitively as contr. with *ginōskō* (1097), to know experientially. Also to perceive or know with the outward senses, to see; to perceive with the eyes of the mind, understand; to see, experience as death, corruption, grief; know, be acquainted with, as a person; esteem; acknowledge or own.

1494. Eidōlothuton; from *eidōlon* (1497), idol, and *thuō* (2380), to sacrifice. Whatever is sacrificed or offered to an idol, such as flesh or heathen sacrifices (Acts 15:29; I Cor. 8:1,4 etc.).

1495. Eidōlolatreia; idolatry. Used only in the N.T. and Patristic Gr. (I Cor. 10:14; Gal. 5:20; Col. 3:5; I Pet. 4:3); from *eidōlon* (1497), idol, and *latreia* (2999), worship. Worship of idols, or false gods. An idolater is *eidōlolatrēs* (1496).

1496. Eidōlolatrēs; from *eidōlon* (1497), idol, and *latris*, a servant, worshipper. Idolater. A servant or worshipper of idols (I Cor. 5:10,11; 6:9; 10:7; Eph. 5:5; Rev. 21:8; 22:15, etc.).

1497. Eidōlon; from *eidos* (1491), a form, appearance. An image or representation whether corporeal or mental or some other thing. In Class. Gr. used for a statue of man or even for a concept of the mind. In the N.T. it stands for an idol or image set up to be worshipped as a god whether intended as a representative of the true God (Acts 7:41) or of a false one (Acts 15:20; I Cor. 12:2; Rev. 9:20). Also stands for a false god, usually worshipped by an image (II Cor. 6:16; I Thess. 1:9; I Jn. 5:21). Paul in I Cor. 8:4 says that an idol is nothing in the world but it cannot mean absolutely nothing. An idol is something in itself or in whatever it represents. Paul means that an idol is not a representation of the true God. Idols may be material as they are sometimes works of men's hands, statues of gold, etc., moon, etc.; but as to their being of any excellency which might require divine worship, they are nothing of that which servile worshippers are pleased to attribute to them. Cf. Isa. 41:24; Hab. 2:18,19.

1504. Eikōn; from *eikō,* to be like, resemble. A bodily representation, an image as of a man made of gold, silver or whatever (Rom. 1:23); a monarch's likeness impressed on a coin (Mt. 22:20; Mk. 12:16; Lk. 20:24); image, resemblance, likeness (Rom. 8:29; I Cor. 11:7; 15:49; Col. 1:15; 3:10). *Eikōn* sometimes may be used as syn. with *homoiōma* (3667), and both may refer to the earthly copies and resemblances of the archetypal things in the heavens. However, there is a distinction: *eikōn,* image, always assumes a prototype, that which it not merely resembles but from which it is drawn. Thus, the reflection of the sun on the water is *eikōn* (Rev. 13:14); and more importantly, the child is *empsuchos* (possessed of a soul), *eikōn,* image of his parents. *Homoiōma* is the result, the likeness or resemblance (Rom. 1:23; 5:14; 6:5; 8:3; Phil. 2:7; Rev. 9:7). *Homoiōsis* (3669), is the process or act of producing a likeness or resemblance (Js. 3:9). However, while in *homoiōma* and *homoiōsis* there is resemblance, it by no means follows that it is derived from what it resembles. There may be a resemblance between two men in no way related to each other. The *eikōn, image,* includes and involves the resemblance of similitude (*homoiōsis*), but the *homoiōsis* does not involve the image. The Son is an *homoiōma* of God in that both are God, but He is also the *eikōn,* the image of God indicating His relation to the Father (II Cor. 4:4; Col. 1:15) in as far as His humanity is concerned. There are two other Gr. words that stand in contr. to *eikōn* and *homoiōma.* They are *charaktēr* (5481), character, and *apaugasma* (541), brightness (used only in Heb. 1:3). *Charaktēr* signifies the image impressed as corresponding with the original or pattern. On account of this idea of close resemblance it has for its syn. *mimēma,* imitation, anything imitated, a copy; *eikōn,* image; *apeikonisma,* representation. On the other hand, *apaugasma* means radiation, not merely reflection. Furthermore, Heb. 1:3 uses *charaktēr,* not *charagma* (5480), because the latter word was used in a narrower sense and rarely denoted the peculiar characteristics of an individual or a people and always prominently suggests the pass. bearing of the subject spoken of. *Charagma* occurs in Acts 17:29; Rev. 13:16,17; 14:9,11; 15:2 T.R.; 16:2; 19:20; 20:4 meaning impression, mark, symbol.

1505. Eilikrineia; purity, sincerity (I Cor. 5:8; II Cor. 1:12; 2:17). Adj.: *eilikrinēs* (1506), sincere.

1506. Eilikrinēs; from *heilē* or *helē,* the shining or splendor of the sun and *krinō* (2919), judge, discern. Sincere; pure, unsullied, free from spot or blemish to such a degree as to bear examination in the full splendor of the sun. In the N.T. generally understood to relate to the lives or wills of Christians, since in Paul it seems to refer to *dokimazō* (1381), to discern. Peter joins it with *dianoia* (1271), understanding, and thus meaning clearness or perspicuity of mind or understanding by which one is able to see all things intelligibly, clearly, and proceed without mistake. Therefore, *eilikrinēs* may be rendered, clear, clearly discerning, of clear judgment or discernment, i.e., spiritually, in all things both of Christian faith and practice (Phil. 1:10, II Pet. 3;1). Another Gr. word with which *eilikrinēs* is continually found in company is *katharos* (2513), pure, clean, free from soil or stain. Some relate *eilikrinēs* to the verb *eliō,* that which is cleansed by much rolling and shaking to and fro in the sieve. According to one etymology, therefore, *eilikrinēs* is the clear and transparent, and, according to another, the purged, winnowed, unmingled. See *katharos* (2513); *koinos* (2839), unclean; *achreios* (888), useless.

1510. Eimi; to be, exist, have existence or being (Jn. 1:1,2,10; 8:58; Heb. 11:6, etc.); denoting the quality, state, condition or situation of a person or thing (Mt. 1:18,19; 2:9,13,15; 3:11; Mk. 1:6; 9:7, etc.); to happen (Mt. 13:40,49; 16:22; Mk. 13:4); to be reckoned or reputed (Mt. 18:17; I Cor. 3:19; I Tim. 1:7); to represent figuratively (Mt. 13:37-39, etc.); to mean, to count important (Mt. 9:13; 12:7; Mk. 9:10; Acts 10:17); with a gen. case it denotes possession or property (Mt. 6:13 T.R.), also with a dat. (Lk. 8:42); with the neg. *ouk* (not), not to be alive (Mt. 2:18); *eimi eis* (in), to be for, become (Mt. 19:5).

1514. Eirēneuō; to live in peace, keep peace toward someone or with someone (Mk. 9:50; Rom. 12:18; II Cor. 13:11; I Thess. 5:13). Syn. thinking the same, *to auto phroneō* (II Cor. 13:11).

1515. Eirēnē; peace, rest. In contr. with strife; denoting the absence or end of strife. Opp. *machaira* (3162), sword (Mt. 10:34); *diamerismos* (1267), division (Lk. 12:51); *laleō* (2980), to speak; *dolos* (1388), guile (I Pet. 3:10); *akatastasia* (181), commotion or confusion (I Cor. 14:33, etc.). *Eirēnē* denotes a state of untroubled, undisturbed, well-being (Js. 3:18). Syn.: *asphaleia* (803), security (I Thess. 5:3, cf. Lk. 11:21; Acts 9:31; 24:2). This is the meaning when used as a form of salutation (Lk. 24:36; Jn. 20:19,21,26) and taking leave (Mk. 5:34; Lk. 8:48; Acts 15:33; 16:36; I Cor. 16:11; Js. 2:16). May mean peace as contr. with strife. Such a state of peace is the object of divine and saving promise and is brought about by God's mercy, granting deliverance and freedom from all the distresses that are experienced as a result of sin. Used together with *eleos* (1656), mercy for the consequences of sin, and also with *charis* (5485), grace, which affects the character of the person. Peace as a Messianic blessing is that state brought about by the grace and loving mind of God wherein the derangement and distress of life caused by sin are removed. Hence, the message of salvation is called the Gospel of peace (Acts 10:36; Rom. 10:15 T.R.; Eph. 2:17; 6:15). It is called the peace of God, not that God needs it, but God gives it (Phil. 4:7; I Thess. 5:23), the peace of Christ (Col. 3:15). It can be the result only of accomplished reconciliation (Rom. 5:1; Eph. 2:16,17), referring to the new relationship between man and God brought about by the atonement (Rom. 5:9,10).

1516. Eirēnikos; adj. pertaining to peace, peaceable or peaceful (Heb. 12:11; Js. 3:17). The reference is to *eirēnē* (1515), peace, as the blessing of salvation.

1517. Eirēnopoieō; to make peace, put an end to strife (only in Col. 1:20).

1518. Eirēnopoios; The one who makes peace in others having first received the peace of God in his own heart (only in Mt. 5:9); not simply one who makes peace between two parties.

1519. Eis; without any accent as a prep. With rough breathing and circumflex, *heis* (1520), (mas.); *mia* (fem.); *hen* with rough breathing and acute accent (neut.); the first cardinal numeral meaning one. However, without the rough breathing and the circumflex, it is merely the prep. which usually governs the accus. with the primary idea of motion into any place or thing; also of motion or direction to, towards, upon any place or thing, etc. The opp. is expressed by *ek* (1537), out of place. which is the primary and the most frequent use meaning into, to, implying motion of any kind. As to time, it implies when, referring to a term or limit, up to, towards, until (Acts 4:3, until tomorrow). Many times in the N.T. it is used to indicate intention, purpose, identity, aim, such as baptism of repentance unto the remission of sins (Mk. 1:4); "baptized into Moses," identified with Moses in what he was doing (I Cor. 10:2). In composition with verbs forming comp. verbs, *eis* implies motion into, as *eisdechomai* (1523), to receive into; motion or direction to, towards, as *eisakouō* (1522), to let words sink into one's ear.

1520. Heis; one with the circumflex accent *heir* (mas.); *mia* (fem.); *hen* (neut.). If it does not have an accent and rough breathing, but only a smooth breathing, it means *eis* (1519), into or unto. This adj. or pron. in the mas. *heis* must be distinguished from the neut. *hen*. Heis means numerically one while *hen* means one in essence; as in Jn. 10:30; "I and the Father are (*hen*) one" in essence although they are two different personalities. Had it said *heis*, it would have been one person. When *hen* does not have a rough breathing and an accent, it is the prep. *en* (1722) meaning in or with.

1523. Eisdechomai; from the prep. *eis* (1519), into, and *dechomai* (1209), to receive. To receive into favor or communion (only in II Cor. 6:17).

1537. Ek; before a vowel; *ex*, a prep. governing the gen. with the primary meaning out of, from, of; spoken of such objects which before were in another but are now separated from it, either in respect of place, time, source, or origin, etc. The direct opp. of *eis* (1519), unto, which means to become part of or to be identified with. Metaphorically, after verbs of motion, direction, etc., it speaks of a state, condition, etc., out of which one comes, is brought, or tends toward. After verbs implying motion of any kind, out of or from any place or object, e.g., verbs of going, coming, sending, throwing, falling, gathering, separating, removing, etc. After verbs implying direction out of or from any place, etc., thus marking the point from which the direction sets off or tends toward. Related meanings: (1) Of time, the beginning of a period of time, a point from which onward anything takes place, etc. (2) Of the origin or source of anything, i.e., the primary, direct, immediate source, in distinction from *apo* (575). This is strictly the primary sense of the gen. case itself, also used in the N.T. (3) When used of persons, it refers to the place, stock, family, condition, etc., out of which one is derived or to which one belongs. (4) Referring to the source, i.e., the person, thing, etc., out of or from which anything proceeds, is derived, to which it pertains. (5) Of the motive, ground, occasion, from which anything proceeds, the incidental, from, out of, i.e., by reason of, because of, in consequence of. (6) It also may speak of the efficient cause, agent, etc: that from which any action or thing proceeds, is produced, effected, from, by, etc. (7) To the manner or mode in which anything is done, etc., out of, from, in, with. (8) To the means, instrument, instrumental cause, from, i.e., by means of, by, through, with, as in Lk. 16:9 by means of the mammon of unrighteousness. (9) When referring to the material, of, out of, from, as in Mt. 27:29, "a crown of thorns," made out of thorns. (10) Referring to a whole in relation to a part, a whole from which a part is spoken, ie., partitively as in I Cor. 12:15,16.

1538. Hekastos; from *hekas*, separate, each, everyone, of any number separately. In construction with pl. verbs, it means distributively, where it is in opp. with a pl. noun implied as in Mt. 18:35 where *hekastos* should not be "everyone" (KJV) but "each one."

1551. Ekdechomai; from *ek* (1537), out, and *dechomai* (1209), to receive. to watch for, expect (Jn. 5:3; I Cor. 16:11; Heb. 11:10); expect, wait for (Acts 17:16; I Cor. 11:33; I Pet. 3:20).

1553. Ekdēmeō; from *ek* (1537), from, or out of, and *dēmos* (1218), people. To go abroad, to part as the parting from the body as the earthly abode of the spirit (II Cor. 5:8) or to be away or absent from the body and present with the Lord.

1556. Ekdikeō; to revenge (Lk. 18:3,5; Rom. 12:19; Rev. 6:10; 19:2); to avenge or punish (II Cor. 10:6).

1557. Ekdikēsis; revenge or vengeance (Lk. 18:7,8; 21:22; Rom. 12:19; II Cor. 7:11); punishment (I Pet. 2:14).

1558. Ekdikos; the one outside of that which is lawful. Lawless, mischievous, Opp. *hosios* (3741), holy. In later Gr. it came to mean he who brings to pass what he believes to be his right, an avenger. Only in the N.T. in Rom. 13:4 and I Thess. 4:6 translated "avenger," in referring to the magistracy, it is the one who carries out the right to its issue.

1561. Ekdochē; from the verb *ekdechomai* (1551), to expect. A looking for, expectation (Heb. 10:27).

1573. Ekkakeō; or *egkakeō*. Denotes moral behavior and used in the sense of being in the midst of misfortune.

To be unfortunate, desperate (II Cor. 4:1). Usually translated "to lose heart" (Lk. 18:1; II Cor. 4:1,16; Gal. 6:9; Eph. 3:13; II Thess 3:13).

1577. Ekklēsia; originally seems to have been derived from *ekkaleō,* to call out. It was a common term for a congregation of the *ekklētoi,* those called out or assembled in the public affairs of a free state; the body of free citizens called together by a herald (*kērux,* 2783). The *ekklētoi,* the called people, constituted the *ekklēsia.* In the N.T. the word is applied to the congregation of the people of Israel (Acts 7:38). On the other hand, of the two terms used in the O.T., *sunagōgē* (4864) seems to have been used to designate the people from Israel in distinction from all other nations (Acts 13:43, cf. Mt. 4:23; 6:2; Js. 2:2; Rev. 2:9; 3:9). But when in Heb. 10:25 the gathering of the Christians is referred to, it is called not *sunagōgē* but *episunagōgē* (1997), with the prep. *epi* (1909), upon, translated "the assembling together." The Christian community was designated for the first time as *ekklēsia* to differentiate it from the Jewish community, *sunagōgē* (Acts 2:47 T.R.). The term *ekklēsia* denotes the N.T. community of the redeemed in its twofold aspect. All who were called by and to Christ in the fellowship of His salvation, the Church worldwide of all times, and only secondarily to an individual church (Mt. 16:18; Acts 2:44,47; 9:31; I Cor. 6:4; 10:32; 11:22; 12:28; 14:4,5,12; 15:9; Gal. 1:13; Phil. 3:6; Col. 1:18,24). Designated Church of God (I Cor. 10:32; 11:22; 15:9; Gal. 1:13; I Tim. 3:5,15); the body of Christ (Eph. 3:21; 5:23,24); exclusively the entire Church (Eph. 1:22; 3:10,21; 5:23-25,27,29,32; Heb. 12:23). The N.T. churches, however, are also confined to particular places (Rom. 16:5; I Cor. 1:2; 16:19; II Cor. 1:1; Col. 4:15; I Thess. 2:14; Phile. 2); to local single churches (Acts 8:1; 11:22; Rom. 16:1; I Thess. 1:1; II Thess. 1:1). *Ekklēsia* does not occur in Mark, Luke, John, II Timothy, Titus, I and II John or Jude.

1586. Eklegomai; mid. voice of *eklegō,* from *ek* (1537), out, and *legō* (3004), To intelligently speak. To choose, select, choose for oneself, not necessarily implying the rejection of what is not chosen but giving favor to the chosen subject, keeping in view a relation to be established between him and the object. It involves preference and choosing from among many. Cf. *epilegomai* (1951), to select; *haireomai* (138), to prefer; *hairetizō* (140), to choose.

1588. Eklektos; chosen, elected; related to *eklegomai* (1586), to choose.

1589. Eklogē; choice, election; related to *eklegomai* (1586), to choose.

1595. Hekousios; adj. voluntary; related to *hekōn;* (1635), willingly. Only in Phile. 14 in which it means willingly, uncompelled, gladly.

1596. Hekousiōs; adv., voluntarily, intentionally. Refers to the sins committed willingly, those done designedly and deliberately in the face of better knowledge (only in Heb. 10:26; I Pet. 5:2).

1598. Ekpeirazō; from the inten. *ek* (1537), out, and *peirazō* (3985), tempt. Try, prove, tempt, put to the test. Sinners are said to tempt God (Mt. 4:7; acts 5:9, *peirazō,* I Cor. 10:9), putting Him to the test, refusing to believe Him or His Word until He has manifested His power. When God is said to tempt (*peirazō*) man (Heb. 11:17, cf. Gen. 22:1; Ex. 15:25; Deut. 12:3,4), in no other sense can He do this (Js. 1:13) but to train in order to elevate him as a result of the self-knowledge which may be won through these temptations (*peirasmoi,* 3986), so that man may emerge from them holier, humbler, stronger than when he entered in (Js. 1:2,12). *Peirazō* is predominantly used to prove someone in order to show he is not approved of God but reprobate, in the hope that he will break down under the proof. Used for Satan's solicitations (Mt. 4:1; I Cor. 7:5; Rev. 2:10).

1603. Eklēroō; from the inten. *ek* (1537), and *plēroō;* 4137), to fulfill. To fulfill entirely (Acts 13:33).

1604. Eklērōsis; from *eklēroō* (1603), to fulfill. A fulfilling, an accomplishment (only in Acts 21:26).

1611. Ekstasis; from *existēmi* (1839); to remove out of its place or state. An ecstasy in which the mind is for a time carried, as it were, out of or beyond itself and lost. Great astonishment, amazement (Mk. 5:42; 16:8; Lk. 5:26; Acts 3:10); sacred ecstasy or rapture of the mind beyond itself when the use of the external senses are suspended and God reveals something in a peculiar manner (Acts 10;10; 11:5; 22:17). See *histēmi* (2476), to stand.

1618. Ektenēs; adj. meaning stretched out, continual, intense (Acts 12:5 T.R.; I Pet. 4:8). Verb: *ekteinō* (1614), to stretch out, extend, as the hand (Mt. 8:3; 12:13, etc.); to cast out, let down, as an anchor from a ship (Acts 27:30). Related words: *ektenōs* (1619), intensely, earnestly (I Pet. 1:22); *ekteneia* (1616), intenseness or continuance (Acts 26:7); *ektenesteron* (1617), the comparative neut. of *ektenēs* used adverbially, more intensely, earnestly (Lk. 22:44 T.R.).

1634. Ekpsuchō; from *ek* (1537), out, and *psuchō* (5594), to breathe. To expire (Acts 5:5,10; 12:23).

1635. Hekōn; willing, unconstrained, gladly. Usually stands opp. to violence or compulsion (only in Rom. 8:20; I Cor. 9:17).

1637. Elaion; oil, originally the express use of the oil of the olive (Lk. 7:46; 10:34). *Elaion agalliaseōs* (20), the oil of gladness, denotes the exhilarating influences of the Holy Spirit typified by oil (Heb. 1:9). As oil is used to give light, so the Holy Spirit enlightens men's hearts concerning their need of God in Jesus Christ. *Elaion* should be distinguished from *muron* (3464), ointment. Ointment has oil as its base to which spice or scent or other aromatic ingredients are added. There is evidence that in ancient times the men were rubbed with oil while women were rubbed with ointment. This distinction clarifies Lk. 7:45,46 in which our Lord is found in the house of the Pharisee telling him, "You did not anoint my head with oil (*elaion*) but she anointed my feet with perfume (*muron*)." Oil represented the common courtesy that would be expressed to a man. It was as if our Lord said to the Pharisee. "You withheld from me a cheap and ordinary courtesy (represented by oil) while this woman bestowed upon me costly and rare homage (represented by *muron*) which she did not put on my head, but on my feet." It was as if he was saying that the least honored part, the feet, received the highest honor, *muron.*

1650. Elegchos; conviction, only in Heb. 11:1; II Tim. 3:16. Implies not merely the charge on the basis of which one is convicted, but also the manifestation of the truth of that charge, the results to be reaped from that charge, and the acknowledgement, if not outwardly, yet inwardly, of its truth on the part of the accused. The verb *elegchō* (1651), to convict, reprove.

1651. Elegchō; to reprove with conviction upon the offender. Contr. *epitimaō* (2008), to rebuke without conviction on the part of the offender. The sub. *elegchos* (1650), conviction, implies not merely the charge, but the truth of the charge and very often also the acknowledgement, if not outwardly, yet inwardly, of its truth on the part of the accused (Heb. 11:1; II Tim. 3:16 T.R.). Contr. *aitia* (156), an accusation, true or false.

1652. Eleeinos; from *eleos* (1656), mercy. Worthy of pity, pitiable, full of misery. In the N.T. used only in I Cor. 15:19; Rev. 3:17.

1653. Eleeō; sometimes *eleaō,* to have pity, be compassionate. To show mercy (*eleos,* 1656), contr. grace, *charis* (5485). To show compassion, extend help for the consequence of sin as opp. to *skiērunomai* (4645), to be hardened.

1654. Eleēmosunē; mercifulness. The result of *eleos* (1656), mercy, which becomes part and parcel of the character of a person. *Eleēmosunē* is the expression of mercy to be contr. with *oiktirmos* (3628), which means more the expression of a sentiment rather than the outward manifestation of character. *Oiktos,* from *oikteirō* (3627) and the sub. *oiktirmos,* only mentally express pity for a situation or a person, while *eleos, eleeō,* mercy, to be merciful, and the sub. *eleēmosunē* refer to the actual helpful action of the pity. Therefore, *oiktirmos* (3628) refers only to the mental and emotional agony for a situation. This is the reason why *eleēmosunē* is consistently translated "alms or almsgiving" although it is derived from *eleos,* mercy, while *oiktirmos* is consistently translated "mercy" (Rom. 12:1; II Cor. 1:3; Phil. 2:1; Col. 3:12; Heb. 10:28). In truth, however, *eleēmosunē* is the result of being *eleēmōn* (1655), merciful, and it is the outward expression of *eleos,* active compassion of mercifulness while *oiktirmos,* although translated "mercy," really has nothing to do with *eleos,* mercy, in its outward manifestation. It is rather inner pity and compassion.

1655. Eleēmōn; compassionate, benevolently merciful, involving thought and action; from *eleos* (1656), mercy (Mt. 5:7; Heb. 2:17), while *oiktirmōn* (3629), involves compassion from sensation (Lk. 6:36; Js. 5:11). Both expressions are used of God in the manifestation of His pardoning and saving grace. *Oiktirmōn* is tenderly compassionate, one who grieves within for the condition and need of another. *Eleos,* from which this adj. is derived, gives expression to the love which is part and parcel of an individual and which finds its emphasis in the expression and the power of that love. The adj. *eleēmōn* occurs only in Mt. 5:7, "blessed are the merciful" ones, not merely those who express acts of mercifulness, but who have this attribute as a result of the indwelling of God within them, being *makarioi* (3107), blessed, because of Christ.

1656. Eleos; mercy. Special and immediate regard to the misery which is the consequence of sins. Contr. *charis* (5485), which is God's free grace and gift displayed in the forgiveness of sins as extended to men in their guilt. God's mercy, *eleos,* is extended for the alleviation of the consequences of sin. The lower creation is the object of God's mercy inasmuch as the burden of man's curse has redounded also upon it (Rom. 8:20-23). But man alone needs God's grace and is capable of receiving it. In God's mind and in the order of our salvation as conceived therein, God's mercy, His benevolent pity for the misery brought about by our sin, His pitying love, precedes His saving grace and continues to be actively demonstrated after the work of His saving grace. There may be certain consequences of our past sinfulness which grace may not eliminate. For these we need God's mercifulness. In Jn. 3:16, God loved in mercy and gave in grace, but God's manifestation of grace goes before His mercy. It is always grace and mercy that we find in the apostolic salutations for as we experience guilt for our sin and receive God's grace, we also need mercy to alleviate the consequences of our sins which may remain unaffected by grace. The guilt and power of sin must be removed through God's grace before the alleviation of the misery of sin can be experienced. The believer is to exercise mercifulness, for he can feel compassion for the misery of sin upon others, but he has no power to exercise grace since that is exclusively God's work. "Blessed are the merciful for they shall receive mercy." (Mt. 5:7). See Js. 2:12,13; I Jn. 4:17.

1657. Eleutheria; freedom, generosity, independence. Opp.: *douleia* (1397), slavery or the state of dependence or having to follow a prescribed course. Freedom is presented as a distinctive blessing of the economy of grace, which, in contrast with the O.T. economy, is represented as including independence of legal restrictions and rules of life (I Cor. 10:29; Gal. 2:4; 5:1,13). In contrast with the present subjection of the creature to the bondage of corruption, freedom represents the future state of the children of God (Rom. 8:21; see also vv. 20,23). The perfect law of freedom in Js. 1:25 is the freedom of generosity, especially in Js. 2:12,13, when the Judge shows his generosity in proportion to the mercifulness of the believers on earth.

1658. Eleutheros; connected with *eleusomai,* the fut. of *erchomai* (2064), I come. One capable of movement, the free one. In the absolute sense: free, unconstrained, unfettered, independent. One who is not dependent upon another, for the most part in a social and political sense. In a relative sense: free, separate from or independent of (Rom. 7:3; I Cor. 9:19). Opp.: *doulos* (1401), slave, whose will and power another directs (Jn. 8:32,33; I Cor. 7:21, 22; 12:13; Gal. 3:28; Eph. 6:8; Col. 3:11, etc.).

1659. Eleutheroō; to make free, liberate, the result of redemption (Jn. 8:32,36; Rom. 6:18;22; 8:2,21; Gal. 5:1).

1670. Helkuō; or *helkō,* to draw without necessarily the notion of force as in *surō* (4951). See Acts 8:3; 14:19; 17:6; Rev. 12:4. To drag, although it may be implied (Acts 16:19; 21:30; Js. 2:6). *Helkuō* is used of Jesus on the cross drawing by His love, not force (Jn. 6:44; 12:32). It is the drawing to a certain point as in Jn. 21:6,11 indicating the drawing of the net while *surō* is merely dragging after one. In Jn. 21:8 *helkuō* gives place to *surō* for nothing is intended there but the dragging of the net.

1677. Ellogeō; to charge, impute, take into account or consideration. Derived from *en,* in or into, and *logos,* an account (Rom. 5:13; Phile. 18).

1679. Elpizō; from *elpis* (1680), hope. To hope, expect with desire (Lk. 6:34; 23:8; 24:21, etc.); hope in the manner of trust, to confide; with prep. *en* (1722), in or with; *eis* (1519), unto; *epi* (1909), on (Jn. 5:45; I Cor. 15:19; II Cor. 1:10; Phil. 2:19, etc.). Without an obj.: to set one's hope upon something, i.e., the hope of future good fortune (I Tim. 6:17).

1680. Elpis; hope. Hope, desire of some good with expectation of obtaining it (Acts 16:19; Rom. 5:4; Tit. 1:2; I Jn. 3:3). The object of hope, the thing hoped for (Rom. 8:24; Heb. 6:18, cf. Gal. 5:5; Col. 1:5; Tit. 2:13; Heb. 7:19). The foundation, or ground of hope (Col. 1:27; I Tim. 1:1). Trust, confidence in someone when used with *eis* (1519), in or unto, following (I Pet. 1:21). Confidence, security (Acts 2:26).

1696. Emmenō; from *en* (1722), in, and *menō* (3306), to remain. To remain, persevere in (Acts 14:22; Gal. 3:10; Heb. 8:9); with topographical reference (Acts 28:30).

1722. En; in, with only the smooth breathing. Distinguished from *hen* with a rough breathing and the accute accent in which case *hen* is the neut. of *heis* (1520), the numeral one. The prep. *en* usually governs the dat., with a primary idea of rest in any place or thing, as also on, at, by. *En,* cf. with *eis* (1519), unto, and *ek* (1537), from, stands between the two, *eis* implying motion into, *en,* in or remaining in, and *ek,* indicating motion out of. Commonly used of place it means remaining, taking place within some definite place or limits, in, on, at, by, etc., as within the house. If spoken of elevated objects, a surface, etc., it may mean in, i.e., on, upon, as on a fig tree, literally, in it (Mk. 11:13), on the mountain *en tō orei* (Lk. 8:32). In a somewhat wider sense, implying simply contact, it means close proximity (Mt. 6:5), on the corners of the streets, near the corners of the streets so that they could be seen by people who passed the intersection at the corners. Used of a number or multitude, as indicating place, it means in, among, with, equivalent to *en mesō,* in the midst (Mt. 2:6; 11:11,21, etc.). When used of persons, by implication it means before, in the presence of (Mk. 8:38). When spoken of that by which one is surrounded, in which one is enveloped, etc., in, with (Mt. 16:27). When used of time, it means when, i.e., a definite point or period, in, during, on, at which anything takes place Mt. 2:1; 3:1; 8:13). When used of time it may also mean how long, i.e., a space or period within which anything takes place, in, within, as "in three days" (Mt. 27:40).

1735. Endechomai; from the prep. *en* (1722), in, upon, and *dechomai* (1209), to receive. As an impersonal verb *endechetai,* it is possible, it may be (Lk. 13:33).

1738. Endikos; fair, just. Syn. *dikaios* (1342), just. *Dikaios* characterizes the subject so far as he or it is one with *dikē* (1349), justice; while *endikos* characterizes the subject so far as he occupies the due relation to *dikē,* justice, or is within the confines of the law. Thus, in Heb. 2:2 it means a just or fair recompense. In Rom. 3:8 *endikon* presupposes that which has been decided justly. *Dikaiōs* is that which leads to the just sentence.

1740. Endoxaxō; used only in II Thess. 1:10,12 in the mid. voice, *endoxazomai,* from *en* (1722), in, and *dox-*

azō (1392), to glorify; in the pass. aor., to appear glorious, to appear and be recognized for all that He is.

1741. Endoxos; glorious, splendid. Neut. pl.: *endoxa* as in Lk. 13:17, works, miracles in which the *doxa* (1391), glory of God and of the Son of God, shone forth manifestly (Jn. 2:11; 11:40, cf. Lk. 7:25). See *sēmeia* (4592), signs; *dunameis* (1411), mighty works; *megaleia* (3167), great works; *paradoxa* (3861), strange works; *thaumasia* (2297), admirable works.

1743. Endunamoō; to strengthen, only in biblical and ecclesiastical Gr., from *en* (1722), in, and *dunamoō* (1412), to strengthen. To make strong, vigorous. Used in the pass., to be strengthened, become strong. In connection with Heb. 11:34 (T.R.), reference is appropriately made to Samson and Hezekiah. Elsewhere only metaphorically or spiritually and in the moral sphere (I Tim. 1:12; II Tim. 4:17; where it is used of the equipment with the power necessary to the office of an apostle). Used also in Acts 9:22; Rom. 4:20; Phil. 4:13; II Tim. 2:1.

1754. Energeō; to be active and energetic, to effect, prove oneself strong (Mt. 14:2; Mk. 6:14; I Cor. 12:6,11; Eph. 1:11,20; 2:2, etc.). In the pass, and mid. *energeomai*, to be effected, accomplished (II Cor. 1:6, cf. II Cor. 4:12). In Js. 5:16 it seems to denote the inspired prayer or the prayer of a righteous man wrought by the operation or energy of the Holy Spirit (cf. Rom. 8:26,27). To be in action, to be acting (II Thess. 2:7), the mid. with the meaning to prove oneself strong or to make oneself felt by energetic working is, except in Phil. 2:13, used of the Apostle Paul when he predicates it to other subjects (Rom. 7:5; II Cor. 1:6; 4:12; Gal. 5:6; Eph. 3:20; Col. 1:29; I Thess. 2:13; II Thess. 2:7).

1755. Energēma; the suffix *-ma* makes it the result or effect of *energeia* (1753), energy. In the N.T. used only in I Cor. 12:6,10 of the results of the energy of God in the believer translated "effects," but actually it is the results energized by God's grace.

1756. Energēs; from *energeia* (1753), energy. Refers to energy, engaged in work, capable of doing, active, powerful (I Cor. 16:9; Phile. 6; Heb. 4:12). In Class Gr. *energēs, energeia* (energy) and the verb *energeō* (1754), to be at work, seem to have been used almost exclusively as medical terms referring to medical treatment and the influence of medicine.

1758. Enechō; from *en* (1722), in or upon, and *echō* (2192), to have. To hold in, endure. With the dat.: to urge, press upon one (Lk. 11:53), to have a quarrel, to spite or have resentment against one, very close to hatred (Mk. 6:19). Deriv.: *enochos* (1777), to be held fast, bound, obliged; with a gen. following: bound, subject to, subject of (Heb. 2:15), guilty, deserving of and subject to punishment (Mt. 26:66; Mk. 3:29; 14:64); bound by sin or guilt, guilty of sin and deserving of punishment (I Cor. 11:27; Js. 2:10).

1764. Enistēmi; from *en* (1722), in, with, and *histēmi* (2476), to stand, be present, instant or at hand (Rom. 8:38; I Cor. 7:26; II Thess 2:2; II Tim. 3:1).

1771. Ennoia; from *en* (1722), in, and *nous* (3563), mind. Intention, purpose, mind (Heb. 4:12; I Pet. 4:1). See *noeō* (3539), to think; *nous* (3563), mind.

1772. Ennomos; from *en* (1722), in, and *nomos* (3551), law. What is within range of law based upon law and governed or determined.by law. Opp.: *paranomos*, not in accordance with the law, which word does not occur in the N.T.; the verb of which, *paranomeō* (3891), to act contrary to the law, occurs in Acts 23:3, and the sub. *paranomia* (3892), wrongdoing, in II Pet. 2:16. *Ennomos* refers to the church (Acts 19:39; I Cor. 9:21, cf. Gal. 6:2).

1778. Entalma; commandment but emphasizing the thing commanded, a commission (Mt. 15:9; Mk. 7:7; Col. 2:22). Verb: *entellomai* (1781), from *en* (1722), in, and *tellō*, to charge, command, emphasizing the thing commanded, versus *entolē* (1785), commandment, which stresses the authority of the one commanding.

1783. Enteuxis; intercession, prayer, address to God for oneself or others (I Tim. 2:1; 4:5) from the verb *entugchanō* (1793), to interpolate with familiarity and freedom of access, to interrupt another in speaking. Coming to God with boldness (*parrhēsia*, 3954).

1785. Entolē; commandment, whether of God or man. Related to *entellomai* (1781), from *en* (1722), in, upon, and *tellō*, to charge, command (Mt. 4:6; Mk. 13:34; Jn. 15:17; Acts 13:47). Syn.: *prostassō* (4367), charge. *Entolē* is the most common of the words meaning commandment. See *diatagma*, (1297), edict, decree; *diatagē* (1296), ordinance, disposition; *entalma* (1778), a religious commandment; *epitagē* (2003), commanding authority, order, command; *paraggelia* (3852), charge. It stresses the authority of the one commanding, while *entalma* (1778) stresses the thing commanded.

1791. Entropē; shame (I Cor. 6:5; 15:34), from the verb *entrepō* (1788), from *en* (1722), in, upon, and *trepō*, to turn, to cause to return upon oneself through shame (Mt. 21:37; Mk. 12:6; Lk. 18:2,4; 20:13; I Cor. 4:14; II Thess. 3:14; Tit. 2:8; Heb. 12:9). Implies something which neither *aidōs* (127), modesty, nor *aischunē* (152), shame, has. It conveys at least a hint of that shame of conduct resulting from an apparent change.

1804. Exaggellō; from *ex* (*ek*, 1537), out, and *aggellō*, to tell, declare. To tell out, declare abroad (I Pet. 2:9).

1805. Exagorazō; from *ex* (*ek*, 1537), out or from, and *agorazō* (59), to buy. To buy or redeem from as applied to our redemption by Christ from the curse and yoke of the law (Gal. 3:13; 4:5). To redeem as spoken of time (Eph. 5:16; Col. 4:5). The same phrase is used in the Gr. version of Dan. 2:8 meaning, "Ye are gaining or protracting time." Similarly to be understood in Eph. 5:16, "because the days are evil," or afflicting, abounding in troubles and persecutions. This sense of the expression is still more evident in Col. 4:5 as "redeeming the time" (KJV) by prudent and blameless conduct, gaining as much time and opportunity as possible in view of persecution and death. The word generally means to buy up, to buy all that is anywhere to be bought and not to allow the suitable moment to pass by unheeded but to make it one's own.

1809. Exaiteō; from *ex* (*ek*, 1537), out, and *aiteō* (154), to require or demand. To claim back, require something to be delivered up. In the mid. voice, *exaiteomai*, to claim back for oneself (Lk. 22:31).

1815. Exanastasis; from *ex* (*ek*, 1537), from, and *anastasis* (386), arising again. The resurrection from among the dead (Phil. 3:11). See *histēmi* (2476), to stand.

1817. Exanistēmi; related to *exanastasis* (1815), from *ex* (*ek*, 1537), out or from, and *anistēmi* (450), to rise up. To rise up from among others (Acts 15:5); trans., to raise up seed from the woman (Mk. 12:19; Lk. 20:28). See *histēmi* (2476), to stand.

1822. Exartizō; from the inten. *ex* (*ek*, 1537), from, and *artios* (739), complete. The verb *artizō*, to put in appropriate condition. To complete entirely, spoken of time (Acts 21:5); to furnish, or fit completely (II Tim. 3:17). Deriv.: *katartizō* (2675), to put a thing in its appropriate position, establish, set up.

1825. Exegeirō; from *ex* (*ek*, 1537), out, and *egeiro* (1453), to raise. To raise up (Rom. 9:17; I Cor. 6:14).

1834. Exēgeomai; from *ex* (*ek*, 1537), out, or emph. and *hēgeomai* (2233), to tell, lead forward. To bring out, declare thoroughly and particularly (Lk. 24:35; Jn. 1:18; Acts 10:8; 15:12, 14; 21:19). From this verb comes the English word "exegesis," the unfolding through teaching.

1839. Existēmi; or *existamai* from *ex* (*ek*, 1537), out, and *histēmi* (2476), to stand. To remove out of its place or state. In the N.T. applied only to the mind, meaning to be out of one's mind, to be beside oneself (II Cor. 5:13); in a neut. or pass. sense, to be transported beyond oneself with astonishment, to be amazed, astounded (Mt. 12:23; Mk. 2:12; 5:42); in an act. or trans. sense, to astonish (Lk. 24:22; Acts 8:9).

1843. Exomologeō; verb made up of three distinct words: *ex* (*ek*, 1537), out of, or *exō* (1854), out; *homou* (3674), together; and *logeō* or *legō* (3004), to reason, speak intelligently. To agree together with God or with one's conscience, and to externalize that which is inside oneself; to profess, express in agreement with, confess. N.T. meanings: To promise (Lk. 22:6). In the mid. voice, *exomologeomai*, to confess as one's own sins (Mt. 3:6; Mk. 1:5; Acts 19:18; Js. 5:16). To profess, confess, as the truth (Phil. 2:11). To confess, acknowledge as belonging to one (Rev. 3:5). With a dat. following, to give praise or glory to, glorify (Mt. 11:25; Lk. 10:21; Rom. 14:11; 15:9).

1849. Exousia; from *exesti* (1832), it is permissible, allowed. Permission, authority, right, liberty, power to do anything (Acts 26:12). As *exesti* denies the presence of a hindrance, it may be used either of the capability or the right to do a certain action. The words *exesti* and *exousia* combine the two ideas of right and might. As far as right, authority, or capability is concerned it involves ability, power, strength (*dunamis*, 1411) as in Mt. 9:8; 28:18. Syn.: *kratos* (2904), dominion (Jude 25) and *dunamis* (Lk. 4:36). *Exousia* denotes the executive power while *archē* (746), rule, represents the authority granting the power (Lk. 20:20). The combined meaning of right and might is indicated in Jn. 5:27; 17:2; 19:10,11. *Exousia* also means justified, rightly supra-ordinated power (Mt. 8:9; Rev. 18:1). In I Cor. 11:10, it is clear from the connection in vv. 6,7 that authority on the head is the same as covering on the head *kalumma* (2571), and the verb *katakaluptō* (2619), to cover wholly, and *akatakaluptos* (177), uncovered. In Tit. 3:1; Rom. 13:1-3 *exousia* in the pl. denotes not so much the magistracy of a court, but the powers which govern and is syn. with *archē* (746), authority; *thronos* (2362), throne; and *kuriotēs* (2963), dominion or government (I Cor. 15:24; Eph. 1:21; 3:10; 6:12; Col. 2:10,15; I Pet. 3:22). In the Pauline passages it probably refers to evil powers who oppose Christ (I Cor. 15:24; Eph. 6:12; Col. 2:15).

1860. Epaggelia; from *epi* (1909), upon, and *aggellō* (32), to report, declare. Primarily a legal term denoting a summons or promise undertaking to do or give something. Used only of the promises of God, except in Acts 23:21. The thing promised, a gift graciously given, not a pledge secured by negotiation (Lk. 24:49; Acts 2:33; Gal. 3:14; Eph. 1:13; Heb. 9:15, etc.). Deriv.: *epaggelma* (1862), a promise made with emphasis on the promise fulfilled, the result of the promise (II Pet. 1:4, 3:13).

1861. Epaggellō; from *epi* (1909), an inten., and *aggellō* (32), to tell, declare. To proclaim as public announcements or decrees; hence to announce a message, summons, or a promise. In the Class. Gr. used more in the sense of announcing a summons, issuing a command for something. In the N.T. used only in the mid. voice, *epaggellomai*, as a deponent verb meaning basically to announce oneself, offer oneself for a responsibility, offer one's services. Used primarily as "to promise" in Mk. 14:11; Acts 7:5; Rom. 4:21; II Pet. 2:19, etc., and "to profess" in I Tim. 2:10; 6:21 with the meaning of pretending. When used with this special meaning, the word and its deriv. refers to God's divine promise of spontaneous salvation. To render a service. (See Acts 1:4, *epaggelian*, 1860, the promise, and also Acts 7:5; Rom. 4:21; Tit. 1:2; Heb. 12:26; Js. 1:12; 2:5). Used absolutely meaning to give a promise (Gal. 3:19; Heb. 6:13; 10:23; 11:11). Deriv.: *proepaggellō*, in the N.T. only in the pass. form; *proepaggellomai* (4279), to proclaim beforehand, promise beforehand; *epaggelia* (1860), proclamation; *epaggelma* (1862), promise or assurance.

1862. Epaggelma; promise, assurance. The suffix *-ma* makes it the result of *epaggellō* (1861), to proclaim. Occurs only in II Pet. 1:4; 3:13. Deriv.: *epaggellō* (1861), to proclaim.

1864. Epagōnizomai; from *epi* (1909), for, and *agōnizomai* (75), to strive, contend earnestly. To fight for or in reference to something, with the dat. of that which gives the occasion (Jude 3).

1871. Epaiteō; from *epi* (1909), an inten., and *aiteō* (154), to ask, implore, claim. To beg, ask for alms (Lk. 16:3). The literal word for "beg." *Ptōchos* (4434), helplessly poor and depending upon others for his survival (Lk. 16:20) translated "poor man" only by inference. A helplessly poor person can survive only begging. *Epaitēs* is one who realizes his inferior position and need and asks as a beggar (the noun derived from *epaiteō*).

1876. Epanagkes; an adv. necessity or necessarily. Derived from *epi* (1909), upon, on account of, and *anagkē* (318), necessity. With the art. it assumes the meaning of the adj., *ta epanagkes*, things of necessity (Acts 15:28).

1879. Epanapauō; or in the pass. from, *epanapauomai*, from *epi* (1909), upon, and *anapauomai* (373), to rest. To rely, to rest, repose oneself upon (Rom. 2:17); to rest with the sense of remaining upon (Lk. 10:6).

1882. Epanorthōsis; from *epanorthoō*, to set right again, correct, from *epi* (1909), an inten., and *anorthoō* (461), to make right. Correction or amendment of what is wrong in a man's life. Occurs only in II Tim. 3:16. See *nouthesia* (3559), admonition; *paideia* (3809), instruction.

1896. Epeidon; from *epi* (1909), upon, and *horaō* (3708), second aor. imper., to look upon favorably (Lk. 1:25) or unfavorably (Acts 4:29).

1905. Eperōtaō; from the inten. *epi* (1909), and *erōtaō* (2065), to ask, inquire of, beg of. In the N.T., to interrogate, inquire of with the accus. *tina* (Mt. 12:10; 17:10; 27:11, etc.); used in the sense of to ask for, demand (Mt. 16:1). Deriv.: *eperōtēma* (1906), inquiry.

1910. Epibainō; from *epi* (1909), upon, to, and *bainō*, to go, go upon, mount, as upon a donkey (Mt. 21:5); to go on shipboard (Acts 21:2,6 T.R.; 27:2); to come to, enter into (Acts 20:18).

1919. Epigeios; from *epi* (1909), upon, and *gē* (1093), the earth. Earthly, being upon the earth (Phil. 2:10; 3:19). Earthly, belonging to the earth or wrought in men upon the earth (Jn. 3:12). Earthly, terrestrial, made of earth (I Cor. 15:40; II Cor. 5:1, cf. Job 4:19). Earthly, arising from the earth and attached to it (Js. 3:15). In the N.T. always opp. *epouranios* (2032), that which pertains to heaven (I Cor. 15:40). In II Cor. 5:1 contr. as an earthly house to the one not made by hands, eternal in the heavens (see also Jn. 3:12; Phil. 2:10). Occurs with a moral import, answering to the moral contr. between earth and heaven (Phil. 3:19, cf. v. 14; Col. 3:2; Js. 3:15, cf. v. 14,16,17).

1922. Epignōsis; *epi* (1909), an inten., and *gnōsis* (1108), knowledge, meaning clear and exact knowledge. It is more inten. than *gnōsis*, because it expresses a more thorough participation in the object of knowledge on the part of the knowing subject. In the N.T. it appears only in the Pauline writings and in Heb. 10:26; II Pet. 1:2,3,8; 2:20, and always refers to knowledge which very powerfully influences the form of the religious life, a knowledge laying claim to personal sympathy and exerting an influence upon the person. When used as an obj. (Eph. 1:17; 4:13; Col. 1:9,10; 2:2; I Tim. 2:4; II Tim. 2:25; 3:7; Tit. 1:1; Heb. 10:26; II Pet. 1:2,3), it evinces the relation of the person knowing to the object of his knowledge (II Pet. 1:8). It affects the religious blessings possessed by the subject (Eph. 1:17; II Pet. 1:2,3) and determines the manifestations of the religious life (II Pet. 2:20). When used without an obj. in a formal sense (Rom. 1:28; Col. 3:10), it gives a more precise definition as a knowledge which is determined by, or which regulates itself according to, etc., so that the difference mentioned in Col. 3:10 disappears. In Col. 2:2,23 meaning discernment in connection with the knowledge of possession of salvation which determines the moral conduct (see Phil. 1:9, the knowledge which enables one to avoid error, cf. Rom. 10:2; 11:33; II Pet. 1:5).

1930. Epidiorthoō; from *epi* (1909), besides, above, and *diorthoō*, to correct. See *diorthōsis* (1357), an amendment, restoration. Occurs only in Tit. 1:5 meaning to proceed in correcting or setting in order.

1932. Epieikeia; clemency or gentleness (Acts 24:4; II Cor. 10:1). Consideration springing from a consciousness of the danger inherent in the assertion of legal rights lest they should be pushed to moral wrongs. The virtue that rectifies and redresses the requisites of justice. The adj. *epieikēs* (1933) occurs in Phil. 4:5; I Tim. 3:3; Tit. 3:2; Js. 3:17; I Pet. 2:18. Contr. *ēpios* (2261), mild. See *anochē* (463), forbearance;

makrothumia (3115), longsuffering; *hupomonē* (5281), patience.

1937. Epithumeō; from *epi* (1909), in, and *thumos* (2372), the mind. To have the affections directed toward anything, desire, long after. To desire in a good sense (Mt. 13:17; Lk. 22:15; I Tim. 3:1; Heb. 6:11; I Pet. 1:12). To desire or long for as a matter of natural course (Lk. 15:16; 16:21; 17:22; Gal. 5:17). To desire in a bad sense as coveting and lusting after (Mt. 5:28; Rom. 7:7; 13:9; I Cor. 10:6; cf. Js. 4:2).

1939. Epithumia; the active and individual desire resulting from *pathos* (3806), the diseased condition of the soul. Occurs many times in the N.T. See *hormē* (3730), an impulse; *orexis* (3715), lust.

1941. Epikaleomai; from *epi* (1909), upon, and *kaleō* (2564), to surname. To be called by a person's name, declared to be dedicated to a person as to the Lord (Acts 15:17; Js. 2:7); to call a person by a name by charging him with an offense (Mt. 10:25); to call upon or invoke; in the mid. voice to call upon a person as a witness (II Cor. 1:23) or to appeal to an authority (Acts 25:25; etc.); to call upon by way of adoration, making use of the name of the Lord (Acts 2:21; Rom. 10:12-14; II Tim. 2:22).

1944. Epikataratos; from *epi* (1909), upon, and *kataratos,* cursed. Used as a verbal adj. from *epikataraomai,* to lay a curse on, or to connect it with anything. One on whom the curse rests or in whom it is realized. See Gal. 3:10 which corresponds with being under the curse and also v. 13.

1949. Epilambanomai; from *epi* (1909), upon, and the mid. form of *lambanō* (2983), to take. With a gen. or more rarely with an accus., to lay of, take, catch hold of (Mt. 14:31; Mk. 8:23; Lk. 9:47; 23:26; Acts 9:27; 16:19, cf. I Tim. 6:12,19). To lay hold of one's words (Lk. 20:20,26). With a gen., to assume, take upon one (Heb. 2:16). The angels mentioned must be the material ones, because the Apostle is speaking only of angels in chapter one and two. The text, therefore, means that when Christ came to redeem us, He did not assume a glorious, awful, and angelic appearance in fire and light or in clouds of thick darkness as He did at Sinai (Ex. 19:18), but that He took upon Himself human nature of the seed of Abraham (Gal. 3:16). For even though He was in the form of God. "(He) . . . did not regard equality with God a thing to be grasped, but emptied Himself, taking the form of a bond-servant, and being made in the likeness of men." (Phil. 2:6,7).

1951. Epilegomai; from *epi* (1909), to, moreover, and *legō* (3004), to say. To choose either in addition or in succession to another. Cf. *eklegomai* (1586), to select out of; *haireomai* (138), to choose in preference; and *hairetizō* (140), to elect in preference.

1957. Epimartureō; from *epi* (1909), inten., and *martureō* (3140), to witness. To testify emphatically, appear as a witness decidedly for anything. Used in I Pet. 5:12; also with the conj. *sun* (4862), together, as *sunepimartureō* (4901), to give additional testimony (Heb. 2:4).

1963. Epinoia; from *epinoeō,* to think upon, from *epi* (1909), upon, and *noeō* (3539), to think. A thought, a device (Acts 8:22). See 3563.

1967. Epiousios; from *epi* (1909), for or into, and *ousia,* being, substance. Occurs only in the Lord's Prayer in Mt. 6:11; Lk. 11:3. It was coined by the evangelist in analogy of *periousios* (4041), from *peri* (4012), beyond, and *ousia,* being or substance, meaning special or peculiar. The Greek church father, Chrysostom, explains the *epiousion arton* (740) as that bread which is needed for our daily support of life. It is that bread which is needful to the *ousia,* substance, of our being, that will sustain us.

1980. Episkeptomai; a deponent verb meaning that it has a mid. or pass. form but it is used in an act. sense. Basically it signifies to look at something, examine closely, inspect, observe. To look upon with mercy, favor, or regard. (Lk. 1:68; 7:16; Acts 15:14; Heb. 2:6); to look after, take care of, tend. Frequently used in the Class Gr. for taking care of or nursing the sick (Mt. 25:36,43; Js. 1:27); to look accurately or diligently (Acts 6:3); to visit, go, or come to see (Lk. 1:78; Acts 7:23, 15:36).

1983. Episkopeō; from *epi* (1909), upon, and *skopeō* (4648), to regard, give attention to. Therefore, the comp. verb means to look upon, observe, examine how it is concerning anything, look after. In the N.T. used in Heb. 12:15; I Pet. 5:2 as to the work of shepherding the flock, an exhortation to elders. See *episkopos* (1985), a bishop, overseer; *episkopē* (1984), the office of a bishop; *allotriepiskopos* (244), a bishop who looks inquisitively into other people's affairs; busybody.

1984. Episkopē; fem., a purely biblical and patristic word. The office of an overseer or bishop in Christ's Church (Acts 1:20; I Tim. 3:1). The word may be derived from *episkeō,* to visit, consider, examine, and provide covering for (Lk. 19:44; I Pet. 2:12). Deriv.: *episkopeō* (1983), to look after.

1985. Episkopos; watcher, overseer. In the N.T. the elders are called *episkopoi* (Acts 20:28), knowing the watchful care which those holding this office are to exercise (cf. I Pet. 5:2). In Phil. 1:1 the *episkopoi,* elsewhere called elders (*presbuteroi,* 4245), are mentioned along with the deacons (*diakonoi,* 1249), and in I Tim. 3:2, cf. v 8. See also Tit. 1:7, cf. v. 5. An elder denotes the dignity of the office, and *episkopos,* bishop or overseer, denotes its duties (cf. I Pet. 5:1,2; see I Pet. 2:25; 5:4). Deriv.: *episkopeō* (1983), to look after.

1994. Epistrephō; from *epi* (1909), to, and *strephō* (4762), to turn. To turn, turn to or towards (Mt. 9:22 T.R.; Mk. 5:30; 8:33; Acts 16:18). To return (Mt. 10:13; 12:44; 24:18; Lk. 2:20 T.R.). Trans., to convert, turn to God and holiness (Lk. 1:16,17; Js. 5:19,20). Intrans., to turn, to be thus converted or turned (Mt. 13:15; Lk. 22:32; Acts 3:19; 9:35; 14:15; 26:18,20). Opp. *apostrephō* (654), to turn away from. Deriv.: *strephō* (4762), to turn.

1995. Epistrophē; a turning oneself around, from *epistrephō* (1994), to turn about. Conversion occurs only in Acts 15:3.

1997. Episunagōgē; from *episunagō* (1996), to gather together, from *epi* (1909), to, and *sunagō* (4863), together, collect. A being gathered together (II Thess. 2:1, cf. I Thess. 4:17). An assembling together at one place (Heb. 10:25). In Heb. 10:25 it does not merely denote the worshipping assembly of the church from which some were likely to absent themselves, but the assembling for corporate worship, not as a solitary or occasional act, but as customary conduct. The verb *egkataleipō* (1459), to desert or leave stranded, to leave neglected or give up or abandon, which term is used of betrayers, is too strong an expression for the mere avoidance of assembling for religious worship (see Heb. 10:25; II Cor. 4:9; II Tim 4:10,16). It refers rather to the separating of oneself from the local Christian community because of the dread of persecution. The prep. *epi* (1909), to, must refer to Christ Himself as the One to which this assembly was attached and, therefore, it would have the meaning of not betraying one's attachment to Jesus Christ and other believers, not avoiding one's own personal responsibility as part of the body of Christ.

1999. Episustasis; from *episunistēmi,* which does not occur in the N.T. and which is made up of the inten. *epi* (1909), and *sunistēmi* (4921), from the conj. *sun,* together, and *histēmi* (2476), to stand. The intrans. verb, in a hostile sense to stand together against, rebel; and in a friendly sense, to stand by or together with, unite together. The sub. *episustasis,* uprising, disturbance, occurs only in a hostile sense in Acts 24:12 (T.R.) and in II Cor. 11:28 referring to all that the Apostle Paul had to encounter which was in opposition to him.

2003. Epitagē; authority, command imposed upon someone or something. Verb: *epitassō* (2004), to command.

2004. Epitassō; from *epi* (1909), over, and *tassō* (5021), to appoint or place appropriately, to appoint over, put in charge; put upon one as a duty, enjoin (Mk. 1:27; 6:27,39, etc.).

2005. Epiteleō; from *epi* (1909), inten., and *teleō* (5055), to finish, complete, perfect (Rom. 15:28; II Cor. 7:1;

8:6,11; Gal. 3:3; Phil. 1:6; Heb. 8:5); to perform, accomplish (Lk. 13:32 T.R.; Heb. 9:6, I Pet. 5:9). Deriv.: see *telos* (5056), end, goal.

2008. Epitimaō; rebuke, but not effectual to bring the offender to conviction, from *epi* (1909), upon, and *timaō* (5091), to evaluate. To punish, rebuke. One, however, may rebuke another without bringing the rebuke to a conviction of any fault on the offender's part, perhaps because there may have not been any fault or because there was fault but the rebuke was insufficient and ineffectual to bring the offender to acknowledge it. Therefore, *epitimaō* is merely the rebuke without any result on the person who is being rebuked. For instance, Peter began to rebuke, *epitimaō,* his Lord (Mt. 16:22; 19:13; Lk. 19:39), but without any effect upon the Lord. The same is true when the penitent robber rebuked (*epitimōn*) his fellow malefactor (Lk. 23:40; Mk. 9:25). Contr. the verb *elegchō* (1651), to reprove with conviction, which refers to effectual rebuke leading, if not to a confession, at least a conviction of sin (Jn. 8:46; 9:16, etc.).

2014. Epiphainō; from *epi* (1909), over, upon or to, and *phainō* (5316), to shine. Trans. to show forth, shine light upon, e.g., upon the surface. Usually used in the pass., to show oneself openly or before the people, to come forward, appear, with the idea of sudden or unexpected appearing. Often used of the gods and hence the significance of the N.T. *epiphaneia* (2015), appearing, the sub. of *epiphainō* (Gen. 35:7; Tit. 2:11; 3:4). The word is often used in Patristic Gr. of the incarnation of Christ. Intrans., to show oneself, e.g., of the break of day (Acts 27:20); to appear, shine, (Lk. 1:79).

2015. Epiphaneia; appearing, from the adj. *epiphanēs* (2016), glorious, illustrious; and the verb *epiphainō* (2014), to appear, from *epi* (1909), over, upon, to, and *phainō* (5316), to shine, shine over or upon, give light to. *Epiphainō* (2014), in the mid. voice in the pass. form, *epiphainomai,* to appear, to manifest oneself. *Epiphaneia* used only by Paul (II Thess. 2:8; I Tim. 6:14; II Tim. 1:10; 4:1,8; Tit. 2:13).

2026. Epoikodomeō; to build upon, from *epi* (1909), upon, and *oikodomeō* (3618), to build. To build upon, superstructure (I Cor. 3:10,12,14; Eph. 2:20); to build up, edify (Acts 20:32 T.R.; Col. 2:7; Jude 20).

2032. Epouranios; from *epi* (1909), upon, in, and *ouranos* (3772), heaven. What pertains to or is in heaven, chiefly of the pods. In Mt. 18:35 the Father, the heavenly One (*epouranios*). The meaning of this word is determined according to the various meanings of heaven. Deriv.: *ouranos* (3772), heaven.

2038. Ergazomai; from *ergon* (2041), to work, labor (Mt. 21:28; Lk. 13:14; Acts 18:3; I Cor. 4:12; I Thess. 2:9, etc.). To perform (Mt. 26:10; Jn. 3:21; 6:28; 9:4, etc.); practice (in a good sense as in Acts 10:35; Rom. 2:10; or evil as in Mt. 7:23; Rom. 13:10; Js. 2:9); be employed in or about (I Cor. 9:13; Rev. 18:17); procure, acquire by labor as the word is frequently applied in Class. Gr. (Mt. 25:16; Jn. 6:27); trade with the idea of gaining (Mt. 25:16).

2041. Ergon; (neut.) work, performance, the result or object of employment, making or working. Sometimes it means work as a single performance (Mt. 26:10; Mk. 14:6; Jn. 7:21; 10:32,33; I Cor. 5:2). Denotes any matter or thing, any object which one may have to do or attain (I Tim. 3:1; II Tim. 4:18); the general object or result of doing and working, an object or result whose attainment or realization is not accomplished by a single act but by accumulated labor and continued work (Rom. 14:20; I Cor. 3:14,15; 9:1); calling or occupation (Acts 14:26; Eph. 4:12; I Thess. 5:13; II Tim. 4:5); labor enjoined by and done for Christ as the spreading of His Gospel and the furthering of His Church; moral conduct (Rom. 2:6; I Cor. 3:13; I Pet. 1:17; etc.). It is especially used in the pl., *ta erga* (Mt. 11:2). In John used of Christ's miracles (Jn. 5:20,36; 7:3, etc.). In Jn. 6:28 "the works of God" must be understood as works such as what God does. On the other hand, v. 29, "the work of God" must be understood as what God requires to be done. The question in v. 28 implies misapprehension of Christ's words which He corrects in v. 29. In the Pauline Epistles those works to which Christians are called are designated not simply as *erga,* but *erga agatha* (18), benevolent works. In James, however, *erga* generally denotes acts in which the man proves his genuineness and his faith (Js. 2:14). Faith is proven by its works (Js. 2:22,25). Elsewhere in the N.T. *ta erga,* the works, usually denotes comprehensively what a man is and how he acts (Rom. 2:6; II Cor. 11:15; II Tim. 4:14; III Jn. 10; Rev. 2:2, 5,6,22,23; 3:1,2,8,15; 14:13; 16:11; 18:6; 20:12,13). The sum total of created things (Heb. 13:21).

2046. Ereō; sometimes *rheō* (4483), or *erō* (2036), to say, declare (Mt. 26:75; Lk. 2:24; 22:13; Jn. 4:18, etc.). To promise (Heb. 13:5); to call (Jn. 15:15). The verbal adj. *rhētos,* spoken, expressly named, and the adv. *rhētōs* (4490), expressly occurs especially in later writers denoting the literalness of the quotation as in I Tim. 4:1 in which case reference is made to the clearness of the statement cited indicating that there is no mystery about it. Contr. *arrhētos* (731), that which cannot or dare not be uttered, unknown, full of mystery (II Cor. 12:4).

2052. Eritheia; or *erithia,* derived from *erithos,* one who works for hire. *Eritheuō* means one who works for hire, usually in the mid. voice, used in a bad sense of those who seek only their own, who take bribes. *Eritheia* is not bribery (seeking after situations of honor), but susceptibility of being bribed or corrupted, selfishness, a self-willed positiveness. In such a state, one is vulnerable to be bribed. Generally speaking, the word means selfishness, self-willed (Phil. 1:16; 2:3). Other N.T. references: Rom. 2:8; II Cor. 12:20; Gal. 5:20; Js. 3:14,16.

2064. Erchomai; to come; opp. *hupagō* (5217), to go. It primarily and property denotes motion from one place to another. N.T. meanings: (1) To come (Mt. 2:2,8; 8:2 T.R.; Mk. 4:22; Lk. 19:18; Acts 19:6). To come to Christ is to believe on Him (Jn. 6:35; 7:37). (2) To go (Mt. 12:9; Lk. 2:44; Jn. 6:17; Acts 13:51; 28:14). (3) To come, referring to time (Lk. 22:7; Gal. 4:4). (4) Yet to come, the future (Mk. 10:30; Lk. 18:30; Jn. 16:13; I Thess. 1:10). *Ho erchomenos,* "the coming One" or "He who is coming" is a title of the Messiah (Mt. 11:3; Lk. 7:19). (5) To be coming, following, next, or instant (Acts 13:44; 18:21). (6) To happen (Jn. 18:4; Phil. 1:12; II Thess. 2:3; Rev. 3:10). (7) To be brought (Mk. 4:21). (8) To come back, return (Jn. 14:18,28). (9) To come to oneself meaning to recover one's sense or understanding (Lk. 15:17).

2065. Erōtaō; ask, with the accus. of a person, to ask him (Jn. 9:21; 16:30); ask for something in the accus. (Mt. 21:24; Mk. 4:10; Lk. 20:3; Jn. 16:23); with *peri* (4012) following, about, concerning (Lk. 9:45; Jn. 18:19); or with the direct question following (Lk. 19:31; Jn. 1:19,21; 5:12; 16:5); introduced by *legōn* (part. of 3004), saying, or the like (Mt. 16:13; Jn. 1:25; 9:2,19); with indirect question following (Jn. 9:15). A very distinct meaning of the verb *erōtaō* is to pray but in distinction from the verb *aiteō* (154). The first provides the most delicate and tender expression for prayer or request with the one asking and the one being asked on an equal level, such as the Lord Jesus asking of the Father. This is made very clear in Jn. 14:13,14 where the word *aiteō* is used in the case of us asking God as an inferior to a superior, leaving it up to Him to do that which pleases Him. In v. 16 when the Lord Jesus is praying to the Father or asking the Father, the verb *erōtaō* is used, also used in Jn. 17:9,15,20. Deriv.: *eperōtaō* (1905), to interrogate, to inquire of; *eperōtēma* (1906), inquiry.

2078. Eschatos; probably connected with *echō* (2192), primarily with reference to place, the extreme, most remote (Acts 1:8; 13:47). With reference to time, the last, generally that which concludes anything (Mt. 12:45; Lk. 11:26; II Pet. 2:20; Rev. 15:1). Denotes the time when the development of God's plan of salvation shall come to a close, the time of the final and decisive judgment (Heb. 1:2; I Pet. 1:20; II Pet. 3:3, etc.). Thus we have the *eschatē hēmera,* the last day (Jn. 6:39,40,44,54; 11:24; 12:48) which refers to the conclusive character of the final time. In the pl., the *eschatai hēmerai,* the last days (Acts 2:17) denote the time and era referred to in the context rather than the time previous to Christ's second advent in II Tim. 3:1; Js. 5:3,7. With reference to rank or order, generally in a bad sense (Lk. 14:9). Of persons, the lowest (Mk. 9:35; Jn. 8:9; I Cor. 4:9). Sometimes denoting a moral lowness (Mt. 19:30; 20:16; Mk. 10:31; Lk. 13:30).

2084. Heteroglōssos; from *heteros* (2087), another, but different, and *glōssa* (1100), a tongue, language. One of another tongue or language (I Cor. 14:21). See *heterodidaskaleō* (2085), to teach a different doctrine; *heterozugeō* (2086), to be yoked differently, unequally; *heterōs* (2088), differently, otherwise.

2085. Heterodidaskaleō; from *heteros* (2087), other but different, and *didaskalia* (1319), doctrine or teaching. To teach a doctrine different from one's own (I Tim. 1:3; 6:3). See *heteroglōssos* (2084), of a different language. Contr.: *allos* (243), numerically another or one coming after.

2086. Heterozugeō; from *heteros* (2087), another, different, and *zugos* (2218), a yoke. To draw the other side of a yoke that is different. To be yoked unequally, particularly in marriage (II Cor. 6:14). See *heteroglōssos* (2084), of a different language. Contr.: *allos* (243), numerically another or one coming after.

2087. Heteros; another, qualitatively (Mt. 6:24; 8:21; 11:3; 12:45; Lk. 7:41; 17:34,35, etc.). Contr. *allos* (243), another numerically or coming after. *Heteros* and *heteros* repeated, one and another different from each other (I Cor. 15:40). Different, altered (Lk. 9:29); other, foreign, strange (Acts 2:4). Deriv.: *heterōs* (2088), adv., otherwise differently; *heteroglōssos* (2084), one of another (different) tongue; *heterodidaskaleō* (2085), to teach a different doctrine than one's own; *heterozugeō* (2086), to be unequally yoked.

2088. Heterōs; adverb of *heteros* (2087), a different one, another of a different quality. Otherwise, differently (Phil. 3:15). See *heteroglōssos* (2084), of a different language. Contr.: *allos* (243), another numerically but not qualitatively different.

2095. Eu; an adv. meaning well, good. In commendations, "Well done!" as in Mt. 25:21; followed by a noun and an adj. as in v. 23, "Well done, servant, a good one." Used extensively as a prefix to comp. verbs with the meaning of well, good, and hence often used as an inten., e.g., *eulogeō* (2127), to eulogize, bless; *eukairia* (2120), good or appropriate opportunity.

2097. Euaggelizō; to evangelize, proclaim the good news, almost always concerning the Son of God as declared in the Gospel (exceptions: Lk. 1:19; I Thess. 3:6; Gal. 1:8). Used in the act. voice, to declare, proclaim (Rev. 10:7; 14:6); in the pass. voice, *euaggelizomai,* of matters to be proclaimed as glad tidings (Lk. 16:16; Gal. 1:11; I Pet. 1:25), of persons to whom the proclamation is made (Mt. 11:5; Lk. 7:22; Heb. 4:2,6; I Pet. 4:6); in the mid. voice especially of the message of salvation with a personal obj., either of the person preached (Acts 5:42; 11:20; Gal. 1:16), or with a prep., of the persons evangelized (Acts 8:4,12; 13:32; 15:35; I Cor. 15:1; II Cor. 11:7; Gal. 1:23; Eph. 2:17; 3:8). Deriv.: *euaggelion* (2098), Gospel; *euaggelistēs* (2099), evangelist; *proeuaggelizomai* (4283), announce good news beforehand (Gal. 3:8).

2098. Euaggelion; gospel. Originally a reward for good news, later becoming the Good News. The Good News of the kingdom of God and salvation through Christ (Mt. 4:23; 9:35; 24:14; 26:13; Mk. 1:1,14; 8:35; 10:29; 13:10; 14:9; 16:15; Acts 15:7; 20:24; I Pet. 4:17); in Paul's epistles used of the basic facts of the death, burial, and resurrection of Christ (I Cor. 15:1-3) and of the interpretation of these facts (Rom. 2:16; Gal. 1:7,11; 2:2).

2099. Euaggelistēs; evangelist, one who declares the Good News (Rom. 10:15). Used of Philip (Acts 21:8; see also 8:4,5,12,35,40); of evangelists along with apostles, prophets, pastors, and teachers (Eph. 4:11); of Timothy (II Tim. 4:5; Phil. 2:22; I Thess. 3:2). The number of evangelists must have been greater than the number suggested by N.T. references (II Cor. 8:18; Phil. 4:3; Col. 1:7; 4:12). Originally *euaggelistēs* denoted a function rather than an office, and there could have been little difference between an apostle and an evangelist, all the apostles being evangelists, but not all evangelists being apostles; they were subordinate to the apostles. In Eph. 4:11 the evangelists are mentioned only after the apostles. They were not just missionaries. A distinction must be made between the office of an evangelist and the work of one. An evangelist is also an author of the Gospel.

2100. Euaresteō; to be well pleasing (Heb. 11:5,6). The pass., to give satisfaction, make content, satisfy (Heb. 13:16). Syn.: *areskō* (700), to make one inclined to, content with.

2101. Euarestos; from *eu* (2095), well, and *arestos* (701), pleasing, agreeable. Well-pleasing, acceptable. Used with reference to God, that which God wills and recognizes (Rom. 12:1,2; Eph. 5:10; Phil. 4:18; Col. 3:20; Heb. 13:21); to persons (Rom. 14:18; II Cor. 5:9); to men and of slaves (Tit. 2:9).

2102. Euarestōs; the adv. of *euarestos* (2101), pleasing, well-pleasing (Heb. 12:28).

2106. Eudokeō; from *eu* (2095), well, good, and *dokeō* (1380), to think. To be well-pleased, to think it good, not merely an understanding of what is right and good as in *dokeō,* but stressing the willingness and freedom of an intention or resolve regarding what is good (Lk. 12:32; Rom. 15:26,27; I Cor. 1:21; Gal. 1:15; Col. 1:19; I Thess. 2:8). To take pleasure in (Mt. 3:17; 12:18; 17:5; I Cor. 10:5; II Cor. 12:10; II Thess. 2:12; Heb. 10:6,8,38; II Pet. 1:17). The noun *eudokia* (2107), good pleasure implying a gracious purpose, a good object with the idea of a resolution showing the willingness with which it is made.

2107. Eudokia; from *eudokeō* (2106), from *eu* (2095), well, good, and *dokeō* (1380), to think, appear. An appearing well or good will, good pleasure (Mt. 11:26; Lk. 10:21), a free will (willingness, pleasure) whose intent is something good; benevolence, gracious purpose. In this sense it is parallel to *eulogia* (2129), blessed. *Eudokia* never denotes good will in the moral sense, not even in II Thess. 1:11. It must be an outcome of *agathōsunē* (19), goodness, the virtue of beneficence even as works are the product of faith. Therefore, the *eudokia,* the good will of *agathōsunē,* denotes that which pleases, goodness, the tendency to the good.

2120. Eikairia; from *eu* (2095), well, good, and *kairos* (2540), time with the meaning of season or a suitable or convenient time. Contr. *chronos* (5550) which relates only to time as a measurement. The right and suitable time or convenient opportunity (Mt. 26:16; Lk. 22:6). Deriv.: *kairos* (2540), time or season; *eukairos* (2121), a convenient, seasonable time, suitable to the time, well-timed; *eukairōs* (2122), an adv., conveniently as far as time is concerned; *eukaireō* (2119), verb, to have convenient time or opportunity.

2124. Eulabeia; godly fear, (Heb. 5:7; 12:28); predominantly used in a good sense, though like *phobos* (5401), fear, it has not altogether escaped being employed in an evil sense. Verb: *eulabeomia* (2125), fearing (Acts 23:10 T.R.; Heb. 11:7); adj.: *eulabēs* (2126), devout (Lk. 2:25; Acts 2:5; 8:2). *Eulabeia* relates to the good and *deilia* (1167), cowardice, the bad with *phobos,* fear or reverence, as the mid. term.

2125. Eulabeomai; from *eulabēs* (2126). To be cautious, thoughtful, circumspect. To be afraid, to be moved or impressed with a natural or religious fear (Acts 23:10 T.R.; Heb. 11:7).

2126. Eulabēs; devout, from *eu* (2095), well, carefully, and *elabon,* second aor. of *lambanō* (2983), to take (Lk. 2:25; Acts 2:5; 8:2). One who takes anything carefully which is held out to him, cautious, circumspect, careful in the worship of god and in his duties toward God. The sub. *eulabeia* (2124), godly fear (Heb. 5:7; 12:28). The verb: *eulabeomai* (2125), to be impressed with a natural or religious fear (Acts 23:10 T.R.; Heb. 11:7). On all three occasions where *eulabēs* occurs it expresses Jewish piety: Lk. 2:25, Simeon; Acts 2:5, those Jews who came from distant places to keep the commanded feasts at Jerusalem; Acts 8:2, those who carry Stephen to his burial, devout Jews who had separated themselves in spirit from the murder of Stephen. *Eulabēs* is the scrupulous worshipper who is careful about changing or writing anything lest he offend.

2127. Eulogeō; to bless, or more accurately to speak well of, from *eu* (2095), good, well, and *legō* (3004), to speak. When the subject is God, His speaking is His action, for God's speaking and acting are the same thing. When God is said to bless us, eulogize us, speak well of us, He acts for our good as He sees what we need most and not what we desire. Therefore, He blesses by interfering. When we bless (eulogize) God we speak well of Him, we laud or praise Him because He deserves it (Lk. 1:64; 2:28; 24:53). When we bless (eulogize) one another, we express good wishes. When we bless as Christ did the loaves and fishes when He miraculously multiplied them (Mt. 14:19; Mk. 6:41; 8:7, Lk. 9:16), and as He did the memorial bread (Mt. 26:26; I Cor. 10:16), and the infants (Mk. 10:16 T.R.) we consecrate them to divine use. Distinguished from *makarizō* (3106), to pronounce blessed, and *makarios* (3107), blessed, indwelt by God.

2127a. Eulogēmenos; blessed, but more accurately one well spoken of and acted upon. From the verb *eulogeō* (2127), to speak well of, one upon whom God has acted or who has experienced the blessing (*eulogian* 2129) of God (Mt. 21:9; 23:39; 25:34; Mk. 11:9,10; Lk. 1:28,42; 13:35; 19:38; Jn. 12:13). The *eulogia* of God is God's action or interference in man's life to bring him to the desired relationship with Himself. Distinguished from *eulogētos* (2128), spoken only of God as inherently worthy to be well-spoken of by man, and from *makarios* (3107) which refers to a permanent state of being and not the particular effect of a certain cause such as *eulogēmenos* would imply. Related to *eulogētos*, worthy to be well-spoken of.

2128. Eulogētos; blessed, derived from *eulogeō* (2127), from *eu* (2095), good or well, and *lego* (3004), to speak; to bless or more accurately to speak well of, to eulogize. Therefore, *eulogētos* means one to be well spoken of, worthy of praise (Mk. 14:61; Lk. 1:68; Rom. 1:25; 9:5; Eph. 1:3; II Cor. 1:3; 11:31; I Pet. 1:3). This adj. ending in *-tos*, has the meaning of "worthy to be praised," and is in all instances ascribed to God. No one is inherently worthy of praise except God. On the other hand, the part. adj. *eulogēmenos* (fem.: *eulogēmenē*) refers to humans who have been well spoken of and acted upon by God. Distinguished from *makarios* (3107), the blessed one possessing God's nature because of Christ and hence fully satisfied as compared to the happy person favored by circumstances. The non-permanent state of happiness is not referred to in the N.T. In Mod. Gr. a happy person is called *eutuchēs*, from *eu*, good or well, and *tuchē*, luck, one who had good luck. The verb *tugchanō* (5177), to happen, to come upon or to be found in a certain state, related to *eutuchia*, happiness, occurs in Lk. 10:30 T.R.; 20:35; Acts 19:11; 24:2; 26:22; 27:3; 28:2; I Cor. 14:10; 15:37; II Tim. 2:10; Heb. 8:6; 11:35.

2129. Eulogia; blessing, from *eulogeō* (2127), to bless, as distinguished from *makarizō* (3106), to declare as indwelt by God and thereby fully satisfied (Lk. 1:48; Js. 5:11). Expressing good wishes, praise, eulogy to God (Rev. 5:12,13; 7:12); commendation to man (Rom. 16:18); the blessing, good word or action of God (Rom. 15:29; Eph. 1:3; Gal. 3:14; Heb. 6:7); consecration, beneficence (II Cor. 9:5,6). Contr. *makarismos*, blessedness or the action of becoming blessed (Rom. 4:6,9; Gal. 4:15).

2132. Eunoeō; to favor, from *eu* (2095), well, and *nous* (3563), mind. To be well affected or well-minded toward another, to be friends (Mt. 5:25). Noun: *eunoia* (2133), benevolence. See *noeō* (3539), to think.

2133. Eunoia; the noun of *eunoeō* (2132), favor. Benevolence, good will (I Cor. 7:3 T.R.; Eph. 6:7). See *noeō* (3539), to think; *nous* (3563), mind.

2141. Euporeō; to prosper, from *eu* (2095), well, *poreō*, to journey (Acts 11:29).

2144. Euprosdektos; from *eu* (2095), well, and *prosdektos*, accepted, acceptable, which in turn is from *prosdechomai* (4327), to receive, accept. Well-accepted, acceptable (Rom. 15:16,31; II Cor. 6:2; 8;12; I Pet. 2:5). A strong affirmation of acceptability, favorably accepted, predicated as *dektos* (1184), of the time of grace (Rom. 15:31; II Cor. 8:12).

2146. Euprosōpeō; from *eu* (2095), well, and *prosōpon* (4383), a face, appearance. Occurs only in Gal. 6:12, to make a fair appearance or show. It presents the contrast between appearance and reality.

2147. Heuriskō; to find, either with a previous search (Mt. 7:7,8) or without (Mt. 27:32). In the pass. voice of Enoch's disappearance (Heb. 11:5), of mountains (Rev. 16:20), of Babylon and its occupants (Rev. 18:21,22). Metaphorically, to find out by injury, or to learn, discover (Lk. 19:48; Jn. 18:38; 19:4,6; Acts 4:21; 13:28; Rom. 7:10; Gal. 2:17; I Pet. 1:7; Rev. 5:4). In the mid. voice. to find for oneself, gain, procure, obtain (Mt. 10:39; 11:29; Lk. 1:30; Acts 7:46; II Tim. 1:18). Deriv.: *aneuriskō* (429), to find out by search, discover, from *ana* (303), up, and *heurisko* as in Lk. 2:16 of the shepherds in searching for and finding Mary and Joseph and the Child; also in Acts 21:4 of Paul searching for and finding the disciples at Tyre.

2150. Eusebeia; from *eu* (2095), well, and *sebomai* (4576), to worship. Devotion, piety toward God (Acts 3:12; I Tim. 2:2; II Pet. 1:6,7). Godliness or the whole of true religion, so named because piety toward God is the foundation and principle part of it (Mt. 22:37,38; I Tim. 4:7,8; 6:6; Heb. 11:6). Related words: *eusebeō* (2151), verb, to exercise piety or true religion (I Tim. 5:4), to worship (Acts 17:23); *eusebēs* (2152), adj., devout, pious, religious, godly (Acts 10:2,7; 22:12; II Pet. 2:9); *eusebōs* (2153), adv., piously, religiously, godly (II Tim. 3:12; Tit. 2:12). All these words originally were often provided with more precise definitions to show to whom the worship was directed. It has the general sense of a pious life or a life which is morally good.

2151. Eusebeō; from *eu* (2095), well, and *sebomai* (4576), to worship, venerate. To be pious, to act as in the fear of God (Acts 17:23; I Tim. 5:4) in which instance it means to fulfill one's duty in reference to, etc., in the fear of God.

2152. Eusebēs; one who reverences aright; pious toward God, parents or others (Acts 10:2,7; 22:12; II Pet. 2:9). Noun: *eusebeia* (2150), godliness, well-directed, piety or worship, used to be called "worthship" (Acts 3:12; I Tim. 2:2; 3:16; 4:7,8; 6:3,5,6,11; II Tim. 3:5; Tit. 1:1; II Pet. 1:3,6,7; 3:11). Adv.: *eusebōs* (2153), in a godly manner (II Tim. 3:12; Tit. 2:12).

2160. Eutrapelia; from *eutrapelos*, which is derived from *eu* (2095), easily, and *etrapon*, second aor. of *trepō*, to turn. One who can easily or readily turn his speech for the purpose of exciting mirth or laughter. A wit, but since such persons are very apt to deviate into mischief-making and clownishness, an *eutrapelos* is sometimes used in a bad sense as a scoffer, a sneerer. In a bad sense it means obscene jesting to which Paul probably refers in Eph. 5:4, the only usage in the N.T.

2165. Euphrainō; from *eu* (2095), well, and *phrēn* (5424), mind. To rejoice, make joyful in mind. In a good and spiritual sense, to rejoice, make joyful (II Cor. 2:2); in the pass., *euphrainomai*, to be glad, joyful (Acts 2:26; Rom. 15:10; Gal. 4:27). To be joyful, merry, in a natural sense (Lk. 15:23,24,29,32) or in a bad sense (Acts 7:41; Lk. 12:19). In Lk. 16:19, refers to the rich man's luxurious and sumptous living. Noun: *euphrosunē* (2167), gladness.

2167. Euphrosunē; from the verb *euphrainō* (2165), to rejoice. Joy, joyfulness, gladness (Acts 2:28; 14:17).

2168. Eucharisteō; to be thankful, to thank. It does not occur in the Septuagint where instead we find *eulogeō* (2127), to speak well of or eulogize, which, in some respects, embraces a more narrow and in others a wider concept than *eucharisteō*. In the N.T. except in Rom. 16:4, used in a religious sense with or without reference to God. In Luke's and Paul's writings, it is followed by God in the dat., *tō Theō*. There is, however, a difference between *eucharisteō* with the dat. and *euchristeō* absolutely or by itself. With the dat. it always stands where there is implied a kindness done, a favor, a *charis* (5485), grace for an undeserved gift received where it appears as thanks for any good experience (Lk. 17:16; Acts 27:35; 28:15; Rom. 14:6; I Cor. 14:18; Col. 1:12; 3:17). The reason for thanks is designated by *huper* (5228), for the sake or on the part of (Rom. 1:8; I Cor. 10:30; Eph. 1:16; 5:20); by *peri* (4012), with respect to, with the gen. (I Cor. 1:4; I Thess. 1:2; II Thess. 1:3; 2:13; Phile. 4); by *epi* (1909), upon, with the dat. (I Cor. 1:4; Phil. 1:3); by *dia* (1223), through, with the accus. (Col. 1:3). Sometimes it is added on with *hoti* (3754), that (Lk. 18:11; Jn. 11:41; Rom. 1:8; I Cor. 1:14; I Thess. 2:13; Rev. 11:17); also used with *ti* (5100), something, and *tina,* someone, *eucharisteō, ti, tina,* thankfully to praise God for something or someone (Rom. 1:21; II Cor. 1:11). This construction, unknown in Class. Gr. has its origin from the absolute use of *eucharisteō*. Syn.: *eulogeō* (2127), to bless, praise, eulogize, meaning praising and glorifying God which is prompted only by God Himself and His revealed glory (Mt. 14:19; 26:26; Mk. 8:6,7; I Cor. 10:16). *Eucharisteō*, from *eu* (2095), good or well, and *charis* (5485), grace, basically means the good response or reception by that which does not deserve grace. Such a response expresses itself in thanksgiving and praise. Deriv.: *eucharistia* (2169), thankfulness, giving of thanks; *eucharistos* (2170), thankful, grateful, well-pleasing.

2169. Eucharistia; thanksgiving from *eu* (2095), well, and *charis* (5485), grace. To receive something as an expression of grace by someone and accept it as if one does not deserve it. From this is derived the verb *eucharisteō* (2168), to be thankful or to give thanks. *Eucharistia*, Eucharist, which is also the word used for Holy Communion, embodies the highest act of thanksgiving for the greatest benefit received from God, the sacrifice of Jesus. It is the grateful acknowledgement of past mercies as distinguished from the earnest seeking of the future.

2170. Eucharistos; from *eu* (2095), well, and *charis* (5485), grace or thanks. Thankful, grateful (Col. 3:15).

2173. Euchrēstos; from *eu* (2095), well, and *chrēstos* (5543), useful. Useful or very useful (II Tim. 2:21; 4:11; Phile. 11). See *chreia* (5532), need, and *chrēstotēs* (5544), kindness.

2192. Echō; have, to hold, hold on, to count, consider, regard, wear (Mt. 3:4; 22:12; Jn. 18:10); to be with child (Mk. 13:17; Rom. 9:10); to possess. Deriv.: *apechō* (568), to receive; *parechō* (3930), to grant; *antechomai* (472), to hold firmly to; *enechō* (1758), to have a grudge against; *katechō* (2722), to hold fast; *metechō* (3348), to share; *nounechōs* (3562), wisely; *anechomai* (430), to bear with; *schēma* (4976), fashion.

2198. Zaō; *zō,* to live, from *zeō* (2204), to be warm. Meanings: (1) To have life, be alive: naturally (Mt. 27:63; Lk. 2:36; Acts 17:28; 22:22, cf. Mk. 16:11; Lk. 24:23; Acts 1:3; Rev. 2:8); spiritually (Gal. 2:20); eternally (Lk. 10:28; Jn. 6:58); spiritually and eternally together (Jn. 6:57; Rom. 1:17; Gal. 3:12). The part. *zōn* is used in a trans. sense and means not only living, but causing to live, vivifying, quickening (Jn. 6:51, cf. vv. 33,50,54,58; Acts 7:38; I Pet. 1:3, cf. Jn. 4:10). The inf. *to,* the, *zēn,* live, with the neut. art. is used as a noun for life (Heb. 2:15). (2) Applied to God who has life independently from anyone and from whom all living beings derive their life and existence (Mt. 16:16; 26:63; Jn. 6:57,69 T.R.; I Thess. 1:9; I Tim. 4:10; 6:17 T.R., Heb. 10:31). (3) Joined with other words it denotes a particular manner of living (Rom. 6:10,11; Gal. 2:19; I Pet. 4:6). In I Pet. 2:24 to "live to righteousness" means to live in all righteousness and holiness as persons justified by the death of Christ (Rom. 6:2,4,6,7,11). To live in the Spirit (Gal. 5:25) is to live under His constant guidance and influence (cf. Rom. 8:15). To live to oneself (II Cor. 5:15) means to live according to one's own evil and corrupt inclinations. (4) To live as recovering from an illness (Jn. 4:50,51,53). The sub. *zōē* (2222), life, is animal life, bare existence as compared to *bios* (979), mental life with consciousness, from which our word "biography" is derived.

2200. Zestos; from *zeō* (2204), to be hot, used figuratively in Rev. 3:15,16.

2204. Zeō; to seethe, bubble, connected with *zēlos* (2205), zeal. The parrotry of the sound of boiling water. In the N.T. only applied spiritually (Acts 18:25; Rom. 12:11).

2205. Zēlos; zeal, used in a good sense (Jn. 2:17; Rom. 10:2; II Cor. 9:2) and, more often, in an evil sense (Acts 5:17; Rom. 13:13; Gal. 5:20; Js. 3:14). Unlike *phthonos* (5355), envy, when used in a good sense, it signifies the honorable emulation with the consequent imitation of that which presents itself to the mind's eye as excellent. According to Aristotle, *zēlos* grieves, not because another has the good, but that one does not have it and seeks to supply such deficiencies in himself. However, *zēlos* may degenerate into a desire to make war upon the good which it beholds in another, and thus to trouble that good and diminish it. This is why we find *zēlos* joined together with *eris* (2054), contention (Rom. 13:13; II Cor. 12:20; Gal. 5:20).

2219. Zumē; leaven, fermenting matter, most probably from *zeō* (2204), to heat, so called from heating, fermentation, the mass of dough (*phurama,* 5445) with which it is mixed (Mt. 13:33; Rom. 11:16; I Cor. 5:6,7). Everywhere in Scripture the word *zumē* represent evil, including Mt. 13:33; Lk. 13:21, if properly understood. The real significance of leaven is shown in I Cor. 5:7 as being destructive and typifies what does not belong originally and essentially to life, that by which it is disturbed and penetrated, namely, sin. It is sin penetrating daily life. First appears in the institution of the Passover (Ex. 12:15,19,20,34,39; 13:3,7) and in the ritual of sacrifices (Ex. 23:18; 34:25; Lev. 2:11; 6:17; 7:13; Deut. 16:3,4; Amos 4:5). All that disgraces the Christian and detracts from his holy newness of life is after the manner of leaven (I Cor. 5:6; Gal. 5:9). Represents false doctrine as opposed to that which has been received (Gal. 5:9). In Lk. 12:1, hypocrisy is named in the same connection with leaven which finds its embodiment in the doctrine covering such conduct. Deriv.: *zumoō* (2220), to leaven, mix with leaven; *azumos* (106), unleavened.

2220. Zumoō; to leaven, mix with leaven (*zumē,* 2219). In the act. voice, to permeate with leaven (I Cor. 5:6; Gal. 5:9). In the pass. voice used intrans., to be leavened or mixed with leaven and thus to ferment (Mt. 13:33; Lk. 13:21). Deriv.: *zumē* (2219), leaven.

2222. Zōe; life, referring to the principle of life in the spirit and soul. Distinguished from *bios* (979), physical life, livelihood, of which *zōē* is the nobler word, expressing all of the highest and best which Christ is (Jn. 14:6; I Jn. 1:2) and which He gives to the saints. The highest blessedness of the creature.

2225. Zōogoneō; from *zōos,* alive, and *gegona,* the perf. mid. of the obsolete *genō,* to form, make. To give birth to living creatures. To vivify, make alive. In the N.T. occurs only in I Tim. 6:13 UBS; Acts 7:19; Lk. 17:33, to retain life.

2226. Zōon; derived from *zaō* (2198), to live. A living creature, an animal (Heb. 13:11; II Pet. 2:12; Rev. 4:6,7, etc.). Sometimes used syn. with *thērion* (2342), a wild beast. However, there is a distinction between the two. Although in the Class. Gr. *zōon* is also designated as a thinking animal to indicate that man also is such, it is not so in the N.T. The fact that man lives does not make him a *zōon,* an animal. He is a living creature but not an animal in the sense of nonthinking animals. Similarly, in spite of the fact that God is living. He is never called a *zōon,* but He is called life itself as is also Jesus Christ (Jn. 1:4; I Jn. 1:2, *zōē,* 2222), the source of life. *Thērion* gives predominance to the lower animal life and is associated with a hellish symbolism.

2227. Zōopoieō; from *zōos,* alive, and *poieō* (4160), to make. Make alive, vivify (Jn. 6:63; I Cor. 15:45; II Cor. 3:6). Used primarily in the N.T. of raising the dead to life (Jn. 5:21; Rom. 4:17; 8:11; I Cor. 15:22,36; I Pet. 3:18). Generally used in reference to salvation, answering to the Pauline connection between righteousness and life (Gal. 3:21).

2233. Hēgeomai; primarily signifies to lead on or forward, from *agō* (71); to bring, lead. To be the chief or principal (Acts 14:12); to preside, govern, rule, whether in a temporal sense (Acts 7:10) or in a spiritual one (Heb. 13:7,17,24, cf. Mt. 2:6; Lk. 22:26). To think, esteem, reckon (Acts 26:2; II Cor. 9:5; Phil. 2:3; I Thess. 5:13, etc.). Deriv.: *exēgeomai* (1834), to bring forth, thoroughly explain; *proēgeomai* (4285), from *pro* (4253), before, and *hēgeomai,* to think. Esteem another before, to prefer or go before another (Rom. 12:10).

2250. Hēmera; the day as distinguished from night, quantitatively as a division of time. Sometimes used, however, of a longer space of time. N.T. meanings: (1) Daytime as distinguished from nighttime (Mt. 20:6,12; Jn. 11:9; Acts 12:18; 26:13; 27:29,33,39). A day in the Eastern way of thinking may be any part of a twenty-four-hour period or the entire twenty-four-hour period. Thus the day in the Eastern calculation of time is considered as a night and a day (*nuchthēmeron,* a unit consisting of a night and a day). Therefore, the three days and three nights of Mt. 12:40 in which Jesus was in the grave should be considered as Friday (being part of the first day), all of Saturday (being the second day), and part of Sunday (being the third day). (2) Figuratively, time for work or labor (Jn. 9:4, cf. Mt. 20:6,12). (3) The day of eternal life, as opp. to the spiritual darkness of our present state (Rom. 13:12). (4) A day including both the day and night, *nuchthēmeron* (Mt. 15:32; 17:1; Acts 28:7,12,14; II Cor. 4:16). (5) In the pl., days means time measured by periods of time as "in those days" (Mt. 3:1, meaning at that time, Lk. 5:35; 17:22; 23:29, etc.). (6) In the pl., days may mean time of life or office (Mt. 2:1; 23:30, Lk. 1:5; 4:25; 17:28). (7) *Ekeinē,* that, *hē,* the, *hēmera,* day, "that day" means that great Day of the Lord, the day of judgment (Mt. 7:22; Lk. 10:12; II Thess. 1:10; II Tim. 1:18; 4:8), also the expressions that day, the last day, the Day of the Lord, the day of judgment all refer to the same thing. (8) In I Cor. 4:3 is man's day which speaks of the opposition to the coming of the Lord. (9) The Day of Christ or of our Lord Jesus (I Cor. 5:5; II Cor. 1:14; Phil. 1:6,10; 2:16; II Thess. 2:2) refers to the day when the Lord Jesus Christ will appear and take His Church unto Himself as described in I Thess. 4:14-17.

2261. Epios; from *hepō,* to follow, as denoting one who readily follows the will of another and is ready to do what he desires or wants (I Thess. 2:7; II Tim. 2:24). Placid, mild, easy, compliant. Contr. *praos* (4235), meek, and *epieikēs* (1933), gentle, tolerant.

2270. Hēsuchazō; to rest from labor (Lk. 23:56); to be quiet, live quietly (I Thess. 4:11); to be silent, quiet from speaking (Lk. 14:4); to acquiesce (Acts 11:18; 21:14). Deriv.: *hēsuchia* (2271), quietness, quiet (II Thess. 3:12); silence, quietness from speaking (Acts 22:2; I Tim. 2:11,12); *hēsuchios* (2272), quiet, peaceable (I Tim. 2:2, I Pet. 3:4).

2281. Thalassa; from *tarassō* (5015), agitate. Some consider it as the sea as contr. with the land (Gen. 1:10; Mt. 23:15; Acts 4:24) or perhaps more strictly as contr. with the shore. Another Gr. word, *pelagos* (3989), is also translated as "sea," but there is a difference. The latter word occurring in Mt. 18:6; Acts 27:5 represents the vast uninterrupted level and expanse of open water.

2288. Thanatos; death. N.T. meanings: (1) Natural or temporal death (Mt. 10:21; 16:28; Lk. 2:26, etc.). In I Jn. 5:16, "a sin leading to death" is a sin which, should a believer continue to engage in, may lead him to premature physical death (Eccl. 7:17; Jer. 14:11,12; 34:18-20; Acts 5:1-11; I Cor. 11:30). (2) Spiritual death (Jn. 5:24; I Jn. 3:14). As spiritual life consists in constant communication with the divine Light and Spirit, who are life; so spiritual death is the separation from their blessed influence. (3) Eternal death (Rom. 6:21,23; Js. 5:20; I Jn. 5:16,17) which in respect to the natural and temporal is called the second death (Rev. 2:11; 20:6,14) and implies everlasting punishment (Rev. 21:8). (4) Plague or pestilence (Ex. 5:3; 9:3,15; Mt. 24:7). *Thanatos* is joined with *limos* (3042), famine (Rev. 6:8, cf. Ezek. 14:21).

2297. Thaumasios; wonderful things, miracles, as provoking admiration and astonishment (Mt. 21:15). See *thaumazō* (2296) (Mt. 8:27; 9:8 T.R., 33; 15:31; Mk. 5:20; Acts 3:12). To the Gr. church fathers and in Mod. Gr. miracles are known as *thaumata* (pl.), a word not used with such meaning in the N.T., although it occurs as *thauma* (2295), astonishment (sing.) in Rev. 17:6. This word was used prior to this period by magicians and impostors of various kinds. See *sēmeion* (4592), sign; *dunamis* (1411), power, mighty work; *megaleios* (3167), great work; *endoxos* (1741), glorious, glorious work; *paradoxos* (3861), strange, astonishing work; *teras* (5059), frightful, terrifying work.

2300. Theaomai; to behold, view attentively, contemplate, indicating the sense of a wondering regard involving a careful and deliberate vision which interprets its object. It involves more than merely seeing (Mt. 6:1; 11:7; 22:11; 23:5; Mk. 16:11,14; Lk. 5:27; 7:24; 23:55; Jn. 1:14,32,38; 4:35; 6:5; 8:10; 11:45; Acts 1:11; 8:18; 21:27; 22:9; Rom. 15:24, I Jn. 1:1; 4:12,14).

2304. Theios; an adj. meaning divine, what is God's especially and what proceeds from Him. Distinguished from *Theos* (2316), God, as indeed *Theiotēs* (2305), divinity, is distinguished from *Theotēs* (2320), Godhead. *Theios* denotes an attribute of God and not the character of God in its totality. See Acts 17:29; II Pet. 1:3,4. In Class. Gr. the adj. denoted the power of God as the noun *Theiotēs* definitely does in Rom. 1:20.

2305. Theiotēs; divinity, only in Rom. 1:20. Syn. *theios* (2304), divine; *dunamis* (1411), power, in II Pet. 1:3, a concept derived from His works. Distinguished from *theotēs* (2320), deity, the personality of God or Godhead, a concept not logically derived at by observing His might, but directly revealed (Col. 2:9).

2307. Thelēma; from the verb *thelō* (2309), to will. The suffix *-ma* indicates that it is the result of the will. Will, not to be conceived as demand, but as an expression or inclination of pleasure towards that which is liked, that which pleases and creates joy. When it denotes God's will, it signifies His gracious disposition toward something. Used to designate what God Himself does of His own good pleasure. It does not occur in Phil., II Thess., I Tim., Tit., Phile., Js., II Jn. or III Jn. As a rule, N.T. usage refers to the will of God. Used only in Lk. 23:25; Jn. 1:13; I Cor. 7:37; Eph. 2:3; II Tim. 2:26; II Pet. 1:21. Nowhere, however, is it a name for the commands of God as such, whether in any particular case or in general. Rather it designates what occurs or what should be done by others as the object of God's good pleasure in the carrying out of the divine purpose or the accomplishment of what He would have, that which He purposes or has purposed, what He regards or does as good (Mt. 18:14; 26:42; Lk. 22:42; Acts 21:14; I Pet. 3:17; 4:19). Paul uses it especially with reference to God's saving purpose (Eph. 1:5,9,11), and in particular to the tracing back of his apostleship to the will of God (I Cor. 1:1; II Cor. 1:1; Gal. 1:4; Col. 1:1; II Tim. 1:1) as bestowed upon him not only by the sovereign, but by the gracious will of God (Gal. 1:15; Eph. 3:7,8; Tit. 1:3). Also used of the carrying out of God's will by others with reference to what God has ordained (Acts 13:22), of the Father's will in redemption as carried out by Christ (Jn. 4:34; 5:30; 6:38-40; 9:31, cf. Heb. 10:7,9,10), and God's will or good pleasure to be carried out by us (Rom. 12:2) with an implied reference to God's judgment (Rom. 2:18; Eph. 5:17; 6:6; Col. 1:9; 4:12, etc.). The pl. occurs only in Acts 13:22; Eph. 2:3.

2309. Thelō; to will. There is a distinction between *thelō* and *boulomai* (1014), to design, to decree. *Thelō* indicates not only willing something, but also pressing on to action. *Boulomai* is deciding, but not pressing on to execute that which is decided. When the sub.

boulēma (1013) is used, not like *thelēma* (2307), it denotes the substance of the law and also the intention underlying the law but not the execution thereof. Thus *boulē* (1012) is counsel, decision, conclusion. In Mod. Gr. this is the name given to a parliament which makes the laws and provides the intent of the law but not the execution of it. *Thelēma* (2307), on the other hand, is resolve and denotes the will of God which must be done. However, *boulē Theou,* the will of God, refers only to God's self-affirmation in His own acting. *Boulomai,* therefore, is not in agreement with the meaning *eudokeō* (2106), to be possessed of good will. *Boulomai* and *thelō* differ as to degree and resolve, and *thelō* in the N.T. denotes elective inclination, love, occurring frequently in biblical Gr. with the accus. of the obj., which is rare with *boulomai.* The refusal is usually rendered by *ou,* not, *thelō,* will, and rarely by *ou boulomai. Thelō* may mean to be about to, but never *boulomai.* This latter word demonstrates resolve, but not necessarily action. Nevertheless, *boulomai* may be used for *thelō,* and *thelō,* though far more rarely, for *boulomai. Thelō,* therefore, means to will as the equivalent of to purpose, to be decided upon seeing one's desire to its execution. It may stand side-by-side with *poieō* (4160), to do, to make (Rom. 7:21; Jn. 8:44; II Cor. 8:11); with *energeō* (1754), to effect (Mt. 8:2; Phil. 2:13). The neg. *ou,* not, and *thelō* means not to will, refuse, oppose (Mt. 18:30; 21:29; 23:37). *Thelō* also means to be inclined (Acts 26:5); to have a mind to, to wish or desire (Jn. 3:8); and with the neg. *ou,* not to be inclined, often to intend not (Mt. 1:19). Used with the inf. of the subject matter following (Mt. 14:5; 26:15, etc.). Used in the sense of to endeavor, desire; rarely by itself as in Mt. 5:42; 12:38; 15:28; 19:17; 20:26,27, etc. It may stand for what one chooses, likes, is inclined to (Mt. 9:13; 12:7; 27:43; Heb. 10:5,8). Deriv.: *thelēma* (2307), will as an expression or inclination of pleasure, passion (Jn. 1:13; I Cor. 7:37; Eph. 2:3); *thelēsis* (2308), the act of the will, pleasure, desire.

2315. Theopneustos; from *Theos,* God, and *pepneustai,* from *pneō* (4154), to breathe. Prompted by God, divinely inspired, occurs only in II Tim. 3:16 in the N.T. In Class. Gr. opp. to *phusikos,* natural, as opp. to divine. In reality the formation of the word should be traced rather to *empneō* (1709), inspire (Acts 9:1), urged by the *pneuma* (4151), spirit, whether one's own, or God's or the spirit world, instead of *pneō,* the root word meaning to breathe or to blow. The simple verb *pneō* is never used of divine action. Neither *empneō* nor *pneō* is used in II Pet. 1:21 but the expression "by the Spirit, the Holy one, being driven or carried (*pheromenoi,* 5342)" referring to those who wrote God's utterances or prophecies.

2316. Theos; God. Originally used by the heathen and adopted in the N.T. as the name of the true God. The most probable deriv. is from the verb *theō,* to place (see *tithēmi,* 5087). The heathen thought the gods were disposers (*thetēres,* placers) and formers of all things. The ancient Greeks used the word both in the sing. and the pl. In the pl., they intimated their belief that elements such as the heavens had their own "disposer or placer," e.g., the god of money called mammon (Mt. 6:24; Lk. 16:9,13). The heavens were the grand objects of divine worship throughout the heathen world as is apparent from the names attributed to the gods by the ancient Greeks. The Scriptures also attest to this (Deut. 4:19; 17:3; II Kgs. 17:16; 23:4,5; Job 31:26,27; Jer. 8:2; 19:13; Zeph. 1:5; Acts 7:42,43). The only gods the Greeks worshipped were the various parts of created nature and especially the heavens, or some demons or intelligences which they supposed resided in them. Orpheus, a legendary poet and musician of ancient Thrace, for instance, had the power of charming animate and inanimate objects with his lyre, and calls almost all the gods of the Greeks demons. The Septuagint constantly translated the Heb. pl. name *Elohim* when used for the true God by the sing. *Theos.* God, never by the pl. *theoi,* gods. The reason for this was that at the time the Septuagint translation was made, Greek idoltary was the prevailing superstition, especially in Egypt under the Ptolemies. Their gods were regarded as demons, i.e., intelligent beings totally separate and distinct from each other. If the translators rendered the name of the true God by the pl. *theoi,* they would have given the heathen under Greek culture an idea of God which was inconsistent with the unity of the divine essence and conformable to their own polytheistic notions. However, by translating the Hebrew *gods* as God, they inculcated the unity of God and at the same time did not deny a plurality of persons in the divine nature. In the N.T. and the Septuagint *Theos,* God, generally answers to the O.T. pl. name *Elohim* and so denotes God, the Trinity. See Mt. 4:7, cf. Deut. 6:16 in the Heb. and the Septuagint; Mt. 4:10, cf. Deut. 6:3; Mt 22:32, cf. Ex. 3:6; Mt. 22:37, cf. Deut. 6:5; Mk. 1:14,15, cf. Dan. 2:44; Mk. 12:29, cf. Deut. 6:4,5; Jn. 1:12, cf. Gen. 6:2; Acts 4:24, cf. Gen. 1:1; Eccl. 12:1 in the Heb.; Acts 10:34, cf. Deut. 10:17. It is applied personally, but very rarely to the Father (Jn. 5:18; 13:3; 16:27,30, cf. vv. 28,29; II Cor. 13:14; Phil. 2:6); to the Son (Mt. 1:23; Jn. 1:1; 20:28; Rom. 9:5; I Tim. 3:16 T.R.; Tit. 2:13; II Pet. 1:1; I Jn. 5:20; etc.); to the Holy Spirit (Lk. 1:35; Acts 5:3,4, cf. I Cor. 3:16,17; 6:19; II Cor. 6:16; also cf. Acts 4:24,25 with Acts 1:16; II Pet 1:21). Also denotes the heathen gods or idols (Acts 14:11; I Cor. 8:5); magistrates (Jn. 10:34,35); by false application to Satan (II Cor. 4:4); to the belly which some people make their god or in which they place their supreme happiness (Phil. 3:19). Many times *Theos* occurs with the definite art. *ho,* but it is not so rendered in the translation because in English we never refer to God as *the God* except if He is designated as belonging to someone specifically such as the God of Abraham, etc. (Mt. 22:32). In many instances when the definite art. *ho* occurs before *Theos,* God, particular reference is made to God the Father, making the distinction in the personalities of the Trinity evident, e.g., in Jn. 1:1b, "And the Word had been (*ēn*) toward (*pros,* 4314) the god, *ton Theon.*" The definite art. here designates "the Father." The Word (*Logos,* 3056) is Jesus Christ in His pre-incarnate existence as one personality of the Trinity and "the God" was God the Father. In the third statement of Jn. 1:1, "and the Word was God," the word "God," *Theos* is without the art. and is used as a predicate, stating the Word was "God" equal in meaning to the adj. "divine." Therefore, *Theos,* not having the definite art. before it cannot be the subj. Only if it did have the definite art. before, it, could it be interchangeable with the subj. *ho Logos,* the Word. Nor could the indefinite art. "a" be added in the English making it "and the Word was a God." This translation would make the verse declare that the Bible teaches polytheism. If so, then the statement in Jn. 1:18 which in Gr. begins with *Theon,* God, without the art. should also be translated, "A God, no man hath seen at any time." Then the question would be; which of the many gods?. In Jn. 1:18 the word *Theos*is used without the art. to indicate not the God as He appeared in a limited spacial environment as in the various theophanies to Moses and others, and finally to mankind in the physical person of the Lord Jesus, but God in His eternity, infinity, totality, and in His essential essence as Spirit. The Creator being larger than any of His creatures cannot possibly be seen in His totality (see I Tim. 6:16). In the grammatical notations the designation *"an"* meaning anarthrous, or without the art. shows when a certain word, and particularly *Theos,* occurs in Gr. without the definite article. When the definite article does occur before a Gr. word, such as *Theos,* God, the abbreviation "art.," is placed in the upper left-hand side of the word to show the article is in the Greek.

2318. Theosebēs; godly, devout; translated "God-fearing" (Jn. 9:31). The noun *theosebeia* (2317) in I Tim. 2:10 translated "godliness" from the noun God, *Theos* (2316), and *sebomai* (4576), worship, venerate (Mt. 15:9; Mk. 7:7; Acts 16:14; 18:7,13; 19:27).

2319. Theostugēs; from *Theos* (2316), God, and *stugeō,* to hate, abhor. Occurs only in Rom. 1:30, translated "haters of God" and could be held syn. with *atheos* (112), destitute of God. The ancient Greeks used to call *theostugēs* someone who turned against God, accusing Him and also His providence when any heavy calamity befell that person.

2320. Theotēs; deity, Godhead as directly revealed; God's personality (Col. 2:9) as distinguished from *theiotēs* (2305) in Rom. 1:20, divinity or divine power and majesty, a concept arrived at by observing God's mighty works.

2323. Therapeuō; heal, but primarily signifies to serve as *therapōn* (2324), an attendant. Noun: *therapeia* (2322), caring, attention (Lk. 12:42), medical service or therapy (Lk. 9:11; Rev. 22:2), also household servants (Mt. 24:45 T.R. [*oiketeia* UBS]; Lk. 12:42). Distinguished from other verbs: *iaomai* (2390), to cure diseases mainly of the body, also used metaphorically; *sōzō* (4982), to save, mostly spiritually but sometimes physically, to rescue; *diasōzō* (1295), to bring safely through, to preserve, maintain. The sub.: *iama* (2386), cure, and *iasis* (2392), the process of curing (Lk. 13:32; Acts 4:22,30). *Therapeuō* means to heal miraculously (Mt. 4:23,24; 10:1,8; Acts 4:14, etc.), not effectively healed (Lk. 8:43).

2324. Therapōn; servant. Verb: *therapeuō* (2323), to heal, cure, serve. Denotes a faithful friend to one who is superior, who solicitously regards his interest or looks after his affairs, not a common or domestic servant (*oiketēs*, 3610). One who serves regardless of whether he is a free man (*eleutheros*, 1658) or a slave (*doulos*, 1401), bound by duty or impelled by love. Thus the services of a *therapōn* are higher than those of a *doulos*, slave. *Therapeuō* (2323) may be used of the physician's watchful attendance of the sick and man's service to God. *Therapōn* approaches more closely the position of *oikonomos* (3623), manager, in God's house.

2334. Theōreō; to gaze, from *theōros*, a spectator, to look with interest and for a purpose, usually indicating the careful observation of details. Distinguished from *blepō* (991), to look, see, to look to someone from whom help is expected, to take care, beware (Mk. 15:47; Lk. 10:18; 23:35; Jn. 20:6,12,14; Heb. 7:4). Used of experience in the sense of partaking of (Jn. 8:51; 17:24). Noun: *theōria* (2335), sight (Lk. 23:48), from which our English word "theory" is derived. Deriv.: *anatheōreō* (333), from *ana* (303), up again, (inten.), and *theōreō*, to view with interest; consider contemplatively (Acts 17:23; Heb. 13:7).

2338. Thēlus; from *thēlē*, the nipple of a woman's breast which Plato deduces from *thallō*, to thrive, because it has this effect on the child. The verb *thēlazō* (2337), therefore, means to give the breast, give suck, suck the breast. The adj. *thēlus*, female or woman, is used in the fem. in Rom. 1:26 and in the neut. in Mt. 19:4; Mk. 10:6; Gal. 3:28.

2342. Thērion; the same as *thēr*, to run, or a wild beast (Mk. 1:13; Acts 10:12 T.R.; 11:6; Rev. 6:8, cf. Rev. 15:1,2). Denotes particularly a venomous animal and is applied to a viper (Acts 28:4,5). May also refer to any kind of beast including the tame species (Heb. 12:20), the same as *zōon* (2226), animal. Paul applies to the Cretans the character of *kaka* (2556), evil, *thēria*, wild beasts (Tit. 1:12). In the Septuagint where sacrifices of beasts are mentioned, they are never mentioned as *thēria*, but as *zōa*, because the bestial element is brought out in *thērion* which is regrettable. Throughout the N.T., however, both *zōon* and *thērion* are rendered by the word "beast." Yet these animals represented by the two words are far removed from one another. The *zōa* or "living creatures" stand before the throne and in them dwells the fullness of all creaturely life, as it gives praise and glory to God (Rev. 4:6-9; 5:6; 6:1, etc.). They constitute a part of the heavenly symbolism. The *thēria*, the first and second beast which rise up, one from the bottomless pit (Rev. 11:7) and the other from the sea (Rev. 13:1), one making war upon the two witnesses and the other opening his mouth in blasphemies, form part of the hellish symbolism. Therefore, *thērion* brings out the predominance of the lower animal life and can never be the name applied to glorious creatures in the very court and presence of heaven. Consequently, *zōa* should always be rendered as living creatures and *thēria* as beasts in Scripture.

2345. Thigganō; touch so that one can exert a modifying influence on something (Col. 2:21; Heb. 11:28; 12:20). Syn.: *haptomai* (680), but stronger; to hurt as in Heb. 11:28. See *psēlaphaō* (5584), to touch lightly (Lk. 24:39; Acts 17:27; Heb. 12:18; I Jn. 1:1).

2347. Thlipsis; from *thlibō* (2346), which in turn is derived from *thlaō*, to break. *Thlibō* means to crush, press, compress, squeeze. *Thlipsis* symbolically means grievous affliction or distress (Mt. 13:21; 24:21; Jn. 16:21; Acts 7:10; 11:19; 14:22; I Cor. 7:28; Js. 1:27), pressure or a burden upon the spirit. Related to *stenochōria* (4730), distress, narrowness, occurring only four times with the connotation of narrowness, from *stenos* (4728), narrow of room, confined space. In three of the four occurrences in the N.T. *stenochōria* is associated with *thlipsis* (Rom. 2:9; 8:35; II Cor. 6:4). *Thlipsis* refers more to being crushed while *stenochōria* refers more to narrowness of room or discomfort.

2348. Thnēskō; to die a natural death (Mt. 2:20: Mk. 15:44; Lk. 8:49). To die a spiritual death (I Tim. 5:6). See *thanatos*, (2288), death.

2349. Thnētos; an adj. from the verb *thnēsko* (2348), to die. Mortal. In Class. Gr. contr. *athanatos*, immortal, which does not occur in the N.T. and which denoted that essential distinction between men and gods which lies at the foundation of all other differences. However, the sub. *athanasia* (110), immortality, occurs in the N.T. in I Cor. 15:53,54; I Tim. 6:16 referring always to the immortality of the body. *Thnētos*, according to the N.T., is a condition of changeability or mortality of the body which is indirect punitive suffering as a result of man's sin. There is no indication whatsoever in the N.T. that this condition of the mortality of the body does not also belong to the Christian who receives Jesus Christ. Mt. 8:17, speaking of Isa. 53:5, refers to the fact that the Lord Jesus on the cross bore upon His body both our spiritual iniquities and our physical sicknesses which resulted from our sin in Adam. When we exercise repentant faith, we are instantly redeemed from our spiritual iniquities and we continue to be so until we meet the Lord face to face. Our redeemed soul remains in an unredeemed body. It is unredeemed because as presently constituted, it is incapable of avoiding suffering, sickness and death. Whenever the body is referred to, even if it is a body that belongs to a Christian (Rom. 6:12; 8:11; I Cor. 15:53,54; II Cor. 4:11;5:4), it is referred to as a mortal body. Our present body, though now mortal, will be redeemed after our resurrection as indicated by Paul in Rom. 8:23. This redemption of our mortal body was accomplished by Christ on the cross, but its effective realization takes place at our resurrection. An equivalent term of *thnētos* is *phthartos* (5349), corruptible (Rom. 1:23; I Cor. 9:25; 15:53; I Pet. 1:18,23).

2354. Thrēneō; from *thrēnos* (2355), lamentation. To lament in an audible manner (Mt. 11:17; Lk. 7:32; 23:27; Jn. 16:20). The sub. *thrēnos* occurs together with *klauthmos* (2805), weeping, in Mt. 2:18 T.R. This demonstration of grief may take the form of a poem such as the beautiful lamentation which David composed over Saul and Jonathan (II Sam. 1:17). The sublime dirge over Tyre is called a *thrēnos* (Ezk. 26:17, cf. II Chron. 35:25; Amos 8:10; Rev. 18:11). It is an outward demonstration of an inner grief, *lupē* (3077), a stronger and more expressive outward demonstration of grief than involved in *pentheō* (3996), to mourn, but not as strong as *koptō* (2875), to strike one's breast in demonstration of grief.

2357. Thrēskos; religious, devout, only in Js. 1:26, the diligent performer of the divinely ascribed duties of the outward service of God. The sub. *thrēskeia* (2356), religion, (Acts 26:5; Col. 2:18; Js. 1:26,27) is predominantly the ceremonial service of religion. It is the external framework whereas *eusebeia* (2150), godliness, is the inward piety of soul. According to James, *thrēskeia*, religion, is not merely ceremonial formality, but acts of mercy, love, and holiness.

2366. Thuella; cyclone, see *pnoē* (4157).

2372. Thumos; anger, wrath, from *thuō*, to move impetuously, particularly as the air or wind; a violent motion, or passion of the mind; as ascribed to God (Rev. 14:10,19; 15:1,7; 19:15); to man (Lk. 4:28; Acts 19:28); to the devil (Rev. 12:12). Found together with *orgē* (3709) (Rom. 2:8, indignation; Eph 4:31, wrath; Col. 3:8, wrath; Rev. 19:15, fierce wrath) which means the more abiding and settled habit of mind, whereas the more passionate and, at the same time, more temporary character of anger and wrath is *thumos*. *Thumos* is an outburst of *orgē* (3709), anger.

2378. Thusia; the act of sacrificing or offering, from *thuō* (2380), to sacrifice. A sacrifice (Lk. 2:24; 13:1; Acts 7:41; Heb. 5:1; 7:27, cf. Eph. 5:2; Heb. 9:26; 10:12). Spoken of the bodies of Christians (Rom. 12:1); of their religious services (I Pet. 2:5); of their praises of God and works of charity to men (Heb. 13:15,16) and to the preachers of the Gospel (Phil. 4:18).

2379. Thusiastērion; an altar of the true God. Contr. *bōmos* (1041), an idol altar.

2380. Thuō; to offer, sacrifice. In a ritualistic sense, primarily to smoke or burn incense (Acts 7:42). Generally, to offer, of bloody and unbloody offerings, and only in a derived sense, to slay (Lk. 15:23,27,30; Acts 10:13; 11:7; Mt. 22:4); to kill (Jn. 10:10).

2390. Iaomai; mid. voice of *iaō*. To heal, cure, restore to bodily health (Lk. 5:17; 6:19; 22:51, etc.); to heal spiritually (Mt. 13:15; Lk. 4:18, T.R.; Jn. 12:40). Pass. voice, to be thus healed (Mt. 8:8,13; 15:28; Mk. 5:29, etc.); to be spiritually healed (I Pet. 2:24). Deriv.; *iasis* (2392), the act or process of healing (Lk. 13:32; Acts 4:22,30); *iama* (2386), the result of healing; used in the pl. in I Cor. 12:9,28,30. Although there are a number of verbs used for healing, there is a distinction in their meaning: *therapeuō* (2323), to heal; *sōzō* (4982), to save, restore (Mk. 5:23; Lk. 8:36); *diasōzō* (1295), to bring safely through (Lk. 7:3). Noun: *iatros* (2395), physician (Mt. 9:12; Mk. 2:17; 5:26; Lk. 4:23; 5:31; 8:43; Col. 4:14) used even in Mod. Gr.

2396. Ide; behold, act. voice, *idou* (2400), mid. voice, imper. moods of *eidon* from *horaō* (3708), to see, calling attention to what may be seen or heard or mentally apprehended in any way.

2397. Idea; or *eidea*. Appearance, only in Mt. 28:3, from *eidō* (1492), to see, equivalent to *eidos* (1491), appearance (Jn. 5:37). Something conceived in the mind without an objective reality. Contr. *morphē* (3444) and *schēma* (4976), form and fashion which have an objective reality. *Idea* implies someone in whose mind an appearance is formed; there must be one forming the idea before the object can become visible. The English word "idea" is derived from the Gr. *idea*.

2398. Idios; properly one's own. Denotes property or peculiar relation (Mk. 15:20; Lk. 2:3 T.R.; 6:41,44; Jn. 1:11,41; 5:43; Acts 1:19; 4:32; Rom. 8:32; 14:4). The phrase *eis* (1519) *ta* and the neut. pl. of *idios* occurring in Jn. 1:11 means to those he was familiar with. This form may be used with *oikēmata*, pl. of *oikēma* (3612), houses or house implied (Jn. 16:32; 19:27). The expression *kat' idian* with the prep. *kata* (2596) with the word *choran* (5561) (place understood) means in a private place, privately, apart (Mt. 14:13,23; 17:1,19; Mk. 4:34, etc.); joined with *kairso* (2540), time, proper or convenient time (Gal. 6:9; I Tim. 2:6; 6:15). Deriv.: *Idiōtēs* (2399), a common man or a private man. Adv.: *idia*, (dat. of *idios*), separately.

2399. Idiōtēs; from *idios* (2398). A common man as opp. either to a man of power or a man of education and learning (I Cor. 14:16); a person in a private station, a private or common man (Acts 4:13); uninstructed, unskilled (I Cor. 14:23,24); plain in speech (II Cor. 11:6, in this text refers both to speech and knowledge). Our English word "idiot" is derived from *idiōtēs*, but has a very different meaning. The Gr. word never signifies, either in the sacred or secular writers, a person deficient in natural capacity for understanding.

2409. Hiereus; priest, a sacred person, as serving at God's altar but not implying that he is also holy, *hagios* (40). Adj.: *hieros* (2413), performing the ordinances, sacred.

2411. Hieron; from *hieros* (2413), sacred, a temple, whether of the true God (Mt. 12:5,6) or of an idol (Acts 19:27). Often includes not only the building but the courts and all the sacred ground or enclosure. See *naos* (3485), temple.

2412. Hieroprepēs; from *hieros* (2413), sacred, and *prepō* (4241), to suit, become. Such as becomes sacred persons, venerable. Only in Tit. 2:3, to act like a sacred person.

2413. Hieros; sacred, not used of persons but of things (I Cor. 9:13) and of the Scriptures (II Tim. 3:15); that which may not be violated, externally related to God but not necessarily having a holy (*hagios*, 40) character. Thus, *hiereus* (2409), priest, is a sacred person as serving at God's altar, but it is not in the least implied that he is a holy person as far as his character is concerned. The true antithesis of *hieros* is *bebēlos* (952), profane (I Tim. 1:9; 4:7; 6:20; II Tim. 2:16; Heb. 12:16). Verb: *bebēloō* (953), to profane (Mt. 12:5; Acts 24:6).

2416. Hierosuleō; from adj. noun *hierosulos* (2417), a sacrilegious person. To commit sacrilege, take to one's own private use what is consecrated to God as in Rom. 2:22. Derived from *hieron* (2413), a sacred place or thing, and *sulaō* (4813), to rob, spoil.

2417. Hierosulos; a robber of a temple, a sacrilegious person; from *hierosuleō* from *hieron* (2413), sacred, and *sulaō* (4813), to rob, spoil. Only in Acts 19:37.

2418. Hierourgeō; from *hieron* (2413), sacred, and *ergon* (2041), work. To perform or be employed in a sacred office. Only in Rom. 15:16 referring to the sacred business of preaching or administering the Gospel.

2425. Hikanos; from *hikanō*, to reach, attain the desired end. Sufficient, fit (II Cor. 2:16; 3:5, etc.); worthy (Mt. 3:11, etc.); adequate, enough (Lk. 22:38; II Cor. 2:6); sufficiently many, great, a considerable number or quantity (Mt. 28:12; Mk. 10:46, etc.). Deriv.: *hikanotēs* (2426), sufficiency, fitness (II Cor. 3:5). Verb: *hikanoō* (2427), to make sufficient or fit, qualify (II Cor. 3:6; Col. 1:12). Syn.: *arketos* (713), enough; *perissos* (4053), abundant; *korennumi* (2880), to satisfy.

2428. Hiketēria; supplication, from *hiketēs*, a suppliant, which comes from *hikomai*, to come, approach, particularly as suppliant, from the act. *hikō*, to come. Equivalent to a supplication or humble and earnest prayer (Heb. 5:7). Related words: *euchē* (2171), wish; *proseuchē* (4335), prayer; *deēsis* (1162), supplication for a particular need; *enteuxis* (1783), intercession; *eucharistia* (2169), thanksgiving; *aitēma* (155), petition.

2433. Hilaskomai; to make reconciliation (Lk. 18:13; Heb. 2:17), and the noun *hilasmos* (2434), propitiation (I Jn. 2:2; 4:10) may have a personal object, the sinner, or an impersonal object, our sins. It provides the satisfaction demanded by God's justice whereby the removal of sins is attained. *Katallassō* (2644), however, signifies not only the removal of the demands of justice but God taking upon Himself the expiation (*hilasmos*, 2434) and establishing a relationship of peace between God and man. While God *katallassei*, reconciles particularly, Christ *hilasketai*, expiates.

2434. Hilasmos; propitiation, only in I Jn. 2:2; 4:10. Deriv.: *hilaskomai* (2433), to propitiate, appease because of Christ's sacrifice. The benefit of Christ's death for man. *Katallagē* (2643), reconciliation, sets forth the benefit of the death of Christ for the sinner, but *hilasmos* indicates not only the benefit of reconciliation, but the manner whereby we were made friends of God. *Hilasmos* refers to Christ as the One who propitiates and offers Himself as the propitiation. He is both the sacrifice and the High Priest sacrificing Himself. (Jn. 1:29,36; I Cor. 5:7; Eph. 5:2; Heb. 10:14; I Pet. 1:19; Rev. 5:6,8).

2435. Hilastērion; mercy seat, viewed as a sub. The lid or covering of the Ark of the Covenant, made of pure gold, on and before which the high priest was to sprinkle the blood of the expiatory sacrifices on the great day of atonement, and where the Lord promised to meet His people (Ex. 25:17,22; 29:42; 30:36; Lev. 16:2,14,15). Paul, by applying this name to Christ in

Rom. 3:25, assures us that Christ was the true mercy seat, the reality of the cover of the Ark of the Covenant (Heb. 9:5). Therefore it means a place of conciliation, of expiation, what the ancients called *thusiastērion* (2379), altar or place of sacrifice. It does not refer to the expiatory sacrifices themselves. Jesus Christ is designated as *hilastērion* in Heb. 9:5 and Rom. 3:25 because He is designated not only as the place where the sinner deposits his sin, but He Himself is the means of expiation. He is not like the high priest of the O.T. whose expiation of the people was accomplished through the blood of another and not of himself (Heb. 9:25). What the Jews called the Capporeth, *hilastērion,* was the principal part of the Holy of Holies. Later it was even termed as "the house of the Capporeth" (I Chr. 28:11). Philo calls the Capporeth "the symbol of the mercy of the power of God."

2436. Hileōs; the Attic for *hilaos,* from *hilaō,* to be propitious (Mt. 16:22; Heb. 8:12). Propitious, favorable, merciful. In the former passage what is translated "God forbid it, Lord" in Gr. is *hielōs soi,* unto you, *Kurie,* Lord, and it is elliptical for *hileōs soi hē,* be Lord, *kurie*. Literally it is "Be merciful to thyself, Lord." In these and such phrases the word *hileōs* implies an invocation of mercy for the overturning of evil, that is to say for the cancellation of the consequence of the evil that others are contemplating to do. See *eleos* (1656), mercy. In modern vernacular we would say, "God forbid." In Heb. 8:12 what is meant is "I will be merciful to their iniquities" or "I will alleviate the results of their iniquities." Opp. *anileōs* (448), without mercy (Js. 2:12 T.R.).

2440. Himation; larger outer garment. In a more restricted sense, it refers to a loose upper garment so large that a man would sometimes sleep in it.

2441. Himatismos; garments stately and costly (Lk. 7:25; 9:29; Jn. 19:24; Acts 20:33; I Tim. 2:9).

2465. Isaggelos; from *isos* (2470), similar or equal, and *aggelos* (32) angel; angel-like (Lk. 20:36, which, if taken in connection with Mk. 12:25, should be translated as "like" instead of "equal"; see also Mt. 22:30. According to this passage, neither mortality nor sexual union pertains either to the sons of the resurrection or to the angels [I Cor. 6:3]. Therefore, the meaning of Jude 6,7; II Pet. 2:4 is that sexual union must not be attributed to the angels).

2473. Isopsuchos; from *isos* (2470), equal, and *psuchē* (5590), soul, mind. To be activated by the same motives, of like character, like-minded (Phil. 2:20).

2476. Histēmi; trans., to set, place (Mt. 4:5; 18:2; Mk. 9:36; Lk. 9:47); intrans., to stand (Mt. 12:46,47; 13:2; 16:28, etc.). To remain, abide, continue (Jn. 8:44); to stand still, stop (Acts 8:38); to make to stand, establish, confirm (Rom. 14:4). In the pass., to be established, stand firm, stand (Mt. 12:25,26; Mk. 3:25,26); to be confirmed (Mt. 18:16; II Cor. 13:1); to appoint (Acts 17:31); to agree, covenant (Mt. 26:15, cf. *epēggeilanto,* 1861, in Mk. 14:11; Lk. 22:5); impute, lay to one's charge (Acts 7:60). Deriv.: *akatastasis* (181); *akatastatos* (182); *anastasis* (386); *anastatoō* (387); *anistēmi* (450); *apokathistēmi* (600); *apokatastasis* (605); *apostasia* (646); *apostasion* (647); *astateō* (790); *aphistēmi* (868); *dichostasia* (1370); *ekstasis* (1611); *enistēmi* (1764); *exanastasis* (1815); *exanistēmi* (1817); *existēmi* (1839); *kathistēmi* (2525); *methistēmi* (3179); *stasis* (4714); *sunistaō* (4921); *hupostasis* (5287).

2479. Ischus; strength, especially physical power as an endowment. Verb: *ischuō* (2480), syn. with *dunamai* (1410), but in the case of the basic *ischus,* there is more emphasis on the actual power. In *dunamis* (1411), there is implied ability or capacity. The stem of *ischus* is linked with *isch-,* strength, and *echō* (2192), I have. *Ischuō,* therefore, may mean to have health, syn. with *hugiainō* (5198), to be healthy, as opp. to *astheneō* (770), to be weak, sick. *Enischuō* (1765), from *en* (1722), in, and *ischuō,* to strengthen; to gain strength (Lk. 22:43; Acts 9:19); *katischuō* (2729), from *kata* (2596), against; to prevail against (Mt. 16:18; Lk. 23:23). The adj. *ischuros* (2478), strong, powerful.

2480. Ischuō; to be strong, from *ischus* (2479), strength (Mt. 9:12; Mk. 2:17). To avail, to be of use, or force (Mt. 5:13; Gal. 5:6; 6:15; Js. 5:16; Heb. 9:17); to be able, can (Mt. 8:28; 26:40; Mk. 5:4; 9:18; Lk. 6:48, etc.); to be strong in body (Mt. 9:12; Mk. 2:17); to have power as of the Gospel (Acts 19:20); to prevail against (Acts 19:16; Rev. 12:8); to be effective, capable of producing results (Mt. 5:13; Gal. 5:6; Heb. 9:17; Js. 5:16); to be whole, healthy, strong (Mt. 9:12; Mk. 2:17). Contr. *dunamai* (1410), denoting a more forceful strength or ability (Js. 5:16). Still stronger forms are *exischuō* (1840), to be thoroughly strong (Eph. 3:18); *katischuō* (2729), negatively, of the powerlessness of the gates of Hades to prevail against the Church (Mt. 16:18; Lk. 21:36; 23:23).

2508. Kathairō; to cleanse, purify, related to *katharos* (2513), pure, clean, without stain, without spot. Occurs only twice in Jn. 15:2 referring to the vine in that the vine dresser cuts off certain branches in order that other branches may bear more fruit. In Heb. 10:2, expiate, redeem, referring to the once-and-for-all initial redemption by Jesus Christ, cleansing the sinner and positioning him in Christ.

2511. Katharizō; in the Attic *kathariō* (Heb. 9:14), from *katharos* (2513), pure. To cleanse, free from filth (Mt. 23:25; Lk. 11:39, cf. Mk. 7:19). To cleanse or make clean from leprosy (Mt. 8:2,3; 10:8), often used in the Septuagint for legal cleansing from leprosy (Lev. 14). To cleanse in the sense of purification, legal or ceremonial (Heb. 9:22,23, cf. Acts 10:15; 11:9), frequently so used in the Septuagint. In a spiritual sense, to purify from the pollution and guilt of sin (Acts 15:9; II Cor. 7:1; Eph. 5:26; Tit. 2:14; Heb. 9:14; Js. 4:8; I Jn. 1:7,9). Deriv.: *katharismos* (2512), purification; *katharotēs* (2514), purity; *perikatharma* (4027), offscouring, refuse; *akathartos* (169), unpurified; *akatharsia* (167), uncleanness; *kathairō* (2508), to cleanse, to purify.

2512. Katharismos; purification. In Class. Gr. *katharmos*. Actually refers to the process of purification, the sacrifice of purification. In Lk. 2:22 the purification of women. In Mk. 1:44; Lk. 5:14; Jn. 2:6 ritual purification. The baptism both of John and the Lord Jesus is designated as *katharismos* in Jn. 3:25, not that the ritual of physical baptism brought about spiritual results or spiritual purification, but only as a parallel in its results. As water cleanses the body, so baptism symbolizes the work of repentance and forgiveness of sin. Its designation as a baptism of repentance unto forgiveness of sins (Mk. 1:4; Lk. 3:3; Acts 2:38) means in identification of the forgiveness of sins. In Heb. 1:3 the word denotes the objective removal of our sins by Jesus Christ (see also Heb. 9:22,23). In II Pet. 1:9 it refers to the actual purification accomplished in man, while in Heb. 1:3 to the propitiation provided by the Lord Jesus.

2513. Katharos; clean, pure, clear, in a natural sense (Mt. 27:59; Jn 13:10; Heb. 10:22; Rev. 15:6; 22:1). Clean in the sense that something is lawful to be eaten or used (Lk. 11:41; Rom. 14:20; Tit. 1:15). In all these passages there is a plain reference to a legal or ceremonial cleanness. Clean or pure in a spiritual sense from the pollution and guilt of sin (Mt. 5:8; Jn. 13:10,11; 15:3; I Tim. 1:5; 3:9; Js. 1:27). Sometimes applied to purity or cleanness from blood or blood guiltiness (Acts 18:6; 20:26). In the physical or nonethical sense, opp. *rhuparos* (4508), dirty (Mt. 27:59; Heb. 10:22; Rev. 15:6). Sometimes the meaning of *katharos* is very close to the meaning of *eilikrinēs* (1506), sincere, or something that has been cleansed by shaking to and fro as in a sieve or in winnowing. *Katharos* describes the purity contemplated under the aspect of that which is free from soil or stain (Js. 1:27). Sometimes seen as the opp. of *koinos* (2839), common as well as *akathartos* (169) unpurified, (Rom. 14:14,20; Heb. 9:13).

2514. Katharotēs; purity, referring to the result of cleansing or purification. *Katharismos* (2512) refers to the process of purification instead of the result. In Heb. 9:13 *katharotēs* is freedom from the guilt of filthiness.

2525. Kathistēmi; from the inten. *kata* (2596), down, and *histēmi* (2476), to set, place. Trans., to set down, bring to (Acts 17:15); to place anywhere in an office, in a condition (Mt. 24:45,47; 25:21,23; Lk. 12:42,44; Acts 6:3); with double accus., to make somebody something, to put in a situation or position (Lk. 12:14; Acts 7:10,27,35; Tit. 1:5; Heb. 5:1; 7:28; 8:3). In Rom. 5:19: "For as through the one man's disobedience the many were made (*katestathēsan*) sinners, even so through the obedience of the One the many will be made (*katastathēsontai*) righteous." Another Gr. word that could have been used is *ginomai* (1096), to become, or in this case, to make. To have used this latter word would have actually meant that God is responsible for making transgressors. As a judge does not make lawbreakers or bear moral responsibility for what they do, so it is with the Lord. God does not make sinners, but He declares them to be so. He set the consequence of the disobedience of man, but He was not responsible for that disobedience. The verb *kathistēmi* used in this regard means that God has set or placed man in a definite place or position, that of the transgressor, but He did not make him a transgressor. The responsibility is entirely man's. Intrans., existing as inactive and unfruitful (II Pet. 1:8). In the present mid. voice, to take a position, come forward, appear (Js. 3:6; 4:4). See *histēmi* (2476), to stand.

2537. Kainos; qualitatively new as contr. with *neos* (3501), numerically new or the last one numerically. Deriv.: *kainotēs* (2538) newness (Rom. 6:4; 7:6); *anakainizō* (340), to renew qualitatively (Heb. 6:6); anakainoō (341), to renew (II Cor. 4:16; Col. 3:10); *anakainōsis* (342), the act of renewing (Rom. 12:2; Tit. 3:5); *egkainizō* (1457), to dedicate, consecrate into a qualitatively new use; hence the N.T. is *kainē diathēkē*, qualitatively new, not merely numerically new, *nea* (3501). See *neos* (3501), new.

2538. Kainotēs; renewal, not simply an experience similar to the past, but a qualitatively different one. Related to *kainos* (2537), new, but qualitatively different. Contr. *neos* (3501), numerically new; and also the verb *ananeoō* (365), to renew, to have a new experience, the same as in the past. See *neotēs* (3503), newness, youthfulness and also *anakainizō* (340); *anakainoō* (341); *anakainōsis* (342); *ananeoō* (365); *egkainizō* (1457); *kainos* (2537).

2540. Kairos; season, time, but not merely as a succession of moments which is *chronos* (5550). *Kairos* implies that which time gives an opportunity to do. Related to *eukairia* (2120), from *eu* (2095), good, and *kairos*, opportune time, opportunity. *Kairos*, however, implies not the convenience of the season, but the necessity of the task at hand whether the time provides a good, convenient opportunity or not. There is really no English equivalent to the word *kairos*, appropriate time, which when used in the pl. with *chronoi* (times), is translated as "seasons," times at which certain foreordained events take place or necessary accomplishments need to take place.

2549. Kakia; wickedness, as an evil habit of the mind, while *ponēria* (4189) is the act. outcoming of the same. *Ponēria* is, therefore, malevolence, the doing of evil and not only of being evil. Contr. *kakos* (2556) with *ponēros* (4190). Deriv.: *kakoētheia* (2550), evil manners or morals (Rom. 1:29), ill-nature, depravity.

2550. Kakoētheia; from *kakos* (2556), bad, evil, and *ēthos*, custom. Occurs only in Rom. 1:29 translated "malice." It actually means ill nature, taking everything with an evil connotation and giving a malicious interpretation of the actions of others. That nature which is evil and makes one suspect evil in others. On the other hand *kakia* (2549), wickedness, is the name not of one vice but of the viciousness out of which all vices spring as the ancients saw it. In the N.T.; however, *kakai* is not so much viciousness as a special form of vice. It is more the evil habit of the mind. Contr. *ponēria* (4189), malevolence, the acting out, the externalization of the evil habit of the mind. Attributing to others and their actions the worst imaginable motives (Rom. 1:29).

2552. Kakopatheia; from *kakopatheō* (2553), to suffer misfortune, hardship. Suffering of evil, a bearing of affliction (Js. 5:10, cf. II Tim. 1:8).

2553. Kakopatheō; from *kakos* (2556), evil, and *paschō* (3958), to suffer. To suffer evil or afflictions, to be afflicted (II Tim. 2:9; Js. 5:13, cf. II Tim. 1:8). To endure, to sustain afflictions (II Tim. 2:3; 4:5).

2554. Kakopoieō; from *kakos* (2556), bad, and *poieō* (4160), to do. To do evil in the moral sense (III Jn. 11, cf. I Pet. 3:17). Equivalent to doing mischief, doing evil, with a reference to the moral offensiveness of that which for another is evil (Mk. 3:4; Lk. 6:9). Opp. *agathopoieō* (15), to do good. The moral character of the mode of action primarily to be considered here is clear from the absence of the object which must be specified if the reference were solely to the harm done.

2555. Kakopoios; evil-doer, the sub. from *kakopoieō*, to do evil. Used as an adj. noun meaning pernicious, injurious, or an evil doer or a malefactor, behaving in a bad way. Used in Jn. 18:30; I Pet. 2:12,14; 3:16 in a moral sense corresponding to behaving in an evil way or doing evil. Only in I Pet. 4:15 it appears in the sense of generally injurious, denoting one who is injurious to the community.

2556. Kakos; evil, wicked, from the verb *chazō* or *chazomai*, to give back, recede, retire, retreat in battle. One that is evil in himself and as such puts others in trouble. Syn.: *ponēros* (4190), malicious indicating willful harm to others, an element not necessarily found in *kakos*. The *kakos* may be content to perish in his own corruption but the *ponēros* (a name also attributed to Satan, Mt. 6:13; Eph. 6:16) is not content unless he is corrupting others as well and drawing them into the same destruction with himself. From this is derived *kakia* (2549), wickedness, iniquity, evil, affliction.

2557. Kakourgos; from *kakoergos*, which is derived from *kakos* (2556), bad, and *ergon* (2041), work. An evil doer, malefactor (Lk. 23:32,33,39; II Tim. 2:9). In the Gr. writers the word is joined with thieves as also in Lk. 23:32. There are some who suggest the deriv. of the word from *kakos*, bad, and *orgē* (3709), anger, in which case the accent is placed on the ultima making it not *kakoúrgos*, but *kakourgós*, making it the opp. of *agathoergos* or *euergos*, well-doer. In this sense, of course, it would be evildoer, malicious, cunning, treacherous.

2559. Kakoō; to harm or do evil to anyone, to ill-treat, plague, injure (Acts 7:6,19; 12:1; 18:10; I Pet. 3:13); to put one into a bad mood against anyone (Acts 14:2). Sub.: *kakōsis* (2561), distress (Acts 7:34).

2560. Kakōs; badly, with *echō* (2192), to have; to have it badly, i.e., to be ill (Mt. 14:35; Mk. 1:32; Lk. 7:2). See *arrhōstos* (732); *astheneia* (769); *asthenēs* (772).

2564. Kaleō; call, with a personal obj., to call anyone, invite (Mt. 20:8; 25:14); of the divine invitation to participate in the blessings of redemption (Rom. 8:30; I Cor. 1:9; Heb. 9:15); to name; in the pass. voice, to be called by name. It suggests either vocation or destination. Noun: *klēsis* (2821), a calling; *klētos* (2822), called. In the Epistles an effectual call (Rom. 1:1,6,7; 8:28; I Cor. 1:2,24, etc.); appointed (Rom. 1:1; I Cor. 1:1). Deriv.: *eiskaleō* (1528), to call in (Acts 10:23); *epikaleomai* (1941), to be called; *metakaleō* (3333), to recall; *proskaleomai* (4341), to invite; *sugkaleō* (4779), to call together; *parakaleō* (3870), to call near, to comfort.

2570. Kalos; constitutionally good without necessarily being benevolent; expresses beauty as a harmonious completeness, balance, proposition.

2572. Kaluptō; to wrap around, as bark, skin, shell or plaster; to cover up. Syn. *kruptō* (2928), to hide (Mt. 8:24; 10:26; Lk. 8:16; 23:30; II Cor. 4:3; Js. 5:20; I Pet. 4:8). Deriv.: *apokaluptō* (601), to unveil, discover, make visible, reveal; *apokalupsis* (602), uncovering, unveiling, disclosure, revelation.

2577. Kamnō; primarily, to work, to be weary from constant work (Heb. 12:3). When used in connection with *astheneō* (770), to be sick, it suggests the common accompaniment of sickness, weariness of mind which may hinder physical recovery. In some mss. it occurs also in Rev. 2:3.

2585. Kapēleuō; to treat as if for personal profit, profiteer. Used only in II Cor. 2:17 translated "peddling." *Kapēleuō,* to adulterate the wine and make it thick like *pēlos* (4081), mud, mire; to make a gain of anything. The *kapēlos* may also be derived from *kapē,* food, victuals, from *kaptō,* to eat; a huckster or petty retail trader, contr. *emporos* (1713), merchant (Mt. 13:45; Rev. 18:3,11,15,23) who sells his wares wholesale. *Kapēlos* is especially the retailer of wine who is exposed to the strong temptation to tamper with it or sell it in short measure in order to make a profit. *Kapēleuō* includes *doloō* (1389), falsify (II Cor. 4:2); adultering not simply for the sake of it but making an unworthy personal gain thereby. Profiteering from God's Word, preaching for money or professing faith for personal gain.

2588. Kardia; heart (Acts 2:26). The Scriptures attributed to the heart thoughts, reasonings, understanding, will, judgment, designs, affections, love, hatred, fear, joy, sorrow and anger since these things can actually affect a man's physical heart. We all know how thoughts and emotions affect our blood pressure. Therefore, the heart is used for the mind in general (Mt. 12:34; Jn. 13:2; Rom. 2:15; 10:9,10; I Pet. 3:4); the understanding (Lk. 3:15; 9:47; Acts 28:27; Rom. 1:21; II Cor. 4:6); the will (Acts 11:23; 13:22; Rom. 10:1); the memory (Lk. 1:66; 2:51); the intention, affection, or desire (Mt. 6:21; 18:35; Mk. 7:6; Lk. 1:17; 8:15; Acts 8:21; I Thess. 2:4); the conscience (I Jn. 3:20,21). It can also mean the middle or inner part, as the heart is of the breast (Mt. 12:40), as the heart of the earth is the inner part of the earth, the grave. Deriv.: *kardiognōstēs* (2589), heart-knower, heart-searcher; *sklērokardia* (4641), hardening of the heart, stubborness.

2589. Kardiognōstēs; from *kardia* (2588), heart, and *gnōstēs* (1109), a knower, which in turn is derived from *gnoō* or *ginōskō* (1097), to know: "The prophet" means, "a knower of hearts, one who knows the hearts," i.e., the most secret thoughts, desires, and intentions (Acts 1:24; 15:8).

2594. Kartereō; to be strong, steadfast, firm, to endure, hold out, bear the burden. Meaning in Heb. 11:27 that he endured severe yet voluntary exile with strength and courage.

2596. Kata; a prep. governing the gen. and accus. with the primary meaning of down, i.e., down from, down upon, down in, etc. With the gen. used of place indicating motion down from, a higher to a lower place (Mt. 8:32; Mk. 5:13; Lk. 8:33). Generally used of motion or direction, upon, towards, through, any place or object in the sense of against (Acts 27:14), of, through, throughout (Lk. 4:14; 23:5); with *holou,* the whole in the adv. phrase *kath' holou,* or one word *katholou,* not at all. After verbs of swearing it has the meaning of upon or by anything (Mt. 26:63; Heb. 6:13,16). Metaphorically, used of the obj. toward or upon which anything tends, aims, etc., upon, in respect to (I Cor. 15:15). With the accus. used of place with verbs of motion either expressed or implied. Used of extension: out, over, through, throughout a place (Lk. 8:39). Used of motion or situation: upon, at, near to, adjacent to (Lk. 10:32); sometimes as *en* (1722), within a place, might be employed though not strictly syn., as in the English phrase "at a house" or "in a house," used interchangeably. Used of time: of a period or point of time upon which, i.e., in, at, during which anything takes place as in Acts 14:1, at the same time. In a distributive sense, derived strictly from the idea of pervading all the parts of a whole; also of place (Heb. 9:5); *kata meros,* i.e., part for part particularly of number, *kath' hena,* one by one (I Cor. 14:31); *kata duo,* two and two (I Cor. 14:27). It may also express the relation in which one thing stands toward another, thus everywhere implying manner (Mt. 9:29; 23:3; Mk. 7:5; Lk. 2:22, etc.). Used of an occasion: by virtue of, because of, for, by, through, where the idea of accordance, adaptedness, still lies at its basis (Mt. 19:3; Acts 3:17, etc.). Used of any general reference, allusion, etc.: in respect to, as to (Rom. 1:3; 9:5; 11:28; Phil. 3:6); of likeness, similitude in which case it is equivalent to like, after the manner of (II Cor. 1:17; Heb. 5:6,10, etc.). It may also refer to the end, aim, purpose, in which case it means towards which anything is directed, for, by way of (II Cor. 11:21; I Tim. 6:3, etc.). In composition *kata* usually used as a prefix implies motion downward as *katabainō* (2597), to go down; against, in a hostile sense, as *katēgoreō* (2723), to speak against; distribution, as *kataklērodoteō* (2624), to distribute the inheritance; in a general sense, down, down upon, and also throughout, but it often cannot be expressed in English and is then simply inten. Sometimes it gives to an intrans. verb a trans. sense, as *katargeō* (2673), to render inoperative.

2597. Katabainō; from *kata* (2596), down, and *bainō,* to go or come; to come down, descend (Mt. 3:16; 7:25, etc.).

2602. Katabolē; from *kataballō* (2598). A casting or laying down. Dejection (Heb. 11:11). *Katabolē kosmou,* the foundation of the world (Mt. 13:35; 25:34).

2604. Kataggeleus; from *kataggellō* (2605), to proclaim. A proclaimer, publisher (only in Acts 17:18).

2605. Kataggellō; from *kata* (2596), inten., and *aggellō* (32), to tell, declare; to declare plainly, openly, or aloud (Acts 4:2; 13:5,38; 16:21; 17:23; Rom. 1:8). Deriv.: *kataggeleus* (2604), a proclaimer, publisher (Acts 17:18).

2607. Kataginōskō; from *kata,* (2596), against, and *ginōskō* (1097), to know. To perceive something concerning one, observe, usually to discern in a bad sense and therefore to discern something against another, to incriminate, condemn (I Jn. 3:20,21), to blame (Gal. 2:11). In the perf. pass.: to be blamed, worthy of blame, reprehensible, justly charged with madness.

2610. Katagōnizomai; from *kata* (2596), against, and *agōnizomai* (75), to contend for victory in the public games. To throw down, subdue (only in Heb. 11:33).

2613. Katadikazō; from *kata* (2596), against, and *dikazō,* to judge, pronounce sentence, which in turn is from *dikē* (1349), judgment. To give judgment against a person, recognize the right against him, pass sentence, condemn (Mt. 12:7,37; Lk. 6:37; Js. 5:6). Opp.: *apoluō* (630), to dismiss as innocent (Mt. 5:31,32; 19:3,7-9; Mk. 10:2,4,11,12; Lk. 6:37; 16:18, etc.); and *dikaioō* (1344), to justify (Mt. 12:7,37; Js. 5:6).

2615. Katadouloō; from the inten. *kata* (2596), and *douloō* (1402), to enslave. To enslave entirely, reduce to absolute slavery (II Cor. 11:20; Gal. 2:4).

2624. Kataklērodoteō; to distribute by or according to lot or for an inheritance (Acts 13:19). The verb *kataklēro* which in Class. Gr. is equivalent to *kataklērodoteō* or *kataklēronomeō,* embraces the two meanings, to distribute or receive by lot.

2631. Katakrima; related to *krinō* (2919), to divide, separate, judge, with the suffix *-ma* which makes it the result of judgment. To be decided against anyone, a condemnatory judgment. Only in Rom. 5:16,18; 8:1. In v. 16 contr. *dikaiōma,* the right given to the believer as a result of his acknowledgement of the right of God in his life. In v. 18 *katakrima* contr. with a more definite *dikaiōsis,* the act of making life righteous, therefore, a judgment of condemnation in the sense of the economy of redemption.

2632. Katakrinō; from *kata* (2596), against, and *krinō* (2919), to judge. To pronounce sentence against, condemn, adjudge to punishment whether temporal (Mt. 20:18; 27:3; Jn. 8:10,11) or eternal (Mk. 16:16); to furnish matter or occasion for condemnation, to prove or show worthy of condemnation (Mt. 12:41,42; Lk. 11:31,32; Heb. 11:7); to punish (II Pet. 2:6); to weaken, enervate, repress; spoken of sin, to take away its condemning power (Rom. 8:3). Deriv.: *krinō* (2919), to judge.

2633. Katakrisis; from *katakrinō* (2632) which is in turn from *kata* (2596), *krinō* (2919), condemnation against anyone. *Katakrisis,* the act of condemnation or the doing of it. Distinguished from *katakrima* (2631) which is the actual condemnation or the judgment itself (II Cor. 3:9; 7:3).

2635. Katalaleō; from *kata* (2596), against, and *laleō* (2980), to speak, speak against, allowing thoughtless words to be spoken (Js. 4:11; I Pet. 2:12; 3:16). Contr.

katalegō from *kata,* against, and *legō* (3004), to say. *Legō* does not only mean to speak what is in one's mind or to mentally consider. *Katalogos,* from the verb *katalegō,* used as the English "catalogue." Contr. *diaballō* (1225), to falsely accuse.

2637. Katalalos; an open slanderer (Rom. 1:30) from the verb *katalaleō* (2635), from *kata* (2596), against, and *laleō* (2980), to speak. To speak evil of, slander with whatever words come to one's mouth without giving thought to them (Js. 4:11; I Pet. 2:12; 3:16). Noun: *katalalia* (2636), evil speaking, slander, insult.

2638. Katalambanō; from *kata* (2596), an inten. and *lambanō* (2983), to take. To seize (Mk. 9:18); to lay hold of, apprehend, but in a figurative sense (Phil. 3:12); to receive, admit (Jn. 1:5 meaning the darkness did not admit or receive the light; cf. vv. 10-12; 3:19. The darkness is here presented as being so thick that the light could not penetrate it); to take, catch unawares (Jn. 8:3f.); to come upon, overtake (Jn. 12:35; I Thess. 5:4); to attain, obtain (Rom. 9:30; I Cor. 9:24); to comprehend mentally (Eph. 3:18). In the mid. voice *katalambanomai,* to perceive, understand, find (Acts 4:13; 25:25).

2643. Katallagē; from *katallassō* (2644), from the inten. *kata* (2596), and *allassō* (236), to change. A change or reconciliation from a state of enmity between persons to one of friendship. It is the result of the *apolutrōsis* (629), redemption, the divine act of salvation, the ceasing of God's wrath.

2644. Katallassō; reconcile. Used of the divine work of redemption denoting that act of redemption insofar as God Himself, by taking upon Himself our sin and becoming an atonement, establishes that relationship of peace with mankind which the demands of His justice have hitherto prevented. In *katallassō,* God is the subject, man the object. While *hilasmos* (2434), propitiation (I Jn. 2:2; 4:10) and *hilaskomai* (2433), to make reconciliation (Lk. 18:13; Heb. 2:17), aim at the averting of God's wrath, *katallassō* implies God has laid aside or withdrawn wrath.

2647. Kataluō; from the inten. *kata* (2596), and *luō* (3089), to loose. To loose, unloose what was before bound or fastened as used in Class. Gr. To refresh oneself, to lodge or be a guest (Lk. 9:12; 19:7). It properly refers to travellers loosening their own burdens or those of their animals when they stay at a house on a journey (Lk. 9:12). To dissolve, demolish, destroy, or throw down as a building or its materials (Mt. 24:2; 26:61; 27:40); as the law and the prophets (Mt. 5:17); as a work (Acts 5:38,39: Rom. 14:20).

2657. Katanoeō; from the inten. *kata* (2596), and *noeō* (3539), to mind. To observe, remark, consider, contemplate (Mt. 7:3; Lk. 12:24,27; 20:23; Acts 7:31; 11:6; 27:39; Heb. 3:1; 10:24). See *noeō* (3539), to understand, and *nous* (3563), mind.

2663. Katapausis; from *katapauō* (2664), to make to cease. As a noun it means a rest (Heb. 3:11,18; 4:1,3,10,11). Used as a dwelling in Acts 7:49.

2664. Katapauō; from the inten. *kata* (2596), and *pauō* (3973), to make to cease. Trans., to cause to rest, give rest (Heb. 4:8); to restrain (Acts 14:18). Intrans., to rest entirely (Heb. 4:4,10).

2671. Katara; from *kata* (2596), against, and *ara* (685), a curse. Opp. *eulogia* (2129), blessing (Js. 3:10). The same antithesis occurs in Gal. 3:10,13; Heb. 6:8; II Pet. 2:14 meaning the curse proceeding from God, the rejection and surrender to punishment, the destruction of judgment. It is equivalent to judgment without mercy in Js. 2:13. The word involves both the sentence of the divine judgment and the ruin therein inflicted, the manifested curse. The expression, "Christ who became for us (*katara*) curse," means the Lord Himself and the curse He bore are not to be separated from each other (II Cor. 5:21).

2672. Kataraomai; from *katara* (2671), a curse. Used only in the mid. voice, to wish anyone evil or ruin, to curse (Mt. 5:44 T.R.; Mk. 11:21; Lk. 6:28; Rom. 12:14; Js. 3:9). In the pass. perf., to be cursed (Mt. 25:41). In the N.T. with the accus., to give one over to ruin (Mt. 5:44 T.R.; Mk. 11:21; Lk. 6:28; Rom. 12:14; Js. 3:9).

2673. Katargeō; from *kata* (2596), an inten., and *argeō* (691), to be idle. The *kata* gives to the intrans. *argeō,* a trans. meaning, make to cease (Lk. 13:7; Heb. 2:14). Paul uses it often to signify more than hindering or cessation from outward activity, to rest, as in Lk. 13:7 where the idle earth does not denote unused or untilled, but unfruitful, land lying fallow, opp. of *energēs* (1756), active. To abrogate, make void, do away with or put an end to the law (Rom. 3:3,31; I Cor. 13:11; 15:24; Gal. 3:17; Eph. 2:15; II Tim. 1:10). With Paul it always denotes a complete, not a temporary or partial ceasing (I Cor. 1:28; 6:13).

2675. Katartizō; from the inten., *kata* (2596), with, and *artizō,* to adjust, fit, finish, derived in turn from *artios* (739), fit, complete. The fundamental meaning, to put a thing in its appropriate position, to establish, set up, equip, arrange. N.T. meanings: to adjust, adapt, dispose of perhaps with great wisdom and propriety (Heb. 10:5; 11:3); to fit (Rom. 9:22); to perfect, finish, complete (Mt. 21:16; I Thess. 3:10; Heb. 13:21; I Pet. 5:10); to instruct fully or perfectly (Lk. 6:40); to refit, repair, mend, applied to nets which have been broken (Mt. 4:21; Mk. 1:19); to reunite in mind and sentiment, to reconcile, opp. schisms, ruptures (I Cor. 1:10); to reduce, restore as it were a disjointed limb (Gal. 6:1). Deriv.: *katartisis* (2676), completion; *prokatartizō* (4294), to perfect beforehand, make right, equip beforehand.

2676. Katartisis; completing, perfecting (II Cor. 13:9). Denotes the process in its progress while *katartismos* (2677) denotes the process as completed.

2677. Katartismos; perfection or completion. Differs from *katartisis* (2676) in that the latter denotes the process in progress while *katartismos* denotes the process as completed (Eph. 4:12).

2699. Katatomē; from the inten. *kata* (2596), and *temnō,* to cut. A cutting away, mangling, concision (only in Phil. 3:2). Paul here uses sarcasm. *Katatomē* and *peritomē* (4061), circumcision, sound alike. *Peritomē,* ordained by the law of Moses, has a spiritual meaning to distinguish the Jews from the Gentiles. If the spiritual meaning is forgotten, then *peritomē,* circumcision, becomes *kataomē,* butchering up, merely cutting away flesh which in itself is of no value. Paul thus calls the Jewish teachers "butchers," because after the coming of Christ they taught that the outward circumcision of the flesh was necessary to salvation while at the same time they were destitute of the circumcision of the heart. This word of the Apostle not only depreciates the carnal circumcision, but seems also to allude to the superstitious cuttings and manglings of the flesh practiced among the heathen (Lev. 21:5).

2710. Katachraomai; from *kata* (2596) denoting ill, and *chraomai* (5530), to use. To use immoderately, abuse (I Cor. 7:31; 9:18).

2711. Katapsuchō; from *kata* (2596), an inten., and *psuchō* (5594), to cool. To cool, to refresh (Lk. 16:24).

2712. Kateidōlos; from *kata* (2596), as an inten., and *eidōlon* (1497), idol. Full of idols (Acts 17:16). It is a peculiar word describing the *deisidaimōn* (1174), superstitious, wholly given up to the worship of false gods.

2722. Katechō; from *kata* (2596), inten., and *echō* (2192), to have, hold, hold fast in a spiritual sense (Lk. 8:15; I Cor. 11:2; 15:2; I Thess. 5:21; Heb. 3:6,14; 10:23, cf. Rom. 7:6); to possess (I Cor. 7:30; II Cor. 6:10); to take possession, seize (Mt. 21:38 T.R., cf. Jn. 5:4 a disease); to take as a place (Lk. 14:9); detain (Lk. 4:42; Phile. 13); restrain, withhold (II Thess. 2:6,7, cf. Rom. 1:18); with prep. *eis* (1519), to bring a ship toward the shore (Acts 27:40).

2723. Katēgoreō; from *kata* (2596), against, and *agoreō* or *agoreuō,* to speak. To speak openly against, to impeach, accuse mainly in a legal sense (Mt. 12:10; Jn. 5:45; Rom. 2:15; Rev. 12:10). Deriv.: *katēgoros* (2725), accuser; *katēgoria* (2724), accusation, incrimination; *katēgōr* used instead of *katēgoros* in Rev. 12:10 (U.B.S.).

2724. Katēgoria; accusation, incrimination, against a person (Lk. 6:7 T.R.; Jn. 18:29; I Tim. 5:19). With the gen. (Tit. 1:6) it does not refer to judicial punishment, but public condemnation.

2725. Katēgoros; accuser (Jn. 8:10 T.R.; Acts 23:30,35; 24:8; 25:16,18). In the Septuagint: he who brought his own complaint, he who accused in his own behalf (Prov. 18:17). In Rev. 12:10 T.R., used instead of *katēgōr*, of the devil.

2730. Katoikeō; from *kata* (2596), inten., and *oikeō* (3611), to dwell. Refers to a certain fixed and durable dwelling. Opp. *paroikeō* (3939), to sojourn, dwell in a place for a time only; to dwell in, inhabit a house or place (Mt. 2:23; 4:13; Lk. 13:4; Acts 1:19). In Acts 2:5 it means sojourn or to dwell in a place for a time as *paroikeō*; to dwell as God in the temple at Jerusalem (Mt. 23:21); to dwell as the fullness of the Godhead in Christ (Col. 1:19); as Christ (Eph. 3:17); and the Holy Ghost (Js. 4:5) in the faithful; as devils possessing a man (Mt. 12:45; Lk. 11:26); as righteousness in the new heavens and the new earth (II Pet. 3:13). Deriv.: *katoikēsis* (2731), a dwelling, habitation (Mk. 5:3); *katoikētērion* (2732), a place of dwelling, a habitation (Eph. 2:22; Rev. 18:2); *katoikia* (2733), a dwelling (Acts 17:26).

2736. Katō; adv. of place from *kata* (2596), down, downwards (Mt. 4:6; Lk. 4:9, etc.), beneath, below (Mk. 14:66; Acts 2:19). Deriv.: *katōteros* (2737), comparative adj. from *katō*, below, lower (Eph. 4:9); *katōterō* (2736), an adv. of the comparative degree from *katō*, under, time and age (Mt. 2:16).

2749. Keimai; to lie, the mid. form of the obsolete *keō* or *keiō*, to cause to lie. N.T. meanings: To lie, be laid (Lk. 2:12,16; 24:12 T.R.; Jn. 11:41 T.R.); to be placed or set (Mt. 5:14; Jn. 2:6; 19:29; Rev. 4:2); to be laid, applied (Mt. 3:10; Lk. 3:9); to be laid, as a foundation (I Cor. 3:11); to be laid up (Lk. 12:19); to be set, appointed (Lk. 2:34; Phil. 1:17; I Thess. 3:3); to be made or promulgated as a law (I Tim. 1:9); to be in the power of anyone (I Jn. 5:19). In Mt. 3:10; Lk. 3:9 in regard to the axe that lies at the root of the trees, it does not simply mean that it is laid there, but it speaks also of the necessity of its being taken up and used. Deriv.: *antikeimai* (480), to lie over against or to oppose.

2756. Kenos; empty, indicating the hollowness of something or somebody. Contr. *mataios* (3152), an ethical sense of vain and aimlessness. In I Thess. 2:1 it means unaccompanied with the demonstration of Spirit and of power. When used not of things but of persons, it predicates not merely an absence and emptiness of good, but, since the moral nature of man endures no vacuum, it indicates the presence of evil (Js. 2:20).

2757. Kenophōnia; from *kenos* (2756), vain, and *phōnē* (5456), a voice. Empty, fruitless speaking. In I Tim. 6:20; II Tim. 2:16 Paul designates the *bebēloi* (952), godless, as *kenophōnia*, destitute or wicked discourses, speeches that are devoid of any divine or spiritual character, fruitless as far as the satisfaction of man's need of salvation and the molding of the Christian life and character are concerned. It is equivalent to the empty, (*kenoi*, 2756), words, (*logoi*, 3056) in Eph. 5:6.

2758. Kenoō; to make empty, to empty, from *kenos* (2756), empty, void. The antithesis of *plēroō* (4137), to fill. Used in Rom. 4:14; I Cor. 1:17; 9:15; II Cor. 9:3; Phil. 2:7. The use in Phil. 2:7 is of extreme theological importance. It refers to Jesus Christ as emptying Himself at the time of His incarnation, denoting the beginning of his self-humiliation in v. 8. In order to understand what is meant by Jesus' emptying Himself, the whole passage of Phil. 2:6-8 must be examined. The two states of the Lord Jesus are spoken of here. In v. 7 the state of His humiliation is referred to as He having taken "the form of a servant," *morphēn* (3444), *doulou* (1401); having become "in the likeness of men," *homoiōmati* (3667), *anthrōpōn* (444). In contr. to this we have His preincarnate, eternal state spoken of in v. 6 as being in the form of God, *morphē* (3444) and *isa* (2470), equal with God. The truth expressed here concerning His preincarnate state is that He had to be equal with God in order to have the form of God. He could not be God the Son without being God. He who showed us the *morphē*, the form of God, the essence of God, had to be equal with God. The fact that He showed us God in the form in which He appeared was not something that He claimed to be without really being that in His essence. If He appeared to be something that He was not in His essence, then that would have been robbery. As to the use of the sub. *harpagmos* (725), robbery or plunder, see the verb *harpazō* (726), to seize, catch, pluck or pull (I Thess. 4:17; II Cor. 12:2,4; Jude 23; Rev. 12:5). As a sub. *harpagmos* is only used in Phil. 2:6. It refers to the form of God in which Christ appeared as not being considered a robber or a taking upon Himself that which did not belong to Him. His whole life was characterized by being *hyparchōn* (5225), continuing to be that which He always was. Prior to His incarnation He was in the form, the essence of God, and after His incarnation, in spite of His voluntary humiliation, He was still in the form of God. But in spite of His essense of deity, He took upon Himself the true essence of a servant, *morphēn doulou*. However, in order to be a servant, He had to become a man and appear in the likeness of men (*en homoiōmati anthrōpōn*). When He became man, He emptied Himself of the proper recognition that He had with the Father and entered into the world of men who did not properly recognize Him for all that He was before and after His incarnation, before and after He became a servant. The part. *labōn* (from *lambanō*, 2983), having taken, the form of the servant, did not displace deity in His personality, but rather He took upon Himself voluntarily something in addition to what He was which caused His improper recognition by men. This proper recognition is called *doxa* (1391), glory, praise, from the verb *dokeō*, (1380), to recognize. Among men, in the form of man and servant, He lacked the recognition that He had with the Father (Jn. 17:5). This voluntary humiliation of Christ began with the incarnation in order to be carried through His crucifixion. In His resurrection He laid aside His form of a servant. The word *kenoō*, to make empty, is used metaphorically as meaning to bring to nought in the sense of not accomplishing what one set out to accomplish as in Rom. 4:14, the faith not accomplishing its purpose. Used in reference to the working of faith and its fruitfulness (I Cor. 15:14) and to the cross of Christ, meaning the cross not accomplishing its purpose, salvation for man (I Cor. 1:17,18). In the same manner, life can be vain or empty, not accomplishing its purpose (I Cor. 9:15; II Cor. 9:3).

2776. Kephalē; the head (Mt. 6:17; 8:20; 10:30); the head, as the top (Mt. 21:42; Lk. 20:17); the head, as the superior (Eph. 5:23), as the husband of the wife (I Cor. 11:3), Christ of the Church (Eph. 4:15,16; Col. 2:19), and of all principality and power (Col. 2:10, cf. Eph. 1:22); so God the Father is designated as the head of Christ in His manifestation as man, or as the divinity is superior to the humanity (I Cor. 11:3).

2782. Kērugma; sermon, message, from *kērussō* (2784), to discharge a herald's office, to cry out, proclaim, preach. With the suffix *-ma* it means the result of preaching, that which is cried by the herald, the command, the communication, the proclamation of the redeeming purpose of God in Christ (Rom. 16:25); the proclamation of Jesus Christ (I Cor. 1:21; 2:4; 15:14; II Tim. 4:17; Tit. 1:3); the message of God to the Ninevites through Jonah (Mt. 12:41; Lk. 11:32).

2783. Kērux; herald, crier. In Class. Gr., a public servant of supreme power both in peace and in war, one who summoned the *ekklēsia* (1577), the town gathering. This word, *ekklēsia*, later became used for the Church. A *kērux*, messenger, was the public crier and reader of state messages such as the conveyor of a declaration of war. In the N.T., except in II Pet. 2:5 where it speaks of Noah as the herald of righteousness, the word denotes one who is employed by God in the work of proclaiming salvation (I Tim. 2:7, cf. vv. 5,6; II Tim. 1:11 where it is conjoined with *apostolos*, 652, apostle). When both designations are used, *kērux* designates the herald according to his commission and work as a proclaimer, while *apostolos*, apostle, points more to the relation to the one who sent him. The authority of the herald or preacher lies in the message he has to bring (II Pet. 2:5), while the apostle is protected by the authority of his Lord who sends him. In I Tim. 2:7; II Tim. 1:11 it is conjoined with *didaskalos* (1320), teacher.

2784. Kērussō; to preach, to be a herald, proclaim (Mt. 3:1; Mk. 1:45; Lk. 4:18,19; 12:3; Acts 10:37; Rom. 2:21; Rev. 5:2). In I Pet. 3:19 there is no reference to evangelizing, but to the act of Christ, after His resurrection, in proclaiming His victory to fallen spirits. To preach the Gospel as a herald (Mt. 24:14; Mk. 13:10; 14:9; 16:15,20; Lk. 8:1; 9:2; 24:47; Acts 8:5; 19:13; 28:31; Rom. 10:14, etc.); to preach the Word (II Tim. 4:2). Deriv.: *prokērussō* (4296), from *pro* (4253), before, and *kērussō,* to proclaim before or ahead (Acts 3:20 T.R.; 13:24); *kērugma* (2782), a proclamation by a herald, denotes preaching, the substance of which is distinct from the act of preaching (Mt. 12:41; Lk. 11:22; Rom. 16:25; I Cor. 1:21; 2:4; 15:14; II Tim. 4:17; Tit. 1:3); *kērux* (2783), a herald used of the preacher of the Gospel (I Tim. 2:7; II Tim. 1:11) and of Noah as a preacher of righteousness (II Pet. 2:5).

2800. Klasis; from *klaō* (2806), to break. The breaking, particularly of the bread in the Lord's Supper (Lk. 24:35; Acts 2:42).

2801. Klasma; in the neut., that which is broken off, indicated by the suffix *-ma,* a fragment, crumb, used only of pieces of bread (Mt. 14:20; 15:37; Mk. 6:43; 8:8,19,20; Lk. 9:17; Jn. 6:12,13.) Deriv.: see *klaō,* to break (2806).

2806. Klaō; to break. In later Gr. it especially came to mean the breaking off of leaves, sprouts, tendrils. *Klados* (2798), the branch (Rom. 11:21). In the N.T. used only of the breaking of bread which was made in thin cakes, not in loaves (Mt. 14:19; 15:36). Applied to the body of Christ broken on the cross (I Cor. 11:24). Denotes the celebration of the Lord's Supper (Acts 20:7,11; I Cor. 10:16). The fellowship of the Lord with His people is described as a table fellowship (Lk. 24:30, cf. Jn. 13:18). Deriv.: *klasis* (2800), the breaking; *klasma* (2801), that which is broken off, fragment, crumb.

2812. Kleptēs; thief, along with *lētēs* (3027), robber, occurring together in Jn. 10:1,8 and appropriating what is not theirs, but the *kleptēs* steals by fraud and in secret (Mt. 24:43; Jn. 12:6) while the *lēstēs* by violence and openly. *Lēstēs,* as the case may have been with the penitent one on a cross near Jesus, may have been a noble person who turned insurgent for some presumed righteous cause, thus seeking by the wrath of man of work out God's righteousness.

2814. Klēma; properly that which is broken off from a plant, from *klaō* (2806), to break; a shoot, young twig, as the shoots of the vine or the branches (Jn. 15:5).

2816. Klēronomeō; to be a *klēronomos* (2818), an heir, to inherit, obtain for an inheritance properly by lot as the children of Israel did the promised land. (Num. 26:55; 33:54; Josh. 14:1,2). See also Mt. 5:5; 19:29; Heb. 1:4,14; 6:12. Deriv.: *klēros* (2819), lot.

2817. Klēronomia; from *klēronomos* (2818), an heir. Inheritance, that which constitutes one as a *klēronomos,* heir. An inheritance by lot. See *klēronomeō* (2816), to inherit (Mt. 21:38; Lk. 12:13; Acts 7:5). As the inheritance of the earthly typified that of the heavenly Canaan, so the latter is often called *klēronomia,* inheritance (Acts 20:32; Eph. 1:14; 5:5; Heb. 9:15, etc.). Heritage (Acts 7:5). Divine salvation, considered both as promised and as already bestowed, is designated an inheritance in the N.T. so far as man, the heir, obtains possession of it. Deriv.: *klēros* (2819), lot.

2818. Klēronomos; one who has a *klēros* (2819), lot, from the verb *nemō,* to hold, have in one's power. It does not mean one to whom a *klēros,* a lot, is allotted, because it is derived from the act. like *oikonomos* (3623), steward. It probably means an heir or inheritor, or an inheritance divided by lot (Mt. 21:38; Mk. 12:7; Lk. 20:14). Applies to the heirs of the heavenly Canaan (Rom. 8:17; Gal. 4:7; Tit. 3:7; Heb. 6:17; Js. 2:5) and to Christ who is appointed heir and possessor, the Lord of all things (Mt. 21:38; Heb. 1:2; etc.). Deriv.: *klēros* (2819), lot.

2819. Klēros; a lot. Meanings: (1) A lot, the stone or mark itself which was cast into the urn or lap (Mt. 27:35; Acts 1:26). The Gr. method of casting lots was in this way: The lots of the several parties properly marked or distinguished were put into a vessel which was violently shaken by one who turned away his face. The lot which first fell upon the ground indicated the man chosen or preferred for the occasion. It seems that the Romans followed the same method. They attributed divine choice to this method. (2) A lot, allotment, part, or share (Acts 1:17 T.R.; 8:21). (3) An inheritance (Acts 26:18, cf. Acts 20:32; Col. 1:12, cf. the noun *klēronomia,* 2817, inheritance). (4) *Klēroi,* in the pl. (I Pet. 5:3) seems to denote those distinct congregations of Christians (cf. Deut. 4:20; 9:29) which fell to the lot, as it were, of different pastors. Deriv.: *klēroō* (2820), to cast lots, determine by lot; *holoklēros* (3648), an entire portion, intact; *klēronomos* (2818), one who has a *klēros,* inheritance or a lot; *klēronomia* (2817), that which constitutes one as heir, inheritance; *klēronomeō* (2816), to be an heir (*klēronomos*); *sugklēronomos* (4789), he who participates in the same inheritance or lot, joint-heir; *kataklērodoteō* (2624), to divide by lot.

2820. Klēroō; to cast lots, determine by lot, i.e., to determine something, or concerning someone. In Eph. 1:11 it means, "to whom the lot has fallen upon us also, as fore-ordained thereto . . ., to be." The entire thought expressed here demands a declaration referring to the present Christian state of those addressed and its actual accomplishment. The Apostle is saying that the lot has fallen upon us now, before the fulfillment of all, to be those who contribute to the praise of His glory as being the first who trusted in Christ.

2821. Klēsis; call, summons, invitation, vocation, from *kaleō* (2564), to call. A calling (Rom. 11:29; I Cor. 1:26; Eph. 4:1). A calling, condition, employment (I. Cor. 7:20).

2822. Klētos; verbal adj. from *kaleō* (2564), to call. Called, invited, welcomed, appointed. One who is called to an office (Rom. 1:1; I Cor. 1:1). The called ones, *klētoi,* are those who have received the divine call, *klēsis* (2821), having conformed to God's saving purpose (Rom. 1:6,7; 8:28; I Cor. 1:2,24), without implying immediate obedience to the call (Mt. 20:16; 22:14, cf. Rev. 17:14). See *eklektos* (1588), elect.

2839. Koinos; defiled, common, unclean; to lie common or open to all; common or belonging to several or of which several are partakers (Acts 2:44; 4:32; Tit. 1:4; Jude 3); unclean of the hands (Mk. 7:2), of meats (Acts 10:14,28; 11:8; Rom. 14:14; Heb. 10:29) such as were common to other nations but were avoided by the Jews as polluted and unclean (Mk. 7:2). Verb: *koinoō* (2840), to make common, unclean.

2840. Koinoō; from *koinos* (2839), common. To make common, unclean, pollute or defile (Mt. 15:11; Acts 21:28; Heb. 9:13; Rev. 21:27 T.R.); to pronounce or call common or unclean (Acts 10:15; 11:9). Related to *miainō* (3392), to defile.

2841. Koinōneō; from *koinos* (2839), lying open to all, common. With a dat. of the thing: to communicate, partake, participate, be a partaker in or of (Rom. 15:27; I Tim. 5:22; I Pet. 4:13; II Jn. 11), as it is also with the gen. in Heb. 2:14. With a dat. of the person: to communicate, distribute, impart (Rom. 12:13; Gal. 6:6; Phil. 4:15).

2842. Koinōnia; fellowship with, participation in anything (I Cor. 10:16); a communion, fellowship, society (Acts 2:42; I Cor. 1:9; II Cor. 6:14; Phile. 6, cf. II Cor. 8:4); communication distribution, alms-giving (Rom. 15:26; II Cor. 9:13; Heb. 13:16).

2844. Koinōnos; from *koinoō* (2840), to make anything common (*koinon,* 2839); a partaker (Mt. 23:30; I Cor. 10:18; II Cor. 1:7; I Pet. 5:1; II Pet. 1:4; see also Phile. 17 where it refers to the participation in Christ or in Gospel blessings). Partner, companion (Lk. 5:10; I Cor. 10:20; Heb. 10:33). Deriv.: *koinos* (2839), common; *koinoō* (2840), to make anything common; *koinōneō* (2841), to share; *koinōnia* (2842), fellowship with, participation in anything; *koinōnikos* (2843), communicative or cultivating a loving fellowship; *sugkoinōneō* (4790), to participate in something with someone; *sug-*

koinōnos (4791), partaker.

2851. Kolasis; from *kolazō* (2849), to punish; punishment (Mt. 25:46); torment (I Jn. 4:18). Distinguished from *timōria* (5098), in Class. Gr. the vindictive character of the punishment as the predominant thought which satisfies the inflicter's sense of outraged justice as defending his own honor or that of the violated law. *Kolasis*, on the other hand, conveys the notion of punishment for the correction and bettering of the offender. It does not always, however, have the same meaning in the N.T., e.g., in Mt. 25:46 *kolasis aiōnios* (166), eternal, does not refer to temporary corrective punishment and discipline, but has more the meaning of *timōria*, punishment, because of the violation of the eternal law of God. It is the punishment with which our Lord threatens the offenders with finality (Mk. 9:43-48). In this sense it does not have the underthought of the bettering of one who endures such punishment. In *kolasis* we have the relation of the punishment to the punished while in *timōria* the relationship is to the punisher himself.

2869. Kopazō; from *kopos* (2873), labor, fatigue; to cease through extreme fatigue or being worn out with labor; to cease, as the wind (Mt. 14:32; Mk. 4:39; 6:51). Deriv.: *kopiaō* (2872), to toil, labor even to exhaustion and weariness (Mt. 6:28; Lk. 5:5, etc.); *kopos* (2873), labor, travail (II Cor. 11:23,27, etc.); trouble, disturbance, uneasiness (Mt. 26:10; Lk. 18:5, etc.).

2873. Kopos; from *kekopa*, the perf. mid. voice of *koptō* (2875), to strike. Labor, travail (II Cor. 11:23,27; I Thess. 2:9; 3:5); trouble, disturbance, uneasiness. Used nineteen times in the N.T. to denote not so much the actual exertion which a man makes, but the weariness which he experiences from that exertion. Used to designate that which we as Christians ought to render to the Lord as labor in the Christian ministry. *Kopos* is to be distinguished from *mochthos* (3449), the everyday word for human labor, and *ponos* (4192), the labor which demands the whole strength of a man exerted to the uttermost if he is to accomplish the task which is before him. Verb: *kopiaō* (2872), labor, toil.

2875. Koptō; to cut off or down (Mt. 21:8; Mk. 11:8); in the mid. voice *koptomai*, to strike or beat one's body, particularly one's breasts, with the hands in lamentation, to lament, wail (Nah. 2:7; Lk. 18:13; 23:48). Used trans. in Lk. 8:52 and intrans. in Lk. 23:27. Used with the inten. prep. *epi* (1909) in Rev. 1:7; 18:9. The strongest form of outward expression of inner grief, *lupē* (3077) and *lupeō* (3076), referring to inner grief without necessarily an outward expression. The two milder words expressing grief outwardly are *pentheō* (3996), to mourn, and *thrēneō* (2354), to wail.

2880. Korennumi; to have enough, abundance (Acts 27:38; I Cor. 4:8). Deriv.: *koros* (2884). A measure equal to ten baths (Gr. *batoi*, 943) or seventy-five gallons (Lk. 16:6).

2886. Kosmikos; worldly, what belongs to the world. In the N.T. it corresponds to the idea of *kosmos* (2889), world (Heb. 9:1). Opp. heavenly and spiritual (v. 11). In Tit. 2:12 "worldly desires" pertain to those desires of the world which estrange a person from God (Eph. 2:1,2).

2887. Kosmios; from *kosmos* (2889), order. Orderly, decent (I Tim. 2:9; 3:2). Derived from *kosmos* which earlier had the sense of ornament. Plato presents a *kosmios* as the citizen who is quiet in the land, who fulfills the duties which are incumbent on him as such and is not disorderly. He associates such persons, even as Paul does, with *sōphrōn* (4998), sensible, self-controlled, one who voluntarily places limitations on his freedom. The virtue of the *kosmios*, however, is not only the propriety of his dress and demeanor, but of his inner life, uttering and expressing itself in the outward conversation. Contr. *semnos* (4586), venerable, this latter person has a grace and dignity not obtained from earth only. While *kosmios* behaves himself well in his earthly citizenship and is an asset, the *semnos* owes his quality to that higher citizenship which is also his. *Semnos* inspires not only respect but reverence and worship. Syn.: *hieroprepēs* (2412), one who acts like a sacred person.

2888. Kosmokratōr; world ruler, from *kosmos* (2889), order or world, and *kratos* (2904), power, authority. A ruler of this world (Eph. 6:12, spoken of evil spirits, cf. Jn. 12:31; 14:30). Contr. *pantokratōr* (3841), the ruler of everything, from *panta pas, pan* (3956), all, and *kratōr*, the one holding authority (II Cor. 6:18; Rev. 1:8; 4:8; 11:17; 15:3; 16:7,14; 19:6,15; 21:22).

2889. Kosmos; world, cosmos from *kosmeō* (2885), to set in order, adorn. That which pertains to space and not time (*aiōn*, 165, age). The sum total of the material universe, the beauty in it; the sum total of persons living in the world.

2897. Kraipalē; from *kra*, the head, an abbreviation of *karēnon* or *kranion* (2898), and *pallō*, to agitate. A headache, a shooting pain or a confusion of the head arising from intemperance in wine or strong liquors. Translated in Lk. 21:34 as "dissipation," the sense of disgust and loathing from overfullness of wine. Related words: *methē* (3178), drunkenness in the abstract; *potos* (4224), a drinking bout leading possibly to excess; *oinophlugia* (3632), excess of wine; *kōmos* (2970), pl., revellings and rioting.

2902. Krateō; from *kratos* (2904), strength. To hold fast (Mt. 26:48,50; Mk. 14:44,46; Acts 3:11); to detain (Acts 2:24); to maintain, retain (Mk. 7:3,4,8; II Thess. 2:15; Heb. 4:14; Rev. 2:13-15,25); to lay hold of or take. In this sense either with a gen. (Mt. 9:25; Mk. 1:31; Lk. 8:54), or with an accus. (Mt. 12:11; 14:3; 22:6; 26:4); to hold, as in the hands (Rev. 2:1); to obtain (Acts 27:13); to hold, restrain (Lk. 24:16); to retain, not to remit, as sins (Jn. 20:23).

2904. Kratos; force, strength, might, more especially manifested power, dominion, from *krateō* (2902), to hold fast. More closely related to *ischus* (2479), strength, than *dunamis* (1411), power. Denotes the presence and significance of force or strength rather than its exercise. Deriv.: *krataios* (2900), adj. describing God's power manifested in the blows and severe punishments which He sends and which man cannot escape (I Pet. 5:6); *krataioō* (2901), to make strong, in the pass. to become strong (Lk. 1:80; 2:40; I Cor. 16:13; Eph. 3:16); *kosmokratōr* (2888), pl., indicating the terrifying power of the rulers of the world (Eph. 6:12); *pantokratōr* (3841), the Almighty, from *panta* (3956), all, and *kratōr*, the ruler, the One who holds everything together (II Cor. 6:18; Rev. 1:8; 4:8; 11:17; 15:3; 16:7,14; 19:6,15; 21:22).

2908. Kreisson; the neut. of *kreissōn* or *kreittōn* (2909), occurs as an adv. in Heb. 12:24 meaning more emphatically; in I Cor. 7:38, more advantageously, more appropriately (cf. v. 35).

2909. Kreissōn; or *kreittōn*, comparative of *agathos* (18), benevolently good. Others make it the comparative from *kratus*, strong, the adj. from *kratos* (2904), power, strength, dominion. Stronger, more powerful, superior or better in strength (Heb. 1:4); better, more excellent (I Cor. 11:17; 12:31 T.R.; etc.); better, more profitable (II Pet. 2:21); better, more favorable (Heb. 12:24).

2917. Krima; the suffix *-ma* indicates the result of *krinō* (2919), to judge, or *krisis* (2920), the act of judging. A solemn judgment, judicial trial (Acts 24:25; Heb. 6:2) or judicial sentence (Rom. 2:2,3, cf. Rom. 5:16); a private judgment, or pronouncement of a private sentence or opinion (Mt. 7:2); being adjudged or sentenced to punishment, condemnation, damnation (Mt. 23:14 T.R.; Lk. 23:40; 24:20; Rom. 3:8; 13:2, etc.); the execution or judgment, punishment (Mt. 23:14 T.R.; Mk. 12:40; Js. 3:1); judicial or legal contest, a lawsuit (I Cor. 6:7); judicial authority, power of judging (Rev. 20:4). Deriv.: *krinō* (2919), to judge.

2919. Krinō; to divide, separate, make a distinction, come to a decision. N.T. meanings: (1) To judge, try in a solemn judicial manner. Spoken of men (Jn. 18:31; Acts 24:6); of God (Acts 17:31; Rom. 3:6); of Christ as the God-Man (II Tim. 4:1, cf. Lk. 19:22). (2) To judge, pass sentence or give one's opinion in a private manner (Mt. 7:1,2; Lk. 6:37; Jn. 8:15). (3) To judge, discern, form a mental judgment or opinion (Lk. 12:57; Jn. 7:24; Acts 4:19; I Cor. 10:15; 11:13). (4) To judge, think, esteem (Acts 16:15; 26:8, cf. Acts 13:46; Rom.

14:5; I Cor. 4:5. In the last two passages the verb seems to denote preferring one to another). (5) To judge properly, determine (Acts 15:19; 16:4; 20:16; 21:25; 25:25; I Cor. 5:3). (6) To adjudge to punishment, condemn (Jn. 3:17,18; 7:51; Acts 13:27, etc.). (7) To furnish matter or occasion for condemnation, to condemn in this sense (Rom. 2:27), cf. *katakrinō* (2632), to condemn (Mt. 12:41,42; Lk. 11:31,32; Heb. 11:7). (8) In the pass.: *krinomai*, to be judged or to be brought or called into judgment, to be called in question (Acts 23:6; 24:21; 26:6); also *krinomai*, to be judged, i.e., to enter into a judicial contest with, to go to law with (Mt. 5:40; I Cor. 6:1,6). (9) In the inf. followed by the prep. *en* (1722), in: *krinetai en* (I Cor. 6:2), to be judged by. Deriv.: *krisis* (2920), separation, judgment; *krima* (2917), the result or issue of judging, the decision arrived at or judgment; *kritēs* (2923), the one who decides or a judge; *kritērion* (2922), an instrument of judging, a court of justice; *kritikos* (2924), one whose business and special gift is to judge; *apokrinomai* (611), the mid. or pass. of *apokrinō*, to be separated, selected to answer, to take occasion to speak; *apokrisis* (612), a decision, answer; *apokrima* (610), an answer against, condemnation; *diakrinō* (1252), separate one from another, divide, part; *diakrisis* (1253), separation, discrimination; *adiakritos* (87), undistinguishable; *egkrinō* (1469), to divide up, place in a series, to rank with; *katakrinō* (2632), decide, judge, pronounce condemnation against anyone; *katakrima* (2631), that which is decided against anyone, a condemnatory judgment; *katakrisis* (2633), the act of condemnation; *eilikrinēs* (1506), tested or judged by the sun, by the light as spotless, pure, clear, sincere; *eilikrineia* (1505), purity, sincerity; *prokrima* (4299), that which is decided ahead of time; *sugkrinō* (4793), to separate and arrange together, combine, unite, compare, measure or estimate; *hupokrinō* (5271), to act out what one is not, act like a hypocrite; *hupokrisis* (5272), pretense, hyprocrisy; *hupokritēs* (5273), a hypocrite; *anupokritos* (505), inexperienced in the art of acting, unhypocritical, genuine.

2920. Krisis; a separation, sundering, judgment, sentence, from *krinō* (2919), to judge. N.T. meanings: (1) Judgment (Jn. 5:22,30; 7:24; 8:16, cf. Jn. 16:11). The final judgment (Mt. 10:15; 12:36,41,42, etc.). Used with the verb *poieō* (4160), to make, to pass judgment or sentence (Jn. 5:27; II Pet. 2:11; Jude 9). (2) In judgment, justice (Mt. 12:20, cf. Mt. 23:23) (3) Judgment of condemnation, condemnation, damnation (Mk. 3:29 T.R.; Jn. 5:24,29); the punishment consequent on condemnation (Mt. 23:33). (4) The cause or ground of condemnation or punishment (Jn. 3:19). (5) A particular court of justice among the Jews consisting of twenty-three men which, before the Roman government was established in Judea, had the power of life and death so far as its jurisdiction extended and punished criminals by strangling or beheading (Mt. 5:21,22). Deriv.: *krinō* (2919), to judge.

2922. Kritērion; from *krinō* (2919), to judge. Judgment, the art, act or authority of judging or determining (I Cor. 6:2); judidical contest or controversy, a lawsuit (I Cor. 6:4); judgment seat, tribunal, court of justice (Js. 2:6).

2923. Kritēs; he who decides, a judge (Mt. 5:25; 12:27; Lk. 18:2; Acts 10:42; 13:20). Deriv.: *krinō* (2919), to judge.

2924. Kritikos; one whose business and special gift is to judge. Used only in Heb. 4:12.

2936. Ktizō; from *ktaō*, or *ktaomai* (2932), in the pass. or mid., to possess. In Homer the word meant to found a city or a habitable place. N.T. meanings: to create, produce from nothing (Mk. 13:19; Col. 1:16; Rev. 4:11); to form out of preexistent matter (I Cor. 11:9); to make, compose (Eph. 2:15); to create and form in a spiritual sense, regeneration or renewal (Eph. 2:10; 4:24). Deriv.: *ktisis* (2937), the founding, creation; *ktisma* (2938), a place founded, built or colonized; *ktistēs* (2939), a settler, founder, inventor.

2937. Ktisis; a founding, i.e., of a city, colonization of a habitable place. Creation in a pass. sense, what is created, the sum total of what is created (Mk. 10:6; 13:19; I Pet. 2:13). Denotes particularly the individual creature or what is created (Rom. 1:25; 8:39; Col. 1:15; Heb. 4:13). The sum total of what God has created, the creation (Mk. 10:6; 13:19; Rom. 1:20; Heb. 9:11; II Pet. 3:4; Rev. 3:14). Refers specifically to mankind as God's creation (Mk. 16:15; Col. 1:23). Cf. *kainē* (2537), qualitatively new with *ktisis*, creation or creature (II Cor. 5:17; Gal. 6:15). Deriv.: *ktizō* (2936), to create, make.

2938. Ktisma; that which is created, from the verb *ktizō* (2936), to build, plant a colony, with the suffix *-ma* the result of building. In the N.T., creature, created thing (I Tim. 4:4; Js. 1:18; Rev. 5:13; 8:9).

2939. Ktistēs; settler, founder, inventor. Only in I Pet. 4:19. A creator.

2955. Kuptō; to bow the head, stoop down (Mk. 1:7; Jn. 8:6,8). Deriv.: *parakuptō* (3879) from *para* (3844), aside; denotes to bend forward, to stoop to look into (Lk. 24:12; Jn. 20:5,11; Js. 1:25; I Pet. 1:12); *anakuptō* (352), from *ana* (303), up, to lift oneself up. Used of the body (Jn. 8:7,10; Lk. 13:11); of the mind, to look up, to be elated (Lk. 21:28).

2960. Kuriakos; belonging to a lord or ruler. Only in I Cor. 11:20; Rev. 1:10 as belonging to Christ, to the Lord, having special reference to Him. Hence, *kuriakē*, which came to mean *kuriakē hēmera*, the day of the Lord, what we call Sunday. It was the day kept in commemoration of Christ's resurrection (Jn. 20:1,24-29; Acts 20:7; I Cor. 16:2). See also Rev. 1:5,18.

2962. Kurios; Lord, wielding authority for good. Contr. *despotēs* (1203), a despot wielding authority over slaves.

2963. Kuriotēs; dominion, from *kurios* (2962), lord, mighty one. Dominion, civil power, authority or magistracy (II Pet. 2:10; Jude 8); a certain order of angels, an abstract term being used for a concrete form (Eph. 1:21; Col. 1:16). Reference is made to evil angelic powers as indicated in II Pet. 2:11, although not in Jude 9. The word is peculiar to N.T. and Patristic Gr. and denotes the kingly glory of Christ.

2970. Kōmos; used in the pl. only in the N.T.; riotings (Rom. 13:13); revelings (Gal. 5:21; I Pet. 4:3). Derived from *Comus*, the god of feasting and reveling. His sacred rights consisted in feasting and drunkenness, in impurity and obscenity of the grossest kind. Actually there were lascivious feastings with songs, music, and drinking wine. Therefore, it always presupposes a festal company and drunken revellers. Related words: *methē* (3178), drunkenness in the abstract sense; *potos* (4224), a drinking bout or banquet giving opportunity for excessive drinking but not necessarily realizing it; *oinophlugia* (3632), excess of wine; *kraipalē* (2897), the sense of overfullness of wine.

2978. Lailaps; whirlwind; see *pnoē* (4157), wind.

2980. Laleō; to talk at random. Sub.: *laliā* (2981), articulated words as contr. with silence or mere sounds or animal cries (Mt. 26:73; Mk. 14:70; Jn. 4:42; 8:43). The dumb man is *alalos* (216), mute (Mk. 7:37; 9:17,25); when restored to speech, *elalēse*, aor. of *laleō* (Mt. 9:33; Lk. 11:14), emphasizing the fact of speech versus speechlessness. When reference is made to those who spoke in tongues whether foreign languages or the Corinthian unknown tongue, it is always referred to as *laleo glōssais* (Mk. 16:17; Acts 2:4; I Cor. 12:30) emphasizing not the content of the speech, but merely that they uttered sounds as far as the hearers were concerned. *Laleō* is ascribed to God (Heb. 1:1,2), indicating not that the content of His speech was meaningless, but that He spoke at all instead of keeping silent. Contr. *legō* (3004), to speak expressing thoughts.

2983. Lambanō; to take in whatever manner. Almost syn. with *dechomai* (1209), to take or receive, and yet distinct from it in that *lambanō* sometimes means to receive as merely a self-prompted action without necessarily signifying a favorable reception (Gal. 2:6). Deriv.: (1) *Analambanō* (353); from *ana* (303), up, and *lambanō* (2983), to take, to take up (Mk. 16:19; Acts 1:2; 20:13,14; Eph. 6:13,16; II Tim. 4:11). (2) *Lēpsis* (3028), or *lēmpsis*, a receiving, related to *lambanō* (Phil. 4:15). (3) *Analēpsis* (354), from *ana* (303), up, a taking up as in reference to Christ's ascension (Lk. 9:51). (4) *Metalamabanō* (3335), from *meta* (3326), with, meaning to have or get a share of, partake of (Heb. 6:7). (5) *Metalē(m)psis* (3336), a participation (I Tim. 4:3) in connection with food. (6) *Paralambanō* (3880), from *para* (3844), beside, thus meaning not only to receive, but denotes to take to or with oneself, as taking a wife (Mt. 1:20,24), or taking a person or persons with one (Mt. 2:13,14,20,21; 4:5,8, etc.); of the removal of persons from earth in judgment (Mt. 24:40,41; Lk. 17:34,35); of the taking of Christ by the soldiers for scourging (Mt. 27:27) and to crucifixion (Jn. 19:16). (7) *Proslambanō* (4355), from *pros* (4314), to; always in the mid. voice signifying a special interest on the part of the receiver, suggesting a welcome (Acts 27:33-36); of persons (Mt. 16:22; Mk. 8:32); for evil purposes (Acts 17:5); for good purposes (18:26). (8) *Proslē(m)psis* (4356), receiving (Rom. 11:15). (9) *Apolambanō* (618), from *apo* (575), from; to receive from another as one's due (Lk. 18:30; 23:41; Rom. 1:27; Col. 3:24; II Jn. 8); without the indication of what is due (Lk. 16:25; Gal. 4:5); to receive back (Lk. 6:34; 15:27); to take apart (Mk. 7:33). (10) *Epilambanō* (1949), from *epi* (1909), upon; in the mid. voice *epilambanomai*, with a gen. or more rarely with an accus., to lay, take, or catch hold of (Mt. 14:31; Mk. 8:23; Lk. 9:47; 23:26; Acts 9:27; 16:19); to lay hold of one's words in order to accuse him (Lk. 20:20,26); with a gen., to assume, to take upon one (Heb. 2:16), which means when Christ came to redeem us, He did not assume a glorious, awful, and angelic appearance in fire and light, clouds and thick darkness, as He did at Sinai (Ex. 19:18; Deut. 4:11,12), but He took upon Himself human nature (Gal. 3:16; Phil. 2:6,7). The adj. derived from *epilambanomai* is *anepilēptos* (423) from the neg. *a* and *epileptos*, blameable which in turn is deriv. from *epilambanomai*, to reprehend, blame. Therefore, the adj. *anepilēptos* means unblamable, blameless, irreprehensible (I Tim. 3:2; 5:7; 6:14). (11) *Katalambanō* (2638), to seize. (12) *Prolambanō* (4301) from *pro* (4253), before; to take before another (I Cor. 11:21), to anticipate, do somewhat beforehand (Mk. 14:8). In the mid. voice, to be taken before one is aware, to be overtaken, surprised as in a fault (Gal. 6:1). (13) *Hupolambanō* (5274) from *hupo* (5259), under; to take under (Acts 1:9); to answer, to take up (Lk. 10:30); to suppose, apprehend, think, to take it (Lk. 7:43; Acts 2:15).

2985. Lampas; a torch. Contr. *luchnos* (3088), lamp. In the East the torch as well as the lamp is fed with oil.

2992. Laos; a people, nation, a number of men joined together by the common bands of society (Lk. 2:10,31,32). The common people, the multitude (Mt. 26:5; 27:64; Lk. 1:10). The society of Christians or of the Christian church (Mt. 1:21; I Pet. 2:9,10). In the Septuagint, it is a title almost totally reserved for the elect people, the Israel of God. Contr. *ethnos* (1484), nation, which signifies the heathen, or Gentiles, as distinguished from the Jews or believers (Mt. 6:32; 10:5,18; 20:19,25; Lk. 2:32; I Cor. 5:1; 12:2; Eph. 2:11; 3:6, etc.). Syn.: *dēmos* (1218), from the verb *deō* (1210), to bind, a people commonly bound together from which comes the word "democracy"; *ochlos* (3793), a disorganized crowd or multitude.

2999. Latreia; service or divine service, from *latreuō* (3000), to worship. Occurs only in Jn. 16:2; Rom. 9:4; 12:1; Heb. 9:1,6. That sacrifice seems especially to be the service denoted is clear from Rom. 9:4; 12:1; Heb. 9:1,6.

3000. Latreuō; to serve; in a religious sense to worship God (Mt. 4:10; Lk. 1:74; 2:37), or creatures (Acts 7:42; Rom. 1:25). It refers particularly to the performing of the Levitical service (Heb. 8:5; 9:9; 10:2; 13:10). Allied to *latris*, a hired servant as opp. to *doulos* (1401), a slave. Therefore, to serve or worship but not out of compulsion.

3004. Legō; to speak by linking and knitting together in connected discourse the inward thoughts and feelings of the mind. Sub.: *logos* (3056), thought, intelligence and also that which expresses it, speech. Contr. *laleō* (2980), to speak, and *lalia* (2981), speech.

3008. Leitourgeō; to minister publicly in sacred office (Acts 13:2; Heb. 10:11); in works of charity (Rom. 15:27). Deriv. from *leitos*, public, and *ergon* (2041), work. Leading in public worship, *latreia* (2999). It came to mean performing of priestly or ministerial functions. To serve God is the duty of all, *latreuō* (3000), but to serve Him in special offices and ministries can be the duty and privilege of only a few who are set apart to the same. Deriv.: *leitourgia* (3009), public ministry whether in sacred offices (Lk. 1:23; Phil. 2:17; Heb. 8:6; 9:21) or in works of charity (II Cor. 9:12; Phil. 2:30) from which are derived the English words "liturgy" and "liturgical"; *leitourgos* (3011), a public officer or minister (Rom. 13:6; 15:16; Phil. 2:25; Heb. 1:7; 8:2); *leitourgikos* (3010), performing public service (Heb. 1:14).

3027. Lēstēs; a robber depriving another of his property openly and by violence. May be a noble person avenging a righteous cause by human wrath such as a guerrilla. Contr. *kleptēs* (2812), thief.

3049. Logizomai; derived from *logos* (3056), reason, word, account. Actually, the verb *legō* (3004) means to put together with one's mind, to count, to occupy oneself with reckonings or calculations. In the N.T. the present in a pass. sense as in Rom. 4:4,5,24; 9:8 also means to reckon, count (I Cor. 13:5). To count something to somebody means to reckon anything to a person, to put to his account, either in his favor or what he must be answerable for (Rom. 4:4, 6,8,11; II Cor. 5:19; II Tim. 4:16). In Rom. 4:11 the expression is used as a term technically applied to God's act of justification which is more fully explained in v. 6. It is that imputation of righteousness whose correlative is freedom from guilt, and the emphasis clearly rests upon "it was reckoned" (Rom. 4:10, 23,24). In Acts 19:27, to esteem or reckon as of no account. Such a meaning is common with Paul (Rom. 2:26; 9:8). When something is counted to somebody for something, it denotes that it is imputed to the person in a substitutionary manner. The expression, "to count someone with somebody," means to number anyone with (Mk. 15:28; Lk. 22:37). *Logizomai* also means to reckon, to value or esteem (Rom. 8:36; I Cor. 4:1; II Cor. 10:2; 12:6); followed by the accus. with the inf. (Rom. 14:14; II Cor. 11:5; Phil. 3:13); followed by *hoti* (3754), that (Heb. 11:19); followed by two accus (Rom. 6:11). To account, to conclude or infer, to believe (Rom. 3:28); to consider (Jn. 11:50). Deriv.: *logismos* (3053), reckoning; *dialogizomai* (1260), to reckon distributively, to settle with one, to ponder, consider; *dialogismos* (1261), calculation, consideration.

3050. Logikos; pertaining to reason and therefore reasonable, or pertaining to speech as reasonable expression. In Rom. 12:1 the reasonable service or worship is to be understood as that service to God which implies intelligent meditation or reflection without heathen practices intimated in I Cor. 12:2 and without the O.T. cultic worship which had become mere thoughtless habit (Isa. 1:12-15). On the other hand, in I Pet. 2:2, *logikon gala*, literally logical milk, cannot possibly mean "reasonable milk." Milk, if taken literally, cannot be reasonable. *Logos*, from which *logikos* is derived, means God's reason or intelligence expressed in human speech (Jn. 1:1,14). Understand *logos* as the Word of God and *logikon gala* becomes the milk of the Word, milk to be found in the Word. The Word of God is spiritual nourishment as milk is physical nourishment. The second adj. *adolon* (97), unadulterated, agrees with this, meaning that the Word of God when not mixed with human error is nourishing. Cf. *adolon*, in II Cor. 4:2, not beguiling the Word of God.

3051. Logion; sentence, declaration, especially the utterance of the oracles of the gods, equivalent to *chrēsmos*. In Acts 7:38; Rom. 3:2; Heb. 5:12; I Pet. 4:11 the expression, *ta logia*, in the neut. pl., means the declaration of God, and differs from *ho logos*, the Word of God, "that which God has to say." The neut. pl. *ta logia* denotes rather the historical manifestations of this Word of God. In I Pet. 4:11 it does not say the Word (*logon*) of God, the object being to give prominence to the contr. between the word and the mere subjectivity of the speaker.

3053. Logismos; from *logizomai* (3049), to reckon. A reckoning, calculation, consideration, reflection. In the Class. writers used of the consideration and reflection preceding and determining conduct, the same meaning as in Jn. 11:50. Syn.: *boulē* (1012), purpose or thought still in the mind, not executed. In this sense the sub. is used in II Cor. 10:5 translated "imaginations." Actually, it is considerations and intentions which are hostile to the Gospel. On the other hand, in Rom. 2:15 used of considerations and reflections following upon conduct.

3056. Logos; intelligence, word as the expression of that intelligence. From *legō* (3004), to speak. Contr. *lalia* (2981), unintelligent sound, noise, or utterance, and *laleō* (2980), to speak without necessarily saying anything intelligent or understanding it as such. *Logos* is the articulate utterance of human language. It can be unspoken as formulation of thought in the mind which in that case stands in contr. to *phōnē* (5456), voice. When the contr. is between intelligent speech by man and unintelligent sounds by animals or inanimate objects, the two contr. words are *logos* and *lalia. Logos,* when it refers to discourse, is regarded as the orderly linking and knitting together in connected arrangement of words of the inward thoughts and feelings of the mind. The animals produce sounds, *laloun,* while God and human beings and those who have intelligence produce thoughtful expressions, *legoun*. In Mk. 2:2; 4:33; 8:32 we have the two words used together. In Mt. 14:27, we have *elalēse,* "He uttered or spoke," *legōn,* saying or giving meaning to the outward speech. The same is true in Heb. 2:2. *Laleō* (2980) expresses the opening of the mouth to speak as opp. to remaining silent (Acts 18:9). A problematic passage is Jn. 8:43 in which we have both *lalia* and *logos* spoken by our Lord. He was debating with the Pharisees. They were listening to what He had to say, but they were not capable of understanding because they did not want to understand. The Lord said to them, "Why do you not understand what I am saying (*lalian*)?" In other words, "What I am saying to you is as if it had no meaning whatsoever." And why did it have no meaning? The reason is explained in the balance of the paragraph, "Even because ye cannot hear my word, (*logon*)," or better still, "Because you cannot understand and obey (*akouō,* 191) my *logon,*" speech with its intended meaning. What the Lord really meant is that those who will not give room in their hearts to His truth will not understand His speech, utterance, the outward form of His language which His Word (*logos*) assumes. Those who are of God hear God's words (*rhēmata, rhēma,* 4487) (Jn. 3:34; 8:47). The word *rhēma* here is equivalent to *lalia*. Jn. 3:34 says that Jesus Christ being sent of God speaks exactly God's utterances which those who are of God understand and those who are not do not understand. The *logos* not being accepted as the intelligent utterance of God, even His speech (*lalia* and *rhēma*) is not known or recognized. In Jn. 1 Jesus Christ in His preincarnate state is called *ho Logos,* the Word, meaning first immaterial intelligence and then the expression of that intelligence in speech that humans could understand. Additional meanings of *logos:* (1) A word (Mt. 8:8,16; Lk. 7:7). (2) A saying, discourse, conversation (Mt. 12:37; 15:12; 19:22; 22:15; 26:1; Jn. 4:39; Acts 5:24). (3) A report, rumor (Mt. 28:15; Lk. 5:15; 7:17, etc.). (4) A common saying, a proverb (Jn. 4:37). (5) The Word of God, whether of the law (Mk. 7:13) or of the Gospel (Mt. 13:19-23; Mk. 2:2; 16:20; Acts 8:4; II Tim. 4:2, etc.). In this regard it sometimes implies the profession and practice of the Gospel (Mt. 13:21; Mk. 4:17; Jn. 8:31; Rev. 1:9; 20:4). (6) Speech, eloquence (I Cor. 2:1; II Cor. 11:6). (7) Ability to speak, utterance (Eph. 6:19). (8) Reason, the faculty of reasoning or discoursing. *Kata logon,* according to reason, reasonably (Acts 18:14). This use was very common among the heathen writers and it is an unbeliever who is speaking in this instance. Cf. *alogos* (249), irrational, without intelligence, unreasonable; and its opp. *logikos* (3050), reasonable. See also *phēmi* (5346), to speak with a prophetic tinge to it.

3058. Loidoreō; to revile, reproach (Jn. 9:28; Acts 23:4; I Cor. 4:12; I Pet. 2:23). Syn.: *blasphēmeō* (987), to revile, to blaspheme (Mt. 27:39; Mk. 15:29; Lk. 22:65; 23:39; Rom. 3:8; 14:16; I Cor. 4:13; Tit. 3:2; II Pet. 2:10; Jude 8) and *oneidizō* (3679), to reproach.

3067. Loutron; bath, answering to the biblical use of *louō* (3068), to bathe, wash. In Eph. 5:26, it is used metaphorically of the Word of God as the instrument of spiritual cleansing. In Tit. 3:5 "the bath of regeneration" brings to mind the close connection between cleansing from sin and regeneration (cf. Jn. 3:8; Rom. 6:4; II Cor. 5:17).

3068. Louō; bathe oneself, used of washing the whole body and not part of it as indicated by *niptō* (3538). Both of these verbs refer to the washing of living persons while *plunō* (4150) refers to the washing of inanimate things.

3076. Lupeomai; or *lupeō,* from *lupē* (3077), sorrow. Used trans., to grieve, to cause to grieve, make sorrowful (II Cor. 2:2,5; 7:8,9; Eph. 4:30), and the mid. or pass. voice *lupeomai,* to be grieved, sorrowful (Mt. 14:9; 17:23; 26:37; Rom. 14:15). This is the most common word expressing grief and opp. *chairō* (5463), to rejoice. This grief, however, is inward unlike the other words, *pentheō* (3996), mourn; *thrēneō* (2354), bewail; and *koptō* (2875), to strike the bosom or beat the breast as an outward sign of an inward grief. Paul expressed the outwardness of the inner grief, *lupē;* therefore, in *lupeō* and the sub. *lupē* (3077), there is no outward manifestation necessary of the inner grief. It depends on whether or not the individual chooses to reveal outwardly his inner grief (Rom. 9:2).

3083. Lutron; a neut. noun, from *luō* (3089), to loose from which is derived *lutroō* (3084), to ransom. Ransom or a price paid for redeeming captives, loosing them from their bonds and setting them at liberty. In Mt. 20:28; Mk. 10:45 it applies spiritually to the ransom paid by Christ for the delivering of men from the bondage of sin and death. Deriv.: *lutrōsis* (3085), the act of redemption or deliverance; *lutrōtēs* (3086), redeemer; *antilutron* (487), ransom; *apolutrōsis* (629), ransoming, redemption as the result of expiation.

3084. Lutroō; literally to bring forward a ransom (*lutron,* 3083). The act. verb used not of him who gives, but of him who receives it; hence to release on receipt of a ransom. In the mid. voice, to release by payment of a ransom, to redeem; in the pass., to be redeemed or ransomed. Therefore, *lutroō* means to receive a ransom. In the N.T. used in the mid. voice in Lk. 24:21; Tit. 2:14; in the pass. in I Pet. 1:18. Denotes that aspect of the Saviour's work wherein He appears as the redeemer of mankind from bondage. This bondage was still regarded quite generally as oppression in Lk. 24:21 because of the deficient understanding of Christ's death on the part of the Emmaus disciples (see Tit. 2:14; I Pet. 1:18). *Lutrōsis* (3085) or *apolutrōsis* (629), redemption and deliverance from suffering; redemption as the result of expiation which is the view of salvation in the N.T. This was foreshadowed in the connection between the sins of Israel and their oppression (see Eph. 1:7; I Pet. 1:18; Tit. 2:14).

3085. Lutrōsis; the act of freeing or releasing, deliverance. Derived from the act. meaning *lutroō* (3084), to release on receipt of a ransom. In biblical Gr., redemption, deliverance, not with reference to the person delivering, but to the person delivered, and, therefore, in a pass. sense like most sub. ending in *-sis* (Lk. 1:68; 2:38). Used of redemption from guilt and punishment of sin brought about by expiation (Heb. 9:12).

3086. Lutrōtēs; redeemer, liberator, from *lutroō* (3084), to redeem. In the N.T. used only in Acts 7:35 of Moses.

3088. Luchnos; a hand lamp fed with oil, not a candle as commonly translated. Contr. *lampas* (2985), torch.

3089. Luō; to loose as opp. to *deō* (1210), to bind. To loose something tied or bound (Mt. 21:2; Mk. 1:7; 11:2,4,5; Lk. 13:15; I Cor. 7:27). Spoken of seals (Rev.

5:2,5 T.R.); to loose, to pronounce or determine not to be bound (Mt. 16:19; 18:18); to break or violate a commandment or law (Mt. 5:19; Jn. 7:23); the Sabbath (Jn. 5:18); the Scripture (Jn. 10:35); to dissolve, destroy (Jn. 2:19; Eph. 2:14; II Pet. 3:10,11, cf. I Jn. 3:8); to break or beat to pieces, as a ship (Acts 27:41). Deriv.: *analuō* (360), to return; *analusis* (359), departure or return; *epiluō* (1956), to loose, dissolve; *epilusis* (1955), exposition, interpretation; *kataluō* (2647), to loose, unloose; *kataluma* (2646), an inn; *akatalutos* (179), not to be dissolved, indissoluable; *apoluō* (630), dismiss.

3100. Mathēteuō; from *mathētēs* (3101), disciple. Governing a dat., to be a disciple or follower of another's doctrine (Mt. 27:57); governing an accus., to make a disciple (Mt. 28:19; Acts 14:21); to instruct (Mt. 13:52) with the purpose of making a disciple. *Mathēteuō* must be distinguished from the verb *matheō* which is not found in the N.T. and which simply means to learn without any attachment to the teacher who teaches. *Mathēteuō* means not only to learn but to become attached to one's teacher and to become his follower in doctrine and conduct of life. Occurs only four times in the N.T.: Mt. 13:52; 27:57; 28:19; Acts 14:21. It is really not sufficient to translate this verb as "learn" but as "making a disciple" in its trans. meaning in the N.T. sense of *mathētēs*. Deriv.: *manthanō* (3129), to cause oneself to know.

3101. Mathētēs; from *matheō*, to learn, not used in the N.T. A learner, pupil. Contr. *didaskalos* (1320), an instructor, a teacher, e.g., in Mt. 10:24 where the learner cannot be higher than the instructor. See also Lk. 6:40. The term is used only in the Gospels and Acts. *Mathētēs* means more in the N.T. than a mere pupil or learner. It means an adherer who accepts the instruction given to him and makes it his rule of conduct, e.g., the disciples of John (Mt. 11:2; Mk. 2:18; Lk. 5:33; 7:18; Jn. 3:25); the disciples of the Pharisees (Mk. 2:18). In Jn. 9:28 the Pharisees told the healed blind man, "You are His disciple, but we are disciples of Moses." Jesus had disciples in the sense that they were His adherents who made His teaching the basis of their conduct. In this sense He had many disciples and He invited all those who believed to become His disciples in this manner (Mt. 5:1; 9:19; 14:22; Lk. 14:26,27,33; Jn. 9:27; 15:8). Besides, however, these believers, there was a smaller select group of twelve Apostles whom Jesus chose to be with Him. They were to teach and exercise power in performing miracles in substantiation of His authority transferred to them. Thus, the twelve are so designated in Mt. 11:1 and the eleven after Judas betrayed Jesus, Mt. 28:16. These were not ordinary disciples, but they were those who were with Him and followed Him (Mt. 5:1; 8:23,25 T.R.; 9:10; 11:1; 14:22). Sometimes they are called the disciples (Mt. 12:1; 14:19; Mk. 2:18; 9:14; Jn. 15:8, etc.). These original twelve were chosen out of the general group of those who were called the followers of Jesus (Mt. 8:21; Lk. 6:13,17; 7:11; Jn. 6:60,66, etc.). The general designation was given as a name to those who believed on Christ (Jn. 8:31). They were disciples but not the 12 disciples (Mt. 10:42; Jn. 8:31; Acts 6:2; 19:9, etc.). The name *mathētai* (pl. of *mathētēs*, Acts 19:1) was applied to John's disciples at Ephesus due to the relationship of John the Baptist to the Messiah. These disciples were utterly ignorant that Jesus was the Messiah (v. 4). Generally speaking, however, the term *mathētai*, disciples, denoted just the followers of Christ, the Messiah. Deriv.: *manthanō* (3129), to learn by putting what one learns into experience.

3106. Makarizō; to pronounce blessed, as indwelt by God, and thus fully satisfied. Used only of the Virgin Mary (Lk. 1:48) and of the persecuted prophets (Js. 5:11). Contr. *eulogeō* (2127), the more common verb in the N.T., to speak well of. The adj. *makarios* (3107), blessed, occurs many times in the N.T., to have the kingdom of God within one's heart because of Christ (Mt. 5:2,11) and as a result to be fully satisfied (Lk. 17:21).

3107. Makarios; blessed, possessing the characteristic of deity, *makariotēs*. It indicates the state of the believer in Christ (Mt. 5:3-11: "Blessed . . . on account of Me"; Lk. 6:20-22, "Blessed . . . for the sake of the Son of Man"). He is indwelt by God because of Christ and as a result is fully satisfied. Contr. *eulogētos* (2128), worthy to be well-spoken of; eulogized from *eulogeō* (2127), to speak well of. *Makarios* differs from happy because happy is the person who has good luck (from the root *hap*, favorable circumstances). A blessed person is one whom God makes fully satisfied, not because of favorable circumstances, but because He indwells the believer through Christ. To be *makarios*, blessed, is equivalent to having God's kingdom within one's heart (Mt. 5:2,11; Lk. 17:21). Aristotle contr. *makarios* to *endeēs* (1729), the needy one. *Makarios* is the one who is in the world yet independent of the world; his satisfaction comes from God and not from favorable circumstances.

3114. Makrothumeō; to suffer long, be long suffering, as opp. to hasty anger or punishment (I Cor. 13:4; I Thess. 5:14; II Pet. 3:9); to forbear (Mt. 18:26,29); to endure patiently as opp. to despondency (Heb. 6:15; Js. 5:7,8); to tarry, delay (Lk. 18:7). *Makrothumeō* is to exercise understanding and patience toward persons while *hupomenō* (5278) is to be patient toward things or circumstances. See *hupomonē* (5281), patience, and *makrothumia* (3115), longsuffering.

3115. Makrothumia; forbearance, longsuffering from the adj. *makrothumos*, longsuffering. The person who has power to avenge himself, yet refrains from the exercise of this power. Derived from *makros* (3117), long, and *thumos* (2372), passion; a long-holding of the mind before it gives room to action or passion. it is patience in respect to persons while *hupomonē* (5281), endurance, is patience toward things or circumstances. In Heb. 6:15 *makrothumeō* (3114) is used of Abraham's longsuffering toward God under the pressure of trying circumstances (Js. 5:7,8). *Makrothumia* and *hupomonē* are often found together (II Cor. 6:4,6; II Tim. 3:10). *Makrothumia* is associated with mercy (*eleos*, 1656) and is used of God (Rom. 2:4; I Pet. 3:20). See *anochē* (463), tolerance.

3116. Makrothumōs; adv. from the adj. *makrothumos*, longsuffering, which does not occur in the N.T., and the sub. *makrothumia* (3115), longsuffering. Verb: *makrothumeō* (3114), to be longsuffering. It is wrong to translate *makrothumōs* "patiently," because patience is exercised toward things and circumstances, while *makrothumia* is exercised toward God or people. When exercised toward another, one suffers long and extends himself to the life of that person wishing to win such a one to a godly life in spite of his sinfulness. This adv. occurs only in Acts 26:3. The basic word *makrothumia* stands in contr. to *hupomonē* (5281), patience or ability to stand under pressure of circumstances and things.

3119. Malakia; disease, from *malakos* (3120), soft, from *malassō*, to soften. An indisposition, infirmity (Mt. 4:23; 9:35; 10:1). Literally, softness; referring to men, delicacy, effeminacy. In Aristotelian ethics opp. *karteria*, patient endurance, weakness. The verb *kartereō* (2594), to endure, is used in Heb. 11:27.

3126. Mamōnas; or *mammōnas*, mammon, the comprehensive word for all kinds of possessions, earnings, and gains, a designation of material value. In Lk. 16:9,11 denotes riches. In Mt. 6:24; Lk. 16:13, mammon is personified by the Lord.

3129. Manthanō; from the obsolete *matheō*, to learn, from which we have the second aor. *emathon* and the inf. *mathein* as well as the aor. part. of *mathōn*. Probably related to *maomai*, to endeavor, to desire, to seek; thus meaning to learn, experience, bring into experience (Acts 23:27; Gal. 3:2). The aor., to have learned anything, to understand it (Phil. 4:11). Answers to the verb *didaskō* (1321), to teach (I Tim. 2:11,12), which denotes instruction concerning the facts and plan of salvation. In this sense it means to cause oneself to know with a moral bearing and responsibility (Jn. 6:45; Phil. 4:9). In Col. 1:6,7 *manthanō* is equivalent to *epigi-*

nōskō (1921), to know more fully. The syn. use is also indicated in II Tim. 3:7 where the two words *manthanō* and *epignōsis* (1922), a full knowledge, are used. In Eph. 4:20 the verb *manthanō* has Christ as the direct obj. He is presented as the object matter and the sum and substance of the Gospel. To become related to Him is to know Him and knowing Him is to know His teaching and abide by it. Deriv.: *mathētēs* (3101), disciple; *mathētria* (3102), a female disciple (Acts 9:36); *mathēteuō* (3100), to make anyone a disciple.

3132. Manteuomai; from *mantis,* a soothsayer, diviner, which is deduced from *mainomai* (3105), to be mad, beside oneself, from the mad extravagant behavior of such persons among the heathen. Such soothsayers raged, foamed and yelled, making strange and terrible noises, sometimes gnashing with their teeth, shaking and trembling, with many such strange motions. Plato calls such people possessed of madness from Muses, which excited and inspired the mind into enthusiastic songs and poems. They were caught up in such ecstasy that they were beside themselves. No one in his right senses was seized with the true spirit of divination. In many instances there was a real possession by the devil, e.g., in the case of the prophetic damsel (Acts 16:16,18). The *manteis* (pl.) were possessed of a mantic fury which displayed itself by the eyes rolling, the mouth foaming, and the hair flying, etc. It is quite possible that these symptoms were sometimes produced, as no doubt they were often aggravated in the seers, Pythonesses, Sibyls, and the like, by the inhalation of vapors or other artificial stimulants. There is no doubt that such belonged to a spiritual world not related to the true God. Their relationship was not with heaven above but with hell below. The Word of God knows nothing of this mantic fury except to condemn it. Paul says in I Cor. 14:32: "The spirits of prophets are subject to prophets" and not to any devilish powers. They speak not in an unknown tongue as the soothsayers, but in understandable languages. The true prophet indeed speaks not of himself, but he is possessed by the Spirit of God (Rev. 1:10); his ecstasy is of God (Acts 11:5), being led of the Holy Spirit (II Pet. 1:21) which is much more than moved by the Holy Spirit as the translations have it. Man is not "beside himself" when he is led by the Spirit, but is wise and discreet when he is filled with the presence of God. However, in the *mantis,* the sorcerer, as Plato testifies, we have one in whom all sense of reason is suspended. Thus the line is drawn broadly and distinctly between a *mantis* and a *prophētēs* (4396), prophet.

3140. Martureō; to be a witness, to bear witness; from *martur* or *martus* (3144), witness. To witness, bear witness, testify (Jn. 1:7,8; 3:26,28; 5:32; 10:25; 15:26,27; Acts 22:5; 23:11; 26:22; I Jn. 5:7); with a dat. to bear witness to, or concern (Mt. 23:31); implying praise or commendation (Lk. 4:22). In the pass. *martureomai,* to be of good report, having good character (Acts 6:3; 10:22; 22:12; Heb. 11:2,39, cf. vv. 4,5). It also means to bear witness to, denoting accent or confirmation (Acts 14:3; Heb. 10:15); the pass. *martureomai,* to implore, beseech, to charge (I Thess 2:11). Deriv.: *martus* (3144), witness.

3141. Marturia; bearing witness, certifying, (Jn. 1:7); witnessing to (Mk. 14:55,56,59; Lk. 22:71); that which anyone witnesses or states concerning a person or thing (Acts 22:18; I Tim. 3:7; Tit. 1:13). Also used of the testimony of John the Baptist concerning Jesus (Jn. 1:19; 5:36; 8:17; 19:35; 21:24); of the declarations of Jesus concerning Himself (Jn. 5:31; 8:13,14). It is a declaration which not only informs but corroborates a testimony borne by a witness who speaks with the authority of one who knows (Jn. 5:34). In I Jn. 5:9,10 the Apostle designates the eternal life possessed by believers as God's gift as they witness testifying of Him (v. 11). In Jn. 3:11,32,33, the testimony of Jesus is that which He declares with the authority of a witness, of one who knows (v. 11). But in Rev. 1:9 the testimony of Jesus is the announcement of the Gospel, the apostolic preaching of Christ as it is determined by the Apostle's testimony (v. 2, "those things that he saw"). This testimony, which especially concerns Christ and which is based upon a knowledge of Him specifically vouchsafed, is also spoken of as the testimony of Jesus (Rev. 12:17; 19:10; 20:4). That *marturia* is used in the N.T. to denote martyrdom is an untenable inference from Rev. 11:7; 12:11. See *martus* (3144), witness.

3142. Marturion; a neut. noun meaning witness; ordinarily, the declaration which confirms or makes known anything (II Cor. 1:12). The things which testify to anything (Js. 5:3). In the Class. Gr. used also for proof. In the N.T. usage it is the witness or the testimony of Christ (I Cor. 1:6, cf. II Tim. 1:8). The meaning is that the preacher bases what he says on his own direct knowledge coincident with reality, and the Gospel is preached as a narrative of actual and practical truth, a declaration of facts. This form of expression distinguishes *marturion* from the work of Christian doctrinal teaching (Acts 4:33; 5:32; II Thess. 1:10; I Tim. 2:6). The preaching of the Gospel in I Cor. 2:1 is called a *marturion,* the witness of God (Acts 7:44; Rev. 15:5). Deriv.: *martus* (3144), witness.

3143. Marturomai; to cause to witness for oneself, to call to witness. To attest, to announce and ratify as truth, to affirm (Acts 20:26; 26:22; Gal. 5:3; Eph. 4:17; I Thess. 2:12).

3144. Martus; witness. Literally, one who remembers, one who has information or knowledge or joint knowledge of anything, and hence, one who can give information, bring to light, or confirm anything (Mt. 18:16; 26:65; Mk. 14:63; Acts 7:58; II Cor. 13:1; I Tim. 5:19; Heb. 10:28). It usually denotes simply that the witness confirms something, though in many cases it also implies that he avoids something and supports his statement on the strength of his own authority (Acts 6:13). In the sense of simply a confirmation (II Cor. 1:23). Of the knowledge or cognizance which the witness possesses (Rom. 1:9; Phil. 1:8; I Thess. 2:5,10; I Tim. 6:12; II Tim. 2:2). In Heb. 12:1 they are described as witnesses who have an experimental knowledge of that which is required of us, faith (Heb. 10:35-37; 11:6ff; 12:2). Peculiar to the N.T. is the designation as *martures* (pl., witnesses) of those who announce the facts of the Gospel and tell its tidings (Acts 1:8; 2:32; 3:15; 10:39; 13:31; Rev. 11:3, etc.). Also *martus* is used as a designation of those who have suffered death in consequence of confessing Christ (of Stephen, Acts 22:20; of Antipas, Rev. 2:13; see also Rev. 17:6). This verse and the previous ones, however, should not be understood as if their witness consisted in their suffering death but rather that their witnessing of Jesus became the cause of their death. The Lord Jesus in Rev. 1:5 is called the Witness, the Faithful One (see also Rev. 3:14; 22:20). Deriv.: *marturion* (3142), the declaration which confirms or makes known anything; *marturia* (3141), certifying, witnessing; *marturomai* (3143), to cause to witness for oneself, to call to witness; *diamarturomai* (1263), to call to witness, to protest, to assert or attest anything; *martureō* (3140), to be witness, to bear witness; *epimartureō* (1957), to testify emphatically.

3151. Mataiologos; from *mataios* (3152) vain, and *legō* (3004), to speak. A vain talker, one idly speaking what is of no use (Tit. 1:10). The sub. *mataiologia* (3150), used in I Tim. 1:6 denotes speaking which lacks reason, worth, and the fruit of divine and eternal life.

3152. Mataios; vain, characterized by aimlessness, leading to no object or end, especially that end being God. It is building houses on sand, chasing the wind, shooting at stars, pursuing one's own shadow. Contr. *kenos* (2756), empty, indicating the hollowness of something or somebody. Sub.: *mataiotēs* (3153), vanity (Rom. 8:20; Eph. 4:17; II Pet. 2:18); *mataiologia* (3150), from *mataios* and *legō* (3004), to speak, vain talking (I Tim. 1:6); *mataiologos* (3151), one who talks vainly (Tit. 1:10). Verb: *mataiomai* (3154), become vain (Rom 1:21); *matēn* (3155), used in the accus. with the prep. *eis* (1519), in (Mt. 15:9; Mk. 7:7), in vain.

3153. Mataiotēs; vanity, nothingness, worth lessness, used in Rom. 8:20 to show the emptiness of the present in contr. with the living fullness of the future (Eph. 4:17; II Pet. 2:18).

3154. Mataioō; to make vain or worthless. In the pass, *mataioomai,* to become vain, destitute of real wisdom (Rom. 1:21), to be perverse, foolish, or act perversely, foolishly. In reality, to get off the right path, to follow foolish or bad courses.

3155. Matēn; an adv., strictly the accus. of *matē,* folly, fault, with the prep. *eis* (1519) in front of it. In vain. In a causal sense, groundless, invalid; and in a final sense, objectless, useless, futile, and according to circumstances may combine both idle and vain. Untrue, false (Mt. 15:9; Mk. 7:7). Deriv.: *mataios* (3152), vain, idle; *mataiotēs* (3153), vanity, nothingness, worthlessness; *mataioō* (3154), to make vain or worthless; *mataiologos* (3151), one who speaks emptiness or vanity.

3163. Machē; fighting, battle. The actual battle of hostile armies as differentiated from *polemos* (4171), war, which embraces the whole course of hostilities. The noun *machē* and *machomai* (3164), to fight, may fall short of the battle although the word may mean that. There are battles of all kinds such as legal battles as in Tit. 3:9 and battles of words as in I Tim. 6:4. Another related word is *stasis* (4714), insurrection or sedition, distinguished from *polemos* (4171), war, with *stasis* being a civil war and *polemos* a foreign one.

3167. Megaleios; from *megas* (3173), great; indicating great works or miracles (Lk. 1:49 T.R.; Acts 2:11) contemplated as outcomings of the greatness (*megaleion*) of God's power and glory. See *sēmeia* (4592), signs; *dunameis* (1411), mighty works; *endoxa* (1741), glorious things; *paradoxa* (3861), strange or extraordinary things; *thaumasia* (2297), astonishing things; *terata* (5059), wonders.

3178. Methē; drunkeness (Lk. 21:34; Rom. 13:13; Gal. 5:21). Used in an abstract sense, contr. *potos* (4224) used in a concrete sense, the drinking bout, the banquet, the symposium, not necessarily excessive but giving opportunity for excess. *Methē* is stronger and expresses a greater excess than *oinōsis,* the influence of wine. The excess of wine in the N.T. is expressed as *oinophlugia* (3632).

3179. Methistēmi; from *meta* (3326), denoting change of place and *histēmi* (2476), to place, stand. To remove from an office (Lk. 16:4; Acts 13:22); to remove, to translate into the kingdom of the Son of God (Col. 1:13); to turn away, pervert (Acts 19:26). Also spelled *methistanō,* from *meta,* denoting change of place and *histanō,* to place; to remove from its place, transfer (I Cor. 13:2).

3180. Methodeia; from *methodos,* method; the following or pursuing of orderly and technical procedure in the handling of a subject. Verb: *methodeuō,* to go systematically to work, to do or pursue something methodically and according to the rules. In the N.T. connected with evil doing, a device, artifice, art, artificial method, or wile (Eph. 4:14; 6:11).

3195. Mellō; signifying intention, about to do something (Acts 3:3; 18:14, etc.); certainty, compulsion or necessity; to be certain to act (Jn. 6:71); almost (Acts 21:27, cf. 26:28); to be about to (Rev. 10:7); to be about to do something often implying the necessity and, therefore, the certainty of what is to take place (Mt. 3:7; 11:14; Eph. 1:21; I Tim. 4:8; 6:19; Heb. 2:5); to be about to do a thing, indicating simply the formation of a design (Acts 5:35; 20:7,13); to be about to be or do, used of purpose, certainty, compulsion or necessity (II Pet. 1:12, *mellōso* [U.B.S.]). Expressed by "shall" or "should" which elsewhere frequently represents part of the fut. tense of the verb expressed by the suffix.

3306. Menō; to remain, dwell. N.T. meanings: intrans., to remain, abide, dwell (Mt. 10:11; Mk. 14:34; Lk. 1:56; Jn. 1:39; 2:12, cf. Jn. 14:10,16; 15:4,7; I Jn. 4:12,15,16); to remain, endure, last (Mt. 11:23; I Cor. 13:13; II Cor. 9:9, cf. Heb. 7:3,24; 10:34); to persevere (I Tim. 2:15, cf. Jn. 15:9,10; I Jn. 4:16); to stand firm or steadfast (Rom. 9:11); to remain alive (Jn. 21:22,23; I Cor. 15:6); trans. with an accus., to wait for (Acts 20:5). Deriv.: *hypomenō* (5278), to remain under, be patient; *hupomonē* (5281), patience toward things and circumstances as distinguished from *makrothumia* (3115), longsuffering or patience toward people.

3311. Merismos; distribution, translated "gifts" In Heb. 2:4 and "dividing asunder" in Heb. 4:12. From *merizō* (3307), to divide, from *meros* (3313), part.

3315. Mesiteuō; to be a mediator between two contending parties (Heb. 6:17); from *mesitēs* (3316), mediator.

3316. Mesitēs; from *mesos* (3319), the middle. A mediator, one who mediates between two parties (Gal. 3:20). Ascribed to Christ (I Tim. 2:5; Heb. 8:6; 9:15; 12:24); to Moses (Gal. 3:19). In Paul's language *mesitēs* is one who unites parties, one who mediates for peace (I Tim. 2:5). Christ is thus called Mediator because in man's behalf He satisfies the claims of God upon man. In Hebrews He is called Mediator clearly in the sense as a surety, one who becomes security for something (Heb. 8:6, cf. Heb. 7:22; 9:15; 12:24). He it is who, with reference to mankind, mediates or guarantees for them a new and better covenant, and with reference to God appears as High Priest (Heb. 7:20-22). What the Epistle to the Hebrews divides into these two elements, the High Priesthood and the Mediatorship of Christ, Paul represents as blended in the Mediatorship (I Tim. 2:5).

3319. Mesos; middle, in the midst. Used of time or place (Mt. 14:24; 25:6; Jn. 1:26; Acts 1:18). With the neut. art. *to, to meson,* the middle part, the midst (Acts 27:27). Used with different prep. as follows: *ek* (1537), from *mesou,* from the midst, from among, away (Mt. 13:49; I Cor. 5:2; II Cor. 6:17; Col. 2:14); *ana* (303), up, *meson,* in or through the midst, between (Mt. 13:25; Mk. 7:31; I Cor. 6:5); *dia* (1223), through, *mesou,* through the midst (Lk. 4:30; 17:11); *eis* (1519), into, *to meson,* in or into the midst (Mk. 14:60; Lk. 5:19; 6:8); *en* (1722), in, *mesō,* in the midst, among (Mt. 18:20; Lk. 2:46; 8:7, etc.).

3326. Meta; a prep. governing the gen. and accus. with the primary significance of amid, in the midst, with, among, implying accompaniment, and thus differing from *sun* (4862), together, which expresses conjunction, union. With the gen, it implies companionship, fellowship, meaning amid, among, as where one is said to be, sit, stand, etc., with or in the midst of others (Mt. 26:58); when followed with a gen. of persons, with, i.e., together with (Lk. 22:28; 24:29; Jn. 6:66); where one is said to do or suffer anything with another, implying joint or mutual action, influence, suffering, etc. (Mt. 2:3; 5:41, etc.); nearness or contiguity (Mt. 21:2); indicates the state or emotion of mind which accompanies the doing of anything, with which one acts (Mt. 28:8); designates an external action, circumstance, or condition with which another action or event is accompanied (Mt. 14:7; 24:31, etc.); implies accord or discord denoting common agreement or disagreement (Lk. 23:12); signifies participation, fellowship (II Cor. 6:15,16). With the accus. *meta* strictly implies motion towards the middle or into the midst of anything and also motion after any person or thing, i.e., either so as to follow and be with a person or to bring a person or thing. After, as spoken of succession either in place or time. In composition *meta* implies fellowship, partnership, as *metadidōmi* (3330), to impart; proximity, contiguity, as *methorion* (3181), border, boundary from *meta* and *horion* (3725), limit, border; motion or direction after, as *methodeia* (3180), from *meta* and *hodeuō* (3593), to travel, to contrive; a device, method; transition, transposition, changeover, as *metabainō* (3327), to go over.

3327. Metabainō; from *meta* (3326), denoting change of place or condition, and *bainō,* to go or come. To pass or go from one place or state to another (Mt. 17:20; Lk. 10:7; Jn. 5:24); to go away, depart (Mt. 8:34; Jn. 13:1; Acts 18:7).

3333. Metakaleō; from *meta* (3326), implying change, and *kaleō* (2564), to call from one place to another, summon. As used in the mid. voice: to call for oneself, to send for, to call here (Acts 7:14; 10:32; 20:17; 34:25).

3337. Metallassō; from *meta* (3326) denoting change of condition, and *allassō* (236), to change. To exchange, to convert from one state to another (Rom. 1:25,26).

3338. Metamellomai; to regret (Mt. 21:29,32; 27:3; II Cor. 7:8; Heb. 7:21). Contr. *metanoeō* (3340), to repent. To express the mere desire that what is done may be undone, accompanied with regrets or even remorse, but with no effective change of heart. An ineffective repentance, *metameleia* (which nowhere occurs in the N.T.) and to which forgiveness of sins is not promised as it is for *metanoia* (3341), repentance. *Metamellomai* means little or nothing more than a selfish dread of the consequence of what one has done whereas *metanoeō* means regret and turning away by a change of heart brought about by God's Spirit.

3339. Metamorphoō; and *metamorphoomai* (mid.), from *meta* (3326), denoting change of condition, and *morphoō* (3445), to form. Used of Jesus' transfiguration on the Mount (Mt. 17:2; Mk. 9:2) involving the miracle of transformation from an earthly form into a supernatural which is denoted by the radiance of the garments, also the countenance, suggesting what the bodies of the righteous may be like in the new age (I Cor. 15:51f). In Rom. 12:2; II Cor. 3:18 the idea of transformation refers to an invisible process in Christians which takes place or begins to take place already during their life in this age. See *metaschēmatizō* (3345), to change one's outward form; *metastrephō* (3344), to turn from; *schēma* (4976), external condition, fashion.

3340. Metanoeō; repent with regret accompanied by a true change of heart toward God. The word means to know *noeō* (3539) after *meta* (3326) as contr. to *pronoeō* (4306), to know ahead (Rom. 12:17; II Cor. 8:21; I Tim. 5:8). *Metanoia* (3341), repentance, is after knowledge as *pronoia* (4307), is foreknowledge (Acts 24:2; Rom. 13:14). It signifies a change of mind consequent to the after knowledge indicating regret for the course pursued and resulting in a wiser view of the past and future. Most importantly, it is distinguished from *metamellomai* (3338), to regret because of the consequences of one's act or acts. Deriv.: *noeō* (3539), to comprehend; *nous* (3563), mind.

3341. Metanoia; a change of mind, repentance from *metanoeō* (3340), to repent. A change or alteration of mind (Heb. 12:17). Repentance, change of mind from evil to good or from worse to better (Mt. 3:11; 9:13 T.R.; Acts 20:21). In the N.T. used with reference to *nous* (3563), mind, as the faculty of moral reflection (Acts 11:18; 20:21; II Cor. 7:9,10; II Tim. 2:25; Heb. 6:1). It is combined with *aphesis* (859), remission of sins, (Lk. 24:47); cf. baptism of repentance (Mt. 3:11; Mk. 1:4; Lk. 3:3; Acts 13:24; 19:4), baptism which identifies one as having repented. For deriv. see *noeō* (3539), to perceive. For a distinction from *metameleia* and *metamellomai* (3338), to change one's mind because of the consequences of one's sin, see *metanoeō* (3340), to change one's mind because of the sinfulness of the sin.

3345. Metaschēmatizō; transfigure, from *meta* (3326), denoting change of condition. Occurs only in I Cor. 4:6; II Cor. 11:13-15; Phil. 3:21. Best illustrated in this way: If one were to change a Dutch garden into an Italian one, this would be *metaschēmatizō*. But if one were to transform a garden into something wholly different, as into a ballfield, it is *metamorphoō* (3339), from *morphē* (3444). It is possible for Satan to *metaschēmatizō*, transform himself into an angel of light; i.e., he can take the whole outward semblance of such, but to any such change it would be impossible to apply the *metamorphoō* for this would imply an internal change, a change not of appearance but of essence, which lies beyond his power. In the *metaschēmatismos*, a transformation of the bodies (Phil. 3:21; I Cor. 15:53) there is to be seen a transition but no absolute dissolution of continuity. The outer physical transformation of believers at the end of the days (I Cor. 15:44ff,51f) is called by Paul in Phil. 3:21 *metaschēmatizō*, but such transformation has already begun in this life from within.

3348. Metechō; from *meta* (3326), with, and *echō* (2192), have. To have together with others, to partake (I Cor. 10:21,30; Heb. 5:13; 7:13). Deriv.: *metochē* (3352), a partaking, participation, fellowship (II Cor. 6:14); *metochos* (3353), a partaker (Heb. 3:1,14; 6:4; 12:8), an associate (Heb. 1:9, all those who believe on Christ, cf. Heb. 2:11; Rom. 8:17); a partner (Lk. 5:7); *summetochos* (4830), from *sun* (4862), together, and *metochos* (3353), partaker; co-partaker (Eph. 3:6; 5:7).

3356. Metriopatheō; to act with moderation; from *metriopathēs*, moderate in his passions, which in its turn is derived from *metrios*, moderate, and *pathos* (3806), passion. In Plutarch, *metriopatheia*, moderation, is the same as *praotēs* or *prautēs* (4240), meekness. With a dat. following, to moderate one's anger towards, to pardon, treat with mildness or meekness (Heb. 5:2).

3367. Mēdeis; not even one, no one, i.e., no one no matter who he may be. Used with moods other than the indicative, i.e., the imper., the subjunctive, and the inf. When the indicative is used, then *oudeis* (3762) is utilized instead of *mēdeis*. Neut.: *mēden*, nothing. Adv.: not at all, in no respect. After verbs of profit or loss, deficiency (Lk. 4:35; II Cor. 11:5; Phil. 4:6). Metaphorically, *mēden ōn*, being nothing, i.e., of no account, no weight of character (Gal. 6:3).

3392. Miainō; to stain with color as the staining of glass. Contr. *molunō* (3435), to besmear or besmirch as with mud or filth, to defile. *Molunō* is not used in a ritual or ceremonial sense as is *miainō*.

3393. Miasma; pollution (II Pet. 2:20); from the verb *miainō* (3392), to defile. The contamination of the world upon the godly as a result of the latter living in it; the result of *miasmos* (3394), the act of polluting.

3394. Miasmos; the act of defiling resulting in *miasma* (3393) as in II Pet. 2:10.

3405. Misthapodosia; from *misthos* (3408), reward, recompense, and *apodidōmi* (591), to render. A recompense, whether a reward (Heb. 10:35; 11:26) or a punishment (Heb. 2:2).

3406. Misthapodotēs; from *misthos* (3408), a reward, and *apodidōmi* (591), to render. A recompenser, a rewarder (Heb. 11:6).

3407. Misthios; hired servant, an adj. related to *misthōtos* (3411), a hireling (Lk. 15:17,19).

3408. Misthos; wages, hire, reward received in this life (Mt. 5:46; 6:2,5,16; Rom. 4:4; I Cor. 9:17,18); of evil rewards (Acts 1:18) to be received hereafter (Mt. 5:12; 10:41; Mk. 9:41; Lk. 6:23,35, etc.).

3411. Misthōtos; an adj. meaning hired. Used as an adj. noun, one who is hired, sometimes indicating one who is not showing real interest in his duty and who is unfaithful; a hireling (Mk. 1:20; Jn. 10:12,13). Related words: *misthios* (3407), hired servant; *misthos* (3408), wages.

3435. Molunō; to defile, besmear or besmirch as with mud or filth (I Cor. 8:7; Rev. 3:4; 14:4). Contr. *miainō* (3392), to stain; *spiloō* (4695), to spot, pollute.

3436. Molusmos; filthiness (II Cor. 7:1); from the verb *molunō* (3435), the act of defilement produced by the body. Cf. *miasmos* (3394), the act of defiling.

3438. Monē; from *menō* (3306), to remain, dwell. A mansion, habitation, abode (Jn. 14:2,23). Also related to *monos* (3441), alone, only, single.

3439. Monogenēs; from *monos* (3441), only, and *genō*, to form, to make, and *ginomai* (1096). To be differentiated from *gennaō* (1080), to beget, generate. *Ginomai* is related to *genos* (1085) as in genealogy, species, family, kindred. *Monogenēs* means the only one of the family as in Lk. 7:12 referring to the only son of his mother; in Lk. 8:42, the daughter of Jairus; in Lk. 9:38, the demoniac boy. Only John uses *monogenēs* to describe the relation of Jesus to God the Father, presenting Him as the unique One, the only One (*monos*) of the family (*genos*), in the discussion of the relationship of the Son to the Father (Jn. 1:14,18; 3:16,18; I Jn. 4:9). Jesus is never called *teknon* (5043), child, *Theou* (2316), of God, as the believers are (Jn. 1:12; 11:52; I Jn. 3:1,2,10; 5:2). Jn. 5:18 reveals Jesus called God His very own, *idion* (2398), Father. To Him He was not a Father as to us. See also Jn. 20:17. He never spoke of God as the common Father of

Him and believers. The term *monogenēs* also occurs in Heb. 11:17. The *genos* from which *genēs* in *monogenēs* is derived means race, stock, family, and *genō* comes from *ginomai,* become, as in Jn. 1:14, ". . . and the Word became (*egeneto*) flesh," in distinction from *gennaō,* to beget, engender or create. The noun from *gennaō* is *gennēma* (1081), the result of birth. But in *monogenēs* we have *genos,* Jesus Christ designated as the only One of the same stock in the relationship of the Son to the Father. He is not to be understood as eternally born of the Father, but only in His humanity was He born. Therefore, *monogenēs* can be held as syn. with the God-Man. Jesus was the only such One ever in distinction with the Holy Spirit, the third person of the Triune God.

3444. Morphē; form. *Morphē* appears together with *schēma* (4976), fashion, whole outward appearance, in Phil. 2:6-8. These two words are objective for the form and the fashion of a thing would exist were it alone in the universe and whether there were any to behold it or not. They do not represent subjective ideas of non-existing entities. Another word *idea* (2397), idea, concept of the mind, is subjective (Mt. 28:3), from *ideō, eidō* (1492), to see, which in turn is from *eidos* (1491), appearance, visible form (Jn. 5:37; Lk. 3:22; 9:29; II Cor. 5:7; I Thess. 5:22). The appearance of *morphē* or *schēma* implies someone to whom this appearance is made. There needs to be a seer before something can be seen. It becomes objectively real by its subjective realization. *Morphē* in Phil. 2:6-8 presumes an objective reality. None could be in the form (*morphē*) of God who was not God. *Morphē* is the reality which can be externalized, not some shape that is the result of pure thought. It is the utterance of the inner life, a life which bespeaks of the existence of God. He who had been from eternity, *en morphē Theou,* in the form of God (Jn. 17:5) took at His incarnation *morphēn doulou,* form of a servant (1401). Nothing appeared that was not in objective reality from the beginning. And the fact that He continued to be God in His humanity is demonstrated by the present part. *huparchōn,* "being" in the form of God. *Huparchō* (5225) means to continue to be that which one was before. In His incarnation He took upon Himself the form (*morphē*) of a servant which is an inner attitude by taking upon Himself the shape (*schēma*) of man. That was the only way He could die for man's salvation. The *schēma,* shape, fashion, is the outward form having to do not with its essential being, but with His appearance. In Mk. 16:12 the expression *en* (1722), in, *hetera* (2087), qualitatively another, *morphē,* form, Christ was transformed (*metemorphōthē,* aor. pass. of *metamorphoō,* 3339) as in Mt. 17:2; Mk. 9:2. The transformation upon the Mount was a prophetic anticipation of that which we shall all experience. This form in which the risen Lord also appeared to two disciples by the way (Lk. 24:13ff) is a human form, but different from that which Jesus bore during His life on earth.

3445. Morphoō; to form, fashion, originally of artists who shape their material into an image. Used only in Gal. 4:19 where the Christian is described as a little child who needs to mature. See *morphē* (3444), form; *schēma* (4976), outward appearance; *metamorphoō* (3339), transform.

3446. Morphōsis; the activity of forming; shaping. In Rom. 2:20 refers to a sketch, summary, corresponding to the high sense of pride with which a Jew who feels himself to be a teacher regards a book of the Law as a physical representation of absolute knowledge, and truth as the true depiction and representation of the idea of a divine form. In II Tim. 3:5 it refers to the external form of the Christian life with no inner power, the mere appearance or mask of pious conduct.

3449. Mochthos; from *mogos,* labor, toil (cf. *mogis,* 3425, with difficulty). Toil, travel, afflicting and wearisome labor. It is the everyday word for that labor which, in one shape or another, is the lot of all of the sinful children of Adam. It is more than *kopos* (2873), labor, and it therefore follows *kopos* in all the three passages wherein it occurs, namely II Cor. 11:27; I Thess. 2:9; II Thess. 3:8. Related words: *ponos* (4192), pain; *zēlos* (2205), zeal; *agōn* (73), conflict.

3454. Muthos; from *mueō,* to instruct. It is the word from which mythology is derived. Commonly rendered as a tale or a fable. There is nothing necessarily false in a myth. It is that which is fabricated by the mind set over against the real and actually true. There may be much *logos* (3056), logic and reasoning, in a myth. In the N.T., however, the word "myth" does not have the meaning of its being a vehicle of some lofty truth as the early use of the word did. Mostly used in the N.T. as a lying fable with all its falsehood and all its pretenses to be what it is not. Thus in I Tim. 4:7 fables are described as *bebēloi* (952), profane, and *graōdeis* (1126), belonging to old women. In Tit. 1:14 Jewish fables; in II Pet. 1:16 *muthoi sesophismenoi* (perf. part. of *sophizō,* 4679, to make wise), the result of sophistry or cunning fables for the purpose of deceiving. In I Tim. 1:4; II Tim. 4:4 the use of the word is equally degrading and contemptuous. Although *logos* (3056) and *muthos* begin together with the thought, intelligence, mind, they part ranks since the first ends in the kingdom of light and truth and the second in the kingdom of darkness and lies.

3464. Muron; ointment, the base of which is *elaion* (1637), oil. It is mixed, however, with aromatic substances and thus is fit for finer uses as by women, men preferring oil. Contr. *elaion* for the distinction between the two and the explanation of Lk. 7:46.

3466. Mustērion; from *mustēs,* a person initiated in sacred mysteries which in turn is derived from *muō,* close, to shut; e.g., the lips or eyes. It is referred to a locking up or that which serves for locking up. In Class. Gr. usually in the pl., *ta mustēria,* the mysteries, as denoting secret politico-religious doctrines, especially of the Eleusinian Mysteries wherein some secret information was communicated to the initiated which was in turn to be kept secret. N.T. meanings: (1) Denotes in general something hidden or not fully manifest. II Thess. 2:7 speaks of "the mystery of lawlessness" which began to work in secret but was not then completely disclosed or manifested. (2) Some sacred thing hidden or secret which is naturally unknown to human reason and is only known by the revelation of God (I Tim. 3:16; see also I Cor. 2:7). When Paul speaks of the mystery of the incarnation as being great, he seems plainly to allude to the famous Eleusinian Mysteries which were distinguished as being small and great, the latter of which were held in the highest reverence among the Greeks and Romans (cf. Eph. 5:32). The term *mustērion* (Rom. 11:25; I Cor. 15:51), denotes what was hidden or unknown until revealed, and thus the Apostle speaks (I Cor. 13:2) of a man understanding all mysteries, i.e., all the revealed truths of the Christian religion which is elsewhere called the mystery of faith (I Tim. 3:9). In Mt. 13:11, "because to them it was not given to know the mysteries of the kingdom of God," it means those things which are not revealed to them by virtue of their not being related to King Jesus. (3) In the writings of Paul the word *mustērion* is sometimes applied in a peculiar sense to the calling of the Gentiles. In Eph. 3:3-6 he styles a mystery and the mystery of Christ, the fact that the Gentiles should be fellow-heirs and of the same body and partakers of Christ by the Gospel. In other generations, such a thing was not made known to the sons of man as it is now revealed to His holy apostles and prophets by the Spirit (cf. Rom. 16:25; Eph. 1:9; 3:9; 6:19; Col. 1:26,27; 4:3). (4) It denotes a spiritual truth couched under an external representation or similitude, and concealed or hidden thereby unless some explanation be given (Mt. 13:11; Mk. 4:11; Lk. 8:10; Eph. 5:32; Rev. 1:20; 17:5,7, and their respective contexts).

3470. Mōmos; blame, fault, used only in II Pet. 2:13, blemish, disgrace. See *amōmos* (299), without blame, without fault.

3473. Mōrologia; from *mōros* (3474), foolish, and *logos* (3056), a word, speech. Foolish talking (Eph. 5:4). It is that type of speech that shows how foolish a person is. Besides this word there are two others that show the sins of the tongue; namely *aischrologia* (148), foul speech, and *eutrapella* (2160), the ability to extricate oneself from difficult situations with witty or clever words.

3474. Mōros; silly, stupid, foolish, from which the English "moron" is derived. Used of persons (Mt. 5:22), morally worthless, a more serious reproach than "raca," as the latter scorns a man's mind and calls him stupid. *Mōros* scorns his heart and character. Used of things (II Tim. 2:23); foolish and ignorant questionings (Tit. 3:9). In Mt. 5:13; Lk. 14:34 it is said of salt that has lost its flavor becoming tasteless. Noun: *mōria* (3472), foolishness as a personal quality (I Cor. 1:8,21,23; 2:14; 3:19). *Mōrologia* (3473), foolish talking (Eph. 5:4), denoting more than mere idle talk, talk of fools which is foolishness and sin together. Verb: *mōrainō* (3471) as used in the causal sense, to make foolish (I Cor. 1:20); in the pass. sense to become foolish (Rom. 1:22).

3485. Naos; habitation of God, from *naiō,* to dwell (Acts 7:48 T.R.; 17:24; I Cor. 6:19). The temple itself is the heart and center of the whole sacred enclosure called *hieron* (2411). *Naos* was the Holy of Holies. The Lord never entered the *naos* during His ministry on earth, the right of such entry being reserved for the Jewish priests alone.

3498. Nekros; dead. Dead, naturally (Mt. 10:8; 11:5, etc.); dead, spiritually, dead in sin, separated from the vivifying grace of God, or more distinctly, having one's soul separated from the enlivening influences of the divine light and spirit as a dead body is from those of the material light and air, and consequently having no hope of life eternal (Mt. 8:22; Eph. 2:1,5; 5:14; Col. 2:13). Thus, sinful practices are called dead works, such as those performed by those who are dead in sin (Heb. 6:1; 9:14). Also dead unto sin, meaning inactive with regard to sin, as a dead man is in respect to bodily functions (Rom. 6:11); a dead faith (Js. 2:17,20 T.R., 26) which means a faith unaccompanied with good works and, therefore, unprofitable (vv. 16,17) and unable to justify (vv. 20,21) and save (v. 14); sin is said to have been dead without the law (Rom. 7:8), i.e., apparently dead and inoperative. Deriv.: *nekrōsis* (3500), a killing, deadness.

3500. Nekrōsis; a killing, from *nekros* (3498), dead, and *nekroō* (3499), to mortify. The act of putting to death (II Cor. 4:10). Always carrying about in the body the putting to death of the Lord Jesus, i.e., being exposed to cruelties resembling those which He sustained in His last sufferings (I Cor. 15:31). It also means deadness (Rom. 4:19).

3501. Neos; new in relation to time as that which has recently come into existence. New under the aspect of quality is *kainos* (2537) which also may indicate the novel and strange. The *kainon* is the *heteron* (2087), the qualitatively new. The *neon* is the *allon* (243), the numerically distinct. *Neos* may be derived from *neō,* to move, agitate, hence one who moves briskly, a young man, so named either because of the activity and vigor, or of the unsettled attitude of that age of life. Young image (Tit. 2:4); new referring to wine, but the same as was had before (Mt. 9:17; Mk. 2:22, etc.); the new man (Col. 3:10). Here both *neos* and *anakainoumenos* (part. of *anakainoō,* to renew, 341) are used. Paul refers to the new nature the believer puts on, but this new nature becomes qualitatively new by the activity of God Himself by His renewing (*anakainoumenon*). Man on his own can only reform (become *neos*), but by God's activity, he becomes *kainos,* qualitatively new. This is the impartation by God of His divine nature in man spoken of in II Cor. 5:17; II Pet. 1:4. See ananeoō (365), to renew, having an experience of the same kind as previously; neotēs (3503), newness.

3502. Neossos; or *nossos,* from *neos* (3501), young. A young bird, a chicken (Lk. 2:24). Deriv.: *neotēs* (3503), youth; *neophutos* (3504), newly planted, a novice.

3503. Neotēs; from *neos* (3501), young, youth, age or time of youth (Mt. 19:20 T.R.; Mk. 10:20; Lk. 18:21; Acts 26:4; I Tim. 4:12). Deriv.: *ananeōō,* to renew (365); *neossos* (3502), a fledgling, a young bird; *neophutos* (3504), newly planted or a novice.

3504. Neophutos; from *neos* (3501), new, and *phutos,* planted. Newly planted, or figuratively one who is but lately converted from Judaism or heathenism to Christianity and newly implanted in the Church; newly instructed or a novice (I Tim. 3:6).

3516. Nēpios; infant, from *nē* (3513), not, and *epō* (2036), to speak; a child not yet able to speak plainly (Mt. 21:16, cf. I Cor. 13:11); a young person underage (Gal. 4:1, cf. v. 3); a child, a babe in ignorance and simplicity (Mt. 11:25; Lk. 10:21; Rom. 2:20); a babe in Christ, a person weak in faith, a beginner, (I Cor. 3:1; Eph. 4:14; Heb. 5:13). Verb: *nēpiazō* (3515), to be an infant (I Cor. 14:20).

3538. Niptō; also *louō* (3068), to bathe, especially the washing of living objects or persons, contr. *plunō* (4150), to wash things. *Niptō,* however, usually expresses the washing of a part of the body, the hands (Mk. 7:3), the feet (Jn. 13:5), the face (Mt. 6:17), the eyes (Jn. 9:7), while *louō,* to bathe oneself, always imples not the washing of a part of the body, but of the whole (Acts 9:37; Heb. 10:22; II Pet. 2:22; Rev. 1:5). The lesson in Jn. 13:9,10 symbolizes justification as the bathing of the whole body, *louō,* while sanctification is the constant need of *niptō,* washing the feet.

3539. Noeō; to perceive, observe, from *nous* (3563), the mind. To perceive with thought coming into consciousness as distinct from the perception of senses. To mark, understand, apprehend, discern. Syn.: *suniēmi* (4920), to put it all together and make out its meaning (Mk. 7:18; 8:17; II Tim. 2:7). Distinguished from *ginōskō* (1097), the relation to the object known instead of merely the act of knowing (Mt. 15:17; 16:9,11; Mk. 7:18; Eph. 3:4,20; I Tim. 1:7; II Tim. 2:7). *Noeō* denotes independently the action of the mind or the heart. If the latter is used referring to the mind, it means to understand, think, reflect (Jn. 12:40). Thus *nous,* mind, is the organ of the spirit and at the same time a function of the heart. Deriv.: *noēma* (3540), the product of the action of the mind; *anoētos* (453), unthought of, inconceivable; *dianoia* (1271), the faculty of thought; *ennoia* (1771), what lies in thought, meaning; *metanoeō* (3340), to repent; *metanoia* (3341), a change of mind, repentance; *noutheteō* (3560), to put in mind, work upon the mind of one, put the mind in its right course, admonish); *nouthesia* (3559), admonition.

3540. Noēma; from *noeō* (3539), to perceive. A thought, concept of the mind (II Cor. 10:5); a device, contrivance (II Cor. 2:11); the understanding, the mind (II Cor. 3:14; 4:4; 11:3; Phil. 4:7). See *nous* (3563), mind.

3544. Nomikos; a person who is learned in the law or legal practice, a lawyer. Appears together with the Parisees (Lk. 7:30; 14:3). Apparently they were from among the Pharisees (Mt. 22:35; Mk. 12:28) and with the scribes. In all places where the word is employed and legal questions come into consideration, the scribes appear as authorities in questions concerning prophecy (Mt. 2:4; 13:52). It may be inferred that "scribes" is the generic name, and *nomikoi,* the lawyers, are the specialized ones skilled in law and jurisprudence. *Nomodidaskalos* (3547), teacher of the law (Lk. 5:17; Acts 5:34), is apparently another name. Probably the members of the Sanhedrin and the Council were learned in the law.

3551. Nomos; law, from *nenoma,* perf. mid. voice of *nemō,* either of distributing, assigning, because the law assigns to everyone his own, or of administering, because it administers all things either by commanding or forbidding. N.T. meanings: (1) A law in general (Rom. 4:15; 5:13). (2) Most frequently, the divine law given by Moses, whether moral, ceremonial, or judicial (Mt. 5:17,18; 7:12; 23:23; Lk. 2:22; Jn. 7:51; 8:5). Sometimes it means the books of Moses or the Pentateuch containing the law (Lk. 24:44; Acts 13:15, cf. Gal. 4:21), or the O.T. in general (Jn. 10:34; 12:34; 15:25; Rom. 3:19; I Cor. 14:21). (3) The Gospel or gospel-method of justification is called the "law of faith," opp. the "law of works" (Rom. 3:27); "the law of the Spirit of life," opp. the law, i.e., power, dominion of sin and death (Rom. 8:2); "the royal law" (Js. 2:8) because it is the law of Christ, our King; "the perfect law, the law of liberty" (Js. 1:25, cf. 2:12) freeing believers from the yoke of ceremonial observances and slavery of sin, opp. the Mosaic law, which made nothing perfect (Heb. 7:19; 10:1). (4) A force or principle of action equivalent to a law (Rom. 7:21,23,25; 8:2). Deriv.: *anomos* (459), without law, lawless; *anomia* (458), lawlessness; *ennomos* (1772), what is within the range of law.

3554. Nosos; the regular word for disease, sickness. Syn.: *astheneia* (769), sickness, weakness; *malakia* (3119), ailment, softness; *arrhōstia,* although only the adj. or adj. noun, *arrhōstos* (732), sick, ill, is found in the N.T. It is a disease of a more grievous kind. It is joined to *malakia* (Mt. 4:23,24, etc.) denoting a slighter infirmity. From *nosos* comes the English "nosology," the classification of diseases. Deriv.: *noseō* (3552), to be sick in body, but also to rave like a person in the delirium of a fever (I Tim. 6:4); *nosēma* (3553), the result of *nosos,* disease (Jn. 5:4 T.R.).

3557. Nosphizomai; from *nosphi,* apart, separated. Mid. voice: to embezzle, keep back (Acts 5:2,3; Tit. 2:10). Applied by Gr. writers to public treasures.

3559. Nouthesia; admonition (I Cor. 10:11; Eph. 6:4; Tit. 3:10), from *nous* (3563), mind, and *thesis,* a putting. The verb *noutheteō* (3560), from *nous,* mind, and *tithēmi* (5087), to put or put into the mind. *Nouthesia* is the training by word of encouragement when it proves sufficient, but also by word of remonstrance, reproof, blame, as required. *Paideia* (3809), instruction, training by act and discipline. *Nouthesia* is the milder term without which *paideia* would be incomplete. *Nouthesia* involves correction by deed as needed. In both words there is the appeal to the reasonable faculties. See *epanorthōsis* (1882), correction.

3560. Noutheteō; from *nous* (3563), mind, and *tithemi* (5087), to put. To put into the mind, instruct, warn, admonish (Acts 20:31; Rom. 15:14; I Cor. 4:14; Col. 1:28; 3:16; I Thess. 5:12). To admonish with reproof (Rom. 15:14; I Thess. 5:14; II Thess. 3:15). See *noeō* (3539), to perceive.

3562. Nounechōs; an adv. from *nounechēs,* wise, discreet, from *nous* (3563), mind, and *echō* (2192), have. Wisely, discreetly, sensibly (Mk. 12:34). See *phronimōs* (5430), prudently; *sophronōs* (4996), with sound mind.

3563. Nous; mind, the organ of mental perception and apprehension, the organ of conscious life, the organ of the consciousness preceding actions or recognizing and judging them, the understanding of word concept, sense. Deriv.: verb, *noeō* (3539), to perceive with the mind as distinct from perception by feeling (Mt. 15:17; 16:9,11; 24:15); *dianoia* (1271), the faculty of thought, from *dianoeō,* to agitate in the mind. Intellectual faculty, understanding or moral reflection. With an evil significance, a consciousness characterized by a perverted moral impulse (Eph. 2:3; 4:18), or with a good significance, the faculty renewed by the Holy Spirit (Mt. 22:37; Mk. 12:30; Lk. 10:27; Heb. 8:10; 10:16; I Pet. 1:13; I Jn. 5:20). *Dianoia* also means a sentiment, disposition, not as a function but as a product in an evil sense (Lk. 1:51; Col. 1:21) or in a good sense (II Pet. 3:1). *Dianoēma* (1270), reflection with machinations (Lk. 11:17); *ennoia* (1771), an idea, consideration which denotes purpose, intention, design, from *en* (1722), in, and *nous,* mind (Heb. 4:12; I Pet. 4:1); *noēma* (3540), thought, a purpose, device of the mind (II Cor. 2:11; 3:14; 4:4; 10:5; 11:3; Phil. 4:7); *epinoia* (1963), a thought by way of evil design (Acts 8:22); *anoētos* (453), not applying the mind, sometimes with moral reproach (Lk. 24:25; Rom. 1:14; Gal. 3:1,3), contr. *sōphron* (4998), self-controlled, one who does not govern his lusts (I Tim 6:9; Tit. 3:3); *katanoeō* (2657), the inten. *kata* (2596) with *noeō,* to perceive, making it the action of the mind in apprehending certain facts about a thing (Mt. 7:3; Lk. 6:41; 12:24,27; 20:33; Acts 7:31,32; 11:6; 27:39; Rom. 4:19; Heb. 3:1; 10:24; Js. 1:23,24); *pronoeō* (4306), from *pro* (4253), before, and *noeō,* to perceive, thus to take thought of before, provide (Rom. 12:17; II Cor. 8:21; I Tim. 5:8); *pronoia* (4307), forethought, providence, provision (Acts 24:2; Rom. 13:14); *huponoeō* (5282) from *hupo* (5259), under, denoting diminution, thus lack of proper knowledge and therefore to suspect, suppose (Acts 13:25; 25:18; 27:27); the noun *huponoia* (5283), suspicion, surmising (I Tim. 6:4); *anoia* (454), without understanding, folly, senselessness (II Tim. 3:9), violent, mad rage or madness resulting from it (Lk. 6:11).

3576. Nōthros; slothful, sluggish. It involves inborn sluggishness which makes a person unfit for activities of the mind or spirit. Syn.: *bradus* (1021), slow; *argos* (692), idle.

3598. Hodos; way, path. A way, a road in which one travels (Mt. 2:12; 8:28; etc., cf. Mt. 4:15; 10:5); a journey (Mk. 2:23; Lk. 2:44; Acts 1:12; I Thess. 3:11); a way, manner of life or action, custom (Acts 14:16; Rom. 3:16; Js. 1:8; Jude 11); particularly with a gen. following, a way leading to, a method or manner of obtaining (Rom. 3:17; Acts 2:28; 16:17, cf. Mt. 21:32; II Pet. 2:21); a way or manner of religion (Acts 24:14, cf. Acts 9:2; 19:9,23; 24:22); the way of the Lord or of God, sometimes denoting the revealed will of God as being shown by God and leading to Him (Mt. 22:16; Acts 13:10; 18:25,26). The ways of the Lord in the pl. signify the directions of His providence in removing the impediments for His reception (Mt. 3:3; Mk. 1:2,3; Lk. 1:76); Christ calls Himself "The Way" (Jn. 14:6) because no one comes to the Father or can approach the divine essence in a future state of blessedness but through Him. Deriv.: *methodeia* (3180), from *methodos,* method, the following or pursuing of orderly and technical procedures in the handling of a subject.

3609. Oikeios; from *oikos* (3624), a house or household. A person of or belonging to a certain household (I Tim. 5:8); a believer, one belonging to the Church which is the household of God (Gal. 6:10; Eph. 2:19). See *oiketēs* (3610), a household servant.

3610. Oiketēs; a domestic servant, from *oikeō* (3611), to dwell in a house. One of the household, of the family, but not one necessarily born in the house, *oikogenēs; oiketeia,* a household of servants (Mt. 24:45, U.B.S.). *Oiketēs* does not bring out the servile relation as strongly as does *doulos* (1401), slave.

3611. Oikeō; from *oikos* (3624), a dwelling. To dwell, inhabit (Rom. 7:17,18,20; 8:9,11; I Cor. 3:16; I Tim. 6:16). Deriv.: *sunoikeō* (4924), from *sun* (4862), together with, and *oikeō,* to dwell; to dwell or cohabit with (I Pet. 3:7).

3612. Oikēma; from *oikeō* (3611), to dwell. A house, a prison (Acts 12:7).

3614. Oikia; a building, house, originally distinguished from *oikos* (3624), a dwelling. *Oikos* had a broader range than *oikia,* being the whole of a deceased person's possessions, what he leaves behind, whereas *oikia* is simply his residence. In the N.T. *oikia* is used literally for house (Mt. 5:15; 7:24ff; 10:12, etc.). Then it came to figuratively mean family, household (Mt. 10:13; 12:25; Mk. 6:4). In Mk. 10:29 *oikia* means the whole family. The word can also mean possession, one's belongings, e.g., in Mk. 12:40 the expression "who devour widows' houses (*oikias*)," means widow's possessions which are so precious and needed. In Mk. 13:35 the expression "the master of the house (*oikias*)" is equivalent to *ho oikodespotēs* (3617) which is commonly translated "the head of the house" (Mt. 24:43). The word *oikia* can also be used figuratively as in Jn. 8:35 as reference to the kingdom of God. The term *oikia* does not refer to a ruling house, but simply to a family. In Jn. 14:2 "In my Father's house (*oikia*) are many dwelling places" (or resting places, *monai,* pl. of *monē,* 3438, resting place), it is to be remembered that from the word *monai* comes also *monos* (3441) which means alone. This may have reference to individual places for families even as they lived on earth. In II Cor. 5:1-10 the metaphorical *oikia tou skēnous* (the house of our tabernacle) denotes first the corruptible body which we have on earth. Its counterpart is *oikodomē* (3619), a building in process of preparation by God, incorruptible, eternal, a house "from heaven," not "in the heavens" as the translation has it. In Phil. 4:22, those of the household of Caesar might mean the ruling family with all its members, but more likely the staff of the imperial household, both slaves and freedmen.

3617. Oikodespotēs; from *oikos* (3624), a house, and *despotēs* (1203), a lord, despot, master; the master of the house (Mt. 10:25; 20:1,11; Mk. 14:14). Verb: *oikodespoteō* (3616), to govern or manage a household or the domestic affairs of a family (I Tim. 5:14).

3618. Oikodomeō; from *oikos,* (3624), a house, and *domeō,* to build. To build a house, tower, town, etc. (Mt. 7:24,26, etc.); to build in a spiritual sense, as the Church (Mt. 16:18, etc.); to profit spiritually, to edify (I Cor. 8:1; 14:4,17); in the pass. voice, in a bad sense, to be built up, emboldened, encouraged (I Cor. 8:10). Deriv.: *oikodomē* (3619), the act of building, but not used in this sense in the N.T., rather used as a building, edifice (Mt. 24:1; Mk. 13:1,2); edification, spiritual profit or advancement (Rom. 14:19; 15:2, etc.); *sunoikodomeō* (4925) from *sun* (4862), together, and *oikodomeō,* to build; to build or build up together (Eph. 2:22).

3619. Oikodomē; from *oikodomeō* (3618),to build. Literally the act of building, building as a process and, hence, also that which is built, the building. N.T. meanings: a building, edifice (Mt. 24:1; Mk. 13:1,2, cf. I Cor. 3:9; II Cor. 5:1; Eph. 2:21); edification spiritual profit or advancement (Rom. 14:19; 15:2; I Cor. 14:3,5; II Cor. 13:10, etc.). Deriv.: *oikos* (3624), a house, a dwelling; *oikeios* (3609), belonging to the house, relative; *oikeō* (3611), to dwell; *paroikos* (3941), sojourner; *oikodomos,* one who builds a house or building (Acts 4:11); *epoikodomeō* (2026), to build upon.

3622. Oikonomia; administration of the house or of property, one's own or another's (Lk. 16:2,3,4); a spiritual dispensation, management, or economy (I Cor. 9:17; Eph. 1:10; 3:2; Col. 1:25). The "dispensation of God" means the administration of divine grace. Act., the administrative activity of the owner or of the steward, and pass., that which is administered, the administration or ordering of the house, the arrangement. "With a view to an administration suitable to the fulness of the times" (Eph. 1:10), the object of *oikonomia,* dispensation, is the relative phrase *hēn proetheto* of v. 9 translated "which he purposed." It is the divine purpose which is said to be administered. The meaning is the administration of God's saving purpose pertaining to the fullness of the times. Therefore, *oikonomia* here is to be taken as pass.

3623. Oikonomos; steward, from *oikos* (3624), house, and *neomai* or *nemō,* to administer; a person who manages the domestic affairs of a family or a minor, a treasurer, a chamberlain of a city; applies to apostles and ministers of the Gospel (I Cor. 4:1; Tit. 1:7), but also to private believers (I Pet. 4:10). Deriv.: *oikonomeō* (3621), verb, to be a steward; *oikonomia* (3622), stewardship, a spiritual dispensation, management (I Cor. 9:17; Eph. 1:10; 3:2; Col. 1:25).

3624. Oikos; a house (Mt. 9:6,7; 11:8); a household, a family dwelling in a house (Lk. 19:9; Acts 10:2; I Cor. 1:16); a family, lineage (Lk. 1:27; 2:4); the house (of God) denotes either the material temple at Jerusalem (Mt. 21:13; Jn. 2:17) or the household of God's people, all who belong to Him (Heb. 3:2,3,5). See *oikia* (3614), a dwelling.

3625. Oikoumenē; from *oikeō* (3611), to inhabit; the inhabited or habitable earth or world (Mt. 24:14; Rom. 10:18); the inhabitants of the world; the Roman Empire (Acts 11:28); a particular inhabited country (Lk. 2:1; Acts 11:28); that country where the seven churches of Asia Minor were settled (Rev. 3:10); the world (Heb. 2:5); the state of the world under the Messiah, or the kingdom of the Messiah. This is the word from which the English word "ecumenical" is derived.

3626. Oikouros; from *oikos* (3624), a house, and *ouros,* a keeper; a keeper at home, to look after domestic affairs with prudence and care (Tit. 2:5).

3631. Oinos; wine derived from grapes. The mention of the bursting of the wine skins in Mt. 9:17; Mk. 2:22; Lk. 5:37 implies fermentation. See also Eph. 5:18, cf. Jn. 2:10; I Tim. 3:8; Tit. 2:3. From the intoxicating effects of wine and the idolatrous use of it among the heathen, wine signifies communion in the intoxicating idolatries of the mystic Babylon (Rev. 14:8, cf. Jer. 51:7). From the Jewish custom of giving a cup of medicated wine to condemned criminals just before their execution to dull their senses, it denotes figuratively the dreadful judgments of God upon sinners (Rev. 14:10; 16:19, cf. Isa. 51:17,21,23; Jer. 25:15). The drinking of wine could be a stumbling block and Paul enjoins abstinence in this respect, as in others, so as to avoid giving an occasion of stumbling to a brother (Rom. 14:21). Contr. I Tim. 5:23 which has an entirely different connection. Cf. the word *gleukos* (1098), sweet new wine, and *sikera* (4608), strong drink.

3639. Olethros; ruin, destruction, from *ollumi* (I Cor. 5:5; I Thess. 5:3; II Thess. 1:9; I Tim. 6:9). The verb as such does not occur, but the comp. *apollumi* (622), to destroy, does. The fundamental thought is not by any means annihilation, but perhaps corruption, an injurious force, which the subject exerts or cannot hinder.

3640. Oligopistos; from *oligos* (3641), little, and *pistis* (4102), faith. Of little faith, having but little faith (Mt. 6:30; 8:26; 14:31; 16:8; Lk. 12:28). Deriv.: *pistos* (4103), a believer.

3642. Oligopsuchos; from *oligos* (3641), small or little, and *psuchē* (5590), soul, mind. Feebleminded or weak-hearted. Only in I Thess. 5:14.

3648. Holoklēros; whole, having all its parts, sound, perfect. From *holos* (3650), all the whole, and *klēros* (2819), a part, share. That which retains all which was allotted to it at the first, wanting nothing for its completeness; bodily, mental and moral entireness. It expresses the perfection of man before the fall (I Thess. 5:23; Js. 1:4). The sub. *holoklēria* (3647), soundness (Acts 3:16). Related to *teleios* (5049), perfect, and *artios* (739), with all its needed parts. The *holoklēros* is one who has preserved, or who, having once lost has now regained his completeness. In the *holoklēros* no grace which ought to be in a Christian man is deficient.

3650. Holos; whole, used as a demonstrative pron. To say "the whole," the noun must have the art., and *holos,* to be placed in the position of predicate. It is declined as a mas. noun such as *anthrōpos* (444), man; e.g., *holon to theros,* the whole summer. It can also be expressed with *holon* at the end, as *to theros hoion,* the summer all of it.

3651. Holotelēs; from *holos* (3650), all, the whole, and *teleō* (5055), to complete. All or the whole, completely or entirely (I Thess. 5:23). Deriv.: see *telos* (5056).

3664. Homolos; like, similar. It denotes coincidence in kind or quality, while *isos* (2470), equal, refers primarily to quantity. In biblical Gr. it means of the same kind, like. The two commandments which form the sum of the law, as on a par with each other (Mt. 22:38,39; Mk. 12:31). It denotes the rest that are of the same kind in Gal. 5:21, after a list of the works of the flesh.

3667. Homoiōma; or *homoiōsis* (3669), likeness, resemblance (Rom. 1:23; 5:14; 6:5; 8:3; Phil. 2:7; Rev. 9:7). While there is resemblance, it by no means follows that one has been derived from the other. There may exist a resemblance between two men who are in no way related to one another. See *eikōn* (1504), image.

3668. Homoiōs; adv., in like manner, likewise (Mt. 22:26; Mk. 4:16; Lk. 3:11; 10:37; Jn. 6:11; I Cor. 7:3,4).

3669. Homoiōsis; likeness (only in Js. 3:9). In its distinction from *eikōn* (1504), image.

3670. Homologeō; from *homou,* together with, or *homoios* (3664), like, and *logos* (3056), thoughtful word, speech. To accent, consent, as used commonly in Class. Gr.; to promise, i.e., to speak the same with or consent to the desire of another (Mt. 14:7); to confess, i.e., to speak agreeable to fact and truth (Jn. 1:20; 9:22; 12:42; Acts 23:8; Heb. 11:13; I Jn. 1:9); to confess, celebrate with public praises (Heb. 13:15); to confess, profess (Mt. 7:23; Tit. 1:16); *homologeō en* (in or with) *tini* (someone or something), meaning to confess or publicly acknowledge anyone (Mt. 10:32;

Lk. 12:8). Deriv.: *ellogeō* (1677), to charge, impute; *homologia* (3671), agreement, understanding, confession; *homologoumenōs* (3672), adv., confessedly or in reality.

3671. Homologia; from *homologeō* (3670), to say the same. A confession, profession or recognition. In Heb. 3:1 Christ is called the Chief Priest of our confession. Used also in II Cor. 9:13; Heb. 10:23. Used absolutely, meaning confession of Christ and to Christ (I Tim. 6:12,13; Heb. 4:14, cf. Rom. 10:10), and also as a vow, especially in the Septuagint.

3672. Homologoumenōs; confessedly (I Tim. 3:16), from *homologeō* (3670), to say the same.

3686. Onoma; name, from *onēmi*, to help, because the name helps us to know the thing; or from *nemō*, to attribute, because a particular name is attributed or given to everything. N.T. meanings: (1) A name (Mt. 1:21,23; 10:2; Mk. 14:32; Lk. 1:26). (2) A name meaning character described by the name (Mt. 10:41,42, cf. Mt. 24:5; Mk. 13:6; Lk. 21:8). (3) Name, fame, reputation (Mk. 6:14). (4) Name as implying authority, dignity (Eph. 1:21; Phil. 2:9). (5) A name as the substitute or representative of a person, hence *onoma* is used for the person himself, whether divine (Mt. 6:9; Jn. 1:12; 2:23; 3:18; Rom. 15:9; Heb. 13:15, etc.) or human (Acts 1:15; Rev. 3:4; 11:13). (6) It gives importance to the confession of a name, or for the sake of the person so confessed (Mt. 10:22; 19:29; 24:9, cf. Mt. 18:5; Mk. 9:37; Acts 4:17), so to be baptized into (*eis*, 1519) the name means to be baptized into the faith or confession of that person and to be identified with his character and purpose (Mt. 28:19; Acts 2:38; 8:16; 10:48). (7) Delegated power and authority (Mt. 7:22; Mk. 16:17; Lk. 10:17; Acts 3:6, cf. 3:16; 4:7,10,12, etc., cf. Eph. 1:21; Phil. 2:9). The promise in Jn. 14:13, "Whatsoever you ask in My name that will I do," means whatever is conformable to His character and to His purpose He will do, not simply what we ask.

3708. Horaō; to see, behold; of bodily vision (Mk. 6:38; Jn. 1:18,46); of mental perception (Rom. 15:21; Col. 2:18); of taking heed (Mt. 8:4; I Thess. 5:15) but not with as great attention as *blepō* (991) (Mk. 13:23,33); of caring for (Mt. 27:4). Noun: *horasis* (3706), the act of seeing, vision (Acts 2:17; Rev. 4:3; 9:17); *horama* (3705), that which is seen (Mt. 17:9; Acts 7:31; 9:10,12; 10:3,17,19; 11:5; 12:9; 16:9,10; 18:9). Deriv.: *aphoraō* (872), to look away from one thing so as to see another, from *apo* (575), from, and *horaō* (Phil. 2:23; Heb. 12:2); *epopteuō* (2029), to observe, from *epi* (1909), upon, and a form of *horaō* (I Pet. 2:12; 3:2); *epoptēs* (2030), noun, one who looks on (II Pet. 1:16), used of one witnessing as a spectator, or overseer.

3709. Orgē; wrath, anger as a state of mind. Contr. *thumos* (2372), indignation, wrath as an outburst of that state of mind with the purpose of revenge. From *oregomai* (3713), to desire eagerly or earnestly. Aristotle says *orgē*, anger, is desire with grief, cf. Mk. 3:5. The Stoics considered it as a desire to punish one who seems to have hurt them in a manner he ought not. The anger, wrath of man (Eph. 4:31; Col. 3:8; Js. 1:19,20), or of God (Heb. 3:11; 4:3); the effect of anger or wrath, i.e., punishment, from man (Rom. 13:4,5) or from God (Rom. 2:5; 3:5; Eph. 5:6; I Thess. 1:10; 5:9). Deriv.: *orgizō* (3710), to provoke to anger, irritate; *orgilos* (3711), prone to anger, passionate (Tit. 1:7).

3715. Orexis; appetite, lust or concupiscence (Rom. 1:27). It is always the reaching out after and toward an object with the purpose of drawing it to itself and appropriating it. Opp. *hormē* (3730), the hostile motion and springing toward an object with the purpose of propelling and repelling it still further from itself.

3717. Orthos; from *orō*, to excite. Straight, erect, upright. To stand straight up from a prostrate position (Acts 14:10). In Heb. 12:13 in a moral sense, straight in opp. to crooked, meaning upright, true, right, good. Syn.: *alēthinos* (228), truthful; *dikaios* (1342), just.

3718. Orthotomeō; from *orthos* (3717), right, and *temnō*, to cut or divide. Only in II Tim. 2:15 meaning rightly dividing.

3724. Horizō; from *horos* (3735), boundary. To bound, put limits to. Transferred from relations of space to those of time, it means to determine the time (Acts 17:26; Heb. 4:7). To establish, determine (Acts 11:29), to resolve, to decree (Lk. 22:22; Acts 2:23). The meaning of determining that one is something or that one is to be something pertains to Acts 10:42; 17:31.

3730. Hormē; purpose and intention of assault or onset, from *hormaō* (3729), to rush violently or impetuously, only in Acts 14:5; Js. 3:4. *Hormē* oftentimes is the whole style of motion and springing toward an object with the purpose of propelling and repelling it still further from itself. Contr. *orexis* (3715), translated as "lust" or "concupiscence" from *oregomai* (3713), to covet after, desire, which is always the reaching out after and toward an object with the purpose of appropriation.

3741. Hosios; holy, righteous, unpolluted with wickedness. Often grouped with *dikaios* (1342), righteous, just (Tit. 1:8) or its corresponding deriv. Deriv.: *hosiōs* (3743), adv., piously; *dikaiōs* (1346), righteously (I Thess. 2:10); *hosiotēs*, (3742), sub., holiness (Lk. 1:75; Eph. 4:24); *dikaiosunē* (1343), righteousness. It cannot be ascertained that *hosios* (Acts 2:27; Heb. 7:26) refers to the one who is holy unto God and *dikaios* (Lk. 1:6; Rom. 1:17; I Jn. 2:1) to the one who is righteous toward his fellow men. The Scriptures recognize that all righteousness has one root, i.e., one's relationship to God. Our righteousness toward men is rooted in our relationship with God. *Hieros* (2413), holy, is related to *hosios*, both referring to the ordinances of right which no law or custom of men has constituted. They rest on the divine constitution of the moral universe and man's relation to this. *Hosios* is one who reverences these everlasting sanctities and recognizes the duty for such reverencing. Opp.: *anosios* (462), one who misses the ordinances of right (I Tim. 1:9; II Tim. 3:2). Thus *hosios* is the performer of the ordinances, but not necessarily *hagios* (40), holy in character.

3742. Hosiotēs; holiness manifesting itself in the discharge of pious duties, in religious and social life; related to *hosios* (3741), holy. Twice in the N.T. joined with *dikaiosunē* (1343), righteousness (Lk. 1:75; Eph. 4:24). *Hosiotēs* is related more to the keeping of the ordinances than the character of life (*hagiotēs*, 41) which denotes the spirit and conduct of one who is joined in fellowship with God. Later *hosiotēs* was used as an ecclesiastical title or term of respect. The term *anosios* (462) is the opp. of *hosios*.

3748. Hostis; *hētis*, fem., *hoti*, neut.; derived from *hos* (3739), he who, and *tis* (5101), anyone, someone. The meaning of *hostis* is virtually the same as the basic relative pron. *hos* or the indefinite pron. *tis*.

3754. Hoti; a conj. meaning that, for, because. When used to introduce a direct statement, it is usually not translated. This is called *hoti* recitative and is equivalent to the English quotation marks; e.g., *humeis*, you (pl.), *legete*, say, *hoti*, to be rendered by a quote, *blasphēmeis*, are blaspheming, *hoti*, because, *eipon*, I said, *Huios*, Son, *tou*, of the, *Theou*, of God, *eimi*, am (Jn. 10:36). The translation is "you say, 'You are blaspheming,' because I said, 'I am the Son of God.'" Observe that in translation in each instance of the introduction by *hoti* of a direct statement, that direct statement begins with a capital letter. *Hoti*, when introducing dependent clauses or indirect statements, will be translated "that," e.g., *ginōsko*, I know, *hoti*, that, *prophētēs* a prophet, *esti*, is; translated "I know that he is a prophet." The *hoti* introduces an indirect statement. *Hoti* is used causally corresponding to the English word "because" (cf. the second *hoti* in Jn. 10:36 above).

3762. Oudeis; not even one, not the least; made up of *ou* (3756), not, and *heis* (1520), one. Not a one. When it is used in the neut., *ouden*, it means nothing or not a thing. When used with the indicative, it is *oudeis*, but with the other moods, the imper., the subjunctive, and the inf., *mēdeis* (3367) is used.

3770. Ouranios; from *ouranos* (3772), heaven; especially of the gods, heavenly. In the N.T. a heavenly host is of angels (Lk. 2:13); a heavenly vision (Acts 26:19). Heavenly Father occurs only in Matthew (Mt. 6:14,26,32; 15:13; 18:35; 23:9).

3772. Ouranos; heaven. The sing. and pl. are used similarly and interchangeably. There is no difference in meaning between them. In the N.T. it means in a physical sense, the over-arching, all-embracing heaven beneath which is the earth and all that is therein. In this not only do the fowls of the air fly (Mt. 6:26; 8:20; 13:32), but the clouds are supported (Mt. 24:30; 26:64; Lk. 12:56), the rain is formed (Js. 5:18); but also the sun, moon and stars are placed in the same celestial expanse (Mk. 13:25; Heb. 11:12). It is also used for that heaven where the residence of God is called by the Psalmist "the holy heaven," or "heaven of holiness," of separation (Ps. 20:6). It is God's dwelling or resting place (Mt. 5:34,45,48); where the blessed angels are (Mk. 13:32); whence Christ descended (Jn. 3:13,31; 6:32,33,38); where after His resurrection and ascension "He sitteth at the right hand of the majesty on high" (Heb. 8:1) and appears in the presence of God for us (Heb. 9:24); and where a reward is reserved for the righteous (Mt. 5:12; I Pet. 1:4). The heavens are used as a name of God in the O.T. (II Chron. 32:20, cf. II Kgs. 19:15; Isa. 37:15,16; Dan. 4:23, 26). *Ouranos,* heaven, is used with the same sense in the N.T. (Mt. 21:25; Mk. 11:30,31; Lk. 15:18,21; 20:4,5; Jn. 3:27). Thus, the kingdom of the heavens, or heaven, is syn. with the kingdom of God (Mt. 19:23,24). In II Cor. 12:2 Paul was raptured to the third heaven and returned. This is called Paradise (v. 4) which is applied to the state of the faithful souls between death and the resurrection where they are admitted to immediate communion with God in Christ, or to a participation of the true Tree of Life which is in the midst of the paradise of God (Lk. 23:43; Rev. 2:7). There is a final heaven which in Heb. 11:16 is referred to as a better country; in 13:14 as a continuing city; and in Rev. 21:2, the holy city, new Jerusalem. This eternal heaven is also called a country that is heavenly (Heb. 11:16). It is the place where the believers are going to receive their inheritance which is incorruptible (I Pet. 1:3-5). See also Mt. 6:19,20; I Cor. 2:9; Col. 3:2; Rev. 21:1-5. Deriv.: *ouranios* (3770), heavenly; *epouranios* (2032), heavenly, what pertains to or is in heaven.

3781. Opheiletēs; from *opheilō* (3784), to owe. A debtor, one who is indebted to another (Mt. 18:24); a debtor, one who is obliged to do something (Rom. 1:14; 8:12; Gal. 5:3); an offender, a trespasser, one who is a debtor or obliged either to reparation or punishment (Mt. 6:12; Lk. 13:4). Deriv.: *opheilēma* (3783), debt.

3782. Opheilē; a debt which must be paid (Mt. 18:32); obligation, a service which one owes anyone (Rom. 13:7; I Cor. 7:3). Only in N.T. Gr. Deriv.: *opheiletēs* (3781), debtor.

3783. Opheilēma; debt, that which is owed, which is strictly due (Rom. 4:4). Also an offense, a trespass which obliges to reparation (Mt. 6:12). The suffix *-ma* makes it that which is owed and makes it syn. with *opheilē* (3782), a debt (Mt. 18:32; Rom. 13:7, cf. Mt. 18:30,34). Deriv.: *opheilō* (3784), to owe; *opheiletēs* (3781), debtor.

3784. Opheilō; ought to, must, out of moral or personal obligation. Contr. *dei* (1163), must, out of intrinsic necessity.

3787. Ophthalmodouleia; from *ophthalmos,* eye, and *douleia* (1397), service. Eye service, implying a mere outward service only, to falsify the eye of man (Eph. 6:6; Col. 3:22).

3793. Ochlos; a multitude, disorganized or unorganized (Mt. 21:8; Lk. 9:38; Acts 14:14). Related words: *laos* (2992), referring usually to Israel; *ethnos* (1484), a heathen nation; *dēmos* (1218), an organized assembly of people.

3800. Opsōnion; from *opson,* meat, and *ōneomai,* to buy. Primarily signifying whatever is bought to be eaten with bread, provisions, supplies for a soldier's pay (I Cor. 9:7). Also Lk. 3:14; Rom. 6:23; II Cor. 11:8.

3804. Pathēma; suffering; from *paschō* (3958), to suffer. The suffix *-ma* makes it that which is suffered. Suffering, affliction (Rom. 8:18; II Cor. 1:5; Col. 1:24; Heb. 2:9). In this last verse, the sufferings of saints are called the sufferings of Christ because they are endured for the sake of Christ and in conformity to His suffering (cf. II Cor. 4:10; Phil. 3:10; I Pet. 4:13). A passion, an affection (Rom. 7:5; Gal. 5:24). In this latter passage, *pathēmata,* (pl.) passions or affections, denotes the bad passions as equivalent to *epithumiai* (1939), desires.

3805. Pathētos; from *patheō* or *pēthō,* to bruise, wound, hurt, suffer; or from *paschō* (3958), to suffer, to undergo pain, inconvenience or punishment. One who can suffer, who should suffer, or having suffered as in Acts 26:23 where it must be understood in this sense. Cf. Lk. 24:26,27. See *pathēma* (3804), suffering.

3806. Pathos; passion; from *pēthō,* to wound, hurt, to suffer. *Pathos* occurs three times in the N.T.; once coordinated with *epithumia* (1939), desire (Col. 3:5), once subordinated to it, *pathos epithumias,* the lust of desire (I Thess. 4:5), and in the third reference, vile affections (Rom. 1:26). These are lusts that dishonor those who indulge in them. *Pathos* is the soul's diseased condition out of which the various lusts spring. *Epithumia* is the active lust or desire springing from the diseased soul while *pathos* is the condition.

3807. Paidagōgos; from *pais* (3816), a child, and *agōgos,* a leader, which in turn is derived from *agō* (71), to lead. An instructor or teacher of children, a schoolmaster, a pedagogue (I Cor. 4:15; Gal. 3:24,25). Originally referred to the slave who conducted the boys from home to the school. Then it became a teacher or an educator. The ancient Greeks regarded a philosopher as a teacher, but not necessarily as *paidagōgos.*

3809. Paideia; originally instruction of children, from *pais* (3816), a child. It evolved to mean chastening because all effectual instruction for the sinful children of men includes and implies chastening, correction. *Paideia* occurs with *epanorthōsis* (1882), rectification, in II Tim. 3:16. In *paideia* there is discipline. See *nouthesia* (3559), instruction mainly by word, while *paideia* is by deed.

3810. Paideutēs; from *paideuō* (3811), to instruct, correct, chastise. An instructor (Rom. 2:20); a corrector, a chastiser (Heb. 12:9).

3811. Paideuō; originally to bring up a child, to educate, used of activity directed toward the moral and spiritual nurture and training of the child, to influence conscious will and action. Derived from *pais* (3816), a child. To instruct, particularly a child or youth (Acts 7:22; 22:3; II Tim. 2:25, cf. Tit. 2:12); to instruct by chastisement (I Tim. 1:20); to correct, chastise (Lk. 23:16,22; I Cor. 11:32; II Cor. 6:9). In a religious sense, to chastise in order to educate someone to conform to divine truth.

3816. Pais; a child in relation to descent; a boy or girl in relation to age; a manservant, attendant, maid in relation to condition. Contr. *paidiskē* (3814), a maidservant (Lk. 12:45). Used of spiritual service to God of Israel (Lk. 1:54); of David (Lk. 1:69; Acts 4:25); of Christ, so declared by God the Father (Mt. 12:18).

3819. Palai; an adv. of time signifying the past in contr. with the present. Meaning in the past, long ago, of olden times, formerly, also much longer ago in distinction from what has just occurred or just appeared. Note the distinction between what is over and gone, passed away, and what has existed for a long time. *Palai* in reality means old, what lies behind (Heb. 1:1). In II Pet. 1:9 what is designated as old sins (*palai*) does not mean as having taken place in the past but as belonging to a past which, in consequence of the cleansing, is over and gone. This differs from Rom. 3:25 where the sins are called previous, *progegonotōn,* and refer to what is past, not indeed long ago, but nevertheless already past for sometime (Mk. 15:44). *Palai* may also mean a great while, now for a long while (Mt. 11:21; Lk. 10:13).

3820. Palaios; old, both of what had been formerly, and of what is of long standing. The O.T. (*hē palaia diathēkē*) referred to in II Cor. 3:14 means the Covenant which was for a long time. In the Pauline Epistles, *ho palaios anthrōpos,* the old man, stands in antithesis with *kainos* (2537), qualitatively new (Rom. 6:6; Eph. 4:22). Here a reference to the past cannot be directly denied. The expression, "our old man" in Rom. 6:6, denotes what we formerly were, what we had been or are said to have been which belongs to the past as distinct from our state of salvation wrought by Christ and appropriated by faith. See *archaios* (744), one who has been from the beginning. *Palaios* is not necessarily from the beginning but just old.

3821. Palaiotēs; age, antiquity, length of time, existing a long time. Used only in Rom. 7:6 referring to the oldness of the letter of the law as compared to the newness of the Spirit. As the Spirit comes in the place of the letter, the letter in relation to the Spirit is something belonging to the past, and if made much of, has no longer any right to be so because it belongs to a time now past and gone (cf. Heb. 8:13).

3822. Palaioō; from *palaios* (3820), old. In the act., to make old (Heb. 8:13). In the pass., to grow old, *palaioomai* or *palaioumai,* (Lk. 12:33; Heb. 1:11).

3824. Paliggenesia; recovery, renovation, a new birth; from *palin* (3825), again, and *ginomai* (1096), to become. Occurs in Mt. 19:28 which refers to the coming state of the whole creation, equivalent to the restoration of all things of Acts 3:21 which will occur when the Son of Man shall come in His glory. The washing of *paliggenesia* (Tit. 3:5) refers to the regeneration of the single soul. See *anagennaō* (313), to beget again.

3831. Panēguris; from *pan,* all, and *aguris,* an assembly, derived from *ageirō,* to assemble. A solemn assembly for purposes of festal rejoicing, and on this account it is found joined continually with *heortē* (1859), feast. Occurs only in Heb. 12:23. Distinguished from *ekklēsia* (1577), church, and *sunagōgē* (4864), synagogue.

3838. Pantelēs; from *pan* (the neut. of *pas,* 3956, any), all, and *telos* (5056), end. Complete; in the expression *eis* (1519), unto, *to panteles* (neut.), unto the completion, completely (Heb. 7:25); at all, in any wise (Lk. 13:11). Deriv.: see *telos* (5056).

3844. Para; a prep. governing the gen., dat., and accus. with the primary meaning of near, nearby; expressing thus the relation of immediate vicinity or proximity which is differently modified according to the force of the different cases. After verbs of motion, as of coming, sending, it has the meaning of from or out from (Lk. 6:19; Jn. 6:46, etc.). With the gen. of persons it denotes the source, author, director, from whom anything proceeds or is derived (Mt. 21:42). With the dat. both of person and thing, it expresses rest or position, near, hard by, with; and with a dat. pl. it means among. With the accus. it expresses motion, nearby, near to a place, etc. It means by the side of anything or along side when it is used after verbs of motion. Sometimes it expresses movement to a place, near to, to, at, after verbs of motion, and so it is equivalent to *pros* (4314) or *eis* (1519) with the accus. (Mt. 15:29, "he came near to the sea."). Sometimes it also expresses the idea of rest or remaining near a place, etc., near by, at, with the dat. Here, however, the idea of previous motion or coming to the place is strictly implied. Contr. *eis* (1519) where it is not implied. Metaphorically, it is used of the ground or reason by or along with which a conclusion follows, by reason of, because of (I Cor. 12:15,16). Related meanings: (1) Motion by or past a place, i.e., a passing by, going beyond. Aside from or contrary to, against (Acts 18:13). (2) Besides, in the sense of except, save, or falling short (II Cor. 11:24 where it means forty stripes except one, or falling short of one). (3) Past, in the sense of beyond, besides, more than (Heb. 11:11), past the proper age. In composition *para-* used as a prefix implies nearness, proximity, near by, as *parakathizō* (3869), to sit down near; motion or direction near to, to, by, as *paraballō* (3846), to throw alongside, to compare; motion by or past any place, a going beyond, as *parerchomai* (3928), I go beyond. It also refers to whatever swerves from the true point, comes short of it, goes beyond it, like the English prefix mis- meaning wrongly, falsely (*parakouō,* to disobey), or like the prefix trans- in transgress (*parabainō,* 3845).

3845. Parabainō; from *para* (3844), beyond, and *bainō,* to go. To step on one side, and translated "to transgress, violate." In the N.T. it always has a moral sense (Mt. 15:2,3; II Jn. 9). To fall from or lose one's station or office by transgression (Acts 1:25). *Parabainō,* transgress, has more of the guilt of willful stepping out of line than *parapiptō* (3895), which is not stepping out of line but falling off.

3846. Paraballō; from *para* (3844), near, and *ballō* (906), to cast, put. To cast or put near. As a term of navigation to arrive or touch at, properly, to bring the ship or ships near or close (Acts 20:15). To compare (Mk. 4:30). Deriv.: *ballō* (906), to cast, place, throw; *parabolē* (3850), parable.

3847. Parabasis; transgression, an act which is excessive. The *parabasis* as the transgression of a commandment distinctly given is more serious than *hamartia* (266), sin (Rom. 2:23; I Tim. 2:14).

3848. Parabatēs; transgressor of the law; used with reference to the imputation of sin so far as it is transgression of the known law, deviation from recognized truth (Rom. 2:25,27; Gal. 2:18; Js. 2:9,11). Syn.: *parabasis* (3847), transgression, trespassing; *paraptōma* (3900), fault, mistake, neglect. Note the difference is between this somewhat involuntary deviation from the straight line and *parabasis* which is willful and knowledgeable deviation.

3850. Parabolē; from *paraballō* which is derived from *para* (3844), near, and *ballō* (906), to cast or put. The following meanings are to be distinguished: (1) A comparison, similitude, or simile in which one thing is compared with another (Mk. 4:10), and particularly spiritual things with natural, by which means such spiritual things are better understood and make the deeper impression on the honest and attentive hearer at the same time that they are concealed from the gross, carnal, and inattentive. See Mt. 13:3 (cf. vv. 9,11,15; 24:32). (2) Because these comparisons have an obscurity in their very nature, the word is used to denote a speech or maxim which is obscure to the person who hears it even though it contains no comparison (Mt. 15:15; Mk. 7:17). (3) Since short parables or comparisons often grow into proverbs, or proverbs often imply a simile or comparison, thus the word denotes a proverb or by-word (Lk. 4:23). (4) It is by some interpreted to mean merely a special doctrine or a weighty, memorable speech (Mt. 22:1; Lk. 14:7; 19:11). (5) A visible type of emblem representing something different from and beyond itself (Heb. 9:9). The Mosaic tabernacle with its services was a parable, a type, emblem, or figurative representation of the good things of Christianity.

3852. Paraggelia; from *para* (3844) an inten., and *aggelia* (31), message. A proclamation, command (Acts 5:28; 16:24). The noun corresponds to the verb *paraggellō* (3853), to command, charge by the apostles (I Thess. 4:2; I Tim. 1:5,18).

3853. Paraggellō; from *para* (3844), beside, and *aggellō* (31), to announce. To pass on an announcement, hence denotes to give the word, order, give a charge, command (Mk. 6:8; Lk. 8:29; 9:21; Acts 5:28; II Thess. 3:4,6,10,12). Deriv.: *paraggelia* (3852), a proclamation strictly used of commands received from a superior and transmitted to others (Acts 16:24; I Thess. 4:2; I Tim. 1:5,18).

3858. Paradechomal; from *para* (3844), at or to, and *dechomai* (1209), to receive. In the N.T., to receive, admit (Acts 16:21; I Tim. 5:19); to receive, embrace with assent and obedience (Mk. 4:20; Acts 22:18); to receive or embrace with peculiar favor (Heb. 12:6 which is a citation from the Septuagint version of Prov. 3:12).

3861. Paradoxos; from *para* (3844), beyond, and *doxa* (1391), opinion, expectation. Something beyond one's expectation, a miracle. In Lk. 5:26, used to express new things, miracles not hitherto seen (Mk. 2:12), and thus beside and beyond all opinion and expectation of men. Related words: *sēmeia* (4592), signs; *dunameis* (1411), miracles; *megaleia* (3167), magnificent things; *endoxa* (1741), glorious things; *thaumasia* (2297), wonderful things; *terata* (5059), terrifying things.

3868. Paraiteomai; from *para* (3844), an inten., and *aiteō* (154), to ask, beg. Never used in the act. sense, but only in the mid. voice, to try to obtain by asking, to beg a person's release, the person addressed being regarded as reluctant, or the thing asked for difficult to obtain. It then came to mean to beg to be excused, to decline, or refuse the thing spoken of. In the N.T., to decline, refuse, avoid with accus. following (Acts 25:11; I Tim. 4:7; 5:11; II Tim. 2:23; Tit. 3:10; Heb. 12:25). With *mē* (3361), not, following with the inf. (Heb. 12:19), to excuse oneself (see also Lk. 14:18,19 used as an inf. and followed by a part. adj.).

3870. Parakaleō; from *para* (3844), by the side, and *kaleō,* to call (2564); to call to one's side, hence aid. Used for every kind of calling to a person which is meant to produce a particular effect; comfort, exhort, desire, call for, beseech with a stronger force than *aiteō* (154). Deriv.: *paraklēsis* (3874), a calling to one's side and aid, hence, an appeal (II Cor. 8:4), an encouragement, exhortation (Acts 4:36; Rom. 12:8), consolation, comfort (Rom. 15:4); *paraklētos* (3875), one called to one's side and aid, counsel for the defense, an advocate, comforter; *sumparakaleō* (4837), with, *sun* (4862), together, to comfort together (Rom. 1:12).

3874. Paraklēsis; from *parakaleō* (3870), from *para* (3844), to, or used as an inten., and *kaleō* (2564), to call. The act of calling toward or hither to help, begging, and also of exhortation, encouragement toward virtue. The entire Scripture is actually a *paraklēsis,* an exhortation or admonition or encouragement for the purpose of strengthening and establishing the believer's possession of redemption (see Rom. 15:4; also Phil. 2:1; Heb. 12:5; 13:22, the purpose of which is to strengthen faith). Paul speaks of his preaching of the Gospel as *paraklēsis* in I Thess. 2:2,3; also Lk 3:18; Acts 13:15; II Cor. 8:4,17. The contents of the letter addressed to the church at Antioch are from the Apostolic Council, *paraklēsis* in Acts 15:31. Comforting words, consolation (Acts 9:31; II Thess. 2:16; Phile. 7). Opp. of tribulation and sufferings in II Cor. 7:4 and conjoined with joy in II Cor. 7:7,13 (see also II Cor. 1:3-7). In Lk. 6:24 used to designate the comfort in heaven to be denied the selfish, rich Christians who preferred to have their physical comfort on earth at the detriment of Christ's work. See the Beatitudes and woes in Lk. 6:20-26. In Lk. 2:25 the Messiah is described as the consolation of Israel which refers to the proclamation of salvation belonging to the department of prophesying (I Cor. 14:3) and appearing as a special gift (*charisma,* 5486) in Rom. 12:8. In Acts 4:36 Barnabas is called "son of encouragement," referring to his prophetic gift manifested especially in the exercise of comforting others. In connection with Acts 13:15; I Tim. 4:13, *paraklēsis* was regarded as based on the reading of a portion of Scripture (Lk. 4:20,21, an expository application of the prophetic word), although this was by no means the whole.

3875. Paraklētos; from *parakaleō* (3870), to call hither, toward, or to speak to, to speak cheerfully to, encourage. It is properly a verbal adj., i.e., he who has been or may be called to help, a helper. Used in the Gr. writers of a legal advisor, pleader, proxy, or advocate, one who comes forward in behalf of and as the representative of another. Thus in I Jn. 2:1, Christ is termed our substitutionary, intercessory advocate. Christ designates the Holy Spirit as Paraclete (Jn. 14:16), and He calls Him *allos* (243), another, which means another of equal quality and not *heteros* (2087), another of a different quality. Therefore, the Holy Spirit is designated by Jesus Christ as equal with Himself, God (I Jn. 2:1). This new Paraclete, the Holy Spirit, was to witness concerning Jesus Christ (Jn. 14:26; 16:7,14) and to glorify Him. The Holy Spirit is called a Paraclete because He undertakes Christ's office in the world while Christ is away from the world as the God-Man. He is also called the Paraclete because He acts as Christ's substitute on earth. When Christ in Jn. 14:16 designates Himself at the same time as the Paraclete, the word must not be understood as applied to Christ in the same sense as in I Jn. 2:1 where it is used with the meaning of our substitutionary Advocate, but rather as He who pleads God's cause with us (see Jn. 14:7-9). The verbs *parakaleō* (3870) and *paraklēsis* (3874), the act or process of comforting or advocating, do not occur at all in the writings of John.

3876. Parakoē; in its strictest sense a failing to hear (*akouō,* 191), or hearing amiss; with the notion of active disobedience which follows this inattentive or careless hearing (cf. Rom. 5:19; II Cor. 10:6; Heb. 2:2).

3887. Paramenō; from *para* (3844), with, and *menō* (3306), to remain. To stay, abide (I Cor. 16:6; Js. 1:25), to remain alive (Heb. 7:23).

3892. Paranomia; from *paranomeō,* which in turn is from *para* (3844), beyond, and *nomos* (3551), a law. A transgression or an offense of the law occurring only in II Pet. 2:16. The verb *paranomeō* (3891) occurs in Acts 23:3. Syn. *anomia* (458), lawlessness, without conformity to the law (Mt. 7:23; I Jn. 3:4). It follows that where there is no law (Rom. 5:13), there may be *hamartia* (266), sin or missing the mark which originally was placed by God, and *adikia* (93), what God expects as a right from us, but not *anomia,* lawlessness, or *paranomia,* transgression or going beyond the law. Paul means in Rom. 5:13 that *hamartia* as *anomia,* sin as lawlessness, cannot be if there is no law which to transgress. Thus, the Gentiles, not having a law (Rom. 2:14), could be charged with sin; but they, sinning without law (Rom. 2:12; 3:21), could not be charged with *anomia,* lawlessness, or *paranomia,* transgression. It is true that behind the Law of Moses which the Gentiles did not have, there is another law, the original law and revelation of the righteousness of God written on the hearts of all (Rom. 2:14,15). Since in no human heart is this original law totally obliterated, all sin, even that of the most ignorant savage, must still in a secondary sense remain as *anomia* or *paranomia,* a violation of this older, though partially obscured, law.

3895. Parapiptō; from *para* (3844), either an inten. or by the side of, and *piptō* (4098), to fall. To fall beside, to fall down or inadvertently. Used only in Heb. 6:6 denoting a side-falling and not conscious and deceitful faithless action, blameworthy and willful carelessness and falling into sin as would be expressed by parabainō (3845), to willfully transgress. Deriv.: *paraptōma* (3900), transgression.

3900. Paraptōma; fault. Sometimes used in profane Gr. when it is intended to designate a sin not of the deepest nature and the worst enormity. In the N.T. it is purposely stepping over. Syn. *parabasis* (3847), which designates sin as the transgression of a known rule of life and as involving guilt (Rom. 5:14,15). Still *paraptōma* is not quite as strong as *parabasis,* used only in Heb. 9:15 in connection with salvation, and elsewhere only when imputation and punishment are referred to (Heb. 2:2); whereas *paraptōma* occurs only in Paul's writings, except for Mt. 6:14,15; 18:35; Mk. 11:25f.; Js. 5:16 and is often used where pardon is spoken of (see Gal. 6:1). *Parabasis* denotes sin objectively viewed as a violation of a known rule of life, whereas in *paraptōma* reference is specially made to the subjective passivity and suffering of him who misses or falls short of the enjoined command. In Gal. 6:1 translated "trespass," indicating a sin involving guilt, a missing of the mark rather than a transgression of the law. Refers to a particular form of sin. Therefore, *paraptōma* has come to be used both of great and serious guilt and generally of all sin, unknown and unintentional (Ps. 19:13; Gal. 6:1). This is simply a missing of that which is right involving little guilt; therefore, it is a missing or failure including the activity and passivity of the acting subject. In Rom. 5:16 it stands in antithesis to *dikaiōma* (1345), righteousness or justification, or a being acquitted from past offences and being able to exercise the right of a child toward God as the legitimate Father (Rom. 5:18). *Paraptōma,* therefore, may be equated to defeat. Like its verb, *parapiptō* (3895), it is used syn. with *hamartia* as the generic word. In Rom. 5:20 *parap-*

tōma is used as the missing of the mark (*hamartia,* 266) and includes both *hamartia* (266) and *parabasis* (3847), transgression. Occurs also in Rom. 5:15,17,18. In Rom. 11:11,12 it means defeat. See Rom. 4:25; 5:16,20; II Cor. 5:19; Eph. 1:7; 2:1; Col. 2:13.

3906. Paratēreō; from *para* (3844), inten. denoting ill, and *tēreō* (5083), keep, observe, especially with sinister intent. To watch narrowly, to observe as the gates of a city (Acts 9:24); to observe a person insidiously (Mk. 3:2; Lk. 6:7; 14:1; 20:20); to observe days scrupulously (Gal. 4:10).

3907. Paratērēsis; from *paratēreō* (3906), attentive watching (Lk. 17:20) as can be observed with the eyes.

3927. Parepidēmos; from *para* (3844), to, at; *epi* (1909), in, among; and *dēmos* (1218), a people. A stranger, sojourner (Heb. 11:13; I Pet. 1:1; 2:11).

3929. Paresis; from the verb *pariēmi* (3935), from *para* (3844), by, and *hiēmi,* to send, place, stand. To put on the side. Putting our sins by, on the side, without punishment as in Rom. 3:25 where it is translated in the A.V. as "remission" which is the English equivalent to *aphesis* (859), forgiveness, deliverance, remission; from *aphiēmi* (863) (*apo,* 575, from, and *hiēmi,* to send, place, put, cause to stand). *Aphiēmi* is to remit or to cause one's sins to stand away from the sinner. This presupposes Christ's sacrifice as punishment for sin which *paresis* does not.

3930. Parechō; from *para* (3844), beside, near, and *echō* (2192), to have, hold. To present as the cheek to be smitten (Lk. 6:29), offer, to hold near. To show oneself (Tit. 2:7). To afford, furnish (Acts 16:16; 19:24; I Tim. 1:4; 6:17). To confer a favor (Lk. 7:4). To afford or show kindness as in Acts 28:2 or equity as in Col. 4:1. In Mt. 26:10; Mk. 14:6 with *kopous* (2873), trouble, to give anyone trouble. In Acts 22:2 with silence, to be still that another may be the better heard in speaking. In Acts 17:31 with faith to anyone, to give proof or demonstration to anyone.

3939. Paroikeō; from *para* (3844), at, and *oikeō* (3611), to dwell. To be a stranger, dwell or sojourn as a stranger, to dwell at a place only for a short time (Lk. 24:18; Heb. 11:9). Deriv.: *paroikia* (3940), sojourning, temporary dwelling in a strange or foreign country (Acts 13:17); applied spiritually in I Pet. 1:17. *Paroikos* (3941), a sojourner, one who dwells in a foreign country, a temporary dweller, not having a settled habitat, the place where he is now (Acts 7:6,29); applied spiritually (Eph. 2:19; I Pet. 2:11). Contr.: *katoikeō* (2730), to dwell in a certain fixed and durable dwelling.

3941. Paroikos; from *paroikeō,* which in turn is from *para* (3844), at, and *oikeō* (3611), to dwell, to be a stranger. A sojourner, one who dwells in a foreign country, a temporary dweller not having a settled habitation in the place where he is now (Acts 7:6,29). Applied spiritually (Eph. 2:19; I Pet. 2:11). Deriv.: *paroikeō* (3939), to dwell near; *paroikia* (3940), foreign residence.

3950. Parorgismos; the irritation, exasperation, embitterment that may spring from *orgē,* wrath, anger as a state of mind; only in Eph. 4:26. *Parogismos* is not *orgē* (3709) although both are translated "anger." The verb *parorgizō* (3949) from the inten. *para* (3844) and *orgizō* (3710), to anger, irritate, means to provoke to violent or bitter anger (Rom. 10:19; Eph. 6:4). It is to be so angry that one is beside (*para*) himself, out of his sound mind; hence it is strictly forbidden in Scripture. Contr. *orgē,* which under certain conditions is to entertain a righteous passion which sometimes involves moderate anger for good which is not only permitted but demanded.

3952. Parousia; from *parōn,* present, presence, a being present, a coming to a place, from the verb *pareimi* (3918) (*para,* 3844, near, with, and *eimi,* 1510, to be). To be present, to be at hand. Opp. of *apousia* (666), absence. *Parousia* is connected with the Second Coming of Christ, as *apokalupsis* (602) and *epiphaneia* (2015). See I Thess. 4:15-17; Js. 5:8; II Pet. 3:4; I Jn. 2:28. The *parousia corresponds* with the *apokalupsis* of the Son of Man (Mt. 24:17,37,39); of Christ (I Cor. 15:23); of our Lord (I Thess. 3:13; 5:23). See also I Thess. 2:19; II Thess. 1:7; I Pet. 1:7. The two expressions are used interchangeably in II Thess. 2:1,2.

3954. Parrēsia; freedom or frankness in speaking. N.T. meanings: freedom in speaking, saying freely all that one thinks, all that he pleases (Jn. 7:13,26; Acts 4:13,29); confidence or boldness, particularly in speaking (Eph. 3:12; 6:19, cf. I Jn. 2:28; 3:21; 4:17; 5:14); plainness, perspicuity of speech (Jn. 10:24; 11:14; 16:25,29; II Cor. 3:12); openness, making speech public (Jn. 18:20); freedom, liberty (Heb. 10:19); denotes being public or publicly known in opposition to being concealed (Jn. 7:4, cf. v. 10; Jn. 11:54, cf. Col. 2:15). Especially in Hebrews and I John, the word particularly denotes the unwaivering, fearless, and unhesitating confidence of faith in communion with God, in fulfilling the duties of the evangelist and holding fast our hope, and in every act which implies a special exercise of faith. *Parrēsia* removes fear and anxiety which characterize man's relation to God. It comes as the result of the ground of guilt being set aside (Heb. 10:19, cf. vv. 17,18; I Jn. 3:21; 4:17) and manifests itself in undoubting confidence in prayer (Heb. 4:16; I Jn. 5:14).

3955. Parrēsiazomai; from *parrēsia* (3954), freedom or frankness in speaking. To speak openly, boldly, and without constraint (Acts 9:27,28; 13:46; Eph. 6:20; I Thess. 2:2, etc.).

3956. Pas; mas.; *pasa,* fem.; *pan,* neut., every, all. It can mean the individual within the totality and the totality of the individuals. It can stand alone as in the case of *pas,* anyone and everyone; *oun,* therefore; *hostis,* who; *akouei,* hears, "Therefore, anyone and everyone who hears" (Mt. 7:24); *panta,* all things individually and in their totality; *di'* (*dia*) through; *autou,* him; *egeneto,* came into existence. It means not only all things in their totality but also each thing within that totality came into existence through Him (Jn. 1:3). It can also stand with a noun without an art., e.g., *pan,* every individual and all of them together; *dendron,* tree; *agathon,* good (Mt. 7:17); meaning every good tree and all the good trees.

3958. Paschō; the opp. of free action, to bar oneself passively from some influence from without; hence, to experience something evil, to suffer (Gal. 3:4). In all other places, to suffer something; experience evil, with the accus. of the obj. (Mt. 16:21; Acts 28:5; II Cor. 1:6; I Pet. 5:10, etc.). However, it occurs usually without an obj., to suffer (Mt. 17:15). In the N.T. it is mostly suffering on behalf of someone (Acts 9:16; II Thess. 1:5; Phil. 1:29, etc.).

3961. Pateō; from *patos,* a path, a beaten way. To tread, trample (Lk. 10:19); to tread as a winepress (Rev. 14:20; 19:15); to trample upon or have in subjection (Lk. 21:24; Rev. 11:2).

3962. Patēr; father. N.T. meanings: (1) A human father (Mt. 2:22; 4:22, etc.). (2) In the pl. *pateres,* for both parents (Heb. 11:23). (3) A remote progenitor (Mt. 3:9; 23:30,32; Lk. 1:32; 11:47, etc.). (4) A person respectable for his age or dignity (Acts 7:2; 22:1). (5) A spiritual father, i.e., one who converts another to the Christian faith and is thus the instrument of his spiritual birth (I Cor. 4:15). When Christ forbids His disciples in Mt. 23:9 to call any man their father upon earth, the meaning seems to be that they should not, with regard to spiritual things, have that implicit faith in any mere man which young children are apt to have in their parents. (6) One whom another resembles in disposition and actions as children usually do their parents (Jn. 8:44). (7) A first author or beginner of anything (Jn. 8:44) where the devil is called the "father of lies." (8) It is spoken of God, essentially denoting the divine essence, or Jehovah, as the Creator of the lights of heaven (Js. 1:17); and as the Father of man by creation (Lk. 3:8). He is thus called the Father of spirits or souls (Heb. 12:9), and by redemption (Mt. 6:9; 7:11; 10:29; Lk. 11:13, etc.). God is also spoken of as a Father in His divine essence as the Father of the human nature of Christ (Mt. 16:17; 24:36; 26:39,42,53; Jn. 6:27,46; 10:30; 14:6-13,16, 20,21,23,24,26,28,31; I Cor. 15:24). As the first person of the Trinity, the Father is so-called to distinguish Him from the Son and the Holy Spirit (Mt. 28:19; Jn. 15:26; 16:28; I Jn. 2:1; 5:7).

3965. Patria; from *patēr* (3962), father. What is called after the father, belongs to or springs from him, family, descendants. In this manner used in Lk. 2:4, "Of the family (or the descendants) of David." Used in a wider sense as a people, nationality or race (Acts 3:25). In Eph. 3:14,15 we have God presented as "the Father" and having only one *patria,* family. This indicates the oneness of God's family, both Jews and Gentiles, both those saints of the O.T. as well as of the N.T., who were all baptized into the body of Christ as is so clearly indicated in Acts 2; 10; 11; 19 and explained in I Cor. 12:13.

3973. Pauō; to stop, make an end. Used chiefly in the mid. voice meaning to come to an end, take one's rest, a willing cessation (contr. the pass. voice which denotes a forced cessation), Lk. 5:4. Used in the act. voice in I Pet. 3:10, to cause to cease. Deriv.: *katapauō* (2664), to rest, from *kata* (2596), down, inten., and *pauō* (3973), to cause to rest, to give rest (Heb. 4:8); also intrans., to rest entirely (Heb. 4:4,10); trans., to restrain (Acts 14:18); *katapausis* (2663), a rest (Heb. 3:11, etc.), a dwelling (Acts 7:49); *akatapaustos* (180), incessant, not to be set at rest, from the neg. *a, kata,* down, and *pauō,* to cease (II Pet. 2:14).

3982. Peithō; to entice or persuade. N.T. meanings: to persuade, followed by an accus. (Acts 13:43; 18:4; 28:23); to seek to persuade or solicit the favor of (Gal. 1:10); to prevail by persuasion (Mt. 28:14; Acts 12:20; 14:19); in the pass. *peithomai,* to be persuaded, assent, believe (Lk. 16:31; 20:6; Acts 17:4; 21:14; 27:11); in the pass. with a dat., to obey, comply with (Acts 5:36,37,40; 23:21; 28:24; Gal. 3:1, etc.); to assure, make confident, to free from fear or doubt (I John 3:19); in the perf. mid. voice *pepoitha,* to be persuaded, trust (Rom. 2:8; Heb. 13:18); with an accus. following, to be persuaded or confident of (Phil. 1:6,25); with a dat. following, to depend upon, trust in, have confidence in (II Cor. 10:7). Deriv.: *pepoithēsis* (4006), confidence, trust; *apeithēs* (545), disobedient; *apeitheō* (544), to be disobedient; *apeitheia* (543), disobedience.

3984. Peira; connected with *peraō,* to penetrate, or from *peirō,* to perforate, pierce through by trying the durability of things or simply passing through. Therefore, it has come to mean experience, trial, attempt, especially when it is used actively (Heb. 11:29), to make an attempt. When used pass., to make the knowledge, to experience (Heb. 11:36). These are the only places the word occurs. It is from this word that *peirasmos* (3986), temptation, is derived, which is an attempt against anyone. However, when it is brought by God it is that the object of temptation may acquire *peira,* experience. See *peirazō* (3985), tempt or test, and *peirasmos* (3986), temptation or testing.

3985. Peirazō; to try, to prove in a good sense (Jn. 6:6; II Cor. 13:5; Heb. 11:17) or in a bad one (Mt. 16:1; 22:18,35; I Cor. 10:9); to tempt, prove by soliciting to sin (Mt. 4:1; I Thess. 3:5; Js. 1:13,14). *Ho peirazōn,* the tempter (Mt. 4:3; I Thess. 3:5). The difference between *dokimazō* (1381) and *peirazō* is that the latter has the intention of proving that one has been evil or to make him evil, whereas the intent of *dokimazō* is to prove someone good and acceptable. *Peirazō* is connected with *peira* (3984), experience (Heb. 11:29,36); or to attempt (Acts 16:7; 24:6); to entangle a person in sin, doing contrary to God's will for him or to discover what good or evil, weakness or strength was in a person (Mt. 16:1; 19:3; 22:18); or knowing it, make it manifest to the one tempted (II Cor. 13:5, examine). Satan tempts (Mt. 4:1; I Cor. 7:5; Rev. 2:10) to show someone unapproved. Satan is called *peirastēs,* tempter (Mt. 4:3; I Thess. 3:5).

3986. Peirasmos; temptation from the Attic *peirasis,* trial. Basically from the noun *peira,* experience. The meaning depends on who tempts. If it is God, it is for the purpose of proving someone and never for the purpose of causing him to fall. If it is the devil who tempts, then it is for the purpose of causing one to fall. See *peirazō* (3985).

3987. Peiraō; related to *peirazō* (3985), to tempt or test. Only in Acts 9:26; 26:21; used in the mid. voice, to try, to take pains. In Class. Gr. when used with the gen. of the person, it meant to try anyone, put him to the test. It has to do primarily with the knowledge to be obtained concerning anyone. In the perf. pass. voice, to have tested, to have tried, to know from experience, to be experienced. Syn.: *epistamai* (1987), to comprehend, be acquainted with.

3989. Pelagos; closely allied with *plax* (4109), *platus* (4116), flat. The vast uninterrupted lull and expanse of open water. Occurs only in Mt. 18:6; Acts 27:5 and translated "sea." Distinguished from *thalassa* (2281) which suggests depth while *pelagos* suggests breadth, may refer to the open sea rather than to the shore or portions of the sea broken by islands and shut in by coasts and headlands. The two words are used together in Mt. 18:6: "it is better for him that a heavy millstone be hung around his neck, and that he be drowned in the depth (*pelagei,* the dat. sign. of *pelagos*) of the sea (*thalassēs,* the gen. of *thalassa*)." Here, however, the depth is implied not by the word *pelagos,* but by the verb *katapontisthē,* drowned, derived from *pontos* (not used in the N.T.) but which is connected with the word *bathos* (899), depth, *buthos* (1037), deep, depth, implying the sea in its perpendicular depth as *pelagos,* the same in its horizontal dimensions and extent. In Class. Gr. *pelagos* also referred to the illimitable sand-flats of the desert.

3993. Penēs; poor but one who can help himself through his own labor (*ponos,* 4192, pain, *poneomai*) (II Cor. 9:9). Contr. *ptōchos* (4434), poor but helpless, one dependent on alms, a beggar (Lk. 16:20).

3996. Pentheō; from *penthos* (3997), mourning. To mourn, grieve, upon the death of a friend (Mk. 16:10; 1 Cor. 5:2; Js. 4:9). Trans. with an accus., to mourn over or for (II Cor. 12:21). This verb expresses mildly the inner grief which in Gr. is designated as *lupē* (3077) and *lupeō* (3076) which in itself does not necessarily denote outwardly the inner grief. The other two words are *thrēneō* (2354), to bewail, and *koptō* (2875), literally to cut or to strike the bosom or beat the breast as an outward sign of inward grief (Lk. 18:13).

4006. Pepolthēsis; from the verb *peithō* (3982), to persuade. Used as trust, confidence (II Cor. 1:15; 3:4; 8:22; 10:2; Eph. 3:12). The object of trust or confidence, that on which one trusts (Phil. 3:4).

4014. Periaireō; from *peri* (4012), around, and *haireomai* (138), to lift up and take away. To take away from around (cf. II Cor. 3:16). Used of the taking away of sin by sacrifice (Heb. 10:11).

4027. Perikatharma; the defilement swept away by cleansing, *katharismos* (2512), the process of purification. Denotes the sacrificial victim laden with guilt, and therefore defiled. The dross discarded in cleaning metal; figuratively, the offscouring of mankind and is thus employed in I Cor. 4:13.

4037. Perimenō; from *peri* (4012), for, and *menō* (3306), to remain, wait. Trans. with an accus., to wait for as in Acts 1:4 where it means waiting for the fulfillment of the promise of the end.

4041. Periousios; from *periousia,* abundance, from *peri* (4012), beyond, and *ousia* (3776), being. Used only in Tit. 2:14 and translated "peculiar people" (KJV), rather it should be considered as people wherein God had a superlative propriety and interest above and besides His common interest to or in all the nations of the world. It should rather be "His treasured people."

4050. Perisseia; an exceeding measure, overflowing, something above the ordinary (Rom. 5:17, II Cor. 8:2; 10:15; Js. 1:21).

4051. Perisseuma; denotes abundance in a slightly more concrete form (II Cor. 8:13,14) where it stands for the gifts in kind supplied by the saints. Of the abundance of the heart (Mt. 12:34; Lk. 6:45); of the pieces left over (Mk. 8:8). Deriv.: *perisseuō* (4052), used intrans. of exceeding a certain number or measure, to be over, to remain of the fragments after feeding the multitude; exist in abundance as of wealth (Lk. 12:15; 21:4); of food (Lk. 15:17); of consolation (II Cor. 1:5); of the effect of a gift sent to meet the needs of saints (II Cor. 9:12); of rejoicing (Phil. 1:26, etc.); to redound to or to turn out abundantly as of the liberal effects of poverty (Rom. 3:7; II Cor. 8:2); to be abundantly furnished, abound in anything, to be preeminent, to excel. Used trans. in the sense to make to abound, to provide a person richly so that he has abundance; as of spiritual truth (Mt. 13:12). *Huperperisseuō* (5248), a strengthened form of *perisseuō* (4052).

4053. Perissos; abundant (Jn. 10:10). With the neut. art. *to perisson* used adverbially with *kata* (2596, according to) being understood, abundantly. With the prep. *ek* (1537), from, *perissou* (gen.), abundantly, of abundance (Mk. 6:51; Eph. 3:20; I Thess. 3:10; 5:13). In the last three passages the prep. *huper* (5228), over, is prefixed making it very emphatic, i.e., exceedingly, above the greatest abundance, superabundantly, over and above, more exceeding (Mt. 5:37); *ek*, out of, *perissou*, moreover (Mk. 14:31); excellent, extraordinary (Mt. 5:47); superfluous (II Cor. 9:1); with the neut. art. *to perisson*, advantage, preogative, privilege (Rom. 3:1). The comparative form is *perissoteros* (4055), more, more abundant, greater (Mt. 23:14; Lk. 12:4,48; 20:47; I Cor. 12:23,24; II Cor. 2:7) in which it means over much; more excellent, greater (Mt. 11:9; Lk. 7:26); the adv. as a comparative *perissoterōs* (4056); more abundantly (Mk. 15:14; II Cor. 1:12, etc.); used in a superlative sense, as comparatives are often used, very much, especially (I Thess. 2:17; Heb. 2:1; 13:19). From *perissos* as an adv. *perissōs* (4057), abundantly, exceedingly (Mk. 10:26; Acts 26:11); more, the more (Mt. 27:23); *huperperissōs* (5249), adv. from *huper*, above, exceedingly, and *perissōs*, abundantly, more exceedingly, superabundantly, above measure (Mk. 7:37); *huperperisseuō* (5248), verb meaning to abound more, super abound (Rom. 5:20); in the mid. voice *huperperisseuomai* (5248), to abound exceedingly, to overflow (II Cor. 7:4); *huperekperissou* (5240), a still further strengthened form meaning exceedingly abundant (Eph. 3:20; I Thess. 3:10; 5:13).

4059. Peritemnō; to cut around, cut off, circumcise. From *peri* (4012), around, about, and *temnō*, to cut off. To cut off around, to circumcise (Lk. 1:59; 2:21; Jn. 7:22, etc.). Spiritually, denotes the mortification of the sins of the flesh (Col. 2:11).

4061. Peritomē; from *peritemnō* (4059), to cut around, circumcise. Refers to circumcision or cutting off the foreskin (Jn. 7:22,23, etc.) It also means the abstract in the place of the concrete, i.e., persons circumcised, the Jews, as opp. the uncircumcised Gentiles (Rom. 3:30; 4:12; Gal. 2:7,8,9; Eph. 2:11). Denotes also spiritual circumcision of the heart and affections (see Deut. 10:16; 30:6; Jer. 4:4) by putting off the body of the sins of the flesh (Rom. 2:29; Col. 2:11); persons who were spiritually circumcised (Phil. 3:3).

4068. Perpereuomai; noun: *perperos*, to vaunt things one has (I Cor. 13:4). Related words: *alazōn* (213), one who vaunts of things which he has not; *huperēphanos* (5244), proud, one who shows himself above his fellows; *hubristēs* (5197), one who takes revenge on others for pleasure; *tuphoō* (5187), to be drunk with pride and set against men and God; *hubristēs* (5197), insolent wrongdoer.

4077. Pēgē; a fountain which either springs up or flows. Fountains of water (Rev. 8:10; 14:7; 16:4). Metaphorically of life-giving doctrine (Jn. 4:14). An emblem of the highest enjoyment (Rev. 7:17; 21:6). Cf. *phrear* (5421), a well or a pit in which water is stored. *Pēgē* also means an issue, flux of blood (Mk. 5:29) which is equivalent to *rhusis* (4511), an issue of blood (Lk. 8:44).

4098. Piptō; to fall. N.T. meanings: (1) To fall, (Mt. 13:4; 15:14,27). (2) To fall down (Mt. 2:11; 4:9; 26:39; Mk. 9:20; Jn. 18:6; Acts 5:10); as a house (Mt. 7:25,27); a tower (Lk. 13:4); or walls (Heb. 11:30). (3) With *epi* (1909), upon, following, to fall upon (Lk. 23:30; Rev. 6:16); as a lot (Acts 1:26). (4) To fall, perish, or be destroyed (Mt. 10:29; Lk. 21:24; I Cor. 10:8; Heb. 3:17). (5) To fail (Lk. 16:17). (6) To fall into sin and a state of disfavor with God (Rom. 11:22; I Cor. 10:12). (7) To fall in judgment, to be condemned and punished (Rom. 14:4). Deriv.: *parapiptō* (3895), to fall beside, to fall down; *paraptōma* (3900), fault, mistake.

4100. Pisteuō; to believe. From *pistis* (4102), faith, belief. N.T. meanings: (1) Trans. with a dat. following, to believe, give credit to (Mt. 21:25,32; 27:42; Jn. 5:46; 12:38). (2) Intrans., to believe, have a mental persuasion (Mt. 8:13; 9:28; Js. 2:19). (3) To believe, be of opinion (Rom. 14:2). (4) *Pisteuomai* in the pass. with an accus., to be entrusted with (Rom. 3:2; I Cor. 9:17; Gal. 2:7; I Thess. 2:4). (5) Followed by the prep. *eis* (1519), unto, to believe in or on Christ implying knowledge or assent to and confidence in Him (Jn. 3:15,16,18; 12:11; 14:1). Also followed by *epi* (1909), on, to believe on, either with an accus. (Rom. 4:5,24) or dat. following (Rom. 9:33; 10:11); or followed by the prep. *en* (1722), in, to believe in, give credit to. (6) Since believing in Christ or in the Gospel is the distinguishing characteristic of a Christian, believing is often used absolutely for believing in Christ (Mk. 16:16,17; Acts 2:44; 4:32; 8:13; 13:12; 19:2, etc.). Deriv.: see *pistos* (4103), faithful.

4102. Pistis; faith. From *peithō* (3982), to persuade. N.T. meanings: (1) Being persuaded, faith, belief. In general it implies such a knowledge of, assent to, and confidence in certain divine truths, especially those of the Gospel, as produces good works (Mt. 8:10; 15:28; Acts 3:16; Rom. 1:17; 3:22,25,28; Gal. 5:6; Heb. 11). Some times, however, simply a knowledge and assent to religious truths without good works and, therefore, false faith (Js. 2:14,17,18,24,26). (2) Miraculous faith or that faith in Christ to which, when the Gospel was first propagated, was annexed the gift of working miracles (Mt. 17:20; 21:21; Mk. 11:22; Lk. 17:6; I Cor. 13:2). (3) The doctrine of faith or of the Gospel promising justification and salvation to a lively faith in Christ (Acts 6:7; 14:27; Rom. 1:5; Gal. 1:23; Eph. 4:5). (4) The Christian religion (Gal. 6:10; Col. 2:7; I Tim. 4:1; Jude 3). (5) Fidelity, faithfulness (Rom. 3:3; Tit. 2:10). (6) Assurance, proof (Acts 17:31). Deriv.: *pistos* (4103), faithful.

4103. Pistos; faithful, with the following meanings: faithful, certain, worthy to be believed (I Tim. 1:15; 3:1; 4:9, etc.); true, just, trust worthy, observant of and steadfast to one's trust, word or promises (Mt. 25:21,23; Lk. 12:42; 16:10; I Cor. 1:9; 4:2; II Cor. 1:18; Eph. 6:21; Rev. 1:5); believing or giving credit to another (Jn. 20:27); one believing in the Gospel of Christ, a believer, a Christian (Acts 10:45; 16:1; II Cor. 6:15; I Tim. 6:2; Tit. 1:6, etc.). Deriv.: *pistoō* (4104), to make faithful; *pistis* (4102), faith; *pisteuō* (4100), to believe; *apistos* (571), an unbeliever, untrustworthy; *apistia* (570), faithlessness, uncertainty; *apisteō* (569), to put no confidence in; *oligopistos* (3640), of little faith.

4104. Pistoō; from *pistos* (4103), faithful. As a verb: to confirm, establish, ascertain, make faithful or certain. In the pass.: *pistoomai* or *pistoumai*, spoken of a person meaning to be confirmed in or assured of (II Tim. 3:14).

4124. Pleonexia; covetousness, the desire for having more or for what he has not. Contr. *philarguria* (5365), avarice to retain. Derived from *pleōn*, more, and *echō* (2192), to have. *Pleonexia* is a larger term which includes *philarguria*, avarice. It is connected with extortioners (I Cor. 5:10); with thefts (Mk. 7:22); with sins of the flesh (Eph. 5:3,5; Col. 3:5). *Pleonexia* may be said to be the root from which these sins grow, the longing of the creature which has forsaken God to fill itself with the lower objects of nature.

4134. Plērēs; from *plaō* or *plēmi*, to fill, compounded perhaps with *rheō* (4482), to flow. N.T. meanings: full, in a pass. sense, filled (Mt. 14:20; 15:37, etc.); abounding or abundant (Jn. 1:14; Acts 9:36); abundant, ample (II Jn. 8); full, complete, perfect (Mk. 4:28). Deriv.: *plēroō* (4137), to make full, to fulfill or complete; *plērōma* (4138), fullness; *plērophoreō* (4135), to fulfill, thoroughly accomplish; *plērophoria* (4136), fullness, completion.

4135. Plērophoreō; found for the most part only in biblical and Patristic Gr.; from *plērēs* (4134), full, and *phoreō* (5409), to fill, or *pherō* (5342), to carry. N.T. meanings: to fulfill, thoroughly accomplish (II Tim. 4:5), equivalent to *plēroō* (4137), to fill up. In the pass.: *plērophoreomai,* to be fulfilled (II Tim. 4:17), being established or being brought to an end and completed, reaching its goal; to be proved fully, to be confirmed with the fullest evidence (Lk. 1:1); to be fully persuaded (Rom. 4:21; 14:5).

4136. Plērophoria; from *plērophoreō* (4135), to fulfill. Perfect certitude, full conviction (I Thess. 1:5), equivalent to *bebaiōsis* (951), confirmation. Fullness, completion (Col. 2:2), or completion of understanding or complete understanding.

4137. Plēroō; from *plērēs* (4134), full. N.T. meanings: to fill, as a net with fish (Mt. 13:48), as a house with a perfumed smell (Jn. 12:3); to fill up, as a valley (Lk. 3:5), or measure (Mt. 23:32); fill up, supply (Phil. 4:19); to fulfill, complete, of time (Mt. 2:15; Lk. 21:24; Jn. 7:8; Acts 24:27), of number (Rev. 6:11), to complete, to perfect (Jn. 15:11; Phil. 2:2); to complete, finish, end (Lk. 7:1); to fulfill, complete, accomplish, perform fully (Mt. 3:15; Lk. 9:31; Acts 12:25; Rom. 13:8; Col. 4:17); to preach or explain fully (Rom. 15:19; Col. 1:25); to accomplish or perform what was foretold or prefigured in the O.T. (Mt. 1:22; 21:4; Jn. 19:24,36); to fully satisfy (Mt. 5:17). When Jesus said that He came not to destroy the law or the prophets but to fulfill, He meant that He came not only to fulfill the types and prophecies by His actions and sufferings, but also to perform perfect obedience to the law of God in His own person and fully to enforce and explain it by His doctrine. Thus He has fully satisfied the requirements of the law. Deriv. *plērēs* (4134), full.

4138. Plērōma; from *plēroō* (4137), to fill. A filling of filling up. N.T. meanings: (1) A fullness, of being full (Mk. 8:20). (2) Something put in to fill up (Mt. 9:16; Mk. 2:21). (3) A fullness, complete number (Rom. 11:12,25). (4) The expression "the fullness of the earth" means all the good things with which the earth is filled or plentifully stored (I Cor. 10:26,28). (5) The fullness of time denotes the completion of a particular period of time before ordained and appointed (Gal. 4:4; Eph. 1:10). (6) Completion. The Church is called the *plērōma* of Christ who fills all in all (Eph. 1:23). It indicates that Christ has filled it with all kinds of gifts and dwells in it and walks in it. (7) A fullness of the Godhead in Christ in Col. 1:19; 2:9 means that in the body of Christ as it was constituted God was in His fullness and not simply in His manifestation. Jesus was fully God and fully man with a body. Deriv.: *plērēs* (4134), full.

4139. Plēsion; adver. neut. of *plēsios,* from *pelas,* near, near to (Jn. 4:5). With the art., it means neighbor, fellow man or fellow creature, indicating primarily an outward nearness or proximity. Occurs in Lk. 10:29, the parable of the Good Samaritan, which teaches that he who is outwardly near us should be the object of our concern in spite of the fact that there are no ties of kindred or nation between us (Mt. 5:43; 19:19; 22:39; Mk. 12:31,33; Rom. 13:9; Js. 2:8).

4147. Plouteō; to be rich, to become rich. Contr. *ploutizō* (4148), to make rich, to enrich. Deriv.: *ploutos* (4149), riches, abundance; *plousios* (4145), rich, abounding; *plousiōs* (4146), (adv.), richly, abundantly.

4150. Plunō; to wash inanimate things (Rev. 7:14). Deriv.: *apoplunō* (637) with the prep. *apō* (575), from, washing the nets (Lk. 5:2). See *niptō* 3538), to wash part of the body, and *louō* (3068), bathe.

4151. Pneuma; primarily denotes the wind, related to *pneō* (4154), to breathe, blow. Breath; the spirit which like the wind is invisible, immaterial and powerful. N.T. uses: the wind (Jn. 3:8; Heb. 1:7); the breath (II Thess. 2:8; Rev. 11:11; 13:15); the immaterial invisible part of man (Lk. 8:55; 24:37,39; Acts 7:59; I Cor. 5:3-5; Heb. 12:23; Js. 2:26; I Pet. 3:19); man, the resurrection body (I Cor. 15:45; I Pet. 3:18); the element in man by which he perceives, reflects, feels, desires (Mt. 5:3; 26:41; Mk. 2:8, etc.); purpose, aim (II Cor. 12:18; Phil. 1:27; Eph. 4:23; Rev. 19:10); the character (Lk. 1:17; Rom. 1:4); moral qualities and activities (Rom. 8:15; 11:8; II Tim. 1:7); the Holy Spirit (Mt. 4:1; Lk. 4:18); the inward man (an expression used only of the believer, Rom. 7:6; II Cor. 4:13); the new life (Rom. 8:4-6,10,16; Heb. 12:9); unclean spirits, demons (Mt. 8:16; Lk. 4:33; I Pet. 3:19); angels (Heb. 1:14); divine gift for service (I Cor. 14:12,32); a vision (Rev. 1:10; 4:2; 17:3; 21:10). Sometimes *pneuma,* spirit, is used without the definite art. and sometimes with it. Any meaning pertaining to the presence or absence of the definite art. must be sought through the context in which it is used. With the definite art. it refers to Jesus' spirit (Jn. 11:33; 13:21) as contr. with the Holy Spirit as the Third Person of the Triune Godhead. In I Cor. 5:3 Paul refers to his spirit and in v. 5 to man's spirit. If not with the art. it may still refer to the Holy Spirit, but it also may refer to the spirit of anyone or to the spirit as contrasted with the body. When the expression is *to Pneuma to agion,* the Spirit, the Holy One, it stresses the character of the person of the Holy Spirit (Mt. 12:32; Mk. 3:29; 12:36, etc.). Spirit is the element in man which gives him the ability to think of God. It is man's vertical window while *psuchē* (5590), soul, is man's horizontal window making him conscious of his environment. The animals do not have a spirit, but they do have a soul. A soul is the element of life whereas the spirit is the element of faith. Whenever the word "spirit" is used it refers to the immaterial part of man including his spirit and soul. Sometimes when just "soul" is used in regard to man, it may refer to his immaterial part including his spirit. But sometimes the word "soul" refers to man's sinful propensities as in Lk. 14:26. In this verse and other similar ones, the translators have rendered *psuchē* as "life," but in reality it refers to man's fallen nature and his sinfulness.

4152. Pneumatikos; spiritual, from *pneuma* (4151), spirit. Opp. of *psuchikos* (5591), an animalistic man, man with his sinful propensities ruling him; *sarkikos* (4559), carnal man. Deriv.: *pneumatikōs* (4153), adv., spiritually.

4153. Pneumatikōs; an adv. from the adj. *pneumatikos* (4152), spiritual. Spiritually, by the assistance of the Holy Spirit (I Cor. 2:14); spiritually emblematically, mystically (Rev. 11:8, cf. Rev. 17:5,7).

4154. Pneō; to blow, breathe, as the wind or air (Mt. 7:25,27; Lk. 12:55; Jn. 3:8; 6:18; Acts 27:40; Rev. 7:1). *Pnoē* (4157), wind, breath (Acts 2:2; 17:25).

4157. Pnoē; derived from *pepnoa,* perf. mid. of *pneō* (4154), to breathe, blow. In Acts 2:2 translated "a wind a blast of wind." In Acts 17:25 it is breath, the air considered as proper for breathing. Syn.: *pneuma* (4151) from *pepneumai,* perf. pass. of *pneō* which in its earthly and natural sense means wind or air in motion. In Acts 2:2 the material blast of wind is differentiated from the spiritual *pneuma* used throughout the chapter to indicate the Holy Spirit. Thus, *pneuma* may mean something material or something purely spiritual such as a spiritual gift or the spirit of man which is the immaterial element in man enabling him to communicate with the Spirit of God. Used only in Jn. 3:8; Heb. 1:7 with the meaning of wind. *Pnoē* conveys the impression of a lighter, gentler motion of the air than *pneuma,* spirit. Related words: *anemos* (417), which is violent wind; *lailaps* (2978), storm, tempest. Its deriv. seems to be *lian* (3029), very much, and *laptō,* to lick or lap up as wolves do water in drinking or as a whirlwind violently licks up, as it were, the dust and all that is in its way. Therefore, *lailaps* actually means a whirlwind, a tornado, a violent storm (Mk. 4:37; Lk. 8:23; II Pet. 2:17). *Thuella* (2366), a hurricane, cyclone, from *thuō,* to move or rush impetuously. Found only in Heb. 12:18. *Thuella* is often a natural phenomenon wilder and fiercer than the *lailaps* itself. In it there is often the mingling in conflict of many opposing winds which makes it a turbulent cyclone. In Mt. 8:24 the word is *seismos* (4578), translated "storm," while its real meaning is "earthquake" as translated in all the other occurrences in the N.T.

4158. Podērēs; a garment reaching down to the feet (Rev. 1:13). Almost the same as *stolē* (4749), long robe.

4160. Poieō; to make, from *poios* (4169), quality. To endow a person or thing with a certain quality; to qualify (Mt. 3:3; 4:19; 5:36; 23:15; Lk. 15:19; Jn. 5:11,15); to make, appoint, constitute (Mk. 3:14; Acts 2:36). Contr. *prassō* (4238), to do, perform. *Poieō* brings out more the object and end of an act while *prassō* brings out more the means by which this object is attained. *Poieō* may well refer to the doing once and for all, the producing and bringing forth something which being produced has an independent existence of its own.

4165. Poimainō; to shepherd, tend. It involves much more than *boskō* (1006), to feed. It implies the whole office of the shepherd, guiding, guarding, folding of the flock as well as leading it to nourishment (Mt. 2:6; Lk. 17:7; Jn. 21:16; Acts 20:28; I Cor. 9:7; I Pet. 5:2; Jude 12; Rev. 2:27).

4166. Poimēn; shepherd (Mt. 9:36; 25:32; Mk. 6:34; Lk. 2:8,15,18,20). Applied spiritually to Christ (Mt. 26:31; Jn. 10:11,12,14,16; Heb. 13:20; I Pet. 2:25) and also given as a designation for a spiritual pastor of the flock (Eph. 4:11).

4167. Poimnē; a flock of sheep (Lk. 2:8; I Cor. 9:7). A spiritual flock of men (Mt. 26:31; Jn. 10:16).

4168. Poimnion; a diminutive of *poimnē*. A flock, properly a little flock. In the N.T. it is applied only spiritually (Lk. 12:32; Acts 20:28,29; I Pet. 5:2,3).

4171. Polemos; from *polus,* much, or many, and *oleō,* to destroy or, according to others, from *palamē,* the hand, which is derived from *pallō* (3823), to shake, move. A war (Mt. 24:6; Mk. 13:7). *Polemos* embraces the whole course of hostilities while *machē* (3163), is the actual stock in arms of hostile armies. Another related word is *stasis* (4714), insurrection, sedition.

4189. Ponēria; from *ponēros* (4190) which means a malicious person in that not only is he evil (*kakos,* 2556), but he expresses that malice and affects others. Therefore, it is malevolence. Contr. *kakia* (2549) which is simply the evil habit of mind without necessarily its being expressed in affecting others. Contr. both words with *kakoētheia* (2550), nature attributing evil to the actions and speech of others.

4190. Ponēros; evil in a moral or spiritual sense; wicked, malicious, mischievous. From the noun *ponos* (4192), labor, sorrow, pain. Distinguished from *kakos* (2556), evil in oneself but not necessarily malicious. *Ponēros* is Satan as the first author of all the mischief in the world (Mt. 6:13; Eph. 6:16). From it is derived *ponēria* (4189), aptness to do shrewd turns, delight in mischief and tragedies, perverseness.

4192. Ponos; from *pepona,* the perf. mid. voice of *penomai,* to labor. Labor (Rev. 21:4); pain, misery (Rev. 16:10; 11). It is labor which does not stop short of demanding the whole strength of man. Contr. *mochthos* (3449) which is the everyday word for labor, and *kopos* (2873) which means not so much the actual exertion which a man makes as the weariness resulting from labor.

4224. Potos; from *pepotai, poō,* to drink. A drinking match, drunken bout (I Pet. 4:3). Contr. *methē* (3178), drunkenness. It is abstract in meaning, it is the opportunity of drinking, the banquet, not necessarily excessive drinking but giving opportunity for excess. Syn.: *oinophlugia* (3632), excess of wine. It marks a step in advance of *methē,* drunkenness. In strict definition it is an insatiate desire for wine, alcoholism. Commonly used for debauchery. No single word rendering is better than this since it is an extravagant indulgence in long, drawn-out drinking bouts which may induce permanent damage on the body. *Oinophlugia* is ascribed to the death of Alexander the Great. *Kōmos* (2970), rioting or reveling and *kraipalē* (2897), the sense of overfullness of wine.

4238. Prassō; to make, perform in general (Acts 26:26; I Thess. 4:11); do good (Acts 26:20; Rom. 2:25); but more commonly, do evil (Lk. 22:23; 23:41; Jn. 3:20; Rom. 13:4, cf. Rom. 9:11; II Cor. 5:10). Whenever the words *prassō* and *poieō* (4160) assume an ethical tinge, the inclination makes itself felt to use *poieō* in a good sense and *prassō* in an evil sense, the latter tendency appearing in a more marked way in the uses of *praxis* (4234), work, action, deed (Lk. 23:51; Rom. 8:13; Col. 3:9); practice, behavior (Mt. 16:27); of office (Rom. 12:4). In all the uses except Mt. 16:27; Phil. 4:9, *prassō* has an evil connotation.

4239. Praus; meek (Mt. 5:5; 21:5; I Pet. 3:4) or *praos* (4235), meek, lowly (Mt. 11:29). See *prautēs* (4240), meekness.

4240. Prautēs; meekness, not in a man's outward behavior only nor in his relations to his fellowman or his mere natural disposition, rather it is an inwrought grace of the soul and the expressions of it are first and chiefly toward God (Mt. 11:29, adj. *praos;* Js. 1:21). That attitude of spirit in which we accept God's dealings with us as good and do not dispute or resist. *Prautēs,* according to Aristotle, is the middle course in being angry, standing between two extremes, getting angry without reason (*orgulotēs*), and not getting angry at all (*aorgēsia*). Therefore, *prautēs* is getting angry at the right time, in the right measure, and for the right reason. *Prautēs* is not readily expressed in English since the term "meekness" suggests weakness, but *prautēs* is a condition of mind and heart which demonstrates gentleness not in weakness but power. It is a virtue born in strength of character.

4244. Presbuterion; presbytery referring to the group of the elders (4245) and also the Jewish people (Lk. 22:66; Acts 22:5; I Tim. 4:14).

4245. Presbus; ambassador. The word, however, more commonly used in the comparative is *presbuteros,* a person who is older, commonly translated "elder" (Lk. 15:25; Jn. 8:9; Acts 2:17; I Tim. 5:1,2; I Pet. 5:5). *Presbuteroi,* pl., ancestors, predecessors (Mt. 15:2; Mk. 7:3,5; Heb. 11:2). Syn.: *archaioi* (744), the original ones (Mt. 5:21,27,33) and also used as a name of dignity, an official position in the senate or as an ambassador. We read of the elders of the Egyptians (Gen. 50:7), Moabites and Midianites (Num. 22:7). These enjoyed the natural dignity of age. We find elders in Israel as the representatives of the people whose decisions held good for the whole people (Ex. 3:16,18; 4:29; 19:7) which were apparently the foremost of the tribes and families according to the rite of the first born (I Kgs. 8:1,3). From among them Moses, at God's command, chose a college of seventy men who should "bear with him the burden of the people" (Num. 11:17, and who, therefore, were no longer the representatives of the people (Ex. 19:7; Deut. 27:1; Josh. 8:10). Later we have the institution of the Sanhedrin made up of seventy (Mt. 26:59; Lk. 7:3; 22:52). In every city also there were elders who had no connection with the members of the Sanhedrin but who were perhaps men chosen from among the people. In the N.T. they are mentioned together with the chief priests and scribes and served as assistants (Mt. 16:21; 26:3; 27:41; Mk. 8:31; 11:27; 14:43,53; 15:1; Lk. 9:22; 20:1; Acts 6:12, etc.). Related to this institution, at least at first, the name *presbuteroi,* elders, was used to designate the *proestōtes,* from the verb *proistēmi* (4291), to stand before or maintain rule over (I Tim. 5:17) within the Christian churches. These were appointed (Tit. 1:5) and ordained (Acts 14:23) everywhere in each church (Acts 14:23) and each town (Tit. 1:5). We have the first notice of them in Acts 11:30 where the disciples at Antioch sent their contributions for their brethren in Judaea to the presbyters in Jerusalem (12:25). In Acts 6 the appointment of the seven so-called deacons as assistants to the apostles leads us to suppose that the Twelve were the beginning of the presbytery. See I Pet. 5:1 which reveals the fellowship between the apostles and elders (Acts 15:2,6; 16:4, cf. Acts 15:4,22,23). In the absence of the apostles they entered upon their work (Acts 20:17,28-30); and the deacons in like manner, though with a narrower sphere of work, were appointed to their side, just as they had been to the apostles. As to the range of their work, hints of it are given in Acts 15; 20:28ff; I Tim. 5:17; Js. 5:14; I Pet. 5:1. The word *presbuteros* also occurs in Acts 21:18, II Jn. 1; III Jn. 1. John calls himself simply *prebuteros,* whether on account of his age (Phile. 9) or his office (I Pet. 5:1), we are not sure. Priority of office usually implies that of age also. In Rev. twenty-four elders appear with the four beasts around God's throne (Rev. 4:4,10; 5:5,6,8,11,14; 7:11,13; 11:16; 14:3; 19:4), representatives of Israel and the nations, or of N.T. churches. See *episkopos* (1985), bishop.

4254. Proagō; from *pro* (4253), before or forth, and *agō* (71), to go. Lead, bring. Used of place, to go before, lead when others follow (Mt. 14:22; 21:9; 26:32; 28:7, etc.); figuratively, in relation to the kingdom of heaven (Mt. 21:31); to go before, precede in time (I Tim. 1:18; 5:24; Heb. 7:18); to bring out or forth (Acts 16:30; 25:26), particularly to condemnation or punishment.

4267. Proginōskō; from *pro* (4253), before, and *ginōskō* (1097), to know. To perceive or recognize beforehand, to know previously, foreknow. The correlative of time is given in the context. Occurs in Acts 26:5; Rom. 8:29; 11:2; I Pet. 1:20; II Pet. 3:17. Distinct meanings: (1) To know before, whether a person (Acts 26:5), or a thing (II Pet. 3:17). (2) To foreknow with approbation, to foreapprove or make a previous choice of, as a peculiar people (Amos 3:2, *ginōskō* in the Septuagint; I Pet. 1:20, cf. Rom. 8:29; 11:2). (3) To ordain before, foreordain (I Pet. 1:20). In Rom. 8:29 it occurs with the verb *proōrise* (4309), did predestinate. This foreknowledge and foreordination in the Scripture is always unto salvation and not unto perdition. Therefore, it could be said that the Lord never foreordains anyone to be lost, but those who are saved as a result of their exercise of faith in the Lord Jesus Christ were known ahead of time and thus chosen unto God (see Hosea 13:5; Amos 3:2; Mt. 7:23; Jn. 10:14; Rom. 11:2; I Cor. 8:3; Gal. 4:9; II Tim. 2:19). The word "knowing" here denotes a previous uniting of oneself with someone. This divine knowledge and divine predestination in Rom. 8:29 is coincident and present in the mind and will of God prior to its manifestation in history resulting in salvation but not in condemnation. The salvation of every believer is known and determined in the mind of God before its actual accomplishment in a historical setting. Thus, *proginōskō*, foreknow, corresponds with the having been chosen before the foundation of the world of Eph. 1:4 and always precedes the *proorizō* (4309), foreordain. *Proginōskō* essentially includes a self-determining on God's part to this fellowship of Himself with the believers (Rom. 8:29) with whom God had beforehand entered into fellowship. However, the *eklegomai,* choose, of Eph. 1:4, merely expresses a determining directed to the objects of the fellowship (I Pet. 1:2).

4268. Prognōsis; foreknowing, prescience, recognizing beforehand, from *pro* (4253), before, and *ginōskō* or *gnōsis* (1108). Foreknowledge. Only in Acts 2:23; I Pet. 1:2. Denotes the foreordained relation of the fellowship of God with the objects of His saving counsel; God's self-determining towards fellowship with the objects of His sovereign counsel preceding the realization thereof. It involves a resolution formed beforehand, though this meaning is foreign to Class. Gr.

4279. Proepaggellō; in the N.T. only in the mid. form, *proepaggellomai,* to proclaim beforehand or promise beforehand (Rom. 1:2). Deriv.: *epaggellō* (1861), to promise or proclaim.

4283. Proeuaggelizomai; form *pro* (4253), before, and *euaggelizomai* (2097), to preach the Gospel or the Good News. Only in Gal. 3:8. To proclaim beforehand a joyful message.

4286. Prothesis; from the verb *protithēmi* (4388), from the prep. *pro* (4253), before, and *tithēmi* (5087), to set, place or lay. A setting forth, setting up, an exposition. It involves purpose, resolve, design. The motion of time is not in the prep. *pro,* before, but the meaning is derived from its literal and local import, a putting forth to view or to openly display. A thought or purpose (Acts 11:23; 27:13). When used of the purpose of God, it exclusively refers to salvation (II Tim. 1:9). Therefore, in Rom. 8:28, "those who are called according to his purpose," *kata prothesin,* must be taken as syn. with eudokeō (2107), indicating that those who are called are called because of God's good pleasure and not because of man deserving it (Eph. 1:8,9). The reference of time is not contained in the word itself, but is expressed by additional words; e.g., Eph. 1:11, *prooristhentes* (4309), "having been afore-appointed"; 3:11, "according to the purpose of the ages" (*aeons,* 165) making it *aiōnios* (166), eternal. N.T. meanings: (1) A setting before (Mt. 12:4; Mk. 2:26; Lk. 6:4; Heb. 9:2). The Septuagint applies this word only to the showbread (II Chr. 13:11; Heb. 9:2) referring not to time but to the position of the loaves set before the Lord on the holy tables. See also Ex. 25:30; 40:23. Since part of the frankincense put upon the bread was to be burned on the altar for a memorial of the bread, even an offering made by fire unto the Lord, and since Aaron and his sons were to eat it in the holy place (see Lev. 24:5-9), it is evident that this bread typified Christ, first presented as a sacrifice to Jehovah and then becoming the spiritual priest to God, even His Father (Rev. 1:6; 5:10; 20:6, cf. I Pet. 2:5). (2) A predetermination, purpose, intent, design of God in calling men in general, Gentiles as well as Jews, to salvation (Rom. 8:28); of gathering together all things in Christ (Eph. 1:9-11); of making the Gentiles fellow-heirs with the Jews of the same body and partakers of His promise in Christ by the Gospel (Eph. 3:6,11, cf. II Tim. 1:9); in choosing one nation rather than another to certain privileges and blessings (Rom. 9:11). All these passages are applied to the purpose of God in the N.T. (3) Predetermination, purpose, resolution of man (Acts 11:23; II Tim. 3:10). (4) Purpose, intent, design, (Acts 27:13).

4287. Prothesmios; and *prothesmia* (fem.), from *pro* (4253), before, and *tithēmi* (5087), to set, place, lay. A before-appointed day or time, the day or time being understood (Gal. 4:2).

4293. Prokataggellō; from *pro* (4253), before, and *kataggellō* (2605), declare, publish. To speak beforehand (Acts 3:18,24; 7:52; II Cor. 9:5).

4294. Prokatartizō; from the prep. *pro* (4253), before, and *katartizō* (2675), to establish, to set up. To perfect or equip beforehand, make right. Used in II Cor. 9:5 of the offerings for the Jerusalem Church which the Apostle wished to find already made up.

4299. Prokrima; from *prokrinō,* to prefer, derived from pro (4253), before, and *krinō* (2919), to judge. In Class. Gr. with reference to place and time, to decide beforehand, prefer before, another being put aside. Used in I Tim. 5:21. *Prokrima* includes an unfavorable prejudgment against one, partiality being included in the attitude of this prejudgment.

4306. Pronoeō; from the prep. *pro* (4253), before, and *noeō* (3539), to think, to comprehend. With a gen. of the person following, to provide for (I Tim. 5:8). In the mid. voice *pronoeomai* with an accus. of the thing, to provide, take thought, to care beforehand for (Rom. 12:17; II Cor. 8:21). See *nous* (3563), mind; the noun *pronoia* (4307), providence.

4307. Pronoia; from *pronoeō* (4306), to know ahead. Providence, care, prudence (Acts 24:2); provision (Rom. 13:14). See *noeō* (3539), to know; *nous* (3563), mind.

4309. Proorizō; to determine or decree beforehand. From *pro* (4253), before, and *horizō* (3724), to determine. Occurs six times: Acts 4:28; Rom. 8:29,30; I Cor. 2:7; Eph. 1:5,11. It is a word that has caused a great deal of division within the Christian Church as if it attributed to God absolute and capricious determination of who would be saved and who would not. A careful examination of each instance of its occurrence is important. (1) In I Cor. 2:7 it has a thing as its object, namely, the wisdom of God. The purpose was our glory which means our proper recognition of what we were. This is in no way condemnatory. In Acts 4:28, the verb is followed by the inf. *genesthai* (1096), to be done. Here reference is made to the actions of Herod and Pontius Pilate in regard to the crucifixion of Jesus Christ in doing only what God knew and permitted them to do. This concerns Jesus Christ and His position in history in that it was not of man but of God. (2) In Romans 8:29 it is used with a personal object, the relative pron. *hous,* whom, in the pl. This personal pron. applies also to the previous verb *proegnō* (4267), foreknew. The translation is "For whom He foreknew, He also predestined." The purpose of this foreordination is expressed in the phrase, "to be conformed to the image of His Son." In Eph. 1:5 the purpose of the foreordination is the adoption, which means the placing of those who were born of God into their proper position (*huiothesia,* 5206), from *huios* (5207), which means "Son" in His personal and voluntary conformity to the character of God, and the verb *tithēmi* (5087), to place. This is not condemnatory but rather beneficient for the believer. In v. 11 it is used again and the purpose of it is explained in v. 12 in the inf., "That we should be to the praise of his glory" (*eis to einai*) "for the purpose of being." This purpose is benevolent. Rom. 8:30 is to be explained by v. 29 in which it is clearly stated that this fore ordination was not capricious or an independent concept or complete in itself. It was conjoined with the verb "foreknew." The important thing for us to consider when the word is used is not who are the objects of this predestination, but what they are predestined to. They are always predestined to salvation, to adoption, or to glory, etc.

4314. Pros; a prep. governing the gen., dat., and accus.; and corresponding in its basic meaning to the primary force of these cases themselves as, for instance, with the gen. implying motion or direction, i.e., from a place, hither; with a dat. rest or remaining by, at, near a place; with the accus. motion or direction towards or to a place. In the N.T. used once with the meaning of pertaining to, i.e., for, for the benefit of (Acts 27:34). With a dat., *pros* marks a place or object by the side of which a person or thing is, i.e., by, at, near, as if in answer to the question where (Mk. 5:11; Lk. 19:37; Jn. 18:16; 20:12; Rev. 1:13). With the accus., *pros* marks the object towards or to which anything moves or is directed. When used of time, it means towards, near, as in Lk. 24:29, near the evening. Denotes the direction, reference, relation, which one object has towards another, i.e., in reference to, in respect to, as to, implying the direction or remote object of an action (Mk. 12:12; Acts 24:16, etc.). When spoken of a rule, norm, standard, it means according to, in conformity with, etc. (Lk. 12:47; II Cor. 5:10, etc.). When it is used of the motive, reason, occasion of an action, it means on account of, because of, for (Mt. 19:8). When it marks the end or result, the aim or purpose of an action, it may be translated "for what," "why," i.e., to what end, for what purpose (Jn. 13:28). Sometimes *pros* with the accus. is used after verbs which express simply rest: at, by, in a place, equivalent to *pros,* with a dat. But in such instances for the most part, the idea of a previous coming to or direction toward that place is either actually expressed or is implied in the context. Mk. 11:4 expresses that the donkey was tied at or by the door. In composition, *pros* imples: (1) motion, direction, reference; towards, to, at, as *prosagō* (4317), to lead towards or to bring toward; (2) accession, addition, thereto; over and above, more, further, as *prosaiteō* (4319), to request further and also used as an inten. as in *prosphilēs* (4375), very beloved; (3) it also implies nearness, a being or remaining near, at, by, as *prosmenō* (4357), to abide near.

4316. Prosagoreuō; from *pros* (4314), to, and *agoreuō,* to speak. To address, to greet. In some instances to designate, give a name to (Heb. 5:10). Used only in the mid. voice in the N.T.

4317. Prosagō; from *pros* (4314), to or towards, and *agō* (71), to bring, come. To bring to, (Lk. 9:41; Acts 16:20; I Pet. 3:18); to come to or toward, to approach (Acts 27:27). Basically to make oneself inclined to one, to surrender oneself to another. Intrans., to come to, to come hither, to approach (Acts 27:27). Subst.: *prosagōgē* (4318), access, approach.

4318. Prosagōgē; from *pros* (4314), to or toward, and *agō* (71), to bring or come. Used intrans., access, approach (Rom. 5:2; Eph. 2:18; 3:12). Syn.: *parrēsia* (3954), boldness or confidence.

4319. Prosaiteō; from *pros* (4314), an inten., toward, and *aiteō* (154), to ask, beg. To ask earnestly, to beg (Mk. 10:46; Lk. 18:35; Jn. 9:8). Syn.: *epaiteō* (1871), to beg.

4322. Prosanaplēroō; from the inten. *pros* (4314), and *anaplēroō* (378), to supply. Used in II Cor. 9:12; 11:9, to supply abundantly.

4327. Prosdechomai; from *pros* (4314), to, and *dechomai* (1209), to receive or accept. To receive or take the spoiling of one's goods with joy (Heb. 10:34); receive; accept as deliverance (Heb. 11:35); receive kindly, as a friend (Lk. 15:2); receive, entertain (Rom. 16:2; Phil. 2:29); receive, admit, as a hope (Acts 24:15); expect, look or wait for (Mk. 15:43; Lk. 2:25,38; 12:36; 23:51; Acts 23:21; Tit. 2:13).

4328. Prosdokaō; from *pros* (4314), toward, and *dokaō,* to look for. Expect, wait for (Mt. 11:3; 24:50; Acts 3:5, etc.). Deriv.: *prosdokia* (4329) from *prosdechomai* (4327), a looking for, expectation (Lk. 21:26; Acts 12:11).

4329. Prosdokia; from *prosdechomai* (4327), to accept, receive, or *prosdokaō* (4328), to wait, expect. A looking for, an expectation (Lk. 21:26; Acts 12:11).

4331. Proseggizō; from *pros* (4314), to, and *eggizō* (1448), to approach. To approach or come near to (Mk. 2:4).

4334. Proserchomai; from *pros* (4314), to, and *erchomai* (2064), to come. To come to, approach as to location (Mt. 5:1; 9:14, 20,28); to come to, approach, draw near spiritually (Heb. 4:16; 7:25; 10:22; 11:6; 12:22); to accede, assent to (I Tim. 6:3). If any man teach otherwise and does not accede to sound words, even the words of our Lord Jesus Christ, he is proud, etc. This relates to those who, after admonition (cf. I Tim. 1:3), persisted in teaching otherwise and did not then accede to sound words.

4335. Proseuchē; prayer; from the prep. *pros* (4314), to, and *euchē* (2171), a prayer, a vow (Js. 5:17). Prayer to God. Contr. *deēsis* (1162), supplication to anyone, not necessarily to God for particular benefits.

4336. Proseuchomai; to pray, vow. A deponent verb, i.e., a verb that has a mid. or pass. form ending in -*omai,* but used in an act. sense. From the prep. *pros* (4314), to, and *euchomai* (2172), to wish, pray. In the N.T. this comp. verb almost totally supplants the simple verb in designating to pray. The combination with a dat. although constant in Class. Gr., in the N.T. occurs only in Mt. 6:6; I Cor. 11:13, the prep. *pros,* to, implying praying to God, whether for the obtaining of good or the averting of evil (Mt. 6:9; 24:20; 26:36,39,44; Lk. 1:10). *Proseuchomai* embraces all that is included in the idea of prayer, thanks, asking, requesting special things; however, the distinctive word for worshipping is not *proseuchomai,* but *proskuneō* (4352) which properly means to crouch, crawl, prostrate oneself to. *Proseuchomai* appears in combination with *aiteomai* (154), to ask (Mk. 11:24; Col. 1:9); with *eucharisteō* (2168), to thank (Col. 1:3; 4:3; I Thess. 5:17). Deriv.: *proseuchē* (4335), prayer.

4339. Prosēlutos; from the obsolete *proseleuthō,* to come to. A stranger, foreigner, one who comes from his own people to another. Used in this sense in the Septuagint (Ex. 22:21; 23:9). The Septuagint also applies it to a stranger or foreigner who came to dwell among the Jews and embraced their religion (Ex. 12:48,49; Lev. 17:8,10,12,15; Num. 9:14, etc.). In the N.T. it is used for a proselyte or convert from heathenism to Judaism (Mt. 23:15; Acts 2:10; 6:5; 13:43). The words of Jesus in Mt. 23:15 have reference to the zeal of the Jews in making proselytes, even at Rome, such zeal being so remarkable about this time that it became proverbial among the Romans. Thus at Pentecost we have those who came from Rome who were both Jews and proselytes (Acts 2:10). There were also a number of Jewish proselytes at Antioch in Syria (Acts 6:5; 11:20).

4341. Proskaleō; pass.: *proskaleomai,* from *pros* (4314), to, and *kaleō* (2564), to call. Call to oneself, bid to come. Used only in the mid. voice (Mt. 10:1; Acts 5:40; Js. 5:14)

God's call to Gentiles through the Gospel (Acts 2:39), the Divine call in entrusting men with the preaching of the Gospel (Acts 13:2; 16:10).

4342. Proskartereō; from *pros* (4314), to, and *kartereō*

(2594), to endure. To tarry, remain somewhere (Mk. 3:9); to continue steadfastly with someone (Acts 8:13); to cleave faithfully to someone (Acts 10:7); refering to those who continually insist on something or stay close to someone (Acts 2:46; Rom. 13:6); used metaphorically of steadfastness and faithfulness in the outgoings of the Christian life, especially in prayer (Acts 1:14; 2:42; 6:4; Rom. 12:12; Col. 4:2).

4350. Proskoptō; from *pros* (4314), to, against, and *koptō* (2875), to cut, strike. Trans., to strike or dash against as the foot against stone (Mt. 4:6; Lk. 4:11). In these passages it is well worth our observation to note that the devil frames his temptation not only by quoting a detached sentence of Scripture without regard to the context, but by applying in a natural sense what was originally spoken in a spiritual sense. In the neut. sense with a dat. following: to dash or beat against, as winds and waters (Mt. 7:27). With a dat., to stumble at or against but in a spiritual sense (Rom. 9:32; I Pet. 2:8). Used in an absolute sense, to stumble (Jn. 11:9,10; Rom. 14:21). Deriv.: *koptō* (2875), to strike, hew, thrust; *apokoptō* (609), to hew off; *proskopē* (4349), stumbling block, offense; *proskomma* (4348), the stumble or offense, hindrance.

4357. Prosmenō; from *pros* (4314), to, with, and *menō* (3306), to remain. To stay at a place (Acts 18:18; I Tim. 1:3); with a dat. of the person following, to remain or continue with (Mt. 15:32; Mk. 8:2). In a spiritual sense, to adhere to (Acts 11:23). With a dat. of the thing, to continue or persevere (I Tim. 5:5).

4382. Prosōpolēpsia; respect of persons, partiality (Rom. 2:11; Eph. 6:9; Col. 3:25; Js. 2:1). The sub. *prosōpolēptēs* (4381), respecter of persons, and the verb *prosōpolēpteō* (4380), to act with respect to persons (Acts 10:34; Js. 2:9). Adv.: *aprosōpolēptōs* (678), without respect of persons or impartially (I Pet. 1:17).

4383. Prosōpon; from *pros* (4314), to, and *ōps*, the eye. In general that part of anything which is turned or presented to the eye of another. N.T. meanings: (1) The face, the countenance (Mt. 6:16,17; 17:2,6; Mk. 14:65, etc.). (2) Face, surface, as of the earth (Lk. 21:35; Acts 17:26). (3) Face, external or outward appearance (Mt. 16:3; Lk. 12:56; II Cor. 5:12; 10:7; Js. 1:11). (4) Person, personal appearance (Mt. 22:16; Mk. 12:14). *En* (1722), in, *prosōpō*, in person meaning in the name or as the representative of and by the authority of (II Cor. 2:10, cf. I Cor. 5:4). (5) A human being (II Cor. 1:11). (6) With the prep. *apo* (575), from, *prosōpou*, from the face or presence of (Acts 3:19; 5:41); from before (Acts 7:45). (7) *Eis* (1519), unto, *prosōpon*, in the presence of or sight, before (II Cor. 8:24). (8) *Kata* (2596), against or before, prosōpon, before the face or presence, before (Lk. 2:31; Acts 3:13; 25:16; Gal. 2:11). (9) *Pro* (4253), before, *prosōpon*, before the fact, before whether of place or time (Mt. 11:10; Lk. 1:76; 9:52; Acts 13:24). Deriv.: *prosōpolēpsia* (4382), respect of persons, partiality.

4384. Protassō; to put a specific command forward for a specific purpose (Acts 17:26). See *tassō* (5021), to place in its category.

4388. Protithēmi; from *pro* (4253), before, forth, and *tithēmi* (5087), to place. To propose, to set forth or before the eyes (Rom. 3:25); to propose, purpose, design beforehand (Rom. 1:13; Eph. 1:9).

4394. Prophēteia; the prophetic rank or work, the office or gift of a prophet. In Rom. 12:6 it is classed with *diakonia* (1248), ministry or serving, and *didaskalia* (1319), teaching as a *charisma* (5486), the result of God's grace or divine enablement to be exercised within the church (I Cor. 12:10; 13:2; I Thess. 5:20; I Tim. 4:14; Rev. 11:6; 19:10). Elsewhere it means prophecy, that which is prophesied, foretold (Mt. 13:14; I Cor. 13:8; 14:6,22; I Tim. 1:18; II Pet. 1:20,21; Rev. 1:3; 22:7,10,18,19). A prophecy is something that any believer may exercise as telling forth God's Word. This, however, does not make him a prophet (*prophētēs*, 4396), which is used in the N.T. in a very restrictive sense, placed side by side with the apostles as the foundation of the N.T. church (Eph. 2:20; 3:5), and also with the evangelists who were the successors of the prophets (I Cor. 12:28; Eph. 4:11). A prophet prophesies; but one who prophesies is not necessarily a prophet. Deriv.: see *prophētēs* (4396), prophet.

4395. Prophēteuō; from *prophētēs* (4396), prophet, from the prep. *pro* (4253), before, forth, and *phēmi* (5346), to tell. To prophesy, to foretell things to come (Mt. 11:13; 15:7; Mk. 7:6; I Pet. 1:10); to declare truths through the inspiration of God's Holy Spirit whether by prediction or not (Lk. 1:67; Acts 2:17,18; 19:6; 21:9; I Cor. 14:1,3-5, etc.). The art of heathen divination, however, uses the word *manteuomai* (3132). The foretelling or fore announcing may be, and often is, of the office of the prophet, but is not of the essence of that office. The *prophētēs*, prophet, is the outspeaker, he who speaks out the counsel of God with the clearness, energy and authority which spring from the consciousness of speaking in God's name and having received a direct message from Him to deliver. Thus one may prophesy without being a prophet in the strict sense of the word. A *prophētēs*, both in the O.T. and N.T., is not primarily one who foretells future things, but who having been taught of God, speaks out His will (Deut. 18:18; Isa. 1; Jer. 1; Ezek. 2; I Cor. 14:3).

4396. Prophētēs; from the prep. *pro* (4253), before or forth. The word was used of soothsayers who announced beforehand the will of the gods with reference to the future, but this is only a secondary and derived sense, for the *pro* must be regarded not as having reference to time meaning before, but rather as local, in the context of space, as in *prophasis* (4392), meaning pretext, what one states or puts forth before another. It means one who speaks openly before anyone and is the technical name for an interpreter of the oracle, of a divine message. This meaning was never lost in Class. Gr. because the gods were thought of as knowing the future. This technical term came also to mean the interpreters of the future. In the O.T., one to whom and through whom God spoke (Num. 12:2, cf. v. 6), also one to whom God made known His mysteries (Amos 3:7,8). Hence, generally, one to whom God revealed His purposes, one to whom God spoke (Gen. 20:7,8,17,18). That prediction of the future, while belonging to the subject matter of prophecy, did not form part of the true concept and is especially plain from the promise given in Deut. 18:15,18-20, cf. Num. 12:8. The earlier name of a prophet indicating foretelling in Heb. meant seer (I Sam. 9:9). It is clear that what really constituted the prophet was immediate communion with God, a divine communication of what the prophet had to declare. This is confirmed by the two terms, "reveal myself" (*apokaluptomai*, 601) and "prophesy" in I Cor. 14:29,30. See also I Pet. 1:12; Eph. 3:5. That the special element of prophesying was not merely predictions but a showing forth of God's will, especially of His saving purpose, is confirmed by I Cor. 14:37. Two things go to make the prophet, an insight granted by God into the divine secrets or mysteries and a communication to others of these secrets. It includes God's concept of grace, but with the warnings, announcements of judgment, etc., pertaining thereto. In the case of the O.T., their preaching was a foretelling of the salvation yet to be accomplished. In the N.T., prophecy was a publication of the salvation already accomplished, so far at least as it did not concern itself with realities still future. Accordingly, in Eph. 2:20; 3:5, the prophets, name side by side with the Apostles (meaning the Twelve and those who are so commissioned by Jesus directly) as the foundation of the N.T. Church, are to be understood as exclusively N.T. prophets, named again in Eph. 4:11 between apostles and evangelists (see I Cor. 12:28). N.T. prophets were for the Christian Church what O.T. prophets were for Israel. They maintained intact the immediate connection between the Church and the God of their salvation. They were messengers or communicators. Such prophets were not ordained in local churches nor do they have successors. The office of a prophet should not be confused with prophecy or the gift of prophecy which pertains to all believers (I Cor. 13:8; 14:3; I Tim. 1:18; 4:14; Rev. 11:6). Hence, the significant admonition in I Thess. 5:20, "do not despise prophecies." One thing must be very carefully remembered—that he who prophesies is not necessarily a prophet in the O.T. or N.T. sense of a restricted office. In the N.T. generally in the pl., *hoi prophētai,* the prophets, denotes the prophets of the O.T. In the sing. *ho prophētēs,* the prophet, is applied to Christ with obvious reference to Deut. 18; Jn. 1:21; 6:14; 7:40; Acts 3:22; 7:37. *Prophētēs* is used of Christ in Mt. 13:57; 14:5; 21:11; Mk. 6:4,15; Lk. 4:24; 7:16,39; 13:33; 24:19; Jn. 4:19,44; 9:17. We read of N.T. prophets in Acts 11:27; 13:1; 15:32; 21:10; I Cor. 12:28,29; 14:29,32,37; Eph. 2:20; 3:5; 4:11; Rev. 11:10; 22:9. The word prophet is used in the general sense of the Cretan poet Epimenides (Tit. 1:12). The fem. *prophētis* (4398) is used in Lk. 2:36; Rev. 2:20. Deriv.: *phemi* (5346), to say with the element of manifestation or enlightening; *prophēteuō* (4395), to prophesy; *prophēteia* (4394), the prophetic rank or work, the office or gift of a prophet; *blasphēmos* (989), blasphemer; *blasphēmia* (988), blasphemy or abuse; *blasphēmeō* (987), to blaspheme, revile, calumniate.

4412. Prōton; the neut. of *prōtos* (4413) used adverbially and signifying first, of time, and that whether in a superlative sense (Mt. 6:33; Mk. 16:9) or more commonly in a comparative sense (Mt. 5:24; 7:5; 8:21). *prōton humōn,* before you (Jn. 15:18); of order, dignity (Rom. 3:2; I Cor. 12:28; I Tim. 2:1; II Pet. 1:20; 3:3).

4413. Prōtos; first, the superlative degree of *prō* (4253), before. Used of time (Jn. 5:4; I Cor. 15:45,47; II Tim. 4:16; Rev. 1:11,17; 2:8); former, before in a comparative sense as first is often used in English (Jn. 1:15,30,42; 8:58; 20:4,8; Lk. 2:2; I Cor. 14:30); of order or situation (Acts 16:12); of dignity, first chief, principal.

4416. Prōtotokos; from *prōtos* (4413), first, and *tiktō* (5088), to bear, bring forth. The firstborn of man or beast (Heb. 11:28). As applied to Christ: (1) In respect of His being the firstborn of the virgin without excluding, however, the following higher sense in which He was eminently the firstborn (Mt. 1:25; Lk. 2:7). (2) He is called the first begotten or the firstborn of the whole creation (Col. 1:15), not only because He is before all things and all things both in heaven and earth were created by Him, but also because He was foreordained to inherit all things and in all things to have the preeminence, because all things were created unto Him or for Him (*eis auton*), as well as by Him (*di'autou*). See Col. 1:16-18. With the same meaning He is spoken of absolutely (*ton prōtotokon*), the firstborn (Heb. 1:6). (3) Christ is also called *prōtotokos ek tōn nekrōn,* the firstborn or first-begotten from the dead in regard to His being the first who rose from the dead, no more to die; being the first to arise to an immortal and incorruptible life. Those who were raised from the dead all died, having had only a sample of the resurrection that is yet to come of which Jesus was the firstborn. The Lord Jesus, however, rose and did not become subject to death again (Col. 1:18; Rev. 1:5, cf. Acts 26:23; Rom. 6:9; I Cor. 15:20,23). (4) This title is applied to Christ in respect of His being the firstborn among many brethren, both in holiness and glory (Rom. 8:29). The above are all the references where *prōtotokos* speaks of Christ. *Prōtotokos* also refers to saints. Saints are called the firstborn because under the law the firstborn were peculiarly appropriated to God and were heirs of a double honor and inheritance (Heb. 12:23, cf. Ex. 4:22). As an adj., *prōtotokos* is joined to *huios* (5207), son, in Mt. 1:25; Lk. 2:7: "and she gave birth to her firstborn son." The firstborn here adds prominence to the virginity of the mother of the Lord Jesus until that particular time (Ex. 13:2, 15; 34:19) where a child is spoken of as opening the womb. According to the laws of the O.T., the firstborn male was holy to Jehovah and had to be redeemed (Num. 18:15; Lk. 2:23,24). The firstborn son also has special rights as the head of the family and heir (Gen. 25:31; 49:3; II Chr. 21:3; cf. Lk. 1:32). As a sub., the firstborn, *ho prōtotokos,* as we saw above, is a name given to Christ with various attributes. In Col. 1:15 Christ holds the same relation to all creation; not that He is included as part of the creation, but that the relation of the whole creation to Him is determined by the fact that He is *prōtotokos,* the firstborn, *pasēs* (3956), of all, *ktiseōs* (2937), creation, so that without Him creation could not be (see v. 16), It is not said of Christ that He was *ktistheis,* created, and not of the creation that it was *techtheisa,* born or brought forth. Christ is spoken of in His relationship to creation as to time. He was before there was any creation whatsoever and was not part of the creation. Such relationship is quite a different and far more general one than that of the precedence of a firstborn, meaning that the firstborn was born before the second, third, etc., were born. This difference in Christ's relationship to the creation is made clear by v. 17, a verse which has no meaning if *prōtotokos* does not denote Christ's superiority in dignity as well as in time. What is said of Him in v. 17, "And He is before all things," shows that *prōtotokos* does not merely imply precedence in point of time, as if Christ were the beginning of a series of creations. In Heb. 1:6 Christ is called *ho prōtotokos,* the firstborn, without any further qualification, and here as in v. 5 a distinction between *huios* (5207), son, and *aggelos* (32), angel, is referred to, and in v. 6 this distinction is recognized. With reference to the angels, we are led to conclude that *prōtotokos* is here used instead of *huios,* son, on account of this superiority, so that we have here before us a mode of expression analogous to that of Col. 1:15, for the relationship of *gegennēka* (1080), of "being born" of God, can no more be applied to the angels than to the *ktisis,* creation, generally. In Heb. 12:23 the Christian Church is called "church of the first-born, which are enrolled in heaven," as holding a relationship to God analagous to that of Israel (Ex. 4:22) where Israel is presented as God's firstborn son, and perhaps as also holding a special relationship to all other creatures (Js. 1:18, cf. Heb. 12:16).

4434. Ptōchos; poor and helpless; one who in his abjectness (*ptōssō*) needs lifting. One who had fallen from a better estate. The *penēs* (3993) may be poor but he earns his bread by daily labor; but the *ptōchos* is so poor that he can only obtain his living by begging. The *penēs* has nothing superfluous, while the *ptōchos* has nothing at all.

4456. Pōroō; from *pōros,* a small piece of stone broken off from a larger one. The verb means to harden, make hard like a stone, or to make callous and insensible to the touch. In the N.T. applied only in a spiritual sense to the hearts or minds of men (Mk. 6:52; 8:17; Jn. 12:40; Rom. 11:7; II Cor. 3:14). Deriv.: *pōrōsis* (4457), hardening.

4457. Pōrōsis; from *pōroō,* to harden, petrify. Used figuratively, hardness, callousness, or blindness (Mk. 3:5; Rom. 11:25; Eph. 4:18).

4472. Rhantizō; from the Class. Gr. *rhainō,* to sprinkle. Sprinkling was the form of transfer of the blood of the sacrifice in order to secure its atoning efficacy, the form of purifying connected with expiation. Sprinkling of persons took place only upon the ratifying of the covenant (Ex. 24:8); upon the consecration of the family of Aaron to the priesthood (Ex. 29:21); in cleansing from leprosy and pollution from a dead body (Lev. 14:7,16; Num. 19:11). The first two cases are dealing with the establishment of a convenant between God and His people and, accordingly, the application of the atoning blood by the mediator. In the last two we have the removal of fellowship with that which is of the nature of judgment against sin. But it is in keeping with the character of the provisional expiation that an operation (the sprinkling) took place only on God's side; on man's side once only at the outset and never afterward except when leprosy and contact with death (as anticipations of judgment) had actually annulled the covenant relation. It is thus that the sprinkling with the blood of Christ in Heb. 12:24 is to be taken in the N.T. It can properly be connected only with Ex. 24 and Num. 19 and is to be understood of sprinkling on both sides (Heb. 9:13,19,21; 10:22), though no mention is made of sprinkling corresponding with that of the holy place or the altar, as once done in the regular O.T. ritual (Heb. 9:12). Deriv.: *rhantismos* (4473), sprinkling.

4473. Rhantismos; from *rhantizō* (4472), to sprinkle. Sprinkling. In the N.T. the blood of Christ corresponds to the blood of sprinkling (Heb. 12:24, cf. Heb. 9:13,14; I Pet. 1:2). Denotes the application of the expiation made by Christ. In the O.T. it is the form of that purification which is accomplished by expiation.

4487. Rhēma; from *rheō,* to speak. A word spoken or uttered (Mt. 12:36; 27:14); a speech or sentence consisting of several words (Mt. 26:75; Mk. 14:72; Lk. 1:38; 2:50, cf. Rom. 10:8; Heb. 6:5; I Pet. 1:25); a word, command (Lk. 5:5); denoting the operative or all-powerful word or command of God (Mt. 4:4; Heb. 1:3; 11:3, cf. Heb. 12:19); a report, account (Mt. 5:11); a thing, matter (Mt. 18:16; Lk. 1:37,65; 2:15). *Rhēma* stands for the subject matter of the word, the thing which is spoken about (Lk. 1:37; 2:15; Acts 10:37; II Cor. 13:1).

4506. Rhuomai; or *rhuō.* Properly denotes to draw with force and violence, to drag, pull, meaning to deliver or to draw out of danger or calamity and to liberate (Mt. 6:13; Lk. 1:74; Rom. 7:24; 11:26; II Tim. 4:17).

4522. Sagēnē; a long-drawn net or sweep-net, the ends of which were spread out by boats so as to cover a large portion of open sea, then drawn together, and all which they contained is enclosed and taken (Mt. 13:47). Contr. *diktuon* (1350), net in a general sense; and *amphiblēstron* (293), casting net.

4559. Sarkikos; carnal, from *sarx* (4561), flesh. Opp. of *pneumatikos* (4152), spiritual. Syn.: *psuchikos* (5591), soulish, with affinity to natural sinful propensities. The person in whom the *sarx,* the flesh, is more the ruling principle even as *psuchikos* and *psuchē* (5590) is for the animalistic instincts. *Sarx* covers that entire domain of our fallen nature made subject to vanity in which sin springs up and moves (Rom. 7:18; 8:5).

4560. Sarkinos; fleshly material, made or consisting of flesh. Occurs only in II Cor. 3:3. Characterized by the suffix *-inos* versus *-ikos* which carries an ethical meaning as in *sarkikos* (4559), with propensities of the flesh unto sin.

4561. Sarx; flesh. N.T. meanings: (1) Flesh, whether of men, beasts, fish, or birds (I Cor. 15:39). (2) The human body (Acts 2:26,31; II Cor. 7:1; Eph. 2:15; 5:29; Col. 2:5). The expression in Jude 7, "went after strange flesh," denotes unnatural homosexual abominations (Rom. 1:27). (3) Man (Mt. 24:22; Lk. 3:6; Acts 2:17; Rom. 3:20; I Cor. 1:29; Gal. 2:20; I Pet. 1:24). In Jn. 1:14 when it speaks of the Word becoming flesh, it means He became man or took human nature upon Himself and became subject to suffering and mortality (I Tim. 3:16; I Jn. 4:2,3). (4) The infirmity of human nature (Heb. 5:7). (5) The corrupt nature of man subject to the filthy appetites and passions (Jn. 3:6; Rom. 7:18; 8:6; Gal. 5:13,16,17,19,24; 6:8). (6) Natural relation or descent (Rom. 1:3; 9:3,5; 11:14). (7) Fleshly and temporal advantages (II Cor. 11:18). (8) Refers to the outward and carnal ordinances of the Mosaic Law (Gal. 3:3). (9) The expression "flesh and blood" means either such infirm bodies as we now have (I Cor. 15:50) in regard to our present weak and corruptible state (Mt. 16:17; Gal. 1:16; Eph. 6:12), or the corruptibility of our present body which will be replaced with incorruptibility (I Cor. 15:50). Deriv.: *sarkikos* (4559), fleshly, carnal; *sarkinos* (4560), made or consisting of flesh without any moral implication of following after fleshly lusts.

4567. Satanas; a Gr. form derived from the Aramaic (Heb.: *Sātān*). An adversary. This is the second name given to the prince of the devils. The other name is *diabolos* (1228), devil, one who casts either himself or something between two in order to separate them, the false accuser. In his name as Satan, he is the opposer, the adversary. *Satanas* is the prince of the fallen angels (Mt. 4:10; Mk. 1:13, etc.) and also used as a collective word for evil spirits or devils (Mt. 12:26; Mk. 3:23,26; Lk. 11:18). Applied by the Lord to Peter considered as opposing the divine plan of man's redemption by Christ's sufferings and death, and thus as joining with Satan (Mt. 16:23; Mk. 8:33).

4573. Sebazomai; from *sebō* or *sebomai* (4576), to worship religiously (Rom. 1:25). Occurs with *latreuō* (3000), to worship as in a cult. *Sebazomai* denotes not merely the act of pious reverence but the act or acts of worship. *Sebastos* (4575), venerable, august. In the N.T. applied to Nero (Acts 25:21,25); Augustus (Acts 27:1). See *sebomai,* (4576), adore, worship.

4574. Sebasma; from *sebazomai* (4573), to worship religiously. The object of worship or veneration (Acts 17:23; II Thess. 2:4). See *sebomai* (4576), to worship religiously.

4576. Sebomai; worship, from the root *seb-,* which originally meant to fall back, before. Such a bodily movement expressed an attitude of respect, being impressed by something great and lofty. Used only in the mid. voice in the N.T., to worship, adore (Mt. 15:9; Mk. 7:7; Acts 16:14; 18:7,13; 19:27). The part. noun *sebomenos,* a worshipper of the true God (Acts 13:43,50; 16:14; 17:4,17). These were Gentile proselytes as expressed in Acts 13:43. See *sebazomai* (4573), to worship religiously.

4578. Seismos; earthquake (Mt. 24:7; Acts 16:26; Rev. 16:18, etc.); see *pnoē* (4157), breath, wind.

4586. Semnos; venerable, from *sebnos* which in turn is from *sebomai* (4576), to worship, venerate. *Semnos* does not merely indicate the earthly dignity (*kosmios,* 2887) lent to a person, but is one who also owes his modesty to that higher citizenship which is also his, being one who inspires not only respect but reverence and worship. There lies something of majestic and awe-inspiring qualities in *semnos* which does not repel but rather invites and attracts (Phil. 4:8; I Tim. 3:8,11; Tit. 2:2). Syn.: *hieroprepēs* (2412), acting like a sacred person.

4587. Semnotēs; decency, from *semnos* (4586). Aristotle defined *semnotēs* as the average or the virtue that lies between two extremes, *authadeia,* related to *authadēs* (829), arrogance, and *areskeia* (699), the sub. of *areskō* (700), to please, or the ignoble seeking to please everybody. The endeavoring at all costs of dignity and truth to stand well with all the world. Therefore, *semnotēs* stands between caring to please nobody and endeavoring at all costs to please everybody. It is the ability to perform well one's duties as a citizen, but in addition showing that the dignity is not from this earth but from heaven, thus to drawing respect and reverence. See I Tim. 2:2; 3:4; Tit. 2:7.

4592. Sēmeion; sign, miracle with an ethical end and purpose. In the pl. miracles which lead to something out of and beyond themselves; finger-posts of God; valuable not so much for what they are as for what they indicate of the grace and power of the doer or of his immediate connection with a higher spiritual world (Mk. 16:20; Acts 14:3; Heb. 2:4). See *dunameis* (1411), mighty works; *megaleia* (3167), great works; *endoxa* (1741), glorious works; *paradoxa* (3861), strange works; *thaumasia* (2297), admirable works; *terata* (5059), terrifying works.

4599. Sthenoō; Stenoō; from *sthenos,* strength. A verb only in I Pet. 5:10. Far more common with the neg., *a,* without, as in *astheneō* (770), to lack in strength or to be sick; *astheneia* (769), disease, infirmity, sickness, weakness; *asthenēs* (772), sick, without strength, weak.

4607. Sikarios; derived from the Latin *sica,* a short dagger. An assassin using a particular weapon and following his trade of blood in a special manner. Only in Acts 21:38. Contr. the general term *phoneus* (5406), murderer, and *anthrōpoktonos* (443), man-slayer.

4608. Sikera; strong drink, any intoxicating liquor, whether wine (Num. 28:7), or more usually, that prepared from grain, fruit, honey, dates, etc., as in Lk. 1:15 where it occurs together with *oinos* (3631), wine. See Lev. 10:9; Deut. 29:6; Judg. 13:4,7,14.

4624. Skandalizō; to commit that which leads to the fall or ruin of anyone. Without reference to the element of misleading, it means to throw anyone unawares into ruin; to give occasion for ungodly conduct resulting in the mischief incurred thereby (Mt. 5:29; 18:8,9; Mk. 9:43,45,47; I Cor. 8:13, cf. Mt. 17:27; Jn. 16:1;

I Cor. 8:13); to craftily entice or lead to ruin, allowing someone to adopt a course in which unperceived he will come to mischief and ruin (Mt. 18:6; Mk. 9:42,43; Lk. 17:2). In the pass., to fall into ruin unawares; to be offended or to be caught or affected by a *skandalon* (4625), trap, or to regard something as a *skandalon*.

4625. Skandalon; the trigger in the trap on which the bait is placed, and which, when touched by the animal, springs and causes it to close causing entrapment. The word and its deriv. belong only to biblical and ecclesiastical Gr. In the O.T. it answers to the word for *pagis* (3803), trap. However, *pagis* always implies a reference simply to the injury lurking or hidden in the ambush and not so much to the suffering; whereas, *skandalon* involves a reference also to the conduct of the person who is thus injured. *Skandalon* always denotes the enticement or occasion leading to conduct which brings with it the ruin of the person in question. In the N.T. the concept of *skandalon* is concerned mainly with the fact that it produces certain behavior which leads to ruin and rarely denotes merely a hidden, unexpected cause of ruin (Rom. 9:33; I Pet. 2:8). In most cases, however, the *skandalon* is something which gives occasion to conduct leading to ruin, the cause; the course of sin leading to ruin or to a fall (Rom. 14:13; I Cor. 1:23; Gal. 5:11; Rev. 2:14). *Ta skandala* are things which lead others to turn away from God's salvation and thus to come to ruin (Mt. 18:7; Lk. 17:1).

4641. Sklērokardia; from *sklēros* (4642), hard, and *kardia* (2588), heart. Hardness of heart, i.e., stubbornness, obstinacy, perverseness (Mt. 19:8; Mk. 10:5; 16:14). Indicates man's condition in his bearing toward God and the revelation of His grace for which He ought to have a willing and receptive place in his heart.

4642. Sklēros; hard (Mt. 25:24), related to touch. An adj. applied to that which through lack of moisture is hard and dry. In the ethical sense, rough, harsh. Contr. *austēros* (840), austere related to the taste (Lk. 19:21). Applies to such things as draw together and contract the tongue, which are harsh and stringent to the palate, a new wine not yet mellowed by age, unripe fruit, etc. *Sklēros* always conveys a grave reproach indicating a harsh, inhuman character which is not the case with *austēros*.

4643. Sklērotēs; from *sklēros* (4642), dry, hard. Hardness, obstinacy, stubborness (Rom. 2:5).

4645. Sklērunō; to make hard or stiff, to harden, make obdurate. In the N.T., applied only figuratively to the heart or mind (Acts 19:9; Rom. 9:18; Heb. 3:13). Joined with the pl. *kardias* (2588), hearts (Heb. 3:8,13,15; 4:7).

4648. Skopeō; used only in the present and imperfect. To look towards an object, to contemplate, give attention to; literally, to spy out (Lk. 11:35; Rom. 16:17; II Cor. 4:18; Gal. 6:1; Phil. 2:4; 3:17). *Skopos* (4649), a scout or spy, also goal, aim, end Phil. 3:14).

4649. Skopos, from *skopeō* (4648), to look toward a goal, give heed. Used as a mark at the goal or end of a race (Phil. 3:14, cf. II Cor. 4:18).

4653. Skotia; darkness (Mt. 10:27; Lk. 12:3; Jn. 6:17; 20:1). Figuratively, like *skotos* (4655), darkness, and with the prevailing associated idea of unhappiness or ruin (Jn. 8:12; 12:35,46). As light is not only the emblem of happiness but is also itself beneficent; darkness in like manner works unhappiness (Jn. 12:35; I Jn. 2:11). Thus, *skotia* is not a figurative term for sin, but the consequences of sin.

4655. Skotos; from *ischō,* to restrain, stop, for when we are overcome by the night we are forced to stop. The exact opp. of *phōs* (5457), light. Physical darkness (Mt. 27:45; Mk. 15:33; Lk. 23:44; II Cor. 4:6, cf. Acts 13:11); spiritual darkness, implying ignornace or error (Jn. 3:19; Rom. 2:19); sin and misery (Mt. 4:16; Lk. 1:79; Acts 26:18; I Thess. 5:4; I Pet. 2:9); also persons in such a state (Eph. 5:8); the works of darkness (Rom. 13:12; Eph. 5:11); such works as are usually practiced by men in darkness or secretly (cf. I Cor. 4:5; I Jn. 1:6). Denotes the infernal spirits as opp. to Christ, the sun or light of righteousness (Lk. 22:53). Eternal misery and damnation (Mt. 8:12; II Pet. 2:17; Jude 13). Syn.: *gnophos* (1105), a thick dark cloud; *zophos* (2217), infernal darkness; *achlus* (887), a thick mist, fog.

4678. Sophia; wisdom, the knowledge of how to regulate one's relationship with God, wisdom which is related to goodness. When one is wise unto God, he is *phronimos* (5429), prudent with others and knows how to regulate circumstances. Adj. or adj. noun: *sophos* (4680), wise; applied to God (Rom. 16:27; I Tim. 1:17; Jude 25) and man, both in respect of true, spiritual and heavenly wisdom (I Cor. 3:18; Eph. 5:15, cf. Mt. 23-34); and also of false or worldly wisdom (Mt. 11:25; Rom. 1:22; I Cor. 1:19-21); skillful, expert (I Cor. 3:10); sensible, judicious (I Cor. 6:5) although this is more frequently expressed by *phronimos,* prudent. Related words: *sophizō* (4679), to make wise, instruct (II Tim. 3:15); *sophizomai,* pass. voice, to devise cunningly or deceitfully (II Pet. 1:16).

4680. Sophos; derived probably from the Heb. *sophim,* signifying watchmen. The Greeks apparently derived their *sophia* from this *sophim.* In the O.T. these watchmen used to ascend to the mountains so that they might see all around (Num. 23:14), but in the absence of mountains, the Greeks just observed the course and motions of the heavens and called themselves *sophoi.* Therefore, in its basic meaning *sophos* is the one who knows how to regulate his course in view of movements of the heavens or of God. N.T. meanings: (1) Wise, as applied both to God (Rom. 16:27; I Tim. 1:17) and man both in respect of truth, i.e., spiritual and heavenly (I Cor. 3:18; Eph. 5:15) and also of false or worldly wisdom (Mt. 11:25; Rom. 1:22; I Cor. 1:19,20,26). (2) Skillful, expert (I Cor. 3:10). In Class. Gr. used of workmen to show their expertise. (3) Prudent, sensible, judicious. To vindicate this quality the Greeks used to speak of a person as *phronimos* (5429) rather than *sophos.* However, it is used in this manner in I Cor. 6:5, and in the comparative degree, wiser, in I Cor. 1:25. See *sophia* (4678), wisdom.

4684. Spatalaō; to live in luxury, the same characteristics as *strēniaō* (4763), to live deliciously, and *truphaō* (5171), to live in pleasure, but with the further notion of waste fulness and prodigality (I Tim. 5:6; Js. 5:5). The *spatalaō* applies to the prodigal son (Lk. 15:13); the *truphaō* to the rich man faring sumptuously every day (Lk. 16:19); *strēniaō* to Jeshurun, when, waxing fat, he kicked (Deut. 32:15).

4690. Sperma; seed for sowing and seed springing; both what is sown as containing the germ of new fruit, and the seed which is growing out of the seed sown. Originally used of plants as seed (Mt. 13:24,27,32, 37,38; II Cor. 9:10); as seed sown and growing, produce. In I Jn. 3:9 the *sperma* of God denotes God's power working the divine life in believers who thence derive the divine nature, and thus it means the Holy Spirit working in the believers (Jn. 1:13). Also figuratively used of living beings as of the seed of the man; of posterity or descendants. In the Class. Gr. terminology, however, it does not strictly signify descendants collectively, and less posterity as a whole, but primarily only the individual, the child, offspring, son or daughter. It is a rare occasion that *sperma* means descendants collectively, that is to say, the children as a whole, the brothers and sisters. In the Bible, however, *sperma* has mostly a collective meaning. In the few places where it is used of an individual (Gen. 4:25; I Sam. 1:11), it includes oneself or represents the progeny (I Sam. 2:20, cf. 1:11). Occurs of a single person (Gen. 21:13; II Sam. 7:12). In Isa. 59:21 it signifies primarily the immediate descendants, the children (Gen. 15:3; 21:13), and hence *sperma* denotes the descendants collectively traced back to one ancestor (Gen. 13:16; 15:13,18; 22:17; 28:14; 32:12, etc.). Therefore, it passes into the meaning of family, stock (II Kgs. 11:1; 25:25; Jer. 41:1), and of Israel collectively (Ezra 9:2). In some instances such as Ps. 37:28; 69:36; Prov. 11:21; Isa. 1:4; 57:4; 65:23, it has the meaning of *gennēma* (1081), offspring, and signifies an ethical spiritual fellowship without reference to relationship of race. Especially is *sperma* used of the people of Israel as descendants of Abraham or Jacob, Israel, with whom Ishmael or Esau and their descendants were not reckoned (Gen. 21:12,13; 28:4,13,14; Ps. 105:6; Isa. 41:8, etc.). Besides these, we find it employed of individual families, such as the family of Aaron, David and others. With these aforementioned exceptions, *sperma* is everywhere a collective concept for which the plural is never used. The word continues in its collective meaning in the N.T. (Rev. 12:17). Thus, it denotes the immediate descendants, children (Mt. 22:24,25; Mk. 12:19-22; Lk. 20:28). The expression of the seed of David (Jn. 7:42; Rom. 1:3; II Tim. 2:8) means progeny, posterity (see II Sam. 7:12; Ps. 89:4; Acts 13:23). Similarly with the term the *sperma* of Abraham (Lk. 1:55; Jn. 8:33,37; Acts 3:25; 7:5,6; Rom. 4:13,16,18, etc.). Where Christ is designated as the progeny or offspring of Abraham, He is referred to as the Messiah, as Isaac is the offspring of Abraham, including and exhibiting in himself that progeny (Rom. 9:7). There are, indeed, *spermata,* seeds, of Abraham, lines of descent, those namely of Ishmael or Esau besides Isaac or Israel; yet the promise does not apply to all the lines of descent, but to one line which alone is always meant by the seed of Abraham, i.e., the Messiah, which henceforward is brought into existence through Christ. To take *spermata* (pl.) as a collective term, and *sperma* (sing.) of an individual person, is foreign to Pauline phraseology. In Gal. 3:16 we must distinguish between one line of progeny and more than one, *sperma,* seed, coll. *spermata,* seeds, lines of descendants, and to bear in mind Gen. 21:12,13 with which Gal. 3:29 very well agrees. That Paul has in mind the several lines of descendants from Abraham is evident in Gal. 4:22.

4695. Spiloō; to defile, spot (Js. 3:6; Jude 23). Close to the meaning of *miainō* (3392), to defile. Related words: *spilos* (4695), a spot, moral blemish (Eph. 5:27; II Pet. 2:13); *aspilos* (784), without spot (I Tim. 6:14; Js. 1:27; I Pet. 1:19; II Pet. 3:14); *spilas* (4694), spot (Jude 12), equivalent to *spilos.*

4714. Stasis; from *histēmi* (2476), to stand. A standing, stability, continuance (Heb. 9:8). An insurrection, sedition or a standing up (Mk. 15:7; Lk. 23:19,25; Acts 19:40; 24:5) referring to a civil insurrection while *polemos* (4171), war, refers to a foreign strife. A contention, dissension, dispute (Acts 15:2; 23:7,10).

4716. Stauros; cross; from *histēmi* (2476) or staō, to stand. A stake for execution, an instrument of torture for punishment, most dreadful and agonizing. It was not abolished until the time of Constantine who put an end to it out of regard to Christianity. Crucifixion was at one and the same time an execution, a pillory, and an instrument of torture. In biblical Gr. occurs only in the N.T. and means: (1) A Roman cross consisting of a straight and erected piece of wood fixed in the earth with a transverse beam fastened across its top and another piece of wood projecting from the upright piece nearer the bottom on which the crucified person's feet were nailed as the cross on which the Lord Jesus suffered (Mt. 27:32,40,42, etc.). (2) It refers to the whole passion of Christ and the merit of His sufferings and death (Gal. 6:14; Eph. 2:16) and also to the doctrine concerning these (I Cor. 1:17; Gal. 6:12). (3) It denotes that portion of affliction which is endured by pious and good men as a trial of their faith and to conform them to the example of their crucified Master (Mt. 10:38; 16:24; Mk. 8:34; 10:21; Lk. 9:23; 14:27). The expressions of taking up or carrying the cross allude to the Roman custom of making the criminal carry the cross on which he was to suffer (Jn. 19:17). When we read of the antagonism to the cross of Christ, we must understand it as antagonism to a redemption which was accomplished by the deepest humiliation, not by the display of power and glory (Phil. 2:5-8; Gal. 6:14). The Pauline way of speaking of Christ's death differs from the Johannine and Petrine writings and the Epistle to the Hebrews. These predicate the blood or the sacrifice of Christ (as Paul himself does elsewhere) what is here proclaimed of the cross. In the cross it is not the idea of sacrifice as such which is emphasized, but the blood of Christ (Col. 1:20) and what Christ experienced from the world as the full measure of His rejection which, however, has become the means of redemption. The cross shows this peculiarity of His death which also was a sacrifice. It makes the manner of His death prominent. Therefore, the blood refers to the sacrifice but the cross refers also to the shame. Deriv.: *stauroō* (4717), to crucify.

4717. Stauroō; from *stauros* (4716), cross. To crucify. It is spoken of the punishment of crucifixion. N.T. meanings: to crucify or fix or nail to a cross (Mt. 20:19; 23:34; 26:2, etc.); to crucify the flesh with the affections and lusts is to mortify them through the faith and love of Christ crucified (Gal. 5:24; 6:14). When Paul says, "The world has been crucified to me, and I to the world," he means that so great was his regard for his crucified Saviour that the world had no longer any more charms for him than the corpse of a crucified malefactor would have, nor did he take any more delight in worldy things than a person expiring on the cross would do in the objects around him. Deriv.: *stauros* (4716), cross; *anastauroō* (388), to crucify again; *sunstauroō* (4957), to crucify with.

4724. Stellō; to send, related to *histēmi* (2476), to set, to place or stand. As such it does not occur in the N.T., but it does occur in many deriv. with a prep., especially *apostellō* (649), send, from and *apostolos* (652), an apostle or one sent from. In its pass. form, *stellomai* with the mid. voice meaning, with an accus. of the prep. *apo* following, it means to avoid or withdraw oneself from, to send oneself away from (II Cor. 8:20; II Thess. 3:6).

4730. Stenochōria; from the verb *stenochōreō* (4729), to straighten or press together in a narrow place. Derived from *stenos* (4728), narrow, and *chōreō* (5562), to be or fit in a space. A narrow place (Rom. 2:9). Symbolically, great distress, straights (Rom. 8:35; II Cor. 6:4; 12:10). Distinguished from *thlipsis* (2347), tribulation. In three of the four occurrences in the N.T. these two words are used together (Rom. 2:9; 8:35; II Cor. 6:4). *Thlipsis* has more the meaning of crushing or affliction and is more serious than *stenochōria* which may refer more to the narrowness of room or being pressed from the sides rather than from the top. *Stenochōria* may be the opp. of *anesis* (425) which figuratively speaking means plenty of room or relaxation.

4735. Stephanos; crown. In Class. Gr. not used of the kingly crown but of the crown of victory in games, of civic worth, military valor, nuptial joy, festal gladness. Woven of oak, ivy, myrtle, olive leaves or flowers. Used as a wreath or the garland. Contr. *diadēma* (1238), diadem, a white linen band encircling the brow to indicate the assumption of royal dignity.

4747. Stoicheion; from *stoichos,* row, and *stoicheō* (4748), to put or go in a row, one of a series. In the pl. *ta stoicheia,* the elements or first principles of matter, the constituent atoms from which other things proceed in order or of which they are composed (II Pet. 3:10,12). Figuratively refers to the elements of first principles of the Christian doctrine (Heb. 5:12). Paul calls the ceremonial ordinances of the Mosaic Law the elements of the world or worldly elements (Gal. 4:3; Col. 2:8,20). In Gal. 4:9 he calls them weak and poor elements when considered merely in themselves and in opposition to the great realities to which they were designed to lead. These elements contain the rudiments of the knowledge of Christ. The law, as a school master, was to bring the Jews to this knowledge (Gal. 3:24). They are called worldly as consisting in outward worldly institutions (Heb. 9:1).

4749. Stolē; from *stellō* (4724), to send. A stately robe reaching to the feet or a train sweeping the ground. More often worn by women (Mk. 12:38; 16:5; Lk. 15:22; 20:46; Rev. 6:11; 7:9,13,14).

4762. Strephō; to turn. Intrans., to turn oneself (Acts 7:42); pass. with mid., to turn oneself (Acts 13:46); in a moral sense, to change, alter, adopt another course (Mt. 18:3). Deriv.: *epistrephō* (1994), to turn toward, turn about to; *apostrephō* (654), to turn away or back;

epistrophē (1995), return.

4763. Strēniaō; to be insolent because of wealth. To act with wantonness and petulance from abundance. There is the notion of strength, vigor, and not effeminacy and self-indulgence in it as there is in *truphaō* (5171), to live in pleasure. Occurs only in Rev. 18:7,9. The noun, *strēnos* (4764), luxury (Rev. 18:3); the comp. verb, *katastrēniaō* (2691) with the prep. *kata* (2596), against, to become lascivious against.

4774. Suggnōmē; from *sun* (4862), with, and *gnōmē* (1106), opinion, sentiment, will. Concession, permission, leave (I Cor. 7:6).

4777. Sugkakopatheō; from *sun* (4862), together with, and *kakopatheō* (2553), to suffer evil or affliction. Only in II Tim. 1:8. To suffer evil or affliction together with.

4779. Sugkaleō; from *sun* (4862), together, and *kaleō* (2564), to call. To call together (Mk. 15:16; Lk. 9:1; 15:6,9; 23:13; Acts 5:21; 10:24; 28:17).

4789. Sugklēronomos; from the conj. *sun* (4862), together, and *klēronomos* (2818), an heir, one who has a lot or who is allotted something. One who participates in the same lot, a joint heir (Rom. 8:17). Refers to a personal equality based on an equality of possession. In Heb. 11:9 it speaks of Isaac and Jacob in their relation to Abraham; in I Pet. 3:7 of women in relation to their husbands being joint heirs of the grace of life; in Eph. 3:6 of the Gentiles being joint heirs with Israel (see also Eph. 1:11).

4790. Sugkoinōneō; from *sun* (4862), together with, and *koinōeō* (2841), to partake. To participate in something with someone. In the N.T. only with a dat. of the thing, as a strengthened form of *koinōneō*, to be common (Phil. 4:14; Eph. 5:11; Rev. 18:4, noun form *sugkoinōnos*). To be a partaker together with others, a fellow or joint partaker, a sharer with (Rom. 11:17; I Cor. 9:23; Phil. 1:7; Rev. 1:9).

4793. Sugkrinō; from *sun* (4862), together, and *krinō* (2919), to judge. Literally, to separate and arrange together, combine, unite. Opp. of *diakrinō* (1252), to separate one from another, divide, part. To compare (II Cor. 10:12); comparing spiritual things with spiritual (I Cor. 2:13).

4832. Summorphos; from *sun* (4862), together with, and *morphē* (3444), form; *morphoō* (3445), to form, fashion. In Rom. 8:29 refers to the conformity of children of God "to the image of His Son" and in Phil. 3:21 of their physical conformity to His body of glory. Deriv.: *summorphoō* (4833), becoming conformed (Phil. 3:10).

4834. Sumpatheō; from *sun* (4862), together with, and *paschō* (3958), to suffer. With a dat., to sympathize with, to be compassionate, have compassion upon (Heb. 4:15; 10:34).

4835. Sumpathēs; from *sumpatheō* (4834), to feel together with. Compassionate, sympathizing, adj. (I Pet. 3:8).

4841. Sumpaschō; from *sun* (4862), together with, and *paschō* (3958), to suffer. To suffer together with (Rom. 8:17; I Cor. 12:26).

4845. Sumplēroō; from *sun* (4862), an inten., and *plēroō* (4137), to fill. Fulfill. The comp. verb, to fill to the brim. Used in the pass., to be filled completely, as with water (Lk. 8:23, cf. Mk. 4:37). In the pass., used of time, to be fulfilled or fully come (Lk. 9:51; Acts 2:1, cf. Jn. 7:8).

4850. Sumpresbuteros; from *sun* (4862), together with, and *presbuteros* (4245), an elder. A fellow elder (I Pet. 5:1). Peter reminds the elders of the dignity of their office that they might not forget its duties (vv. 2,3).

4851. Sumpherō; from *sun* (4862), together, and *pherō* (5342), to bring. To bring together (Acts 19:19); absolutely or with a dat. following, to be profitable, advantageous, to conduce or bring together for the benefit of another. Used either personally (I Cor. 6:12; 10:23; II Cor. 8:10) or impersonally meaning that it is advantageous (Mt. 5:29; 19:10). The neut. part. *to* (neut. def. art.), the, *sumpheron*, advantage, profit, benefit (I Cor. 7:35; 10:33; 12:7; Heb. 12:10). See *pherō* (5342), bring.

4854. Sumphutos; from *sun* (4862), together, and *phuō* (5453), to become, to increase. Growing at the same time, growing together, growing over (Lk. 8:7; Rom. 6:5, to be explained in accordance with vv. 4,5). It means not merely homogeneousness, but a being combined and united one with another.

4861. Sumpsuchos; from *sun* (4862), together, and *psuchē* (5590), soul. Joined together in soul or sentiment, unanimous (Phil. 2:2). It signifies community of life and love. Deriv.: *psuchē* (5590), soul; *psuchikos* (5591), soulish or driven by one's natural instinct; *apsuchos* (895), from the negative *a*, and *psuchē*, soul, without a soul, lifeless; *isopsuchos* (2473), equal-souled or like-minded; *dipsuchos* (1374), double-souled or double-minded.

4862. Sun; together as a prep. governing only the dat., with, implying a nearer and closer connection than the conj. *meta* (3326), with. When *sun* demonstrates connection, consort, as arising from likeness of doing or suffering from a common lot or event, it means in like manner with (Rom. 6:8). When used, however, of connection arising from possession, it means being entrusted with anything (I Cor. 15:10). Implies a joint working, cooperation, and when it does, it speaks of a means, instrument, with, through, by virtue of (I Cor. 5:4); also addition, accession, like the English "with" equivalent to besides, over and above (Lk. 24:21). In composition *sun* implies society, companionship, consort, with, together, as the English prefix con-; also therewith, withal, as in *sunagō* (4863), to gather together. Denotes completeness, all together, round about, on every side, wholly, and in this way it becomes an inten. as in *sugkaluptō* (4780), to cover altogether.

4863. Sunagō; from *sun* (4862), and *agō* (71), to lead, from which comes *sunagōgē* (4864), synagogue. It has a much gentler meaning than *sullegō* (4816), to gather together. To take in, lodge, entertain (Mt. 25:35). The difference between the two words is demonstrated in Mt. 13:28 when the verb *sullegō* is used for collecting the tares, and the word *sunagō* is used for gathering together the wheat in the barn in v. 30.

4864. Sunagōgē; from *sunagō* (4863), to lead together, assemble. A gathering, congregation, synagogue. The congregation of Israel was designated by the term *sunagōgē* or *ekklēsia* (1577), church. As the word was used, it did not imply the natural unity of the people, but a community established in a special way and for a special object. In the N.T. where *ekklēsia*, church, is adopted as the name for God's Church, i.e., the congregation of the saved, *sunagōgē* is used to designate the fellowship only in Rev. 2:9; 3:9, where the unbelieving Jews as a body are called the "synagogue of Satan" Jn. 8:44 calls them the "children of Satan." See also Acts 14:1; 17:1; 18:7. The synagogue of Satan is set as opp. to the church of God. A synagogue was finally designated as the Sabbath assembly of the Jews (Acts 13:43). In Js. 2:2 a synagogue is used to designate the worshipping assembly of the Jewish Christians. In other places in the N.T. it is used as the assembly place of the Jews.

4865. Sunagōnizomai; from *sun* (4862), together, and *agōnizomai* (75), to contend for victory in the public games. To fight in company with, assist in fight, help to fight (Rom. 15:30). The word is chosen with reference to the opposers from whom the Apostle desired to be delivered (v. 31), not like *agōnizomai* (Col. 4:12). Neither words are to be thought of as wrestling with God (Gen. 32).

4888. Sundoxazō; from *sun* (4862), together, and *doxazō* (1392), to glorify. To glorify together (Rom. 8:17).

4889. Sundoulos; from *sun* (4862), together, and *doulos* (1401), slave. A fellow slave found in the same natural conditions (Mt. 18:28,29,31,33; 24:49); a servant of the same Lord (Col. 1:7; 4:7; Rev. 6:11); of angels (Rev. 19:10; 22:9).

4891. Sunegeirō; from *sun* (4862), together, and *egeirō* (1453), to raise. To awaken together, both with cooperation and common activity. In the N.T. it occurs first in Eph. 2:6 where our being "raised up together with Christ" is referred to. The revivification of Christ, His giving them a new life (Rom. 6:10), involves at the same time revivifying anew those that are His. It refers to the delivery from the state into which they have been brought by sin and which brought death to them (Rom. 6:4,10). Therefore, the *sun,* together, in *sunegeirō,* expresses not merely the similarity of the deliverance, the divine work of salvation, raising us up from the death of sin to new life in Christ, but it affirms that it is an effect not specially and newly appearing, but connected with Christ's resurrection, taking place and included in it and also proceeding from it. It also refers to an effect brought about on God's part through His death and resurrection and our appropriation of that and the symbolism of it in baptism (Rom. 6:4). It has a similar meaning in Col. 2:12; 3:1. Practically, the meaning coincides with being justified (Rom. 4:25; 5:1; Col. 2:12,13).

4893. Suneidēsis; conscience. Not derived from *suneidenai tini* (dat. of *tis,* 5101, with someone), to know together with someone; but from *suneidenai,* to know together, *heautō* (1438), with oneself, that is to say, to be one's own witness, one's own consciousness coming forward as witness. It denotes an abiding consciousness whose nature it is to bear witness to the subject regarding his own conduct in a moral sense (Tit. 1:15). It is self-consciousness. Syn.: *sunesis* (4907), mentally putting it together, refers to the presentiment of an obligation bearing witness to itself in the consciousness. *Sunesis* is that which generally precedes action, therefore *sunesis* is moral obligation. However, in the N.T. there is something of the meaning of *sunesis* in the *suneidēsis* in that the latter is not merely the testimony of one's own conduct borne by consciousness (Rom. 9:1), but at the same time also the testimony concerning duty (Rom. 1:19,21,32; 2:15; II Cor. 1:12). Where there is knowledge of and acquaintance with God, conscience is specially determined thereby; hence "conscience of God" (I Pet. 2:19) which means the testimony a man must bear to himself in regard to God or whatever such as an idol in I Cor. 8:7. Inasmuch as man is compelled to testify to himself concerning his duty toward God and his relation thereto, *suneidēsis,* conscience, is the bearer of the religious need (Heb. 9:9; 10:2), and accordingly it has the duty of confirming the truth of divine and saving revelation as intended to meet and satisfy the religious need (Heb. 9:9,14; II Cor. 4:2; 5:11). Conscience, accordingly, is the awareness man has of himself in his relation to God, manifesting itself in the form of a testimony that is the result of the action of the spirit in the heart (Acts 23:1; 24:16; II Tim. 1:3; Heb. 9:9,14; 10:2). Hence the obligation (I Tim. 1:5,19; 3:9). As a result of the consciousness of sins, purification is needed (Heb. 9:14), the removal of the evil conscience (Heb. 10:22). Thus, the conscience of God coincides with the Spirit of God in man (Rom. 9:1, cf. Rom. 1:9; II Tim. 1:3).

4894. Suneidō; or *suneideō, suneidon,* the second aorist of *sunoraō* from *sun* (4862), together, and *horaō* (3708), to see. Also *sunoida,* from sun, and *oida,* or *eidō* (1492), to know intuitively. To know together with, to know what others know or do, intend to do, or have done. A precise definition would be to be conscious in oneself or to be one's own witness. The word used by Paul in I Cor. 4:4 is equal to being compelled to testify against oneself. The verb *suneideō* is used also in Acts 5:2; 12:12; 14:6. From this verb is derived the noun *suneidēsis* (4893), translated "conscience" or the subject's own consciousness in which he bears witness to himself and appears as his own witness.

4907. Sunesis; insight, the critical faculty of how to evaluate anything, people, things circumstances (Mk. 12:33; Lk. 2:47; I Cor. 1:19; Eph. 3:4; Col. 1:9; 2:2; II Tim. 2:7).

4908. Sunetos; intelligent, sagacious, penetrating. Having *sunesis* (4907), the critical faculty of discernment (Mt. 11:25; Lk. 10:21; Acts 13:7; I Cor. 1:19).

4912. Sunechō; from *sun* (4862), inten., and *echō* (2192), to have. To hold fast (Lk. 22:63); to straiten, confine (Lk. 8:45; 19:43). Mid. voice: *sunechomai,* to be in a mental strait (Lk. 12:50; Acts 18:5; Phil. 1:23); to constrain, bind (II Cor. 5:14); to stop the ears (Acts 7:57). Pass. voice: *sunechomai,* to be detained, afflicted with, to be sick of (Mt. 4:24; Lk. 4:38; Acts 28:8); to be under the influence of (Lk. 8:37).

4920. Suniēmi; from *sun* (4862), together or together with, and *hiēmi,* to send or put. To bring together. When the word is confined to the sphere of mental perception it means to hear, notice, perceive, recognize, understand, put it all together and make sense out of it. Thus, it strictly denotes the collecting together of the single features of an object into a whole, as collecting the pieces of the puzzle and putting them together. According to Aristotle it is a syn. of *manthanō* (3129), to learn, to understand, and differs from *noeō* (3539), to merely perceive. *Manthanō* involves the capability of knowing and suniēmi involves the activity of knowing (Mt. 15:16; Mk. 8:17; Lk. 24:45). The difference between *ginōskō* (1097), to know, knowledge acquired by reflection and consideration, is that *suniēmi* involves immediate knowledge (Lk. 8:9,10; 18:34) even as the verb *oida,* derived from *eidō* (1492). Therefore, it means moral reflection, pondering or laying to heart (Eph. 5:17). It involves moral or religious conduct and is attributed to the heart (Mk. 6:52; 8:17; Acts 28:27). The adj. *sunetos* (4908), judicious, and *asunetos* (801), nonjudicious, are also used with the same moral significance. The verb is seldom used with an obj. In a weakened sense, the verb means to notice, heed, hear, or listen to.

4921. Sunistēmi; or *sunistaō* made up of *sun* (4862), together with, and *histēmi* (2476) or *histao,* to set, place. To set or place together with. In the perf. act. joined with a dat., to stand together with (Lk. 9:32); to stand together, stand (II Pet. 3:5) referring to the earth standing out of the water and in the water in its first formation (Gen. 1:6) and at the height of the flood (Gen. 8:2); to consist, subsist (Col. 1:17); to commend, recommend or make acceptable or illustrious (Rom. 3:5; 5:8; II Cor. 4:2; 10:18; 12:11); to commend, recommend, commit to the care or kindness of another (Rom. 16:1); to show, prove, approve, manifest (II Cor. 6:4; 7:11; Gal. 2:18).

4930. Sunteleia; from *sunteleō* (4931), from *sun* (4862), used as an inten., and *teleō* (5055), to complete or to accomplish. A termination, completion. In the N.T. used only in the expressions *sunteleia tou aiōnos,* "the completion of the age" (Mt. 13:39,40,49; 24:3; 28:20) and *tōn aiōnōn,* "of the ages" (Heb. 9:26).

4931. Sunteleō; from *sun* (4862), together, an inten., and *teleō* (5055), to finish; finish entirely, make an end of (Mt. 7:28; Lk. 4:13); of time (Lk. 4:2; Acts 21:27); to accomplish, perform (Mk. 13:4; Rom. 9:28); to complete (Heb. 8:8). Deriv.: *sunteleia* (4930), a finishing, consummation, end (Mt. 13:39; Heb. 9:26, etc.); not the termination but the heading up of events to the appointed climax. Deriv.: *telos* (5056).

4933. Suntēreō; from *sun* (4862), together with, used as an inten., and *tēreō,* to guard, keep. To preserve, keep safe, close. In Lk. 2:19, contr. *diatēreō* (1301) in v. 51 to the words of the shepherds. In Mk. 6:20, used of the preservation of John the Baptist from Herodias. In Mt. 9:17 (in some mss. Lk. 5:38) used of the preservation of wineskins.

4951. Surō; to draw, drag, whether of things (Jn. 21:8) or persons (Acts 8:3; 14:19; 17:6). It involves the notion of violence which is not necessarily expressed in *helkuō* (1670), to attract. *Surō* has the sense of dragging something or someone with no will of its own, like pulling in a fish already hooked or pulling a dead body.

4954. Sussōmos; united in one body, from *sun* (4862), together, and *sōma* (4983), body. United in one body, that is, members of the body of Christ (Eph. 3:6). *Sōma* used elsewhere of the Church, meaning incorporated with the Church.

4957. Sustauroō; from *sun* (4862), together with, and *stauroō* (4717), to crucify. To crucify together with, whether bodily (Mt. 27:44; Mk. 15:32; Jn. 19:32), or spiritually by mortifying our worldly and fleshly lusts by the cross of Christ (Rom. 6:6; Gal. 2:20).

4964. Suschēmatizō; from *sun* (4862), together with, and *schēmatizō*, to fashion, from *schēma* (4976), external form. With a dat. following; to conform to (Rom. 12:2; I Pet. 1:14). In Rom. 12:2 we have mē, not, and *suschēmatizesthe,* with this age, i.e., do not fall in with the external and fleeting fashions of this age nor be yourselves fashioned to them, but undergo a deep inner change (*metamorphousthe,* 3339) by the qualitative renewing (*anakainōsei,* 341) of your mind as the Spirit of God alone can work in you (II Cor. 3:18).

4976. Schēma; from *eschēmai*, perf. pass. of *echō* (2192), have. Fashion, external form, appearance (I Cor. 7:31), possibly from *skēma* from the scene of the theater. The *schema* of Phil. 2:8 is Jesus' whole outward appearance in which there was no difference between the Incarnate Son and the other children of men. It was the mode of His manifestation. The phrase in Phil. 2:8, "and being found in appearance (*schēmati*) as a man," brings foward the distinction of *schēma* with *morphē* (3444), essence. The verity of the incarnation that He was God and continued to be God is expressed with *morphē*. The verb for this is *labōn* (*lambanō*, 2983) "took upon him," aor. act. part., having taken on His own initiative and power the form of a servant, *doulou* (1401). The words that follow, *kai schēmati euretheis* (*heuriskō*, 2147), "and found in fashion as a man," declare the outward facts which came under the knowledge of His fellowmen with an emphasis on the verb *euretheis*, "when He was found." The *schēma* here signifies the whole outward appearance. In no physical way was He found different from other children of men in contrast to His *morphē* which was the externalization of His inner character which was without sin. Deriv.: *metaschēmatizō* (3345), to change the external shape. Contr. *metamorphoō* (3339), change both internal and external. See *morphoō* (3445), to fashion.

4978. Schisma; schism, from *schizō* (4977), to split, tear. To be divided in mind, sentiment, and so into factions (Mt. 9:16; Mk. 2:21; Jn. 7:43; 9:16; 10:19; I Cor. 1:10; 11:18; 12:25). Contr. *hairesis* (139), heresy, which indicates a tendency opp. the accepted doctrine or practice.

4982. Sōzō; to save, and the noun *sōtēria* (4991), salvation. Salvation in regard to: (1) material and temporal deliverance from danger, suffering, etc. (Mt. 8:25; Mk. 13:20; Lk. 23:35; Jn. 12:27; I Tim. 2:15; II Tim. 4:18); sickness (Mt. 9:22; Mk. 5:34; Lk. 8:48; Js. 5:15); preservation (Jude 5); (2) the spiritual and eternal salvation granted immediately by God to those who believe on Christ (Acts 2:47; 16:31; Rom. 8:24; Eph. 2:5,8; I Tim. 2:4; II Tim. 1:9; Tit. 3:5); human agency in this (Rom. 11:14; I Cor. 7:16; 9:22); (3) the present experience of God's power to deliver from the bondage of sin (Mt. 1:21; Rom. 5:10; I Cor. 15:2; Heb. 7:25; Js. 1:21; I Pet. 3:21); human agency in this (I Tim. 4:16); (4) the future deliverance of believers at the Second Coming (Rom. 5:9); (5) the deliverance of Israel (Rom. 11:26); (6) all the blessings inclusively of God on men in Christ (Lk. 19:10; Jn. 10:9; I Cor. 10:33; I Tim. 1:15); (7) those who endure to the end the time of the Great Tribulation (Mt. 10:22; Mk. 13:13); (8) the individual believer who through losing his reward at the Judgment Seat of Christ will not lose his salvation (I Cor. 3:15; 5:5); (9) the deliverance of the nations at the millenium (Rev. 21:24). Deriv.: *diasōzō* (1295), to rescue; *sōtēria* (4991), salvation; *sōtēr* (4990), Saviour; *sōtērion* (4992), salvation; *sōtērios* (4992), saving.

4983. Sōma; body. Various meanings: (1) A corporeal body, whether of a man (Mt. 6:25; 10:28) or of some other creature (Js. 3:3); either living or dead (Mt. 14:12; 27:58; Heb. 13:11). (2) In the pl. often used in the Gr. writers for the bodies of men taken in war and reduced to slavery, thus meaning slaves as applied in Rev. 18:13. (3) The Church, in respect of Christ who is the head of this body and supplies its spiritual life and motion (Eph. 1:23; 4:16; Col. 1:18; 2:19); in respect of believers who are mystical members of one body (Rom. 12:5; I Cor. 12:12ff). (4) An organized body, as of vegetables (I Cor. 15:37,38). (5) A body, material substance (I Cor. 15:40). (6) Substance or reality as opposed to shadows or types (Col. 2:17). The body is the vessel of the spiritual part of man which is called *psuchē*, distinguished from *pneuma* (4151) which only man possesses (I Thess. 5:23). A separation of the physical from the spiritual is possible (Lk. 12:4; II Cor. 12:2,3) and is accomplished at death. With reference to this separation, the body may be regarded as the covering, the dwelling place (II Cor. 5:1-4; 5:6,8). The *sōma psuchikon* (5591), soulish body, means that body which is driven and directed by the natural sinful instincts of man while the *sōma pneumatikon* (4152) is our new resurrection body which will be governed only by our God-given spirit which enables us to communicate with God (I Cor. 15:35-44). Deriv.: *sōmatikos* (4984), bodily or corporeal; *sussōmos* (4954), united in one body.

4984. Sōmatikos; from *sōma* (4983), body. An adj. meaning bodily, corporeal (I Tim. 4:8). Contr. *asōmatos,* without body (Lk. 3:22). As an adv., *sōmatikōs* (4985), bodily, occurs in Col. 2:9 where the reference is to *sōma,* body, denoting the manifestation of human nature as in all the texts where the body of Christ is spoken about.

4990. Sōtēr; from *sōzō* (4982), to save. A saviour, deliverer, preserver. Used of God (Lk. 1:47; I Tim. 1:1; 2:3; 4:10; Tit. 1:3; 2:10; 3:4; Jude 25); of Christ (Lk. 2:11; Jn. 4:42; Acts 5:31; 13:23); of Israel (Eph. 5:23; Phil. 3:20); of His return to receive the Church to Himself (Tit. 1:4; 2:13; 3:6; II Pet. 1:1, etc.).

4991. Sōtēria; from *sōzō* (4982), to save. Deliverance, preservation, salvation. Used of material and temporal deliverance (Lk. 1:69,71; Acts 7:25; 27:34; Phil. 1:19; Heb. 11:7); of spiritual and eternal deliverance (Acts 4:12; Rom. 1:16; 10:10; Eph. 1:13); of the present experience of God's power to deliver (Phil. 2:12; I Pet. 1:9); of the future deliverance at the *parousia* (3952), the Second Coming of Christ (Lk. 1:71; II Thess. 2:13; Rev. 12:10); inclusively of all the blessing of God (II Cor. 6:2; Heb. 5:9; I Pet. 1:9,10; Jude 3); occasionally standing for the Saviour (Lk. 19:9; Jn. 4:22)
ascriptions of praise to God (Rev. 7:10) and as to what He bestows (Rev. 19:1).

4992. Sōtērion; always with the neut. art. *to* while *sōtēria* (4991), salvation, is fem. Used as an adj. noun in Lk. 2:30; 3:6 where it stands for the Saviour (*sōtēr,* 4990) as with *sōtēria;* in Acts 28:28; in Eph. 6:17 meaning the hope of salvation as in *sōtēria* and is metaphorically described as a helmet. *Sōtērios,* adj., related to *sōzō* (4982), saving, bringing salvation, and describing God's grace (Tit. 2:11).

4998. Sōphrōn; discreet, one who has a sound mind (*sōas,* sound; *phrenes,* 5424, cognitive faculties) (I Tim. 3:2; Tit. 2:2,5); a person who limits his own freedom and ability with proper thinking, demonstrating self-government with proper restraint on all the passions and desires; one who voluntarily places limitations on his freedom. Deriv.: *sōphroneō* (4993), verb; to be sober-minded, to prudently restrict one's freedom, to be discreet (Mk. 5:15; Lk. 8:35; Rom. 12:3; II Cor. 5:13; Tit. 2:6; I Pet. 4:7); *sōphronizō* (4994), to teach to be discreet (Tit. 2:4); *sōphronismos* (4995), accomplishing discreetness in someone (II Tim. 1:7); *sōphrosunē* (4997), the virtue of discreetness (Acts 26:25; I Tim. 2:9, 15); *sōphronōs* (4996), adv., discreetly (Tit. 2:12); *sōphronismos,* a sound, collected mind (II Tim. 1:7). *Sōphrōn* is the exact antithesis of *hubristēs* (5197) whose insolence and contempt of others break forth in acts of wantonness and outrage.

5001. Tagma; an order, regular method. See *tassō* (5021), to categorize, place in one's proper order (only in I Cor. 15:23).

5010. Taxis; an arrangement, order, regularity (Lk. 1:18; I Cor. 14:40; Col. 2:5; Heb. 5:6,10, etc.). See *tassō* (5021), to place in one's proper order.

5011. Tapeinos; humble, lowly (Mt. 11:29; Lk. 1:52; Rom. 12:16; II Cor. 7:6; 10:1; Js. 1:9; 4:6; I Pet. 5.5). The sinner is *tapeinos* when he recognizes his sinfulness which is his true condition; the unfallen creature when merely recognizing that his is a creature; Jesus in His incarnate state in recognizing His absolute dependence on the Father. Thus, the grace of *tapeinophro-*

sunē (5012), humility, is a necessity for mankind, but also belongs to the highest angel before the throne since he is a creature. In His incarnation and humanity Jesus becomes the pattern of all humility. Only as a man does Jesus claim to be *tapeinos*, humble.

5012. Tapeinophrosunē; humility, lowliness of mind, the esteeming of ourselves small inasmuch as we are so; the real estimate of ourselves (Acts 20:19; Eph. 4:2; Phil. 2:3; Col. 2:18,23; 3:12; I Pet. 5:5). For the sinner *tapeinophrosunē* involves the confession of sin as his true condition. For the unfallen creature it is the acknowledgment not of sinfulness but of creatureliness, of absolute dependence, having nothing, but receiving all things of God. Related to *tapeinos* (5011), humble, lowly; *tapeinoō* (5013), to humble; *tapeinōsis* (5014), the act of humiliation. See also *prautēs* (4240), meekness.

5013. Tapeinoō; to humble, bring about a recognition of one's sinfulness, to be recognized as a mere creature (Mt. 18:4; II Cor. 12:21; Js. 4:10; I Pet. 5:6); to abase (Mt. 23:12; Lk. 14:11; 18:14; Phil. 4:12); to bring low (Lk. 3:5). In the case of Jesus' incarnation (Phil. 2:8), He brought about the recognition of His humanity by demonstrating His absolute dependence on His Father.

5014. Tapeinōsis; the act of humiliation. In Lk. 1:48 the Virgin Mary is stated as possessed of *tapeinōsin*, the recognition of her sinfulness and therefore humility. In Acts 8:33 on the eunuch's *tapeinōsis*, recognition of his sinfulness, the due judgment was lifted. In Phil. 3:21 *tapeinōsis* is translated "humble state" referring to our present body being a sinful one. In Js. 1:10 the rich is made low (*tapeinōsis*) in his recognition that his riches should not be considered as a cover-up for his sinfulness.

5020. Tartaroō; *tartaros*, found only in its verbal form in II Pet. 2:4 meaning to consign to Tartarus, which is neither Sheol of the O.T. nor Hades of the N.T., nor Gehenna or hell, but the place where certain angels are confined, reserved unto judgment. This punishment for these angels is because of their special sin.

5021. Tassō; to place, set, appoint, order (Mt. 28:16; Acts 22:10; 28:23); to set in order or in its proper category (Lk. 7:8; Rom. 13:1); to dispose, adapt (Acts 13:48). Derived from the noun *taxis* (5010), an arrangement (Lk. 1:8; I Cor. 14:40; Col. 2:5; Heb. 5:6,10; 6:20; 7:11,17,21); *tagma* (5001), an order, regular method (I Cor. 15:23). All the deriv. have inherent in them order and categorization, classification. *Anatassomai* (392), to compose in an orderly manner (Lk. 1:1); *apotassō* or *apotassomai* (657), to set in its proper category away from oneself (*apo*) (Mk. 6:46; Lk. 9:61; 14:33; Acts 18:18,21; II Cor. 2:13); *diatassō* (1299), from *dia*, emphatic, and *tassō*, to order, regulate, set in order, issue orderly and detailed instructions (Mt. 11:1; Lk. 3:13; 8:55; 17:9,10; Acts 7:44; 18:2; 20:13; 23:31; 24:23; I Cor. 7:17; 9:14; 11:34; 16:1; Gal. 3:19; Tit. 1:5). The noun is *diatagē* (1296), an order, disposition, appointment (Acts 7:35; Rom. 13:2); *diatagma* (1297), commandment (Heb. 11:23); *epitagē* (2003), authority, command (Rom. 16:26; I Cor. 7:6,25; II Cor. 8:8; I Tim. 1:1; Tit. 1:3; 2:15) a commandment imposed on one, from *epitassō* (2004), from *epi*, upon, and *tassō* to order (Mk. 1:27; 6:27,39; 9:25; Lk. 4:36; 8:25,31; 14:22; Acts 23:2; Phile. 8); *prostassō* (4367), from *pros*, to, and *tassō*, a specific command for a specific person (Mt. 1:24; 8:4; 21:6; Mk. 1:44; Lk. 5:14; Acts 10:33,48); *hupotassō* (5293) from *hupo*, under, and *tassō*, to place under; *hupotagē* (5292), submission; *protassō* and *protassomai* (4384), from *pro*, before, and *tassō*, to before-ordain (Acts 17:26); *taktos* (5002), appointed (Acts 12:21); *ataktos* (813), unruly (I Thess. 5:14); *atakteō* (812), to behave in a disorderly manner (II Thess. 3:6,11).

5040. Teknion; a little child, diminutive of *teknon* (5043). Used only figuratively and always in the pl. A term of affection by a teacher to his disciples (Jn. 13:33; Gal. 4:19; I Jn. 2:1,12,28; 3:7,18; 4:4; 5:21).

5043. Teknon; child, related to *tiktō* (5088), to beget, bear. Used both in the natural and the figurative senses giving prominence to the fact of birth, whereas *huios* (5207), son in a generic sense, stresses the dignity and character of the relationship. In the narrative of His human birth, Jesus Christ is never designated as *teknon* (Mt. 1:21,23,25; Lk. 1:31; 2:7), or *teknon Theou*, a child of God, but always *ho Huios*, the Son or the Son of God or the Son of Man. He was not born *tiktō*, of God, in which case He would be inferior and posterior to the Father, nor of man only. Only His mother called Him *teknon* (Lk. 2:48) as she viewed Him in His humanity. Jesus never presents Himself in His God-Man consciousness as a *teknon* of man or of God. He was only *huios*, denoting relationship of character with the Father God, not giving the idea He was a mere child of the Father. He was Mary's *teknon* but God's Son, *huios*. When speaking of Elizabeth and Zachariah, it was said of them that they had no child, *teknon* (Lk. 1:7).

5046. Teleios; perfect from *teleō*, to complete, from *telos* (5056), goal, purpose. Adult, full-grown, of full age as opp. to little children. This image of fully completed growth as contr. with infancy and childhood underlies the ethical use of *teleioi*, being set over against the babes in Christ (I Cor. 2:6; 14:20; Eph. 4:13, 14; Phil. 3:15; Heb. 5:14). Can be used in a relative or absolute sense (Mt. 5:48; 19:21), i.e., God's perfection is absolute; man's is relative reaching the goal set for him by God with each individual different according to one's God-given ability. The *teleios* is one who has attained his moral end, the goal for which he was intended, namely, to be a man obedient in Christ. It may be true though, that having reached this attainment, other and higher ends will open up before him to have Christ formed in him more and more. When one is *teleios*, is does not mean that he has had all of the grace available bestowed upon him. *Teleiotēs* (5047), perfection, is not a static state. In a physical or literal sense, used of spotless sacrifices, involving animals or objects wherein nothing is deficient; also as a full year, perfect work, or something done as it ought to be (I Cor. 13:10; Js. 1:4). *To*, the, *teleion*, complete one, in contr. with *to ek merous* (3313), that which in part indicates the ultimate goal in heaven as contr. with something that can have only partial fulfillment on earth. In I Jn. 4:18 *he*, the, *teleia agapē*, perfect love, means the love that is not wanting, the love which accomplishes its goal. Frequently it means full growth, either of men or beasts (I Cor. 2:6; 14:20; Phil. 8:12,15; Eph. 4:13; Heb. 5:14). Also generally, means what is highest and preeminent (Heb. 9:11; Js. 1:25). When used in a moral sense referring to God's expectation of us, completely blameless. A perfect gift in Js. 1:17 means that which meets the need of a person. In Js. 1:4, "that you may be perfect" means that you may not be morally lacking. It has similar meaning in Mt. 5:48; 19:21; Rom. 12:2; Col. 1:28; 4:12; Js. 3:2. *Holotelēs* (3651), complete to the end (I Thess. 5:23) holding a connecting link between *holos* (3650), whole, and *holoklēros* (3648), complete in every part, and *teleios*, to the end. *Teleios* is not to be confused with *anamartētos*, without sin or sinless (361).

5047. Teleiotēs; from *teleios* (5046), perfect. Perfection or perfectness, stressing the actual accomplishment of the end in view (Col. 3:14; Heb. 6:1); not sinlessness which would have been *anamartēsia*, never used in the N.T. although the adj. *anamartētos* (361) is used in Jn. 8:7 (T.R.) Deriv.: *telos* (5056), end, goal.

5048. Teleioō; from *teleios* (5046), perfect. To complete, finish (Jn. 4:34; 5:36; 17:4; Acts 20:24; Heb. 7:19; 9:9; 10:1,14). To complete, accomplish, of time (Lk. 2:43); of prophecy (Jn. 19:28). In the pass. *teleiōmai* (5048), to be made perfect or complete only in the sense of reaching one's prescribed goal (II Cor. 12:9; Phil. 3:12; Heb. 11:40; 12:23; Js. 2:22); *teleiōsai*, to make Christ perfect (Heb. 2:10); to consecrate Him by sufferings to His office (Heb. 5:9; 7:28, cf. Ex. 29:34; Lev. 8:22,28,33; 21:10) and fully to qualify and enable Him to discharge it (cf. Heb. 2:17,18; 4:15; 5:1,2). See also Lk. 13:32 referring to Christ's death. Deriv.: *telos* (5056), end, goal.

5049. Teleiōs; adv. from *telos* (5056), end, goal. Perfectly, entirely, to the end in the sense of accomplishment of the hope (I Pet. 1:13).

5050. Teleiōsis; fem., completion, successful issue, the attainment of a perfect whole, a *teleion* (5046) which needs nothing further to complete it (Heb. 7:11,19). Also the fulfillment of a promise (Lk. 1:45). Contr. *teleiotēs* (5047), completeness which refers to the attainment to be reached while *teleiōsis* refers to the completeness as an attainment already reached. Deriv.: *telos* (5056), end, goal.

5051. Teleiotēs; from *teleios* (5046), what achieves its goal. A completer, perfecter, one who brings something through to the goal so as to win and receive the prize (Heb. 12:2).

5052. Telesphoreō; from *telos* (5056), end, goal, perfection, and *phoreō* (5409), to bring, bear. To bring to its intended perfection or goal as the seed does the fruit (Lk. 8:14).

5053. Teleutaō; from *teleutē* (5054), an end, accomplishment. To end, finish, accomplish (not used in this manner in the N.T.). In Mt. 2:19; 9:18 to end one's life, to die. Deriv.: *telos* (5056), end, goal.

5054. Teleutē; from *teleō* (5055), to end, finish. An end, accomplishment (not used in this manner in the N.T.) In Mt. 2:15 the end of life, death, decease.

5055. Teleō; from *telos* (5056), end, goal. To make an end or accomplishment, to complete anything, not merely to end it, but to bring it to perfection or its destined goal, to carry it through. Generally it means to carry out a thing, (Mt. 11:1; 13:53, etc); to accomplish (Lk. 2:39, 18:31; 22:37, etc.); to go over (Mt. 10:23); to end, finish, fulfill time (Rev. 20:3,5,7); to pay tribute (Mt. 17:24; Rom. 13:6). Frequently it speaks of fulfilling or answering promises and prayers. When it speaks of definite periods of time it means to pass, spend, fulfill. In the pass., to be completed or fulfilled (Jn. 19:28,30; Rev. 15:1,8; 17:17; 20:3,5,7) with the meaning of the perfect accomplishment of that work whereby the Scripture is fulfilled, not merely to filfil (Lk. 18:31; 22:37; Acts 13:29; Rev. 10:7). As the greatness of Christ's power is fully manifested in the sphere of human weakness (II Cor. 12:9). When the word does not refer to the production or attainment of the object, it means to perform, execute, carry out (Lk. 12:50; Rom. 2:27; Gal. 5:16; Js. 2:8). See *teleutē* (5054); *teleutaō* (5053); *telesphoreō* (5052); *teleiōtēs* (5051); *teleiōsis* (5050); *teleiōs* (5049); *teleioō* (5048); *teleiotēs* (5047); and *teleios* (5046).

5056. Telos; neut. usually with *to,* the definite art, end, goal. The limit, either at which a person or thing ceases to be what he or it was up to that point or at which previous activities ceased (II Cor. 3:13; I Pet. 4:7). It does not, as is commonly supposed, mean the extinction, end, termination with reference to time, but the goal reached, the completion or conclusion at which anything arrives, either as issue or ending and including the termination of what went before; or as a result, acme, consummation, e.g., when we speak of the end of the war, we speak of victory. When we speak of *telos andros,* the end of man, we speak of the full age of man; also used of the ripening of the seed. It never denotes merely an end as to time, a termination in and for itself, for which another word, *teleutē* (5054), death, is always used. The issue, end, conclusion (Mt. 24:14; 26:58; Mk. 13:7; Lk. 21:9; Acts 2:17; I Cor. 10:11; II Tim. 3:1; Js. 5:11; I Pet. 4:7,17) in which case *telos* means the termination of the present course and condition of the world. In I Cor. 15:24; Heb. 7:3 it means the goal reached, the beginning of a new order of things. The adv. phrase *eis telos* means to the last or to the conclusion of that spoken of, as in Jn. 13:1 where reference is made to Christ's work of love (see also Mt. 10:22; 24:13; Mk. 13:13); or it may mean at last or in the end, finally (Lk. 18:5). In the gen. meaning until, with *heōs* (2193), *achri* (891), *mechri* (3360) and the gen. *telous,* until the end (I Cor. 1:8; Heb. 3:6 T.R., 14; 6:11; Rev. 2:26). *To,* the, *telos,* finally (I Pet. 3:8). Refers to the goal reached, the end (Rom. 6:21,22; 13:10; II Cor. 11:15; Phil. 3:16; I Tim. 1:5; Heb. 6:8; I Pet. 1:9). In Rom. 10:4 (see also vv. 3,5; Acts 13:39) *telos* denotes the final end, the conclusion which the dominion of the law has found in Christ. Adv. phrases, *eis telos,* in I Thess. 2:16 means completely; *heōs telous* in II Cor. 1:13 means completely as contr. with *apo merous* (3313), (in part, not completely in v. 14). *Telos,* also means toll or tax (Mt. 17:25; Rom. 13:7). Deriv.: *telōnes* (5057), a collector of *telē* (5056), taxes; *telōnion* (5058), a custom house (Mt. 9:9; Mk. 2:14; Lk. 5:27); *teleō* (5055); *epiteleō* (2005); *sunteleō* (4931); *sunteleia* (4930); *pantelēs* (3838); *teleios* (5046); *teleiotēs* (5047); *teleioō* (5048); *teleiōsis* (5050); *teleiōtes* (5051); *teleutaō* (5053); *telesphoreō* (5052).

5059. Teras; often associated with *sēmeion* (4592), sign, and usually translated as "wonder." These two words refer not to different classes of miracles, but to different qualities of the same miracle. *Teras* is derived from *tēreō,* to watch, as being that which for its extraordinary character is apt to be observed and kept in the memory. It is a miracle regarded as startling, imposing, amazing, frequently used elsewhere for strange appearances in the heavens. Related words: *dunamis* (1411); *megaleios* (3167); *endoxos* (1741); *paradoxos* (3861); *thaumasios* (2297).

5083. Tēreō; to keep, watch (Mt. 27:36,54; 28:4; Acts 12:6; 16:23; 24:23; 25:4,21); to reserve with unhappy results (II Pet. 2:4,9,17; 3:7; Jude 6,13) or with the possibility of either deliverance or execution (Acts 25:21); to preserve as opp. to leaving (Jude 6); to observe, as commands, ordinances, traditions, a law, etc. (Mt. 19:17; 23:3, etc.). Deriv.: *tērēsis* (5084); *paratēreō* (3906); *paratērēsis* (3907); *diatēreō* (1301); *diatērēsis.*

5084. Tērēsis; custody, from *tēreō* (5083), to keep. A prison, hold (Acts 4:3), of the imprisonment of the apostles (Acts 5:18). A keeping or observance of commandments (I Cor. 7:19).

5087. Tithēmi; to set, place, lay. To place, put, lay (Mt. 5:15; 14:3; Mk. 6:29,56; 10:16; Lk. 6:48); to put or lay down (Lk. 19:21,22); to put or set on, as food upon a table (Jn. 2:10); to lay by, reserve (I Cor. 16:2); to put off, lay aside (Jn. 13:4); to appoint, assign (Mt. 24:51; Lk. 12:46); to appoint, constitute, ordain (Jn. 15:16; Acts 13:47; 20:28; Rom. 4:17; I Tim. 2:7; II Tim. 1:11; Heb. 1:2); to make, render (I Cor. 9:18); in the second aor. mid., to purpose, propose, design (Acts 19:21); to give advice or counsel, advise (Acts 27:12). Deriv.: *anatithēmi* (394), to lay upon, attribute something to someone; *anathema* (331), a thing devoted to destruction, ruin, a consecrated gift; *diatithēmi* (1303), to place separately, appoint anyone to a place, arrange and dispose of one's effects by will and testament; *diathēkē* (1242), testament; *protithēmi* (4388), to set or lay before; *prothesis* (4286), a setting forth, setting up, an exposition, purpose, resolve, design; *prothesmios* (4287), before appointed.

5088. Tiktō; to bring forth (Lk. 1:57; Jn. 16:21; Heb. 11:11 T.R.; Rev. 12:2,4) or be born, as said of the Child Jesus (Mt. 2:2; Lk. 2:11); used metaphorically of lust as bringing forth sin (Js. 1:15). See *apokueō* (616), to bring forth; *gennaō* (1080), to give birth. Deriv.: *teknon* (5043), child.

5098. Timōria; a noun meaning punishment, only in Heb. 10:29, from *timōreō* (5097), to punish, derived from *timē* (5092), revenge, punishment and *horaō* (3708), to see, inspect. The verb *timōreō* is used only twice (Acts 22:5; 26:11). In *timōria,* in Class. Gr. the vindictiveness of the punishment is the predominant thought, a punishment satisfying the inflicter's sense of outraged justice, as defending his own honor or that of a violated law. From its etymology, the guardianship or protection of honor. Contr. *kolasis* (2851), to torment, which has more the notion of punishment rather than the correction and rehabilitation of the offender.

5100. Tis; without an accent used as an indefinite pron. meaning someone, anyone, a certain one; and in the neut. *ti,* something.

5101. Tis; or *ti,* with the accent can be used as interrogative pron. meaning who or what. Without the accent, used as an indefinite pron. (5100), someone, something.

5171. Truphaō; to live in luxury, pleasure; noun *truphē* (5172), luxury (Lk. 7:25; II Pet. 2:13). Deriv. verb: *entruphaō* (1792), to revel (II Pet. 2:13). As in *strēniaō* (4763) and *spatalaō* (4684), *truphaō* and the inten. *entruphao* have the notion of excess, wantonness, dissolute attitude, self-indulgence, prodigal living, but with special emphasis of self-indulgence (Js. 5:5). Includes the notion of insolence only as a secondary and rarer meaning.

5179. Tupos; type as a constituent element of a parable or model of some reality which was yet to appear, a prototype or that which was yet to be developed and evolved, e.g., the ordinances and institutions in the O.T. were, in their inward essence, types of the N.T. The first era serves as a type of the second. Cf. *sumbolon,* a symbol, which does not occur in the N.T. Whereas, however, the outline or archetype or model of some reality which was yet to appear was called *tupos, sumbolon* was an equivalent, a visible sign of what is invisible, e.g., the tares in the parable of the wheat and the tares (Mt. 13:24-30; 36-43) are a symbol of the activity of the devil and his agents in one's spiritual life. A symbol is an outward manifestation of something inward, an emblem of what is higher. These two constituent elements of the parables are to be joined with the verb *allēgoria,* allegory from the verb *allēgoreō* (238) found only in Gal. 4:24, which in turn is from *allos* (243), another, and *agoreō,* to speak. Therefore, to allegorize is to speak symbolically about one thing whereas something somewhat different is meant, of which the thing spoken is the emblem or representative. Therefore, an allegory is the mark, the indication of outward similarity, and also the internal relationship and connection of things. It is a counterpart and reappearance of what has the same shape, either in the world of matter or of mind. Thus, the enemy was an allegory of Satan; the book of the Revelation is full of allegories, and when our Lord spoke of Herod, "Tell that fox," He was using an allegory. Distinct meanings of *tupos:* a mark, impression made by striking, and used with this meaning to indicate the print of the nails on Jesus' hands and feet (Jn. 20:25); a form, figure, image (Acts 7:43); a pattern or model of a building (Acts 7:44; Heb. 8:5, referring to Ex. 25:40); a pattern, example (Phil. 3:17; I Thess. 1:7; Tit. 2:7); a figure, emblem, representative, type (Rom. 5:14, cf. I Cor. 10:6,11); a form of a writing (Acts 23:25); a form of doctrine (Rom. 6:17). Deriv.: *hupotupōsis* (5296), pattern; *antitupos* (499), an antitype, counterpart.

5180. Tuptō; to strike, smite with the hand, stick, or other instrument (Mt. 27:30; Mk. 15:19; Lk. 6:29; 18:13; 22:64 T.R.; 23:48; Acts 23:2,3); to beat (Mt. 24:49; Lk. 12:45; Acts 18:17; 21:32); to smite, strike, punish (Acts 23:3); to hurt, wound spiritually (I Cor. 8:12). Deriv.: *tupos* (5179), stroke, the impression left by striking, a trace or print; *antitupos* (499), that which gives a counterstroke, similar, like, antitype; *hupotupōsis* (5296), a design or outline of a representation, pattern.

5187. Tuphoō; to raise or make a smoke, from *tuphos,* smoke, symbolizing pride, insolence; in the pass. *tuphoōmai,* to be drunk with pride with a heart lifted up not only against man, but against God (I Tim. 3:6; 6:4; II Tim. 3:4).

5197. Hubristēs; insolent wrongdoer to others for the pleasure which the affliction of the wrong imparts (Rom. 1:30; I Tim. 1:13). Noun: *hubris* (5196), injury, injurious treatment (Acts 27:10,21; II Cor. 12:10). Verb: *hubrizō* (5195), to treat injuriously, reproach (Mt. 22:6; Lk. 11:45; 18:32; Acts 14:5; I Thess. 2:2).

5198. Hugiainō; to be healthy, sound, physically well (English: hygiene). *Hugia,* health, does not occur in the N.T. *Hugiēs* (5199), healthy, is translated "whole" (Mt. 12:13; 15:31; Mk. 3:5 T.R.; 5:34; Lk. 6:10 T.R.; Jn. 5:4 T.R.,6,9,11,14,15; 7:23; Acts 4:10; Tit. 2:8). In Acts 27:34 what is translated "preservation" is *sōtēria* (4991), salvation, meaning safety.

5199. Hugiēs; sound, healthy, perhaps from *hugros,* moist, as sound, healthy bodies are. N.T. meanings: sound, whole, in health (Mt. 12:13; 15:31; Mk. 5:34; Jn. 5:9; Acts 4:10); of sound speech or doctrine, wholesome, right (Tit. 2:8).

5206. Huiothesia; adoption. Receiving into the relationship of a child, from *huios* (5207), son, and *tithēmi* (5087), to place. Used by Paul in Rom. 9:4 with reference to the filial relationship into which Israel was admitted by election to God (Deut. 14:1). In Rom. 8:15; Gal. 4:5; Eph. 1:5 used with reference to the N.T. adoption, answering to the Pauline *tekna Theou,* children of God, in the sense of belonging to God. See *teknon* (5043), child, and also *huios.* In Rom. 8:23, *huiothesia* denotes the adoption as it regards the future (see Rev. 21:7), and in contr. with the slavery of corruption (v. 21) of the present. It is questionable whether *huiothesia,* the receiving into the relationship of children, denotes also the relationship itself as based upon adoption. In no case is it ever equivalent to *huiotēs,* sonship. Cf. Eph. 1:5 where it is precisely "adoption" which illustrates the greatness of divine love in making a stranger, such as a sinner to be a real son. Whereas *huiothesia* places a person in the position of a son, *huiotēs* is the quality or character of a son. The expression here "to fore-appoint," *proorisas eis huiothesian,* means to appoint beforehand to adoption.

5207. Huios; son, distinguished from *teknon* (5043), child. In I Jn. 1:3,7; 2:22-24; 3:8,23; 4:9,10,14,15; 5:5,9-13,20 *huios* is reserved for the Son of God. *Huios* primarily signifies the relation of offspring to parent and not simply the birth as indicated by *teknon* which is derived from *tiktō,* to give birth to (Jn. 9:18-20; Gal. 4:30). Used metaphorically of prominent moral characteristics (Mt. 5:9,45; 8:12; 13:38; Mk. 2:19; 3:17; Lk. 6:35, 10:6; 16:8; 20:36; Jn. 12:36; 17:12; Acts 10:36; II Cor. 6:18; Eph. 2:2). In the N.T. used of male offspring (Gal. 4:30); legitimate offspring (Heb. 12:8); descendants, irrespective of sex (Rom. 9:27); friends (Mt. 9:15); generally demonstrating behavior or character (Mt. 23:15,31; Lk. 6:35; 20:36; Jn. 17:12; Acts 4:36; 13:10; Rom. 8:14,19; Gal. 3:26; Eph. 2:2). The difference between believers as children, *tekna,* of God and as sons, *huioi,* is brought out in Rom. 8:14-21. *Tekna* refers to those who were born of God and *huioi* refers to those who show maturity acting as sons. When just the basic relationship as a born-again child of God is referred to, it is expressed as *tekna* (Rom. 8:16). *Huios* gives evidence of the dignity of one's relationship and likeness to God's character. In Jn. 1:12 *tekna* is used of new believers, not *huioi.* The expression "Son of God," *huios Theou,* is used of Jesus as a manifestation of His relationship with the Father or the expression of His character. The Lord Jesus is never called *teknon Theou,* a child of God, as believers are. Jesus used either the full title (Jn. 5:25; 11:4) or more frequently "the Son" *ho Huios,* which is to be understood as an abbreviation of the Son of God, not the Son of Man which He always expressed in full (Lk. 10:22; Jn. 5:19, etc.) stressing the characteristic of humanity apart from sin. In Acts 13:33 (see also Ps. 2:7), the birth of Christ in His humanity and His sinless conformity to the Father's character is expressed not with *teknon,* but with *huios.*

5215. Humnos; a song in honor of God. It also came to mean praise to men. Whereas a psalm is the story of man's deliverance or a commemoration of mercies received, a hymn is a magnificant telling forth how great someone or something is (Lk. 1:46-55, 66-79; Acts 4:24; 16:25). It is a direct address of praise and glory to God. According to Augustine a hymn has three characteristics: It must be sung; it must be praise; it must be to God. The word "hymn" nowhere occurs in the writings of the Apostolic Fathers because it was used as a praise to heathen deities and thus the early Christians instinctively shrank from it. In Eph. 5:19; Col. 3:16 it occurs with *psalmos* (5568) and *hōdē* (5603), spiritual song, any kind of song (Eph. 5:19; Col. 3:16; Rev. 5:9; 14:3; 15:3).

5218. Hupakoē; obedience, unknown in Class. Gr. from *hupakouō* (5219), to obey, listen to something, hearken. Generally in the N.T. it refers to obedience (Rom. 6:16). Elsewhere it always refers to obedience to God's will in a special sense, of willing subjection to that which, in the sphere of divine revelation, is right (Rom. 6:16; see also Rom. 5:19; Heb. 5:8). More especially, it refers to subjection to the saving will of God revealed in Christ and referred to as obedience to the truth (I Pet. 1:22); obedience of faith (Rom. 1:5; 16:26) or obedience unto faith or by faith (Acts 6:7; II Cor. 10:5); the obedience that is demanded by Christ (II Cor. 10:5). The word also stands alone as a mode of the manifestation of Christian faith (Rom. 15:18; 16:19; II Cor. 7:15; 10:6; Phile. 21; I Pet. 1:2,14).

5219. Hupakouō; from *hupo* (5259), under, and *akouō* (191), to hear. To listen to something, hearken (Acts 12:13); mostly it means to obey, give heed, follow, yield, of servants, soldiers, pupils (Mt. 8:27; Mk. 1:27; 4:41; Lk. 8:25; 17:6; Eph. 6:1,5; Col. 3:20,22; I Pet. 3:6; Rom. 6:16,17); refers to the manifestation of faith as revealed in the humble acceptance of the Gospel message (Acts 6:7; Rom. 6:17; 10:16; II Thess. 1:8; 3:14; Heb. 5:9; 11:8); also denotes the continuous subjection of faith under the preached Word, the keeping of the Word in believing obedience (II Cor. 7:15; Phil. 2:12).

5225. Huparchō; from *hupo* (5259), under, and *archō* (757), to begin; to be, to subsist, to rule (Lk. 7:25; 8:41; 16:23; Acts 21:20; 27:34). In Phil. 2:6 *huparchōn* (present part.), refers to continuing to be what He was before, God or in the form of God, in contr. to *hōn* (present part.) *eimi* (1510) in Jn. 1:18, "who is in the bosom of the Father," referring to the same state of being as the immaterial *Logos* (Word, Jn. 1:1) before becoming *ginomai* (1096), something new, i.e., flesh, which He was not before. In Phil. 2:6 it denotes an existence or condition both previous to the circumstances mentioned and continuing after, referring to the deity of Christ previous to His incarnation and its continuance at and after the event of His birth. With a dat. following, it denotes property or possession (Acts 3:6, cf. Acts 4:37; 28:7; II Pet. 1:8); *ta huparchonta* (5224), the belongings, possessions, things one had before and continues to have (Mt. 19:21; 24:47; Lk. 8:3; Acts 4:32, etc.).

5228. Huper; for, syn. with *anti* (473), on behalf of. Includes both equivalence and exchange when it comes to the death of Christ for us as equal to our need and in our behalf or stead, showing His acceptance by the Father.

5233. Huperbainō; from *huper* (5228), beyond, and *bainō,* to go, used only in I Thess. 4:6 with the meaning of inconsiderate overreaching.

5244. Huperēphanos; proud, from *huper* (5228), over, and *phainomai,* appear. One who shows himself above his fellow men in honor preferring himself.

5255. Hupēkoos; obedient to the will of God (Acts 7:39), from *hupakouō* (5219), which comes from *hupo* (5259), under, and *akouō* (191), to hear. Like *hupakouō* it means the obedience required in believing (II Cor. 2:9); of Christ in that He was obedient to the law (Phil. 2:8) and as man (Gal. 4:4; Heb. 5:8) shed His blood for our sins. This *hupēkoos* has only a remote reference to Jn. 10:18 as having received the commandment from the Father.

5257. Hupēretēs; subordinate, servant, attendant, or officer in general. From *hupo* (5259), under, and *eretēs,* literally meaning a rower; the subordinate official who waits to accomplish the commands of his superior; an inferior minister who performed certain defined functions for Paul and Barnabas (Acts 13:5). Allied to the meaning of *diakonos* (1249), deacon, and contr. to *doulos* (1401), slave; *therapōn* (2324), servant, healer, and *oiketēs* (3610), domestic servant.

5259. Hupo; a prep. governing the gen. and accus.; in the Class. Gr. also the dat.; with a primary meaning of under. When used with the gen. it refers to from, under, from which anything comes forth. With pass. verbs and the gen. of persons it means by. Used of time it means at, during. In composition in comp. words *hupo* implies: (1) place, i.e., beneath, as *hupoballō* (5260), to throw under or cast under; (2) subjection, dependence, the being under any person or thing, as *hupandros* (5220), under a husband, *hupotasso* (5293), to place under; (3) succession, being behind, after, as *hupoleipō* (5275), one or something left behind, *hupomenō* (5278), to remain under; (4) *hupo* in composition also implies something done or happening underhand, covertly, unperceived, without noise or notice; also a little, somewhat by degrees as for instance *huponoeō* (5282), to let be understood little by little.

5261. Hupogrammos; from *hupo* (5259), before, and *graphō* (1125), to write, used only in biblical and later Class. Gr. meaning a writing copy, pattern (I Pet. 2:21). This sub. is related to the verb *hupographō,* to write under, meaning writing a copy, to teach to write, since the writing copy of the teacher was to be followed by the scholars.

5264. Hupodechomai; from *hupo* (5259), under, and *dechomai* (1209), to receive. To receive hospitably and kindly (Lk. 10:38; 19:6; Acts 17:7; Js. 2:25).

5267. Hupodikos; from *hupo* (5259), under, and *dikē* (1349), judgment, justice. One who comes under *dikē,* justice, and is thus guilty. Opp. *endikos,* the one who occupies the due relation to justice. *Hupodikos* denotes one who is bound to do or suffer what is imposed for the sake of justice because he has neglected to do what is right. Therefore, it denotes one who is under obligation to make compensation (Rom. 3:19).

5271. Hupokrinō; to pretend, from the prep. *hupo* (5259), under, indicating secrecy, and *krinō* (2919), to judge. To divide, separate. In its original, literal sense to divide secretly. Originally syn. to *apokrinomai* (611), to devise a proper answer. In its primary meaning to inquire, distinguish, get under the meaning of dreams, expound and interpret them. Later, it came to mean to represent, act, or simulate anything as an actor. It arose from the application of the word in Attic Gr. to persons in a play, and then to men generally who act a part or pretend to be what they are not, to present oneself, to simulate, to distinguish oneself. Used in Lk. 20:20. See *hupokrisis* (5272), hypocrisy; *hupokritēs* (5273), hypocrite; *anupokritos* (505), one without hypocrisy.

5273. Hupokritēs; from *hupokrinomai* (5271), to act as a hypocrite. An expounder or interpreter of dreams, and then an actor, and consequently a hypocrite. That is what they used to call a stage player who acted under a mask impersonating a character. A counterfeit, a man who assumes and speaks or acts under a feigned character (Mt. 6:2,5,16, etc.). A conjecturer, guesser, diviner (Mt. 16:3 T.R.; Lk. 12:56). The Greeks used to call an expounder of dreams a hypocrite. Deriv.: *krinō* (2919), to judge.

5278. Hupomenō; from *hupo* (5259), under, and *menō* (3306), to remain. To remain under, i.e., to endure or sustain a load of miseries, adversities, persecutions or provocations in faith and patience (Mt. 10:22; 24:13; Rom. 12:12; I Cor. 13:7; II Tim. 2:10,12; Heb. 12:2, etc.); to remain privately, stay behind (Lk. 2:43; Acts 17:14). *Hupomonē* (5281), patience toward things or circumstances, contr. to *makrothumia* (3115), longsuffering which is patience toward people.

5280. Hupomnēsis; to be reminded by, from *hupo* (5259), under, and *mimnēskō* (3403), to remind, recall someone (II Tim. 1:5; II Pet. 1:13; 3:1). Contr. *anamnēsis* (364), recollection, remembering again, vanished impressions by a definite act of will in the consciousness; an act of the recollection of the death of Christ in the celebration of the Eucharist in the early church (Lk. 22:19; I Cor. 11:24,25; Heb. 10:3).

5281. Hupomonē; patience, endurance as to things or circumstances as contr. to *makrothumia* (3115), longsuffering, endurance toward people. From *hupo* (5259), under, and *menō* (3306), to abide. *Hupomonē* is associated with hope (I Thess. 1:3) and refers to the quality that does not surrender to circumstances or succumb under trial.

5282. Huponoeō; from the prep. *hupo* (5259), under, denoting diminution and *noeō* (3539), to think. To suppose, suspect (Acts 13:25; 25:18; 27:27). See also *nous* (3563), mind. Noun: *huponoia* (5283), suspicion.

5283. Huponoia; from the verb *huponoeō* (5282), to suppose, suspect. A suspicion, surmise (I Tim. 6:4). See *noeō* (3539), to think; *nous* (3563), mind.

5287. Hupostasis; from *huphistamai,* to be placed or stand under. In general, somewhat put under; therefore, used for a basis or foundation; subsistence, existence; frequently applied by the church fathers as a distinct person in the Godhead (Heb. 1:3); applied to the mind, firm confidence, constancy (II Cor. 9:4; 11:17; Heb. 3:14); confidence or confident expectation (Heb. 11:1). See *histēmi* (2476), to stand.

5293. Hupotassō; to place in an orderly fashion under, *hupo* (5259), under, and *tassō* (5021), to order. Noun: *hupotagē* (5292), submission, dependent position (II Cor. 9:13; Gal. 2:5; I Tim. 2:11; 3:4). Originally, it showed one's relation to superiors, either compulsory or voluntary subordination. If compulsory, the main idea may be that of either power or conquest on the one side or lack of freedom on the other. In the N.T. the verb does not immediately carry with it the thought of obedience. In the act. the verb occurs in Rom. 8:20: "Became subject or was given up to futility" (Rom. 5:12). All the other act. statements are Christological, with Christ having supreme rule. The mid. voice used in the pass. aor. occurs once in the sense of compulsion and means to have one submit (Lk. 10:17,20).

5296. Hupotupōsis; from *hupotupoō,* to draw a sketch or first draft as painters when they begin a picture. A delineation, sketch, concise representation or form (II Tim. 1:13); a pattern, example (I Tim. 1:16). See *tupos* (5179), type; *antitupos* (499), antitype.

5316. Phainō, phainomai; to shine (Jn. 1:5; 5:35; II Pet. 1:19; I Jn. 2:8; Rev. 1:16; 8:12; 21:23). In the pass., to appear, be conspicuous, shine (Mt. 24:27, cf. Phil. 2:15); to appear, be seen (Mt. 1:20; 2:13,19); to appear, seem (Mt. 6:5,16; 23:28, cf. Lk. 24:11); to seem, appear, be thought (Mk. 14:64). In the mid., to appear in judgment (I Pet. 4:18). It indicates how a matter phenomenally shows and presents itself with no necessary assumption of any beholder at all. Suggests something may shine without anybody necessarily seeing it, contr. to something that exists but does not shine. *Nooumenon* is that which is conceived in the mind but does not have any objective existence and does not necessarily manifest itself. *Phainomenon* is that which manifests itself, appears or shines (*phainetai*), and must have a reality behind it. It cannot be just the figment of the imagination. Therefore, *phainomai* is often syn. with *eimi* (1510), be, and *ginomai* (1096), become (Mt. 2:7; 13:26), but it may also have no substance, yet presupposes one. *Dokeō* (1380), think, has in contr. the subjective estimate which may be formed of a thing, not the objective showing and seeming which it may actually possess. One may *dokei,* think something, which may not have an objective reality. The Docetic heresy owes its name from this verb. It taught that Christ's body was not real but imaginary. However, something that shines, *phainei,* must exist objectively.

5318. Phaneros; from *phainomai* or *phainō* (5316), to shine, to make to shine or to cause to appear. *Phaneros* means apparent, manifest, plain (Gal. 5:19; I Tim. 4:15; I Jn. 3:10); apparent, manifest with the idea of being known (Mt. 12:16; Mk. 3:12; Lk. 8:17; Acts 4:16; 7:13; Phil. 1:13); apparent in the sense of being public, open (Mt. 6:4,6,18 T.R.); publicly famous or eminent (Mk. 6:14); apparent in the sense of seeming in the expression *en tō,* in the, *phanerō,* appearance or outward show (Rom. 2:28). Deriv.: *phōs* (5457), light; *phaneroō* (5319), to make manifest, make known, show; *phanerōsis* (5321), manifestation, making known; *epiphainō* (2014), to make visible, celebrated, distinguished, renowned; *epiphaneia* (2015), manifestation.

5319. Phaneroō; to make manifest, make known, show. In the N.T, syn. *apokaluptō* (601), to reveal, take the lid off. Therefore, in this sense it means to denote the act of divine revelation (Jn. 17:6; Rom. 1:19; 3:21; 16:26; Col. 1:26; 4:4; II Tim. 1:10; Tit. 1:3; Heb. 9:8; I Jn. 1:2; 4:9, etc.). It differs from *apokaluptō* as "to exhibit" differs from "to disclose," so that in relation to each other *apokaluptō* must precede *phaneroō* (I Cor. 3:13). *Apokaluptō* refers only to the obj. revealed, but *phaneroō* refers to those to whom the revelation is made (cf. Eph. 3:5; Col. 1:26; 3:4; 4:4; Tit. 1:3). Note the combination in Eph. 3:3, "by a revelation was known to me the mystery." *Phaneroō* signifies also to make visible, to show (Jn. 2:11; 21:1); to make known (Jn. 7:4; 17:6; Rom. 1:19; II Cor. 2:14); to make public (I Cor. 4:5; Col. 4:4). The pass. means to become or be made visible or manifest (Mk. 4:22; Jn. 3:21; 9:3; II Cor. 4:10,11; Eph. 5:13; Heb. 9:8; I Jn. 2:19; Rev. 3:18; 15:4); to appear (Mk. 16:12,14; Jn. 21:14; II Cor. 5:10; II Tim. 1:10; Heb. 9:26; I Pet. 1:20; 5:4; I Jn. 1:2; 2:28; 3:2,5,8; 4:9); to be made known, or to be known (Jn. 1:31; Rom. 3:21; 16:26; II Cor. 3:3; 5:11; 7:12; Col. 1:26; 4:4; Tit. 1:3).

5321. Phanerōsis; manifestation, only in I Cor. 12:7; II Cor. 4:2. The verb *phaneroō* (5319), to make manifest, is continuously employed of *apokalupsis* (602), revelation, and *epiphaneia* (2015), appearing, of the first coming of Christ (I Tim. 3:16; Heb. 9:26; I Pet. 1:20; I Jn. 1:2); and of the Second Coming (Col. 3:4; I Pet. 5:4; I Jn. 3:2); other uses (Jn. 2:11; 21:1). The word *phanerōsis,* however, does not attain to the meaning of either *apokalupsis,* revelation, or *epiphaneia,* appearing, as to the Second Coming.

5337. Phaulos; vile, refuse, evil, wicked, foul. Someone or something good-for-nothing from which nothing good can come; worthless, mediocre, unimportant. Distinguished from *katos* (2556), bad, and *ponēros* (4190), malevolent.

5338. Pheggos; the light of the moon or the other luminaries of the night (Mt. 24:29; Mk. 13:24; Lk. 11:33 T.R.). Contr. *phōs* (5457), light; *phōstēr* (5458), luminary.

5342. Pherō; to bear fruit (Mk. 4:8; Jn. 12:24); to bear, bring (Mt. 14:18, etc.); sustain, uphold (Heb. 1:3); endure (Heb. 12:20); sustain (Heb. 13:13); bear with (Rom. 9:22); cause to come (Mt. 17:17; Mk. 1:32; 7:32); bring as an accusation (Jn. 18:29; Acts 25:7 T.R.); lead in a certain direction (Acts 12:10). Pass.: *pheromai,* to be carried, brought (Acts 2:2); to be driven as persons in a storm (Acts 27:15,17); to be borne away or actuated by the Holy Spirit (II Pet. 1:21); to be carried, proceed (Heb. 6:1); to be produced, proved, or made apparent in a forensic sense as in a court of justice (Heb. 9:16). Deriv.: *anapherō* (399), (*ana,* 303, up), to carry or bring up (Mt. 17:1; Mk. 9:2; Lk. 24:51); to bring up sacrifices on the altar (Heb. 7:27); to bear sins by imputation, in reality or as the ancient sacrifices did typically (Heb. 9:28; I Pet. 2:24); *apopherō* (667) (*apo,* 575, from), to carry away (Mk. 15:1; Lk. 16:22; I Cor. 16:3; Rev. 17:3; 21:10); *eispherō* (1533) (*eis,* 1519, in or to), to bring to or into (Acts 17:20; Heb. 13:11); *ekpherō* (1627) (*ek,* 1537, out), to bring or carry out (Acts 5:15; I Tim. 6:7), to carry out to burial (Acts 5:6,9,10), bring forth, produce as the earth (Heb. 6:8); *epipherō* (2018) (*epi,* 1909, upon, besides, or against), to bring, carry to (Acts 19:12), inflict wrath or vengeance (Rom. 3:5), add or superadd (Phil. 1:16 T.R.); bring against as an accusation (Acts 25:18; Jude 9); *propherō* (4393), (*pro,* 4253, forth), bring forth or out, produce (Lk. 6:45); *prospherō* (4374) (*pros,* 4314, to), to bring to (Mt. 4:24; 5:23, etc.), to bring to or before as a magistrate (Lk. 12:11; 23:14), to offer, tender, proffer, as money for a benefit to be received (Acts 8:18), to offer to God as oblations or sacrifices (Mt. 5:24; 8:4, etc.). In the mid. voice infin. *prospheresthai tini* (dat., to someone) literally to offer oneself to anyone, i.e., to behave towards, deal with or treat him (Heb. 12:7); *diapherō* (1308) (*dia,* 1223, denoting transition or separation), to carry through (Mk. 11:16), to carry abroad or to publish throughout (Acts 13:49). In the pass.: *diapheromai,* to be carried, driven, or tossed different ways, hither and thither or up and down (Acts 27:27). Governing a gen., to differ (Rom. 2:18; I Cor. 15:41; Gal. 4:1; Phil. 1:10); to excel, be of more importance or value than (Mt. 6:26, 10:31; 12:12; Lk. 12:7,24). Impersonally, *diapherei,* makes a difference, is of consequence, is important (Gal. 2:6). Related words: *diaphoros* (1313), different, diverse (Rom. 12:6; Heb. 9:10), excellent, and the comparative *diaphoroteros,* more excellent (Heb. 1:4; 8:6); *prosphora* (4376), an offering, the act of offering to God (Heb. 10:10), an oblation, the thing offered (Acts 21:26; 24:17; Eph. 5:2; Heb. 10:5,8,14,18). See *sumpherō* (4851), to be profitable for; *phoros* (5411), tribute; *phortion* (5413), burden.

5346. Phēmi; to say, to speak, from which is derived *prophētes* (4396), prophet. Related to *phaō*, to speak, say or shine. It has the sense of affirmation. See *laleō* (2980), to speak; *legō* (3004), to say.

5349. Phthartos; from *ptheiro* (5351), to corrupt. Corruptible, the essential quality of the body of man, equivalent to *thnētos* (2349), mortal, used in I Cor. 15:53,54 with a clear indication that this characteristic will be changed to incorruptibility, the characteristic of the believer's resurrection body. Used as an adj. to indicate degenerating man (Rom. 1:23), the temporal character of a crown won on this earth (I Cor. 9:25), and the physical means which cannot bring spiritual salvation (I Pet. 1:18,23).

5351. Phtheirō; to corrupt, destroy. Related to *phthino* or *phthiō*, which does not occur in the N.T. but from which *phthinopōron*, autumn, is derived (see *phthinopōrinos*, 5352, pertaining to the fall season). In the N.T. used in general to denote corruption, destruction. To destroy, punish with destruction (I Cor. 3:17); to corrupt, spoil, vitiate, in a moral or spiritual sense (I Cor. 3:17; 15:33, etc.); to corrupt, i.e., to seduce to evil company or corrupt opinions (II Cor. 7:2; 11:3).

5355. Phthonos; envy, pain felt and malignity conceived at the sight of excellence or happiness; malice. It may be derived from *phthinō*, to decay, wither, pine away (Prov. 14:30). *Phthonos*, unlike *zēlos* (2205), zeal, is incapable of good and is used always with an evil meaning.

5358. Philagathos; from *philos* (5384), friend, and *agathos* (18), benevolently good. One who loves and practices with self-denial what is good (Tit. 1:8). It combines not only the liking to be kind but also the liking to do good. The word stands in contradistinction to *philoiktirmōn* which means one who has or likes to have sympathetic feelings without necessarily externalizing those in good actions. Deriv.: *aphilagathos* (865), the opp. of *philagathos*.

5360. Philadelphia; from *philos* (5384), friend, and *adelphos* (80), brother. In the N.T. used of the love of Christians one to another, brotherly love, out of a common spiritual life (Rom. 12:10; I Thess. 4:9; Heb. 13:1; I Pet. 1:22; II Pet. 1:7).

5361. Philadelphos; from *philos* (5384), friend, and *adelphos* (80), brother. In a wider sense it meant to love one's fellow countrymen. In the strictly Christian sense of brother (I Pet. 3:8), used as a more comprehensive word in line with the meaning of the other adj. distinguishing the Christians from other people. *Philadelphoi* (pl.) sums up the bearing of Christians to each other, and the adj. which follows describes what their behavior should be to those who are without (see I Pet. 3:9,13).

5363. Philanthrōpia; from *philos* (5384), friend, and *anthrōpos* (444), man. Human friendship. Denotes that apparent and ready goodwill usually manifest in a friendly, considerate demeanor, and especially in the practice of hospitality, readiness to help, tenderheartedness, cherishing and maintaining fellowship. *Philanthrōpia*, which is used in English as "philanthropy," is that disposition which does not always think of self, but takes thought for others, their needs and wishes. The philanthropist serves his fellow citizens, protects the oppressed, is mindful of the erring, gentle to the conquered, and self-renouncing in reference to his rights. The word does not occur in the Septuagint. In the N.T. it occurs as a sub. in Acts 28:2 referring to the hospitable reception of the shipwrecked. Philanthropy does not occur in the list of Israelitish or Christian virtues. This social virtue in the N.T. is expressed with the words *agapē* (26) and *philadelphia* (5360), brotherly love, which occupy the place of social righteousness. It is actually one further step to nobleness to be possessed of *philadelphia*, because one considers man as his brother while *philanthrōpia* considers him only as a fellow human being. In Acts 27:3 the word is used as an adv., *philanthrōpōs* (5364), of the human treatment of Paul. In Tit. 3:4 we have the philanthropy of God as a Saviour which means His manifestation in the salvation of man.

5365. Philarguria; love of money, from *philos* (5384), friend or loving, and *arguros* (696), silver, money. To retain that which one has, and by accumulating, to multiply it. *Philarguria* may be regarded as a type of *pleonexia* (4124), covetousness.

5367. Philautos; from *philos* (5384), loving, and *autos* (846), himself. In reality it is not the one who simply loves himself but one who loves himself more than he ought to, involving self-conceit and selfishness (II Tim. 3:2). A person who is characterized by an undue sparing of self and whose primary concern is that things be easy and pleasant for himself. Contr. *authadēs* (829), insolent, one who is harsh and rigorous towards others. The *philautos* is one who loves his life so much that he seeks ignobly to save it.

5368. Phileō; to love with the meaning of having common interests with another (Mt. 10:37; Jn. 5:20, etc.). Contr. *agapaō* (25), taking interest in somebody. To befriend.

5373. Philia; friendship, from *phileō*, having common interests with. Only in Js. 4:4.

5399. Phobeō; from *phobos* (5401), in the Class. Gr. to cause to run away, terrify, frighten. In the N.T. used in the pass. form *phobeomai*, to be terrified, afraid, whether intrans. (Mt. 14:27,30, etc.), or trans., with an accus., to be afraid of, fear (Mt. 14:5; 21:26,46; Lk. 12:5; Heb. 11:23,27), or joined with an inf. (Mt. 1:20; 2:22, etc.). Trans., with an accus.: to fear revenge (Mk. 6:20; Lk. 1:50; Acts 10:2; Eph. 5:33).

5401. Phobos; fear (Mt. 14:26). Capable of a good interpretation (Eph. 5:21) in which case it is syn. with *eulabeia* (2124), godly fear, reverence, or *deilia* (1167), fearfulness, timidity, shrinking for fear. Verb: *phebomai*, to flee, run away from. Adj.: *phoberos* (5398), dreadful, terrible, horrid.

5406. Phoneus; from *phonos* (5408), murder. A murderer (Mt. 22:7; I Pet. 4:15; Rev. 21:8). Two other words translated also as "murderer" have distinctive features: (1) *anthrōpoktonos* (443), from *anthrōpos* (444), a man, and *ektona*, the perf. mid. of *kteinō*, to slay. Manslayer corresponds to the exact meaning. (2) *Sikarios* (4607), an assassin hired to kill somebody. *Phoneus* has the most vague use of all three words.

5411. Phoros; from *pephora*, perf. mid. of *pherō* (5342), to bring. Tribute brought into the prince's treasury (Lk. 20:22; 23:2; Rom. 13:6,7). Related words: *phoreō* (5409), to bear, carry (I Cor. 15:49), to wear (Mt. 11:8; Jn. 19:5; Js. 2:3); *antilambanomai* (482), to help; *antilēpsis* (484), help, relief.

5413. Phortion; the diminutive of *phortos* (5414), a burden, load, from *pherō* (*5342*), to bear; the goods or merchandise carried by a ship (Acts 27:10). Used in the N.T. only figuratively as the burden of Christ's commandments (Mt. 11:30); the burden of ceremonial observances rigorously exacted and increased by human traditions (Mt. 23:4; Lk. 11:46); sin and the punishment of it (Gal. 6:5). See also *phortizō* (5412), to load, burden (Mt. 11:28; Lk. 11:46).

5421. Phrear; a well or pit for water dug in the earth and thus strictly distinguished from *pēgē* (4077), fountain, though a well may also be called a fountain. In Lk. 14:5; Jn. 4:11,12 the depth of the well and in Rev. 9:1,2 *Hades* (86), the bottomless pit.

5424. Phrēn; pl., *phrenes*, only in I Cor. 14:20 translated "thinking," as also *nous* (3563), mind; *sunesis* (4907), putting it together; and *dianoia* (1271), penetrating mind. *Phrenes* (pl.) used in connection with Paul's discussion regarding speaking without being understood. *Phrenes* was regarded early as the seat of intellectual and spiritual activity. It was the diaphragm which determined the strength of the breath and hence also the human spirit and its emotions. It precisely refers to the ability not only to think, but also to control one's thoughts or one's inner attitude of mind. It is the heart as the seat of passions as well as the mind as the seat of mental faculties.

5426. Phroneō; to think, implying not only thinking but

also the affections, will, or moral consideration. Related to *phrenes* (5424) as contr. with *nous* (3563), mind. In the Scripture it is applied most commonly to the actions of the will and affections. Trans. with an accus., to mind, set the affections on (Mt. 16:23; Rom. 8:5; 12:16; Phil. 3:19; Col. 3:2). Intrans., to be affected (II Cor. 13:11). To think, be of opinion (Acts 28:22; Rom. 12:3; I Cor. 4:6 T.R.). *Phronēma* (5427), the result of *phronēsis* (5428), a minding. Adv.: *phronimōs* (5429), prudently (Lk. 16:8).

5428. Phronēsis; prudence, the knowledge of how to regulate one's relationships and dealings with other people. It skillfully adapts its means to the attainment of the ends which it desires without consideration to the ends themselves being good or not. Adj.: *phronimos* (5429), prudent. Deriv.: *aphrosunē* (877), senselessness, related to *aphrōn* (878), imprudent, without reason, from *a,* without, and *phrenes* (5424), mind and heart; one who lacks mental sanity and sobriety, reckless and lacking the common sense perception of the reality of things natural and spiritual.

5429. Phronimos; prudent, sensible, practically wise in relationships with others (Mt. 7:24; 10:16; 24:45; 25:2,4,8,9; Lk. 12:42; 16:8; I Cor. 10:15). In an evil sense, thinking oneself to be prudent judging by one's self-complacency (Rom. 11:25; 12:16; used ironically in I Cor. 4:10; II Cor. 11:19).

5438. Phulakē; from *phulassō* (5442), to keep. A keeping, guarding or watching (Lk. 2:8); a guard, a number of sentinels (Acts 12;10); a prison (Mt. 14:3,10); a hold, a dwelling (Rev. 18:2); a cage of birds (Rev. 18:2); as a division of time, a watch, the night being divided into four watches (*phulakai*): 6-9 p.m.; 9-12 midnight; 12-3 a.m.; 3-6 a.m.; then began the first hour of the day at 6 a.m. and so on (see Mt. 20:1-16). Deriv.: *phulakizō* (5439), to imprison (Acts 22:19); *phulax* (5441), a keeper, sentinel (Acts 5:23; 12:6, 19).

5442. Phulassō; or *phulattō,* to keep or preserve from danger of harm (Jn. 12:25; 17:12, etc.). To guard, watch (Lk. 2:8; 11:21, etc.); to observe a commandment, law, etc. (Mt. 19:20; Lk. 11:28, etc.). In the mid. voice, to beware (II Pet. 3:17). Deriv.: *phulakē* (5438), a prison, hold.

5453. Phuō; intrans., to become, increase (Heb. 12:15). Trans., to produce; pass., to become, to grow (Lk. 8:6,8).

5456. Phōnē; from the obsolete *phaō* or *phō,* to speak. Plutarch call it "that which brings light upon that which is thought of in the mind." The voice explains that which one has in his own mind for others. It is variably translated in Jn. 3:8 as "sound"; Mt. 2:18 and Rev. 6:1 as "voice." *Phōnē* is the cry of the living creature. Sometimes ascribed to God (Mt. 3:17); to men (Mt. 3:3); to animals (Mt. 26:34), to inanimate objects (I Cor. 14:7); to the trumpet (Mt. 24:31 T.R.); to the wind (Jn. 3:8); to the thunder (Rev. 6:1). *Phōnē* is something that definitely can be heard by others. Contr. *logos* (3056), saying or a rational utterance of the mind, whether spoken (*prophorikos,* with utterance as in Dan. 7:11), or unspoken (*endiathetos,* remaining with oneself), of which the latter meaning is equivalent to reason and which can only be predicated of men who can think. Therefore, *logos,* thought or expressed thought, is something that only intelligent beings can exercise and it can be either spoken or unspoken. Thus Jesus Christ in His preincarnate state is called *Logos,* intelligence, but also the expression of that intelligence in terms that could make us understand what was in the mind of God eternally.

5457. Phōs; light of the sun or of the day. Contr. *pheggos* (5338), the light of the moon or the other luminaries of the night (Mt. 24:29; Mk. 13:24; Lk. 11:33). *Phōs* is never kindled and therefore, never quenched, but *luchnos* (3088), is kindled by the hands of another.

5458. Phōstēr; a heavenly body, a luminary, mainly the sun and moon (Phil. 2:15; Rev. 21:11).

5461. Phōtizō; related to *phōs* (5457), light. To enlighten, give light to (Lk. 11:36; Rev. 18:1, cf. Rev. 21:23; 22:5); to enlighten, give light to in a spiritual sense (Jn. 1:9; Eph. 1:18; Heb. 6:4; 10:32); to instruct, to make to see or understand (Eph. 3:9); to bring to light (I Cor. 4:5; II Tim. 1:10).

5462. Phōtismos; enlightening, the illumination going forth from something, the light proceeding therefrom. From *phōtizō* (5461), to enlighten. As a sub., light, luster, illumination (II Cor. 4:4,6 where it is applied spiritually).

5463. Chairō; to rejoice, related to *charis* (5485), grace, as if joy is a direct result of God's grace. It may also be related to the Heb. word meaning a young sheep or lamb indicating the skipping and frisking of a lamb for joy. To rejoice, be glad (Mt. 5:12; 18:13, etc.); with the same meaning in the second aor. pass., *echarēn,* and second fut. pass., *charēsomai* (Mt. 2:10; Mk. 14:11; Lk. 1:14; Jn. 16:20). The imper. *chaire,* and in the pl. *chairete* are applied even in Mod Gr. as terms of salutation or of wishing happiness to another corresponding to our hello (Mt. 28:9; Lk. 1:28); used deceitfully (Mt. 26:49); ironically (Mt. 27:29; Mk. 15:18; Jn. 19:3). II John 10,11 forbid that such salutation should be given to heretical teachers. In the pl. *chairete* is also applied as a form of salutation equal to farewell, adieu, good-by (II Cor. 13:11). The inf. *chairein* is used as a form of salutation at the beginning of a letter indicating the wish of health, happiness (Acts 15:23; 23:26; Js. 1:1). The noun *chara* (5479), joy, delight, gladness. Syn.: *euphrainō* (2165), to cheer, gladden; *agalliaō* (21), to exult, rejoice greatly.

5479. Chara; joy in general from *chairō* (5463), to rejoice (Mt. 2:10; 13:20; 25:21,23; Lk. 15:7,10; II Cor. 7:4; Heb. 13:17; Js. 4:9; I Pet. 1:8). Cause or matter of joy or rejoicing (Lk. 2:10; Phil. 4:1; I Thess. 2:19,20). Syn.: *agalliasis* (20), exultation, exuberant joy; *euphrosunē* (2167), good cheer, mirth, gladness of heart.

5480. Charagma; engraving, impression, mark, symbol. Distinguished from *charaktēr* (5481), the representation of a person. The difference between *charaktēr* and *apaugasma* (541), effulgence, both occurring in Heb. 1:3, is discussed fully under *eikōn* (1504), image, in its contr. with *homoiōsis* (3669), resemblance; and *homoiōma* (3667), likeness.

5481. Charaktēr; representation, express image (English, character). Occurs only in Heb. 1:3 where it is translated "express image," referring to the person of Jesus Christ. Distinguished from *charagma* (5480), graven mark. For the distinction between these two and also the contr. between *charaktēr* and *apaugasma* (541), brightness, appearing in Heb. 1:3, see *eikōn* (1504), image.

5483. Charizomai; as a deponent verb, a pass. form which is used act.; to do a person a favor, be kind to. With the dat. (Gal. 3:18), in the N.T. sense of *charis* (5485), grace, meaning to be gracious to. With the accus. of the thing, to give or bestow a thing willingly as a gift. With the dat. of a person (Lk. 7:21; Acts 27:24; Rom. 8:32; Phil. 2:9); for an end proposed by the receiver, to yield to his will (Acts 25:11,16). The end in view must be inferred from the context (Acts 3:14). The most common meaning peculiar to the N.T. is to pardon, graciously to remit a person's sin (Col. 2:13) in which *charis,* grace, must be viewed as the opp. of *hamartia* (266), sin. With the accus. only. *Charizomai* means to forgive something (II Cor. 2:10; 12:13); with the dat. only, to forgive anyone, to be gracious to (Eph. 4:32; Col. 3:13). II Cor. 2:7 uses it without any obj. with the meaning to offer. In Lk. 7:42,43 it means simply to give. In the pass., especially in the aor. *echaristhēn,* and the fut., *charisthēsomai,* to be kindly treated, to be pleasingly dealt with (Acts 3:14; I Cor. 2:12; Phil. 1:29; Phile. 22).

5485. Charis; from *chairō* (5463), to rejoice, or *chara* (5479), joy, favor, acceptance, a kindness granted or desired, a benefit, thanks, gratitude, grace. A favor done without expectation of return; absolute freeness of the lovingkindness of God to men finding its only motive in the bounty and freeheartedness of the Giver; unearned and unmerited favor. *Charis* stands in direct antithesis to *erga,* works, the two being mutually exclusive. God's grace affects man's sinfulness and not only forgives the repentant sinner, but brings joy and thankfulness to him. In contr. to *charis* stands *eleos*

(1656), mercy, which is concerned not with sin itself, as does *charis,* but with the misery brought upon the sinner as a consequence of that sin.

5486. Charisma; a gift of grace. An undeserved benefit from God. Derived from *charis,* grace, and the suffix *-ma,* indicating the result of grace.

5487. Charitoō; only in Scripture and in later post-Christian Gr., from the basic Gr. word *charis* (5485), grace. Trans., with an accus., to make accepted or acceptable, make lovely or deserving of love, amiable (Eph. 1:6). To be acceptable, favored, highly favored as in Lk. 1:28 meaning to bestow grace upon, as distinct from *charizomai,* to confer grace. It really does not mean to show favor to, but to give grace to, since Mary was to bear Jesus Christ in her womb, the whole treasure of God's grace.

5500. Cheirotoneō; from *cheir* (5495), hand, and *tetona,* perf. mid. of *teinō,* to extend, stretch out. To elect or choose to an office by lifting up the hand; to choose to vote (II Cor. 8:19); to appoint to an office without votes (Acts 14:23).

5509. Chitōn; a close-fitting inner vest, an inner garment (Mt. 5:40; Lk. 6:29, etc.). Used with *himation* (2440), an outer cloak in Lk. 6:29. In the pl., used generally for garments or clothes (Mk. 14:63) and equivalent to *himatia* in Mt. 26:65. Contr. *himatismos* (2441); *chlamus* (5511); *stolē* (4749), and *podēres* (4158).

5511. Chlamus; a garment of dignity and office. The purple robe with which our Lord was arrayed in scorn by the mockers in Pilate's Judgment Hall (Mt. 27:28-31). *Chlamus* was constantly used as a garment of dignity and office and, when put over the shoulders of someone, was an indication that he was assuming a magistracy. Perhaps it was the cast-off cloak of some high Roman officer which they put over the body of Jesus to mock Him as if He were an official person. Contr. *himation* (2440); *chitōn* (5509); *himatismos* (2441); *stolē* (4749); *podērēs* (4158).

5517. Choikos; from *choos,* earth, dust. Earthly, made of earth or dust (I Cor. 15:47-49).

5530. Chraomai; the mid. voice of *chraō* (5531), to borrow, receive for use. With a dat., to use, make use of, and, more literally, to hand, from *cheir* (5495), hand (Acts 27:17; I Cor. 7:31, etc.); to behave toward, to treat (English, to handle) (Acts 27:3). See *chreia* (5532) and *chrēstotēs* (5544).

5531. Chraō; perhaps from *cheir* (5495), the hand. To lend, furnish as a loan or to put into another's hands (Lk. 11:5); the mid. voice, *chraomai* (5530), to borrow, receive for use. With a dat., to use, make use of, handle (Acts 27:17; I Cor. 7:31, etc.); to treat, behave towards (Acts 27:3). Deriv.: *chrēsis* (5540), noun, use, manner of using (Rom. 1:26,27); *euchrēstos* (2173), from *eu* (2095), well, or as an inten., and *chrēstos* (5543), useful, very useful (II Tim. 2:21; 4:11; Phile. 11). Contr. *achrēstos* (890), of no use, unprofitable (Phile. 11); *apochrēsis* (671), from *apochraomai,* to abuse, consume by use, from *apo,* from, or used as inten., and *chraomai,* to use, using or use (Col. 2:22) bearing the meaning of *chrēsis,* referring to the things that could not be used without rendering them unfit for further use. See *katachraomai* (2710), to abuse, misuse.

5532. Chreia; from *chraomai,* to use. Occasion, use, need, necessity (Acts 20:34; Rom. 12:13; Phil. 2:25, etc.); a necessary business or affair (Acts 6:3). Deriv.: *achrēstos* (890), unprofitable, useless; *euchrēstos* (2173), useful (Phile. 11); *chrē* (5534), there is need or occasion; *chrēzō* (5535), to need; *chrēma* (5536), something useful, riches or money; *chrēmatizō* (5537), to give divine directions or information, the same as to utter oracles; *chrēmatismos* (5538), a divine answer or oracle; *chrēsimos* (5539), useful, profitable; *chrēsis* (5540), use; *chrēstotēs* (5544), benignity, kindness.

5534. Chrē; an impersonal verb used by shortening it for *chrēsis,* from *chreia* (5532), need, necessity. It is translated "it is becoming" or "it is appropriate" (Js. 3:10). See *chrēstotēs* (5544), benignity.

5535. Chrēzō; from *chreia* (5532), need, necessity. Governing a gen., to have need of, want (Mt. 6:32; Rom. 16:2, etc.). See *chrēstotēs* (5544), benignity.

5536. Chrēma; from *kechrēmai,* the perf. of *chraomai* (5530), to handle. Something useful or capable of being used. In the pl., riches, wealth (Mk. 10:23,24 T.R.; Lk. 18:24). In both the sing. and pl. it means money (Acts 4:37; 8:18,20; 24:26). Contr. *chreia* (5532), need; *chrēstotēs* (5544), usefulness, gentleness.

5537. Chrēmatizō; from *chrēma* (5536), an affair, business, from *chraomai* (5530), to use. To have a business affair or dealings, manage a business. To be called or named (Acts 11:26; Rom. 7:3). Particularly in the N.T. it means to utter oracles, give divine directions or information (Heb. 12:25). To be directed or warned by God or as by a divine oracle (Mt. 2:12; 2:22; Acts 10:22; Heb. 8:5; 11:7), or things revealed by divine oracle (Lk. 2:26). Related to *kechrēmai,* the perf. pass. of *chraō,* uttering a divine oracle. See *chreia* (5532), need; *chrēstotēs* (5544) usefulness, gentleness.

5538. Chrēmatismos; the perf. pass. of *chrēmatizō* (5537) to utter an oracle. A divine answer or oracle (Rom. 11:4).

5539. Chrēsimos; from *chrēsis* (5540), use. Useful, profitable (II Tim. 2:14). See *chreia* (5532); *chrēstotēs* (5544).

5540. Chrēsis; from *chraomai* (5530), to use. Use, manner of using (Rom. 1:26,27). See *chreia* (5532), need; *chrēstotēs* (5544).

5543. Chrēstos; from *chraomai* (5530), to furnish what is needed. Useful, profitable, good as opp. to bad (I Cor. 15:33); good, kind, obliging, gracious (Lk. 6:35; Eph. 4:32; I Pet. 2:3); of a yoke, gentle, easy (Mt. 11:30). See *chrēstotēs* (5544), and deriv. under *chreia* (5532).

5544. Chrēstotēs; benignity, kindness (Rom. 2:4; 3:12; 11:22; II Cor. 6:6; Gal. 5:22; Eph. 2:7; Col. 3:12; Tit. 3:4). It is joined to *philanthrōpia* (5363), philanthropy; *anochē* (463), forbearance (Rom. 2:4), and opp. to *apotomia* (663), severity or cutting it short and quickly (Rom. 11:22). *Chrēstotēs* is translated as "good" (Rom. 3:12), "kindness" (II Cor. 6:6; Eph. 2:7; Col. 3:12; Tit. 3:4); "gentleness" (Gal. 5:22). It is the grace which pervades the whole nature, mellowing all which would have been harsh and austere. Thus, wine is *chrēstos* (5543), mellowed with age (Lk. 5:39); Christ's yoke is *chrēstos,* as having nothing harsh or galling about it (Mt. 11:30). Contr. *agathōsunē* (19), it pertains to character without the necessary altruistic externalization found in *agathōsunē,* active benignity. *Chrēstotēs* has only the harmlessness of the dove, not the wisdom of the serpent which *agathōsunē* may have indicated in sharpness and rebuke. Related words: *chrēstos,* kind or good in oneself, mellow (Mt. 11:30; Lk. 5:39; 6:35; Rom. 2:4; I Cor. 15:33; Eph. 4:32; I Pet. 2:3).

5545. Chrisma; the anointing (Ex. 30:25; 40:9; Lev. 21:10). The specially-prepared anointing oil was called *chrisma,* anointing, *hagion* (39), holy. See *chrio* (5548), to rub over, anoint. Only in I Jn. 2:20,27 where it signifies an anointing which had been experienced, a communication and reception of the Spirit (cf. Jn. 16:13). *Chrisma* is not merely a figurative name for the Spirit as seen from the expression *chrisma echete* ("you have an anointing" v. 20) and *elabete* ("you received" v. 27). The word seems chosen in order to give prominence, on the one hand, to what the readers had experienced, and on the other hand, by referring to the O.T. practice, and especially to Christ, to remind them of their calling and mark (I Pet. 2:5,9).

5546. Christianos; Christian, a name given to the disciples or followers of Christ (see *mathētēs,* 3101, disciple of Jesus Christ), and first adopted at Antioch. It does not occur in the N.T. as a name commonly used by Christians themselves (Acts 11:26; 26:28; I Pet. 4:16). In Acts 11:26 the verb used for "were called" is not *ōnomasthēsan* (3687), but *chrēmatisai,* the inf. of *chrēmatizō* (5537) which means to be directed by God as if by divine oracle. This same verb was used by the magi from the East who were divinely informed not to return to tell Herod where the baby Jesus was

(Mt. 2:12,22). See also Acts 10:22; Heb. 8:5; 11:7 where the same verb is used. Thus the believers first became known as Christians not as an appellation of ridicule as commonly taught, but by divine direction. See *chriō* (5548), to anoint.

5547. Christos; anointed, from *chriō* (5548), to anoint, a term used in the O.T. applied to everyone anointed with the holy oil, primarily to the high priesthood (Lev. 4:3,5,16; 6:22, etc.). Also a name applied to others acting as redeemers. As an appellative and with the art. *ho,* the, *Christos,* Christ, occurs chiefly in the Gospels. Without the art. and as a proper noun alone, in the Gospels only in Mk. 9:41 (cf. Acts 24:24); elsewhere only in the connection of Jesus Christ (Mt. 1:16), "Jesus called the Christ." In the Pauline Epistles and in I Peter, Christ is used as a proper name (Rom. 5:8; 6:4,8; 8:10,34; 9:1; I Pet. 1:11,19; 2:21; 3:16,18). As to the different uses in the N.T. besides the name of our Lord, it denotes the Christian Church or that society of which Christ is the head (I Cor. 12:12). The body of Christ means the Church because Christ is the head of the body (I Cor. 12:27; Gal. 3:24,28; Col. 1:24). It also means the doctrine of Christ (Eph. 4:20); the benefits (Heb. 3:14); and the Christian temper or disposition arising from a sound Christian faith (Gal. 4:19, cf. II Cor. 3:14; Eph. 3:17; Phil. 2:5). Deriv.: *antichristos* (500), an opponent of Christ or the one who takes the place of Christ; *christianos* (5546), Christian.

5548. Chriō; to anoint with a sacred or religious meaning. From this is derived *Christos,* the Anointed One, Christ (Lk. 4:18; Acts 4:27; 10:38; II Cor. 1:21; Heb. 1:9). Contr. *aleiphō* (218), to cover over, rub, used with mundane significance involving oil or ointment (Mt. 6:17; Mk. 6:13; 16:1; Lk. 7:38,46; Jn. 11:2; 12:3; Js. 5:14).

5550. Chronos; time as succession or measurement of moments as in chronometer, a meter of *chronos,* of the passing moments without any moral impact as to the opportunity and accomplishment in that time as indicated by *kairos* (2540), the time of opportunities. *Chronos* has only length, not challenge of accomplishment, as *kairos. Chronos* embraces all possible *kairos,* and is often used as the larger and more inclusive term, but not the converse. In the N.T. used only in the pl., *chronoi,* together with *kairoi,* times and opportunities or seasons (Acts 1:7; I Thess. 5:1).

5568. Psalmos; psalm, from *psaō,* actually a touching, and then a touching of the harp or other stringed instruments with the finger or with the plectrum; later known as the instrument itself, and finally it became known as the song sung with the musical accompaniment. This latest stage of its meaning was adopted in the Septuagint. In all probability the psalms of Eph. 5:19; Col. 3:16 are the inspired psalms of the Hebrew Canon. The word certainly designates these on all other occasions when it occurs in the N.T., with the one possible exception of I Cor. 14:26. These are the old songs to which new hymns and praises are added (Rev. 5:9). See *hymn* (5215); *ōdē* (5603) song of praise.

5569. Pseudadelphos; from *pseudēs* (5571), false, and *adelphos* (80), brother; a false brother. In Gal. 2:4 it denotes those who had become members of the Christian church, sharers in its fellowship of life and love, but in reality were not so inwardly, and therefore, had no right to be counted as brothers. They had the companionship of the brothers but the real kinship of spiritual life was missing (see II Cor. 11:26).

5572. Pseudodidaskalos; from *pseudō,* to deceive, or the mid. or pass. voice *pseudomai,* to lie, and *didaskalos* (1320), a teacher. A false teacher or one who pretends to have the character of a Christian teacher and teaches false doctrine (II Pet. 2:1).

5580. Pseudochristos; from *pseudēs* (5571), false, and *Christos* (5547), Christ (Mt. 24:24; Mk. 13:22). The false Christ does not deny the being of Christ. On the contrary, he builds on the world's expectations of such a person, but he blasphemously appropriates these to himself and affirms that he is the foretold One in whom God's promises and men's expectations are fulfilled. Contr. *antichristos* (500), antichrist, who denies that there is a Christ, the *pseudochristos* affirms himself to be the Christ. Both are against the Christ of God. The final antichrist will be a pseudochrist as well. He will usurp to himself Christ's offices, presenting himself to the world as the true center of its hopes, the satisfier of all its needs and the healer of all its ills. He will be a pseudo christ and antichrist in one.

5584. Psēlaphaō; feel on the surface, feeling for or after an object without any actual coming in contact with it at all; groping in the dark (Lk. 24:39; Acts 17:27; Heb. 12:18; I Jn. 1:1). See *haptomai* (680); *haptō* (681); *thigganō* (2345).

5588. Psithuristēs; from *psithurizō,* to whisper; a whisperer, a secret slanderer, versus *katalalos* (2637), a backbiter who does his slandering openly (Rom. 1:29,30). Deriv.: *psithurismos* (5587) (II Cor. 12:20), a whisperer, slanderer.

5590. Psuchē; soul, that immaterial part of man held in common with animals. Contr. *sōma* (4983), body and *pneuma* (4151), spirit (I Thess. 5:23). The *psuchē* no less than the *sarx,* flesh, belongs to the lower region of man's being. Sometimes *psuchē* stands for the immaterial part of man made up of the soul, *psuchē* in the restrictive sense of the animus, the life element, and the *pneuma,* spirit. But animals are not said to possess a spirit; this is only in man, giving him the ability to communicate with God.

5591. Psuchikos; pertaining to the natural, animal, as distinguished from spiritual or glorified nature of man. From *psuchē* (5590), soul, the part of the immaterial life held in common with the animals, as contr. with spirit, *pneuma* (4151), only in man, enabling him to communicate with God. I Cor. 15:44 refers to a body *psuchikon,* an animalistic or physical body governed by the soul or animal or fallen instinct of man, and a body *pneumatikon* (4152), spiritual, governed by the divine quality in man, the spirit. Rendered as natural in I Cor. 2:14; I Cor. 15:44,46 and sensual in Js. 3:15; Jude 19. The term *psuchikos* is not a word of honor even as *sarkikos* (4559), carnal.

5594. Psuchō; from *psuchos,* cold. Derived from a word meaning to compress, condense, concrete, which is the property of coldness. Therefore, *psuchō* means to cool or refrigerate as with cool air. It is from this verb that *psuchē* (5590), which has come to mean soul, is derived. It is to refresh with cool air and naturally to breathe. Hence *psuchē* is the breath of a living creature, animal life, and the verb *psuchō,* in the pass. *psuchomai,* means to be cool, to grow cool or cold in a spiritual sense, as in Christian love (Mt. 24:12).

5603. Ōdē; song, contracted from *aoidē,* which in turn comes from *aeidō* or *adō* (103), to sing, confess, praise. The original use of singing among both believers and idolaters was in the confessions and praises of the respective gods. Paul qualifies it in Eph. 5:19; Col. 3:16 as spiritual songs in association with psalms and hymns, because *ōdē* by itself might mean any kind of song, as of battle, harvest, festal, whereas *psalmos* (5568), psalm, from its Heb. use, and *hymnos* (5215), hymn, from its Gr. use, did not require any such qualifying adj. It is a harmonious song (Rev. 5:9; 14:3; 15:3).

5604. Ōdin; from *odunē,* grief, sorrow. Used usually in the pl. and meaning pains of labor, distress, woe, compared to the pain which a woman experiences in childbirth (Mt. 24:8; Mk. 13:8). In Acts 2:24 the *ōdinas thanatou,* the cords or snares of death. Deriv.: *ōdinō* (5605), to be in pain.

5605. Ōdinō; from *ōdin* (5604). Intrans., to be in pain as when a woman is in travail (Gal. 4:27; Rev. 12:2, in both cases applied spiritually to the Church); trans., with an accus., to travail in birth of, to be in labor with (Gal. 4:19 where Paul applies it in a spiritual sense to himself with respect to the Galatian converts).

5610. Hōra; hour. N.T. meanings: (1) Time, season, particular time (Mk. 11:11; Jn. 4:23; 5:35; 12:23; 17:1; I Jn. 2:18, cf. Mk. 14:35; Rev. 3:10; 14:7,15). (2) A short time (Jn. 5:35; I Thess. 2:17; Phile. 15). (3) Denotes the day or time of day (Mt. 14:15). The *hōra* *pollē* (much hour or much time) in Mk. 6:35 means either a great part of the day already past or yet remaining. The *ēdē* (2235), already, in this verse forces us to adopt the first meaning, a great part of the day already past. (4) An hour, the twelfth part of daylight, or the time the sun is above the horizon, e.g., the third hour means 9:00 a.m., and the eleventh hour means 5 p.m. (Mt. 20:3,5,6 T.R.,9,12; Jn. 19:14). (5) The right time, the time fixed, the time determined upon or demanded, the fit time such as the time of judgment (Rev. 14:7), the time for harvest (v. 15), of temptation (3:10). Also used in this manner in Mt. 26:45; Jn. 4:21,23. Often Christ's hour is spoken of as the time of His sufferings and death (Mt. 26:18; Jn. 7:30; 8:20; 13:1).

5611. Hōraios; beautiful, from *hōra* (5610), hour. Time indicating timely, fair, proper, good timing (only in Mt. 23:27; Acts 3:2,10; Rom. 10:15).

5613. Hōs; as, used with numerals, it means about (Mk. 5:13; 8:9; Jn. 1:39; 6:19; 11:18; Acts 1:15; Rev. 8:1). Distinguished from *hōsei* (5616), which indicates greater indefiniteness.

5616. Hōsei; as if, used before numerals and denotes about, nearly, something like, with some what of an indication of greater indefiniteness than *hōs* (5613) (Mt. 14:21; Lk. 3:23, etc.).

The New American Standard
CONCORDANCE
to the Old and New Testaments

This is a collection of the principal **proper nouns** and **key words** in Scripture. The following format is used: Descriptive phrases and references are listed under each **proper noun.** If the descriptive phrases are numbered, this indicates different individuals or identities. **Key words** are immediately followed by explanatory words or synonyms. Under each **key word** examples are listed with text and reference. The **key word** is abbreviated in the text to its first letter, e.g., "abide" is "**a**". Variants add suffixes, e.g., "abides" appears as "**a-s**" and "abiding" appears as "**a-ing**".

A

AARON
brother of Moses Ex 4:14
spokesman for Moses Ex 4:28;7:1-2
as priest Ex 28:1;29:44
rod of Num 17:8; Heb 9:4
critical of Moses Num 12:1
death Deut 10:6

ABANDON *leave*
LORD has **a-ed** us Judg 6:13
not **a** His people 1 Sam 12:22
a the remnant 2 Kin 21:14
not **a** my soul to Ps 16:10
not **a** His people Ps 94:14
a-ed My inheritance Jer 12:7
a my soul to Hades Acts 2:27

ABASE *humble*
man will be **a-d** Is 2:11
lofty will be **a-d** Is 10:33
a the haughtiness Is 13:11
a-d before all Mal 2:9

ABATED *decreased*
water was **a** Gen 8:8
his vigor **a** Deut 34:7

ABBA *father*
A! Father Mark 14:36
we cry out, **A**! Rom 8:15

ABEL
son of Adam Gen 4:2
shepherd Gen 4:2
favored by God Gen 4:4
slain by Cain Gen 4:8
called righteous Matt 23:35

ABHOR *despise, detest*
associates **a** me Job 19:19
greatly **a-red** Israel Ps 78:59
nations will **a** him Prov 24:24
To the One **a-red** Is 49:7
A what is evil Rom 12:9

ABIB
early name of first month of Hebrew calendar Ex 34:18
month of Passover and Unleavened Bread Deut 16:1

ABIDE *remain, stay*
LORD **a-s** forever Ps 9:7
a in Thy tent Ps 15:1
a in the shadow Ps 91:1
wrath of God **a-s** John 3:36
a in My word John 8:31
If you **a** in Me John 15:7
a in My love John 15:9
now **a** faith 1 Cor 13:13
word . . . LORD **a-s** 1 Pet 1:25
love of God **a** 1 John 3:17
God **a-s** in us 1 John 4:12

ABIHU
son of Aaron Ex 6:23
priest Ex 28:1
disobeyed God Lev 10:1
judged by God Lev 10:2

ABIJAH
1 *son of Samuel* 1 Sam 8:2
2 *son of Jeroboam* 1 Kin 14:1
3 *son of Becher* 1 Chr 7:8
4 *line of Eleazar* 1 Chr 24:10
5 *king of Judah* 2 Chr 12:16
6 *Hezekiah's mother* 2 Chr 29:1
7 *priest* Neh 10:7;12:4

ABILITY *power, strength*
According to their **a** Ezra 2:69
a for serving Dan 1:4
a to conceive Heb 11:11

ABIMELECH
1 *king of Gerar* Gen 20:1-18
2 *king of Gerar* Gen 26:1ff
3 *king of Shechem* Judg 9:1ff
4 *priest* 1 Chr 18:16
5 *Psalm title* Ps 34

ABNER
Saul's commander 1 Sam 17:55
loyal to David 2 Sam 3:12ff
killed by Joab 2 Sam 3:27
mourned by David 2 Sam 3:32

ABODE *habitation*
a of righteousness Jer 31:23
Our **a** with him John 14:23
their proper **a** Jude 6

ABOLISH
not come to **a** Matt 5:17
a-ing in His flesh Eph 2:15
who **a-ed** death 2 Tim 1:10

ABOMINABLE *detestable*
committed **a** deeds Ps 14:1
your beauty **a** Ezek 16:25
a idolatries 1 Pet 4:3
unbelieving and **a** Rev 21:8

ABOMINATION *hated thing*
a to the Egyptians Ex 8:26
a into your house Deut 7:26
seen their **a-s** Deut 29:17
a to the LORD Prov 3:32
all their **a-s** Ezek 33:29
a of desolation Matt 24:15
a-s of the earth Rev 17:5

ABRAHAM
covenant Gen 17:1-8
promise of Isaac Gen 17:19
asked the LORD Gen 18:22ff
offers Isaac Gen 22:9,10
death Gen 25:8
righteousness of Rom 4:3-9

ABRAHAM'S BOSOM
rabbinic terminology for Paradise Luke 16:22

ABRAM
called of God Gen 12:1-3
rescued Lot Gen 14:14-16
covenant with God Gen 15:18
name changed Gen 17:5

ABSALOM
son of David 2 Sam 13:1
his revolt 2 Sam 15:1-2
popular 2 Sam 15:6
slain by Joab 2 Sam 18:15

ABSENT *being away*
we are **a** one from Gen 31:49
a in body 1 Cor 5:3
a from the LORD 2 Cor 5:6
a from the body 2 Cor 5:8

ABSTAIN *refrain from*
a from wine Num 6:3
a-ing from foods 1 Tim 4:3
a from wickedness 2 Tim 2:19
a from fleshly lusts 1 Pet 2:11

ABUNDANCE *plenty, surplus*
seven years of **a** Gen 41:34
a of all things Deut 28:47
a of Thy house Ps 36:8
a of counselors Prov 24:6
he who loves **a** Eccl 5:10
delight yourself in **a** Is 55:2
one has an **a** Luke 12:15
the **a** of grace Rom 5:17

ABUNDANT *enough, plenteous*
come . . . find **a** water 2 Chr 32:4
a righteousness Job 37:23
a in lovingkindness Ps 86:5
comfort is **a** 2 Cor 1:5

ABUSE (n) *insulting speech*
hurling **a** at Him Matt 27:39
was hurling **a** Luke 23:39

ABUSE (v) *hurt, molest*
a-d her all night Judg 19:25
uncircumcised . . . **a** me 1 Chr 10:4

ABUSIVE *filthy, vulgar, hurtful*
a speech from your Col 3:8
strife, **a** language 1 Tim 6:4

ABYSS *deep, depth*
depart into the **a** Luke 8:31
descend into the **a** Rom 10:7
angel of the **a** Rev 9:11

key of the a Rev 20:1

ACCEPT *receive*
a the work of Deut 33:11
a good from God Job 2:10
the LORD **a-ed** Job Job 42:9
hear the word and **a** Mark 4:20
God has **a-ed** him Rom 14:3
a one another Rom 15:7

ACCEPTABLE *pleasing*
my heart Be **a** Ps 19:14
sacrifice, **a** to God Rom 12:1
a to the saints Rom 15:31
now is the **a** time 2 Cor 6:2
to God an **a** service Heb 12:28
sacrifices **a** to God 1 Pet 2:5

ACCESS *approach, entry*
grant you free **a** Zech 3:7
our **a** in one Spirit Eph 2:18

ACCOMPLISH *perform, realize*
a-ed deliverance 1 Sam 11:13
shall **a** my desire 1 Kin 5:9
God . . . **a-es** *all things* Ps 57:2
has **a-ed** His wrath Lam 4:11
a-ed redemption Luke 1:68
a His work John 4:34
I am **a-ing** a work Acts 13:41
man can **a** much James 5:16

ACCOUNT (n) *reckoning, record*
the **a** of the heavens Gen 2:4
Thou hast taken **a** of Ps 56:8
On whose **a** *has* this Jon 1:8
settled **a-s** with Matt 25:19
who will give an **a** Heb 13:17

ACCOUNT (v) *reckon*
do not **a** *this* sin Num 12:11
I am **a-ed** wicked Job 9:29
are **a-ed** as nothing Dan 4:35

ACCURSED *damned*
camp of Israel **a** Josh 6:18
be *thought* **a** Is 65:20
Depart . . . **a** ones Matt 25:41
let him be **a** Gal 1:8
in greed, **a** children 2 Pet 2:14

ACCUSATION *charge of wrong*
wrote an **a** against Ezra 4:6
find a ground of **a** Dan 6:4
What **a** do you John 18:29
a against my nation Acts 28:19
Do not receive an **a** 1 Tim 5:19

ACCUSE *testify against*
a-d his brother Deut 19:18
a-s you in judgment Is 54:17
He was being **a-d** Matt 27:12
a-ing . . . vehemently Luke 23:10
a you before the John 5:45
not **a-d** of dissipation Titus 1:6
unjustly **a-ing** us 3 John 10

ACCUSER *complainant*
they act as my **a-s** Ps 109:4
instructing his **a-s** Acts 23:30
when the **a-s** stood Acts 25:18
a of our brethren Rev 12:10

ACHAIA
province of Greece Acts 18:12; Rom 15:26; 1 Cor 16:15

ACHAN
stole from Jericho Josh 7:1
executed by people Josh 7:25

ACKNOWLEDGE *confess*
I **a-d** my sin Ps 32:5
all your ways **a** Him Prov 3:6
Pharisees **a** them all Acts 23:8
see fit to **a** God Rom 1:28

ACQUAINTANCE *friend*
dread to my **a-s** Ps 31:11
removed my **a-s** far Ps 88:8
relatives and **a-s** Luke 2:44
And all His **a-s** Luke 23:49

ACQUIRE *get, purchase*
a property in it Gen 34:10
have **a-d** Ruth Ruth 4:10
a wise counsel Prov 1:5
Do not **a** gold Matt 10:9

ACQUIT *declare innocent*
not **a** me of my guilt Job 10:14
A me of hidden *faults* Ps 19:12
You will not be **a-ted** Jer 49:12

ACT (n) *deed, work*
a detestable **a** Lev 20:13
mighty **a-s** as Thine Deut 3:24
every abominable **a** Deut 12:31
over the rebellious **a** Mic 7:18

ACT (v) *behave*
they refuse to **a** Prov 21:7
I **a-ed** ignorantly 1 Tim 1:13
So speak and so **a** James 2:12
are **a-ing** faithfully 3 John 5

ACTION *behavior, work*
a-s are weighed 1 Sam 2:3
a-s of a . . . harlot Ezek 16:30
plan or **a** should be Acts 5:38
gird your minds for **a** 1 Pet 1:13

ADAM
1 *first man* Gen 2:20
fall of man Gen 3:6,7
type of Christ Rom 5:14
compared to Jesus 1 Cor 15:22
2 *site in Jordan Valley* Josh 3:16

ADAR
twelfth month of Hebrew calendar Ezra 6:15
Purim observed Esth 3:7; 9:19ff

ADMINISTRATION *management*
a of the province Dan 3:12
healings, helps, **a-s** 1 Cor 12:28
in our **a** of this 2 Cor 8:20
a of the mystery Eph 3:9

ADMONISH *warn*
prophets . . . had **a-ed** Neh 9:26
How shall I **a** you Lam 2:13
not cease to **a** each Acts 20:31
able also to **a** one Rom 15:14
a-ing one another Col 3:16
a him as a brother 2 Thess 3:15

ADONIJAH
1 *son of David* 2 Sam 3:4
aspired to throne 1 Kin 1:5ff
pardoned 1 Kin 1:52ff
executed 1 Kin 2:25
2 *Levite* 2 Chr 17:8
3 *of the restoration* Neh 10:16

ADOPTION *acceptance*
spirit of **a** as sons Rom 8:15
to whom belongs . . . **a** Rom 9:4
receive the **a** as sons Gal 4:5
predestined us to **a** Eph 1:5

ADORN *array, clothe*
A yourself with Job 40:10
as a bride **a-s** herself Is 61:10
a-ed with beautiful Luke 21:5
women to **a** 1 Tim 2:9
a the doctrine of God Titus 2:10
as a bride **a-ed** Rev 21:2

ADULTERER
a and the adulteress Lev 20:10
eye of the **a** waits Job 24:15
associate with **a-s** Ps 50:18
a-s, nor effeminate 1 Cor 6:9
a-s God will judge Heb 13:4

ADULTERESS
a shall surely be Lev 20:10
a who flatters with Prov 2:16
mouth of an **a** Prov 22:14
You **a** wife, who Ezek 16:32
they are **a-es** Ezek 23:45
shall be called an **a** Rom 7:3

ADULTERY
shall not commit **a** Ex 20:14
man who commits **a** Lev 20:10
a-ies of faithless Jer 3:8
worn out by **a-ies** Ezek 23:43
committed **a** with her Matt 5:28
Do not commit **a** Luke 18:20
eyes full of **a** 2 Pet 2:14

ADVERSARY *foe, opponent*
an **a** to your **a-ies** Ex 23:22
an **a** to Solomon 1 Kin 11:14
Lest my **a-ies** rejoice Ps 13:4
a-ies and my enemies Ps 27:2
there are many **a-ies** 1 Cor 16:9
consume the **a-ies** Heb 10:27
Your **a**, the devil 1 Pet 5:8

ADVICE *counsel*
forsook the **a** 1 Kin 12:13
a of the cunning Job 5:13
they took his **a** Acts 5:40
have followed my **a** Acts 27:21

ADVISER *counselor*
with his **a** Ahuzzath Gen 26:26
Pharaoh's wisest **a-s** Is 19:11

ADVOCATE *defender, witness*
my **a** is on high Job 16:19
A with the Father 1 John 2:1

AFFECTION *devotion, love*
set His **a** to love Deut 10:15
in your own **a-s** 2 Cor 6:12
a of Christ Jesus Phil 1:8
fond **a** for you 1 Thess 2:8

AFFLICT (v) *oppress, trouble*
a with hard labor Ex 1:11
not **a** any widow Ex 22:22
Egyptians . . . **a-ed** us Deut 26:6
the wicked **a** them 2 Sam 7:10
They **a-ed** his feet Ps 105:18
will **a** you no longer Nah 1:12
were sick or **a-ed** Acts 5:16
are **a-ed** in every 2 Cor 4:8
those who **a** you 2 Thess 1:6
a-ed, ill-treated Heb 11:37

AFFLICTED (n) *troubled*
to catch the **a** Ps 10:9
justice to the **a** Ps 82:3
LORD supports the **a** Ps 147:6
days of the **a** Prov 15:15
good news to the **a** Is 61:1

AFFLICTION *oppression*
the land of my **a** Gen 41:52
the bread of **a** Deut 16:3
LORD saw the **a** 2 Kin 14:26
afflicted in their **a** Job 36:15
Look upon my **a** Ps 25:18
a or persecution Mark 4:17
healed of her **a** Mark 5:29
a-s await me Acts 20:23
out of much **a** 2 Cor 2:4
great ordeal of **a** 2 Cor 8:2
to suffer **a** 1 Thess 3:4

AFRAID *dreading, fearful*
a because . . . naked Gen 3:10
a to look at God Ex 3:6
a and fainthearted Deut 20:8
Whoever is **a** Judg 7:3
not **a** of the snow Prov 31:21
a of man who dies Is 51:12
a to take Mary Matt 1:20
were **a** of Him Mark 11:18
Do not be **a**, Mary Luke 1:30
a of those who kill Luke 12:4
a of the people Luke 22:2

a, lest as the serpent — 2 Cor 11:3

AGED *old*
Wisdom is . . . **a** men — Job 12:12
a are among us — Job 15:10
refined, **a** wine — Is 25:6
Paul, the **a** — Philem 9

AGONY *anguish*
a has seized me — 2 Sam 1:9
A like . . . childbirth — Jer 50:43
in **a** in this flame — Luke 16:24
in **a** He was praying — Luke 22:44
the **a** of death — Acts 2:24

AGREE *consent*
if two of you **a** — Matt 18:19
did you not **a** — Matt 20:13
Jews had already **a-d** — John 9:22
have **a-d** together — Acts 5:9
words . . . Prophets **a** — Acts 15:15
a with sound words — 1 Tim 6:3

AGREEMENT *accord*
an **a** in writing — Neh 9:38
Saul was in hearty **a** — Acts 8:1
a has the temple — 2 Cor 6:16
three are in **a** — 1 John 5:8

AGRIPPA
1 *Herod Agrippa I* see **HEROD**
2 *Herod Agrippa II* see **HEROD**

AHAB
1 *king of Israel* — 1 Kin 16:28
son of Omri — 1 Kin 16:29
married Jezebel — 1 Kin 16:31
idolater — 1 Kin 16:33
2 *false prophet* — Jer 29:21,22

AHASUERUS
1 *Persian king, Xerxes I* — Ezra 4:6; Book of Esther
2 *father of Darius the Mede* — Dan 9:1

AHAZ
1 *son of Jotham* — 2 Kin 15:38
king of Judah — 2 Kin 16:2
2 *line of Jonathan* — 1 Chr 8:35

AHIJAH / AHIAH
1 *prophet of Shiloh* — 1 Kin 14:2
2 *of Issachar* — 1 Kin 15:27
3 *son of Jerahmeel* — 1 Chr 2:25
4 *the Pelonite* — 1 Chr 11:36
5 *under Nehemiah* — Neh 10:26

AI
place near Bethel — Gen 12:8
defeat of Israelites — Josh 7:5
captured — Josh 8:23, 29

AIJALON
1 *city of refuge* — Josh 10:12
Levitical city — Josh 21:24
2 *valley* — Josh 19:42
3 *Zebulunite town* — Judg 12:12

ALABASTER *whitish stone*
stones, and **a** — 1 Chr 29:2
pillars of **a** — Song 5:15
brought an **a** vial — Luke 7:37

ALERT (n) *watch, watchful*
be on the **a** — Matt 24:42
keeping **a** in it — Col 4:2
be **a** and sober — 1 Thess 5:6

ALEXANDER
1 *son of Simon of Cyrene* — Mark 15:21
2 *of priestly family* — Acts 4:6
3 *Ephesian Jew* — Acts 19:33
4 *apostate teacher* — 1 Tim 1:20
5 *enemy of Paul* — 2 Tim 4:14

ALEXANDRIAN
1 *of Alexandria* — Acts 6:9
2 *ship* — Acts 27:6; 28:11
3 *Apollos* — Acts 18:24

ALIEN *foreigner, stranger*
love for the **a** — Deut 10:19
give it to the **a** — Deut 14:21
Our houses to **a-s** — Lam 5:2
a-s in a foreign land — Acts 7:6
no longer . . . **a-s** — Eph 2:19
he lived as an **a** — Heb 11:9
I urge you as **a-s** — 1 Pet 2:11

ALIVE
Is your father still **a** — Gen 43:7
down **a** to Sheol — Num 16:33
go down **a** to Sheol — Ps 55:15
when He was . . . **a** — Matt 27:63
heard . . . He was **a** — Mark 16:11
presented Himself **a** — Acts 1:3
yet the spirit is **a** — Rom 8:10
all shall be made **a** — 1 Cor 15:22
made us **a** together — Eph 2:5
a in the spirit — 1 Pet 3:18
I am **a** forevermore — Rev 1:18

ALLEGIANCE *loyalty*
pledged **a** to King — 1 Chr 29:24
he pledged his **a** — Ezek 17:18

ALLIANCE *agreement*
formed a marriage **a** — 1 Kin 3:1
after an **a** is made — Dan 11:23

ALLIED *joined*
a . . . by marriage — 2 Chr 18:1
throne of . . . **a** — Ps 94:20

ALLOT *apportion, divide*
only **a** it to Israel — Josh 13:6
a Him a portion — Is 53:12
a-ted to each . . . faith — Rom 12:3

ALLOTMENT *portion*
an **a** from Pharaoh — Gen 47:22
as a perpetual **a** — Num 18:19
Jacob is the **a** — Deut 32:9
set apart the . . . **a** — Ezek 48:20

ALLOW *permit*
not **a** the destroyer — Ex 12:23
whether his body **a-s** — Lev 15:3
a Thy Holy One — Ps 16:10
Nor **a** Thy Holy One — Acts 2:27
not be **a-ed** to live — Acts 22:22
a you to be tempted — 1 Cor 10:13
not **a** a woman — 1 Tim 2:12

ALMIGHTY *all-powerful*
I am God **A** — Gen 17:1
vision of the **A** — Num 24:4
A has afflicted me — Ruth 1:21
limits of the **A** — Job 11:7
A was yet with me — Job 29:5
destruction from . . . **A** — Joel 1:15
Lord God, the **A** — Rev 4:8
the **A**, reigns — Rev 19:6

ALMS *charity*
therefore you give **a** — Matt 6:2
a may be in secret — Matt 6:4
a to the *Jewish* — Acts 10:2
bring **a** to my nation — Acts 24:17

ALOUD *joyfully, piercingly*
crying **a** as she — 2 Sam 13:19
read **a** from the book — Neh 13:1
I will cry **a** — Ps 77:1
Sing **a** with gladness — Jer 31:7
The king called **a** — Dan 5:7
began to weep **a** — Acts 20:37

ALPHA
first letter of Gr. alphabet — Rev 1:8
title of Jesus Christ — Rev 21:6
expresses eternalness of God — Rev 22:13

ALTAR *place of sacrifice*
offerings on the **a** — Gen 8:20
Moses built an **a** — Ex 17:15
Gideon built an **a** — Judg 6:24
erect an **a** to — 2 Sam 24:18
go to the **a** of God — Ps 43:4
offering at the **a** — Matt 5:23
a that sanctifies — Matt 23:19
golden **a** of incense — Heb 9:4
we have an **a** — Heb 13:10
horns of the golden **a** — Rev 9:13

AMASA
1 *son of Abigail* — 1 Chr 2:17
Absalom's commander — 2 Sam 17:25
pardoned — 2 Sam 19:13
2 *an Ephraimite* — 2 Chr 28:12

AMAZED *astonished, astounded*
are **a** at His rebuke — Job 26:11
a at His teaching — Mark 1:22
heard Him were **a** — Luke 2:47
were **a** and marveled — Acts 2:7
whole earth was **a** — Rev 13:3

AMAZIAH
1 *king of Judah* — 2 Kin 12:21
son of Joash — 2 Kin 14:1
2 *a Simeonite* — 1 Chr 4:34
3 *son of Hilkiah* — 1 Chr 6:45
4 *a priest of Bethel* — Amos 7:10

AMBASSADOR *envoy*
a-s of peace weep — Is 33:7
a-s for Christ — 2 Cor 5:20
an **a** in chains — Eph 6:20

AMBUSH (n) *cover, hiding place*
a for the city — Josh 8:2
rise from *your* **a** — Josh 8:7
Israel set men in **a** — Judg 20:29
a . . . behind them — 2 Chr 13:13
Place men in **a** — Jer 51:12

AMBUSH (v) *lie in wait*
going to **a** the city — Josh 8:4
a the innocent — Prov 1:11
a their own lives — Prov 1:18

AMEN *so be it*
people shall say, **A** — Deut 27:16
the Lord forever! **A** — Ps 89:52
glory forever . . . **A** — Phil 4:20
the **A**, the faithful — Rev 3:14
A, Come, Lord Jesus — Rev 22:20

AMMONITES
tribes E of Jordan — Gen 19:38
defeated Israel — Judg 3:13
hired Arameans — 2 Sam 10:6
fought against Judah — 2 Kin 24:2

AMNON
1 *eldest son of David* — 2 Sam 3:2
raped his sister — 2 Sam 13:2ff
ordered killed — 2 Sam 13:28
2 *line of Judah* — 1 Chr 4:20

AMON
1 *Ahab's governor* — 1 Kin 22:26
2 *king of Judah* — 2 Kin 21:18-26
3 *of the Nethinims* — Neh 7:59
4 *Egyptian deity* — Jer 46:25

AMOS
prophet to Israel — Book of Amos

AMRAM
1 *father of Moses* — Ex 6:18-20; 1 Chr 23:13
2 *son of Bani* — Ezra 10:34

ANAK / ANAKIM
pre-Israelite tribe of Palestine — Num 13:22-33
giants — Deut 2:10; Josh 14:15

ANANIAS
1 *deceived Jerusalem church* — Acts 5:1-5
2 *Damascus Christian* — Acts 9:10,17
3 *high priest* — Acts 23:2

ANCESTORS *forefathers*
blessings of my **a** — Gen 49:26

the **a** have set Deut 19:14
iniquities of their **a** Jer 11:10

ANCHOR

they weighed **a** Acts 27:13
they cast four **a-s** Acts 27:29
an **a** of the soul Heb 6:19

ANCIENT *aged, old*

of the **a** mountains Deut 33:15
the records are **a** 1 Chr 4:22
keep to the **a** path Job 22:15
O **a** doors Ps 24:9
A of Days Dan 7:9
the **a-s** were told Matt 5:21
from **a** generations Acts 15:21
not spare the **a** world 2 Pet 2:5

ANDREW

fisherman Matt 4:18
brother of Peter Matt 4:18
receives Jesus John 1:40-42
apostle Luke 6:14

ANGEL *divine messenger*

send His **a** before Gen 24:7
a-s . . . were ascending Gen 28:12
an **a** to Jerusalem 1 Chr 21:15
bread of **a-s** Ps 78:25
a of His presence Is 63:9
a who was speaking Zech 4:4
give His **a-s** charge Matt 4:6
a Gabriel was sent Luke 1:26
they are like **a-s** Luke 20:36
two **a-s** in white John 20:12
like the face of an **a** Acts 6:15
worship of the **a-s** Col 2:18
entertained **a-s** Heb 13:2
God did not spare **a-s** 2 Pet 2:4
a of the church Rev 2:1

ANGEL OF THE LORD

a called to Abraham Gen 22:15
a took his stand Num 22:22
I have seen the **a** Judg 6:22
a destroying 1 Chr 21:12
a encamps around those Ps 34:7
a commanded him Matt 1:24
a appeared to Joseph Matt 2:13
a . . . opened the gates Acts 5:19

ANGER *indignation, wrath*

My **a** will be kindled Ex 22:24
Moses' **a** burned Ex 32:19
a with their idols 1 Kin 16:13
a kills the simple Job 5:2
not turn back His **a** Job 9:13
a is but for a moment Ps 30:5
He who is slow to **a** Prov 14:29
a man *given* to **a** Prov 22:24
a of the LORD Is 5:25
sun go down . . . **a** Eph 4:26
put . . . aside: **a** Col 3:8
slow to **a** James 1:19

ANGRY *enraged, indignant*

Why are you **a** Gen 4:6
lest He become **a** Ps 2:12
a man stirs up strife Prov 29:22
a beyond measure Is 64:9
and **a** no more Ezek 16:42
a with his brother Matt 5:22
Be **a** . . . do not sin Eph 4:26
a with this generation Heb 3:10

ANGUISH *distress, pain*

writhed in great **a** Esth 4:4
My heart is in **a** Ps 55:4
land of distress and **a** Is 30:6
A has seized us Jer 6:24
and **a** of heart 2 Cor 2:4

ANNIHILATE *destroy*

to **a** all the Jews Esth 3:13
My enemy **a-d** them Lam 2:22
to destroy and **a** Dan 11:44
let it be **a-d** Zech 11:9

ANNOUNCE *proclaim*

Who **a-s** peace Is 52:7
I shall **a** My words Jer 18:2
a-ing to . . . disciples John 20:18
a-d . . . the Righteous Acts 7:52

ANOINT (v) *sprinkle oil upon*

a them and ordain Ex 28:41
a Aaron and his sons Ex 30:30
LORD **a-ed** you king 1 Sam 15:17
a-ed my head with oil Ps 23:5
a the most holy *place* Dan 9:24
has **a-ed** My body Mark 14:8
did not **a** My head Luke 7:46
and **a-ed** my eyes John 9:11
a-ed . . . feet of Jesus John 12:3
a-ing him with oil James 5:14

ANOINTED (adj) *consecrated*

if the **a** priest sins Lev 4:3
not touch My **a** 1 Chr 16:22
a cherub who Ezek 28:14
the two **a** ones Zech 4:14

ANOINTED (n) *consecrated one*

walk before My **a** 1 Sam 2:35
he is the LORD's **a** 1 Sam 24:10
against His **A** Ps 2:2

ANOINTING (adj) *consecration*

spices for the **a** oil Ex 25:6
shall be a holy **a** oil Ex 30:31
for the LORD's **a** oil Lev 10:7

ANOINTING (n) *consecration*

a shall qualify them Ex 40:15
a from the Holy 1 John 2:20
His **a** teaches you 1 John 2:27

ANSWER (n) *response*

consider what **a** I 1 Chr 21:12
the king sent an **a** Ezra 4:17
Who gives a right **a** Prov 24:26
amazed at . . . His **a-s** Luke 2:47

ANSWER (v) *respond*

anyone who will **a** you Job 5:1
The LORD **a-ed** me Ps 118:5
king **a-ed** and said Dan 2:8
Jesus **a-ing** said Matt 3:15
who **a-s** back to God Rom 9:20

ANT *insect*

to the **a,** O sluggard Prov 6:6
a-s are not a strong Prov 30:25

ANTELOPE *animal*

Like an **a** in a net Is 51:20

ANTICHRIST *foe of Christ*

a-s have arisen 1 John 2:18
This is the **a** 1 John 2:22
the *spirit* of the **a** 1 John 4:3
deceiver and the **a** 2 John 7

ANTIOCH

1 *city in Syria* Acts 6:5;11:19,26
2 *city in Galatia* Acts 13:14; 14:19

ANTIPAS

1 *Pergamum martyr* Rev 2:13
2 *Herod Antipas*
see **HEROD**

ANXIOUS *concerned, worried*

and become **a** for us 1 Sam 9:5
not be **a** in . . . drought Jer 17:8
my spirit is **a** to Dan 2:3
not be **a** for your life Matt 6:25
not be **a** for tomorrow Matt 6:34
be **a** beforehand Mark 13:11
a can add a *single* Luke 12:25
Be **a** for nothing Phil 4:6

APOLLOS

Alexandrian Jew Acts 18:24
taught at Ephesus Acts 18:24
taught at Corinth 1 Cor 3:4,6

APOSTASY *faithlessness*

a-ies are numerous Jer 5:6
Turned away in . . . **a** Jer 8:5
I will heal their **a** Hos 14:4
unless the **a** comes 2 Thess 2:3

APOSTLE *one sent with authority*

the twelve **a-s** Matt 10:2
called *as* an **a** Rom 1:1
an **a** of Gentiles Rom 11:13
fit to be called an **a** 1 Cor 15:9
men are false **a-s** 2 Cor 11:13
He gave some *as* **a-s** Eph 4:11
Jesus, the **A** and Heb 3:1
a-s of the Lamb Rev 21:14

APOSTLESHIP *office of apostle*

received grace and **a** Rom 1:5
seal of my **a** 1 Cor 9:2
Peter in *his* **a** to Gal 2:8

APPEAL *ask, entreat*

standing and **a-ing** Acts 16:9
I **a** to Caesar Acts 25:11
Paul **a-ed** to be held Acts 25:21
a-ed to . . . Emperor Acts 25:25
a to *him* as a father 1 Tim 5:1
love's sake I . . . **a** Philem 9

APPEAR *become visible*

LORD **a-ed** to Abram Gen 12:7
glory of the LORD **a-ed** Ex 16:10
a-ed on the wings 2 Sam 22:11
and **a-ed** to many Matt 27:53
a-ed to them tongues Acts 2:3
we must all **a** before 2 Cor 5:10
a-ing of the glory Titus 2:13
shall **a** a second time Heb 9:28
Chief Shepherd **a-s** 1 Pet 5:4
not **a-ed** as yet 1 John 3:2

APPETITE *desire, hunger*

our **a** is gone Num 11:6
man of *great* **a** Prov 23:2
a is not satisfied Eccl 6:7
enlarged his **a** like Hab 2:5
whose god is *their* **a** Phil 3:19

APPLE *fruit*

as the **a** of the eye Ps 17:8
Like **a-s** of gold Prov 25:11
Refresh me with **a-s** Song 2:5
touches the **a** of His Zech 2:8

APPOINT *assign, commission*

shall **a** *as a penalty* Ex 21:23
I will **a** over you Lev 26:16
to **a** their relatives 1 Chr 15:16
a magistrates and Ezra 7:25
there is a harvest **a-ed** Hos 6:11
a-ed a preacher and 1 Tim 2:7
For the Law **a-s** men Heb 7:28

APPROVAL *consent*

loved the **a** of men John 12:43
give hearty **a** to Rom 1:32
men of old gained **a** Heb 11:2

APPROVE *accept, condone*

the Lord does not **a** Lam 3:36
too pure to **a** evil Hab 1:13
standing by **a-ing** Acts 22:20
and **a-d** by men Rom 14:18
present yourself **a-d** 2 Tim 2:15

AQUILA

a native of Pontus Acts 18:2
Corinthian Christian Acts 18:18
co-worker with Paul Rom 16:3

ARAB

1 *town in Judah* Josh 15:52
2 *ethnic identity* 1 Kin 10:15; Neh 2:19; Is 13:20

ARABAH

1 *desert steppe* Is 35:1,6; Jer 52:7
2 *Jordan rift valley* Deut 1:1; Josh 3:17
3 *Dead Sea* Josh 3:16; 2 Kin 14:25

ARABIA
land SE of Israel / Judah Is 21:13; Ezek 30:5; Gal 1:17;4:25

ARAM
1 *son of Shem* Gen 10:22,23
2 *line of Asher* 1 Chr 7:34
3 *ancestor of Jesus, shortened to Ram* Ruth 4:19; Matt 1:3; Luke 3:33
4 *Syria and N Mesopotamia* Num 23:7; 1 Kin 11:25; 2 Kin 13:19; Is 7:8

ARAMAIC
Semitic language 2 Kin 18:26; Ezra 4:7; Is 36:11; Dan 2:4

ARAMEANS
tribes of Aram 2 Sam 8:5; 1 Kin 20:20; 2 Kin 24:2

ARARAT
kingdom and mountain range in Armenia Gen 8:4; 2 Kin 19:37; Jer 51:27

ARAUNAH
Jebusite owner of threshing floor on Mt. Moriah 2 Sam 24:16,18
David purchases threshing floor for altar and later temple 2 Sam 24:23,24

ARCHANGEL
voice of *the* a 1 Thess 4:16
But Michael the a Jude 9

ARCHER *bowman*
the **a-s** hit him 1 Sam 31:3
a-s shot King Josiah 2 Chr 35:23
a-s equipped with bows Ps 78:9
an **a** who wounds Prov 26:10

ARGUE *dispute, question*
I will **a** my ways Job 13:15
hastily to **a** *a your case* Prov 25:8
Pharisees . . . **a** with Mark 8:11
scribes **a-ing** with Mark 9:14
a-ing with the . . . *Jews* Acts 9:29

ARGUMENT *disagreement*
Please hear my **a** Job 13:6
mouth are no **a-s** Ps 38:14
a arose among them Luke 9:46

ARIEL
1 *a Moabite* 2 Sam 23:20; 1 Chr 11:22
2 *applied to Jerusalem* Is 29:1ff
3 *sent by Ezra* Ezra 8:16

ARISE *rise, stand*
A, walk about the Gen 13:17
will **a** and play Deut 31:16
arose and tore his robe Job 1:20
when God **a-s** Job 31:14
A, O LORD; save me Ps 3:7
Though war **a** Ps 27:3
A, my darling Song 2:13
a-n *anyone* greater Matt 11:11
false prophets will **a** Matt 24:11
arose from the dead Acts 10:41
a from the dead Eph 5:14

ARK *chest, vessel*
a of gopher wood Gen 6:14
into the **a** to Noah Gen 7:9
a of acacia wood Ex 37:1
a of the covenant Josh 4:7
Noah entered the **a** Matt 24:38
a of His covenant Rev 11:19

ARM (n) *part of body*
the everlasting **a-s** Deut 33:27
a without strength Job 26:2
a seal on your **a** Song 8:6
be carried in the **a-s** Is 60:4
took . . . in His **a-s** Mark 10:16
with an uplifted **a** Acts 13:17

ARM (v) *mobilize*
A men from among Num 31:3
a-ed for battle Num 32:29
a-ed with iron 2 Sam 23:7
a yourselves also 1 Pet 4:1

ARMED (adj) *mobilized*
the **a** men went Josh 6:13
their **a** camps 1 Sam 28:1
So the **a** men left 2 Chr 28:14
like an **a** man Prov 6:11

ARMOR *protective device*
a joint of the **a** 1 Kin 22:34
strip off his outer **a** Job 41:13
put on . . . **a** of light Rom 13:12
full **a** of God Eph 6:11

ARMY *host, warriors*
not go out with the **a** Deut 24:5
like the **a** of God 1 Chr 12:22
a ready for battle 2 Chr 26:11
exceedingly great **a** Ezek 37:10
a-ies . . . in heaven Rev 19:14
and against His **a** Rev 19:19

AROUSE *raise, stir*
A Thyself to help me Ps 59:4
a-s for you the spirits Is 14:9
a-d one from the north Is 41:25
He will **a** *His* zeal Is 42:13
LORD has **a-d** the spirit Jer 51:11
Jews **a-d** the devout Acts 13:50

ARREST *restrain*
he **a-ed** Jeremiah Jer 37:13
Herod had John **a-ed** Matt 14:3
and clubs to **a** Me Matt 26:55
proceeded to **a** Peter Acts 12:3

ARROGANCE *pride*
your **a** has come 2 Kin 19:28
Pride and **a** and Prov 8:13
a, pride, and fury Is 16:6
a of your heart Jer 49:16
you boast in your **a** James 4:16

ARROGANT *proud*
a men have risen up Ps 86:14
But a fool is **a** Prov 14:16
a toward the LORD Jer 48:26
Knowledge makes **a** 1 Cor 8:1
speaking . . . **a** *words* 2 Pet 2:18

ARROW *dart, missile*
shot an **a** past him 1 Sam 20:36
a-s of the Almighty Job 6:4
make ready their **a** Ps 11:2
broke the flaming **a-s** Ps 76:3
sword and a sharp **a** Prov 25:18
tongue is a deadly **a** Jer 9:8
deadly **a-s** of famine Ezek 5:16

ART *craft*
with their secret **a-s** Ex 7:22
the perfumers' **a** 2 Chr 16:14

ARTAXERXES
Persian king Ezra 4:7,8;7:1,12; Neh 2:1;5:14

ARTEMIS
Greek goddess Acts 19:24ff

ASA
1 *king of Judah* 1 Kin 15:8-24; 2 Chr 14:8-15
2 *a Levite* 1 Chr 9:16

ASCEND *go up*
a into the hill Ps 24:3
If I **a** to heaven Ps 139:8
Who has **a-ed** into Prov 30:4
breath of man **a-s** Eccl 3:21
has **a-ed** into heaven John 3:13
Son of Man **a-ing** John 6:62
a-ed to the Father John 20:17
who **a-ed** far above Eph 4:10

ASCENT *hill, rise*
by the **a** of Heres Judg 8:13
a of the . . . Olives 2 Sam 15:30
Song of **A-s** Ps 120-134

ASH
but dust and **a-es** Gen 18:27
from the **a** heap 1 Sam 2:8
a-es on her head 2 Sam 13:19
a-es were poured 1 Kin 13:5
proverbs of **a-es** Job 13:12
repent in dust and **a-es** Job 42:6
garland instead of **a-es** Is 61:3
roll in **a-es** Jer 6:26
sackcloth and **a-es** Luke 10:13
a-es of a heifer Heb 9:13

ASHAMED *embarrassed*
naked and were not **a** Gen 2:25
Let me never be **a** Ps 71:1
a of Me . . . My words Mark 8:38
a when He comes Luke 9:26
not **a** of the gospel Rom 1:16
a of the testimony 2 Tim 1:8
God is not **a** Heb 11:16
let him not feel **a** 1 Pet 4:16

ASHDOD
Philistine city Josh 15:47; 1 Sam 5:1,6; Amos 1:8

ASHER
1 *eighth son of Jacob* Gen 35:26;49:20
2 *tribe of Israel* Num 1:41;13:13; Rev 7:6
3 *town in hill country* Josh 17:7

ASHERAH
Canaanite goddess and symbol Deut 16:21; Judg 6:25
Asherim (pl) 1 Kin 14:15; Mic 5:14
Asheroth (pl) Judg 3:7; 2 Chr 19:3

ASHKELON
Philistine city Judg 1:18; 2 Sam 1:20; Jer 47:5; Zeph 2:4

ASHTORETH
1 *Near Eastern goddess* 1 Kin 11:5,33; 2 Kin 23:13
Ashtaroth (pl) Judg 2:13; 1 Sam 7:4;31:10
2 *town of Bashan in E Manasseh* Deut 1:4; Josh 13:12

ASIA
Roman province of Asia Minor Acts 6:9; Rom 16:5; Rev 1:4

ASK *appeal, beg, inquire*
whatever you **a** Ruth 3:11
Two things I **a-ed** Prov 30:7
A a sign for yourself Is 7:11
A rain from the LORD Zech 10:1
Give to him who **a-s** Matt 5:42
A, and it shall be Matt 7:7
a . . . believing Matt 21:22
pray and **a**, believe Mark 11:24
Jews **a** for signs 1 Cor 1:22
let him **a** of God James 1:5

ASLEEP *dead, resting*
sound **a** . . . exhausted Judg 4:21
they fall **a** Ps 90:5
not died, but is **a** Matt 9:24
in the stern, **a** Mark 4:38
Lazarus . . . fallen **a** John 11:11
said this, he fell **a** Acts 7:60
fallen **a** in Jesus 1 Thess 4:14

ASSEMBLE *gather*
a all the congregation Lev 8:3
David **a-d** all Israel 1 Chr 13:5
peoples may be **a-d** Is 43:9
A . . . on the mountains Amos 3:9
I will . . . **a** all of you Mic 2:12
whole city **a-d** to Acts 13:44
a-d to make war Rev 19:19

ASSEMBLY *congregation*
holy **a** on the seventh Ex 12:16
the people of the **a** Lev 16:33

a before the rock	Num 20:10
a of the righteous	Ps 1:5
hate the **a** of evildoers	Ps 26:5
the **a** was divided	Acts 23:7
general **a** and church	Heb 12:23
comes into your **a**	James 2:2

ASSOCIATE (n) *colleague*

All my **a-s** abhor me	Job 19:19
high priest and . . . **a-s**	Acts 5:21

ASSOCIATE (v) *identify with*

shall they **a** with	1 Kin 11:2
a with adulterers	Ps 50:18
not **a** with a man	Prov 22:24
dared to **a** with them	Acts 5:13
but **a** with the lowly	Rom 12:16
not **a** with him	2 Thess 3:14

ASSURANCE *confirmation*

no one has **a** of life	Job 24:22
a of understanding	Col 2:2
full **a** of hope	Heb 6:11
full **a** of faith	Heb 10:22
a of *things* hoped for	Heb 11:1

ASSYRIA

kingdom name from Asshur	Gen 10:22; 1 Chr 1:17
empire in upper Mesopotamia	2 Kin 19:17; Is 19:24; Jer 2:36

ASTONISHED *amazed*

will be **a** and hiss	1 Kin 9:8
a at His teaching	Matt 22:33
listeners were **a**	Mark 6:2
were utterly **a**	Mark 7:37
they were all **a**	Luke 1:63

ASTOUNDED *astonished*

prophets will be **a**	Jer 4:9
a at the vision	Dan 8:27
were completely **a**	Mark 5:24

ASTRAY *erring, wandering*

a like a lost sheep	Ps 119:176
like sheep have gone **a**	Is 53:6
led My people **a**	Jer 23:32
lead the elect **a**	Mark 13:22
a from the faith	1 Tim 6:21
go **a** in their heart	Heb 3:10
My bond-servants **a**	Rev 2:20

ATHENS

leading Greek city	Acts 17:15ff

ATONEMENT *expiation, reconcilliation*

by which **a** was made	Ex 29:33
shall make **a** for him	Lev 4:35
a before the LORD	Lev 14:31
how can I make **a**	2 Sam 21:3
make **a** for iniquity	Dan 9:24

ATTACK (n) *assault*

at the first **a**	2 Sam 17:9
king ready for the **a**	Job 15:24
joined in the **a**	Acts 24:9

ATTACK (v) *assault, fall upon*

lest he come and **a**	Gen 32:11
adversary who **a-s**	Num 10:9
and **a-ed** the camp	Judg 8:11
a the Philistines	1 Sam 23:2
it **a-ed** the plant	Jon 4:7
no man will **a** you	Acts 18:10

ATTEND *pay attention to*

a to your priesthood	Num 18:7
thousands were **a-ing**	Dan 7:10
who **a** regularly	1 Cor 9:13
a to . . . business	1 Thess 4:11
ears **a** to their prayer	1 Pet 3:12

ATTENDANT *helper, servant*

the **a** of Moses	Num 11:28
king's **a-s**, who served	Esth 2:2
a-s of . . . bridegroom	Mark 2:19

ATTENTION *heed, regard*

no **a** to false words	Ex 5:9
pays **a** to falsehood	Prov 29:12
they do not pay **a**	Is 5:12
pay **a** to myths	1 Tim 1:4
a to the . . . reading	1 Tim 4:13

ATTIRE *covering, dress*

in his military **a**	2 Sam 20:8
cupbearers . . . **a**	2 Chr 9:4
Him in holy **a**	2 Chr 20:21

ATTITUDE *frame of mind*

see your father's **a**	Gen 31:5
a of the righteous	Luke 1:17
Have this **a** in	Phil 2:5
have a different **a**	Phil 3:15

AUGUSTUS

name of Caesar Octavianus	Luke 2:1
see **CAESAR**	

AUTHORITY *power, right*

submit . . . to her **a**	Gen 16:9
put . . . your **a** on him	Num 27:20
Who gave Him **a**	Job 34:13
entrust him with your **a**	Is 22:21
as *one* having **a**	Matt 7:29
a on earth to forgive	Matt 9:6
a over unclean spirits	Matt 10:1
All **a** . . . given to Me	Matt 28:18
Son of Man has **a**	Luke 5:24
no **a** except from God	Rom 13:1
majesty, dominion . . . **a**	Jude 25
give **a** over . . . nations	Rev 2:26

AVENGE *get revenge*

He will **a** the blood	Deut 32:43
the LORD **a** me	1 Sam 24:12
Shall I not **a** Myself	Jer 5:9
I will **a** their blood	Joel 3:21
a-ing our blood	Rev 6:10

AVENGER *one seeking revenge*

The blood **a** himself	Num 35:19
lest the **a** of blood	Deut 19:6
a of their *evil* deeds	Ps 99:8
God, an **a** who brings	Rom 13:4
Lord is *the* **a**	1 Thess 4:6

AWAKE *be attentive, become alert*

awoke from his sleep	Gen 28:16
A, a, Deborah	Judg 5:12
Thy likeness when I **a**	Ps 17:15
dream when one **a-s**	Ps 73:20
arouse or **a-n** *my* love	Song 2:7
He **a-ns** My ear	Is 50:4
A, a, put on strength	Is 51:9
A, drunkards . . . weep	Joel 1:5
that I may **a-n** him	John 11:11
hour for you to **a-n**	Rom 13:11

AWE *fear, reverence*

stand in **a** of Him	Ps 33:8
in **a** of Thy words	Ps 119:161
in **a** of My name	Mal 2:5
feeling a sense of **a**	Acts 2:43

AWESOME *fearful*

How **a** is this place	Gen 28:17
angel of God, very **a**	Judg 13:6
great and **a** God	Neh 1:5
God is **a** majesty	Job 37:22
As **a** as an army	Song 6:4
a day of the LORD	Joel 2:31

AZARIAH

1 *ancestor of Samuel*	1 Chr 6:36
2 *official of Solomon*	1 Kin 4:2
3 *son of Nathan*	1 Kin 4:5
4 *prophet*	2 Chr 15:1-8
5 *two sons of king Jehoshaphat*	2 Chr 21:2
6 *king of Judah, also* **Uzziah**	2 Kin 15:1; 2 Chr 26:1
7 *high priest*	1 Chr 6:10
8 *family of Merari*	2 Chr 29:12
9 *son of Hilkiah*	1 Chr 6:13,14
10 *original name of Abed-nego*	Dan 1:7
the name of twelve other individuals in the OT	

B

BAAL

1 *Canaanite god(s)*	Num 22:41; Judg 6:25; 1 Kin 18:40
2 *line of Reuben*	1 Chr 5:5
3 *personal name*	1 Chr 8:30
4 *place name*	1 Chr 4:33

BAASHA

king of Israel	1 Kin 15:16,32

BABEL *a city*

founded by Nimrod later called Babylon	Gen 10:10;11:9

BABY *infant*

b leaped . . . her womb	Luke 1:41
b wrapped in cloths	Luke 2:12
b as He lay	Luke 2:16

BABYLON *city*

1 *on the Euphrates*	2 Kin 17:24; Jer 20:4; Ezek 29:18; Dan 4:29
2 *symbolic of godlessness*	Rev 14:8;17:5

BAD *evil, wrong, spoiled*

b report of the land	Num 13:32
basket had very **b** figs	Jer 24:2
if your eye is **b**	Matt 6:23
b tree bears **b** fruit	Matt 7:18
B company corrupts	1 Cor 15:33

BAG *sack*

fill their **b-s**	Gen 42:25
in the shepherd's **b**	1 Sam 17:40
silver in two **b-s**	2 Kin 5:23
carrying *his* **b** of seed	Ps 126:6
b of . . . weights	Mic 6:11
Carry no purse, no **b**	Luke 10:4

BAGGAGE *bags, supplies*

stayed with the **b**	1 Sam 25:13
prepare . . . yourself **b**	Ezek 12:3

BAKE *cook*

b-d unleavened bread	Gen 19:3
b-d food for Pharaoh	Gen 40:17
they **b-d** the dough	Ex 12:39
B what you will **b**	Ex 16:23
grain offering **b-d**	Lev 2:4
b twelve cakes	Lev 24:5
taste of cakes **b-d**	Num 11:8
fire to **b** bread	Is 44:15

BAKER *cook*

b for the king	Gen 40:1
cooks and **b-s**	1 Sam 8:13
from the **b-s'** street	Jer 37:21
oven heated by the **b**	Hos 7:4

BALAAM

diviner	Num 22:5-31;23:5; Josh 13:22; Rev 2:14

BALAK

king of Moab	Num 22:4; Mic 6:5

BALANCE *scale*

shall have just **b-s**	Lev 19:36
b-s . . . with my iniquity	Job 6:2
False **b** is an	Prov 11:1
mountains in a **b**	Is 40:12

BALD *hairless*

if . . . head becomes **b**	Lev 13:41
every head is **b**	Jer 48:37
head was made **b**	Ezek 29:18

BALSAM *aromatic gum*

tops of the **b** trees	2 Sam 5:24
like a bed of **b**	Song 5:13

BAN *set apart to God, cursed*

city . . . under the **b**	Josh 6:17
destroy . . . under the **b**	Josh 7:12
who violated the **b**	1 Chr 2:7
consign Jacob to the **b**	Is 43:28

BAND *bond* or *group*
b-s *shall be* of silver Ex 27:10
skillfully woven **b** Ex 28:8
saw a marauding **b** 2 Kin 13:21
b of destroying angels Ps 78:49
b-s of the yoke Is 58:6

BANISH *exile*
b-ed one may not 2 Sam 14:14
assemble the **b-ed** Is 11:12
gaiety . . . is **b-ed** Is 24:11
where I shall **b** them Ezek 4:13

BANNER *flag, standard*
set up our **b-s** Ps 20:5
b to those who fear Ps 60:4
b over me is love Song 2:4
as an army with **b-s** Song 6:4

BANQUET *dinner, feast*
b lasting seven days Esth 1:5
brought me to *his* **b** Song 2:4
lavish **b** for all Is 25:6
place of honor at **b-s** Matt 23:6
Herod . . . gave a **b** Mark 6:21

BAPTISM *symbolic washing*
Sadducees coming . . . **b** Matt 3:7
b of repentance Mark 1:4
b with which I am Mark 10:38
with the **b** of John Luke 7:29
a **b** to undergo Luke 12:50
through **b** into death Rom 6:4
one faith, one **b** Eph 4:5
buried with Him in **b** Col 2:12

BAPTIZE *wash symbolically*
b . . . Holy Spirit Matt 3:11
tax-gatherers . . . **b-d** Luke 3:12
Jesus also was **b-d** Luke 3:21
sent me to **b** in water John 1:33
b-ing more disciples John 4:1
b-d with the Holy Acts 1:5
he arose and was **b-d** Acts 9:18
household . . . been **b-d** Acts 16:15
John **b-d** with the Acts 19:4
b-d into Christ Jesus Rom 6:3
b-d into Moses 1 Cor 10:2
b-d into one body 1 Cor 12:13
b-d for the dead 1 Cor 15:29

BARABBAS
robber Matt 27:16; Luke 23:18
released by Pilate Matt 27:26

BARBARIAN *non-Hellenic*
obligation . . . to **b-s** Rom 1:14
who speaks a **b** 1 Cor 14:11
b, Scythian, slave Col 3:11

BAREFOOT *without sandals*
priests walk **b** Job 12:19
gone naked and **b** Is 20:3

BAR-JESUS
magician Acts 13:6
also **Elymas**

BARLEY *grain*
land of wheat and **b** Deut 8:8
beginning . . . **b** harvest Ruth 1:22
stinkweed instead . . . **b** Job 31:40
has five **b** loaves John 6:9

BARN *farm building*
b-s are torn down Joel 1:17
seed still in the **b** Hag 2:19
nor gather into **b-s** Matt 6:26
tear down my **b-s** Luke 12:18

BARNABAS
Cyprian by birth Acts 4:36
introduced Paul Acts 9:27
co-worker with Paul Acts 13:2,7
separated from Paul Acts 15:39

BARREN *childless, sterile*
Sarai was **b** Gen 11:30
but Rachel was **b** Gen 29:31
Shout . . . O **b** one Is 54:1

Blessed are the **b** Luke 23:29

BARSABBAS
1 *Apostolic candidate, also called Joseph and Justus* Acts 1:23
2 *colleague of Paul, also called Judas* Acts 15:22

BARTHOLOMEW
apostle Matt 10:3; Luke 6:14; Acts 1:13

BARTIMAEUS
healed by Jesus Mark 10:46

BARUCH
1 *scribe* Jer 36:26;43:6
2 *priest* Neh 3:20
3 *a Judean* Neh 11:5

BASEMATH
1 *Esau's wife* Gen 26:34
2 *daughter of Solomon* 1 Kin 4:15

BASHAN
land E of Jordan Num 21:33; Josh 13:11; Is 2:13

BATH *measure of capacity*
two thousand **b-s** 1 Kin 7:26
100 **b-s** of oil Ezra 7:22
only one **b** *of wine* Is 5:10
a tenth of a **b** from Ezek 45:14

BATHSHEBA
wife of Uriah 2 Sam 11:3
taken by David 2 Sam 11:4
wife of David 2 Sam 11:27
mother of Solomon 2 Sam 12:24

BATTLE (n) *conflict, war*
b is the LORD's 1 Sam 17:47
b is . . . God's 2 Chr 20:15
scents the **b** from afar Job 39:25
with strength for **b** Ps 18:39
noise of **b** is in Jer 50:22
another king in **b** Luke 14:31
horses prepared for **b** Rev 9:7

BATTLE (v) *fight*
b against the sons Judg 20:14
drew near to **b** 1 Sam 7:10
about to go to **b** 1 Chr 12:19
nations . . . to **b** Zech 14:2

BEACH *coast*
multitude . . . on the **b** Matt 13:2
Jesus stood on the **b** John 21:4
down on the **b** Acts 21:5

BEAM *log*
like a weaver's **b** 2 Sam 21:19
one was felling a **b** 2 Kin 6:5
b-s, the thresholds 2 Chr 3:7
b-s of His . . . chambers Ps 104:3

BEAR (n) *animal*
b came and took 1 Sam 17:34
b robbed of . . . cubs Prov 17:12
the **b** will graze Is 11:7
resembling a **b** Dan 7:5

BEAR (v) *sustain, carry, produce*
too great to **b** Gen 4:13
not **b** false witness Ex 20:16
LORD . . . **b-s** our burden Ps 68:19
b the penalty Ezek 23:49
John **bore** witness John 1:15
it **b-s** much fruit John 12:24
you *will* **b** witness John 15:27
b-ing His own cross John 19:17
b fruit for God Rom 7:4
Spirit . . . **b-s** witness Rom 8:16
B . . . another's burdens Gal 6:2
b the sins of many Heb 9:28
bore our sins 1 Pet 2:24

BEARD *whiskers*
infection . . . on the **b** Lev 13:29
seized *him* by . . . **b** 1 Sam 17:35
shaved . . . their **b-s** 2 Sam 10:4

until your **b-s** grow 1 Chr 19:5

BEARER *carrier*
the **b-s** of the ark 2 Sam 6:13
strength of . . . **b-s** Neh 4:10
b of good news Is 40:9

BEAST *animal, creature*
God formed every **b** Gen 2:19
Noah and all the **b-s** Gen 8:1
b of the forest Ps 50:10
b also had four heads Dan 7:6
they worshiped the **b** Rev 13:4
mark of the **b** Rev 16:2

BEAT *hit, strike*
b-ing a Hebrew Ex 2:11
b out what she Ruth 2:17
B your plowshares Joel 3:10
b Him with their Matt 26:67
b-ing His head with Mark 15:19
b-ing his breast Luke 18:13
b-en us in public Acts 16:37
stopped **b-ing** Paul Acts 21:32

BEAUTIFUL *lovely, pleasing*
daughters . . . were **b** Gen 6:2
Rachel was **b** Gen 29:17
foliage of **b** trees Lev 23:40
Most **b** among women Song 1:8
Branch . . . will be **b** Is 4:2
Your **b** sheep Jer 13:20
enter the **B** Land Dan 11:41
How **b** are the feet Rom 10:15

BEAUTY
Your **b** . . . is slain 2 Sam 1:19
behold the **b** of the LORD Ps 27:4
Zion . . . perfection of **b** Ps 50:2
b is vain Prov 31:30
see the King in His **b** Is 33:17

BED *pallet*
My **b** will comfort me Job 7:13
remember . . . on my **b** Ps 63:6
in **b** with a fever Matt 8:14
take up your **b** Matt 9:6
lamp . . . under a **b** Mark 4:21

BEELZEBUL
N.T. prince of the demons Matt 12:27; Luke 11:15

BEERSHEBA
well / town in Negev Gen 21:31; Judg 20:1
home of Abraham Gen 22:19
home of Isaac Gen 26:23

BEG *appeal, ask*
children wander . . . **b** Ps 109:10
b-s during . . . harvest Prov 20:4
b You to look at Luke 9:38
I am ashamed to **b** Luke 16:3
who used to sit and **b** John 9:8
b-ging them to leave Acts 16:39

BEGINNING *origin, starting*
In the **b** God created Gen 1:1
b was insignificant Job 8:7
fear of the LORD . . . **b** Ps 111:10
The **b** of the gospel Mark 1:1
In the **b** was the Word John 1:1
This **b** of *His* signs John 2:11
He is the **b** Col 1:18
the **b** and the end Rev 21:6

BEGOTTEN (adj) *born*
b from the Father John 1:14
the only **b** God John 1:18
gave His only **b** Son John 3:16
only **b** Son of God John 3:18
offering . . . only **b** Heb 11:17
sent His only **b** Son 1 John 4:9

BEHAVE *act*
David **b-d** himself 1 Sam 18:30
b-ing as a madman 1 Sam 21:14
b properly as in Rom 13:13
blamelessly we **b-d** 1 Thess 2:10

BEHAVIOR *conduct*
instruction in wise **b** Prov 1:3
reverent in their **b** Titus 2:3
holy . . . in all *your* **b** 1 Pet 1:15
the **b** of their wives 1 Pet 3:1

BEHEADED *cut off the head*
killed him and **b** him 2 Sam 4:7
John **b** in the prison Matt 14:10
John, whom I **b** Mark 6:16
b because of the Rev 20:4

BEHEMOTH
hippopotamus Job 40:15

BEING *existence, life*
man became a living **b** Gen 2:7
a . . . **b** coming up 1 Sam 28:13
wisdom in the . . . **b** Job 38:36
truth in the . . . **b** Ps 51:6
four living **b-s** Ezek 1:5
resembled a . . . **b** Dan 10:16

BEL
Babylonian god, related to Baal Jer 50:2;51:44

BELA
1 *king of Edom* Gen 36:32
2 *son of Benjamin* Gen 46:21; 1 Chr 8:1
3 *a Rubenite* 1 Chr 5:8
4 *city of the plain near the Dead Sea* Gen 14:2,8
also **ZOAR**

BELIEVE *have faith, trust*
he **b-d** in the LORD Gen 15:6
did not **b** in God Ps 78:22
you **b** that I am able Matt 9:28
ask in prayer, **b-ing** Matt 21:22
repent and **b** Mark 1:15
they **b-d** . . . Scripture John 2:22
whoever **b-s** in Him John 3:16
will you **b** My words John 5:47
who **b-s** has eternal John 6:47
men will **b** in Him John 11:48
b in the light John 12:36
not see, and *yet* **b-d** John 20:29
B in the Lord Jesus Acts 16:31
Abraham **b-d** God Rom 4:3
how shall they **b** Rom 10:14
love . . . **b-s** all 1 Cor 13:7
whom I have **b-d** 2 Tim 1:12
comes to God must **b** Heb 11:6
demons also **b** James 2:19
do not **b** every spirit 1 John 4:1

BELIEVERS *faithful ones*
all the circumcised **b** Acts 10:45
example to all the **b** 1 Thess 1:7
toward you **b** 1 Thess 2:10

BELLY *stomach*
On your **b** . . . you go Gen 3:14
crawls on its **b** Lev 11:42
b of the sea monster Matt 12:40

BELOVED *dearly loved*
b of the LORD dwell Deut 33:12
gives to His **b** *even* Ps 127:2
b is like a gazelle Song 2:9
This is My **b** Son Matt 3:17
your upbuilding, **b** 2 Cor 12:19
stand firm . . . my **b** Phil 4:1
Luke, the **b** physician Col 4:14
slave, a **b** brother Philem 16
the called, **b** in God Jude 1

BELSHAZZAR
ruler of Babylon Dan 5:1;7:1

BELT *waistband*
the **b** of the strong Job 12:21
Paul's **b** and bound Acts 21:11

BELTESHAZZAR
Daniel's Babylonian name Dan 1:7;2:26;5:12;10:1

BENAIAH
1 *son of Jehoiada* 2 Sam 8:18
captain of David 2 Sam 23:23
2 *Levitical singer* 1 Chr 15:18,20
3 *a priest* 1 Chr 15:24;16:5
the name of nine other individuals in the OT

BENEFIT *blessing, profit*
no return for the **b** 2 Chr 32:25
forget none of His **b-s** Ps 103:2
His **b-s** toward me Ps 116:12
the **b** of circumcision Rom 3:1

BEN-HADAD
1 *Ben-hadad I* 1 Kin 15:18-21
2 *Ben-hadad II* 1 Kin 20,22
3 *Ben-hadad III* 2 Kin 8:7-15;13:22

BENJAMIN
1 *son of Jacob* Gen 35:18
2 *tribe* Num 2:22
3 *of clan of Jediael* 1 Chr 7:10
4 *of the restoration* Neh 3:23

BEREA
city in Macedonia visited by Paul Acts 17:10,13

BEREAVE *deprive, make sad*
be **b-d** of you both Gen 27:45
b . . . of your children Lev 26:22
I will **b** *them* Jer 15:7
longer **b** your nation Ezek 36:14

BERODACH-BALADAN
king of Babylon 2 Kin 20:12
also **Merodach-Baladan**

BESEECH *ask earnestly*
LORD, I **b** Thee Ps 116:4
do save, we **b** Thee Ps 118:25
leper came . . . **b-ing** Mark 1:40
b the Lord of the Luke 10:2

BESIEGE *assail, surround*
When you **b** a city Deut 20:19
enemies **b** them 2 Chr 6:28
was **b-ing** Jerusalem Jer 32:2
b-d . . . with bitterness Lam 3:5

BESTOWED *granted*
that the Spirit was **b** Acts 8:18
which He freely **b** Eph 1:6
b on Him the name Phil 2:9
love the Father has **b** 1 John 3:1

BETHANY
1 *E of Jerusalem* Matt 21:17
home of Mary, Martha and Lazarus John 11:1,18
2 *where John baptized* John 1:28

BETHEL
town in Benjamin Gen 12:8
N of Jerusalem Josh 8:17

BETHESDA
pool in Jerusalem John 5:2

BETH-HORON
1 *famous battle site pass NW of Jerusalem* Josh 10:10,11
2 *two towns at both ends of mountain pass* Josh 16:3,5

BETHLEHEM
1 *town S of Jerusalem* Gen 35:19
home of Ruth and Boaz Ruth 4:11
birthplace of Jesus Matt 2:1
2 *Zebulunite village* Josh 19:15

BETHPHAGE
village on the Mount of Olives Matt 21:1; Mark 11:1

BETHSAIDA
village on Sea of Galilee Mark 8:22; Luke 9:10
home of Philip, Andrew and Peter John 1:44

BETH-SHAN / BETH-SHEAN
city at junction of Jezreel and Jordan valleys Josh 17:11; 1 Kin 4:12; 1 Chr 7:29

BETH-SHEMESH
1 *city of Judah* Josh 15:10
2 *Issachar border city* Josh 19:22
3 *city of Naphtali* Josh 19:38

BETRAY *break faith with, expose*
do not **b** the fugitive Is 16:3
wine **b-s** the haughty Hab 2:5
how to **b** Him Mark 14:11
one . . . will **b** Me Mark 14:18
Judas, are you **b-ing** Luke 22:48

BETROTH *promise to wed*
You shall **b** a wife Deut 28:30
I will **b** you to Me Hos 2:19
Mary had been **b-ed** Matt 1:18
I **b-ed** you to one 2 Cor 11:2

BEZALEL
1 *architect of tabernacle* Ex 31:1ff
2 *Israelite* Ezra 10:30

BEZER
1 *son of Zophah* 1 Chr 7:37
2 *city of refuge* Josh 20:8

BIND *fasten, secure*
bound his son Isaac Gen 22:9
b them as a sign Deut 6:8
b-s up their wounds Ps 147:3
B up the testimony Is 8:16
b up the brokenhearted Is 61:1
shall **b** on earth Matt 16:19
and **bound** Him John 18:12
bound . . . a thousand Rev 20:2

BIRD *fowl*
eat any clean **b** Deut 14:20
b-s of the heavens Ps 8:8
snare of a **b** catcher Hos 9:8
b-s . . . *have* nests Luke 9:58

BIRTH *event of being born*
A time to give **b** Eccl 3:2
You gave me **b** Jer 2:27
b of Jesus Christ Matt 1:18
rejoice at his **b** Luke 1:14
a man blind from **b** John 9:1

BIRTHDAY *day of birth*
was Pharaoh's **b** Gen 40:20
Herod's **b** came Matt 14:6
his **b** . . . banquet Mark 6:21

BIRTHRIGHT *first-born rights*
First sell me your **b** Gen 25:31
He took away my **b** Gen 27:36
sold his own **b** Heb 12:16

BITHYNIA
territory on the Bosporus in Asia Minor Acts 16:7; 1 Pet 1:1

BITTER *painful, unpleasant*
b with hard labor Ex 1:14
waters of Marah . . . **b** Ex 15:23
b speech *as* their arrow Ps 64:3
substitute **b** for sweet Is 5:20
Strong drink is **b** Is 24:9
fresh and **b** *water* James 3:11

BITTERNESS *unpleasantness*
in the **b** of my soul Job 10:1
because of the **b** Is 38:15
full of cursing and **b** Rom 3:14
all **b** . . . be put away Eph 4:31
no root of **b** Heb 12:15

BLAME *fault, responsibility*
let me bear the **b** Gen 43:9
bear the **b** . . . forever Gen 44:32

BLAMELESS *faultless*
show Thyself **b** 2 Sam 22:26
just *and* **b** *man* is a Job 12:4
His way is **b** Ps 18:30

b will inherit good Prov 28:10
holy and **b** before Him Eph 1:4
in the Law, found **b** Phil 3:6
spotless and **b** 2 Pet 3:14

BLASPHEME *curse*
enemies . . . to **b** 2 Sam 12:14
name is continually **b-d** Is 52:5
This *fellow* **b-s** Matt 9:3
b-s . . . Holy Spirit Mark 3:29
force them to **b** Acts 26:11
name of God is **b-d** Rom 2:24
taught not to **b** 1 Tim 1:20

BLASPHEMY *cursing, profanity*
b against the Spirit Matt 12:31
b-ies they utter Mark 3:28
You . . . heard the **b** Mark 14:64
man . . . speaks **b-ies** Luke 5:21
stone You . . . for **b** John 10:33

BLEMISH *imperfection, spot*
there is no **b** in you Song 4:7
six lambs without **b** Ezek 46:4
Himself without **b** Heb 9:14
stains and **b-es** 2 Pet 2:13

BLESS (v) *bestow favor or praise*
God **b-ed** the . . . day Gen 2:3
LORD **b-ed** the sabbath Ex 20:11
and **b** Thine inheritance Ps 28:9
LORD will **b** His people Ps 29:11
B the LORD Ps 103:2
generous will be **b-ed** Prov 22:9
rise up and **b** her Prov 31:28
b-ed of My Father Matt 25:34
He **b-ed** *the food* Mark 6:41
b . . . who curse you Luke 6:28
you are **b-ed** if you John 13:17
b . . . who persecute Rom 12:14
we **b** *our* Lord James 3:9

BLESSED (adj) *favored, happy*
b be God Most High Gen 14:20
B are you, O Israel Deut 33:29
How **b** is the man Ps 127:5
b . . . who finds wisdom Prov 3:13
nations will call you **b** Mal 3:12
B are the poor in Matt 5:3
B *is* the . . . kingdom Mark 11:10
B among women *are* Luke 1:42
more **b** to give Acts 20:35
looking for . . . **b** hope Titus 2:13

BLESSING (n) *God's favor*
you shall be a **b** Gen 12:2
a **b** and a curse Deut 11:26
curse into a **b** Neh 13:2
b of the LORD be upon Ps 129:8
showers of **b** Ezek 34:26
pour out for you a **b** Mal 3:10
cup of **b** which we 1 Cor 10:16
inherit a **b** 1 Pet 3:9
honor and glory and **b** Rev 5:12

BLIND (adj) *sightless*
misleads a **b** *person* Deut 27:18
To open **b** eyes Is 42:7
b . . . guides a **b** man Matt 15:14
b beggar *named* Mark 10:46
b man was sitting Luke 18:35
I was **b**, now I see John 9:25

BLIND (n) *without sight*
block before the **b** Lev 19:14
I was eyes to the **b** Job 29:15
the **b** receive sight Matt 11:5
a guide to the **b** Rom 2:19

BLIND (v) *make sightless*
b-s the clear-sighted Ex 23:8
bribe to **b** my eyes 1 Sam 12:3
has **b-ed** the minds 2 Cor 4:4
darkness has **b-ed** 1 John 2:11

BLOOD
Whoever sheds man's **b** Gen 9:6
bridegroom of **b** Ex 4:25
b shall be a sign Ex 12:13
not eat . . . any **b** Lev 3:17
b did not reveal Matt 16:17
covenant in My **b** Luke 22:20
sweat . . . drops of **b** Luke 22:44
Field of **B** Acts 1:19
the moon into **b** Acts 2:20
justified by His **b** Rom 5:9
sharing in the **b** 1 Cor 10:16
redemption . . . His **b** Eph 1:7
b, as of a lamb 1 Pet 1:19
b of the saints Rev 17:6

BLOODGUILTINESS
no **b** on his account Ex 22:2
b shall be forgiven Deut 21:8
Deliver me from **b** Ps 51:14

BLOODSHED *killing, murder*
abhors the man of **b** Ps 5:6
Men of **b** hate Prov 29:10
the **b** of Jerusalem Is 4:4
b follows **b** Hos 4:2

BLOSSOM *bloom*
the almond tree **b-s** Eccl 12:5
Israel will **b** and sprout Is 27:6
arrogance has **b-ed** Ezek 7:10

BLOT *erase*
I will **b** out man Gen 6:7
b me . . . from Thy book Ex 32:32
b out their name Deut 9:14
b out all my iniquities Ps 51:9
works . . . be **b-ted** out Ezek 6:6

BLUE *color*
tent of **b** and purple Ex 26:36
ephod all of **b** Ex 28:31
royal robes of **b** Esth 8:15

BOANERGES
name of James and John Mark 3:17

BOAST (n) *bragging*
soul shall make its **b** Ps 34:2
the **b** of our hope Heb 3:6

BOAST (v) *brag, glory*
B no more so 1 Sam 2:3
b in the LORD Ps 34:2
who **b-s** of his gifts Prov 25:14
not **b** about tomorrow Prov 27:1
let not a rich man **b** Jer 9:23
b in God Rom 2:17
who **b** in the Law Rom 2:23
b . . . my weaknesses 2 Cor 12:9
it **b-s** of great things James 3:5

BOAT *watercraft*
slip by like reed **b-s** Job 9:26
left the **b** and their Matt 4:22
Peter got out of . . . **b** Matt 14:29
filled both of the **b-s** Luke 5:7
disciples into the **b** John 6:22

BOAZ
1 *husband of Ruth* Ruth 4:13
grandfather of David Ruth 4:17ff
2 *temple pillar* 2 Chr 3:17

BODY *corpse, flesh*
b cleaves to the earth Ps 44:25
perfume upon My **b** Matt 26:12
this is My **b** Mark 14:22
did not find His **b** Luke 24:23
b of sin . . . done away Rom 6:6
present your **b-ies** Rom 12:1
b-ies are members 1 Cor 6:15
b is a temple 1 Cor 6:19
you are Christ's **b** 1 Cor 12:27
b to be burned 1 Cor 13:3
absent from the **b** 2 Cor 5:8
one **b** and one Spirit Eph 4:4
building up of the **b** Eph 4:12
transform the **b** Phil 3:21
b be preserved 1 Thess 5:23
bore . . . sins in His **b** 1 Pet 2:24

BOLDNESS *confidence*
word of God with **b** Acts 4:31
b and . . . access Eph 3:12
with **b** the mystery Eph 6:19

BOND *band, restraint*
neither **b** nor free 2 Kin 14:26
b of the covenant Ezek 20:37
with **b-s** of love Hos 11:4
in the **b** of peace Eph 4:3

BONDAGE *servitude, slavery*
Israel sighed . . . **b** Ex 2:23
the **b** of iniquity Acts 8:23
sold into **b** to sin Rom 7:14

BOND-SERVANT *servant, slave*
b-s of . . . Most High Acts 16:17
Paul, a **b** of Christ Rom 1:1
b . . . be quarrelsome 2 Tim 2:24
b of God . . . apostle Titus 1:1
His **b-s** . . . serve Him Rev 22:3

BONDSLAVE *servant, slave*
state of His **b** Luke 1:48
a **b** of Jesus Christ Col 4:12
Urge **b-s** to be subject Titus 2:9
use it as **b-s** of God 1 Pet 2:16

BONE
now **b** of my **b-s** Gen 2:23
the **b-s** of Joseph Josh 24:32
my **b-s** are dismayed Ps 6:2
can these **b-s** live Ezek 37:3
dead men's **b-s** Matt 23:27
Not a **b** . . . be broken John 19:36

BOOK *scroll*
blot me . . . from Thy **b** Ex 32:32
found the **b** of the 2 Kin 22:8
seal up the **b** Dan 12:4
not contain the **b-s** John 21:25
names are in the **b** Phil 4:3
worthy to open the **b** Rev 5:2
Lamb's **b** of life Rev 21:27

BOOK OF LIFE
God's book with names of righteous Ps 69:28; Phil 4:3; Rev 13:8;17:8;20:15

BOOTHS *shelters*
b for his livestock Gen 33:17
live in **b** for seven Lev 23:42
in **b** during the feast Neh 8:14

BOOTY *loot, plunder*
b that remained Num 31:32
Swift is the **b** Is 8:1
divide the **b** with Is 53:12
have his *own* life as **b** Jer 38:2

BORDER *boundary*
enlarge your **b-s** Ex 34:24
b of . . . city of refuge Num 35:26
the Jordan as *a* **b** Deut 3:17
God extends your **b** Deut 12:20
peace in your **b-s** Ps 147:14

BORN *brought into life*
mountains were **b** Ps 90:2
child will be **b** to us Is 9:6
b King of the Jews Matt 2:2
those **b** of women Luke 7:28
b not of blood John 1:13
unless one is **b** again John 3:3
b of the Spirit John 3:6
to one untimely **b** 1 Cor 15:8
loves is **b** of God 1 John 4:7

BORROW *use temporarily*
if a man **b-s** *anything* Ex 22:14
you shall not **b** Deut 28:12
b-s and does not pay Ps 37:21
wants to **b** from you Matt 5:42

BOSOM *breast*
iniquity in my **b** Job 31:33
take fire in his **b** Prov 6:27

to Abraham's **b** Luke 16:22
the **b** of the Father John 1:18

BOTTOMLESS *without bottom*
key of the **b** pit Rev 9:1
he opened the **b** pit Rev 9:2

BOUND (adj) *fastened, tied*
Foolishness is **b** up Prov 22:15
cast **b** into the . . . fire Dan 3:24
A wife is **b** as long 1 Cor 7:39

BOUND (n) *boundary, limit*
utmost **b** of . . . hills Gen 49:26
set **b-s** for the people Ex 19:12
b-s . . . the mountain Ex 19:23

BOUNDARY *border, limit*
b-ies of the peoples Deut 32:8
the **b-ies** of the earth Ps 74:17
set for the sea its **b** Prov 8:29
the **b** of the widow Prov 15:25

BOUNTY *generous gift*
to his royal **b** 1 Kin 10:13
crowned . . . with Thy **b** Ps 65:11
over the **b** of the LORD Jer 31:12

BOW (n) *rainbow*
set My **b** in the cloud Gen 9:13

BOW (n) *shooting device*
his **b** remained firm Gen 49:24
a **b** of bronze 2 Sam 22:35
not trust in my **b** Ps 44:6
b-s are shattered Jer 51:56

BOW (v) *bend, worship*
nations **b** down to Gen 27:29
Israel **b-ed** *in* Gen 47:31
to Him you shall **b** 2 Kin 17:36
My soul is **b-ed** down Ps 57:6
nations will **b** down Zeph 2:11
He **b-ed** His head John 19:30
every knee shall **b** Rom 14:11

BOWELS *entrails, innards*
a disease of your **b** 2 Chr 21:15
smote him in his **b** 2 Chr 21:18
b gushed out Acts 1:18

BOWL *dish, jug*
golden **b** is crushed Eccl 12:6
from sacrificial **b-s** Amos 6:6
dips with Me in . . . **b** Mark 14:20
b-s full of the wrath Rev 15:7

BOX *container*
b with the golden 1 Sam 6:11
sashes, perfume **b-es** Is 3:20
Judas had the . . . **b** John 13:29

BOX *type of tree*
b tree and the cypress Is 41:19

BOY *child, lad*
she left the **b** Gen 21:15
let the **b-s** live Ex 1:17
Traded a **b** for a harlot Joel 3:3
b was cured at once Matt 17:18

BRANCH *bough*
David a righteous **B** Jer 23:5
b-es *fit* for scepters Ezek 19:11
birds . . . in its **b-es** Luke 13:19
b-es of the palm John 12:13
b . . . not bear fruit John 15:2
you are the **b-es** John 15:5
be holy, the **b-es** Rom 11:16

BREAD *food*
eat unleavened **b** Ex 12:20
rain **b** from heaven Ex 16:4
He will bless your **b** Ex 23:25
b of the Presence Ex 25:30
not live by **b** alone Deut 8:3
b of heaven Ps 105:40
b *eaten* in secret Prov 9:17
eat the **b** of idleness Prov 31:27
Cast your **b** . . . waters Eccl 11:1
Give us . . . daily **b** Matt 6:11
gives you the true **b** John 6:32
I am the **b** of life John 6:35

BREAK *divide, shatter*
b down your pride Lev 26:19
never **b** My covenant Judg 2:1
soft tongue **b-s** the Prov 25:15
reed He will not **b** Is 42:3
I **broke** your yoke Jer 2:20
waves were **b-ing** Mark 4:37
she **broke** the vial Mark 14:3
their nets *began* to **b** Luke 5:6
b-ing the Sabbath John 5:18
did not **b** His legs John 19:33
your **b-ing** the Law Rom 2:23

BREAST *bosom*
orphan from the **b** Job 24:9
upon my mother's **b-s** Ps 22:9
b-s are like . . . fawns Song 7:3
reclining on Jesus' **b** John 13:23
girded across His **b** Rev 1:13

BREASTPIECE *breast covering*
a **b** and an ephod Ex 28:4
make a **b** of judgment Ex 28:15
they bound the **b** Ex 39:21

BREASTPLATE *breast armor*
righteousness like a **b** Is 59:17
b of faith and love 1 Thess 5:8
like **b-s** of iron Rev 9:9

BREATH *air, spirit, wind*
the **b** of life Gen 2:7
days are *but* a **b** Job 7:16
man is a mere **b** Ps 39:11
b came into them Ezek 37:10
give **b** to the image Rev 13:15

BREATHE *inhale and exhale*
Abraham **b-d** his last Gen 25:8
such as **b** out violence Ps 27:12
garden **b** . . . *fragrance* Song 4:16
b on these slain Ezek 37:9
He **b-d** His last Mark 15:39
He **b-d** on them John 20:22

BRETHREN *brothers*
beating . . . his **b** Ex 2:11
His **b** Will return Mic 5:3
sinning against . . . **b** 1 Cor 8:12
dangers . . . false **b** 2 Cor 11:26
Peace be to the **b** Eph 6:23
faithful **b** in Christ Col 1:2
the love of the **b** 1 Thess 4:9
my **b**, do not swear James 5:12
accuser of our **b** Rev 12:10

BRIBE *illegal gift*
b blinds . . . clear-sighted Ex 23:8
nor take a **b** Deut 10:17
who hates **b-s** will Prov 15:27
b corrupts the heart Eccl 7:7
Everyone loves a **b** Is 1:23

BRICK *clay block*
they used **b** for stone Gen 11:3
straw to make **b** as Ex 5:7
deliver . . . quota of **b-s** Ex 5:18
burning incense on **b-s** Is 65:3

BRIDE *newlywed*
as a **b** adorns herself Is 61:10
the voice of the **b** Jer 7:34
b out of her *bridal* Joel 2:16
He who has the **b** John 3:29
b . . . of the Lamb Rev 21:9

BRIDEGROOM *newlywed*
a **b** of blood to me Ex 4:25
As a **b** decks himself Is 61:10
voice of the **b** Jer 7:34
attendants of the **b** Matt 9:15
out to meet the **b** Matt 25:1

BRIDLE (n) *head harness*
My **b** in your lips 2 Kin 19:28
a **b** for the donkey Prov 26:3
up to the horses' **b-s** Rev 14:20

BRIGHT *shining*
b in the skies Job 37:21
night is as **b** as Ps 139:12
B eyes gladden Prov 15:30
b cloud . . . them Matt 17:5
b light . . . flashed Acts 22:6
the **b** morning star Rev 22:16

BRIMSTONE *sulfur*
b and fire from Gen 19:24
b and burning wind Ps 11:6
rained fire and **b** Luke 17:29
tormented with . . . **b** Rev 14:10
lake of fire and **b** Rev 20:10

BRING *carry, lead*
shall **b** forth children Gen 3:16
b two of every *kind* Gen 6:19
B the ark of God 1 Sam 14:18
Kings will **b** gifts Ps 68:29
B water for the thirsty Is 21:14
B the whole tithe Mal 3:10
b-ing . . . a paralytic Matt 9:2
not . . . to **b** peace Matt 10:34
brought forth a son Luke 1:57
I **b** you good news Luke 2:10
b-ing salvation Titus 2:11

BROKEN *crushed, separated*
My spirit is **b** Job 17:1
A **b** and contrite heart Ps 51:17
they have **b** Thy law Ps 119:126
silver cord is **b** Eccl 12:6
bind up the **b** Ezek 34:16
Scripture . . . be **b** John 10:35
Not a bone . . . **b** John 19:36
Branches were **b** off Rom 11:19

BROKENHEARTED *grieving*
LORD is near to the **b** Ps 34:18
He heals the **b** Ps 147:3
sent me to bind . . . **b** Is 61:1

BRONZE *metal*
implements of **b** Gen 4:22
made a **b** serpent Num 21:9
bend a bow of **b** 2 Sam 22:35
third kingdom of **b** Dan 2:39
costly wood and **b** Rev 18:12

BROOD *group, offspring*
b of sinful men Num 32:14
You **b** of vipers Matt 3:7
hen *gathers* her **b** Luke 13:34

BROOK *stream, wadi*
stones from the **b** 1 Sam 17:40
by the **b** Cherith 1 Kin 17:5
deer pants for . . . **b-s** Ps 42:1
wisdom . . . bubbling **b** Prov 18:4

BROTHER *male sibling*
Am I my **b-'s** Gen 4:9
b-s were jealous Gen 37:11
b-s to dwell together Ps 133:1
b is born for Prov 17:17
b-s of a poor man Prov 19:7
b will deliver up **b** Matt 10:21
behold, His . . . **b-s** Matt 12:46
not forgive his **b** Matt 18:35
b of yours was dead Luke 15:32
left . . . wife or **b-s** Luke 18:29
b shall rise again John 11:23
b goes to law with **b** 1 Cor 6:6
my **b** to stumble 1 Cor 8:13
yet hates his **b** 1 John 2:9

BROTHERHOOD
the covenant of **b** Amos 1:9
love the **b**, fear God 1 Pet 2:17

BRUISE (n) *wound*
for wound, **b** for **b** Ex 21:25
Only **b-s**, welts, and raw Is 1:6

the **b** He has inflicted Is 30:26

BRUISE (v) *batter, crush*
b him on the heel Gen 3:15
b-s me with a tempest Job 9:17

BUILD *construct, form*
Noah **built** an altar Gen 8:20
let us **b** . . . a city Gen 11:4
b for Me a house 1 Chr 17:12
b-ing . . . house of God 2 Chr 3:3
has **built** up Zion Ps 102:16
Unless the LORD **b-s** Ps 127:1
a time to **b** up Eccl 3:3
built his house upon Matt 7:24
I will **b** My church Matt 16:18
being **built** together Eph 2:22
stones . . . being **built** 1 Pet 2:5

BUILDER *fashioner, maker*
Solomon's **b-s** 1 Kin 5:18
b-s had laid the Ezra 3:10
the **b-s** rejected Matt 21:42
architect and **b** is Heb 11:10

BUILDING *structure*
reconstructing this **b** Ezra 5:4
b that *was* in front Ezek 41:12
what wonderful **b-s** Mark 13:1
you are . . . God's **b** 1 Cor 3:9
have a **b** from God 2 Cor 5:1
whole **b**, being fitted Eph 2:21

BUL
eighth month of Hebrew calendar 1 Ki 6:38

BULL *animal*
b of the sin offering Lev 4:20
b without blemish Ezek 45:18
blood of **b-s** and Heb 10:4

BULRUSH *marsh plant*
b in a single day Is 9:14
b-es by the Nile Is 19:7

BURDEN (n) *load, weight*
b-s of the Egyptians Ex 6:6
the **b** of the people Num 11:17
who daily bears our **b** Ps 68:19
b-s hard to bear Luke 11:46
Bear one another's **b-s** Gal 6:2

BURDEN (v) *weigh down*
b-ed Me with your sins Is 43:24
were **b-ed** excessively 2 Cor 1:8
not **b** you myself 2 Cor 12:16
the church be **b-ed** 1 Tim 5:16

BURIAL *interment*
give me a **b** site Gen 23:4
even have a *proper* **b** Eccl 6:3
to prepare Me for **b** Matt 26:12
b custom of the Jews John 19:40

BURN (v) *consume, kindle*
Jacob's anger **b-ed** Gen 30:2
bush was **b-ing** Ex 3:2
Moses' anger **b-ed** Ex 32:19
did not **b** any cities Josh 11:13
to **b** their sons Jer 7:31
not to **b** the scroll Jer 36:25
will **b** up the chaff Luke 3:17
my body to be **b-ed** 1 Cor 13:3
works will be **b-ed** 2 Pet 3:10
lake of fire . . . **b-s** Rev 19:20

BURNING (adj)
Thy **b** anger Ex 15:7
b lips and a wicked Prov 26:23
b heat of famine Lam 5:10
b anger of the LORD Zeph 2:2

BURNISHED *polished*
gleamed like **b** bronze Ezek 1:7
feet . . . like **b** bronze Rev 1:15

BURST *break*
great deep **b** open Gen 7:11
wine will **b** the skins Luke 5:37
b his fetters Luke 8:29
he **b** open Acts 1:18

BURY *place in earth*
b-ied at . . . old age Gen 15:15
that I may **b** my dead Gen 23:4
b-ied the bones of Josh 24:32
go and **b** my father Matt 8:21
devout . . . **b-ied** Stephen Acts 8:2
that He was **b-ied** 1 Cor 15:4
b-ied . . . in baptism Col 2:12

BUSH *shrub*
boy under . . . the **b-es** Gen 21:15
the **b** was burning Ex 3:2
who dwelt in the **b** Deut 33:16
like a **b** in the desert Jer 17:6

BUSINESS *occupation, work*
until I . . . told my **b** Gen 24:33
carry on the *king's* **b** Esth 3:9
attend to your . . . **b** 1 Thess 4:11
engage in **b** James 4:13

BUSYBODIES *meddlers*
no work . . . like **b** 2 Thess 3:11
gossips and **b** 1 Tim 5:13

BUTTER
steps . . . bathed in **b** Job 29:6
smoother than **b** Ps 55:21
milk produces **b** Prov 30:33

BUYER *purchaser*
Bad, bad, says the **b** Prov 20:14
the **b** like the seller Is 24:2
Let not the **b** rejoice Ezek 7:12

C

CAESAR
1 *Roman emperor* Matt 22:17,21; Mark 12:14; John 19:12
2 *Augustus* Luke 2:1
3 *Tiberius* Luke 3:1; John 19:12
4 *Claudius* Acts 11:28;17:7;18:2
5 *Nero* Acts 25:12;26:32; Phil 4:22

CAESAREA
Roman coastal city Acts 8:40;10:1;21:16;25:4

CAESAREA PHILIPPI
city at base of Mt. Hermon Matt 16:13; Mark 8:27

CAIAPHAS
high priest Matt 26:57; Luke 3:2; John 11:49ff

CAIN
son of Adam Gen 4:1
tiller of the ground Gen 4:2
killed his brother Gen 4:8
marked by sign Gen 4:15

CALAMITY *adversity, trouble*
day of my **c** 2 Sam 22:19
sorry over the **c** 1 Chr 21:15
c from God is Job 31:23
stumble in *time of* **c** Prov 24:16
beginning to work **c** Jer 25:29

CALEB
1 *aide to Moses* Num 13:30
son of Jephunneh Num 32:12
received Hebron Josh 14:13
2 *son of Hezron* 1 Chr 2:18

CALF *animal*
tender and choice **c** Gen 18:7
c and the young lion Is 11:6
skip about like **c-ves** Mal 4:2
bring the fattened **c** Luke 15:23
blood of . . . **c-ves** Heb 9:12

CALL *address, summon, name*
God **c-ed** the light day Gen 1:5
c upon the name Gen 4:26
c-s up the dead Deut 18:11
c upon the LORD Ps 18:3
those who **c** evil good Is 5:20
c His name Immanuel Is 7:14
who is **c-ed** Christ Matt 1:16
to **c** the righteous Matt 9:13
c-s his own sheep John 10:3
c Me Teacher and John 13:13
God has not **c-ed** 1 Thess 4:7

CALLING *summoning*
the **c** of assemblies Is 1:13
the **c** of God Rom 11:29
For consider your **c** 1 Cor 1:26
with a holy **c** 2 Tim 1:9
His **c** and choosing 2 Pet 1:10

CALM *still*
be **c**, have no fear Is 7:4
sea may become **c** Jon 1:11
it became perfectly **c** Matt 8:26
you ought to keep **c** Acts 19:36

CAMEL *animal*
dismounted . . . the **c** Gen 24:64
his wives upon **c-s** Gen 31:17
a garment of **c-'s** hair Matt 3:4
c . . . eye of a needle Matt 19:24
clothed with **c-'s** hair Mark 1:6

CAMP (n) *lodging area*
This is God's **c** Gen 32:2
people out of the **c** Ex 19:17
outside the **c** seven Num 31:19
the **c** of the saints Rev 20:9

CAMP (v) *settle*
you shall **c** in front Ex 14:2
they shall also **c** Num 1:50
Israel **c-ed** at Gilgal Josh 5:10
c around My house Zech 9:8

CANAAN
1 *son of Ham* Gen 9:18,25
2 *Syro-Palestine* Gen 13:12;42:5; Ex 16:35
3 *language (Hebrew)* Is 19:18
see also **HEBREW**
see also **JUDEAN**

CANAL *water way*
c-s will emit a stench Is 19:6
rivers *and* wide **c-s** Is 33:21
the Nile **c-s** dry Ezek 30:12
in front of the **c** Dan 8:3

CAPERNAUM
city on Sea of Galilee Matt 4:13; Luke 4:23

CAPITAL *top part of column*
height of the other **c** 1 Kin 7:16
c on the top of each 2 Chr 3:15
c-s . . . were on top 2 Chr 4:12

CAPITAL *city*
Susa the **c** Esth 2:3

CAPTAIN *leader*
c of the bodyguard Gen 39:1
the **c-s** of hundreds Num 31:14
c of the host of Josh 5:14
the **c** of the ship Acts 27:11

CAPTIVE *prisoner*
first-born of the **c** Ex 12:29
restores his **c** people Ps 14:7
hast led **c** *Thy* **c-s** Ps 68:18
release to the **c-s** Luke 4:18
every thought **c** 2 Cor 10:5
having been held **c** 2 Tim 2:26

CAPTIVITY *imprisonment*
restore you from **c** Deut 30:3
land of their **c** 2 Chr 6:37
had come from the **c** Ezra 8:35
destined for **c** Rev 13:10

CAPTURE *seize, take*
they **c-d** and looted Gen 34:29

c-d all his cities Deut 2:34
Can anyone c him Job 40:24
it c-s nothing at all Amos 3:5

CARAVAN *expedition*
a c of Ishmaelites Gen 37:25
The c-s of Tema Job 6:19
O c-s of Dedanites Is 21:13

CARCASS *corpse*
down upon the c-es Gen 15:11
one who touches . . . c Lev 11:39
c-es shall be food Deut 28:26
c-es of their . . . idols Jer 16:18

CARE (n) *concern*
into the c of . . . sons Gen 30:35
put him in my c Gen 42:37
friends and receive c Acts 27:3
c for one another 1 Cor 12:25

CARE (v) *have concern for*
He c-d for him Deut 32:10
c for My sheep Ezek 34:12
and took c of him Luke 10:34
take c of the church 1 Tim 3:5
he c-s for you 1 Pet 5:7

CAREFUL *watchful, on guard*
I not be c to speak Num 23:12
c to observe all Deut 6:25
you shall be c to do Deut 8:1
be c not to drink Judg 13:4
be c how you walk Eph 5:15

CARELESS *thoughtless*
a fool is . . . c Prov 14:16
food, and c ease Ezek 16:49
that every c word Matt 12:36

CARMEL
1 *range of hills* 1 Kin 18:42; 2 Kin 4:25
2 *town in Judah* 1 Sam 15:12;25:5,40

CARPENTER *craftsman*
c-s and stonemasons 2 Sam 5:11
to the masons and c-s Ezra 3:7
this the c-'s son Matt 13:55
c, the son of Mary Mark 6:3

CARRY *bear*
LORD . . . c-ied you Deut 1:31
Spirit . . . will c you 1 Kin 18:12
c *them* in His bosom Is 40:11
our sorrows He c-ied Is 53:4
c-ied away . . . diseases Matt 8:17
C no purse, no bag Luke 10:4
the cross to c Luke 23:26
c out the desire of Gal 5:16

CAST *throw*
one who c-s a spell Deut 18:11
Joshua c lots for Josh 18:10
c *lots* for the orphans Job 6:27
Do not c me away Ps 51:11
c you out of My sight Jer 7:15
will c out demons Mark 16:17
c Him out of . . . city Luke 4:29
c fire upon . . . earth Luke 12:49
clothing they c lots John 19:24
but c them into hell 2 Pet 2:4
c their crowns before Rev 4:10

CATCH *seize, trap*
shall c his wife Judg 21:21
to c the afflicted Ps 10:9
C the foxes for us Song 2:15
caught in My snare Ezek 12:13
will be c-ing men Luke 5:10
caught in adultery John 8:3
who c-es the wise 1 Cor 3:19
child was **caught** up Rev 12:5

CATTLE *domestic animals*
c and creeping things Gen 1:24
the first-born of c Ex 12:29
defect from the c Lev 22:19
c on a thousand hills Ps 50:10
no c in the stalls Hab 3:17

CAVE *shelter*
buried him in the c Gen 25:9
escaped to the c 1 Sam 22:1
by fifties in a c 1 Kin 18:4
hid . . . in the c-s Rev 6:15

CEASE *stop*
you shall c *from labor* Ex 23:12
poor will never c Deut 15:11
He makes wars to c Ps 46:9
make this proverb c Ezek 12:23
c-d to kiss My feet Luke 7:45
tongues, they will c 1 Cor 13:8
pray without c-ing 1 Thess 5:17

CEDAR *tree, wood*
with the c wood Lev 14:6
c-s beside the waters Num 24:6
all the c-s of Lebanon Is 2:13
the height of c-s Amos 2:9

CELEBRATE *rejoice*
may c a feast to Me Ex 5:1
you shall c it in Lev 23:41
C the Passover 2 Kin 23:21
all Israel were c-ing 1 Chr 13:8
to c *the feast* 2 Chr 30:23

CENSER *incense container*
c-s for yourselves Num 16:6
his c in his hand Ezek 8:11
holding a golden c Rev 8:3
angel took the c Rev 8:5

CENSUS *population roll*
c of . . . congregation Num 1:2
number of the c 1 Chr 21:5
c which . . . David 2 Chr 2:17
the first c taken Luke 2:2
in the days of the c Acts 5:37

CENT *money*
paid up the last c Matt 5:26
sparrows . . . for a c Matt 10:29
amount to a c Mark 12:42

CENTURION *captain*
Jesus said to the c Matt 8:13
summoning the c Mark 15:44
soldiers and c-s Acts 21:32
gave orders to the c Acts 24:23

CEPHAS
apostle Peter John 1:42; 1 Cor 1:12;15:5; Gal 2:11

CERTIFICATE *permit, record*
a c of divorce Deut 24:1
a c of divorce Matt 5:31
c of debt Col 2:14

CHAFF *husk*
consumes them as c Ex 15:7
c which the wind drives Ps 1:4
make the hills like c Is 41:15
c from the summer Dan 2:35
burn up the c Matt 3:12

CHAIN *band*
bound . . . bronze c-s Judg 16:21
he drew c-s of gold 1 Kin 6:21
whose hands are c-s Eccl 7:26
c-s fell off his hands Acts 12:7
great c in his hand Rev 20:1

CHALDEANS
inhabitants of Chaldea Gen 11:28; 2 Kin 24:2; Job 1:17; Jer 24:5; Dan 5:11

CHAMBER *room*
entered his c Gen 43:30
in his cool roof c Judg 3:20
c-s of the storehouse Neh 10:38
bridegroom . . . his c Ps 19:5
to the c-s of death Prov 7:27
c-s in the heavens Amos 9:6

CHAMPION *fighter*
c, the Philistine 1 Sam 17:23

a Savior and a C Is 19:20
like a dread c Jer 20:11

CHANGE (n) *alteration*
gave c-s of garments Gen 45:22
had a c of heart Ex 14:5
two c-s of clothes 2 Kin 5:23
Until my c comes Job 14:14
a c of law Heb 7:12

CHANGE (v) *alter, transform*
and c-d my wages Gen 31:7
He c-s a wilderness Ps 107:35
Ethiopian c his skin Jer 13:23
He who c-s the times Dan 2:21
LORD c-d His mind Amos 7:6
I, the LORD, do not c Mal 3:6
shall all be c-d 1 Cor 15:51

CHANNEL *furrow*
Who has cleft a c Job 38:25
c-s of water appeared Ps 18:15
heart is *like* c-s Prov 21:1
sent out its c-s Ezek 31:4

CHANT *sing*
David c-ed . . . this 2 Sam 1:17
Jeremiah c-ed a 2 Chr 35:25
daughters . . . shall c Ezek 32:16

CHARACTER
and proven c, hope Rom 5:4
Let your c be free Heb 13:5

CHARGE (n) *responsibility*
under Joseph's c Gen 39:23
keep the c of the LORD Lev 8:35
c of his household Matt 24:45
allotted to your c 1 Pet 5:3

CHARGE (n) *accusation*
far from a false c Ex 23:7
bring c-s against Acts 19:38
c against God's elect Rom 8:33

CHARGE (n) *cost*
gospel without c 1 Cor 9:18

CHARGE (v) *command*
Abimelech c-d all Gen 26:11
I c-d your judges Deut 1:16
Moses c-d us with a Deut 33:4
I solemnly c you 1 Tim 5:21

CHARGE (v) *exact a price*
not c him interest Ex 22:25
c that to my account Philem 18

CHARIOT *wagon*
Joseph prepared . . . c Gen 46:29
appeared a c of fire 2 Kin 2:11
Some *boast* in c-s Ps 20:7
c-s of God are myriads Ps 68:17
I will cut off the c Zech 9:10

CHARIOTEERS *warriors*
David killed 700 c 2 Sam 10:18
7,000 c and 40,000 1 Chr 19:18
with horses and c Ezek 39:20

CHARITY *alms*
give that . . . as c Luke 11:41
and give to c Luke 12:33
deeds of . . . c Acts 9:36

CHARM *beauty*
A bribe is a c Prov 17:8
C is deceitful Prov 31:30
with *all* your c-s Song 7:6

CHASTE *pure*
c . . . behavior 1 Pet 3:2
kept themselves c Rev 14:4

CHASTEN *discipline*
Man is also c-ed Job 33:19
Nor c me in Thy wrath Ps 6:1
c-ed every morning Ps 73:14
who c-s the nations Ps 94:10

CHASTISE *punish*
Thou hast **c-d** me — Jer 31:18
I will **c** all of them — Hos 5:2

CHEAT *deceive*
your father has **c-ed** — Gen 31:7
c with . . . scales — Amos 8:5

CHEBAR
river in Babylonia — Ezek 3:15

CHEERFUL
countenance and be **c** — Job 9:27
joyful heart . . . a **c** — Prov 15:13
c heart . . . feast — Prov 15:15
God loves a **c** giver — 2 Cor 9:7

CHEMOSH
god of Moab — Judg 11:24; 1 Kin 11:7

CHERETHITES
1 *tribe on Philistine plain* — 1 Sam 30:14; Ezek 25:16
2 *David's bodyguards* — 2 Sam 8:18;15:18; 1 Kin 1:38

CHERISH *love*
or the wife you **c** — Deut 13:6
the wife he **c-es** — Deut 28:54
men **c** themselves — Acts 24:15
c-es it, just as Christ — Eph 5:29

CHERUB *celestial being*
He rode on a **c** — 2 Sam 22:11
one **c** . . . ten cubits — 1 Kin 6:26
c stretched out his — Ezek 10:7

CHERUBIM *plural of cherub*
He stationed the **c** — Gen 3:24
c had *their* wings — Ex 37:9
c appeared to have — Ezek 10:8

CHEST *box*
the priest took a **c** — 2 Kin 12:9
money in the **c** — 2 Kin 12:10
levies . . . into the **c** — 2 Chr 24:10

CHIEF *head, prominent*
c-s of the sons of — Gen 36:15
the **c-s** of Edom — Gen 36:43
of the thirty **c** men — 2 Sam 23:13
c of the magicians — Dan 4:9
C Shepherd appears — 1 Pet 5:4

CHILD
Train up a **c** in — Prov 22:6
discipline from the **c** — Prov 23:13
with **c** by the Holy — Matt 1:18
take the **C** and His — Matt 2:13
He called a **c** to — Matt 18:2
a woman with **c** — 1 Thess 5:3

CHILDBIRTH
multiply . . . pain in **c** — Gen 3:16
as of a woman in **c** — Ps 48:6
pains of **c** come — Hos 13:13
suffers the pains of **c** — Rom 8:22

CHILDLESS
I am **c**, and the heir — Gen 15:2
They shall die **c** — Lev 20:20
c among women — 1 Sam 15:33
and died **c** — Luke 20:29

CHILDREN
pain . . . bring forth **c** — Gen 3:16
Are these all the **c** — 1 Sam 16:11
c are a gift — Ps 127:3
c rise up and bless — Prov 31:28
slew all the male **c** — Matt 2:16
stones to raise up **c** — Matt 3:9
and become like **c** — Matt 18:3
bringing **c** to Him — Mark 10:13
C, obey your parents — Eph 6:1
kill her **c** with — Rev 2:23

CHINNERETH / CHINNEROTH
1 *lake* — Num 34:11; Josh 12:3
also **Sea of Galilee**
also **Lake of Gennesaret**
also **Sea of Tiberius**
2 *city of Naphtali* — Deut 3:17; Josh 19:35
3 *plain near Galilee* — Josh 11:2; 1 Kin 15:20

CHISLEV
ninth month of Hebrew calendar — Neh 1:1; Zech 7:1

CHOICE *option* or *best*
Saul, a **c** . . . *man* — 1 Sam 9:2
c men of Israel — 2 Sam 10:9
And eat its **c** fruits — Song 4:16
God's gracious **c** — Rom 11:5

CHOIR *chorus*
c proceeded to the — Neh 12:38
two **c-s** took their — Neh 12:40

CHOOSE *select, take*
C men for us — Ex 17:9
whom the LORD **c-s** — Num 16:7
C wise . . . discerning — Deut 1:13
refuse evil and **c** good — Is 7:15
not God **c** the poor — James 2:5

CHOP *cut*
who **c-s** your wood — Deut 29:11
c-ped down . . . altars — 2 Chr 34:7
C down the tree — Dan 4:14

CHOSE *selected*
God has **c-n** you — Deut 7:6
I **c** David to be — 1 Kin 8:16
when I **c** Israel — Ezek 20:5
c twelve of them — Luke 6:13
has **c-n** the weak — 1 Cor 1:27

CHOSEN *elected, selected*
Moses His **c** one — Ps 106:23
My **c** *one in whom* — Is 42:1
Israel My **c** *one* — Is 45:4
c ones shall inherit — Is 65:9
My Son, *My* **C** One — Luke 9:35
c of God, holy and — Col 3:12
you are a **c** race — 1 Pet 2:9

CHRIST *Messiah*
birth of Jesus **C** was — Matt 1:18
both LORD and **C** — Acts 2:36
fellow heirs with **C** — Rom 8:17
are one body in **C** — Rom 12:5
judgment seat of **C** — 2 Cor 5:10
faith in **C** Jesus — Gal 2:16
as sons through Jesus **C** — Eph 1:5
to live is **C** — Phil 1:21
C, who is our life — Col 3:4
dead in **C** shall — 1 Thess 4:16
coming of . . . **C** — 2 Thess 2:1
Advocate . . . Jesus **C** — 1 John 2:1
with **C** for a thousand — Rev 20:4

CHRISTIAN *follower of Christ*
first called **C-s** in — Acts 11:26
me to become a **C** — Acts 26:28
suffers as a **C** — 1 Pet 4:16

CHRONICLES *book of register*
1 *of kings of Israel* — 1 Kin 14:19;15:31; 2 Kin 14:28;15:26
2 *of kings of Judah* — 1 Kin 14:29;15:23; 2 Kin 15:36;24:5
3 *of kings of Media / Persia* — Esth 10:2

CHURCH *assembly, congregation*
I will build my **c** — Matt 16:18
tell it to the **c** — Matt 18:17
shepherd the **c** — Acts 20:28
c-es of the Gentiles — Rom 16:4
woman . . . speak in **c** — 1 Cor 14:35
to the **c-es** of Judea — Gal 1:22
Christ . . . head of the **c** — Eph 5:23
persecutor of the **c** — Phil 3:6
Spirit says to the **c-es** — Rev 2:11

CILICIA
region in SE Asia Minor — Acts 15:41;21:39;27:5

CINNAMON *spice*
and of fragrant **c** — Ex 30:23
myrrh, aloes and **c** — Prov 7:17
and **c** and spice — Rev 18:13

CIRCUMCISE *be pure* or *cut off*
every male . . . be **c-d** — Gen 17:10
Abraham **c-d** his son — Gen 21:4
C then your heart — Deut 10:16
God will **c** . . . heart — Deut 30:6
C yourselves . . . LORD — Jer 4:4
came to **c** the child — Luke 1:59
c-d the eighth day — Phil 3:5

CIRCUMCISION *act of purity*
because of the **c** — Ex 4:26
c is . . . of the heart — Rom 2:29
if you receive **c** — Gal 5:2
if I still preach **c** — Gal 5:11
we are the *true* **c** — Phil 3:3
c made without hands — Col 2:11
those of the **c** — Titus 1:10

CISTERN *reservoir*
a **c** collecting water — Lev 11:36
water from your . . . **c** — Prov 5:15
wheel at the **c** is — Eccl 12:6
prophet from the **c** — Jer 38:10

CITADEL *fortress*
in the **c** of Susa — Dan 8:2
c-s of Jerusalem — Amos 2:5
Proclaim on the **c-s** — Amos 3:9
tramples on our **c-s** — Mic 5:5

CITIES OF REFUGE
1 *Kedesh in Naphtali* — Josh 20:7
2 *Shechem in Ephraim* — Josh 20:7
3 *Hebron (Kiriath-arba)* — Josh 20:7
4 *Bezer in Reuben* — Josh 20:8
5 *Ramoth-gilead, Gad* — Josh 20:8
6 *Golan in Manasseh* — Josh 20:8

CITIZEN *resident*
your fellow **c-s** — Ezek 33:12
fellow **c-s** who talk — Ezek 33:30
c-s hated him — Luke 19:14
c of no insignificant — Acts 21:39
fellow **c-s** with the — Eph 2:19

CLAIM *demand*
Let darkness . . . **c** it — Job 3:5
Do not **c** honor in — Prov 25:6
c-ing to be someone — Acts 8:9

CLAN *family, tribe*
c of the household — Judg 9:1
and by your **c-s** — 1 Sam 10:19
among . . . **c-s** of Judah — Mic 5:2
I will make the **c-s** — Zech 12:6

CLAP *applaud*
c-ped their hands — 2 Kin 11:12
c-s his hands among — Job 34:37
rivers **c** their hands — Ps 98:8
trees . . . will **c** — Is 55:12

CLAUDIA
Roman Christian — 2 Tim 4:21

CLAY
dwell in houses of **c** — Job 4:19
Father, We are the **c** — Is 64:8
c in the potter's hand — Jer 18:6
the **c** to his eyes — John 9:6

CLEAN *cleansed, washed*
animals that are not **c** — Gen 7:2
eat in a **c** place — Lev 10:14
pronounce him **c** — Lev 13:28
Create in me a **c** heart — Ps 51:10
You can make me **c** — Matt 8:2
things are **c** for you — Luke 11:41
c because of the word — John 15:3

CLEANSE *purify, wash*
To **c** the house then — Lev 14:49
I have **c-d** my heart — Prov 20:9

- I am willing; be **c-d** — Matt 8:3
- *the* lepers are **c-d** — Matt 11:5
- not eat unless they **c** — Mark 7:4
- let us **c** ourselves — 2 Cor 7:1
- **C** . . . you sinners — James 4:8
- blood . . . **c-s** us — 1 John 1:7

CLEAR *make free* or *plain*

- **c** away many nations — Deut 7:1
- **C** the way for the LORD — Is 40:3
- **c** His threshing floor — Matt 3:12
- Christ had made **c** — 2 Pet 1:14
- river . . . **c** as crystal — Rev 22:1

CLEAVE *cling, divide*

- shall **c** to his wife — Gen 2:24
- tongue **c-s** to my jaws — Ps 22:15
- **c** to Thy testimonies — Ps 119:31
- shall **c** to his wife — Eph 5:31

CLEFT *crevice*

- in the **c** of the rock — Judg 15:8
- the **c-s** of the cliffs — Is 2:21
- who live in the **c-s** — Obad 3

CLEVER *smart*

- **c** in their own sight — Is 5:21
- cleverness of the **c** — 1 Cor 1:19

CLIFF *crag*

- nest is set in the **c** — Num 24:21
- On the **c** he dwells — Job 39:28
- **c-s** are a refuge — Ps 104:18

CLIMB *ascend*

- I will **c** the palm tree — Song 7:8
- the one who **c-s** — Jer 48:44
- **c-ed** . . . a sycamore — Luke 19:4
- **c-s** up . . . other way — John 10:1

CLING *cleave*

- **c** to the LORD — Josh 23:8
- My soul **c-s** to Thee — Ps 63:8
- Stop **c-ing** to Me — John 20:17
- **c** to what is good — Rom 12:9

CLOAK *coat, mantle*

- Give me the **c** — Ruth 3:15
- neither bread nor **c** — Is 3:7
- fringe of His **c** — Matt 9:20
- Wrap your **c** around — Acts 12:8

CLOSE *shut, stop*

- and the LORD **c-d** — Gen 7:16
- floodgates . . . were **c-d** — Gen 8:2
- earth **c-d** over them — Num 16:33
- have **c-d** their eyes — Acts 28:27
- every mouth . . . **c-d** — Rom 3:19
- **c-s** his heart — 1 John 3:17

CLOTH *fabric*

- spread over *it* a **c** — Num 4:6
- is wrapped in a **c** — 1 Sam 21:9
- with embroidered **c** — Ezek 16:10
- in the linen **c** — Mark 15:46

CLOTHE *array, dress*

- **C** me with skin — Job 10:11
- O Zion; **C** yourself — Is 52:1
- naked . . . you **c-d** Me — Matt 25:36
- are splendidly **c-d** — Luke 7:25
- **c-d** with power — Luke 24:49
- **c** . . . with humility — 1 Pet 5:5
- **c-d** in the white robes — Rev 7:13

CLOTHES *garments*

- **c** of her captivity — Deut 21:13
- your **c** have not worn — Deut 29:5
- and worn-out **c** on — Josh 9:5
- and changed his **c** — 2 Sam 12:20
- without wedding **c** — Matt 22:12
- And tearing his **c** — Mark 14:63

CLOTHING *clothes, raiment*

- reduce . . . her **c** — Ex 21:10
- **c** did not wear out — Deut 8:4
- and the body than **c** — Matt 6:25
- in sheep's **c** — Matt 7:15
- His **c** *became* white — Luke 9:29

- sister is without **c** — James 2:15

CLOUD *mist*

- set My bow in the **c** — Gen 9:13
- in a pillar of **c** — Ex 13:21
- **c** where God *was* — Ex 20:21
- **c** covered . . . mountain — Ex 24:15
- voice came out . . . **c** — Mark 9:7
- Son . . . coming in **c-s** — Mark 13:26
- in a **c** with power — Luke 21:27
- and a **c** received Him — Acts 1:9

COAST

- **c** of the Great Sea — Josh 9:1
- along the **c** of Asia — Acts 27:2

COASTLAND

- inhabitants of this **c** — Is 20:6
- to the **c-s** of Kittim — Jer 2:10
- **c-s** shake at the — Ezek 26:15
- **c-s** of the nations — Zeph 2:11

COAT *cloak*

- opening . . . **c** of mail — Ex 28:32
- with his **c** torn — 2 Sam 15:32
- have your **c** also — Matt 5:40

COBRA *snake*

- deadly poison of **c-s** — Deut 32:33
- To the venom of **c-s** — Job 20:14
- tread upon the . . . **c** — Ps 91:13

COCK *bird*

- The strutting **c** — Prov 30:31
- before a **c** crows — Matt 26:34
- **c** shall not crow — John 13:38

COFFIN *bier*

- in a **c** in Egypt — Gen 50:26
- and touched the **c** — Luke 7:14

COHORT *military unit*

- the whole *Roman* **c** — Matt 27:27
- called the Italian **c** — Acts 10:1
- of the Augustan **c** — Acts 27:1

COIN *money*

- Show Me the **c** — Matt 22:19
- woman . . . loses one **c** — Luke 15:8
- He poured out . . . **c-s** — John 2:15

COLLAPSE *fall*

- grass **c-s** into the flame — Is 5:24
- pathways will **c** — Ezek 38:20
- ancient hills **c-d** — Hab 3:6

COLLEAGUES *co-workers*

- the rest of his **c** — Ezra 4:7
- and your **c** — Ezra 6:6

COLLECT *exact, take*

- **c-ed** his strength — Gen 48:2
- cistern **c-ing** water — Lev 11:36
- **c** captives like sand — Hab 1:9
- **c-ed** a tenth from — Heb 7:6

COLLECTION *acquisition*

- let your **c** *of idols* — Is 57:13
- no **c-s** be made — 1 Cor 16:2

COLT *foal*

- camels and their **c-s** — Gen 32:15
- Even on a **c** — Zech 9:9
- and a **c** with her — Matt 21:2
- on a donkey's **c** — John 12:15

COLUMN *pillar, text*

- in a **c** of smoke — Judg 20:40
- and marble **c-s** — Esth 1:6
- read three . . . **c-s** — Jer 36:23

COMFORT (n) *consolation*

- mourning without **c** — Job 30:28
- **c** in my affliction — Ps 119:50
- **c** of the Holy Spirit — Acts 9:31
- and God of all **c** — 2 Cor 1:3
- your **c** and salvation — 2 Cor 1:6

COMFORT (v) *console, cheer*

- relatives came to **c** — 1 Chr 7:22
- Thy rod . . . they **c** me — Ps 23:4
- I, am He who **c-s** you — Is 51:12
- To **c** all who mourn — Is 61:2
- he is being **c-ed** — Luke 16:25
- **c** one another — 1 Thess 4:18

COMFORTER *consoler*

- Sorry **c-s** are you all — Job 16:2
- **c-s**, but I found none — Ps 69:20
- She has no **c** — Lam 1:9
- Where will I seek **c-s** — Nah 3:7

COMING (n) *arrival*

- Joseph's **c** at noon — Gen 43:25
- the day of His **c** — Mal 3:2
- **c** of the Son of Man — Matt 24:37
- Christ's at His **c** — 1 Cor 15:23
- **c** of the LORD is — James 5:8
- the promise of His **c** — 2 Pet 3:4

COMMAND (n) *order*

- the **c** of the LORD — Lev 24:12
- disobeyed the **c** — 1 Kin 13:21
- to the king's **c** — 2 Chr 35:10
- no **c** of the Lord — 1 Cor 7:25
- could not bear the **c** — Heb 12:20

COMMAND (v) *declare, order*

- I **c-ed** you not to eat — Gen 3:11
- may **c** his children — Gen 18:19
- speak all that I **c** you — Ex 7:2
- the angel . . . **c-ed** — Matt 1:24
- **c** that these stones — Matt 4:3
- **c-s** even the winds — Luke 8:25

COMMANDER *captain, general*

- the **c-s** of Israel — Judg 5:9
- **c** of Saul's army — 2 Sam 2:8
- his chariot **c-s** — 1 Kin 9:22
- **c** for the peoples — Is 55:4
- the **C** of the host — Dan 8:11
- and the flesh of **c-s** — Rev 19:18

COMMANDMENT *instruction*

- and keep My **c-s** — Ex 20:6
- the Ten **C-s** — Ex 34:28
- **c** of the LORD is pure — Ps 19:8
- the **c** of your father — Prov 6:20
- which is the great **c** — Matt 22:36
- A new **c** I give — John 13:34
- will keep My **c-s** — John 14:15
- I have kept . . . **c-s** — John 15:10
- keep the **c-s** of God — Rev 14:12

COMMEND *praise, present*

- So I **c-ed** pleasure — Eccl 8:15
- I **c** you to God — Acts 20:32
- food will not **c** us — 1 Cor 8:8
- to **c** ourselves again — 2 Cor 3:1

COMMISSION *appoint*

- **c** him in their sight — Num 27:19
- He **c-ed** Joshua — Deut 31:23
- king has **c-ed** me — 1 Sam 21:2
- **c** it against the people — Is 10:6

COMMIT *entrust, practice*

- **c-ted** to Joseph's — Gen 39:22
- shall not **c** adultery — Ex 20:14
- I **c** my spirit — Ps 31:5
- **C** your way to the LORD — Ps 37:5
- Do not **c** adultery — Luke 18:20
- I **c** My spirit — Luke 23:46
- everyone who **c-s** sin — John 8:34
- who **c-ted** no sin — 1 Pet 2:22

COMPANION *comrade, friend*

- are you striking your **c** — Ex 2:13
- brought thirty **c-s** — Judg 14:11
- And a **c** of ostriches — Job 30:29
- **c** of fools will suffer — Prov 13:20
- your **c** and your wife — Mal 2:14
- Paul and his **c-s** — Acts 13:13

COMPARE *contrast, like*

- none to **c** with Thee — Ps 40:5
- to what shall I **c** — Matt 11:16

c the kingdom of — Luke 13:20
be **c-d** with the glory — Rom 8:18

COMPASS

outlines it with a **c** — Is 44:13
four points of the **c** — Dan 11:4

COMPASSION *concern, love*

God . . . grant you **c** — Gen 43:14
whom I will show **c** — Ex 33:19
in Thy great **c** — Neh 9:19
have **c** on the poor — Ps 72:13
have **c** on Zion — Ps 102:13
His **c-s** never fail — Lam 3:22
He felt **c** for them — Matt 9:36
put on a heart of **c** — Col 3:12
Lord is full of **c** — James 5:11

COMPASSIONATE *loving*

your God is a **c** God — Deut 4:31
c, Slow to anger — Neh 9:17
He is gracious and **c** — Joel 2:13
a gracious and **c** God — Jon 4:2

COMPETE *strive*

can you **c** with horses — Jer 12:5
everyone who **c-s** — 1 Cor 9:25
c-s as an athlete — 2 Tim 2:5

COMPLAIN *murmur*

c-ed to Abimelech — Gen 21:25
c in the bitterness — Job 7:11
I will **c** and murmur — Ps 55:17
Do not **c**, brethren — James 5:9

COMPLAINT *grumbling*

c-s of . . . Israel — Num 14:27
couch will ease my **c** — Job 7:13
today my **c** is rebellion — Job 23:2
hospitable . . . without **c** — 1 Pet 4:9

COMPLETE (adj) *full, total*

a sabbath of **c** rest — Ex 35:2
be seven **c** sabbaths — Lev 23:15
not . . . a **c** destruction — Jer 5:10
you have been made **c** — Col 2:10
joy may be made **c** — 1 John 1:4

COMPLETE (v) *finish, fulfill*

God **c-d** His work — Gen 2:2
C the week of this — Gen 29:27
C your work quota — Ex 5:13
your days are **c** — 2 Sam 7:12
thousand years are **c-d** — Rev 20:7

COMPOSE *write*

c words against you — Job 16:4
have **c-d** songs for — Amos 6:5
The first account I **c-d** — Acts 1:1

COMPOSE *make calm*

c-d and quieted my — Ps 131:2
I **c** *my soul* — Is 38:13

CONCEAL *cover, hide*

man **c-s** knowledge — Prov 12:23
They do not *even* **c** *it* — Is 3:9
Do not **c** *it but* — Jer 50:2
was **c-ed** from them — Luke 9:45

CONCEIT *pride*

selfishness or empty **c** — Phil 2:3
he is **c-ed** — 1 Tim 6:4
c-ed, lovers of — 2 Tim 3:4

CONCEIVE *become pregnant*

Sarah **c-d** and bore a — Gen 21:2
c-d all this people — Num 11:12
sin my mother **c-d** me — Ps 51:5
when lust has **c-d** — James 1:15

CONCERN *have care*

master does not **c** — Gen 39:8
the LORD was **c-ed** — Ex 4:31
Thou art **c-ed** about — Job 7:17
c-ed about the poor — John 12:6
not **c-ed** about oxen — 1 Cor 9:9

CONCUBINE *secondary wife*

Ephraim . . . took a **c** — Judg 19:1
Now Saul had a **c** — 2 Sam 3:7
king left ten **c-s** — 2 Sam 15:16
three hundred **c-s** — 1 Kin 11:3
in charge of the **c-s** — Esth 2:14

CONDEMN *discredit, judge*

c-ing the wicked — 1 Kin 8:32
my mouth will **c** me — Job 9:20
he who **c-s** Me — Is 50:9
will **c** Him to death — Mark 10:33
do not **c**, and you — Luke 6:37
our heart **c-s** us — 1 John 3:20

CONDEMNATION *judgment*

receive greater **c** — Mark 12:40
same sentence of **c** — Luke 23:40
Their **c** is just — Rom 3:8
no **c** . . . in Christ — Rom 8:1
c upon themselves — Rom 13:2
c . . . by the devil — 1 Tim 3:6

CONDUCT (n) *behavior*

queen's **c** . . . known — Esth 1:17
who are upright in **c** — Ps 37:14
sensual **c** of . . . men — 2 Pet 2:7
holy **c** and godliness — 2 Pet 3:11

CONDUCT (v) *behave*

c-s himself arrogantly — Job 15:25
c . . . same spirit — 2 Cor 12:18
C . . . with wisdom — Col 4:5
c yourselves in fear — 1 Pet 1:17

CONDUIT *channel*

c of the upper pool — 2 Kin 18:17
at the end of the **c** — Is 7:3

CONFESS *acknowledge*

c-ing the sins of — Neh 1:6
c my transgressions — Ps 32:5
c Me before men — Matt 10:32
c-ing their sins — Mark 1:5
c with your mouth — Rom 10:9
If we **c** our sins — 1 John 1:9

CONFIDENCE *boldness, trust*

What is this **c** — 2 Kin 18:19
they lost their **c** — Neh 6:16
LORD will be your **c** — Prov 3:26
proud **c** is this — 2 Cor 1:12
c in me may abound — Phil 1:26
no **c** in the flesh — Phil 3:3

CONFINE *imprison, limit*

who were **c-d** in jail — Gen 40:5
he does not **c** it — Ex 21:29
be **c-d** in prison — Is 24:22
c-d in the court — Jer 33:1

CONFIRM *establish, strengthen*

LORD **c** His word — 1 Sam 1:23
c Thine inheritance — Ps 68:9
c the work of our — Ps 90:17
C-ing the word of His — Is 44:26
c-ed . . . by the signs — Mark 16:20
who shall also **c** you — 1 Cor 1:8

CONFLICT *contention*

one of great **c** — Dan 10:1
in **c** with the LORD — Jer 50:24
experiencing . . . **c** — Phil 1:30
source of . . . **c-s** — James 4:1

CONFORMED *being like*

c . . . image of His Son — Rom 8:29
not be **c** to . . . world — Rom 12:2
being **c** to His death — Phil 3:10

CONFOUND *confuse*

LORD **c-ed** them — Josh 10:10
c their strategy — Is 19:3
c-ing the Jews — Acts 9:22

CONFRONT *challenge, face*

snares of death **c-ed** — 2 Sam 22:6
Days of affliction **c** — Job 30:27
Arise, O LORD, **c** him — Ps 17:13
the elders **c-ed** *Him* — Luke 20:1

CONFUSE *perplex*

c their language — Gen 11:7
Send . . . and **c** them — Ps 144:6
They are **c-d** by wine — Is 28:7

CONFUSION *disorder*

into great **c** — Deut 7:23
Jerusalem was in **c** — Acts 21:31
not *a God* of **c** — 1 Cor 14:33

CONGREGATION *assembly*

all the **c** of Israel — Ex 12:3
c shall stone him — Num 15:35
strife of the **c** — Num 27:14
c of the godly ones — Ps 149:1
the **c** of the disciples — Acts 6:2
In the midst of the **c** — Heb 2:12

CONQUER *be victorious*

c-ed all the country — Gen 14:7
but could not **c** it — Is 7:1
c through Him — Rom 8:37
out **c-ing**, and to **c** — Rev 6:2

CONSCIENCE *moral obligation*

always a blameless **c** — Acts 24:16
also for **c'** sake — Rom 13:5
their **c** being weak is — 1 Cor 8:7
seared in their own **c** — 1 Tim 4:2
keep a good **c** — 1 Pet 3:16

CONSECRATE (v) *sanctify*

sons of Israel **c** — Ex 28:38
garments shall be **c-d** — Ex 29:21
c it and all its — Ex 40:9
c-s his house as holy — Lev 27:14
he shall **c** his head — Num 6:11
C yourselves — Josh 3:5
have **c-d** this house — 1 Kin 9:3

CONSECRATED (adj) *sanctified*

touch any **c** thing — Lev 12:4
c people . . . LORD — Deut 26:19
there is **c** bread — 1 Sam 21:4
c ones were purer — Lam 4:7
ate the **c** bread — Matt 12:4

CONSIDER *observe, think, regard*

were **c-ed** unclean — Neh 7:64
C my groaning — Ps 5:1
he who **c-s** the helpless — Ps 41:1
c the work of His hands — Is 5:12
C the ravens, for — Luke 12:24
c your calling — 1 Cor 1:26
c how to stimulate — Heb 10:24

CONSOLATION *comfort*

c-s of God too small — Job 15:11
Thy **c-s** delight my — Ps 94:19
is any **c** of love — Phil 2:1

CONSOLE *soothe, comfort*

Esau is **c-ing** himself — Gen 27:42
servants to **c** him — 2 Sam 10:2
c-d . . . comforted — Job 42:11
c them concerning — John 11:19

CONSPIRACY *plot, scheme*

the **c** was strong — 2 Sam 15:12
found **c** in Hoshea — 2 Kin 17:4
from the **c-ies** of man — Ps 31:20

CONSPIRE *plot against*

have **c-d** against me — 1 Sam 22:8
c-d against my — 2 Kin 10:9
c together against — Ps 83:3
Amos . . . **c-d** against — Amos 7:10

CONSTELLATION *star configuration*

a **c** in its season — Job 38:32
c-s Will not flash — Is 13:10

CONSTRUCT *build*

c a sanctuary for Me — Ex 25:8
c siegeworks — Deut 20:20

CONSULT *confer with*

c-ed with the elders — 1 Kin 12:6

C the mediums Is 8:19
Without **c-ing** Me Is 30:2
people **c** their wooden Hos 4:12
not . . . **c** with flesh Gal 1:16

CONSUME *destroy, devour*
c-d . . . purchase price Gen 31:35
the bush was not **c-d** Ex 3:2
c-d the burnt offering Lev 9:24
great fire will **c** us Deut 5:25
c the cedars Judg 9:15
c-d by Thine anger Ps 90:7
fire **c-ing** the stubble Joel 2:5
Zeal . . . will **c** John 2:17
c your flesh like fire James 5:3

CONTEMPT *scorn*
He pours **c** on nobles Job 12:21
With pride and **c** Ps 31:18
treating Him with **c** Luke 23:11
your brother with **c** Rom 14:10

CONTEND *strive*
c with him in battle Deut 2:24
c-ed . . . vigorously Judg 8:1
c with the Almighty Job 40:2
Who will **c** with me Is 50:8
I will not **c** forever Is 57:16
he **c-ed** with God Hos 12:3
c . . . for the faith Jude 3

CONTENT *satisfied*
Nor will he be **c** Prov 6:35
c with your wages Luke 3:14
c with weaknesses 2 Cor 12:10
have learned to be **c** Phil 4:11
c with what you have Heb 13:5

CONTENTION *strife*
object of **c** to our Ps 80:6
puts an end to **c-s** Prov 18:18
the **c-s** of a wife Prov 19:13
Strife exists and **c** Hab 1:3

CONTRARY *against*
c to the command Num 24:13
for the wind was **c** Matt 14:24
grafted **c** to nature Rom 11:24
c to the teaching Rom 16:17
c to sound teaching 1 Tim 1:10

CONTRIBUTE *give*
Josiah **c-d** to the 2 Chr 35:7
c yearly one third Neh 10:32
c-ing to their support Luke 8:3
c-ing to . . . the saints Rom 12:13

CONTRIBUTION *gift, offering*
to raise a **c** for Me Ex 25:2
as a **c** to the LORD Lev 7:14
c-s, the first fruits Neh 12:44
a **c** for the poor Rom 15:26
liberality of your **c** 2 Cor 9:13

CONTRITE *sorrowful, repentant*
broken and a **c** heart Ps 51:17
humble and **c** of spirit Is 66:2

CONTROL (n) *order, rule*
people were out of **c** Ex 32:25
was it not under . . . **c** Acts 5:4
children under **c** 1 Tim 3:4

CONTROL (v) *rule, subdue*
he **c-led** himself and Gen 43:31
Joseph could not **c** Gen 45:1
Haman **c-led** himself Esth 5:10

CONTROVERSY *dispute*
wise man has a **c** Prov 29:9
LORD has a **c** with the Jer 25:31
shun foolish **c-ies** Titus 3:9

CONVERSION *change*
c of the Gentiles Acts 15:3

CONVERTED *changed*
sinners will be **c** Ps 51:13
unless you are **c** Matt 18:3

perceive . . . and be **c** John 12:40

CONVICT *condemn, judge*
one of you **c-s** Me John 8:46
c . . . concerning sin John 16:8
he is **c-ed** by all 1 Cor 14:24
to **c** all the ungodly Jude 15

CONVINCED *persuaded*
c that John was a Luke 20:6
c that neither death Rom 8:38
c in the Lord Jesus Rom 14:14
c of better things Heb 6:9

CONVOCATION *assembly, conclave*
sabbath . . . a holy **c** Lev 23:3
shall have a holy **c** Num 29:7

CONVULSION *paroxysm, spasm*
threw him into a **c** Mark 9:20
a **c** with foaming Luke 9:39

COOK *prepare food*
Jacob had **c-ed** stew Gen 25:29
you shall **c** and eat Deut 16:7

COPY *facsimile*
c of this law on a Deut 17:18
c of . . . law of Moses Josh 8:32
c of the edict Esth 8:13
mere **c** of the true Heb 9:24

CORBAN *offering*
C (that is . . .) Mark 7:11

CORD *band, rope*
c-s of Sheol 2 Sam 22:6
c-s of affliction Job 36:8
c-s of death Ps 18:4
silver **c** is broken Eccl 12:6
the **c-s** of falsehood Is 5:18
a scourge of **c-s** John 2:15

CORNELIUS
centurion, believer Acts 10:1ff

CORNER *angle, intersection*
the chief **c** *stone* Ps 118:22
lurks by every **c** Prov 7:12
on the street **c-s** Matt 6:5
the chief **c** *stone* Mark 12:10
four **c-s** of the earth Rev 7:1

CORNERSTONE *support stone*
who laid its **c** Job 38:6
the **c** of her tribes Is 19:13
costly **c** *for* the Is 28:16
From them . . . the **c** Zech 10:4

CORPSE *dead body*
made unclean by a **c** Lev 22:4
Their **c-s** will rise Is 26:19
a mass of **c-s** Nah 3:3
boy . . . like a **c** Mark 9:26

CORRECT *reprove*
c him with the rod 2 Sam 7:14
He who **c-s** a scoffer Prov 9:7
C your son, and he Prov 29:17
C me, O LORD Jer 10:24
gentleness **c-ing** 2 Tim 2:25

CORRUPT (adj) *evil, rotten*
the earth was **c** Gen 6:11
detestable and **c** Job 15:16
They are **c** Ps 14:1
all of them, are **c** Jer 6:28

CORRUPT (v) *make evil*
a bribe **c-s** the heart Eccl 7:7
c-ed your wisdom Ezek 28:17
have **c-ed** the covenant Mal 2:8
Bad company **c-s** 1 Cor 15:33
harlot who was **c-ing** Rev 19:2

CORRUPTION *decay, evil*
their **c** is in them Lev 22:25
no negligence or **c** Dan 6:4
from the flesh reap **c** Gal 6:8

c that is in the world 2 Pet 1:4
slaves of **c** 2 Pet 2:19

COST *expense, price*
c of their lives Num 16:38
let the **c** be paid Ezra 6:4
calculate the **c** Luke 14:28
water . . . without **c** Rev 22:6

COUCH *bed, pallet*
he went up to my **c** Gen 49:4
falling on the **c** Esth 7:8
dissolve my **c** with my Ps 6:6
sprawl on their **c-es** Amos 6:4

COUNCIL *assembly*
not enter into their **c** Gen 49:6
the **c** of the holy ones Ps 89:7
the **c** of My people Ezek 13:9
to their **c** *chamber* Luke 22:66
conferred with his **c** Acts 25:12

COUNCIL
Sanhedrin Matt 26:59
Jewish governing body Mark 15:1,43; Luke 23:50

COUNSEL (n) *advice, opinion*
I shall give you **c** Ex 18:19
To Him belong **c** Job 12:13
not walk in the **c** Ps 1:1
Listen to **c** and Prov 19:20
the **c** of His will Eph 1:11

COUNSEL (v) *advise*
he **c-ed** rebellion Deut 13:5
I **c** that all Israel 2 Sam 17:11
How do you **c** *me* 1 Kin 12:6
c you with My eye Ps 32:8

COUNSELOR *adviser*
the king and his **c-s** Ezra 7:15
c-s walk barefoot Job 12:17
abundance of **c-s** Prov 11:14
Wonderful C, Mighty Is 9:6
who became His **c** Rom 11:34

COUNT *consider, number*
c the stars, if you Gen 15:5
could not be **c-ed** 1 Kin 8:5
my prayer be **c-ed** Ps 141:2
was **c-ed** among us Acts 1:17
as some **c** slowness 2 Pet 3:9

COUNTENANCE *appearance*
why has your **c** fallen Gen 4:6
LORD lift up His **c** Num 6:26
light of Thy **c** Ps 4:6
an angry **c** Prov 25:23

COUNTRYMAN *citizen*
not hate . . . fellow **c** Lev 19:17
among your **c-men** Deut 17:15
a man and his **c** Deut 25:11
my fellow **c-men** and Rom 11:14

COURAGE *heart, valor*
he lost **c** 2 Sam 4:1
and do not lose **c** 2 Chr 15:7
let your heart take **c** Ps 27:14
Take **c**, My son Matt 9:2
Take **c**, it is I Matt 14:27
c; I have overcome John 16:33
we are of good **c** 2 Cor 5:8

COURIER *messenger*
c-s went throughout 2 Chr 30:6
letters . . . by **c-s** Esth 3:13
One **c** runs to meet Jer 51:31

COURT *area, hall, tribunal*
c of the tabernacle Ex 27:9
a day in Thy **c-s** Ps 84:10
c of the LORD's house Jer 26:2
c of the guardhouse Jer 39:15
then you have law **c-s** 1 Cor 6:4
drag you into **c** James 2:6

COURTYARD *compound, enclosure*
a well in his **c** 2 Sam 17:18
c of the high priest Matt 26:58
Peter . . . in the **c** Mark 14:66

COVENANT *binding agreement*
establish My **c** Gen 6:18
for a sign of a **c** Gen 9:13
ark of the **c** Num 10:33
My **c** of peace Num 25:12
book of the **c** 2 Kin 23:2
who keep His **c** Ps 103:18
I will make a new **c** Jer 31:31
forsake the holy **c** Dan 11:30
a **c** with Assyria Hos 12:1
cup . . . is the new **c** Luke 22:20
c which God made Acts 3:25
this is My **c** with Rom 11:27
servants of a new **c** 2 Cor 3:6
strangers to the **c-s** Eph 2:12
guarantee . . . better **c** Heb 7:22
ark of His **c** Rev 11:19

COVER (n)
c of porpoise skin Num 4:14
the **c** of a couch Amos 3:12

COVER (v) *hide, protect*
and **c** up his blood Gen 37:26
Whose sin is **c-ed** Ps 32:1
He will **c** you with Ps 91:4
love **c-s** all Prov 10:12
c-ed . . . with sackcloth Jon 3:6
to the hills, **C** us Luke 23:30
c a multitude of sins James 5:20
love **c-s** a multitude 1 Pet 4:8

COVERING *canopy*
made . . . loin **c-s** Gen 3:7
spread a cloud for a **c** Ps 105:39
sackcloth their **c** Is 50:3
given to her for a **c** 1 Cor 11:15
freedom as a **c** 1 Pet 2:16

COVET *crave, desire*
not **c** your neighbor's Ex 20:17
You shall not **c** Deut 5:21
I **c-ed** them and took Josh 7:21
They **c** fields and then Mic 2:2
c-ed no one's silver Acts 20:33

CRAFTINESS *shrewdness*
the wise in their **c** 1 Cor 3:19
not walking in **c** 2 Cor 4:2
by **c** in deceitful Eph 4:14

CRAFTSMAN *artisan*
the hands of the **c** Deut 27:15
all the **c-men** and 2 Kin 24:14
idol, a **c** casts it Is 40:19
business to . . . **c-men** Acts 19:24
c of any craft will Rev 18:22

CRAG *protrusion, rock*
sharp **c** on the one 1 Sam 14:4
Upon the rocky **c** Job 39:28
clefts of the **c-s** Is 57:5

CREATE *form, make*
c-d the heavens Gen 1:1
c-d man in His Gen 1:27
C in me a clean Ps 51:10
C-ing the praise of Is 57:19
one God **c-d** us Mal 2:10
c-d . . . for good works Eph 2:10
c-d in righteousness Eph 4:24
Thou didst **c** all Rev 4:11

CREATION
beginning of **c** Mark 10:6
preach . . . to all **c** Mark 16:15
whole **c** groans Rom 8:22
beginning of **c** 2 Pet 3:4

CREATOR *Maker*
Remember . . . your **C** Eccl 12:1
The **C** of Israel Is 43:15
rather than the **C** Rom 1:25
to a faithful **C** 1 Pet 4:19

CREATURE *created being*
every living **c** that Gen 1:21
winged **c** will make Eccl 10:20
and crawling **c-s** Rom 1:23
in Christ . . . new **c** 2 Cor 5:17
as **c-s** of instinct 2 Pet 2:12

CREDITOR *lender*
not to act as a **c** to Ex 22:25
every **c** shall release Deut 15:2
Let the **c** seize all Ps 109:11
My **c-s** did I sell you Is 50:1

CRIME *vice*
be a lustful **c** Job 31:11
committed no **c** Dan 6:22
full of bloody **c-s** Ezek 7:23
not of such **c-s** Acts 25:18

CRIMINAL *lawbreaker*
crucified . . . the **c-s** Luke 23:33
imprisonment as a **c** 2 Tim 2:9

CRIMSON *deep red*
purple, **c** and violet 2 Chr 2:7
like **c** . . . be like wool Is 1:18

CRIPPLED *lame*
a son **c** in his feet 2 Sam 4:4
enter life **c** or lame Matt 18:8
bring . . . **c** and blind Luke 14:21

CROOKED *evil, twisted*
and **c** generation Deut 32:5
to their **c** ways Ps 125:5
What is **c** cannot be Eccl 1:15
make **c** the straight Acts 13:10
c and perverse Phil 2:15

CROP *yield of produce*
old things from the **c** Lev 25:22
c-s to the grasshopper Ps 78:46
c began to sprout Amos 7:1
share of the **c-s** 2 Tim 2:6

CROSS (n) *execution device*
take his **c** and Matt 10:38
to bear His **c** Mark 15:21
take up his **c** daily Luke 9:23
standing by the **c** John 19:25
hanging Him on a **c** Acts 5:30
c of Christ should 1 Cor 1:17
word of the **c** is 1 Cor 1:18
boast, except in the **c** Gal 6:14
even death on a **c** Phil 2:8
blood of His **c** Col 1:20
endured the **c** Heb 12:2

CROSS (v) *pass over*
you **c** the Jordan Deut 12:10
c-ed opposite Jericho Josh 3:16
kept **c-ing** the ford 2 Sam 19:18
Jesus had **c-ed** over Mark 5:21
c-ing over to Acts 21:2

CROUCH *bow, stoop*
sin is **c-ing** at the Gen 4:7
Beneath Him **c** the Job 9:13
Nothing . . . but to **c** Is 10:4

CROWD *multitude*
because of the **c** Mark 2:4
c of tax-gatherers Luke 5:29
they stirred up the **c** Acts 17:8

CROWN (n) *royal emblem* or *top*
on the **c** of the head Gen 49:26
the **c** of their king 2 Sam 12:30
he set the royal **c** Esth 2:17
wife is the **c** of Prov 12:4
gray head is a **c** Prov 16:31
c of the drunkards Is 28:3
a **c** of thorns Matt 27:29
receive the **c** of life James 1:12
c-s before the throne Rev 4:10
golden **c** on His head Rev 14:14

CROWN (v) *to place crown on*
c him with glory Ps 8:5

Who **c-s** you with Ps 103:4
head **c-s** you like Song 7:5
c-ed him with glory Heb 2:7

CRUCIFY *to execute on a cross*
scourge and **c** *Him* Matt 20:19
Let Him be **c-ied** Matt 27:22
Jesus . . . been **c-ied** Matt 28:5
c your King John 19:15
Paul was not **c-ied** 1 Cor 1:13
preach Christ **c-ied** 1 Cor 1:23
not have **c-ied** the 1 Cor 2:8
c-ied with Christ Gal 2:20
world . . . **c-ied** to me Gal 6:14
their Lord was **c-ied** Rev 11:8

CRUEL *fierce, harsh*
their . . . **c** bondage Ex 6:9
c man does . . . harm Prov 11:17
compassion . . . is **c** Prov 12:10
c and have no mercy Jer 6:23
people has become **c** Lam 4:3

CRUMBS *morsels*
dogs feed on the **c** Matt 15:27
on the children's **c** Mark 7:28

CRUSH *demolish, destroy*
a foot may **c** them Job 39:15
saves . . . **c-ed** in spirit Ps 34:18
lying tongue . . . **c-es** Prov 26:28
by **c-ing** My people Is 3:15
c-ed for our iniquities Is 53:5
LORD was pleased To **c** Is 53:10
who **c** the needy Amos 4:1
c Satan under . . . feet Rom 16:20

CRYSTAL *glass*
awesome gleam of **c** Ezek 1:22
sea of glass like **c** Rev 4:6
water . . . clear as **c** Rev 22:1

CUBIT *linear measure*
ark three hundred **c-s** Gen 6:15
length was nine **c-s** Deut 3:11
gallows fifty **c-s** high Esth 5:14
the altar by **c-s** Ezek 43:13
add a *single* **c** to Matt 6:27

CUD *previously swallowed food*
chews the **c** Lev 11:3
not chew **c**, it is Lev 11:7
chews the **c** Deut 14:6

CULT *religious ritual*
be a **c** prostitute Deut 23:17
male **c** prostitutes 1 Kin 14:24
male **c** prostitutes 2 Kin 23:7

CULTIVATE *till*
no man to **c** the Gen 2:5
Eden to **c** it Gen 2:15
servants shall **c** 2 Sam 9:10
and **c** faithfulness Ps 37:3

CUPBEARER *royal official*
c spoke to Pharaoh Gen 41:9
his **c-s**, and his 1 Kin 10:5
c-s and their attire 2 Chr 9:4
c to the king Neh 1:11

CURE *heal*
c him of his leprosy 2 Kin 5:3
c you of your wound Hos 5:13
they could not **c** him Matt 17:16
that . . . time He **c-d** Luke 7:21

CURSE (n) *condemning oath*
upon myself a **c** Gen 27:12
c on Mount Ebal Deut 11:29
c to My chosen ones Is 65:15
they will become a **c** Jer 44:12
will be no more **c** Zech 14:11
become a **c** for us Gal 3:13

CURSE (v) *condemn verbally*
who **c-s** you I will **c** Gen 12:3
You shall not **c** God Ex 22:28
not **c** a deaf man Lev 19:14

c-d the . . . anointed 2 Sam 19:21
c-d the day of his *birth* Job 3:1
began to **c** and Mark 14:71
with it we **c** men James 3:9

CURTAIN *covering, drape*
on the edge of the **c** Ex 26:4
heaven like a *tent* **c** Ps 104:2
c-s of your dwellings Is 54:2
c-s of the land of Hab 3:7

CUSH
1 *area of W Asia* Gen 2:13
2 *patriarch* Gen 10:6,8
3 *region S of Egypt* Is 20:3
4 *a Benjamite* Ps 7:title

CUSTODY *prison, protection*
they put him in **c** Num 15:34
into the **c** of Hegai Esth 2:3
John . . . taken into **c** Matt 4:12
holding Jesus in **c** Luke 22:63

CUSTOM *manner* or *tax*
it became a **c** in Judg 11:39
not pay tribute, **c** Ezra 4:13
burial **c** of the Jews John 19:40
c-s . . . not lawful Acts 16:21
c-s of our fathers Acts 28:17
whom tax *is due;* **c** Rom 13:7

CUT *destroy, divide*
c off from the earth Ex 9:15
c down their Asherim Ex 34:13
LORD **c** off . . . lips Ps 12:3
tongue will be **c** Prov 10:31
C off your hair and Jer 7:29
were **c-ting** branches Matt 21:8
and **c** off his ear Matt 26:51
were **c** to the quick Acts 7:54
you . . . will be **c** off Rom 11:22

CYMBAL *musical instrument*
castanets and **c-s** 2 Sam 6:5
loud-sounding **c-s** 1 Chr 15:16
with loud **c-s** Ps 150:5
or a clanging **c** 1 Cor 13:1

CYPRESS *tree*
cedar and **c** timber 1 Kin 5:10
c and algum timber 2 Chr 2:8
Our rafters, **c-es** Song 1:17
Wail, O **c**, for the Zech 11:2

CYPRUS
Mediterranean island Is 23:1; Acts 11:19;15:39;21:16

CYRENE
NW African port Mark 15:21; Luke 23:26; Acts 2:10;11:20

CYRUS
king of Persia 2 Chr 36:22; Is 45:1
decreed to rebuild Temple Ezra 1:1;5:13

D

DAGON
god of Philistines Judg 16:23; 1 Sam 5:4

DAMAGE (n) *destruction*
any **d** may be found 2 Kin 12:5
the **d-s** of the house 2 Kin 12:6
d and great loss Acts 27:10
incurred this **d** and Acts 27:21

DAMAGE (v) *destroy, hurt*
it will **d** the revenue Ezra 4:13
and **d-ing** to kings Ezra 4:15
enemy has **d-d** Ps 74:3
Lest anyone **d** it Is 27:3

DAMASCUS
city of Aram (Syria) Gen 14:15; Acts 9:3,27

DAN
1 *son of Jacob* Gen 30:6;49:16
2 *tribal area* Josh 19:40; Judg 18:2
3 *city in N Palestine* Josh 19:47

DANCE (n) *rhythmic movement*
timbrels . . . with **d-ing** Ex 15:20
they sing in the **d-s** 1 Sam 29:5
shall rejoice in the **d** Jer 31:13
music and **d-ing** Luke 15:25

DANCE (v) *move rhythmically*
from those who **d-d** Judg 21:23
David was **d-ing** 2 Sam 6:14
and a time to **d** Eccl 3:4
Herodias **d-d** before Matt 14:6

DANGER *peril*
not only is there **d** Acts 19:27
often in **d** of death 2 Cor 11:23
d-s from . . . Gentiles 2 Cor 11:26

DANIEL
1 *son of David and Abigail* 1 Chr 3:1
2 *priest* Ezra 8:2
3 *prophet* Ezek 14:14; Dan 1:6
also **BELTESHAZZAR**

DARIUS
1 *Darius the Mede* Dan 5:31
2 *Darius I* Ezra 4:5; Hag 1:1
3 *Darius II* Neh 12:22

DARK *dim, shadow*
not in **d** sayings Num 12:8
d places of the land Ps 74:20
it was still **d** John 20:1
shining in a **d** place 2 Pet 1:19

DARKNESS *gloom, shadow*
blind . . . gropes in **d** Deut 28:29
are silenced in **d** 1 Sam 2:9
illumines my **d** 2 Sam 22:29
those who dwelt in **d** Ps 107:10
as light excels **d** Eccl 2:13
people who walk in **d** Is 9:2
into the outer **d** Matt 22:13
those who sit in **d** Luke 1:79
turn from **d** to light Acts 26:18
has light with **d** 2 Cor 6:14
unfruitful deeds of **d** Eph 5:11
in Him there is no **d** 1 John 1:5

DARLING *love*
you are, my **d** Song 1:15
Arise, my **d** Song 2:13
my **d**, My dove Song 5:2

DAUGHTER
d-s were born to them Gen 6:1
if a man sells his **d** Ex 21:7
inheritance to his **d** Num 27:8
Kings' **d-s** are among Ps 45:9
the **d** of my people Jer 9:1
mother against **d** Luke 12:53

DAVID
anointed 1 Sam 16:13
killed Goliath 1 Sam 17:50
fled from Saul 1 Sam 19:18
spared Saul 1 Sam 26:9
king of Judah and Israel 2 Sam 2:4;5:3
covenant with God 2 Sam 7:8
death 1 Kin 2:10

DAWN (n) *daylight*
at the approach of **d** Judg 19:25
caused the **d** to know Job 38:12
rise before **d** and Ps 119:147
wings of the **d** Ps 139:9
As the **d** is spread Joel 2:2

DAWN (v) *become light*
the day began to **d** Judg 19:26
when morning **d-s** Ps 46:5
d toward the first Matt 28:1
until the day **d-s** 2 Pet 1:19

DAY *light*
God called the light **d** Gen 1:5
come on a festive **d** 1 Sam 25:8
d . . . LORD has made Ps 118:24
d-s of your youth Eccl 12:1
d of the LORD is near Is 13:6
has despised the **d** Zech 4:10
the **d** of His coming Mal 3:2
Give us this **d** Matt 6:11
judge . . . the last **d** John 12:48
perfect it until the **d** Phil 1:6
d of the Lord 1 Thess 5:2
d is as a thousand 2 Pet 3:8

DAY OF ATONEMENT
month is the **d** Lev 23:27
for it is a **d** Lev 23:28

DAZZLING *blinding, bright*
My beloved is **d** Song 5:10
Like **d** heat Is 18:4
near . . . in **d** apparel Luke 24:4

DEACONS *officer, server*
overseers and **d** Phil 1:1
D likewise *must be* 1 Tim 3:8
let them serve as **d** 1 Tim 3:10
Let **d** be husbands 1 Tim 3:12
served well as **d** 1 Tim 3:13

DEAD *without life*
you are a **d** man Gen 20:3
dealt with the **d** Ruth 1:8
forgotten as a **d** man Ps 31:12
d do not praise Ps 115:17
Your **d** will live Is 26:19
not weep for the **d** Jer 22:10
rising from the **d** Mark 9:10
d shall hear the John 5:25
resurrection of the **d** Acts 23:6
first-born from the **d** Col 1:18
living and the **d** 2 Tim 4:1
to those who are **d** 1 Pet 4:6
I was **d** . . . I am alive Rev 1:18
Hades gave up the **d** Rev 20:13

DEAF *without hearing*
makes *him* dumb or **d** Ex 4:11
not curse a **d** man Lev 19:14
the **d** shall hear Is 29:18
and *the* **d** hear Matt 11:5
the **d** to hear Mark 7:37
d and dumb spirit Mark 9:25

DEAL *allot, barter, treat*
let us **d** wisely Ex 1:10
have you **d-t** with us Ex 14:11
d-t with mediums 2 Kin 21:6
who **d** treacherously Ps 25:3
has **d-t** bountifully Ps 116:7
who **d** faithfully Prov 12:22
Everyone **d-s** falsely Jer 6:13
has **d-t** with me Luke 1:25

DEALINGS *actions, relations*
no **d** with anyone Judg 18:7
no **d** with Samaritans John 4:9
of the Lord's **d** James 5:11

DEAR *beloved*
Is Ephraim My **d** son Jer 31:20
my life . . . as **d** to Acts 20:24
had become very **d** 1 Thess 2:8

DEATH *cessation of life*
d encompassed me 2 Sam 22:5
d for his own sin 2 Chr 25:4
D rather than my pains Job 7:15
no mention of Thee in **d** Ps 6:5
the shadow of **d** Ps 23:4
doomed to **d** Ps 102:20
d of His godly ones Ps 116:15
who hate me love **d** Prov 8:36
love is as strong as **d** Song 8:6
D cannot praise Thee Is 38:18
no pleasure in the **d** Ezek 18:32
d is better to me Jon 4:3
let him be put to **d** Matt 15:4
shall not taste **d** Matt 16:28
passed out of **d** John 5:24
he shall never see **d** John 8:51

sickness is not unto **d** John 11:4
d by hanging Him Acts 10:39
d reigned from Adam Rom 5:14
wages of sin is **d** Rom 6:23
d, where . . . victory 1 Cor 15:55
even **d** on a cross Phil 2:8
He might taste **d** Heb 2:9
passed out of **d** 1 John 3:14
Be faithful until **d** Rev 2:10
had the name **D** Rev 6:8

DEBATE *dispute*
d-d . . . themselves Mark 1:27
dissension and **d** Acts 15:2
had been much **d** Acts 15:7

DEBORAH
1 *nurse of Rebekah* Gen 35:8
2 *prophetess, judge* Judg 4:4ff

DEBT *obligation*
and pay your **d** 2 Kin 4:7
exaction of every **d** Neh 10:31
sureties for **d-s** Prov 22:26
forgive us our **d-s** Matt 6:12

DEBTOR *borrower*
restores to the **d** Ezek 18:7
forgiven our **d-s** Matt 6:12
had two **d-s** Luke 7:41
his master's **d-s** Luke 16:5

DECAY *corruption*
own eyes see his **d** Job 21:20
Holy One to . . . **d** Acts 2:27
did not undergo **d** Acts 13:37

DECEASED *dead*
wife of the **d** shall Deut 25:5
the widow of the **d** Ruth 4:5
the sister of the **d** John 11:39

DECEIT *falsehood, deception*
full of curses and **d** Ps 10:7
in whose spirit . . . no **d** Ps 32:2
D is in the heart Prov 12:20
he lays up **d** Prov 26:24
houses are full of **d** Jer 5:27
house of Israel . . . **d** Hos 11:12
d, sensuality, envy Mark 7:22
full of envy . . . **d** Rom 1:29
the lusts of **d** Eph 4:22
nor was any **d** found 1 Pet 2:22

DECEIVE *cheat, mislead*
have you **d-d** me Gen 29:25
Jacob **d-d** Laban Gen 31:20
d-s his companion Lev 6:2
Do not **d** me 2 Kin 4:28
who **d-s** his neighbor Prov 26:19
your heart had **d-d** you Obad 3
they keep **d-ing** Rom 3:13
Let no one **d** you Eph 5:6
d-ing and being **d-d** 2 Tim 3:13

DECEIVER *liar*
as a **d** in his sight Gen 27:12
as **d-s** and yet true 2 Cor 6:8
d and the antichrist 2 John 7

DECEPTION *falsehood*
their mind prepares **d** Job 15:35
last **d** will be worse Matt 27:64
philosophy and empty **d** Col 2:8
reveling in their **d-s** 2 Pet 2:13

DECISION *judgment, resolution, choice*
d is from the LORD Prov 16:33
in the valley of **d** Joel 3:14
My **d** is to gather Zeph 3:8
majority reached a **d** Acts 27:12

DECLARE *explain, proclaim*
Moses **d-d** to . . . sons Lev 23:44
d Thy faithfulness Ps 30:9
d Thy lovingkindness Ps 92:2
Who has **d-d** *this* Is 41:26
d-s the LORD Amos 4:11
He will **d** all things John 4:25

d-d the Son of God Rom 1:4

DECREASE *abate, subside*
the water **d-d** steadily Gen 8:5
not let their cattle **d** Ps 107:38
increase . . . I must **d** John 3:30

DECREE (n) *judgment, order*
issued a **d** to rebuild Ezra 5:13
and **d** of the king Esth 2:8
devises mischief by **d** Ps 94:20
delivering the **d-s** Acts 16:4
to the **d-s** of Caesar Acts 17:7

DECREE (v) *decide, determine*
been **d-d** against her Esth 2:1
will also **d** a thing Job 22:28
And rulers **d** justice Prov 8:15
Seventy weeks . . . **d-d** Dan 9:24

DEDICATE *consecrate, devote*
D yourselves today Ex 32:29
I wholly **d** the silver Judg 17:3
d-d by . . . David 1 Kin 7:51
David . . . **d-d** these 1 Chr 18:11
d-d part . . . the spoil 1 Chr 26:27
d-ing it to Him 2 Chr 2:4

DEDICATION *consecration*
the **d** of the altar 2 Chr 7:9
celebrated the **d** of Ezra 6:16
d of the wall Neh 12:27
d of the image Dan 3:2
assembled for the **d** Dan 3:3

DEED *action* or *document*
What is this **d** Gen 44:15
for our evil **d-s** Ezra 9:13
abominable **d-s** Ps 14:1
prophet mighty in **d** Luke 24:19
their **d-s** were evil John 3:19
d-s of the flesh are Gal 5:19
for every good **d** Titus 3:1
I know your **d-s** Rev 2:2

DEEP (adj) *far ranging, profound*
d sleep falls on men Job 4:13
Thy judgments are . . . **d** Ps 36:6
casts into a **d** sleep Prov 19:15
into **d** darkness Jer 13:16
the well is **d** John 4:11

DEEP (n) *abyss, depth*
fountains of the . . . **d** Gen 7:11
the **d** lying beneath Deut 33:13
surface of the **d** is Job 38:30
The **d-s** also trembled Ps 77:16
the springs of the **d** Prov 8:28

DEFEAT *conquer, overthrow*
d-ed . . . and pursued Gen 14:15
able to **d** them Num 22:6
sons of Israel **d-ed** Josh 12:7
d the Arameans 2 Kin 13:17
d-ed the Philistines 1 Chr 18:1
d-ed the entire army Jer 37:10

DEFECT (n) *blemish, spot*
No one who has a **d** Lev 21:18
one ram without **d** Num 6:14
no **d** in him 2 Sam 14:25
in whom was no **d** Dan 1:4

DEFECT (v) *rebel, disobey*
d to his master 1 Chr 12:19
many **d-ed** to him 2 Chr 15:9
you have deeply **d-ed** Is 31:6

DEFEND *protect*
LORD of hosts will **d** Zech 9:15
d-ed him and took Acts 7:24
or else **d-ing** them Rom 2:15
are **d-ing** ourselves 2 Cor 12:19

DEFILE *pollute, profane*
astray . . . **d-s** herself Num 5:29
d-d the priesthood Neh 13:29
d-d Thy holy temple Ps 79:1
those **d** the man Matt 15:18

is what **d-s** the man Mark 7:20
conscience . . . is **d-d** 1 Cor 8:7
d-s the entire body James 3:6

DEFRAUD *deprive, wrong, cheat*
whom have I **d-ed** 1 Sam 12:3
To **d** a man Lam 3:36
Do not **d** Mark 10:19
no one keep **d-ing** Col 2:18

DEITY *God, gods*
of strange **d-ies** Acts 17:18
fulness of **D** dwells Col 2:9

DELAY *hinder, linger, stall*
Do not **d** me Gen 24:56
Moses **d-ed** to come Ex 32:1
shall not **d** to pay Deut 23:21
in case I am **d-ed** 1 Tim 3:15

DELICACIES *fancy foods*
eat of their **d** Ps 141:4
Do not desire his **d** Prov 23:3
Those who ate **d** Lam 4:5

DELIGHT (n) *pleasure*
I have no **d** in you 2 Sam 15:26
his **d** is in the law Ps 1:2
commandments . . . **d** Ps 119:143
my **d** in the sons of Prov 8:31
a just weight is His **d** Prov 11:1
the **d** of kings Prov 16:13
call the sabbath a **d** Is 58:13

DELIGHT (v) *desire*
d in . . . offerings 1 Sam 15:22
d to revere Thy name Neh 1:11
d in the Almighty Job 22:26
D yourself in the LORD Ps 37:4
Who **d** in doing evil Prov 2:14
takes no **d** in fools Eccl 5:4
I **d** in loyalty Hos 6:6
d-s . . . unchanging love Mic 7:18
d-ing . . . self-abasement Col 2:18

DELIVER *give, rescue, save*
come down to **d** them Ex 3:8
d the manslayer Num 35:25
can this one **d** 1 Sam 10:27
He will **d** you Job 5:19
none who can **d** Is 43:13
d us from evil Matt 6:13
d Him up to you Matt 26:15
d-ed over to death 2 Cor 4:11
The Lord will **d** me 2 Tim 4:18

DELIVERANCE *salvation*
by a great **d** Gen 45:7
given this great **d** Judg 15:8
with songs of **d** Ps 32:7
a God of **d-s** Ps 68:20

DELIVERER *savior*
the LORD raised up a **d** Judg 3:9
my fortress and my **d** Ps 18:2
d-s . . . ascend Mount Obad 21
D . . . come from Zion Rom 11:26

DEMAND *order, require*
husband may **d** of him Ex 21:22
but I **d** one thing 2 Sam 3:13
captors **d-ed** of us Ps 137:3
do not **d** it back Luke 6:30
d-ing of Him a sign Luke 11:16

DEMETRIUS
1 *Ephesian smith* Acts 19:24,38
2 *a Christian* 3 John 12

DEMOLISH *destroy*
d all . . . high places Num 33:52
he **d-ed** its stones 2 Kin 23:15
to **d** its strongholds Is 23:11

DEMON *devil*
sacrificed to **d-s** Deut 32:17
daughters to the **d-s** Ps 106:37
after the **d** was cast Matt 9:33
d-s also believe James 2:19

not to worship **d-s** Rev 9:20

DEMONIACS *possessed ones*

d, epileptics Matt 4:24
the *incident* of the **d** Matt 8:33

DEMON-POSSESSED

many who were **d** Matt 8:16
a dumb man, **d** Matt 9:32
to the **d** man Mark 5:16
sayings of one **d** John 10:21

DEMONSTRATE *show*

God **d-s** His own love Rom 5:8
to **d** His wrath Rom 9:22
d-d yourselves to be 2 Cor 7:11
d His . . . patience 1 Tim 1:16

DEN *abode*

remains in its **d** Job 37:8
From the **d-s** of lions Song 4:8
the viper's **d** Is 11:8
cast into the lions' **d** Dan 6:7
it a robbers' **d** Mark 11:17

DENARIUS

Roman silver coin Matt 20:2,9
a day's wage Luke 20:24
Denarii *(pl)* John 6:7;12:5

DENOUNCE *accuse, slander*

And come, **d** Israel Num 23:7
the LORD has not **d-d** Num 23:8
let us **d** him Jer 20:10

DENY *conceal, refuse, disavow*

Sarah **d-ied** *it* Gen 18:15
lest you **d** your God Josh 24:27
and **d-ing** the LORD Is 59:13
whoever shall **d** Me Matt 10:33
has **d-ied** the faith 1 Tim 5:8
deeds they **d** *Him* Titus 1:16
d-ies the Son 1 John 2:23

DEPART *leave*

scepter shall not **d** Gen 49:10
to **d** from evil is Job 28:28
His spirit **d-s** Ps 146:4
his folly will not **d** Prov 27:22
I never knew you; **d** Matt 7:23
d from Me, all you Luke 13:27
D from your country Acts 7:3
d and be with Christ Phil 1:23

DEPEND *rely, rest*

d-ed on the weapons Is 22:8
you did not **d** on Him Is 22:11
d the whole Law Matt 22:40

DEPORTATION *exile*

after the **d** to Matt 1:12
to the **d** to Babylon Matt 1:17

DEPOSE *release, remove*

d you from your office Is 22:19
d-d from his royal Dan 5:20

DEPOSIT (n) *security*

in regard to a **d** Lev 6:2
d which was entrusted Lev 6:4

DEPOSIT (v) *place, put*

d them in the tent Num 17:4
d *it* in your town Deut 14:28
d . . . in the temple Ezra 5:15
had **d-ed** the scroll Jer 36:20

DEPRAVED *degenerate*

over to a **d** mind Rom 1:28
men of **d** mind 2 Tim 3:8

DEPRIVE *take away*

d the needy of justice Is 10:2
d-d of . . . my years Is 38:10
d-ing one another 1 Cor 7:5
d-d of the truth 1 Tim 6:5

DEPTH *abyss, deep*

hand are the **d-s** Ps 95:4
went down to the **d-s** Ps 107:26
sins Into the **d-s** Mic 7:19
it had no **d** of soil Mark 4:5
nor height, nor **d** Rom 8:39
even the **d-s** of God 1 Cor 2:10

DEPUTY *proconsul, assistant*

he was the only **d** 1 Kin 4:19
Solomon's . . . **d-ies** 1 Kin 5:16
a **d** was king 1 Kin 22:47

DESCEND *go down*

angels of God . . . **d-ing** Gen 28:12
His glory will not **d** Ps 49:17
breath of . . . **d-s** Eccl 3:21
shall **d** to Hades Matt 11:23
Spirit **d-ing** . . . dove John 1:32
d into the abyss Rom 10:7
who **d-ed** . . . ascended Eph 4:10

DESCENDANT *seed, offering*

your **d-s** I will give Gen 12:7
will raise up your **d** 2 Sam 7:12
So shall your **d-s** be Rom 4:18
to the **d** of Abraham Heb 2:16

DESCRIBE *explain*

you shall **d** the land Josh 18:6
man, **d** the temple Ezek 43:10
who had seen it **d-d** Mark 5:16

DESECRATE *defile*

d the sanctuary Dan 11:31
tried to **d** the temple Acts 24:6

DESERT (n) *wilderness*

d plains of Jericho Josh 5:10
better to live in a **d** Prov 21:19
in the **d** a highway Is 40:3
Rivers in the **d** Is 43:19
like a bush in the **d** Jer 17:6
he lived in the **d-s** Luke 1:80

DESERT (v) *abandon, forsake*

d-ed to the king 2 Kin 25:11
who had **d-ed** them Acts 15:38
but all **d-ed** me 2 Tim 4:16
I will never **d** you Heb 13:5

DESERVE *earn, merit*

with him as he **d-ed** Judg 9:16
done this **d-s** to die 2 Sam 12:5
He is **d-ing** of death Matt 26:66
receiving what we **d** Luke 23:41

DESIGN *creation, plan*

d-s for work in gold Ex 31:4
makers of **d-s** Ex 35:35
execute any **d** which 2 Chr 2:14
All their deadly **d-s** Jer 18:23

DESIGNATE *appoint*

if he **d-s** her for Ex 21:9
one whom I **d** to 1 Sam 16:3
were **d-d** by name 1 Chr 16:41
being **d-d** by God Heb 5:10

DESIRE (n) *appetite, craving*

d . . . for your husband Gen 3:16
poor from *their* **d** Job 31:16
the **d-s** of your heart Ps 37:4
d of the righteous Prov 10:24
d of your eyes Ezek 24:16
d and my prayer Rom 10:1
d-s of the flesh Eph 2:3
d to depart and be Phil 1:23
evil **d,** and greed Col 3:5

DESIRE (v) *crave, wish*

your heart **d-s** Deut 14:26
as much as you **d** 1 Sam 2:16
I **d** to argue with God Job 13:3
not **d** his delicacies Prov 23:3
righteous men **d-d** Matt 13:17
d the greater gifts 1 Cor 12:31
d . . . a good showing Gal 6:12
d a better *country* Heb 11:16

DESOLATE *lonely, waste*

your sanctuaries **d** Lev 26:31
sons of the **d** one Is 54:1
high places will be **d** Ezek 6:6
loaves in a **d** place Matt 15:33
homestead be made **d** Acts 1:20
children of the **d** Gal 4:27

DESOLATION *ruin, waste*

a **d** and a curse 2 Kin 22:19
D is left in the city Is 24:12
d-s of many generations Is 61:4
the abomination of **d** Dan 11:31
day of . . . **d** Zeph 1:15
her **d** is at hand Luke 21:20

DESPAIR (n) *grief*

words of one in **d** Job 6:26
my soul is in **d** Ps 42:6
Why are you in **d** Ps 43:5

DESPAIR (v) *grieve*

Saul then will **d** 1 Sam 27:1
I . . . **d-ed** of all Eccl 2:20
we **d-ed** even of life 2 Cor 1:8
but not **d-ing** 2 Cor 4:8

DESPISE *reject, scorn*

d-d his birthright Gen 25:34
those who **d** Me 1 Sam 2:30
not **d** the discipline Job 5:17
hate and **d** falsehood Ps 119:163
Fools **d** wisdom and Prov 1:7
have we **d-d** Thy name Mal 1:6
not **d** one of these Matt 18:10
do you **d** . . . church 1 Cor 11:22

DESPOIL *injure, lay waste*

d-ed all the cities 2 Chr 14:14
the wicked who **d** me Ps 17:9
plundered and **d-ed** Is 42:22

DESTINE *appoint*

is **d-d** for the sword Job 15:22
d you for the sword Is 65:12
things **d-d** to perish Col 2:22
not **d-d** us for wrath 1 Thess 5:9

DESTITUTE *deprived, needy*

prayer of the **d** Ps 102:17
the land is **d** Ezek 32:15
being **d,** afflicted Heb 11:37

DESTROY *abolish, ruin, waste*

to **d** all flesh Gen 6:17
lest I **d** you 1 Sam 15:6
wouldst Thou **d** me Job 10:8
seek my life to **d** it Ps 40:14
the wicked, He will **d** Ps 145:20
that which **d-s** kings Prov 31:3
shepherds . . . are **d-ing** Jer 23:1
He will **d** mighty men Dan 8:24
who is able to **d** Matt 10:28
You come to **d** us Mark 1:24
seeking . . . to **d** Him Mark 11:18
d the temple and Mark 15:29
D this temple, and John 2:19
to save and to **d** James 4:12
heavens will be **d-ed** 2 Pet 3:12
d the works of the 1 John 3:8

DESTRUCTION *calamity, ruin*

the **d** of my kindred Esth 8:6
God apportion **d** Job 21:17
Your tongue devises **d** Ps 52:2
Pride *goes* before **d** Prov 16:18
called the City of **D** Is 19:18
d of the daughter of Lam 2:11
broad that leads to **d** Matt 7:13
whose end is **d** Phil 3:19
penalty of eternal **d** 2 Thess 1:9
bringing swift **d** upon 2 Pet 2:1

DETERMINE *decide*

to **d** whether he laid Ex 22:8
his days are **d-d** Job 14:5
d-d *their* appointed Acts 17:26
but rather **d** this Rom 14:13
d-d to know nothing 1 Cor 2:2

DETEST *despise, loathe*
carcasses you shall **d** Lev 11:11
not **d** an Egyptian Deut 23:7
I **d** his citadels Amos 6:8

DEVASTATE *destroy, lay waste*
d-d the nations 2 Kin 19:17
Until cities are **d-d** Is 6:11
the LORD . . . **d-s** it Is 24:1
my tents are **d-d** Jer 4:20
d . . . pride of Egypt Ezek 32:12

DEVICE *plan, scheme*
By their own **d-s** Ps 5:10
not promote his *evil* **d** Ps 140:8
a man of evil **d-s** Prov 14:17
in their **d-s** you walk Mic 6:16

DEVIL *demon, Satan*
tempted by the **d** Matt 4:1
one of you is a **d** John 6:70
you son of the **d** Acts 13:10
firm against . . . the **d** Eph 6:11
serpent . . . the **d** Rev 12:9
d . . . into the lake Rev 20:10

DEVISE *design, scheme, plot*
d-d against the Jews Esth 9:25
d-s mischief by decree Ps 94:20
d-s evil continually Prov 6:14
man who **d-s** evil Prov 12:2
He **d-s** wicked schemes Is 32:7
do not **d** evil in Zech 7:10
d futile things Acts 4:25

DEVOTE *commit, dedicate*
shall **d** to the LORD Ex 13:12
d . . . to the law 2 Chr 31:4
d-ing . . . to prayer Acts 1:14
d-d to one another Rom 12:10
D yourselves to prayer Col 4:2

DEVOTED *set apart (to God), cursed*
d to destruction Lev 27:28
Every **d** thing in Num 18:14
d to destruction 1 Sam 15:21
d thing in Israel Ezek 44:29

DEVOTION *consecration*
his deeds of **d** 2 Chr 32:32
excessive **d** *to books* Eccl 12:12
the **d** of your youth Jer 2:2

DEVOUR *consume, swallow*
wild beast **d-ed** him Gen 37:20
the sword **d** forever 2 Sam 2:26
fire from . . . **d-ed** Ps 18:8
love all words that **d** Ps 52:4
has **d-ed** your prophets Jer 2:30
d widows' houses Mark 12:40
bite . . . **d** one another Gal 5:15

DEVOUT *God-fearing*
d men are taken away Is 57:1
was righteous and **d** Luke 2:25
d men, from every Acts 2:5
the **d** women Acts 13:50

DIALECT *language*
in the Hebrew **d** Acts 21:40
the Hebrew **d** Acts 22:2

DIAMOND *jewel*
a sapphire and a **d** Ex 28:18
With a **d** point Jer 17:1

DICTATION *spoken words*
at the **d** of Jeremiah Jer 36:4
written at the **d** of Jer 36:27
book at Jeremiah's **d** Jer 45:1

DIE *decease, expire*
you shall surely **d** Gen 2:17
Where you **d**, I will **d** Ruth 1:17
Curse God and **d** Job 2:9
even wise men **d** Ps 49:10
fools **d** for lack of Prov 10:21
and the fool alike **d** Eccl 2:16
to **d** with You Matt 26:35
child has not **d-d** Mark 5:39
grain of wheat . . . **d-s** John 12:24
d-d for the ungodly Rom 5:6
we who **d-d** to sin Rom 6:2
for whom Christ **d-d** Rom 14:15
I **d** daily 1 Cor 15:31
I **d-d** to the Law Gal 2:19
to **d** is gain Phil 1:21
Jesus **d-d** and rose 1 Thess 4:14
these **d-d** in faith Heb 11:13
who **d** in the Lord Rev 14:13

DIFFICULT *hard*
too **d** for the LORD Gen 18:14
test Solomon with **d** 2 Chr 9:1
anything too **d** for Me Jer 32:27
speech or **d** language Ezek 3:5
solving of **d** problems Dan 5:12
last days **d** times 2 Tim 3:1

DIG *excavate, till*
opens a pit, or **d-s** Ex 21:33
you can **d** copper Deut 8:9
they **d** into houses Job 24:16
dug through the wall Ezek 8:8
dug a wine press Matt 21:33
until I **d** around it Luke 13:8

DIGNITY *majesty, decorum*
Preeminent in **d** Gen 49:3
What honor or **d** has Esth 6:3
all godliness and **d** 1 Tim 2:2
must be men of **d** 1 Tim 3:8

DILIGENCE *effort*
carried out with all **d** Ezra 6:12
Watch . . . with all **d** Prov 4:23
lagging behind in **d** Rom 12:11
show the same **d** Heb 6:11

DIM *cloudy, dark*
eye was not **d** Deut 34:7
eyesight . . . to grow **d** 1 Sam 3:2
d because of grief Job 17:7
windows grow **d** Eccl 12:3

DIMINISH *dwindle, reduce*
you shall **d** its price Lev 25:16
d their inheritance Num 26:54
are **d-ed** and bowed Ps 107:39

DINAH
daughter of Jacob Gen 34:1,3
raped by Shechem Gen 34:2,5

DINE *eat*
men are to **d** with Gen 43:16
to **d** with a ruler Prov 23:1
came and were **d-ing** Matt 9:10

DINNER *meal*
I have prepared . . . **d** Matt 22:4
because of . . . **d** guests Mark 6:26
was giving a big **d** Luke 14:16

DIP *plunge*
d-ped the tunic in Gen 37:31
d your piece of bread Ruth 2:14
d-ped . . . seven times 2 Kin 5:14
d-ped . . . with Me Matt 26:23
who **d-s** with Me Mark 14:20
robe **d-ped** in blood Rev 19:13

DIRECT *arrange, guide, order*
LORD **d-s** his steps Prov 16:9
d your heart in the Prov 23:19
has **d-ed** the Spirit Is 40:13
I **d-ed** the churches 1 Cor 16:1
d their entire body James 3:3

DIRGE *lament*
for you as a **d** Amos 5:1
we sang a **d** Luke 7:32

DISAPPEAR *vanish*
For the faithful **d** Ps 12:1
When the grass **d-s** Prov 27:25
old is ready to **d** Heb 8:13

DISASTER *calamity*
d was close to them Judg 20:34
d on this people Jer 6:19
because of all its **d-s** Jer 19:8
In the day of their **d** Obad 13

DISBELIEVE *doubt*
Jews who **d-d** stirred Acts 14:2
for those who **d** 1 Pet 2:7

DISCERNMENT *judgment*
blessed be your **d** 1 Sam 25:33
asked for yourself **d** 1 Kin 3:11
not a people of **d** Is 27:11
knowledge and all **d** Phil 1:9

DISCHARGE *emission*
a **d** from his body Lev 15:2
leper or who has a **d** Lev 22:4
everyone having a **d** Num 5:2
d, or who is a leper 2 Sam 3:29
the **d** of your blood Ezek 32:6

DISCIPLE *student, learner*
to listen as a **d** Is 50:4
His twelve **d-s** Matt 10:1
d is not above his Matt 10:24
d-s left Him . . . fled Matt 26:56
Your **d-s** do not fast Mark 2:18
Passover . . . My **d-s** Mark 14:14
gaze on His **d-s** Luke 6:20
he cannot be My **d** Luke 14:26
d-s believed in Him John 2:11
wash the **d-s** feet John 13:5
d whom He loved John 19:26
d-s were first called Acts 11:26

DISCIPLINE (n) *chastisement*
the **d** of the LORD Deut 11:2
d of the Almighty Job 5:17
The rod of **d** Prov 22:15
to see your good **d** Col 2:5
d . . . of little profit 1 Tim 4:8

DISCIPLINE (v) *chastise*
as a man **d-s** his son Deut 8:5
d-d you with whips 1 Kin 12:11
D your son while Prov 19:18
d-d by the Lord 1 Cor 11:32
father does not **d** Heb 12:7

DISCLOSE *reveal*
without **d-ing** it to 1 Sam 20:2
Esther had **d-d** what Esth 8:1
will **d** Myself to him John 14:21
d the motives of 1 Cor 4:5
secrets . . . are **d-d** 1 Cor 14:25

DISCOURAGE *dishearten*
d-ing the sons of Num 32:7
people of the land **d-d** Ezra 4:4
d-d with the work Neh 6:9

DISCOVER *find, uncover*
strength was not **d-ed** Judg 16:9
d the depths of God Job 11:7
man may not **d** Eccl 7:14
shamed . . . he is **d-ed** Jer 2:26

DISCRETION *understanding*
LORD give you **d** 1 Chr 22:12
sound wisdom and **d** Prov 3:21
woman who lacks **d** Prov 11:22
Daniel replied with **d** Dan 2:14

DISCUSS *converse, reason*
d matters of justice Jer 12:1
d among themselves Matt 16:7
What were you **d-ing** Mark 9:33
d-ed together what Luke 6:11

DISEASE *sickness*
none of the **d-s** on you Ex 15:26
harmful **d-s** of Egypt Deut 7:15
d-d . . . not healed Ezek 34:4
heals all your **d-s** Ps 103:3
various **d-s** and pains Matt 4:24
power . . . to heal **d-s** Luke 9:1

DISGRACE *reproach, shame*
a **d** to us Gen 34:14
nakedness, it is a **d** Lev 20:17
sin is a **d** to Prov 14:34
not **d** the throne Jer 14:21
and bear your **d** Ezek 16:52

DISGUISE *change, conceal*
d-d his sanity 1 Sam 21:13
Arise now, and **d** 1 Kin 14:2
king of Israel **d-d** 1 Kin 22:30
he **d-s** his face Job 24:15
d-ing . . . as apostles 2 Cor 11:13

DISHONEST *untruthful*
order to get **d** gain Ezek 22:27
cheat with **d** scales Amos 8:5

DISHONOR (n) *disgrace, shame*
to see the king's **d** Ezra 4:14
Fill their faces with **d** Ps 83:16
man conceals **d** Prov 12:16

DISHONOR (v) *disgrace, shame*
who **d-s** his father Deut 27:16
be ashamed and **d-ed** Ps 35:4
and you **d** Me John 8:49
bodies might be **d-ed** Rom 1:24
do you **d** God Rom 2:23

DISOBEDIENCE *rebellion*
the one man's **d** Rom 5:19
in the sons of **d** Eph 2:2
d received a just Heb 2:2
same example of **d** Heb 4:11

DISPERSE *spread*
d them in Jacob Gen 49:7
d-d . . . the peoples Esth 3:8
d them among the Ezek 20:23
who are **d-d** abroad James 1:1

DISPLAY *declare, show*
to **d** her beauty Esth 1:11
d-ed Thy splendor Ps 8:1
d their sin like Is 3:9
works of God . . . **d-ed** John 9:3

DISPLEASE *annoy, trouble*
if it is **d-ing** to you Num 22:34
d-ing in the sight 1 Sam 8:6
may not **d** the lords 1 Sam 29:7
d-ing in His sight Is 59:15
it greatly **d-d** Jonah Jon 4:1

DISPOSSESS *remove*
d-ed the Amorites Num 21:32
Esau **d-ed** them Deut 2:12
He will assuredly **d** Josh 3:10
d-ing the nations Acts 7:45

DISPUTE (n) *controversy*
When they have a **d** Ex 18:16
bring the **d-s** to God Ex 18:19
d in your courts Deut 17:8
a great **d** among Acts 28:29

DISPUTE (v) *contend, debate*
wished to **d** with Him Job 9:3
with Israel he will **d** Mic 6:2
without . . . **d-ing** Phil 2:14
He **d-d** with the devil Jude 9

DISSENSION *division, disagreement*
great **d** and debate Acts 15:2
d between the Acts 23:7
those who cause **d-s** Rom 16:17
without wrath and **d** 1 Tim 2:8

DISSOLVE *melt*
dost **d** me in a storm Job 30:22
I **d** my couch with Ps 6:6
d-d in tears Is 15:3
And the hills **d** Nah 1:5

DISTANCE *far away*
sister stood at a **d** Ex 2:4
following . . . at a **d** Matt 26:58
welcomed . . . from a **d** Heb 11:13

DISTINCTION *difference*
the LORD makes a **d** Ex 11:7
d between the holy Lev 10:10
He made no **d** Acts 15:9
for there is no **d** Rom 3:22
d-s among yourselves James 2:4

DISTINGUISH (v) *discern*
I **d** between good 2 Sam 19:35
not **d** the sound Ezra 3:13
d . . . the righteous Mal 3:18
d-ing of spirits 1 Cor 12:10

DISTORT *pervert*
who **d-s** the justice Deut 27:19
my garment is **d-ed** Job 30:18
d the gospel of Christ Gal 1:7

DISTRESS *adversity, trouble*
day of my **d** Gen 35:3
When you are in **d** Deut 4:30
I am in great **d** 2 Sam 24:14
refuge in the day of **d** Jer 16:19
I am in **d** Lam 1:20
d for every soul Rom 2:9
assisted those in **d** 1 Tim 5:10
widows in their **d** James 1:27

DISTRIBUTE *apportion*
d-d by lot in Shiloh Josh 19:51
to **d** their kinsmen Neh 13:13
d it to the poor Luke 18:22
d-ing to each one 1 Cor 12:11

DISTRICT *area, province*
the **d** of Jerusalem Neh 3:12
d around the Jordan Matt 3:5
d of Galilee Mark 1:28
the **d-s** of Libya Acts 2:10

DISTURB *annoy, bother*
no one **d** his bones 2 Kin 23:18
d them and destroy Esth 9:24
being greatly **d-ed** Acts 4:2
one who is **d-ing** you Gal 5:10

DIVIDE *apportion, separate*
that **d-s** the hoof Deut 14:6
D the living child 1 Kin 3:25
d my garments among Ps 22:18
d-d up His garments Matt 27:35
d-d his wealth Luke 15:12

DIVINATION *witchcraft*
nor practice **d** or Lev 19:26
witchcraft, used **d** 2 Chr 33:6
false vision, **d** Jer 14:14
falsehood and lying **d** Ezek 13:6
a spirit of **d** met us Acts 16:16

DIVINE (adj) *pertaining to deity*
in whom . . . **d** spirit Gen 41:38
I see a **d** being 1 Sam 28:13
power and **d** nature Rom 1:20
is the **d** response Rom 11:4

DIVINE (v) *practice divination*
d-d that the LORD Gen 30:27
d-ing lies for them Ezek 22:28
prophets **d** for money Mic 3:11

DIVINER *seer, conjurer*
called for the . . . **d-s** 1 Sam 6:2
The **d** and the elder Is 3:2
your **d-s** deceive you Jer 29:8
d-s will be embarrassed Mic 3:7
d-s see lying visions Zech 10:2

DIVISION *dissension, portion*
d between My people Ex 8:23
divided..into **d-s** 1 Chr 23:6
d in the multitude John 7:43
no **d-s** among you 1 Cor 1:10
d of soul and spirit Heb 4:12

DIVORCE (n) *separation*
a certificate of **d** Deut 24:1
given her a writ of **d** Jer 3:8
For I hate **d** Mal 2:16

DIVORCE (v) *separate*
he cannot **d** her Deut 22:19
husband **d-s** his wife Jer 3:1
man to **d** his wife Matt 19:3
Whoever **d-s** his Mark 10:11

DOCTRINE *teaching*
Teaching as **d-s** the Matt 15:9
every wind of **d** Eph 4:14
to teach strange **d-s** 1 Tim 1:3
to exhort in sound **d** Titus 1:9

DOCUMENT *manuscript*
the **d** which you sent Ezra 4:18
And on the sealed **d** Neh 9:38
Darius signed the **d** Dan 6:9

DOMAIN *estate*
give You all this **d** Luke 4:6
the **d** of darkness Col 1:13
keep their own **d** Jude 6

DOMINION *authority, rule*
Thine is the **d** 1 Chr 29:11
places of His **d** Ps 103:22
d will be from sea Zech 9:10
and power and **d** Eph 1:21
glory and the **d** forever Rev 1:6

DONKEY *ass*
a wild **d** of a man Gen 16:12
Balaam . . . to the **d** Num 22:29
the foal of a **d** Zech 9:9
you will find a **d** Matt 21:2
and mounted on a **d** Matt 21:5
a dumb **d**, speaking 2 Pet 2:16

DOOR *entrance, opening*
crouching at the **d** Gen 4:7
Uriah slept at the **d** 2 Sam 11:9
over the **d** of my lips Ps 141:3
shut your **d**, pray Matt 6:6
I am the **d** John 10:9
before you an open **d** Rev 3:8
I stand at the **d** Rev 3:20

DOORKEEPER *guard*
d-s have gathered 2 Kin 22:4
eunuchs who were **d-s** Esth 6:2
commanded the **d** Mark 13:34
To him the **d** opens John 10:3

DOORPOST
put it on the two **d-s** Ex 12:7
write them on the **d-s** Deut 6:9
on the seat by the **d** 1 Sam 1:9
Waiting at my **d-s** Prov 8:34

DOORWAY *entrance, opening*
the **d** of the tent Judg 4:20
d-s and doorposts 1 Kin 7:5
at my neighbor's **d** Job 31:9
chamber with its **d** Ezek 40:38

DOUBT (n) *unbelief*
life shall hang in **d** Deut 28:66
why do **d-s** arise Luke 24:38

DOUBT (v) *disbelieve*
why did you **d** Matt 14:31
not **d** in his heart Mark 11:23
d-s is condemned Rom 14:23
who **d-s** is like the James 1:6

DOVE *bird*
he sent out a **d** Gen 8:8
had wings like a **d** Ps 55:6
eyes are *like* **d-s** Song 1:15
descending as a **d** Matt 3:16
descending as a **d** John 1:32
selling the **d-s** John 2:16

DOWNFALL *collapse*
became the **d** of 2 Chr 28:23
noise of their **d** Jer 49:21

DOWNPOUR *rain*
the **d** and the rain Job 37:6
d of waters swept Hab 3:10

DOWRY *bequest*
must pay a **d** for her Ex 22:16
to the **d** for virgins Ex 22:17
d to his daughter 1 Kin 9:16

DRACHMA
Greek silver coin Neh 7:70-72; Matt 17:24

DRAG *draw, pull*
grasshopper **d-s** Eccl 12:5
D them off like sheep Jer 12:3
the dogs to **d** off Jer 15:3
Paul and **d-ged** Acts 14:19
d you into court James 2:6

DRAGON *monster, serpent*
d who *lives* in the sea Is 27:1
Who pierced the **d** Is 51:9
d stood before the Rev 12:4
he laid hold of the **d** Rev 20:2

DRAW *haul, pull*
out to **d** water Gen 24:13
drew him out of the Ex 2:10
but are **d-n** away Deut 30:17
He **d-s** up the drops Job 36:27
d near to my soul Ps 69:18
They are **d-ing** back Jer 46:5
redemption is **d-ing** Luke 21:28
d all men to Myself John 12:32
D near to God James 4:8

DRAWERS *servants*
wood and **d** of water Josh 9:21

DREAD (n) *fear*
in **d** . . . of Israel Ex 1:12
in **d** night and day Deut 28:66
d of the Jews Esth 8:17
they are in great **d** Ps 14:5
d comes like a storm Prov 1:27

DREAD (v) *fear*
what I **d** befalls me Job 3:25
Whom shall I **d** Ps 27:1
whose two kings you **d** Is 7:16
are **d-ed** and feared Hab 1:7

DREAM (n) *vision*
had a **d,** and behold Gen 28:12
man was relating a **d** Judg 7:13
flies away like a **d** Job 20:8
like a **d,** a vision Is 29:7
visions and **d-s** Dan 1:17
to Joseph in a **d** Matt 2:13

DREAM (v) *see a vision*
asleep and **d-ed** Gen 41:5
like those who **d** Ps 126:1
when a hungry man **d-s** Is 29:8
Your old men will **d** Joel 2:28

DRENCH *soak, wet*
d you with my tears Is 16:9
head is **d-ed** with dew Song 5:2
d-ed with the dew Dan 4:33

DRINK (n) *refreshment*
gave the lad a **d** Gen 21:19
or wine, or strong **d** Deut 14:26
to desire strong **d** Prov 31:4
thirsty . . . gave Me **d** Matt 25:35
My blood is true **d** John 6:55
thirsty, give him a **d** Rom 12:20

DRINK (v)
he **drank** of the wine Gen 9:21
Do not **d** wine Lev 10:9
d from the brook 1 Kin 17:6
they all **drank** from Mark 14:23
after **d-ing** old *wine* Luke 5:39
who eats and **d-s** 1 Cor 11:29
ground that **d-s** the Heb 6:7

DRIVE *chase, defeat*
Thou hast **d-n** me Gen 4:14
and **drove** them away Ex 2:17
angel . . . **d-ing** *them* on Ps 35:5
d hard all your workers Is 58:3
drove *them* all out John 2:15
to **d** the ship Acts 27:39

DROSS *metallic waste*
of the earth *like* **d** Ps 119:119
Take away the **d** Prov 25:4
silver has become **d** Is 1:22
Israel has become **d** Ezek 22:18

DROUGHT *dryness*
Like heat in **d** Is 25:5
in regard to the **d** Jer 14:1
I called for a **d** Hag 1:11

DROWNED *suffocated*
d in the Red Sea Ex 15:4
he be **d** in the depth Matt 18:6
were **d** in the sea Mark 5:13

DRUNK *intoxicated*
arrows **d** with blood Deut 32:42
d, but not with wine Is 29:9
made . . . **d** in My wrath Is 63:6
not get **d** with wine Eph 5:18
I saw the woman **d** Rev 17:6

DRUNKARD *intoxicated person*
a glutton and a **d** Deut 21:20
song of the **d-s** Ps 69:12
Awake, **d-s,** and weep Joel 1:5
a reviler, or a **d** 1 Cor 5:11

DRY (adj) *parched, scorched*
let the **d** land appear Gen 1:9
In a **d** and weary land Ps 63:1
Better is a **d** morsel Prov 17:1
O **d** bones, hear Ezek 37:4

DRY (v) *scorch, wither*
My strength is **dried** Ps 22:15
d up . . . streams Ps 74:15
I **d** up the sea Is 50:2
new wine **dries** up Joel 1:10
dries up . . . rivers Nah 1:4

DUE (adj) *proper, right*
In **d** time their foot Deut 32:35
food in **d** season Ps 104:27
d penalty of their Rom 1:27

DUE (n) *what is owed*
as *their* **d** forever Lev 7:34
be the priests' **d** Deut 18:3
Indeed it is Thy **d** Jer 10:7

DULL *heavy, stupid*
eyes are **d** from wine Gen 49:12
Their ears **d** Is 6:10
people . . . become **d** Matt 13:15
become **d** of hearing Heb 5:11

DUMB *silent, unable to speak*
who makes *him* **d** Ex 4:11
I was **d** and silent Ps 39:2
behold, a **d** man Matt 9:32
and the **d** to speak Mark 7:37
astray to the **d** idols 1 Cor 12:2

DUNG *waste*
sweeps away **d** 1 Kin 14:10
dove's **d** for five 2 Kin 6:25
give you cow's **d** Ezek 4:15
their flesh like **d** Zeph 1:17

DUNGEON *prison*
put me into the **d** Gen 40:15
captive . . . in the **d** Ex 12:29
prisoners from the **d** Is 42:7
Jeremiah . . . into the **d** Jer 37:16

DUST *dirt, earth*
God formed man of **d** Gen 2:7
And **d** shall you eat Gen 3:14
repent in **d** and ashes Job 42:6
d before the wind Ps 18:42
Will the **d** praise Thee Ps 30:9
shake off the **d** of Matt 10:14
the **d** of your city Luke 10:11
d on their heads Rev 18:19

DUTY *responsibility*
perform your **d** Gen 38:8
charged with any **d** Deut 24:5
the **d** of a husband's Deut 25:7
his **d** to his wife 1 Cor 7:3

DWELL *abide, live*
father of those who **d** Gen 4:20
Behold, I am **d-ing** 1 Chr 17:1
No evil **d-s** with Thee Ps 5:4
d on Thy holy hill Ps 15:1
I will **d** in the house Ps 23:6
have **d-t** in Jerusalem Jer 35:11
flesh, and **d-t** among John 1:14
of God **d-s** in you 1 Cor 3:16
Christ may **d** in your Eph 3:17
mind **d** on these things Phil 4:8

DWELLING *habitation*
earth shall be your **d** Gen 27:39
name there for His **d** Deut 12:5
place for Thy **d** 1 Kin 8:13
into the eternal **d-s** Luke 16:9
might find a **d** place Acts 7:46

E

EAGLE *bird*
bore you on **e-s'** wings Ex 19:4
the **e** swoops down Deut 28:49
swifter than **e-s** 2 Sam 1:23
with wings like **e-s** Is 40:31
the face of an **e** Ezek 1:10
was like a flying **e** Rev 4:7

EAR *hearing*
heard with our **e-s** 2 Sam 7:22
the **e** test words Job 12:11
and incline your **e** Ps 45:10
e of the wise seeks Prov 18:15
let your **e** receive Jer 9:20
He who has **e-s** to Matt 11:15
and cut off his **e** Matt 26:51
fingers into his **e-s** Mark 7:33
their **e-s** tickled 2 Tim 4:3
He who has an **e** Rev 2:7

EARRING *ornament*
brought . . . **e-s** Ex 35:22
e-s and necklaces Num 31:50
Like an **e** of gold Prov 25:12
her **e-s** and jewelry Hos 2:13

EARTH *land, world*
God created the . . . **e** Gen 1:1
Judge of all the **e** Gen 18:25
the **e** is the LORD's Ex 9:29
way of all the **e** Josh 23:14
foundation of the **e** Job 38:4
saints . . . in the **e** Ps 16:3
give birth to the **e** Ps 90:2
He established the **e** Ps 104:5
the **e** remains forever Eccl 1:4
made the **e** tremble Is 14:16
the vault of the **e** Is 40:22
the **e** is My footstool Is 66:1
e shone with His Ezek 43:2
make the **e** dark Amos 8:9
e will be devoured Zeph 3:8
shall inherit the **e** Matt 5:5
you shall bind on **e** Matt 16:19
on **e** peace among Luke 2:14
glorified . . . on the **e** John 17:4
man is from the **e** 1 Cor 15:47
e and heaven fled Rev 20:11

EARTHENWARE *pottery*
bird in an **e** vessel Lev 14:5
holy water in an **e** Num 5:17
shatter them like **e** Ps 2:9
buy a potter's **e** jar Jer 19:1
vessels of . . . **e** 2 Tim 2:20

EARTHQUAKE *temblor*
LORD *was* not . . . **e** 1 Kin 19:11
punished with . . . **e** Is 29:6
be famines and **e-s** Matt 24:7
there was a great **e** Rev 6:12
killed in the **e** Rev 11:13

EAST *direction of compass*
spread out . . . to the **e** Gen 28:14
directed an **e** wind Ex 10:13
sons of the **e** were Judg 7:12
With the **e** wind Thou Ps 48:7
offspring from the **e** Is 43:5
faces toward the **e** Ezek 8:16
Jerusalem on the **e** Zech 14:4
saw His star in the **e** Matt 2:2
kings from the **e** Rev 16:12

EASY *without difficulty*
knowledge is **e** to him Prov 14:6
My yoke is **e**, and Matt 11:30

EAT *consume, dine, feast*
shall not **e** from it Gen 3:17
they **ate** every plant Ex 10:15
not **e** . . . blood Lev 19:26
e and be satisfied Ps 22:26
not **e** the bread of Prov 31:27
words . . . I **ate** them Jer 15:16
e this scroll Ezek 3:1
e-ing grass like cattle Dan 4:33
e with unwashed Matt 15:20
Take, **e**; this is My Matt 26:26
sinners and **e-s** with Luke 15:2
e . . . at My table Luke 22:30
He took it and **ate** Luke 24:43
e the flesh of . . . Son John 6:53
Peter, kill and **e** Acts 10:13
e-s . . . judgment 1 Cor 11:29

EBAL
1 *son of Shobal* Gen 36:23
2 *son of Joktan* 1 Chr 1:22
also Obal Gen 10:28
3 *mountain near Shechem* Deut 11:29

EBER
1 *line of Shem* Gen 10:21-24
progenitor of Jocktanide Arabs Gen 10:25-30
progenitor of Hebrews Gen 11:16ff
2 *a Gadite* 1 Chr 5:13
3 *son of Elpaal* 1 Chr 8:12
4 *son of Shashak* 1 Chr 8:22
5 *priest* Neh 12:20
see also **HEBER**

EDEN
1 *garden of God* Gen 2:15
2 *city area* 2 Kin 19:12; Ezek 27:23
3 *son of Joah* 2 Chr 29:12

EDICT *decree*
the king's **e-s** Ezra 8:36
a royal **e** be issued Esth 1:19
king's command and **e** Esth 9:1
afraid of the king's **e** Heb 11:23

EDIFICATION *building up*
his good, to his **e** Rom 15:2
speaks to men for **e** 1 Cor 14:3

EDOM
1 *name of Esau* Gen 25:30
2 *Edomites* Num 20:18,20
3 *region or country* Gen 32:3; Judg 11:17
see also **SEIR**

EDUCATED *taught*
be **e** three years Dan 1:5
Moses was **e** in all Acts 7:22
e under Gamaliel Acts 22:3

EFFEMINATE *womanlike*
e, nor homosexuals 1 Cor 6:9

EGYPT
country in NE Africa Gen 12:10;37:25
source of food Gen 42:1,2
on the Nile Ex 4:19;7:5
conflict with Moses Ex 7:8ff
scene of Passover Ex 12:1-36

ELAH
1 *Edomite* Gen 36:41
2 *valley SW of Jerusalem* 1 Sam 17:2
3 *father of Shimei* 1 Kin 4:18
4 *king of Israel* 1 Kin 16:8-10
5 *father of Hoshea* 2 Kin 15:30
6 *son of Caleb* 1 Chr 4:15
7 *son of Uzzi* 1 Chr 9:8

ELAM
1 *son of Shem* Gen 10:22
2 *son of Shashak* 1 Chr 8:24
3 *Korahite Levite* 1 Chr 26:3
4 *head of restoration family* Ezra 2:7; Neh 7:12
5 *head of restoration family* Ezra 2:31; Neh 7:34
6 *chief of people* Neh 10:14
7 *priest* Neh 12:42
8 *region E of Babylonia* Is 21:2; Dan 8:2

ELATH / ELOTH *city*
at Gulf of Aqabah near Ezion-geber 2 Kin 14:22

ELDER *aged, older person*
words of her **e** son Gen 27:42
the **e-s** of Israel Ex 17:6
sits among the **e-s** Prov 31:23
tradition of the **e-s** Matt 15:2
chief priests and **e-s** Matt 27:12
scribes . . . **e-s** came Mark 11:27
Council of **e-s** of Luke 22:66
e-s of the church Acts 20:17
I saw twenty-four **e-s** Rev 4:4

ELEAZAR
1 *son of Aaron* Ex 6:23
high priest Num 20:25-28
2 *son of Abinadab* 1 Sam 7:1
3 *son of Dodo* 2 Sam 23:9
4 *a Levite* 1 Chr 23:22
5 *son of Phinehas* Ezra 8:33
6 *son of Parosh* Ezra 10:18-25
7 *priest* Neh 12:27
8 *ancestor of Jesus* Matt 1:15

ELECT *chosen*
sake of the **e** Matt 24:22
to lead the **e** astray Mark 13:22
justice for His **e** Luke 18:7
against God's **e** Rom 8:33

ELI
high priest 1 Sam 1:9;2:12;3:6;4:18

ELIAKIM
1 *son of Hilkiah* 2 Kin 18:18;19:2
2 *son of Josiah* 2 Kin 23:34
3 *priest* Neh 12:41
4 *ancestor of Jesus* Matt 1:13
5 *ancestor of Jesus* Luke 3:30,31

ELIEZER
1 *Abraham's servant* Gen 15:2
2 *son of Moses* 1 Chr 23:15
3 *son of Becher* 1 Chr 7:8
4 *priest* 1 Chr 15:24
5 *son of Zichri* 1 Chr 27:16
6 *a prophet* 2 Chr 20:37
7 *served under Ezra* Ezra 8:16
8 *son of Jeshua* Ezra 10:18
9 *Levite* Ezra 10:10,23
10 *son Harim* Ezra 10:10,31
11 *ancestor of Jesus* Luke 3:29

ELIHU
1 *son of Tohu* 1 Sam 1:1
2 *Manassite captain* 1 Chr 12:20
3 *temple gatekeeper* 1 Chr 26:1
4 *officer of Judah* 1 Chr 27:18
5 *one of Job's friends* Job 32:17

ELIJAH
1 *prophet* 1 Kin 17:1
aided by widow 1 Kin 17:8ff
revived child 1 Kin 17:23
defeats prophets 1 Kin 18:20ff
flees Jezebel 1 Kin 19:4-8
chooses Elisha 1 Kin 19:19-21
taken up 2 Kin 2:1-11
2 *Benjamite* 1 Chr 8:27
3 *son of Harim* Ezra 10:21
4 *son of Elam* Ezra 10:26

ELIMINATE *remove*
e harmful beasts Lev 26:6
I am going to **e** Jer 16:9
stomach, and is **e-d** Mark 7:19

ELISHA
prophet 2 Kin 6:12
called 1 Kin 19:19-21
Elijah's successor 2 Kin 2:1ff
miracle of oil 2 Kin 4:1-7
revived child 2 Kin 4:8-37
death 2 Kin 13:20

ELIZABETH
mother of John the Baptist Luke 1:7, 13,41,57

ELUL
sixth month of Hebrew calendar Neh 6:15

EMBALM *preserve*
to **e** his father Gen 50:2
he was **e-ed** and Gen 50:26

EMBITTERED *resentful*
the people were **e** 1 Sam 30:6
e them against the Acts 14:2

EMBRACE *clasp, hug*
Esau ran . . . and **e-d** Gen 33:4
e . . . a foreigner Prov 5:20
A time to **e** Eccl 3:5
ran and **e-d** him Luke 15:20

EMERALD *precious stone*
ruby, topaz and **e** Ex 28:17
throne, like an **e** Rev 4:3

EMINENT *renowned*
nor anything **e** Ezek 7:11
the most **e** apostles 2 Cor 11:5
inferior to . . . **e** 2 Cor 12:11

EMISSION *issuance*
man has a seminal **e** Lev 15:16
nocturnal **e** Deut 23:10

EMMAUS
village by Jerusalem Luke 24:13

EMPTY (adj) *containing nothing*
Now the pit was **e** Gen 37:24
did not return **e** 2 Sam 1:22
sent widows away **e** Job 22:9
deceive you with **e** Eph 5:6
avoid . . . **e** chatter 2 Tim 2:16

EMPTY (v) *remove contents*
e-ing their sacks Gen 42:35
they **e** the house Lev 14:36
I **e-ied** them out as Ps 18:42
therefore **e** their net Hab 1:17
e the golden *oil* Zech 4:12
but **e-ied** Himself Phil 2:7

ENCAMP *abide, lodge*
the tabernacle **e-s** Num 1:51
and **e-ed** together Josh 11:5
a host **e** against me Ps 27:3
angel of the LORD **e-s** Ps 34:7

ENCIRCLE *go around*
entirely **e-ing** the sea 2 Chr 4:3
he **e-d** the Ophel 2 Chr 33:14
cords . . . have **e-d** me Ps 119:61
Who **e** yourselves with Is 50:11

ENCOMPASS *surround*
waves of death **e** 2 Sam 22:5
e-ing the walls of 1 Kin 6:5

e-ed . . . with bitterness Lam 3:5
Water **e-ed** me to the Jon 2:5

ENCOURAGE *strengthen*
charge Joshua and **e** Deut 3:28
e-d him in God 1 Sam 23:16
e them in the work Ezra 6:22
Paul was **e-ing** them Acts 27:33
e one another 1 Thess 5:11
e the young women Titus 2:4

END (n) *extremity, goal, result*
e of all flesh has Gen 6:13
one **e** of the heavens Deut 4:32
from beginning to **e** 1 Sam 3:12
very **e-s** of the earth Ps 2:8
wicked come to an **e** Ps 7:9
e is the way of death Prov 14:12
The **e** is coming Ezek 7:2
who endures to . . . **e** Matt 24:13
kingdom . . . no **e** Luke 1:33
He loved . . . to the **e** John 13:1
Christ . . . **e** of the law Rom 10:4
beginning and the **e** Rev 21:6

END (v) *complete, stop*
border **e-ed** at the sea Josh 15:4
words of Job are **e-ed** Job 31:40
summer is **e-ed** Jer 8:20
days there were **e-ed** Acts 21:5
it **e-s** up being burned Heb 6:8

ENDOW *provide a gift*
God has **e-ed** me Gen 30:20
e-ed with discretion 2 Chr 2:12
to **e** those who love Prov 8:21
e-ed with salvation Zech 9:9

ENDURE *persevere*
will be able to **e** Ex 18:23
that I should **e** Job 6:11
while the sun **e-s** Ps 72:5
May his name **e** Ps 72:17
and your name will **e** Is 66:22
Can your heart **e** Ezek 22:14
the one who has **e-d** Matt 10:22
who **e-s** to the end Mark 13:13
e-s all things 1 Cor 13:7
discipline that you **e** Heb 12:7
blessed who **e-d** James 5:11

ENEMY *foe*
delivered your **e-ies** Gen 14:20
a man finds his **e** 1 Sam 24:19
consider me Thine **e** Job 13:24
presence of my **e-ies** Ps 23:5
e has persecuted my Ps 143:3
If your **e** is hungry Prov 25:21
love your **e-ies,** and Matt 5:44
e of all righteousness Acts 13:10
e . . . be abolished 1 Cor 15:26
an **e** of God James 4:4

ENGAGE *be involved, betroth*
virgin who is not **e-d** Ex 22:16
the girl who is **e-d** Deut 22:25
e-d in their work 1 Chr 9:33
e-d to . . . Joseph Luke 1:27
to **e** in good deeds Titus 3:8

ENGEDI
spring and town near Dead Sea 1 Sam 23:29;24:1; Song 1:14

ENGRAVE *inscribe*
shall **e** the two stones Ex 28:11
e-d on the tablets Ex 32:16
e an inscription Zech 3:9
letters **e-d** on stones 2 Cor 3:7

ENGRAVINGS *carvings*
like the **e** of a seal Ex 28:36
the **e** of a signet Ex 39:30
carved **e** of cherubim 1 Kin 6:29

ENLARGE *extend, increase*
May God **e** Japheth Gen 9:27
Thou wilt **e** my heart Ps 119:32
Sheol has **e-d** its Is 5:14
He **e-s** his appetite Hab 2:5

ENMITY *hostility*
e Between you and Gen 3:15
had everlasting **e** Ezek 35:5
at **e** with each other Luke 23:12
sorcery, **e-ies,** strife Gal 5:20
abolishing . . . the **e** Eph 2:15

ENOCH
1 *son of Cain* Gen 4:17
2 *city* Gen 4:17
3 *Methuselah's father* Gen 5:22
walked with God Gen 5:24

ENRAGE *anger*
e-d and curse their Is 8:21
jealousy **e-s** a man Prov 6:34
he became very **e-d** Matt 2:16
dragon was **e-d** with Rev 12:17

ENRICH *make wealthy*
king will **e** the 1 Sam 17:25
Thou dost greatly **e** Ps 65:9
You **e-ed** the kings Ezek 27:33

ENSLAVE *subjugate*
you have been **e-d** Is 14:3
e-d and mistreated Acts 7:6
if he **e-s** you 2 Cor 11:20
e-d to various lusts Titus 3:3

ENSNARE *catch*
An evil man is **e-d** Prov 12:13
e him who adjudicates Is 29:21

ENTANGLE *ensnare*
camel **e-ing** her ways Jer 2:23
No soldier . . . **e-s** 2 Tim 2:4
sin which . . . **e-s** us Heb 12:1

ENTER *go in*
you shall **e** the ark Gen 6:18
He **e-s** into judgment Job 22:4
E His gates with Ps 100:4
E the rock and hide Is 2:10
He **e-s** into peace Is 57:2
Spirit **e-ed** me and Ezek 2:2
not **e** the kingdom Matt 5:20
E by the narrow gate Matt 7:13
afraid as they **e-ed** Luke 9:34
e into the kingdom John 3:5
not **e** by the door John 10:1
shall not **e** My rest Heb 3:11

ENTHRONED *exalt, make king*
e *above* the cherubim 2 Sam 6:2
LORD who is **e** *above* 1 Chr 13:6
e upon the praises of Ps 22:3
who sits **e** from of old Ps 55:19
Who is **e** on high Ps 113:5

ENTICE *deceive, seduce*
E your husband Judg 14:15
Who will **e** Ahab 2 Chr 18:19
if sinners **e** you Prov 1:10
e-d by his own lust James 1:14
e-ing unstable souls 2 Pet 2:14

ENTREAT *appeal, ask*
E the LORD that He Ex 8:8
Moses **e-ed** the LORD Ex 32:11
Please **e** the LORD 1 Kin 13:6
gain if we **e** Him Job 21:15
centurion . . . **e-ing** Him Matt 8:5
demons *began* to **e** Matt 8:31
they were **e-ing** Him Luke 8:31
I **e-ed** the Lord 2 Cor 12:8
e you to walk in a Eph 4:1

ENVIOUS *covetous*
e of the arrogant Ps 73:3
not be **e** of evil men Prov 24:1
is your eye **e** Matt 20:15
And you are **e** James 4:2

ENVIRONS *outskirts, suburbs*
the **e** of Jerusalem Jer 32:44
devour all his **e** Jer 50:32
Bethlehem . . . its **e** Matt 2:16

ENVOY *agent, messenger*
e-s of the rulers 2 Chr 32:31
faithful **e** *brings* Prov 13:17
sent your **e-s** a great Is 57:9
his **e-s** to Egypt Ezek 17:15

ENVY (n) *jealousy*
full of **e,** murder Rom 1:29
preaching . . . from **e** Phil 1:15
out of which arise **e** 1 Tim 6:4
life in malice and **e** Titus 3:3
e and all slander 1 Pet 2:1

ENVY (v) *be discontent, jealous*
Philistines **e-ied** him Gen 26:14
e a man of violence Prov 3:31
not let your heart **e** Prov 23:17
e-ing one another Gal 5:26

EPHAH
1 *bushel, measure of capacity* Lev 5:11; Num 5:15
2 *son of Midian* Gen 25:4; 1 Chr 1:33
3 *Caleb's concubine* 1 Chr 2:46
4 *son of Jahdai* 1 Chr 2:47

EPHESUS
city of Asia Minor Acts 18:19; 1 Cor 16:8; Rev 1:11;2:1

EPHOD
1 *priestly garment* Ex 28:6; 1 Sam 23:9; 2 Sam 6:14
2 *father of Hanniel* Num 34:23

EPHRAIM
1 *son of Joseph* Gen 41:52;48:17
2 *tribe* Josh 16:5; Judg 7:24
3 *northern kingdom* Is 7:2-17; Hos 4:17;9:3-17
4 *city* 2 Sam 13:23; John 11:54

EPHRATH(AH)
1 *Bethlehem* Gen 35:19;48:7; Ruth 4:11; Mic 5:2
2 *wife of Caleb* 1 Chr 2:19,50
3 *territory* Ps 132:6

EPICUREAN
a Greek philosophy Acts 17:18

EPOCHS *ages, seasons*
the times and the **e** Dan 2:21
to know times or **e** Acts 1:7

EQUIPMENT *implements*
the **e** for the service Ex 39:40
e for his chariots 1 Sam 8:12
e of a foolish Zech 11:15

EQUITY *equality, fairness*
eyes look with **e** Ps 17:2
hast established **e** Ps 99:4
justice and **e** Prov 1:3
e *and* every good Prov 2:9

ERROR *mistake, sin*
can discern *his* **e-s** Ps 19:12
like an **e** which goes Eccl 10:5
e against the LORD Is 32:6
e of unprincipled 2 Pet 3:17
the spirit of **e** 1 John 4:6
rushed . . . into the **e** Jude 11

ESARHADDON
Assyrian king 2 Kin 19:37; Ezra 4:2; Is 37:38

ESAU
son of Isaac Gen 25:25
twin of Jacob Gen 25:26
skillful hunter Gen 25:27
sold birthright Gen 25:34
despised Jacob Gen 27:41
reconciled with Jacob Gen 33:4

ESCAPE (n) *deliverance, refuge*
there will be no **e** Job 11:20
is no **e** for me Ps 142:4
Let there be no **e** Jer 50:29
provide . . . **e** 1 Cor 10:13

ESCAPE (v) *elude*
slave who has **e-d** Deut 23:15
let no one **e** *or* 2 Kin 9:15
tells lies will not **e** Prov 19:5
how shall we **e** Is 20:6
nothing at all **e-s** Joel 2:3
how shall we **e** if Heb 2:3
it **e-s** their notice 2 Pet 3:5

ESTABLISH *confirm, found*
I will **e** My covenant Gen 17:19
how God **e-es** them Job 37:15
my ways may be **e-ed** Ps 119:5
e-ed in lovingkindness Is 16:5
to **e** the heavens Is 51:16
we **e** the Law Rom 3:31
e-ed in the truth 2 Pet 1:12

ESTATE *domain* or *standard*
restore your . . . **e** Job 8:6
us in our low **e** Ps 136:23
squandered his **e** Luke 15:13

ESTHER
Hadassah, Hebrew name
cousin of Mordecai Esth 2:7
Persian queen Esth 2:16-18

ETERNAL *everlasting*
e God is a dwelling Deut 33:27
An **e** decree Jer 5:22
cast into the **e** fire Matt 18:8
guilty of an **e** sin Mark 3:29
He may give **e** life John 17:2
gift of God is **e** life Rom 6:23
e weight of glory 2 Cor 4:17
Now to the King **e** 1 Tim 1:17
source of **e** salvation Heb 5:9
through the **e** Spirit Heb 9:14
kept us in **e** bonds Jude 6

ETERNITY *perpetuity*
set **e** in their heart Eccl 3:11
from **e** I am He Is 43:13
Jesus from all **e** 2 Tim 1:9
to the day of **e** 2 Pet 3:18

ETHANIM
seventh month of Hebrew calendar 1 Ki 8:2

ETHIOPIA
NE African country Esth 1:1; Ps 68:31; Nah 3:9; Zeph 3:10

EUNUCH *castrated male, official*
seven **e-s** who served Esth 1:10
Neither let the **e** say Is 56:3
children, and *the* **e-s** Jer 41:16
made **e-s** by men Matt 19:12
an Ethiopian **e** Acts 8:27

EUPHRATES
river of Mesopotamia Gen 2:14; Jer 13:5;46:10; Rev 9:14;16:12

EVANGELIST *proclaimer of good news*
house of Philip the **e** Acts 21:8
and some *as* **e-s** Eph 4:11
do the work of an **e** 2 Tim 4:5

EVE
first woman Gen 2:22
wife of Adam Gen 2:23
deceived by serpent Gen 3:1-7
named by Adam Gen 3:20

EVERLASTING *eternal*
e covenant between Gen 9:16
the LORD, the **E** God Gen 21:33
are the **e** arms Deut 33:27
e to **e**, Thou art God Ps 90:2
lovingkindness is **e** Ps 106:1
From **e** I was Prov 8:23
The **E** God, the LORD Is 40:28
LORD for an **e** light Is 60:20
loved you with an **e** Jer 31:3

EVIDENCE *facts, testimony*
the **e** of witnesses Num 35:30
on the **e** of two Deut 19:15
not able to give **e** Ezra 2:59
and giving **e** Acts 17:3

EVIL *bad, wicked, wrong*
man's heart is **e** Gen 8:21
keep . . . from every **e** Deut 23:9
discern good and **e** 2 Sam 14:17
I fear no **e** Ps 23:4
repay me **e** for good Ps 35:12
turn away from **e** Prov 3:7
run rapidly to **e** Prov 6:18
returns **e** for good Prov 17:13
committed two **e-s** Jer 2:13
deliver us from **e** Matt 6:13
If you then, being **e** Luke 11:13
who does **e** hates the John 3:20
love of money is . . . **e** 1 Tim 6:10
tongue . . . restless **e** James 3:8

EVILDOER *wicked one*
LORD repay the **e** 2 Sam 3:39
e-s will be cut off Ps 37:9
e listens to wicked Prov 17:4
Offspring of **e-s** Is 1:4
is godless and an **e** Is 9:17
depart . . . you **e-s** Luke 13:27
punishment of **e-s** 1 Pet 2:14

EVIL-MERODACH
king of Babylon 2 Kin 25:27; Jer 52:31

EWE *female sheep*
seven **e** lambs Gen 21:28
e lamb without Lev 14:10
poor man's **e** lamb 2 Sam 12:4
e-s with suckling Ps 78:71
like a flock of **e-s** Song 6:6

EXACT (adj) *certain, correct*
e amount of money Esth 4:7
e meaning of all this Dan 7:16
know the **e** truth Luke 1:4
a more **e** knowledge Acts 24:22

EXACT (v) *collect*
let him **e** a fifth Gen 41:34
he shall not **e** it Deut 15:2
He **e-ed** the silver 2 Kin 23:25
You are **e-ing** usury Neh 5:7
e a tribute of grain Amos 5:11

EXALT *extol, honor, lift*
He is highly **e-ed** Ex 15:1
e-ed be God 2 Sam 22:47
He is **e-ed** in power Job 37:23
let us **e** His name Ps 34:3
e-ed far above all gods Ps 97:9
city is **e-ed** Prov 11:11
my God; I will **e** Thee Is 25:1
E that which is low Ezek 21:26
e-ed to . . . right hand Acts 2:33
be **e-ed** in my body Phil 1:20
He will **e** you James 4:10

EXAMINE *investigate, search*
Thou dost **e** him every Job 7:18
E me, O LORD, and try Ps 26:2
e-ing the Scriptures Acts 17:11
e-d by scourging Acts 22:24
a man **e** himself 1 Cor 11:28

EXAMPLE *model, pattern*
the **e** of his father 2 Chr 17:3
I gave you an **e** John 13:15
e of those who 1 Tim 4:12
e of disobedience Heb 4:11
be **e-s** to the flock 1 Pet 5:3
made them an **e** 2 Pet 2:6

EXCEL *be superior, surpass*
e in . . . wickedness Jer 5:28
wisdom **e-s** folly Eccl 2:13
you may **e** . . . more 1 Thess 4:1

EXCELLENCE *surpassing quality*
greatness of Thine **e** Ex 15:7
are a woman of **e** Ruth 3:11
if there is any **e** Phil 4:8
proclaim the **e-ies** of 1 Pet 2:9

EXCELLENT *outstanding*
e wife is the crown Prov 12:4
He has done **e** things Is 12:5
e governor Felix Acts 23:26
a still more **e** way 1 Cor 12:31
a more **e** name Heb 1:4

EXCLUDE *put out, shut out*
e-d from . . . assembly Ezra 10:8
e-d all foreigners Neh 13:3
e you for My name's Is 66:5
e-d from the life of Eph 4:18

EXCUSE *justification*
began to make **e-s** Luke 14:18
no **e** for their sin John 15:22
they are without **e** Rom 1:20

EXECUTE *carry out*
e-d the justice of Deut 33:21
He has **e-d** judgment Ps 9:16
e vengeance on the Ps 149:7
Lord will **e** His word Rom 9:28
e judgment upon all Jude 15

EXERCISE *perform*
man has **e-d** authority Eccl 8:9
e-s lovingkindness Jer 9:24
e authority over Matt 20:25
e-s self-control in all 1 Cor 9:25

EXHAUSTED *used up, wearied*
sound asleep and **e** Judg 4:21
too **e** to follow 1 Sam 30:21
of flour was not **e** 1 Kin 17:16
Their strength is **e** Jer 51:30

EXHORTATION *urging*
with many other **e-s** Luke 3:18
given them much **e** Acts 20:2
who exhorts, in his **e** Rom 12:8
this word of **e** Heb 13:22

EXILE *banishment* or *capture*
Israel away into **e** 2 Kin 17:6
people of the **e** were Ezra 4:1
captivity of the **e-s** Neh 7:6
into **e** from Jerusalem Esth 2:6
e will soon be set free Is 51:14
Israel went into **e** Ezek 39:23

EXODUS *departure*
e of . . . Israel Heb 11:22

EXPANSE *firmament, vastness*
e of the heavens Gen 1:20
e of the waters Job 37:10
in His mighty **e** Ps 150:1
from above the **e** Ezek 1:25

EXPECTATION *anticipation*
your **e** is false Job 41:9
e of the wicked Prov 10:28
to my earnest **e** Phil 1:20
e of judgment Heb 10:27

EXPECTED *awaited*
Are You the **E** One Matt 11:3
Are You the **E** One Luke 7:20

EXPERIENCE *undergo*
all who had not **e-d** Judg 3:1
Thy people **e** hardship Ps 60:3
e-s Thy judgments Is 26:9
e-d mockings and Heb 11:36

EXPERT *very skillful*
an **e** in warfare 2 Sam 17:8
be like an **e** warrior Jer 50:9
an **e** in all customs Acts 26:3

EXPOSE *disclose, reveal*
shame . . . be **e-d** Is 47:3
He will **e** your sins Lam 4:22
deeds should be **e-d** John 3:20
would **e** their infants Acts 7:19
are **e-d** by the light Eph 5:13

EXTEND *enlarge, stretch out*
God **e-s** . . . border Deut 12:20
e-ed lovingkindness Ezra 7:28
e-s her hand to the Prov 31:20
I **e** peace to her Is 66:12
boundary shall **e** Ezek 47:17

EXTENT *amount* or *degree*
the **e** of my days Ps 39:4
e that you did it to Matt 25:40
such an **e** that Jesus Mark 1:45

EXTERMINATE *destroy*
planned to **e** us 2 Sam 21:5
He will **e** its sinners Is 13:9

EXTERNAL *outward*
not with **e** service Col 3:22
adornment be . . . **e** 1 Pet 3:3

EXTINGUISH *put out*
they will **e** my coal 2 Sam 14:7
not **e** the lamp of 2 Sam 21:17
my days are **e-ed** Job 17:1
when *I* **e** you Ezek 32:7
e all the flaming Eph 6:16

EXTOL *praise*
God, and I will **e** Him Ex 15:2
I will **e** Thee, O LORD Ps 30:1
I will **e** Thee, my God Ps 145:1
We will **e** your love Song 1:4

EXTORTION *stealing*
practicing . . . **e** Jer 22:17
practiced **e**, robbed Ezek 18:18

EXULT *rejoice*
heart **e-s** in the LORD 1 Sam 2:1
Let the field **e** 1 Chr 16:32
e-ed when evil befell Job 31:29
let them **e** before God Ps 68:3
I will **e** in the LORD Hab 3:18
e in our tribulations Rom 5:3

EXULTATION *jubilation*
e like the nations Hos 9:1
joy or crown of **e** 1 Thess 2:19
may rejoice with **e** 1 Pet 4:13

EYE *organ of sight*
e-s are dull from Gen 49:12
e for **e**, tooth for Ex 21:24
his **e** was not dim Deut 34:7
right in his own **e-s** Judg 17:6
open his **e-s** that he 2 Kin 6:17
e-s of the LORD 2 Chr 16:9
Haughty **e-s**, a lying Prov 6:17
e . . . mocks a father Prov 30:17
To open blind **e-s** Is 42:7
e-s will bitterly weep Jer 13:17
have **e-s** to see but Ezek 12:2
e for an **e**, and a Matt 5:38
e . . . you to stumble Matt 18:9
lamp . . . is your **e** Luke 11:34
the clay to his **e-s** John 9:6
e-s of your heart may Eph 1:18
e-s full of adultery 2 Pet 2:14
the lust of the **e-s** 1 John 2:16
God, who has **e-s** like Rev 2:18
His **e-s** *are* a flame Rev 19:12

EYEWITNESSES *observers*
e . . . of the word Luke 1:2
e of His majesty 2 Pet 1:16

EZEKIEL
Hebrew prophet Ezek 1:1
called by God Ezek 1:1,3
spoke to Israel Ezek 14:1ff
taken captive Ezek 33:21
spoke to false prophets Ezek 34:2ff
spoke to nations Ezek 35:2ff
restored temple Ezek 40:1ff

EZRA
priest Ezra 7:1-5
scribe Ezra 7:6
sent by king Ezra 7:14,21
brought exiles Ezra 8:1-14
Nehemiah's colleague Neh 8:2-6

F

FACE *countenance*
sweat of your **f** You Gen 3:19
Abram fell on his **f** Gen 17:3
speak to Moses **f** to **f** Ex 33:11
skin of his **f** shone Ex 34:30
hide Thy **f** from me Ps 13:1
Who seek Thy **f** Ps 24:6
His **f** to shine upon us Ps 67:1
makes a cheerful **f** Prov 15:13
set My **f** against you Jer 44:11
had the **f** of an eagle Ezek 1:10
fast . . . wash your **f** Matt 6:17
they spat in His **f** Matt 26:67
like the **f** of an angel Acts 6:15
His **f** was like the sun Rev 1:16

FACT *truth*
f may be confirmed Matt 18:16
are undeniable **f-s** Acts 19:36
f is to be confirmed 2 Cor 13:1

FACTIONS *divisions*
be **f** among you 1 Cor 11:19
dissensions, **f** Gal 5:20

FAIL *be spent* or *fall short*
He will not **f** you Deut 4:31
none of his words **f** 1 Sam 3:19
no man's heart **f** 1 Sam 17:32
not one word . . . **f-ed** 1 Kin 8:56
my strength **f-s** me Ps 38:10
the olive should **f** Hab 3:17
faith may not **f** Luke 22:32
Love never **f-s** 1 Cor 13:8

FAINTHEARTED *weak*
Do not be **f** Deut 20:3
encourage the **f** 1 Thess 5:14

FAITH *belief, trust*
because you broke **f** Deut 32:51
Who keeps **f** forever Ps 146:6
will live by his **f** Hab 2:4
Jesus seeing their **f** Matt 9:2
f as a mustard seed Matt 17:20
Your **f** has saved you Luke 7:50
Increase our **f** Luke 17:5
man full of **f** Acts 6:5
of **f** to the Gentiles Acts 14:27
sanctified by **f** in Me Acts 26:18
justified by **f** Rom 5:1
if I have all **f** 1 Cor 13:2
your **f** also is vain 1 Cor 15:14
we walk by **f** 2 Cor 5:7
live by **f** in the Son Gal 2:20
saved through **f** Eph 2:8
joy in the **f** Phil 1:25
stability of your **f** Col 2:5
breastplate of **f** 1 Thess 5:8
fall away from the **f** 1 Tim 4:1
they upset the **f** 2 Tim 2:18
sound in the **f** Titus 1:13
full assurance of **f** Heb 10:22
By **f** Enoch was taken Heb 11:5
perfecter of **f** Heb 12:2
ask in **f** James 1:6
prayer offered in **f** James 5:15
the **f** of the saints Rev 13:10

FAITHFUL *loyal, trustworthy*
the **f** God, who keeps Deut 7:9
heart **f** before Thee Neh 9:8
LORD preserves the **f** Ps 31:23
f witness will not lie Prov 14:5
the LORD who is **f** Is 49:7
God is **f** 1 Cor 1:9
F is He who calls 1 Thess 5:24
He considered me **f** 1 Tim 1:12
entrust to **f** men 2 Tim 2:2
souls to a **f** Creator 1 Pet 4:19
Be **f** until death Rev 2:10
called **F** and True Rev 19:11

FAITHFULNESS *loyalty*
kindness and **f** Gen 47:29
A God of **f** Deut 32:4
make known Thy **f** Ps 89:1
f to all generations Ps 100:5
and mercy and **f** Matt 23:23
kindness, goodness, **f** Gal 5:22

FAITHLESS *unbelieving*
what **f** Israel did Jer 3:6
O **f** daughter Jer 31:22
Their heart is **f** Hos 10:2
If we are **f** 2 Tim 2:13

FALL *descend* or *fail*
deep sleep to **f** upon Gen 2:21
devices let them **f** Ps 5:10
dread . . . had **f-en** Ps 105:38
wicked will **f** Prov 11:5
a righteous man **f-s** Prov 24:16
Assyrian will **f** Is 31:8
Babylon has **f-en** Jer 51:8
f down and worship Dan 3:5
f-ing on his knees Mark 1:40
all may **f** . . . I will Mark 14:29
appointed for the **f** Luke 2:34
watching Satan **f** Luke 10:18
sinned and **f** short Rom 3:23
have **f-en** asleep 1 Cor 15:6
f-en from grace Gal 5:4
rich **f** into temptation 1 Tim 6:9
rocks, **F** on us Rev 6:16

FALSE *deceitful, dishonest*
not bear a **f** report Ex 23:1
I hate every **f** way Ps 119:104
But a **f** witness Prov 12:17
f witness will not go Prov 19:5
f scale is not good Prov 20:23
F and foolish *visions* Lam 2:14
not bear **f** witness Matt 19:18
f Christs and **f** Matt 24:24
men are **f** apostles 2 Cor 11:13
the **f** circumcision Phil 3:2
and the **f** prophet Rev 20:10

FALSEHOOD *deception*
lifted up his soul to **f** Ps 24:4
delight in **f** Ps 62:4
I hate and despise **f** Ps 119:163
Bread obtained by **f** Prov 20:17
prophesying **f** in My Jer 14:14
laying aside **f** Eph 4:25

FAMILY *household, relatives*
f-ies from the ark Gen 8:19
f may redeem him Lev 25:49
f-ies of the Levites Num 3:20
my **f** is the least Judg 6:15
f-ies like a flock Ps 107:41
God of all the **f-ies** Jer 31:1
every **f** in heaven Eph 3:15
upsetting whole **f-ies** Titus 1:11

FAMINE *shortage of food*
a **f** in the land Gen 12:10
seven years of **f** Gen 41:27
In **f** He will redeem Job 5:20
keep them alive in **f** Ps 33:19
f and pestilence Jer 14:12
f and wild beasts Ezek 5:17
f-s and earthquakes Matt 24:7
plagues and **f-s** Luke 21:11
mourning and **f** Rev 18:8

FAMISHED *hungry, parched*
for I am **f** Gen 25:30
strength is **f** Job 18:12
honorable men are **f** Is 5:13

FAMOUS *well-known*
f in Bethlehem Ruth 4:11

men of valor, **f** men 1 Chr 5:24

FARM *agricultural land*

consume the **f** land Amos 7:4
one to his own **f** Matt 22:5
or **f-s**, for My sake Mark 10:29

FARMER *husbandman*

Does the **f** plow Is 28:24
will be your **f-s** Is 61:5
f-s . . . put to shame Jer 14:4
the **f** to mourning Amos 5:16

FASHION *create, form*

f-ed into a woman Gen 2:22
f us in the womb Job 31:15
He who **f-s** the hearts Ps 33:15
f a graven image Is 44:9
I am **f-ing** calamity Jer 18:11

FAST (n) *food abstinence*

Proclaim a **f** 1 Kin 21:9
you call this a **f** Is 58:5
Consecrate a **f** Joel 1:14
f was already over Acts 27:9

FAST (v) *abstain from food*

and David **f-ed** 2 Sam 12:16
maidens also will **f** Esth 4:16
you **f** for contention Is 58:4
had **f-ed** forty days Matt 4:2
whenever you **f** Matt 6:16
disciples do not **f** Mark 2:18
I **f** twice a week Luke 18:12
had **f-ed** and prayed Acts 13:3

FASTING *food abstinence*

times of **f** Esth 9:31
weak from **f** Ps 109:24
to be seen **f** by men Matt 6:16
by prayer and **f** Matt 17:21
Pharisees were **f** Mark 2:18

FATE *destiny*

appalled at his **f** Job 18:20
one **f** befalls them Eccl 2:14
f for the righteous Eccl 9:2
one **f** for all men Eccl 9:3

FATHER *God* or *parent*

leave his **f** . . . mother Gen 2:24
f of a multitude Gen 17:4
Honor your **f** Ex 20:12
who strikes his **f** Ex 21:15
Is not He your **F** Deut 32:6
your **f-'s** instruction Prov 1:8
son makes a **f** glad Prov 10:1
Eternal **F**, Prince of Is 9:6
F who sees in secret Matt 6:4
Our **F** who art in Matt 6:9
does the will of My **F** Matt 7:21
in My **F-'s** kingdom Matt 26:29
in the glory of His **F** Mark 8:38
be in my **F-'s** *house* Luke 2:49
F, hallowed be Thy Luke 11:2
F, forgive them Luke 23:34
begotten from the **F** John 1:14
F . . . bears witness John 8:18
the **f** of lies John 8:44
I and the **F** are one John 10:30
In my **F-'s** house are John 14:2
F is the vinedresser John 15:1
ask the **F** for John 16:23
I ascend to My **F** John 20:17
one God and **F** of all Eph 4:6

FATHER-IN-LAW

she sent to her **f** Gen 38:25
returned to Jethro his **f** Ex 4:18
f of Caiaphas John 18:13

FATHERLESS *orphan*

father of the **f** Ps 68:5
He supports the **f** Ps 146:9
fields of the **f** Prov 23:10
f and the widow Ezek 22:7

FAULT *error, offense*

found no **f** in him 1 Sam 29:3
let no one find **f** Hos 4:4
does He still find **f** Rom 9:19
grumblers, finding **f** Jude 16

FAVOR *kind regard*

Noah found **f** Gen 6:8
I will grant . . . **f** Ex 3:21
show no **f** to them Deut 7:2
Why have I found **f** Ruth 2:10
show **f** to Thy land Ps 85:1
obtains **f** . . . LORD Prov 8:35
f is like a cloud Prov 16:15
found **f** with God Luke 1:30
in **f** with God and Luke 2:52
seeking the **f** of men Gal 1:10

FEAR (n) *awe, dread, reverence*

no **f** of God in Gen 20:11
f of the LORD is clean Ps 19:9
f . . . is the beginning Ps 111:10
afraid of sudden **f** Prov 3:25
f . . . prolongs life Prov 10:27
f of man brings a Prov 29:25
guards shook for **f** Matt 28:4
men fainting for **f** Luke 21:26
for **f** of the Jews John 7:13
no **f** of God before Rom 3:18
in weakness and in **f** 1 Cor 2:3
with **f** and trembling Eph 6:5
through **f** of death Heb 2:15
love casts out **f** 1 John 4:18

FEAR (v) *be afraid, revere*

the midwives **f-ed** God Ex 1:21
Moses said . . . Do not **f** Ex 14:13
may learn to **f** Me Deut 4:10
not **f** other gods 2 Kin 17:37
I **f** no evil Ps 23:4
Whom shall I **f** Ps 27:1
who **f-s** the LORD Prov 31:30
Rather, **f** God Eccl 5:7
Take courage, **f** not Is 35:4
Do not **f**, for I am Is 41:10
shall **f** and tremble Jer 33:9
f-ed the multitude Matt 14:5
who did not **f** God Luke 18:2
slavery leading to **f** Rom 8:15
I **f** for you Gal 4:11
let us **f** lest Heb 4:1

FEARFUL *terrifying*

it is a **f** thing Ex 34:10
were **f** and amazed Luke 8:25
may be **f** *of sinning* 1 Tim 5:20

FEAST *celebration*

a **f** to the LORD Ex 12:14
godless jesters at a **f** Ps 35:16
hate . . . appointed **f-s** Is 1:14
a wedding **f** Matt 22:2
seeking Him at the **f** John 7:11
celebrate the **f** 1 Cor 5:8
f with you without Jude 12

FEASTS

1 **Feast of Booths** Lev 23:24; Deut 16:16; 2 Chr 8:13
also **Feast of Ingathering**
2 **Feast of Dedication** John 10:22
3 **Feast of Harvest** Ex 23:16
also **Feast of Weeks**
also **Feast of Pentecost**
4 **Feast of Ingathering** Ex 23:16
also **Feast of Booths**
5 **Feast of Passover** Ex 34:25; Luke 2:41
6 **Feast of Unleavened Bread** Ex 23:15; Luke 22:1
7 **Feast of Weeks** Ex 34:22; Deut 16:10,16
also **Feast of Harvest**
also **Feast of Pentecost**
8 **Feast of Pentecost** Acts 2:1; 20:16; 1 Cor 16:8
also **Feast of Harvest**
also **Feast of Weeks**

FEED *eat, supply*

fed you with manna Deut 8:3
f him sparingly 1 Kin 22:27
He **f-s** on ashes Is 44:20
f you on knowledge Jer 3:15
He **fed** me this scroll Ezek 3:2
I will **f** My flock Ezek 34:15
dogs **f** on the Matt 15:27
hungry, and **f** You Matt 25:37
enemy is hungry, **f** Rom 12:20

FELIX

Roman procurator Acts 23:26;24:25;25:14

FELL *came upon, collapsed*

fire of the LORD **f** 1 Kin 18:38
the lot **f** on Jonah Jon 1:7
He **f** asleep Luke 8:23
he **f** to the ground Acts 9:4
Holy Spirit **f** upon Acts 10:44
star **f** from heaven Rev 8:10

FELLOW *companion*

oil of joy above Thy **f-s** Ps 45:7
your **f** exiles Ezek 11:15
beat his **f** slaves Matt 24:49
f heirs with Christ Rom 8:17
Gentiles are **f** heirs Eph 3:6
brother and **f** worker Phil 2:25
f worker in the 1 Thes 3:2
I am a **f** servant of Rev 22:9

FELLOWSHIP *companionship*

had sweet **f** together Ps 55:14
f . . . Holy Spirit 2 Cor 13:14
right hand of **f** Gal 2:9
f of His sufferings Phil 3:10
f is with the Father 1 John 1:3

FEMALE *girl, woman*

and **f** He created Gen 1:27
a **f** slave Ex 21:7
f from the flock Lev 5:6
likeness of male or **f** Deut 4:16
neither male nor **f** Gal 3:28

FERTILE *productive*

a **f** land Neh 9:25
the **f** valley Is 28:4
in **f** soil Ezek 17:5

FERVENT *ardent*

being **f** in spirit Acts 18:25
f in spirit, serving Rom 12:11
keep **f** in your love 1 Pet 4:8

FESTIVAL *celebration*

celebrate a great **f** Neh 8:12
I reject your **f-s** Amos 5:21
turn your **f-s** into Amos 8:10
during the **f**, lest Matt 26:5

FESTUS, PORCIUS

Roman procurator of Judea Acts 24:27; 25:14,23; 26:25

FEVER *inflammation*

bones burn with **f** Job 30:30
in bed with a **f** Matt 8:14
from a high **f** Luke 4:38
He rebuked the **f** Luke 4:39

FIELD *productive land*

let me go to the **f** Ruth 2:2
f of the sluggard Prov 24:30
the lilies of the **f** Matt 6:28
the **f** is the world Matt 13:38
Two men . . . in the **f** Luke 17:36
f-s . . . white for John 4:35
F of Blood Acts 1:19

FIERCE *violent*

anger, for it is **f** Gen 49:7
Wrath is **f** Prov 27:4
see a **f** people Is 33:19
a **f** gale of wind Mark 4:37
scorched with **f** heat Rev 16:9
f wrath of God Rev 19:15

FIERY *burning*

LORD sent **f** serpents Num 21:6

with **f** heat Deut 28:22
His arrows **f** shafts Ps 7:13
f ordeal among you 1 Pet 4:12

FIG *fruit*
they sewed **f** leaves Gen 3:7
a piece of **f** cake 1 Sam 30:12
nor **f-s** from thistles Matt 7:16
the **f** tree withered Matt 21:19
f-s from thorns Luke 6:44
under the **f** tree John 1:48
Can a **f** tree James 3:12

FIGHT *struggle*
Hebrews were **f-ing** Ex 2:13
LORD will **f** for you Ex 14:14
stars **fought** from Judg 5:20
and **f** our battles 1 Sam 8:20
f for your brothers Neh 4:14
f-ing against God Acts 5:39
fought the good **f** 2 Tim 4:7
so you **f** and quarrel James 4:2

FILIGREE *ornamental work*
f *settings* of gold Ex 28:13
cords on the two **f** Ex 28:25

FILL (n) *satisfaction, fullness*
eat your **f** Lev 25:19
They drink their **f** Ps 36:8
drink our **f** of love Prov 7:18
its **f** of their blood Jer 46:10

FILL (v) *make full*
and **f** the earth Gen 1:28
Can you **f** his skin Job 41:7
was **f-ing** with smoke Is 6:4
I am **f-ed** with power Mic 3:8
God of hope **f** you Rom 15:13

FILTHY *offensive, foul*
are full of **f** vomit Is 28:8
like a **f** garment Is 64:6
clothed . . . **f** garments Zech 3:3
let the one who is **f** Rev 22:11

FILTHINESS *disgusting foulness*
not washed . . . his **f** Prov 30:12
your **f** is lewdness Ezek 24:13
no **f** and silly talk Eph 5:4
putting aside all **f** James 1:21

FIND *discover, uncover*
not **found** a helper Gen 2:20
But Noah **found** favor Gen 6:8
sin will **f** you out Num 32:23
he who **f-s** me **f-s** life Prov 8:35
who **f-s** a wife **f-s** Prov 18:22
f gladness and joy Is 35:10
few . . . who **f** it Matt 7:14
has **found** his life Matt 10:39
f rest for your souls Matt 11:29
f-ing one pearl Matt 13:46
f a colt tied Mark 11:2
found . . . sleeping Mark 14:40
seek, and you shall **f** Luke 11:9
found the Messiah John 1:41
was **found** worthy Rev 5:4

FINISH *complete*
Moses **f-ed** the work Ex 40:33
Solomon **f-ed** the 2 Chr 7:11
It is **f-ed** John 19:30
I may **f** my course Acts 20:24
f doing it also 2 Cor 8:11
wrath of God is **f-ed** Rev 15:1

FIRE *burning* or *flame*
the **f** and the knife Gen 22:6
bush . . . burning with **f** Ex 3:2
pillar of **f** by night Ex 13:21
offered strange **f** Num 3:4
f of the LORD fell 1 Kin 18:38
a chariot of **f** 2 Kin 2:11
jealousy burn like **f** Ps 79:5
Is not My word like **f** Jer 23:29
the Holy Spirit and **f** Matt 3:11
with unquenchable **f** Matt 3:12
tongues as of **f** Acts 2:3
lake that burns with **f** Rev 21:8

FIREBRAND *burning wood*
who throws **F-s** Prov 26:18
you were like a **f** Amos 4:11

FIREPAN *used in worship*
a **f** full of coals Lev 16:12
the **f-s** of pure gold 2 Chr 4:22

FIRM *established, steadfast*
his bow remained **f** Gen 49:24
stood **f** on dry ground Josh 3:17
making my footsteps **f** Ps 40:2
He made **f** the skies Prov 8:28
stand **f** in the faith 1 Cor 16:13
f foundation of God 2 Tim 2:19
hope **f** until the end Heb 3:6

FIRST-BORN *oldest*
Sidon, his **f** Gen 10:15
the **f** bore a son Gen 19:37
I am Esau your **f** Gen 27:19
LORD killed every **f** Ex 13:15
birth to her **f** son Luke 2:7
church of the **f** Heb 12:23
f of the dead Rev 1:5

FISH
rule over the **f** Gen 1:26
Their **f** stink Is 50:2
a great **f** to swallow Jon 1:17
loaves and two **f** Matt 14:17
snake instead of a **f** Luke 11:11
net *full* of **f** John 21:8

FISHERMEN *fishers*
f will lament Is 19:8
for they were **f** Matt 4:18
the **f** had gotten out Luke 5:2

FISHERS *fishermen*
make you **f** of men Matt 4:19
become **f** of men Mark 1:17

FIX *make firm, secure*
I will **f** your boundary Ex 23:31
f-ed her hope on God 1 Tim 5:5
f-ing . . . eyes on Jesus Heb 12:2
f your hope 1 Pet 1:13

FIXED *established*
the **f** festivals 1 Chr 23:31
f order of the moon Jer 31:35
is a great chasm **f** Luke 16:26

FLAME *fire*
ascended in the **f** Judg 13:20
f . . . the wicked Ps 106:18
f of the LORD Song 8:6
his Holy One a **f** Is 10:17
crackling of a **f** Joel 2:5
f of a burning thorn Acts 7:30
eyes *are* a **f** of fire Rev 19:12

FLAMING *burning*
the **f** sword Gen 3:24
f fire by night Is 4:5
eyes were like **f** Dan 10:6
angels in a **f** fire 2 Thess 1:7

FLASK *utensil*
take this **f** of oil 2 Kin 9:1
took oil in **f-s** Matt 25:4

FLATTER
Nor **f** *any* man Job 32:21
f with their tongue Ps 5:9
adulterous who **f-s** Prov 2:16
who **f-s** his neighbor Prov 29:5

FLAX *plant*
the **f** was in bud Ex 9:31
looks for wool and **f** Prov 31:13
made from combed **f** Is 19:9

FLEE *escape, run away*
arise, **f** to Haran Gen 27:43
F *as* a bird Ps 11:1
f from Thy presence Ps 139:7
rulers have **fled** Is 22:3
f to Egypt Matt 2:13
left Him and **fled** Matt 26:56
fled from the tomb Mark 16:8
f from idolatry 1 Cor 10:14
f from youthful lusts 2 Tim 2:22
and heaven **fled** Rev 20:11

FLEECE *wool*
put a **f** of wool Judg 6:37
dry only on the **f** Judg 6:39
warmed with the **f** Job 31:20

FLEET *group of ships*
Solomon . . . built a **f** 1 Kin 9:26
sent . . . with the **f** 1 Kin 9:27

FLESH *body, meat*
f of my **f** Gen 2:23
shall become one **f** Gen 2:24
from my **f** I shall see Job 19:26
heart and my **f** sing Ps 84:2
All **f** is grass Is 40:6
the **f** is weak Matt 26:41
spirit . . . not have **f** Luke 24:39
the Word became **f** John 1:14
born of the **f** is **f** John 3:6
who eats My **f** John 6:56
children of the **f** Rom 9:8
thorn in the **f** 2 Cor 12:7
desires of the **f** Eph 2:3
filled with their **f** Rev 19:21

FLESHLY *carnal*
not in **f** wisdom 2 Cor 1:12
His **f** body Col 1:22
abstain from **f** lusts 1 Pet 2:11

FLIES *insects*
sent . . . swarms of **f** Ps 78:45
swarm of **f** *And* gnats Ps 105:31
Dead **f** make a Eccl 10:1

FLOCK *goats, sheep*
a keeper of **f-s** Gen 4:2
Thy people like a **f** Ps 77:20
He will tend His **f** Is 40:11
scattered My **f** Jer 23:2
over their **f** by night Luke 2:8
shall become one **f** John 10:16
f of God among you 1 Pet 5:2

FLOOD *overflowing of water*
I am bringing the **f** Gen 6:17
f came upon the earth Gen 7:17
end . . . with a **f** Dan 9:26
the **f-s** came Matt 7:25
f . . . destroyed Luke 17:27

FLOOR *ground, level*
threshing **f** of Atad Gen 50:11
go down to the . . . **f** Ruth 3:3
the **f** . . . with gold 1 Kin 6:30
His threshing **f** Matt 3:12
fell . . . from the third **f** Acts 20:9

FLOUR *ground grain*
measures of fine **f** Gen 18:6
only a handful of **f** 1 Kin 17:12
f . . . not exhausted 1 Kin 17:16

FLOW *pour forth*
river **f-ed** out of Eden Gen 2:10
f-ing with milk and Ex 3:8
eyelids **f** with water Jer 9:18
hills will **f** with milk Joel 3:18
f of her blood Mark 5:29
f . . . living waters John 7:38

FLOWER *blossom*
As a **f** of the field Ps 103:15
f-s have *already* Song 2:12
to the fading **f** Is 28:1
glory like the **f** 1 Pet 1:24

FLUTE *musical instrument*
tambourine, **f**, and 1 Sam 10:5

playing on **f-s** 1 Kin 1:40
the f or on the harp 1 Cor 14:7
musicians . . . **f-players** Rev 18:22

FLY *soar*
let birds f above Gen 1:20
a raven, and it **flew** Gen 8:7
As sparks f upward Job 5:7
f-ies away like a dream Job 20:8
glory will f away Hos 9:11
heard an eagle **f-ing** Rev 8:13
the birds which f Rev 19:17

FOAL *colt*
ties *his* f to the vine Gen 49:11
f of a wild donkey Job 11:12
f of a beast of burden Matt 21:5

FOE *enemy*
before your **f-s** 1 Chr 21:12
A f and an enemy Esth 7:6
iniquity of my **f-s** Ps 49:5
the evil to my **f-s** Ps 54:5
avenge . . . His **f-s** Jer 46:10

FOLLOW *imitate, pursue*
not f other gods Deut 6:14
turn back from **f-ing** Ruth 1:16
f the LORD your God 1 Sam 12:14
who f . . . wickedness Ps 119:150
bloodshed **f-s** Hos 4:2
He said to them, **F** Matt 4:19
left . . . and **f-ed** Matt 4:20
his cross, and f Me Matt 16:24
multitude was **f-ing** Mark 5:24
allowed no one to f Mark 5:37
and they f Me John 10:27
Peter . . . **f-ing** Jesus John 18:15
f-ing after . . . lusts Jude 16
ones who f the Lamb Rev 14:4

FOLLOWERS *disciples*
His f . . . *began* asking Mark 4:10

FOOD *bread, meat*
shall be f for you Gen 1:29
tree was good for f Gen 3:6
in giving them f Ruth 1:6
it is deceptive f Prov 23:3
his f was locusts Matt 3:4
life more than f Matt 6:25
f is to do the will John 4:34
My flesh is true f John 6:55

FOOL *unwise person*
The f has said in his Ps 14:1
F-s despise wisdom Prov 1:7
f multiplies words Eccl 10:14
The prophet is a f Hos 9:7
shall say, You f Matt 5:22
f-s and blind men Matt 23:17
wise, they became **f-s** Rom 1:22
f-s for Christ's sake 1 Cor 4:10

FOOLISH *silly, unwise*
O f and unwise Deut 32:6
a f son is a grief Prov 10:1
False and f *visions* Lam 2:14
f took their lamps Matt 25:3
O f men and slow Luke 24:25
let him become f 1 Cor 3:18
You f Galatians Gal 3:1
do not be f Eph 5:17

FOOLISHNESS *folly*
folly of fools is f Prov 14:24
mouth is speaking f Is 9:17
f of God is wiser 1 Cor 1:25
is f before God 1 Cor 3:19

FOOT *part of body*
she lay at his **feet** Ruth 3:14
six toes on each f 2 Sam 21:20
lamp to my **feet** Ps 119:105
their **feet** run to evil Prov 1:16
signals with his **feet** Prov 6:13
beautiful . . . your **feet** Song 7:1
feet . . . polished bronze Dan 10:6
dust of your **feet** Matt 10:14
Bind . . . hand and f Matt 22:13
kissing His **feet** Luke 7:38
anointed the **feet** John 12:3
the disciples' **feet** John 13:5
beautiful . . . the **feet** Rom 10:15
Satan under . . . **feet** Rom 16:20

FOOTSTOOL *foot support*
the f of our God 1 Chr 28:2
worship at His f Ps 99:5
Thine enemies a f Ps 110:1
the earth is My f Is 66:1
sit down by my f James 2:3

FORBID *prohibit*
if her father should f Num 30:5
f-ding to pay taxes Luke 23:2
do not f to speak 1 Cor 14:39
men who f marriage 1 Tim 4:3
he **f-s** those who 3 John 10

FORCE (n) *power, strength*
with a heavy f Num 20:20
captains of the **f-s** 2 Kin 25:23
use f against you Neh 13:21
commanders of the **f-s** Jer 43:5
with f and with Ezek 34:4
not take. . .by f Luke 3:14

FORCE (v) *compel*
are **f-d** into bondage Neh 5:5
man **f-d** to labor Job 7:1
f you to go one mile Matt 5:41
f them to blaspheme Acts 26:11
f-d to appeal to Acts 28:19

FORCED LABOR *work as tax*
Canaanites to f Josh 17:13
was over the f 2 Sam 20:24
will be put to f Prov 12:24

FORCED LABORERS
Solomon levied f 1 Kin 5:13
Solomon raised as f 2 Chr 8:8
men will become f Is 31:8

FORD *shallow place*
the f of the Jabbok Gen 32:22
the **f-s** of the Jordan Judg 12:5
f-s . . . been seized Jer 51:32

FOREFATHER *ancestor*
iniquity of their **f-s** Lev 26:40
Your first f sinned Is 43:27
I swore to your **f-s** Jer 11:5
Abraham, our f Rom 4:1
the way my **f-s** did 2 Tim 1:3

FOREIGN *alien, strange*
Put away the f gods Gen 35:2
sojourner in a f land Ex 2:22
sell her to a f people Ex 21:8
drank f waters 2 Kin 19:24
married f women Ezra 10:2
f armies to flight Heb 11:34

FOREIGNER *alien, stranger*
no f is to eat of it Ex 12:43
sell it to a f Deut 14:21
charge . . . a f Deut 23:20
since I am a f Ruth 2:10
a f in their sight Job 19:15
f-s entered his gate Obad 11

FOREKNOWLEDGE
plan and f of God Acts 2:23
f of God the Father 1 Pet 1:2

FOREMOST *first*
f commandment Matt 22:38
among whom I am f 1 Tim 1:15

FORERUNNER *one who goes before*
Jesus . . . as a f for Heb 6:20

FORETOLD *predicted*
the Holy Spirit f Acts 1:16
just as Isaiah f Rom 9:29

FOREVER *always, eternally*
not strive with man f Gen 6:3
throne shall be . . . f 1 Chr 17:14
the LORD abides f Ps 9:7
LORD sits as King f Ps 29:10
riches are not f Prov 27:24
One Who lives f Is 57:15
Christ is to remain f John 12:34
He is able to save f Heb 7:25
Son, made perfect f Heb 7:28
they shall reign f Rev 22:5

FORGET *forsake, neglect*
God has made me f Gen 41:51
lest you f the LORD Deut 6:12
f-got the God who Deut 32:18
God **f-s** . . . iniquity Job 11:6
nations who f God Ps 9:17
needy . . . be **f-gotten** Ps 9:18
Do not f the afflicted Ps 10:12
they **f-got** His deeds Ps 78:11
do not f my teaching Prov 3:1
you will f the shame Is 54:4
My people f My name Jer 23:27
f-ing what *lies* behind Phil 3:13
f your work and Heb 6:10

FORGIVE *pardon*
f the transgression Gen 50:17
f their sin Ex 32:32
f our sins Ps 79:9
f us our debts Matt 6:12
authority . . . to f sins Matt 9:6
f-gave him the debt Matt 18:27
can f sins but God Mark 2:7
he who is **f-n** little Luke 7:47
Father, f them Luke 23:34
whom you f 2 Cor 2:10
f-ing each other Eph 4:32
righteous to f us 1 John 1:9

FORGIVENESS *pardon*
a God of f Neh 9:17
there is f with Thee Ps 130:4
poured out . . . for f Matt 26:28
repentance for f Luke 24:47
f of our trespasses Eph 1:7
the f of sins Col 1:14
there is no f Heb 9:22

FORM (n) *appearance, shape*
beautiful of f and Gen 29:17
the f of the LORD Num 12:8
like the f of a man Is 44:13
in a different f Mark 16:12
bodily f like a dove Luke 3:22
f of corruptible man Rom 1:23
existed in the f of God Phil 2:6

FORM (v) *fashion, shape*
f-ed man of dust Gen 2:7
f my inward parts Ps 139:13
One **f-ing** light Is 45:7
who **f-s** mountains Amos 4:13
f-s the spirit of man Zech 12:1
plot was **f-ed** against Acts 20:3
Christ is **f-ed** in you Gal 4:19

FORMLESS *without form*
earth was f and void Gen 1:2
behold, *it was* f Jer 4:23

FORNICATION *sexual sin*
f-s, thefts, false Matt 15:19
were not born of f John 8:41
strangled and from f Acts 15:29

FORNICATORS
neither **f**, nor 1 Cor 6:9
f . . . God will judge Heb 13:4

FORSAKE *leave, neglect*
not fail you or f you Josh 1:5
f-sook the law of the 2 Chr 12:1
f Him, He will f you 2 Chr 15:2
God has not **f-n** us Ezra 9:9
why hast Thou **f-n** me Ps 22:1
Your sons have **f-n** Me Jer 5:7

f the idols of Egypt Ezek 20:8
hast Thou **f-n** Me Matt 27:46
persecuted . . . not **f-n** 2 Cor 4:9
f-ing . . . assembling Heb 10:25
nor will I ever f you Heb 13:5

FORTRESS *stronghold*
God is my strong f 2 Sam 22:33
my rock and my f Ps 18:2
My refuge and my f Ps 91:2
wealth is his f Prov 10:15
f-es will be destroyed Hos 10:14

FORTY *number*
f days nd f nights Gen 7:4
flood . . . for f days Gen 7:17
ate the manna f years Ex 16:35
with the LORD f days Ex 34:28
fasted f days and f Matt 4:2
f days being tempted Mark 1:13

FOUNDATION *establishment, base*
f-s of heaven were 2 Sam 22:8
the f of His throne Ps 97:2
the earth upon its **f-s** Ps 104:5
an everlasting f Prov 10:25
cornerstone *for* the f Is 28:16
a f upon the rock Luke 6:48
the firm f of God 2 Tim 2:19
a f of repentance Heb 6:1

FOUNDED *established*
the day it was f Ex 9:18
f it upon the seas Ps 24:2
by wisdom f the earth Prov 3:19
f His vaulted dome Amos 9:6
f upon the rock Matt 7:25

FOUNTAIN *spring, well*
f-s of the great deep Gen 7:11
is the f of life Ps 36:9
The f of wisdom Prov 18:4
f of living waters Jer 2:13

FOWL *bird*
and fattened f 1 Kin 4:23
things and winged f Ps 148:10

FOX *small animal*
three hundred **f-es** Judg 15:4
f-es that are ruining Song 2:15
like **f-es** among ruins Ezek 13:4
The **f-es** have holes Matt 8:20
Go and tell that f Luke 13:32

FRAGRANCE *pleasant aroma*
oils have a pleasing f Song 1:3
given forth *their* f Song 2:13
f like *the cedars* Hos 14:6
we are a f of Christ 2 Cor 2:15

FRANKINCENSE *spice*
spices with pure f Ex 30:34
f and the spices 1 Chr 9:29
trees of f Song 4:14
gold and f and myrrh Matt 2:11

FREE *at liberty*
she is not to go f Ex 21:7
let the oppressed go f Is 58:6
shall make you f John 8:32
who has died is **f-d** Rom 6:7
the f gift of God Rom 6:23
f from the law Rom 8:2
Christ set us f Gal 5:1
whether slave or f Eph 6:8

FREEDOM *liberty*
proclaim . . . f to Is 61:1
f of the glory Rom 8:21
you were called to f Gal 5:13
do not use your f as 1 Pet 2:16

FRESH *new, recently prepared*
found a f jawbone Judg 15:15
anointed with f oil Ps 92:10
f water from your Prov 5:15
new wine into f Mark 2:22
f and bitter *water* James 3:11

FRIEND *companion, comrade*
man speaks to his f Ex 33:11
f-s are my scoffers Job 16:20
loved ones and my **f-s** Ps 38:11
A f loves at all Prov 17:17
Wealth adds . . . **f-s** Prov 19:4
confidence in a f Mic 7:5
F, your sins are Luke 5:20
f of the bridegroom John 3:29
his life for his **f-s** John 15:13
You are My **f-s**, if John 15:14

FRIENDSHIP
the f of God Job 29:4
f with the world James 4:4

FRIGHTEN *terrify*
to f *them* away Deut 28:26
Thou dost f me Job 7:14
I was **f-ed** and fell Dan 8:17
Him and were **f-ed** Mark 6:50
wars, do not be **f-ed** Mark 13:7

FRINGE *edge*
the **f-s** of His ways Job 26:14
touched the f of His Matt 9:20

FROGS *amphibians*
smite . . . with f Ex 8:2
f which destroyed Ps 78:45
land swarmed with f Ps 105:30
unclean spirits like f Rev 16:13

FRONTALS *prayer bands*
they shall be as f Deut 6:8
f on your forehead Deut 11:18

FRUIT *growth, produce*
f trees bearing f Gen 1:11
she took from its f Gen 3:6
the f of the womb Gen 30:2
offering of first **f-s** Lev 2:12
its f in its season Ps 1:3
eat its choice **f-s** Song 4:16
eaten the f of lies Hos 10:13
know . . . by their **f-s** Matt 7:16
bad tree bears bad f Matt 7:17
the f of the Spirit Gal 5:22
f in every good work Col 1:10

FRUITFUL *productive*
be f and multiply Gen 9:7
were f and increased Ex 1:7
gather a f harvest Ps 107:37
into the f land Jer 2:7
f labor for me Phil 1:22

FRUSTRATE *conteract*
to f their cousel Ezra 4:5
He **f-s** the plotting Job 5:12
plans are **f-d** Prov 15:22

FUEL *that which burns*
people are like f Is 9:19
You will be f Ezek 21:32

FUGITIVE *one who flees*
do not betray the f Is 16:3
Meet the f with bread Is 21:14
gather the **f-s** Jer 49:5

FULFILL *complete*
to f the word 2 Chr 36:21
May the LORD f all Ps 20:5
f-ing His word Ps 148:8
the prophet was **f-ed** Matt 2:17
to abolish, but to f Matt 5:17
f-ed in the kingdom Luke 22:16
Scripture . . . be **f-ed** John 13:18
husband f his duty 1 Cor 7:3
f the law of Christ Gal 6:2

FULFILLMENT *completion*
the f of every vision Ezek 12:23
f of what had been Luke 1:45
f of *the* law Rom 13:10

FULLER *one who bleaches cloth*
of the **f-s'** field 2 Kin 18:17
like **f-s'** soap Mal 3:2

FULNESS *completeness*
Thy presence is f of Ps 16:11
the f of the Gentiles Rom 11:25
f of the time came Gal 4:4
all the f of God Eph 3:19
f to dwell in Him Col 1:19
the f of Deity dwells Col 2:9

FURIOUS *angry*
Pharaoh was f Gen 41:10
became f and very Neh 4:1
king became . . . f Dan 2:12

FURNACE *oven*
As silver tried in a f Ps 12:6
the f of affliction Is 48:10
into the midst of a f Dan 3:6
cast them into the f Matt 13:42

FURY *anger*
brother's f subsides Gen 27:44
terrify them in His f Ps 2:5
plucked up in f Ezek 19:12
the f of a fire Heb 10:27

FUTILE *useless, vain*
go after f things 1 Sam 12:21
devise f things Acts 4:25
f in . . . speculations Rom 1:21

FUTURE *that which is ahead*
discern their f Deut 32:29
no f for the evil Prov 24:20
is hope for your f Jer 31:17
foundation for the f 1 Tim 6:19

G

GABRIEL
angel of high rank Dan 8:16;9:21; Luke 1:19,26

GAD
1 *son of Jacob* Gen 30:11;35:26
2 *tribe of* Num 1:25;2:14
3 *valley* 2 Sam 24:5
4 *seer, prophet* 2 Sam 24:11,18

GAIN (n) *profit, increase*
hate dishonest g Ex 18:21
Ill-gotten **g-s** do not Prov 10:2
who rejects unjust g Is 33:15
to die is g Phil 1:21
fond of sordid g 1 Tim 3:8

GAIN (v) *acquire*
have **g-ed** the victory Ps 98:1
he will g knowledge Prov 19:25
g-s the whole world Matt 16:26
that I may g Christ Phil 3:8

GAIUS
1 *Macedonian* Acts 19:29
2 *companion of Paul* Acts 20:4
3 *Corinthian believer* 1 Cor 1:14
4 *addressee of 3 John* 3 John 1

GALATIA
Roman province in Asia Minor 1 Cor 16:1; 2 Tim 4:10

GALE *storm*
dust before a g Is 17:13
a fierce g of wind Mark 4:37

GALILEE
1 *district in N Palestine* Josh 21:32; 1 Kin 9:11; Matt 2:22; Acts 10:37
2 *Sea of* Matt 4:18; Mark 7:31
also **Sea of Chinnereth**
also **Lake of Gennesaret**
also **Sea of Tiberias**

GALL *bitter herb, bitterness*
gave me g for my food Ps 69:21
drink . . . with g Matt 27:34

the **g** of bitterness Acts 8:23

GALLOWS *for hanging*
Have a **g** . . . made Esth 5:14
hanged . . . on the **g** Esth 7:10
his sons . . . on the **g** Esth 9:25

GAMALIEL
1 *head of tribe* Num 2:20;7:54
2 *Pharisee* Acts 5:34;22:3

GARDEN *planted area*
God walking in the **g** Gen 3:8
from the **g** of Eden Gen 3:23
Make my **g** breathe Song 4:16
tabernacle like a **g** Lam 2:6
the **g** a new tomb John 19:41

GARLAND *ornament*
a **g** instead of ashes Is 61:3
brought . . . **g-s** to the Acts 14:13

GARMENT *clothing, dress*
God made **g-s** of skin Gen 3:21
in **g-s** of fine linen Gen 41:42
divide my **g-s** among Ps 22:18
g-s of glowing colors Is 63:1
g as white as snow Matt 28:3
I just touch His **g-s** Mark 5:28
spread their **g-s** Mark 11:8
dividing up His **g-s** Luke 23:34
clothed in white **g-s** Rev 3:5

GARRISON *defense*
g of the Philistines 1 Sam 13:4
the **g** . . . trembled 1 Sam 14:15
set **g-s** in the land 2 Chr 17:2

GATE *entry way*
is the **g** of heaven Gen 28:17
g-s with thanksgiving Ps 100:4
enter the **g-s** of Sheol Is 38:10
Enter . . . narrow **g** Matt 7:13
g-s of Hades shall Matt 16:18
did not open the **g** Acts 12:14

GATEKEEPERS *guards*
g for the camp 1 Chr 9:18
The sons of the **g** Ezra 2:42
g, and the singers Neh 10:39

GATES OF JERUSALEM
alternate names in italics
1 **Beautiful Gate** Acts 3:10
East Gate
2 **Benjamin Gate** Jer 20:2; Zech 14:10
Sheep Gate
Inspection Gate
3 **Corner Gate** 2 Kin 14:13; 2 Chr 26:9
4 **East Gate** Neh 3:29; Ezek 10:19;44:1
Beautiful Gate
5 **Ephraim Gate** 2 Kin 14:13; Neh 8:16
Middle Gate
Old Gate
6 **First Gate** Zech 14:10
7 **Fish Gate** 2 Chr 33:14; Neh 3:3
8 **Foundation Gate** 2 Chr 23:5
Gate of Sur
9 **Fountain Gate** Neh 2:14;12:37
"gate between two walls" 2 Kin 25:4; Jer 39:4
10 **Guard, Gate of the** Neh 12:39
Inspection Gate
11 **Horse Gate** 2 Chr 23:15; Neh 3:28
12 **Inspection Gate** Neh 3:31
Gate of the Guard
Benjamin Gate
13 **Middle Gate** Jer 39:3
Ephraim Gate
14 **Old Gate** Neh 3:6;12:39
Ephraim Gate
15 **Refuse Gate** Neh 2:13;12:31
16 **Sheep Gate** Neh 3:1
Benjamin Gate
17 **Sur, Gate of** 2 Kin 11:6
Foundation Gate
18 **Valley Gate** 2 Chr 26:9; Neh 3:13
19 **Water Gate** Neh 3:26;8:1,3

GATHER *assemble, collect*
g-ed to his people Gen 25:8
g stubble for straw Ex 5:12
G My godly ones Ps 50:5
g all nations and Is 66:18
hen **g-s** her chicks Matt 23:37
elders . . . were **g-ed** Matt 26:3
g . . . His elect Mark 13:27

GAZA
Philistine city Gen 10:19; Judg 16:1; Jer 47:5

GAZE (n) *view, glance*
Turn Thy **g** away from Ps 39:13
let your **g** be fixed Prov 4:25
I lifted my **g** and Dan 8:3
turning His **g** on His Luke 6:20

GAZE (v) *look, stare*
man . . . **g-ing** at her Gen 24:21
and **g** after Moses Ex 33:8
LORD **g-d** upon the Ps 102:19
g-ing . . . into the sky Acts 1:10

GAZELLE *animal*
swift as the **g-s** 1 Chr 12:8
a **g** Or a young stag Song 2:17
like a hunted **g** Is 13:14

GEHAZI
servant of Elisha 2 Kin 4:12;5:20;8:4

GENEALOGY *family record*
found the book of . . . **g** Neh 7:5
g of Jesus Christ Matt 1:1
and endless **g-ies** 1 Tim 1:4
whose **g** is not traced Heb 7:6

GENERATION *age, period*
this evil **g** Deut 1:35
faithfulness to all **g-s** Ps 100:5
salvation to all **g-s** Is 51:8
this **g** seek for a sign Mark 8:12
g-s . . . not made known Eph 3:5
and perverse **g** Phil 2:15

GENEROUS *bountiful*
g will be blessed Prov 22:9
because I am **g** Matt 20:15
g . . . ready to share 1 Tim 6:18

GENNESARET
1 *lake* Luke 5:1
also **Sea of Chinnereth**
also **Sea of Galilee**
also **Sea of Tiberius**
2 *land or district* Matt 14:34; Mark 6:53

GENTILES *foreigners, non-Jews*
Galilee of the **G** Matt 4:15
deliver . . . to the **G** Matt 20:19
revelation to the **G** Luke 2:32
Why did the **G** rage Acts 4:25
preach . . . among the **G** Gal 1:16

GENTLE *compassionate, mild*
g answer turns away Prov 15:1
I was like a **g** lamb Jer 11:19
Blessed are the **g** Matt 5:5
G, and mounted on Matt 21:5
a **g** and quiet spirit 1 Pet 3:4

GENTLENESS *kindness*
and a spirit of **g** 1 Cor 4:21
and **g** of Christ 2 Cor 10:1
g, self-control Gal 5:23
humility and **g**, with Eph 4:2

GERIZIM
mountain near Shechem Deut 11:29; Josh 8:33

GERSHOM
1 *son of Moses* Ex 2:22;18:3
2 *son of Levi* 1 Chr 6:16,43
3 *line of Phinehas* Ezra 8:2

GETHSEMANE
garden on Mount of Olives Matt 26:36; Mark 14:32

GIANT
were born to the **g** 2 Sam 21:22
from the **g-s** 1 Chr 20:6

GIBEON
town in Benjamin Josh 9:3,17; 1 Kin 3:5; 1 Chr 8:29

GIDEON
son of Joash Judg 6:11, 36
judge Judg 8:4-21

GIFT *present*
the sacred **g-s** Num 18:32
children are a **g** Ps 127:3
g of the Holy Spirit Acts 2:38
impart . . . spiritual **g** Rom 1:11
g of God is eternal Rom 6:23
desire . . . greater **g-s** 1 Cor 12:31

GIHON
1 *river of Eden* Gen 2:13
2 *Jerusalem spring* 2 Chr 32:30

GILBOA
mountain 2 Sam 1:6
where Saul died 2 Sam 21:12

GILEAD
1 *son of Machir* Num 36:1
2 *descendant of Gad* 1 Chr 5:14
3 *father of Jephthah* Judg 11:1
4 *land E of Jordan* Num 32:29
5 *mountain* Judg 7:3
6 *city* Hos 6:8

GILGAL
1 *in Arabah* Deut 11:30
2 *encampment in Jordan Valley* Josh 5:9; 1 Sam 7:16
near Jericho Josh 5:8,10
3 *in N Judah* Josh 15:7
4 *in Galilee* Josh 12:23
5 *village near Bethel* 2 Kin 2:1

GIRDLE *belt, waistband*
man with a leather **g** 2 Kin 1:8
binds . . . with a **g** Job 12:18
with a golden **g** Rev 1:13

GIRL *maiden*
the **g** and consult Gen 24:57
sold a **g** for wine Joel 3:3
the **g** has not died Matt 9:24

GIVE *bestow, yield*
g-n you every plant Gen 1:29
gave me from . . . tree Gen 3:12
in the land . . . God **g-s** Ex 20:12
g him to the LORD 1 Sam 1:11
G ear to my prayer Ps 17:1
G me neither poverty Prov 30:8
a son will be **g-n** Is 9:6
gave birth to a Son Matt 1:25
G us this day Matt 6:11
g-ing thanks, He Matt 15:36
authority . . . been **g-n** Matt 28:18
what shall a man **g** Mark 8:37
body which is **g-n** Luke 22:19
gave His only . . . Son John 3:16
not as the world **g-s** John 14:27
gave up His spirit John 19:30
what I do have I **g** Acts 3:6
more blessed to **g** Acts 20:35
was **g-n** me a thorn 2 Cor 12:7
always **g-ing** thanks Eph 5:20
who **gave** Himself 1 Tim 2:6
to be **g-n** a mark Rev 13:16

GLADNESS *joy*
celebrate . . . with **g** Neh 12:27
g . . . for the Jews Esth 8:17
Serve the LORD with **g** Ps 100:2
g and sincerity of Acts 2:46
With the oil of **g** Heb 1:9

GLASS *crystal*
or **g** cannot equal Job 28:17

sea of **g** like crystal Rev 4:6

GLEAN *gather, pick*
Nor shall you **g** Lev 19:10
Do not go to **g** Ruth 2:8
she **g-ed** in the field Ruth 2:17
they **g** the vineyard Job 24:6
g-ing ears of grain Is 17:5

GLOOM *darkness*
cloud and thick **g** Deut 4:11
The land of utter **g** Job 10:22
darkness and **g** and Heb 12:18
and your joy to **g** James 4:9

GLORIFY *honor, worship*
g Thy name forever Ps 86:12
Let the LORD be **g-ied** Is 66:5
g your Father Matt 5:16
shepherds . . . **g-ing** Luke 2:20
Jesus . . . not yet **g-ied** John 7:39
Father, **g** Thy name John 12:28
God is **g-ied** in Him John 13:31
were all **g-ing** God Acts 4:21
Gentiles to **g** God Rom 15:9
g God in your body 1 Cor 6:20
did not **g** Himself Heb 5:5

GLORIOUS *exalted, great*
g name be blessed Neh 9:5
G things are spoken Ps 87:3
resting place will be **g** Is 11:10
the law great and **g** Is 42:21
g gospel of . . . God 1 Tim 1:11

GLORY (n) *honor, splendor*
show me Thy **g** Ex 33:18
while My **g** is passing Ex 33:22
Tell of His **g** 1 Chr 16:24
King of **g** may come Ps 24:7
exchanged their **g** Ps 106:20
earth is full of His **g** Is 6:3
their **g** into shame Hos 4:7
Solomon in all his **g** Matt 6:29
g of the Lord shone Luke 2:9
G . . . in the highest Luke 2:14
He comes in His **g** Luke 9:26
do not seek My **g** John 8:50
short of the **g** of God Rom 3:23
all to the **g** of God 1 Cor 10:31
eternal weight of **g** 2 Cor 4:17
body of His **g** Phil 3:21
crowned Him with **g** Heb 2:7
unfading crown of **g** 1 Pet 5:4

GLORY (v) *exalt*
and **g** in thy praise 1 Chr 16:35
G in His holy name Ps 105:3
in Him they will **g** Jer 4:2
I . . . have cause to **g** Phil 2:16

GLUTTON *excessive eater*
g . . . come to poverty Prov 23:21
a companion of **g-s** Prov 28:7
evil beasts, lazy **g-s** Titus 1:12

GNASH *grind*
They **g-ed** at me Ps 35:16
He will **g** his teeth Ps 112:10
They hiss and **g** Lam 2:16
g-ing their teeth Acts 7:54

GO *move, proceed*
Let My people **g** Ex 7:16
God who **g-es** before Deut 1:30
where you **g,** I will **g** Ruth 1:16
the way he should **g** Prov 22:6
g one mile, **g** . . . two Matt 5:41
G into all . . . world Mark 16:15
I **g** to prepare a John 14:2
night is almost **gone** Rom 13:12

GOADS *inducements*
wise men are like **g** Eccl 12:11
kick against the **g** Acts 26:14

GOAL *end, object*
press on toward the **g** Phil 3:14

g . . . is love 1 Tim 1:5

GOAT *animal*
curtains of **g-s'** *hair* Ex 26:7
g for a sin offering Num 15:27
quilt of **g-s'** *hair* 1 Sam 19:13
g *had* a . . . horn Dan 8:5
shaggy **g** *represents* Dan 8:21
sheep from the **g-s** Matt 25:32
blood of **g-s** . . . bulls Heb 9:13

GOD *Deity, Eternal One*
In the beginning **G** Gen 1:1
G formed man of dust Gen 2:7
G sent him out Gen 3:23
tablets were **G-'s** work Ex 32:16
G is my . . . fortress 2 Sam 22:33
G of my salvation Ps 18:46
In **G** . . . put my trust Ps 56:4
Search me, O **G** Ps 139:23
word of **G** is tested Prov 30:5
I am **G** and not man Hos 11:9
Will a man rob **G** Mal 3:8
G descending . . . dove Matt 3:16
they shall see **G** Matt 5:8
What . . . **G** has joined Matt 19:6
kingdom of **G** is at Mark 1:15
My **G,** why hast Mark 15:34
You the Son of **G** Luke 22:70
the Word was **G** John 1:1
the Lamb of **G** John 1:29
G so loved the world John 3:16
G is spirit John 4:24
obey **G** rather than Acts 5:29
judgment of **G** Rom 2:2
are a temple of **G** 1 Cor 3:16
full armor of **G** Eph 6:11
one **G** . . . one mediator 1 Tim 2:5
word of **G** is . . . sharper Heb 4:12
impossible . . . **G** to lie Heb 6:18
G is love 1 John 4:8
great supper of **G** Rev 19:17

GODDESS *female deity*
Ashtoreth the **g** of 1 Kin 11:5
great **g** Artemis Acts 19:27
blasphemers of . . . **g** Acts 19:37

GODLESS *pagan, without God*
hope of the **g** will Job 8:13
joy of . . . **g** momentary Job 20:5
g man destroys his Prov 11:9
hands of **g** men Acts 2:23
become of the **g** 1 Pet 4:18

GODLINESS *holiness*
in all **g** and dignity 1 Tim 2:2
the mystery of **g** 1 Tim 3:16
g is profitable 1 Tim 4:8
g, brotherly kindness 2 Pet 1:7

GODLY *holy*
keeps . . . His **g** ones 1 Sam 2:9
g man ceases to be Ps 12:1
not forsake His **g** ones Ps 37:28
and **g** sincerity 2 Cor 1:12
to live **g** in Christ 2 Tim 3:12
rescue the **g** from 2 Pet 2:9

GOD(S) *false deity, idols*
no other **g-s** before Me Ex 20:3
New **g-s** were chosen Judg 5:8
cast their **g-s** into Is 37:19
bowed . . . to other **g-s** Jer 22:9
no other **g** who is Dan 3:29
g-s . . . become like Acts 14:11
the **g** of this world 2 Cor 4:4

GOG
1 *a Reubenite* 1 Chr 5:4
2 *prince of Meshech and Tubal* Ezek 38:2
3 *symbol of godless nations* Rev 20:8

GOLAN
city of refuge Josh 21:27
a Levitical city 1 Chr 6:71

GOLD *precious metal*
g of that land is good Gen 2:12

mercy seat of pure **g** Ex 25:17
more desirable than **g** Ps 19:10
to Him gifts of **g** Matt 2:11
Do not acquire **g** Matt 10:9
coveted no . . . **g** Acts 20:33
city was pure **g** Rev 21:18

GOLDSMITH *gold craftsman*
g-s and . . . merchants Neh 3:32
g, and he makes it Is 46:6

GOLGOTHA
site of Crucifixion Matt 27:33; Mark 15:22

GOLIATH
Philistine giant 1 Sam 17:4,23; 21:9

GOMER
1 *son of Japheth* Gen 10:2
2 *group of people* Ezek 38:6
3 *wife of Hosea* Hos 1:3

GOMORRAH
city of Jordan plain Gen 10:19; 14:10;19:24
probably S of Dead Sea Is 13:19; 2 Pet 2:6

GOOD *complete, right, commendable*
God saw that it was **g** Gen 1:18
Do not withhold **g** Prov 3:27
joyful heart is **g** Prov 17:22
feed in . . . **g** pasture Ezek 34:18
Seek **g** and not evil Amos 5:14
Well done, **g** and Matt 25:23
sown on the **g** soil Mark 4:20
Salt is **g** Mark 9:50
No one is **g** except Luke 18:19
I am the **g** shepherd John 10:11
perseverance in . . . **g** Rom 2:7
nothing **g** . . . in me Rom 7:18
work together for **g** Rom 8:28
overcome evil . . . **g** Rom 12:21
g hope by grace 2 Thess 2:16
Fight the **g** fight 1 Tim 6:12

GOODNESS *excellence, value*
My **g** pass before you Ex 33:19
Surely **g** . . . will follow Ps 23:6
How great is Thy **g** Ps 31:19
kindness, **g** Gal 5:22
every desire for **g** 2 Thess 1:11

GOSHEN
1 *district of Egypt in Nile Delta* Gen 45:10; 47:6,27
2 *S Judah region* Josh 10:41
3 *town in Judah* Josh 15:51

GOSPEL *good news*
proclaiming the **g** of Matt 4:23
not ashamed of the **g** Rom 1:16
if our **g** is veiled 2 Cor 4:3
distort the **g** of Christ Gal 1:7
g of your salvation Eph 1:13
g of peace Eph 6:15
the hope of the **g** Col 1:23
eternal **g** to preach Rev 14:6

GOSSIP *one who spreads rumors*
associate with a **g** Prov 20:19
malice; *they are* **g-s** Rom 1:29
g-s and busybodies 1 Tim 5:13

GOVERN *rule*
light to **g** the day Gen 1:16
light to **g** the night Gen 1:16
when the judges **g-ed** Ruth 1:1

GOVERNMENT *authority, rule*
g . . . on His shoulders Is 9:6
be no end to . . . *His* **g** Is 9:7

GOVERNOR *ruler*
not offer it to your **g** Mal 1:8
brought before **g-s** Matt 10:18
g was quite amazed Matt 27:14
Pilate was **g** of Judea Luke 3:1
g over Egypt Acts 7:10

GRACE *benevolence, favor*
G is poured upon Thy Ps 45:2
g of God was upon Luke 2:40
full of g and truth John 1:14
g abounded . . . more Rom 5:20
g of our Lord Jesus Rom 16:20
My g is sufficient 2 Cor 12:9
justified by His g Titus 3:7
to the throne of g Heb 4:16
g to the humble James 4:6

GRACIOUS *kind*
God be g to you Gen 43:29
g to whom I will be Ex 33:19
a g and . . . God Neh 9:31
Be g to me, O LORD Ps 6:2
and g, Slow to anger Ps 86:15
g to a poor man Prov 19:17
be g to . . . remnant Amos 5:15

GRAFT *insert, join*
I might be **g-ed** in Rom 11:19
God is able to g Rom 11:23
g-ed into their own Rom 11:24

GRANDCHILDREN
G are the crown of Prov 17:6
widow has . . . or g 1 Tim 5:4

GRANDDAUGHTER
g-s, and all his Gen 46:7
g of Omri king of 2 Kin 8:26

GRANDSON
g might fear the LORD Deut 6:2
sons and thirty **g-s** Judg 12:14
master's g shall eat 2 Sam 9:10

GRAPE *fruit*
nor eat . . . dried **g-s** Num 6:3
of **g-s** you drank Deut 32:14
when the g harvest is Is 24:13
G-s are not gathered Matt 7:16
g-s from a briar Luke 6:44

GRASSHOPPER *insect*
the g in its kinds Lev 11:22
we became like **g-s** Num 13:33
inhabitants are like **g-s** Is 40:22

GRATITUDE *thankfulness*
overflowing with g Col 2:7
is received with g 1 Tim 4:4
let us show g Heb 12:28

GRAVE *sepulchre, tomb*
pillar of Rachel's g Gen 35:20
throat is an open g Ps 5:9
I will open your **g-s** Ezek 37:12
I will prepare your g Nah 1:14
made the g secure Matt 27:66

GRAVEN *sculptured*
make . . . a g image Deut 4:23
ashamed who serve g Ps 97:7
praise to g images Is 42:8

GRAY *color*
g hair . . . in sorrow Gen 42:38
with the man of g Deut 32:25
Both the **g-haired** Job 15:10
when *I am* old and g Ps 71:18
g head is a crown Prov 16:31

GREAT *big, excellent, grand*
made . . . two g lights Gen 1:16
make you a g nation Gen 12:2
lovingkindness is g Ps 57:10
your iniquity is g Jer 30:15
g day of the LORD Zeph 1:14
rejoiced . . . with g joy Matt 2:10
woman . . . faith is g Matt 15:28
good news of a g joy Luke 2:10
reward is g in Luke 6:23
because of His g love Eph 2:4
so g a salvation Heb 2:3
we have a g . . . priest Heb 4:14
so g a cloud of Heb 12:1
g supper of God Rev 19:17
a g white throne Rev 20:11

GREATEST *most important*
who is the g among Luke 22:26
g of these is love 1 Cor 13:13
least to the g Heb 8:11

GREED *excessive desire*
caught by *their* . . . g Prov 11:6
every form of g Luke 12:15
wickedness, g, evil Rom 1:29
a pretext for g 1 Thess 2:5
a heart trained in g 2 Pet 2:14

GREEDY *craving*
had g desires Num 11:4
g man curses Ps 10:3
Everyone is g for Jer 6:13

GREEKS
people of Greece Joel 3:6; Acts 16:1,3; Rom 1:16; 1 Cor 12:13

GRIEF *heartache, sorrow*
weeps because of g Ps 119:28
foolish son is a g Prov 17:25
acquainted with g Is 53:3
our **g-s** He Himself Is 53:4
joy and not with g Heb 13:17

GRIEVE *mourn, sorrow*
was **g-d** in His heart Gen 6:6
Do not be **g-d** Neh 8:10
g-d Him in the desert Ps 78:40
g-d His Holy Spirit Is 63:10
g-d at their hardness Mark 3:5
Peter was **g-d** John 21:17
not g the Holy Spirit Eph 4:30

GROAN *cry, moan*
From the city men g Job 24:12
man rules, people g Prov 29:2
wounded will g Jer 51:52
whole creation **g-s** Rom 8:22

GROANING *crying*
God heard their g Ex 2:24
O LORD, Consider my g Ps 5:1
g of the prisoner Ps 79:11
g-s of a wounded Ezek 30:24
g-s too deep for Rom 8:26

GROPE *move about blindly*
you shall g at noon Deut 28:29
They g in darkness Job 12:25
g like . . . blind men Is 59:10
g for Him and find Acts 17:27

GROUND *earth, land, soil*
Cursed is the g Gen 3:17
a spirit from the g Is 29:4
finger wrote on the g John 8:6
standing is holy g Acts 7:33
g that drinks the rain Heb 6:7

GROUNDED *established*
hope . . . is firmly g 2 Cor 1:7
rooted and g in love Eph 3:17

GROW *develop, increase*
Moses had **g-n** up Ex 2:11
You are **g-n** fat Deut 32:15
my spirit **g-s** faint Ps 77:3
sun and moon g dark Joel 3:15
lilies of the field g Matt 6:28
love will g cold Matt 24:12
Child continued to g Luke 2:40
grew strong in faith Rom 4:20
as your faith **g-s** 2 Cor 10:15
g in the grace 2 Pet 3:18

GROWTH *increase*
new g is seen Prov 27:25
God who causes the g 1 Cor 3:7

GRUDGE *hostile feeling*
Esau bore a g Gen 27:41
nor bear any g Lev 19:18
Herodias had a g Mark 6:19

GRUMBLE *complain*
they **g-d** against Moses Ex 17:3
the congregation g Num 14:36
g-d in their tents Ps 106:25
scribes *began* to g Luke 15:2
g among yourselves John 6:43

GUARD (n) *keeper*
dost set a g over me Job 7:12
be a g for them Ezek 38:7
g-s shook for fear Matt 28:4
Him away under g Mark 14:44

GUARD (v) *keep watch*
g the way to the tree Gen 3:24
g-ed the threshold 2 Kin 12:9
Discretion will g you Prov 2:11
soldier . . . was **g-ing** Acts 28:16
shall g your hearts Phil 4:7
g . . . from idols 1 John 5:21

GUARDIAN *overseer*
g-s of *the children* 2 Kin 10:1
under **g-s** and Gal 4:2
G of your souls 1 Pet 2:25

GUEST *visitor*
Herod and his . . . **g-s** Mark 6:22
Where . . . My g room Mark 14:14
to the invited **g-s** Luke 14:7
g of a . . . sinner Luke 19:7

GUIDE (n) *advisor, director*
The righteous is a g Prov 12:26
Woe to . . . blind **g-s** Matt 23:16
You blind **g-s**, who Matt 23:24
are a g to the blind Rom 2:19

GUIDE (v) *direct, lead*
LORD alone **g-d** him Deut 32:12
He **g-s** me in the paths Ps 23:3
g us until death Ps 48:14
my mind was **g-ing** *me* Eccl 2:3
blind . . . **g-s** a blind Matt 15:14
g you into . . . truth John 16:13
unless someone **g-s** Acts 8:31

GUILE *deceit*
in whom is no g John 1:47
all malice and all g 1 Pet 2:1
lips from speaking g 1 Pet 3:10

GUILT *offence*
be free from g Num 5:31
according to his g Deut 25:2
charge me with a g 2 Sam 3:8
our g has grown Ezra 9:6
land is full of g Jer 51:5
must bear their g Hos 10:2
I find no g in Him John 18:38

GUILTY *charged* or *condemned*
he sins and becomes g Lev 6:4
murderer . . . g of Num 35:31
as one who is g 2 Sam 14:13
g by the blood Ezek 22:4
g of an eternal sin Mark 3:29
has become g of all James 2:10

H

HABITATION *abode, dwelling*
from Thy holy h Deut 26:15
a rock of h Ps 71:3
h-s of violence Ps 74:20
live in a peaceful h Is 32:18
holy and glorious h Is 63:15
laid waste his h Jer 10:25
a h of shepherds Jer 33:12

HABOR
river in Mesopotamia 2 Kin 17:6;18:11; 1 Chr 5:26

HADAD
1 *son of Ishmael* Gen 25:15; 1 Chr 1:30
2 *king of Edom, son of Bedad* Gen 36:35,36; 1 Chr 1:46,47
3 *a king of Edom* Gen 36:39; 1 Chr 1:50,51

4 *Edomite prince* 1 Kin 11:14ff

HADASSAH
Esther's Hebrew name Esth 2:7

HADES *hell, place of dead*
shall descend to **H** Matt 11:23
in **H** he lifted up Luke 16:23
abandoned to **H** Rev 1:18

HAGAR
Sarah's handmaiden Gen 16:1
Abraham's slave wife Gen 16:3
mother of Ishmael Gen 16:15

HAGGITH
David's wife 2 Sam 3:4
mother of Adonijah 1 Kin 1:11

HAIL (n) *pieces of ice*
rained **h** on the land Ex 9:23
storehouses of the **h** Job 38:22
gave them **h** for rain Ps 105:32
plague of the **h** Rev 16:21

HAIL (v) *greetings*
H, Rabbi Matt 26:49
H, King of . . . Jews Matt 27:29

HAILSTONES *pieces of ice*
who died from the **h** Josh 10:11
H and coals of fire Ps 18:13
you, O **h**, will fall Ezek 13:11
h . . . one hundred Rev 16:21

HALLELUJAH *praise Yahweh*
H! Salvation and Rev 19:1
H! Her smoke rises Rev 19:3
Amen. **H** Rev 19:4
H! For the Lord our Rev 19:6

HALLOWED *consecrated, holy*
H be Thy name Matt 6:9

HAM
1 *son of Noah* Gen 5:32;9:18
2 *city* Gen 14:5
3 *poetic name for Egypt* Ps 105:27;106:22

HAMMER *mallet, tool*
and seized a **h** Judg 4:21
neither **h** nor axe 1 Kin 6:7
smash with . . . **h-s** Ps 74:6
like a **h** which Jer 23:29

HAMON-GOG
valley where army of Gog is defeated Ezek 39:11,15

HANANIAH
1 *son of Zerubbabel* 1 Chr 3:19
2 *son of Shishak* 1 Chr 8:24
3 *musician* 1 Chr 25:4,23
4 *in Uzziah's army* 2 Chr 26:11
5 *repaired wall* Neh 3:30
6 *overseer of palace* Neh 7:2
7 *false prophet* Jer 28:15
8 *Shadrach* Dan 1:6,7
name of six other individuals

HAND *part of body*
cover you with My **h** Ex 33:22
sling was in his **h** 1 Sam 17:40
They pierced my **h-s** Ps 22:16
the hollow of His **h** Is 40:12
clay in the potter's **h** Jer 18:6
not let your left **h** Matt 6:3
the right **h** of God Mark 16:19
into the **h-s** of men Luke 9:44
into Thy **h-s** I Luke 23:46
not made with **h-s** 2 Cor 5:1
lifting up holy **h-s** 1 Tim 2:8
h-s of . . . God Heb 10:31

HANDMAID *female servant, slave*
save the son of Thy **h** Ps 86:16
the son of Thy **h** Ps 116:16
her **h-s** are moaning Nah 2:7

HANDSOME *attractive*
a choice and **h** *man* 1 Sam 9:2
ruddy, with a **h** 1 Sam 17:42

HANG *attach, suspend*
h you on a tree Gen 40:19
h up the veil Ex 40:8
h-ed is accursed of Deut 21:23
h-ing in an oak 2 Sam 18:10
they **h-ed** Haman Esth 7:10
he . . . **h-ed** himself Matt 27:5
millstone were **hung** Luke 17:2
h-ing Him on a cross Acts 5:30
who **h-s** on a tree Gal 3:13

HANNAH
mother of Samuel 1 Sam 2:21

HAPPINESS *joy*
give **h** to his wife Deut 24:5
eat your bread in **h** Eccl 9:7
I have forgotten **h** Lam 3:17

HAPPY *blessed, joyful*
Leah said, **H** am I Gen 30:13
h . . . man whom God Job 5:17
h . . . who keeps the Prov 29:18

HARAN
1 *brother of Abraham* Gen 11:27
father of Lot Gen 11:31
2 *Gershonite Levite* 1 Chr 23:9
3 *Mesopotamian city* Gen 11:32;27:43

HARDEN *make hard, callous*
h Pharaoh's heart Ex 7:3
dust **h-s** into a mass Job 38:38
who **h-s** *his* neck Prov 29:1
h-s whom He Rom 9:18
minds were **h-ed** 2 Cor 3:14
Do not **h** your hearts Heb 3:15

HARDSHIP *difficulty*
H after **h** is with me Job 10:17
people experience **h** Ps 60:3
afflictions, in **h-s** 2 Cor 6:4
our labor and **h** 1 Thess 2:9
Suffer **h** with *me* 2 Tim 2:3

HAREM *royal wives' quarters*
best place in the **h** Esth 2:9
the court of the **h** Esth 2:11
from the **h** to the Esth 2:13
to the second **h** Esth 2:14

HARLOT *prostitute*
thought she *was* a **h** Gen 38:15
the hire of a **h** Deut 23:18
h whose name was Josh 2:1
Dressed as a **h** Prov 7:10
city has become a **h** Is 1:21
Traded a boy for a **h** Joel 3:3
to a **h** is one body 1 Cor 6:16
Mother of **H-s** Rev 17:5

HARLOTRY *prostitution*
with child by **h** Gen 38:24
profaned by **h** Lev 21:7
uncovered her **h-ies** Ezek 23:18
children of **h** Hos 1:2
spirit of **h** Hos 5:4

HARM (n) *evil, hurt*
pillar to me, for **h** Gen 31:52
h to this people Ex 5:22
Do not devise **h** Prov 3:29
great **h** to yourselves Jer 44:7
the fire without **h** Dan 3:25
did me much **h** 2 Tim 4:14

HARM (v) *damage, hurt*
David seeks to **h** 1 Sam 24:9
planning to **h** me Neh 6:2
have not **h-ed** me Dan 6:22
in order to **h** you Acts 18:10
is there to **h** you 1 Pet 3:13

HAR-MAGEDON
hill of Megiddo Rev 16:16

HARMONY *agreement*
what **h** has Christ 2 Cor 6:15
live in **h** in the Phil 4:2

HARP *musical instrument*
my **h** is turned to Job 30:31
praises . . . with a **h** Ps 33:2
Awake, **h** and lyre Ps 57:8
gaiety of the **h** ceases Is 24:8
holding **h-s** of God Rev 15:2

HARSH *difficult, hard*
man was **h** and evil 1 Sam 25:3
h word stirs up anger Prov 15:1
A **h** vision Is 21:2
under **h** servitude Lam 1:3

HARVEST *reap and gather*
Seedtime and **h** Gen 8:22
fruits of the wheat **h** Ex 34:22
you reap your **h** Deut 24:19
like rain in **h** Prov 26:1
the gladness of **h** Is 9:3
time of **h** will come Jer 51:33
Lord of the **h** Matt 9:38
h is the end of the Matt 13:39
fields . . . white for **h** John 4:35
h of the earth is Rev 14:15

HASTEN *accelerate*
h-ed after deceit Job 31:5
H to me, O God Ps 70:5
they **h** to shed blood Prov 1:16
bird **h-s** to the snare Prov 7:23
eye **h-s** after wealth Prov 28:22
h-ing . . . day of God 2 Pet 3:12

HATE *despise, loathe*
you **h** discipline Ps 50:17
who **h** the LORD Ps 81:15
I **h** every false way Ps 119:104
fools **h** knowlege Prov 1:22
spares his rod **h-s** Prov 13:24
H evil, love good Amos 5:15
For I **h** divorce Mal 2:16
good to those who **h** Luke 6:27
you will be **h-d** Luke 21:17
he who **h-s** his life John 12:25
Esau I **h-d** Rom 9:13
h-ing one another Titus 3:3
yet **h-s** his brother 1 John 2:9

HATRED *hate, ill will*
h for my love Ps 109:5
H stirs up strife Prov 10:12
who conceals **h** *has* Prov 10:18

HAUGHTY *proud*
nor my eyes **h** Ps 131:1
H eyes, a lying Prov 6:17
h spirit before Prov 16:18
Proud, **H**, Scoffer Prov 21:24
wine betrays the **h** Hab 2:5
do not be **h** in mind Rom 12:16

HAVILAH
1 *second son of Cush* Gen 10:7
2 *son of Jokian* Gen 10:29; 1 Chr 1:23
3 *region encompassed by one of Eden's rivers* Gen 2:11
4 *area in W Arabia* Gen 25:18

HAZOR
1 *Canaanite city in N Palestine* Josh 11:11
2 *town of the Negev* Josh 15:23
3 *Benjamite city* Neh 11:33
4 *desert kingdom* Jer 49:33

HEAD *chief* or *part of body*
bruise you on the **h** Gen 3:15
anointed my **h** with oil Ps 23:5
gray **h** is a crown Prov 16:31
coals on his **h** Prov 25:22
had four **h-s** Dan 7:6
an oath by your **h** Matt 5:36
nowhere to lay His **h** Matt 8:20
h of John the Baptist Matt 14:8
not a hair of your **h** Luke 21:18
crown . . . on His **h** John 19:2

God is the **h** of 1 Cor 11:3
husband is the **h** Eph 5:23

HEAL *make well, restore*
will **h** their land 2 Chr 7:14
h-s the brokenhearted Ps 147:3
a time to **h** Eccl 3:3
H me, O LORD Jer 17:14
will **h** their apostasy Hos 14:4
h-ed all who were Matt 8:16
H *the* sick, raise Matt 10:8
h him on . . . Sabbath Mark 3:2
Physician, **h** yourself Luke 4:23
you may be **h-ed** James 5:16
fatal wound was **h-ed** Rev 13:3

HEALING *producing health* or *wholeness*
be **h** to your body Prov 3:8
h to the bones Prov 16:24
sorrow is beyond **h** Jer 8:18
There is no **h** for Jer 46:11
their leaves for **h** Ezek 47:12
h every kind of Matt 4:23
gifts of **h** 1 Cor 12:9
h of the nations Rev 22:2

HEALTH *soundness, wholeness*
no **h** in my bones Ps 38:3
restore you to **h** Jer 30:17
and be in good **h** 3 John 2

HEAR *listen*
h-d the sound of Gen 3:10
God **h-d** their groaning Ex 2:24
H, O Israel Deut 6:4
h the wisdom of 1 Kin 4:34
h Thou in heaven 1 Kin 8:30
Will God **h** his cry Job 27:9
who dost **h** prayer Ps 65:2
h Thy lovingkindness Ps 143:8
poor **h-s** no rebuke Prov 13:8
deaf shall **h** words Is 29:18
bones, **h** the word Ezek 37:4
ears to **h,** let him **h** Matt 11:15
h of wars and Mark 13:7
he who **h-s** My word John 5:24
does not **h** sinners John 9:31
sheep **h** My voice John 10:27
we **h-d** of your faith Col 1:4
anyone **h-s** My voice Rev 3:20

HEARING *listening*
in the LORD's **h** 1 Sam 8:21
in the **h** of a fool Prov 23:9
fulfilled in your **h** Luke 4:21
I will give you a **h** Acts 23:35
become dull of **h** Heb 5:11

HEART *mind* or *seat of emotions*
intent of man's **h** is Gen 8:21
I will harden his **h** Ex 4:21
LORD looks at the **h** 1 Sam 16:7
fool has said in his **h** Ps 14:1
meditation of my **h** Ps 19:14
My **h** is like wax Ps 22:14
and a contrite **h** Ps 51:17
Thy word . . . in my **h** Ps 119:11
Deceit is in the **h** Prov 12:20
A joyful **h** is good Prov 17:22
bribe corrupts the **h** Eccl 7:7
a new **h** and a new Ezek 18:31
uncircumcised in **h** Ezek 44:7
are the pure in **h** Matt 5:8
adultery . . . in his **h** Matt 5:28
and humble in **h** Matt 11:29
h is far . . . from Me Matt 15:8
pondering . . . in her **h** Luke 2:19
pierced to the **h** Acts 2:37
who searches the **h-s** Rom 8:27
tablets of human **h-s** 2 Cor 3:3
melody with your **h** Eph 5:19
intentions of the **h** Heb 4:12

HEAVEN *place of God* or *sky*
God created the **h-s** Gen 1:1
shut up the **h-s** Deut 11:17
thunder in the **h-s** 1 Sam 2:10
fire came . . . from **h** 2 Kin 1:14
make windows in **h** 2 Kin 7:2
walks . . . vault of **h** Job 22:14
I consider Thy **h-s** Ps 8:3
h and earth praise Ps 69:34
lights in the **h-s** Ezek 32:8
open . . . windows of **h** Mal 3:10
kingdom of **h** is at Matt 3:2
voice out of the **h-s** Matt 3:17
Father who art in **h** Matt 6:9
shall be loosed in **h** Matt 16:19
great signs from **h** Luke 21:11
Him go into **h** Acts 1:11
up to the third **h** 2 Cor 12:2
citizenship is in **h** Phil 3:20
there was war in **h** Rev 12:7
new **h** and a new Rev 21:1

HEAVENLY *related to God*
h Father is perfect Matt 5:48
h Father knows that Matt 6:32
h host praising God Luke 2:13
I tell you **h** things John 3:12
Him in the **h** *places* Eph 2:6
partakers of a **h** Heb 3:1
shadow of the **h** Heb 8:5

HEAVY *burdensome, hard to lift*
Moses' hands were **h** Ex 17:12
servitude was **h** on Neh 5:18
h drinkers of wine Prov 23:20
A stone is **h** Prov 27:3
Jerusalem a **h** stone Zech 12:3
eyes were very **h** Mark 14:40

HEBREW(S)
1 *people* Gen 14:13; Ex 1:15;9:13; Jon 1:9
2 *language* John 19:17; Acts 22:2;26:14
see also **JUDEAN**
see also **CANAAN**

HEBRON
1 *site of Sarah's death* Gen 23:2
visited by spies Num 13:22
destroyed Josh 10:37
city of refuge Josh 20:7
residence of David 2 Sam 2:1
2 *son of Kohath* Ex 6:18
3 *son of Mareshah* 1 Chr 2:42

HEEL *back of foot*
bruise him on the **h** Gen 3:15
on to Esau's **h** Gen 25:26
his **h** against Me John 13:18

HEIFER *young cow*
unblemished red **h** Num 19:2
plowed with my **h** Judg 14:18
Egypt is a pretty **h** Jer 46:20
Like a stubborn **h** Hos 4:16

HEIGHT *elevation, heaven, sky*
in the **h** of heaven Job 22:12
from His holy **h** Ps 102:19
Praise Him in the **h-s** Ps 148:1
As the heavens for **h** Prov 25:3
ascend above the **h-s** Is 14:14
nor **h,** nor depth Rom 8:39

HEIR *person who inherits*
in my house is my **h** Gen 15:3
has he no **h-s** Jer 49:1
h-s also, **h-s** of God Rom 8:17
an **h** through God Gal 4:7
h-s of the kingdom James 2:5

HELIOPOLIS
ancient Egyptian city Jer 43:13 *also* **ON**

HELL *place of dead*
go into the fiery **h** Matt 5:22
soul and body in **h** Matt 10:28
to be cast into **h** Mark 9:47
set on fire by **h** James 3:6
cast them into **h** 2 Pet 2:4
see also **HADES** *and* **SHEOL**

HELMET *headpiece*
bronze **h** on his 1 Sam 17:5
h of salvation Is 59:17
take the **h** of Eph 6:17

HELP (n) *assistance, relief*
h is not within me Job 6:13
He is our **h** and our Ps 33:20
present **h** in trouble Ps 46:1
I cried for **h** Jon 2:2
gifts of . . . **h-s** 1 Cor 12:28

HELP (v) *aid, assist*
h-ing the Hebrew Ex 1:16
the LORD **h-ed** David 2 Sam 8:6
I will **h** you Is 41:13
Lord, **h** me Matt 15:25
h my unbelief Mark 9:24
must **h** the weak Acts 20:35
Spirit also **h-s** our Rom 8:26
earth **h-ed** the Rev 12:16

HELPER *one who assists*
h of the orphan Ps 10:14
be Thou my **h** Ps 30:10
Behold, God is my **h** Ps 54:4
give you another **H** John 14:16
H, the Holy Spirit John 14:26

HELPLESS *weak*
the **h** has hope Job 5:16
who considers the **h** Ps 41:1
while we were still **h** Rom 5:6

HEMORRHAGE *bleeding*
suffering from a **h** Matt 9:20
a **h** for twelve years Mark 5:25
her **h** stopped Luke 8:44

HERB *dried plant*
bread and bitter **h-s** Ex 12:8
fade like the green **h** Ps 37:2
h-s of . . . mountains Prov 27:25
sweet-scented **h-s** Song 5:13

HERD *cattle, flock*
first-born of your **h** Deut 12:6
h, or flock taste a Jon 3:7
h of many swine Matt 8:30

HERITAGE *what is inherited*
the **h** decreed to him Job 20:29
my **h** is beautiful Ps 16:6
their land as a **h** Ps 136:21
inherit the desolate **h-s** Is 49:8
you who pillage My **h** Jer 50:11

HERMES
1 *Greek god* Acts 14:12
2 *Roman Christian* Rom 16:14

HERMON
mountain region in
N Palestine Josh 11:17; Ps 42:6;133:3
N boundary of Promised Land Deut 3:8

HEROD
1 **Herod the Great**
king of Judea Matt 2:1
ruled during Jesus' birth Matt 2:1ff
2 **Herod Archelaus**
son of Herod the Great Matt 2:22
3 **Herod Antipas**
son of Herod the Great Matt 14:1
tetrarch of Galilee Luke 3:1
ruled at time of Jesus'
ministry Luke 13:31;23:7,8,11
executed John the Baptist Matt 14:10; Mark 6:27
4 **Herod Philip I**
brother of Herod Antipas
son of Herod the Great Mark 6:17
5 **Herod Philip II**
son of Herod the Great Luke 3:1
6 **Herod Agrippa I**
grandson of Herod the Great Acts 12:1
ruler of Judea and Samaria
persecuted the early church Acts 12:2-23
7 **Herod Agrippa II**
son of Agrippa I Acts 25:13
tetrarch of N Palestine

heard Paul's testimony Acts 25:23ff;26:1ff

HERODIANS

influential Jews favoring Herod Matt 22:16; Mark 3:6

HERODIAS

wife of Herod Antipas Matt 14:3; Mark 6:17
requested head of John the Baptist Matt 14:8; Mark 6:24

HETH

1 *son of Canaan* Gen 10:15
2 *Hebrew eponym for Hittites* Gen 23:10

HEZEKIAH

king of Judah 2 Kin 18:1
reformer 2 Kin 18:4
warrior 2 Kin 18:7,8
builder 2 Kin 20:20

HIDE *conceal, cover*

man and his wife **hid** Gen 3:8
I **h** from Abraham Gen 18:17
Moses **hid** his face Ex 3:6
h-ing my iniquity Job 31:33
H me in the shadow Ps 17:8
Do not **h** Thy face Ps 27:9
sees evil *and* **h-s** Prov 27:12
hid your talent Matt 25:25
nothing is **h-den** Mark 4:22
Jesus **hid** Himself John 8:59
h us from . . . Him Rev 6:16

HIDING PLACE

Clouds are a **h** Job 22:14
He lurks in a **h** Ps 10:9
Thou art my **h** Ps 32:7
uncovered his **h-s** Jer 49:10

HIGH PLACE

worship place of God or idols Num 22:41; 1 Sam 9:12-14

HIGH PRIEST

first in hierarchy Ex 27:21
under Aaron Ex 28:1,2
enters Holy of Holies Ex 28:29,30; Heb 9:7
head of Sanhedrin Matt 26:57; Acts 5:21
Jesus as High Priest Heb 3:1;5:5-9

HIGHWAY *road*

h from Egypt to Is 19:23
the **H** of Holiness Is 35:8
a **h** for our God Is 40:3
Go out into the **h-s** Luke 14:23

HILKIAH

1 *father of Eliakim* 2 Kin 18:18
2 *high priest* 2 Kin 22:4-14
3 *Merarite Levite* 1 Chr 6:45
4 *son of Hosah* 1 Chr 26:11
5 *was with Ezra* Neh 8:4
6 *returned from exile* Neh 12:7

HILL *mountain*

the **h** of God 1 Sam 10:5
dwell on Thy holy **h** Ps 15:1
cattle . . . thousand **h-s** Ps 50:10
h-s, Fall on us Hos 10:8
city set on a **h** Matt 5:14
h . . . brought low Luke 3:5
h-s, Cover us Luke 23:30

HINDER *delay, impede, restrain*

h meditation before Job 15:4
do not **h** them Luke 18:16
h-ed you from obeying Gal 5:7
prayers . . . not be **h-ed** 1 Pet 3:7

HINNOM

1 *valley SW of Jerusalem* Josh 15:8; Neh 11:30
2 *person for whom valley named* 2 Kin 23:10; Jer 7:31

HIRAM / HURAM

1 *king of Tyre* 1 Kin 5:1ff; 2 Chr 2:3,11
2 *skilled craftsman* 1 Kin 7:14; 2 Chr 4:11

HIRE (n) *wages*

it came for its **h** Ex 22:15
the **h** of a harlot Deut 23:18

HIRE (v) *engage for labor*

h . . . for bread 1 Sam 2:5
h-d the Arameans 2 Sam 10:6
to **h** . . . chariots 1 Chr 19:6
he who **h-s** a fool Prov 26:10
to **h** laborers for Matt 20:1

HIRED (adj) *employed*

as a **h** man, as if Lev 25:40
oppress a **h** servant Deut 24:14
as one of your **h** Luke 15:19

HIRELING *employee*

h . . . not a shepherd John 10:12
because he is a **h** John 10:13

HITTITES

1 *people in Palestine in patriarchal age* Gen 15:20;49:29
2 *inhabitants of Aram during Israelite monarchy* 2 Kin 7:6; 2 Chr 8:7

HIVITES

people dispossessed by the Israelites Ex 23:28; 2 Sam 24:7

HOLD *grasp, retain*

Moses **held** his hand Ex 17:11
h fast to Him Deut 11:22
heart **h** fast my words Prov 4:4
Take **h** of instruction Prov 4:13
h fast My covenant Is 56:4
h fast the word 1 Cor 15:2
h-ing to the mystery 1 Tim 3:9
h of the eternal 1 Tim 6:12
He **held** seven stars Rev 1:16

HOLIDAY *period of leisure*

a feast and a **h** Esth 8:17
a **h** for rejoicing Esth 9:19
mourning into a **h** Esth 9:22

HOLINESS *sacredness*

majestic in **h** Ex 15:11
H befits Thy house Ps 93:5
the Highway of **H** Is 35:8
unblamable in **h** 1 Thess 3:13
we may share His **h** Heb 12:10

HOLY *sacred, sanctified*

standing is **h** ground Ex 3:5
sabbath . . . keep it **h** Ex 20:8
you are a **h** people Deut 7:6
ten thousand **h** ones Deut 33:2
h like the LORD 1 Sam 2:2
His **h** dwelling 2 Chr 30:27
Jerusalem, the **h** city Neh 11:1
Zion, My **h** mountain Ps 2:6
to His **h** land Ps 78:54
bless His **h** name Ps 145:21
H, H, H, is the LORD Is 6:3
the **H** One of Israel Is 30:15
righteous and **h** man Mark 6:20
the **H** One of God Luke 4:34
in the **h** Scriptures Rom 1:2
with a **h** kiss Rom 16:16
lifting up **h** hands 1 Tim 2:8
with a **h** calling 2 Tim 1:9
I saw the **h** city Rev 21:2

HOLY OF HOLIES

most holy place in the Tabernacle / Temple Ex 26:33,34; 2 Chr 3:8

HOLY SPIRIT

Third Person of the Godhead Matt 28:19; 2 Cor 13:14
Helper John 14:16,26
Giver of gifts Rom 12:6-8; 1 Cor 12:8-11
fruit of the Spirit Gal 5:22

HOMAGE *act of reverence*

my people shall do **h** Gen 41:40
did **h** to the LORD 1 Chr 29:20
and paid **h** to Haman Esth 3:2
did **h** to Daniel Dan 2:46

HOME *place of dwelling*

God makes a **h** Ps 68:6
man is not at **h** Prov 7:19
to his eternal **h** Eccl 12:5
Go **h** to your people Mark 5:19
let him eat at **h** 1 Cor 11:34
at **h** with the Lord 2 Cor 5:8

HOMER *measure of capacity*

a **h** of barley Lev 27:16
a **h** of seed Is 5:10
from a **h** of wheat Ezek 45:13

HOMOSEXUALS

effeminate, nor **h** 1 Cor 6:9
immoral men and **h** 1 Tim 1:10

HONEST *respectable, truthful*

we are **h** men Gen 42:11
painful are **h** words Job 6:25
an **h** and good heart Luke 8:15

HONEY *syrup*

with milk and **h** Ex 3:8
is sweeter than **h** Judg 14:18
sweet as **h** in my Ezek 3:3
locusts and wild **h** Matt 3:4

HONOR (n) *glory, great respect*

both riches and **h** 1 Kin 3:13
stripped my **h** from Job 19:9
is not without **h** Matt 13:57
glory and **h** and Rom 2:10
marriage *be held* in **h** Heb 13:4
blessing and **h** and Rev 5:13

HONOR (v) *show respect*

H your father Ex 20:12
h the aged Lev 19:32
who **h** Me I will **h** 1 Sam 2:30
A son **h-s** *his* father Mal 1:6
may be **h-ed** by men Matt 6:2
h-s Me with . . . lips Matt 15:8
does not **h** the Son John 5:23
fear God, **h** the king 1 Pet 2:17

HONORABLE *respectable*

the elder and **h** man Is 9:15
one vessel for **h** use Rom 9:21
whatever is **h** Phil 4:8

HOOK *fastener*

into pruning **h-s** Is 2:4
My **h** in your nose Is 37:29
h-s into your jaws Ezek 38:4

HOPE (n) *expectation*

Where now is my **h** Job 17:15
My **h** is in Thee Ps 39:7
Thou art my **h** Ps 71:5
while there is **h** Prov 19:18
the **h** of Israel Jer 17:13
our **h** has perished Ezek 37:11
h does not disappoint Rom 5:5
rejoicing in **h** Rom 12:12
may the God of **h** Rom 15:13
now abide faith, **h** 1 Cor 13:13
h of righteousness Gal 5:5
the **h** of His calling Eph 1:18
the **h** of glory Col 1:27
the **h** of salvation 1 Thess 5:8
h of eternal life Titus 3:7
to a living **h** 1 Pet 1:3

HOPE (v) *expect with confidence*

I will **h** in Him Job 13:15
For I **h** in Thee Ps 38:15
We **h** for justice Is 59:11
are **h-ing** for light Jer 13:16
Gentiles will **h** Matt 12:21
h-s all things 1 Cor 13:7
first to **h** in Christ Eph 1:12
I **h** in the Lord Jesus Phil 2:19
of *things* **h-d** for Heb 11:1

HOREB

another name for Mount Sinai Ex 3:1; Deut 4:10; Ps 106:19

HORITES
inhabitants of Mount Seir in Edom Gen 14:6;36:29

HORN
caught . . . by his **h-s** Gen 22:13
h-s of the altar Ex 29:12
you shall sound a **h** Lev 25:9
with the ram's **h** Josh 6:5
h of my salvation 2 Sam 22:3
the **h**, flute, lyre Dan 3:5
it had ten **h-s** Dan 7:7

HORROR *terror*
h overwhelms me Is 21:4
object of **h** Jer 49:13
clothed with **h** Ezek 7:27
cup of **h** Ezek 23:33

HORSE *animal*
bites the **h-'s** heels Gen 49:17
h-s and chariots of 2 Kin 6:17
A **h** is a false hope Ps 33:17
whip is for the **h** Prov 26:3
slaves *riding* on **h-s** Eccl 10:7
behold, a black **h** Rev 6:5

HORSEMEN *cavalry, horse rider*
Pharaoh, his **h** and Ex 14:9
chariots and **h** 1 Kin 10:26
h riding on Ezek 23:12
H charging, Swords Nah 3:3
armies of the **h** Rev 9:16

HOSANNA *acclamation of praise*
H to the Son of Matt 21:9
H in the highest Mark 11:10
H! Blessed is He John 12:13

HOSHEA
1 *name of Joshua* Num 13:8,16
2 *king of Israel* 2 Kin 15:30;17:6
3 *Ephraim's officer* 1 Chr 27:20
4 *signer of covenant* Neh 10:23

HOSPITABLE *friendly*
h, able to teach 1 Tim 3:2
h, loving what is Titus 1:8
h to one another 1 Pet 4:9

HOSPITALITY *openness to guests*
practicing **h** Rom 12:13
show **h** to strangers Heb 13:2

HOST *army, multitude*
all the **h** of heaven Deut 4:19
captain . . . LORD's **h** Josh 5:15
LORD of **h-s**, He is Ps 24:10
of the heavenly **h** Luke 2:13

HOSTILE *antagonistic*
h to . . . Jesus Acts 26:9
set on the flesh is **h** Rom 8:7
h to all men 1 Thess 2:15

HOUR *time period*
healed that *very* **h** Matt 8:13
the **h** is at hand Matt 26:45
ninth **h** Jesus cried Mark 15:34
save Me from this **h** John 12:27
the **h** has come John 17:1
the **h** of testing Rev 3:10

HOUSE *home* or *temple*
born in my **h** is my Gen 15:3
the **h** of slavery Ex 20:2
consecrates his **h** Lev 27:14
as for me and my **h** Josh 24:15
Set your **h** in order 2 Kin 20:1
h of God forsaken Neh 13:11
h like the spider's Job 27:18
Holiness befits Thy **h** Ps 93:5
LORD builds the **h** Ps 127:1
in My **h** of prayer Is 56:7
O **h** of Israel Jer 18:6
his **h** upon the rock Matt 7:24
devour widow's **h-s** Mark 12:40
In My Father's **h** John 14:2
h for a holy 1 Pet 2:5

HOUSEHOLD *family, home*
stole the **h** idols Gen 31:19
each one with his **h** Ex 1:1
like a head of a **h** Matt 13:52
are of God's **h** Eph 2:19
manages his own **h** 1 Tim 3:4
in the **h** of God 1 Tim 3:15

HOUSETOP *roof*
As grass on the **h-s** 2 Kin 19:26
lonely bird on a **h** Ps 102:7
upon the **h-s** Matt 10:27
Peter went . . . the **h** Acts 10:9

HULDAH
a Hebrew prophetess 2 Kin 22:14; 2 Chr 34:22

HUMAN *mankind, person*
the life of any **h** Lev 24:17
guilt of **h** blood Prov 28:17
tablets of **h** hearts 2 Cor 3:3

HUMBLE (adj) *gentle, modest*
Moses was very **h** Num 12:3
h will inherit Ps 37:11
with the **h** is wisdom Prov 11:2
H, and mounted on Zech 9:9
gentle and **h** in Matt 11:29
grace to the **h** James 4:6

HUMBLE (v) *make low*
refuse to **h** yourself Ex 10:3
He might **h** you Deut 8:2
h . . . and pray 2 Chr 7:14
h-s . . . as this child Matt 18:4
H yourselves 1 Pet 5:6

HUMILIATE *embarrass*
h-d who seek my hurt Ps 71:24
Neither feel **h-d** Is 54:4
His opponents . . . **h-d** Luke 13:17

HUMILIATION *embarrassment*
h has overwhelmed me Ps 44:15
go away together in **h** Is 45:16
let our **h** cover us Jer 3:25
In **h** His judgment Acts 8:33

HUMILITY *self-abasement*
before honor . . . **h** Prov 15:33
with **h** of mind Phil 2:3
clothe . . . with **h** 1 Pet 5:5

HUNGER (n) *craving, starvation*
in **h**, in thirst Deut 28:48
man will suffer **h** Prov 19:15
h is not satisfied Is 29:8
sleeplessness, in **h** 2 Cor 6:5

HUNGER (v) *crave, need food*
the righteous to **h** Prov 10:3
are those who **h** Matt 5:6
to Me shall not **h** John 6:35
They shall **h** no more Rev 7:16

HUNGRY *empty, needing food*
people are **h** and 2 Sam 17:29
If your enemy is **h** Prov 25:21
when a **h** man dreams Is 29:8
He then became **h** Matt 4:2
disciples became **h** Matt 12:1
For I was **h** Matt 25:35
if your enemy is **h** Rom 12:20

HUNT *pursue, seek*
to **h** for game Gen 27:5
h-s a partridge 1 Sam 26:20
evil **h** the violent Ps 140:11
H-ed me down like Lam 3:52
companions **h-ed** for Mark 1:36

HUNTER *seeker of game*
Nimrod a mighty **h** Gen 10:9
became a skillful **h** Gen 25:27

HURAM
a Benjamite 1 Chr 8:5
see also **HIRAM / HURAM**

HURT (n) *damage, harm, wound*
Who delight in my **h** Ps 70:2
hoarded . . . to his **h** Eccl 5:13
your brother is **h** Rom 14:15

HURT (v) *cause pain, wound*
not allow him to **h** Gen 31:7
may be **h** by them Eccl 10:9
will not **h** or destroy Is 11:9
their power to **h** men Rev 9:10

HUSBAND *family head, spouse*
desire . . . your **h** Gen 3:16
crown of her **h** Prov 12:4
divorces her **h** and Mark 10:12
have had five **h-s** John 4:18
if her **h** dies Rom 7:2
have her own **h** 1 Cor 7:2
unbelieving **h** is 1 Cor 7:14
h is the head of Eph 5:23
H-s, love your wives Eph 5:25
h-s of . . . one wife 1 Tim 3:12

HYMN *song of praise*
h-s of thanksgiving Neh 12:46
after singing a **h** Matt 26:30
singing **h-s** of praise Acts 16:25
psalms and **h-s** and Eph 5:19

HYPOCRISY *pretense*
full of **h** and Matt 23:28
love be without **h** Rom 12:9
without **h** James 3:17

HYPOCRITE *a pretender*
as the **h-s** do Matt 6:2
and Pharisees, **h-s** Matt 23:13
You **h**, first take Luke 6:42

HYSSOP *fragrant plant*
bunch of **h** and dip it Ex 12:22
scarlet string and **h** Lev 14:4
Purify me with **h** Ps 51:7
upon *a branch of* **h** John 19:29

I

I AM
related to name of God in Hebrew
I WHO **I** Ex 3:14
I has sent me Ex 3:14
I the LORD Ex 6:2
I the LORD your God Lev 19:3
I the first Is 44:6
I the Son of God Matt 27:43
Jesus said, **I** Mark 14:62
believe that **I** *He* John 8:24
will know that **I** *He* John 8:28
before Abraham . . . **I** John 8:58
believe that **I** *He* John 13:19
I the Alpha and Rev 1:8
I the first and Rev 1:17

ICHABOD
1 *son of Phinehas* 1 Sam 4:19,20
grandson of Eli 1 Sam 14:3
2 *name commemorates departed glory from Israel* 1 Sam 4:21,22

IDOL *false deity, image*
not make . . . an **i** Ex 20:4
Do not turn to **i-s** Lev 19:4
who makes an **i** or Deut 27:15
who blesses an **i** Is 66:3
abstain from . . . **i-s** Acts 15:20
guard . . . from **i-s** 1 John 5:21

IDOLATRY *idol worship*
flee from **i** 1 Cor 10:14
i, sorcery, enmities Gal 5:20
and abominable **i-ies** 1 Pet 4:3

IGNORANCE *lack of knowledge*
you worship in **i** Acts 17:23
i that is in them Eph 4:18

silence the **i** of — 1 Pet 2:15

IGNORANT *without knowledge*
I was senseless and **i** — Ps 73:22
not **i** of his schemes — 2 Cor 2:11
and **i** speculations — 2 Tim 2:23

ILL *unhealthy, sick*
woman who is **i** — Lev 15:33
became mortally **i** — Is 38:1
lunatic, and is . . . **i** — Matt 17:15
healed many . . . **i** — Mark 1:34

ILLEGITIMATE *bastard*
No one of **i** birth — Deut 23:2
borne **i** children — Hos 5:7
you are **i** children — Heb 12:8

ILLUMINE *light up*
God **i-s** my darkness — Ps 18:28
fire to **i** by night — Ps 105:39
glory of God has **i-d** — Rev 21:23
God shall **i** them — Rev 22:5

IMAGE *copy, likeness*
make man in Our **i** — Gen 1:26
i of God He made — Gen 9:6
burn their graven **i-s** — Deut 7:5
worshiped a molten **i** — Ps 106:19
made an **i** of gold — Dan 3:1
i and glory of God — 1 Cor 11:7
i of the invisible — Col 1:15
the **i** of the beast — Rev 13:15

IMITATORS *followers*
be **i** of me — 1 Cor 4:16
be **i** of God — Eph 5:1
i of the churches — 1 Thess 2:14

IMMANUEL
1 *son born to a virgin* — Is 7:14
a sign to King Ahaz — Is 8:8
2 *title of Jesus* — Matt 1:23

IMMORAL *lewd, unchaste*
with **i** people — 1 Cor 5:9
the **i** man sins — 1 Cor 6:18
i men . . . liars — 1 Tim 1:10
i or godless person — Heb 12:16
and **i** persons — Rev 21:8

IMMORALITY *immoral acts*
no **i** in your midst — Lev 20:14
except for **i** — Matt 19:9
Flee **i** — 1 Cor 6:18
abstain from . . . **i** — 1 Thess 4:3
the wine of her **i** — Rev 17:2

IMMORTALITY *everlasting life*
must put on **i** — 1 Cor 15:53
alone possess **i** — 1 Tim 6:16
life and **i** to light — 2 Tim 1:10

IMPATIENT *restless*
the people became **i** — Num 21:4
should I not be **i** — Job 21:4
my soul was **i** with — Zech 11:8

IMPERISHABLE *indestructible*
wreath, but we an **i** — 1 Cor 9:25
will be raised **i** — 1 Cor 15:52
inheritance . . . *is* **i** — 1 Pet 1:4

IMPOSE *force upon*
i-d hard labor on us — Deut 26:6
whatever you **i** on — 2 Kin 18:14
you **i** heavy rent — Amos 5:11
i-d until a time of — Heb 9:10

IMPRISON *jail, restrict*
i-ed him at Riblah — 2 Kin 23:33
i his princes at will — Ps 105:22
not **i** their survivors — Obad 14
I used to **i** and beat — Acts 22:19

IMPRISONMENT *confinement*
in **i-s**, in tumults — 2 Cor 6:5
Remember my **i** — Col 4:18
even to **i** as a — 2 Tim 2:9

IMPURE *unclean*
her **i** discharge — Lev 15:25
eating . . . with **i** hands — Mark 7:2
no immoral or **i** person — Eph 5:5

IMPURITY *uncleanness*
menstrual **i** for seven — Lev 15:19
i-ies of the sons of — Lev 16:19
the **i** of the nations — Ezra 6:21
as slaves to **i** — Rom 6:19
of **i** with greediness — Eph 4:19

INCENSE *fragrant substance*
burn frangrant **i** on — Ex 30:7
gold pans, full of **i** — Num 7:86
My altar, to burn **i** — 1 Sam 2:28
i on the high places — 2 Kin 14:4
i before the LORD — 1 Chr 23:13
golden altar of **i** — Heb 9:4
the smoke of the **i** — Rev 8:4

INCEST *ilicit sexual relations*
they . . . committed **i** — Lev 20:12

INCITE *stir up*
i-d David against — 2 Sam 24:1
Jezebel . . . **i-d** him — 1 Kin 21:25
I will **i** Egyptians — Is 19:2
who **i-s** the people — Luke 23:14

INCOME *wages*
i of the wicked — Prov 10:16
i with injustice — Prov 16:8
abundance *with its* **i** — Eccl 5:10

INCORRUPTIBLE *not impure*
glory of the **i** God — Rom 1:23
Christ with *a love* **i** — Eph 6:24

INCREASE (n) *multiplication*
the **i** of your herd — Deut 7:13
the **i** of your house — 1 Sam 2:33
the LORD give you **i** — Ps 115:14
i of *His* government — Is 9:7

INCREASE (v) *multiply*
If riches **i**, do not — Ps 62:10
the righteous **i** — Prov 28:28
i-ing in wisdom — Luke 2:52
i-ng in . . . knowledge — Col 1:10
Lord cause . . . to **i** — 1 Thess 3:12

INDIGNANT *be angry*
i toward His enemies — Is 66:14
the ten became **i** — Matt 20:24
Jesus . . . was **i** — Mark 10:14
i because Jesus had — Luke 13:14

INDIGNATION *anger*
God who has **i** — Ps 7:11
Pour out Thine **i** — Ps 69:24
lips are filled with **i** — Is 30:27
didst fill me with **i** — Jer 15:17
stand before His **i** — Nah 1:6

INFANT *child*
carries a nursing **i** — Num 11:12
an **i** *who lives* — Is 65:20
tongue of the **i** — Lam 4:4
the mouth of **i-s** — Matt 21:16

INFERIOR *lower in status*
I am not **i** to you — Job 12:3
i against the honorable — Is 3:5
i to . . . apostles — 2 Cor 12:11

INFINITE *unlimited*
His understanding is **i** — Ps 147:5

INFLICT *strike, impose*
frogs . . . He had **i-ed** — Ex 8:12
i all these curses — Deut 30:7
i-s pain, and gives — Job 5:18
i-ed many blows — Acts 16:23

INHABIT *dwell*
no one would **i** — Job 15:28
She shall be **i-ed** — Is 44:26

build houses and **i** — Is 65:21
those **i-ing** the desert — Jer 9:26
who **i** the coastlands — Ezek 39:6
but not **i** *them* — Zeph 1:13

INHABITANT *resident*
i-s of the cities — Gen 19:25
cities . . . without **i** — Is 6:11
ruins Without **i** — Jer 4:7
i-s of Jerusalem — Zech 12:10

INHERIT *receive a legacy*
shall **i** *it* forever — Ex 32:13
humble will **i** the land — Ps 37:11
The naive **i** folly — Prov 14:18
gentle . . . **i** the earth — Matt 5:5
do to **i** the earth — Luke 10:25
not **i** the kingdom — 1 Cor 6:9
might **i** a blessing — 1 Pet 3:9

INHERITANCE *bequest, legacy*
the LORD is his **i** — Deut 10:9
the nations as Thine **i** — Ps 2:8
will He forsake His **i** — Ps 94:14
man leaves an **i** — Prov 13:22
Thine **i** a reproach — Joel 2:17
A man and his **i** — Mic 2:2
the **i** will be ours — Mark 12:7
we . . . obtained an **i** — Eph 1:11
the **i** of the saints — Col 1:12

INIQUITY *injustice, wickedness*
the **i** of the fathers — Deut 5:9
O LORD, Pardon my **i** — Ps 25:11
my **i** I did not hide — Ps 32:5
blot out all my **i-ies** — Ps 51:9
sows **i** will reap — Prov 22:8
the workers of **i** — Is 31:2
die for his own **i** — Jer 31:30
the bondage of **i** — Acts 8:23
the *very* world of **i** — James 3:6

INJURE *harm, wrong*
who seek to **i** me — Ps 38:12
i-d your neighbors — Ezek 22:12
nothing shall **i** you — Luke 10:19
do you **i** one another — Acts 7:26

INJURY *wound*
there is no *further* **i** — Ex 21:22
because of my **i** — Jer 10:19
no **i** . . . was found — Dan 6:23

INJUSTICE *inequity, unfairness*
do no **i** in judgment — Lev 19:15
there **i** on my tongue — Job 6:30
They devise **i-s** — Ps 64:6
is no **i** with God — Rom 9:14

INK *writing liquid*
I wrote them with **i** — Jer 36:18
with pen and **i** — 3 John 13

INN *lodge for travelers*
no room . . . in the **i** — Luke 2:7
brought him to . . . **i** — Luke 10:34

INNKEEPER *traveler's host*
gave them to the **i** — Luke 10:35

INNOCENCE *blamelessness*
wash my hands in **i** — Ps 26:6
be incapable of **i** — Hos 8:5

INNOCENT *blameless*
do not kill the **i** — Ex 23:7
the blood of the **i** — Deut 19:13
i before the LORD — 2 Sam 3:28
that shed **i** blood — Prov 6:17
and **i** as doves — Matt 10:16
betraying **i** blood — Matt 27:4
i of this Man's — Matt 27:24
holy, **i**, undefiled — Heb 7:26

INQUIRE *ask, seek*
to **i** of the LORD — Gen 25:22
I of God, please — Judg 18:5
David **i-d** of . . . LORD — 1 Sam 23:2
you come to **i** of Me — Ezek 20:3

i . . . where the Christ — Matt 2:4

INSANE *mad*
a demon and is i — John 10:20
I speak as if i — 2 Cor 11:23

INSCRIBE *carve, write*
were **i-d** in a book — Job 19:23
i it on a scroll — Is 30:8
and i a city on it — Ezek 4:1
i *it* on tablets — Hab 2:2

INSCRIPTION *writing*
could not read the i — Dan 5:8
I will engrave an i — Zech 3:9
Pilate wrote an i — John 19:19
i, To An Unknown — Acts 17:23

INSECTS
swarms of i on you — Ex 8:21
all other winged i — Lev 11:23

INSIGHT *discernment*
a counselor with i — 1 Chr 26:14
according to his i — Prov 12:8
i with understanding — Dan 9:22
not gained any i — Mark 6:52
In all wisdom and i — Eph 1:8

INSOLENT *arrogant*
acts with i pride — Prov 21:24
haters of God, i — Rom 1:30

INSPIRED *stimulated, breathed out*
the love we i in you — 2 Cor 8:7
All Scripture is i — 2 Tim 3:16

INSTRUCTION *teaching*
will walk in My i — Ex 16:4
Heed i and be wise — Prov 8:33
i-s to His twelve — Matt 11:1
written for our i — Rom 15:4
i of the Lord — Eph 6:4
goal of our i is love — 1 Tim 1:5
i about washings — Heb 6:2

INSULT (n) *affront, indignity*
i-s of the nations — Ezek 34:29
casting the same i — Matt 27:44
and cast **i-s** at you — Luke 6:22
evil, or i for i — 1 Pet 3:9

INSULT (v) *treat with scorn*
and do not i her — Ruth 2:15
to i the LORD — 2 Chr 32:17
times you have **i-ed** — Job 19:3
i-ed the Spirit of — Heb 10:29

INTEGRITY *honesty*
In the i of my heart — Gen 20:5
dealt in truth and i — Judg 9:19
He who walks with i — Ps 15:2
have walked in my i — Ps 26:1
The i of the upright — Prov 11:3

INTELLIGENCE *mental ability*
He deprives of i — Job 12:24
gave them . . . i — Dan 1:17
Paulus, a man of i — Acts 13:7

INTELLIGENT *bright, smart*
was i and beautiful — 1 Sam 25:3
mind of the i seeks — Prov 15:14
from *the* wise and i — Matt 11:25

INTENTION *aim, goal*
the **i-s** of the heart — 1 Chr 29:18
i of your heart — Acts 8:22
kind i of His will — Eph 1:5

INTERCEDE *plead, mediate*
i-d for the people — Num 21:7
who can i for him — 1 Sam 2:25
And **i-d** for the — Is 53:12
do not i with Me — Jer 7:16
Spirit Himself **i-s** — Rom 8:26

INTERCOURSE *copulation*
not have i with — Lev 18:20
not have i . . . animal — Lev 18:23
husband has had i — Num 5:20

INTEREST *concern* or *usury*
not charge him i — Ex 22:25
not take usurious i — Lev 25:36
i to a foreigner — Deut 23:20
his money at i — Ps 15:5
mind on God's **i-s** — Matt 16:23
money . . . with i — Matt 25:27
he has a morbid i — 1 Tim 6:4

INTERMARRY
And i with us — Gen 34:9
shall not i with — Deut 7:3
i with the peoples — Ezra 9:14

INTERPRETATION *explanation*
i-s belong to God — Gen 40:8
make its i known — Dan 5:16
the i of tongues — 1 Cor 12:10
of one's own i — 2 Pet 1:20

INTIMATE *close*
my i friends have — Job 19:14
i with the upright — Prov 3:32
separates i friends — Prov 16:28

INVADE *attack*
king of Assyria **i-d** — 2 Kin 17:5
nation had **i-d** my land — Joel 1:6
Assyrian **i-s** our land — Mic 5:5

INVALIDATE *nullify*
i-d the word of God — Matt 15:6
i-ing the word of — Mark 7:13
does not i a covenant — Gal 3:17

INVESTIGATE *examine*
the judges shall i — Deut 19:18
the plot was **i-d** — Esth 2:23
i, and to seek wisdom — Eccl 7:25
having **i-d** everything — Luke 1:3

INVISIBLE *unseen*
His i attributes — Rom 1:20
image of the i God — Col 1:15
visible and i — Col 1:16
eternal, immortal, i — 1 Tim 1:17

INVITE *request*
i-d us to impoverish — Judg 14:15
you shall i Jesse — 1 Sam 16:3
i-d all the king's — 2 Sam 13:23
I am **i-d** by her — Esth 5:12
did not i Me in — Matt 25:43
i *the* poor — Luke 14:13

IRON *metal*
was an i bedstead — Deut 3:11
whose stones are i — Deut 8:9
had i chariots — Judg 1:19
made the i float — 2 King 6:6
break them . . . rod of i — Ps 2:9
from the i furnace — Jer 11:4
as strong as i — Dan 2:40
rule . . . rod of i — Rev 19:15

ISAAC
birth, son of Abraham — Gen 21:3
offered for sacrifice — Gen 22:2
took Rebekah as wife — Gen 24
father of twins — Gen 25:26
blessed Jacob — Gen 27:1-40

ISAIAH
prophet of Judah — Is 1:1
son of Amoz — 2 Kin 19:2
called — Is 6:8ff
under four kings — Is 1:1

ISCARIOT
geographical identity of Judas — Mark 3:19; John 12:4; 13:26

ISHMAEL
1 *son of Abraham* — Gen 16:11;17:18;25:17
2 *son of Nethaniah* — 2 Kin 25:23
3 *line of Jonathan* — 1 Chr 8:38;9:44
4 *Zebadiah's father* — 2 Chr 19:11
5 *son of Jehohanan* — 2 Chr 23:1
6 *son of Pashhur* — Ezra 10:22

ISRAEL
1 *Jacob* — Gen 32:28-32;35:10;37:3
2 *line of Jacob* — Gen 34:7
tribal nation — Ex 1:7;4:22; Num 10:29
3 *united kingdom* — 1 Sam 15:35; 1 Kin 4:1
4 *northern kingdom* — 1 Kin 14:19;15:9; 2 Kin 10:29
5 *under Roman rule* — Luke 2:32; John 1:49; Rom 9:6

ISSACHAR
1 *son of Jacob* — Gen 30:18;49:14
2 *tribe* — Num 1:29; Josh 21:28; Rev 7:7
3 *Levite* — 1 Chr 26:5

ISSUE (n) *outflow, out go, matter*
first i of the womb — Num 3:12
offspring and i — Is 22:24
like the i of horses — Ezek 23:20
concerning this i — Acts 15:2

ISSUE (v) *go forth, put forth*
Moses **i-d** a command — Ex 36:6
shall i from you — 2 Kin 20:18
decree was **i-d** in — Esth 3:15
i-d a proclamation — Dan 5:29

ITURAEA
region N of Palestine tetrarchy of Philip — Luke 3:1

IVORY *elephant tusk*
a great throne of i — 1 Kin 10:18
silver, i and apes — 2 Chr 9:21
Out of i palaces — Ps 45:8
every article of i — Rev 18:12

J

JABAL
son of Lamech — Gen 4:20
father of herders

JABBOK
tributary of Jordan — Gen 32:22; Num 21:24; Josh 12:2; Judg 11:13,22

JACKALS *wild dogs*
j in their . . . palaces — Is 13:22
ruins, A haunt of j — Jer 9:11
a lament like the j — Mic 1:8

JACOB
1 *son of Isaac* — Gen 25:26
brother of Esau — Gen 25:27
obtained birthright — Gen 25:33
fled to Aram — Gen 28:5,6
marriage — Gen 29:1ff
wrestled angel — Gen 32:24ff
name changed — Gen 35:9,10
went down to Egypt — Gen 46:4ff
death and burial — Gen 49:28ff
2 *father of Joseph* — Matt 1:15,16

JAIL *place of confinement*
put him into the j — Gen 39:20
in j in the house — Jer 37:15
put them in . . . j — Acts 5:18

JAILER *warden*
sight of the chief j — Gen 39:21
chief j did not — Gen 39:23
the j to guard them — Acts 16:23

JAIRUS
ruler of synagogue — Mark 5:22; Luke 8:41

JAMES
1 *son of Zebedee* — Matt 4:21
brother of John — Matt 10:2
called as apostle — Matt 10:2ff
martyred — Acts 12:2
2 *son of Alphaeus* — Matt 10:3
called as apostle — Matt 10:3ff

3 *brother of Jesus* Matt 13:55; Mark 6:3
church leader Acts 12:17;15:13
4 *Judas' father* Luke 6:16

JASHAR
book quoted in Bible Josh 10:13; 2 Sam 1:18

JASPER *precious stone*
fourth row . . . a **j** Ex 28:20
the onyx, and the **j** Ezek 28:13
was like a **j** stone Rev 4:3
of crystal-clear **j** Rev 21:11

JAVAN
Hebrew word for Greeks Gen 10:2,4;
or Greece 1 Chr 1:5,7; Is 66:19; Ezek 27:13,19

JAVELIN *spear*
Stretch out the **j** Josh 8:18
j *slung* between his 1 Sam 17:6
flashing spear and **j** Job 39:23
seize *their* . . . **j** Jer 50:42

JAWBONE
j of a donkey Judg 15:15
threw the **j** from Judg 15:17

JEALOUS *envious, zealous*
your God, am a **j** God Ex 20:5
whose name is **J**, is Ex 34:14
j with My jealousy Num 25:11
He is a **j** God Josh 24:19
j and avenging God Nah 1:2
j for Jerusalem Zech 1:14
Jews, becoming **j** Acts 17:5
I will make you **j** Rom 10:19
love is kind . . . not **j** 1 Cor 13:4

JEBUS
Jerusalem Judg 19:10,11; 1 Chr 11:4,5

JEBUSITES
clan or tribe Gen 10:16
inhabitants of Jebus Ex 3:8,17; Josh 15:63; 2 Sam 24:16,18; Ezra 9:1; Zech 9:7

JECONIAH
variant of Jehoiachin's name 1 Chr 3:16,17; Esth 2:6

JEHOAHAZ
1 *son of Jehu* 2 Kin 10:35
king of Israel 2 Kin 13:1ff
2 *son of Josiah* 2 Kin 23:30-34
king of Judah 2 Kin 23:30
3 *son of Jehoram* 2 Chr 21:17

JEHOASH
1 *king of Judah* 2 Kin 11:21
son of Ahaziah 2 Kin 12:1-18
2 *king of Israel* 2 Kin 13:10
son of Jehoahaz 2 Kin 13:25;14:13

JEHOIACHIN
son of Jehoiakim 2 Kin 24:6
king of Judah 2 Kin 24:8-15; 2 Chr 36:8,9; Jer 52:31,33

JEHOIAKIM
son of King Josiah 2 Kin 23:34; 2 Chr 36:4
king of Judah 2 Kin 23:36; 2 Chr 36:5; Jer 22:18; Dan 1:2
father of Jehoiachin 2 Kin 24:6

JEHORAM
1 *son of Ahab* 2 Kin 3:1
king of Israel 2 Kin 3:6
2 *priest* 2 Chr 17:8
3 *Jehoshaphat's son* 2 Kin 8:16
king of Judah 2 Kin 8:25,29
see also **JORAM**

JEHOSHAPHAT
1 *son of Ahilud* 2 Sam 8:16
2 *son of Paruah* 1 Kin 4:17
3 *son of Asa* 1 Kin 15:24
king of Judah 1 Kin 22:2-51; 2 Chr 17:1-12
4 *father of Jehu* 2 Kin 9:2,14
5 *wadi E of Jerusalem* Joel 3:2,12

JEHU
1 *prophet, son of Hanani* 1 Kin 16:1,7,12; 2 Chr 19:2
2 *king of Israel* 1 Kin 19:16; 2 Kin 9:14,30; 2 Chr 22:7
3 *man of Judah* 1 Chr 2:38
4 *Simeonite* 1 Chr 4:35
5 *Benjamite* 1 Chr 12:3

JEREMIAH
1 *lived in Libnah* 2 Kin 23:31
2 *man of Manasseh* 1 Chr 5:24
3 *three individuals who joined David* 1 Chr 12:4,10,13
4 *prophet* Jer 1:1
called Jer 1:2-10
put in stocks Jer 20:2,3
life threatened Jer 26
put in prison Jer 32:2;37:13ff
taken to Egypt Jer 43:1-6
5 *son of Habazziniah* Jer 35:3
6 *priest* Neh 10:2
7 *priest from Babylon* Neh 12:1

JERICHO
city in Jordan Valley Josh 3:16
N of Dead Sea Josh 6:1; Luke 18:35

JEROBOAM
1 *Solomon's warrior* 1 Kin 11:28
first king of N Kingdom 1 Kin 12:26,27; 2 Chr 10:13
made gold calves 1 Kin 12:28
2 *son of Joash* 2 Kin 14:27
king of Israel 2 Kin 14:28,29

JERUSALEM
city called Salem Gen 14:18
city called Jebus Judg 1:21;19:10
David's capital 2 Sam 5:5,6
capital of united kingdom 1 Kin 2:36;11:42
site of temple 1 Kin 6:2;8:6,12
destroyed by Babylonians Jer 52:12-14
rebuilt by remnant Neh 2:11-20;12:27
city of Roman period Luke 13:34; Acts 11:2,22
new Jerusalem Rev 3:12;21:2,10

JESHUA
1 *line of Aaron* 1 Chr 24:11
2 *under Kore* 2 Chr 31:15
3 *high priest* Ezra 3:2; Neh 7:7
4 *of Pahath-moab* Ezra 2:6; Neh 7:11
5 *part of remnant* Ezra 2:40; Neh 7:43
6 *aided Ezra* Neh 8:7
7 *village in Judah* Neh 11:26
also **Joshua**

JESSE
father of David 1 Sam 16:1,8; 2 Sam 20:1; 1 Kin 12:16; 1 Chr 2:12,13

JESUS
1 *name of the Lord* Matt 1:21; Luke 1:31
birth in Bethlehem Matt 1:18-25; Luke 2:1-7
youth in Nazareth Matt 2:19ff
baptized Matt 3:13ff; Mark 1:9ff; Luke 3:21; John 1:31ff
tempted Matt 4:1-11; Luke 4:1ff
called disciples Matt 4:18ff; Mark 1:16ff; Luke 5:1ff
transfigured Matt 17:1ff; Mark 9:2ff
triumphal entry to Jerusalem Matt 21:1ff; Luke 19:29ff
crucified Matt 27:31ff; Mark 15:20ff; Luke 23:26ff; John 19:16ff
resurrected Christ Matt 28:1ff; Mark 16:1ff; Luke 24:13ff; John 20:11ff
ascended to the Father Mark 16:19; Acts 1:9ff
2 *Jewish Christian called Justus* Col 4:11

JETHRO
priest of Midian Ex 3:1
Moses' father-in-law Ex 4:18;18:1-12

JEW(S)
originally an inhabitant of Judah, a Judean 2 Kin 16:6
Judean shortened to Jew during exile 2 Kin 25:25
synonym for Hebrew Ezra 4:12,23; Neh 4:1,2; Esth 4:3,7; Jer 34:9
later term for all Israelites Matt 27:11;
in the land Mark 7:3; Luke 23:51;
and in Diaspora John 4:9; Acts 22:3; Rom 3:1; Gal 3:28; Rev 2:9

JEWEL *precious stone*
precious than **j-s** Prov 3:15
better than **j-s** Prov 8:11
adorns . . . her **j-s** Is 61:10
the **J** of *his* kingdom Dan 11:20

JEZEBEL
1 *wife of Ahab* 1 Kin 21:5ff; 2 Kin 9:7ff
2 *woman at Thyatira* Rev 2:20

JEZREEL
1 *valley and plain* Josh 17:16; Judg 6:33; Hos 1:5
2 *fortified town* Josh 19:18; 1 Kin 18:45; 2 Kin 8:29;9:30
3 *descendant of Etam* 1 Chr 4:3
4 *son of Hosea* Hos 1:4

JOAB
1 *son of Zeruiah* 2 Sam 8:16
David's nephew 2 Sam 17:25
David's commander 2 Sam 20:23; 1 Chr 11:6
2 *son of Seraiah* 1 Chr 4:14
3 *father of those returning from captivity* Ezra 2:6;8:9; Neh 7:11

JOASH
1 *father of Gideon* Judg 6:11,31
2 *son of Ahab* 1 Kin 22:26; 2 Chr 18:25
3 *son of Ahaziah* 2 Kin 11:2
king of Judah 2 Chr 24:1-4
4 *son of Jehoahaz* 2 Kin 13:9
king of Israel 2 Kin 13:25
5 *line of Shelah* 1 Chr 4:22
6 *son of Becher* 1 Chr 7:8
7 *a Benjamite* 1 Chr 12:3
8 *official of David* 1 Chr 27:28

JOB *occupation*
workmen . . . **j** to **j** 2 Chr 34:13

JOEL
1 *son of Samuel* 1 Sam 8:2
2 *line of Simeon* 1 Chr 4:35
3 *line of Reuben* 1 Chr 5:4
4 *chief of Gadites* 1 Chr 5:12
5 *ancestor of Samuel* 1 Chr 6:36
6 *son of Izrahiah* 1 Chr 7:3
7 *brother of Nathan* 1 Chr 11:38
8 *Gershonite Levite* 1 Chr 15:7;26:22
9 *son of Pedaiah* 1 Chr 27:20
10 *Kohathite Levite* 2 Chr 29:12
11 *son of Nebo* Ezra 10:43
12 *son of Zichri* Neh 11:9
13 *prophet* Joel 1:1; Acts 2:16

JOHN
1 *father of Peter* John 1:42
2 *the Baptist* Matt 3:1
baptizing Matt 3:13
beheaded Mark 6:25
birth foretold Luke 1:13
son of Zacharias Luke 1:57ff
praised by Jesus Luke 7:28
preached John 1:15
3 *the apostle* Matt 10:2
called by Jesus Matt 4:21
Sons of Thunder Mark 3:17
request refused Mark 10:35ff
assigned the care of Mary John 19:26,27
with Peter Acts 3:1,3
4 *Jewish leader* Acts 4:6
5 *Mark, evangelist* Acts 12:12,25

JOIN *bring together, couple*
do not **j** your hand Ex 23:1
j field to field Is 5:8
j . . . in hypocrisy Dan 11:34
God . . . **j-ed** together Matt 19:6

- **j-ed** him . . . believed — Acts 17:34
- **j** . . . *me* in suffering — 2 Tim 1:8

JONATHAN

- 1 *son of Gershom* — Judg 18:30
- 2 *son of King Saul* — 1 Sam 13:16;14:49
- *friend of David* — 1 Sam 18:1
- 3 *son of Abiathar* — 2 Sam 15:36
- 4 *son of Shimei* — 2 Sam 21:21
- 5 *son of Jada* — 1 Chr 2:32
- 6 *son of Shagee* — 1 Chr 11:34
- 7 *official of David* — 1 Chr 27:25
- 8 *David's uncle* — 1 Chr 27:32

JOPPA

- *seaport W of Jerusalem* — 2 Chr 2:16; Ezra 3:7; Jon 1:3; Acts 9:36

JORAM

- 1 *son of Toi* — 2 Sam 8:10
- 2 *son of Ahab* — 2 Kin 8:16
- *king of Israel* — 2 Kin 8:25
- 3 *line of Eliezer* — 1 Chr 26:25
- 4 *son of Jehoshaphat* — Matt 1:8
- *king of Judah*
- *see also* **JEHORAM**

JORDAN

- 1 *river in Palestine* — Gen 32:10; Josh 3:17; Judg 8:4; 2 Kin 5:10; Matt 3:6
- 2 *valley* — Gen 13:10,11

JOSEPH

- 1 *son of Jacob* — Gen 30:23,24
- *put in prison* — Gen 40:3
- *prime minister* — Gen 41:41
- *revealed himself* — Gen 45:4
- *death* — Gen 50:26
- 2 *father of spy* — Num 13:7ff
- 3 *son of Asaph* — 1 Chr 25:9
- 4 *son of Bani* — Ezra 10:42
- 5 *son of Shebaniah* — Neh 12:14
- 6 *husband of Mary* — Matt 1:18;2:13; John 6:42
- 7 *brother of Jesus* — Matt 13:55
- 8 *brother of James the Less* — Matt 27:56
- *also* **Joses**
- 9 *of Arimathea* — Matt 27:57ff
- *in Sanhedrin (Council)* — Mark 15:43
- *disciple of Jesus* — John 19:38
- *provided tomb* — Matt 27:57
- 10 *ancestor of Jesus* — Luke 3:24
- 11 *ancestor of Jesus* — Luke 3:30
- 12 *surname Barsabbas* — Acts 1:23
- 13 *Barnabas* — Acts 4:36

JOSHUA

- 1 *Moses' successor* — Deut 31:23
- *chosen by God* — Num 27:18
- *encouraged by God* — Josh 1:1-9
- *charged Israel* — Josh 23:1ff
- *death* — Josh 24:29
- 2 *of Beth-shemesh* — 1 Sam 6:14
- 3 *governor* — 2 Kin 23:8
- 4 *high priest* — Hag 1:1,12; Zech 3:1ff
- *also* **Jeshua**

JOURNEY *traveling, trip*

- Let us take our **j** — Gen 33:12
- day's **j** on the other — Num 11:31
- seek . . . a safe **j** — Ezra 8:21
- a bag for *your* **j** — Matt 10:10
- Sabbath day's **j** away — Acts 1:12
- on frequent **j-s** — 2 Cor 11:26

JOY *delight, happiness*

- shouted aloud for **j** — Ezra 3:12
- see His face with **j** — Job 33:26
- Restore to me the **j** — Ps 51:12
- godly ones sing for **j** — Ps 132:9
- Everlasting **j** will be — Is 61:7
- their mourning into **j** — Jer 31:13
- enter into the **j** — Matt 25:21
- **j** in heaven over one — Luke 15:7
- **j** in the Holy Spirit — Rom 14:17
- love, **j**, peace — Gal 5:22
- make my **j** complete — Phil 2:2

JOYFUL *feeling gladness*

- be altogether **j** — Deut 16:15
- **j** with gladness — Ps 21:6
- shall reap with **j** — Ps 126:5
- **j** heart is good — Prov 17:22

JUBILANT *elated*

- no . . . **j** shouting — Is 16:10
- Is this your **j** *city* — Is 23:7
- because you are **j** — Jer 50:11
- they may become **j** — Jer 51:39

JUBILEE, YEAR OF

- *return of ancestral possessions every fiftieth year*
- *year of liberty* — Lev 25:8ff

JUDAH

- 1 *son of Jacob* — Gen 29:35;37:26;44:14;49:8,10
- 2 *tribe* — Num 1:27; Judg 1:8; 2 Sam 2:4; 1 Kin 12:20
- 3 *border city* — Josh 19:34
- 4 *S kingdom* — 1 Kin 14:21; 1 Chr 9:1; Ps 60:7; Jer 20:4
- 5 *ancestor of Kadmiel* — Ezra 2:40
- 6 *urged by Ezra to put away foreign wife* — Ezra 10:23
- 7 *Benjamite* — Neh 11:9
- 8 *Levite who returned from captivity* — Neh 12:8
- 9 *participant in wall dedication* — Neh 12:34
- 10 *musician* — Neh 12:36

JUDAISM *Jewish way of life*

- manner of life in **J** — Gal 1:13
- advancing in **J** — Gal 1:14

JUDAS

- 1 *Iscariot* — Matt 10:4
- *used by Satan* — Luke 22:3
- *son of Simon* — John 6:71
- *treasurer* — John 13:29
- *betrayed Jesus* — John 18:2
- 2 *Jesus' brother* — Matt 13:55; Mark 6:3
- 3 *apostle* — Luke 6:16; Acts 1:13
- 4 *Judas of Galilee* — Acts 5:37
- 5 *of Damascus* — Acts 9:11
- 6 *Barsabbas* — Acts 15:22,27

JUDE

- *brother of Jesus* — Matt 13:55; Mark 6:3
- *brother of James* — Jude 1

JUDEA

- *Roman province in Palestine based on earlier Judah* — Matt 2:1; Mark 1:5; Luke 2:4

JUDEAN

- *language (Hebrew)* — 2 Kin 18:26,28; Is 36:11, 13
- *see also* **CANAAN**
- *see also* **HEBREW**

JUDGE (n) *leader*

- **J** of all the earth — Gen 18:25
- prince or a **j** over us — Ex 2:14
- Lord was with the **j** — Judg 2:18
- For God Himself is **j** — Ps 50:6
- unrighteous **j** said — Luke 18:6
- one Lawgiver and **J** — James 4:12

JUDGE (v) *pass judgment*

- Lord **j** between you — Gen 16:5
- Lord will **j** . . . earth — 1 Sam 2:10
- coming to **j** the earth — Ps 98:9
- He will **j** the poor — Is 11:4
- not **j** lest you be **j-d** — Matt 7:1
- Law . . . not **j** a man — John 7:51
- not come to **j** the — John 12:47
- adulterers God will **j** — Heb 13:4

JUDGMENT *condemnation*

- I will execute **j-s** — Ex 12:12
- partiality in **j** — Deut 1:17
- will not stand in the **j** — Ps 1:5
- in the day of **j** — Matt 10:15
- **j**, that the light — John 3:19
- resurrection of **j** — John 5:29
- after this *comes* **j** — Heb 9:27
- not fall under **j** — James 5:12
- kept for the day of **j** — 2 Pet 3:7
- to execute **j** upon all — Jude 15
- His **j-s** are true — Rev 19:2

JUNIPER *tree*

- slept under a **j** tree — 1 Kin 19:5
- The **j**, the box tree — Is 60:13
- like a **j** in the — Jer 48:6

JUST *fair, right*

- shall have **j** balances — Lev 19:36
- a man be **j** with God — Job 25:4
- Hear a **j** cause, O Lord — Ps 17:1
- He is **j** and endowed — Zech 9:9
- My judgment is **j** — John 5:30
- *the* **j** for *the* unjust — 1 Pet 3:18

JUSTICE *fairness, righteousness*

- shall not distort **j** — Deut 16:19
- Does God pervert **j** — Job 8:3
- **j** to the afflicted — Job 36:6
- Righteousness and **j** — Ps 89:14
- do not understand **j** — Prov 28:5
- **j** is turned back — Is 59:14
- let **j** roll down — Amos 5:24
- **j** and mercy and — Matt 23:23
- acknowledged . . . **j** — Luke 7:29
- grant to your slaves **j** — Col 4:1

JUSTIFICATION *vindication*

- because of our **j** — Rom 4:25
- **j** of life to all men — Rom 5:18

JUSTIFY *declare guiltless*

- how . . . **j** ourselves — Gen 44:16
- they **j** the righteous — Deut 25:1
- he **j-ied** himself — Job 32:2
- wishing to **j** himself — Luke 10:29
- these He also **j-ied** — Rom 8:30
- God . . . **j-ies** — Rom 8:33
- seeking to be **j-ied** — Gal 2:17

JUTTAH

- *Levitical city in Judah* — Josh 15:55;21:16

K

KADESH / KADESH-BARNEA

- *desert oasis in Negev* — Gen 14:7
- *Israelite encampment* — Num 13:26;33:37

KEDESH

- 1 *city of Naphtali* — Josh 12:22
- 2 *city in S Judah* — Josh 15:23
- 3 *city of refuge, in Galilee* — Josh 20:7
- 4 *city of Issachar* — 1 Chr 6:72

KEEPER *guard, protector*

- Am I my brother's **k** — Gen 4:9
- been **k-s** of livestock — Gen 46:32
- The Lord is your **k** — Ps 121:5
- I, the Lord, am its **k** — Is 27:3

KENITE(S)

- *Canaanite tribe* — Gen 15:19; Num 24:21
- *tribe of metal-workers* — Judg 4:11; 1 Sam 15:6

KENIZZITE

- *Canaanite tribe in S Palestine and Edom* — Gen 15:19; Num 32:12; Josh 14:14

KETURAH

- *second wife of Abraham* — Gen 25:1,4; 1 Chr 1:32,33

KEY *unlocking tool*

- **k-s** of the kingdom — Matt 16:19
- the **k** of knowledge — Luke 11:52
- **k-s** of death and of — Rev 1:18
- **k** of the bottomless pit — Rev 9:1

KID *young goat*

- a **k** from the flock — Gen 38:17
- not boil a **k** . . . milk — Ex 34:26
- prepare a **k** for you — Judg 13:15

never given me a **k** Luke 15:29

KIDRON
brook and valley between Jerusalem and Mount of Olives 2 Sam 15:23; 2 Kin 23:6; 2 Chr 29:16; John 18:1

KILL *take life*
for Cain **k-ed** him Gen 4:25
k-ed every first-born Ex 13:15
who **k-s** a man shall Lev 24:21
LORD **k-s** and makes 1 Sam 2:6
Am I God, to **k** 2 Kin 5:7
he **k-s** the innocent Ps 10:8
A time to **k** Eccl 3:3
unable to **k** the Matt 10:28
k-ed, and be raised Luke 9:22
do you seek to **k** Me John 7:19
Arise, Peter, **k** and Acts 10:13
the letter **k-s**, but 2 Cor 3:6
k a third of mankind Rev 9:15

KIND (adj) *good, tender*
be **k** to this people 2 Chr 10:7
He Himself is **k** Luke 6:35
love is **k** 1 Cor 13:4
be **k** to one another Eph 4:32

KIND (n) *group, variety*
fruit after their **k** Gen 1:11
plant all **k-s** of trees Lev 19:23
all **k-s** of evil Matt 5:11
k-s of tongues 1 Cor 12:28
every **k** of impurity Eph 4:19

KINDLE *cause to burn*
anger . . . was **k-d** Num 11:10
His breath **k-s** coals Job 41:21
man to **k** strife Prov 26:21
all you who **k** a fire Is 50:11
k-d a fire in Zion Lam 4:11

KINDNESS *tenderness*
teaching of **k** is on Prov 31:26
to love **k**, And to Mic 6:8
with deeds of **k** Acts 9:36
k and . . . of God Rom 11:22
joy, peace, patience, **k** Gal 5:22
compassion, **k** Col 3:12
tasted the **k** of the 1 Pet 2:3
godliness, brotherly **k** 2 Pet 1:7

KINDRED *relative*
her people or her **k** Esth 2:10
destruction of my **k** Esth 8:6
no one . . . of **k** spirit Phil 2:20

KING *monarch, regent*
the **k-'s** highway Num 20:17
no **k** in Israel Judg 17:6
appoint a **k** for us 1 Sam 8:5
annointed David **k** 2 Sam 5:3
my **K** and my God Ps 5:2
The LORD is **K** forever Ps 10:16
Who is the **k** of glory Ps 24:8
By me **k-s** reign Prov 8:15
The Creator . . . your **K** Is 43:15
O **K** of the nations Jer 10:7
born **K** of the Jews Matt 2:2
Are You the **K** of Matt 27:11
your **K** is coming John 12:15
K of **k-s** and Lord 1 Tim 6:15
God, honor the **k** 1 Pet 2:17

KINGDOM *domain, monarchy*
his **k** was Babel Gen 10:10
to Me a **k** of priests Ex 19:6
will establish his **k** 1 Chr 28:7
the **k** is the LORD's Ps 22:28
Sing to God, O **k-s** Ps 68:32
an everlasting **k** Ps 145:13
k of heaven is at Matt 3:2
showed Him . . . **k-s** Matt 4:8
Thy **k** come Matt 6:10
sons of the **k** Matt 13:38
keys of the **k** Matt 16:19
in My Father's **k** Matt 26:29
enter the **k** of God Mark 10:24
cannot see the **k** of John 3:3
k of His beloved Son Col 1:13
to His heavenly **k** 2 Tim 4:18
heirs of the **k** James 2:5

KINSMAN *relative*
of my master's **k** Gen 24:48
he took his **k-men** Gen 31:23
a man has no **k** Lev 25:26
Naomi had a **k** of her Ruth 2:1
k-men stand afar off Ps 38:11
Herodion, my **k** Rom 16:11

KIRIATHAIM
1 *Reubenite city* Num 32:37; Josh 13:19
2 *Levitical city* 1 Chr 6:76

KIRIATH-ARBA
old name of Hebron Gen 23:2; Josh 14:15;15:13,54; Judg 1:10
city of Refuge Josh 20:7

KISHON
battle scene Judg 4:7
river Judg 4:13;5:21
priests of Baal slain on its bank 1 Kin 18:40

KISS (n) *expression of affection*
threw a **k** from my Job 31:27
the **k-es** of his mouth Song 1:2
You gave Me no **k** Luke 7:45
betraying . . . with a **k** Luke 22:48
with a holy **k** Rom 16:16
with a **k** of love 1 Pet 5:14

KISS (v) *express affection*
come close and **k** Gen 27:26
let me **k** my father 1 Kin 19:20
I would **k** you Song 8:1
Whomever I . . . **k** Mark 14:44
not . . . to **k** my feet Luke 7:45

KITTIM
1 *grandson of Japheth* Gen 10:4; 1 Chr 1:7
2 *island of Cyprus* Num 24:24; Jer 2:10; Dan 11:30

KNEAD *work dough* or *clay*
took flour, **k-ed** it 1 Sam 28:24
the women **k** dough Jer 7:18

KNEEL *bend, rest on knee*
made the camels **k** Gen 24:11
people **k-ed** to drink Judg 7:6
k before the LORD Ps 95:6
k-ed . . . before Him Matt 27:29
man ran . . . **knelt** Mark 10:17
He **knelt** down Luke 22:41

KNIFE *cutting instrument*
k to slay his son Gen 22:10
jaw teeth *like* **k-ves** Prov 30:14
with a scribe's **k** Jer 36:23

KNIT *joined together*
Jonathan was **k** to 1 Sam 18:1
k me together with Job 10:11
his thighs are **k** Job 40:17
His hand they are **k** Lam 1:14
k together in love Col 2:2

KNOCK *smite, strike*
his knees began **k-ing** Dan 5:6
k, and it shall be Matt 7:7
stand outside and **k** Luke 13:25
he **k-ed** at the door Acts 12:13
at the door and **k** Rev 3:20

KNOW *experience, understand*
like one of Us, **k-ing** Gen 3:22
make **k-n** the statutes Ex 18:16
k that my Redeemer Job 19:25
He **k-s** the secrets Ps 44:21
k that I am God Ps 46:10
made **k-n** His salvation Ps 98:2
Try me and **k** my Ps 139:23
left hand **k** what Matt 6:3
k . . . by their fruits Matt 7:20
I never **knew** you Matt 7:23
God **k-s** your hearts Luke 16:15
you shall **k** the truth John 8:32
I **k** My own John 10:14
k-ing that His hour John 13:1
k that I love You John 21:15
and **k** all mysteries 1 Cor 13:2
who **knew** no sin 2 Cor 5:21
k the love of Christ Eph 3:19
value of **k-ing** Christ Phil 3:8
k . . . I have believed 2 Tim 1:12
k . . . eternal life 1 John 5:13
I **k** your deeds Rev 2:2

KNOWLEDGE *information*
tree of the **k** of good Gen 2:9
LORD is a God of **k** 1 Sam 2:3
anyone teach God **k** Job 21:22
k is too wonderful Ps 139:6
the beginning of **k** Prov 1:7
fools hate **k** Prov 1:22
Wise . . . store up **k** Prov 10:14
k increases power Prov 24:5
would He teach **k** Is 28:9
in accordance with **k** Rom 10:2
K makes arrogant 1 Cor 8:1
k, it will be done 1 Cor 13:8
have no **k** of God 1 Cor 15:34
love . . . surpasses **k** Eph 3:19
treasures of . . . **k** Col 2:3
grow in . . . grace and **k** 2 Pet 3:18

KOR *measure of capacity*
k-s of fine flour 1 Kin 4:22
20,000 **k-s** of barley 2 Chr 2:10
100 **k-s** of wheat Ezra 7:22
a bath from *each* **k** Ezek 45:14

KORAH
1 *son of Esau* Gen 36:5
2 *opposed Moses* Num 16:8,16
3 *son of Hebron* 1 Chr 2:43
4 *a Kohathite* 1 Chr 6:37

L

LABAN
1 *Abraham's kinsman Rachel's father* Gen 24:29; Gen 29:10,16
2 *place in the desert* Deut 1:1

LABOR (n) *work* or *childbirth*
fruits of your **l-s** Ex 23:16
their **l** to the locust Ps 78:46
bread of painful **l-s** Ps 127:2
like a woman in **l** Is 42:14
in **l** and hardship 2 Cor 11:27
fruitful **l** for me Phil 1:22
faith and **l** of love 1 Thess 1:3

LABOR (v) *toil, work*
Six days you shall **l** Ex 20:9
l in vain who build Ps 127:1
for whom am I **l-ing** Eccl 4:8
l-ed over you in vain Gal 4:11

LABORER *workman*
l-s for his vineyard Matt 20:1
Call the **l-s** and pay Matt 20:8
l-s into His harvest Luke 10:2
l is worthy of his Luke 10:7

LACHISH
city in Judah Josh 10:3; 2 Kin 14:19

LACK (n) *deficiency, need*
where there is no **l** Judg 18:10
for **l** of instruction Prov 5:23
for **l** of a shepherd Ezek 34:5
l of self-control 1 Cor 7:5

LACK (v) *be deficient, need*
shall not **l** anything Deut 8:9
l-ing in counsel Deut 32:28
man **l-ing** sense Prov 7:7
One thing you **l** Mark 10:21
not **l-ing** in any gift 1 Cor 1:7
if any . . . **l-s** wisdom James 1:5

LAISH
1 *a Benjamite* 1 Sam 25:44; 2 Sam 3:15
2 *place in N Palestine later called Dan* Judg 18:27,29

LAMB *young sheep*
l for the burnt Gen 22:7
shall redeem with a l Ex 34:20
l without defect Lev 14:10
will dwell with the l Is 11:6
l . . . led to slaughter Is 53:7
wolf and the l shall Is 65:25
Behold, the **L** of God John 1:29
Tend My **l-s** John 21:15
l before its shearer Acts 8:32
Worthy is the **L** Rev 5:12
blood of the **L** Rev 12:11

LAME *crippled, disabled*
was l in both feet 2 Sam 9:13
feet to the l Job 29:15
Then the l will leap Is 35:6
the l walk Matt 11:5
l from his mother's Acts 14:8

LAMENT (n) *dirge, wail*
this l over Saul 2 Sam 1:17
chanted a l 2 Chr 35:25
I must make a l Mic 1:8

LAMENT (v) *mourn, wail*
house of Israel **l-ed** 1 Sam 7:2
her gates will l Is 3:26
fisherman will l Is 19:8
And l over you Ezek 27:32
weep and l over her Rev 18:9

LAMENTATION *weeping, mourning*
great . . . sorrowful l Gen 50:10
in Ramah, **L** *and* Jer 31:15
your sons into l Amos 8:10
made loud l over him Acts 8:2

LAMP *light*
l-s of pure gold 2 Chr 4:20
his l goes out Job 18:6
Thy word is a l Ps 119:105
commandment is a l Prov 6:23
l of the body is the Matt 6:22
l-s in the upper room Acts 20:8
l shining in a dark 2 Pet 1:19
seven **l-s** of fire Rev 4:5

LAMPSTAND *candlestick*
l of pure gold Ex 25:31
and a chair and a l 2 Kin 4:10
puts it on a l Luke 8:16
will remove your l Rev 2:5

LAND *country, earth*
let the dry l appear Gen 1:9
I have given this l Gen 15:18
out of the l of Egypt Ex 6:13
l flowing with milk Deut 6:3
in to possess the l Josh 1:11
will heal their l 2 Chr 7:14
the l of the living Job 28:13
will inherit the l Ps 37:11
l be born in one day Is 66:8
l is filled with blood Ezek 9:9
smite the l with a Mal 4:6
darkness . . . all the l Matt 27:45
owned a tract of l Acts 4:37

LANGUAGE *speech, word*
according to his l Gen 10:5
earth used the same l Gen 11:1
speech or difficult l Ezek 3:5
in figurative l John 16:25
speak in his own l Acts 2:6
many kinds of **l-s** 1 Cor 14:10

LANGUISH *faint*
l-ed because of the Gen 47:13
My soul **l-es** for Ps 119:81
never l again Jer 31:12
refresh . . . who **l-es** Jer 31:25

LAODICEANS
people of Laodicea Col 4:16

LAPIS LAZULI *precious stone*
polishing *was* like l Lam 4:7
like l in appearance Ezek 1:26
the jasper; The l Ezek 28:13

LAST *final, utmost*
breathed his l Gen 25:8
In the l days Is 2:2
The l Adam 1 Cor 15:45
at the l trumpet 1 Cor 15:52
in these l days Heb 1:2
it is the l hour 1 John 2:18
the first and the l Rev 1:17

LATIN
language of the Roman Empire
one of three languages written on Jesus' cross John 19:20

LAUGH *be amused, mock*
Why did Sarah l Gen 18:13
will l at violence Job 5:22
l at your calamity Prov 1:26
weep, and a time to l Eccl 3:4
began **l-ing** at Him Matt 9:24

LAUGHINGSTOCK *derision*
l among the peoples Ps 44:14
was not Israel a l Jer 48:27
I have become a l Lam 3:14

LAUGHTER *amusement*
God has made l for Gen 21:6
Even in l the heart Prov 14:13
Sorrow is better than l Eccl 7:3

LAVER *wash basin*
make a l of bronze Ex 30:18
set the l between Ex 40:7
anoint the l Ex 40:11

LAW *scripture, statute*
tablets with the l Ex 24:12
Moses wrote this l Deut 31:9
walk in My l 2 Chr 6:16
l . . . is perfect Ps 19:7
I delight in Thy l Ps 119:70
abolish the **L** or the Matt 5:17
Our **L** . . . not judge John 7:51
by a l of faith Rom 3:27
L brings . . . wrath Rom 4:15
not under l Rom 6:14
the **L** is holy Rom 7:12
L . . . become our tutor Gal 3:24
thus fulfill the l Gal 6:2
L . . . nothing perfect Heb 7:19

LAWFUL *legal, right*
not l for him to eat Matt 12:4
Is it l to heal Matt 12:10
l . . . man to divorce Mark 10:2
All things are l 1 Cor 6:12

LAWGIVER *lawmaker*
The LORD is our l Is 33:22
one **L** and Judge James 4:12

LAWLESS *illegal, without law*
l one will be 2 Thess 2:8
are l and rebellious 1 Tim 1:9
from every l deed Titus 2:14

LAWYER *interpreter of law*
a l, asked Him *a* Matt 22:35
one of the **l-s** said Luke 11:45
Woe to you **l-s** Luke 11:52

LAYMAN *non-ecclesiastic person*
l shall not eat *them* Ex 29:33
married to a l Lev 22:12
l who comes near Num 3:10

LAZARUS
1 *beggar* Luke 16:20-25
2 *brother of Mary and Martha* John 11:1,2,5,11,43

LAZY *idle, slothful*
Because they are l Ex 5:8
You are l, *very* l Ex 5:17
You wicked, l slave Matt 25:26
beasts, l gluttons Titus 1:12

LEAD (n) *metal*
They sank like l Ex 15:10
an iron stylus and l Job 19:24
l is consumed by Jer 6:29
l in the furnace Ezek 22:18

LEAD (v) *direct, guide*
God **led** the people Ex 13:18
cloud by day to l Ex 13:21
l-s me beside quiet Ps 23:2
L me in Thy truth Ps 25:5
led captive *Thy* Ps 68:18
little boy will l Is 11:6
lamb that is **led** to Is 53:7
not l us into Matt 6:13
l the elect astray Mark 13:22
led Him . . . crucify Mark 15:20
and **l-s** them out John 10:3
led by the Spirit Rom 8:14
led captive a host Eph 4:8
that **l-s** to salvation 2 Tim 3:15

LEADER *director, guide*
Let us appoint a l Num 14:4
one l of every tribe Num 34:18
l over My people 1 Kin 14:7
the l as the servant Luke 22:26
Obey your **l-s** Heb 13:17

LEADING (adj) *chief, noted*
gathered l men Ezra 7:28
number . . . l women Acts 17:4
l men of the Jews Acts 28:17

LEAH
wife of Jacob Gen 29:23,30
mother of Reuben, Simeon, Levi and Judah Gen 29:32-35

LEAN (adj) *thin*
seven l . . . ugly cows Gen 41:20
my flesh has grown l Ps 109:24
and the l sheep Ezek 34:20

LEAN (v) *incline, rest*
may l against them Judg 16:26
l . . . own understanding Prov 3:5
l on the God of Israel Is 48:2

LEAP *jump, spring*
l-ing and dancing 2 Sam 6:16
I can l over a wall Ps 18:29
baby **l-ed** in her Luke 1:41
and l *for joy* Luke 6:23
l-ed up and *began* Acts 14:10

LEARN *get knowledge*
l to fear the LORD Deut 31:13
I may l Thy statutes Ps 119:71
have I **l-ed** wisdom Prov 30:3
will they l war Is 2:4
l from Me Matt 11:29
l-ed to be content Phil 4:11
He **l-ed** obedience Heb 5:8

LEARNING (n) *knowledge*
increase *his* l Prov 9:9
l of the Egyptians Acts 7:22
great l is driving Acts 26:24

LEATHER *animal skin*
man with a l girdle 2 Kin 1:8
a l belt about his Matt 3:4
and *wore* a l belt Mark 1:6

LEAVE *abandon, depart, forsake*
shall l his father Gen 2:24
arise, l this land Gen 31:13
not l me defenseless Ps 141:8
kindness and truth l Prov 3:3
l the ninety-nine Matt 18:12
Peace I l with you John 14:27
I am **l-ing** . . . world John 16:28

LEAVEN *yeast*
no l found in your Ex 12:19
not be baked with l Lev 6:17
seven days no l shall Deut 16:4
heaven is like l Matt 13:33
little l leavens the 1 Cor 5:6

LEBANON
mountain range N of Israel Josh 9:1; Judg 3:3; 1 Kin 5:6
showing God's greatness Ps 29:6
symbol of prosperity Ps 92:12

LEGAL *lawful*
has a l matter Ex 24:14
Give me l protection Luke 18:3

LEGION *division, group, large number*
twelve **l-s** of angels Matt 26:53
My name is L Mark 5:9
man who had . . . l Mark 5:15
L; for many demons Luke 8:30

LEND *loan*
l-ing them money Neh 5:10
l-s . . . on interest Ezek 18:13
l, expecting nothing Luke 6:35
l me three loaves Luke 11:5

LENDER *loaner*
becomes the **l-'s** slave Prov 22:7
l like the borrower Is 24:2

LEOPARD *animal*
l will lie down with Is 11:6
Or the l his spots Jer 13:23
beast . . . was like a l Rev 13:2

LEPER *one having leprosy*
As for the l Lev 13:45
King Uzziah . . . a l 2 Chr 26:21
cleanse *the* **l-s** Matt 10:8
home of Simon the l Mark 14:3

LEPROSY *infectious disease*
of l on the skin Lev 13:2
mark of l on a Lev 14:34
an infection of l Deut 24:8
cure him of his l 2 Kin 5:3
his l was cleansed Matt 8:3

LETTER *epistle* or *symbol*
a l sent to Solomon 2 Chr 2:11
smallest l or stroke Matt 5:18
You are our l 2 Cor 3:2
large **l-s** I am writing Gal 6:11

LEVEL *flat, plain*
lead me in a l path Ps 27:11
path of the righteous l Is 26:7
stood on a l place Luke 6:17

LEVI
1 *son of Jacob* Gen 34:25
2 *tribe* Num 1:49; Rev 7:7
3 *two ancestors of Jesus* Luke 3:24,29
4 *apostle* Mark 2:14; Luke 5:27,29

LEVITES
descendants of Levi Ex 6:19,25
charged with the care of the sanctuary Num 1:50; 3:41

LEWDNESS *lascivious, lust*
land . . . full of l Lev 19:29
not commit this l Ezek 16:43
I will uncover her l Hos 2:10

LIAR *one telling lies*
who . . . prove me a l Job 24:25
a poor man than a l Prov 19:22
hypocrisy of **l-s** 1 Tim 4:2
we make Him a l 1 John 1:10

LIBERTY *freedom*
I will walk at l Ps 119:45
proclaim l to captives Is 61:1
spy out our l Gal 2:4
the *law* of l James 1:25

LIBNAH
1 *place in wilderness* Num 33:21
2 *Canaanite city* Josh 10:29; 2 Kin 23:31
a Levitical city 1 Chr 6:57

LIE (n) *false statement*
tells **l-s** will perish Prov 19:9
prophesy a l to you Jer 27:10
the father of **l-s** John 8:44
truth of God for a l Rom 1:25
no l is of the truth 1 John 2:21

LIE (v) *make false statement*
l-d to Him with their Ps 78:36
l-d about the LORD Jer 5:12
l to the Holy Spirit Acts 5:3
not l to one another Col 3:9
impossible . . . God to l Heb 6:18

LIE (v) *recline*
when you l down Deut 11:19
she **lay** at his feet Ruth 3:14
Saul **lay** sleeping 1 Sam 26:7
makes me l down Ps 23:2
lying in a manger Luke 2:12

LIFE *living* or *salvation*
the breath of l Gen 2:7
l for l Ex 21:23
l . . . is in the blood Lev 17:11
Our l for yours Josh 2:14
my l is *but* breath Job 7:7
the springs of l Prov 4:23
way of l and . . . death Jer 21:8
to everlasting l Dan 12:2
anxious for your l Matt 6:25
loses his l for My Matt 16:25
His l a ransom for Matt 20:28
to inherit eternal l Mark 10:17
but have eternal l John 3:16
out of death into l John 5:24
I am the bread of l John 6:35
lays down his l John 10:11
resurrection and . . . l John 11:25
truth, and the l John 14:6
lay down his l for John 15:13
walk in newness of l Rom 6:4
the Spirit gives l 2 Cor 3:6
Christ, who is our l Col 3:4
an undisciplined l 2 Thess 3:11
receive . . . crown of l James 1:12
book of l of the lamb Rev 13:8

LIFEBLOOD
I will require your l Gen 9:5
poured out their l Is 63:6
l of the innocent Jer 2:34

LIFETIME *length of life*
Throughout his l 2 Chr 34:33
His favor is for a l Ps 30:5
my l of futility Eccl 7:15
as the l of a tree Is 65:22

LIFT *exalt, raise*
l up your staff and Ex 14:16
One who **l-s** my head Ps 3:3
I Will l up my eyes Ps 121:1
Spirit **l-ed** me up Ezek 3:14
Son of Man be **l-ed** John 3:14
He was **l-ed** up Acts 1:9
l-ing up holy hands 1 Tim 2:8

LIGHT *brightness, lamp*
Let there be l Gen 1:3
Israel had l in Ex 10:23
LORD is my l Ps 27:1
And a l to my path Ps 119:105
like the l of dawn Prov 4:18
walk in the l of the Is 2:5
stars for l by night Jer 31:35
the l of the world Matt 5:14
l of revelation to Luke 2:32
There was the true l John 1:9
I am the l John 8:12
while you have . . . l John 12:35
l of the gospel 2 Cor 4:4
walk as children of l Eph 5:8
Father of **l-s** James 1:17

if we walk in the l 1 John 1:7

LIGHTNING *flash of light*
thunder and l flashes Ex 19:16
He spreads His l Job 36:30
makes l for the rain Jer 10:13
l . . . from the east Matt 24:27
appearance . . . like l Matt 28:3

LIKENESS *similarity*
according to Our l Gen 1:26
the l of sinful flesh Rom 8:3
made in the l of men Phil 2:7

LILY *flower*
The l of the valleys Song 2:1
blossom like the l Hos 14:5
l-ies of the field Matt 6:28

LIMIT *end, extent*
there is no l 1 Chr 22:16
no l to windy words Job 16:3
set a l for the rain Job 28:26
no l to the treasure Nah 2:9

LINEN *type of cloth*
makes l garments Prov 31:24
buy . . . a l waistband Jer 13:1
left the l sheet Mark 14:52
wrapped Him . . . l Mark 15:46
saw the l wrappings John 20:5
clothed in fine l Rev 19:14

LINTEL *horizontal crosspiece*
blood on the l Ex 12:23
l *and* five-sided 1 Kin 6:31

LION *wild animal*
Judah is a **l-'s** whelp Gen 49:9
hunt me like a l Job 10:16
tear my soul like a l Ps 7:2
are bold as a l Prov 28:1
cast into the **l-s'** Dan 6:16
like a roaring l 1 Pet 5:8

LIQUOR *alcoholic drink*
concerning wine and l Mic 2:11
drink no wine or l Luke 1:15

LISTEN *hear, heed*
Pharaoh will not l Ex 7:4
l to His voice Deut 4:30
l . . . commandments Deut 11:27
L to your father Prov 23:22
draw near to l Eccl 5:1
L to Me, O Jacob Is 48:12
L . . . another parable Matt 21:33
l-ing to the word Luke 5:1
My Son . . . l to Him Luke 9:35

LITERATURE *writings*
teach them the l Dan 1:4
every *branch of* l Dan 1:17

LIVE (v) *reside* or *be alive*
eat, and l forever Gen 3:22
does not l by bread Deut 8:3
my Redeemer **l-s** Job 19:25
Listen, that you may l Is 55:3
can these bones l Ezek 37:3
righteous will l by Hab 2:4
not l on bread alone Matt 4:4
l even if he dies John 11:25
because I l John 14:19
shall l by faith Rom 1:17
Christ died and **l-d** Rom 14:9
no longer I who l Gal 2:20
to l is Christ Phil 1:21
worship Him who **l-s** Rev 4:10

LIVER *internal organ*
the lobe of the l Ex 29:13
l of the sin offering Lev 9:10
pierces through his l Prov 7:23
he looks at the l Ezek 21:21

LIVESTOCK *domestic animals*
was very rich in l Gen 13:2
their l to Joseph Gen 47:17

l of Egypt died Ex 9:6
large number of l Num 32:1

LIVING (adj) *alive*
man became a l being Gen 2:7
voice of the l god Deut 5:26
Divide the l child 1 Kin 3:25
Son of the l God Matt 16:16
given you l water John 4:10
I am the l bread John 6:51
l and holy sacrifice Rom 12:1
became a l soul 1 Cor 15:45
temple of the l God 2 Cor 6:16
word of God is l Heb 4:12

LIVING (n) *what is alive*
mother of all *the* l Gen 3:20
land of the l Job 28:13
that the l may know Dan 4:17
God . . . of the l Matt 22:32
judge the l and the 1 Pet 4:5

LOAD *burden*
in all their **l-s** Num 4:27
I alone bear the l Deut 1:12
My l is light Matt 11:30

LOAN *something lent*
your neighbor a l Deut 24:10
rich with **l-s** Hab 2:6

LOATHSOME *detestable*
l to the Egyptians Gen 46:34
like l food to me Job 6:7
l and malignant sore Rev 16:2

LOCK (n) *tuft of hair*
seven **l-s** of my hair Judg 16:13
flowing **l-s** of . . . head Song 7:5
a l of my head Ezek 8:3

LOCK (v) *secure, shut*
l the door behind 2 Sam 13:17
l-ed quite securely Acts 5:23
l up . . . the saints Acts 26:10

LOCUST *grasshopper*
wind brought the **l-s** Ex 10:13
you may eat: the l Lev 11:22
leap like the l Job 39:20
like the swarming l Nah 3:17
food was **l-s** and wild Matt 3:4

LODGE *dwell, spend the night*
where you l, I will l Ruth 1:16
drank and **l-d** there Judg 19:4
In his neck **l-s** Job 41:22
l in the wilderness Ps 55:7

LODGING (adj) *dwelling*
fodder at the l place Gen 42:27
about at the l place Ex 4:24
A wayfarers' l place Jer 9:2

LOFTINESS *elevation, haughtiness*
l of man will be Is 2:11
l of your dwelling Obad 3

LOG *beam, wood*
he who splits **l-s** Eccl 10:9
l out of your own eye Matt 7:5

LOINS *groin*
with your l girded Ex 12:11
Gird up your l 2 Kin 4:29
l are full of anguish Is 21:3
having girded your l Eph 6:14

LONELY *alone, isolated*
I am l and afflicted Ps 25:16
makes a home for the l Ps 68:6
How l sits the city Lam 1:1
to a l place and rest Mark 6:31

LONG (adj) *extended*
there was a l war 2 Sam 3;1
L life is in her Prov 3:16
you make l prayers Matt 23:14
if a man has l hair 1 Cor 11:14

LONG (v) *desire, want*
Who l for death Job 3:21
my soul **l-s** for Thee Is 26:9
l-ing to be fed Luke 16:21
I l to see you Rom 1:11
angels l to look 1 Pet 1:12
l for the pure milk 1 Pet 2:2

LOOK *see, stare*
Do not l behind you Gen 19:17
afraid to l at God Ex 3:6
LORD **l-s** at . . . heart 1 Sam 16:7
L upon my affliction Ps 25:18
The sea **l-ed** and fled Ps 114:3
not l on the wine Prov 23:31
l eagerly for Him Is 8:17
l to the Holy One Is 17:7
l on Me . . . pierced Zech 12:10
plow and **l-ing** back Luke 9:62
l on the fields John 4:35
l on Him . . . pierced John 19:37
l-ing for the blessed Titus 2:13

LORD *personal name of God*
Old Testament
Different Hebrew words are translated as Lord
LORD *(Yahweh)* Gen 4:1; Ex 3:2,15; Ps 23:1; Is 40:31; Ezek 11:23
Lord GOD *(Adonai Yahweh)* Gen 15:2; 2 Sam 7:18,19; Is 1:24; Ezek 28:6; Hab 3:19
LORD God *(Yahweh Elohim)* Gen 2:4; Ps 59:5; 68:18; Jer 15:16; Jon 1:9
Lord *(Adonai)* Gen 18:27; Ex 4:10; Josh 3:11; Ps 68:19; Mic 4:13
LORD GOD *(Yah Yahweh)* Is 12:2
New Testament
Different Greek words are translated as Lord
Lord *(Kyrios, refers to either the Father or the Son)* Matt 1:20; John 11:2; Acts 5:19; 2 Cor 5:6; 1 Thess 4:16
Lord *(Despotes)* Luke 2:29; Acts 4:24; Rev 6:10
Lord God *(Kyrios Theos, refers to either* the Father *or the Son)* Luke 1:32; Rev 1:8;11:17;16:7;18:8
Lord Jesus *(Kyrios Iesous)* Mark 16:19; Luke 24:3; Acts 4:33;7:59
Lord Jesus Christ *(Kyrios Iesous Christos)* Acts 15:26; Rom 1:7;5:1; 1 Cor 1:10; Eph 1:2,3; 1 Thess 5:9; James 2:1

LORD *human master, ruler*
Hear us, my l Gen 23:6
not my l be angry Gen 31:35
Moses, my l Num 11:28
l-s of . . . Philistines Judg 16:27
counsel of my l Ezra 10:3
l-s of the nations Is 16:8
his l commanded Matt 18:25
write to my l Acts 25:26

LOSE *mislay, suffer loss*
do not l courage 2 Chr 15:7
lost their confidence Neh 6:16
stars l their Joel 2:10
his life shall l it Matt 10:39
not l his reward Mark 9:41
whoever **l-s** his life Luke 9:24

LOST (adj) *missing, ruined*
like a l sheep Ps 119:176
have become l sheep Jer 50:6
l sheep . . . of Israel Matt 10:6
the wine is l Mark 2:22

LOST (n) *without God*
I will seek the l Ezek 34:16
sent only to the l Matt 15:24

LOT *portion* or *decision process*
one l for the LORD Lev 16:8
clothing they cast **l-s** Ps 22:18
your l with us Prov 1:14
let us cast **l-s** Jon 1:7
tear it, but cast **l-s** John 19:24
l fell to Matthias Acts 1:26

LOUD *great, noisy*
very l trumpet sound Ex 19:16
with a l shout Ezra 3:13
Jesus cried . . . l voice Matt 27:50
heard . . . a l voice Rev 1:10

LOVE (n) *compassion, devotion*
l covers all Prov 10:12
in unchanging l Mic 7:18
l will grow cold Matt 24:12
abide in My l John 15:10
Greater l has no one John 15:13
demonstrates His . . . l Rom 5:8
separate us from . . . l Rom 8:39
l edifies 1 Cor 8:1
l is kind 1 Cor 13:4
l of Christ controls 2 Cor 5:14
through l serve one Gal 5:13
speaking . . . truth in l Eph 4:15
l of money is a root 1 Tim 6:10
for l is from God 1 John 4:7
God is l 1 John 4:16
l casts out fear 1 John 4:18
have left your first l Rev 2:4

LOVE (v)
who l Me and keep My Ex 20:6
l your neighbor as Lev 19:18
l the LORD your God Deut 6:5
the LORD **l-d** Israel 1 Kin 10:9
I l Thy testimonies Ps 119:119
LORD **l-s** He reproves Prov 3:12
Do not l sleep Prov 20:13
A time to l Eccl 3:8
Hate evil, l good Amos 5:15
l your enemies Matt 5:44
l to stand and pray Matt 6:5
God so **l-d** the world John 3:16
you l one another John 13:34
l-s a cheerful giver 2 Cor 9:7
Husbands, l . . . wives Eph 5:25
Do not l the world 1 John 2:15
whom I l, I reprove Rev 3:19

LOVERS *one who desires, loves*
l have been crushed Jer 22:20
I called to my l Lam 1:19
I will go after my l Hos 2:5
l of pleasure . . . l of 2 Tim 3:4

LOVINGKINDNESS *compassion*
His l is upon Israel Ezra 3:11
abundant in l and Ps 86:15
sing of the l of the Ps 89:1
By l and truth Prov 16:6
with everlasting l Is 54:8

LOWLY *humble, little*
He sets on high . . . l Job 5:11
He regards the l Ps 138:6
associate with the l Rom 12:16

LOYALTY *faithfulness*
Is this your l 2 Sam 16:17
proclaims his own l Prov 20:6
I delight in l Hos 6:6

LUKE
associate of Paul 2 Tim 4:11; Philem 24
author of Luke and Acts Luke 1:1; Acts 1:1
physician Col 4:14

LUKEWARM *tepid*
because you are l Rev 3:16

LUST *sinful desire*
looks . . . woman to l Matt 5:28
from youthful **l-s** 2 Tim 2:22
You l and do not James 4:2
l of the eyes 1 John 2:16

LUXURY *extravagance*
L is not fitting for Prov 19:10
clothed and live in l Luke 7:25

LYDIA
1 *seller of purple dyes and goods* Acts 16:14,40

2 *region on the W coast of Asia Minor* Jer 46:9

LYING (adj) *false*
with a l tongue Ps 109:2
hatred *has* l lips Prov 10:18
l pen of the scribes Jer 8:8
and l divination Ezek 13:6

LYRE *stringed instrument*
play the l and pipe Gen 4:21
prophesy with **l-s** 1 Chr 25:1
Awake, harp and l Ps 57:8

M

MACHPELAH
cave near Hebron Gen 23:17,19
Sarah's burial place Gen 23:19
Abraham buried there Gen 25:9
burial place of Jacob, Isaac, Rebekah, and Leah Gen 49:29ff;50:13

MAD *insane*
makes a wise man **m** Eccl 7:7
nations are going **m** Jer 51:7

MADMAN *insane person*
behaving as a **m** 1 Sam 21:14
m who prophesies Jer 29:26

MAGDALENE
Mary Matt 27:56,61
from village of Magdala Mark 15:40,47; John 20:1,18

MAGI
wise men from Persia who visited Jesus, Mary, and Joseph Matt 2:1,7,16

MAGIC *sorcery*
practicing **m** Acts 8:9
who practiced **m** Acts 19:19

MAGICIAN *sorcerer, wizard*
called for . . . **m-s** Gen 41:8
the **m-s** of Egypt Ex 7:11
of any **m**, conjurer or Dan 2:10
found a certain **m** Acts 13:6

MAGISTRATE
appear before the **m** Luke 12:58
to the chief **m-s** Acts 16:20

MAGNIFY *extol, praise*
name . . . be **m-ied** 2 Sam 7:26
Thou dost **m** him Job 7:17
O **m** the LORD with me Ps 34:3
hast **m-ied** Thy word Ps 138:2
Jesus was . . . **m-ied** Acts 19:17
I **m** my ministry Rom 11:13

MAGOG
1 *son of Japheth* 1 Chr 1:5
2 *region in Asia Minor or further N ruled by Gog* Ezek 38:2;39:6

MAHANAIM
city in Trans-Jordan Josh 13:26,30
Levitical city 1 Chr 6:80

MAID *servant girl*
Hagar, Sarai's **m** Gen 16:8
gave my **m** to my Gen 30:18
I am Ruth your **m** Ruth 3:9
way of a man . . . a **m** Prov 30:19

MAIDENS *young women*
at the Nile . . . her **m** Ex 2:5
m . . . tambourines Ps 68:25

MAIDSERVANT *female slave*
do . . . to your **m** Deut 15:17
give Thy **m** a son 1 Sam 1:11
let your **m** speak 2 Sam 14:12
while your **m** slept 1 Kin 3:20

MAJESTIC *dignified, grand*
Who is like Thee, **m** Ex 15:11
with His **m** voice Job 37:4
How **m** is Thy name Ps 8:1
They are the **m** ones Ps 16:3
m is His work Ps 111:3
by the **M** Glory 2 Pet 1:17

MAJESTY *grandeur*
Around God is . . . **m** Job 37:22
He is clothed with **m** Ps 93:1
The **m** of our God Is 35:2
right hand of the **M** Heb 1:3
revile angelic **m-ies** Jude 8

MAKER *creator*
Where is God my **M** Job 35:10
kneel before . . . our **M** Ps 95:6
M of heaven and Ps 115:15
I, the LORD, am the **m** Is 44:24

MALCHUS
servant whose ear was cut off by Peter John 18:10

MALE
m and female He Gen 1:27
lamb . . . unblemished **m** Ex 12:5
likeness of **m** or Deut 4:16
slew . . . **m** children Matt 2:16
made . . . **m** and female Matt 19:4
neither **m** nor female Gal 3:28

MALICE *evil, mischief*
perceived their **m** Matt 22:18
leaven of **m** and 1 Cor 5:8
wrath, **m**, slander Col 3:8
putting aside all **m** 1 Pet 2:1

MAMMON *wealth*
serve God and **m** Matt 6:24
m of unrighteousness Luke 16:9

MAMRE
1 *Abraham's dwelling place near Hebron* Gen 13:18
2 *Amorite chieftain* Gen 14:24

MAN *male, humanity*
make **m** in Our image Gen 1:26
God formed **m** of dust Gen 2:7
Elisha the **m** of God 2 Kin 5:8
blessed is the **m** Ps 1:1
m is a mere breath Ps 39:11
Will a **m** rob God Mal 3:8
light . . . before **men** Matt 5:16
fishers of **men** Mark 1:17
Sabbath . . . for **m** Mark 2:27
what is a **m** profited Luke 9:25
a **m**, sent from God John 1:6
How can a **m** be born John 3:4
a . . . **m** of Macedonia Acts 16:9
as is common to **m** 1 Cor 10:13
m . . . leave his father Eph 5:31

MANASSEH
1 *son of Joseph* Gen 41:51;46:20
2 *tribe and area* Num 13:11; Josh 17:1
3 *king of Judah* 2 Kin 21:1,11
4 *Pahath-moab's son* Ezra 10:30
5 *son of Hashum* Ezra 10:33

MANDRAKES *love fruit*
found **m** in the field Gen 30:14
m . . . fragrance Song 7:13

MANGER *feeding trough*
spend . . . at your **m** Job 39:9
the **m** is clean Prov 14:4
laid Him in a **m** Luke 2:7

MANIFEST *reveal, known*
I **m-ed** Thy name John 17:6
became **m** to those Rom 10:20
made **m** to God 2 Cor 5:11
m-ed to His saints Col 1:26

MANKIND *the human race*
All **m** is stupid Jer 51:17
Authority over all **m** John 17:2
His love for **m** Titus 3:4
kill a third of **m** Rev 9:15

MANNA *food of the desert*
Israel named it **m** Ex 16:31
m was like coriander Num 11:7
He rained down **m** Ps 78:24
Our fathers ate the **m** John 6:31

MANSLAYER
for the **m** to flee to Num 35:6
m might flee there Deut 4:42
the **m** who kills any Josh 20:3

MANTLE *cloak, garment*
threw his **m** on him 1 Kin 19:19
the **m** of Elijah 2 Kin 2:13
as a **m** Thou wilt roll Heb 1:12

MARCH *pace, walk*
m around . . . seven times Josh 6:4
m everyone in his path Joel 2:8

MARDUK
chief Babylonian god Jer 50:2

MARESHAH
1 *father of Hebron* 1 Chr 2:42
2 *son of Laadah* 1 Chr 4:21
3 *town in Judah* 2 Chr 11:5-8

MARK *sign, spot*
m on the foreheads Ezek 9:4
m on his forehead Rev 14:9
m of the beast Rev 19:20

MARK, JOHN
author of Gospel of Mark accompanied Paul and Barnabas Acts 13:5;15:37
cousin of Barnabas Col 4:10

MARKET *selling* or *trading place*
was the **m** of nations Is 23:3
coastlands were . . . **m** Ezek 27:15
idle in the **m** place Matt 20:3
sold in the meat **m** 1 Cor 10:25

MARRIAGE *wedlock*
a **m** alliance with 1 Kin 3:1
nor are given in **m** Matt 22:30
m *be held* in honor Heb 13:4
m supper of the Lamb Rev 19:9

MARRY *join in wedlock*
m-ied foreign wives Ezra 10:10
m-ies a divorced Matt 5:32
better not to **m** Matt 19:10
neither **m**, nor are Mark 12:25
better to **m** than to 1 Cor 7:9

MARTHA
sister of Lazarus and Mary John 11:1,5

MARVEL *be amazed, wonder*
Jesus heard . . . **m-ed** Matt 8:10
the multitude **m-ed** Matt 15:31
Do not **m** that I said John 3:7
m at the sight Acts 7:31

MARY
1 *mother of Jesus* Matt 1:16
2 *Mary Magdalene* Matt 27:56; Mark 15:40
3 *mother of James and Joseph* Matt 27:56; Mark 16:1
4 *sister of Martha and Lazarus* John 11:1
5 *mother of Mark* Acts 12:12
6 *wife of Clopas* John 19:25
7 *Roman believer* Rom 16:6

MASTER *lord, ruler*
God of . . . **m** Abraham Gen 24:12
m shall pierce his ear Ex 21:6
can serve two **m-s** Matt 6:24
death no longer is **m** Rom 6:9
obedient to . . . your **m-s** Eph 6:5
a **M** in heaven Col 4:1

MATTHEW
tax-gatherer Matt 9:9;10:3

apostle Matt 10:3; Luke 6:15

MATTHIAS
replaced Judas Acts 1:23,26

MATURE *full grown* or *stable*
then the **m** grain Mark 4:28
those who are **m** 1 Cor 2:6
your thinking be **m** 1 Cor 14:20
food is for the **m** Heb 5:14
let us press on to **m-ity** Heb 6:1

MEAL *prepared food*
a **m** for enjoyment Eccl 10:19
washed before . . . **m** Luke 11:38
m-s together with Acts 2:46
for a *single* **m** Heb 12:16

MEASURE (n) *amount*
a full and just **m** Deut 25:15
good **m**, pressed Luke 6:38
to each a **m** of faith Rom 12:3
m of Christ's gift Eph 4:7

MEASURE (v) *determine extent*
he stopped **m-ing** *it* Gen 41:49
m their former work Is 65:7
he **m-ed** the gate Ezek 40:13
rod to **m** the city Rev 21:15

MEAT *flesh, food*
Who will give us **m** Num 11:4
LORD . . . you **m** Num 11:18
from **m** sacrificed Acts 21:25
good not to eat **m** Rom 14:21
m sacrificed . . . idols 1 Cor 10:28

MEDE(S)
ancient Indo-Europeans of NW Iran Dan 5:31;11:1

MEDIA
country of the Medes Ezra 6:2; Esth 1:18; Is 21:2

MEDIATOR *intermediary*
by the agency of a **m** Gal 3:19
one **m** . . . between God 1 Tim 2:5
Jesus . . . **m** of a new Heb 12:24

MEDITATE *ponder*
Isaac went out to **m** Gen 24:63
His law he **m-s** day Ps 1:2
M in your heart Ps 4:4
I **m** on Thee in the Ps 63:6

MEDITATION *deep reflection*
m . . . Be acceptable Ps 19:14
m be pleasing to Him Ps 104:34
my **m** all the day Ps 119:97

MEDIUM *summons spirits*
not turn to **m-s** or Lev 19:31
m . . . be put to death Lev 20:27
a **m**, or a spiritist Deut 18:11
woman who is a **m** 1 Sam 28:7
will resort to . . . **m-s** Is 19:3

MEEKNESS *gentleness*
cause of truth and **m** Ps 45:4
m and . . . of Christ 2 Cor 10:1

MEETING *assembly*
house of **m** for all Job 30:23
midst of Thy **m** place Ps 74:4

MEGIDDO
strategic city between Manasseh and Issachar Josh 12:21; 2 Kin 9:27
plain in Jezreel Valley 2 Chr 35:22; Zech 12:11

see also **HAR-MAGEDON**

MELCHIZEDEK
1 *king of Salem* Gen 14:18,19
priest Ps 110:4
2 *type of undying priesthood* Heb 5:6,10;6:20;7:1ff

MELODY *tune*
lyre . . . the sound of **m** Ps 98:5
singing . . . making **m** Eph 5:19

MEMORIAL *commemoration*
this is My **m-name** Ex 3:15
in a book as a **m** Ex 17:14
stones . . . become a **m** Josh 4:7
ascended as a **m** Acts 10:4

MEMORY *remembrance*
M of him perishes Job 18:17
cut off their **m** Ps 109:15
m of the righteous Prov 10:7
spoken of in **m** of Mark 14:9

MEMPHIS
city in Egypt Is 19:13; Jer 46:19; Ezek 30:13

MENSTRUAL
m impurity for seven Lev 15:19
a woman during . . . **m** Ezek 18:6

MENSTRUATION
in the days of her **m** Lev 12:2
like her bed at **m** Lev 15:26

MERCHANDISE *products for sale*
and your **m** Ezek 27:33
a house of **m** John 2:16

MERCHANT *buyer / seller*
m-s procured *them* 1 Kin 10:28
A **m**, in whose hands Hos 12:7
m seeking . . . pearls Matt 13:45
m-s of the earth Rev 18:3

MERCIFUL *compassionate*
God **m** and gracious Ps 86:15
the LORD is . . . and **m** Ps 145:8
The **m** man . . . good Prov 11:17
Blessed are the **m** Matt 5:7
as your Father is **m** Luke 6:36
m to me, the sinner Luke 18:13

MERCY *compassion*
Great are Thy **m-ies** Ps 119:156
in His **m** He redeemed Is 63:9
m to *the* poor Dan 4:27
the orphan finds **m** Hos 14:3
they shall receive **m** Matt 5:7
tender **m** of our God Luke 1:78
m on whom I have **m** Rom 9:15
by the **m-ies** of God Rom 12:1
God, being rich in **m** Eph 2:4

MERCY SEAT *covering over ark*
a **m** of pure gold Ex 25:17
put the **m** on the ark Ex 26:34
in front of the **m** Ex 30:6
sprinkle it on the **m** Lev 16:15
overshadowing the **m** Heb 9:5

MERIBAH
1 *fountain of Rephidim* Ex 17:7
2 *fountain of Kadesh-Barnea* Num 27:14

MERODACH-BALADAN
king of Babylon Is 39:1
also **Berodach-Baladan**

MERRY *joyful, lively*
David . . . making **m** 1 Chr 15:29
wine makes life **m** Eccl 10:19
eat, drink *and* be **m** Luke 12:19
m with my friends Luke 15:29

MESHA
1 *territorial boundary in Arabia* Gen 10:30
2 *Moabite king* 2 Kin 3:4
3 *man of Judah* 1 Chr 2:42
4 *a Benjamite* 1 Chr 8:9

MESOPOTAMIA
land of Tigris and Euphrates Rivers Deut 23:4; Judg 3:8; 1 Chr 19:6; Acts 7:2

MESSAGE *communication*
m from God for you Judg 3:20
m . . . with authority Luke 4:32
m and my preaching 1 Cor 2:4
m we have heard 1 John 1:5

MESSENGER *one sent*
My **m** whom I send Is 42:19
m of the LORD of hosts Mal 2:7
I send My **m** before Matt 11:10
m-s of the churches 2 Cor 8:23
m of Satan 2 Cor 12:7

MESSIAH
anointed one Dan 9:25,26; John 1:41;4:25
Greek: Christ

METHUSELAH
son of Enoch Gen 5:21
grandfather of Noah Gen 5:25ff

MICAH
1 *an Ephraimite* Judg 17:1
2 *line of Reuben* 1 Chr 5:5
3 *father of Abdon* 2 Chr 34:20
4 *prophet* Jer 26:18; Mic 1:1
name of several other people

MICAIAH
1 *prophet* 1 Kin 22:8-26
2 *father of Achbor* 2 Kin 22:12
3 *wife of Rehoboam* 2 Chr 13:2
4 *under Jehoshaphat* 2 Chr 17:7
5 *line of Asaph* Neh 12:35
6 *under Nehemiah* Neh 12:41
7 *son of Gemariah* Jer 36:11

MICHAEL
1 *an archangel* Dan 10:21;12:1; Jude 9; Rev 12:7
2 *Jehoshaphat's son prince of Judah* 2 Chr 21:2
3 *army captain* 1 Chr 12:20
4 *line of Gershom* 1 Chr 6:40
name of seven other people

MIDIAN
1 *a son of Abraham* Gen 25:1,2
2 *land SE of Canaan in desert* Ex 2:15; Num 31:8; Judg 8:28

MIDIANITES
people of Midian Gen 37:36; Num 31:2; Judg 7:7

MIDWIFE *aids childbirth*
m . . . tied a scarlet Gen 38:28
before the **m** can get Ex 1:19

MIGDOL
1 *Israelite camp near Red Sea* Ex 14:2; Num 33:7
2 *town in Egypt* Jer 44:1

MIGHTY *powerful*
a **m** hunter before Gen 10:9
m . . . awesome God Deut 10:17
m men of valor 1 Chr 12:8
The LORD **m** in battle Ps 24:8
a **m** king will rule Is 19:4
m in the Scriptures Acts 18:24
the **m** hand of God 1 Pet 5:6

MILCOM
god of Ammonites 1 Kin 11:5,33; 2 Kin 23:13

MILE *distance, measurement*
one **m**, go with him Matt 5:41
m-s from Jerusalem Luke 24:13

MILK
land flowing with **m** Ex 3:8
m produces butter Prov 30:33
m to drink, not 1 Cor 3:2
pure **m** of the word 1 Pet 2:2

MILL *grinding stones*
sound of the . . . **m** Eccl 12:4
at the grinding **m** Lam 5:13
women . . . at the **m** Matt 24:41

MILLO
1 *fort near Shechem Beth-millo* Judg 9:6,20
2 *fortress in Jerusalem* 2 Sam 5:9; 1 Kin 9:15,24; 1 Chr 11:8; 2 Chr 32:5

MILLSTONE *grinding stone*
upper **m** in pledge Deut 24:6
woman threw . . . **m** Judg 9:53
m be hung around Matt 18:6
stone like a great **m** Rev 18:21

MIND *memory, thought*
God tries the . . . **m-s** Ps 7:9
Recall it to **m** Is 46:8
Let his **m** be changed Dan 4:16
He opened . . . **m-s** Luke 24:45
to a depraved **m** Rom 1:28
m set on the flesh Rom 8:7
the **m** of Christ 1 Cor 2:16
m-s were hardened 2 Cor 3:14
with humility of **m** Phil 2:3

MINDFUL *aware*
Lord be **m** of me Ps 40:17
He is **m** that we are Ps 103:14
LORD has been **m** Ps 115:12
m of the . . . faith 2 Tim 1:5

MINISTER (n) *one who serves*
m-s before the ark 1 Chr 16:4
spoken of *as* **m-s** Is 61:6
a **m** of Christ Jesus Rom 15:16
is Christ then a **m** Gal 2:17
I was made a **m** Eph 3:7
faithful **m** in the Eph 6:21
His **m-s** a flame of Heb 1:7
a **m** in the sanctuary Heb 8:2

MINISTER (v) *give help, serve*
to **m** as priest to Me Ex 28:1
not stand to **m** 1 Kin 8:11
to the LORD, To **m** Is 56:6
angels were **m-ing** Mark 1:13
follow Him and **m** Mark 15:41

MINISTRY *service*
He began His **m** Luke 3:23
to the **m** of the word Acts 6:4
m of the Spirit 2 Cor 3:8
m of reconciliation 2 Cor 5:18
fulfill your **m** 2 Tim 4:5
a more excellent **m** Heb 8:6

MIRACLE *supernatural event*
Work a **m** Ex 7:9
I will perform **m-s** Ex 34:10
m-s had occurred Matt 11:21
He could do no **m** Mark 6:5
perform a **m** in My Mark 9:39
this **m** of healing Acts 4:22
works **m-s** among you Gal 3:5
wonders and . . . **m-s** Heb 2:4

MIRIAM
1 *sister of Moses and Aaron* Ex 15:20; Num 12:4,10;20:1
2 *line of Ezrah* 1 Chr 4:17

MIRROR *image reflector*
see in a **m** dimly 1 Cor 13:12
natural face in a **m** James 1:23

MISCARRIAGE *aborted fetus*
so that she has a **m** Ex 21:22
m-s of a woman Ps 58:8

MISERABLE *bad, unhappy*
loathe this **m** food Num 21:5
m and chronic Deut 28:59
Be **m** and mourn James 4:9
m and poor and blind Rev 3:17

MISERY *sorrow, suffering*
conscious of my **m** Job 10:15
Destruction and **m** Rom 3:16

MISFORTUNE *adversity*
M will not come Jer 5:12
m which He has Jer 26:13

The day of his **m** Obad 12

MISHAEL
1 *of family of Kohath* Ex 6:22; Lev 10:4
2 *associate of Ezra* Neh 8:4
3 *Daniel's friend* Dan 1:6,7,11,19;2:17
also **Meshach**

MISLEAD *lead astray*
m-s a blind *person* Deut 27:18
m-led My people Ezek 13:10
that no one **m-s** you Mark 13:5
m-ing our nation Luke 23:2

MISSILES *what is thrown or shot*
m of the evil *one* Eph 6:16

MISTREAT *treat badly, wrong*
not **m** . . . the stranger Jer 22:3
slaves . . . **m-ed** them Matt 22:6
mocked and **m-ed** Luke 18:32
m and to stone them Acts 14:5

MISTRESS *woman in charge*
her **m** was despised Gen 16:4
m of the house 1 Kin 17:17
the maid like her **m** Is 24:2
the **m** of sorceries Nah 3:4

MIZRAIM
1 *son of Ham* Gen 10:6
father of nations Gen 10:13
2 *Heb. for Egypt* 1 Chr 1:8,11

MOAB
1 *son of Lot* Gen 19:37
2 *country E of the Dead Sea* Ex 15:15; Josh 24:9; Ruth 1:2; 2 Kin 3:7; Ps 60:8; Jer 48:1

MOCK *ridicule, scorn*
lads . . . **m-ed** him 2 Kin 2:23
Fools **m** at sin Prov 14:9
soldiers also **m-ed** Luke 23:36
God is not **m-ed** Gal 6:7

MOCKERY *ridicule*
a **m** of the Egyptians Ex 10:2
made a **m** of me Num 22:29
a **m** of justice Prov 19:28
m *and* insinuations Hab 2:6

MOLECH
god of the Ammonites Lev 18:21; Jer 32:35

MOLTEN *cast metal*
made it into a **m** calf Ex 32:4
make . . . no **m** gods Ex 34:17
destroy . . . **m** images Num 33:52
capitals of **m** bronze 1 Kin 7:16
his **m** images are Jer 10:14

MONEY *currency*
take double *the* **m** Gen 43:12
not sell her for **m** Deut 21:14
loves **m** will not be Eccl 5:10
no **m** in their belt Mark 6:8
m in the bank Luke 19:23
love of **m** is a root 1 Tim 6:10

MONEYCHANGERS
the tables of the **m** Matt 21:12
coins of the **m** John 2:15

MONSTER *enormous animal*
created . . . sea **m-s** Gen 1:21
sea, or the sea **m** Job 7:12
sea **m-s** in the waters Ps 74:13
belly of the sea **m** Matt 12:40

MOON
m and . . . were bowing Gen 37:9
the **m** stopped Josh 10:13
beautiful as . . . **m** Song 6:10
the **m** into blood Joel 2:31
m will not . . . light Matt 24:29

MORALS *principles*
Bad . . . good **m** 1 Cor 15:33

MORIAH
land / mountain where Abraham offered Isaac Gen 22:2
threshing floor of Araunah (Ornan) 2 Sam 24:18
site of Temple 2 Chr 3:1

MORTAL *what eventually dies*
not trust . . . In **m** man Ps 146:3
life to your **m** bodies Rom 8:11
m . . . immortality 1 Cor 15:53
in our **m** flesh 2 Cor 4:11

MOSES
birth Ex 2:1-3
in Pharaoh's care Ex 2:5-10
killed an Egyptian Ex 2:11,12
exiled Ex 2:15
called by God Ex 3:1-22
opposed Pharaoh Ex 5:11
crossed Red Sea Ex 14
Ten Commandments Ex 20:1-18
saw Canaan Deut 3:23ff;34:1ff
death Deut 31:14;34:5

MOTH *insect*
crushed before the **m** Job 4:19
The **m** will eat them Is 50:9
like a **m** to Ephraim Hos 5:12
m and rust destroy Matt 6:19

MOTHER *parent*
leave . . . and his **m** Gen 2:24
m of all *the* living Gen 3:20
Honor . . . and your **m** Ex 20:12
a grief to his **m** Prov 10:1
When His **m** Mary Matt 1:18
take . . . and His **m** Matt 2:13
Who is My **m** Matt 12:48
Honor your . . . **m** Matt 19:19
Behold, your **m** John 19:27

MOTHER-IN-LAW
who lies with his **m** Deut 27:23
Orpah kissed her **m** Ruth 1:14
m lying sick in bed Matt 8:14

MOTIVES *attitudes, intentions*
LORD weighs the **m** Prov 16:2
disclose the **m** of 1 Cor 4:5
than from pure **m** Phil 1:17
ask with wrong **m** James 4:3

MOUND *bank of earth, hill*
cities . . . on their **m-s** Josh 11:13
throw up a **m** 2 Kin 19:32
against the seige **m-s** Jer 33:4

MOUNT (n) *hill, mountain*
In the **m** of the LORD Gen 22:14
Israel at **M** Carmel 1 Kin 18:19
M Zion which He Ps 78:68
M of Olives . . . split Zech 14:4

MOUNT (v) *climb up*
to **m** his chariot 2 Chr 10:18
m up *with* wings Is 40:31
My fury will **m** up Ezek 38:18
m-ed on a donkey Zech 9:9
m-ed on a donkey Matt 21:5

MOUNTAIN
sacrifice on the **m** Gen 31:54
from His holy **m** Ps 3:4
lovely on the **m-s** Is 52:7
m-s will melt Mic 1:4
the **m** will move Zech 14:4
m-s, Fall on us Luke 23:30
withdrew . . . to the **m** John 6:15
faith . . . remove **m-s** 1 Cor 13:2

MOURN *grieve, lament*
m her father and Deut 21:13
A time to **m** Eccl 3:4
comfort all who **m** Is 61:2
Blessed . . . who **m** Matt 5:4
shall **m** and weep Luke 6:25
Be miserable and **m** James 4:9

MOUTH
has made man's **m** Ex 4:11
m condemns you Job 15:6
From the **m** of infants Ps 8:2
Let the words of my **m** Ps 19:14
your **m** is lovely Song 4:3
out of the **m** of God Matt 4:4
confess with your **m** Rom 10:9

MOVE *change position, stir*
Spirit of God . . . **m-ing** Gen 1:2
pillar of cloud **m-d** Ex 14:19
I shall not be **m-d** Ps 10:6
m-d with compassion Mark 1:41
He was deeply **m-d** John 11:33
m-d by the . . . Spirit 2 Pet 1:21

MULE *animal*
mounted his **m** 2 Sam 13:29
Absalom . . . on *his* **m** 2 Sam 18:9
ride on the king's **m** 1 Kin 1:44

MULTIPLY *increase*
Be fruitful and **m** Gen 1:22
the fool **m-ies** words Eccl 10:14
He **m-ies** lies and Hos 12:1
and peace be **m-ied** 2 Pet 1:2

MULTITUDE *crowd, number*
father of a **m** of Gen 17:4
send the **m-s** away Matt 14:15
He summoned the **m** Mark 8:34
cover a **m** of sins James 5:20
love covers a **m** of 1 Pet 4:8

MURDER *premeditated killing*
You shall not **m** Ex 20:13
Whoever commits **m** Matt 5:21
m-ed the prophets Matt 23:31
full of envy, **m** Rom 1:29

MURDERER *killer*
m shall be put to Num 35:30
m from . . . beginning John 8:44
this man is a **m** Acts 28:4
no **m** has eternal 1 John 3:15

MUSIC *harmony, melody*
instruments of **m** 1 Chr 15:16
m to the LORD 2 Chr 7:6
m upon the lyre Ps 92:3
heard **m** and Luke 15:25

MUSICIAN *one skilled in music*
m, a mighty man 1 Sam 16:18
the **m-s** after *them* Ps 68:25
harpists and **m-s** Rev 18:22

MUSTARD *type of plant*
kingdom . . . like a **m** Matt 13:31
faith as a **m** seed Matt 17:20
It is like a **m** seed Luke 13:19

MUZZLE *gag*
shall not **m** the ox Deut 25:4
guard . . . as with a **m** Ps 39:1

MYRIADS *countless*
chariots . . . are **m** Ps 68:17
m of angels Heb 12:22
number . . . was **m** Rev 5:11

MYRRH *spice*
aromatic gum . . . **m** Gen 43:11
Dripping with . . . **m** Song 5:13
frankincense and **m** Matt 2:11
mixture of **m** and John 19:39

MYRTLE *type of plant*
the **m**, and the olive Is 41:19
among the **m** trees Zech 1:11

MYSTERY *hidden truth, secret*
no **m** baffles you Dan 4:9
God's wisdom in a **m** 1 Cor 2:7
into the **m** of Christ Eph 3:4
the **m** of the gospel Eph 6:19
the **m** of the faith 1 Tim 3:9

MYTHS *fables*
to pay attention to **m** 1 Tim 1:4
will turn aside to **m** 2 Tim 4:4
attention to Jewish **m** Titus 1:14

N

NADAB
1 *son of Aaron* Ex 6:23
2 *king of Israel* 1 Kin 14:20
3 *son of Shammai* 1 Chr 2:28
4 *son of Jehiel* 1 Chr 8:29,30

NAHOR
1 *Abram's grandfather* Gen 11:24ff
2 *brother of Abram* Gen 11:27;22:23
3 *city in N Mesopotamia* Gen 24:10

NAILED (v) *attached*
you **n** to a cross Acts 2:23
n it to the cross Col 2:14

NAILS (n) *finger ends* or *pins*
and trim her **n** Deut 21:12
fasten it with **n** Jer 10:4
imprint of the **n** John 20:25

NAIVE *simple, not suspicious*
prudence to the **n** Prov 1:4
n believes everything Prov 14:15
the **n** becomes wise Prov 21:11
goes astray or is **n** Ezek 45:20

NAKED *unclothed*
n and . . . not ashamed Gen 2:25
n I shall return there Job 1:21
n . . . you clothed Me Matt 25:36

NAKEDNESS *nudity*
the **n** of his father Gen 9:22
n of . . . father's sister Lev 18:12
Your **n** . . . be uncovered Is 47:3
shame of your **n** Rev 3:18

NAME *designation, title*
man gave **n-s** to all Gen 2:20
takes His **n** in vain Ex 20:7
blot out his **n** Deut 29:20
How majestic is Thy **n** Ps 8:1
sing praises to Thy **n** Ps 18:49
LORD, that is My **n** Is 42:8
Hallowed be Thy **n** Matt 6:9
such child in My **n** Matt 18:5
n-s are recorded Luke 10:20
will come in My **n** Luke 21:8
baptized in the **n** Acts 2:38
other **n** under heaven Acts 4:12
n-s are in the book Phil 4:3

NAOMI
woman of Bethlehem Ruth 1:1
Ruth's mother-in-law Ruth 1:4,6

NAPHTALI
1 *son of Jacob* Gen 30:8
2 *tribe / district* Num 13:14; 1 Chr 2:2; Rev 7:6

NARD *fragrant ointment*
henna with **n** plants Song 4:13
perfume of pure **n** John 12:3

NATHANAEL
disciple of Jesus John 1:49

NATION *government, people*
make you a great **n** Gen 12:2
priests and a holy **n** Ex 19:6
scatter . . . the **n-s** Lev 26:33
the **n-s** in an uproar Ps 2:1
n-s . . . fear the name Ps 102:15
N will not lift up sword Is 2:4
glory among the **n-s** Is 66:19
n should not perish John 11:50
men, from every **n** Acts 2:5
tongue . . . people and **n** Rev 5:9

NATURAL *normal*
died a **n** death Ezek 44:31
n man . . . not accept 1 Cor 2:14
is sown a **n** body 1 Cor 15:44

NAZARENE
1 *of Nazareth* John 18:7
2 *follower of Jesus* Acts 24:5

NAZARETH
town of Galilee Matt 2:23
home of Joseph, Mary, and Jesus Luke 4:16; John 1:45

NAZIRITE
1 *one consecrated to God* Num 6:2,19,20
2 *religious vow* Judg 13:5,7; Amos 2:11,12

NEBO
1 *Moabite town* Num 32:38
2 *mountain where Moses viewed promised land* Deut 32:49; 34:1
3 *Babylonian god* Is 46:1
4 *town W of Jordan* Ezra 2:29; Neh 7:33
5 *Jew whose sons married foreign wives* Ezra 10:43

NEBUCHADNEZZAR
king of Babylon 2 Kin 24:1,10
captured Judah 1 Chr 6:15; Ezra 2:1

NECKLACE *neck ornament*
n around his neck Gen 41:42
earrings and **n-s** Num 31:50
pride is their **n** Ps 73:6

NEED *necessity, obligation*
sufficient for his **n** Deut 15:8
ministered to . . . **n-s** Acts 20:34
n-s of the saints 2 Cor 9:12
supply all your **n-s** Phil 4:19

NEEDLE
the eye of a **n** Matt 19:24
n than for a rich Mark 10:25

NEEDY *destitute, poor*
to your **n** and poor Deut 15:11
a father to the **n** Job 29:16
n will not always be Ps 9:18
the LORD hears the **n** Ps 69:33
n will lie down in Is 14:30

NEGEV
S desert region Gen 12:9; Judg 1:9; Jer 32:44

NEGLECT *disregard, ignore*
You **n-ed** the Rock Deut 32:18
who **n-s** discipline Prov 15:32
n so great a salvation Heb 2:3
n to show hospitality Heb 13:2
do not **n** doing good Heb 13:16

NEHEMIAH
1 *Jewish exile* Ezra 2:2; Neh 7:7
2 *son of Azbuk* Neh 3:16
3 *son of Hacaliah* Neh 1:1
rebuilt walls Neh 3:1ff
governor of Jerusalem Neh 8:9

NEIGHBOR *one living nearby*
not covet . . . **n-'s** wife Ex 20:17
shall love your **n** Lev 19:18
make your **n-s** drink Hab 2:15
love your **n**, and Matt 5:43
And who is my **n** Luke 10:29
love your **n** as Gal 5:14

NEPHILIM
people of great stature Gen 6:4; Num 13:33

NEST
n is set in the cliff Num 24:21
n among the stars Obad 4
birds . . . *have* **n-s** Matt 8:20

NET *snare*
a **n** for my steps Ps 57:6
an antelope in a **n** Is 51:20
casting a **n** into Matt 4:18

left the **n-s** and Mark 1:18
n *full* of fish John 21:8

NEW *fresh, recent*
nothing **n** under the Eccl 1:9
a **n** spirit within Ezek 11:19
n wine into old Mark 2:22
A **n** commandment John 13:34
he is a **n** creature 2 Cor 5:17
a **n** and living way Heb 10:20
making all things **n** Rev 21:5

NEWS *report, tidings*
a day of good **n** 2 Kin 7:9
Good **n** puts fat on Prov 15:30
the **n** about Jesus Matt 14:1
n about Him went Mark 1:28
n of a great joy Luke 2:10
n of your faith 1 Thess 3:6

NICODEMUS
Pharisee John 3:1,4,9
in Sanhedrin John 7:50; 19:39

NIGHT *darkness*
darkness He called **n** Gen 1:5
pillar of fire by **n** Ex 13:21
meditate . . . day and **n** Josh 1:8
make **n** into day Job 17:12
At **n** my soul longs Is 26:9
over their flock by **n** Luke 2:8
a thief in the **n** 1 Thess 5:2
tormented day and **n** Rev 20:10

NILE
river of Egypt Gen 41:1; Ex 1:22;7:20; Is 23:10

NINEVAH
capital of Assyria 2 Kin 19:36
visited by Jonah Jon 1:1ff

NISAN
first month of the Hebrew calendar Neh 2:1; Esth 3:7

NOAH
1 *son of Lamech* Gen 5:28,29
father of Shem, Ham, Japeth Gen 5:32
built an ark Gen 6:14-22
saved from Flood Gen 6:9;7:15;8:1;8:13
promised by God Gen 9:9-17
2 *daughter of Zelophehad* Num 26:33;27:1;36:11

NOBLE *lofty, renowned one*
king's most **n** princes Esth 6:9
speak **n** things Prov 8:6
all the **n-s** of Judah Jer 39:6

NOBLEMAN *man of high rank*
the house of the **n** Job 21:28
A certain **n** went to Luke 19:12

NOMADS *desert wanderers*
n of the desert bow Ps 72:9

NORTH *direction of compass*
stretches out the **n** Job 26:7
king of the **N** will Dan 11:13
three gates on the **n** Rev 21:13

NOSTRILS *nose*
breathed into his **n** Gen 2:7
breath of His **n** 2 Sam 22:16
breath of God . . . my **n** Job 27:3

NOURISH *feed, sustain*
n-es and cherishes it Eph 5:29
constantly **n-ed** on 1 Tim 4:6
she might be **n-ed** Rev 12:6

NULLIFY *annul, make void*
LORD **n-ies** the counsel Ps 33:10
unbelief will not **n** Rom 3:3
the promise is **n-ied** Rom 4:14
n the grace of God Gal 2:21

NUMBER (n) *group, total*
their **n** according to Num 29:21
the **n** of the stars Ps 147:4
increasing in **n** daily Acts 16:5
his **n** is six hundred Rev 13:18

NUMBER (v) *count, enumerate*
n . . . by their armies Num 1:3
Thou dost **n** my steps Job 14:16
hairs . . . all **n-ed** Matt 10:30

NURSE (n) *attendant*
Deborah, Rebekah's **n** Gen 35:8
and call a **n** for you Ex 2:7
n carries a nursing Num 11:12
n in the bedroom 2 Kin 11:2

NURSE (v) *suckle an infant*
Sarah . . . **n** children Gen 21:7
the child and **n-d** him Ex 2:9
morning to **n** my son 1 Kin 3:21
who **n** babes in Mark 13:17
breasts . . . never **n** Luke 23:29

O

OAK *type of tree*
by the **o-s** of Mamre Gen 13:18
the diviners' **o** Judg 9:37
o-s of righteousness Is 61:3
strong as the **o-s** Amos 2:9

OATH *declaration, vow*
confirm the **o** which Deut 9:5
free from the **o** Josh 2:20
make no **o** at all Matt 5:34
priests without an **o** Heb 7:21

OBADIAH
1 *in Ahab's court* 1 Kin 18:3ff
2 *Gadite warrior* 1 Chr 12:8,9
3 *sent to teach* 2 Chr 17:7
4 *Levite, of Merari* 2 Chr 34:12
5 *son of Jehiel* Ezra 8:9
6 *signer of covenant* Neh 10:1,5
7 *prophet* Obad 1
name of five other Old Testament people

OBED
1 *son of Ruth / Boaz* Ruth 4:17
ancestor of Jesus Matt 1:5; Luke 3:32
2 *son of Ephlal* 1 Chr 2:37
3 *warrior* 1 Chr 11:26,47
4 *temple gatekeeper* 1 Chr 26:1,7
5 *father of Azariah* 2 Chr 23:1

OBEDIENCE *submission*
the **o** of the peoples Gen 49:10
pretend **o** to me 2 Sam 22:45
the **o** of the One Rom 5:19
leading to **o** of faith Rom 16:26
in **o** to the truth 1 Pet 1:22

OBEY *follow commands* or *orders*
have **o-ed** My voice Gen 22:18
o My voice and keep Ex 19:5
o the LORD Deut 27:10
to **o** is better than 1 Sam 15:22
and the sea **o** Him Matt 8:27
o God rather than Acts 5:29
o your parents Eph 6:1
O your leaders Heb 13:17
may **o** Jesus Christ 1 Pet 1:2

OBJECT *implement* or *goal*
struck . . . an iron **o** Num 35:16
an **o** of loathing to Ps 88:8
o like a great sheet Acts 10:11
god or **o** of worship 2 Thess 2:4

OBLIGATION *duty*
o toward the LORD Num 32:22
for his daily **o-s** 2 Chr 31:16
under **o**, not to the Rom 8:12
o to keep the . . . Law Gal 5:3

OBSERVE *keep* or *notice*
surely **o** My sabbaths Ex 31:13
o all My statutes Lev 19:37
you may **o** discretion Prov 5:2
the ant . . . **O** her ways Prov 6:6
O how the lilies Matt 6:28
the word . . . **o** it Luke 11:28
o days and months Gal 4:10

OBSTACLE *hindrance*
Remove *every* **o** out of Is 57:14
an **o** or a stumbling Rom 14:13

OBSTINATE *stubborn*
you are an **o** people Ex 33:3
made his heart **o** Deut 2:30
Israel is . . . **o** Ezek 3:7
disobedient and **o** Rom 10:21

OBTAIN *get possession of*
o children through Gen 16:2
finds a wife . . . **o-s** Prov 18:22
may **o** eternal life Matt 19:16
o the gift of God Acts 8:20
for **o-ing** salvation 1 Thess 5:9

ODIOUS *offensive*
o in Pharaoh's sight Ex 5:21
o to the Philistines 1 Sam 13:4

OFFEND *insult* or *violate*
I will not **o** *anymore* Job 34:31
A brother **o-ed** *is* Prov 18:19
Pharisees were **o-ed** Matt 15:12

OFFENSE *anger* or *transgression*
of my *own* **o-s** Gen 41:9
they took **o** at Him Matt 13:57
of the **o** of Adam Rom 5:14
and a rock of **o** 1 Pet 2:8

OFFER (v) *give, present*
o him . . . as a burnt Gen 22:2
O to God a sacrifice Ps 50:14
my mouth **o-s** praises Ps 63:5
o both gifts and Heb 5:1
o-ed Himself Heb 9:14
prayer **o-ed** in faith James 5:15
o . . . spiritual sacrifices 1 Pet 2:5

OFFERING (n) *contribution*
freewill **o** to the LORD Ex 35:29
o of first fruits Lev 2:12
your worthless **o-s** Is 1:13
presenting your **o** Matt 5:23
any **o** for sin Heb 10:18

OFFERINGS
1 **Burnt Offering** Gen 22:13; Lev 1:17
2 **Drink Offering** Phil 2:17; 2 Tim 4:6
also **Libation**
3 **Freewill Offering** Ex 35:29; Lev 7:16
4 **Grain Offering** Lev 9:4; Josh 22:29
also **Meal Offering**
5 **Guilt Offering** Lev 5:6; Num 6:12
6 **Heave Offering** Ex 29:27,28
7 **Libation Offering** Num 6:15,17;28:9,10
also **Drink Offering**
8 **Meal Offering** 2 Kin 16:15; Ps 40:6
also **Grain Offering**
9 **Ordination Offering** Lev 8:28,31
10 **Peace Offering** Lev 4:31; Num 6:14
11 **Sin Offering** Ex 29:14; Ezek 46:20
12 **Thank Offering** 2 Chr 33:16; Jer 33:11
13 **Votive Offering** Deut 12:26;23:18
14 **Wave Offering** Lev 14:12; Num 18:18

OFFICE *function* or *position*
wield the staff of **o** Judg 5:14
priests in their **o-s** 2 Chr 35:2
sitting in the tax **o** Luke 5:27
to the **o** of overseer 1 Tim 3:1

OFFICIAL *one in authority*
o-s in the palace 2 Kin 20:18
o of the synagogue Luke 8:41

OFFSPRING *descendants*
o in place of Abel Gen 4:25
bring forth **o** from Is 65:9
Being . . . the **o** of God Acts 17:29

you are Abraham's **o** Gal 3:29
and the **o** of David Rev 22:16

OIL
o for lighting Ex 25:6
anointed my head . . . **o** Ps 23:5
the **o** of joy Ps 45:7
prudent took **o** in Matt 25:4
not anoint . . . with **o** Luke 7:46

OLD *aged, obsolete*
too **o** to have a Ruth 1:12
honor of **o** men Prov 20:29
o men will dream Joel 2:28
wine into **o** wineskins Matt 9:17
o self was crucified Rom 6:6
o things passed away 2 Cor 5:17
serpent of **o** . . . devil Rev 12:9

OLIVE *tree* or *fruit*
freshly picked **o** leaf Gen 8:11
land of **o** oil and Deut 8:8
cherubim of **o** wood 1 Kin 6:23
children like **o** plants Ps 128:3

OLIVES, MOUNT OF
mountain E of Jerusalem 2 Sam 15:30; Zech 14:4; Matt 24:3; Mark 11:1
place where Jesus prayed Matt 26:30; Luke 22:39-41

OMEGA
last letter of Gr. alphabet Rev 1:8
title of Jesus Christ Rev 21:6
expresses eternalness of God Rev 22:13

OMEN *foretells a future event*
who interprets **o-s** Deut 18:10
took this as an **o** 1 Kin 20:33

OMER *dry measure*
take an **o** apiece Ex 16:16
o is a tenth of an Ex 16:36

OMRI
1 *king of Israel* 1 Kin 16:22ff
2 *a Benjamite* 1 Chr 7:8
3 *line of Perez* 1 Chr 9:4
4 *son of Michael* 1 Chr 27:18

ONE *single unit*
shall become **o** flesh Gen 2:24
God, the LORD is **o** Deut 6:4
Holy **O** of Israel Ps 71:22
Are You the . . . **O** Matt 11:3
I . . . Father are **o** John 10:30
they may all be **o** John 17:21
o body in Christ Rom 12:5
o died for all 2 Cor 5:14
o Lord, **o** faith Eph 4:5
o God . . . **o** mediator 1 Tim 2:5
husband of **o** wife 1 Tim 3:2

ONYX *precious stone*
bdellium and the **o** Gen 2:12
o, and the jasper Ezek 28:13

OPEN (adj) *not shut, exposed*
throat is an **o** grave Ps 5:9
Better is **o** rebuke Prov 27:5
before you an **o** door Rev 3:8

OPEN (v) *expose, free, unfasten*
eyes will be **o-ed** Gen 3:5
Ezra **o-ed** the book Neh 8:5
O Lord, **o** my lips Ps 51:15
O my eyes, that I Ps 119:18
To **o** blind eyes Is 42:7
o . . . windows of heaven Mal 3:10
o-ed a door of faith Acts 14:27
and **o-s** the door Rev 3:20

OPHEL
citadel on S slope of Temple Mount in Jeruslaem 2 Chr 27:3; 33:14; Neh 3:27
home of temple servants (Nethinim) Neh 3:26; 11:21

OPPOSE *contend, resist*
o the Prince of Dan 8:25
o-d the ordinance of Rom 13:2
men also **o** the truth 2 Tim 3:8
God is **o-d** to the James 4:6

OPPOSITION *hostility*
you . . . know My **o** Num 14:34
these are in **o** Gal 5:17
gospel . . . much **o** 1 Thess 2:2

OPPRESS (v) *trouble, tyrannize*
enslaved and **o-ed** Gen 15:13
Egyptians are **o-ing** Ex 3:9
not **o** your neighbor Lev 19:13
woman **o-ed** in 1 Sam 1:15
do not **o** the widow Zech 7:10
healing all . . . **o-ed** Acts 10:38
the rich who **o** you James 2:6

OPPRESSED (n) *afflicted*
stronghold for the **o** Ps 9:9
justice for the **o** Ps 146:7
let the **o** go free Is 58:6
devour . . . **o** in secret Hab 3:14
vengeance for the **o** Acts 7:24

OPPRESSION *affliction*
Do not trust in **o** Ps 62:10
o makes a . . . man mad Eccl 7:7
and water of **o** Is 30:20
o of My people Acts 7:34

OPPRESSOR *one who afflicts*
And crush the **o** Ps 72:4
a great **o** lacks Prov 28:16
punish all their **o-s** Jer 30:20

ORACLE *revelation*
The **o** of Balaam Num 24:3
o concerning Babylon Is 13:1
the **o** of the LORD Jer 23:33
and misleading **o-s** Lam 2:14
entrusted with the **o-s** Rom 3:2

ORDAIN *invest, set apart*
anoint . . . and **o** them Ex 28:41
o Aaron and his sons Ex 29:9
o-ed His covenant Ps 111:19
law as **o-ed** by angels Acts 7:53

ORDEAL *difficulty, trial*
great **o** of affliction 2 Cor 8:2
at the fiery **o** 1 Pet 4:12

ORDER (n) *arrangement*
Set your house in **o** 2 Kin 20:1
fixed **o** of the moon Jer 31:35
the **o** of Melchizedek Heb 5:6

ORDER (v) *command* or *request, arrange*
I will **o** *my prayer* Ps 5:3
o-ed him to tell no Luke 5:14
confidence . . . to **o** you Philem 8

ORDINANCE *statute*
o of the Passover Ex 12:43
they rejected My **o-s** Lev 26:43
o-s of the heavens Job 38:33
opposed the **o** of God Rom 13:2

ORDINATION
Aaron's ram of **o** Ex 29:26
and the **o** offering Lev 7:37
period of your **o** Lev 8:33

ORIGIN *beginning, source*
of Jewish **o** Esth 6:13
o is from antiquity Is 23:7
Your **o** and your Ezek 16:3

ORNAN
Jebusite owner of threshing floor on Mount Moriah 1 Chr 21:15,18
sells threshing floor to David for altar and temple 1 Chr 21:25,28

ORPHAN *fatherless child*
not afflict any . . . **o** Ex 22:22
justice for the **o** Deut 10:18

helper of the **o** Ps 10:14
may plunder the **o-s** Is 10:2
Leave . . . **o-s** behind Jer 49:11
visit **o-s** and widows James 1:27

OSTRICH *bird*
the **o** and the owl Lev 11:16
a companion of **o-es** Job 30:29
cruel Like **o-es** Lam 4:3
mourning like the **o-es** Mic 1:8

OUTCAST *rejected*
the **o-s** of Israel Ps 147:2
Hide the **o-s** Is 16:3
called you an **o** Jer 30:17
o-s from . . . synagogue John 16:2

OUTCRY *strong cry* or *protest*
no **o** in our streets Ps 144:14
o is heard among the Jer 50:46
a *single* **o** arose Acts 19:34

OUTSIDER *stranger*
o may not come near Num 18:4
toward **o-s** 1 Thess 4:12

OUTSTRETCHED *extended*
redeem . . . with an **o** arm Ex 6:6
war . . . with an **o** hand Jer 21:5

OVEN *baking, cooking vessel*
appeared a . . . **o** Gen 15:17
make them as a fiery **o** Ps 21:9

OVERCOME *conquer, master*
a man **o** with wine Jer 23:9
I have **o** the world John 16:33
but **o** evil with good Rom 12:21
have **o** the evil one 1 John 2:13
who **o-s** shall inherit Rev 21:7

OVERFLOW *flood, inundate*
My cup **o-s** Ps 23:5
waters shall **o** the Is 28:17
I am **o-ing** with joy 2 Cor 7:4
o-ing with gratitude Col 2:7

OVERLAID *decorate, spread*
o . . . with gold 1 Kin 6:28
vessel **o** with silver Prov 26:23
o with gold . . . silver Hab 2:19

OVERPOWER *subdue*
deceive you and **o** you Obad 7
Hades shall not **o** Matt 16:18
attacks him and **o-s** Luke 11:22

OVERSEER *director, leader*
o in the house of Jer 29:26
the **o-s** and deacons Phil 1:1
the office of **o** 1 Tim 3:1
o . . . above reproach Titus 1:7

OVERSHADOW *engulf, obscure*
Most High . . . **o** you Luke 1:35
o-ing the mercy seat Heb 9:5

OWE *be indebted*
Pay . . . what you **o** Matt 18:28
O nothing to anyone Rom 13:8
that you **o** to me Philem 19

OWL *bird*
the **o**, the sea gull Deut 14:15
o of the waste places Ps 102:6
houses . . . full of **o-s** Is 13:21

OWN (adj) *belonging to*
man in His **o** image Gen 1:27
led . . . His **o** people Ps 78:52
in his **o** language Acts 2:6

OWN (n) *belonging to*
He came to His **o** John 1:11
provide for his **o** 1 Tim 5:8

OWNER *possessor*
restitution to its **o** Ex 22:12
when the **o** . . . comes Matt 21:40

who were **o-s** of land Acts 4:34

OX *bull used as draft animal*
oxen and donkeys Gen 12:16
servant or his **o** Ex 20:17
horns of the wild **oxen** Ps 22:21
not muzzle the **o** 1 Tim 5:8

P

PACT *agreement*
Sheol we . . . made a **p** Is 28:15
p with Sheol shall Is 28:18

PADDAN-ARAM
NW Mesopotamia Gen 25:20
home of Laban Gen 28:5
birthplace of most of Jacob's sons Gen 35:22-26

PAIN *discomfort, hurt*
multiply Your **p** Gen 3:16
p-s came upon her 1 Sam 4:19
rejoice in unsparing **p** Job 6:10
rest from your **p** Is 14:3
Your **p** is incurable Jer 30:15
bring **p** to my soul Lam 3:51
suffering great **p** Matt 8:6
no longer be . . . **p** Rev 21:4

PALACE *royal residence*
build . . . royal **p** 2 Chr 2:12
to the king's **p** Esth 2:8
Out of ivory **p-s** Ps 45:8
A **p** of strangers Is 25:2
luxury . . . royal **p-s** Luke 7:25

PALLET *bed, mat*
they let down the **p** Mark 2:4
take up your **p** and Mark 2:9

PALM *type of tree*
the city of **p** trees Deut 34:3
flourish like the **p** Ps 92:12
branches of the **p** John 12:13

PANGS *sudden pains*
beginning of birth **p** Mark 13:8
like birth **p** 1 Thess 5:3

PANIC *fear*
P seized them there Ps 48:6
P and pitfall have Lam 3:47
great **p** . . . will fall Zech 14:13

PANT *breathe rapidly*
deer **p-s** for the water Ps 42:1
my soul **p-s** for Thee Ps 42:1
I will both gasp and **p** Is 42:14

PAPYRUS *reed plant*
p . . . without marsh Job 8:11
Even in **p** vessels Is 18:2

PARABLE *story for illustration*
speak a **p** to Ezek 17:2
p of the sower Matt 13:18
heard His **p-s** Matt 21:45
p from the fig tree Mark 13:28
spoke by way of a **p** Luke 8:4

PARADISE
abode of the righteous dead Luke 23:43; 2 Cor 12:4

PARALYTIC
said to the **p**--Rise Matt 9:6
p, carried by four Mark 2:3

PARDON *forgive, release*
he will not **p** your Ex 23:21
May the . . . LORD **p** 2 Chr 30:18
O LORD, **P** my iniquity Ps 25:11
He will abundantly **p** Is 55:7
p, and you will be Luke 6:37

PARENTS *father and mother*
rise up against **p** Matt 10:21
left house or . . . **p** Luke 18:29
evil, disobedient to **p** Rom 1:30
Children, obey your **p** Eph 6:1
disobedient to **p** 2 Tim 3:2

PARTAKERS *participators*
do not be **p** with Eph 5:7
become **p** of Christ Heb 3:14
p of the Holy Spirit Heb 6:4
p of *the* divine nature 2 Pet 1:4

PARTIAL *favoring*
not be **p** to the poor Lev 19:15
you shall not be **p** Deut 16:19
now be **p** to no one Job 32:21
You are not **p** Matt 22:16

PARTIALITY *favoritism*
show **p** in judgment Deut 1:17
p is not good Prov 28:21
God shows no **p** Gal 2:6

PARTICIPATE *take part*
not **p** . . . deeds of Eph 5:11
p-s in his evil deeds 2 John 11
may not **p** in her sins Rev 18:4

PARTNER *comrade*
is a **p** with a thief Prov 29:24
been **p-s** with them Matt 23:30
regard me a **p** Philem 17

PASS *proceed*
LORD will **p** over the Ex 12:23
My glory is **p-ing** by Ex 33:22
words shall not **p** Matt 24:35
this cup **p** from Me Matt 26:39
p-ed out of death John 5:24
old things **p-ed** away 2 Cor 5:17

PASSION *desire, lust*
p is rottenness to Prov 14:30
over to degrading **p-s** Rom 1:26
flesh with its **p-s** Gal 5:24
dead to . . . **p** Col 3:5
not in lustful **p** 1 Thess 4:5

PASSOVER
Israel's firstborn protected from the plague of death prior to the exodus from Egypt Ex 12:1-30
Feast commemorating Israelite exodus and protection from death Ex 12:42,43; Lev 23:5; Num 9:2,12,14; Matt 26:2,18; John 19:14; Acts 12:4

PASTORS *shepherds of people*
and some *as* **p** Eph 4:11

PASTURE (n) *grazing field*
lie down in green **p-s** Ps 23:2
sheep of Thy **p** Ps 79:13

PASTURE (v) *feed, graze*
Moses . . . **p-ing** the flock Ex 3:1
They will **p** on it Zeph 2:7
So I **p-d** the flock Zech 11:7

PATCH *mending cloth*
p of unshrunk cloth Matt 9:16
p pulls away from it Mark 2:21

PATH *way*
snake in the **p** Gen 49:17
the **p** of life Ps 16:11
a light to my **p** Ps 119:105
p of the upright is Prov 15:19
Make His **p-s** straight Matt 3:3

PATIENCE *endurance*
try the **p** of men Is 7:13
in **p**, in kindness 2 Cor 6:6
love, joy, peace, **p** Gal 5:22
exhort, with great **p** 2 Tim 4:2
endure it with **p** 1 Pet 2:20

PATIENT *bearing, enduring*
Love is **p**, love is 1 Cor 13:4
p when wronged 2 Tim 2:24
Lord . . . is **p** toward 2 Pet 3:9

PATRIARCH *father of clan*
regarding the **p** David Acts 2:29
the twelve **p-s** Acts 7:8
Abraham, the **p**, gave Heb 7:4

PAUL
heritage Acts 21:39;22:3; Phil 3:5
persecuted believers Acts 7:58;8:1,3;9:1,2
conversion and call Acts 9:1-19
name changed Acts 13:9
Jerusalem council Acts 15:2-6
missionary journeys Acts 13:1ff;15:36ff; 18:23ff
apostolic defense Acts 11:5ff; Gal 1:13ff
arrest and imprisonment Acts 21:33; 22:24-28:31
defense Acts 22:1ff;24:10ff; 25:10,11
final journey to Rome Acts 27,28

PAVEMENT *paved road*
on a **p** of stone 2 Kin 16:17
mosaic **p** of porphyry Esth 1:6
place called The **P** John 19:13

PAY *give what is due*
thief . . . **p** double Ex 22:7
p Thee my vows Ps 66:13
P back what you Matt 18:28
Never **p** back evil Rom 12:17
p the penalty 2 Thess 1:9

PEACE *calmness, tranquility*
grant **p** in the land Lev 26:6
made **p** with David 1 Chr 19:19
for the **p** of Jerusalem Ps 122:6
a time for **p** Eccl 3:8
Prince of **P** Is 9:6
p . . . like a river Is 66:12
have withdrawn My **p** Jer 16:5
not come to bring **p** Matt 10:34
P I leave with you John 14:27
we have **p** with God Rom 5:1
love, joy, **p** Gal 5:22
He Himself is our **p** Eph 2:14
gospel of **p** Eph 6:15
p of God . . . surpasses Phil 4:7
p through the blood Col 1:20
take **p** from the earth Rev 6:4

PEACEMAKERS
Blessed are the **p** Matt 5:9

PEARL *precious gem*
wisdom is above . . . **p-s** Job 28:18
p-s before swine Matt 7:6
one **p** of great value Matt 13:46

PENALTY *punishment*
you will bear the **p** Ezek 23:49
pay the **p** of eternal 2 Thess 1:9

PENIEL
where Jacob wrestled with God Gen 32:30

PENTECOST
Jewish feast held 50 days after Passover Acts 20:16; 1 Cor 16:8
coming of the Holy Spirit Acts 2:1

PENUEL
1 *tower destroyed* Judg 8:17
rebuilt 1 Kin 12:25
2 *father of Gedor* 1 Chr 4:4
3 *son of Shashak* 1 Chr 8:25

PEOPLE *group, nation*
they are one **p** Gen 11:6
Let My **p** go Ex 5:1
blessed above all **p-s** Deut 7:14
Forgive Thy **p** Israel Deut 21:8
LORD loves His **p** 2 Chr 2:11
We are His **p** Ps 100:3
LORD will judge His **p** Ps 135:14
p whom I formed Is 43:21
they feared the **p** Luke 20:19
should die for the **p** John 11:50
not rejected His **p** Rom 11:2

every tribe and **p** Rev 13:7

PERCEIVE *be aware, discern*
p-d all the wisdom 1 Kin 10:4
listening, but do not **p** Is 6:9
p-ing in Himself Mark 5:30
p with their heart John 12:40

PERDITION *damnation*
the son of **p** John 17:12

PEREZ
son of Judah Gen 38:29

PERFECT (adj) *flawless*
His work is **p** Deut 32:4
law of the LORD is **p** Ps 19:7
heavenly Father is **p** Matt 5:48
p bond of unity Col 3:14
be **p** and complete James 1:4
p love casts out 1 John 4:18

PERFECTED *completed*
is **p** in weakness 2 Cor 12:9
love is **p** with us 1 John 4:17

PERFORM *carry out*
I will **p** miracles Ex 34:10
p-s righteous deeds Ps 103:6
p a miracle in My Mark 9:39
John **p-ed** no sign John 10:41
p-ing great wonders Acts 6:8

PERFUME *fragrant oil*
and **p** make the heart Prov 27:9
instead of sweet **p** Is 3:24
p upon My body Matt 26:12
anointed . . . with **p** Luke 7:46
prepared . . . **p-s** Luke 23:56

PERISH *be destroyed*
we **p**, we are dying Num 17:12
weapons . . . **p-ed** 2 Sam 1:27
if I **p**, I **p** Esth 4:16
the wicked will **p** Ps 1:6
rod of his fury will **p** Prov 22:8
little ones **p** Matt 18:14
p, but have eternal John 3:16
for any to **p** 2 Pet 3:9

PERMANENT *lasting*
it is a **p** ordinance Lev 6:18
p right of redemption Lev 25:32
use them as **p** slaves Lev 25:46
p home for the ark 1 Chr 28:2

PERMISSION *consent*
p they had from Cyrus Ezra 3:7
He gave them **p** Mark 5:13
he had given him **p** Acts 21:40

PERMIT *allow*
not **p-ting** . . . demons Mark 1:34
p the children Mark 10:14
Spirit . . . did not **p** Acts 16:7
if the Lord **p-s** 1 Cor 16:7

PERPETUAL *lasting*
p incense before the Ex 30:8
as a **p** covenant Ex 31:16
for a **p** priesthood Ex 40:15
may sleep a **p** sleep Jer 51:39

PERSECUTE *afflict, oppress*
Why do you **p** me Job 19:22
has **p-d** my soul Ps 143:3
pray for those who **p** Matt 5:44
p you in this city Matt 10:23
why are you **p-ing** Me Acts 9:4
used to **p** the church Gal 1:13

PERSECUTION *oppression*
p arises because of Mark 4:17
p arose against the Acts 8:1
a **p** against Paul Acts 13:50
distress, or **p**, or Rom 8:35

PERSEVERANCE *persistence*
by **p** in doing good Rom 2:7
tribulation brings . . . **p** Rom 5:3
for your **p** and faith 2 Thess 1:4
p of the saints Rev 14:12

PERSUADE *convince, prevail on*
a ruler may be **p-d** Prov 25:15
trying to **p** Jews and Acts 18:4
p-s men to worship Acts 18:13
you will **p** me Acts 26:28

PERVERSE *corrupt*
a **p** and crooked Deut 32:5
A **p** heart shall depart Ps 101:4
mind will utter **p** Prov 23:33
and **p** generation Phil 2:15

PERVERT *distort, misdirect*
not **p** the justice Ex 23:6
Does God **p** justice Job 8:3
have **p-ed** their way Jer 3:21

PESTILENCE *epidemic, plague*
LORD sent a **p** 2 Sam 24:15
sword, famine, and **p** Jer 27:13
p and mourning and Rev 18:8

PETER
heritage and occupation Matt 4:18; John 1:42,44
called by Jesus Matt 1:17; Mark 3:16
names: Cephas, Simon Matt 4:18; Mark 3:16; John 1:42; Acts 15:14
walked on water Matt 14:28ff
confessed Jesus as Messiah Matt 16:16; Luke 9:20
on mount of Transfiguration Matt 17:1ff; Mark 9:2ff
denied Jesus Matt 26:70; Mark 14:70; Luke 22:58
at Pentecost Acts 2
apostle of Christ Gal 2:8; 1 Pet 1:1; 2 Pet 1:1

PETITION *request, supplication*
God . . . grant your **p** 1 Sam 1:17
p to any god or man Dan 6:7
p-s . . . be made 1 Tim 2:1

PHARAOH *title of Egyptian kings*
1 **Pharaoh,** *time of Abraham* Gen 12:15ff
2 **Pharaoh,** *time of Joseph* Gen 37:36; 39:1-50:26
3 **Pharaoh,** *during oppression* Ex 1:8-2:23
4 **Pharaoh,** *during the Exodus* Ex 5:1-12:41
5 **Pharaoh,** *father of Bithiah* 1 Chr 4:17
6 **Pharaoh,** *time of David* 1 Kin 11:14ff
7 **Pharaoh,** *whose daughter married Solomon* 1 Kin 3:1;7:8;9:16
8 **Shishak,** *time of Rehoboam* 1 Kin 14:25,26
9 **So,** *time of Hoshea* 2 Kin 17:4
10 **Tirhakah,** *time of Hezekiah* 2 Kin 19:9; Is 37:9
11 **Neco,** *slew Josiah* 2 Kin 23:29,33,34
12 **Hophra,** *subject of prophecy* Jer 44:30

PHARISEES
Jewish religious party Matt 3:7;23:13; Mark 2:18;7:3; Luke 11:42;16:14; John 3:1;11:47

PHILIP
1 *Herod Philip I, son of Herod the Great* Mark 6:17
2 *Herod Philip II, son of Herod the Great* Luke 3:1
3 *Philip the apostle* Matt 10:3; Mark 3:18; Luke 6:14; John 1:43ff; Acts 1:13
4 *Philip the evangelist* Acts 6:5;8:5,29;21:8

PHILIPPI
Macedonian city Acts 16:12;20:6

PHILIPPIANS
people of Philippi Phil 4:15

PHILISTIA
coastal area of SW Palestine Ex 15:14; Ps 60:8; 83:7

PHILISTINES
people of Philistia Gen 10:14; Josh 13:2; Judg 13:1; 1 Sam 4:2

PHOEBE
Cenchrea (Corinth) deaconess commended by Paul Rom 16:1

PHOENICIA
coastal land N of Land of Israel Acts 11:19;21:2
visited by Paul Acts 15:3

PHYLACTERIES *prayer bands*
as **p** on your forehead Ex 13:16
they broaden their **p** Matt 23:5

PHYSICIAN
all worthless **p-s** Job 13:4
healthy who need a **p** Matt 9:12
P, heal yourself Luke 4:23
Luke, the beloved **p** Col 4:14

PIERCE *penetrate*
master shall **p** his ear Ex 21:6
They **p-d** my hands Ps 22:16
He was **p-d** through Is 53:5
whom they have **p-d** Zech 12:10
sword will **p** . . . soul Luke 2:35
p-d His side John 19:34

PIETY *reverence*
learn to practice **p** 1 Tim 5:4
because of His **p** Heb 5:7

PILATE, PONTIUS
Roman governor of Judea Matt 27:2; Luke 3:1
presided at Jesus' trial Matt 27:11ff; Mark 15:2ff; Luke 23:1ff; John 18:28-38
warned by his wife Matt 27:19
orders Jesus' crucifixion Matt 27:24ff; Mark 15:15; Luke 23:24,25; John 19:15,16

PILLAR *column* or *memorial*
became a **p** of salt Gen 19:26
p of fire by night Ex 13:21
set up . . . a **p** 2 Sam 18:18
feet like **p-s** of fire Rev 10:1

PILOT *steersman*
sailors, and your **p-s** Ezek 27:27
the **p** and . . . captain Acts 27:11
inclination of the **p** James 3:4

PINION *wing*
p and plumage of Job 39:13
cover you with His **p-s** Ps 91:4

PINNACLE *highest point*
had Him . . . on the **p** Matt 4:5
p of the temple Luke 4:9

PIT *deep hole, dungeon*
full of tar **p-s** Gen 14:10
Joseph . . . not in the **p** Gen 37:29
redeems . . . from the **p** Ps 103:4
silenced me in the **p** Lam 3:53
to **p-s** of darkness 2 Pet 2:4
the bottomless **p** Rev 9:1

PITCH (n) *tar*
inside and out with **p** Gen 6:14
covered it over . . . **p** Ex 2:3

PITCH (v) *set up*
p-ed his tent in the Gen 31:25
he will **p** the tents Dan 11:45
tabernacle . . . Lord **p-ed** Heb 8:2

PITCHER *container*
torches inside the **p-s** Judg 7:16
Fill four **p-s** 1 Kin 18:33
carrying a **p** of Mark 14:13

PITHOM
Egyptian storage city built by Hebrew slaves Ex 1:11

PITY (n) *sympathy*
she had **p** on him Ex 2:6
shall not show **p** Deut 19:21
I will not show **p** Jer 13:14
No eye looked with **p** Ezek 16:5
take **p** on us Mark 9:22

PITY (v) *have compassion*
eye shall not **p** them Deut 7:16
most to be **p-ied** 1 Cor 15:19

PLAGUE *contagious disease*
no **p** will befall you Ex 12:13
Remove Thy **p** from Ps 39:10
p of the hail Rev 16:21
the seven last **p-s** Rev 21:9

PLAIN *flat area*
p in . . . Shinar Gen 11:2
desert **p-s** of Jericho Josh 4:13
the **p** of Megiddo 2 Chr 35:22
broad **p** of the earth Rev 20:9

PLAN *design, scheme*
tabernacle . . . its **p** Ex 26:30
P-s *formed* long ago Is 25:1
follow our own **p-s** Jer 18:12
p and foreknowledge Acts 2:23

PLANT (n) *growth from soil*
every **p** yielding seed Gen 1:29
eat the **p-s** of the Gen 3:18
hail . . . struck every **p** Ex 9:25
God appointed a **p** Jon 4:6

PLANT (v) *put into soil*
God **p-ed** a garden Gen 2:8
p . . . trees for food Lev 19:23
shall **p** a vineyard Deut 28:30
A time to **p** Eccl 3:2
her earnings she **p-s** Prov 31:16
I **p-ed**, Apollos 1 Cor 3:6

PLATTER *shallow dish*
on a **p** the head of Matt 14:8
his head on a **p** Mark 6:28

PLAY *take part*
who **p** the lyre Gen 4:21
p-ed the fool 1 Sam 26:21
P skillfully with a Ps 33:3
not **p** the harlot Hos 3:3
We **p-ed** the flute Matt 11:17

PLEAD *appeal, beseech*
p-ed with the LORD Deut 3:23
LORD . . . **p** their case Prov 22:23
P for the widow Is 1:17
Elijah . . . **p-s** with God Rom 11:2

PLEASANT *pleasing*
despised the **p** land Ps 106:24
P words are a Prov 16:24
sleep . . . is **p** Eccl 5:12
Speak to us **p** words Is 30:10

PLEASE *satisfy*
it **p** Thee to bless 2 Sam 7:29
Thou art **p-d** with me Ps 41:11
sacrifices . . . not **p** Him Hos 9:4
how he may **p** his 1 Cor 7:33
p all men in all 1 Cor 10:33
striving to **p** men Gal 1:10
to walk and **p** God 1 Thess 4:1
impossible to **p** Heb 11:6

PLEASURE *gratification*
old, shall I have **p** Gen 18:12
He who loves **p** *will* Prov 21:17
work for *His* good **p** Phil 2:13
lovers of **p** rather 2 Tim 3:4
passing **p-s** of sin Heb 11:25

PLEDGE *promise*
cloak as a **p** Ex 22:26
those who give **p-s** Prov 22:26
the Spirit as a **p** 2 Cor 5:5
p of our inheritance Eph 1:14

PLOT *plan, scheme*
wicked **p-s** against Ps 37:12
you have **p-ted** *evil* Prov 30:32
Jews **p-ted** together Acts 9:23

PLOW *dig the soil*
not **p** with an ox Deut 22:10
sluggard does not **p** Prov 20:4
his hand to the **p** Luke 9:62
ought to **p** in hope 1 Cor 9:10

PLOWSHARES *blade of plow*
their swords into **p** Is 2:4
your **p** into swords Joel 3:10

PLUMB LINE *vertical line*
the **p** of emptiness Is 34:11
p In the midst of My Amos 7:8
when they see the **p** Zech 4:10

PLUNDER (n) *booty, loot*
took no **p** in silver Judg 5:19
you will become **p** Hab 2:7
wealth will become **p** Zeph 1:13

PLUNDER (v) *rob*
will **p** the Egyptians Ex 3:22
stouthearted were **p-ed** Ps 76:5
he will **p** his house Matt 12:29

POISON *lethal substance*
P . . . under their lips Ps 140:3
given us **p-ed** water Jer 8:14
turned justice into **p** Amos 6:12

POLL TAX *income and head tax*
collect customs or **p** Matt 17:25
give a **p** to Caesar Matt 22:17

POLLUTE *contaminate*
blood **p-s** the land Num 35:33
earth is also **p-d** Is 24:5

POMEGRANATE *fruit*
golden bell and a **p** Ex 28:34
p-s of blue and purple Ex 39:24
juice of my **p-s** Song 8:2
the fig tree, the **p** Hag 2:19

POOL *pond*
of the upper **p** 2 Kin 18:17
rock into a **p** Ps 114:8
land will become a **p** Is 35:7
in the **p** of Siloam John 9:7

POOR *impoverished, needy*
p will never cease Deut 15:11
raises the **p** from the 1 Sam 2:8
lest you become **p** Prov 20:13
not rob the **p** Prov 22:22
are the **p** in spirit Matt 5:3
a **p** widow came Mark 12:42
p you always have Mark 14:7
sake He became **p** 2 Cor 8:9
not God choose the **p** James 2:5

POPULATE *increase number*
P the earth abundantly Gen 9:7
whole earth was **p-d** Gen 9:19

POPULATION *people*
with all *his* great **p** Is 16:14
deported an entire **p** Amos 1:6

PORPOISE SKIN
covering of **p-s** above Ex 26:14
put sandals of **p** on Ezek 16:10

PORTICO *porch*
in the **p** of Solomon John 10:23
one accord in . . . **p** Acts 5:12

POSSESS *control, take*
give . . . this land to **p** Gen 15:7
are to **p** their land Lev 20:24
go in and **p** the land Deut 1:8
p-ed by Beelzebul Mark 3:22
p-ed with demons Luke 8:27
do not **p** silver and Acts 3:6

POSSESSION *ownership*
for an everlasting **p** Gen 17:8
you shall be My own **p** Ex 19:5
people for His own **p** Deut 4:20
full of Thy **p-s** Ps 104:24
charge of all his **p-s** Matt 24:47
selling their . . . **p-s** Acts 2:45

POSSIBLE *can be done*
all things are **p** Matt 19:26
p with God Luke 18:27

POSTERITY *descendants*
P will serve Him Ps 22:30
p of the wicked Ps 37:38

POTSHERD *piece of pottery*
p to scrape himself Job 2:8
is dried up like a **p** Ps 22:15

POTTER *one who molds clay*
clay say to the **p** Is 45:9
and Thou our **p** Is 64:8
as it pleased the **p** Jer 18:4
Throw it to the **p** Zech 11:13

POTTER'S FIELD
burial place bought with Judas money Matt 27:3ff

POUR *cause to flow*
p me out like milk Job 10:10
P out your heart Ps 62:8
I will **p** out My Spirit Is 44:3
P out Thy wrath Jer 10:25
p out . . . a blessing Mal 3:10
p-ed it upon His Matt 26:7
p forth of My Spirit Acts 2:17

POVERTY *destitution, want*
glutton . . . come to **p** Prov 23:21
neither **p** nor riches Prov 30:8
through His **p** might 2 Cor 8:9

POWER *authority, strength*
to show you My **p** Ex 9:16
from the **p** of Sheol Ps 49:15
p of the tongue Prov 18:21
the **p** of the sword Jer 18:21
→ Not by might nor . . . **p** Zech 4:6
Thine is . . . the **p** Matt 6:13
clothed with **p** from Luke 24:49
you shall receive **p** Acts 1:8
gospel . . . **p** of God Rom 1:16
the **p** of our Lord 1 Cor 5:4
p of Christ . . . dwell 2 Cor 12:9
prince of the **p** of Eph 2:2
p of His resurrection Phil 3:10
timidity, but of **p** 2 Tim 1:7
quenched the **p** of Heb 11:34
p-s . . . been subjected 1 Pet 3:22

POWERLESS *without strength*
p before this great 2 Chr 20:12
He might render **p** Heb 2:14

PRACTICE (n) *custom, habit*
evil of their **p-s** Ps 28:4
disclosing their **p-s** Acts 19:18
laid aside . . . *evil* **p-s** Col 3:9

PRACTICE (v) *engage in*
keep . . . statutes and **p** Lev 20:8
He who **p-s** deceit Ps 101:7
p-ing hospitality Rom 12:13
learn to **p** piety 1 Tim 5:4
the one who **p-s** sin 1 John 3:8

PRAISE (n) *acclamation, honor*
offering of **p** Lev 19:24
sing **p-s** to Him 1 Chr 16:9
songs of **p** . . . hymns Neh 12:46
From Thee . . . my **p** Ps 22:25
sound His **p** abroad Ps 66:8
makes Jerusalem a **p** Is 62:7
his **p** is not from men Rom 2:29
a sacrifice of **p** Heb 13:15
Give **p** to our God Rev 19:5

PRAISE (v) *extol, glorify*
I will **p** Him Ex 15:2

greatly to be **p-d** 1 Chr 16:25
My lips will **p** Thee Ps 63:3
heavens will **p** Thy Ps 89:5
P Him, sun and moon Ps 148:3
P Him with trumpet Ps 150:3
Death cannot **p** Thee Is 38:18
I **p** Thee, O Father Matt 11:25
heavenly host **p-ing** Luke 2:13
disciples began to **p** Luke 19:37

PRAY *ask, worship*
Abraham **p-ed** to Gen 20:17
For this boy I **p-ed** 1 Sam 1:27
found *courage* to **p** 1 Chr 17:25
For to Thee do I **p** Ps 5:2
P for . . . Jerusalem Ps 122:6
We earnestly **p** Jon 1:14
p for . . . persecute Matt 5:44
by Himself to **p** Matt 14:23
p and ask, believe Mark 11:24
Lord, teach us to **p** Luke 11:1
they ought to **p** Luke 18:1
I have **p-ed** for you Luke 22:32
p-ed with fasting Acts 14:23
if I **p** in a tongue 1 Cor 14:14
p without ceasing 1 Thess 5:17
p-ing in the . . . Spirit Jude 20

PRAYER
I have heard your **p** 2 Chr 7:12
And my **p** is pure Job 16:17
LORD receives my **p** Ps 6:9
Give ear to my **p** Ps 55:1
ask in **p**, believing Matt 21:22
you make long **p-s** Matt 23:14
whole night in **p** Luke 6:12
My house . . . of **p** Luke 19:46
offering **p** with joy Phil 1:4
but in everything by **p** Phil 4:6
p-s of the saints Rev 5:8

PREACH *exhort, proclaim*
Jesus began to **p** Matt 4:17
as you go, **p** Matt 10:7
teach and **p** in their Matt 11:1
p the gospel to all Mark 16:15
p the kingdom of Luke 4:43
p . . . the good news Acts 13:32
how shall they **p** Rom 10:15
we **p** Christ crucified 1 Cor 1:23
He . . . **p-ed** peace Eph 2:17
p the word 2 Tim 4:2

PREACHER *one who proclaims*
hear without a **p** Rom 10:14
appointed a **p** and an 1 Tim 2:7
Noah, a **p** of 2 Pet 2:5

PRECEPTS *commandments*
All His **p** are sure Ps 111:7
meditate on Thy **p** Ps 119:15
as doctrines the **p** of Matt 15:9

PREDESTINED *foreordained*
purpose **p** to occur Acts 4:28
foreknew, He also **p** Rom 8:29
God **p** before the ages 1 Cor 2:7
p us to adoption Eph 1:5
p according to His Eph 1:11

PREEMINENT *foremost*
P in dignity Gen 49:3

PREFECTS *Persian officials*
shatter governors . . . **p** Jer 51:23
the satraps, the **p** Dan 3:3

PREGNANT *with child*
womb of . . . **p** woman Eccl 11:5
And her womb ever **p** Jer 20:17
ripped open . . . **p** Amos 1:13
Elizabeth . . . became **p** Luke 1:24

PREPARE *make ready*
p a savory dish Gen 27:4
p a table before me Ps 23:5
P to meet your God Amos 4:12
will **p** Your way Matt 11:10

to **p** Me for burial Matt 26:12
p-d spices and Luke 23:56
I go to **p** a place John 14:2
worlds were **p-d** by Heb 11:3

PRESENCE *appearance*
My **p** shall go *with* Ex 33:14
in the **p** of my enemies Ps 23:5
the light of Thy **p** Ps 44:3
tremble at Thy **p** Is 64:2
the **p** of His glory Jude 24
the **p** of the Lamb Rev 14:10

PRESENT (n) *gift*
a **p** for his brother Gen 32:13
sent a **p** to the king 2 Kin 16:8
and a **p** to Hezekiah Is 39:1

PRESENT (v) *give, offer*
p you with a crown of Prov 4:9
you **p** the blind for Mal 1:8
p Him to the Lord Luke 2:22
p yourselves to God Rom 6:13
p your bodies a Rom 12:1
p you before Him holy Col 1:22

PRESERVE *protect*
no son to **p** my 2 Sam 18:18
P me, O God Ps 16:1
Do **p** my soul Ps 86:2
LORD **p-s** the simple Ps 116:6
p-d ones of Israel Is 49:6
p the unity of the Eph 4:3
be **p-d** complete 1 Thess 5:23

PRETEND *deceive, feign*
p to be a mourner 2 Sam 14:2
p to be another 1 Kin 14:5
p-s to be poor Prov 13:7
spies who **p-ed** to Luke 20:20

PREY *what is hunted*
birds of **p** came Gen 15:11
lion tearing the **p** Ezek 22:25
no longer be a **p** to Ezek 34:28

PRICE *cost, value*
their redemption **p** Num 18:16
p of the pardoning of Is 27:9
it is the **p** of blood Matt 27:6
p of his wickedness Acts 1:18
kept back *some* . . . **p** Acts 5:2
bought with a **p** 1 Cor 7:23

PRIDE *exaggerated self-esteem*
P *goes* before Prov 16:18
you an everlasting **p** Is 60:15
p of Israel testifies Hos 5:5
envy, slander, **p** Mark 7:22
boastful **p** of life 1 John 2:16

PRIEST *intermediary*
a **p** of God Most Gen 14:18
a kingdom of **p-s** Ex 19:6
Aaron's sons, the **p-s** Lev 1:5
p . . . make atonement Lev 4:31
Thou art a **p** forever Ps 110:4
show yourself to the **p** Matt 8:4
faithful high **p** Heb 2:17
have a great high **p** Heb 4:14
Thou art a **p** forever Heb 5:6

PRIESTHOOD *office of priest*
for a perpetual **p** Ex 40:15
have defiled the **p** Neh 13:29
His **p** permanently Heb 7:24
royal **p**, a holy nation 1 Pet 2:9

PRIME *period of full maturity*
die in the **p** of life 1 Sam 2:33
p of life . . . fleeing Eccl 11:10

PRINCE *ruler*
Who made you a **p** Ex 2:14
p-s of the tribes 1 Chr 29:6
Do not trust in **p-s** Ps 146:3
Father, **P** of Peace Is 9:6
to death the **P** of life Acts 3:15
p of . . . the air Eph 2:2

PRISON *jail*
Put this man in **p** 1 Kin 22:27
my soul out of **p** Ps 142:7
beheaded in the **p** Matt 14:10
I was in **p**, and Matt 25:36
opened . . . the **p** Acts 5:19
spirits *now* in **p** 1 Pet 3:19

PRISONER *one who is confined*
sets the **p-s** free Ps 146:7
a notorious **p** Matt 27:16
p of the law of sin Rom 7:23
Paul, a **p** of Christ Philem 1

PRIZE *reward*
one receives the **p** 1 Cor 9:24
p of the upward call Phil 3:14

PROCEED *go forth*
p from evil to evil Jer 9:3
p-s out of the mouth Matt 4:4
p-s from . . . Father John 15:26

PROCLAIM *announce, declare*
p . . . name of the LORD Ex 33:19
P good tidings 1 Chr 16:23
p liberty to captives Is 61:1
he *began* to **p** Jesus Acts 9:20
first to **p** light Acts 26:23
p . . . eternal life 1 John 1:2

PROCLAMATION *declaration*
a **p** was circulated Ex 36:6
made **p** to the spirits 1 Pet 3:19

PRODUCE (n) *yield of the soil*
land will yield its **p** Lev 25:19
tithe all the **p** Deut 14:22
earth has yielded its **p** Ps 67:6
precious **p** of . . . soil James 5:7

PRODUCE (v) *bring forth*
milk **p-s** butter Prov 30:33
cannot **p** bad fruit Matt 7:18
they **p** quarrels 2 Tim 2:23
faith **p-s** endurance James 1:3

PROFANE *defile, desecrate*
p My holy name Lev 20:3
is **p-d** by harlotry Lev 21:7
and **p-d** My sabbaths Ezek 22:8
p-d your sanctuaries Ezek 28:18
to **p** the covenant Mal 2:10

PROFESS *confess, declare*
P-ing to be wise Rom 1:22
They **p** to know God Titus 1:16

PROFIT (n) *benefit, gain*
labor there is **p** Prov 14:23
no **p** for the charmer Eccl 10:11
not seeking my . . . **p** 1 Cor 10:33
business . . . make a **p** James 4:13

PROFIT (v) *reap an advantage*
p . . . my destruction Job 30:13
what does it **p** a Mark 8:36
the flesh **p-s** nothing John 6:63
it **p-s** me nothing 1 Cor 13:3

PROMISE (n) *agreement, pledge*
p of the Holy Spirit Acts 2:33
the **p** made by God Acts 26:6
the **p** is nullified Rom 4:14
children of the **p** Rom 9:8
commandment . . . a **p** Eph 6:2
heirs of the **p** Heb 6:17
precious . . . **p-s** 2 Pet 1:4
the **p** of His coming 2 Pet 3:4

PRONOUNCE *declare officially*
shall **p** him clean Lev 13:23
I will **p** My judgments Jer 1:16
Pilate **p-d** sentence Luke 23:24
God . . . **p-d** judgment Rev 18:20

PROOF *evidence*
furnished **p** to all Acts 17:31

p of your love 2 Cor 8:24
p of the Christ 2 Cor 13:3

PROPERTY *goods* or *land, possession*
acquire **p** in it Gen 34:10
p . . . too great Gen 36:7
buys a slave as *his* **p** Lev 22:11
who owned much **p** Matt 19:22
selling their **p** and Acts 2:45
things . . . common **p** Acts 4:32

PROPHECY *proclamation from God*
seal up vision and **p** Dan 9:24
p . . . fulfilled Matt 13:14
have *the gift of* **p** 1 Cor 13:2
no **p** . . . of human will 2 Pet 1:21
the spirit of **p** Rev 19:10

PROPHESY *predict, proclaim*
to **p** with lyres 1 Chr 25:1
he never **p-ies** good 2 Chr 18:7
P over these bones Ezek 37:4
sons and . . . will **p** Joel 2:28
did we . . . **p** in Your Matt 7:22
P to us . . . Christ Matt 26:68
speaking . . . **p-ing** Acts 19:6
who **p-ies** edifies 1 Cor 14:4

PROPHET *spokesman for God*
Aaron shall be your **p** Ex 7:1
I will raise up a **p** Deut 18:18
summon all . . . **p-s** 2 Kin 10:19
vision of . . . the **p** 2 Chr 32:32
written by the **p** Matt 2:5
persecuted the **p-s** Matt 5:12
Beware . . . false **p-s** Matt 7:15
He . . . receives a **p** Matt 10:41
the **p** Jesus Matt 21:11
p of the Most High Luke 1:76
great **p** has arisen Luke 7:16
Are you the **P** John 1:21
a Jewish false **p** Acts 13:6
All are not **p-s** 1 Cor 12:29
and some *as* **p-s** Eph 4:11
beast and . . . false **p** Rev 20:10

PROPHETESS *speaker for God*
Miriam the **p** Ex 15:20
Deborah, a **p** Judg 4:4
there was a **p**, Anna Luke 2:36
calls herself a **p** Rev 2:20

PROPHETIC *predictive*
not . . . **p** utterances 1 Thess 5:20
p word . . . sure 2 Pet 1:19

PROPITIATION *atonement*
a **p** in His blood Rom 3:25
p for the sins Heb 2:17
He himself is the **p** 1 John 2:2
p for our sins 1 John 4:10

PROSELYTE *convert*
both Jews and **p-s** Acts 2:10
a **p** from Antioch Acts 6:5
God-fearing **p-s** Acts 13:43

PROSPER *flourish, succeed*
I will surely **p** you Gen 32:12
David was **p-ing** 1 Sam 18:14
they built and **p-ed** 2 Chr 14:7
His ways **p** at all Ps 10:5
they **p** who love you Ps 122:6

PROSPERITY *success, wealth*
my **p** has passed away Job 30:15
soul will abide in **p** Ps 25:13
saw the **p** of the wicked Ps 73:3
know how to live in **p** Phil 4:12

PROSTITUTE *harlot*
Where . . . temple **p** Gen 38:21
male cult **p-s** in the 1 Kin 14:24
an adulterer and a **p** Is 57:3

PROTECT *guard, shield*
The LORD will **p** him Ps 41:2
LORD **p-s** the strangers Ps 146:9
LORD . . . **p** Jerusalem Is 31:5
He will . . . **p** you 2 Thess 3:3
p-ed by the power of 1 Pet 1:5

PROTECTION *safe-keeping*
p has been removed Num 14:9
For wisdom is **p** Eccl 7:12
p from the storm Is 4:6
let him rely on My **p** Is 27:5

PROUD *arrogant*
heart becomes **p** Deut 8:14
recompense to the **p** Ps 94:2
eyes and a **p** heart Prov 21:4
daughters of Zion are **p** Is 3:16
opposed to the **p** James 4:6

PROVERB *adage, short saying*
become . . . a **p** Deut 28:37
spoke 3,000 **p-s** 1 Kin 4:32
To understand a **p** Prov 1:6
quote this **p** to Me Luke 4:23

PROVIDE *furnish, supply*
p for Himself . . . lamb Gen 22:8
p for . . . redemption Lev 25:24
p bread from heaven Neh 9:15
p . . . way of escape 1 Cor 10:13
not **p** for his own 1 Tim 5:8

PROVINCE *district* or *territory*
rulers of the **p-s** 1 Kin 20:17
holiday for the **p-s** Esth 2:18
whole **p** of Babylon Dan 2:48
arrived in the **p** Acts 25:1

PROVISION *supply, requirement*
bread of their **p** was Josh 9:5
bless her **p** Ps 132:15
p-s of the law Matt 23:23
no **p** for the flesh Rom 13:14

PROVOKE *evoke, excite*
images to **p** Me 1 Kin 14:9
who **p** God are secure Job 12:6
love . . . is not **p-d** 1 Cor 13:4,5
not **p** your children Eph 6:4

PRUDENT *careful, wise*
a **p** man conceals Prov 12:16
p wife is from the Prov 19:14
the **p** took oil in Matt 25:4
you are **p** in Christ 1 Cor 4:10

PRUNING *cutting*
spears into **p** hooks Is 2:4

PSALMS *sacred songs*
shout . . . with **p** Ps 95:2
P must be fulfilled Luke 24:44
speaking . . . in **p** Eph 5:19

PUNISH *chastise, penalize*
p them for their sin Ex 32:34
and are **p-ed** for it Prov 22:3
will **p** your iniquity Lam 4:22
p Him and release Luke 23:16
p all disobedience 2 Cor 10:6

PUNISHMENT *penalty*
My **p** is too great Gen 4:13
p of the sword Job 19:29
fear involves **p** 1 John 4:18
the **p** of eternal fire Jude 7

PURCHASE *buy*
p-d with His . . . blood Acts 20:28
p for God with Thy Rev 5:9

PURE *genuine, undefiled*
be **p** before his Maker Job 4:17
My teaching is **p** Job 11:4
pleasant words are **p** Prov 15:26
As **p** as the sun Song 6:10
Blessed are the **p** in Matt 5:8
whatever is **p** Phil 4:8
p milk of the word 1 Pet 2:2
the city was **p** gold Rev 21:18

PURGE *remove*
p . . . evil from among Deut 13:5
Many will be **p-d** Dan 12:10

PURIFICATION *cleansing*
Jewish custom of **p** John 2:6
He . . . made **p** of sins Heb 1:3

PURIFY *make clean*
p-ied these waters 2 Kin 2:21
P me with hyssop Ps 51:7
p . . . a people Titus 2:14
p-ied your souls 1 Pet 1:22

PURIM
Jewish festival Esth 9:26ff

PURITY *not corrupted*
who loves **p** of heart Prov 22:11
love, faith *and* **p** 1 Tim 4:12
with **p** in doctrine Titus 2:7

PURPLE *color*
a veil of blue and **p** Ex 26:31
clothed Daniel with **p** Dan 5:29
a seller of **p** fabrics Acts 16:14
clothed in **p** and Rev 17:4

PURPOSE *intention, reason*
p of shedding blood Ezek 22:9
rejected God's **p** Luke 7:30
for this **p** I have Acts 26:16
according to *His* **p** Rom 8:28

PURSE *bag, pouch*
gold from the **p** Is 46:6
Carry no **p**, no bag Luke 10:4
p-s . . . do not wear Luke 12:33

PURSUE *chase, follow*
p the manslayer Deut 19:6
They **p** my honor Job 30:15
the enemy **p** my soul Ps 7:5
Seek peace, and **p** it Ps 34:14
Adversity **p-s** Prov 13:21
p-s righteousness Prov 21:21
p righteousness 2 Tim 2:22
P peace with . . . men Heb 12:14

PUT *place*
p enmity Between Gen 3:15
He **p** a new song Ps 40:3
p on the Lord Jesus Rom 13:14
p on the new self Eph 4:24
P on the full armor Eph 6:11

Q

QUAIL *type of bird*
q-s came up and Ex 16:13
q from the sea Num 11:31

QUAKE *shake, tremble*
The mountains **q-d** Judg 5:5
made the land **q** Ps 60:2
The earth **q-d** Ps 68:8
q at Thy presence Is 64:1

QUALITY *character*
test the **q** of each 1 Cor 3:13
imperishable **q** of a 1 Pet 3:4

QUANTITY *amount*
large **q-ies** of cedar 1 Chr 22:4
a great **q** of fish Luke 5:6

QUARANTINE *isolate*
shall **q** the article Lev 13:50
q the house for Lev 14:38

QUARREL (n) *altercation*
if men have a **q** Ex 21:18
So abandon the **q** Prov 17:14
are **q-s** among you 1 Cor 1:11
the source of **q-s** James 4:1

QUARREL (v) *contend, fight*
did not **q** over it Gen 26:22
Why do you **q** with me Ex 17:2

any fool will **q** Prov 20:3
those who **q** with you Is 41:12

QUEEN *female sovereign*

when the **q** of Sheba 1 Kin 10:1
king saw Esther the **q** Esth 5:2
The **Q** of *the* South Matt 12:42
Candace, **q** of the Acts 8:27

QUENCH *extinguish*

donkeys **q** their thirst Ps 104:11
waters cannot **q** love Song 8:7
not **q** the Spirit 1 Thess 5:19
q-ed . . . power of fire Heb 11:34

QUESTION (n) *inquiry, problem*

Was it not just a **q** 1 Sam 17:29
answered all her **q-s** 2 Chr 9:2
Jesus asked . . . a **q** Matt 22:41
in controversial **q-s** 1 Tim 6:4

QUESTION (v) *ask*

q-ed the priests 2 Chr 31:9
Jeremiah and **q-ed** Jer 38:27
He *began* to **q** them Mark 9:33
to **q** Him closely on Luke 11:53
Q those who have John 18:21

QUICK (adj) *rapid*

is **q**-tempered exalts Prov 14:29
q to hear, slow to James 1:19

QUICK (n) *deepest feelings*

cut to the **q** and Acts 5:33
were cut to the **q** Acts 7:54

QUIET *calm, still*

he knew no **q** within Job 20:20
me beside **q** waters Ps 23:2
God, do not remain **q** Ps 83:1
and **q-ed** my soul Ps 131:2
will be **q in His love** Zeph 3:17
Be **q**, and come out Mark 1:25
lead a . . . **q** life 1 Tim 2:2
gentle and **q** spirit 1 Pet 3:4

QUIVER *case for holding arrows*

your **q** and your bow Gen 27:3
man whose **q** is full Ps 127:5
hidden Me in His **q** Is 49:2
q is like an open grave Jer 5:16
fill the **q-s** Jer 51:11

QUOTA *portion assigned*

complete your work **q** Ex 5:13
deliver the **q** of bricks Ex 5:18

QUOTE *repeat a passage*

who **q-s** proverbs Ezek 16:44
will **q** this proverb Luke 4:23

R

RAAMSES / RAMESES

where Joseph settled Gen 47:11
Egyptian store-city built by Hebrew slaves Ex 1:11
origin of exodus Ex 12:37; Num 33:3,5

RABBI / RABBONI

respectful form of address Matt 23:7;26:25; Mark 10:51
master, teacher John 1:49;6:25;11:8;20:16

RACA *worthless fool*

shall say . . . **R** Matt 5:22

RACE (n) *nation, people*

r has intermingled Ezra 9:2
mongrel **r** will dwell Zech 9:6
advantage of our **r** Acts 7:19
you are a chosen **r** 1 Pet 2:9

RACE (n) *competition of speed*

r is not to . . . swift Eccl 9:11
in a **r** all run, but 1 Cor 9:24
r . . . set before us Heb 12:1

RACHEL

Jacob's wife Gen 29:18,28
mother of Joseph and Benjamin Gen 30:25;35:24;46:19

RADIANCE *brightness*

a **r** around Him Ezek 1:27
His **r** is like Hab 3:4
r of His glory Heb 1:3

RAFTS *boats*

r *to go* by sea 1 Kin 5:9
bring it to you on **r** 2 Chr 2:16

RAGE (n) *violent anger*

Haman was filled . . . **r** Esth 3:5
with **r** as they heard Luke 4:28

RAGE (v) *be very angry*

r-s against the LORD Prov 19:3
foolish man . . . **r-s** Prov 29:9
Why . . . Gentiles **r** Acts 4:25

RAHAB

1 *harlot in Jericho* Josh 2:1
assisted spies Josh 2:4-7
family spared Josh 2:13,14;6:22,23
ancestor of Jesus Matt 1:5
example of faith Heb 11:31; James 2:25
2 *symbolic for sea monster* Job 9:13;26:12; Ps 89:10
3 *symbolic for Egypt* Ps 87:4; Is 30:7

RAIN (n)

God had not sent **r** Gen 2:5
r fell upon the earth Gen 7:12
I shall give you **r-s** Lev 26:4
no **r** in the land 1 Kin 17:7
r is over *and* gone Song 2:11
anger a flooding **r** Ezek 13:13
r on *the* righteous Matt 5:45
ground . . . drinks the **r** Heb 6:7

RAIN (v) *fall down, pour*

r bread from heaven Ex 16:4
the LORD **r-ed** hail Ex 9:23
it **r-ed** fire and Luke 17:29
not **r** . . . for three James 5:17

RAINBOW *colored arc in sky*

appearance of the **r** Ezek 1:28
a **r** around the throne Rev 4:3
r was upon his head Rev 10:1

RAISE *elevate, lift*

will **r** up a prophet Deut 18:18
LORD **r-d** up judges Judg 2:16
r-s the poor from 1 Sam 2:8
He will **r** us up Hos 6:2
He will be **r-d** up Matt 20:19
three days I will **r** John 2:19
Jesus God **r-d** up Acts 2:32
r-d a spiritual 1 Cor 15:44
r-d us up with Him Eph 2:6
God is able to **r** *men* Heb 11:19

RAISIN *dried grapes*

clusters of **r-s** 2 Sam 16:1
Sustain me with **r** Song 2:5
and love **r** cakes Hos 3:1

RAM *male sheep*

Abraham . . . took the **r** Gen 22:13
a **r** without defect Lev 5:15
the **r** of atonement Num 5:8
r which had two horns Dan 8:3

RAMPART *bulwark, embankment*

and **r-s** for security Is 26:1
Whose **r** *was* the sea Nah 3:8
station myself on the **r** Hab 2:1

RANK *position*

men of **r** are a lie Ps 62:9
He . . . has a higher **r** Josh 1:15
a Man . . . higher **r** John 1:30

RANSOM (n) *payment*

give a **r** for himself Ex 30:12
not take **r** for Num 35:31
wicked is a **r** for Prov 21:18
His life a **r** for Matt 20:28
gave Himself as a **r** 1 Tim 2:6

RANSOM (v) *redeem*

Thou hast **r-ed** me Ps 31:5
R me because of my Ps 69:18
LORD has **r-ed** Jacob Jer 31:11
I will **r** them from Hos 13:14

RAVAGE *devastate*

famine will **r** the Gen 41:30
mice that **r** the land 1 Sam 6:5
r-ing the church Acts 8:3

RAVEN *type of bird*

he sent out a **r** Gen 8:7
young **r-s** which cry Ps 147:9
Consider the **r-s** Luke 12:24

RAVINE *gorge*

settle on the steep **r-s** Is 7:19
smooth *stones* of the **r** Is 57:6
Every **r** shall be filled Luke 3:5

RAZOR *instrument for shaving*

no **r** shall pass over Num 6:5
no **r** shall come upon Judg 13:5
A **r** has never come Judg 16:17
Like a sharp **r** Ps 52:2

READY *equipped, prepared*

and **r** to forgive Ps 86:5
Let Thy hand be **r** Ps 119:173
Make **r** the way Matt 3:3
you be **r** too Matt 24:44
be **r** in season 2 Tim 4:2
r to make a defense 1 Pet 3:15

REALM *area, kingdom*

ruler over the **r** of Dan 4:17
kingdom is not . . . **r** John 18:36

REAP *cut, gather*

when you **r** . . . harvest Lev 19:9
iniquity will **r** vanity Prov 22:8
they **r** the whirlwind Hos 8:7
neither do they **r** Matt 6:26
neither sow nor **r** Luke 12:24
sows . . . another **r-s** John 4:37
r eternal life Gal 6:8
your sickle and **r** Rev 14:15

REAPER *harvester*

after the **r-s** Ruth 2:3
will overtake the **r** Amos 9:13
the **r-s** are angels Matt 13:39

REASON (n) *explanation*

this **r** the Father John 10:17
this **r** I found mercy 1 Tim 1:16
For this **r**, rejoice Rev 12:12

REASON (v) *analyze, argue*

upright would **r** with Job 23:7
let us **r** together Is 1:18
Pharisees began to **r** Luke 5:21
r-ing in . . . synagogue Acts 17:17
as a child, **r** as a 1 Cor 13:11

REBEKAH

wife of Isaac Gen 24:67;26:8
mother of Esau and Jacob Gen 25:21ff

REBEL (n) *rebellious one*

Your rulers are **r-s** Is 1:23
called a **r** from birth Is 48:8
their princes are **r-s** Hos 9:15

REBEL (v) *revolt*

not **r** against the Num 14:9
r-led against . . . words Ps 107:11
r-led against Me Ezek 20:21

REBELLION *insurrection*

he has counseled **r** Deut 13:5
I know your **r** Deut 31:27
my **r** and my sin Job 13:23
children of **r** Is 57:4

REBUILD *restore*
- **r** the house of the Ezra 1:3
- let us **r** the wall Neh 2:17
- **r** it in three days Matt 26:61
- **r** the tabernacle Acts 15:16

REBUKE (n) *reprimand*
- amazed at His **r** Job 26:11
- At Thy **r** they fled Ps 104:7
- the poor hears no **r** Prov 13:8

REBUKE (v) *scold*
- **r** me not in Thy wrath Ps 38:1
- LORD **r** you, Satan Zech 3:2
- **r-d** the winds Matt 8:26
- He **r-d** the fever Luke 4:39
- Do not sharply **r** 1 Tim 5:1
- reprove, **r**, exhort 2 Tim 4:2

RECEIVE *encounter, take*
- The LORD **r-s** my prayer Ps 6:9
- **r** me to glory Ps 73:24
- man **r-s** a bribe Prov 17:23
- freely you **r-d** Matt 10:8
- *the* blind **r** sight Matt 11:5
- ask . . . you shall **r** Matt 21:22
- **r-d** up into heaven Mark 16:19
- This man **r-s** sinners Luke 15:2
- **r** you to Myself John 14:3
- **R** the Holy Spirit John 20:22
- you shall **r** power Acts 1:8
- **r** the crown of life James 1:12
- **r-d** the mark of Rev 19:20

RECKONED *accounted for*
- **r** it to him as Gen 15:6
- **r** among the nations Num 23:9
- his wage is not **r** Rom 4:4
- **r** . . . as righteousness James 2:23

RECLINE *lean, lie down*
- **r** on beds of ivory Amos 6:4
- **r** on the grass Matt 14:19
- **r** *at the table* in Luke 13:29
- **r-ing** on Jesus' John 13:23

RECOGNIZE *be aware, know*
- he did not **r** him Gen 27:23
- Saul **r-d** David's 1 Sam 26:17
- **r** that He is near Matt 24:33
- I did not **r** Him John 1:31

RECOMPENSE (n) *reward*
- the **r** of the wicked Ps 91:8
- **r** to the proud Ps 94:2
- **r** of God will come Is 35:4
- received a just **r** Heb 2:2

RECOMPENSE (v) *compensate*
- LORD has **r-d** me 2 Sam 22:25
- He will **r** the evil Ps 54:5
- But if you do **r** Me Joel 3:4

RECONCILE *bring together*
- **r-d** to your brother Matt 5:24
- be **r-d** to God 2 Cor 5:20
- **r** them both in one Eph 2:16
- **r** all . . . to Himself Col 1:20

RECORD (n) *document, register*
- the **r-s** are ancient 1 Chr 4:22
- **r-s** of the kings 2 Chr 33:18
- discover in . . . **r** books Ezra 4:15
- I found the . . . **r** Neh 7:5

RECORD (v) *register, write*
- **r-ed** their starting Num 33:2
- **R** the vision Hab 2:2
- are **r-ed** in heaven Luke 10:20

RED *color*
- first came forth **r** Gen 25:25
- water . . . **r** as blood 2 Kin 3:22
- they are **r** like crimson Is 1:18
- the sky is **r** Matt 16:2
- a great **r** dragon Rev 12:3

RED SEA
- *Hebrew: Sea of Reeds* Ex 10:19
- *body of water between Egypt and Sinai* Ex 13:18; Ps 106:9

REDEEM *buy back*
- I will also **r** you Ex 6:6
- family may **r** him Lev 25:49
- God will **r** my soul Ps 49:15
- He will **r** Israel Ps 130:8
- Christ **r-ed** us Gal 3:13
- He might **r** those Gal 4:5

REDEEMER *one who buys back*
- left you without a **r** Ruth 4:14
- know that my **R** lives Job 19:25
- my rock and my **R** Ps 19:14
- your **R** is the Holy Is 41:14
- our Father, Our **R** Is 63:16
- Their **R** is strong Jer 50:34

REDEMPTION *deliverance*
- **r** of the land Lev 25:24
- *have* my right of **r** Ruth 4:6
- **r** of his soul is Ps 49:8
- **r** . . . in Christ Jesus Rom 3:24
- **r** of our body Rom 8:23
- **r** through His blood Eph 1:7
- obtained eternal **r** Heb 9:12

REED *tall marsh grass*
- set *it* among the **r-s** Ex 2:3
- bruised **r** He will Is 42:3
- the **r** . . . to beat Him Matt 27:30
- and put it on a **r** Matt 27:48

REFINE *purify*
- **r-d** seven times Ps 12:6
- in order to **r** Dan 11:35
- **R** them as silver Zech 13:9
- **r** them like gold Mal 3:3
- gold **r-d** by fire Rev 3:18

REFRESH *renew, replenish*
- you may **r** yourselves Gen 18:5
- **R** me with apples Song 2:5
- times of **r-ing** may Acts 3:19
- **r** my heart in Christ Philem 20

REFUGE *protection, shelter*
- in whom I take **r** 2 Sam 22:3
- God is our **r** Ps 46:1
- **r** in the LORD Ps 118:8
- the **r** of lies Is 28:17
- who have fled for **r** Heb 6:18

REFUSE (n) *waste*
- be made a **r** heap Ezra 6:11
- corpses lay like **r** Is 5:25
- its waters toss up **r** Is 57:20
- sell . . . **r** of the wheat Amos 8:6

REFUSE (v) *decline*
- **r** to let My people go Ex 10:4
- his hands **r** to work Prov 21:25
- **r-d** to be comforted Matt 2:18
- can **r** the water Acts 10:47
- not **r** Him who is Heb 12:25

REFUTE *prove wrong*
- **R** me if you can Job 33:5
- he . . . **r-d** the Jews Acts 18:28
- to **r** those who Titus 1:9

REGAIN *recover*
- **r-ed** their sight Matt 20:34
- *want* to **r** my sight Mark 10:51
- he might **r** his sight Acts 9:12

REGARD (n) *respect*
- LORD had **r** for Abel Gen 4:4
- **r** to the prayer 1 Kin 8:28
- have **r** for his Maker Is 17:7
- **r** for the humble Luke 1:48

REGARD (v) *esteem, respect*
- If I **r** wickedness Ps 66:18
- Yet He **r-s** the lowly Ps 138:6
- who **r-s** reproof Prov 15:5
- you **r** one another Phil 2:3
- did not **r** equality Phil 2:6

REGENERATION *renewal*
- **r** when the Son Matt 19:28
- the washing of **r** Titus 3:5

REGION *area*
- **r** of the Jordan Josh 22:10
- the **r-s** of Galilee Matt 2:22
- to the **r** of Judea Mark 10:1
- same **r** . . . shepherds Luke 2:8

REGISTER *enroll, record*
- **r** . . . people of Israel 2 Sam 24:4
- to **r** for the census Luke 2:3

REIGN *rule*
- LORD shall **r** forever Ex 15:18
- Shall Saul **r** over 1 Sam 11:12
- The LORD **r-s** Ps 93:1
- will **r** righteously Is 32:1
- death **r-ed** . . . Adam Rom 5:14
- He must **r** until 1 Cor 15:25
- also **r** with Him 2 Tim 2:12
- He will **r** forever Rev 11:15
- will **r** with Him Rev 20:6

REJECT *decline, refuse*
- have **r-ed** the LORD Num 11:20
- will **r** you forever 1 Chr 28:9
- A fool **r-s** his Prov 15:5
- have **r-ed** this word Is 30:12
- **r-ed** My ordinances Ezek 20:13
- they **r-ed** the law Amos 2:4
- the builders **r-ed** Matt 21:42
- who **r-s** you **r-s** Me Luke 10:16
- He who **r-s** Me John 12:48

REJOICE *be glad*
- **r** before the LORD Lev 23:40
- I **r** in Thy salvation 1 Sam 2:1
- my soul shall **r** Ps 35:9
- king will **r** in God Ps 63:11
- Let us **r** and be glad Ps 118:24
- I **r** at Thy word Ps 119:162
- God will **r** over you Is 62:5
- **r** at his birth Luke 1:14
- multitude was **r-ing** Luke 13:17
- you would have **r-d** John 14:28
- **r-ing** in hope Rom 12:12
- **R** in the Lord Phil 4:4
- I **r** in my sufferings Col 1:24
- **r**, O heavens Rev 12:12

RELATIONS *sexual intercourse*
- **r** with his wife Eve Gen 4:1
- had no **r** with a man Judg 11:39
- we may have **r** with Judg 19:22
- had **r** with Hannah 1 Sam 1:19

RELATIVE *kinsman*
- and to my **r-s** Gen 24:4
- The man is our **r** Ruth 2:20
- among his *own* **r-s** Mark 6:4
- your **r** Elizabeth has Luke 1:36

RELEASE (n) *liberation*
- a **r** through the land Lev 25:10
- **r** to the captives Luke 4:18

RELEASE (v) *set free*
- he **r-d** Barabbas Matt 27:26
- **r** for you the King Mark 15:9
- wanting to **r** Jesus Luke 23:20
- efforts to **r** Him John 19:12
- you **r-d** from a wife 1 Cor 7:27
- **r-d** us from our sins Rev 1:5
- **R** the four angels Rev 9:14

RELIGION *system of belief*
- about their own **r** Acts 25:19
- sect of our **r** Acts 26:5
- pure and undefiled **r** James 1:27

RELIGIOUS *devout, pious*
- **r** in all respects Acts 17:22
- thinks . . . to be **r** James 1:26

RELY *depend, trust*
- **r-ied** on the LORD 2 Chr 16:8

who . . . **r** on horses Is 31:1
r on his God Is 50:10
You **r** on your sword Ezek 33:26
r upon the Law Rom 2:17

REMAIN *abide, be left*
While the earth **r-s** Gen 8:22
R . . . in his place Ex 16:29
r-s yet . . . youngest 1 Sam 16:11
dove . . . **r-ed** upon John 1:32
not **r** in darkness John 12:46
not **r** on the cross John 19:31
let her **r** unmarried 1 Cor 7:11
He **r-s** faithful 2 Tim 2:13

REMEMBER *recall, recollect*
God **r-ed** Noah Gen 8:1
I will **r** My covenant Gen 9:15
R the sabbath day Ex 20:8
R also your Creator Eccl 12:1
O LORD, **R** me Jer 15:15
sin I will **r** no more Jer 31:34
R Lot's wife Luke 17:32
r the words of Acts 20:35
to **r** the poor Gal 2:10

REMEMBRANCE *memory*
Thy **r**, O LORD Ps 135:13
Put Me in **r** Is 43:26
a book of **r** was Mal 3:16
do this in **r** of Me Luke 22:19
in **r** of Me 1 Cor 11:25

REMNANT *remaining part*
preserve for you a **r** Gen 45:7
prayer for the **r** 2 Kin 19:4
an escaped **r** Ezra 9:8
A **r** will return Is 10:21
the **r** of Israel Jer 6:9
a **r** of the Spirit Mal 2:15
r that will be saved Rom 9:27

REMOVE *take away* or *off*
r-d all the idols 1 Kin 15:12
He **r-d** the high 2 Kin 18:4
r the heart of stone Ezek 36:26
r this cup from Me Luke 22:42
R the stone John 11:39

RENEW *make new, revive*
r a steadfast spirit Ps 51:10
r-ed like the eagle Ps 103:5
R our days as of old Lam 5:21
inner man . . . **r-ed** 2 Cor 4:16

RENOWN *fame*
men of **r** Gen 6:4
a people, for **r** Jer 13:11
shame into . . . and **r** Zeph 3:19

REPAY *pay back*
you thus **r** the LORD Deut 32:6
so God has **repaid** Judg 1:7
LORD **r** the evildoer 2 Sam 3:39
repaid me evil for Ps 109:5
r their iniquity Jer 16:18
in secret will **r** Matt 6:4
is Mine, I will **r** Rom 12:19
no one **r-s** . . . evil 1 Thess 5:15

REPENT *change mind*
that He should **r** Num 23:19
r in dust and ashes Job 42:6
have refused to **r** Jer 5:3
R, for the kingdom Matt 3:2
r-ed long ago in Matt 11:21
r and believe Mark 1:15
one sinner who **r-s** Luke 15:7
R, . . . be baptized Acts 2:38
all . . . should **r** Acts 17:30
r and turn to God Acts 26:20

REPENTANCE *penitence*
with water for **r** Matt 3:11
baptism of **r** Mark 1:4
r for forgiveness Luke 24:47
r without regret 2 Cor 7:10
r from dead works Heb 6:1

to come to **r** 2 Pet 3:9

REPHAIM
1 *pre-Israelite people of Palestine* Gen 14:5; 15:20
people of large stature
2 *valley near Jerusalem* Josh 15:8; 2 Sam 23:13

REPRESENTATIVE *substitute*
people's **r** before God Ex 18:19
the king's **r** Neh 11:24

REPROACH (n) *dishonor*
taken away my **r** Gen 30:23
a **r** on all Israel 1 Sam 11:2
with dishonor . . . **r** Prov 18:3
not fear the **r** of Is 51:7
the **r** of Christ Heb 11:26

REPROACH (v) *accuse, rebuke*
to **r** the living God 2 Kin 19:4
My heart does not **r** Job 27:6
enemies have **r-ed** me Ps 102:8
He . . . to **r** the cities Matt 11:20
He **r-ed** them for Mark 16:14

REPROOF *correction, rebuke*
spurned all my **r** Prov 1:30
regards **r** is prudent Prov 15:5
who hates **r** will Prov 15:10
and **r** give wisdom Prov 29:15
for teaching, for **r** 2 Tim 3:16

REPROVE *correct, rebuke*
r your neighbor Lev 19:17
LORD loves He **r-s** Prov 3:12
Do not **r** a scoffer Prov 9:8
r him in private Matt 18:15
r, rebuke, exhort 2 Tim 4:2
whom I love, I **r** Rev 3:19

REPTILE *snake*
and the sand **r** Lev 11:30
r-s of the earth Mic 7:17
r-s and creatures James 3:7

REPUTATION *character, esteem*
seven men of good **r** Acts 6:3
a **r** for good works 1 Tim 5:10

REQUEST *desire, petition*
my people as my **r** Esth 7:3
the **r** of his lips Ps 21:2
He gave them their **r** Ps 106:15
r-s be made known to Phil 4:6

REQUIRE *demand, insist*
r your lifeblood Gen 9:5
God **r** from you Deut 10:12
as each day **r-d** Ezra 3:4
your soul is **r-d** Luke 12:20
r-d of stewards 1 Cor 4:2

REQUIREMENT *necessity*
r-s of the Lord Luke 1:6
r of the Law Rom 8:4
law of physical **r** Heb 7:16

RESCUE *deliver, redeem*
O LORD, **r** my soul Ps 6:4
R the weak and needy Ps 82:4
He delivers and **r-s** Dan 6:27
r the godly from 2 Pet 2:9

RESIDE *dwell, live*
stranger who **r-s** Lev 19:34
a son of man **r** in it Jer 49:18
r-d in . . . Nazareth Matt 2:23
those who **r** as aliens 1 Pet 1:1

RESIST *oppose, withstand*
not **r** him who is Matt 5:39
r-ing the Holy Spirit Acts 7:51
he who **r-s** authority Rom 13:2
R the devil James 4:7

RESPECT (n) *regard*
no **r** for the old Deut 28:50

where is My **r** Mal 1:6
please *Him* in all **r-s** Col 1:10
to your masters . . . **r** 1 Pet 2:18

RESPECT (v) *esteem*
They will **r** my son Matt 21:37
not fear God nor **r** Luke 18:4
R what is right Rom 12:17
wife . . . **r** her husband Eph 5:33

REST (n) *remainder*
r turned and fled Judg 20:45
the **r** of the exiles Ezra 6:16
the **r** of your days Prov 19:20
to the **r** . . . parables Luke 8:10

REST (n) *tranquility*
r from our work Gen 5:29
sabbath of solemn **r** Lev 16:31
God gives you **r** Josh 1:13
Return to your **r** Ps 116:7
I will give you **r** Matt 11:28
no **r** for my spirit 2 Cor 2:13
no **r** day and night Rev 14:11

REST (v) *settled, refresh*
the ark **r-ed** upon Gen 8:4
glory . . . LORD **r-ed** Ex 24:16
Spirit **r-ed** upon Num 11:25
R in the LORD Ps 37:7
government will **r** on Is 9:6
r-ed on the seventh Heb 4:4
r from their labors Rev 14:13

RESTING PLACE
dove found no **r** Gen 8:9
This is My **r** forever Ps 132:14
Do not destroy his **r** Prov 24:15
r will be glorious Is 11:10

RESTITUTION *reparation*
owner . . . make **r** Ex 21:34
make **r** in full Num 5:7
r for the lamb 2 Sam 12:6

RESTORE *reestablish, replace*
son he had **r-d** to 2 Kin 8:1
r His righteousness Job 33:26
He **r-s** my soul Ps 23:3
R to me the joy Ps 51:12
O God, **r** us Ps 80:3
the LORD **r-s** Zion Is 52:8
R us to Thee Lam 5:21
his hand was **r-d** Mark 3:5

RESTRAIN *hold back*
the rain . . . was **r-ed** Gen 8:2
who can **r** Him Job 11:10
who **r-s** his lips Prov 10:19
Wilt Thou **r** Thyself Is 64:12
R your voice from Jer 31:16
r-ed the crowds Acts 14:18

RESURRECTION
who say . . . no **r** Matt 22:23
r of the righteous Luke 14:14
being sons of the **r** Luke 20:36
r of judgment John 5:29
the **r** and the life John 11:25
r of the dead Acts 24:21
if there is no **r** 1 Cor 15:13
power of His **r** Phil 3:10
hope through the **r** 1 Pet 1:3
This is the first **r** Rev 20:5

RETRIBUTION *punishment*
days of **r** have come Hos 9:7
stumbling block . . . **r** Rom 11:9
dealing out **r** to 2 Thess 1:8

RETURN *go back* or *repay*
to dust you shall **r** Gen 3:19
clouds **r** after the Eccl 12:2
a remnant . . . will **r** Is 10:22
r-ed to Galilee Luke 4:14
Repent . . . and **r** Acts 3:19
not **r-ing** evil for 1 Pet 3:9

REVEAL *expose, make known*
God had **r-ed** Himself Gen 35:7
He **r-s** mysteries Job 12:22
glory . . . will be **r-ed** Is 40:5
r this mystery Dan 2:47
r them to babes Matt 11:25
blood did not **r** *this* Matt 16:17
Son of Man is **r-ed** Luke 17:30
glory . . . to be **r-ed** Rom 8:18
to **r** His Son in me Gal 1:16
lawlessness is **r-ed** 2 Thess 2:3

REVELATION *divine disclosure*
a **r** to Thy servant 2 Sam 7:27
the **r** ended Dan 7:28
r to the Gentiles Luke 2:32
the **r** of the mystery Rom 16:25
through a **r** of Jesus Gal 1:12
by **r** . . . made known Eph 3:3
The **R** of Jesus Rev 1:1

REVENGE *vengeance*
take our **r** on him Jer 20:10
Never take . . . **r** Rom 12:19

REVERE *adore, venerate*
r My sanctuary Lev 19:30
nations will **r** Thee Is 25:3

REVERENCE *respect, awe*
Worship . . . with **r** Ps 2:11
bow in **r** for Thee Ps 5:7
in **r** prepared an ark Heb 11:7
service with **r** and Heb 12:28

REVILE *use abusive language*
Do you **r** God's high Acts 23:4
are **r-d**, we bless 1 Cor 4:12
r-d for the name of 1 Pet 4:14
r angelic majesties Jude 8

REVIVE *bring back to life*
they **r** the stones Neh 4:2
r us again Ps 85:6
r me in Thy ways Ps 119:37
r-d your concern Phil 4:10

REVOLT *rebellion*
incited **r** within it Ezra 4:15
Speaking . . . and **r** Is 59:13
stirred up a **r** Acts 21:38

REWARD *prize*
emptiness . . . his **r** Job 15:31
r for the righteous Ps 58:11
The **r** of humility Prov 22:4
His **r** is with Him Is 62:11
your **r** in heaven Matt 5:12
not lose his **r** Matt 10:42
looking to the **r** Heb 11:26
receive a full **r** 2 John 8

RIB *bone*
took one of his **r-s** Gen 2:21
r-s *were* in its mouth Dan 7:5

RICH (adj) *wealthy*
Abram was very **r** Gen 13:2
LORD makes poor . . . **r** 1 Sam 2:7
woe to you who are **r** Luke 6:24
being **r** in mercy Eph 2:4
r in good works 1 Tim 6:18

RICH (n) *wealthy*
r shall not pay more Ex 30:15
the **r** above the poor Job 34:19
r among the people Ps 45:12
The **r** and the poor Prov 22:2

RICHES *wealth*
R do not profit Prov 11:4
who trusts in his **r** Prov 11:28
neither poverty nor **r** Prov 30:8
deceitfulness of **r** Matt 13:22
r of His grace Eph 1:7
r of Christ Eph 3:8
His **r** in glory Phil 4:19
Your **r** have rotted James 5:2

RIDDLE *puzzle*
propound a **r** Judg 14:12
my **r** on the harp Ps 49:4
wise and their **r-s** Prov 1:6
propound a **r** Ezek 17:2

RIGHT (adj) *correct* or *direction*
r in the sight of Deut 12:25
r in his own eyes Judg 17:6
r eye makes you Matt 5:29
what your **r** hand is Matt 6:3
Sit at My **r** hand Matt 22:44
the **r** hand of God Mark 16:19
r hand of fellowship Gal 2:9
forsaking the **r** way 2 Pet 2:15

RIGHT (n) *due, prerogative*
her conjugal **r-s** Ex 21:10
r of redemption Lev 25:32
the **r-s** of the poor Prov 29:7
r-s of the afflicted Prov 31:9
my **r** in the gospel 1 Cor 9:18

RIGHTEOUS (adj) *virtuous*
Noah was a **r** man Gen 6:9
LORD is the **r** one Ex 9:27
God is a **r** judge Ps 7:11
for David a **r** Branch Jer 23:5
LORD our God is **r** Dan 9:14
ninety-nine **r** Luke 15:7
coming of the **R** One Acts 7:52
none **r**, not even one Rom 3:10
many will be made **r** Rom 5:19
prayer of a **r** man James 5:16

RIGHTEOUS (n) *moral one*
assembly of the **r** Ps 1:5
LORD tests the **r** Ps 11:5
LORD loves the **r** Ps 146:8
the **r** will flourish Prov 11:28
way of the **r** is Is 26:7
they sell the **r** for Amos 2:6
sends rain on *the* **r** Matt 5:45
r into eternal life Matt 25:46

RIGHTEOUSNESS
reckoned it . . . as **r** Gen 15:6
will repay . . . his **r** 1 Sam 26:23
in the paths of **r** Ps 23:3
judge the world in **r** Ps 96:13
His **r** endures forever Ps 111:3
R exalts a nation Prov 14:34
wrapped me with . . . **r** Is 61:10
The LORD our **r** Jer 23:6
to rain **r** on you Hos 10:12
to fulfill all **r** Matt 3:15
kingdom and His **r** Matt 6:33
you enemy of all **r** Acts 13:10
through one act of **r** Rom 5:18
breastplate of **r** Eph 6:14
the crown of **r** 2 Tim 4:8
peaceful fruit of **r** Heb 12:11
not achieve the **r** James 1:20
suffer for . . . **r** 1 Pet 3:14

RING *jewelry, ornament*
make four gold **r-s** Ex 25:26
took his signet **r** Esth 3:10
As a **r** of gold Prov 11:22
finger **r-s**, nose **r-s** Is 3:21

RIOT *tumult, uprising*
lest a **r** occur Matt 26:5
a **r** was starting Matt 27:24
accused of a **r** Acts 19:40

RIPE *fully developed*
old man of **r** age Gen 35:29
produced **r** grapes Gen 40:10
harvest . . . is **r** Rev 14:15

RISE *go up, issue forth*
mist used to **r** from Gen 2:6
scepter shall **r** Num 24:17
witnesses **r** up Ps 35:11
nation will **r** Matt 24:7
r-n, just as He said Matt 28:6
children will **r** up Mark 13:12
R and walk Luke 5:23
R and pray Luke 22:46
Lord has really **r-n** Luke 24:34

RIVER
r flowed out of Eden Gen 2:10
r of Thy delights Ps 36:8
the **r-s** of Babylon Ps 137:1
r-s in the desert Is 43:20
peace . . . like a **r** Is 66:12
baptized . . . Jordan **R** Mark 1:5
r-s of living water John 7:38
r of the water of life Rev 22:1

ROAR (n) *loud deep sound*
the sound of the **r** 1 Kin 18:41
young lions' **r** Zech 11:3
pass away with a **r** 2 Pet 3:10

ROAR (v) *utter a deep sound*
a voice **r-s** Job 37:4
Let the sea **r** Ps 96:11
LORD will **r** from Jer 25:30
a lion **r** in the Amos 3:4

ROAST *cook*
grain **r-ed** in the fire Lev 2:14
r-ed the . . . *animals* 2 Chr 35:13
slothful man . . . **r** Prov 12:27

ROB *steal*
bear **r-bed** of her Prov 17:12
Do not **r** the poor Prov 22:22
Will a man **r** God Mal 3:8
do you **r** temples Rom 2:22
I **r-bed** . . . churches 2 Cor 11:8

ROBBER *thief*
she lurks as a **r** Prov 23:28
become a den of **r-s** Jer 7:11
crucified two **r-s** Mark 15:27
he fell among **r-s** Luke 10:30
r-s of temples Acts 19:37

ROBBERY *theft*
not vainly hope in **r** Ps 62:10
I hate **r** in the Is 61:8
they are full of **r** Matt 23:25
you are full of **r** Luke 11:39

ROBE *cloak, garment*
cut off . . . Saul's **r** 1 Sam 24:4
justice was like a **r** Job 29:14
r of righteousness Is 61:10
put a scarlet **r** on Matt 27:28
walk . . . in long **r-s** Mark 12:38
wearing a white **r** Mark 16:5
bring . . . the best **r** Luke 15:22
washed their **r-s** Rev 7:14
a **r** dipped in blood Rev 19:13

ROCK *stone*
the cleft of the **r** Ex 33:22
struck the **r** twice Num 20:11
R of his salvation Deut 32:15
LORD is my **r** 2 Sam 22:2
engraved in the **r** Job 19:24
my **r** and my fortress Ps 18:2
r and my Redeemer Ps 19:14
set my feet upon a **r** Ps 40:2
a **r** to stumble over Is 8:14
an everlasting **R** Is 26:4
his house upon the **r** Matt 7:24
upon this **r** I will Matt 16:18
the **r-s** were split Matt 27:51
hewn out in the **r** Mark 15:46
a **r** of offense Rom 9:33

ROD *staff, stick*
fresh **r-s** of poplar Gen 30:37
r of Aaron Num 17:8
break them with a **r** Ps 2:9
Thy **r** and Thy staff Ps 23:4
who spares his **r** Prov 13:24
The **r** of discipline Prov 22:15
r of My anger Is 10:5
rule them with a **r** Rev 19:15

ROME
Italian city Acts 2:10

Roman Empire capital Acts 18:2
Paul held there Acts 28:14,16

ROOF

brought . . . to the **r** Josh 2:6
r . . . woman bathing 2 Sam 11:2
removed the **r** above Mark 2:4
r and let him down Luke 5:19

ROOT (n) *source*

the **r** of Jesse Is 11:10
of money is a **r** 1 Tim 6:10
no **r** of bitterness Heb 12:15
the **R** of David Rev 5:5

ROOT (v) *establish* or *tear out*

r out your Asherim Mic 5:14
r-ed and grounded in Eph 3:17

ROPE *cord*

them down by a **r** Josh 2:15
bound . . . two new **r-s** Judg 15:13
he snapped the **r-s** Judg 16:12
Instead of a belt, a **r** Is 3:24

ROSE (n) *flower*

I am the **r** of Sharon Song 2:1

ROTTENNESS *decay*

passion is **r** to Prov 14:30
r to the house of Hos 5:12

ROYAL *kingly*

captured the **r** city 2 Sam 12:26
all the **r** offspring 2 Kin 11:1
put on her **r** robes Esth 5:1
And a **r** diadem Is 62:3
roof of the **r** palace Dan 4:29
a certain **r** official John 4:46
fulfilling the **r** law James 2:8
a **r** priesthood 1 Pet 2:9

RUDDY *reddish in complexion*

he was **r** 1 Sam 16:12
a youth, and **r** 1 Sam 17:42
beloved is . . . and **r** Song 5:10

RUIN (n) *destruction*

shall be a **r** forever Deut 13:16
the perpetual **r-s** Ps 74:3
Jerusalem in **r-s** Ps 79:1
r of the poor is Prov 10:15
fool's mouth is his **r** Prov 18:7

RUIN (v) *destroy*

to **r** him without Job 2:3
the grain is **r-ed** Joel 1:10
skins will be **r-ed** Luke 5:37

RULE (n) *authority, government*

to establish his **r** 1 Chr 18:3
against the **r** of 2 Chr 21:8
will walk by this **r** Gal 6:16
above all **r** and Eph 1:21
according to the **r-s** 2 Tim 2:5

RULE (v) *govern*

r over the fish Gen 1:26
Gideon, **R** over us Judg 8:22
godless men . . . not **r** Job 34:30
The sun to **r** by day Ps 136:8
By me princes **r** Prov 8:16
women **r** over them Is 3:12
r over the Gentiles Rom 15:12
peace of Christ **r** Col 3:15
r them with a rod Rev 2:27

RULER *king, monarch*

Joseph was the **r** Gen 42:6
no chief . . . or **r** Prov 6:7
your **r-s** have fled Is 22:3
Most High God is **r** Dan 4:32
come forth a **R** Matt 2:6
r of the demons Matt 9:34
r-s of the Gentiles Mark 10:42
the **r** of this world John 12:31
be subject to **r-s** Titus 3:1

RUMOR *gossip, hearsay*

r will be *added* to **r** Ezek 7:26
wars and **r-s** of wars Matt 24:6

RUSHES *marshy plant*

Can the **r** grow Job 8:11
reeds and **r** will rot Is 19:6

RUST *corrosion*

in which there is **r** Ezek 24:6
moth and **r** destroy Matt 6:19
r will be a witness James 5:3

RUTH

Moabitess Ruth 1:4
Naomi's daughter-in-law Ruth 1:14ff
married Boaz Ruth 4:13
in Messianic line Matt 1:5

RUTHLESS *cruel*

Reprove the **r** Is 1:17
song of the **r** is Is 25:5
most **r** of the Ezek 28:7

S

SABAOTH

Lord of Sabaoth is same as Lord of Hosts Rom 9:29; James 5:4

SABBATH *day of rest*

Remember the **s** day Ex 20:8
LORD bless the **s** day Ex 20:11
keep My **s-s** and Lev 26:2
Observe the **s** day Deut 5:12
call the **s** a delight Is 58:13
My **s-s** to be a sign Ezek 20:12
is Lord of the **S** Matt 12:8
S was made for man Mark 2:27
on the **S** to do good Mark 3:4
a **S** day's journey Acts 1:12
are read every **S** Acts 13:27
S rest for the people Heb 4:9

SABBATICAL YEAR

seventh year of rest Lev 25:5

SACKCLOTH *coarse cloth*

put **s** on his loins Gen 37:34
gird on **s** and lament 2 Sam 3:31
with fasting, **s**, and Dan 9:3
sun became black as **s** Rev 6:12

SACRED *consecrated, holy*

took all the **s** things 2 Kin 12:18
perform **s** services 1 Cor 9:13
table and the **s** bread Heb 9:2

SACRIFICE (n) *offering of a life*

Jacob offered a **s** Gen 31:54
a Passover **s** to Ex 12:27
s-s of righteousness Ps 4:5
loyalty rather than **s** Hos 6:6
compassion . . . not **s** Matt 9:13
a living and holy **s** Rom 12:1
by the **s** of Himself Heb 9:26
s-s God is pleased Heb 13:16
offer up spiritual **s-s** 1 Pet 2:5

SACRIFICE (v) *offer a life*

we may **s** to the Lord Ex 5:3
s on it your burnt Ex 20:24
when you **s** a sacrifice Lev 22:29
even **s-d** their sons Ps 106:37
s-ing to the Baals Hos 11:2
lamb had to be **s-d** Luke 22:7
they **s** to demons 1 Cor 10:20

SADDUCEES

Jewish religious party Matt 3:7;16:11,12; Mark 12:18; Acts 5:17;23:6-8

SAIL (n) *canvas for wind*

Nor spread out the **s** Is 33:23
s was . . . embroidered Ezek 27:7

SAIL (v) *proceed by boat*

they **s-ed** to Cyprus Acts 13:4
to **s** past Ephesus Acts 20:16
set **s** from Crete Acts 27:21

SAILOR *mariner, seaman*

s-s . . . knew the sea 1 Kin 9:27
s-s and your pilots Ezek 27:27
every passenger and **s** Rev 18:17

SAINTS *ones faithful to God*

s . . . in the earth Ps 16:3
the **s** of the Highest Dan 7:22
s . . . fallen asleep Matt 27:52
intercedes for the **s** Rom 8:27
s will judge the 1 Cor 6:2
perseverance of the **s** Rev 14:12

SALEM

Jerusalem Gen 14:18; Ps 76:2; Heb 7:1,2

SALOME

1 *wife of Zebedee* Mark 15:40
mother of James and John at open tomb Mark 16:1
2 *daughter of Herodias* Matt 14:6ff; Mark 6:22-26

SALT *preservative*

became a pillar of **s** Gen 19:26
and sowed it with **s** Judg 9:45
be eaten without **s** Job 6:6
the **s** of the earth Matt 5:13
can **s** water produce James 3:12

SALT SEA

the Dead Sea Gen 14:3; Num 34:3

SALT, VALLEY OF

S of Dead Sea 2 Sam 8:13; 2 Chr 25:11

SALVATION *deliverance*

For Thy **s** I wait Gen 49:18
He has become my **s** Ex 15:2
S belongs to the LORD Ps 3:8
my light and my **s** Ps 27:1
lift up the cup of **s** Ps 116:13
helmet of **s** on His Is 59:17
S is from the LORD Jon 2:9
eyes have seen Thy **s** Luke 2:30
s in no one else Acts 4:12
now is the day of **s** 2 Cor 6:2
take the helmet of **s** Eph 6:17
work out your **s** with Phil 2:12
that leads to **s** 2 Tim 3:15
who will inherit **s** Heb 1:14
neglect so great a **s** Heb 2:3
S to our God who Rev 7:10

SAMARIA

1 *capital of N kingdom* 1 Kin 16:24; 2 Chr 18:9
2 *another name for N kingdom* 1 Kin 13:32; 2 Kin 17:24; Hos 8:5; Amos 3:9; Obad 19
3 *region of central hill country* John 4:4-7; Acts 8:1ff

SAMSON

a Hebrew judge Judg 13:24
weak in character Judg 14:1ff
slave of passion Judg 16:1ff
great strength Judg 16:5,12

SAMUEL

son of Elkanah and Hannah 1 Sam 1:20
dedicated to God 1 Sam 1:21ff
called by God 1 Sam 3:1-18
judge 1 Sam 7:15-17
opposed monarchy 1 Sam 8:6
anointed Saul 1 Sam 10:1
anointed David 1 Sam 16:12
death 1 Sam 25:1

SANCTIFICATION *holiness, consecration*

resulting in **s** Rom 6:22
righteousness and **s** 1 Cor 1:30
will of God, your **s** 1 Thess 4:3
s by the Spirit 2 Thess 2:13
s without which no Heb 12:14

SANCTIFY *set apart to God*

S to Me every Ex 13:2

the LORD who **s-ies** Lev 22:32
They will **s** My name Is 29:23
will **s** the Holy One Is 29:23
And **s** My sabbaths Ezek 20:20
S them in the truth John 17:17
husband is **s-ied** 1 Cor 7:14
s Christ as Lord 1 Pet 3:15

SANCTUARY *place of worship*
construct a **s** for Me Ex 25:8
revere My **s** Lev 19:30
utensils of the **s** 1 Chr 9:29
into the **s** of God Ps 73:17
Praise God in His **s** Ps 150:1
beautify . . . My **s** Is 60:13
a minister in the **s** Heb 8:2

SANDAL *footwear*
s has not worn out Deut 29:5
fit to remove His **s-s** Matt 3:11
two tunics, or **s-s** Matt 10:10

SAPPHIRE *precious stone*
a **s** and a diamond Ex 28:18
Inlaid with **s-s** Song 5:14
foundations . . . in **s-s** Is 54:11

SARAH / SARAI
wife of Abraham Gen 11:29
barren Gen 11:30
beautiful Gen 12:11
gave birth to Isaac Gen 21:2,3
death Gen 23:2

SATAN
Titles:
Abaddon Rev 9:11
accuser Ps 109:6; Rev 12:10
adversary 1 Pet 5:8
Apollyon Rev 9:11
Beelzebul Matt 10:25; Mark 3:22
Belial 2 Cor 6:15
deceiver of the world Rev 12:9
devil Matt 4:1,5;25:41; John 6:70;13:2; Eph 4:27;6:11; 1 Tim 3:6,7; Rev 2:10;20:2,10
dragon Rev 12:9
enemy Matt 13:28,39
evil one Matt 13:19,38; John 17:15; 1 John 2:13,14
father of lies John 8:44
god of this world 2 Cor 4:4
liar John 8:44
murderer John 8:44
prince of the air Eph 2:2
ruler of the demons Matt 9:34; Mark 3:22
ruler of this world John 12:31;14:30;16:11
serpent of old Rev 12:9

SATISFY *make content*
eat and not be **s-ied** Lev 26:26
s-ied their desire Ps 78:30
hunger is not **s-ied** Is 29:8
to **s** the multitude Mark 15:15

SATRAPS *Persian officials*
to the king's **s** Ezra 8:36
the **s**, the governors Esth 8:9
commissioners and **s** Dan 6:4

SAUL
1 *son of Kish* 1 Sam 9:1,2
anointed 1 Sam 10:1ff
first king 1 Sam 11:15
rejected as king 1 Sam 15:11ff
jealous of David 1 Sam 18:6ff
death 1 Sam 31:4ff
2 *apostle, see* **PAUL**

SAVE *deliver, rescue*
s-d by the LORD Deut 33:29
S with Thy right hand Ps 60:5
Turn to Me, and be **s-d** Is 45:22
he will **s** his life Ezek 18:27
will **s** His people Matt 1:21
Son . . . has come to **s** Matt 18:11
faith has **s-d** you Luke 7:50
world should be **s-d** John 3:17
Father, **s** Me from John 12:27
be **s-d** by His life Rom 5:10
Jesus came . . . to **s** 1 Tim 1:15
One who is able to **s** James 4:12
the righteous is **s-d** 1 Pet 4:18

SAVIOR *one who saves*
My **s**, Thou dost 2 Sam 22:3
forgot God their **S** Ps 106:21
send them a **S** and a Is 19:20
righteous God and a **S** Is 45:21
S, who is Christ Luke 2:11
the **S** of the world John 4:42
as a Prince and a **S** Acts 5:31
S of all men 1 Tim 4:10
appearing of our **S** 2 Tim 1:10
our great God and **S** Titus 2:13
kingdom of our . . . **S** 2 Pet 1:11

SAVORY *appetizing*
prepare a **s** dish for Gen 27:4
mother made **s** food Gen 27:14

SAWS *cutting tools*
set *them* under **s** 2 Sam 12:31
cut *them* with **s** 1 Chr 20:3

SCALE *for measuring weight*
with accurate **s-s** Job 31:6
false **s** is not good Prov 20:23
been weighed on the **s-s** Dan 5:27
with dishonest **s-s** Amos 8:5
justify wicked **s-s** Mic 6:11
a pair of **s-s** in his Rev 6:5

SCAPEGOAT *for removal of sin*
lot for the **s** fell Lev 16:10
released the goat . . . **s** Lev 16:26

SCARLET *bright red*
tied a **s** *thread* Gen 38:28
s thread . . . window Josh 2:18
lips are like a **s** Song 4:3
sins are as **s** Is 1:18
put a **s** robe on Him Matt 27:28

SCATTER *spread, sprinkle*
s among the nations Lev 26:33
Brimstone is **s-ed** on Job 18:15
s-ing the sheep of Jer 23:1
s him like dust Matt 21:44
sheep . . . shall be **s-ed** Matt 26:31

SCEPTER *symbol of authority*
s shall not depart Gen 49:10
s . . . rise from Israel Num 24:17
A **s** of uprightness Ps 45:6
The **s** of rulers Is 14:5
s of His kingdom Heb 1:8

SCOFFER *mocker*
My friends are my **s-s** Job 16:20
sit in the seat of **s-s** Ps 1:1
He who corrects a **s** Prov 9:7
Behold, you **s-s** Acts 13:41

SCORCHING *burning*
words are as a **s** fire Prov 16:27
s heat or sun strike Is 49:10
appointed a **s** east wind Jon 4:8
s heat of the day Matt 20:12

SCORN *treat with contempt*
s-ed . . . his salvation Deut 32:15
and **s-s** a mother Prov 30:17

SCORPION *poisonous spider*
serpents and **s-s** Deut 8:15
discipline . . . with **s-s** 1 Kin 12:11
tread upon . . . **s-s** Luke 10:19
not give him a **s** Luke 11:12
s-s . . . have power Rev 9:3

SCOURGE (n) *whip*
the **s** of the tongue Job 5:21
arouse a **s** against Is 10:26
He made a **s** of cords John 2:15

SCOURGE (v) *flog, whip*
s and crucify *Him* Matt 20:19
having Jesus **s-d** Matt 27:26
lawful for you to **s** Acts 22:25
He **s-s** every son Heb 12:6

SCREEN *conceal, separate*
s the ark with the veil Ex 40:3
s-ed off the ark Ex 40:21

SCRIBE *copier, writer*
and Sheva was **s** 2 Sam 20:25
then the king's **s** 2 Chr 24:11
Ezra the **s** stood Neh 8:4
lying pen of the **s-s** Jer 8:8
chief priests and **s-s** Matt 2:4
and not as the **s-s** Mark 1:22
Where is the **s** 1 Cor 1:20

SCRIPTURE
understanding . . . **S-s** Matt 22:29
S-s . . . be fulfilled Mark 14:49
S has been fulfilled Luke 4:21
You search the **S-s** John 5:39
S cannot be broken John 10:35
mighty in the **S-s** Acts 18:24
what does the **S** say Rom 4:3
S is inspired by God 2 Tim 3:16

SCROLL *parchment*
these curses on a **s** Num 5:23
Take a **s** and write Jer 36:2
eat this **s**, and go Ezek 3:1
like a **s** . . . rolled Rev 6:14

SEA *body of salt water*
waters He called **s-s** Gen 1:10
s, or the **s** monster Job 7:12
founded it upon the **s-s** Ps 24:2
rebukes the **s** and Nah 1:4
walking on the **s** Matt 14:26
s *began* to be stirred John 6:18
s of glass like crystal Rev 4:6

SEACOAST *seashore*
remnant of the **s** Ezek 25:16
inhabitants of the **s** Zeph 2:5
s will be pastures Zeph 2:6

SEAL (n) *mark, stamp*
Your **s** and your cord Gen 38:18
the engravings of a **s** Ex 28:21
the **s** of perfection Ezek 28:12
witness has set his **s** John 3:33
s of God on their Rev 9:4

SEAL (v) *mark, secure*
s-ed . . . his seal 1 Kin 21:8
s *it* . . . king's signet Esth 8:8
a spring **s-ed** up Song 4:12
to **s** up vision Dan 9:24
s up the book until Dan 12:4

SEARCH *examine, inquire*
LORD **s-es** all hearts 1 Chr 28:9
S me, O God, and Ps 139:23
LORD, **s** the heart Jer 17:10
s for the Child Matt 2:13
You **s** the Scriptures John 5:39

SEASHORE *sea coast*
sand that is on the **s** Josh 11:4
the **s** in abundance 1 Kin 4:20
he stood on . . . **s** Rev 13:1

SEASON *time of the year*
rains in their **s** Lev 26:4
grain in its **s** Job 5:26
its fruit in its **s** Ps 1:3
in **s** *and* out of **s** 2 Tim 4:2

SEAT (n) *chair, stool*
mercy **s** of pure gold Ex 25:17
sit in the **s** of scoffers Ps 1:1
sit in the **s** of gods Ezek 28:2
s-s in the synagogues Matt 23:6
before . . . judgment **s** Rom 14:10

SEAT (v) *sit*
s-ed at His feet Luke 10:39

coming, **s-ed** . . . colt John 12:15
s-ed at the right hand Col 3:1

SECRET *what is hidden*
sets *it* up in **s** Deut 27:15
the **s-s** of wisdom Job 11:6
the **s-s** of the heart Ps 44:21
bread *eaten* in **s** Prov 9:17
A gift in **s** subdues Prov 21:14
have not spoken in **s** Is 45:19
alms may be in **s** Matt 6:4
Father who sees in **s** Matt 6:4
God will judge the **s-s** Rom 2:16

SECT *faction, party*
s of the Sadducees Acts 5:17
s of the Pharisees Acts 15:5
s of the Nazarenes Acts 24:5

SECURE *safe, stable*
overthrows the **s** Job 12:19
be **s** on their land Ezek 34:27
s in the mountain Amos 6:1
made the grave **s** Matt 27:66

SEDUCE *entice, persuade*
if a man **s-s** a virgin Ex 22:16
s you from . . . LORD Deut 13:10
s-d them to do evil 2 Kin 21:9
lips she **s-s** him Prov 7:21

SEED *descendant* or *plant*
sow your **s** uselessly Lev 26:16
establish your **s** Ps 89:4
O **s** of Abraham Ps 105:6
s to the sower Is 55:10
like a mustard **s** Matt 13:31
went out to sow his **s** Luke 8:5
s is the word of God Luke 8:11
s which is perishable 1 Pet 1:23
His **s** abides in him 1 John 3:9

SEEK *pursue, search for*
s the LORD your God Deut 4:29
pray, and **s** My face 2 Chr 7:14
S peace, and pursue it Ps 34:14
s me will find me Prov 8:17
man **s-s** only evil Prov 17:11
s wisdom and an Eccl 7:25
I will **s** the lost Ezek 34:16
time to **s** the LORD Hos 10:12
S good and not evil Amos 5:14
s first His kingdom Matt 6:33
s, and you shall find Matt 7:7
he who **s-s,** finds Luke 11:10
I do not **s** My glory John 8:50
s-ing the things above Col 3:1

SEER *prophet*
prophets . . . every **s** 2 Kin 17:13
Who say to the **s-s** Is 30:10
Go, you **s,** flee away Amos 7:12
s-s will be ashamed Mic 3:7

SEIZE *grasp, take*
mother shall **s** him Deut 21:19
Babylon has been **s-d** Jer 50:46
and **s** her plunder Ezek 29:19
fields and then **s** *them* Mic 2:2
seeking . . . to **s** Him John 7:30

SELA
rock city in Edom Judg 1:36; Is 16:1;42:11
also **Joktheel** 2 Kin 14:7
later known as Petra

SELAH
musical, liturgical Ps 3:2,4,8;20:3;60:4;
or pausal sign Ps 81:7; Hab 3:3,9,13

SELF-CONTROL
s and the judgment Acts 24:25
your lack of **s** 1 Cor 7:5
gentleness, **s** Gal 5:23
without **s,** brutal 2 Tim 3:3
in *your* knowledge, **s** 2 Pet 1:6

SELFISH *self-centered*
the bread of a **s** man Prov 23:6
s ambition in your James 3:14

SELL *barter, trade*
s me your birthright Gen 25:31
s me food for money Deut 2:28
s the oil and pay 2 Kin 4:7
sold a girl for wine Joel 3:3
sold all that he had Matt 13:46
s-ing their property Acts 2:45
sold into bondage Rom 7:14

SENATE
Sanhedrin Acts 5:21

SEND *convey, dispatch*
s rain on the earth Gen 7:4
he **sent** out a raven Gen 8:7
Whom shall I **s** Is 6:8
Lord God has **sent** Me Is 48:16
He has **sent** Me Luke 4:18
s-ing His own Son Rom 8:3
not **s** her husband 1 Cor 7:13
s him . . . in peace 1 Cor 16:11
God **sent** forth His Son Gal 4:4

SENSUALITY
deceit, **s,** envy Mark 7:22
promiscuity and **s** Rom 13:13
themselves over to **s** Eph 4:19
the wealth of her **s** Rev 18:3

SENTENCE *judgment*
s is by the decree Dan 4:17
escape the **s** of hell Matt 23:33
Pilate pronounced **s** Luke 23:24
to the **s** of death Luke 24:20

SEPARATE *divide, set apart*
God **s-d** the light Gen 1:4
They **s** with the lip Ps 22:7
s-s intimate friends Prov 16:28
let no man **s** Matt 19:6
Who shall **s** us from Rom 8:35

SEPARATION *division, isolation*
of his **s** to the LORD Num 6:6
his **s** he is holy Num 6:8
his **s** was defiled Num 6:12
have made a **s** Is 59:2

SERAPHIM
celestial beings Is 6:2,6

SERPENT *snake*
s was more crafty Gen 3:1
they turned into **s-s** Ex 7:12
be shrewd as **s-s** Matt 10:16
will pick up **s-s** Mark 16:18
Moses lifted up the **s** John 3:14

SERVANT *helper, slave*
s of **s-s** He shall be Gen 9:25
Thy **s** is listening 1 Sam 3:9
to shine upon Thy **s** Ps 31:16
s-s of a new covenant 2 Cor 3:6
they **s-s** of Christ 2 Cor 11:23
s of Christ Jesus 1 Tim 4:6

SERVE *help, work for*
shall **s** the LORD Ex 23:25
s Him with . . . heart Josh 22:5
you shall **s** strangers Jer 5:19
God whom we **s** is Dan 3:17
s God and mammon Matt 6:24
If anyone **s-s** Me John 12:26
through love **s** one Gal 5:13

SERVICE *ministry, work*
s of righteous Is 32:17
spiritual **s** of worship Rom 12:1
for the work of **s** Eph 4:12
s with reverence Heb 12:28

SETTLED *arranged* or *inhabited*
Lot **s** in the cities Gen 13:12
cloud **s** over the Num 9:18
assault shall be **s** Deut 21:5
word is **s** in heaven Ps 119:89
mountains were **s** Prov 8:25
s in the lawful Acts 19:39

SEVEN *number*
Jacob served **s** years Gen 29:20
For **s** women . . . one man Is 4:1
will be **s** weeks Dan 9:25
s other spirits more Matt 12:45
forgive . . . **s** times Matt 18:21
John to the **s** churches Rev 1:4
s golden lampstands Rev 1:12

SEVERE *difficult, hard*
famine was **s** Gen 12:10
a very **s** pestilence Ex 9:3
s and lasting plagues Deut 28:59
s judgments against Ezek 14:21
a **s** earthquake had Matt 28:2

SEW *fasten, join*
s-ed fig leaves together Gen 3:7
s-ed sackcloth over Job 16:15
a time to **s** together Eccl 3:7
women who **s** *magic* Ezek 13:18

SEXUAL
not in **s** promiscuity Rom 13:13
from **s** immorality 1 Thess 4:3

SHACKLES *fetters*
will tear off your **s** Nah 1:13
s broken in pieces Mark 5:4
with chains and **s** Luke 8:29

SHADE *protection*
cover him with **s** Job 40:22
The LORD is your **s** Ps 121:5
lived under its **s** Ezek 31:6
over Jonah to be a **s** Jon 4:6
nest under its **s** Mark 4:32

SHADOW *image of shade*
days . . . like a **s** 1 Chr 29:15
the **s** of Thy wings Ps 17:8
in the **s** . . . Almighty Ps 91:1
the **s-s** flee away Song 2:17
his **s** might fall on Acts 5:15
s of the heavenly Heb 8:5

SHAKE *quiver, tremble*
made all my bones **s** Job 4:14
s my head at you Job 16:4
peace will not be **s-n** Is 54:10
s off the dust Matt 10:14
A reed **s-n** by the Matt 11:7
heavens will be **s-n** Luke 21:26
he **shook** the creature Acts 28:5
voice **shook** the earth Heb 12:26

SHAME *disgrace, dishonor*
wicked be put to **s** Ps 31:17
my reproach and my **s** Ps 69:19
s to his mother Prov 29:15
wise men are put to **s** Jer 8:9
worthy to suffer **s** Acts 5:41
glory is in their **s** Phil 3:19
put Him to open **s** Heb 6:6

SHARE (n) *portion*
them take their **s** Gen 14:24
s from My offerings Lev 6:17
give me the **s** Luke 15:12
I do my **s** Col 1:24

SHARE (v) *partake, participate*
stranger does not **s** Prov 14:10
s in the inheritance Prov 17:2
s all good things Gal 6:6
may **s** His holiness Heb 12:10
s the sufferings of 1 Pet 4:13

SHARON
coastal plain in central Israel Is 33:9; 65:10

SHATTER *break, burst*
s-ed every tree of the Ex 9:25
the mighty are **s-ed** 1 Sam 2:4
s them like earthenware Ps 2:9
s the doors of bronze Is 45:2
iron crushes and **s-s** Dan 2:40

SHAVE *cut* or *scrape*
he shall **s** his head Lev 14:9
s off the seven Judg 16:19
s-d off half of 2 Sam 10:4
will **s** with a razor Is 7:20

SHEAF *bundle of grain stalks*
s-ves in the field Gen 37:7
s of the first fruits Lev 23:10
among the **s-ves** Ruth 2:15

SHEARER *wool cutter*
silent before its **s-s** Is 53:7
lamb before its **s** Acts 8:32

SHEBA
1 *son of Raamah* Gen 10:7
2 *son of Joktan* Gen 10:28
3 *grandson of Abraham* Gen 25:3
4 *Simeonite town* Josh 19:2
5 *a Benjamite* 2 Sam 20:1-7
6 *a Gadite* 1 Chr 5:13
7 *kingdom* Job 6:19; Ps 72:10,15; Jer 6:20
8 *Queen of* 2 Chr 9:1ff

SHEBAT
eleventh month of Hebrew calendar Zech 1:7

SHECHEM
1 *city in Ehpraim hill country* Gen 12:6;33:18; 1 Chr 7:28
city of refuge Josh 20:7
2 *son of Hamor* Gen 34:2
3 *line of Manasseh* Num 26:31
4 *son of Shemida* 1 Chr 7:19

SHED *pour out*
Whoever **s-s** man's Gen 9:6
s streams of water Ps 119:136
hasten to **s** blood Prov 1:16
will not **s** its light Is 13:10
bribes to **s** blood Ezek 22:12
s-ding of blood Heb 9:22

SHEEP *animal*
Rachel came with . . . **s** Gen 29:9
not be like **s** Num 27:17
s of His pasture Ps 100:3
All of us like **s** Is 53:6
will care for My **s** Ezek 34:12
lost **s** of . . . Israel Matt 10:6
my **s** which was lost Luke 15:6
His life for the **s** John 10:11
s hear My voice John 10:27
Tend My **s** John 21:17
Shepherd of the **s** Heb 13:20

SHEEPFOLDS *enclosure*
s for the flocks 2 Chr 32:28
lie down among the **s** Ps 68:13
took him from the **s** Ps 78:70

SHEEPSKINS *coverings*
they went about in **s** Heb 11:37

SHEET
hammered out gold **s-s** Ex 39:3
s over *his* naked Mark 14:51
object like a great **s** Acts 10:11

SHELTER *cover, refuge*
under the **s** of my Gen 19:8
in the **s** of Thy wings Ps 61:4
a **s** from the storm Is 32:2
made a **s** for himself Jon 4:5

SHEOL
place of the dead Gen 37:35; Job 7:9; Ps 49:15; Prov 15:11; Is 38:10; Ezek 32:27; Hab 2:5

SHEPHERD (n)
The LORD is my **s** Ps 23:1
Like a **s** He Is 40:11
s-s after My own heart Jer 3:15
for lack of a **s** Ezek 34:5
sheep without a **s** Matt 9:36
strike down the **s** Matt 26:31
s-s . . . in the fields Luke 2:8
I am the good **s** John 10:11
the great **S** Heb 13:20
the Chief **S** 1 Pet 5:4

SHEPHERD (v)
s My people 2 Sam 5:2
S My sheep John 21:16
to **s** the church Acts 20:28
s the flock of God 1 Pet 5:2

SHIBBOLETH
test word for identification Judg 12:6

SHIELD *protection*
Abram, I am a **s** Gen 15:1
He is a **s** to all 2 Sam 22:31
My **s** is with God Ps 7:10
the **s** of faith Eph 6:16

SHILOH
1 *Messianic title* Gen 49:10
2 *town N of Bethel* Josh 18:1
site of tabernacle Judg 18:31

SHINE *be radiant, glow*
his face **shone** Ex 34:29
His face **s** on you Num 6:25
Thy face to **s** *upon us* Ps 80:3
light **s** before men Matt 5:16
lamp **s-ing** in a dark 2 Pet 1:19
light is . . . **s-ing** 1 John 2:8

SHIP *boat*
a haven for **s-s** Gen 49:13
to the sea in **s-s** Ps 107:23
like merchant **s-s** Prov 31:14
escape from the **s** Acts 27:30

SHOOT *new growth*
s will spring from Is 11:1
like a tender **s** Is 53:2
His **s-s** will sprout Hos 14:6

SHORT *lacking*
Is My hand so **s** Is 50:2
days shall be cut **s** Matt 24:22
s of the grace Heb 12:15

SHOUT *cry out loudly*
s with a great **s** Josh 6:5
the people **s-ed** with Ezra 3:11
s for joy Ps 35:27
S joyfully to God Ps 66:1

SHOW *manifest, reveal*
land . . . I will **s** you Gen 12:1
s me Thy glory Ex 33:18
s Thy lovingkindness Ps 17:7
S us the Father John 14:9
God **s-s** no partiality Gal 2:6
if you **s** partiality James 2:9

SHOWBREAD
tables of **s** 1 Chr 28:16
s is *set* . . . table 2 Chr 13:11

SHOWER *abundant flow*
roar of a *heavy* **s** 1 Kin 18:41
Like **s-s** that water Ps 72:6
be **s-s** of blessing Ezek 34:26
A **s** is coming Luke 12:54

SHREWD *cunning*
frustrates . . . the **s** Job 5:12
be **s** as serpents Matt 10:16

SHRINE *object* or *place of worship*
built yourself a **s** Ezek 16:24
tear down your **s-s** Ezek 16:39
who made silver **s-s** Acts 19:24

SIBBOLETH
test word for identification Judg 12:6

SICKLE *cutting tool*
who wields the **s** Jer 50:16
sharp **s** in His hand Rev 14:14
Put in your **s** Rev 14:15

SICKNESS *illness*
remove from you . . . **s** Deut 7:15
every kind of **s** Matt 4:23
authority over . . . **s** Matt 10:1
s is not unto death John 11:4

SIDON
1 *son of Canaan* Gen 10:15; 1 Chr 1:13
2 *Phoenician port* Gen 10:19; Is 23:4; Ezek 28:22

SIEGE *encirclement*
city came under **s** 2 Kin 24:10
their **s** towers Is 23:13
s against Jerusalem Jer 6:6
build a **s** wall Ezek 4:2

SIGHT *perception, vision*
pleasing to the **s** Gen 2:9
precious in My **s** Is 43:4
blind receive **s** Matt 11:5
three days without **s** Acts 9:9
by faith, not by **s** 2 Cor 5:7

SIGN *indication* or *wonder*
a **s** for Cain Gen 4:15
s of the covenant Gen 9:12
blood shall be a **s** Ex 12:13
Ask a **s** for yourself Is 7:11
an everlasting **s** Is 55:13
a **s** from You Matt 12:38
s of Your coming Matt 24:3
s-s in sun and moon Luke 21:25
beginning of *His* **s-s** John 2:11
s of circumcision Rom 4:11
Jews ask for **s-s** 1 Cor 1:22
tongues are for a **s** 1 Cor 14:22
s-s . . . false wonders 2 Thess 2:9

SIGNET *seal*
examine . . . whose **s** Gen 38:25
engravings of a **s** Ex 39:14
s rings of his nobles Dan 6:17

SILAS
co-worker with Paul Acts 15:22,32,40;16:19,25

SILENCE *quietness*
My soul *waits* in **s** Ps 62:1
war will be **s-d** Jer 50:30
s the ignorance 1 Pet 2:15
s in heaven Rev 8:1

SILENT *quiet*
LORD, do not keep **s** Ps 35:22
A time to be **s** Eccl 3:7
But Jesus kept **s** Matt 26:63
women keep **s** 1 Cor 14:34

SILOAM
1 *tower in Jerusalem* Luke 13:4
2 *water pool in Jeru.* John 9:7,11

SILVER *precious metal*
rich in . . . **s** Gen 13:2
took no plunder in **s** Judg 5:19
as **s** is refined Ps 66:10
in settings of **s** Prov 25:11
The **s** is Mine Hag 2:8
not acquire . . . **s** Matt 10:9
thirty pieces of **s** Matt 26:15

SIMEON
1 *son of Jacob* Gen 29:33
2 *tribe* Num 1:23; Rev 7:7
3 *devout Jew* Luke 2:25
4 *ancestor of Jesus* Luke 3:30
5 *Christian prophet* Acts 13:1
6 *Simon Peter* Acts 15:14

SIMON
1 *apostle* Matt 4:18; Mark 1:16
2 *the Zealot* Matt 10:4; Mark 3:18; Luke 6:15
3 *brother of Jesus* Matt 13:55; Mark 6:3
4 *leper* Matt 26:6; Mark 14:3
5 *a Pharisee* Luke 7:40,43

6 *of Cyrene carried Jesus' cross* Matt 27:32; Mark 15:21; Luke 23:26
7 *father of Judas* John 6:71;13:2
8 *Magus sorcerer* Acts 8:9,13,18
9 *the tanner* Acts 9:43;10:6,32

SIN (n) *transgression*
please forgive my **s** Ex 10:17
atonement for your **s** Ex 32:30
s will find you out Num 32:23
s of divination 1 Sam 15:23
the **s-s** of my youth Ps 25:7
s my mother conceived Ps 51:5
Fools mock at **s** Prov 14:9
bore the **s** of many Is 53:12
an eternal **s** Mark 3:29
forgive us our **s-s** Luke 11:4
takes away the **s** John 1:29
wash away your **s-s** Acts 22:16
wages of **s** is death Rom 6:23
died for our **s-s** 1 Cor 15:3
Him who knew no **s** 2 Cor 5:21
pleasures of **s** Heb 11:25
confess our **s-s** 1 John 1:9
s is lawlessness 1 John 3:4

SIN (v) *transgress*
When a leader **s-s** Lev 4:22
s against the LORD 1 Sam 14:34
Job did not **s** Job 1:22
s against Thee Ps 119:11
I have **s-ned** Luke 15:18
s no more John 8:11
all have **s-ned** Rom 3:23
that you may not **s** 1 John 2:1

SIN
1 *wilderness in Sinai* Ex 16:1; Num 33:11,12
2 *Egyptian city* Ezek 30:15,16

SINAI
1 *mountain* Ex 19:11; Lev 26:46; Num 28:6
where Law received Ex 31:18
2 *desert wilderness* Ex 16:1;19:1; Num 1:19;9:5

SINCERE *without deceit*
be **s** and blameless Phil 1:10
mindful of the **s** faith 2 Tim 1:5
s love . . . brethren 1 Pet 1:22

SINEW *strength* or *tendon*
with bones and **s-s** Job 10:11
neck is an iron **s** Is 48:4
will put **s-s** on you Ezek 37:6

SING
s to the LORD Ex 15:1
s-ing and dancing 1 Sam 18:6
I will **s** praises 2 Sam 22:50
S to Him a new song Ps 33:3
the righteous **s-s** Prov 29:6
after **s-ing** a hymn Mark 14:26
sang a new song Rev 5:9

SINGERS
these are the **s** 1 Chr 9:33
male and female **s** Eccl 2:8

SINK *descend, fall*
do not let me **s** Ps 69:14
so shall Babylon **s** Jer 51:64

SINNER *wrongdoer*
He instructs **s-s** Ps 25:8
if **s-s** entice you Prov 1:10
one **s** destroys much Eccl 9:18
a friend of . . . **s-s** Matt 11:19
one **s** who repents Luke 15:7
merciful to me . . . **s** Luke 18:13
while we were yet **s-s** Rom 5:8
came . . . to save **s-s** 1 Tim 1:15

SISTER
She is my **s** Gen 12:19
We have a little **s** Song 8:8
a **s** called Mary Luke 10:39
younger women . . . **s-s** 1 Tim 5:2

SIT *recline, rest*
Moses **sat** to judge Ex 18:13
S at My right hand Ps 110:1
lonely **s-s** the city Lam 1:1
who **s** in darkness Luke 1:79
where the harlot **s-s** Rev 17:15

SIVAN
third month of Hebrew calendar Esth 8:9

SKILL *proficiency*
filled them with **s** Ex 35:35
the heavens with **s** Ps 136:5
s-ed in destruction Ezek 21:31

SKIN *covering*
garments of **s** Gen 3:21
s of his face shone Ex 34:29
My **s** turns black Job 30:30
will burst the **s-s** Mark 2:22

SKIP *hop, leap*
children **s** about Job 21:11
Lebanon **s** like a calf Ps 29:6
go forth and **s** Mal 4:2

SKULL *bony framework of head*
head, crushing his **s** Judg 9:53
the **s** and the feet 2 Kin 9:35
Place of a **S** Matt 27:33

SKY *heavens*
sun stopped in . . . **s** Josh 10:13
the **s** grew black 1 Kin 18:45
for the **s** is red Matt 16:2
will appear in the **s** Matt 24:30
s was shut up Luke 4:25
gazing . . . into the **s** Acts 1:10

SLANDER (n) *defamation*
spreads **s** is a fool Prov 10:18
s-s, gossip 2 Cor 12:20
and **s** be put away Eph 4:31

SLANDER (v) *defame*
He does not **s** Ps 15:3
Whoever secretly **s-s** Ps 101:5
Do not **s** a slave Prov 30:10

SLANDERER *defamer*
s separates . . . friends Prov 16:28
s-s, haters of God Rom 1:30

SLAUGHTER (n) *brutal killing*
great **s** at Gibeon Josh 10:10
lamb led to the **s** Jer 11:19
as a sheep to **s** Acts 8:32
in a day of **s** James 5:5

SLAUGHTER (v) *kill*
shall **s** the bull Ex 29:11
shall **s** the lamb Lev 14:25
Who **s** the children Is 57:5
s-ed My children Ezek 16:21

SLAVE *bond servant*
The Hebrew **s** Gen 39:17
s at forced labor Gen 49:15
sold *in* a **s** sale Lev 25:42
Is Israel a **s** Jer 2:14
S-s rule over us Lam 5:8
good and faithful **s** Matt 25:21
shall be **s** of all Mark 10:44
is the **s** of sin John 8:34
neither **s** nor free Gal 3:28
as **s-s** of Christ Eph 6:6

SLAVERY *servitude*
from the house of **s** Ex 13:3
ransomed you from . . . **s** Mic 6:4
received a spirit of **s** Rom 8:15
to a yoke of **s** Gal 5:1

SLAY *destroy, kill*
knife to **s** his son Gen 22:10
s-s the foolish Job 5:2
Though He **s** me Job 13:15
s her with thirst Hos 2:3
Lamb that was **slain** Rev 5:12

SLEEP (n) *rest*
caused a deep **s** Gen 2:21
Do not love **s** Prov 20:13
a spirit of deep **s** Is 29:10
s fled from him Dan 6:18

SLEEP (v) *slumber*
why dost Thou **s** Ps 44:23
neither slumber nor **s** Ps 121:4
who **s-s** in harvest Prov 10:5
found them **s-ing** Matt 26:43
we shall not all **s** 1 Cor 15:51

SLUGGARD *lazy one*
to the ant, O **s** Prov 6:6
the **s** craves Prov 13:4
s buries his hand Prov 26:15

SLUMBER *sleep*
s in their beds Job 33:15
He . . . will not **s** Ps 121:3
None **s-s** or sleeps Is 5:27
Dreamers . . . love to **s** Is 56:10

SMILE *grin*
I **s-d** on them Job 29:24
that I may **s** *again* Ps 39:13
she **s-s** at the future Prov 31:25

SMITE *hit, strike*
s . . . with frogs Ex 8:2
sun will not **s** you Ps 121:6
righteous **s** me Ps 141:5
s the earth Rev 11:6

SMOKE *mist, vapor*
Sinai *was* all in **s** Ex 19:18
like **s** they vanish Ps 37:20
temple was filling with **s** Is 6:4
s rises up forever Rev 19:3

SNAKE *serpent*
horned **s** in the path Gen 49:17
a **s** bites him Amos 5:19
s instead of a fish Luke 11:11

SNARE *trap*
gods shall be a **s** Judg 2:3
s-s of death 2 Sam 22:6
laid a **s** for me Ps 119:110
caught in My **s** Ezek 12:13
s of the devil 1 Tim 3:7

SNOW *ice flakes*
storehouses of the **s** Job 38:22
be whiter than **s** Ps 51:7
He gives **s** like wool Ps 147:16
Like **s** in summer Prov 26:1
as white as **s** Matt 28:3

SOBER *serious, temperate*
words of **s** truth Acts 26:25
be alert and **s** 1 Thess 5:6
Be of **s** *spirit* 1 Pet 5:8

SODOM
city S of Dead Sea Gen 10:19
home of Lot Gen 19:1,4
destroyed by God Gen 19:24

SODOMITE
one guilty of unnatural sexual practices 1 Kin 22:46

SOIL *earth, ground*
first fruits of your **s** Ex 23:19
he loved the **s** 2 Chr 26:10
fell into the good **s** Mark 4:8

SOJOURN *visit temporarily*
S in this land Gen 26:3
stranger **s-s** with you Ex 12:48
s . . . land of Moab Ruth 1:1

SOJOURNER
s in a foreign land Ex 2:22
are s-s before Thee 1 Chr 29:15
oppressed the s Ezek 22:29

SOLDIER *military man*
s-s took Him away Mark 15:16
s-s also mocked Luke 23:36
s-s pierced His side John 19:34
a devout s Acts 10:7
good s of Christ 2 Tim 2:3

SOLEMN *deeply earnest, serious*
sabbath of s rest Lev 16:31
have a s assembly Num 29:35
sworn s oaths Ezek 21:23
bound . . . a s oath Acts 23:14

SOLOMON
1 *son of David* 2 Sam 12:24
king of Israel 1 Kin 1:43
ruled wisely 1 Kin 4:29,34
built the Temple 1 Kin 6:2;9:1
international fame 1 Kin 10:1
ruled foolishly 1 Kin 11:6
death 1 Kin 11:43
2 *Song of Solomon*

SON *male descendant*
the s-s of Noah Gen 9:18
O Absalom, my s 2 Sam 18:33
to be a s to Me 1 Chr 28:6
s-s of God shouted Job 38:7
Thou art My S Ps 2:7
Discipline your s Prov 19:18
bear a s . . . Immanuel Is 7:14
Egypt I called My s Hos 11:1
she gave birth to a S Matt 1:25
This is My beloved S Matt 3:17
I am the S of God Matt 27:43
S of Man . . . suffer Mark 8:31
If You are the S Luke 4:3
man had two s-s Luke 15:11
only begotten S John 3:16
S also gives life John 5:21
sending His own S Rom 8:3
image of His S Rom 8:29
not spare His own S Rom 8:32
fellowship with His S 1 Cor 1:9
if a s, then an heir Gal 4:7
abide in the S 1 John 2:24
He who has the S 1 John 5:12

SON-IN-LAW
the s of the Timnite Judg 15:6
be the king's s 1 Sam 18:18
s of Sanballat Neh 13:28

SON OF GOD
Messianic title indicating deity of Jesus Christ
Matt 4:3;8:29;16:16; Mark 1:20;3:11;14:61; Luke 1:35; John 3:18;11:27; Acts 8:37

SON OF MAN
Messianic title of Jesus Christ
Matt 8:20;9:6; Mark 2:10; 10:33; Luke 12:10;18:31

SONG *melody, music*
Lord is my . . . s Ex 15:2
gives s-s in the night Job 35:10
s-s of deliverance Ps 32:7
Sing to Him a new s Ps 33:3
Praise the Lord in s Is 12:5
not drink wine with s Is 24:9
hymns . . . spiritual s-s Eph 5:19

SORCERER *witch*
interprets . . . or a s Deut 18:10
witness against the s-s Mal 3:5
immoral persons . . . s-s Rev 21:8

SORCERY *witchcraft*
practiced s 2 Chr 33:6
idolatry, s, enmities Gal 5:20
deceived by your s Rev 18:23

SORDID *filthy*
fond of s gain 1 Tim 3:8
the sake of s gain Titus 1:11
not for s gain 1 Pet 5:2

SORROW *grief, sadness*
down to Sheol in s Gen 42:38
life is spent with s Ps 31:10
man of s-s Is 53:3
s is beyond healing Jer 8:18
s . . . turned to joy John 16:20
if I cause you s 2 Cor 2:2

SOUL *life, spirit*
her s was departing Gen 35:18
humble your s-s Lev 16:29
not abandon my s Ps 16:10
my s pants for Thee Ps 42:1
Bless . . . Lord, O my s Ps 103:1
who is wise wins s-s Prov 11:30
s who sins will die Ezek 18:4
unable to kill the s Matt 10:28
My s is . . . grieved Matt 26:38
and forfeit his s Mark 8:36
My s exalts the Lord Luke 1:46
your s is required Luke 12:20
an anchor of the s Heb 6:19
war against the s 1 Pet 2:11

SOUND (n) *noise*
s of Thee in . . . garden Gen 3:10
s of war in the camp Ex 32:17
s of a great army 2 Kin 7:6
s of many waters Ezek 43:2

SOUND (v) *express*
s His praise abroad Ps 66:8
s an alarm Joel 2:1
trumpet will s 1 Cor 15:52

SOURCE *origin*
the s of sapphires Job 28:6
s of eternal salvation Heb 5:9
s of quarrels James 4:1

SOVEREIGNTY *authority*
His s rules over all Ps 103:19
s from Damascus Is 17:3
s will be uprooted Dan 11:4

SOW *plant, spread*
you may s the land Gen 47:23
who s in tears Ps 126:5
who s-s iniquity will Prov 22:8
birds . . . do not s Matt 6:26
s-ed spiritual things 1 Cor 9:11
whatever a man s-s Gal 6:7

SOWER *planter*
seed to the s Is 55:10
s went out to sow Matt 13:3
s sows the word Mark 4:14

SPARE *save* or *be lenient*
did not s their soul Ps 78:50
who s-s his rod Prov 13:24
No man s-s his brother Is 9:19
not s His own Son Rom 8:32
I will not s *anyone* 2 Cor 13:2
God did not s angels 2 Pet 2:4

SPEAK *proclaim, tell*
God **spoke** to Noah Gen 8:15
God s-s with man Deut 5:24
S of all His wonders 1 Chr 16:9
and a time to s Eccl 3:7
the dumb to s Mark 7:37
s that . . . we know John 3:11
s with other tongues Acts 2:4
If I s with tongues 1 Cor 13:1

SPEAR *weapon*
leaning on his s 2 Sam 1:6
s-s into pruning hooks Is 2:4
pruning hooks into s-s Joel 3:10
pierced . . . with a s John 19:34

SPECK *particle*
regarded as a s of Is 40:15
s out of your eye Matt 7:4

SPEECH *message, word*
I am slow of s Ex 4:10
His s was smoother Ps 55:21
in cleverness of s 1 Cor 1:17
I am unskilled in s 2 Cor 11:6

SPELL *incantation*
one who casts a s Deut 18:11
skillful caster of s-s Ps 58:5
power of your s-s Is 47:9

SPICE
s and the oil Ex 35:28
mix in the s-s Ezek 24:10
prepared s-s and Luke 23:56
wrappings with . . . s-s John 19:40

SPIES *clandestine persons*
we are not s Gen 42:31
two men as s Josh 2:1
David sent out s 1 Sam 26:4
welcomed the s Heb 11:31

SPIN *make thread*
nor do they s Matt 6:28
neither toil nor s Luke 12:27

SPIRIT
S rested upon them Num 11:26
God sent an evil s Judg 9:23
renew a steadfast s Ps 51:10
my s grows faint Ps 77:3
a haughty s before Prov 16:18
the S lifted me up Ezek 3:14
his s was troubled Dan 2:1
are the poor in s Matt 5:3
authority over . . . s-s Matt 10:1
put My S upon Him Matt 12:18
blasphemy . . . the S Matt 12:31
yielded up *His* s Matt 27:50
S like a dove Mark 1:10
born of . . . the S John 3:5
worship in s and John 4:24
gave up His s John 19:30
pour forth of My S Acts 2:17
Jesus, receive my s Acts 7:59
power of the S Rom 15:19
taught by the S 1 Cor 2:13
pray with the s 1 Cor 14:15
walk by the S Gal 5:16
fruit of the S is love Gal 5:22
one body and one S Eph 4:4
be filled with the S Eph 5:18
not quench the S 1 Thess 5:19
division of soul and s Heb 4:12
the s-s *now* in prison 1 Pet 3:19
S who bears witness 1 John 5:7

SPIRIT OF GOD
the S was moving Gen 1:2
S came upon him 1 Sam 10:10
a vision by the S Ezek 11:24
S descending as a Matt 3:16
being led by the S Rom 8:14
S dwells in you 1 Cor 3:16
worship in the S Phil 3:3

SPIRIT OF THE LORD
S came upon him Judg 3:10
S departed from 1 Sam 16:14
filled with . . . the S Mic 3:8
S is upon Me Luke 4:18

SPIRITIST *medium*
not turn to . . . s-s Lev 19:31
s . . . be put to death Lev 20:27
removed . . . the s-s 2 Kin 23:24

SPIRITUAL *of the spirit*
the Law is s Rom 7:14
s service of worship Rom 12:1
raised a s body 1 Cor 15:44
with every s blessing Eph 1:3
hymns and s songs Eph 5:19
offer up s sacrifices 1 Pet 2:5

SPIT
began to s at Him Mark 14:65
and s upon Luke 18:32

He **spat** on . . . ground John 9:6
I will **s** you out Rev 3:16

SPLENDOR *magnificence*

the moon going in **s** Job 31:26
displayed Thy **s** Ps 8:1
Thy **s** and Thy majesty Ps 45:3
clothed with **s** Ps 104:1
s covers the heavens Hab 3:3

SPLIT *divide*

He **s** the rock Is 48:21
valleys will be **s** Mic 1:4
Mount . . . will be **s** Zech 14:4
sky was **s** apart Rev 6:14

SPOIL *booty, pillage*

he divides the **s** Gen 49:27
the **s** of the cities Deut 2:35
widows may be their **s** Is 10:2
for **s** to the nations Ezek 25:7

SPONGE *absorbent matter*

taking a **s**, he filled Matt 27:48
a **s** with sour wine Mark 15:36

SPOT *speck*

Or the leopard his **s-s** Jer 13:23
no **s** or wrinkle Eph 5:27

SPOTLESS *no defects*

unblemished and **s** 1 Pet 1:19
s and blameless 2 Pet 3:14

SPRING (adj) *period, season*

has been no **s** rain Jer 3:3
Like the **s** rain Hos 6:3
s crop began to sprout Amos 7:1

SPRING (n) *water source*

went down to the **s** Gen 24:16
stop all **s-s** of water 2 Kin 3:19
s-s of the deep . . . fixed Prov 8:28
the **s-s** of salvation Is 12:3
s of the water of life Rev 21:6

SPRING (v) *jump, leap*

S up, O well Num 21:17
Truth **s-s** from the Ps 85:11
s-ing up to eternal John 4:14

SPRINKLE *scatter*

take its blood and **s** Ex 29:16
s some of the blood Lev 4:6
s *it* seven times Lev 4:17
s some of the oil Lev 14:16

SPY *investigate*

Moses sent . . . to **s** Num 13:17
to **s** out Jericho Josh 6:25
spied out Bethel Judg 1:23
s out our liberty Gal 2:4

STAFF *rod*

s of God in his hand Ex 4:20
Thy **s**, they comfort Ps 23:4
or sandals, or a **s** Matt 10:10
a mere **s**; no bread Mark 6:8

STAIN *blemish*

s of your iniquity Jer 2:22
without **s** . . . reproach 1 Tim 6:14

STAND *maintain position*

s before the LORD Deut 10:8
O sun, **s** still Josh 10:12
word of our God **s-s** Is 40:8
will **s** on the Mount Zech 14:4
s-ing by the cross John 19:25
why do you **s** looking Acts 1:11
s by your faith Rom 11:20
s firm in the faith 1 Cor 16:13
I **s** at the door Rev 3:20

STANDARD *banner* or *rule*

set up their own **s-s** Ps 74:4
set up My **s** Is 49:22
s of the Law Acts 22:12
s of sound words 2 Tim 1:13

STAR *heavenly body*

He made the **s-s** Gen 1:16
morning **s-s** sang Job 38:7
s-s for light by night Jer 31:35
His **s** in the east Matt 2:2
s fell from heaven Rev 8:10
the bright morning **s** Rev 22:16

STATE *position, condition*

s of expectation Luke 3:15
of our humble **s** Phil 3:21
s has become worse 2 Pet 2:20

STATURE *height*

was growing in **s** 1 Sam 2:26
in wisdom and **s** Luke 2:52
he was small in **s** Luke 19:3
measure of the **s** Eph 4:13

STATUTE *law, rule*

My **s-s** and My laws Gen 26:5
a perpetual **s** Ex 29:9
Teach me Thy **s-s** Ps 119:26
not walked in My **s-s** Ezek 5:7

STEADFAST *established, firm*

be **s** and not fear Job 11:15
renew a **s** spirit Ps 51:10
s in righteousness Prov 11:19
be **s**, immovable 1 Cor 15:58

STEAL *rob, take*

You shall not **s** Ex 20:15
be in want and **s** Prov 30:9
thieves break in . . . **s** Matt 6:19
Do not **s** Mark 10:19

STEPHEN

deacon Acts 6:5,8
martyred Acts 7:59;8:2

STEPS *distance* or *movements*

dost number my **s** Job 14:16
His **s** do not slip Ps 37:31
s lay hold of Sheol Prov 5:5
in the **s** of the faith Rom 4:12
follow in His **s** 1 Pet 2:21

STEWARDSHIP *responsibility*

an account of your **s** Luke 16:2
a **s** entrusted to me 1 Cor 9:17
s of God's grace Eph 3:2

STIFFEN *make rigid*

s your neck no more Deut 10:16
do not **s** your neck 2 Chr 30:8
have **s-ed** their necks Jer 19:15

STIMULATE *excite*

how to **s** my body Eccl 2:3
s one another to Heb 10:24

STING *pain*

where is your **s** 1 Cor 15:55
s of death is sin 1 Cor 15:56

STIR *agitate*

S up Thyself Ps 35:23
man **s-s** up strife Prov 29:22
s-red up the water John 5:4

STOCKS *confinement*

put my feet in the **s** Job 13:27
Jeremiah from the **s** Jer 20:3
their feet in the **s** Acts 16:24

STOMACH *part of body*

s will be satisfied Prov 18:20
s of the fish Jon 1:17
s was made bitter Rev 10:10

STONE (n) *rock*

they used brick for **s** Gen 11:3
two **s** tablets Ex 34:1
five smooth **s-s** 1 Sam 17:40
Water wears . . . **s-s** Job 14:19
foot against a **s** Ps 91:12
in Zion a **s** Is 28:16
serving wood and **s** Ezek 20:32
foot against a **s** Matt 4:6
rolled away the **s** Matt 28:2
s-s will cry out Luke 19:40
six **s** waterpots John 2:6
first to throw a **s** John 8:7
Remove the **s** John 11:39
s-s, wood, hay 1 Cor 3:12
A **s** of stumbling 1 Pet 2:8

STONE (v) *throw stones*

people will **s** us Luke 20:6
seeking to **s** You John 11:8
went on **s-ing** Stephen Acts 7:59
they **s-d** Paul Acts 14:19

STORE *accumulate*

s up the grain Gen 41:35
His sin is **s-d** up Hos 13:12
place to **s** my crops Luke 12:17
s-d up your treasure James 5:3

STOREHOUSE *storage place*

s-s of the snow Job 38:22
wind from His **s-s** Jer 10:13
tithe into the **s** Mal 3:10

STORK *bird*

the **s**, the heron Lev 11:19
the **s** in the sky Jer 8:7
wings of a **s** Zech 5:9

STORM *tempest, whirlwind*

A refuge from the **s** Is 25:4
will come like a **s** Ezek 38:9
a great **s** on the sea Jon 1:4
mists driven by a **s** 2 Pet 2:17

STRANGE *foreign*

offered **s** fire Lev 10:1
no **s** god among you Ps 81:9
to teach **s** doctrines 1 Tim 1:3
went after **s** flesh Jude 7

STRANGER *alien, sojourner*

a **s** and a sojourner Gen 23:4
shall not wrong a **s** Ex 22:21
LORD protects the **s-s** Ps 146:9
violence to the **s** Jer 22:3
I was a **s** Matt 25:35
hospitality to **s-s** Heb 13:2

STRAW *stalk of grain*

s to make brick Ex 5:7
s for the horses 1 Kin 4:28
as **s** before the wind Job 21:18
wood, hay, **s** 1 Cor 3:12

STREAM *current, flow*

planted by **s-s** of water Ps 1:3
The **s** of God Ps 65:9
like a rushing **s** Is 59:19

STREET *road, way*

Wisdom shouts in . . . **s** Prov 1:20
race madly in the **s-s** Nah 2:4
on the **s** corners Matt 6:5
s of the city . . . gold Rev 21:21

STRENGTH *force, power*

The LORD is my **s** Ex 15:2
was no **s** in him 1 Sam 28:20
My **s** is dried up Ps 22:15
The LORD is my **s** Ps 28:7
God is our refuge . . . **s** Ps 46:1
s of my salvation Ps 140:7
your **s** to women Prov 31:3
s to the weary Is 40:29
Strangers devour his **s** Hos 7:9
s which God supplies 1 Pet 4:11

STRENGTHEN *make strong*

David **s-ed** himself 1 Sam 30:6
s-ed weak hands Job 4:3
s the feeble Is 35:3
s the sick Ezek 34:16
s your brothers Luke 22:32
Him who **s-s** me Phil 4:3
s your hearts 2 Thess 2:17

who has **s-ed** me 1 Tim 1:12

STRIFE *discord, quarrel*
s between . . . herdsmen Gen 13:7
the s of tongues Ps 31:20
Hatred stirs up s Prov 10:12
fool's lips bring s Prov 18:6
of envy, murder, s Rom 1:29
and s among you 1 Cor 3:3
enmities, s, jealousy Gal 5:20

STRIKE *hit*
you shall s the rock Ex 17:6
s the timbrel Ps 81:2
you s your foot Ps 91:12
S a scoffer Prov 19:25
let us s at him Jer 18:18
S the Shepherd Zech 13:7
s . . . the shepherd Matt 26:31

STRIVE *contend, struggle*
not s with man forever Gen 6:3
He will not always s Ps 103:9
and **s-ing** after wind Eccl 1:14
we labor and s 1 Tim 4:10
s-ing against sin Heb 12:4

STRONG *powerful, steadfast*
a very s west wind Ex 10:19
Be s and courageous Deut 31:6
God is . . . s fortress 2 Sam 22:33
The LORD s and mighty Ps 24:8
s drink a brawler Prov 20:1
their Redeemer is s Prov 23:11
love is as s as death Song 8:6
Their Redeemer is s Jer 50:34
act like men, be s 1 Cor 16:13
be s in the Lord Eph 6:10
I saw a s angel Rev 5:2

STRONGHOLD *fortress, refuge*
David lived in the s 2 Sam 5:9
s and my refuge 2 Sam 22:3
For God is my s Ps 59:9
my salvation, My s Ps 62:2
a s to the upright Prov 10:29

STRUGGLE (n) *conflict*
the days of my s Job 14:14
our s is not against Eph 6:12
have shared my s Phil 4:3

STRUGGLE (v) *contend*
children **s-d** together Gen 25:22
men s . . . each other Ex 21:22

STUBBLE *short stumps*
gather s for straw Ex 5:12
fire consumes s Is 5:24
give birth to s Is 33:11
house of Esau . . . s Obad 18

STUBBORN *obstinate*
Pharaoh's heart is s Ex 7:14
you are a s people Deut 9:6
s . . . generation Ps 78:8
house of Israel is s Ezek 3:7

STUMBLE *fall, trip*
your foot will not s Prov 3:23
a rock to s over Is 8:14
arrogant one will s Jer 50:32
eye makes you s Matt 5:29
a stone of **s-ing** Rom 9:33
all s in many *ways* James 3:2

STUMBLING BLOCK *obstacle*
s before the blind Lev 19:14
s of iniquity Ezek 44:12
You are a s to Me Matt 16:23
to Jews a s 1 Cor 1:23
s of the cross Gal 5:11

STUPID *foolish, senseless*
s and the senseless Ps 49:10
I am more s than Prov 30:2
they are altogether s Jer 10:8

STYLUS *marking/writing device*
an iron s and lead Job 19:24
with an iron s Jer 17:1

SUBDUE *conquer, overcome*
fill the earth, and s Gen 1:28
the land was **s-d** Josh 18:1
s nations before him Is 45:1

SUBJECT (adj) *under authority*
s to forced labor Judg 1:30
demons are s to us Luke 10:17
church is s to Christ Eph 5:24
s to . . . husbands Titus 2:5
be s to the Father Heb 12:9

SUBJECT (v)
s him to a slave's Lev 25:39
creation was **s-ed** Rom 8:20
them s themselves 1 Cor 14:34
all things are **s-ed** 1 Cor 15:28

SUBJECTION *under authority*
kingdom . . . in s Ezek 17:14
He continued in s Luke 2:51
s to the governing Rom 13:1
all things in s 1 Cor 15:27

SUBMISSIVE *yielding*
Servants, be s 1 Pet 2:18
s to . . . husbands 1 Pet 3:5

SUBMIT *yield to*
Foreigners s to me Ps 18:44
s yourself to decrees Col 2:20
S therefore to God James 4:7

SUBSTITUTE
s shall become holy Lev 27:10
s darkness for light Is 5:20
s bitter for sweet Is 5:20

SUCCESS *accomplishment*
grant me s today Gen 24:12
hands cannot attain s Job 5:12
Daniel enjoyed s Dan 6:28

SUFFER *experience pain*
s the fate of all Num 16:29
Son of Man must s Mark 8:31
s and rise again Luke 24:46
we s with *Him* Rom 8:17
if one member **s-s** 1 Cor 12:26
s-ing for the gospel 2 Tim 1:8
Christ also **s-ed** 1 Pet 2:21

SUFFERINGS *distresses*
s of this present Rom 8:18
sharers of our s 2 Cor 1:7
fellowship of His s Phil 3:10
rejoice in my s Col 1:24
share the s of Christ 1 Pet 4:13

SUMMER *season*
Thou hast made s Ps 74:17
Like snow in s Prov 26:1
know that s is near Matt 24:32

SUMMIT *peak, top*
Like the s of Lebanon Jer 22:6
hide on the s Amos 9:3

SUN *heavenly body*
the s stood still Josh 10:13
chariots of the s 2 Kin 23:11
God is a s Ps 84:11
s will not smite Ps 121:6
new under the s Eccl 1:9
shine forth as the s Matt 13:43
signs in the s Luke 21:25
not let the s go down Eph 4:26
clothed with the s Rev 12:1

SUNRISE *appearance of sun*
toward the s Num 3:38
Jordan toward the s Josh 1:15

SUNSET
Passover . . . at s Deut 16:6
dawn and the s shout Ps 65:8

SUNSHINE
Through s after rain 2 Sam 23:4
dazzling heat in the s Is 18:4

SUPPER *meal*
made Him a s John 12:2
eat the Lord's S 1 Cor 11:20
marriage s of the Rev 19:9
the great s of God Rev 19:17

SUPPLICATION *petition*
Make s to the LORD Ex 9:28
LORD has heard my s Ps 6:9
poor man utters **s-s** Prov 18:23
seek *Him by* . . . **s-s** Dan 9:3
by prayer and s Phil 4:6

SUPPORT (n) *strength*
the LORD was my s 2 Sam 22:19
gave him strong s 1 Chr 11:10
Both supply and s Is 3:1
worthy of his s Matt 10:10

SUPPORT (v) *uphold*
Hur **s-ed** his hands Ex 17:12
will He s . . . evildoers Job 8:20
He **s-s** the fatherless Ps 146:9
ought to s such men 3 John 8

SURETY *liability, security*
I myself will be s Gen 43:9
s for Thy servant Ps 119:122
s for a stranger Prov 11:15

SURFACE *exterior*
s of the deep Gen 1:2
ark floated on the s Gen 7:18
water was on the s Gen 8:9

SURPASS *excel*
you s in beauty Ezek 32:19
s-ing riches of His Eph 2:7
which **s-es** knowledge Eph 3:19

SURRENDER *yield*
s me into his hand 1 Sam 23:11
How can I s you Hos 11:8

SURROUND *encircle*
s him with favor Ps 5:12
Sheol **s-ed** me Ps 18:5
s me with songs Ps 32:7
witnesses **s-ing** us Heb 12:1

SURVIVE *outlive*
your household will s Jer 38:17
how can we s Ezek 33:10

SURVIVORS *continued to live*
inheritance for . . . s Judg 21:17
out of . . . Zion s 2 Kin 19:31
left us a few s Is 1:9
imprison their s Obad 14

SUSTAIN *provide for*
land could not s Gen 13:6
LORD **s-s** the righteous Ps 37:17
He will s you Ps 55:22
S . . . with raisin cakes Song 2:5

SWALLOW (n) *bird*
the s a nest Ps 84:3
like a s in *its* Prov 26:2

SWALLOW (v) *take in*
earth may s us up Num 16:34
He will s up death Is 25:8
great fish to s Jonah Jon 1:17
s-ed up in victory 1 Cor 15:54

SWEAR *take oath, vow*
s by the LORD Gen 24:3
oath which I **swore** Gen 26:3
person **s-s** thoughtlessly Lev 5:4
not s falsely Lev 19:12
sworn by My holiness Ps 89:35
s by My name Jer 12:16
who **s-s** by heaven Matt 23:22

began to . . . **s** Matt 26:74
brethren do not **s** James 5:12

SWEAT *perspiration*
By the **s** of your face Gen 3:19
s . . . like drops of Luke 22:44

SWEET *fresh, pleasant*
waters became **s** Ex 15:25
s psalmist of Israel 2 Sam 23:1
who had **s** fellowship Ps 55:14
s are Thy words Ps 119:103
your sleep will be **s** Prov 3:24
Stolen water is **s** Prov 9:17
it was **s** as honey Ezek 3:3

SWINDLER *cheater*
cursed be the **s** Mal 1:14
a drunkard, or a **s** 1 Cor 5:11
revilers, nor **s-s** 1 Cor 6:10

SWINE *pig*
gold in a **s-'s** snout Prov 11:22
Who eat **s-'s** flesh Is 65:4
your pearls before **s** Matt 7:6
Send us into the **s** Mark 5:12

SWORD *weapon with blade*
flaming **s** . . . turned Gen 3:24
the **s** shall bereave Deut 32:25
A **s** for the LORD Judg 7:20
fell on his **s** 1 Chr 10:5
tongue a sharp **s** Ps 57:4
as a two-edged **s** Prov 5:4
teeth are *like* **s-s** Prov 30:14
the power of the **s** Jer 18:21
s-s into plowshares Mic 4:3
s of the Spirit Eph 6:17
than any two-edged **s** Heb 4:12
s of My mouth Rev 2:16

SYCAMORE *tree*
olive and **s** trees 1 Chr 27:28
plentiful as **s-s** 2 Chr 1:15
grower of **s** figs Amos 7:14
climbed up into a **s** Luke 19:4

SYNAGOGUE *assembly*
pray in the **s-s** Matt 6:5
He went into their **s** Matt 12:9
flogged in *the* **s-s** Mark 13:9
chief seats in . . . **s-s** Luke 20:46
outcasts from the **s** John 16:2
taught in **s-s** John 18:20
reasoning in the **s** Acts 17:17
but are a **s** of Satan Rev 2:9

T

TABERNACLE *assembly and area for sacrificial worship*
dwelling place of God among the Israelites Ex 25:8
construction directed by God Ex 25:9
contained Ark of the Covenant Ex 25:10
phrases used in connection with the tabernacle:
house of the LORD Ex 23:19;34:26; Deut 23:18
tabernacle of the house of God 1 Chr 6:48
tabernacle of the tent of meeting Ex 39:40;40:6,29
tabernacle or tent of the testimony Ex 38:21; Num 1:50,53
tent of meeting Ex 29:32;30:26; 38:30,43;40:2,6,7

TABLE *furniture*
gold **t** before the LORD Lev 24:6
Thou doest prepare a **t** Ps 23:5
crumbs . . . master's **t** Matt 15:27
t-s . . . moneychangers Matt 21:12
dogs under the **t** Mark 7:28
drink at My **t** Luke 22:30
in order to serve **t-s** Acts 6:2
t of the Lord 1 Cor 10:21

TABLET *writing surface*
give you the stone **t-s** Ex 24:12
t-s of the testimony Ex 31:18
the **t** of their heart Jer 17:1
t-s of human hearts 2 Cor 3:3

TABOR
1 *mountain* Judg 4:6,12
2 *city in Zebulun* 1 Chr 6:77
3 *oak in Benjamin* 1 Sam 10:3

TAIL
grasp *it* by its **t** Ex 4:4
the foxes **t** to **t** Judg 15:4
cuts off head and **t** Is 9:14
t-s like scorpions Rev 9:10

TALENT
measure of weight Ex 38:27; 2 Sam 12:30
measure of money Matt 18:24;25:15,25

TALK (n) *conversation, speech*
argue with useless **t** Job 15:3
no . . . silly **t** Eph 5:4
their **t** will spread 2 Tim 2:17

TALK (v) *converse, speak*
God **t-ed** with him Gen 17:3
lips **t** of trouble Prov 24:2
who **t** about you Ezek 33:30
Paul kept on **t-ing** Acts 20:9

TAMAR
1 *Judah's daughter-in-law* Gen 38:6ff
2 *daughter of David* 2 Sam 13:1
3 *daughter of Absalom* 2 Sam 14:27
4 *town near the Dead Sea* 1 Kin 9:18; Ezek 47:19;48:28

TAMARISK *tree*
a **t** tree at Beersheba Gen 21:33
under the **t** tree 1 Sam 22:6

TAMBOURINE
accompanied by . . . **t** Is 5:12
gaiety of **t-s** ceases Is 24:8

TARES *weeds*
t . . . among the wheat Matt 13:25
gather up the **t** Matt 13:30
parable of the **t** Matt 13:36

TARSHISH
1 *lineage of Japheth* Gen 10:4
2 *ships of* 1 Ki 10:22;22:48; 2 Chr 9:21; Ps 48:7
3 *line of Benjamin* 1 Chr 7:6-10
4 *Persian official* Esth 1:14
5 *city* Is 66:19; Jon 1:3

TASKMASTERS *overseers*
appointed **t** over them Ex 1:11
Pharaoh commanded . . . **t** Ex 5:6

TASTE *test flavor*
As the palate **t-s** Job 34:3
O **t** and see Ps 34:8
shall not **t** death Matt 16:28
t death for everyone Heb 2:9
t-d . . . heavenly gift Heb 6:4

TAUNT *object of ridicule*
a **t** among all Deut 28:37
I have become their **t** Job 30:9

TAX *charge, tribute*
a **t** for LORD Num 31:28
money for the king's **t** Neh 5:4
sitting in the **t** office Matt 9:9
pay **t-es** to Caesar Luke 20:22
t to whom **t** *is due* Rom 13:7

TAX-GATHERER *tax collector*
t-s do the same Matt 5:46
many **t-s** and sinners Matt 9:10
Matthew the **t** Matt 10:3
he was a chief **t** Luke 19:2

TEACH *instruct*
t you what . . . to say Ex 4:12
Can anyone **t** God Job 21:22
T me Thy paths Ps 25:4
T me to do Thy will Ps 143:10
He *began* to **t** them Matt 5:2
t-ing . . . in parables Mark 4:2
Lord, **t** us to pray Luke 11:1
Spirit will **t** you Luke 12:12
t strange doctrines 1 Tim 1:3
allow a woman to **t** 1 Tim 2:12

TEACHER *instructor*
will behold your **T** Is 30:20
T, I will follow You Matt 8:19
not above his **t** Matt 10:24
the **t** of Israel John 3:10
call Me **T** and Lord John 13:13
t of the immature Rom 2:20
t of the Gentiles 1 Tim 2:7
false **t-s** among you 2 Pet 2:1

TEACHING (n) *instruction*
t drop as the rain Deut 32:2
your mother's **t** Prov 1:8
amazed at His **t** Matt 7:28
My **t** is not Mine John 7:16
contrary to sound **t** 1 Tim 1:10

TEAR *crying*
my **t-s** in Thy bottle Ps 56:8
sow in **t-s** shall reap Ps 126:5
drench you with my **t-s** Is 16:9
eyes a fountain of **t-s** Jer 9:1
His feet with her **t-s** Luke 7:38
God . . . wipe every **t** Rev 7:17

TEBETH
name of the tenth month in Hebrew calendar Esth 2:16

TEL-ABIB
place in Babylonia Ezek 3:15
Jewish exiles located there

TEMPER *anger*
always loses his **t** Prov 29:11
the ruler's **t** rises Eccl 10:4

TEMPEST *storm*
bruises me with a **t** Job 9:17
stormy wind *and* **t** Ps 55:8
t of destruction Is 28:2
on the day of **t** Amos 1:14

TEMPLE *structure for worship*
doorpost of the **t** 1 Sam 1:9
LORD is in His holy **t** Ps 11:4
meditate in His **t** Ps 27:4
pinnacle of the **t** Matt 4:5
veil of the **t** Luke 23:45
Destroy this **t**, and John 2:19
you are a **t** of God 1 Cor 3:16
t of the Holy Spirit 1 Cor 6:19
the Lamb, are its **t** Rev 21:22

TEMPT *test, try*
And **t-ed** God in the Ps 106:14
being **t-ed** by Satan Mark 1:13
lest Satan **t** you 1 Cor 7:5
t-ed beyond what 1 Cor 10:13
Himself does not **t** James 1:13

TEMPTATION *testing, trial*
not lead us into **t** Matt 6:13
not enter into **t** Matt 26:41
time of **t** fall away Luke 8:13
t has overtaken you 1 Cor 10:13
the godly from **t** 2 Pet 2:9

TEND *take care of*
t his father's flock 1 Sam 17:15
He will **t** His flock Is 40:11
T My lambs John 21:15
T My sheep John 21:17

TENDER *gentle, young*
t and choice calf Gen 18:7
your heart was **t** 2 Kin 22:19
like a **t** shoot Is 53:2
t mercy of our God Luke 1:78

TENT *mobile shelter*
Abram moved his t Gen 13:18
man, living in **t-s** Gen 25:27
t-s of the destroyers Job 12:6
dwell in Thy t forever Ps 61:4
grumbled in their **t-s** Ps 106:25
Like a shepherd's t Is 38:12

TENT OF MEETING
perhaps the same as the Tabernacle or at certain periods a separate meeting place Ex 33:7; Lev 1:1; Num 7:5

TERAPHIM
household gods, idols 2 Kin 23:24; Zech 10:2

TERRIFY *frighten*
t-ied by the sword 1 Chr 21:30
t me by visions Job 7:14
t them with Thy storm Ps 83:15
t you by my letters 2 Cor 10:9

TERRITORY *country, land*
smite your whole t Ex 8:2
God enlarges your t Deut 19:8
t of . . . inheritance Josh 19:10
will possess the t Obad 19

TERROR *intense fear*
Sounds of t are in Job 15:21
t-s of thick darkness Job 24:17
t-s of Sheol came Ps 116:3
t-s and great signs Luke 21:11

TEST (n) *trial*
put God to the t Ps 78:18
put Him to the t Luke 10:25
Spirit . . . to the t Acts 5:9
you fail the t 2 Cor 13:5

TEST (v) *try*
God **t-ed** Abraham Gen 22:1
Why do you t the LORD Ex 17:2
T my mind and my Ps 26:2
word of God is **t-ed** Prov 30:5
t the spirits to see 1 John 4:1

TESTIFY *give witness*
nor shall you t Ex 23:2
them t against him 1 Kin 21:10
our sins t against us Is 59:12
Jesus Himself **t-ied** John 4:44

TESTIMONY *witness*
into the ark the t Ex 25:16
two tablets of the t Ex 31:18
t of the LORD is sure Ps 19:7
t-ies are righteous Ps 119:144
t against Jesus Matt 26:59
t of two men is true John 8:17
t concerning Christ 1 Cor 1:6
ashamed of the t 2 Tim 1:8

THANK (v) *express gratitude*
my song I shall t Him Ps 28:7
God, I t Thee Luke 18:11
I t God always 1 Cor 1:4

THANKS (n) *gratitude*
give t to the LORD 1 Chr 16:7
It is good to give t Ps 92:1
giving t, He broke Matt 15:36
a cup and given t Matt 26:27
not cease giving t Eph 1:16
always to give t 2 Thess 1:3

THANKSGIVING *gratitude*
the sacrifice of t Lev 7:12
with the voice of t Ps 26:7
His presence with t Ps 95:2
supplication with t Phil 4:6
t and honor and Rev 7:12

THEFT *robbery*
be sold for his t Ex 22:3
t-s, murders Mark 7:21

THICKET *underbrush*
ram caught in the t Gen 22:13
the t of the Jordan Jer 50:44

THIEF *robber*
that t shall die Deut 24:7
partner with a t Prov 29:24
companions of **t-ves** Is 1:23
enter . . . like a t Joel 2:9
t comes . . . to steal John 10:10
a t in the night 1 Thess 5:2

THIGH *part of leg*
hand under my t Gen 24:2
socket of Jacob's t Gen 32:25
Thy sword on *Thy* t Ps 45:3
on His t . . . a name Rev 19:16

THINK *ponder, reflect*
as he **t-s** . . . so he is Prov 23:7
not t . . . to abolish Matt 5:17
not to t more highly Rom 12:3
t as a child 1 Cor 13:11
t-s he is something Gal 6:3
beyond all that we . . . t Eph 3:20

THIRD *ordinal number*
morning, a t day Gen 1:13
raised . . . the t day Matt 16:21
raised on the t day 1 Cor 15:4
to the t heaven 2 Cor 12:2

THIRST (n) *craving, dryness*
for my t . . . vinegar Ps 69:21
donkeys quench . . . t Ps 104:11

THIRST (v) *have a craving*
My soul **t-s** for God Ps 42:2
not hunger or t Is 49:10
Every one who **t-s**, come Is 55:1
t for righteousness Matt 5:6
in Me shall never t John 6:35
no more, neither t Rev 7:16

THORN *sharp point*
Both **t-s** and thistles Gen 3:18
as **t-s** in your sides Num 33:55
as a hedge of **t-s** Prov 15:19
lily among the **t-s** Song 2:2
have reaped **t-s** Jer 12:13
fell among the **t-s** Matt 13:7
a crown of **t-s** Matt 27:29
a burning t bush Acts 7:30
t in the flesh 2 Cor 12:7

THOUGHT *concept, idea*
t-s of his heart Gen 6:5
knows the **t-s** of man Ps 94:11
My **t-s** are not your **t-s** Is 55:8
Jesus knowing . . . **t-s** Matt 9:4
heart come evil **t-s** Matt 15:19
every t captive 2 Cor 10:5

THREAD *string*
cord of scarlet t Josh 2:18
lips . . . a scarlet t Song 4:3

THREE *number*
Job's t friends Job 2:11
or t have gathered Matt 18:20
deny Me t times Matt 26:34
t days I will raise John 2:19

THRESH *beat out*
ox while he is **t-ing** Deut 25:4
like dust at **t-ing** 2 Kin 13:7
will t the mountains Is 41:15
Arise and t Mic 4:13

THRESHING FLOOR
winnows . . . at the t Ruth 3:2
David bought . . . t 2 Sam 24:24
clear His t Matt 3:12

THROAT *part of neck*
t is an open grave Ps 5:9
my t is parched Ps 69:3
has enlarged its t Is 5:14
t is an open grave Rom 3:13

THRONE *seat of sovereign*
sitting on His t 1 Kin 22:19
LORD's t is in heaven Ps 11:4
Thy t is established Ps 93:2
it is the t of God Matt 5:34
sit upon twelve **t-s** Matt 19:28
Thy t . . . is forever Heb 1:8
to the t of grace Heb 4:16
a great white t Rev 20:11

THRUST *cast, push*
He shall t them out Josh 23:5
t away like thorns 2 Sam 23:6
Nor to t aside Prov 18:5
LORD has t . . . down Jer 46:15

THUMMIM
kept in high priest's breastplate for determining will of God Ex 28:30; Lev 8:8; Deut 33:8; Ezra 2:63; Neh 7:65

THUNDER (n)
LORD sent . . . t Ex 9:23
But His mighty t Job 26:14
the hiding place of t Ps 81:7
be punished with t Is 29:6
sound of loud t Rev 14:2

THUNDER (v)
t in the heavens 1 Sam 2:10
you t with a voice Job 40:9
LORD also **t-ed** Ps 18:13

TIBERIAS
city on W shore of Sea of Galilee John 6:23
Sea of John 6:1;21:1
also **Sea of Chinnereth**
also **Sea of Galilee**
also **Lake of Gennesaret**

TIDINGS *information, news*
t of His salvation 1 Chr 16:23
not fear evil t Ps 112:7
bring glad t of good Rom 10:15

TILLER *cultivator*
Cain was a t Gen 4:2
a t of the ground Zech 13:5

TIMBER *wood*
cedar and cypress t 1 Kin 9:11
whatever t you need 2 Chr 2:16
t of Lebanon Song 3:9

TIMBREL *musical instrument*
with songs, with t Gen 31:27
strike the t Ps 81:2
Praise Him with t Ps 150:4

TIME *day, period, season*
t-s are in Thy hand Ps 31:15
for a t, **t-s**, and half Dan 12:7
t to seek the LORD Hos 10:12
My t is at hand Matt 26:18
deny Me three **t-s** Luke 22:61
My t is not yet John 7:6
not . . . you to know **t-s** Acts 1:7
is the acceptable t 2 Cor 6:2
for the t is near Rev 1:3

TIMOTHY
companion of Paul Acts 17:15;18:5; Phil 1:1; Col 1:1; Heb 13:23

TITHE (n) *tenth*
all the t of the land Lev 27:30
a t of the t Num 18:26
t into the storehouse Mal 3:10
t-s of all that I get Luke 18:12
mortal men receive **t-s** Heb 7:8

TITHE (v) *pay a tithe*
shall surely t all Deut 14:22
you t mint and dill Matt 23:23

TITUS
co-worker with Paul 2 Cor 2:13;8:23; Gal 2:1

TOIL (n) *labor, work*
the t of our hands Gen 5:29

t is not *in* vain 1 Cor 15:58

TOIL (v) *work hard*
I have **t-ed** in vain Is 49:4
they do not **t** nor Matt 6:28

TOMB *grave, sepulchre*
from womb to **t** Job 10:19
you have hewn a **t** Is 22:16
like whitewashed **t-s** Matt 23:27
laid Him in a **t** Mark 15:46
Lazarus out of the **t** John 12:17
outside the **t** John 20:11

TONGUE *speech, talk*
flatter with their **t** Ps 5:9
their **t** a sharp sword Ps 57:4
t of the wise Prov 12:18
soft **t** breaks . . . bone Prov 25:15
t is a deadly arrow Jer 9:8
impediment of his **t** Mark 7:35
and his **t** loosed Luke 1:64
no one . . . tame the **t** James 3:8

TONGUE *language*
speak with new **t-s** Mark 16:17
speak with other **t-s** Acts 2:4
t-s of men . . . angels 1 Cor 13:1
if I pray in a **t** 1 Cor 14:14
every tribe and **t** Rev 5:9

TOOL *work instrument*
among your **t-s** Deut 23:13
nor any iron **t** 1 Kin 6:7
iron into a cutting **t** Is 44:12

TOOTH
teeth white from Gen 49:12
eye for eye, **t** for **t** Ex 21:24
and a **t** for a **t** Matt 5:38

TOPAZ *precious stone*
ruby, **t**, and emerald Ex 39:10
t of Ethiopia Job 28:19
the ninth, **t** Rev 21:20

TORMENT (n) *pain, torture*
this place of **t** Luke 16:28
their **t** was like Rev 9:5
the fear of her **t** Rev 18:15

TORMENT (v) *annoy, harass*
long will you **t** me Job 19:2
t us before the time Matt 8:29
do not **t** me Luke 8:28

TORRENT *flood*
The ancient **t** Judg 5:21
t-s of destruction 2 Sam 22:5
t-s of ungodliness Ps 18:4
like an overflowing **t** Is 30:28

TOUCH *feel, handle*
not eat . . . or **t** it Gen 3:3
an angel **t-ing** him 1 Kin 19:5
not **t** My anointed Ps 105:15
T nothing unclean Is 52:11
t the fringe of His Matt 14:36
not to **t** a woman 1 Cor 7:1

TOWER *fortress structure*
t whose top *will reach* Gen 11:4
Count her **t-s** Ps 48:12
name . . . strong **t** Prov 18:10
and built a **t** Matt 21:33

TRADERS *merchants*
Midianite **t** passed Gen 37:28
king's **t** procured 2 Chr 1:16
in a city of **t** Ezek 17:4
increased your **t** Nah 3:16

TRADITION *custom*
sake of your **t** Matt 15:3
hold to the **t** of men Mark 7:8
hold . . . to the **t-s** 1 Cor 11:2
my ancestral **t-s** Gal 1:14

TRAIN *guide, instruct*
T up a child Prov 22:6
will they **t** for war Mic 4:3
t-ed to discern good Heb 5:14
heart **t-ed** in greed 2 Pet 2:14

TRAMPLE *crush, hurt*
t-s down the waves Job 9:8
let him **t** my life Ps 7:5
didst **t** the nations Hab 3:12
Jerusalem . . . **t-d** Luke 21:24

TRANCE *daze, dream*
he fell into a **t** Acts 10:10
in a **t** I saw a vision Acts 11:5
fell into a **t** Acts 22:17

TRANSFIGURED *changed*
He was **t** before them Matt 17:2

TRANSFORM *change*
t-ed by the renewing Rom 12:2
t-ed into the same 2 Cor 3:18
who will **t** the body Phil 3:21

TRANSGRESS *break, overstep*
you **t** the covenant Josh 23:16
rulers also **t-ed** Jer 2:8
they **t-ed** laws Is 24:5
disciples **t** the Matt 15:2

TRANSGRESSION *trespass, sin*
forgives iniquity, **t** Ex 34:7
removed our **t-s** from Ps 103:12
love covers all **t-s** Prov 10:12
pierced . . . for our **t-s** Is 53:5
not forgive your **t-s** Matt 6:15
dead in our **t-s** Eph 2:5

TRANSGRESSOR *sinner*
teach **t-s** Thy ways Ps 51:13
numbered with the **t-s** Is 53:12
a **t** of the law James 2:11

TRANSLATED
t and read before me Ezra 4:18
Immanuel . . . **t** means Matt 1:23
Golgotha, which is **t** Mark 15:22
Messiah . . . **t** means John 1:41

TRAVAIL *intense pain*
t-ed nor given birth Is 23:4
woman is in **t** John 16:21

TRAVEL *journey*
t by day and by night Ex 13:21
who **t** on the road Judg 5:10
Jesus . . . *began* **t-ing** Luke 24:15

TREAD *walk on*
They **t** wine presses Job 24:11
as the potter **t-s** clay Is 41:25
t upon serpents Luke 10:19
t-s the wine press Rev 19:15

TREASURE (n) *valuable thing*
t-s of the sand Deut 33:19
the LORD is his **t** Is 33:6
for where your **t** is Matt 6:21
have **t** in heaven Matt 19:21
t in earthen vessels 2 Cor 4:7
stored up your **t** James 5:3

TREASURE (v) *value greatly*
I have **t-d** the words Job 23:12
Thy word have I **t-d** Ps 119:11
t my commandments Prov 7:1

TREASURY *place of valuables*
t of the LORD Josh 6:19
paid from the royal **t** Ezra 6:4
fill their **t-ies** Prov 8:21
into the temple **t** Matt 27:6

TREATY *agreement, contract*
Let there be a **t** 1 Kin 15:19
go, break your **t** 2 Chr 16:3

TREE *woody plant*
fruit **t-s** bearing Gen 1:11
t of life Gen 2:9
hang him on a **t** Deut 21:22
said to the olive **t** Judg 9:8
she is a **t** of life Prov 3:18
like a **t** planted by Jer 17:8
under his fig **t** Mic 4:4
good **t** bears good Matt 7:17
the fig **t** withered Matt 21:19
eat of the **t** of life Rev 2:7

TREMBLE *shake*
T before Him 1 Chr 16:30
T, and do not sin Ps 4:4
make the heavens **t** Is 13:13
His soul **t-s** Is 15:4
my inward parts **t-d** Hab 3:16

TRESPASS *fault, sin*
Saul died for his **t** 1 Chr 10:13
caught in any **t** Gal 6:1
dead in your **t-es** Eph 2:1

TRIAL *testing*
if we are on **t** today Acts 4:9
which was a **t** to you Gal 4:14
perseveres under **t** James 1:12

TRIBE *common ancestry*
twelve **t-s** of Israel Gen 49:28
a man of each **t** Num 1:4
t-s of the LORD Ps 122:4
judging . . . twelve **t-s** Luke 22:30
men from every **t** Rev 5:9

TRIBULATION *affliction*
will be a great **t** Matt 24:21
world you have **t** John 16:33
exult in our **t-s** Rom 5:3
my **t-s** on your behalf Eph 3:13
out of the great **t** Rev 7:14

TRIBUTE *tax*
sons of Israel sent **t** Judg 3:15
impose a . . . **t** or toll Ezra 7:24
exact a **t** of grain Amos 5:11

TRIUMPH *victory*
the righteous **t** Prov 28:12
His **t** in Christ 2 Cor 2:14
mercy **t-s** over James 2:13

TROUBLE (n) *affliction*
forget all my **t** Gen 41:51
man is born for **t** Job 5:7
Look upon . . . my **t** Ps 25:18
very present help in **t** Ps 46:1
remember his **t** no Prov 31:7
t is heavy upon him Eccl 8:6
day has enough **t** Matt 6:34

TROUBLE (v) *bother, disturb*
t you in the land Num 33:55
t-s his own house Prov 11:29
also **t** the hearts Ezek 32:9
Herod . . . was **t-d** Matt 2:3
why **t** the Teacher Mark 5:35
your heart be **t-d** John 14:1

TRUE *actual, real, reliable*
gets a **t** reward Prov 11:18
There was the **t** light John 1:9
gives you . . . **t** bread John 6:32
let God be found **t** Rom 3:4
This testimony is **t** Titus 1:13
t grace of God 1 Pet 5:12
faithful and **t** Witness Rev 3:14

TRUMPET *wind instrument*
t-s of rams' horns Josh 6:6
Praise Him with **t** Ps 150:3
do not sound a **t** Matt 6:2
at the last **t** 1 Cor 15:52
voice like . . . a **t** Rev 1:10

TRUST (n) *confidence, hope*
whose **t** a spider's web Job 8:14
In God . . . put my **t** Ps 56:11
put My **t** in Him Heb 2:13

TRUST (v) *commit to*
t in the LORD Ps 4:5
Than to t in man Ps 118:8
t-s in his riches Prov 11:28
not t in a neighbor Mic 7:5
not t in ourselves 2 Cor 1:9

TRUTH *genuineness, honesty*
walk before Me in t 1 Kin 2:4
speaks t in his heart Ps 15:2
Thy word is t Ps 119:160
Buy t, and do not Prov 23:23
full of grace and t John 1:14
worship in . . . t John 4:24
t shall make you free John 8:32
the way, and the t John 14:6
exchanged the t of Rom 1:25
t of the gospel Gal 2:5
speaking the t in love Eph 4:15
the word of t 2 Tim 2:15
the t is not in us 1 John 1:8

TUMULT *disturbance*
t of the peoples Ps 65:7
A sound of t Is 13:4
t of waters Jer 51:16

TUNIC *cloak, garment*
a varicolored t Gen 37:3
the holy linen t Lev 16:4
or even two t-s Matt 10:10

TURBAN *headdress*
a t of fine linen Ex 28:39
justice was like . . . a t Job 29:14
Remove the t Ezek 21:26

TURMOIL *tumult*
treasure and t with Prov 15:16
rest from your . . . t Is 14:3
ill repute, full of t Ezek 22:5

TURTLEDOVE *bird*
t for a sin offering Lev 12:6
the voice of the t Song 2:12

TUTOR *teacher*
t-s in Christ 1 Cor 4:15
Law . . . become our t Gal 3:24

TWELVE *number*
t tribes of Israel Gen 49:28
t legions of angels Matt 26:53
when He became t Luke 2:42
a crown of t stars Rev 12:1

TWILIGHT *darkness, dusk*
lamb . . . offer at t Ex 29:39
waits for the t Job 24:15
midday as in the t Is 59:10

TWINKLING *flicker*
in the t of an eye 1 Cor 15:52

TWINS *pair, two*
t in her womb Gen 25:24
T of a gazelle Song 4:5

TWO-EDGED *with two edges*
than any t sword Heb 4:12
His mouth . . . t sword Rev 1:16

U

UGLY *unsightly*
u and gaunt cows Gen 41:4
seven lean . . . u cows Gen 41:27

UNBELIEF *lack of faith*
wondered at their u Mark 6:6
help my u Mark 9:24
continue in their u Rom 11:23

UNBELIEVER *non-believer*
a place with the u-s Luke 12:46
wife who is an u 1 Cor 7:12
ungifted men or u-s 1 Cor 14:23
bound . . . with u-s 2 Cor 6:14
worse than an u 1 Tim 5:8

UNBLEMISHED *without defect*
shall be an u male Ex 12:5
u and spotless 1 Pet 1:19

UNCEASING *continuous*
u complaint in his Job 33:19
sorrow and u grief Rom 9:2

UNCIRCUMCISED
But an u male Gen 17:14
u heart . . . humbled Lev 26:41
the nations are u Jer 9:26
who is physically u Rom 2:27
the gospel to the u Gal 2:7

UNCIRCUMCISION
has become u Rom 2:25
who are called U Eph 2:11
the u of your flesh Col 2:13

UNCLEAN *not clean* or *not holy*
touches any u thing Lev 5:2
u in their practices Ps 106:39
man of u lips Is 6:5
authority over u Matt 10:1
u spirits entered Mark 5:13
eaten anything . . . u Acts 10:14
nothing is u in itself Rom 14:14

UNCOVER *expose*
to u her nakedness Lev 18:7
u his feet and Ruth 3:4
head u-ed while 1 Cor 11:5

UNDEFILED *uncorrupted*
holy, innocent, u Heb 7:26
marriage bed *be* u Heb 13:4
pure and u religion James 1:27
imperishable and u 1 Pet 1:4

UNDERGARMENTS
u next to his flesh Lev 6:10
linen u shall be on Ezek 44:18

UNDERSTAND *comprehend*
u-s every intent 1 Chr 28:9
To u a proverb Prov 1:6
do not u justice Prov 28:5
u that the vision Dan 8:17
Hear, and u Matt 15:10
to u the Scriptures Luke 24:45
Why do you not u John 8:43
none who u-s Rom 3:11
things hard to u 2 Pet 3:16

UNDERSTANDING
a wise and u people Deut 4:6
servant an u heart 1 Kin 3:9
Holy One is u Prov 9:10

UNDISCIPLINED
in an u manner 2 Thess 3:7
leading an u life 2 Thess 3:11

UNDISTURBED *peaceful*
land was u for forty Judg 8:28
an u habitation Is 33:20

UNFADING *lasting*
u crown of glory 1 Pet 5:4

UNFAITHFUL *faithless*
u to her husband Num 5:27
very u to the LORD 2 Chr 28:19
u to our God Ezra 10:2

UNFAITHFULNESS *faithlessness*
u . . . they committed Lev 26:40
to Babylon for their u 1 Chr 9:1
the u of the exiles Ezra 9:4

UNFATHOMABLE
How . . . u His ways Rom 11:33
u riches of Christ Eph 3:8

UNFRUITFUL *not productive*
the land is u 2 Kin 2:19
my mind is u 1 Cor 14:14
u deeds of darkness Eph 5:11

UNGODLY *sinful, wicked*
who justifies the u Rom 4:5
Christ died for the u Rom 5:6
destruction of u men 2 Pet 3:7
their own u lusts Jude 18

UNHOLY *not holy*
no *longer* consider u Acts 10:15
for the u and profane 1 Tim 1:9

UNITED *joined, union*
u as one man Judg 20:11
become u with *Him* Rom 6:5
love, u in spirit Phil 2:2
not u by faith Heb 4:2

UNITY *united, union*
dwell together in u Ps 133:1
perfected in u John 17:23
all attain to the u Eph 4:13
perfect bond of u Col 3:14

UNJUST *unfair*
u man is abominable Prov 29:27
For God is not u Heb 6:10
the just for *the* u 1 Pet 3:18

UNKNOWN *not known*
To An U God Acts 17:23
as u yet well-known 2 Cor 6:9

UNLEAVENED *non-fermented*
and baked u bread Gen 19:3
you shall eat u bread Ex 12:15
first day of U Bread Matt 26:17
you are *in fact* u 1 Cor 5:7

UNLOVED *not loved*
that Leah was u Gen 29:31
loved and the u Deut 21:15
Under an u woman Prov 30:23

UNMARRIED *single*
I say to the u 1 Cor 7:8
let her remain u 1 Cor 7:11

UNPRINCIPLED *unscrupulous*
conduct of u men 2 Pet 2:7
error of u men 2 Pet 3:17

UNPROFITABLE *without value*
u and worthless Titus 3:9
grief . . . u for you Heb 13:17

UNPUNISHED *not punished*
not leave him u Ex 20:7
shall go u Ex 21:19
not let him go u 1 Kin 2:9

UNQUENCHABLE
burn . . . with u fire Matt 3:12
into the u fire Mark 9:43

UNRESTRAINED *uncontrolled*
the people are u Prov 29:18
with u persecution Is 14:6

UNRIGHTEOUS *evil, wicked*
u man his thoughts Is 55:7
rain on . . . *the* u Matt 5:45
u in a . . . little thing Luke 16:10
God . . . is not u Rom 3:5
u shall not inherit 1 Cor 6:9

UNRIGHTEOUSNESS *evil*
have no part in u 2 Chr 19:7
no u in Him Ps 92:15
not rejoice in u 1 Cor 13:6
cleanse us from all u 1 John 1:9
All u is sin 1 John 5:17

UNSEARCHABLE *inscrutable*
His greatness is u Ps 145:3
u are His judgments Rom 11:33

UNSKILLED *without training*
I am u in speech Ex 6:12
u in speech, yet I 2 Cor 11:6

UNSTABLE *unreliable*
Her ways are **u** Prov 5:6
u in all his ways James 1:8
enticing **u** souls 2 Pet 2:14

UNWILLING *reluctant*
u to move the ark 2 Sam 6:10
they were **u** to come Matt 22:3
He was **u** to drink Matt 27:34
u to be obedient Acts 7:39

UNWISE *foolish*
foolish and **u** people Deut 32:6
walk, not as **u** men Eph 5:15

UNWORTHY *not deserving*
u of . . . lovingkindness Gen 32:10
We are **u** slaves Luke 17:10
u of eternal life Acts 13:46

UPRIGHT *honest, just*
the death of the **u** Num 23:10
blameless and **u** man Job 1:8
u will behold His face Ps 11:7
God made men **u** Eccl 7:29
Stand **u** on your feet Acts 14:10

UPROAR *loud noise*
Why . . . such an **u** 1 Kin 1:41
nations in an **u** Ps 2:1
there arose a great **u** Acts 23:9

UPROOT *tear out*
He will **u** Israel 1 Kin 14:15
He has **u-ed** my hope Job 19:10
u-ed and be planted Luke 17:6

URIAH
1 *husband of Bathsheba* 2 Sam 11:3;12:9
2 *priest under Ezra* Neh 8:4
3 *priest under Ahaz* Is 8:2
also **Urijah** 2 Kin 16:10ff
4 *time of Jeremiah* Jer 26:20

URIM
kept in high priest's breastplate for determining the will of God
Ex 28:30; Lev 8:8; Num 27:21

USEFUL *beneficial*
man be **u** to himself Job 22:2
u to me for service 2 Tim 4:11

USELESS *worthless*
they have become **u** Rom 3:12
without works is **u** James 2:20

USURY *interest*
leave off this **u** Neh 5:10
by interest and **u** Prov 28:8

UTENSILS *vessels*
table also and its **u** Ex 31:8
u of the sanctuary 1 Chr 9:29

UTTERANCE *expression*
was giving them **u** Acts 2:4
u may be given Eph 6:19
through prophetic **u** 1 Tim 4:14

V

VAIN *empty* or *profane*
name of . . . God in **v** Ex 20:7
labor in **v** who build Ps 127:1
our preaching is **v** 1 Cor 15:14

VALIANT *brave, strong*
these . . . **v** warriors Judg 20:46
be a **v** man for me 1 Sam 18:17
even all the **v** men 1 Chr 28:1
He drags off the **v** Job 24:22

VALLEY *ravine*
v of the Jordan Gen 13:10
the **v** of Aijalon Josh 10:12
v of the shadow of Ps 23:4
The lily of the **v-s** Song 2:1
v of the dead bodies Jer 31:40
v . . . full of bones Ezek 37:1

VALOR *bravery*
mighty man of **v** 1 Sam 16:18
mighty men of **v** 1 Chr 12:8

VALUE *worth*
you are of more **v** Matt 10:31
one pearl of great **v** Matt 13:46
v of knowing Christ Phil 3:8

VANISH *disappear*
When a cloud **v-es** Job 7:9
sky will **v** like smoke Is 51:6
v-ed from . . . sight Luke 24:31

VANITY *futility, pride*
will reap **v** Prov 22:8
V of **v-ies**! All is **v** Eccl 1:2
arrogant *words* of **v** 2 Pet 2:18

VAPOR *smoke*
causes the **v-s** to Ps 135:7
Is a fleeting **v** Prov 21:6
You are *just* a **v** James 4:14

VARICOLORED *multicolored*
made him a **v** tunic Gen 37:3

VAULT *arched cover*
the **v** of heaven Job 22:14
the **v** of the earth Is 40:22

VEGETABLE *plant*
like a **v** garden Deut 11:10
Better . . . dish of **v-s** Prov 15:17
weak eats **v-s** *only* Rom 14:2

VEGETATION *plant life*
earth brought forth **v** Gen 1:12
ate up all **v** Ps 105:35
wither all their **v** Is 42:15

VEIL *cover, curtain*
a **v** over his face Ex 34:33
v of the sanctuary Lev 4:6
Remove your **v** Is 47:2
v of the temple Matt 27:51
enters within the **v** Heb 6:19

VENGEANCE *revenge*
not take **v** Lev 19:18
V is Mine Deut 32:35
God . . . executes **v** 2 Sam 22:48
LORD takes **v** on His Nah 1:2
V is Mine, I will Heb 10:30

VESSEL *utensil*
Go, borrow **v-s** 2 Kin 4:3
treasure in . . . **v-s** 2 Cor 4:7
be a **v** for honor 2 Tim 2:21
as with a weaker **v** 1 Pet 3:7

VIAL *small container*
alabaster **v** of Matt 26:7
she broke the **v** Mark 14:3

VICTORIOUS *triumphant*
A **v** warrior Zeph 3:17
v from the beast Rev 15:2

VICTORY *triumph*
LORD brought . . . **v** 2 Sam 23:10
the glory and the **v** 1 Chr 29:11
gained the **v** for Him Ps 98:1
v belongs to . . . LORD Prov 21:31
He leads justice to **v** Matt 12:20
swallowed up in **v** 1 Cor 15:54
v that has overcome 1 John 5:4

VILLAGE *small town*
land of unwalled **v-s** Ezek 38:11
Go into the **v** Matt 21:2
entered a certain **v** Luke 10:38

VINDICATE *justify*
will **v** His people Deut 32:36
V the weak Ps 82:3
wisdom is **v-d** by Matt 11:19

VINE *stem of plant*
trees said to the **v** Judg 9:12
every man . . . his **v** 1 Kin 4:25
like a fruitful **v** Ps 128:3
mother was like a **v** Ezek 19:10
Israel is a luxuriant **v** Hos 10:1
fruit of the **v** Matt 26:29
I am the true **v** John 15:1

VINEDRESSER *gardener*
v-s and plowmen 2 Kin 25:12
My Father is the **v** John 15:1

VINEGAR *sour liquid*
he shall drink no **v** Num 6:3
bread in the **v** Ruth 2:14
gave me **v** to drink Ps 69:21
Like **v** to the teeth Prov 10:26

VINE-GROWERS
rented it out to **v** Matt 21:33
and destroy the **v** Mark 12:9

VINEYARD *grapevines*
Noah . . . planted a **v** Gen 9:20
shelter in a **v** Is 1:8
ruined My **v** Jer 12:10
laborers for his **v** Matt 20:1
Who plants a **v** 1 Cor 9:7

VIOLATE *assault* or *break*
shall not **v** his word Num 30:2
who **v-d** the ban 1 Chr 2:7
If they **v** My statutes Ps 89:31

VIOLENCE *destructive action*
earth was filled with **v** Gen 6:11
implements of **v** Gen 49:5
such as breathe out **v** Ps 27:12
drink the wine of **v** Prov 4:17
He had done no **v** Is 53:9
not mistreat *or* do **v** Jer 22:3

VIPER *snake*
v-'s tongue slays him Job 20:16
hand on the **v-'s** den Is 11:8
v and flying serpent Is 30:6
You brood of **v-s** Matt 3:7

VIRGIN *unmarried maiden*
very beautiful, a **v** Gen 24:16
if a man seduces a **v** Ex 22:16
v shall be with child Matt 1:23
kept her a **v** Matt 1:25
comparable to ten **v-s** Matt 25:1
v-'s name was Mary Luke 1:27
if a **v** should marry 1 Cor 7:28

VISIBLE *manifest, seen*
He should become **v** Acts 10:40
becomes **v** is light Eph 5:13
things which are **v** Heb 11:3

VISION *dream, foresight*
to Abram in a **v** Gen 15:1
Where there is no **v** Prov 29:18
prophets find No **v** Lam 2:9
I saw **v-s** of God Ezek 1:1
in a night **v** Dan 2:19
young men . . . see **v-s** Joel 2:28
Tell the **v** to no one Matt 17:9
young men . . . see **v-s** Acts 2:17

VISIT *come* or *go to see*
v-ing the iniquity of Ex 20:5
Thou dost **v** the earth Ps 65:9
you did not **v** Me Matt 25:43
For He has **v-ed** us Luke 1:68
v orphans . . . widows James 1:27

VOICE *sound, speech*
have obeyed My **v** Gen 22:18
Thou wilt hear my **v** Ps 5:3
the **v** of my teachers Prov 5:13
Give ear . . . hear my **v** Is 28:23
A **v** is calling Is 40:3
v came from heaven Dan 4:31
v . . . out of the cloud Mark 9:7
v of one crying in Luke 3:4
v of the Son of God John 5:25

v has gone out | Rom 10:18
v of *the* archangel | 1 Thess 4:16
His v shook . . . earth | Heb 12:26
if anyone hears My v | Rev 3:20

VOID *empty, invalid*
was formless and v | Gen 1:2
make v the counsel | Jer 19:7
faith is made v | Rom 4:14
cross . . . be made v | 1 Cor 1:17

VOTIVE *dedicated*
his offering is a v | Lev 7:16
choice v offerings | Deut 12:11

VOW *solemn promise*
Jacob made a v | Gen 28:20
v of a Nazirite | Num 6:2
I shall pay my **v-s** | Ps 22:25
not make false **v-s** | Matt 5:33
he was keeping a v | Acts 18:18

VULTURE *bird*
not eat . . . the v | Deut 14:12
the **v-s** will gather | Matt 24:28
the **v-s** be gathered | Luke 17:37

W

WAFER *thin cake of bread*
w-s with honey | Ex 16:31
one unleavened **w** | Num 6:19

WAGE *salary*
God has given . . . **w-s** | Gen 30:18
w-s of the righteous | Prov 10:16
w is not reckoned | Rom 4:4
the **w-s** of sin | Rom 6:23
worthy of his **w-s** | 1 Tim 5:18

WAIL *lament, mourn*
w with a broken spirit | Is 65:14
w, son of man | Ezek 21:12
I must lament and **w** | Mic 1:8
W, O inhabitants of | Zeph 1:11
weeping and **w-ing** | Mark 5:38

WALK *follow, go along*
w-ing in the garden | Gen 3:8
W before Me | Gen 17:1
w in My instruction | Ex 16:4
w-ed forty years | Josh 5:6
w before Me in truth | 1 Kin 2:4
W about Zion | Ps 48:12
fool **w-s** in darkness | Eccl 2:14
w in the light | Is 2:5
w and not . . . weary | Is 40:31
w-ed with Me in peace | Mal 2:6
Rise, and **w** | Matt 9:5
w-ed on the water | Matt 14:29
w in newness of life | Rom 6:4
we **w** by faith | 2 Cor 5:7
w by the Spirit | Gal 5:16
w in love | Eph 5:2
w as children of light | Eph 5:8
if we **w** in the light | 1 John 1:7

WALL *structure*
living on the **w** | Josh 2:15
So we built the **w** | Neh 4:6
I can leap over a **w** | Ps 18:29
w-s of Jerusalem | Jer 39:8
you whitewashed **w** | Acts 23:3
w-s of Jericho fell | Heb 11:30
a great and high **w** | Rev 21:12

WANDER *roam*
w in the wilderness | Num 32:13
I would **w** far away | Ps 55:7
people **w** like sheep | Zech 10:2
w-ed . . . the faith | 1 Tim 6:10

WANDERER *roamer*
a **w** on the earth | Gen 4:12
an exile and a **w** | Is 49:21
w-s among . . . nations | Hos 9:17

WAR *battle, conflict*
when they see **w** | Ex 13:17
land . . . rest from **w** | Josh 11:23
He makes **w-s** to cease | Ps 46:9
the weapons of **w** | Ps 76:3
A time for **w** | Eccl 3:8
w-s . . . rumors of **w-s** | Matt 24:6
w against the law | Rom 7:23
w in your members | James 4:1
judges and wages **w** | Rev 19:11

WARN *give notice*
w the people | Ex 19:21
not . . . **w** the wicked | Ezek 33:8
w-ed . . . in a dream | Matt 2:12
w you whom to fear | Luke 12:5
Moses was **w-ed** | Heb 8:5

WARRIOR *soldier*
The LORD is a **w** | Ex 15:3
O valiant **w** | Judg 6:12
w from his youth | 1 Sam 17:33
w-s will flee naked | Amos 2:16

WASH *bathe, clean*
w your feet, and rest | Gen 18:4
w in the Jordan | 2 Kin 5:10
W . . . from my iniquity | Ps 51:2
w-ed off your blood | Ezek 16:9
do not **w** their hands | Matt 15:2
ceremonially **w-ed** | Luke 11:38
w the disciples' feet | John 13:5
w away your sins | Acts 22:16
w-ed . . . saints' feet | 1 Tim 5:10
who **w** their robes | Rev 22:14

WASTE (n) *wilderness*
land was laid **w** | Ex 8:24
land into a salt **w** | Ps 107:34
altars may become **w** | Ezek 6:6
Egypt . . . become a **w** | Joel 3:19

WASTE (v) *destroy, use up*
he **w-d** his seed | Gen 38:9
w away the eyes | Lev 26:16
sick man **w-s** away | Is 10:18
perfume been **w-d** | Mark 14:4

WASTE PLACE *barren region*
w-s of the wealthy | Is 5:17
Seek Me in a **w** | Is 45:19
like the ancient **w-s** | Ezek 26:20
w-s will be rebuilt | Ezek 36:10

WATCHMAN *one who guards*
w keeps awake in vain | Ps 127:1
w-men for . . . morning | Ps 130:6
W, how far gone is | Is 21:11
I set **w-men** over you | Jer 6:17
Ephraim *was* a **w** | Hos 9:8

WATER (n) *flood, liquid*
flood of **w** came | Gen 7:6
w of bitterness | Num 5:18
W wears away stones | Job 14:19
poured out like **w** | Ps 22:14
Stolen **w** is sweet | Prov 9:17
bread on the . . . **w-s** | Eccl 11:1
come to the **w-s** | Is 55:1
fountain of living **w-s** | Jer 2:13
knees . . . like **w** | Ezek 7:17
baptize you with **w** | Matt 3:11
a cup of cold **w** | Matt 10:42
walked on the **w** | Matt 14:29
no **w** for My feet | Luke 7:44
one is born of **w** | John 3:5
given you living **w** | John 4:10
John baptized with **w** | Acts 1:5
of **w** with the word | Eph 5:26
by **w** and blood | 1 John 5:6

WATER (v) *make moist*
to **w** the garden | Gen 2:10
I will **w** your camels | Gen 24:46
w their father's flock | Ex 2:16
that **w** the earth | Ps 72:6
Apollos **w-ed** | 1 Cor 3:6

WAVES *billows*
w of death | 2 Sam 22:5
tramples down the **w** | Job 9:8
Thy **w** have rolled | Ps 42:7
w were breaking | Mark 4:37
wild **w** of the sea | Jude 13

WAX *paraffin*
My heart is like **w** | Ps 22:14
Like **w** before the fire | Mic 1:4

WAY *manner* or *path*
all His **w-s** are just | Deut 32:4
blameless . . . His **w** | 2 Sam 22:33
from your evil **w-s** | 2 Kin 17:13
w of the righteous | Ps 1:6
Commit your **w** to | Ps 37:5
is the **w** of death | Prov 14:12
Clear the **w** | Is 40:3
w of the wicked | Jer 12:1
Make ready the **w** | Matt 3:3
w is broad that leads | Matt 7:13
teach . . . **w** of God | Mark 12:14
into the **w** of peace | Luke 1:79
I am the **w** | John 14:6
belonging to the **W** | Acts 9:2
the **w** of salvation | Acts 16:17
the **w** of escape | 1 Cor 10:13
new and living **w** | Heb 10:20
the **w** of the truth | 2 Pet 2:2

WEAK *feeble*
I shall become **w** | Judg 16:17
Rescue the **w** | Ps 82:4
but the flesh is **w** | Matt 26:41
must help the **w** | Acts 20:35
who is **w** in faith | Rom 14:1
God . . . chosen the **w** | 1 Cor 1:27

WEALTH *riches*
a man of great **w** | Ruth 2:1
who trust in their **w** | Ps 49:6
Honor . . . from you **w** | Prov 3:9
W adds many friends | Prov 19:4
A **w** of salvation | Is 33:6
the **w** of all nations | Hag 2:7
w of their liberality | 2 Cor 8:2
rich by her **w** | Rev 18:19

WEAPON *armament*
girded on his **w-s** | Deut 1:41
flee from the iron **w** | Job 20:24
turn back the **w-s** | Jer 21:4
w-s of righteousness | 2 Cor 6:7

WEARY *tired*
the people were **w** | 1 Sam 14:28
w with my crying | Ps 69:3
water to a **w** soul | Prov 25:25
sustain the **w** one | Is 50:4
all who are **w** | Matt 11:28
w of doing good | 2 Thess 3:13

WEAVE *interlace*
Thou didst **w** me | Ps 139:13
w the spider's web | Is 59:5
after **w-ing** a crown | Matt 27:29

WEB *woven work*
loom and the **w** | Judg 16:14
trust a spider's **w** | Job 8:14

WEDDING *marriage*
had no **w** songs | Ps 78:63
day of his **w** | Song 3:11
come to the **w** feast | Matt 22:4
a **w** in Cana | John 2:1

WEEK *period of time*
Complete the **w** of | Gen 29:27
Seventy **w-s** | Dan 9:24
first *day* of the **w** | Matt 28:1
I fast twice a **w** | Luke 18:12

WEEP *cry, sorrow*
sought *a place* to **w** | Gen 43:30
do not mourn or **w** | Neh 8:9
My eye **w-s** to God | Job 16:20
widows could not **w** | Ps 78:64
w day and night | Jer 9:1

w-ing and gnashing Matt 13:42
he . . . **wept** bitterly Matt 26:75
saw the city . . . **wept** Luke 19:41
w for yourselves Luke 23:28
Jesus **wept** John 11:35
why are you **w-ing** John 20:13
w with . . . who **w** Rom 12:15

WEIGH *measure out*
actions are **w-ed** 1 Sam 2:3
LORD **w-s** the motives Prov 16:2

WEIGHT
a full and just **w** Deut 25:15
w to the wind Job 28:25
bag of deceptive **w-s** Mic 6:11

WELCOME *gladly receive*
no prophet is **w** Luke 4:24
multitude **w-d** Him Luke 8:40
who fears Him . . . **w** Acts 10:35
she . . . **w-d** the spies Heb 11:31

WELL *water shaft*
sat down by a **w** Ex 2:15
w of Bethlehem 1 Chr 11:17
A **w** of fresh water Song 4:15
Jacob's **w** was there John 4:6

WELL-PLEASED *satisfied*
in whom I am **w** Matt 3:17
in Thee I am **w** Luke 3:22
God was not **w** 1 Cor 10:5

WEST *direction*
very strong **w** wind Ex 10:19
east is from the **w** Ps 103:12
gather you from the **w** Is 43:5

WHEAT *grain*
days of **w** harvest Gen 30:14
first fruits of the **w** Ex 34:22
plant **w** in rows Is 28:25
gather His **w** into Matt 3:12
to sift you like **w** Luke 22:31
unless a grain of **w** John 12:24

WHEEL *circular disk*
the **w** . . . is crushed Eccl 12:6
w-s like a whirlwind Is 5:28
one **w** were within Ezek 1:16
rattling of the **w** Nah 3:2

WHIRLWIND
take . . . Elijah by a **w** 2 Kin 2:1
comes on like a **w** Prov 1:27
chariots like the **w** Jer 4:13
they reap the **w** Hos 8:7

WHISPER *talk quietly*
who hate me **w** Ps 41:7
w a prayer Is 26:16
your speech shall **w** Is 29:4

WHISTLE *shrill sound*
And will **w** for it Is 5:26
LORD will **w** for the fly Is 7:18
I will **w** for them Zech 10:8

WHITEWASHED *wall covering*
like **w** tombs Matt 23:27
you **w** wall Acts 23:3

WICK *candle thread*
extinguished like a **w** Is 43:17
a smoldering **w** Matt 12:20

WICKED *evil, ungodly*
condemn the **w** Deut 25:1
counsel of the **w** Ps 1:1
the **w** spurned God Ps 10:13
devises **w** plans Prov 6:18
When a **w** man dies Prov 11:7
no peace for the **w** Is 48:22
taking . . . some **w** men Acts 17:5
righteous and the **w** Acts 24:15

WICKEDNESS *evil*
w of man was great Gen 6:5
eat the bread of **w** Prov 4:17
w of My people Jer 7:12
You have plowed **w** Hos 10:13
repent of this **w** Acts 8:22
spiritual *forces* of **w** Eph 6:12

WIDOW *husband is dead*
Remain a **w** Gen 38:11
sent **w-s** away empty Job 22:9
judge for the **w-s** Ps 68:5
devour **w-s'** houses Matt 23:14
Honor **w-s** 1 Tim 5:3
visit orphans . . . **w-s** James 1:27

WIFE *married woman*
cleave to his **w** Gen 2:24
w of your youth Prov 5:18
An excellent **w** Prov 31:10
who divorces his **w** Matt 5:32
have his own **w** 1 Cor 7:2
head of the **w** Eph 5:23
husband of one **w** 1 Tim 3:2
w-ves, be submissive 1 Pet 3:1
w of the Lamb Rev 21:9

WILDERNESS *barren area*
water in the **w** Gen 16:7
journey into the **w** Ex 5:3
forty years in the **w** Deut 29:5
roadway in the **w** Is 43:19
Have I been a **w** Jer 2:31
preaching in the **w** Matt 3:1
into the **w** . . . tempted Matt 4:1
crying in the **w** Mark 1:3
manna in the **w** John 6:31

WILL *desire, purpose*
delight to do Thy **w** Ps 40:8
Thy **w** be done Matt 6:10
the **w** of My Father Matt 7:21
not My **w**, but Luke 22:42
nor of the **w** of man John 1:13
what the **w** of God Rom 12:2
knowledge of His **w** Col 1:9
come to do Thy **w** Heb 10:9

WIN *succeed*
wise **w-s** souls Prov 11:30
we will **w** him over Matt 28:14
that I might **w** Jews 1 Cor 9:20

WIND
caused a **w** to pass Gen 8:1
scorched by . . . **w** Gen 41:27
will inherit **w** Prov 11:29
they sow the **w** Hos 8:7
w and the sea obey Mark 4:41
He rebuked the **w** Luke 8:24
violent, rushing **w** Acts 2:2
every **w** of doctrine Eph 4:14
driven by strong **w-s** James 3:4

WINDOW *opening*
enter through the **w-s** Joel 2:9
open . . . **w-s** of heaven Mal 3:10
sitting on the **w** sill Acts 20:9
basket through a **w** 2 Cor 11:33

WINE *strong drink*
Do not drink **w** Lev 10:9
overflow with new **w** Prov 3:10
W is a mocker Prov 20:1
love is better than **w** Song 1:2
new **w** into old Matt 9:17
made the water **w** John 4:46
full of sweet **w** Acts 2:13
not get drunk with **w** Eph 5:18
not addicted to **w** 1 Tim 3:3

WINESKINS *animal skin bag*
these **w** . . . were new Josh 9:13
Like new **w** Job 32:19
wine into fresh **w** Matt 9:17

WINGS
bore you on eagles' **w** Ex 19:4
He spread His **w** Deut 32:11
under whose **w** Ruth 2:12
with **w** like eagles Is 40:31
healing in its **w** Mal 4:2
chicks under her **w** Matt 23:37

WINK *blink*
w maliciously Ps 35:19
w-s with his eyes Prov 6:13

WINNOW *scatter*
king **w-s** the wicked Prov 20:26
You will **w** them Is 41:16
His **w-ing** fork Matt 3:12

WINTER *season*
And summer and **w** Gen 8:22
the **w** is past Song 2:11
even spend the **w** 1 Cor 16:6

WISDOM *discernment*
the spirit of **w** Ex 28:3
w has two sides Job 11:6
the beginning of **w** Ps 111:10
Fools despise **w** Prov 1:7
w given to Him Mark 6:2
kept increasing in **w** Luke 2:52
any of you lacks **w** James 1:5

WISE *judicious, prudent*
making **w** the simple Ps 19:7
w in your own eyes Prov 3:7
the words of the **w** Prov 22:17
He is not a **w** son Hos 13:13

WITCHCRAFT *magic, sorcery*
who practices **w** Deut 18:10
practiced **w** and 2 Kin 21:6

WITHER *dry up*
its leaf does not **w** Ps 1:3
earth mourns *and* **w-s** Is 24:4
the leaf shall **w** Jer 8:13
with a **w-ed** hand Mark 3:1
the fig tree **w-ed** Mark 11:20

WITNESS (n) *testimony*
This heap is a **w** Gen 31:48
is **w** between us Judg 11:10
w to all the nations Matt 24:14
He came for a **w** John 1:7
My **w** is true John 8:14
you shall be My **w-es** Acts 1:8
For God is my **w** Phil 1:8
w of God is greater 1 John 5:9
Christ, the faithful **w** Rev 1:5

WITNESS (v) *testify*
not bear false **w** Ex 20:16
w against you today Deut 4:26
John bore **w** John 1:32
bear **w** of Me John 15:26
Spirit . . . bears **w** Rom 8:16
three that bear **w** 1 John 5:8

WOLF *animal*
w will dwell with Is 11:6
the midst of **w-ves** Matt 10:16
w snatches them John 10:12

WOMAN *female, lady*
She shall be called **W** Gen 2:23
a **w** of excellence Ruth 3:11
gracious **w** attains Prov 11:16
a contentious **w** Prov 25:24
looks on a **w** to lust Matt 5:28
w-en . . . grinding Matt 24:41
Blessed among **w-en** Luke 1:42
W, behold, your son John 19:26
not to touch a **w** 1 Cor 7:1
w is the glory of 1 Cor 11:7
His Son, born of a **w** Gal 4:4
w clothed with . . . sun Rev 12:1

WOMB
nations . . . in your **w** Gen 25:23
LORD . . . closed her **w** 1 Sam 1:5
from **w** to tomb Job 10:19
formed you from the **w** Is 44:2
baby leaped in . . . **w** Luke 1:41

WONDER *marvel, sign*
- consider the w-s of — Job 37:14
- tell of all Thy w-s — Ps 9:1
- His w-s in the deep — Ps 107:24
- w-s in the sky — Joel 2:30
- were filled with w — Acts 3:10

WOOL *cloth* or *hair*
- of w and linen — Deut 22:11
- put a fleece of w on — Judg 6:37
- They will be like w — Is 1:18
- hair . . . like pure w — Dan 7:9
- white like white w — Rev 1:14

WORD *message, speech*
- to the w of Moses — Lev 10:7
- declare to you the w — Deut 5:5
- Thy w . . . confirmed — 2 Chr 6:17
- *no* limit to windy w-s — Job 16:3
- Thy w is a lamp — Ps 119:105
- w of God is tested — Prov 30:5
- despised the w — Is 5:24
- w-s of a sealed book — Is 29:11
- speak My w in truth — Jer 23:28
- every w that proceeds — Matt 4:4
- these w-s of Mine — Matt 7:24
- the W was God — John 1:1
- the W became flesh — John 1:14
- w-s of eternal life — John 6:68
- abide in My w — John 8:31
- glorifying the w — Acts 13:48
- hearing by the w — Rom 10:17
- the w of the cross — 1 Cor 1:18
- fulfilled in one w — Gal 5:14
- the w of truth — 2 Tim 2:15
- w of God is living — Heb 4:12
- doers of the w — James 1:22
- pure milk of the w — 1 Pet 2:2
- the W of Life — 1 John 1:1
- The W of God — Rev 19:13

WORK (n) *act, deed, labor*
- God completed His w — Gen 2:2
- His w is perfect — Deut 32:4
- see the w-s of God — Ps 66:5
- Commit your w-s to — Prov 16:3
- His w on Mount Zion — Is 10:12
- the w-s of Christ — Matt 11:2
- the w of the Law — Rom 2:15
- faith apart from w-s — Rom 3:28
- for the w of service — Eph 4:12
- began a good w — Phil 1:6
- rich in good w-s — 1 Tim 6:18
- faith without w-s — James 2:20

WORK (v) *perform, produce*
- You shall w six days — Ex 34:21
- those who w iniquity — Ps 28:3
- Who . . . w-s wonders — Ps 72:18
- not w for the food — John 6:27
- w together for good — Rom 8:28
- w out your salvation — Phil 2:12
- anyone will not w — 2 Thess 3:10

WORKER *laborer*
- O w of deceit — Ps 52:2
- w-s of iniquity — Prov 10:29
- God's fellow w-s — 1 Cor 3:9
- beware . . . evil w-s — Phil 3:2
- pure, w-s at home — Titus 2:5

WORKMAN *craftsman*
- a skillful w — Ex 38:23
- approved . . . as a w — 2 Tim 2:15

WORLD *earth, humanity*
- foundations of . . . w — 2 Sam 22:16
- He will judge the w — Ps 9:8
- the light of the w — Matt 5:14
- Go into all the w — Mark 16:15
- gains the whole w — Luke 9:25
- God so loved the w — John 3:16
- Savior of the w — John 4:42
- the light of the w — John 8:12
- overcome the w — John 16:33
- sin entered . . . the w — Rom 5:12
- reconciling the w — 2 Cor 5:19
- unstained by the w — James 1:27
- Do not love the w — 1 John 2:15

WORLDLY *earthly*
- w fables fit only — 1 Tim 4:7
- avoid w . . . chatter — 2 Tim 2:16

WORM *creeping animal*
- But I am a w — Ps 22:6
- God appointed a w — Jon 4:7
- their w does not die — Mark 9:48

WORMWOOD
- 1 *a bitter plant* — Deut 29:18
- 2 *used figuratively* — Prov 5:4; Amos 6:12; Rev 8:11

WORSHIP *bow, revere*
- not w any other god — Ex 34:14
- you shall w Him — Deut 6:13
- W the LORD — Ps 2:11
- earth will w Thee — Ps 66:4
- w in spirit and truth — John 4:24
- w in the Spirit — Phil 3:3
- w Him who lives — Rev 4:10
- who w the beast — Rev 14:11

WORTHLESS *useless*
- all w physicians — Job 13:4
- w man digs up evil — Prov 16:27
- your faith is w — 1 Cor 15:17
- man's religion is w — James 1:26

WORTHY *having merit*
- sin w of death — Deut 21:22
- w of his support — Matt 10:10
- is not w of Me — Matt 10:37
- w of the gospel — Phil 1:27
- world was not w — Heb 11:38
- W is the Lamb — Rev 5:12

WOUND *injury*
- My w is incurable — Job 34:6
- binds up their w-s — Ps 147:3
- bandaged . . . his w-s — Luke 10:34
- by His w-s you were — 1 Pet 2:24
- fatal w was healed — Rev 13:3

WRAPPINGS *cloth coverings*
- bound . . . with w — John 11:44
- linen w lying *there* — John 20:5

WRATH *anger, indignation*
- Nor chasten . . . in Thy w — Ps 6:1
- Pour out Thy w — Ps 79:6
- turns away w — Prov 15:1
- spent My w upon — Ezek 5:13
- from the w to come — Matt 3:7
- w of God abides on — John 3:36
- God who inflicts w — Rom 3:5
- w of God will come — Col 3:6
- the w of the Lamb — Rev 6:16

WRETCHED *miserable*
- in to this w place — Num 20:5
- W man that I am — Rom 7:24

WRITE *inscribe*
- Moses, W this in a — Ex 17:14
- W them on the tablet — Prov 3:3
- he **wrote** the dream — Dan 7:1
- w a certificate — Mark 10:4
- with His finger **wrote** — John 8:6
- w . . . King of the Jews — John 19:21
- W in a book — Rev 1:11

WRITINGS *literary works*
- not believe his w — John 5:47
- known the sacred w — 2 Tim 3:15

WRITTEN *inscribed*
- w by . . . God — Ex 31:18
- w in the law — 2 Chr 23:18
- remembrance was w — Mal 3:16
- w by the prophet — Matt 2:5
- about whom it is w — Matt 11:10
- Law w in . . . hearts — Rom 2:15
- name has not been w — Rev 13:8
- w in the Lamb's — Rev 21:27

WRONG *do evil, harm*
- not w a stranger — Ex 22:21
- not w one another — Lev 25:14
- I . . . have done w — 2 Sam 24:17
- Love does no w — Rom 13:10

Y

YAHWEH
- *see* **YHWH** *and* **LORD**

YEAR *time period*
- atonement . . . every y — Lev 16:34
- fiftieth y . . . jubilee — Lev 25:11
- the y of remission — Deut 15:9
- crowned the y with — Ps 65:11
- length of . . . y-s — Prov 3:2
- favorable y of the LORD — Is 61:2
- thirty y-s of age — Luke 3:23
- y of the LORD — Luke 4:19
- priest *enters,* once a y — Heb 9:7
- sacrifices y by y — Heb 10:1
- y-s as one day — 2 Pet 3:8
- reign . . . thousand y-s — Rev 20:6

YEARLING *one year old*
- a y ewe lamb — Lev 14:10
- With y calves — Mic 6:6

YHWH
- *Hebrew tetragrammaton for name of God, probably pronounced Yahweh*
- *Derived from Hebrew verb meaning "to be"*
- Translated usually as LORD
- *see also* **LORD**
- *see also introductory material to NASB*

YIELD *produce*
- no longer y its — Gen 4:12
- land . . . y its produce — Lev 25:19
- Which y-s its fruit — Ps 1:3
- y-ed up *His* spirit — Matt 27:50
- not y in subjection — Gal 2:5
- y-s the peaceful — Heb 12:11

YOKE *wooden bar*
- break his y from — Gen 27:40
- iron y on . . . neck — Deut 28:48
- made our y hard — 1 Kin 12:4
- the y of their burden — Is 9:4
- Take My y upon — Matt 11:29
- to a y of slavery — Gal 5:1

YOUNG *of an early age, youthful*
- he sent y men — Ex 24:5
- or two y pigeons — Lev 15:29
- glory of y men is — Prov 20:29
- y men stumble — Is 40:30
- like a y lion — Hos 5:14
- finding a y donkey — John 12:14
- y men . . . visions — Acts 2:17
- urge the y men — Titus 2:6

YOUTH *young person*
- evil from his y — Gen 8:21
- fresher than in y — Job 33:25
- the sins of my y — Ps 25:7
- confidence from my y — Ps 71:5
- your y is renewed — Ps 103:5
- the wife of your y — Prov 5:18
- y-s grow weary — Is 40:30
- the reproach of my y — Jer 31:19
- life from my y up — Acts 26:4

Z

ZEAL *fervor, passion*
- kill them in his z — 2 Sam 21:2
- my z for the LORD — 2 Kin 10:16
- z has consumed me — Ps 119:139
- *Thy* z for the people — Is 26:11
- have a z for God — Rom 10:2
- your z for me — 2 Cor 7:7

ZEALOT
- *member of radical Jewish nationalist party*
- Matt 10:4; Mark 3:18; Luke 6:15; Acts 1:13

ZEALOUS *fervent*

z for the LORD 1 Kin 19:10
all **z** for the Law Acts 21:20
z of . . . *gifts* 1 Cor 14:12
z for good deeds Titus 2:14
be **z** . . . and repent Rev 3:19

ZECHARIAH

1 *son of Jeiel* 1 Chr 9:35-37
2 *priest with ark* 1 Chr 15:24
3 *son of Isshiah* 1 Chr 24:25
4 *father of Iddo* 1 Chr 27:21
5 *son of Benaiah* 2 Chr 20:14
6 *son of Jehoshaphat* 2 Chr 21:2
7 *son of Jehoida* 2 Chr 24:20
8 *prophet* 2 Chr 26:5
9 *priest under Ezra* Neh 12:41
10 *minor prophet* Zech 1:1

ZIN

wilderness in Negev Num 13:21; Deut 32:51; Josh 15:1,3

ZION

1 *hill / City of David which is Jerusalem* 2 Sam 5:7; 1 Chr 11:5
2 *after Temple built, name extended to top of hill, Mount Zion* Is 8:18;18:7; Mic 4:7
3 *applied to all of Jerusalem as city spreads* 2 Kin 19:21; Ps 69:35; Is 1:8
4 *used in the corporate sense for for the people and land* Ps 97:8;149:2; Is 3:16;8:14;59:20; Joel 2:23; Zech 9:9; Rom 9:33; 1 Pet 2:3
5 *used eschatologically for heavenly Jerusalem* Is 60:14; Heb 12:22; Rev 14:1

ZIPPORAH

wife of Moses Ex 2:21;4:25

ZIV

name of the second month in Hebrew calendar 1 Kin 6:1,37

GUIDE TO TRANSLITERATION—FROM GREEK TO ENGLISH WITH MODERN GREEK PRONUNCIATION

Capital Letter	Small Letter	Greek Name	Trans-literation	Phonetic Sound	Example
Α	α	alpha	a	a	as in father
Β	β	vēta	b	v	as in victory
Γ	γ	ghamma	g	gh	as in gh (soft gutteral)
Δ	δ	thelta	d	th	as in there
Ε	ϵ	epsilon	e	e	as in met
Ζ	ζ	zēta	z	z	as in zenith
Η	η	ēta	ē	ee	as in the
Θ	θ	thēta	th	th	as in thin
Ι	ι	iōta	i	i	as in pin or machine
Κ	κ	kappa	k	k	as in kill (soft accent)
Λ	λ	lamvtha	l	l	as in land
Μ	μ	mee	m	m	as in mean
Ν	ν	nee	n	n	as in now
Ξ	ξ	xi	x	x	as in wax
Ο	ο	omicron	o	o	as in obey
Π	π	pi	p	p	as in pet (soft accent)
Ρ	ρ	rhō	rh,r	rh	as in Rhine
				r	as in fur
Σ	σ,ς*	sighma	s	s	as in sit
Τ	τ	taf	t	t	as in tell (soft accent)
Υ	υ	eepsilon	ē	ee	as in Easter
Φ	φ	phi	ph	ph	as in graphic
Χ	χ	hi	h	h	as in heel, but heavily aspirated
Ψ	ψ	psi	ps	ps	as in hips
Ω	ω	omega	oo	o	as in Austin

* At end of words

Guide to Transliteration—Greek to English

COMBINATIONS OF CONSONANTS

γγ	ghamma	+	ghamma = gg	as in go
γκ	ghamma	+	kappa = gk	as in go
γχ	ghamma	+	hi = gh	as in gh

DIPHTHONGS (DOUBLE VOWELS)

AI	αι alpha + iōta	= ai as in air
AY	αυ alpha + eepsilon	= au, ou as in aft or average
EI	ει epsilon + iōta	= ei as in ear
EY	ευ epsilon + eepsilon	= ef as in effort or every
HY	ηυ ēta + eepsilon	= ēf, almost as in if or iv
OI	οι omicron + iōta	= ē as in eel
OY	ου omicron + eepsilon	= ou as in group
YI	υι upsilon + iōta	= ē as in eel

BREATHINGS (Occur only with initial vowels)

(ʼ) Smooth, not transliterated or pronounced. When words begin with vowels, it may occur at the beginning of words with every vowel or double vowel (diphthong). ἔργον—ergon, work; εὐχή—euchē, vow.

(ʽ) Rough = h. When words begin with vowels, it may occur at the beginning of words with every vowel or double vowel (diphthong). No distinction in pronunciation from the smooth breathing. To indicate the rough breathing we use h in the transliteration.

(ῥ) Rho = r.
(ὑ) Eepsilon = u.
When these begin a word, they always have the rough breathing. There they are transliterated rh, hu, respectively. ῥέω—rheō, flow; ὑπομονή—hupomonē, patience.

* Iōta subscript is silent.
† In our transliteration we cannot distinguish between vowels with and without iōta subscript.

A CONCISE

DICTIONARY

OF THE WORDS IN

THE HEBREW BIBLE;

WITH THEIR RENDERINGS

IN THE

AUTHORIZED ENGLISH VERSION.

BY

JAMES STRONG, S.T.D., LL.D.

PREFACE.

THIS work, although prepared as a companion to the Exhaustive Concordance, to which it is specially adapted, is here paged and printed so that it can be bound separately, in the belief that a brief and simple Dictionary of the Biblical Hebrew and Chaldee will be useful to students and others, who do not care at all times to consult a more copious and elaborate Lexicon; and it will be particularly serviceable to many who are unable to turn conveniently and rapidly, amid the perplexities and details of foreign characters with which the pages of Gesenius and Fürst bristle, to the fundamental and essential points of information that they are seeking. Even scholars will find here, not only all of a strictly verbal character which they most frequently want in ordinary consultation of a lexicon, but numerous original suggestions, relations, and distinctions, carefully made and clearly put, which are not unworthy of their attention, especially in the affinities of roots and the classification of meanings. The portable form and moderate cost of the book, it is hoped, will facilitate its use with all classes. The vocabulary is complete as to the ground-forms that actually occur in the biblical text (or *Kethib*), with the pointing that properly belongs to them. Their designation by numbers will especially aid those who are not very familiar with the original language, and the Anglicizing and pronunciation of the words will not come amiss to multitudes who have some acquaintance with it. The addition of the renderings in the common version will greatly contribute to fixing and extending the varied significations and applications of the Hebrew and Chaldee words, as well as to correcting their occasionally wrong translations. On this account, as well as for the sake of precision and to prevent repetition, the use of the same terms in the preceding definitions has been avoided wherever practicable. The design of the volume, being purely *lexical*, does not include grammatical, archæological, or exegetical details, which would have swelled its size and encumbered its plan.

By observing the subjoined directions, in the associated use of the Main Concordance, the reader will have substantially a Concordance-Dictionary of the Authorized Version and the Hebrew Bible.

PLAN OF THE BOOK.

1. All the original words are treated in their alphabetical Hebrew order, and are numbered regularly from the first to the last, each being known throughout by its appropriate number. This renders reference easy without recourse to the Hebrew characters.

2. Immediately after each word is given its exact equivalent in English letters, according to the system of transliteration laid down in the scheme here following, which is substantially that adopted in the Common English Version, only more consistently and uniformly carried out; so that the word could readily be turned back again into Hebrew from the form thus given it.

3. Next follows the precise pronunciation, according to the usual English mode of sounding syllables, so plainly indicated that none can fail to apprehend and apply it. The most approved sounds are adopted, as laid down in the annexed scheme of articulation, and in such a way that any good Hebraist would immediately recognize the word if so pronounced, notwithstanding the minor variations current among scholars in this respect.

4. Then ensues a tracing of the etymology, radical meaning, and applied signification of the word, justly but tersely analyzed and expressed, with any other important peculiarities in this regard.

5. In the case of proper names, the same method is pursued, and at this point the regular mode of Anglicizing it, after the general style of the Common English Version, is given, and a few words of explanation are added to identify it.

6. Finally (after the punctuation-mark :—) are given all the different renderings of the word in the Authorized English Version, arranged in the alphabetical order of the leading terms, and conveniently condensed according to the explanations given below.

By searching out these various renderings in the MAIN CONCORDANCE, to which this Dictionary is designed as a companion, and noting the passages to which the same number corresponding to that of any given Hebrew word is attached in the marginal column, the reader, whether acquainted with the original language or not, will obtain a complete *Hebrew Concordance* also, expressed in the words of the Common English Version. This is an advantage which no other Concordance or Lexicon affords.

HEBREW ARTICULATION.

THE following explanations are sufficient to show the method of transliterating Hebrew words into English adopted in this *Dictionary*.

1. The Hebrew is read *from right to left*. The Alphabet consists of 22 letters (and their variations), which are all regarded as *consonants*, being enunciated by the aid of certain "points" or marks, mostly beneath the letters, and which serve as *vowels*. There is no distinction of *capitals*, *italics*, etc.

2. The letters are as follows:

No.	Form.	Name.		Transliteration and Power.
1.	א	'Aleph	(*aw'-lef*)	ʾ unappreciable
2.	ב	Bêyth	(*bayth*)	**b**
3.	ג	Gîymel	(*ghee'-mel*)	**g** hard = γ
4.	ד	Dâleth	(*daw'-leth*)	**d** [cent
5.	ה	Hê'	(*hay*)	**h**, often quies-
6.	ו	Vâv	(*vawv*)	**v**, or **w** quies-
7.	ז	Zayin	(*zah'-yin*)	**z**, as in *zeal* [cent
8.	ח	Chêyth	(*khayth*)	German **ch** = χ [(nearly *kh*)
9.	ט	Têyth	(*tayth*)	**ṭ** = ת [cent
10.	י	Yôwd	(*yode*)	**y**, often quies-
11.	כ, final ך	Kaph	(*caf*)	**k** = ק
12.	ל	Lâmed	(*law'-med*)	**l**
13.	מ, final ם	Mêm	(*mame*)	**m**
14.	נ, final ן	Nûwn	(*noon*)	**n**
15.	ס	Çâmek	(*saw'-mek*)	**ç** = *s* sharp = שׂ
16.	ע	'Ayin	(*ah'-yin*)	ʿ peculiar *
17.	פ, final ף	Phê'	(*fay*)	**ph** = *f* = φ
	פּ	Pê'	(*pay*)	**p**
18.	צ, final ץ	Tsâdêy	(*tsaw-day'*)	**ts**
19.	ק	Qôwph	(*cofe*)	**q** = *k* = כ
20.	ר	Rêysh	(*raysh*)	**r**
21.	שׂ	Sîyn	(*seen*)	**s** sharp = ס = σ
	שׁ	Shîyn	(*sheen*)	**sh**
22.	ת	Thâv	(*thawv*)	**th**, as in THin
	תּ	Tâv	(*tawv*)	**t** = ט = τ [= ϑ

3. The *vowel-points* are the following:

Form.*	Name.		Representation and Power.
(ָ)	Qâmêts	(*caw-mates'*)	**â**, as in *All*
(ַ)	Pattach	(*pat'-takh*)	**a**, as in *mAn*, (*fār*)
(ֲ)	Shᵉvâ'-Pattach	(*she-vaw' pat'-takh*)	**ă**, as in *hAt*
(ֵ)	Tsêrêy	(*tsay-ray'*)	**ê**, as in *thEy* = η
(ֶ)	Çegôwl	(*seg-ole'*)	**e**, as in *thEir*; **e**, as in *mEn* = ε
(ֱ)	Shᵉvâ'-Çegôwl	(*she-vaw' seg-ole'*)	**ĕ**, as in *mEt*
(ְ)	Shᵉvâ' †	(*she-vaw'*)	ᵉ obscure, as in [*avErage*; silent, as *e* in *madE*
(ִ)	Chîyriq	(*khee'-rik*)	**î**, as in *machIne* ‡; **i**, as in *supplIant*, [(*mīsery*, *hĭt*)
(ֹ)	Chôwlem §	(*kho'-lem*)	**ô**, as in *no* = ω
(ָ)	Short Qâmêts ‖		**o**, as in *nOr* = ο
(ֳ)	Shᵉvà'-Qâmêts	(*she-vaw' caw-mates'*)	**ŏ**, as in *not*
(ּ)	Shûwrêq *	(*shoo-rake'*)	**û**, as in *crUel*
(ֻ)	Qîbbûts *	(*kib'-boots*)	**u**, as in *fUll*, *rūde*

4. A point in the bosom of a letter is called *Dâgêsh'*, and is of two kinds, which must be carefully distinguished.

a. Dâgêsh *lenè* occurs only in the letters ב, ג, ד, כ, פ, ת, (technically vocalized *Bᵉgad'-Kᵉphath'*,) when they *begin* a clause or sentence, or are preceded by a consonant *sound;* and simply has the effect of removing their aspiration.†

b. Dâgêsh *fortè* may occur in any letter except א, ה, ח, ע or ר; it is equivalent to *doubling* the letter, and at the same time it removes the aspiration of a Bᵉgad-Kᵉphath letter.‡

5. The *Maqqêph'* (־), like a *hyphen*, unites words only for purposes of pronunciation (by removing the primary accent from all except the last of them), but does not affect their meaning or their grammatical construction.

---

* The letter *'Ayin*, owing to the difficulty experienced by Occidentals in pronouncing it accurately (it is a deep guttural sound, like that made in *gargling*), is generally neglected (i.e. passed over silently) in reading. We have represented it to the eye (but not exactly to the ear) by the Greek *rough breathing* (for distinctness and typographical convenience, a reversed *apostrophe*) in order to distinguish it from *'Âleph*, which is likewise treated as silent, being similarly represented by the Greek *smooth breathing* (the *apostrophe*).

* The parenthesis-marks ( ) are given here in order to show the place of the vowel-points, whether below, above, or in the middle of the letter.

† *Silent Shᵉvâ'* is not represented by any mark in our method of transliteration, as it is understood whenever there is no other vowel-point.

‡ *Chîyriq* is thus long only when it is followed by a quiescent *yôwd* (either expressed or implied).

§ *Chôwlem* is written *fully* only over *Vâv*, which is then quiescent (*w*); but when used "defectively" (without the *Vâv*) it may be written either over the left-hand corner of the letter to which it belongs, or over the right-hand corner of the following one.

‖ Short *Qâmêts* is found only in *unaccented syllables ending with a consonant sound.*

* *Shûwrêq* is written only in the bosom of *Vâv*. Sometimes it is said to be "defectively" written (without the *Vâv*), and then takes the form of *Qibbûts*, which in such cases is called *vicarious*.

† In our system of transliteration Dâgêsh *lenè* is represented only in the letters פ and ת, because elsewhere it does not affect the pronunciation (with most Hebraists).

‡ A point in the bosom of ה is called *Mappîyq* (*map-peek'*). It occurs only in the final vowelless letter of a few words, and we have represented it by *hh*. A Dâgêsh *fortè* in the bosom of ו may easily be distinguished from the vowel *Shûwrêq* by noticing that in the former case the letter has a proper vowel-point accompanying it.

It should be noted that both kinds of Dâgêsh are often omitted in writing (being then said to be *implied*), but (in the case at least of Dâgêsh *fortè*) the word is (by most Hebraists) pronounced the same as if it were present.

ABBREVIATIONS EMPLOYED.

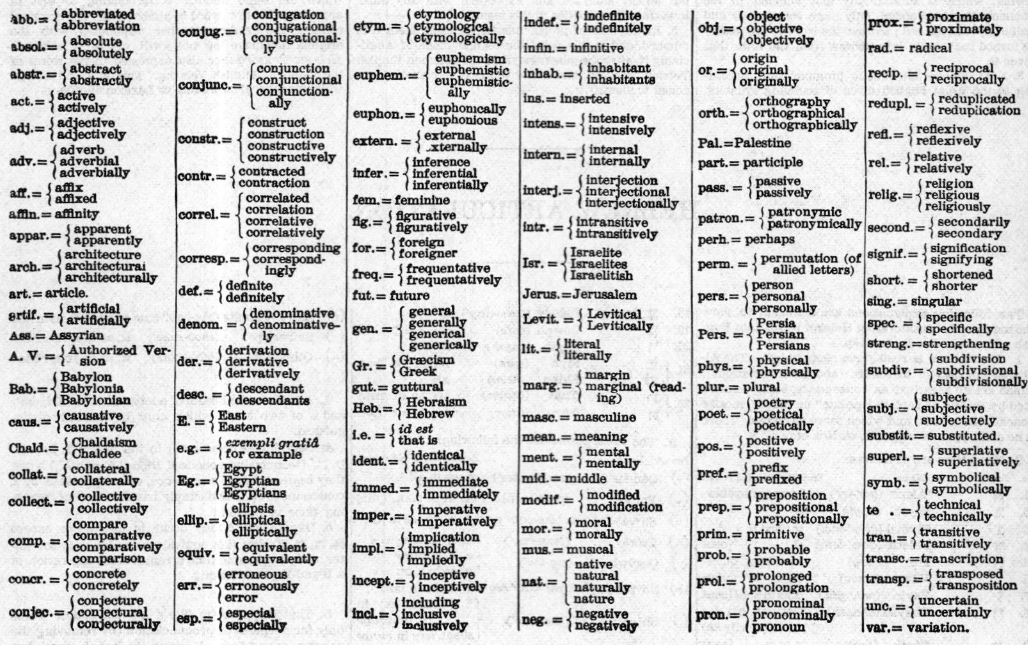

abb. = abbreviated, abbreviation
absol. = absolute, absolutely
abstr. = abstract, abstractly
act. = active, actively
adj. = adjective, adjectively
adv. = adverb, adverbial, adverbially
aff. = affix, affixed
affin. = affinity
appar. = apparent, apparently
arch. = architecture, architectural, architecturally
art. = article.
artif. = artificial, artificially
Ass. = Assyrian
A. V. = Authorized Version
Bab. = Babylon, Babylonia, Babylonian
caus. = causative, causatively
Chald. = Chaldaism, Chaldee
collat. = collateral, collaterally
collect. = collective, collectively
comp. = compare, comparative, comparatively, comparison
concr. = concrete, concretely
conjec. = conjecture, conjectural, conjecturally
conjug. = conjugation, conjugational, conjugationally
conjunc. = conjunction, conjunctional, conjunctionally
constr. = construct, construction, constructive, constructively
contr. = contracted, contraction
correl. = correlated, correlation, correlative, correlatively
corresp. = corresponding, correspondingly
def. = definite, definitely
denom. = denominative, denominatively
der. = derivation, derivative, derivatively
desc. = descendant, descendants
E. = East, Eastern
e.g. = *exempli gratiâ*, for example
Eg. = Egypt, Egyptian, Egyptians
ellip. = ellipsis, elliptical, elliptically
equiv. = equivalent, equivalently
err. = erroneous, erroneously, error
esp. = especial, especially
etym. = etymology, etymological, etymologically
euphem. = euphemism, euphemistic, euphemistically
euphon. = euphonically, euphonious
extern. = external, externally
infer. = inference, inferential, inferentially
fem. = feminine
fig. = figurative, figuratively
for. = foreign, foreigner
freq. = frequentative, frequentatively
fut. = future
gen. = general, generally, generical, generically
Gr. = Græcism, Greek
gut. = guttural
Heb. = Hebraism, Hebrew
i.e. = *id est*, that is
ident. = identical, identically
immed. = immediate, immediately
imper. = imperative, imperatively
impl. = implication, implied, impliedly
incept. = inceptive, inceptively
incl. = including, inclusive, inclusively
indef. = indefinite, indefinitely
infin. = infinitive
inhab. = inhabitant, inhabitants
ins. = inserted
intens. = intensive, intensively
intern. = internal, internally
interj. = interjection, interjectional, interjectionally
intr. = intransitive, intransitively
Isr. = Israelite, Israelites, Israelitish
Jerus. = Jerusalem
Levit. = Levitical, Levitically
lit. = literal, literally
marg. = margin, marginal (reading)
masc. = masculine
mean. = meaning
ment. = mental, mentally
mid. = middle
modif. = modified, modification
mor. = moral, morally
mus. = musical
nat. = native, natural, naturally, nature
neg. = negative, negatively
obj. = object, objective, objectively
or. = origin, original, originally
orth. = orthography, orthographical, orthographically
Pal. = Palestine
part. = participle
pass. = passive, passively
patron. = patronymic, patronymically
perh. = perhaps
perm. = permutation (of allied letters)
pers. = person, personal, personally
Pers. = Persia, Persian, Persians
phys. = physical, physically
plur. = plural
poet. = poetry, poetical, poetically
pos. = positive, positively
pref. = prefix, prefixed
prep. = preposition, prepositional, prepositionally
prim. = primitive
prob. = probable, probably
prol. = prolonged, prolongation
pron. = pronominal, pronominally, pronoun
prox. = proximate, proximately
rad. = radical
recip. = reciprocal, reciprocally
redupl. = reduplicated, reduplication
refl. = reflexive, reflexively
rel. = relative, relatively
relig. = religion, religious, religiously
second. = secondarily, secondary
signif. = signification, signifying
short. = shortened, shorter
sing. = singular
spec. = specific, specifically
streng. = strengthening
subdiv. = subdivision, subdivisional, subdivisionally
subj. = subject, subjective, subjectively
substit. = substituted.
superl. = superlative, superlatively
symb. = symbolical, symbolically
te . = technical, technically
tran. = transitive, transitively
transc. = transcription
transp. = transposed, transposition
unc. = uncertain, uncertainly
var. = variation.

SIGNS EMPLOYED.

+ (*addition*) denotes a rendering in the A. V. of one or more Heb. words in connection with the one under consideration.

× (*multiplication*) denotes a rendering in the A. V. that results from an idiom peculiar to the Heb.

° (*degree*), appended to a Heb. word, denotes a vowel-pointing corrected from that of the text. (This mark is set in Heb. Bibles over syllables in which the vowels of the marg. have been inserted instead of those properly belonging to the text.)

( ) (*parenthesis*), in the renderings from the A. V., denotes a word or syllable sometimes given in connection with the principal word to which *it* is annexed.

[ ] (*bracket*), in the rendering from the A. V., denotes the inclusion of an additional word in the Heb.

Italics, at the end of a rendering from the A. V., denote an explanation of the variations from the usual form.

HEBREW AND CHALDEE DICTIONARY

ACCOMPANYING

THE EXHAUSTIVE CONCORDANCE.

א

1. אָב **'âb**, *awb;* a prim. word; *father* in a lit. and immed., or fig. and remote application):—chief, (fore-) father ([-less]), × patrimony, principal. Comp. names in "Abi-".

2. אַב **'ab** (Chald.), *ab;* corresp. to 1:—father.

3. אֵב **'êb**, *abe;* from the same as 24; a *green* plant:—greenness, fruit.

4. אֵב **'êb** (Chald.), *abe;* corresp. to 3:—fruit.

אֹב **'ôb**. See 178.

5. אֲבַגְתָא **'Ăbagthâ'**, *ab-ag-thaw';* of for. or.; *Abagtha,* a eunuch of Xerxes:—Abagtha.

6. אָבַד **'âbad**, *aw-bad';* a prim. root; prop. to *wander* away, i.e. *lose* oneself; by impl. to *perish* (caus. *destroy*):—break, destroy (-uction), + not escape, fail, lose, (cause to, make) perish, spend, × and surely, take, be undone, × utterly, be void of, have no way to flee.

7. אֲבַד **'ăbad** (Chald.), *ab-ad';* corresp. to 6:—destroy, perish.

8. אֹבֵד **'ôbêd**, *o-bade';* act. part. of 6; (concr.) *wretched* or (abstr.) *destruction:*—perish.

9. אֲבֵדָה **'ăbêdâh**, *ab-ay-daw';* from 6; concr. something *lost;* abstr. *destruction,* i.e. Hades:—lost. Comp. 10.

10. אֲבַדֹּה **'ăbaddôh**, *ab-ad-do';* the same as 9, miswritten for 11; a *perishing:*—destruction.

11. אֲבַדּוֹן **'ăbaddôwn**, *ab-ad-done';* intens. from 6; abstr. a *perishing;* concr. Hades:—destruction.

12. אַבְדָן **'abdân**, *ab-dawn';* from 6; a *perishing:*—destruction.

13. אָבְדַן **'obdân**, *ob-dawn';* from 6; a *perishing:*—destruction.

14. אָבָה **'âbâh**, *aw-baw';* a prim. root; to *breathe* after, i.e. (fig.) to *be acquiescent:*—consent, rest content, will, be willing.

15. אָבֶה **'âbeh**, *aw-beh';* from 14; *longing:*—desire.

16. אֵבֶה **'êbeh**, *ay-beh';* from 14 (in the sense of *bending* towards); the *papyrus:*—swift.

17. אֲבוֹי **'ăbôwy**, *ab-o'ee;* from 14 (in the sense of *desiring*); *want:*—sorrow.

18. אֵבוּס **'êbûwç**, *ay-booce';* from 75; a *manger* or *stall:*—crib.

19. אִבְחָה **'ibchâh**, *ib-khaw';* from an unused root (appar. mean. to *turn*); *brandishing* of a sword:—point.

20. אֲבַטִּחַ **'ăbaṭṭîyach**, *ab-at-tee'-akh;* of uncert. der.; a *melon* (only plur.):—melon.

21. אֲבִי **'Ăbîy**, *ab-ee';* from 1; *fatherly; Abi,* Hezekiah's mother:—Abi.

22. אֲבִיאֵל **'Ăbîy'êl**, *ab-ee-ale';* from 1 and 410; *father* (i.e. *possessor*) *of God; Abiel,* the name of two Isr.:—Abiel.

23. אֲבִיאָסָף **'Ăbîy'âçâph**, *ab-ee-aw-sawf';* from 1 and 622; *father of gathering* (i.e. *gatherer*); *Abiasaph,* an Isr.:—Abiasaph.

24. אָבִיב **'âbîyb**, *aw-beeb';* from an unused root (mean. to *be tender*); *green,* i.e. a young *ear* of grain; hence the name of the month *Abib* or Nisan:—Abib, ear, green ears of corn.

25. אֲבִי גִבְעוֹן **'Ăbîy Gib'ôwn**, *ab-ee' ghib-one';* from 1 and 1391; *father* (i.e. *founder*) *of Gibon; Abi-Gibon,* perh. an Isr.:—father of Gibeon.

26. אֲבִיגַיִל **'Ăbîygayil**, *ab-ee-gah'-yil,* or shorter אֲבִיגַל **'Ăbîygal**, *ab-ee-gal';* from 1 and 1524; *father* (i.e. *source*) *of joy; Abigail* or *Abigal,* the name of two Israelitesses:—Abigal.

27. אֲבִידָן **'Ăbîydân**, *ab-ee-dawn';* from 1 and 1777; *father of judgment* (i.e. *judge*); *Abidan,* an Isr.:—Abidan.

28. אֲבִידָע **'Ăbîydâ'**, *ab-ee-daw';* from 1 and 3045; *father of knowledge* (i.e. *knowing*); *Abida,* a son of Abraham by Keturah:—Abida, Abidah.

29. אֲבִיָּה **'Ăbîyâh**, *ab-ee-yaw';* or prol. אֲבִיָּהוּ **'Ăbîyâhûw**, *ab-ee-yaw'-hoo;* from 1 and 3050; *father* (i.e. *worshipper*) *of Jah; Abijah,* the name of several Isr. men and two Israelitesses:—Abiah, Abijah.

30. אֲבִיהוּא **'Ăbîyhûw'**, *ab-ee-hoo';* from 1 and 1931; *father* (i.e. *worshipper*) *of Him* (i.e. *God*); *Abihu,* a son of Aaron:—Abihu.

31. אֲבִיהוּד **'Ăbîyhûwd**, *ab-ee-hood';* from 1 and 1935; *father* (i.e. *possessor*) *of renown; Abihud,* the name of two Isr.:—Abihud.

32. אֲבִיהַיִל **'Ăbîyhayil**, *ab-ee-hah'-yil;* or (more correctly) אֲבִיחַיִל **'Ăbîychayil**, *ab-ee-khah'-yil;* from 1 and 2428; *father* (i.e. *possessor*) *of might; Abihail* or *Abichail,* the name of three Isr. and two Israelitesses:—Abihail.

33. אֲבִי הָעֶזְרִי **'Ăbîy hâ-'Ezrîy**, *ab-ee'-haw-ez-ree';* from 44 with the art. inserted; *father of the Ezrite;* an *Abiezrite* or descendant of Abiezer:—Abiezrite.

34. אֶבְיוֹן **'ebyôwn**, *eb-yone';* from 14, in the sense of *want* (espec. in feeling); *destitute:*—beggar, needy, poor (man).

35. אֲבִיּוֹנָה **'ăbîyôwnâh**, *ab-ee-yo-naw';* from 14; provocative of *desire;* the *caper* berry (from its *stimulative* taste):—desire.

אֲבִיחַיִל **'Ăbîychayil**. See 32.

36. אֲבִיטוּב **'Ăbîyṭûwb**, *ab-ee-toob';* from 1 and 2898; *father of goodness* (i.e. *good*); *Abitub,* an Isr.:—Abitub.

37. אֲבִיטַל **'Ăbîyṭâl**, *ab-ee-tal';* from 1 and 2919; *father of dew* (i.e. *fresh*); *Abital,* a wife of King David:—Abital.

38. אֲבִיָּם **'Ăbîyâm**, *ab-ee-yawm';* from 1 and 3220; *father of* (the) *sea* (i.e. *seaman*); *Abijam* (or Abijah), a king of Judah:—Abijam.

39. אֲבִימָאֵל **'Ăbîymâ'êl**, *ab-ee-maw-ale';* from 1 and an elsewhere unused (prob. for.) word; *father of Mael* (appar. some Arab tribe); *Abimael,* a son of Joktan:—Abimael.

40. אֲבִימֶלֶךְ **'Ăbîymelek**, *ab-ee-mel'-ek;* from 1 and 4428; *father of* (the) *king; Abimelek,* the name of two Philistine kings and of two Isr.:—Abimelech.

41. אֲבִינָדָב **'Ăbîynâdâb**, *ab-ee-naw-dawb';* from 1 and 5068; *father of generosity* (i.e. *liberal*); *Abinadab,* the name of four Isr.:—Abinadab.

42. אֲבִינֹעַם **'Ăbîynô'am**, *ab-ee-no'-am;* from 1 and 5278; *father of pleasantness* (i.e. *gracious*); *Abinoam,* an Isr.:—Abinoam.

אֲבִינֵר **'Ăbîynêr**. See 74.

43. אֶבְיָסָף **'Ebyâçâph**, *eb-yaw-sawf';* contr. from 23; *Ebjasaph,* an Isr.:—Ebiasaph.

44. אֲבִיעֶזֶר **'Ăbîy'ezer**, *ab-ee-ay'-zer;* from 1 and 5829; *father of help* (i.e. *helpful*); *Abiezer,* the name of two Isr.:—Abiezer.

45. אֲבִי־עַלְבוֹן **'Ăbîy-'albôwn**, *ab-ee-al-bone';* from 1 and an unused root of unc. der.; prob. *father of strength* (i.e. *valiant*); *Abialbon,* an Isr.:—Abialbon.

46. אָבִיר **'âbîyr**, *aw-beer';* from 82; *mighty* (spoken of God):—mighty (one).

47. אַבִּיר **'abbîyr**, *ab-beer';* for 46:—angel, bull, chiefest, mighty (one), stout [-hearted], strong (one), valiant.

48. אֲבִירָם **'Ăbîyrâm**, *ab-ee-rawm';* from 1 and 7311; *father of height* (i.e. *lofty*); *Abiram,* the name of two Isr.:—Abiram.

49. אֲבִישַׁג **'Ăbîyshag**, *ab-ee-shag';* from 1 and 7686; *father of error* (i.e. *blundering*); *Abishag,* a concubine of David:—Abishag.

50. אֲבִישׁוּעַ **'Ăbîyshûwac**, *ab-ee-shoo'-ah;* from 1 and 7771; *father of plenty* (i.e. *prosperous*); *Abishua,* the name of two Isr.:—Abishua.

51. אֲבִישׁוּר **'Ăbîyshûwr**, *ab-ee-shoor';* from 1 and 7791; *father of* (the) *wall* (i.e. perh. *mason*); *Abishur,* an Isr.:—Abishur.

52. אֲבִישַׁי **'Ăbîyshay**, *ab-ee-shah'ee;* or (shorter) אַבְשַׁי **'Abshay**, *ab-shah'ee;* from 1 and 7862; *father of a gift* (i.e. prob. *generous*); *Abishai,* an Isr.:—Abishai.

53. אֲבִישָׁלוֹם **'Ăbîyshâlôwm**, *ab-ee-shaw-lome';* or (short.) אַבְשָׁלוֹם **'Abshâlôwm**, *ab-shaw-lome';* from 1 and 7965; *father of peace* (i.e. *friendly*); *Abshalom,* a son of David; also (the fuller form) a later Isr.:—Abishalom, Absalom.

54. אֶבְיָתָר **'Ebyâthâr**, *eb-yaw-thawr';* contr. from 1 and 3498; *father of abundance* (i.e. *liberal*); *Ebjathar,* an Isr.:—Abiathar.

55. אָבַךְ **'âbak**, *aw-bak';* a prim. root; prob. to *coil* upward:—mount up.

56. אָבַל **'âbal**, *aw-bal';* a prim. root; to *bewail:*—lament, mourn.

57. אָבֵל **'âbêl**, *aw-bale';* from 56; *lamenting:*—mourn (-er, -ing).

58. אָבֵל **'âbêl**, *aw-bale';* from an unused root (mean. to *be grassy*); a *meadow:*—plain. Comp. also the prop. names beginning with Abel-.

59. אָבֵל **'Âbêl**, *aw-bale';* from 58; a *meadow; Abel,* the name of two places in Pal.:—Abel.

60. אֵבֶל **'êbel**, *ay'-bel;* from 56; *lamentation:*—mourning.

61. אֲבָל **'ăbâl**, *ab-awl';* appar. from 56 through the idea of *negation; nay,* i.e. *truly* or *yet:*—but, indeed, nevertheless, verily.

62. אָבֵל בֵּית־מַעֲכָה **'Âbêl Bêyth-Ma'âkâh**, *aw-bale' bayth ma-a-kaw';* from 58 and 1004 and 4601; *meadow of Beth-Maakah; Abel of Beth-maakah,* a place in Pal.:—Abel-beth-maachah, Abel of Beth-maachah.

63. אָבֵל הַשִּׁטִּים **'Âbêl hash-Shiṭṭîym,** *aw-bale' hash-shit-teem';* from 58 and the plur. of 7848, with the art. ins.; *meadow of the acacias; Abel hash-Shittim,* a place in Pal.:—Abel-shittim.

64. אָבֵל כְּרָמִים **'Âbêl Kᵉrâmîym,** *aw-bale' ker-aw-meem';* from 58 and the plur. of 3754; *meadow of vineyards; Abel-Keramim,* a place in Pal.:—plain of the vineyards.

65. אָבֵל מְחוֹלָה **'Âbêl Mᵉchôwlâh,** *aw-bale' mekh-o-law';* from 58 and 4246; *meadow of dancing; Abel-Mecholah,* a place in Pal.:—Abel-meholah.

66. אָבֵל מַיִם **'Âbêl Mayim,** *aw-bale' mah'-yim;* from 58 and 4325; *meadow of water; Abel-Majim,* a place in Pal.:—Abel-maim.

67. אָבֵל מִצְרַיִם **'Âbêl Mitsrayim,** *aw-bale' mits-rah'-yim;* from 58 and 4714; *meadow of Egypt; Abel-Mitsrajim,* a place in Pal.:—Abel-mizraim.

68. אֶבֶן **'eben,** *eh'-ben;* from the root of 1129 through the mean. to *build; a stone:*—+carbuncle, + mason, + plummet, [chalk-, hail-, head-, sling-] stone (-ny), (divers) weight (-s).

69. אֶבֶן **'eben** (Chald.), *eh'-ben;* corresp. to 68:—stone.

70. אֹבֶן **'ôben,** *o'-ben;* from the same as 68; *a pair of stones* (only dual); a potter's *wheel* or a midwife's *stool* (consisting alike of two horizontal disks with a support between):—wheel, stool.

71. אֲבָנָה **'Ăbânâh,** *ab-aw-naw';* perh. fem. of 68; *stony; Abanah,* a river near Damascus:—Abana. Comp. 549.

72. אֶבֶן הָעֵזֶר **'Eben hâ-'ezer,** *eh'-ben haw-e'-zer;* from 68 and 5828 with the art. ins.; *stone of the help; Eben-ha-Ezer,* a place in Pal.:—Ebenezer.

73. אַבְנֵט **'abnêṭ,** *ab-nate';* of uncert. deriv.; a *belt:*—girdle.

74. אַבְנֵר **'Abnêr,** *ab-nare';* or (fully) אֲבִינֵר **'Ăbîynêr,** *ab-ee-nare';* from 1 and 5216; *father of light* (i.e. *enlightening*); *Abner,* an Isr.:—Abner.

75. אָבַס **'âbaç,** *aw-bas';* a prim. root; to *fodder:*—fatted, stalled.

76. אֲבַעְבֻּעָה **'ăba'bû'âh,** *ab-ah-boo-aw';* (by redupl.) from an unused root (mean. to *belch* forth); an inflammatory *pustule* (as *eruption*):—blains.

77. אֶבֶץ **'Ebets,** *eh'-bets;* from an unused root prob. mean. to *gleam; conspicuous; Ebets,* a place in Pal.:—Abez.

78. אִבְצָן **'Ibtsân,** *ib-tsawn';* from the same as 76; *splendid; Ibtsan,* an Isr.:—Ibzan.

79. אָבַק **'âbaq,** *aw-bak';* a prim. root; prob. to *float* away (as vapor), but used only as denom. from 80; to *bedust,* i.e. *grapple:*—wrestle.

80. אָבָק **'âbâq,** *aw-bawk';* from root of 79; light *particles* (as *volatile*):—(small) dust, powder.

81. אֲבָקָה **'ăbâqâh,** *ab-aw-kaw';* fem. of 80:—powder.

82. אָבַר **'âbar,** *aw-bar';* a prim. root; to *soar:*—fly.

83. אֵבֶר **'êber,** *ay-ber';* from 82; a *pinion:*—[long-] wing (-ed).

84. אֶבְרָה **'ebrâh,** *eb-raw';* fem. of 83:—feather, wing.

85. אַבְרָהָם **'Abrâhâm,** *ab-raw-hawm';* contr. from 1 and an unused root (prob. mean. to *be populous*); *father of a multitude; Abraham,* the later name of Abram:—Abraham.

86. אַבְרֵךְ **'abrêk,** *ab-rake';* prob. an Eg. word mean. *kneel:*—bow the knee.

87. אַבְרָם **'Abrâm,** *ab-rawm';* contr. from 48; *high father; Abram,* the original name of Abraham:—Abram.

אַבְשַׁי **'Abshay.** See 52.

אַבְשָׁלוֹם **'Abshâlôwm.** See 53.

88. אֹבֹת **'ôbôth,** *o-both';* plur. of 178; water-*skins; Oboth,* a place in the Desert:—Oboth.

89. אָגֵא **'Âgê',** *aw-gay';* of uncert. der. [comp. 90]; *Agê,* an Isr.:—Agee.

90. אֲגַג **'Ăgag,** *ag-ag';* or אֲגָג **'Ăgâg,** *ag-awg';* of uncert. der. [comp. 89]; *flame; Agag,* a title of Amalekitish kings:—Agag.

91. אֲגָגִי **'Ăgâgîy,** *ag-aw-ghee';* patrial or patron. from 90; an *Agagite* or descendant (subject) of Agag:—Agagite.

92. אֲגֻדָּה **'ăguddâh,** *ag-ood-daw';* fem. pass. part. of an unused root (mean. to *bind*); a *band, bundle, knot,* or *arch:*—bunch, burden, troop.

93. אֱגוֹז **'ĕgôwz,** *eg-oze';* prob. of Pers. or.; a *nut:*—nut.

94. אָגוּר **'Âgûwr,** *aw-goor';* pass. part. of 103; *gathered* (i.e. *received* among the sages); *Agur,* a fanciful name for Solomon:—Agur.

95. אֲגוֹרָה **'ăgôwrâh,** *ag-o-raw';* from the same as 94; prop. something *gathered,* i.e. perh. a *grain* or *berry;* used only of a small (silver) *coin:*—piece [of] silver.

96. אֶגֶל **'egel,** *eh'-ghel;* from an unused root (mean. to *flow* down or together as drops); a *reservoir:*—drop.

97. אֶגְלַיִם **'Eglayim,** *eg-lah'-yim;* dual of 96; a *double pond; Eglajim,* a place in Moab:—Eglaim.

98. אֲגַם **'ăgam,** *ag-am';* from an unused root (mean. to *collect* as water); a *marsh;* hence a *rush* (as growing in swamps); hence a *stockade* of reeds:—pond, pool, standing [water].

99. אָגֵם **'âgêm,** *aw-game';* prob. from the same as 98 (in the sense of *stagnant* water); fig. *sad:*—pond.

100. אַגְמוֹן **'agmôwn,** *ag-mone';* from the same as 98; a marshy *pool* [others from a different root, a *kettle*]; by impl. a *rush* (as growing there); collect. a *rope* of rushes:—bulrush, caldron, hook, rush.

101. אַגָּן **'aggân,** *ag-gawn';* prob. from 5059; a *bowl* (as *pounded* out hollow):—basin, cup, goblet.

102. אַגָּף **'aggâph,** *ag-gawf';* prob. from 5062 (through the idea of *impending*); a *cover* or *heap;* i.e. (only plur.) *wings* of an army, or *crowds* of troops:—bands.

103. אָגַר **'âgar,** *aw-gar';* a prim. root; to *harvest:*—gather.

104. אִגְּרָא **'iggᵉrâ'** (Chald.), *ig-er-aw';* of Pers. or.; an *epistle* (as carried by a state courier or postman):—letter.

105. אֲגַרְטָל **'ăgarṭâl,** *ag-ar-tawl';* of uncert. der.; a *basin:*—charger.

106. אֶגְרֹף **'egrôph,** *eg-rofe';* from 1640 (in the sense of *grasping*); the *clenched* hand:—fist.

107. אִגֶּרֶת **'iggereth,** *ig-eh'-reth;* fem. of 104; an *epistle:*—letter.

108. אֵד **'êd,** *ade;* from the same as 181 (in the sense of *enveloping*); a *fog:*—mist, vapor.

109. אָדַב **'âdab,** *aw-dab';* a prim. root; to *languish:*—grieve.

110. אַדְבְּאֵל **'Adbᵉ'êl,** *ad-beh-ale';* prob. from 109 (in the sense of *chastisement*) and 410; *disciplined of God; Adbeël,* a son of Ishmael:—Adbeel.

111. אֲדַד **'Ădad,** *ad-ad';* prob. an orth. var. for 2301; *Adad* (or Hadad), an Edomite:—Hadad.

112. אִדּוֹ **'Iddôw,** *id-do;* of uncert. der.; *Iddo,* an Isr.:—Iddo.

אֱדוֹם **'Ĕdôwm.** See 123.

אֱדוֹמִי **'Ĕdôwmîy.** See 30.

113. אָדוֹן **'âdôwn,** *aw-done',* or (short.) אָדֹן **'âdôn,** *aw-done';* from an unused root (mean. to *rule*); *sovereign,* i.e. *controller* (human or divine):—lord, master, owner. Comp. also names beginning with "Adoni-".

114. אַדּוֹן **'Addôwn,** *ad-done';* prob. intens. for 113; *powerful; Addon,* appar. an Isr.:—Addon.

115. אֲדוֹרַיִם **'Ădôwrayim,** *ad-o-rah'-yim;* dual from 142 (in the sense of *eminence*); *double mound; Adorajim,* a place in Pal.:—Adoraim.

116. אֱדַיִן **'ĕdayin** (Chald.), *ed-ah'-yin;* of uncert. der.; *then* (of time):—now, that time, then.

117. אַדִּיר **'addîyr,** *ad-deer';* from 142; *wide* or (gen.) *large;* fig. *powerful:*—excellent, famous, gallant, glorious, goodly, lordly, mighty (-ier one), noble, principal, worthy.

118. אֲדַלְיָא **'Ădalyâ',** *ad-al-yaw';* of Pers. der. *Adalja,* a son of Haman:—Adalia.

119. אָדַם **'âdam,** *aw-dam';* to *show blood* (in the face), i.e. *flush* or turn rosy:—be (dyed made) red (ruddy).

120. אָדָם **'âdâm,** *aw-dawm';* from 119; *ruddy,* i.e. a *human being* (an individual or the species, *mankind,* etc.):— × another, + hypocrite, + common sort, × low, man (mean, of low degree), person.

121. אָדָם **'Âdâm,** *aw-dawm';* the same as 120 *Adam,* the name of the first man, also of a place in Pal.:—Adam.

122. אָדֹם **'âdôm,** *aw-dome';* from 119; *rosy:*—red ruddy.

123. אֱדֹם **'Ĕdôm,** *ed-ome';* or (fully) אֱדוֹם **'Ĕdôwm,** *ed-ome';* from 122; *red* [see Gen. 25 : 25]; *Edom,* the elder twin-brother of Jacob hence the region (Idumæa) occupied by him:—Edom Edomites, Idumea.

124. אֹדֶם **'ôdem,** *o'-dem;* from 119; *redness,* i.e. the *ruby, garnet,* or some other red gem:—sardius.

125. אֲדַמְדָּם **'ădamdâm,** *ad-am-dawm';* redupl. from 119; *reddish:*—(somewhat) reddish.

126. אַדְמָה **'Admâh,** *ad-maw';* contr. for 127 *earthy; Admah,* a place near the Dead Sea:—Admah.

127. אֲדָמָה **'ădâmâh,** *ad-aw-maw';* from 119; *soil* (from its gen. *redness*):—country, earth, ground, husband [-man] (-ry), land.

128. אֲדָמָה **'Ădâmâh,** *ad-aw-maw';* the same as 127; *Adamah,* a place in Pal.:—Adamah.

אַדְמוֹנִי **'admôwnîy.** See 132.

129. אֲדָמִי **'Ădâmîy,** *ad-aw-mee';* from 127 *earthy; Adami,* a place in Pal.:—Adami.

130. אֱדֹמִי **'Ĕdômîy,** *ed-o-mee';* or (fully) אֱדוֹמִי **'Ĕdôwmîy,** *ed-o-mee';* patron. from 123; an *Edomite,* or desc. from (or inhab. of) Edom:—Edomite. See 726.

131. אֲדֻמִּים **'Ădummîym,** *ad-oom-meem';* plur. of 121; *red spots; Adummim,* a pass in Pal.:—Adummim.

132. אַדְמֹנִי **'admônîy,** *ad-mo-nee',* or (fully) אַדְמוֹנִי **'admôwnîy,** *ad-mo-nee';* from 119; *reddish* (of the hair or the complexion):—red, ruddy.

133. אַדְמָתָא **'Admâthâ',** *ad-maw-thaw';* prob. of Pers. der.; *Admatha,* a Pers. nobleman:—Admatha.

134. אֶדֶן **'eden,** *eh'-den;* from the same as 113 (in the sense of *strength*); a *basis* (of a building, a column, etc.):—foundation, socket.

אָדֹן **'âdôn.** See 113.

135. אַדָּן **'Addân,** *ad-dawn';* intens. from the same as 134; *firm; Addan,* an Isr.:—Addan.

136. אֲדֹנָי **'Ădônây,** *ad-o-noy';* an emphatic form of 113; the *Lord* (used as a prop. name of God only):—(my) Lord.

137. אֲדֹנִי־בֶזֶק **'Ădônîy-Bezeq,** *ad-o''-nee-beh'-zek;* from 113 and 966; *lord of Bezek; Adoni-Bezek,* a Canaanitish king:—Adoni-bezek.

138. אֲדֹנִיָּה **'Ădônîyâh,** *ad-o-nee-yaw';* or. (prol.) אֲדֹנִיָּהוּ **'Ădônîyâhûw,** *ad-o-nee-yaw'-hoo;* from 113 and 3050; *lord* (i.e. worshipper) of Jah; *Adonijah,* the name of three Isr.:—Adonijah.

139. אֲדֹנִי־צֶדֶק **'Ădônîy-Tsedeq,** *ad-o''-nee-tseh'-dek;* from 113 and 6664; *lord of justice; Adoni-Tsedek,* a Canaanitish king:—Adoni-zedec.

140. אֲדֹנִיקָם **'Ădônîyqâm,** *ad-o-nee-kawm';* from 113 and 6965; *lord of rising* (i.e. *high*); *Adonikam,* the name of one or two Isr.:—Adonikam.

41. אֲדֹנִירָם **'Ădônîyrâm**, *ad-o-nee-rawm'*; from 113 and 7311; *lord of height; Adoniram*, ı Isr.:—Adoniram.

42. אָדַר **'âdar**, *aw-dar'*; a prim. root; to *expand*, i.e. *be great* or (fig.) *magnificent*:—(be-)me) glorious, honourable.

43. אֲדָר **'Ădâr**, *ad-awr'*; prob. of for. der.; perh. mean. *fire; Adar*, the 12th Heb. month:—dar.

44. אֲדָר **'Ădâr** (Chald.), *ad-awr'*; corresp. to 143:—Adar.

45. אֶדֶר **'eder**, *eh'-der*; from 142; *amplitude*, i.e. (concr.) a *mantle*; also (fig.) *splendor*:—odly, robe.

46. אַדָּר **'Addâr**, *ad-dawr'*; intens. from 142; *ample; Addar*, a place in Pal.; also an Isr.:—ddar.

47. אִדַּר **'iddar** (Chald.), *id-dar'*; intens. from a root corresp. to 142; *ample*, i.e. a *thresh-g-floor*:—threshingfloor.

48. אֲדַרְגָּזֵר **'ădargâzêr** (Chald.), *ad-ar''-gaw-zare'*; from the same as 147, and 1505; *chief diviner*, or *astrologer*:—judge.

49. אַדְרַזְדָּא **'adrazdâ'** (Chald.), *ad-raz-daw'*; prob. of Pers. or.; *quickly* or *carefully*:—diligently.

50. אֲדַרְכֹּן **'ădarkôn**, *ad-ar-kone'*; of Pers. or.; a *daric* or Pers. coin:—dram.

51. אֲדֹרָם **'Ădôrâm**, *ad-o-rawm'*; contr. for 141; *Adoram* (or Adoniram), an Isr.:—doram.

52. אַדְרַמֶּלֶךְ **'Adrammelek**, *ad-ram-meh'-lek*; from 142 and 4428; *splendor of* (the) *ng; Adrammelek*, the name of an Assyr. idol, also a son of Sennacherib:—Adrammelech.

53. אֶדְרָע **'edra'** (Chald.), *ed-raw'*; an orth. var. for 1872; an *arm*, i.e. (fig.) *power*:—force.

54. אֶדְרֶעִי **'edre'îy**, *ed-reh'-ee*; from the equivalent of 153; *mighty; Edrei*, the name of wo places in Pal.:—Edrei.

55. אַדֶּרֶת **'addereth**, *ad-deh'-reth*; fem. of 117; something *ample* (as a *large* vine, a *wide* ress); also the same as 145:—garment, glory, goodly, antle, robe.

56. אָדַשׁ **'âdash**, *aw-dash'*; a prim. root; to *tread* out (grain):—thresh.

57. אָהַב **'âhab**, *aw-hab'*; or אָהֵב **'âhêb**, *aw-habe'*; a prim. root; to *have affection* for exually or otherwise):—(be-) love (-d, -ly, -r), like, riend.

58. אַהַב **'ahab**, *ah'-hab*; from 157; *affection* (in a good or a bad sense):—love (-r).

59. אֹהַב **'ôhab**, *o'-hab*; from 156; mean. the same as 158:—love.

60. אַהֲבָה **'ahăbâh**, *ă-hab-aw'*; fem. of 158 and mean. the same:—love.

61. אֹהַד **'Ôhad**, *o'-had*; from an unused root mean. to *be united; unity; Ohad*, an Isr.:—had.

62. אֲהָהּ **'ăhâhh**, *ă-haw'*; appar. a prim. word expressing *pain* exclamatorily; *Oh!*:—ah, las.

63. אַהֲוָא **'Ahăvâ'**, *ă-hav-aw'*; prob. of for. or.; *Ahava*, a river of Babylonia:—Ahava.

64. אֵהוּד **'Êhûwd**, *ay-hood'*; from the same as 161; *united; Ehud*, the name of two or hree Isr.:—Ehud.

65. אֱהִי **'ĕhîy**, *e-hee'*; appar. an orth. var. for 346; *where*:—I will be (Hos. 13 : 10, 14) *which is often the rendering of the same Heb. form from* 1961].

66. אָהַל **'âhal**, *aw-hal'*; a prim. root; to *be clear*:—shine.

67. אָהַל **'âhal**, *aw-hal'*; a denom. from 168; to *tent*:—pitch (remove) a tent.

68. אֹהֶל **'ôhel**, *o'-hel*; from 166; a *tent* (as *clearly* conspicuous from a distance):—covering, dwelling) (place), home, tabernacle, tent.

69. אֹהֶל **'Ôhel**, *o'-hel*; the same as 168; *Ohel*, an Isr.:—Ohel.

170. אָהֳלָה **'Ohŏlâh**, *ŏ-hol-aw'*; in form a fem. of 168, but in fact for אָהֳלָהּ **'Ohŏlâhh**, *ŏ-hol-aw'*; from 168; *her tent* (i.e. idolatrous *sanctuary*); *Oholah*, a symbol. name for Samaria:—Aholah.

171. אָהֳלִיאָב **'Ohŏlîy'âb**, *ŏ''-hol-e-awb'*; from 168 and 1; *tent of* (his) *father*; *Oholiab*, an Isr.:—Aholiab.

172. אָהֳלִיבָה **'Ohŏlîybâh**, *ŏ''-hol-ee-baw'*; (similarly with 170) for אָהֳלִיבָהּ **'Ohŏlîybâhh**, *ŏ''-hol-e-baw'*; from 168; *my tent* (is) *in her*; *Oholibah*, a symbol. name for Judah:—Aholibah.

173. אָהֳלִיבָמָה **'Ohŏlîybâmâh**, *ŏ''-hol-e-baw-maw'*; from 168 and 1116; *tent of* (the) *height; Oholibamah*, a wife of Esau:—Aholibamah.

174. אֲהָלִים **'ăhâlîym**, *ă-haw-leem'*; or (fem.) אֲהָלוֹת **'ăhâlôwth**, *ă-haw-loth'* (only used thus in the plur.); of for. or.; *aloe* wood (i.e. sticks):—(tree of lign-) aloes.

175. אַהֲרוֹן **'Ahărôwn**, *ă-har-one'*; of uncert. deriv.; *Aharon*, the brother of Moses:—Aaron.

176. אוֹ **'ôw**, *o*; presumed to be the "constr." or genitival form of אַו **'av**, *av*, short. for 185; *desire* (and so prob. in Prov. 31 : 4); hence (by way of alternative) *or*, also *if*:—also, and, either, if, at the least, × nor, or, otherwise, then, whether.

177. אוּאֵל **'Ûw'êl**, *oo-ale'*; from 176 and 410; *wish of God; Uel*, an Isr.:—Uel.

178. אוֹב **'ôwb**, *obe*; from the same as 1 (appar. through the idea of *prattling* a father's name); prop. a *mumble*, i.e. a water-*skin* (from its hollow sound); hence a *necromancer* (ventriloquist, as from a jar):—bottle, familiar spirit.

179. אוֹבִיל **'Ôwbîyl**, *o-beel'*; prob. from 56; *mournful; Obil*, an Ishmaelite:—Obil.

180. אוּבָל **'ûwbâl**, *oo-bawl'*; or (short.) אֻבָל **'ûbâl**, *oo-bawl'*; from 2986 (in the sense of 2988); a *stream*:—river.

181. אוּד **'ûwd**, *ood*; from an unused root mean. to *rake* together; a *poker* (for *turning* or *gathering* embers):—(fire-) brand.

182. אוֹדוֹת **'ôwdôwth**, *o-dōth'*; or (short.) אֹדוֹת **'ôdôwth**, *o-dōth'* (only thus in the plur.); from the same as 181; *turnings* (i.e. *occasions*); (adv.) on *account* of:—(be-) cause, concerning, sake.

183. אָוָה **'âvâh**, *aw-vaw'*; a prim. root; to *wish* for:—covet, (greatly) desire, be desirous, long, lust (after).

184. אָוָה **'âvâh**, *aw-vaw'*; a prim. root; to *extend* or *mark* out:—point out.

185. אַוָּה **'avvâh**, *av-vaw'*; from 183; *longing*:—desire, lust after, pleasure.

186. אוּזַי **'Ûwzay**, *oo-zah'ee*; perh. by perm. for 5813, *strong; Uzai*, an Isr.:—Uzai.

187. אוּזָל **'Ûwzâl**, *oo-zâwl'*; of uncert. der.; *Uzal*, a son of Joktan:—Uzal.

188. אוֹי **'ôwy**, *ō'ee*; prob. from 183 (in the sense of *crying* out after); *lamentation*; also interj. *Oh!*:—alas, woe.

189. אֱוִי **'Ĕvîy**, *ev-ee'*; prob. from 183; *desirous; Evi*, a Midianitish chief:—Evi.

אוֹיֵב **'ôwyêb**. See 341.

190. אוֹיָה **'ôwyâh**, *o-yaw'*; fem. of 188:—woe.

191. אֱוִיל **'ĕvîyl**, *ev-eel'*; from an unused root (mean. to be *perverse*); (fig.) *silly*:—fool (-ish) (man).

192. אֱוִיל מְרֹדַךְ **'Ĕvîyl Merôdak**, *ev-eel' mer-o-dak'*; of Chald. deriv. and prob. mean. *soldier of Merodak; Evil-Merodak*, a Babylonian king:—Evil-merodach.

193. אוּל **'ûwl**, *ool*; from an unused root mean. to *twist*, i.e. (by impl.) *be strong*; the *body* (as being *rolled* together); also *powerful*:—mighty, strength.

194. אוּלַי **'ûwlay**, *oo-lah'ee*; or (short.) אֻלַי **'ûlay**, *oo-lah'ee*; from 176; *if not*; hence *perhaps*:—if so be, may be, peradventure, unless.

195. אוּלַי **'Ûwlay**, *oo-lah'ee*: of Pers. der.; the *Ulai* (or Eulæus), a river of Persia:—Ulai.

196. אֱוִלִי **'ĕvîlîy**, *ev-ee-lee'*; from 191; *silly, foolish*; hence (mor.) *impious*:—foolish.

197. אוּלָם **'ûwlâm**, *oo-lawm'*; or (short.) אֻלָם **'ûlâm**, *oo-lawm'*; from 481 (in the sense of *tying*); a *vestibule* (as *bound* to the building):—porch.

198. אוּלָם **'Ûwlâm**, *oo-lawm'*; appar. from 481 (in the sense of *dumbness*); *solitary; Ulam*, the name of two Isr.:—Ulam.

199. אוּלָם **'ûwlâm**, *oo-lawm'*; appar. a variation of 194; *however* or *on the contrary*:—as for, but, howbeit, in very deed, surely, truly, wherefore.

200. אִוֶּלֶת **'ivveleth**, *iv-veh'-leth*; from the same as 191; *silliness*:—folly, foolishly (-ness).

201. אוֹמָר **'Ôwmâr**, *o-mawr'*; from 559; *talkative; Omar*, a grandson of Esau:—Omar.

202. אוֹן **'ôwn**, *ōne*; prob. from the same as 205 (in the sense of *effort*, but successful); *ability, power*, (fig.) *wealth*:—force, goods, might, strength, substance.

203. אוֹן **'Ôwn**, *ōne*; the same as 202; *On*, an Isr.:—On.

204. אוֹן **'Ôwn**, *ōne*; or (short.) אֹן **'Ôn**, *ōne*; of Eg. der.; *On*, a city of Egypt:—On.

205. אָוֶן **'âven**, *aw'-ven*; from an unused root perh. mean. prop. to *pant* (hence to *exert* oneself, usually in vain; to *come to naught*); strictly *nothingness*; also *trouble, vanity, wickedness*; spec. an *idol*:—affliction, evil, false, idol, iniquity, mischief, mourners (-ing), naught, sorrow, unjust, unrighteous, vain, vanity, wicked (-ness.) Comp. 369.

206. אָוֶן **'Âven**, *aw'-ven*; the same as 205; *idolatry; Aven*, the contemptuous synonym of three places, one in Cœle-Syria, one in Egypt (On), and one in Pal. (Bethel):—Aven. See also 204, 1007.

207. אוֹנוֹ **'Ôwnôw**, *o-no'*; or (short.) אֹנוֹ **'Ônôw**, *o-no'*; prol. from 202; *strong; Ono*, a place in Pal.:—Ono.

208. אוֹנָם **'Ôwnâm**, *o-nawm'*; a var. of 209; *strong; Onum*, the name of an Edomite and of an Isr.:—Onam.

209. אוֹנָן **'Ôwnân**, *o-nawn'*; a var. of 207; *strong; Onan*, a son of Judah:—Onan.

210. אוּפָז **'Ûwphâz**, *oo-fawz'*; perh. a corruption of 211; *Uphaz*, a famous gold region:—Uphaz.

211. אוֹפִיר **'Ôwphîyr**, *o-feer'*; or (short.) אֹפִיר **'Ôphîyr**, *o-feer'*; and אוֹפִר **'Ôwphîr**, *o-feer'*; of uncert. deriv.; *Ophir*, the name of a son of Joktan, and of a gold region in the East:—Ophir.

212. אוֹפָן **'ôwphân**, *o-fawn'*; or (short.) אֹפָן **'ôphân**, *o-fawn'*; from an unused root mean. to *revolve*; a *wheel*:—wheel.

אוֹפִר **'Ôwphîr**. See 211.

213. אוּץ **'ûwts**, *oots*; a prim. root; to *press*; (by impl.) to *be close, hurry, withdraw*:—(make) haste (-n, -y), labor, be narrow.

214. אוֹצָר **'ôwtsâr**, *o-tsaw'*; from 686; a *depository*:—armory, cellar, garner, store (-house), treasure (-house) (-y).

215. אוֹר **'ôwr**, *ore*; a prim. root; to *be* (caus. *make*) *luminous* (lit. and metaph.):—× break of day, glorious, kindle, (be, en-, give, show) light (-en, -ened), set on fire, shine.

216. אוֹר **'ôwr**, *ore*; from 215; *illumination* or (concr.) *luminary* (in every sense, including *lightning, happiness*, etc.):—bright, clear, + day, light (-ning), morning, sun.

217. אוּר **'ûwr**, *oor*; from 215; *flame*, hence (in the plur.) the *East* (as being the region of light):—fire, light. See also 224.

218. אוּר **'Ûwr**, *oor*; the same as 217; *Ur*, a place in Chaldæa; also an Isr.:—Ur.

219. אוֹרָה **'ôwrâh**, *o-raw'*; fem. of 216; *luminousness*, i.e. (fig.) *prosperity*; also a plant (as being *bright*):—herb light.

220. אֲוֵרָה **'âvêrâh**, *av-ay-raw';* by transp. for 723; a *stall:*—cote.

221. אוּרִי **'Ûwrîy**, *oo-ree';* from 217; *fiery; Uri,* the name of three Isr.:—Uri.

222. אוּרִיאֵל **'Ûwrîy'êl**, *oo-ree-ale';* from 217 and 410; *flame of God; Uriel,* the name of two Isr.:—Uriel.

223. אוּרִיָּה **'Ûwrîyâh**, *oo-ree-yaw';* or (prol.) אוּרִיָּהוּ **'Ûwrîyâhûw**, *oo-ree-yaw'-hoo;* from 217 and 3050; *flame of Jah; Urijah,* the name of one Hittite and five Isr.:—Uriah, Urijah.

224. אוּרִים **'Ûwrîym**, *oo-reem';* plur. of 217; *lights; Urim,* the oracular brilliancy of the figures in the high-priest's breastplate:—Urim.

אוֹרְנָה **'Owrenâh**. See 728.

225. אוּת **'ûwth**, *ooth;* a prim. root; prop. to *come,* i.e. (impl.) to *assent:*—consent.

226. אוֹת **'ôwth**, *ōth;* prob. from 225 (in the sense of *appearing*); a *signal* (lit. or fig.), as a *flag, beacon, monument, omen, prodigy, evidence,* etc.:—mark, miracle, (en-) sign, token.

227. אָז **'âz**, *awz;* a demonstrative adv.; *at that time* or *place;* also as a conj., *therefore:*—beginning, for, from, hitherto, now, of old, once, since, then, at which time, yet.

228. אֲזָא **'ăzâ'** (Chald.), *az-aw';* or אֲזָה **'ăzâh** (Chald.), *az-aw';* to *kindle;* (by impl.) to *heat:*—heat, hot.

229. אֶזְבַּי **'Ezbay**, *ez-bah'ee;* prob. from 231; *hyssop-like; Ezbai,* an Isr.:—Ezbai.

230. אֲזַד **'ăzad** (Chald.), *az-awd';* of uncert. der.; *firm:*—be gone.

231. אֵזוֹב **'êzôwb**, *ay-zobe';* prob. of for. der.; *hyssop:*—hyssop.

232. אֵזוֹר **'êzôwr**, *ay-zore';* from 246; something *girt;* a *belt,* also a *band:*—girdle.

233. אֲזַי **'ăzay**, *az-ah'ee;* prob. from 227; *at that time:*—then.

234. אַזְכָּרָה **'azkârâh**, *az-kaw-raw';* from 2142; a *reminder;* spec. *remembrance-offering:*—memorial.

235. אָזַל **'âzal**, *aw-zal';* a prim. root; to *go away,* hence to *disappear:*—fail, gad about, go to and fro [*but in Ezek.* 27 : 19 *the word is rendered by many* "from Uzal," *by others* "yarn"], be gone (spent).

236. אֲזַל **'ăzal** (Chald.), *az-al';* the same as 235; to *depart:*—go (up).

237. אֶזֶל **'ezel**, *eh'-zel;* from 235; *departure; Ezel,* a memorial stone in Pal.:—Ezel.

238. אָזַן **'âzan**, *aw-zan';* a prim. root; prob. to *expand;* but used only as a denom. from 241; to *broaden out the ear* (with the hand), i.e. (by impl.) to *listen:*—give (perceive by the) ear, hear (-ken). See 239.

239. אָזַן **'âzan**, *aw-zan';* a prim. root [rather ident. with 238 through the idea of *scales* as if two ears]; to *weigh,* i.e. (fig.) *ponder:*—give good heed.

240. אָזֵן **'âzên**, *aw-zane';* from 238; a *spade* or *paddle* (as having a *broad* end):—weapon.

241. אֹזֶן **'ôzen**, *o'-zen;* from 238; *broadness,* i.e. (concr.) the *ear* (from its form in man):—+advertise, audience, +displease, ear, hearing, +show.

242. אֻזֵּן שֶׁאֱרָה **'Uzzên She'ĕrâh**, *ooz-zane' sheh-er-aw';* from 238 and 7609; *plat of Sheerah* (i.e. settled by him); *Uzzen-Sheërah,* a place in Pal.:—Uzzen-sherah.

243. אַזְנוֹת תָּבוֹר **'Aznôwth Tâbôwr**, *az-nōth' taw-bore';* from 238 and 8396; *flats* (i.e. *tops*) *of Tabor* (i.e. situated on it); *Aznoth-Tabor,* a place in Pal.:—Aznoth-tabor.

244. אָזְנִי **'Ozniy**, *oz-nee';* from 241; *having* (quick) *ears; Ozni,* an Isr.; also an *Oznite* (collect.), his desc.:—Ozni, Oznites.

245. אֲזַנְיָה **'Ăzanyâh**, *az-an-yaw';* from 238 and 3050; *heard by Jah; Azanjah,* an Isr.:—Azaniah.

246. אֲזִקִּים **'ăziqqîym**, *az-ik-keem';* a var. for 2131; *manacles:*—chains.

247. אָזַר **'âzar**, *aw-zar';* a prim. root; to *belt:*—bind (compass) about, gird (up, with).

248. אֶזְרוֹעַ **'ezrôwa'**, *ez-ro'-ă;* a var. for 2220; the *arm:*—arm.

249. אֶזְרָח **'ezrâch**, *ez-rawkh';* from 2224 (in the sense of *springing up*); a spontaneous *growth,* i.e. *native* (tree or persons):—bay tree, (home-) born (in the land), of the (one's own) country (nation).

250. אֶזְרָחִי **'Ezrâchîy**, *ez-raw-khee';* patron. from 2246; an *Ezrachite* or desc. of Zerach:—Ezrahite.

251. אָח **'âch**, *awkh;* a prim. word; a *brother* (used in the widest sense of literal relationship and metaph. affinity or resemblance [like 1]):—another, brother (-ly), kindred, like, other. Comp. also the prop. names beginning with "Ah-" or "Ahi-".

252. אָח **'ach** (Chald.), *akh;* corresp. to 251:—brother.

253. אָח **'âch**, *awkh;* a var. for 162; *Oh!* (expressive of grief or surprise):—ah, alas.

254. אָח **'âch**, *awkh;* of uncert. der.; a fire-*pot* or chafing-dish:—hearth.

255. אֹחַ **'ôach**, *o'-akh;* prob. from 253; a *howler* or lonesome wild animal:—doleful creature.

256. אַחְאָב **'Ach'âb**, *akh-awb';* once (by contr.) אֶחָב **'Echâb** (Jer. 29 : 22), *ekh-awb';* from 251 and 1; *brother* [i.e. *friend*] *of* (his) *father; Achab,* the name of a king of Israel and of a prophet at Babylon:—Ahab.

257. אַחְבָּן **'Achbân**, *akh-bawn';* from 251 and 995; *brother* (i.e. *possessor*) *of understanding; Achban,* an Isr.:—Ahban.

258. אָחַד **'âchad**, *aw-khad';* perh. a prim. root; to *unify,* i.e. (fig.) *collect* (one's thoughts):—go one way or other.

259. אֶחָד **'echâd**, *ekh-awd';* a numeral from 258; prop. *united,* i.e. *one;* or (as an ordinal) *first:*—a, alike, alone, altogether, and, any (-thing), apiece, a certain, [dai-] ly, each (one), + eleven, every, few, first, + highway, a man, once, one, only, other, some, together.

260. אָחוּ **'âchûw**, *aw'-khoo;* of unc. (perh. Eg.) der.; a *bulrush* or any marshy grass (particularly that along the Nile):—flag, meadow.

261. אֵחוּד **'Êchûwd**, *ay-khood';* from 258; *united; Echud,* the name of three Isr.:—Ehud.

262. אַחְוָה **'achvâh**, *akh-vaw';* from 2331 (in the sense of 2324); an *utterance:*—declaration.

263. אַחֲוָה **'achăvâh** (Chald.), *akh-av-aw';* corresp. to 262; *solution* (of riddles):—showing.

264. אַחֲוָה **'achăvâh**, *akh-av-aw';* from 251; *fraternity:*—brotherhood.

265. אֲחוֹחַ **'Ăchôwach**, *akh-o'-akh;* by redupl. from 251; *brotherly; Achoach,* an Isr.:—Ahoah.

266. אֲחוֹחִי **'Ăchôwchîy**, *akh-o-khee';* patron. from 264; an *Achochite* or desc. of Achoach:—Ahohite.

267. אֲחוּמַי **'Ăchûwmay**, *akh-oo-mah'ee;* perh. from 251 and 4325; *brother* (i.e. *neighbour*) *of water; Achumai,* an Isr.:—Ahumai.

268. אָחוֹר **'âchôwr**, *aw-khore';* or (short.) אָחֹר **'âchôr**, *aw-khore';* from 299; the *hinder* part; hence (adv.) *behind, backward;* also (as facing north) the *West:*—after (-ward), back (part, -side, -ward), hereafter, (be-) hind (-er part), time to come, without.

269. אָחוֹת **'achôwth**, *aw-khōth';* irreg. fem. of 251; a *sister* (used very widely [like 250], lit. and fig.):—(an-) other, sister, together.

270. אָחַז **'âchaz**, *aw-khaz';* a prim. root; to *seize* (often with the accessory idea of holding in possession):— + be affrighted, bar, (catch, lay, take) hold (back), come upon, fasten, handle, portion, (get, have or take) possess (-ion).

271. אָחָז **'Âchâz**, *aw-khawz';* from 270; *possessor; Achaz,* the name of a Jewish king and of an Isr.:—Ahaz.

272. אֲחֻזָּה **'ăchuzzâh**, *akh-ooz-zaw';* fem. pas part. from 270; something *seized,* i. a *possession* (esp. of land):—possession.

273. אַחְזַי **'Achzay**, *akh-zah'ee;* from 270; *seize Achzai,* an Isr.:—Ahasai.

274. אֲחַזְיָה **'Ăchazyâh**, *akh-az-yaw';* or (pro אֲחַזְיָהוּ **'Ăchazyâhûw**, *akh-az-yaw'-ho* from 270 and 3050; *Jah has seize Achazjah,* the name of a Jewish and an Isr. king: Ahaziah.

275. אֲחֻזָּם **'Ăchuzzâm**, *akh-ooz-zawm';* fro 270; *seizure; Achuzzam,* an Isr.:—Ah zam.

276. אֲחֻזַּת **'Ăchuzzath**, *akh-ooz-zath';* a var. 272; *possession; Achuzzath,* a Phili tine:—Ahuzzath.

277. אֲחִי **'Ăchîy**, *akh-ee';* from 251; *brotherl Achi,* the name of two Isr.:—Ahi.

278. אֵחִי **'Êchîy**, *ay-khee';* prob. the same 277; *Echi,* an Isr.:—Ehi.

279. אֲחִיאָם **'Ăchîy'âm**, *akh-ee-awm';* from 2 and 517; *brother of the mother* (i. *uncle*); *Achiam,* an Isr.:—Ahiam.

280. אֲחִידָה **'ăchîydâh** (Chald.), *akh-ee-daw* corresp. to 2420, an *enigma:*—har sentence.

281. אֲחִיָּה **'Ăchîyâh**, *akh-ee-yaw';* or (pro אֲחִיָּהוּ **'Ăchîyâhûw**, *akh-ee-yaw'-ho* from 251 and 3050; *brother* (i.e. *worshi per*) *of Jah; Achijah,* the name of nine Isr.:—Ahia Ahijah.

282. אֲחִיהוּד **'Ăchîyhûwd**, *akh-ee-hood';* fro 251 and 1935; *brother* (i.e. *possesso of renown; Achihud,* an Isr.:—Ahihud.

283. אַחְיוֹ **'Achyôw**, *akh-yo';* prol. from 25 *brotherly; Achio,* the name of thre Isr.:—Ahio.

284. אֲחִיחֻד **'Ăchîychûd**, *akh-ee-khood';* fro 251 and 2330; *brother of a riddle* (i. *mysterious*); *Achichud,* an Isr.:—Ahihud.

285. אֲחִיטוּב **'Ăchîyṭûwb**, *akh-ee-toob';* fro 251 and 2898; *brother of goodnes Achitub,* the name of several priests:—Ahitub.

286. אֲחִילוּד **'Ăchîylûwd**, *akh-ee-lood';* fro 251 and 3205; *brother of one born Achilud,* an Isr.:—Ahilud.

287. אֲחִימוֹת **'Ăchîymôwth**, *akh-ee-mōth* from 251 and 4191; *brother of death Achimoth,* an Isr.:—Ahimoth.

288. אֲחִימֶלֶךְ **'Ăchîymelek**, *akh-ee-meh'-lek* from 251 and 4428; *brother of* (the *king; Achimelek,* the name of an Isr. and of a Hit tite:—Ahimelech.

289. אֲחִימַן **'Ăchîyman**, *akh-ee-man';* o אֲחִימָן **'Ăchîymân**, *akh-ee-mawn';* fro 251 and 4480; *brother of a portion* (i. *gift*); *Achiman,* the name of an Anakite and of a Isr.:—Ahiman.

290. אֲחִימַעַץ **'Ăchîyma'ats**, *akh-ee-mah'-ats* from 251 and the equiv. of 4619 *brother of anger; Achimaats,* the name of thre Isr.:—Ahimaaz.

291. אַחְיָן **'Achyân**, *akh-yawn';* from 251; *broth erly; Achjan,* an Isr.:—Ahian.

292. אֲחִינָדָב **'Ăchîynâdâb**, *akh-ee-naw-dawb* from 251 and 5068; *brother of liberal ity; Achinadab,* an Isr.:—Ahinadab.

293. אֲחִינֹעַם **'Ăchîynô'am**, *akh-ee-no'-am* from 251 and 5278; *brother of pleas antness; Achinoam,* the name of two Israelitesses:— Ahinoam.

294. אֲחִיסָמָךְ **'Ăchîyçâmâk**, *akh-ee-saw mawk';* from 251 and 5564; *brothe of support; Achisamak,* an Isr.:—Ahisamach.

295. אֲחִיעֶזֶר **'Ăchîy'ezer**, *akh-ee-eh'-zer;* fro 251 and 5828; *brother of help: Achi ezer,* the name of two Isr.:—Ahiezer.

296. אֲחִיקָם **'Ăchîyqâm**, *akh-ee-kawm';* fro 251 and 6965; *brother of rising* (i. *high*); *Achikam,* an Isr.:—Ahikam.

297. אֲחִירָם **'Ăchîyrâm**, *akh-ee-rawm';* fro 251 and 7311; *brother of height* (i. *high*); *Achiram,* an Isr.:—Ahiram.

98. אֲחִירָמִי **'Âchîyrâmîy,** *akh-ee-raw-mee';* patron. from 297; an *Achiramite* or esc. (collect.) of Achiram:—Ahiramites.

99. אֲחִירַע **'Ăchîyra',** *akh-ee-rah';* from 251 and 7451; *brother of wrong; Achira,* n Isr.:—Ahira.

00. אֲחִישַׁחַר **'Achîyshachar,** *akh-ee-shakh'-ar;* from 251 and 7837; *brother of* he) *dawn; Achishachar,* an Isr.:—Ahishar.

01. אֲחִישָׁר **'Ăchîyshâr,** *akh-ee-shawr';* from 251 and 7891; *brother of* (the) *singer;* .*chishar,* an Isr.:—Ahishar.

02. אֲחִיתֹפֶל **'Ăchîythôphel,** *akh-ee-tho'-fel;* from 251 and 8602; *brother of folly;* *chithophel,* an Isr.:—Ahithophel.

03. אַחְלָב **'Achlâb,** *akh-lawb';* from the same root as 2459; *fatness* (i.e. *fertile*); *Ach-b,* a place in Pal.:—Ahlab.

04. אַחְלַי **'Achlay,** *akh-lah'ee;* the same as 305; *wishful; Achlai,* the name of an Israel-ess and of an Isr.:—Ahlai.

05. אַחֲלַי **'achălay,** *akh-al-ah'ee;* or אַחֲלֵי **'achălêy,** *akh-al-ay':* prob. from 253 nd a var. of 3863; *would that!:*—O that, would God.

06. אַחְלָמָה **'achlâmâh,** *akh-law'-maw;* perh. from 2492 (and thus *dream-stone*); a em, prob. the *amethyst:*—amethyst.

07. אַחְמְתָא **'Achmᵉthâ',** *akh-me-thaw';* of Pers. der.; *Achmetha* (i.e. *Ecbatana*), ne summer capital of Persia:—Achmetha.

08. אַחַסְבַּי **'Achaçbay,** *akh-as-bah'ee;* of uncert. der.; *Achasbai,* an Isr.:—Ahasbai.

09. אָחַר **'âchar,** *aw-khar';* a prim. root; to *loiter* (i.e. *be behind*); by impl. to *pro-rastinate:*—continue, defer, delay, hinder, be late lack), stay (there), tarry (longer).

10. אַחַר **'achar,** *akh-ar';* from 309; prop. the *hind* part; gen. used as an adv. or conj., *fter* (in various senses):—after (that, -ward), again, , away from, back (from, -side), behind, beside, by, ollow (after, -ing), forasmuch, from, hereafter, hind-: end, + out (over) live, + persecute, posterity, pur-ing, remnant, seeing, since, thence [-forth], when, ith.

11. אַחַר **'achar** (Chald.), *akh-ar';* corresp. to 310; *after:*—[here-] after.

12. אַחֵר **'achêr,** *akh-air';* from 309; prop. *hinder;* gen. *next, other,* etc.:—(an-) her (man), following, next, strange.

13. אַחֵר **'Achêr,** *akh-air';* the same as 312; *Acher,* an Isr.:—Aher.

14. אַחֲרוֹן **'achărôwn,** *akh-ar-one';* or (short.) אַחֲרֹן **'achărôn,** *akh-ar-one';* from 309; *hinder;* gen. *late* or *last;* spec. (as fac-g the east) *western:*—after (-ward), to come, fol-wing, hind (-er, -ermost, -most), last, latter, rere-ard, ut(ter)most.

15. אַחְרַח **'Achrach,** *akh-rakh';* from 310 and 251, *after* (his) *brother: Achrach,* an r.:—Aharah.

16. אֲחַרְחֵל **'Ăcharchêl,** *akh-ar-kale';* from 310 and 2426; *behind* (the) *intrench-ent* (i.e. *safe*); *Acharchel,* an Isr.:—Aharhel.

17. אָחֳרִי **'ochŏrîy** (Chald.), *okh-or-ee';* from 311; *other:*—(an-) other.

18. אָחֳרֵין **'ochŏrêyn** (Chald.), *okh-or-ane';* or (short.) אָחֳרֵן **'ochŏrên** (Chald.), *kh-or-ane';* from 317; *last:*—at last.

19. אַחֲרִית **'achărîyth,** *akh-ar-eeth';* from 310; the *last* or *end,* hence the *future;* also *osterity:*—(last, latter) end (time), hinder (utter) nost, length, posterity, remnant, residue, reward.

20. אַחֲרִית **'achărîyth** (Chald.), *akh-ar-eeth';* from 311; the same as 319; *later:*—atter.

21. אָחֳרָן **'ochŏrân** (Chald.), *okh-or-awn';* from 311; the same as 317; *other:*—(an-) ther.

אָחֳרֵן **'ochŏrên.** See 318.

22. אֲחֹרַנִּית **'ăchôrannîyth,** *akh-o-ran-neeth';* prol. from 268; *backwards:*—back ward, again).

323. אֲחַשְׁדַּרְפַּן **'ăchashdarpan,** *akh-ash-dar-pan';* of Pers. der.; a *satrap* or governor of a main province (of Persia):—lieutenant.

324. אֲחַשְׁדַּרְפַּן **ăchashdarpan** (Chald.), *akh-ash-dar-pan';* corresp. to 323:—prince.

325. אֲחַשְׁוֵרוֹשׁ **'Ăchashvêrôwsh,** *akh-ash-vay-rōsh';* or (short.) אֲחַשְׁרֹשׁ **'Achashrôsh,** *akh-ash-rōsh'* (Esth. 10 : 1); of Pers. or.; *Achashverosh* (i.e. Ahasuerus or Artaxerxes, but in this case Xerxes), the title (rather than name) of a Pers. king:—Ahasuerus.

326. אֲחַשְׁתָּרִי **'ăchashtârîy,** *akh-ash-taw-ree';* prob. of Pers. der.; an *achastarite* (i.e. courier); the designation (rather than name) of an Isr.:—Haakashtari [*includ. the art.*].

327. אֲחַשְׁתְּרָן **'ăchastârân,** *akh-ash-taw-rawn';* of Pers. r.; a *mule:*—camel.

328. אַט **'aṭ,** *at;* from an unused root perh. mean. to *move softly;* (as a noun) a *necromancer* (from their soft incantations), (as an adv.) *gently:*—charmer, gently, secret, softly.

329. אָטָד **'âṭâd,** *aw-tawd';* from an unused root prob. mean. to *pierce* or *make fast;* a *thorn*-tree (espec. the *buckthorn*):—Atad, bramble, thorn.

330. אֵטוּן **'êṭûwn,** *ay-toon';* from an unused root (prob. mean. to *bind*); prop. *twisted* (yarn), i.e. *tapestry:*—fine linen.

331. אָטַם **'âṭam,** *aw-tam';* a prim. root; to *close* (the lips or ears); by anal. to *contract* (a window by bevelled jambs):—narrow, shut, stop.

332. אָטַר **'âṭar,** *aw-tar';* a prim. root; to *close* up:—shut.

333. אָטֵר **'Âṭêr,** *aw-tare';* from 332; *maimed;* *Ater,* the name of three Isr.:—Ater.

334. אִטֵּר **'iṭṭêr,** *it-tare';* from 332; *shut* up, i.e. *impeded* (as to the use of the right hand):— + left-handed.

335. אַי **'ay,** *ah'ee;* perh. from 370; *where?* hence *how?:*—how, what, whence, where, whether, which (way).

336. אִי **'îy,** *ee;* prob. ident. with 335 (through the idea of a *query*); *not:*—island (Job 22 : 30).

337. אִי **'îy,** *ee;* short. from 188; *alas!:*—woe.

338. אִי **'îy,** *ee;* prob. ident. with 337 (through the idea of a *doleful* sound); a *howler* (used only in the plural), i.e. any solitary wild creature:—wild beast of the islands.

339. אִי **'îy,** *ee;* from 183; prop. a *habitable* spot (as *desirable*); dry *land,* a *coast,* an *island:*—country, isle, island.

340. אָיַב **'âyab,** *aw-yab';* a prim. root; to *hate* (as one of an opposite tribe or party); hence to *be hostile:*—be an enemy.

341. אֹיֵב **'ôyêb,** *o-yabe';* or (fully) אוֹיֵב **'ôwyêb,** *o-yabe';* act. part. of 340; *hating;* an *adversary:*—enemy, foe.

342. אֵיבָה **'êybâh,** *ay-baw';* from 340; *hostility:*—enmity, hatred.

343. אֵיד **'êyd,** *ade;* from the same as 181 (in the sense of *bending* down); *oppression;* by impl. *misfortune, ruin:*—calamity, destruction.

344. אַיָּה **'ayâh,** *ah-yaw';* perh. from 337; the *screamer,* i.e. a *hawk:*—kite, vulture.

345. אַיָּה **'Ayâh,** *ah-yaw';* the same as 344; *Ajah,* the name of two Isr.:—Aiah, Ajah.

346. אַיֵּה **'ayêh,** *ah-yay';* prol. from 335; *where?:*—where.

347. אִיּוֹב **'Îyôwb,** *ee-yobe';* from 340; *hated* (i.e. *persecuted*); *Ijob,* the patriarch famous for his patience:—Job.

348. אִיזֶבֶל **'Îyzebel,** *ee-zeh'-bel;* from 336 and 2083; *chaste; Izebel,* the wife of king Ahab:—Jezebel.

349. אֵיךְ **'êyk,** *ake;* also אֵיכָה **'êykâh,** *ay-kaw';* and אֵיכָכָה **'êykâkâh,** *ay-kaw'-kah;* prol. from 335; *how?* or *how!;* also *where:*—how, what.

350. אִי־כָבוֹד **Îy-kâbôwd,** *ee-kaw-bode';* from 336 and 3519; (there is) *no glory,* i.e. *inglorious; Ikabod,* a son of Phineas:—I-chabod.

351. אֵיכֹה **'êykôh,** *ay-kō;* prob. a var. for 349, but not as an interrogative; *where:*—where.

אֵיכָה **'êykâh;** אֵיכָכָה **'êykâkâh.** See 349.

352. אַיִל **'ayîl,** *ah'-yil;* from the same as 193; prop. *strength;* hence anything *strong;* spec. a *chief* (politically); also a *ram* (from his strength); a *pilaster* (as a strong support); an *oak* or other strong tree:—mighty (man), lintel, oak, post. ram, tree.

353. אֱיָל **'ĕyâl,** *eh-yawl';* a var. of 352; *strength.*—strength.

354. אַיָּל **'ayâl,** *ah-yawl';* an intens. form of 352 (in the sense of *ram*); a *stag* or *male* deer:—hart.

355. אַיָּלָה **'ayâlâh,** *ah-yaw-law';* fem. of 354; a *doe* or female deer:—hind.

356. אֵילוֹן **'Êylôwn,** *ay-lone';* or (short.) אֵלוֹן **'Êlôwn,** *ay-lone';* or אֵילֹן **'Êylôn,** *ay-lone';* from 352; *oak-grove; Elon,* the name of a place in Pal., and also of one Hittite, two Isr.:—Elon.

357. אַיָּלוֹן **'Ayâlôwn,** *ah-yaw-lone';* from 354. *deer-field; Ajalon,* the name of five places in Pal.:—Aijalon, Ajalon.

358. אֵילוֹן בֵּית חָנָן **'Êylôwn Bêyth Châ-nân,** *ay-lone' bayth-chaw-nawn';* from 356, 1004, and 2603; *oak-grove of* (the) *house of favor; Elon of Beth-chanan,* a place in Pal.:—Elon-beth-hanan.

359. אֵילוֹת **'Êylôwth,** *ay-lōth';* or אֵילַת **'Êylath,** *ay-lath';* from 352; *trees* or a *grove* (i.e. palms); *Eloth* or *Elath,* a place on the Red Sea:—Elath, Eloth.

360. אֱיָלוּת **'ĕyâlûwth,** *eh-yaw-looth';* fem. of 353; *power;* by impl. *protection:*—strength.

361. אֵילָם **'êylâm,** *ay-lawm';* or (short.) אֵלָם **'êlâm,** *ay-lawm';* or (fem.) אֵלַמָּה **'êlammâh,** *ay-lam-maw';* prob. from 352; a *pil-lar-space* (or colonnade), i.e. a *pale* (or portico):—arch.

362. אֵילִם **'Êylîm,** *ay-leem';* plur. of 352; palm-*trees; Elim,* a place in the Desert:—Elim.

363. אִילָן **'îylân** (Chald.), *ee-lawn';* corresp. to 356; a *tree:*—tree.

364. אֵיל פָּארָן **'Êyl Pâ'rân,** *ale paw-rawn';* from 352 and 6290; *oak of Paran; El-Paran,* a portion of the district of Paran:—El-paran.

אֵילֹן **'Êylôn.** See 356.

365. אַיֶּלֶת **'ayeleth,** *ah-yeh'-leth;* the same as 355; a *doe:*—hind, Aijeleth.

אַיִם **'ayim.** See 368.

366. אָיֹם **'âyôm,** *aw-yome';* from an unused root (mean. to *frighten*); *frightful:*—terrible.

367. אֵימָה **'êymâh,** *ay-maw';* or (short.) אֵמָה **'êmah,** *ay-maw';* from the same as 366; *fright;* concr. an *idol* (as a bugbear):—dread, fear, horror, idol, terrible, terror.

368. אֵימִים **'Êymîym,** *ay-meem';* plur. of 367; *terrors; Emim,* an early Canaanitish (or Moabitish) tribe:—Emims.

369. אַיִן **'ayin,** *ah'-yin;* as if from a prim. root mean. to *be nothing* or *not exist;* a *non-entity;* gen. used as a neg. particle:—else, except, fail, [father-] less, be gone, in [-curable], neither, never, no (where), none, nor (any, thing), not, nothing, to nought, past, un [-searchable], well-nigh, without. Comp. 370.

370. אַיִן **'ayin,** *ah-yin';* prob. ident. with 369 in the sense of *query* (comp. 336);—*where?* (only in connection with prep. pref., *whence*):—whence, where.

371. אִין **'îyn,** *een;* appar. a short. form of 369, but (like 370) interrog.; is it *not?:*—not

372. אִיעֶזֶר **'Îy'ezer,** *ee-eh'-zer;* from 336 and 5829; *helpless; Iezer,* an Isr.:—Jeezer.

373. אִיעֶזְרִי **'Îy'ezrîy**, *ee-ez-ree';* patron. from 372; an *Iezrite* or desc. of Iezer:—Jezerite.

374. אֵיפָה **'êyphâh**, *ay-faw';* or (short.) אֵפָה **'êphâh**, *ay-faw';* of Eg. der.; an *ephah* or measure for grain; hence a *measure* in gen.:—ephah, (divers) measure (-s).

375. אֵיפֹה **'êyphôh**, *ay-fō';* from 335 and 6311; *what place?;* also (of time) *when?;* or (of means) *how?:*—what manner, where.

376. אִישׁ **'îysh**, *eesh;* contr. for 582 [or perh. rather from an unused root mean. to *be extant*]; a *man* as an individual or a male person; often used as an adjunct to a more definite term (and in such cases frequently not expressed in translation):—also, another, any (man), a certain, + champion, consent, each, every (one), fellow, [foot-, husband-] man, (good-, great, mighty) man, he, high (degree), him (that is), husband, man [-kind], + none, one, people, person, + steward, what (man) soever, whoso (-ever), worthy. Comp. 802.

377. אִישׁ **'îysh**, *eesh;* denom. from 376; to *be a man*, i.e. act in a manly way:—show (one) self a man.

378. אִישׁ־בֹּשֶׁת **'Îysh-Bôsheth**, *eesh-bō'-sheth;* from 376 and 1322; *man of shame; Ish-Bosheth*, a son of King Saul:—Ish-bosheth.

379. אִישְׁהוֹד **'Îyshhôwd**, *eesh-hode';* from 376 and 1935; *man of renown; Ishod*, an Isr.:—Ishod.

380. אִישׁוֹן **'îyshôwn**, *ee-shone';* dimin. from 376; the *little man* of the eye; the *pupil* or *ball;* hence the *middle* (of night):—apple [of the eye], black, obscure.

אִישׁ־חַי **'Îysh-Chay**. See 381.

381. אִישׁ־חַיִל **'îysh-Chayil**, *eesh-khah'-yil;* from 376 and 2428; *man of might;* by defect. transcription (2 Sam. 23 : 20) אִישׁ־חַי **'Îsh-Chay**, *eesh-khah'ee;* as if from 376 and 2416; *living man; Ish-chail* (or *Ish-chai*), an Isr.:—a valiant man.

382. אִישׁ־טוֹב **'Îysh-Tôwb**, *eesh-tobe';* from 376 and 2897; *man of Tob; Ish-Tob*, a place in Pal.:—Ish-tob.

אִישַׁי **'Îshay**. See 3448.

אִיתוֹן **'îthôwn**. See 2978.

383. אִיתַי **'îythay** (Chald.), *ee-thah'ee;* corresp. to 3426; prop. *entity;* used only as a particle of affirmation, there *is:*—art thou, can, do ye, have, it be, there is (are), × we will not.

384. אִיתִיאֵל **'Îythîy'êl**, *eeth-ee-ale';* perh. from 837 and 410; *God has arrived; Ithiel*, the name of an Isr., also of a symb. person:—Ithiel.

385. אִיתָמָר **'Îythâmâr**, *eeth-aw-mawr';* from 339 and 8558; *coast of* the *palm*-tree; *Ithamar*, a son of Aaron:—Ithamar.

386. אֵיתָן **'êythân**, *ay-thawn';* or (short.) אֵתָן **'êthân**, *ay-thawn';* from an unused root (mean. to *continue*); *permanence;* hence (concr.) *permanent;* spec. a *chieftain:*—hard, mighty, rough, strength, strong.

387. אֵיתָן **'Êythân**, *ay-thawn';* the same as 386; *permanent; Ethan*, the name of four Isr.:—Ethan.

388. אֵיתָנִים **Êythânîym**, *ay-thaw-neem';* plur. of 386; always with the art.; the *permanent* brooks; *Ethanim*, the name of a month:—Ethanim.

389. אַךְ **'ak**, *ak;* akin to 403; a particle of affirmation, *surely;* hence (by limitation) *only:*—also, in any wise, at least, but, certainly, even, howbeit, nevertheless, notwithstanding, only, save, surely, of a surety, truly, verily, + wherefore, yet (but).

390. אַכַּד **'Akkad**, *ak-kad';* from an unused root prob. mean. to *strengthen;* a *fortress; Accad*, a place in Bab.:—Accad.

391. אַכְזָב **'akzâb**, *ak-zawb';* from 3576; *falsehood;* by impl. *treachery:*—liar, lie.

392. אַכְזִיב **'Akzîyb**, *ak-zeeb';* from 391; *deceitful* (in the sense of a winter-torrent which *fails* in summer); *Akzib*, the name of two places in Pal.:—Achzib.

393. אַכְזָר **'akzâr**, *ak-zawr';* from an unused root (appar. mean. to *act harshly*); *violent;* by impl. *deadly;* also (in a good sense) *brave:*—cruel, fierce.

394. אַכְזָרִי **'akzârîy**, *ak-zaw-ree';* from 393; *terrible:*—cruel (one).

395. אַכְזְרִיּוּת **'akzᵉrîyûwth**, *ak-ze-ree-ooth';* from 394; *fierceness:*—cruel.

396. אֲכִילָה **'ăkîylâh**, *ak-ee-law';* fem. from 398; something *eatable*, i.e. *food:*—meat.

397. אָכִישׁ **'Âkîysh**, *aw-keesh';* of uncert. der.; *Akish*, a Philistine king:—Achish.

398. אָכַל **'âkal**, *aw-kal';* a prim. root; to *eat* (lit. or fig.):— × at all, burn up, consume, devour (-er, up), dine, eat (-er, up), feed (with), food, × freely, × in . . . wise (-deed, plenty), (lay) meat, × quite.

399. אֲכַל **'ăkal** (Chald.), *ak-al';* corresp. to 398:—+ accuse, devour, eat.

400. אֹכֶל **'ôkel**, *o'-kel;* from 398; *food:*—eating, food, meal [-time], meat, prey, victuals.

401. אֻכָל **'Ûkâl**, *oo-kawl';* or אֻכָּל **'Ukkâl**, *ook-kawl';* appar. from 398; *devoured; Ucal*, a fancy name:—Ucal.

402. אָכְלָה **'oklâh**, *ok-law';* fem. of 401; *food:*—consume, devour, eat, food, meat.

403. אָכֵן **'âkên**, *aw-kane';* from 3559 [comp. 3651]; *firmly;* fig. *surely;* also (advers.) *but:*—but, certainly, nevertheless, surely, truly, verily.

404. אָכַף **'âkaph**, *aw-kaf';* a prim. root; appar. mean. to *curve* (as with a burden); to *urge:*—crave.

405. אֶכֶף **'ekeph**, *eh'-kef;* from 404; a *load;* by impl. a *stroke* (others *dignity*):—hand.

406. אִכָּר **'ikkâr**, *ik-kawr';* from an unused root mean. to *dig;* a *farmer:*—husbandman, ploughman.

407. אַכְשָׁף **'Akshâph**, *ak-shawf';* from 3784; *fascination; Acshaph*, a place in Pal.:—Achshaph.

408. אַל **'al**, *al;* a neg. particle [akin to 3808]; *not* (the qualified negation, used as a deprecative); once (Job 24 : 25) as a noun, *nothing:*—nay, neither, + never, no, nor, not, nothing [worth], rather than.

409. אַל **'al** (Chald.), *al;* corresp. to 408:—not.

410. אֵל **'êl**, *ale;* short. from 352; *strength;* as adj. *mighty;* espec. the *Almighty* (but used also of any *deity*):—God (god), × goodly, × great, idol, might (-y one), power, strong. Comp. names in "-el."

411. אֵל **'êl**, *ale;* a demonstr. particle (but only in a plur. sense) *these* or *those:*—these, those. Comp. 428.

412. אֵל **'êl** (Chald.), *ale;* corresp. to 411:—these.

413. אֵל **'êl**, *ale;* (but used only in the shortened constr. form אֶל **'el**, *el*); a prim. particle, prop. denoting motion *towards*, but occasionally used of a quiescent position, i.e. *near, with* or *among;* often in general, *to:*—about, according to, after, against, among, as for, at, because (-fore, -side), both . . . and, by, concerning, for, from, × hath, in (-to), near, (out) of, over, through, to (-ward), under, unto, upon, whether, with (-in).

414. אֵלָא **'Êlâ'**, *ay-law';* a var. of 424; *oak; Ela*, an Isr.:—Elah.

415. אֵל אֱלֹהֵי יִשְׂרָאֵל **'Êl 'ělôhêy Yisrâ'êl**, *ale el-o-hay' yis-raw-ale';* from 410 and 430 and 3478; the *mighty God of Jisrael; El-Elohi-Jisrael*, the title given to a consecrated spot by Jacob:—El-elohe-israel.

416. אֵל בֵּית־אֵל **'Êl Bêyth-'Êl**, *ale bayth-ale';* from 410 and 1008; the *God of Bethel; El-Bethel*, the title given to a consecrated spot by Jacob:—El-beth-el.

417. אֶלְגָּבִישׁ **'elgâbîysh**, *el-gaw-beesh';* from 410 and 1378; *hail* (as if a *great pearl*):—great hail [-stones].

418. אַלְגּוּמִּים **'algûwmmîym**, *al-goom-meem';* by transp. for 484; sticks of *algum* wood:—algum [trees].

419. אֶלְדָּד **'Eldâd**, *el-dâd';* from 410 and 178
God has loved; Eldad, an Isr.:—Eldad

420. אֶלְדָּעָה **'Eldâ'âh**, *el-daw-aw';* from 410 an 3045; *God of knowledge; Eldaah*, son of Midian:—Eldaah.

421. אָלָה **'âlâh**, *aw-law';* a prim. root [rathe ident. with 422 through the idea of *inv cation*]; to *bewail:*—lament.

422. אָלָה **'âlâh**, *aw-law';* a prim. root; prop. t *adjure*, i.e. (usually in a bad sense) *in precate:*—adjure, curse, swear.

423. אָלָה **'âlâh**, *aw-law';* from 422; an *imprec tion:*—curse, cursing, execration, oat swearing.

424. אֵלָה **'êlâh**, *ay-law';* fem. of 352; an *oak* c other strong tree:—elm, oak, teil tree

425. אֵלָה **'Êlâh**, *ay-law';* the same as 424; *Ela* the name of an Edomite, of four Isr., an also of a place in Pal.:—Elah.

426. אֱלָהּ **'ělâhh** (Chald.), *el-aw';* corresp. t 433; *God:*—God, god.

427. אַלָּה **'allâh**, *al-law';* a var. of 424:—oak.

428. אֵלֶּה **'êl-leh**, *ale'-leh;* prol. from 411; *these* c *those:*—an- (the) other; one sort, s some, such, them, these (same), they, this, thos thus, which, who (-m).

429. אֵלֶּה **'êlleh** (Chald.), *ale'-leh;* corresp. t 428:—these.

אֱלֹהַּ **'ělôahh**. See 433.

430. אֱלֹהִים **'ělôhîym**, *el-o-heem';* plur. of 43 *gods* in the ordinary sense; but spe used (in the plur. thus, esp. with the art.) of the s preme *God;* occasionally applied by way of defe ence to *magistrates;* and sometimes as a superl tive:—angels, × exceeding, God (gods) (-dess, -ly × (very) great, judges, × mighty.

431. אֲלוּ **'ălûw** (Chald.), *al-oo';* prob. prol. fro 412; *lo!:*—behold.

432. אִלּוּ **'illûw**, *il-loo';* prob. from 408; *nay*, i. (softened) *if:*—but if, yea though.

433. אֱלוֹהַּ **'ělôwahh**, *el-o'-ah;* rarely (short אֱלֹהַּ **'ělôahh**, *el-o'-ah;* prob. prol. (emphat from 410; a *deity* or the *Deity:*—Go god. See 430.

434. אֱלוּל **'ělûwl**, *el-ool';* for 457; good for *not ing:*—thing of nought.

435. אֱלוּל **'Ělûwl**, *el-ool';* prob. of for. der.; *Elu* the sixth Jewish month:—Elul.

436. אֵלוֹן **'êlôwn**, *ay-lone';* prol. from 352; a *oak* or other strong tree:—plain. See als 356.

437. אַלּוֹן **'allôwn**, *al-lone';* a var. of 436:—oak.

438. אַלּוֹן **'Allôwn**, *al-lone';* the same as 43 *Allon*, an Isr., also a place in Pal.:- Allon.

439. אַלּוֹן בָּכוּת **'Allôwn Bâkûwth**, *al-lone baw-kooth';* from 437 and a va of 1068; *oak of weeping; Allon-Bakuth*, a monumen tal tree:—Allon-bachuth.

440. אֵלוֹנִי **'Êlôwnîy**, *ay-lo-nee';* or rathe (short.) אֵלֹנִי **'Êlônîy**, *ay-lo-nee'* patron. from 438; an *Elonite* or desc. (collect.) c Elon:—Elonites.

441. אַלּוּף **'allûwph**, *al-loof';* or (short.) אַלֻּף **'allûph**, *al-loof';* from 502; *familiar* a *friend*, also *gentle;* hence a *bullock* (as being tame applied, although masc., to a *cow*); and so a *chief tain* (as notable like neat cattle):—captain, duke (chief) friend, governor, guide, ox.

442. אָלוּשׁ **'Âlûwsh**, *aw-loosh';* of uncert. der *Alush*, a place in the Desert:—Alush.

443. אֶלְזָבָד **'Elzâbâd**, *el-zaw-bawd';* from 41 and 2064; *God has bestowed; Elzabad* the name of two Isr.:—Elzabad.

444. אָלַח **'âlach**, *aw-lakh';* a prim. root; to *mud dle*, i.e. (fig. and intrans.) to *turn* (mor ally) *corrupt:*—become filthy.

445. אֶלְחָנָן **'Elchânân**, *el-khaw-nawn';* fro 410 and 2603; *God (is) gracious; Elcha nan*, an Isr.:—Elkanan.

אֵלִי **'Êlîy**. See 1017.

446. אֱלִיאָב **'Ĕlîy'âb**, *el-ee-awb'*; from 410 and 1; *God of* (his) *father; Eliab*, the name of six Isr.:—Eliab.

447. אֱלִיאֵל **'Ĕlîy'êl**, *el-ee-ale'*; from 410 repeated; *God of* (his) *God; Eliel*, the name of nine Isr.:—Eliel.

448. אֱלִיאָתָה **'Ĕlîy'âthâh**, *el-ee-aw-thaw'*; or (contr.) אֱלִיָּתָה **'Ĕlîyâthâh**, *el-ee-yaw-thaw'*; from 410 and 225; *God of* (his) *consent; Eliathah*, an Isr.:—Eliathah.

449. אֱלִידָד **'Ĕlîydâd**, *el-ee-dawd'*; from the same as 419; *God of* (his) *love; Elidad*, an Isr.:—Elidad.

450. אֶלְיָדָע **'Elyâdâ'**, *el-yaw-daw'*; from 410 and 3045; *God* (is) *knowing; Eljada*, the name of two Isr. and of an Aramaean leader:—Eliada.

451. אַלְיָה **'alyâh**, *al-yaw'*; from 422 (in the orig. sense of *strength*); the *stout* part, i.e. the fat *tail* of the Oriental sheep:—rump.

452. אֵלִיָּה **'Êlîyâh**, *ay-lee-yaw'*; or prol. אֵלִיָּהוּ **'Êlîyâhûw**, *ay-lee-yaw'-hoo*; from 410 and 3050; *God of Jehovah; Elijah*, the name of the famous prophet and of two other Isr.:—Elijah, Eliah.

453. אֱלִיהוּ **'Ĕlîyhûw**, *el-ee-hoo'*; or (fully) אֱלִיהוּא **'Ĕlîyhûw'**, *el-ee-hoo'*; from 410 and 1931; *God of him; Elihu*, the name of one of Job's friends, and of three Isr.:—Elihu.

454. אֶלְיְהוֹעֵינַי **'Ely^{e}hôw'êynay**, *el-ye-ho-ay-nah'ee*; or (short.) אֶלְיוֹעֵינַי **'Elyôw'êynay**, *el-yo-ay-nah'ee*; from 413 and 3068 and 5869; *towards Jehovah* (are) *my eyes; Eljehoenai* or *Eljoenai*, the name of seven Isr.:—Elihoenai, Elionai.

455. אֶלְיַחְבָּא **'Elyachbâ'**, *el-yakh-baw'*; from 410 and 2244; *God will hide; Eljachba*, an Isr.:—Eliahbah.

456. אֱלִיחֹרֶף **'Ĕlîychôreph**, *el-ee-kho'-ref*; from 410 and 2779; *God of autumn; Elichoreph*, an Isr.:—Elihoreph.

457. אֱלִיל **'ĕlîyl**, *el-eel'*; appar. from 408; good for *nothing*, by anal. *vain* or *vanity*; spec. an *idol*:—idol, no value, thing of nought.

458. אֱלִימֶלֶךְ **'Ĕlîymelek**, *el-ee-meh'-lek*; from 410 and 4428; *God of* (the) *king; Elimelek*, an Isr.:—Elimelech.

459. אִלֵּין **'illêyn** (Chald.), *il-lane'*; or shorter אִלֵּן **'illên**, *il-lane'*; prol. from 412; *these*:—the, these.

460. אֶלְיָסָף **'Elyâçâph**, *el-yaw-sawf'*; from 410 and 3254; *God* (is) *gatherer; Eljasaph*, the name of two Isr.:—Eliasaph.

461. אֱלִיעֶזֶר **'Ĕlîy'ezer**, *el-ee-eh'-zer*; from 410 and 5828; *God of help; Eliezer*, the name of a Damascene and of ten Isr.:—Eliezer.

462. אֱלִיעֵינַי **'Ĕlîy'êynay**, *el-ee-ay-nah'ee*; prob. contr. for 454; *Elienai*, an Isr.:—Elienai.

463. אֱלִיעָם **'Ĕlîy'âm**, *el-ee-awm'*; from 410 and 5971; *God of* (the) *people; Eliam*, an Isr.:—Eliam.

464. אֱלִיפַז **'Ĕlîyphaz**, *el-ee-faz'*; from 410 and 6337; *God of gold; Eliphaz*, the name of one of Job's friends, and of a son of Esau:—Eliphaz.

465. אֱלִיפָל **'Ĕlîyphâl**, *el-ee-fawl'*; from 410 and 6419; *God of judgment; Eliphal*, an Isr.:—Eliphal.

466. אֱלִיפְלֵהוּ **'Ĕlîyph^{e}lêhûw**, *el-ee-fe-lay'-hoo*; from 410 and 6395; *God of his distinction; Eliphelehu*, an Isr.:—Elipheleh.

467. אֱלִיפֶלֶט **'Ĕlîyphelet**, *el-ee-feh'-let*; or (short.) אֶלְפֶּלֶט **'Elpelet**, *el-peh'-let*; from 410 and 6405; *God of deliverance; Eliphelet* or *Elpelet*, the name of six Isr.:—Eliphalet, Eliphelet, Elpalet.

468. אֱלִיצוּר **'Ĕlêytsûwr**, *el-ee-tsoor'*; from 410 and 6697; *God of* (the) *rock; Elitsur*, an Isr.:—Elizur.

469. אֱלִיצָפָן **'Ĕlîytsâphân**, *el-ee-tsaw-fawn'*; or (short.) אֶלְצָפָן **'Eltsâphân**, *el-tsaw-fawn'*; from 410 and 6845; *God of treasure; Elitsaphan* or *Eltsaphan*, an Isr.:—Elizaphan, Elzaphan.

470. אֱלִיקָא **'Ĕlîyqâ'**, *el-ee-kaw'*; from 410 and 6958; *God of rejection; Elika*, an Isr.:—Elika.

471. אֶלְיָקִים **'Elyâqîym**, *el-yaw-keem'*; from 410 and 6965; *God of raising; Eljakim*, the name of four Isr.:—Eliakim.

472. אֱלִישֶׁבַע **'Ĕlîysheba'**, *el-ee-sheh'-bah*; from 410 and 7651 (in the sense of 7650); *God of* (the) *oath; Elisheba*, the wife of Aaron:—Elisheba.

473. אֱלִישָׁה **'Ĕlîyshâh**, *el-ee-shaw'*; prob. of for. der.; *Elishah*, a son of Javan:—Elishah.

474. אֱלִישׁוּעַ **'Ĕlîyshûwa'**, *el-ee-shoo'-ah*; from 410 and 7769; *God of supplication* (or *of riches*); *Elishua*, a son of King David:—Elishua.

475. אֶלְיָשִׁיב **'Elyâshîyb**, *el-yaw-sheeb'*; from 410 and 7725; *God will restore; Eljashib*, the name of six Isr.:—Eliashib.

476. אֱלִישָׁמָע **'Ĕlîyshâmâ'**, *el-ee-shaw-maw'*; from 410 and 8085; *God of hearing; Elishama*, the name of seven Isr.:—Elishama.

477. אֱלִישָׁע **'Ĕlîyshâ'**, *el-ee-shaw'*; contr. for 474; *Elisha*, the famous prophet:—Elisha.

478. אֱלִישָׁפָט **'Ĕlîyshâphât**, *el-ee-shaw-fawt'*; from 410 and 8199; *God of judgment; Elishaphat*, an Isr.:—Elishaphat.

אֱלִיָּתָה **'Ĕlîyâthâh**. See 448.

479. אִלֵּךְ **'illêk** (Chald.), *il-lake'*; prol. from 412; *these*:—these, those.

480. אַלְלַי **'al^{e}lay**, *al-le-lah'ee*; by redupl. from 421; *alas!*:—woe.

481. אָלַם **'âlam**, *aw-lam'*; a prim. root; to *tie* fast; hence (of the mouth) to be *tongue-tied*:—bind, be dumb, put to silence.

482. אֵלֶם **'êlem**, *ay'-lem*; from 481; *silence* (i.e. mute justice):—congregation. Comp. 3128.

אֵלָם **'êlâm**. See 361.

אָלֻם **'âlûm**. See 485.

483. אִלֵּם **'illêm**, *il-lame'*; from 481; *speechless*:—dumb (man).

484. אַלְמֻגִּים **'almuggîym**, *al-moog-gheem'*; prob. of for. der. (used thus only in the plur.); *almug* (i.e. prob. sandal-wood) sticks:—almug trees. Comp. 418.

485. אֲלֻמָּה **'ălummâh**, *al-oom-maw'*; or (masc.) אָלֻם **'âlûm**, *aw-loom'*; pass. part. of 481; something *bound*; a *sheaf*:—sheaf.

486. אַלְמוֹדָד **'Almôwdâd**, *al-mo-dawd'*; prob. of for. der.:—*Almodad*, a son of Joktan:—Almodad.

487. אַלַּמֶּלֶךְ **'Allammelek**, *al-lam-meh'-lek*; from 427 and 4428; *oak of* (the) *king; Allammelek*, a place in Pal.:—Alammelech.

488. אַלְמָן **'almân**, *al-mawn'*; prol. from 481 in the sense of *bereavement; discarded* (as a divorced person):—forsaken.

489. אַלְמֹן **'almôn**, *al-mone'*; from 481 as in 488; *bereavement*:—widowhood.

490. אַלְמָנָה **'almânâh**, *al-maw-naw'*; fem. of 488; a *widow*; also a *desolate* place:—desolate house (palace), widow.

491. אַלְמָנוּת **'almânûwth**, *al-maw-nooth'*; fem. of 488; concr. a *widow*; abstr. *widowhood*:—widow, widowhood.

492. אַלְמֹנִי **'almônîy**, *al-mo-nee'*; from 489 in the sense of *concealment*; *some* one (i.e. *so and so*, without giving the name of the person or place):—one, and such.

אִלֵּן **'illên**. See 459.

אֵלֹנִי **'Êlônîy**. See 440.

493. אֶלְנַעַם **'Elna'am**, *el-nah'-am*; from 410 and 5276; *God* (is his) *delight; Elnaam*, an Isr.:—Elnaam.

494. אֶלְנָתָן **'Elnâthân**, *el-naw-thawn'*; from 410 and 5414; *God* (is the) *giver; Elnathan*, the name of four Isr.:—Elnathan.

495. אֶלָּסָר **'Ellâçâr**, *el-law-sawr'*; prob. of for. der.; *Ellasar*, an early country of Asia:—Ellasar.

496. אֶלְעָד **'El'âd**, *el-awd'*; from 410 and 5749; *God has testified; Elad*, an Isr.:—Elead.

497. אֶלְעָדָה **'El'âdâh**, *el-aw-daw'*; from 410 and 5710; *God has decked; Eladah*, an Isr.:—Eladah.

498. אֶלְעוּזַי **'El'ûwzay**, *el-oo-zah'ee*; from 410 and 5756 (in the sense of 5797); *God* (is) *defensive; Eluzai*, an Isr.:—Eluzai.

499. אֶלְעָזָר **'El'âzâr**, *el-aw-zawr'*; from 410 and 5826; *God* (is) *helper; Elazar*, the name of seven Isr.:—Eleazar.

500. אֶלְעָלֵא **'El'âlê'**, *el-aw-lay'*; or (more properly) אֶלְעָלֵה **'El'âlêh**, *el-aw-lay'*; from 410 and 5927; *God* (is) *going up; Elale* or *Elaleh*, a place east of the Jordan:—Elealeh.

501. אֶלְעָשָׂה **'El'âsâh**, *el-aw-saw'*; from 410 and 6213; *God has made; Elasah*, the name of four Isr.:—Elasah, Eleasah.

502. אָלַף **'âlaph**, *aw-lof'*; a prim. root, to *associate* with; hence to *learn* (and caus. to *teach*):—learn, teach, utter.

503. אָלַף **'âlaph**, *aw-laf'*; denom. from 505; caus. to *make a thousandfold*:—bring forth thousands.

504. אֶלֶף **'eleph**, *eh'-lef*; from 502; a *family*; also (from the sense of *yoking* or *taming*) an *ox* or *cow*:—family, kine, oxen.

505. אֶלֶף **'eleph**, *eh'-lef*; prop. the same as 504; hence (an ox's head being the first letter of the alphabet, and this eventually used as a numeral) a *thousand*:—thousand.

506. אֲלַף **'âlaph** (Chald.), *al-af'*; or אֶלֶף **'eleph**, (Chald.), *eh'-lef*; corresp. to 505:—thousand.

507. אֶלֶף **'Eleph**, *eh'-lef*; the same as 505; *Eleph*, a place in Pal.:—Eleph.

אַלֻּף **'allûph**. See 441.

אֶלְפֶּלֶט **'Elpelet**. See 467.

508. אֶלְפַּעַל **'Elpa'al**, *el-pah'-al*; from 410 and 6466; *God* (is) *act; Elpaal*, an Isr.:—Elpaal.

509. אָלַץ **'âlats**, *aw-lats'*; a prim. root; to *press*:—urge.

אֶלְצָפָן **'Eltsâphân**. See 469.

510. אַלְקוּם **'alqûwm**, *al-koom'*; prob. from 408 and 6965; a *non-rising* (i.e. *resistlessness*):—no rising up.

511. אֶלְקָנָה **'Elqânâh**, *el-kaw-naw'*; from 410 and 7069; *God has obtained; Elkanah*, the name of seven Isr.:—Elkanah.

512. אֶלְקֹשִׁי **'Elqôshîy**, *el-ko-shee'*; patrial from a name of uncert. der.; an *Elkoshite* or native of Elkosh:—Elkoshite.

513. אֶלְתּוֹלַד **'Eltôwlad**, *el-to-lad'*; prob. from 410 and a masc. form of 8435 [comp. 8434]; *God* (is) *generator; Eltolad*, a place in Pal.:—Eltolad.

514. אֶלְתְּקֵא **'Elt^{e}qê**, *el-te-kay'*; or (more prop.) אֶלְתְּקֵה **'Elt^{e}qêh**, *el-te-kay'*; of uncert. der.; *Eltekeh* or *Elteke*, a place in Pal.:—Eltekeh.

515. אֶלְתְּקֹן **'Elt^{e}qôn**, *el-te-kone'*; from 410 and 8626; *God* (is) *straight; Eltekon*, a place in Pal.:—Eltekon.

516. אַל תַּשְׁחֵת **'Al tashchêth**, *al tash-kayth'*; from 408 and 7843; *Thou must not destroy*; prob. the opening words of a popular song:—Al-taschith.

517. אֵם **'êm**, *ame*; a prim. word; a *mother* (as the *bond* of the family); in a wide sense (both lit. and fig.) [like 1]:—dam, mother, × parting.

518. אִם **'îm**, *eem;* a prim. particle; used very widely as demonstr., *lo!;* interrog., *whether?;* or conditional, *if, although;* also *Oh that!, when;* hence as a neg., *not:*—(and, can-, doubtless, if, that) (not), + but, either, + except, + more (-over if, than), neither, nevertheless, nor, oh that, or, + save (only, -ing), seeing, since, sith, + surely (no more, none, not), though, + of a truth, + unless, + verily, when, whereas, whether, while, + yet.

519. אָמָה **'âmâh**, *aw-maw';* appar. a prim. word; a *maid-servant* or female slave:—(hand-) bondmaid (-woman,) maid (-servant).

אֵמָה **'êmâh**. See 367.

520. אַמָּה **'ammâh**, *am-maw';* prol. from 517; prop. a *mother* (i.e. *unit*) of measure, or the *fore-arm* (below the elbow), i.e. a *cubit;* also a door-*base* (as a *bond* of the entrance):—cubit, + hundred [*by exchange for* 3967], measure, post.

521. אַמָּה **'ammâh** (Chald.), *am-maw';* corresp. to 520:—cubit.

522. אַמָּה **'Ammâh**, *am-maw';* the same as 520; *Ammah,* a hill in Pal.:—Ammah.

523. אֻמָּה **ummâh**, *oom-maw';* from the same as 517; a *collection,* i.e. community of persons:—nation, people.

524. אֻמָּה **'ummâh** (Chald.), *oom-maw';* corresp. to 523:—nation.

525. אָמוֹן **'âmôwn**, *aw-mone';* from 539, prob. in the sense of *training; skilled,* i.e. an architect [like 542]:—one brought up.

526. אָמוֹן **'Âmôwn**, *aw-mone';* the same as 525; *Amon,* the name of three Isr.:—Amon.

527. אָמוֹן **'âmôwn**, *aw-mone';* a var. for 1995; a *throng* of people:—multitude.

528. אָמוֹן **'Âmôwn**, *aw-mone';* of Eg. der.; *Amon* (i.e. Ammon or Amn), a deity of Egypt (used only as an adjunct of 4996):—multitude, populous.

529. אֵמוּן **'êmûwn**, *ay-moon';* from 539; *established,* i.e. (fig.) *trusty;* also (abstr.) *trustworthiness:*—faith (-ful), truth.

530. אֱמוּנָה **'ĕmûwnâh**, *em-oo-naw';* or (short.) אֱמֻנָה **'ĕmûnâh**, *em-oo-naw';* fem. of 529; lit. *firmness;* fig. *security;* mor. *fidelity:*—faith (-ful, -ly, -ness, [man]), set office, stability, steady, truly, truth, verily.

531. אָמוֹץ **'Âmôwts**, *aw-mohts';* from 553; *strong; Amots,* an Isr.:—Amoz.

532. אָמִי **'Âmîy**, *aw-mee';* an abbrev. for 526; *Ami,* an Isr.:—Ami.

אֲמִינוֹן **'Ămîynôwn**. See 550.

533. אַמִּיץ **'ammîyts**, *am-meets';* or (short.) אַמִּץ **'ammîts**, *am-meets';* from 553; *strong* or (abstr.) *strength:*—courageous, mighty, strong (one).

534. אָמִיר **'âmîyr**, *aw-meer';* appar. from 559 (in the sense of *self-exaltation*); a *summit* (of a tree or mountain):—bough, branch.

535. אָמַל **'âmal**, *aw-mal';* a prim. root; to *droop;* by impl. to *be sick,* to *mourn:*—languish, be weak, wax feeble.

536. אֻמְלַל **'umlal**, *oom-lal';* from 535; *sick:*—weak.

537. אֲמֵלָל **'ămêlâl**, *am-ay-lawl';* from 535; *languid:*—feeble.

538. אֲמָם **'Ămâm**, *am-awm';* from 517; *gathering*-spot; *Amam,* a place in Pal.:—Amam.

539. אָמַן **'âman**, *aw-man';* a prim. root; prop. to *build up* or *support;* to *foster* as a parent or nurse; fig. to *render* (or *be*) *firm* or faithful, to *trust* or believe, to be *permanent* or quiet; mor. to *be true* or certain; once (Isa. 30 : 21; by interch. for 541) to *go to the right hand:*—hence assurance, believe, bring up, establish, + fail, be faithful (of long continuance, stedfast, sure, surely, trusty, verified), nurse, (-ing father), (put), trust, turn to the right.

540. אֲמַן **'ăman** (Chald.), *am-an';* corresp. to 539:—believe, faithful, sure.

541. אָמַן **'âman**, *aw-man';* denom. from 3225; to take the *right hand* road:—turn to the right. See 539.

542. אָמָּן **'âmân**, *aw-mawn';* from 539 (in the sense of *training*); an *expert:*—cunning workman.

543. אָמֵן **'âmên**, *aw-mane';* from 539; *sure;* abstr. *faithfulness;* adv. *truly:*—Amen, so be it, truth.

544. אֹמֶן **'ômen**, *oh-men';* from 539; *verity:*—truth.

545. אָמְנָה **'omnâh**, *om-naw';* fem. of 544 (in the spec. sense of *training*); *tutelage:*—brought up.

546. אָמְנָה **'omnâh**, *om-naw';* fem. of 544 (in its usual sense); adv. *surely:*—indeed.

547. אֹמְנָה **'ômᵉnâh**, *o-me-naw';* fem. act. part. of 544 (in the orig. sense of *supporting*); a *column:*—pillar.

548. אֲמָנָה **'ămânâh**, *am-aw-naw';* fem. of 543; something *fixed,* i.e. a *covenant,* an *allowance:*—certain portion, sure.

549. אֲמָנָה **'Ămânâh**, *am-aw-naw';* the same as 548; *Amanah,* a mountain near Damascus:—Amana.

אֱמֻנָה **'ĕmûnâh**. See 530.

550. אַמְנוֹן **'Amnôwn**, *am-nohn';* or אֲמִינוֹן **'Ămîynôwn**, *am-ee-nohn';* from 539; *faithful; Amnon* (or Aminon), a son of David:—Amnon.

551. אָמְנָם **'omnâm**, *om-nawm';* adv. from 544; *verily:*—indeed, no doubt, surely, (it is, of a) true (-ly, -th).

552. אֻמְנָם **'umnâm**, *oom-nawm';* an orth. var. of 551:—in (very) deed; of a surety.

553. אָמֵץ **'âmats**, *aw-mats';* a prim. root; to *be alert,* phys. (on foot) or ment. (in courage):—confirm, be courageous (of good courage, stedfastly minded, strong, stronger), establish, fortify, harden, increase, prevail, strengthen (self), make strong (obstinate, speed).

554. אָמֹץ **'âmôts**, *aw-mohts';* prob. from 553; of a *strong* color, i.e. *red* (others *fleet*):—bay.

555. אֹמֶץ **'ômets**, *o'-mets;* from 553; *strength:*—stronger.

אַמִּץ **'ammîts**. See 533.

556. אַמְצָה **'amtsâh**, *am-tsaw';* from 553; *force:*—strength.

557. אַמְצִי **'Amtsîy**, *am-tsee';* from 553; *strong, Amtsi,* an Isr.:—Amzi.

558. אֲמַצְיָה **'Ămatsyâh**, *am-ats-yaw';* or אֲמַצְיָהוּ **'Ămatsyâhûw**, *am-ats-yaw'-hoo;* from 553 and 3050; *strength of Jah; Amatsjah,* the name of four Isr.:—Amaziah.

559. אָמַר **'âmar**, *aw-mar';* a prim. root; to *say* (used with great latitude):—answer, appoint, avouch, bid, boast self, call, certify, challenge, charge, + (at the, give) command (-ment), commune, consider, declare, demand, × desire, determine, × expressly, × indeed, × intend, name, × plainly, promise, publish, report, require, say, speak (against, of), × still, × suppose, talk, tell, term, × that is, × think, use [speech], utter, × verily, × yet.

560. אֲמַר **'ămar** (Chald.), *am-ar';* corresp. to 559:—command, declare, say, speak, tell.

561. אֵמֶר **'êmer**, *ay'-mer;* from 559; something *said:*—answer, × appointed unto him, saying, speech, word.

562. אֹמֶר **'ômer**, *o'-mer;* the same as 561:—promise, speech, thing, word.

563. אִמַּר **'immar** (Chald.), *im-mar';* perh. from 560 (in the sense of *bringing forth*); a *lamb:*—lamb.

564. אִמֵּר **'Immêr**, *im-mare';* from 559; *talkative; Immer,* the name of five Isr.:—Immer.

565. אִמְרָה **'imrâh**, *im-raw';* or אֶמְרָה **'emrâh**, *em-raw';* fem. of 561, and mean. the same:—commandment, speech, word.

566. אִמְרִי **'Imrîy**, *im-ree';* from 564; *wordy; Imri,* the name of two Isr.:—Imri.

567. אֱמֹרִי **'Ĕmôrîy**, *em-o-ree';* prob. a patr[onymic] from an unused name derived from [5]59 in the sense of *publicity,* i.e. prominence; thus [a] *mountaineer;* an *Emorite,* one of the Canaanit[e] tribes:—Amorite.

568. אֲמַרְיָה **'Ămaryâh**, *am-ar-yaw';* or (pro[l].) אֲמַרְיָהוּ **'Ămaryâhûw**, *am-ar-yaw'-ho[o];* from 559 and 3050; *Jah has said* (i[.e.] promised); *Amarjah,* the name of nine Isr.:—Am[a]riah.

569. אַמְרָפֶל **'Amrâphel**, *am-raw-fel';* of uncer[tain] (perh. for.) der.; *Amraphel,* a king [of] Shinar:—Amraphel.

570. אֶמֶשׁ **'emesh**, *eh'-mesh;* time *past,* i.e. *ye[s]terday* or *last night:*—former time, ye[s]terday (-night).

571. אֱמֶת **'emeth**, *eh'-meth;* contr. from 53[9]; *stability;* fig. *certainty, truth, tru[st]worthiness:*—assured (-ly), establishment, faithfu[l], right, sure, true (-ly, -th), verity.

572. אַמְתַּחַת **'amtachath**, *am-takh'-ath;* fro[m] 4969; prop. something *expansive,* i[.e.] a *bag:*—sack.

573. אֲמִתַּי **'Ămittay**, *am-it-tah'ee;* from 57[1]; *veracious; Amittai,* an Isr.:—Amittai.

574. אֵמְתָנִי **'emtânîy** (Chald.), *em-taw-nee* from a root corresp. to that of 497[5]; *well-loined* (i.e. burly) or *mighty:*—terrible.

575. אָן **ân**, *awn;* or אָנָה **'ânâh**, *aw'-naw* contr. from 370; *where?;* hence *whither* *when?;* also *hither* and *thither:*—+ any (no) whithe[r], now, where, whither (-soever).

אֹן **'ôn**. See 204.

576. אֲנָא **'ănâ'** (Chald.), *an-aw';* or [אֲנָ]ה **'ănâh** (Chald.), *an-aw';* corresp. [to] 589; *I:*—I, as for me.

577. אָנָּא **'ânnâ'**, *awn'-naw;* or אָנָּה **'ânnâ[h]** *awn'-naw;* appar. contr. from 160 an[d] 4994: *oh now!:*—I (me) beseech (pray) thee, O.

אֲנָה **'ănâh**. See 576.

אָנָה **'ânâh**. See 575.

578. אָנָה **'ânâh**, *aw-naw';* a prim. root; [to] *groan:*—lament, mourn.

579. אָנָה **'ânâh**, *aw-naw';* a prim. root [perh.] rather ident. with 578 through the idea o[f] *contraction* in anguish]; to *approach;* hence to *mee[t]* in various senses:—befall, deliver, happen, seek quarrel.

אָנָּה **'ânnâh**. See 577.

580. אֲנוּ **'ănûw**, *an-oo';* contr. for 587; *we:*—we.

אֹנוֹ **Ônôw**. See 207.

581. אִנּוּן **'innûwn** (Chald.), *in-noon';* or (fem.) אִנִּין **'inníyn** (Chald.), *in-neen';* corresp. [to] 1992; *they:*— × are, them, these.

582. אֱנוֹשׁ **'ĕnôwsh**, *en-oshe';* from 605; prop. [a] *mortal* (and thus differing from th[e] more dignified 120); hence a *man* in gen. (singl[e] or collect.):—another, × [blood-] thirsty, certai[n] chap [-man], divers, fellow, × in the flower of the[ir] age, husband, (certain, mortal) man, people, perso[n], servant, some (× of them), + stranger, thos[e] + their trade. It is often unexpressed in the Eng[lish] Version, especially when used in apposition with a[n]other word. Comp. 376.

583. אֱנוֹשׁ **'Ĕnôwsh**, *en-ohsh';* the same as 58[2]; *Enosh,* a son of Seth:—Enos.

584. אָנַח **'ânach**, *aw-nakh';* a prim. root; t[o] *sigh:*—groan, mourn, sigh.

585. אֲנָחָה **'ănâchâh**, *an-aw-khaw';* from 58[4]; *sighing:*—groaning, mourn, sigh.

586. אֲנַחְנָא **'ănachnâ'** (Chald.), *an-akh'-naw;* [or] אֲנַחְנָה **'ănachnâh** (Chald.), *an-akh-naw* corresp. to 587; *we:*—we.

587. אֲנַחְנוּ **'ănachnûw**, *an-akh'-noo,* appa[r.] from 595; *we:*—ourselves, us, we.

588. אֲנָחֲרָת **'Ănâchărâth**, *an-aw-kha-rawth* prob. from the same root as 5170; [a] *gorge* or narrow pass; *Anacharath,* a place in Pal.:—Anaharath.

589. אֲנִי **'ănîy**, *an-ee'*; contr. from 595; *I*:—I, (as for) me, mine, myself, we, × which, × who.

590. אֳנִי **'ŏnîy**, *on-ee'*; prob. from 579 (in the sense of *conveyance*); a *ship* or (collect.) a *fleet*:—galley, navy (of ships).

591. אֳנִיָּה **'ŏnîyâh**, *on-ee-yaw'*; fem. of 590; a *ship*:—ship ([-men]).

592. אֲנִיָּה **'ănîyâh**, *an-ee-yaw'*; from 578; *groaning*:—lamentation, sorrow.

אִנִּין **'innîyn**. See 581.

593. אֲנִיעָם **'Ănîy'âm**, *an-ee-awm'*; from 578 and 5971; *groaning of* (the) *people*; *Aniam*, an Isr.:—Aniam.

594. אֲנָךְ **'ănâk**, *an-awk'*; prob. from an unused root mean. to *be narrow*; according to most a plumb-*line*, and to others a *hook*:—plumb-line.

595. אָנֹכִי **'ânôkîy**, *aw-no-kee'* (sometimes *aw-no'-kee*); a prim. pron.; *I*:—I, me, × which.

596. אָנַן **'ânan**, *aw-nan'*; a prim. root; to *mourn*, i.e. *complain*:—complain.

597. אָנַס **'ânaç**, *aw-nas'*; to *insist*:—compel.

598. אֲנַס **'ănaç** (Chald.), *an-as'*; corresp. to 597; fig. to *distress*:—trouble.

599. אָנַף **'ânaph**, *aw-naf'*; a prim. root; to *breathe* hard, i.e. *be enraged*:—be angry (displeased).

600. אֱנַף **'ănaph** (Chald.), *an-af'*; corresp. to 639 (only in the plur. as a sing.); the *face*:—face, visage.

601. אֲנָפָה **'ănâphâh**, *an-aw-faw'*; from 599; an unclean bird, perh. the *parrot* (from its *irascibility*):—heron.

602. אָנַק **'ânaq**, *aw-nak'*; a prim. root; to *shriek*:—cry, groan.

603. אֲנָקָה **'ănâqâh**, *an-aw-kaw'*, from 602; *shrieking*:—crying out, groaning, sighing.

604. אֲנָקָה **'ănâqâh**, *an-aw-kaw'*; the same as 603; some kind of lizard, prob. the *gecko* (from its *wail*):—ferret.

605. אָנַשׁ **'ânash**, *aw-nash'*; a prim. root; to *be frail*, *feeble*, or (fig.) *melancholy*:—desperate (-ly wicked), incurable, sick, woeful.

606. אֱנָשׁ **'ĕnâsh** (Chald.), *en-awsh'*; or אֱנַשׁ **'ĕnash** (Chald.), *en-ash'*; corresp. to 582; a *man*:—man, + whosoever.

אַנְתְּ **'ant**. See 859.

607. אַנְתָּה **'antâh** (Chald.), *an-taw'*; corresp. to 859; *thou*:—as for thee, thou.

608. אַנְתּוּן **'antûwn** (Chald.), *an-toon'*; plur. of 607; *ye*:—ye.

609. אָסָא **'Âçâ'**, *aw-saw'*; of uncert. der.; *Asa*, the name of a king and of a Levite:—Asa.

610. אָסוּךְ **'âçûwk**, *aw-sook'*; from 5480; *anointed*, i.e. an oil-*flask*:—pot.

611. אָסוֹן **'âçôwn**, *aw-sone'*; of uncert. der.; *hurt*:—mischief.

612. אֵסוּר **'êçûwr**, *ay-soor'*; from 631; a *bond* (espec. *manacles* of a prisoner):—band, + prison.

613. אֱסוּר **'ĕçûwr** (Chald.), *es-oor'*; corresp. to 612:—band, imprisonment.

614. אָסִיף **'âçîyph**, *aw-seef'*; or אָסִף **'âçîph**, *aw-seef'*; from 622; *gathered*, i.e. (abstr.) a *gathering* in of crops:—ingathering.

615. אָסִיר **'âçîyr**, *aw-sere'*; from 631; *bound*, i.e. a *captive*:—(those which are) bound, prisoner.

616. אַסִּיר **'aççîyr**, *as-sere'*; for 615:—prisoner.

617. אַסִּיר **'Aççîyr**, *as-sere'*; the same as 616; *prisoner*; *Assir*, the name of two Isr.:—Assir.

618. אָסָם **'âçâm**, *aw-sawm'*; from an unused root mean. to *heap* together; a *storehouse* (only in the plur.):—barn, storehouse.

619. אַסְנָה **'Açnâh**, *as-naw'*; of uncert. der.; *Asnah*, one of the Nethinim:—Asnah.

620. אָסְנַפַּר **'Oçnappar**, *os-nap-par'*; of for. der.; *Osnappar*, an Assyrian king:—Asnapper.

621. אָסְנַת **'Âçᵉnath**, *aw-se-nath'*; of Eg. der.; *Asenath*, the wife of Joseph:—Asenath.

622. אָסַף **'âçaph**, *aw-saf'*; a prim. root; to *gather* for any purpose; hence to *receive*, *take away*, i.e. remove (destroy, leave behind, put up, restore, etc.):—assemble, bring, consume, destroy, fetch, gather (in, together, up again), × generally, get (him), lose, put all together, receive, recover [another from leprosy], (be) rereward, × surely, take (away, into, up), × utterly, withdraw.

623. אָסָף **'Âçâph**, *aw-sawf'*; from 622; *collector*; *Asaph*, the name of three Isr., and of the family of the first:—Asaph.

אָסִף **'âçiph**. See 614.

624. אָסֻף **'âçûph**, *aw-soof'*; pass. part. of 622; *collected* (only in the plur.), i.e. a *collection* (of offerings):—threshold, Asuppim.

625. אֹסֶף **'ôçeph**, *o'-sef*; from 622; a *collection* (of fruits):—gathering.

626. אֲסֵפָה **'ăçêphâh**, *as-ay-faw'*; from 622; a *collection* of people (only adv.):— × together.

627. אֲסֻפָּה **'ăçuppâh**, *as-up-paw'*; fem. of 624; a *collection* of (learned) men (only in the plur.):—assembly.

628. אֲסַפְסֻף **'açpᵉçûph**, *as-pes-oof'*; by redupl. from 624; *gathered up together*, i.e. a promiscuous *assemblage* (of people):—mixt multitude.

629. אָסְפַּרְנָא **'oçparnâ'** (Chald.), *os-par-naw'*; of Pers. der.; *diligently*:—fast, forthwith, speed (-ily).

630. אַסְפָּתָא **'Açpâthâ'**, *as-paw-thaw'*; of Pers. der.; *Aspatha*, a son of Haman:—Aspatha.

631. אָסַר **'âçar**, *aw-sar'*; a prim. root; to *yoke* or *hitch*; by anal. to *fasten* in any sense, to *join* battle:—bind, fast, gird, harness, hold, keep, make ready, order, prepare, prison (-er), put in bonds, set in array, tie.

632. אֱסָר **'ĕçâr**, *es-awr'*; or אִסָּר **'iççâr**, *is-sawr'*; from 631; an *obligation* or *vow* (of abstinence):—binding, bond.

633. אֱסָר **'ĕçâr** (Chald.), *es-awr'*; corresp. to 632 in a legal sense; an *interdict*:—decree.

634. אֵסַר־חַדּוֹן **'Êçar-Chaddôwn**, *ay-sar' chad-dohn'*; of for. der.; *Esar-chaddon*, an Assyr. king:—Esar-haddon.

635. אֶסְתֵּר **'Eçtêr**, *es-tare'*; of Pers. der.; *Ester*, the Jewish heroine:—Esther.

636. אָע **'â'** (Chald.), *aw*; corresp. to 6086; a *tree* or *wood*:—timber, wood.

637. אַף **'aph**, *af*; a prim. particle; mean. *accession* (used as an adv. or conj.); *also* or *yea*; adversatively *though*:—also, + although, and (furthermore, yet), but, even, + how much less (more, rather than), moreover, with, yea.

638. אַף **'aph** (Chald.), *af*; corresp. to 637:—also.

639. אַף **'aph**, *af*; from 599; prop. the *nose* or *nostril*; hence the *face*, and occasionally a *person*; also (from the rapid breathing in passion) *ire*:—anger (-gry), + before, countenance, face, + forbearing, forehead, + [long-] suffering, nose, nostril, snout, × worthy, wrath.

640. אָפַד **'âphad**, *aw-fad'*; a prim. root [rather a denom. from 646]; to *gird* on (the ephod):—bind, gird.

אֵפֹד **'êphôd**. See 646.

641. אֵפֹד **'Êphôd**, *ay-fode'*; the same as 646 short.; *Ephod*, an Isr.:—Ephod.

642. אֲפֻדָּה **'êphuddâh**, *ay-food-daw'*; fem. of 646; a *girding* on (of the ephod); hence gen. a *plating* (of metal):—ephod, ornament.

643. אַפֶּדֶן **'appeden**, *ap-peh'-den*; appar. of for. der.; a *pavilion* or palace-tent:—palace.

644. אָפָה **'âphâh**, *aw-faw'*; a prim. root; to *cook*, espec. to *bake*:—bake, (-r, [-meats]).

אֵפָה **'êphâh**. See 374.

645. אֵפוֹ **'ephôw**, *ay-fo'*; or אֵפוֹא **'êphôw'**, *ay-fo'*; from 6311; strictly a demonstrative particle, *here*; but used of time, *now* or *then*:—here, now, where?

646. אֵפוֹד **'êphôwd**, *ay-fode'*; rarely אֵפֹד **'êphôd**, *ay-fode'*; prob. of for. der.; a *girdle*; spec. the *ephod* or high-priest's shoulder-piece; also gen. an *image*:—ephod.

647. אֲפִיחַ **'Ăphîyach**, *af-ee'-akh*; perh. from 6315; *breeze*; *Aphiach*, an Isr.:—Aphiah.

648. אָפִיל **'âphîyl**, *aw-feel'*; from the same as 651 (in the sense of *weakness*); *unripe*:—not grown up.

649. אַפַּיִם **'Appayim**, *ap-pah'-yim*; dual of 639; *two nostrils*; *Appajim*, an Isr.:—Appaim.

650. אָפִיק **'âphîyq**, *aw-feek'*; from 622; prop. *containing*, i.e. a *tube*; also a *bed* or *valley* of a stream; also a *strong* thing or a *hero*:—brook, channel, mighty, river, + scale, stream, strong piece.

אֹפִיר **'Ôphîyr**. See 211.

651. אָפֵל **'âphêl**, *aw-fale'*; from an unused root mean. to *set* as the sun; *dusky*:—very dark.

652. אֹפֶל **'ôphel**, *o'-fel*; from the same as 651; *dusk*:—darkness, obscurity, privily.

653. אֲפֵלָה **'ăphêlâh**, *af-ay-law'*; fem. of 651; *duskiness*, fig. *misfortune*; concr. *concealment*:—dark, darkness, gloominess, × thick.

654. אֶפְלָל **'Ephlâl**, *ef-lawl'*; from 6419; *judge*; *Ephlal*, an Isr.:—Ephlal.

655. אֹפֶן **'ôphen**, *o'-fen*; from an unused root mean. to *revolve*; a *turn*, i.e. a *season*:— + fitly.

אֹפָן **'ôphân**. See 212.

656. אָפֵס **'âphêç**, *aw-face'*; a prim. root; to *disappear*, i.e. *cease*:—be clean gone (at an end, brought to nought), fail.

657. אֶפֶס **'epheç**, *eh'-fes*; from 656; *cessation*, i.e. an *end* (espec. of the earth); often used adv. *no further*; also (like 6466) the *ankle* (in the dual), as being the extremity of the leg or foot:—ankle, but (only), end, howbeit, less than nothing, nevertheless (where), no, none (beside), not (any, -withstanding), thing of nought, save (-ing), there, uttermost part, want, without (cause).

658. אֶפֶס דַּמִּים **'Epheç Dammîym**, *eh'-fes dam-meem'*; from 657 and the plur. of 1818; *boundary of blood-drops*; *Ephes-Dammim*, a place in Pal.:—Ephes-dammim.

659. אֶפַע **'êpha'**, *eh'-fah*; from an unused root prob. mean. to *breathe*; prop. a *breath*, i.e. *nothing*:—of nought.

660. אֶפְעֶה **'eph'eh**, *ef-eh'*; from 659 (in the sense of *hissing*); an *asp* or other venomous serpent:—viper.

661. אָפַף **'âphaph**, *aw-faf'*; a prim. root; to *surround*:—compass.

662. אָפַק **'âphaq**, *aw-fak'*; a prim. root; to *contain*, i.e. (reflex.) *abstain*:—force (oneself), restrain.

663. אֲפֵק **'Ăphêq**, *af-ake'*; or אֲפִיק **'Ăphîyq**, *af-eek'*; from 662 (in the sense of *strength*); *fortress*; *Aphek* (or *Aphik*), the name of three places in Pal.:—Aphek, Aphik.

664. אֲפֵקָה **'Ăphêqâh**, *af-ay-kaw'*; fem. of 663; *fortress*; *Aphekah*, a place in Pal.:—Aphekah.

665. אֵפֶר **'êpher**, *ay'-fer*; from an unused root mean. to *bestrew*; *ashes*:—ashes.

666. אֲפֵר **'ăphêr**, *af-ayr'*; from the same as 665 (in the sense of *covering*); a *turban*:—ashes.

667. אֶפְרֹחַ **'ephrôach**, *ef-ro'-akh*; from 6524 (in the sense of *bursting* the shell); the *brood* of a bird:—young (one).

668. אַפִּרְיוֹן **'appiryôwn**, *ap-pir-yone'*; prob. of Eg. der.; a *palanquin*:—chariot.

669. אֶפְרַיִם **'Ephrayim**, *ef-rah'-yim*; dual of a masc. form of 672; *double fruit*; *Ephrajim*, a son of Joseph; also the tribe descended from him, and its territory:—Ephraim Ephraimites

670. אֲפָרְסָי **'Âphârçay** (Chald.), *af-aw-re-sah'-ee;* of for. or. (only in the plur.); an *Apharesite* or inhabitant of an unknown region of Assyria:—Apharsite.

671. אֲפָרְסְכָי **'Ăpharçekay** (Chald.), *af-ar-sek-ah'ee;* or אֲפָרְסַתְכָי **'Ăpharçathkay** (Chald.), *af-ar-sath-kah'ee;* of for. or. (only in the plur.); an *Apharsekite* or *Apharsathkite*, an unknown Assyrian tribe:—Apharsachites, Apharsathchites.

672. אֶפְרָת **'Ephrâth**, *ef-rawth';* or אֶפְרָתָה **'Ephrâthâh**, *ef-raw'-thaw;* from 6509; *fruitfulness; Ephrath*, another name for Bethlehem; once (Psa. 132 : 6) perh. for *Ephraim;* also of an Israelitish woman:—Ephrath, Ephratah.

673. אֶפְרָתִי **'Ephrâthîy**, *ef-rawth-ee';* patrial from 672; an *Ephrathite* or an *Ephraimite:*—Ephraimite, Ephrathite.

674. אַפְּתֹם **'appᵉthôm** (Chald.), *ap-pe-thome';* of Pers. or.; *revenue;* others *at the last:*—revenue.

675. אֶצְבּוֹן **'Etsbôwn**, *ets-bone';* or אֶצְבֹּן **'Etsbôn**, *ets-bone';* of uncert. der.; *Etsbon*, the name of two Isr.:—Ezbon.

676. אֶצְבַּע **'etsba'**, *ets-bah';* from the same as 6648 (in the sense of *grasping*); some thing to *seize* with, i.e. a *finger;* by anal. a *toe:*—finger, toe.

677. אֶצְבַּע **'etsba'** (Chald.), *ets-bah';* corresp. to 676:—finger, toe.

678. אָצִיל **'âtsîyl**, *aw-tseel';* from 680 (in its secondary sense of *separation*); an *extremity* (Isa. 41 : 9), also a *noble:*—chief man, noble.

679. אַצִּיל **'atstsîyl**, *ats-tseel';* from 680 (in its primary sense of *uniting*); a *joint* of the hand (i.e. *knuckle*); also (accord. to some) a *party-wall* (Ezek. 41 : 8):—[arm] hole, great.

680. אָצַל **'âtsal**, *aw-tsal';* a prim. root; prop. to *join;* used only as a denom. from 681; to *separate;* hence to *select, refuse, contract:*—keep, reserve, straiten, take.

681. אֵצֶל **'êtsel**, *ay'-tsel;* from 680 (in the sense of *joining*); a *side;* (as a prep.) *near:*—at, (hard) by, (from) (beside), near (unto), toward, with. See also 1018.

682. אָצַל **'Âtsêl**, *aw-tsale';* from 680; *noble; Atsel*, the name of an Isr., and of a place in Pal.:—Azal, Azel.

683. אֲצַלְיָהוּ **'Ătsalyâhûw**, *ats-al-yaw'-hoo;* from 680 and 3050 prol.; *Jah has reserved; Atsaljah*, an Isr.:—Azaliah.

684. אֹצֶם **'Ôtsem**, *o'-tsem;* from an unused root prob. mean. to *be strong; strength* (i.e. *strong*); *Otsem*, the name of two Isr.:—Ozem.

685. אֶצְעָדָה **'ets'âdâh**, *ets-aw-daw';* a var. from 6807; prop. a *step-chain;* by anal. a *bracelet:*—bracelet, chain.

686. אָצַר **'âtsar**, *aw-tsar;* a prim. root; to *store* up:—(lay up in) store, (make) treasure (-r).

687. אֵצֶר **'Êtser**, *ay'-tser;* from 686; *treasure; Etser*, an Idumæan:—Ezer.

688. אֶקְדָּח **'eqdâch**, *ek-dawkh';* from 6916; *burning*, i.e. a *carbuncle* or other fiery gem:—carbuncle.

689. אַקּוֹ **'aqqôw**, *ak-ko';* prob. from 602; *slender*, i.e. the *ibex:*—wild goat.

690. אֲרָא **'Ărâ'**, *ar-aw';* prob. for 738; *lion; Ara*, an Isr.:—Ara.

691. אֶרְאֵל **'er'êl**, *er-ale';* prob. for 739; a h... (collect.):—valiant one.

692. אַרְאֵלִי **'Ar'êlîy**, *ar-ay-lee';* from 691; *heroic; Areli* (or an *Arelite*, collect.), an Isr. and his desc.:—Areli, Arelites.

693. אָרַב **'ârab**, *aw-rab';* a prim. root; to *lurk:*—(lie in) ambush (-ment), lay (lie in) wait.

694. אֲרָב **'Ărâb**, *ar-awb';* from 693; *ambush; Arab*, a place in Pal.:—Arab.

695. אֶרֶב **'ereb**, *eh'-reb;* from 693; *ambuscade:*—den, lie in wait.

696. אֹרֶב **'ôreb**, *o'-reb:* the same as 695:—wait.

אַרְבֵּאל **'Arbê'l.** See 1009.

697. אַרְבֶּה **'arbeh**, *ar-beh';* from 7235; a *locust* (from its rapid *increase*):—grasshopper, locust.

698. אָרֳבָה **'orŏbâh**, *or-ob-aw';* fem. of 696 (only in the plur.); *ambuscades:*—spoils.

699. אֲרֻבָּה **'ărubbâh**, *ar-oob-baw';* fem. part. pass. of 693 (as if for *lurking*); a *lattice;* (by impl.) a *window, dove-cot* (because of the pigeon-holes), *chimney* (with its apertures for smoke), *sluice* (with openings for water):—chimney, window.

700. אֲרֻבּוֹת **'Ărubbôwth**, *ar-oob-both;* plur. of 699; *Arubboth*, a place in Pal.:—Aruboth.

701. אַרְבִּי **'Arbîy**, *ar-bee';* patrial from 694; an *Arbite* or native of Arab:—Arbite.

702. אַרְבַּע **'arba'**, *ar-bah';* masc. אַרְבָּעָה **'arbâ'âh**, *ar-baw-aw';* from 7251; *four:*—four.

703. אַרְבַּע **'arba'** (Chald.), *ar-bah';* corresp. to 702:—four.

704. אַרְבַּע **'Arba'**, *ar-bah';* the same as 702; *Arba*, one of the Anakim:—Arba.

אַרְבָּעָה **'arbâ'âh.** See 702.

705. אַרְבָּעִים **'arbâ'îym**, *ar-baw-eem';* multiple of 702; *forty:*—forty.

706. אַרְבַּעְתַּיִם **'arba'tayim**, *ar-bah-tah'-yim;* dual of 702; *fourfold:*—fourfold.

707. אָרַג **'ârag**, *aw-rag';* a prim. root; to *plait* or *weave:*—weaver (-r).

708. אֶרֶג **'ereg**, *eh'-reg;* from 707; a *weaving;* a *braid;* also a *shuttle:*—beam, weaver's shuttle.

709. אַרְגֹּב **'Argôb**, *ar-gobe';* from the same as 7263; *stony; Argob*, a district of Pal.:—Argob.

710. אַרְגְּוָן **'argᵉvân**, *arg-ev-awn';* a var. for 713; *purple:*—purple.

711. אַרְגְּוָן **'argᵉvân** (Chald.), *arg-ev-awn';* corresp. to 710:—scarlet.

712. אַרְגָּז **'argâz**, *ar-gawz';* perh. from 7264 (in the sense of being *suspended*); a *box* (as a pannier):—coffer.

713. אַרְגָּמָן **'argâmân**, *ar-gaw-mawn';* of for. or.; *purple* (the color or the dyed stuff):—purple.

714. אַרְדְּ **'Ard**, *ard;* from an unused root prob. mean. to *wander; fugitive; Ard*, the name of two Isr.:—Ard.

715. אַרְדּוֹן **'Ardôwn**, *ar-dohn';* from the same as 714; *roaming; Ardon*, an Isr.:—Ardon.

716. אַרְדִּי **'Ardîy**, *ar-dee';* patron. from 714; an *Ardite* (collect.) or desc. of Ard:—Ardites.

717. אָרָה **'ârâh**, *aw-raw';* a prim. root; to *pluck:*—gather, pluck.

718. אֲרוּ **'ărûw** (Chald.), *ar-oo';* prob. akin to 431; *lo!:*—behold, lo.

719. אַרְוַד **'Arvad**, *ar-vad';* prob. from 7300; a refuge for the *roving; Arvad*, an island-city of Pal.:—Arvad.

720. אֲרוֹד **'Ărôwd**, *ar-ode';* an orth. var. of 719; *fugitive; Arod*, an Isr.:—Arod.

721. אַרְוָדִי **'Arvâdîy**, *ar-vaw-dee';* patrial from 719; an *Arvadite* or citizen of Arvad:—Arvadite.

722. אֲרוֹדִי **'Ărôwdîy**, *ar-o-dee';* patron. from 721; an *Arodite* or desc. of Arod:—Arodi, Arodites.

723. אֻרְוָה **'urvâh**, *oor-vaw';* or, אֲרָיָה **'ărâyâh**, *ar-aw-yah';* from 717 (in the sense of *feeding*); a *herding-place* for an animal:—stall.

724. אֲרוּכָה **'ărûwkâh**, *ar-oo-kaw';* or אֲרֻכָה **'ărûkâh**, *ar-oo-kaw';* fem. pass. part. of 748 (in the sense of *restoring* to soundness); *wholeness* (lit. or fig.):—health, made up, perfected.

725. אֲרוּמָה **'Ărûwmâh**, *ar-oo-maw':* a var. of 7316; *height; Arumah*, a place in Pal.:—Arumah.

726. אֲרוֹמִי° **'Ărôwmîy**, *ar-o-mee';* a clerical error for 130; an *Edomite* (as in the marg.):—Syrian.

727. אָרוֹן **'ârôwn**, *aw-rone';* or אָרֹן **'ârôn**, *aw-rone';* from 717 (in the sense of *gathering*); a *box:*—ark, chest, coffin.

728. אֲרַוְנָה **'Ăravnâh**, *ar-av-naw';* or (by transp.) אוֹרְנָה° **'Ôwrnâh**, *ore-naw';* or אַרְנִיָּה° **'Arnîyah**, *ar-nee-yaw';* all by orth. var. for 771; *Aravnah* (or *Arnijah* or *Ornah*), a Jebusite:—Araunah.

729. אָרַז **'âraz**, *aw-raz';* a prim. root; to be *firm;* used only in the pass. participle as a denom. from 730; of *cedar:*—made of cedar.

730. אֶרֶז **'erez**, *eh'-rez;* from 729; a *cedar* tree (from the tenacity of its roots):—cedar (tree).

731. אַרְזָה **'arzâh**, *ar-zaw';* fem. of 730; *cedar wainscoting:*—cedar work.

732. אָרַח **'ârach**, *aw-rakh';* a prim. root; to *travel:*—go, wayfaring (man).

733. אָרַח **'Ârach**, *aw-rakh';* from 732; *way-faring; Arach*, the name of three Isr.:—Arah.

734. אֹרַח **'ôrach**, *o'-rakh;* from 732; a well trodden *road* (lit. or fig.); also a *caravan:*—manner, path, race, rank, traveller, troop, [by-, high-] way.

735. אֹרַח **'ôrach** (Chald.), *o'-rakh;* corresp. to 734; a *road:*—way.

736. אֹרְחָה **'ôrᵉchâh**, *o-rekh-aw';* fem. act. part. of 732; a *caravan:*—(travelling) company.

737. אֲרֻחָה **'ărûchâh**, *ar-oo-khaw';* fem. pass. part. of 732 (in the sense of *appointing*); a *ration* of food:—allowance, diet, dinner, victuals.

738. אֲרִי **'ărîy**, *ar-ee';* or (prol.) אַרְיֵה **'aryêh**, *ar-yay';* from 717 (in the sense of *violence*); a *lion:*—(young) lion, + pierce [*from the marg.*].

739. אֲרִיאֵל **'ărîy'êl**, *ar-ee-ale';* or אֲרִאֵל **'ărî'êl**, *ar-ee-ale';* from 738 and 410; *lion of God*, i.e. *heroic:*—lionlike men.

740. אֲרִיאֵל **'Ărî'êl**, *ar-ee-ale';* the same as 739; *Ariel*, a symb. name for Jerusalem, also the name of an Isr.:—Ariel.

741. אֲרִאֵיל **'ărî'êyl**, *ar-ee-ale';* either by transposition for 739 or, more prob., an orth. var. for 2025; the *altar* of the Temple:—altar.

742. אֲרִידַי **'Ărîyday**, *ar-ee-dah'-ee;* of Pers. or.; *Aridai*, a son of Haman:—Aridai.

743. אֲרִידָתָא **'Ărîydâthâ'**, *ar-ee-daw-thaw';* of Pers. or.; *Aridatha*, a son of Haman:—Aridatha.

אַרְיֵה **'aryêh.** See 738.

744. אַרְיֵה **'aryêh** (Chald.), *ar-yay';* corresp. to 738:—lion.

745. אַרְיֵה **'Aryêh**, *ar-yay';* the same as 738; *lion; Arjeh*, an Isr.:—Arieh.

אֲרָיָה **'ărâyâh.** See 723.

746. אַרְיוֹךְ **'Ăryôwk**, *ar-yoke';* of for. or.; *Arjok*, the name of two Babylonians:—Arioch.

747. אֲרִיסַי **'Ărîyçay**, *ar-ee-sah'-ee;* of Pers. or.; *Arisai*, a son of Haman:—Arisai.

748. אָרַךְ **'ârak**, *aw-rak';* a prim. root; to be (caus. *make*) *long* (lit. or fig.):—defer, draw out, lengthen, (be, become, make, pro-) long, + (out-, over-) live, tarry (long).

749. אֲרַךְ **'ărak** (Chald.), *ar-ak';* prop. corresp. to 748, but used only in the sense of *reaching* to a given point; to *suit:*—be meet.

750. אָרֵךְ **'ârêk** *aw-rake';* from 748; *long:*—long [-suffering, -winged], patient, slow [to anger].

751. אֶרֶךְ **'Erek**, *eh'-rek;* from 748; *length; Erech*, a place in Bab.:—Erech.

752. אָרֹךְ **'ârôk**, *aw-roke';* from 748; *long:*—long.

753. אֹרֶךְ **'ôrek**, *o'-rek;* from 748; *length:*—+ forever, length, long.

754. אַרְכָּא **'arkâ'** (Chald.), *ar-kaw';* or אַרְכָּה **'arkâh** (Chald.), *arkaw';* from 749; *length:*—lengthening, prolonged.

755. אַרְכֻבָּה **'arkûbâh** (Chald.), *ar-koo-baw'* from an unused root corresp. to 7392 (in the sense of *bending* the knee); the *knee:*—knee.

אֲרֻכָה **'ărûkâh**. See 724.

756. אַרְכְּוַי **'Arkvay** (Chald.), *ar-kev-ah'ee;* patrial from 751; an *Arkevite* (collect.) or native of Erek:—Archevite.

757 אַרְכִּי **'Arkîy**, *ar-kee';* patrial from another place (in Pal.) of similar name with 751; an *Arkite* or native of Erek:—Archi, Archite.

758. אֲרָם **'Ărâm**, *arawm';* from the same as 759; the *highland; Aram* or Syria, and its inhabitants; also the name of a son of Shem, a grandson of Nahor, and of an Isr.:—Aram, Mesopotamia, Syria, Syrians.

759. אַרְמוֹן **'armôwn**, *ar-mone';* from an unused root (mean. to *be elevated*); a *citadel* (from its *height*):—castle, palace. Comp. 2038.

760. אֲרַם צוֹבָה **'Ăram Tsôbâh**, *ar-am' tso-baw';* from 758 and 6678; *Aram of Tsoba* (or Cœle-Syria):—Aram-zobah.

761. אֲרַמִּי **'Ărammîy**, *ar-am-mee';* patrial from 758; an *Aramite* or Aramæan:—Syrian, Aramitess.

762. אֲרָמִית **'Ărâmîyth**, *ar-aw-meeth';* fem. of 761; (only adv.) *in Aramæan:*—in the Syrian language (tongue), in Syriack.

763. אֲרַם נַהֲרַיִם **'Ăram Nahărayim**, *ar-am' nah-har-ah'-yim;* from 758 and the dual of 5104; *Aram of* (the) *two rivers* (Euphrates and Tigris) or Mesopotamia:—Aham-naharaim, Mesopotamia.

764. אַרְמֹנִי **'Armônîy**, *ar-mo-nee';* from 759; *palatial; Armoni*, an Isr.:—Armoni.

765. אֲרָן **'Ărân**, *ar-awn';* from 7442; *stridulous; Aran*, an Edomite:—Aran.

766. אֹרֶן **'ôren**, *o'-ren;* from the same as 765 (in the sense of *strength*); the *ash* tree (from its toughness):—ash.

767. אֹרֶן **'Ôren**, *o'-ren;* the same as 766; *Oren*, an Isr.:—Oren.

אָרֹן **'ârôn**. See 727.

768. אַרְנֶבֶת **'arnebeth**, *ar-neh'-beth;* of uncert. der.; the *hare:*—hare.

769. אַרְנוֹן **'Arnôwn**, *ar-nohn';* or אַרְנֹן **'Arnôn**, *ar-nohn';* from 7442; a *brawling* stream; the *Arnon*, a river east of the Jordan; also its territory:—Arnon.

אַרְנִיָּה° **'Arnîyah**. See 728.

770. אַרְנָן **'Arnân**, *ar-nawn';* prob. from the same as 769; *noisy; Arnan*, an Isr.:—Arnan.

771. אָרְנָן **'Ornân**, *or-nawn';* prob. from 766; *strong; Ornan*, a Jebusite:—Ornan. See 728.

772. אֲרַע **'ăra'** (Chald.), *ar-ah';* corresp. to 776; the *earth;* by impl. (fig.) *low:*—earth, inferior.

773. אַרְעִית **'ar'îyth** (Chald.), *arh-eeth';* fem. of 772; the *bottom:*—bottom.

774. אַרְפָּד **'Arpâd**, *ar-pawd';* from 7502; *spread* out; *Arpad*, a place in Syria:—Arpad, Arphad.

775. אַרְפַּכְשַׁד **'Arpakshad**, *ar-pak-shad';* prob. of for. or.; *Arpakshad*, a son of Noah; also the region settled by him:—Arphaxad.

776. אֶרֶץ **'erets**, *eh'-rets;* from an unused root prob. mean. to *be firm;* the *earth* (at large, or partitively a *land*):— × common, country, earth, field, ground, land, × nations, way, + wilderness, world.

777. אַרְצָא **'artsâ'**, *ar-tsaw';* from 776; *earthiness; Artsa*, an Isr.:—Arza.

778. אֲרַק **'ăraq** (Chald.), *ar-ak';* by transmutation for 772; the *earth:*—earth.

779. אָרַר **'ârar**, *aw-rar';* a prim. root; to *execrate:*— × bitterly curse.

780. אֲרָרַט **'Ărâraṭ**, *ar-aw-rat';* of for. or.; *Ararat* (or rather Armenia):—Ararat, Armenia.

781. אָרַשׂ **'âras**, *aw-ras';* a prim. root; to *engage* for matrimony:—betroth, espouse.

782. אֲרֶשֶׁת **'ăresheth**, *ar-eh'-sheth;* from 781 (in the sense of *desiring* to possess); a *longing* for:—request.

783. אַרְתַּחְשַׁשְׁתָּא **'Artachshashtâ'**, *ar-takh-shash-taw';* or אַרְתַּחְשַׁשְׁתְּא **'Artachshasht'**, *ar-takh-shasht';* or by perm. אַרְתַּחְשַׁסְתְּא **'Artachshaçt'**, *ar-takh-shast';* of for. or.; *Artachshasta* (or Artaxerxes), a title (rather than name) of several Pers. kings:—Artaxerxes.

784. אֵשׁ **'êsh**, *aysh;* a prim. word; *fire* (lit. or fig.):—burning, fiery, fire, flaming, hot.

785. אֶשׁ **'êsh** (Chald.), *aysh;* corresp. to 784:—flame.

786. אִשׁ **'îsh**, *eesh;* ident. (in or. and formation) with 784; *entity;* used only adv., there *is* or *are:*—are there, none can. Comp. 3426.

787. אשׁ **'ôsh** (Chald.), *ohsh;* corresp. (by transp. and abb.) to 803; a *foundation:*—foundation.

788. אַשְׁבֵּל **'Ashbêl**, *ash-bale';* prob. from the same as 7640; *flowing; Ashbel*, an Isr.:—Ashbel.

789. אַשְׁבֵּלִי **'Ashbêlîy**, *ash-bay-lee';* patron. from 788; an *Ashbelite* (collect.) or desc. of Ashbel:—Ashbelites.

790. אֶשְׁבָּן **'Eshbân**, *esh-bawn';* prob. from the same as 7644; *vigorous; Eshban*, an Idumæan:—Eshban.

791. אַשְׁבֵּעַ **'Ashbêa'**, *ash-bay'-ah;* from 7650; *adjurer; Asbeă*, an Isr.:—Ashbea.

792. אֶשְׁבַּעַל **'Eshba'al**, *esh-bah'-al;* from 376 and 1168; *man of Baal; Eshbaal* (or Ishbosheth), a son of King Saul:—Eshbaal.

793. אֶשֶׁד **'eshed**, *eh'-shed;* from an unused root mean. to *pour;* an *outpouring:*—stream.

794. אֲשֵׁדָה **'ăshêdâh**, *ash-ay-daw';* fem. of 793; a *ravine:*—springs.

795. אַשְׁדּוֹד **'Ashdôwd**, *ash-dode';* from 7703; *ravager; Ashdod*, a place in Pal.:—Ashdod.

796. אַשְׁדּוֹדִי **'Ashdôwdîy**, *ash-do-dee';* patrial from 795; an *Ashdodite* (often collect.) or inhabitant of Ashdod:—Ashdodites, of Ashdod.

797. אַשְׁדּוֹדִית **'Ashdôwdîyth**, *ash-do-deeth';* fem. of 796; (only adv.) *in the language of Ashdod:*—in the speech of Ashdod.

798. אַשְׁדּוֹת הַפִּסְגָּה **'Ashdôwth hap-Piçgâh**, *ash-doth' hap-pis-gaw';* from the plur. of 794 and 6449 with the art. interposed; *ravines of the Pisgah; Ashdoth-Pisgah*, a place east of the Jordan:—Ashdoth-pisgah.

799. אֶשְׁדָּת **'eshdâth**, *esh-dawth';* from 784 and 1881; a *fire-law:*—fiery law.

800. אֶשָּׁה **'eshshâh**, *esh-shaw';* fem. of 784; *fire:*—fire.

801. אִשָּׁה **'ishshâh**, *ish-shaw';* the same as 800, but used in a liturgical sense; prop. a *burnt-offering;* but occasionally of any *sacrifice:*—(offering, sacrifice), (made) by fire.

802. אִשָּׁה **'ishshâh**, *ish-shaw';* fem. of 376 or 582; irregular plur. נָשִׁים **nâshîym**, *naw-sheem';* a *woman* (used in the same wide sense as 582):—[adulter]ess, each, every, female, × many, + none, one, + together, wife, woman. Often unexpressed in English.

803. אֲשׁוּיָה° **'ăshûwyâh**, *ash-oo-yah';* fem. pass. part. from an unused root mean. to *found; foundation:*—foundation.

804. אַשּׁוּר **'Ashshûwr**, *ash-shoor';* or אַשֻּׁר **'Ashshûr**, *ash-shoor';* appar. from 833 (in the sense of *successful*); *Ashshur*, the second son of Shem; also his desc. and the country occupied by them (i.e. Assyria), its region and its empire:—Asshur, Assur, Assyria, Assyrians. See 838.

805. אֲשׁוּרִי **'Ăshûwrîy**, *ash-oo-ree';* or אַשּׁוּרִי **'Ashshûwrîy**, *ash-shoo-ree';* from a patrial word of the same form as 804; an *Ashurite* (collect.) or inhab. of Ashur, a district in Pal.:—Asshurim, Ashurites.

806. אַשְׁחוּר **'Ashchûwr**, *ash-khoor';* prob. from 7835; *black; Ashchur*, an Isr.:—Ashur.

807. אֲשִׁימָא **'Ăshîymâ'**, *ash-ee-maw';* of for. or.; *Ashima*, a deity of Hamath:—Ashima.

אֲשֵׁירָה **'ăshêyrah**. See 842.

808. אָשִׁישׁ **'âshîysh**, *aw-sheesh';* from the same as 784 (in the sense of *pressing* down firmly; comp. 803); a (ruined) *foundation:*—foundation.

809. אֲשִׁישָׁה **'ăshîyshâh**, *ash-ee-shaw';* fem. of 808; something closely *pressed* together, i.e. a *cake* of raisins or other comfits:—flagon.

810. אֶשֶׁךְ **'eshek**, *eh'-shek;* from an unused root (prob. mean. to *bunch* together); a *testicle* (as a *lump*):—stone.

811. אֶשְׁכּוֹל **'eshkôwl**, *esh-kole';* or אֶשְׁכֹּל **'eshkôl**, *esh-kole';* prob. prol. from 810; a *bunch of grapes* or other fruit:—cluster (of grapes).

812. אֶשְׁכֹּל **'Eshkôl**, *esh-kole';* the same as 811; *Eshcol*, the name of an Amorite, also of a valley in Pal.:—Eshcol.

813. אַשְׁכְּנַז **'Ashknaz**, *ash-ken-az';* of for. or.; *Ashkenaz*, a Japhethite, also his desc.:—Ashkenaz.

814. אֶשְׁכָּר **'eshkâr**, *esh-cawr';* for 7939; a *gratuity:*—gift, present.

815. אֶשֶׁל **'êshel**, *ay'-shel;* from a root of uncert. signif.; a *tamarisk* tree; by extens. a *grove* of any kind:—grove, tree.

816. אָשַׁם **'âsham**, *aw-sham';* or אָשֵׁם **'âshêm**, *aw-shame';* a prim. root; to *be guilty;* by impl. to *be punished* or *perish:*— × certainly, be (-come, made) desolate, destroy, × greatly, be (-come, found, hold) guilty, offend (acknowledge offence), trespass.

817. אָשָׁם **'âshâm**, *aw-shawm';* from 816; *guilt;* by impl. a *fault;* also a *sin-offering:*—guiltiness, (offering for) sin, trespass (offering).

818. אָשֵׁם **'âshêm**, *aw-shame';* from 816; *guilty;* hence *presenting a sin-offering:*—one which is faulty, guilty.

819 אַשְׁמָה **'ashmâh**, *ash-maw';* fem. of 817; *guiltiness*, a *fault*, the *presentation of a sin-offering:*—offend, sin, (cause of) trespass (-ing, offering).

אַשְׁמוּרָה **'ashmûrâh**. See 821.

820. אַשְׁמָן **'ashmân**, *ash-mawn';* prob. from 8081; a *fat* field:—desolate place.

821. אַשְׁמֻרָה **'ashmûrâh**, *ash-moo-raw';* or אַשְׁמוּרָה **'ashmûwrâh**, *ash-moo-raw';* or אַשְׁמֹרֶת **'ashmôreth**, *ash-mo'-reth;* (fem.) from 8104; a night *watch:*—watch.

822. אֶשְׁנָב **'eshnâb**, *esh-nawb';* appar. from an unused root (prob. mean. to *leave interstices*); a latticed *window:*—casement, lattice.

823. אַשְׁנָה **'Ashnâh**, *ash-naw';* prob. a var. for 3466; *Ashnah*, the name of two places in Pal.:—Ashnah.

824. אֶשְׁעָן **'Esh'ân**, *esh-awn';* from 8172; *support; Eshan*, a place in Pal.:—Eshean.

825. אַשָּׁף **'ashshâph**, *ash-shawf';* from an unused root (prob. mean. to *lisp*, i.e. *practise enchantment*); a *conjurer:*—astrologer.

826. אַשָּׁף **'ashshâph** (Chald.), *ash-shawf';* corresp. to 825:—astrologer.

827. אַשְׁפָּה **'ashpâh**, *ash-paw';* perh. (fem.) from the same as 825 (in the sense of *covering*); a *quiver* or arrow-case:—quiver.

828. אַשְׁפְּנַז **'Ashpnaz**, *ash-pen-az';* of for. or.; *Ashpenaz*, a Bab. eunuch:—Ashpenaz.

829. אֶשְׁפָּר **'eshpâr**, *esh-pawr';* of uncert. der.; a measured *portion:*—good piece (of flesh).

830. אַשְׁפֹּת **'ashpôth**, *ash-pohth'*; or אַשְׁפּוֹת **'ashpôwth**, *ash-pohth'*; or (contr.) שְׁפֹת **shephôth**, *shef-ohth'*; plur. of a noun of the same form as 827, from 8192 (in the sense of *scraping*); a heap of *rubbish* or *filth*:—dung (hill).

831. אַשְׁקְלוֹן **'Ashqelôwn**, *ash-kel-one'*; prob. from 8254 in the sense of *weighing*-place (i.e. *mart*); *Ashkelon*, a place in Pal.:—Ashkelon, Askalon.

832. אֶשְׁקְלוֹנִי **'Eshqelôwnîy**, *esh-kel-o-nee'*; patrial from 831; an *Ashkelonite* (collect.) or inhab. of Ashkelon:—Eshkalonites.

833. אָשַׁר **'âshar**, *aw-shar'*; or אָשֵׁר **'âshêr**, *aw-share'*; a prim. root; to *be straight* (used in the widest sense, espec. to *be level, right, happy*); fig. to *go forward, be honest, prosper*:—(call, be) bless (-ed, happy), go, guide, lead, relieve.

834. אֲשֶׁר **'ăsher**, *ash-er'*; a prim. rel. pron. (of every gend. and numb.); *who, which, what, that*; also (as adv. and conjunc.) *when, where, how, because, in order that*, etc.:— × after, × alike, as (soon as), because, × every, for, + forasmuch, + from whence, + how (-soever), × if, (so) that ([thing] which, wherein), × though, + until, + whatsoever, when, where (+ -as, -in, -of, -on, -soever, -with), which, whilst, + whither (-soever), who (-m, -soever, -se). As it is indeclinable, it is often accompanied by the personal pron. expletively, used to show the connection.

835. אֶשֶׁר **'esher**, *eh'-sher*; from 833; *happiness*; only in masc. plur. constr. as interjec., how *happy!*:—blessed, happy.

836. אָשֵׁר **'Âshêr**, *aw-share'*; from 833; *happy*; *Asher*, a son of Jacob, and the tribe descended from him, with its territory; also a place in Pal.:—Asher.

837. אֹשֶׁר **'ôsher**, *o'-sher*; from 833; *happiness*:—happy.

838. אָשֻׁר **'âshûr**, *aw-shoor'*; or אַשֻּׁר **ashshûr**, *ash-shoor'*; from 833 in the sense of *going*; a *step*:—going, step.

839. אֲשֻׁר **'ăshûr**, *ash-oor'*; contr. for 8391; the *cedar* tree or some other light elastic wood:—Ashurite.

אַשֻּׁר **'Ashshûr**. See 804, 838.

840. אֲשַׂרְאֵל **'Ăsar'êl**, *as-ar-ale'*; by orth. var. from 833 and 410; *right of God*; *Asarel*, an Isr.:—Asareel.

841. אֲשַׂרְאֵלָה **'Ăsar'êlâh**, *as-ar-ale'-aw*; from the same as 840; *right towards God*; *Asarelah*, an Isr.:—Asarelah. Comp. 3480.

842. אֲשֵׁרָה **'ăshêrâh**, *ash-ay-raw'*; or אֲשֵׁירָה **'ăshêyrâh**, *ash-ay-raw'*; from 833; *happy*; *Asherah* (or Astarte) a Phœnician goddess; also an *image* of the same:—grove. Comp. 6253.

843. אָשֵׁרִי **'Âshêrîy**, *aw-shay-ree'*; patron. from 836; an *Asherite* (collect.) or desc. of Asher:—Asherites.

844. אַשְׂרִיאֵל **'Asrîy'êl**, *as-ree-ale'*; an orth. var. for 840; *Asriel*, the name of two Isr.:—Ashriel, Asriel.

845. אַשְׂרִאֵלִי **'Asrî'êlîy**, *as-ree-ale-ee'*; patron. from 844; an *Asrielite* (collect.) or desc. of Asriel:—Asrielites.

846. אֻשַּׁרְנָא **'ushsharnâ'** (Chald.), *oosh-ar-naw'*; from a root corresp. to 833; a *wall* (from its uprightness):—wall.

847. אֶשְׁתָּאֹל **'Eshtâ'ôl**, *esh-taw-ole'*; or אֶשְׁתָּאוֹל **'Eshtâ'ôwl**, *esh-taw-ole'*; prob. from 7592; *intreaty*; *Eshtaol*, a place in Pal.:—Eshtaol.

848. אֶשְׁתָּאֻלִי **'Eshtâ'ûlîy**, *esh-taw-oo-lee'*; patrial from 847; an *Eshtaolite* (collect.) or inhab. of Eshtaol:—Eshtaulites.

849. אֶשְׁתַּדּוּר **'eshtaddûwr** (Chald.), *esh-tad-dure'*; from 7712 (in a bad sense); *rebellion*:—sedition.

850. אֶשְׁתּוֹן **'Eshtôwn**, *esh-tone'*; prob. from the same as 7764; *restful*; *Eshton*, an Isr.:—Eshton.

851. אֶשְׁתְּמֹעַ **'Eshtemôa'**, *esh-tem-o'-ah*; or אֶשְׁתְּמוֹעַ **'Eshtemôwa'**, *esh-tem-o'-ah*; or אֶשְׁתְּמֹה **'Eshtemôh**, *esh-tem-o'*; from 8085 (in the sense of *obedience*); *Eshtemoa* or *Eshtemoh*, a place in Pal.:—Eshtemoa, Eshtemoh.

אַתְ **'ath**. See 859.

852. אָת **'âth** (Chald.), *awth*; corresp. to 226; a *portent*:—sign.

853. אֵת **'êth**, *ayth*; appar. contr. from 226 in the demonstr. sense of *entity*; prop. *self* (but gen. used to point out more def. the object of a verb or prep., *even* or *namely*):—[*as such unrepresented in English*.]

854. אֵת **'êth**, *ayth*; prob. from 579; prop. *nearness* (used only as a prep. or adv.), *near*; hence gen. *with, by, at, among*, etc.:—against, among, before, by, for, from, in (-to), (out) of, with. Often with another prep. prefixed.

855. אֵת **'êth**, *ayth*; of uncert. der.; a *hoe* or other digging implement:—coulter, plowshare.

אַתָּ **'attâ**. See 859.

אָתָא **'âthâ'**. See 857.

856. אֶתְבַּעַל **'Ethba'al**, *eth-bah'-al*; from 854 and 1168; *with Baal*; *Ethbaal*, a Phœnician king:—Ethbaal.

857. אָתָה **'âthâh**, *aw-thaw'*; or אָתָא **'âthâ'**, *aw-thaw'*; a prim. root [collat. to 225 contr.]; to *arrive*:—(be-, things to) come (upon), bring.

858. אָתָה **'âthâh** (Chald.), *aw-thaw'*; or אָתָא **'âthâ'** (Chald.), *aw-thaw'*; corresp. to 857:—(be-) come, bring.

859. אַתָּה **'attâh**, *at-taw'*; or (short.) אַתָּ **'attâ**, *at-taw'*; or אַתְ **'ath**, *ath*; fem. (irreg.) sometimes אַתִּי **'attîy**, *at-tee'*; plur. masc. אַתֶּם **'attem**, *at-tem'*; fem. אַתֶּן **'atten**, *at-ten'*; or אַתֵּנָה **'attênâh**, *at-tay'-naw*; or אַתֵּנָּה **'attennâh**, *at-tane'-naw*; a prim. pron. of the sec. pers.; *thou* and *thee*, or (plur.) *ye* and *you*:—thee, thou, ye, you.

860. אָתוֹן **'âthôwn**, *aw-thone'*; prob. from the same as 386 (in the sense of *patience*); a female *ass* (from its docility):—(she) ass.

861. אַתּוּן **'attûwn** (Chald.), *at-toon'*; prob. from the corresp. to 784; prob. a *fire-place*, i.e. *furnace*:—furnace.

862. אַתּוּק **'attûwq**, *at-tooke'*; or אַתִּיק **'attîyq**, *at-teek'*; from 5423 in the sense of *decreasing*; a *ledge* or offset in a building:—gallery.

אַתִּי **'attîy**. See 859.

863. אִתַּי **'Ittay**, *it-tah'ee*; or אִיתַי **'Iythay**, *ee-thah'ee*; from 854; *near*; *Ittai* or *Ithai*, the name of a Gittite and of an Isr.:—Ithai, Ittai.

864. אֵתָם **'Êthâm**, *ay-thawm'*; of Eg. der.; *Etham*, a place in the Desert:—Etham.

אַתֶּם **'attem**. See 859.

865. אֶתְמוֹל **'ethmôwl**, *eth-mole'*; or אִתְמוֹל **'ithmôwl**, *ith-mole'*; or אֶתְמוּל **'ethmûwl**, *eth-mool'*; prob. from 853 or 854 and 4136; *heretofore*; def. *yesterday*:— + before (that) time, + heretofore, of late (old), + times past, yester[day].

אַתֶּן **atten**. See 859.

866. אֶתְנָה **'ethnâh**, *eth-naw'*; from 8566; a *present* (as the price of harlotry):—reward.

אַתֵּנָה **'attênâh**, or אַתֵּנָּה **'attennâh**. See 859.

867. אֶתְנִי **'Ethnîy**, *eth-nee'*; perh. from 866; *munificence*; *Ethni*, an Isr.:—Ethni.

868. אֶתְנַן **'ethnan**, *eth-nan'*; the same as 866; a *gift* (as the price of harlotry or idolatry):—hire, reward.

869. אֶתְנַן **'Ethnan**, *eth-nan'*; the same as 868 in the sense of 867; *Ethnan*, an Isr.:—Ethnan.

870. אֲתַר **'ăthar** (Chald.), *ath-ar'*; from a roo corresp. to that of 871; a *place*; (adv *after*:—after, place.

871. אֲתָרִים **'Âthârîym**, *ath-aw-reem'*; plu from an unused root (prob. mean. t *step*); *places*; *Atharim*, a place near Pal.:—spies.

ב

872. בְּאָה **be'âh**, *bě-aw'*; from 935; an *entrance* t a building:—entry.

873. בִּאוּשׁ **bî'ûwsh** (Chald.) *be-oosh'*; from 888 *wicked*:—bad.

874. בָּאַר **bâ'ar**, *baw-ar'*; a prim. root; to *dig* by anal. to *engrave*; fig. to *explain*:—de clare, (make) plain (-ly).

875. בְּאֵר **be'êr**, *bě-ayr'*; from 874; a *pit*; espec. *well*:—pit, well.

876. בְּאֵר **Be'êr**, *bě-ayr'*; the same as 875; *Beër*, place in the Desert, also one in Pal.:— Beer.

877. בֹּאר **bô'r**, *bore*; from 874; a *cistern*:—cistern

878. בְּאֵרָא **Be'êrâ'**, *bě-ay-raw'*; from 875; a *well* *Beëra*, an Isr.:—Beera.

879. בְּאֵר אֵלִים **Be'êr 'Êlîym**, *bě-ayr' ay-leem* from 875 and the plur. of 410; *wel of heroes*; *Beër-Elim*, a place in the Desert:—Beer elim.

880. בְּאֵרָה **Be'êrâh**, *bě-ay-raw'*; the same a 878; *Beërah*, an Isr.:—Beerah.

881. בְּאֵרוֹת **Be'êrôwth**, *bě-ay-rohth'*; fem. plur of 875; *wells*; *Beëroth*, a place in Pal.:— Beeroth.

882. בְּאֵרִי **Be'êrîy**, *bě-ay-ree'*; from 875; *foun tained*; *Beëri*, the name of a Hittite an of an Isr.:—Beeri.

883. בְּאֵר לַחַי רֹאִי **Be'êr la-Chay Rô'îy** *bě-ayr' lakh-ah'ee ro-ee'*; fror 875 and 2416 (with pref.) and 7203; *well of a livin (One) my Seer*; *Beër-Lachai-Roï*, a place in the Des ert:—Beer-lahai-roi.

884. בְּאֵר שֶׁבַע **Be'êr Sheba'**, *bě-ayr' sheh'-bah* from 875 and 7651 (in the sense o 7650); *well of an oath*; *Beër-Sheba*, a place in Pal.:— Beer-shebah.

885. בְּאֵרֹת בְּנֵי־יַעֲקָן **Be'êrôth Benêy-Ya'ăqan**, *bě-ay-roth' bě-nay yah-a-can'*; from the fem. plur. of 875, and the plur contr. of 1121, and 3292; *wells of* (the) *sons of Jaakan Beeroth-Bene-Jaakan*, a place in the Desert:—Beerot of the children of Jaakan.

886. בְּאֵרֹתִי **Be'êrôthîy**, *bě-ay-ro-thee'*; patria from 881; a *Beërothite* or inhab. o Beëroth:—Beerothite.

887. בָּאַשׁ **bâ'ash**, *baw-ash'*; a prim. root; t *smell* bad; fig. to *be offensive* morally:— (make to) be abhorred (had in abomination, loath some, odious), (cause a, make to) stink (-ing savour) × utterly.

888. בְּאֵשׁ **be'êsh** (Chald.), *bě-aysh'*; corresp. t 887:—displease.

889. בְּאֹשׁ **be'ôsh**, *bě-oshe'*; from 877; a *stench*:— stink.

890. בָּאְשָׁה **bo'shâh**, *bosh-aw'*; fem. of 889 *stink-weed* or any other noxious o useless plant:—cockle.

891. בְּאֻשִׁים **be'ûshîym**, *bě-oo-sheem'*; plur. o 889; *poison-berries*:—wild grapes.

892. בָּבָה **bâbâh**, *baw-baw'*; fem. act. part. o an unused root mean. to *hollow* out something *hollowed* (as a *gate*), i.e. the *pupil* of th eye:—apple [of the eye].

893. בֵּבַי **Bêbay**, *bay-bah'ee*; prob. of for. or. *Bebai*, an Isr.:—Bebai.

894. בָּבֶל **Bâbel**, *baw-bel'*; from 1101; *confusion* *Babel* (i.e. Babylon), including Babylon and the Bab. empire:—Babel, Babylon.

895. בָּבֶל **Bâbel** (Chald.), *baw-bel'*; corresp. t 894:—Babylon.

896. בַּבְלִי **Bablîy** (Chald.), *bab-lee'*; patrial fror 895; a *Babylonian*:—Babylonia.

7. בַּג **bag**, *bag;* a Pers. word; *food:*—spoil [*from the marg. for* 957.]

8. בָּגַד **bâgad**, *baw-gad';* a prim. root; to *cover* (with a garment); fig. to *act covertly;* by pl. to *pillage:*—deal deceitfully (treacherously, unthfully), offend, transgress (-or), (depart), treachous (dealer, -ly, man), unfaithful (-ly, man), × very.

9. בֶּגֶד **beged**, *behg'-ed;* from 898; a *covering,* i.e. clothing; also *treachery* or *pillage:*—parel, cloth (-es, -ing), garment, lap, rag, raiment, be, × very [treacherously], vesture, wardrobe.

0. בֹּגְדוֹת **bôgᵉdôwth**, *bohg-ed-ōhth;* fem. plur. act. part. of 898; *treacheries:*—treachous.

1. בָּגוֹד **bâgôwd**, *baw-gode';* from 898; *treacherous:*—treacherous.

2. בִּגְוַי **Bigvay**, *big-vah'ee;* prob. of for. or.; *Bigvai,* an Isr.:—Bigvai.

3. בִּגְתָא **Bigthâʼ**, *big-thaw';* of Pers. der.; *Bigtha,* a eunuch of Xerxes:—Bigtha.

4. בִּגְתָן **Bigthân**, *big-thawn';* or בִּגְתָנָא **Bigthânâʼ**, *big-thaw'-naw;* of similar riv. to 903; *Bigthan* or *Bigthana,* a eunuch of rxes:—Bigthan, Bigthana.

5. בַּד **bad**, *bad;* from 909; prop. *separation;* by impl. a *part* of the body, *branch* of a tree, r for carrying; fig. *chief* of a city; espec. (with ep. pref.) as adv., *apart, only, besides:*—alone, art, bar, besides, branch, by self, of each alike, expt, only, part, staff, strength.

6. בַּד **bad**, *bad;* perh. from 909 (in the sense of *divided* fibres); flaxen *thread* or yarn; nce a *linen* garment:—linen.

7. בַּד **bad**, *bad;* from 908; a *brag* or *lie;* also a *liar:*—liar, lie.

8. בָּדָא **bâdâʼ**, *baw-daw';* a prim. root; (fig.) to *invent:*—devise, feign.

9. בָּדַד **bâdad**, *baw-dad';* a prim. root; to *divide,* i.e. (reflex.) *be solitary:*—alone.

0. בָּדָד **bâdâd**, *baw-dawd';* from 909; *separate;* adv. *separately:*—alone, desolate, only, litary.

1. בְּדַד **Bᵉdad**, *bed-ad';* from 909; *separation; Bedad,* an Edomite:—Bedad.

2. בֵּדְיָה **Bêdᵉyâh**, *bay-dĕ-yaw';* prob. shortened for 5662; *servant of Jehovah; Bedejah,* Isr.:—Bedeiah.

3. בְּדִיל **bᵉdîyl**, *bed-eel';* from 914; *alloy* (because *removed* by smelting); by anal. *n:*—+ plummet, tin.

4. בָּדַל **bâdal**, *baw-dal';* a prim. root; to *divide* (in var. senses lit. or fig., *separate, stinguish, differ, select,* etc.):—(make, put) difference, divide (asunder), (make) separate (self, -ation), ver (out), × utterly.

5. בָּדָל **bâdâl**, *baw-dawl';* from 914; a *part:*—piece.

6. בְּדֹלַח **bᵉdôlach**, *bed-o'-lakh;* prob. from 914; something in *pieces,* i.e. *bdellium,* a agrant) gum (perh. *amber*); others a *pearl:*—bdelm.

7. בְּדָן **Bᵉdân**, *bed-awn';* prob. short. for 5658; *servile; Bedan,* the name of two Isr.:—edan.

8. בָּדַק **bâdaq**, *baw-dak';* a prim. root; to *gap* open; used only as a denom. from 919; to *end* a breach:—repair.

9. בֶּדֶק **bedeq**, *beh'-dek;* from 918; a *gap* or *leak* (in a building or a ship):—breach, calker.

0. בִּדְקַר **Bidqar**, *bid-car';* prob. from 1856 with prep. pref.; *by stabbing,* i.e. *assassin; dkar,* an Isr.:—Bidkar.

1. בְּדַר **bᵉdar** (Chald.), *bed-ar';* corresp. (by transp.) to 6504; to *scatter:*—scatter.

2. בֹּהוּ **bôhûw**, *bo'-hoo;* from an unused root (mean. to *be empty*); a *vacuity,* i.e. (superdally) an undistinguishable *ruin:*—emptiness, void.

3. בַּהַט **bahat**, *bah'-hat;* from an unused root (prob. mean. to *glisten*); white *marble* or rh. *alabaster:*—red [marble].

4. בְּהִילוּ **bᵉhîylûw** (Chald.), *bĕ-hee-loo';* from 927; a *hurry;* only adv. *hastily:*—in aste.

925. בָּהִיר **bâhîyr**, *baw-here';* from an unused root (mean. to *be bright*); *shining:*—bright.

926. בָּהַל **bâhal**, *baw-hal';* a prim. root; to *tremble* inwardly (or *palpitate*), i.e. (fig.) *be* (caus. *make*) (suddenly) *alarmed* or *agitated;* by impl. to *hasten* anxiously:—be (make) affrighted (afraid, amazed, dismayed, rash), (be, get, make) haste (-n, -y, -ily), (give) speedy (-ily), thrust out, trouble, vex.

927. בְּהַל **bᵉhal** (Chald.), *bĕ-hal';* corresp. to 926; to *terrify, hasten:*—in haste, trouble.

928. בֶּהָלָה **behâlâh**, *beh-haw-law';* from 926; *panic, destruction:*—terror, trouble.

929. בְּהֵמָה **bᵉhêmâh**, *bĕ-hay-maw';* from an unused root (prob. mean. to be *mute*); prop. a *dumb* beast; espec. any large quadruped or *animal* (often collect.):—beast, cattle.

930. בְּהֵמוֹת **bᵉhêmôwth**, *bĕ-hay-mōhth';* in form a plur. of 929, but really a sing. of Eg. der.; a *water-ox,* i.e. the *hippopotamus* or Nile-horse:—Behemoth.

931. בֹּהֶן **bôhen**, *bo'-hen;* from an unused root appar. mean. to *be thick;* the *thumb* of the hand or *great toe* of the foot:—thumb, great toe.

932. בֹּהַן **Bôhan**, *bo'-han;* an orth. var. of 931; *thumb; Bohan,* an Isr.:—Bohan.

933. בֹּהַק **bôhaq**, *bo'-hak;* from an unused root mean. to *be pale;* white *scurf:*—freckled spot.

934. בֹּהֶרֶת **bôhereth**, *bo-heh'-reth;* fem. act. part. of the same as 925; a *whitish* spot on the skin:—bright spot.

935. בּוֹא **bôwʼ**, *bo;* a prim. root; to *go* or *come* (in a wide variety of applications):—abide, apply, attain, × be, befall, + besiege, bring (forth, in, into, to pass), call, carry, × certainly, (cause, let, thing for) to come (against, in, out, upon, to pass), depart, × doubtless again, + eat, + employ, (cause to) enter (in, into, -tering, -trance, -try), be fallen, fetch, + follow, get, give, go (down, in, to war), grant, + have, × indeed, [in-]vade, lead, lift [up], mention, pull in, put, resort, run (down), send, set, × (well) stricken [in age], × surely, take (in), way.

בּוּב **bûwb**. See 892, 5014.

936. בּוּז **bûwz**, *booz;* a prim. root; to *disrespect:*—contemn, despise, × utterly.

937. בּוּז **bûwz**, *booz;* from 936; *disrespect:*—contempt (-uously), despised, shamed.

938. בּוּז **Bûwz**, *booz;* the same as 937; *Buz,* the name of a son of Nahor, and of an Isr.:—Buz.

939. בּוּזָה **bûwzâh**, *boo-zaw';* fem. pass. part. of 936; something *scorned;* an object of *contempt:*—despised.

940. בּוּזִי **Bûwzîy**, *boo-zee';* patron. from 938; a *Buzite* or desc. of Buz:—Buzite.

941. בּוּזִי **Bûwzîy**, *boo-zee';* the same as 940, *Buzi,* an Isr.:—Buzi.

942. בַּוַּי **Bavvay**, *bav-vah'ee;* prob. of Pers. or.; *Bavvai,* an Isr.:—Bavai.

943. בּוּךְ **bûwk**, *book;* a prim. root; to *involve* (lit. or fig.):—be entangled (perplexed).

944. בּוּל **bûwl**, *bool;* for 2981; *produce* (of the earth, etc.):—food, stock.

945. בּוּל **Bûwl**, *bool;* the same as 944 (in the sense of *rain*); *Bul,* the eighth Heb. month:—Bul.

בּוּם **bûwm**. See 1116.

946. בּוּנָה **Bûwnâh**, *boo-naw';* from 995; *discretion; Bunah,* an Isr.:—Bunah.

בּוּנִי **Bûwnîy**. See 1138.

947. בּוּס **bûwç**, *boos;* a prim. root; to *trample* (lit. or fig.):—loath, tread (down, under [foot]), be polluted.

948. בּוּץ **bûwts**, *boots;* from an unused root (of the same form) mean. to *bleach,* i.e. (intrans.) *be white;* prob. *cotton* (of some sort):—fine (white) linen.

949. בּוֹצֵץ **Bôwtsêts**, *bo-tsates';* from the same as 948; *shining; Botsets,* a rock near Michmash:—Bozez.

950. בּוּקָה **bûwqâh**, *boo-kaw';* fem. pass. part. of an unused root (mean. to *be hollow*); *emptiness* (as adj.):—empty.

951. בּוֹקֵר **bôwkêr**, *bo-kare';* prop. act. part. from 1239 as denom. from 1241; a *cattle-tender:*—herdman.

952. בּוּר **bûwr**, *boor;* a prim. root; to *bore,* i.e. (fig.) *examine:*—declare.

953. בּוֹר **bôwr**, *bore;* from 952 (in the sense of 877); a pit *hole* (espec. one used as a *cistern* or *prison*):—cistern, dungeon, fountain, pit, well.

954. בּוּשׁ **bûwsh**, *boosh;* a prim. root; prop. to *pale,* i.e. by impl. to *be ashamed;* also (by impl.) to *be disappointed,* or *delayed:*—(be, make, bring to, cause, put to, with, a-) shame (-d), be (put to) confounded (-fusion), become dry, delay, be long.

955. בּוּשָׁה **bûwshâh**, *boo-shaw';* fem. part. pass. of 954; *shame:*—shame.

956. בּוּת **bûwth** (Chald.), *booth;* appar. denom. from 1005; to *lodge* over night:—pass the night.

957. בַּז **baz**, *baz;* from 962; *plunder:*—booty, prey, spoil (-ed).

958. בָּזָא **bâzâʼ**, *baw-zaw';* a prim. root; prob. to *cleave:*—spoil.

959. בָּזָה **bâzâh**, *baw-zaw';* a prim. root; to *disesteem:*—despise, disdain, contemn (-ptible), + think to scorn, vile person.

960. בָּזֹה **bâzôh**, *baw-zo';* from 959; *scorned:*—despise.

961. בִּזָּה **bizzâh**, *biz-zaw';* fem. of 957; *booty:*—prey, spoil.

962. בָּזַז **bâzaz**, *baw-zaz';* a prim. root; to *plunder:*—catch, gather, (take) for a prey, rob (-ber), spoil, take (away, spoil), × utterly.

963. בִּזָּיוֹן **bizzâyôwn**, *biz-zaw-yone';* from 959:—*disesteem:*—contempt.

964. בִּזְיוֹתְיָה **bizyôwthᵉyâh**, *biz-yo-thĕ-yaw';* from 959 and 3050; *contempts of Jah; Bizjothjah,* a place in Pal.:—Bizjothjah.

965. בָּזָק **bâzâq**, *baw-zawk';* from an unused root mean. to *lighten;* a *flash* of lightning:—flash of lightning.

966. בֶּזֶק **Bezeq**, *beh'-zek;* from 965; *lightning; Bezek,* a place in Pal.:—Bezek.

967. בָּזַר **bâzar**, *baw-zar';* a prim. root; to *disperse:*—scatter.

968. בִּזְּתָא **Bizthâʼ**, *biz-thaw';* of Pers. or.; *Biztha,* a eunuch of Xerxes:—Biztha.

969. בָּחוֹן **bâchôwnʼ**, *baw-khone';* from 974; an *assayer* of metals:—tower.

970. בָּחוּר **bâchûwr**, *baw-khoor';* or בָּחֻר **bâchûr**, *baw-khoor';* part. pass. of 977; prop. *selected,* i.e. a *youth* (often collect.):—(choice) young (man), chosen, × hole.

בְּחוּרוֹת **bᵉchûwrôwth**. See 979.

בַּחוּרִים **Bachûwrîym**. See 980.

971. בַּחִין° **bachîyn**, *bakh-een';* another form of 975; a watch-*tower* of besiegers:—tower.

972. בָּחִיר **bâchîyr**, *baw-kheer';* from 977; *select:*—choose, chosen one, elect.

973. בָּחַל **bâchal**, *baw-khal';* a prim. root; to *loathe:*—abhor, get hastily [*from the marg. for* 926].

974. בָּחַן **bâchan**, *baw-khan';* a prim. root; to *test* (espec. metals); gen. and fig. to *investigate:*—examine, prove, tempt, try (trial).

975. בַּחַן **bachan**, *bakh'-an;* from 974 (in the sense of keeping a *look-out*); a watch-*tower:*—tower.

976. בֹּחַן **bôchan**, *bo'-khan;* from 974; *trial:*—tried.

977. בָּחַר **bâchar**, *baw-khar';* a prim. root; prop. to *try,* i.e. (by impl.) *select:*—acceptable, appoint, choose (choice), excellent, join, be rather, require.

בָּחֻר **bâchûr**. See 970.

978. בַּחֲרוּמִי **Bachărûwmîy**, *bakh-ar-oo-mee';* patrial from 980 (by transp.); a *Bacharumite* or inhab. of Bachurim:—Baharumite.

979. בְּחֻרוֹת **bᵉchûrôwth**, *bekh-oo-rothe';* or בְּחוּרוֹת **bᵉchûwrôwth**, *bekh-oo-roth';* fem. plur. of 970; also (masc. plur.) בְּחֻרִים **bᵉchûrîym**, *bekh-oo-reem';* *youth* (collect. and abstr.):—young men, youth.

980. בַּחֻרִים **Bachûrîym**, *bakh-oo-reem'*; or בַּחוּרִים **Bachûwrîym**, *bakh-oo-reem'*; masc. plur. of 970; *young men; Bachurim*, a place in Pal.:—Bahurim.

981. בָּטָא **bâṭâ'**, *baw-taw'*; or בָּטָה **bâṭâh**, *baw-taw'*; a prim. root; to *babble*; hence to *vociferate* angrily:—pronounce, speak (unadvisedly).

982. בָּטַח **bâṭach**, *baw-takh'*; a prim. root; prop. to *hie* for refuge [but not so *precipitately* as 2620]; fig. to *trust*, be *confident* or *sure*:—be bold (confident, secure, sure), careless (one, woman), put confidence, (make to) hope, (put, make to) trust.

983. בֶּטַח **beṭach**, *beh'-takh*; from 982; prop. a place of *refuge*; abstr. *safety*, both the fact (*security*) and the feeling (*trust*); often (adv. with or without prep.) *safely*:—assurance, boldly, (without) care (-less), confidence, hope, safe (-ly, -ty), secure, surely.

984. בֶּטַח **Beṭach**, *beh'-takh*; the same as 983; *Betach*, a place in Syria:—Betah.

985. בִּטְחָה **biṭchâh**, *bit-khaw'*; fem. of 984; *trust*:—confidence.

986. בִּטָּחוֹן **biṭṭâchôwn**, *bit-taw-khone'*; from 982; *trust*:—confidence, hope.

987. בַּטֻּחוֹת **baṭṭûchôwth**, *bat-too-khōth'*; fem. plur. from 982; *security*:—secure.

988. בָּטֵל **bâṭêl**, *baw-tale'*; a prim. root; to *desist* from labor:—cease.

989. בְּטֵל **beṭêl** (Chald.), *bet-ale'*; corresp. to 988; to *stop*:—(cause, make to), cease, hinder.

990. בֶּטֶן **beṭen**, *beh'-ten*; from an unused root prob. mean. to *be hollow*; the *belly*, espec. the *womb*; also the *bosom* or *body* of anything:—belly, body, + as they be born, + within, womb.

991. בֶּטֶן **Beṭen**, *beh'-ten*; the same as 990; *Beten*, a place in Pal.:—Beten.

992. בֹּטֶן **bôṭen**, *bo'-ten*; from 990; (only in plur.) a *pistachio*-nut (from its form):—nut.

993. בְּטֹנִים **Beṭônîym**, *bet-o-neem'*; prob. plur. from 992; *hollows; Betonim*, a place in Pal.:—Betonim.

994. בִּי **bîy**, *bee*; perh. from 1158 (in the sense of *asking*); prop. a *request*; used only adv. (always with "my Lord"); *Oh that!; with leave*, or *if it please*:—alas, O, oh.

995. בִּין **bîyn**, *bene*; a prim. root; to *separate* mentally (or *distinguish*), i.e. (gen.) *understand*:—attend, consider, be cunning, diligently, direct, discern, eloquent, feel, inform, instruct, have intelligence, know, look well to, mark, perceive, be prudent, regard, (can) skill (-ful), teach, think, (cause, make to, get, give, have) understand (-ing), view, (deal) wise (-ly, man).

996. בֵּין **bêyn**, *bane* (sometimes in the plur. masc. or fem.); prop. the constr. contr. form of an otherwise unused noun from 995; a *distinction*; but used only as a prep., *between* (repeated before each noun, often with other particles); also as a conj., *either . . . or*:—among, asunder, at, between (-twixt . . . and), + from (the widest), × in, out of, whether (it be . . . or), within.

997. בֵּין **bêyn** (Chald.), *bane*; corresp. to 996:—among, between.

998. בִּינָה **bîynâh**, *bee-naw'*; from 995; *understanding*:—knowledge, meaning, × perfectly, understanding, wisdom.

999. בִּינָה **bîynâh** (Chald.), *bee-naw'*; corresp. to 998:—knowledge.

1000. בֵּיצָה **bêytsâh**, *bay-tsaw'*; from the same as 948; an *egg* (from its whiteness):—egg.

1001. בִּירָא **bîyrâ'** (Chald.), *bee-raw'*; corresp. to 1002; a *palace*:—palace.

1002. בִּירָה **bîyrâh**, *bee-raw'*; of for. or.; a *castle* or *palace*:—palace.

1003. בִּירָנִית **bîyrânîyth**, *bee-raw-neeth'*; from 1002; a *fortress*:—castle.

1004. בַּיִת **bayith**, *bah'-yith*; prob. from 1129 abbrev.; a *house* (in the greatest var. of applications, espec. *family*, etc.):—court, daughter, door, + dungeon, family, + forth of, × great as would contain, hangings, home[born], [winter]house (-hold), inside (-ward), palace, place, + prison, + steward, + tablet, temple, web, + within (-out).

1005. בַּיִת **bayith** (Chald.), *bah-yith*; corresp. to 1004:—house.

1006. בַּיִת **Bayith**, *bah'-yith*; the same as 1004; *Bajith*, a place in Pal.:—Bajith.

1007. בֵּית אָוֶן **Bêyth 'Âven**, *bayth aw'-ven*; from 1004 and 205; *house of vanity; Beth-Aven*, a place in Pal.:—Beth-aven.

1008. בֵּית־אֵל **Bêyth-'Êl**, *bayth-ale'*; from 1004 and 410; *house of God; Beth-El*, a place in Pal.:—Beth-el.

1009. בֵּית אַרְבֵּאל **Bêyth 'Arbê'l**, *bayth arbale'*; from 1004 and 695 and 410; *house of God's ambush; Beth-Arbel*, a place in Pal.:—Beth-Arbel.

1010. בֵּית בַּעַל מְעוֹן **Bêyth Ba'al Me'ôwn**, *bayth bah'-al mĕ-own'*; from 1004 and 1168 and 4583; *house of Baal* of (the) *habitation of* [appar. by transp.]; or (shorter) בֵּית מְעוֹן **Bêyth Me'ôwn**, *bayth mĕ-own'*; *house of habitation of* (Baal); *Beth-Baal-Meön*, a place in Pal.:—Beth-baal-meon. Comp. 1186 and 1194.

1011. בֵּית בִּרְאִי **Bêyth Bir'îy**, *bayth bir-ee'*; from 1004 and 1254; *house of a creative* one; *Beth-Biri*, a place in Pal.:—Beth-birei.

1012. בֵּית בָּרָה **Bêyth Bârâh**, *bayth baw-raw'*; prob. from 1004 and 5679; *house of* (the) *ford; Beth-Barah*, a place in Pal.:—Beth-barah.

1013. בֵּית־גָּדֵר **Bêyth-Gâdêr**, *bayth-gaw-dare'*; from 1004 and 1447; *house of* (the) *wall; Beth-Gader*, a place in Pal.:—Beth-gader.

1014. בֵּית גָּמוּל **Bêyth Gâmûwl**, *bayth gaw-mool'*; from 1004 and the pass. part. of 1576; *house of* (the) *weaned; Beth-Gamul*, a place E. of the Jordan:—Beth-gamul.

1015. בֵּית דִּבְלָתַיִם **Bêyth Diblâthayim**, *bayth dib-law-thah'-yim*; from 1004 and the dual of 1690; *house of* (the) *two figcakes; Beth-Diblathajim*, a place E. of the Jordan:—Beth-diblathaim.

1016. בֵּית־דָּגוֹן **Bêyth-Dâgôwn**, *bayth-daw-gohn'*; from 1004 and 1712; *house of Dagon; Beth-Dagon*, the name of two places in Pal.:—Beth-dagon.

1017. בֵּית הָאֱלִי **Bêyth hâ-'Èlîy**, *bayth haw-el-ee'*; patrial from 1008 with the art. interposed; a *Beth-elite*, or inhab. of Bethel:—Bethelite.

1018. בֵּית הָאֵצֶל **Bêyth hâ-'êtsel**, *bayth haw-ay'-tsel*; from 1004 and 681 with the art. interposed; *house of the side; Beth-ha-Etsel*, a place in Pal.:—Beth-ezel.

1019. בֵּית הַגִּלְגָּל **Bêyth hag-Gilgâl**, *bayth hag-gil-gawl'*; from 1004 and 1537 with the article interposed; *house of the Gilgal* (or *rolling*); *Beth-hag-Gilgal*, a place in Pal.:—Beth-gilgal.

1020. בֵּית הַיְשִׁימוֹת **Bêyth ha-Yeshîymôwth**, *bayth hah-yesh-ee-mōth'*; from 1004 and the plur. of 3451 with the art. interposed; *house of the deserts; Beth-ha-Jeshimoth*, a town E. of the Jordan:—Beth-jeshimoth.

1021. בֵּית הַכֶּרֶם **Bêyth hak-Kerem**, *bayth hak-keh'-rem*; from 1004 and 3754 with the art. interposed; *house of the vineyard; Beth-hak-Kerem*, a place in Pal.:—Beth-haccerem.

1022. בֵּית הַלַּחְמִי **Bêyth hal-Lachmîy**, *bayth hal-lakh-mee'*; patrial from 1035 with the art. ins.; a *Beth-lechemite*, or native of Bethlechem:—Bethlehemite.

1023. בֵּית הַמֶּרְחָק **Bêyth ham-Merchâq**, *bayth ham-mer-khawk'*; from 1004 and 4801 with the art. interposed; *house of the breadth; Beth-ham-Merchak*, a place in Pal.:—place that was far off.

1024. בֵּית הַמַּרְכָּבוֹת **Bêyth ham-Markâbôwth**, *bayth ham-mar-kaw-both'*; or (short.) בֵּית מַרְכָּבוֹת **Bêyth Markâbôwth**, *bayth mar-kaw-both'*; from 1004 and the plur. of 4818 (with or without the art. interposed); *place of* (the) *chariots; Beth-ham-Markaboth* or *Beth-Markaboth*, a place in Pal.:- Beth-marcaboth.

1025. בֵּית הָעֵמֶק **Bêyth hâ-'Êmeq**, *bay[th] haw-Ay'-mek*; from 1004 a[nd] 6010 with the art. interposed; *house of the vall[ey]; Beth-ha-Emek*, a place in Pal.:—Beth-emek.

1026. בֵּית הָעֲרָבָה **Bêyth hâ-'Ărâbâh**, *ba[yth] haw-ar-aw-baw'*; from 1004 [and] 6160 with the art. interposed; *house of the Dese[rt]; Beth-ha-Arabah*, a place in Pal.:—Beth-arabah.

1027. בֵּית הָרָם **Bêyth hâ-Râm**, *bayth h[aw-] rawm'*; from 1004 and 7311 w[ith] the art. interposed; *house of the height; Beth-ha-Ra[m]*, a place E. of the Jordan:—Beth-aram.

1028. בֵּית הָרָן **Bêyth hâ-Rân**, *bayth h[aw-] rawn'*; prob. for 1027; *Beth-ha-Ra[n]*, a place E. of the Jordan:—Beth-haran.

1029. בֵּית הַשִּׁטָּה **Bêyth hash-Shiṭṭ[âh]**, *bayth hash-shit-taw'*; fr[om] 1004 and 7848 with the art. interposed; *house of [the] acacia; Beth-hash-Shittah*, a place in Pal.:—Be[th-] shittah.

1030. בֵּית הַשִּׁמְשִׁי **Bêyth hash-Shimsh[îy]**, *bayth hash-shim-shee'*; patr[ial] from 1053 with the art. inserted; a *Beth-shimshite*, inhab. of Bethshemesh:—Bethshemite.

1031. בֵּית חָגְלָה **Bêyth Choglâh**, *bayth ch[og-] law'*; from 1004 and the same [as] 2295; *house of a partridge; Beth-Choglah*, a place [in] Pal.:—Beth-hoglah.

1032. בֵּית חוֹרוֹן **Bêyth Chôwrôwn**, *ba[yth] kho-rone'*; from 1004 and 2[356]; *house of hollowness; Beth-Choron*, the name of [two] adjoining places in Pal.:—Beth-horon.

בֵּית חָנָן **Bêyth Chânân**. See 358.

1033. בֵּית כַּר **Bêyth Kar**, *bayth kar*; fr[om] 1004 and 3733; *house of pastu[re]; Beth-Car*, a place in Pal.:—Beth-car.

1034. בֵּית לְבָאוֹת **Bêyth Lebâ'ôwth**, *ba[yth] leb-aw-ōth'*; from 1004 and [the] plur. of 3833; *house of lionesses; Beth-Lebaoth*, [a] place in Pal.:—Beth-lebaoth. Comp. 3822.

1035. בֵּית לֶחֶם **Bêyth Lechem**, *bayth l[eh'-] khem*; from 1004 and 3899; *ho[use] of bread; Beth-Lechem*, a place in Pal.:—Beth-lehe[m].

1036. בֵּית לְעַפְרָה **Bêyth le-'Aphrâh**, *ba[yth] lĕ-af-raw'*; from 1004 and [the] fem. of 6083 (with prep. interposed); *house to* (i.e. [of]) *dust; Beth-le-Aphrah*, a place in Pal.:—house [of] Aphrah.

1037. בֵּית מִלּוֹא **Bêyth Millôw'**, *bayth m[il-] lo'*; or בֵּית מִלֹּא **Bêyth M[il]lô'**, *bayth mil-lo'*; from 1004 and 4407; *house of* (t[he]) *rampart; Beth-Millo*, the name of two citadels[:—] house of Millo.

1038. בֵּית מַעֲכָה **Bêyth Ma'âkâh**, *ba[yth] mah-ak-aw'*; from 1004 and 4[601]; *house of Maakah; Beth-Maakah*, a place in Pal[.:—] Beth-maachah.

1039. בֵּית נִמְרָה **Bêyth Nimrâh**, *bayth n[im-] raw'*; from 1004 and the fem. [of] 5246; *house of* (the) *leopard; Beth-Nimrah*, a pl[ace] east of the Jordan:—Beth-nimrah. Comp. 5247.

1040. בֵּית עֶדֶן **Bêyth 'Êden**, *bayth ay'-d[en]*; from 1004 and 5730; *house of pl[ea]sure; Beth-Eden*, a place in Syria:—Beth-eden.

1041. בֵּית עַזְמָוֶת **Bêyth 'Azmâveth**, *bay[th] az-maw'-veth*; from 1004 a[nd] 5820; *house of Azmaveth*, a place in Pal.:—Beth-[az]maveth. Comp. 5820.

1042. בֵּית עֲנוֹת **Bêyth 'Ănôwth**, *bayth a[n-] ōth'*; from 1004 and a plur. fr[om] 6030; *house of replies; Beth-Anoth*, a place in Pal. [:—] Beth-anoth.

1043. בֵּית עֲנָת **Bêyth 'Ănâth**, *bayth an-awth'*; an orth. var. for 1042; *Beth-Ana[th]*, a place in Pal.:—Beth-anath.

1044. בֵּית עֵקֶד **Bêyth 'Êqed**, *bayth ay'-k[ed]*; from 1004 and a deriv. of 61[24]; *house of* (the) *binding* (for sheep-shearing); *Be[th-] Eked*, a place in Pal.:—shearing-house.

045. בֵּית עַשְׁתָּרוֹת **Bêyth ʻAshtârôwth**, *bayth ash-taw-rōth'*; from 004 and 6252; *house of Ashtoreths; Beth-Ashtaroth*, a place in Pal.:—house of Ashtaroth. Comp. 1203, 252.

046. בֵּית פֶּלֶט **Bêyth Peleṭ**, *bayth peh'-let*; from 1004 and 6412; *house of escape; Beth-Palet*, a place in Pal.:—Beth-palet.

047. בֵּית פְּעוֹר **Bêyth Peʻôwr**, *bayth pĕ-ore'*; from 1004 and 6465; *house of Peor; eth-Peor*, a place E. of the Jordan:—Beth-peor.

048. בֵּית פַּצֵּץ **Bêyth Patstsêts**, *bayth pats-tsates'*; from 1004 and a der. from 327; *house of dispersion; Beth-Patstsets*, a place in al.:—Beth-pazzez.

049. בֵּית צוּר **Bêyth Tsûwr**, *bayth tsoor'*; from 1004 and 6697; *house of* (the) *ock; Beth-Tsur*, a place in Pal.:—Beth-zur.

050. בֵּית רְחוֹב **Bêyth Rechôwb**, *bayth rĕ-khobe'*; from 1004 and 7339; *house* (the) *street; Beth-Rechob*, a place in Pal.:—Beth-ehob.

051. בֵּית רָפָא **Bêyth Râphâʼ**, *bayth raw-faw'*; from 1004 and 7497; *house of he) giant; Beth-Rapha*, an Isr.:—Beth-rapha.

052. בֵּית שְׁאָן **Bêyth Sheʼân**, *bayth shĕ-awn'*; or בֵּית שָׁן **Bêyth Shân**, *bayth shawn'*; from 1004 and 7599; *house of ease; Beth-hean* or *Beth-Shan*, a place in Pal.:—Beth-shean, eth-Shan.

053. בֵּית שֶׁמֶשׁ **Bêyth Shemesh**, *bayth sheh'-mesh*; from 1004 and 8121; *house* (the) *sun; Beth-Shemesh*, a place in Pal.:—Beth-emesh.

054. בֵּית תַּפּוּחַ **Bêyth Tappûwach**, *bayth tap-poo'-akh*; from 1004 and 8598; *ouse of* (the) *apple; Beth-Tappuach*, a place in al.:—Beth-tappuah.

055. בִּיתָן **bîythân**, *bee-thawn'*; prob. from 1004; a *palace* (i.e. *large house*):—alace.

056. בָּכָא **Bâkâʼ**, *baw-kaw'*; from 1058; *weeping; Baca*, a valley in Pal.:—Baca.

057. בָּכָא **bâkâʼ**, *baw-kaw'*; the same as 1056; the *weeping* tree (some gum-distilling ee, perh. the *balsam*):—mulberry tree.

058. בָּכָה **bâkâh**, *baw-kaw'*; a prim. root; to *weep*; gen. to *bemoan*:—× at all, be-ail, complain, make lamentation, × more, mourn, sore, × with tears, weep.

059. בֶּכֶה **bekeh**, *beh'-keh*; from 1058; a *weeping*:—× sore.

060. בְּכוֹר **bekôwr**, *bek-ore'*; from 1069; *first-born*; hence *chief*:—eldest (son), first-orn (-ling).

061. בִּכּוּר **bikkûwr**, *bik-koor'*; from 1069; the *first-fruits* of the crop:—first fruit ipe [fig.]), hasty fruit.

062. בְּכוֹרָה **bekôwrâh**, *bek-o-raw'*; or (short.) בְּכֹרָה **bekôrâh**, *bek-o-raw'*; fem. of 1060; the *firstling* of man or beast; abstr. *imogeniture*:—birthright, firstborn (-ling).

063. בִּכּוּרָה **bikkûwrâh**, *bik-koo-raw'*; fem. of 1061; the *early* fig:—firstripe ruit).

064. בְּכוֹרַת **Bekôwrath**, *bek-o-rath'*; fem. of 1062; *primogeniture; Bekorath*, an r.:—Bechorath.

065. בְּכִי **bekîy**, *bek-ee'*; from 1058; a *weeping*; by analogy, a *dripping*:—overflowing, sore, (continual) weeping, wept.

066. בֹּכִים **Bôkîym**, *bo-keem'*; plur. act. part. of 1058; (with the art.) the *weepers; Bom*, a place in Pal.:—Bochim.

067. בְּכִירָה **bekîyrâh**, *bek-ee-raw'*; fem. from 1069; the *eldest* daughter:—firstborn.

068. בְּכִית **bekîyth**, *bek-eeth'*; from 1058; a *weeping*:—mourning.

069. בָּכַר **bâkar**, *baw-kar'*; a prim. root; prop. to *burst* the womb, i.e. (caus.) *bear* or *ake early fruit* (of woman or tree); also (as denom. om 1061) to *give the birthright*:—make firstborn, be rstling, bring forth first child (new fruit).

1070. בֶּכֶר **beker**, *beh'-ker*; from 1069 (in the sense of *youth*); a young *camel*:—dromedary.

1071. בֶּכֶר **Beker**, *beh'-ker*; the same as 1070; *Beker*, the name of two Isr.:—Becher.

1072. בִּכְרָה **bikrâh**, *bik-raw'*; fem. of 1070; a young *she-camel*:—dromedary.

בְּכֹרָה **bekôrâh**. See 1062.

1073. בַּכֻּרָה **bakkûrâh**, *bak-koo-raw'*; by orth. var. for 1063; a *first-ripe* fig:—first-ripe.

1074. בֹּכְרוּ **Bôkerûw**, *bo-ker-oo'*; from 1069; *first-born; Bokeru*, an Isr.:—Bocheru.

1075. בִּכְרִי **Bikrîy**, *bik-ree'*; from 1069; *youthful; Bikri*, an Isr.:—Bichri.

1076. בַּכְרִי **Bakrîy**, *bak-ree'*; patron. from 1071; a *Bakrite* (collect.) or desc. of Beker:—Bachrites.

1077. בַּל **bal**, *bal*; from 1086; prop. a *failure*; by impl. *nothing*; usually (adv.) *not* at all; also *lest*:—lest, neither, no, none (that . . .), not (any), nothing.

1078. בֵּל **Bêl**, *bale*; by contr. for 1168; *Bel*, the Baal of the Babylonians:—Bel.

1079. בָּל **bâl** (Chald.), *bawl*; from 1080; prop. *anxiety*, i.e. (by impl.) the *heart* (as its seat):—heart.

1080. בְּלָא **belâʼ** (Chald.), *bel-aw'*; corresp. to 1086 (but used only in a mental sense); to *afflict*:—wear out.

1081. בַּלְאֲדָן **Balʼădân**, *bal-ad-awn'*; from 1078 and 113 (contr.); *Bel* (is his) *lord; Baladan*, the name of a Bab. prince:—Baladan.

1082. בָּלַג **bâlag**, *baw-lag'*; a prim. root; to *break off* or *loose* (in a favorable or unfavorable sense), i.e. *desist* (from grief) or *invade* (with destruction):—comfort, (recover) strength (-en).

1083. בִּלְגָּה **Bilgâh**, *bil-gaw'*; from 1082; *desistance; Bilgah*, the name of two Isr.:—Bilgah.

1084. בִּלְגַּי **Bilgay**, *bil-gah'ee*; from 1082; *desistant; Bilgai*, an Isr.:—Bilgai.

1085. בִּלְדַּד **Bildad**, *bil-dad'*; of uncert. der.; *Bildad*, one of Job's friends:—Bildad.

1086. בָּלָה **bâlâh**, *baw-law'*; a prim. root; to *fail*; by impl. to *wear out, decay* (caus. *consume, spend*):—consume, enjoy long, become (make, wax) old, spend, waste.

1087. בָּלֶה **bâleh**, *baw-leh'*; from 1086; *worn out*:—old.

1088. בָּלָה **Bâlâh**, *baw-law'*; fem. of 1087; *failure; Balah*, a place in Pal.:—Balah.

1089. בָּלַהּ **bâlahh**, *baw-lah'*; a prim. root [rather by transp. for 926]; to *palpitate*; hence (caus.) to *terrify*:—trouble.

1090. בִּלְהָה **Bilhâh**, *bil-haw'*; from 1089; *timid; Bilhah*, the name of one of Jacob's concubines; also of a place in Pal.:—Bilhah.

1091. בַּלָּהָה **ballâhâh**, *bal-law-haw'*; from 1089; *alarm*; hence *destruction*:—terror, trouble.

1092. בִּלְהָן **Bilhân**, *bil-hawn'*; from 1089; *timid; Bilhan*, the name of an Edomite and of an Isr.:—Bilhan.

1093. בְּלוֹ **belôw** (Chald.), *bel-o'*; from a root corresp. to 1086; *excise* (on articles consumed):—tribute.

1094. בְּלוֹא **belôwʼ**, *bel-o'*; or (fully) בְּלוֹי **belôwy**, *bel-o'ee*; from 1086; (only in plur. constr.) *rags*:—old.

1095. בֵּלְטְשַׁאצַּר **Bêlteshaʼtstsar**, *bale-tesh-ats-tsar'*; of for. der.; *Belteshatstsar*, the Bab. name of Daniel:—Belteshazzar.

1096. בֵּלְטְשַׁאצַּר **Bêlteshaʼtstsar** (Chald.), *bale-tesh-ats-tsar'*; corresp. to 1095:—Belteshazzar.

1097. בְּלִי **belîy**, *bel-ee'*; from 1086; prop. *failure*, i.e. *nothing* or *destruction*; usually (with prep.) *without, not yet, because not, as long as*, etc.:—corruption, ig[norantly], for lack of, where no . . . is, so that no, none, not, un[awares], without.

1098. בְּלִיל **belîyl**, *bel-eel'*; from 1101; *mixed*, i.e. (spec.) *feed* (for cattle):—corn, fodder, provender.

1099. בְּלִימָה **belîymâh**, *bel-ee-mah'*; from 1097 and 4100; (as indef.) *nothing whatever*:—nothing.

1100. בְּלִיַּעַל **belîyaʻal**, *bel-e-yah'-al*; from 1097 and 3276; *without profit, worthlessness*; by extens. *destruction, wickedness* (often in connection with 376, 802, 1121, etc.):—Belial, evil, naughty, ungodly (men), wicked.

1101. בָּלַל **bâlal**, *baw-lal'*; a prim. root; to *overflow* (spec. with oil); by impl. to *mix*; also (denom. from 1098) to *fodder*:—anoint, confound, × fade, mingle, mix (self), give provender, temper.

1102. בָּלַם **bâlam**, *baw-lam'*; a prim. root; to *muzzle*:—be held in.

1103. בָּלַס **bâlaç**, *baw-las'*; a prim. root; to *pinch* sycamore figs (a process necessary to ripen them):—gatherer.

1104. בָּלַע **bâlaʻ**, *baw-lah'*; a prim. root; to *make away with* (spec. by *swallowing*); gen. to *destroy*:—cover, destroy, devour, eat up, be at end, spend up, swallow down (up).

1105. בֶּלַע **belaʻ**, *beh'-lah*; from 1104; a *gulp*; fig. *destruction*:—devouring, that which he hath swallowed up.

1106. בֶּלַע **Belaʻ**, *beh'-lah*; the same as 1105; *Bela*, the name of a place, also of an Edomite and of two Isr.:—Bela.

1107. בִּלְעֲדֵי **bilʻădêy**, *bil-ad-ay'*; or בַּלְעֲדֵי **balʻădêy**, *bal-ad-ay'*; constr. plur. from 1077 and 5703; *not till*, i.e. (as prep. or adv.) *except, without, besides*:—beside, not (in), save, without.

1108. בַּלְעִי **Balʻîy**, *bel-ee'*; patronym. from 1106: a *Belaite* (collect.) or desc. of Bela:—Belaites.

1109. בִּלְעָם **Bilʻâm**, *bil-awm'*; prob. from 1077 and 5971; *not* (of the) *people*, i.e. *foreigner*; *Bilam*, a Mesopotamian prophet; also a place in Pal.:—Balaam, Bileam.

1110. בָּלַק **bâlaq**, *baw-lak'*; a prim. root; to *annihilate*:—(make) waste.

1111. בָּלָק **Bâlâq**, *baw-lawk'*; from 1110; *waster; Balak*, a Moabitish king:—Balak.

1112. בֵּלְשַׁאצַּר **Bêlshaʼtstsar**, *bale-shats-tsar'*; or בֵּלְאשַׁצַּר **Bêlʼshatstsar**, *bale-shats-tsar'*; of for. or. (comp. 1095); *Belshatstsar*, a Bab. king:—Belshazzar.

1113. בֵּלְשַׁאצַּר **Bêlshaʼtstsar** (Chald.), *bale-shats-tsar'*; corresp. to 1112:—Belshazzar.

1114. בִּלְשָׁן **Bilshân**, *bil-shawn'*; of uncert. der.; *Bilshan*, an Isr.:—Bilshan.

1115. בִּלְתִּי **biltîy**, *bil-tee'*; constr. fem. of 1086 (equiv. to 1097); prop. a *failure of*, i.e. (used only as a neg. particle, usually with prep. pref.) *not, except, without, unless, besides, because not, until*, etc.:—because un[satiable], beside, but, + continual, except, from, lest, neither, no more, none, not, nothing, save, that no, without.

1116. בָּמָה **bâmâh**, *baw-maw'*; from an unused root (mean. to *be high*); an *elevation*:—height, high place, wave.

1117. בָּמָה **Bâmâh**, *baw-maw'*; the same as 1116; *Bamah*, a place in Pal.:—Bamah. See also 1120.

1118. בִּמְהָל **Bimhâl**, *bim-hawl'*; prob. from 4107 with prep. pref.; *with pruning; Bimhal*, an Isr.:—Bimhal.

1119. בְּמוֹ **bemôw**, *bem-o'*; prol. for prep. pref.; *in, with, by*, etc.:—for, in, into, through.

1120. בָּמוֹת **Bâmôwth**, *baw-mōth'*; plur. of 1116; *heights*; or (fully) בָּמוֹת בַּעַל **Bâmôwth Baʻal**, *baw-mōth' bah'-al*; from the same and 1168; *heights of Baal; Bamoth* or *Bamoth-Baal*, a place E. of the Jordan:—Bamoth, Bamoth-baal.

1121. בֵּן **bên**, *bane*; from 1129; a *son* (as a *builder* of the family name), in the widest sense (of lit. and fig. relationship, including *grandson, subject, nation, quality* or *condition*, etc., [like 1, 251, etc.]):—+ afflicted, age, [Ahoh-] [Ammon-] [Hachmon-] [Lev-]ite, [anoint-]ed one, appointed to, (+) arrow, [Assyr-] [Babylon-] [Egypt-] [Grec-]ian, one born, bough, branch, breed, + (young) bullock, + (young) calf, × came up in, child, colt, × common, × corn, daughter, × of first, + firstborn, foal, + very fruitful, + postage, × in, + kid, + lamb, (+) man, meet, + mighty, + nephew, old, (+) people, + rebel, + robber, × servant born, × soldier, son, + spark, + steward, + stranger, × surely, them of, + tumultuous one, + valiant[-est], whelp, worthy, young (one), youth.

1122. בֵּן **Bên**, *bane;* the same as 1121; *Ben,* an Isr.:—Ben.

1123. בֵּן **bên** (Chald.), *bane;* corresp. to 1121:—child, son, young.

1124. בְּנָא **benâ'** (Chald.), *ben-aw';* or בְּנָה **benâh** (Chald.), *ben-aw';* corresp. to 1129; to *build:*—build, make.

1125. בֶּן־אֲבִינָדָב **Ben-'Âbîynâdâb,** *ben-ab-ee''-naw-dawb';* from 1121 and 40; (the) *son of Abinadab; Ben-Abinadab,* an Isr.:—the son of Abinadab.

1126. בֶּן־אוֹנִי **Ben-'Ôwnîy,** *ben-o-nee';* from 1121 and 205; *son of my sorrow; Ben-Oni,* the original name of Benjamin:—Ben-oni.

1127. בֶּן־גֶּבֶר **Ben-Geber,** *ben-gheh'-ber;* from 1121 and 1397; *son of* (the) *hero; Ben-Geber,* an Isr.:—the son of Geber.

1128. בֶּן־דֶּקֶר **Ben-Deqer,** *ben-deh'-ker;* from 1121 and a der. of 1856; *son of piercing* (or *of a lance*); *Ben-Deker,* an Isr.:—the son of Dekar.

1129. בָּנָה **bânâh,** *baw-naw';* a prim. root; to *build* (lit. and fig.):—(begin to) build (-er), obtain children, make, repair, set (up), × surely.

1130. בֶּן־הֲדַד **Ben-Hădad,** *ben-had-ad';* from 1121 and 1908; *son of Hadad; Ben-Hadad,* the name of several Syrian kings:—Ben-hadad.

1131. בִּנּוּי **Binnûwy,** *bin-noo'ee;* from 1129; *built* up; *Binnui,* an Isr.:—Binnui.

1132. בֶּן־זוֹחֵת **Ben-Zôwchêth,** *ben-zo-khayth';* from 1121 and 2105; *son of Zocheth; Ben-Zocheth,* an Isr.:—Ben-zoketh.

1133. בֶּן־חוּר **Ben-Chûwr,** *ben-khoor';* from 1121 and 2354; *son of Chur; Ben-Chur,* an Isr.:—the son of Hur.

1134. בֶּן־חַיִל **Ben-Chayil,** *ben-khah'-yil;* from 1121 and 2428; *son of might; Ben-Chail,* an Isr.:—Ben-hail.

1135. בֶּן־חָנָן **Ben-Chânân,** *ben-khaw-nawn';* from 1121 and 2605; *son of Chanan; Ben-Chanan,* an Isr.:—Ben-hanan.

1136. בֶּן־חֶסֶד **Ben-Cheçed,** *ben-kheh'-sed;* from 1121 and 2617; *son of kindness; Ben-Chesed,* an Isr.:—the son of Hesed.

1137. בָּנִי **Bânîy,** *baw-nee';* from 1129; *built; Bani,* the name of five Isr.:—Bani.

1138. בֻּנִּי **Bunnîy,** *boon-nee';* or (fuller) בּוּנִי **Bûwnîy,** *boo-nee';* from 1129; *built; Bunni* or *Buni,* an Isr.:—Bunni.

1139. בְּנֵי־בְרַק **Benêy-Beraq,** *ben-ay'-ber-ak';* from the plur. constr. of 1121 and 1300; *sons of lightning, Bene-berak,* a place in Pal.:—Bene-barak.

1140. בִּנְיָה **binyâh,** *bin-yaw';* fem. from 1129; a *structure:*—building.

1141. בְּנָיָה **Benâyâh,** *ben-aw-yaw';* or (prol.) בְּנָיָהוּ **Benâyâhûw,** *ben-aw-yaw'-hoo;* from 1129 and 3050; *Jah has built; Benajah,* the name of twelve Isr.:—Benaiah.

1142. בְּנֵי יַעֲקָן **Benêy Ya'ăqân,** *ben-ay' yah-ak-awn';* from the plur. of 1121 and 3292; *sons of Yaakan; Bene-Jaakan,* a place in the Desert:—Bene-jaakan.

1143. בֵּנַיִם **bênayim,** *bay-nah'-yim;* dual of 996; a *double interval,* i.e. the space between two armies:—+ champion.

1144. בִּנְיָמִין **Binyâmîyn,** *bin-yaw-mene';* from 1121 and 3225; *son of* (the) *right hand; Binjamin,* youngest son of Jacob; also the tribe descended from him, and its territory:—Benjamin.

1145. בֶּן־יְמִינִי **Ben-yemîynîy,** *ben-yem-ee-nee';* sometimes (with the art. ins.) בֶּן־הַיְמִינִי **Ben-ha-yemînîy,** *ben-hah-yem-ee-nee';* with 376 ins. (1 Sam. 9 : 1) בֶּן־אִישׁ יְמִינִי **Ben-'îysh Yemîynîy,** *ben-eesh' yem-ee-nee'; son of a man of Jemini;* or short. (1 Sam. 9 : 4; Esth. 2 : 5) אִישׁ יְמִינִי **'Îysh Yemîynîy,** *eesh yem-ee-nee'; a man of Jemini;* or (1 Sam. 20 : 1) simply יְמִינִי **Yemînîy,** *yem-ee-nee'; a Jeminite;* (plur. בְּנֵי יְמִינִי **Benîy Yemîynîy,** *ben-ay' yem-ee-nee';*) patron. from 1144; a *Benjaminite,* or descendant of Benjamin:—Benjamite, of Benjamin.

1146. בִּנְיָן **binyân,** *bin-yawn';* from 1129; an *edifice:*—building.

1147. בִּנְיָן **binyân** (Chald.), *bin-yawn';* corresp. to 1146:—building.

1148. בְּנִינוּ **Benîynûw,** *ben-ee-noo';* prob. from 1121 with pron. suff.; *our son; Beninu,* an Isr.:—Beninu.

1149. בְּנַס **benaç** (Chald.), *ben-as';* of uncert. affin.; to *be enraged:*—be angry.

1150. בִּנְעָא **Bin'â',** *bin-aw';* or בִּנְעָה **Bin'âh,** *bin-aw';* of uncert. der.; *Bina* or *Binah,* an Isr.:—Binea, Bineah.

1151. בֶּן־עַמִּי **Ben-'Ammîy,** *ben-am-mee';* from 1121 and 5971 with pron. suff.; *son of my people; Ben-Ammi,* a son of Lot:—Ben-ammi.

1152. בְּסוֹדְיָה **Beçôwdeyâh,** *bes-o-deh-yaw';* from 5475 and 3050 with prep. pref.; *in* (the) *counsel of Jehovah; Besodejah,* an Isr.:—Besodeiah.

1153. בְּסַי **Beçay,** *bes-ah'-ee;* from 947; *domineering; Besai,* one of the Nethinim:—Besai.

1154. בֶּסֶר **beçer,** *beh'-ser;* from an unused root mean. to *be sour;* an *immature* grape:—unripe grape.

1155. בֹּסֶר **bôçer,** *bo'-ser;* from the same as 1154:—sour grape.

1156. בְּעָא **be'â'** (Chald.), *beh-aw';* or בְּעָה **be'âh** (Chald.), *beh-aw';* corresp. to 1158; to *seek* or *ask:*—ask, desire, make [petition], pray, request, seek.

1157. בְּעַד **be'ad,** *beh-ad';* from 5704 with prep. pref.; *in up to* or *over against;* gen. *at, beside, among, behind, for,* etc.:—about, at, by (means of), for, over, through, up (-on), within.

1158. בָּעָה **bâ'âh,** *baw-aw';* a prim. root; to *gush* over, i.e. to *swell;* (fig.) to *desire* earnestly; by impl. to *ask:*—cause, inquire, seek up, swell out, boil.

1159. בָּעוּ **bâ'ûw** (Chald.), *baw-oo';* from 1156; a *request:*—petition.

1160. בְּעוֹר **Be'ôwr,** *beh-ore';* from 1197 (in the sense of *burning*); a *lamp; Beör,* the name of the father of an Edomitish king; also of that of Balaam:—Beor.

1161. בִּעוּתִים **bi'ûwthîym,** *be-oo-theme';* masc. plur. from 1204; *alarms:*—terrors.

1162. בֹּעַז **Bô'az,** *bo'-az;* from an unused root of uncert. mean.; *Boaz,* the ancestor of David; also the name of a pillar in front of the temple:—Boaz.

1163. בָּעַט **bâ'aṭ,** *baw-at';* a prim. root; to *trample* down, i.e. (fig.) *despise:*—kick.

1164. בְּעִי **be'îy,** *beh-ee';* from 1158; a *prayer:*—grave.

1165. בְּעִיר **be'îyr,** *beh-ere';* from 1197 (in the sense of *eating*): cattle:—beast, cattle.

1166. בָּעַל **bâ'al,** *baw-al';* a prim. root; to *be master;* hence (as denom. from 1167) to *marry:*—Beulah have dominion (over), be husband, marry (-ried, × wife).

1167. בַּעַל **ba'al,** *bah'-al;* from 1166; a *master;* hence a *husband,* or (fig.) *owner* (often used with another noun in modifications of this latter sense):—+ archer, + babbler, + bird, captain, chief man, + confederate, + have to do, + dreame those to whom it is due, + furious, those that a given to it, great, + hairy, he that hath it, hav + horseman, husband, lord, man, + married, ma ter, person, + sworn, they of.

1168. בַּעַל **Ba'al,** *bah'-al;* the same as 1167; *Baa* a Phœnician deity:—Baal, [*plur.*] B alim.

1169. בְּעֵל **be'êl** (Chald.), *beh-ale';* corresp. 1167:—+ chancellor.

1170. בַּעַל בְּרִית **Ba'al Berîyth,** *bah'-al be eeth';* from 1168 and 1285; *Ba of* (the) *covenant; Baal-Berith,* a special deity of th Shechemites:—Baal-berith.

1171. בַּעַל גָּד **Ba'al Gâd,** *bah'-al gawd;* fro 1168 and 1409; *Baal of Fortun Baal-Gad,* a place in Syria:—Baal-gad.

1172. בַּעֲלָה **ba'ălâh,** *bah-al-aw';* fem. of 116 a *mistress:*—that hath, mistress.

1173. בַּעֲלָה **Ba'ălâh,** *bah-al-aw';* the same 1172; *Baalah,* the name of thre places in Pal.:—Baalah.

1174. בַּעַל הָמוֹן **Ba'al Hâmôwn,** *bah'- haw-mone';* from 1167 and 199 *possessor of a multitude; Baal-Hamon,* a place Pal.:—Baal-hamon.

1175. בְּעָלוֹת **Be'âlôwth,** *beh-aw-lōth';* plur. 1172; *mistresses; Beäloth,* a place Pal.:—Bealoth, in Aloth [*by mistake for a plur. fro 5927 with prep. pref.*].

1176. בַּעַל זְבוּב **Ba'al Zebûwb,** *bah'-al ze oob';* from 1168 and 2070; *Ba of* (the) *Fly; Baal-Zebub,* a special deity of th Ekronites:—Baal-zebub.

1177. בַּעַל חָנָן **Ba'al Chânân,** *bah'-al kha nawn';* from 1167 and 2603; *posse sor of grace; Baal-Chanan,* the name of an Edomit also of an Isr.:—Baal-hanan.

1178. בַּעַל חָצוֹר **Ba'al Châtsôwr,** *bah'- khaw-tsore';* from 1167 and modif. of 2691; *possessor of a village; Baal-Chats* a place in Pal.:—Baal-hazor.

1179. בַּעַל חֶרְמוֹן **Ba'al Chermôwn,** *bah'- kher-mone';* from 1167 a 2768; *possessor of Hermon; Baal-Chermon,* a pla in Pal.:—Baal-hermon.

1180. בַּעֲלִי **Ba'ălîy,** *bah-al-ee';* from 1167 wit pron. suff.; *my master; Baali,* a sy bolical name for Jehovah:—Baali.

1181. בַּעֲלֵי בָמוֹת **Ba'ălêy Bâmôwth,** *ba al-ay' baw-mōth';* from t plur. of 1168 and the plur. of 1116; *Baals of* (th *heights; Baale-Bamoth,* a place E. of the Jordan: lords of the high places.

1182. בְּעֶלְיָדָע **Be'elyâdâ',** *beh-el-yaw-daw';* fro 1168 and 3045; *Baal has know Beëljada,* an Isr.:—Beeliada.

1183. בְּעַלְיָה **Be'alyâh,** *beh-al-yaw';* from 11 and 3050; *Jah* (is) *master; Bealja* an Isr.:—Bealiah.

1184. בַּעֲלֵי יְהוּדָה **Ba'ălêy Yehûwdâh,** *ba al-ay' yeh-hoo-daw';* from t plur. of 1167 and 3068; *masters of Judah; Baale-J hudah,* a place in Pal.:—Baale of Judah.

1185. בַּעֲלִיס **Ba'ălîç,** *bah-al-ece';* prob. from der. of 5965 with prep. pref.; *in exu tation; Baalis,* an Ammonitish king:—Baalis.

1186. בַּעַל מְעוֹן **Ba'al Me'ôwn,** *bah-al me one';* from 1168 and 4583; *Baal* (the) *habitation* (of) [comp. 1010]; *Baal-Meön,* a pla E. of the Jordan:—Baal-meon.

1187. בַּעַל פְּעוֹר **Ba'al Pe'ôwr,** *bah'-al peh-ore* from 1168 and 6465; *Baal of Peo Baal-Peör,* a Moabitish deity:—Baal-peor.

1188. בַּעַל פְּרָצִים **Ba'al Perâtsîym,** *bah'- per-aw-tseem';* from 1167 a the plur. of 6556; *possessor of breaches; Baal-Pe tsim,* a place in Pal.:—Baal-perazim.

1189. בַּעַל צְפוֹן **Ba'al Tsephôwn,** *bah'-al tse one';* from 1168 and 6828 (in t sense of *cold*) [according to others an Eg. form Typhon, the destroyer]; *Baal of winter; Baal-T phon,* a place in Egypt:—Baal-zephon.

1190. בַּעַל שָׁלִשָׁה **Baʻal Shâlîshâh**, *bah'-al shaw-lee-shaw'*; from 1168 and 8031; *Baal of Shalishah; Baal-Shalishah*, a place in Pal.:—Baal-shalisha.

1191. בַּעֲלָת **Baʻălâth**, *bah-al-awth'*; a modif. of 1172; *mistressship; Baalath*, a place in Pal.:—Baalath.

1192. בַּעֲלַת בְּאֵר **Baʻălath Beʼêr**, *bah-al-ath' beh-ayr'*; from 1172 and 875; *mistress of a well; Baalath-Beër*, a place in Pal.:—Baalath-beer.

1193. בַּעַל תָּמָר **Baʻal Tâmâr**, *bah'-al taw-mawr'*, from 1167 and 8558; *possessor of* (the) *palm-tree; Baal-Tamar*, a place in Pal.:—Baal-tamar.

1194. בְּעֹן **Beʻôn**, *beh-ohn'*; prob. a contr. of 1010; *Beön*, a place E. of the Jordan:—Beon.

1195. בַּעֲנָא **Baʻănâʼ**, *bah-an-aw'*; the same as 1196; *Baana*, the name of four Isr.:—Baana, Baanah.

1196. בַּעֲנָה **Baʻănâh**, *bah-an-aw'*; from a der. of 6031 with prep. pref.; *in affliction:—Baanah*, the name of four Isr.:—Baanah.

1197. בָּעַר **bâʻar**, *baw-ar'*; a prim. root; to *kindle*, i.e. *consume* (by fire or by eating); also (as denom. from 1198) to *be (-come) brutish:*—be brutish, bring (put, take) away, burn, (cause to) eat (up), feed, heat, kindle, set ([on fire]), waste.

1198. בַּעַר **baʻar**, *bah'-ar*; from 1197; prop. *food* (as *consumed*); i.e. (by exten.) of cattle *brutishness;* (concr.) *stupid:*—brutish (person), foolish.

1199. בָּעֲרָא **Bâʻărâʼ**, *bah-ar-aw'*; from 1198; *brutish; Baara*, an Israelitish woman:—Baara.

1200. בְּעֵרָה **beʻêrâh**, *bĕ-ay-raw'*; from 1197; a *burning:*—fire.

1201. בַּעְשָׁא **Baʻshâʼ**, *bah-shaw'*; from an unused root mean. to *stink; offensiveness: Basha*, a king of Israel:—Baasha.

1202. בַּעֲשֵׂיָה **Baʻăsêyâh**, *bah-as-ay-yaw'*; from 6213 and 3050 with prep. pref.; *in* (the) *work of Jah; Baasejah*, an Isr.:—Baaseiah.

1203. בְּעֶשְׁתְּרָה **Beʻeshterâh**, *beh-esh-ter-aw'*; from 6251 (as sing. of 6252) with prep. pref.; *with Ashtoreth; Beështerah*, a place E. of the Jordan:—Beeshterah.

1204. בָּעַת **bâʻath**, *baw-ath'*; a prim. root; to *fear:*—affright, be (make) afraid, terrify, trouble.

1205. בְּעָתָה **beʻâthâh**, *beh-aw-thaw'*; from 1204; *fear:*—trouble.

1206. בֹּץ **bôts**, *botse*; prob. the same as 948; *mud* (as *whitish* clay):—mire.

1207. בִּצָּה **bitstsâh**, *bits-tsaw'*; intens. from 1206; a *swamp:*—fen, mire (-ry place).

1208. בָּצוֹר **bâtsôwr**, *baw-tsore'*; from 1219; *inaccessible*, i.e. *lofty:*—vintage [*by confusion with* 1210].

1209. בֵּצַי **Bêtsay**, *bay-tsah'ee*; perh. the same as 1153; *Betsai*, the name of two Isr.:—Bezai.

1210. בָּצִיר **bâtsîyr**, *baw-tseer'*; from 1219; *clipped*, i.e. the *grape crop:*—vintage.

1211. בֶּצֶל **betsel**, *beh'-tsel*; from an unused root appar. mean. to *peel;* an *onion:*—onion.

1212. בְּצַלְאֵל **Betsalʼêl**, *bets-al-ale'*; prob. from 6738 and 410 with prep. pref.; *in* (the) *shadow* (i.e. protection) *of God; Betsalel;* the name of two Isr.:—Bezaleel.

1213. בַּצְלוּת **Batslûwth**, *bats-looth'*; or

בַּצְלִית **Batslîyth**, *bats-leeth'*; from the same as 1211; a *peeling; Batsluth* or *Batslith;* an Isr.:—Bazlith, Bazluth.

1214. בָּצַע **bâtsaʻ**, *baw-tsah'*; a prim. root; to *break* off, i.e. (usually) *plunder;* fig. to *finish*, or (intrans.) *stop:*—(be) covet (-ous), cut (off), finish, fulfill, gain (greedily), get, be given to [covetousness], greedy, perform, be wounded.

1215. בֶּצַע **betsaʻ**, *beh'-tsah*; from 1214; *plunder;* by extens. *gain* (usually unjust):—covetousness, (dishonest) gain, lucre, profit.

1216. בָּצֵק **bâtsêq**, *baw-tsake'*; a prim. root; perh. to *swell* up, i.e. *blister:*—swell.

1217. בָּצֵק **bâtsêq**, *baw-tsake'*; from 1216; *dough* (as *swelling* by fermentation):—dough, flour.

1218. בָּצְקַת **Botsqath**, *bots-cath'*; from 1216; a *swell* of ground; *Botscath*, a place in Pal.:—Bozcath, Boskath.

1219. בָּצַר **bâtsar**, *baw-tsar'*; a prim. root; to *clip* off; spec. (as denom. from 1210) to *gather* grapes; also to *be isolated* (i.e. *inaccessible* by height or fortification):—cut off, (de-) fenced, fortify, (grape) gather (-er), mighty things, restrain, strong, wall (up), withhold.

1220. בֶּצֶר **betser**, *beh'-tser*; from 1219; strictly a *clipping*, i.e. *gold* (as *dug* out):—gold defence.

1221. בֶּצֶר **Betser**, *beh'-tser*; the same as 1220. an *inaccessible* spot; *Betser*, a place in Pal.; also an Isr.:—Bezer.

1222. בְּצַר **betsar**, *bets-ar'*; another form for 1220; *gold:*—gold.

1223. בָּצְרָה **botsrâh**, *bots-raw'*; fem. from 1219; an *enclosure*, i.e. *sheep-fold:*—Bozrah.

1224. בָּצְרָה **Botsrâh**, *bots-raw'*; the same as 1223; *Botsrah*, a place in Edom:—Bozrah.

1225. בִּצָּרוֹן **bitstsârôwn**, *bits-tsaw-rone'*; masc. intens. from 1219; a *fortress:*—stronghold.

1226. בַּצֹּרֶת **batstsôreth**, *bats-tso'-reth*; fem. intens. from 1219; *restraint* (of rain), i.e. *drought:*—dearth, drought.

1227. בַּקְבּוּק **Baqbûwq**, *bak-book'*; the same as 1228; *Bakbuk*, one of the *Nethinim:*—Bakbuk.

1228. בַּקְבֻּק **baqbûk**, *bak-book'*; from 1238; a *bottle* (from the gurgling in *emptying*):—bottle, cruse.

1229. בַּקְבֻּקְיָה **Baqbukyâh**, *bak-book-yaw'*; from 1228 and 3050; *emptying* (i.e. *wasting*) *of Jah; Bakbukjah*, an Isr.:—Bakbukiah.

1230. בַּקְבַּקַּר **Baqbaqqar**, *bak-bak-kar'*; redupl. from 1239; *searcher; Bakbakkar*, an Isr.:—Bakbakkar.

1231. בֻּקִּי **Buqqîy**, *book-kee'*; from 1238; *wasteful; Bukki*, the name of two Isr.:—Bukki.

1232. בֻּקִּיָּה **Buqqîyâh**, *book-kee-yaw'*; from 1238 and 3050; *wasting of Jah; Bukkijah*, an Isr.:—Bukkiah.

1233. בְּקִיעַ **beqîyaʻ**, *bek-ee'-ah*; from 1234; a *fissure:*—breach, cleft.

1234. בָּקַע **bâqaʻ**, *baw-kah'*; a prim. root; to *cleave;* gen. to *rend, break, rip* or *open:*—make a breach, break forth (into, out, in pieces, through, up), be ready to burst, cleave (asunder), cut out, divide, hatch, rend (asunder), rip up, tear, win.

1235. בֶּקַע **beqaʻ**, *beh'-kah*; from 1234; a *section* (half) of a shekel, i.e. a *beka* (a weight and a coin):—bekah, half a shekel.

1236. בִּקְעָא **biqʻâʼ** (Chald.), *bik-aw'*; corresp. to 1237:—plain.

1237. בִּקְעָה **biqʻâh**, *bik-aw'*; from 1234; prop. a *split*, i.e. a wide level *valley* between mountains:—plain, valley.

1238. בָּקַק **bâqaq**, *baw-kah'*; a prim. root; to *pour* out, i.e. to *empty*, fig. to *depopulate;* by anal. to *spread* out (as a fruitful vine):—(make) empty (out), fail, × utterly, make void.

1239. בָּקַר **bâqar**, *baw-kar'*; a prim. root; prop. to *plough*, or (gen.) *break* forth, i.e. (fig.) to *inspect, admire, care for, consider:*—(make) inquire (-ry), (make) search, seek out.

1240. בְּקַר **beqar** (Chald.), *bek-ar'*; corresp. to 1239:—inquire, make search.

1241. בָּקָר **bâqâr**, *baw-kawr'*; from 1239; a *beeve* or animal of the ox kind of either gender (as used for *ploughing*); collect. a *herd:*—beeve, bull (+ -ock), + calf, + cow, great [cattle], + heifer, herd, kine, ox.

1242. בֹּקֶר **bôqer**, *bo'-ker*; from 1239; prop. *dawn* (as the *break* of day); gen. *morning:*—(+) day, early, morning, morrow.

1243. בַּקָּרָה **baqqârâh**, *bak-kaw-raw'*; intens. from 1239; a *looking after:*—seek out.

1244. בִּקֹּרֶת **biqqôreth**, *bik-ko'-reth*; from 1239; prop. *examination*, i.e. (by impl.) *punishment:*—scourged.

1245. בָּקַשׁ **bâqash**, *baw-kash'*; a prim. root; to *search* out (by any method, spec. in worship or prayer); by impl. to *strive after:*—ask, beg, beseech, desire, enquire, get, make inquisition, procure, (make) request, require, seek (for).

1246. בַּקָּשָׁה **baqqâshâh**, *bak-kaw-shaw'*; from 1245; a *petition:*—request.

1247. בַּר **bar** (Chald.), *bar*; corresp. to 1121; a *son, grandson*, etc.:— × old, son.

1248. בַּר **bar**, *bar*; borrowed (as a title) from 1247; the *heir* (apparent to the throne):—son.

1249. בַּר **bar**, *bar*; from 1305 (in its various senses); *beloved;* also *pure, empty:*—choice, clean, clear, pure.

1250. בָּר **bâr**, *bawr*; or

בַּר **bar**, *bar*; from 1305 (in the sense of *winnowing*): *grain* of any kind (even while standing in the field); by extens. the open *country:*—corn, wheat.

1251. בַּר **bar** (Chald.), *bar*; corresp. to 1250; a *field:*—field.

1252. בֹּר **bôr**, *bore*; from 1305; *purity:*—cleanness, pureness.

1253. בֹּר **bôr**, *bore*; the same as 1252; vegetable *lye* (from its *cleansing*); used as a *soap* for washing, or a *flux* for metals:— × never so, purely.

1254. בָּרָא **bârâʼ**, *baw-raw'*; a prim. root; (absol.) to *create;* (qualified) to *cut* down (a wood), *select, feed* (as formative processes):—choose, create (creator), cut down, dispatch, do, make (fat).

1255. בְּרֹאדַךְ בַּלְאֲדָן **Berôʼdak Balʼădân**, *ber-o-dak' bal-ad-awn'*; a var. of 4757; *Berodak-Baladan*, a Bab. king:—Berodach-baladan.

בִּרְאִי **Birʼîy**. See 1011.

1256. בְּרָאיָה **Berâʼyâh**, *ber-aw-yaw'*; from 1254 and 3050; *Jah has created; Berajah*, an Isr.:—Beraiah.

1257. בַּרְבֻּר **barbûr**, *bar-boor'*; by redupl. from 1250; a *fowl* (as fattened on *grain*):—fowl.

1258. בָּרַד **bârad**, *baw-rad'*; a prim. root, to *hail:*—hail.

1259. בָּרָד **bârâd**, *baw-rawd'*; from 1258; *hail:*—hail ([stones]).

1260. בֶּרֶד **Bered**, *beh'-red*; from 1258; *hail; Bered*, the name of a place south of Pal., also of an Isr.:—Bered.

1261. בָּרֹד **bârôd**, *baw-rode'*; from 1258; *spotted* (as if with *hail*):—grisled.

1262. בָּרָה **bârâh**, *baw-raw'*; a prim. root; to *select;* also (as denom. from 1250) to *feed;* also (as equiv. to 1305) to *render clear* (Eccl. 3 : 18):—choose, (cause to) eat, manifest, (give) meat.

1263. בָּרוּךְ **Bârûwk**, *baw-rook'*; pass. part. from 1288; *blessed; Baruk*, the name of three Isr.:—Baruch.

1264. בְּרֹמִים **berôwm**, *ber-ome'*; prob. of for. or. *damask* (stuff of variegated thread):—rich apparel.

1265. בְּרוֹשׁ **berôwsh**, *ber-ōsh'*; of uncert. der.; a *cypress* (?) tree; hence a *lance* or a *musical* instrument (as made of that wood):—fir (tree).

1266. בְּרוֹת **berôwth**, *ber-ōth'*; a var. of 1265; the *cypress* (or some elastic tree):—fir.

1267. בָּרוּת **bârûwth**, *baw-rooth'*; from 1262; *food:*—meat.

1268. בֵּרוֹתָה **Bêrôwthâh**, *bay-ro-thaw'*; or

בֵּרֹתַי **Bêrôthay**, *bay-ro-thah'ee*; prob. from 1266; *cypress* or *cypresslike; Berothah* or *Berothai*, a place north of Pal.:—Berothah, Berothai.

1269. בִּרְזוֹת° **Birzôwth**, *beer-zoth'*; prob. fem. plur. from an unused root (appar. mean. to *pierce*); *holes; Birzoth*, an Isr.:– Birzavith [*from the marg.*].

1270. בַּרְזֶל **barzel**, *bar-zel'*; perh. from the root of 1269; *iron* (as *cutting*); by extens. an iron *implement:*—(ax) head, iron.

1271. בַּרְזִלַּי **Barzillay**, *bar-zil-lah'ee;* from 1270; *iron* hearted; *Barzillai*, the name of three Isr.:—Barzillai.

1272. בָּרַח **bârach**, *baw-rakh'*; a prim. root; to *bolt*, i.e. fig. to *flee* suddenly:—chase (away); drive away, fain, flee (away), put to flight, make haste, reach, run away, shoot.

בָּרִחַ **bârîach**. See 1281.

1273. בַּרְחֻמִי **Barchûmîy**, *bar-khoo-mee'*; by transp. for 978; a *Barchumite*, or native of *Bachurim:*—Barhumite.

1274. בְּרִי **berîy**, *ber-ee'*; from 1262; *fat:*—fat.

1275. בֵּרִי **Bêrîy**, *bay-ree'*; prob. by contr. from 882; *Beri*, an Isr.:—Beri.

1276. בֵּרִי **Bêrîy**, *bay-ree'*; of uncert. der.; (only in the plur. and with the art.) the *Berites*, a place in Pal.:—Berites.

1277. בָּרִיא **bârîy'**, *baw-ree'*; from 1254 (in the sense of 1262); *fatted* or *plump:*—fat ([fleshed], -ter), fed, firm, plenteous, rank.

1278. בְּרִיאָה **berîy'âh**, *ber-ee-aw'*; fem. from 1254; a *creation*, i.e. a *novelty:*—new thing.

1279. בִּרְיָה **biryâh**, *beer-yaw'*; fem. from 1262; *food:*—meat.

1280. בְּרִיחַ **berîyach**, *ber-ee'-akh;* from 1272; a *bolt:*—bar, fugitive.

1281. בָּרִיחַ **bârîyach**, *baw-ree'-akh;* or (short.) בָּרִחַ **bârîach**, *baw-ree'-akh;* from 1272; a *fugitive*, i.e. the *serpent* (as *fleeing*), and the constellation by that name:—crooked, noble, piercing.

1282. בָּרִיחַ **Bârîyach**, *baw-ree'-akh;* the same as 1281; *Bariach*, an Isr.:—Bariah.

1283. בְּרִיעָה **Berîyʻâh**, *ber-ee'-aw;* appar. from the fem. of 7451 with prep. pref.; *in trouble; Beriah*, the name of four Isr.:—Beriah.

1284. בְּרִיעִי **Berîyʻîy**, *ber-ee-ee';* patron. from 1283; a *Beriite* (collect.) or desc. of Beriah:—Beerites.

1285. בְּרִית **berîyth**, *ber-eeth';* from 1262 (in the sense of *cutting* [like 1254]); a *compact* (because made by passing between *pieces* of flesh):—confederacy, [con-]feder[-ate], covenant, league.

1286. בְּרִית **Berîyth**, *ber-eeth';* the same as 1285; *Berith*, a Shechemitish deity:—Berith.

1287. בֹּרִית **bôrîyth**, *bo-reeth';* fem. of 1253; vegetable *alkali:*—sope.

1288. בָּרַךְ **bârak**, *baw-rak';* a prim. root; to *kneel;* by impl. to *bless* God (as an act of adoration), and (vice-versa) man (as a benefit); also (by euphemism) to *curse* (God or the king, as treason):—× abundantly, × altogether, × at all, blaspheme, bless, congratulate, curse, × greatly, × indeed, kneel (down), praise, salute, × still, thank.

1289. בְּרַךְ **berak** (Chald.), *ber-ak';* corresp. to 1288:—bless, kneel.

1290. בֶּרֶךְ **berek**, *beh'-rek;* from 1288; a *knee:*—knee.

1291. בֶּרֶךְ **berek** (Chald.), *beh'-rek;* corresp. to 1290:—knee.

1292. בָּרַכְאֵל **Bârak'êl**, *baw-rak-ale';* from 1288 and 410, *God has blessed; Barakel*, the father of one of Job's friends:—Barachel.

1293. בְּרָכָה **Berâkâh**, *ber-aw-kaw';* from 1288; *benediction;* by impl. *prosperity:*—blessing, liberal, pool, present.

1294. בְּרָכָה **Berâkâh**, *ber-aw-kaw';* the same as 1293; *Berakah*, the name of an Isr., and also of a valley in Pal.:—Berachah.

1295. בְּרֵכָה **berêkâh**, *ber-ay-kaw';* from 1288; a *reservoir* (at which camels *kneel* as a resting-place):—(fish-) pool.

1296. בֶּרֶכְיָה **Berekyâh**, *beh-rek-yaw';* or בֶּרֶכְיָהוּ **Berekyâhûw**, *beh-rek-yaw'-hoo;* from 1290 and 3050; *knee* (i.e. *blessing*) of *Jah; Berekjah*, the name of six Isr.:—Berachiah, Berechiah.

1297. בְּרַם **beram**, (Chald.) *ber-am';* perh. from 7313 with prep. pref.; prop. *highly*, i.e. *surely;* but used adversatively, *however:*—but, nevertheless, yet.

1298. בֶּרַע **Beraʻ**, *beh'-rah;* of uncert. der.; *Bera*, a Sodomitish king:—Bera.

1299. בָּרַק **bâraq**, *baw-rak';* a prim. root; to *lighten* (lightning):—cast forth.

1300. בָּרָק **bârâq**, *baw-rawk';* from 1299; *lightning;* by anal. a *gleam;* concr. a *flashing* sword:—bright, glitter (-ing, sword), lightning.

1301. בָּרָק **Bârâq**, *baw-rawk';* the same as 1300; *Barak*, an Isr.:—Barak.

1302. בַּרְקוֹס **Barqôwç**, *bar-kose';* of uncert. der.; *Barkos*, one of the Nethimim:—Barkos.

1303. בַּרְקָן **barqân**, *bar-kawn';* from 1300; a *thorn* (perh. as burning *brightly*):—brier.

1304. בָּרֶקֶת **bâreqeth**, *baw-reh'-keth;* or בָּרְקַת **bârekath**, *baw-rek-ath';* from 1300; a gem (as *flashing*), perh. the *emerald:*—carbuncle.

1305. בָּרַר **bârar**, *baw-rar';* a prim. root; to *clarify* (i.e. *brighten*), *examine, select:*—make bright, choice, chosen, cleanse (be clean), clearly, polished, (shew self) pure (-ify), purge (out).

1306. בִּרְשַׁע **Birshaʻ**, *beer-shah';* prob. from 7562 with prep. pref.; *with wickedness; Birsha*, a king of Gomorrah:—Birsha.

1307. בֵּרֹתִי **Bêrôthîy**, *bay-ro-thee';* patrial from 1268; a *Berothite*, or inhabitant of Berothai:—Berothite.

1308. בְּשׂוֹר **Besôwr**, *bes-ore';* from 1319; *cheerful; Besor*, a stream of Pal.:—Besor.

1309. בְּשׂוֹרָה **besôwrâh**, *bes-o-raw';* or (short.) בְּשֹׂרָה **besôrâh**, *bes-o-raw';* fem. from 1319; glad *tidings;* by impl. *reward for good news:*—reward for tidings.

1310. בָּשַׁל **bâshal**, *baw-shal';* a prim. root; prop. to *boil* up; hence to *be done* in cooking; fig. to *ripen:*—bake, boil, bring forth, is ripe, roast, seethe, sod (be sodden).

1311. בָּשֵׁל **bâshêl**, *baw-shale';* from 1310; *boiled:*—× at all, sodden.

1312. בִּשְׁלָם **Bishlâm**, *bish-lawm';* of for. der.; *Bishlam*, a Pers.:—Bishlam.

1313. בָּשָׂם **bâsâm**, *baw-sawm';* from an unused root mean. to *be fragrant;* [comp. 5561] the *balsam* plant:—spice.

1314. בֶּשֶׂם **besem**, *beh'-sem;* or בֹּשֶׂם **bôsem**, *bo'-sem;* from the same as 1313; *fragrance;* by impl. *spicery;* also the *balsam* plant:—smell, spice, sweet (odour).

1315. בָּשְׂמַת **Bosmath**, *bos-math';* fem. of 1314 (the second form); *fragrance; Bosmath*, the name of a wife of Esau, and of a daughter of Solomon:—Bashemath, Basmath.

1316. בָּשָׁן **Bâshân**, *baw-shawn';* of uncert. der.; *Bashan* (often with the art.), a region E. of the Jordan:—Bashan.

1317. בָּשְׁנָה **boshnâh**, *bosh-naw';* fem. from 954; *shamefulness:*—shame.

1318. בָּשַׁס **bâshaç**, *baw-shas';* a prim. root; to *trample* down:—tread.

1319. בָּשַׂר **bâsar**, *baw-sar';* a prim. root; prop. to *be fresh*, i.e. *full* (*rosy*, fig. *cheerful*); to *announce* (glad news):—messenger, preach, publish, shew forth, (bear, bring, carry, preach, good, tell good) tidings.

1320. בָּשָׂר **bâsâr**, *baw-sawr';* from 1319; *flesh* (from its *freshness*); by extens. *body, person;* also (by euphem.) the *pudenda* of a man:—body, [fat, lean] flesh [-ed], kin, [man-] kind, + nakedness, self, skin.

1321. בְּשַׂר **besar** (Chald.), *bes-ar';* corresp. to 1320:—flesh.

בְּשֹׂרָה **besôrâh**. See 1309.

1322. בֹּשֶׁת **bôsheth**, *bo'-sheth;* from 954; *shame* (the feeling and the condition, as well as its cause); by impl. (spec.) an *idol:*—ashamed, confusion, + greatly, (put to) shame (-ful thing).

1323. בַּת **bath**, *bath;* from 1129 (as fem. of 1121); a *daughter* (used in the same wide sense as other terms of relationship, lit. and fig.):—apple [of the eye], branch, company, daughter, × first, × old, + owl, town, village.

1324. בַּת **bath**, *bath;* prob. from the same as 1327; a *bath* or Heb. measure (as a means of *division*) of liquids:—bath.

1325. בַּת **bath** (Chald.), *bath;* corresp. to 1324:—bath.

1326. בָּתָה **bâthâh**, *baw-thaw';* prob. an orth. var. for 1327; *desolation:*—waste.

1327. בַּתָּה **battâh**, *bat-taw';* fem. from an unused root (mean. to *break* in pieces); *desolation:*—desolate.

1328. בְּתוּאֵל **Bethûw'êl**, *beth-oo-ale';* appar. from the same as 1326 and 410; *destroyed of God; Bethuel*, the name of a nephew of Abraham, and of a place in Pal.:—Bethuel. Comp. 1329.

1329. בְּתוּל **Bethûwl**, *beth-ool';* for 1328; *Bethul* (i.e. *Bethuel*), a place in Pal.:—Bethuel.

1330. בְּתוּלָה **bethûwlâh**, *beth-oo-law';* fem. pass. part. of an unused root mean. to *separate;* a *virgin* (from her *privacy*); sometimes (by continuation) a *bride;* also (fig.) a *city* or *state:*—maid, virgin.

1331. בְּתוּלִים **bethûwlîym**, *beth-oo-leem';* masc. plur. of the same as 1330; (collect. and abstr.) *virginity;* by impl. and concr. the *tokens* of it:—× maid, virginity.

1332. בִּתְיָה **Bithyâh**, *bith-yaw';* from 1323 and 3050; *daughter* (i.e. worshipper) *of Jah; Bithjah*, an Eg. woman:—Bithiah.

1333. בָּתַק **bâthaq**, *baw-thak';* a prim. root; to *cut* in pieces:—thrust through.

1334. בָּתַר **bâthar**, *baw-thar';* a prim. root, to *chop* up:—divide.

1335. בֶּתֶר **bether**, *beh'-ther;* from 1334; a *section:*—part, piece.

1336. בֶּתֶר **Bether**, *beh'-ther;* the same as 1335; *Bether*, a (craggy) place in Pal.:—Bether.

1337. בַּת רַבִּים **Bath Rabbîym**, *bath rabbeem';* from 1323 and a masc. plur. from 7227; the *daughter* (i.e. *city*) *of Rabbah:*—Bath-rabbim.

1338. בִּתְרוֹן **Bithrôwn**, *bith-rone';* from 1334; (with the art.) the *craggy* spot; *Bithron*, a place E. of the Jordan:—Bithron.

1339. בַּת־שֶׁבַע **Bath-Shebaʻ**, *bath-sheh'-bah;* from 1323 and 7651 (in the sense of 7650); *daughter of an oath; Bath-Sheba*, the mother of Solomon:—Bath-sheba.

1340. בַּת־שׁוּעַ **Bath-Shûwaʻ**, *bath-shoo'-ah;* from 1323 and 7771; *daughter of wealth; Bath-shua*, the same as 1339:—Bath-shua.

ג

1341. גֵּא **gê'**, *gay';* for 1343; *haughty:*—proud.

1342. גָּאָה **gâ'âh**, *gaw-aw';* a prim. root; to *mount* up; hence in gen. to *rise*, (fig.) be *majestic:*—gloriously, grow up, increase, be risen, triumph.

1343. גֵּאֶה **gê'eh**, *gay-eh';* from 1342; *lofty;* fig. *arrogant:*—proud.

1344. גֵּאָה **gê'âh**, *gay-aw';* fem. from 1342; *arrogance:*—pride.

1345. גְּאוּאֵל **Ge'ûw'êl**, *gheh-oo-ale';* from 1342 and 410; *majesty of God; Geüel*, an Isr.:—Geuel.

1346. גַּאֲוָה **ga'ăvâh**, *gah-av-aw'*; from 1342; *arrogance* or *majesty*; by impl. (concr.) *ornament*:—excellency, haughtiness, highness, pride, proudly, swelling.

1347. גָּאוֹן **gâ'ôwn**, *gaw-ohn'*; from 1342; the same as 1346:—arrogancy, excellency (-lent), majesty, pomp, pride, proud, swelling.

1348. גֵּאוּת **gê'ûwth**, *gay-ooth'*; from 1342; the same as 1346:—excellent things, lifting up, majesty, pride, proudly, raging.

1349. גַּאֲיוֹן **ga'ăyôwn**, *gah-ăh-yone'*; from 1342: *haughty*:—proud.

1350. גָּאַל **gâ'al**, *gaw-al'*; a prim. root, to *redeem* (according to the Oriental law of kinship), i.e. to *be the next of kin* (and as such to *buy back* a relative's property, *marry* his widow, etc.):—× in any wise, × at all, avenger, deliver, (do, perform the part of near, next) kinsfolk (-man), purchase, ransom, redeem (-er), revenger.

1351. גָּאַל **gâ'al**, *gaw-al'*; a prim. root, [rather ident. with 1350, through the idea of *freeing*, i.e. *repudiating*]; to *soil* or (fig.) *desecrate*:—defile, pollute, stain.

1352. גֹּאֶל **gô'el**, *go'-el*; from 1351; *profanation*:—defile.

1353. גְּאֻלָּה **ge'ullâh**, *gheh-ool-law'*; fem. pass. part. of 1350; *redemption* (including the right and the object); by impl. *relationship*:—kindred, redeem, redemption, right.

1354. גַּב **gab**, *gab*; from an unused root mean. to *hollow* or *curve*; the *back* (as *rounded* [comp. 1460 and 1479]; by anal. the *top* or *rim*, a *boss*, a *vault*, *arch* of eye, *bulwarks*, etc.:—back, body, boss, eminent (higher) place, [eye] brows, nave, ring.

1355. גַּב **gab** (Chald.), *gab*; corresp. to 1354:—back.

1356. גֵּב **gêb**, *gabe*; from 1461; a *log* (as *cut* out); also *well* or *cistern* (as *dug*):—beam, ditch, pit.

1357. גֵּב **gêb**, *gabe*; prob. from 1461 [comp. 1462]; a *locust* (from its *cutting*):—locust.

1358. גֹּב **gôb** (Chald.), *gobe*; from a root corresp. to 1461; a *pit* (for wild animals) (as *cut* out):—den.

1359. גֹּב **Gôb**, *gobe*; or (fully)
גּוֹב **Gôwb**, *gobe'*; from 1461; *pit*; *Gob*, a place in Pal.:—Gob.

1360. גֶּבֶא **gebe**, *geh'-beh*; from an unused root mean. prob. to *collect*; a *reservoir*; by anal. a *marsh*:—marish, pit.

1361. גָּבַהּ **gâbahh**, *gaw-bah'*; a prim. root; to *soar*, i.e. *be lofty*; fig. to *be haughty*:—exalt, be haughty, be (make) high (-er), lift up, mount up, be proud, raise up great height, upward.

1362. גָּבָהּ **gâbâhh**, *gaw-bawh'*; from 1361; *lofty* (lit. or fig.):—high, proud.

1363. גֹּבַהּ **gôbahh**, *go'-bah*; from 1361; *elation*, *grandeur*, *arrogance*:—excellency, haughty, height, high, loftiness, pride.

1364. גָּבֹהַּ **gâbôahh**, *gaw-bo'-ah*; or (fully)
גָּבוֹהַּ **gâbôwahh**, *gaw-bo'-ah*; from 1361; *elevated* (or *elated*), *powerful*, *arrogant*:—haughty, height, high (-er), lofty, proud, × exceeding proudly.

1365. גַּבְהוּת **gabhûwth**, *gab-hooth'*; from 1361; *pride*:—loftiness, lofty.

1366. גְּבוּל **gebûwl**, *gheb-ool'*; or (short.)
גְּבֻל **gebûl**, *gheb-ool'*; from 1379; prop. a *cord* (as *twisted*), i.e. (by impl.) a *boundary*; by extens. the *territory* inclosed:—border, bound, coast, × great, landmark, limit, quarter, space.

1367. גְּבוּלָה **gebûwlâh**, *gheb-oo-law'*; or (short.)
גְּבֻלָה **gebûlâh**, *gheb-oo-law'*; fem. of 1366; a *boundary*, *region*:—border, bound, coast, landmark, place.

1368. גִּבּוֹר **gibbôwr**, *ghib-bore'*; or (short.)
גִּבֹּר **gibbôr**, *ghib-bore'*; intens. from the same as 1397; *powerful*; by impl. *warrior*, *tyrant*:—champion, chief, × excel, giant, man, mighty (man, one), strong (man), valiant man.

1369. גְּבוּרָה **gebûwrâh**, *gheb-oo-raw'*; fem. pass. part. from the same as 1368; *force* (lit. or fig.); by impl. *valor*, *victory*:—force, mastery, might, mighty (act, power), power, strength.

1370. גְּבוּרָה **gebûwrâh** (Chald.), *gheb-oo-raw'*; corresp. to 1369; *power*:—might.

1371. גִּבֵּחַ **gibbêach**, *ghib-bay'-akh*; from an unused root mean. to *be high* (in the forehead); *bald* in the forehead:—forehead bald.

1372. גַּבַּחַת **gabbachath**, *gab-bakh'-ath*; from the same as 1371; *baldness* in the forehead; by anal. a *bare spot* on the right side of cloth:—bald forehead, × without.

1373. גַּבַּי **Gabbay**, *gab-bah'ee*; from the same as 1354; *collective*:—*Gabbai*, an Isr.:—Gabbai.

1374. גֵּבִים **Gêbîym**, *gay-beem'*; plur. of 1356; *cisterns*; *Gebim*, a place in Pal.:—Gebim.

1375. גְּבִיעַ **gebîyaʻ**, *gheb-ee'-ah*; from an unused root (mean. to *be convex*); a *goblet*; by anal. the *calyx* of a flower:—house, cup, pot.

1376. גְּבִיר **gebîyr**, *gheb-eer'*; from 1396; a *master*:—lord.

1377. גְּבִירָה **gebîyrâh**, *gheb-ee-raw'*; fem. of 1376; a *mistress*:—queen.

1378. גָּבִישׁ **gâbîysh**, *gaw-beesh'*; from an unused root (prob. mean. to *freeze*); *crystal* (from its resemblance to *ice*):—pearl.

1379. גָּבַל **gâbal**, *gaw-bal'*; a prim. root; prop. to *twist* as a rope; only (as a denom. from 1366) to *bound* (as by a line):—be border, set (bounds about).

1380. גְּבַל **Gebal**, *gheb-al'*; from 1379 (in the sense of a *chain* of hills); a *mountain*; *Gebal*, a place in Phœnicia:—Gebal.

1381. גְּבָל **Gebâl**, *gheb-awl'*; the same as 1380; *Gebal*, a region in Idumæa:—Gebal.

גְּבֻלָה **gebûlâh**. See 1367.

1382. גִּבְלִי **Giblîy**, *ghib-lee'*; patrial from 1380; a *Gebalite*, or inhab. of Gebal:—Giblites, stone-squarer.

1383. גַּבְלֻת **gablûth**, *gab-looth'*; from 1379; a twisted *chain* or *lace*:—end.

1384. גִּבֵּן **gibbên**, *gib-bane'*; from an unused root mean. to be *arched* or *contracted*; *hunch-backed*:—crookbackt.

1385. גְּבִינָה **gebînah**, *gheb-ee-naw'*; fem. from the same as 1384; *curdled* milk:—cheese.

1386. גַּבְנֹן **gabnôn**, *gab-nohn'*; from the same as 1384; a *hump* or *peak* of hills:—high.

1387. גֶּבַע **Gebaʻ**, *gheh'-bah*; from the same as 1375, a *hillock*; *Geba*, a place in Pal.:—Gaba, Geba, Gibeah.

1388. גִּבְעָא **Gibʻâ'**, *ghib-aw'*; by perm. for 1389; a *hill*; *Giba*, a place in Pal.:—Gibeah.

1389. גִּבְעָה **gibʻâh**, *ghib-aw'*; fem. from the same as 1387; a *hillock*:—hill, little hill.

1390. גִּבְעָה **Gibʻâh**, *ghib-aw'*; the same as 1389; *Gibah*; the name of three places in Pal.:—Gibeah, the hill.

1391. גִּבְעוֹן **Gibʻôwn**, *ghib-ohn'*; from the same as 1387; *hilly*; *Gibon*, a place in Pal.:—Gibeon.

1392. גִּבְעֹל **gibʻôl**, *ghib-ole'*; prol. from 1375; the *calyx* of a flower:—bolled.

1393. גִּבְעֹנִי **Gibʻônîy**, *ghib-o-nee'*; patrial from 1391; a *Gibonite*, or inhab. of Gibon:—Gibeonite.

1394. גִּבְעַת **Gibʻath**, *ghib-ath'*; from the same as 1375; *hilliness*; *Gibath*:—Gibeath.

1395. גִּבְעָתִי **Gibʻâthîy**, *ghib-aw-thee'*; patrial from 1390; a *Gibathite*, or inhab. of Gibath:—Gibeathite.

1396. גָּבַר **gâbar**, *gaw-bar'*; a prim. root; to *be strong*; by impl. to *prevail*, *act insolently*:—exceed, confirm, be great, be mighty, prevail, put to more [strength], strengthen, be stronger, be valiant.

1397. גֶּבֶר **geber**, *gheh'-ber*; from 1396; prop. a *valiant* man or *warrior*; gen. a *person* simply:—every one, man, × mighty.

1398. גֶּבֶר **Geber**, *gheh'-ber*; the same as 1397; *Geber*, the name of two Isr.:—Geber.

1399. גְּבַר **gebar**, *gheb-ar'*; from 1396; the same as 1397; a person:—man.

1400. גְּבַר **gebar** (Chald.), *gheb-ar'*; corresp. to 1399:—certain, man.

1401. גִּבָּר **gibbâr** (Chald.), *ghib-bawr'*; intens. of 1400; *valiant*, or *warrior*:—mighty.

1402. גִּבָּר **Gibbâr**, *ghib-bawr'*; intens. of 1399; *Gibbar*, an Isr.:—Gibbar.

גְּבֻרָה **gebûrâh**. See 1369.

1403. גַּבְרִיאֵל **Gabrîy'êl**, *gab-ree-ale'*; from 1397 and 410; *man of God*; *Gabriel*, an archangel:—Gabriel.

1404. גְּבֶרֶת **gebereth**, *gheb-eh'-reth*; fem. of 1376; *mistress*:—lady, mistress.

1405. גִּבְּתוֹן **Gibbethôwn**, *ghib-beth-one'*; intens. from 1389; a *hilly* spot; *Gibbethon*, a place in Pal.:—Gibbethon.

1406. גָּג **gâg**, *gawg*; prob. by redupl. from 1342; a *roof*; by anal. the *top* of an altar:—roof (of the house), (house) top (of the house).

1407. גַּד **gad**, *gad*; from 1413 (in the sense of *cutting*); *coriander* seed (from its furrows):—coriander.

1408. גַּד **Gad**, *gad*; a var. of 1409; *Fortune*, a Bab. deity:—that troop.

1409. גָּד **gâd**, *gawd*; from 1464 (in the sense of *distributing*); *fortune*:—troop.

1410. גָּד **Gâd**, *gawd*; from 1464; *Gad*, a son of Jacob, includ. his tribe and its territory; also a prophet:—Gad.

1411. גְּדָבָר **gedâbâr** (Chald.), *ghed-aw-bawr'*; corresp. to 1489; a *treasurer*:—treasurer.

1412. גֻּדְגֹּדָה **Gudgôdâh**, *gud-go'-daw*; by redupl. from 1413 (in the sense of *cutting*) *cleft*; *Gudgodah*, a place in the Desert:—Gudgodah.

1413. גָּדַד **gâdad**, *gaw-dad'*; a prim. root [comp. 1464]; to *crowd*; also to *gash* (as if by *pressing* into):—assemble (selves by troops), gather (selves together, self in troops), cut selves.

1414. גְּדַד **gedad** (Chald.), *ghed-ad'*; corresp. to 1413; to *cut down*:—hew down.

גְּדוּדָה **gedûdâh**. See 1417.

1415. גָּדָה **gâdâh**, *gaw-daw'*; from an unused root (mean. to *cut* off); a *border* of a river (as *cut* into by the stream):—bank.

גַּדָּה **Gaddâh**. See 2693.

1416. גְּדוּד **gedûwd**, *ghed-ood'*; from 1413; a *crowd* (espec. of soldiers):—army, band (of men), company, troop (of robbers).

1417. גְּדוּד **gedûwd**, *ghed-ood'*; or (fem.)
גְּדֻדָה **gedûdâh**, *ghed-oo-daw'*; from 1413; a *furrow* (as *cut*):—furrow.

1418. גְּדוּדָה **gedûwdâh**, *ghed-oo-daw'*; fem. part. pass. of 1413; an *incision*:—cutting.

1419. גָּדוֹל **gâdôwl**, *gaw-dole'*; or (short.)
גָּדֹל **gâdôl**, *gaw-dole'*; from 1431; *great* (in any sense); hence *older*; also *insolent*:—+ aloud, elder (-est), + exceeding (-ly), + far, (man of) great (man, matter, thing, -er, -ness), high, long, loud, mighty, more, much, noble, proud thing, × sore, (×) very.

1420. גְּדוּלָה **gedûwlâh**, *ghed-oo-law'*; or (short.) גְּדֻלָּה **gedullâh**, *ghed-ool-law'*; or (less accurately)
גְּדוּלָּה **gedûwllâh**, *ghed-ool-law'*; fem. of 1419; *greatness*; (concr.) *mighty acts*:—dignity, great things (-ness), majesty.

1421. גִּדּוּף **giddûwph**, *ghid-doof'*; or (short.)
גִּדֻּף **giddûph**, *ghid-doof'*; and (fem.)
גִּדּוּפָה **giddûphâh**, *ghid-doo-faw'*; or
גִּדֻּפָה **giddûphâh**, *ghid-doo-faw'*; from 1422; *vilification*:—reproach, reviling.

1422. גְּדוּפָה **gᵉdûwphâh**, *ghed-oo-faw'*; fem. pass. part. of 1442; a *revilement:*—taunt.

גְּדוֹר **Gᵉdôwr.** See 1446.

1423. גְּדִי **gᵉdîy**, *ghed-ee'*; from the same as 1415; a young *goat* (from *browsing*):—kid.

1424. גָּדִי **Gâdîy**, *gaw-dee'*; from 1409; *fortunate; Gadi*, an Isr.:—Gadi.

1425. גָּדִי **Gâdîy**, *gaw-dee'*; patron. from 1410; a *Gadite* (collect.) or desc. of Gad:—Gadites, children of Gad.

1426. גַּדִּי **Gaddîy**, *gad-dee'*; intens. for 1424; *Gaddi*, an Isr.:—Gaddi.

1427. גַּדִּיאֵל **Gaddîy'êl**, *gad-dee-ale'*; from 1409 and 410; *fortune of God; Gaddiel*, an Isr.:—Gaddiel.

1428. גִּדְיָה° **gidyâh**, *ghid-yaw'*; or

גַּדְיָה° **gadyâh**, *gad-yaw'*; the same as 1415; a river *brink:*—bank.

1429. גְּדִיָּה **gᵉdîyâh**, *ghed-ee-yaw'*; fem. of 1423; a young female *goat:*—kid.

1430. גָּדִישׁ **gâdîysh**, *gaw-deesh'*; from an unused root (mean. to *heap* up); a *stack* of sheaves; by anal. a *tomb:*—shock (stack) (of corn), tomb.

1431. גָּדַל **gâdal**, *gaw-dal'*; a prim. root; prop. to *twist* [comp. 1434], i.e. to *be* (caus. *make*) *large* (in various senses, as in body, mind, estate or honor, also in pride):—advance, boast, bring up, exceed, excellent, be (-come, do, give, make, wax), great (-er, come to . . . estate, + things), grow (up), increase, lift up, magnify (-ifical), be much set by, nourish (up), pass, promote, proudly [spoken], tower.

1432. גָּדֵל **gâdêl**, *gaw-dale'*; from 1431; *large* (lit. or fig.):—great, grew.

1433. גֹּדֶל **gôdel**, *go'-del*; from 1431; *magnitude* (lit. or fig.):—greatness, stout (-ness).

1434. גְּדִל **gᵉdîl**, *ghed-eel'*; from 1431 (in the sense of *twisting*); *thread*, i.e. a *tassel* or *festoon:*—fringe, wreath.

1435. גִּדֵּל **Giddêl**, *ghid-dale'*; from 1431; *stout; Giddel*, the name of one of the Nethinim, also of one of "Solomon's servants":—Giddel.

גָּדֹל **gâdôl.** See 1419.

גְּדֻלָּה **gᵉdullâh.** See 1420.

1436. גְּדַלְיָה **Gᵉdalyâh**, *ghed-al-yaw'*; or (prol.)

גְּדַלְיָהוּ **Gᵉdalyâhûw**, *ghed-al-yaw'-hoo*; from 1431 and 3050; *Jah has become great; Gedaljah*, the name of five Isr.:—Gedaliah.

1437. גִּדַּלְתִּי **Giddaltîy**, *ghid-dal'-tee*; from 1431; *I have made great; Giddalti*, an Isr.:—Giddalti.

1438. גָּדַע **gâdaʻ**, *gaw-dah'*; a prim. root; to *fell* a tree; gen. to *destroy* anything:—cut (asunder, in sunder, down, off), hew down.

1439. גִּדְעוֹן **Gidʻôwn**, *ghid-ohn'*; from 1438; *feller* (i.e. *warrior*); *Gidon*, an Isr.:—Gideon.

1440. גִּדְעֹם **Gidʻôm**, *ghid-ohm'*; from 1438; a *cutting* (i.e. *desolation*); *Gidom*, a place in Pal.:—Gidom.

1441. גִּדְעֹנִי **Gidʻônîy**, *ghid-o-nee'*; from 1438; *warlike* [comp. 1439]; *Gidoni*, an Isr.:—Gideoni.

1442. גָּדַף **gâdaph**, *gaw-daf'*; a prim. root; to *hack* (with words), i.e. *revile:*—blaspheme, reproach.

גִּדּוּף **giddûph**, and

גִּדּוּפָה **giddûphâh.** See 1421.

1443. גָּדַר **gâdar**, *gaw-dar'*; a prim. root; to *wall* in or around:—close up, fence up, hedge, inclose, make up [a wall], mason, repairer.

1444. גֶּדֶר **geder**, *gheh'-der*; from 1443; a *circumvallation:*—wall.

1445. גֶּדֶר **Geder**, *gheh'-der*; the same as 1444; *Geder*, a place in Pal.:—Geder.

1446. גְּדֹר **Gᵉdôr**, *ghed-ore'*; or (fully)

גְּדוֹר **Gᵉdôwr**, *ghed-ore'*; from 1443; *inclosure; Gedor*, a place in Pal.; also the name of three Isr.:—Gedor.

1447. גָּדֵר **gâdêr**, *gaw-dare'*; from 1443; a *circumvallation;* by impl. an *inclosure:*—fence, hedge, wall.

1448. גְּדֵרָה **gᵉdêrâh**, *ghed-ay-raw'*; fem. of 1447; *inclosure* (espec. for flocks):—[sheep-] cote (fold) hedge, wall.

1449. גְּדֵרָה **Gᵉdêrâh**, *ghed-ay-raw'*; the same as 1448; (with the art.) *Gederah*, a place in Pal.:—Gederah, hedges.

1450. גְּדֵרוֹת **Gᵉdêrôwth**, *ghed-ay-rohth'*; plur. of 1448; *walls; Gederoth*, a place in Pal.:—Gederoth.

1451. גְּדֵרִי **Gᵉdêrîy**, *ghed-ay-ree'*; patrial from 1445; a *Gederite*, or inhab. of Geder:—Gederite.

1452. גְּדֵרָתִי **Gᵉdêrâthîy**, *ghed-ay-raw-thee'*; patrial from 1449; a *Gederathite*, or inhab. of Gederah:—Gederathite.

1453. גְּדֵרֹתַיִם **Gᵉdêrôthayim**, *ghed-ay-ro-thah'-yim*; dual of 1448; *double wall; Gederothajim*, a place in Pal.:—Gederothaim.

1454. גֵּה **gêh**, *gay*; prob. a clerical error for 2088; *this:*—this.

1455. גָּהָה **gâhâh**, *gaw-haw'*; a prim. root; to *remove* (a bandage from a wound, i.e. *heal* it):—cure.

1456. גֵּהָה **gêhâh**, *gay-haw'*; from 1455; a *cure:*—medicine.

1457. גָּהַר **gâhar**, *gaw-har'*; a prim. root; to *prostrate* oneself:—cast self down, stretch self.

1458. גַּו **gav**, *gav*; another form for 1460; the *back:*—back.

1459. גַּו **gav** (Chald.), *gav*; corresp. to 1460; the *middle:*—midst, same, there- (where-) in.

1460. גֵּו **gêv** *gave*; from 1342 [corresp. to 1354]; the *back;* by anal. the *middle:*— + among, back, body.

1461. גּוּב **gûwb**, *goob*; a prim. root; to *dig:*—husbandman.

1462. גּוֹב **gôwb**, *gobe*; from 1461; the *locust* (from its *grubbing* as a larve):—grasshopper, × great.

1463. גּוֹג **Gôwg**, *gohg*; of uncert. der.; *Gog*, the name of an Isr., also of some northern nation:—Gog.

1464. גּוּד **gûwd**, *goode*; a prim. root [akin to 1413]; to *crowd* upon, i.e. *attack:*—invade, overcome.

1465. גֵּוָה **gêvâh**, *gay-vaw'*; fem. of 1460; the *back*, i.e. (by extens.) the *person:*—body.

1466. גֵּוָה **gêvah**, *gay-vaw'*; the same as 1465; *exaltation;* (fig.) *arrogance:*—lifting up, pride.

1467. גֵּוָה **gêvâh** (Chald.), *gay-vaw'*; corresp. to 1466:—pride.

1468. גּוּז **gûwz**, *gooz*; a prim. root [comp. 1494]; prop. to *shear* off; but used only in the (fig.) sense of *passing* rapidly:—bring, cut off.

1469. גּוֹזָל **gôwzâl**, *go-zawl'*; or (short.)

גֹּזָל **gôzâl**, *go-zawl'*; from 1497; a *nestling* (as being comparatively *nude* of feathers):—young (pigeon).

1470. גּוֹזָן **Gôwzân**, *go-zawn'*; prob. from 1468; a *quarry* (as a place of *cutting* stones); *Gozan*, a province of Assyria:—Gozan.

1471. גּוֹי **gôwy**, *go'ee*; rarely (short.)

גֹּי **gôy**, *go'-ee*; appar. from the same root as 1465 (in the sense of *massing*); a foreign *nation;* hence a *Gentile;* also (fig.) a *troop* of animals, or a *flight* of locusts:—Gentile, heathen, nation, people.

1472. גְּוִיָּה **gᵉvîyâh**, *ghev-ee-yaw'*; prol. for 1465; a *body*, whether alive or dead:—(dead) body, carcase, corpse.

1473. גּוֹלָה **gôwlâh**, *go-law'*; or (short.)

גֹּלָה **gôlah**, *go-law'*; act. part. fem. of 1540; *exile;* concr. and coll. *exiles:*—(carried away), captive (-ity), removing.

1474. גּוֹלָן **Gôwlân**, *go-lawn'*; from 1473; *captive; Golan*, a place east of the Jordan:—Golan.

1475. גּוּמָּץ **gûwmmâts**, *goom-mawts'*; of uncert. der.; a *pit:*—pit.

1476. גּוּנִי **Gûwnîy**, *goo-nee'*; prob. from 1598; *protected; Guni*, the name of two Isr.:—Guni.

1477. גּוּנִי **Gûwnîy**, *goo-nee'*; patron. from 1476; a *Gunite* (collect. with art. pref.) or desc. of Guni:—Gunites.

1478. גָּוַע **gâvaʻ**, *gaw-vah'*; a prim. root; to *breathe* out, i.e. (by impl.) *expire:*—die, be dead, give up the ghost, perish.

1479. גּוּף **gûwph**, *goof*; a prim. root; prop. to *hollow* or *arch*, i.e. (fig.) *close;* to *shut:*—shut.

1480. גּוּפָה **gûwphâh**, *goo-faw'*; from 1479; a *corpse* (as *closed* to sense):—body.

1481. גּוּר **gûwr**, *goor*; a prim. root; prop. to *turn* aside from the road (for a lodging or any other purpose), i.e. *sojourn* (as a guest); also to *shrink, fear* (as in a *strange* place); also to *gather* for hostility (as *afraid*):—abide, assemble, be afraid, dwell, fear, gather (together), inhabitant, remain, sojourn, stand in awe, (be) stranger, × surely.

1482. גּוּר **gûwr**, *goor*; or (short.)

גֻּר **gûr**, *goor*; perh. from 1481; a *cub* (as still *abiding* in the lair), espec. of the lion:—whelp, young one.

1483. גּוּר **Gûwr**, *goor*; the same as 1482; *Gur*, a place in Pal.:—Gur.

1484. גּוֹר **gôwr**, *gore*; or (fem.)

גֹּרָה **gôrah**, *go-raw'*; a var. of 1482:—whelp.

1485. גּוּר־בַּעַל **Gûwr-Baʻal**, *goor-bah'-al*; from 1481 and 1168; *dwelling of Baal; Gur-Baal*, a place in Arabia:—Gur-baal.

1486. גּוֹרָל **gôwrâl**, *go-rawl'*; or (short.)

גֹּרָל **gôral**, *go-ral'*; from an unused root mean. to *be rough* (as stone); prop. a *pebble*, i.e. a *lot* (small stones being used for that purpose); fig. a *portion* or *destiny* (as if determined by lot):—lot.

1487. גּוּשׁ **gûwsh**, *goosh*; or rather (by perm.)

גִּישׁ **gîysh**, *gheesh*; of uncert. der.; a *mass* of earth:—clod.

1488. גֵּז **gêz**, *gaze*; from 1494; a *fleece* (as *shorn*); also mown *grass:*—fleece, mowing, mown grass.

1489. גִּזְבָּר **gizbâr**, *ghiz-bawr'*; of for. der.; *treasurer:*—treasurer.

1490. גִּזְבָּר **gizbâr** (Chald.), *ghiz-bawr'*; corresp. to 1489:—treasurer.

1491. גָּזָה **gâzâh**, *gaw-zaw'*; a prim. root [akin to 1468]; to *cut* off, i.e. *portion* out:—take.

1492. גַּזָּה **gazzâh**, *gaz-zaw'*; fem. from 1494; a *fleece:*—fleece.

1493. גִּזוֹנִי **Gizôwnîy**, *ghee-zo-nee'*; patrial from the unused name of a place appar. in Pal.; a *Gizonite* or inhab. of Gizoh:—Gizonite.

1494. גָּזַז **gâzaz**, *gaw-zaz'*; a prim. root [akin to 1468]; to *cut* off; spec. to *shear* a flock, or *shave* the hair; fig. to *destroy* an enemy:—cut off (down), poll, shave, ([sheep-]) shear (-er).

1495. גָּזֵז **Gâzêz** *gaw-zaze'*; from 1494; *shearer; Gazez*, the name of two Isr.:—Gazez.

1496. גָּזִית **gâzîyth**, *gaw-zeeth'*; from 1491; something *cut*, i.e. *dressed* stone:—hewed, hewn stone, wrought.

1497. גָּזַל **gâzal**, *gaw-zal'*; a prim. root; to *pluck* off; spec. to *flay, strip* or *rob:*—catch, consume, exercise [robbery], pluck (off), rob, spoil, take away (by force, violence), tear.

1498. גָּזֵל **gâzêl**, *gaw-zale'*; from 1497; *robbery*, or (concr.) *plunder:*—robbery, thing taken away by violence.

1499. גֵּזֶל **gêzel**, *ghe'-zel*; from 1497; *plunder*, i.e. *violence:*—violence, violent perverting.

גֹּזָל **gôzâl.** See 1469.

500. גְּזֵלָה **gᵉzêlâh**, *ghez-ay-law'*; fem. of 1498 and mean. the same:—that (he had bbed) [which he took violently away], spoil, vioence.

501. גָּזָם **gâzâm**, *gaw-zawm'*; from an unused root mean. to *devour*; a kind of *locust*:—lmer-worm.

502. גַּזָּם **Gazzâm**, *gaz-zawm'*; from the same as 1501; *devourer*:—*Gazzam*, one of the Neinim:—Gazzam.

503. גֶּזַע **gezaʻ**, *geh'-zah*; from an unused root mean. to *cut* down (trees); the *trunk* or *ump* of a tree (as felled or as planted):—stem, stock.

504. גָּזַר **gâzar**, *gaw-zar'*; a prim. root; to *cut* down or off; (fig.) to *destroy, divide, ex ude* or *decide*:—cut down (off), decree, divide, natch.

505. גְּזַר **gᵉzar** (Chald.), *ghez-ar'*; corresp. to 1504; to *quarry; determine*:—cut out, oothsayer.

506. גֶּזֶר **gezer**, *gheh'-zer*; from 1504; something *cut* off; a *portion*:—part, piece.

507. גֶּזֶר **Gezer**, *gheh'-zer*; the same as 1506; *Gezer*, a place in Pal.:—Gazer, Gezer.

508. גִּזְרָה **gizrâh**, *ghiz-raw'*; fem. of 1506; the *figure* or person (as if *cut* out); also an *nclosure* (as *separated*):—polishing, separate place.

509. גְּזֵרָה **gᵉzêrâh**, *ghez-ay-raw'*; from 1504; a *desert* (as *separated*):—not inhabited.

510. גְּזֵרָה **gᵉzêrâh** (Chald.), *ghez-ay-raw'*; from 1505 (as 1504); a *decree*:—decree.

511. גִּזְרִי **Gizrîy** (in the marg.), *ghiz-ree'*; patrial from 1507; a *Gezerite* (collect.) or nhab. of Gezer; but better (as in the text) by transp.

גִּרְזִי **Girzîy**, *gher-zee'*; patrial of 1630; a *Girzite* (collect.) or member of a native ribe in Pal.:—Gezrites.

גִּחוֹן **Gîchôwn**. See 1521.

512. גָּחוֹן **gâchôwn**, *gaw-khone'*; prob. from 1518; the external *abdomen, belly* (as he *source* of the fœtus [comp. 1521]):—belly.

גֵּחֲזִי **Gêchăzîy**. See 1522.

גָּחֹל **gâchol**. See 1513.

513. גֶּחֶל **gechel**, *geh'-khel*; or (fem.)

גַּחֶלֶת **gacheleth**, *gah-kheh'-leth*; from an unused root mean. to *glow* or *kindle*; *n ember*:—(burning) coal.

514. גַּחַם **Gacham**, *gah'-kham*; from an unused root mean. to *burn; flame; Gacham*, a on of Nahor:—Gaham.

515. גַּחַר **Gachar**, *gah'-khar*; from an unused root mean. to *hide; lurker; Gachar*, one f the Nethinim:—Gahar.

גּוֹי **gôy**. See 1471.

516. גַּיְא **gay'**, *gah'ee*; or (short.)

גַּי **gay**, *gah'ee*; prob. (by transm.) from the same root as 1466 (abbrev.); a *gorge* (from s *lofty* sides; hence narrow, but not a gully or winer-torrent):—valley.

517. גִּיד **gîyd**, *gheed*; prob. from 1464; a *thong* (as *compressing*); by anal. a *tendon*:—inew.

518. גִּיחַ **gîyach**, *ghee'-akh*; or (short.)

גֹּחַ **gôach**, *go'-akh*; a prim. root; to *gush* forth (as water), gen. to *issue*:—break orth, labor to bring forth, come forth, draw up, take ut.

519. גִּיחַ **gîyach** (Chald.), *ghee'-akh*; or (short.)

גּוּחַ **gûwach** (Chald.), *goo'-akh*; corresp. to 1518; to *rush* forth:—strive.

520. גִּיחַ **Gîyach**, *ghee'-akh*; from 1518; a *fountain; Giach*, a place in Pal.:—Giah.

521. גִּיחוֹן **Gîychôwn**, *ghee-khone'*; or (short.)

גִּחוֹן **Gîchôwn**, *ghee-khone'*; from 1518; *stream; Gichon*, a river of Paradise; lso a valley (or pool) near Jerusalem:—Gihon.

522. גֵּיחֲזִי **Gêychăzîy**, *gay-khah-zee'*; or

גֵּחֲזִי **Gêchăzîy**, *gay-khah-zee'*; appar from 1516 and 2372; *valley of a visionry; Gechazi*, the servant of Elisha:—Gehazi.

1523. גִּיל **gîyl**, *gheel*; or (by perm.)

גּוּל **gûwl**, *gool*; a prim. root; prop. to *spin* round (under the influence of any violent emotion), i.e. usually *rejoice*, or (as *cringing*) *fear*:—be glad, joy, be joyful, rejoice.

1524. גִּיל **gîyl**, *gheel*; from 1523; a *revolution* (of time, i.e. an *age*); also *joy*:—× exceedingly, gladness, × greatly, joy, rejoice (-ing), sort.

1525. גִּילָה **gîylâh**, *ghee-law'*; or

גִּילַת **gîylath**, *ghee-lath'*; fem. of 1524; *joy*:—joy, rejoicing.

גִּילֹה **Gîylôh**. See 1542.

1526. גִּילֹנִי **Gîylônîy**, *ghee-lo-nee'*; patrial from 1542; a *Gilonite* or inhab. of Giloh:—Gilonite.

1527. גִּינַת **Gîynath**, *ghee-nath'*; of uncert. der.; *Ginath*, an Isr.:—Ginath.

1528. גִּיר **gîyr** (Chald.), *gheer*; corresp. to 1615; *lime*:—plaster.

גֵּיר **gêyr**. See 1616.

1529. גֵּישָׁן **Gêyshân**, *gay-shawn'*; from the same as 1487; *lumpish; Geshan*, an Isr.:—Geshan.

1530. גַּל **gal**, *gal*; from 1556; something *rolled*, i.e. a *heap* of stone or dung (plur. *ruins*); by anal. a *spring* of water (plur. *waves*):—billow, heap, spring, wave.

1531. גֹּל **gôl**, *gole*; from 1556; a *cup* for oil (as *round*):—bowl.

גְּלָא **gᵉlâ'**. See 1541.

1532. גַּלָּב **gallâb**, *gal-lawb'*; from an unused root mean. to *shave*; a *barber*:—barber.

1533. גִּלְבֹּעַ **Gilbôaʻ**, *ghil-bo'-ah*; from 1530 and 1158; *fountain of ebullition; Gilboa*, a mountain of Pal.:—Gilboa.

1534. גַּלְגַּל **galgal**, *gal-gal'*; by redupl. from 1556; a *wheel*; by anal. a *whirlwind*; also *dust* (as *whirled*):—heaven, rolling thing, wheel.

1535. גַּלְגַּל **galgal** (Chald.), *gal-gal'*; corresp. to 1534; a *wheel*:—wheel.

1536. גִּלְגָּל **gilgâl**, *ghil-gawl'*; a var. of 1534:—wheel.

1537. גִּלְגָּל **Gilgâl**, *ghil-gawl'*; the same as 1536 (with the art. as a prop. noun); *Gilgal*, the name of three places in Pal.:—Gilgal. See also 1019.

1538. גֻּלְגֹּלֶת **gulgôleth**, *gul-go'-leth*; by redupl. from 1556; a *skull* (as *round*); by impl. a *head* (in enumeration of persons):—head, every man, poll, skull.

1539. גֶּלֶד **geled**, *ghe'-led*; from an unused root prob. mean. to *polish*; the (human) *skin* (as *smooth*):—skin.

1540. גָּלָה **gâlâh**, *gaw-law'*; a prim. root; to *denude* (espec. in a disgraceful sense); by impl. to *exile* (captives being usually *stripped*); fig. to *reveal*:—+ advertise, appear, bewray, bring, (carry, lead, go) captive (into captivity), depart, disclose, discover, exile, be gone, open, × plainly, publish, remove, reveal, × shamelessly, shew, × surely, tell, uncover.

1541. גְּלָה **gᵉlâh** (Chald.), *ghel-aw'*; or

גְּלָא **gᵉlâ'** (Chald.), *ghel-aw'*; corresp. to 1540:—bring over, carry away, reveal.

גֹּלָה **gôlâh**. See 1473.

1542. גִּלֹה **Gîlôh**, *ghee-lo'*; or (fully)

גִּילֹה **Gîylôh**, *ghee-lo'*; from 1540; *open; Giloh*, a place in Pal.:—Giloh.

1543. גֻּלָּה **gullâh**, *gool-law'*; fem. from 1556; a *fountain, bowl* or *globe* (all as *round*):—bowl, pommel, spring.

1544. גִּלּוּל **gillûwl**, *ghil-lool'*; or (short.)

גִּלֻּל **gillûl**, *ghil-lool'*; from 1556; prop. a *log* (as *round*); by impl. an *idol*:—idol.

1545. גְּלוֹם **gᵉlôwm**, *ghel-ome'*; from 1563; *clothing* (as *wrapped*):—clothes.

1546. גָּלוּת **gâlûwth**, *gaw-looth'*; fem. from 1540; *captivity*; concr. *exiles* (collect.):—(they that are carried away) captives (-ity.)

1547. גָּלוּת **gâlûwth** (Chald.), *gaw-looth'*; corresp. to 1546:—captivity.

1548. גָּלַח **gâlach**, *gaw-lakh'*; a prim. root; prop. to *be bald*, i.e. (caus.) to *shave*; fig. to *lay waste*:—poll, shave (off).

1549. גִּלָּיוֹן **gîllâyôwn**, *ghil-law-yone'*; or

גִּלְיוֹן **gilyôwn**, *ghil-yone'*; from 1540; a *tablet* for writing (as *bare*); by anal. a *mirror* (as a *plate*):—glass, roll.

1550. גָּלִיל **gâlîyl**, *gaw-leel'*; from 1556; a *valve* of a folding door (as *turning*); also a *ring* (as *round*):—folding, ring.

1551. גָּלִיל **Gâlîyl**, *gaw-leel'*; or (prol.)

גָּלִילָה **Gâlîylâh**, *gaw-lee-law'*; the same as 1550; a *circle* (with the art.); *Galil* (as a special *circuit*) in the North of Pal.:—Galilee.

1552. גְּלִילָה **gᵉlîylâh**, *ghel-ee-law'*; fem. of 1550; a *circuit* or *region*:—border, coast, country.

1553. גְּלִילוֹת **Gᵉlîylôwth**, *ghel-ee-lowth'*; plur. of 1552; *circles; Geliloth*, a place in Pal.:—Geliloth.

1554. גַּלִּים **Gallîym**, *gal-leem'*; plur. of 1530; *springs; Gallim*, a place in Pal.:—Gallim.

1555. גָּלְיַת **Golyath**, *gol-yath'*; perh. from 1540; *exile; Golyath*, a Philistine:—Goliath.

1556. גָּלַל **gâlal**, *gaw-lal'*; a prim. root; to *roll* (lit. or fig.):—commit, remove, roll (away, down, together), run down, seek occasion, trust, wallow.

1557. גָּלָל **gâlâl**, *gaw-lawl'*; from 1556; *dung* (as in *balls*):—dung.

1558. גָּלָל **gâlâl**, *gaw-lawl'*; from 1556; a *circumstance* (as *rolled* around); only used adv., on *account* of:—because of, for (sake).

1559. גָּלָל **Gâlâl**, *gaw-lawl'*; from 1556, in the sense of 1560; *great; Galal*, the name of two Isr.:—Galal.

1560. גְּלָל **gᵉlâl** (Chald.), *ghel-awl'*; from a root corresp. to 1556; *weight* or *size* (as if *rolled*):—great.

1561. גֵּלֶל **gêlel**, *gay'-lel*; a var. of 1557; *dung* (plur. *balls* of dung):—dung.

1562. גִּלֲלַי **Gilălay**, *ghe-lal-ah'ee*; from 1561; *dungy; Gilalai*, an Isr.:—Gilalai.

1563. גָּלַם **gâlam**, *gaw-lam'*; a prim. root; to *fold*:—wrap together.

1564. גֹּלֶם **gôlem**, *go'-lem*; from 1563; a *wrapped* (and unformed *mass*, i.e. as the *embryo*):—substance yet being unperfect.

1565. גַּלְמוּד **galmûwd**, *gal-mood'*; prob. by prol. from 1563; *sterile* (as *wrapped* up too hard); fig. *desolate*:—desolate, solitary.

1566. גָּלַע **gâlaʻ**, *gaw-lah'*; a prim. root; to *be obstinate*:—(inter-) meddle (with).

1567. גַּלְעֵד **Galʻêd**, *gal-ade'*; from 1530 and 5707; *heap of testimony; Galed*, a memorial cairn E. of the Jordan:—Galeed.

1568. גִּלְעָד **Gilʻâd**, *ghil-awd'*; prob. from 1567; *Gilad*, a region E. of the Jordan; also the name of three Isr.:—Gilead, Gileadite.

1569. גִּלְעָדִי **Gilʻâdîy**, *ghil-aw-dee'*; patron. from 1568; a *Giladite* or desc. of Gilad:—Gileadite.

1570. גָּלַשׁ **gâlash**, *gaw-lash'*; a prim. root; prob. to *caper* (as a goat):—appear.

1571. גַּם **gam**, *gam*; by contr. from an unused root mean. to *gather*; prop. *assemblage*; used only adv. *also, even, yea, though*; often repeated as correl. *both . . . and*:—again, alike, also, (so much) as (soon), both (so) . . . and, but, either . . . or, even, for all, (in) likewise (manner), moreover, nay . . . neither, one, then (-refore), though, what, with, yea.

1572. גָּמָא **gâmâ'**, *gaw-maw'*; a prim. root (lit. or fig.) to *absorb*:—swallow, drink.

1573. גֹּמֶא **gôme'**, *go'-meh*; from 1572; prop. an *absorbent*, i.e. the *bulrush* (from its *porosity*); spec. the *papyrus*:—(bul-) rush.

1574. גֹּמֶד **gômed**, *go'-med*; from an unused root appar. mean. to *grasp*; prop. a *span*:—cubit.

1575. גַּמָּד **gammâd**, *gam-mawd'*; from the same as 1574; a *warrior* (as *grasping* weapons):—Gammadims.

1576. גְּמוּל **gᵉmûwl**, *ghem-ool'*; from 1580; *treatment*, i.e. an *act* (of good or ill); by impl. *service* or *requital*:— + as hast served, benefit, desert, deserving, that which he hath given, recompence, reward.

1577. גָּמוּל **gâmûwl**, *gaw-mool'*; pass. part. of 1580; *rewarded*; *Gamul*, an Isr.:—Gamul. See also 1014.

1578. גְּמוּלָה **gᵉmûwlâh**, *ghem-oo-law'*; fem. of 1576; mean. the same:—deed, recompence, such a reward.

1579. גִּמְזוֹ **Gimzôw**, *ghim-zo'*; of uncert. der.; *Gimzo*, a place in Pal.:—Gimzo.

1580. גָּמַל **gâmal**, *gaw-mal'*; a prim. root; to *treat* a person (well or ill), i.e. *benefit* or *requite*; by impl. (of *toil*) to *ripen*, i.e. (spec.) to *wean*:—bestow on, deal bountifully, do (good), recompense, requite, reward, ripen, + serve, wean, yield.

1581. גָּמָל **gâmâl**, *gaw-mawl'*; appar. from 1580 (in the sense of *labor* or *burden-bearing*): a *camel*:—camel.

1582. גְּמַלִּי **Gᵉmalliy**, *ghem-al-lee'*; prob. from 1581; *camel-driver*; *Gemalli*, an Isr.:—Gemalli.

1583. גַּמְלִיאֵל **Gamlîy'êl**, *gam-lee-ale'*; from 1580 and 410; *reward of God*; *Gamliel*, an Isr.:—Gamaliel.

1584. גָּמַר **gâmar**, *gaw-mar'*; a prim. root; to *end* (in the sense of *completion* or *failure*):—cease, come to an end, fail, perfect, perform.

1585. גְּמַר **gᵉmar** (Chald.), *ghem-ar'*; corresp. to 1584:—perfect.

1586. גֹּמֶר **Gômer**, *go'-mer*; from 1584; *completion*; *Gomer*, the name of a son of Japheth and of his desc.; also of a Hebrewess:—Gomer.

1587. גְּמַרְיָה **Gᵉmaryâh**, *ghem-ar-yaw'*; or
גְּמַרְיָהוּ **Gᵉmaryâhûw**, *ghem-ar-yaw'-hoo*; from 1584 and 3050; *Jah has perfected*; *Gemarjah*, the name of two Isr.:—Gemariah.

1588. גַּן **gan**, *gan*; from 1598; a *garden* (as *fenced*):—garden.

1589. גָּנַב **gânab**, *gaw-nab'*; a prim. root; to *thieve* (lit. or fig.); by impl. to *deceive*:—carry away, × indeed, secretly bring, steal (away), get by stealth.

1590. גַּנָּב **gannâb**, *gaw-nab'*; from 1589; a *stealer*:—thief.

1591. גְּנֵבָה **gᵉnêbâh**, *ghen-ay-baw'*; from 1589; *stealing*, i.e. (concr.) something *stolen*:—theft.

1592. גְּנֻבַת **Gᵉnûbath**, *ghen-oo-bath'*; from 1589; *theft*; *Genubath*, an Edomitish prince:—Genubath.

1593. גַּנָּה **gannâh**, *gan-naw'*; fem. of 1588; a *garden*:—garden.

1594. גִּנָּה **ginnâh**, *ghin-naw'*; another form for 1593:—garden.

1595. גֶּנֶז **genez**, *gheh'-nez*; from an unused root mean. to *store*; *treasure*; by impl. a *coffer*:—chest, treasury.

1596. גְּנַז **gᵉnaz** (Chald.), *ghen-az'*; corresp. to 1595; *treasure*:—treasure.

1597. גִּנְזַךְ **ginzak**, *ghin-zak'*; prol. from 1595; a *treasury*:—treasury.

1598. גָּנַן **gânan**, *gaw-nan'*; a prim. root; to *hedge* about, i.e. (gen.) *protect*:—defend.

1599. גִּנְּתוֹן **Ginnᵉthôwn**, *ghin-neth-ōne*; or
גִּנְּתוֹ **Ginnᵉthôw**, *ghin-neth-o'*; from 1598; *gardener*; *Ginnethon* or *Ginnetho*, an Isr.:—Ginnetho, Ginnethon.

1600. גָּעָה **gâ'âh**, *gaw-aw'*; a prim. root; to *bellow* (as cattle):—low.

1601. גֹּעָה **Gô'âh**, *go-aw'*; fem. act. part. of 1600; *lowing*; *Goah*, a place near Jerus.:—Goath.

1602. גָּעַל **gâ'al**, *gaw-al'*; a prim. root; to *detest*; by impl. to *reject*:—abhor, fail, lothe, vilely cast away.

1603. גַּעַל **Ga'al**, *gah'-al*; from 1602; *loathing*; *Gaal*, an Isr.:—Gaal.

1604. גֹּעַל **gô'al**, *go'-al*; from 1602; *abhorrence*:—loathing.

1605. גָּעַר **gâ'ar**, *gaw-ar'*; a prim. root; to *chide*:—corrupt, rebuke, reprove.

1606. גְּעָרָה **gᵉ'ârâh**, *gheh-aw-raw'*; from 1605; a *chiding*:—rebuke (-ing), reproof.

1607. גָּעַשׁ **gâ'ash**, *gaw-ash'*; a prim. root to *agitate* violently:—move, shake, toss, trouble.

1608. גַּעַשׁ **Ga'ash**, *ga'-ash*; from 1607; a *quaking*; *Gaash*, a hill in Pal.:—Gaash.

1609. גַּעְתָּם **Ga'tâm**, *gah-tawm'*; of uncert. der.; *Gatam*, an Edomite:—Gatam.

1610. גַּף **gaph**, *gaf*; from an unused root mean. to *arch*; the *back*; by extens. the *body* or self:— + highest places, himself.

1611. גַּף **gaph** (Chald.), *gaf*; corresp. to 1610:—a *wing*:—wing.

1612. גֶּפֶן **gephen**, *gheh'-fen*; from an unused root mean. to *bend*; a *vine* (as *twining*), esp. the grape:—vine, tree.

1613. גֹּפֶר **gôpher**, *go'-fer*; from an unused root, prob. mean. to *house in*; a kind of tree or wood (as used for *building*), appar. the *cypress*:—gopher.

1614. גָּפְרִית **gophrîyth**, *gof-reeth'*; prob. fem. of 1613; prop. cypress-*resin*; by anal. *sulphur* (as equally inflammable):—brimstone.

1615. גִּר **gîr**, *gheer*; perh. from 3564; *lime* (from being *burned* in a kiln:—chalk [-stone].

1616. גֵּר **gêr**, *gare*; or (fully)
גֵּיר **gêyr**, *gare*; from 1481; prop. a *guest*; by impl. a *foreigner*:—alien, sojourner, stranger.
גּוּר **gûr**. See 1482.

1617. גֵּרָא **Gêrâ'**, *gay-raw'*; perh. from 1626; a *grain*; *Gera*, the name of six Isr.:—Gera.

1618. גָּרָב **gârâb**, *gaw-rawb'*; from an unused root mean. to *scratch*; *scurf* (from *itching*):—scab, scurvy.

1619. גָּרֵב **Gârêb**, *gaw-rabe'*; from the same as 1618; *scabby*; *Gareb*, the name of an Isr., also of a hill near Jerus.:—Gareb.

1620. גַּרְגַּר **gargar**, *gar-gar'*; by redupl. from 1641; a *berry* (as if a pellet of *rumination*):—berry.

1621. גַּרְגְּרוֹת **gargᵉrôwth**, *gar-gher-owth'*; fem. plur. from 1641; the *throat* (as used in *rumination*):—neck.

1622. גִּרְגָּשִׁי **Girgâshîy**, *ghir-gaw-shee'*; patrial from an unused name [of uncert. der.]; a *Girgashite*, one of the native tribes of Canaan:—Girgashite, Girgasite.

1623. גָּרַד **gârad**, *gaw-rad'*; a prim. root; to *abrade*:—scrape.

1624. גָּרָה **gârâh**, *gaw-raw'*; a prim. root; prop. to *grate*, i.e. (fig.) to *anger*:—contend, meddle, stir up, strive.

1625. גֵּרָה **gêrâh**, *gay-raw'*; from 1641; the *cud* (as *scraping* the throat):—cud.

1626. גֵּרָה **gêrâh**, *gay-raw'*; from 1641 (as in 1625); prop. (like 1620) a *kernel* (round as if *scraped*), i.e. a *gerah* or small weight (and coin):—gerah.
גֹּרָה **gôrâh**. See 1484.

1627. גָּרוֹן **gârôwn**, *gaw-rone'*; or (short.)
גָּרֹן **gârôn**, *gaw-rone'*; from 1641; the *throat* [comp. 1621] (as *roughened* by swallowing):— × aloud, mouth, neck, throat.

1628. גֵּרוּת **gêrûwth**, *gay-rooth'*; from 1481; a (temporary) *residence*:—habitation.

1629. גָּרַז **gâraz**, *gaw-raz'*; a prim. root; to *cut* off:—cut off.

1630. גְּרִזִים **Gᵉrîzîym**, *gher-ee-zeem'*; plur. of an unused noun from 1629 [comp. 1511], *cut up* (i.e. *rocky*); *Gerizim*, a mountain of Pal.:—Gerizim.

1631. גַּרְזֶן **garzen**, *gar-zen'*; from 1629; an *axe*:—ax.

1632. גָּרֹל **gârôl**, *gaw-role'*; from the same as 1486; *harsh*:—man of great [*as in the marg. which reads* 1419].
גּוֹרָל **gôrâl**. See 1486.

1633. גָּרַם **gâram**, *gaw-ram'*; a prim. root; to be *spare* or *skeleton-like*; used only as a denom. from 1634; (caus.) to *bone*, i.e. *denude* (by extens. *craunch*) the bones:—gnaw the bones, break.

1634. גֶּרֶם **gerem**, *gheh'-rem*; from 1633; a *bone* (as the *skeleton* of the body); hence *self*, i.e. (fig.) *very*:—bone, strong, top.

1635. גְּרַם **gerem** (Chald.), *gheh'-rem*; corresp. to 1634; a *bone*:—bone.

1636. גַּרְמִי **Garmîy**, *gar-mee'*; from 1634; *bony*, i.e. *strong*:—Garmite.

1637. גֹּרֶן **gôren**, *go'-ren*; from an unused root mean. to *smooth*; a threshing-*floor* (as made *even*); by anal. any open *area*:—(barn, corn, threshing-) floor, (threshing-, void) place.
גָּרֹן **gârôn**. See 1627.

1638. גָּרַס **gâraç**, *gaw-ras'*; a prim. root; to *crush*; also (intrans. and fig.) to *dissolve*:—break.

1639. גָּרַע **gâra'**, *gaw-rah'*; a prim. root; to *scrape* off; by impl. to *shave*, *remove*, *lessen* or *withhold*:—abate, clip, (di-) minish, do (take) away, keep back, restrain, make small, withdraw.

1640. גָּרַף **gâraph**, *gaw-raf'*; a prim. root; to *bear* off violently:—sweep away.

1641. גָּרַר **gârar**, *gaw-rar'*; a prim. root; to *drag* off roughly; by impl. to *bring up* the cud (i.e. *ruminate*); by anal. to *saw*:—catch, chew, × continuing, destroy, saw.

1642. גְּרָר **Gᵉrâr**, *gher-awr'*; prob. from 1641; a *rolling* country; *Gerar*, a Philistine city:—Gerar.

1643. גֶּרֶשׂ **geres**, *gheh'-res*; from an unused root mean. to *husk*; a *kernel* (collect.), i.e. *grain*:—beaten corn.

1644. גָּרַשׁ **gârash**, *gaw-rash'*; a prim. root; to *drive* out from a possession; espec. to *expatriate* or *divorce*:—cast up (out), divorced (woman), drive away (forth, out), expel, × surely put away, trouble, thrust out.

1645. גֶּרֶשׁ **geresh**, *gheh'-resh*; from 1644; *produce* (as if *expelled*):—put forth.

1646. גְּרֻשָׁה **gᵉrûshâh**, *gher-oo-shaw'*; fem. pass. part. of 1644; (abstr.) *dispossession*:—exaction.

1647. גֵּרְשֹׁם **Gêrᵉshôm**, *gay-resh-ome'*; for 1648; *Gereshom*, the name of four Isr.:—Gershom.

1648. גֵּרְשׁוֹן **Gêrᵉshown**, *gay-resh-one'*; or
גֵּרְשׁוֹם **Gêrᵉshôwm**, *gay-resh-ome'*; from 1644; a *refugee*; *Gereshon* or *Gereshom*, an Isr.:—Gershon, Gershom.

1649. גֵּרְשֻׁנִּי **Gerᵉshunnîy**, *gay-resh-oon-nee'*; patron. from 1648; a *Gereshonite* or desc. of Gereshon:—Gershonite, sons of Gershon.

1650. גְּשׁוּר **Gᵉshûwr**, *ghesh-oor'*; from an unused root (mean. to *join*); *bridge*; *Geshur*, a district of Syria:—Geshur, Geshurite.

1651. גְּשׁוּרִי **Gᵉshûwrîy**, *ghe-shoo-ree'*; patrial from 1650; a *Geshurite* (also collect.) or inhab. of Geshur:—Geshuri, Geshurites.

1652. גָּשַׁם **gâsham**, *gaw-sham'*; a prim. root; to *shower* violently:—(cause to) rain.

1653. גֶּשֶׁם **geshem**, *gheh'-shem*; from 1652; a *shower*:—rain, shower.

1654. גֶּשֶׁם **Geshem**, *gheh'-shem*; or (prol.)
גַּשְׁמוּ **Gashmûw**, *gash-moo'*; the same as 1653; *Geshem* or *Gashmu*, an Arabian:—Geshem, Gashmu.

1655. גֶּשֶׁם **geshem** (Chald.), *gheh'-shem*; appar. the same as 1653; used in a peculiar sense, the *body* (prob. for the [fig.] idea of a *hard rain*):—body.

1656. גֹּשֶׁם **gôshem**, *go'-shem;* from 1652; equiv. to 1653:—rained upon.
גַּשְׁמוּ **Gashmûw**. See 1654.
1657. גֹּשֶׁן **Gôshen**, *go'-shen;* prob. of Eg. or.; *Goshen*, the residence of the Isr. in Egypt; lso a place in Pal.:—Goshen.
1658. גִּשְׁפָּא **Gishpâ'**, *ghish-paw';* of uncert. der.; *Gishpa*, an Isr.:—Gispa.
1659. גָּשַׁשׁ **gâshash**, *gaw-shash';* a prim. root; appar. to *feel* about:—grope.
1660. גַּת **gath**, *gath;* prob. from 5059 (in the sense of *treading* out grapes); a wine-*press* (or at for holding the grapes in pressing them):—wine-) press (fat).
1661. גַּת **Gath**, *gath;* the same as 1660; *Gath*, a Philistine city:—Gath.
1662. גַּת־הַחֵפֶר **Gath-ha-Chêpher**, *gath-hah-khay'-fer;* or (abridged)
גִּתָּה־חֵפֶר **Gittâh-Chêpher**, *ghit-taw-khay'-fer;* from 1660 and 2658 with ne art. ins.; *wine-press of (the) well; Gath-Chepher*, place in Pal.:—Gath-kephr, Gittah-kephr.
1663. גִּתִּי **Gittîy**, *ghit-tee';* patrial from 1661; a *Gittite* or inhab. of Gath:—Gittite.
1664. גִּתַּיִם **Gittayim**, *ghit-tah'-yim;* dual of 1660; *double wine-press; Gittajim*, a lace in Pal.:—Gittaim.
1665. גִּתִּית **Gittîyth**, *ghit-teeth';* fem. of 1663; a *Gittite* harp:—Gittith.
1666. גֶּתֶר **Gether**, *gheh'-ther;* of uncert. der.; *Gether*, a son of Aram, and the region ettled by him:—Gether.
1667. גַּת־רִמּוֹן **Gath-Rimmôwn**, *gath-rim-mone';* from 1660 and 7416; *wine-ress of* (the) *pomegranate; Gath-Rimmon*, a place in al.:—Gath-rimmon.

ד

1668. דָּא **dâ'** (Chald.), *daw;* corresp. to 2088; *this:*—one . . . another, this.
1669. דָּאַב **dâ'ab**, *daw-ab';* a prim. root; to *pine:*—mourn, sorrow (-ful).
1670. דְּאָבָה **de'âbâh**, *dĕh-aw-baw';* from 1669; prop. *pining;* by anal. *fear:*—sorrow.
1671. דְּאָבוֹן **de'âbôwn**, *dĕh-aw-bone';* from 1669; *pining:*—sorrow.
1672. דָּאַג **dâ'ag**, *daw-ag';* a prim. root; *be anxious:*—be afraid (careful, sorry), sorrow, ake thought.
1673. דֹּאֵג **Dô'êg**, *do-ayg';* or (fully)
דּוֹאֵג **Dôw'êg**, *do-ayg';* act. part. of 1672; *anxious; Doëg*, an Edomite:—Doeg.
1674. דְּאָגָה **de'âgâh**, *dĕh-aw-gaw';* from 1672; *anxiety:*—care (-fulness), fear, heaviness, sorrow.
1675. דָּאָה **dâ'âh**, *daw-aw';* a prim. root; to *dart*, i.e. *fly* rapidly:—fly.
1676. דָּאָה **dâ'âh**, *daw-aw';* from 1675; the *kite* (from its rapid *flight*):—vulture. See 7201.
1677. דֹּב **dôb**, *dobe;* or (fully)
דּוֹב **dôwb**, *dobe;* from 1680; the *bear* (as slow):—bear.
1678. דֹּב **dôb** (Chald.), *dobe;* corresp. to 1677:—bear.
1679. דֹּבֶא **dôbe'**, *do'-beh;* from an unused root (comp. 1680) (prob. mean. to *be sluggish*, .e. *restful*); *quiet:*—strength.
1680. דָּבַב **dâbab**, *daw-bab';* a prim. root (comp. 1679); to *move* slowly, i.e. *glide:*—cause o speak.
1681. דִּבָּה **dibbâh**, *dib-baw';* from 1680 (in the sense of *furtive* motion); *slander:*—defaming, evil report, infamy, slander.
1682. דְּבוֹרָה **debôwrâh**, *deb-o-raw';* or (short.)
דְּבֹרָה **debôrâh**, *deb-o-raw';* from 1696 (in the sense of *orderly* motion); the *bee* from its *systematic* instincts):—bee.

1683. דְּבוֹרָה **Debôwrâh**, *deb-o-raw';* or (short.)
דְּבֹרָה **Debôrâh**, *deb-o-raw';* the same as 1682; *Deborah*, the name of two Hebrewesses:—Deborah.
1684. דְּבַח **debach** (Chald.), *deb-akh';* corresp. to 2076; to *sacrifice* (an animal):—offer [sacrifice].
1685. דְּבַח **debach** (Chald.), *deb-akh';* from 1684; a *sacrifice:*—sacrifice.
1686. דִּבְיוֹן **dibyôwn**, *dib-yone';* in the marg. for the textual reading
חֶרְיוֹן **cheryôwn**, *kher-yone';* both (in the plur. only and) of uncert. der.; prob. some cheap vegetable, perh. a bulbous root:—dove's dung.
1687. דְּבִיר **debîyr**, *deb-eer';* or (short.)
דְּבִר **debîr**, *deb-eer';* from 1696 (appar. in the sense of *oracle*); the *shrine* or innermost part of the sanctuary:—oracle.
1688. דְּבִיר **Debîyr**, *deb-eer';* or (short.)
דְּבִר **Debîr** (Josh. 13 : 26 [but see 3810]), *deb-eer';* the same as 1687; *Debir*, the name of an Amoritish king and of two places in Pal.:—Debir.
1689. דִּבְלָה **Diblâh**, *dib-law';* prob. an orth. err. for 7247; *Diblah*, a place in Syria:—Diblath.
1690. דְּבֵלָה **debêlâh**, *deb-ay-law';* from an unused root (akin to 2082) prob. mean. to *press* together; a *cake* of pressed figs:—cake (lump) of figs.
1691. דִּבְלַיִם **Diblayim**, *dib-lah'-yim;* dual from the masc. of 1690; *two cakes; Diblajim*, a symbol. name:—Diblaim.
דִּבְלָתַיִם **Diblâthayim**. See 1015.
1692. דָּבַק **dâbaq**, *daw-bak';* a prim. root; prop. to *impinge*, i.e. *cling* or *adhere;* fig. to *catch* by pursuit:—abide fast, cleave (fast together), follow close (hard after), be joined (together), keep (fast), overtake, pursue hard, stick, take.
1693. דְּבַק **debaq** (Chald.), *deb-ak';* corresp. to 1692; to *stick* to:—cleave.
1694. דֶּבֶק **debeq**, *deh'-bek;* from 1692; a *joint;* by impl. *solder:*—joint, solder.
1695. דָּבֵק **dâbêq**, *daw-bake';* from 1692; *adhering:*—cleave, joining, stick closer.
1696. דָּבַר **dâbar**, *daw-bar';* a prim. root; perh. prop. to *arrange;* but used fig. (of words) to *speak;* rarely (in a destructive sense) to *subdue:*—answer, appoint, bid, command, commune, declare, destroy, give, name, promise, pronounce, rehearse, say, speak, be spokesman, subdue, talk, teach, tell, think, use [entreaties], utter, × well, × work.
1697. דָּבָר **dâbâr**, *daw-bawr';* from 1696; a *word;* by impl. a *matter* (as *spoken* of) or *thing;* adv. a *cause:*—act, advice, affair, answer, × any such (thing), + because of, book, business, care, case, cause, certain rate, + chronicles, commandment, × commune (-ication), + concern [-ing], + confer, counsel, + dearth, decree, deed, × disease, due, duty, effect, + eloquent, errand, [evil favoured-] ness, + glory, + harm, hurt, + iniquity, + judgment, language, + lying, manner, matter, message, [no] thing, oracle, × ought, × parts, + pertaining, + please, portion, + power, promise, provision, purpose, question, rate, reason, report, request, × (as hast) said, sake, saying, sentence, + sign, + so, some [uncleanness], somewhat to say, + song, speech, × spoken, talk, task, + that, × there done, thing (concerning), thought, + thus, tidings, what [-soever], + wherewith, which, word, work.
1698. דֶּבֶר **deber**, *deh'-ber;* from 1696 (in the sense of *destroying*); a *pestilence:*—murrain, pestilence, plague.
1699. דֹּבֶר **dôber**, *do'-ber;* from 1696 (in its original sense); a *pasture* (from its *arrangement* of the flock):—fold, manner.
דְּבִר **debîr** or **Debîr**. See 1687, 1688.
1699'. דִּבֵּר **dibbêr**, *dib-bare';* for 1697:—word.
1700. דִּבְרָה **dibrâh**, *dib-raw';* fem. of 1697; a *reason*, *suit* or *style:*—cause, end, estate, order, regard.

1701. דִּבְרָה **dibrâh** (Chald.), *dib-raw';* corresp. to 1700:—intent, sake.
דְּבֹרָה **debôrâh** or **Debôrâh**. See 1682, 1683.
1702. דֹּבְרָה **dôberâh**, *do-ber-aw';* fem. act. part. of 1696 in the sense of *driving* [comp. 1699]; a *raft:*—float.
1703. דַּבָּרָה **dabbârâh**, *dab-baw-raw';* intens. from 1696; a *word:*—word.
1704. דִּבְרִי **Dibrîy**, *dib-ree';* from 1697; *wordy; Dibri*, an Isr.:—Dibri.
1705. דָּבְרַת **Dâberath**, *daw-ber-ath';* from 1697 (perh. in the sense of 1699); *Daberath*, a place in Pal.:—Dabareh, Daberath.
1706. דְּבַשׁ **debash**, *deb-ash';* from an unused root mean. to *be gummy;* *honey* (from its *stickiness*); by anal. *syrup:*—honey ([-comb]).
1707. דַּבֶּשֶׁת **dabbesheth**, *dab-beh'-sheth;* intens. from the same as 1706; a sticky *mass*, i.e. the *hump* of a camel:—hunch [of a camel].
1708. דַּבֶּשֶׁת **Dabbesheth**, *dab-beh'-sheth;* the same as 1707; *Dabbesheth*, a place in Pal.:—Dabbesheth.
1709. דָּג **dâg**, *dawg;* or (fully)
דָּאג° **dâ'g** (Neh. 13 : 16), *dawg;* from 1711; a *fish* (as *prolific*); or perh. rather from 1672 (as *timid*); but still better from 1672 (in the sense of *squirming*, i.e. moving by the vibratory action of the tail); a *fish* (often used collect.):—fish.
1710. דָּגָה **dâgâh**, *daw-gaw';* fem. of 1709, and mean. the same:—fish.
1711. דָּגָה **dâgâh**, *daw-gaw';* a prim. root; to *move rapidly;* used only as a denom. from 1709; to *spawn*, i.e. *become numerous:*—grow.
1712. דָּגוֹן **Dâgôwn**, *daw-gohn';* from 1709; the *fish-god; Dagon*, a Philistine deity:—Dagon.
1713. דָּגַל **dâgal**, *daw-gal';* a prim. root; to *flaunt*, i.e. *raise a flag;* fig. to *be conspicuous:*—(set up, with) banners, chiefest.
1714. דֶּגֶל **degel**, *deh'-gel;* from 1713; a *flag:*—banner, standard.
1715. דָּגָן **dâgân**, *daw-gawn';* from 1711; prop. *increase*, i.e. *grain:*—corn ([floor]), wheat.
1716. דָּגַר **dâgar**, *daw-gar';* a prim. root; to *brood* over eggs or young:—gather, sit.
1717. דַּד **dad**, *dad;* appar. from the same as 1730; the *breast* (as the seat of *love*, or from its shape):—breast, teat.
1718. דָּדָה **dâdâh**, *daw-daw';* a doubtful root; to *walk gently:*—go (softly, with).
1719. דְּדָן **Dedân**, *ded-awn';* or (prol.)
דְּדָנֶה **Dedâneh** (Ezek. 25 : 13), *deh-daw'-neh;* of uncert. der.; *Dedan*, the name of two Cushites and of their territory:—Dedan.
1720. דְּדָנִים **Dedânîym**, *ded-aw-neem';* plur. of 1719 (as patrial); *Dedanites*, the desc. or inhab. of Dedan:—Dedanim.
1721. דֹּדָנִים **Dôdânîym**, *do-daw-neem';* or (by orth. err.)
רֹדָנִים **Rôdânîym** (1 Chron. 1 : 7), *ro-daw-neem';* a plur. of uncert. der.; *Dodanites*, or desc. of a son of Javan:—Dodanim.
1722. דְּהַב **dehab** (Chald.), *deh-hab';* corresp. to 2091; *gold:*—gold (-en).
1723. דַּהֲוָא **Dahăvâ'** (Chald.), *dah-hav-aw';* of uncert. der.; *Dahava*, a people colonized in Samaria:—Dehavites.
1724. דָּהַם **dâham**, *daw-ham';* a prim. root (comp. 1740); to *be dumb*, i.e. (fig.) *dumbfounded:*—be astonished.
1725. דָּהַר **dâhar**, *daw-har';* a prim. root; to *curvet* or move irregularly:—pranse.
1726. דַּהֲהַר **dahăhar**, *dah-hah-har';* by redupl. from 1725; a *gallop:*—pransing.
דּוֹאֵג **Dôw'êg**. See 1673.
1727. דּוּב **dûwb**, *doob;* a prim. root; to *mope*, i.e. (fig.) *pine:*—sorrow.
דּוֹב **dôwb**. See 1677.

1728. דַּוָּג **davvâg**, *dav-vawg'*; an orth. var. of 1709 as a denom. [1771]; a *fisherman:*—fisher.

1729. דּוּגָה **dûwgâh**, *doo-gaw'*; fem. from the same as 1728; prop. *fishery*, i.e. a *hook* for fishing:—fish [hook].

1730. דּוֹד **dôwd**, *dode*; or (short.)

דֹּד **dôd**, *dode*; from an unused root mean. prop. to *boil*, i.e. (fig.) to *love*; by impl. a *love-token, lover, friend*; spec. an *uncle:*—(well-) beloved, father's brother, love, uncle.

1731. דּוּד **dûwd**, *dood*; from the same as 1730; a *pot* (for *boiling*); also (by resemblance of shape) a *basket:*—basket, caldron, kettle, (seething) pot.

1732. דָּוִד **Dâvîd**, *daw-veed'*; rarely (fully)

דָּוִיד **Dâvîyd**, *daw-veed'*; from the same as 1730; *loving*; *David*, the youngest son of Jesse.—David.

1733. דּוֹדָה **dôwdâh**, *do-daw'*; fem. of 1730; an *aunt:*—aunt, father's sister, uncle's wife.

1734. דּוֹדוֹ **Dôwdôw**, *do-do'*; from 1730; *loving*; *Dodo*, the name of three Isr.:—Dodo.

1735. דּוֹדָוָהוּ **Dôwdâvâhûw**, *do-daw-vaw'-hoo*; from 1730 and 3050; *love of Jah*; *Dodavah*, an Isr.:—Dodavah.

1736. דּוּדַי **dûwday**, *doo-dah'-ee*; from 1731; a *boiler* or *basket*; also the *mandrake* (as *aphrodisiac*):—basket, mandrake.

1737. דּוֹדַי **Dôwday**, *do-dah'ee*; formed like 1736; *amatory*; *Dodai*, an Isr.:—Dodai.

1738. דָּוָה **dâvâh**, *daw-vaw'*; a prim. root; to *be sick* (as if in menstruation):—infirmity.

1739. דָּוֶה **dâveh**, *daw-veh'*; from 1738; *sick* (espec. in menstruation):—faint, menstruous cloth, she that is sick, having sickness.

1740. דּוּחַ **dûwach**, *doo'-akh*; a prim. root; to *thrust* away; fig. to *cleanse:*—cast out, purge, wash.

1741. דְּוַי **devay**, *dev-ah'ee*; from 1739; *sickness*; fig. *loathing:*—languishing, sorrowful.

1742. דַּוָּי **davvây**, *dav-voy'*; from 1739; *sick*; fig. *troubled:*—faint.

דָּוִיד **Dâvîyd**. See 1732.

1743. דּוּךְ **dûwk**, *dook*; a prim. root; to *bruise* in a mortar:—beat.

1744. דּוּכִיפַת **dûwkîyphath**, *doo-kee-fath'*; of uncert. der.; the *hoopoe* or else the *grouse:*—lapwing.

1745. דּוּמָה **dûwmâh**, *doo-maw'*; from an unused root mean. to *be dumb* (comp. 1820); *silence*; fig. *death:*—silence.

1746. דּוּמָה **Dûwmâh**, *doo-maw'*; the same as 1745; *Dumah*, a tribe and region of Arabia:—Dumah.

1747. דּוּמִיָּה **dûwmîyâh**, *doo-me-yaw'*; from 1820; *stillness*; adv. *silently*; abstr. *quiet, trust:*—silence, silent, waiteth.

1748. דּוּמָם **dûwmâm**, *doo-mawm'*; from 1826; *still*; adv. *silently:*—dumb, silent, quietly wait.

דּוּמֶשֶׂק° **Dûwmesheq**. See 1833.

1749. דּוֹנַג **dôwnag**, *do-nag'*; of uncert. der.; *wax:*—wax.

1750. דּוּץ **dûwts**, *doots*; a prim. root; to *leap:*—be turned.

1751. דּוּק **dûwq** (Chald.), *dook*; corresp. to 1854; to *crumble:*—be broken to pieces.

1752. דּוּר **dûwr**, *dure*; a prim. root; prop. to *gyrate* (or move in a circle), i.e. to *remain:*—dwell.

1753. דּוּר **dûwr** (Chald.), *dure*; corresp. to 1752; to *reside:*—dwell.

1754. דּוּר **dûwr**, *dure*; from 1752; a *circle, ball* or *pile:*—ball, turn, round about.

1755. דּוֹר **dôwr**, *dore*; or (short.)

דֹּר **dôr**, *dore*; from 1752; prop. a *revolution* of time, i.e. an *age* or generation; also a *dwelling:*—age, × evermore, generation, [n-]ever, posterity.

1756. דּוֹר **Dôwr**, *dore*; or (by perm.)

דֹּאר **Dô'r** (Josh. 17 : 11; 1 Kings 4 : 11), *dore*; from 1755; *dwelling*; *Dor*, a place in Pal.:—Dor.

1757. דּוּרָא **Dûwrâ'** (Chald.), *doo-raw'*; prob. from 1753; *circle* or *dwelling*; *Dura*, a place in Bab.:—Dura.

1758. דּוּשׁ **dûwsh**, *doosh*; or

דּוֹשׁ **dôwsh**, *dōsh*; or

דִּישׁ **dîysh**, *deesh*; a prim. root; to *trample* or *thresh:*—break, tear, thresh, tread out (down), at grass [Jer. 50 : 11, *by mistake for* 1877].

1759. דּוּשׁ **dûwsh** (Chald.), *doosh*; corresp. to 1758; to *trample:*—tread down.

1760. דָּחָה **dâchâh**, *daw-khaw'*; or

דָּחַח **dâchach** (Jer. 23 : 12), *daw-khakh'*; a prim. root; to *push* down:—chase, drive away (on), overthrow, outcast, × sore, thrust, totter.

1761. דַּחֲוָה **dachăvâh** (Chald.), *dakh-av-aw'*; from the equiv. of 1760; prob. a musical *instrument* (as being *struck*):—instrument of music.

1762. דְּחִי **dechîy**, *deh-khee'*; from 1760; a *push*, i.e. (by impl.) a *fall:*—falling.

1763. דְּחַל **dechal** (Chald.), *deh-khal'*; corresp. to 2119; to *slink*, i.e. (by impl.) to *fear*, or (caus.) *be formidable:*—make afraid, dreadful, fear, terrible.

1764. דֹּחַן **dôchan**, *do'-khan*; of uncert. der.; *millet:*—millet.

1765. דָּחַף **dâchaph**, *daw-khaf'*; a prim. root; to *urge*, i.e. *hasten:*—(be) haste (-ned), pressed on.

1766. דָּחַק **dâchaq**, *daw-khak'*; a prim. root; to *press*, i.e. *oppress:*—thrust, vex.

1767. דַּי **day**, *dahee*; of uncert. der.; *enough* (as noun or adv.), used chiefly with prep. in phrases:—able, according to, after (ability), among, as (oft as), (more than) enough, from, in, since, (much as is) sufficient (-ly), too much, very, when.

1768. דִּי **dîy** (Chald.), *dee*; appar. for 1668; *that*, used as rel., conj., and espec. (with prep.) in adv. phrases; also as a prep. *of:*—× as, but, for (-asmuch +), + now, of, seeing, than, that, therefore, until, + what (-soever), when, which, whom, whose.

1769. דִּיבוֹן **Dîybôwn**, *dee-bone'*; or (short.)

דִּיבֹן **Dîybôn**, *dee-bone'*; from 1727; *pining:*—*Dibon*, the name of three places in Pal.:—Dibon. [*Also, with 1410 added,* Dibon-gad.]

1770. דִּיג **dîyg**, *deeg*; denom. from 1709; to *fish:*—fish.

1771. דַּיָּג **dayâg**, *dah-yawg'*; from 1770; a *fisherman:*—fisher.

1772. דַּיָּה **dayâh**, *dah-yaw'*; intens. from 1675; a *falcon* (from its *rapid* flight):—vulture.

1773. דְּיוֹ **deyôw**, *deh-yo'*; of uncert. der.; *ink:*—ink.

1774. דִּי זָהָב **Dîy zâhâb**, *dee zaw-hawb'*; as if from 1768 and 2091; *of gold*; *Dizahab*, a place in the Desert:—Dizahab.

1775. דִּימוֹן **Dîymôwn**, *dee-mone'*; perh. for 1769; *Dimon*, a place in Pal.:—Dimon.

1776. דִּימוֹנָה **Dîymôwnâh**, *dee-mo-naw'*; fem. of 1775; *Dimonah*, a place in Pal.:—Dimonah.

1777. דִּין **dîyn**, *deen*; or (Gen. 6 : 3)

דּוּן **dûwn**, *doon*; a prim. root [comp. 113]; to *rule*; by impl. to *judge* (as umpire); also to *strive* (as at law):—contend, execute (judgment), judge, minister judgment, plead (the cause), at strife, strive.

1778. דִּין **dîyn** (Chald.), *deen*; corresp. to 1777; to *judge:*—judge.

1779. דִּין **dîyn**, *deen*; or (Job 19 : 29)

דּוּן **dûwn**, *doon*; from 1777; *judgment* (the suit, justice, sentence or tribunal); by impl. also *strife:*—cause, judgment, plea, strife.

1780. דִּין **dîyn** (Chald.), *deen*; corresp. to 1779:—judgment.

1781. דַּיָּן **dayân**, *dah-yawn'*; from 1777; a *judge* or *advocate:*—judge.

1782. דַּיָּן **dayân** (Chald.), *dah-yawn'*; corresp. to 1781:—judge.

1783. דִּינָה **Dîynâh**, *dee-naw'*; fem. of 1779; *justice*; *Dinah*, the daughter of Jacob:—Dinah.

1784. דִּינַי **Dîynay** (Chald.), *dee-nah'ee*; patrial from an uncert. prim.; a *Dinaite* or inhab. of some unknown Ass. province:—Dinaite.

דִּיפַת **Dîyphath**. See 7384.

1785. דָּיֵק **dâyêq**, *daw-yake'*; from a root corresp. to 1751; a *battering-tower:*—fort.

1786. דַּיִשׁ **dayîsh**, *dah'-yish*; from 1758; *threshing*-time:—threshing.

1787. דִּישׁוֹן **Dîyshôwn**,

דִּישֹׁן **Dîyshôn**,

דִּשׁוֹן **Dîshôwn**, or

דִּשֹׁן **Dîshôn**, *dee-shone'*; the same as 1788; *Dishon*, the name of two Edomites:—Dishon.

1788. דִּישֹׁן **dîyshôn**, *dee-shone'*; from 1758; the *leaper*, i.e. an *antelope:*—pygarg.

1789. דִּישָׁן **Dîyshân**, *dee-shawn'*; another form of 1787; *Dishan*, an Edomite:—Dishan, Dishon.

1790. דַּךְ **dak**, *dak*; from an unused root (comp. 1794); *crushed*, i.e. (fig.) *injured:*—afflicted, oppressed.

1791. דֵּךְ **dêk** (Chald.), *dake*; or

דָּךְ **dâk** (Chald.), *dawk*; prol. from 1668; *this:*—the same, this.

1792. דָּכָא **dâkâ'**, *daw-kaw'*; a prim. root (comp. 1794); to *crumble*; trans. to *bruise* (lit. or fig.):—beat to pieces, break (in pieces), bruise, contrite, crush, destroy, humble, oppress, smite.

1793. דַּכָּא **dakkâ'**, *dak-kaw'*; from 1792; *crushed* (lit. *powder*, or fig. *contrite*):—contrite, destruction.

1794. דָּכָה **dâkâh**, *daw-kaw'*; a prim. root (comp. 1790, 1792); to *collapse* (phys. or mentally):—break (sore), contrite, crouch.

1795. דַּכָּה **dakkâh**, *dak-kaw'*; from 1794 like 1793; *mutilated:*— + wounded.

1796. דֳּכִי **dŏkîy**, *dok-ee'*; from 1794; a *dashing* of surf:—wave.

1797. דִּכֵּן **dikkên** (Chald.), *dik-kane'*; prol. from 1791; *this:*—same, that, this.

1798. דְּכַר **dekar** (Chald.), *dek-ar'*; corresp. to 2145; prop. a *male*, i.e. of sheep:—ram.

1799. דִּכְרוֹן **dikrôwn** (Chald.), *dik-rone'*; or

דָּכְרָן **dokrân**, *dok-rawn'* (Chald.); corresp. to 2146; a *register:*—record.

1800. דַּל **dal**, *dal*; from 1809; prop. *dangling*, i.e. (by impl.) *weak* or *thin:*—lean, needy, poor (man), weaker.

1801. דָּלַג **dâlag**, *daw-lag'*; a prim. root; to *spring:*—leap.

1802. דָּלָה **dâlâh**, *daw-law'*; a prim. root (comp. 1809); prop. to *dangle*, i.e. to *let down* a bucket (for *drawing* out water); fig. to *deliver:*—draw (out), × enough, lift up.

1803. דַּלָּה **dallâh**, *dal-law'*; from 1802; prop. something *dangling*, i.e. a loose *thread* or *hair*; fig. *indigent:*—hair, pining sickness, poor (-est sort).

1804. דָּלַח **dâlach**, *daw-lakh'*; a prim. root; to *roil* water:—trouble.

1805. דְּלִי **delîy**, *del-ee'*; or

דָּלִי **dŏlîy**, *dol-ee'*; from 1802; a *pail* or *jar* (for *drawing* water):—bucket.

1806. דְּלָיָה **Delâyâh**, *del-aw-yaw'*; or (prol.)

דְּלָיָהוּ **Delâyâhhûw**, *del-aw-yaw'-hoo*; from 1802 and 3050; *Jah has delivered*; *Delajah*, the name of five Isr.:—Dalaiah, Delaiah.

1807. דְּלִילָה **Delîylâh**, *del-ee-law'*; from 1809; *languishing:*—*Delilah*, a Philistine woman:—Delilah.

1808. דָּלִיָּה **dâlîyâh**, *daw-lee-yaw'*; from 1802; something *dangling*, i.e. a *bough:*—branch.

1809. דָּלַל **dâlal**, *daw-lal'*; a prim. root (comp. 1802); to *slacken* or *be feeble*; fig. to *be oppressed:*—bring low, dry up, be emptied, be not equal, fail, be impoverished, be made thin.

310. דִּלְעָן **Dilʻân**, *dil-awn'*; of uncert. der.; *Dilan*, a place in Pal.:—Dilean.

311. דָּלַף **dâlaph**, *daw-laf'*; a prim. root; to *drip*; by impl. to *weep*:—drop through, elt, pour out.

312. דֶּלֶף **deleph**, *deh'-lef*; from 1811; a *dripping*:—dropping.

313. דַּלְפוֹן **Dalphôwn**, *dal-fone'*; from 1811; *dripping*; *Dalphon*, a son of Haman:—alphon.

314. דָּלַק **dâlaq**, *daw-lak'*; a prim. root; to *flame* (lit. or fig.):—burning, chase, inflame, ndle, persecute (-or), pursue hotly.

315. דְּלַק **delaq** (Chald.), *del-ak'*; corresp. to 1814:—burn.

316. דַּלֶּקֶת **dalleqeth**, *dal-lek'-keth*; from 1814; a *burning* fever:—inflammation.

317. דֶּלֶת **deleth**, *deh'-leth*; from 1802; something *swinging*, i.e. the *valve* of a door:—door wo-leaved), gate, leaf, lid. [In Psa. 141:3, *dâl*, irreg.]

318. דָּם **dâm**, *dawm*; from 1826 (comp. 119); *blood* (as that which when shed causes eath) of man or an animal; by anal. the *juice* of the rape; fig. (espec. in the plur.) *bloodshed* (i.e. *drops* blood):—blood (-y, -guiltiness, [-thirsty]), + in-ocent.

319. דָּמָה **dâmâh**, *daw-maw'*; a prim. root; to *compare*; by impl. to *resemble*, *liken*, nsider:—compare, devise, (be) like (-n), mean, ink, use similitudes.

320. דָּמָה **dâmâh**, *daw-maw'*; a prim. root; to *be dumb* or *silent*; hence to *fail* or erish; trans. to *destroy*:—cease, be cut down (off), estroy, be brought to silence, be undone, × utterly.

321. דְּמָה **demâh** (Chald.), *dem-aw'*; corresp. to 1819; to *resemble*:—be like.

322. דֻּמָּה **dummâh**, *doom-maw'*; from 1820; *desolation*; concr. *desolate*:—destroy.

323. דְּמוּת **demûwth**, *dem-ooth'*; from 1819; *resemblance*; concr. *model*, *shape*; adv. *ke*:—fashion, like (-ness, as), manner, similitude.

324. דְּמִי **demîy**, *dem-ee'*; or

דֳּמִי **dŏmîy**, *dom-ee'*; from 1820; *quiet*:—cutting off, rest, silence.

825. דִּמְיוֹן **dimyôwn**, *dim-yone'*; from 1819; *resemblance*:—× like.

826. דָּמַם **dâmam**, *daw-mam'*; a prim. root [comp. 1724, 1820]; to *be dumb*; by impl. *be astonished*, to *stop*; also to *perish*:—cease, be ut down (off), forbear, hold peace, quiet self, rest, e silent, keep (put to) silence, be (stand) still, tarry, ait.

827. דְּמָמָה **demâmâh**, *dem-aw-maw'*; fem. from 1826; *quiet*:—calm, silence, still.

828. דֹּמֶן **dômen**, *do'-men*; of uncert. der.; *manure*:—dung.

829. דִּמְנָה **Dimnâh**, *dim-naw'*; fem. from the same as 1828; a *dung-heap*; *Dimnah*, a lace in Pal.:—Dimnah.

830. דָּמַע **dâmaʻ**, *daw-mah'*; a prim. root; to *weep*:—× sore, weep.

831. דֶּמַע **demaʻ**, *deh'-mah*; from 1830; a *tear*; fig. *juice*:—liquor.

832. דִּמְעָה **dimʻâh**, *dim-aw'*; fem. of 1831; *weeping*:—tears.

833. דְּמֶשֶׁק **demesheq**, *dem-eh'-shek*; by orth. var. from 1834; *damask* (as a fabric of Damascus):—in Damascus.

834. דַּמֶּשֶׂק **Dammeseq**, *dam-meh'-sek*; or

דּוּמֶשֶׂק **Dûwmeseq**, *doo-meh'-sek*; or

דַּרְמֶשֶׂק **Darmeseq**, *dar-meh'-sek*; of for. or.; *Damascus*, a city of Syria:—Damascus.

1835. דָּן **Dân**, *dawn*; from 1777; *judge*; *Dan*, one of the sons of Jacob; also the tribe descended from him, and its territory; likewise a place n Pal. colonized by them:—Dan.

1836. דֵּן **dên** (Chald.), *dane*; an orth. var. of 1791; *this*:—[afore-] time, + after this manner, here [-after], one . . . another, such, there [-fore], these, this (matter), + thus, where [-fore], which.

דָּנִאֵל **Dânîʼêl**. See 1841.

1837. דַּנָּה **Dannâh**, *dan-naw'*; of uncert. der.; *Dannah*, a place in Pal.:—Dannah.

1838. דִּנְהָבָה **Dinhâbâh**, *din-haw-baw'*; of uncert. der.; *Dinhabah*, an Edomitish town:—Dinhaban.

1839. דָּנִי **Dânîy**, *daw-nee'*; patron. from 1835; a *Danite* (often collect.) or desc. (or inhab.) of Dan:—Danites, of Dan.

1840. דָּנִיֵּאל **Dânîyêʼl**, *daw-nee-yale'*; in Ezek.

דָּנִאֵל **Dânîʼêl**, *daw-nee-ale'*; from 1835 and 410; *judge of God*; *Daniel* or *Danijel*, the name of two Isr.:—Daniel.

1841. דָּנִיֵּאל **Dânîyêʼl** (Chald.), *daw-nee-yale'*; corresp. to 1840; *Danijel*, the Heb. prophet:—Daniel.

1842. דָּן יַעַן **Dân Yaʻan**, *dawn yah'-an*; from 1835 and (appar.) 3282; *judge of purpose*; *Dan-Jaan*, a place in Pal.:—Dan-jaan.

1843. דֵּעַ **dêaʻ**, *day'-ah*; from 3045; *knowledge*:—knowledge, opinion.

1844. דֵּעָה **dêʻâh**, *day-aw'*; fem. of 1843; *knowledge*:—knowledge.

1845. דְּעוּאֵל **Deʻûwʼêl**, *deh-oo-ale'*; from 3045 and 410; *known of God*; *Deüel*, an Isr.:—Deuel.

1846. דָּעַךְ **dâʻak**, *daw-ak'*; a prim. root; to *be extinguished*; fig. to *expire* or *be dried up*:—be extinct, consumed, put out, quenched.

1847. דַּעַת **daʻath**, *dah'-ath*; from 3045; *knowledge*:—cunning, [ig-] norantly, know (-ledge), [un-] awares (wittingly).

1848. דֳּפִי **dŏphîy**, *dof'-ee*; from an unused root (mean. to *push* over); a *stumbling-block*:—slanderest.

1849. דָּפַק **dâphaq**, *daw-fak'*; a prim. root; to *knock*; by anal. to *press* severely:—beat, knock, overdrive.

1850. דָּפְקָה **Dophqâh**, *dof-kaw'*; from 1849; a *knock*; *Dophkah*, a place in the Desert:—Dophkah.

1851. דַּק **daq**, *dak*; from 1854; *crushed*, i.e. (by impl.) *small* or *thin*:—dwarf, lean [-fleshed], very little thing, small, thin.

1852. דֹּק **dôq**, *doke*; from 1854; something *crumbling*, i.e. *fine* (as a *thin* cloth):—curtain.

1853. דִּקְלָה **Diqlâh**, *dik-law'*; of for. or.; *Diklah*, a region of Arabia:—Diklah.

1854. דָּקַק **dâqaq**, *daw-kak'*; a prim. root [comp. 1915]; to *crush* (or intrans.) *crumble*:—beat in pieces (small), bruise, make dust, (into) × powder, (be, very) small, stamp (small).

1855. דְּקַק **deqaq** (Chald.), *dek-ak'*; corresp. to 1854; to *crumble* or (trans.) *crush*:—break to pieces.

1856. דָּקַר **dâqar**, *daw-kar'*; a prim. root; to *stab*; by anal. to *starve*; fig. to *revile*:—pierce, strike (thrust) through, wound.

1857. דֶּקֶר **Deqer**, *deh'-ker*; from 1856; a *stab*; *Deker*, an Isr.:—Dekar.

1858. דַּר **dar**, *dar*; appar. from the same as 1865; prop. a *pearl* (from its sheen as rapidly *turned*); by anal. *pearl-stone*, i.e. mother-of-pearl or alabaster:—× white.

1859. דָּר **dâr** (Chald.), *dawr*; corresp. to 1755; an *age*:—generation.

דֹּר **dôr**. See 1755.

1860. דְּרָאוֹן **derâʼôwn**, *der-aw-one'*; or

דֵּרָאוֹן **dêrâʼôwn**, *day-raw-one'*; from an unused root (mean. to *repulse*); an object of *aversion*:—abhorring, contempt.

1861. דָּרְבוֹן **dorbôwn**, *dor-bone'* [also *dor-bawn'*]; of uncert. der.; a *goad*:—goad.

1862. דַּרְדַּע **Dardaʻ**, *dar-dah'*; appar. from 1858 and 1843; *pearl of knowledge*; *Darda*, an Isr.:—Darda.

1863. דַּרְדַּר **dardar**, *dar-dar'*; of uncert. der.; a *thorn*:—thistle.

1864. דָּרוֹם **dârôwm**, *daw-rome'*; of uncert. der.; the *south*; poet. the *south wind*:—south.

1865. דְּרוֹר **derôwr**, *der-ore'*; from an unused root (mean. to *move rapidly*); *freedom*; hence *spontaneity* of outflow, and so *clear*:—liberty, pure.

1866. דְּרוֹר **derôwr**, *der-ore'*; the same as 1865, applied to a bird; the *swift*, a kind of swallow:—swallow.

1867. דָּרְיָוֶשׁ **Dârᵉyâvêsh**, *daw-reh-yaw-vaysh'*; of Pers. or.; *Darejavesh*, a title (rather than name) of several Persian kings:—Darius.

1868. דָּרְיָוֶשׁ **Dârᵉyâvêsh** (Chald.), *daw-reh-yaw-vaysh'*; corresp. to 1867:—Darius.

1869. דָּרַךְ **dârak**, *daw-rak'*; a prim. root; to *tread*; by impl. to *walk*; also to *string* a bow (by treading on it in bending):—archer, bend, come, draw, go (over), guide, lead (forth), thresh, tread (down), walk.

1870. דֶּרֶךְ **derek**, *deh'-rek*; from 1869; a *road* (as *trodden*); fig. a *course* of life or *mode* of action, often adv.:—along, away, because of, + by, conversation, custom, [east-] ward, journey, manner, passenger, through, toward, [high-] [path-] way [-side], whither [-soever].

1871. דַּרְכְּמוֹן **darkᵉmôwn**, *dar-kem-one'*; of Pers. or.; a "*drachma*," or coin:—dram.

1872. דְּרָע **deraʻ** (Chald.), *der-aw'*; corresp. to 2220; an *arm*:—arm.

1873. דָּרַע **Dâraʻ**, *daw-rah'*; prob. contr. from 1862; *Dara*, an Isr.:—Dara.

1874. דַּרְקוֹן **Darqôwn**, *dar-kone'*; of uncert. der.; *Darkon*, one of "Solomon's servants":—Darkon.

1875. דָּרַשׁ **dârash**, *daw-rash'*; a prim. root; prop. to *tread* or *frequent*; usually to *follow* (for pursuit or search); by impl. to *seek* or *ask*; spec. to *worship*:—ask, × at all, care for, × diligently, inquire, make inquisition, [necro-] mancer, question, require, search, seek [for, out], × surely.

1876. דָּשָׁא **dâshâ**, *daw-shaw'*; a prim. root; to *sprout*:—bring forth, spring.

1877. דֶּשֶׁא **desheʼ**, *deh'-sheh*; from 1876; a *sprout*; by anal. *grass*:—(tender) grass, green, (tender) herb.

1878. דָּשֵׁן **dâshên**, *daw-shane'*; a prim. root; to *be fat*; trans. to *fatten* (or regard as fat); spec. to *anoint*; fig. to *satisfy*; denom. (from 1880) to *remove* (fat) *ashes* (of sacrifices):—accept, anoint, take away the (receive) ashes (from), make (wax) fat.

1879. דָּשֵׁן **dâshên**, *daw-shane'*; from 1878; *fat*; fig. *rich*, *fertile*:—fat.

1880. דֶּשֶׁן **deshen**, *deh'-shen*; from 1878; the *fat*; abstr. *fatness*, i.e. (fig.) *abundance*; spec. the (fatty) *ashes* of sacrifices:—ashes, fatness.

1881. דָּת **dâth**, *dawth*; of uncert. (perh. for.) der.: a royal *edict* or statute:—commandment, commission, decree, law, manner.

1882. דָּת **dâth** (Chald.), *dawth*; corresp. to 1881; decree, law.

1883. דֶּתֶא **detheʼ** (Chald.), *deh'-thay*; corresp. to 1877:—tender grass.

1884. דְּתָבָר **dethâbâr** (Chald.), *deth-aw-bawr'*; of Pers. or.; mean. one *skilled in law*; a *judge*:—counsellor.

1885. דָּתָן **Dâthân**, *daw-thawn'*; of uncert. der.; *Dathan*, an Isr.:—Dathan.

1886. דֹּתָן **Dôthân**, *do'-thawn*; or (Chaldaizing dual)

דֹּתַיִן **Dôthayin** (Gen. 37 : 17), *do-thah'-yin*; of uncert. der.; *Dothan*, a place in Pal.:—Dothan.

ה

1887. הֵא **hêʼ**, *hay*; a prim. particle; *lo!*:—behold, lo.

1888. הֵא **hêʼ** (Chald.), *hay*; or

הָא **hâʼ** (Chald.), *haw*; corresp. to 1887:—even, lo.

1889. הֶאָח **heâch**, *heh-awkh'*; from 1887 and 253; *aha!*:—ah, aha, ha.

הָאֲרָרִי **Hâʼrârîy**. See 2043.

1890. הַבְהָב **habhâb**, *hab-hawb'*; by redupl. from 3051; *gift* (in sacrifice), i.e. *holocaust*:—offering.

1891. הָבַל **hâbal**, *haw-bal'*; a prim. root; to *be vain* in act, word, or expectation; spec. to *lead astray*:—be (become, make) vain.

1892. הֶבֶל **hebel**, *heh'-bel*; or (rarely in the abs.)
הֲבֵל **hăbêl**, *hab-ale'*; from 1891; *emptiness* or *vanity*; fig. something *transitory* and *unsatisfactory*; often used as an adv.:— × altogether, vain, vanity.

1893. הֶבֶל **Hebel**, *heh'-bel*; the same as 1892; *Hebel*, the son of Adam:—Abel.

1894. הֹבֶן **hôben**, *ho'-ben*; only in plur., from an unused root mean. to *be hard*; *ebony*:—ebony.

1895. הָבַר **hâbar**, *haw-bar'*; a prim. root of uncert. (perh. for.) der.; to *be a horoscopist*:— + (astro-) loger.

1896. הֵגֵא **Hêgêʼ**, *hay-gay'*; or (by perm.)
הֵגַי **Hêgay**, *hay-gah'ee*; prob. of Pers. or.; *Hege* or *Hegai*, a eunuch of Xerxes:—Hegai, Hege.

1897. הָגָה **hâgâh**, *haw-gaw'*; a prim. root [comp. 1901]; to *murmur* (in pleasure or anger); by impl. to *ponder*:—imagine, meditate, mourn, mutter, roar, × sore, speak, study, talk, utter.

1898. הָגָה **hâgâh**, *haw-gaw'*; a prim. root; to *remove*;—stay, take away.

1899. הֶגֶה **hegeh**, *heh'-geh*; from 1897; a *muttering* (in sighing, thought, or as thunder):—mourning, sound, tale.

1900. הָגוּת **hâgûwth**, *haw-gooth'*; from 1897; *musing*:—meditation.

1901. הָגִיג **hâgîyg**, *haw-gheeg'*; from an unused root akin to 1897; prop. a *murmur*, i.e. *complaint*:—meditation, musing.

1902. הִגָּיוֹן **higgâyôwn**, *hig-gaw-yone'*; intens. from 1897; a *murmuring* sound, i.e. a musical notation (prob. similar to the modern *affettuoso* to indicate solemnity of movement); by impl. a *machination*:—device, Higgaion, meditation, solemn sound.

1903. הָגִין **hâgîyn**, *haw-gheen'*; of uncert. der.; perh. *suitable* or *turning*:—directly.

1904. הָגָר **Hâgâr**, *haw-gawr'*; of uncert. (perh. for.) der.; *Hagar*, the mother of Ishmael:—Hagar.

1905. הַגְרִי **Hagrîy**, *hag-ree'*; or (prol.)
הַגְרִיא **Hagrîʼ**, *hag-ree'*; perh. patron. from 1904; a *Hagrite* or member of a certain Arabian clan:—Hagarene, Hagarite, Haggeri.

1906. הֵד **hêd**, *hade*; for 1959; a *shout*:—sounding again.

1907. הַדָּבָר **haddâbâr** (Chald.), *had-daw-bawr'*; prob. of for. or.; a *vizier*:—counsellor.

1908. הֲדַד **Hădad**, *had-ad'*; prob. of for. or. [comp. 111]; *Hadad*, the name of an idol, and of several kings of Edom:—Hadad.

1909. הֲדַדְעֶזֶר **Hădadʻezer**, *had-ad-eh'-zer*; from 1908 and 5828; *Hadad* (is his) *help*; *Hadadezer*, a Syrian king:—Hadadezer. Comp. 1928.

1910. הֲדַדְרִמּוֹן **Hădadrimmôwn**, *had-ad-rim-mone'*; from 1908 and 7417; *Hadad-Rimmon*, a place in Pal.:—Hadad-rimmon.

1911. הָדָה **hâdâh**, *haw-daw'*; a prim. root [comp. 3034]; to *stretch forth* the hand:—put.

1912. הֹדוּ **Hôdûw**, *ho'-doo*; of for. or.; *Hodu* (i.e. Hindû-stan):—India.

1913. הֲדוֹרָם **Hădôwrâm**, *had-o-rawm'*; or
הֲדֹרָם **Hădôrâm**, *had-o-rawm'*; prob. of for. der.; *Hadoram*, a son of Joktan, and the tribe descended from him:—Hadoram.

1914. הִדַּי **Hidday**, *hid-dah'ee*; of uncert. der.; *Hiddai*, an Isr.:—Hiddai.

1915. הָדַךְ **hâdak**, *haw-dak'*; a prim. root [comp. 1854]; to *crush* with the foot:—tread down.

1916. הֲדֹם **hădôm**, *had-ome'*; from an unused root mean. to *stamp* upon; a *footstool*:—[foot-] stool.

1917. הַדָּם **haddâm** (Chald.), *had-dawm'*; from a root corresp. to that of 1916; something *stamped* to pieces, i.e. a *bit*:—piece.

1918. הֲדַס **hădaç**, *had-as'*; of uncert. der.; the *myrtle*:—myrtle (tree).

1919. הֲדַסָּה **Hădaççâh**, *had-as-saw'*; fem. of 1918; *Hadassah* (or Esther):—Hadassah.

1920. הָדַף **hâdaph**, *haw-daf'*; a prim. root; to *push* away or down:—cast away (out), drive, expel, thrust (away).

1921. הָדַר **hâdar**, *haw-dar'*; a prim. root; to *swell* up (lit. or fig., act. or pass.); by impl. to *favor* or *honour*, *be high* or *proud*:—countenance, crooked place, glorious, honour, put forth.

1922. הֲדַר **hădar** (Chald.), *had-ar'*; corresp. to 1921; to *magnify* (fig.):—glorify, honour.

1923. הֲדַר **hădar** (Chald.), *had-ar'*; from 1922; *magnificence*:—honour, majesty.

1924. הֲדַר **Hădar**, *had-ar'*; the same as 1926; *Hadar*, an Edomite:—Hadar.

1925. הֶדֶר **heder**, *heh'-der*; from 1921; *honour*; used (fig.) for the *capital* city (Jerusalem):—glory.

1926. הָדָר **hâdâr**, *haw-dawr'*; from 1921; *magnificence*, i.e. ornament or splendor:—beauty, comeliness, excellency, glorious, glory, goodly, honour, majesty.

1927. הֲדָרָה **hădârâh**, *had-aw-raw'*; fem. of 1926; *decoration*:—beauty, honour.

הֲדֹרָם **Hădôrâm**. See 1913.

1928. הֲדַרְעֶזֶר **Hădarʻezer**, *had-ar-eh'-zer*; from 1924 and 5828; *Hadar* (i.e. *Hadad*, 1908) is his *help*; *Hadarezer* (i.e. Hadadezer, 1909), a Syrian king:—Hadarezer.

1929. הָהּ **hâhh**, *haw*; a short. form of 162; *ah!* expressing grief:—woe worth.

1930. הוֹ **hôw**, *ho*; by perm. from 1929; *oh!*:—alas.

1931. הוּא **hûwʼ**, *hoo*; of which the fem. (beyond the Pentateuch) is
הִיא **hîyʼ**, *he*; a prim. word, the third pers. pron. sing., *he* (*she* or *it*); only expressed when emphatic or without a verb; also (intens.) *self*, or (esp. with the art.) the *same*; sometimes (as demonstr.) *this* or *that*; occasionally (instead of copula) *as* or *are*:—he, as for her, him (-self), it, the same, she (herself), such, that (. . . it), these, they, this, those, which (is), who.

1932. הוּא **hûw** (Chald.), *hoo*; or (fem.)
הִיא **hîyʼ** (Chald.), *he*; corresp. to 1931:— × are, it, this.

1933. הָוָא **hâvâʼ**, *haw-vaw'*; or
הָוָה **hâvâh**, *haw-vaw'*; a prim. root [comp. 183, 1961] supposed to mean prop. to *breathe*; to *be* (in the sense of existence):—be, × have.

1934. הָוָא **hăvâʼ** (Chald.), *hav-aw'*; or
הֲוָה **hăvâh** (Chald.), *hav-aw'*; corresp. to 1933; to *exist*; used in a great variety of applications (especially in connection with other words):—be, become, + behold, + came (to pass), + cease, + cleave, + consider, + do, + give, + have + judge, + keep, + labour, + mingle (self), + put, + see, + seek, + set, + slay, + take heed, tremble, + walk, + would.

1935. הוֹד **hôwd**, *hode*; from an unused root; *grandeur* (i.e. an imposing form and appearance):—beauty, comeliness, excellency, glorious, glory, goodly, honour, majesty.

1936. הוֹד **Hôwd**, *hode*; the same as 1935; *Hod*, an Isr.:—Hod.

1937. הוֹדְוָה **Hôwdᵉvâh**, *ho-dev-aw'*; a form of 1938; *Hodevah* (or Hodevjah), an Isr.:—Hodevah.

1938. הוֹדַוְיָה **Hôwdavyâh**, *ho dav-yaw'*; from 1935 and 3050; *majesty of Jah*; *Hodavjah*, the name of three Isr.:—Hodaviah.

1939. הוֹדַיְוָהוּ **Howdayᵉvâhûw**, *ho-dah-yeh-vaw'-hoo*; a form of 1938; *Hodajvah*, an Isr.:—Hodaiah.

1940. הוֹדִיָּה **Hôwdîyâh**, *ho-dee-yaw'*; a form for the fem. of 3064; a *Jewess*:—Hodiah.

1941. הוֹדִיָּה **Hôwdîyâh**, *ho-dee-yaw'*; a fo[rm] of 1938; *Hodijah*, the name of th[ree] Isr.:—Hodijah.

הָוָה **hâvâh**. See 1933.

הָוָה **hăvâh**. See 1934.

1942. הַוָּה **havvâh**, *hav-vaw'*; from 1933 (in t[he] sense of eagerly *coveting* and *rushi*[ng] upon; by impl. of *falling*); *desire*; also *ruin*:—cala[m]ity, iniquity, mischief, mischievous (thing), naugh[ti]ness, naughty, noisome, perverse thing, substan[ce], very wickedness.

1943. הֹוָה **hôvâh**, *ho-vaw'*; another form f[or] 1942; *ruin*:—mischief.

1944. הוֹהָם **Hôwhâm**, *ho-hawm'*; of unce[rt.] der.; *Hoham*, a Canaanitish king:[—] Hoham.

1945. הוֹי **hôwy**, *hoh'ee*; a prol. form of 1[929] [akin to 188]; *oh!*:—ah, alas, ho, O, woe.

1946. הוּךְ **hûwk** (Chald.), *hook*; corresp. to 19[80]; to *go*; caus. to *bring*:—bring agai[n], come, go (up).

1947. הוֹלֵלָה **hôwlêlâh**, *ho-lay-law'*; fem. a[ct.] part. of 1984; *folly*:—madness.

1948. הוֹלֵלוּת **hôwlêlûwth**, *ho-lay-looth'*; fr[om] act. part. of 1984; *folly*:—madness.

1949. הוּם **hûwm**, *hoom*; a prim. root [com[p.] 2000]; to *make an uproar*, or *agita*[te] greatly:—destroy, move, make a noise, put, ring aga[in].

1950. הוֹמָם **Hôwmâm**, *ho-mawm'*; from 20[00]; *raging*; *Homam*, an Edomitish chie[f]tain:—Homam. Comp. 1967.

1951. הוּן **hûwn**, *hoon*; a prim. root; prop. to *naught*, i.e. (fig.) to *be* (caus. *act*) *light*: be ready.

1952. הוֹן **hôwn**, *hone*; from the same as 1951 [in] the sense of 202; *wealth*; by im[pl.] *enough*:—enough, + for nought, riches, substan[ce], wealth.

1953. הוֹשָׁמָע **Hôwshâmâʻ**, *ho-shaw-maw'*; from 3068 and 8085; *Jehovah h[as] heard*; *Hoshama*, an Isr.:—Hoshama.

1954. הוֹשֵׁעַ **Hôwshêaʻ**, *ho-shay'-ah*; from 346[7]; *deliverer*; *Hosheä*, the name of fi[ve] Isr.:—Hosea, Hoshea, Oshea.

1955. הוֹשַׁעְיָה **Hôwshaʻyâh**, *ho-shah-yaw'*; from 3467 and 3050; *Jah has save[d]*; *Hoshajah*, the name of two Isr.:—Hoshaiah.

1956. הוֹתִיר **Hôwthîyr**, *ho-theer'*; from 349[8]; *he has caused to remain*; *Hothir*, a[n] Isr.:—Hothir.

1957. הָזָה **hâzâh**, *haw-zaw'*; a prim. root [com[p.] 2372]; to *dream*:—sleep.

1958. הִי **hîy**, *he*; for 5092; *lamentation*:—woe.

הִיא **hîyʼ**. See 1931, 1932.

1959. הֵידָד **hêydâd**, *hay-dawd'*; from an unuse[d] root (mean. to *shout*); *acclamation*: shout (-ing).

1960. הֻיְּדָה **huyᵉdâh**, *hoo-yed-aw'*; from th[e] same as 1959; prop. an *acclaim*, i.e. *choir* of singers:—thanksgiving.

1961. הָיָה **hâyâh**, *haw-yaw'*; a prim. root [comp. 1933]; to *exist*, i.e. *be* or *become*, *come t[o] pass* (always emphatic, and not a mere copula or auxi[li]ary):—beacon, × altogether, be (-come, accomplishe[d], committed, like), break, cause, come (to pass), continue, do, faint, fall, + follow, happen, × hav[e], last, pertain, quit (one-)self, require, × use.

1962. הַיָּה **hayâh**, *hah-yaw'*; another form fo[r] 1943; *ruin*:—calamity.

1963. הֵיךְ **hêyk**, *hake*; another form for 34[63]; *how?*:—how.

1964. הֵיכָל **hêykâl**, *hay-kawl'*; prob. from 32[01] (in the sense of *capacity*); a large pub[]lic building, such as a *palace* or *temple*:—palace, temple.

1965. הֵיכַל **hêykal** (Chald.), *hay-kal'*; corresp. to 1964:—palace, temple.

1966. הֵילֵל **hêylêl**, *hay-lale'*; from 1984 (in the sense of *brightness*); the *morning-star*:—lucifer.

67. הֵימָם **Hêymâm**, *hay-mawm'*; another form for 1950; *Hemam*, an Idumæan:—
emam.

68. הֵימָן **Hêymân**, *hay-mawn'*; prob. from 539; *faithful*; *Heman*, the name of at
ast two Isr.:—Heman.

69. הִין **hîyn**, *heen*; prob. of Eg. or.; a *hin* or liquid measure:—hin.

70. הָכַר **hâkar**, *haw-kar'*; a prim. root; appar. to *injure*:—make self strange.

71. הַכָּרָה **hakkârâh**, *hak-kaw-raw'*; from 5234; *respect*, i.e. partiality:—shew.

הַל **hal**. See 1973.

72. הָלָא **hâlâʼ**, *haw-law'*; prob. denom. from 1973; to *remove* or be *remote*:—cast far
t.

73. הָלְאָה **hâlᵉâh**, *haw-leh-aw'*; from the prim. form of the art. [הַל **hal**]; *to the dis-*
nce, i.e. *far away*; also (of time) *thus far*:—back,
yond, (hence-) forward, hitherto, thenceforth,
onder.

74. הִלּוּל **hillûwl**, *hil-lool'*; from 1984 (in the sense of *rejoicing*); a *celebration* of
anksgiving for harvest:—merry, praise.

75. הַלָּז **hallâz**, *hal-lawz'*; from 1976; *this* or *that*:—side, that, this.

76. הַלָּזֶה **hallâzeh**, *hal-law-zeh'*; from the art. [see 1973] and 2088; *this very*:—
is.

77. הַלֵּזוּ **hallêzûw**, *hal-lay-zoo'*; another form of 1976; *that*:—this.

78. הָלִיךְ **hâlîyk**, *haw-leek'*; from 1980; a *walk*, i.e. (by impl.) a *step*:—step.

79. הֲלִיכָה **hălîykâh**, *hal-ee-kaw'*; fem. of 1978; a *walking*; by impl. a *proces-*
on or *march*, a *caravan*:—company, going, walk,
ay.

980. הָלַךְ **hâlak**, *haw-lak'*; akin to 3212; a prim. root; to *walk* (in a great variety of ap-
lications, lit. and fig.):—(all) along, apace, behave
elf), come, (on) continually, be conversant, depart,
- be eased, enter, exercise (self), + follow, forth,
orward, get, go (about, abroad, along, away, for-
ard, on, out, up and down), + greater, grow, be
ont to haunt, lead, march, × more and more, move
self), needs, on, pass (away), be at the point, quite,
n (along), + send, speedily, spread, still, surely,
- tale-bearer, + travel (-ler), walk (abroad, on,
o and fro, up and down, to places), wander, wax,
ay-] faring man, × be weak, whirl.

981. הֲלַךְ **hălak** (Chald.), *hal-ak'*; corresp. to 1980 [comp. 1946]; to *walk*:—walk.

982. הֵלֶךְ **hêlek**, *hay'-lek*; from 1980; prop. a *journey*, i.e. (by impl.) a *wayfarer*; also
flowing:—× dropped, traveller.

983. הֲלָךְ **hălâk** (Chald.), *hal-awk'*; from 1981; prop. a *journey*, i.e. (by impl.) *toll* on
oods at a road:—custom.

984. הָלַל **hâlal**, *haw-lal'*; a prim. root; to *be clear* (orig. of sound, but usually of color);
o shine; hence to *make a show*, to *boast*; and thus to
e (clamorously) *foolish*; to *rave*; causat. to *cele-*
rate; also to *stultify*:—(make) boast (self), celebrate,
ommend, (deal, make), fool (-ish, -ly), glory, give
light], be (make, feign self) mad (against), give in
marriage, [sing, be worthy of] praise, rage, renowned,
hine.

985. הִלֵּל **Hillêl**, *hil-layl'*; from 1984; *praising* (namely God); *Hillel*, an Isr.:—Hillel.

986. הָלַם **hâlam**, *haw-lam'*; a prim. root; to *strike* down; by impl. to *hammer*, *stamp*,
onquer, *disband*:—beat (down), break (down), over-
ome, smite (with the hammer).

987. הֵלֶם **Hêlem**, *hay'-lem*; from 1986; *smiter*; *Helem*, the name of two Isr.:—Helem.

988. הֲלֹם **hălôm**, *hal-ome'*; from the art. [see 1973]; *hither*:—here, hither (-[to]),
hither.

989. הַלְמוּת **halmûwth**, *hal-mooth'*; from 1986; a *hammer* (or *mallet*):—ham-
er.

1990. הָם **Hâm**, *hawm*; of uncert. der.; *Ham*, a region of Pal.:—Ham.

1991. הֵם **hêm**, *haym*; from 1993; *abundance*, i.e. *wealth*:—any of theirs.

1992. הֵם **hêm**, *haym*; or (prol.)

הֵמָּה **hêmmâh**, *haym'-maw*; masc. plur. from 1931; *they* (only used when emphatic):—it, like, × (how, so) many (soever, more as) they (be), (the) same, × so, × such, their, them, these, they, those, which, who, whom, withal, ye.

1993. הָמָה **hâmâh**, *haw-maw'*; a prim. root [comp. 1949]; to *make a loud sound* (like Engl. "hum"); by impl. to *be in great commotion* or *tumult*, to *rage*, *war*, *moan*, *clamor*:—clamorous, concourse, cry aloud, be disquieted, loud, mourn, be moved, make a noise, rage, roar, sound, be troubled, make in tumult, tumultuous, be in an uproar.

1994. הִמּוֹ **himmôw** (Chald.), *him-mo'*; or (prol.)

הִמּוֹן **himmôwn** (Chald.) *him-mone'*; corresp. to 1992; *they*:—× are, them, those.

1995. הָמוֹן **hâmôwn**, *haw-mone'*; or

הָמֹן **hâmôn** (Ezek. 5 : 7), *haw-mone'*; from 1993; a *noise*, *tumult*, *crowd*; also *disquietude*, *wealth*:—abundance, company, many, multitude, multiply, noise, riches, rumbling, sounding, store, tumult.

הַמֹּלֶכֶת **ham-môleketh**. See 4447.

1996. הֲמוֹן גּוֹג **Hămôwn Gôwg**, *ham-one' gohg*; from 1995 and 1463; the *multitude of Gog*; the fanciful name of an emblematic place in Pal.:—Hamon-gog.

1997. הֲמוֹנָה **Hămôwnâh**, *ham-o-naw'*; fem. of 1995; *multitude*; *Hamonah*, the same as 1996:—Hamonah.

הֲמוּנֵךְ° **hămûwnêk**. See 2002.

1998. הֶמְיָה **hemyâh**, *hem-yaw'*; from 1993; *sound*:—noise.

1999. הֲמֻלָּה **hămullâh**, *ham-ool-law'*; or (too fully)

הֲמוּלָּה **hămûwllâh** (Jer. 11 : 16), *ham-ool-law'*; fem. pass. part. of an unused root mean. to *rush* (as rain with a windy roar); a *sound*:—speech, tumult.

הַמֶּלֶךְ **ham-melek**. See 4429.

2000. הָמַם **hâmam**, *haw-mam'*; a prim. root [comp. 1949, 1993]; prop. to *put in commotion*; by impl. to *disturb*, *drive*, *destroy*:—break, consume, crush, destroy, discomfit, trouble, vex.

הָמֹן **hâmôn**. See 1995.

2001. הָמָן **Hâmân**, *haw-mawn'*; of for. der.; *Haman*, a Pers. vizier:—Haman.

2002. הַמְנִיךְ **hamnîyk** (Chald.), *ham-neek'*; but the text is

הֲמוּנֵךְ° **hămûwnêk**, *ham-oo-nayk'*; of for. or.; a *necklace*:—chain.

2003. הָמָס **hâmâç**, *haw-mawce'*; from an unused root appar. mean. to *crackle*; a dry *twig* or *brushwood*:—melting.

2004. הֵן **hên**, *hane*; fem. plur. from 1931; *they* (only used when emphatic):—× in, such like, (with) them, thereby, therein, (more than) they, wherein, in which, whom, withal.

2005. הֵן **hên**, *hane*; a prim. particle; *lo!*; also (as expressing surprise) *if*:—behold, if, lo, though.

2006. הֵן **hên** (Chald.), *hane*; corresp. to 2005: *lo!* also *there* [-fore], [un-] *less*, *whether*, *but*, *if*:—(that) if, or, whether.

2007. הֵנָּה **hênnâh**, *hane'-naw*; prol. for 2004; *themselves* (often used emphat. for the copula, also in indirect relation):—× in, × such (and such things), their, (into) them, thence, therein, these, they (had), on this side, those, wherein.

2008. הֵנָּה **hênnâh**, *hane'-naw*; from 2004; *hither* or *thither* (but used both of place and time):—here, hither [-to], now, on this (that) side, + since, this (that) way, thitherward, + thus far, to . . . fro, + yet.

2009. הִנֵּה **hinnêh**, *hin-nay'*; prol. for 2005; *lo!*:—behold, lo, see.

2010. הֲנָחָה **hănâchâh**, *han-aw-khaw'*; from 5117; *permission* of rest, i.e. *quiet*:—release.

2011. הִנֹּם **Hinnôm**, *hin-nome'*; prob. of for. or.; *Hinnom*, appar. a Jebusite:—Hinnom.

2012. הֵנַע **Hênaʻ**, *hay-nah'*; prob. of for. der. *Hena*, a place appar. in Mesopotamia:—Hena.

2013. הָסָה **hâçâh**, *haw-saw'*; a prim. root; to *hush*:—hold peace (tongue), (keep) silence, be silent, still.

2014. הֲפֻגָה **hăphûgâh**, *haf-oo-gaw'*; from 6313; *relaxation*:—intermission.

2015. הָפַךְ **haphak**, *haw-fak'*; a prim. root; to *turn* about or over; by impl. to *change*, *overturn*, *return*, *pervert*:—× become, change, come, be converted, give, make [a bed], overthrow (-turn), perverse, retire, tumble, turn (again, aside, back, to the contrary, every way).

2016. הֶפֶךְ **hephek**, *heh'-fek*; or

הֵפֶךְ **hêphek**, *hay'-fek*; from 2015; a *turn*, i.e. the *reverse*:—contrary.

2017. הֹפֶךְ **hôphek**, *ho'-fek*; from 2015; an *upset*, i.e. (abstr.) *perversity*:—turning of things upside down.

2018. הֲפֵכָה **hăphêkâh**, *haf-ay-kaw'*; fem. of 2016; *destruction*:—overthrow.

2019. הֲפַכְפַּךְ **hăphakpak**, *haf-ak-pak'*; by redupl. from 2015; *very perverse*:—froward.

2020. הַצָּלָה **hatstsâlâh**, *hats-tsaw-law'*; from 5337; *rescue*:—deliverance.

2021. הֹצֶן **hôtsen**, *ho'-tsen*; from an unused root mean. appar. to *be sharp* or *strong*; a *weapon* of war:—chariot.

2022. הַר **har**, *har*; a short. form of 2042; a *mountain* or *range* of hills (sometimes used fig.):—hill (country), mount (-ain), × promotion.

2023. הֹר **Hôr**, *hore*; another form for 2022; *mountain*; *Hor*, the name of a peak in Idumæa and of one in Syria:—Hor.

2024. הָרָא **Hârâʼ**, *haw-raw'*; perh. from 2022; *mountainousness*; *Hara*, a region of Media:—Hara.

2025. הַרְאֵל **har'êl**, *har-ale'*; from 2022 and 410; *mount of God*; fig. the *altar* of burnt-offering:—altar. Comp. 739.

2026. הָרַג **hârag**, *haw-rag'*; a prim. root; to *smite* with deadly intent:—destroy, out of hand, kill, murder (-er), put to [death], make [slaughter], slay (-er), × surely.

2027. הֶרֶג **hereg**, *heh'-reg*; from 2026; *slaughter*:—be slain, slaughter.

2028. הֲרֵגָה **hărêgâh**, *har-ay-gaw'*; fem. of 2027; *slaughter*:—slaughter.

2029. הָרָה **hârâh**, *haw-raw'*; a prim. root; to *be* (or *become*) *pregnant*, *conceive* (lit. or fig.):—been, be with child, conceive, progenitor.

2030. הָרֶה **hâreh**, *haw-reh'*; or

הָרִי **hârîy** (Hos. 14 : 1), *haw-ree'*; from 2029; *pregnant*:—(be, woman) with child, conceive, × great.

2031. הַרְהֹר **harhôr** (Chald.), *har-hor'*; from a root corresp. to 2029; a mental *conception*:—thought.

2032. הֵרוֹן **hêrôwn**, *hay-rone'*; or

הֵרָיוֹן **hêrâyôwn**, *hay-raw-yone'*; from 2029; *pregnancy*:—conception.

2033. הֲרוֹרִי **Hărôwrîy**, *har-o-ree'*; another form for 2043; a *Harorite* or mountaineer:—Harorite.

2034. הֲרִיסָה **hărîyçâh**, *har-ee-saw'*; from 2040; something *demolished*:—ruin.

2035. הֲרִיסוּת **hărîyçûwth**, *har-ee-sooth'*; from 2040; *demolition*:—destruction.

2036. הֹרָם **Hôrâm**, *ho-rawm'*; from an unused root (mean. to *tower* up); *high; Horam*, a Canaanitish king:—Horam.

2037. הָרֻם **Hârûm**, *haw-room'*; pass. part. of the same as 2036; *high; Harum*, an Isr.:—Harum.

2038. הַרְמוֹן **harmôwn**, *har-mone'*; from the same as 2036; a *castle* (from its height):—palace.

2039. הָרָן **Hârân**, *haw-rawn'*; perh. from 2022; *mountaineer; Haran*, the name of two men:—Haran.

2040. הָרַס **hâraç**, *haw-ras'*; a prim. root; to *pull* down or in pieces, *break, destroy*:—beat down, break (down, through), destroy, overthrow, pluck down, pull down, ruin, throw down, × utterly.

2041. הֶרֶס **hereç**, *heh'-res*; from 2040; *demolition*:—destruction.

2042. הָרָר **hârâr**, *haw-rawr'*; from an unused root mean. to *loom* up; a *mountain*:—hill, mount (-ain).

2043. הֲרָרִי **Hărârîy** *hah-raw-ree'*; or
הָרָרִי **Hârârîy** (2 Sam. 23 : 11), *haw-raw-ree'*; or
הָאֲרָרִי **Hâ'rârîy** (2 Sam. 23 : 34, last clause), *haw-raw-ree'*; appar. from 2042; a *mountaineer*:—Hararite.

2044. הָשֵׁם **Hâshêm**, *haw-shame'*; perh. from the same as 2828; *wealthy; Hashem*, an Isr.:—Hashem.

2045. הַשְׁמָעוּת **hâshmâ'ûwth**, *hashmaw-ooth'*; from 8085; *announcement*:—to cause to hear.

2046. הִתּוּךְ **hittûwk**, *hit-took'*; from 5413; a *melting*:—is melted.

2047. הֲתָךְ **Hăthâk**, *hath-awk'*; prob. of for. or.; *Hathak*, a Pers. eunuch:—Hatach.

2048. הָתַל **hâthal**, *haw-thal'*; a prim. root; to *deride*; by impl. to *cheat*:—deal deceitfully, deceive, mock.

2049. הָתֹל **hâthôl**, *haw-thole'*; from 2048 (only in plur. collect.); a *derision*:—mocker.

2050. הָתַת **hâthath'**, *haw-thath'*; a prim. root; prop. to *break* in upon, i.e. to *assail*:—imagine mischief.

ו

2051. וְדָן **Vᵉdân**, *ved-awn'*; perh. for 5730; *Vedan* (or Aden), a place in Arabia:—Dan also.

2052. וָהֵב **Vâhêb**, *vaw-habe'*; of uncert. der.; *Vaheb*, a place in Moab:—what he did.

2053. וָו **vâv**, *vaw*; prob. a *hook* (the name of the sixth Heb. letter):—hook.

2054. וָזָר **vâzâr**, *vaw-zawr'*; presumed to be from an unused root mean. to *bear* guilt; *crime*:—× strange.

2055. וַיְזָתָא **Vayᵉzâthâ'**, *vah-yez-aw'-thaw*; of for. or.; *Vajezatha*, a son of Haman:—Vajezatha.

2056. וָלָד **vâlâd**, *vaw-lawd'*; for 3206; a *boy*:—child.

2057. וַנְיָה **Vanyâh**, *van-yaw'*; perh. for 6043; *Vanjah*, an Isr.:—Vaniah.

2058. וָפְסִי **Vophçîy**, *vof-see'*; prob. from 3254; *additional; Vophsi*, an Isr.:—Vophsi.

2059. וַשְׁנִי **Vashnîy**, *vash-nee'*; prob. from 3461; *weak; Vashni*, an Isr.:—Vashni.

2060. וַשְׁתִּי **Vashtîy**, *vash-tee'*; of Pers. or.; *Vashti*, the queen of Xerxes:—Vashti.

ז

2061. זְאֵב **zᵉ'êb**, *zeh-abe'*; from an unused root mean. to *be yellow*; a *wolf*:—wolf.

2062. זְאֵב **Zᵉ'êb**, *zeh-abe'*; the same as 2061; *Zeëb*, a Midianitish prince:—Zeeb.

2063. זֹאת **zô'th**, *zothe'*; irreg. fem. of 2089; *this* (often used adv.):—hereby (-in, -with), it, likewise, the one (other, same), she, so (much), such (deed), that, therefore, these, this (thing), thus.

2064. זָבַד **zâbad**, *zaw-bad'*; a prim. root; to *confer*:—endure.

2065. זֶבֶד **zebed**, *zeh'-bed*; from 2064; a *gift*:—dowry.

2066. זָבָד **Zâbâd**, *zaw-bawd'*; from 2064; *giver; Zabad*, the name of seven Isr.:—Zabad.

2067. זַבְדִּי **Zabdîy**, *zab-dee'*; from 2065; *giving; Zabdi*, the name of four Isr.:—Zabdi.

2068. זַבְדִּיאֵל **Zabdîy'êl**, *zab-dee-ale'*; from 2065 and 410; *gift of God; Zabdiel*, the name of two Isr.:—Zabdiel.

2069. זְבַדְיָה **Zᵉbadyâh**, *zeb-ad-yaw'*; or
זְבַדְיָהוּ **Zᵉbadyâhûw**, *zeb-ad-yaw'-hoo*; from 2064 and 3050; *Jah has given; Zebadjah*, the name of nine Isr.:—Zebadiah.

2070. זְבוּב **zᵉbûwb**, *zeb-oob'*; from an unused root (mean. to *flit*); a *fly* (espec. one of a stinging nature):—fly.

2071. זָבוּד **Zâbûwd**, *zaw-bood'*; from 2064; *given; Zabud*, an Isr.:—Zabud.

2072. זַבּוּד **Zabbûwd**, *zab-bood'*; a form of 2071; *given; Zabbud*, an Isr.:—Zabbud.

2073. זְבוּל **zᵉbûwl**, *ze-bool'*; or
זְבֻל **zᵉbûl**, *zeb-ool'*; from 2082; a *residence*:—dwell in, dwelling, habitation.

2074. זְבוּלוּן **Zᵉbûwlûwn**, *zeb-oo-loon'*; or
זְבֻלוּן **Zᵉbûlûwn**, *zeb-oo-loon'*; or
זְבוּלֻן **Zᵉbûwlûn**, *zeb-oo-loon'*; from 2082; *habitation; Zebulon*, a son of Jacob; also his territory and tribe:—Zebulun.

2075. זְבוּלֹנִי **Zᵉbûwlônîy**, *zeb-oo-lo-nee'*; patron. from 2074; a *Zebulonite* or desc. of Zebulun:—Zebulonite.

2076. זָבַח **zâbach**, *zaw-bakh'*; a prim. root; to *slaughter* an animal (usually in sacrifice):—kill, offer, (do) sacrifice, slay.

2077. זֶבַח **zebach**, *zeh'-bakh*; from 2076; prop. a *slaughter*, i.e. the *flesh* of an animal; by impl. a *sacrifice* (the victim or the act):—offer (-ing), sacrifice.

2078. זֶבַח **Zebach**, *zeh'-bakh*; the same as 2077; *sacrifice; Zebach*, a Midianitish prince:—Zebah.

2079. זַבַּי **Zabbay**, *zab-bah'ee*; prob. by orth. err. for 2140; *Zabbai* (or Zaccai), an Isr.:—Zabbai.

2080. זְבִידָה **Zᵉbîydâh**, *zeb-ee-daw'*; fem. from 2064; *giving; Zebidah*, an Israelitess:—Zebudah.

2081. זְבִינָא **Zᵉbîynâ'**, *zeb-ee-naw'*; from an unused root (mean. to *purchase*); *gainfulness; Zebina*, an Isr.:—Zebina.

2082. זָבַל **zâbal**, *zaw-bal'*; a prim. root; appar. prop. to *inclose*, i.e. to *reside*:—dwell with.

2083. זְבֻל **Zᵉbûl**, *zeb-ool'*; the same as 2073; *dwelling; Zebul*, an Isr.:—Zebul. Comp. 2073.

זְבֻלוּן **Zᵉbûlûwn**. See 2074.

2084. זְבַן **zᵉban** (Chald.), *zeb-an'*; corresp. to the root of 2081; to *acquire* by purchase:—gain.

2085. זָג **zâg**, *zawg*; from an unused root prob. mean. to *inclose*; the *skin* of a grape:—husk.

2086. זֵד **zêd**, *zade'*; from 2102; *arrogant*:—presumptuous, proud.

2087. זָדוֹן **zâdôwn**, *zaw-done'*; from 2102; *arrogance*:—presumptuously, pride, proud (man).

2088. זֶה **zeh**, *zeh*; a prim. word; the masc. demonst. pron., *this* or *that*:—he, × hence, × here, it (-self), × now, × of him, the one . . . the other, × than the other, (× out of) the (self) same, such (an one) that, these, this (hath, man), on this side . . . on that side, × thus, very, which. Comp. 2063, 2090, 2097, 2098.

2089. זֶה **zeh** (1 Sam. 17 : 34), *zeh*; by perm. for 7716; a *sheep*:—lamb.

2090. זֹה **zôh**, *zo*; for 2088; *this* or *that*:—as well as another, it, this, that, thus and thus.

2091. זָהָב **zâhâb**, *zaw-hawb'*; from an unus root mean. to *shimmer*; *gold*; fig. som thing *gold-colored* (i.e. *yellow*), as *oil*, a *clear sky* gold (-en), fair weather.

2092. זָהַם **zâham**, *zaw-ham'*; a prim. root; to *rancid*, i.e. (trans.) to *loathe*:—abhor.

2093. זַהַם **Zaham**, *zah'-ham*; from 2092; *loo ing; Zaham*, an Isr.:—Zaham.

2094. זָהַר **zâhar**, *zaw-har'*; a prim. root; *gleam*; fig. to *enlighten* (by caution) admonish, shine, teach, (give) warn (-ing).

2095. זְהַר **zᵉhar** (Chald.), *zeh-har'*; corresp. 2094; (pass.) *be admonished*:—take he

2096. זֹהַר **zôhar**, *zo'-har*; from 2094; *brilliancy* brightness.

2097. זוֹ **zôw**, *zo*; for 2088; *this* or *that*:—th this.

2098. זוּ **zûw**, *zoo*; for 2088; *this* or *that*:—th this, × wherein, which, whom.

2099. זִו **Zîv**, *zeev'*; prob. from an unused r mean. to *be prominent*; prop. *brightn* [comp. 2122], i.e. (fig.) the month of *flowers*; *Ziv* (c resp. to Ijar or May):—Zif.

2100. זוּב **zûwb**, *zoob*; a prim. root; to *flow* fre (as water), i.e. (spec.) to *have a* (sexu *flux*; fig. to *waste* away; also to *overflow*:—flo gush out, have a (running) issue, pine away, run.

2101. זוֹב **zôwb**, *zobe*; from 2100; a seminal menstrual *flux*:—issue.

2102. זוּד **zûwd**, *zood*; or (by perm.)
זִיד **zîyd**, *zeed*; a prim. root; to *seethe*; fig. *be insolent*:—be proud, deal proudly, p sume, (come) presumptuously, sod.

2103. זוּד **zûwd** (Chald.), *zood*; corresp. to 2102; *be proud*:—in pride.

2104. זוּזִים **Zûwzîym**, *zoo-zeem'*; plur. pr from the same as 2123; *prominent*; *Z zites*, an aboriginal tribe of Pal.:—Zuzims.

2105. זוֹחֵת **Zôwchêth**, *zo-khayth'*; of unce or.; *Zocheth*, an Isr.:—Zoheth.

2106. זָוִית **zâvîyth**, *zaw-veeth'*; appar. from t same root as 2099 (in the sense of *pr minence*); an *angle* (as *projecting*), i.e. (by impl.) *corner-column* (or *anta*):—corner (stone).

2107. זוּל **zûwl**, *zool*; a prim. root [comp. 215 prob. to *shake* out, i.e. (by impl.) to *sc ter* profusely; fig. to *treat lightly*:—lavish, despise.

2108. זוּלָה **zûwlâh**, *zoo-law'*; from 2107; pr *scattering*, i.e. *removal*; used adv. *cept*:—beside, but, only, save.

2109. זוּן **zûwn** *zoon*; a prim. root; perh. pr to *be plump*, i.e. (trans.) to *nourish*:—fe

2110. זוּן **zûwn** (Chald.), *zoon*; corresp. to 2109; feed.

2111. זוּעַ **zûwa'**, *zoo'-ah*; a prim. root; prop. *shake* off, i.e. (fig.) to *agitate* (as wi fear):—move, tremble, vex.

2112. זוּעַ **zûwa'** (Chald.), *zoo'-ah*; corresp. 2111; to *shake* (with fear):—tremble.

2113. זְוָעָה **zᵉvâ'âh**, *zev-aw-aw'*; from 2111; *ag tation, fear*:—be removed, trouble, ve ation. Comp. 2189.

2114. זוּר **zûwr**, *zoor*; a prim. root; to *turn* asi (espec. for lodging); hence to *be a fo eigner, strange, profane*; spec. (act. part.) to *comm adultery*:—(come from) another (man, place), fanne go away, (e-) strange (-r, thing, woman).

2115. זוּר **zûwr**, *zoor*; a prim. root [comp. 669 to *press* together, *tighten*:—close, crus thrust together.

2116. זוּרֶה **zûwreh**, *zoo-reh'*; from 2115; *trodde* on:—that which is crushed.

2117. זָזָא **zâzâ'**, *zaw-zaw'*; prob. from the root of 2123; *prominent; Zaza*, an Isr.:—Zaza.

2118. זָחַח **zâchach**, *zaw-khakh'*; a prim. root; *shove* or *displace*:—loose.

2119. זָחַל **zâchal**, *zaw-khal'*; a prim. root; *crawl*; by impl. to *fear*:—be afraid, se pent, worm.

2120. זֹחֶלֶת **Zôcheleth**, *zo-kheh'-leth*; fem. ac part. of 2119; *crawling* (i.e. *serpent Zocheleth*, a boundary stone in Pal.:—Zoheleth.

121. זֵידוֹן **zêydôwn**, *zay-dohn'*; from 2102; *boiling* of water, i.e. *wave*:—proud.

122. זִיו **zîyv** (Chald.), *zeev*; corresp. to 2099; (fig.) *cheerfulness*:—brightness, counte-ance.

123. זִיז **zîyz**, *zeez*; from an unused root appar. mean. to *be conspicuous*; *fulness* of the east; also a moving *creature*:—abundance, wild east.

124. זִיזָא **Zîyzâ'**, *zee-zaw'*, appar. from the same as 2123; *prominence*, *Ziza*, the ame of two Isr.:—Ziza.

125. זִיזָה **Zîyzâh**, *zee-zaw'*; another form for 2124; *Zizah*, an Isr.:—Zizah.

126. זִינָא **Zîynâ'**, *zee-naw'*; from 2109; well *fed*; or perh. an orth. err. for 2124; *Zina*, an r.:—Zina.

127. זִיעַ **Zîya'**, *zee'-ah*; from 2111; *agitation*; *Zia*, an Isr.:—Zia.

128. זִיף **Zîyph**, *zeef*; from the same as 2203; *flowing*; *Ziph*, the name of a place in al.; also of an Isr.:—Ziph.

129. זִיפָה **Zîyphâh**, *zee-faw'*; fem. of 2128; a *flowing*; *Ziphah*, an Isr.:—Ziphah.

130. זִיפִי **Zîyphîy**, *zee-fee'*; patrial from 2128; a *Ziphite* or inhab. of Ziph:—Ziphim, iphite.

131. זִיקָה **zîyqâh** (Isa. 50 : 11), *zee-kaw'* (fem.); and
זִק **zîq**, *zeek*; or
זֵק **zêq**, *zake*; from 2187; prop. what *leaps* forth, i.e. *flash* of fire, or a burning *arrow*; lso (from the orig. sense of the root) a *bond*:—chain, etter, firebrand, spark.

132. זַיִת **zayith**, *zah'-yith*; prob. from an unused root [akin to 2099]; an *olive* (as yielding *lluminating* oil), the tree, the branch or the berry:—live (tree, -yard), Olivet.

133. זֵיתָן **Zêythân**, *zay-thawn'*; from 2132; *olive* grove; *Zethan*, an Isr.:—Zethan.

134. זַךְ **zak**, *zak*; from 2141; *clear*:—clean, pure.

135. זָכָה **zâkâh**, *zaw-kaw'*; a prim. root [comp. 2141]; to *be translucent*; fig. to *be innocent*:—be (make) clean, cleanse, be clear, count ure.

136. זָכוּ **zâkûw** (Chald.), *zaw-koo'*; from a root corresp. to 2135; *purity*:—innocency.

137. זְכוּכִית **zᵉkûwkîyth**, *zek-oo-keeth'*; from 2135; prop. *transparency*, i.e. *glass*:—rystal.

138. זָכוּר **zâkûwr**, *zaw-koor'*; prop. pass. part. of 2142, but used for 2145; a *male* (of nan or animals):—males, men-children.

139. זַכּוּר **Zakkûwr**, *zak-koor'*; from 2142; *mindful*; *Zakkur*, the name of seven sr.:—Zaccur, Zacchur.

140. זַכַּי **Zakkay**, *zak-kah'ee*; from 2141; *pure*; *Zakkai*, an Isr.:—Zaccai.

141. זָכַךְ **zâkak**, *zaw-kak'*; a prim. root [comp. 2135]; to *be transparent* or *clean* (phys. or mor.):—be (make) clean, be pure (-r).

142. זָכַר **zâkar**, *zaw-kar'*; a prim. root; prop. to *mark* (so as to be recognized), i.e. to *remember*; by impl. to *mention*; also (as denom. from 2145) to *be male*:—× burn [incense], × earnestly, be male, (make) mention (of), be mindful, recount, record (-er), remember, make to be remembered, bring (call, come, keep, put) to (in) remembrance, × still, think on, × well.

2143. זֵכֶר **zêker**, *zay'-ker*; or
זֶכֶר **zeker**, *zeh'-ker*, from 2142; a *memento*, abstr. *recollection* (rarely if ever); by impl. *commemoration*:—memorial, memory, remembrance, scent.

2144. זֶכֶר **Zeker**, *zeh'-ker*; the same as 2143; *Zeker*, an Isr.:—Zeker.

2145. זָכָר **zâkâr**, *zaw-kawr'*; from 2142; prop. *remembered*, i.e. a *male* (of man or animals, as being the most noteworthy sex):—× him, male, man (child, -kind).

2146. זִכְרוֹן **zikrôwn**, *zik-rone'*; from 2142; a *memento* (or memorable thing, day or writing):—memorial, record.

2147. זִכְרִי **Zikrîy**, *zik-ree'*; from 2142; *memorable*; *Zicri*, the name of twelve Isr.:—Zichri.

2148. זְכַרְיָה **Zᵉkaryâh**, *zek-ar-yaw'*; or
זְכַרְיָהוּ **Zᵉkaryâhûw**, *zek-ar-yaw'-hoo*; from 2142 and 3050; *Jah has remembered*; *Zecarjah*, the name of twenty-nine Isr.:—Zachariah, Zechariah.

2149. זֻלּוּת **zullûwth**, *zool-looth'*; from 2151; prop. a *shaking*, i.e. perh. a *tempest*:—vilest.

2150. זַלְזַל **zalzal**, *zal-zal'*; by redupl. from 2151; *tremulous*, i.e. a *twig*:—sprig.

2151. זָלַל **zâlal**, *zaw-lal'*; a prim. root [comp. 2107]; to *shake* (as in the wind), i.e. to *quake*; fig. to *be loose* morally, *worthless* or *prodigal*:—blow down, glutton, riotous (eater), vile.

2152. זַלְעָפָה **zal'âphâh**, *zal-aw-faw'*; or
זִלְעָפָה **zil'âphâh**, *zil-aw-faw'*; from 2196; a *glow* (of wind or anger); also a *famine* (as *consuming*):—horrible, horror, terrible.

2153. זִלְפָּה **Zilpâh**, *zil-paw'*; from an unused root appar. mean. to *trickle*, as myrrh; fragrant *dropping*; *Zilpah*, Leah's maid:—Zilpah.

2154. זִמָּה **zimmâh**, *zim-maw'*; or
זַמָּה **zammâh**, *zam-maw'*; from 2161; a *plan*, espec. a bad one:—heinous crime, lewd (-ly, -ness), mischief, purpose, thought, wicked (device, mind, -ness).

2155. זִמָּה **Zimmâh**, *zim-maw'*; the same as 2154; *Zimmah*, the name of two Isr.:—Zimmah.

2156. זְמוֹרָה **zᵉmôwrâh**, *zem-o-raw'*; or
זְמֹרָה **zᵉmôrâh**, *zem-o-raw'* (fem.); and
זְמֹר **zᵉmôr**, *zem-ore'* (masc.): from 2168; a *twig* (as *pruned*):—vine, branch, slip.

2157. זַמְזֹם **Zamzôm**, *zam-zome'*; from 2161; *intriguing*; a *Zamzumite*, or native tribe of Pal.:—Zamzummim.

2158. זָמִיר **zâmîyr**, *zaw-meer'*; or
זָמִר **zâmîr**, *zaw-meer'*; and (fem.)
זְמִרָה **zᵉmîrâh**, *zem-ee-raw'*; from 2167; a *song* to be accompanied with instrumental music:—psalm (-ist), singing, song.

2159. זָמִיר **zâmîyr**, *zaw-meer'*; from 2168; a *twig* (as *pruned*):—branch.

2160. זְמִירָה **Zᵉmîyrâh**, *zem-ee-raw'*; fem. of 2158; *song*; *Zemirah*, an Isr.:—Zemira.

2161. זָמַם **zâmam**, *zaw-mam'*; a prim. root; to *plan*, usually in a bad sense:—consider, devise, imagine, plot, purpose, think (evil).

2162. זָמָם **zâmâm**, *zaw-mawm'*; from 2161; a *plot*:—wicked device.

2163. זָמַן **zâman**, *zaw-man'*; a prim. root; to *fix* (a time):—appoint.

2164. זְמַן **zᵉman** (Chald.), *zem-an'*; corresp. to 2163; to *agree* (on a time and place):—prepare.

2165. זְמָן **zᵉmân**, *zem-awn'*; from 2163; an *appointed* occasion:—season, time.

2166. זְמָן **zᵉmân** (Chald.), *zem-awn'*; from 2165; the same as 2165:—season, time.

2167. זָמַר **zâmar**, *zaw-mar'*; a prim. root [perh. ident. with 2168 through the idea of *striking* with the fingers]; prop. to *touch* the strings or parts of a musical instrument, i.e. *play* upon it; to make *music*, accompanied by the voice; hence to *celebrate* in song and music:—give praise, sing forth praises, psalms.

2168. זָמַר **zâmar**, *zaw-mar'*; a prim. root [comp. 2167, 5568, 6785]; to *trim* (a vine):—prune.

2169. זֶמֶר **zemer**, *zeh'-mer*; appar. from 2167 or 2168; a *gazelle* (from its lightly *touching* the ground):—chamois.

2170. זְמָר **zᵉmâr** (Chald.), *zem-awr'*; from a root corresp. to 2167; instrumental *music*:—musick.

זָמִר **zâmîr**. See 2158.

זְמֹר **zᵉmôr**. See 2156.

2171. זַמָּר **zammâr** (Chald.), *zam-mawr'*; from the same as 2170; an instrumental *musician*:—singer.

2172. זִמְרָה **zimrâh**, *zim-raw'*; from 2167; a *musical* piece or *song* to be accompanied by an instrument:—melody, psalm.

2173 זִמְרָה **zimrâh**, *zim-raw'*; from 2168; *pruned* (i.e. *choice*) fruit:—best fruit.

זְמִרָה **zᵉmîrâh**. See 2158.

זְמֹרָה **zᵉmôrâh**. See 2156.

2174. זִמְרִי **Zimrîy**, *zim-ree'*; from 2167; *musical*; *Zimri*, the name of five Isr., and of an Arabian tribe:—Zimri.

2175. זִמְרָן **Zimrân**, *zim-rawn'*; from 2167; *musical*; *Zimran*, a son of Abraham by Keturah:—Zimran.

2176. זִמְרָת **zimrâth**, *zim-rawth'*; from 2167; instrumental *music*; by impl. *praise*:—song.

2177. זַן **zan**, *zan*; from 2109; prop. *nourished* (or fully *developed*), i.e. a *form* or *sort*:—divers kinds, × all manner of store.

2178. זַן **zan** (Chald.), *zan*; corresp. to 2177; *sort*:—kind.

2179. זָנַב **zânab**, *zaw-nab'*; a prim. root mean. to *wag*; used only as a denom. from 2180; to *curtail*, i.e. *cut* off the rear:—smite the hindmost.

2180. זָנָב **zânâb**, *zaw-nawb'*; from 2179 (in the orig. sense of *flapping*); the *tail* (lit. or fig.):—tail.

2181. זָנָה **zânâh**, *zaw-naw'*; a prim. root [highly *fed* and therefore *wanton*]; to *commit adultery* (usually of the female, and less often of simple fornication, rarely of involuntary ravishment); fig. to *commit idolatry* (the Jewish people being regarded as the spouse of Jehovah):—(cause to) commit fornication, × continually, × great, (be an, play the) harlot, (cause to be, play the) whore, (commit, fall to) whoredom, (cause to) go a-whoring, whorish.

2182. זָנוֹחַ **Zânôwach**, *zaw-no'-akh*; from 2186; *rejected*; *Zanoach*, the name of two places in Pal.:—Zanoah.

2183. זָנוּן **zânûwn**, *zaw-noon'*; from 2181; *adultery*; fig. *idolatry*:—whoredom.

2184. זְנוּת **zᵉnûwth**, *zen-ooth'*; from 2181; *adultery*, i.e. (fig.) *infidelity*, *idolatry*:—whoredom.

2185. זֹנוֹת **zônôwth**, *zo-noth'*; regarded by some as if from 2109 or an unused root, and applied to military *equipments*; but evidently the fem. plur. act. part. of 2181; *harlots*:—armour.

2186. זָנַח **zânach**, *zaw-nakh'*; a prim. root mean. to *push* aside, i.e. *reject*, *forsake*, *fail*:—cast away (off), remove far away (off).

2187. זָנַק **zânaq**, *zaw-nak'*; a prim. root; prop. to *draw together* the feet (as an animal about to dart upon its prey), i.e. to *spring* forward:—leap.

2188. זֵעָה **zê'âh**, *zay-aw'*; from 2111 (in the sense of 3154); *perspiration*:—sweat.

2189. זַעֲוָה **za'ăvâh**, *zah-av-aw'*; by transp. for 2113; *agitation*, *maltreatment*:—× removed, trouble.

2190. זַעֲוָן **Za'ăvân**, *zah-av-awn'*; from 2111; *disquiet*; *Zaavan*, an Idumæan:—Zaavan.

2191. זְעֵיר **zᵉ'êyr**, *zeh-ayr'*; from an unused root [akin (by perm.) to 6819], mean. to *dwindle*; *small*:—little.

2192. זְעֵיר **zᵉ'êyr** (Chald.), *zeh-ayr'*; corresp. to 2191:—*little*.

2193. זָעַךְ **zâ'ak**, *zaw-ak'*; a prim. root; to *extinguish*:—be extinct.

2194. זָעַם **zâ'am**, *zaw-am'*; a prim. root; prop. to *foam* at the mouth, i.e. to *be enraged*:—abhor, abominable, (be) angry, defy, (have) indignation.

2195. זַעַם **za'am**, *zah'-am;* from 2194; strictly *froth* at the mouth, i.e. (fig.) *fury* (espec. of God's displeasure with sin):—angry, indignation, rage.

2196. זָעַף **zâ'aph**, *zaw-af';* a prim. root; prop. to *boil* up, i.e. (fig.) to *be peevish* or *angry:*—fret, sad, worse liking, be wroth.

2197. זַעַף **za'aph**, *zah'-af;* from 2196; *anger:*—indignation, rage (-ing), wrath.

2198. זָעֵף **zâ'êph**, *zaw-afe';* from 2196; *angry:*—displeased.

2199. זָעַק **zâ'aq**, *zaw-ak';* a prim. root; to *shriek* (from anguish or danger); by anal. (as a herald) to *announce* or *convene* publicly:—assemble, call (together), (make a) cry (out), come with such a company, gather (together), cause to be proclaimed.

2200. זְעִק **ze'iq** (Chald.), *zeh'-eek;* corresp. to 2199; to *make an outcry:*—cry.

2201. זַעַק **za'aq**, *zah'-ak;* and (fem.)

זְעָקָה **ze'âqâh**, *zeh-aw-kaw';* from 2199; a *shriek* or *outcry:*—cry (-ing).

2202. זִפְרֹן **Ziphrôn**, *zi-frone';* from an unused root (mean. to *be fragrant*); *Ziphron,* a place in Pal.:—Ziphron.

2203. זֶפֶת **zepheth**, *zeh'-feth;* from an unused root (mean. to *liquify*); *asphalt* (from its tendency to *soften* in the sun):—pitch.

זִק **zîq**, or זֵק **zêq**. See 2131.

2204. זָקֵן **zâqên**, *zaw-kane';* a prim. root; to *be old:*—aged man, be (wax) old (man).

2205. זָקֵן **zâqên**, *zaw-kane';* from 2204; *old:*—aged, ancient (man), elder (-est), old (man, men and . . . women), senator.

2206. זָקָן **zâqân**, *zaw-kawn';* from 2204; the *beard* (as indicating *age*):—beard.

2207. זֹקֶן **zôqen**, *zo'-ken;* from 2204; old *age:*—age.

2208. זָקֻן **zâqûn**, *zaw-koon';* prop. pass. part. of 2204 (used only in the plur. as a noun); *old* age:—old age.

2209. זִקְנָה **ziqnâh**, *zik-naw';* fem. of 2205; old *age:*—old (age).

2210 זָקַף **zâqaph**, *zaw-kaf';* a prim. root; to *lift,* i.e. (fig.) *comfort:*—raise (up).

2211. זְקַף **zeqaph** (Chald.), *zek-af';* corresp. to 2210; to *hang,* i.e. *impale:*—set up.

2212. זָקַק **zâqaq**, *zaw-kak';* a prim. root; to *strain,* (fig.) *extract, clarify:*—fine, pour down, purge, purify, refine.

2213. זֵר **zêr**, *zare;* from 2237 (in the sense of *scattering*); a *chaplet* (as *spread* around the top), i.e. (spec.) a border *moulding:*—crown.

2214. זָרָא **zârâ'**, *zaw-raw';* from 2114 (in the sense of *estrangement*) [comp. 2219]; *disgust:*—loathsome.

2215. זָרַב **zârab**, *zaw-rab';* a prim. root; to *flow* away:—wax warm.

2216. זְרֻבָּבֶל **Zerubbâbel**, *zer-oob-baw-bel';* from 2215 and 894; *descended of* (i.e. from) *Babylon,* i.e. born there; *Zerubbabel,* an Isr.:—Zerubbabel.

2217. זְרֻבָּבֶל **Zerubbâbel** (Chald.), *zer-oob-baw-bel';* corresp. to 2216:—Zerubbabel.

2218. זֶרֶד **Zered**, *zeh'-red;* from an unused root mean. to *be exuberant* in growth; lined with *shrubbery; Zered,* a brook E. of the Dead Sea:—Zared, Zered.

2219. זָרָה **zârâh**, *zaw-raw';* a prim root [comp. 2114; to *toss* about; by impl. to *diffuse, winnow:*—cast away, compass, disperse, fan, scatter (away), spread, strew, winnow.

2220. זְרוֹעַ **zerôwa'**, *zer-o'-ah;* or (short.)

זְרֹעַ **zerôa'**, *zer-o'-ah;* and (fem.)

זְרוֹעָה **zerôw'âh**, *zer-o-aw';* or

זְרֹעָה **zerô'âh**, *zer-o-aw';* from 2232; the *arm* (as *stretched* out), or (of animals) the *foreleg;* fig. *force:*—arm, + help, mighty, power, shoulder, strength.

2221. זֵרוּעַ **zêrûwa'**, *zay-roo'-ah;* from 2232; something *sown,* i.e. a *plant:*—sowing, thing that is sown.

2222. זַרְזִיף **zarzîyph**, *zar-zeef';* by redupl. from an unused root mean. to *flow;* a *pouring rain:*—water.

זְרוֹעָה **zerôw'âh**. See 2220.

2223. זַרְזִיר **zarzîyr**, *zar-zeer';* by redupl. from 2115; prop. tightly *girt,* i.e. prob. a *racer,* or some fleet animal (as being *slender* in the waist):— + greyhound.

2224. זָרַח **zârach**, *zaw-rakh';* a prim. root; prop. to *irradiate* (or shoot forth beams), i.e. to *rise* (as the sun); spec. to *appear* (as a symptom of leprosy):—arise, rise (up), as soon as it is up.

2225. זֶרַח **zerach**, *zeh'-rakh;* from 2224; a *rising* of light:—rising.

2226. זֶרַח **Zerach**, *zeh'-rakh;* the same as 2225: *Zerach,* the name of three Isr., also of an Idumæan and an Ethiopian prince:—Zarah, Zerah.

2227. זַרְחִי **Zarchîy**, *zar-khee';* patron. from 2226; a *Zarchite* or desc. of Zerach:—Zarchite.

2228. זְרַחְיָה **Zerachyâh**, *zer-akh-yaw';* from 2225 and 3050; *Jah has risen; Zerachjah,* the name of two Isr.:—Zerahiah.

2229. זָרַם **zâram**, *zaw-ram';* a prim. root; to *gush* (as water):—carry away as with a flood, pour out.

2230. זֶרֶם **zerem**, *zeh'-rem;* from 2229; a *gush* of water:—flood, overflowing, shower, storm, tempest.

2231. זִרְמָה **zirmâh**, *zir-maw';* fem. of 2230; a *gushing* of fluid (semen):—issue.

2232. זָרַע **zâra'**, *zaw-rah';* a prim. root; to *sow;* fig. to *disseminate, plant, fructify:*—bear, conceive seed, set with, sow (-er), yield.

2233. זֶרַע **zera'**, *zeh'-rah;* from 2232; *seed;* fig. *fruit, plant, sowing-time, posterity:*—× carnally, child, fruitful, seed (-time), sowing-time.

2234. זְרַע **zera'** (Chald.), *zer-ah';* corresp. to 2233; *posterity:*—seed.

זְרֹעַ **zerôa'**. See 2220.

2235. זֵרֹעַ **zêrôa'**, *zay-ro'-ah;* or

זֵרָעֹן **zêrâ'ôn**, *zay-raw-ohn';* from 2232; something *sown* (only in the plur.), i.e. a *vegetable* (as food):—pulse.

זְרֹעָה **zerô'âh**. See 2220.

2236. זָרַק **zâraq**, *zaw-rak';* a prim. root; to *sprinkle* (fluid or solid particles):—be here and there, scatter, sprinkle, strew.

2237. זָרַר **zârar**, *zaw-rar';* a prim. root [comp. 2114]; perh. to *diffuse,* i.e. (spec.) to *sneeze:*—sneeze.

2238. זֶרֶשׁ **Zeresh**, *zeh'-resh;* of Pers. or.; *Zeresh,* Haman's wife:—Zeresh.

2239. זֶרֶת **zereth**, *zeh'-reth;* from 2219; the *spread* of the fingers, i.e. a *span:*—span.

2240. זַתּוּא **Zattûw'**, *zat-too';* of uncert. der.; *Zattu,* an Isr.:—Zattu.

2241. זֵתָם **Zêthâm**, *zay-thawm';* appar. a var. for 2133; *Zetham,* an Isr.:—Zetham.

2242. זֵתַר **Zêthar**, *zay-thar';* of Pers. or.; *Zethar,* a eunuch of Xerxes:—Zethar.

ח

2243. חֹב **chôb**, *khobe;* by contr. from 2245; prop. a *cherisher,* i.e. the *bosom:*—bosom.

2244. חָבָא **châbâ'**, *khaw-baw';* a prim. root [comp. 2245]; to *secrete:*— × held, hide (self), do secretly.

2245. חָבַב **châbab**, *khaw-bab';* a prim. root [comp. 2244, 2247]; prop. to *hide* (as in the bosom), i.e. to *cherish* (with affection):—love.

2246. חֹבָב **Chôbâb**, *kho-bawb';* from 2245; *cherished; Chobab,* father-in-law of Moses:—Hobab.

2247. חָבָה **châbah**, *khaw-bah';* a prim. root [comp. 2245]; to *secrete:*—hide (self).

2248. חֲבוּלָה **chăbûwlâh** (Chald.), *khab-oo-law';* from 2255; prop. *overthrown,* i.e. (morally) *crime:*—hurt.

2249. חָבוֹר **Châbôwr**, *khaw-bore';* from 22[illegible] *united; Chabor,* a river of Assyria: Habor.

2250. חַבּוּרָה **chabbûwrâh**, *khab-boo-raw';* [illegible]

חַבֻּרָה **chabbûrâh**, *khab-boo-raw';* or

חֲבֻרָה **chăbûrâh**, *khab-oo-raw';* fro[m] 2266; prop. *bound* (with stripes), i.e. *weal* (or black-and-blue mark itself):—bluene[ss], bruise, hurt, stripe, wound.

2251. חָבַט **châbaṭ**, *khaw-bat';* a prim. root; [to] *knock* out or off:—beat (off, out), thres[h].

2252. חֲבַיָּה **Chăbayâh**, *khab-ah-yaw';* or

חֲבָיָה **Chăbâyâh**, *khab-aw-yaw';* fro[m] 2247 and 3050; *Jah has hidden; Chab[a]jah,* an Isr.:—Habaiah.

2253. חֶבְיוֹן **chebyôwn**, *kheb-yone';* from 224[7]; a *concealment:*—hiding.

2254. חָבַל **châbal**, *khaw-bal';* a prim. root; [to] *wind* tightly (as a rope), i.e. to *bin[d];* spec. by a *pledge;* fig. to *pervert, destroy;* also [to] *writhe* in pain (espec. of parturition):— × at a[ll], band, bring forth, (deal) corrupt (-ly), destroy, o[f]fend, lay to (take a) pledge, spoil, travail, × ver[y], withhold.

2255. חֲבַל **chăbal** (Chald.), *khab-al';* corresp. [to] 2254; to *ruin:*—destroy, hurt.

2256. חֶבֶל **chebel**, *kheh'-bel;* or

חֵבֶל **chêbel**, *khay'-bel;* from 2254; a *ro[pe]* (as *twisted*), espec. a measuring *line;* b[y] impl. a *district* or *inheritance* (as *measured*); [or] *noose* (as of *cords*); fig. a *company* (as if *tied* t[o]gether); also a *throe* (espec. of parturition); als[o] *ruin:*—band, coast, company, cord, country, destru[c]tion, line, lot, pain, pang, portion, region, rope, snar[e], sorrow, tackling.

2257. חֲבַל **chăbal** (Chald.), *khab-al';* from 225[5]; *harm* (personal or pecuniary):—damag[e], hurt.

2258. חֲבֹל **chăbôl**, *khab-ole';* or (fem.)

חֲבֹלָה **chăbôlâh**, *khab-o-law';* from 225[4]; a *pawn* (as security for debt):—pledg[e].

2259. חֹבֵל **chôbêl**, *kho-bale';* act. part. from 22[54] (in the sense of handling *ropes*); *sailor:*—pilot, shipmaster.

2260. חִבֵּל **chibbêl**, *khib-bale';* from 2254 (in th[e] sense of furnished with *ropes*); *mast:*—mast.

2261. חֲבַצֶּלֶת **chăbatstseleth**, *khab-ats-tseh'-leth;* of uncert. der.; prob. *meadow saffron:*—rose.

2262. חֲבַצִּנְיָה **Chăbatstsanyâh**, *khab-ats-tsan-yaw';* of uncert. der.; *Chabatstsanjah,* a Rechabite:—Habazaniah.

2263. חָבַק **châbaq**, *khaw-bak';* a prim. root; [to] *clasp* (the hands or in embrace):—em[]brace, fold.

2264. חִבֻּק **chibbûq**, *khib-book';* from 2263; a *clasp[]ing* of the hands (in idleness):—fold.

2265. חֲבַקּוּק **Chăbaqqûwq**, *khab-ak-kook';* b[y] redupl. from 2263; *embrace; Chabak[]kuk,* the prophet:—Habakkuk.

2266. חָבַר **châbar**, *khaw-bar';* a prim. root; [to] *join* (lit. or fig.); spec. (by means o[f] spells) to *fascinate:*—charm (-er), be compact, coupl[e] (together), have fellowship with, heap up, join (sel[f] together), league.

2267. חֶבֶר **cheber**, *kheh'-ber;* from 2266; a *so[]ciety;* also a *spell:*— + charmer (-ing), company, enchantment, × wide.

2268. חֶבֶר **Cheber**, *hheh'-ber;* the same as 2267; *community; Cheber,* the name of a Ken[]ite and of three Isr.:—Heber.

2269. חֲבַר **chăbar** (Chald.), *khab-ar';* from a ro[ot] corresp. to 2266; an *associate:*—compa[n]ion, fellow.

2270. חָבֵר **châbêr**, *khaw-bare';* from 2266; a[n] *associate:*—companion, fellow, kn[it] together.

2271. חַבָּר **chabbâr**, *khab-bawr';* from 2266; [a] *partner:*—companion.

72. חֲבַרְבֻּרָה **chăbarbûrâh**, *khab-ar-boo-raw'*; by redupl. from 2266; a
'eak (like a *line*), as on the tiger:—spot.

73. חַבְרָה **chabrâh** (Chald.), *khab-raw'*; fem. of 2269; an *associate*:—other.

74. חֶבְרָה **chebrâh**, *kheb-raw'*; fem. of 2267; *association*:—company.

75. חֶבְרוֹן **Chebrôwn**, *kheb-rone'*; from 2267; seat of *association*; *Chebron*, a place
Pal., also the name of two Isr.:—Hebron.

76. חֶבְרוֹנִי **Chebrôwnîy**, *kheb-ro-nee'*; or

חֶבְרֹנִי **Chebrônîy**, *kheb-ro-nee'*; patron. from 2275; *Chebronite* (collect.), an in-
.b. of Chebron:—Hebronites.

77. חֶבְרִי **Chebrîy**, *kheb-ree'*; patron. from 2268; a *Chebrite* (collect.) or desc. of
.eber:—Heberites.

78. חֲבֶרֶת **chăbereth**, *khab-eh'-reth*; fem. of 2270; a *consort*:—companion.

79. חֹבֶרֶת **chôbereth**, *kho-beh'-reth*; fem. act. part. of 2266; a *joint*:—which coup-
h, coupling.

80. חָבַשׁ **châbash**, *khaw-bash'*; a prim. root; to *wrap* firmly (espec. a turban, com-
ess, or *saddle*); fig. to *stop*, to *rule*:—bind (up),
'd about, govern, healer, put, saddle, wrap about.

81. חֲבִת **chăbêth**, *khaw-bayth'*; from an unused root prob. mean. to *cook* [comp.
27]; something *fried*, prob. a griddle-*cake*:—pan.

82. חַג **chag**, *khag*; or

חָג **châg**, *khawg*; from 2287; a *festival*, or a *victim* therefor:—(solemn) feast (day),
crifice, solemnity.

83. חָגָא **châgâ'**, *khaw-gaw'*; from an unused root mean. to *revolve* [comp. 2287]; prop.
rtigo, i.e. (fig.) *fear*:—terror.

84. חָגָב **châgâb**, *khaw-gawb'*; of uncert. der.; a *locust*:—locust.

85. חָגָב **Châgâb**, *khaw-gawb'*; the same as 2284; *locust*; *Chagab*, one of the Neth-
im:—Hagab.

86. חֲגָבָא **Chăgâbâ'**, *khag-aw-baw'*; or

חֲגָבָה **Chăgâbâh**, *khag-aw-baw'*; fem. of 2285; *locust*; *Chagaba* or *Chagabah*,
ıe of the Nethinim:—Hagaba, Hagabah.

87. חָגַג **châgag**, *khaw-gag'*; a prim. root [comp. 2283, 2328]; prop. to move in a *circle*, i.e.
pec.) to *march* in a sacred procession, to *observe* a
stival; by impl. to *be giddy*:—celebrate, dance, (keep,
ɔld) a (solemn) feast (holiday), reel to and fro.

88. חֲגָו **chăgâv**, *khag-awv'*; from an unused root mean. to take *refuge*; a *rift* in
ɔcks:—cleft.

89. חָגוֹר **châgôwr**, *khaw-gore'*; from 2296; *belted*:—girded with.

90. חֲגוֹר **chăgôwr**, *khag-ore'*; or

חֲגֹר **chăgôr**, *khag-ore'*; and (fem.)

חֲגוֹרָה **chăgôwrâh**, *khag-o-raw'*; or

חֲגֹרָה **chăgôrâh**, *khag-o-raw'*; from 2296; a *belt* (for the waist):—apron, armour,
rd (-le).

91. חַגִּי **Chaggîy**, *khag-ghee'*; from 2287; *festive*; *Chaggi*, an Isr.; also (patron.) a
'haggite, or desc. of the same:—Haggi, Haggites.

92. חַגַּי **Chaggay**, *khag-gah'ee*; from 2282; *festive*; *Chaggai*, a Heb. prophet:—Haggai.

93. חַגִּיָּה **Chaggîyâh**, *khag-ghee-yaw'*; from 2282 and 3050; *festival of Jah*; *Chaggi-
ah*, an Isr.:—Haggiah.

94. חַגִּית **Chaggîyîth**, *khag-gheeth'*; fem. of 2291; *festive*; *Chaggith*, a wife of
avid:—Haggith.

95. חָגְלָה **Choglâh**, *khog-law'*; of uncert. der.; prob. a *partridge*; *Choglah*, an Israel-
ess:—Hoglah. See also 1031.

96. חָגַר **châgar**, *khaw gar'*; a prim. root; to *gird* on (as a belt, armor, etc.):—be able
o put on, be afraid, appointed, gird, restrain, × on
very side.

297. חַד **chad**, *khad*; abridged from 259; *one*:—one.

2298. חַד **chad** (Chald.), *khad*; corresp. to 2297; as card. *one*; as art. *single*; as ord. *first*; adv. *at once*:—a, first, one, together.

2299. חַד **chad**, *khad*; from 2300; *sharp*:—sharp.

2300. חָדַד **châdad**, *khaw-dad'*; a prim. root; to *be* (caus. *make*) *sharp* or (fig.) *severe*:—be fierce, sharpen.

2301. חֲדַד **Chădad**, *khad-ad'*; from 2300; *fierce*; *Chadad*, an Ishmaelite:—Hadad.

2302. חָדָה **châdâh**, *khaw-daw'*; a prim. root; to *rejoice*:—make glad, be joined, rejoice.

2303. חַדּוּד **chaddûwd**, *khad-dood'*; from 2300; a *point*:—sharp.

2304. חֶדְוָה **chedvâh**, *khed-vaw'*; from 2302; *rejoicing*:—gladness, joy.

2305. חֶדְוָה **chedvâh** (Chald.), *khed-vaw'*; corresp. to 2304:—*joy*.

2306. חֲדִי **chădîy** (Chald.), *khad-ee'*; corresp. to 2373; a *breast*:—breast.

2307. חָדִיד **Châdîyd**, *khaw-deed'*; from 2300; a *peak*; *Chadid*, a place in Pal.:—Hadid.

2308. חָדַל **châdal**, *khaw-dal'*; a prim. root; prop. to *be flabby*, i.e. (by impl.) *desist*; (fig.) *be lacking* or *idle*:—cease, end, fail, forbear, forsake, leave (off), let alone, rest, be unoccupied, want.

2309. חֶדֶל **chedel**, *kheh'-del*; from 2308; *rest*, i.e. the state of the *dead*:—world.

2310. חָדֵל **châdêl**, *khaw-dale'*; from 2308; *vacant*, i.e. *ceasing* or *destitute*:—he that forbeareth, frail, rejected.

2311. חַדְלַי **Chadlay**, *khad-lah'ee*; from 2309; *idle*; *Chadlai*, an Isr.:—Hadlai.

2312. חֵדֶק **chêdeq**, *khay'-dek*; from an unused root mean. to *sting*; a *prickly* plant:—brier, thorn.

2313. חִדֶּקֶל **Chiddeqel**, *khid-deh'-kel*; prob. of for. or.; the *Chiddekel* (or Tigris) river:—Hiddekel.

2314. חָדַר **châdar**, *khaw-dar'*; a prim. root; prop. to *inclose* (as a room), i.e. (by anal.) to *beset* (as in a siege):—enter a privy chamber.

2315. חֶדֶר **cheder**, *kheh'-der*; from 2314; an *apartment* (usually lit.):—([bed] inner) chamber, innermost (-ward) part, parlour, + south, × within.

2316. חֲדַר **Chădar**, *khad-ar'*; another form for 2315; *chamber*; *Chadar*, an Ishmaelite:—Hadar.

2317. חַדְרָךְ **Chadrâk**, *khad-rawk'*; of uncert. der.; *Chadrak*, a Syrian deity:—Hadrach.

2318. חָדַשׁ **châdash**, *khaw-dash'*; a prim. root; to *be new*; caus. to *rebuild*:—renew, repair.

2319. חָדָשׁ **châdâsh**, *khaw-dawsh'*; from 2318; *new*:—fresh, new thing.

2320. חֹדֶשׁ **chôdesh**, *kho'-desh*; from 2318; the *new* moon; by impl. a *month*:—month (-ly), new moon.

2321. חֹדֶשׁ **Chôdesh**, *kho'-desh*; the same as 2320; *Chodesh*, an Israelitess:—Hodesh.

2322. חֲדָשָׁה **Chădâshâh**, *khad-aw-shaw'*; fem. of 2319; *new*; *Chadashah*, a place in Pal.:—Hadashah.

2323. חֲדַת **chădath** (Chald.), *khad-ath'*; corresp. to 2319; *new*:—new.

2324. חֲוָא **chăvâ'** (Chald.), *khav-aw'*; corresp. to 2331; to *show*:—shew.

2325. חוּב **chûwb**, *khoob*; also

חָיַב **châyab**, *khaw-yab'*; a prim. root; prop. perh. to *tie*, i.e. (fig. and reflex.) to *owe*, or (by impl.) to *forfeit*:—make endanger.

2326. חוֹב **chôwb**, *khobe*; from 2325; *debt*:—debtor.

2327. חוֹבָה **chôwbâh**, *kho-baw'*; fem. act. part. of 2247; *hiding* place; *Chobah*, a place in Syria:—Hobah.

2328. חוּג **chûwg**, *khoog*; a prim. root [comp. 2287]; to describe a *circle*:—compass.

2329. חוּג **chûwg**, *khoog*; from 2328; a *circle*:—circle, circuit, compass.

2330. חוּד **chûwd**, *khood*; a prim. root; prop. to *tie* a knot, i.e. (fig.) to *propound* a riddle:—put forth.

2331. חָוָה **châvâh**, *khaw-vah'*; a prim. root; [comp. 2324, 2421]; prop. to *live*; by impl. (intens.) to *declare* or *show*:—show.

2332. חַוָּה **Chavvâh**, *khav-vaw'*; causat. from 2331; *life-giver*; *Chavvah* (or Eve), the first woman:—Eve.

2333. חַוָּה **chavvâh**, *khav-vaw'*; prop. the same as 2332 (*life-giving*, i.e. *living-place*); by impl. an encampment or *village*:—(small) town.

2334. חַוּוֹת יָעִיר **Chavvôwth Yâ'îyr**, *khav-vothe' yaw-eer'*; from the plur. of 2333 and a modification of 3265; *hamlets of Jair*, a region of Pal.:—[Bashan-] Havoth-jair.

2335. חוֹזַי **Chôwzay**, *kho-zah'ee*; from 2374; *visionary*; *Chozai*, an Isr.:—the seers.

2336. חוֹחַ **chôwach**, *kho'-akh*; from an unused root appar. mean. to *pierce*; a *thorn*; by anal. a *ring* for the nose:—bramble, thistle, thorn.

2337. חָוָח **châvâch**, *khaw-vawkh'*; perh. the same as 2336; a *dell* or *crevice* (as if *pierced* in the earth):—thicket.

2338. חוּט **chûwṭ** (Chald.), *khoot*; corresp. to the root of 2339, perh. as a denom.; to *string* together, i.e. (fig.) to *repair*:—join.

2339. חוּט **chûwṭ**, *khoot*; from an unused root prob. mean. to *sew*; a *string*; by impl. a measuring *tape*:—cord, fillet, line, thread.

2340. חִוִּי **Chivvîy**, *khiv-vee'*; perh. from 2333; a *villager*; a *Chivvite*, one of the aboriginal tribes of Pal.:—Hivite.

2341. חֲוִילָה **Chăvîylâh**, *khav-ee-law'*; prob. from 2342; *circular*; *Chavilah*, the name of two or three eastern regions; also perh. of two men:—Havilah.

2342. חוּל **chûwl**, *khool*; or

חִיל **chîyl**, *kheel*; a prim. root; prop. to *twist* or *whirl* (in a circular or spiral manner), i.e. (spec.) to *dance*, to *writhe* in pain (espec. of parturition) or fear; fig. to *wait*, to *pervert*:—bear, (make to) bring forth, (make to) calve, dance, drive away, fall grievously (with pain), fear, form, great, grieve, (be) grievous, hope, look, make, be in pain, be much (sore) pained, rest, shake, shapen, (be) sorrow (-ful), stay, tarry, travail (with pain), tremble, trust, wait carefully (patiently), be wounded.

2343. חוּל **Chûwl**, *khool*; from 2342; a *circle*; *Chul*, a son of Aram; also the region settled by him:—Hul.

2344. חוֹל **chôwl**, *khole*; from 2342; *sand* (as *round* or whirling particles):—sand.

2345. חוּם **chûwm**, *khoom*; from an unused root mean. to *be warm*, i.e. (by impl.) *sunburnt* or *swarthy* (blackish):—brown.

2346. חוֹמָה **chôwmâh**, *kho-maw'*; fem. act. part. of an unused root appar. mean. to *join*; a *wall* of protection:—wall, walled.

2347. חוּס **chûwç**, *khoos*; a prim. root; prop. to *cover*, i.e. (fig.) to *compassionate*:—pity, regard, spare.

2348. חוֹף **chôwph**, *khofe*; from an unused root mean. to *cover*; a *cove* (as a *sheltered* bay):—coast [of the sea], haven, shore, [sea-] side.

2349. חוּפָם **Chûwphâm**, *khoo-fawm'*; from the same as 2348; *protection*; *Chupham*, an Isr.:—Hupham.

2350. חוּפָמִי **Chûwphâmîy**, *khoo-faw-mee'*; patron. from 2349; a *Chuphamite* or desc. of Chupham:—Huphamites.

2351. חוּץ **chûwts**, *khoots*; or (short.)

חֻץ **chûts**, *khoots*; (both forms fem. in the plur.) from an unused root mean. to *sever*; prop. *separate* by a wall, i.e. *outside*, *outdoors*:—abroad, field, forth, highway, more, out (-side, -ward), street, without.

חוֹק **chôwq**. See 2436.

חוֹקֹק **Chûwqôq**. See 2712.

2352. חוּר **chûwr**, *khoor;* or (short.)
חֻר **chûr**, *khoor;* from an unused root prob. mean. to *bore;* the *crevice* of a serpent; the *cell* of a prison:—hole.

2353. חוּר **chûwr**, *khoor;* from 2357; *white* linen:—white.

2354. חוּר **Chûwr**, *khoor;* the same as 2353 or 2352; *Chur,* the name of four Isr. and one Midianite:—Hur.

2355. חוֹר **chôwr**, *khore;* the same as 2353; *white* linen:—network. Comp. 2715.

2356. חוֹר **chôwr**, *khore;* or (short.)
חֹר **chôr**, *khore;* the same as 2352; a *cavity, socket, den:*—cave, hole.

2357. חָוַר **châvar**, *khaw-var';* a prim. root; to *blanch* (as with shame):—wax pale.

2358. חִוָּר **chivvâr** (Chald.), *khiv-vawr';* from a root corresp. to 2357; *white:*—white.
חוֹרוֹן **Chôwrôwn.** See 1032.
חוֹרִי **chôwrîy.** See 2753.

2359. חוּרִי **Chûwrîy**, *khoo-ree';* prob. from 2353; *linen*-worker; *Churi,* an Isr.:—Huri.

2360. חוּרַי **Chûwray**, *khoo-rah'ee;* prob. an orth. var. for 2359; *Churai,* an Isr.:—Hurai.

2361. חוּרָם **Chûwrâm**, *khoo-rawm';* prob. from 2353; *whiteness,* i.e. noble; *Churam,* the name of an Isr. and two Syrians:—Huram. Comp. 2438.

2362. חַוְרָן **Chavrân**, *khav-rawn';* appar. from 2357 (in the sense of 2352); *cavernous; Chavran,* a region E. of the Jordan:—Hauran.

2363. חוּשׁ **chûwsh**, *koosh;* a prim. root; to *hurry;* fig. to *be eager* with excitement or enjoyment:—(make) haste (-n), ready.

2364. חוּשָׁה **Chûwshâh**, *khoo-shaw';* from 2363; *haste; Chushah,* an Isr.:—Hushah.

2365. חוּשַׁי **Chûwshay**, *khoo-shah'ee;* from 2363; *hasty; Chushai,* an Isr.:—Hushai.

2366. חוּשִׁים **Chûwshîym**, *khoo-sheem';* or
חֻשִׁים **Chûshîym**, *khoo-shem';* or
חֻשִׁם **Chûshîm**, *khoo-sheem';* plur. from 2363; *hasters; Chushim,* the name of three Isr.:—Hushim.

2367. חוּשָׁם **Chûwshâm**, *khoo-shawm';* or
חֻשָׁם **Chûshâm**, *khoo-shawm';* from 2363; *hastily; Chusham,* an Idumæan:—Husham.

2368. חוֹתָם **chôwthâm**, *kho-thawm';* or
חֹתָם **chôthâm**, *kho-thawm';* from 2856; a *signature*-ring:—seal, signet.

2369. חוֹתָם **Chôwthâm**, *kho-thawm',* the same as 2368; *seal; Chotham,* the name of two Isr.:—Hotham, Hothan.

2370. חֲזָא **chăzâ'** (Chald.), *khaz-aw';* or
חֲזָה **chăzâh** (Chald.), *khaz-aw';* corresp. to 2372; to *gaze* upon; mentally to *dream, be usual* (i.e. *seem*):—behold, have [a dream], see, be wont.

2371. חֲזָאֵל **Chăzâ'êl**, *khaz-aw-ale';* or
חֲזָהאֵל **Chăzâh'êl**, *khaz-aw-ale';* from 2372 and 410; *God has seen; Chazaël,* a king of Syria:—Hazael.

2372. חָזָה **châzâh**, *khaw-zaw';* a prim. root; to *gaze* at; mentally to *perceive, contemplate* (with pleasure); spec. to *have a vision of:*—behold, look, prophesy, provide, see.

2373. חָזֶה **châzeh**, *khaw-zeh';* from 2372; the *breast* (as most *seen* in front):—breast.

2374. חֹזֶה **chôzeh**, *kho-zeh';* act. part. of 2372; a *beholder* in vision; also a *compact* (as *looked upon* with approval):—agreement, prophet, see that, seer, [star-] gazer.
חֲזָהאֵל **Chăzâh'êl.** See 2371.

2375. חֲזוֹ **Chăzow**, *khaz-o';* from 2372; *seer; Chazo,* a nephew of Abraham:—Hazo.

2376. חֵזֵו **chêzev** (Chald.), *khay'-zev;* from 2370; a *sight:*—look, vision.

2377. חָזוֹן **châzôwn**, *khaw-zone';* from 2372; a *sight* (mentally), i.e. a *dream, revelation,* or *oracle:*—vision.

2378. חָזוֹת **châzôwth**, *khaw-zooth';* from 2372; a *revelation:*—vision.

2379. חֲזוֹת **chăzôwth** (Chald.), *khaz-oth';* from 2370; a *view:*—sight.

2380. חָזוּת **châzûwth**, *khaw-zooth';* from 2372; a *look;* hence (fig.) striking *appearance, revelation,* or (by impl.) *compact:*—agreement, notable (one), vision.

2381. חֲזִיאֵל **Chăzîy'êl**, *khaz-ee-ale';* from 2372 and 410; *seen of God; Chaziel,* a Levite:—Haziel.

2382. חֲזָיָה **Chăzâyâh**, *khaz-aw-yaw';* from 2372 and 3050; *Jah has seen; Chazajah,* an Isr.:—Hazaiah.

2383. חֶזְיוֹן **Chezyôwn**, *khez-yone';* from 2372; *vision; Chezjon,* a Syrian:—Hezion.

2384. חִזָּיוֹן **chizzâyôwn**, *khiz-zaw-yone';* from 2372; a *revelation,* espec. by *dream:*—vision.

2385. חֲזִיז **châzîyz**, *khaw-zeez';* from an unused root mean. to *glare;* a *flash* of lightning:—bright cloud, lightning.

2386. חֲזִיר **châzîyr**, *khaz-eer';* from an unused root prob. mean. to *inclose;* a *hog* (perh. as *penned*):—boar, swine.

2387. חֵזִיר **Chêzîyr**, *khay-zeer';* from the same as 2386; perh. *protected; Chezir,* the name of two Isr.:—Hezir.

2388. חָזַק **châzaq**, *khaw-zak';* a prim. root; to *fasten* upon; hence to *seize, be strong* (fig. *courageous,* causat. *strengthen, cure, help, repair, fortify*), *obstinate;* to *bind, restrain, conquer:*—aid, amend, × calker, catch, cleave, confirm, be constant, constrain, continue, be of good (take) courage (-ous, -ly), encourage (self), be established, fasten, force, fortify, make hard, harden, help, (lay) hold (fast), lean, maintain, play the man, mend, become (wax) mighty, prevail, be recovered, repair, retain, seize, be (wax) sore, strengthen (self), be stout, be (make, shew, wax) strong (-er), be sure, take (hold), be urgent, behave self valiantly, withstand.

2389. חָזָק **châzâq**, *khaw-zawk';* from 2388; *strong* (usu. in a bad sense, *hard, bold, violent*):—harder, hottest, + impudent, loud, mighty, sore, stiff [-hearted], strong (-er).

2390. חָזֵק **châzêq**, *khaw-zake';* from 2388; *powerful:*— × wax louder. stronger.

2391. חֵזֶק **chêzeq**, *khay'-zek;* from 2388; *help:*—strength.

2392. חֹזֶק **chôzeq**, *kho'-zek;* from 2388; *power:*—strength.

2393. חֶזְקָה **chezqâh**, *khez-kaw';* fem. of 2391; prevailing *power:*—strength (-en self), (was) strong.

2394. חָזְקָה **chozqâh**, *khoz-kaw';* fem. of 2392; *vehemence* (usu. in a bad sense):—force, mightily, repair. sharply.

2395. חִזְקִי **Chizqîy**, *khiz-kee';* from 2388; *strong; Chizki,* an Isr.:—Hezeki.

2396. חִזְקִיָּה **Chizqîyâh**, *khiz-kee-yaw';* or
חִזְקִיָּהוּ **Chizqîyâhûw**, *khiz-kee-yaw'-hoo;* also
יְחִזְקִיָּה **Yechizqîyâh**, *yekh-iz-kee-yaw';* or
יְחִזְקִיָּהוּ **Yechizqîyâhûw**, *yekh-iz-kee-yaw'-hoo;* from 2388 and 3050; *strengthened of Jah; Chizkijah,* a king of Judah, also the name of two other Isr.:—Hezekiah, Hizkiah, Hizkijah. Comp. 3169.

2397. חָח **châch**, *khawkh;* once (Ezek. 29 : 4)
חָחִי **châchîy**, *khakh-ee';* from the same as 2336; a *ring* for the nose (or lips):—bracelet, chain, hook.
חָחִי **châchîy.** See 2397.

2398. חָטָא **châţâ'**, *khaw-taw';* a prim. root; pro[perly] to *miss;* hence (fig. and gen.) to *si[n]* by infer. to *forfeit, lack, expiate, repent,* (causat.) *lead astray, condemn:*—bear the blame, cleanse, commit [sin], by fault, harm he hath done, loss, mis[s], (make) offend (-er), offer for sin, purge, purify (self), make reconciliation, (cause, make) sin (-ful, -ness), trespass.

2399. חֵטְא **chêţ'**, *khate;* from 2398; a *crime* or i[ts] *penalty:*—fault, × grievously, offenc[e], (punishment of) sin.

2400. חַטָּא **chaţţâ'**, *khat-taw';* intens. from 239[8]; a *criminal,* or one accounted *guilty:*—offender, sinful, sinner.

2401. חֲטָאָה **chăţâ'âh**, *khat-aw-aw';* fem. o[f] 2399; an *offence,* or a *sacrifice* for it:—sin (offering), sinful.

2402. חַטָּאָה **chaţţâ'âh** (Chald.), *khat-taw-aw';* corresp. to 2401; an *offence,* and th[e] *penalty* or *sacrifice* for it:—sin (offering).

2403. חַטָּאָה **chaţţâ'âh**, *khat-taw-aw';* or
חַטָּאת **chaţţâ'th**, *khat-tawth';* from 239[8]; an *offence* (sometimes habitual *sinful[ness]*), and its penalty, occasion, sacrifice, or expia[tion]; also (concr.) an *offender:*—punishment (of sin), purifying (-fication for sin), sin (-ner, offering).

2404. חָטַב **châţab**, *khaw-tab';* a prim. root; t[o] *chop* or *carve* wood:—cut down, he[w] (-er), polish.

2405. חֲטֻבָה **chăţûbâh**, *khat-oo-baw';* fem. pas[s.] part. of 2404; prop. a *carving;* henc[e] a *tapestry* (as figured):—carved.

2406. חִטָּה **chiţţâh**, *khit-taw';* of uncert. der.; *wheat,* whether the grain or th[e] plant:—wheat (-en).

2407. חַטּוּשׁ **Chaţţûwsh**, *khat-toosh';* from a[n] unused root of uncert. signif.; *Chat[]tush,* the name of four or five Isr.:—Hattush.

2408. חֲטִי **chăţîy** (Chald.), *khat-ee';* from a roo[t] corresp. to 2398; an *offence:*—sin.

2409. חַטָּיָא **chaţţâyâ'** (Chald.), *khat-taw-yaw';* from the same as 2408; an *expiation:*—sin offering.

2410. חֲטִיטָא **Chăţîyţa'**, *khat-ee-taw';* from a[n] unused root appar. mean. to *dig out; explorer; Chatita,* a temple porter:—Hatita.

2411. חַטִּיל **Chaţţîyl**, *khat-teel';* from an unuse[d] root appar. mean. to *wave; fluctuating; Chattil,* one of "Solomon's servants":—Hattil.

2412. חֲטִיפָא **Chăţîyphâ'**, *khat-ee-faw';* fro[m] 2414; *robber; Chatipha,* one of th[e] Nethinim:—Hatipha.

2413. חָטַם **châţam**, *khaw-tam';* a prim. root; t[o] *stop:*—refrain.

2414. חָטַף **châţaph**, *khaw-taf';* a prim. root; t[o] *clutch;* hence to *seize* as a prisoner:—catch.

2415. חֹטֶר **chôţer**, *kho'-ter;* from an unused roo[t] of uncert. signif.; a *twig:*—rod.

2416. חַי **chay**, *khah'ee;* from 2421; *alive;* henc[e] *raw* (flesh); *fresh* (plant, water, year), *strong;* also (as noun, espec. in the fem. sing. and masc. plur.) *life* (or living thing), whether lit. o[r] fig.:— + age, alive, appetite, (wild) beast, company, congregation, life (-time), live (-ly), living (creature, thing), maintenance, + merry, multitude, + (be) old, quick, raw, running, springing, troop.

2417. חַי **chay** (Chald.), *khah'ee;* from 2418; *alive;* also (as noun in plur.) *life:*—life, tha[t] liveth, living.

2418. חֲיָא **chăyâ'** (Chald.), *khah-yaw';* or
חֲיָה **chăyâh** (Chald.), *khah-yaw';* corresp. to 2421; to *live:*—live, keep alive.

2419. חִיאֵל **Chîy'êl**, *khee-ale';* from 2416 and 410; *living of God; Chiel,* an Isr.:—Hiel.
חָיָב **châyab.** See 2325.

2420. חִידָה **chîydâh**, *khee-daw';* from 2330; a *puzzle;* hence a *trick, conundrum, sen[]tentious maxim:*—dark saying (sentence, speech), hard question, proverb, riddle.

421. חָיָה **châyâh**, *khaw-yaw'*; a prim. root [comp. 2331, 2424]; to *live*, whether lit. or g.; causat. to *revive*:—keep (leave, make) alive, certainly, give (promise) life, (let, suffer to) live, ourish up, preserve (alive), quicken, recover, reair, restore (to life), revive, (× God) save (alive, life, ves), × surely, be whole.

422. חָיֶה **châyeh**, *khaw-yeh'*; from 2421; *vigorous*:—lively.

423. חֵיוָא **chêyvâ'** (Chald.), *khay-vaw'*; from 2418; an *animal*:—beast.

424. חַיּוּת **chayûwth**, *khah-yooth'*; from 2421; *life*:— × living.

425. חָיַי **châyay**, *khaw-yah'ee*; a prim. root [comp. 2421]; to *live*; causat. to *revive*:—ve, save life.

426. חֵיל **chêyl**, *khale*; or (short.)

חֵל **chêl**, *khale*; a collat. form of 2428; an *army*; also (by anal.) an *intrenchment*:—rmy, bulwark, host, + poor, rampart, trench, wall.

חֵיל **chiyl**. See 2342.

427. חִיל **chîyl**, *kheel*; and (fem.)

חִילָה **chîylâh**, *khee-law'*; from 2342; a *throe* (espec. of childbirth):—pain, pang, orrow.

428. חַיִל **chayil**, *khah'-yil*; from 2342; prob. a *force*, whether of men, means or other esources; an *army*, *wealth*, *virtue*, *valor*, *strength*:—ble, activity, (+) army, band of men (soldiers), comany, (great) forces, goods, host, might, power, riches, rength, strong, substance, train, (+) valiant (-ly), alour, virtuous (-ly), war, worthy (-ily).

429. חַיִל **chayil** (Chald.), *khah'-yil*; corresp. to 2428; an *army*, or *strength*:—aloud, army, most [mighty], power.

430. חֵילָה **chêylâh**, *khay-law'*; fem. of 2428; an *intrenchment*:—bulwark.

431. חֵילָם **Chêylâm**, *khay-lawm'*; or

חֵלְאָם **Chêl'âm**, *khay-lawm'*; from 2428; *fortress*; *Chelam*, a place E. of Pal.:—Ielam.

432. חִילֵן **Chîylên**, *khee-lane'*; from 2428; *fortress*; *Chilen*, a place in Pal.:—Iilen.

433. חִין **chîyn**, *kheen*; another form for 2580; *beauty*:—comely.

434. חַיִץ **chayits**, *khah'-yits*; another form for 2351; a *wall*:—wall.

435. חִיצוֹן **chîytsôwn**, *khee-tsone'*; from 2434; prop. the (outer) *wall side*; hence *exerior*; fig. *secular* (as opposed to sacred):—outer, utward, utter, without.

436. חֵיק **chêyq**, *khake*, or

חֵק **chêq**, *khake*; and

חוֹק **chôwq**, *khoke*; from an unused root, appar. mean. to *inclose*; the *bosom* (lit. r fig.):—bosom, bottom, lap, midst, within.

437. חִירָה **Chîyrâh**, *khee-raw'*; from 2357 in the sense of *splendor*; *Chirah*, an Adullame:—Hirah.

438. חִירָם **Chîyrâm**, *khee-rawm'*, or

חִירוֹם **Chîyrôwm**, *khee-rome'*; another form of 2361; *Chiram* or *Chirom*, the ame of two Tyrians:—Hiram, Huram.

439. חִישׁ **chîysh**, *kheesh*; another form for 2363; to *hurry*:—make haste.

440. חִישׁ **chîysh**, *kheesh*; from 2439; prop. a *hurry*; hence (adv.) *quickly*:—soon.

441. חֵךְ **chêk**, *khake*; prob. from 2596 in the sense of *tasting*; prop. the *palate* or nside of the mouth; hence the *mouth* itself (as the rgan of speech, taste and kissing):—(roof of the) nouth, taste.

442. חָכָה **châkâh**, *khaw-kaw'*; a prim. root [appar. akin to 2707 through the idea of *iercing*]; prop. to *adhere* to; hence to await:—long, arry, wait.

2443. חַכָּה **chakkâh**, *khak-kaw'*; prob. from 2442; a *hook* (as *adhering*):—angle, hook.

2444. חֲכִילָה **Chakîylâh**, *khak-ee-law'*; from the same as 2447; *dark*; *Chakilah*, a hill in Pal.:—Hachilah.

2445. חַכִּים **chakkîym** (Chald.), *khak-keem'*; from a root corresp. to 2449; *wise*, i.e. a *Magian*:—wise.

2446. חֲכַלְיָה **Chăkalyâh**, *khak-al-yaw'*; from the base of 2447 and 3050; *darkness* of *Jah*; *Chakaljah*, an Isr.:—Hachaliah.

2447. חַכְלִיל **chaklîyl**, *khak-leel'*; by redupl. from an unused root appar. mean. to *be dark*; darkly *flashing* (only of the eyes); in a good sense, *brilliant* (as stimulated by wine):—red.

2448. חַכְלִלוּת **chaklilûwth**, *khak-lee-looth'*; from 2447; *flash* (of the eyes); in a bad sense, *blearedness*:—redness.

2449. חָכַם **châkam**, *khaw-kam'*; a prim. root, to *be wise* (in mind, word or act):—× exceeding, teach wisdom, be (make self, shew self) wise, deal (never so) wisely, make wiser.

2450. חָכָם **châkâm**, *khaw-kawm'*; from 2449; *wise*, (i.e. intelligent, skilful or artful):—cunning (man), subtil, ([un-]), wise ([hearted], man).

2451. חָכְמָה **chokmâh**, *khok-maw'*; from 2449; *wisdom* (in a good sense):—skilful, wisdom, wisely, wit.

2452. חָכְמָה **chokmâh** (Chald.), *khok-maw'*; corresp. to 2451; *wisdom*:—wisdom.

2453. חַכְמוֹנִי **Chakmôwnîy**, *khak-mo-nee'*; from 2449; *skilful*; *Chakmoni*, an Isr.:—Hachmoni, Hachmonite.

2454. חָכְמוֹת **chokmôwth**, *khok-môth'*; or

חַכְמוֹת **chakmôwth**, *khak-môth'*; collat. forms of 2451; *wisdom*:—wisdom, every wise [woman].

חֵל **chêl**. See 2426.

2455. חֹל **chôl**, *khole*; from 2490; prop. *exposed*; hence *profane*:—common, profane (place), unholy.

2456. חָלָא **châlâ'**, *khaw-law'*; a prim. root [comp. 2470]; to *be sick*:—be diseased.

2457. חֶלְאָה **chel'âh**, *khel-aw'*; from 2456; prop. *disease*; hence *rust*:—scum.

2458. חֶלְאָה **Chel'âh**, *khel-aw'*; the same as 2457; *Chelah*, an Israelitess:—Helah.

2459. חֶלֶב **cheleb**, *kheh'-leb*; or

חֵלֶב **chêleb**, *khay'-leb*; from an unused root mean. to *be fat*; *fat*, whether lit. or fig.; hence the *richest* or *choice* part:— × best, fat (-ness), × finest, grease, marrow.

2460. חֵלֶב **Chêleb**, *khay'-leb*; the same as 2459; *fatness*; *Cheleb*, an Isr.:—Heleb.

2461. חָלָב **châlâb**, *khaw-lawb'*; from the same as 2459; *milk* (as the *richness* of kine):—+ cheese, milk, sucking.

2462. חֶלְבָּה **Chelbâh**, *khel-baw'*; fem. of 2459; *fertility*; *Chelbah*, a place in Pal.:—Helbah.

2463. חֶלְבּוֹן **Chelbôwn**, *khel-bone'*; from 2459; *fruitful*; *Chelbon*, a place in Syria:—Helbon.

2464. חֶלְבְּנָה **chelbenâh**, *khel-ben-aw'*; from 2459; *galbanum*, an odorous gum (as if *fatty*):—galbanum.

2465. חֶלֶד **cheled**, *kheh'-led*; from an unused root appar. mean. to *glide* swiftly; *life* (as a *fleeting* portion of time); hence the *world* (as *transient*):—age, short time, world.

2466. חֵלֶד **chêled**, *khay'-led*; the same as 2465; *Cheled*, an Isr.:—Heled.

2467. חֹלֶד **chôled**, *kho'-led*; from the same as 2465; a *weasel* (from its *gliding* motion):—weasel.

2468. חֻלְדָּה **Chuldâh**, *khool-daw'*; fem. of 2467; *Chuldah*, an Israelitess:—Huldah.

2469. חֶלְדַּי **Chelday**, *khel-dah'-ee*; from 2466; *worldliness*; *Cheldai*, the name of two Isr.:—Heldai.

2470. חָלָה **châlâh**, *khaw-law'*; a prim. root [comp. 2342, 2470, 2490]; prop. to *be rubbed* or *worn*; hence (fig.) to *be weak*, *sick*, *afflicted*; or (causat.) to *grieve*, *make sick*; also to *stroke* (in flattering), *entreat*:—beseech, (be) diseased, (put to) grief, be grieved, (be) grievous, infirmity, intreat, lay to, put to pain, × pray, make prayer, be (fall, make) sick, sore, be sorry, make suit (× supplication), woman in travail, be (become) weak, be wounded.

2471. חַלָּה **challâh**, *khal-law'*; from 2490; a *cake* (as usually *punctured*):—cake.

2472. חֲלוֹם **chălôwm**, *khal-ome'*; or (short.)

חֲלֹם **chălôm**, *khal-ome'*; from 2492; a *dream*:—dream (-er).

2473. חֹלוֹן **Chôlôwn**, *kho-lone'*; or (short.)

חֹלֹן **Chôlôn**, *kho-lone'*; prob. from 2344, *sandy*; *Cholon*, the name of two places in Pal.:—Holon.

2474. חַלּוֹן **challôwn**, *khal-lone'*; a *window* (as *perforated*):—window.

2475. חֲלוֹף **chălôwph**, *khal-ofe'*; from 2498; prop *surviving*, by impl. (collect.) *orphans*:— × destruction.

2476. חֲלוּשָׁה **chălûwshâh**, *khal-oo-shaw'*; fem. pass. part. of 2522; *defeat*:—being overcome.

2477. חֲלַח **Chălach**, *khal-akh'*; prob. of for. or.; *Chalach*, a region of Assyria:—Halah.

2478. חַלְחוּל **Chalchûwl**, *khal-khool'*; by redupl. from 2342; *contorted*; *Chalchul*, a place in Pal.:—Halhul.

2479. חַלְחָלָה **chalchâlâh**, *khal-khaw-law'*; fem. from the same as 2478; *writhing* (in childbirth); by impl. *terror*:—(great, much) pain.

2480. חָלַט **châlat**, *khaw-lat'*; a prim. root; to *snatch* at:—catch.

2481. חֲלִי **chălîy**, *khal-ee'*; from 2470; a *trinket* (as *polished*):—jewel, ornament.

2482. חֲלִי **Chălîy**, *khal-ee'*; the same as 2481; *Chali*, a place in Pal.:—Hali.

2483. חֳלִי **chŏlîy**, *khol-ee'*; from 2470; *malady*, *anxiety*, *calamity*:—disease, grief, (is) sick (-ness).

2484. חֶלְיָה **chelyâh**, *khel-yaw'*; fem. of 2481; a *trinket*:—jewel.

2485. חָלִיל **châlîyl**, *khaw-leel'*; from 2490; a *flute* (as *perforated*):—pipe.

2486. חָלִילָה **châlîylâh**, *khaw-lee'-law*; or

חָלִלָה **châlîlâh**, *khaw-lee'-law*; a directive from 2490; lit. *for a profaned* thing; used (interj.) *far be it!*:—be far, (× God) forbid.

2487. חֲלִיפָה **chălîyphâh**, *khal-ee-faw'*; from 2498; *alternation*:—change, course.

2488. חֲלִיצָה **chălîytsâh**, *khal-ee-tsaw'*; from 2502; *spoil*:—armour.

2489. חֵלְכָא **chêlekâ'**, *khay-lek-aw'*; or

חֵלְכָה **chêlekâh**, *khay-lek-aw'*; appar. from an unused root prob. mean. to *be dark* or (fig.) *unhappy*; a *wretch*, i.e. unfortunate:—poor.

2490. חָלַל **châlal**, *khaw-lal'*; a prim. root [comp. 2470]; prop. to *bore*, i.e. (by impl.) to *wound*, to *dissolve*; fig. to *profane* (a person, place or thing), to *break* (one's word), to *begin* (as if by an "opening wedge"); denom. (from 2485) to *play* (the flute):—begin (× men began), defile, × break, defile, × eat (as common things), × first, × gather the grape thereof, × take inheritance, pipe, player on instruments, pollute, (cast as) profane (self), prostitute, slay (slain), sorrow, stain, wound.

2491. חָלָל **châlâl**, *khaw-lawl'*; from 2490; *pierced* (espec. to death); fig. *polluted*:—kill, profane, slain (man), × slew, (deadly) wounded.

חָלִלָה **châlîlâh**. See 2486.

2492. חָלַם **châlam**, *khaw-lam'*; a prim. root; prop. to *bind* firmly, i.e. (by impl.) to *be* (causat. to *make*) *plump;* also (through the fig. sense of *dumbness*) to *dream:*—(cause to) dream (-er), be in good liking, recover.

2493. חֵלֶם **chêlem** (Chald.), *khay'-lem;* from a root corresp. to 2492; a *dream:*—dream.

2494. חֵלֶם **Chêlem**, *khay'-lem;* from 2492; a *dream; Chelem*, an Isr.:—Helem. Comp. 2469.

2495. חַלָּמוּת **challâmûwth**, *khal-law-mooth';* from 2492 (in the sense of *insipidity*); prob. *purslain:*—egg.

2496. חַלָּמִישׁ **challâmîysh**, *khal-law-meesh';* prob. from 2492 (in the sense of *hardness*); *flint:*—flint (-y), rock.

2497. חֵלֹן **Chêlôn**, *khay-lone'*, from 2428; *strong Chelon*, an Isr.:—Helon

2498. חָלַף **châlaph**, *khaw-laf';* a prim. root; prop. to *slide* by, i.e. (by impl.) to *hasten* away, *pass* on, *spring* up, *pierce* or *change:*—abolish, alter, change, cut off, go on forward, grow up, be over, pass (away, on, through), renew, sprout, strike through.

2499. חֲלַף **chălaph** (Chald.), *khal-af';* corresp. to 2498; to *pass* on (of time):—pass.

2500. חֵלֶף **chêleph**, *khay'-lef;* from 2498; prop. *exchange;* hence (as prep.) *instead* of:—× for.

2501. חֵלֶף **Cheleph**, *kheh'-lef;* the same as 2500; *change; Cheleph*, a place in Pal.:—Heleph.

2502. חָלַץ **châlats**, *khaw-lats';* a prim. root; to *pull* off; hence (intens.) to *strip*, (reflex.) to *depart;* by impl. to *deliver, equip* (for fight); *present, strengthen:*—arm (self), (go, ready) armed (× man, soldier), deliver, draw out, make fat, loose, (ready) prepared, put off, take away, withdraw self.

2503. חֶלֶץ **Chelets**, *kheh'-lets;* or חֵלֶץ **Chêlets**, *khay'-lets;* from 2502; perh. *strength; Chelets*, the name of two Isr.:—Helez.

2504. חָלָץ **châlâts**, *khaw-lawts';* from 2502 (in the sense of *strength*); only in the dual; the *loins* (as the seat of vigor):—loins, reins.

2505. חָלַק **châlaq**, *khaw-lak';* a prim. root; to *be smooth* (fig.); by impl. (as smooth stones were used for *lots*) to *apportion* or *separate:*—deal, distribute, divide, flatter, give, (have, im-) part (-ner), take away a portion, receive, separate self, (be) smooth (-er).

2506. חֵלֶק **chêleq**, *khay'-lek;* from 2505; prop. *smoothness* (of the tongue); also an *allotment:*—flattery, inheritance, part, × partake, portion.

2507. חֵלֶק **Chêleq**, *khay'-lek;* the same as 2506; *portion; Chelek*, an Isr.:—Helek.

2508. חֲלָק **chălâq** (Chald.), *khal-awk';* from a root corresp. to 2505; a *part:*—portion.

2509. חָלָק **châlâq**, *khaw-lawk';* from 2505; *smooth* (espec. of tongue):—flattering, smooth.

2510. חָלָק **Châlâq**, *khaw-lawk';* the same as 2509; *bare; Chalak*, a mountain of Idumæa:—Halak.

2511. חַלָּק **challâq**, *khal-lawk';* from 2505; *smooth:*—smooth.

2512. חַלֻּק **challuq**, *khal-look';* from 2505; *smooth:*—smooth.

2513. חֶלְקָה **chelqâh**, *khel-kaw';* fem. of 2506; prop. *smoothness;* fig. *flattery;* also an *allotment:*—field, flattering (-ry), ground, parcel, part, piece of land ([ground]), plat, portion, slippery place, smooth (thing).

2514. חֲלַקָּה **chălaqqâh**, *khal-ak-kaw';* fem. from 2505; *flattery:*—flattery.

2515. חֲלֻקָּה **chăluqqâh**, *khal-ook-kaw';* fem. of 2512; a *distribution:*—division.

2516. חֶלְקִי **Chelqîy**, *khel-kee';* patron. from 2507; a *Chelkite* or desc. of Chelek:—Helkites.

2517. חֶלְקַי **Chelqay**, *khel-kah'ee;* from 2505; *apportioned; Chelkai*, an Isr.:—Helkai.

2518. חִלְקִיָּה **Chilqîyâh**, *khil-kee-yaw';* or חִלְקִיָּהוּ **Chilqîyâhûw**, *khil-kee-yaw'-hoo;* from 2506 and 3050; *portion of Jah; Chilhijah*, the name of eight Isr.:—Hilkiah.

2519. חֲלַקְלַקָּה **chălaqlaqqâh**, *khal-ak-lak-kaw';* by redupl. from 2505; prop. something *very smooth;* i.e. a *treacherous* spot; fig. *blandishment:*—flattery, slippery.

2520. חֶלְקַת **Chelqath**, *khel-kath';* a form of 2513; *smoothness; Chelkath*, a place in Pal.:—Helkath.

2521. חֶלְקַת הַצֻּרִים **Chelqath hats-Tsûrîym**, *khel-kath' hats-tsoo-reem';* from 2520 and the plur. of 6697, with the art. inserted; *smoothness of the rocks; Chelkath Hats-tsurim*, a place in Pal.:—Helkath-hazzurim.

2522. חָלַשׁ **châlash**, *khaw-lash';* a prim. root; to *prostrate;* by impl. to *overthrow, decay:*—discomfit, waste away, weaken.

2523. חַלָּשׁ **challâsh**, *khal-lawsh';* from 2522; *frail:*—weak.

2524. חָם **châm**, *khawm;* from the same as 2346; a *father-in-law* (as in *affiniiy*):—father in law.

2525. חָם **châm**, *khawm;* from 2552; *hot:*—hot, warm.

2526. חָם **Châm**, *khawm;* the same as 2525; *hot* (from the tropical habitat); *Cham*, a son of Noah; also (as a patron.) his desc. or their country:—Ham.

2527. חֹם **chôm**, *khome;* from 2552; *heat:*—heat, to be hot (warm).

2528. חֱמָא **chĕmâ'** (Chald.), *khem-aw';* or חֲמָה **chămâh** (Chald.), *kham-aw';* corresp. to 2534; *anger:*—fury. חֵמָא **chêmâ'**. See 2534.

2529. חֶמְאָה **chem'âh**, *khem-aw';* or (short.) חֵמָה **chêmâh**, *khay-maw';* from the same root as 2346; curdled *milk* or *cheese:*—butter.

2530. חָמַד **châmad**, *khaw-mad';* a prim. root; to *delight* in:—beauty, greatly beloved, covet, delectable thing, (× great) delight, desire, goodly, lust, (be) pleasant (thing), precious (thing).

2531. חֶמֶד **chemed**, *kheh'-med;* from 2530; *delight:*—desirable, pleasant.

2532. חֶמְדָּה **chemdâh**, *khem-daw';* fem. of 2531; *delight:*—desire, goodly, pleasant, precious.

2533. חֶמְדָּן **Chemdân**, *khem-dawn';* from 2531; *pleasant; Chemdan*, an Idumæan:—Hemdan.

2534. חֵמָה **chêmâh**, *khay-maw';* or (Dan. 11:44) חֵמָא **chêmâ'**, *khay-maw';* from 3179; *heat;* fig. *anger, poison* (from its *fever*):—anger, bottles, hot displeasure, furious (-ly, -ry), heat, indignation, poison, rage, wrath (-ful). See 2529.

2535. חַמָּה **chammâh**, *kham-maw';* from 2525; *heat;* by impl. the *sun:*—heat, sun.

2536. חַמּוּאֵל **Chammûw'êl**, *kham-moo-ale';* from 2535 and 410; *anger of God; Chammuel*, an Isr.:—Hamuel.

2537. חֲמוּטַל **Chămûwṭal**, *kham-oo-tal';* or חֲמִיטַל **Chămîyṭal**, *kham-ee-tal';* from 2524 and 2919; *father-in-law of dew; Chamutal* or *Chamital*, an Israelitess:—Hamutal.

2538. חָמוּל **Châmûwl**, *khaw-mool';* from 2550; *pitied; Chamul*, an Isr.:—Hamul.

2539. חָמוּלִי **Châmûwlîy**, *khaw-moo-lee';* patron. from 2538; a *Chamulite* (collect.) or desc. of Chamul:—Hamulites.

2540. חַמּוֹן **Chammôwn**, *kham-mone';* from 2552; *warm* spring; *Chammon*, the name of two places in Pal.:—Hammon.

2541. חָמוֹץ **châmôwts**, *khaw-motse';* from 2556; prop. *violent;* by impl. a *robber:*—oppressed.

2542. חַמּוּק **chammûwq**, *kham-mook';* fro 2559; a *wrapping*, i.e. *drawers:*—joint

2543. חֲמוֹר **chămôwr**, *kham-ore';* or (short.) חֲמֹר **chămôr**, *kham-ore;* from 2560; a ma ass (from its dun *red*):—(he) ass.

2544. חֲמוֹר **Chămôwr**, *kham-ore';* the same 2543; *ass; Chamor*, a Canaanite: Hamor.

2545. חֲמוֹת **chămôwth**, *kham-ōth';* or (short.) חֲמֹת **chămôth**, *kham-ōth';* fem. of 252 a *mother-in-law:*—mother in law.

2546. חֹמֶט **chômeṭ**, *kho'-met;* from an unuse root prob. mean. to *lie low;* a *lizard* (*creeping*):—snail.

2547. חֻמְטָה **Chumṭâh**, *khoom-taw';* fem. 2546; *low; Chumtah*, a place in Pal.:— Humtah.

2548. חָמִיץ **châmîyts**, *khaw-meets';* from 255 *seasoned*, i.e. *salt* provender:—clean.

2549. חֲמִישִׁי **chămîyshîy**, *kham-ee-shee';* or חֲמִשִּׁי **chamishshîy**, *kham-ish-shee';* or from 2568; *fifth;* also a *fifth:*—fif (part).

2550. חָמַל **châmal**, *khaw-mal';* a prim. root; *commiserate;* by impl. to *spare:*—hav compassion, (have) pity, spare.

2551. חֶמְלָה **chemlâh**, *khem-law';* from 255 *commiseration:*—merciful, pity.

2552. חָמַם **châmam**, *khaw-mam';* a prim. roo to *be hot* (lit. or fig.):—enflame self, ge (have) heat, be (wax) hot, (be, wax) warm (self, at).

2553. חַמָּן **chammân**, *kham-mawn';* from 255 a *sun*-pillar:—idol, image.

2554. חָמַס **châmaç**, *khaw-mas';* a prim. root; t *be violent;* by impl. to *maltreat:*—mak bare, shake off, violate, do violence, take away vio lently, wrong, imagine wrongfully.

2555. חָמָס **châmâç**, *khaw-mawce';* from 2554 *violence;* by impl. *wrong;* by meton. un just *gain:*—cruel (-ty), damage, false, injustice, × op pressor, unrighteous, violence (against, done), violen (dealing), wrong.

2556. חָמֵץ **châmêts**, *khaw-mates';* a prim. root to *be pungent;* i.e. in taste (*sour*, i.e. li *fermented*, or fig. *harsh*), in color (*dazzling*):—crue (man), dyed, be grieved, leavened.

2557. חָמֵץ **châmêtz**, *khaw-mates';* from 2556 *ferment*, (fig.) *extortion:*—leaven, lea vened (bread).

2558. חֹמֶץ **chômets**, *kho'-mets;* from 2556; *vine gar:*—vinegar.

2559. חָמַק **châmaq**, *khaw-mak';* a prim. root prop. to *enwrap;* hence to *depart* (i.e turn about):—go about, withdraw self.

2560. חָמַר **châmar**, *khaw-mar';* a prim. root prop. to *boil* up; hence to *ferment* (wit scum); to *glow* (with redness); as denom. (from 2564 to *smear* with pitch:—daub, foul, be red, trouble

2561. חֶמֶר **chemer**, *kheh'-mer;* from 2560; *win* (as *fermenting*):—× pure, red wine.

2562. חֲמַר **chămar** (Chald.), *kham-ar';* corresp to 2561; *wine:*—wine. חֲמֹר **chămôr**. See 2543.

2563. חֹמֶר **chômer**, *kho'-mer;* from 2560; prop a *bubbling* up, i.e. of water, a *wave;* of earth, *mire* or *clay* (cement); also a *heap;* hence a *chomer* or dry measure:—clay, heap, homer, mire, motion, mortar.

2564. חֵמָר **chêmâr**, *khay-mawr';* from 2560; *bitumen* (as *rising* to the surface):— slime (-pit).

2565. חֲמֹרָה **chămôrâh**, *kham-o-raw';* from 2560 [comp. 2563]; a *heap:*—heap.

2566. חַמְרָן **Chamrân**, *kham-rawn';* from 2560; *red; Chamran*, an Idumæan:—Amran.

2567. חָמַשׁ **châmash**, *khaw-mash';* a denom. from 2568; to *tax a fifth:*—take up the fifth part.

568. חָמֵשׁ **châmêsh**, *khaw-maysh'*; masc.

חֲמִשָּׁה **chămishshâh**, *kham-ish-shaw'*; a prim. numeral; *five:*—fif [-teen], fth, five (× apiece).

569. חֹמֶשׁ **chômesh**, *kho'-mesh*; from 2567; a *fifth* tax:—fifth part.

570. חֹמֶשׁ **chômesh**, *kho'-mesh;* from an unused root prob. mean. to *be stout;* the bdomen (as *obese*):—fifth [rib].

571. חָמֻשׁ **châmûsh**, *khaw-moosh';* pass. part. of the same as 2570; *staunch*, i.e. able odied *soldiers:*—armed (men), harnessed.

חֲמִשָּׁה **chămishshâh**. See 2568.

חֲמִשִׁי **chămishshîy**. See 2549.

572. חֲמִשִּׁים **chămishshîym**, *kham-ish-sheem';* multiple of 2568; *fifty:*—fty.

573. חֵמֶת **chêmeth**, *khay'-meth;* from the same as 2346; a skin *bottle* (as *tied* up):—ottle.

574. חֲמָת **Chămâth**, *kham-awth';* from the same as 2346; *walled; Chamath*, a place Syria:—Hamath, Hemath.

חֲמֹת **chămôth**. See 2545.

575. חַמַּת **Chammath**, *kham-math';* a var. for the first part of 2576; *hot* springs; *Chammath*, a place in Pal.:—Hammath.

576. חַמֹּת דֹּאר **Chammôth Dôʼr**, *kham-moth' dore;* from the plur. of 535 and 1756; *hot* springs *of Dor; Chammath-Dor*, place in Pal.:—Hamath-Dor.

577. חֲמָתִי **Chămâthîy**, *kham-aw-thee';* patrial from 2574; a *Chamathite* or native f *Chamath:*—Hamathite.

578. חֲמַת צוֹבָה **Chămath Tsôwbâh**, *kham-ath' tso-baw';* from 2574 nd 6678; *Chamath of Tsobah; Chamath-Tsobah;* rob. the same as 2574:—Hamath-Zobah.

579. חֲמַת רַבָּה **Chămath Rabbâh**, *kham-ath' rab-baw';* from 2574 and 7237; *hamath of Rabbah; Chamath-Rabbah*, prob. the ame as 2574.

580. חֵן **chên**, *khane;* from 2603; *graciousness*, i.e. subj. (*kindness, favor*) or objective *beauty*):—favour, grace (-ious), pleasant, precious, well-] favoured.

581. חֵן **Chên**, *khane;* the same as 2580; *grace; Chen*, a fig. name for an Isr.:—Hen.

582. חֵנָדָד **Chênâdâd**, *khay-naw-dawd';* prob. from 2580 and 1908; *favor of Hadad; henadad*, an Isr.:—Henadad.

583. חָנָה **chânâh**, *khaw-naw';* a prim. root [comp. 2603]; prop. to *incline;* by impl. o *decline* (of the slanting rays of evening); spec. to *itch* a tent; gen. to *encamp* (for abode or siege):—bide (in tents), camp, dwell, encamp, grow to an end, e, pitch (tent), rest in tent.

584. חַנָּה **Channâh**, *khan-naw';* from 2603; *favored; Channah*, an Israelitess:—Hannah.

585. חֲנוֹךְ **Chănôwk**, *khan-oke';* from 2596; *initiated; Chanok*, an antediluvian atriach:—Enoch.

586. חָנוּן **Chânûwn**, *khaw-noon';* from 2603; *favored; Chanun*, the name of an Ammonite and of two Isr.:—Hanun.

587. חַנּוּן **channûwn**, *khan-noon';* from 2603; *gracious:*—gracious.

588. חָנוּת **chânûwth**, *khaw-nooth';* from 2583; prop. a *vault* or *cell* (with an arch); by mpl. a *prison:*—cabin.

589. חַנּוֹת **channôwth**, *khan-nōth';* from 2603 (in the sense of *prayer*); *supplication:*—e gracious, intreated.

590. חָנַט **chânaṭ**, *khaw-nat';* a prim. root; to *spice;* by impl. to *embalm;* also to *ipen:*—embalm, put forth.

591. חִנְטָא **chinṭâʼ** (Chald.), *khint-taw';* corresp. to 2406; *wheat:*—wheat.

2592. חַנִּיאֵל **Channîyʼêl**, *khan-nee-ale';* from 2603 and 410; *favor of God; Channiel*, the name of two Isr.:—Hanniel.

2593. חָנִיךְ **chânîyk**, *kaw-neek';* from 2596; *initiated;* i.e. *practised:*—trained.

2594. חֲנִינָה **chănîynâh**, *khan-ee-naw';* from 2603; *graciousness:*—favour.

2595. חֲנִית **chănîyth**, *khan-eeth';* from 2583; a *lance* (for *thrusting*, like *pitching* a tent):—javelin, spear.

2596. חָנַךְ **chânak**, *khaw-nak';* a prim. root; prop. to *narrow* [comp. 2614]; fig. to *initiate* or *discipline:*—dedicate, train up.

2597. חֲנֻכָּא **chănukkâʼ** (Chald.), *chan-ook-kaw';* corresp. to 2598; *consecration:*—dedication.

2598. חֲנֻכָּה **chănukkâh**, *khan-ook-kaw';* from 2596; *initiation*, i.e. *consecration:*—dedicating (-tion).

2599. חֲנֹכִי **Chănôkîy**, *khan-o-kee';* patron. from 2585; a *Chanokite* (collect.) or desc. of Chanok:—Hanochites.

2600. חִנָּם **chinnâm**, *khin-nawm';* from 2580; *gratis*, i.e. devoid of cost, reason or advantage:—without a cause (cost, wages), causeless, to cost nothing, free (-ly), innocent, for nothing (nought), in vain.

2601. חֲנַמְאֵל **Chănamʼêl**, *khan-am-ale';* prob. by orth. var. for 2606; *Chanamel*, an Isr.:—Hanameel.

2602. חֲנָמָל **chănâmâl**, *khan-aw-mawl';* of uncert. der.; perh. the *aphis* or plant-louse:—frost.

2603. חָנַן **chânan**, *khaw-nan';* a prim. root [comp. 2583]; prop. to *bend* or stoop in kindness to an inferior; to *favor, bestow;* causat. to *implore* (i.e. move to favor by petition):—beseech, × fair, (be, find, shew) favour (-able), be (deal, give, grant (gracious (-ly), intreat, (be) merciful, have (shew) mercy (on, upon), have pity upon, pray, make supplication, × very.

2604. חֲנַן **chănan** (Chald.), *khan-an';* corresp. to 2603; to *favor* or (causat.) to *entreat:*—shew mercy, make supplication.

2605. חָנָן **Chânân**, *khaw-nawn';* from 2603; *favor; Chanan*, the name of seven Isr.:—Canan.

2606. חֲנַנְאֵל **Chănanʼêl**, *khan-an-ale';* from 2603 and 410; *God has favored; Chananel*, prob. an Isr., from whom a tower of Jerusalem was named:—Hananeel.

2607. חֲנָנִי **Chănânîy**, *khan-aw-nee';* from 2603; *gracious; Chanani*, the name of six Isr.:—Hanani.

2608. חֲנַנְיָה **Chănanyâh**, *khan-an-yaw';* or

חֲנַנְיָהוּ **Chănanyâhûw**, *khan-an-yaw'-hoo;* from 2603 and 3050; *Jah has favored; Chananjah*, the name of thirteen Isr.:—Hananiah.

2609. חָנֵס **Chânêç**, *khaw-nace';* of Eg. der.; *Chanes*, a place in Egypt:—Hanes.

2610. חָנֵף **chânêph**, *khaw-nafe';* a prim. root; to *soil*, espec. in a moral sense:—corrupt, defile, × greatly, pollute, profane.

2611. חָנֵף **chânêph**, *khaw-nafe';* from 2610; *soiled* (i.e. with sin), *impious:*—hypocrite (-ical).

2612. חֹנֶף **chôneph**, *kho'-nef;* from 2610; moral *filth*, i.e. *wickedness:*—hypocrisy.

2613. חֲנֻפָה **chănûphâh**, *khan-oo-faw';* fem. from 2610; *impiety:*—profaneness.

2614. חָנַק **chânaq**, *khaw-nak';* a prim. root [comp. 2596]; to *be narrow;* by impl. to *throttle*, or (reflex.) to *choke* oneself to death (by a rope):—hang self, strangle.

2615. חַנָּתֹן **Channâthôn**, *khan-naw-thone';* prob. from 2603; *favored; Channathon*, a place in Pal.:—Hannathon.

2616. חָסַד **châçad**, *khaw-sad';* a prim. root; prop. perh. to *bow* (the neck only [comp. 2603] in courtesy to an equal), i.e. to *be kind;* also (by euphem. [comp. 1288], but rarely) to *reprove:*—shew self merciful, put to shame.

2617. חֶסֶד **cheçed**, *kheh'-sed;* from 2616; *kindness;* by impl. (towards God) *piety;* rarely (by opp.) *reproof*, or (subject.) *beauty:*—favour, good deed (-liness, -ness), kindly, (loving-) kindness, merciful (kindness), mercy, pity, reproach, wicked thing.

2618. חֶסֶד **Cheçed**, *kheh'-sed;* the same as 2617; *favor; Chesed*, an Isr.:—Hesed.

2619. חֲסַדְיָה **Chăçadyâh**, *khas-ad-yaw';* from 2617 and 3050; *Jah has favored; Chasadjah*, an Isr.:—Hasadiah.

2620. חָסָה **châçâh**, *khaw-saw';* a prim. root; to *flee* for protection [comp. 982]; fig. to *confide* in:—have hope, make refuge, (put) trust.

2621. חֹסָה **Chôçâh**, *kho-saw';* from 2620; *hopeful; Chosah*, an Isr.; also a place in Pal.:—Hosah.

2622. חָסוּת **châçûwth**, *khaw-sooth';* from 2620; *confidence:*—trust.

2623. חָסִיד **châçîyd**, *khaw-seed';* from 2616; prop. *kind*, i.e. (religiously) *pious* (a saint):—godly (man), good, holy (one), merciful, saint, [un-] godly.

2624. חֲסִידָה **chăçîydâh**, *khas-ee-daw';* fem. of 2623; the *kind* (maternal) bird, i.e. a *stork:*—× feather, stork.

2625. חָסִיל **châçîyl**, *khaw-seel';* from 2628; the *ravager*, i.e. a *locust:*—caterpillar.

2626. חֲסִין **chăçîyn**, *khas-een';* from 2630; prop. *firm*, i.e. (by impl.) *mighty:*—strong.

2627. חַסִּיר **chaççîyr** (Chald.), *khas-seer';* from a root corresp. to 2637; *deficient:*—wanting.

2628. חָסַל **châçal**, *khaw-sal';* a prim. root; to *eat* off:—consume.

2629. חָסַם **châçam**, *khaw-sam';* a prim. root; to *muzzle;* by anal. to *stop* the nose:—muzzle, stop.

2630. חָסַן **châçan**, *khaw-san';* a prim. root; prop. to (be) *compact;* by impl. to *hoard:*—lay up.

2631. חֲסַן **chăçan** (Chald.), *khas-an';* corresp. to 2630; to *hold* in occupancy:—possess.

2632. חֵסֶן **chêçen** (Chald.), *khay'-sen;* from 2631; *strength:*—power.

2633. חֹסֶן **chôçen**, *kho'-sen;* from 2630; *wealth:*—riches, strength, treasure.

2634. חָסֹן **châçôn**, *khaw-sone';* from 2630; *powerful:*—strong.

2635. חֲסַף **chăçaph** (Chald.), *khas-af';* from a root corresp. to that of 2636; a *clod:*—clay.

2636. חַסְפַּס **chaçpaç**, *khas-pas';* redupl. from an unused root mean. appar. to *peel;* a *shred* or *scale:*—round thing.

2637. חָסֵר **châçêr**, *khaw-sare';* a prim. root to *lack;* by impl. to *fail, want, lessen:*—be abated, bereave, decrease, (cause to) fail, (have) lack, make lower, want.

2638. חָסֵר **châçêr**, *khaw-sare';* from 2637; *lacking;* hence *without:*—destitute, fail lack, have need, void, want.

2639. חֶסֶר **cheçer**, *kheh'-ser;* from 2637; *lack;* hence *destitution:*—poverty, want.

2640. חֹסֶר **chôçer**, *kho'-ser;* from 2637; *poverty:*—in want of.

2641. חַסְרָה **Chaçrâh**, *khas-raw';* from 2637; *want:*—Chasrah, an Isr.:—Hasrah.

2642. חֶסְרוֹן **cheçrôwn**, *khes-rone';* from 2637; *deficiency:*—wanting.

2643. חַף **chaph**, *khaf;* from 2653 (in the moral sense of *covered* from soil); *pure:*—innocent.

2644. חָפָא **châphâʼ**, *khaw-faw';* an orth. var. of 2645; prop. to *cover*, i.e. (in a sinister sense) to *act covertly:*—do secretly.

2645. חָפָה **châphâh**, *khaw-faw';* a prim. root [comp. 2644, 2653]; to *cover;* by impl. to *veil*, to *incase, protect:*—ceil, cover, overlay.

2646. חֻפָּה **chuppâh**, *khoop-paw';* from 2645; a *canopy:*—chamber, closet, defence.

2647. חֻפָּה **Chuppâh**, *khoop-*
2646;

2648. חָפַז **châphaz**, *khaw-faz'*; a prim. root; prop. to *start* up suddenly, i.e. (by impl.) to *hasten* away, to *fear*:—(make) haste (away), tremble.

2649. חִפָּזוֹן **chîppâzôwn**, *khip-paw-zone'*; from 2648; *hasty flight*:—haste.

2650. חֻפִּים **Chuppîym**, *khoop-peem'*; plur. of 2646 [comp. 2349]; *Chuppim*, an Isr.:—Huppim.

2651. חֹפֶן **chôphen**, *kho'-fen*; from an unused root of uncert. signif.; a *fist* (only in the dual):—fists, (both) hands, hand [-ful].

2652. חׇפְנִי **Chophnîy**, *khof-nee'*; from 2651; perh. *pugilist*; *Chophni*, an Isr.:—Hophni.

2653. חֹפַף **chôphaph**, *khaw-faf'*; a prim. root [comp. 2645, 3182]; to *cover* (in protection):—cover.

2654. חָפֵץ **châphêts**, *khaw-fates'*; a prim. root; prop. to *incline* to; by impl. (lit. but rarely) to *bend*; fig. to *be pleased* with, *desire*:—× any at all, (have, take) delight, desire, favour, like, move, be (well) pleased, have pleasure, will, would.

2655. חָפֵץ **châphêts**, *khaw-fates'*; from 2654; *pleased* with:—delight in, desire, favour, please, have pleasure, whosoever would, willing, wish.

2656. חֵפֶץ **chêphets**, *khay'-fets*; from 2654; *pleasure*; hence (abstr.) *desire*; concr. a *valuable* thing; hence (by extens.) a *matter* (as something in mind):—acceptable, delight (-some), desire, things desired, matter, pleasant (-ure), purpose, willingly.

2657. חֶפְצִי בָּהּ **Chephtsîy bâhh**, *khef-tsee' baw*; from 2656 with suffixes; *my delight* (is) *in her*; *Cheptsi-bah*, a fanciful name for Pal.:—Hephzi-bah.

2658. חָפַר **châphar**, *khaw-far'*; a prim. root; prop. to *pry* into; by impl. to *delve*, to *explore*:—dig, paw, search out, seek.

2659. חָפֵר **châphêr**, *khaw-fare'*; a prim. root [perh. rath. the same as 2658 through the idea of *detection*]; to *blush*; fig. to *be ashamed*, *disappointed*; causat. to *shame*, *reproach*:—be ashamed, be confounded, be brought to confusion (unto shame), come (be put to) shame, bring reproach.

2660. חֵפֶר **Chêpher**, *khay'-fer*; from 2658 or 2659; a *pit* or *shame*; *Chepher*, a place in Pal.; also the name of three Isr.:—Hepher.

2661. חֲפֹר **chăphôr**, *khaf-ore'*; from 2658; a *hole*; only in connection with 6512, which ought rather to be joined as one word, thus

חֲפַרְפֵּרָה **chăpharpêrâh**, *khaf-ar-pay-raw'*; by redupl. from 2658; a *burrower*, i.e. prob. a *rat*:— + mole.

2662. חֶפְרִי **Chephrîy**, *khef-ree'*; patron. from 2660; a *Chephrite* (collect.) or desc. of *Chepher*:—Hepherites.

2663 חֲפָרַיִם **Chăphârayîm**, *khaf-aw-rah'-yim*; dual of 2660; *double pit*; *Chapharajim*, a place in Pal.:—Haphraim.

חֲפַרְפֵּרָה **chăpharpêrâh**. See 2661.

2664. חָפַשׂ **châphas**, *khaw-fas'*; a prim. root; to *seek*; causat. to *conceal* oneself (i.e. let be sought), or *mask*:—change, (make) diligent (search), disguise self, hide, search (for, out).

2665. חֵפֶשׂ **chêphes**, *khay'-fes*; from 2664; something *covert*, i.e. a *trick*:—search.

2666. חָפַשׁ **châphash**, *khaw-fash'*; a prim. root; to *spread* loose, fig. to *manumit*:—be free.

2667. חֹפֶשׁ **Chôphesh**, *kho'-fesh*; from 2666; something *spread* loosely, i.e. a *carpet*:—precious.

2668. חֻפְשָׁה **chuphshâh**, *khoof-shaw'*; from 2666; *liberty* (from slavery):—freedom.

2669. חׇפְשׁוּת **chôphshûwth**, *khof-shooth'*; and

חׇפְשִׁית **chophshîyth**, *khof-sheeth'*; from 2666; *prostration* by sickness (with 1004, a *hospital*):—several.

2670. חׇפְשִׁי **chophshîy**, *khof-shee'*; from 2666; *exempt* (from bondage, tax or care):—free, liberty.

2671. חֵץ **chêts**, *khayts*; from 2686; prop. a *piercer*, i.e. an *arrow*; by impl. a *wound*; fig. (of God) thunder-*bolt*; (by interchange for 6086) the *shaft* of a spear:— + archer, arrow, dart, shaft, staff, wound.

חֻץ **chûts**. See 2351.

2672. חָצַב **châtsab**, *khaw-tsab'*; or

חָצֵב **châtsêb**, *khaw-tsabe'*; a prim. root; to *cut* or carve (wood, stone or other material); by impl. to *hew*, *split*, *square*, *quarry*, *engrave*:—cut, dig, divide, grave, hew (out, -er), make, mason.

2673. חָצָה **châtsâh**, *khaw-tsaw'*; a prim. root [comp. 2686]; to *cut* or *split* in two; to *halve*:—divide, × live out half, reach to the midst, part.

2674. חָצוֹר **Châtsôwr**, *khaw-tsore'*; a collect. form of 2691; *village*; *Chatsor*, the name (thus simply) of two places in Pal. and of one in Arabia:—Hazor.

2675. חָצוֹר חֲדַתָּה **Châtsôwr Chădattâh**, *khaw-tsore' khad-at-taw'*; from 2674 and a Chaldaizing form of the fem. of 2319 [comp. 2323]; *new Chatsor*, a place in Pal.:—Hazor, Hadattah [*as if two places*].

2676. חָצוֹת **châtsôwth**, *khaw-tsoth'*; from 2673; the *middle* (of the night):—mid [-night].

2677. חֵצִי **chêtsîy**, *khay-tsee'*; from 2673; the *half* or *middle*:—half, middle, mid [-night], midst, part, two parts.

2678. חִצִּי **chitstsîy**, *khits-tsee'*; or

חֵצִי **chêtsîy**, *chay-tsee'*; prol. from 2671; an *arrow*:—arrow.

2679. חֲצִי הַמְּנֻחוֹת **Chătsîy ham-Menûchôwth**, *chat-tsee' ham-men-oo-khoth'*; from 2677 and the plur. of 4496, with the art. interposed; *midst of the resting-places*; *Chatsi-ham-Menuchoth*, an Isr.:—half of the Manahethites.

2680. חֲצִי הַמְּנַחְתִּי **Chătsîy ham-Menachtîy**, *khat-see' ham-men-akh-tee'*; patron. from 2679; a *Chatsi-ham-Menachtite* or desc. of Chatsi-ham-Menuchoth:—half of the Manahethites.

2681. חָצִיר **châtsîyr**, *khaw-tseer'*; a collat. form of 2691; a *court* or *abode*:—court.

2682. חָצִיר **châtsîyr**, *khaw-tseer'*; perh. orig. the same as 2681, from the *greenness* of a court-yard; *grass*; also a *leek* (collect.):—grass, hay, herb, leek.

2683. חֵצֶן **chêtsen**, *khay'-tsen*; from an unused root mean. to hold *firmly*; the *bosom* (as *comprised* between the arms):—bosom.

2684. חֹצֶן **chôtsen**, *kho'-tsen*; a collat. form of 2683, and mean. the same:—arm, lap.

2685. חֲצַף **chătsaph** (Chald.), *khats-af'*; a prim. root; prop. to *shear* or cut close; fig. to *be severe*:—hasty, be urgent.

2686. חָצַץ **châtsats**, *khaw-tsats'*; a prim. root [comp. 2673]; prop. to *chop* into, pierce or sever; hence to *curtail*, to *distribute* (into ranks); as denom. from 2671, to *shoot* an arrow:—archer, × bands, cut off in the midst.

2687. חָצָץ **châtsâts**, *khaw-tsawts'*; from 2687; prop. something *cutting*; hence *gravel* (as *grit*); also (like 2671) an *arrow*:—arrow, gravel (stone).

2688. חַצְצוֹן תָּמָר **Chatsetsôwn Tâmâr**, *khats-ets-one' taw-mawr'*; or

חַצְצֹן תָּמָר **Chatsătsôn Tâmâr**, *khats-ats-one' taw-mawr'*; from 2686 and 8558; *division* [i.e. perh. *row*] *of* (the) *palm-tree*; *Chatsetson-tamar*, a place in Pal.:—Hazezon-tamar.

2689. חֲצֹצְרָה **chătsôtsrâh**, *khats-o-tser-aw'*; by redupl. from 2690; a *trumpet* (from its *sundered* or quavering note):—trumpet (-er).

2690. חָצַר **châtsar**, *khaw-tsar'*; a prim. root prop. to *surround* with a stockade, and thus *separate* from the open country; but used only in the redupl. form

חֲצֹצֵר **chătsôtsêr**, *khast-o-tsare'*; or (Chron. 5 : 12)

חֲצֹרֵר **chătsôrêr**, *hhats-o-rare'*; as denom. from 2689; to *trumpet*, i.e. blow on that instrument:—blow, sound, trumpeter.

2691. חָצֵר **châtsêr**, *khaw-tsare'* (masc. and fem.); from 2690 in its original sense; a *yard* (as *inclosed* by a fence); also a *hamlet* (as similarly *surrounded* with walls):—court, tower, village.

2692. חֲצַר אַדָּר **Chătsar Addâr**, *khats-ar' ad-dawr'*; from 2691 and 146; (the) *village of Addar*; *Chatsar-Addar*, a place in Pal.:—Hazar-addar.

2693. חֲצַר גַּדָּה **Chătsar Gaddâh**, *khats-ar' gad-daw'*; from 2691 and a fem. of 1408; (the) *village of* (female) *Fortune*; *Chatsar Gaddah*, a place in Pal.:—Hazar-gaddah.

2694. חֲצַר הַתִּיכוֹן **Chătsar hat-Tîykôwn**, *khats-ar' hat-tee-kone'*; from 2691 and 8484 with the art. interposed; *village of the middle*; *Chatsar-hat-Tikon*, a place in Pal.:—Hazar hatticon.

2695. חֶצְרוֹ **Chetsrôw**, *khets-ro'*; by an orth. var. for 2696; *inclosure*; *Chetsro*, an Isr.:—Hezro, Hezrai.

2696. חֶצְרוֹן **Chetsrôwn**, *khets-rone'*; from 2691; *court-yard*; *Chetsron*, the name of a place in Pal.; also of two Isr.:—Hezron.

2697. חֶצְרוֹנִי **Chetsrôwnîy**, *khets-ro-nee'*; patron. from 2696; a *Chetsronite* or (collect.) desc. of Chetsron:—Hezronites.

2698. חֲצֵרוֹת **Chătsêrowth**, *khats-ay-roth'*; fem. plur. of 2691; *yards*; *Chatseroth*, a place in Pal.:—Hazeroth.

2699. חֲצֵרִים **Chătsêrîym**, *khats-ay-reem'*; plur. masc. of 2691; *yards*; *Chatserim*, a place in Pal.:—Hazerim.

2700. חֲצַרְמָוֶת **Chătsarmâveth**, *khats-ar-maw'-veth*; from 2691 and 4194; *village of death*; *Chatsarmaveth*, a place in Arabia:—Hazarmaveth.

2701. חֲצַר סוּסָה **Chătsar Çûwçâh**, *khats-ar' soo-saw'*; from 2691 and 5484; *village of cavalry*; *Chatsar-Susah*, a place in Pal.:—Hazar-susah.

2702. חֲצַר סוּסִים **Chătsar Çûwçîym**, *khats-ar' soo-seem'*; from 2691 and the plur. of 5488; *village of horses*; *Chatsar-Susim*, a place in Pal.:—Hazar-susim.

2703. חֲצַר עֵינוֹן **Chătsar 'Êynôwn**, *khats-ar' ay-none'*; from 2691 and a der. of 5869; *village of springs*; *Chatsar-Enon*, a place in Pal.:—Hazar-enon.

2704. חֲצַר עֵינָן **Chătsar 'Êynân**, *khats-ar' ay-nawn'*; from 2691 and the same as 5881; *village of springs*; *Chatsar-Enan*, a place in Pal.:—Hazar-enan.

2705. חֲצַר שׁוּעָל **Chătsar Shûw'âl**, *khats-ar' shoo-awl'*; from 2691 and 7776; *village of* (the) *fox*; *Chatsar-Shual*, a place in Pal.:—Hazar-shual.

חֵק **chêq**. See 2436.

2706. חֹק **chôq**, *khoke*; from 2710; an *enactment*; hence an *appointment* (of time, space, quantity, labor or usage):—appointed, bound, commandment, convenient, custom, decree (-d), due, law, measure, × necessary, ordinance (-nary), portion, set time, statute, task.

2707. חָקָה **châqah**, *khaw-kaw'*; a prim. root; to *carve*; by impl. to *delineate*; also to *intrench*:—carved work, portrayed, set a print.

2708. חֻקָּה **chuqqâh**, *khook-kaw'*; fem. of 2706, and mean. substantially the same:—appointed, custom, manner, ordinance, site, statute.

2709. חֲקוּפָא **Chăqûwphâ'**, *khah-oo-faw'*; from an unused root prob. mean. to *bend*; *crooked*; *Chakupha*, one of the Nethinim:—Hakupha.

710. חָקַק **châqaq**, *khaw-kak'*; a prim. root; prop. to *hack*, i.e. *engrave* (Judg. 5 : 14, o *be a scribe* simply); by impl. to *enact* (laws being ut in stone or metal tablets in primitive times) or gen.) *prescribe*:—appoint, decree, governor, grave, awgiver, note, pourtray, print, set.

711. חֵקֶק **chêqeq**, *khay'-kek*; from 2710; an *enactment*, a *resolution*:—decree, thought.

712. חֻקֹּק **Chuqqôq**, *khook-koke'*; or (fully)

חוּקֹק **Chûwqôq**, *khoo-koke'*; from 2710; *appointed*; *Chukkok* or *Chukok*, a lace in Pal.:—Hukkok, Hukok.

713. חָקַר **châqar**, *khaw-kar'*; a prim. root; prop. to *penetrate*; hence to *examine* ntimately:—find out, (make) search (out), seek (out), ound, try.

714. חֵקֶר **chêqer**, *khay'-ker*; from 2713; *examination*, *enumeration*, *deliberation*:—nding out, number, [un-] search (-able, -ed out, -ing).

715. חֹר **chôr**, *khore*; or (fully)

חוֹר **chôwr**, *khore*; from 2787; prop. *white* or *pure* (from the *cleansing* or *shining* ower of fire [comp. 2751]); hence (fig.) *noble* (in ank):—noble.

חֻר **chûr**. See 2352.

716. חֶרֶא **chere'**, *kheh'-reh*; from an unused (and vulg.) root prob. mean. to *evacuate* the bowels; xcrement:—dung. Also חֲרִי° **chărîy**, *khar-ee'*.

717. חָרַב **chârab**, *khaw-rab'*; or

חָרֵב **chârêb**, *khaw-rabe'*; a prim. root; to *parch* (through drought), i.e. (by anal.) o *desolate*, *destroy*, *kill*:—decay, (be) desolate, destroy (-er), (be) dry (up), slay, × surely, (lay, lie, nake) waste.

718. חֲרַב **chărab** (Chald.), *khar-ab'*; a root corresp. to 2717; to *demolish*:—destroy.

719. חֶרֶב **chereb**, *kheh'-reb*; from 2717; *drought*; also a *cutting* instrument (from its *detructive* effect), as a *knife*, *sword*, or other sharp implement:—axe, dagger, knife, mattock, sword, tool.

720. חָרֵב **chârêb**, *khaw-rabe'*; from 2717; *parched* or *ruined*:—desolate, dry, vaste.

721. חֹרֶב **chôreb**, *kho'-reb*; a collat. form of 2719; *drought* or *desolation*:—desolation, rought, dry, heat, × utterly, waste.

722. חֹרֵב **Chôrêb**, *kho-rabe'*; from 2717; *desolate*; *Choreb*, a (gen.) name for the Sinaic mountains:—Horeb.

723. חָרְבָּה **chorbâh**, *khor-baw'*; fem. of 2721; prop. *drought*, i.e. (by impl.) a *desolaion*:—decayed place, desolate (place, -tion), destrucion, (laid) waste (place).

724. חָרָבָה **chârâbâh**, *khaw-raw-baw'*; fem. of 2720; a *desert*:—dry (ground, land).

725. חֲרָבוֹן **chărâbôwn**, *khar-aw-bone'*; from 2717; parching *heat*:—drought.

726. חַרְבוֹנָא **Charbôwnâ'**, *khar-bo-naw'*; or

חַרְבוֹנָה **Charbôwnâh**, *khar-bo-naw'*; of Pers. or.; *Charbona* or *Charbonah*, eunuch of Xerxes:—Harbona, Harbonah.

727. חָרַג **chârag**, *khaw-rag'*; a prim. root; prop. to *leap* suddenly, i.e. (by impl.) to e *dismayed*:—be afraid.

728. חַרְגֹּל **chargôl**, *khar-gole'*; from 2727; the *leaping* insect, i.e. a *locust*:—beetle.

729. חָרַד **chârad**, *khaw-rad'*; a prim. root; to *shudder* with terror; hence to *fear*; also o *hasten* (with anxiety):—be (make) afraid, be careul, discomfit, fray (away), quake, tremble.

730. חָרֵד **chârêd**, *khaw-rade'*; from 2729; *fearful*; also *reverential*:—afraid, trembling.

731. חֲרָדָה **chărâdâh**, *khar-aw-daw'*; fem. of 2730; *fear*, *anxiety*:—care, × exceedngly, fear, quaking, trembling.

732. חֲרָדָה **Chărâdâh**, *khar-aw-daw'*; the same as 2731; *Charadah*, a place in the Deert:—Haradah.

733. חֲרֹדִי **Chărôdîy**, *khar-o-dee'*; patrial from a deriv. of 2729 [comp. 5878]; a *Charodite*, or inhab. of *Charod*:—Harodite.

2734. חָרָה **chârâh**, *khaw-raw'*; a prim. root [comp. 2787]; to *glow* or grow warm; fig. (usually) to *blaze* up, of anger, zeal, jealousy:—be angry, burn, be displeased, × earnestly, fret self, grieve, be (wax) hot, be incensed, kindle, × very, be wroth. See 8474.

2735. חֹר הַגִּדְגָּד **Chôr hag-Gidgâd**, *khore hag-ghid-gawd'*; from 2356 and a collat. (masc.) form of 1412, with the art. interposed; *hole of the cleft*; *Chor-hag-Gidgad*, a place in the Desert:—Hor-hagidgad.

2736. חַרְהֲיָה **Charhăyâh**, *khar-hah-yaw'*; from 2734 and 3050; *fearing Jah*; *Charhajah*, an Isr.:—Harhaiah.

2737. חָרוּז **chârûwz**, *khaw-rooz'*; from an unused root mean. to *perforate*; prop. *pierced*, i.e. a *bead* of pearl, gems or jewels (as strung):—chain.

2738. חָרוּל **chârûwl**, *khaw-rool'*; or (short.)

חָרֻל **chârûl**, *khaw-rool'*; appar. pass. part. of an unused root prob. mean. to *be prickly*; prop. *pointed*, i.e. a *bramble* or other thorny weed:—nettle.

חֹרֹון **chôrôwn**. See 1032, 2772.

2739. חֲרוּמַף **chărûwmaph**, *khar-oo-maf'*; from pass. part. of 2763 and 639; *snub-nosed*; *Charumaph*, an Isr.:—Harumaph.

2740. חָרוֹן **chârôwn**, *khaw-rone'*; or (short.)

חָרֹן **chârôn**, *khaw-rone'*; from 2734; a *burning* of anger:—sore displeasure, fierce (-ness), fury, (fierce) wrath (-ful).

2741. חֲרוּפִי **Chărûwphîy**, *khar-oo-fee'*; a patrial from (prob.) a collat. form of 2756; a *Charuphite* or inhab. of Charuph (or Chariph):—Haruphite.

2742. חָרוּץ **chârûwts**, *khaw-roots'*; or

חָרֻץ **chârûts**, *khaw-roots'*; pass. part. of 2782; prop. *incised* or (act.) *incisive*; hence (as noun masc. or fem.) a *trench* (as dug), *gold* (as mined), a *threshing-sledge* (having sharp teeth); (fig.) *determination*; also *eager*:—decision, diligent, (fine) gold, pointed things, sharp, threshing instrument, wall.

2743. חָרוּץ **Chârûwts**, *khaw-roots'*; the same as 2742; *earnest*; *Charuts*, an Isr.:—Haruz.

2744. חַרְחוּר **Charchûwr**, *khar-khoor'*; a fuller form of 2746; *inflammation*; *Charchur*, one of the Nethinim:—Harhur.

2745. חַרְחַס **Charchaç**, *khar-khas'*; from the same as 2775; perh. *shining*; *Charchas*, an Isr.:—Harhas.

2746. חַרְחֻר **charchûr**, *khar-khoor'*; from 2787; *fever* (as *hot*):—extreme burning.

2747. חֶרֶט **cheret**, *kheh'-ret*; from a prim. root mean. to *engrave*; a *chisel* or *graver*; also a *style* for writing:—graving tool, pen.

חָרִט **chârit**. See 2754.

2748. חַרְטֹם **chartôm**, *khar-tome'*; from the same as 2747; a *horoscopist* (as *drawing* magical lines or circles):—magician.

2749. חַרְטֹם **chartôm** (Chald.), *khar-tome'*; the same as 2748:—magician.

2750. חֳרִי **chŏrîy**, *khor-ee'*; from 2734; a *burning* (i.e. intense) anger:—fierce, × great, heat.

חֲרִי° **chărîy**. See 2716.

2751. חֹרִי **chôrîy**, *kho-ree'*; from the same as 2353; *white* bread:—white.

2752. חֹרִי **Chôrîy**, *kho-ree'*; from 2356; *cave-dweller* or troglodyte; a *Chorite* or aboriginal Idumæan:—Horims, Horites.

2753. חֹרִי **Chôrîy**, *kho-ree'*; or

חוֹרִי **Chôwrîy**, *kho-ree'*; the same as 2752; *Chori*, the name of two men:—Hori.

2754. חָרִיט **chârîyt**, *khaw-reet'*; or

חָרִט **chârit**, *khaw-reet'*; from the same as 2747; prop. *cut* out (or *hollow*), i.e. (by impl.) a *pocket*:—bag, crisping pin.

2755. חֲרֵי־יוֹנִים **chărêy-yôwnîym**, *khar-ay'-yo-neem'*; from the plur. of 2716 and the plur. of 3123; *excrements of doves* [or perh. rather the plur. of a single word

חֲרָאיוֹן **chărâ'yôwn**, *khar-aw-yone'*; of similar or uncert. deriv.], prob. a kind of vegetable:—doves' dung.

2756. חָרִיף **Chârîyph**, *khaw-reef'*; from 2778; *autumnal*; *Chariph*, the name of two Isr.:—Hariph.

2757. חָרִיץ **chârîyts**, *khaw-reets'*; or

חָרִץ **chârîts**, *khaw-reets'*; from 2782; prop. *incisure* or (pass.) *incised* [comp. 2742]; hence a *threshing-sledge* (with *sharp* teeth): also a *slice* (as cut):— + cheese, harrow.

2758. חָרִישׁ **chârîysh**, *khaw-reesh'*; from 2790; *ploughing* or its season:—earing (time), ground.

2759. חֲרִישִׁי **chărîyshîy**, *khar-ee-shee'*; from 2790 in the sense of *silence*; *quiet*, i.e. *sultry* (as noun fem. the *sirocco* or hot east wind):—vehement.

2760. חָרַךְ **chârak**, *khaw-rak'*; a prim. root; to *braid* (i.e. to *entangle* or snare) or *catch* (game) in a net:—roast.

2761. חֲרַךְ **chărak** (Chald.), *khar-ak'*; a root prob. allied to the equiv. of 2787; to *scorch*:—singe.

2762. חֶרֶךְ **cherek**, *kheh'-rek*; from 2760; prop. a *net*, i.e. (by anal.) *lattice*:—lattice.

חָרֻל **chârûl**. See 2738.

2763. חָרַם **charam**, *khaw-ram'*; a prim. root; to *seclude*; spec. (by a ban) to *devote* to relig. uses (espec. destruction); phys. and reflex. to be *blunt* as to the nose:—make accursed, consecrate, (utterly) destroy, devote, forfeit, have a flat nose, utterly (slay, make away).

2764. חֵרֶם **chêrem**, *khay'-rem*; or (Zech. 14 : 11)

חֶרֶם **cherem**, *kheh'-rem*; from 2763; phys. (as *shutting in*) a *net* (either lit. or fig.); usually a *doomed* object; abstr. *extermination*:—(ac-) curse (-d, -d thing), dedicated thing, things which should have been utterly destroyed, (appointed to) utter destruction, devoted (thing), net.

2765. חֳרֵם **Chŏrêm**, *khor-ame'*; from 2763; *devoted*; *Chorem*, a place in Pal.:—Horem.

2766. חָרִם **Chârîm**, *khaw-reem'*; from 2763; *snub-nosed*; *Charim*, an Isr.:—Harim.

2767. חָרְמָה **Chormâh**, *khor-maw'*; from 2763; *devoted*; *Chormah*, a place in Pal.:—Hormah.

2768. חֶרְמוֹן **Chermôwn**, *kher-mone'*; from 2763; *abrupt*; *Chermon*, a mount of Pal.:—Hermon.

2769. חֶרְמוֹנִים **Chermôwnîym**, *kher-mo-neem'*; plur. of 2768; *Hermons*, i.e. its peaks:—the Hermonites.

2770. חֶרְמֵשׁ **chermêsh**, *kher-mashe'*; from 2763; a *sickle* (as *cutting*):—sickle.

2771. חָרָן **Chârân**, *kaw-rawn'*; from 2787; *parched*; *Charan*, the name of a man and also of a place:—Haran.

חָרֹן **chârôn**. See 2740.

2772. חֹרֹנִי **Chôrônîy**, *kho-ro-nee'*; patrial from 2773; a *Choronite* or inhab. of Choronaim:—Horonite.

2773. חֹרֹנַיִם **Chôrônayim**, *kho-ro-nah'-yim*; dual of a deriv. from 2356; *double cave-town*; *Choronajim*, a place in Moab:—Horonaim.

2774. חַרְנֶפֶר **Charnepher**, *khar-neh'-fer*; of uncert. der.; *Charnepher*, an Isr.:—Harnepher.

2775. חֶרֶס **chereç**, *kheh'-res*; or (with a directive enclitic)

חַרְסָה **charçâh**, *khar'-saw*; from an unused root mean. to *scrape*; the *itch*; also [perh. from the mediating idea of 2777] the *sun*:—itch, sun.

2776. חֶרֶס **Chereç**, *kheh'-res*; the same as 2775; *shining*; *Cheres*, a mount. in Pal.:—Heres.

2777. חַרְסוּת **charçûwth**, *khar*- 2775

used for scraping); a *potsherd*, i.e. (by impl.) a *pottery;* the name of a gate at Jerus.:—east.

2778. חָרַף **châraph**, *khaw-raf';* a prim. root; to *pull* off, i.e. (by impl.) to *expose* (as by *stripping*); spec. to *betroth* (as if a surrender); fig. to *carp at*, i.e. *defame;* denom. (from 2779) to spend the *winter:*—betroth, blaspheme, defy, jeopard, rail, reproach, upbraid.

2779. חֹרֶף **chôreph**, *kho'-ref;* from 2778; prop. the *crop* gathered, i.e. (by impl.) the *autumn* (and winter) season; fig. *ripeness* of age:—cold, winter ([-house]), youth.

2780. חָרֵף **Chârêph**, *khaw-rafe';* from 2778; *reproachful; Chareph*, an Isr.:—Hareph.

2781. חֶרְפָּה **cherpâh**, *kher-paw';* from 2778; *contumely, disgrace*, the *pudenda:*—rebuke, reproach (-fully), shame.

2782. חָרַץ **chârats**, *khaw-rats';* a prim root; prop. to *point* sharply, i.e. (lit.) to *wound;* fig. to *be alert*, to *decide:*—bestir self, decide, decree, determine, maim, move.

2783. חֲרַץ **chărats** (Chald.), *khar-ats';* from a root corresp. to 2782 in the sense of *vigor;* the *loin* (as the seat of strength):—loin.

חָרֻץ **chârûts**. See 2742.

2784. חַרְצֻבָּה **chartsubbâh**, *khar-tsoob-baw';* of uncert. der.; a *fetter;* fig. a *pain:*—band.

חָרִיץ **chârîts**. See 2757.

2785. חַרְצַן **chartsan**, *khar-tsan';* from 2782; a *sour* grape (as *sharp* in taste):—kernel.

2786. חָרַק **châraq**, *khaw-rak';* a prim. root; to *grate* the teeth:—gnash.

2787. חָרַר **chârar**, *khaw-rar';* a prim. root; to *glow*, i.e. lit. (to *melt, burn, dry* up) or fig. (to *show* or *incite passion:*—be angry, burn, dry, kindle.

2788. חָרֵר **chârêr**, *khaw-rare';* from 2787; *arid:*—parched place.

2789. חֶרֶשׂ **cheres**, *kheh'-res;* a collat. form mediating between 2775 and 2791; a piece of *pottery:*—earth (-en), (pot-) sherd, + stone.

2790. חָרַשׁ **chârash**, *khaw-rash';* a prim. root; to *scratch*, i.e. (by impl.) to *engrave, plough;* hence (from the use of tools) to *fabricate* (of any material); fig. to *devise* (in a bad sense); hence (from the idea of secrecy) to be *silent*, to *let alone;* hence (by impl.) to *be deaf* (as an accompaniment of dumbness):— × altogether, cease, conceal, be deaf, devise, ear, graven, imagine, leave off speaking, hold peace, plow (-er, -man), be quiet, rest, practise secretly, keep silence, be silent, speak not a word, be still, hold tongue, worker.

2791. חֶרֶשׁ **cheresh**, *kheh'-resh;* from 2790; magical *craft;* also *silence:*—cunning, secretly.

2792. חֶרֶשׁ **Cheresh**, *kheh'-resh;* the same as 2791:—*Cheresh*, a Levite:—Heresh.

2793. חֹרֶשׁ **chôresh**, *kho'-resh;* from 2790; a *forest* (perh. as furnishing the material for fabric):—bough, forest, shroud, wood.

2794. חֹרֵשׁ **chôrêsh**, *kho-rashe';* act. part. of 2790; a *fabricator* or mechanic:—artificer.

2795. חֵרֵשׁ **chêrêsh**, *khay-rashe';* from 2790; *deaf* (whether lit. or spir.):—deaf.

2796. חָרָשׁ **chârâsh**, *khaw-rawsh';* from 2790; a *fabricator* of any material:—artificer, (+) carpenter, craftsman, engraver, maker, + mason, skilful, (+) smith, worker, workman, such as wrought.

2797. חַרְשָׁא **Charshâ'**, *khar-shaw';* from 2792; *magician; Charsha*, one of the Nethinim:—Harsha.

2798. חֲרָשִׁים **Chărâshîym**, *khar-aw-sheem';* plur. of 2796; *mechanics*, the name of a valley in Jerus.:—Charashim, craftsmen.

2799. חֲרֹשֶׁת **chărôsheth**, *khar-o'-sheth;* from 2790; mechanical *work:*—carving, cutting.

2800. חֲרֹשֶׁת **Chărôsheth**, *khar-o'-sheth;* the same as 2799; *Charosheth*, a place in Pal.:—Harosheth.

2801. חָרַת **chârath**, *khaw-rath';* a prim. root; to *engrave:*—graven.

2802. חֶרֶת **Chereth**, *kheh'-reth;* from 2801 [but equiv. to 2793]; *forest; Chereth*, a thicket in Pal.:—Hereth.

2803. חָשַׁב **châshab**, *khaw-shab';* a prim. root; prop. to *plait* or interpenetrate, i.e. (lit.) to *weave* or (gen.) to *fabricate;* fig. to *plot* or contrive (usually in a malicious sense); hence (from the mental effort) to *think, regard, value, compute:*—(make) accoun[t] (of), conceive, consider, count, cunning (man, work, workman), devise, esteem, find out, forecast, hold, imagine, impute, invent, be like, mean, purpose, reckon (-ing be made), regard, think.

2804. חֲשַׁב **chăshab** (Chald.), *khash-ab';* corresp. to 2803; to *regard:*—repute.

2805. חֵשֶׁב **chêsheb**, *khay'-sheb;* from 2803; a *belt* or strap (as being interlaced):—curious girdle.

2806. חַשְׁבַּדָּנָה **Chashbaddânâh**, *khash-bad-daw'-naw;* from 2803 and 1777; *considerate judge; Chasbaddanah*, an Isr.:—Hasbadana.

2807. חֲשֻׁבָה **Chăshûbâh**, *khash-oo-baw';* from 2803; *estimation; Chashubah*, an Isr.:—Hashubah.

2808. חֶשְׁבּוֹן **cheshbôwn**, *khesh-bone';* from 2803; prop. *contrivance;* by impl. *intelligence:*—account, device, reason.

2809. חֶשְׁבּוֹן **Cheshbôwn**, *khesh-bone';* the same as 2808; *Cheshbon*, a place E. of the Jordan:—Heshbon.

2810. חִשָּׁבוֹן **chishshâbôwn**, *khish-shaw-bone';* from 2803; a *contrivance*, i.e. actual (a warlike *machine*) or mental (a *machination*):—engine, invention.

2811. חֲשַׁבְיָה **Chăshabyâh**, *khash-ab-yaw';* or

חֲשַׁבְיָהוּ **Chăshabyâhûw**, *khash-ab-yaw'-hoo;* from 2803 and 3050; *Jah has regarded; Chashabjah*, the name of nine Isr.:—Hashabiah.

2812. חֲשַׁבְנָה **Chăshabnâh**, *khash-ab-naw';* fem. of 2808; *inventiveness; Chashnah*, an Isr.:—Hashabnah.

2813. חֲשַׁבְנְיָה **Chăshabneyâh**, *khash-ab-neh-yaw';* from 2808 and 3050; *thought of Jah; Chashabnejah*, the name of two Isr.:—Hashabniah.

2814. חָשָׁה **châshâh**, *khaw-shaw';* a prim. root; to *hush* or keep quiet:—hold peace, keep silence, be silent, (be) still.

2815. חַשּׁוּב **Chashshûwb**, *khash-shoob';* from 2803; *intelligent; Chashshub*, the name of two or three Isr.:—Hashub, Hasshub.

2816. חֲשׁוֹךְ **chăshôwk** (Chald.), *khash-oke';* from a root corresp. to 2821; the *dark:*—darkness.

2817. חֲשׂוּפָא **Chăsûwphâ'**, *khas-oo-faw';* or

חֲשֻׂפָא **Chăsûphâ'**, *khas-oo-faw';* from 2834; *nakedness; Chasupha*, one of the Nethinim:—Hashupha, Hasupha.

חָשׁוּק **châshûwq**. See 2838.

2818. חֲשַׁח **chăshach** (Chald.), *khash-akh';* a collat. root to one corresp. to 2363 in the sense of *readiness;* to *be necessary* (from the idea of *convenience*) or (transit.) to *need:*—careful, have need of.

2819. חַשְׁחוּת **chashchûwth**, *khash-khooth';* from a root corresp. to 2818; *necessity:*—be needful.

חֲשֵׁיכָה **chăshêykâh**. See 2825.

חֻשִׁים **Chûshîym**. See 2366.

2820. חָשַׂךְ **châsak**, *khaw-sak';* a prim root; to *restrain* or (reflex.) *refrain;* by impl. to *refuse, spare, preserve;* also (by interch. with 2821) to *observe:*—assuage, × darken, forbear, hinder, hold back, keep (back), punish, refrain, reserve, spare, withhold.

2821. חָשַׁךְ **châshak**, *khaw-shak';* a prim. root to *be dark* (as *withholding* light); transit. to *darken:*—be black, be (make) dark, darken, cause darkness, be dim, hide.

2822. חֹשֶׁךְ **chôshek**, *kho-shek';* from 2821; th[e] *dark;* hence (lit.) *darkness;* fig. *misery*, *destruction, death, ignorance, sorrow, wickedness:*—dark (-ness), night, obscurity.

2823. חָשֹׁךְ **châshôk**, *khaw-shoke';* from 282[1]; *dark* (fig. i.e. *obscure*):—mean.

2824. חֶשְׁכָה **cheshkâh**, *khesh-kaw';* from 2821; *darkness:*—dark.

2825. חֲשֵׁכָה **chăshêkâh**, *khash-ay-kaw';* or

חֲשֵׁיכָה **chăshêkâh**, *khash-ay-kaw'* from 2821; *darkness;* fig. *misery:*—darkness.

2826. חָשַׁל **châshal**, *khaw-shal';* a prim. root to *make* (intrans. *be*) *unsteady*, i.e. *weak:*—feeble.

2827. חֲשַׁל **chăshal** (Chald.), *khash-al';* a roo[t] corresp. to 2826; to *weaken*, i.e. *crush:*—subdue.

2828. חָשֻׁם **Châshûm**, *khaw-shoom';* from th[e] same as 2831; *enriched; Chashum*, th[e] name of two or three Isr.:—Hashum.

חֻשָׁם **Chûshâm**. See 2367.

חֻשִׁם **Chûshîm**. See 2366.

2829. חֶשְׁמוֹן **Cheshmôwn**, *khesh-mone';* th[e] same as 2831; *opulent; Cheshmon*, place in Pal.:—Heshmon.

2830. חַשְׁמַל **chashmal**, *khash-mal';* of uncert. der.; prob. *bronze* or polished spec[u]trum metal:—amber.

2831. חַשְׁמַן **chashman**, *khash-man';* from a[n] unused root (prob. mean. *firm* o[r] *capacious* in resources); appar. *wealthy:*—princes.

2832. חַשְׁמֹנָה **Chashmônâh**, *khash-mo-naw';* fem. of 2831; *fertile; Chasmonah*, [a] place in the Desert:—Hashmonah.

2833. חֹשֶׁן **chôshen**, *kho'-shen;* from an unuse[d] root prob. mean. to *contain* or *sparkle*; perh. a *pocket* (as holding the Urim and Thummim) or *rich* (as containing gems), used only of the *gorge[t]* of the highpriest:—breastplate.

2834. חָשַׂף **châsaph**, *khaw-saf';* a prim. root to *strip* off, i.e. gen. to *make naked* (fo[r]) exertion or in disgrace), to *drain* away or *bail up* (a liquid):—make bare, clean, discover, draw out, take, uncover.

2835. חָשִׂף **châsîph**, *khaw-seef';* from 2834; prop. *drawn off*, i.e. separated; hence [a] small *company* (as divided from the rest):—little flock.

2836. חָשַׁק **châshaq**, *khaw-shak';* a prim. root to *cling*, i.e. *join*, (fig.) to *love, delight* in; ellipt. (or by interch. for 2820) to *deliver:*—have a de[-]light, (have a) desire, fillet, long, set (in) love.

2837. חֵשֶׁק **chêsheq**, *khay'-shek;* from 2836; *de[-]light:*—desire, pleasure.

2838. חָשֻׁק **châshûq**, *khaw-shook';* or

חָשׁוּק **châshûwq**, *khaw-shook';* pass. part of 2836; *attached*, i.e. a fence-*rail* o[r] rod connecting the posts or pillars:—fillet.

2839. חִשֻּׁק **chishshûq**, *khish-shook';* from 2836; *conjoined*, i.e. a wheel-*spoke* or rod con[-]necting the hub with the rim:—felloe.

2840. חִשֻּׁר **chishshûr**, *khish-shoor';* from a[n] unused root mean. to *bind* together; *combined*, i.e. the *nave* or hub of a wheel (as holding the spokes together):—spoke.

2841. חַשְׁרָה **chashrâh**, *khash-raw';* from the same as 2840; prop. a *combination* or gathering, i.e. of watery *clouds:*—dark.

חֲשֻׂפָא **Chăsûphâ'**. See 2817.

2842. חֲשַׁשׁ **châshash**, *khaw-shash';* by var. for 7179; dry *grass:*—chaff.

2843. חֻשָׁתִי **Chûshâthîy**, *khoo-shaw-thee';* pa[-]tron. from 2364; a *Chushathite* or desc. of Chushah:—Hushathite.

2844. חַת **chath**, *khath;* from 2865; concr. *crushed;* also *afraid;* abstr. *terror:*—broken, dismayed, dread, fear.

2845. חֵת **Chêth**, *khayth;* from 2865; *terror; Cheth*, an aboriginal Canaanite:—Heth.

2846. חָתָה **châthâh**, *khaw-thaw';* a prim. root; to lay *hold* of; espec. to *pick* up fire:—heap, take (away).

2847. חִתָּה **chittâh**, *khit-taw';* from 2865; *fear:*—terror.

2848. חִתּוּל **chittûwl**, *khit-tool';* from 2853; *swathed*, i.e. a *bandage:*—roller.

2849. חַתְחַת **chathchath**, *khath-khath';* from 2844; *terror:*—fear.

2850. חִתִּי **Chittîy**, *khit-tee';* patron. from 2845; a *Chittite*, or desc. of Cheth:—Hittite, Hittites.

2851. חִתִּית **chittîyth**, *khit-teeth';* from 2865; *fear:*—terror.

2852. חָתַךְ **châthak**, *khaw-thak';* a prim. root; prop. to *cut* off, i.e. (fig.) to *decree:*—determine.

2853. חָתַל **châthal**, *khaw-thal';* a prim. root; to *swathe:*— × at all, swaddle.

2854. חֲתֻלָּה **châthullâh**, *khath-ool-law';* from 2853; a *swathing* cloth (fig.):—swaddling band.

2855. חֶתְלֹן **Chethlôn**, *kheth-lone';* from 2853; *enswathed; Chethlon*, a place in Pal.:—Hethlon.

2856. חָתַם **châtham**, *khaw-tham';* a prim. root; to *close* up; espec. to *seal:*—make an end, mark, seal (up), stop.

2857. חֲתַם **chătham** (Chald.), *khath-am';* a root corresp. to 2856; to *seal:*—seal.

חֹתָם **chôthâm**. See 2368.

2858. חֹתֶמֶת **chôthemeth**, *kho-the-meth;* fem. act. part. of 2856; a *seal:*—signet.

2859. חָתַן **châthan**, *khaw-than';* a prim. root; to *give* (a daughter) *away* in marriage; hence (gen.) to *contract affinity* by marriage:—join in affinity, father in law, make marriages, mother in law, son in law.

2860. חָתָן **châthân**, *khaw-thawn';* from 2859; a *relative* by marriage (espec. through the bride); fig. a *circumcised* child (as a species of religious espousal):—bridegroom, husband, son in law.

2861. חֲתֻנָּה **chăthunnâh**, *khath-oon-naw';* from 2859; a *wedding:*—espousal.

2862. חָתַף **châthaph**, *khaw-thaf';* a prim. root; to *clutch:*—take away.

2863. חֶתֶף **chetheph**, *kheh'-thef;* from 2862; prop. *rapine;* fig. *robbery:*—prey.

2864. חָתַר **châthar**, *khaw-thar';* a prim. root; to *force* a passage, as by burglary; fig. with oars:—dig (through), row.

2865. חָתַת **châthath**, *khaw-thath';* a prim. root; prop. to *prostrate;* hence to *break* down, either (lit.) by violence, or (fig.) by confusion and fear:—abolish, affright, be (make) afraid, amaze, beat down, discourage, (cause to) dismay, go down, scare, terrify.

2866. חֲתַת **chăthath**, *khath-ath';* from 2865; *dismay:*—casting down.

2867. חֲתַת **Chăthath**, *khath-ath';* the same as 2866; *Chathath*, an Isr.:—Hathath.

ט

2868. טְאֵב **ṭᵉʼêb** (Chald.), *teh-abe';* a prim. root; to *rejoice:*—be glad.

2869. טָב **ṭâb** (Chald.), *tawb;* from 2868; the same as 2896; *good:*—fine, good.

2870. טָבְאֵל **ṭâbᵉʼêl**, *taw-beh-ale';* from 2895 and 410; *pleasing* (to) *God; Tabeel*, the name of a Syrian and of a Persian:—Tabeal, Tabeel.

2871. טָבוּל **ṭâbûwl**, *taw-bool';* pass. part. of 2881; prop. *dyed*, i.e. a *turban* (prob. as of colored stuff):—dyed attire.

2872. טַבּוּר **ṭabbûwr**, *tab-boor';* from an unused root mean. to *pile* up; prop. *accumulated;* i.e. (by impl.) a *summit:*—middle, midst.

2873. טָבַח **ṭâbach**, *taw-bakh';* a prim. root; to *slaughter* (animals or men):—kill, (make) slaughter, slay.

2874. טֶבַח **ṭebach**, *teh'-bakh;* from 2873; prop. something *slaughtered;* hence a *beast* (or *meat*, as butchered); abstr. *butchery* (or concr. a place of slaughter):— × beast, slaughter, × slay, × sore.

2875. טֶבַח **Tebach**, *teh'-bakh;* the same as 2874; *massacre; Tebach*, the name of a Mesopotamian and of an Isr.:—Tebah.

2876. טַבָּח **ṭabbâch**, *tab-bawkh';* from 2873; prop. a *butcher;* hence a *lifeguardsman* (because acting as executioner); also a *cook* (as usually slaughtering the animal for food):—cook, guard.

2877. טַבָּח **ṭabbâch** (Chald.), *tab-bawkh';* the same as 2876; a *lifeguardsman:*—guard.

2878. טִבְחָה **ṭibchâh**, *tib-khaw';* fem. of 2874 and mean. the same:—flesh, slaughter.

2879. טַבָּחָה **ṭabbâchâh**, *tab-baw-khaw';* fem. of 2876; a female *cook:*—cook.

2880. טִבְחַת **Tibchath**, *tib-khath';* from 2878; *slaughter; Tibchath*, a place in Syria:—Tibhath.

2881. טָבַל **ṭâbal**, *taw-bal';* a prim. root; to *dip:*—dip, plunge.

2882. טְבַלְיָהוּ **Tᵉbalyâhûw**, *teb-al-yaw'-hoo;* from 2881 and 3050; *Jah has dipped; Tebaljah*, an Isr.:—Tebaliah.

2883. טָבַע **ṭâbaʻ**, *taw-bah';* a prim. root; to *sink:*—drown, fasten, settle, sink.

2884. טַבָּעוֹת **Tabbâʻôwth**, *tab-baw-othe';* plur. of 2885; *rings; Tabbaoth*, one of the Nethinim:—Tabbaoth.

2885. טַבַּעַת **ṭabbaʻath**, *tab-bah'-ath;* from 2883; prop. a *seal* (as *sunk* into the wax), i.e. *signet* (for sealing); hence (gen.) a *ring* of any kind:—ring.

2886. טַבְרִמּוֹן **Tabrimmôwn**, *tab-rim-mone';* from 2895 and 7417; *pleasing* (to) *Rimmon; Tabrimmon*, a Syrian:—Tabrimmon.

2887. טֵבֵת **Têbeth**, *tay'-beth;* prob. of for. der.; *Tebeth*, the tenth Heb. month:—Tebeth.

2888. טַבַּת **Tabbath**, *tab-bath';* of uncert. der.; *Tabbath*, a place E. of the Jordan:—Tabbath.

2889. טָהוֹר **ṭâhôwr**, *taw-hore';* or

טָהֹר **ṭâhôr**, *taw-hore';* from 2891; *pure* (in a phys., chem., cerem. or moral sense):—clean, fair, pure (-ness).

2890. טְהוֹר **ṭᵉhôwr**, *teh-hore';* from 2891; *purity:*—pureness.

2891. טָהֵר **ṭâhêr**, *taw-hare';* a prim. root; prop. to *be bright;* i.e. (by impl.) to *be pure* (phys. *sound, clear, unadulterated;* Levit. *uncontaminated;* mor. *innocent* or *holy*):—be (make, make self, pronounce) clean, cleanse (self), purge, purify (-ier, self).

2892. טֹהַר **ṭôhar**, *to'-har;* from 2891; lit. *brightness;* ceremon. *purification:*—clearness, glory, purifying.

2893. טָהֳרָה **ṭohŏrâh**, *toh-or-aw';* fem. of 2892; cerem. *purification;* moral *purity:*— × is cleansed, cleansing, purification (-fying).

2894. טוּא **ṭûwʼ**, *too;* a prim. root; to *sweep away:*—sweep.

2895. טוֹב **ṭowb**, *tobe;* a prim. root, to *be* (trans. *do* or *make*) *good* (or *well*) in the widest sense:—be (do) better, cheer, be (do, seem) good, (make) goodly, × please, (be, do, go, play) well.

2896. טוֹב **ṭôwb**, *tobe;* from 2895; *good* (as an adj.) in the widest sense; used likewise as a noun, both in the masc. and the fem., the sing. and the plur. (*good*, a *good* or *good* thing, a *good* man or woman; the *good*, *goods* or *good* things, *good* men or women), also as an adv. (*well*):—beautiful, best, better, bountiful, cheerful, at ease, × fair (word), (be in) favour, fine, glad, good (deed, -lier, -liest, -ly, -ness, -s), graciously, joyful, kindly, kindness, liketh (best), loving, merry, × most, pleasant, + pleaseth, pleasure, precious, prosperity, ready, sweet, wealth, welfare, (be) well ([-favoured]).

2897. טוֹב **Ṭôwb**, *tobe;* the same as 2896; *good; Tob*, a region appar. E. of the Jordan:—Tob.

2898. טוּב **ṭûwb**, *toob;* from 2895; *good* (as a noun), in the widest sense, espec. *goodness* (superl. concr. the *best*), *beauty, gladness, welfare:*—fair, gladness, good (-ness, thing, -s), joy, go well with.

2899. טוֹב אֲדֹנִיָּהוּ **Ṭôwb Ădônîyâhûw**, *tobe ado-nee-yah'-hoo;* from 2896 and 138; *pleasing* (to) *Adonijah; Tob-Adonijah*, an Isr.:—Tob-adonijah.

2900. טוֹבִיָּה **Ṭôwbîyâh**, *to-bee-yaw';* or

טוֹבִיָּהוּ **Ṭôwbîyâhûw**, *to-bee-yaw'-hoo;* from 2896 and 3050; *goodness of Jehovah; Tobijah*, the name of three Isr. and of one Samaritan:—Tobiah, Tobijah.

2901. טָוָה **ṭâvâh**, *taw-vaw';* a prim. root; to *spin:*—spin.

2902. טוּחַ **ṭûwach**, *too'-akh;* a prim. root; to *smear*, espec. with lime:—daub, overlay, plaister, smut.

2903. טוֹפָפָה **ṭôwphâphâh**, *to-faw-faw';* from an unused root mean. to *go around* or *bind;* a *fillet* for the forehead:—frontlet.

2904. טוּל **ṭûwl**, *tool;* a prim. root; to *pitch* over or *reel;* hence (transit.) to *cast* down or out:—carry away, (utterly) cast (down, forth, out), send out.

2905. טוּר **ṭûwr**, *toor;* from an unused root mean. to *range* in a reg. manner; a *row;* hence a *wall:*—row.

2906. טוּר **ṭûwr** (Chald.), *toor;* corresp. to 6697; a *rock* or hill:—mountain.

2907. טוּשׂ **ṭûws**, *toos;* a prim. root; to *pounce* as a bird of prey:—haste.

2908. טְוָת **ṭᵉvâth** (Chald.), *tev-awth';* from a root corresp. to 2901; *hunger* (as *twisting*):—fasting.

2909. טָחָה **ṭâchâh**, *taw-khaw';* a prim. root; to *stretch* a bow, as an *archer:*—[bow-] shot.

2910. טוּחָה **ṭûwchâh**, *too-khaw';* from 2909 (or 2902) in the sense of *overlaying;* (in the plur. only) the *kidneys* (as being *covered*); hence (fig.) the inmost *thought:*—inward parts.

2911. טְחוֹן **ṭᵉchôwn**, *tekh-one';* from 2912; a hand *mill;* hence a *millstone:*—to grind.

2912. טָחַן **ṭâchan**, *taw-khan';* a prim. root; to *grind* meal; hence to *be a concubine* (that being their employment):—grind (-er).

2913. טַחֲנָה **ṭachănâh**, *takh-an-aw';* from 2912; a hand *mill;* hence (fig.) *chewing:*—grinding.

2914. טְחֹר **ṭᵉchôr**, *tekh-ore';* from an unused root mean. to *burn;* a *boil* or ulcer (from the inflammation), espec. a tumor in the anus or pudenda (the piles):—emerod.

2915. טִיחַ **ṭîyach**, *tee'-akh;* from (the equiv. of) 2902; mortar or *plaster:*—daubing.

2916. טִיט **ṭîyṭ**, *teet;* from an unused root mean. appar. to *be sticky* [rath. perh. a denom. from 2894, through the idea of dirt to be *swept* away]; *mud* or *clay;* fig. *calamity:*—clay, dirt, mire.

2917. טִין **ṭîyn** (Chald.), *teen;* perh. by interch. for a word corresp. to 2916; *clay:*—miry.

2918. טִירָה **ṭîyrâh**, *tee-raw';* fem. of (an equiv. to) 2905; a *wall;* hence a *fortress* or a *hamlet:*—(goodly) castle, habitation, palace, row.

2919. טַל **ṭal**, *tal;* from 2926; *dew* (as *covering* vegetation):—dew.

2920. טַל **ṭal** (Chald.), *tal;* the same as 2919:—dew.

2921. טָלָא **ṭâlâʼ**, *taw-law';* a prim. root; prop. to *cover* with pieces; i.e. (by impl.) to *spot* or *variegate* (as tapestry):—clouted, with divers colours, spotted.

2922. טְלָא **ṭᵉlâʼ**, *tel-aw';* appar. from 2921 in the (orig.) sense of *covering* (for protection); a *lamb* [comp. 2924]:—lamb.

2923. טְלָאִים **Ṭᵉlâ'îym**, *tel-aw-eem'*; from the plur. of 2922; *lambs; Telaim*, a place in Pal.:—Telaim.

2924. טָלֶה **ṭâleh**, *taw-leh'*; by var. for 2922; a *lamb:*—lamb.

2925. טַלְטֵלָה **ṭalṭêlâh**, *tal-tay-law'*; from 2904; *overthrow* or *rejection:*—captivity.

2926. טָלַל **ṭâlal**, *taw-lal'*; a prim. root; prop. to *strew* over, i.e. (by impl.) to *cover* in or *plate* (with beams):—cover.

2927. טְלַל **ṭᵉlal** (Chald.), *tel-al'*; corresp. to 2926; to *cover* with shade:—have a shadow.

2928. טֶלֶם **Ṭelem**, *teh'-lem*; from an unused root mean. to *break* up or treat violently; *oppression; Telem*, the name of a place in Idumæa, also of a temple doorkeeper:—Telem.

2929. טַלְמוֹן **Ṭalmôwn**, *tal-mone'*; from the same as 2728; *oppressive; Talmon*, a temple doorkeeper:—Talmon.

2930. טָמֵא **ṭâmê'**, *taw-may'*; a prim. root; to *be foul*, espec. in a cerem. or mor. sense (*contaminated*):—defile (self), pollute (self), be (make, make self, pronounce) unclean, × utterly.

2931. טָמֵא **ṭâmê'**, *taw-may'*; from 2930; *foul* in a relig. sense:—defiled, + infamous, polluted (-tion), unclean.

2932. טֻמְאָה **ṭum'âh**, *toom-aw'*; from 2930; relig. *impurity:*—filthiness, unclean (-ness).

2933. טָמָה **ṭâmâh**, *taw-maw'*; a collat. form of 2930; to *be impure* in a relig. sense:—be defiled, be reputed vile.

2934. טָמַן **ṭâman**, *taw-man'*; a prim. root; to *hide* (by *covering* over):—hide, lay privily, in secret.

2935. טֶנֶא **ṭene'**, *teh'-neh*; from an unused root prob. mean. to *weave*; a *basket* (of interlaced osiers):—basket.

2936. טָנַף **ṭânaph**, *taw-naf'*; a prim. root; to *soil:*—defile.

2937. טָעָה **ṭâ'âh**, *taw-aw'*; a prim. root; to *wander*; causat. to *lead astray:*—seduce.

2938. טָעַם **ṭâ'am**, *taw-am'*; a prim. root; to *taste*; fig. to *perceive:*— × but, perceive, taste.

2939. טְעֵם **ṭᵉ'am** (Chald.), *teh-am'*; corresp. to 2938; to *taste*; causat. to *feed:*—make to eat, feed.

2940. טַעַם **ṭa'am**, *tah'-am*; from 2938; prop. a *taste*, i.e. (fig.) *perception*; by impl. *intelligence*; transit. a *mandate:*—advice, behaviour, decree, discretion, judgment, reason, taste, understanding.

2941. טַעַם **ṭa'am** (Chald.), *tah'-am*; from 2939; prop. a *taste*, i.e. (as in 2940) a judicial *sentence:*—account, × to be commanded, commandment, matter.

2942. טְעֵם **ṭᵉ'êm** (Chald.), *teh-ame'*; from 2939, and equiv. to 2941; prop. *flavor*; fig. *judgment* (both subj. and obj.); hence *account* (both subj. and obj.):— + chancellor, + command, commandment, decree, + regard, taste, wisdom.

2943. טָעַן **ṭâ'an**, *taw-an'*; a prim. root; to *load* a beast:—lade.

2944. טָעַן **ṭâ'an**, *taw-an'*; a prim. root; to *stab:*—thrust through.

2945. טַף **ṭaph**, *taf*; from 2952 (perh. referring to the *tripping* gait of children); a *family* (mostly used collect. in the sing.):—(little) children (ones), families.

2946. טָפַח **ṭâphach**, *taw-fakh'*; a prim. root; to *flatten* out or *extend* (as a tent); fig. to *nurse* a child (as *promotive* of growth); or perh. a denom. from 2947, from *dandling* on the palms:—span, swaddle.

2947. טֶפַח **ṭêphach**, *tay'-fakh*; from 2946; a *spread* of the hand, i.e. a *palm-breadth* (not "span" of the fingers); archit. a *corbel* (as a supporting palm):—coping, hand-breadth.

2948. טֹפַח **ṭôphach**, *to'-fakh*; from 2946 (the same as 2947):—hand-breadth (broad).

2949. טִפֻּחַ **ṭippûch**, *tip-pookh'*; from 2946; *nursing:*—span long.

2950. טָפַל **ṭâphal**, *taw-fal'*; a prim. root; prop. to *stick* on as a patch; fig. to *impute* falsely:—forge (-r), sew up.

2951. טִפְסַר **ṭiphçar**, *tif-sar'*; of for. der.; a military *governor:*—captain.

2952. טָפַף **ṭâphaph**, *taw-faf'*; a prim. root; appar. to *trip* (with short steps) coquettishly:—mince.

2953. טְפַר **ṭᵉphar** (Chald.), *tef-ar'*; from a root corresp. to 6852, and mean. the same as 6856; a finger-*nail*; also a *hoof* or *claw:*—nail.

2954. טָפַשׁ **ṭâphash**, *taw-fash'*; a prim. root; prop. appar. to *be thick*; fig. to *be stupid:*—be fat.

2955. טָפַת **Ṭâphath**, *taw-fath'*; prob. from 5197; a *dropping* (of ointment); *Taphath*, an Israelitess:—Taphath.

2956. טָרַד **ṭârad**, *taw-rad'*; a prim. root; to *drive* on; fig. to *follow* close:—continual.

2957. טְרַד **ṭᵉrad** (Chald.), *ter-ad'*; corresp. to 2956; to *expel:*—drive.

2958. טְרוֹם **ṭᵉrôwm**, *ter-ome'*; a var. of 2962; *not yet:*—before.

2959. טָרַח **ṭârach**, *taw-rakh'*; a prim. root; to *overburden:*—weary.

2960. טֹרַח **ṭôrach**, *to'-rakh*; from 2959; a *burden:*—cumbrance, trouble.

2961. טָרִי **ṭârîy**, *taw-ree'*; from an unused root appar. mean. to *be moist*; prop. *dripping*; hence *fresh* (i.e. recently made such):—new, putrefying.

2962. טֶרֶם **ṭerem**, *teh'-rem*; from an unused root appar. mean. to *interrupt* or *suspend*; prop. *non-occurrence*; used adv. *not yet* or *before:*—before, ere, not yet.

2963. טָרַף **ṭâraph**, *taw-raf'*; a prim. root; to *pluck* off or *pull* to pieces; causat. to *supply* with food (as in morsels):—catch, × without doubt, feed, ravin, rend in pieces, × surely, tear (in pieces).

2964. טֶרֶף **ṭereph**, *teh'-ref*; from 2963; something *torn*, i.e. a fragment, e.g. a *fresh* leaf, *prey, food:*—leaf, meat, prey, spoil.

2965. טָרָף **ṭârâph**, *taw-rawf'*; from 2963; recently *torn* off, i.e. *fresh:*—pluckt off.

2966. טְרֵפָה **ṭᵉrêphâh**, *ter-ay-faw'*; fem. (collect.) of 2964; *prey*, i.e. flocks devoured by animals:—ravin, (that which was) torn (of beasts, in pieces).

2967. טַרְפְּלַי **Ṭarpᵉlay** (Chald.), *tar-pel-ah'ee*; from a name of for. der.; a *Tarpelite* (collect.) or inhab. of Tarpel, a place in Assyria:—Tarpelites.

י

2968. יָאַב **yâ'ab**, *yaw-ab'*; a prim. root; to *desire:*—long.

2969. יָאָה **yâ'âh**, *yaw-aw'*; a prim. root; to *be suitable:*—appertain.

יְאוֹר **yᵉ'ôwr**. See 2975.

2970. יַאֲזַנְיָה **Ya'ăzanyâh**, *yah-az-an-yaw'*; or
יַאֲזַנְיָהוּ **Ya'ăzanyâhûw**, *yah-az-an-yaw'-hoo*; from 238 and 3050; *heard of Jah; Jaazanjah*, the name of four Isr.:—Jaazaniah. Comp. 3153.

2971. יָאִיר **Yâ'îyr**, *yaw-ere'*; from 215; *enlightener; Jaïr*, the name of four Isr.:—Jair.

2972. יָאִרִי **Yâ'îrîy**, *yaw-ee-ree'*; patron. from 2971; a *Jaïrite* or desc. of Jair:—Jairite.

2973. יָאַל **yâ'al**, *yaw-al'*; a prim. root; prop. to *be slack*, i.e. (fig.) to *be foolish:*—dote, be (become, do) foolish (-ly).

2974. יָאַל **yâ'al**, *yaw-al'*; a prim. root [prob. rather the same as 2973 through the idea of mental *weakness*]; prop. to *yield*, espec. *assent*; hence (pos.) to *undertake* as an act of volition:—assay, begin, be content, please, take upon, × willingly, would.

2975. יְאֹר **yᵉ'ôr**, *yeh-ore'*; of Eg. or.; a *channel*, e.g. a fosse, canal, shaft; spec. the *Nile*, as the one river of Egypt, including its collat. trenches; also the *Tigris*, as the main river of Assyria:—brook, flood, river, stream.

2976. יָאַשׁ **yâ'ash**, *yaw-ash'*; a prim. root; to *desist*, i.e. (fig.) to *despond:*—(cause to) despair, one that is desperate, be no hope.

2977. יֹאשִׁיָּה **Yô'shîyâh**, *yo-shee-yaw'*; or
יֹאשִׁיָּהוּ **Yô'shîyâhûw**, *yo-she-yaw'-hoo*; from the same root as 803 and 3050; *founded of Jah; Joshijah*, the name of two Isr.:—Josiah.

2978. יְאִתוֹן **yᵉ'îthôwn**, *yeh-ee-thone'*; from 857; an *entry:*—entrance.

2979. יְאָתְרַי **yᵉ'âthᵉray**, *yeh-aw-ther-ah'ee*; from the same as 871; *stepping; Jeätherai*, an Isr.:—Jeaterai.

2980. יָבַב **yâbab**, *yaw-bab*; a prim. root; to *bawl:*—cry out.

2981. יְבוּל **yᵉbûwl**, *yeb-ool'*; from 2986; *produce*, i.e. a *crop* or (fig.) *wealth:*—fruit, increase.

2982. יְבוּס **Yᵉbûwç**, *yeb-oos'*; from 947; *trodden*, i.e. threshing-place; *Jebus*, the aboriginal name of Jerus.:—Jebus.

2983. יְבוּסִי **Yᵉbûwçîy**, *yeb-oo-see'*; patrial from 2982; a *Jebusite* or inhab. of Jebus:—Jebusite (-s).

2984. יִבְחָר **Yibchar**, *yib-khar'*; from 977; *choice*; *Jibchar*, an Isr.:—Ibhar.

2985. יָבִין **Yâbîyn**, *yaw-bene'*; from 995; *intelligent*; *Jabin*, the name of two Canaanitish kings:—Jabin.

יָבֵישׁ **Yâbêysh**. See 3003.

2986. יָבַל **yâbal**, *yaw-bal'*; a prim. root; prop. to *flow*; causat. to *bring* (espec. with pomp):—bring (forth), carry, lead (forth).

2987. יְבַל **yᵉbal** (Chald.), *yeb-al'*; corresp. to 2986; to *bring:*—bring, carry.

יֹבֵל **yôbêl**. See 3104.

2988. יָבָל **yâbâl**, *yaw-bawl'*; from 2986; a *stream:*—[water-] course, stream.

2989. יָבָל **Yâbâl**, *yaw-bawl'*; the same as 2988; *Jabal*, an antediluvian:—Jabal.

יוֹבֵל **yôbêl**. See 3104.

2990. יַבֶּל **yabbêl**, *yab-bale'*; from 2986; having *running* sores:—wen.

2991. יִבְלְעָם **Yiblᵉ'âm**, *yib-leh-awm'*; from 1104 and 5971; *devouring people; Jibleäm*, a place in Pal.:—Ibleam.

2992. יָבַם **yâbam**, *yaw-bam'*; a prim. root of doubtful mean.; used only as a denom. from 2993; to *marry* a (deceased) brother's widow:—perform the duty of a husband's brother, marry.

2993. יָבָם **yâbâm**, *yaw-bawm'*; from (the orig. of) 2992; a *brother-in-law:*—husband's brother.

2994. יְבֶמֶת **yᵉbêmeth**, *yeb-ay'-meth*; fem. part. of 2992; a *sister-in-law:*—brother's wife, sister in law.

2995. יַבְנְאֵל **Yabnᵉ'êl**, *yab-neh-ale'*; from 1129 and 410; *built of God; Jabneël*, the name of two places in Pal.:—Jabneel.

2996. יַבְנֶה **Yabneh**, *yab-neh'*; from 1129; a *building*; *Jabneh*, a place in Pal.:—Jabneh.

2997. יִבְנְיָה **Yibnᵉyâh**, *yib-neh-yaw'*; from 1129 and 3050; *built of Jah; Jibnejah*, an Isr.:—Ibneiah.

2998. יִבְנִיָּה **Yibnîyâh**, *yib-nee-yaw'*; from 1129 and 3050; *building of Jah; Jibnijah*, an Isr.:—Ibnijah.

2999. יַבֹּק **Yabbôq**, *yab-boke'*; prob. from 1238; *pouring* forth; *Jabbok*, a river E. of the Jordan:—Jabbok.

3000. יְבֶרֶכְיָהוּ **Yᵉberekyâhûw**, *yeb-eh-rek-yaw'-hoo*; from 1288 and 3050; *blessed of Jah; Jeberekjah*, an Isr.:—Jeberechiah.

3001. יָבֵשׁ **yâbêsh**, *yaw-bashe'*; a prim. root; to *be ashamed, confused* or *disappointed*; also (as failing) to *dry* up (as water) or *wither* (as herbage):—be ashamed, clean, be confounded, (make) dry (up), (do) shame (-fully), × utterly, wither (away).

3002. יָבֵשׁ **yâbêsh**, *yaw-bashe'*; from 3001: *dry:*—dried (away), dry.

3003. יָבֵשׁ **Yâbêsh**, *yaw-bashe'*; the same as 3002 (also

יָבֵישׁ **Yâbêysh**, *yaw-bashe'*; often with the addition of 1568, i.e. *Jabesh of Gilad*); *Jabesh*, the name of an Isr. and of a place in Pal.:—Jabesh ([-Gilead]).

3004. יַבָּשָׁה **yabbâshâh**, *yab-baw-shaw'*; from 3001; *dry* ground:—dry (ground, land).

3005. יִבְשָׂם **Yibsâm**, *yib-sawm'*; from the same as 1314; *fragrant; Jibsam*, an Isr.:—Jibsam.

3006. יַבֶּשֶׁת **yabbesheth**, *yab-beh'-sheth*; a var. of 3004; *dry* ground:—dry land.

3007. יַבֶּשֶׁת **yabbesheth** (Chald.), *yab-beh'-sheth*; corresp. to 3006; *dry* land:—earth.

3008. יִגְאָל **Yigʼâl**, *yig-awl'*; from 1350; *avenger; Jigal*, the name of three Isr.:—Igal, Igeal.

3009. יָגַב **yâgab**, *yaw-gab'*; a prim. root; to *dig* or plough:—husbandman.

3010. יָגֵב **yâgêb**, *yaw-gabe'*; from 3009; a ploughed *field:*—field.

3011. יָגְבְּהָה **Yogbᵉhâh**, *yog-beh-haw'*; fem. from 1361; *hillock; Jogbehah*, a place E. of the Jordan:—Jogbehah.

3012. יִגְדַּלְיָהוּ **Yigdalyâhûw**, *yig-dal-yaw'-hoo*; from 1431 and 3050; *magnified of Jah; Jigdaljah*, an Isr.:—Igdaliah.

3013. יָגָה **yâgâh**, *yaw-gaw'*; a prim. root; to *grieve:*—afflict, cause grief, grieve, sorrowful, vex.

3014. יָגָה **yâgâh**, *yaw-gaw'*; a prim. root [prob. rather the same as 3013 through the common idea of *dissatisfaction*]; to *push* away:—be removed.

3015. יָגוֹן **yâgôwn**, *yaw-gohn'*; from 3013; *affliction:*—grief, sorrow.

3016. יָגוֹר **yâgôwr**, *yaw-gore'*; from 3025; *fearful:*—afraid, fearest.

3017. יָגוּר **Yâgûwr**, *yaw-goor'*; prob. from 1481; a *lodging; Jagur*, a place in Pal.:—Jagur.

3018. יְגִיעַ **yᵉgîyaʻ**, *yeg-ee'-ah*; from 3021; *toil;* hence a *work, produce, property* (as the result of labor):—labour, work.

3019. יָגִיעַ **yâgîyaʻ**, *yaw-ghee'-ah*; from 3021; *tired:*—weary.

3020. יָגְלִי **Yoglîy**, *yog-lee'*; from 1540; *exiled; Jogli*, an Isr.:—Jogli.

3021. יָגַע **yâgaʻ**, *yaw-gah'*; a prim. root; prop. to *gasp;* hence to *be exhausted*, to *tire*, to *toil:*—faint, (make to) labour, (be) weary.

3022. יָגָע **yâgâʻ**, *yaw-gaw'*; from 3021; *earnings* (as the product of toil):—that which he laboured for.

3023. יָגֵעַ **yâgêaʻ**, *yaw-gay'-ah*; from 3021; *tired;* hence (trans.) *tiresome:*—full of labour, weary.

3024. יְגִעָה **yᵉgîʻâh**, *yeg-ee-aw'*; fem. of 3019; *fatigue:*—weariness.

3025. יָגֹר **yâgôr**, *yaw-gore'*; a prim. root; to *fear:*—be afraid, fear.

3026. יְגַר שָׂהֲדוּתָא **Yᵉgar Sahădûwthâʼ** (Chald.), *yegar' sah-had-oo-thaw'*; from a word derived from an unused root (mean. to *gather*) and a der. of a root corresp. to 7717; *heap of the testimony; Jegar-Sahadutha*, a cairn E. of the Jordan:—Jegar-Sahadutha.

3027. יָד **yâd**, *yawd*; a prim. word; a *hand* (the *open* one [indicating *power, means, direction*, etc.], in distinction from 3709, the *closed* one); used (as noun, adv., etc.) in a great variety of applications, both lit. and fig., both proximate and remote [as follow]:—(+ be) able, × about, + armholes, at, axletree, because of, beside, border, × bounty, + broad, [broken-] handed, × by, charge, coast, + consecrate, + creditor, custody, debt, dominion, × enough, + fellowship, force, × from, hand [-staves, -y work], × he, himself, × in, labour, + large, ledge, [left-] handed, means, × mine, ministry, near, × of, × order, ordinance, × our, parts, pain, power, × presumptuously, service, side, sore, state, stay, draw with strength, stroke, + swear, terror, × thee, × by them, × themselves, × thine own, × thou, through, × throwing, + thumb, times, × to, × under, × us, × wait on, [way-] side, where, + wide, × with (him, me, you), work, + yield, × yourselves.

3028. יַד **yad** (Chald.), *yad*; corresp. to 3027:—hand, power.

3029. יְדָא **yᵉdâʼ** (Chald.), *yed-aw'*; corresp. to 3034; to *praise:*—(give) thank (-s).

3030. יִדְאֲלָה **Yidălâh**, *yid-al-aw'*; of uncert. der. *Jidalah*, a place in Pal.:—Idalah.

3031. יִדְבָּשׁ **Yidbâsh**, *yid-bawsh'*; from the same as 1706; perh. *honeyed; Jidbash*, an Isr.:—Idbash.

3032. יָדַד **yâdad**, *yaw-dad'*; a prim. root; prop. to *handle* [comp. 3034], i.e. to *throw*, e.g. lots:—cast.

3033. יְדִדוּת **yᵉdîdûwth**, *yed-ee-dooth'*; from 3039; prop. *affection;* concr. a *darling* object:—dearly beloved.

3034. יָדָה **yâdâh**, *yaw-daw'*; a prim. root; used only as denom. from 3027; lit. to *use* (i.e. hold out) *the hand;* phys. to *throw* (a stone, an arrow) at or away; espec. to *revere* or *worship* (with extended hands); intens. to *bemoan* (by wringing the hands):—cast (out), (make) confess (-ion), praise, shoot, (give) thank (-ful, -s, -sgiving).

3035. יִדּוֹ **Yiddôw**, *yid-do'*; from 3034; *praised; Jiddo*, an Isr.:—Iddo.

3036. יָדוֹן **Yâdôwn**, *yaw-done'*; from 3034; *thankful; Jadon*, an Isr.:—Jadon.

3037. יַדּוּעַ **Yaddûwaʻ**, *yad-doo'-ah*; from 3045; *knowing; Jaddua*, the name of two Isr.:—Jaddua.

3038. יְדוּתוּן **Yᵉdûwthûwn**, *yed-oo-thoon'*; or

יְדֻתוּן **Yᵉdûthûwn**, *yed-oo-thoon'*; or

יְדִיתוּן **Yᵉdîythûwn**, *yed-ee-thoon'*; prob. from 3034; *laudatory; Jeduthun*, an Isr.:—Jeduthun.

3039. יְדִיד **yᵉdîyd**, *yed-eed'*; from the same as 1730; *loved:*—amiable, (well-) beloved, loves.

3040. יְדִידָה **Yᵉdîydâh**, *yed-ee-daw'*; fem. of 3039; *beloved; Jedidah*, an Israelitess:—Jedidah.

3041. יְדִידְיָה **Yᵉdîydᵉyâh**, *yed-ee-deh-yaw'*; from 3039 and 3050; *beloved of Jah; Jedidejah*, a name of Solomon:—Jedidiah.

3042. יְדָיָה **Yᵉdâyâh**, *yed-aw-yaw'*; from 3034 and 3050; *praised of Jah; Jedajah*, the name of two Isr.:—Jedaiah.

3043. יְדִיעֲאֵל **Yᵉdîyʻăʼêl**, *yed-ee-ah-ale'*; from 3045 and 410; *knowing God; Jediaël*, the name of three Isr.:—Jediael.

3044. יִדְלָף **Yidlâph**, *yid-lawf'*; from 1811; *tearful; Jidlaph*, a Mesopotamian:—Jidlaph.

3045. יָדַע **yâdaʻ**, *yaw-dah'*; a prim. root; to *know* (prop. to ascertain by *seeing*); used in a great variety of senses, fig., lit., euphem. and infer. (including *observation, care, recognition;* and causat. *instruction, designation, punishment*, etc.) [as follow]:—acknowledge, acquaintance (-ted with), advise, answer, appoint, assuredly, be aware, [un-] awares, can [-not], certainly, for a certainty, comprehend, consider, × could they, cunning, declare, be diligent, (can, cause to) discern, discover, endued with, familiar friend, famous, feel, can have, be [ig-] norant, instruct, kinsfolk, kinsman, (cause to, let, make) know, (come to give, have, take) knowledge, have [knowledge], (be, make, make to be, make self) known, + be learned, + lie by man, mark, perceive, privy to, × prognosticator, regard, have respect, skilful, shew, can (man of) skill, be sure, of a surety, teach, (can) tell, understand, have [understanding], × will be, wist, wit, wot.

3046. יְדַע **yᵉdaʻ** (Chald.), *yed-ah'*; corresp. to 3045:—certify, know, make known, teach.

3047. יָדָע **Yâdâʻ**, *yaw-daw'*; from 3045; *knowing; Jada*, an Isr.:—Jada.

3048. יְדַעְיָה **Yᵉdaʻyâh**, *yed-ah-yaw'*; from 3045 and 3050; *Jah has known; Jedajah*, the name of two Isr.:—Jedaiah.

3049. יִדְּעֹנִי **yiddᵉʻônîy**, *yid-deh-o-nee'*; from 3045; prop. a *knowing* one; spec. a *conjurer;* (by impl.) a *ghost:*—wizard.

3050. יָהּ **Yâhh**, *yaw*; contr. for 3068, and mean. the same; *Jah*, the sacred name:—Jah, the Lord, most vehement. Cp. names in "-iah," "-jah."

3051. יָהַב **yâhab**, *yaw-hab'*; a prim. root; to *give* (whether lit. or fig.); gen. to *put;* imper. (reflex.) *come:*—ascribe, bring, come on, give, go, set, take.

3052. יְהַב **yᵉhab** (Chald.), *yeh-hab'*; corresp. to 3051:—deliver, give, lay, + prolong, pay, yield.

3053. יְהָב **yᵉhâb**, *yeh-hawb'*; from 3051; prop. what is *given* (by Providence), i.e. a *lot:*—burden.

3054. יָהַד **yâhad**, *yaw-had'*; denom. from a form corresp. to 3061; to *Judaize*, i.e. become Jewish:—become Jews.

3055. יְהֻד **Yᵉhûd**, *yeh-hood'*; a briefer form of one corresp. to 3061; *Jehud*, a place in Pal.:—Jehud.

3056. יֶהְדַּי **Yehday**, *yeh-dah'ee*; perh. from a form corresp. to 3061; *Judaistic; Jehdai*, an Isr.:—Jehdai.

3057. יְהֻדִיָּה **Yᵉhûdîyâh**, *yeh-hoo-dee-yaw'*; fem. of 3064; *Jehudijah*, a Jewess:—Jehudijah.

3058. יֵהוּא **Yêhûwʼ**, *yay-hoo'*; from 3068 and 1931; *Jehovah (is) He; Jehu*, the name of five Isr.:—Jehu.

3059. יְהוֹאָחָז **Yᵉhôwʼâchâz**, *yeh-ho-aw-khawz'*; from 3068 and 270; *Jehovah-seized; Jehoächaz*, the name of three Isr.:—Jehoahaz. Comp. 3099.

3060. יְהוֹאָשׁ **Yᵉhôwʼâsh**, *yeh-ho-awsh'*; from 3068 and (perh.) 784; *Jehovah-fired; Jehoäsh*, the name of two Isr. kings:—Jehoash Comp. 3101.

3061. יְהוּד **Yᵉhûwd** (Chald.), *yeh-hood'*; contr. from a form corresp. to 3063; prop. *Judah*, hence *Judæa:*—Jewry, Judah, Judea.

3062. יְהוּדָאִי **Yᵉhûwdâʼîy** (Chald.), *yeh-hoo-daw-ee'*; patrial from 3061; a *Jehudaïte* (or Judaite), i.e. Jew:—Jew.

3063. יְהוּדָה **Yᵉhûwdâh**, *yeh-hoo-daw'*; from 3034; *celebrated; Jehudah* (or Judah), the name of five Isr.; also of the tribe descended from the first, and of its territory:—Judah.

3064. יְהוּדִי **Yᵉhûwdîy**, *yeh-hoo-dee'*; patron. from 3063; a *Jehudite* (i.e. Judaite or Jew), or desc. of Jehudah (i.e. Judah):—Jew.

3065. יְהוּדִי **Yᵉhûwdîy**, *yeh-hoo-dee'*; the same as 3064; *Jehudi*, an Isr.:—Jehudi.

3066. יְהוּדִית **Yᵉhûwdîyth**, *yeh-hoo-deeth'*; fem. of 3064; the *Jewish* (used adv.) language:—in the Jews' language.

3067. יְהוּדִית **Yᵉhûwdîyth**, *yeh-hoo-deeth'*; the same as 3066; *Jewess; Jehudith*, a Canaanitess:—Judith.

3068. יְהֹוָה **Yᵉhôvâh**, *yeh-ho-vaw'*; from 1961; (the) self-*Existent* or Eternal; *Jehovah*, Jewish national name of God:—Jehovah, the Lord. Comp. 3050, 3069.

3069. יְהֹוִה **Yᵉhôvîh**, *yeh-ho-vee'*; a var. of 3068 [used after 136, and pronounced by Jews as 430, in order to prevent the repetition of the same sound, since they elsewhere pronounce 3068 as 136]:—God.

3070. יְהֹוָה יִרְאֶה **Yᵉhôvâh yireh**, *yeh-ho-vaw' yir-eh'*; from 3068 and 7200; *Jehovah will see* (to it); *Jehovah-Jireh*, a symbolical name for Mt. Moriah:—Jehovah-jireh.

3071. יְהֹוָה נִסִּי **Yᵉhôvâh niççîy**, *yeh-ho-vaw' nis-see'*; from 3068 and 5251 with pron. suffix.; *Jehovah (is) my banner; Jehovah-Nissi*, a symbolical name of an altar in the Desert.—Jehovah-nissi.

3072. יְהֹוָה צִדְקֵנוּ **Yᵉhôvâh tsidqênûw**, *yeh-ho-vaw' tsid-kay'-noo*; from 3068 and 6664 with pron. suffix.; *Jehovah (is) our right; Jehovah-Tsidkenu*, a symbolical epithet of the Messiah and of Jerus.:—the Lord our righteousness.

3073. יְהוָֹה שָׁלוֹם **Y^{e}hôvâh shâlôwm**, *yeh-ho-vaw' shaw-lome'*; from 3068 and 7965; *Jehovah* (is) *peace; Jehovah-Shalom*, a symbolical name of an altar in Pal.:—Jehovah-shalom.

3074. יְהוָֹה שָׁמָּה **Y^{e}hôvâh shâmmâh**, *yeh-ho-vaw' shawm'-maw*; from 3068 and 8033 with directive enclitic; *Jehovah* (is) *thither; Jehovah-Shammah*, a symbol. title of Jerus.:—Jehovah-shammah.

3075. יְהוֹזָבָד **Y^{e}hôwzâbâd**, *yeh-ho-zaw-bawd'*; from 3068 and 2064; *Jehovah-endowed; Jehozabad*, the name of three Isr.:—Jehozabad. Comp. 3107.

3076. יְהוֹחָנָן **Y^{e}hôwchânân**, *yeh-ho-khaw-nawn'*; from 3068 and 2603; *Jehovah-favored; Jehochanan*, the name of eight Isr.:—Jehohanan, Johanan. Comp. 3110.

3077. יְהוֹיָדָע **Y^{e}hôwyâdâʻ**, *yeh-ho-yaw-daw'*; from 3068 and 3045; *Jehovah-known; Jehojada*, the name of three Isr.:—Jehoiada. Comp. 3111.

3078. יְהוֹיָכִין **Y^{e}hôwyâkîyn**, *yeh-ho-yaw-keen'*; from 3068 and 3559; *Jehovah will establish; Jehojakin*, a Jewish king:—Jehoiachin. Comp. 3112.

3079. יְהוֹיָקִים **Y^{e}hôwyâqîym**, *yeh-ho-yaw-keem'*; from 3068 abbrev. and 6965; *Jehovah will raise; Jehojakim*, a Jewish king:—Jehoiakim. Comp. 3113.

3080. יְהוֹיָרִיב **Y^{e}hôwyârîyb**, *yeh-ho-yaw-reeb'*; from 3068 and 7378; *Jehovah will contend; Jehojarib*, the name of two Isr.:—Jehoiarib. Comp. 3114.

3081. יְהוּכַל **Y^{e}hûwkal**, *yeh-hoo-kal'*; from 3201; *potent; Jehukal*, an Isr.:—Jehucal. Comp. 3116.

3082. יְהוֹנָדָב **Y^{e}hôwnâdâb**, *yeh-ho-naw-dawb'*; from 3068 and 5068; *Jehovah-largessed; Jehonadab*, the name of an Isr. and of an Arab:—Jehonadab, Jonadab. Comp. 3122.

3083. יְהוֹנָתָן **Y^{e}hôwnâthân**, *yeh-ho-naw-thawn'*; from 3068 and 5414; *Jehovah-given; Jehonathan*, the name of four Isr.:—Jonathan. Comp. 3129.

3084. יְהוֹסֵף **Y^{e}hôwçêph**, *yeh-ho-safe'*; a fuller form of 3130; *Jehoseph* (i.e. Joseph), a son of Jacob:—Joseph.

3085. יְהוֹעַדָּה **Y^{e}hôwʻaddâh**, *yeh-ho-ad-daw'*; from 3068 and 5710; *Jehovah-adorned; Jehoäddah*, an Isr.:—Jehoada.

3086. יְהוֹעַדִּין **Y^{e}hôwʻaddîyn**, *yeh-ho-ad-deen'*; or

יְהוֹעַדָּן **Y^{e}hôwaddân**, *yeh-ho-ad-dawn'*; from 3068 and 5727; *Jehovah-pleased; Jehoäddin* or *Jehoäddan*, an Israelitess:—Jehoaddan.

3087. יְהוֹצָדָק **Y^{e}hôwtsâdâq**, *yeh-ho-tsaw-dawk'*; from 3068 and 6663; *Jehovah-righted; Jehotsadak*, an Isr.:—Jehozadek, Josedech. Comp. 3136.

3088. יְהוֹרָם **Y^{e}hôwrâm**, *yeh-ho-rawm'*; from 3068 and 7311; *Jehovah-raised; Jehoram*, the name of a Syrian and of three Isr.:—Jehoram, Joram. Comp. 3141.

3089. יְהוֹשֶׁבַע **Y^{e}hôwshebaʻ**, *yeh-ho-sheh'-bah*; from 3068 and 7650; *Jehovah-sworn; Jehosheba*, an Israelitess:—Jehosheba. Comp. 3090.

3090. יְהוֹשַׁבְעַת **Y^{e}hôwshabʻath**, *yeh-ho-shab-ath'*; a form of 3089; *Jehoshabath*, an Israelitess:—Jehoshabeath.

3091. יְהוֹשׁוּעַ **Y^{e}hôwshûwaʻ**, *yeh-ho-shoo'-ah*; or

יְהוֹשֻׁעַ **Y^{e}hôwshûʻa**, *yeh-ho-shoo'-ah*; from 3068 and 3467; *Jehovah-saved; Jehoshuä* (i.e. Joshua), the Jewish leader:—Jehoshua, Jehoshuah, Joshua. Comp. 1954, 3442.

3092. יְהוֹשָׁפָט **Y^{e}hôwshâphâṭ**, *yeh-ho-shaw-fawt'*; from 3068 and 8199; *Jehovah-judged; Jehoshaphat*, the name of six Isr.; also of a valley near Jerus.:—Jehoshaphat. Comp. 3146.

3093. יָהִיר **yâhîyr**, *yaw-here'*; prob. from the same as 2022; *elated;* hence *arrogant:*—haughty, proud.

3094. יְהַלֶּלְאֵל **Y^{e}hallel'êl**, *yeh-hal-lel-ale'*; from 1984 and 410; *praising God; Jehalleiel*, the name of two Isr.:—Jehaleleel, Jehalelel.

3095. יַהֲלֹם **yahălôm**, *yah-hal-ome'*; from 1986 (in the sense of *hardness*); a precious stone, prob. *onyx:*—diamond.

3096. יַהַץ **Yahats**, *yah'-hats*; or

יַהְצָה **Yahtsâh**, *yah'-tsaw*; or (fem.)

יַהְצָה **Yahtsâh**, *yah-tsaw'*; from an unused root mean. to *stamp;* perh. *threshing*-floor; *Jahats* or *Jahtsah*, a place E. of the Jordan:—Jahaz, Jahazah, Jahzah.

3097. יוֹאָב **Yôw'âb**, *yo-awb'*; from 3068 and 1; *Jehovah-fathered; Joäb*, the name of three Isr.:—Joab.

3098. יוֹאָח **Yôw'âch**, *yo-awkh'*; from 3068 and 251; *Jehovah-brothered; Joach*, the name of four Isr.:—Joah.

3099. יוֹאָחָז **Yôw'âchâz**, *yo-aw-khawz'*; a form of 3059; *Joächaz*, the name of two Isr.:—Jehoahaz, Joahaz.

3100. יוֹאֵל **Yôw'êl**, *yo-ale'*; from 3068 and 410; *Jehovah* (is his) *God; Joël*, the name of twelve Isr.:—Joel.

3101. יוֹאָשׁ **Yôw'âsh**, *yo-awsh'*; or

יֹאָשׁ **Yô'âsh** (2 Chron. 24 : 1), *yo-awsh'*; a form of 3060; *Joäsh*, the name of six Isr.:—Joash.

3102. יוֹב **Yôwb**, *yobe*; perh. a form of 3103, but more prob. by err. transc. for 3487; *Job*, an Isr.:—Job.

3103. יוֹבָב **Yôwbâb**, *yo-bawb'*; from 2980; *howler; Jobab*, the name of two Isr. and of three foreigners:—Jobab.

3104. יוֹבֵל **yôwbêl**, *yo-bale'*; or

יֹבֵל **yôbêl**, *yo-bale'*; appar. from 2986; the *blast* of a horn (from its *continuous* sound); spec. the *signal* of the silver trumpets; hence the instrument itself and the festival thus introduced:—jubile, ram's horn, trumpet.

3105. יֻבַל **yûwbal**, *yoo-bal'*; from 2986; a *stream:*—river.

3106. יוּבָל **Yûwbâl**, *yoo-bawl'*; from 2986; *stream; Jubal*, an antediluvian:—Jubal.

3107. יוֹזָבָד **Yôwzâbâd**, *yo-zaw-bawd'*; a form of 3075; *Jozabad*, the name of ten Isr:—Josabad, Jozabad.

3108. יוֹזָכָר **Yôwzâkâr**, *yo-zaw-kawr'*; from 3068 and 2142; *Jehovah-remembered; Jozacar*, an Isr.:—Jozachar.

3109. יוֹחָא **Yôwchâ'**, *yo-khaw'*; prob. from 3068 and a var. of 2421; *Jehovah-revived; Jocha*, the name of two Isr.:—Joha.

3110. יוֹחָנָן **Yôwchânân**, *yo-khaw-nawn'*; a form of 3076; *Jochanan*, the name of nine Isr.:—Johanan.

יוּטָה **Yûwṭâh**. See 3194.

3111. יוֹיָדָע **Yôwyâdâʻ**, *yo-yaw-daw'*; a form of 3077; *Jojada*, the name of two Isr.:—Jehoiada, Joiada.

3112. יוֹיָכִין **Yôwyâkîyn**, *yo-yaw-keen'*; a form of 3078; *Jojakin*, an Isr. king:—Jehoiachin.

3113. יוֹיָקִים **Yôwyâqîym**, *yo-yaw-keem'*; a form of 3079; *Jojakim*, an Isr.:—Joiakim. Comp. 3137.

3114. יוֹיָרִיב **Yôwyârîyb**, *yo-yaw-reeb'*; a form of 3080; *Jojarib*, the name of four Isr.:—Joiarib.

3115. יוֹכֶבֶד **Yôwkebed**, *yo-keh'-bed*; from 3068 contr. and 3513; *Jehovah-gloried; Jokebed*, the mother of Moses:—Jochebed.

3116. יוּכַל **Yûwkal**, *yoo-kal'*; a form of 3081; *Jukal*, an Isr.:—Jucal.

3117. יוֹם **yôwm**, *yome*; from an unused root mean. to *be hot;* a *day* (as the *warm* hours), whether lit. (from sunrise to sunset, or from one sunset to the next), or fig. (a space of time defined by an associated term), [often used adv.]:—age, + always, + chronicles, continually (-ance), daily, ([birth-], each, to) day, (now a, two) days (agone), + elder, × end, + evening, + (for) ever (-lasting, -more), × full, life, as (so) long as (. . . live), (even) now, + old, + outlived, + perpetually, presently, + remaineth, × required, season, × since, space, then, (process of) time, + as at other times, + in trouble, weather, (as) when, (a, the, within a) while (that), × whole (+ age), (full) year (-ly), + younger.

3118. יוֹם **yôwm** (Chald.), *yome*; corresp. to 3117; a *day:*—day (by day), time.

3119. יוֹמָם **yôwmâm**, *yo-mawm'*; from 3117; *daily:*—daily, (by, in the) day (-time).

3120. יָוָן **Yâvân**, *yaw-vawn'*; prob. from the same as 3196; *effervescing* (i.e. hot and active); *Javan*, the name of a son of Joktan, and of the race (*Ionians*, i.e. Greeks) descended from him, with their territory; also of a place in Arabia:—Javan.

3121. יָוֵן **yâvên**, *yaw-ven'*; from the same as 3196; prop. *dregs* (as *effervescing*); hence *mud:*—mire, miry.

3122. יוֹנָדָב **Yôwnâdâb**, *yo-naw-dawb'*; a form of 3082; *Jonadab*, the name of an Isr. and of a Rechabite:—Jonadab.

3123. יוֹנָה **yôwnâh**, *yo-naw'*; prob. from the same as 3196; a *dove* (appar. from the *warmth* of their mating):—dove, pigeon.

3124. יוֹנָה **Yônâh**, *yo-naw'*; the same as 3123; *Jonah*, an Isr.:—Jonah.

3125. יְוָנִי **Y^{e}vânîy**, *yev-aw-nee'*; patron. from 3121; a *Jevanite*, or desc. of Javan:—Grecian.

3126. יוֹנֵק **yôwnêq**, *yo-nake'*; act. part. of 3243; a *sucker;* hence a *twig* (of a tree felled and sprouting):—tender plant.

3127. יוֹנֶקֶת **yôwneqeth**, *yo-neh'-keth*; fem. of 3126; a *sprout:*—(tender) branch, young twig.

3128. יוֹנַת אֵלֶם רְחֹקִים **yôwnath 'êlem r^{e}chôqîym**, *yo-nath' ay'-lem rekh-o-keem'*; from 3123 and 482 and the plur. of 7350; *dove of* (the) *silence* (i.e. *dumb* Israel) *of* (i.e. among) *distances* (i.e. strangers); the title of a ditty (used for a name of its melody):—Jonath-elem-rechokim.

3129. יוֹנָתָן **Yôwnâthân**, *yo-naw-thawn'*; a form of 3083; *Jonathan*, the name of ten Isr.:—Jonathan.

3130. יוֹסֵף **Yôwçêph**, *yo-safe'*; fut. of 3254; *let him add* (or perh. simply act. part. *adding*); *Joseph*, the name of seven Isr.:—Joseph. Comp. 3084.

3131. יוֹסִפְיָה **Yôwçiphyâh**, *yo-sif-yaw'*; from act. part. of 3254 and 3050; *Jah* (is) *adding; Josiphjah*, an Isr.:—Josiphiah.

3132. יוֹעֵאלָה **Yôwʻê'lâh**, *yo-ay-law'*; perh. fem. act. part. of 3276; *furthermore; Joelah*, an Isr.:—Joelah.

3133. יוֹעֵד **Yôwʻêd**, *yo-ade'*; appar. act. part. of 3259; *appointer; Joed*, an Isr.:—Joed.

3134. יוֹעֶזֶר **Yôwʻezer**, *yo-eh'-zer*; from 3068 and 5828; *Jehovah* (is his) *help; Joezer*, an Isr.:—Joezer.

3135. יוֹעָשׁ **Yôwʻâsh**, *yo-awsh'*; from 3068 and 5789; *Jehovah-hastened; Joash*, the name of two Isr.:—Joash.

3136. יוֹצָדָק **Yôwtsâdâq**, *yo-tsaw-dawk'*; a form of 3087; *Jotsadak*, an Isr.:—Jozadak.

3137. יוֹקִים **Yôwqîym**, *yo-keem'*; a form of 3113; *Jokim*, an Isr.:—Jokim.

3138. יוֹרֶה **yôwreh**, *yo-reh'*; act. part. of 3384; *sprinkling;* hence a *sprinkling* (or autumnal showers):—first rain, former [rain].

3139. יוֹרָה **Yôwrâh**, *yo-raw'*; from 3384; *rainy; Jorah*, an Isr.:—Jorah.

3140. יוֹרַי **Yôwray**, *yo-rah'-ee*; from 3384; *rainy; Jorai*, an Isr.:—Jorai.

3141. יוֹרָם **Yôwrâm**, *yo-rawm'*; a form of 3088; *Joram*, the name of three Isr. and one Syrian:—Joram.

3142. יוּשַׁב חֶסֶד **Yûwshab Cheçed**, *yoo-shab' kheh'-sed*; from 7725 and 2617; *kindness will be returned; Jushab-Chesed*, an Isr.:—Jushab-hesed.

3143. יוֹשִׁבְיָה **Yôwshibyâh**, *yo-shib-yaw'*; from 3427 and 3050; *Jehovah will cause to dwell; Joshibjah*, an Isr.:—Josibiah.

3144. יוֹשָׁה **Yôwshâh**, *yo-shaw'*; prob. a form of 3145; *Joshah*, an Isr.:—Joshah.

3145. יוֹשַׁוְיָה **Yôwshavyâh**, *yo-shav-yaw'*; from 3068 and 7737; *Jehovah-set; Joshavjah*, an Isr.:—Joshaviah. Comp. 3144.

3146. יוֹשָׁפָט **Yôwshâphâṭ**, *yo-shaw-fawt'*; a form of 3092; *Joshaphat*, an Isr.:—Joshaphat.

3147. יוֹתָם **Yôwthâm**, *yo-thawm'*; from 3068 and 8535; *Jehovah* (is) *perfect; Jotham*, the name of three Isr.:—Jotham.

3148. יוֹתֵר **yôwthêr**, *yo-thare'*; act. part. of 3498; prop. *redundant;* hence *over and above*, as adj., noun, adv. or conj. [as follows]:—better, more (-over), over, profit.

3149. יְזַוְאֵל **Yᵉzav'êl**, *yez-av-ale'*; from an unused root (mean. to *sprinkle*) and 410; *sprinkled of God; Jezavel*, an Isr.:—Jeziel [*from the marg.*].

3150. יִזִּיָּה **Yizzîyâh**, *yiz-zee-yaw'*; from the same as the first part of 3149 and 3050; *sprinkled of Jah; Jizzijah*, an Isr.:—Jeziah.

3151. יָזִיז **Yâzîyz** *yaw-zeez'*; from the same as 2123; *he will make prominent; Jaziz*, an Isr.:—Jaziz.

3152. יִזְלִיאָה **Yizlîy'ah**, *yiz-lee-aw'*; perh. from an unused root (mean. to *draw up*); *he will draw out; Jizliah*, an Isr.:—Jezliah.

3153. יְזַנְיָה **Yᵉzanyâh**, *yez-an-yaw'*; or

יְזַנְיָהוּ **Yᵉzanyâhûw**, *yez-an-yaw'-hoo*; prob. for 2970; *Jezanjah*, an Isr.:—Jezaniah.

3154. יֶזַע **yezaʻ**, *yeh'-zah*; from an unused root mean to *ooze; sweat*, i.e. (by impl.) a *sweating* dress:—any thing that causeth sweat.

3155. יִזְרָח **Yizrâch**, *yiz-rawkh'*; a var. for 250; a *Jizrach* (i.e. Ezrachite or Zarchite) or desc. of Zerach:—Izrahite.

3156. יִזְרַחְיָה **Yizrachyâh**, *yiz-rakh-yaw'*; from 2224 and 3050; *Jah will shine; Jizrachjah*, the name of two Isr.:—Izrahiah, Jezrahiah.

3157. יִזְרְעֶאל **Yizrᵉʻê'l**, *yiz-reh-ale'*; from 2232 and 410; *God will sow; Jizreël*, the name of two places in Pal. and of two Isr.:—Jezreel.

3158. יִזְרְעֵאלִי **Yizrᵉʻê'lîy**, *yiz-reh-ay-lee'*; patron. from 3157; a *Jizreëlite* or native of Jizreel:—Jezreelite.

3159. יִזְרְעֵאלִית **Yizrᵉʻê'lîyth**, *yiz-reh-ay-leeth'*; fem. of 3158; a *Jezreëlitess*:—Jezreelitess.

3160. יְחֻבָּה **Yᵉchubbâh**, *yekh-oob-baw'*; from 2247; *hidden; Jechubbah*, an Isr.:—Jehubbah.

3161. יָחַד **yâchad**, *yaw-khad'*; a prim. root; to be (or become) *one*:—join, unite.

3162. יַחַד **yachad**, *yakh'-ad*; from 3161; prop. a *unit*, i.e. (adv.) *unitedly*:—alike, at all (once), both, likewise, only, (al-) together, withal.

3163. יַחְדּוֹ **Yachdôw**, *yakh-doe'*; from 3162 with pron. suffix; *his unity*, i.e. (adv.) *together; Jachdo*, an Isr.:—Jahdo.

3164. יַחְדִּיאֵל **Yachdîy'êl**, *yakh-dee-ale'*; from 3162 and 410; *unity of God; Jachdiël*, an Isr.:—Jahdiel.

3165. יֶחְדִּיָּהוּ **Yechdîyâhûw**, *yekh-dee-yaw'-hoo*; from 3162 and 3050; *unity of Jah; Jechdijah*, the name of two Isr.:—Jehdeiah.

יְחַוְאֵל **Yᵉchav'êl**. See 3171.

3166. יַחֲזִיאֵל **Yachăzîy'êl**, *yakh-az-ee-ale'*; from 2372 and 410; *beheld of God; Jachaziël*, the name of five Isr.:—Jahaziel, Jahziel.

3167. יַחְזְיָה **Yachzᵉyâh**, *yakh-zeh-yaw'*; from 2372 and 3050; *Jah will behold; Jachzejah*, an Isr.:—Jahaziah.

3168. יְחֶזְקֵאל **Yᵉchezqê'l**, *yekh-ez-kale'*; from 2388 and 410; *God will strengthen; Jechezkel*, the name of two Isr.:—Ezekiel, Jehezekel.

3169. יְחִזְקִיָּה **Yᵉchizqîyâh**, *yekh-iz-kee-yaw'*; or

יְחִזְקִיָּהוּ **Yᵉchizqîyâhûw**, *yekh-iz-kee-yaw'-hoo*; from 3388 and 3050; *strengthened of Jah; Jechizkijah*, the name of five Isr.:—Hezekiah, Jehizkiah. Comp. 2396.

3170. יַחְזֵרָה **Yachzêrâh**, *yakh-zay-raw'*; from the same as 2386; perh. *protection; Jachzerah*, an Isr.:—Jahzerah.

3171. יְחִיאֵל **Yᵉchîy'êl**, *yekh-ee-ale'*; or (2 Chron. 29 : 14)

יְחַוְאֵל **Yᵉchav'êl**, *yekh-av-ale'*; from 2421 and 410; *God will live; Jechiël* (or *Jechavel*), the name of eight Isr.:—Jehiel.

3172. יְחִיאֵלִי **Yᵉchîy'êlîy**, *yekh-ee-ay-lee'*; patron. from 3171; a *Jechiëlite* or desc. of Jechiel:—Jehieli.

3173. יָחִיד **yâchîyd**, *yaw-kheed'*; from 3161; prop. *united*, i.e. *sole;* by impl. *beloved;* also *lonely;* (fem.) the *life* (as not to be replaced):—darling, desolate, only (child, son), solitary.

3174. יְחִיָּה **Yᵉchîyâh**, *yekh-ee-yaw'*; from 2421 and 3050; *Jah will live; Jechijah*, an Isr.:—Jehiah.

3175. יָחִיל **yâchîyl**, *yaw-kheel'*; from 3176; *expectant*:—should hope.

3176. יָחַל **yâchal**, *yaw-chal'*; a prim. root; to *wait;* by impl. to *be patient, hope*:—(cause to, have, make to) hope, be pained, stay, tarry, trust, wait.

3177. יַחְלְאֵל **Yachlᵉ'êl**, *yakh-leh-ale'*; from 3176 and 410; *expectant of God; Jachleël*, an Isr.:—Jahleel.

3178. יַחְלְאֵלִי **Yachlᵉ'êlîy**, *yakh-leh-ay-lee'*; patron. from 3177; a *Jachleëlite* or desc. of Jachleel:—Jahleelites.

3179. יָחַם **yâcham**, *yaw-kham'*; a prim. root; prob. to *be hot;* fig. to *conceive*:—get heat, be hot, conceive, be warm.

3180. יַחְמוּר **yachmûwr**, *yakh-moor'*; from 2560; a kind of *deer* (from the color; comp. 2543):—fallow deer.

3181. יַחְמַי **Yachmay**, *yakh-mah'-ee*; prob. from 3179; *hot; Jachmai*, an Isr.:—Jahmai.

3182. יָחֵף **yâchêph**, *yaw-khafe'*; from an unused root mean. to *take off the shoes; unsandalled*:—barefoot, being unshod.

3183. יַחְצְאֵל **Yachtsᵉ'êl**, *yakh-tseh-ale'*; from 2673 and 410; *God will allot; Jachtseël*, an Isr.:—Jahzeel. Comp. 3185.

3184. יַחְצְאֵלִי **Yachtsᵉ'êlîy**, *yakh-tseh-ay-lee'*; patron. from 3183; a *Jachtseëlite* (collect.) or desc. of Jachtseel:—Jahzeelites.

3185. יַחְצִיאֵל **Yachtsîy'êl**, *yakh-tsee-ale'*; from 2673 and 410; *allotted of God; Jachtsiël*, an Isr.:—Jahziel. Comp. 3183.

3186. יָחַר **yâchar**, *yaw-khar'*; a prim. root; to *delay*:—tarry longer.

3187. יָחַשׂ **yâchas**, *yaw-khas'*; a prim. root; to *sprout;* used only as denom. from 3188; to *enroll* by pedigree:—(number after, number throughout the) genealogy (to be reckoned), be reckoned by genealogies.

3188. יַחַשׂ **yachas**, *yakh'-as*; from 3187; a *pedigree* or family list (as *growing* spontaneously):—genealogy.

3189. יַחַת **Yachath**, *yakh'-ath*; from 3161; *unity; Jachath*, the name of four Isr.:—Jahath.

3190. יָטַב **yâṭab**, *yaw-tab'*; a prim. root; to be (causat.) *make well*, lit. (*sound, beautiful*) or fig. (*happy, successful, right*):—be accepted, amend, use aright, benefit, be (make) better, seem best, make cheerful, be comely, + be content, diligent (-ly), dress, earnestly, find favour, give, be glad, do (be, make) good ([-ness]), be (make) merry, please (+ well), shew more [kindness], skilfully, × very small, surely, make sweet, thoroughly, tire, trim, very, be (can, deal, entreat, go, have) well [said, seen].

3191. יְטַב **yᵉṭab** (Chald.), *yet-ab'*; corresp. to 3190:—seem good.

3192. יָטְבָה **Yoṭbâh**, *yot-baw'*; from 3190; *pleasantness; Jotbah*, a place in Pal.:—Jotbah.

3193. יָטְבָתָה **Yoṭbâthâh**, *yot-baw'-thaw*; from 3192; *Jotbathah*, a place in the Desert:—Jotbath, Jotbathah.

3194. יֻטָּה **Yuṭṭâh**, *yoot-taw'*; or

יוּטָה **Yûwṭâh**, *yoo-taw'*; from 5186; *extended; Juttah* (or *Jutah*), a place in Pal.:—Juttah.

3195. יְטוּר **Yᵉṭûwr**, *yet-oor'*; prob. from the same as 2905; *encircled* (i.e. inclosed); *Jetur*, a son of Ishmael:—Jetur.

3196. יַיִן **yayin**, *yah'-yin*; from an unused root mean. to *effervesce; wine* (as fermented); by impl. *intoxication*:—banqueting, wine, wine [-bibber].

3197. יַךְ **yak**, *yak*; by err. transc. for 3027; a *hand* or *side*:—[way-] side.

יָכוֹל **yâkôwl**. See 3201.

יְכוֹנְיָה **Yᵉkôwnᵉyâh**. See 3204.

3198. יָכַח **yâkach**, *yaw-kahh'*; a prim. root; to *be right* (i.e. correct); recip. to *argue;* causat. to *decide, justify* or *convict*:—appoint, argue, chasten, convince, correct (-ion), daysman, dispute, judge, maintain, plead, reason (together), rebuke, reprove (-r), surely, in any wise.

יְכִילְיָה **Yᵉkîylᵉyâh**. See 3203.

3199. יָכִין **Yâkîyn**, *yaw-keen'*; from 3559; *he* (or *it*) *will establish; Jakin*, the name of three Isr. and of a temple pillar:—Jachin.

3200. יָכִינִי **Yâkîynîy**, *yaw-kee-nee'*; patron. from 3199; a *Jakinite* (collect.) or desc. of Jakin:—Jachinites.

3201. יָכֹל **yâkôl**, *yaw-kole'*; or (fuller)

יָכוֹל **yâkôwl**, *yaw-kole'*; a prim. root; to *be able*, lit. (*can, could*) or mor. (*may, might*):—be able, any at all (ways), attain, can (away with, [-not]), could, endure, might, overcome, have power, prevail, still, suffer.

3202. יְכֵל **yᵉkêl** (Chald.), *yek-ale'*; or

יְכִיל **yᵉkîyl** (Chald.), *yek-eel'*; corresp. to 3201:—be able, can, couldest, prevail.

3203. יְכָלְיָה **Yᵉkolyâh**, *yek-ol-yaw'*; and

יְכָלְיָהוּ **Yᵉkolyâhûw**, *yek-ol-yaw'-hoo*; or (2 Ch. 26 : 3)

יְכִילְיָה **Yᵉkîylᵉyâh**, *yek-ee-leh-yaw'*; from 3201 and 3050; *Jah will enable; Jekoljah* or *Jekiljah*, an Israelitess:—Jecholiah, Jecoliah.

3204. יְכָנְיָה **Yᵉkonyâh**, *yek-on-yaw'*; and

יְכָנְיָהוּ **Yᵉkonyâhûw**, *yek-on-yaw'-hoo*; or (Jer. 27 : 20)

יְכוֹנְיָה **Yᵉkôwnᵉyâh**, *yek-o-neh-yaw'*; from 3559 and 3050; *Jah will establish; Jekonjah*, a Jewish king:—Jeconiah. Comp. 3659.

3205. יָלַד **yâlad**, *yaw-lad'*; a prim. root; to *bear* young; causat. to *beget;* med. to *act as midwife;* spec. to *show lineage*:—bear, beget, birth ([-day]), born, (make to) bring forth (children, young), bring up, calve, child, come, be delivered (of a child), time of delivery, gender, hatch, labour, (do the office of a) midwife, declare pedigrees, be the son of, (woman in, woman that) travail (-eth, -ing woman).

3206. יֶלֶד **yeled**, *yeh'-led*; from 3205; something *born*, i.e. a *lad* or *offspring*:—boy, child, fruit, son, young man (one).

3207. יַלְדָּה **yaldâh**, *yal-daw'*; fem. of 3206; a *lass*:—damsel, girl.

3208. יַלְדוּת **yaldûwth**, *yal-dooth'*; abstr. from 3206; *boyhood* (or *girlhood*):—childhood, youth.

3209. יִלּוֹד **yillôwd**, *yil-lode'*; pass. from 3205; *born*:—born.

3210. יָלוֹן **Yâlôwn**, *yaw-lone'*; from 3885; *lodging; Jalon*, an Isr.:—Jalon.

3211. יָלִיד **yâlîyd**, *yaw-leed'*; from 3205; *born*:—([home-]) born, child, son.

3212. יָלַךְ **yâlak**, *yaw-lak'*; a prim. root [comp. 1980]; to *walk* (lit. or fig.); causat. to *carry* (in various senses):— × again, away, bear, bring, carry (away), come (away), depart, flow, + follow (-ing), get (away, hence, him), (cause to, make) go (away, -ing, -ne, one's way, out), grow, lead (forth), let down, march, prosper, + pursue, cause to run, spread, take away ([-journey]), vanish, (cause to) walk (-ing), wax, × be weak.

3213. יָלַל **yâlal**, *yaw-lal'*; a prim. root; to *howl* (with a wailing tone) or *yell* (with a boisterous one):—(make to) howl, be howling.

3214. יְלֵל **yᵉlêl**, *yel-ale'*; from 3213; a *howl*;—howling.

3215. יְלָלָה **yᵉlâlâh**, *yel-aw-law'*; fem. of 3214; a *howling*:—howling.

3216. יָלַע **yâlaʻ**, *yaw-lah'*; a prim. root; to *blurt* or utter inconsiderately:—devour.

3217. יַלֶּפֶת **yallepheth**, *yal-leh'-feth*; from an unused root appar. mean. to *stick* or *scrape*; *scurf* or *tetter*:—scabbed.

3218. יֶלֶק **yeleq**, *yeh'-lek*; from an unused root mean. to *lick* up; a *devourer*; spec. the young *locust*:—cankerworm, caterpillar.

3219. יַלְקוּט **yalqûwṭ**, *yal-koot'*; from 3950; a travelling *pouch* (as if for gleanings):—scrip.

3220. יָם **yâm**, *yawm*; from an unused root mean. to *roar*; a *sea* (as breaking in *noisy* surf) or large body of water; spec. (with the art.) the *Mediterranean*; sometimes a large *river*, or an artificial *basin*; locally, the *west*, or (rarely) the *south*:—sea (× -faring man, [-shore]), south, west (-ern, side, -ward).

3221. יָם **yâm** (Chald.), *yawm*; corresp. to 3220:—sea.

3222. יֵם **yêm**, *yame*; from the same as 3117; a *warm* spring:—mule.

3223. יְמוּאֵל **Yᵉmûwʼêl**, *yem-oo-ale'*; from 3117 and 410; *day of God*; *Jemuel*, an Isr.:—Jemuel.

3224. יְמִימָה **Yᵉmîymâh**, *yem-ee-maw'*; perh. from the same as 3117; prop. *warm*, i.e. *affectionate*; hence *dove* [comp. 3123]; *Jemimah*, one of Job's daughters:—Jemimah.

3225. יָמִין **yâmîyn**, *yaw-meen'*; from 3231; the *right* hand or side (leg, eye) of a person or other object (as the *stronger* and more dexterous); locally, the *south*:— + left-handed, right (hand, side), south.

3226. יָמִין **Yâmîyn**, *yaw-meen'*; the same as 3225; *Jamin*, the name of three Isr.:—Jamin. See also 1144.

3227. יְמִינִי **yᵉmîynîy**, *yem-ee-nee'*; for 3225; *right*:—(on the) right (hand).

3228. יְמִינִי **Yᵉmîynîy**, *yem-ee-nee'*; patron. from 3226; a *Jeminite* (collect.) or desc. of Jamin:—Jaminites. See also 1145.

3229. יִמְלָא **Yimlâʼ**, *yeem-law'*; or
יִמְלָה **Yimlâh**, *yim-law'*; from 4390; *full*; *Jimla* or *Jimlah*, an Isr.:—Imla, Imlah.

3230. יַמְלֵךְ **Yamlêk**, *yam-lake'*; from 4427; *he will make king*; *Jamlek*, an Isr.:—Jamlech.

3231. יָמַן **yâman**, *yaw-man'*; a prim. root; to *be* (phys.) *right* (i.e. firm); but used only as denom. from 3225 and transit., to *be right-handed* or *take the right-hand* side:—go (turn) to (on, use) the right hand.

3232. יִמְנָה **Yimnâh**, *yim-naw'*; from 3231; *prosperity* (as betokened by the *right* hand); *Jimnah*, the name of two Isr.; also (with the art.) of the posterity of one of them:—Imna, Imnah, Jimnah, Jimnites.

3233. יְמָנִי **yᵉmânîy**, *yem-aw-nee'*; from 3231; *right* (i.e. at the right hand):—(on the) right (hand).

3234. יִמְנָע **Yimnâʻ**, *yim-naw'*; from 4513; *he will restrain*; *Jimna*, an Isr.:—Imna.

3235. יָמַר **yâmar**, *yaw-mar'*; a prim. root; to *exchange*; by impl. to *change places*:—boast selves, change.

3236. יִמְרָה **Yimrâh**, *yim-raw'*; prob. from 3235; *interchange*; *Jimrah*, an Isr.:—Imrah.

3237. יָמַשׁ **yâmash**, *yaw-mash'*; a prim. root; to *touch*:—feel.

3238. יָנָה **yânâh**, *yaw-naw'*; a prim. root; to *rage* or *be violent*; by impl. to *suppress*, to *maltreat*:—destroy, (thrust out by) oppress (-ing, -ion, -or), proud, vex, do violence.

3239. יָנוֹחַ **Yânôwach**, [*yaw-no'-akh*; or (with enclitic)
יָנוֹחָה **Yânôwchâh**, *yaw-no'-khaw*; from 3240; *quiet*; *Janoăch* or *Janochah*, a place in Pal.:—Janoah, Janohah.

יָנוּם **Yânûm**. See 3241.

3240. יָנַח **yânach**, *yaw-nakh'*; a prim. root; to *deposit*; by impl. to *allow to stay*:—bestow, cast down, lay (down, up), leave (off), let alone (remain), pacify, place, put, set (down), suffer, withdraw, withhold. (The Hiphil forms with the *dagesh* are here referred to, in accordance with the older grammarians; but if any distinction of the kind is to be made, these should rather be referred to 5117, and the others here.)

3241. יָנִים **Yânîym**, *yaw-neem'*; from 5123; *asleep*; *Janim*, a place in Pal.:—Janum [*from the marg.*].

3242. יְנִיקָה **yᵉnîyqâh**, *yen-ee-kaw'*; from 3243; a *sucker* or sapling:—young twig.

3243. יָנַק **yânaq**, *yaw-nak'*; a prim. root; to *suck*; causat. to *give milk*:—milch, nurse (-ing mother), (give, make to) suck (-ing child, -ling).

3244. יַנְשׁוּף **yanshûwph**, *yan-shoof'*; or
יַנְשׁוֹף **yanshôwph**, *yan-shofe'*; appar. from 5398; an unclean (aquatic) bird; prob. the *heron* (perh. from its *blowing* cry, or because the *night*-heron is meant [comp. 5399]):—(great) owl.

3245. יָסַד **yâçad**, *yaw-sad'*; a prim. root; to *set* (lit. or fig.); intens. to *found*; reflex. to *sit* down together, i.e. *settle*, *consult*:—appoint, take counsel, establish, (lay the, lay for a) found (-ation), instruct, lay, ordain, set, × sure.

3246. יְסֻד **yᵉçûd**, *yes-ood'*; from 3245; a *foundation* (fig. i.e. *beginning*):— × began.

3247. יְסוֹד **yᵉçôwd**, *yes-ode'*; from 3245; a *foundation* (lit. or fig.):—bottom, foundation, repairing.

3248. יְסוּדָה **yᵉçûwdâh**, *yes-oo-daw'*; fem. of 3246; a *foundation*:—foundation.

3249. יָסוּר **yâçûwr**, *yaw-soor'*; from 5493; *departing*:—they that depart.

3250. יִסּוֹר **yiççôwr**, *yis-sore'*; from 3256; a *reprover*:—instruct.

3251. יָסַךְ **yâçak**, *yaw-sak'*; a prim. root; to *pour* (intrans.):—be poured.

3252. יִסְכָּה **Yiçkâh**, *yis-kaw'*; from an unused root mean. to *watch*; *observant*; *Jiskah*, sister of Lot:—Iscah.

3253. יִסְמַכְיָהוּ **Yiçmakyâhûw**, *yis-mak-yaw-hoo'*; from 5564 and 3050; *Jah will sustain*; *Jismakjah*, an Isr.:—Ismachiah.

3254. יָסַף **yâçaph**, *yaw-saf'*; a prim. root; to *add* or *augment* (often adv. to *continue* to do a thing):—add, × again, × any more, × cease, × come more, + conceive again, continue, exceed, × further, × gather together, get more, give moreover, × henceforth, increase (more and more), join, × longer (bring, do, make, much, put), × (the, much, yet) more (and more), proceed (further), prolong, put, be [strong-] er, × yet, yield.

3255. יְסַף **yᵉçaph** (Chald.), *yes-af'*; corresp. to 3254:—add.

3256. יָסַר **yâçar**, *yaw-sar'*; a prim. root; to *chastise*, lit. (with blows) or fig. (with words); hence to *instruct*:—bind, chasten, chastise, correct, instruct, punish, reform, reprove, sore, teach.

3257. יָע **yâʻ**, *yaw*; from 3261; a *shovel*:—shovel.

3258. יַעְבֵּץ **Yaʻbêts**, *yah-bates'*; from an unused root prob. mean. to *grieve*; *sorrowful*; *Jabets*, the name of an Isr., and also of a place in Pal.:—Jabez.

3259. יָעַד **yâʻad**, *yaw-ad'*; a prim. root; to *fix* upon (by agreement or appointment); by impl. to *meet* (at a stated time), to *summon* (to trial), to *direct* (in a certain quarter or position), to *engage* (for marriage):—agree, (make an) appoint (-ment, a time), assemble (selves), betroth, gather (selves, together), meet (together), set (a time).

יֶעְדּוֹ **Yeʻdôw**. See 3260.

3260. יֶעְדִּי **Yeʻdîy**, *yed-ee'*; from 3259; *appointed*; *Jedi*, an Isr.:—Iddo [*from the marg.*] See 3035.

3261. יָעָה **yâʻâh**, *yaw-aw'*; a prim. root; appa to *brush* aside:—sweep away.

3262. יְעוּאֵל **Yᵉʻûwʼêl**, *yeh-oo-ale'*; from 3261 ar 410; *carried away of God*; *Jeüel*, t name of four Isr.:—Jehiel, Jeiel, Jeuel. Comp. 327

3263. יְעוּץ **Yᵉʻûwts**, *yeh-oots'*; from 5779; *cou sellor*; *Jeüts*, an Isr.:—Jeuz.

3264. יָעוֹר **yâʻôwr**, *yaw-ore'*; a var. of 3293; *forest*:—wood.

3265. יָעוּר **Yâʻûwr**, *yaw-oor'*; appar. pass. pa of the same as 3293; *wooded*; *Jaü* an Isr.:—Jair [*from the marg.*].

3266. יְעוּשׁ **Yᵉʻûwsh**, *yeh-oosh'*; from 5789; *hast Jeüsh*, the name of an Edomite and four Isr.:—Jehush, Jeush. Comp. 3274.

3267. יָעַז **yâʻaz**, *yaw-az'*; a prim. root; to be *bol* or *obstinate*:—fierce.

3268. יַעֲזִיאֵל **Yaʻăzîyʼêl**, *yah-az-ee-ale'*; fro 3267 and 410; *emboldened of God*; *J aziël*, an Isr.:—Jaaziel.

3269. יַעֲזִיָּהוּ **Yaʻăzîyâhûw**, *yah-az-ee-yau hoo*; from 3267 and 3050; *emboldene of Jah*; *Jaazijah*, an Isr.:—Jaaziah.

3270. יַעֲזֵיר **Yaʻăzêyr**, *yah-az-ayr'*; or
יַעְזֵר **Yaʻzêr**, *yah-zare'*; from 5826; *helpfu Jaazer* or *Jazer*, a place E. of the Jo dan:—Jaazer, Jazer.

3271. יָעַט **yâʻaṭ**, *yaw-at'*; a prim. root; *clothe*:—cover.

3272. יְעַט **yᵉʻaṭ** (Chald.), *yeh-at'*; corresp. to 328 to *counsel*; reflex. to *consult*:—counse lor, consult together.

3273. יְעִיאֵל **Yᵉʻîyʼêl**, *yeh-ee-ale'*; from 3261 ar 410; *carried away of God*; *Jeïel*, th name of six Isr.:—Jeiel, Jehiel. Comp. 3262.

יָעִיר **Yâʻîyr**. See 3265.

3274. יְעִישׁ **Yᵉʻîysh**, *yeh-eesh'*; from 5789; *hasty Jeïsh*, the name of an Edomite and a Isr.:—Jeush [*from the marg.*]. Comp. 3266.

3275. יַעְכָּן **Yaʻkân**, *yah-kawn'*; from the sam as 5912; *troublesome*; *Jakan*, an Isr.:- Jachan.

3276. יָעַל **yâʻal**, *yaw-al'*; a prim. root; prop. t *ascend*; fig. to *be valuable* (obj. *usefu* subj. *benefited*):— × at all, set forward, can do good (be, have) profit (-able).

3277. יָעֵל **yâʻêl**, *yaw-ale'*; from 3276; an *ibex* (a *climbing*):—wild goat.

3278. יָעֵל **Yâʻêl**, *yaw-ale'*; the same as 3277; *Jaë* a Canaanite:—Jael.

3279. יַעֲלָא **Yaʻălâʼ**, *yah-al-aw'*; or
יַעֲלָה **Yaʻălâh**, *yah-al-aw'*; the same a 3280 or direct from 3276; *Jaala* o *Jaalah*, one of the Nethinim:—Jaala, Jaalah.

3280. יַעֲלָה **yaʻălâh**, *yah-al-aw'*; fem. of 3277:- roe.

3281. יַעְלָם **Yaʻlâm**, *yah-lawm'*; from 5956; *oc cult*; *Jalam*, an Edomite:—Jalam.

3282. יַעַן **yaʻan**, *yah'-an*; from an unused roo mean. to *pay attention*; prop. *heed*; by impl. *purpose* (sake or account); used adv. to indi cate the *reason* or cause:—because (that), foras much (+ as), seeing then, + that, + whereas, + why.

3283. יָעֵן **yâʻên**, *yaw-ane'*; from the same a 3282; the *ostrich* (prob. from its *answer ing* cry:—ostrich.

3284. יַעֲנָה **yaʻănâh**, *yah-an-aw'*; fem. of 3283 and mean. the same:— + owl.

3285. יַעֲנַי **Yaʻănay**, *yah-an-ah'ee*; from the same as 3283; *responsive*; *Jaanai*, ar Isr.:—Jaanai.

3286. יָעַף **yâʻaph**, *yaw-af'*; a prim. root; to *tire* (as if from wearisome *flight*):—faint, cause to fly, (be) weary (self).

3287. יָעֵף **yâʻêph**, *yaw-afe'*; from 3286; *fatigued*; fig. *exhausted*:—faint, weary.

3288. יְעָף **yᵉʻâph**, *yeh-awf'*; from 3286; *fatigue* (adv. utterly *exhausted*):—swiftly.

3289. יָעַץ **yâʻats**, *yaw-ats'*; a prim. root; to *advise*; reflex. to *deliberate* or *resolve*:— advertise, take advice, advise (well), consult, (give take) counsel (-lor), determine, devise, guide, pur pose.

3290. יַעֲקֹב **Yaʻăqôb**, *yah-ak-obe'*; from 6117; *heel*-catcher (i.e. supplanter); *Jaakob*, the Israelitish patriarch:—Jacob.

3291. יַעֲקֹבָה **Yaʻăqôbâh**, *yah-ak-o'-baw*; from 3290; *Jaakobah*, an Isr.:—Jaakobah.

3292. יַעֲקָן **Yaʻăqân**, *yah-ak-awn'*; from the same as 6130; *Jaakan*, an Idumæan:—Jaakan. Comp. 1142.

3293. יַעַר **yaʻar**, *yah'-ar*; from an unused root prob. mean. to *thicken* with verdure; a *copse* of bushes; hence a *forest*; hence *honey* in the *comb* (as hived in trees):—[honey-] comb, forest, wood.

3294. יַעְרָה **Yaʻrâh**, *yah-raw'*; a form of 3295; *Jarah*, an Isr.:—Jarah.

3295. יַעֲרָה **yaʻărâh**, *yah-ar-aw'*; fem. of 3293, and mean. the same:—[honey-] comb, forest.

3296. יַעֲרֵי אֹרְגִים **Yaʻărêy ʼOregîym**, *yah-ar-ay' o-reg-eem'*; from the plur. of 3293 and the masc. plur. part. act. of 707; *woods of weavers*; *Jaare-Oregim*, an Isr.:—Jaare-oregim.

3297. יְעָרִים **Yeʻârîym**, *yeh-aw-reem'* plur. of 3293; *forests*; *Jeärim*, a place in Pal.:—Jearim. Comp. 7157.

3298. יַעֲרֶשְׁיָה **Yaʻăreshyâh**, *yah-ar-esh-yaw'*; from an unused root of uncert. signif. and 3050; *Jaareshjah*, an Isr.:—Jaresiah.

3299. יַעֲשׂוּ **Yaʻăsûw**, *yah-as-oo'*; from 6213; *they will do*; *Jaasu*, an Isr.:—Jaasau.

3300. יַעֲשִׂיאֵל **Yaʻăsîyʼêl**, *yah-as-ee-ale'*; from 6213 and 410; *made of God*; *Jaasiel*, an Isr.:—Jaasiel, Jasiel.

3301. יִפְדְּיָה **Yiphdeyâh**, *yif-deh-yaw'*; from 6299 and 3050; *Jah will liberate*; *Jiphdejah*, an Isr.:—Iphedeiah.

3302. יָפָה **yâphâh**, *yaw-faw'*; a prim. root; prop. to *be bright*, i.e. (by impl.) *beautiful*:—be beautiful, be (make self) fair (-r), deck.

3303. יָפֶה **yâpheh**, *yaw-feh'*; from 3302; *beautiful* (lit. or fig.):—+ beautiful, beauty, comely, fair (-est, one), + goodly, pleasant, well.

3304. יְפֵה־פִיָּה **yephêh-phîyâh**, *yef-eh' fee-yaw'*; from 3302 by redupl.; *very beautiful*:—very fair.

3305. יָפוֹ **Yâphô**, *yaw-fo'*; or

יָפוֹא **Yâphôwʼ** (Ezra 3 : 7), *yaw-fo'*; from 3302; *beautiful*; *Japho*, a place in Pal.:—Japha, Joppa.

3306. יָפַח **yâphach**, *yaw-fakh'*; a prim. root; prop. to *breathe* hard, i.e. (by impl.) to *sigh*:—bewail self.

3307. יָפֵחַ **yâphêach**, *yaw-fay'-akh*; from 3306; prop. *puffing*, i.e. (fig.) *meditating*:—such as breathe out.

3308. יֳפִי **yŏphîy**, *yof-ee'*; from 3302; *beauty*:—beauty.

3309. יָפִיעַ **Yâphîyaʻ**, *yaw-fee'-ah*; from 3313; *bright*; *Japhia*, the name of a Canaanite, an Isr., and a place in Pal.:—Japhia.

3310. יַפְלֵט **Yaphlêṭ**, *yaf-late'*; from 6403; *he will deliver*; *Japhlet*, an Isr.:—Japhlet.

3311. יַפְלֵטִי **Yaphlêṭîy**, *yaf-lay-tee'*; patron. from 3310; a *Japhletite* or desc. of Japhlet:—Japhleti.

3312. יְפֻנֶּה **Yephunneh**, *yef-oon-neh'*; from 6437; *he will be prepared*; *Jephunneh*, the name of two Isr.:—Jephunneh.

3313. יָפַע **yâphaʻ**, *yaw-fah'*; a prim. root; to *shine*:—be light, shew self, (cause to) shine (forth).

3314. יִפְעָה **yiphʻâh**, *yif-aw'*; from 3313; *splendor* or (fig.) *beauty*:—brightness.

3315. יֶפֶת **Yepheth**, *yeh'-feth*; from 6601; *expansion*; *Jepheth*, a son of Noah; also his posterity:—Japheth.

3316. יִפְתָּח **Yiphtâch**, *yif-tawkh'*; from 6605; *he will open*; *Jiphtach*, an Isr.; also a place in Pal.:—Jephthah, Jiphtah.

3317. יִפְתַּח־אֵל **Yiphtach-ʼêl**, *yif-tach-ale'*; from 6605 and 410; *God will open*; *Jiphtach-el*, a place in Pal.:—Jiphthah-el.

3318. יָצָא **yâtsâʼ**, *yaw-tsaw'*; a prim. root; to *go* (causat. *bring*) *out*, in a great variety of applications, lit. and fig., direct and proxim.:—× after, appear, × assuredly, bear out, × begotten, break out, bring forth (out, up), carry out, come (abroad, out, thereat, without), + be condemned, depart (-ing, -ure), draw forth, in the end, escape, exact, fail, fall (out), fetch forth (out), get away (forth, hence, out), (able to, cause to, let) go abroad (forth, on, out), going out, grow, have forth (out), issue out, lay (lie) out, lead out, pluck out, proceed, pull out, put away, be risen, × scarce, send with commandment, shoot forth, spread, spring out, stand out, × still, × surely, take forth (out), at any time, × to [and fro], utter.

3319. יְצָא **yetsâʼ** (Chald.), *yets-aw'*; corresp. to 3318:—finish.

3320. יָצַב **yâtsab**, *yaw-tsab'*; a prim. root; to *place* (any thing so as to stay); reflex. to *station*, *offer*, *continue*:—present selves, remaining, resort, set (selves), (be able to, can, with-) stand (fast, forth, -ing, still, up).

3321. יְצֵב **yetsêb** (Chald.), *yets-abe'*; corresp. to 3320; to *be firm*; hence to *speak surely*:—truth.

3322. יָצַג **yâtsag**, *yaw-tsag'*; a prim. root; to *place* permanently:—establish, leave, make, present, put, set, stay.

3323. יִצְהָר **yitshâr**, *yits-hawr'*; from 6671; *oil* (as producing *light*); fig. *anointing*:—+ anointed, oil.

3324. יִצְהָר **Yitshâr**, *yits-hawr'*; the same as 3323; *Jitshar*, an Isr.:—Izhar.

3325. יִצְהָרִי **Yitshârîy**, *yits-haw-ree'*; patron. from 3324; a *Jitsharite* or desc. of Jitshar:—Izeharites, Izharites.

3326. יָצוּעַ **yâtsûwaʻ**, *yaw-tsoo'-ah*; pass. part. of 3331; *spread*, i.e. a *bed*; (arch.) an *extension*, i.e. *wing* or *lean-to* (a single story or collect.):—bed, chamber, couch.

3327. יִצְחָק **Yitschâq**, *yits-khawk'*; from 6711; *laughter* (i.e. *mockery*); *Jitschak* (or Isaac), son of Abraham:—Isaac. Comp. 3446.

3328. יִצְחַר **Yitschar**, *yits-khar'*; from the same as 6713; *he will shine*; *Jitschar*, an Isr.:—and Zehoar [*from the marg.*].

3329. יָצִיא **yâtsîyʼ**, *yaw-tsee'*; from 3318; *issue*, i.e. offspring:—those that came forth.

3330. יַצִּיב **yatstsîyb** (Chald.), *yats-tseeb'*; from 3321; *fixed*, *sure*; concr. *certainty*:—certain (-ty), true, truth.

יָצִיעַ **yâtsîyaʻ**. See 3326.

3331. יָצַע **yâtsaʻ**, *yaw-tsah'*; a prim. root; to *strew* as a surface:—make [one's] bed, × lie, spread.

3332. יָצַק **yâtsaq**, *yaw-tsak'*; a prim. root; prop. to *pour* out (trans. or intrans.); by impl. to *melt* or *cast* as metal; by extens. to *place* firmly, to *stiffen* or grow hard:—cast, cleave fast, be (as) firm, grow, be hard, lay out, molten, overflow, pour (out), run out, set down, stedfast.

3333. יְצֻקָה **yetsûkâh**, *yets-oo-kaw'*; pass. part. fem. of 3332; *poured* out, i.e. *run* into a mould:—when it was cast.

3334. יָצַר **yâtsar**, *yaw-tsar'*; a prim. root; to *press* (intrans.), i.e. *be narrow*; fig. *be in distress*:—be distressed, be narrow, be straitened (in straits), be vexed.

3335. יָצַר **yâtsar**, *yaw-tsar'*; prob. identical with 3334 (through the *squeezing* into shape); ([comp. 3331]); to *mould* into a form; espec. as a *potter*; fig. to *determine* (i.e. form a resolution):—× earthen, fashion, form, frame, make (-r), potter, purpose.

3336. יֵצֶר **yêtser**, *yay'-tser*; from 3335; a *form*; fig. *conception* (i.e. purpose):—frame, thing framed, imagination, mind, work.

3337. יֵצֶר **Yêtser**, *yay'-tser*; the same as 3336; *Jetser*, an Isr.:—Jezer.

3338. יָצֻר **yâtsûr**, *yaw-tsoor'*; pass. part. of 3335; *structure*, i.e. limb or part:—member.

3339. יִצְרִי **Yitsrîy**, *yits-ree'*; from 3335; *formative*; *Jitsri*, an Isr.:—Isri.

3340. יִצְרִי **Yitsrîy**, *yits-ree'*; patron. from 3337; a *Jitsrite* (collect.) or desc. of Jetser:—Jezerites.

3341. יָצַת **yâtsath**, *yaw-tsath'*; a prim. root; to *burn* or *set on fire*; fig. to *desolate*:—burn (up), be desolate, set (on) fire ([fire]), kindle.

3342. יֶקֶב **yeqeb**, *yeh'-keb*; from an unused root mean. to *excavate*; a *trough* (as dug out); spec. a wine-*vat* (whether the lower one, into which the juice drains; or the upper, in which the grapes are crushed):—fats, presses, press-fat, wine (-press).

3343. יְקַבְצְאֵל **Yeqabtseʼêl**, *yek-ab-tseh-ale'*; from 6908 and 410; *God will gather*; *Jekabtseël*, a place in Pal.:—Jekabzeel. Comp. 6909.

3344. יָקַד **yâqad**, *yaw-kad'*; a prim. root; to *burn*:—(be) burn (-ing), × from the hearth, kindle.

3345. יְקַד **yeqad** (Chald.), *yek-ad'*; corresp. to 3344:—burning.

3346. יְקֵדָא **yeqêdâʼ** (Chald.), *yek-ay-daw'*; from 3345; a *conflagration*:—burning.

3347. יָקְדְעָם **Yoqdeʻâm**, *yok-deh-awm'*; from 3344 and 5971; *burning of* (the) *people*; *Jokdeäm*, a place in Pal.:—Jokdeam.

3348. יָקֶה **Yâqeh**, *yaw-keh'*; from an unused root prob. mean. to *obey*; *obedient*; *Jakeh*, a symbolical name (for Solomon):—Jakeh.

3349. יִקָּהָה **yiqqâhâh**, *yik-kaw-haw'*; from the same as 3348; *obedience*:—gathering, to obey.

3350. יְקוֹד **yeqôwd**, *yek-ode'*; from 3344; a *burning*:—burning.

3351. יְקוּם **yeqûwm**, *yek-oom'*; from 6965; prop. *standing* (extant), i.e. by impl. a *living thing*:—(living) substance.

3352. יָקוֹשׁ **yâqôwsh**, *yaw-koshe'*; from 3369; prop. *entangling*; hence a *snarer*:—fowler.

3353. יָקוּשׁ **yâqûwsh**, *yaw-koosh'*; pass. part. of 3369; prop. *entangled*, i.e. by impl. (intrans.) a *snare*, or (trans.) a *snarer*:—fowler, snare.

3354. יְקוּתִיאֵל **Yeqûwthîyʼêl**, *yek-ooth-ee'-ale*; from the same as 3348 and 410; *obedience of God*; *Jekuthiël*, an Isr.:—Jekuthiel.

3355. יָקְטָן **Yoqṭân**, *yok-tawn'*; from 6994; *he will be made little*; *Joktan*, an Arabian patriarch:—Joktan.

3356. יָקִים **Yâqîym**, *yaw-keem'*; from 6965; *he will raise*; *Jakim*, the name of two Isr.:—Jakim. Comp. 3079.

3357. יַקִּיר **yaqqîyr**, *yak-keer'*; from 3365; *precious*:—dear.

3358. יַקִּיר **yaqqîyr** (Chald.) *yak-keer'*; corresp. to 3357:—noble, rare.

3359. יְקַמְיָה **Yeqamyâh**, *yek-am-yaw'*; from 6965 and 3050; *Jah will rise*; *Jekamjah*, the name of two Isr.:—Jekamiah. Comp. 3079.

3360. יְקַמְעָם **Yeqamʻâm**, *yek-am'-awm*; from 6965 and 5971; (the) *people will rise*; *Jekamam*, an Isr.:—Jekameam. Comp. 3079, 3361.

3361. יָקְמְעָם **Yoqmeʻâm**, *yok-meh-awm'*; from 6965 and 5971; (the) *people will be raised*; *Jokmeäm*, a place in Pal.:—Jokmeam. Comp. 3360, 3362.

3362. יָקְנְעָם **Yoqneʻâm**, *yok-neh-awm'*; from 6969 and 5971; (the) *people will be lamented*; *Jokneäm*, a place in Pal.:—Jokneam.

3363. יָקַע **yâqaʻ**, *yaw-kah'*; a prim. root; prop. to *sever* oneself, i.e. (by impl.) to *be dislocated*; fig. to *abandon*; causat. to *impale* (and thus allow to drop to pieces by *rotting*):—be alienated, depart, hang (up), be out of joint.

3364. יָקַץ **yâqats**, *yaw-kats'*; a prim. root; to *awake* (intrans.):—(be) awake (-d).

יָקַף **yâqaph**. See 5362.

3365. יָקַר **yâqar**, *yaw-kar'*; a prim. root; prop. appar. to *be heavy*, i.e. (fig.) *valuable*; causat. to *make rare* (fig. to *inhibit*):—be (make) precious, be prized, be set by, withdraw.

3366. יְקָר **yeqâr**, *yek-awr'*; from 3365; *value*, i.e. (concr.) *wealth*; abstr. *costliness*, *dignity*:—honour, precious (things), price.

3367. יְקָר **yeqâr** (Chald.), *yek-awr';* corresp. to 3366:—glory, honour.

3368. יָקָר **yâqâr**, *yaw-kawr';* from 3365; *valuable* (obj. or subj.):—brightness, clear, costly, excellent, fat, honourable women, precious, reputation.

3369. יָקֹשׁ **yâqôsh**, *yaw-koshe';* a prim. root; to *ensnare* (lit. or fig.):—fowler (lay a) snare.

3370. יָקְשָׁן **Yoqshân**, *yok-shawn';* from 3369; *insidious; Jokshan*, an Arabian patriarch:—Jokshan.

3371. יָקְתְאֵל **Yoqtheʼêl**, *yok-theh-ale';* prob. from the same as 3348 and 410; *veneration of God* [comp. 3354]; *Joktheël*, the name of a place in Pal., and of one in Idumæa:—Joktheel.

יָרָא **yârâʼ**. See 3384.

3372. יָרֵא **yârêʼ**, *yaw-ray';* a prim. root; to *fear;* mor. to *revere;* caus. to *frighten:*—affright, be (make) afraid, dread (-ful), (put in) fear (-ful, -fully, -ing). (be had in) reverence (-end), × see, terrible (act, -ness, thing).

3373. יָרֵא **yârêʼ**, *yaw-ray';* from 3372; *fearing;* mor. *reverent:*—afraid, fear (-ful).

3374. יִרְאָה **yirʼâh**, *yir-aw';* fem. of 3373; *fear* (also used as infin.); mor. *reverence:*—× dreadful, × exceedingly, fear (-fulness).

3375. יִרְאוֹן **Yirôwn**, *yir-ohn';* from 3372; *fearfulness; Jiron*, a place in Pal.:—Iron.

3376. יִרְאִיָּיה **Yirʼîyâyh**, *yir-ee-yaw';* from 3373 and 3050; *fearful of Jah; Jirijah*, an Isr.:—Irijah.

3377. יָרֵב **Yârêb**, *yaw-rabe';* from 7378; *he will contend; Jareb*, a symbolical name for Assyria:—Jareb. Comp. 3402.

3378. יְרֻבַּעַל **Yerubbaʻal**, *yer-oob-bah'-al;* from 7378 and 1168; *Baal will contend; Jerubbaal*, a symbol. name of Gideon:—Jerubbaal.

3379. יָרָבְעָם **Yârobʻâm**, *yaw-rob-awm';* from 7378 and 5971; (the) *people will contend; Jarobam*, the name of two Isr. kings:—Jeroboam.

3380. יְרֻבֶּשֶׁת **Yerubbesheth**, *yer-oob-beh'-sheth;* from 7378 and 1322; *shame* (i.e. the idol) *will contend; Jerubbesheth*, a symbol. name for Gideon:—Jerubbesheth.

3381. יָרַד **yârad**, *yaw-rad';* a prim. root; to *descend* (lit. to *go downwards;* or conventionally to a lower region, as the shore, a boundary, the enemy, etc.; or fig. to *fall*); causat. to *bring down* (in all the above applications):—× abundantly, bring down, carry down, cast down, (cause to) come (-ing) down, fall (down), get down, go (-ing) down (-ward), hang down, × indeed, let down, light (down), put down (off), (cause to, let) run down, sink, subdue, take down.

3382. יֶרֶד **Yered**, *yeh'-red;* from 3381; a *descent; Jered*, the name of an antediluvian, and of an Isr.:—Jared.

3383. יַרְדֵּן **Yardên**, *yar-dane';* from 3381; a *descender; Jarden*, the principal river of Pal.:—Jordan.

3384. יָרָה **yârâh**, *yaw-raw';* or (2 Chr. 26 : 15)

יָרָא **yârâʼ**, *yaw-raw';* a prim. root; prop. to *flow* as water (i.e. to *rain*); trans. to *lay* or *throw* (espec. an arrow, i.e. to *shoot*); fig. to *point* out (as if by *aiming* the finger), to *teach:*—(+) archer, cast, direct, inform, instruct, lay, shew, shoot, teach (-er, -ing), through.

3385. יְרוּאֵל **Yerûwʼêl**, *yer-oo-ale';* from 3384 and 410: *founded of God; Jeruel*, a place in Pal.:—Jeruel

3386. יָרוֹחַ **Yârôwach**, *yaw-ro'-akh;* perh. denom. from 3394; (born at the) *new moon; Jaroäch*, an Isr.:—Jaroah.

3387. יָרוֹק **yârôwq**, *yaw-roke';* from 3417; *green*, i.e. an herb:—green thing.

3388. יְרוּשָׁא **Yerûwshâʼ**, *yer-oo-shaw';* or

יְרוּשָׁה **Yerûwshâh**, *yer-oo-shaw';* fem. pass. part. of 3423; *possessed; Jerusha* or *Jerushah*, an Israelitess:—Jerusha, Jerushah.

3389. יְרוּשָׁלַםִ **Yerûwshâlaim**, *yer-oo-shaw-lah'-im;* rarely

יְרוּשָׁלַיִם **Yerûwshâlayim**, *yer-oo-shaw-lah'-yim;* a dual (in allusion to its two main hills [the true pointing, at least of the former reading, seems to be that of 3390]); prob. from (the pass. part. of) 3384 and 7999; *founded peaceful; Jerushalaïm* or *Jerushalem*, the capital city of Pal.:—Jerusalem.

3390. יְרוּשְׁלֵם **Yerûwshâlêm** (Chald.), *yer-oo-shaw-lame';* corresp. to 3389:—Jerusalem.

3391. יֶרַח **yerach**, *yeh'-rakh;* from an unused root of uncert. signif.; a *lunation*, i.e. *month:*—month, moon.

3392. יֶרַח **Yerach**, *yeh'-rakh;* the same as 3391; *Jerach*, an Arabian patriarch:—Jerah.

3393. יְרַח **yerach** (Chald.), *yeh-rakh';* corresp. to 3391; a *month:*—month.

3394. יָרֵחַ **yârêach**, *yaw-ray'-akh;* from the same as 3391; the *moon:*—moon.

יְרֵחוֹ **Yerêchôw**. See 3405.

3395. יְרֹחָם **Yerôchâm**, *yer-o-khawm';* from 7355; *compassionate; Jerocham*, the name of seven or eight Isr.:—Jeroham.

3396. יְרַחְמְאֵל **Yerachmeʼêl**, *yer-akh-meh-ale';* from 7355 and 410; *God will compassionate; Jerachmeël*, the name of three Isr.:—Jerahmeel.

3397. יְרַחְמְאֵלִי **Yerachmeʼêlîy**, *yer-akh-meh-ay-lee';* patron. from 3396; a *Jerachmeëlite* or desc. of Jerachmeel:—Jerahmeelites.

3398. יַרְחָע **Yarchâʻ**, *yar-khaw';* prob. of Eg. or.; *Jarcha*, an Eg.:—Jarha.

3399. יָרַט **yâraṭ**, *yaw-rat';* a prim. root; to *precipitate* or *hurl* (*rush*) headlong; (intrans.) to *be rash:*—be perverse, turn over.

3400. יְרִיאֵל **Yerîyʼêl**, *yer-ee-ale';* from 3384 and 410; *thrown of God; Jeriël*, an Isr.:—Jeriel. Comp. 3385.

3401. יָרִיב **yârîyb**, *yaw-rebe';* from 7378; lit. *he will contend;* prop. adj. *contentious;* used as noun, an *adversary:*—that contend (-eth), that strive.

3402. יָרִיב **Yârîyb**, *yaw-rebe';* the same as 3401; *Jarib*, the name of three Isr.:—Jarib.

3403. יְרִיבַי **Yerîybay**, *yer-eeb-ah'ee;* from 3401; *contentious; Jeribai*, an Isr.:—Jeribai.

3404. יְרִיָּה **Yerîyâh**, *yer-ee-yaw';* or

יְרִיָּהוּ **Yerîyâhûw**, *yer-ee-yaw'-hoo;* from 3384 and 3050; *Jah will throw; Jerijah*, an Isr.:—Jeriah, Jerijah.

3405. יְרִיחוֹ **Yerîychôw**, *yer-ee-kho';* or

יְרֵחוֹ **Yerêchôw** *yer-ay-kho';* or var. (1 Kings 16 : 34)

יְרִיחֹה **Yerîychôh**, *yer-ee-kho';* perh. from 3394; *its month;* or else from 7306; *fragrant; Jericho* or *Jerecho*, a place in Pal.:—Jericho.

3406. יְרִימוֹת **Yerîymôwth**, *yer-ee-mohth';* or

יְרֵימוֹת **Yerêymôwth**, *yer-ay-mohth';* or

יְרֵמוֹת **Yerêmôwth**, *yer-ay-mohth';* fem. plur. from 7311; *elevations; Jerimoth* or *Jeremoth*, the name of twelve Isr.:—Jeremoth, Jerimoth, and Ramoth [*from the marg.*].

3407. יְרִיעָה **yerîyʻâh**, *yer-ee-aw';* from 3415; a *hanging* (as *tremulous*):—curtain.

3408. יְרִיעוֹת **Yerîyʻôwth**, *yer-ee-ohth';* plur. of 3407; *curtains; Jerioth*, an Israelitess:—Jerioth.

3409. יָרֵךְ **yârêk**, *yaw-rake';* from an unused root mean. to *be soft;* the *thigh* (from its fleshy *softness*); by euphem. the *generative parts;* fig. a *shank, flank, side:*—× body, loins, shaft, side, thigh.

3410. יַרְכָא **yarkâʼ** (Chald.), *yar-kaw';* corresp. to 3411; a *thigh:*—thigh.

3411. יְרֵכָה **yerêkâh**, *yer-ay-kaw';* fem. of 3409; prop. the *flank;* but used only fig., the *rear* or *recess:*—border, coast, part, quarter, side.

3412. יַרְמוּת **Yarmûwth**, *yar-mooth';* from 7311; *elevation; Jarmuth*, the name of two places in Pal.:—Jarmuth.

יְרֵמוֹת **Yerêmôwth**. See 3406.

3413. יְרֵמַי **Yerêmay**, *yer-ay-mah'ee;* from 7311; *elevated; Jeremai*, an Isr.:—Jeremai.

3414. יִרְמְיָה **Yirmeyâh**, *yir-meh-yaw';* or

יִרְמְיָהוּ **Yirmeyâhûw**, *yir-meh-yaw'-hoo;* from 7311 and 3050; *Jah will rise; Jirmejah*, the name of eight or nine Isr.:—Jeremiah.

3415. יָרַע **yâraʻ**, *yaw-rah';* a prim. root; prop. to *be broken* up (with any violent action), i.e. (fig.) to *fear:*—be grievous [*only Isa. 15 : 4; the rest belong to 7489*].

3416. יִרְפְּאֵל **Yirpeʼêl**, *yir-peh-ale';* from 7495 and 410; *God will heal; Jirpeël*, a place in Pal.:—Irpeel.

3417. יָרַק **yâraq**, *yaw-rak';* a prim. root; to *spit:*—× but, spit.

3418. יֶרֶק **yereq**, *yeh'-rek;* from 3417 (in the sense of *vacuity* of color); prop. *pallor*, i.e. hence the yellowish *green* of young and sickly vegetation; concr. *verdure*, i.e. grass or vegetation:—grass, green (thing).

3419. יָרָק **yârâq**, *yaw-rawk';* from the same as 3418; prop. *green;* concr. a *vegetable:*—green, herbs.

יַרְקוֹן **Yarqôwn**. See 4313.

3420. יֵרָקוֹן **yêrâqôwn**, *yay-raw-kone';* from 3418; *paleness*, whether of persons (from fright), or of plants (from drought):—mildew, paleness.

3421. יָרְקְעָם **Yorqeʻâm**, *yor-keh-awm';* from 7324 and 5971; *people will be poured forth; Jorkeäm*, a place in Pal.:—Jorkeam.

3422. יְרַקְרַק **yeraqraq**, *yer-ak-rak';* from the same as 3418; *yellowishness:*—greenish, yellow.

3423. יָרַשׁ **yârash**, *yaw-rash';* or

יָרֵשׁ **yârêsh**, *yaw-raysh';* a prim. root; to *occupy* (by *driving* out previous tenants, and *possessing* in their place); by impl. to *seize*, to *rob*, to *inherit;* also to *expel*, to *impoverish*, to *ruin:*—cast out, consume, destroy, disinherit, dispossess, drive (-ing) out, enjoy, expel, × without fail, (give to, leave for) inherit (-ance, -or), + magistrate, be (make) poor, come to poverty, (give to, make to) possess, get (have) in (take) possession, seize upon, succeed, × utterly.

3424. יְרֵשָׁה **yerêshâh**, *yer-ay-shaw';* from 3423; *occupancy:*—possession.

3425. יְרֻשָּׁה **yerushshâh**, *yer-oosh-shaw';* from 3423; something *occupied;* a *conquest;* also a *patrimony:*—heritage, inheritance, possession.

3426. יֵשׁ **yêsh**, *yaysh;* perh. from an unused root mean. to *stand* out, or *exist; entity;* used adv. or as a copula for the substantive verb (1961); there *is* or *are* (or any other form of the verb to *be*, as may suit the connection):—(there) are, (he, it, shall, there, there may, there shall, there should) be, thou do, had, hast, (which) hath, (I, shalt, that) have, (he, it, there) is, substance, it (there) was, (there) were, ye will, thou wilt, wouldest.

3427. יָשַׁב **yâshab**, *yaw-shab';* a prim. root; prop. to *sit* down (spec. as judge. in ambush, in quiet); by impl. to *dwell*, to *remain;* causat. to *settle*, to *marry:*—(make to) abide (-ing), continue, (cause to, make to) dwell (-ing), ease self, endure, establish, × fail, habitation, haunt, (make to) inhabit (-ant), make to keep [house], lurking, × marry (-ing), (bring again to) place, remain, return, seat, set (-tle), (down-) sit (-down, still, -ting down, -ting [place] -uate), take, tarry.

3428. יֶשֶׁבְאָב **Yeshebʼâb**, *yeh-sheb-awb';* from 3427 and 1; *seat of* (his) *father; Jeshebab*, an Isr.:—Jeshebeab.

3429. יֹשֵׁב בַּשֶּׁבֶת **Yôshêb bash-Shebeth**, *yo-shabe' bash-sheh'-beth;* from the act. part. of 3427 and 7674, with a prep. and the art. interposed; *sitting in the seat; Josheb-bash-Shebeth*, an Isr.:—that sat in the seat.

3430. יֹשְׁבוֹ בְּנֹב **Yishbôw beNôb**, *yish-bo' beh-nobe;* from 3427 and 5011, with a pron. suffix and a prep. interposed; *his dwelling (is) in Nob; Jishbo-be-Nob,* a Philistine:—Ishbi-benob [*from the marg.*].

3431. יִשְׁבַּח **Yishbach**, *yish-bakh';* from 7623; *he will praise; Jishbach,* an Isr.:—Ishbah.

3432. יָשֻׁבִי **Yâshûbîy**, *yaw-shoo-bee';* patron. from 3437; a *Jashubite,* or desc. of Jashub:—Jashubites.

3433. יָשֻׁבִי לֶחֶם **Yâshûbîy Lechem**, *yaw-shoo'-bee leh'-khem;* from 7725 and 3899; *returner of bread; Jashubi-Lechem,* an Isr.:—Jashubi-lehem. [Prob. the text should be pointed יֹשְׁבֵי לֶחֶם **Yôshebêy Lechem**, *yo-sheh-bay' leh'-khem,* and rendered "(they were) inhabitants of Lechem," i.e. of Beth-lehem (by contraction). Comp. 3902.]

3434. יָשָׁבְעָם **Yâshobʻâm**, *yaw-shob-awm';* from 7725 and 5971; *people will return; Jashobam,* the name of two or three Isr.:—Jashobeam.

3435. יִשְׁבָּק **Yishbâq**, *yish-bawk';* from an unused root corresp. to 7662; *he will leave; Jishbak,* a son of Abraham:—Ishbak.

3436. יָשְׁבְּקָשָׁה **Yoshbeqâshâh**, *yosh-bek-aw-shaw';* from 3427 and 7186; a *hard seat; Joshbekashah,* an Isr.:—Joshbekashah.

3437. יָשׁוּב **Yâshûwb**, *yaw-shoob';* or יָשִׁיב **Yâshîyb**, *yaw-sheeb';* from 7725; *he will return; Jashub,* the name of two Isr.:—Jashub.

3438. יִשְׁוָה **Yishvâh**, *yish-vaw';* from 7737; *he will level; Jishvah,* an Isr.:—Ishvah, Isvah.

3439. יְשׁוֹחָיָה **Yeshôwchâyâh**, *yesh-o-khaw-yaw';* from the same as 3445 and 3050; *Jah will empty; Jeshochajah,* an Isr.:—Jeshoaiah.

3440. יִשְׁוִי **Yishvîy**, *yish-vee';* from 7737; *level; Jishvi,* the name of two Isr.:—Ishuai, Ishvi, Isui, Jesui.

3441. יִשְׁוִי **Yishvîy**, *yish-vee';* patron. from 3440; a *Jishvite* (collect.) or desc. of Jishvi:—Jesuites.

3442. יֵשׁוּעַ **Yêshûwaʻ**, *yay-shoo'-ah;* for 3091; *he will save; Jeshua,* the name of ten Isr., also of a place in Pal.:—Jeshua.

3443. יֵשׁוּעַ **Yêshûwaʻ** (Chald.), *yay-shoo'-ah;* corresp. to 3442:—Jeshua.

3444. יְשׁוּעָה **yeshûwʻâh**, *yesh-oo'-aw;* fem. pass. part. of 3467; something *saved,* i.e. (abstr.) *deliverance;* hence *aid, victory, prosperity:*—deliverance, health, help (-ing), salvation, save, saving (health), welfare.

3445. יֶשַׁח **yeshach**, *yeh'-shakh;* from an unused root mean. to *gape* (as the empty stomach); *hunger:*—casting down.

3446. יִשְׂחָק **Yischâq**, *yis-khawk';* from 7831; *he will laugh; Jischak,* the heir of Abraham:—Isaac. Comp. 3327.

3447. יָשַׁט **yâshaṭ**, *yaw-shat';* a prim. root; to *extend:*—hold out.

3448. יִשַׁי **Yîshay**, *yee-shah'ee;* by Chald. אִישַׁי **'Îyshay**, *ee-shah'ee;* from the same as 3426; *extant; Jishai,* David's father:—Jesse.

יָשִׁיב **Yâshîyb.** See 3437.

3449. יִשִּׁיָּה **Yishshîyâh**, *yish-shee-yaw';* or יִשִּׁיָּהוּ **Yishshîyâhûw**, *yish-shee-yaw'-hoo;* from 5383 and 3050; *Jah will lend; Jishshijah,* the name of five Isr.:—Ishiah, Isshiah, Ishijah, Jesiah.

3450. יְשִׂימָאֵל **Yesîymâ'êl**, *yes-eem-aw-ale';* from 7760 and 410; *God will place; Jesimaël,* an Isr.:—Jesimael.

3451. יְשִׁימָה **yeshîymâh**, *yesh-ee-maw';* from 3456; *desolation:*—let death seize [*from the marg.*].

3452. יְשִׁימוֹן **yeshîymôwn**, *yesh-ee-mone';* from 3456; a *desolation:*—desert, Jeshimon, solitary, wilderness.

יְשִׁימוֹת **yeshîymôwth.** See 1020, 3451.

3453. יָשִׁישׁ **yâshîysh**, *yaw-sheesh';* from 3486; an *old* man:—(very) aged (man), ancient, very old.

3454. יְשִׁישַׁי **Yeshîyshay**, *yesh-ee-shah'ee;* from 3453; *aged; Jeshishai,* an Isr.:—Jeshishai.

3455. יָשַׂם **yâsam**, *yaw-sam';* a prim root; to *place;* intrans. to *be placed:*—be put (set).

3456. יָשַׁם **yâsham**, *yaw-sham';* a prim. root; to *lie waste:*—be desolate.

3457. יִשְׁמָא **Yishmâ'**, *yish-maw';* from 3456; *desolate; Jishma,* an Isr.:—Ishma.

3458. יִשְׁמָעֵאל **Yishmâʻê'l**, *yish-maw-ale';* from 8085 and 410; *God will hear; Jishmaël,* the name of Abraham's oldest son, and of five Isr.:—Ishmael.

3459. יִשְׁמָעֵאלִי **Yishmâʻê'lîy**, *yish-maw-ay-lee';* patron. from 3458; a *Jishmaëlite* or desc. of Jishmael:—Ishmaelite.

3460. יִשְׁמַעְיָה **Yishmaʻyâh**, *yish-mah-yaw';* or יִשְׁמַעְיָהוּ **Yishmaʻyâhûw**, *yish-mah-yaw'-hoo;* from 8085 and 3050; *Jah will hear; Jishmajah,* the name of two Isr.:—Ishmaiah.

3461. יִשְׁמְרַי **Yishmeray**, *yish-mer-ah'ee;* from 8104; *preservative; Jishmerai,* an Isr.:—Ishmerai.

3462. יָשֵׁן **yâshên**, *yaw-shane';* a prim. root; prop. to *be slack* or *languid,* i.e. (by impl.) *sleep* (fig. to *die*); also to *grow old, stale* or *inveterate:*—old (store), remain long, (make to) sleep.

3463. יָשֵׁן **yâshên**, *yaw-shane';* from 3462; *sleepy:*—asleep, (one out of) sleep (-eth, -ing), slept.

3464. יָשֵׁן **Yâshên**, *yaw-shane';* the same as 3463; *Jashen,* an Isr.:—Jashen.

3465. יָשָׁן **yâshân**, *yaw-shawn';* from 3462; *old:*—old.

3466. יְשָׁנָה **Yeshânâh**, *yesh-aw-naw';* fem. of 3465; *Jeshanah,* a place in Pal.:—Jeshanah.

3467. יָשַׁע **yâshaʻ**, *yaw-shah';* a prim. root; prop. to *be open, wide* or *free,* i.e. (by impl.) to *be safe;* causat. to *free* or *succor:*— × at all, avenging, defend, deliver (-er), help, preserve, rescue, be safe, bring (having) salvation, save (-iour), get victory.

3468. יֶשַׁע **yeshaʻ**, *yeh'-shah;* or יֵשַׁע **yêshaʻ**, *yay'-shah;* from 3467; *liberty, deliverance, prosperity:*—safety, salvation, saving.

3469. יִשְׁעִי **Yishʻîy**, *yish-ee';* from 3467; *saving; Jishi,* the name of four Isr.:—Ishi.

3470. יְשַׁעְיָה **Yeshaʻyâh**, *yesh-ah-yaw';* or יְשַׁעְיָהוּ **Yeshaʻyâhûw**, *yesh-ah-yaw'-hoo;* from 3467 and 3050; *Jah has saved; Jeshajah,* the name of seven Isr.:—Isaiah, Jesaiah, Jeshaiah.

3471. יָשְׁפֵה **yâshephêh**, *yaw-shef-ay';* from an unused root mean. to *polish;* a gem supposed to be *jasper* (from the resemblance in name):—jasper.

3472. יִשְׁפָּה **Yishpâh**, *yish-paw';* perh. from 8192; *he will scratch; Jishpah,* an Isr.:—Ispah.

3473. יִשְׁפָּן **Yishpân**, *yish-pawn';* prob. from the same as 8227; *he will hide; Jishpan,* an Isr.:—Ishpan.

3474. יָשַׁר **yâshar**, *yaw-shar';* a prim. root; to *be straight* or *even;* fig. to *be* (causat. to *make*) *right, pleasant, prosperous:*—direct, fit, seem good (meet), + please (well), be (esteem, go) right (on), bring (look, make, take the) straight (way), be upright (-ly).

3475. יֵשֶׁר **Yêsher**, *yay'-sher;* from 3474; the *right; Jesher,* an Isr.:—Jesher.

3476. יֹשֶׁר **yôsher**, *yo'-sher;* from 3474; the *right:*—equity, meet, right, upright (-ness).

3477. יָשָׁר **yâshâr**, *yaw-shawr';* from 3474; *straight* (lit. or fig.):—convenient, equity, Jasher, just, meet (-est), + pleased well right (-eous), straight, (most) upright (-ly, -ness).

3478. יִשְׂרָאֵל **Yisrâ'êl**, *yis-raw-ale';* from 8280 and 410; *he will rule as God; Jisraël,* a symbolical name of Jacob; also (typically) of his posterity:—Israel.

3479. יִשְׂרָאֵל **Yisrâ'êl** (Chald.), *yis-raw-ale'* corresp. to 3478:—Israel.

3480. יְשַׂרְאֵלָה **Yesar'êlâh**, *yes-ar-ale'-aw;* by var. from 3477 and 410 with directive enclitic; *right towards God; Jesarelah,* an Isr.:—Jesharelah. Comp. 841.

3481. יִשְׂרְאֵלִי **Yisre'êlîy**, *yis-reh-ay-lee';* patron. from 3478; a *Jisreëlite* or desc. of Jisrael:—of Israel, Israelite.

3482. יִשְׂרְאֵלִית **Yisre'êlîyth**, *yis-reh-ay-leeth';* fem. of 3481; a *Jisreëlitess* or female desc. of Jisrael:—Israelitish.

3483. יִשְׁרָה **yishrâh**, *yish-raw';* fem. of 3477; *rectitude:*—uprightness.

3484. יְשֻׁרוּן **Yeshûrûwn**, *yesh-oo-roon';* from 3474; *upright; Jeshurun,* a symbol. name for Israel:—Jeshurun.

3485. יִשָּׂשכָר **Yissâskâr**, *yis-saw-kawr'* (strictly *yis-saws-kawr'*); from 5375 and 7939; *he will bring a reward; Jissaskar,* a son of Jacob:—Issachar.

3486. יָשֵׁשׁ **yâshêsh**, *yaw-shaysh';* from an unused root mean. to *blanch; gray-haired,* i.e. an *aged* man:—stoop for age.

3487. יַת **yath** (Chald.), *yath;* corresp. to 853; a sign of the object of a verb: + whom.

3488. יְתִב **yethîyb** (Chald.), *yeth-eeb';* corresp. to 3427; to *sit* or *dwell:*—dwell, (be) set, sit.

3489. יָתֵד **yâthêd**, *yaw-thade';* from an unused root mean. to *pin* through or *fast;* a *peg:*—nail, paddle, pin, stake.

3490. יָתוֹם **yâthôwm**, *yaw-thome';* from an unused root mean. to *be lonely;* a *bereaved* person:—fatherless (child), orphan.

3491. יָתוּר **yâthûwr**, *yaw-thoor';* pass. part. of 3498; prop. what is *left,* i.e. (by impl.) a *gleaning:*—range.

3492. יַתִּיר **Yattîyr**, *yat-teer';* from 3498; *redundant; Jattir,* a place in Pal.:—Jattir.

3493. יַתִּיר **yattîyr** (Chald.) *yat-teer';* corresp. to 3492; *preeminent;* adv. *very:*—exceeding (-ly), excellent.

3494. יִתְלָה **Yithlâh**, *yith-law';* prob. from 8518; it *will hang,* i.e. be high; *Jithlah,* a place in Pal.:—Jethlah.

3495. יִתְמָה **Yithmâh**, *yith-maw';* from the same as 3490; *orphanage; Jithmah,* an Isr.:—Ithmah.

3496. יַתְנִיאֵל **Yathnîy'êl**, *yath-nee-ale';* from an unused root mean. to *endure,* and 410; *continued of God; Jathniël,* an Isr.:—Jathniel.

3497. יִתְנָן **Yithnân**, *yith-nawn';* from the same as 8577; *extensive; Jithnan,* a place in Pal.:—Ithnan.

3498. יָתַר **yâthar**, *yaw-thar';* a prim. root; to *jut* over or *exceed;* by impl. to *excel;* (intrans.) to *remain* or *be left;* causat. to *leave, cause to abound, preserve:*—excel, leave (a remnant), left behind, too much, make plenteous, preserve, (be, let) remain (-der, -ing, -nant), reserve, residue, rest.

3499. יֶתֶר **yether**, *yeh'-ther;* from 3498; prop. an *overhanging,* i.e. (by impl.) an *excess, superiority, remainder;* also a small *rope* (as hanging free):— + abundant, cord, exceeding, excellency (-ent), what they leave, that hath left, plentifully, remnant, residue, rest, string, with.

3500. יֶתֶר **Yether**, *yeh'-ther;* the same as 3499 *Jether,* the name of five or six Isr. and of one Midianite:—Jether, Jethro. Comp. 3503.

3501. יִתְרָא **Yithrâ'**, *yith-raw';* by var. for 3502; *Jithra,* an Isr. (or Ishmaelite):—Ithra.

3502. יִתְרָה **yithrâh**, *yith-raw'*; fem. of 3499; prop. *excellence*, i.e. (by impl.) *wealth*:—abundance, riches.

3503. יִתְרוֹ **Yithrôw**, *yith-ro'*; from 3499 with pron. suffix; *his excellence; Jethro*, Moses' father-in-law:—Jethro. Comp. 3500.

3504. יִתְרוֹן **yithrôwn**, *yith-rone'*; from 3498; *preeminence, gain*:—better, excellency (-leth), profit (-able).

3505. יִתְרִי **Yithrîy**, *yith-ree'*; patron. from 3500; a *Jithrite* or desc. of Jether:—Ithrite.

3506. יִתְרָן **Yithrân**, *yith-rawn'*; from 3498; *excellent; Jithran*, the name of an Edomite and of an Isr.:—Ithran.

3507. יִתְרְעָם **Yithreʿâm**, *yith-reh-awm'*; from 3499 and 5971; *excellence of people; Jithreäm*, a son of David:—Ithream.

3508. יֹתֶרֶת **yôthereth**, *yo-theh'-reth*; fem. act. part. of 3498; the *lobe* or *flap* of the liver (as if redundant or outhanging):—caul.

3509. יְתֵת **Yethêth**, *yeh-thayth'*; of uncert. der.; *Jetheth*, an Edomite:—Jetheth.

כ

3510. כָּאַב **kâʼab**, *kaw-ab'*; a prim. root; prop. to feel *pain*; by impl. to *grieve*; fig. to *spoil*:—grieving, mar, have pain, make sad (sore), (be) sorrowful.

3511. כְּאֵב **keʼêb**, *keh-abe'*; from 3510; *suffering* (phys. or mental), *adversity*:—grief, pain, sorrow.

3512. כָּאָה **kâʼâh**, *kaw-aw'*; a prim. root; to *despond*: causat. to *deject*:—broken, be grieved, make sad.

3513. כָּבַד **kâbad**, *kaw-bad'*; or

כָּבֵד **kâbêd**, *kaw-bade'*; a prim. root; to *be heavy*, i.e. in a bad sense (*burdensome, severe, dull*) or in a good sense (*numerous, rich, honorable*); causat. to *make weighty* (in the same two senses):—abounding with, more grievously afflict, boast, be chargeable, × be dim, glorify, be (make) glorious (things), glory, (very) great, be grievous, harden, be (make) heavy, be heavier, lay heavily, (bring to, come to, do, get, be had in) honour (self), (be) honourable (man), lade, × more be laid, make self many, nobles, prevail, promote (to honour), be rich, be (go) sore, stop.

3514. כֹּבֶד **kôbed**, *ko'-bed*; from 3513; *weight, multitude, vehemence*:—grievousness, heavy, great number.

3515. כָּבֵד **kâbêd**, *kaw-bade'*; from 3513; *heavy*; fig. in a good sense (*numerous*) or in a bad sense (*severe, difficult, stupid*):—(so) great, grievous, hard (-ened), (too) heavy (-ier), laden, much, slow, sore, thick.

3516. כָּבֵד **kâbêd**, *kaw-bade'*; the same as 3515; the *liver* (as the *heaviest* of the viscera):—liver.

כָּבֹד **kâbôd**. See 3519.

3517. כְּבֵדֻת **kebêdûth**, *keb-ay-dooth'*; fem. of 3515; *difficulty*:— × heavily.

3518. כָּבָה **kâbâh**, *kaw-baw'*; a prim. root; to *expire* or (causat.) to *extinguish* (fire, light, anger):—go (put) out, quench.

3519. כָּבוֹד **kâbôwd**, *kaw-bode'*; rarely

כָּבֹד **kâbôd**, *kaw-bode'*; from 3513; prop. *weight*; but only fig. in a good sense, *splendor* or *copiousness*:—glorious (-ly), glory, honour (-able).

3520. כְּבוּדָּה **kebûwddâh**, *keb-ood-daw'*; irreg. fem. pass. part. of 3513; *weightiness*, i.e. *magnificence, wealth*:—carriage, all glorious, stately.

3521. כָּבוּל **Kâbûwl**, *kaw-bool'*; from the same as 3525 in the sense of *limitation; sterile; Cabul*, the name of two places in Pal.:—Cabul.

3522. כַּבּוֹן **Kabbôwn**, *kab-bone'*; from an unused root mean. to *heap up*; *hilly; Cabbon*, a place in Pal.:—Cabbon.

3523. כְּבִיר **kebîyr**, *keb-eer'*; from 3527 in the orig. sense of *plaiting*; a *matrass* (of intertwined materials):—pillow.

3524. כַּבִּיר **kabbîyr**, *kab-beer'*; from 3527; *vast*, whether in extent (fig. of power, *mighty*; of time, *aged*), or in number, *many*:—+ feeble, mighty, most, much, strong, valiant.

3525. כֶּבֶל **kebel**, *keh'-bel*; from an unused root mean. to *twine* or braid together; a *fetter*:—fetter.

3526. כָּבַס **kâbaç**, *kaw-bas'*; a prim. root; to *trample*; hence to *wash* (prop. by stamping with the feet), whether lit. (including the *fulling* process) or fig.:—fuller, wash (-ing).

3527. כָּבַר **kâbar**, *kaw-bar'*; a prim. root; prop. to *plait* together, i.e. (fig.) to *augment* (espec. in number or quantity, to *accumulate*):—in abundance, multiply.

3528. כְּבָר **kebâr**, *keb-awr'*; from 3527; prop. *extent* of time, i.e. a *great while*; hence *long ago, formerly, hitherto*:—already, (seeing that which), now.

3529. כְּבָר **Kebâr**, *keb-awr'*; the same as 3528; *length; Kebar*, a river of Mesopotamia:—Chebar. Comp. 2249.

3530. כִּבְרָה **kibrâh**, *kib-raw'*; fem. of 3528; prop. *length*, i.e. a *measure* (of uncert. dimension):— × little.

3531. כְּבָרָה **kebârâh**, *keb-aw-raw'*; from 3527 in its orig. sense; a *sieve* (as netted):—sieve.

3532. כֶּבֶשׂ **kebes**, *keh-bes'*; from an unused root mean. to *dominate*; a *ram* (just old enough to *butt*):—lamb, sheep.

3533. כָּבַשׁ **kâbash**, *kaw-bash'*; a prim. root; to *tread* down; hence neg. to *disregard*; pos. to *conquer, subjugate, violate*:—bring into bondage, force, keep under, subdue, bring into subjection.

3534. כֶּבֶשׁ **kebesh**, *keh'-besh*; from 3533; a *footstool* (as trodden upon):—footstool.

3535. כִּבְשָׂה **kibsâh**, *kib-saw'*; or

כַּבְשָׂה **kabsâh**, *kab-saw'*; fem. of 3532; a *ewe*:—(ewe) lamb.

3536. כִּבְשָׁן **kibshân**, *kib-shawn'*; from 3533; a smelting *furnace* (as *reducing* metals):—furnace.

3537. כַּד **kad**, *kad*; from an unused root mean. to *deepen*; prop. a *pail*; but gen. of earthenware; a *jar* for domestic purposes:—barrel, pitcher.

3538. כְּדַב **kedab** (Chald.), *ked-ab'*; from a root corresp. to 3576; *false*:—lying.

3539. כַּדְכֹּד **kadkôd**, *kad-kode'*; from the same as 3537 in the sense of *striking fire* from a metal forged; a *sparkling* gem, prob. the ruby:—agate.

3540. כְּדָרְלָעֹמֶר **Kedorlâʿômer**, *ked-or-law-o'-mer*; of for. or.; *Kedorlaomer*, an early Pers. king:—Chedorlaomer.

3541. כֹּה **kôh**, *ko*; from the prefix *k* and 1931; prop. *like this*, i.e. by impl. (of manner) *thus* (or *so*); also (of place) *here* (or *hither*); or (of time) *now*:—also, here, + hitherto, like, on the other side, so (and much), such, on that manner, (on) this (manner, side, way, way and that way), + mean while, yonder.

3542. כָּה **kâh** (Chald.), *kaw*; corresp. to 3541:—hitherto.

3543. כָּהָה **kâhâh**, *kaw-haw'*; a prim. root; to *be weak*, i.e. (fig.) to *despond* (causat. *rebuke*), or (of light, the eye) to *grow dull*:—darken, be dim, fail, faint, restrain, × utterly.

3544. כֵּהֶה **kêheh**, *kay-heh'*; from 3543; *feeble, obscure*:—somewhat dark, darkish, wax dim, heaviness, smoking.

3545. כֵּהָה **kêhâh**, *kay-haw'*; fem. of 3544; prop. a *weakening*; fig. *alleviation*, i.e. cure:—healing.

3546. כְּהַל **kehal** (Chald.), *keh-hal'*; a root corresp. to 3201 and 3557; to *be able*:—be able, could.

3547. כָּהַן **kâhan**, *kaw-han'*; a prim. root, appar. mean. to *mediate* in religious services; but used only as denom. from 3548; to *officiate* as a priest; fig. to *put on regalia*:—deck, be (do the office of a, execute the, minister in the) priest ('s office).

3548. כֹּהֵן **kôhên**, *ko-hane'*; act. part. of 3547; lit. one *officiating*, a *priest*; also (by courtesy) an *acting priest* (although a layman):—chief ruler, × own, priest, prince, principal officer.

3549. כָּהֵן **kâhên** (Chald.), *kaw-hane'*; corresp. to 3548:—priest.

3550. כְּהֻנָּה **kehunnâh**, *keh-hoon-naw'*; from 3547; *priesthood*:—priesthood, priest's office.

3551. כַּו **kav** (Chald.), *kav*; from a root corresp. to 3854 in the sense of *piercing*; a *window* (as a perforation):—window.

3552. כּוּב **Kûwb**, *koob*; of for. der.; *Kub*, a country near Egypt:—Chub.

3553. כּוֹבַע **kôwbaʿ**, *ko'-bah*; from an unused root mean. to be *high* or *rounded*; a *helmet* (as *arched*):—helmet. Comp. 6959.

3554. כָּוָה **kâvâh**, *kaw-vaw'*; a prim. root; prop. to *prick* or *penetrate*; hence to *blister* (as smarting or eating into):—burn.

כּוֹחַ **kôwach**. See 3581.

3555. כְּוִיָּה **keviyâh**, *kev-ee-yaw'*; from 3554; a *branding*:—burning.

3556. כּוֹכָב **kôwkâb**, *ko-kawb'*; prob. from the same as 3522 (in the sense of *rolling*) or 3554 (in the sense of *blazing*); a *star* (as *round* or as *shining*); fig. a *prince*:—star ([-gazer]).

3557. כּוּל **kûwl**, *kool*; a prim. root; prop. to *keep in*; hence to *measure*; fig. to *maintain* (in various senses):—(be able to, can) abide, bear. comprehend, contain, feed, forbearing, guide, hold (-ing in), nourish (-er), be present, make provision, receive, sustain, provide sustenance (victuals).

3558. כּוּמָז **kûwmâz**, *koo-mawz'*; from an unused root mean. to *store away*; a *jewel* (prob. gold beads):—tablet.

3559. כּוּן **kûwn**, *koon*; a prim. root; prop. to *be erect* (i.e. stand perpendicular); hence (causat.) to *set up*, in a great variety of applications, whether lit. (*establish, fix, prepare, apply*), or fig. (*appoint, render sure, proper* or *prosperous*):—certain (-ty), confirm, direct, faithfulness, fashion, fasten, firm, be fitted, be fixed, frame, be meet, ordain, order, perfect, (make) preparation, prepare (self), provide, make provision, (be, make) ready, right, set (aright, fast, forth), be stable, (e-) stablish, stand, tarry, × very deed.

3560. כּוּן **Kûwn**, *koon*; prob. from 3559; *established; Kun*, a place in Syria:—Chun.

3561. כַּוָּן **kavvân**, *kav-vawn'*; from 3559; something *prepared*, i.e. a sacrificial *wafer*:—cake.

3562. כּוֹנַנְיָהוּ **Kôwnanyâhûw**, *ko-nan-yaw'-hoo*; from 3559 and 3050; *Jah has sustained; Conanjah*, the name of two Isr.:—Conaniah, Cononiah. Comp. 3663.

3563. כּוֹס **kôwç**, *koce*; from an unused root mean. to *hold* together; a *cup* (as a container), often fig. a *lot* (as if a potion); also some unclean bird, prob. an *owl* (perh. from the cup-like cavity of its eye):—cup, (small) owl. Comp. 3599.

3564. כּוּר **kûwr**, *koor*; from an unused root mean. prop. to *dig* through; a *pot* or *furnace* (as if excavated):—furnace. Comp. 3600.

כּוֹר **kôwr**. See 3733.

3565. כּוֹר עָשָׁן **Kôwr ʿÂshân**, *kore aw-shawn'*; from 3564 and 6227; *furnace of smoke; Cor-Ashan*, a place in Pal.:—Chor-ashan.

3566. כּוֹרֶשׁ **Kôwresh**, *ko'-resh*; or (Ezra 1 : 1 [last time], 2)

כֹּרֶשׁ **Kôresh**, *ko'-resh*; from the Pers.; *Koresh* (or Cyrus), the Pers. king:—Cyrus.

3567. כּוֹרֶשׁ **Kôwresh** (Chald.), *ko'-resh*; corresp. to 3566:—Cyrus.

3568. כּוּשׁ **Kûwsh**, *koosh;* prob. of for. or.; *Cush* (or Ethiopia), the name of a son of Ham, and of his territory; also of an Isr.:—Chush, Cush, Ethiopia.

3569. כּוּשִׁי **Kûwshîy**, *koo-shee';* patron. from 3568; a *Cushite*, or desc. of Cush:—Cushi, Cushite, Ethiopian (-s).

3570. כּוּשִׁי **Kûwshîy**, *koo-shee';* the same as 3569; *Cushi*, the name of two Isr.:—Cushi.

3571. כּוּשִׁית **Kûwshîyth**, *koo-sheeth';* fem. of 3569; a *Cushite woman:*—Ethiopian.

3572. כּוּשָׁן **Kûwshân**, *koo-shawn';* perh. from 3568; *Cushan*, a region of Arabia:—Cushan.

3573. כּוּשַׁן רִשְׁעָתַיִם **Kûwshan Rish'âthâyim**, *koo-shan' rish-aw-thah'-yim;* appar. from 3572 and the dual of 7564; *Cushan of double wickedness; Cushan-Rishathajim*, a Mesopotamian king:—Chushan-rishathayim.

3574. כּוֹשָׁרָה **kôwshârâh**, *ko-shaw-raw';* from 3787; *prosperity;* in plur. *freedom:*—× chain.

3575. כּוּת **Kûwth**, *kooth;* or (fem.)

כּוּתָה **Kûwthâh**, *koo-thaw';* of for. or.; *Cuth* or *Cuthah*, a province of Assyria:—Cuth.

3576. כָּזַב **kâzab**, *kaw-zab';* a prim. root; to *lie* (i.e. *deceive*), lit. or fig.:—fail, (be found a, make a) liar, lie, lying, be in vain.

3577. כָּזָב **kâzâb**, *kaw-zawb';* from 3576; *falsehood;* lit. (*untruth*) or fig. (*idol*):—deceitful, false, leasing, + liar, lie, lying.

3578. כֹּזְבָא **Kôzᵉbâ'**, *ko-zeb-aw';* from 3576; *fallacious; Cozeba*, a place in Pal.:—Choseba.

3579. כָּזְבִּי **Kozbîy**, *koz-bee';* from 3576; *false; Cozbi*, a Midianitess:—Cozbi.

3580. כְּזִיב **Kᵉzîyb**, *kez-eeb';* from 3576; *falsified; Kezib*, a place in Pal.:—Chezib.

3581. כֹּחַ **kôach**, *ko'-akh;* or (Dan. 11 : 6)

כּוֹחַ **kôwach**, *ko'-akh;* from an unused root mean. to *be firm; vigor*, lit. (*force*, in a good or a bad sense) or fig. (*capacity, means, produce*); also (from its hardiness) a large *lizard:*—ability, able, chameleon, force, fruits, might, power (-ful), strength, substance, wealth.

3582. כָּחַד **kâchad**, *kaw-khad';* a prim. root; to *secrete*, by act or word; hence (intens.) to *destroy:*—conceal, cut down (off), desolate, hide.

3583. כָּחַל **kâchal**, *kaw-khal';* a prim. root; to *paint* (with stibium):—paint.

3584. כָּחַשׁ **kâchash**, *kaw-khash';* a prim. root; to *be untrue*, in word (to *lie, feign, disown*) or deed (to *disappoint, fail, cringe*):—deceive, deny, dissemble, fail, deal falsely, be found liars, (be-) lie, lying, submit selves.

3585. כַּחַשׁ **kachash**, *kakh'-ash;* from 3584; lit. a *failure* of flesh, i.e. *emaciation;* fig. *hypocrisy:*—leanness, lies, lying.

3586. כֶּחָשׁ **kechâsh**, *kekh-awsh';* from 3584; *faithless:*—lying.

3587. כִּי **kîy**, *kee;* from 3554; a *brand* or *scar:*—burning.

3588. כִּי **kîy**, *kee;* a prim. particle [the full form of the prepositional prefix] indicating *causal* relations of all kinds, antecedent or consequent; (by impl.) very widely used as a rel. conj. or adv. [as below]; often largely modified by other particles annexed:—and, + (forasmuch, inasmuch, where-) as, assured [-ly], + but, certainly, doubtless, + else, even, + except, for, how, (because, in, so, than) that, + nevertheless, now, rightly, seeing, since, surely, then, therefore, + (al-) though, + till, truly, + until, when, whether, while, whom, yea, yet.

3589. כִּיד **kîyd**, *keed;* from a prim. root mean. to *strike:* a *crushing;* fig. *calamity:*—destruction.

3590. כִּידוֹד **kîydôwd**, *kee-dode';* from the same as 3589 [comp. 3539]; prop. something *struck* off, i.e. a *spark* (as struck):—spark.

3591. כִּידוֹן **kîydôwn**, *kee-dohn';* from the same as 3589; prop. something to *strike* with, i.e. a *dart* (perh. smaller than 2595):—lance, shield, spear, target.

3592. כִּידוֹן **Kîydôwn**, *kee-dohn';* the same as 3591; *Kidon*, a place in Pal.:—Chidon.

3593. כִּידוֹר **kîydôwr**, *kee-dore';* of uncert. der.; perh. *tumult:*—battle.

3594. כִּיּוּן **Kîyûwn**, *kee-yoon';* from 3559; prop. a *statue*, i.e. idol; but used (by euphemism) for some heathen deity (perh. corresp. to Priapus or Baal-peor):—Chiun.

3595. כִּיּוֹר **kîyôwr**, *kee-yore';* or

כִּיֹּר **kîyôr**, *kee-yore';* from the same as 3564; prop. something *round* (as *excavated* or *bored*), i.e. a chafing-*dish* for coals or a *caldron* for cooking; hence (from similarity of form) a *washbowl;* also (for the same reason) a *pulpit* or platform:—hearth, laver, pan, scaffold.

3596. כִּילַי **kîylay**, *kee-lah'ee;* or

כֵּלַי **kêlay**, *kay-lah'ee;* from 3557 in the sense of *withholding; niggardly:*—churl.

3597. כֵּילַף **kêylaph**, *kay-laf';* from an unused root mean. to *clap* or strike with noise; a *club* or sledge-hammer:—hammer.

3598. כִּימָה **Kîymâh**, *kee-maw';* from the same as 3558; a *cluster* of stars, i.e. the *Pleiades:*—Pleiades, seven stars.

3599. כִּיס **kîyç**, *keece;* a form for 3563; a *cup;* also a *bag* for money or weights:—bag, cup, purse.

3600. כִּיר **kîyr**, *keer;* a form for 3564 (only in the dual); a cooking *range* (consisting of two parallel stones, across which the boiler is set):—ranges for pots.

כִּיֹּר **kîyôr**. See 3595.

3601. כִּישׁוֹר **kîyshôwr**, *kee-shore';* from 3787; lit. a *director*, i.e. the *spindle* or shank of a distaff (6418), by which it is twirled:—spindle.

3602. כָּכָה **kâkâh**, *kaw'-kaw;* from 3541; *just so*, referring to the previous or following context:—after that (this) manner, this matter, (even) so, in such a case, thus.

3603. כִּכָּר **kikkâr**, *kik-kawr';* from 3769; a *circle*, i.e. (by impl.) a circumjacent *tract* or region, espec. the *Ghôr* or valley of the Jordan; also a (round) *loaf;* also a *talent* (or large [round] coin):—loaf, morsel, piece, plain, talent.

3604. כִּכֵּר **kikkêr** (Chald.), *kik-kare';* corresp. to 3603; a *talent:*—talent.

3605. כֹּל **kôl**, *kole;* or (Jer. 33 : 8)°

כּוֹל **kôwl**, *kole;* from 3634; prop. the *whole;* hence *all, any* or *every* (in the sing. only, but often in a plur. sense):—(in) all (manner, [ye]), altogether, any (manner), enough, every (one, place, thing), howsoever, as many as, [no-] thing, ought, whatsoever, (the) whole, whoso (-ever).

3606. כֹּל **kôl** (Chald.), *kole;* corresp. to 3605:—all, any, + (forasmuch) as, + be- (for this) cause, every, + no (manner, -ne), + there (where) -fore, + though, what (where, who) -soever, (the) whole.

3607. כָּלָא **kâlâ'**, *kaw-law';* a prim. root; to *restrict*, by act (*hold* back or in) or word (*prohibit*):—finish, forbid, keep (back), refrain, restrain, retain, shut up, be stayed, withhold.

3608. כֶּלֶא **kele'**, *keh'-leh;* from 3607; a *prison:*—prison. Comp. 3610, 3628.

3609. כִּלְאָב **Kil'âb**, *kil-awb';* appar. from 3607 and 1; *restraint of* (his) *father; Kilab*, an Isr.:—Chileab.

3610. כִּלְאַיִם **kil'ayim**, *kil-ah'-yim;* dual of 3608 in the original sense of *separation; two heterogeneities:*—divers seeds (-e kinds), mingled (seed).

3611. כֶּלֶב **keleb**, *keh'-leb;* from an unused root mean. to *yelp*, or else to *attack;* a *dog;* hence (by euphemism) a male *prostitute:*—dog.

3612. כָּלֵב **Kâlêb**, *kaw-labe';* perh. a form of 3611, or else from the same root in the sense of *forcible; Caleb*, the name of three Isr.:—Caleb.

3613. כָּלֵב אֶפְרָתָה **Kâlêb 'Ephrâthâh**, *kaw-labe' ef-raw'-thaw;* from 3612 and 672; *Caleb-Ephrathah*, a place in Eg. (if the text is correct):—Caleb-ephrathah.

3614. כָּלִבּוֹ° **Kâlibbôw**, *kaw-lib-bo';* prob. by err. transc. for

כָּלֵבִי **Kâlêbîy**, *kaw-lay-bee';* patron. from 3612; a *Calebite* or desc. of Caleb:—of the house of Caleb.

3615. כָּלָה **kâlâh**, *kaw-law';* a prim. root; to *end*, whether intrans. (to *cease, be finished, perish*) or trans. (to *complete, prepare, consume*):—accomplish, cease, consume (away), determine, destroy (utterly), be (when . . . were) done, (be an) end (of), expire, (cause to) fail, faint, finish, fulfil, × fully, × have, leave (off), long, bring to pass, wholly reap, make clean riddance, spend, quite take away, waste.

3616. כָּלֶה **kâleh**, *kaw-leh';* from 3615; *pining:*—fail.

3617. כָּלָה **kâlâh**, *kaw-law';* from 3615; a *completion;* adv. *completely;* also *destruction:*—altogether, (be, utterly) consume (-d), consummation (-ption), was determined, (full, utter) end, riddance.

3618. כַּלָּה **kallâh**, *kal-law';* from 3634; a *bride* (as if *perfect*); hence a *son's wife:*—bride, daughter-in-law, spouse.

כְּלוּא **kᵉlûw'**. See 3628.

3619. כְּלוּב **kᵉlûb**, *kel-oob';* from the same as 3611; a bird-*trap* (as furnished with a *clap*-stick or treadle to spring it); hence a *basket* (as resembling a wicker cage):—basket, cage.

3620. כְּלוּב **Kᵉlûwb**, *kel-oob';* the same as 3619; *Kelub*, the name of two Isr.:—Chelub.

3621. כְּלוּבַי **Kᵉlûwbay**, *kel-oo-bay'ee;* a form of 3612; *Kelubai*, an Isr.:—Chelubai.

3622. כְּלוּהַי **Kᵉlûwhay**, *kel-oo-hah'ee;* from 3615; *completed; Keluhai*, an Isr.:—Chelluh.

3623. כְּלוּלָה **kᵉlûwlâh**, *kel-oo-law';* denom. pass. part. from 3618; *bridehood* (only in the plur.):—espousal.

3624. כֶּלַח **kelach**, *keh'-lakh;* from an unused root mean. to *be complete; maturity:*—full (old) age.

3625. כֶּלַח **Kelach**, *keh'-lakh;* the same as 3624; *Kelach*, a place in Assyria:—Calah.

3626. כָּל־חֹזֶה **Kol-Chôzeh**, *kol-kho-zeh';* from 3605 and 2374; *every seer; Col-Chozeh*, an Isr.:—Col-hozeh.

3627. כְּלִי **kᵉlîy**, *kel-ee';* from 3615; something *prepared*, i.e. any *apparatus* (as an implement, utensil, dress, vessel or weapon):—armour ([-bearer]), artillery, bag, carriage, + furnish, furniture, instrument, jewel, that is made of, × one from another, that which pertaineth, pot, + psaltery, sack, stuff, thing, tool, vessel, ware, weapon, + whatsoever.

3628. כְּלִיא **kᵉlîy'**, *kel-ee';* or

כְּלוּא **kᵉlûw'**, *kel-oo';* from 3607 [comp. 3608]; a *prison:*—prison.

3629. כִּלְיָה **kilyâh**, *kil-yaw';* fem. of 3627 (only in the plur.); a *kidney* (as an essential *organ*); fig. the *mind* (as the interior self):—kidneys, reins.

3630. כִּלְיוֹן **Kilyôwn**, *kil-yone';* a form of 3631; *Kiljon*, an Isr.:—Chilion.

3631. כִּלָּיוֹן **killâyôwn**, *kil-law-yone';* from 3615; *pining, destruction:*—consumption, failing.

3632. כָּלִיל **kâlîyl**, *kaw-leel';* from 3634; *complete;* as noun, the *whole* (spec. a sacrifice *entirely consumed*); as adv. *fully:*—all, every whit, flame, perfect (-ion), utterly, whole burnt offering (sacrifice), wholly.

3633. כַּלְכֹּל **Kalkôl**, *kal-kole';* from 3557; *sustenance; Calcol*, an Isr.:—Calcol, Chalcol.

3634. כָּלַל **kâlal**, *kaw-lal';* a prim. root; to *complete:*—(make) perfect.

3635. כְּלַל **kᵉlal** (Chald.), *kel-al'*; corresp. to 3634; to *complete:*—finish, make (set) up.

3636. כְּלָל **Kᵉlâl**, *kel-awl'*; from 3634; *complete; Kelal*, an Isr.:—Chelal.

3637. כָּלַם **kâlam**, *kaw-lawm'*; a prim. root; prop. to *wound;* but only fig., to *taunt* or *insult:*—be (make) ashamed, blush, be confounded, be put to confusion, hurt, reproach, (do, put to) shame.

3638. כִּלְמַד **Kilmâd**, *kil-mawd'*; of for. der.; *Kilmad*, a place appar. in the Assyrian empire:—Chilmad.

3639. כְּלִמָּה **kᵉlimmâh**, *kel-im-maw'*; from 3637; *disgrace:*—confusion, dishonour, reproach, shame.

3640. כְּלִמּוּת **kᵉlimmûwth**, *kel-im-mooth'*; from 3639; *disgrace:*—shame.

3641. כַּלְנֶה **Kalneh**, *kal-neh'*; or

כַּלְנֵה **Kalnêh**, *kal-nay'*; also

כַּלְנוֹ **Kalnôw**, *kal-no'*; of for. der.; *Calneh* or *Calno*, a place in the Assyrian empire:—Calneh, Calno. Comp. 3656.

3642. כָּמַהּ **kâmahh**, *kaw-mah'*; a prim. root; to *pine* after:—long.

3643. כִּמְהָם **Kimhâm**, *kim-hawm'*; from 3642; *pining; Kimham*, an Isr.:—Chimham.

3644. כְּמוֹ **kᵉmôw**, *kem-o'*; or

כָּמוֹ **kâmôw**, *kaw-mo'*; a form of the pref. *k*, but used separately [comp. 3651]; *as, thus, so:*—according to, (such) as (it were, well as), in comparison of, like (as, to, unto), thus, when, worth.

3645. כְּמוֹשׁ **Kᵉmôwsh**, *kem-oshe'*; or (Jer. 48 : 7)

כְּמִישׁ **Kᵉmîysh**, *kem-eesh'*; from an unused root mean. to *subdue;* the *powerful; Kemosh*, the god of the Moabites:—Chemosh.

3646. כַּמֹּן **kammôn**, *kam-mone'*; from an unused root mean. to *store up* or *preserve;* "*cummin*" (from its use as a *condiment*):—cummin.

3647. כָּמַס **kâmaç**, *kaw-mas'*; a prim. root; to *store* away, i.e. (fig.) in the memory:—lay up in store.

3648. כָּמַר **kâmar**, *kaw-mar'*; a prim. root; prop. to *intertwine* or *contract*, i.e. (by impl.) to *shrivel* (as with heat); fig. to *be* deeply *affected* with passion (love or pity):—be black, be kindled, yearn.

3649. כָּמָר **kâmâr**, *kaw-mawr'*; from 3648; prop. an *ascetic* (as if *shrunk* with self-maceration), i.e. an idolatrous *priest* (only in plur.):—Chemarims, (idolatrous) priests.

3650. כִּמְרִיר **kimrîyr**, *kim-reer'*; redupl. from 3648; *obscuration* (as if from *shrinkage* of light), i.e. an *eclipse* (only in plur.):—blackness.

3651. כֵּן **kên**, *kane;* from 3559; prop. *set* upright; hence (fig. as adj.) *just;* but usually (as adv. or conj.) *rightly* or *so* (in various applications to manner, time and relation; often with other particles):— + after that (this, -ward, -wards), as . . . as, + [for-] asmuch as yet, + be (for which) cause, + following, howbeit, in (the) like (manner, -wise), × the more, right, (even) so, state, straightway, such (thing), surely, + there (where) -fore, this, thus, true, well, × you.

3652. כֵּן **kên** (Chald.), *kane;* corresp. to 3651; *so:*—thus.

3653. כֵּן **kên**, *kane;* the same as 3651, used as a noun; a *stand*, i.e. pedestal or station:—base, estate, foot, office, place, well.

3654. כֵּן **kên**, *kane;* from 3661 in the sense of *fastening;* a *gnat* (from infixing its sting; used only in plur. [and irreg. in Exod. 8 : 17, 18; Heb. 13 : 14]):—lice, × manner.

3655. כָּנָה **kânâh**, *kaw-naw'*; a prim. root; to *address* by an additional name; hence, to *eulogize:*—give flattering titles, surname (himself).

3656. כַּנֶּה **Kanneh**, *kan-neh'*; for 3641; *Canneh*, a place in Assyria:—Canneh

3657. כַּנָּה **kannâh**, *kan-naw'*; from 3661; a *plant* (as *set*):— × vineyard.

3658. כִּנּוֹר **kinnôwr**, *kin-nore'*; from an unused root mean. to *twang;* a *harp:*—harp.

3659. כָּנְיָהוּ **Konyâhûw**, *kon-yaw'-hoo;* for 3204; *Conjah*, an Isr. king:—Coniah.

3660. כְּנֵמָא **kᵉnêmâ'** (Chald.), *ken-ay-maw'*; corresp. to 3644; *so* or *thus:*—so, (in) this manner (sort), thus.

3661. כָּנַן **kânan**, *kaw-nan'*; a prim. root; to *set* out, i.e. *plant:*— × vineyard.

3662. כְּנָנִי **Kᵉnânîy**, *ken-aw-nee';* from 3661; *planted; Kenani*, an Isr.:—Chenani.

3663. כְּנַנְיָה **Kᵉnanyâh**, *ken-an-yaw';* or

כְּנַנְיָהוּ **Kᵉnanyâhûw**, *ken-an-yaw'-hoo;* from 3661 and 3050; *Jah has planted; Kenanjah*, an Isr.:—Chenaniah.

3664. כָּנַס **kânaç**, *kaw-nas';* a prim. root; to *collect;* hence, to *enfold:*—gather (together), heap up, wrap self.

3665. כָּנַע **kânaʻ**, *kaw-nah';* a prim. root; prop. to *bend* the knee; hence to *humiliate, vanquish:*—bring down (low), into subjection, under, humble (self), subdue.

3666. כִּנְעָה **kinʻâh**, *kin-aw';* from 3665 in the sense of *folding* [comp. 3664]; a *package:*—wares.

3667. כְּנַעַן **Kᵉnaʻan**, *ken-ah'-an;* from 3665; *humiliated; Kenaan*, a son of Ham; also the country inhabited by him:—Canaan, merchant, traffick.

3668. כְּנַעֲנָה **Kᵉnaʻănâh**, *ken-ah-an-aw';* fem. of 3667; *Kenaanah*, the name of two Isr.:—Chenaanah.

3669. כְּנַעֲנִי **Kᵉnaʻănîy**, *ken-ah-an-ee';* patrial from 3667; a *Kenaanite* or inhabitant of Kenaan; by impl. a *pedlar* (the Canaanites standing for their neighbors the Ishmaelites, who conducted mercantile caravans):—Canaanite, merchant, trafficker.

3670. כָּנַף **kânaph**, *kaw-naf';* a prim. root; prop. to *project* laterally, i.e. prob. (reflex.) to *withdraw:*—be removed.

3671. כָּנָף **kânâph**, *kaw-nawf';* from 3670; an *edge* or *extremity;* spec. (of a bird or army) a *wing*, (of a garment or bed-clothing) a *flap*, (of the earth) a *quarter*, (of a building) a *pinnacle:*— + bird, border, corner, end, feather [-ed], × flying, + (one an-) other, overspreading, × quarters, skirt, × sort, uttermost part, wing ([-ed]).

3672. כִּנְּרוֹת **Kinnᵉrôwth**, *kin-ner-ōth';* or

כִּנֶּרֶת **Kinnereth**, *kin-neh'-reth;* respectively plur. and sing. fem. from the same as 3658; perh. *harp*-shaped; *Kinneroth* or *Kinnereth*, a place in Pal.:—Chinnereth, Chinneroth, Cinneroth.

3673. כָּנַשׁ **kânash** (Chald.), *kaw-nash';* corresp. to 3664; to *assemble:*—gather together.

3674. כְּנָת **kᵉnâth**, *ken-awth';* from 3655; a *colleague* (as having the same title):—companion.

3675. כְּנָת **kᵉnâth** (Chald.), *ken-awth';* corresp. to 3674:—companion.

3676. כֵּס **kêç**, *kace;* appar. a contr. for 3678, but prob. by err. transc. for 5251:—sworn.

3677. כֶּסֶא **keçeʼ**, *keh'-seh;* or

כֶּסֶה **keçeh**, *keh'-seh;* appar. from 3680; prop. *fulness* or the *full moon*, i.e. its festival:—(time) appointed.

3678. כִּסֵּא **kiççêʼ**, *kis-say';* or

כִּסֵּה **kiççêh**, *kis-say';* from 3680; prop. *covered*, i.e. a *throne* (as *canopied*):—seat, stool, throne.

3679. כַּסְדַּי **Kaçday**, *kas-dah'ee;* for 3778:—Chaldean.

3680. כָּסָה **kâçâh**, *kaw-saw';* a prim. root; prop. to *plump*, i.e. *fill up* hollows; by impl. to *cover* (for clothing or secrecy):—clad self, close, clothe, conceal, cover (self), (flee to) hide, overwhelm. Comp. 3780.

כֶּסֶה **keçeh**. See 3677.

כִּסֵּה **kiççêh**. See 3678.

3681. כָּסוּי **kâçûwy**, *kaw-soo'ee;* pass. part. of 3680; prop. *covered*, i.e. (as noun) a *covering:*—covering.

3682. כְּסוּת **kᵉçûwth**, *kes-ooth';* from 3680; a *cover* (garment); fig. a *veiling:*—covering, raiment, vesture.

3683. כָּסַח **kâçach**, *kaw-sakh';* a prim. root; to *cut off:*—cut down (up).

3684. כְּסִיל **kᵉçîyl**, *kes-eel';* from 3688; prop. *fat*, i.e. (fig.) stupid or *silly:*—fool (-ish).

3685. כְּסִיל **Kᵉçîyl**, *kes-eel';* the same as 3684; any notable *constellation;* spec. *Orion* (as if a *burly* one):—constellation, Orion.

3686. כְּסִיל **Kᵉçîyl**, *kes-eel';* the same as 3684; *Kesil*, a place in Pal.:—Chesil.

3687. כְּסִילוּת **kᵉçîylûwth**, *kes-eel-ooth';* from 3684; *silliness:*—foolish.

3688. כָּסַל **kâçal**, *kaw-sal';* a prim. root; prop. to *be fat*, i.e. (fig.) *silly:*—be foolish.

3689. כֶּסֶל **keçel**, *keh'-sel;* from 3688; prop. *fatness*, i.e. by impl. (lit.) the *loin* (as the seat of the leaf *fat*) or (gen.) the *viscera;* also (fig.) *silliness* or (in a good sense) *trust:*—confidence, flank, folly, hope, loin.

3690. כִּסְלָה **kiçlâh**, *kis-law';* fem. of 3689; in a good sense, *trust;* in a bad one, *silliness:*—confidence, folly.

3691. כִּסְלֵו **Kiçlêv**, *kis-lave';* prob. of for. or.; *Kisleu*, the 9th Heb. month:—Chisleu.

3692. כִּסְלוֹן **Kiçlôwn**, *kis-lone';* from 3688; *hopeful; Kislon*, an Isr.:—Chislon.

3693. כְּסָלוֹן **Kᵉçâlôwn**, *kes-aw-lone';* from 3688; *fertile; Kesalon*, a place in Pal.:—Chesalon.

3694. כְּסֻלּוֹת **Kᵉçullôwth**, *kes-ool-lōth';* fem. plur. of pass. part. of 3688; *fattened, Kesulloth*, a place in Pal.:—Chesulloth.

3695. כַּסְלֻחִים **Kaçlûchîym**, *kas-loo'-kheem;* a plur. prob. of for. der.; *Casluchim*, a people cognate to the Eg.:—Casluhim.

3696. כִּסְלֹת תָּבֹר **Kiçlôth Tâbôr**, *kis-lōth' taw-bore';* from the fem. plur. of 3689 and 8396; *flanks of Tabor; Kisloth-Tabor*, a place in Pal.:—Chisloth-tabor.

3697. כָּסַם **kâçam**, *kaw-sam';* a prim. root; to *shear:*— × only, poll. Comp. 3765.

3698. כֻּסֶּמֶת **kuççemeth**, *koos-seh'-meth;* from 3697; *spelt* (from its bristliness as if just *shorn*):—fitches, rie.

3699. כָּסַס **kâçaç**, *kaw-sas';* a prim. root; to *estimate:*—make count.

3700. כָּסַף **kâçaph**, *kaw-saf';* a prim. root; prop. to become *pale*, i.e. (by impl.) to *pine* after; also to *fear:*—[have] desire, be greedy, long, sore.

3701. כֶּסֶף **keçeph**, *keh'-sef;* from 3700; *silver* (from its *pale* color); by impl. *money:*—money, price, silver (-ling).

3702. כְּסַף **kᵉçaph** (Chald.), *kes-af';* corresp. to 3701:—money, silver.

3703. כָּסִפְיָא **Kâçiphyâʼ**, *kaw-sif-yaw';* perh. from 3701; *silvery; Casiphja*, a place in Bab.:—Casiphia.

3704. כֶּסֶת **keçeth**, *keh'-seth;* from 3680; a *cushion* or pillow (as *covering* a seat or bed):—pillow.

3705. כְּעַן **kᵉʻan** (Chald.), *keh-an';* prob. from 3652; *now:*—now.

3706. כְּעֶנֶת **kᵉʻeneth** (Chald.), *keh-eh'-neth;* or

כְּעֶת **kᵉʻeth** (Chald.), *keh-eth';* fem. of 3705; *thus* (only in the formula "and *so forth*"):—at such a time.

3707. כָּעַס **kâʻaç**, *kaw-as';* a prim. root; to *trouble;* by impl. to *grieve, rage, be indignant:*—be angry, be grieved, take indignation, provoke (to anger, unto wrath), have sorrow, vex, be wroth.

3708. כַּעַס **kaʻaç**, *kah'-as;* or (in Job)

כַּעַשׂ **kaʻas**, *kah'-as;* from 3707; *vexation:*—anger, angry, grief, indignation, provocation, provoking, × sore, sorrow, spite, wrath.

כְּעֶת **kᵉʻeth**. See 3706.

3709. כַּף **kaph**, *kaf;* from 3721; the hollow *hand* or palm (so of the *paw* of an animal, of the *sole*, and even of the *bowl* of a dish or sling, the *handle* of a bolt, the *leaves* of a palm-tree); fig. *power:*—branch, + foot, hand ([-ful], -dle, [-led]), hollow, middle, palm, paw, power, sole, spoon.

3710. כֵּף **kêph**, *kafe;* from 3721; a hollow *rock:*—rock.

3711. כָּפָה **kâphâh**, *kaw-faw';* a prim. root; prop. to *bend*, i.e. (fig.) to *tame* or subdue:—pacify.

3712. כִּפָּה **kippâh**, *kip-paw';* fem. of 3709; a *leaf* of a palm-tree:—branch.

3713. כְּפוֹר **k^{e}phôwr**, *kef-ore';* from 3722; prop. a *cover*, i.e. (by impl.) a *tankard* (or *covered* goblet); also white *frost* (as *covering* the ground):—bason, hoar (-y) frost.

3714. כָּפִיס **kâphîyç**, *kaw-fece';* from an unused root mean. to *connect;* a *girder:*—beam.

3715. כְּפִיר **k^{e}phîyr**, *kef-eer';* from 3722; a *village* (as *covered* in by walls); also a young *lion* (perh. as *covered* with a mane):—(young) lion, village. Comp. 3723.

3716. כְּפִירָה **K^{e}phîyrâh**, *kef-ee-raw';* fem. of 3715; the *village* (always with the art.); *Kephirah*, a place in Pal.:—Chephirah.

3717. כָּפַל **kâphal**, *kaw-fal';* a prim. root; to *fold* together; fig. to *repeat:*—double.

3718. כֶּפֶל **kephel**, *keh'-fel;* from 3717; a *duplicate:*—double.

3719. כָּפַן **kâphan**, *kaw-fan';* a prim. root; to *bend:*—bend.

3720. כָּפָן **kâphân**, *kaw-fawn';* from 3719; *hunger* (as making to *stoop* with emptiness and pain):—famine.

3721. כָּפַף **kâphaph**, *kaw-faf';* a prim. root; to *curve:*—bow down (self).

3722. כָּפַר **kâphar**, *kaw-far';* a prim. root; to *cover* (spec. with bitumen); fig. to *expiate* or *condone*, to *placate* or *cancel:*—appease, make (an) atonement, cleanse, disannul, forgive, be merciful, pacify, pardon, to *pitch*, purge (away), put off, (make) reconcile (-liation).

3723. כָּפָר **kâphâr**, *kaw-fawr';* from 3722; a *village* (as *protected* by walls):—village. Comp. 3715.

3724. כֹּפֶר **kôpher**, *ko'-fer;* from 3722; prop. a *cover*, i.e. (lit.) a *village* (as *covered* in); (spec.) *bitumen* (as used for *coating*), and the *henna* plant (as used for *dyeing*); fig. a *redemption*-price:—bribe, camphire, pitch, ransom, satisfaction, sum of money, village.

3725. כִּפֻּר **kippûr**, *kip-poor';* from 3722; *expiation* (only in plur.):—atonement.

3726. כְּפַר הָעַמּוֹנִי **K^{e}phar hâ-ʿAmmôwnîy**, *kef-ar' haw-am-mo-nee';* from 3723 and 5984, with the art. interposed; *village of the Ammonite; Kefar-ha-Ammoni*, a place in Pal.:—Chefar-haamonai.

3727. כַּפֹּרֶת **kappôreth**, *kap-po'-reth;* from 3722; a *lid* (used only of the *cover* of the sacred Ark):—mercy seat.

3728. כָּפַשׁ **kâphash**, *kaw-fash';* a prim. root; to *tread* down; fig. to *humiliate:*—cover.

3729. כְּפַת **k^{e}phath** (Chald.), *kef-ath';* a root of uncert. correspondence; to *fetter:*—bind.

3730. כַּפְתֹּר **kaphtôr**, *kaf-tore';* or (Am. 9 : 1)

כַּפְתּוֹר **kaphtôwr**, *kaf-tore';* prob. from an unused root mean. to *encircle;* a *chaplet;* but used only in an architectonic sense, i.e. the *capital* of a column, or a wreath-like *button* or *disk* on the candelabrum:—knop, (upper) lintel.

3731. כַּפְתֹּר **Kaphtôr**, *kaf-tore';* or (Am. 9 : 7)

כַּפְתּוֹר **Kaphtôwr**, *kaf-tore';* appar. the same as 3730; *Caphtor* (i.e. a *wreath*-shaped island), the original seat of the Philistines:—Caphtor.

3732. כַּפְתֹּרִי **Kaphtôrîy**, *kaf-to-ree';* patrial from 3731; a *Caphtorite* (collect.) or native of Caphtor:—Caphthorim, Caphtorim (-s).

3733. כַּר **kar**, *kar;* from 3769 in the sense of *plumpness;* a *ram* (as *full-grown* and *fat*), including a *battering-ram* (as *butting*); hence a *meadow* (as *for sheep*); also a *pad* or camel's saddle (as *puffed out*):—captain, furniture, lamb, (large) pasture, ram. See also 1033, 3746.

3734. כֹּר **kôr**, *kore;* from the same as 3564; prop. a deep round *vessel*, i.e. (spec.) a *cor* or measure for things dry:—cor, measure. Chald. the same.

3735. כָּרָא **kârâʾ** (Chald.), *kaw-raw';* prob. corresp. to 3738 in the sense of *piercing* (fig.); to *grieve:*—be grieved.

3736. כַּרְבֵּל **karbêl**, *kar-bale';* from the same as 3525; to *gird* or *clothe:*—clothed.

3737. כַּרְבְּלָא **karb^{e}lâʾ** (Chald.), *kar-bel-aw';* from a verb corresp. to that of 3736; a *mantle:*—hat.

3738. כָּרָה **kârâh**, *kaw-raw';* a prim. root; prop. to *dig;* fig. to *plot;* gen. to *bore* or open:—dig, × make (a banquet), open.

3739. כָּרָה **kârâh**, *kaw-raw';* usually assigned as a prim. root, but prob. only a special application of 3738 (through the common idea of *planning* implied in a bargain); to *purchase:*—buy, prepare.

3740. כֵּרָה **kêrâh**, *kay-raw';* from 3739; a *purchase:*—provision.

3741. כָּרָה **kârâh**, *kaw-raw';* fem. of 3733; a *meadow:*—cottage.

3742. כְּרוּב **k^{e}rûwb**, *ker-oob';* of uncert. der.; a *cherub* or imaginary figure:—cherub, [*plur.*] cherubims.

3743. כְּרוּב **K^{e}rûwb**, *ker-oob';* the same as 3742; *Kerub*, a place in Bab.:—Cherub.

3744. כָּרוֹז **kârôwz** (Chald.), *kaw-roze';* from 3745; a *herald:*—herald.

3745. כְּרַז **k^{e}raz** (Chald.), *ker-az';* prob. of Greek or. (κηρύσσω); to *proclaim:*—make a proclamation.

3746. כָּרִי **kârîy**, *kaw-ree';* perh. an abridged plur. of 3733 in the sense of *leader* (of the flock); a *life-guardsman:*—captains, Cherethites [*from the marg.*].

3747. כְּרִית **K^{e}rîyth**, *ker-eeth';* from 3772; a *cut; Kerith*, a brook of Pal.:—Cherith.

3748. כְּרִיתוּת **k^{e}rîythûwth**, *ker-ee-thooth';* from 3772; a *cutting* (of the matrimonial bond), i.e. *divorce:*—divorce (-ment).

3749. כַּרְכֹּב **karkôb**, *kar-kobe';* expanded from the same as 3522; a *rim* or top margin:—compass.

3750. כַּרְכֹּם **karkôm**, *kar-kome';* prob. of for. or.; the *crocus:*—saffron.

3751. כַּרְכְּמִישׁ **Kark^{e}mîysh**, *kar-kem-eesh';* of for. der.; *Karkemish*, a place in Syria:—Carchemish.

3752. כַּרְכַּס **Karkaç**, *kar-kas';* of Pers. or.; *Karkas*, a eunuch of Xerxes:—Carcas.

3753. כִּרְכָּרָה **karkârâh**, *kar-kaw-raw';* from 3769; a *dromedary* (from its *rapid* motion as if *dancing*):—swift beast.

3754. כֶּרֶם **kerem**, *keh'-rem;* from an unused root of uncert. mean.; a *garden* or *vineyard:*—vines, (increase of the) vineyard (-s), vintage. See also 1021.

3755. כֹּרֵם **kôrêm**, *ko-rame';* act. part. of an imaginary denom. from 3754; a *vinedresser:*—vine dresser [*as one or two words*].

3756. כַּרְמִי **Karmîy**, *kar-mee';* from 3754; *gardener; Karmi*, the name of three Isr.:—Carmi.

3757. כַּרְמִי **Karmîy**, *kar-mee';* patron. from 3756; a *Karmite* or desc. of *Karmi:*—Carmites.

3758. כַּרְמִיל **karmîyl**, *kar-mele';* prob. of for. or.; *carmine*, a deep red:—crimson.

3759. כַּרְמֶל **karmel**, *kar-mel';* from 3754; a planted *field* (garden, orchard, vineyard or park); by impl. garden *produce:*—full (green) ears (of corn), fruitful field (place), plentiful (field).

3760. כַּרְמֶל **Karmel**, *kar-mel';* the same as 3759; *Karmel*, the name of a hill and of a town in Pal.:—Carmel, fruitful (plentiful) field, (place).

3761. כַּרְמְלִי **Karm^{e}lîy**, *kar-mel-ee';* patron from 3760; a *Karmelite* or inhab. of Karmel (the town):—Carmelite.

3762. כַּרְמְלִית **Karm^{e}lîyth**, *kar-mel-eeth';* fem of 3761; a *Karmelitess* or female inhab. of Karmel:—Carmelitess.

3763. כְּרָן **K^{e}rân**, *ker-awn';* of uncert. der.; *Keran*, an aboriginal Idumæan:—Cheran.

3764. כׇּרְסֵא **korçêʾ** (Chald.), *kor-say';* corresp. to 3678; a *throne:*—throne.

3765. כִּרְסֵם **kirçêm**, *kir-same';* from 3697; to *lay waste:*—waste.

3766. כָּרַע **kâraʿ**, *kaw-rah';* a prim. root; to *bend* the knee; by impl. to *sink*, to *prostrate:*—bow (down, self), bring down (low), cast down, couch, fall, feeble, kneeling, sink, smite (stoop) down, subdue, × very.

3767. כָּרָע **kârâʿ**, *kaw-raw';* from 3766; the *leg* (from the knee to the ankle) of men or locusts (only in the dual):—leg.

3768. כַּרְפַּס **karpaç**, *kar-pas';* of for. or.; *byssus* or fine vegetable wool:—green.

3769. כָּרַר **kârar**, *kaw-rar';* a prim. root; to *dance* (i.e. *whirl*):—dance (-ing).

3770. כְּרֵשׂ **k^{e}rês**, *ker-ace';* by var. from 7164; the *paunch* or belly (as *swelling* out):—belly.

כֹּרֶשׁ **Kôresh.** See 3567.

3771. כַּרְשְׁנָא **Karsh^{e}nâʾ**, *kar-shen-aw';* of for. or.; *Karshena*, a courtier of Xerxes:—Carshena.

3772. כָּרַת **kârath**, *kaw-rath';* a prim. root; to *cut* (off, down or asunder); by impl. to *destroy* or *consume;* spec. to *covenant* (i.e. make an alliance or bargain, orig. by cutting flesh and passing between the pieces):—be chewed, be con- [feder-] ate, covenant, cut (down, off), destroy, fail, feller, be freed, hew (down), make a league ([covenant]), × lose, perish, × utterly, × want.

3773. כָּרֻתָה **kârûthâh**, *kaw-rooth-aw';* pass. part. fem. of 3772; something *cut*, i.e. a hewn *timber:*—beam.

3774. כְּרֵתִי **K^{e}rêthîy**, *ker-ay-thee';* prob. from 3772 in the sense of *executioner;* a *Kerethite* or *life-guardsman* [comp. 2876] (only collect. in the sing. as plur.):—Cherethims, Cherethites.

3775. כֶּשֶׂב **keseb**, *keh'-seb;* appar. by transp. for 3532; a young *sheep:*—lamb, sheep.

3776. כִּשְׂבָּה **kisbâh**, *kis-baw';* fem. of 3775; a young *ewe:*—lamb.

3777. כֶּשֶׂד **Kesed**, *keh'-sed;* from an unused root of uncert. mean.; *Kesed*, a relative of Abraham:—Chesed.

3778. כַּשְׂדִּי **Kasdîy**, *kas-dee'* (occasionally with enclitic

כַּשְׂדִּימָה **Kasdîymâh**, *kas-dee'-maw;* *towards* the *Kasdites:*—into Chaldea), patron. from 3777 (only in the plur.); a *Kasdite*, or desc. of Kesed; by impl. a *Chaldæan* (as if so descended); also an *astrologer* (as if proverbial of that people:—Chaldeans, Chaldees, inhabitants of Chaldea.

3779. כַּשְׂדַּי **Kasday** (Chald.), *kas-dah'ee;* corresp. to 3778; a *Chaldæan* or inhab. of Chaldæa; by impl. a *Magian* or professional astrologer:—Chaldean.

3780. כָּשָׂה **kâsâh**, *kaw-saw';* a prim. root; to *grow fat* (i.e. be *covered* with flesh):—be covered. Comp. 3680.

3781. כַּשִּׁיל **kashshîyl**, *kash-sheel';* from 3782; prop. a *feller*, i.e. an *axe:*—ax.

3782. כָּשַׁל **kâshal**, *kaw-shal';* a prim. root; to *totter* or *waver* (through weakness of the legs, espec. the ankle); by impl. to *falter*, *stumble*, faint or fall:—bereave [*from the marg.*], cast down, be decayed, (cause to) fail, (cause, make to) fall (down, -ing), feeble, be (the) ruin (-ed, of), (be) overthrown, (cause to) stumble, × utterly, be weak.

3783. כִּשָּׁלוֹן **kishshâlôwn**, *kish-shaw-lone';* from 3782; prop. a *tottering*, i.e. *ruin:*—fall.

3784. כָּשַׁף **kâshaph**, *kaw-shaf'*; a prim. root; prop. to *whisper* a spell, i.e. to *inchant* or practise magic:—sorcerer, (use) witch (-craft).

3785. כֶּשֶׁף **kesheph**, *keh'-shef*; from 3784; *magic:*—sorcery, witchcraft.

3786. כַּשָּׁף **kashshâph**, *kash-shawf'*; from 3784; a *magician:*—sorcerer.

3787. כָּשֵׁר **kâshêr**, *kaw-share'*; a prim. root prop. to be *straight* or *right;* by impl. to *be acceptable;* also to *succeed* or prosper:—direct, be right, prosper.

3788. כִּשְׁרוֹן **kishrôwn**, *kish-rone'*; from 3787; *success, advantage:*—equity, good, right.

3789. כָּתַב **kâthab**, *kaw-thab'*; a prim. root; to *grave;* by impl. to *write* (describe, inscribe, prescribe, subscribe):—describe, record, prescribe, subscribe, write (-ing, -ten).

3790. כְּתַב **k^ethab** (Chald.), *keth-ab'*; corresp. to 3789:—write (-ten).

3791. כָּתָב **kâthâb**, *kaw-thawb'*; from 3789; something *written*, i.e. a *writing, record* or *book:*—register, scripture, writing.

3792. כְּתָב **k^ethâb** (Chald.), *keth-awb'*; corresp. to 3791:—prescribing, writing (-ten).

3793. כְּתֹבֶת **k^ethôbeth**, *keth-o'-beth*; from 3789; a *letter* or other *mark* branded on the skin:—× any [mark].

3794. כִּתִּי **Kittîy**, *kit-tee'*; or

כִּתִּיִּי **Kittiyîy**, *kit-tee-ee'*; patrial from an unused name denoting Cyprus (only in the plur.); a *Kittite* or Cypriote; hence an *islander* in gen., i.e. the Greeks or Romans on the shores opposite Pal.:—Chittim, Kittim.

3795. כָּתִית **kâthîyth**, *kaw-theeth'*; from 3807; *beaten*, i.e. pure (oil):—beaten.

3796. כֹּתֶל **kôthel**, *ko'-thel*; from an unused root mean. to *compact;* a *wall* (as *gathering* inmates):—wall.

3797. כְּתַל **k^ethal** (Chald.), *keth-al'*; corresp. to 3796:—wall.

3798. כִּתְלִישׁ **Kithlîysh**, *kith-leesh'*; from 3796 and 376; *wall of a man; Kithlish*, a place in Pal.:—Kithlish.

3799. כָּתַם **kâtham**, *kaw-tham'*; a prim. root; prop. to *carve* or *engrave*, i.e. (by impl.) to *inscribe* indelibly:—mark.

3800. כֶּתֶם **kethem**, *keh'-them*; from 3799; prop. something *carved* out, i.e. *ore;* hence *gold* (pure as originally mined):—([most] fine, pure) gold (-en wedge).

3801. כְּתֹנֶת **k^ethôneth**, *keth-o'-neth*; or

כֻּתֹּנֶת **kuttôneth**, *koot-to'-neth*; from an unused root mean. to *cover* [comp. 3802]; a *shirt:*—coat, garment, robe.

3802. כָּתֵף **kâthêph**, *kaw-thafe'*; from an unused root mean. to *clothe;* the *shoulder* (proper, i.e. upper end of the arm; as being the spot where the garments hang); fig. *side-piece* or lateral projection of anything:—arm, corner, shoulder (-piece), side, undersetter.

3803. כָּתַר **kâthar**, *kaw-thar'*; a prim. root; to *enclose;* hence (in a friendly sense) to *crown*, (in a hostile one) to *besiege;* also to *wait* (as restraining oneself):—beset round, compass about, be crowned inclose round, suffer.

3804. כֶּתֶר **kether**, *keh'-ther*; from 3803; prop. a *circlet*, i.e. a *diadem:*—crown.

3805. כֹתֶרֶת **kôthereth**, *ko-theh'-reth*; fem. act. part. of 3803; the *capital* of a column:—chapiter.

3806. כָּתַשׁ **kâthash**, *kaw-thash'*; a prim. root; to *butt* or *pound:*—bray.

3807. כָּתַת **kâthath**, *kaw-thath'*; a prim. root; to *bruise* or violently *strike:*—beat (down, to pieces), break in pieces, crushed, destroy, discomfit, smite, stamp.

ל

3808. לֹא **lô'**, *lo*; or

לוֹא **lôw'**, *lo*; or

לֹה **lôh** (Deut. 3 : 11), *lo*; a prim. particle; *not* (the simple or abs. negation); by impl. *no;* often used with other particles (as follows):—× before, + or else, ere, + except, ig [-norant], much. less, nay, neither, never, no ([-ne], -r, [-thing]), (× as though . . . , [can-], for) not (out of), of nought, otherwise, out of, + surely, + as truly as, + of a truth, + verily, for want, + whether, without.

3809. לָא **lâ'** (Chald.), *law;* or

לָה **lâh** (Chald.) (Dan. 4 : 32), *law;* corresp. to 3808:—or even, neither, no (-ne, -r), ([can-]) not, as nothing, without.

לֻא **lû'**. See 3863.

3810. לֹא דְבַר **Lô' D^ebar**, *lo deb-ar'*; or

לוֹ דְבַר **Lôw D^ebar** (2 Sam. 9 : 4, 5), *lo deb-ar'*; or

לִדְבִר **Lidbir** (Josh. 13 : 26), *lid-beer'* [prob. rather

לֹדְבַר° **Lôd^ebar**, *lo-deb-ar'*]; from 3808 and 1699; *pastureless; Lo-Debar*, a place in Pal.:—Debir, Lo-debar.

3811. לָאָה **lâ'âh**, *law-aw'*; a prim. root; to *tire;* (fig.) to *be* (or *make*) *disgusted:*—faint, grieve, lothe, (be, make) weary (selves).

3812. לֵאָה **Lê'âh**, *lay-aw'*; from 3811; *weary; Leah*, a wife of Jacob:—Leah.

לְאוֹם **l^e'owm**. See 3816.

3813. לָאַט **lâ'aṭ**, *law-at'*; a prim. root; to *muffle:*—cover.

3814. לָאט **lâ'ṭ**, *lawt*; from 3813 (or perh. for act. part. of 3874); prop. *muffled*, i.e. *silently:*—softly.

3815. לָאֵל **Lâ'êl**, *law-ale'*; from the prep. pref. and 410; (belonging) *to God; Laël* an Isr.:—Lael.

3816. לְאֹם **l^eôm**, *leh-ome'*; or

לְאוֹם **l^e'ôwm**, *leh-ome'*; from an unused root mean. to *gather;* a *community:*—nation, people.

3817. לְאֻמִּים **L^e'ummîym**, *leh-oom-meem'*; plur. of 3816; *communities; Leüm mim*, an Arabian:—Leummim.

3818. לֹא עַמִּי **Lô' 'Ammîy**, *lo am-mee'*; from 3808 and 5971 with pron. suffix; *not my people; Lo-Ammi*, the symbol. name of a son of Hosea:—Lo-ammi.

3819. לֹא רֻחָמָה **Lô' Rûchâmâh**, *lo roo-khaw-maw'*; from 3808 and 7355; *not pitied; Lo-Ruchamah*, the symbol. name of a daughter of Hosea:—Lo-ruhamah.

3820. לֵב **lêb**, *labe;* a form of 3824; the *heart;* also used (fig.) very widely for the feelings, the will and even the intellect; likewise for the *centre* of anything:— + care for, comfortably, consent, × considered, courag [-eous], friend [-ly], ([broken-], [hard-], [merry-], [stiff-], [stout-], double) heart ([-ed]), × heed, × I, kindly, midst, mind (-ed), × regard ([-ed]), × themselves, × unawares, understanding, × well, willingly, wisdom.

3821. לֵב **lêb** (Chald.), *labe;* corresp. to 3820:—heart.

3822. לְבָאוֹת **L^ebâ'ôwth**, *leb-aw-ōth'*; plur. of 3833; *lionesses; Lebaoth*, a place in Pal.:—Lebaoth. See also 1034.

3823. לָבַב **lâbab**, *law-bab'*; a prim. root; prop. *to be enclosed* (as if with *fat*); by impl. (as denom. from 3824) to *unheart*, i.e. (in a good sense) *transport* (with love), or (in a bad sense) *stultify;* also (as denom. from 3834) to *make cakes:*—make cakes, ravish, be wise.

3824. לֵבָב **lêbâb**, *lay-bawb'*; from 3823: the *heart* (as the most interior organ); used also like 3820:— + bethink themselves, breast, comfortably, courage, ([faint], [tender-] heart ([-ed]), midst, mind, × unawares, understanding.

3825. לְבַב **l^ebab** (Chald.), *leb-ab'*; corresp. to 3824:—heart.

לְבִבָה **l^ebîbâh**. See 3834.

3826. לִבָּה **libbâh**, *lib-baw'*; fem. of 3820; the *heart:*—heart.

3827. לַבָּה **labbâh**, *lab-baw'*; for 3852; *flame:*—flame.

3828. לְבוֹנָה **l^ebôwnâh**, *leb-o-naw'*; or

לְבֹנָה **l^ebônâh**, *leb-o-naw'*; from 3836; *frankincense* (from its *whiteness* or perh. that of its smoke):—(frank-) incense.

3829. לְבוֹנָה **L^ebôwnâh**, *leb-o-naw'*; the same as 3828; *Lebonah*, a place in Pal.:—Lebonah.

3830. לְבוּשׁ **l^ebûwsh**, *leb-oosh'*; or

לְבֻשׁ **l^ebûsh**, *leb-oosh'*; from 3847; a *garment* (lit. or fig.); by impl. (euphem.) a *wife:*—apparel, clothed with, clothing, garment, raiment, vestment, vesture.

3831. לְבוּשׁ **l^ebûwsh** (Chald.), *leb-oosh'*; corresp. to 3830:—garment.

3832. לָבַט **lâbaṭ**, *law-bat'*; a prim. root; to *overthrow;* intrans. to *fall:*—fall.

לֻבִּי **Lubbîy**. See 3864.

3833. לָבִיא **lâbîy'**, *law-bee'*; or (Ezek. 19 : 2)

לְבִיָּא **l^ebiyâ'**, *leb-ee-yaw'*; irreg. masc. plur.

לְבָאִים **l^ebâ'îym**, *leb-aw-eem'*; irreg. fem. plur.

לְבָאוֹת **l^ebâ'ôwth**, *leb-aw-ōth'*; from an unused root mean. to *roar;* a *lion* (prop. a lioness as the fiercer [although not a *roarer;* comp. 738]):—(great, old, stout) lion, lioness, young [lion].

3834. לָבִיבָה **lâbîybâh**, *law-bee-baw'*; or rather

לְבִבָה **l^ebîbâh**, *leb-ee-baw'*; from 3823 in its orig. sense of *fatness* (or perh. of *folding*); a *cake* (either as *fried* or *turned*):—cake.

3835. לָבַן **lâban**, *law-ban'*; a prim. root; to *be* (or become) *white;* also (as denom. from 3843) to *make bricks:*—make brick, be (made, make) white (-r).

3836. לָבָן **lâbân**, *law-bawn'*; or (Gen. 49 : 12)

לָבֵן **lâbên**, *law-bane'*; from 3835; *white:*—white.

3837. לָבָן **Lâbân**, *law-bawn'*; the same as 3836; *Laban*, a Mesopotamian; also a place in the Desert:—Laban.

לַבֵּן **Labbên**. See 4192.

3838. לְבָנָא **L^ebânâ'**, *leb-aw-naw'*; or

לְבָנָה **L^ebânâh**, *leb-aw-naw'*; the same as 3842; *Lebana* or *Lebanah*, one of the Nethinim:—Lebana, Lebanah.

3839. לִבְנֶה **libneh**, *lib-neh'*; from 3835; some sort of *whitish* tree, perh. the *storax:*—poplar.

3840. לִבְנָה **libnâh**, *lib-naw'*; from 3835; prop. *whiteness*, i.e. (by impl.) *transparency:*—paved.

3841. לִבְנָה **Libnâh**, *lib-naw'*; the same as 3839; *Libnah*, a place in the Desert and one in Pal.:—Libnah.

3842. לְבָנָה **l^ebânâh**, *leb-aw-naw'*; from 3835; prop. (the) *white*, i.e. the *moon:*—moon. See also 3838.

3843. לְבֵנָה **l^ebênâh**, *leb-ay-naw'*; from 3835; a *brick* (from the *whiteness* of the clay):—(altar of) brick, tile.

לְבֹנָה **l^ebônâh**. See 3828.

3844. לְבָנוֹן **L^ebânôwn**, *leb-aw-nohn'*; from 3825; (the) *white* mountain (from its snow); *Lebanon*, a mountain range in Pal.:—Lebanon.

3845. לִבְנִי **Libnîy**, *lib-nee'*; from 3835; *white; Libni*, an Isr.:—Libni.

3846. לִבְנִי **Libnîy**, *lib-nee'*; patron. from 3845; a *Libnite* or desc. of Libni (collect.):—Libnites.

3847. לָבַשׁ **lâbash**, *law-bash'*; or

לָבֵשׁ **lâbêsh**, *law-bashe'*; a prim. root; prop. *wrap* around, i.e. (by impl.) to *put on* a garment or *clothe* (oneself, or another), lit. or fig.:—(in) apparel, arm, array (self), clothe (self), come upon, put (on, upon), wear.

3848. לְבַשׁ **lᵉbash** (Chald.), *leb-ash';* corresp. to 3847:—clothe.

לְבוּשׁ **lᵉbûsh.** See 3830.

3849. לֹג **lôg**, *lohg;* from an unused root appar. mean. to *deepen* or *hollow* [like 3537]; a *log* or measure for liquids:—log [of oil].

3850. לֹד **Lôd**, *lode;* from an unused root of uncert. signif.; *Lod*, a place in Pal.:—Lod.

לִדְבִר **Lidbîr.** See 3810.

3851. לַהַב **lahab**, *lah'-hab;* from an unused root mean. to *gleam;* a *flash;* fig. a sharply polished *blade* or *point* of a weapon:—blade, bright, flame, glittering.

3852. לֶהָבָה **lehâbâh**, *leh-aw-baw';* or

לַהֶבֶת **lahebeth**, *lah-eh'-beth;* fem. of 3851, and mean. the same:—flame (-ming), head [of a spear].

3853. לְהָבִים **Lᵉhâbîym**, *leh-haw-beem';* plur. of 3851; *flames; Lehabim*, a son of Mizrain, and his descend.:—Lehabim.

3854. לַהַג **lahag**, *lah'-hag;* from an unused root mean. to *be eager;* intense mental *application:*—study.

3855. לַהַד **Lahad**, *lah'-had;* from an unused root mean. to *glow* [comp. 3851] or else to *be earnest* [comp. 3854]; *Lahad*, an Isr.:—Lahad.

3856. לָהַהּ **lâhahh**, *law-hah';* a prim. root mean. prop. to *burn*, i.e. (by impl.) to *be rabid* (fig. *insane*); also (from the *exhaustion* of frenzy) to *languish:*—faint, mad.

3857. לָהַט **lâhaṭ**, *law-hat';* a prim. root; prop. to *lick*, i.e. (by impl.) to *blaze:*—burn (up), set on fire, flaming, kindle.

3858. לַהַט **lahaṭ**, *lah'-hat;* from 3857; a *blaze;* also (from the idea of *enwrapping*) *magic* (as *covert*):—flaming, enchantment.

3859. לָהַם **lâham**, *law-ham';* a prim. root; prop. to *burn* in, i.e. (fig.) to *rankle:*—wound.

3860. לָהֵן **lâhên**, *law-hane';* from the pref. prep. mean. *to* or *for* and 2005; pop. *for if;* hence *therefore:*—for them [*by mistake for prep. suffix*].

3861. לָהֵן **lâwhên** (Chald.), *law-hane';* corresp. to 3860; *therefore;* also *except:*—but, except, save, therefore, wherefore.

3862. לַהֲקָה **lahăqâh**, *lah-hak-aw';* prob. from an unused root mean. to *gather;* an *assembly:*—company.

לוֹא **lôw'.** See 3808.

3863. לוּא **lûw'**, *loo;* or

לֻא **lû'**, *loo;* or

לוּ **lûw**, *loo;* a conditional particle; *if;* by impl. (interj. as a wish) *would that!:*—if (haply), peradventure, I pray thee, though, I would, would God (that).

3864. לוּבִי **Lûwbîy**, *loo-bee';* or

לֻבִּי **Lubbîy** (Dan. 11 : 43), *loob-bee';* patrial from a name prob. derived from an unused root mean. to *thirst*, i.e. a *dry* region; appar. a *Libyan* or inhab. of interior Africa (only in plur.):—Lubim (-s), Libyans.

3865. לוּד **Lûwd**, *lood;* prob. of for. der.; *Lud*, the name of two nations:—Lud, Lydia.

3866. לוּדִי **Lûwdîy**, *loo-dee';* or

לוּדִיִּי **Lûwdîyîy**, *loo-dee-ee';* patrial from 3865; a *Ludite* or inhab. of Lud (only in plur.):—Ludim, Lydians.

3867. לָוָה **lâvâh**, *law-vaw';* a prim. root; prop. to *twine*, i.e. (by impl.) to *unite*, to *remain;* also to *borrow* (as a form of *obligation*) or (caus.) to *lend:*—abide with, borrow (-er), cleave, join (self), lend (-er).

3868. לוּז **lûwz**, *looz;* a prim. root; to *turn* aside [comp. 3867, 3874 and 3885], i.e. (lit.) to *depart*, (fig.) *be perverse:*—depart, froward, perverse (-ness).

3869. לוּז **lûwz**, *looz;* prob. of for. or; some kind of *nut*-tree, perh. the *almond:*—hazel.

3870. לוּז **Lûwz**, *looz;* prob. from 3869 (as growing there); *Luz*, the name of two places in Pal.:—Luz.

3871. לוּחַ **lûwach**, *loo'-akh;* or

לֻחַ **lûach**, *loo'-akh;* from a prim. root; prob. mean. to *glisten;* a *tablet* (as *polished*), of stone, wood or metal:—board, plate, table.

3872. לוּחִית **Lûwchîyth**, *loo-kheeth';* or

לֻחוֹת° **Lûchôwth** (Jer. 48 : 5), *loo-khoth';* from the same as 3871; *floored; Luchith*, a place E. of the Jordan:—Luhith.

3873. לוֹחֵשׁ **Lôwchêsh**, *lo-khashe';* act. part. of 3907; (the) *enchanter; Lochesh*, an Isr.:—Hallohesh, Haloshesh [*includ. the art.*].

3874. לוּט **lûwṭ**, *loot;* a prim. root; to *wrap* up:—cast, wrap.

3875. לוֹט **lôwṭ**, *lote;* from 3874; a *veil:*—covering.

3876. לוֹט **Lôwṭ**, *lote;* the same as 3875; *Lot*, Abraham's nephew:—Lot.

3877. לוֹטָן **Lôwṭân**, *lo-tawn';* from 3875; *covering; Lotan*, an Idumæan:—Lotan.

3878. לֵוִי **Lêvîy**, *lay-vee';* from 3867; *attached; Levi*, a son of Jacob:—Levi. See also 3879, 3881.

3879. לֵוִי **Lêvîy** (Chald.), *lay-vee';* corresp. to 3880:—Levite.

3880. לִוְיָה **livyâh**, *liv-yaw';* from 3867; something *attached*, i.e. a *wreath:*—ornament.

3881. לֵוִיִּי **Lêvîyîy**, *lay-vee-ee';* or

לֵוִי **Lêvîy**, *lay-vee';* patron. from 3878; a *Leviite* or desc. of Levi:—Levite.

3882. לִוְיָתָן **livyâthân**, *liv-yaw-thawn';* from 3867; a *wreathed* animal, i.e. a *serpent* (espec. the *crocodile* or some other large sea-monster); fig. the constellation of the *dragon;* also as a symbol of *Bab.:*—leviathan, mourning.

3883. לוּל **lûwl**, *lool;* from an unused root mean. to *fold* back; a *spiral* step:—winding stair. Comp. 3924.

3884. לוּלֵא **lûwlê'**, *loo-lay';* or

לוּלֵי **lûwlêy**, *loo lay';* from 3863 and 3808; *if not:*—except, had not, if (... not), unless, were it not that.

3885. לוּן **lûwn**, *loon;* or

לִין **lîyn**, *leen;* a prim. root; to *stop* (usually over night); by impl. to *stay* permanently; hence (in a bad sense) to be *obstinate* (espec. in words, to *complain*):—abide (all night), continue, dwell, endure, grudge, be left, lie all night, (cause to) lodge (all night, in, -ing, this night), (make to) murmur, remain, tarry (all night, that night).

3886. לוּעַ **lûwa'**, *loo'-ah;* a prim. root; to *gulp;* fig. to *be rash:*—swallow down (up).

3887. לוּץ **lûwts**, *loots;* a prim. root; prop. to *make mouths* at, i.e. to *scoff;* hence (from the effort to pronounce a foreign language) to *interpret*, or (gen.) *intercede:*—ambassador, have in derision, interpreter, make a mock, mocker, scorn (-er, -ful), teacher.

3888. לוּשׁ **lûwsh**, *loosh;* a prim. root; to *knead:*—knead.

3889. לוּשׁ° **Lûwsh**, *loosh;* from 3888; *kneading; Lush*, a place in Pal.:—Laish [*from the marg.*]. Comp. 3919.

3890. לְוָת **lᵉvâth** (Chald.), *lev-awth';* from a root corresp. to 3867; prop. *adhesion*, i.e. (as prep.) *with:*—× thee.

לֻחֹת **Lûchôwth.** See 3872.

לָז **lâz**, and

לָזֶה **lâzeh.** See 1975 and 1976.

3891. לְזוּת **lᵉzûwth**, *lez-ooth';* from 3868; *perverseness:*—perverse.

3892. לַח **lach**, *lakh;* from an unused root mean. to *be new; fresh*, i.e. unused or undried:—green, moist.

3893. לֵחַ **lêach**, *lay'-akh;* from the same as 3892; *freshness*, i.e. vigor:—natural force.

לֻחַ **lûach.** See 3871.

3894. לָחוּם **lâchûwm**, *law-khoom';* or

לָחֻם **lâchûm**, *law-khoom';* pass. part. of 3898; prop. *eaten*, i.e. *food;* also *flesh*, i.e. *body:*—while ... is eating, flesh.

3895. לְחִי **lᵉchîy**, *lekh-ee';* from an unused root mean. to *be soft;* the *cheek* (from its *fleshiness*); hence the *jaw*-bone:—cheek (bone), jaw (bone).

3896. לֶחִי **Lechîy**, *lekh'-ee;* a form of 3895; *Lechi*, a place in Pal.:—Lehi. Comp. also 7437.

3897. לָחַךְ **lâchak**, *law-khak';* a prim. root; to *lick:*—lick (up).

3898. לָחַם **lâcham**, *law-kham';* a prim. root; to *feed* on; fig. to *consume;* by impl. to *battle* (as *destruction*):—devour, eat, × ever, fight (-ing), overcome, prevail, (make) war (-ring).

3899. לֶחֶם **lechem**, *lekh'-em;* from 3898; *food* (for man or beast), espec. *bread*, or *grain* (for making it):—([shew-]) bread, × eat, food, fruit, loaf, meat, victuals. See also 1036.

3900. לְחֶם **lᵉchem** (Chald.), *lekh-em';* corresp. to 3899:—feast.

3901. לָחֶם **lâchem**, *law-khem';* from 3898; *battle:*—war.

לָחֻם **lâchûm.** See 3894.

3902. לַחְמִי **Lachmîy**, *lakh-mee';* from 3899; *foodful; Lachmi*, a Philis.; or rather prob. a brief form (or perh. err. transc.) for 1022:—Lahmi. See also 3433.

3903. לַחְמָס **Lachmâç**, *lakh-maws';* prob. by err. transc. for

לַחְמָם° **Lachmâm**, *lakh-mawm';* from 3899; *food-like; Lachmam* or *Lachmas*, a place in Pal.:—Lahmam.

3904. לְחֵנָה **lᵉchênâh** (Chald.), *lekh-ay-naw';* from an unused root of uncert. mean.; a *concubine:*—concubine.

3905. לָחַץ **lâchats**, *law-khats';* a prim. root; prop. to *press*, i.e. (fig.) to *distress:*—afflict, crush, force, hold fast, oppress (-or), thrust self.

3906. לַחַץ **lachats**, *lakh'-ats;* from 3905; *distress:*—affliction, oppression.

3907. לָחַשׁ **lâchash**, *law-khash';* a prim. root; to *whisper;* by impl. to *mumble* a spell (as a magician):—charmer, whisper (together).

3908. לַחַשׁ **lachash**, *lakh'-ash;* from 3907; prop. a *whisper*, i.e. by impl. (in a good sense) a private *prayer*, (in a bad one) an *incantation;* concr. an *amulet:*—charmed, earring, enchantment, orator, prayer.

3909. לָט **lâṭ**, *lawt;* a form of 3814 or else part. from 3874; prop. *covered*, i.e. *secret;* by impl. *incantation;* also *secrecy* or (adv.) *covertly:*—enchantment, privily, secretly, softly.

3910. לֹט **lôṭ**, *lote;* prob. from 3874; a gum (from its *sticky* nature), prob. *ladanum:*—myrrh.

3911. לְטָאָה **lᵉṭâ'âh**, *let-aw-aw';* from an unused root mean. to *hide;* a kind of *lizard* (from its *covert* habits):—lizard.

3912. לְטוּשִׁם **Lᵉṭûwshîm**, *let-oo-sheem';* masc. plur. of pass. part. of 3913; *hammered* (i.e. *oppressed*) ones; *Letushim*, an Arabian tribe:—Letushim.

3913. לָטַשׁ **lâṭash**, *law-tash';* a prim. root; prop. to *hammer* out (an edge), i.e. to *sharpen:*—instructer, sharp (-en), whet.

3914. לֹיָה **lôyâh**, *lo-yaw';* a form of 3880; a *wreath:*—addition.

3915. לַיִל **layil**, *lah'-yil;* or (Isa. 21 : 11)

לֵיל **lêyl**, *lale;* also

לַיְלָה **layᵉlâh**, *lah'-yel-aw;* from the same as 3883; prop. a *twist* (away of the light), i.e. *night;* fig. *adversity:*—([mid-]) night (season).

3916. לֵילְיָא **leylᵉyâ'** (Chald.), *lay-leh-yaw';* corresp. to 3915:—night.

3917. לִילִית **lîylîyth**, *lee-leeth'*; from 3915; a *night* spectre:—screech owl.

3918. לַיִשׁ **layish**, *lah'-yish*; from 3888 in the sense of *crushing*; a lion (from his destructive *blows*):—(old) lion.

3919. לַיִשׁ **Layish**, *lah'-yish*; the same as 3918; *Laïsh*, the name of two places in Pal.:—Laish. Comp. 3889.

3920. לָכַד **lâkad**, *law-kad'*; a prim. root; to *catch* (in a net, trap or pit); gen. to *capture* or *occupy*; also to *choose* (by lot); fig. to *cohere*:— × at all, catch (self), be frozen, be holden, stick together, take.

3921. לֶכֶד **leked**, *leh'-ked*; from 3920; something to *capture* with, i.e. a *noose*:—being taken.

3922. לֵכָה **lêkâh**, *lay-kaw'*; from 3212; a *journey*; *Lekah*, a place in Pal.:—Lecah.

3923. לָכִישׁ **Lâchîysh**, *law-keesh'*; from an unused root of uncert. mean.; *Lakish*, a place in Pal.:—Lachish.

3924. לֻלָאָה **lûlâ'âh**, *loo-law-aw'*; from the same as 3883; a *loop*:—loop.

3925. לָמַד **lâmad**, *law-mad'*; a prim. root; prop. to *goad*, i.e. (by impl.) to *teach* (the rod being an Oriental *incentive*):—[un-] accustomed, × diligently, expert, instruct, learn, skilful, teach (-er, -ing).

לִמֻּד **limmûd**. See 3928.

3926. לְמוֹ **lᵉmôw**, *lem-o'*; a prol. and separable form of the pref. prep.; *to* or *for*:—at, for, to, upon.

3927. לְמוּאֵל **Lᵉmûw'êl**, *lem-oo-ale'*; or
לְמוֹאֵל **Lᵉmôw'êl**, *lem-o-ale'*; from 3926 and 410; (belonging) *to God*; *Lemuël* or *Lemoël*, a symbol. name of Solomon:—Lemuel.

3928. לִמּוּד **limmûwd**, *lim-mood'*; or
לִמֻּד **limmûd**, *lim-mood'*; from 3925; *instructed*:—accustomed, disciple, learned, taught, used.

3929. לֶמֶךְ **Lemek**, *leh'-mek*; from an unused root of uncert. mean.; *Lemek*, the name of two antediluvian patriarchs:—Lamech.

3930. לֹעַ **lôaʻ**, *lo'ah* from 3886; the *gullet*:—throat.

3931. לָעַב **lâʻab**, *law-ab'*; a prim. root; to *deride*:—mock.

3932. לָעַג **lâʻag**, *law-ag'*; a prim. root; to *deride*; by impl. (as if imitating a foreigner) to *speak unintelligibly*:—have in derision, laugh (to scorn), mock (on), stammering.

3933. לַעַג **laʻag**, *lah'-ag*; from 3932; *derision*, *scoffing*:—derision, scorn (-ing).

3934. לָעֵג **lâʻêg**, *law-ayg'*; from 3932; a *buffoon*; also a *foreigner*:—mocker, stammering.

3935. לַעְדָּה **Laʻdâh**, *lah-daw'*; from an unused root of uncert. mean.; *Ladah*, an Isr.:—Laadah.

3936. לַעְדָּן **Laʻdân**, *lah-dawn'*; from the same as 3935; *Ladan*, the name of two Isr.:—Laadan.

3937. לָעַז **lâʻaz**, *law-az'*; a prim. root; to *speak in a foreign tongue*:—strange language.

3938. לָעַט **lâʻaṭ**, *law-at'*; a prim. root; to *swallow* greedily; causat. to *feed*:—feed.

3939. לַעֲנָה **laʻănâh**, *lah-an-aw'*; from an unused root supposed to mean to *curse*; *wormwood* (regarded as *poisonous*, and therefore *accursed*):—hemlock, wormwood.

3940. לַפִּיד **lappîyd**, *lap-peed'*; or
לַפִּד **lappîd**, *lap-peed'*; from an unused root prob. mean. to *shine*; a *flambeau*, *lamp* or *flame*:—(fire-) brand, (burning) lamp, lightning, torch.

3941. לַפִּידוֹת **Lappîydôwth**, *lap-pee-dōth'*; fem. plur. of 3940; *Lappidoth*, the husband of Deborah:—Lappidoth.

3942. לִפְנַי **liphnay**, *lif-nah'ee*; from the pref. prep. (*to* or *for*) and 6440; *anterior*:—before.

3943. לָפַת **lâphath**, *law-fath'*; a prim. root; prop. to *bend*, i.e. (by impl.) to *clasp*; also (reflex.) to *turn* around or aside:—take hold, turn aside (self).

3944. לָצוֹן **lâtsôwn**, *law-tsone'*; from 3887; *derision*:—scornful (-ning).

3945. לָצַץ **lâtsats**, *law-tsats'*; a prim. root; to *deride*:—scorn.

3946. לַקּוּם **Laqqûwm** *lak-koom'*; from an unused root thought to mean to *stop* up by a barricade; perh. *fortification*; *Lakkum*, a place in Pal.:—Lakum.

3947. לָקַח **lâqach**, *law-kakh'*; a prim. root; to *take* (in the widest variety of applications):—accept, bring, buy, carry away, drawn, fetch, get, infold, × many, mingle, place, receive (-ing), reserve, seize, send for, take (away, -ing, up), use, win.

3948. לֶקַח **leqach**, *leh'-kakh*; from 3947; prop. something *received*, i.e. (mentally) *instruction* (whether on the part of the teacher or hearer); also (in an act. and sinister sense) *inveiglement*:—doctrine, learning, fair speech.

3949. לִקְחִי **Liqchîy**, *lik-khee'*; from 3947; *learned*; *Likchi*, an Isr.:—Likhi.

3950. לָקַט **lâqaṭ**, *law-kat'*; a prim. root; prop. to *pick* up, i.e. (gen.) to *gather*; spec. to *glean*:—gather (up), glean.

3951. לֶקֶט **leqeṭ**, *leh'-ket*; from 3950; the *gleaning*:—gleaning.

3952. לָקַק **lâqaq**, *law-kak'*; a prim. root; to *lick* or *lap*:—lap, lick.

3953. לָקַשׁ **lâqash**, *law-kash'*; a prim. root; to *gather* the *after* crop:—gather.

3954. לֶקֶשׁ **leqesh**, *leh'-kesh*; from 3953; the *after crop*:—latter growth.

3955. לְשַׁד **lᵉshad**, *lesh-ad'*; from an unused root of uncert. mean.; appar. *juice*, i.e. (fig.) *vigor*; also a sweet or fat *cake*:—fresh, moisture.

3956. לָשׁוֹן **lâshôwn**, *law-shone'*; or
לָשֹׁן **lâshôn**, *law-shone'*; also (in plur.) fem.
לְשֹׁנָה **lᵉshônâh**, *lesh-o-naw'*; from 3960; the *tongue* (of man or animals), used lit. (as the instrument of licking, eating, or speech), and fig. (speech, an ingot, a fork of flame, a cove of water):— + babbler, bay, + evil speaker, language, talker, tongue, wedge.

3957. לִשְׁכָּה **lishkâh**, *lish-kaw'*; from an unused root of uncert. mean.; a *room* in a building (whether for storage, eating, or lodging):—chamber, parlour. Comp. 5393.

3958. לֶשֶׁם **leshem**, *leh'-shem*; from an unused root of uncert. mean.; a *gem*, perh. the *jacinth*:—ligure.

3959. לֶשֶׁם **Leshem**, *leh'-shem*; the same as 3958; *Leshem*, a place in Pal.:—Leshem.

3960. לָשַׁן **lâshan**, *law-shan'*; a prim. root; prop. to *lick*; but used only as a denom. from 3956; to *wag the tongue*, i.e. to *calumniate*:—accuse, slander.

3961. לִשָּׁן **lishshân** (Chald.) *lish-shawn'*; corresp. to 3956; *speech*, i.e. a *nation*:—language.

3962. לֶשַׁע **Leshaʻ**, *leh'-shah*; from an unused root thought to mean to *break* through; a boiling *spring*; *Lesha*, a place prob. E. of the Jordan:—Lasha.

3963. לֶתֶךְ **lethek**, *leh'-thek*; from an unused root of uncert. mean.; a *measure* for things dry:—half homer.

מ

מַה־ **ma-**, or
מָה־ **mâ-**. See 4100.

3964. מָא **mâ'** (Chald.) *maw*; corresp. to 4100; (as indef.) *that*:— + what.

3965. מַאֲבוּס **maʼăbûwç**, *mah-ab-ooce'*; from 75; a *granary*:—storehouse.

3966. מְאֹד **mᵉʼôd**, *meh-ode'*; from the same as 181; prop. *vehemence*, i.e. (with or without prep.) *vehemently*; by impl. *wholly*, *speedily*, etc. (often with other words as an intensive or superlative; espec. when repeated):—diligently, especially, exceeding (-ly), far, fast, good, great (-ly), × louder and louder, might (-ily, -y), (so) much, quickly, (so) sore, utterly, very (+ much, sore), well.

3967. מֵאָה **mê'âh**, *may-aw'*; or
מֵאיָה **mê'yâh**, *may-yaw'*; prob. a prim. numeral; a *hundred*; also as a multiplicative and a fraction:—hundred ([-fold], -th), + sixscore.

3968. מֵאָה **Mê'âh**, *may-aw'*; the same as 3967; *Meäh*, a tower in Jerus.:—Meah.

3969. מְאָה **mᵉ'âh** (Chald.), *meh-aw'*; corresp. to 3967:—hundred.

3970. מַאֲוַי **maʼăvay**, *mah-av-ah'ee*; from 183; a *desire*:—desire.

מוֹאל **môw'l**. See 4136.

3971. מאוּם **m'ûwm**, *moom*; usually
מוּם **mûwm**, *moom*; as if pass. part. from an unused root prob. mean. to *stain*; a *blemish* (phys. or mor.):—blemish, blot, spot.

3972. מְאוּמָה **mᵉʼûwmâh**, *meh-oo'-maw*; appar. a form of 3971; prop. a *speck* or *point*, i.e. (by impl.) *something*; with neg. *nothing*:—fault, + no (-ught), ought, somewhat, any ([no-]) thing.

3973. מָאוֹס **mâ'ôwç**, *maw-oce'*; from 3988; *refuse*:—refuse.

3974. מָאוֹר **mâ'ôwr**, *maw-ore'*; or
מָאֹר **mâ'ôr**, *maw-ore'*; also (in plur.) fem.
מְאוֹרָה **mᵉ'ôwrâh**, *meh-o-raw'*; or
מְאֹרָה **mᵉ'ôrâh**, *meh-o-raw'*; from 215; prop. a *luminous* body or *luminary*, i.e. (abstr.) *light* (as an element); fig. *brightness*, i.e. *cheerfulness*; spec. a *chandelier*:—bright, light.

3975. מְאוּרָה **mᵉʼûwrâh**, *meh-oo-raw'*; fem. pass. part. of 215; something *lighted*, i.e. an *aperture*; by impl. a *crevice* or *hole* of a serpent):—den.

3976. מֹאזֵן **mô'zên**, *mo-zane'*; from 239; (only in the dual) a pair of *scales*:—balances.

3977. מֹאזֵן **mô'zên** (Chald.) *mo-zane'*; corresp. to 3976:—balances.

מֵאיָה **mê'yâh**. See 3967.

3978. מַאֲכָל **maʼăkâl**, *mah-ak-awl'*; from 398; an *eatable* (includ. provender, flesh and fruit):—food, fruit, ([bake-]) meat (-s), victual.

3979. מַאֲכֶלֶת **maʼăkeleth**, *mah-ak-eh'-leth*; from 398; something to *eat* with, i.e. a *knife*:—knife.

3980. מַאֲכֹלֶת **maʼăkôleth**, *mah-ak-o'-leth*; from 398; something *eaten* (by fire), i.e. *fuel*:—fuel.

3981. מַאֲמָץ **maʼămâts**, *mah-am-awts'*; from 553; *strength*, i.e. (plur.) *resources*:—force.

3982. מַאֲמַר **maʼămar**, *mah-am-ar'*; from 559; something (authoritatively) *said*, i.e. an *edict*:—commandment, decree.

3983. מֵאמַר **mê'mar** (Chald.), *may-mar'*; corresp. to 3982:—appointment, word.

3984. מָאן **mâ'n** (Chald.), *mawn*; prob. from a root corresp. to 579 in the sense of an *inclosure* by sides; a *utensil*:—vessel.

3985. מָאֵן **mâ'ên**, *maw-ane'*; a prim. root; to *refuse*:—refuse, × utterly.

3986. מָאֵן **mâ'ên**, *maw-ane'*; from 3985; *unwilling*:—refuse.

3987. מֵאֵן **mê'ên**, *may-ane'*; from 3985; *refractory*:—refuse.

3988. מָאַס **mâ'aç**, *maw-as'*; a prim. root; to *spurn*; also (intrans.) to *disappear*:—abhor, cast away (off), contemn, despise, disdain, (become) loathe (-some), melt away, refuse, reject, reprobate, × utterly, vile person.

3989. מַאֲפֶה **maʼăpheh**, *mah-af-eh'*; from 644; something *baked*, i.e. a *batch*:—baken.

3990. מַאֲפֵל **maʼăphêl**, *mah-af-ale'*; from the same as 651; something *opaque*:—darkness.

3991. מַאְפֵּלְיָה **maʼphêlᵉyâh**, *mah-af-ay-leh-yaw'*; prol. fem. of 3990; *opaqueness*:—darkness.

3992. מָאַר **mâ'ar**, *maw-ar'*, a prim. root; to *be bitter* or (causat.) to *embitter*, i.e. *be painful*:—fretting, picking.

מָאֹר **mâ'ôr**. See 3974.

3993. מַאֲרָב **ma'ărâb**, *mah-ar-awb'*; from 693; an *ambuscade*:—lie in ambush, ambushment, lurking place, lying in wait.

3994. מְאֵרָה **me'êrâh**, *meh-ay-raw'*; from 779; an *execration*:—curse.

מְאֹרָה **me'ôrâh**. See 3974.

3995. מִבְדָּלָה **mibdâlâh**, *mib-daw-law'*; from 914; a *separation*, i.e. (concr.) a *separate* place:—separate.

3996. מָבוֹא **mâbôw'**, *maw-bo'*; from 935; an *entrance* (the place or the act); spec. (with or without 8121) *sunset* or the *west*; also (adv. with prep.) *towards*:—by which came, as cometh, in coming, as men enter into, entering, entrance into, entry, where goeth, going down, + westward. Comp. 4126.

3997. מְבוֹאָה **mebôwâh**, *meb-o-aw'*; fem. of 3996; a *haven*:—entry.

3998. מְבוּכָה **mebûwkâh**, *meb-oo-kaw'*; from 943; *perplexity*:—perplexity,

3999. מַבּוּל **mabbûwl**, *mab-bool'*; from 2986 in the sense of *flowing*; a *deluge*:—flood.

4000. מָבוֹן **mâbôwn**, *maw-bone'*; from 995; *instructing*:—taught.

4001. מְבוּסָה **mebûwçâh**, *meb-oo-saw'*; from 947; a *trampling*:—treading (trodden) down (under foot).

4002. מַבּוּעַ **mabbûwa'**, *mab-boo'-ah*; from 5042; a *fountain*:—fountain, spring.

4003. מְבוּקָה **mebûwqâh**, *meb-oo-kah'*; from the same as 950; *emptiness*:—void.

4004. מִבְחוֹר **mibchôwr**, *mib-khore'*; from 977; *select*, i.e. well fortified:—choice.

4005. מִבְחָר **mibchâr**, *mib-khawr'*; from 977; *select*, i.e. best:—choice (-st), chosen.

4006. מִבְחָר **Mibchâr**, *mib-khawr'*; the same as 4005; *Mibchar*, an Isr.:—Mibhar.

4007. מַבָּט **mabbâṭ**, *mab-bawt'*; or

מֶבָּט **mebbâṭ**, *meb-bawt'*; from 5027; something *expected*, i.e. (abstr.) *expectation*:—expectation.

4008. מִבְטָא **mibṭâ'**, *mib-taw'*; from 981; a rash *utterance* (hasty vow):—(that which . . .) uttered (out of).

4009. מִבְטָח **mibṭâch**, *mib-tawkh'*; from 982; prop. a *refuge*, i.e. (obj.) *security*, or (subj.) *assurance*:—confidence, hope, sure, trust.

4010. מַבְלִיגִית **mablîygîyth**, *mab-leeg-eeth'*; from 1082; *desistance* (or rather *desolation*):—comfort self.

4011. מִבְנֶה **mibneh**, *mib-neh'*; from 1129; a *building*:—frame.

4012. מְבֻנַּי **Mebunnay**, *meb-oon-nah'ee*; from 1129; *built* up; *Mebunnai*, an Isr.:—Iebunnai.

4013. מִבְצָר **mibtsâr**, *mib-tsawr'*; also (in plur.) fem. (Dan. 11 : 15)

מִבְצָרָה **mibtsârâh**, *mib-tsaw-raw'*; from 1219; a *fortification*, *castle*, or *fortified* city; fig. a *defender*:—(de-, most) fenced, fortress, (most) strong (hold).

4014. מִבְצָר **Mibtsâr**, *mib-tsawr'*; the same as 4013; *Mibtsar*, an Idumæan:—Mibzar.

מִבְצָרָה **mibtsârâh**. See 4013.

4015. מִבְרָח **mibrâch**, *mib-rawkh'*; from 1272; a *refugee*:—fugitive.

4016. מָבֻשׁ **mâbûsh**, *maw-boosh'*; from 954; (plur.) the (male) *pudenda*:—secrets.

4017. מִבְשָׂם **Mibsâm**, *mib-sawm'*; from the same as 1314; *fragrant*; *Mibsam*, the name of an Ishmaelite and of an Isr.:—Mibsam.

4018. מְבַשְּׁלָה **mebashshelâh**, *meb-ash-shel-aw'*; from 1310; a cooking *hearth*:—boiling-place.

מָג **Mâg**. See 7248, 7249.

4019. מַגְבִּישׁ **Magbîysh**, *mag-beesh'*; from the same as 1378; *stiffening*; *Magbish*, an Isr., or a place in Pal.:—Magbish.

4020. מִגְבָּלָה **migbâlâh**, *mig-baw-law'*; from 1379; a *border*:—end.

4021. מִגְבָּעָה **migbâ'âh**, *mig-baw-aw'*; from the same as 1389; a *cap* (as *hemispherical*):—bonnet.

4022. מֶגֶד **meged**, *meh'-ghed*; from an unused root prop. mean. to *be eminent*; prop. a *distinguished* thing; hence something *valuable*, as a product or fruit:—pleasant, precious fruit (thing).

4023. מְגִדּוֹן **Megiddôwn** (Zech. 12 : 11), *meg-id-dōne'*; or

מְגִדּוֹ **Megiddôw**, *meg-id-do'*; from 1413; *rendezvous*; *Megiddon* or *Megiddo*, a place in Pal.:—Megiddo, Megiddon.

4024. מִגְדּוֹל **Migdôwl**, *mig-dole'*; or

מִגְדֹּל **Migdôl**, *mig-dole'*; prob. of Eg. or.; *Migdol*, a place in Eg.:—Migdol, tower.

4025. מַגְדִּיאֵל **Magdîy'êl**, *mag-dee-ale'*; from 4022 and 410; *preciousness of God*; *Magdiël*, an Idumæan:—Magdiel.

4026. מִגְדָּל **migdâl**, *mig-dawl'*; also (in plur.) fem.

מִגְדָּלָה **migdâlâh**, *mig-daw-law'*; from 1431; a *tower* (from its size or height); by anal. a *rostrum*; fig. a (pyramidal) *bed* of flowers:—castle, flower, pulpit, tower. Comp. the names following.

מִגְדֹּל **Migdôl**. See 4024.

מִגְדָּלָה **migdâlâh**. See 4026.

4027. מִגְדַּל־אֵל **Migdal-'Êl**, *mig-dal-ale'*; from 4026 and 410; *tower of God*; *Migdal-El*, a place in Pal.:—Migdal-el.

4028. מִגְדַּל־גָּד **Migdal-Gâd**, *migdal-gawd'*; from 4026 and 1408; *tower of Fortune*; *Migdal-Gad*, a place in Pal.:—Migdal-gad.

4029. מִגְדַּל־עֵדֶר **Migdal-'Êder**, *mig-dal'-ay'-der*; from 4026 and 5739; *tower of a flock*; *Migdal-Eder*, a place in Pal.:—Migdal-eder, tower of the flock.

4030. מִגְדָּנָה **migdânâh**, *mig-daw-naw'*; from the same as 4022; *preciousness*, i.e. a *gem*:—precious thing, present.

4031. מָגוֹג **Mâgôwg**, *maw-gogue'*; from 1463; *Magog*, a son of Japheth; also a barbarous northern region:—Magog.

4032. מָגוֹר **mâgôwr**, *maw-gore'*; or (Lam. 2 : 22)

מָגוּר **mâgûwr**, *maw-goor'*; from 1481 in the sense of *fearing*; a *fright* (obj. or subj.):—fear, terror. Comp. 4036.

4033. מָגוּר **mâgûwr**, *maw-goor'*; or

מָגֻר **mâgûr**, *maw-goor'*; from 1481 in the sense of *lodging*; a temporary *abode*; by extens. a permanent *residence*:—dwelling, pilgrimage, where sojourn, be a stranger. Comp. 4032.

4034. מְגוֹרָה **megôwrâh**, *meg-o-raw'*; fem. of 4032; *affright*:—fear.

4035. מְגוּרָה **megûwrâh**, *meg-oo-raw'*; fem. of 4032 or of 4033; a *fright*; also a *granary*:—barn, fear.

4036. מָגוֹר מִסָּבִיב **Mâgôwr miç-Çâbîyb**, *maw-gore' mis-saw-beeb'*; from 4032 and 5439 with the prep. inserted; *affright from around*; *Magor-mis-Sabib*, a symbol. name of Pashur:—Magor-missabib.

4037. מַגְזֵרָה **magzêrâh**, *mag-zay-raw'*; from 1504; a *cutting* implement, i.e. a *blade*:—axe.

4038. מַגָּל **maggâl**, *mag-gawl'*; from an unused root mean. to *reap*; a *sickle*:—sickle.

4039. מְגִלָּה **megillâh**, *meg-il-law'*; from 1556; a *roll*:—roll, volume.

4040. מְגִלָּה **megillâh** (Chald.), *meg-il-law'*; corresp. to 4039:—roll.

4041. מְגַמָּה **megammâh**, *meg-am-maw'*; from the same as 1571; prop. *accumulation*, i.e. *impulse* or *direction*:—sup up.

4042. מָגַן **mâgan**, *maw-gan'*; a denom. from 4043; prop. to *shield*; *encompass* with; fig. to *rescue*, to *hand* safely *over* (i.e. *surrender*):—deliver.

4043. מָגֵן **mâgên**, *maw-gane'*; also (in plur.) fem.

מְגִנָּה **meginnâh**, *meg-in-naw'*; from 1598; a *shield* (i.e. the small one or *buckler*); fig. a *protector*; also the scaly *hide* of the crocodile:—× armed, buckler, defence, ruler, + scale, shield.

4044. מְגִנָּה **meginnâh**, *meg-in-naw'*; from 4042; a *covering* (in a bad sense), i.e. *blindness* or obduracy:—sorrow. See also 4043.

4045. מִגְעֶרֶת **mig'ereth**, *mig-eh'-reth*; from 1605; *reproof* (i.e. curse):—rebuke.

4046. מַגֵּפָה **maggêphâh**, *mag-gay-faw'*; from 5062; a *pestilence*; by anal. *defeat*:—(× be) plague (-d), slaughter, stroke.

4047. מַגְפִּיעָשׁ **Magpîy'âsh**, *mag-pee-awsh'*; appar. from 1479 or 5062 and 6211; *exterminator of* (the) *moth*; *Magpiash*, an Isr.:—Magpiash.

4048. מָגַר **mâgar**, *maw-gar'*; a prim. root; to *yield up*; intens. to *precipitate*:—cast down, terror.

4049. מְגַר **megar** (Chald.), *meg-ar'*; corresp. to 4048; to *overthrow*:—destroy.

4050. מְגֵרָה **megêrâh**, *meg-ay-raw'*; from 1641; a *saw*:—axe, saw.

4051. מִגְרוֹן **Migrôwn**, *mig-rone'*; from 4048; *precipice*; *Migron*, a place in Pal.:—Migron.

4052. מִגְרָעָה **migrâ'âh**, *mig-raw-aw'*; from 1639; a *ledge* or offset:—narrowed rest.

4053. מִגְרָפָה **migrâphâh**, *mig-raw-faw'*; from 1640; something *thrown off* (by the spade), i.e. a *clod*:—clod.

4054. מִגְרָשׁ **migrâsh**, *mig-rawsh'*; also (in plur.) fem. (Ezek. 27 : 28)

מִגְרָשָׁה **migrâshâh**, *mig-raw-shaw'*; from 1644; a *suburb* (i.e. open country whither flocks are *driven* for pasture); hence the *area* around a building, or the *margin* of the sea:—cast out, suburb.

4055. מַד **mad**, *mad*; or

מֵד **mêd**, *made*; from 4058; prop. *extent*, i.e. *height*; also a *measure*; by impl. a *vesture* (as measured); also a *carpet*:—armour, clothes, garment, judgment, measure, raiment, stature.

4056. מַדְבַּח **madbach** (Chald.), *mad-bakh'*; from 1684; a sacrificial *altar*:—altar.

4057. מִדְבָּר **midbâr**, *mid-bawr'*; from 1696 in the sense of *driving*; a *pasture* (i.e. open field, whither cattle are driven); by impl a *desert*; also *speech* (including its organs):—desert, south, speech, wilderness.

4058. מָדַד **mâdad**, *maw-dad'*; a prim. root; prop. to *stretch*; by impl. to *measure* (as if by *stretching* a line); fig. to *be extended*:—measure, mete, stretch self.

4059. מִדַּד **middad**, *mid-dad'*; from 5074; *flight*:—be gone.

4060. מִדָּה **middâh**, *mid-daw'*; fem. of 4055; prop. *extension*, i.e. height or breadth; also a *measure* (including its standard); hence a *portion* (as measured) or a *vestment*; spec. *tribute* (as measured):—garment, measure (-ing, meteyard, piece, size, (great) stature, tribute, wide.

4061. מִדָּה **middâh** (Chald.), *mid-daw'*; or

מִנְדָּה **mindâh** (Chald.), *min-daw'*; corresp. to 4060; *tribute* in money:—toll, tribute.

4062. מַדְהֵבָה **madhêbâh**, *mad-hay-baw'*; perh. from the equiv. of 1722; *gold-making*, i.e. *exactress*:—golden city.

4063. מֶדֶו **medev**, *meh'-dev*; from an unused root mean. to *stretch*; prop. *extent*, i.e. *measure*; by impl. a *dress* (as measured):—garment.

4064. מַדְוֶה **madveh**, *mad-veh'*; from 1738; *sickness*:—disease.

4065. מַדּוּחַ **maddûwach**, *mad-doo'-akh*, from 5080; *seduction*:—cause of banishment.

4066. מָדוֹן **mâdôwn**, *maw-dohn'*; from 1777; a *contest* or quarrel:—brawling, contention (-ous), discord, strife. Comp. 4079, 4090.

4067. מָדוֹן **mâdôwn**, *maw-dohn'*; from the same as 4063; *extensiveness*, i.e. height:—stature.

4068. מָדוֹן **Mâdôwn**, *maw-dohn'*; the same as 4067; *Madon*, a place in Pal.:—Madon.

4069. מַדּוּעַ **maddûwaʿ**, *mad-doo'-ah*; or
מַדֻּעַ **maddûaʿ**, *mad-doo'-ah*; from 4100 and the pass. part. of 3045; *what* (is) *known?*; i.e. (by impl.) (adv.) *why?*:—how, wherefore, why.

4070. מְדוֹר **m^{e}dôwr** Chald.), *med-ore'*; or
מְדֹר **m^{e}dôr** (Chald.), *med-ore'*; or
מְדָר **m^{e}dâr** (Chald.), *med-awr'*; from 1753; a *dwelling*:—dwelling.

4071. מְדוּרָה **m^{e}dûwrâh**, *med-oo-raw'*; or
מְדֻרָה **m^{e}dûrâh**, *med-oo-raw'*; from 1752 in the sense of *accumulation*; a *pile* of fuel:—pile (for fire).

4072. מִדְחֶה **midcheh**, *mid-kheh'*; from 1760; *overthrow*:—ruin.

4073. מְדַחְפָה **m^{e}dachphâh**, *med-akh-faw'*; from 1765; a *push*, i.e. ruin:—overthrow.

4074. מָדַי **Mâday**, *maw-dah'ee*; of for. der.; *Madai*, a country of central Asia:—Madai, Medes, Media.

4075. מָדַי **Mâday**, *maw-dah'ee*; patrial from 4074; a *Madian* or native of Madai:—Mede.

4076. מָדַי **Mâday** (Chald.), *maw-dah'ee*; corresp. to 4074:—Mede (-s).

4077. מָדַי **Mâday** (Chald.), *maw-dah'ee*; corresp. to 4075:—Median.

4078. מַדַּי **madday**, *mad-dah'ee*; from 4100 and 1767; *what* (is) *enough*, i.e. *sufficiently*:—sufficiently.

4079. מִדְיָן **midyân**, *mid-yawn'*; a var. for 4066:—brawling, contention (-ous).

4080. מִדְיָן **Midyân** ,*mid-yawn'*; the same as 4079; *Midjan*, a son of Abraham; also his country and (collect.) his descend.:—Midian, Midianite.

4081. מִדִּין **Middîyn**, *mid-deen'*; a var. for 4080:—Middin.

4082. מְדִינָה **m^{e}dîynâh**, *med-ee-naw'*; from 1777; prop. a *judgeship*, i.e. *jurisdiction*; by impl. a *district* (as ruled by a judge); gen. a *region*:—(× every) province.

4083. מְדִינָה **m^{e}dîynâh** (Chald.), *med-ee-naw'*; corresp. to 4082:—province.

4084. מִדְיָנִי **Midyânîy**, *mid-yaw-nee'*; patron. or patrial from 4080; a *Midjanite* or descend. (native) of Midjan:—Midianite. Comp. 4092.

4085. מְדֹכָה **m^{e}dôkâh**, *med-o-kaw'*; from 1743; a *mortar*:—mortar.

4086. מַדְמֵן **Madmên**, *mad-mane'*; from the same as 1828; *dunghill*; *Madmen*, a place in Pal.:—Madmen.

4087. מַדְמֵנָה **madmênâh**, *mad-may-naw'*; fem. from the same as 1828; a *dunghill*:—dunghill.

4088. מַדְמֵנָה **Madmênâh**, *mad-may-naw'*; the same as 4087; *Madmenah*, a place in Pal.:—Madmenah.

4089. מַדְמַנָּה **Madmannâh**, *mad-man-naw'*; a var. for 4087; *Madmannah*, a place in Pal.:—Madmannah.

4090. מְדָן **m^{e}dân**, *med-awn'*; a form of 4066:—discord, strife.

4091. מְדָן **M^{e}dân**, *med-awn'*; the same as 4090; *Medan*, a son of Abraham:—Medan.

4092. מְדָנִי **M^{e}dânîy**, *med-aw-nee'*; a var. of 4084:—Midianite.

4093. מַדָּע **maddâʿ**, *mad-daw'*; or
מַדַּע **maddaʿ**, *mad-dah'*; from 3045; *intelligence* or *consciousness*:—knowledge, science, thought.
מֹדָע **môdâʿ**. See 4129.
מַדֻּעַ **madûaʿ**. See 4069.

4094. מַדְקָרָה **madqârâh**, *mad-kaw-raw'*; from 1856; a *wound*:—piercing.
מְדֹר **m^{e}dôr**. See 4070.

4095. מַדְרֵגָה **madrêgâh**, *mad-ray-gaw'*; from an unused root mean. to *step*; prop. a *step*; by impl. a *steep* or inaccessible place:—stair, steep place.
מְדֻרָה **m^{e}dûrâh**. See 4071.

4096. מִדְרָךְ **midrâk**, *mid-rawk'*; from 1869; a *treading*, i.e. a place for stepping on:—[foot-] breadth.

4097. מִדְרָשׁ **midrâsh**, *mid-rawsh'*; from 1875; prop. an *investigation*, i.e. (by impl.) a *treatise* or elaborate compilation:—story.

4098. מְדֻשָּׁה **m^{e}dushshâh**, *med-oosh-shaw'*; from 1758; a *threshing*, i.e. (concr. and fig.) *down-trodden* people:—threshing.

4099. מְדָתָא **M^{e}dâthâ**, *med-aw-thaw'*; of Pers. or.; *Medatha*, the father of Haman:—Hammedatha [*includ. the art.*].

4100. מָה **mâh**, *maw*; or מַה **mah**, *mah*; or
מָ **mâ**, *maw*; or מַ **ma**, *mah*; also
מֶה **meh**, *meh*; a prim. particle; prop. interrog. *what?* (includ. *how? why? when?*); but also exclam. *what!* (includ. *how!*), or indef. *what* (includ. *whatever*, and even rel. *that which*); often used with prefixes in various adv. or conj. senses:—how (long, oft, [-soever]), [no-] thing, what (end, good, purpose, thing), whereby (-fore, -in, -to, -with), (for) why.

4101. מָה **mâh** (Chald.), *maw*; corresp. to 4100:—how great (mighty), that which, what (-soever), why.

4102. מָהַהּ **mâhahh**, *maw-hah'*; appar. a denom. from 4100; prop. to *question* or hesitate, i.e. (by impl.) to *be reluctant*:—delay, linger, stay selves, tarry.

4103. מְהוּמָה **m^{e}hûwmâh**, *meh-hoo-maw'*; from 1949; *confusion* or uproar:—destruction, discomfiture, trouble, tumult, vexation, vexed.

4104. מְהוּמָן **M^{e}hûwmân**, *meh-hoo-mawn'*; of Pers. or.; *Mehuman*, a eunuch of Xerxes:—Mehuman.

4105. מְהֵיטַבְאֵל **M^{e}hêyṭab'êl**, *meh-hay-tab-ale'*; from 3190 (augmented) and 410; *bettered of God*; *Mehetabel*, the name of an Edomitish man and woman:—Mehetabeel, Mehetabel.

4106. מָהִיר **mâhîyr**, *maw-here'*; or
מָהִר **mâhîr**, *maw-here'*; from 4116; *quick*; hence *skilful*:—diligent, hasty, ready.

4107. מָהַל **mâhal**, *maw-hal'*; a prim. root; prop. to *cut down* or *reduce*, i.e. by impl. to *adulterate*:—mixed.

4108. מַהְלֵךְ **mahlêk**, *mah-lake'*; from 1980; a *walking* (plur. collect.), i.e. *access*:—place to walk.

4109. מַהֲלָךְ **mahălâk**, *mah-hal-awk'*; from 1980; a *walk*, i.e. a *passage* or a *distance*:—journey, walk.

4110. מַהֲלָל **mahălâl**, *mah-hal-awl'*; from 1984; *fame*:—praise.

4111. מַהֲלַלְאֵל **Mahălal'êl**, *mah-hal-al-ale'*; from 4110 and 410; *praise of God*; *Mahalalel*, the name of an antediluvian patriarch and of an Isr.:—Mahalaleel.

4112. מַהֲלֻמָּה **mahălummâh**, *mah-hal-oom-maw'*; from 1986; a *blow*:—stripe, stroke.

4113. מַהֲמֹרָה **mahămôrâh**, *mah-ham-o-raw'*; from an unused root of uncert. mean.; perh. an *abyss*:—deep pit.

4114. מַהְפֵּכָה **mahpêkâh**, *mah-pay-kaw'*; from 2015; a *destruction*:—when . . . overthrew, overthrow (-n).

4115. מַהְפֶּכֶת **mahpeketh**, *mah-peh'-keth*; from 2015; a *wrench*, i.e. the *stocks*:—prison, stocks.

4116. מָהַר **mâhar**, *maw-har'*; a prim. root; prop. to *be liquid* or *flow* easily, i.e. (by impl.); to *hurry* (in a good or a bad sense); often used (with another verb) adv. *promptly*:—be carried headlong, fearful, (cause to make, in, make) haste (-n, -ily, (be) hasty, (fetch, make ready) × quickly, rash, × shortly, (be so) × soon, make speed, × speedily, × straightway, × suddenly, swift.

4117. מָהַר **mâhar**, *maw-har'*; a prim. root (perh. rather the same as 4116 through the idea of *readiness* in assent): to *bargain* (for a wife), i.e. to *wed*:—endow, × surely.

4118. מַהֵר **mahêr**, *mah-hare'*; from 4116; prop. *hurrying*; hence (adv.) *in a hurry*:—hasteth, hastily, at once, quickly, soon, speedily, suddenly.
מָהִר **mâhîr**. See 4106.

4119. מֹהַר **môhar**, *mo'-har*; from 4117; a *price* (for a wife):—dowry.

4120. מְהֵרָה **m^{e}hêrâh**, *meh-hay-raw'*; fem. of 4118; prop. a *hurry*; hence (adv.) *promptly*:—hastily, quickly, shortly, soon, make (with) speed (-ily), swiftly.

4121. מַהֲרַי **Mahăray**, *mah-har-ah'ee*; from 4116; *hasty*; *Maharai*, an Isr.:—Maharai.

4122. מַהֵר שָׁלָל חָשׁ בַּז **Mahêr Shâlâl Châsh Baz**, *mah-hare' shaw-lawl' khawsh baz*; from 4118 and 7998 and 2363 and 957; *hasting* (is he [the enemy] to the) *booty*, *swift* (to the) *prey*; *Maher-Shalal-Chash-Baz*; the symbol. name of the son of Isaiah:—Maher-shalal-hash-baz.

4123. מַהֲתַלָּה **mahăthallâh**, *mah-hath-al-law'*; from 2048; a *delusion*:—deceit.

4124. מוֹאָב **Môw'âb**, *mo-awb*; from a prol. form of the prep. pref. *m-* and 1; *from* (her [the mother's]) *father*; *Moäb*, an incestuous son of Lot; also his territory and desc.:—Moab.

4125. מוֹאָבִי **Môw'âbîy**, *mo-aw-bee'*; fem.
מוֹאָבִיָּה **Môw'âbîyah**, *mo-aw-bee-yaw'*; or
מוֹאָבִית **Môwâbîyth**, *mo-aw-beeth'*; patron. from 4124; a *Moäbite* or *Moäbitess*, i.e. a desc. from Moab:—(woman) of Moab, Moabite (-ish, -ss).
מוֹאל **môw'l**. See 4136.

4126. מוֹבָא **môwbâ'**, *mo-baw'*; by transp. for 3996; an *entrance*:—coming.

4127. מוּג **mûwg**, *moog*; a prim. root; to *melt*, i.e. lit. (to *soften*, flow down, *disappear*), or fig. (to *fear*, *faint*):—consume, dissolve, (be) faint (-hearted), melt (away), make soft.

4128. מוּד **mûwd**, *mood*; a prim. root; to *shake*:—measure.

4129. מוֹדַע **môwdaʿ**, *mo-dah'*; or rather
מֹדָע **môdâʿ**, *mo-daw'*; from 3045; an *acquaintance*:—kinswoman.

4130. מוֹדַעַת **môwda'ath**, *mo-dah'-ath*; from 3045; *acquaintance*:—kindred.

4131. מוֹט **môwṭ**, *mote*; a prim. root; to *waver*, by impl. to *slip*, *shake*, *fall*:—be carried, cast, be out of course, be fallen in decay, × exceedingly, fall (-ing down), be (re-) moved, be ready shake, slide, slip.

4132. מוֹט **môwṭ**, *mote*; from 4131; a *wavering*, i.e. *fall*; by impl. a *pole* (as shaking); hence a *yoke* (as essentially a bent pole):—bar, be moved, staff, yoke.

4133. מוֹטָה **môwṭâh**, *mo-taw';* fem. of 4132; a *pole;* by impl. an ox-*bow;* hence a *yoke* (either lit. or fig.):—bands, heavy, staves, yoke.

4134. מוּךְ **mûwk**, *mook;* a prim. root; to *become thin,* i.e. (fig.) *be impoverished:*—be (waxen) poor (-er).

4135. מוּל **mûwl**, *mool;* a prim. root; to *cut short,* i.e. *curtail* (spec. the prepuce, i.e. to *circumcise*); by impl. to *blunt;* fig. to *destroy:*—circumcise (-ing, selves), cut down (in pieces), destroy, × must needs.

4136. מוּל **mûwl**, *mool;* or
מוֹל **môwl** (Deut. 1 : 1), *mole;* or
מוֹאל **môw'l** (Neh. 12 : 38), *mole;* or
מֻל **mûl** (Num. 22 : 5), *mool;* from 4135; prop. *abrupt,* i.e. a *precipice;* by impl. the *front;* used only adv. (with prep. pref.) *opposite:*—(over) against, before, [fore-] front, from, [God-] ward, toward, with.

4137. מוֹלָדָה **Môwlâdâh**, *mo-law-daw';* from 3205; *birth; Moladah,* a place in Pal.:—Moladah.

4138. מוֹלֶדֶת **môwledeth**, *mo-leh'-deth;* from 3205; *nativity* (plur. *birth-place*); by impl. *lineage, native country;* also *offspring, family:*—begotten, born, issue, kindred, native (-ity).

4139. מוּלָה **mûwlâh**, *moo-law';* from 4135; *circumcision:*—circumcision.

4140. מוֹלִיד **Môwlîyd**, *mo-leed';* from 3205; *genitor; Molid,* an Isr.:—Molid.

מוּם **muwm**. See 3971.

מוֹמֻכָן° **Môwmûkân**. See 4462.

4141. מוּסָב **mûwçâb**, *moo-sawb';* from 5437; a *turn,* i.e. *circuit* (of a building):—winding about.

4142. מוּסַבָּה **mûwçabbâh**, *moo-sab-baw';* or
מֻסַבָּה **mûçabbâh**, *moo-sab-baw';* fem. of 4141; a *reversal,* i.e. the *backside* (of a gem), *fold* (of a double-leaved door), *transmutation* (of a name):—being changed, inclosed, be set, turning.

4143. מוּסָד **mûwçâd**, *moo-sawd';* from 3245; a *foundation:*—foundation.

4144. מוֹסָד **môwçâd**, *mo-sawd';* from 3245; a *foundation:*—foundation.

4145. מוּסָדָה **mûwçâdâh**, *moo-saw-daw';* fem. of 4143; a *foundation;* fig. an *appointment:*—foundation, grounded. Comp. 4328.

4146. מוֹסָדָה **môwçâdâh**, *mo-saw-daw';* or
מֹסָדָה **môçâdâh** *mo-saw-daw';* fem. of 4144; a *foundation:*—foundation.

4147. מוֹסֵר **môwçêr**, *mo-sare';* also (in plur.) fem.
מוֹסֵרָה **môwçêrâh**, *mo-say-raw';* or
מֹסְרָה **môçᵉrâh**, *mo-ser-aw';* from 3256; prop. *chastisement,* i.e. (by impl.) a *halter;* fig. *restraint:*—band, bond.

4148. מוּסָר **mûwçâr**, *moo-sawr';* from 3256; prop. *chastisement;* fig. *reproof, warning* or *instruction;* also *restraint:*—bond, chastening ([-eth]), chastisement, check, correction, discipline, doctrine, instruction, rebuke.

4149. מוֹסֵרָה **Môwçêrâh**, *mo-say-raw';* or (plur.)
מֹסְרוֹת **Môçᵉrôwth**, *mo-ser-othe';* fem. of 4147; *correction* or *corrections; Moserah* or *Moseroth,* a place in the Desert:—Mosera, Moseroth.

4150. מוֹעֵד **môwʻêd**, *mo-ade';* or
מֹעֵד **môʻêd** *mo-ade';* or (fem.)
מוֹעָדָה **môwʻâdâh** (2 Chron. 8 : 13), *mo-aw-daw';* from 3259; prop. an *appointment,* i.e. a fixed *time* or season; spec. a *festival;* conventionally a *year;* by implication, an *assembly* (as convened for a definite purpose); technically the *congregation;* by extension, the *place of meeting;* also a *signal* (as appointed beforehand):—appointed (sign, time), (place of, solemn) assembly, congregation, (set, solemn) feast, (appointed, due) season, solemn (-ity), synagogue, (set) time (appointed).

4151. מוֹעָד **môwʻâd**, *mo-awd';* from 3259; prop. an *assembly* [as in 4150]; fig. a *troop:*—appointed time.

4152. מוּעָדָה **mûwʻâdâh**, *moo-aw-daw';* from 3259; an *appointed* place, i.e. *asylum:*—appointed.

4153. מוֹעַדְיָה **Môwʻadyâh**, *mo-ad-yaw';* from 4151 and 3050; *assembly of Jah; Moädjah,* an Isr.:—Moadiah. Comp. 4573.

4154. מוּעֶדֶת **mûwʻedeth**, *moo-ay'-deth;* fem. pass. part. of 4571; prop. *made to slip,* i.e. *dislocated:*—out of joint.

4155. מוּעָף **mûwʻâph**, *moo-awf';* from 5774; prop. *covered,* i.e. *dark;* abstr. *obscurity,* i.e. *distress:*—dimness.

4156. מוֹעֵצָה **môwʻêtsâh**, *mo-ay-tsaw';* from 3289; a *purpose:*—counsel, device.

4157. מוּעָקָה **mûwʻâqâh**, *moo-aw-kaw';* from 5781; *pressure,* i.e. (fig.) *distress:*—affliction.

4158. מוֹפַעַת° **Môwphaʻath** (Jer. 48 : 21), *mo-fah'-ath;* or
מֵיפַעַת **mêyphaath**, *may-fah'-ath;* or
מֵפַעַת **mêphaath**, *may-fah'-ath;* from 3313; *illuminative; Mophaath* or *Mephaath,* a place in Pal.:—Mephaath.

4159. מוֹפֵת **môwphêth**, *mo-faith';* or
מֹפֵת **môphêth**, *mo-faith';* from 3302 in the sense of *conspicuousness;* a *miracle;* by impl. a *token* or *omen:*—miracle, sign, wonder (-ed at).

4160. מוּץ **mûwts**, *moots;* a prim. root; to *press,* i.e. (fig.) to *oppress:*—extortioner.

4161. מוֹצָא **môwtsâʼ**, *mo-tsaw';* or
מֹצָא **môtsâʼ**, *mo-tsaw';* from 3318; a *going forth,* i.e. (the act) an *egress,* or (the place) an *exit;* hence a *source* or *product;* spec. *dawn,* the *rising* of the sun (the *East*), *exportation, utterance,* a *gate,* a *fountain,* a *mine,* a *meadow* (as producing grass):—brought out, bud, that which came out, east, going forth, goings out, that which (thing that) is gone out, outgoing, proceeded out, spring, vein, [water-] course [springs].

4162. מוֹצָא **môwtsâʼ**, *mo-tsaw';* the same as 4161; *Motsa,* the name of two Isr.:—Moza.

4163. מוֹצָאָה **môwtsâʼâh**, *mo-tsaw-aw';* fem. of 4161; a family *descent;* also a *sewer* [marg.; comp. 6675]:—draught house; going forth.

4164. מוּצַק **mûwtsaq**, *moo-tsak';* or
מוּצָק **mûwtsâq**, *moo-tsawk';* from 3332; *narrowness;* fig. *distress:*—anguish, is straitened, straitness.

4165. מוּצָק **mûwtsâq**, *moo-tsawk';* from 5694; prop. *fusion,* i.e. lit. a *casting* (of metal); fig. a *mass* (of clay):—casting, hardness.

4166. מוּצָקָה **mûwtsâqâh**, *moo-tsaw-kaw';* or
מֻצָקָה **mûtsâqâh**, *moo-tsaw-kaw';* from 3332; prop. something *poured* out, i.e. a *casting* (of metal); by impl. a *tube* (as cast):—when it was cast, pipe.

4167. מוּק **mûwq**, *mook;* a prim. root; to *jeer,* i.e. (intens.) *blaspheme:*—be corrupt.

4168. מוֹקֵד **môwqêd**, *mo-kade';* from 3344; a *fire* or *fuel;* abstr. a *conflagration:*—burning, hearth.

4169. מוֹקְדָה° **môwqᵉdâh**, *mo-ked-aw';* fem. of 4168; *fuel:*—burning.

4170. מוֹקֵשׁ **môwqêsh**, *mo-kashe';* or
מֹקֵשׁ **môqêsh**, *mo-kashe';* from 3369; a *noose* (for catching animals) (lit. or fig.); by impl. a *hook* (for the nose):—be ensnared, gin, (is) snare (-d), trap.

4171. מוּר **mûwr**, *moor;* a prim. root; to *alter;* by impl. to *barter,* to *dispose of:*—× at all, (ex-) change, remove.

4172. מוֹרָא **môwrâʼ**, *mo-raw';* or
מֹרָא **môrâʼ**, *mo-raw';* or
מֹרָה **môrâh** (Psa. 9 : 20), *mo-raw';* from 3372; *fear;* by impl. a *fearful* thing or deed:—dread, (that ought to be) fear (-ed), terribleness, terror.

4173. מוֹרַג **môwrag**, *mo-rag';* or
מֹרַג **môrag**, *mo-rag';* from an unused root mean. to *triturate;* a threshing *sledge:*—threshing instrument.

4174. מוֹרָד **môwrâd**, *mo-rawd';* from 3381; a *descent;* arch. an ornamental *appendage,* perh. a *festoon:*—going down, steep place, thin work.

4175. מוֹרֶה **môwreh**, *mo-reh';* from 3384; an *archer;* also *teacher* or *teaching;* also the *early rain* [see 3138]:—(early) rain.

4176. מוֹרֶה **Môwreh**, *mo-reh';* or
מֹרֶה **Môreh**, *mo-reh';* the same as 4175; *Moreh,* a Canaanite; also a hill (perh. named from him):—Moreh.

4177. מוֹרָה **môwrâh**, *mo-raw';* from 4171 in the sense of *shearing;* a *razor:*—razor.

4178. מוֹרָט **môwrâṭ**, *mo-rawt';* from 3399; *obstinate,* i.e. independent:—peeled.

4179. מוֹרִיָּה **Môwrîyâh**, *mo-ree-yaw';* or
מֹרִיָּה **Môrîyâh**, *mo-ree-yaw';* from 7200 and 3050; *seen of Jah; Morijah,* a hill in Pal.:—Moriah.

4180. מוֹרָשׁ **môwrâsh**, *mo-rawsh';* from 3423; a *possession;* fig. *delight:*—possession, thought.

4181. מוֹרָשָׁה **môwrâshâh**, *mo-raw-shaw';* fem. of 4180; a *possession:*—heritage, inheritance, possession.

4182. מוֹרֶשֶׁת גַּת **Môwresheth Gath**, *mo-reh'-sheth gath;* from 3423 and 1661; *possession of Gath; Moresheth-Gath,* a place in Pal.:—Moresheth-gath.

4183. מוֹרַשְׁתִּי **Morashtîy**, *mo-rash-tee';* patrial from 4182; a *Morashtite* or inhab. of Moresheth-Gath:—Morashthite.

4184. מוּשׁ **mûwsh**, *moosh;* a prim. root; to *touch:*—feel, handle.

4185. מוּשׁ **mûwsh**, *moosh;* a prim. root [perh. rather the same as 4184 through the idea of receding by *contact*]; to *withdraw* (both lit. and fig., whether intrans. or trans.):—cease, depart, go back, remove, take away.

4186. מוֹשָׁב **môwshâb**, *mo-shawb';* or
מֹשָׁב **môshâb**, *mo-shawb';* from 3427; a *seat;* fig. a *site;* abstr. a *session;* by extension an *abode* (the place or the time); by impl. *population:*—assembly, dwell in, dwelling (-place), wherein (that) dwelt (in), inhabited place, seat, sitting, situation, sojourning.

4187. מוּשִׁי **Mûwshîy**, *moo-shee';* or
מֻשִּׁי **Mushshîy**, *mush-shee';* from 4184; *sensitive; Mushi,* a Levite:—Mushi.

4188. מוּשִׁי **Mûwshîy**, *moo-shee';* patron. from 4187; a *Mushite* (collect.) or desc. of Mushi:—Mushites.

4189. מוֹשְׁכָה **môwshᵉkâh**, *mo-shek-aw';* act part. fem. of 4900; something *drawing,* i.e. (fig.) a *cord:*—band.

4190. מוֹשָׁעָה **môwshâʻâh**, *mo-shaw-aw';* from 3467; *deliverance:*—salvation.

4191. מוּת **mûwth**, *mooth;* a prim. root; to *die* (lit. or fig.); causat. to *kill:*—× at all, × crying, (be) dead (body, man, one), (put to, worthy of) death, destroy (-er), (cause to, be like to, must) die, kill, necro [-mancer], × must needs, slay, × surely, × very suddenly, × in [no] wise.

4192. מוּת **Mûwth** (Psa. 48 : 14), *mooth;* or

מוּת לַבֵּן **Mûwth lab-bên**, *mooth lab-bane';* from 4191 and 1121 with the prep. and art. interposed; "*To die for the son*", prob. the title of a popular song:—death, Muthlabben.

4193. מוֹת **môwth** (Chald.), *mohth;* corresp. to 4194; *death:*—death.

4194. מָוֶת **mâveth**, *maw'-veth;* from 4191; *death* (nat. or violent); concr. the *dead*, their place or state (*hades*); fig. *pestilence, ruin:*—(be) dead ([-ly]), death, die (-d).

מוּת לַבֵּן **Mûwth lab-bên.** See 4192.

4195. מוֹתָר **môwthar**, *mo-thar';* from 3498; lit. *gain;* fig. *superiority:*—plenteousness, preeminence, profit.

4196. מִזְבֵּחַ **mizbêach**, *miz-bay'-akh;* from 2076; an *altar:*—altar.

4197. מֶזֶג **mezeg**, *meh'-zeg;* from an unused root mean. to *mingle* (water with wine); *tempered* wine:—liquor.

4198. מָזֶה **mâzeh**, *maw-zeh';* from an unused root mean. to *suck* out; *exhausted:*—burnt.

4199. מִזָּה **Mizzâh**, *miz-zaw';* prob. from an unused root mean. to *faint* with fear; *terror; Mizzah*, an Edomite:—Mizzah.

4200. מֶזֶו **mezev**, *meh'-zev;* prob. from an unused root mean. to *gather* in; a *granary:*—garner.

4201. מְזוּזָה **m^{e}zûwzâh**, *mez-oo-zaw';* or

מְזֻזָה **m^{e}zûzâh**, *mez-oo-zaw';* from the same as 2123; a *door-post* (as *prominent*):—(door, side) post.

4202. מָזוֹן **mâzôwn**, *maw-zone';* from 2109; *food:*—meat, victual.

4203. מָזוֹן **mâzôwn** (Chald.), *maw-zone';* corresp. to 4202:—meat.

4204. מָזוֹר **mâzôwr**, *maw-zore';* from 2114 in the sense of *turning aside* from truth; *treachery*, i.e. a *plot:*—wound.

4205. מָזוֹר **mâzôwr**, *maw-zore';* or

מָזֹר **mâzôr**, *maw-zore';* from 2115 in the sense of *binding* up; a *bandage*, i.e. remedy; hence a *sore* (as needing a compress):—bound up, wound.

מְזֻזָה **m^{e}zûzâh.** See 4201.

4206. מָזִיחַ **mâzîyach**, *maw-zee'-akh;* or

מֵזַח **mêzach**, *may-zakh';* from 2118; a *belt* (as movable):—girdle, strength.

4207. מַזְלֵג **mazlêg**, *maz-layg';* or (fem.)

מִזְלָגָה **mizlâgâh**, *miz-law-gaw';* from an unused root mean. to *draw* up; a *fork:*—fleshhook.

4208. מַזָּלָה **mazzâlâh**, *maz-zaw-law';* appar. from 5140 in the sense of *raining;* a *constellation*, i.e. Zodiacal sign (perh. as affecting the weather):—planet. Comp. 4216.

4209. מְזִמָּה **m^{e}zimmâh**, *mez-im-maw';* from 2161; a *plan*, usually evil (*machination*), sometimes good (*sagacity*):—(wicked) device, discretion, intent, witty invention, lewdness, mischievous (device), thought, wickedly.

4210. מִזְמוֹר **mizmôwr**, *miz-more';* from 2167; prop. instrumental *music;* by impl. a *poem* set to notes:—psalm.

4211. מַזְמֵרָה **mazmêrâh**, *maz-may-raw';* from 2168; a *pruning-knife:*—pruning-hook.

4212. מְזַמְּרָה **m^{e}zamm^{e}râh**, *mez-am-mer-aw';* from 2168; a *tweezer* (only in the plur.):—snuffers.

4213. מִזְעָר **miz'âr**, *miz-awr';* from the same as 2191; *fewness;* by impl. as superl. *diminutiveness:*—few, × very.

מָזֹר **mâzôr.** See 4205.

4214. מִזְרֶה **mizreh**, *miz-reh';* from 2219; a winnowing *shovel* (as scattering the chaff):—fan.

4215. מְזָרֶה **m^{e}zâreh**, *mez-aw-reh';* appar. from 2219; prop. a *scatterer*, i.e. the north *wind* (as dispersing clouds; only in plur.):—north.

4216. מַזָּרָה **mazzârâh**, *maz-zaw-raw';* appar. from 5144 in the sense of *distinction;* some noted *constellation* (only in the plur.), perh. collect. the *zodiac:*—Mazzoroth. Comp. 4208.

4217. מִזְרָח **mizrâch**, *miz-rawkh';* from 2224; *sunrise*, i.e. the *east:*—east (side, -ward), (sun-) rising (of the sun).

4218. מִזְרָע **mizrâ'**, *miz-raw';* from 2232; a planted *field:*—thing sown.

4219. מִזְרָק **mizrâq**, *miz-rawk';* from 2236; a *bowl* (as if for sprinkling):—bason, bowl.

4220. מֵחַ **mêach**, *may'-akh;* from 4229 in the sense of *greasing; fat;* fig. *rich:*—fatling (one).

4221. מֹחַ **môach**, *mo'-akh;* from the same as 4220; *fat*, i.e. marrow:—marrow.

4222. מָחָא **mâchâ'**, *maw-khaw';* a prim. root; to *rub* or *strike* the hands together (in exultation):—clap.

4223. מְחָא **m^{e}châ'** (Chald.), *mekh-aw';* corresp. to 4222; to *strike* in pieces; also to *arrest;* spec. to *impale:*—hang, smite, stay.

4224. מַחֲבֵא **machăbê'**, *makh-ab-ay';* or

מַחֲבֹא **machăbô'**, *makh-ab-o';* from 2244; a *refuge:*—hiding (lurking) place.

4225. מַחְבֶּרֶת **machbereth**, *makh-beh'-reth;* from 2266; a *junction*, i.e. seam or sewed piece:—coupling.

4226. מְחַבְּרָה **m^{e}chabb^{e}râh**, *mekh-ab-ber-aw';* from 2266; a *joiner*, i.e. brace or cramp:—coupling, joining.

4227. מַחֲבַת **machăbath**, *makh-ab-ath';* from the same as 2281; a *pan* for baking in:—pan.

4228. מַחֲגֹרֶת **machăgôreth**, *makh-ag-o'-reth;* from 2296; a *girdle:*—girding.

4229. מָחָה **mâchâh**, *maw-khaw';* a prim. root; prop. to *stroke* or *rub;* by impl. to *erase;* also to *smooth* (as if with oil), i.e. *grease* or make fat; also to *touch*, i.e. reach to:—abolish, blot out, destroy, full of marrow, put out, reach unto, × utterly, wipe (away, out).

4230. מְחוּגָה **m^{e}chûwgâh**, *mekh-oo-gaw';* from 2328; an instrument for marking a circle, i.e. *compasses:*—compass.

4231. מָחוֹז **mâchôwz**, *maw-khoze';* from an unused root mean. to *enclose;* a *harbor* (as *shut* in by the shore):—haven.

4232. מְחוּיָאֵל **M^{e}chûwyâ'êl**, *mekh-oo-yaw-ale';* or

מְחִיָּיאֵל **M^{e}chîyyâ'êl**, *mekh-ee-yaw-ale';* from 4229 and 410; *smitten of God; Mechujael* or *Mechijael*, an antediluvian patriarch:—Mehujael.

4233. מַחֲוִים **Machăvîym**, *makh-av-eem';* appar. a patrial, but from an unknown place (in the plur. only for a sing.); a *Machavite* or inhab. of some place named Machaveh:—Mahavite.

4234. מָחוֹל **mâchôwl**, *maw-khole';* from 2342; a (round) *dance:*—dance (-cing).

4235. מָחוֹל **Mâchôwl**, *maw-khole';* the same as 4234; *dancing; Machol*, an Isr.:—Mahol.

מְחוֹלָה **m^{e}chôwlâh.** See 65, 4246.

4236. מַחֲזֶה **machăzeh**, *makh-az-eh';* from 2372; a *vision:*—vision.

4237. מֶחֱזָה **mechĕzâh**, *mekh-ez-aw';* from 2372; a *window:*—light.

4238. מַחֲזִיאוֹת **Machăzîy'ôwth**, *makh-az-ee-oth';* fem. plur. from 2372; *visions; Machazioth*, an Isr.:—Mahazioth.

4239. מְחִי **m^{e}chîy**, *mekh-ee';* from 4229; a *stroke*, i.e. battering-*ram:*—engines.

4240. מְחִידָא **M^{e}chîydâ'**, *mekh-ee-daw';* from 2330; *junction; Mechida*, one of the Nethinim:—Mehida.

4241. מִחְיָה **michyâh**, *mikh-yaw';* from 2421; *preservation of life;* hence *sustenance;* also the live flesh, i.e. the *quick:*—preserve life, quick, recover selves, reviving, sustenance, victuals.

מְחִיָּיאֵל **M^{e}chîyyâ'êl.** See 4232.

4242. מְחִיר **m^{e}chîyr**, *mekh-eer';* from an unused root mean. to *buy; price, payment, wages:*—gain, hire, price, sold, worth.

4243. מְחִיר **M^{e}chîyr**, *mekh-eer';* the same as 4242; *price; Mechir*, an Isr.:—Mehir.

4244. מַחְלָה **Machlâh**, *makh-law';* from 2470; *sickness; Machlah*, the name appar. of two Israelitesses:—Mahlah.

4245. מַחֲלֶה **machăleh**, *makh-al-eh';* or (fem.)

מַחֲלָה **machălâh**, *makh-al-aw';* from 2470; *sickness:*—disease, infirmity, sickness.

4246. מְחוֹלָה **m^{e}chôwlâh**, *mekh-o-law';* fem. of 4234; a *dance:*—company, dances (-cing).

4247. מְחִלָּה **m^{e}chillâh**, *mekh-il-law';* from 2490; a *cavern* (as if excavated):—cave.

4248. מַחְלוֹן **Machlôwn**, *makh-lone';* from 2470; *sick; Machlon*, an Isr.:—Mahlon.

4249. מַחְלִי **Machlîy**, *makh-lee';* from 2470; *sick; Machli*, the name of two Isr.:—Mahli.

4250. מַחְלִי **Machlîy**, *makh-lee';* patron. from 4249; a *Machlite* or (collect.) desc. of Machli:—Mahlites.

4251. מַחְלֻי **machlûy**, *makh-loo'ee;* from 2470; a *disease:*—disease.

4252. מַחֲלָף **machălâph**, *makh-al-awf';* from 2498; a (sacrificial) *knife* (as *gliding* through the flesh):—knife.

4253. מַחְלָפָה **machlâphâh**, *makh-law-faw';* from 2498; a *ringlet* of hair (as *gliding* over each other):—lock.

4254. מַחֲלָצָה **machălâtsâh**, *makh-al-aw-tsaw';* from 2502; a *mantle* (as easily *drawn off*):—changeable suit of apparel, change of raiment.

4255. מַחְלְקָה **machl^{e}qâh** (Chald.), *makh-lek-aw';* corresp. to 4256; a *section* (of the Levites):—course.

4256. מַחֲלֹקֶת **machălôqeth**, *makh-al-o'-keth;* from 2505; a *section* (of Levites, people or soldiers):—company, course, division, portion. See also 5555.

4257. מַחֲלַת **machălath**, *makh-al-ath';* from 2470; *sickness; Machalath*, prob. the title (initial word) of a popular song:—Mahalath.

4258. מַחֲלַת **Machălath**, *makh-al-ath';* the same as 4257; *sickness; Machalath*, the name of an Ishmaelitess and of an Israelitess:—Mahalath.

4259. מְחֹלָתִי **M^{e}chôlâthîy**, *mekh-o-law-thee';* patrial from 65; a *Mecholathite* or inhab. of Abel-Mecholah:—Mecholathite.

4260. מַחֲמָאָה **machămâ'âh**, *makh-am-aw-aw';* a denom. from 2529; something *buttery* (i.e. unctuous and pleasant), as (fig.) *flattery:*— × than butter.

4261. מַחְמָד **machmâd**, *makh-mawd';* from 2530; *delightful;* hence a *delight*, i.e. object of affection or desire:—beloved, desire, goodly, lovely, pleasant (thing).

4262. מַחְמֻד **machmûd**, *makh-mood';* or

מַחְמוּד **machmûwd**, *makh-mood';* from 2530; *desired;* hence a *valuable:*—pleasant thing.

4263. מַחְמָל **machmâl**, *makh-mawl';* from 2550; prop. *sympathy;* (by paronomasia with 4261) *delight:*—pitieth.

4264. מַחֲנֶה **machăneh**, *makh-an-eh';* from 2583; an *encampment* (of travellers or troops); hence an *army*, whether lit. (of soldiers) or fig. (of dancers, angels, cattle, locusts, stars; or even the sacred courts):—army, band, battle, camp, company, drove, host, tents.

4265. מַחֲנֵה־דָן **Machănêh-Dân**, *makh-an-ay'-dawn;* from 4264 and 1835; *camp of Dan; Machaneh-Dan*, a place in Pal.:—Mahaneh-dan.

4266. מַחֲנַיִם **Machănayim**, *makh-an-ah'-yim;* dual of 4264; *double camp; Machanajim*, a place in Pal.:—Mahanaim.

4267. מַחֲנַק **machănaq**, *makh-an-ak';* from 2614; *choking:*—strangling.

4268. מַחֲסֶה **machăçeh**, *makh-as-eh';* or
מַחְסֶה **machçeh**, *makh-seh';* from 2620; a *shelter* (lit. or fig.):—hope, (place of) refuge, shelter, trust.

4269. מַחְסוֹם **machçôwm**, *makh-sohm';* from 2629; a *muzzle:*—bridle.

4270. מַחְסוֹר **machçôwr**, *makh-sore';* or
מַחְסֹר **machçôr**, *makh-sore';* from 2637; *deficiency;* hence *impoverishment:*—lack, need, penury, poor, poverty, want.

4271. מַחְסֵיָה **Machçêyâh**, *makh-say-yaw';* from 4268 and 3050; *refuge of* (i.e. *in*) *Jah; Machsejah*, an Isr.:—Maaseiah.

4272. מָחַץ **mâchats**, *maw-khats';* a prim. root; to *dash* asunder; by impl. to *crush, smash* or violently *plunge;* fig. to *subdue* or *destroy:*—dip, pierce (through), smite (through), strike through, wound.

4273. מַחַץ **machats**, *makh'-ats;* from 4272; a *contusion:*—stroke.

4274. מַחְצֵב **machtsêb**, *makh-tsabe';* from 2672; prop. a *hewing;* concr. a *quarry:*—hewed (-n).

4275. מֶחֱצָה **mechĕtsâh**, *mekh-ets-aw';* from 2673; a *halving:*—half.

4276. מַחֲצִית **machătsîyth**, *makh-ats-eeth';* from 2673; a *halving* or the *middle:*—half (so much), mid [-day].

4277. מָחַק **mâchaq**, *maw-khak';* a prim. root; to *crush:*—smite off.

4278. מֶחְקָר **mechqâr**, *mekh-kawr';* from 2713; prop. *scrutinized*, i.e. (by impl.) a *recess:*—deep place.

4279. מָחָר **mâchar**, *maw-khar';* prob. from 309; prop. *deferred*, i.e. the *morrow;* usually (adv.) *tomorrow;* indef. *hereafter:*—time to come, tomorrow.

4280. מַחֲרָאָה **machărâ'âh**, *makh-ar-aw-aw';* from the same as 2716; a *sink:*—draught house.

4281. מַחֲרֵשָׁה **machărêshâh**, *makh-ar-ay-shaw';* from 2790; prob. a *pick-axe:*—mattock.

4282. מַחֲרֶשֶׁת **machăresheth**, *makh-ar-eh'-sheth;* from 2790; prob. a *hoe:*—share.

4283. מָחֳרָת **mochŏrâth**, *mokh-or-awth';* or
מָחֳרָתָם **mochŏrâthâm** (1 Sam. 30 : 17), *mokh-or-aw-thawm';* fem. from the same as 4279; the *morrow* or (adv.) *tomorrow:*—morrow, next day.

4284. מַחֲשָׁבָה **machăshâbâh**, *makh-ash-aw-baw';* or
מַחֲשֶׁבֶת **machăshebeth**, *makh-ash-eh'-beth;* from 2803; a *contrivance*, i.e. (concr.) a *texture, machine*, or (abstr.) *intention, plan* (whether bad, a *plot;* or good, *advice*):—cunning (work), curious work, device (-sed), imagination, invented, means, purpose, thought.

4285. מַחְשָׁךְ **machshâk**, *makh-shawk';* from 2821; *darkness;* concr. a *dark place:*—dark (-ness, place).

4286. מַחְשֹׂף **machsôph**, *makh-sofe';* from 2834; a *peeling:*—made appear.

4287. מַחַת **Machath**, *makh'-ath;* prob. from 4229; *erasure; Machath*, the name of two Isr.:—Mahath.

4288. מְחִתָּה **mᵉchittâh**, *mekh-it-taw';* from 2846; prop. a *dissolution;* concr. a *ruin*, or (abstr.) *consternation:*—destruction, dismaying, ruin, terror.

4289. מַחְתָּה **machtâh**, *makh-taw';* the same as 4288 in the sense of *removal;* a *pan* for live coals:—censer, firepan, snuffdish.

4290. מַחְתֶּרֶת **machtereth**, *makh-teh'-reth;* from 2864; a *burglary;* fig. *unexpected examination:*—breaking up, secret search.

4291. מְטָא **mᵉṭâ'** (Chald.), *met-aw';* or
מְטָה **mᵉṭâh** (Chald.), *met-aw';* appar. corresp. to 4672 in the intrans. sense of being found *present;* to *arrive, extend* or *happen:*—come, reach.

4292. מַטְאֲטֵא **maṭ'ăṭê'**, *mat-at-ay';* appar. a denom. from 2916; a *broom* (as removing *dirt* [comp. Engl. "to dust", i.e. remove dust]):—besom.

4293. מַטְבֵּחַ **maṭbêach**, *mat-bay'-akh;* from 2873; *slaughter:*—slaughter.

4294. מַטֶּה **maṭṭeh**, *mat-teh';* or (fem.)
מַטָּה **maṭṭâh**, *mat-taw';* from 5186; a *branch* (as *extending*); fig. a *tribe;* also a *rod*, whether for chastising (fig. *correction*), ruling (a *sceptre*), throwing (a *lance*), or walking (a *staff;* fig. a *support* of life, e.g. bread):—rod, staff, tribe.

4295. מַטָּה **maṭṭâh**, *mat'-taw;* from 5786 with directive enclitic appended; *downward, below* or *beneath;* often adv. with or without prefixes:—beneath, down (-ward), less, very low, under (-neath).

4296. מִטָּה **miṭṭâh**, *mit-taw';* from 5186; a *bed* (as *extended*) for sleeping or eating; by anal. a *sofa, litter* or *bier:*—bed ([-chamber]), bier.

4297. מֻטֶּה **muṭṭeh**, *moot-teh';* from 5186; a *stretching*, i.e. *distortion* (fig. *iniquity*):—perverseness.

4298. מֻטָּה **muṭṭâh**, *moot-taw';* from 5186; *expansion:*—stretching out.

4299. מַטְוֶה **maṭveh**, *mat-veh';* from 2901; something *spun:*—spun.

4300. מְטִיל **mᵉṭîyl**, *met-eel';* from 2904 in the sense of *hammering* out; an iron *bar* (as *forged*):—bar.

4301. מַטְמוֹן **maṭmôwn**, *mat-mone';* or
מַטְמֹן **maṭmôn**, *mat-mone';* or
מַטְמֻן **maṭmûn**, *mat-moon';* from 2934; a *secret* storehouse; hence a *secreted* valuable (buried); gen. *money:*—hidden riches, (hid) treasure (-s).

4302. מַטָּע **maṭṭâᶜ**, *mat-taw';* from 5193; something *planted*, i.e. the place (a *garden* or vineyard), or the thing (a *plant*, fig. of men); by impl. the act, *planting:*—plant (-ation, -ing).

4303. מַטְעַם **maṭᶜam**, *mat-am';* or (fem.)
מַטְעַמָּה **maṭᶜammâh**, *mat-am-maw';* from 2938; a *delicacy:*—dainty (meat), savoury meat.

4304. מִטְפַּחַת **miṭpachath**, *mit-pakh'-ath;* from 2946; a wide *cloak* (for a woman):—vail, wimple.

4305. מָטַר **mâṭar**, *maw-tar';* a prim. root; to *rain:*—(cause to) rain (upon).

4306. מָטָר **mâṭâr**, *maw-tawr';* from 4305; *rain:*—rain.

4307. מַטָּרָא **maṭṭârâ'**, *mat-taw-raw';* or
מַטָּרָה **maṭṭârâh**, *mat-taw-raw';* from 5201; a *jail* (as a *guard*-house); also an *aim* (as being closely *watched*):—mark, prison.

4308. מַטְרֵד **Maṭrêd**, *mat-rade';* from 2956; *propulsive; Matred*, an Edomitess:—Matred.

4309. מַטְרִי **Maṭrîy**, *mat-ree';* from 4305; *rainy; Matri*, an Isr.:—Matri.

4310. מִי **mîy**, *me;* an interrog. pron. of persons, as 4100 is of things, *who?* (occasionally, by a peculiar idiom, of things); also (indef.) *whoever;* often used in oblique construction with pref. or suff.:—any (man), × he, × him, + O that! what, which, who (-m, -se, -soever), + would to God.

4311. מֵידְבָא **Mêydᵉbâ'**, *may-deb-aw';* from 4325 and 1679; *water of quiet; Medeba*, a place in Pal.:—Medeba.

4312. מֵידָד **Mêydâd**, *may-dawd';* from 3032 in the sense of *loving; affectionate; Medad*, an Isr.:—Medad.

4313. מֵי הַיַּרְקוֹן **Mêy hay-Yarqôwn**, *may hah''ee-yar-kone';* from 4325 and 3420 with the art. interposed; *water of the yellowness; Me-haj-Jarkon*, a place in Pal.:—Me-jarkon.

4314. מֵי זָהָב **Mêy Zâhâb**, *may zaw-hawb';* from 4325 and 2091, *water of gold; Me-Zahab*, an Edomite:—Mezahab.

4315. מֵיטָב **mêyṭâb**, *may-tawb';* from 3190; the *best* part:—best.

4316. מִיכָא **Mîykâ'**, *mee-kaw';* a var. for 4318; *Mica*, the name of two Isr.:—Micha.

4317. מִיכָאֵל **Mîykâ'êl**, *me-kaw-ale';* from 4310 and (the pref. der. from) 3588 and 410; *who* (is) *like God?; Mikael*, the name of an archangel and of nine Isr.:—Michael.

4318. מִיכָה **Mîykâh**, *mee-kaw';* an abbrev. of 4320; *Micah*, the name of seven Isr.:—Micah, Micaiah, Michah.

4319. מִיכָהוּ **Mîykâhûw**, *me-kaw'-hoo;* a contr. for 4321; *Mikehu*, an Isr. prophet:—Micaiah (2 Chron. 18 : 8).

4320. מִיכָיָה **Mîykâyâh**, *me-kaw-yaw';* from 4310 and (the pref. der. from) 3588 and 3050; *who* (is) *like Jah?; Micajah*, the name of two Isr.:—Micah, Michaiah. Comp. 4318.

4321. מִיכָיְהוּ **Mîykâyᵉhûw**, *me-kaw-yeh-hoo';* or
מִכָיְהוּ **Mikâyᵉhûw** (Jer. 36 : 11), *me-kaw-yeh-hoo';* abbrev. for 4322; *Mikajah*, the name of three Isr.:—Micah, Micaiah, Michaiah.

4322. מִיכָיָהוּ **Mîykâyâhûw**, *me-kaw-yaw'-hoo;* for 4320; *Mikajah*, the name of an Isr. and an Israelitess:—Michaiah.

4323. מִיכַל **mîykâl**, *me-kawl';* from 3201; prop. a *container*, i.e. a *streamlet:*—brook.

4324. מִיכַל **Mîykâl**, *me-kawl';* appar. the same as 4323; *rivulet; Mikal*, Saul's daughter:—Michal.

4325. מַיִם **mayim**, *mah'-yim;* dual of a prim. noun (but used in a sing. sense); *water;* fig. *juice;* by euphem. *urine, semen:*— + piss, wasting, water (-ing, [-course, -flood, -spring]).

4326. מִיָּמִן **Mîyâmîn**, *me-yaw-meen';* a form for 4509; *Mijamin*, the name of three Isr.:—Miamin, Mijamin.

4327. מִין **mîyn**, *meen;* from an unused root mean. to *portion* out; a *sort*, i.e. *species:*—kind. Comp. 4480.

4328. מְיֻסָּדָה **mᵉyuççâdâh**, *meh-yoos-saw-daw';* prop. fem. pass. part. of 3245; something *founded*, i.e. a *foundation:*—foundation.

4329. מֵיסַךְ **mêyçâk**, *may-sawk';* from 5526; a *portico* (as *covered*):—covert.

מֵיפַעַת **Mêyphaᶜath**. See 4158.

4330. מִיץ **mîyts**, *meets;* from 4160; *pressure:*—churning, forcing, wringing.

4331. מֵישָׁא **Mêyshâ'**, *may-shaw';* from 4185; *departure; Mesha*, a place in Arabia; also an Isr.:—Mesha.

4332. מִישָׁאֵל **Mîyshâ'êl**, *mee-shaw-ale';* from 4310 and 410 with the abbrev. insep. rel. [see 834] interposed; *who* (is) *what God* (is)?; *Mishaël*, the name of three Isr.:—Mishael.

4333. מִישָׁאֵל **Mîyshâ'êl** (Chald.), *mee-shaw-ale';* corresp. to 4332; *Mishaël*, an Isr.:—Mishael.

4334. מִישׁוֹר **mîyshôwr**, *mee-shore';* or
מִישֹׁר **mîyshôr**, *mee-shore';* from 3474; a *level*, i.e. a *plain* (often used [with the art. pref.] as a prop. name of certain districts); fig. *concord;* also *straightness*, i.e. (fig.) *justice* (sometimes adv. *justly*):—equity, even place, plain, right (-eously), (made) straight, uprightness.

4335. מֵישַׁךְ **Mêyshak**, *may-shak';* borrowed from 4336; *Meshak*, an Isr.:—Meshak.

4336. מֵישַׁךְ **Mêyshak** (Chald.), *may-shak';* of for. or. and doubtful signif.; *Meshak*, the Bab. name of 4333:—Meshak.

4337. מֵישַׁע **Mêyshâᶜ**, *may-shah';* from 3467; *safety; Mesha*, an Isr.:—Mesha.

4338. מֵישַׁע **Mêyshaᶜ**, *may-shaw';* a var. for 4337; *safety; Mesha*, a Moabite:—Mesha.

4339. מֵישָׁר **mêyshâr**, *may-shawr';* from 3474; *evenness*, i.e. (fig.) *prosperity* or *con-*

cord; also *straightness,* i.e. (fig.) *rectitude* (only in plur. with sing. sense; often adv.):—agreement, aright, that are equal, equity, (things that are) right (-eously, things), sweetly, upright (-ly, -ness).

4340. מֵיתָר **mêythâr,** *may-thawr';* from 3498; a *cord* (of a tent) [comp. 3499] or the *string* (of a bow):—cord, string.

4341. מַכְאֹב **mak'ôb,** *mak-obe';* sometimes מַכְאוֹב **mak'ôwb,** *mak-obe';* also (fem. Isa. 53 : 3) מַכְאֹבָה **mak'ôbâh,** *mak-o-baw';* from 3510; *anguish* or (fig.) *affliction:*—grief, pain, sorrow.

4342. מַכְבִּיר **makbîyr,** *mak-beer';* trans. part. of 3527; *plenty:*—abundance.

4343. מַכְבֵּנָא **Makbênâ',** *mak-bay-naw';* from the same as 3522; *knoll; Macbena,* a place in Pal. settled by him:—Machbenah.

4344. מַכְבַּנַּי **Makbannay,** *mak-ban-nah'ee;* patrial from 4343; a *Macbannite* or native of Macbena:—Machbanai.

4345. מַכְבֵּר **makbêr,** *mak-bare';* from 3527 in the sense of *covering* [comp. 3531]; a *grate:*—grate.

4346. מַכְבָּר **makbâr,** *mak-bawr';* from 3527 in the sense of *covering;* a cloth (as *netted* [comp. 4345]):—thick cloth.

4347. מַכָּה **makkâh,** *mak-kaw';* or (masc.) מַכֶּה **makkeh,** *mak-keh';* (plur. only) from 5221; a *blow* (in 2 Chron. 2 : 10, of the flail); by impl. a *wound;* fig. *carnage,* also *pestilence:*—beaten, blow, plague, slaughter, smote, × sore, stripe, stroke, wound ([-ed]).

4348. מִכְוָה **mikvâh,** *mik-vaw';* from 3554; a *burn:*—that burneth, burning.

4349. מָכוֹן **mâkôwn,** *maw-kone';* from 3559; prop. a *fixture,* i.e. a *basis;* gen. a *place,* esp. as an *abode:*—foundation, habitation, (dwelling-, settled) place.

4350. מְכוֹנָה **mᵉkôwnâh,** *mek-o-naw';* or מְכֹנָה **mᵉkônâh,** *mek-o-naw';* fem. of 4349; a *pedestal,* also a *spot:*—base.

4351. מְכוּרָה **mᵉkûwrâh,** *mek-oo-raw';* or מְכֹרָה **mᵉkôrâh,** *mek-o-raw';* from the same as 3564 in the sense of *digging; origin* (as if a mine):—birth, habitation, nativity.

4352. מָכִי **Mâkîy,** *maw-kee';* prob. from 4134; *pining; Maki,* an Isr.:—Machi.

4353. מָכִיר **Mâkîyr,** *maw-keer';* from 4376; *salesman; Makir,* an Isr.:—Machir.

4354. מָכִירִי **Mâkîyrîy,** *maw-kee-ree';* patron. from 4353; a *Makirite* or descend. of Makir:—of Machir.

4355. מָכַךְ **mâkak,** *maw-kak';* a prim. root; to *tumble* (in ruins); fig. to *perish:*—be brought low, decay.

4356. מִכְלָאָה **miklâ'âh,** *mik-law-aw';* or מִכְלָה **miklâh,** *mik-law';* from 3607; a *pen* (for flocks):—([sheep-]) fold. Comp. 4357.

4357. מִכְלָה **miklâh,** *mik-law';* from 3615; *completion* (in plur. concr. adv. *wholly*):—perfect. Comp. 4356.

4358. מִכְלוֹל **miklôwl,** *mik-lole';* from 3634; *perfection* (i.e. concr. adv. *splendidly*):—most gorgeously, all sorts.

4359. מִכְלָל **miklâl,** *mik-lawl';* from 3634; *perfection* (of beauty):—perfection.

4360. מִכְלֻל **miklûl,** *mik-lool';* from 3634; something *perfect,* i.e. a splendid *garment:*—all sorts.

4361. מַכֹּלֶת **makkôleth,** *mak-ko'-leth;* from 398; *nourishment:*—food.

4362. מִכְמַן **mikman,** *mik-man';* from the same as 3646 in the sense of *hiding; treasure* (as *hidden*):—treasure.

4363. מִכְמָס **Mikmâç** (Ezra 2 : 27; Neh. 7 : 31), *mik-maws';* or מִכְמָשׁ **Mikmâsh,** *mik-mawsh';* or מִכְמַשׁ **Mikmash** (Neh. 11 : 31), *mik-mash';* from 3647; *hidden; Mikmas* or *Mikmash,* a place in Pal.:—Mikmas, Mikmash.

4364. מַכְמָר **makmâr,** *mak-mawr';* or מִכְמֹר **mikmôr,** *mik-more';* from 3648 in the sense of *blackening* by heat; a (hunter's) *net* (as *dark* from concealment):—net.

4365. מִכְמֶרֶת **mikmereth,** *mik-meh'-reth;* or מִכְמֹרֶת **mikmôreth,** *mik-mo'-reth;* fem. of 4364; a (fisher's) *net:*—drag, net.

מִכְמָשׁ **Mikmâsh.** See 4363.

4366. מִכְמְתָת **Mikmᵉthâth,** *mik-meth-awth';* appar. from an unused root mean. to *hide; concealment; Mikmethath,* a place in Pal.:—Michmethath.

4367. מַכְנַדְבַי **Maknadbay,** *mak-nad-bah'ee:* from 4100 and 5068 with a particle interposed; *what* (is) *like* (a) *liberal* (man)?; *Maknadbai,* an Isr.:—Machnadebai.

מְכֹנָה **mᵉkônâh.** See 4350.

4368. מְכֹנָה **Mᵉkônâh,** *mek-o-naw';* the same as 4350; a *base; Mekonah,* a place in Pal.:—Mekonah.

4369. מְכֻנָה **mᵉkûnâh,** *mek-oo-naw';* the same as 4350; a *spot:*—base.

4370. מִכְנָס **miknâç,** *mik-nawce';* from 3647 in the sense of *hiding;* (only in dual) *drawers* (from *concealing* the private parts):—breeches.

4371. מֶכֶס **mekeç,** *meh'-kes;* prob. from an unused root mean. to *enumerate;* an *assessment* (as based upon a *census*):—tribute.

4372. מִכְסֶה **mikçeh,** *mik-seh';* from 3680; a *covering,* i.e. weather-*boarding:*—covering.

4373. מִכְסָה **mikçâh,** *mik-saw';* fem. of 4371; an *enumeration;* by impl. a *valuation:*—number, worth.

4374. מְכַסֶּה **mᵉkaççeh,** *mek-as-seh';* from 3680; a *covering,* i.e. *garment;* spec. a *coverlet* (for a bed), an *awning* (from the sun); also the *omentum* (as covering the intestines):—clothing, to cover, that which covereth.

4375. מַכְפֵּלָה **Makpêlâh,** *mak-pay-law';* from 3717; a *fold; Makpelah,* a place in Pal.:—Machpelah.

4376. מָכַר **mâkar,** *maw-kar';* a prim. root; to *sell,* lit. (as merchandise, a daughter in marriage, into slavery), or fig. (to *surrender*):—× at all, sell (away, -er, self).

4377. מֶכֶר **meker,** *meh'-ker;* from 4376; *merchandise;* also *value:*—pay, price, ware.

4378. מַכָּר **makkâr,** *mak-kawr';* from 5234; an *acquaintance:*—acquaintance.

4379. מִכְרֶה **mikreh,** *mik-reh';* from 3738; a *pit* (for salt):—[salt-] pit.

4380. מְכֵרָה **mᵉkêrâh,** *mek-ay-raw';* prob. from the same as 3564 in the sense of *stabbing;* a *sword:*—habitation.

מְכֹרָה **mᵉkôrâh.** See 4351.

4381. מִכְרִי **Mikrîy,** *mik-ree';* from 4376; *salesman; Mikri,* an Isr.:—Michri.

4382. מְכֵרָתִי **Mᵉkêrâthîy,** *mek-ay-raw-thee';* patrial from an unused name (the same as 4380) of a place in Pal.; a *Mekerathite,* or inhab. of Mekerah:—Mecherathite.

4383. מִכְשׁוֹל **mikshôwl,** *mik-shole';* or מִכְשֹׁל **mikshôl,** *mik-shole';* masc. from 3782; a *stumbling-block,* lit. or fig. (*obstacle, enticement* [spec. an idol], *scruple*):—caused to fall, offence, × [no-] thing offered, ruin, stumbling-block.

4384. מַכְשֵׁלָה **makshêlâh,** *mak-shay-law';* fem. from 3782; a *stumbling-block,* but only fig. (*fall, enticement* [idol]):—ruin, stumbling-block.

4385. מִכְתָּב **miktâb,** *mik-tawb';* from 3789; a thing *written,* the *characters,* or a *document* (letter, copy, edict, poem):—writing.

4386. מְכִתָּה **mᵉkittâh,** *mek-it-taw';* from 3807; a *fracture:*—bursting.

4387. מִכְתָּם **miktâm,** *mik-tawm';* from 3799; an *engraving,* i.e. (techn.) a *poem:*—Michtam.

4388. מַכְתֵּשׁ **maktêsh,** *mak-taysh';* from 3806; a *mortar;* by anal. a *socket* (of a tooth):—hollow place, mortar.

4389. מַכְתֵּשׁ **Maktêsh,** *mak-taysh';* the same as 4388; *dell;* the *Maktesh,* a place in Jerus.:—Maktesh.

מֻל **mûl.** See 4136.

4390. מָלֵא **mâlê',** *maw-lay';* or מָלָא **mâlâ'** (Esth. 7 : 5), *maw-law';* a prim. root, to *fill* or (intrans.) *be full* of, in a wide application (lit. and fig.):—accomplish, confirm, + consecrate, be at an end, be expired, be fenced, fill, fulfil, (be, become, × draw, give in, go) full (-ly, -ly set, tale), [over-] flow, fulness, furnish, gather (selves, together), presume, replenish, satisfy, set, space, take a [hand-] full, + have wholly.

4391. מְלָא **mᵉlâ'** (Chald.), *mel-aw';* corresp. to 4390; to *fill:*—fill, be full.

4392. מָלֵא **mâlê',** *maw-lay';* from 4390; *full* (lit. or fig.) or *filling* (lit.); also (concr.) *fulness;* adv. *fully:*—× she that was with child, fill (-ed, -ed with), full (-ly), multitude, as is worth.

4393. מְלֹא **mᵉlô',** *mel-o';* rarely מְלוֹא **mᵉlôw',** *mel-o';* or מְלוֹ **mᵉlôw** (Ezek. 41 : 8), *mel-o';* from 4390; *fulness* (lit. or fig.):—× all along, × all that is (there-) in, fill, (× that whereof . . . was) full, fulness, [hand-] full, multitude.

מִלֹּא **Millô'.** See 4407.

4394. מִלֻּא **millû',** *mil-loo';* from 4390; a *fulfilling* (only in plur.), i.e. (lit.) a *setting* (of gems), or (techn.) *consecration* (also concr. a dedicatory *sacrifice*):—consecration, be set.

4395. מְלֵאָה **mᵉlê'âh,** *mel-ay-aw';* fem. of 4392; something *fulfilled,* i.e. *abundance* (of produce):—(first of ripe) fruit, fulness.

4396. מִלֻּאָה **millû'âh,** *mil-loo-aw';* fem. of 4394; a *filling,* i.e. *setting* (of gems):—inclosing, setting.

4397. מַלְאָךְ **mal'âk,** *mal-awk';* from an unused root mean. to *despatch* as a deputy; a *messenger;* spec. of God, i.e. an *angel* (also a prophet, priest or teacher):—ambassador, angel, king, messenger.

4398. מַלְאַךְ **mal'ak** (Chald.), *mal-ak';* corresp. to 4397; an *angel:*—angel.

4399. מְלָאכָה **mᵉlâ'kâh,** *mel-aw-kaw';* from the same as 4397; prop. *deputyship,* i.e. ministry; gen. *employment* (never servile) or work (abstr. or concr.); also *property* (as the result of *labor*):—business, + cattle, + industrious, occupation, (+ -pied), + officer, thing (made), use, (manner of) work ([-man], -manship).

4400. מַלְאֲכוּת **mal'ăkûwth,** *mal-ak-ooth';* from the same as 4397; a *message:*—message.

4401. מַלְאָכִי **Mal'âkîy,** *mal-aw-kee';* from the same as 4397; *ministrative; Malaki,* a prophet:—Malachi.

4402. מִלֵּאת **millê'th,** *mil-layth';* from 4390; *fulness,* i.e. (concr.) a *plump* socket (of the eye):—× fitly.

4403. מַלְבּוּשׁ **malbûwsh,** *mal-boosh';* or מַלְבֻּשׁ **malbûsh,** *mal-boosh';* from 3847; a *garment,* or (collect.) *clothing:*—apparel, raiment, vestment.

4404. מַלְבֵּן **malbên,** *mal-bane';* from 3835 (denom.); a *brick-kiln:*—brickwork.

4405. מִלָּה **millâh,** *mil-law';* from 4448 (plur. masc. as if from מִלֶּה **milleh,** *mil-leh'*); a *word;* collect. a *discourse;* fig. a *topic:*—+ answer, by-word, matter, any thing (what) to say, to speak (-ing), speak, talking, word.

4406. מִלָּה **millâh** (Chald.), *mil-law';* corresp. to 4405; a *word, command, discourse,* or *subject:*—commandment, matter, thing, word.

מְלוֹ **m^elôw**. See 4393.

מְלוֹא **m^elôw'**. See 4393.

4407. מִלּוֹא **millôw'**, *mil-lo';* or

מִלֹּא **mil-lô'** (2 Kings 12 : 20), *mil-lo';* from 4390; a *rampart* (as *filled* in), i.e. the *citadel:*—Millo. See also 1037.

4408. מַלּוּחַ **mallûwach**, *mal-loo'-akh;* from 4414; *sea-purslain* (from its *saltness*):—mallows.

4409. מַלּוּךְ **Mallûwk**, *mal-luke';* or

מַלּוּכִי° **Mallûwkîy** (Neh. 12 : 14), *mal-loo-kee';* from 4427; *regnant; Malluk,* the name of five Isr.:—Malluch, Melichu [*from the marg.*].

4410. מְלוּכָה **m^elûwkâh**, *mel-oo-kaw';* fem. pass. part. of 4427; something *ruled,* i.e. a *realm:*—kingdom, king's, × royal.

4411. מָלוֹן **mâlôwn**, *maw-lone';* from 3885; a *lodgment,* i.e. *caravanserai* or *encampment:*—inn, place where . . . lodge, lodging (place).

4412. מְלוּנָה **m^elûwnâh**, *mel-oo-naw';* fem. from 3885; a *hut,* a *hammock:*—cottage, lodge.

4413. מַלּוֹתִי **Mallôwthîy**, *mal-lo'-thee;* appar. from 4448; *I have talked* (i.e. *loquacious*):—*Mallothi,* an Isr.:—Mallothi.

4414. מָלַח **mâlach**, *maw-lakh';* a prim. root; prop. to *rub* to pieces or pulverize; intrans. to *disappear* as dust; also (as denom. from 4417) to *salt* whether intern. (to *season* with salt) or extern. (to *rub* with salt):— × at all, salt, season, temper together, vanish away.

4415. מְלַח **m^elach** (Chald.), *mel-akh';* corresp. to 4414; to *eat* salt, i.e. (gen.) *subsist:*— + have maintenance.

4416. מְלַח **m^elach** (Chald.), *mel-akh';* from 4415; *salt:*— + maintenance, salt.

4417. מֶלַח **melach**, *meh'-lakh;* from 4414; prop. *powder,* i.e. (spec.) *salt* (as easily pulverized and dissolved:—salt ([-pit]).

4418. מָלָח **mâlâch**, *maw-lawkh';* from 4414 in its orig. sense; a *rag* or old garment:—rotten rag.

4419. מַלָּח **mallâch**, *mal-lawkh';* from 4414 in its second. sense; a *sailor* (as following "the salt"):—mariner.

4420. מְלֵחָה **m^elêchâh**, *mel-ay-khaw';* from 4414 (in its denom. sense); prop. *salted* (i.e. land [776 being understood]), i.e. a *desert:*—barren land (-ness), salt [land].

4421. מִלְחָמָה **milchâmâh**, *mil-khaw-maw';* from 3898 (in the sense of *fighting*); a *battle* (i.e. the *engagement*); gen. *war* (i.e. *warfare*):—battle, fight, (-ing), war ([-rior]).

4422. מָלַט **mâlat**, *maw-lat';* a prim. root; prop. to *be smooth,* i.e. (by impl.) to *escape* (as if by *slipperiness*); causat. to *release* or *rescue;* spec. to *bring forth* young, *emit* sparks:—deliver (self), escape, lay, leap out, let alone, let go, preserve, save, × speedily, × surely.

4423. מֶלֶט **melet**, *meh'-let;* from 4422, *cement* (from its plastic *smoothness*):—clay.

4424. מְלַטְיָה **M^elatyâh**, *mel-at-yaw';* from 4423 and 3050; (whom) *Jah has delivered; Melatjah,* a Gibeonite:—Melatiah.

4425. מְלִילָה **m^elîylâh**, *mel-ee-law';* from 4449 (in the sense of *cropping* [comp. 4135]); a *head* of grain (as *cut* off):—ear.

4426. מְלִיצָה **m^elîytsâh**, *mel-ee-tsaw';* from 3887; an *aphorism;* also a *satire:*—interpretation, taunting.

4427. מָלַךְ **mâlak**, *maw-lak';* a prim. root; to *reign;* incept. to *ascend the throne;* causat. to *induct* into royalty; hence (by impl.) to *take counsel:*—consult, × indeed, be (make, set a, set up) king, be (make) queen, (begin to, make to) reign (-ing), rule, × surely.

4428. מֶלֶךְ **melek**, *meh'-lek;* from 4427; a *king:*—king, royal.

4429. מֶלֶךְ **Melek**, *meh'-lek;* the same as 4428; *king; Melek,* the name of two Isr.:—Melech, Hammelech [*by includ. the art.*].

4430. מֶלֶךְ **melek** (Chald.), *meh'-lek;* corresp. to 4428; a *king:*—king, royal.

4431. מְלַךְ **m^elak** (Chald.), *mel-ak';* from a root corresp. to 4427 in the sense of *consultation; advice:*—counsel.

4432. מֹלֶךְ **Môlek**, *mo'-lek;* from 4427; *Molek* (i.e. king), the chief deity of the Ammonites:—Molech. Comp. 4445.

4433. מַלְכָּא **malkâ'** (Chald.), *mal-kaw';* corresp. to 4436; a *queen:*—queen.

4434. מַלְכֹּדֶת **malkôdeth**, *mal-ko'-deth;* from 3920; a *snare:*—trap.

4435. מִלְכָּה **Milkâh**, *mil-kaw';* a form of 4436; *queen; Milcah,* the name of a Hebrewess and of an Isr.:—Milcah.

4436. מַלְכָּה **malkâh**, *mal-kaw';* fem. of 4428; a *queen:*—queen.

4437. מַלְכוּ **malkûw** (Chald.), *mal-koo';* corresp. to 4438; *dominion* (abstr. or concr.):—kingdom, kingly, realm, reign.

4438. מַלְכוּת **malkûwth**, *mal-kooth';* or

מַלְכֻת **malkûth**, *mal-kooth';* or (in plur.)

מַלְכֻיָה **malkûyâh**, *mal-koo-yâh';* from 4427; a *rule;* concr. a *dominion:*—empire, kingdom, realm, reign, royal.

4439. מַלְכִּיאֵל **Malkîy'êl**, *mal-kee-ale';* from 4428 and 410; *king of* (i.e. appointed by) *God; Malkiël,* an Isr.:—Malchiel.

4440. מַלְכִּיאֵלִי **Malkîy'êlîy**, *mal-kee-ay-lee';* patron. from 4439; a *Malkiëlite* or desc. of Malkiel:—Malchielite.

4441. מַלְכִּיָּה **Malkîyâh**, *mal-kee-yaw';* or

מַלְכִּיָּהוּ **Malkîyâhûw** (Jer. 38 : 6), *mal-kee-yaw'-hoo;* from 4428 and 3050; *king of* (i.e. appointed by) *Jah; Malkijah,* the name of ten Isr.:—Malchiah, Malchijah.

4442. מַלְכִּי־צֶדֶק **Malkîy-Tsedeq**, *mal-kee-tseh'-dek;* from 4428 and 6664; *king of right; Malki-Tsedek,* an early king in Pal.:—Melchizedek.

4443. מַלְכִּירָם **Malkîyrâm**, *mal-kee-rawm';* from 4428 and 7311; *king of* a *high* one (i.e. of exaltation); *Malkiram,* an Isr.:—Malchiram.

4444. מַלְכִּישׁוּעַ **Malkîyshûwa'**, *mal-kee-shoo'-ah;* from 4428 and 7769; *king of wealth; Malkishua,* an Isr.:—Malchishua.

4445. מַלְכָּם **Malkâm**, *mal-kawm';* or

מִלְכּוֹם **Milkôwm**, *mil-kome';* from 4428 for 4432; *Malcam* or *Milcom,* the national idol of the Ammonites:—Malcham, Milcom.

4446. מְלֶכֶת **m^eleketh**, *mel-eh'-keth;* from 4427; a *queen:*—queen.

4447. מֹלֶכֶת **Môleketh**, *mo-leh'-keth;* fem. act. part. of 4427; *queen; Moleketh,* an Israelitess:—Hammoleketh [*includ. the art.*].

4448. מָלַל **mâlal**, *maw-lal';* a prim. root; to *speak* (mostly poet.) or *say:*—say, speak, utter.

4449. מְלַל **m^elal** (Chald.), *mel-al';* corresp. to 4448; to *speak:*—say, speak (-ing).

4450. מִלֲלַי **Milălay**, *mee-lal-ah'ee;* from 4448; *talkative; Milalai,* an Isr.:—Milalai.

4451. מַלְמָד **malmâd**, *mal-mawd';* from 3925; a *goad* for oxen:—goad.

4452. מָלַץ **mâlats**, *maw-lats';* a prim. root; to *be smooth,* i.e. (fig.) *pleasant:*—be sweet.

4453. מֶלְצָר **meltsâr**, *mel-tsawr';* of Pers. der.; the *butler* or other officer in the Bab. court:—Melzar.

4454. מָלַק **mâlaq**, *maw-lak';* a prim. root; to *crack* a joint; by impl. to *wring* the neck of a fowl (without separating it):—wring off.

4455. מַלְקוֹחַ **malqôwach**, *mal-ko'-akh;* from 3947; trans. (in dual) the *jaws* (as taking food); intrans. *spoil* [and captives] (as taken):—booty, jaws, prey.

4456. מַלְקוֹשׁ **malqôwsh**, *mal-koshe';* from 3953; the spring *rain* (comp. 3954); fig. *eloquence:*—latter rain.

4457. מֶלְקָח **melqâch**, *mel-kawkh';* or

מַלְקָח **malqâch**, *mal-kawkh';* from 3947; (only in dual) *tweezers:*—snuffers, tongs.

4458. מֶלְתָּחָה **meltâchâh**, *mel-taw-khaw';* from an unused root mean. to *spread* out; a *wardrobe* (i.e. room where clothing is *spread*):—vestry.

4459. מַלְתָּעָה **maltâ'âh**, *mal-taw-aw';* transp. for 4973; a *grinder,* i.e. back *tooth:*—great tooth.

4460. מַמְּגֻרָה **mamm^egûrâh**, *mam-meg-oo-raw';* from 4048 (in the sense of *depositing*); a *granary:*—barn.

4461. מֵמַד **mêmad**, *may-mad';* from 4058; a *measure:*—measure.

4462. מְמוּכָן **M^emûwkân**, *mem-oo-kawn';* or (transp.)

מוֹמֻכָן° **Môwmûkân** (Esth. 1 : 16), *mo-moo-kawn';* of Pers. der.; *Memucan* or *Momucan,* a Pers. satrap:—Memucan.

4463. מָמוֹת **mâmôwth**, *maw-mothe';* from 4191; a mortal *disease;* concr. a *corpse:*—death.

4464. מַמְזֵר **mamzêr**, *mam-zare';* from an unused root mean. to *alienate;* a *mongrel,* i.e. born of a Jewish father and a heathen mother:—bastard.

4465. מִמְכָּר **mimkâr**, *mim-kawr';* from 4376; *merchandise;* abstr. a *selling:*— × ought, (that which cometh of) sale, that which . . . sold, ware.

4466. מִמְכֶּרֶת **mimkereth**, *mim-keh'-reth;* fem. of 4465; a *sale:*— + sold as.

4467. מַמְלָכָה **mamlâkâh**, *mam-law-kaw';* from 4427; *dominion,* i.e. (abstr.) the estate (*rule*) or (concr.) the country (*realm*):—kingdom, king's, reign, royal.

4468. מַמְלָכוּת **mamlâkûwth**, *mam-law-kooth';* a form of 4467 and equiv. to it:—kingdom, reign.

4469. מַמְסָךְ **mamçâk**, *mam-sawk';* from 4537; *mixture,* i.e. (spec.) wine *mixed* (with water or spices):—drink-offering, mixed wine.

4470. מֶמֶר **memer**, *meh'-mer;* from an unused root mean. to *grieve; sorrow:*—bitterness.

4471. מַמְרֵא **Mamrê'**, *mam-ray';* from 4754 (in the sense of *vigor*); *lusty; Mamre,* an Amorite:—Mamre.

4472. מַמְרֹר **mamrôr**, *mam-rore';* from 4843; a *bitterness,* i.e. (fig.) calamity:—bitterness.

4473. מִמְשַׁח **mimshach**, *mim-shakh';* from 4886, in the sense of *expansion; outspread* (i.e. with outstretched wings):—anointed.

4474. מִמְשָׁל **mimshâl**, *mim-shawl';* from 4910; a *ruler* or (abstr.) *rule:*—dominion, that ruled.

4475. מֶמְשָׁלָה **memshâlâh**, *mem-shaw-law';* fem. of 4474; *rule;* also (concr. in plur.) a *realm* or a *ruler:*—dominion, government, power, to rule.

4476. מִמְשָׁק **mimshâq**, *mim-shawk';* from the same as 4943; a *possession:*—breeding.

4477. מַמְתַּק **mamtaq**, *mam-tak';* from 4985; something *sweet* (lit. or fig.):—(most) sweet.

4478. מָן **mân**, *mawn;* from 4100; lit. a *whatness* (so to speak), i.e. *manna* (so called from the question about it):—manna.

4479. מָן **mân** (Chald.), *mawn;* from 4101; *who* or *what* (prop. interrog., hence also indef. and rel.):—what, who (-msoever, + -so).

4480. מִן **min**, *min;* or

מִנִּי **minnîy**, *min-nee';* or

מִנֵּי **minnêy** (constr. plur.), *min-nay'* (Isa. 30 : 11); for 4482; prop. a *part of;* hence (prep.), *from* or *out of* in many senses (as follows):—above, after, among, at, because of, by (reason of), from (among), in, × neither, × nor, (out) of, over, since, × then, through, × whether, with.

4481. מִן **min** (Chald.), *min;* corresp. to 4480:—according, after, + because, + before, by, for, from, × him, × more than, (out) of, part, since, × these, to, upon, + when.

4482. מֵן **mên**, *mane;* from an unused root mean. to *apportion;* a *part;* hence a musical *chord* (as parted into strings):—in [the same] (Psa. 68 : 23), stringed instrument (Psa. 150 : 4), whereby (Psa. 45 : 8 [*defective plur.*]).

4483. מְנָא **m^enâ'** (Chald.), *men-aw';* or

מְנָה **m^enâh** (Chald.), *men-aw';* corresp. to 4487; to *count, appoint:*—number, ordain, set.

4484. מְנֵא **menê'** (Chald.), *men-ay';* pass. part. of 4483; *numbered:*—Mene.

4485. מַנְגִּינָה **mangîynâh**, *man-ghee-naw';* from 5059; a *satire:*—music.

מִנְדָּה **mindâh**. See 4061.

4486. מַנְדַּע **manda'** (Chald.), *man-dah';* corresp. to 4093; *wisdom* or *intelligence:*—knowledge, reason, understanding.

מְנָה **m^enâh**. See 4483.

4487. מָנָה **mânâh**, *maw-naw';* a prim. root; prop. to *weigh* out; by impl. to *allot* or constitute officially; also to *enumerate* or enroll:—appoint, count, number, prepare, set, tell.

4488. מָנֶה **mâneh**, *maw-neh';* from 4487; prop. a fixed *weight* or measured amount, i.e. (techn.) a *maneh* or mina:—maneh, pound.

4489. מֹנֶה **môneh**, *mo-neh';* from 4487; prop. something *weighed* out, i.e. (fig.) a *portion* of time, i.e. an *instance:*—time.

4490. מָנָה **mânâh**, *maw-naw';* from 4487; prop. something *weighed* out, i.e. (gen.) a *division;* spec. (of food) a *ration;* also a *lot:*—such things as belonged, part, portion.

4491. מִנְהָג **minhâg**, *min-hawg';* from 5090; the *driving* (of a chariot):—driving.

4492. מִנְהָרָה **minhârâh**, *min-haw-raw';* from 5102; prop. a *channel* or fissure, i.e. (by impl.) a *cavern:*—den.

4493. מָנוֹד **mânôwd**, *maw-node';* from 5110; a *nodding* or *toss* (of the head in derision):—shaking.

4494. מָנוֹחַ **mânôwach**, *maw-no'-akh;* from 5117; *quiet*, i.e. (concr.) a *settled spot*, or (fig.) a *home:*—(place of) rest.

4495. מָנוֹחַ **Mânôwach**, *maw-no'-akh;* the same as 4494; *rest; Manoäch*, an Isr.:—Manoah.

4496. מְנוּחָה **menûwchâh**, *men-oo-khaw';* or

מְנֻחָה **m^enûchâh**, *men-oo-khaw';* fem. of 4495; *repose* or (adv.) *peacefully;* fig. *consolation* (spec. *matrimony*); hence (concr.) an *abode:*—comfortable, ease, quiet, rest (-ing place), still.

4497. מָנוֹן **mânôwn**, *maw-nohn';* from 5125; a *continuator*, i.e. *heir:*—son.

4498. מָנוֹס **mânôwç**, *maw-noce';* from 5127; a *retreat* (lit. or fig.); abstr. a *fleeing:*—× apace, escape, way to flee, flight, refuge.

4499. מְנוּסָה **m^enuwçâh**, *men-oo-saw';* or

מְנֻסָה **m^enûçâh**, *men-oo-saw';* fem. of 4498; *retreat:*—fleeing, flight.

4500. מָנוֹר **mânôwr**, *maw-nore';* from 5214; a *yoke* (prop. for *ploughing*), i.e. the *frame* of a loom:—beam.

4501. מְנוֹרָה **menôwrâh**, *men-o-raw';* or

מְנֹרָה **m^enôrâh**, *men-o-raw';* fem. of 4500 (in the orig. sense of 5216); a *chandelier:*—candlestick.

4502. מִנְּזָר **minn^ezâr**, *min-ez-awr';* from 5144; a *prince:*—crowned.

4503. מִנְחָה **minchâh**, *min-khaw';* from an unused root mean. to *apportion*, i.e. *bestow; a donation;* euphem. *tribute;* spec. a sacrificial *offering* (usually bloodless and voluntary):—gift, oblation, (meat) offering, present, sacrifice.

4504. מִנְחָה **minchâh** (Chald.), *min-khaw';* corresp. to 4503; a sacrificial *offering:*—oblation, meat offering.

מְנֻחָה **m^enûchâh**. See 4496.

מְנֻחוֹת **M^enûchôwth**. See 2679.

4505. מְנַחֵם **M^enachêm**, *men-akh-ame';* from 5162; *comforter; Menachem*, an Isr.:—Menahem.

4506. מָנַחַת **Mânachath**, *maw-nakh'-ath;* from 5117; *rest; Manachath*, the name of an Edomite and of a place in Moab:—Manahath.

מְנַחְתִּי **M^enachtîy**. See 2680.

4507. מְנִי **M^eniy**, *men-ee';* from 4487; the *Apportioner*, i.e. Fate (as an idol):—number.

מִנִּי **minnîy**. See 4480, 4482.

4508. מִנִּי **Minnîy**, *min-nee';* of for. der.; *Minni*, an Armenian province:—Minni.

מְנָיוֹת **m^enâyôwth**. See 4521.

4509. מִנְיָמִין **Minyâmîyn**, *min-yaw-meen';* from 4480 and 3225; *from* (the) *right hand; Minjamin*, the name of two Isr.:—Miniamin. Comp. 4326.

4510. מִנְיָן **minyân** (Chald.), *min-yawn';* from 4483; *enumeration:*—number.

4511. מִנִּית **Minnîyth**, *min-neeth';* from the same as 4482; *enumeration; Minnith*, a place E. of the Jordan:—Minnith.

4512. מִנְלֶה **minleh**, *min-leh';* from 5239; *completion*, i.e. (in produce) *wealth:*—perfection.

מְנֻסָה **m^enûçâh**. See 4499.

4513. מָנַע **mâna'**, *maw-nah';* a prim. root; to *debar* (neg. or pos.) from benefit or injury:—deny, keep (back), refrain, restrain, withhold.

4514. מַנְעוּל **man'ûwl**, *man-ool';* or

מַנְעֻל **man'ûl**, *man-ool';* from 5274; a *bolt:*—lock.

4515. מִנְעָל **man'âl**, *man-awl';* from 5274; a *bolt:*—shoe.

4516. מַנְעַם **man'am**, *man-am';* from 5276; a *delicacy:*—dainty.

4517. מְנַעְנַע **m^ena'na'**, *men-ah-ah';* from 5128; a *sistrum* (so called from its *rattling* sound):—cornet.

4518. מְנַקִּית **m^enaqqîyth**, *men-ak-keeth';* from 5352; a *sacrificial basin* (for holding blood):—bowl.

מְנֹרָה **m^enôrâh**. See 4501.

4519. מְנַשֶּׁה **M^enashsheh**, *men-ash-sheh';* from 5382; *causing to forget; Menashsheh*, a grandson of Jacob, also the tribe desc. from him, and its territory:—Manasseh.

4520. מְנַשִּׁי **M^enashshîy**, *men-ash-shee';* from 4519; a *Menashshite* or desc. of Menashsheh:—of Manasseh, Manassites.

4521. מְנָת **m^enâth**, *men-awth';* from 4487; an *allotment* (by courtesy, law or providence):—portion.

4522. מַס **maç**, *mas;* or

מִס **miç**, *mees;* from 4549; prop. a *burden* (as causing to *faint*), i.e. a *tax* in the form of forced *labor:*—discomfited, levy, task [-master], tribute (-tary).

4523. מָס **mâç**, *mawce;* from 4549; *fainting*, i.e. (fig.) *disconsolate:*—is afflicted.

4524. מֵסַב **mêçab**, *may-sab';* plur. masc.

מְסִבִּים **m^eçibbîym**, *mes-ib-beem';* or fem.

מְסִבּוֹת **m^eçibbôwth**, *mes-ib-bohth';* from 5437; a *divan* (as *enclosing* the room); abstr. (adv.) *around:*—that compass about, (place) round about, at table.

מוּסַבָּה **mûçabbâh**. See 4142.

4525. מַסְגֵּר **maçgêr**, *mas-gare';* from 5462; a *fastener*, i.e. (of a person) a *smith*, (of a thing) a *prison:*—prison, smith.

4526. מִסְגֶּרֶת **miçgereth**, *mis-gheh'-reth;* from 5462; something *enclosing*, i.e. a *margin* (of a region, of a panel); concr. a *stronghold:*—border, close place, hole.

4527. מַסַּד **maççad**, *mas-sad';* from 3245; a *foundation:*—foundation.

מוֹסָדָה **môçâdâh**. See 4146.

4528. מִסְדְּרוֹן **miçd^erôwn**, *mis-der-ohn';* from the same as 5468; a *colonnade* or internal portico (from its *rows* of pillars):—porch.

4529. מָסָה **mâçâh**, *maw-saw';* a prim. root; to *dissolve:*—make to consume away, (make to) melt, water.

4530. מִסָּה **miççâh**, *mis-saw';* from 4549 (in the sense of *flowing*); *abundance*, i.e. (adv.) *liberally:*—tribute.

4531. מַסָּה **maççâh**, *mas-saw';* from 5254; a *testing*, of men (judicial) or of God (querulous):—temptation, trial.

4532. מַסָּה **Maççâh**, *mas-saw';* the same as 4531; *Massah*, a place in the Desert:—Massah.

4533. מַסְוֶה **maçveh**, *mas-veh';* appar. from an unused root mean. to *cover;* a *veil:*—vail.

4534. מְסוּכָה **m^eçûwkâh**, *mes-oo-kaw';* for 4881; a *hedge:*—thorn hedge.

4535. מַסָּח **maççâch**, *mas-sawkh';* from 5255 in the sense of *staving* off; a *cordon*, (adv.) or (as) a military *barrier:*—broken down.

4536. מִסְחָר **miçchâr**, *mis-khawr';* from 5503; *trade:*—traffic.

4537. מָסַךְ **mâçak**, *maw-sak';* a prim. root; to *mix*, espec. wine (with spices):—mingle.

4538. מֶסֶךְ **meçek**, *meh'-sek;* from 4537; a *mixture*, i.e. of wine with spices:—mixture.

4539. מָסָךְ **mâçâk**, *maw-sawk';* from 5526; a *cover*, i.e. *veil:*—covering, curtain, hanging.

4540. מְסֻכָּה **m^eçukkâh**, *mes-ook-kaw';* from 5526; a *covering*, i.e. garniture:—covering.

4541. מַסֵּכָה **maççêkâh**, *mas-say-kaw';* from 5258; prop. a *pouring* over, i.e. *fusion* of metal (espec. a *cast* image); by impl. a *libation*, i.e. league; concr. a *coverlet* (as if *poured* out):—covering, molten (image), vail.

4542. מִסְכֵּן **miçkên**, *mis-kane';* from 5531; *indigent:*—poor (man).

4543. מִסְכְּנָה **miçk^enâh**, *mis-ken-aw';* by transp. from 3664; a *magazine:*—store (-house), treasure.

4544. מִסְכֵּנֻת **miçkênûth**, *mis-kay-nooth';* from 4542; *indigence:*—scarceness.

4545. מַסֶּכֶת **maççeketh**, *mas-seh'-keth;* from 5259 in the sense of *spreading* out; something *expanded*, i.e. the *warp* in a loom (as *stretched* out to receive the woof):—web.

4546. מְסִלָּה **m^eçillâh**, *mes-il-law';* from 5549; a *thoroughfare* (as *turnpiked*), lit. or fig.; spec. a *viaduct*, a *staircase:*—causeway, course, highway, path, terrace.

4547. מַסְלוּל **maçlûwl**, *mas-lool';* from 5549; a *thoroughfare* (as turnpiked):—highway.

4548. מַסְמֵר **maçmêr**, *mas-mare';* or

מִסְמֵר **miçmêr**, *mis-mare';* also (fem.)

מַסְמְרָה **maçm^erâh**, *mas-mer-aw';* or

מִסְמְרָה **miçm^erâh**, *mis-mer-aw';* or even

מַשְׂמְרָה **masm^erâh** (Eccles. 12 : 11), *mas-mer-aw';* from 5568; a *peg* (as *bristling* from the surface):—nail.

4549. מָסַס **mâçaç**, *maw-sas'*; a prim. root; to *liquefy*; fig. to *waste* (with disease), to *faint* (with fatigue, fear or grief):—discourage, faint, be loosed, melt (away), refuse, × utterly.

4550. מַסַּע **maççaʻ**, *mas-sah'*; from 5265; a *departure* (from *striking* the tents), i.e. march (not necessarily a single day's travel); by impl. a *station* (or point of *departure*):—journey (-ing).

4551. מַסָּע **maççâʻ**, *mas-saw'*; from 5265 in the sense of *projecting*; a *missile* (spear or arrow); also a *quarry* (whence stones are, as it were, *ejected*):—before it was brought, dart.

4552. מִסְעָד **miçʻâd**, *mis-awd'*; from 5582; a *balustrade* (for stairs):—pillar.

4553. מִסְפֵּד **miçpêd**, *mis-pade'*; from 5594; a *lamentation*:—lamentation, one mourneth, mourning, wailing.

4554. מִסְפּוֹא **miçpôwʼ**, *mis-po'*; from an unused root mean. to *collect*; *fodder*:—provender.

4555. מִסְפָּחָה **miçpâchâh**, *mis-paw-khaw'*; from 5596; a *veil* (as *spread* out):—kerchief.

4556. מִסְפַּחַת **miçpachath**, *mis-pakh'-ath*; from 5596; *scurf* (as *spreading* over the surface):—scab.

4557. מִסְפָּר **miçpâr**, *mis-pawr'*; from 5608; a *number*, def. (arithmetical) or indef. (large, *innumerable*; small, a *few*); also (abstr.) *narration*:— + abundance, account, × all, × few, [in-] finite, (certain) number (-ed), tale, telling, + time.

4558. מִסְפָּר **Miçpâr**, *mis-pawr'*; the same as 4457; *number*; *Mispar*, an Isr.:—Mizpar. Comp. 4559.

מֹסֵרוֹת **Môçêrowth**. See 4149.

4559. מִסְפֶּרֶת **Miçpereth**, *mis-peh'-reth*; fem. of 4457; *enumeration*; *Mispereth*, an Isr.:—Mispereth. Comp. 4458.

4560. מָסַר **mâçar**, *maw-sar'*; a prim. root; to *sunder*, i.e. (trans.) *set apart*, or (reflex.) *apostatize*:—commit, deliver.

4561. מֹסָר **môçâr**, *mo-sawr'*; from 3256; *admonition*:—instruction.

4562. מָסֹרֶת **mâçôreth**, *maw-so'-reth*; from 631; a *band*:—bond.

4563. מִסְתּוֹר **miçtôwr**, *mis-tore'*; from 5641; a *refuge*:—covert.

4564. מַסְתֵּר **maçtêr**, *mas-tare'*; from 5641; prop. a *hider*, i.e. (abstr.) a hiding, i.e. *aversion*:—hid.

4565. מִסְתָּר **miçtâr** *mis-tawr'*; from 5641; prop. a *concealer*, i.e. a *covert*:—secret (-ly, place).

מְעָא **meʻâʼ**. See 4577.

4566. מַעְבָּד **maʻbâd**, *mah-bawd'*; from 5647; an *act*:—work.

4567. מַעְבָד **maʻbâd** (Chald.), *mah-bawd'*; corresp. to 4566; an *act*:—work.

4568. מַעֲבֶה **maʻăbeh**, *mah-ab-eh'*; from 5666; prop. *compact* (part of soil), i.e. *loam*:—clay.

4569. מַעֲבָר **maʻăbâr**, *mah-ab-awr'*; or fem.

מַעֲבָרָה **maʻăbârâh**, *mah-ab-aw-raw'*; from 5674; a *crossing*-place (of a river, a *ford*; of a mountain, a *pass*); abstr. a *transit*, i.e. (fig.) *overwhelming*:—ford, place where . . . pass, passage.

4570. מַעְגָּל **maʻgâl**, *mah-gawl'*; or fem.

מַעְגָּלָה **maʻgâlâh**, *mah-gaw-law'*; from the same as 5696; a *track* (lit. or fig.); also a *rampart* (as *circular*):—going, path, trench, way ([-side]).

4571. מָעַד **mâʻad**, *maw-ad'*; a prim. root; to *waver*:—make to shake, slide, slip.

מֹעֵד **môʻêd**. See 4150.

4572. מַעֲדַי **Maʻăday**, *mah-ad-ah'ee*; from 5710; *ornamental*; *Maadai*, an Isr.:—Maadai.

4573. מַעַדְיָה **Maʻadyâh**, *mah-ad-yaw'*; from 5710 and 3050; *ornament of Jah*; *Maadjah*, an Isr.:—Maadiah. Comp. 4153.

4574. מַעֲדָן **maʻădân**, *mah-ad-awn'*; or (fem.)

מַעֲדַנָּה **maʻădannâh**, *mah-ad-an-naw'*; from 5727; a *delicacy* or (abstr.) *pleasure* (adv. *cheerfully*):—dainty, delicately, delight.

4575. מַעֲדַנָּה **maʻădannâh**, *mah-ad-an-naw'*; by transp. from 6029; a *bond*, i.e. *group*:—influence.

4576. מַעְדֵּר **maʻdêr**, *mah-dare'*; from 5737; a (weeding) *hoe*:—mattock.

4577. מְעָה **meʻâh** (Chald.), *meh-aw'*; or

מְעָא **meʻâʼ** (Chald.), *meh-aw'*; corresp. to 4578; only in plur. the *bowels*:—belly.

4578. מֵעָה **mêʻâh**, *may-aw'*; from an unused root prob. mean. to *be soft*; used only in plur. the *intestines*, or (collect.) the *abdomen*, fig. *sympathy*; by impl. a *vest*; by extens. the *stomach*, the *uterus* (or of men, the seat of generation), the *heart* (fig.):—belly, bowels, × heart, womb.

4579. מֵעָה **mêʻâh**, *may-aw'*; fem. of 4578; the *belly*, i.e. (fig.) interior:—gravel.

4580. מָעוֹג **mâʻôwg**, *maw-ogue'*; from 5746; a *cake* of bread (with 3934 a *table-buffoon*, i.e. *parasite*):—cake, feast.

4581. מָעוֹז **mâʻôwz**, *maw-oze'* (also

מָעוּז **mâʻûwz**, *maw-ooz'*); or

מָעֹז **mâʻôz**, *maw-oze'* (also

מָעֻז **mâʻûz**, *maw-ooz'*); from 5810; a *fortified* place; fig. a *defence*:—force, fort (-ress), rock, strength (-en), (× most) strong (hold).

4582. מָעוֹךְ **Mâʻôwk**, *maw-oke'*; from 4600; *oppressed*; *Maok*, a Philistine:—Maoch.

4583. מָעוֹן **mâʻôwn**, *maw-ohn'*; or

מָעִין **mâʻîyn** (1 Chron. 4 : 41), *maw-een'*; from the same as 5772; an *abode*, of God (the Tabernacle or the Temple), men (their home) or animals (their lair); hence a *retreat* (asylum):—den, dwelling ([-] place), habitation.

4584. מָעוֹן **Mâʻôwn**, *maw-ohn'*; the same as 4583; a *residence*; *Maon*, the name of an Isr. and of a place in Pal.:—Maon, Maonites. Comp. 1010, 4586.

4585 מְעוֹנָה **meʻôwnâh**, *meh-o-naw'*; or

מְעֹנָה **meʻônâh**, *meh-o-naw'*; fem. of 4583, and mean. the same:—den, habitation, (dwelling) place, refuge.

4586. מְעוּנִי **Meʻûwnîy**, *meh-oo-nee'*; or

מְעִינִי **Meʻîynîy**, *meh-ee-nee'*; prob. patrial from 4584; a *Meünite*, or inhab. of Maon (only in plur.):—Mehunim (-s), Meunim.

4587. מְעוֹנֹתַי **Meʻôwnôthay**, *meh-o-no-thah'ee*; plur. of 4585; *habitative*; *Meonothai*, an Isr.:—Meonothai.

4588. מָעוּף **mâʻûwph**, *maw-oof'*; from 5774 in the sense of *covering* with shade [comp. 4155]; *darkness*:—dimness.

4589. מָעוֹר **mâʻôwr**, *maw-ore'*; from 5783; *nakedness*, i.e. (in plur.) the *pudenda*:—nakedness.

מָעֹז **mâʻôz**. See 4583.

מָעֻז **mâʻûz**. See 4583.

4590. מַעַזְיָה **Maʻazyâh**, *mah-az-yaw'*; or

מַעַזְיָהוּ **Maʻazyâhûw**, *mah-az-yaw'-hoo*; prob. from. 5756 (in the sense of *protection*) and 3050; *rescue of Jah*; *Maazjah*, the name of two Isr.:—Maaziah.

4591. מָעַט **mâʻaṭ**, *maw-at'*; a prim. root; prop. to *pare* off, i.e. *lessen*; intrans. to *be* (or caus. to *make*) *small* or *few* (or fig. *ineffective*):—suffer to decrease, diminish, (be, × borrow a, give, make) few (in number, -ness), gather least (little), be (seem) little, (× give the) less, be minished, bring to nothing.

4592. מְעַט **meʻaṭ**, *meh-at'*; or

מְעָט **meʻâṭ**, *meh-awt'*; from 4591; a *little* or *few* (often adv. or compar.):—almost, (some, very) few (-er, -est), lightly, little (while), (very) small (matter, thing), some, soon, × very.

4593. מָעֹט **mâʻôṭ**, *maw-ote'*; pass. adj. of 4591; *thinned* (as to the edge), i.e. *sharp*:—wrapped up.

4594. מַעֲטֶה **maʻăṭeh**, *mah-at-eh'*; from 5844; a *vestment*:—garment.

4595. מַעֲטָפָה **maʻăṭâphâh**, *mah-at-aw-faw'*; from 5848; a *cloak*:—mantle.

4596. מְעִי **meʻîy**, *meh-ee'*; from 5753; a *pile* of rubbish (as *contorted*), i.e. a *ruin* (comp. 5856):—heap.

4597. מָעַי **Mâʻai**, *maw-ah'ee*; prob. from 4578; *sympathetic*; *Maai*, an Isr.:—Maai.

4598. מְעִיל **meʻîyl**, *meh-eel'*; from 4603 in the sense of *covering*; a *robe* (i.e. upper and outer *garment*):—cloke, coat, mantle, robe.

מֵעִים **mêʻîym**. See 4578.

מְעִין **meʻîyn** (Chald.). See 4577.

4599. מַעְיָן **maʻyân**, *mah-yawn'*; or

מַעְיְנוֹ **maʻyenôw** (Psa. 114 : 8), *mah-yen-o'*; or (fem.)

מַעְיָנָה **maʻyânâh**, *mah-yaw-naw'*; from 5869 (as a denom. in the sense of a *spring*); a *fountain* (also collect.), fig. a *source* (of satisfaction):—fountain, spring, well.

מְעִינִי **Meʻîynîy**. See 4586.

4600. מָעַךְ **mâʻak**, *maw-ak'*; a prim. root; to *press*, i.e. to *pierce*, *emasculate*, *handle*:—bruised, stuck, be pressed.

4601. מַעֲכָה **Maʻăkâh**, *mah-ak-aw'*; or

מַעֲכָת **Maʻăkâth** (Josh. 13 : 13), *mah-ak-awth'*; from 4600; *depression*; *Maakah* (or *Maakath*), the name of a place in Syria, also of a Mesopotamian, of three Isr., and of four Israelitesses and one Syrian woman:—Maachah, Maachathites. See also 1038.

4602. מַעֲכָתִי **Maʻăkâthîy**, *mah-ak-aw-thee'*; patrial from 4601; a *Maakathite*, or inhab. of Maakah:—Maachathite.

4603. מָעַל **mâʻal**, *maw-al'*; a prim. root; prop. to *cover* up; used only fig. to *act covertly*, i.e. *treacherously*:—transgress, (commit, do a) trespass (-ing).

4604. מַעַל **maʻal**, *mah'-al*; from 4603; *treachery*, i.e. sin:—falsehood, grievously, sore, transgression, trespass, × very.

4605. מַעַל **maʻal**, *mah'-al*; from 5927; prop. the *upper* part, used only adv. with pref. *upward*, *above*, *overhead*, *from the top*, etc.:—above, exceeding (-ly), forward, on (× very) high, over, up (-on, -ward), very.

מֵעַל **mêʻal**. See 5921.

4606. מֵעָל **mêʻâl** (Chald.), *may-awl'*; from 5954; (only in plur. as sing.) the *setting* (of the sun):—going down.

4607. מֹעַל **môʻal**, *mo'-al*; from 5927; a *raising* (of the hands):—lifting up.

4608. מַעֲלֶה **maʻăleh**, *mah-al-eh'*; from 5927; an *elevation*, i.e. (concr.) *acclivity* or *platform*; abstr. (the relation or state) a *rise* or (fig.) *priority*:—ascent, before, chiefest, cliff, that goeth up, going up, hill, mounting up, stairs.

4609. מַעֲלָה **maʻălâh**, *mah-al-aw'*; fem. of 4608; *elevation*, i.e. the act (lit. a *journey* to a higher place, fig. a *thought* arising), or (concr.) the condition (lit. a *step* or *grade-mark*, fig. a *superiority* of station); spec. a climactic *progression* (in certain Psalms):—things that come up, (high) degree, deal, go up, stair, step, story.

4610. מַעֲלֵה עַקְרַבִּים **Ma'ălêh 'Aqrabbîym**, *mah-al-ay' ak-rab-beem'*; from 4608 and (the plur. of) 6137; *Steep of Scorpions*, a place in the Desert:—Maaleh-accrabim, the ascent (going up) of Akrabbim.

4611. מַעֲלָל **ma'ălâl**, *mah-al-awl'*; from 5953; an *act* (good or bad):—doing, endeavour, invention, work.

4612. מַעֲמָד **ma'ămâd**, *mah-am-awd'*; from 5975; (fig.) a *position:*—attendance, office, place, state.

4613. מָעֳמָד **mo'ŏmâd**, *moh-om-awd'*; from 5975; lit. a *foothold:*—standing.

4614. מַעֲמָסָה **ma'ămâçâh**, *mah-am-aw-saw'*; from 6006; *burdensomeness:*—burdensome.

4615. מַעֲמָק **ma'ămâq**, *mah-am-awk'*; from 6009; a *deep:*—deep, depth.

4616. מַעַן **ma'an**, *mah'-an*; from 6030; prop. *heed*, i.e. *purpose*; used only adv., *on account of* (as a motive or an aim), teleologically *in order that:*—because of, to the end (intent) that, for (to, . . . 's sake), + lest, that, to.

4617. מַעֲנֶה **ma'ăneh**, *mah-an-eh'*; from 6030; a *reply* (favorable or contradictory):—answer, × himself.

4618. מַעֲנָה **ma'ănâh**, *mah-an-aw'*; from 6031, in the sense of *depression* or *tilling*; a *furrow:*— + acre, furrow.

מְעֹנָה **me'ônâh**. See 4585.

4619. מַעַץ **Ma'ats**, *mah'-ats*; from 6095; *closure*; *Maats*, an Isr.:—Maaz.

4620. מַעֲצֵבָה **ma'ătsêbâh**, *mah-ats-ay-baw'*; from 6087; *anguish:*—sorrow.

4621. מַעֲצָד **ma'ătsâd**, *mah-ats-awd'*; from an unused root mean. to *hew*; an *axe:*—ax, tongs.

4622. מַעְצוֹר **ma'tsôwr**, *mah-tsore'*; from 6113; obj. a *hindrance:*—restraint.

4623. מַעְצָר **ma'tsâr**, *mah-tsawr'*; from 6113; subj. *control:*—rule.

4624. מַעֲקֶה **ma'ăqeh**, *mah-ak-eh'*; from an unused root mean. to *repress*; a *parapet:*—battlement.

4625. מַעֲקָשׁ **ma'ăqâsh**, *mah-ak-awsh'*; from 6140; a *crook* (in a road):—crooked thing.

4626. מַעַר **ma'ar**, *mah'-ar*; from 6168; a *nude* place, i.e. (lit.) the *pudenda*, or (fig.) a vacant *space:*—nakedness, proportion.

4627. מַעֲרָב **ma'ărâb**, *mah-ar-awb'*; from 6148, in the sense of *trading*; *traffic*; by impl. mercantile *goods:*—market, merchandise.

4628. מַעֲרָב **ma'ărâb**, *mah-ar-awb'*; or (fem.)

מַעֲרָבָה **ma'ărâbâh**, *mah-ar-aw-baw'*; from 6150, in the sense of *shading*; the *west* (as the region of the *evening* sun):—west.

4629. מַעֲרֶה **ma'ăreh**, *mah-ar-eh'*; from 6168; a *nude* place, i.e. a *common:*—meadows.

4630. מַעֲרָה **ma'ărâh**, *mah-ar-aw'*; fem. of 4629; an *open* spot:—army [*from the marg.*].

4631. מְעָרָה **me'ârâh**, *meh-aw-raw'*; from 5783; a *cavern* (as dark):—cave, den, hole.

4632. מְעָרָה **Me'ârâh**, *meh-aw-raw'*; the same as 4631; *cave*; *Meärah*, a place in Pal.:—Mearah.

4633. מַעֲרָךְ **ma'ărâk**, *mah-ar-awk'*; from 6186; an *arrangement*, i.e. (fig.) mental *disposition:*—preparation.

4634. מַעֲרָכָה **ma'ărâkâh**, *mah-ar-aw-kaw'*; fem. of 4633; an *arrangement*; concr. a *pile*; spec. a military *array:*—army, fight, be set in order, ordered place, rank, row.

4635. מַעֲרֶכֶת **ma'ăreketh**, *mah-ar-eh'-keth*; from 6186; an *arrangement*, i.e. (concr.) a *pile* (of loaves):—row, shewbread.

4636. מַעֲרֹם **ma'ărôm**, *mah-ar-ome'*; from 6191, in the sense of *stripping*; *bare:*—naked.

4637. מַעֲרָצָה **ma'ărâtsâh**, *mah-ar-aw-tsaw'*; from 6206; *violence:*—terror.

4638. מַעֲרָת **Ma'ărâth**, *mah-ar-awth'*; a form of 4630; *waste*; *Maarath*, a place in Pal.:—Maarath.

4639. מַעֲשֶׂה **ma'ăseh**, *mah-as-eh'*; from 6213; an *action* (good or bad); gen. a *transaction*; abstr. *activity*; by impl. a *product* (spec. a *poem*) or (gen.) *property:*—act, art, + bakemeat, business, deed, do (-ing), labour, thing made, ware of making, occupation, thing offered, operation, possession, × well, ([handy-, needle-, net-]) work, (-ing, -manship), wrought.

4640. מַעֲשַׂי **Ma'say**, *mah-as-ah'ee*; from 6213; *operative*; *Maasai*, an Isr.:—Maasiai.

4641. מַעֲשֵׂיָה **Ma'ăsêyâh**, *mah-as-ay-yaw'*; or

מַעֲשֵׂיָהוּ **Ma'ăsêyâhûw**, *mah-as-ay-yaw'-hoo*; from 4639 and 3050; *work of Jah*; *Maasejah*, the name of sixteen Isr.:—Maaseiah.

4642. מַעֲשַׁקָּה **ma'ăshaqqâh**, *mah-ash-ak-kaw'*; from 6231; *oppression:*—oppression, × oppressor.

4643. מַעֲשֵׂר **ma'ăsêr**, *mah-as-ayr'*; or

מַעֲשַׂר **ma'ăsar**, *mah-as-ar'*; and (in plur.) fem.

מַעַשְׂרָה **ma'asrâh**, *mah-as-raw'*; from 6240; a *tenth*; espec. a *tithe:*—tenth (part), tithe (-ing).

4644. מֹף **Môph** *mofe*; of Eg. or.; *Moph*, the capital of Lower Egypt:—Memphis. Comp. 5297.

מְפִבֹשֶׁת **Mephîbôsheth**. See 4648.

4645. מִפְגָּע **miphgâ'**, *mif-gaw'*; from 6293; an *object of attack:*—mark.

4646. מַפָּח **mappâch**, *map-pawkh'*; from 5301; a *breathing out* (of life), i.e. expiring:—giving up.

4647. מַפֻּחַ **mappûach**, *map-poo'-akh*; from 5301; the *bellows* (i.e. *blower*) of a forge:—bellows.

4648. מְפִיבֹשֶׁת **Mephîybôsheth**, *mef-ee-bo'-sheth*; or

מְפִבֹשֶׁת **Mephîbôsheth**, *mef-ee-bo'-sheth*; prob. from 6284 and 1322; *dispeller of shame* (i.e. of Baal); *Mephibosheth*, the name of two Isr.:—Mephibosheth.

4649. מֻפִּים **Muppîym**, *moop-peem'*; a plur. appar. from 5130; *wavings*; *Muppim*, an Isr.:—Muppim. Comp. 8206.

4650. מֵפִיץ **mêphîyts**, *may-feets'*; from 6327; a *breaker*, i.e. mallet:—maul.

4651. מַפָּל **mappâl**, *map-pawl'*; from 5307; a *falling* off, i.e. chaff; also something *pendulous*, i.e. a flap:—flake, refuse.

4652. מִפְלָאָה **miphlâ'âh**, *mif-law-aw'*; from 6381; a *miracle:*—wondrous work.

4653. מִפְלַגָּה **miphlaggâh**, *mif-lag-gaw'*; from 6385; a *classification:*—division.

4654. מַפָּלָה **mappâlâh**, *map-paw-law'*; or

מַפֵּלָה **mappêlâh**, *map-pay-law'*; from 5307; something *fallen*, i.e. a *ruin:*—ruin (-ous).

4655. מִפְלָט **miphlâṭ**, *mif-lawt'*; from 6403; an *escape:*—escape.

4656. מִפְלֶצֶת **miphletseth**, *mif-leh'-tseth*; from 6426; a *terror*, i.e. an idol:—idol.

4657. מִפְלָשׂ **miphlâs**, *mif-lawce'*; from an unused root mean. to *balance*; a *poising:*—balancing.

4658. מַפֶּלֶת **mappeleth**, *map-peh'-leth*; from 5307; *fall*, i.e. *decadence*; concr. a *ruin*; spec. a *carcase:*—carcase, fall, ruin.

4659. מִפְעָל **miph'âl**, *mif-awl'*; or (fem.)

מִפְעָלָה **miph'âlâh**, *mif-aw-law'*; from 6466; a *performance:*—work.

4660. מַפָּץ **mappâts**, *map-pawts'*; from 5310; a *smiting* to pieces:—slaughter.

4661. מַפֵּץ **mappêts**, *map-pates'*; from 5310; a *smiter*, i.e. a war *club:*—battle ax.

4662. מִפְקָד **miphqâd**, *mif-kawd'*; from 6485; an *appointment*, i.e. *mandate*; concr. a designated *spot*; spec. a *census:*—appointed place, commandment, number.

4663. מִפְקָד **Miphqâd**, *mif-kawd'*; the same as 4662; *assignment*; *Miphkad*, the name of a gate in Jerus.:—Miphkad.

4664. מִפְרָץ **miphrâts**, *mif-rawts'*; from 6555; a *break* (in the shore), i.e. a *haven:*—breach.

4665. מִפְרֶקֶת **miphreketh**, *mif-reh'-keth*; from 6561; prop. a *fracture*, i.e. *joint* (*vertebra*) of the neck:—neck.

4666. מִפְרָשׂ **miphrâs**, *mif-rawce'*; from 6566; an *expansion:*—that which . . . spreadest forth, spreading.

4667. מִפְשָׂעָה **miphsâ'âh**, *mif-saw-aw'*; from 6585; a *stride*, i.e. (by euphem.) the *crotch:*—buttocks.

מֹפֵת **môphêth**. See 4159.

4668. מַפְתֵּחַ **maphtêach**, *maf-tay'-akh*; from 6605; an *opener*, i.e. a *key:*—key.

4669. מִפְתָּח **miphtâch**, *mif-tawkh'*; from 6605; an *aperture*, i.e. (fig.) *utterance:*—opening.

4670. מִפְתָּן **miphtân**, *mif-tawn'*; from the same as 6620; a *stretcher*, i.e. a *sill:*—threshold.

4671. מֹץ **môts**, *motes*; or

מוֹץ **môwts** (Zeph. 2 : 2), *motes*; from 4160; *chaff* (as *pressed* out, i.e. *winnowed* or [rather] threshed loose):—chaff.

4672. מָצָא **mâtsâ'**, *maw-tsaw'*; a prim. root; prop. to *come* forth to, i.e. *appear* or *exist*; trans. to *attain*, i.e. *find* or *acquire*; fig. to *occur*, *meet* or *be present:*— + be able, befall, being, catch, × certainly, (cause to) come (on, to, to hand), deliver, be enough (cause to) find (-ing, occasion, out), get (hold upon), × have (here), be here, hit, be left, light (up-) on, meet (with), × occasion serve, (be) present, ready, speed, suffice, take hold on.

מֹצָא **môtsâ'**. See 4161.

4673. מַצָּב **matstsâb**, *mats-tsawb'*; from 5324; a fixed *spot*; fig. an *office*, a military *post:*—garrison, station, place where . . . stood.

4674. מֻצָּב **mutstsâb**, *moots-tsawb'*; from 5324; a *station*, i.e. military *post:*—mount.

4675. מַצָּבָה **matstsâbâh**, *mats-tsaw-baw'*; or

מִצָּבָה **mitstsâbâh**, *mits-tsaw-baw'*; fem. of 4673; a military *guard:*—army, garrison.

4676. מַצֵּבָה **matstsêbâh**, *mats-tsay-baw'*; fem. (causat.) part. of 5324; something *stationed*, i.e. a *column* or (memorial *stone*); by anal. an *idol:*—garrison, (standing) image, pillar.

4677. מְצֹבָיָה **Metsôbâyâh**, *mets-o-baw-yaw'*; appar. from 4672 and 3050; *found of Jah*; *Metsobajah*, a place in Pal.:—Mesobaite.

4678. מַצֶּבֶת **matstsebeth**, *mats-tseh'-beth*; from 5324; something *stationary*, i.e. a monumental *stone*; also the *stock* of a tree:—pillar, substance.

4679. מְצַד **metsad**, *mets-ad'*; or

מְצָד **metsâd**, *mets-awd'*; or (fem.)

מְצָדָה **metsâdâh**, *mets-aw-daw'*; from 6679; a *fastness* (as a *covert* of ambush):—castle, fort, (strong) hold, munition.

מְצֻדָה **metsûdâh**. See 4686.

4680. מָצָה **mâtsâh**, *maw-tsaw'*; a prim. root; to *suck* out; by impl. to *drain*, to *squeeze* out:—suck, wring (out).

4681. מֹצָה **Môtsâh**, *mo-tsaw'*; act. part. fem. of 4680; *drained*; *Motsah*, a place in Pal.:—Mozah.

4682. מַצָּה **matstsâh**, *mats-tsaw'*; from 4711 in the sense of *greedily* devouring for sweetness; prop. *sweetness*; concr. *sweet* (i.e. not soured or bittered with yeast); spec. an *unfermented cake* or loaf, or (ellipt.) the festival of *Passover* (because no leaven was then used):—unleavened (bread, cake), without leaven.

4683. מַצָּה **matstsâh**, *mats-tsaw'*; from 5327; a *quarrel:*—contention, debate, strife.

684. מַצְהָלָה **matshâlâh**, *mats-haw-law';* from 6670; a *whinnying* (through mpatience for battle or lust):—neighing.

685. מָצוֹד **mâtsôwd**, *maw-tsode';* or (fem.)
מְצוֹדָה **m^{e}tsôwdâh**, *mets-o-daw';* or
מְצֹדָה **m^{e}tsôdâh**, *mets-o-daw';* from 6679; a *net* (for *capturing* animals or shes); also (by interch. for 4679) a *fastness* or besieging) *tower:*—bulwark, hold, munition, net, nare.

686. מָצוּד **mâtsûwd**, *maw-tsood';* or (fem.)
מְצוּדָה **m^{e}tsûwdâh**, *mets-oo-daw';* or
מְצֻדָה **m^{e}tsûdâh**, *mets-oo-daw';* for 4685; a *net*, or (abstr.) *capture;* also a *fastess:*—castle, defence, fort (-ress), (strong) hold, be unted, net, snare, strong place.

687. מִצְוָה **mitsvâh**, *mits-vaw';* from 6680; a *command*, whether human or divine ollect. the *Law*):—(which was) commanded (-ment), w, ordinance, precept.

688. מְצוֹלָה **m^{e}tsôwlâh**, *mets-o-law';* or
מְצֹלָה **m^{e}tsôlâh**, *mets-o-law';* also
מְצוּלָה **m^{e}tsûwlâh**, *mets-oo-law';* or
מְצֻלָה **m^{e}tsûlâh**, *mets-oo-law';* from the same as 6683; a *deep* place (of water r mud):—bottom, deep, depth.

689. מָצוֹק **mâtsôwq**, *maw-tsoke';* from 6693; a *narrow* place, i.e. (abstr. and fig.) *nfinement* or *disability:*—anguish, distress, straitess.

690. מָצוּק **mâtsûwq**, *maw-tsook';* or
מָצֻק **mâtsûq**, *maw-tsook';* from 6693; something *narrow*, i.e. a *column* or *hillop:*—pillar, situate.

691. מְצוּקָה **m^{e}tsûwqâh**, *mets-oo-kaw';* or
מְצֻקָה **m^{e}tsûqâh**, *mets-oo-kaw';* fem. of 4690; *narrowness*, i.e. (fig.) *trouble:*—nguish, distress.

692. מָצוֹר **mâtsôwr**, *maw-tsore';* or
מָצוּר **mâtsûwr**, *maw-tsoor';* from 6696; something *hemming* in, i.e. (obj.) a *ound* (of besiegers), (abstr.) a *siege*, (fig.) *distress;* (subj.) a *fastness:*—besieged, bulwark, defence, nced, fortress, siege, strong (hold), tower.

693. מָצוֹר **mâtsôwr**, *maw-tsore';* the same as 4692 in the sense of a *limit; Egypt* (as e *border* of Pal.):—besieged places, defence, fortied.

694. מְצוּרָה **m^{e}tsûwrâh**, *mets-oo-raw';* or
מְצֻרָה **m^{e}tsûrâh**, *mets-oo-raw';* fem. of 4692; a *hemming* in, i.e. (obj.) a *mound* f siege), or (subj.) a *rampart* (of protection), bstr.) *fortification:*—fenced (city), fort, munition, trong hold.

695. מַצּוּת **matstsûwth**, *mats-tsooth';* from 5327; a *quarrel:*—that contended.

696. מֵצַח **mêtsach**, *may'-tsakh;* from an unused root mean. to be *clear*, i.e. *conspicous;* the *forehead* (as *open* and *prominent*):—brow, orehead, + impudent.

697. מִצְחָה **mitschâh**, *mits-khaw';* from the same as 4696; a *shin-piece* of armor s *prominent*), only plur.:—greaves.
מְצֹלָה **m^{e}tsôlah**. See 4688.
מְצֻלָה **m^{e}tsûlâh**. See 4688.

698. מְצִלָּה **m^{e}tsillâh**, *mets-il-law';* from 6750; a *tinkler*, i.e. a *bell:*—bell.

699. מְצֻלָּה **m^{e}tsullâh**, *mets-ool-law';* from 6751; *shade:*—bottom.

700. מְצֵלֶת **m^{e}tsêleth**, *mets-ay'-leth;* from 6750; (only dual) double *tinklers*, i.e. ymbals:—cymbals.

701. מִצְנֶפֶת **mitsnepheth**, *mits-neh'-feth;* from 6801; a *tiara*, i.e. official *turban* of a king or high priest):—diadem, mitre.

702. מַצָּע **matstsâʻ**, *mats-tsaw';* from 3331; a *couch:*—bed.

4703. מִצְעָד **mitsʻâd**, *mits-awd';* from 6805; a *step;* fig. *companionship:*—going, step.

4704. מִצְּעִירָה **mitstseʻîyrâh**, *mits-tseh-ee-raw';* fem. of 4705; prop. *littleness:* concr. *diminutive:*—little.

4705. מִצְעָר **mitsʻâr**, *mits-awr';* from 6819; *petty* (in size or number); adv. a *short* (time):—little one (while), small.

4706. מִצְעָר **Mitsʻâr**, *mits-awr';* the same as 4705; *Mitsar*, a peak of Lebanon:—Mizar.

4707. מִצְפֶּה **mitspeh**, *mits-peh';* from 6822; an *observatory*, espec. for military purposes:—watch tower.

4708. מִצְפֶּה **Mitspeh**, *mits-peh';* the same as 4707; *Mitspeh*, the name of five places in Pal.:—Mizpeh, watch tower. Comp. 4709.

4709. מִצְפָּה **Mitspah**, *mits-paw';* fem. of 4708; *Mitspah*, the name of two places in Pal.:—Mitspah. [This seems rather to be only an orth. var. of 4708 when "in pause".]

4710. מִצְפֻּן **mitspûn**, *mits-poon';* from 6845; a *secret* (place or thing, perh. *treasure*):—hidden thing.

4711. מָצַץ **mâtsats**, *maw-tsats';* a prim. root; to *suck:*—milk.
מוּצָקָה **mûtsâqâh**. See 4166.

4712. מֵצַר **mêtsar**, *may-tsar';* from 6896; something *tight*, i.e. (fig.) *trouble:*—distress, pain, strait.
מָצֻק **mâtsûq**. See 4690.
מְצֻקָה **m^{e}tsûqâh**. See 4691.
מְצֻרָה **m^{e}tsûrâh**. See 4694.

4713. מִצְרִי **Mitsrîy**, *mits-ree';* from 4714; a *Mitsrite*, or inhab. of Mitsrajim:—Egyptian, of Egypt.

4714. מִצְרַיִם **Mitsrayim**, *mits-rah'-yim;* dual of 4693; *Mitsrajim*, i.e.Upper and Lower Egypt:—Egypt, Egyptians, Mizraim.

4715. מִצְרֵף **mitsrêph**, *mits-rafe';* from 6884; a *crucible:*—fining pot.

4716. מַק **maq**, *mak;* from 4743; prop. a *melting*, i.e. *putridity:*—rottenness, stink.

4717. מַקָּבָה **maqqâbâh**, *mak-kaw-baw';* from 5344; prop. a *perforatrix*, i.e. a *hammer* (as *piercing*):—hammer.

4718. מַקֶּבֶת **maqqebeth**, *mak-keh'-beth;* from 5344; prop. a *perforator*, i.e. a *hammer* (as *piercing*); also (intrans.) a *perforation*, i.e. a *quarry:*—hammer, hole.

4719. מַקֵּדָה **Maqqêdâh**, *mak-kay-daw';* from the same as 5348 in the denom. sense of *herding* (comp. 5349); *fold; Makkedah*, a place in Pal.:—Makkedah.

4720. מִקְדָּשׁ **miqdâsh**, *mik-dawsh';* or
מִקְּדָשׁ **miqq^{e}dâsh** (Exod. 15 : 17), *mik-ked-awsh';* from 6942; a *consecrated* thing or place, espec. a *palace*, *sanctuary* (whether of Jehovah or of idols) or *asylum:*—chapel, hallowed part, holy place, sanctuary.

4721. מַקְהֵל **maqhêl**, *mak-hale';* or (fem.)
מַקְהֵלָה **maqhêlâh**, *mak-hay-law';* from 6950; an *assembly:*—congregation.

4722. מַקְהֵלֹת **Maqhêlôth**, *mak-hay-loth';* plur. of 4721 (fem.); *assemblies; Makheloth*, a place in the Desert:—Makheloth.

4723. מִקְוֶה **miqveh**, *mik-veh';* or
מִקְוֵה **miqvêh** (1 Kings 10 : 28), *mik-vay';* or
מִקְוֵא° **miqvêʼ** (2 Chron. 1 : 16), *mik-vay';* from 6960; something *waited* for, i.e. *confidence* (obj. or subj.); also a *collection*, i.e. (of water) a *pond*, or (of men and horses) a *caravan* or *drove:*—abiding, gathering together, hope, linen yarn, plenty [of water], pool.

4724. מִקְוָה **miqvâh**, *mik-vaw';* fem. of 4723; a *collection*, i.e. (of water) a *reservoir:*—ditch.

4725. מָקוֹם **mâqôwm**, *maw-kome';* or
מָקֹם **mâqôm**, *maw-kome';* also (fem.)
מְקוֹמָה° **m^{e}qôwmâh**, *mek-o-mah';* or
מְקֹמָה **m^{e}qômâh**, *mek-o-mah';* from 6965; prop. a *standing*, i.e. a *spot;* but used widely of a *locality* (gen. or spec.); also (fig.) of a *condition* (of body or mind):—country, × home, × open, place, room, space, × whither [-soever].

4726. מָקוֹר **mâqôwr**, *maw-kore';* or
מָקֹר **mâqôr**, *maw-kore';* from 6979; prop. something *dug*, i.e. a (gen.) *source* (of water, even when naturally flowing; also of tears, blood [by euphem. of the female *pudenda*]; fig. of happiness, wisdom, progeny):—fountain, issue, spring, well (-spring).

4727. מִקָּח **miqqâch**, *mik-kawkh';* from 3947; *reception:*—taking.

4728. מַקָּחָה **maqqâchâh**, *mak-kaw-khaw';* from 3947; something *received*, i.e. *merchandise* (purchased):—ware.

4729. מִקְטָר **miqṭâr**, *mik-tawr';* from 6999; something to *fume* (incense) on, i.e. a *hearth* place:—to burn . . . upon.
מְקַטְּרָה **m^{e}qaṭṭ^{e}râh**. See 6999.

4730. מִקְטֶרֶת **miqṭereth**, *mik-teh'-reth;* fem. of 4729; something to *fume* (incense) in, i.e. a *coal-pan:*—censer.

4731. מַקֵּל **maqqêl**, *mak-kale';* or (fem.)
מַקְּלָה **maqq^{e}lâh**, *mak-kel-aw';* from an unused root mean. appar. to *germinate;* a *shoot*, i.e. *stick* (with leaves on, or for walking, striking, guiding, divining):—rod, ([hand-]) staff.

4732. מִקְלוֹת **Miqlôwth**, *mik-lohth'* (or perh. *mik-kel-ohth'*); plur. of (fem.) 4731; *rods; Mikloth*, a place in the Desert:—Mikloth.

4733. מִקְלָט **miqlâṭ**, *mik-lawt';* from 7038 in the sense of *taking* in; an *asylum* (as a *receptacle*):—refuge.

4734. מִקְלַעַת **miqlaʻath**, *mik-lah'-ath;* from 7049; a *sculpture* (prob. in bass-relief):—carved (figure), carving, graving.
מָקֹם **mâqôm**. See 4725.
מְקוֹמָה **m^{e}qômâh**. See 4725.

4735. מִקְנֶה **miqneh**, *mik-neh';* from 7069; something *bought*, i.e. *property*, but only live *stock;* abstr. *acquisition:*—cattle, flock, herd, possession, purchase, substance.

4736. מִקְנָה **miqnâh**, *mik-naw';* fem. of 4735; prop. a *buying*, i.e. *acquisition;* concr. a piece of *property* (land or living); also the *sum* paid:—(he that is) bought, possession, piece, purchase.

4737. מִקְנֵיָהוּ **Miqnêyâhûw**, *mik-nay-yaw'-hoo;* from 4735 and 3050; *possession of Jah; Miknejah*, an Isr.:—Mikneiah.

4738. מִקְסָם **miqçâm**, *mik-sawm';* from 7080; an *augury:*—divination.

4739. מָקַץ **Mâqats**, *maw-kats';* from 7112; *end; Makats*, a place in Pal.:—Makaz.

4740. מַקְצוֹעַ **maqtsôwaʻ**, *mak-tso'-ah;* or
מַקְצֹעַ **maqtsôaʻ**, *mak-tso'-ah;* or (fem.)
מַקְצֹעָה **maqtsôʻâh**, *mak-tso-aw';* from 7106 in the denom. sense of *bending*. an *angle* or recess:—corner, turning.

4741. מַקְצֻעָה **maqtsûʻâh**, *mak-tsoo-aw';* from 7106; a *scraper*, i.e. a carving *chisel:*—plane.

4742. מְקֻצְעָה **m^{e}qutsʻâh**, *mek-oots-aw';* from 7106 in the denom. sense of *bending;* an *angle:*—corner.

4743. מָקַק **mâqaq**, *maw-kak';* a prim. root; to *melt;* fig. to *flow, dwindle, vanish:*—consume away, be corrupt, dissolve, pine away.
מָקֹר **mâqôr**. See 4726.

4744. מִקְרָא **miqrâʼ**, *mik-raw';* from 7121; something *called* out, i.e. a public *meeting* (the act, the persons, or the place); also a *rehearsal:*—assembly, calling, convocation, reading.

4745. מִקְרֶה **miqreh**, *mik-reh';* from 7136; something *met* with, i.e. an *accident* or *fortune:*—something befallen, befalleth, chance, event, hap (-peneth).

4746. מְקָרֶה **mᵉqâreh**, *mek-aw-reh'*; from 7136; prop. something meeting, i.e. a frame (of timbers):—building.

4747. מְקֵרָה **mᵉqêrâh**, *mek-ay-raw'*; from the same as 7119; a cooling off:— × summer.

מֹקֵשׁ **môqêsh**. See 4170.

4748. מִקְשֶׁה **miqsheh**, *mik-sheh'*; from 7185 in the sense of knotting up round and hard; something turned (rounded), i.e. a curl (of tresses):— × well [set] hair.

4749. מִקְשָׁה **miqshâh**, *mik-shaw'*; fem. of 4748; rounded work, i.e. moulded by hammering (repoussé):—beaten (out of one piece, work), upright, whole piece.

4750. מִקְשָׁה **miqshâh**, *mik-shaw'*; denom. from 7180; lit. a cucumbered field, i.e. a cucumber patch:—garden of cucumbers.

4751. מַר **mar**, *mar*; or (fem.)

מָרָה **mârâh**, *maw-raw'*; from 4843; bitter (lit. or fig.); also (as noun) bitterness, or (adv.) bitterly:— + angry, bitter (-ly, -ness), chafed, discontented, × great, heavy.

4752. מַר **mar**, *mar*; from 4843 in its orig. sense of distillation; a drop:—drop.

4753. מֹר **môr**, *more*; or

מוֹר **môwr**, *more*; from 4843; myrrh (as distilling in drops, and also as bitter):—myrrh.

4754. מָרָא **mârâ'**, *maw-raw'*; a prim. root; to rebel; hence (through the idea of maltreating) to whip, i.e. lash (self with wings, as the ostrich in running):—be filthy, lift up self.

4755. מָרָא **Mârâ'**, *maw-raw'*; for 4751 fem.; bitter; Mara, a symbol. name of Naomi:—Mara.

4756. מָרֵא **mârê'** (Chald.), *maw-ray'*; from a root corresp. to 4754 in the sense of domineering; a master:—lord, Lord.

מֹרָא **môrâ'**. See 4172.

4757. מְרֹאדַךְ בַּלְאֲדָן **Mᵉrô'dak Bal'âdân**, *mer-o-dak' bal-aw-dawn'*; of for. der.; Merodak-Baladan, a Bab. king:—Merodach-baladan. Comp. 4781.

4758. מַרְאֶה **mar'eh**, *mar-eh'*; from 7200; a view (the act of seeing); also an appearance (the thing seen), whether (real) a shape (espec. if handsome, comeliness; often plur. the looks), or (mental) a vision:— × apparently, appearance (-reth), × as soon as beautiful (-ly), countenance, fair, favoured, form, goodly, to look (up) on (to), look [-eth], pattern, to see, seem, sight, visage, vision.

4759. מַרְאָה **mar'âh**, *mar-aw'*; fem. of 4758; a vision; also (causat.) a mirror:—looking glass, vision.

4760. מֻרְאָה **mur'âh**, *moor-aw'*; appar. fem. pass. causat. part. of 7200; something conspicuous, i.e. the craw of a bird (from its prominence):—crop.

מֵרְאוֹן **Mᵉr'ôwn**. See 8112.

4761. מַרְאָשָׁה **mar'âshâh**, *mar-aw-shaw'*; denom. from 7218; prop. headship, i.e. (plur. for collect.) dominion:—principality.

4762 מַרְאֵשָׁה **Mar'êshâh**, *mar-ay-shaw'*; or

מָרֵשָׁה **Marêshâh**, *mar-ay-shaw'*; formed like 4761; summit; Mareshah, the name of two Isr. and of a place in Pal.:—Mareshah.

4763. מְרַאֲשָׁה **mᵉra'ăshâh**, *mer-ah-ash-aw'*; formed like 4761; prop. a headpiece, i.e. (plur. for adv.) at (or as) the head-rest (or pillow):—bolster, head, pillow. Comp. 4772.

4764. מֵרָב **Mêrâb**, *may-rawb'*; from 7231; increase; Merab, a daughter of Saul:—Merab.

4765. מַרְבַד **marbad**, *mar-bad'*; from 7234; a coverlet:—covering of tapestry.

4766. מַרְבֶּה **marbeh**, *mar-beh'*; from 7235; prop. increasing; as noun, greatness, or (adv.) greatly:—great, increase.

4767. מִרְבָּה **mirbâh**, *meer-baw'*; from 7235; abundance, i.e. a great quantity:—much.

4768. מַרְבִּית **marbîyth**, *mar-beeth'*; from 7235; a multitude; also offspring; spec. interest (on capital):—greatest part, greatness, increase, multitude.

4769. מַרְבֵּץ **marbêts**, *mar-bates'*; from 7257; a reclining place, i.e. fold (for flocks):—couching place, place to lie down.

4770. מַרְבֵּק **marbêq**, *mar-bake'*; from an unused root mean. to tie up; a stall (for cattle):— × fat (-ted), stall.

מֹרַג **môrag**. See 4173.

4771. מַרְגּוֹעַ **margôwa'**, *mar-go'-ah*; from 7280; a resting place:—rest.

4772. מַרְגְּלָה **margᵉlâh**, *mar-ghel-aw'*; denom. from 7272; (plur. for collect.) a footpiece, i.e. (adv.) at the foot, or (direct.) the foot itself:—feet. Comp. 4763.

4773. מַרְגֵּמָה **margêmâh**, *mar-gay-maw'*; from 7275; a stone-heap:—sling.

4774. מַרְגֵּעָה **margê'âh**, *mar-gay-aw'*; from 7280; rest:—refreshing.

4775. מָרַד **mârad**, *maw-rad'*; a prim. root; to rebel:—rebel (-lious).

4776. מְרַד **mᵉrad** (Chald.), *mer-ad'*; from a root corresp. to 4775; rebellion:—rebellion.

4777. מֶרֶד **mered**, *meh'-red*; from 4775; rebellion:—rebellion.

4778. מֶרֶד **Mered**, *meh'-red*; the same as 4777; Mered, an Isr.:—Mered.

4779. מָרָד **mârâd** (Chald.), *maw-rawd'*; from the same as 4776; rebellious:—rebellious.

4780. מַרְדּוּת **mardûwth**, *mar-dooth'*; from 4775; rebelliousness:— × rebellious.

4781. מְרֹדָךְ **Mᵉrôdâk**, *mer-o-dawk'*; of for. der.; Merodak, a Bab. idol:—Merodach. Comp. 4757.

4782. מָרְדְּכַי **Mordᵉkay**, *mor-dek-ah'ee*; of for. der.; Mordecai, an Isr.:—Mordecai.

4783. מֻרְדָּף **murdâph**, *moor-dawf'*; from 7291; persecuted:—persecuted.

4784. מָרָה **mârâh**, *maw-raw'*; a prim. root; to be (caus. make) bitter (or unpleasant); (fig.) to rebel (or resist; causat. to provoke):—bitter, change, be disobedient, disobey, grievously, provocation, provoke (-ing), (be) rebel (against, -lious).

4785. מָרָה **Mârâh**, *maw-raw'*; the same as 4751 fem.; bitter; Marah, a place in the Desert:—Marah.

מֹרֶה **Môreh**. See 4175.

4786. מֹרָה **môrâh**, *mo-raw'*; from 4843; bitterness, i.e. (fig.) trouble:—grief.

4787. מָרָּה **morrâh**, *mor-raw'*; a form of 4786; trouble:—bitterness.

4788. מָרוּד **mârûwd**, *maw-rood'*; from 7300 in the sense of maltreatment; an outcast; (abstr.) destitution:—cast out, misery.

4789. מֵרוֹז **Mêrôwz**, *may-roze'*; of uncert. der.; Meroz, a place in Pal.:—Meroz.

4790. מְרוֹחַ **mᵉrôwach**, *mer-o-akh'*; from 4799; bruised, i.e. emasculated:—broken.

4791. מָרוֹם **mârôwm**, *maw-rome'*; from 7311; altitude, i.e. concr. (an elevated place), abstr. (elevation), fig. (elation), or adv. (aloft):—(far) above, dignity, haughty, height, (most, on) high (one, place), loftily, upward.

4792. מֵרוֹם **Mêrôwm**, *may-rome'*; formed like 4791; height; Merom, a lake in Pal.:—Merom.

4793. מֵרוֹץ **mêrôwts**, *may-rotes'*; from 7323; a run (the trial of speed):—race.

4794. מְרוּצָה **mᵉrûwtsâh**, *mer-oo-tsaw'*; or

מְרֻצָה **mᵉrûtsâh**, *mer-oo-tsaw'*; fem. of 4793; a race (the act), whether the manner or the progress:—course, running. Comp. 4835.

4795. מָרוּק **mârûwq**, *maw-rook'*; from 4838 prop. rubbed; but used abstr., a rubbing (with perfumery):—purification.

מְרוֹר **mᵉrôwr**. See 4844.

מְרוֹרָה **mᵉrôwrâh**. See 4846.

4796. מָרוֹת **Mârôwth**, *maw-rohth'*; plur. o 4751 fem.; bitter springs; Maroth, place in Pal.:—Maroth.

4797. מִרְזַח **mirzach**, *meer-zakh'*; from an unused root mean. to scream; a cry, i.e. (of joy), a revel:—banquet.

4798. מַרְזֵחַ **marzêach**, *mar-zay'-akh*; forme like 4797; a cry, i.e. (of grief) a lamentation:—mourning.

4799. מָרַח **mârach**, *maw-rakh'*; a prim. root prop. to soften by rubbing or pressure hence (medicinally) to apply as an emollient:—lay fo a plaister.

4800. מֶרְחָב **merchâb**, *mer-khawb'*; from 7337 enlargement, either lit. (an ope space, usually in a good sense), or fig. (liberty):—breadth, large place (room).

4801. מֶרְחָק **merchâq**, *mer-khawk'*; from 7368 remoteness, i.e. (concr.) a distan place; often (adv.) from afar:— (a-, dwell in, very far (country, off). See also 1023.

4802. מַרְחֶשֶׁת **marchesheth**, *mar-kheh'-sheth* from 7370; a stew-pan:—fryingpan

4803. מָרַט **mâraṭ**, *maw-rat'*; a prim. root; t polish; by impl. to make bald (th head), to gall (the shoulder); also, to sharpen:—bright, furbish, (have his) hair (be) fallen off, peeled pluck off (hair).

4804. מְרַט **mᵉraṭ** (Chald.), *mer-at'*; corresp. t 4803; to pull off:—be plucked.

4805. מְרִי **mᵉrîy**, *mer-ee'*; from 4784; bitterness i.e. (fig.) rebellion; concr. bitter, or re bellious:—bitter, (most) rebel (-lion, -lious).

4806. מְרִיא **mᵉrîy'**, *mer-ee'*; from 4754 in the sens of grossness, through the idea of dom neering (comp. 4756); stall-fed; often (as noun) beeve:—fat (fed) beast (cattle, -ling).

4807. מְרִיב בַּעַל **Mᵉrîyb Ba'al**, *mer-eeb' bah' al*; from 7378 and 1168; quarrelle of Baal; Merib-Baal, an epithet of Gideon:—Merib baal. Comp. 4810.

4808. מְרִיבָה **mᵉrîybâh**, *mer-ee-baw'*; fro 7378; quarrel:—provocation, strife.

4809. מְרִיבָה **Mᵉrîybâh**, *mer-ee-baw'*; the sam as 4808; Meribah, the name of tw places in the Desert:—Meribah.

4810. מְרִי בַעַל **Mᵉrîy Ba'al**, *mer-ee' bah'-al* from 4805 and 1168; rebellion o (i.e. against) Baal; Meri-Baal, an epithet of Gid eon:—Meri-baal. Comp. 4807.

4811. מְרָיָה **Mᵉrâyâh**, *mer-aw-yaw'*; from 4784 rebellion; Merajah, an Isr.:—Meraiah Comp. 3236.

מֹרִיָּה **Môrîyâh**. See 4179.

4812. מְרָיוֹת **Mᵉrâyôwth**, *mer-aw-yohth'*; plur of 4811; rebellious; Merajoth, th name of two Isr.:—Meraioth.

4813. מִרְיָם **Miryâm**, *meer-yawm'*; from 4805 rebelliously; Mirjam, the name of tw Israelitesses:—Miriam.

4814. מְרִירוּת **mᵉrîyrûwth**, *mer-ee-rooth* from 4843; bitterness, i.e. (fig grief:—bitterness.

4815. מְרִירִי **mᵉrîyrîy**, *mer-ee-ree'*; from 4843 bitter, i.e. poisonous:—bitter.

4816. מֹרֶךְ **môrek**, *mo'-rek*; perh. from 7401 softness, i.e. (fig.) fear:—faintness.

4817. מֶרְכָּב **merkâb**, *mer-kawb'*; from 7392; chariot; also a seat (in a vehicle):—chariot, covering, saddle.

4818. מֶרְכָּבָה **merkâbâh**, *mer-kaw-baw'*; fem of 4817; a chariot:—chariot. See als 1024.

4819. מַרְכֹּלֶת **markôleth**, *mar-ko'-leth*; fron 7402; a mart:—merchandise.

4820. מִרְמָה **mirmâh**, *meer-maw'*; from 7411 in the sense of *deceiving*; *fraud*:—craft, deceit (-ful, -fully), false, feigned, guile, subtilly, treachery.

4821. מִרְמָה **Mirmâh**, *meer-maw'*; the same as 4820; *Mirmah*, an Isr.:—Mirma.

4822. מְרֵמוֹת **Mᵉrêmôwth**, *mer-ay-mohth'*; plur. from 7311; *heights*; *Meremoth*, the name of two Isr.:—Meremoth.

4823. מִרְמָס **mirmâç**, *meer-mawce'*; from 7429; *abasement* (the act or the thing):—tread (down) -ing, (to be) trodden (down) under foot.

4824. מֵרֹנֹתִי **Mêrônôthîy**, *may-ro-no-thee'*; patrial from an unused noun; a *Meronothite*, or inhab. of some (otherwise unknown) Meronoth:—Meronothite.

4825. מֶרֶס **Mereç**, *meh'-res*; of for. der.; *Meres*, a Pers.:—Meres.

4826. מַרְסְנָא **Marçᵉnâ'**, *mar-sen-aw'*; of for. der.; *Marsena*, a Pers.:—Marsena.

4827. מֵרַע **mêraʻ**, *may-rah'*; from 7489; used as (abstr.) noun, *wickedness*:—do mischief.

4828. מֵרֵעַ **mêrêaʻ**, *may-ray'-ah*; from 7462 in the sense of *companionship*; a *friend*:—companion, friend.

4829. מִרְעֶה **mirʻeh**, *meer-eh'*; from 7462 in the sense of *feeding*; *pasture* (the place or the act); also the *haunt* of wild animals:—feeding place, pasture.

4830. מִרְעִית **mirʻîyth**, *meer-eeth'*; from 7462 in the sense of *feeding*; *pasturage*; concr. a *flock*:—flock, pasture.

4831. מַרְעֲלָה **Marʻălâh**, *mar-al-aw'*; from 7477; perh. *earthquake*; *Maralah*, a place in Pal.:—Maralah.

4832. מַרְפֵּא **marpê'**, *mar-pay'*; from 7495; prop. *curative*, i.e. lit. (concr.) a *medicine*, or (abstr.) a *cure*; fig. (concr.) *deliverance*, or (abstr.) *placidity*:—([in-]) cure (-able), healing (-lth), remedy, sound, wholesome, yielding.

4833. מִרְפָּשׂ **mirpâs**, *meer-paws'*; from 7515; *muddled* water:—that which . . . have fouled.

4834. מָרַץ **mârats**, *maw-rats'*; a prim. root; prop. to *press*, i.e. (fig.) to be *pungent* or vehement; to *irritate*:—embolden, be forcible, grievous, sore.

4835. מְרֻצָה **mᵉrûtsâh**, *mer-oo-tsaw'*; from 7533; *oppression*:—violence. See also 4794.

4836. מַרְצֵעַ **martsêaʻ**, *mar-tsay'-ah*; from 7527; an *awl*:—aul.

4837. מַרְצֶפֶת **martsepheth**, *mar-tseh'-feth*; from 7528; a *pavement*:—pavement.

4838. מָרַק **mâraq**, *maw-rak'*; a prim. root; to *polish*; by impl. to *sharpen*; also to *rinse*:—bright, furbish, scour.

4839. מָרָק **mârâq**, *maw-rawk'*; from 4838; *soup* (as if a *rinsing*):—broth. See also 6564.

4840. מֶרְקָח **merqâch**, *mer-kawkh'*; from 7543; a *spicy* herb:— × sweet.

4841. מֶרְקָחָה **merqâchâh**, *mer-kaw-khaw'*, fem. of 4840; abstr. a *seasoning* (with spicery); concr. an *unguent-kettle* (for preparing spiced oil):—pot of ointment, × well.

4842. מִרְקַחַת **mirqachath**, *meer-kakh'-ath*; from 7543; an aromatic *unguent*; also an *unguent-pot*:—prepared by the apothecaries' art, compound, ointment.

4843. מָרַר **mârar**, *maw-rar'*; a prim. root; prop. to *trickle* [see 4752]; but used only as a denom. from 4751; to *be* (causat. make) *bitter* (lit. or fig.):—(be, be in, deal, have, make) bitter (-ly, -ness), be moved with choler, (be, have sorely, it) grieved (-eth), provoke, vex.

4844. מְרֹר **mᵉrôr**, *mer-ore'*; or

מְרוֹר **mᵉrôwr**, *mer-ore'*; from 4843; a *bitter* herb:—bitter (-ness).

4845. מְרֵרָה **mᵉrêrâh**, *mer-ay-raw'*; from 4843; *bile* (from its bitterness):—gall.

4846. מְרֹרָה **mᵉrôrâh**, *mer-o-raw'*; or

מְרוֹרָה **mᵉrôwrâh**, *mer-o-raw'*; from 4843; prop. *bitterness*; concr. a *bitter thing*; spec. *bile*; also *venom* (of a serpent):—bitter (thing), gall.

4847. מְרָרִי **Mᵉrârîy**, *mer-aw-ree'*; from 4843; *bitter*; *Merari*, an Isr.:—Merari. See also 4848.

4848. מְרָרִי **Mᵉrârîy**, *mer-aw-ree'*; from 4847; a *Merarite* (collect.), or desc. of Merari:—Merarites.

מָרֵשָׁה **Mârêshâh**. See 4762.

4849. מִרְשַׁעַת **mirshaʻath**, *meer-shah'-ath*; from 7561; a female *wicked doer*:—wicked woman.

4850. מְרָתַיִם **Mᵉrâthayim**, *mer-aw-thah'-yim*; dual of 4751 fem.; *double bitterness*; *Merathajim*, an epithet of Babylon:—Merathaim.

4851. מַשׁ **Mash**, *mash*; of for. der.; *Mash*, a son of Aram, and the people desc. from him:—Mash.

4852. מֵשָׁא **Mêshâ'**, *may-shaw'*; of for. der.; *Mesha*, a place in Arabia:—Mesha.

4853. מַשָּׂא **massâ'**, *mas-saw'*; from 5375; a *burden*; spec. *tribute*, or (abstr.) *porterage*; fig. an *utterance*, chiefly a *doom*, espec. *singing*; mental, *desire*:—burden, carry away, prophecy, × they set, song, tribute.

4854. מַשָּׂא **Massâ'**, *mas-saw'*; the same as 4853; *burden*; *Massa*, a son of Ishmael:—Massa.

4855. מַשָּׁא **mashshâ'**, *mash-shaw'*; from 5383; a *loan*; by impl. *interest* on a debt:—exaction, usury.

4856. מַשֹּׂא **massô'**, *mas-so'*; from 5375; *partiality* (as a *lifting* up):—respect.

4857. מַשְׁאָב **mash'âb**, *mash-awb'*; from 7579; a *trough* for cattle to drink from:—place of drawing water.

מְשֹׁאָה **mᵉshô'âh**. See 4875.

4858. מַשָּׂאָה **massâ'âh**, *mas-saw-aw'*; from 5375; a *conflagration* (from the *rising* of smoke):—burden.

4859. מַשָּׁאָה **mashshâ'âh**, *mash-shaw-aw'*; fem. of 4855; a *loan*:— × any [-thing], debt.

מַשֻּׁאָה **mashshû'âh**. See 4876.

4860. מַשָּׁאוֹן **mashshâ'ôwn**, *mash-shaw-ohn'*; from 5377; *dissimulation*:—deceit.

4861. מִשְׁאָל **Mish'âl**, *mish-awl'*; from 7592; *request*; *Mishal*, a place in Pal.:—Mishal, Misheal. Comp. 4913.

4862. מִשְׁאָלָה **mish'âlâh**, *mish-aw-law'*; from 7592; a *request*:—desire, petition.

4863. מִשְׁאֶרֶת **mish'ereth**, *mish-eh'-reth*; from 7604 in the orig. sense of *swelling*; a *kneading-trough* (in which the dough *rises*):—kneading trough, store.

4864. מַשְׂאֵת **mas'êth**, *mas-ayth'*; from 5375; prop. (abstr.) a *raising* (as of the hands in prayer), or *rising* (of flame); fig. an *utterance*; concr. a *beacon* (as *raised*); a *present* (as taken), *mess*, or *tribute*; fig. a *reproach* (as a burden):—burden, collection, sign of fire, (great) flame, gift, lifting up, mess, oblation, reward.

מֹשָׁב **môshâb**. See 4186.

מְשֻׁבָה **mᵉshûbâh**. See 4878.

4865. מִשְׁבְּצָה **mishbᵉtsâh**, *mish-bets-aw'*; from 7660; a *brocade*; by anal. a (reticulated) *setting* of a gem:—ouch, wrought.

4866. מִשְׁבֵּר **mishbêr**, *mish-bare'*; from 7665; the *orifice* of the womb (from which the fœtus *breaks* forth):—birth, breaking forth.

4867. מִשְׁבָּר **mishbâr**, *mish-bawr'*; from 7665; a *breaker* (of the sea):—billow, wave.

4868. מִשְׁבָּת **mishbâth**, *mish-bawth'*; from 7673; *cessation*, i.e. destruction:—sabbath.

4869. מִשְׂגָּב **misgâb**, *mis-gawb'*; from 7682; prop. a *cliff* (or other *lofty* or *inaccessible* place); abstr. *altitude*; fig. a *refuge*:—defence, high fort (tower), refuge.

4869; *Misgab*, a place in Moab:—Misgab.

4870'. מִשְׁגֶּה **mishgeh**, *mish-gay'*; from 7686; an *error*:—oversight.

4871. מָשָׁה **mâshâh**, *maw-shaw'*; a prim. root; to *pull* out (lit. or fig.):—draw (out). draw (out).

4872. מֹשֶׁה **Môsheh**, *mo-sheh'*; from 4871; *drawing* out (of the water), i.e. *rescued*; *Mosheh*, the Isr. lawgiver:—Moses.

4873. מֹשֶׁה **Môsheh** (Chald.), *mo-sheh'*; corresp. to 4872:—Moses.

4874. מַשֶּׁה **mashsheh**, *mash-sheh'*; from 5383; a *debt*:— + creditor.

4875. מְשׁוֹאָה **mᵉshôw'âh**, *mesh-o-aw'*; or

מְשֹׁאָה **mᵉshô'âh**, *mesh-o-aw'*; from the same as 7722; (a) *ruin*, abstr. (the act) or concr. (the wreck):—desolation, waste.

4876. מַשּׁוּאָה **mashshûw'âh**, *mash-shoo-aw'*; or

מַשֻּׁאָה **mashshû'âh**, *mash-shoo-aw'*; for 4875; *ruin*:—desolation, destruction.

4877. מְשׁוֹבָב **Mᵉshôwbâb**, *mesh-o-bawb'*; from 7725; *returned*; *Meshobab*, an Isr.:—Meshobab.

4878. מְשׁוּבָה **mᵉshûwbâh**, *mesh-oo-baw'*; or

מְשֻׁבָה **mᵉshûbâh**, *mesh-oo-baw'*; from 7725; *apostasy*:—backsliding, turning away.

4879. מְשׁוּגָה **mᵉshûwgâh**, *mesh-oo-gaw'*; from an unused root mean. to *stray*; *mistake*:—error.

4880. מָשׁוֹט **mâshôwṭ**, *maw-shote'*; or

מִשּׁוֹט **mishshôwṭ**, *mish-shote'*; from 7751; an *oar*:—oar.

4881. מְשׂוּכָה **mᵉsûwkâh**, *mes-oo-kaw'*; or

מְשֻׂכָה **mᵉsûkâh**, *mes-oo-kaw'*; from 7753; a *hedge*:—hedge.

4882. מְשׁוּסָה **mᵉshûwçâh**, *mesh-oo-saw'*; from an unused root mean. to *plunder*; *spoliation*:—spoil.

4883. מַשּׂוֹר **massôwr**, *mas-sore'*; from an unused root mean. to *rasp*; a *saw*:—saw.

4884. מְשׂוּרָה **mᵉsûwrâh**, *mes-oo-raw'*; from an unused root mean. appar. to *divide*; a *measure* (for liquids):—measure.

4885. מָשׂוֹשׂ **mâsôws**, *maw-soce'*; from 7797; *delight*, concr. (the cause or object) or abstr. (the feeling):—joy, mirth, rejoice.

4886. מָשַׁח **mâshach**, *maw-shakh'*; a prim. root; to *rub* with oil, i.e. to *anoint*; by impl. to *consecrate*; also to *paint*:—anoint, paint.

4887. מְשַׁח **mᵉshach** (Chald.), *mesh-akh'*; from a root corresp. to 4886; *oil*:—oil.

4888. מִשְׁחָה **mishchâh**, *meesh-khaw'*; or

מָשְׁחָה **moshchâh**, *mosh-khaw'*; from 4886; *unction* (the act); by impl. a consecratory *gift*:—(to be) anointed (-ing), ointment.

4889. מַשְׁחִית **mashchîyth**, *mash-kheeth'*; from 7843; *destructive*, i.e. (as noun) *destruction*, lit. (spec. a *snare*) or fig. (*corruption*):—corruption, (to) destroy (-ing), destruction, trap, × utterly.

4890. מִשְׂחָק **mischâq**, *mis-khawk'*; from 7831; a *laughing-stock*:—scorn.

4891. מִשְׁחָר **mishchâr**, *mish-khawr'*; from 7836 in the sense of day *breaking*; *dawn*: morning.

4892. מַשְׁחֵת **mashchêth**, *mash-khayth'*; for 4889; *destruction*:—destroying.

4893. מִשְׁחָת **mishchâth**, *mish-khawth'*; or

מָשְׁחָת **moshchâth**, *mosh-khawth'*; from 7843; *disfigurement*:—corruption, marred.

4894. מִשְׁטוֹחַ **mishṭôwach**, *mish-to'-akh*; or

מִשְׁטַח **mishṭach**, *mish-takh'*; from 7849; a *spreading*-place:—(to) spread (forth, -ing, upon).

4895. מַשְׂטֵמָה **masṭêmâh**, *mas-tay-maw'*; from the same as 7850; *enmity*:—hatred.

4896. מִשְׁטָר **mishṭâr**, *mish-tawr'*; from 7860; *jurisdiction:*—dominion.

4897. מֶשִׁי **meshîy**, *meh'-shee*; from 4871; *silk* (as *drawn* from the cocoon):—silk.

מֻשִׁי **Mûshîy**. See 4187.

4898. מְשֵׁיזַבְאֵל **Meshêyzab'êl**, *mesh-ay-zab-ale'*; from an equiv. to 7804 and 410; *delivered of God; Meshezabel*, an Isr.:—Meshezabeel.

4899. מָשִׁיחַ **mâshîyach**, *maw-shee'-akh*; from 4886; *anointed;* usually a *consecrated* person (as a king, priest, or saint); spec. the *Messiah:*—anointed, Messiah.

4900. מָשַׁךְ **mâshak**, *maw-shak'*; a prim. root; to *draw*, used in a great variety of applications (includ. to *sow*, to *sound*, to *prolong*, to *develop*, to *march*, to *remove*, to *delay*, to *be tall*, etc.):—draw (along, out), continue, defer, extend, forbear, × give, handle, make (pro-, sound) long, × sow, scatter, stretch out.

4901. מֶשֶׁךְ **meshek**, *meh'-shek*; from 4900; a *sowing;* also a *possession:*—precious, price.

4902. מֶשֶׁךְ **Meshek**, *meh'-shek;* the same in form as 4901, but prob. of for. der.; *Meshek*, a son of Japheth, and the people desc. from him:—Mesech, Meshech.

4903. מִשְׁכַּב **mishkab** (Chald.), *mish-kab'*; corresp. to 4904; a *bed:*—bed.

4904. מִשְׁכָּב **mishkâb**, *mish-kawb'*; from 7901; a *bed* (fig. a *bier*); abstr. *sleep;* by euphem. carnal *intercourse:*—bed ([-chamber]), couch, lieth (lying) with.

מְשֻׁכָּה **mesûkâh**. See 4881.

4905. מַשְׂכִּיל **maskîyl**, *mas-keel'*; from 7919; *instructive*, i.e. a *didactic* poem:—Maschil.

מַשְׁכִּים **mashkîym**. See 7925.

4906. מַשְׂכִּית **maskîyth**, *mas-keeth'*; from the same as 7906; a *figure* (carved on stone, the wall, or any object); fig. *imagination:*—conceit, image (-ry), picture, × wish.

4907. מִשְׁכַּן **mishkan** (Chald.), *mish-kan'*; corresp. to 4908; *residence:*—habitation.

4908. מִשְׁכָּן **mishkân**, *mish-kawn'*; from 7931; a *residence* (includ. a shepherd's *hut*, the *lair* of animals, fig. the *grave;* also the *Temple*); spec. the *Tabernacle* (prop. its wooden walls):—dwelleth, dwelling (place), habitation, tabernacle, tent.

4909. מַשְׂכֹּרֶת **maskôreth**, *mas-koh'-reth;* from 7936; *wages* or a *reward:*—reward, wages.

4910. מָשַׁל **mâshal**, *maw-shal'*; a prim. root; to *rule:*—(have, make to have) dominion, governor, × indeed, reign, (bear, cause to, have) rule (-ing, -r), have power.

4911. מָשַׁל **mâshal**, *maw-shal'*; denom. from 4912; to *liken*, i.e. (trans.) to use figurative language (an allegory, adage, song or the like); intrans. to *resemble:*—be (-come) like, compare, use (as a) proverb, speak (in proverbs), utter.

4912. מָשָׁל **mâshâl**, *maw-shawl'*; appar. from 4910 in some orig. sense of *superiority* in mental action; prop. a pithy *maxim*, usually of a metaphorical nature; hence a *simile* (as an adage, poem, discourse):—byword, like, parable, proverb.

4913. מָשָׁל **Mâshâl**, *maw-shawl'*; for 4861; *Mashal*, a place in Pal.:—Mashal.

4914. מְשֹׁל **meshôwl**, *mesh-ol'*; from 4911; a *satire:*—byword.

4915. מֹשֶׁל **môshel**, *mo'-shel;* (1) from 4910; *empire;* (2) from 4911; a *parallel:*—dominion, like.

מִשְׁלוֹשׁ **mishlôwsh**. See 7969.

4916. מִשְׁלוֹחַ **mishlôwach**, *mish-lo'-akh;* or

מִשְׁלֹחַ **mishlôach**, *mish-lo'-akh;* also

מִשְׁלָח **mishlâch**, *mish-lawkh'*; from 7971; a *sending* out, i.e. (abstr.) *presentation* (favorable), or *seizure* (unfavorable); also (concr.) a place of *dismissal*, or a *business* to be discharged:—to lay, to put, sending (forth), to set.

4917. מִשְׁלַחַת **mishlachath**, *mish-lakh'-ath;* fem. of 4916; a *mission*, i.e. (abstr. and favorable) *release*, or (concr. and unfavorable) an *army:*—discharge, sending.

4918. מְשֻׁלָּם **Meshullâm**, *mesh-ool-lawm'*; from 7999; *allied; Meshullam*, the name of seventeen Isr.:—Meshullam.

4919. מְשִׁלֵּמוֹת **Meshillêmôwth**, *mesh-il-lay-mohth'*; plur. from 7999; *reconciliations:*—*Meshillemoth*, an Isr.:—Meshillemoth. Comp. 4921.

4920. מְשֶׁלֶמְיָה **Meshelemyâh**, *mesh-eh-lem-yaw'*; or

מְשֶׁלֶמְיָהוּ **Meshelemyâhûw**, *mesh-eh-lem-yaw'-hoo*; from 7999 and 3050; *ally of Jah; Meshelemjah*, an Isr.:—Meshelemiah.

4921. מְשִׁלֵּמִית **Meshillêmîyth**, *mesh-il-lay-meeth'*; from 7999; *reconciliation; Meshillemith*, an Isr.:—Meshillemith. Comp. 4919.

4922. מְשֻׁלֶּמֶת **Meshullemeth**, *mesh-ool-leh'-meth;* fem. of 4918; *Meshullemeth*, an Israelitess:—Meshullemeth.

4923. מְשַׁמָּה **meshammâh**, *mesh-am-maw'*; from 8074; a *waste* or *amazement:*—astonishment, desolate.

4924. מַשְׁמָן **mashmân**, *mash-mawn'*; from 8080; *fat*, i.e. (lit. and abstr.) *fatness;* but usually (fig. and concr.) a *rich* dish, a *fertile* field, a *robust* man:—fat (one, -ness, -test, -test place).

4925. מִשְׁמַנָּה **Mishmannâh**, *mish-man-naw'*; from 8080; *fatness; Mashmannah*, an Isr.:—Mishmannah.

4926. מִשְׁמָע **mishmâ'**, *mish-maw'*; from 8085; a *report:*—hearing.

4927. מִשְׁמָע **Mishmâ'**, *mish-maw'*; the same as 4926; *Mishma*, the name of a son of Ishmael, and of an Isr.:—Mishma.

4928. מִשְׁמַעַת **mishma'ath**, *mish-mah'-ath;* fem. of 4926; *audience*, i.e. the royal *court;* also *obedience*, i.e. (concr.) a *subject:*—bidding, guard, obey.

4929. מִשְׁמָר **mishmâr**, *mish-mawr'*; from 8104; a *guard* (the man, the post, or the *prison*); fig. a *deposit;* also (as observed) a *usage* (abstr.), or an *example* (concr.):—diligence, guard, office, prison, ward, watch.

4930. מַשְׂמְרָה **masmerâh**, *mas-mer-aw'*; for 4548 fem.; a *peg:*—nail.

4931. מִשְׁמֶרֶת **mishmereth**, *mish-meh'-reth;* fem. of 4929; *watch*, i.e. the act (*custody*) or (concr.) the *sentry*, the *post;* obj. *preservation*, or (concr.) *safe;* fig. *observance*, i.e. (abstr.) *duty*, or (obj.) a *usage* or *party:*—charge, keep, to be kept, office, ordinance, safeguard, ward, watch.

4932. מִשְׁנֶה **mishneh**, *mish-neh'*; from 8138; prop. a *repetition*, i.e. a *duplicate* (*copy* of a document), or a *double* (in amount); by impl. a *second* (in order, rank, age, quality or location):—college, copy, double, fatlings, next, second (order), twice as much.

4933. מְשִׁסָּה **mechiççâh**, *mesh-is-saw'*; from 8155; *plunder:*—booty, spoil.

4934. מִשְׁעוֹל **mish'ôwl**, *mish-ole'*; from the same as 8168; a *hollow*, i.e. a narrow passage:—path.

4935. מִשְׁעִי **mish'îy**, *mish-ee'*; prob. from 8159; *inspection:*—to supple.

4936. מִשְׁעָם **Mish'âm**, *mish-awm'*; appar. from 8159; *inspection; Misham*, an Isr.:—Misham.

4937. מִשְׁעֵן **mish'ên**, *mish-ane'*; or

מִשְׁעָן **mish'ân**, *mish-awn'*; from 8172; a *support* (concr.), i.e. (fig.) a *protector* or *sustenance:*—stay.

4938. מִשְׁעֵנָה **mish'ênâh**, *mish-ay-naw'*; or

מִשְׁעֶנֶת **mish'eneth**, *mish-eh'-neth;* fem. of 4937; *support* (abstr.), i.e. (fig.) *sustenance* or (concr.) a *walking-stick:*—staff.

4939. מִשְׂפָּח **mispâch**, *mis-pawkh'*; from 5596; *slaughter:*—oppression.

4940. מִשְׁפָּחָה **mishpâchâh**, *mish-paw-khaw'*; from 8192 [comp. 8198]; a *family*, i.e. circle of relatives; fig. a *class* (of persons), a *species* (of animals) or *sort* (of things); by extens. a *tribe* or *people:*—family, kind (-red).

4941. מִשְׁפָּט **mishpâṭ**, *mish-pawt'*; from 8199; prop. a *verdict* (favorable or unfavorable) pronounced judicially, espec. a *sentence* or formal decree (human or [partic.] divine *law*, individual or collect.), includ. the act, the place, the suit, the crime, and the penalty; abstr. *justice*, includ. a partic. *right*, or *privilege* (statutory or customary), or even a *style:*— + adversary, ceremony, charge, × crime, custom, desert, determination, discretion, disposing, due, fashion, form, to be judged, judgment, just (-ice, -ly), (manner of) law (-ful), manner, measure, (due) order, ordinance, right, sentence, usest, × worthy, + wrong.

4942. מִשְׁפָּת **mishpâth**, *mish-pawth'*; from 8192; a *stall* for cattle (only dual):—burden, sheepfold.

4943. מֶשֶׁק **mesheq**, *meh'-shek;* from an unused root mean. to *hold; possession:*— + steward.

4944. מַשָּׁק **mashshâq**, *mash-shawk'*; from 8264; a *traversing*, i.e. rapid *motion:*—running to and fro.

4945. מַשְׁקֶה **mashqeh**, *mash-keh'*; from 8248; prop. *causing to drink*, i.e. a *butler;* by impl. (intrans.) *drink* (itself); fig. a *well-watered* region:—butler (-ship), cupbearer, drink (-ing), fat pasture, watered.

4946. מִשְׁקוֹל **mishqôwl**, *mish-kole'*; from 8254; *weight:*—weight.

4947. מַשְׁקוֹף **mashqôwph**, *mash-kofe'*; from 8259 in its orig. sense of *overhanging;* a *lintel:*—lintel, upper door post.

4948. מִשְׁקָל **mishqâl**, *mish-kawl'*; from 8254; *weight* (numerically estimated); hence, *weighing* (the act):—(full) weight.

4949. מִשְׁקֶלֶת **mishqeleth**, *mish-keh'-leth;* or

מִשְׁקֹלֶת **mishqôleth**, *mish-ko'-leth;* fem. of 4948 or 4947; a *weight*, i.e. a *plummet* (with line attached):—plummet.

4950. מִשְׁקָע **mishqâ'**, *mish-kaw'*; from 8257; a *settling* place (of water), i.e. a pond:—deep.

4951. מִשְׂרָה **misrâh**, *mis-raw'*; from 8280; *empire:*—government.

4952. מִשְׁרָה **mishrâh**, *mish-raw'*; from 8281 in the sense of *loosening; maceration*, i.e. steeped *juice:*—liquor.

4953. מַשְׁרוֹקִי **mashrôwqîy** (Chald.), *mash-ro-kee'*; from a root corresp. to 8319; a (musical) *pipe* (from its *whistling* sound):—flute.

4954. מִשְׁרָעִי **Mishrâ'îy**, *mish-raw-ee'*; patrial from an unused noun from an unused root; prob. mean. to *stretch* out; *extension;* a *Mishraite*, or inhab. (collect.) of Mishra:—Mishraites.

4955. מִשְׂרָפָה **misrâphâh**, *mis-raw-faw'*; from 8313; *combustion*, i.e. *cremation* (of a corpse), or *calcination* (of lime):—burning.

4956. מִשְׂרְפוֹת מַיִם **Misrephôwth mayim**, *mis-ref-ohth' mah'-yim;* from the plur. of 4955 and 4325; *burnings of water; Misrephoth-Majim*, a place in Pal.:—Misrephoth-mayim.

4957. מַשְׂרֵקָה **Masrêqâh**, *mas-ray-kaw'*; a form for 7796 used denom.; *vineyard; Masrekah*, a place in Idumæa:—Masrekah.

4958. מַשְׂרֵת **masrêth**, *mas-rayth'*; appar. from an unused root mean. to *perforate*, i.e. hollow out; a *pan:*—pan.

4959. מָשַׁשׁ **mâshash**, *maw-shash'*; a prim. root; to *feel* of; by impl. to *grope:*—feel, grope, search.

4960. מִשְׁתֶּה **mishteh**, *mish-teh'*; from 8354; *drink;* by impl. *drinking* (the act); also (by impl.), a *banquet* or (gen.) *feast:*—banquet, drank, drink, feast ([-ed], -ing).

4961. מִשְׁתֵּה **mishteh** (Chald.), *mish-teh'*; corresp. to 4960; a *banquet:*—banquet.

4962. מַת **math**, *math;* from the same as 4970; prop. an *adult* (as of full length); by impl. a *man* (only in the plur.):— + few, × friends, men, persons, × small.

4963. מַתְבֵּן **mathbên**, *math-bane'*; denom. from 8401; *straw* in the heap:—straw.

4964. מֶתֶג **metheg**, *meh'-theg*; from an unused root mean. to *curb*; a *bit*:—bit, bridle.

4965. מֶתֶג הָאַמָּה **Metheg hâ-'Ammâh**, *meh'-theg haw-am-maw'*; from 4964 and 520 with the art. interposed; *bit of the metropolis; Metheg-ha-Ammah* an epithet of Gath:—Metheg-ammah.

4966. מָתוֹק **mâthôwq**, *maw-thoke'*; or

מָתוּק **mâthûwq**, *maw-thook'*; from 4985; *sweet*:—sweet (-er, -ness).

4967. מְתוּשָׁאֵל **Methûwshâ'êl**, *meth-oo-shaw-ale'*; from 4962 and 410, with the rel. interposed; *man who* (is) *of God; Methushaël*, an antediluvian patriarch:—Methusael.

4968. מְתוּשֶׁלַח **Methûwshelach**, *meth-oo-sheh'-lakh*; from 4962 and 7973; *man of a dart; Methushelach*, an antediluvian patriarch:—Methuselah.

4969. מָתַח **mâthach**, *maw-thakh'*; a prim. root; to *stretch* out:—spread out.

4970. מָתַי **mâthay**, *maw-thah'ee*; from an unused root mean. to *extend*; prop. *extent* (of time); but used only adv. (espec. with other particles pref.), *when* (either rel. or interrog.):—long, when.

מְתִים **methîym**. See 4962.

4971. מַתְכֹּנֶת **mathkôneth**, *math-ko'-neth*; or

מַתְכֻּנֶת **mathkûneth**, *math-koo'-neth*; from 8505 in the transferred sense of *measuring; proportion* (in size, number or ingredients):—composition, measure, state, tale.

4972. מַתְּלָאָה **matt**e**lâ'âh**, *mat-tel-aw-aw'*; from 4100 and 8513; *what a trouble!*:—what a weariness.

4973. מְתַלְּעָה **m**e**thall**e**'âh**, *meth-al-leh-aw'*; contr. from 3216; prop. a *biter*, i.e. a *tooth*:—cheek (jaw) tooth, jaw.

4974. מְתֹם **m**e**thôm**, *meth-ohm'*; from 8552; *wholesomeness*; also (adv.) *completely*:—men [*by reading* 4962], soundness.

מֶתֶן **Methen**. See 4981.

4975. מֹתֶן **môthen**, *mo'-then*; from an unused root mean. to be *slender*; prop. the *waist* or small of the back; only in plur. the *loins*:—+ greyhound, loins, side.

4976. מַתָּן **mattân**, *mat-tawn'*; from 5414; a *present*:—gift, to give, reward.

4977. מַתָּן **Mattân**, *mat-tawn'*; the same as 4976; *Mattan*, the name of a priest of Baal, and of an Isr.:—Mattan.

4978. מַתְּנָא **matt**e**nâ'** (Chald.), *mat-ten-aw'*; corresp. to 4979:—gift.

4979. מַתָּנָה **mattânâh**, *mat-taw-naw'*; fem. of 4976; a *present*; spec. (in a good sense) a sacrificial *offering*, (in a bad sense) a *bribe*:—gift.

4980. מַתָּנָה **Mattânâh**, *mat-taw-naw'*; the same as 4979; *Mattanah*, a place in the Desert:—Mattanah.

4981. מִתְנִי **Mithnîy**, *mith-nee'*; prob. patrial from an unused noun mean. *slenderness*; a *Mithnite*, or inhab. of Methen:—Mithnite.

4982. מַתְּנַי **Matt**e**nay**, *mat-ten-ah'ee*; from 4976; *liberal; Mattenai*, the name of three Isr.:—Mattenai.

4983. מַתַּנְיָה **Mattanyâh**, *mat-tan-yaw'*; or

מַתַּנְיָהוּ **Mattanyâhûw**, *mat-tan-yaw'-hoo*; from 4976 and 3050; *gift of Jah; Mattanjah*, the name of ten Isr.:—Mattaniah.

מָתְנַיִם **mothnayim**. See 4975.

4984. מִתְנַשֵּׂא **mithnassê'**, *mith-nas-say'*; from 5375; (used as abstr.) supreme *exaltation*:—exalted.

4985. מָתַק **mâthaq**, *maw-thak'*; a prim. root; to *suck*; by impl. to *relish*, or (intrans.) *be sweet*:—be (made, × take) sweet.

4986. מֶתֶק **metheq**, *meh'-thek*; from 4985; fig. *pleasantness* (of discourse):—sweetness.

4987. מֹתֶק **môtheq**, *mo'-thek*; from 4985; *sweetness*:—sweetness.

4988. מָתָק **mâthâq**, *maw-thawk'*; from 4985; a *dainty*, i.e. (gen.) *food*:—feed sweetly.

4989. מִתְקָה **Mithqâh**, *mith-kaw'*; fem. of 4987; *sweetness; Mithkah*, a place in the Desert:—Mithcah.

4990. מִתְרְדָת **Mithr**e**dâth**, *mith-red-awth'*; of Pers. origin; *Mithredath*, the name of two Persians:—Mithredath.

4991. מַתָּת **mattâth**, *mat-tawth'*; fem. of 4976 abbrev.; a *present*:—gift, reward.

4992. מַתַּתָּה **Mattattâh**, *mat-tat-taw'*; for 4993; *gift of Jah; Mattattah*, an Isr.:—Mattathah.

4993. מַתִּתְיָה **Mattithyâh**, *mat-tith-yaw'*; or

מַתִּתְיָהוּ **Mattithyâhûw**, *mat-tith-yaw'-hoo*; from 4991 and 3050; *gift of Jah; Mattithjah*, the name of four Isr.:—Mattithiah.

נ

4994. נָא **nâ'**, *naw*; a prim. particle of incitement and entreaty, which may usually be rendered *I pray, now* or *then*; added mostly to verbs (in the Imperat. or Fut.), or to interj., occasionally to an adv. or conj.:—I beseech (pray) thee (you), go to, now, oh.

4995. נָא **nâ'**, *naw*; appar. from 5106 in the sense of *harshness* from refusal; prop. *tough*, i.e. *uncooked* (flesh):—raw.

4996. נֹא **Nô'**, *no*; of Eg. origin; *No* (i.e. *Thebes*), the capital of Upper Egypt:—No. Comp. 528.

4997. נֹאד **nô'd**, *node*; or

נֹאוד **nô'wd**, *node*; also (fem.)

נֹאדָה **nô'dâh**, *no-daw'*; from an unused root of uncert. signif.; a (skin or leather) *bag* (for fluids):—bottle.

נֶאְדָּרִי **ne'dârîy**. See 142.

4998. נָאָה **nâ'âh**, *naw-aw'*; a prim. root; prop. to *be at home*, i.e. (by impl.) to be *pleasant* (or *suitable*), i.e. *beautiful*:—be beautiful, become, be comely.

4999. נָאָה **nâ'âh**, *naw-aw'*; from 4998; a *home*; fig. a *pasture*:—habitation, house, pasture, pleasant place.

5000. נָאוֶה **nâ'veh**, *naw-veh'*; from 4998 or 5116; *suitable*, or *beautiful*:—becometh, comely, seemly.

5001. נָאַם **nâ'am**, *naw-am'*; a prim. root; prop. to *whisper*, i.e. (by impl.) to *utter* as an oracle:—say.

5002. נְאֻם **n**e**'ûm**, *neh-oom'*; from 5001; an *oracle*:—(hath) said, saith.

5003. נָאַף **nâ'aph**, *naw-af'*; a prim. root; to *commit adultery*; fig. to *apostatize*:—adulterer (-ess), commit (-ing) adultery, woman that breaketh wedlock.

5004. נִאֻף **nî'ûph**, *nee-oof'*; from 5003; *adultery*:—adultery.

5005. נַאֲפוּף **na'âphûwph**, *nah-af-oof'*; from 5003; *adultery*:—adultery.

5006. נָאַץ **nâ'ats**, *naw-ats'*; a prim. root; to *scorn*; or (Eccles. 12 : 5) by interch. for 5132, to *bloom*:—abhor, (give occasion to) blaspheme, contemn, despise, flourish, × great, provoke.

5007. נְאָצָה **n**e**'âtsâh**, *neh-aw-tsaw'*; or

נֶאָצָה **ne'âtsâh**, *neh-aw-tsaw'*; from 5006; *scorn*:—blasphemy.

5008. נָאַק **nâ'aq**, *naw-ak'*; a prim. root; to *groan*:—groan.

5009. נְאָקָה **n**e**'âqâh**, *neh-aw-kaw'*; from 5008; a *groan*:—groaning.

5010. נָאַר **nâ'ar**, *naw-ar'*; a prim. root; to *reject*:—abhor, make void.

5011. נֹב **Nôb**, *nobe*; the same as 5108; *fruit; Nob*, a place in Pal.:—Nob.

5012. נָבָא **nâbâ'**, *naw-baw'*; a prim. root; to *prophesy*, i.e. speak (or sing) by inspiration (in prediction or simple discourse):—prophesy (-ing), make self a prophet.

5013. נְבָא **n**e**bâ'** (Chald.), *neb-aw'*; corresp. to 5012:—prophesy.

5014. נָבַב **nâbab**, *naw-bab'*; a prim. root; to *pierce*; to *be hollow*, or (fig.) *foolish*:—hollow, vain.

5015. נְבוֹ **N**e**bôw**, *neb-o'*; prob. of for. der.; *Nebo*, the name of a Bab. deity, also of a mountain in Moab, and of a place in Pal.:—Nebo.

5016. נְבוּאָה **n**e**bûw'âh**, *neb-oo-aw'*; from 5012; a *prediction* (spoken or written):—prophecy.

5017. נְבוּאָה **n**e**bûw'âh** (Chald.), *neb-oo-aw*; corresp. to 5016; inspired *teaching*:—prophesying.

5018. נְבוּזַרְאֲדָן **N**e**bûwzar'adân**, *neb-oo-zar-ad-awn'*; of for. or.; *Nebuzaradan*, a Bab. general:—Nebuzaradan.

5019. נְבוּכַדְנֶאצַּר **N**e**bûwkadne'tstsar**, *neb-oo-kad-nets-tsar'*; or

נְבֻכַדְנֶאצַּר **N**e**bûkadne'tstsar** (2 Kings 24 : 1, 10), *neb-oo-kad-nets-tsar'*; or

נְבוּכַדְנֶצַּר **N**e**bûwkadnetstsar** (Esth. 2 : 6; Dan. 1 : 18), *neb-oo-kad-nets-tsar'*; or

נְבוּכַדְרֶאצַּר **N**e**bûwkadre'tstsar**, *neb-oo-kad-rets-tsar'*; or

נְבוּכַדְרֶאצּוֹר **N**e**bûwkadre'tstsôwr** (Ezra 2 : 1; Jer. 49 : 28), *neb-oo-kad-rets-tsore'*; of for. der.; *Nebukadnetstsar* (or *-retstsar*, or *-retstsor*), king of Babylon:—Nebuchadnezzar, Nebuchadrezzar.

5020. נְבוּכַדְנֶצַּר **N**e**bûwkadnetstsar** (Chald.), *neb-oo-kad-nets-tsar'*; corresp. to 5019:—Nebuchadnezzar.

5021. נְבוּשַׁזְבָּן **N**e**bûwshazbân**, *neb-oo-shaz-bawn'*; of for. der.; *Nebushazban*, Nebuchadnezzar's chief eunuch:—Nebushazban.

5022. נָבוֹת **Nâbôwth**, *naw-both'*; fem. plur. from the same as 5011; *fruits; Naboth*, an Isr.:—Naboth.

5023. נְבִזְבָּה **n**e**bizbâh** (Chald.), *neb-iz-baw'*; of uncert. der.; a *largess*:—reward.

5024. נָבַח **nâbach**, *naw-bakh'*; a prim. root; to *bark* (as a dog):—bark.

5025. נֹבַח **Nôbach**, *no'-bach*; from 5024; a *bark; Nobach*, the name of an Isr., and of a place E. of the Jordan:—Nobah.

5026. נִבְחַז **Nibchaz**, *nib-khaz'*; of for. or.; *Nibchaz*, a deity of the Avites:—Nibhaz.

5027. נָבַט **nâbaṭ**, *naw-bat'*; a prim. root; to *scan*, i.e. look intently at; by impl. to *regard* with pleasure, favor or care:—(cause to) behold, consider, look (down), regard, have respect, see.

5028. נְבָט **N**e**bâṭ**, *neb-awt'*; from 5027; *regard; Nebat*, the father of Jeroboam I:—Nebat.

5029. נְבִיא **n**e**bîy'** (Chald.), *neb-ee'*; corresp. to 5030; a *prophet*:—prophet.

5030. נָבִיא **nâbîy'**, *naw-bee'*; from 5012; a *prophet* or (gen.) *inspired* man:—prophecy, that prophesy, prophet.

5031. נְבִיאָה **n**e**bîy'âh**, *neb-ee-yaw'*; fem. of 5030; a *prophetess* or (gen.) *inspired* woman; by impl. a *poetess*; by association a *prophet's wife*:—prophetess.

5032. נְבָיוֹת **N**e**bâyôwth**, *neb-aw-yoth'*; or

נְבָיֹת **N**e**bâyôth**, *neb-aw-yoth'*; fem. plur. from 5107; *fruitfulnesses; Nebajoth*, a son of Ishmael, and the country settled by him:—Nebaioth, Nebajoth.

5033. נֵבֶךְ **nêbek**, *nay'-bek*; from an unused root mean. to *burst* forth; a *fountain*:—spring.

5034. נָבֵל **nâbêl**, *naw-bale'*; a prim. root; to *wilt*; gen. to *fall away, fail, faint*; fig. to *be foolish* or (mor.) *wicked*; causat. to *despise, disgrace*:—disgrace, dishonour, lightly esteem, fade (away, -ing), fall (down, -ling, off), do foolishly, come to nought, × surely, make vile, wither.

5035. נֶבֶל **nebel**, *neh'-bel*; or

נֵבֶל **nêbel**, *nay'-bel*; from 5034; a *skin-bag* for liquids (from *collapsing* when empty);

hence, a *vase* (as similar in shape when full); also a *lyre* (as having a body of like form):—bottle, pitcher, psaltery, vessel, viol.

5036. נָבָל **nâbâl**, *naw-bawl'*; from 5034; *stupid; wicked* (espec. *impious*):—fool (-ish, -ish man, -ish woman), vile person.

5037. נָבָל **Nâbâl**, *naw-bawl'*; the same as 5036; *dolt; Nabal*, an Isr.:—Nabal.

5038. נְבֵלָה **nᵉbêlâh**, *neb-ay-law'*; from 5034; a *flabby* thing, i.e. a *carcase* or *carrion* (human or bestial, often collect.); fig. an *idol*:—(dead) body, (dead) carcase, dead of itself, which died, (beast) that (which) dieth of itself.

5039. נְבָלָה **nᵉbâlâh**, *neb-aw-law'*; fem. of 5036; *foolishness*, i.e. (mor.) *wickedness*; concr. a *crime*; by extens. *punishment*:—folly, vile, villany.

5040. נַבְלוּת **nablûwth**, *nab-looth'*; from 5036; prop. *disgrace*, i.e. the (female) *pudenda*:—lewdness.

5041. נְבַלָּט **Nᵉballâṭ**, *neb-al-lawt'*; appar. from 5036 and 3909; *foolish secrecy; Neballat*, a place in Pal.:—Neballat.

5042. נָבַע **nâbaʻ**, *naw-bah'*; a prim. root; to *gush* forth; fig. to *utter* (good or bad words); spec. to *emit* (a foul odor):—belch out, flowing, pour out, send forth, utter (abundantly).

5043. נֶבְרְשָׁא **nebrᵉshâʼ** (Chald.), *neb-reh-shaw'*; from an unused root mean. to *shine*; a *light*; plur. (collect.) a *chandelier*:—candlestick.

5044. נִבְשָׁן **Nibshân**, *nib-shawn'*; of uncert. der.; *Nibshan*, a place in Pal.:—Nibshan.

5045. נֶגֶב **negeb**, *neh'-gheb*; from an unused root mean. to *be parched*; the *south* (from its drought); spec. the *Negeb* or southern district of Judah, occasionally, *Egypt* (as south to Pal.):—south (country, side, -ward).

5046. נָגַד **nâgad**, *naw-gad'*; a prim. root; prop. to *front*, i.e. stand boldly out opposite; by impl. (causat.), to *manifest*; fig. to *announce* (always by word of mouth to one present); spec. to *expose, predict, explain, praise*:—bewray, × certainly, certify, declare (-ing), denounce, expound, × fully, messenger, plainly, profess, rehearse, report, shew (forth), speak, × surely, tell, utter.

5047. נְגַד **nᵉgad** (Chald.), *neg-ad'*; corresp. to 5046; to *flow* (through the idea of *clearing* the way):—issue.

5048. נֶגֶד **neged**, *neh'-ghed*; from 5046; a *front*, i.e. part opposite; spec. a *counterpart*, or mate; usually (adv., espec. with prep.) *over against* or *before*:—about, (over) against, × aloof, × far (off), × from, over, presence, × other side, sight, × to view.

5049. נֶגֶד **neged** (Chald.), *neh'-ghed*; corresp. to 5048; *opposite*:—toward.

5050. נָגַהּ **nâgahh**, *naw-găh'*; a prim. root; to *glitter*; causat. to *illuminate*:—(en-) lighten, (cause to) shine.

5051. נֹגַהּ **nôgahh**, *no'-găh*; from 5050; *brilliancy* (lit. or fig.):—bright (-ness), light, (clear) shining.

5052. נֹגַהּ **Nôgahh**, *no'-găh*; the same as 5051; *Nogah*, a son of David:—Nogah.

5053. נֹגַהּ **nôgahh** (Chald.), *no'-găh*; corresp. to 5051; *dawn*:—morning.

5054. נְגֹהָה **nᵉgôhâh**, *neg-o-haw'*; fem. of 5051; *splendor*:—brightness.

5055. נָגַח **nâgach**, *naw-gakh'*; a prim. root; to *but* with the horns; fig. to *war* against:—gore, push (down, -ing).

5056. נַגָּח **naggâch**, *nag-gawkh'*; from 5055; *butting*, i.e. *vicious*:—used (wont) to push.

5057. נָגִיד **nâgîyd**, *naw-gheed'*; or

נָגִד **nâgid**, *naw-gheed'*; from 5046; a *commander* (as occupying the *front*), civil, military or religious; gen. (abstr. plur.), *honorable* themes:—captain, chief, excellent thing, (chief) governor, leader, noble, prince, (chief) ruler.

5058. נְגִינָה **nᵉgîynâh**, *neg-ee-naw'*; or

נְגִינַת **nᵉgîynath** (Psa. 61 : title), *neg-ee-nath'*; from 5059; prop. instrumental *music*; by impl. a stringed *instrument*; by extens. a *poem* set to music; spec. an *epigram*:—stringed instrument, musick, Neginoth [*plur.*], song.

5059. נָגַן **nâgan**, *naw-gan'*; a prim. root; prop. to *thrum*, i.e. *beat* a tune with the fingers; espec. to *play* on a stringed instrument; hence (gen.) to *make music*:—player on instruments, sing to the stringed instruments, melody, ministrel, play (-er, -ing).

5060. נָגַע **nâgaʻ**, *naw-gah'*; a prim. root; prop. to *touch*, i.e. *lay the hand upon* (for any purpose; euphem., to *lie with* a woman); by impl. to *reach* (fig. to *arrive, acquire*); violently, to *strike* (punish, defeat, destroy, etc.):—beat, (× be able to) bring (down), cast, come (nigh), draw near (nigh), get up, happen, join, near, plague, reach (up), smite, strike, touch.

5061. נֶגַע **negaʻ**, *neh'-gah*; from 5060; a *blow* (fig. *infliction*); also (by impl.) a *spot* (concr. a *leprous* person or dress):—plague, sore, stricken, stripe, stroke, wound.

5062. נָגַף **nâgaph**, *naw-gaf'*; a prim. root; to *push, gore, defeat, stub* (the toe), *inflict* (a disease):—beat, dash, hurt, plague, slay, smite (down), strike, stumble, × surely, put to the worse.

5063. נֶגֶף **negeph**, *neh'-ghef*; from 5062; a *trip* (of the foot); fig. an *infliction* (of disease):—plague, stumbling.

5064. נָגַר **nâgar**, *naw-gar'*; a prim. root; to *flow*; fig. to *stretch* out; causat. to *pour* out or down; fig. to *deliver* over:—fall, flow away, pour down (out), run, shed, spilt, trickle down.

5065. נָגַשׂ **nâgas**, *naw-gas'*; a prim. root; to *drive* (an animal, a workman, a debtor, an army); by impl. to *tax, harass, tyrannize*:—distress, driver, exact (-or), oppress (-or), × raiser of taxes, taskmaster.

5066. נָגַשׁ **nâgash**, *naw-gash'*; a prim. root; to *be* or *come* (causat. *bring*) *near* (for any purpose); euphem. to *lie with* a woman; as an enemy, to *attack*; relig. to *worship*; causat. to *present*; fig. to *adduce* an argument; by reversal, to *stand back*:—(make to) approach (nigh), bring (forth, hither, near), (cause to) come (hither, near, nigh), give place, go hard (up), (be, draw, go) near (nigh), offer, overtake, present, put, stand.

5067. נֵד **nêd**, *nade*; from 5110 in the sense of *piling* up; a *mound*, i.e. *wave*:—heap.

5068. נָדַב **nâdab**, *naw-dab'*; a prim. root; to *impel*; hence to *volunteer* (as a soldier), to *present* spontaneously:—offer freely, be (give, make, offer self) willing (-ly).

5069. נְדַב **nᵉdab** (Chald.), *ned-ab'*; corresp. to 5068; *be* (or *give*) *liberal* (*-ly*):—(be minded of . . . own) freewill (offering), offer freely (willingly).

5070. נָדָב **Nâdâb**, *naw-dawb'*; from 5068; *liberal; Nadab*, the name of four Isr.:—Nadab.

5071. נְדָבָה **nᵉdâbâh**, *ned-aw-baw'*; from 5068; prop. (abstr.) *spontaneity*, or (adj.) *spontaneous*; also (concr.) a *spontaneous* or (by infer., in plur.) *abundant* gift:—free (-will) offering, freely, plentiful, voluntary (-ily, offering), willing (-ly, offering).

5072. נְדַבְיָה **Nᵉdabyâh**, *ned-ab-yaw'*; from 5068 and 3050; *largess of Jah; Nedabjah*, an Isr.:—Nedabiah.

5073. נִדְבָּךְ **nidbâk** (Chald.), *nid-bawk'*; from a root mean. to *stick*; a *layer* (of building materials):—row.

5074. נָדַד **nâdad**, *naw-dad'*; a prim. root; prop. to *wave* to and fro (rarely to *flap* up and down); fig. to *rove, flee*, or (caus.) to *drive* away:—chase (away), × could not, depart, flee (× apace, away), (re-) move, thrust away, wander (abroad, -er, -ing).

5075. נְדַד **nᵉdad** (Chald.), *ned-ad'*; corresp. to 5074; to *depart*:—go from.

5076. נָדֻד **nâdûd**, *naw-dood'*; pass. part. of 5074; prop. *tossed*; abstr. a *rolling* (on the bed):—tossing to and fro.

5077. נָדָה **nâdâh**, *naw-daw'*; or

נָדָא **nâdâʼ** (2 Kings 17 : 21), *naw-daw'*; a prim. root; prop. to *toss*; fig. to *exclude* i.e. banish, postpone, prohibit:—cast out, drive, put far away.

5078. נֵדֶה **nêdeh**, *nay'-deh*; from 5077 in the sense of freely *flinging* money; a *bounty* (for prostitution):—gifts.

5079. נִדָּה **niddâh**, *nid-daw'*; from 5074; prop. *rejection*; by impl. *impurity*, espec. personal (menstruation) or moral (idolatry, incest):—× far, filthiness, × flowers, menstruous (woman), put apart, × removed (woman), separation, set apart, unclean (-ness, thing, with filthiness).

5080. נָדַח **nâdach**, *naw-dakh'*; a prim. root; to *push* off; used in a great variety of applications, lit. and fig. (to expel, mislead, strike, inflict etc.):—banish, bring, cast down (out), chase, compel, draw away, drive (away, out, quite), fetch a stroke, force, go away, outcast, thrust away (out), withdraw.

5081. נָדִיב **nâdîyb**, *naw-deeb'*; from 5068; prop. *voluntary*, i.e. generous; hence, *magnanimous*; as noun, a *grandee* (sometimes a *tyrant*):—free, liberal (things), noble, prince, willing ([hearted]).

5082. נְדִיבָה **nᵉdîybâh**, *ned-ee-baw'*; fem. of 5081; prop. *nobility*, i.e. reputation:—soul.

5083. נָדָן **nâdân**, *naw-dawn'*; prob. from an unused root mean. to *give*; a *present* (for prostitution):—gift.

5084. נָדָן **nâdân**, *naw-dawn'*; of uncert. der.; a *sheath* (of a sword):—sheath.

5085. נִדְנֶה **nidneh** (Chald.), *nid-neh'*; from the same as 5084; a *sheath*; fig. the *body* (as the receptacle of the soul):—body.

5086. נָדַף **nâdaph**, *naw-daf'*; a prim. root; to *shove* asunder, i.e. *disperse*:—drive (away, to and fro), thrust down, shaken, tossed to and fro.

5087. נָדַר **nâdar**, *naw-dar'*; a prim. root; to *promise* (pos., to do or give something to God):—(make a) vow.

5088. נֶדֶר **neder**, *neh'-der*; or

נֵדֶר **nêder**, *nay'-der*; from 5087; a *promise* (to God); also (concr.) a thing *promised*:—vow ([-ed]).

5089. נֹהַּ **nôahh**, *no'-ăh*; from an unused root mean. to *lament*; *lamentation*:—wailing.

5090. נָהַג **nâhag**, *naw-hag'*; a prim. root; to *drive* forth (a person, an animal or chariot), i.e. *lead, carry away*; reflex. to *proceed* (i.e. impel or guide oneself); also (from the *panting* induced by effort), to *sigh*:—acquaint, bring (away), carry away, drive (away), lead (away, forth), (be) guide, lead (away, forth).

5091. נָהָה **nâhâh**, *naw-haw'*; a prim. root; to *groan*, i.e. *bewail*; hence (through the idea of *crying* aloud) to *assemble* (as if on proclamation):—lament, wail.

5092. נְהִי **nᵉhîy**, *neh-hee'*; from 5091; an *elegy*:—lamentation, wailing.

5093. נִהְיָה **nihyâh**, *nih-yaw'*; fem. of 5092; *lamentation*:—doleful.

5094. נְהִיר **nᵉhîyr** (Chald.), *neh-heere'*; or

נְהִירוּ **nehîyrûw** (Chald.), *neh-hee-roo'*; from the same as 5105; *illumination*, i.e. (fig.) wisdom:—light.

5095. נָהַל **nâhal**, *naw-hal'*; a prim. root; prop. to run with a *sparkle*, i.e. *flow*; hence (trans.) to *conduct*, and (by infer.) to *protect, sustain*:—carry, feed, guide, lead (gently, on).

5096. נַהֲלָל **Nahălâl**, *năh-hal-awl'*; or

נַהֲלֹל **Nahălôl**, *năh-hal-ole'*; the same as 5097; *Nahalal* or *Nahalol*, a place in Pal.:—Nahalal, Nahallal, Nahalol.

5097. נַהֲלֹל **nahălôl**, *năh-hal-ole'*; from 5095; *pasture*:—bush.

5098. נָהַם **nâham**, *naw-ham'*; a prim. root; to *growl*:—mourn, roar (-ing).

5099. נַהַם **naham**, *năh'-ham*; from 5098; a *snarl*:—roaring.

5100. נְהָמָה **nᵉhâmâh**, *neh-haw-maw';* fem. of 5099; *snarling:*—disquietness, roaring.

5101. נָהַק **nâhaq**, *naw-hak';* a prim. root; to *bray* (as an ass), *scream* (from hunger):—bray.

5102. נָהַר **nâhar**, *naw-har';* a prim. root; to *sparkle*, i.e. (fig.) *be cheerful;* hence (from the *sheen* of a running stream) to *flow*, i.e. (fig.) *assemble:*—flow (together), be lightened.

5103. נְהַר **nᵉhar** (Chald.), *neh-har';* from a root corresp. to 5102; a *river*, espec. the Euphrates:—river, stream.

5104. נָהָר **nâhâr**, *naw-hawr';* from 5102; a *stream* (includ. the *sea;* espec. the Nile, Euphrates, etc.); fig., *prosperity:*—flood, river.

5105. נְהָרָה **nᵉhârâh**, *neh-haw-raw';* from 5102 in its orig. sense; *daylight:*—light.

5106. נוּא **nûw'**, *noo;* a prim. root; to *refuse, forbid, dissuade*, or *neutralize:*—break, disallow, discourage, make of none effect.

5107. נוּב **nûwb**, *noob;* a prim. root; to *germinate*, i.e. (fig.) to (causat. *make*) *flourish;* also (of words), to *utter:*—bring forth (fruit), make cheerful, increase.

5108. נוֹב° **nôwb**, *nobe;* or

נֵיב **nêyb**, *nabe;* from 5107; *produce*, lit. or fig.:—fruit.

5109. נוֹבַי° **Nôwbay**, *no-bah'ee;* from 5108; *fruitful; Nobai*, an Isr.:—Nebai [*from the marg.*].

5110. נוּד **nûwd**, *nood;* a prim. root; to *nod*, i.e. *waver;* fig. to *wander, flee, disappear;* also (from *shaking* the head in sympathy), to *console, deplore*, or (from *tossing* the head in scorn) *taunt:*—bemoan, flee, get, mourn, make to move, take pity, remove, shake, skip for joy, be sorry, vagabond, way, wandering.

5111. נוּד **nûwd** (Chald.), *nood;* corresp. to 5116; to *flee:*—get away.

5112. נוֹד **nôwd**, *node* [only defect.

נֹד **nôd**, *node*]; from 5110; *exile:*—wandering.

5113. נוֹד **Nôwd**, *node;* the same as 5112; *vagrancy; Nod*, the land of Cain:—Nod.

5114. נוֹדָב **Nôwdâb**, *no-dawb';* from 5068; *noble; Nodab*, an Arab tribe:—Nodab.

5115. נָוָה **nâvâh**, *naw-vaw';* a prim. root; to *rest* (as at home); causat. (through the implied idea of *beauty* [comp. 5116]), to *celebrate* (with praises):—keep at home, prepare an habitation.

5116. נָוֶה **nâveh**, *naw-veh';* or (fem.)

נָוָה **nâvâh**, *naw-vaw';* from 5115; (adj.) *at home;* hence (by impl. of satisfaction) *lovely;* also (noun) a *home*, of God (temple), men (residence), flocks (pasture), or wild animals (*den*):—comely, dwelling (place), fold, habitation, pleasant place, sheepcote, stable, tarried.

5117. נוּחַ **nûwach**, *noo'-akh;* a prim. root; to *rest*, i.e. *settle* down; used in a great variety of applications, lit. and fig., intrans., trans. and causat. (to *dwell, stay, let fall, place, let alone, withdraw, give comfort*, etc.):—cease, be confederate, lay, let down, (be) quiet, remain, (cause to, be at, give, have, make to) rest, set down. Comp. 3241.

5118. נוּחַ **nûwach**, *noo'-akh;* or

נוֹחַ **nôwach**, *no'-akh;* from 5117; *quiet:*—rest (-ed, -ing place).

5119. נוֹחָה **Nôwchâh**, *no-chaw';* fem. of 5118; *quietude; Nochah*, an Isr.:—Nohah.

5120. נוּט **nûwṭ**, *noot;* to *quake:*—be moved.

5121. נָוִית° **Nâvîyth**, *naw-veeth';* from 5115; *residence; Navith*, a place in Pal.:—Naioth [*from the marg.*].

5122. נְוָלוּ **nᵉvâlûw** (Chald.), *nev-aw-loo';* or

נְוָלִי **nᵉvâlîy** (Chald.), *nev-aw-lee';* from an unused root prob. mean. to be *foul;* a *sink:*—dunghill.

5123. נוּם **nûwm**, *noom;* a prim. root; to *slumber* (from drowsiness):—sleep, slumber.

5124 נוּמָה **nûwmâh**, *noo-maw';* from 5123; *sleepiness:*—drowsiness.

5125. נוּן **nûwn**, *noon;* a prim. root; to *resprout*, i.e. propagate by shoots; fig., to *be perpetual:*—be continued.

5126. נוּן **Nûwn**, *noon;* or

נוֹן **Nôwn** (1 Chron. 7 : 27), *nohn;* from 5125; *perpetuity; Nun* or *Non*, the father of Joshua:—Non, Nun.

5127. נוּס **nûwç**, *noos;* a prim. root; to *flit*, i.e. *vanish* away (subside, escape; causat. chase, impel, deliver):— × abate, away, be displayed, (make to) flee (away, -ing), put to flight, × hide, lift up a standard.

5128. נוּעַ **nûwaʻ**, *noo'-ah;* a prim. root; to *waver*, in a great variety of applications, lit. and fig. (as subjoined):—continually, fugitive, × make to [go] up and down, be gone away, (be) move (-able, -d), be promoted, reel, remove, scatter, set, shake, sift, stagger, to and fro, be vagabond, wag, (make) wander (up and down).

5129. נוֹעַדְיָה **Nôwʻadyâh**, *no-ad-yaw';* from 3259 and 3050; *convened of Jah; Noädjah*, the name of an Isr., and a false prophetess:—Noadiah.

5130. נוּף **nûwph**, *noof;* a prim. root; to *quiver* (i.e. *vibrate* up and down, or *rock* to and fro); used in a great variety of applications (includ. sprinkling, beckoning, rubbing, bastinadoing, sawing, waving, etc.):—lift up, move, offer, perfume, send, shake, sift, strike, wave.

5131. נוֹף **nôwph**, *nofe;* from 5130; *elevation:*—situation. Comp. 5297.

5132. נוּץ **nûwts**, *noots;* a prim. root; prop. to *flash;* hence, to *blossom* (from the brilliancy of color); also, to *fly* away (from the quickness of motion):—flee away, bud (forth).

5133. נוֹצָה **nôwtsâh**, *no-tsaw';* or

נֹצָה **nôtsâh**, *no-tsaw';* fem. act. part. of 5327 in the sense of *flying;* a *pinion* (or wing feather); often (collect.) *plumage:*—feather (-s), ostrich.

5134. נוּק **nûwq**, *nook;* a prim. root; to *suckle:*—nurse.

5135. נוּר **nûwr** (Chald.), *noor;* from an unused root (corresp. to that of 5216) mean. to *shine; fire:*—fiery, fire.

5136. נוּשׁ **nûwsh**, *noosh;* a prim. root; to *be sick*, i.e. (fig.) *distressed:*—be full of heaviness.

5137. נָזָה **nâzâh**, *naw-zaw';* a prim. root; to *spirt*, i.e. *besprinkle* (espec. in expiation):—sprinkle.

5138. נָזִיד **nâzîyd**, *naw-zeed';* from 2102; something *boiled*, i.e. *soup:*—pottage.

5139. נָזִיר **nâzîyr**, *naw-zeer';* or

נָזִר **nâzîr**, *naw-zeer';* from 5144; *separate*, i.e. consecrated (as *prince*, a *Nazirite*); hence (fig. from the latter) an *unpruned* vine (like an unshorn Nazirite):—Nazarite [*by a false alliteration with Nazareth*], separate (-d), vine undressed.

5140. נָזַל **nâzal**, *naw-zal';* a prim. root; to *drip*, or *shed* by trickling:—distil, drop, flood, (cause to) flow (-ing), gush out, melt, pour (down), running water, stream.

5141. נֶזֶם **nezem**, *neh'-zem;* from an unused root of uncert. mean.; a nose-*ring:*—earring, jewel.

5142. נְזַק **nᵉzaq** (Chald.), *nez-ak';* corresp. to the root of 5143; to *suffer* (causat. *inflict*) *loss:*—have (en-) damage, hurt (-ful).

5143. נֵזֶק **nêzeq**, *nay'-zek;* from an unused root mean. to *injure; loss:*—damage.

5144. נָזַר **nâzar**, *naw-zar';* a prim. root; to *hold aloof*, i.e. (intrans.) *abstain* (from food and drink, from impurity, and even from divine worship [i.e. *apostatize*]); spec. to *set apart* (to sacred purposes), i.e. *devote:*—consecrate, separate (-ing, self).

5145. נֶזֶר **nezer**, *neh'-zer;* or

נֵזֶר **nêzer**, *nay'-zer;* from 5144; prop. something *set apart*, i.e. (abstr.) *dedication* (of a priest or Nazirite); hence (concr.) unshorn *locks;* also (by impl.) a *chaplet* (espec. of royalty):—consecration, crown, hair, separation.

5146. נֹחַ **Nôach**, *no'-akh;* the same as 5118; *rest; Noäch*, the patriarch of the flood:—Noah.

5147. נַחְבִּי **Nachbîy**, *nakh-bee';* from 2247; *occult; Nachbi*, an Isr.:—Nakbi.

5148. נָחָה **nâchâh**, *naw-khaw';* a prim. root; to *guide;* by impl. to *transport* (into exile, or as colonists):—bestow, bring, govern, guide, lead (forth), put, straiten.

5149. נְחוּם **Nᵉchûwm**, *neh-khoom';* from 5162; *comforted; Nechum*, an Isr.:—Nehum.

5150. נִחוּם **nichûwm**, *nee-khoom';* or

נִחֻם **nichûm**, *nee-khoom';* from 5162; prop. *consoled;* abstr. *solace:*—comfort (-able), repenting.

5151. נַחוּם **Nachûwm**, *nakh-oom';* from 5162; *comfortable; Nachum*, an Isr. prophet:—Nahum.

5152. נָחוֹר **Nâchôwr**, *naw-khore';* from the same as 5170; *snorer; Nachor*, the name of the grandfather and a brother of Abraham:—Nahor.

5153. נָחוּשׁ **nâchûwsh**, *naw-khoosh';* appar. pass. part. of 5172 (perh. in the sense of *ringing*, i.e. bell-metal; or from the *red* color of the throat of a serpent [5175, as denom.] when hissing); *coppery*, i.e. (fig.) hard:—of brass.

5154. נְחוּשָׁה **nᵉchûwshâh**, *nekh-oo-shaw';* or

נְחֻשָׁה **nᵉchûshâh**, *nekh-oo-shaw';* fem. of 5153; *copper:*—brass, steel. Comp. 5176.

5155. נְחִילָה **nᵉchîylah**, *nekh-ee-law';* prob. denom. from 2485; a *flute:*—[*plur.*] Nehiloth.

5156. נְחִיר **nᵉchîyr**, *nekh-eer';* from the same as 5170; a *nostril:*—[*dual*] nostrils.

5157. נָחַל **nâchal**, *naw-khal';* a prim. root; to *inherit* (as a [fig.] mode of descent), or (gen.) to *occupy;* causat. to *bequeath*, or (gen.) *distribute, instate:*—divide, have ([inheritance]), take as an heritage, (cause to, give to, make to) inherit, (distribute for, divide [for, for an, by], give for, have, leave for, take [for]) inheritance, (have in, cause to, be made to) possess (-ion).

5158. נַחַל **nachal**, *nakh'-al;* or (fem.)

נַחְלָה **nachlâh** (Psa. 124 : 4), *nakh'-law;* or

נַחֲלָה **nachălâh** (Ezek. 47 : 19; 48 : 28), *nakh-al-aw';* from 5157 in its orig. sense; a *stream*, espec. a winter *torrent;* (by impl.) a (narrow) *valley* (in which a brook runs); also a *shaft* (of a mine):—brook, flood, river, stream, valley.

5159. נַחֲלָה **nachălâh**, *nakh-al-aw';* from 5157 (in its usual sense); prop. something *inherited*, i.e. (abstr.) *occupancy*, or (concr.) an *heirloom;* gen. an *estate, patrimony* or *portion:*—heritage, to inherit, inheritance, possession. Comp. 5158.

5160. נַחֲלִיאֵל **Nachălîyʼêl**, *nakh-al-ee-ale';* from 5158 and 410; *valley of God; Nachaliël*, a place in the Desert:—Nahaliel.

5161. נֶחֱלָמִי **Nechĕlâmîy**, *nekh-el-aw-mee';* appar. a patron. from an unused name (appar. pass. part. of 2492); *dreamed;* a *Nechelamite*, or descend. of Nechlam:—Nehelamite.

5162. נָחַם **nâcham**, *naw-kham';* a prim. root; prop. to *sigh*, i.e. *breathe* strongly; by impl. to *be sorry*, i.e. (in a favorable sense) to *pity, console* or (reflex.) *rue;* or (unfavorably) to *avenge* (oneself):—comfort (self), ease [one's self], repent (-er, -ing, self).

5163. נַחַם **Nacham**, *nakh'-am;* from 5162; *consolation; Nacham*, an Isr.:—Naham.

5164. נֹחַם **nôcham**, *no'-kham;* from 5162; *ruefulness*, i.e. desistance:—repentance.

5165. נֶחָמָה **nechâmâh**, *nekh-aw-maw';* from 5162; *consolation:*—comfort.

5166. נְחֶמְיָה **Nᵉchemyâh**, *nekh-em-yaw';* from 5162 and 3050; *consolation of Jah; Nechemjah*, the name of three Isr.:—Nehemiah.

5167. נַחֲמָנִי **Nachămânîy**, *nakh-am-aw-nee';* from 5162; *consolatory; Nachamani*, an Isr.:—Nahamani.

5168. נַחְנוּ **nachnûw**, *nakh-noo';* for 587; *we:*—we.

5169. נָחַץ **nâchats**, *naw-khats'*; a prim. root; to *be urgent*:—require haste.

5170. נַחַר **nachar**, *nakh'-ar*; and (fem.)

נַחֲרָה **nachărâh**, *nakh-ar-aw'*; from an unused root mean. to *snort* or *snore*; a *snorting*:—nostrils, snorting.

5171. נַחֲרַי **Nachăray**, *nakh-ar-ah'ee*; or

נַחְרַי **Nachray**, *nakh-rah'ee*; from the same as 5170; *snorer*; *Nacharai* or *Nachrai*, an Isr.:—Naharai, Nahari.

5172. נָחַשׁ **nâchash**, *naw-khash'*; a prim. root; prop. to *hiss*, i.e. *whisper* a (magic) spell; gen. to *prognosticate*:— × certainly, divine, enchanter, (use) × enchantment, learn by experience, × indeed, diligently observe.

5173. נַחַשׁ **nachash**, *nakh'-ash*; from 5172; an *incantation* or *augury*:—enchantment.

5174. נְחָשׁ **n^{e}châsh** (Chald.) *nekh-awsh'*; corresp. to 5154; *copper*:—brass.

5175. נָחָשׁ **nâchâsh**, *naw-khawsh'*; from 5172; a *snake* (from its *hiss*):—serpent.

5176. נָחָשׁ **Nâchâsh**, *naw-khawsh'*; the same as 5175; *Nachash*, the name of two persons appar. non-Isr.:—Nahash.

נְחֻשָׁה **n^{e}chûshâh**. See 5154.

5177. נַחְשׁוֹן **Nachshôwn**, *nakh-shone'*; from 5172; *enchanter*; *Nachshon*, an Isr.:—Naashon, Nahshon.

5178. נְחֹשֶׁת **n^{e}chôsheth**, *nekh-o'-sheth*; for 5154; *copper*; hence, something made of that metal, i.e. *coin*, a *fetter*; fig. *base* (as compared with gold or silver):—brasen, brass, chain, copper, fetter (of brass), filthiness, steel.

5179. נְחֻשְׁתָּא **N^{e}chushtâ'**, *nekh-oosh-taw'*; from 5178; *copper*; *Nechushta*, an Israelitess:—Nehushta.

5180. נְחֻשְׁתָּן **N^{e}chushtân**, *nekh-oosh-tawn'*; from 5178; something made *of copper*, i.e. the copper *serpent* of the Desert:—Nehushtan.

5181. נָחַת **nâchath**, *naw-khath'*; a prim. root; to *sink*, i.e. *descend*; causat., to *press* or *lead* down:—be broken, (cause to) come down, enter, go down, press sore, settle, stick fast.

5182. נְחַת **n^{e}chath** (Chald.), *nekh-ath'*; corresp. to 5181; to *descend*; causat., to *bring away*, *deposit*, *depose*:—carry, come down, depose, lay up, place.

5183. נַחַת **nachath**, *nakh'-ath*; from 5182; a *descent*, i.e. imposition, unfavorable (*punishment*) or favorable (*food*); also (intrans.; perh. from 5117), *restfulness*:—lighting down, quiet (-ness), to rest, be set on.

5184. נַחַת **Nachath**, *nakh'-ath*; the same as 5183; *quiet*; *Nachath*, the name of an Edomite and of two Isr.:—Nahath.

5185. נָחֵת **nâchêth**, *naw-khayth'*; from 5181; *descending*:—come down.

5186. נָטָה **nâṭâh**, *naw-taw'*; a prim. root; to *stretch* or spread out; by impl. to *bend* away (includ. mor. deflection); used in a great variety of application (as follows):— + afternoon, apply, bow (down, -ing), carry aside, decline, deliver, extend, go down, be gone, incline, intend, lay, let down, offer, outstretched, overthrown, pervert, pitch, prolong, put away, shew, spread (out), stretch (forth, out), take (aside), turn (aside, away), wrest, cause to yield.

5187. נְטִיל **n^{e}ṭîyl**, *net-eel'*; from 5190; *laden*:—that bear.

5188. נְטִיפָה **n^{e}ṭîyphâh**, *net-ee-faw'*; from 5197; a *pendant* for the ears (espec. of pearls):—chain, collar.

5189. נְטִישָׁה **n^{e}ṭîyshâh**, *net-ee-shaw'*; from 5203; a *tendril* (as an offshoot):—battlement, branch, plant.

5190. נָטַל **nâṭal**, *naw-tal'*; a prim root; to *lift*; by impl. to *impose*:—bear, offer, take up.

5191. נְטַל **n^{e}ṭal** (Chald.), *net-al'*; corresp. to 5190; to *raise*:—take up.

5192. נֵטֶל **nêṭel**, *nay'-tel*; from 5190; a *burden*:—weighty.

5193. נָטַע **nâṭaʻ**, *naw-tah'*; a prim. root; prop. to *strike* in, i.e. *fix*; spec. to *plant* (lit. or fig.):—fastened, plant (-er).

5194. נֶטַע **neṭaʻ**, *neh'-tah*; from 5193; a *plant*; collect., a *plantation*; abstr., a *planting*:—plant.

5195. נָטִיעַ **nâṭîaʻ**, *naw-tee'-ah*; from 5193; a *plant*:—plant.

5196. נְטָעִים **N^{e}ṭâʻîym**, *net-aw-eem'*; plur. of 5194; *Netaïm*, a place in Pal.:—plants.

5197. נָטַף **nâṭaph**, *naw-taf'*; a prim. root; to *ooze*, i.e. *distil* gradually; by impl. to *fall in drops*; fig. to *speak* by inspiration:—drop (-ping), prophesy (-et).

5198. נָטָף **nâṭâph**, *naw-tawf'*; from 5197; a *drop*; spec., an aromatic *gum* (prob. *stacte*):—drop, stacte.

5199. נְטֹפָה **N^{e}ṭôphâh**, *net-o-faw'*; from 5197; *distillation*; *Netophah*, a place in Pal.:—Netophah.

5200. נְטֹפָתִי **N^{e}ṭôphâthîy**, *net-o-faw-thee'*; patron. from 5199; a *Netophathite*, or inhab. of Netophah:—Netophathite.

5201. נָטַר **nâṭar**, *naw-tar'*; a prim. root; to *guard*; fig., to *cherish* (anger):—bear grudge, keep (-er), reserve.

5202. נְטַר **n^{e}ṭar** (Chald.), *net-ar'*; corresp. to 5201; to *retain*:—keep.

5203. נָטַשׁ **nâṭash**, *naw-tash'*; a prim. root; prop. to *pound*, i.e. *smite*; by impl. (as if beating out, and thus expanding) to *disperse*; also, to *thrust* off, down, out or upon (includ. *reject*, *let alone*, *permit*, *remit*, etc.):—cast off, drawn, let fall, forsake, join [battle], leave (off), lie still, loose, spread (self) abroad, stretch out, suffer.

5204. נִי **nîy**, *nee*; a doubtful word; appar. from 5091; *lamentation*:—wailing.

5205. נִיד **nîyd**, *need*; from 5110; *motion* (of the lips in speech):—moving.

5206. נִידָה **nîydâh**, *nee-daw'*; fem. of 5205; *removal*, i.e. exile:—removed.

5207. נִיחוֹחַ **nîychôwach**, *nee-kho'-akh*; or

נִיחֹחַ **nîychôach**, *nee-kho'-akh*; from 5117; prop. *restful*, i.e. *pleasant*; abstr. *delight*:—sweet (odour).

5208. נִיחוֹחַ **nîychôwach** (Chald.), *nee-kho'-akh*; or (shorter)

נִיחֹחַ **nîychôach** (Chald.), *nee-kho'-akh*; corresp. to 5207; *pleasure*:—sweet odour (savour).

5209. נִין **nîyn**, *neen*; from 5125; *progeny*:—son.

5210. נִינְוֵה **Nîyn^{e}vêh**, *nee-nev-ay'*; of for. or.; *Nineveh*, the capital of Assyria:—Nineveh.

5211. נִיס **nîyç**, *neece*; from 5127; *fugitive*:—that fleeth.

5212. נִיסָן **Nîyçân**, *nee-sawn'*; prob. of for. or.; *Nisan*, the first month of the Jewish sacred year:—Nisan.

5213. נִיצוֹץ **nîytsôwts**, *nee-tsotes'*; from 5340; a *spark*:—spark.

5214. נִיר **nîyr**, *neer*; a root prob. ident. with that of 5216, through the idea of the *gleam* of a fresh furrow; to *till* the soil:—break up.

5215. נִיר **nîyr**, *neer*; or

נִר **nîr**, *neer*; from 5214; prop. *ploughing*, i.e. (concr.) freshly *ploughed* land:—fallow ground, ploughing, tillage.

5216. נִיר **nîyr**, *neer*; or

נִר **nîr**, *neer*; also

נֵיר **nêyr**, *nare*; or

נֵר **nêr**, *nare*; or (fem.)

נֵרָה **nêrâh**, *nay-raw'*; from a prim. root [see 5214; 5135] prop. mean. to *glisten*; a *lamp* (i.e. the burner) or *light* (lit. or fig.):—candle, lamp, light.

5217. נָכָא **nâkâ'**, *naw-kaw'*; a prim. root; to *smite*, i.e. *drive away*:—be viler.

5218. נָכֵא **nâkê'**, *naw-kay'*; or

נָכָא **nâkâ'**, *naw-kaw'*; from 5217; *smitten*, i.e. (fig.) *afflicted*:—broken, stricken, wounded.

5219. נְכֹאת **n^{e}kô'th**, *nek-ohth'*; from 5218; prop. a *smiting*, i.e. (concr.) an aromatic *gum* [perh. *styrax*] (as *powdered*):—spicery (-ces).

5220. נֶכֶד **neked**, *neh'-ked*; from an unused root mean. to *propagate*; *offspring*:—nephew, son's son.

5221. נָכָה **nâkâh**, *naw-kaw'*; a prim. root; to *strike* (lightly or severely, lit. or fig.):—beat, cast forth, clap, give [wounds], × go forward, × indeed, kill, make [slaughter], murderer, punish, slaughter, slay (-er, -ing), smite (-r, -ing), strike, be stricken, (give) stripes, × surely, wound.

5222. נֵכֶה **nêkeh**, *nay-keh'*; from 5221; a *smiter*, i.e. (fig.) *traducer*:—abject.

5223. נָכֶה **nâkeh**, *naw-keh'*; *smitten*, i.e. (lit.) maimed, or (fig.) dejected:—contrite, lame.

5224. נְכוֹ **N^{e}kôw**, *nek-o'*; prob. of Eg. or.; *Neko* an Eg. king:—Necho. Comp. 6549.

5225. נָכוֹן **Nâkôwn**, *naw-kone'*; from 3559; *prepared*; *Nakon*, prob. an Isr.:—Nachon.

5226. נֵכַח **nêkach**, *nay'-kakh*; from an unused root mean. to *be straightforward*; prop. the *fore* part; used adv., *opposite*:—before, over against.

5227. נֹכַח **nôkach**, *no'-kakh*; from the same as 5226; prop., the *front* part; used adv. (espec. with prep.), *opposite*, *in front of*, *forward*, *in behalf of*:—(over) against, before, direct [-ly], for, right (on).

5228. נָכֹחַ **nâkôach**, *naw-ko'-akh*; from the same as 5226; *straightforward*, i.e. (fig.), *equitable*, *correct*, or (abstr.), *integrity*:—plain, right, uprightness.

5229. נְכֹחָה **n^{e}kôchâh**, *nek-o-khaw'*; fem. of 5228; prop. *straightforwardness*, i.e. (fig.) *integrity*, or (concr.) *a truth*:—equity, right (thing), uprightness.

5230. נָכַל **nâkal**, *naw-kal'*; a prim root; to *defraud*, i.e. *act treacherously*:—beguile, conspire, deceiver, deal subtilly.

5231. נֵכֶל **nêkel**, *nay'-kel*; from 5230; *deceit*:—wile.

5232. נְכַס **n^{e}kaç** (Chald.), *nek-as'*; corresp. to 5233:—goods.

5233. נֶכֶס **nekeç**, *neh'-kes*; from an unused root mean. to *accumulate*; *treasure*:—riches, wealth.

5234. נָכַר **nâkar**, *naw-kar'*; a prim. root; prop. to *scrutinize*, i.e. look intently at; hence (with *recognition* implied), to *acknowledge*, *be acquainted with*, *care for*, *respect*, *revere*, or (with *suspicion* implied), to *disregard*, *ignore*, *be strange* toward, *reject*, *resign*, *dissimulate* (as if ignorant or disowning):—acknowledge, × could, deliver, discern, dissemble, estrange, feign self to be another, know, take knowledge (notice), perceive, regard, (have) respect, behave (make) self strange (-ly).

5235. נֶכֶר **neker**, *neh'-ker*; or

נֹכֶר **nôker**, *no'-ker*; from 5234; something *strange*, i.e. unexpected *calamity*:—strange.

5236. נֵכָר **nêkâr**, *nay-kawr'*; from 5234; *foreign*, or (concr.) a *foreigner*, or (abstr.) *heathendom*:—alien, strange (+ -er).

5237. נָכְרִי **nokrîy**, *nok-ree'*; from 5235 (second form); *strange*, in a variety of degrees and applications (*foreign*, *non-relative*, *adulterous*, *different*, *wonderful*):—alien, foreigner, outlandish, strange (-r, woman).

5238. נְכֹת **n^{e}kôth**, *nek-ōth'*; prob. for 5219; *spicery*, i.e. (gen.) *valuables*:—precious things.

5239. נָלָה **nâlâh**, *naw-law'*; appar. a prim. root; to *complete*:—make an end.

5240. נְמִבְזֶה **n^{e}mibzeh**, *nem-ib-zeh'*; from 959; *despised*:—vile.

5241. נְמוּאֵל **Nᵉmûwʼêl**, *nem-oo-ale'*; appar. for 3223; *Nemuel*, the name of two Isr.:—Nemuel.

5242. נְמוּאֵלִי **Nᵉmûwʼêlîy**, *nem-oo-ay-lee'*; from 5241; a *Nemuelite*, or desc. of Nemuel:—Nemuelite.

5243. נָמַל **nâmal**, *naw-mal'*; a prim. root; to *become clipped* or (spec.) *circumcised*:—(branch to) be cut down (off), circumcise.

5244. נְמָלָה **nᵉmâlâh**, *nem-aw-law'*; fem. from 5243; an *ant* (prob. from its almost *bisected* form):—ant.

5245. נְמַר **nᵉmar** (Chald.), *nem-ar'*; corresp. to 5246:—leopard.

5246 נָמֵר **nâmêr**, *naw-mare'*; from an unused root mean. prop. to *filtrate*, i.e. *be limpid* [comp. 5247 and 5249]; and thus to *spot* or *stain* as if by dripping; a *leopard* (from its stripes):—leopard.

נִמְרֹד **Nimrôd**. See 5248.

5247. נִמְרָה **Nimrâh**, *nim-raw'*; from the same as 5246; *clear* water; *Nimrah*, a place E. of the Jordan:—Nimrah. See also 1039, 5249.

5248. נִמְרוֹד **Nimrôwd**, *nim-rode'*; or

נִמְרֹד **Nimrôd**, *nim-rode'*; prob. of for. or.; *Nimrod*, a son of Cush:—Nimrod.

5249. נִמְרִים **Nimrîym**, *nim-reem'*; plur. of a masc. corresp. to 5247; *clear* waters; *Nimrim*, a place E. of the Jordan:—Nimrim. Comp. 1039.

5250. נִמְשִׁי **Nimshîy**, *nim-shee'*; prob. from 4871; *extricated*; *Nimshi*, the (grand-) father of Jehu:—Nimshi.

5251. נֵס **nêç**, *nace*; from 5264; a *flag*; also a *sail*; by impl. a *flagstaff*; gen. a *signal*; fig. a *token*:—banner, pole, sail, (en-) sign, standard.

5252. נְסִבָּה **nᵉçibbâh**, *nes-ib-baw'*; fem. part. pass. of 5437; prop. an *environment*, i.e. *circumstance* or *turn* of affairs:—cause.

5253. נָסַג **nâçag**, *naw-sag'*; a prim. root; to *retreat*:—departing away, remove, take (hold), turn away.

נְסָה **nᵉçâh**. See 5375.

5254. נָסָה **nâçâh**, *naw-saw'*; a prim. root; to *test*; by impl. to *attempt*:—adventure, assay, prove, tempt, try.

5255. נָסַח **nâçach**, *naw-sakh'*; a prim. root; to *tear* away:—destroy, pluck, root.

5256. נְסַח **nᵉçach** (Chald.), *nes-akh'*; corresp. to 5255:—pull down.

5257. נְסִיךְ **nᵉçîyk**, *nes-eek'*; from 5258; prop. something *poured* out, i.e. a *libation*; also a molten *image*; by impl. a *prince* (as *anointed*):—drink offering, duke, prince (-ipal).

5258. נָסַךְ **nâçak**, *naw-sak'*; a prim. root; to *pour* out, espec. a libation, or to *cast* (metal); by anal. to *anoint* a king:—cover, melt, offer, (cause to) pour (out), set (up).

5259. נָסַךְ **nâçak**, *naw-sak'*; a prim. root [prob. identical with 5258 through the idea of fusion]; to *interweave*, i.e. (fig.) to *overspread*:—that is spread.

5260. נְסַךְ **nᵉçak** (Chald.), *nes-ak'*; corresp. to 5258; to *pour* out a libation:—offer.

5261. נְסַךְ **nᵉçak** (Chald.), *nes-ak'*; corresp. to 5262; a *libation*:—drink offering.

5262. נֶסֶךְ **neçek**, *neh'-sek*; or

נֵסֶךְ **nêcek**, *nay'-sek*; from 5258; a *libation*; also a *cast idol*:—cover, drink offering, molten image.

נִסְמָן **niçmân**. See 5567.

5263. נָסַס **nâçac**, *naw-sas'*; a prim. root; to *wane*, i.e. *be sick*.

5264. נָסַס **nâçaç**, *naw-sas'*; a prim. root; to *gleam* from afar, i.e. to *be conspicuous* as a signal; or rather perh. a denom. from 5251 [and ident. with 5263, through the idea of a flag as *fluttering* in the wind]; to *raise a beacon*:—lift up as an ensign, standard bearer.

5265. נָסַע **nâçaʻ**, *naw-sah'*; a prim. root; prop. to *pull* up, espec. the tent-pins, i.e. *start* on a journey:—cause to blow, bring, get, (make to) go (away, forth, forward, onward, out), (take) journey, march, remove, set aside (forward), × still, be on his (go their) way.

5266. נָסַק **nâçaq**, *naw-sak'*; a prim. root; to *go* up:—ascend.

5267. נְסַק **nᵉçaq** (Chald.), *nes-ak'*; corresp. to 5266:—take up.

5268. נִסְרֹךְ **Niçrôk**, *nis-roke'*; of for. or.; *Nisrok*, a Bab. idol:—Nisroch.

5269. נֵעָה **Nêʻâh**, *nay-aw'*; from 5128; *motion*; *Neäh*, a place in Pal.:—Neah.

5270. נֹעָה **Nôʻâh**, *no-aw'*; from 5128; *movement*; *Noäh*, an Israelitess:—Noah.

5271. נָעוּר **nâʻûwr**, *naw-oor'*; or

נָעֻר **nâʻûr**, *naw-oor'*; and (fem.)

נְעֻרָה **nᵉʻûrâh**, *neh-oo-raw'*; prop. pass. part. from 5288 as denom.; (only in plur. collect. or emphat.) *youth*, the state (*juvenility*) or the persons (*young* people):—childhood, youth.

5272. נְעִיאֵל **Nᵉʻîyʼêl**, *neh-ee-ale'*; from 5128 and 410; *moved of God*; *Neïel*, a place in Pal.:—Neiel.

5273. נָעִים **nâʻîym**, *naw-eem'*; from 5276; *delightful* (obj. or subj., lit. or fig.):—pleasant (-ure), sweet.

5274. נָעַל **nâʻal**, *naw-al'*; a prim. root; prop. to *fasten* up, i.e. with a bar or cord; hence (denom. from 5275), to *sandal*, i.e. furnish with slippers:—bolt, inclose, lock, shod, shut up.

5275. נַעַל **naʻal**, *neh'-al*; or (fem.)

נַעֲלָה **naʻălâh**, *nah-al-aw'*; from 5274; prop. a sandal *tongue*; by extens. a *sandal* or slipper (sometimes as a symbol of occupancy, a refusal to marry, or of something valueless):—dryshod, (pair of) shoe ([-latchet], -s).

5276. נָעֵם **nâʻêm**, *naw-ame'*; a prim. root; to *be agreeable* (lit. or fig.):—pass in beauty, be delight, be pleasant, be sweet.

5277. נַעַם **Naʻam**, *nah'-am*; from 5276; *pleasure*; *Naam*, an Isr.:—Naam.

5278. נֹעַם **noʻam**, *no'-am*; from 5276; *agreeableness*, i.e. *delight*, *suitableness*, *splendor* or *grace*:—beauty, pleasant (-ness).

5279. נַעֲמָה **Naʻămâh**, *nah-am-aw'*; fem. of 5277; *pleasantness*; *Naamah*, the name of an antediluvian woman, of an Ammonitess, and of a place in Pal.:—Naamah.

5280. נַעֲמִי **Naʻămîy**, *nah-am-ee'*; patron. from 5283; a *Naamanite*, or desc. of Naaman (collect.):—Naamites.

5281. נָעֳמִי **Noʻŏmîy**, *nŏ-om-ee'*; from 5278; *pleasant*; *Noömi*, an Israelitess:—Naomi.

5282. נַעֲמָן **naʻămân**, *nah-am-awn'*; from 5276; *pleasantness* (plur. as concr.):—pleasant.

5283. נַעֲמָן **Naʻămân**, *nah-am-awn'*; the same as 5282; *Naaman*, the name of an Isr. and of a Damascene:—Naaman.

5284. נַעֲמָתִי **Naʻămâthîy**, *nah-am-aw-thee'*; patrial from a place corresp. in name (but not ident.) with 5279; a *Naamathite*, or inhab. of Naamah:—Naamathite.

5285. נַעֲצוּץ **naʻătsûwts**, *nah-ats-oots'*; from an unused root mean. to *prick*; prob. a *brier*; by impl. a *thicket* of thorny bushes:—thorn.

5286. נָעַר **nâʻar**, *naw-ar'*; a prim. root; to *growl*:—yell.

5287. נָעַר **nâʻar**, *naw-ar'*; a prim. root [prob. ident. with 5286, through the idea of the *rustling* of mane, which usually accompanies the lion's roar]; to *tumble* about:—shake (off, out, self), overthrow, toss up and down.

5288. נַעַר **naʻar**, *nah'-ar*; from 5287; (concr.) a *boy* (as active), from the age of infancy to adolescence; by impl. a *servant*; also (by interch. of sex), a *girl* (of similar latitude in age):—babe, boy, child, damsel [*from the marg.*], lad, servant, young (man).

5289. נַעַר **naʻar**, *nah'-ar*; from 5287 in its der. sense of *tossing* about; a *wanderer*:—young one.

5290. נֹעַר **nôʻar**, *no'-ar*; from 5287; (abstr.) *boyhood* [comp. 5288]:—child, youth.

נָעֻר **nâʻûr**. See 5271.

5291. נַעֲרָה **naʻărâh**, *nah-ar-aw'*; fem. of 5288; a *girl* (from infancy to adolescence):—damsel, maid (-en), young (woman).

5292. נַעֲרָה **Naʻărâh**, *nah-ar-aw'*; the same as 5291; *Naarah*, the name of an Israelitess, and of a place in Pal.:—Naarah, Naarath.

נְעֻרָה **nᵉʻûrâh**. See 5271.

5293. נַעֲרַי **Naʻăray**, *nah-ar-ah'ee*; from 5288; *youthful*; *Naarai*, an Isr.:—Naarai.

5294. נְעַרְיָה **Nᵉʻaryâh**, *neh-ar-yaw'*; from 5288 and 3050; *servant of Jah*; *Neärjah*, the name of two Isr.:—Neariah.

5295. נַעֲרָן **Naʻărân**, *nah-ar-awn'*; from 5288; *juvenile*; *Naaran*, a place in Pal.:—Naaran.

5296. נְעֹרֶת **nᵉʻôreth**, *neh-o'-reth*; from 5287; something *shaken* out, i.e. *tow* (as the refuse of flax):—tow.

נַעֲרָתָה **Naʻărâthâh**. See 5292.

5297. נֹף **Nôph**, *nofe*; a var. of 4644; *Noph*, the capital of Upper Egypt:—Noph.

5298. נֶפֶג **Nepheg**, *neh'-feg*; from an unused root prob. mean. to *spring* forth; a *sprout*; *Nepheg*, the name of two Isr.:—Nepheg.

5299. נָפָה **nâphâh**, *naw-faw'*; from 5130 in the sense of *lifting*; a *height*; also a *sieve*:—border, coast, region, sieve.

5300. נְפוּשְׁסִים **Nᵉphûwshᵉçîym**, *nef-oo-shes-eem'*; for 5304; *Nephushesim*, a Temple-servant:—Nephisesim [*from the marg.*].

5301. נָפַח **nâphach**, *naw-fakh'*; a prim. root; to *puff*, in various applications (lit., to *inflate*, *blow* hard, *scatter*, *kindle*, *expire*; fig., to *disesteem*):—blow, breath, give up, cause to lose [life], seething, snuff.

5302. נֹפַח **Nôphach**, *no'-fakh*; from 5301; a *gust*; *Nophach*, a place in Moab:—Nophah.

5303. נְפִיל **nᵉphîyl**, *nef-eel'*; or

נְפִל **nᵉphil**, *nef-eel'*; from 5307; prop., a *feller*, i.e. a *bully* or *tyrant*:—giant.

5304. נְפִיסִים **Nᵉphîyçîym**, *nef-ee-seem'*; plur. from an unused root mean. to *scatter*; *expansions*; *Nephisim*, a Temple-servant:—Nephusim [*from the marg.*].

5305. נָפִישׁ **Nâphîysh**, *naw-feesh'*; from 5314; *refreshed*; *Naphish*, a son of Ishmael, and his posterity:—Naphish.

5306. נֹפֶךְ **nôphek**, *no'-fek*; from an unused root mean. to *glisten*; *shining*; a gem, prob. the *garnet*:—emerald.

5307. נָפַל **nâphal**, *naw-fal'*; a prim. root; to *fall*, in a great variety of applications (intrans. or causat., lit. or fig.):—be accepted, cast (down, self, [lots], out), cease, die, divide (by lot), (let) fail, (cause to, let, make, ready to) fall (away, down, -en, -ing), fell (-ing), fugitive, have [inheritance], inferior, be judged [*by mistake for* 6419], lay (along), (cause to) lie down, light (down), be (× hast) lost, lying, overthrow, overwhelm, perish, present (-ed, -ing), (make to) rot, slay, smite out, × surely, throw down.

5308. נְפַל **nᵉphal** (Chald.), *nef-al'*; corresp. to 5307:—fall (down), have occasion.

5309. נֶפֶל **nephel**, *neh'-fel*; or

נֵפֶל **nêphel**, *nay'-fel*; from 5307; something *fallen*, i.e. an *abortion*:—untimely birth.

נְפִל **nᵉphîl**. See 5303.

5310. נָפַץ **nâphats**, *naw-fats'*; a prim. root; to *dash* to pieces, or *scatter*:—be beaten in sunder, break (in pieces), broken, dash (in pieces), cause to be discharged, dispersed, be overspread, scatter.

5311. נֶפֶץ **nephets**, *neh'-fets*; from 5310; a *storm* (as dispersing):—scattering.

5312. נְפַק **nᵉphaq** (Chald.), *nef-ak'*; a prim. root; to *issue*; causat., to *bring out*:—come (go, take) forth (out).

5313. נִפְקָא **niphqâ'** (Chald.), *nif-kaw'*; from 5312; an *outgo*, i.e. expense:—expense.

5314. נָפַשׁ **nâphash**, *naw-fash'*; a prim. root; to *breathe;* pass., to *be breathed* upon, i.e. (fig.) *refreshed* (as if by a current of air):—(be) refresh selves (-ed).

5315. נֶפֶשׁ **nephesh**, *neh'-fesh*; from 5314; prop. a *breathing* creature, i.e. *animal* or (abstr.) *vitality;* used very widely in a lit., accommodated or fig. sense (bodily or mental):—any, appetite, beast, body, breath, creature, × dead (-ly), desire, × [dis-] contented, × fish, ghost, + greedy, he, heart (-y), (hath, × jeopardy of) life (× in jeopardy), lust, man, me, mind, mortally, one, own, person, pleasure, (her-, him-, my-, thy-) self, them (your) -selves, + slay, soul, + tablet, they, thing, (× she) will, × would have it.

5316. נֶפֶת **nepheth**, *neh'-feth;* for 5299; a *height:*—country.

5317. נֹפֶת **nôpheth**, *no'-feth;* from 5130 in the sense of *shaking* to pieces; a *dripping* i.e. of *honey* (from the comb):—honeycomb.

5318. נֶפְתּוֹחַ **Nephtôwach**, *nef-to'-akh;* from 6605; *opened*, i.e. a *spring; Nephtoäch*, a place in Pal.:—Neptoah.

5319. נַפְתּוּל **naphtûwl**, *naf-tool';* from 6617; prop. *wrestled;* but used (in the plur.) trans., a *struggle:*—wrestling.

5320. נַפְתֻּחִים **Naphtûchîym**, *naf-too-kheem;* plur. of for. or.; *Naphtuchim*, an Eg. tribe:—Naptuhim.

5321. נַפְתָּלִי **Naphtâlîy**, *naf-taw-lee';* from 6617; *my wrestling; Naphtali*, a son of Jacob, with the tribe descended from him, and its territory:—Naphtali.

5322. נֵץ **nêts**, *nayts;* from 5340; a *flower* (from its *brilliancy*); also a *hawk* (from its *flashing* speed):—blossom, hawk.

5323. נָצָא **nâtsâ'**, *naw-tsaw';* a prim. root; to *go away:*—flee.

5324. נָצַב **nâtsab**, *naw-tsab';* a prim. root; to *station*, in various applications (lit. or fig.):—appointed, deputy, erect, establish, × Huzzah [*by mistake for a prop. name*], lay, officer, pillar, present, rear up, set (over, up), settle, sharpen, stablish, (make to) stand (-ing, still, up, upright), best state.

נְצִב **nᵉtsib**. See 5333.

5325. נִצָּב **nitstsâb**, *nits-tsawb';* pass. part. of 5324; *fixed*, i.e. a *handle:*—haft.

5326. נִצְבָּה **nitsbâh** (Chald.), *nits-baw';* from a root corresp. to 5324; *fixedness*, i.e. *firmness:*—strength.

5327. נָצָה **nâtsâh**, *naw-tsaw';* a prim. root; prop. to *go forth*, i.e. (by impl.) to *be expelled*, and (consequently) *desolate;* causat. to *lay waste;* also (spec.), to *quarrel:*—be laid waste, ruinous, strive (together).

נֹצָה **nôtsâh**. See 5133.

5328. נִצָּה **nitstsâh**, *nits-tsaw';* fem. of 5322; a *blossom:*—flower.

נְצוּרָה **nᵉtsûwrâh**. See 5341.

5329. נָצַח **nâtsach**, *naw-tsakh';* a prim. root; prop. to *glitter* from afar, i.e. to be *eminent* (as a superintendent, espec. of the Temple services and its music); also (as denom. from 5331), to *be permanent:*—excel, chief musician (singer), oversee (-r), set forward.

5330. נְצַח **nᵉtsach** (Chald.), *nets-akh';* corresp. to 5329; to *become chief:*—be preferred.

5331. נֶצַח **netsach**, *neh'-tsakh;* or

נֵצַח **nêtsach**, *nay'-tsakh;* from 5329; prop. a *goal*, i.e. the bright object at a distance travelled towards; hence (fig.), *splendor*, or (subj.) *truthfulness*, or (obj.) *confidence;* but usually (adv.), *continually* (i.e. to the most distant point of view):—alway (-s), constantly, end, (+ n-) ever (more), perpetual, strength, victory.

5332. נֵצַח **Nêtsach**, *nay'-tsakh;* prob. ident. with 5331, through the idea of *brilliancy* of color; *juice* of the grape (as blood red):—blood, strength.

5333. נְצִיב **nᵉtsîyb**, *nets-eeb';* or

נְצִב **nᵉtsib**, *nets-eeb';* from 5324; something *stationary*, i.e. a *prefect*, a military *post*, a *statue:*—garrison, officer, pillar.

5334. נְצִיב **Nᵉtsîyb**, *nets-eeb';* the same as 5333; *station; Netsib*, a place in Pal.:—Nezib.

5335. נְצִיחַ **nᵉtsîyach**, *nets-ee'-akh;* from 5329; *conspicuous; Netsiach*, a Temple servant:—Neziah.

5336. נָצִיר° **nâtsîyr**, *naw-tsere';* from 5341; prop. *conservative;* but used pass., *delivered:*—preserved.

5337. נָצַל **nâtsal**, *naw-tsal';* a prim. root; to *snatch* away, whether in a good or a bad sense:— × at all, defend, deliver (self), escape, × without fail, part, pluck, preserve, recover, rescue, rid, save, spoil, strip, × surely, take (out).

5338. נְצַל **nᵉtsal** (Chald.), *nets-al';* corresp. to 5337; to *extricate:*—deliver, rescue.

5339. נִצָּן **nitstsân**, *nits-tsawn';* from 5322; a *blossom:*—flower.

5340. נָצַץ **nâtsats**, *naw-tsats';* a prim. root; to *glare*, i.e. *be bright*-colored:—sparkle.

5341. נָצַר **nâtsar**, *naw-tsar';* a prim. root; to *guard*, in a good sense (to *protect, maintain, obey*, etc.) or a bad one (to *conceal*, etc.):—besieged, hidden thing, keep (-er, -ing), monument, observe, preserve (-r), subtil, watcher (-man).

5342. נֵצֶר **nêtser**, *nay'-tser;* from 5341 in the sense of *greenness* as a striking color; a *shoot;* fig., a *descendant:*—branch.

5343. נְקֵא **nᵉqê'** (Chald.), *nek-ay';* from a root corresp. to 5352; *clean:*—pure.

5344. נָקַב **nâqab**, *naw-kab';* a prim. root; to *puncture*, lit. (to *perforate*, with more or less violence) or fig. (to *specify, designate, libel*):—appoint, blaspheme, bore, curse, express, with holes, name, pierce, strike through.

5345. נֶקֶב **neqeb**, *neh'-keb;* a *bezel* (for a gem):—pipe.

5346. נֶקֶב **Neqeb**, *neh'-keb;* the same as 5345; *dell; Nekeb*, a place in Pal.:—Nekeb.

5347. נְקֵבָה **nᵉqêbâh**, *nek-ay-baw';* from 5344; *female* (from the sexual form):—female, woman.

5348. נָקֹד **nâqôd**, *naw-kode';* from an unused root mean. to *mark* (by *puncturing* or *branding*); *spotted:*—speckled.

5349. נֹקֵד **nôqêd**, *no-kade';* act. part. from the same as 5348; a *spotter* (of sheep or cattle), i.e. the owner or tender (who thus marks them):—herdman, sheepmaster.

5350. נִקֻּד **niqqud**, *nik-kood';* from the same as 5348; a *crumb* (as *broken* to spots); also a *biscuit* (as *pricked*):—cracknel, mouldy.

5351. נְקֻדָּה **nᵉquddâh**, *nek ood-daw';* fem. of 5348; a *boss:*—stud.

5352. נָקָה **nâqâh**, *naw-kaw';* a prim. root; to *be* (or *make*) *clean* (lit. or fig.); by impl. (in an adverse sense) to *be bare*, i.e. *extirpated:*—acquit × at all, × altogether, be blameless, cleanse, (be) clear (-ing), cut off, be desolate, be free, be (hold) guiltless, be (hold) innocent, × by no means, be quit, be (leave) unpunished, × utterly, × wholly.

5353. נְקוֹדָא **Nᵉqôwdâ'**, *nek-o-daw';* fem. of 5348 (in the fig. sense of *marked*); *distinction; Nekoda*, a Temple-servant:—Nekoda.

5354. נָקַט **nâqat**, *naw-kat';* a prim. root; to *loathe:*—weary.

5355. נָקִי **nâqîy**, *naw-kee';* or

נָקִיא **nâqîy'** (Joel 4 : 19; Jonah 1 : 14), *naw-kee';* from 5352; *innocent:*—blameless, clean, clear, exempted, free, guiltless, innocent, quit.

5356. נִקָּיוֹן **niqqâyôwn**, *nik-kaw-yone';* or

נִקָּיֹן **niqqâyôn**, *nik-kaw-yone';* from 5352; *clearness* (lit. or fig.):—cleanness, innocency.

5357. נָקִיק **nâqîyq**, *naw-keek';* from an unused root mean. to *bore;* a *cleft:*—hole.

5358. נָקַם **nâqam**, *naw-kam';* a prim. root; to *grudge*, i.e. *avenge* or *punish:*—avenge (-r, self), punish, revenge (self), × surely, take vengeance.

5359. נָקָם **nâqâm**, *naw-kawm';* from 5358; *revenge:*— + avenged, quarrel, vengeance.

5360. נְקָמָה **nᵉqâmâh**, *nek-aw-maw';* fem. of 5359; *avengement*, whether the act or the passion:— + avenge, revenge (-ing), vengeance.

5361. נָקַע **nâqaʿ**, *naw-kah';* a prim. root; to *feel aversion:*—be alienated.

5362. נָקַף **nâqaph**, *naw-kaf';* a prim. root; to *strike* with more or less violence (*beat, fell, corrode*); by impl. (of attack) to *knock together*, i.e. *surround* or *circulate:*—compass (about, -ing), cut down, destroy, go round (about), inclose, round.

5363. נֹקֶף **nôqeph**, *no'-kef;* from 5362; a *threshing* (of olives):—shaking.

5364. נִקְפָּה **niqpâh**, *nik-paw';* from 5362; prob. a *rope* (as *encircling*):—rent.

5365. נָקַר **nâqar**, *naw-kar';* a prim. root; to *bore* (*penetrate, quarry*):—dig, pick out, pierce, put (thrust) out.

5366. נְקָרָה **nᵉqârâh**, *nek-aw-raw';* from 5365; a *fissure:*—cleft, clift.

5367. נָקַשׁ **nâqash**, *naw-kash';* a prim. root; to *entrap* (with a noose), lit. or fig.:—catch. (lay a) snare.

5368. נְקַשׁ **nᵉqash** (Chald.), *nek-ash';* corresp. to 5367; but used in the sense of 5362; to *knock:*—smote.

נֵר **nêr**, נִיר **nîr**. See 5215, 5216.

5369. נֵר **Nêr**, *nare;* the same as 5216; *lamp; Ner*, an Isr.:—Ner.

5370. נֵרְגַל **Nêrgal**, *nare-gal';* of for. or.; *Nergal*, a Cuthite deity:—Nergal.

5371. נֵרְגַל שַׁרְאֶצֶר **Nêrgal Sharʾetser**, *nare-gal' shar-eh'-tser;* from 5370 and 8272; *Nergal-Sharetser*, the name of two Bab.:—Nergal-sharezer.

5372. נִרְגָּן **nirgân**, *neer-gawn';* from an unused root mean. to *roll* to pieces; a *slanderer:*—talebearer, whisperer.

5373. נֵרְדְּ **nêrd**, *nayrd;* of for. or.; *nard*, an aromatic:—spikenard.

נֵרָה **nêrâh**. See 5216.

5374. נֵרִיָּה **Nêrîyâh**, *nay-ree-yaw';* or

נֵרִיָּהוּ **Nêrîyâhûw**, *nay-ree-yaw'-hoo;* from 5216 and 3050; *light of Jah; Nerijah*, an Isr.:—Neriah.

5375. נָשָׂא **nâsâ'**, *naw-saw';* or

נָסָה **nâçâh** (Psa. 4 : 6 [7]), *naw-saw';* a prim. root; to *lift*, in a great variety of applications, lit. and fig., absol. and rel. (as follows):—accept, advance, arise, (able to, [armour], suffer to) bear (-er, up), bring (forth), burn, carry (away), cast, contain, desire, ease, exact, exalt (self), extol, fetch, forgive, furnish, further, give, go on, help, high, hold up, honourable (+ man), lade, lay, lift (self) up, lofty, marry, magnify, × needs, obtain, pardon, raise (up), receive, regard, respect, set (up), spare, stir up, + swear, take (away, up), × utterly, wear, yield.

5376. נְשָׂא **nᵉsâ'** (Chald.), *nes-aw';* corresp. to 5375:—carry away, make insurrection, take.

5377. נָשָׁא **nâshâ'**, *naw-shaw';* a prim. root; to *lead astray*, i.e. (mentally) to *delude*, or (morally) to *seduce:*—beguile, deceive, × greatly, × utterly.

5378. נָשָׁא **nâshâ'**, *naw-shaw';* a prim. root [perh. ident. with 5377, through the idea of *imposition*]; to *lend* on interest; by impl. to *dun* for debt:—× debt, exact, giver of usury.

נָשִׂא **nâsîʾ**. See 5387.

נְשֻׂאָה **nᵉsûʾâh**. See 5385.

5379. נִשֵּׂאת **nissêʾth**, *nis-sayth';* pass. part. fem. of 5375; something *taken*, i.e. a *present:*—gift.

5380. נָשַׁב **nâshab**, *naw-shab';* a prim. root; to *blow;* by impl. to *disperse:*—(cause to) blow, drive away.

5381. נָשַׂג **nâsag**, *naw-sag'*; a prim. root; to *reach* (lit. or fig.):—ability, be able, attain (unto), (be able to, can) get, lay at, put, reach, remove, wax rich, × surely, (over-) take (hold of, on, upon).

5382. נָשָׁה **nâshâh**, *naw-shaw'*; a prim. root; to *forget;* fig., to *neglect;* causat., to *remit, remove:*—forget, deprive, exact.

5383. נָשָׁה **nâshâh**, *naw-shaw'*; a prim. root [rather ident. with 5382, in the sense of 5378]; to *lend* or (by reciprocity) *borrow* on security or interest:—creditor, exact, extortioner, lend, usurer, lend on (taker of) usury.

5384. נָשֶׁה **nâsheh**, *naw-sheh'*; from 5382, in the sense of *failure; rheumatic* or *crippled* (from the incident to Jacob):—which shrank.

5385. נְשׂוּאָה **nᵉsûw'âh**, *nes-oo-aw'*; or rather נְשֻׂאָה **nᵉsû'âh**, *nes-oo-aw'*; fem. pass. part. of 5375; something *borne*, i.e. a *load:*—carriage.

5386. נְשִׁי **nᵉshîy**, *nesh-ee'*; from 5383; a *debt:*—debt.

5387. נָשִׂיא **nâsîy'**, *naw-see'*; or נָשִׂא **nâsî'**, *naw-see'*; from 5375; prop. an *exalted* one, i.e. a *king* or *sheik;* also a rising *mist:*—captain, chief, cloud, governor, prince, ruler, vapour.

5388. נְשִׁיָּה **nᵉshîyâh**, *nesh-ee-yaw'*; from 5382; *oblivion:*—forgetfulness.

נָשִׁים **nâshîym**. See 802.

5389. נָשִׁין **nâshîyn** (Chald.), *naw-sheen'*; irreg. plur. fem. of 606:—women.

5390. נְשִׁיקָה **nᵉshîyqâh**, *nesh-ee-kaw'*; from 5401; a *kiss:*—kiss.

5391. נָשַׁךְ **nâshak**, *naw-shak'*; a prim. root; to *strike* with a sting (as a serpent); fig., to *oppress* with interest on a loan:—bite, lend upon usury.

5392. נֶשֶׁךְ **neshek**, *neh'-shek;* from 5391; *interest* on a debt:—usury.

5393. נִשְׁכָּה **nishkâh**, *nish-kaw';* for 3957; a *cell:*—chamber.

5394. נָשַׁל **nâshal**, *naw-shal'*; a prim. root; to *pluck* off, i.e. *divest, eject,* or *drop:*—cast (out), drive, loose, put off (out), slip.

5395. נָשַׁם **nâsham**, *naw-sham'*; a prim. root; prop. to *blow* away, i.e. *destroy:*—destroy.

5396. נִשְׁמָא **nishmâ'** (Chald.), *nish-maw'*; corresp. to 5397; vital *breath:*—breath.

5397. נְשָׁמָה **nᵉshâmâh**, *nesh-aw-maw'*; fr. 5395; a *puff*, i.e. *wind*, angry or vital *breath*, divine *inspiration, intellect.* or (concr.) an *animal:*—blast, (that) breath (-eth), inspiration, soul, spirit.

5398. נָשַׁף **nâshaph**, *naw-shaf'*; a prim. root; to *breeze*, i.e. *blow* up fresh (as the wind):—blow.

5399. נֶשֶׁף **nesheph**, *neh'-shef;* from 5398; prop. a *breeze*, i.e. (by impl.) *dusk* (when the evening breeze prevails):—dark, dawning of the day (morning), night, twilight.

5400. נָשַׂק **nâsaq**, *naw-sak'*; a prim. root; to *catch* fire:—burn, kindle.

5401. נָשַׁק **nâshaq**, *naw-shak'*; a prim. root [ident. with 5400, through the idea of *fastening* up; comp. 2388, 2836]; to *kiss*, lit. or fig. (*touch*); also (as a mode of *attachment*), to *equip* with weapons:—armed (men), rule, kiss, that touched.

5402. נֶשֶׁק **nesheq**, *neh'-shek;* or נֵשֶׁק **nêsheq**, *nay'-shek;* from 5401; military *equipment*, i.e. (collect.) *arms* (offensive or defensive), or (concr.) an *arsenal:*—armed men, armour (-y), battle, harness, weapon.

5403. נְשַׁר **nᵉshar** (Chald.), *nesh-ar';* corresp. to 5404; an *eagle:*—eagle.

5404. נֶשֶׁר **nesher**, *neh'-sher;* from an unused root mean. to *lacerate;* the *eagle* (or other large bird of prey):—eagle.

5405. נָשַׁת **nâshath**, *naw-shath'*; a prim. root; prop. to *eliminate*, i.e. (intrans.) to *dry up:*—fail.

נְתִבָה **nᵉthîbâh**. See 5410.

5406. נִשְׁתְּוָן **nishtᵉvân**, *nish-tev-awn';* prob. of Pers. or.; an *epistle:*—letter.

5407. נִשְׁתְּוָן **nishtᵉvân** (Chald.), *nish-tev-awn';* corresp. to 5406:—letter.

נָתוּן° **Nathûwn**. See 5411.

5408. נָתַח **nâthach**, *naw-thakh';* a prim. root; to *dismember:*—cut (in pieces), divide, hew in pieces.

5409. נֵתַח **nêthach**, *nay'-thakh;* from 5408; a *fragment:*—part, piece.

5410. נָתִיב **nâthîyb**, *naw-theeb';* or (fem.) נְתִיבָה **nᵉthîybâh**, *neth-ee-baw';* or נְתִבָה **nᵉthîbâh** (Jer. 6 : 16), *neth-ee-baw';* from an unused root mean. to *tramp;* a (beaten) *track:*—path ([-way]), × travel [-ler], way.

5411. נָתִין **Nâthîyn**, *naw-theen';* or נָתוּן° **Nâthûwn** (Ezra 8 : 17), *naw-thoon'* (the prop. form, as pass. part.), from 5414; one *given*, i.e. (in the plur. only) the *Nethinim*, or Temple-servants (as *given* up to that duty):—Nethinims.

5412. נְתִין **Nᵉthîyn** (Chald.), *netheen';* corresp. to 5411:—Nethinims.

5413. נָתַךְ **nâthak**, *naw-thak';* a prim. root; to *flow* forth (lit. or fig.); by impl. to *liquefy:*—drop, gather (together), melt, pour (forth, out).

5414. נָתַן **nâthan**, *naw-than';* a prim. root; to *give*, used with great latitude of application (*put, make*, etc.):—add, apply, appoint, ascribe, assign, × avenge, × be ([healed]), bestow, bring (forth, hither), cast, cause, charge, come, commit consider, count, + cry, deliver (up), direct, distribute do, × doubtless, × without fail, fasten, frame, × get, give (forth, over, up), grant, hang (up), × have, × indeed, lay (unto charge, up), (give) leave, lend, let (out), + lie, lift up, make, + O that, occupy, offer, ordain, pay, perform, place, pour, print, × pull, put (forth), recompense, render, requite, restore, send (out), set (forth), shew, shoot forth (up). + sing, + slander, strike, [sub-] mit, suffer, × surely, × take, thrust, trade, turn, utter, + weep, × willingly, + withdraw, + would (to) God, yield.

5415. נְתַן **nᵉthan** (Chald.), *neth-an';* corresp. to 5414; *give:*—bestow, give, pay.

5416. נָתָן **Nâthân**, *naw-thawn';* from 5414; *given; Nathan*, the name of five Isr.:—Nathan.

5417. נְתַנְאֵל **Nᵉthanê'l**, *neth-an-ale';* from 5414 and 410; *given of God; Nethanel*, the name of ten Isr.:—Nethaneel.

5418. נְתַנְיָה **Nᵉthanyâh**, *neth-an-yaw';* or נְתַנְיָהוּ **Nᵉthanyâhûw**, *neth-an-yaw'-hoo;* from 5414 and 3050; *given of Jah; Nethanjah*, the name of four Isr.:—Nethaniah.

5419. נְתַן־מֶלֶךְ **Nᵉthan-Melek**, *neth-an' meh'-lek;* from 5414 and 4428; *given of* (the) *king; Nethan-Melek*, an Isr.:—Nathan-melech.

5420. נָתַס **nâthaç**, *naw-thas';* a prim. root; to *tear* up:—mar.

5421. נָתַע **nâtha'**, *naw-thah';* for 5422; to *tear* out:—break.

5422. נָתַץ **nâthats**, *naw-thats';* a prim. root; to *tear* down:—beat down, break down (out), cast down, destroy, overthrow, pull down, throw down.

5423. נָתַק **nâthaq**, *naw-thak';* a prim. root; to *tear* off:—break (off), burst, draw (away), lift up, pluck (away, off), pull (out), root out.

5424. נֶתֶק **netheq**, *neh'-thek;* from 5423; *scurf:*—(dry) scall.

5425. נָתַר **nâthar**, *naw-thar';* a prim. root; to *jump*, i.e. *be* violently *agitated;* causat., to *terrify, shake* off, *untie:*—drive asunder, leap, (let) loose, × make, move, undo.

5426. נְתַר **nᵉthar** (Chald.), *neth-ar';* corresp. to 5425:—shake off.

5427. נֶתֶר **nether**, *neh'-ther;* from 5425; mineral *potash* (so called from *effervescing* with acid):—nitre.

5428. נָתַשׁ **nâthash**, *naw-thash';* a prim. root; to *tear* away:—destroy, forsake, pluck (out, up, by the roots), pull up, root out (up), × utterly.

ס

5429. סְאָה **çᵉ'âh**, *seh-aw';* from an unused root mean. to *define;* a *seäh*, or certain measure (as *determinative*) for grain:—measure.

5430. סְאוֹן **çᵉ'ôwn**, *seh-own';* from 5431; perh. a military *boot* (as a protection from *mud*):—battle.

5431. סָאַן **çâ'an**, *saw-an';* a prim. root; to *be miry;* used only as denom. from 5430; to *shoe*, i.e. (act. part.) a *soldier* shod:—warrior.

5432. סַאסְּאָה° **ça'çᵉ'âh**, *sah-seh-aw';* for 5429; *measurement*, i.e. *moderation:*—measure.

5433. סָבָא **çâbâ'**, *saw-baw';* a prim. root; to *quaff* to satiety, i.e. *become tipsy:*—drunkard, fill self, Sabean, [wine-] bibber.

5434. סְבָא **Çᵉbâ'**, *seb-aw';* of for. or.; *Seba*, a son of Cush, and the country settled by him:—Seba.

5435. סֹבֶא **çôbe'**, *so'-beh;* from 5433; *potation*, concr. (*wine*), or abstr. (*carousal*):—drink, drunken, wine.

5436. סְבָאִי **Çᵉbâ'îy**, *seb-aw-ee';* patrial from 5434; a *Sebaite*, or inhab. of Seba:—Sabean.

5437. סָבַב **çâbab**, *saw-bab';* a prim. root; to *revolve, surround* or *border;* used in various applications, lit. and fig. (as follows):—bring, cast, fetch, lead, make, walk, × whirl, × round about, be about on every side, apply, avoid, beset (about), besiege, bring again, carry (about), change, cause to come about, × circuit, (fetch a) compass (about, round), drive, environ, × on every side, beset (close, come, compass, go, stand) round about, remove, return, set, sit down, turn (self) (about, aside, away, back).

5438. סִבָּה **çibbâh**, *sib-baw';* from 5437; a (providential) *turn* (of affairs):—cause.

5439. סָבִיב **çâbîyb**, *saw-beeb';* or (fem.) סְבִיבָה **çᵉbîybâh**, *seb-ee-baw';* from 5437; (as noun) a *circle, neighbor*, or *environs;* but chiefly (as adv., with or without prep.) *around:*—(place, round) about, circuit, compass, on every side.

5440. סָבַךְ **çâbak**, *saw-bak';* a prim. root; to *entwine:*—fold together, wrap.

5441. סֹבֶךְ **çôbek**, *so'-bek;* from 5440; a *copse:*—thicket.

5442. סְבָךְ **çᵉbâk**, *seb-awk';* from 5440; a *copse:*—thick (-et).

5443. סַבְּכָא **çabbᵉkâ'** (Chald.), *sab-bek-aw';* or שַׂבְּכָא **sabbᵉkâ'** (Chald.), *sab-bek-aw';* from a root corresp. to 5440; a *lyre:*—sackbut.

5444. סִבְּכַי **Çibbᵉkay**, *sib-bek-ah'ee;* from 5440; *copse-like; Sibbecai*, an Isr.:—Sibbecai, Sibbechai.

5445. סָבַל **çâbal**, *saw-bal';* a prim. root; to *carry* (lit. or fig.), or (reflex.) *be burdensome;* spec. to *be gravid:*—bear, be a burden, carry, strong to labour.

5446. סְבַל **çᵉbal** (Chald.), *seb-al';* corresp. to 5445; to *erect:*—strongly laid.

5447. סֵבֶל **çêbel**, *say'-bel;* from 5445; a *load* (lit. or fig.):—burden, charge.

5448. סֹבֶל **çôbel**, *so'-bel* [only in the form סֻבָּל **çubbâl**, *soob-bawl'*]; from 5445; a *load* (fig.):—burden.

5449. סַבָּל **çabbâl**, *sab-bawl';* from 5445; a *porter:*—(to bear, bearer of) burden (-s).

5450. סְבָלָה **çᵉbâlâh**, *seb-aw-law';* from 5447; *porterage:*—burden.

5451. סִבֹּלֶת **çibbôleth**, *sib-bo'-leth;* for 7641; an *ear* of grain:—Sibboleth.

5452. סְבַר **çᵉbar** (Chald.), *seb-ar';* a prim. root; to *bear in mind*, i.e. *hope:*—think.

5453. סִבְרַיִם **Çibrayim**, *sib-rah'-yim;* dual from a root corresp. to 5452; *double hope; Sibrajim*, a place in Syria:—Sibraim.

5454. סַבְתָּא **Çabtâʼ**, *sab-taw'*; or

סַבְתָּה **Çabtâh**, *sab-taw'*; prob. of for. der.; *Sabta* or *Sabtah*, the name of a son of Cush, and the country occupied by his posterity:—Sabta, Sabtah.

5455. סַבְתְּכָא **Çabtᵉkâʼ**, *sab-tek-aw'*; prob. of for. der.; *Sabteca*, the name of a son of Cush, and the region settled by him:—Sabtecha, Sabtechah.

5456. סָגַד **çâgad**, *saw-gad'*; a prim. root; to *prostrate* oneself (in homage):—fall down.

5457. סְגִד **çᵉgîd** (Chald.), *seg-eed'*; corresp. to 5456:—worship.

5458. סְגוֹר **çᵉgôwr**, *seg-ore'*; from 5462; prop. *shut up*, i.e. the *breast* (as inclosing the heart); also *gold* (as generally *shut* up safely):—caul, gold.

5459. סְגֻלָּה **çᵉgullâh**, *seg-ool-law'*; fem. pass. part. of an unused root mean. to *shut up*; *wealth* (as closely *shut* up):—jewel, peculiar (treasure), proper good, special.

5460. סְגַן **çᵉgan** (Chald.), *seg-an'*; corresp. to 5461:—governor.

5461. סָגָן **çâgân**, *saw-gawn'*; from an unused root mean. to *superintend*; a *præfect* of a province:—prince, ruler.

5462. סָגַר **çâgar**, *saw-gar'*; a prim. root; to *shut* up; fig. to *surrender*:—close up, deliver (up), give over (up), inclose, × pure, repair, shut (in, self, out, up, up together), stop, × straitly.

5463. סְגַר **çᵉgar** (Chald.), *seg-ar'*; corresp. to 5462:—shut up.

5464. סַגְרִיד **çagrîyd**, *sag-reed'*; prob. from 5462 in the sense of *sweeping* away; a pouring rain:—very rainy.

5465. סַד **çad**, *sad*; from an unused root mean. to *estop*; the *stocks*:—stocks.

5466. סָדִין **çâdîyn**, *saw-deen'*; from an unused root mean. to *envelop*; a *wrapper*, i.e. *shirt*:—fine linen, sheet.

5467. סְדֹם **Çᵉdôm**, *sed-ome'*; from an unused root mean. to *scorch*; *burnt* (i.e. *volcanic* or *bituminous*) district; *Sedom*, a place near the Dead Sea:—Sodom.

5468. סֶדֶר **çeder**, *seh'-der*; from an unused root mean. to *arrange*; *order*:—order.

5469. סַהַר **çahar**, *sah'-har*; from an unused root mean. to *be round*; *roundness*:—round.

5470. סֹהַר **çôhar**, *so'-har*; from the same as 5469; a *dungeon* (as *surrounded* by walls):—prison.

5471. סוֹא **Çôwʼ**, *so*; of for. der.; *So*, an Eg. king:—So.

5472. סוּג **çûwg**, *soog*; a prim. root; prop. to *flinch*, i.e. (by impl.) to *go back*, lit. (to *retreat*) or fig. (to *apostatize*):—backslider, drive, go back, turn (away, back).

5473. סוּג **çûwg**, *soog*; a prim. root [prob. rather ident. with 5472 through the idea of *shrinking* from a hedge; comp. 7735]; to *hem* in, i.e. *bind*:—set about.

סוּג° **çûwg**. See 5509.

5474. סוּגַר **çûwgar**, *soo-gar'*; from 5462; an *inclosure*, i.e. *cage* (for an animal):—ward.

5475. סוֹד **çôwd**, *sode*; from 3245; a *session*, i.e. *company* of persons (in close deliberation); by impl. *intimacy*, *consultation*, a *secret*:—assembly, counsel, inward, secret (counsel).

5476. סוֹדִי **Çôwdîy**, *so-dee'*; from 5475; a *confidant*; *Sodi*, an Isr.:—Sodi.

5477. סוּחַ **Çûwach**, *soo'-akh*; from an unused root mean. to *wipe* away; *sweeping*; *Suăch*, an Isr.:—Suah.

5478. סוּחָה **çûwchâh**, *soo-khaw'*; from the same as 5477; something *swept* away, i.e. *filth*:—torn.

סוּט **çûwṭ**. See 7750.

5479. סוֹטַי **Çôwṭay**, *so-tah'ee*; from 7750; *roving*; *Sotai*, one of the Nethinim:—Sotai.

5480. סוּךְ **çûwk**, *sook*; a prim. root; prop. to *smear* over (with oil), i.e. *anoint*:—anoint (self), × at all.

סוֹלְלָה **çôwlᵉlâh**. See 5550.

5481. סוּמְפּוֹנְיָה **çûwmpôwnᵉyâh** (Chald.), *soom-po-neh-yaw'*; or

סוּמְפֹּנְיָה **çûwmpônᵉyâh** (Chald.), *soom-po-neh-yaw'*; or

סִיפֹנְיָא° **çîyphônᵉyâʼ** (Dan. 3:10) (Chald.), *see-fo-neh-yaw'*; of Greek origin (συμφωνία); a *bagpipe* (with a double pipe):—dulcimer.

5482. סְוֵנֵה **Çᵉvênêh**, *sev-ay-nay'* [rather to be written

סְוֵנָה **Çᵉvênâh**, *sev-ay'-naw*; for

סְוֵן **Çᵉvên**, *sev-ane'*; i.e. *to Seven*]; of Eg. der.; *Seven*, a place in Upper Eg.:—Syene.

5483. סוּס **çûwç**, *soos*; or

סֻס **çûç**, *soos*; from an unused root mean. to *skip* (prop. for joy); a *horse* (as leaping); also a *swallow* (from its rapid *flight*):—crane, horse ([-back, -hoof]). Comp. 6571.

5484. סוּסָה **çûwçâh**, *soo-saw'*; fem. of 5483; a *mare*:—company of horses.

5485. סוּסִי **Çûwçîy**, *soo-see'*; from 5483; *horse-like*; *Susi*, an Isr.:—Susi.

5486. סוּף **çûwph**, *soof*; a prim. root; to *snatch* away, i.e. *terminate*:—consume, have an end, perish, × be utterly.

5487. סוּף **çûwph** (Chald.), *soof*; corresp. to 5486; to *come to an end*:—consume, fulfil.

5488. סוּף **çûwph**, *soof*; prob. of Eg. or.; a *reed*, espec. the *papyrus*:—flag, Red [sea], weed. Comp. 5489.

5489. סוּף **Çûwph**, *soof*; for 5488 (by ellipsis of 3220); the *Reed* (*Sea*):—Red sea.

5490. סוֹף **çôwph**, *sofe*; from 5486; a *termination*:—conclusion, end, hinder part.

5491. סוֹף **çôwph** (Chald.), *sofe*; corresp. to 5490:—end.

5492. סוּפָה **çûwphâh**, *soo-faw'*; from 5486; a *hurricane*:—Red Sea, storm, tempest, whirlwind, Red sea.

5493. סוּר **çûwr**, *soor*; or

שׂוּר **sûwr** (Hos. 9:12), *soor*; a prim. root; to *turn* off (lit. or fig.):—be [-head], bring, call back, decline, depart, eschew, get [you], go (aside), × grievous, lay away (by), leave undone, be past, pluck away, put (away, down), rebel, remove (to and fro), revolt, × be sour, take (away, off), turn (aside, away, in), withdraw, be without.

5494. סוּר **çûwr**, *soor*; prob. pass. part. of 5493; *turned* off, i.e. *deteriorated*:—degenerate.

5495. סוּר **Çûwr**, *soor*; the same as 5494; *Sur*, a gate of the Temple:—Sur.

5496. סוּת **çûwth**, *sooth*; perh. denom. from 7898; prop. to *prick*, i.e. (fig.) stimulate; by impl. to *seduce*:—entice, move, persuade, provoke, remove, set on, stir up, take away.

5497. סוּת **çûwth**, *sooth*; prob. from the same root as 4533; *covering*, i.e. *clothing*:—clothes.

5498. סָחַב **çâchab**, *saw-khab'*; a prim. root; to *trail* along:—draw (out), tear.

5499. סְחָבָה **çᵉchâbâh**, *seh-khaw-baw'*; from 5498; a *rag*:—cast clout.

5500. סָחָה **çâchâh**, *saw-khaw'*; a prim. root; to *sweep* away:—scrape.

5501. סְחִי **çᵉchîy**, *seh khee'*; from 5500; *refuse* (as *swept* off):—offscouring.

סָחִישׁ **çâchîysh**. See 7823.

5502. סָחַף **çâchaph**, *saw-khaf'*; a prim. root; to *scrape* off:—sweep (away).

5503. סָחַר **çâchar**, *saw-khar'*; a prim. root; to *travel* round (spec. as a *pedlar*); intens. to *palpitate*:—go about, merchant (-man), occupy with, pant, trade, traffick.

5504. סַחַר **çachar**, *sakh'-ar*; from 5503; *profit* (from trade):—merchandise.

5505. סָחָר **çâchar**, *saw-khar'*; from 5503; an *emporium*; abstr. *profit* (from trade):—mart, merchandise.

5506. סְחֹרָה **çᵉchôrâh**, *sekh-o-raw'*; from 5503; *traffic*:—merchandise.

5507. סֹחֵרָה **çôchêrâh**, *so-khay-raw'*; prop. act. part. fem. of 5503; something *surrounding* the person, i.e. a *shield*:—buckler.

5508. סֹחֶרֶת **çôchereth**, *so-kheh'-reth*; similar to 5507; prob. a (black) *tile* (or *tessara*) for laying borders with:—black marble.

סֵט **çêṭ**. See 7750.

5509. סִיג **çîyg**, *seeg*; or

סוּג° **çûwg** (Ezek. 22:18), *soog*; from 5472 in the sense of *refuse*; *scoria*:—dross.

5510. סִיוָן **Çîyvân**, *see-vawn'*; prob. of Pers. or.; *Sivan*, the third Heb. month:—Sivan.

5511. סִיחוֹן **Çîychôwn**, *see-khone'*; or

סִיחֹן **Çîychôn**, *see-khone'*; from the same as 5477; *tempestuous*; *Sichon*, an Amoritish king:—Sihon.

5512. סִין **Çîyn**, *seen*; of uncert. der.; *Sin*, the name of an Eg. town and (prob.) desert adjoining:—Sin.

5513. סִינִי **Çîynîy**, *see-nee'*; from an otherwise unknown name of a man; a *Sinite*, or descend. of one of the sons of Canaan:—Sinite.

5514. סִינַי **Çîynay**, *see-nah'ee*; of uncert. der.; *Sinai*, a mountain of Arabia:—Sinai.

5515. סִינִים **Çîynîym**, *see-neem'*; plur. of an otherwise unknown name; *Sinim*, a distant Oriental region:—Sinim.

5516. סִיסְרָא **Çîyçᵉrâʼ**, *see-ser-aw'*; of uncert. der.; *Sisera*, the name of a Canaanitish king and of one of the Nethinim:—Sisera.

5517. סִיעָא **Çîyʻâʼ**, *see-ah'*; or

סִיעֲהָא **Çîyʻăhâʼ**, *see-ah-haw'*; from an unused root mean. to *converse*; *congregation*; *Sia*, or *Siaha*, one of the Nethinim:—Sia, Siaha.

סִיפֹנְיָא° **çîyphônᵉyâʼ**. See 5481.

5518. סִיר **çîyr**, *seer*; or (fem.)

סִירָה **çîyrâh**, *see-raw'*; or

סִרָה **çirâh** (Jer. 52:18), *see-raw'*; from a prim. root mean. to *boil* up; a *pot*; also a *thorn* (as springing up rapidly); by impl. a *hook*:—caldron, fishhook, pan, ([wash-]) pot, thorn.

5519. סָךְ **çâk**, *sawk*; from 5526; prop. a *thicket* of men, i.e. a *crowd*:—multitude.

5520. סֹךְ **çôk**, *soke*; from 5526; a *hut* (as of *entwined* boughs); also a *lair*:—covert, den, pavilion, tabernacle.

5521. סֻכָּה **çukkâh**, *sook-kaw'*; fem. of 5520; a *hut* or *lair*:—booth, cottage, covert, pavilion, tabernacle, tent.

5522. סִכּוּת **çikkûwth**, *sik-kooth'*; fem. of 5519; an (idolatrous) *booth*:—tabernacle.

5523. סֻכּוֹת **Çukkôwth**, *sook-kohth'*; or

סֻכֹּת **Çukkôth**, *sook-kohth'*; plur. of 5521; *booths*; *Succoth*, the name of a place in Egypt and of three in Pal.:—Succoth.

5524. סֻכּוֹת בְּנוֹת **Çukkôwth bᵉnôwth**, *sook-kohth' ben-ohth'*; from 5523 and the (irreg.) plur. of 1323; *booths of* (*the*) *daughters*; *brothels*, i.e. idolatrous *tents* for impure purposes:—Succoth-benoth.

5525. סֻכִּי **Çukkîy**, *sook-kee'*; patrial from an unknown name (perh. 5520); a *Sukkite*, or inhab. of some place near Eg. (i.e. *hut-dwellers*):—Sukkiims.

5526. סָכַךְ **çâkak**, *saw-kak'*; or

שָׂכַךְ **sâkak** (Exod. 33:22), *saw-kak'*; a prim. root; prop. to *entwine* as a screen; by impl. to *fence* in, *cover* over, (fig.) *protect*:—cover, defence, defend, hedge in, join together, set, shut up.

5527. סְכָכָה **Çᵉkâkâh**, *sek-aw-kaw'*; from 5526; *inclosure; Secacah*, a place in Pal.:—Secacah.

5528. סָכַל **çâkal**, *saw-kal'*; for 3688; to *be silly*:—do (make, play the, turn into) fool (-ish, -ishly, -ishness).

5529. סֶכֶל **çekel**, *seh'-kel*; from 5528; *silliness*; concr. and collect. *dolts*:—folly.

5530. סָכָל **çâkâl**, *saw-kawl'*; from 5528; *silly*:—fool (-ish), sottish.

5531. סִכְלוּת **çiklûwth**, *sik-looth'*; or

שִׂכְלוּת **siklûwth** (Eccl. 1 : 17), *sik-looth'*; from 5528; *silliness*:—folly, foolishness.

5532. סָכַן **çâkan**, *saw-kan'*; a prim. root; to *be familiar* with; by impl. to *minister* to, *be serviceable* to, to *cherish*, *be customary*:—acquaint (self), be advantage, × ever, (be, [un-]) profit (-able), treasurer, be wont.

5533. סָכַן **çâkan**, *saw-kan'*; prob. a denom. from 7915; prop. *to cut*, i.e. *damage*; also to *grow* (caus. *make*) *poor*:—endanger, impoverish.

5534. סָכַר **çâkar**, *saw-kar'*; a prim. root; to *shut* up; by impl. to *surrender*:—stop, give over. See also 5462; 7936.

5535. סָכַת **çâkath**, *saw-kath'*; a prim. root; to *be silent*; by impl. to *observe* quietly:—take heed.

סֻכֹּת **Çukkôth**. See 5523.

5536. סַל **çal**, *sal*; from 5549; prop. a willow *twig* (as *pendulous*), i.e. an *osier*; but only as woven into a *basket*:—basket.

5537. סָלָא **çâlâ'**, *saw-law'*; a prim. root; to *suspend* in a balance, i.e. *weigh*:—compare.

5538. סִלָּא **Çillâ'**, *sil-law'*; from 5549; an *embankment; Silla*, a place in Jerus.:—Silla.

5539. סָלַד **çâlad**, *saw-lad'*; a prim. root; prob. to *leap* (with joy), i.e. *exult*:—harden self.

5540. סֶלֶד **Çeled**, *seh'-led*; from 5539; *exultation; Seled*, an Isr.:—Seled.

5541. סָלָה **çâlâh**, *saw-law'*; a prim. root; to *hang* up, i.e. *weigh*, or (fig.) *contemn*:—tread down (under foot), value.

5542. סֶלָה **çelâh**, *seh'-law*; from 5541; *suspension* (of music), i.e. *pause*:—Selah.

5543. סַלּוּ **Çallûw**, *sal-loo'*; or

סַלּוּא **Çallûw'**, *sal-loo'*; or

סָלוּא **Çâlûw**, *saw-loo'*; or

סַלַּי **Çallay**, *sal-lah'ee*; from 5541; *weighed*; *Sallu* or *Sallai*, the name of two Isr.:—Sallai, Sallu, Salu.

5544. סִלּוֹן **çillôwn**, *sil-lone'*; or

סַלּוֹן **callôwn**, *sal-lone'*; from 5541; a *prickle* (as if *pendulous*):—brier, thorn.

5545. סָלַח **çâlach**, *saw-lakh'*; a prim. root; to *forgive*:—forgive, pardon, spare.

5546. סַלָּח **callâch**, *sal-lawkh'*; from 5545; *placable*:—ready to forgive.

סַלַּי **Çallay**. See 5543.

5547. סְלִיחָה **çelîychâh**, *sel-ee-khaw'*; from 5545; *pardon*:—forgiveness, pardon.

5548. סַלְכָה **Çalkâh**, *sal-kaw'*; from an unused root mean. to *walk; walking; Salcah*, a place E. of the Jordan:—Salcah, Salchah.

5549. סָלַל **çâlal**, *saw-lal'*; a prim. root; to *mound* up (espec. a turnpike); fig. to *exalt*; reflex. to *oppose* (as by a dam):—cast up, exalt (self), extol, make plain, raise up.

5550. סֹלְלָה **çôlᵉlâh**, *so-lel-aw'*; or

סוֹלְלָה **çôwlᵉlâh**, *so-lel-aw'*; act. part. fem. of 5549, but used pass.; a military *mound*, i.e. *rampart* of besiegers:—bank, mount.

5551. סֻלָּם **çullâm**, *sool-lawm'*; from 5549; a *stair-case*:—ladder.

5552. סַלְסִלָּה **çalçillâh**, *sal-sil-law'*; from 5541; a *twig* (as *pendulous*):—basket.

5553. סֶלַע **çelaʽ**, *seh'-lah*; from an unused root mean. to be *lofty*; a craggy *rock*, lit. or fig. (a *fortress*):—(ragged) rock, stone (-ny), strong hold.

5554. סֶלַע **Çelaʽ**, *seh'-lah*; the same as 5553; *Sela*, the rock-city of Idumæa:—rock, Sela (-h).

5555. סֶלַע הַמַּחְלְקוֹת **Çelaʽ ham-machlᵉqôwth**, *seh'-lah ham-makh-lek-ōth'*; from 5553 and the plur. of 4256 with the art. interposed; *rock of the divisions; Sela-ham-Machlekoth*, a place in Pal.:—Sela-hammalekoth.

5556. סָלְעָם **çolʽâm**, *sol-awm'*; appar. from the same as 5553 in the sense of *crushing* as with a rock, i.e. consuming; a kind of *locust* (from its *destructiveness*):—bald locust.

5557. סָלַף **çâlaph**, *saw-laf'*; a prim. root; prop. to *wrench*, i.e. (fig.) to *subvert*:—overthrow, pervert.

5558. סֶלֶף **çeleph**, *seh'-lef*; from 5557; *distortion*, i.e. (fig.) *viciousness*:—perverseness.

5559. סְלִק **çᵉlîq** (Chald.), *sel-eek'*; a prim. root; to *ascend*:—come (up).

5560. סֹלֶת **çôleth**, *so'-leth*; from an unused root mean. to *strip; flour* (as *chipped* off):—(fine) flour, meal.

5561. סַם **çam**, *sam*; from an unused root mean. to *smell* sweet; an *aroma*:—sweet (spice).

5562. סַמְגַּר נְבוֹ **Çamgar Nᵉbôw**, *sam-gar' neb-o'*; of for. or.; *Samgar-Nebo*, a Bab. general:—Samgar-nebo.

5563. סְמָדַר **çᵉmâdar**, *sem-aw-dar'*; of uncert. der.; a vine *blossom*; used also adv. *abloom*:—tender grape.

5564. סָמַךְ **çâmak**, *saw-mak'*; a prim. root; to *prop* (lit. or fig.); reflex. to *lean* upon or *take hold* of (in a favorable or unfavorable sense):—bear up, establish, (up-) hold, lay, lean, lie hard, put, rest self, set self, stand fast, stay (self), sustain.

5565. סְמַכְיָהוּ **Çᵉmakyâhûw**, *sem-ak-yaw'-hoo*; from 5564 and 3050; *supported of Jah; Semakjah*, an Isr.:—Semachiah.

5566. סֶמֶל **çemel**, *seh'-mel*; or

סֵמֶל **çêmel**, *say'-mel*; from an unused root mean. to *resemble*; a *likeness*:—figure, idol, image.

5567. סָמַן **çâman**, *saw-man'*; a prim. root; to *designate*:—appointed.

5568. סָמַר **çâmar**, *saw-mar'*; a prim. root; to *be erect*, i.e. *bristle* as hair:—stand up, tremble.

5569. סָמָר **çâmâr**, *saw-mawr'*; from 5568; *bristling*, i.e. *shaggy*:—rough.

5570. סְנָאָה **Çᵉnâ'âh**, *sen-aw-aw'*; from an unused root mean. to *prick; thorny; Senaah*, a place in Pal.:—Senaah, Hassenaah [*with the art.*].

סְנֻאָה **çᵉnû'âh**. See 5574.

5571. סַנְבַלַּט **Çanballaṭ**, *san-bal-lat'*; of for. or.; *Sanballat*, a Pers. satrap of Samaria:—Sanballat.

5572. סְנֶה **çᵉneh**, *sen-eh'*; from an unused root mean. to *prick*; a *bramble*:—bush.

5573. סֶנֶה **Çeneh**, *seh'-neh*; the same as 5572; *thorn; Seneh*, a crag in Pal.:—Seneh.

סַנָּה **Çannâh**. See 7158.

5574. סְנוּאָה **Çᵉnûw'âh**, *sen-oo-aw'*; or

סְנֻאָה **Çᵉnû'âh**, *sen-oo-aw'*; from the same as 5570; *pointed*; (used with the art. as a prop. name) *Senuah*, the name of two Isr.:—Hasenuah [*includ. the art.*], Senuah.

5575. סַנְוֵר **çanvêr**, *san-vare'*; of uncert. der.; (in plur.) *blindness*:—blindness.

5576. סַנְחֵרִיב **Çanchêrîyb**, *san-khay-reeb'*; of for. or.; *Sancherib*, an Ass. king:—Sennacherib.

5577. סַנְסִן **çançîn**, *san-seen'*; from an unused root mean. to be *pointed*; a *twig* (as *tapering*):—bough.

5578. סַנְסַנָּה **Çançannâh**, *san-san-naw'*; fem. of a form of 5577; a *bough; Sansannah*, a place in Pal.:—Sansannah.

5579. סְנַפִּיר **çᵉnappîyr**, *sen-ap-peer'*; of uncert. der.; a *fin* (collect.):—fins.

5580. סָס **çâç**, *sawce*; from the same as 5483; a *moth* (from the *agility* of the fly):—moth.

סוּס **çûç**. See 5483.

5581. סִסְמַי **Çiçmay**, *sis-mah'ee*; of uncert. der.; *Sismai*, an Isr.:—Sisamai.

5582. סָעַד **çâʽad**, *saw-ad'*; a prim. root; to *support* (mostly fig.):—comfort, establish, hold up, refresh self, strengthen, be upholden.

5583. סְעַד **çᵉʽad** (Chald.), *seh-ad'*; corresp. to 5582; to *aid*:—helping.

5584. סָעָה **çâʽâh**, *saw-aw'*; a prim. root; to *rush*:—storm.

5585. סָעִיף **çâʽîyph**, *saw-eef'*; from 5586; a *fissure* (of rocks); also a *bough* (as *subdivided*):—(outmost) branch, clift, top.

5586. סָעַף **çâʽaph**, *saw-af'*; a prim. root; prop. to *divide* up; but used only as denom. from 5585, to *disbranch* (a tree):—top.

5587. סָעִף **çâʽiph**, *saw-eef'*; or

שָׂעִף **sâʽiph**, *saw-eef'*; from 5586; *divided* (in mind), i.e. (abstr.) a *sentiment*:—opinion.

5588. סֵעֵף **çêʽêph**, *say-afe'*; from 5586; *divided* (in mind), i.e. (concr.) a *skeptic*:—thought.

5589. סְעַפָּה **çᵉʽappâh**, *seh-ap-paw'*; fem. of 5585; a *twig* or *branch*:—bough. Comp. 5634.

5590. סָעַר **çâʽar**, *saw-ar'*; a prim. root; to *rush* upon; by impl. to *toss* (trans. or intrans., lit. or fig.):—be (toss with) tempest (-uous), be sore troubled, come out as a (drive with the, scatter with a) whirlwind.

5591. סַעַר **çaʽar**, *sah'-ar*; or (fem.)

סְעָרָה **çᵉʽârâh**, *seh-aw-raw'*; from 5590; a *hurricane*:—storm (-y), tempest, whirlwind.

5592. סַף **çaph**, *saf*; from 5605, in its original sense of *containing*; a *vestibule* (as a *limit*); also a *dish* (for holding blood or wine):—bason, bowl, cup, door (post), gate, post, threshold.

5593. סַף **Çaph**, *saf*; the same as 5592; *Saph*, a Philistine:—Saph. Comp. 5598.

5594. סָפַד **çâphad**, *saw-fad'*; a prim. root; prop. to *tear* the hair and *beat* the breasts (as Orientals do in grief); gen. to *lament*; by impl. to *wail*:—lament, mourn (-er), wail.

5595. סָפָה **çâphâh**, *saw-faw'*; a prim. root; prop. to *scrape* (lit. to *shave*; but usually fig.) together (i.e. to *accumulate* or *increase*) or away (i.e. to *scatter*, *remove* or *ruin*; intrans. to *perish*):—add, augment, consume, destroy, heap, join, perish, put.

5596. סָפַח **çâphach**, *saw-fakh'*; or

שָׂפַח **sâphach** (Isa. 3 : 17), *saw-fakh'*; a prim. root; prop. to *scrape* out, but in certain peculiar senses (of *removal* or *association*):—abiding, gather together, cleave, put, smite with a scab.

5597. סַפַּחַת **çappachath**, *sap-pakh'-ath*; from 5596; the *mange* (as making the hair fall off):—scab.

5598. סִפַּי **Çippay**, *sip-pah'ee*; from 5592; *basonlike; Sippai*, a Philistine:—Sippai. Comp. 5593.

5599. סָפִיחַ **çâphîyach**, *saw-fee'-akh*; from 5596; something (spontaneously) *falling* off, i.e. a *self-sown* crop; fig. a *freshet*:—(such) things as (which) grow (of themselves), which groweth of its own accord (itself).

5600. סְפִינָה **çᵉphîynâh**, *sef-ee-naw'*; from 5603; a (sea-going) *vessel* (as *ceiled* with a deck):—ship.

5601. סַפִּיר **cappîyr**, *sap-peer'*; from 5608; a *gem* (perh. as used for *scratching* other substances), prob. the *sapphire*:—sapphire.

5602. סֵפֶל **çêphel**, *say'-fel*; from an unused root mean. to *depress*; a *basin* (as *deepened* out):—bowl, dish.

5603. סָפַן çâphan, *saw-fan'*; a prim. root; to *hide* by covering; spec. to *roof* (pass. part. as noun, a *roof*) or *wainscot*; fig. to *reserve*:—cieled, cover, seated.

5604. סִפֻּן çippûn, *sip-poon'*; from 5603; a *wainscot*:—cieling.

5605. סָפַף çâphaph, *saw-faf'*; a prim. root; prop. to *snatch* away, i.e. *terminate*; but used only as denom. from 5592 (in the sense of a *vestibule*), to *wait at* the *threshold*:—be a doorkeeper.

5606. סָפַק çâphaq, *saw-fak'*; or

שָׂפַק sâphaq (1 Kings 20 : 10; Job 27 : 23; Isa. 2 : 6), *saw-fak'*; a prim. root; to *clap* the hands (in token of compact, derision, grief, indignation or punishment); by impl. of satisfaction, to *be enough*; by impl. of excess, to *vomit*:—clap, smite, strike, suffice, wallow.

5607. סֵפֶק çêpheq, *say'-fek*; or

שֶׂפֶק sepheq (Job 20 : 22; 36 : 18), *seh'-fek*; from 5606; *chastisement*; also *satiety*:—stroke, sufficiency.

5608. סָפַר çâphar, *saw-far'*; a prim. root; prop. to *score* with a mark as a tally or record, i.e. (by impl.) to *inscribe*, and also to *enumerate*; intens. to *recount*, i.e. *celebrate*:—commune, (ac-) count, declare, number, + penknife, reckon, scribe, shew forth, speak, talk, tell (out), writer.

5609. סְפַר çᵉphar (Chald.), *sef-ar'*; from a root corresp. to 5608; a *book*:—book, roll.

5610. סְפָר çᵉphâr, *sef-awr'*; from 5608; a *census*:—numbering.

5611. סְפָר Çᵉphâr, *sef-awr'*; the same as 5610; *Sephar*, a place in Arabia:—Sephar.

5612. סֵפֶר çêpher, *say'-fer*; or (fem.)

סִפְרָה çiphrâh (Psa. 56 : 8 [9]), *sif-raw'*; from 5608; prop. *writing* (the art or a document); by impl. a *book*:—bill, book, evidence, × learn [-ed] (-ing), letter, register, scroll.

5613. סָפֵר çâphêr (Chald.), *saw-fare'*; from the same as 5609; a *scribe* (secular or sacred):—scribe.

5614. סְפָרָד Çᵉphârâd, *sef-aw-rawd'*; of for. der.; *Sepharad*, a region of Ass.:—Sepharad.

סִפְרָה çiphrâh. See 5612.

5615. סְפֹרָה çᵉphôrâh, *sef-o-raw'*; from 5608; a *numeration*:—number.

5616. סְפַרְוִי Çᵉpharvîy, *sef-ar-vee'*; patrial from 5617; a *Sepharvite* or inhab. of Sepharvain:—Sepharvite.

5617. סְפַרְוַיִם Çᵉpharvayim (dual), *sef-ar-vah'-yim*; or

סְפָרִים Çᵉphârîym (plur.), *sef-aw-reem'*; of for. der.; *Sepharvajim* or *Spharim*, a place in Ass.:—Sepharvaim.

5618. סֹפֶרֶת Çôphereth, *so-feh'-reth*; fem. act. part. of 5608; a *scribe* (prop. female); *Sophereth*, a temple servant:—Sophereth.

5619. סָקַל çâqal, *saw-kal'*; a prim. root; prop. to *be weighty*; but used only in the sense of *lapidation* or its contrary (as if a *delapidation*):—(cast, gather out, throw) stone (-s), × surely.

5620. סַר çar, *sar*; from 5637 contr.; *peevish*:—heavy, sad.

5621. סָרָב çârâb, *saw-rawb'*; from an unused root mean. to *sting*; a thistle:—brier.

5622. סַרְבַּל çarbal (Chald.), *sar-bal'*; of uncert. der.; a *cloak*:—coat.

5623. סַרְגּוֹן Çargôwn, *sar-gōne'*; of for. der.; *Sargon*, an Ass. king:—Sargon.

5624. סֶרֶד Çered, *seh'-red*; from a prim. root mean. to *tremble*; *trembling*; *Sered*, an Isr.:—Sered.

5625. סַרְדִּי Çardîy, *sar-dee'*; patron. from 5624; a *Seredite* (collect.) or desc. of Sered:—Sardites.

5626. סִרָה Çîrâh, *see-raw'*; from 5493; *departure*; *Sirah*, a cistern so-called:—Sirah. See also 5518.

5627. סָרָה çârâh, *saw-raw'*; from 5493; *apostasy*, *crime*; fig. *remission*:— × continual, rebellion, revolt ([-ed]), turn away, wrong.

5628. סָרַח çarach, *saw-rakh'*; a prim. root; to *extend* (even to *excess*):—exceeding, hand, spread, stretch self, banish.

5629. סֶרַח çerach, *seh'-rakh*; from 5628; a *redundancy*:—remnant.

5630. סִרְיֹן çiryôn, *sir-yone'*; for 8302; a coat of *mail*:—brigandine.

5631. סָרִיס çârîyç, *saw-reece'*; or

סָרִס çârîç, *saw-reece'*; from an unused root mean. to *castrate*; a *eunuch*; by impl. *valet* (espec. of the female apartments), and thus a *minister* of state:—chamberlain, eunuch, officer. Comp. 7249.

5632. סָרֵךְ çârêk (Chald.), *saw-rake'*; of for. or.; an *emir*:—president.

5633. סֶרֶן çeren, *seh'-ren*; from an unused root of unc. mean.; an *axle*; fig. a *peer*:—lord, plate.

5634. סַרְעַפָּה çarʻappâh, *sar-ap-paw'*; for 5589; a *twig*:—bough.

5635. סָרַף çâraph, *saw-raf'*; a prim. root; to *cremate*, i.e. to *be* (near) *of kin* (such being privileged to kindle the pyre):—burn.

5636. סַרְפָּד çarpâd, *sar-pawd'*; from 5635: a *nettle* (as stinging like a *burn*):—brier.

5637. סָרַר çârar, *saw-rar'*; a prim. root; to *turn* away, i.e. (morally) *be refractory*:— × away, backsliding, rebellious, revolter (-ing), slide back, stubborn, withdrew.

5638. סְתָו° çᵉthâv, *seth-awv'*; from an unused root mean. to *hide*; *winter* (as the dark season):—winter.

5639. סְתוּר Çᵉthûwr, *seth-oor'*; from 5641; *hidden*; *Sethur*, an Isr.:—Sethur.

5640. סָתַם çâtham, *saw-tham'*; or

שָׂתַם sâtham (Num. 24 : 15), *saw-tham'*; a prim. root; to *stop* up; by impl. to *repair*; fig. to *keep secret*:—closed up, hidden, secret, shut out (up), stop.

5641. סָתַר çâthar, *saw-thar'*; a prim. root; to *hide* (by covering), lit. or fig.:—be absent, keep close, conceal, hide (self), (keep) secret, × surely.

5642. סְתַר çᵉthar (Chald.), *seth-ar'*; corresp. to 5641; to *conceal*; fig. to *demolish*:—destroy, secret thing.

5643. סֵתֶר çêther, *say'-ther*; or (fem.)

סִתְרָה çithrâh (Deut. 32 : 38), *sith-raw'*; from 5641; a *cover* (in a good or a bad, a lit. or a fig. sense):—backbiting, covering, covert, × disguise [-th], hiding place, privily, protection, secret (-ly, place).

5644. סִתְרִי Çithrîy, *sith-ree'*; from 5643; *protective*; *Sithri*, an Isr.:—Zithri.

ע

5645. עָב ʻâb, *awb* (masc. and fem.); from 5743; prop. an *envelope*, i.e. *darkness* (or *density*, 2 Chron. 4 : 17); spec. a (scud) *cloud*; also a *copse*:—clay, (thick) cloud, × thick, thicket. Comp. 5672.

5646. עָב ʻâb, *awb*; or

עֹב ʻôb, *obe*; from an unused root mean. to *cover*; prop. equiv. to 5645; but used only as an arch. term, an *architrave* (as *shading* the pillars):—thick (beam, plant).

5647. עָבַד ʻâbad, *aw-bad'*; a prim. root; to *work* (in any sense); by impl. to *serve*, *till*, (caus.) *enslave*, etc.:— × be, keep in bondage, be bondmen, bond-service, compel, do, dress, ear, execute, + husbandman, keep, labour (-ing man), bring to pass, (cause to, make to) serve (-ing, self), (be, become) servant (-s), do (use) service, till (-er), transgress [*from margin*], (set a) work, be wrought, worshipper.

5648. עֲבַד ʻăbad (Chald.), *ab-ad'*; corresp. to 5647; to *do*, *make*, *prepare*, *keep*, etc.:— × cut, do, execute, go on, make, move, work.

5649. עֲבַד ʻăbad (Chald.), *ab-ad'*; from 5648; a *servant*:—servant.

5650. עֶבֶד ʻebed, *eh'-bed*; from 5647; a *servant*:— × bondage, bondman, [bond-] servant, (man-) servant.

5651. עֶבֶד ʻEbed, *eh'-bed*; the same as 5650; *Ebed*, the name of two Isr.:—Ebed.

5652. עֲבָד ʻăbâd, *ab-awd'*; from 5647; a *deed*:—work.

5653. עַבְדָּא ʻAbdâʼ, *ab-daw'*; from 5647; *work*; *Abda*, the name of two Isr.:—Abda.

5654. עֹבֵד אֱדוֹם ʻÔbêd ʼĔdôwm, *o-bade' edome'*; from the act. part. of 5647 and 123; *worker of Edom*; *Obed-Edom*, the name of five Isr.:—Obed-edom.

5655. עַבְדְאֵל ʻAbdᵉʼêl, *ab-deh-ale'*; from 5647 and 410; *serving God*; *Abdeël*, an Isr.:—Abdeel. Comp. 5661.

5656. עֲבֹדָה ʻăbôdâh, *ab-o-daw'*; or

עֲבוֹדָה ʻăbôwdâh, *ab-o-daw'*; from 5647; *work* of any kind:—act, bondage, + bondservant, effect, labour, ministering (-try), office, service (-ile, -itude), tillage, use, work, × wrought.

5657. עֲבֻדָּה ʻăbuddâh, *ab-ood-daw'*; pass. part. of 5647; something *wrought*, i.e. (concr.) *service*:—household, store of servants.

5658. עַבְדּוֹן ʻAbdôwn, *ab-dohn'*; from 5647; *servitude*; *Abdon*, the name of a place in Pal. and of four Isr.:—Abdon. Comp. 5683.

5659. עַבְדוּת ʻabdûwth, *ab-dooth'*; from 5647; *servitude*:—bondage.

5660. עַבְדִּי ʻAbdîy, *ab-dee'*; from 5647; *serviceable*; *Abdi*, the name of two Isr.:—Abdi.

5661. עַבְדִיאֵל ʻAbdîyʼêl, *ab-dee-ale'*; from 5650 and 410; *servant of God*; *Abdiël*, an Isr.:—Abdiel. Comp. 5655.

5662. עֹבַדְיָה ʻÔbadyâh, *o-bad-yaw'*; or

עֹבַדְיָהוּ ʻÔbadyâhûw, *o-bad-yaw'-hoo*; act. part. of 5647 and 3050; *serving Jah*; *Obadjah*, the name of thirteen Isr.:—Obadiah.

5663. עֶבֶד מֶלֶךְ ʻEbed Melek, *eh'-bed meh'-lek*; from 5650 and 4428; *servant of a king*; *Ebed-Melek*, a eunuch of king Zedekeah:—Ebed-melech.

5664. עֲבֵד נְגוֹ ʻĂbêd Nᵉgôw, *ab-ade' neg-o'*; the same as 5665; *Abed-Nego*, the Bab. name of one of Daniel's companions:—Abed-nego.

5665. עֲבֵד נְגוֹא ʻĂbêd Nᵉgôwʼ (Chald.), *ab-ade' neg-o'*; of for. or.; *Abed-Nego*, the name of Azariah:—Abed-nego.

5666. עָבָה ʻâbâh, *aw-baw'*; a prim. root; to *be dense*:—be (grow) thick (-er).

5667. עֲבוֹט ʻăbôwṭ, *ab-ote'*; or

עֲבֹט ʻăbôṭ, *ab-ote'*; from 5670; a *pawn*:—pledge.

5668. עָבוּר ʻâbûwr, *aw-boor'*; or

עָבֻר ʻâbûr, *aw-boor'*; pass. part. of 5674; prop. *crossed*, i.e. (abstr.) *transit*; used only adv. on *account* of, in *order* that:—because of, for (. . . 's sake), (intent) that, to.

5669. עָבוּר **ʽâbûwr**, *aw-boor'*; the same as 5668; *passed*, i.e. *kept* over; used only of *stored* grain:—old corn.

5670. עָבַט **ʽâbaṭ**, *aw-bat'*; a prim. root; to *pawn;* caus. to *lend* (on security); fig. to *entangle:*—borrow, break [*ranks*], fetch [*a pledge*], lend, × surely.

5671. עַבְטִיט **ʽabṭîyṭ**, *ab-teet'*; from 5670; something *pledged*, i.e. (collect.) *pawned goods:*—thick clay [*by a false etym.*].

5672. עֲבִי **ʽăbîy**, *ab-ee'*; or

עֳבִי **ʽŏbîy**, *ob-ee'*; from 5666; *density*, i.e. *depth* or *width:*—thick (-ness). Comp. 5645.

5673. עֲבִידָה **ʽăbîydâh** (Chald.), *ab-ee-daw'*; from 5648; *labor* or *business:*—affairs, service, work.

5674. עָבַר **ʽâbar**, *aw-bar'*; a prim. root; to *cross* over; used very widely of any *transition* (lit. or fig.; trans., intrans., intens. or causat.); spec. to *cover* (in copulation):—alienate, alter, × at all, beyond, bring (over, through), carry over, (over-) come (on, over), conduct (over), convey over, current, deliver, do away, enter, escape, fail, gender, get over, (make) go (away, beyond, by, forth, his way, in, on, over, through), have away (more), lay, meddle, overrun, make partition, (cause to, give, make to, over) pass (-age, along, away, beyond, by, -enger, on, out, over, through), (cause to, make) + proclaim (-amation), perish, provoke to anger, put away, rage, + raiser of taxes, remove, send over, set apart, + shave, cause to (make) sound, × speedily, × sweet smelling, take (away), (make to) transgress (-or), translate, turn away, [way-] faring man, be wrath.

5675. עֲבַר **ʽăbar** (Chald.), *ab-ar'*; corresp. to 5676:—beyond, this side.

5676. עֵבֶר **ʽêber**, *ay'-ber*; from 5674; prop. a region *across;* but used only adv. (with or without a prep.) on the *opposite* side (espec. of the Jordan; usually mean. the *east*):—× against, beyond, by, × from, over, passage, quarter, (other, this) side, straight.

5677. עֵבֶר **ʽÊber**, *ay'-ber*; the same as 5676; *Eber*, the name of two patriarchs and four Isr.:—Eber, Heber.

5678. עֶבְרָה **ʽebrâh**, *eb-raw'*; fem. of 5676; an *outburst* of passion:—anger, rage, wrath.

5679. עֲבָרָה **ʽăbârâh**, *ab-aw-raw'*; from 5674; a *crossing*-place:—ferry, plain [*from the marg.*].

5680. עִבְרִי **ʽIbrîy**, *ib-ree'*; patron. from 5677; an *Eberite* (i.e. Hebrew) or desc. of Eber:—Hebrew (-ess, woman).

5681. עִבְרִי **ʽIbrîy**, *ib-ree'*; the same as 5680; *Ibri*, an Isr.:—Ibri.

5682. עֲבָרִים **ʽĂbârîm**, *ab-aw-reem'*; plur. of 5676; regions *beyond; Abarim*, a place in Pal.:—Abarim, passages.

5683. עֶבְרֹן **ʽEbrôn**, *eb-rone'*; from 5676; *transitional; Ebron*, a place in Pal.:—Hebron. Perh. a clerical error for 5658.

5684. עֶבְרֹנָה **ʽEbrônâh**, *eb-raw-naw'*; fem. of 5683; *Ebronah*, a place in the Desert:—Ebronah.

5685. עָבַשׁ **ʽâbash**, *aw-bash'*; a prim. root; to *dry* up:—be rotten.

5686. עָבַת **ʽâbath**, *aw-bath'*; a prim. root; to *interlace*, i.e. (fig.) to *pervert:*—wrap up.

5687. עָבֹת **ʽâbôth**, *aw-both'*; or

עָבוֹת **ʽâbôwth**, *aw-both'*; from 5686; *intwined*, i.e. *dense:*—thick.

5688. עֲבֹת **ʽăbôth**, *ab-oth'*; or

עֲבוֹת **ʽăbôwth**, *ab-oth'*; or (fem.)

עֲבֹתָה **ʽăbôthâh**, *ab-oth-aw'*; the same as 5687; something *intwined*, i.e. a *string, wreath* or *foliage:*—band, cord, rope, thick bough (branch), wreathen (chain).

5689. עָגַב **ʽâgab**, *aw-gab'*; a prim. root; to *breathe* after, i.e. to *love* (sensually):—dote, lover.

5690. עֶגֶב **ʽegeb**, *eh'-gheb*; from 5689; *love* (concr.), i.e. *amative* words:—much love, very lovely.

5691. עֲגָבָה **ʽăgâbâh**, *ag-aw-baw'*; from 5689; *love* (abstr.), i.e. *amorousness:*—inordinate love.

5692. עֻגָּה **ʽuggâh**, *oog-gaw'*; from 5746; an *ash-cake* (as *round*):—cake (upon the hearth).

עָגוֹל **ʽâgôwl**. See 5696.

5693. עָגוּר **ʽâgûwr**, *aw-goor'*; pass. part. [but with act. sense] of an unused root mean. to *twitter;* prob. the *swallow:*—swallow.

5694. עָגִיל **ʽâgîyl**, *aw-gheel'*; from the same as 5696; something *round*, i.e. a *ring* (for the ears):—earring.

5695. עֵגֶל **ʽêgel**, *ay'-ghel*; from the same as 5696; a (male) *calf* (as *frisking* round), espec. one nearly grown (i.e. a *steer*):—bullock, calf.

5696. עָגֹל **ʽâgôl**, *aw-gole'*; or

עָגוֹל **ʽâgôwl**, *aw-gole'*; from an unused root mean. to *revolve, circular:*—round.

5697. עֶגְלָה **ʽeglâh**, *eg-law'*; fem. of 5695; a (female) *calf*, espec. one nearly grown (i.e. a *heifer*):—calf, cow, heifer.

5698. עֶגְלָה **ʽEglâh**, *eg-law'*; the same as 5697; *Eglah*, a wife of David:—Eglah.

5699. עֲגָלָה **ʽăgâlâh**, *ag-aw-law'*; from the same as 5696; something *revolving*, i.e. a wheeled *vehicle:*—cart, chariot, wagon.

5700. עֶגְלוֹן **ʽEglôwn**, *eg-lawn'*; from 5695; *vituline; Eglon*, the name of a place in Pal. and of a Moabitish king:—Eglon.

5701. עָגַם **ʽâgam**, *aw-gam'*; a prim. root; to *be sad:*—grieve.

5702. עָגַן **ʽâgan**, *aw-gan'*; a prim. root; to *debar*, i.e. from marriage:—stay.

5703. עַד **ʽad**, *ad*; from 5710; prop. a (peremptory) *terminus*, i.e. (by impl.) *duration*, in the sense of *advance* or *perpetuity* (substantially as a noun, either with or without a prep.):—eternity, ever (-lasting, -more), old, perpetually, + world without end.

5704. עַד **ʽad**, *ad*; prop. the same as 5703 (used as a prep., adv. or conj.; especially with a prep.); *as far* (or *long*, or *much*) *as*, whether of space (*even unto*) or time (*during, while, until*) or degree (*equally with*):—against, and, as, at, before, by (that), even (to), for (-asmuch as), [hither-] to, + how long, into, as long (much) as, (so) that, till, toward, until, when, while, (+ as) yet.

5705. עַד **ʽad** (Chald.), *ad*; corresp. to 5704; × and, at, for, [hither-] to, on, till, (un-) to, until, within.

5706. עַד **ʽad**, *ad*; the same as 5703 in the sense of the *aim* of an attack; *booty:*—prey.

5707. עֵד **ʽêd**, *ayd*; from 5749 contr.; concr. a *witness;* abstr. *testimony;* spec. a *recorder*, i.e. *prince:*—witness.

5708. עֵד **ʽêd**, *ayd*; from an unused root mean. to *set* a period [comp. 5710, 5749]; the *menstrual* flux (as periodical); by impl. (in plur.) *soiling:*—filthy.

עֹד **ʽôd**. See 5750.

5709. עֲדָא **ʽădâʼ** (Chald.), *ad-aw'*; or

עֲדָה **ʽădâh** (Chald.), *ad-aw'*; corresp. to 5710:—alter, depart, pass (away), remove, take (away).

עֹדֵד **ʽÔdêd**. See 5752.

5710. עָדָה **ʽâdâh**, *aw-daw'*; a prim. root; to *advance*, i.e. *pass* on or *continue;* causat. to *remove;* spec. to *bedeck* (i.e. bring an ornament upon):—adorn, deck (self), pass by, take away.

5711. עָדָה **ʽÂdâh**, *aw-daw'*; from 5710; *ornament; Adah*, the name of two women:—Adah.

5712. עֵדָה **ʽêdâh**, *ay-daw'*; fem. of 5707 in the orig. sense of *fixture;* a stated *assemblage* (spec. a *concourse*, or gen. a *family* or *crowd*):—assembly, company, congregation, multitude, people, swarm. Comp. 5713.

5713. עֵדָה **ʽêdâh**, *ay-daw'*; fem. of 5707 in its techn. sense; *testimony:*—testimony, witness. Comp. 5712.

5714. עִדּוֹ **ʽIddôw**, *id-do'*; or

עִדּוֹא **ʽIddôwʼ**, *id-do'*; or

עִדִּיא **ʽIddîyʼ**, *id-dee'*; from 5710; *timely; Iddo* (or *Iddi*), the name of five Isr.:—Iddo. Comp. 3035, 3260.

5715. עֵדוּת **ʽêdûwth**, *ay-dooth'*; fem. of 5707; *testimony:*—testimony, witness.

5716. עֲדִי **ʽădîy**, *ad-ee'*; from 5710 in the sense of *trappings; finery;* gen. an *outfit;* spec. a *headstall:*—× excellent, mouth, ornament.

5717. עֲדִיאֵל **ʽĂdîyʼêl**, *ad-ee-ale'*; from 5716 and 410; *ornament of God; Adiël*, the name of three Isr.:—Adiel.

5718. עֲדָיָה **ʽĂdâyâh**, *ad-aw-yaw'*; or

עֲדָיָהוּ **ʽĂdâyâhûw**, *ad-aw-yaw'-hoo;* from 5710 and 3050; *Jah has adorned; Adajah*, the name of eight Isr.:—Adaiah.

5719. עָדִין **ʽâdîyn**, *aw-deen'*; from 5727; *voluptuous:*—given to pleasures.

5720. עָדִין **ʽÂdîyn**, *aw-deen'*; the same as 5719; *Adin*, the name of two Isr.:—Adin.

5721. עֲדִינָא **ʽĂdîynâʼ**, *ad-ee-naw'*; from 5719; *effeminacy; Adina*, an Isr.:—Adina.

5722. עֲדִינוֹ **ʽădîynôw**, *ad-ee-no'*; prob. from 5719 in the orig. sense of *slender* (i.e. a *spear*); *his spear:*—Adino.

5723. עֲדִיתַיִם **ʽĂdîythayim**, *ad-ee-thah'-yim;* dual of a fem. of 5706; *double prey; Adithajim*, a place in Pal.:—Adithaim.

5724. עַדְלַי **ʽAdlay**, *ad-lah'ee*; prob. from an unused root of uncert. mean.; *Adlai*, an Isr.:—Adlai.

5725. עֲדֻלָּם **ʽĂdullâm**, *ad-ool-lawm'*; prob. from the pass. part. of the same as 5724; *Adullam*, a place in Pal.:—Adullam.

5726. עֲדֻלָּמִי **ʽĂdullâmîy**, *ad-ool-law-mee'*; patrial from 5725; an *Adullamite* or native of Adullam:—Adullamite.

5727. עָדַן **ʽâdan**, *aw-dan'*; a prim. root; to be *soft* or *pleasant;* fig. and reflex. to *live voluptuously:*—delight self.

5728. עֲדֶן **ʽăden**, *ad-en'*; or

עֲדֶנָּה **ʽădennâh**, *ad-en'-naw;* from 5704 and 2004; *till now:*—yet.

5729. עֶדֶן **ʽEden**, *eh'-den*; from 5727; *pleasure; Eden*, a place in Mesopotamia:—Eden.

5730. עֵדֶן **ʽêden**, *ay'-den*; or (fem.)

עֶדְנָה **ʽednâh**, *ed-naw'*; from 5727; *pleasure:*—delicate, delight, pleasure. See also 1040.

5731. עֵדֶן **ʽÊden**, *ay'-den*; the same as 5730 (masc.); *Eden*, the region of Adam's home:—Eden.

5732. עִדָּן **ʽiddân** (Chald.), *id-dawn'*; from a root corresp. to that of 5708; a set *time;* techn. a *year:*—time.

5733. עַדְנָא **ʽAdnâʼ**, *ad-naw'*; from 5727; *pleasure; Adna*, the name of two Isr.:—Adna.

5734. עַדְנָה **ʽAdnâh**, *ad-naw'*; from 5727; *pleasure; Adnah*, the name of two Isr.:—Adnah.

5735. עֲדְעָדָה **ʽĂdʽâdâh**, *ad-aw-daw'*; from 5712; *festival; Adadah*, a place in Pal.:—Adadah.

5736. עָדַף **ʽâdaph**, *aw-daf'*; a prim. root; to *be* (causat. *have*) *redundant:*—be more, odd number, be (have) over (and above), overplus, remain.

5737. עָדַר **ʽâdar**, *aw-dar'*; a prim. root; to *arrange*, as a battle, a vineyard (to *hoe*); hence to *muster*, and so to *miss* (or find *wanting*):—dig, fail, keep (rank), lack.

5738. עֶדֶר **ʽEder**, *eh'-der*; from 5737; an *arrangement* (i.e. drove); *Eder*, an Isr.:—Ader.

5739. עֵדֶר **ʽêder**, *ay'-der*; from 5737; an *arrangement*, i.e. *muster* (of animals):—drove, flock, herd.

5740. עֵדֶר **ʻÊder**, *ay'-der;* the same as 5739; *Eder*, the name of an Isr. and of two places in Pal.:—Edar, Eder.

5741. עַדְרִיאֵל **ʻAdrîyʼêl**, *ad-ree-ale';* from 5739 and 410; *flock of God; Adriel*, an Isr.:—Adriel.

5742. עָדָשׁ **ʻâdâsh**, *aw-dawsh';* from an unused root of uncert. mean.; a *lentil:*—lentile.

עַוָּא **ʻAvvâʼ.** See 5755.

5743. עוּב **ʻûwb**, *oob;* a prim. root; to be *dense* or *dark*, i.e. to *becloud:*—cover with a cloud.

5744. עוֹבֵד **ʻÔwbêd**, *o-bade';* act. part. of 5647; *serving; Obed*, the name of five Isr.:—Obed.

5745. עוֹבָל **ʻÔwbâl**, *o-bawl';* of for. der.; *Obal*, a son of Joktan:—Obal.

5746. עוּג **ʻûwg**, *oog;* a prim. root; prop. to *gyrate;* but used only as denom. from 5692, to *bake* (round cakes on the hearth):—bake.

5747. עוֹג **ʻÔwg**, *ogue;* prob. from 5746; *round; Og*, a king of Bashan:—Og.

5748. עוּגָב **ʻûwgâb**, *oo-gawb';* or

עֻגָּב **ʻûggâb**, *oog-gawb';* from 5689 in the orig. sense of *breathing;* a *reed*-instrument of music:—organ.

5749. עוּד **ʻûwd**, *ood;* a prim. root; to *duplicate* or *repeat;* by impl. to *protest, testify* (as by reiteration); intens. to *encompass, restore* (as a sort of reduplication):—admonish, charge, earnestly, lift up, protest, call (take) to record, relieve, rob, solemnly, stand upright, testify, give warning, (bear, call to, give, take to) witness.

5750. עוֹד **ʻôwd**, *ode;* or

עֹד **ʻôd**, *ode;* from 5749; prop. *iteration* or *continuance;* used only adv. (with or without prep.), *again, repeatedly, still, more:*—again, × all life long, at all, besides, but, else, further (-more), henceforth, (any) longer, (any) more (-over), × once, since, (be) still, when, (good, the) while (having being), (as, because, whether, while) yet (within).

5751. עוֹד **ʻôwd** (Chald.), *ode;* corresp. to 5750:—while.

5752. עוֹדֵד **ʻÔwdêd**, *o-dade';* or

עֹדֵד **ʻÔdêd**, *o-dade';* from 5749; *reiteration; Oded*, the name of two Isr.:—Oded.

5753. עָוָה **ʻâvâh**, *aw-vaw';* a prim. root; to *crook*, lit. or fig. (as follows):—do amiss, bow down, make crooked, commit iniquity, pervert, (do) perverse (-ly), trouble, × turn, do wickedly, do wrong.

5754. עַוָּה **ʻavvâh**, *av-vaw';* intens. from 5753 abbrev.; *overthrow:*—× overturn.

5755. עִוָּה **ʻIvvâh**, *iv-vaw';* or

עַוָּא **ʻAvvâʼ** (2 Kings 17 : 24), *av-vaw';* for 5754; *Ivvah* or *Avva*, a region of Ass.:—Ava, Ivah.

עָוֹן **ʻâvôwn.** See 5771.

5756. עוּז **ʻûwz**, *ooz;* a prim. root; to *be strong;* causat. to *strengthen*, i.e. (fig.) to *save* (by flight):—gather (self, self to flee), retire.

5757. עַוִּי **ʻAvvîy**, *av-vee';* patrial from 5755; an *Avvite* or native of Avvah (only plur.):—Avims, Avites.

5758. עִוְיָא **ʻivyâʼ** (Chald.), *iv-yaw';* from a root corresp. to 5753; *perverseness:*—iniquity.

5759. עֲוִיל **ʻăvîyl**, *av-eel';* from 5764; a *babe:*—young child, little one.

5760. עֲוִיל **ʻăvîyl**, *av-eel';* from 5765; *perverse* (morally):—ungodly.

5761. עַוִּים **ʻAvvîym**, *av-veem';* plur. of 5757; *Avvim* (as inhabited by Avvites), a place in Pal. (with the art. pref.):—Avim.

5762. עֲוִית **ʻĂvîyth**, *av-veeth';* or [perh.

עַיּוֹת° **ʻAyôwth**, *ah-yōth'*, as if plur. of 5857]

עַיּוּת° **ʻAyûwth**, *ah-yōth';* from 5753; *ruin; Avvith* (or *Avvoth*), a place in Pal.:—Avith.

5763. עוּל **ʻûwl**, *ool;* a prim. root; to *suckle*, i.e. *give milk:*—milch, (ewe great) with young.

5764. עוּל **ʻûwl**, *ool;* from 5763; a *babe:*—sucking child, infant.

5765. עָוַל **ʻâval**, *aw-val';* a prim. root; to *distort* (morally):—deal unjustly, unrighteous.

עוֹל **ʻôwl.** See 5923.

5766. עֶוֶל **ʻevel**, *eh'-vel;* or

עָוֶל **ʻâvel**, *aw'-vel;* and (fem.)

עַוְלָה **ʻavlâh**, *av-law';* or

עוֹלָה **ʻôwlâh**, *o-law';* or

עֹלָה **ʻôlâh**, *o-law';* from 5765; (moral) *evil:*—iniquity, perverseness, unjust (-ly), unrighteousness (-ly), wicked (-ness).

5767. עַוָּל **ʻavvâl**, *av-vawl';* intens. from 5765; *evil* (morally):—unjust, unrighteous, wicked.

עוֹלָה **ʻôwlâh.** See 5930.

5768. עוֹלֵל **ʻôwlêl**, *o-lale';* or

עֹלָל **ʻôlâl**, *o-lawl';* from 5763; a *suckling:*—babe, (young) child, infant, little one.

5769. עוֹלָם **ʻôwlâm**, *o-lawm';* or

עֹלָם **ʻôlâm**, *o-lawm';* from 5956; prop. *concealed*, i.e. the *vanishing* point; gen. time *out of mind* (past or fut.), i.e. (practically) *eternity;* freq. adv. (espec. with prep. pref.) *always:*—alway (-s), ancient (time), any more, continuance, eternal, (for, [n-]) ever (-lasting, -more, of old), lasting, long (time), (of) old (time), perpetual, at any time, (beginning of the) world (+ without end). Comp. 5331, 5703.

5770. עָוַן° **ʻâvan**, *aw-van';* denom. from 5869; to *watch* (with jealousy):—eye.

5771. עָוֹן **ʻâvôn**, *aw-vone';* or

עָוֺון **ʻâvôwn** (2 Kings 7 : 9; Psa. 51 : 5 [7]), *aw-vone';* from 5753; *perversity*, i.e. (moral) *evil:*—fault, iniquity, mischief, punishment (of iniquity), sin.

5772. עוֹנָה **ʻôwnâh**, *o-naw';* from an unused root appar. mean. to *dwell* together; (sexual) *cohabitation:*—duty of marriage.

5773. עַוְעֶה **ʻavʻeh**, *av-eh';* from 5753; *perversity:*—× perverse.

5774. עוּף **ʻûwph**, *oof;* a prim root; to *cover* (with wings or obscurity); hence (as denom. from 5775) to *fly;* also (by impl. of dimness) to *faint* (from the darkness of swooning):—brandish, be (wax) faint, flee away, fly (away), × set, shine forth, weary.

5775. עוֹף **ʻôwph**, *ofe;* from 5774; a *bird* (as *covered* with feathers, or rather as *covering* with wings), often collect.:—bird, that flieth, flying, fowl.

5776. עוֹף **ʻôwph** (Chald.), *ofe;* corresp. to 5775:—fowl.

5777. עוֹפֶרֶת **ʻôwphereth**, *o-feh'-reth;* or

עֹפֶרֶת **ʻôphereth**, *o-feh'-reth;* fem. part. act. of 6080; *lead* (from its *dusty* color):—lead.

5778. עוֹפַי° **ʻÔwphay**, *o-fah'-ee;* from 5775; *birdlike; Ephai*, an Isr.:—Ephai [*from marg.*].

5779. עוּץ **ʻûwts**, *oots;* a prim. root; to *consult:*—take advice ([counsel] together).

5780. עוּץ **ʻÛwts**, *oots;* appar. from 5779; *consultation; Uts*, a son of Aram, also a Seirite, and the regions settled by them:—Uz.

5781. עוּק **ʻûwq**, *ook;* a prim. root; to *pack:*—be pressed.

5782. עוּר **ʻûwr**, *oor;* a prim. root [rather ident. with 5783 through the idea of *opening* the eyes]; to *wake* (lit. or fig.):—(a-) wake (-n, up), lift up (self), × master, raise (up), stir up (self).

5783. עוּר **ʻûwr**, *oor;* a prim. root; to (*be*) *bare:*—be made naked.

5784. עוּר **ʻûwr** (Chald.), *oor; chaff* (as the *naked* husk):—chaff.

5785. עוֹר **ʻôwr**, *ore;* from 5783; *skin* (as *naked*); by impl. *hide, leather:*—hide, leather, skin.

5786. עָוַר **ʻâvar**, *aw-var';* a prim. root [rather denom. from 5785 through the idea of a *film* over the eyes]; to *blind:*—blind, put out. See also 5895.

5787. עִוֵּר **ʻivvêr**, *iv-vare';* intens. from 5786; *blind* (lit. or fig.):—blind (men, people).

עוֹרֵב **ʻôwrêb.** See 6159.

5788. עִוָּרוֹן **ʻivvârôwn**, *iv-vaw-rone';* and (fem.)

עַוֶּרֶת **ʻavvereth**, *av-veh'-reth;* from 5787; *blindness:*—blind (-ness).

5789. עוּשׁ **ʻûwsh**, *oosh;* a prim. root; to *hasten:*—assemble self.

5790. עוּת **ʻûwth**, *ooth;* for 5789; to *hasten*, i.e. *succor:*—speak in season.

5791. עָוַת **ʻâvath**, *aw-vath';* a prim. root; to *wrest:*—bow self, (make) crooked, falsifying, overthrow, deal perversely, pervert, subvert, turn upside down.

5792. עַוָּתָה **ʻavvâthâh**, *av-vaw-thaw';* from 5791; *oppression:*—wrong.

5793. עוּתַי **ʻÛwthay**, *oo-thah'-ee;* from 5790; *succoring; Uthai*, the name of two Isr.:—Uthai.

5794. עַז **ʻaz**, *az;* from 5810; *strong, vehement, harsh:*—fierce, + greedy, mighty, power, roughly, strong.

5795. עֵז **ʻêz**, *aze;* from 5810; a she-*goat* (as *strong*), but masc. in plur. (which also is used ellipt. for *goats' hair*):—(she) goat, kid.

5796. עֵז **ʻêz** (Chald.), *aze;* corresp. to 5795:—goat.

5797. עֹז **ʻôz**, *oze;* or (fully)

עוֹז **ʻôwz**, *oze;* from 5810; *strength* in various applications (*force, security, majesty, praise*):—boldness, loud, might, power, strength, strong.

5798. עֻזָּא **ʻUzzâʼ**, *ooz-zaw';* or

עֻזָּה **ʻUzzâh**, *ooz-zaw';* fem. of 5797; *strength; Uzza* or *Uzzah*, the name of five Isr.:—Uzza, Uzzah.

5799. עֲזָאזֵל **ʻăzâʼzêl**, *az-aw-zale';* from 5795 and 235; *goat of departure;* the *scape-goat:*—scapegoat.

5800. עָזַב **ʻâzab**, *aw-zab';* a prim. root; to *loosen*, i.e. *relinquish, permit*, etc.:—commit self, fail, forsake, fortify, help, leave (destitute, off), refuse, × surely.

5801. עִזָּבוֹן **ʻizzâbôwn**, *iz-zaw-bone';* from 5800 in the sense of *letting go* (for a price, i.e. *selling*); *trade*, i.e. the place (*mart*) or the payment (*revenue*):—fair, ware.

5802. עַזְבּוּק **ʻAzbûwq**, *az-book';* from 5794 and the root of 950; *stern depopulator; Azbuk*, an Isr.:—Azbuk.

5803. עַזְגָּד **ʻAzgâd**, *az-gawd';* from 5794 and 1409; *stern troop; Azgad*, an Isr.:—Azgad.

5804. עַזָּה **ʻAzzâh**, *az-zaw';* fem. of 5794; *strong; Azzah*, a place in Pal.:—Azzah, Gaza.

5805. עֲזוּבָה **ʻăzûwbâh**, *az-oo-baw';* fem. pass. part. of 5800; *desertion* (of inhabitants):—forsaking.

5806. עֲזוּבָה **ʻĂzûwbâh**, *az-oo-baw';* the same as 5805; *Azubah*, the name of two Israelitesses:—Azubah.

5807. עֱזוּז **ʻĕzûwz**, *ez-ooz';* from 5810; *forcibleness:*—might, strength.

5808. עִזּוּז **ʻizzûwz**, *iz-zooz';* from 5810; *forcible*, collect. and concr. an *army:*—power, strong.

5809. עַזּוּר **ʻAzzûwr**, *az-zoor';* or

עַזֻּר **ʻAzzûr**, *az-zoor';* from 5826; *helpful; Azzur*, the name of three Isr.:—Azur, Azzur.

5810. עָזַז **ʻâzaz**, *aw-zaz'*; a prim. root; to *be stout* (lit. or fig.):—harden, impudent, prevail, strengthen (self), be strong.

5811. עָזָז **ʻÂzâz**, *aw-zawz'*; from 5810; *strong*; *Azaz*, an Isr.:—Azaz.

5812. עֲזַזְיָהוּ **ʻĂzazyâhûw**, *az-az-yaw'-hoo*; from 5810 and 3050; *Jah has strengthened*; *Azazjah*, the name of three Isr.:—Azaziah.

5813. עֻזִּי **ʻUzzîy**, *ooz-zee'*; from 5810; *forceful*; *Uzzi*, the name of six Isr.:—Uzzi.

5814. עֻזִּיָּא **ʻUzzîyâʼ**, *ooz-zee-yaw'*; perh. for 5818; *Uzzija*, an Isr.:—Uzzia.

5815. עֲזִיאֵל **ʻĂzîyʼêl**, *az-ee-ale'*; from 5756 and 410; *strengthened of God*; *Aziël*, an Isr.:—Aziel. Comp. 3268.

5816. עֻזִּיאֵל **ʻUzzîyʼêl**, *ooz-zee-ale'*; from 5797 and 410; *strength of God*; *Uzziël*, the name of six Isr..—Uzziel.

5817. עָזִּיאֵלִי **ʻOzzîyʼêlîy**, *oz-zee-ay-lee'*; patron. from 5816; an *Uzziëlite* (collect.) or desc. of Uzziel:—Uzzielites.

5818. עֻזִּיָּה **ʻUzzîyâh**, *ooz-zee-yaw'*; or

עֻזִּיָּהוּ **ʻUzzîyâhûw**, *ooz-zee-yaw'-hoo*; from 5797 and 3050; *strength of Jah*; *Uzzijah*, the name of five Isr.:—Uzziah.

5819. עֲזִיזָא **ʻĂzîyzâʼ**, *az-ee-zaw'*; from 5756; *strengthfulness*; *Aziza*, an Isr.:—Aziza.

5820. עַזְמָוֶת **ʻAzmâveth**, *az-maw'-veth*; from 5794 and 4194; *strong* one *of death*; *Azmaveth*, the name of three Isr. and of a place in Pal.:—Azmaveth. See also 1041.

5821. עַזָּן **ʻAzzân**, *az-zawn'*; from 5794; *strong* one; *Azzan*, an Isr.:—Azzan.

5822. עָזְנִיָּה **ʻozniyâh**, *oz-nee-yaw'*; prob. fem. of 5797; prob. the *sea-eagle* (from its *strength*):—ospray.

5823. עָזַק **ʻâzaq**, *aw-zak'*; a prim. root; to *grub* over:—fence about.

5824. עִזְקָא **ʻizqâʼ** (Chald.), *iz-kaw'*; from a root corresp. to 5823; a *signet*-ring (as engraved):—signet.

5825. עֲזֵקָה **ʻĂzêqâh**, *az-ay-kaw'*; from 5823; *tilled*; *Azekah*, a place in Pal.:—Azekah.

5826. עָזַר **ʻâzar**, *aw-zar'*; a prim. root; to *surround*, i.e. *protect* or *aid*:—help, succour.

5827. עֶזֶר **ʻEzer**, *eh'-zer*; from 5826; *help*; *Ezer*, the name of two Isr.:—Ezer. Comp. 5829.

5828. עֵזֶר **ʻêzer**, *ay'-zer*; from 5826; *aid*:—help.

5829. עֵזֶר **ʻÊzer**, *ay'-zer*; the same as 5828; *Ezer*, the name of four Isr.:—Ezer. Comp. 5827.

עַזֻּר **ʻAzzûr**. See 5809.

5830. עֶזְרָא **ʻEzrâʼ**, *ez-raw'*; a var. of 5833; *Ezra*, an Isr.:—Ezra.

5831. עֶזְרָא **ʻEzrâʼ** (Chald.), *ez-raw'*; corresp. to 5830; *Ezra*, an Isr.:—Ezra.

5832. עֲזַרְאֵל **ʻĂzarʼêl**, *az-ar-ale'*; from 5826 and 410; *God has helped*; *Azarel*, the name of five Isr.:—Azarael, Azareel.

5833. עֶזְרָה **ʻezrâh**, *ez-raw'*; or

עֶזְרָת **ʻezrâth** (Psa. 60 : 11 [13]; 108 : 12 [13]), *ez-rawth'*; fem. of 5828; *aid*:—help (-ed, -er).

5834. עֶזְרָה **ʻEzrâh**, *ez-raw'*; the same as 5833; *Ezrah*, an Isr.:—Ezrah.

5835. עֲזָרָה **ʻăzârâh**, *az-aw-raw'*; from 5826 in its orig. mean. of *surrounding*; an *inclosure*; also a *border*:—court, settle.

5836. עֶזְרִי **ʻEzrîy**, *ez-ree'*; from 5828; *helpful*; *Ezri*, an Isr.:—Ezri.

5837. עַזְרִיאֵל **ʻAzrîyʼêl**, *az-ree-ale'*; from 5828 and 410; *help of God*; *Azriël*, the name of three Isr.:—Azriel.

5838. עֲזַרְיָה **ʻĂzaryâh**, *az-ar-yaw'*; or

עֲזַרְיָהוּ **ʻĂzaryâhûw**, *az-ar-yaw'-hoo*; from 5826 and 3050; *Jah has helped*; *Azarjah*, the name of nineteen Isr.:—Azariah.

5839. עֲזַרְיָה **ʻĂzaryâh** (Chald.), *az-ar-yaw'*; corresp. to 5838; *Azarjah*, one of Daniel's companions:—Azariah.

5840. עַזְרִיקָם **ʻAzrîyqâm**, *az-ree-kawm'*; from 5828 and act. part. of 6965; *help of an enemy*; *Azrikam*, the name of four Isr.:—Azrikam.

5841. עַזָּתִי **ʻAzzâthîy**, *az-zaw-thee'*; patrial from 5804; an *Azzathite* or inhab. of Azzah:—Gazathite, Gazite.

5842. עֵט **ʻêṭ**, *ate*; from 5860 (contr.) in the sense of *swooping*, i.e. *side-long stroke*; a *stylus* or marking stick:—pen.

5843. עֵטָא **ʻêṭâʼ** (Chald.), *ay-taw'*; from 3272; *prudence*:—counsel.

5844. עָטָה **ʻâṭâh**, *aw-taw'*; a prim. root; to *wrap*, i.e. *cover*, *veil*, *clothe* or *roll*:—array self, be clad, (put a) cover (-ing, self), fill, put on, × surely, turn aside.

5845. עֲטִין **ʻăṭîyn**, *at-een'*; from an unused root mean. appar. to *contain*; a *receptacle* (for milk, i.e. *pail*; fig. *breast*):—breast.

5846. עֲטִישָׁה **ʻăṭîyshâh**, *at-ee-shaw'*; from an unused root mean. to *sneeze*; *sneezing*:—sneezing.

5847. עֲטַלֵּף **ʻăṭallêph**, *at-al-lafe'*; of uncert. der.; a *bat*:—bat.

5848. עָטַף **ʻâṭaph**, *aw-taf'*; a prim. root; to *shroud*, i.e. *clothe* (whether trans. or reflex.); hence (from the idea of *darkness*) to *languish*:—cover (over), fail, faint, feebler, hide self, be overwhelmed, swoon.

5849. עָטַר **ʻâṭar**, *aw-tar'*; a prim. root; to *encircle* (for attack or protection); espec. to *crown* (lit. or fig.):—compass, crown.

5850. עֲטָרָה **ʻăṭârâh**, *at-aw-raw'*; from 5849; a *crown*:—crown.

5851. עֲטָרָה **ʻĂṭârâh**, *at-aw-raw'*; the same as 5850; *Atarah*, an Israelitess:—Atarah.

5852. עֲטָרוֹת **ʻĂṭârôwth**, *at-aw-rōth'*; or

עֲטָרֹת **ʻĂṭârôth**, *at-aw-rōth'*; plur. of 5850; *Ataroth*, the name (thus simply) of two places in Pal.:—Ataroth.

5853. עַטְרוֹת אַדָּר **ʻAṭrôwth ʼAddâr**, *at-rōth' ad-dawr'*; from the same as 5852 and 146; *crowns of Addar*; *Atroth-Addar*, a place in Pal.:—Ataroth-adar (-addar).

5854. עַטְרוֹת בֵּית יוֹאָב **ʻAṭrôwth bêyth Yôwʼâb**, *at-rōth' bayth yo-awb'*; from the same as 5852 and 1004 and 3097; *crowns of* the *house of Joäb*; *Atroth-beth-Joäb*, a place in Pal.:—Ataroth the house of Joab.

5855. עַטְרוֹת שׁוֹפָן **ʻAṭrôwth Shôwphân**, *at-rōth' sho-fawn'*; from the same as 5852 and a name otherwise unused [being from the same as 8226] mean. *hidden*; *crowns of Shophan*; *Atroth-Shophan*, a place in Pal.:—Atroth, Shophan [*as if two places*].

5856. עִי **ʻîy**, *ee*; from 5753; a *ruin* (as if overturned):—heap.

5857. עַי **ʻAy**, *ah'ee*; or (fem.)

עַיָּא **ʻAyâʼ** (Neh. 11 : 31), *ah-yaw'*; or

עַיָּת **ʻAyâth** (Isa. 10 : 28), *ah-yawth'*; for 5856; *Ai*, *Aja* or *Ajath*, a place in Pal.:—Ai, Aija, Aijath, Hai.

5858. עֵיבָל **ʻÊybâl**, *ay-bawl'*; perh. from an unused root prob. mean. to be *bald*; *bare*; *Ebal*, a mountain of Pal.:—Ebal.

עַיָּה **ʻAyâh**. See 5857.

5859. עִיּוֹן **ʻIyôwn**, *ee-yone'*; from 5856; *ruin*; *Ijon*, a place in Pal.:—Ijon.

5860. עִיט **ʻîyṭ**, *eet*; a prim. root; to *swoop* down upon (lit. or fig.):—fly, rail.

5861. עַיִט **ʻayiṭ**, *ah'-yit*; from 5860; a *hawk* or other bird of prey:—bird, fowl, ravenous (bird).

5862. עֵיטָם **ʻÊyṭâm**, *ay-tawm'*; from 5861; *hawk-ground*; *Etam*, a place in Pal.:—Etam.

5863. עִיֵּי הָעֲבָרִים **ʻIyêy hâ-ʻĂbârîym**, *ee-yay' haw-ab-aw-reem'*; from the plur. of 5856 and the plur. of the act. part. of 5674 with the art. interposed; *ruins of the passers*; *Ije-ha-Abarim*, a place near Pal.:—Ije-abarim.

5864. עִיִּים **ʻIyîym**, *ee-yeem'*; plur. of 5856; *ruins*; *Ijim*, a place in the Desert:—Iim.

5865. עֵילוֹם **ʻêylôwm**, *ay-lome'*; for 5769:—ever.

5866. עִילַי **ʻÎylay**, *ee-lah'ee*; from 5927; *elevated*; *Ilai*, an Isr.:—Ilai.

5867. עֵילָם **ʻÊylâm**, *ay-lawm'*; or

עוֹלָם **ʻÔwlâm** (Ezra 10 : 2; Jer. 49 : 36), *o-lawm'*; prob. from 5956; *hidden*, i.e. *distant*; *Elam*, a son of Shem, and his descend., with their country; also of six Isr.:—Elam.

5868. עֲיָם **ʻăyâm**, *ah-yawm'*; of doubtful or. and authenticity; prob. mean. *strength*:—mighty.

5869. עַיִן **ʻayin**, *ah'-yin*; prob. a prim. word; an *eye* (lit. or fig.); by anal. a *fountain* (as the *eye* of the landscape):—affliction, outward appearance, + before, + think best, colour, conceit, + be content, countenance, + displease, eye ([-brow], [-d], -sight), face, + favour, fountain, furrow [*from the marg.*], × him, + humble, knowledge, look, (+ well), × me, open (-ly), + (not) please, presence, + regard, resemblance, sight, × thee, × them, + think, × us, well, × you (-rselves).

5870. עַיִן **ʻayin** (Chald.), *ah'-yin*; corresp. to 5869; an *eye*:—eye.

5871. עַיִן **ʻAyin**, *ah'-yin*; the same as 5869; *fountain*; *Ajin*, the name (thus simply) of two places in Pal.:—Ain.

5872. עֵין גֶּדִי **ʻÊyn Gedîy**, *ane geh'-dee*; from 5869 and 1423; *fountain of a kid*; *En-Gedi*, a place in Pal.:—En-gedi.

5873. עֵין גַּנִּים **ʻÊyn Gannîym**, *ane gan-neem'*; from 5869 and the plur. of 1588; *fountain of gardens*; *En-Gannim*, a place in Pal.:—En-gannim.

5874. עֵין־דֹּאר **ʻÊyn-Dôʼr**, *ane-dore'*; or

עֵין דּוֹר **ʻÊyn Dôwr**, *ane dore*; or

עֵין־דֹּר **ʻÊyn-Dôr**, *ane-dore'*; from 5869 and 1755; *fountain of dwelling*; *En-Dor*, a place in Pal.:—En-dor.

5875. עֵין הַקּוֹרֵא **ʻÊyn haq-Qôwrêʼ**, *ane hak-ko-ray'*; from 5869 and the act. part. of 7121; *fountain of One calling*; *En-hak-Korè*, a place near Pal.:—En-hakhore.

עֵינוֹן **ʻÊynôwn**. See 2703.

5876. עֵין חַדָּה **ʻÊyn Chaddâh**, *ane khad-daw'*; from 5869 and the fem. of a der. from 2300; *fountain of sharpness*; *En-Chaddah*, a place in Pal.:—En-haddah.

5877. עֵין חָצוֹר **ʻÊyn Châtsôwr**, *ane khaw-tsore'*; from 5869 and the same as 2674; *fountain of a village*; *En-Chatsor*, a place in Pal.:—En-hazor.

5878. עֵין חֲרֹד **ʻÊyn Charôd**, *ane khar-ode'*; from 5869 and a der. of 2729; *fountain of trembling*; *En-Charod*, a place in Pal.:—well of Harod.

5879. עֵינַיִם **ʻÊynayim**, *ay-nah'-yim*; or

עֵינָם **ʻÊynâm**, *ay-nawm'*; dual of 5869; *double fountain*; *Enajim* or *Enam*, a place in Pal.:—Enaim, openly (Gen. 38 : 21).

5880. עֵין מִשְׁפָּט **ʻÊyn Mishpâṭ**, *ane mish-pawt'*; from 5869 and 4941; *fountain of judgment*; *En-Mishpat*, a place near Pal.:—En-mishpat.

5881. עֵינָן **ʻÊynân**, *ay-nawn'*; from 5869; *having eyes*; *Enan*, an Isr.:—Enan. Comp. 2704.

5882. עֵין עֶגְלַיִם **ʻÊyn ʻEglayim**, *ane eg-lah'-yim*; from 5869 and the dual of 5695; *fountain of two calves*; *En-Eglajim*, a place in Pal.:—En-eglaim.

5883. עֵין רֹגֵל **ʻÊyn Rôgêl**, *ane ro-gale'*; from 5869 and the act. part. of 7270; *fountain of a traveller*; *En-Rogel*, a place near Jerus.:—En-rogel.

5884. עֵין רִמּוֹן **ʻÊyn Rimmôwn**, *ane rim-mone'*; from 5869 and 7416; *fountain of a pomegranate; En-Rimmon*, a place in Pal.:—En-rimmon.

5885. עֵין שֶׁמֶשׁ **ʻÊyn Shemesh**, *ane sheh'-mesh*; from 5869 and 8121; *fountain of the sun; En-Shemesh*, a place in Pal.:—En-shemesh.

5886. עֵין תַּנִּים **ʻÊyn Tannîym**, *ane tan-neem'*; from 5869 and the plur. of 8565; *fountain of jackals; En-Tannim*, a pool near Jerus.:—dragon well.

5887. עֵין תַּפּוּחַ **ʻÊyn Tappûwach**, *ane tap-poo'-akh*; from 5869 and 8598; *fountain of an apple*-tree; *En-Tappuăch*, a place in Pal.:—En-tappuah.

5888. עָיֵף **ʻâyêph**, *aw-yafe'*; a prim. root; to *languish*:—be wearied.

5889. עָיֵף **ʻâyêph**, *aw-yafe'*; from 5888; *languid*:—faint, thirsty, weary.

5890. עֵיפָה **ʻêyphâh**, *ay-faw'*; fem. from 5774; *obscurity* (as if from *covering*):—darkness.

5891. עֵיפָה **ʻÊyphâh**, *ay-faw'*; the same as 5890; *Ephah*, the name of a son of Midian, and of the region settled by him; also of an Isr. and of an Israelitess:—Ephah.

5892. עִיר **ʻiyr**, *eer*; or (in the plur.)
עָר **ʻâr**, *awr*; or
עָיַר **ʻâyar** (Judg. 10 : 4), *aw-yar'*; from 5782 a *city* (a place guarded by *waking* or a watch) in the widest sense (even of a mere *encampment* or *post*):—Ai [*from marg.*], city, court [*from marg.*], town.

5893. עִיר **ʻÎyr**, *eer*; the same as 5892; *Ir*, an Isr.:—Ir.

5894. עִיר **ʻiyr** (Chald.), *eer*; from a root corresp. to 5782; a *watcher*, i.e. an *angel* (as guardian):—watcher.

5895. עַיִר **ʻayir**, *ah'-yeer*; from 5782 in the sense of *raising* (i.e. *bearing* a burden); prop. a young *ass* (as just broken to a load); hence an ass-*colt*:—(ass) colt, foal, young ass.

5896. עִירָא **ʻÎyrâʼ**, *ee-raw'*; from 5782; *wakefulness; Ira*, the name of three Isr.:—Ira.

5897. עִירָד **ʻÎyrâd**, *ee-rawd'*; from the same as 6166; *fugitive; Irad*, an antediluvian:—Irad.

5898. עִיר הַמֶּלַח **ʻÎyr ham-Melach**, *eer ham-meh'-lakh*; from 5892 and 4417 with the art. of substance interp.; *city of* (*the*) *salt; Ir-ham-Melach*, a place near Pal.:—the city of salt.

5899. עִיר הַתְּמָרִים **ʻÎyr hat-Tᵉmârîym**, *eer hat-tem-aw-reem'*; from 5892 and the plur. of 8558 with the art. interp.; *city of the palmtrees; Ir-hat-Temarim*, a place in Pal.:—the city of palmtrees.

5900. עִירוּ **ʻÎyrûw**, *ee-roo'*; from 5892; a *citizen; Iru*, an Isr.:—Iru.

5901. עִירִי **ʻÎyrîy**, *ee-ree'*; from 5892; *urbane; Iri*, an Isr.:—Iri.

5902. עִירָם **ʻÎyrâm**, *ee-rawm'*; from 5892; *city-wise; Iram*, an Idumæan:—Iram.

5903. עֵירֹם **ʻêyrôm**, *ay-rome'*; or
עֵרֹם **ʻêrôm**, *ay-rome'*; from 6191; *nudity*:—naked (-ness).

5904. עִיר נָחָשׁ **ʻÎyr Nâchâsh**, *eer naw-khawsh'*; from 5892 and 5175; *city of a serpent; Ir-Nachash*, a place in Pal.:—Ir-nahash.

5905. עִיר שֶׁמֶשׁ **ʻÎyr Shemesh**, *eer sheh'-mesh*; from 5892 and 8121; *city of the sun; Ir-Shemesh*, a place in Pal.:—Ir-shemesh.

5906. עַיִשׁ **ʻAyish**, *ah'-yish*; or
עָשׁ **ʻÂsh**, *awsh*; from 5789; the constellation of the Great *Bear* (perh. from its *migration* through the heavens):—Arcturus.
עַיָּת **ʻAyâth**. See 5857.

5907. עַכְבּוֹר **ʻAkbôwr**, *ak-bore'*; prob. for 5909; *Akbor*, the name of an Idumæan and two Isr.:—Achbor.

5908. עַכָּבִישׁ **ʻakkâbîysh**, *ak-kaw-beesh'*; prob. from an unused root in the lit. sense of *entangling*; a *spider* (as *weaving* a network):—spider.

5909. עַכְבָּר **ʻakbâr**, *ak-bawr'*; prob. from the same as 5908 in the secondary sense of *attacking*; a *mouse* (as *nibbling*):—mouse.

5910. עַכּוֹ **ʻAkkôw**, *ak-ko'*; appar. from an unused root mean. to *hem* in; *Akko* (from its situation on a *bay*):—Accho.

5911. עָכוֹר **ʻÂkôwr**, *aw-kore'*; from 5916; *troubled; Akor*, the name of a place in Pal.:—Achor.

5912. עָכָן **ʻÂkân**, *aw-kawn'*; from an unused root mean. to *trouble; troublesome; Akan*, an Isr.:—Achan. Comp. 5917.

5913. עָכַס **ʻâkaç**, *aw-kas'*; a prim. root; prop. to *tie*, spec. with fetters; but used only as denom. from 5914; to *put on anklets*:—make a tinkling ornament.

5914. עֶכֶס **ʻekeç**, *eh'-kes*; from 5913; a *fetter*; hence an *anklet*:—stocks, tinkling ornament.

5915. עַכְסָה **ʻAkçâh**, *ak-saw'*; fem. of 5914; *anklet; Aksah*, an Israelitess:—Achsah.

5916. עָכַר **ʻâkar**, *aw-kar'*; a prim. root; prop. to *roil* water; fig. to *disturb* or *afflict*:—trouble, stir.

5917. עָכָר **ʻÂkâr**, *aw-kawr'*; from 5916; *troublesome; Akar*, an Isr.:—Achar. Comp. 5912.

5918. עָכְרָן **ʻOkrân**, *ok-rawn'*; from 5916; *muddler; Okran*, an Isr.:—Ocran.

5919. עַכְשׁוּב **ʻakshûwb**, *ak-shoob'*; prob. from an unused root mean. to *coil*; an *asp* (from lurking *coiled* up):—adder.

5920. עַל **ʻal**, *al*; from 5927; prop. the *top*; spec. the *Highest* (i.e. *God*); also (adv.) *aloft, to Jehovah*:—above, high, most High.

5921. עַל **ʻal**, *al*; prop. the same as 5920 used as a prep. (in the sing. or plur., often with pref., or as conj. with a particle following); *above, over, upon*, or *against* (yet always in this last relation with a downward aspect) in a great variety of applications (as follow):—above, according to (-ly), after, (as) against, among, and, × as, at, because of, beside (the rest of), between, beyond the time, × both and, by (reason of), × had the charge of, concerning for, in (that), (forth, out) of, (from) (off), (up-) on, over, than, through (-out), to, touching, × with.

5922. עַל **ʻal** (Chald.), *al*; corresp. to 5921:—about, against, concerning, for, [there-] fore, from, in, × more, of, (there-, up-) on, (in-) to, + why with.

5923. עֹל **ʻôl**, *ole*; or
עוֹל **ʻôwl**, *ole*; from 5953; a *yoke* (as *imposed* on the neck), lit. or fig.:—yoke.

5924. עֵלָּא **ʻêllâʼ** (Chald.), *ale-law'*; from 5922; *above*:—over.

5925. עֻלָּא **ʻUllâʼ**, *ool-law'*; fem. of 5923; *burden; Ulla*, an Isr.:—Ulla.

5926. עִלֵּג **ʻillêg**, *il-layg'*; from an unused root mean. to *stutter; stuttering*:—stammerer.

5927. עָלָה **ʻâlâh**, *aw-law'*; a prim. root; to *ascend*, intrans. (*be high*) or act. (*mount*); used in a great variety of senses, primary and secondary, lit. and fig. (as follow):—arise (up), (cause to) ascend up, at once, break [*the day*] (up), bring (up), (cause to) burn, carry up, cast up, + shew, climb (up), (cause to, make to) come (up), cut off, dawn, depart, exalt, excel, fall, fetch up, get up, (make to) go (away, up), grow (over), increase, lay, leap, levy, lift (self) up, light, [make] up, × mention, mount up, offer, make to pay, + perfect, prefer, put (on), raise, recover, restore, (make to) rise (up), scale, set (up), shoot forth (up), (begin to) spring (up), stir up, take away (up), work.

5928. עֲלָה **ʻălâh** (Chald.), *al-aw'*; corresp. to 5930; a *holocaust*:—burnt offering.

5929. עָלֶה **ʻâleh**, *aw-leh'*; from 5927; a *leaf* (as *coming up* on a tree); collect. *foliage*:—branch, leaf.

5930. עֹלָה **ʻôlâh**, *o-law'*; or
עוֹלָה **ʻôwlâh**, *o-law'*; fem. act. part. of 5927; a *step* or (collect. *stairs*, as *ascending*); usually a *holocaust* (as *going up* in smoke):—ascent, burnt offering (sacrifice), go up to. See also 5766.

5931. עִלָּה **ʻillâh** (Chald.), *il-law'*; fem. from a root corresp. to 5927; a *pretext* (as *arising* artificially):—occasion.

5932. עַלְוָה **ʻalvâh**, *al-vaw'*; for 5766; moral *perverseness*:—iniquity.

5933. עַלְוָה **ʻAlvâh**, *al-vaw'*; or
עַלְיָה **ʻAlyâh**, *al-yaw'*; the same as 5932; *Alvah* or *Aljah*, an Idumæan:—Aliah, Alvah.

5934. עָלוּם **ʻâlûwm**, *aw-loom'*; pass. part. of 5956 in the denom. sense of 5958; (only in plur. as abstr.) *adolescence*; fig. *vigor*:—youth.

5935. עַלְוָן **ʻAlvân**, *al-vawn'*; or
עַלְיָן **ʻAlyân**, *al-yawn'*; from 5927; *lofty; Alvan* or *Aljan*, an Idumæan:—Alian, Alvan.

5936. עֲלוּקָה **ʻălûwqâh**, *al-oo-kaw'*; fem. pass. part. of an unused root mean. to *suck*; the *leech*:—horse-leech.

5937. עָלַז **ʻâlaz**, *aw-laz'*; a prim. root; to *jump* for joy, i.e. *exult*:—be joyful, rejoice, triumph.

5938. עָלֵז **ʻâlêz**, *aw-laze'*; from 5937; *exultant*:—that rejoiceth.

5939. עֲלָטָה **ʻălâṭâh**, *al-aw-taw'*; fem. from an unused root mean. to *cover*; *dusk*:—dark, twilight.

5940. עֱלִי **ʻĕlîy**, *el-ee'*; from 5927; a *pestle* (as *lifted*):—pestle.

5941. עֵלִי **ʻÊlîy**, *ay-lee'*; from 5927; *lofty; Eli*, an Isr. high-priest:—Eli.

5942. עִלִּי **ʻillîy**, *il-lee'*; from 5927; *high*, i.e. compar.:—upper.

5943. עִלַּי **ʻillay** (Chald.), *il-lah'ee*; corresp. to 5942; *supreme* (i.e. *God*):—(most) high.
עַלְיָה **ʻAlyâh**. See 5933.

5944. עֲלִיָּה **ʻălîyâh**, *al-ee-yaw'*; fem. from 5927; something *lofty*, i.e. a *stair-way*; also a *second-story* room (or even one on the roof); fig. the *sky*:—ascent, (upper) chamber, going up, loft, parlour.

5945. עֶלְיוֹן **ʻelyôwn**, *el-yone'*; from 5927; an *elevation*, i.e. (adj.) *lofty* (compar.); as title, the *Supreme*:—(Most, on) high (-er, -est), upper (-most).

5946. עֶלְיוֹן **ʻelyôwn** (Chald.), *el-yone'*; corresp. to 5945; the *Supreme*:—Most high.

5947. עַלִּיז **ʻallîyz**, *al-leez'*; from 5937; *exultant*:—joyous, (that) rejoice (-ing).

5948. עֲלִיל **ʻălîyl**, *al-eel'*; from 5953 in the sense of *completing*; prob. a *crucible* (as *working* over the metal):—furnace.

5949. עֲלִילָה **ʻălîylâh**, *al-ee-law'*; or
עֲלִלָה **ʻălilâh**, *al-ee-law'*; from 5953 in the sense of *effecting*; an *exploit* (of God), or a *performance* (of man, often in a bad sense); by impl. an *opportunity*:—act (-ion), deed, doing, invention, occasion, work.

5950. עֲלִילִיָּה **ʻălîylîyâh**, *al-ee-lee-yaw'*; for 5949; (miraculous) *execution*:—work.
עַלְיָן **ʻAlyân**. See 5935.

5951. עֲלִיצוּת **ʻălîytsûwth**, *al-ee-tsooth'*; from 5970; *exultation*:—rejoicing.

5952. עַלִּית **ʻallîyth**, *al-leeth'*; from 5927; a *second-story* room:—chamber. Comp. 5944.

5953. עָלַל **ʻâlal**, *aw-lal'*; a prim. root; to *effect* thoroughly; spec. to *glean* (also fig.); by impl. (in a bad sense) to *overdo*, i.e. maltreat, be saucy to, pain, impose (also lit.):—abuse, affect, × child, defile, do, glean, mock, practise, throughly, work (wonderfully).

5954. עֲלַל **ʻălal** (Chald.), *al-al'*; corresp. to 5953 (in the sense of *thrusting* oneself in), to *enter;* caus. to *introduce:*—bring in, come in, go in.

עֹלָל **ʻôlâl**. See 5768.

עֲלִלָה **ʻălîlâh**. See 5949.

5955. עֹלֵלָה **ʻôlêlâh**, *o-lay-law'*; fem. act. part. of 5953; only in plur. *gleanings;* by extens. *gleaning-time:*—(gleaning) (of the) grapes, grapegleanings.

5956. עָלַם **ʻâlam**, *aw-lam'*; a prim. root; to *veil* from sight, i.e. *conceal* (lit. or fig.):—× any ways, blind, dissembler, hide (self), secret (thing).

5957. עָלַם **ʻâlam** (Chald.), *aw-lam'*; corresp. to 5769; *remote* time, i.e. the *future* or *past* indefinitely; often adv. *forever:*—for ([n-]) ever (lasting), old.

5958. עֶלֶם **ʻelem**, *eh'lem;* from 5956; prop. something *kept out of sight* [comp. 5959], i.e. a *lad:*—young man, stripling.

עֹלָם **ʻôlâm**. See 5769.

5959. עַלְמָה **ʻalmâh**, *al-maw'*; fem. of 5958; a *lass* (as *veiled* or private):—damsel, maid, virgin.

5960. עַלְמוֹן **ʻAlmôwn**, *al-mone'*; from 5956; *hidden; Almon,* a place in Pal. See also 5963.

5961. עֲלָמוֹת **ʻĂlâmôwth**, *al-aw-mōth'*; plur. of 5959; prop. *girls,* i.e. the *soprano* or female voice, perh. *falsetto:*—Alamoth.

עַלְמוּת **ʻalmûwth**. See 4192.

5962. עַלְמִי **ʻAlmîy** (Chald.), *al-mee'*; patrial from a name corresp. to 5867 contr.; an *Elamite* or inhab. of Elam:—Elamite.

5963. עַלְמֹן דִּבְלָתָיְמָה **ʻAlmôn Diblâthâ-yᵉmâh**, *al-mone' dib-law-thaw'-yem-aw;* from the same as 5960 and the dual of 1690 [comp. 1015] with enclitic of direction; *Almon towards Diblathajim; Almon-Diblathajemah,* a place in Moab:—Almon-dilathaim.

5964. עָלֶמֶת **ʻÂlemeth**, *aw-leh'-meth;* from 5956; a *covering; Alemeth,* the name of a place in Pal. and of two Isr.:—Alameth, Alemeth.

5965. עָלַס **ʻâlaç**, *aw-las'*; a prim. root; to *leap* for joy, i.e. *exult, wave* joyously:—× peacock, rejoice, solace self.

5966. עָלַע **ʻâlaʻ**, *aw-lah'*; a prim. root; to *sip* up:—suck up.

5967. עֲלַע **ʻălaʻ** (Chald.), *al-ah'*; corresp. to 6763; a *rib:*—rib.

5968. עָלַף **ʻâlaph**, *aw-laf'*; a prim. root; to *veil* or *cover;* fig. to *be languid:*—faint, overlaid, wrap self.

5969. עֻלְפֶּה **ʻulpeh**, *ool-peh';* from 5968; an *envelope,* i.e. (fig.) *mourning:*—fainted.

5970. עָלַץ **ʻâlats**, *aw-lats'*; a prim. root; to *jump* for joy, i.e. *exult:*—be joyful, rejoice, triumph.

5971. עַם **ʻam**, *am;* from 6004; a *people* (as a congregated *unit*); spec. a *tribe* (as those of Israel); hence (collect.) *troops* or *attendants;* fig. a *flock:*—folk, men, nation, people.

5972. עַם **ʻam** (Chald.), *am;* corresp. to 5971:—people.

5973. עִם **ʻim**, *eem;* from 6004; adv. or prep., *with* (i.e. in *conjunction* with), in varied applications; spec. *equally with;* often with prep. pref. (and then usually unrepresented in English):—accompanying, against, and, as (× long as), before, beside, by (reason of), for all, from (among, between), in, like, more than, of, (un-) to, with (-al).

5974. עִם **ʻim** (Chald.), *eem;* corresp. to 5973:—by, from, like, to (-ward), with.

5975. עָמַד **ʻâmad**, *aw-mad'*; a prim. root; to *stand,* in various relations (lit. and fig., intrans. and trans.):—abide (behind), appoint, arise, cease, confirm, continue, dwell, be employed, endure, establish, leave, make, ordain, be [over], place, (be) present (self), raise up, remain, repair, + serve, set (forth, over, -tle, up), (make to, make to be at a, with-) stand (by, fast, firm, still, up), (be at a) stay (up), tarry.

5976 עָמַד **ʻâmad**, *aw-mad'*; for 4571; to *shake:*—be at a stand.

5977. עֹמֶד **ʻômed**, *o'-med;* from 5975; a *spot* (as being *fixed*):—place, (+ where) stood, upright.

5978. עִמָּד **ʻimmâd**, *im-mawd'*; prol. for 5973; along *with:*—against, by, from, in, + me, + mine, of, + that I take, unto, upon, with (-in).

עַמֻּד **ʻammûd**. See 5982.

5979. עֶמְדָּה **ʻemdâh**, *em-daw';* from 5975; a *station,* i.e. domicile:—standing.

5980. עֻמָּה **ʻummâh**, *oom-maw';* from 6004; *conjunction,* i.e. *society;* mostly adv. or prep. (with prep. pref.), *near, beside, along with:*—(over) against, at, beside, hard by, in points.

5981. עֻמָּה **ʻUmmâh**, *oom-maw';* the same as 5980; *association; Ummah,* a place in Pal.:—Ummah.

5982. עַמּוּד **ʻammûwd**, *am-mood';* or

עַמֻּד **ʻammûd**, *am-mood';* from 5975; a *column* (as *standing*); also a *stand,* i.e. platform:—× apiece, pillar.

5983. עַמּוֹן **ʻAmmôwn**, *am-mone';* from 5971; *tribal,* i.e. *inbred; Ammon,* a son of Lot; also his posterity and their country:—Ammon, Ammonites.

5984. עַמּוֹנִי **ʻAmmôwnîy**, *am-mo-nee';* patron. from 5983; an *Ammonite* or (adj.) *Ammonitish:*—Ammonite (-s).

5985. עַמּוֹנִית **ʻAmmôwnîyth**, *am-mo-neeth';* fem. of 5984; an *Ammonitess:*—Ammonite (-ss).

5986. עָמוֹס **ʻÂmôwç**, *aw-moce';* from 6006; *burdensome; Amos,* an Isr. prophet:—Amos.

5987. עָמוֹק **ʻÂmôwq**, *aw-moke';* from 6009; *deep; Amok,* an Isr.:—Amok.

5988. עַמִּיאֵל **ʻAmmîyʼêl**, *am-mee-ale';* from 5971 and 410; *people of God; Ammiël,* the name of three or four Isr.:—Ammiel.

5989. עַמִּיהוּד **ʻAmmîyhûwd**, *am-mee-hood';* from 5971 and 1935; *people of splendor; Ammihud,* the name of three Isr.:—Ammihud.

5990. עַמִּיזָבָד **ʻAmmîyzâbâd**, *am-mee-zaw-bawd';* from 5971 and 2064; *people of endowment; Ammizabad,* an Isr.:—Ammizabad.

5991. עַמִּיחוּר **ʻAmmîychûwr**, *am-mee-khoor';* from 5971 and 2353; *people of nobility; Ammichur,* a Syrian prince:—Ammihud [*from the marg.*].

5992. עַמִּינָדָב **ʻAmmîynâdâb**, *am-mee-naw-dawb';* from 5971 and 5068; *people of liberality; Amminadab,* the name of four Isr.:—Amminadab.

5993. עַמִּי נָדִיב **ʻAmmîy Nâdîyb**, *am-mee' naw-deeb';* from 5971 and 5081; *my people* (is) *liberal; Ammi-Nadib,* prob. an Isr.:—Amminadib.

5994. עֲמִיק **ʻămîyq** (Chald.), *am-eek';* corresp. to 6012; *profound,* i.e. unsearchable:—deep.

5995. עָמִיר **ʻâmîyr**, *aw-meer';* from 6014; a *bunch* of grain:—handful, sheaf.

5996. עַמִּישַׁדַּי **ʻAmmîyshadday**, *am-mee-shad-dah'ee;* from 5971 and 7706; *people of* (the) *Almighty; Ammishaddai,* an Isr.:—Ammishaddai.

5997. עָמִית **ʻâmîyth**, *aw-meeth';* from a prim. root mean. to *associate; companionship;* hence (concr.) a *comrade* or kindred man:—another, fellow, neighbour.

5998. עָמַל **ʻâmal**, *aw-mal';* a prim. root; to *toil,* i.e. *work severely* and with irksomeness:—[take] labour (in).

5999. עָמָל **ʻâmâl**, *aw-mawl';* from 5998; *toil,* i.e. *wearing effort;* hence *worry,* wheth. of body or mind:—grievance (-vousness), iniquity, labour, mischief, miserable (-sery), pain (-ful), perverseness, sorrow, toil, travail, trouble, wearisome, wickedness.

6000. עָמָל **ʻÂmâl**, *aw-mawl';* the same as 5999; *Amal,* an Isr.:—Amal.

6001. עָמֵל **ʻâmêl**, *aw-male';* from 5998; *toiling* concr. a *laborer;* fig. *sorrowful:*—that laboureth, that is a misery, had taken [labour], wicked, workman.

6002. עֲמָלֵק **ʻĂmâlêq**, *am-aw-lake';* prob. of for. or.; *Amalek,* a descend. of Esau; also his posterity and their country:—Amalek.

6003. עֲמָלֵקִי **ʻĂmâlêqîy**, *am-aw-lay-kee';* patron. from 6002; an *Amalekite* (or collect. the *Amalekites*) or desc. of Amalek:—Amalekite (-s).

6004. עָמַם **ʻâmam**, *aw-mam';* a prim. root; to *associate;* by impl. to *overshadow* (by *huddling* together):—become dim, hide.

6005. עִמָּנוּאֵל **ʻImmânûwʼêl**, *im-maw-noo-ale';* from 5973 and 410 with suff. pron. ins.; *with us* (is) *God; Immanuel,* a typ. name of Isaiah's son:—Immanuel.

6006. עָמַס **ʻâmaç**, *aw-mas';* or

עָמַשׂ **ʻâmas**, *aw-mas';* a prim. root; to *load,* i.e. *impose* a burden (or fig. infliction):—be borne, (heavy) burden (self), lade, load, put.

6007. עֲמַסְיָה **ʻĂmaçyâh**, *am-as-yaw';* from 6006 and 3050; *Jah has loaded; Amasjah,* an Isr.:—Amasiah.

6008. עַמְעָד **ʻAmʻâd**, *am-awd';* from 5971 and 5703; *people of time; Amad,* a place in Pal.:—Amad.

6009. עָמַק **ʻâmaq**, *aw-mak';* a prim. root; to *be* (causat. *make*) *deep* (lit. or fig.):—(be, have, make, seek) deep (-ly), depth, be profound.

6010. עֵמֶק **ʻêmeq**, *ay'-mek;* from 6009; a *vale* (i.e. broad *depression*):—dale, vale, valley [*often used as a part of proper names*]. See also 1025.

6011. עֹמֶק **ʻômeq**, *o'-mek;* from 6009; *depth:*—depth.

6012. עָמֵק **ʻâmêq**, *aw-make';* from 6009; *deep* (lit. or fig.):—deeper, depth, strange.

6013. עָמֹק **ʻâmôq**, *aw-moke';* from 6009; *deep* (lit. or fig.):—(× exceeding) deep (thing)

6014. עָמַר **ʻâmar**, *aw-mar';* a prim. root; prop. appar. to *heap;* fig. to *chastise* (as if *piling* blows); spec. (as denom. from 6016) to *gather* grain:—bind sheaves, make merchandise of.

6015. עֲמַר **ʻămar** (Chald.), *am-ar';* corresp. to 6785; *wool:*—wool.

6016. עֹמֶר **ʻômer**, *o'-mer;* from 6014; prop. a *heap,* i.e. a *sheaf;* also an *omer,* as a dry measure:—omer, sheaf.

6017. עֲמֹרָה **ʻĂmôrâh**, *am-o-raw';* from 6014; a (ruined) *heap; Amorah,* a place in Pal.:—Gomorrah.

6018. עָמְרִי **ʻOmrîy**, *om-ree';* from 6014; *heaping; Omri,* an Isr.:—Omri.

6019. עַמְרָם **ʻAmrâm**, *am-rawm';* prob. from 5971 and 7311; *high people; Amram,* the name of two Isr.:—Amram.

6020. עַמְרָמִי **ʻAmrâmîy**, *am-raw-mee';* patron. from 6019; an *Amramite* or desc. of Amram:—Amramite.

עָמַשׂ **ʻâmas**. See 6006.

6021. עֲמָשָׂא **ʻĂmâsâʼ**, *am-aw-saw';* from 6006; *burden; Amasa,* the name of two Isr.:—Amasa.

6022. עֲמָשַׂי **ʻĂmâsay**, *am-aw-sah'ee;* from 6006; *burdensome; Amasai,* the name of three Isr.:—Amasai.

6023. עֲמַשְׁסַי **ʻĂmashçay**, *am-ash-sah'ee;* prob. from 6006; *burdensome; Amashsay,* an Isr.:—Amashai.

6024. עֲנָב **ʻĂnâb**, *an-awb';* from the same as 6025; *fruit; Anab,* a place in Pal.:—Anab.

6025. עֵנָב **ʻênâb**, *ay-nawb';* from an unused root prob. mean. to *bear* fruit; a *grape:*—(ripe) grape, wine.

6026. עָנַג **ʻânag**, *aw-nag';* a prim. root; to be *soft* or pliable, i.e. (fig.) *effeminate* or luxurious:—delicate (-ness), (have) delight (self), sport self.

6027. עֹנֶג **ʻôneg**, *o'-neg;* from 6026; *luxury:*—delight, pleasant.

6028. עָנֹג **ʻânôg**, *aw-nogue';* from 6026; *luxurious:*—delicate.

6029. עָנַד **ʻânad**, *aw-nad'*; a prim. root; to *lace* fast:—bind, tie.

6030. עָנָה **ʻânâh**, *aw-naw'*; a prim. root; prop. to *eye* or (gen.) to *heed*, i.e. *pay attention;* by impl. to *respond;* by extens. to *begin* to *speak;* spec. to *sing, shout, testify, announce:*—give account, afflict [*by mistake for* 6031], (cause to, give) answer, bring low [*by mistake for* 6031], cry, hear, Leannoth, lift up, say, × scholar, (give a) shout, sing (together by course), speak, testify, utter, (bear) witness. See also 1042, 1043.

6031. עָנָה **ʻânâh**, *aw-naw'*; a prim. root [possibly rather ident. with 6030 through the idea of *looking* down or *browbeating*]; to *depress* lit. or fig., trans. or intrans. (in various applications, as follow):—abase self, afflict (-ion, self), answer [*by mistake for* 6030], chasten self, deal hardly with, defile, exercise, force, gentleness, humble (self), hurt, ravish, sing [*by mistake for* 6030], speak [*by mistake for* 6030], submit self, weaken, × in any wise.

6032. עֲנָה **ʻănâh** (Chald.), *an-aw'*; corresp. to 6030:—answer, speak.

6033. עֲנָה **ʻănâh** (Chald.), *an-aw'*; corresp. to 6031:—poor.

6034. עֲנָה **ʻĂnâh**, *an-aw'*; prob. from 6030; an *answer; Anah*, the name of two Edomites and one Edomitess:—Anah.

6035. עָנָו **ʻânâv**, *aw-nawv'*; or [by intermixture with 6041]

עָנָיו **ʻânâyv**, *aw-nawv'*; from 6031; *depressed* (fig.), in mind (*gentle*) or circumstances (*needy*, espec. *saintly*):—humble, lowly, meek, poor°. Comp. 6041.

6036. עָנוּב **ʻÂnûwb**, *aw-noob'*; pass. part. from the same as 6025; *borne* (as fruit); *Anub*, an Isr.:—Anub.

6037. עַנְוָה **ʻanvâh**, *an-vaw'*; fem. of 6035; *mildness* (royal); also (concr.) *oppressed:*—gentleness, meekness.

6038. עֲנָוָה **ʻănâvâh**, *an-aw-vaw'*; from 6035; *condescension*, human and subj. (*modesty*), or divine and obj. (*clemency*):—gentleness, humility, meekness.

6039. עֱנוּת **ʻĕnûwth**, *en-ooth'*; from 6031; *affliction:*—affliction.

6040. עֳנִי **ʻŏnîy**, *on-ee'*; from 6031; *depression*, i.e. misery:—afflicted (-ion), trouble.

6041. עָנִי **ʻânîy**, *aw-nee'*; from 6031; *depressed*, in mind or circumstances [practically the same as 6035, although the marg. constantly disputes this, making 6035 subj. and 6041 obj.]:—afflicted, humble°, lowly°, needy, poor.

6042. עֻנִּי **ʻUnnîy**, *oon-nee'*; from 6031; *afflicted; Unni*, the name of two Isr.:—Unni.

6043. עֲנָיָה **ʻĂnâyâh**, *an-aw-yaw'*; from 6030; *Jah has answered; Anajah*, the name of two Isr.:—Anaiah.

עָנִיו **ʻânâyv**. See 6035.

6044. עָנִים **ʻÂnîym**, *aw-neem'*; for plur. of 5869; *fountains; Anim*, a place in Pal.:—Anim.

6045. עִנְיָן **ʻinyân**, *in-yawn'*; from 6031; *ado*, i.e. (gen.) *employment* or (spec.) an *affair:*—business, travail.

6046. עָנֵם **ʻÂnêm**, *aw-name'*; from the dual of 5869; *two fountains; Anem*, a place in Pal.:—Anem.

6047. עֲנָמִים **ʻĂnâmîm**, *an-aw-meem'*; as if plur. of some Eg. word; *Anamim*, a son of Mizraim and his desc., with their country:—Anamim.

6048. עֲנַמֶּלֶךְ **ʻĂnammelek**, *an-am-meh'-lek*; of for. or.; *Anammelek*, an Assyrian deity:—Anammelech.

6049. עָנַן **ʻânan**, *aw-nan'*; a prim. root; to *cover;* used only as denom. from 6051, to *cloud over;* fig. to *act covertly*, i.e. practise magic:—× bring, enchanter, Meonemin, observe (-r of) times, soothsayer, sorcerer.

6050. עֲנַן **ʻănan** (Chald.), *an-an'*; corresp. to 6051:—cloud.

6051. עָנָן **ʻânân**, *aw-nawn'*; from 6049; a *cloud* (as *covering* the sky), i.e. the *nimbus* or thunder-cloud:—cloud (-y).

6052. עָנָן **ʻÂnân**, *aw-nawn'*; the same as 6051; *cloud; Anan*, an Isr.:—Anan.

6053. עֲנָנָה **ʻănânâh**, *an-aw-naw'*; fem. of 6051; *cloudiness:*—cloud.

6054. עֲנָנִי **ʻĂnânîy**, *an-aw-nee'*; from 6051; *cloudy; Anani*, an Isr.:—Anani.

6055. עֲנַנְיָה **ʻĂnanyâh**, *an-an-yaw'*; from 6049 and 3050; *Jah has covered; Ananjah*, the name of an Isr. and of a place in Pal.:—Ananiah.

6056. עֲנַף **ʻănaph** (Chald.), *an-af'*; or

עֶנֶף **ʻeneph** (Chald.), *eh'-nef*; corresp. to 6057:—bough, branch.

6057. עָנָף **ʻânâph**, *aw-nawf'*; from an unused root mean. to *cover;* a *twig* (as *covering* the limbs):—bough, branch.

6058. עָנֵף **ʻânêph**, *aw-nafe'*; from the same as 6057; *branching:*—full of branches.

6059. עָנַק **ʻânaq**, *aw-nak'*; a prim. root; prop. to *choke;* used only as denom. from 6060, to *collar*, i.e. adorn with a necklace; fig. to *fit out* with supplies:—compass about as a chain, furnish, liberally.

6060. עֲנָק **ʻânâq**, *aw-nawk'*; from 6059; a *necklace* (as if *strangling*):—chain.

6061. עֲנָק **ʻÂnâq**, *aw-nawk'*; the same as 6060; *Anak*, a Canaanite:—Anak.

6062. עֲנָקִי **ʻĂnâqîy**, *an-aw-kee'*; patron. from 6061; an *Anakite* or desc. of Anak:—Anakim.

6063. עָנֵר **ʻÂnêr**, *aw-nare'*; prob. for 5288; *Aner*, an Amorite, also a place in Pal.:—Aner.

6064. עָנַשׁ **ʻânash**, *aw-nash'*; a prim. root; prop. to *urge;* by impl. to *inflict* a penalty, spec. to *fine:*—amerce, condemn, punish, × surely.

6065. עֲנַשׁ **ʻănash** (Chald.), *an-ash'*; corresp. to 6066; a *mulct:*—confiscation.

6066. עֹנֶשׁ **ʻônesh**, *o'-nesh*; from 6064; a *fine:*—punishment, tribute.

עֶנֶת **ʻeneth**. See 3706.

6067. עֲנָת **ʻĂnâth**, *an-awth'*; from 6030; *answer; Anath*, an Isr.:—Anath.

6068. עֲנָתוֹת **ʻĂnâthôwth**, *an-aw-thōth'*; plur. of 6067; *Anathoth*, the name of two Isr., also of a place in Pal.:—Anathoth.

6069. עַנְתֹתִי **ʻAnthôthîy**, *an-tho-thee'*; or

עַנְּתוֹתִי **ʻAnnethôwthîy**, *an-ne-tho-thee'*; patrial from 6068; an *Antothite* or inhab. of Anathoth:—of Anathoth, Anethothite, Anetothite, Antothite.

6070. עַנְתֹתִיָּה **ʻAnthôthîyâh**, *an-tho-thee-yaw'*; from the same as 6068 and 3050; *answers of Jah; Anthothijah*, an Isr.:—Antothijah.

6071. עָסִיס **ʻâçîyç**, *aw-sees'*; from 6072; *must* or fresh grape-juice (as just *trodden* out):—juice, new (sweet) wine.

6072. עָסַס **ʻâçaç**, *aw-sas'*; a prim. root; to *squeeze* out juice; fig. to *trample:*—tread down.

6073. עֳפֶא **ʻŏpheʼ**, *of-eh'*; from an unused root mean. to *cover;* a *bough* (as covering the tree):—branch.

6074. עֳפִי **ʻŏphîy** (Chald.), *of-ee'*; corresp. to 6073; a *twig;* bough, i.e. (collect.) *foliage:*—leaves.

6075. עָפַל **ʻâphal**, *aw-fal'*; a prim. root; to *swell;* fig. *be elated:*—be lifted up, presume.

6076. עֹפֶל **ʻôphel**, *o'-fel*; from 6075; a *tumor;* also a *mound*, i.e. fortress:—emerod, fort, strong hold, tower.

6077. עֹפֶל **ʻÔphel**, *o'-fel*; the same as 6076; *Ophel*, a ridge in Jerus.:—Ophel.

6078. עָפְנִי **ʻOphnîy**, *of-nee'*; from an unused noun [denoting a place in Pal.; from an unused root of uncert. mean.]; an *Ophnite* (collect.) or inhab. of Ophen:—Ophni.

6079. עַפְעַף **ʻaphʻaph**, *af-af'*; from 5774; an *eyelash* (as *fluttering*); fig. morning *ray:*—dawning, eye-lid.

6080. עָפַר **ʻâphar**, *aw-far'*; a prim. root; mean. either to *be gray* or perh. rather to *pulverize;* used only as denom. from 6083, to *be dust:*—cast [dust].

6081. עֵפֶר **ʻÊpher**, *ay'-fer*; prob. a var. of 6082; *gazelle; Epher*, the name of an Arabian and of two Isr.:—Epher.

6082. עֹפֶר **ʻôpher**, *o'-fer*; from 6080; a *fawn* (from the *dusty* color):—young roe [hart].

6083. עָפָר **ʻâphâr**, *aw-fawr'*; from 6080; *dust* (as *powdered* or *gray*); hence *clay, earth, mud:*—ashes, dust, earth, ground, morter, powder, rubbish.

עָפְרָה **ʻAphrâh**. See 1035.

6084. עָפְרָה **ʻOphrâh**, *of-raw'*; fem. of 6082; *female fawn; Ophrah*, the name of an Isr. and of two places in Pal.:—Ophrah.

6085. עֶפְרוֹן **ʻEphrôwn**, *ef-rone'*; from the same as 6081; *fawn-like; Ephron*, the name of a Canaanite and of two places in Pal.:—Ephron, Ephrain [*from the marg.*].

עֹפֶרֶת **ʻôphereth**. See 5777.

6086. עֵץ **ʻêts**, *ates*; from 6095; a *tree* (from its *firmness*); hence *wood* (plur. *sticks*):—+ carpenter, gallows, helve, + pine, plank, staff, stalk, stick, stock, timber, tree, wood.

6087. עָצַב **ʻâtsab**, *aw-tsab'*; a prim. root; prop. to *carve*, i.e. *fabricate* or *fashion;* hence (in a bad sense) to *worry, pain* or *anger:*—displease, grieve, hurt, make, be sorry, vex, worship, wrest.

6088. עֲצַב **ʻătsab** (Chald.), *ats-ab'*; corresp. to 6087; to *afflict:*—lamentable.

6089. עֶצֶב **ʻetseb**, *eh'-tseb*; from 6087; an earthen *vessel;* usually (painful) *toil;* also a *pang* (whether of body or mind):—grievous, idol, labor, sorrow.

6090. עֹצֶב **ʻôtseb**, *o'-tseb*; a var. of 6089; an *idol* (as fashioned); also *pain* (bodily or mental):—idol, sorrow, × wicked.

6091. עָצָב **ʻâtsâb**, *aw-tsawb'*; from 6087; an (idolatrous) *image:*—idol, image.

6092. עָצֵב **ʻâtsêb**, *aw-tsabe'*; from 6087; a (hired) *workman:*—labour.

6093. עִצָּבוֹן **ʻitstsâbôwn**, *its-tsaw-bone'*; from 6087; *worrisomeness*, i.e. *labor* or *pain:*—sorrow, toil.

6094. עַצֶּבֶת **ʻatstsebeth**, *ats-tseh'-beth*; from 6087; an *idol;* also a *pain* or *wound:*—sorrow, wound.

6095. עָצָה **ʻâtsâh**, *aw-tsaw'*; a prim. root; prop. to *fasten* (or *make firm*), i.e. to *close* (the eyes):—shut.

6096. עָצֶה **ʻâtseh**, *aw-tseh'*; from 6095; the *spine* (as giving *firmness* to the body):—back bone.

6097. עֵצָה **ʻêtsâh**, *ay-tsaw'*; fem. of 6086; *timber:*—trees.

6098. עֵצָה **ʻêtsâh**, *ay-tsaw'*; from 3289; *advice;* by impl. *plan;* also *prudence:*—advice, advisement, counsel ([-lor]), purpose.

6099. עָצוּם **ʻâtsûwm**, *aw-tsoom'*; or

עָצֻם **ʻâtsûm**, *aw-tsoom'*; pass. part. of 6105; *powerful* (spec. a *paw*); by impl. *numerous:*— + feeble, great, mighty, must, strong.

6100. עֶצְיוֹן גֶּבֶר **ʻEtsyôwn** (shorter

עֶצְיֹן **ʻEtsyôn**) **Geber**, *ets-yone' gheh'-ber*; from 6096 and 1397; *backbone-like of a man; Etsjon-Geber*, a place on the Red Sea:—Ezion-gaber, Ezion-geber.

6101. עָצַל **ʻâtsal**, *aw-tsal'*; a prim. root; to *lean* idly, i.e. to be *indolent* or *slack:*—be slothful.

6102. עָצֵל **ʻâtsêl**, *aw-tsale'*; from 6101; *indolent:*—slothful, sluggard.

6103. עַצְלָה **ʻatslâh**, *ats-law'*; fem. of 6102; (as abstr.) *indolence:*—slothfulness.

6104. עַצְלוּת **ʻatslûwth**, *ats-looth'*; from 6101; *indolence:*—idleness.

6105. עָצַם **ʻâtsam**, *aw-tsam'*; a prim. root; to *bind* fast, i.e. *close* (the eyes); intrans.

to be (causat. *make*) *powerful* or *numerous;* denom. (from 6106) to *craunch* the bones:—break the bones, close, be great, be increased, be (wax) mighty (-ier), be more, shut, be (-come, make) strong (-er).

6106. עֶצֶם **ʻetsem**, *eh'-tsem;* from 6105; a *bone* (as *strong*); by extens. the *body;* fig. the *substance,* i.e. (as pron.) *selfsame:*—body, bone, × life, (self-) same, strength, × very.

6107. עֶצֶם **ʻEtsem**, *eh'-tsem;* the same as 6106; *bone; Etsem,* a place in Pal.:—Azem, Ezem.

6108. עֹצֶם **ʻôtsem**, *o'-tsem;* from 6105; *power;* hence *body:*—might, strong, substance.

עָצֻם **ʻâtsûm**. See 6099.

6109. עָצְמָה **ʻotsmâh**, *ots-maw';* fem. of 6108; *powerfulness;* by extens. *numerousness:*—abundance, strength.

6110. עַצֻּמָה **ʻatstsumâh**, *ats-tsoo-maw';* fem. of 6099; a *bulwark,* i.e. (fig.) *argument:*—strong.

6111. עַצְמוֹן **ʻAtsmôwn**, *ats-mone';* or עַצְמֹן **ʻAtsmôn**, *ats-mone';* from 6107; *bone-like; Atsmon,* a place near Pal.:—Azmon.

6112. עֵצֶן **ʻêtsen**, *ay'-tsen;* from an unused root mean. to *be sharp* or *strong;* a *spear:*—Eznite [*from the marg.*].

6113. עָצַר **ʻâtsar**, *aw-tsar';* a prim. root; to *inclose;* by anal. to *hold back;* also to *maintain, rule, assemble:*— × be able, close up, detain, fast, keep (self close, still), prevail, recover, refrain, × reign, restrain, retain, shut (up), slack, stay, stop, withhold (self).

6114. עֶצֶר **ʻetser**, *eh'-tser;* from 6113; *restraint:*— + magistrate.

6115. עֹצֶר **ʻôtser**, *o'-tser;* from 6113; *closure;* also *constraint:*— × barren, oppression, × prison.

6116. עֲצָרָה **ʻătsârâh**, *ats-aw-raw';* or עֲצֶרֶת **ʻătsereth**, *ats-eh'-reth;* from 6113; an *assembly,* espec. on a *festival* or *holiday:*—(solemn) assembly (meeting).

6117. עָקַב **ʻâqab**, *aw-kab';* a prim. root; prop. to *swell* out or up; used only as denom. from 6119, to *seize by the heel;* fig. to *circumvent* (as if *tripping* up the heels); also to *restrain* (as if holding by the heel):—take by the heel, stay, supplant, × utterly.

6118. עֵקֶב **ʻêqeb**, *ay'-keb;* from 6117 in the sense of 6119; a *heel,* i.e. (fig.) the *last* of anything (used adv. *for ever*); also *result,* i.e. *compensation;* and so (adv. with prep. or rel.) on *account* of:— × because, by, end, for, if, reward.

6119. עָקֵב **ʻâqêb**, *aw-kabe';* or (fem.) עִקְּבָה **ʻiqqᵉbâh**, *ik-keb-aw';* from 6117; a *heel* (as *protuberant*); hence a *track;* fig. the *rear* (of an army):—heel, [horse-] hoof, last, lier in wait [*by mistake for* 6120], (foot-) step.

6120. עָקֵב **ʻâqêb**, *aw-kabe';* from 6117 in its denom. sense; a *lier in wait:*—heel [*by mistake for* 6119].

6121. עָקֹב **ʻâqôb**, *aw-kobe';* from 6117; in the orig. sense, a *knoll* (as *swelling up*); in the denom. sense (trans.) *fraudulent* or (intrans.) *tracked:*—crooked, deceitful, polluted.

6122. עָקְבָה **ʻoqbâh**, *ok-baw';* fem. of an unused form from 6117 mean. a *trick; trickery:*—subtilty.

6123. עָקַד **ʻâqad**, *aw-kad';* a prim. root; to *tie* with thongs:—bind.

עֵקֶד **ʻÊqed**. See 1044.

6124. עָקֹד **ʻâqôd**, *aw-kode';* from 6123; *striped* (with *bands*):—ring straked.

6125. עָקָה **ʻâqâh**, *aw-kaw';* from 5781; *constraint:*—oppression.

6126. עַקּוּב **ʻAqqûwb**, *ak-koob';* from 6117; *insidious; Akkub,* the name of five Isr.:—Akkub.

6127. עָקַל **ʻâqal**, *aw-kal';* a prim. root; to *wrest:*—wrong.

6128. עֲקַלְקַל **ʻăqalqal**, *ak-al-kal';* from 6127; *winding:*—by [-way], crooked way.

6129. עֲקַלָּתוֹן **ʻăqallâthôwn**, *ak-al-law-thone';* from 6127; *tortuous:*—crooked.

6130. עָקָן **ʻÂqân**, *aw-kawn';* from an unused root mean. to *twist; tortuous; Akan,* an Idumæan:—Akan. Comp. 3292.

6131. עָקַר **ʻâqar**, *aw-kar';* a prim. root; to *pluck* up (espec. by the roots); spec. to *hamstring;* fig. to *exterminate:*—dig down, hough, pluck up, root up.

6132. עֲקַר **ʻăqar** (Chald.), *ak-ar';* corresp. to 6131:—pluck up by the roots.

6133. עֵקֶר **ʻêqer**, *ay'-ker;* from 6131; fig. a *transplanted* person, i.e. naturalized citizen:—stock.

6134. עֵקֶר **ʻÊqer**, *ay'-ker;* the same as 6133; *Eker,* an Isr.:—Eker.

6135. עָקָר **ʻâqâr**, *aw-kawr';* from 6131; *sterile* (as if *extirpated* in the generative organs):—(× male or female) barren (woman).

6136. עִקַּר **ʻiqqar** (Chald.), *ik-kar';* from 6132; a *stock:*—stump.

6137. עַקְרָב **ʻaqrâb**, *ak-rawb';* of uncert. der.; a *scorpion;* fig. a *scourge* or knotted whip:—scorpion.

6138. עֶקְרוֹן **ʻEqrôwn**, *ek-rone';* from 6131; *eradication; Ekron,* a place in Pal.:—Ekron.

6139. עֶקְרוֹנִי **ʻEqrôwnîy**, *ek-ro-nee';* or עֶקְרֹנִי **ʻEqrônîy**, *ek-ro-nee';* patrial from 6138; an *Ekronite* or inhab. of Ekron:—Ekronite.

6140. עָקַשׁ **ʻâqash**, *aw-kash';* a prim. root; to *knot* or *distort;* fig. to *pervert* (act or declare perverse):—make crooked, (prove, that is) perverse (-rt).

6141. עִקֵּשׁ **ʻiqqêsh**, *ik-kashe';* from 6140; *distorted;* hence *false:*—crooked, froward, perverse.

6142. עִקֵּשׁ **ʻIqqêsh**, *ik-kashe';* the same as 6141; *perverse; Ikkesh,* an Isr.:—Ikkesh.

6143. עִקְּשׁוּת **ʻiqqᵉshûwth**, *ik-kesh-ooth';* from 6141; *perversity:*— × froward.

עָר **ʻâr**. See 5892.

6144. עָר **ʻÂr**, *awr;* the same as 5892; a *city; Ar,* a place in Moab:—Ar.

6145. עָר **ʻâr**, *awr;* from 5782; a *foe* (as *watchful* for mischief):—enemy.

6146. עָר **ʻâr** (Chald.), *awr;* corresp. to 6145:—enemy.

6147. עֵר **ʻÊr**, *ayr;* from 5782; *watchful; Er,* the name of two Isr.:—Er.

6148. עָרַב **ʻârab**, *aw-rab';* a prim. root; to *braid,* i.e. *intermix;* techn. to *traffic* (as if by barter); also to *give* or *be security* (as a kind of exchange):—engage, (inter-) meddle (with), mingle (self), mortgage, occupy, give pledges, be (-come, put in) surety, undertake.

6149. עָרֵב **ʻârêb**, *aw-rabe';* a prim. root [rather identical with 6148 through the idea of close *association*]; to be *agreeable:*—be pleasant (-ing), take pleasure in, be sweet.

6150. עָרַב **ʻârab**, *aw-rab';* a prim. root [rather identical with 6148 through the idea of *covering* with a texture]; to *grow dusky* at sundown:—be darkened, (toward) evening.

6151. עֲרַב **ʻărab** (Chald.), *ar-ab';* corresp. to 6148; to *commingle:*—mingle (self), mix.

6152. עֲרָב **ʻĂrâb**, *ar-awb';* or עֲרַב **ʻĂrab**, *ar-ab';* from 6150 in the fig. sense of *sterility; Arab* (i.e. *Arabia*), a country E. of Pal.:—Arabia.

6153. עֶרֶב **ʻereb**, *eh'-reb;* from 6150; *dusk:*— + day, even (-ing, tide), night.

6154. עֵרֶב **ʻêreb**, *ay'-reb;* or עֶרֶב **ʻereb** (1 Kings 10 : 15), (with the art. pref.), *eh'-reb;* from 6148; the *web* (or transverse threads of cloth); also a *mixture,* (or *mongrel* race):—Arabia, mingled people, mixed (multitude), woof.

6155. עָרָב **ʻârâb**, *aw-rawb';* from 6148; a *willow* (from the use of osiers as wattles):—willow.

6156. עָרֵב **ʻârêb**, *aw-rabe';* from 6149; *pleasant:*—sweet.

6157. עָרֹב **ʻârôb**, *aw-robe';* from 6148; a *mosquito* (from its *swarming*):—divers sorts of flies, swarm.

6158. עֹרֵב **ʻôrêb**, *o-rabe';* or עוֹרֵב **ʻôwrêb**, *o-rabe';* from 6150; a *raven* (from its *dusky* hue):—raven.

6159. עֹרֵב **ʻôrêb**, *o-rabe';* or עוֹרֵב **ʻôwrêb**, *o-rabe';* the same as 6158; *Oreb,* the name of a Midianite and of a cliff near the Jordan:—Oreb.

6160. עֲרָבָה **ʻărâbâh**, *ar-aw-baw';* from 6150 (in the sense of *sterility*); a *desert;* espec. (with the art. pref.) the (generally) sterile valley of the Jordan and its continuation to the Red Sea:—Arabah, champaign, desert, evening, heaven, plain, wilderness. See also 1026.

6161. עֲרֻבָּה **ʻărubbâh**, *ar-oob-baw';* fem. pass. part. of 6148 in the sense of a *bargain* or *exchange;* something given as *security,* i.e. (lit.) a *token* (of safety) or (metaph.) a *bondsman;*—pledge, surety.

6162. עֲרָבוֹן **ʻărâbôwn**, *ar-aw-bone';* from 6148 (in the sense of *exchange*); a *pawn* (given as security):—pledge.

6163. עֲרָבִי **ʻĂrâbîy**, *ar-aw-bee';* or עַרְבִי **ʻArbîy**, *ar-bee';* patrial from 6152; an *Arabian* or inhab. of Arab (i.e. Arabia):—Arabian.

6164. עַרְבָתִי **ʻArbâthîy**, *ar-baw-thee';* patrial from 1026; an *Arbathite* or inhab. of (Beth-) Arabah:—Arbathite.

6165. עָרַג **ʻârag**, *aw-rag';* a prim. root; to *long* for:—cry, pant.

6166. עֲרָד **ʻĂrâd**, *ar-awd';* from an unused root mean. to *sequester* itself; *fugitive; Arad,* the name of a place near Pal., also of a Canaanite and an Isr.:—Arad.

6167. עֲרָד **ʻărâd** (Chald.), *ar-awd';* corresp. to 6171; an *onager:*—wild ass.

6168. עָרָה **ʻârâh**, *aw-raw';* a prim. root; to *be* (caus. *make*) *bare;* hence to *empty, pour* out, *demolish:*—leave destitute, discover, empty, make naked, pour (out), rase, spread self, uncover.

6169. עָרָה **ʻârâh**, *aw-raw';* fem. from 6168; a *naked* (i.e. level) plot:—paper reed.

6170. עֲרוּגָה **ʻărûwgâh**, *ar-oo-gaw';* or עֲרֻגָה **ʻărûgâh**, *ar-oo-gaw';* fem. pass. part. of 6165; something *piled* up (as if [fig.] *raised* by mental aspiration), i.e. a *parterre:*—bed, furrow.

6171. עָרוֹד **ʻârôwd**, *aw-rode';* from the same as 6166; an *onager* (from his *lonesome* habits):—wild ass.

6172. עֶרְוָה **ʻervâh**, *er-vaw';* from 6168; *nudity,* lit. (espec. the *pudenda*) or fig. (*disgrace, blemish*):—nakedness, shame, unclean (-ness).

6173. עַרְוָה **ʻarvâh** (Chald.), *ar-vaw';* corresp. to 6172; *nakedness,* i.e. (fig.) *impoverishment:*—dishonour.

6174. עָרוֹם **ʻârôwm**, *aw-rome';* or עָרֹם **ʻârôm**, *aw-rome';* from 6191 (in its orig. sense); *nude,* either partially or totally:—naked.

6175. עָרוּם **ʻârûwm**, *aw-room';* pass. part. of 6191; *cunning* (usually in a bad sense):—crafty, prudent, subtil.

6176. עֲרוֹעֵר **ʻărôwʻêr**, *ar-o-ayr';* or עַרְעָר **ʻarʻâr**, *ar-awr';* from 6209 redupl.; a *juniper* (from its *nudity* of situation):—heath.

6177. עֲרוֹעֵר **ʻĂrôwʻêr**, *ar-o-ayr';* or עֲרֹעֵר **ʻĂrôʻêr**, *ar-o-ayr';* or עַרְעוֹר **ʻArʻôwr**, *ar-ore';* the same as 6176; *nudity* of situation; *Aroër,* the name of three places in or near Pal.:—Aroer.

6178. עָרוּץ **ʽârûwts**, *aw-roots'*; pass. part. of 6206; *feared*, i.e. (concr.) a *horrible place* or *chasm*:—cliffs.

6179. עֵרִי **ʽÊrîy**, *ay-ree'*; from 5782; *watchful*; *Eri*, an Isr.:—Eri.

6180. עֵרִי **ʽÊrîy**, *ay-ree'*; patron. of 6179; an *Erite* (collect.) or desc. of Eri:—Erites.

6181. עֶרְיָה **ʽeryâh**, *er-yaw'*; for 6172; *nudity*:—bare, naked, × quite.

6182. עֲרִיסָה **ʽărîyçâh**, *ar-ee-saw'*; from an unused root mean. to *comminute*; *meal*:—dough.

6183. עָרִיף **ʽârîyph**, *aw-reef'*; from 6201; the *sky* (as *drooping* at the horizon):—heaven.

6184. עָרִיץ **ʽârîyts**, *aw-reets'*; from 6206; *fearful*, i.e. *powerful* or *tyrannical*:—mighty, oppressor, in great power, strong, terrible, violent.

6185. עֲרִירִי **ʽărîyrîy**, *ar-e-ree'*; from 6209; *bare*, i.e. destitute (of children):—childless.

6186. עָרַךְ **ʽârak**, *aw-rak'*; a prim. root; to set in a *row*, i.e. *arrange*, put in *order* (in a very wide variety of applications):—put (set) (the battle, self) in array, compare, direct, equal, esteem, estimate, expert [in war], furnish, handle, join [battle], ordain, (lay, put, reckon up, set) (in) order, prepare, tax, value.

6187. עֵרֶךְ **ʽêrek**, *eh'-rek*; from 6186; a *pile*, *equipment*, *estimate*:—equal, estimation, (things that are set in) order, price, proportion, × set at, suit, taxation, × valuest.

6188. עָרֵל **ʽârêl**, *aw-rale'*; a prim. root; prop. to *strip*; but used only as denom. from 6189; to *expose* or *remove* the *prepuce*, whether lit. (to *go naked*) or fig. (to *refrain* from using):—count uncircumcised, foreskin to be uncovered.

6189. עָרֵל **ʽârêl**, *aw-rale'*; from 6188; prop. *exposed*, i.e. projecting loose (as to the prepuce); used only techn. *uncircumcised* (i.e. still having the prepuce uncurtailed):—uncircumcised (person).

6190. עָרְלָה **ʽorlâh**, *or-law'*; fem. of 6189; the *prepuce*:—foreskin, + uncircumcised.

6191. עָרַם **ʽâram**, *aw-ram'*; a prim. root; prop. to *be* (or *make*) *bare*; but used only in the der. sense (through the idea perh. of *smoothness*) to *be cunning* (usually in a bad sense):—× very, beware, take crafty [counsel], be prudent, deal subtilly.

6192. עָרַם **ʽâram**, *aw-ram'*; a prim. root; to *pile* up:—gather together.

6193. עֹרֶם **ʽôrem**, *o'-rem*; from 6191; a *stratagem*:—craftiness.

עֵרֹם **ʽÊrôm**. See 5903.

עָרֹם **ʽârôm**. See 6174.

6194. עָרֵם **ʽârêm** (Jer. 50 : 26), *aw-rame'*; or (fem.)

עֲרֵמָה **ʽărêmâh**, *ar-ay-maw'*; from 6192; a *heap*; spec. a *sheaf*:—heap (of corn), sheaf.

6195. עָרְמָה **ʽormâh**, *or-maw'*; fem. of 6193; *trickery*; or (in a good sense) *discretion*:—guile, prudence, subtilty, wilily, wisdom.

עֲרֵמָה **ʽarêmâh**. See 6194.

6196. עַרְמוֹן **ʽarmôwn**, *ar-mone'*; prob. from 6191; the *plane* tree (from its *smooth* and shed bark):—chestnut tree.

6197. עֵרָן **ʽÊrân**, *ay-rawn'*; prob. from 5782; *watchful*; *Eran*, an Isr.:—Eran.

6198. עֵרָנִי **ʽÊrânîy**, *ay-raw-nee'*; patron. from 6197; an *Eranite* or desc. (collect.) of Eran:—Eranites.

עַרְעוֹר **ʽArʽôwr**. See 6177.

6199. עַרְעָר **ʽarʽâr**, *ar-awr'*; from 6209; *naked*, i.e. (fig.) *poor*:—destitute. See also 6176.

עֲרֹעֵר **ʽĂrôʽêr**. See 6177.

6200. עֲרֹעֵרִי **ʽĂrôʽêrîy**, *ar-o-ay-ree'*; patron. from 6177; an *Aroërite* or inhab. of Aroër:—Aroerite.

6201. עָרַף **ʽâraph**, *aw-raf'*; a prim. root; to *droop*; hence to *drip*:—drop (down).

6202. עָרַף **ʽâraph**, *aw-raf'*; a prim. root [rather ident. with 6201 through the idea of *sloping*]; prop. to *bend* downward; but used only as a denom. from 6203, to *break the neck*; hence (fig.) to *destroy*:—that is beheaded, break down, break (cut off, strike off) neck.

6203. עֹרֶף **ʽôreph**, *o-ref'*; from 6202; the *nape* or back of the neck (as *declining*); hence the *back* generally (whether lit. or fig.):—back ([stiff-]) neck ([-ed]).

6204. עָרְפָּה **ʽOrpâh**, *or-paw'*; fem. of 6203; *mane*; *Orpah*, a Moabitess:—Orpah.

6205. עֲרָפֶל **ʽărâphel**, *ar-aw-fel'*; prob. from 6201; *gloom* (as of a *lowering* sky):—(gross, thick) dark (cloud, -ness).

6206. עָרַץ **ʽârats**, *aw-rats'*; a prim. root; to *awe* or (intrans.) to *dread*; hence to *harass*:—be affrighted (afraid, dread, feared, terrified), break, dread, fear, oppress, prevail, shake terribly.

6207. עָרַק **ʽâraq**, *aw-rak'*; a prim. root; to *gnaw*, i.e. (fig.) *eat* (by hyberbole); also (part.) a *pain*:—fleeing, sinew.

6208. עַרְקִי **ʽArqîy**, *ar-kee'*; patrial from an unused name mean. a *tush*; an *Arkite* or inhab. of Erek:—Arkite.

6209. עָרַר **ʽârar**, *aw-rar'*; a prim. root; to *bare*; fig. to *demolish*:—make bare, break, raise up [*perh. by clerical error for* RAZE], × utterly.

6210. עֶרֶשׂ **ʽeres**, *eh'-res*; from an unused root mean. perh. to *arch*; a *couch* (prop. with a *canopy*):—bed (-stead), couch.

6211. עָשׁ **ʽâsh**, *awsh*; from 6244; a *moth*:—moth. See also 5906.

6211′. עֲשַׂב **ʽăsab** (Chald.), *as-ab'*; 6212:—grass.

6212. עֶשֶׂב **ʽeseb**, *eh'-seb*; from an unused root mean. to *glisten* (or *be green*); *grass* (or any tender shoot):—grass, herb.

6213. עָשָׂה **ʽâsâh**, *aw-saw'*; a prim. root; to *do* or *make*, in the broadest sense and widest application (as follows):—accomplish, advance, appoint, apt, be at, become, bear, bestow, bring forth, bruise, be busy, × certainly, have the charge of, commit, deal (with), deck, + displease, do, (ready) dress (-ed), (put in) execute (-ion), exercise, fashion, + feast, [fight-] ing man, + finish, fit, fly, follow, fulfil, furnish, gather, get, go about, govern, grant, great, + hinder, hold ([a feast]), × indeed, + be industrious, + journey, keep, labour, maintain, make, be meet, observe, be occupied, offer, + officer, pare, bring (come) to pass, perform, practise, prepare, procure, provide, put, requite, × sacrifice, serve, set, shew, × sin, spend, × surely, take, × throughly, trim, × very, + vex, be [warr-] ior, work (-man), yield, use.

6214. עֲשָׂהאֵל **ʽĂsâhʼêl**, *as-aw-ale'*; from 6213 and 410; *God has made*; *Asahel*, the name of four Isr.:—Asahel.

6215. עֵשָׂו **ʽÊsâv**, *ay-saw'*; appar. a form of the pass. part. of 6213 in the orig. sense of *handling*; *rough* (i.e. sensibly *felt*); *Esav*, a son of Isaac, including his posterity:—Esau.

6216. עָשׁוֹק **ʽâshôwq**, *aw-shoke'*; from 6231; *oppressive* (as noun, a *tyrant*):—oppressor.

6217. עָשׁוּק **ʽâshûwq**, *aw-shook'*; or

עָשֻׁק **ʽâshûq**, *aw-shook'*; pass. part. of 6231; used in plur. masc. as abstr. *tyranny*:—oppressed (-ion). [*Doubtful.*]

6218. עָשׂוֹר **ʽâsôwr**, *aw-sore'*; or

עָשֹׂר **ʽâsôr**, *aw-sore'*; from 6235; *ten*; by abbrev. ten *strings*, and so a *decachord*:—(instrument of) ten (strings, -th).

6219. עָשׁוֹת **ʽâshôwth**, *aw-shôth'*; from 6245; *shining*, i.e. polished:—bright.

6220. עַשְׁוָת **ʽAshvâth**, *ash-vawth'*; for 6219; *bright*; *Ashvath*, an Isr.:—Ashvath.

6221. עֲשִׂיאֵל **ʽĂsîyʼêl**, *as-ee-ale'*; from 6213 and 410; *made of God*; *Asiël*, an Isr.:—Asiel.

6222. עֲשָׂיָה **ʽĂsâyâh**, *aw-saw-yaw'*; from 6213 and 3050; *Jah has made*; *Asajah*, the name of three or four Isr.:—Asaiah.

6223. עָשִׁיר **ʽâshîyr**, *aw-sheer'*; from 6238; *rich*, whether lit. or fig. (*noble*):—rich (man)

6224. עֲשִׂירִי **ʽăsîyrîy**, *as-ee-ree'*; from 6235; *tenth*; by abbrev. *tenth month* or (fem.) *part*:—tenth (part).

6225. עָשַׁן **ʽâshan**, *aw-shan'*; a prim. root; to *smoke*, whether lit. or fig.:—be angry (be on a) smoke.

6226. עָשֵׁן **ʽâshên**, *aw-shane'*; from 6225; *smoky*:—smoking.

6227. עָשָׁן **ʽâshân**, *aw-shawn'*; from 6225: *smoke*, lit. or fig. (*vapor, dust, anger*):—smoke (-ing).

6228. עָשָׁן **ʽÂshân**, *aw-shawn'*; the same as 6227; *Ashan*, a place in Pal.:—Ashan.

6229. עָשַׂק **ʽâsaq**, *aw-sak'*; a prim. root (ident. with 6231); to *press upon*, i.e. *quarrel*:—strive with.

6230. עֵשֶׂק **ʽêseq**, *ay'-sek*; from 6229; *strife*:—Esek.

6231. עָשַׁק **ʽâshaq**, *aw-shak'*; a prim. root (comp. 6229); to *press* upon, i.e. *oppress*, *defraud*, *violate*, *overflow*:—get deceitfully, deceive, defraud, drink up, (use) oppress ([-ion], -or), do violence (wrong).

6232. עֵשֶׁק **ʽÊsheq**, *ay-shek'*; from 6231; *oppression*; *Eshek*, an Isr.:—Eshek.

6233. עֹשֶׁק **ʽôsheq**, *o'-shek*; from 6231; *injury*, *fraud*, (subj.) *distress*, (concr.) *unjust gain*:—cruelly, extortion, oppression, thing [deceitfully gotten].

עָשֻׁק **ʽâshûq**. See 6217.

6234. עָשְׁקָה **ʽoshqâh**, *osh-kaw'*; fem. of 6233; *anguish*:—oppressed.

6235. עֶשֶׂר **ʽeser**, *eh'-ser*; masc.

עֲשָׂרָה **ʽăsârâh**, *as-aw-raw'*; from 6237; *ten* (as an *accumulation* to the extent of the digits):—ten, [fif-, seven-] teen.

6236. עֲשַׂר **ʽăsar** (Chald.), *as-ar'*; masc.

עַשְׂרָה **ʽasrâh** (Chald.), *as-raw'*; corresp. to 6235; *ten*:—ten, + twelve.

6237. עָשַׂר **ʽâsar**, *aw-sar'*; a prim. root (ident. with 6238); to *accumulate*; but used only as denom. from 6235; to *tithe*, i.e. take or give a tenth:—× surely, give (take) the tenth, (have, take) tithe (-ing, -s), × truly.

6238. עָשַׁר **ʽâshar**, *aw-shar'*; a prim. root; prop. to *accumulate*; chiefly (spec.) to *grow* (caus. *make*) *rich*:—be (-come, en-, make, make self, wax) rich, make [1 Kings 22 : 48 *marg.*]. See 6240.

6239. עֹשֶׁר **ʽôsher**, *o'-sher*; from 6238; *wealth*:—× far [richer], riches.

6240. עָשָׂר **ʽâsâr**, *aw-sawr'*; for 6235; *ten* (only in combination), i.e. *-teen*; also (ordinal) *-teenth*:—[eigh-, fif-, four-, nine-, seven-, six-, thir-] teen (-th), + eleven (-th), + sixscore thousand, + twelve (-th).

עָשׂוֹר **ʽâsôr**. See 6218.

6241. עִשָּׂרוֹן **ʽissârôwn**, *is-saw-rone'*; or

עִשָּׂרֹן **ʽissârôn**, *is-saw-rone'*; from 6235; (fractional) a *tenth* part:—tenth deal.

6242. עֶשְׂרִים **ʽesrîym**, *es-reem'*; from 6235; *twenty*; also (ordinal) *twentieth*:—[six-] score, twenty (-ieth).

6243. עֶשְׂרִין **ʽesrîyn** (Chald.), *es-reen'*; corresp. to 6242:—twenty.

6244. עָשֵׁשׁ **ʽâshêsh**, *aw-shaysh'*; a prim. root; prob. to *shrink*, i.e. *fail*:—be consumed.

6245. עָשַׁת **ʽâshath**, *aw-shath'*; a prim. root; prob. to be *sleek*, i.e. *glossy*; hence (through the idea of *polishing*) to *excogitate* (as if *forming* in the mind):—shine, think.

6246. עֲשִׁת **ʽăshîth** (Chald.), *ash-eeth'*; corresp. to 6245; to *purpose*:—think.

6247. עֶשֶׁת **ʽesheth**, *eh'-sheth*; from 6245; a *fabric*:—bright.

6248. עַשְׁתּוּת **ʽashtûwth**, *ash-tooth'*; from 6245; *cogitation*:—thought.

6249. עַשְׁתֵּי **ʽashtêy**, *ash-tay'*; appar. masc. plur. constr. of 6247 in the sense of an *after-*

thought; (used only in connection with 6240 in lieu of 259) *eleven* or (ordinal) *eleventh:*— + eleven (-th).

6250. עֶשְׁתֹּנָה **ʻeshtônâh**, *esh-to-naw';* from 6245; *thinking:*—thought.

6251. עַשְׁתְּרָה **ʻashterâh**, *ash-ter-aw';* prob. from 6238; *increase:*—flock.

6252. עַשְׁתָּרוֹת **ʻAshtârôwth**, *ash-taw-rōth',* or

עַשְׁתָּרֹת **ʻAshtârôth**, *ash-taw-rōth';* plur. of 6251; *Ashtaroth,* the name of a Sidonian deity, and of a place E. of the Jordan:—Ashtaroth, Astaroth. See also 1045, 6253, 6255.

6253. עַשְׁתֹּרֶת **ʻAshtôreth**, *ash-to'-reth;* prob. for 6251; *Ashtoreth,* the Phœnician goddess of love (and *increase*):—Ashtoreth.

6254. עַשְׁתְּרָתִי **ʻAshterâthîy**, *ash-ter-aw-thee';* patrial from 6252; an *Ashterathite* or inhab. of Ashtaroth:—Ashterathite.

6255. עַשְׁתְּרֹת קַרְנַיִם **ʻAshterôth Qarnayim**, *ash-ter-ōth' kar-nah'-yim;* from 6252 and the dual of 7161; *Ashtaroth of* (the) *double horns* (a symbol of the deity); *Ashteroth-Karnaïm,* a place E. of the Jordan:—Ashtoreth Karnaim.

6256. עֵת **ʻêth**, *ayth;* from 5703; *time,* espec. (adv. with prep.) *now, when,* etc.:— + after, [al-] ways, × certain, + continually, + evening, long, (due) season, so [long] as, [even-, evening-, noon-] tide, ([meal-], what) time, when.

6257. עָתַד **ʻâthad**, *aw-thad';* a prim. root; to *prepare:*—make fit, be ready to become.

עַתֻּד **ʻattûd**. See 6260.

6258. עַתָּה **ʻattâh**, *at-taw';* from 6256; at *this time,* whether adv., conj. or expletive:—henceforth, now, straightway, this time, whereas.

6259. עָתוּד **ʻâthûwd**, *aw-thood';* pass. part. of 6257; *prepared:*—ready, treasures.

6260. עַתּוּד **ʻattûwd**, *at-tood';* or

עַתֻּד **ʻattûd**, *at-tood';* from 6257; *prepared,* i.e. *full grown;* spoken only (in plur.) of *he-goats,* or (fig.) *leaders* of the people:—chief one, (he) goat, ram.

6261. עִתִּי **ʻittîy**, *it-tee';* from 6256; *timely:*—fit.

6262. עַתַּי **ʻAttay**, *at-tah'ee;* for 6261; *Attai,* the name of three Isr.:—Attai.

6263. עֲתִיד **ʻăthîyd** (Chald.), *ath-eed';* corresp. to 6264; *prepared:*—ready.

6264. עָתִיד **ʻâthîyd**, *aw-theed';* from 6257; *prepared;* by impl. *skilful;* fem. plur. the *future;* also *treasure:*—things that shall come, ready, treasures.

6265. עֲתָיָה **ʻĂthâyâh**, *ath-aw-yaw';* from 5790 and 3050; *Jah has helped; Athajah,* an Isr.:—Athaiah.

6266. עָתִיק **ʻâthîyq**, *aw-theek';* from 6275; prop. *antique,* i.e. *venerable* or *splendid:*—durable.

6267. עַתִּיק **ʻattîyq**, *at-teek';* from 6275; *removed,* i.e. *weaned;* also *antique:*—ancient, drawn.

6268. עַתִּיק **ʻattîyq** (Chald.), *at-teek';* corresp. to 6267; *venerable:*—ancient.

6269. עֲתָךְ **ʻĂthâk**, *ath-awk';* from an unused root mean. to *sojourn; lodging; Athak,* a place in Pal.:—Athach.

6270. עַתְלַי **ʻAthlay**, *ath-lah'ee;* from an unused root mean. to *compress; constringent; Athlai,* an Isr.:—Athlai.

6271. עֲתַלְיָה **ʻĂthalyâh**, *ath-al-yaw';* or

עֲתַלְיָהוּ **ʻĂthalyâhûw**, *ath-al-yaw'-hoo;* from the same as 6270 and 3050; *Jah has constrained; Athaljah,* the name of an Israelitess and two Isr.:—Athaliah.

6272. עָתַם **ʻâtham**, *aw-tham';* a prim. root; prob. to *glow,* i.e. (fig.) *be desolated:*—be darkened.

6273. עָתְנִי **ʻOthnîy**, *oth-nee';* from an unused root mean. to *force; forcible; Othni,* an Isr.:—Othni.

6274. עָתְנִיאֵל **ʻOthnîyʼêl**, *oth-nee-ale';* from the same as 6273 and 410; *force of God; Othniël,* an Isr.:—Othniel.

6275. עָתַק **ʻâthaq**, *aw-thak';* a prim. root; to *remove* (intrans. or trans.); fig. to *grow old;* spec. to *transcribe:*—copy out, leave off, become (wax) old, remove.

6276. עָתֵק **ʻâthêq**, *aw-thake';* from 6275; *antique,* i.e. *valued:*—durable.

6277. עָתָק **ʻâthâq**, *aw-thawk';* from 6275 in the sense of *license; impudent:*—arrogancy, grievous (hard) things, stiff.

6278. עֵת קָצִין **ʻÊth Qâtsîyn**, *ayth kaw-tseen';* from 6256 and 7011; *time of a judge; Eth-Katsin,* a place in Pal.:—Ittah-kazin [*by includ. directive enclitic*].

6279. עָתַר **ʻâthar**, *aw-thar';* a prim. root [rather denom. from 6281]; to burn *incense* in worship, i.e. *intercede* (recipr. *listen* to prayer):—intreat, (make) pray (-er).

6280. עָתַר **ʻâthar**, *aw-thar';* a prim. root; to *be* (caus. *make*) *abundant:*—deceitful, multiply.

6281. עֶתֶר **ʻEther**, *eh'-ther;* from 6280; *abundance; Ether,* a place in Pal.:—Ether.

6282. עָתָר **ʻâthâr**, *aw-thawr';* from 6280; *incense* (as increasing to a *volume* of smoke); hence (from 6279) a *worshipper:*—suppliant, thick.

6283. עֲתֶרֶת **ʻăthereth**, *ath-eh'-reth;* from 6280; *copiousness:*—abundance.

פ

פֹּא **pôʼ**. See 6311.

6284. פָּאָה **pâʼâh**, *paw-aw';* a prim. root; to *puff,* i.e. *blow* away:—scatter into corners.

6285. פֵּאָה **pêʼâh**, *pay-aw';* fem. of 6311; prop. *mouth* in a fig. sense, i.e. *direction, region, extremity:*—corner, end, quarter, side.

6286. פָּאַר **pâʼar**, *paw-ar';* a prim. root; to *gleam,* i.e. (causat.) *embellish;* fig. to *boast;* also to *explain* (i.e. make clear) oneself; denom. from 6288, to *shake* a tree:—beautify, boast self, go over the boughs, glorify (self), glory, vaunt self.

6287. פְּאֵר **peʼêr**, *peh-ayr';* from 6286; an *embellishment,* i.e. fancy *head-dress:*—beauty, bonnet, goodly, ornament, tire.

6288. פְּאֹרָה **peʼôrâh**, *peh-o-raw';* or

פֹּרָאה **pôrâʼh**, *po-raw';* or

פֻּארָה **pûʼrâh**, *poo-raw';* from 6286; prop. *ornamentation,* i.e. (plur.) *foliage* (includ. the limbs) as *bright* green:—bough, branch, sprig.

6289. פָּארוּר **pâʼrûwr**, *paw-roor';* from 6286; prop. *illuminated,* i.e. a *glow;* as noun, a *flush* (of anxiety):—blackness.

6290. פָּארָן **Pâʼrân**, *paw-rawn';* from 6286; *ornamental; Paran,* a desert of Arabia:—Paran.

6291. פַּג **pag**, *pag;* from an unused root mean. to *be torpid,* i.e. *crude;* an *unripe* fig:—green fig.

6292. פִּגּוּל **piggûwl**, *pig-gool';* or

פִּגֻּל **piggûl**, *pig-gool';* from an unused root mean. to *stink;* prop. *fetid,* i.e. (fig.) *unclean* (ceremonially):—abominable (-tion, thing).

6293. פָּגַע **pâgaʻ**, *paw-gah';* a prim. root; to *impinge,* by accident or violence, or (fig.) by importunity:—come (betwixt), cause to entreat, fall (upon), make intercession, intercessor, intreat, lay, light [upon], meet (together), pray, reach, run.

6294. פֶּגַע **pegaʻ**, *peh'-gah;* from 6293; *impact* (casual):—chance, occurrent.

6295. פַּגְעִיאֵל **Pagʻîyʼêl**, *pag-ee-ale';* from 6294 and 410; *accident of God; Pagiël,* an Isr.:—Pagiel.

6296. פָּגַר **pâgar**, *paw-gar';* a prim. root; to *relax,* i.e. become *exhausted:*—be faint.

6297. פֶּגֶר **peger**, *peh'-gher;* from 6296; a *carcase* (as *limp*), whether of man or beast; fig. an idolatrous *image:*—carcase, corpse, dead body.

6298. פָּגַשׁ **pâgash**, *paw-gash';* a prim. root; to *come in contact with,* whether by accident or violence; fig. to *concur:*—meet (with, together).

6299. פָּדָה **pâdâh**, *paw-daw';* a prim. root; to *sever,* i.e. *ransom;* gener. to *release, preserve:*— × at all, deliver, × by any means, ransom, (that are to be, let be) redeem (-ed), rescue, × surely.

6300. פְּדַהְאֵל **Pedahʼêl**, *ped-ah-ale';* from 6299 and 410; *God has ransomed; Pedahel,* an Isr.:—Pedahel.

6301. פְּדָהצוּר **Pedâhtsûwr**, *ped-aw-tsoor';* from 6299 and 6697; a *rock* (i.e. God) *has ransomed; Pedahtsur,* an Isr.:—Pedahzur.

6302. פָּדוּי **pâdûwy**, *paw-doo'ee;* pass. part. of 6299; *ransomed* (and so occurring under 6299); as abstr. (in plur. masc.) a *ransom:*—(that are) to be (that were) redeemed.

6303. פָּדוֹן **Pâdôwn**, *paw-done';* from 6299; *ransom; Padon,* one of the Nethinim:—Padon.

6304. פְּדוּת **pedûwth**, *ped-ooth';* or

פְּדֻת **pedûth**, *ped-ooth';* from 6929; *distinction;* also *deliverance:*—division, redeem, redemption.

6305. פְּדָיָה **Pedâyâh**, *ped-aw-yaw';* or

פְּדָיָהוּ **Pedâyâhûw**, *ped-aw-yaw'-hoo;* from 6299 and 3050; *Jah has ransomed; Pedajah,* the name of six Isr.:—Pedaiah.

6306. פִּדְיוֹם **pidyôwm**, *pid-yome';* or

פִּדְיֹם **pidyôm**, *pid-yome';* also

פִּדְיוֹן **pidyôwn**, *pid-yone';* or

פִּדְיֹן **pidyôn**, *pid-yone';* from 6299; a *ransom:*—ransom, that were redeemed, redemption.

6307. פַּדָּן **Paddân**, *pad-dawn';* from an unused root mean. to *extend;* a *plateau;* or

פַּדַּן אֲרָם **Paddan ʼĂrâm**, *pad-dan' ar-awm';* from the same and 758; the *table-land of Aram; Paddan* or *Paddan-Aram,* a region of Syria:—Padan, Padan-aram.

6308. פָּדַע **pâdaʻ**, *paw-dah';* a prim. root; to *retrieve:*—deliver.

6309. פֶּדֶר **peder**, *peh'-der;* from an unused root mean. to *be greasy; suet:*—fat.

פְּדֻת **pedûth**. See 6304.

6310. פֶּה **peh**, *peh;* from 6284; the *mouth* (as the means of *blowing*), whether lit. or fig. (particularly *speech*); spec. *edge, portion* or *side;* adv. (with prep.) *according to:*—accord (-ing as, -ing to), after, appointment, assent, collar, command (-ment), × eat, edge, end, entry, + file, hole, × in, mind, mouth, part, portion, × (should) say (-ing), sentence, skirt, sound, speech, × spoken, talk, tenor, × to, + two-edged, wish, word.

6311. פֹּה **pôh**, *po;* or

פֹּא **pôʼ** (Job 38 : 11), *po;* or

פּוֹ **pôw**, *po;* prob. from a prim. insep. particle פּ **p** (of demonstrative force) and 1931; *this place* (French *içi*), i.e. *here* or *hence:*—here, hither, the one (other, this, that) side.

פּוֹא **pôwʼ**. See 375.

6312. פּוּאָה **Pûwʼâh**, *poo-aw';* or

פֻּוָּה **Puvvâh**, *poov-vaw';* from 6284; *blast; Puäh* or *Puvvah,* the name of two Isr.:—Phuvah, Pua, Puah.

6313. פּוּג **pûwg**, *poog;* a prim. root; to *be sluggish:*—cease, be feeble, faint, be slacked.

6314. פּוּגָה **pûwgâh**, *poo-gaw';* from 6313; *intermission:*—rest.

פֻּוָּה **Puvvâh**. See 6312.

6315. פּוּחַ **pûwach**, *poo'-akh;* a prim. root; to *puff,* i.e. blow with the breath or air; hence to *fan* (as a breeze), to *utter,* to *kindle* (a fire), to *scoff:*—blow (upon), break, puff, bring into a snare, speak, utter.

6316. פּוּט **Pûwt**, *poot;* of for. or.; *Put,* a son of Ham, also the name of his descendants or their region, and of a Persian tribe:—Phut, Put.

6317. פּוּטִיאֵל **Pûwṭîy'êl**, *poo-tee-ale'*; from an unused root (prob. mean. to *disparage*) and 410; *contempt of God; Putiël*, an Isr.:—Putiel.

6318. פּוֹטִיפַר **Pôwṭîyphar**, *po-tee-far'*; of Eg. der.; *Potiphar*, an Eg.:—Potiphar.

6319. פּוֹטִי פֶרַע **Pôwṭîy Phera'**, *po'-tee feh'-rah*; of Eg. der.; *Poti-Phera*, an Eg.:—Poti-pherah.

6320. פּוּךְ **pûwk**, *pook*; from an unused root mean. to *paint*; *dye* (spec. *stibium* for the eyes):—fair colours, glistering, paint [-ed] (-ing).

6321. פּוֹל **pôwl**, *pole*; from an unused root mean. to *be thick*; a *bean* (as *plump*):—beans.

6322. פּוּל **Pûwl**, *pool*; of for. or.; *Pul*, the name of an Ass. king and of an Ethiopian tribe:—Pul.

6323. פּוּן **pûwn**, *poon*; a prim. root mean. to *turn*, i.e. *be perplexed*:—be distracted.

6324. פּוּנִי **Pûwnîy**, *poo-nee'*; patron. from an unused name mean. a *turn*; a *Punite* (collect.) or desc. of an unknown Pun:—Punites.

6325. פּוּנֹן **Pûwnôn**, *poo-none'*; from 6323; *perplexity*; *Punon*, a place in the Desert:—Punon.

6326. פּוּעָה **Pûw'âh**, *poo-aw'*; from an unused root mean. to *glitter*; *brilliancy*; *Puäh*, an Israelitess:—Puah.

6327. פּוּץ **pûwts**, *poots*; a prim. root; to *dash* in pieces, lit. or fig. (espec. to *disperse*):—break (dash, shake) in (to) pieces, cast (abroad), disperse (selves), drive, retire, scatter (abroad), spread abroad.

6328. פּוּק **pûwq**, *pook*; a prim. root; to *waver*:—stumble, move.

6329. פּוּק **pûwq**, *pook*; a prim. root [rather ident. with 6328 through the idea of *dropping* out; comp. 5312]; to *issue*, i.e. *furnish*; causat. to *secure*; fig. to *succeed*:—afford, draw out, further, get, obtain.

6330. פּוּקָה **pûwqâh**, *poo-kaw'*; from 6328; a *stumbling-block*:—grief.

6331. פּוּר **pûwr**, *poor*; a prim. root; to *crush*:—break, bring to nought, × utterly take.

6332. פּוּר **Pûwr**, *poor*; also (plur.)
פּוּרִים **Pûwrîym**, *poo-reem'*; or
פֻּרִים **Purîym**, *poo-reem'*; from 6331; a *lot* (as by means of a *broken* piece):—Pur, Purim.

6333. פּוּרָה **pûwrâh**, *poo-raw'*; from 6331; a *wine-press* (as *crushing* the grapes):—winepress.

פּוּרִים **Pûwrîym**. See 6332.

6334. פּוֹרָתָא **Pôwrâthâ'**, *po-raw-thaw'*; of Pers. or.; *Poratha*, a son of Haman:—Poratha.

6335. פּוּשׁ **pûwsh**, *poosh*; a prim. root; to *spread*; fig. *act proudly*:—grow up, be grown fat, spread selves, be scattered.

6336. פּוּתִי **Pûwthîy**, *poo-thee'*; patron. from an unused name mean. a *hinge*; a *Puthite* (collect.) or descend. of an unknown Puth:—Puhites [*as if from* 6312].

6337. פָּז **pâz**, *pawz*; from 6338; *pure* (gold); hence *gold* itself (as refined):—fine (pure) gold.

6338. פָּזַז **pâzaz**, *paw-zaz'*; a prim. root; to *refine* (gold):—best [gold].

6339. פָּזַז **pâzaz**, *paw-zaz'*; a prim. root [rather ident. with 6338]; to *solidify* (as if by *refining*); also to *spring* (as if *separating* the limbs):—leap, be made strong.

6340. פָּזַר **pâzar**, *paw-zar'*; a prim. root; to *scatter*, whether in enmity or bounty:—disperse, scatter (abroad).

6341. פַּח **pach**, *pakh*; from 6351; a (metallic) *sheet* (as *pounded* thin); also a spring *net* (as spread out like a *lamina*):—gin, (thin) plate, snare.

6342. פָּחַד **pâchad**, *paw-kkad'*; a prim. root: to *be startled* (by a sudden alarm); hence to *fear* in general:—be afraid, stand in awe, (be in) fear, make to shake.

6343. פַּחַד **pachad**, *pakh'-ad*; from 6342; a (sudden) *alarm* (prop. the object feared, by impl. the feeling):- -dread (-ful), fear, (thing) great [fear, -ly feared], terror.

6344. פַּחַד **pachad**, *pakh'-ad*; the same as 6343; a *testicle* (as a cause of *shame* akin to fear):—stone.

6345. פַּחְדָּה **pachdâh**, *pakh-daw'*; fem. of 6343; *alarm* (i.e. *awe*):—fear.

6346. פֶּחָה **pechâh**, *peh-khaw'*; of for. or.; a *prefect* (of a city or small district):—captain, deputy, governor.

6347. פֶּחָה **pechâh** (Chald.), *peh-khaw'*; corresp. to 6346:—captain, governor.

6348. פָּחַז **pâchaz**, *paw-khaz'*; a prim. root; to *bubble* up or *froth* (as boiling water), i.e. (fig.) to *be unimportant*:—light.

6349. פַּחַז **pachaz**, *pakh'-az*; from 6348; *ebullition*, i.e. froth (fig. lust):—unstable.

6350. פַּחֲזוּת **pachăzûwth**, *pakh-az-ooth'*; from 6348; *frivolity*:—lightness.

6351. פָּחַח **pâchach**, *paw-khakh'*; a prim. root; to *batter* out; but used only as denom. from 6341, to *spread a net*:—be snared.

6352. פֶּחָם **pechâm**, *peh-khawm'*; perh. from an unused root prob. mean. to *be black*; a *coal*, whether charred or live:—coals.

6353. פֶּחָר **pechâr** (Chald.), *peh-khawr'*; from an unused root prob. mean. to *fashion*; a *potter*:—potter.

6354. פַּחַת **pachath**, *pakh'-ath*; prob. from an unused root appar. mean. to *dig*; a *pit*, espec. for catching animals:—hole, pit, snare.

6355. פַּחַת מוֹאָב **Pachath Môw'âb**, *pakh'-ath mo-awb'*; from 6354 and 4124; *pit of Moäb*; *Pachath-Moäb*, an Isr.:—Pahath-moab.

6356. פְּחֶתֶת **p^{e}chetheth**, *pekh-eh'-theth*; from the same as 6354; a *hole* (by mildew in a garment):—fret inward.

6357. פִּטְדָה **piṭdâh**, *pit-daw'*; of for. der.; a *gem*, prob. the *topaz*:—topaz.

6358. פָּטוּר **pâṭûwr**, *paw-toor'*; pass. part. of 6362; *opened*, i.e. (as noun) a *bud*:—open.

6359. פָּטִיר **pâṭîyr**, *paw-teer'*; from 6362; *open*, i.e. *unoccupied*:—free.

6360. פַּטִּישׁ **paṭṭîysh**, *pat-teesh'*; intens. from an unused root mean. to *pound*; a *hammer*:—hammer.

6361. פַּטִּישׁ **paṭṭîysh** (Chald.), *pat-teesh'*; from a root corresp. to that of 6360; a *gown* (as if *hammered* out wide):—hose.

6362. פָּטַר **pâṭar**, *paw-tar'*; a prim. root; to *cleave* or burst through, i.e. (caus.) to *emit*, whether lit. or fig. (*gape*):—dismiss, free, let (shoot) out, slip away.

6363. פֶּטֶר **peṭer**, *peh'-ter*; or
פִּטְרָה **piṭrâh**, *pit-raw'*; from 6362; a *fissure*, i.e. (concr.) *firstling* (as *opening* the matrix):—firstling, openeth, such as open.

6364. פִּי־בֶסֶת **Pîy-Beceth**, *pee beh'-seth*; of Eg. or.; *Pi-Beseth*, a place in Eg.:—Pi-beseth.

6365. פִּיד **pîyd**, *peed*; from an unused root prob. mean. to *pierce*; (fig.) *misfortune*:—destruction, ruin.

6366. פֵּיָה **pêyâh**, *pay-aw'*; or
פִּיָה **pîyâh**, *pee-yaw'*; fem. of 6310; an *edge*:—(two-) edge (-d).

6367. פִּי הַחִירֹת **Pi ha-Chîyrôth**, *pee hah-khee-rōth'*; from 6310 and the fem. plur. of a noun (from the same root as 2356), with the art. interp.; *mouth of the gorges*; *Pi-ha-Chiroth*, a place in Eg.:—Pi-hahiroth. [In Num. 14 : 19 without Pi-.]

6368. פִּיחַ **pîyach**, *pee'-akh*; from 6315; a *powder* (as easily *puffed* away), i.e. *ashes* or *dust*:—ashes.

6369. פִּיכֹל **Pîykôl**, *pee-kole'*; appar. from 6310 and 3605; *mouth of all*; *Picol*, a Philistine:—Phichol.

6370. פִּילֶגֶשׁ **pîylegesh**, *pee-leh'-ghesh*; or
פִּלֶגֶשׁ **pîlegesh**, *pee-leh'-ghesh*; of uncert. der.; a *concubine*; also (masc.) a *paramour*:—concubine, paramour.

6371. פִּימָה **pîymâh**, *pee-maw'*: prob. from an unused root mean. to *be plump*; *obesity*:—collops.

6372. פִּינְחָס **Pîyn^{e}châç**, *pee-nekh-aws'*; appar. from 6310 and a var. of 5175; *mouth of a serpent*; *Pinechas*, the name of three Isr.:—Phinehas.

6373. פִּינֹן **pîynôn**, *pee-none'*; prob. the same as 6325; *Pinon*, an Idumæan:—Pinon.

6374. פִּיפִיָּה **pîyphîyâh**, *pee-fee-yaw'*; for 6366, an *edge* or *tooth*:—tooth, × two-edged.

6375. פִּיק **pîyq**, *peek*; from 6329; a *tottering*:—smite together.

6376. פִּישׁוֹן **Pîyshôwn**, *pee-shone'*; from 6335; *dispersive*; *Pishon*, a river of Eden:—Pison.

6377. פִּיתוֹן **Pîythôwn**, *pee-thone'*; prob. from the same as 6596; *expansive*; *Pithon*, an Isr.:—Pithon.

6378. פַּךְ **pak**, *pak*; from 6379; a *flask* (from which a liquid may *flow*):—box, vial.

6379. פָּכָה **pâkâh**, *paw-kaw'*; a prim. root; to *pour*:—run out.

6380. פֹּכֶרֶת צְבָיִים **Pôkereth Ts^{e}bâyîym**, *po-keh'-reth tseb-aw-yeem'*; from the act. part. (of the same form as the first word) fem. of an unused root (mean. to *entrap*) and plur. of 6643; *trap of gazelles*; *Pokereth-Tsebajim*, one of the "servants of Solomon":—Pochereth of Zebaim.

6381. פָּלָא **pâlâ'**, *paw-law'*; a prim. root; prop. perh. to *separate*, i.e. *distinguish* (lit. or fig.); by impl. to *be* (causat. *make*) *great*, *difficult*, *wonderful*:—accomplish, (arise . . . too, be too) hard, hidden, things too high, (be, do, do a, shew) marvellous (-ly, -els, things, work), miracles, perform, separate, make singular, (be, great, make) wonderful (-ers, -ly, things, works), wondrous (things, works, -ly).

6382. פֶּלֶא **pele'**, *peh'-leh*; from 6381; a *miracle*:—marvellous thing, wonder (-ful, -fully).

6383. פִּלְאִי **pil'îy**, *pil-ee'*; or
פָּלִיא **pâlîy'**, *paw-lee'*; from 6381; *remarkable*:—secret, wonderful.

6384. פַּלֻּאִי **Pallû'îy**, *pal-loo-ee'*; patron. from 6396; a *Palluïte* (collect.) or desc. of Pallu:—Palluites.

פְּלָאיָה **P^{e}lâ'yâh**. See 6411.

פִּלְאֶסֶר **Pil'eçer**. See 8407.

6385. פָּלַג **pâlag**, *paw-lag'*; a prim. root; to *split* (lit. or fig.):—divide.

6386. פְּלַג **p^{e}lag** (Chald.), *pel-ag'*; corresp. to 6385:—divided.

6387. פְּלַג **p^{e}lag** (Chald.), *pel-ag'*; from 6386; a *half*:—dividing.

6388. פֶּלֶג **peleg**, *peh'-leg*; from 6385; a *rill* (i.e. small *channel* of water, as in irrigation):—river, stream.

6389. פֶּלֶג **Peleg**, *pek'-leg*; the same as 6388; *earthquake*; *Peleg*, a son of Shem:—Peleg.

6390. פְּלַגָּה **p^{e}laggâh**, *pel-ag-gaw'*; from 6385; a *runlet*, i.e. *gully*:—division, river.

6391. פְּלֻגָּה **p^{e}luggâh**, *pel-oog-gaw'*; from 6385; a *section*:—division.

6392. פְּלֻגָּה **p^{e}luggâh** (Chald.), *pel-oog-gaw'*; corresp. to 6391:—division.

פִּלֶגֶשׁ **pîlegesh**. See 6370.

6393. פְּלָדָה **p^{e}lâdâh**, *pel-aw-daw'*; from an unused root mean. to *divide*; a *cleaver*, i.e. iron *armature* (of a chariot):—torch.

6394. פִּלְדָּשׁ **Pildâsh**, *pil-dawsh';* of uncert. der.; *Pildash*, a relative of Abraham:—Pildash.

6395. פָּלָה **pâlâh**, *paw-law';* a prim. root; to *distinguish* (lit. or fig.):—put a difference, show marvellous, separate, set apart, sever, make wonderfully.

6396. פַּלּוּא **Pallûw'**, *pal-loo';* from 6395; *distinguished; Pallu*, an Isr.:—Pallu, Phallu.

6397. פְּלוֹנִי **Pelôwnîy**, *pel-o-nee';* patron. from an unused name (from 6395) mean. *separate;* a *Pelonite* or inhab. of an unknown Palon:—Pelonite.

6398. פָּלַח **pâlach**, *paw-lakh';* a prim. root; to *slice*, i.e. *break* open or *pierce:*—bring forth, cleave, cut, shred, strike through.

6399. פְּלַח **pelach** (Chald.), *pel-akh';* corresp. to 6398; to *serve* or worship:—minister, serve.

6400. פֶּלַח **pelach**, *peh'-lakh;* from 6398; a *slice:*—piece.

6401. פִּלְחָא **Pilchâ'**, *pil-khaw';* from 6400; *slicing; Pilcha*, an Isr.:—Pilcha.

6402. פָּלְחָן **polchân** (Chald.), *pol-khawn';* from 6399; *worship:*—service.

6403. פָּלַט **pâlaṭ**, *paw-lat';* a prim. root; to *slip* out, i.e. *escape;* causat. to *deliver:*—calve, carry away safe, deliver, (cause to) escape.

6404. פֶּלֶט **Peleṭ**, *peh'-let;* from 6403; *escape; Pelet*, the name of two Isr.:—Pelet. See also 1046.

פָּלֵט **pâlêṭ**. See 6412.

6405. פַּלֵּט **pallêṭ**, *pal-late';* from 6403; *escape:*—deliverance, escape.

פְּלֵטָה **pelêṭâh**. See 6413.

6406. פַּלְטִי **Palṭîy**, *pal-tee';* from 6403; *delivered; Palti*, the name of two Isr.:—Palti, Phalti.

6407. פַּלְטִי **Palṭîy**, *pal-tee';* patron. from 6406; a *Paltite* or desc. of Palti:—Paltite.

6408. פִּלְטַי **Pilṭay**, *pil-tah'ee;* for 6407; *Piltai*, an Isr.:—Piltai.

6409. פַּלְטִיאֵל **Palṭîy'êl**, *pal-tee-ale';* from the same as 6404 and 410; *deliverance of God; Paltiël*, the name of two Isr.:—Paltiel, Phaltiel.

6410. פְּלַטְיָה **Pelaṭyâh**, *pel-at-yaw';* or

פְּלַטְיָהוּ **Pelaṭyâhûw**, *pel-at-yaw'-hoo;* from 6403 and 3050; *Jah has delivered; Pelatjah*, the name of four Isr.:—Pelatiah.

פָּלִיא **pâlîy'**. See 6383.

6411. פְּלָיָה **Pelâyâh**, *pel-aw-yaw';* or

פְּלָאיָה **Pelâ'yâh**, *pel-aw-yaw';* from 6381 and 3050; *Jah has distinguished; Pelajah*, the name of three Isr.:—Pelaiah.

6412. פָּלִיט **pâlîyṭ**, *paw-leet';* or

פָּלֵיט **pâlêyṭ**, *paw-late';* or

פָּלֵט **pâlêṭ**, *paw-late';* from 6403; a *refugee:*—(that have) escape (-d, -th), fugitive.

6413. פְּלֵיטָה **pelêyṭâh**, *pel-ay-taw';* or

פְּלֵטָה **pelêṭâh**, *pel-ay-taw';* fem. of 6412; *deliverance;* concr. an *escaped* portion:—deliverance, (that is) escape (-d), remnant.

6414. פָּלִיל **pâlîyl**, *paw-leel';* from 6419; a *magistrate:*—judge.

6415. פְּלִילָה **pelîylâh**, *pel-ee-law';* fem. of 6414; *justice:*—judgment.

6416. פְּלִילִי **pelîylîy**, *pel-ee-lee';* from 6414; *judicial:*—judge.

6417. פְּלִילִיָּה **pelîylîyâh**, *pel-ee-lee-yaw';* fem. of 6416; *judicature:*—judgment.

6418. פֶּלֶךְ **pelek**, *peh'-lek;* from an unused root mean. to *be round;* a *circuit* (i.e. *district*); also a *spindle* (as *whirled*); hence a *crutch:*—(di-) staff, part.

6419. פָּלַל **pâlal**, *paw-lal';* a prim. root; to *judge* (officially or mentally); by extens. to *intercede, pray:*—intreat, judge (-ment), (make) pray (-er, -ing), make supplication.

6420. פָּלָל **Pâlâl**, *paw-lawl';* from 6419; *judge; Palal*, an Isr.:—Palal.

6421. פְּלַלְיָה **Pelalyâh**, *pel-al-yaw';* from 6419 and 3050; *Jah has judged; Pelaljah*, an Isr.:—Pelaliah.

6422. פַּלְמוֹנִי **palmôwnîy**, *pal-mo-nee';* prob. for 6423; a *certain* one, i.e. so-and-so:—certain.

פִּלְנְאֶסֶר **Pilne'eçer**. See 8407.

6423. פְּלֹנִי **pelônîy**, *pel-o-nee';* from 6395; *such* a one, i.e. a specified *person:*—such.

פִּלְנֶסֶר **Pilneçer**. See 8407.

6424. פָּלַס **pâlaç**, *paw-las';* a prim. root; prop. to *roll* flat, i.e. *prepare* (a road); also to *revolve*, i.e. *weigh* (mentally):—make, ponder, weigh.

6425. פֶּלֶס **peleç**, *peh'-les;* from 6424; a *balance:*—scales, weight.

פְּלֶסֶר **Peleçer**. See 8407.

6426. פָּלַץ **pâlats**, *paw-lats';* a prim. root; prop. perh. to *rend*, i.e. (by impl.) to *quiver:*—tremble.

6427. פַּלָּצוּת **pallâtsûwth**, *pal-law-tsooth';* from 6426; *affright:*—fearfulness, horror, trembling.

6428. פָּלַשׁ **pâlash**, *paw-lash';* a prim. root; to *roll* (in dust):—roll (wallow) self.

6429. פְּלֶשֶׁת **Pelesheth**, *pel-eh'-sheth;* from 6428; *rolling*, i.e. *migratory; Pelesheth*, a region of Syria:—Palestina, Palestine, Philistia, Philistines.

6430. פְּלִשְׁתִּי **Pelishtîy**, *pel-ish-tee';* patrial from 6429; a *Pelishtite* or inhab. of Pelesheth:—Philistine.

6431. פֶּלֶת **Peleth**, *peh'-leth;* from an unused root mean. to *flee; swiftness; Peleth*, the name of two Isr.:—Peleth.

6432. פְּלֵתִי **Pelêthîy**, *pel-ay-thee';* from the same form as 6431; a *courier* (collect.) or official *messenger:*—Pelethites.

6433. פֻּם **pûm** (Chald.), *poom;* prob. for 6310; the *mouth* (lit. or fig.):—mouth.

6434. פֵּן **pên**, *pane;* from an unused root mean. to *turn;* an *angle* (of a street or wall):—corner.

6435. פֵּן **pên**, *pane;* from 6437; prop. *removal;* used only (in the constr.) adv. as conj. *lest:*—(lest) (peradventure), that . . . not.

6436. פַּנַּג **pannag**, *pan-nag';* of uncert. der.; prob. *pastry:*—Pannag.

6437. פָּנָה **pânâh**, *paw-naw';* a prim. root; to *turn;* by impl. to *face*, i.e. *appear, look*, etc.:—appear, at [even-] tide, behold, cast out, come on, × corner, dawning, empty, go away, lie, look, mark, pass away, prepare, regard, (have) respect (to), (re-) turn (aside, away, back, face, self), × right [early].

פָּנֶה **pâneh**. See 6440.

6438. פִּנָּה **pinnâh**, *pin-naw';* fem. of 6434; an *angle;* by impl. a *pinnacle;* fig. a *chieftain:*—bulwark, chief, corner, stay, tower.

6439. פְּנוּאֵל **Penûw'êl**, *pen-oo-ale';* or (more prop.)

פְּנִיאֵל **Penîy'êl**, *pen-ee-ale';* from 6437 and 410; *face of God; Penuël* or *Peniël*, a place E. of Jordan; also (as Penuel) the name of two Isr.:—Peniel, Penuel.

פָּנִי° **pânîy**. See 6443.

6440. פָּנִים **pânîym**, *paw-neem';* plur. (but always as sing.) of an unused noun

[פָּנֶה **pâneh**, *paw-neh';* from 6437]; the *face* (as the part that *turns*); used in a great variety of applications (lit. and fig.); also (with prep. pref.) as a prep. (*before*, etc.):— + accept, a- (be-) fore (-time), against, anger, × as (long as), at, + battle, + because (of), + beseech, countenance, edge, + employ, endure, + enquire, face, favour, fear of, for, forefront (-part), form (-er time, -ward), from, front, heaviness, × him (-self), + honourable, + impudent, + in, it, look [-eth] (-s), × me, + meet, × more than, mouth, of, off, (of) old (time), × on, open, + out of, over against, the partial, person, + please, presence, propect, was purposed, by reason, of, + regard, right forth, + serve, × shewbread, sight, state, straight, + street, × thee, × them (-selves), through (+ -out), till, time (-s) past, (un-) to (-ward), + upon, upside (+ down), with (-in, + -stand), × ye, × you.

6441. פְּנִימָה **penîymâh**, *pen-ee'-maw;* from 6440 with directive enclitic; *faceward*, i.e. *indoors:*—(with-) in (-ner part, -ward).

6442. פְּנִימִי **penîymîy**, *pen-ee-mee';* from 6440; *interior:*—(with-) in (-ner, -ward).

6443. פָּנִין **pânîyn**, *paw-neen';* or

פָּנִי° **pânîy**, *paw-nee';* from the same as 6434; prob. a *pearl* (as *round*):—ruby.

6444. פְּנִנָּה **Peninnâh**, *pen-in-naw';* prob. fem. from 6443 contr.; *Peninnah*, an Israelitess:—Peninnah.

6445. פָּנַק **pânaq**, *paw-nak';* a prim. root; to *enervate:*—bring up.

6446. פַּס **paç**, *pas;* from 6461; prop. the *palm* (of the hand) or *sole* (of the foot) [comp. 6447]; by impl. (plur.) a *long and sleeved* tunic (perh. simply a *wide* one; from the orig. sense of the root, i.e. of *many breadths*):—(divers) colours.

6447. פַּס **paç** (Chald.), *pas;* from a root corresp. to 6461; the *palm* (of the hand, as being *spread* out):—part.

6448. פָּסַג **pâçag**, *paw-sag';* a prim. root; to *cut up*, i.e. (fig.) *contemplate:*—consider.

6449. פִּסְגָּה **Piçgâh**, *pis-gaw';* from 6448; a *cleft; Pisgah*, a mt. E. of Jordan:—Pisgah.

6450. פַּס דַּמִּים **Paç Dammîym**, *pas dam-meem';* from 6446 and the plur. of 1818; *palm* (i.e. *dell*) *of bloodshed; Pas-Dammim*, a place in Pal.:—Pas-dammim. Comp. 658.

6451. פִּסָּה **piççâh**, *pis-saw';* from 6461; *expansion*, i.e. *abundance:*—handful.

6452. פָּסַח **pâçach**, *paw-sakh';* a prim. root; to *hop*, i.e. (fig.) *skip* over (or *spare*); by impl. to *hesitate;* also (lit.) to *limp*, to *dance:*—halt, become lame, leap, pass over.

6453. פֶּסַח **peçach**, *peh'-sakh;* from 6452; a *pretermission*, i.e. *exemption;* used only tech. of the Jewish *Passover* (the festival or the victim):—passover (offering).

6454. פָּסֵחַ **Pâçêach**, *paw-say'-akh;* from 6452; *limping; Paseäch*, the name of two Isr.:—Paseah, Phaseah.

6455. פִּסֵּחַ **piççêach**, *pis-say'-akh;* from 6452; *lame:*—lame.

6456. פְּסִיל **peçîyl**, *pes-eel';* from 6458; an *idol:*—carved (graven) image, quarry.

6457. פָּסַךְ **Pâçak**, *paw-sak';* from an unused root mean. to *divide; divider; Pasak*, an Isr.:—Pasach.

6458. פָּסַל **pâçal**, *paw-sal';* a prim. root; to *carve*, whether wood or stone:—grave, hew.

6459. פֶּסֶל **peçel**, *peh'-sel;* from 6458; an *idol:*—carved (graven) image.

6460. פְּסַנְטֵרִין **peçanṭêrîyn** (Chald.), *pes-an-tay-reen';* or

פְּסַנְתֵּרִין **peçantêrîyn**, *pes-an-tay-reen';* a transliteration of the Gr. ψαλτήριον *psaltêriŏn;* a *lyre:*—psaltery.

6461. פָּסַס **pâçaç**, *paw-sas';* a prim. root; prob. to *disperse*, i.e. (intrans.) *disappear:*—cease.

6462. פִּסְפָּה **Piçpâh**, *pis-paw';* perh. from 6461; *dispersion; Pispah*, an Isr.:—Pispah.

6463. פָּעָה **pâ'âh**, *paw-aw';* a prim. root; to *scream:*—cry.

6464. פָּעוּ **Pâ'ûw**, *paw-oo';* or

פָּעִי **Pâ'îy**, *paw-ee';* from 6463; *screaming; Paü* or *Paï*, a place in Edom:—Pai, Pau.

6465. פְּעוֹר **Peʿôwr**, *peh-ore'*; from 6473; a *gap*; *Peör*, a mountain E. of Jordan; also (for 1187) a deity worshipped there:—Peor. See also 1047.

פְּעִי **Pâʿîy**. See 6464.

6466. פָּעַל **pâʿal**, *paw-al'*; a prim. root; to *do* or *make* (systematically and habitually), espec. to *practise*:—commit, [evil-] do (-er), make (-r), ordain, work (-er), wrought.

6467. פֹּעַל **pôʿal**, *po'-al*; from 6466; an *act* or *work* (concr.):—act, deed, do, getting, maker, work.

6468. פְּעֻלָּה **peʿullâh**, *peh-ool-law'*; fem. pass. part. of 6466; (abstr.) *work*:—labour, reward, wages, work.

6469. פְּעֻלְּתַי **Peʿullʿthay**, *peh-ool-leh-thah'ee*; from 6468; *laborious*; *Peüllethai*, an Isr.:—Peulthai.

6470. פָּעַם **pâʿam**, *paw-am'*; a prim. root; to *tap*, i.e. beat regularly; hence (gen.) to *impel* or *agitate*:—move, trouble.

6471. פַּעַם **paʿam**, *pah'-am*; or (fem.)

פַּעֲמָה **paʿămâh**, *pah-am-aw'*; from 6470; a *stroke*, lit. or fig. (in various applications, as follow):—anvil, corner, foot (-step), going, [hundred-] fold, × now, (this) + once, order, rank, step, + thrice, ([often-], second, this, two) time (-s), twice, wheel.

6472. פַּעֲמֹן **paʿămôn**, *pah-am-one'*; from 6471; a *bell* (as *struck*):—bell.

6473. פָּעַר **pâʿar**, *paw-ar'*; a prim. root; to *yawn*, i.e. *open* wide (lit. or fig.):—gape, open (wide).

6474. פַּעֲרַי **Paʿăray**, *pah-ar-ah'ee*; from 6473; *yawning*; *Paarai*, an Isr.:—Paarai.

6475. פָּצָה **pâtsâh**, *paw-tsaw'*; a prim. root; to *rend*, i.e. *open* (espec. the mouth):—deliver, gape, open, rid, utter.

6476. פָּצַח **pâtsach**, *paw-tsakh'*; a prim. root; to *break* out (in joyful sound):—break (forth, forth into joy), make a loud noise.

6477. פְּצִירָה **petsîyrâh**, *pets-ee-raw'*; from 6484; *bluntness*:— + file.

6478. פָּצַל **pâtsal**, *paw-tsal'*; a prim. root; to *peel*:—pill.

6479. פְּצָלָה **petsâlâh**, *pets-aw-law'*; from 6478; a *peeling*:—strake.

6480. פָּצַם **pâtsam**, *paw-tsam'*; a prim. root; to *rend* (by earthquake):—break.

6481. פָּצַע **pâtsaʿ**, *paw-tsah'*; a prim. root; to *split*, i.e. *wound*:—wound.

6482. פֶּצַע **petsaʿ**, *peh'-tsah*; from 6481; a *wound*:—wound (-ing).

פַּצֵּץ **Patstsets**. See 1048.

6483. פִּצֵּץ **Pitstsêts**, *pits-tsates'*; from an unused root mean. to *dissever*; *dispersive*; *Pitstsets*, a priest:—Apses [*includ. the art.*].

6484. פָּצַר **pâtsar**, *paw-tsar'*; a prim. root; to *peck* at, i.e. (fig.) *stun* or *dull*:—press, urge, stubbornness.

6485. פָּקַד **pâqad**, *paw-kad'*; a prim. root; to *visit* (with friendly or hostile intent); by anal. to *oversee*, *muster*, *charge*, *care for*, *miss*, *deposit*, etc.:—appoint, × at all, avenge, bestow, (appoint to have the, give a) charge, commit, count, deliver to keep, be empty, enjoin, go see, hurt, do judgment, lack, lay up look, make × by any means, miss, number, officer, (make) overseer have (the) oversight, punish, reckon, (call to) remember (-brance), set (over), sum, × surely, visit, want.

פִּקֻּד **piqqûd**. See 6490.

6486. פְּקֻדָּה **pequddâh**, *pek-ood-daw'*; fem. pass. part. of 6485; *visitation* (in many senses, chiefly official):—account, (that have the) charge, custody, that which ... laid up, numbers, office (-r), ordering, oversight, + prison, reckoning, visitation.

6487. פִּקָּדוֹן **piqqâdôwn**, *pik-kaw-done'*; from 6485; a *deposit*:—that which was delivered (to keep), store.

6488. פְּקִדֻת **peqîdûth**, *pek-ee-dooth'*; from 6496; *supervision*:—ward.

6489. פְּקוֹד **Peqôwd**, *pek-ode'*; from 6485; *punishment*; *Pekod*, a symbol. name for Bab.:—Pekod.

6490. פִּקּוּד **piqqûwd**, *pik-kood'*; or

פִּקֻּד **piqqûd**, *pik-kood'*; from 6485; prop. *appointed*, i.e. a *mandate* (of God; plur. only, collect. for the *Law*):—commandment, precept, statute.

6491. פָּקַח **pâqach**, *paw-kakh'*; a prim. root; to *open* (the senses, espec. the eyes); fig. to *be observant*:—open.

6492. פֶּקַח **Peqach**, *peh'-kakh*; from 6491; *watch*; *Pekach*, an Isr. king:—Pekah.

6493. פִּקֵּחַ **piqqêach**, *pik-kay'-akh*; from 6491; *clear-sighted*; fig. *intelligent*:—seeing, wise.

6494. פְּקַחְיָה **Peqachyâh**, *pek-akh-yaw'*; from 6491 and 3050; *Jah has observed*; *Pekachjah*, an Isr. king:—Pekahiah.

6495. פְּקַח־קוֹחַ **peqach-qôwach**, *pek-akh-ko'-akh*; from 6491 redoubled; *opening* (of a dungeon), i.e. *jail-delivery* (fig. *salvation* from sin):—opening of the prison.

6496. פָּקִיד **pâqîyd**, *paw-keed'*; from 6485; a *superintendent* (civil, military or religious):—which had the charge, governor, office, overseer, [that] was set.

6497. פֶּקַע **peqaʿ**, *peh'-kah*; from an unused root mean. to *burst*; only used as an architect. term of an ornament similar to 6498, a *semi-globe*:—knop.

6498. פַּקֻּעָה **paqqûʿâh**, *pak-koo-aw'*; from the same as 6497; the *wild cucumber* (from *splitting* open to shed its seeds):—gourd.

6499. פַּר **par**, *par*; or

פָּר **pâr**, *pawr*; from 6565; a *bullock* (appar. as *breaking* forth in wild strength, or perh. as *dividing* the hoof):—(+ young) bull (-ock), calf, ox.

6500. פָּרָא **pârâʾ**, *paw-raw'*; a prim. root; to *bear fruit*:—be fruitful.

6501. פֶּרֶא **pereʾ**, *peh'-reh*; or

פֶּרֶה **pereh** (Jer. 2 : 24), *peh'-reh*; from 6500 in the secondary sense of *running* wild; the *onager*:—wild (ass).

פֹּרָאה **pôrâʾh**. See 6288.

6502. פִּרְאָם **Pirʾâm**, *pir-awm'*; from 6501; *wildly*; *Piram*, a Canaanite:—Piram.

6503. פַּרְבָּר **Parbâr**, *par-bawr'*; or

פַּרְוָר **Parvâr**, *par-vawr'*; of for or.; *Parbar* or *Parvar*, a quarter of Jerus.:—Parbar, suburb.

6504. פָּרַד **pârad**, *paw-rad'*; a prim. root; to *break* through, i.e. *spread* or *separate* (oneself):—disperse, divide, be out of joint, part, scatter (abroad), separate (self), sever self, stretch, sunder.

6505. פֶּרֶד **pered**, *peh'-red*; from 6504; a *mule* (perh. from his *lonely* habits):—mule.

6506. פִּרְדָּה **pirdâh**, *pir-daw'*; fem. of 6505; a *she-mule*:—mule.

6507. פְּרֻדָה **perûdâh**, *per-oo-daw'*; fem. pass. part. of 6504; something *separated*, i.e. a *kernel*:—seed.

6508. פַּרְדֵּס **pardêç**, *par-dace'*; of for. or.; a *park*:—forest, orchard.

6509. פָּרָה **pârâh**, *paw-raw'*; a prim. root; to *bear fruit* (lit. or fig.):—bear, bring forth (fruit), (be, cause to be, make) fruitful, grow, increase.

6510. פָּרָה **pârâh**, *paw-raw'*; fem. of 6499; a *heifer*:—cow, heifer, kine.

6511. פָּרָה **Pârâh**, *paw-raw'*; the same as 6510; *Parah*, a place in Pal.:—Parah.

פֶּרֶה **pereh**. See 6501.

6512. פֵּרָה **pêrâh**, *pay-raw'*; from 6331; a *hole* (*as broken*, i.e. dug):— + mole. Comp. 2661.

6513. פֻּרָה **Pûrâh**, *poo-raw*; for 6288; *foliage*; *Purah*, an Isr.:—Phurah.

6514. פְּרוּדָא **Perûwdâʾ**, *per-oo-daw'*; or

פְּרִידָא **Perîydâʾ**, *per-ee-daw'*; from 6504; *dispersion*; *Peruda* or *Perida*, one of "Solomon's servants":—Perida, Peruda.

°פְּרוֹזִי **perôwzîy**. See 6521.

6515. פָּרוּחַ **Pârûwach**, *paw-roo'-akh*; pass. part. of 6524; *blossomed*; *Paruäch*, an Isr.:—Paruah.

6516. פַּרְוַיִם **Parvayim**, *par-vah'-yim*; of for. or.; *Parvajim*, an Oriental region:—Parvaim.

6517. פָּרוּר **pârûwr**, *paw-roor'*; pass. part. of 6565 in the sense of *spreading* out [comp. 6524]; a *skillet* (as *flat or deep*):—pan, pot.

פַּרְוָר **Parvâr**. See 6503.

6518. פָּרָז **pâraz**, *paw-rawz'*; from an unused root mean. to *separate*, i.e. *decide*; a *chieftain*:—village.

6519. פְּרָזָה **perâzâh**, *per-aw-zaw'*; from the same as 6518; an *open* country:—(unwalled) town (without walls), unwalled village.

6520. פְּרָזוֹן **perâzôwn**, *per-aw-zone'*; from the same as 6518; *magistracy*, i.e. *leadership* (also concr. *chieftains*):—village.

6521. פְּרָזִי **perâzîy**, *per-aw-zee'*; or

°פְּרוֹזִי **perôwzîy**, *per-o-zee'*; from 6519; a *rustic*:—village.

6522. פְּרִזִּי **Perîzzîy**, *per-iz-zee'*; for 6521; inhab. *of the open country*; a *Perizzite*, one of the Canaanitish tribes:—Perizzite.

6523. פַּרְזֶל **parzel** (Chald.), *par-zel'*; corresp. to 1270; *iron*:—iron.

6524. פָּרַח **pârach**, *paw-rakh'*; a prim. root; to *break* forth as a bud, i.e. *bloom*; gen. to *spread*; spec. to *fly* (as extending the wings); fig. to *flourish*:— × abroad, × abundantly, blossom, break forth (out), bud, flourish, make fly, grow, spread, spring (up).

6525. פֶּרַח **perach**, *peh'-rakh*; from 6524; a *calyx* (nat. or artif.); gen. *bloom*:—blossom, bud, flower.

6526. פִּרְחַח **pirchach**, *pir-khakh'*; from 6524; *progeny*, i.e. a *brood*:—youth.

6527. פָּרַט **pâraṭ**, *paw-rat'*; a prim. root; to *scatter* words, i.e. *prate* (or *hum*):—chant.

6528. פֶּרֶט **pereṭ**, *peh'-ret*; from 6527; a *stray* or *single* berry:—grape.

6529. פְּרִי **perîy**, *per-ee'*; from 6509; *fruit* (lit. or fig.):—bough, ([first-]) fruit ([-ful]), reward.

פְּרִידָא **Perîydâʾ**. See 6514.

פֻּרִים **Pûrîym**. See 6332.

6530. פְּרִיץ **perîyts**, *per-eets'*; from 6555; *violent*, i.e. a *tyrant*:—destroyer, ravenous, robber.

6531. פֶּרֶךְ **perek**, *peh'-rek*; from an unused root mean. to *break apart*; *fracture*, i.e. *severity*:—cruelty, rigour.

6532. פֹּרֶכֶת **pôreketh**, *po-reh'-keth*; fem. act. part. of the same as 6531; a *separatrix*, i.e. (the sacred) *screen*:—vail.

6533. פָּרַם **pâram**, *paw-ram'*; a prim. root; to *tear*:—rend.

6534. פַּרְמַשְׁתָּא **Parmashtâʾ**, *par-mash-taw'*; of Pers. or.; *Parmashta*, a son of Haman:—Parmasta.

6535. פַּרְנַךְ **Parnak**, *par-nak'*; of uncert. der.; *Parnak*, an Isr.:—Parnach.

6536. פָּרַס **pâraç**, *paw-ras'*; a prim. root; to *break* in pieces, i.e. (usually without violence) to *split*, *distribute*:—deal, divide, have hoofs, part, tear.

6537. פְּרַס **peraç** (Chald.), *per-as'*; corresp. to 6536; to *split* up:—divide, [U-] pharsin.

6538. פֶּרֶס **pereç**, *peh'-res*; from 6536; a *claw*; also a kind of *eagle*:—claw, ossifrage.

6539. פָּרַס **Pâraç**, *paw-ras';* of for. or.; *Paras* (i.e. *Persia*), an Eastern country, including its inhab.:—Persia, Persians.

6540. פָּרַס **Pâraç** (Chald.), *paw-ras';* corresp. to 6539:—Persia, Persians.

6541. פַּרְסָה **parçâh**, *par-saw';* fem. of 6538; a *claw* or split *hoof:*—claw, [cloven-] footed, hoof.

6542. פַּרְסִי **Parçîy**, *par-see';* patrial from 6539; a *Parsite* (i.e. *Persian*), or inhab. of Peres:—Persian.

6543. פַּרְסִי **Parçîy** (Chald.), *par-see';* corresp. to 6542:—Persian.

6544. פָּרַע **pâraʻ**, *paw-rah';* a prim. root; to *loosen;* by impl. to *expose, dismiss;* fig. *absolve, begin:*—avenge, avoid, bare, go back, let, (make) naked, set at nought, perish, refuse, uncover.

6545. פֶּרַע **peraʻ**, *peh'-rah;* from 6544; the *hair* (as *dishevelled*):—locks.

6546. פַּרְעָה **parʻâh**, *par-aw';* fem. of 6545 (in the sense of *beginning*); *leadership* (plur. concr. *leaders*):— + avenging, revenge.

6547. פַּרְעֹה **Parʻôh**, *par-o';* of Eg. der.; *Paroh*, a gen. title of Eg. kings:—Pharaoh.

6548. פַּרְעֹה חָפְרַע **Parʻôh Chophraʻ**, *par-o' khof-rah';* of Eg. der.; *Paroh-Chophra*, an Eg. king:—Pharaoh-hophra.

6549. פַּרְעֹה נְכֹה **Parʻôh Nᵉkôh**, *par-o' nek-o';* or

פַּרְעֹה נְכוֹ **Parʻôh Nᵉkôw**, *par-o' nek-o';* of Eg. der.; *Paroh-Nekoh* (or *-Neko*), an Eg. king:—Pharaoh-necho, Pharaoh-nechoh.

6550. פַּרְעֹשׁ **parʻôsh**, *par-oshe';* prob. from 6544 and 6211; a *flea* (as the *isolated insect*):—flea.

6551. פַּרְעֹשׁ **Parʻôsh**, *par-oshe';* the same as 6550; *Parosh*, the name of four Isr.:—Parosh, Pharosh.

6552. פִּרְעָתוֹן **Pirʻâthôwn**, *pir-aw-thone';* from 6546; *chieftaincy; Pirathon*, a place in Pal.:—Pirathon.

6553. פִּרְעָתוֹנִי **Pirʻâthôwnîy**, *pir-aw-tho-nee';* or

פִּרְעָתֹנִי **Pirʻâthônîy**, *pir-aw-tho-nee';* patrial from 6552; a *Pirathonite* or inhab. of Pirathon:—Pirathonite.

6554. פַּרְפַּר **Parpar**, *par-par';* prob. from 6565 in the sense of *rushing; rapid; Parpar*, a river of Syria:—Pharpar.

6555. פָּרַץ **pârats**, *paw-rats';* a prim. root; to *break* out (in many applications, direct and indirect, lit. and fig.):—× abroad, (make a) breach, break (away, down, -er, forth, in, up), burst out come (spread) abroad, compel, disperse, grow, increase, open, press, scatter, urge.

6556. פֶּרֶץ **perets**, *peh'-rets;* from 6555; a *break* (lit. or fig.):—breach, breaking forth (in), × forth, gap.

6557. פֶּרֶץ **Perets**, *peh'-rets;* the same as 6556; *Perets*, the name of two Isr.:—Perez, Pharez.

6558. פַּרְצִי **Partsîy**, *par-tsee';* patron. from 6557; a *Partsite* (collect.) or desc. of Perets:—Pharzites.

6559. פְּרָצִים **pᵉrâtsîym**, *per-aw-tseem';* plur. of 6556; *breaks; Peratsim*, a mountain in Pal.:—Perazim.

6560. פֶּרֶץ עֻזָּא **Perets ʻUzzâʼ**, *peh'-rets ooz-zaw';* from 6556 and 5798; *break of Uzza; Perets-Uzza*, a place in Pal.:—Perez-uzza.

6561. פָּרַק **pâraq**, *paw-rak';* a prim. root; to *break* off or *craunch;* fig. to *deliver:*—break (off), deliver, redeem, rend (in pieces), tear in pieces.

6562. פְּרַק **pᵉraq** (Chald.), *per-ak';* corresp. to 6561; to *discontinue:*—break off.

6563. פֶּרֶק **pereq**, *peh'-rek;* from 6561; *rapine;* also a *fork* (in roads):—crossway, robbery.

6564. פָּרָק° **pârâq**, *paw-rawk';* from 6561; *soup* (as full of *crumbed* meat):—broth. See also 4832.

6565. פָּרַר **pârar**, *paw-rar';* a prim. root; to *break* up (usually fig., i.e. to *violate, frustrate*):— × any ways, break (asunder), cast off, cause to cease, × clean, defeat, disannul, disappoint, dissolve, divide, make of none effect, fail, frustrate, bring (come) to nought, × utterly, make void.

6566. פָּרַשׂ **pâras**, *paw-ras';* a prim. root; to *break* apart, *disperse*, etc.:—break, chop in pieces, lay open, scatter, spread (abroad, forth, selves, out), stretch (forth, out).

6567. פָּרַשׁ **pârash**, *paw-rash';* a prim. root; to *separate*, lit. (to *disperse*) or fig. (to *specify*); also (by impl.) to *wound:*—scatter, declare, distinctly, shew, sting.

6568. פְּרַשׁ **pᵉrash** (Chald.), *per-ash';* corresp. to 6567; to *specify:*—distinctly.

6569. פֶּרֶשׁ **peresh**, *peh'-resh;* from 6567; *excrement* (as *eliminated*):—dung.

6570. פֶּרֶשׁ **Peresh**, *peh'-resh;* the same as 6569; *Peresh*, an Isr.:—Peresh.

6571. פָּרָשׁ **pârâsh**, *paw-rawsh';* from 6567; a *steed* (as *stretched* out to a vehicle, not single nor for mounting [comp. 5483]); also (by impl.) a *driver* (in a chariot), i.e. (collect.) cavalry:—horseman.

6572. פַּרְשֶׁגֶן **parshegen**, *par-sheh'-ghen;* or

פַּתְשֶׁגֶן **pathshegen**, *path-sheh'-gen;* of for. or.; a *transcript:*—copy.

6573. פַּרְשֶׁגֶן **parshegen** (Chald.), *par-sheh'-ghen;* corresp. to 6572:—copy.

6574. פַּרְשְׁדֹן **parshᵉdôn**, *par-shed-one';* perh. by compounding 6567 and 6504 (in the sense of *straddling*) [comp. 6576]; the *crotch* (or *anus*):—dirt.

6575. פָּרָשָׁה **pârâshâh**, *paw-raw-shaw';* from 6567; *exposition:*—declaration, sum.

6576. פַּרְשֵׁז **parshêz**, *par-shaze';* a root appar. formed by compounding 6567 and that of 6518 [comp. 6574]; to *expand:*—spread.

6577. פַּרְשַׁנְדָּתָא **Parshandâthâʼ**, *par-shan-daw-thaw';* of Pers. or.; *Parshandatha*, a son of Haman:—Parshandatha.

6578. פְּרָת **Pᵉrâth**, *per-awth';* from an unused root mean. to *break* forth; *rushing; Perath* (i.e. *Euphrates*), a river of the East:—Euphrates.

פֹּרָת **pôrâth**. See 6509.

6579. פַּרְתַּם **partam**, *par-tam';* of Pers. or.; a *grandee:*—(most) noble, prince.

6580. פַּשׁ **pash**, *pash;* prob. from an unused root mean. to *disintegrate; stupidity* (as a result of *grossness* or of *degeneracy*):—extremity.

6581. פָּשָׂה **pâsâh**, *paw-saw';* a prim. root; to *spread:*—spread.

6582. פָּשַׁח **pâshach**, *paw-shakh';* a prim. root; to *tear* in pieces:—pull in pieces.

6583. פַּשְׁחוּר **Pashchûwr**, *pash-khoor';* prob. from 6582; *liberation; Pashchur*, the name of four Isr.:—Pashur.

6584. פָּשַׁט **pâshaṭ**, *paw-shat';* a prim. root; to *spread* out (i.e. *deploy* in hostile array); by anal. to *strip* (i.e. *unclothe, plunder, flay*, etc.):—fall upon, flay, invade, make an invasion, pull off, put off, make a road, run upon, rush, set, spoil, spread selves (abroad), strip (off, self).

6585. פָּשַׂע **pâsaʻ**, *paw-sah';* a prim. root; to *stride* (from *spreading* the legs), i.e. *rush* upon:—go.

6586. פָּשַׁע **pâshaʻ**, *paw-shah';* a prim. root [rather ident. with 6585 through the idea of *expansion*]; to *break* away (from just authority), i.e. *trespass, apostatize, quarrel:*—offend, rebel, revolt, transgress (-ion, -or).

6587. פֶּשַׂע **pesaʻ**, *peh'-sah;* from 6585; a *stride:*—step.

6588. פֶּשַׁע **peshaʻ**, *peh'-shah;* from 6586; a *revolt* (national, moral or religious):—rebellion, sin, transgression, trespass.

6589. פָּשַׂק **pâsaq**, *paw-sak';* a prim. root; to *dispart* (the feet or lips), i.e. *become licentious:*—open (wide).

6590. פְּשַׁר **pᵉshar** (Chald.), *pesh-ar';* corresp. to 6622; to *interpret:*—make [interpretations], interpreting.

6591. פְּשַׁר **pᵉshar** (Chald.), *pesh-ar';* from 6590; an *interpretation;*—interpretation.

6592. פֵּשֶׁר **pêsher**, *pay'-sher;* corresp. to 6591:—interpretation.

6593. פִּשְׁתֶּה **pishteh**, *pish-teh';* from the same as 6580 as in the sense of *comminuting; linen* (i.e. the thread, as *carded*):—flax, linen.

6594. פִּשְׁתָּה **pishtâh**, *pish-taw';* fem. of 6593; *flax;* by impl. a *wick:*—flax, tow.

6595. פַּת **path**, *path;* from 6626; a *bit:*—meat, morsel, piece.

6596. פֹּת **pôth**, *pohth;* or

פֹּתָה **pothâh** (Ezek. 13 : 19), *po-thaw';* from an unused root mean. to *open;* a *hole*, i.e. *hinge* or the female *pudenda:*—hinge, secret part.

פְּתָאִי **pᵉthâʼîy**. See 6612.

6597. פִּתְאוֹם **pithʼôwm**, *pith-ome';* or

פִּתְאֹם **pithʼôm**, *pith-ome';* from 6621; *instantly:*—straightway, sudden (-ly).

6598. פַּתְבַּג **pathbag**, *pathbag';* of Pers. or.; a *dainty:*—portion (provision) of meat.

6599. פִּתְגָּם **pithgâm**, *pith-gawm';* of Pers. or.; a (judicial) *sentence:*—decree, sentence.

6600. פִּתְגָּם **pithgâm** (Chald.), *pith-gawm';* corresp. to 6599; a *word, answer, letter* or *decree:*—answer, letter, matter, word.

6601. פָּתָה **pâthâh**, *paw-thaw';* a prim. root; to *open*, i.e. *be* (causat. *make*) *roomy;* usually fig. (in a mental or moral sense) to *be* (causat. *make*) *simple* or (in a sinister way) *delude:*—allure, deceive, enlarge, entice, flatter, persuade, silly (one).

6602. פְּתוּאֵל **Pᵉthûwʼêl**, *peth-oo-ale';* from 6601 and 410; *enlarged of God; Pethuël*, an Isr.:—Pethuel.

6603. פִּתּוּחַ **pittûwach**, *pit-too'-akh;* or

פִּתֻּחַ **pittûach**, *pit-too'-akh;* pass. part. of 6605; *sculpture* (in low or high relief or even intaglio):—carved (work) (are, en-) grave (-ing, -n).

6604. פְּתוֹר **Pᵉthôwr**, *peth-ore';* of for. or.; *Pethor*, a place in Mesopotamia:—Pethor.

6605. פָּתַח **pâthach**, *paw-thakh';* a prim. root; to *open* wide (lit. or fig.); spec. to *loosen, begin, plough, carve;*—appear, break forth, draw (out), let go free, (en-) grave (-n), loose (self), (be, be set) open (-ing), put off, ungird, unstop, have vent.

6606. פְּתַח **pᵉthach** (Chald.), *peth-akh';* corresp to 6605; to *open:*—open.

6607. פֶּתַח **pethach**, *peh'-thakh;* from 6605; an *opening* (lit.), i.e. *door* (*gate*) or *entrance way:*—door, entering (in), entrance (-ry), gate, opening, place.

6608. פֵּתַח **pêthach**, *pay'-thakh;* from 6605; *opening* (fig.) i.e. *disclosure:*—entrance.

פָּתֻחַ **pâthûach**. See 6603.

6609. פְּתִיחָה **pᵉthîkhâh**, *peth-ee-khaw';* from 6605; something *opened*, i.e. a *drawn* sword:—drawn sword.

6610. פִּתְחוֹן **pithchôwn**, *pith-khone';* from 6605; *opening* (the act):—open (-ing).

6611. פְּתַחְיָה **Pᵉthachyâh**, *peth-akh-yaw';* from 6605 and 3050; *Jah has opened; Pethachjah*, the name of four Isr.:—Pethakiah.

6612. פְּתִי **pᵉthîy**, *peth-ee';* or

פֶּתִי **pethiy**, *peh'-thee;* or

פְּתָאִי **pᵉthâʼîy**, *peth-aw-ee';* from 6601; *silly* (i.e. *seducible*):—foolish, simple (-icity, one).

6613. פְּתַי **pᵉthay** (Chald.), *peth-ah'ee;* from a root corresp. to 6601; *open*, i.e. (as noun) *width:*—breadth.

6614. פְּתִיגִיל **pᵉthîygîyl**, *peth-eeg-eel';* of uncert. der.; prob. a figured *mantle* for holidays:—stomacher.

6615. פְּתַיּוּת **pᵉthayûwth**, *peth-ah-yooth';* from 6612; *silliness* (i.e. *seducibility*):—simple.

6616. פָּתִיל **pâthîyl**, *paw-theel';* from 6617; *twine:*—bound, bracelet, lace, line, ribband, thread, wire.

6617. פָּתַל **pâthal**, *paw-thal';* a prim. root; to *twine*, i.e. (lit.) to *struggle* or (fig.) *be* (morally) *tortuous:*—(shew self) froward, shew self unsavoury, wrestle.

6618. פְּתַלְתֹּל **pᵉthaltôl**, *peth-al-tole';* from 6617; *tortuous* (i.e. crafty):—crooked.

6619. פִּתֹם **Pîthôm**, *pee-thome';* of Eg. der.; *Pithom*, a place in Eg.:—Pithom.

6620. פֶּתֶן **pethen**, *peh'-then;* from an unused root mean. to *twist;* an *asp* (from its *contortions*):—adder.

6621. פֶּתַע **petha'**, *peh'-thah;* from an unused root mean. to *open* (the eyes); a *wink*, i.e. *moment* [comp. 6597] (used only [with or without prep.] adv. *quickly* or *unexpectedly*):—at an instant suddenly, × very.

6622. פָּתַר **pâthar**, *paw-thar';* a prim. root; to *open* up, i.e. (fig.) *interpret* (a dream):—interpret (-ation, -er).

6623. פִּתְרוֹן **pithrôwn**, *pith-rone';* or

פִּתְרֹן **pithrôn**, *pith-rone';* from 6622; *interpretation* (of a dream):—interpretation.

6624. פַּתְרוֹס **Pathrôwç**, *path-roce';* of Eg. der.; *Pathros*, a part of Eg.:—Pathros.

6625. פַּתְרֻסִי **Pathrûçîy**, *path-roo-see';* patrial from 6624; a *Pathrusite*, or inhab. of Pathros:—Pathrusim.

פַּתְשֶׁגֶן **pathshegen**. See 6572.

6626. פָּתַת **pâthath**, *paw-thath';* a prim. root; to *open*, i.e. *break:*—part.

צ

6627. צָאָה **tsâ'âh**, *tsaw-aw';* from 3318; *issue*, i.e. (human) *excrement:*—that (which) cometh from (out).

צֹאָה **tsô'âh**. See 6675.

צְאוֹן° **tsᵉ'ôwn**. See 6629.

6628. צֶאֶל **tse'el**, *tseh'-el;* from an unused root mean. to *be slender;* the *lotus* tree:—shady tree.

6629. צֹאן **tsô'n**, *tsone;* or

צְאוֹן° **tsᵉ'ôwn** (Psa. 144 : 13), *tseh-one';* from an unused root mean. to *migrate;* a collect. name for a *flock* (of sheep or goats); also fig. (of men):—(small) cattle, flock (+ -s), lamb (+ -s), sheep ([-cote, -fold, -shearer, -herds]).

6630. צַאֲנָן **Tsa'ănân**, *tsah-an-awn';* from the same as 6629 used denom.; *sheep pasture; Zaanan*, a place in Pal.:—Zaanan.

6631. צֶאֱצָא **tse'ĕtsâ'**, *tseh-ets-aw';* from 3318; *issue*, i.e. *produce*, *children:*—that which cometh forth (out), offspring.

6632. צָב **tsâb**, *tsawb;* from an unused root mean. to *establish;* a *palanquin* or *canopy* (as a *fixture*); also a species of *lizard* (prob. as clinging *fast*):—covered, litter, tortoise.

6633. צָבָא **tsâbâ'**, *tsaw-baw';* a prim. root; to *mass* (an army or servants):—assemble, fight, perform, muster, wait upon, war.

6634. צְבָא **tsᵉbâ'** (Chald.), *tseb-aw';* corresp. to 6633 in the fig. sense of *summoning* one's wishes; to *please:*—will, would.

6635. צָבָא **tsâbâ'**, *tsaw-baw';* or (fem.)

צְבָאָה **tsᵉbâ'âh**, *tseb-aw-aw';* from 6633; a *mass* of persons (or fig. things), espec. reg. organized for war (an *army*); by impl. a *campaign*, lit. or fig (spec. *hardship*, *worship*):—appointed time, (+) army, (+) battle, company, host, service, soldiers, waiting upon, war (-fare).

6636. צְבֹאִים **Tsᵉbô'iym**, *tseb-o-eem';* or (more correctly)

צְבִיִּים° **Tsᵉbîyîym**, *tseb-ee-yeem';* or

צְבִיִּם° **Tsᵉbîyîm**, *tseb-ee-yeem';* plur. of 6643; *gazelles; Tseboïm* or *Tsebijim*, a place in Pal.:—Zeboiim, Zeboim.

6637. צֹבֵבָה **Tsôbêbâh**, *tso-bay-baw';* fem. act. part. of the same as 6632; the *canopier* (with the art.); *Tsobebah*, an Israelitess:—Zobebah.

6638. צָבָה **tsâbâh**, *tsaw-baw';* a prim. root; to *amass*, i.e. *grow turgid;* spec. to *array* an army against:—fight, swell.

6639. צָבֶה **tsâbeh**, *tsaw-beh';* from 6638; *turgid:*—swell.

צֹבָה **Tsôbâh**. See 6678.

6640. צְבוּ **tsᵉbûw** (Chald.), *tseb-oo';* from 6634; prop. *will;* concr. an *affair* (as a matter of *determination*):—purpose.

6641. צָבוּעַ **tsâbûwa'**, *tsaw-boo'-ah;* pass. part. of the same as 6648; *dyed* (in stripes), i.e. the *hyena:*—speckled.

6642. צָבַט **tsâbaṭ**, *tsaw-bat';* a prim. root; to *grasp*, i.e. *hand* out:—reach.

6643. צְבִי **tsᵉbîy**, *tseb-ee';* from 6638 in the sense of *prominence;* *splendor* (as *conspicuous*); also a *gazelle* (as *beautiful*):—beautiful (-ty), glorious (-ry), goodly, pleasant, roe (-buck).

6644. צִבְיָא **Tsibyâ'**, *tsib-yaw';* for 6645; *Tsibja*, an Isr.:—Zibia.

6645. צִבְיָה **Tsibyâh**, *tsib-yaw';* for 6646; *Tsibjah*, an Israelitess:—Zibiah.

6646. צְבִיָּה **tsᵉbîyâh**, *tseb-ee-yaw';* fem. of 6643; a *female* gazelle:—roe.

צְבִיִּים° (or צְבִיִּם) **Tsᵉbîyîym**. See 6636.

צְבָיִם° **Tsᵉbâyîm**. See 6380.

6647. צְבַע **tsᵉba'** (Chald.), *tseb-ah';* a root corresp. to that of 6648; to *dip:*—wet.

6648. צֶבַע **tseba'**, *tseh'-bah;* from an unused root mean. to *dip* (into coloring fluid); a *dye:*—divers, colours.

6649. צִבְעוֹן **Tsib'ôwn**, *tsib-one';* from the same as 6648; *variegated; Tsibon*, an Idumæan:—Zibeon.

6650. צְבֹעִים **Tsᵉbô'îym**, *tseb-o-eem';* plur. of 6641; *hyenas; Tseboïm*, a place in Pal.:—Zeboim.

6651. צָבַר **tsâbar**, *tsaw-bar';* a prim. root; to *aggregate:*—gather (together), heap (up), lay up.

6652. צִבֻּר **tsibbûr**, *tsib-boor';* from 6551; a *pile:*—heap.

6653. צֶבֶת **tsebeth**, *tseh'-beth;* from an unused root appar. mean. to *grip;* a *lock* of stalks:—handful.

6654. צַד **tsad**, *tsad;* contr. from an unused root mean. to *sidle* off; a *side;* fig. an *adversary:*—(be-) side.

6655. צַד **tsad** (Chald.), *tsad;* corresp. to 6654; used adv. (with prep.) at or upon the *side* of:—against, concerning.

6656. צְדָא **tsᵉdâ'** (Chald.), *tsed-aw';* from an unused root corresp. to 6658 in the sense of *intentness;* a (sinister) *design:*—true.

6657. צְדָד **Tsᵉdâd**, *tsed-awd';* from the same as 6654; a *siding; Tsedad*, a place near Pal.:—Zedad.

6658. צָדָה **tsâdâh**, *tsaw-daw';* a prim. root; to *chase;* by impl. to *desolate:*—destroy, hunt, lie in wait.

צֵדָה **tsêdâh**. See 6720.

6659. צָדוֹק **Tsâdôwq**, *tsaw-doke';* from 6663; *just; Tsadok*, the name of eight or nine Isr.:—Zadok.

6660. צְדִיָּה **tsᵉdîyâh**, *tsed-ee-yaw';* from 6658; *design* [comp. 6656]:—lying in wait.

6661. צִדִּים **Tsiddîym**, *tsid-deem';* plur. of 6654; *sides; Tsiddim* (with the art.), a place in Pal.:—Ziddim.

6662. צַדִּיק **tsaddîyq**, *tsad-deek';* from 6663; *just:*—just, lawful, righteous (man).

צִדֹנִי° **Tsîdônîy**. See 6722.

6663. צָדַק **tsâdaq**, *tsaw-dak';* a prim. root; to *be* (causat. *make*) *right* (in a moral or forensic sense):—cleanse, clear self, (be, do) just (-ice, -ify, -ify self), (be, turn to) righteous (-ness).

6664. צֶדֶק **tsedeq**, *tseh'-dek;* from 6663; the *right* (nat., mor. or legal); also (abstr.) *equity* or (fig.) *prosperity:*— × even, (× that which is altogether) just (-ice), ([un-]) right (-eous) (cause, -ly, -ness).

6665. צִדְקָה **tsidqâh** (Chald.), *tsid-kaw';* corresp. to 6666; *beneficence:*—righteousness.

6666. צְדָקָה **tsᵉdâqâh**, *tsed-aw-kaw';* from 6663; *rightness* (abstr.), subj. (*rectitude*), obj. (*justice*), mor. (*virtue*) or fig. (*prosperity*):—justice, moderately, right (-eous) (act, -ly, -ness).

6667. צִדְקִיָּה **Tsidqîyâh**, *tsid-kee-yaw';* or

צִדְקִיָּהוּ **Tsidqîyâhûw**, *tsid-kee-yaw'-hoo;* from 6664 and 3050; *right of Jah; Tsidkijah*, the name of six Isr.:—Zedekiah, Zidkijah.

6668. צָהַב **tsâhab**, *tsaw-hab';* a prim. root; to *glitter*, i.e. *be golden* in color:— × fine.

6669. צָהֹב **tsâhôb**, *tsaw-obe';* from 6668; *golden* in color:—yellow.

6670. צָהַל **tsâhal**, *tsaw-hal';* a prim. root; to *gleam*, i.e. (fig.) *be cheerful;* by transf. to *sound* clear (of various animal or human expressions):—bellow, cry aloud (out), lift up, neigh, rejoice, make to shine, shout.

6671. צָהַר **tsâhar**, *tsaw-har';* a prim. root; to *glisten;* used only as denom. from 3323, to *press* out *oil:*—make oil.

6672. צֹהַר **tsôhar**, *tso'-har;* from 6671; a *light* (i.e. *window*); dual *double light*, i.e. *noon:*—midday, noon (-day, -tide), window.

6673. צַו **tsav**, *tsav;* or

צָו **tsâv**, *tsawv;* from 6680; an *injunction:*—commandment, precept.

6674. צוֹא **tsôw'**, *tso;* or

צֹא **tsô'**, *tso;* from an unused root mean. to *issue;* *soiled* (as if *excrementitious*):—filthy.

6675. צוֹאָה **tsôw'âh**, *tso-aw';* or

צֹאָה **tsô'âh**, *tso-aw';* fem. of 6674; *excrement;* gen. *dirt;* fig. *pollution:*—dung, filth (-iness). Marg. for 2716.

6676. צַוַּאר **tsavva'r** (Chald.), *tsav-var';* corresp. to 6677:—neck.

6677. צַוָּאר **tsavvâ'r**, *tsav-vawr';* or

צַוָּר **tsavvâr** (Neh. 3 : 5), *tsav-vawr';* or

צַוְּרֹן **tsavvârôn** (Cant. 4 : 9), *tsav-vaw-rone';* or (fem.)

צַוָּארָה **tsavvâ'râh** (Mic. 2 : 3), *tsav-vaw-raw';* intens. from 6696 in the sense of *binding;* the back of the *neck* (as that on which burdens are *bound*):—neck.

6678. צוֹבָא **Tsôwbâ'**, *tso-baw';* or

צוֹבָה **Tsôwbâh**, *tso-baw';* or

צֹבָה **Tsôbâh**, *tso-baw';* from an unused root mean. to *station;* a *station; Zoba* or *Zobah*, a region of Syria:—Zoba, Zobah.

6679. צוּד **tsûwd**, *tsood;* a prim. root; to *lie* alongside (i.e. in wait); by impl. to *catch* an animal (fig. men); (denom. from 6718) to *victual* (for a journey):—chase, hunt, sore, take (provision).

6680. צָוָה **tsâvâh**, *tsaw-vaw';* a prim. root; (intens.) to *constitute*, *enjoin:*—appoint, (for-) bid, (give a) charge, (give a, give in, send with) command (-er, -ment), send a messenger, put, (set) in order.

6681. צָוַח **tsâvach**, *tsaw-vakh';* a prim. root; to *screech* (exultingly):—shout.

6682. צְוָחָה **tsᵉvâchâh**, *tsev-aw-khaw';* from 6681; a *screech* (of anguish):—cry (-ing).

6683. צוּלָה **tsûwlâh**, *tsoo-law';* from an unused root mean. to *sink;* an *abyss* (of the sea):—deep.

6684. צוּם **tsûwm**, *tsoom;* a prim. root; to *cover* over (the mouth), i.e. to *fast:*— × at all, fast.

6685. צוֹם **tsôwm**, *tsome;* or

צֹם **tsôm**, *tsome;* from 6684; a *fast:*—fast (-ing).

6686. צוּעָר **Tsûwʽâr**, *tsoo-awr'*; from 6819; *small; Tsuär*, an Isr.:—Zuar.

6687. צוּף **tsûwph**, *tsoof*; a prim. root; to *overflow*:—(make to over-) flow, swim.

6688. צוּף **tsûwph**, *tsoof*; from 6687; *comb* of honey (from *dripping*):—honeycomb.

6689. צוּף **Tsûwph**, *tsoof*; or

צוֹפַי **Tsôwphay**, *tso-fah'ee*; or

צִיף° **Tsîyph**, *tseef*; from 6688; *honey-comb; Tsuph* or *Tsophai* or *Tsiph*, the name of an Isr. and of a place in Pal.:—Zophai, Zuph.

6690. צוֹפַח **Tsôwphach**, *tso-fakh'*; from an unused root mean. to *expand, breadth; Tsophach*, an Isr.:—Zophah.

צוֹפַי **Tsôwphay**. See 6689.

6691. צוֹפַר **Tsôwphar**, *tso-far'*; from 6852; *departing; Tsophar*, a friend of Job:—Zophar.

6692. צוּץ **tsûwts**, *tsoots*; a prim. root; to *twinkle*, i.e. *glance*; by anal. to *blossom* (fig. *flourish*):—bloom, blossom, flourish, shew self.

6693. צוּק **tsûwq**, *tsook*; a prim. root; to *compress*, i.e. (fig.) *oppress, distress*:—constrain, distress, lie sore, (op-) press (-or), straiten.

6694. צוּק **tsûwq**, *tsook*; a prim. root [rather ident. with 6693 through the idea of *narrowness* (of orifice)]; to *pour* out, i.e. (fig.) *smelt, utter*:—be molten, pour.

6695. צוֹק **tsôwq**, *tsoke*; or (fem.)

צוּקָה **tsûwqâh**, *tsoo-kaw'*; from 6693; a *strait*, i.e. (fig.) *distress*:—anguish, × troublous.

6696. צוּר **tsûwr**, *tsoor*; a prim. root; to *cramp*, i.e. *confine* (in many applications, lit. and fig., formative or hostile):—adversary, assault, beset, besiege, bind (up), cast, distress, fashion, fortify, inclose, lay siege, put up in bags.

6697. צוּר **tsûwr**, *tsoor*; or

צֻר **tsûr**, *tsoor*; from 6696; prop. a *cliff* (or sharp rock, as *compressed*); gen. a *rock* or *boulder*; fig. a *refuge*; also an *edge* (as *precipitous*):—edge, × (mighty) God (one), rock, × sharp, stone, × strength, × strong. See also 1049.

6698. צוּר **Tsûwr**, *tsoor*; the same as 6697; *rock; Tsur*, the name of a Midianite and of an Isr.:—Zur.

צוֹר **Tsôwr**. See 6865.

צַוָּר **tsavvâr**. See 6677.

6699. צוּרָה **tsûwrâh**, *tsoo-raw'*; fem. of 6697; a *rock* (Job 28 : 10); also a *form* (as if *pressed* out):—form, rock.

צַוָּרֹן **tsavvârôn**. See 6677.

6700. צוּרִיאֵל **Tsûwrîy'êl**, *tsoo-ree-ale'*; from 6697 and 410; *rock of God; Tsuriël*, an Isr.:—Zuriel.

6701. צוּרִישַׁדַּי **Tsûwrîyshadday**, *tsoo-ree-shad-dah'ee*; from 6697 and 7706; *rock of* (the) *Almighty; Tsurishaddai*, an Isr.:—Zurishaddai.

6702. צוּת **tsûwth**, *tsooth*; a prim. root; to *blaze*:—burn.

6703. צַח **tsach**, *tsakh*; from 6705; *dazzling*, i.e. *sunny, bright*, (fig.) *evident*:—clear, dry, plainly, white.

צִחָא **Tsichâ'**. See 6727.

6704. צִחֶה **tsicheh**, *tsee-kheh'*; from an unused root mean. to *glow; parched*:—dried up.

6705. צָחַח **tsâchach**, *tsaw-khakh'*; a prim. root; to *glare*, i.e. *be dazzling* white:—be whiter.

6706. צְחִיחַ **tsᵉchîyach**, *tsekh-ee'-akh*; from 6705; *glaring*, i.e. *exposed* to the bright sun:—higher place, top.

6707. צְחִיחָה **tsᵉchîychâh**, *tsekh-ee-khaw'*; fem. of 6706; a *parched* region, i.e. the *desert*:—dry land.

6708. צְחִיחִי° **tsᵉchîychîy**, *tsekh-ee-khee'*; from 6706; *bare spot*, i.e. in the *glaring* sun:—higher place.

6709. צַחֲנָה **tsachănâh**, *tsakh-an-aw'*; from an unused root mean. to *putrefy; stench*:—ill savour.

6710. צַחְצָחָה **tsachtsâchâh**, *tsakh-tsaw-khaw'*; from 6705; a *dry* place, i.e. *desert*:—drought.

6711. צָחַק **tsâchaq**, *tsaw-khak'*; a prim. root; to *laugh* outright (in merriment or scorn); by impl. to *sport*:—laugh, mock, play, make sport.

6712. צְחֹק **tsᵉchôq**, *tsekh-oke'*; from 6711; *laughter* (in pleasure or derision):—laugh (-ed to scorn).

6713. צַחַר **tsachar**, *tsakh'-ar*; from an unused root mean. to *dazzle; sheen*, i.e. *whiteness*:—white.

6714. צֹחַר **Tsôchar**, *tso'-khar*; from the same as 6713; *whiteness; Tsochar*, the name of a Hittite and of an Isr.:—Zohar. Comp. 3328.

6715. צָחֹר **tsâchôr**, *tsaw-khore'*; from the same as 6713; *white*:—white.

6716. צִי **tsîy**, *tsee*; from 6680; a *ship* (as a *fixture*):—ship.

6717. צִיבָא **Tsîybâ'**, *tsee-baw'*; from the same as 6678; *station; Tsiba*, an Isr.:—Ziba.

6718. צַיִד **tsayid**, *tsah'-yid*; from a form of 6679 and mean. the same; the *chase*; also *game* (thus taken); (gen.) *lunch* (espec. for a journey):—× catcheth, food, × hunter, (that which he took in) hunting, venison, victuals.

6719. צַיָּד **tsayâd**, *tsah'-yawd*; from the same as 6718; a *huntsman*:—hunter.

6720. צֵידָה **tsêydâh**, *tsay-daw'*; or

צֵדָה **tsêdâh**, *tsay-daw'*; fem. of 6718; *food*:—meat, provision, venison, victuals.

6721. צִידוֹן **Tsîydôwn**, *tsee-done'*; or

צִידֹן **Tsîydôn**, *tsee-done'*; from 6679 in the sense of *catching* fish; *fishery; Tsidon*, the name of a son of Canaan, and of a place in Pal.:—Sidon, Zidon.

6722. צִידֹנִי (or צִדֹנִי°) **Tsîydônîy**, *tsee-do-nee'*; patrial from 6721; a *Tsidonian* or inhab. of Tsidon:—Sidonian, of Sidon, Zidonian.

6723. צִיָּה **tsîyâh**, *tsee-yaw'*; from an unused root mean. to *parch; aridity*; concr. a *desert*:—barren, drought, dry (land, place), solitary place, wilderness.

6724. צִיוֹן **tsîyôwn**, *tsee-yone'*; from the same as 6723; a *desert*:—dry place.

6725. צִיּוּן **tsîyûwn**, *tsee-yoon'*; from the same as 6723 in the sense of *conspicuousness* [comp. 5329]; a monumental or guiding *pillar*:—sign, title, waymark.

6726. צִיּוֹן **Tsîyôwn**, *tsee-yone'*; the same (reg.) as 6725; *Tsijon* (as a permanent *capital*), a mountain of Jerus.:—Zion.

6727. צִיחָא **Tsîychâ'**, *tsee-khaw'*; or

צִחָא **Tsîchâ'**, *tsee-khaw'*; as if fem. of 6704; *drought; Tsicha*, the name of two Nethinim:—Ziha.

6728. צִיִּי **tsîyîy**, *tsee-ee'*; from the same as 6723; a *desert-dweller*, i.e. *nomad* or wild *beast*:—wild beast of the desert, that dwell in (inhabiting) the wilderness.

6729. צִינֹק **tsîynôq**, *tsee-noke'*; from an unused root mean. to *confine*; the *pillory*:—stocks.

6730. צִיעֹר **Tsîyʽôr**, *tsee-ore'*; from 6819; *small; Tsior*, a place in Pal.:—Zior.

צִיף° **Tsîyph**. See 6689.

6731. צִיץ **tsîyts**, *tseets*; or

צִץ **tsîts**, *tseets*; from 6692; prop. *glistening*, i.e. a burnished *plate*; also a *flower* (as *bright* colored); a *wing* (as *gleaming* in the air):—blossom, flower, plate, wing.

6732. צִיץ **Tsîyts**, *tseets*; the same as 6731; *bloom; Tsits*, a place in Pal.:—Ziz.

6733. צִיצָה **tsîytsâh**, *tsee-tsaw'*; fem. of 6731; a *flower*:—flower

6734. צִיצִת **tsîytsîth**, *tsee-tseeth'*; fem. of 6731; a *floral* or *wing*-like projection, i.e. a *fore-lock* of hair, a *tassel*:—fringe, lock.

צִיקְלַג **Tsîyqᵉlag**. See 6860.

6735. צִיר **tsîyr**, *tseer*; from 6696; a *hinge* (as *pressed* in turning); also a *throe* (as a phys. or mental *pressure*); also a *herald* or errand-doer (as *constrained* by the principal):—ambassador, hinge, messenger, pain, pang, sorrow. Comp. 6736.

6736. צִיר **tsîyr**, *tseer*; the same as 6735; a *form* (of beauty; as if *pressed* out, i.e. carved); hence an (idolatrous) *image*:—beauty, idol.

6737. צָיַר **tsâyar**, *tsaw-yar'*; a denom. from 6735 in the sense of *ambassador*; to *make an errand*, i.e. *betake* oneself:—make as if . . . had been ambassador.

6738. צֵל **tsêl**, *tsale*; from 6751; *shade*, whether lit. or fig.:—defence, shade (-ow).

6739. צְלָא **tsᵉlâ'** (Chald.), *tsel-aw'*; prob. corresp. to 6760 in the sense of *bowing; pray*:—pray.

6740. צָלָה **tsâlâh**, *tsaw-law'*; a prim. root; to *roast*:—roast.

6741. צִלָּה **Tsillâh**, *tsil-law'*; fem. of 6738; *Tsillah*, an antediluvian woman:—Zillah.

6742. צְלוּל° **tsᵉlûwl**, *tsel-ool'*; from 6749 in the sense of *rolling*; a (round or flattened) *cake*:—cake.

6743. צָלַח **tsâlach**, *tsaw-lakh'*; or

צָלֵחַ **tsâlêach**, *tsaw-lay'-akh*; a prim. root; to *push* forward, in various senses (lit. or fig., trans. or intrans.):—break out, come (mightily), go over, be good, be meet, be profitable, (cause to, effect, make to, send) prosper (-ity, -ous, -ously).

6744. צְלַח **tsᵉlach** (Chald.), *tsel-akh'*; corresp. to 6743; to *advance* (trans. or intrans.):—promote, prosper.

6745. צֵלָחָה **tsêlâchâh**, *tsay-law-khaw'*; from 6743; something *protracted* or flattened out, i.e. a *platter*:—pan.

6746. צְלֹחִית **tsᵉlôchîyth**, *tsel-o-kheeth'*; from 6743; something *prolonged* or tall, i.e. a *vial* or salt-*cellar*:—cruse.

6747. צַלַּחַת **tsallachath**, *tsal-lakh'-ath*; from 6743; something *advanced* or deep, i.e. a *bowl*; fig. the *bosom*:—bosom, dish.

6748. צָלִי **tsâlîy**, *tsaw-lee'*; pass. part. of 6740; *roasted*:—roast.

6749. צָלַל **tsâlal**, *tsaw-lal'*; a prim. root; prop. to *tumble* down, i.e. *settle* by a waving motion:—sink. Comp. 6750, 6751.

6750. צָלַל **tsâlal**, *tsaw-lal'*; a prim. root [rather ident. with 6749 through the idea of *vibration*]; to *tinkle*, i.e. *rattle* together (as the ears in *reddening* with shame, or the teeth in *chattering* with fear):—quiver, tingle.

6751. צָלַל **tsâlal**, *tsaw-lal'*; a prim. root [rather ident. with 6749 through the idea of *hovering* over (comp. 6754)]; to *shade*, as twilight or an opaque object:—begin to be dark, shadowing.

6752. צֵלֶל **tsêlel**, *tsay'-lel*; from 6751; *shade*:—shadow.

6753. צְלֶלְפּוֹנִי **Tsᵉlelpôwnîy**, *tsel-el-po-nee'*; from 6752 and the act. part. of 6437; *shade-facing; Tselelponi*, an Israelitess:—Hazelelponi [*includ. the art.*].

6754. צֶלֶם **tselem**, *tseh'-lem*; from an unused root mean. to *shade*; a *phantom*, i.e. (fig.) *illusion, resemblance*; hence a representative *figure*, espec. an *idol*:—image, vain shew.

6755. צֶלֶם **tselem** (Chald.), *tseh'-lem*; or

צְלֵם **tsᵉlem** (Chald.), *tsel-em'*; corresp. to 6754; an idolatrous *figure*:—form, image.

6756. צַלְמוֹן **Tsalmôwn**, *tsal-mone'*; from 6754; *shady; Tsalmon*, the name of a place in Pal. and of an Isr.:—Zalmon.

6757. צַלְמָוֶת **tsalmâveth**, *tsal-maw'-veth*; from 6738 and 4194; *shade of death*, i.e. the *grave* (fig. *calamity*):—shadow of death.

6758. צַלְמֹנָה **Tsalmônâh**, *tsal-mo-naw'*; fem. of 6757; *shadiness; Tsalmonah*, a place in the Desert:—Zalmonah.

6759. צַלְמֻנָּע **Tsalmunnâʻ**, *tsal-moon-naw'*; from 6738 and 4513; *shade has been denied; Tsalmunna*, a Midianite:—Zalmunna.

6760. צָלַע **tsâlaʻ**, *tsaw-lah'*; a prim. root; prob. to *curve*; used only as denom. from 6763, to *limp* (as if *one-sided*):—halt.

6761. צֶלַע **tselaʻ**, *tseh'-lah*; from 6760; a *limping* or *fall* (fig.):—adversity, halt (-ing).

6762. צֶלַע **Tselaʻ**, *tseh'-lah*; the same as 6761; *Tsela*, a place in Pal.:—Zelah.

6763. צֵלָע **tsêlâʻ**, *tsay-law'*; or (fem.)

צַלְעָה **tsalʻâh**, *tsal-aw'*; from 6760; a *rib* (as *curved*), lit. (of the body) or fig. (of a door, i.e. *leaf*); hence a *side*, lit. (of a person) or fig. (of an object or the sky, i.e. *quarter*); arch. a (espec. floor or ceiling) *timber* or *plank* (single or collect., i.e. a *flooring*):—beam, board, chamber, corner, leaf, plank, rib, side (chamber).

6764. צָלָף **Tsâlâph**, *tsaw-lawf'*; from an unused root of unknown mean.; *Tsalaph*, an Isr.:—Zalaph.

6765. צְלָפְחָד **Tseᵉlophchâd**, *tsel-of-chawd'*; from the same as 6764 and 259; *Tselophchad*, an Isr.:—Zelophehad.

6766. צֶלְצַח **Tseltsach**, *tsel-tsakh'*; from 6738 and 6703; *clear shade; Tseltsach*, a place in Pal.:—Zelzah.

6767. צְלָצַל **tseᵉlâtsal**, *tsel-aw-tsal'*; from 6750 redupl.; a *clatter*, i.e. (abstr.) *whirring* (of wings); (concr.) a *cricket*; also a *harpoon* (as *rattling*), a *cymbal* (as *clanging*):—cymbal, locust, shadowing, spear.

6768. צֶלֶק **Tseleq**, *tseh'-lek*; from an unused root mean. to *split*; *fissure; Tselek*, an Isr.:—Zelek.

6769. צִלְּתַי **Tsillᵉthay**, *tsil-leth-ah'ee*; from the fem. of 6738; *shady; Tsillethai*, the name of two Isr.:—Zilthai.

צֹם **tsôm**. See 6685.

6770. צָמֵא **tsâmêʼ**, *tsaw-may'*; a prim. root; to *thirst* (lit. or fig.):—(be a-, suffer) thirst (-y).

6771. צָמֵא **tsâmêʼ**, *tsaw-may'*; from 6770; *thirsty* (lit. or fig.):—(that) thirst (-eth, -y).

6772. צָמָא **tsâmâʼ**, *tsaw-maw'*; from 6770; *thirst* (lit. or fig.):—thirst (-y).

6773. צִמְאָה **tsimʼâh**, *tsim-aw'*; fem. of 6772; *thirst* (fig. of *libidinousnes*):—thirst.

6774. צִמָּאוֹן **tsimmâʼôwn**, *tsim-maw-one'*; from 6771; a *thirsty* place, i.e. *desert*:—drought, dry ground, thirsty land.

6775. צָמַד **tsâmad**, *tsaw-mad'*; a prim. root; to *link*, i.e. *gird*; fig. to *serve*, (mentally) *contrive*:—fasten, frame, join (self).

6776. צֶמֶד **tsemed**, *tseh'-med*; a *yoke* or *team* (i.e. pair); hence an *acre* (i.e. day's task for a yoke of cattle to plough):—acre, couple, × together, two [asses], yoke (of oxen).

6777. צַמָּה **tsammâh**, *tsam-maw'*; from an unused root mean. to *fasten on*; a *veil*:—locks.

6778. צַמּוּק **tsammûwq**, *tsam-mook'*; from 6784; a cake of *dried* grapes:—bunch (cluster) of raisins.

6779. צָמַח **tsâmach**, *tsaw-makh'*; a prim. root; to *sprout* (trans. or intrans., lit. or fig.):—bear, bring forth, (cause to, make to) bud (forth), (cause to, make to) grow (again, up), (cause to) spring (forth, up).

6780. צֶמַח **tsemach**, *tseh'-makh*; from 6779; a *sprout* (usually concr.), lit. or fig.:—branch, bud, that which (where) grew (upon), spring (-ing).

6781. צָמִיד **tsâmîyd**, *tsaw-meed'*; or

צָמִד **tsâmîd**, *tsaw-meed'*; from 6775; a *bracelet* or *arm-clasp*; gen. a *lid*:—bracelet, covering.

6782. צַמִּים **tsammîym**, *tsam-meem'*; from the same as 6777; a *noose* (as *fastening*); fig. *destruction*:—robber.

6783. צְמִיתֻת **tsᵉmîythûth**, *tsem-ee-thooth'*; or

צְמִתֻת **tsᵉmîthûth**, *tsem-ee-thooth'*; from 6789; *excision*, i.e. *destruction*; used only (adv.) with prep. pref. *to extinction*, i.e. *perpetually*:—ever.

6784. צָמַק **tsâmaq**, *tsaw-mak'*; a prim. root; to *dry* up:—dry.

6785. צֶמֶר **tsemer**, *tseh'-mer*; from an unused root prob. mean. to *be shaggy*; *wool*:—wool (-len).

6786. צְמָרִי **Tsᵉmârîy**, *tsem-aw-ree'*; patrial from an unused name of a place in Pal.; a *Tsemarite* or branch of the Canaanites:—Zemarite.

6787. צְמָרַיִם **Tsᵉmârayim**, *tsem-aw-rah'-yim*; dual of 6785; *double fleece; Tsemarajim*, a place in Pal.:—Zemaraim.

6788. צַמֶּרֶת **tsammereth**, *tsam-meh'-reth*; from the same as 6785; *fleeciness*, i.e. *foliage*:—highest branch, top.

6789. צָמַת **tsâmath**, *tsaw-math'*; a prim. root; to *extirpate* (lit. or fig.):—consume, cut off, destroy, vanish.

צְמִתֻת **tsᵉmîthûth**. See 6783.

6790. צִן **Tsîn**, *tseen*; from an unused root mean. to *prick*; a *crag; Tsin*, a part of the Desert:—Zin.

6791. צֵן **tsên**, *tsane*; from an unused root mean. to *be prickly*; a *thorn*; hence a *thorn-hedge*:—thorn.

6792. צֹנֵא **tsônêʼ**, *tso-nay'*; or

צֹנֶה **tsôneh**, *tso-neh'*; for 6629; a *flock*:—sheep.

6793. צִנָּה **tsinnâh**, *tsin-naw'*; fem. of 6791; a *hook* (as *pointed*); also a (large) *shield* (as if guarding by *prickliness*); also *cold* (as *piercing*):—buckler, cold, hook, shield, target.

6794. צִנּוּר **tsinnûwr**, *tsin-noor'*; from an unused root perh. mean. to *be hollow*; a *culvert*:—gutter, water-spout.

6795. צָנַח **tsânach**, *tsaw-nakh'*; a prim. root; to *alight*; (trans.) to *cause to descend*, i.e. *drive* down:—fasten, light [from off].

6796. צָנִין **tsânîyn**, *tsaw-neen'*; or

צָנִן **tsânîn**, *tsaw-neen'*; from the same as 6791; a *thorn*:—thorn.

6797. צָנִיף **tsânîyph**, *tsaw-neef'*; or

צָנוֹף° **tsânôwph**, *tsaw-nofe'*; or (fem.)

צְנִיפָה **tsânîyphâh**, *tsaw-nee-faw'*; from 6801; a *head-dress* (i.e. piece of cloth *wrapped* around):—diadem, hood, mitre.

6798. צָנַם **tsânam**, *tsaw-nam'*; a prim. root; to *blast* or *shrink*:—withered.

6799. צְנָן **Tsᵉnân**, *tsen-awn'*; prob. for 6630; *Tsenan*, a place near Pal.:—Zenan.

צָנִן **tsânîn**. See 6796.

6800. צָנַע **tsânaʻ**, *tsaw-nah'*; a prim. root; to *humiliate*:—humbly, lowly.

6801. צָנַף **tsânaph**, *tsaw-naf'*; a prim. root; to *wrap*, i.e. *roll* or *dress*:—be attired, × surely, violently turn.

6802. צְנֵפָה **tsᵉnêphâh**, *tsen-ay-faw'*; from 6801; a *ball*:— × toss.

6803. צִנְצֶנֶת **tsintseneth**, *tsin-tseh'-neth*; from the same as 6791; a *vase* (prob. a vial *tapering* at the top):—pot.

6804. צַנְתָּרָה **tsantârâh**, *tsan-taw-raw'*; prob. from the same as 6794; a *tube*:—pipe.

6805. צָעַד **tsâʻad**, *tsaw-ad'*; a prim. root; to *pace*, i.e. *step* regularly; (upward) to *mount*; (along) to *march*; (down and caus.) to *hurl*:—bring, go, march (through), run over.

6806. צַעַד **tsaʻad**, *tsah'-ad*; from 6804; a *pace* or regular *step*:—pace, step.

6807. צְעָדָה **tseᵉʻâdâh**, *tseh-aw-daw'*; fem. of 6806; a *march*; (concr.) an (ornamental) *ankle-chain*:—going, ornament of the legs.

6808. צָעָה **tsâʻâh**, *tsaw-aw'*; a prim. root; to *tip* over (for the purpose of *spilling* or *pouring* out), i.e. (fig.) *depopulate*; by impl. to *imprison* or *conquer*; (reflex.) to *lie down* (for coition):—captive exile, travelling, (cause to) wander (-er).

צָעוֹר° **tsâʻôwr**. See 6810.

6809. צָעִיף **tsâʻîyph**, *tsaw-eef'*; from an unused root mean. to *wrap* over; a *veil*:—vail.

6810. צָעִיר **tsâʻîyr**, *tsaw-eer'*; or

צָעוֹר° **tsâʻôwr**, *tsaw-ore'*; from 6819; *little*; (in number) *few*; (in age) *young*, (in value) *ignoble*:—least, little (one), small (one), + young (-er, -est).

6811. צָעִיר **Tsâʻîyr**, *tsaw-eer'*; the same as 6810; *Tsaïr*, a place in Idumæa:—Zair.

6812. צְעִירָה **tseᵉʻîyrâh**, *tseh-ee-raw'*; fem. of 6810; *smallness* (of age), i.e. *juvenility*:—youth.

6813. צָעַן **tsâʻan**, *tsaw-an'*; a prim. root; to *load* up (beasts), i.e. to *migrate*:—be taken down.

6814. צֹעַן **Tsôʻan**, *tso'-an*; of Eg. der.; *Tsoän*, a place in Eg.:—Zoan.

6815. צַעֲנַנִּים **Tsaʻănannîym**, *tsah-an-an-neem'*; or (dual)

צַעֲנַיִם° **Tsaʻănayim**, *tsah-an-ah'-yim*; plur. from 6813; *removals; Tsaanannim* or *Tsaanajim*, a place in Pal.:—Zaannannim, Zaanaim.

6816. צַעְצֻעַ **tsaʻtsûaʻ**, *tsah-tsoo'-ah*; from an unused root mean. to *bestrew* with carvings; *sculpture*:—image [work].

6817. צָעַק **tsâʻaq**, *tsaw-ak'*; a prim. root; to *shriek*; (by impl.) to *proclaim* (an assembly):— × at all, call together, cry (out), gather (selves) (together).

6818. צַעֲקָה **tsaʻăqâh**, *tsah-ak-aw'*; from 6817; a *shriek*:—cry (-ing).

6819. צָעַר **tsâʻar**, *tsaw-ar'*; a prim. root; to *be small*, i.e. (fig.) *ignoble*:—be brought low, little one, be small.

6820. צֹעַר **Tsôʻar**, *tso'-ar*; from 6819; *little; Tsoär*, a place E. of the Jordan:—Zoar.

6821. צָפַד **tsâphad**, *tsaw-fad'*; a prim. root; to *adhere*:—cleave.

6822. צָפָה **tsâphâh**, *tsaw-faw'*; a prim. root; prop. to *lean* forward, i.e. to *peer* into the distance; by impl. to *observe, await*:—behold, espy, look up (well), wait for, (keep the) watch (-man).

6823. צָפָה **tsâphâh**, *tsaw-faw'*; a prim. root [prob. rather ident. with 6822 through the idea of *expansion* in outlook transf. to act]; to *sheet* over (espec. with metal):—cover, overlay.

6824. צָפָה **tsâphâh**, *tsaw-faw'*; from 6823; an *inundation* (as *covering*):— × swimmest.

6825. צְפוֹ **Tsᵉphôw**, *tsef-o'*; or

צְפִי **Tsᵉphîy**, *tsef-ee'*; from 6822; *observant; Tsepho* or *Tsephi*, an Idumæan:—Zephi, Zepho.

6826. צִפּוּי **tsippûwy**, *tsip-poo'ee*; from 6823; *encasement* (with metal):—covering, overlaying.

6827. צְפוֹן **Tsᵉphôwn**, *tsef-one'*; prob. for 6837; *Tsephon*, an Isr.:—Zephon.

6828. צָפוֹן **tsâphôwn**, *tsaw-fone'*; or

צָפֹן **tsâphôn**, *tsaw-fone'*; from 6845; prop. *hidden*, i.e. *dark*; used only of the *north* as a quarter (*gloomy* and *unknown*):—north (-ern, side, -ward, wind).

6829. צָפוֹן **Tsâphôwn**, *tsaw-fone'*; the same as 6828; *boreal; Tsaphon*, a place in Pal.:—Zaphon.

6830. צְפוֹנִי **tsᵉphôwnîy**, *tsef-o-nee'*; from 6828; *northern*:—northern.

6831. צְפוֹנִי **Tsᵉphôwnîy**, *tsef-o-nee'*; patron. from 6827; a *Tsephonite*, or (collect.) descend. of Tsephon:—Zephonites.

6832. צְפוּעַ° **tsᵉphûwaʻ**, *tsef-oo'-ah*; from the same as 6848; *excrement* (as *protruded*):—dung.

6833. צִפּוֹר **tsippôwr**, *tsip-pore'*; or

צִפֹּר **tsippôr**, *tsip-pore'*; from 6852; a little *bird* (as *hopping*):—bird, fowl, sparrow.

6834. צִפּוֹר **Tsippôwr**, *tsip-pore'*; the same as 6833; *Tsippor*, a Moabite:—Zippor.

6835. צַפַּחַת **tsappachath**, *tsap-pakh'-ath*; from an unused root mean. to *expand*; a *saucer* (as *flat*):—cruse.

6836. צְפִיָּה **tsephîyâh**, *tsef-ee-yaw'*; from 6822; *watchfulness*:—watching.

6837. צִפְיוֹן **Tsiphyôwn**, *tsif-yone'*; from 6822; *watch*-tower; *Tsiphjon*, an Isr.:—Ziphion. Comp. 6827.

6838. צַפִּיחִת **tsappîychîth**, *tsap-pee-kheeth'*; from the same as 6835; a flat thin *cake*:—wafer.

6839. צֹפִים **Tsôphîym**, *tso-feem'*; plur. of act. part. of 6822; *watchers*; *Tsophim*, a place E. of the Jordan:—Zophim.

6840. צָפִין° **tsâphîyn**, *tsaw-feen'*; from 6845; a *treasure* (as *hidden*):—hid.

6841. צְפִיר **tsephîyr** (Chald.), *tsef-eer'*; corresp. to 6842; a he-*goat*:—he [goat].

6842. צָפִיר **tsâphîyr**, *tsaw-feer'*; from 6852; a male *goat* (as *prancing*):—(he) goat.

6843. צְפִירָה **tsephîyrâh**, *tsef-ee-raw'*; fem. formed like 6842; a *crown* (as *encircling* the head); also a *turn* of affairs (i.e. *mishap*):—diadem, morning.

6844. צָפִית **tsâphîyth**, *tsaw-feeth'*; from 6822; a *sentry*:—watchtower.

6845. צָפַן **tsâphan**, *tsaw-fan'*; a prim. root; to *hide* (by *covering* over); by impl. to *hoard* or *reserve*; fig. to *deny*; spec. (favorably) to *protect*, (unfavorably) to *lurk*:—esteem, hide (-den one, self), lay up, lurk (be set) privily, (keep) secret (-ly, place).

צָפֹן **tsâphôn**. See 6828.

6846. צְפַנְיָה **Tsephanyâh**, *tsef-an-yaw'*; or

צְפַנְיָהוּ **Tsephanyâhûw**, *tsef-an-yaw'-hoo*; from 6845 and 3050; *Jah has secreted*; *Tsephanjah*, the name of four Isr.:—Zephaniah.

6847. צָפְנַת פַּעְנֵחַ **Tsophnath Paʿnêach**, *tsof-nath' pah-nay'-akh*; of Eg. der.; *Tsophnath-Paneäch*, Joseph's Eg. name:—Zaphnath-paaneah.

6848. צֶפַע **tsephaʿ**, *tseh'-fah*; or

צִפְעֹנִי **tsiphʿônîy**, *tsif-o-nee'*; from an unused root mean. to *extrude*; a *viper* (as *thrusting* out the tongue, i.e. *hissing*):—adder, cockatrice.

6849. צְפִעָה **tsephîʿâh**, *tsef-ee-aw'*; fem. from the same as 6848; an *outcast* thing:—issue.

צִפְעֹנִי **tsiphʿônîy**. See 6848.

6850. צָפַף **tsâphaph**, *tsaw-faf'*; a prim. root; to *coo* or *chirp* (as a bird):—chatter, peep, whisper.

6851. צַפְצָפָה **tsaphtsâphâh**, *tsaf-tsaw-faw'*; from 6687; a *willow* (as growing in *overflowed* places):—willow tree.

6852. צָפַר **tsâphar**, *tsaw-far'*; a prim. root; to *skip* about, i.e. *return*:—depart early.

6853. צְפַר **tsephar** (Chald.), *tsef-ar'*; corresp. to 6833; a *bird*.—bird.

צִפֹּר **tsippôr**. See 6833.

6854. צְפַרְדֵּעַ **tsephardêaʿ**, *tsef-ar-day'-ah*; from 6852 and a word elsewhere unused mean. a *swamp*; a *marsh-leaper*, i.e. *frog*:—frog.

6855. צִפֹּרָה **Tsippôrâh**, *tsip-po-raw'*; fem. of 6833; *bird*; *Tsipporah*, Moses' wife:—Zipporah.

6856. צִפֹּרֶן **tsippôren**, *tsip-po'-ren*; from 6852 (in the denom. sense [from 6833] of *scratching*); prop. a *claw*, i.e. (human) *nail*; also the *point* of a style (or pen, tipped with adamant):—nail, point.

6857. צְפַת **Tsephath**, *tsef-ath'*; from 6822; *watch*-tower; *Tsephath*, a place in Pal.:—Zephath.

6858. צֶפֶת **tsepheth**, *tseh'-feth*; from an unused root mean. to *encircle*; a *capital* of a column:—chapiter.

6859. צְפָתָה **Tsephâthâh**, *tsef-aw'-thaw*; the same as 6857; *Tsephathah*, a place in Pal.:—Zephathah.

צִץ **tsîts**. See 6732.

6860. צִקְלַג **Tsiqlâg**, *tsik-lag'*; or

צִיקְלַג **Tsîyqelag** (1 Chron. 12 : 1, 20), *tsee-kel-ag'*; of uncert. der.; *Tsiklag* or *Tsikelag*, a place in Pal.:—Ziklag.

6861. צִקְלֹן **tsiqlôn**, *tsik-lone'*; from an unused root mean. to *wind*; a *sack* (as *tied* at the mouth):—husk.

6862. צַר **tsar**, *tsar*; or

צָר **tsâr**, *tsawr*; from 6887; *narrow*; (as a noun) a *tight* place (usually fig., i.e. *trouble*); also a *pebble* (as in 6864); (trans.) an *opponent* (as *crowding*):—adversary, afflicted (-tion), anguish, close, distress, enemy, flint, foe, narrow, small, sorrow, strait, tribulation, trouble.

6863. צֵר **Tsêr**, *tsare*; from 6887; *rock*; *Tser*, a place in Pal.:—Zer.

6864. צֹר **tsôr**, *tsore*; from 6696; a *stone* (as if *pressed* hard or to a point); (by impl. of use) a *knife*:—flint, sharp stone.

6865. צֹר **Tsôr**, *tsore*; or

צוֹר **Tsôwr**, *tsore*; the same as 6864; a *rock*; *Tsor*, a place in Pal.:—Tyre, Tyrus.

צֻר **tsûr**. See 6697.

6866. צָרַב **tsârab**, *tsaw-rab'*; a prim. root; to *burn*:—burn.

6867. צָרֶבֶת **tsârebeth**, *tsaw-reh'-beth*; from 6866; *conflagration* (of fire or disease):—burning, inflammation.

6868. צְרֵדָה **Tserêdâh**, *tser-ay-daw'*; or

צְרֵדָתָה **Tserêdâthâh**, *tser-ay-daw'-thaw*; appar. from an unused root mean. to *pierce*; *puncture*; *Tseredah*, a place in Pal.:—Zereda, Zeredathah.

6869. צָרָה **tsârâh**, *tsaw-raw'*; fem. of 6862; *tightness* (i.e. fig. *trouble*); trans. a female *rival*:—adversary, adversity, affliction, anguish, distress, tribulation, trouble.

6870. צְרוּיָה **Tserûwyâh**, *tser-oo-yaw'*; fem. part. pass. from the same as 6875; *wounded*; *Tserujah*, an Israelitess:—Zeruiah.

6871. צְרוּעָה **Tserûwʿâh**, *tser-oo-aw'*; fem. pass. part. of 6879; *leprous*; *Tseruäh*, an Israelitess:—Zeruah.

6872. צְרוֹר **tserôwr**, *tser-ore'*; or (shorter)

צְרֹר **tserôr**, *tser-ore'*; from 6887; a *parcel* (as *packed* up); also a *kernel* or *particle* (as if a *package*):—bag, × bendeth, bundle, least grain, small stone.

6873. צָרַח **tsârach**, *tsaw-rakh'*; a prim. root; to *be clear* (in tone, i.e. *shrill*), i.e. to *whoop*:—cry, roar.

6874. צְרִי **Tserîy**, *tser-ee'*; the same as 6875; *Tseri*, an Isr.:—Zeri. Comp. 3340.

6875. צְרִי **tserîy**, *tser-ee'*; or

צֳרִי **tsŏrîy**, *tsor-ee'*; from an unused root mean. to *crack* [as by *pressure*], hence to *leak*; *distillation*, i.e. *balsam*:—balm.

6876. צֹרִי **Tsôrîy**, *tso-ree'*; patrial from 6865; a *Tsorite* or inhab. of Tsor (i.e. *Syrian*):—(man) of Tyre.

6877. צְרִיחַ **tserîyach**, *tser-ee'-akh*; from 6873 in the sense of *clearness* of vision; a *citadel*:—high place, hold.

6878. צֹרֶךְ **tsôrek**, *tso'-rek*; from an unused root mean. to *need*; *need*:—need.

6879. צָרַע **tsâraʿ**, *tsaw-rah'*; a prim. root; to *scourge*, i.e. (intrans. and fig.) to *be stricken with leprosy*:—leper, leprous.

6880. צִרְעָה **tsirʿâh**, *tsir-aw'*; from 6879; a *wasp* (as *stinging*):—hornet.

6881. צָרְעָה **Tsorʿâh**, *tsor-aw'*; appar. another form for 6880; *Tsorah*, a place in Pal.:—Zareah, Zorah, Zoreah.

6882. צָרְעִי **Tsorʿîy**, *tsor-ee'*; or

צָרְעָתִי **Tsorʿâthîy**, *tsor-aw-thee'*; patrial from 6881; a *Tsorite* or *Tsorathite*, i.e. inhab. of Tsorah:—Zorites, Zareathites, Zorathites.

6883. צָרַעַת **tsâraʿath**, *tsaw-rah'-ath*; from 6879; *leprosy*:—leprosy.

6884. צָרַף **tsâraph**, *tsaw-raf'*; a prim. root; to *fuse* (metal), i.e. *refine* (lit. or fig.):—cast, (re-) fine (-er), founder, goldsmith, melt, pure, purge away, try.

6885. צֹרְפִי **Tsôrephîy**, *tso-ref-ee'*; from 6884; *refiner*; *Tsorephi* (with the art.), an Isr.:—goldsmith's.

6886. צָרְפַת **Tsârephath**, *tsaw-ref-ath'*; from 6884; *refinement*; *Tsarephath*, a place in Pal.:—Zarephath.

6887. צָרַר **tsârar**, *tsaw-rar'*; a prim. root; to *cramp*, lit. or fig., trans. or intrans. (as follows):—adversary, (be in) afflict (-ion), besiege, bind (up), (be in, bring) distress, enemy, narrower, oppress, pangs, shut up, be in a strait (trouble), vex.

6888. צְרֵרָה **Tserêrâh**, *tser-ay-raw'*; appar. by erroneous transcription for 6868; *Tsererah* for *Tseredah*:—Zererath.

6889. צֶרֶת **Tsereth**, *tseh'-reth*; perh. from 6671; *splendor*; *Tsereth*, an Isr.:—Zereth.

6890. צֶרֶת הַשַּׁחַר **Tsereth hash-Shachar**, *tseh'-reth hash-shakh'-ar*; from the same as 6889 and 7837 with the art. interposed; *splendor of the dawn*; *Tsereth-hash-Shachar*, a place in Pal.:—Zareth-shahar.

6891. צָרְתָן **Tsârethân**, *tsaw-reth-awn'*; perh. for 6868; *Tsarethan*, a place in Pal.:—Zarthan.

ק

6892. קֵא **qêʾ**, *kay*; or

קִיא **qîyʾ**, *kee*; from 6958; *vomit*:—vomit.

6893. קָאַת **qâʾath**, *kaw-ath'*; from 6958; prob. the *pelican* (from *vomiting*):—cormorant.

6894. קַב **qab**, *kab*; from 6895; a *hollow*, i.e. vessel used as a (dry) *measure*:—cab.

6895. קָבַב **qâbab**, *kaw-bab'*; a prim. root; to *scoop* out, i.e. (fig.) to *malign* or *execrate* (i.e. *stab* with words):—× at all, curse.

6896. קֵבָה **qêbâh**, *kay-baw'*; from 6895; the *paunch* (as a *cavity*) or first stomach of ruminants:—maw.

6897. קֹבָה **qôbâh**, *ko'-baw*; from 6895; the *abdomen* (as a cavity):—belly.

6898. קֻבָּה **qubbâh**, *koob-baw'*; from 6895; a *pavilion* (as a domed *cavity*):—tent.

6899. קִבּוּץ **qibbûwts**, *kib-boots'*; from 6908; a *throng*:—company.

6900. קְבוּרָה **qebûwrâh**, *keb-oo-raw'*; or

קְבֻרָה **qebûrâh**, *keb-oo-raw'*; fem. pass. part. of 6912; *sepulture*; (concr.) a *sepulchre*:—burial, burying place, grave, sepulchre.

6901. קָבַל **qâbal**, *kaw-bal'*; a prim. root; to *admit*, i.e. *take* (lit. or fig.):—choose, (take) hold, receive, (under-) take.

6902. קְבַל **qebal** (Chald.), *keb-al'*; corresp. to 6901; to *acquire*:—receive, take.

6903. קְבֵל **qebêl** (Chald.), *keb-ale'*; or

קֳבֵל **qŏbêl** (Chald.), *kob-ale'*; corresp. to 6905; (adv.) *in front of*; usually (with other particles) *on account of*, *so as*, *since*, *hence*:—+ according to, + as, + because, before, + for this cause, + forasmuch as, + by this means, over against, by reason of, + that, + therefore, + though, + wherefore.

6904. קֹבֶל **qôbel**, *ko'-bel*; from 6901 in the sense of *confronting* (as standing *opposite* in order to receive); a *battering*-ram:—war.

6905. קָבָל **qâbâl**, *kaw-bawl'*; from 6901 in the sense of *opposite* [see 6904]; the *presence*, i.e. (adv.) *in front of*:—before.

6906. קָבַע **qâbaʿ**, *kaw-bah'*; a prim. root; to *cover*, i.e. (fig.) *defraud*:—rob, spoil.

6907. קֻבַּעַת **qubbaʻath**, *koob-bah'-ath;* from 6906; a *goblet* (as deep like a *cover*):—dregs.

6908. קָבַץ **qâbats**, *kaw-bats';* a prim. root; to *grasp*, i.e. *collect:*—assemble (selves), gather (bring) (together, selves together, up), heap, resort, × surely, take up.

6909. קַבְצְאֵל **Qabtseʼêl**, *kab-tseh-ale';* from 6908 and 410; *God has gathered; Kabtseël*, a place in Pal.:—Kabzeel. Comp. 3343.

6910. קְבֻצָה **qebûtsâh**, *keb-oo-tsaw';* fem. pass. part. of 6908; a *hoard:*— × gather.

6911. קִבְצַיִם **Qibtsayim**, *kib-tsah'-yim;* dual from 6908; a *double heap; Kibtsajim*, a place in Pal.:—Kibzaim.

6912. קָבַר **qâbar**, *kaw-bar';* a prim. root; to *inter:*— × in any wise, bury (-ier).

6913. קֶבֶר **qeber**, *keh'-ber;* or (fem.)

קִבְרָה **qibrâh**, *kib-raw';* from 6912; a *sepulchre:*—burying place, grave, sepulchre.

קְבֻרָה **qebûrâh**. See 6900.

6914. קִבְרוֹת הַתַּאֲוָה **Qibrôwth hat-Taʼăvâh**, *kib-rōth' hat-tah-av-aw';* from the fem. plur. of 6913 and 8378 with the art. interposed; *graves of the longing; Kibroth-hat-Taavh*, a place in the Desert:—Kibroth-hattaavah.

6915. קָדַד **qâdad**, *kaw-dad';* a prim. root; to *shrivel* up, i.e. *contract* or *bend* the body (or neck) in deference:—bow (down) (the) head, stoop.

6916. קִדָּה **qiddâh**, *kid-daw';* from 6915; *cassia* bark (as in *shrivelled* rolls):—cassia.

6917. קָדוּם **qâdûwm**, *kaw-doom';* pass. part. of 6923; a *pristine* hero:—ancient.

6918. קָדוֹשׁ **qâdôwsh**, *kaw-doshe';* or

קָדֹשׁ **qâdôsh**, *kaw-doshe';* from 6942; *sacred* (ceremonially or morally); (as noun) *God* (by eminence), an *angel*, a *saint*, a *sanctuary:*—holy (One), saint.

6919. קָדַח **qâdach**, *kaw-dakh';* a prim. root to *inflame:*—burn, kindle.

6920. קַדַּחַת **qaddachath**, *kad-dakh'-ath;* from 6919; *inflammation*, i.e. febrile disease:—burning ague, fever.

6921. קָדִים **qâdîym**, *kaw-deem';* or

קָדִם **qâdîm**, *kaw-deem';* from 6923; the *fore* or front part; hence (by orientation) the *East* (often adv. *eastward*, for brevity the *east wind*):—east (-ward, wind).

6922. קַדִּישׁ **qaddîysh** (Chald.), *kad-deesh';* corresp. to 6918.—holy (One), saint.

6923. קָדַם **qâdam**, *kaw-dam';* a prim. root; to *project* (one self), i.e. *precede;* hence to *anticipate*, *hasten*, *meet* (usually for help):—come (go, [flee]) before, + disappoint, meet, prevent.

6924. קֶדֶם **qedem**, *keh'-dem;* or

קֵדְמָה **qêdmâh**, *kayd'-maw;* from 6923; the *front*, of place (absol. the *fore part*, rel. the *East*) or time (*antiquity*); often used adv. (*before*, *anciently*, *eastward*):—aforetime, ancient (time), before, east (end, part, side, -ward), eternal, × ever (-lasting), forward, old, past. Comp. 6926.

6925. קֳדָם **qŏdâm** (Chald.), *kod-awm';* or

קְדָם **qedâm** (Chald.) (Dan. 7 : 13), *ked-awm';* corresp. to 6924; *before:*—before, × from, × I (thought), × me, + of, × it pleased, presence.

קָדִם **qâdîm**. See 6921.

6926. קִדְמָה **qidmâh**, *kid-maw';* fem. of 6924; the *forward* part (or rel.) *East* (often adv. *on the east* or *in front*):—east (-ward).

6927. קַדְמָה **qadmâh**, *kad-maw';* from 6923; *priority* (in time); also used adv. (*before*):—afore, antiquity, former (old) estate.

6928. קַדְמָה **qadmâh** (Chald.), *kad-maw';* corresp. to 6927; *former* time:—afore [-time], ago.

קֵדְמָה **qêdmâh**. See 6924.

6929. קֵדְמָה **Qêdemâh**, *kayd'-maw;* from 6923; *precedence; Kedemah*, a son of Ishmael:—Kedemah.

6930. קַדְמוֹן **qadmôwn**, *kad-mone';* from 6923; *eastern:*—east.

6931. קַדְמוֹנִי **qadmôwnîy**, *kad-mo-nee';* or

קַדְמֹנִי **qadmônîy**, *kad-mo-nee';* from 6930; (of time) *anterior* or (of place) *oriental:*—ancient, they that went before, east, (thing of) old.

6932. קְדֵמוֹת **Qedêmôwth**, *ked-ay-mothe';* from 6923; *beginnings; Kedemoth*, a place in eastern Pal.:—Kedemoth.

6933. קַדְמַי **qadmay** (Chald.), *kad-mah'ee;* from a root corresp. to 6923; *first:*—first.

6934. קַדְמִיאֵל **Qadmîyʼêl**, *kad-mee-ale';* from 6924 and 410; *presence of God; Kadmiël*, the name of three Isr.:—Kadmiel.

קַדְמֹנִי **qadmônîy**. See 6931.

6935. קַדְמֹנִי **Qadmônîy**, *kad-mo-nee';* the same as 6931; *ancient*, i.e. aboriginal; *Kadmonite* (collect.), the name of a tribe in Pal.:—Kadmonites.

6936. קָדְקֹד **qodqôd**, *kod-kode';* from 6915; the *crown* of the head (as the part most *bowed*):—crown (of the head), pate, scalp, top of the head.

6937. קָדַר **qâdar**, *kaw-dar';* a prim. root; to *be ashy*, i.e. *dark*-colored; by impl. to *mourn* (in sackcloth or sordid garments):—be black (-ish), be (make) dark (-en), × heavily, (cause to) mourn.

6938. קֵדָר **Qêdâr**, *kay-dawr';* from 6937; *dusky* (of the skin or the tent); *Kedar*, a son of Ishmael; also (collect.) *bedawin* (as his descendants or representatives):—Kedar.

6939. קִדְרוֹן **Qidrôwn**, *kid-rone';* from 6937; *dusky* place; *Kidron*, a brook near Jerus.:—Kidron.

6940. קַדְרוּת **qadrûwth**, *kad-rooth';* from 6937; *duskiness:*—blackness.

6941. קְדֹרַנִּית **qedôranniyth**, *ked-o-ran-neeth';* adv. from 6937; *blackish ones* (i.e. *in sackcloth*); used adv. in *mourning* weeds:—mournfully.

6942. קָדַשׁ **qâdash**, *kaw-dash';* a prim. root; to *be* (causat. *make*, *pronounce* or *observe* as) *clean* (ceremonially or morally):—appoint, bid, consecrate, dedicate, defile, hallow, (be, keep) holy (-er, place), keep, prepare, proclaim, purify, sanctify (-ied one, self), × wholly.

6943. קֶדֶשׁ **Qedesh**, *keh'-desh;* from 6942; a *sanctum; Kedesh*, the name of four places in Pal.:—Kedesh.

6944. קֹדֶשׁ **qôdesh**, *ko'-desh;* from 6942; a *sacred* place or thing; rarely abstr. *sanctity:*—consecrated (thing), dedicated (thing), hallowed (thing), holiness, (× most) holy (× day, portion, thing), saint, sanctuary.

6945. קָדֵשׁ **qâdêsh**, *kaw-dashe';* from 6942; a (quasi) *sacred* person, i.e. (techn.) a (male) *devotee* (by prostitution) to licentious idolatry:—sodomite, unclean.

6946. קָדֵשׁ **Qâdêsh**, *kaw-dashe';* the same as 6945; *sanctuary; Kadesh*, a place in the Desert:—Kadesh. Comp. 6947.

קָדֹשׁ **qâdôsh**. See 6918.

6947. קָדֵשׁ בַּרְנֵעַ **Qâdêsh Barneaʻ**, *kaw-dashe' bar-nay'-ah;* from the same as 6946 and an otherwise unused word (appar. compounded of a correspondent to 1251 and a deriv. of 5128) mean. *desert of a fugitive; Kadesh of* (the) *Wilderness of Wandering; Kadesh-Barneä*, a place in the Desert:—Kadesh-barnea.

6948. קְדֵשָׁה **qedêshâh**, *ked-ay-shaw';* fem. of 6945; a female *devotee* (i.e. *prostitute*):—harlot, whore.

6949. קָהָה **qâhâh**, *kaw-haw';* a prim. root; to be *dull:*—be set on edge, be blunt.

6950. קָהַל **qâhal**, *kaw-hal';* a prim. root; to *convoke:*—assemble (selves) (together), gather (selves) (together).

6951. קָהָל **qâhâl**, *kaw-hawl';* from 6950; *assemblage* (usually concr.):—assembly, company, congregation, multitude.

6952. קְהִלָּה **qehillâh**, *keh-hil-law';* from 6950; an *assemblage:*—assembly, congregation.

6953. קֹהֶלֶת **qôheleth**, *ko-heh'-leth;* fem. of act. part. from 6950; a (female) *assembler* (i.e. lecturer); abstr. *preaching* (used as a "nom de plume", *Koheleth*):—preacher.

6954. קְהֵלָתָה **Qehêlâthâh**, *keh-hay-law'-thaw;* from 6950; *convocation; Kehelathah*, a place in the Desert:—Kehelathah.

6955. קְהָת **Qehâth**, *keh-hawth';* from an unused root mean. to *ally* oneself; *allied; Kehath*, an Isr.:—Kohath.

6956. קֳהָתִי **Qŏhâthîy**, *ko-haw-thee';* patron. from 6955; a *Kohathite* (collect.) or desc. of Kehath:—Kohathites.

6957. קַו **qav**, *kav;* or

קָו **qâv**, *kawv;* from 6960 [comp. 6961]; a *cord* (as *connecting*), espec. for measuring; fig. a *rule;* also a *rim*, a musical *string* or *accord:*—line. Comp. 6978.

6958. קוֹא **qôwʼ**, *ko;* or

קָיָה **qâyâh** (Jer. 25 : 27), *kaw-yaw';* a prim. root; to *vomit:*—spue (out), vomit (out, up, up again).

6959. קוֹבַע **qôwbaʻ**, *ko'-bah* or *ko-bah';* a form collat. to 3553; a *helmet:*—helmet.

6960. קָוָה **qâvâh**, *kaw-vaw';* a prim. root; to *bind* together (perh. by *twisting*), i.e. *collect;* (fig.) to *expect:*—gather (together), look, patiently, tarry, wait (for, on, upon).

6961. קָוֶה **qâveh**, *kaw-veh';* from 6960; a (measuring) *cord* (as if for *binding*):—line.

קֹוחַ **qôwach**. See 6495.

6962. קוּט **qûwṭ**, *koot;* a prim. root; prop. to *cut off*, i.e. (fig.) *detest:*—be grieved, lothe self.

6963. קוֹל **qôwl**, *kole;* or

קֹל **qôl**, *kole;* from an unused root mean. to *call* aloud; a *voice* or *sound:*— + aloud, bleating, crackling, cry (+ out), fame, lightness, lowing, noise, + hold peace, [pro-] claim, proclamation, + sing, sound, + spark, thunder (-ing), voice, + yell.

6964. קוֹלָיָה **Qôwlâyâh**, *ko-law-yaw';* from 6963 and 3050; *voice of Jah; Kolajah*, the name of two Isr.:—Kolaiah.

6965. קוּם **qûwm**, *koom;* a prim. root; to *rise* (in various applications, lit., fig., intens. and caus.):—abide, accomplish, × be clearer, confirm, continue, decree, × be dim, endure, × enemy, enjoin, get up, make good, help, hold, (help to) lift up (again), make, × but newly, ordain, perform, pitch, raise (up), rear (up), remain, (a-) rise (up) (again, against), rouse up, set (up), (e-) stablish, (make to) stand (up), stir up, strengthen, succeed, (as-, make) sure (-ly), (be) up (-hold, -rising).

6966. קוּם **qûwm** (Chald.), *koom;* corresp. to 6965:—appoint, establish, make, raise up self, (a-) rise (up), (make to) stand, set (up).

6967. קוֹמָה **qôwmâh**, *ko-maw';* from 6965; *height:*— × along, height, high, stature, tall.

6968. קוֹמְמִיּוּת **qôwmemîyûwth**, *ko-mem-ee-yooth';* from 6965; *elevation*, i.e. (adv.) *erectly* (fig.):—upright.

6969. קוּן **qûwn**, *koon;* a prim. root; to *strike* a musical note, i.e. *chant* or *wail* (at a funeral):—lament, mourning woman.

6970. קוֹעַ **Qôwaʻ**, *ko'-ah;* prob. from 6972 in the orig. sense of *cutting* off; *curtailment; Koä*, a region of Bab.:—Koa.

6971. קוֹף **qôwph**, *kofe;* or

קֹף **qôph**, *kofe;* prob. of for. or.; a *monkey:*—ape.

6972. קוּץ **qûwts**, *koots;* a prim. root; to *clip* off; used only as denom. from 7019; to *spend the harvest* season:—summer.

6973. קוּץ **qûwts**, *koots;* a prim. root [rather ident. with 6972 through the idea of *severing* oneself from (comp. 6962)]; to be (caus. *make*) *dis-*

usted or *anxious*:—abhor, be distressed, be grieved, oathe, vex, be weary.

974. קוּץ **qûwts**, *koots*; a prim. root [rather ident. with 6972 through the idea of *bruptness* in starting up from sleep (comp. 3364)]; o *awake* (lit. or fig.):—arise, (be) (a-) wake, watch.

975. קוֹץ **qôwts**, *kotse*; or

קֹץ **qôts**, *kotse*; from 6972 (in the sense of *pricking*); a *thorn*:—thorn.

976. קוֹץ **Qôwts**, *kotse*; the same as 6975; *Kots*, the name of two Isr.:—Koz, Hakkoz *includ. the art.*].

977. קְוֻצָּה **qᵉvutstsâh**, *kev-oots-tsaw'*; fem. pass. part. of 6972 in its orig. sense; a *orelock* (as *shorn*):—lock.

978. קַו־קַו **qav-qav**, *kav-kav'*; from 6957 (in the sense of a *fastening*); *stalwart*:— meted out.

979. קוּר **qûwr**, *koor*; a prim. root; to *trench*; by impl. to *throw forth*; also (denom. rom 7023) to *wall up*, whether lit. (to *build* a wall) r fig. (to *estop*):—break down, cast out, destroy, dig.

980. קוּר **qûwr**, *koor*; from 6979; (only plur.) *trenches*, i.e. a *web* (as if so formed):—veb.

981. קוֹרֵא **Qôwrê'**, *ko-ray'*; or

קֹרֵא **Qôrê'** (1 Chron. 26 : 1), *ko-ray'*; act. part. of 7121; *crier*; *Korè*, the name of wo Isr.:—Kore.

982. קוֹרָה **qôwrâh**, *ko-raw'*; or

קֹרָה **qôrâh**, *ko-raw'*; from 6979; a *rafter* (forming *trenches* as it were); by impl. *roof*:—beam, roof.

983. קוֹשׁ **qôwsh**, *koshe*; a prim. root; to *bend*; used only as denom. for 3369, to *set a rap*:—lay a snare.

984. קוּשָׁיָהוּ **qûwshâyâhûw**, *koo-shaw-yaw'-hoo*; from the pass. part. of 6983 and 050; *entrapped of Jah*; *Kushajah*, an Isr.:—Kushiah.

985. קַט **qat**, *kat*; from 6990 in the sense of *abbreviation*; a *little*, i.e. (adv.) *merely*:—ery.

986. קֶטֶב **qeṭeb**, *keh'-teb*; from an unused root mean. to *cut* off; *ruin*:—destroying, lestruction.

987. קֹטֶב **qôṭeb**, *ko'-teb*; from the same as 6986; *extermination*:—destruction.

988. קְטוֹרָה **qᵉṭôwrâh**, *ket-o-raw'*; from 6999; *perfume*:—incense.

989. קְטוּרָה **Qᵉṭûwrâh**, *ket-oo-raw'*; fem. pass. part. of 6999; *perfumed*; *Keturah*, a wife of Abraham:—Keturah.

990. קָטַט **qâṭaṭ**, *kaw-tat'*; a prim. root; to *clip* off, i.e. (fig.) *destroy*:—be cut off.

991. קָטַל **qâṭal**, *kaw-tal'*; a prim. root; prop. to *cut* off, i.e. (fig.) *put to death*:—kill, slay.

992. קְטַל **qᵉṭal** (Chald.), *ket-al'*; corresp. to 6991; to *kill*:—slay.

993. קֶטֶל **qeṭel**, *keh'-tel*; from 6991; a violent *death*:—slaughter.

994. קָטֹן **qâṭôn**, *kaw-tone'*; a prim. root [rather denom. from 6996]; to *diminish*, i.e. *be* (caus. *make*) *diminutive* or (fig.) *of no account*:—be (make) small (thing), be not worthy.

995. קֹטֶן **qôṭen**, *ko'-ten*; from 6994; a *pettiness*, i.e. the *little finger*:—little finger.

996. קָטָן **qâṭân**, *kaw-tawn'*; or

קָטֹן **qâṭôn**, *kaw-tone'*; from 6962; *abbreviated*, i.e. *diminutive*, lit. (in quantity, size or number) or fig. (in age or importance):—least, ess (-ser), little (one), small (-est, one, quantity, hing), young (-er, -est).

997. קָטָן **Qâṭân**, *kaw-tawn'*; the same as 6996; *small*; *Katan*, an Isr.:—Hakkatan [*inlud. the art.*].

998. קָטַף **qâṭaph**, *kaw-taf'*; a prim. root; to *strip* off:—crop off, cut down (up), pluck.

6999. קָטַר **qâṭar**, *kaw-tar'*; a prim. root [rather ident. with 7000 through the idea of fumigation in a *close* place and perh. thus *driving* out the occupants]; to *smoke*, i.e. turn into fragrance by fire (espec. as an act of worship):—burn (incense, sacrifice) (upon), (altar for) incense, kindle, offer (incense, a sacrifice).

7000. קָטַר **qâṭar**, *kaw-tar'*; a prim. root; to *inclose*:—join.

7001. קְטַר **qᵉṭar** (Chald.), *ket-ar'*; from a root corresp. to 7000; a *knot* (as *tied* up), i.e. (fig.) a *riddle*; also a *vertebra* (as if a knot):—doubt, joint.

7002. קִטֵּר **qiṭṭêr**, *kit-tare'*; from 6999; *perfume*:—incense.

7003. קִטְרוֹן **Qiṭrôwn**, *kit-rone'*; from 6999; *fumigative*; *Kitron*, a place in Pal.:—Kitron.

7004. קְטֹרֶת **qᵉṭôreth**, *ket-o'-reth*; from 6999; a *fumigation*:—(sweet) incense, perfume.

7005. קַטָּת **Qaṭṭâth**, *kat-tawth'*; from 6996; *littleness*, *Kattath*, a place in Pal.:—Kattath.

7006. קָיָה **qâyâh**, *kaw-yaw'*; a prim. root; to *vomit*:—spue.

7007. קַיִט **qâyiṭ** (Chald.), *kah'-yit*; corresp. to 7019; *harvest*:—summer.

7008. קִיטוֹר **qîyṭôwr**, *kee-tore'*; or

קִיטֹר **qîyṭôr**, *kee-tore'*; from 6999; a *fume*, i.e. *cloud*:—smoke, vapour.

7009. קִים **qîym**, *keem*; from 6965; an *opponent* (as *rising* against one), i.e. (collect.) enemies:—substance.

7010. קְיָם **qᵉyâm** (Chald.), *keh-yawm'*; from 6966; an *edict* (as *arising* in law):—decree, statute.

7011. קַיָּם **qayâm** (Chald.), *kah-yawm'*; from 6966; *permanent* (as *rising* firmly):—stedfast, sure.

7012. קִימָה **qîymâh**, *kee-maw'*; from 6965; an *arising*:—rising up.

קִימוֹשׁ **Qîymôwsh**. See 7057.

7013. קַיִן **qayin**, *kah'-yin*; from 6969 in the orig. sense of *fixity*; a *lance* (as *striking fast*):—spear.

7014. קַיִן **Qayin**, *kah'-yin*; the same as 7013 (with a play upon the affinity to 7069); *Kajin*, the name of the first child, also of a place in Pal., and of an Oriental tribe:—Cain, Kenite (-s).

7015. קִינָה **qîynâh**, *kee-naw'*; from 6969; a *dirge* (as accompanied by *beating* the breasts or on instruments):—lamentation.

7016. קִינָה **Qîynâh**, *kee-naw'*; the same as 7015; *Kinah*, a place in Pal.:—Kinah.

7017. קֵינִי **Qêynîy**, *kay-nee'*; or

קִינִי **Qîynîy** (1 Chron. 2 : 55), *kee-nee'*; patron. from 7014; a *Kenite* or member of the tribe of Kajin:—Kenite.

7018. קֵינָן **Qêynân**, *kay-nawn'*; from the same as 7064; *fixed*; *Kenan*, an antediluvian:—Cainan, Kenan.

7019. קַיִץ **qayits**, *kah'-yits*; from 6972; *harvest* (as *the crop*), whether the product (grain or fruit) or the (dry) season:—summer (fruit, house).

7020. קִיצוֹן **qîytsôwn**, *kee-tsone'*; from 6972; *terminal*:—out- (utter-) most.

7021. קִיקָיוֹן **qîyqâyôwn**, *kee-kaw-yone'*; perh. from 7006; the *gourd* (as *nauseous*):—gourd.

7022. קִיקָלוֹן **qîyqâlôwn**, *kee-kaw-lone'*; from 7036; intense *disgrace*:—shameful spewing.

7023. קִיר **qîyr**, *keer*; or

קִר **qîr** (Isa. 22 : 5), *keer*; or (fem.)

קִירָה **qîyrâh**, *kee-raw'*; from 6979; a *wall* (as built in a *trench*):— + mason, side, town, × very, wall.

7024. קִיר **Qîyr**, *keer*; the same as 7023; *fortress*; *Kir*, a place in Ass.; also one in Moab:—Kir. Comp. 7025.

7025. קִיר חֶרֶשׂ **Qîyr Cheres**, *keer kheh'-res*; or (fem. of the latter word)

קִיר חֲרֶשֶׂת **Qîyr Chăreseth**, *keer khareh'-seth*; from 7023 and 2789; *fortress of earthenware*; *Kir-Cheres* or *Kir-Chareseth*, a place in Moab:—Kir-haraseth, Kir-hareseth, Kir-haresh, Kir-heres.

7026. קֵירֹס **Qêyrôç**, *kay-roce'*; or

קֵרֹס **Qêrôç**, *kay-roce'*; from the same as 7166; *ankled*; *Keros*, one of the Nethinim:—Keros.

7027. קִישׁ **Qîysh**, *keesh*; from 6983; a *bow*; *Kish*, the name of five Isr.:—Kish.

7028. קִישׁוֹן **Qîyshôwn**, *kee-shone'*; from 6983; *winding*; *Kishon*, a river of Pal.:—Kishon, Kison.

7029. קִישִׁי **Qîyshîy**, *kee-shee'*; from 6983; *bowed*; *Kishi*, an Isr.:—Kishi.

7030. קִיתָרֹס° **qîytharôç** (Chald.), *kee-thaw-roce'*; of Gr. origin (κίθαρις); a *lyre*:—harp.

7031. קַל **qal**, *kal*; contr. from 7043; *light*; (by impl.) *rapid* (also adv.):—light, swift (-ly).

7032. קָל **qâl** (Chald.), *kawl*; corresp. to 6963:—sound, voice.

קֹל **qôl**. See 6963.

7033. קָלָה **qâlâh**, *kaw-law'*; a prim. root [rather ident. with 7034 through the idea of *shrinkage* by heat]; to *toast*, i.e. *scorch* partially or slowly:—dried, loathsome, parch, roast.

7034. קָלָה **qâlâh**, *kaw-law'*; a prim. root; to *be light* (as implied in *rapid* motion), but fig. only (*be* [caus. *hold*] *in contempt*):—base, contemn, despise, lightly esteem, set light, seem vile.

7035. קָלַהּ° **qâlahh**, *kaw-lah'*; for 6950; to *assemble*:—gather together.

7036. קָלוֹן **qâlôwn**, *kaw-lone'*; from 7034; *disgrace*; (by impl.) the *pudenda*:—confusion, dishonour, ignominy, reproach, shame.

7037. קַלַּחַת **qallachath**, *kal-lakh'-ath*; appar. but a form for 6747; a *kettle*:—caldron.

7038. קָלַט **qâlaṭ**, *kaw-lat'*; a prim. root; to *maim*:—lacking in his parts.

7039. קָלִי **qâlîy**, *kaw-lee'*; or

קָלִיא **qâlîy'**, *kaw-lee'*; from 7033; *roasted* ears of grain:—parched corn.

7040. קַלַּי **Qallay**, *kal-lah'ee*; from 7043; *frivolous*; *Kallai*, an Isr.:—Kallai.

7041. קֵלָיָה **Qêlâyâh**, *kay-law-yaw'*; from 7034; *insignificance*; *Kelajah*, an Isr.:—Kelaiah.

7042. קְלִיטָא **Qᵉlîyṭâ'**, *kel-ee-taw'*; from 7038; *maiming*; *Kelita*, the name of three Isr.:—Kelita.

7043. קָלַל **qâlal**, *kaw-lal'*; a prim. root; to *be* (caus. *make*) *light*, lit. (*swift*, *small*, *sharp*, etc.) or fig. (*easy*, *trifling*, *vile*, etc.):—abate, make bright, bring into contempt, (ac-) curse, despise, (be) ease (-y, -ier), (be a, make, make somewhat, move, seem a, set) light (-en, -er, -ly, -ly afflict, -ly esteem, thing), × slight [-ly], be swift (-er), (be, be more, make, re-) vile, whet.

7044. קָלָל **qâlâl**, *kaw-lawl'*; from 7043; *brightened* (as if *sharpened*):—burnished, polished.

7045. קְלָלָה **qᵉlâlâh**, *kel-aw-law'*; from 7043; *vilification*:—(ac-) curse (-d, -ing).

7046. קָלַס **qâlaç**, *kaw-las'*; a prim. root; to *disparage*, i.e. ridicule:—mock, scoff, scorn.

7047. קֶלֶס **qeleç**, *keh'-les*; from 7046; a *laughing-stock*:—derision.

7048. קַלָּסָה **qallâçâh**, *kal-law-saw'*; intens. from 7046; *ridicule*:—mocking.

7049. קָלַע **qâlaʻ**, *kaw-lah'*; a prim. root; to *sling*; also to carve (as if a *circular* motion, or into *light* forms):—carve, sling (out).

7050. קֶלַע **qelaʻ**, *keh'-lah*; from 7049; a *sling*; also a (door) *screen* (as if *slung* across), or the *valve* (of the door) itself:—hanging, leaf, sling.

7051. קַלָּע **qallâʻ**, *kal-law'*; intens. from 7049; a *slinger*:—slinger.

7052. קְלֹקֵל **q^{e}lôqêl**, *kel-o-kale'*; from 7043; *insubstantial*:—light.

7053. קִלְּשׁוֹן **qill^{e}shôwn**, *kil-lesh-one'*; from an unused root mean. to *prick*; a *prong*, i.e. hay-fork:—fork.

7054. קָמָה **qâmâh**, *kaw-maw'*; fem. of act. part. of 6965; something that *rises*, i.e. a *stalk* of grain:—(standing) corn, grown up, stalk.

7055. קְמוּאֵל **Q^{e}mûw'êl**, *kem-oo-ale'*; from 6965 and 410; *raised of God*; *Kemuël*, the name of a relative of Abraham, and of two Isr.:—Kemuel.

7056. קָמוֹן **Qâmôwn**, *kaw-mone'*; from 6965; an *elevation*; *Kamon*, a place E. of the Jordan:—Camon.

7057. קִמּוֹשׁ **qimmôwsh**, *kim-moshe'*; or קִימוֹשׁ **qîymôwsh**, *kee-moshe'*; from an unused root mean. to *sting*; a *prickly* plant:—nettle. Comp. 7063.

7058. קֶמַח **qemach**, *keh'-makh*; from an unused root prob. mean. to *grind*; *flour*:—flour, meal.

7059. קָמַט **qâmaṭ**, *kaw-mat'*; a prim. root; to *pluck*, i.e. destroy:—cut down, fill with wrinkles.

7060. קָמַל **qâmal**, *kaw-mal'*; a prim. root; to *wither*:—hew down, wither.

7061. קָמַץ **qâmats**, *kaw-mats'*; a prim. root; to *grasp* with the hand:—take an handful

7062. קֹמֶץ **qômets**, *ko'-mets*; from 7061; a *grasp*, i.e. *handful*:—handful.

7063. קִמָּשׁוֹן **qimmâshôwn**, *kim-maw-shone'*; from the same as 7057; a *prickly* plant:—thorn.

7064. קֵן **qên**, *kane*; contr. from 7077; a *nest* (as *fixed*), sometimes includ. the *nestlings*; fig. a *chamber* or *dwelling*:—nest, room.

7065. קָנָא **qânâ'**, *kaw-naw'*; a prim. root; to *be* (caus. *make*) *zealous*, i.e. (in a bad sense) *jealous* or *envious*:—(be) envy (-ious), be (move to, provoke to) jealous (-y), × very, (be) zeal (-ous).

7066. קְנָא **q^{e}nâ'** (Chald.), *ken-aw'*; corresp. to 7069; to *purchase*:—buy.

7067. קַנָּא **qannâ'**, *kan-naw'*; from 7065; *jealous*:—jealous. Comp. 7072.

7068. קִנְאָה **qin'âh**, *kin-aw'*; from 7065; *jealousy* or *envy*:—envy (-ied), jealousy, × sake, zeal.

7069. קָנָה **qânâh**, *kaw-naw'*; a prim. root; to *erect*, i.e. *create*; by extens. to *procure*, espec. by purchase (caus. *sell*); by impl. to *own*:—attain, buy (-er), teach to keep cattle, get, provoke to jealousy, possess (-or), purchase, recover, redeem, × surely, × verily.

7070. קָנֶה **qâneh**, *kaw-neh'*; from 7069; a *reed* (as *erect*); by resemblance a *rod* (espec. for measuring), *shaft*, *tube*, *stem*, the *radius* (of the arm), *beam* (of a steelyard):—balance, bone, branch, calamus, cane, reed, × spearman, stalk.

7071. קָנָה **Qânâh**, *kaw-naw'*; fem. of 7070; *reediness*; *Kanah*, the name of a stream and of a place in Pal.:—Kanah.

7072. קַנּוֹא **qannôw'**, *kan-no'*; for 7067; *jealous* or *angry*:—jealous.

7073. קְנַז **Q^{e}naz**, *ken-az'*; prob. from an unused root mean. to *hunt*; *hunter*; *Kenaz*, the name of an Edomite and of two Isr.:—Kenaz.

7074. קְנִזִּי **Q^{e}nizzîy**, *ken-iz-zee'*; patron. from 7073; a *Kenizzite* or desc. of Kenaz:—Kenezite, Kenizzites.

7075. קִנְיָן **qinyân**, *kin-yawn'*; from 7069; *creation*, i.e. (concr.) *creatures*; also *acquisition*, *purchase*, *wealth*:—getting, goods, × with money, riches, substance.

7076. קִנָּמוֹן **qinnâmôwn**, *kin-naw-mone'*; from an unused root (mean. to *erect*); *cinnamon* bark (as in *upright* rolls):—cinnamon.

7077. קָנַן **qânan**, *kaw-nan'*; a prim. root; to *erect*; but used only as denom. from 7064; to *nestle*, i.e. *build* or *occupy* as a nest:—make . . . nest.

7078. קֶנֶץ **qenets**, *keh'-nets*; from an unused root prob. mean. to *wrench*; *perversion*:—end.

7079. קְנָת **Q^{e}nâth**, *ken-awth'*; from 7069; *possession*; *Kenath*, a place E. of the Jordan:—Kenath.

7080. קָסַם **qâçam**, *kaw-sam'*; a prim. root; prop. to *distribute*, i.e. *determine* by lot or magical scroll; by impl. to *divine*:—divine (-r, -ation), prudent, soothsayer, use [divination].

7081. קֶסֶם **qeçem**, *keh'-sem*; from 7080; a *lot*; also *divination* (includ. its *fee*), *oracle*:—(reward of) divination, divine sentence, witchcraft.

7082. קָסַס **qâçaç**, *kaw-sas'*; a prim. root; to *lop* off:—cut off.

7083. קֶסֶת **qeçeth**, *keh'-seth*; from the same as 3563 (or as 7185); prop. a *cup*, i.e. an *ink-stand*:—inkhorn.

7084. קְעִילָה **Q^{e}'îylâh**, *keh-ee-law'*; perh. from 7049 in the sense of *inclosing*; *citadel*; *Keïlah*, a place in Pal.:—Keilah.

7085. קַעֲקַע **qa'ăqa'**, *kah-ak-ah'*; from the same as 6970; an *incision* or gash:—+ mark.

7086. קְעָרָה **q^{e}'ârâh**, *keh-aw-raw'*; prob. from 7167; a *bowl* (as *cut* out hollow):—charger, dish.

קֹף **qôph**. See 6971.

7087. קָפָא **qâphâ'**, *kaw-faw'*; a prim. root; to *shrink*, i.e. *thicken* (as unracked wine, curdled milk, clouded sky, frozen water):—congeal, curdle, dark°, settle.

7088. קָפַד **qâphad**, *kaw-fad'*; a prim. root; to *contract*, i.e. roll together:—cut off.

7089. קְפָדָה **q^{e}phâdâh**, *kef-aw-daw'*; from 7088; *shrinking*, i.e. terror:—destruction.

7090. קִפּוֹד **qippôwd**, *kip-pode'*; or קִפֹּד **qippôd**, *kip-pode'*; from 7088; a species of bird, perh. the *bittern* (from its *contracted* form):—bittern.

7091. קִפּוֹז **qippôwz**, *kip-poze'*; from an unused root mean. to *contract*, i.e. *spring* forward; an *arrow-snake* (as *darting* on its prey):—great owl.

7092. קָפַץ **qâphats**, *kaw-fats'*; a prim. root; to *draw together*, i.e. close; by impl. to *leap* (by *contracting* the limbs); spec. to *die* (from *gathering* up the feet):—shut (up), skip, stop, take out of the way.

7093. קֵץ **qêts**, *kates*; contr. from 7112; an *extremity*; adv. (with prep. pref.) *after*:—+ after, (utmost) border, end, [in-] finite, × process.

קוֹץ **qôts**. See 6975.

7094. קָצַב **qâtsab**, *kaw-tsab'*; a prim. root; to *clip*, or (gen.) *chop*:—cut down, shorn.

7095. קֶצֶב **qetseb**, *keh'-tseb*; from 7094; *shape* (as if *cut* out); *base* (as if there *cut* off):—bottom, size.

7096. קָצָה **qâtsâh**, *kaw-tsaw'*; a prim. root; to *cut* off; (fig.) to *destroy*; (partially) to *scrape* off:—cut off, cut short, scrape (off).

7097. קָצֶה **qâtseh**, *kaw-tseh'*; or (neg. only) קֵצֶה **qêtseh**, *kay'-tseh*; from 7096; an *extremity* (used in a great variety of applications and idioms; comp. 7093):— × after, border, brim, brink, edge, end, [in-] finite, frontier, outmost coast, quarter, shore, (out-) side, × some, ut (-ter-) most (part).

7098. קָצָה **qâtsâh**, *kaw-tsaw'*; fem. of 7097; a *termination* (used like 7097):—coast, corner, (selv-) edge, lowest, (uttermost) part.

7099. קֶצֶו **qetsev**, *keh'-tsev*; and (fem.) קִצְוָה **qitsvâh**, *kits-vaw'*; from 7096; a *limit* (used like 7097, but with less variety):—end, edge, uttermost part.

7100. קֶצַח **qetsach**, *keh'-tsakh*; from an unused root appar. mean. to *incise*; *fennel-flower* (from its *pungency*):—fitches.

7101. קָצִין **qâtsîyn**, *kaw-tseen'*; from 7096 in the sense of *determining*; a *magistrate* (as *deciding*) or other *leader*:—captain, guide, prince, ruler. Comp. 6278.

7102. קְצִיעָה **q^{e}tsîy'âh**, *kets-ee-aw'*; from 7106; *cassia* (as *peeled*; plur. the *bark*):—cassia.

7103. קְצִיעָה **Q^{e}tsîy'âh**, *kets-ee-aw'*; the same as 7102; *Ketsiah*, a daughter of Job:—Kezia.

7104. קְצִיץ **Q^{e}tsîyts**, *kets-eets'*; from 7112; *abrupt*; *Keziz*, a valley in Pal.:—Keziz.

7105. קָצִיר **qâtsîyr**, *kaw-tseer'*; from 7114; *severed*, i.e. *harvest* (as *reaped*), the crop, the time, the reaper, or fig.; also a *limb* (of a tree, or simply *foliage*):—bough, branch, harvest (man).

7106. קָצַע **qâtsa'**, *kaw-tsah'*; a prim. root; to *strip* off, i.e. (partially) *scrape*; by impl. to *segregate* (as an angle):—cause to scrape, corner.

7107. קָצַף **qâtsaph**, *kaw-tsaf'*; a prim. root; to *crack* off, i.e. (fig.) *burst* out in rage:—(be) anger (-ry), displease, fret self, (provoke to) wrath (come), be wroth.

7108. קְצַף **q^{e}tsaph** (Chald.), *kets-af'*; corresp. to 7107; to *become enraged*:—be furious.

7109. קְצַף **q^{e}tsaph** (Chald.), *kets-af'*; from 7108; *rage*:—wrath.

7110. קֶצֶף **qetseph**, *keh'-tsef*; from 7107; a *splinter* (as *chipped* off); fig. *rage* or *strife*:—foam, indignation, × sore, wrath.

7111. קְצָפָה **q^{e}tsâphâh**, *kets-aw-faw'*; from 7107; a *fragment*:—bark [-ed].

7112. קָצַץ **qâtsats**, *kaw-tsats'*; a prim. root; to *chop* off (lit. or fig.):—cut (asunder, in pieces, in sunder, off), × utmost.

7113. קְצַץ **q^{e}tsats** (Chald.), *kets-ats'*; corresp. to 7112:—cut off.

7114. קָצַר **qâtsar**, *kaw-tsar'*; a prim. root; to *dock* off, i.e. *curtail* (trans. or intrans., lit. or fig.); espec. to *harvest* (grass or grain):— × at all, cut down, much discouraged, grieve, harvestman, lothe, mourn, reap (-er), (be, wax) short (-en, -er), straiten, trouble, vex.

7115. קֹצֶר **qôtser**, *ko'-tser*; from 7114; *shortness* (of spirit), i.e. impatience:—anguish.

7116. קָצֵר **qâtsêr**, *kaw-tsare'*; from 7114; *short* (whether in size, number, life, strength or temper):—few, hasty, small, soon.

7117. קְצָת **q^{e}tsâth**, *kets-awth'*; from 7096; a *termination* (lit. or fig.); also (by impl.) a *portion*; adv. (with prep. pref.) *after*:—end, part, × some.

7118. קְצָת **q^{e}tsâth** (Chald.), *kets-awth'*; corresp. to 7117:—end, partly.

7119. קַר **qar**, *kar*; contr. from an unused root mean. to *chill*; *cool*; fig. *quiet*:—cold, excellent [*from the marg.*].

קִיר **qîr**. See 7023.

7120. קֹר **qôr**, *kore*; from the same as 7119; *cold*:—cold.

7121. קָרָא **qârâ'**, *kaw-raw'*; a prim. root [rather ident. with 7122 through the idea of *accosting* a person met]; to *call* out to (i.e. prop. *address* by name, but used in a wide variety of applications):—bewray [self], that are bidden, call (for, forth, self, upon), cry (unto), (be) famous, guest, invite, mention, (give) name, preach, (make) proclaim (-ation), pronounce, publish, read, renowned, say.

7122. קָרָא **qârâ'**, *kaw-raw'*; a prim. root; to *encounter*, whether accidentally or in a hostile manner:—befall, (by) chance, (cause to) come (upon), fall out, happen, meet.

7123. קְרָא **q^{e}râ'** (Chald.), *ker-aw'*; corresp. to 7121: call, cry, read.

7124. קֹרֵא **qôrê'**, *ko-ray'*; prop. act. part. of 7121; a *caller*, i.e. *partridge* (from its *cry*):—partridge. See also 6981.

7125. קִרְאָה **qîr'âh**, *keer-aw'*; from 7122; an *encountering*, accidental, friendly or hostile (also adv. *opposite*):— × against (he come), help, meet, seek, × to, × in the way.

7126. קָרַב **qârab**, *kaw-rab'*; a prim. root; to *approach* (caus. *bring near*) for whatever purpose:—(cause to) approach, (cause to) bring (forth, near), (cause to) come (near, nigh), (cause to) draw near (nigh), go (near), be at hand, join, be near, offer, present, produce, make ready, stand, take.

7127. קְרֵב **qerêb** (Chald.), *ker-abe'*; corresp. to 7126:—approach, come (near, nigh), draw near.

7128. קְרָב **qerâb**, *ker-awb'*; from 7126; hostile *encounter*:—battle, war.

7129. קְרָב **qerâb** (Chald.), *ker-awb'*; corresp. to 7128:—war.

7130. קֶרֶב **qereb**, *keh'-reb*; from 7126; prop. the *nearest* part, i.e. the *centre*, whether lit., fig. or adv. (espec. with prep.):— × among, × before, bowels, × unto charge, + eat (up), × heart, × him, × in, inward (× -ly, part, -s, thought), midst, + out of, purtenance, × therein, × through, × within self.

7131. קָרֵב **qârêb**, *kaw-rabe'*; from 7126; *near*:—approach, come (near, nigh), draw near.

קָרֹב **qârôb**. See 7138.

7132. קְרָבָה **qerâbâh**, *ker-aw-baw'*; from 7126; *approach*:—approaching, draw near.

7133. קׇרְבָּן **qorbân**, *kor-bawn'*; or

קֻרְבָּן **qurbân**, *koor-bawn'*; from 7126; something *brought near* the altar, i.e. a sacrificial *present*:—oblation, that is offered, offering.

7134. קַרְדֹּם **qardôm**, *kar-dome'*; perh. from 6923 in the sense of *striking* upon; an *axe*:—ax.

7135. קָרָה **qârâh**, *kaw-raw'*; fem. of 7119; *coolness*:—cold.

7136. קָרָה **qârâh**, *kaw-raw'*; a prim. root; to *light upon* (chiefly by accident); caus. to *bring about;* spec. to *impose* timbers (for roof or floor):—appoint, lay (make) beams, befall, bring, come (to pass unto), floor, [hap] was, happen (unto), meet, send good speed.

7137. קָרֶה **qâreh**, *kaw-reh'*; from 7136; an (unfortunate) *occurrence*, i.e. some accidental (ceremonial) *disqualification*:—uncleanness that chanceth.

קֹרָה **qôrâh**. See 6982.

7138. קָרוֹב **qârôwb**, *kaw-robe'*; or

קָרֹב **qârôb**, *kaw-robe'*; from 7126; *near* (in place, kindred or time):—allied, approach, at hand, + any of kin, kinsfolk (-sman), (that is) near (of kin), neighbour, (that is) next, (them that come) nigh (at hand), more ready, short (-ly).

7139. קָרַח **qârach**, *kaw-rakh'*; a prim. root; to *depilate*:—make (self) bald.

7140. קֶרַח **qerach**, *keh'-rakh*; or

קֹרַח **qôrach**, *ko'-rakh*; from 7139; *ice* (as if bald, i.e. *smooth*); hence, *hail;* by resemblance, rock *crystal*:—crystal, frost, ice.

7141. קֹרַח **Qôrach**, *ko'-rakh*; from 7139; *ice; Korach*, the name of two Edomites and three Isr.:—Korah.

7142. קֵרֵחַ **qêrêach**, *kay-ray'-akh*; from 7139; *bald* (on the back of the head):—bald (head).

7143. קָרֵחַ **Qârêach**, *kaw-ray'-akh*; from 7139; *bald; Kareäch*, an Isr.:—Careah, Kareah.

7144. קׇרְחָה **qorchâh**, *kor-khaw'*; or

קׇרְחָא **qorchâ'** (Ezek. 27 : 31), *kor-khaw'*; from 7139; *baldness*:—bald (-ness), × utterly.

7145. קׇרְחִי **Qorchîy**, *kor-khee'*; patron. from 7141; a *Korchite* (collect.) or desc. of Korach:—Korahite, Korathite, sons of Kore, Korhite.

7146. קָרַחַת **qârachath**, *kaw-rakh'-ath*; from 7139; a *bald* spot (on the back of the head); fig. a *threadbare* spot (on the back side of the cloth):—bald head, bare within.

7147. קְרִי **qerîy**, *ker-ee'*; from 7136; hostile *encounter*:—contrary.

7148. קָרִיא **qârîy'**, *kaw-ree'*; from 7121; *called*, i.e. *select*:—famous, renowned.

7149. קִרְיָא **qiryâ'** (Chald.), *keer-yaw'*; or

קִרְיָה **qiryâh** (Chald.), *keer-yaw'*; corresp. to 7151:—city.

7150. קְרִיאָה **qerîy'âh**, *ker-ee-aw'*; from 7121; a *proclamation*:—preaching.

7151. קִרְיָה **qiryâh**, *kir-yaw'*; from 7136 in the sense of *flooring*, i.e. building; a *city*:—city.

7152. קְרִיּוֹת **Qerîyôwth**, *ker-ee-yōth'*; plur. of 7151; *buildings; Kerioth*, the name of two places in Pal.:—Kerioth, Kirioth.

7153. קִרְיַת אַרְבַּע **Qiryath 'Arbaʻ**, *keer-yath' ar-bah'*; or (with the art. interposed)

קִרְיַת הָאַרְבַּע **Qiryath hâ-'Arbaʻ** (Neh. 11 : 25), *keer-yath' haw-ar-bah'*; from 7151 and 704 or 702; *city of Arba*, or *city of the four* (giants); *Kirjath-Arba* or *Kirjath-ha-Arba*, a place in Pal.:—Kirjath-arba.

7154. קִרְיַת בַּעַל **Qiryath Baʻal**, *keer-yath' bah'-al*; from 7151 and 1168; *city of Baal; Kirjath-Baal*, a place in Pal.:—Kirjath-baal.

7155. קִרְיַת חֻצוֹת **Qiryath Chûtsôwth**, *keer-yath' khoo-tsōth'*; from 7151 and the fem. plur. of 2351; *city of streets; Kirjath-Chutsoth*, a place in Moab:—Kirjath-huzoth.

7156. קִרְיָתַיִם **Qiryâthayim**, *keer-yaw-thah'-yim*; dual of 7151; *double city; Kirjathaïm*, the name of two places in Pal.:—Kiriathaim, Kirjathaim.

7157. קִרְיַת יְעָרִים **Qiryath Yeʻârîym**, *keer-yath' yeh-aw-reem'*; or (Jer. 26 : 20) with the art. interposed; or (Josh. 18 : 28) simply the former part of the word; or

קִרְיַת עָרִים **Qiryath ʻÂrîym**, *keer-yath' aw-reem'*; from 7151 and the plur. of 3293 or 5892; *city of forests*, or *city of towns; Kirjath-Jeärim* or *Kirjath-Arim*, a place in Pal.:—Kirjath, Kirjath-jearim, Kirjath-arim.

7158. קִרְיַת סַנָּה **Qiryath Çannâh**, *keer-yath' san-naw'*; or

קִרְיַת סֵפֶר **Qiryath Çêpher**, *keer-yath' say'-fer*; from 7151 and a simpler fem. from the same as 5577, or (for the latter name) 5612; *city of branches*, or *of a book; Kirjath-Sannah* or *Kirjath-Sepher*, a place in Pal.:—Kirjath-sannah, Kirjath-sepher.

7159. קָרַם **qâram**, *kaw-ram'*; a prim. root; to *cover*:—cover.

7160. קָרַן **qâran**, *kaw-ran'*; a prim. root; to *push* or gore; used only as denom. from 7161, to *shoot out horns;* fig. *rays*:—have horns, shine.

7161. קֶרֶן **qeren**, *keh'-ren*; from 7160; a *horn* (as *projecting*); by impl. a *flask, cornet;* by resembl. an elephant's *tooth* (i.e. *ivory*), a *corner* (of the altar), a *peak* (of a mountain), a *ray* (of light); fig. *power*:— × hill, horn.

7162. קֶרֶן **qeren** (Chald.), *keh'-ren*; corresp. to 7161; a *horn* (lit. or for sound):—horn, cornet.

7163. קֶרֶן הַפּוּךְ **qeren hap-pûwk**, *keh'-ren hap-pook'*; from 7161 and 6320; *horn of cosmetic; Keren-hap-Puk*, one of Job's daughters:—Keren-happuch.

7164. קָרַס **qâraç**, *kaw-ras'*; a prim. root; prop. to *protrude;* used only as denom. from 7165 (for alliteration with 7167), to *hunch*, i.e. be humpbacked:—stoop.

7165. קֶרֶס **qereç**, *keh'-res*; from 7164; a *knob* or belaying-pin (from its swelling *form*):—tache.

קֵרֹס **Qêrôç**. See 7026.

7166. קַרְסֹל **qarçôl**, *kar-sole'*; from 7164; an *ankle* (as a *protuberance* or joint):—foot.

7167. קָרַע **qâraʻ**, *kaw-rah'*; a prim. root; to *rend*, lit. or fig. (*revile, paint* the eyes, as if enlarging them):—cut out, rend, × surely, tear.

7168. קֶרַע **qeraʻ**, *keh'-rah*; from 7167; a *rag*:—piece, rag.

7169. קָרַץ **qârats**, *kaw-rats'*; a prim. root; to *pinch*, i.e. (partially) to *bite* the lips, *blink* the eyes (as a gesture of malice), or (fully) to *squeeze* off (a piece of clay in order to mould a vessel from it):—form, move, wink.

7170. קְרַץ **qerats** (Chald.), *ker-ats'*; corresp. to 7171 in the sense of a *bit* (to "eat the *morsels* of" any one, i.e. *chew* him up [fig.] by *slander*):— + accuse

7171. קֶרֶץ **qerets**, *keh'-rets*; from 7169; *extirpation* (as if by *constriction*):—destruction.

7172. קַרְקַע **qarqaʻ**, *kar-kah'*; from 7167; *floor* (as if a pavement of pieces or *tesseræ*), of a building or the sea:—bottom, (× one side of the) floor.

7173. קַרְקַע **Qarqaʻ**, *kar-kah'*; the same as 7172; *ground-floor; Karka* (with the art. pref.), a place in Pal.:—Karkaa.

7174. קַרְקֹר **Qarqôr**, *kar-kore'*; from 6979; *foundation; Karkor*, a place E. of the Jordan:—Karkor.

7175. קֶרֶשׁ **qeresh**, *keh'-resh*; from an unused root mean. to *split* off; a *slab* or *plank;* by impl. a *deck* of a ship:—bench, board.

7176. קֶרֶת **qereth**, *keh'-reth*; from 7136 in the sense of building; a *city*:—city.

7177. קַרְתָּה **Qartâh**, *kar-taw'*; from 7176; *city; Kartah*, a place in Pal.:—Kartah.

7178. קַרְתָּן **Qartân**, *kar-tawn'*; from 7176; *city-plot; Kartan*, a place in Pal.:—Kartan.

7179. קַשׁ **qash**, *kash*; from 7197; *straw* (as *dry*):—stubble.

7180. קִשֻּׁא **qishshû'**, *kish-shoo'*; from an unused root (mean. to be *hard*); a *cucumber* (from the difficulty of *digestion*):—cucumber.

7181. קָשַׁב **qâshab**, *kaw-shab'*; a prim. root; to *prick up* the ears, i.e. *hearken*:—attend, (cause to) hear (-ken), give heed, incline, mark (well), regard.

7182. קֶשֶׁב **qesheb**, *keh'-sheb*; from 7181; a *hearkening*:— × diligently, hearing, much heed, that regarded.

7183. קַשָּׁב **qashshâb**, *kash-shawb'*; or

קַשֻּׁב **qashshûb**, *kash-shoob'*; from 7181; *hearkening*:—attent (-ive).

7184. קָשָׂה **qâsâh**, *kaw-saw'*; or

קַסְוָה **qasvâh**, *kas-vaw'*; from an unused root mean. to be *round;* a *jug* (from its shape):—cover, cup.

7185. קָשָׁה **qâshâh**, *kaw-shaw'*; a prim. root; prop. to *be dense*, i.e. tough or *severe* (in various applications):—be cruel, be fiercer, make grievous, be ([ask a], be in, have, seem, would) hard (-en, [labour], -ly, thing), be sore, (be, make) stiff (-en, [-necked]).

7186. קָשֶׁה **qâsheh**, *kaw-sheh'*; from 7185; *severe* (in various applications):—churlish, cruel, grievous, hard ([-hearted], thing), heavy, + impudent, obstinate, prevailed, rough (-ly), sore, sorrowful, stiff ([-necked]), stubborn, + in trouble.

7187. קְשׁוֹט **qeshôwṭ** (Chald.), *kesh-ote'*; or

קְשֹׁט **qeshôṭ** (Chald.), *kesh-ote'*; corresp. to 7189; *fidelity*:—truth.

7188. קָשַׁח **qâshach**, *kaw-shakh'*; a prim. root; to *be* (caus. *make*) *unfeeling*:—harden.

7189. קֹשֶׁט **qôsheṭ**, *ko'-shet*; or

קֹשְׁט **qôshṭ**, *kōsht*; from an unused root mean. to *balance; equity* (as evenly *weighed*), i.e. *reality*:—certainty, truth.

קשֹׁט **qôshôṭ**. See 7187.

7190. קְשִׁי **qeshîy**, *kesh-ee'*; from 7185; *obstinacy*:—stubbornness.

7191. קִשְׁיוֹן **Qishyôwn**, *kish-yone'*; from 7190; *hard ground; Kishjon*, a place in Pal.:—Kishion, Kesbon.

7192. קְשִׂיטָה **qesîyṭah**, *kes-ee-taw'*; from an unused root (prob. mean. to *weigh* out); an *ingot* (as definitely *estimated* and stamped for a coin):—piece of money (silver).

7193. קַשְׂקֶשֶׂת **qasqeseth**, *kas-keh'-seth*; by redupl. from an unused root mean. to *shale* off as bark; a *scale* (of a fish); hence a coat of *mail* (as composed of or covered with jointed *plates* of metal):—mail, scale.

7194. קָשַׁר **qâshar**, *kaw-shar'*; a prim. root; to *tie*, phys. (*gird, confine, compact*) or ment. (in *love, league*):—bind (up), (make a) conspire (-acy, -ator), join together, knit, stronger, work [treason].

7195. קֶשֶׁר **qesher**, *keh'-sher;* from 7194; an (unlawful) *alliance:*—confederacy, conspiracy, treason.

7196. קִשֻּׁר **qishshûr**, *kish-shoor';* from 7194; an (ornamental) *girdle* (for women):—attire, headband.

7197. קָשַׁשׁ **qâshash**, *kaw-shash';* a prim. root; to *become sapless* through drought; used only as denom. from 7179; to *forage* for straw, stubble or wood; fig. to *assemble:*—gather (selves) (together).

7198. קֶשֶׁת **qesheth**, *keh'-sheth;* from 7185 in the orig. sense (of 6983) of *bending;* a *bow,* for *shooting* (hence fig. *strength*) or the *iris:*—× arch (-er), + arrow, bow ([-man, -shot]).

7199. קַשָּׁת **qashshâth**, *kash-shawth';* intens. (as denom.) from 7198; a *bowman:*—× archer.

ר

7200. רָאָה **râ'âh**, *raw-aw';* a prim. root; to *see,* lit. or fig. (in numerous applications, direct and implied, trans., intrans. and causat.):—advise self, appear, approve, behold, × certainly, consider, discern, (make to) enjoy, have experience, gaze, take heed, × indeed, × joyfully, lo, look (on, one another, one on another, one upon another, out, up, upon), mark, meet, × be near, perceive, present, provide, regard, (have) respect, (fore-, cause to, let) see (-r, -m, one another), shew (self), × sight of others, (e-) spy, stare, × surely, × think, view, visions.

7201. רָאָה **râ'âh**, *raw-aw';* from 7200; a *bird* of prey (prob. the *vulture,* from its sharp *sight*):—glede. Comp. 1676.

7202. רָאֶה **râ'eh**, *raw-eh';* from 7200; *seeing,* i.e. experiencing:—see.

7203. רֹאֶה **rô'eh**, *ro-eh';* act. part. of 7200; a *seer* (as often rendered); but also (abstr.) a *vision:*—vision.

7204. רֹאֵה **Rô'êh**, *ro-ay';* for 7203; *prophet; Roëh,* an Isr.:—Haroeh [*includ. the art.*].

7205. רְאוּבֵן **R^e'ûwbên**, *reh-oo-bane';* from the imper. of 7200 and 1121; *see ye a son; Reüben,* a son of Jacob:—Reuben.

7206. רְאוּבֵנִי **R^e'ûwbênîy**, *reh-oo-bay-nee';* patron. from 7205; a *Reübenite* or desc. of Reüben:—children of Reuben, Reubenites.

7207. רַאֲוָה **ra'ăvâh**, *rah-av-aw';* from 7200; *sight,* i.e. satisfaction:—behold.

7208. רְאוּמָה **R^e'ûwmâh**, *reh-oo-maw';* fem. pass. part. of 7213; *raised; Reümah,* a Syrian woman:—Reumah.

7209. רְאִי **r^e'îy**, *reh-ee';* from 7200; a *mirror* (as *seen*):—looking glass.

7210. רֳאִי **rô'îy**, *ro-ee';* from 7200; *sight,* whether abstr. (*vision*) or concr. (a *spectacle*):—gazingstock, look to, (that) see (-th).

7211. רְאָיָה **R^e'âyâh**, *reh-aw-yaw';* from 7200 and 3050; *Jah has seen; Reäjah,* the name of three Isr.:—Reaia, Reaiah.

7212. רְאִית **r^e'îyth**, *reh-eeth';* from 7200; *sight:*—beholding.

7213. רָאַם **râ'am**, *raw-am';* a prim. root; to *rise:*—be lifted up.

7214. רְאֵם **r^e'êm**, *reh-ame';* or

רְאֵים **r^e'êym**, *reh-ame';* or

רֵים **rêym**, *rame;* or

רֵם **rêm**, *rame;* from 7213; a wild *bull* (from its *conspicuousness*):—unicorn.

7215. רָאמָה **râ'mâh**, *raw-maw';* from 7213: something *high* in value, i.e. perh. *coral:*—coral.

7216. רָאמוֹת **Râ'môwth**, *raw-môth';* or

רָאמֹת **Râmôth**, *raw-môth';* plur. of 7215; *heights; Ramoth,* the name of two places in Pal.:—Ramoth.

7217. רֵאשׁ **rê'sh** (Chald.), *raysh;* corresp. to 7218; the *head;* fig. the *sum:*—chief, head, sum.

7218. רֹאשׁ **rô'sh**, *roshe;* from an unused root appar. mean. to *shake;* the *head* (as most easily *shaken*), whether lit. or fig. (in many applications, of place, time, rank, etc.):—band, beginning, captain, chapiter, chief (-est place, man, things), company, end, × every [man], excellent, first, forefront, ([be-]) head, height, (on) high (-est part, [priest]), × lead, × poor, principal, ruler, sum, top.

7219. רֹאשׁ **rô'sh**, *roshe;* or

רוֹשׁ **rôwsh** (Deut. 32 : 32), *roshe;* appar. the same as 7218; a poisonous *plant,* prob. the *poppy* (from its conspicuous *head*); gen. *poison* (even of serpents):—gall, hemlock, poison, venom.

7220. רֹאשׁ **Rô'sh**, *roshe;* prob. the same as 7218; *Rosh,* the name of an Isr. and of a for. nation:—Rosh.

רֵאשׁ **rê'sh**. See 7389.

7221. רִאשָׁה **rî'shâh**, *ree-shaw';* from the same as 7218; a *beginning:*—beginning.

7222. רֹאשָׁה **rô'shâh**, *ro-shaw';* fem. of 7218; the *head:*—head [-stone].

7223. רִאשׁוֹן **rî'shôwn**, *ree-shone';* or

רִאשֹׁן **rî'shôn**, *ree-shone';* from 7221; *first,* in place, time or rank (as adj. or noun):—ancestor, (that were) before (-time), beginning, eldest, first, fore [-father] (-most), former (thing), of old time, past.

7224. רִאשֹׁנִי **rî'shônîy**, *ree-sho-nee';* from 7223; *first:*—first.

7225. רֵאשִׁית **rê'shîyth**, *ray-sheeth';* from the same as 7218; the *first,* in place, time, order or rank (spec. a *firstfruit*):—beginning, chief (-est), first (-fruits, part, time), principal thing.

7226. רַאֲשֹׁת **ra'ăshôth**, *rah-ash-ôth';* from 7218; a *pillow* (being for the *head*):—bolster.

7227. רַב **rab**, *rab;* by contr. from 7231; *abundant* (in quantity, size, age, number, rank, quality):—(in) abound (-undance, -ant, -antly), captain, elder, enough, exceedingly, full, great (-ly, man, one), increase, long (enough, [time]), (do, have) many (-ifold, things, a time), ([ship-]) master, mighty, more, (too, very) much, multiply (-tude), officer, often [-times], plenteous, populous, prince, process [of time], suffice (-ient).

7228. רַב **rab**, *rab;* by contr. from 7232; an *archer* [or perh. the same as 7227]:—archer.

7229. רַב **rab** (Chald.), *rab;* corresp. to 7227:—captain, chief, great, lord, master, stout.

רִב **rîb**. See 7378.

7230. רֹב **rôb**, *robe;* from 7231; *abundance* (in any respect):—abundance (-antly), all, × common [sort], excellent, great (-ly, -ness, number), huge, be increased, long, many, more in number, most, much, multitude, plenty (-ifully), × very [age].

7231. רָבַב **râbab**, *raw-bab';* a prim. root; prop. to *cast* together [comp. 7241], i.e. *increase,* espec. in number; also (as denom. from 7233) to *multiply by the myriad:*—increase, be many (-ifold), be more, multiply, ten thousands.

7232. רָבַב **râbab**, *raw-bab';* a prim. root [rather ident. with 7231 through the idea of *projection*]; to *shoot* an arrow:—shoot.

7233. רְבָבָה **r^ebâbâh**, *reb-aw-baw';* from 7231; *abundance* (in number), i.e. (spec.) a *myriad* (whether def. or indef.):—many, million, × multiply, ten thousand.

7234. רָבַד **râbad**, *raw-bad';* a prim. root; to *spread:*—deck.

7235. רָבָה **râbâh**, *raw-baw';* a prim. root; to *increase* (in whatever respect):—[bring in] abundance (× -antly), + archer [*by mistake for* 7232], be in authority, bring up, × continue, enlarge, excel, exceeding (-ly), be full of, (be, make) great (-er, -ly, × -ness), grow up, heap, increase, be long, (be, give, have, make, use) many (a time), (any, be, give, give the, have) more (in number), (ask, be, be so, gather, over, take, yield) much (greater, more), (make to) multiply, nourish, plenty (-eous), × process [of time], sore, store, thoroughly, very.

7236. רְבָה **r^ebâh** (Chald.), *reb-aw';* corresp. to 7235:—make a great man, grow.

7237. רַבָּה **Rabbâh**, *rab-baw';* fem. of 7227: *great; Rabbah,* the name of two places in Pal., E. and W.:—Rabbah, Rabbath.

7238. רְבוּ **r^ebûw** (Chald.), *reb-oo';* from a root corresp. to 7235; *increase* (of dignity):—greatness, majesty.

7239. רִבּוֹ **ribbôw**, *rib-bo';* from 7231; or

רִבּוֹא **ribbôw'**, *rib-bo';* from 7231; a *myriad,* i.e. indef *large number:*—great things, ten ([eight] -een, [for] -ty, + sixscore, + threescore, × twenty, [twen] -ty) thousand.

7240. רִבּוֹ **ribbôw** (Chald.), *rib-bo';* corresp. to 7239:— × ten thousand times ten thousand.

7241. רָבִיב **râbîyb**, *raw-beeb';* from 7231; a *rain* (as an *accumulation* of drops):—shower.

7242. רָבִיד **râbîyd**, *raw-beed';* from 7234; a *collar* (as *spread* around the neck):—chain.

7243. רְבִיעִי **r^ebîy'îy**, *reb-ee-ee';* or

רְבִעִי **r^ebî'îy**, *reb-ee-ee';* from 7251; *fourth;* also (fractionally) a *fourth:*—foursquare, fourth (part).

7244. רְבִיעַי **r^ebîy'ay** (Chald.), *reb-ee-ah'ee;* corresp. to 7243:—fourth.

7245. רַבִּית **Rabbîyth**, *rab-beeth';* from 7231; *multitude; Rabbith,* a place in Pal.:—Rabbith.

7246. רָבַךְ **râbak**, *raw-bak';* a prim. root; to *soak* (bread in oil):—baken, (that which is) fried.

7247. רִבְלָה **Riblâh**, *rib-law';* from an unused root mean. to *be fruitful; fertile; Riblah,* a place in Syria:—Riblah.

7248. רַב־מָג **Rab-Mâg**, *rab-mawg';* from 7227 and a for. word for a Magian; *chief Magian; Rab-Mag,* a Bab. official:—Rab-mag.

7249. רַב־סָרִיס **Rab-Çârîyç**, *rab-saw-reece';* from 7227 and a for. word for a eunuch; *chief chamberlain; Rab-Saris,* a Bab. official:—Rab-saris.

7250. רָבַע **râba'**, *raw-bah';* a prim. root; to *squat* or *lie* out flat, i.e. (spec.) in copulation:—let gender, lie down.

7251. רָבַע **râba'**, *raw-bah';* a prim. root [rather ident. with 7250 through the idea of *sprawling* "at all fours" (or possibly the reverse is the order of deriv.); comp. 702]; prop. to *be four* (sided); used only as denom. of 7253; to *be quadrate:*—(four-) square (-d).

7252. רֶבַע **reba'**, *reh'-bah;* from 7250; *prostration* (for sleep):—lying down.

7253. רֶבַע **reba'**, *reh'-bah;* from 7251; a *fourth* (part or side):—fourth part, side, square.

7254. רֶבַע **Reba'**, *reh'-bah;* the same as 7253; *Reba,* a Midianite:—Reba.

7255. רֹבַע **rôba'**, *ro'-bah;* from 7251; a *quarter;*—fourth part.

7256. רִבֵּעַ **ribbêa'**, *rib-bay'-ah;* from 7251; a descendant of the *fourth* generation, i.e. *great great grandchild:*—fourth.

רְבִעִי **r^ebîy'îy**. See 7243.

7257. רָבַץ **râbats**, *raw-bats';* a prim. root; to *crouch* (on all four legs folded, like a recumbent animal); by impl. to *recline, repose brood, lurk, imbed:*—crouch (down), fall down, make a fold, lay, (cause to, make to) lie (down), make to rest, sit.

7258. רֵבֶץ **rebets**, *reh'-bets;* from 7257; a *couch* or place of repose:—where each lay, lie down in, resting place.

259. רִבְקָה **Ribqâh**, *rib-kaw'*; from an unused root prob. mean. to *clog* by tying up he fetlock; *fettering* (by beauty); *Ribkah*, the wife f Isaac:—Rebekah.

260. רַבְרַב **rabrab** (Chald.), *rab-rab'*; from 7229; *huge* (in size); *domineering* (in haracter):—(very) great (things).

261. רַבְרְבָן **rabr**e**bân** (Chald.), *rab-reb-awn'*; from 7260; a *magnate*:—lord, prince.

262. רַבְשָׁקֵה **Rabshâqêh**, *rab-shaw-kay'*; from 7227 and 8248; *chief butler*; abshakeh, a Bab. official:—Rabshakeh.

263. רֶגֶב **regeb**, *reh'-gheb*; from an unused root mean. to *pile* together; a *lump* of clay:—lod.

264. רָגַז **râgaz**, *raw-gaz'*; a prim. root; to *quiver* (with any violent emotion, espec. nger or fear):—be afraid, stand in awe, disquiet, fall ut, fret, move, provoke, quake, rage, shake, tremle, trouble, be wroth.

265. רְגַז **r**e**gaz** (Chald.), *reg-az'*; corresp. to 7264:—provoke unto wrath.

266. רְגַז **r**e**gaz** (Chald.), *reg-az'*; from 7265; violent *anger*:—rage.

267. רֹגֶז **rôgez**, *ro'-ghez*; from 7264; *commotion*, *restlessness* (of a horse), *crash* (of thuner), *disquiet*, *anger*:—fear, noise, rage, trouble ing), wrath.

268. רַגָּז **raggâz**, *rag-gawz'*; intens. from 7264; *timid*:—trembling.

269. רָגְזָה **rogzâh**, *rog-zaw'*; fem. of 7267; *trepidation*:—trembling.

270. רָגַל **râgal**, *raw-gal'*; a prim. root; to *walk* along; but only in spec. applications, to econnoitre, to *be a tale-bearer* (i.e. slander); also (as enom. from 7272) to *lead about*:—backbite, search, lander, (e-) spy (out), teach to go, view.

271. רְגַל **r**e**gal** (Chald.), *reg-al'*; corresp. to 7272:—foot.

272. רֶגֶל **regel**, *reh'-gel*; from 7270; a *foot* (as used in *walking*); by impl. a *step*; by uphem. the *pudenda*:—× be able to endure, × acording as, × after, × coming, × follow, ([broken-]) oot ([-ed, -stool]), × great toe, × haunt, × journey, g, + piss, + possession, time.

273. רגלי **raglîy**, *rag-lee'*; from 7272; a *footman* (soldier):—(on) foot (-man).

274. רֹגְלִים **Rôg**e**lîym**, *ro-gel-eem'*; plur. of act. part. of 7270; *fullers* (as *tramping* the loth in washing); *Rogelim*, a place E. of the Joran:—Rogelim.

275. רָגַם **râgam**, *raw-gam'*; a prim. root [comp. 7263, 7321, 7551]; to *cast* together (stones), e. to *lapidate*:— × certainly, stone.

276. רֶגֶם **Regem**, *reh'-gem*; from 7275; stone-*heap*; *Regem*, an Isr.:—Regem.

277. רִגְמָה **rigmâh**, *rig-maw'*; fem. of the same as 7276; a *pile* (of stones), i.e. (fig.) a *hrong*:—council.

278. רֶגֶם מֶלֶךְ **Regem Melek**, *reh'-gem meh'-lek*; from 7276 and 4428; *king's eap*; *Regem-Melek*, an Isr.:—Regem-melech.

279. רָגַן **râgan**, *raw-gan'*; a prim. root; to *grumble*, i.e. *rebel*:—murmur.

280. רָגַע **râga'**, *raw-gah'*; a prim. root; prop. to *toss* violently and suddenly (the sea with vaves, the skin with boils); fig. (in a favorable maner) to *settle*, i.e. quiet; spec. to *wink* (from the notion of the eye-lids):—break, divide, find ease, be a noment, (cause, give, make to) rest, make suddenly.

281. רֶגַע **rega'**, *reh'-gah*; from 7280; a *wink* (of the eyes), i.e. a very *short space* of ime:—instant, moment, space, suddenly.

282. רָגֵעַ **râgêa'**, *raw-gay'-ah*; from 7280; *restful*, i.e. peaceable:—that are quiet.

283. רָגַשׁ **râgash**, *raw-gash'*; a prim. root; to *be tumultuous*:—rage.

284. רְגַשׁ **r**e**gash** (Chald.), *reg-ash'*; corresp. to 7283; to *gather* tumultuously:—assemble together).

7285. רֶגֶשׁ **regesh**, *reh'-ghesh*; or (fem.)

רִגְשָׁה **rigshâh**, *rig-shaw'*; from 7283; a tumultuous *crowd*:—company, insurrection.

7286. רָדַד **râdad**, *raw-dad'*; a prim. root; to *tread* in pieces, i.e. (fig.) to *conquer*, or (spec.) to *overlay*:—spend, spread, subdue.

7287. רָדָה **râdâh**, *raw-daw'*; a prim. root; to *tread* down, i.e. *subjugate*; spec. to *crumble* off:—(come to, make to) have dominion, prevail against, reign, (bear, make to) rule. (-r, over), take.

7288. רַדַּי **Radday**, *rad-dah'ee*; intens. from 7287; *domineering*; *Raddai*, an Isr.:—Raddai.

7289. רָדִיד **râdîyd**, *raw-deed'*; from 7286 in the sense of *spreading*; a *veil* (as expanded):—vail, veil.

7290. רָדַם **râdam**, *raw-dam'*; a prim. root; to *stun*, i.e. *stupefy* (with sleep or death):—(be fast a-, be in a deep, cast into a dead, that) sleep (-er, -eth).

7291. רָדַף **râdaph**, *raw-daf'*; a prim. root; to *run after* (usually with hostile intent; fig. [of time] *gone by*):—chase, put to flight, follow (after, on), hunt, (be under) persecute (-ion, -or), pursue (-r).

7292. רָהַב **râhab**, *raw-hab'*; a prim. root; to *urge* severely, i.e. (fig.) *importune*, *embolden*, *capture*, *act insolently*:—overcome, behave self proudly, make sure, strengthen.

7293. רַהַב **rahab**, *rah'-hab*; from 7292; *bluster* (-*er*):—proud, strength.

7294. רַהַב **Rahab**, *rah'-hab*; the same as 7293; *Rahab* (i.e. *boaster*), an epithet of Egypt:—Rahab.

7295. רָהָב **râhâb**, *raw-hawb'*; from 7292; *insolent*:—proud.

7296. רֹהַב **rôhab**, *ro'-hab*; from 7292; *pride*:—strength.

7297. רָהָה **râhâh**, *raw-haw'*; a prim. root; to *fear*:—be afraid.

7298. רַהַט **rahaṭ**, *rah'-hat*; from an unused root appar. mean. to *hollow out*; a *channel* or watering-box; by resemblance a *ringlet* of hair (as forming parallel lines):—gallery, gutter, trough.

7299. רֵו **rêv** (Chald.), *rave*; from a root corresp. to 7200; *aspect*:—form.

רוּב° **rûwb**. See 7378.

7300. רוּד **rûwd**, *rood*; a prim. root; to *tramp* about, i.e. *ramble* (free or disconsolate):—have the dominion, be lord, mourn, rule.

7301. רָוָה **râvâh**, *raw-vaw'*; a prim. root; to *slake* the thirst (occasionally of other appetites):—bathe, make drunk, (take the) fill, satiate, (abundantly) satisfy, soak, water (abundantly).

7302. רָוֶה **râveh**, *raw-veh'*; from 7301; *sated* (with drink):—drunkenness, watered.

7303. רוֹהֲגָה° **Rôwhăgâh**, *ro-hag-aw'*; from an unused root prob. mean. to *cry out*; *outcry*; *Rohagah*, an Isr.:—Rohgah.

7304. רָוַח **râvach**, *raw-vakh'*; a prim. root [rather ident. with 7306]; prop. to *breathe* freely, i.e. *revive*; by impl. to *have ample room*:—be refreshed, large.

7305. רֶוַח **revach**, *reh'-vakh*; from 7304; *room*, lit. (an *interval*) or fig. (*deliverance*):—enlargement, space.

7306. רוּחַ **rûwach**, *roo'-akh*; a prim. root; prop. to *blow*, i.e. *breathe*; only (lit.) to *smell* or (by impl. *perceive* (fig. to *anticipate*, *enjoy*):—accept, smell, × touch, make of quick understanding.

7307. רוּחַ **rûwach**, *roo'-akh*; from 7306; *wind*; by resemblance *breath*, i.e. a sensible (or even violent) exhalation; fig. *life*, *anger*, *unsubstantiality*; by extens. a *region* of the sky; by resemblance *spirit*, but only of a rational being (includ. its expression and functions):—air, anger, blast, breath, × cool, courage, mind, × quarter, × side, spirit ([-ual]), tempest, × vain, ([whirl-]) wind (-y).

7308. רוּחַ **rûwach** (Chald.), *roo'-akh*; corresp. to 7307:—mind, spirit, wind.

7309. רְוָחָה **r**e**vâchâh**, *rev-aw-khaw'*; fem. of 7305; *relief*:—breathing, respite.

7310. רְוָיָה **r**e**vâyâh**, *rev-aw-yaw'*; from 7301; *satisfaction*:—runneth over, wealthy.

7311. רוּם **rûwm**, *room*; a prim. root; to *be high* act. to *rise* or *raise* (in various applications, lit. or fig.):—bring up, exalt (self), extol, give, go up, haughty, heave (up), (be, lift up on, make on, set up on, too) high (-er, one), hold up, levy, lift (-er) up, (be) lofty, (× a-) loud, mount up, offer (up), + presumptuously, (be) promote (-ion), proud, set up, tall (-er), take (away, off, up), breed worms.

7312. רוּם **rûwm**, *room*; or

רֻם **rûm**, *room*; from 7311; (lit.) *elevation* or (fig.) *elation*:—haughtiness, height, × high.

7313. רוּם **rûwm** (Chald.), *room*; corresp. to 7311; (fig. only):—extol, lift up (self), set up.

7314. רוּם **rûwm** (Chald.), *room*; from 7313; (lit.) *altitude*:—height.

7315. רוֹם **rôwm**, *rome*; from 7311; *elevation*, i.e. (adv.) *aloft*:—on high.

7316. רוּמָה **Rûwmâh**, *roo-maw'*; from 7311; *height*; *Rumah*, a place in Pal.:—Rumah.

7317. רוֹמָה **rôwmâh**, *ro-maw'*; fem. of 7315; *elation*, i.e. (adv.) *proudly*:—haughtily.

7318. רוֹמָם **rôwmâm**, *ro-mawm'*; from 7426; *exaltation*, i.e. (fig. and spec.) *praise*:—be extolled.

7319. רוֹמְמָה **rôwm**e**mâh**, *ro-mem-aw'*; fem. act. part. of 7426; *exaltation*, i.e. *praise*:—high.

7320. רוֹמַמְתִּי עֶזֶר **Rôwmamtîy 'Ezer** (or

רֹמַמְתִּי **Rômamtîy**), *ro-mam'-tee eh'-zer*; from 7311 and 5828; *I have raised* up a *help*; *Romamti-Ezer*, an Isr.:—Romamti-ezer.

7321. רוּעַ **rûwa'**, *roo-ah'*; a prim. root; to *mar* (espec. by breaking); fig. to *split* the ears (with sound), i.e. *shout* (for alarm or joy):—blow an alarm, cry (alarm, aloud, out), destroy, make a joyful noise, smart, shout (for joy), sound an alarm, triumph.

7322. רוּף **rûwph**, *roof*; a prim. root; prop. to *triturate* (in a mortar), i.e. (fig.) to *agitate* (by concussion):—tremble.

7323. רוּץ **rûwts**, *roots*; a prim. root; to *run* (for whatever reason, espec. to *rush*):—break down, divide speedily, footman, guard, bring hastily, (make) run (away, through), post, stretch out.

7324. רוּק **rûwq**, *rook*; a prim. root; to *pour* out (lit. or fig.), i.e. *empty*:— × arm, cast out, draw (out), (make) empty, pour forth (out).

7325. רוּר **rûwr**, *roor*; a prim. root; to *slaver* (with spittle), i.e. (by analogy) to *emit* a fluid (ulcerous or natural):—run.

7326. רוּשׁ **rûwsh**, *roosh*; a prim. root; to *be destitute*:—lack, needy, (make self) poor (man).

רוֹשׁ **rôwsh**. See 7219.

7327. רוּת **Rûwth**, *rooth*; prob. for 7468; *friend*; *Ruth*, a Moabitess:—Ruth.

7328. רָז **râz** (Chald.), *rawz*; from an unused root prob. mean. to *attenuate*, i.e. (fig.) *hide*; a *mystery*:—secret.

7329. רָזָה **râzâh**, *raw-zaw'*; a prim. root; to *emaciate*, i.e. *make* (*become*) *thin* (lit. or fig.):—famish, wax lean.

7330. רָזֶה **râzeh**, *raw-zeh'*; from 7329; *thin*:—lean.

7331. רְזוֹן **R**e**zôwn**, *rez-one'*; from 7336; *prince*; *Rezon*, a Syrian:—Rezon.

7332. רָזוֹן **râzôwn**, *raw-zone'*; from 7329; *thinness*:—leanness, × scant.

7333. רָזוֹן **râzôwn**, *raw-zone'*; from 7336; a *dignitary*:—prince.

7334. רָזִי **râzîy**, *raw-zee'*; from 7329; *thinness*:—leanness.

7335. רָזַם **râzam**, *raw-zam'*; a prim. root; to *twinkle* the eye (in mockery):—wink.

7336. רָזַן **râzan**, *raw-zan'*; a prim. root; prob. to be *heavy*, i.e. (fig.) *honorable*:—prince, ruler.

7337. רָחַב **râchab**, *raw-khab'*; a prim. root; to *broaden* (intrans. or trans., lit. or fig.):—be an en- (make) large (-ing), make room, make (open) wide.

7338. רַחַב **rachab**, *rakh'-ab*; from 7337; a *width*:—breadth, broad place.

7339. רְחֹב **rechôb**, *rekh-obe'*; or

רְחוֹב **rechôwb**, *rekh-obe'*; from 7337; a *width*, i.e. (concr.) *avenue* or *area*:—broad place (way), street. See also 1050.

7340. רְחֹב **Rechôb**, *rekh-obe'*; or

רְחוֹב **Rechôwb**, *rekh-obe'*; the same as 7339; *Rechob*, the name of a place in Syria, also of a Syrian and an Isr.:—Rehob.

7341. רֹחַב **rôchab**, *ro'-khab*; from 7337; *width* (lit. or fig.):—breadth, broad, largeness, thickness, wideness.

7342. רָחָב **râchâb**, *raw-khawb'*; from 7337; *roomy*, in any (or every) direction, lit. or fig.:—broad, large, at liberty, proud, wide.

7343. רָחָב **Râchâb**, *raw-khawb'*; the same as 7342; *proud*; *Rachab*, a Canaanitess:—Rahab.

7344. רְחֹבוֹת **Rechôbôwth**, *rekh-o-bōth'*; or

רְחֹבֹת **Rechôbôth**, *rekh-o-bōth'*; plur. of 7339; *streets*; *Rechoboth*, a place in Assyria and one in Pal.:—Rehoboth.

7345. רְחַבְיָה **Rechabyâh**, *rekh-ab-yaw'*; or

רְחַבְיָהוּ **Rechabyâhûw**, *rekh-ab-yaw'-hoo*; from 7337 and 3050; *Jah has enlarged*; *Rechabjah*, an Isr.:—Rehabiah.

7346. רְחַבְעָם **Rechabʻâm**, *rekh-ab-awm'*; from 7337 and 5971; a *people has enlarged*; *Rechabam*, an Isr. king:—Rehoboam.

רְחֹבֹת **Rechôbôth**. See 7344.

7347. רֵחֶה **rêcheh**, *ray-kheh'*; from an unused root mean. to *pulverize*; a *mill*-stone:—mill (stone).

רְחוֹב **Rechôwb**. See 7339, 7340.

7348. רְחוּם **Rechûwm**, *rekh-oom'*; a form of 7349; *Rechum*, the name of a Pers. and of three Isr.:—Rehum.

7349. רַחוּם **rachûwm**, *rakh-oom'*; from 7355; *compassionate*:—full of compassion, merciful.

7350. רָחוֹק **râchôwq**, *raw-khoke'*; or

רָחֹק **râchôq**, *raw-khoke'*; from 7368; *remote*, lit. or fig., of place or time; spec. *precious*; often used adv. (with prep.):—(a-) far (abroad, off), long ago, of old, space, great while to come.

7351. רְחִיט° **rechîyṭ**, *rekh-eet'*; from the same as 7298; a *panel* (as resembling a *trough*):—rafter.

7352. רַחִיק **rachîyq** (Chald.), *rakh-eek'*; corresp. to 7350:—far.

7353. רָחֵל **râchêl**, *raw-khale'*; from an unused root mean. to *journey*; a *ewe* [the *females* being the predominant element of a flock] (as a good *traveller*):—ewe, sheep.

7354. רָחֵל **Râchêl**, *raw-khale'*; the same as 7353; *Rachel*, a wife of Jacob:—Rachel.

7355. רָחַם **râcham**, *raw-kham'*; a prim. root; to *fondle*; by impl. to *love*, espec. to *compassionate*:—have compassion (on, upon), love, (find, have, obtain, shew) mercy (-iful, on, upon), (have) pity, Ruhamah, × surely.

7356. רַחַם **racham**, *rakh'-am*; from 7355; *compassion* (in the plur.); by extens. the *womb* (as *cherishing* the fœtus); by impl. a *maiden*:—bowels, compassion, damsel, tender love, (great, tender) mercy, pity, womb.

7357. רַחַם **Racham**, *rakh'-am*; the same as 7356; *pity*; *Racham*, an Isr.:—Raham.

7358. רֶחֶם **rechem**, *rekh'-em*; from 7355; the *womb* [comp. 7356]:—matrix, womb.

7359. רְחֵם **rechêm** (Chald.), *rekh-ame'*; corresp. to 7356; (plur.) *pity*:—mercy.

7360. רָחָם **râchâm**, *raw-khawm'*; or (fem.)

רָחָמָה **râchâmâh**, *raw-khaw-maw'*; from 7355; a kind of *vulture* (supposed to be *tender* towards its young):—gier-eagle.

7361. רַחֲמָה **rachămâh**, *rakh-am-aw'*; fem. of 7356; a *maiden*:—damsel.

7362. רַחְמָנִי **rachmânîy**, *rakh-maw-nee'*; from 7355; *compassionate*:—pitiful.

7363. רָחַף **râchaph**, *raw-khaf'*; a prim. root; to *brood*, by impl. to *be relaxed*:—flutter, move, shake.

7364. רָחַץ **râchats**, *raw-khats'*; a prim. root; to *lave* (the whole or a part of a thing):—bathe (self), wash (self).

7365. רְחַץ **rechats** (Chald.), *rekh-ats'*; corresp. to 7364 [prob. through the accessory idea of *ministering* as a servant at the bath]; to *attend* upon:—trust.

7366. רַחַץ **rachats**, *rakh'-ats*; from 7364; a *bath*:—wash[-pot].

7367. רַחְצָה **rachtsâh**, *rakh-tsaw'*; fem. of 7366; a *bathing* place:—washing.

7368. רָחַק **râchaq**, *raw-khak'*; a prim. root; to *widen* (in any [direction], i.e. (intrans.) *recede* or (trans.) *remove* (lit. or fig., of place or relation):—(a-, be, cast, drive, get, go, keep [self], put, remove, be too, [wander], withdraw) far (away, off), loose, × refrain, very, (be) a good way (off).

7369. רָחֵק **râchêq**, *raw-khake'*; from 7368; *remote*:—that are far.

רָחֹק **râchôq**. See 7350.

7370. רָחַשׁ **râchash**, *raw-khash'*; a prim. root; to *gush*:—indite.

7371. רַחַת **rachath**, *rakh'-ath*; from 7306; a *winnowing*-fork (as *blowing* the chaff away):—shovel.

7372. רָטַב **râṭab**, *raw-tab'*; a prim. root; to *be moist*:—be wet.

7373. רָטֹב **râṭôb**, *raw-tobe'*; from 7372; *moist* (with sap):—green.

7374. רֶטֶט **reṭeṭ**, *reh'-tet*; from an unused root mean. to *tremble*; *terror*:—fear.

7375. רֻטֲפַשׁ **rûwṭaphash**, *roo-taf-ash'*; a root compounded from 7373 and 2954; to *be rejuvenated*:—be fresh.

7376. רָטַשׁ **râṭash**, *raw-tash'*; a prim. root; to *dash* down:—dash (in pieces).

7377. רִי **rîy**, *ree*; from 7301; *irrigation*, i.e. a *shower*:—watering.

7378. רִיב **rîyb**, *reeb*; or

רוּב° **rûwb**, *roob*; a prim. root; prop. to *toss*, i.e. *grapple*; mostly fig. to *wrangle*, i.e. *hold a controversy*; (by impl.) to *defend*:—adversary, chide, complain, contend, debate, × ever, × lay wait, plead, rebuke, strive, × thoroughly.

7379. רִיב **rîyb**, *reeb*; or

רִב **rîb**, *reeb*; from 7378; a *contest* (personal or legal):— + adversary, cause, chiding, contend (-tion), controversy, multitude [*from the marg.*], pleading, strife, strive (-ing), suit.

7380. רִיבַי **Rîybay**, *ree-bah'ee*; from 7378; *contentious*; *Ribai*, an Isr.:—Ribai.

7381. רֵיחַ **rêyach**, *ray'-akh*; from 7306; *odor* (as if *blown*):—savour, scent, smell.

7382. רֵיחַ **rêyach** (Chald.), *ray'-akh*; corresp. to 7381:—smell.

רֵים **rêym**. See 7214.

רֵיעַ **rêyaʻ**. See 7453.

7383. רִיפָה **rîyphâh**, *ree-faw'*; or

רִפָה **rîphâh**, *ree-faw'*; from 7322; (only plur.), *grits* (as *pounded*):—ground corn, wheat.

7384. רִיפַת **Rîyphath**, *ree-fath'*; or (prob. by orth. error)

דִּיפַת **Dîyphath**, *dee-fath'*; of for. or *Riphath*, a grandson of Japheth an his desc.:—Riphath.

7385. רִיק **rîyq**, *reek*; from 7324; *emptiness*; fig. a *worthless* thing; adv. *in vain*:—empty, to no purpose, (in) vain (thing), vanity.

7386. רֵיק **rêyq**, *rake*; or (shorter)

רֵק **rêq**, *rake*; from 7324; *empty*; fig. *worthless*:—emptied (-ty), vain (fellow, man).

7387. רֵיקָם **rêyqâm**, *ray-kawm'*; from 7386; *emptily*; fig. (obj.) *ineffectually*, (subj.) *undeservedly*:—without cause, empty, in vain, void.

7388. רִיר **rîyr**, *reer*; from 7325; *saliva*; by resemblance *broth*:—spittle, white [of an egg].

7389. רֵישׁ **rêysh**, *raysh*; or

רֵאשׁ **rê'sh**, *raysh*; or

רִישׁ **rîysh**, *reesh*; from 7326; *poverty*:—poverty.

7390. רַךְ **rak**, *rak*; from 7401; *tender* (lit. or fig.); by impl. *weak*:—faint [-hearted], soft, tender ([-hearted], one), weak.

7391. רֹךְ **rôk**, *roke*; from 7401; *softness* (fig.):—tenderness.

7392. רָכַב **râkab**, *raw-kab'*; a prim. root; to *ride* (on an animal or in a vehicle); caus. to *place upon* (for riding or gen.), to *despatch*:—bring (on [horse-] back), carry, get [oneself] up, on [horse-] back, put, (cause to, make to) ride (in a chariot, on, -r), set.

7393. רֶכֶב **rekeb**, *reh'-keb*; from 7392; a *vehicle*; by impl. a *team*; by extens. *cavalry*; by analogy a *rider*, i.e. the upper millstone:—chariot, (upper) millstone, multitude [*from the marg.*], wagon.

7394. רֵכָב **Rêkâb**, *ray-kawb'*; from 7392; *rider*; *Rekab*, the name of two Arabs and of two Isr.:—Rechab.

7395. רַכָּב **rakkâb**, *rak-kawb'*; from 7392; a *charioteer*:—chariot man, driver of a chariot, horseman.

7396. רִכְבָּה **rikbâh**, *rik-baw'*; fem. of 7393; a *chariot* (collect.):—chariots.

7397. רֵכָה **Rêkâh**, *ray-kaw'*; prob. fem. from 7401; *softness*; *Rekah*, a place in Pal.:—Rechah.

7398. רְכוּב **rekûwb**, *rek-oob'*; from pass. part. of 7392; a *vehicle* (as *ridden* on):—chariot.

7399. רְכוּשׁ **rekûwsh**, *rek-oosh'*; or

רְכֻשׁ **rekûsh**, *rek-oosh'*; from pass. part. of 7408; *property* (as *gathered*):—good, riches, substance.

7400. רָכִיל **râkîyl**, *raw-keel'*; from 7402; a *scandal-monger* (as *travelling* about):—slander, carry tales, talebearer.

7401. רָכַךְ **râkak**, *raw-kak'*; a prim. root; to *soften* (intrans. or trans.), used fig.:—(be) faint ([-hearted]), mollify, (be, make) soft (-er), be tender.

7402. רָכַל **râkal**, *raw-kal'*; a prim. root; to *travel* for trading:—(spice) merchant.

7403. רָכָל **Râkâl**, *raw-kawl'*; from 7402; *merchant*; *Rakal*, a place in Pal.:—Rachal.

7404. רְכֻלָּה **rekullâh**, *rek-ool-law'*; fem. pass. part. of 7402; *trade* (as *peddled*):—merchandise, traffic.

7405. רָכַס **râkaç**, *raw-kas'*; a prim. root; to *tie*:—bind.

7406. רֶכֶס **rekeç**, *reh'-kes*; from 7405; a *mountain ridge* (as of *tied* summits):—rough place.

7407. רֹכֶס **rôkeç**, *ro'-kes*; from 7405; a *snare* (as of *tied* meshes):—pride.

7408. רָכַשׁ **râkash**, *raw-kash'*; a prim. root; to *lay up*, i.e. collect:—gather, get.

7409. רֶכֶשׁ **rekesh**, *reh'-kesh*; from 7408; a *relay* of animals on a post-route (as *stored up* for that purpose); by impl. a *courser*:—dromedary, mule, swift beast.

רְכֻשׁ **rekûsh**. See 7399.

רֵם **rêm**. See 7214.

410. רָם **Râm**, *rawm;* act. part. of 7311; *high; Ram*, the name of an Arabian and of an r.:—Ram. See also 1027.

רוּם **rûm**. See 7311.

411. רָמָה **râmâh**, *raw-maw';* a prim. root; to *hurl;* spec. to *shoot;* fig. to *delude* or *etray* (as if causing to fall):—beguile, betray, [bow-] an, carry, deceive, throw.

412. רְמָה **remâh** (Chald.), *rem-aw';* corresp. to 7411; to *throw, set,* (fig.) *assess:*—cast own), impose.

413. רָמָה **râmâh**, *raw-maw';* fem. act. part. of 7311; a *height* (as a seat of idolatry):—gh place.

414. רָמָה **Râmâh**, *raw-maw';* the same as 7413; *Ramah*, the name of four places Pal.:—Ramah.

415. רִמָּה **rimmâh**, *rim-maw';* from 7426 in the sense of *breeding* [comp. 7311]; a *mag-t* (as rapidly *bred*), lit. or fig.:—worm.

416. רִמּוֹן **rimmôwn**, *rim-mone';* or

רִמֹּן **rimmôn**, *rim-mone';* from 7426; a *pomegranate*, the tree (from its *upright* owth) or the fruit (also an artificial ornament):—omegranate.

417. רִמּוֹן **Rimmôwn**, *rim-mone';* or (shorter)

רִמֹּן **Rimmôn**, *rim-mone';* or

רִמּוֹנוֹ **Rimmôwnôw** (1 Chron. 6 : 62 [77]), *rim-mo-no';* the same as 7416; *immon*, the name of a Syrian deity, also of five aces in Pal :—Remmon, Rimmon. The addition methoar" (Josh. 19 : 13) is

הַמְּתֹאָר **ham-methô'âr**, *ham-meth-o-awr';* pass. part. of 8388 with the t.; *the* (one) *marked off*, i.e. *which pertains;* mis-ken for part of the name.

רָמוֹת **Râmôwth**. See 7418, 7433.

418. רָמוֹת־נֶגֶב **Râmôwth-Negeb**, *raw-mōth-neh'-gheb;* or

רָמַת נֶגֶב **Râmath Negeb**, *raw'-math neh'-gheb;* from the plur. or con-ruct. of 7413 and 5045; *heights* (or *height*) *of* the *uth; Ramoth-Negeb* or *Ramath-Negeb*, a place in d.:—south Ramoth, Ramath of the south.

419. רָמוּת **râmûwth**, *raw-mooth';* from 7311; a *heap* (of carcases):—height.

420. רֹמַח **rômach**, *ro'-makh;* from an unused root mean. to *hurl;* a *lance* (as *thrown*); pec. the iron *point:*—buckler, javelin, lancet, spear.

421. רַמִּי **rammîy**, *ram-mee';* for 761; a *Ramite*, i.e. Aramæan:—Syrian.

422. רַמְיָה **Ramyâh**, *ram-yaw';* from 7311 and 3050; *Jah has raised; Ramjah*, an r.:—Ramiah.

423. רְמִיָּה **remîyâh**, *rem-ee-yaw';* from 7411; *remissness, treachery:*—deceit (-ful, lly), false, guile, idle, slack, slothful.

424. רַמָּךְ **rammâk**, *ram-mawk';* of for. or.; a brood *mare:*—dromedary.

425. רְמַלְיָהוּ **Remalyâhûw**, *rem-al-yaw'-hoo;* from an unused root and 3050 (perh. ean. to *deck*); *Jah has bedecked; Remaljah*, an Isr.:—emaliah.

426. רָמַם **râmam**, *raw-mam';* a prim. root; to *rise* (lit. or fig.):—exalt, get [oneself] up, t up (self), mount up.

427. רֹמֵמֻת **rômêmûth**, *ro-may-mooth';* from the act. part. of 7426; *exaltation:*—ting up of self.

רִמֹּן **rimmôn**. See 7416.

428. רִמֹּן פֶּרֶץ **Rimmôn Perets**, *rim-mone' peh'-rets;* from 7416 and 6556; *omegranate of the breach; Rimmon-Perets*, a place the Desert:—Rimmon-parez.

429. רָמַס **râmaç**, *raw-mas';* a prim. root; to *tread* upon (as a potter, in walking or ousively):—oppressor, stamp upon, trample (under et), tread (down, upon).

7430. רָמַשׂ **râmas**, *raw-mas';* a prim. root; prop. to *glide* swiftly, i.e. to *crawl* or *move* with short steps; by analogy to *swarm:*—creep, move.

7431. רֶמֶשׂ **remes**, *reh'-mes;* from 7430; a *reptile* or any other rapidly moving animal:—that creepeth, creeping (moving) thing.

7432. רֶמֶת **Remeth**, *reh'-meth;* from 7411; *height; Remeth*, a place in Pal.:—Remeth.

7433. רָמֹת (or רָאמוֹת **Râmôwth**) גִּלְעָד **Râmôth Gilʻâd** (2 Chron. 22 : 5), *raw-mōth' gil-awd';* from the plur. of 7413 and 1568; *heights of Gilad; Ramoth-Gilad*, a place E. of the Jordan:—Ramoth-gilead, Ramoth in Gilead. See also 7216.

7434. רָמַת הַמִּצְפֶּה **Râmath ham-Mitspeh**, *raw-math' ham-mits-peh';* from 7413 and 4707 with the art. interp.; *height of the watch-*tower; *Ramath-ham-Mitspeh*, a place in Pal.:—Ramath-mizpeh.

7435. רָמָתִי **Râmâthîy**, *raw-maw-thee';* patron. of 7414; a *Ramathite* or inhab. of Ramah:—Ramathite.

7436. רָמָתַיִם צוֹפִים **Râmâthayim Tsôwphîym**, *raw-maw-thah'-yim tso-feem';* from the dual of 7413 and the plur. of the act. part. of 6822; *double height of watchers; Ramathajim-Tsophim*, a place in Pal.:—Ramathaim-zophim.

7437. רָמַת לֶחִי **Râmath Lechîy**, *raw'-math lekh'-ee;* from 7413 and 3895; *height of a jaw-bone; Ramath-Lechi*, a place in Pal.:—Ramath-lehi.

רָן **Rân**. See 1028.

7438. רֹן **rôn**, *rone;* from 7442; a *shout* (of deliverance):—song.

7439. רָנָה **rânâh**, *raw-naw';* a prim. root; to *whiz:*—rattle.

7440. רִנָּה **rinnâh**, *rin-naw';* from 7442; prop. a *creaking* (or shrill sound), i.e. *shout* (of joy or grief):—cry, gladness, joy, proclamation, rejoicing, shouting, sing (-ing), triumph.

7441. רִנָּה **Rinnâh**, *rin-naw';* the same as 7440; *Rinnah*, an Isr.:—Rinnah.

7442. רָנַן **rânan**, *raw-nan';* a prim. root; prop. to *creak* (or emit a stridulous sound), i.e. to *shout* (usually for joy):—aloud for joy, cry out, be joyful, (greatly, make to) rejoice, (cause to) shout (for joy), (cause to) sing (aloud, for joy, out), triumph.

7443. רֶנֶן **renen**, *reh'-nen;* from 7442; an *ostrich* (from its *wail*):—× goodly.

7444. רַנֵּן **rannên**, *ran-nane';* intens. from 7442; *shouting* (for joy):—singing.

7445. רְנָנָה **renânâh**, *ren-aw-naw';* from 7442; a *shout* (for joy):—joyful (voice), singing, triumphing.

7446. רִסָּה **Riççâh**, *ris-saw';* from 7450; a *ruin* (as *dripping* to pieces); *Rissah*, a place in the Desert:—Rissah.

7447. רָסִיס **râçîyç**, *raw-sees';* from 7450; prop. *dripping* to pieces, i.e. a *ruin;* also a dew-*drop:*—breach, drop.

7448. רֶסֶן **reçen**, *reh'-sen;* from an unused root mean. to *curb;* a *halter* (as *restraining*); by impl. the *jaw:*—bridle.

7449. רֶסֶן **Reçen**, *reh'-sen;* the same as 7448; *Resen*, a place in Ass.:—Resen.

7450. רָסַס **râçaç**, *raw-sas';* a prim. root; to *comminute;* used only as denom. from 7447, to *moisten* (with drops):—temper.

7451. רַע **raʻ**, *rah;* from 7489; *bad* or (as noun) *evil* (nat. or mor.):—adversity, affliction, bad, calamity, + displease (-ure), distress, evil ([-favouredness], man, thing), + exceedingly, × great, grief (-vous), harm, heavy, hurt (-ful), ill (favoured), + mark, mischief (-vous), misery, naught (-ty), noisome, + not please, sad (-ly), sore, sorrow, trouble, vex, wicked (-ly, -ness, one), worse (-st), wretchedness, wrong. [Incl. fem. רָעָה **râʻâh**; as adj. or noun.]

7452. רֵעַ **rêaʻ**, *ray'-ah;* from 7321; a *crash* (of thunder), *noise* (of war), *shout* (of joy):—× aloud, noise, shouted.

7453. רֵעַ **rêaʻ**, *ray'-ah;* or

רֵיעַ **rêyaʻ**, *ray'-ah;* from 7462; an *associate* (more or less close):—brother, companion, fellow, friend, husband, lover, neighbour, × (an-) other.

7454. רֵעַ **rêaʻ**, *ray'-ah;* from 7462; a *thought* (as *association* of ideas):—thought.

7455. רֹעַ **rôaʻ**, *ro'-ah;* from 7489; *badness* (as *marring*), phys. or mor.:—× be so bad, badness, (× be so) evil, naughtiness, sadness, sorrow, wickedness.

7456. רָעֵב **râʻêb**, *raw-abe';* a prim. root; to *hunger:*—(suffer to) famish, (be, have, suffer, suffer to) hunger (-ry).

7457. רָעֵב **râʻêb**, *raw-abe';* from 7456; *hungry* (more or less intensely):—hunger bitten, hungry.

7458. רָעָב **râʻâb**, *raw-awb';* from 7456; *hunger* (more or less extensive):—dearth, famine, + famished, hunger.

7459. רְעָבוֹן **reʻâbôwn**, *reh-aw-bone';* from 7456; *famine:*—famine.

7460. רָעַד **râʻad**, *raw-ad';* a prim. root; to *shudder* (more or less violently):—tremble.

7461. רַעַד **raʻad**, *rah'-ad;* or (fem.)

רְעָדָה **reʻâdâh**, *reh-aw-daw';* from 7460; a *shudder:*—fear, trembling.

7462. רָעָה **râʻâh**, *raw-aw';* a prim. root; to *tend* a flock, i.e. *pasture* it; intrans. to *graze* (lit. or fig.); gen. to *rule;* by extens. to *associate* with (as a friend):—× break, companion, keep company with, devour, eat up, evil entreat, feed, use as a friend, make friendship with, herdman, keep [sheep] (-er), pastor, + shearing house, shepherd, wander, waste.

7463. רֵעֶה **rêʻeh**, *ray-eh';* from 7462; a (male) *companion:*—friend.

7464. רֵעָה **rêʻâh**, *ray'-aw;* fem. of 7453; a female *associate:*—companion, fellow.

7465. רֹעָה **rôʻâh**, *ro-aw';* for 7455; *breakage:*—broken, utterly.

7466. רְעוּ **Reʻûw**, *reh-oo';* for 7471 in the sense of 7453; *friend; Reü*, a postdiluvian patriarch:—Reu.

7467. רְעוּאֵל **Reʻûwʼêl**, *reh-oo-ale';* from the same as 7466 and 410; *friend of God; Reüel*, the name of Moses' father-in-law, also of an Edomite and an Isr.:—Raguel, Reuel.

7468. רְעוּת **reʻûwth**, *reh-ooth';* from 7462 in the sense of 7453; a female *associate;* gen. an *additional* one:—+ another, mate, neighbour.

7469. רְעוּת **reʻûwth**, *reh-ooth';* prob. from 7462; a *feeding* upon, i.e. grasping after:—vexation.

7470. רְעוּת **reʻûwth** (Chald.), *reh-ooth';* corresp. to 7469; *desire:*—pleasure, will.

7471. רְעִי **reʻîy**, *reh-ee';* from 7462; *pasture:*—pasture.

7472. רֵעִי **Rêʻîy**, *ray-ee';* from 7453; *social; Reï*, an Isr.:—Rei.

7473. רֹעִי **rôʻîy**, *ro-ee';* from act. part. of 7462; *pastoral;* as noun, a *shepherd:*—shepherd.

7474. רַעְיָה **raʻyâh**, *rah-yaw';* fem. of 7453; a female *associate:*—love.

7475. רַעְיוֹן **raʻyôwn**, *rah-yone';* from 7462 in the sense of 7469; *desire:*—vexation.

7476. רַעְיוֹן **raʻyôwn** (Chald.), *rah-yone';* corresp. to 7475; a *grasp*, i.e. (fig.) mental *conception:*—cogitation, thought.

7477. רָעַל **râʻal**, *raw-al';* a prim. root; to *reel*, i.e. (fig.) to *brandish:*—terribly shake.

7478. רַעַל **raʻal**, *rah'-al;* from 7477; a *reeling* (from intoxication):—trembling.

7479. רַעֲלָה **raʻălâh**, *rah-al-aw';* fem. of 7478; a long *veil* (as *fluttering*):—muffler.

7480. רְעֵלָיָה **Reʻêlâyâh**, *reh-ay-law-yaw';* from 7477 and 3050; *made to tremble* (i.e. *fearful*) *of Jah; Reëlajah*, an Isr.:—Reeliah.

7481. רָעַם **râʻam**, *raw-am';* a prim. root; to *tumble*, i.e. *be* violently *agitated;* spec.

to *crash* (of thunder); fig. to *irritate* (with anger):—make to fret, roar, thunder, trouble.

7482. רַעַם **ra'am**, *rah'-am;* from 7481; a *peal* of thunder:—thunder.

7483. רַעְמָה **ra'mâh**, *rah-maw';* fem. of 7482; the *mane* of a horse (as *quivering* in the wind):—thunder.

7484. רַעְמָה **Ra'mâh**, *rah-maw';* the same as 7483; *Ramah*, the name of a grandson of Ham, and of a place (perh. founded by him):—Raamah.

7485. רַעַמְיָה **Ra'amyâh**, *rah-am-yaw';* from 7481 and 3050; *Jah has shaken; Raamjah*, an Isr.:—Raamiah.

7486. רַעְמְסֵס **Ra'm^eçêç**, *rah-mes-ace';* or

רַעַמְסֵס **Ra'amçêç**, *rah-am-sace';* of Eg. or.; *Rameses* or *Raamses*, a place in Egypt:—Raamses, Rameses.

7487. רַעֲנַן **ra'ânan** (Chald.), *rah-aw-nan';* corresp. to 7488; *green*, i.e. (fig.) *prosperous:*—flourishing.

7488. רַעֲנָן **ra'ănân**, *rah-an-awn';* from an unused root mean. *to be green; verdant;* by anal. *new;* fig. *prosperous:*—green, flourishing.

7489. רָעַע **râ'a'**, *raw-ah';* a prim. root; prop. to *spoil* (lit. by *breaking* to pieces); fig. to *make* (or *be*) *good for nothing*, i.e. *bad* (phys., soc. or mor.):—afflict, associate selves [*by mistake for* 7462], break (down, in pieces), + displease, (be, bring, do) evil (doer, entreat, man), show self friendly [*by mistake for* 7462], do harm, (do) hurt, (behave self, deal) ill, × indeed, do mischief, punish, still, vex, (do) wicked (doer, -ly), be (deal, do) worse.

7490. רְעַע **r^e'a'** (Chald.), *reh-ah';* corresp. to 7489:—break, bruise.

7491. רָעַף **râ'aph**, *raw-af';* a prim. root; to *drip:*—distil, drop (down).

7492. רָעַץ **râ'ats**, *raw-ats';* a prim. root; to *break* in pieces; fig. *harass:*—dash in pieces, vex.

7493. רָעַשׁ **râ'ash**, *raw-ash;* a prim. root; to *undulate* (as the earth, the sky, etc.; also a field of grain), partic. through fear; spec. to *spring* (as a locust):—make afraid, (re-) move, quake, (make to) shake, (make to) tremble.

7494. רַעַשׁ **ra'ash**, *rah'-ash;* from 7493; *vibration, bounding, uproar:*—commotion, confused noise, earthquake, fierceness, quaking, rattling, rushing, shaking.

7495. רָפָא **râphâ'**, *raw-faw';* or

רָפָה **râphâh**, *raw-faw';* a prim. root; prop. to *mend* (by stitching), i.e. (fig.) to *cure:*—cure, (cause to) heal, physician, repair, × thoroughly, make whole. See 7503.

7496. רָפָא **râphâ'**, *raw-faw';* from 7495 in the sense of 7503; prop. *lax*, i.e. (fig.) a *ghost* (as *dead;* in plur. only):—dead, deceased.

7497. רָפָא **râphâ'**, *raw-faw';* or

רָפָה **râphâh**, *raw-faw';* from 7495 in the sense of *invigorating;* a *giant:*—giant, Rapha, Rephaim (-s). See also 1051.

7498. רָפָא **Râphâ'**, *raw-faw';* or

רָפָה **Râphâh**, *raw-faw';* prob. the same as 7497; *giant; Rapha* or *Raphah*, the name of two Isr.:—Rapha.

7499. רְפֻאָה **r^ephû'âh**, *ref-oo-aw';* fem. pass. part. of 7495; a *medicament:*—heal [-ed], medicine.

7500. רִפְאוּת **riph'ûwth**, *rif-ooth';* from 7495; a *cure:*—health.

7501. רְפָאֵל **R^ephâ'êl**, *ref-aw-ale';* from 7495 and 410; *God has cured; Rephaël*, an Isr.:—Rephael.

7502. רָפַד **râphad**, *raw-fad';* a prim. root; to *spread* (a bed); by impl. to *refresh:*—comfort, make [a bed], spread.

7503. רָפָה **râphâh**, *raw-faw';* a prim. root; to *slacken* (in many applications, lit. or fig.):—abate, cease, consume, draw [toward evening], fail, (be) faint, be (wax) feeble, forsake, idle, leave, let alone (go, down), (be) slack, stay, be still, be slothful, (be) weak (-en). See 7495.

7504. רָפֶה **râpheh**, *raw-feh';* from 7503; *slack* (in body or mind):—weak.

רָפָה **râphâh**, **Râphâh**. See 7497, 7498.

רִפָּה **riphâh**. See 7383.

7505. רָפוּא **Râphûw'**, *raw-foo';* pass. part. of 7495; *cured; Raphu*, an Isr.:—Raphu.

7506. רֶפַח **Rephach**, *reh'-fakh;* from an unused root appar. mean. to *sustain; support; Rephach*, an Isr.:—Rephah.

7507. רְפִידָה **r^ephîydâh**, *ref-ee-daw';* from 7502; a *railing* (as *spread* along):—bottom.

7508. רְפִידִים **R^ephîydîym**, *ref-ee-deem';* plur. of the masc. of the same as 7507; *ballusters; Rephidim*, a place in the Desert:—Rephidim.

7509. רְפָיָה **R^ephâyâh**, *ref-aw-yaw';* from 7495 and 3050; *Jah has cured; Rephajah*, the name of five Isr.:—Rephaiah.

7510. רִפְיוֹן **riphyôwn**, *rif-yone';* from 7503; *slackness:*—feebleness.

7511. רָפַס **râphaç**, *raw-fas';* a prim. root; to *trample*, i.e. *prostrate:*—humble self, submit self.

7512. רְפַס **r^ephaç** (Chald.), *ref-as';* corresp. to 7511:—stamp.

7513. רַפְסֹדָה **raphçôdâh**, *raf-so-daw';* from 7511; a *raft* (as *flat* on the water):—flote.

7514. רָפַק **râphaq**, *raw-fak';* a prim. root; to *recline:*—lean.

7515. רָפַשׂ **râphas**, *raw-fas';* a prim. root; to *trample*, i.e. *roil* water:—foul, trouble.

7516. רֶפֶשׁ **rephesh**, *reh'-fesh;* from 7515; *mud* (as *roiled*):—mire.

7517. רֶפֶת **repheth**, *reh'-feth;* prob. from 7503; a *stall* for cattle (from their *resting* there):—stall.

7518. רַץ **rats**, *rats;* contr. from 7533; a *fragment:*—piece.

7519. רָצָא **râtsâ'**, *raw-tsaw';* a prim. root; to *run;* also to *delight* in:—accept, run.

7520. רָצַד **râtsad**, *raw-tsad';* a prim. root; prob. to *look askant*, i.e. (fig.) *be jealous:*—leap.

7521. רָצָה **râtsâh**, *raw-tsaw';* a prim. root; to *be pleased with;* spec. to *satisfy* a debt:—(be) accept (-able), accomplish, set affection, approve, consent with, delight (self), enjoy, (be, have a) favour (-able), like, observe, pardon, (be, have, take) please (-ure), reconcile self.

7522. רָצוֹן **râtsôwn**, *raw-tsone';* or

רָצֹן **râtsôn**, *raw-tsone';* from 7521; *delight* (espec. as shown):—(be) acceptable (-ance, -ed), delight, desire, favour, (good) pleasure, (own, self, voluntary) will, as . . . (what) would.

7523. רָצַח **râtsach**, *raw-tsakh';* a prim. root; prop. to *dash* in pieces, i.e. *kill* (a human being), espec. to *murder:*—put to death, kill, (man-) slay (-er), murder (-er).

7524. רֶצַח **retsach**, *reh'-tsakh;* from 7523; a *crushing;* spec. a *murder-cry:*—slaughter, sword.

7525. רִצְיָא **Ritsyâ'**, *rits-yaw';* from 7521; *delight; Ritsjah*, an Isr.:—Rezia.

7526. רְצִין **R^etsîyn**, *rets-een';* prob. for 7522; *Retsin*, the name of a Syrian and of an Isr.:—Rezin.

7527. רָצַע **râtsa'**, *raw-tsah';* a prim. root; to *pierce:*—bore.

7528. רָצַף **râtsaph**, *raw-tsaf';* a denom. from 7529; to *tessellate*, i.e. embroider (as if with bright stones):—pave.

7529. רֶצֶף **retseph**, *reh'-tsef;* for 7565; a red-hot *stone* (for baking):—coal.

7530. רֶצֶף **Retseph**, *reh'-tsef;* the same as 7529; *Retseph*, a place in Ass.:—Rezeph.

7531. רִצְפָּה **ritspâh**, *rits-paw';* fem. of 7529; a hot *stone;* also a tessellated *pavement:*—live coal, pavement.

7532. רִצְפָּה **Ritspâh**, *rits-paw';* the same as 7531; *Ritspah*, an Israelitess:—Rizpah.

7533. רָצַץ **râtsats**, *raw-tsats';* a prim. root; to *crack* in pieces, lit. or fig.:—break, bruise, crush, discourage, oppress, struggle together.

7534. רַק **raq**, *rak;* from 7556 in its orig. sense; *emaciated* (as if *flattened* out):—lean ([-fleshed]), thin.

7535. רַק **raq**, *rak;* the same as 7534 as a noun; prop. *leanness*, i.e. (fig.) limitation; only adv. *merely*, or conj. *although:*—but, even, except, howbeit howsoever, at the least, nevertheless, nothing but, notwithstanding, only, save, so [that], surely, yet (so), in any wise.

7536. רֹק **rôq**, *roke;* from 7556; *spittle:*—spit (-ting, -tle).

7537. רָקַב **râqab**, *raw-kab';* a prim. root; to *decay* (as by worm-eating):—rot.

7538. רָקָב **râqâb**, *raw-kawb';* from 7537; *decay* (by *caries*):—rottenness (thing).

7539. רִקָּבוֹן **riqqâbôwn**, *rik-kaw-bone';* from 7538; *decay* (by *caries*):—rotten.

7540. רָקַד **râqad**, *raw-kad';* a prim. root; prop. to *stamp*, i.e. to *spring* about (wildly or for joy):—dance, jump, leap, skip.

7541. רַקָּה **raqqâh**, *rak-kaw';* fem. of 7534; prop. *thinness*, i.e. the *side* of the head:—temple.

7542. רַקּוֹן **Raqqôwn**, *rak-kone';* from 7534; *thinness; Rakkon*, a place in Pal.:—Rakkon.

7543. רָקַח **râqach**, *raw-kakh';* a prim. root; to *perfume:*—apothecary, compound, make [ointment], prepare, spice.

7544. רֶקַח **reqach**, *reh'-kakh;* from 7543; prop. *perfumery*, i.e. (by impl.) *spicery* (for flavor):—spiced.

7545. רֹקַח **rôqach**, *ro'-kakh;* from 7542; an aromatic:—confection, ointment.

7546. רַקָּח **raqqâch**, *rak-kawkh';* from 7543; a male *perfumer:*—apothecary.

7547. רִקֻּחַ **raqqûach**, *rak-koo'-akh;* from 7543; *scented* substance:—perfume.

7548. רַקָּחָה **raqqâchâh**, *rak-kaw-khaw';* fem. of 7547; a female *perfumer:*—confectioner.

7549. רָקִיעַ **râqîya'**, *raw-kee'-ah;* from 7554; prop. an *expanse*, i.e. the *firmament* or (apparently) visible arch of the sky:—firmament.

7550. רָקִיק **râqîyq**, *raw-keek';* from 7556 in its orig. sense; a thin *cake:*—cake, wafer.

7551. רָקַם **râqam**, *raw-kam';* a prim. root; to *variegate* color, i.e. *embroider;* by impl. to *fabricate:*—embroiderer, needlework, curious work.

7552. רֶקֶם **Reqem**, *reh'-kem;* from 7551; *versi-color; Rekem*, the name of a place in Pal., also of a Midianite and an Isr.:—Rekem.

7553. רִקְמָה **riqmâh**, *rik-maw';* from 7551; *variegation* of color; spec. *embroidery:*—broidered (work), divers colours, (raiment of) needlework (on both sides).

7554. רָקַע **râqa'**, *raw-kah';* a prim. root; to *pound* the earth (as a sign of passion); by analogy to *expand* (by hammering); by impl. to *overlay* (with thin sheets of metal):—beat, make broad, spread abroad (forth, over, out, into plates), stamp, stretch.

7555. רִקֻּעַ **riqqûa'**, *rik-koo'-ah;* from 7554; *beaten* out, i.e. a (metallic) *plate:*—broad.

7556. רָקַק **râqaq**, *raw-kak';* a prim. root; to *spit:*—spit.

7557. רַקַּת **Raqqath**, *rak-kath';* from 7556 in its orig. sense of *diffusing;* a *beach* (as expanded shingle); *Rakkath*, a place in Pal.:—Rakkath.

7558. רִשְׁיוֹן **rîshyôwn**, *rish-yone';* from an unused root mean. to *have leave;* a *permit:*—grant.

7559. רָשַׁם **râsham**, *raw-sham';* a prim. root; to *record:*—note.

7560. רְשַׁם **r^esham** (Chald.), *resh-am';* corresp. to 7559:—sign, write.

7561. רָשַׁע **râsha'**, *raw-shah';* a prim. root; to *be* (caus. *do* or *declare*) *wrong;* by impl.

to *disturb, violate*:—condemn, make trouble, vex, be (commit, deal, depart, do) wicked (-ly, -ness).

7562. רֶשַׁע **reshaʻ**, *reh'-shah*; from 7561; a *wrong* (espec. moral):—iniquity, wicked (-ness).

7563. רָשָׁע **râshâʻ**, *raw-shaw'*; from 7561; morally *wrong*; concr. an (actively) *bad person*:— + condemned, guilty, ungodly, wicked (man), that did wrong.

7564. רִשְׁעָה **rishʻâh**, *rish-aw'*; fem. of 7562; *wrong* (espec. moral):—fault, wickedly (-ness).

7565. רֶשֶׁף **resheph**, *reh'-shef*; from 8313; a live *coal*; by analogy *lightning*; fig. an *arrow* (as *flashing* through the air); spec. *fever*:—arrow, (burning) coal, burning heat, + spark, hot thunderbolt.

7566. רֶשֶׁף **Resheph**, *reh'-shef*; the same as 7565; *Resheph*, an Isr.:—Resheph.

7567. רָשַׁשׁ **râshash**, *raw-shash'*; a prim. root; to *demolish*:—impoverish.

7568. רֶשֶׁת **resheth**, *reh'-sheth*; from 3423; a *net* (as *catching* animals):—net [-work].

7569. רַתּוֹק **rattôwq**, *rat-toke'*; from 7576; a *chain*:—chain.

7570. רָתַח **râthach**, *raw-thakh'*; a prim. root; to *boil*:—boil.

7571. רֶתַח **rethach**, *reh'-thakh*; from 7570; a *boiling*:— × [boil] well.

7572. רַתִּיקָה **rattîyqâh**, *rat-tee-kaw'*; from 7576; a *chain*:—chain.

7573. רָתַם **râtham**, *raw-tham'*; a prim. root; to *yoke* up (to the pole of a vehicle):—bind.

7574. רֶתֶם **rethem**, *reh'-them*; or

רֹתֶם **rôthem**, *ro'-them*; from 7573; the Spanish *broom* (from its pole-like stems):—juniper (tree).

7575. רִתְמָה **Rithmâh**, *rith-maw'*; fem. of 7574; *Rithmah*, a place in the Desert:—Rithmah.

7576. רָתַק **râthaq**, *raw-thak'*; a prim. root; to *fasten*:—bind.

7577. רְתֻקָה **rethûqâh**, *reth-oo-kaw'*; fem. pass. part. of 7576; something *fastened*, i.e. a *chain*:—chain.

7578. רְתֵת **rethêth**, *reth-ayth'*; for 7374; *terror*:—trembling.

ש

7579. שָׁאַב **shâʼab**, *shaw-ab'*; a prim. root; to *bale* up water:—(woman to) draw (-er, water).

7580. שָׁאַג **shâʼag**, *shaw-ag'*; a prim. root; to *rumble* or *moan*:— × mightily, roar.

7581. שְׁאָגָה **sheʼâgâh**, *sheh-aw-gaw'*; from 7580; a *rumbling* or *moan*:—roaring.

7582. שָׁאָה **shâʼâh**, *shaw-aw'*; a prim. root; to *rush*; by impl. to *desolate*:—be desolate, (make a) rush (-ing), (lay) waste.

7583. שָׁאָה **shâʼâh**, *shaw-aw'*; a prim. root [rather ident. with 7582 through the idea of *whirling* to giddiness]; to *stun*, i.e. (intrans.) *be astonished*:—wonder.

7584. שַׁאֲוָה **shaʼăvâh**, *shah-av-aw'*; from 7582; a *tempest* (as *rushing*):—desolation.

7585. שְׁאוֹל **sheʼôwl**, *sheh-ole'*; or

שְׁאֹל **sheʼôl**, *sheh-ole'*; from 7592; *hades* or the world of the dead (as if a *subterranean retreat*), includ. its accessories and inmates:—grave, hell, pit.

7586. שָׁאוּל **Shâʼûwl**, *shaw-ool'*; pass. part. of 7592; *asked*; *Shaül*, the name of an Edomite and two Isr.:—Saul, Shaul.

7587. שָׁאוּלִי **Shâʼûwlîy**, *shaw-oo-lee'*; patron. from 7856; a *Shaülite* or desc. of Shaul:—Shaulites.

7588. שָׁאוֹן **shâʼôwn**, *shaw-one'*; from 7582; *uproar* (as of *rushing*); by impl. *destruction*:— × horrible, noise, pomp, rushing, tumult (× -uous).

7589. שְׁאָט **sheʼâṭ**, *sheh-awt'*; from an unused root mean. to *push* aside; *contempt*:—despite (-ful).

7590. שָׁאט **shâʼṭ**, *shawt*; for act. part. of 7750 [comp. 7589]; one *contemning*:—that (which) despise (-d).

7591. שְׁאִיָּה **sheʼîyâh**, *sheh-ee-yaw'*; from 7582; *desolation*:—destruction.

7592. שָׁאַל **shâʼal**, *shaw-al'*; or

שָׁאֵל **shâʼêl**, *shaw-ale'*; a prim. root; to *inquire*; by impl. to *request*; by extens. to *demand*:—ask (counsel, on), beg, borrow, lay to charge, consult, demand, desire, × earnestly, enquire, + greet, obtain leave, lend, pray, request, require, + salute, × straitly, × surely, wish.

7593. שְׁאֵל **sheʼêl** (Chald.), *sheh-ale'*; corresp. to 7592:—ask, demand, require.

7594. שְׁאָל **Sheʼâl**, *sheh-awl'*; from 7592; *request*; *Sheäl*, an Isr.:—Sheal.

שְׁאֹל **sheʼôl**. See 7585.

7595. שְׁאֵלָא **sheʼêlâʼ** (Chald.), *sheh-ay-law'*; from 7593; prop. a *question* (at law), i.e. judicial *decision* or mandate:—demand.

7596. שְׁאֵלָה **sheʼêlâh**, *sheh-ay-law'*; or

שֵׁלָה **shêlâh** (1 Sam. 1 : 17), *shay-law'*; from 7592; a *petition*; by impl. a *loan*:—loan, petition, request.

7597. שְׁאַלְתִּיאֵל **Sheʼaltîyʼêl**, *sheh-al-tee-ale'*; or

שַׁלְתִּיאֵל **Shaltîyʼêl**, *shal-tee-ale'*; from 7592 and 410; *I have asked God*; *Sheältiël*, an Isr.:—Shalthiel, Shealtiel.

7598. שְׁאַלְתִּיאֵל **Sheʼaltîyʼêl** (Chald.), *sheh-al-tee-ale'*; corresp. to 7597:—Shealtiel.

7599. שָׁאַן **shâʼan**, *shaw-an'*; a prim. root; to *loll*, i.e. *be peaceful*:—be at ease, be quiet rest. See also 1052.

7600. שַׁאֲנָן **shaʼănân**, *shah-an-awn'*; from 7599; *secure*; in a bad sense, *haughty*:—that is at ease, quiet, tumult. Comp. 7946.

7601 שָׁאַס **shâʼaç**, *shaw-as'*; a prim. root; to *plunder*:—spoil.

7602. שָׁאַף **shâʼaph**, *shaw-af'*; a prim. root; to *inhale* eagerly; fig. to *covet*; by impl. to *be angry*; also to *hasten*:—desire (earnestly), devour, haste, pant, snuff up, swallow up.

7603. שְׂאֹר **seʼôr**, *seh-ore'*; from 7604; *barm* or yeast-cake (as *swelling* by fermentation):—leaven.

7604. שָׁאַר **shâʼar**, *shaw-ar'*; a prim. root; prop. to *swell* up, i.e. *be* (caus. *make*) *redundant*:—leave, (be) left, let, remain, remnant, reserve, the rest.

7605. שְׁאָר **sheʼâr**, *sheh-awr'*; from 7604; a *remainder*:— × other, remnant, residue, rest.

7606. שְׁאָר **sheʼâr** (Chald.), *sheh-awr'*; corresp. to 7605:— × whatsoever more, residue, rest.

7607. שְׁאֵר **sheʼêr**, *sheh-ayr'*; from 7604; *flesh* (as *swelling* out), as living or for food; gen. *food* of any kind; fig. *kindred* by blood:—body, flesh, food, (near) kin (-sman, -swoman), near (nigh) [of kin].

7608. שַׁאֲרָה **shaʼărâh**, *shah-ar-aw'*; fem. of 7607; female *kindred* by blood:—near kinswomen.

7609. שֶׁאֱרָה **Sheʼĕrâh**, *sheh-er-aw'*; the same as 7608; *Sheërah*, an Israelitess:—Sherah.

7610. שְׁאָר יָשׁוּב **Sheʼâr Yâshûwb**, *sheh-awr' yaw-shoob'*; from 7605 and 7725; *a remnant will return*; *Sheär-Jashub*, the symbol. name of one of Isaiah's sons:—Shear-jashub.

7611. שְׁאֵרִית **sheʼêrîyth**, *sheh-ay-reeth'*; from 7604; a *remainder* or residual (surviving, final) portion:—that had escaped, be left, posterity, remain (-der), remnant, residue, rest.

7612. שֵׁאת **shêʼth**, *shayth*; from 7582; *devastation*:—desolation.

7613. שְׂאֵת **seʼêth**, *seh-ayth'*; from 5375; an *elevation* or leprous scab; fig. *elation* or cheerfulness; *exaltation* in rank or character:—be accepted, dignity, excellency, highness, raise up self, rising.

7614. שְׁבָא **Shebâʼ**, *sheb-aw'*; of for. or.; *Sheba*, the name of three early progenitors of tribes and of an Ethiopian district:—Sheba, Sabeans.

7615. שְׁבָאִי **Shebâʼîy**, *sheb-aw-ee'*; patron. from 7614; a *Shebaïte* or desc. of Sheba:—Sabean.

7616. שְׁבָב **shâbâb**, *shaw-bawb'*; from an unused root mean. to *break* up; a *fragment*, i.e. *ruin*:—broken in pieces.

7617. שָׁבָה **shâbâh**, *shaw-baw'*; a prim. root; to *transport* into captivity:—(bring away, carry, carry away, lead, lead away, take) captive (-s), drive (take) away.

7618. שְׁבוּ **shebûw**, *sheb-oo'*; from an unused root (prob. ident. with that of 7617 through the idea of *subdivision* into flashes or streamers [comp. 7632]) mean. to *flame*; a *gem* (from its sparkle), prob. the *agate*:—agate.

7619. שְׁבוּאֵל **Shebûwʼêl**, *sheb-oo-ale'*; or

שׁוּבָאֵל **Shûwbâʼêl**, *shoo-baw-ale'*; from 7617 (abbrev.) or 7725 and 410; *captive* (or *returned*) *of God*; *Shebuël* or *Shubaël*, the name of two Isr.:—Shebuel, Shubael.

7620. שָׁבוּעַ **shâbûwaʻ**, *shaw-boo'-ah*; or

שָׁבֻעַ **shâbûaʻ**, *shaw-boo'-ah*; also (fem.)

שְׁבֻעָה **shebûʻâh**, *sheb-oo-aw'*; prop. pass. part. of 7650 as a denom. of 7651; lit. *sevened*, i.e. a *week* (spec. of years):—seven, week.

7621. שְׁבוּעָה **shebûwʻâh**, *sheb-oo-aw'*; fem. pass. part. of 7650; prop. something *sworn*, i.e. an *oath*:—curse, oath, × sworn.

7622. שְׁבוּת **shebûwth**, *sheb-ooth'*; or

שְׁבִית **shebîyth**, *sheb-eeth'*; from 7617; *exile*: concr. *prisoners*; fig. a *former state* of prosperity:—captive (-ity).

7623. שָׁבַח **shâbach**, *shaw-bakh'*; a prim. root; prop. to *address* in a loud tone, i.e. (spec.) *loud*; fig. to *pacify* (as if by words):—commend, glory, keep in, praise, still, triumph.

7624. שְׁבַח **shebach** (Chald.), *sheb-akh'*; corresp. to 7623; to *adulate*, i.e. *adore*:—praise.

7625. שְׁבַט **shebaṭ** (Chald.), *sheb-at'*; corresp. to 7626; a *clan*:—tribe.

7626. שֵׁבֶט **shêbeṭ**, *shay'-bet*; from an unused root prob. mean. to *branch* off; a *scion*, i.e. (lit.) a *stick* (for punishing, writing, fighting, ruling, walking, etc.) or (fig.) a *clan*:— × correction, dart, rod, sceptre, staff, tribe.

7627. שְׁבָט **Shebâṭ**, *sheb-awt'*; of for. or.; *Shebat*, a Jewish month:—Sebat.

7628. שְׁבִי **shebîy**, *sheb-ee'*; from 7618; *exiled*; *captured*; as noun, *exile* (abstr. or concr. and collect.); by extens. *booty*:—captive (-ity), prisoners, × take away, that was taken.

7629. שֹׁבִי **Shôbîy**, *sho-bee'*; from 7617; *captor*; *Shobi*, an Ammonite:—Shobi.

7630. שֹׁבַי **Shôbay**, *sho-bah'ee*; for 7629; *Shobai*, an Isr.:—Shobai.

7631. שְׂבִיב **sebîyb** (Chald.), *seb-eeb'*; corresp. to 7632:—flame.

7632. שָׁבִיב **shâbîyb**, *shaw-beeb'*; from the same as 7616; *flame* (as *split* into tongues):—spark.

7633. שִׁבְיָה **shibyâh**, *shib-yaw'*; fem. of 7628; *exile* (abstr. or concr. and collect.):—captives (-ity).

7634. שָׁבְיָה **Shobyâh**, *shob-yaw'*; fem. of the same as 7629; *captivation*; *Shobjah*, an Isr.:—Shachia [*from the marg.*].

7635. שָׁבִיל **shâbîyl**, *shaw-beel'*; from the same as 7640; a *track* or passage-way (as if *flowing* along):—path.

7636. שָׁבִיס **shâbîyç**, *shaw-beece'*; from an unused root mean. to *interweave*; a *netting* for the hair:—caul.

7637. שְׁבִיעִי **shebîyʻîy**, *sheb-ee-ee'*; or

שְׁבִעִי **shebiʻîy**, *sheb-ee-ee'*; ordinal from 7657; *seventh:*—seventh (time).

שְׁבִית **shebîyth**. See 7622.

7638. שָׂבָךְ **sâbâk**, *saw-bawk'*; from an unused root mean. to *intwine;* a *netting* (ornament to the capital of a column):—net.

שַׂבְּכָא **sabbekâʼ**. See 5443.

7639. שְׂבָכָה **sebâkâh**, *seb-aw-kaw'*; fem. of 7638; a *net-work*, i.e. (in hunting) a *snare*, (in arch.) a *ballustrade;* also a *reticulated* ornament to a pillar:—checker, lattice, network, snare, wreath (-enwork).

7640. שֹׁבֶל **shôbel**, *show'-bel;* from an unused root mean. to *flow;* a lady's *train* (as *trailing* after her):—leg.

7641. שִׁבֹּל **shibbôl**, *shib-bole* ; or (fem.)

שִׁבֹּלֶת **shibbôleth**, *shib-bo'-leth;* from the same as 7640; a *stream* (as *flowing*); also an *ear* of grain (as *growing* out); by anal. a *branch:*—branch, channel, ear (of corn), ([water-]) flood, Shibboleth. Comp. 5451.

7642. שַׁבְלוּל **shablûwl**, *shab-lool';* from the same as 7640; a *snail* (as if *floating* in its own slime):—snail.

שִׁבֹּלֶת **shibbôleth**. See 7641.

7643. שְׂבָם **Sebâm**, *seb-awm';* or (fem.)

שִׂבְמָה **Sibmâh**, *sib-maw';* prob. from 1313; *spice; Sebam* or *Sibmah*, a place in Moab:—Shebam, Shibmah, Sibmah.

7644. שֶׁבְנָא **Shebnâʼ**, *sheb-naw';* or

שֶׁבְנָה **Shebnâh**, *sheb-naw';* from an unused root mean. to *grow; growth; Shebna* or *Shebnah*, an Isr.:—Shebna, Shebnah.

7645. שְׁבַנְיָה **Shebanyâh**, *sheb-an-yaw';* or

שְׁבַנְיָהוּ **Shebanyâhûw**, *sheb-an-yaw'-hoo;* from the same as 7644 and 3050; *Jah has grown* (i.e. *prospered*); *Shebanjah*, the name of three or four Isr.:—Shebaniah.

7646. שָׂבַע **sâbaʻ**, *saw-bah';* or

שָׂבֵעַ **sâbêaʻ**, *saw-bay'-ah;* a prim. root; to *sate*, i.e. *fill* to satisfaction (lit. or fig.):—have enough, fill (full, self, with), be (to the) full (of), have plenty of, be satiate, satisfy (with), suffice, be weary of.

7647. שָׂבָע **sâbâʻ**, *saw-baw';* from 7646; *copiousness:*—abundance, plenteous (-ness, -ly).

7648. שֹׂבַע **sôbaʻ**, *so'-bah;* from 7646; *satisfaction* (of food or [fig.] joy):—fill, full (-ness), satisfying, be satisfied.

7649. שָׂבֵעַ **sâbêaʻ**, *saw-bay'-ah;* from 7646; *satiated* (in a pleasant or disagreeable sense):—full (of), satisfied (with).

7650. שָׁבַע **shâbaʻ**, *shaw-bah';* a prim. root; prop. to *be complete*, but used only as a denom. from 7651; to *seven* oneself, i.e. *swear* (as if by repeating a declaration seven times):—adjure, charge (by an oath, with an oath), feed to the full [*by mistake for* 7646], take an oath, × straitly, (cause to, make to) swear.

7651. שֶׁבַע **shebaʻ**, *sheh'-bah;* or (masc.)

שִׁבְעָה **shibʻâh**, *shib-aw';* from 7650; a prim. cardinal number; *seven* (as the sacred *full* one); also (adv.) *seven times;* by impl. a *week;* by extens. an *indefinite* number:—(+ by) seven ([-fold], -s, [-teen, -teenth], -th, times). Comp. 7658.

7652. שֶׁבַע **shebaʻ**, *sheh'-bah;* the same as 7651; *seven; Sheba*, the name of a place in Pal., and of two Isr.:—Sheba.

שָׁבֻעַ **shâbûaʻ**. See 7620.

7653. שִׂבְעָה **sibʻâh**, *sib-aw';* fem. of 7647; *satiety:*—fulness.

7654. שָׂבְעָה **sobʻâh**, *sob-aw';* fem. of 7648; *satiety:*—(to have) enough, × till . . . be full, [un-] satiable, satisfy, × sufficiently.

שִׁבְעָה **shibʻâh**. See 7651.

7655. שִׁבְעָה **shibʻâh** (Chald.), *shib-aw';* corresp. to 7651:—seven (times).

7656. שִׁבְעָה **Shibʻâh**, *shib-aw';* masc. of 7651; *seven (-th); Shebah*, a well in Pal.:—Shebah.

שְׁבֻעָה **shebûʻâh**. See 7620.

שְׁבִעִי **shebîyʻîy**. See 7637.

7657. שִׁבְעִים **shibʻîym**, *shib-eem';* multiple of 7651; *seventy:*—seventy, threescore and ten (+ -teen).

7658. שִׁבְעָנָה **shibʻânâh**, *shib-aw-naw';* prol. for the masc. of 7651; *seven:*—seven.

7659. שִׁבְעָתַיִם **shibʻâthayim**, *shib-aw-thah'-yim;* dual (adv.) of 7651; *seven-times:*—seven (-fold, times).

7660. שָׁבַץ **shâbats**, *shaw-bats';* a prim. root; to *interweave* (colored) threads in squares; by impl. (*of reticulation*) to *inchase* gems in gold:—embroider, set.

7661. שָׁבָץ **shâbâts**, *shaw-bawts';* from 7660; *intanglement*, i.e. (fig.) *perplexity:*—anguish.

7662. שְׁבַק **shebaq** (Chald.), *sheb-ak';* corresp. to the root of 7733; to *quit*, i.e. allow to remain:—leave, let alone.

7663. שָׂבַר **sâbar**, *saw-bar';* erroneously

שָׁבַר **shâbar** (Neh. 2 : 13, 15), *shaw-bar';* a prim. root; to *scrutinize;* by impl. (of *watching*) to *expect* (with hope and patience):—hope, tarry, view, wait.

7664. שֵׂבֶר **sêber**, *say'-ber;* from 7663; *expectation:*—hope.

7665. שָׁבַר **shâbar**, *shaw-bar';* a prim. root; to *burst* (lit. or fig.):—break (down, off, in pieces, up), broken ([-hearted]), bring to the birth, crush, destroy, hurt, quench, × quite, tear, view [*by mistake for* 7663].

7666. שָׁבַר **shâbar**, *shaw-bar';* denom. from 7668; to *deal* in grain:—buy, sell.

7667. שֶׁבֶר **sheber**, *sheh'-ber;* or

שֵׁבֶר **shêber**, *shay'-ber;* from 7665; a *fracture*, fig. *ruin;* spec. a *solution* (of a dream):—affliction, breach, breaking, broken [-footed, -handed], bruise, crashing, destruction, hurt, interpretation, vexation.

7668. שֶׁבֶר **sheber**, *sheh'-ber;* the same as 7667; *grain* (as if *broken* into kernels):—corn, victuals.

7669. שֶׁבֶר **Sheber**, *sheh'-ber;* the same as 7667; *Sheber*, an Isr.:—Sheber.

7670. שִׁבְרוֹן **shibrôwn**, *shib-rone';* from 7665; *rupture*, i.e. a *pang;* fig. *ruin:*—breaking, destruction.

7671. שְׁבָרִים **Shebârîym**, *sheb-aw-reem';* plur. of 7667; *ruins; Shebarim*, a place in Pal.:—Shebarim.

7672. שְׁבַשׁ **shebash** (Chald.), *sheb-ash';* corresp. to 7660; to *intangle*, i.e. *perplex:*—be astonished.

7673. שָׁבַת **shâbath**, *shaw-bath';* a prim. root; to *repose*, i.e. *desist* from exertion; used in many impl. relations (caus., fig. or spec.):—(cause to, let, make to) cease, celebrate, cause (make) to fail, keep (sabbath), suffer to be lacking, leave, put away (down), (make to) rest, rid, still, take away.

7674. שֶׁבֶת **shebeth**, *sheh'-beth;* from 7673; *rest*, *interruption*, *cessation:*—cease, sit still, loss of time.

7675. שֶׁבֶת **shebeth**, *sheh'-beth;* infin. of 3427; prop. *session;* but used also concr. an *abode* or *locality:*—place, seat. Comp. 3429.

7676. שַׁבָּת **shabbâth**, *shab-bawth';* intens. from 7673; *intermission*, i.e. (spec.) the *Sabbath:*—(+ every) sabbath.

7677. שַׁבָּתוֹן **shabbâthôwn**, *shab-baw-thone';* from 7676; a *sabbatism* or special holiday:—rest, sabbath.

7678. שַׁבְּתַי **Shabbethay**, *shab-beth-ah'ee;* from 7676; *restful; Shabbethai*, the name of three Isr.:—Shabbethai.

7679. שָׂגָא **sâgâʼ**, *saw-gaw';* a prim. root; to *grow*, i.e. (caus.) to *enlarge*, (fig.) *laud:*—increase, magnify.

7680. שְׂגָא **segâʼ** (Chald.), *seg-aw';* corresp. to 7679; to *increase:*—grow, be multiplied.

7681. שָׁגֵא **Shâgêʼ**, *shaw-gay';* prob. from 7686; *erring; Shagè*, an Isr.:—Shage.

7682. שָׂגַב **sâgab**, *saw-gab';* a prim. root; to *be* (caus. *make*) *lofty*, espec. *inaccessible;* by impl. *safe*, *strong;* used lit. and fig.:—defend, exalt, be excellent, (be, set on) high, lofty, be safe, set up (on high), be too strong.

7683. שָׁגַג **shâgag**, *shaw-gag';* a prim. root; to *stray*, i.e. (fig.) *sin* (with more or less apology):— × also for that, deceived, err, go astray, sin ignorantly.

7684. שְׁגָגָה **shegâgâh**, *sheg-aw-gaw';* from 7683; a *mistake* or inadvertent *transgression:*—error, ignorance, at unawares, unwittingly.

7685. שָׂגָה **sâgâh**, *saw-gaw';* a prim. root; to *enlarge* (espec. upward, also fig.):—grow (up), increase.

7686. שָׁגָה **shâgâh**, *shaw-gaw';* a prim. root; to *stray* (caus. *mislead*), usually (fig.) to *mistake*, espec. (mor.) to *transgress;* by extens. (through the idea of intoxication) to *reel*, (fig.) *be enraptured:*—(cause to) go astray, deceive, err, be ravished, sin through ignorance, (let, make to) wander.

7687. שְׂגוּב **Segûwb**, *seg-oob';* from 7682; *aloft; Segub*, the name of two Isr.:—Segub.

7688. שָׁגַח **shâgach**, *shaw-gakh';* a prim. root; to *peep*, i.e. *glance* sharply at:—look (narrowly).

7689. שַׂגִּיא **saggîyʼ**, *sag-ghee';* from 7679; (superlatively) *mighty:*—excellent, great.

7690. שַׂגִּיא **saggîyʼ** (Chald.), *sag-ghee';* corresp. to 7689; *large* (in size, quantity or number, also adv.):—exceeding, great (-ly), many, much, sore, very.

7691. שְׁגִיאָה **shegîyʼâh**, *sheg-ee-aw';* from 7686; a moral *mistake:*—error.

7692. שִׁגָּיוֹן **shiggâyôwn**, *shig-gaw-yone';* or

שִׁגָּיֹנָה **shiggâyônâh**, *shig-gaw-yo-naw';* from 7686; prop. *aberration*, i.e. (tech.) a *dithyramb* or rambling poem:—Shiggaion, Shigionoth.

7693. שָׁגַל **shâgal**, *shaw-gal';* a prim. root; to *copulate* with:—lie with, ravish.

7694. שֵׁגָל **shêgâl**, *shay-gawl';* from 7693; a *queen* (from cohabitation):—queen.

7695. שֵׁגָל **shêgâl** (Chald.), *shay-gawl';* corresp. to 7694; a (legitimate) *queen:*—wife.

7696. שָׁגַע **shâgaʻ**, *shaw-gah';* a prim. root; to *rave* through insanity:—(be, play the) mad (man).

7697. שִׁגָּעוֹן **shiggâʻôwn**, *shig-gaw-yone';* from 7696; *craziness:*—furiously, madness.

7698. שֶׁגֶר **sheger**, *sheh'-ger;* from an unused root prob. mean. to *eject;* the *fœtus* (as finally *expelled*):—that cometh of, increase.

7699. שַׁד **shad**, *shad;* or

שֹׁד **shôd**, *shode;* prob. from 7736 (in its orig. sense) contr.; the *breast* of a woman or animal (as *bulging*):—breast, pap, teat.

7700. שֵׁד **shêd**, *shade;* from 7736; a *dæmon* (as *malignant*):—devil.

7701. שֹׁד **shôd**, *shode;* or

שׁוֹד **shôwd** (Job 5 : 21), *shode;* from 7736; *violence*, *ravage:*—desolation, destruction, oppression, robbery, spoil (-ed, -er, -ing), wasting.

7702. שָׂדַד **sâdad**, *saw-dad'*; a prim. root; to *abrade*, i.e. *harrow* a field:—break clods, harrow.

7703. שָׁדַד **shâdad**, *shaw-dad'*; a prim. root; prop. to *be burly*, i.e. (fig.) *powerful* (pass. *impregnable*); by impl. to *ravage:*—dead, destroy (-er), oppress, robber, spoil (-er), × utterly, (lay) waste.

7704. שָׂדֶה **sâdeh**, *saw-deh'*; or

שָׂדַי **sâday**, *saw-dah'ee*; from an unused root mean. to *spread* out; a *field* (as flat):—country, field, ground, land, soil, × wild.

7705. שִׁדָּה **shiddâh**, *shid-dah'*; from 7703; a *wife* (as *mistress* of the house):— × all sorts, musical instrument.

7706. שַׁדַּי **Shadday**, *shad-dah'ee*; from 7703; the *Almighty:*—Almighty.

7707. שְׁדֵיאוּר **Shᵉdêy'ûwr**, *shed-ay-oor'*; from the same as 7704 and 217; *spreader of light; Shedejur*, an Isr.:—Shedeur.

7708. שִׂדִּים **Siddîym**, *sid-deem'*; plur. from the same as 7704; *flats; Siddim*, a valley in Pal.:—Siddim.

7709. שְׁדֵמָה **shᵉdêmâh**, *shed-ay-maw'*; appar. from 7704; a cultivated *field:*—blasted, field.

7710. שָׁדַף **shâdaph**, *shaw-daf'*; a prim. root; to *scorch:*—blast.

7711. שְׁדֵפָה **shᵉdêphâh**, *shed-ay-faw'*; or

שִׁדָּפוֹן **shiddâphôwn**, *shid-daw-fone'*; from 7710; *blight:*—blasted (-ing).

7712. שְׁדַר **shᵉdar** (Chald.), *shed-ar'*; a prim. root; to *endeavor:*—labour.

7713. שְׂדֵרָה **sᵉdêrâh**, *sed-ay-raw'*; from an unused root mean. to *regulate*; a *row*, i.e. *rank* (of soldiers), *story* (of rooms):—board, range.

7714. שַׁדְרַךְ **Shadrak**, *shad-rak'*; prob. of for. or.; *Shadrak*, the Bab. name of one of Daniel's companions:—Shadrach.

7715. שַׁדְרַךְ **Shadrak** (Chald.), *shad-rak'*; the same as 7714:—Shadrach.

7716. שֶׂה **seh**, *seh*; or

שֵׂי **sêy**, *say*; prob. from 7582 through the idea of *pushing* out to graze; a member of a flock, i.e. a *sheep* or *goat:*—(lesser, small) cattle, ewe, lamb, sheep.

7717. שָׂהֵד **sâhêd**, *saw-hade'*; from an unused root mean. to *testify*; a *witness:*—record.

7718. שֹׁהַם **shôham**, *sho'-ham*; from an unused root prob. mean. to *blanch*; a gem, prob. the *beryl* (from its *pale* green color):—onyx.

7719. שֹׁהַם **Shôham**, *sho'-ham*; the same as 7718; *Shoham*, an Isr.:—Shoham.

7720. שַׂהֲרֹן **sahărôn**, *sah-har-one'*; from the same as 5469; a round *pendant* for the neck:—ornament, round tire like the moon.

שָׁו° **shav**. See 7723.

7721. שׂוֹא **sôw'**, *so*; from an unused root (akin to 5375 and 7722) mean. to *rise*; a *rising:*—arise.

7722. שׁוֹא **shôw'**, *sho*; or (fem.)

שׁוֹאָה **shôw'âh**, *sho-aw'*; or

שֹׁאָה **shô'âh**, *sho-aw'*; from an unused root mean. to *rush* over; a *tempest*; by impl. *devastation:*—desolate (-ion), destroy, destruction, storm, wasteness.

7723. שָׁוְא **shâv'**, *shawv*; or

שַׁו° **shav**, *shav*; from the same as 7722 in the sense of *desolating*; *evil* (as *destructive*), lit. (*ruin*) or mor. (espec. *guile*); fig. *idolatry* (as false, subj.), *uselessness* (as deceptive, obj.; also adv. in vain):—false (-ly), lie, lying, vain, vanity.

7724. שְׁוָא **Shᵉvâ'**, *shev-aw'*; from the same as 7723; *false; Sheva*, an Isr.:—Sheva.

7725. שׁוּב **shûwb**, *shoob*; a prim. root; to *turn* back (hence, away) trans. or intrans., lit. or fig. (not necessarily with the idea of *return* to the starting point); gen. to *retreat*; often adv. *again:*—([break, build, circumcise, dig, do anything, do evil, feed, lay down, lie down, lodge, make, rejoice, send, take, weep]) × again, (cause to) answer (+ again), × in any case (wise), × at all, averse, bring (again, back, home again), call [to mind], carry again (back), cease, × certainly, come again (back) × consider, + continually, convert, deliver (again), + deny, draw back, fetch home again, × fro, get [oneself] (back) again, × give (again), go again (back, home), [go] out, hinder, let, [see] more, × needs, be past, × pay, pervert, pull in again, put (again, up again), recall, recompense, recover, refresh, relieve, render (again), × repent, requite, rescue, restore, retrieve, (cause to, make to) return, reverse, reward, + say nay, send back, set again, slide back, still, × surely, take back (off), (cause to, make to) turn (again, self again, away, back, back again, backward, from, off), withdraw.

שׁוּבָאֵל **Shûwbâ'êl**. See 7619.

7726. שׁוֹבָב **shôwbâb**, *sho-bawb'*; from 7725; *apostate*, i.e. idolatrous:—backsliding, frowardly, turn away [*from marg.*].

7727. שׁוֹבָב **Shôwbâb**, *sho-bawb'*; the same as 7726; *rebellious; Shobab*, the name of two Isr.:—Shobab.

7728. שׁוֹבֵב **shôwbêb**, *sho-babe'*; from 7725; *apostate*, i.e. heathenish or (actually) heathen:—backsliding.

7729. שׁוּבָה **shûwbâh**, *shoo-baw'*; from 7725; a *return:*—returning.

7730. שׂוֹבֶךְ **sôwbek**, *so'-bek*; for 5441; a *thicket*, i.e. interlaced branches:—thick boughs.

7731. שׁוֹבָךְ **Shôwbâk**, *sho-bawk'*; perh. for 7730; *Shobak*, a Syrian:—Shobach.

7732. שׁוֹבָל **Shôwbâl**, *sho-bawl'*; from the same as 7640; *overflowing; Shobal*, the name of an Edomite and two Isr.:—Shobal.

7733. שׁוֹבֵק **Shôwbêq**, *sho-bake'*; act. part. from a prim. root mean. to *leave* (comp. 7662); *forsaking; Shobek*, an Isr.:—Shobek.

7734. שׂוּג **sûwg**, *soog*; a prim. root; to *retreat:*—turn back.

7735. שׂוּג **sûwg**, *soog*; a prim. root; to *hedge* in:—make to grow.

7736. שׁוּד **shûwd**, *shood*; a prim. root; prop. to *swell* up, i.e. fig. (by impl. of *insolence*) to *devastate:*—waste.

שׁוֹד **shôwd**. See 7699, 7701.

7737. שָׁוָה **shâvâh**, *shaw-vaw'*; a prim. root; prop. to *level*, i.e. *equalize*; fig. to *resemble*; by impl. to *adjust* (i.e. counterbalance, be suitable, compose, place, yield, etc.):—avail, behave, bring forth, compare, countervail, (be, make) equal, lay, be (make, a-) like, make plain, profit, reckon.

7738. שָׁוָה **shâvâh**, *shaw-vaw'*; a prim. root; to *destroy:*— × substance [*from the marg.*].

7739. שְׁוָה **shᵉvâh** (Chald.), *shev-aw'*; corresp. to 7737; to *resemble:*—make like.

7740. שָׁוֵה **Shâvêh**, *shaw-vay'*; from 7737; *plain; Shaveh*, a place in Pal.:—Shaveh.

7741. שָׁוֵה קִרְיָתַיִם **Shâvêh Qiryâthayim**, *shaw-vay' kir-yaw-thah'-yim*; from the same as 7740 and the dual of 7151; *plain of a double city; Shaveh-Kirjathajim*, a place E. of the Jordan:—Shaveh Kiriathaim.

7742. שׂוּחַ **sûwach**, *soo'-akh*; a prim. root; to *muse* pensively:—meditate.

7743. שׁוּחַ **shûwach**, *shoo'-akh*; a prim. root; to *sink*, lit. or fig.:—bow down, incline, humble.

7744. שׁוּחַ **Shûwach**, *shoo'-akh*; from 7743; *dell; Shûach*, a son of Abraham:—Shuah.

7745 שׁוּחָה **shûwchâh**, *shoo-khaw'*; from 7743; a *chasm:*—ditch, pit.

7746. שׁוּחָה **Shûwchâh**, *shoo-khaw'*; the same as 7745; *Shuchah*, an Isr.:—Shuah.

7747. שׁוּחִי **Shuchîy**, *shoo-khee'*; patron. from 7744; a *Shuchite* or desc. of Shuach:—Shuhite.

7748. שׁוּחָם **Shûwchâm**, *shoo-khawm'*; from 7743; *humbly; Shucham*, an Isr.:—Shuham.

7749. שׁוּחָמִי **Shûwchâmîy**, *shoo-khaw-mee'*; patron. from 7748; a *Shuchamite* (collect.):—Shuhamites.

7750. שׂוּט **sûwṭ**, *soot*; or (by perm.)

סוּט **çûwṭ**, *soot*; a primitive root; to *detrude*, i.e. (intrans. and fig.) *become derelict* (wrongly practise; namely, idolatry):—turn aside to.

7751. שׁוּט **shûwṭ**, *shoot*; a prim. root; prop. to *push* forth; (but used only fig.) to *lash*, i.e. (the sea with oars) to *row*; by impl. to *travel:*—go (about, through, to and fro), mariner, rower, run to and fro.

7752. שׁוֹט **shôwṭ**, *shote*; from 7751; a *lash* (lit. or fig.):—scourge, whip.

7753. שׂוּךְ **sûwk**, *sook*; a prim. root; to *entwine*, i.e. *shut* in (for formation, protection or restraint):—fence, (make an) hedge (up).

7754. שׂוֹךְ **sôwk**, *soke*; or (fem.)

שׂוֹכָה **sôwkâh**, *so-kaw'*; from 7753; a *branch* (as *interleaved*):—bough.

7755. שׂוֹכֹה **Sôwkôh**, *so-ko'*; or

שֹׂכֹה **Sôkôh**, *so-ko'*; or

שׂוֹכוֹ **Sôwkôw**, *so-ko'*; from 7753; *Sokoh* or *Soko*, the name of two places in Pal.:—Shocho, Shochoh, Sochoh, Soco, Socoh.

7756. שׂוּכָתִי **Sûwkâthîy**, *soo-kaw-thee'*; prob. patron. from a name corresp. to 7754 (fem.); a *Sukathite* or desc. of an unknown Isr. named Sukah:—Suchathite.

7757. שׁוּל **shûwl**, *shool*; from an unused root mean. to *hang* down; a *skirt*; by impl. a bottom *edge:*—hem, skirt, train.

7758. שׁוֹלָל **shôwlâl**, *sho-lawl'*; or

שֵׁילָל **shêylâl** (Mic. 1 : 8), *shay-lawl'*; from 7997; *nude* (espec. bare-foot); by impl. *captive:*—spoiled, stripped.

7759. שׁוּלַמִּית **Shûwlammîyth**, *shoo-lam-meeth'*; from 7999; *peaceful* (with the art. always pref., making it a pet name); the *Shulammith*, an epithet of Solomon's queen:—Shulamite.

7760. שׂוּם **sûwm**, *soom*; or

שִׂים **sîym**, *seem*; a prim. root; to *put* (used in a great variety of applications, lit., fig., infer. and ellip.):— × any wise, appoint, bring, call [a name], care, cast in, change, charge, commit, consider, convey, determine, + disguise, dispose, do, get, give, heap up, hold, impute, lay (down, up), leave, look, make (out), mark, + name, × on, ordain, order, + paint, place, preserve, purpose, put (on), + regard, rehearse, reward, (cause to) set (on, up), shew, + stedfastly, take, × tell, + tread down, ([over-]) turn, × wholly, work.

7761. שׂוּם **sûwm** (Chald.), *soom*; corresp. to 7760:— + command, give, lay, make, + name, + regard, set.

7762. שׁוּם **shûwm**, *shoom*; from an unused root mean. to *exhale*; *garlic* (from its rank odor):—garlic.

7763. שׁוֹמֵר **Shôwmêr**, *sho-mare'*; or

שֹׁמֵר **Shômêr**, *sho-mare'*; act. part. of 8104; *keeper; Shomer*, the name of two Isr.:—Shomer.

7764. שׁוּנִי **Shûwnîy**, *shoo-nee'*; from an unused root mean. to *rest*; *quiet; Shuni*, an Isr.:—Shuni.

7765. שׁוּנִי **Shûwnîy**, *shoo-nee'*; patron. from 7764; a *Shunite* (collect.) or desc. of Shuni:—Shunites.

7766. שׁוּנֵם **Shûwnêm**, *shoo-name'*; prob. from the same as 7764; *quietly; Shunem*, a place in Pal.:—Shunem.

7767. שׁוּנַמִּית **Shûwnammîyth**, *shoo-nam-meeth'*; patrial from 7766; a *Shunammitess*, or female inhab. of Shunem:—Shunamite.

7768. שָׁוַע **shâva'**, *shaw-vah'*; a prim. root; prop. to *be free;* but used only causat. and reflex. to *halloo* (for help, i.e. *freedom* from some trouble):—cry (aloud, out), shout.

7769. שׁוַע **shuwa'**, *shoo'-ah;* from 7768; a *halloo:*—cry, riches.

7770. שׁוּעַ **Shûwa'**, *shoo'-ah;* the same as 7769; *Shuä*, a Canaanite:—Shua, Shuah.

7771. שׁוֹעַ **shôwa'**, *sho'-ah;* from 7768 in the orig. sense of *freedom;* a *noble*, i.e. *liberal*, *opulent;* also (as noun in the derived sense) a *halloo:*—bountiful, crying, rich.

7772. שׁוֹעַ **Shôwa'**, *sho'-ah;* the same as 7771; *rich; Shoä*, an Oriental people:—Shoa.

7773. שֶׁוַע **sheva'**, *sheh'-vah;* from 7768; a *halloo:*—cry.

7774. שׁוּעָא **Shûw'â'**, *shoo-aw';* from 7768; *wealth; Shuä*, an Israelitess:—Shua.

7775. שַׁוְעָה **shav'âh**, *shav-aw';* fem. of 7773; a *hallooing:*—crying.

7776. שׁוּעָל **shûw'âl**, *shoo-awl';* or

שֻׁעָל **shû'âl**, *shoo-awl';* from the same as 8168; a *jackal* (as a *burrower*):—fox.

7777. שׁוּעָל **Shûw'âl**, *shoo-awl';* the same as 7776; *Shuäl*, the name of an Isr. and of a place in Pal.:—Shual.

7778. שׁוֹעֵר **shôw'êr**, *sho-are';* or

שֹׁעֵר **shô'êr**, *sho-are';* act. part. of 8176 (as denom. from 8179); a *janitor:*—door-keeper, porter.

7779. שׁוּף **shûwph**, *shoof;* a prim. root; prop. to *gape*, i.e. *snap* at; fig. to *overwhelm:*—break, bruise, cover.

7780. שׁוֹפָךְ **Shôwphâk**, *sho-fawk';* from 8210; *poured; Shophak*, a Syrian:—Shophach.

7781. שׁוּפָמִי **Shûwphâmîy**, *shoo-faw-mee';* patron. from 8197; a *Shuphamite* (collect.) or desc. of Shephupham:—Shuphamite.

שׁוֹפָן **Shôwphân**. See 5855.

7782. שׁוֹפָר **shôwphâr**, *sho-far';* or

שֹׁפָר **shôphâr**, *sho-far';* from 8231 in the orig. sense of *incising;* a *cornet* (as giving a *clear* sound) or curved horn:—cornet, trumpet.

7783. שׁוּק **shûwq**, *shook;* a prim. root; to *run* after or over, i.e. *overflow:*—overflow, water.

7784. שׁוּק **shûwq**, *shook;* from 7783; a *street* (as *run over*):—street.

7785. שׁוֹק **shôwq**, *shoke;* from 7783; the (lower) *leg* (as a *runner*):—hip, leg, shoulder, thigh.

7786. שׂוּר **sûwr**, *soor;* a prim. root; prop. to *vanquish;* by impl. to *rule* (caus. *crown*):—make princes, have power, reign. See 5493.

7787. שׂוּר **sûwr**, *soor;* a prim. root [rather ident. with 7786 through the idea of *reducing* to pieces; comp. 4883]; to *saw:*—cut.

7788. שׁוּר **shûwr**, *shoor;* a prim. root; prop. to *turn*, i.e. *travel* about (as a harlot or a merchant):—go, sing. See also 7891.

7789. שׁוּר **shûwr**, *shoor;* a prim. root [rather ident. with 7788 through the idea of *going round* for inspection]; to *spy* out, i.e. (gen.) *survey*, (for evil) *lurk for*, (for good) *care for:*—behold, lay wait, look, observe, perceive, regard, see.

7790. שׁוּר **shûwr**, *shoor;* from 7789; a *foe* (as *lying in wait*):—enemy.

7791. שׁוּר **shûwr**, *shoor;* from 7788; a *wall* (as *going about*):—wall.

7792. שׁוּר **shûwr** (Chald.), *shoor;* corresp. to 7791:—wall.

7793. שׁוּר **Shûwr**, *shoor;* the same as 7791; *Shur*, a region of the Desert:—Shur.

7794. שׁוֹר **shôwr**, *shore;* from 7788; a *bullock* (as a *traveller*):—bull (-ock), cow, ox, wall [*by mistake for* 7791].

7795. שׂוֹרָה **sôwrâh**, *so-raw';* from 7786 in the prim. sense of 5493; prop. a *ring*, i.e. (by analogy) a *row* (adv.):—principal.

שׂוֹרֵק **sôwrêq**. See 8321.

7796. שׂוֹרֵק **Sôwrêq**, *so-rake';* the same as 8321; a *vine; Sorek*, a valley in Pal.:—Sorek.

7797. שׂוּשׂ **sûws**, *soos;* or

שִׂישׂ **sîys**, *sece;* a prim. root; to *be bright*, i.e. *cheerful:*—be glad, × greatly, joy, make mirth, rejoice.

7798. שַׁוְשָׁא **Shavshâ'**, *shav-shaw';* from 7797; *joyful; Shavsha*, an Isr.:—Shavsha.

7799. שׁוּשַׁן **shûwshan**, *shoo-shan';* or

שׁוֹשָׁן **shôwshân**, *sho-shawn';* or

שֹׁשָׁן **shôshân**, *sho-shawn';* and (fem.)

שׁוֹשַׁנָּה **shôwshannâh**, *sho-shan-naw';* from 7797; a *lily* (from its *whiteness*), as a flower or arch. ornament; also a (straight) *trumpet* (from the *tubular* shape):—lily, Shoshannim.

7800. שׁוּשַׁן **Shûwshan**, *shoo-shan';* the same as 7799; *Shushan*, a place in Persia:—Shushan.

7801. שׁוּשַׁנְכִי **Shûwshankîy** (Chald.), *shoo-shan-kee';* of for. or.; a *Shushankite* (collect.) or inhab. of some unknown place in Ass.:—Susanchites.

7802. שׁוּשַׁן עֵדוּת **Shûwshan 'Êdûwth**, *shoo-shan' ay-dooth';* or (plur. of former)

שׁוֹשַׁנִּים עֵדוּת **Shôwshannîym 'Êdûwth**, *sho-shan-neem' ay-dooth';* from 7799 and 5715; *lily* (or *trumpet*) *of assemblage; Shushan-Eduth* or *Shoshannim-Eduth*, the title of a popular song:—Shoshannim-Eduth, Shushan-eduth.

שׁוּשַׁק **Shûwshaq**. See 7895.

7803. שׁוּתֶלַח **Shûwthelach**, *shoo-theh'-lakh;* prob. from 7582 and the same as 8520; *crash of breakage; Shuthelach*, the name of two Isr.:—Shuthelah.

7804. שְׁזַב **sh^ezab** (Chald.), *shez-ab';* corresp. to 5800; to *leave*, i.e. (caus.) *free:*—deliver.

7805. שָׁזַף **shâzaph**, *shaw-zaf';* a prim. root; to *tan* (by sun-burning); fig. (as if by a piercing ray) to *scan:*—look up, see.

7806. שָׁזַר **shâzar**, *shaw-zar';* a prim. root; to *twist* (a thread of straw):—twine.

7807. שַׁח **shach**, *shakh;* from 7817; *sunk*, i.e. *downcast:*— + humble.

7808. שֵׂחַ **sêach**, *say'-akh;* for 7879; *communion*, i.e. (reflex.) *meditation:*—thought.

7809. שָׁחַד **shâchad**, *shaw-khad';* a prim. root; to *donate*, i.e. *bribe:*—hire, give a reward.

7810. שַׁחַד **shachad**, *shakh'-ad;* from 7809; a *donation* (venal or redemptive):—bribe (-ry), gift, present, reward.

7811. שָׂחָה **sâchâh**, *saw-khaw';* a prim. root; to *swim;* caus. to *inundate:*—(make to) swim.

7812. שָׁחָה **shâchâh**, *shaw-khaw';* a prim. root; to *depress*, i.e. *prostrate* (espec. reflex. in homage to royalty or God):—bow (self) down, crouch, fall down (flat), humbly beseech, do (make) obeisance, do reverence, make to stoop, worship.

7813. שָׂחוּ **sâchûw**, *saw'-khoo;* from 7811; a *pond* (for *swimming*):—to swim in.

7814. שְׂחוֹק **s^echôwq**, *sekh-oke';* or

שְׂחֹק **s^echôq**, *sekh-oke';* from 7832; *laughter* (in merriment or defiance):—derision, laughter (-ed to scorn, -ing), mocked, sport.

7815. שְׁחוֹר **sh^echôwr**, *shekh-ore';* from 7835; *dinginess*, i.e. perh. *soot:*—coal.

שִׁחוֹר **shîchôwr**. See 7883.

שָׁחוֹר **shâchôwr**. See 7838.

7816. שְׁחוּת **sh^echûwth**, *shekh-ooth';* from 7812; *pit:*—pit.

7817. שָׁחַח **shâchach**, *shaw-khakh';* a prim. root; to *sink* or *depress* (reflex. or caus.):—bend, bow (down), bring (cast) down, couch, humble self, be (bring) low, stoop.

7818. שָׂחַט **sâchaṭ**, *saw-khat';* a prim. root; to *tread* out, i.e. *squeeze* (grapes):—press.

7819. שָׁחַט **shâchaṭ**, *shaw-khat';* a prim. root; to *slaughter* (in sacrifice or massacre):—kill, offer, shoot out, slay, slaughter.

7820. שׁחט **shâchaṭ**, *shaw-khat';* a prim. root [rather ident. with 7819 through the idea of *striking*]; to *hammer* out:—beat.

7821. שְׁחִיטָה **sh^echîyṭâh**, *shekh-ee-taw';* from 7819; *slaughter:*—killing.

7822. שְׁחִין **sh^echîyn**, *shekh-een';* from an unused root prob. mean. to *burn; inflammation*, i.e. an *ulcer:*—boil, botch.

7823. שָׁחִיס **shâchîyç**, *shaw-khece';* or

סָחִישׁ **çâchîysh**, *saw-kheesh';* from an unused root appar. mean. to *sprout*, *after-growth:*—(that) which springeth of the same.

7824. שָׁחִיף **shâchîyph**, *shaw-kheef';* from the same as 7828; a *board* (as *chipped* thin):—cieled with.

7825. שְׁחִית **sh^echîyth**, *shekh-eeth';* from 7812; a *pit*-fall (lit. or fig.):—destruction, pit.

7826. שַׁחַל **shachal**, *shakh'-al;* from an unused root prob. mean. to *roar;* a *lion* (from his characteristic *roar*):—(fierce) lion.

7827. שְׁחֵלֶת **sh^echêleth**, *shekh-ay'-leth;* appar from the same as 7826 through some obscure idea, perh. that of *peeling* off by concussion of sound; a *scale* or shell, i.e. the aromatic *mussel:*—onycha.

7828. שַׁחַף **shachaph**, *shakh'-af;* from an unused root mean. to *peel*, i.e. *emaciate;* the *gull* (as *thin*):—cuckoo.

7829. שַׁחֶפֶת **shachepheth**, *shakh-eh'-feth;* from the same as 7828; *emaciation:*—consumption.

7830. שַׁחַץ **shachats**, *shakh'-ats;* from an unused root appar. mean. to *strut; haughtiness* (as evinced by the attitude):— × lion, pride.

7831. שַׁחֲצוֹם **Shachatsôwm**, *shakh-ats-ome';* from the same as 7830; *proudly; Shachatsom*, a place in Pal.:—Shahazimah [*from the marg.*].

7832. שָׂחַק **sâchaq**, *saw-khak';* a prim. root; to *laugh* (in pleasure or detraction); by impl. to *play;*—deride, have in derision, laugh, make merry, mock (-er), play, rejoice, (laugh to) scorn, be in (make) sport.

7833. שָׁחַק **shâchaq**, *shaw-khak';* a prim. root; to *comminute* (by trituration or attrition):—beat, wear.

7834. שַׁחַק **shachaq**, *shakh'-ak;* from 7833; a *powder* (as *beaten* small); by anal. a thin *vapor;* by extens. the *firmament:*—cloud, small dust, heaven, sky.

שְׂחֹק **s^echôq**. See 7814.

7835. שָׁחַר **shâchar**, *shaw-khar';* a prim. root [rather ident. with 7836 through the idea of the *duskiness* of early dawn]; to *be dim* or dark (in color):—be black.

7836. שָׁחַר **shâchar**, *shaw-khar';* a prim. root; prop. to *dawn*, i.e. (fig.) *be* (up) *early* at any task (with the impl. of earnestness); by extens. to *search* for (with painstaking):—[do something] betimes, enquire early, rise (seek) betimes, seek diligently) early, in the morning).

7837. שַׁחַר **shachar**, *shakh'-ar;* from 7836; *dawn* (lit., fig. or adv.):—day (-spring), early, light, morning, whence riseth.

שִׁחוֹר **Shîchôr**. See 7883.

7838. שָׁחֹר **shâchôr**, *shaw-khore';* or

שָׁחוֹר **shâchôwr**, *shaw-khore';* from 7835 prop. *dusky*, but also (absol.) *jetty:*—black.

7839. שַׁחֲרוּת **shachărûwth**, *shakh-ar-ooth'*; from 7836; a *dawning*, i.e. (fig.) *juvenescence:*—youth.

7840. שְׁחַרְחֹרֶת **shᵉcharchôreth**, *shekh-ar-kho'-reth*; from 7835; *swarthy:*—black.

7841. שְׁחַרְיָה **Shᵉcharyâh**, *shekh-ar-yaw'*; from 7836 and 3050; *Jah has sought; Shecharjah*, an Isr.:—Shehariah.

7842. שַׁחֲרַיִם **Shachărayim**, *shakh-ar-ah'-yim*; dual of 7837; *double dawn; Shacharajim*, an Isr.:—Shaharaim.

7843. שָׁחַת **shâchath**, *shaw-khath'*; a prim. root; to *decay*, i.e. (caus.) *ruin* (lit. or fig.):—batter, cast off, corrupt (-er, thing), destroy (-er, -uction), lose, mar, perish, spill, spoiler, × utterly, waste (-r).

7844. שְׁחַת **shᵉchath** (Chald.), *shekh-ath'*; corresp. to 7843:—corrupt, fault.

7845. שַׁחַת **shachath**, *shakh'-ath*; from 7743; a *pit* (espec. as a trap); fig. *destruction:*—corruption, destruction, ditch, grave, pit.

7846. שֵׂט **sêṭ**, *sayte*; or סֵט **çêṭ**, *sayt*; from 7750; a *departure* from right, i.e. *sin:*—revolter, that turn aside.

7847. שָׂטָה **sâṭâh**, *saw-taw'*; a prim. root; to *deviate* from duty:—decline, go aside, turn.

7848. שִׁטָּה **shiṭṭâh**, *shit-taw'*; fem. of a deriv. [only in the plur. שִׁטִּים **shiṭṭîym**, *shit-teem'*, mean. the *sticks* of wood] from the same as 7850; the *acacia* (from its *scourging* thorns):—shittah, shittim. See also 1029.

7849. שָׁטַח **shâṭach**, *shaw-takh'*; a prim. root; to *expand:*—all abroad, enlarge, spread, stretch out.

7850. שֹׁטֵט **shôṭêṭ**, *sho-tate'*; act. part. of an otherwise unused root mean. (prop. to *pierce;* but only as a denom. from 7752) to *flog;* a *goad:*—scourge.

7851. שִׁטִּים **Shiṭṭîym**, *shit-teem'*; the same as the plur. of 7848; *acacia* trees; *Shittim*, a place E. of the Jordan:—Shittim.

7852. שָׂטַם **sâṭam**, *saw-tam'*; a prim. root; prop. to *lurk* for, i.e. *persecute:*—hate, oppose self against.

7853. שָׂטַן **sâṭan**, *saw-tan'*; a prim. root; to *attack*, (fig.) *accuse:*—(be an) adversary, resist.

7854. שָׂטָן **sâṭân**, *saw-tawn'*; from 7853; an *opponent;* espec. (with the art. pref.) *Satan*, the arch-enemy of good:—adversary, Satan, withstand.

7855. שִׂטְנָה **siṭnâh**, *sit-naw'*; from 7853; *opposition* (by letter):—accusation.

7856. שִׂטְנָה **Siṭnâh**, *sit-naw'*; the same as 7855; *Sitnah*, the name of a well in Pal.:—Sitnah.

7857. שָׁטַף **shâṭaph**, *shaw-taf'*; a prim. root; to *gush;* by impl. to *inundate, cleanse;* by anal. to *gallop, conquer:*—drown, (over-) flow (-whelm), rinse, run, rush, (throughly) wash (away).

7858. שֶׁטֶף **sheṭeph**, *sheh'-tef*; or שֵׁטֶף **shêṭeph**, *shay'-tef*; from 7857; a *deluge* (lit. or fig.):—flood, outrageous, overflowing.

7859. שְׁטַר **shᵉṭar** (Chald.), *shet-ar'*; of uncert. der.: a *side:*—side.

7860. שֹׁטֵר **shôṭêr**, *sho-tare'*; act. part. of an otherwise unused root prob. mean. to *write;* prop. a *scribe*, i.e. (by anal. or impl.) an official *superintendent* or *magistrate:*—officer, overseer, ruler.

7861. שִׁטְרַי° **Shiṭray**, *shit-rah'ee*; from the same as 7860; *magisterial; Shitrai*, an Isr.:—Shitrai.

7862. שַׁי **shay**, *shah'ee*; prob. from 7737; a *gift* (as *available*):—present.

7863. שִׂיא **siy'**, *see*; from the same as 7721 by perm.; *elevation:*—excellency.

7864. שְׁיָא° **Shᵉyâ'**, *sheh-yaw'*; for 7724; *Sheja*, an Isr.:—Sheva [*from the marg.*].

7865. שִׂיאֹן **Sîy'ôn**, *see-ohn'*; from 7863; *peak; Sion*, the summit of Mt. Hermon:—Sion.

7866. שִׁיאוֹן **Shîy'ôwn**, *shee-ohn'*; from the same as 7722; *ruin; Shijon*, a place in Pal.:—Shihon.

7867. שִׂיב **sîyb**, *seeb*; a prim. root; prop. to *become aged*, i.e. (by impl.) to *grow gray:*—(be) grayheaded.

7868. שִׂיב **sîyb** (Chald.), *seeb*; corresp. to 7867:—elder.

7869. שֵׂיב **sêyb**, *sabe*; from 7867; old *age:*—age.

7870. שִׁיבָה **shîybâh**, *shee-baw'*; by perm. from 7725; a *return* (of property):—captivity.

7871. שִׁיבָה **shîybâh**, *shee-baw'*; from 3427; *residence:*—while . . . lay.

7872. שֵׂיבָה **sêybâh**, *say-baw'*; fem. of 7869; old *age:*—(be) gray (grey, hoar, -y) hairs (head, -ed), old age.

7873. שִׂיג **sîyg**, *seeg*; from 7734; a *withdrawal* (into a private place):—pursuing.

7874. שִׂיד **sîyd**, *seed*; a prim. root prob. mean. to *boil* up (comp. 7736); used only as denom. from 7875; to *plaster:*—plaister.

7875. שִׂיד **sîyd**, *seed*; from 7874; *lime* (as *boiling* when slacked):—lime, plaister.

7876. שָׁיָה **shâyâh**, *shaw-yaw'*; a prim. root; to *keep* in memory:—be unmindful. [Render Deut. 32 : 18, " A Rock bore thee, *thou must recollect;* and (yet) thou hast forgotten," etc.]

7877. שִׁיזָא **Shîyzâ'**, *shee-zaw'*; of unknown der.; *Shiza*, an Isr.:—Shiza.

7878. שִׂיחַ **sîyach**, *see'-akh*; a prim. root; to *ponder*, i.e. (by impl.) *converse* (with oneself, and hence aloud) or (trans.) *utter:*—commune, complain, declare, meditate, muse, pray, speak, talk (with).

7879. שִׂיחַ **sîyach**, *see'-akh*; from 7878; a *contemplation;* by impl. an *utterance:*—babbling, communication, complaint, meditation, prayer, talk.

7880. שִׂיחַ **sîyach**, *see'-akh*; from 7878; a *shoot* (as if *uttered* or put forth), i.e. (gen.) *shrubbery:*—bush, plant, shrub.

7881. שִׂיחָה **sîychâh**, *see-khaw'*; fem. of 7879; *reflection;* by extens. *devotion:*—meditation, prayer.

7882. שִׁיחָה **shîychâh**, *shee-khaw'*; for 7745; a *pit*-fall:—pit.

7883. שִׁיחוֹר **Shîychôwr**, *shee-khore'*; or שִׁחוֹר **Shîchôwr**, *shee-khore'*; or שִׁחֹר **Shîchôr**, *shee-khore'*; prob. from 7835; *dark*, i.e. *turbid; Shichor*, a stream of Egypt:—Shihor, Sihor.

7884. שִׁיחוֹר לִבְנָת **Shîychôwr Libnâth**, *shee-khore' lib-nawth'*; from the same as 7883 and 3835; *darkish whiteness; Shichor-Libnath*, a stream of Pal.:—Shihor-libnath.

7885. שַׁיִט **shayiṭ**, *shah'-yit*; from 7751; an *oar;* also (comp. 7752) a *scourge*° (fig.):—oar, scourge.

7886. שִׁילֹה **Shîylôh**, *shee-lo'*; from 7951; *tranquil; Shiloh*, an epithet of the Messiah:—Shiloh.

7887. שִׁילֹה **Shîylôh**, *shee-lo'*; or שִׁלֹה **Shîlôh**, *shee-lo'*; or שִׁילוֹ **Shîylôw**, *shee-lo'*; or שִׁלוֹ **Shîlôw**, *shee-lo'*; from the same as 7886; *Shiloh*, a place in Pal.:—Shiloh.

7888. שִׁילוֹנִי **Shîylôwnîy**, *shee-lo-nee'*; or שִׁילֹנִי **Shîylônîy**, *shee-lo-nee'*; or שִׁלֹנִי **Shîlônîy**, *shee-lo-nee'*; from 7887; a *Shilonite* or inhab. of Shiloh:—Shilonite.

שֵׁילָל **shêylâl**. See 7758.

7889. שִׁימוֹן **Shîymôwn**, *shee-mone'*; appar. for 3452; *desert; Shimon*, an Isr.:—Shimon.

7890. שַׁיִן **shayin**, *shah'-yin*; from an unused root mean. to *urinate; urine:*—piss.

7891. שִׁיר **shîyr**, *sheer*; or (the orig. form) שׁוּר° **shûwr** (1 Sam. 18 : 6), *shoor*; a prim. root [rather ident. with 7788 through the idea of *strolling* minstrelsy]; to *sing:*—behold [*by mistake for* 7789], sing (-er, -ing man, -ing woman).

7892. שִׁיר **shîyr**, *sheer*; or fem. שִׁירָה **shîyrâh**, *shee-raw'*; from 7891; a *song;* abstr. *singing:*—musical (-ick), × sing (-er, -ing), song.

שִׂישׂ **sîys**. See 7797.

7893. שַׁיִשׁ **shayish**, *shah'-yish*; from an unused root mean. to *bleach*, i.e. *whiten; white*, i.e. *marble:*—marble. See 8336.

7894. שִׁישָׁא **Shîyshâ'**, *shee-shaw'*; from the same as 7893; *whiteness; Shisha*, an Isr.:—Shisha.

7895. שִׁישַׁק **Shîyshaq**, *shee-shak'*; or שׁוּשַׁק° **Shûwshaq**, *shoo-shak'*; of Eg. der.; *Shishak*, an Eg. king:—Shishak.

7896. שִׁית **shîyth**, *sheeth*; a prim. root; to *place* (in a very wide application):—apply, appoint, array, bring, consider, lay (up), let alone, × look, make, mark, put (on), + regard, set, shew, be stayed, × take.

7897. שִׁית **shîyth**, *sheeth*; from 7896; a *dress* (as *put* on):—attire.

7898. שַׁיִת **shayith**, *shah'-yith*; from 7896; *scrub* or *trash*, i.e. wild *growth* of weeds or briers (as if *put* on the field):—thorns.

7899. שֵׂךְ **sêk**, *sake*; from 5526 in the sense of 7753; a *brier* (as of a hedge):—prick.

7900. שֹׂךְ **sôk**, *soke*; from 5526 in the sense of 7753; a *booth* (as *interlaced*):—tabernacle.

7901. שָׁכַב **shâkab**, *shaw-kab'*; a prim. root; to *lie* down (for rest, sexual connection, decease or any other purpose):— × at all, cast down, ([over-]) lay (self) (down), (make to) lie (down, down to sleep, still, with), lodge, ravish, take rest, sleep, stay.

7902. שְׁכָבָה **shᵉkâbâh**, *shek-aw-baw'*; from 7901; a *lying* down (of dew, or for the sexual act):— × carnally, copulation, × lay, seed.

7903. שְׁכֹבֶת **shᵉkôbeth**, *shek-o'-beth*; from 7901; a (sexual) *lying* with:— × lie.

7904. שָׁכָה **shâkâh**, *shaw-kaw'*; a prim. root; to *roam* (through lust):—in the morning [*by mistake for* 7925].

7905. שֻׂכָּה **sukkâh**, *sook-kaw'*; fem. of 7900 in the sense of 7899; a *dart* (as pointed like a *thorn*):—barbed iron.

7906. שֵׂכוּ **Sêkûw**, *say'-koo*; from an unused root appar. mean. to *surmount;* an *observatory* (with the art.); *Seku*, a place in Pal.:—Sechu.

7907. שֶׂכְוִי **sekvîy**, *sek-vee'*; from the same as 7906; *observant*, i.e. (concr.) the *mind:*—heart.

7908. שְׁכוֹל **shᵉkôwl**, *shek-ole'*; infin. of 7921; *bereavement:*—loss of children, spoiling.

7909. שַׁכּוּל **shakkuwl**, *shak-kool'*; or שַׁכֻּל **shakkul**, *shak-kool'*; from 7921; *bereaved:*—barren, bereaved (robbed) of children (whelps).

7910. שִׁכּוֹר **shikkôwr**, *shik-kore'*; or שִׁכֹּר **shikkôr**, *shik-kore'*; from 7937; *into 'cated*, as a state or a habit:—drunk (-ard, -en, -en man).

7911. שָׁכַח **shâkach**, *shaw-kakh'*; or שָׁכֵחַ **shâkêach**, *shaw-kay'-akh*, a prim. root; to *mislay*, i.e. to *be oblivious of*, from want of memory or attention:— × at all, (cause to) forget.

7912. שְׁכַח **shᵉkach** (Chald.), *shek-akh'*; corresp. to 7911 through the idea of disclosure of a *covered* or *forgotten* thing; to *discover* (lit. or fig.):—find.

7913. שָׁכֵחַ **shâkêach**, *shaw-kay'-akh*; from 7911; *oblivious*:—forget.

7914. שְׂכִיָּה **sᵉkîyâh**, *sek-ee-yaw'*; fem. from the same as 7906; a *conspicuous* object:—picture.

7915. שַׂכִּין **sakkîyn**, *sak-keen'*; intens. perh. from the same as 7906 in the sense of 7753; a *knife* (as *pointed* or edged):—knife.

7916. שָׂכִיר **sâkîyr**, *saw-keer'*; from 7936; a man *at wages* by the day or year:—hired (man, servant), hireling.

7917. שְׂכִירָה **sᵉkîyrâh**, *sek-ee-raw'*; fem. of 7916; a *hiring*:—that is hired.

7918. שָׁכַךְ **shâkak**, *shaw-kak'*; a prim. root; to *weave* (i.e. *lay*) a trap; fig. (through the idea of *secreting*) to *allay* (passions; phys. *abate* a flood):—appease, assuage, make to cease, pacify, set.

7919. שָׂכַל **sâkal**, *saw-kal'*; a prim. root; to *be* (caus. *make* or *act*) *circumspect* and hence *intelligent*:—consider, expert, instruct, prosper, (deal) prudent (-ly), (give) skill (-ful), have good success, teach, (have, make to) understand (-ing), wisdom, (be, behave self, consider, make) wise (-ly), guide wittingly.

7920. שְׂכַל **sᵉkal** (Chald.), *sek-al'*; corresp. to 7919:—consider.

7921. שָׁכֹל **shâkôl**, *shaw-kole'*; a prim. root; prop. to *miscarry*, i.e. *suffer abortion*; by anal. to *bereave* (lit. or fig.):—bereave (of children), barren, cast calf (fruit, young), be (make) childless, deprive, destroy, × expect, lose children, miscarry, rob of children, spoil.

7922. שֶׂכֶל **sekel**, *seh'-kel*; or

שֵׂכֶל **sêkel**, *say'-kel*; from 7919; *intelligence*; by impl. *success*:—discretion, knowledge, policy, prudence, sense, understanding, wisdom, wise.

שַׁכֻּל **shakkûl**. See 7909.

שִׂכְלוּת **siklûwth**. See 5531.

7923. שִׁכֻּלִים **shikkûlîym**, *shik-koo-leem'*; plur. from 7921; *childlessness* (by continued bereavements):—to have after loss of others.

7924. שָׂכְלְתָנוּ **soklᵉthânûw** (Chald.), *sok-leth-aw-noo'*; from 7920; *intelligence*:—understanding.

7925. שָׁכַם **shâkam**, *shaw-kam'*; a prim. root; prop. to *incline* (the shoulder to a burden); but used only as denom. from 7926; lit. to *load up* (on the back of man or beast), i.e. to *start early* in the morning:—(arise, be up, get [oneself] up, rise up) early (betimes), morning.

7926. שְׁכֶם **shᵉkem**, *shek-em'*; from 7925; the *neck* (between the shoulders) as the place of burdens; fig. the *spur* of a hill:—back, × consent, portion, shoulder.

7927. שְׁכֶם **Shᵉkem**, *shek-em'*; the same as 7926; *ridge*; *Shekem*, a place in Pal.:—Shechem.

7928. שֶׁכֶם **Shekem**, *sheh'-kem*; for 7926; *Shekem*, the name of a Hivite and two Isr.:—Shechem.

7929. שִׁכְמָה **shikmâh**, *shik-maw'*; fem. of 7926; the *shoulder*-bone:—shoulder blade.

7930. שִׁכְמִי **Shikmîy**, *shik-mee'*; patron. from 7928; a *Shikmite* (collect.), or desc. of Shekem:—Shichemites.

7931. שָׁכַן **shâkan**, *shaw-kan'*; a prim. root [appar. akin (by transm.) to 7901 through the idea of *lodging*; comp. 5531, 7925]; to *reside* or permanently stay (lit. or fig.):—abide, continue, (cause to, make to) dwell (-er), have habitation, inhabit, lay, place, (cause to) remain, rest, set (up).

7932. שְׁכַן **shᵉkan** (Chald.), *shek-an'*; corresp. to 7931:—cause to dwell, have habitation.

7933. שֶׁכֶן **sheken**, *sheh'-ken*; from 7931; a *residence*:—habitation.

7934. שָׁכֵן **shâkên**, *shaw-kane'*; from 7931; a *resident*; by extens. a fellow-*citizen*:—inhabitant, neighbour, nigh.

7935. שְׁכַנְיָה **Shᵉkanyâh**, *shek-an-yaw'*; or (prol.)

שְׁכַנְיָהוּ **Shᵉkanyâhûw**, *shek-an-yaw'-hoo*; from 7931 and 3050; *Jah has dwelt*; *Shekanjah*, the name of nine Isr.:—Shecaniah, Shechaniah.

7936. שָׂכַר **sâkar**, *saw-kar'*; or (by perm.)

סָכַר **çâkar** (Ezra 4 : 5), *saw-kar'*; a prim. root [appar. akin (by prosthesis) to 3739 through the idea of temporary *purchase*; comp. 7937]; to *hire*:—earn wages, hire (out self), reward, × surely.

7937. שָׁכַר **shâkar**, *shaw-kar'*; a prim root; to *become tipsy*; in a qualified sense, to *satiate* with a stimulating drink or (fig.) influence:—(be filled with) drink (abundantly), (be, make) drunk (-en), be merry. [Superlative of 8248.]

7938. שֶׂכֶר **seker**, *seh'-ker*; from 7936; *wages*:—reward, sluices.

7939. שָׂכָר **sâkâr**, *saw-kawr'*; from 7936; *payment* of contract; concr. *salary*, *fare*, *maintenance*; by impl. *compensation*, *benefit*:—hire, price, reward [-ed], wages, worth.

7940. שָׂכָר **Sâkar**, *saw-kar'*; the same as 7939; *recompense*; *Sakar*, the name of two Isr.:—Sacar.

7941. שֵׁכָר **shêkâr**, *shay-kawr'*; from 7937; an *intoxicant*, i.e. intensely alcoholic *liquor*:—strong drink, + drunkard, strong wine.

שִׁכֹּר **shikkôr**. See 7910.

7942. שִׁכְּרוֹן **Shikkᵉrôwn**, *shik-ker-one'*; for 7943; *drunkenness*; *Shikkeron*, a place in Pal.:—Shicron.

7943. שִׁכָּרוֹן **shikkârôwn**, *shik-kaw-rone'*; from 7937; *intoxication*:—(be) drunken (-ness).

7944. שַׁל **shal**, *shal*; from 7952 abbrev.; a *fault*:—error.

7945. שֶׁל **shel**, *shel*; for the rel. 834; used with prep. pref., and often followed by some pron. aff.; on *account* of, *whatsoever*, *whichsoever*:—cause, sake.

7946. שַׁלְאֲנָן **shal'ănân**, *shal-an-awn'*; for 7600; *tranquil*:—being at ease.

7947. שָׁלַב **shâlab**, *shaw-lab'*; a prim. root; to *space* off; intens. (*evenly*) to *make equidistant*:—equally distant, set in order.

7948. שָׁלָב **shâlâb**, *shaw-lawb'*; from 7947; a *spacer* or raised *interval*, i.e. the *stile* in a frame or panel:—ledge.

7949. שָׁלַג **shâlag**, *shaw-lag'*; a prim. root; prop. mean. to be *white*; used only as denom. from 7950; to be *snow-white* (with the linen clothing of the slain):—be as snow.

7950. שֶׁלֶג **sheleg**, *sheh'-leg*; from 7949; *snow* (prob. from its *whiteness*):—snow (-y).

7951. שָׁלָה **shâlâh**, *shaw-law'*; or

שָׁלַו **shâlav** (Job 3 : 26), *shaw-lav'*; a prim. root; to be *tranquil*, i.e. *secure* or *successful*:—be happy, prosper, be in safety.

7952. שָׁלָה **shâlâh**, *shaw-law'*; a prim. root [prob. rather ident. with 7953 through the idea of *educing*]; to *mislead*:—deceive, be negligent.

7953. שָׁלָה **shâlâh**, *shaw-law'*; a prim. root [rather cognate (by contr.) to the base of 5394, 7997 and their congeners through the idea of *extracting*]; to *draw* out or off, i.e. *remove* (the soul by death):—take away.

7954. שְׁלָה **shᵉlâh** (Chald.), *shel-aw'*; corresp. to 7951; to *be secure*:—at rest.

שִׁלֹה **Shilôh**. See 7887.

7955. שָׁלָה **shâlâh** (Chald.), *shaw-law'*; from a root corresp. to 7952; a *wrong*:—thing amiss.

שֵׁלָה **shêlâh**. See 7596.

7956. שֵׁלָה **Shêlâh**, *shay-law'*; the same as 7596 (shortened); *request*; *Shelah*, the name of a postdiluvian patriarch and of an Isr.:—Shelah.

7957. שַׁלְהֶבֶת **shalhebeth**, *shal-heh'-beth*; from the same as 3851 with sibilant pref.; a *flare* of fire:—(flaming) flame.

שָׁלַו **shâlav**. See 7951.

7958. שְׂלָו **sᵉlâv**, *sel-awv'*; or

שְׂלָיו **sᵉlâyv**, *sel-awv'*; by orth. var. from 7951 through the idea of *sluggishness*; the *quail* collect. (as *slow* in flight from its weight):—quails.

7959. שֶׁלֶו **shelev**, *sheh'-lev*; from 7951; *security*:—prosperity.

שִׁלוֹ **Shîlôw**. See 7887.

7960. שָׁלוּ **shâlûw** (Chald.), *shaw-loo'*; or

שָׁלוּת **shâlûwth** (Chald.), *shaw-looth'*; from the same as 7955; a *fault*:—error, × fail, thing amiss.

7961. שָׁלֵו **shâlêv**, *shaw-lave'*; or

שָׁלֵיו **shâlêyv**, *shaw-lave'*; fem.

שְׁלֵוָה **shᵉlêvâh**, *shel-ay-vaw'*; from 7951; *tranquil*; (in a bad sense) *careless*; abstr. *security*:—(being) at ease, peaceable, (in) prosper (-ity), quiet (-ness), wealthy.

7962. שַׁלְוָה **shalvâh**, *shal-vaw'*; from 7951; *security* (genuine or false):—abundance, peace (-ably), prosperity, quietness.

7963. שְׁלֵוָה **shᵉlêvâh** (Chald.), *shel-ay-vaw'*; corresp. to 7962; *safety*:—tranquillity. See also 7961.

7964. שִׁלּוּחַ **shillûwach**, *shil-loo'-akh*; or

שִׁלֻּחַ **shillûach**, *shil-loo'-akh*; from 7971; (only in plur.) a *dismissal*, i.e. (of a wife) *divorce* (espec. the document); also (of a daughter) *dower*:—presents, have sent back.

7965. שָׁלוֹם **shâlôwm**, *shaw-lome'*; or

שָׁלֹם **shâlôm**, *shaw-lome'*; from 7999; *safe*, i.e. (fig.) *well*, *happy*, *friendly*; also (abstr.) *welfare*, i.e. health, prosperity, peace:—× do, familiar, × fare, favour, + friend, × greet, (good) health, (× perfect, such as be at) peace (-able, -ably), prosper (-ity, -ous), rest, safe (-ly), salute, welfare, (× all is, be) well, × wholly.

7966. שִׁלּוּם **shillûwm**, *shil-loom'*; or

שִׁלֻּם **shillûm**, *shil-loom'*; from 7999; a *requital*, i.e. (secure) *retribution*, (venal) a *fee*:—recompense, reward.

7967. שַׁלּוּם **Shallûwm**, *shal-loom'*; or (shorter)

שַׁלֻּם **Shallûm**, *shal-loom'*; the same as 7966; *Shallum*, the name of fourteen Isr.:—Shallum.

שְׁלוֹמִית **Shᵉlôwmîyth**. See 8019.

7968. שַׁלּוּן **Shallûwn**, *shal-loon'*; prob. for 7967; *Shallun*, an Isr.:—Shallum.

7969. שָׁלוֹשׁ **shâlôwsh**, *shaw-loshe'*; or

שָׁלֹשׁ **shâlôsh**, *shaw-loshe'*; masc.

שְׁלוֹשָׁה **shᵉlôwshâh**, *shel-o-shaw'*; or

שְׁלֹשָׁה **shᵉlôshâh**, *shel-o-shaw'*; a prim. number; *three*; occasionally (ordinal) *third*, or (multipl.) *thrice*:—+ fork, + often [-times], third, thir [-teen, -teenth], three, + thrice. Comp. 7991.

7970. שְׁלוֹשִׁים **shᵉlôwshîym**, *shel-o-sheem'*; or

שְׁלֹשִׁים **shᵉlôshîym**, *shel-o-sheem'*; multiple of 7969; *thirty*; or (ordinal) *thirtieth*:—thirty, thirtieth. Comp. 7991.

שָׁלוּת **shâlûwth**. See 7960.

7971. שָׁלַח **shâlach**, *shaw-lakh'*; a prim. root; to *send* away, for, or out (in a great variety of applications):—× any wise, appoint, bring (on the way), cast (away, out), conduct, × earnestly, forsake, give (up), grow long, lay, leave, let depart (down, go, loose), push away, put (away, forth, in, out), reach forth, send (away, forth, out), set, shoot (forth, out), sow, spread, stretch forth (out).

7972. שְׁלַח **shᵉlach** (Chald.), *shel-akh'*; corresp. to 7971:—put, send.

7973. שֶׁלַח **shelach**, *sheh'-lakh;* from 7971; a *missile* of attack, i.e. *spear;* also (fig.) a *shoot* of growth, i.e. *branch:*—dart, plant, × put off, sword, weapon.

7974. שֶׁלַח **Shelach**, *sheh'-lakh;* the same as 7973; *Shelach,* a postdiluvian patriarch:—Salah, Shelah. Comp. 7975.

7975. שִׁלֹחַ **Shilôach**, *shee-lo'-akh;* or (in imitation of 7974)

שֶׁלַח **Shelach** (Neh. 3 : 15), *sheh'-lakh;* from 7971; *rill; Shiloäch,* a fountain of Jerus.:—Shiloah, Siloah.

שִׁלֻּחַ **shillûach**. See 7964.

7976. שִׁלֻּחָה **shilluchâh**, *shil-loo-khaw';* fem. of 7964; a *shoot:*—branch.

7977. שִׁלְחִי **Shilchîy**, *shil-khee';* from 7973; *missive,* i.e. *armed; Shilchi,* an Isr.:—Shilhi.

7978. שִׁלְחִים **Shilchîym**, *shil-kheem';* plur. of 7973; *javelins* or *sprouts; Shilchim,* a place in Pal.:—Shilhim.

7979. שֻׁלְחָן **shulchân**, *shool-khawn';* from 7971; a *table* (as *spread* out); by impl. a *meal:*—table.

7980. שָׁלַט **shâlaṭ**, *shaw-lat';* a prim. root; to *dominate,* i.e. *govern;* by impl. to *permit:*—(bear, have) rule, have dominion, give (have) power.

7981. שְׁלֵט **sheleṭ** (Chald.), *shel-ate';* corresp. to 7980:—have the mastery, have power, bear rule, be (make) ruler.

7982. שֶׁלֶט **sheleṭ**, *sheh'-let;* from 7980; prob. a *shield* (as *controlling,* i.e. protecting the person):—shield.

7983. שִׁלְטוֹן **shilṭôwn**, *shil-tone';* from 7980; a *potentate:*—power.

7984. שִׁלְטוֹן **shilṭôwn** (Chald.), *shil-tone';* or

שִׁלְטֹן **shilṭôn**, *shil-tone';* corresp. to 7983:—ruler.

7985. שָׁלְטָן **sholṭân** (Chald.), *shol-tawn';* from 7981; *empire* (abstr. or concr.):—dominion.

7986. שַׁלֶּטֶת **shalleṭeth**, *shal-leh'-teth;* fem. from 7980; a *vixen:*—imperious.

7987. שְׁלִי **shelîy**, *shel-ee';* from 7951; *privacy:*—+ quietly.

7988. שִׁלְיָה **shilyâh**, *shil-yaw';* fem. from 7953; a *fœtus* or *babe* (as *extruded* in birth):—young one.

שְׂלָיו **selâyv**. See 7958.

שַׁלֵיו **shalêyv**. See 7961.

7989. שַׁלִּיט **shallîyṭ**, *shal-leet';* from 7980; *potent;* concr. a *prince* or *warrior:*—governor, mighty, that hath power, ruler.

7990. שַׁלִּיט **shallîyṭ** (Chald.), *shal-leet';* corresp. to 7989; *mighty;* abstr. *permission;* concr. a *premier:*—captain, be lawful, rule (-r).

7991. שָׁלִישׁ **shâlîysh**, *shaw-leesh';* or

שָׁלוֹשׁ **shâlôwsh** (1 Chron. 11 : 11; 12 : 18), *shaw-loshe';* or

שָׁלֹשׁ **shâlôsh** (2 Sam. 23 : 13), *shaw-loshe';* from 7969; a *triple,* i.e. (as a musical instrument) a *triangle* (or perh. rather *three*-stringed lute); also (as an indef. great quantity) a *three*-fold measure (perh. a *treble* ephah); also (as an officer) a general of the *third* rank (upward, i.e. the highest):—captain, instrument of musick, (great) lord, (great) measure, prince, three [*from the marg.*].

7992. שְׁלִישִׁי **shelîyshîy**, *shel-ee-shee';* ordinal from 7969; *third;* fem. a *third* (part); by extens. a *third* (day, year or time); spec. a *third*-story cell):—third (part, rank, time), three (years old).

7993. שָׁלַךְ **shâlak**, *shaw-lak';* a prim. root; to *throw* out, down or away (lit. or fig.):—adventure, cast (away, down, forth, off, out), hurl, pluck, throw.

7994. שָׁלָךְ **shâlâk**, *shaw-lawk';* from 7993; *bird of prey,* usually thought to be the *pelican* (from *casting* itself into the sea):—cormorant.

7995. שַׁלֶּכֶת **shalleketh**, *shal-leh'-keth;* from 7993; a *felling* (of trees):—when cast.

7996. שַׁלֶּכֶת **Shalleketh**, *shal-leh'-keth;* the same as 7995; *Shalleketh,* a gate in Jerus.:—Shalleketh.

7997. שָׁלַל **shâlal**, *shaw-lal';* a prim. root; to *drop* or *strip;* by impl. to *plunder:*—let fall, make self a prey, × of purpose, (make a, [take]) spoil.

7998. שָׁלָל **shâlâl**, *shaw-lawl';* from 7997; *booty:*—prey, spoil.

7999. שָׁלַם **shâlam**, *shaw-lam';* a prim. root; to *be safe* (in mind, body or estate); fig. to *be* (caus. *make*) *completed;* by impl. to *be friendly;* by extens. to *reciprocate* (in various applications):—make amends, (make an) end, finish, full, give again, make good, (re-) pay (again), (make) (to) (be at) peace (-able), that is perfect, perform, (make) prosper (-ous), recompense, render, requite, make restitution, restore, reward, × surely.

8000. שְׁלַם **shelam** (Chald.), *shel-am';* corresp. to 7999; to *complete,* to *restore:*—deliver, finish.

8001. שְׁלָם **shelâm** (Chald.), *shel-awm';* corresp. to 7965; *prosperity:*—peace.

8002. שֶׁלֶם **shelem**, *sheh'-lem;* from 7999; prop. *requital,* i.e. a (voluntary) sacrifice in *thanks:*—peace offering.

8003. שָׁלֵם **shâlêm**, *shaw-lame';* from 7999; *complete* (lit. or fig.); espec. *friendly:*—full, just, made ready, peaceable, perfect (-ed), quiet, Shalem [*by mistake for a name*], whole.

8004. שָׁלֵם **Shâlêm**, *shaw-lame';* the same as 8003; *peaceful; Shalem,* an early name of Jerus.:—Salem.

שָׁלֹם **shâlôm**. See 7965.

8005. שִׁלֵּם **shillêm**, *shil-lame';* from 7999; *requital:*—recompense.

8006. שִׁלֵּם **Shillêm**, *shil-lame';* the same as 8005; *Shillem,* an Isr.:—Shillem.

שִׁלֻּם **shillûm**. See 7966.

שַׁלֻּם **Shallûm**. See 7967.

8007. שַׂלְמָא **Salmâ'**, *sal-maw';* prob. for 8008; *clothing; Salma,* the name of two Isr.:—Salma.

8008. שַׂלְמָה **salmâh**, *sal-maw';* transp. for 8071; a *dress:*—clothes, garment, raiment.

8009. שַׂלְמָה **Salmâh**, *sal-maw';* the same as 8008; *clothing; Salmah,* an Isr.:—Salmon. Comp. 8012.

8010. שְׁלֹמֹה **Shelômôh**, *shel-o-mo';* from 7965; *peaceful; Shelomoh,* David's successor:—Solomon.

8011. שִׁלֻּמָה **shillumâh**, *shil-loo-maw';* fem. of 7966; *retribution:*—reward.

8012. שַׂלְמוֹן **Salmôwn**, *sal-mone';* from 8008; *investiture; Salmon,* an Isr.:—Salmon. Comp. 8009.

8013. שְׁלֹמוֹת **Shelômôwth**, *shel-o-mōth';* fem. plur. of 7965; *pacifications; Shelomoth,* the name of two Isr.:—Shelomith [*from the marg.*], Shelomoth. Comp. 8019.

8014. שַׂלְמַי **Salmay**, *sal-mah'ee;* from 8008; *clothed; Salmai,* an Isr.:—Shalmai.

8015. שְׁלֹמִי **Shelômîy**, *shel-o-mee';* from 7965; *peaceable; Shelomi,* an Isr.:—Shelomi.

8016. שִׁלֵּמִי **Shillêmîy**, *shil-lay-mee';* patron. from 8006; a *Shilemite* (collect.) or desc. of Shillem:—Shillemites.

8017. שְׁלֻמִיאֵל **Shelumîy'êl**, *shel-oo-mee-ale';* from 7965 and 410; *peace of God; Shelumiël,* an Isr.:—Shelumiel.

8018. שֶׁלֶמְיָה **Shelemyâh**, *shel-em-yaw';* or

שֶׁלֶמְיָהוּ **Shelemyâhuw**, *shel-em-yaw'-hoo;* from 8002 and 3050; *thank-offering of Jah; Shelemjah,* the name of nine Isr.:—Shelemiah.

8019. שְׁלֹמִית **Shelômîyth**, *shel-o-meeth';* or

שְׁלוֹמִית **Shelôwmîyth** (Ezra 8 : 10), *shel-o-meeth';* from 7965; *peaceableness; Shelomith,* the name of five Isr. and three Israelitesses:—Shelomith.

8020. שַׁלְמַן **Shalman**, *shal-man';* of for. der.; *Shalman,* a king appar. of Assyria:—Shalman. Comp. 8022.

8021. שַׁלְמֹן **shalmôn**, *shal-mone';* from 7999; a *bribe:*—reward.

8022. שַׁלְמַנְאֶסֶר **Shalman'eçer**, *shal-man-eh'-ser;* of for. der.; *Shalmaneser,* an Ass. king:—Shalmaneser. Comp. 8020.

8023. שִׁלֹנִי **Shilônîy**, *shee-lo-nee';* the same as 7888; *Shiloni,* an Isr.:—Shiloni.

8024. שֵׁלָנִי **Shêlânîy**, *shay-law-nee';* from 7956; a *Shelanite* (collect.), or desc. of Shelah:—Shelanites.

8025. שָׁלַף **shâlaph**, *shaw-laf';* a prim. root; to *pull* out, up or off:—draw (off), grow up, pluck off.

8026. שֶׁלֶף **sheleph**, *sheh'-lef;* from 8025; *extract; Sheleph,* a son of Jokthan:—Sheleph.

8027. שָׁלַשׁ **shâlash**, *shaw-lash';* a prim. root perh. orig. to *intensify,* i.e. *treble;* but appar. used only as denom. from 7969, to *be* (caus. *make*) *triplicate* (by restoration, in portions, strands, days or years):—do the third time, (divide into, stay) three (days, -fold, parts, years old).

8028. שֶׁלֶשׁ **Shelesh**, *sheh'-lesh;* from 8027; *triplet; Shelesh,* an Isr.:—Shelesh.

שָׁלֹשׁ **shâlôsh**. See 7969.

8029. שִׁלֵּשׁ **shillêsh**, *shil-laysh';* from 8027; a desc. of the *third* degree, i.e. *great grandchild:*—third [generation].

8030. שִׁלְשָׁה **Shilshâh**, *shil-shaw';* fem. from the same as 8028; *triplication; Shilshah,* an Isr.:—Shilshah.

8031. שָׁלִשָׁה **Shâlîshâh**, *shaw-lee-shaw';* fem. from 8027; *trebled* land; *Shalishah,* a place in Pal.:—Shalisha.

שְׁלֹשָׁה **shâlôshâh**. See 7969.

8032. שִׁלְשׁוֹם **shilshôwm**, *shil-shome';* or

שִׁלְשֹׁם **shilshôm**, *shil-shome';* from the same as 8028; *trebly,* i.e. (in time) *day before yesterday:*—+ before (that time, -time), excellent things [*from the marg.*], + heretofore, three days, + time past.

שְׁלֹשִׁים **sh^elôshîym**. See 7970.

שַׁלְתִּיאֵל **Shaltîy'êl**. See 7597.

8033. שָׁם **shâm**, *shawm;* a prim. particle [rather from the rel. 834]; *there* (transf. to time) *then;* often *thither,* or *thence:*—in it, + thence, there (-in, + of, + out), + thither, + whither.

8034. שֵׁם **shêm**, *shame;* a prim. word [perh. rather from 7760 through the idea of definite and conspicuous *position;* comp. 8064]; an *appellation,* as a mark or memorial of individuality; by impl. *honor, authority, character:*— + base, [in-] fame [-ous], name (-d), renown, report.

8035. שֵׁם **Shêm**, *shame;* the same as 8034; *name; Shem,* a son of Noah (often includ. his posterity):—Sem, Shem.

8036. שֻׁם **shum** (Chald.), *shoom;* corresp. to 8034:—name.

8037. שַׁמָּא **Shammâ'**, *sham-maw';* from 8074; *desolation; Shamma,* an Isr.:—Shamma.

8038. שֶׁמְאֵבֶר **Shem'êber**, *shem-ay'-ber;* appar. from 8034 and 83; *name of pinion,* i.e. *illustrious; Shemeber,* a king of Zeboim:—Shemeber.

8039. שִׁמְאָה **Shim'âh**, *shim-aw';* perh. for 8093; *Shimah,* an Isr.:—Shimah. Comp. 8043.

8040. שְׂמֹאול **s^emô'wl**, *sem-ole';* or

שְׂמֹאל **s^emô'l**, *sem-ole';* a prim. word [rather perh. from the same as 8071 (by insertion of א) through the idea of *wrapping* up]; prop. *dark* (as *enveloped*), i.e. the *north;* hence (by orientation) the *left* hand:—left (hand, side).

8041. שָׂמַאל **sâma'l**, *saw-mal';* a prim. root [rather denom. from 8040]; to use the *left* hand or pass in that direction):—(go, turn) (on the, to the) left.

8042. שְׂמָאלִי **semâ'lîy**, *sem-aw-lee'*; from 8040; situated on the *left* side:—left.

8043. שִׁמְאָם **Shim'âm**, *shim-awm'*; for 8089 [comp. 88]; *Shimam*, an Isr.:—Shimeam.

8044. שַׁמְגַּר **Shamgar**, *sham-gar'*; of uncert. der.; *Shamgar*, an Isr. judge:—Shamgar.

8045. שָׁמַד **shâmad**, *shaw-mad'*; a prim. root; to *desolate*:—destroy (-uction), bring to nought, overthrow, perish, pluck down, × utterly.

8046. שְׁמַד **shemad** (Chald.), *shem-ad'*; corresp. to 8045:—consume.

שָׁמֶה **shâmeh**. See 8064.

8047. שַׁמָּה **shammâh**, *sham-maw'*; from 8074; *ruin*; by impl. *consternation*:—astonishment, desolate (-ion), waste, wonderful thing.

8048. שַׁמָּה **Shammâh**, *sham-maw'*; the same as 8047; *Shammah*, the name of an Edomite and four Isr.:—Shammah.

8049. שַׁמְהוּת **Shamhûwth**, *sham-hooth'*; for 8048; *desolation*; *Shamhuth*, an Isr.:—Shamhuth.

8050. שְׁמוּאֵל **Shemûw'êl**, *shem-oo-ale'*; from the pass. part. of 8085 and 410; *heard of God*; *Shemuël*, the name of three Isr.:—Samuel, Shemuel.

שְׁמוֹנֶה **shemôwneh**. See 8083.

שְׁמוֹנָה **shemôwnâh**. See 8083.

שְׁמוֹנִים **shemôwnîym**. See 8084.

8051. שַׁמּוּעַ **Shammûwaʻ**, *sham-moo'-ah*; from 8074; *renowned*; *Shammua*, the name of four Isr.:—Shammua, Shammuah.

8052. שְׁמוּעָה **shemûwʻâh**, *shem-oo-aw'*; fem. pass. part. of 8074; something *heard*, i.e. an *announcement*:—bruit, doctrine, fame, mentioned, news, report, rumor, tidings.

8053. שָׁמוּר° **Shâmûwr**, *shaw-moor'*; pass. part. of 8103; *observed*; *Shamur*, an Isr.:—Shamir [*from the marg.*].

8054. שַׁמּוֹת **Shammôwth**, *sham-mōth'*; plur. of 8047; *ruins*; *Shammoth*, an Isr.:—Shamoth.

8055. שָׂמַח **sâmach**, *saw-makh'*; a prim. root; prob. to *brighten* up, i.e. (fig.) *be* (caus. *make*) *blithe* or *gleesome*:—cheer up, be (make) glad, (have, make) joy (-ful), be (make) merry, (cause to, make to) rejoice. × very.

8056. שָׂמֵחַ **sâmêach**, *saw-may'-akh*; from 8055; *blithe* or *gleeful*:—(be) glad, joyful, (making) merry ([-hearted], -ily), rejoice (-ing).

8057. שִׂמְחָה **simchâh**, *sim-khaw'*; from 8056; *blithesomeness* or *glee*, (religious or festival):—× exceeding (-ly), gladness, joy (-fulness), mirth, pleasure, rejoice (-ing).

8058. שָׁמַט **shâmaṭ**, *shaw-mat'*; a prim. root; to *fling* down; incipiently to *jostle*; fig. to *let alone*, *desist*, *remit*:—discontinue, overthrow, release, let rest, shake, stumble, throw down.

8059. שְׁמִטָּה **shemiṭṭâh**, *shem-it-taw'*; from 8058; *remission* (of debt) or *suspension* of labor):—release.

8060. שַׁמַּי **Shammay**, *sham-mah'ee*; from 8073; *destructive*; *Shammai*, the name of three Isr.:—Shammai.

8061. שְׁמִידָע **Shemîydâʻ**, *shem-ee-daw'*; appar. from 8034 and 3045; *name of knowing*; *Shemida*, an Isr.:—Shemida, Shemidah.

8062. שְׁמִידָעִי **Shemîydâʻîy**, *shem-ee-daw-ee'*; patron. from 8061; a *Shemidaïte* (collect.) or desc. of Shemida:—Shemidaites.

8063. שְׂמִיכָה **semîykâh**, *sem-ee-kaw'*; from 5564; a *rug* (as *sustaining* the Oriental sitter):—mantle.

8064. שָׁמַיִם **shâmayim**, *shaw-mah'-yim*; dual of an unused sing.

שָׁמֶה **shâmeh**, *shaw-meh'*; from an unused root mean. to *be lofty*; the *sky* (as *aloft*; the dual perh. alluding to the visible arch in which the clouds move, as well as to the higher ether where the celestial bodies revolve):—air, × astrologer, heaven (-s).

8065. שָׁמַיִן **shâmayin** (Chald.), *shaw-mah'-yin*; corresp. to 8064:—heaven.

8066. שְׁמִינִי **shemîynîy**, *shem-ee-nee'*; from 8083; *eight*:—eight.

8067. שְׁמִינִית **shemîynîyth**, *shem-ee-neeth'*; fem. of 8066; prob. an *eight*-stringed lyre:—Sheminith.

8068. שָׁמִיר **shâmîyr**, *shaw-meer'*; from 8104 in the orig. sense of *pricking*; a *thorn*; also (from its *keenness* for scratching) a gem, prob. the *diamond*:—adamant (stone), brier, diamond.

8069. שָׁמִיר **Shâmîyr**, *shaw-meer'*; the same as 8068; *Shamir*, the name of two places in Pal.:—Shamir. Comp. 8053.

8070. שְׁמִירָמוֹת **Shemîyrâmôwth**, *shem-ee-raw-mōth'*; or

שְׁמָרִימוֹת° **Shemârîymôwth**, *shem-aw-ree-mōth'*; prob. from 8034 and plur. of 7413; *name of heights*; *Shemiramoth*, the name of two Isr.:—Shemiramoth.

8071. שִׂמְלָה **simlâh**, *sim-law'*; perh. by perm. for the fem. of 5566 (through the idea of a *cover* assuming the shape of the object beneath); a *dress*, espec. a *mantle*:—apparel, cloth (-es, -ing), garment, raiment. Comp. 8008.

8072. שַׂמְלָה **Samlâh**, *sam-law'*; prob. for the same as 8071; *Samlah*, an Edomite:—Samlah.

8073. שַׁמְלַי° **Shamlay**, *sham-lah'ee*; for 8014; *Shamlai*, one of the Nethinim:—Shalmai [*from the marg.*].

8074. שָׁמֵם **shâmêm**, *shaw-mame'*; a prim. root; to *stun* (or intrans. *grow numb*), i.e. *devastate* or (fig.) *stupefy* (both usually in a passive sense):—make amazed, be astonied, (be an) astonish (-ment), (be, bring into, unto, lay, lie, make) desolate (-ion, places), be destitute, destroy (self), (lay, lie, make) waste, wonder.

8075. שְׁמַם **shemam** (Chald.), *shem-am'*; corresp. to 8074:—be astonied.

8076. שָׁמֵם **shâmêm**, *shaw-mame'*; from 8074; *ruined*:—desolate.

8077. שְׁמָמָה **shemâmâh**, *shem-aw-maw'*; or

שִׁמֲמָה **shimămâh**, *shee-mam-aw'*; fem. of 8076; *devastation*; fig. *astonishment*:—(laid, × most) desolate (-ion), waste.

8078. שִׁמָּמוֹן **shimmâmôwn**, *shim-maw-mone'*; from 8074; *stupefaction*:—astonishment.

8079. שְׂמָמִית **semâmîyth**, *sem-aw-meeth'*; prob. from 8074 (in the sense of *poisoning*); a *lizard* (from the superstition of its *noxiousness*):—spider.

8080. שָׁמַן **shâman**, *shaw-man'*; a prim. root; to *shine*, i.e. (by anal.) *be* (caus. *make*) *oily* or *gross*:—become (make, wax) fat.

8081. שֶׁמֶן **shemen**, *sheh'-men*; from 8080; *grease*, espec. liquid (as from the olive, often perfumed); fig. *richness*:—anointing, × fat (things), × fruitful, oil ([-ed]), ointment, olive, + pine.

8082. שָׁמֵן **shâmên**, *shaw-mane'*; from 8080; *greasy*, i.e. *gross*; fig. *rich*:—fat, lusty, plenteous.

8083. שְׁמֹנֶה **shemôneh**, *shem-o-neh'*; or

שְׁמוֹנֶה **shemôwneh**, *shem-o-neh'*; fem.

שְׁמֹנָה **shemônâh**, *shem-o-naw'*; or

שְׁמוֹנָה **shemôwnâh**, *shem-o-naw'*; appar. from 8082 through the idea of *plumpness*; a cardinal number, *eight* (as if a *surplus* above the "perfect" seven); also (as ordinal) *eighth*:—eight ([-een, -eenth]), eighth.

8084. שְׁמֹנִים **shemônîym**, *shem-o-neem'*; or

שְׁמוֹנִים **shemôwnîym**, *shem-o-neem'*; mult. from 8083; *eighty*; also *eightieth*:—eighty (-ieth), fourscore.

8085. שָׁמַע **shâmaʻ**, *shaw-mah'*; a prim. root; to *hear* intelligently (often with impl. of attention, obedience, etc.; caus. to *tell*, etc.):—× attentively, call (gather) together, × carefully, × certainly, consent, consider, be content, declare, × diligently, discern, give ear, (cause to, let, make to) hear (-ken, tell), × indeed, listen, make (a) noise, (be) obedient, obey, perceive, (make a) proclaim (-ation), publish, regard, report, shew (forth), (make a) sound, × surely, tell, understand, whosoever [heareth], witness.

8086. שְׁמַע **shemaʻ** (Chald.), *shem-ah'*; corresp. to 8085:—hear, obey.

8087. שֶׁמַע **Shemaʻ**, *sheh'-mah*; for the same as 8088; *Shema*, the name of a place in Pal. and of four Isr.:—Shema.

8088. שֵׁמַע **shêmaʻ**, *shay'-mah*; from 8085; something *heard*, i.e. a *sound*, *rumor*, *announcement*; abstr. *audience*:—bruit, fame, hear (-ing), loud, report, speech, tidings.

8089. שֹׁמַע **shômaʻ**, *sho'-mah*; from 8085; a *report*:—fame.

8090. שְׁמָע **Shemâʻ**, *shem-aw'*; for 8087; *Shema*, a place in Pal.:—Shema.

8091. שָׁמָע **Shâmâʻ**, *shaw-maw'*; from 8085; *obedient*; *Shama*, an Isr.:—Shama.

8092. שִׁמְעָא **Shimʻâ'**, *shim-aw'*; for 8093; *Shima*, the name of four Isr.:—Shimea, Shimei, Shamma.

8093. שִׁמְעָה **Shimʻâh**, *shim-aw'*; fem. of 8088; *annunciation*; *Shimah*, an Isr.:—Shimeah.

8094. שְׁמָעָה **Shemâʻâh**, *shem-aw-aw'*; for 8093; *Shemaah*, an Isr.:—Shemaah.

8095. שִׁמְעוֹן **Shimʻôwn**, *shim-ōne'*; from 8085: *hearing*; *Shimon*, one of Jacob's sons, also the tribe desc. from him:—Simeon.

8096. שִׁמְעִי **Shimʻîy**, *shim-ee'*; from 8088; *famous*; *Shimi*, the name of twenty Isr.:—Shimeah [*from the marg.*], Shimei, Shimhi, Shimi.

8097. שִׁמְעִי **Shimʻîy**, *shim-ee'*; patron. from 8096; a *Shimite* (collect.) or desc. of Shimi:—of Shimi, Shimites.

8098. שְׁמַעְיָה **Shemaʻyâh**, *shem-aw-yaw'*; or

שְׁמַעְיָהוּ **Shemaʻyâhûw**, *shem-aw-yaw'-hoo*; from 8085 and 3050; *Jah has heard*; *Shemajah*, the name of twenty-five Isr.:—Shemaiah.

8099. שִׁמְעֹנִי **Shimʻônîy**, *shim-o-nee'*; patron. from 8095; a *Shimonite* (collect.) or desc. of Shimon:—tribe of Simeon, Simeonites.

8100. שִׁמְעַת **Shimʻâth**, *shim-awth'*; fem. of 8088; *annunciation*; *Shimath*, an Ammonitess:—Shimath.

8101. שִׁמְעָתִי **Shimʻâthîy**, *shim-aw-thee'*; patron. from 8093; a *Shimathite* (collect.) or desc. of Shimah:—Shimeathites.

8102. שֶׁמֶץ **shemets**, *sheh'-mets*; from an unused root mean. to *emit* a sound; an *inkling*:—a little.

8103. שִׁמְצָה **shimtsâh**, *shim-tsaw'*; fem. of 8102; scornful *whispering* (of hostile spectators):—shame.

8104. שָׁמַר **shâmar**, *shaw-mar'*; a prim. root; prop. to *hedge* about (as with thorns), i.e. *guard*; gen. to *protect*, *attend to*, etc.:—beware, be circumspect, take heed (to self), keep (-er, self), mark, look narrowly, observe, preserve, regard, reserve, save (self), sure, (that lay) wait (for), watch (-man).

8105. שֶׁמֶר **shemer**, *sheh'-mer*; from 8104; something *preserved*, i.e. the *settlings* (plur. only) of wine:—dregs, (wines on the) lees.

8106. שֶׁמֶר **Shemer**, *sheh'-mer*; the same as 8105; *Shemer*, the name of three Isr.:—Shamer, Shemer.

8107. שִׁמֻּר **shimmûr**, *shim-moor'*; from 8104; an *observance*:—× be (much) observed.

שֹׁמֵר **Shômêr**. See 7763.

8108. שָׁמְרָה **shomrâh**, *shom-raw'*; fem. of an unused noun from 8104 mean. a *guard*; *watchfulness*:—watch.

8109. שְׁמֻרָה **shemûrâh**, *shem-oo-raw'*; fem. of pass. part. of 8104; something *guarded*, i.e. an *eye-lid*:—waking.

8110. שִׁמְרוֹן **Shimrôwn**, *shim-rone'*; from 8105 in its orig. sense; *guardianship*; *Shimron*, the name of an Isr. and of a place in Pal.:—Shimron.

8111. שֹׁמְרוֹן **Shômerown**, *sho-mer-ōne'*; from the act. part. of 8104; *watch-station; Shomeron*, a place in Pal.:—Samaria.

8112. שִׁמְרוֹן מְראוֹן **Shimrôwn Merô'wn**, *shim-rone' mer-one'*; from 8110 and a der. of 4754; *guard of lashing; Shimron-Meron*, a place in Pal.:—Shimon-meron.

8113. שִׁמְרִי **Shimrîy**, *shim-ree'*; from 8105 in its orig. sense; *watchful; Shimri*, the name of four Isr.:—Shimri.

8114. שְׁמַרְיָה **Shemaryâh**, *shem-ar-yaw'*; or

שְׁמַרְיָהוּ **Shemaryâhûw**, *shem-ar-yaw'-hoo*; from 8104 and 3050; *Jah has guarded; Shemarjah*, the name of four Isr.:—Shamariah, Shemariah.

שְׁמָרִימוֹת° **Shemârîymôwth**. See 8070.

8115. שָׁמְרַיִן **Shomrayin** (Chald.), *shom-rah'-yin*; corresp. to 8111; *Shomraïn*, a place in Pal.:—Samaria.

8116. שִׁמְרִית **Shimrîyth**, *shim-reeth'*; fem. of 8113; *female guard; Shimrith*, a Moabitess:—Shimrith.

8117. שִׁמְרֹנִי **Shimrônîy**, *shim-ro-nee'*; patron. from 8110; a *Shimronite* (collect.) or desc. of Shimron:—Shimronites.

8118. שֹׁמְרֹנִי **Shômerônîy**, *sho-mer-o-nee'*; patrial from 8111; a *Shomeronite* (collect.) or inhab. of Shomeron:—Samaritans.

8119. שִׁמְרָת **Shimrâth**, *shim-rawth'*; from 8104; *guardship; Shimrath*, an Isr.:—Shimrath.

8120. שְׁמַשׁ **shemash** (Chald.), *shem-ash'*; corresp. to the root of 8121 through the idea of *activity* implied in day-light; to *serve*:—minister.

8121. שֶׁמֶשׁ **shemesh**, *sheh'-mesh*; from an unused root mean. to be *brilliant*; the *sun*; by impl. the *east*; fig. a *ray*, i.e. (arch.) a notched *battlement*:— + east side (-ward), sun ([rising]), + west (-ward), window. See also 1053.

8122. שֶׁמֶשׁ **shemesh** (Chald.), *sheh'-mesh*; corresp. to 8121; the *sun*:—sun.

8123. שִׁמְשׁוֹן **Shimshôwn**, *shim-shone'*; from 8121; *sunlight; Shimshon*, an Isr.:—Samson.

שִׁמְשִׁי **Shimshîy**. See 1030.

8124. שִׁמְשַׁי **Shimshay** (Chald.), *shim-shah'ee*; from 8122; *sunny; Shimshai*, a Samaritan:—Shimshai.

8125. שַׁמְשְׁרַי **Shamsheray**, *sham-sher-ah'ee*; appar. from 8121; *sunlike; Shamsherai*, an Isr.:—Shamsherai.

8126. שֻׁמָתִי **Shûmâthîy**, *shoo-maw-thee'*; patron. from an unused name from 7762 prob. mean. *garlic*-smell; a *Shumathite* (collect.) or desc. of Shumah:—Shumathites.

8127. שֵׁן **shên**, *shane*; from 8150; a *tooth* (as *sharp*); spec. (for 8143) *ivory*; fig. a *cliff*:—crag, × forefront, ivory, × sharp, tooth.

8128. שֵׁן **shên** (Chald.), *shane*; corresp. to 8127; a *tooth*:—tooth.

8129. שֵׁן **Shên**, *shane*; the same as 8127; *crag; Shen*, a place in Pal.:—Shen.

8130. שָׂנֵא **sânê'**, *saw-nay'*; a prim. root; to *hate* (personally):—enemy, foe, (be) hate (-ful, -r), odious, × utterly.

8131. שְׂנֵא **senê'** (Chald.), *sen-ay'*; corresp. to 8130:—hate.

8132. שָׁנָא **shânâ'**, *shaw-naw'*; a prim. root; to *alter*:—change.

8133. שְׁנָא **shenâ'** (Chald.), *shen-aw'*; corresp. to 8132:—alter, change, (be) diverse.

שְׁנָא **shênâ'**. See 8142.

8134. שִׁנְאָב **Shin'âb**, *shin-awb'*; prob. from 8132 and 1; a *father has turned; Shinab*, a Canaanite:—Shinab.

8135. שִׂנְאָה **sin'âh**, *sin-aw'*; from 8130; *hate*:—+ exceedingly, hate (-ful, -red).

8136. שִׁנְאָן **shin'ân**, *shin-awn'*; from 8132; *change*, i.e. *repetition*:— × angels.

8137. שֶׁנְאַצַּר **Shenatstsar**, *shen-ats-tsar'*; appar. of Bab. or.; *Shenatstsar*, an Isr.:—Senazar.

8138. שָׁנָה **shânâh**, *shaw-naw'*; a prim. root; to *fold*, i.e. *duplicate* (lit. or fig.); by impl. to *transmute* (trans. or intrans.):—do (speak, strike) again, alter, double, (be given to) change, disguise, (be) diverse, pervert, prefer, repeat, return, do the second time.

8139. שְׁנָה **shenâh** (Chald.), *shen-aw'*; corresp. to 8142:—sleep.

8140. שְׁנָה **shenâh** (Chald.), *shen-aw'*; corresp. to 8141:—year.

8141. שָׁנֶה **shâneh** (in plur. only), *shaw-neh'*; or (fem.)

שָׁנָה **shânâh**, *shaw-naw'*; from 8138; a *year* (as a *revolution* of time):—+ whole age, × long, + old, year (× -ly).

8142. שֵׁנָה **shênâh**, *shay-naw'*; or

שֵׁנָא **shênâ'** (Psa. 127 : 2), *shay-naw'*; from 3462; *sleep*:—sleep.

8143. שֶׁנְהַבִּים **shenhabbîym**, *shen-hab-beem'*; from 8127 and the plur. appar. of a for. word; prob. *tooth of elephants*, i.e. *ivory tusk*:—ivory.

8144. שָׁנִי **shânîy**, *shaw-nee'*; of uncert. der.; *crimson*, prop. the insect or its color, also stuff dyed with it:—crimson, scarlet (thread).

8145. שֵׁנִי **shênîy**, *shay-nee'*; from 8138; prop. *double*, i.e. *second*; also adv. *again*:—again, either [of them], (an-) other, second (time).

8146. שָׂנִיא **sânîy'**, *saw-nee'*; from 8130; *hated*:—hated.

8147. שְׁנַיִם **shenayim**, *shen-ah'-yim*; dual of 8145; fem.

שְׁתַּיִם **shettayim**, *shet-tah'-yim*; *two*; also (as ordinal) *twofold*:—both, couple, double, second, twain, + twelfth, + twelve, + twenty (sixscore) thousand, twice, two.

8148. שְׁנִינָה **shenîynâh**, *shen-ee-naw'*; from 8150; something *pointed*, i.e. a *gibe*:—byword, taunt.

8149. שְׁנִיר **Shenîyr**, *shen-eer'*; or

שְׂנִיר **Senîyr**, *sen-eer'*; from an unused root mean. to *be pointed; peak; Shenir* or *Senir*, a summit of Lebanon:—Senir, Shenir.

8150. שָׁנַן **shânan**, *shaw-nan'*; a prim. root; to *point* (trans. or intrans.); intens. to *pierce*; fig. to *inculcate*:—prick, sharp (-en), teach diligently, whet.

8151. שָׁנַס **shânaç**, *shaw-nas'*; a prim. root; to *compress* (with a belt):—gird up.

8152. שִׁנְעָר **Shinʻâr**, *shin-awr'*; prob. of for. der.; *Shinar*, a plain in Bab.:—Shinar.

8153. שְׁנָת **shenâth**, *shen-awth'*; from 3462; *sleep*:—sleep.

8154. שָׁסָה **shâçâh**, *shaw-saw'*; or

שָׁשָׂה **shâsâh** (Isa. 10 : 13), *shaw-saw'*; a prim. root; to *plunder*:—destroyer, rob, spoil (-er).

8155. שָׁסַס **shâçaç**, *shaw-sas'*; a prim. root; to *plunder*:—rifle, spoil.

8156. שָׁסַע **shâçaʻ**, *shaw-sah'*; a prim. root; to *split* or *tear*; fig. to *upbraid*:—cleave, (be) cloven ([footed]), rend, stay.

8157. שֶׁסַע **sheçaʻ**, *sheh'-sah*; from 8156; a *fissure*:—cleft, clovenfooted.

8158. שָׁסַף **shâçaph**, *shaw-saf'*; a prim. root; to *cut* in pieces, i.e. slaughter:—hew in pieces.

8159. שָׁעָה **shâʻâh**, *shaw-aw'*; a prim. root; to *gaze* at or about (prop. for help); by impl. to *inspect, consider, compassionate, be nonplussed* (as looking around in amazement) or *bewildered*:—depart, be dim, be dismayed, look (away), regard, have respect, spare, turn.

8160. שָׁעָה **shâʻâh** (Chald.), *shaw-aw'*; from a root corresp. to 8159; prop. a *look*, i.e. a *moment*:—hour.

שְׂעוֹר **seʻôwr**. See 8184.

שְׂעוֹרָה **seʻôwrâh**. See 8184.

8161. שַׁעֲטָה **shaʻățâh**, *shah'-at-aw*; fem. from an unused root mean. to *stamp*; a *clatter* (of hoofs):—stamping.

8162. שַׁעַטְנֵז **shaʻaṭnêz**, *shah-at-naze'*; prob. of for. der.; *linsey-woolsey*, i.e. cloth of linen and wool carded and spun together:—garment of divers sorts, linen and woollen.

8163. שָׂעִיר **sâʻîyr**, *saw-eer'*; or

שָׂעִר **sâʻir**, *saw-eer'*; from 8175; *shaggy*; as noun, a *he-goat*; by anal. a *faun*:—devil, goat, hairy, kid, rough, satyr.

8164. שָׂעִיר **sâʻîyr**, *saw-eer'*; formed the same as 8163; a *shower* (as *tempestuous*):—small rain.

8165. שֵׂעִיר **Sêʻîyr**, *say-eer'*; formed like 8163; *rough; Seïr*, a mountain of Idumæa and its aboriginal occupants, also one in Pal.:—Seir.

8166. שְׂעִירָה **seʻîyrâh**, *seh-ee-raw'*; fem. of 8163; a *she-goat*:—kid.

8167. שְׂעִירָה **Seʻîyrâh**, *seh-ee-raw'*; formed as 8166; *roughness; Seïrah*, a place in Pal.:—Seirath.

8168. שֹׁעַל **shôʻal**, *sho'-al*; from an unused root mean. to *hollow* out; the *palm*; by extens. a *handful*:—handful, hollow of the hand.

שֻׁעָל **shûʻâl**. See 7776.

8169. שַׁעַלְבִים **Shaʻalbîym**, *shah-al-beem'*; or

שַׁעֲלַבִּין **Shaʻălabbîyn**, *shah-al-ab-been'*; plur. from 7776; *fox-holes; Shaalbim* or *Shaalabbin*, a place in Pal.:—Shaalabbin, Shaalbim.

8170. שַׁעַלְבֹנִי **Shaʻalbônîy**, *shah-al-bo-nee'*; patrial from 8169; a *Shaalbonite* or inhab. of Shaalbin:—Shaalbonite.

8171. שַׁעֲלִים **Shaʻălîym**, *shah-al-eem'*; plur. of 7776; *foxes; Shaalim*, a place in Pal.:—Shalim.

8172. שָׁעַן **shâʻan**, *shaw-an'*; a prim. root; to *support* one's self:—lean, lie, rely, rest (on, self), stay.

8173. שָׁעַע **shâʻaʻ**, *shaw-ah'*; a prim. root; (in a good acceptation) to *look* upon (with complacency), i.e. *fondle, please* or *amuse* (self); (in a bad one) to *look* about (in dismay), i.e. *stare*:—cry (out) [*by confusion with* 7768], dandle, delight (self), play, shut.

שָׂעִף **sâʻiph**. See 5587.

8174. שַׁעַף **Shaʻaph**, *shah'-af*; from 5586; *fluctuation; Shaaph*, the name of two Isr.:—Shaaph.

8175. שָׂעַר **sâʻar**, *saw-ar'*; a prim. root; to *storm*; by impl. to *shiver*, i.e. *fear*:—be (horribly) afraid, fear, hurl as a storm, be tempestuous, come like (take away as with) a whirlwind.

8176. שָׁעַר **shâʻar**, *shaw-ar'*; a prim. root; to *split* or *open*, i.e. (lit., but only as denom. from 8179) to *act as gate-keeper* (see 7778); (fig.) to *estimate*:—think.

8177. שְׂעַר **seʻar** (Chald.), *seh-ar'*; corresp. to 8181; *hair*:—hair.

8178. שַׂעַר **saʻar**, *sah'-ar*; from 8175; a *tempest*; also a *terror*:—affrighted, × horribly, × sore, storm. See 8181.

8179. שַׁעַר **shaʻar**, *shah'-ar*; from 8176 in its orig. sense; an *opening*, i.e. *door* or *gate*:—city, door, gate, port (× -er).

8180. שַׁעַר **shaʻar**, *shah'-ar*; from 8176; a *measure* (as a *section*):—[hundred-] fold.

שָׂעִר **sâʻir**. See 8163.

8181. שֵׂעָר **sêʻâr**, *say-awr'*; or

שַׂעַר **saʻar** (Isa. 7 : 20), *sah'-ar*; from 8175 in the sense of *dishevelling; hair* (as if *tossed* or *bristling*):—hair (-y), × rough.

שֹׁעֵר **shôʻêr**. See 7778.

8182. שֹׁעָר **shôʻâr**, *sho-awr'*; from 8176; *harsh* or *horrid*, i.e. *offensive*:—vile.

8183. שְׂעָרָה **seʻârâh**, *seh-aw-raw'*; fem. of 8178; a *hurricane*:—storm, tempest.

8184. שְׂעֹרָה s^eʻôrâh, *seh-o-raw'*; or **שְׂעוֹרָה s^eʻôwrâh**, *seh-o-raw'* (fem. mean. the *plant*); and (masc. mean. the *grain*); also **שְׂעֹר s^eʻôr**, *seh-ore'*; or **שְׂעוֹר s^eʻôwr**, *seh-ore'*; from 8175 in the sense of *roughness*; *barley* (as *villose*):—barley.

8185. שַׂעֲרָה saʻărâh, *sah-ar-aw'*; fem. of 8181; *hairiness*:—hair.

8186. שַׁעֲרוּרָה shaʻărûwrâh, *shah-ar-oo-raw'*; or **שַׁעֲרִרִיָּה° shaʻărîyrîyâh**, *shah-ar-ee-ree-yaw'*; or **שַׁעֲרֻרִת shaʻărûrîth**, *shah-ar-oo-reeth'*; fem. from 8176 in the sense of 8175; something *fearful*:—horrible thing.

8187. שְׁעַרְיָה Sheʻaryâh, *sheh-ar-yaw'*; from 8176 and 3050; *Jah has stormed*; *Shearjah*, an Isr.:—Sheariah.

8188. שְׂעֹרִים S^eʻôrîym, *seh-o-reem'*; masc. plur. of 8184; *barley grains*; *Seörim*, an Isr.:—Seorim.

8189. שַׁעֲרַיִם Shaʻărayim, *shah-ar-ah'-yim*; dual of 8179; *double gates*; *Shaarajim*, a place in Pal.:—Shaaraim.

שַׁעֲרִירִיָּה° shaʻărîyrîyâh. See 8186.

שַׁעֲרֻרִת shaʻărûrîth. See 8186.

8190. שַׁעַשְׁגַז Shaʻashgaz, *shah-ash-gaz'*; of Pers. der.; *Shaashgaz*, a eunuch of Xerxes:—Shaashgaz.

8191. שַׁעְשֻׁעַ shaʻshûaʻ, *shah-shoo'-ah*; from 8173; *enjoyment*:—delight, pleasure.

8192. שָׁפָה shâphâh, *shaw-faw'*; a prim. root; to *abrade*, i.e. *bare*:—high, stick out.

8193. שָׂפָה sâphâh, *saw-faw'*; or (in dual and plur.) **שֶׂפֶת sepheth**, *sef-eth'*; prob. from 5595 or 8192 through the idea of *termination* (comp. 5490); the *lip* (as a natural boundary); by impl. *language*; by anal. a *margin* (of a vessel, water, cloth, etc.):—band, bank, binding, border, brim, brink, edge, language, lip, prating, ([sea-]) shore, side, speech, talk, [vain] words.

8194. שָׁפָה shâphâh, *shaw-faw'*; from 8192 in the sense of *clarifying*; a *cheese* (as strained from the whey):—cheese.

8195. שְׁפוֹ Sh^ephôw, *shef-o'*; or **שְׁפִי Sh^ephîy**, *shef-ee'*; from 8192; *baldness* [comp. 8205]; *Shepho* or *Shephi*, an Idumaean:—Shephi, Shepho.

8196. שְׁפוֹט sh^ephôwṭ, *shef-ote'*; or **שְׁפוּט sh^ephûwṭ**, *shef-oot'*; from 8199; a judicial *sentence*, i.e. *punishment*:—judgment.

8197. שְׁפוּפָם Sh^ephûwphâm, *shef-oo-fawm'*; or **שְׁפוּפָן Sh^ephûwphân**, *shef-oo-fawn'*; from the same as 8207; *serpent-like*; *Shephupham* or *Shephuphan*, an Isr.:—Shephuphan, Shupham.

8198. שִׁפְחָה shiphchâh, *shif-khaw'*; fem. from an unused root mean. to *spread* out (as a *family*; see 4940); a *female slave* (as a member of the *household*):—(bond-, hand-) maid (-en, -servant), wench, bondwoman, womanservant.

8199. שָׁפַט shâphaṭ, *shaw-fat'*; a prim. root; to *judge*, i.e. pronounce *sentence* (for or against); by impl. to *vindicate* or *punish*; by extens. to *govern*; pass. to *litigate* (lit. or fig.):— + avenge, × that condemn, contend, defend, execute (judgment), (be a) judge (-ment), × needs, plead, reason, rule.

8200. שְׁפַט sh^ephaṭ (Chald.), *shef-at'*; corresp. to 8199; to *judge*:—magistrate.

8201. שֶׁפֶט shepheṭ, *sheh'-fet*; from 8199; a *sentence*, i.e. *infliction*:—judgment.

8202. שָׁפָט Shâphâṭ, *shaw-fawt'*; from 8199; *judge*; *Shaphat*, the name of four Isr.:—Shaphat.

8203. שְׁפַטְיָה Sh^ephaṭyâh, *shef-at-yaw'*; or **שְׁפַטְיָהוּ Sh^ephaṭyâhûw**, *shef-at-yaw'-hoo*; from 8199 and 3050; *Jah has judged*; *Shephatjah*, the name of ten Isr.:—Shephatiah.

8204. שִׁפְטָן Shiphṭân, *shif-tawn'*; from 8199; *judge-like*; *Shiphtan*, an Isr.:—Shiphtan.

8205. שְׁפִי sh^ephîy, *shef-ee'*; from 8192; *bareness*; concr. a *bare* hill or plain:—high place, stick out.

8206. שֻׁפִּים Shuppîym, *shoop-peem'*; plur. of an unused noun from the same as 8207 and mean. the same; *serpents*; *Shuppim*, an Isr.:—Shuppim.

8207. שְׁפִיפֹן sh^ephîyphôn, *shef-ee-fone'*; from an unused root mean. the same as 7779; a kind of *serpent* (as *snapping*), prob. the *cerastes* or horned adder:—adder.

8208. שָׁפִיר Shaphîyr, *shaf-eer'*; from 8231; *beautiful*; *Shaphir*, a place in Pal.:—Saphir.

8209. שַׁפִּיר shappîyr (Chald.), *shap-peer'*; intens. of a form corresp. to 8208; *beautiful*:—fair.

8210. שָׁפַךְ shâphak, *shaw-fak'*; a prim. root; to *spill* forth (blood, a libation, liquid metal; or even a solid, i.e. to *mound* up); also (fig.) to *expend* (life, soul, complaint, money, etc.); intens. to *sprawl* out:—cast (up), gush out, pour (out), shed (-der, out), slip.

8211. שֶׁפֶךְ shephek, *sheh'-fek*; from 8210; an *emptying* place, e.g. an ash-*heap*:—are poured out.

8212. שָׁפְכָה shophkâh, *shof-kaw'*; fem. of a der. from 8210; a *pipe* (for *pouring* forth, e.g. wine), i.e. the *penis*:—privy member.

8213. שָׁפֵל shâphêl, *shaw-fale'*; a prim. root; to *depress* or *sink* (espec. fig. to *humiliate*, intrans. or trans.):—abase, bring (cast, put) down, debase, humble (self), be (bring, lay, make, put) low (-er).

8214. שְׁפַל sh^ephal (Chald.), *shef-al'*; corresp. to 8213:—abase, humble, put down, subdue.

8215. שְׁפַל sh^ephal (Chald.), *shef-al'*; from 8214; *low*:—basest.

8216. שֵׁפֶל shêphel, *shay'-fel*; from 8213; an *humble* rank:—low estate (place).

8217. שָׁפָל shâphâl, *shaw-fawl'*; from 8213; *depressed*, lit. or fig.:—base (-st), humble, low (-er, -ly).

8218. שִׁפְלָה shiphlâh, *shif-law'*; fem. of 8216; *depression*:—low place.

8219. שְׁפֵלָה sh^ephêlâh, *shef-ay-law'*; from 8213; *Lowland*, i.e. (with the art.) the maritime slope of Pal.:—low country, (low) plain, vale (-ley).

8220. שִׁפְלוּת shiphlûwth, *shif-looth'*; from 8213; *remissness*:—idleness.

8221. שְׁפָם Sh^ephâm, *shef-awm'*; prob. from 8192; *bare* spot; *Shepham*, a place in or near Pal.:—Shepham.

8222. שָׂפָם sâphâm, *saw-fawm'*; from 8193; the *beard* (as a *lip-piece*):—beard, (upper) lip.

8223. שָׁפָם Shâphâm, *shaw-fawm'*; formed like 8221; *baldly*; *Shapham*, an Isr.:—Shapham.

8224. שִׂפְמוֹת Siphmôwth, *sif-mōth'*; fem. plur. of 8221; *Siphmoth*, a place in Pal.:—Siphmoth.

8225. שִׁפְמִי Shiphmîy, *shif-mee'*; patrial from 8221; a *Shiphmite* inhab. of Shepham:—Shiphmite.

8226. שָׂפַן sâphan, *saw-fan'*; a prim. root; to *conceal* (as a valuable):—treasure.

8227. שָׁפָן shâphân, *shaw-fawn'*; from 8226; a species of *rock-rabbit* (from its *hiding*), i.e. prob. the *hyrax*:—coney.

8228. שֶׁפַע shephaʻ, *sheh'-fah*; from an unused root mean. to *abound*; *resources*:—abundance.

8229. שִׁפְעָה shiphʻâh, *shif-aw'*; fem. of 8228; *copiousness*:—abundance, company, multitude.

8230. שִׁפְעִי Shiphʻîy, *shif-ee'*; from 8228; *copious*; *Shiphi*, an Isr.:—Shiphi.

שָׂפַק sâphaq. See 5606.

8231. שָׁפַר shâphar, *shaw-far'*; a prim. root; to *glisten*, i.e. (fig.) *be* (caus. *make*) *fair*:—× goodly.

8232. שְׁפַר sh^ephar (Chald.), *shef-ar'*; corresp. to 8231; to *be beautiful*:—be acceptable, please, + think good.

8233. שֶׁפֶר shepher, *sheh'-fer*; from 8231; *beauty*:—× goodly.

8234. שֶׁפֶר Shepher, *sheh'-fer*; the same as 8233; *Shepher*, a place in the Desert:—Shapper.

שׁוֹפָר shôphâr. See 7782.

8235. שִׁפְרָה shiphrâh, *shif-raw'*; from 8231; *brightness*:—garnish.

8236. שִׁפְרָה Shiphrâh, *shif-raw'*; the same as 8235; *Shiphrah*, an Israelitess:—Shiphrah.

8237. שַׁפְרוּר° shaphrûwr, *shaf-roor'*; from 8231; *splendid*, i.e. a *tapestry* or *canopy*:—royal pavilion.

8238. שְׁפַרְפַר sh^epharphar (Chald.), *shef-ar-far'*; from 8231; the *dawn* (as *brilliant* with aurora):— × very early in the morning.

8239. שָׁפַת shâphath, *shaw-fath'*; a prim. root; to *locate*, i.e. (gen.) *hang* on or (fig.) *establish*, *reduce*:—bring, ordain, set on.

8240. שָׁפָת shâphâth, *shaw-fawth'*; from 8239; a (double) *stall* (for cattle); also a (two-pronged) *hook* (for flaying animals on):—hook, pot.

8241. שֶׁצֶף shetseph, *sheh'-tsef*; from 7857 (for alliteration with 7110); an *outburst* (of anger):—little.

8242. שַׂק saq, *sak*; from 8264; prop. a *mesh* (as allowing a liquid to *run* through), i.e. coarse loose cloth or *sacking* (used in mourning and for bagging); hence a *bag* (for grain, etc.):—sack (-cloth, -clothes).

8243. שָׁק shâq (Chald.), *shawk*; corresp. to 7785; the *leg*:—leg.

8244. שָׂקַד sâqad, *saw-kad'*; a prim. root; to *fasten*:—bind.

8245. שָׁקַד shâqad, *shaw-kad'*; a prim. root; to *be alert*, i.e. *sleepless*; hence to *be on the lookout* (whether for good or ill):—hasten, remain, wake, watch (for).

8246. שָׁקַד shâqad, *shaw-kad'*; a denom. from 8247; to *be* (intens. *make*) *almond-shaped*:—make like (unto, after the fashion of) almonds.

8247. שָׁקֵד shâqêd, *shaw-kade'*; from 8245; the *almond* (tree or nut; as being the *earliest* in bloom):—almond (tree).

8248. שָׁקָה shâqâh, *shaw-kaw'*; a prim. root; to *quaff*, i.e. (caus.) to *irrigate* or *furnish a potion* to:—cause to (give, give to, let, make to) drink, drown, moisten, water. See 7937, 8354.

8249. שִׁקֻּו shiqqûv, *shik-koov'*; from 8248; (plur. collect.) a *draught*:—drink.

8250. שִׁקּוּי shiqqûwy, *shik-koo'ee*; from 8248; a *beverage*; *moisture*, i.e. (fig.) *refreshment*:—drink, marrow.

8251. שִׁקּוּץ shiqqûwts, *shik-koots'*; or **שִׁקֻּץ shiqqûts**, *shik-koots'*; from 8262; *disgusting*, i.e. *filthy*; espec. *idolatrous* or (concr.) an *idol*:—abominable filth (idol, -ation), detestable (thing).

8252. שָׁקַט shâqaṭ, *shaw-kat'*; a prim. root; to *repose* (usually fig.):—appease, idleness, (at, be at, be in, give) quiet (-ness), (be at, be in, give, have, take) rest, settle, be still.

8253. שֶׁקֶט sheqeṭ, *sheh'-ket*; from 8252; *tranquillity*:—quietness.

8254. שָׁקַל shâqal, *shaw-kal'*; a prim. root; to *suspend* or *poise* (espec. in trade):—pay, receive (-r), spend, × throughly, weigh.

8255. שֶׁקֶל **sheqel**, *sheh'-kel;* from 8254; prob. a *weight;* used as a commercial standard:—shekel.

8256. שָׁקָם **shâqâm**, *shaw-kawm';* or (fem.)

שִׁקְמָה **shiqmâh**, *shik-maw';* of uncert. der.; a *sycamore* (usually the tree):—sycamore (fruit, tree).

8257. שָׁקַע **shâqaʻ**, *shaw-kah'* (abbrev. ° Am. 8 : 8); a prim. root; to *subside;* by impl. *to be overflowed, cease;* caus. to *abate, subdue:*—make deep, let down, drown, quench, sink.

8258. שְׁקַעְרוּרָה **sheqaʻrûwrâh**, *shek-ah-roo-raw';* from 8257; a *depression:*—hollow strake.

8259. שָׁקַף **shâqaph**, *shaw-kaf';* a prim. root; prop. to *lean out* (of a window), i.e. (by impl.) *peep* or *gaze* (pass. *be a spectacle*):—appear, look (down, forth, out).

8260. שֶׁקֶף **sheqeph**, *sheh'-kef;* from 8259; a *loophole* (for *looking out*), to admit light and air:—window.

8261. שָׁקֻף **shâqûph**, *shaw-koof';* pass. part. of 8259; an *embrasure* or opening [comp. 8260] with bevelled jam:—light, window.

8262. שָׁקַץ **shâqats**, *shaw-kats';* a prim. root; to *be filthy,* i.e. (intens.) to *loathe, pollute:*—abhor, make abominable, have in abomination, detest, × utterly.

8263. שֶׁקֶץ **sheqets**, *sheh'-kets;* from 8262; *filth,* i.e. (fig. and spec.) an *idolatrous* object:—abominable (-tion).

שִׁקֻּץ **shiqqûts**. See 8251.

8264. שָׁקַק **shâqaq**, *shaw-kak';* a prim. root; to *course* (like a beast of prey); by impl. to *seek greedily:*—have appetite, justle one against another, long, range, run (to and fro).

8265. שָׂקַר **sâqar**, *saw-kar';* a prim. root; to *ogle,* i.e. *blink* coquettishly:—wanton.

8266. שָׁקַר **shâqar**, *shaw-kar';* a prim. root; to *cheat,* i.e. *be untrue* (usually in words):—fail, deal falsely, lie.

8267. שֶׁקֶר **sheqer**, *sheh'-ker;* from 8266; an *untruth;* by impl. a *sham* (often adv.):—without a cause, deceit (-ful), false (-hood, -ly), feignedly, liar, + lie, lying, vain (thing), wrongfully.

8268. שֹׁקֶת **shôqeth**, *sho'-keth;* from 8248; a *trough* (for *watering*):—trough.

8269. שַׂר **sar**, *sar;* from 8323; a *head* person (of any rank or class):—captain (that had rule), chief (captain), general, governor, keeper, lord, ([-task-]) master, prince (-ipal), ruler, steward.

8270. שֹׁר **shôr**, *shore;* from 8324; a *string* (as *twisted* [comp. 8306]), i.e. (spec.) the umbilical cord (also fig. as the centre of strength):—navel.

8271. שְׁרֵא **sherê'** (Chald.), *sher-ay';* a root corresp. to that of 8293; to *free, separate;* fig. to *unravel, commence;* by impl. (of unloading beasts) to *reside:*—begin dissolve, dwell, loose.

8272. שַׁרְאֶצֶר **Shar'etser**, *shar-eh'-tser;* of for. der.; *Sharetser*, the name of an Ass. and an Isr.:—Sharezer.

8273. שָׁרָב **shârâb**, *shaw-rawb';* from an unused root mean. to *glare;* quivering *glow* (of the air), espec. the *mirage:*—heat, parched ground.

8274. שֵׁרֵבְיָה **Shêrêbyâh**, *shay-rayb-yaw';* from 8273 and 3050; *Jah has brought heat; Sherebjah*, the name of two Isr.:—Sherebiah.

8275. שַׁרְבִיט **sharbîyt**, *shar-beet';* for 7626; a *rod* of empire:—sceptre.

8276. שָׂרַג **sârag**, *saw-rag';* a prim. root; to *intwine:*—wrap together, wreath.

8277. שָׂרַד **sârad**, *saw-rad';* a prim. root; prop. to *puncture* [comp. 8279], i.e. (fig. through the idea of *slipping* out) to *escape* or survive:—remain.

8278. שְׂרָד **serâd**, *ser-awd';* from 8277; *stitching* (as *pierced* with a needle):—service.

8279. שֶׂרֶד **sered**, *seh'-red;* from 8277; a (carpenter's) *scribing-awl* (for *pricking* or scratching measurements):—line.

8280. שָׂרָה **sârâh**, *saw-raw';* a prim. root; to *prevail:*—have power (as a prince).

8281. שָׁרָה **shârâh**, *shaw-raw';* a prim. root; to *free:*—direct.

8282. שָׂרָה **sârâh**, *saw-raw';* fem. of 8269; a *mistress,* i.e. female noble:—lady, princess, queen.

8283. שָׂרָה **Sârâh**, *saw-raw';* the same as 8282; *Sarah*, Abraham's wife:—Sarah.

8284. שָׁרָה **shârâh**, *shaw-raw';* prob. fem. of 7791; a *fortification* (lit. or fig.):—sing [*by mistake for* 7891], wall.

8285. שֵׁרָה **shêrâh**, *shay-raw';* from 8324 in its orig. sense of *pressing;* a wrist-*band* (as *compact* or *clasping*):—bracelet.

8286. שְׂרוּג **Serûwg**, *ser-oog';* from 8276; *tendril; Serug*, a postdiluvian patriarch:—Serug.

8287. שָׁרוּחֶן **Shârûwchen**, *shaw-roo-khen';* prob. from 8281 (in the sense of *dwelling* [comp. 8271]) and 2580; *abode of pleasure; Sharuchen*, a plac in Pal.:—Sharuhen.

8288. שְׂרוֹךְ **serôwk**, *ser-oke';* from 8308; a *thong* (as *laced* or *tied*):—([shoe-]) latchet.

8289. שָׁרוֹן **Shârôwn**, *shaw-rone';* prob. abridged from 3474; *plain; Sharon*, the name of a place in Pal.:—Lasharon, Sharon.

8290. שָׁרוֹנִי **Shârôwnîy**, *shaw-ro-nee';* patrial from 8289; a *Sharonite* or inhab. of Sharon:—Sharonite.

8291. שַׂרוּק **sarûwq**, *sar-ook';* pass. part. from the same as 8321; a *grapevine:*—principal plant. See 8320, 8321.

8292. שְׁרוּקָה **sherûwqâh**, *sher-oo-kaw';* or (by perm.)

שְׁרִיקָה **sherîyqâh**, *sher-ee-kaw';* fem. pass. part. of 8319; a *whistling* (in scorn); by anal. a *piping:*—bleating, hissing.

8293. שֵׁרוּת° **shêrûwth**, *shay-rooth';* from 8281 abbrev.; *freedom:*—remnant.

8294. שֶׂרַח **Serach**, *seh'-rakh;* by perm. for 5629; *superfluity; Serach*, an Israelitess:—Sarah, Serah.

8295. שָׂרַט **sâraṭ**, *saw-rat';* a prim. root: to *gash:*—cut in pieces, make [cuttings] pieces.

8296. שֶׂרֶט **sereṭ**, *seh'-ret;* and

שָׂרֶטֶת **sâreṭeth**, *saw-reh'-teth;* from 8295; an *incision:*—cutting.

8297. שָׂרַי **Sâray**, *saw-rah'ee;* from 8269; *dominative; Sarai*, the wife of Abraham:—Sarai.

8298. שָׁרַי **Shâray**, *shaw-rah'ee;* prob. from 8324; *hostile; Sharay*, an Isr.:—Sharai.

8299. שָׂרִיג **sârîyg**, *saw-reeg';* from 8276; a *tendril* (as *intwining*):—branch.

8300. שָׂרִיד **sârîyd**, *saw-reed',* from 8277; a *survivor:*— × alive, left, remain (-ing), remnant, rest.

8301. שָׂרִיד **Sârîyd**, *suw-reed';* the same as 8300; *Sarid*, a place in Pal.:—Sarid.

8302. שִׁרְיוֹן **shiryôwn**, *shir-yone';* or

שִׁרְיֹן **shiryôn**, *shir-yone';* and

שִׁרְיָן **shiryân**, *shir-yawn';* also (fem.)

שִׁרְיָה **shiryâh**, *shir-yaw';* and

שִׁרְיֹנָה **shiryônâh**, *shir-yo-naw';* from 8281 in the orig. sense of *turning;* a *corslet* (as if *twisted*):—breastplate, coat of mail, habergeon, harness. See 5030.

8303. שִׁרְיוֹן **Shiryôwn**, *shir-yone';* and

שִׂרְיֹן **Siryôn**, *sir-yone';* the same as 8302 (i.e. *sheeted* with snow); *Shirjon* or *Sirjon*, a peak of the Lebanon:—Sirion.

8304. שְׂרָיָה **Serâyâh**, *ser-aw-yaw';* or

שְׂרָיָהוּ **Serâyâhûw**, *ser-aw-yaw'-hoo;* from 8280 and 3050; *Jah has prevailed; Serajah*, the name of nine Isr.:—Seraiah.

8305. שְׂרִיקָה **serîyqâh**, *ser-ee-kaw';* from the same as 8321 in the orig. sense of *piercing; hetchelling* (or combing flax), i.e. (concr.) *tow* (by extens. *linen* cloth):—fine.

8306. שָׁרִיר **shârîyr**, *shaw-reer';* from 8324 in the orig. sense as in 8270 (comp. 8326); a *cord,* i.e. (by anal.) *sinew:*—navel.

8307. שְׁרִירוּת **sherîyrûwth**, *sher-ee-rooth';* from 8324 in the sense of *twisted,* i.e. *firm; obstinacy:*—imagination, lust.

8308. שָׂרַךְ **sârak**, *saw-rak';* a prim. root; to *interlace:*—traverse.

8309. שְׁרֵמָה° **sherêmâh**, *sher-ay-maw';* prob. by orth. error for 7709; a *common:*—field.

8310. שַׂרְסְכִים **Sarçekîym**, *sar-seh-keem';* of for. der.; *Sarsekim*, a Bab. general:—Sarsechim.

8311. שָׂרַע **sâraʻ**, *saw-rah';* a prim. root; to *prolong,* i.e. (reflex.) *be deformed* by excess of members:—stretch out self, (have any) superfluous thing.

8312. שַׂרְעַף **sarʻaph**, *sar-af';* for 5587; *cogitation:*—thought.

8313. שָׂרַף **sâraph**, *saw-raf';* a prim. root; to *be* (caus. *set*) *on fire:*—(cause to, make a) burn ([-ing], up), kindle, × utterly.

8314. שָׂרָף **sârâph**, *saw-rawf';* from 8313; *burning,* i.e. (fig.) *poisonous* (serpent); spec. a *saraph* or symbol. creature (from their copper color):—fiery (serpent), seraph.

8315. שָׂרָף **Sâraph**, *saw-raf';* the same as 8314; *Saraph*, an Isr.:—Saraph.

8316. שְׂרֵפָה **serêphâh**, *ser-ay-faw';* from 8313; *cremation:*—burning.

8317. שָׁרַץ **shârats**, *shaw-rats';* a prim. root; to *wriggle,* i.e. (by impl.) *swarm* or *abound:*—breed (bring forth, increase) abundantly (in abundance), creep, move.

8318. שֶׁרֶץ **sherets**, *sheh'-rets;* from 8317; a *swarm,* i.e. active mass of minute animals:—creep (-ing thing), move (-ing creature).

8319. שָׁרַק **shâraq**, *shaw-rak';* a prim. root; prop. to *be shrill,* i.e. to whistle or *hiss* (as a call or in scorn):—hiss.

8320. שָׂרֻק **sâruq**, *saw-rook';* from 8319; *bright red* (as *piercing* to the sight), i.e. *bay:*—speckled. See 8291.

8321. שֹׂרֵק **sôrêq**, *so-rake';* or

שׂוֹרֵק **sôwrêq**, *so-rake';* and (fem.)

שֹׂרֵקָה **sôrêqâh**, *so-ray-kaw';* from 8319 in the sense of *redness* (comp. 8320); a *vine* stock (prop. one yielding *purple* grapes, the richest variety):—choice (-st, noble) wine. Comp. 8291.

8322. שְׁרֵקָה **sherêqâh**, *sher-ay-kaw';* from 8319; a *derision:*—hissing.

8323. שָׂרַר **sârar**, *saw-rar';* a prim. root; to *have* (trans. *exercise;* reflex. *get*) *dominion:*—× altogether, make self a prince, (bear) rule.

8324. שָׁרַר **shârar**, *shaw-rar';* a prim. root; to *be hostile* (only act. part. an *opponent*):—enemy.

8325. שָׁרָר **Shârâr**, *shaw-rawr';* from 8324; *hostile; Sharar*, an Isr.:—Sharar.

8326. שֹׁרֶר **shôrer**, *sho'-rer;* from 8324 in the sense of *twisting* (comp. 8270); the umbilical *cord,* i.e. (by extens.) a *bodice:*—navel.

8327. שָׁרַשׁ **shârash**, *shaw-rash';* a prim. root; to *root,* i.e. strike into the soil, or (by impl.) to pluck from it:—(take, cause to take) root (out).

8328. שֶׁרֶשׁ **sheresh**, *sheh'-resh;* from 8327; a *root* (lit. or fig.):—bottom, deep, heel, root.

8329. שֶׁרֶשׁ **Sheresh**, *sheh'-resh;* the same as 8328; *Sheresh*, an Isr.:—Sharesh.

8330. שֹׁרֶשׁ **shôresh** (Chald.), *sho'-resh;* corresp. to 8328:—root.

8331. שַׁרְשָׁה **sharshâh**, *shar-shaw';* from 8327; a *chain* (as *rooted,* i.e. *linked*):—chain. Comp. 8333.

8332. שְׁרֹשׁוּ° **sherôshûw** (Chald.), *sher-o-shoo';* from a root corresp. to 8327; *eradication,* i.e. (fig.) *exile:*—banishment.

8333. שַׁרְשְׁרָה sharsherâh, *shar-sher-aw'*; from 8327 [comp. 8331]; a *chain;* (arch.) prob. a *garland:*—chain.

8334. שָׁרַת shârath, *shaw-rath'*; a prim. root; to *attend* as a menial or worshipper; fig. to *contribute* to:—minister (unto), (do) serve (-ant, -ice, -itor), wait on.

8335. שָׁרֵת shârêth, *shaw-rayth'*; infin. of 8334; *service* (in the Temple):—minister (-ry).

8336. שֵׁשׁ shêsh, *shaysh;* or (for alliteration with 4897)

שְׁשִׁי sheshiy, *shesh-ee'*; for 7893; *bleached* stuff, i.e. *white* linen or (by anal.) marble:— × blue, fine ([twined]) linen, marble, silk.

8337. שֵׁשׁ shêsh, *shaysh;* masc.

שִׁשָּׁה shishshâh, *shish-shaw'*; a prim. number; *six* (as an overplus [see 7797] beyond five or the fingers of the hand); as ord. *sixth:*—six ([-teen, -teenth]), sixth.

8338. שָׁשָׁא shâwshâw, *shaw-shaw'*; a prim. root; appar. to *annihilate:*—leave but the sixth part [*by confusion with* 8341].

8339. שֵׁשְׁבַּצַּר Shêshbatstsar, *shaysh-bats-tsar'*; of for. der.; *Sheshbatstsar*, Zerubbabel's Pers. name:—Sheshbazzar.

8340. שֵׁשְׁבַּצַּר Shêshbatstsar (Chald.), *shaysh-bats-tsar'*; corresp. to 8339:—Sheshbazzar.

שָׂשָׂה shâsâh. See 8154.

8341. שָׁשָׁה shâshâh, *shaw-shaw'*; a denom. from 8337; to *sixth* or divide into sixths:—give the sixth part.

8342. שָׂשׂוֹן sâsôwn, *saw-sone';* or

שָׂשֹׂן sâsôn, *saw-sone'*; from 7797; *cheerfulness;* spec. *welcome:*—gladness, joy, mirth, rejoicing.

8343. שָׁשַׁי Shâshay, *shaw-shah'ee*; perh. from 8336; *whitish; Shashai*, an Isr.:—Shashai.

8344. שֵׁשַׁי Shêshay, *shay-shah'ee*; prob. for 8343; *Sheshai*, a Canaanite:—Sheshai.

8345. שִׁשִּׁי shishshîy, *shish-shee'*; from 8337; *sixth*, ord. or (fem.) fractional:—sixth (part).

8346. שִׁשִּׁים shishshîym, *shish-sheem'*; multiple of 8337; *sixty:*—sixty, three score.

8347. שֵׁשַׁךְ Shêshak, *shay-shak'*; of for. der.; *Sheshak*, a symbol. name of Bab.:—Sheshach.

8348. שֵׁשָׁן Shêshân, *shay-shawn'*; perh. for 7799; *lily; Sheshan*, an Isr.:—Sheshan.

שׁשָׁן Shôshân. See 7799.

8349. שָׁשַׁק Shâshaq, *shaw-shak'*; prob. from the base of 7785; *pedestrian; Shashak*, an Isr.:—Shashak.

8350. שָׁשַׁר shâshar, *shaw-shar'*; perh. from the base of 8324 in the sense of that of 8320; *red* ochre (from its *piercing* color):—vermillion.

8351. שֵׁת shêth (Num. 24 : 17), *shayth;* from 7582; *tumult:*—Sheth.

8352. שֵׁת Shêth, *shayth;* from 7896; *put*, i.e. *substituted; Sheth*, third son of Adam:—Seth, Sheth.

8353. שֵׁת shêth (Chald.), *shayth;* or

שִׁת shîth (Chald.), *sheeth;* corresp. to 8337:—six (-th).

8354. שָׁתָה shâthâh, *shaw-thaw'*; a prim. root; to *imbibe* (lit. or fig.):— × assuredly, banquet, × certainly, drink (-er, -ing), drunk (× -ard), surely. [Prop. intensive of 8248.]

8355. שְׁתָה shethâh (Chald.), *sheth-aw'*; corresp. to 8354:—drink.

8356. שָׁתָה shâthâh, *shaw-thaw'*; from 7896; a *basis*, i.e. (fig.) political or moral *support:*—foundation, purpose.

8357. שֵׁתָה shêthâh, *shay-thaw'*; from 7896; the *seat* (of the person):—buttock.

8358. שְׁתִי shethîy, *sheth-ee'*; from 8354; *intoxication:*—drunkenness.

8359. שְׁתִי shethîy, *sheth-ee'*; from 7896; a *fixture*, i.e. the *warp* in weaving:—warp.

8360. שְׁתִיָּה shethîyâh, *sheth-ee-yaw'*; fem. of 8358; *potation:*—drinking.

שְׁתַּיִם shettayim. See 8147.

8361. שִׁתִּין shittîyn (Chald.), *shit-teen'*; corresp. to 8346 [comp. 8353]; *sixty:*—threescore.

8362. שָׁתַל shâthal, *shaw-thal'*; a prim. root; to *transplant:*—plant.

8363. שְׁתִל shethîyl, *sheth-eel'*; from 8362; a *sprig* (as if *transplanted*), i.e. *sucker:*—plant.

8364. שֻׁתַלְחִי Shûthalchîy, *shoo-thal-kee'*; patron. from 7803; a *Shuthalchite* (collect.) or desc. of Shuthelach:—Shuthalhites.

שָׂתַם sâtham. See 5640.

8365. שָׁתַם shâtham, *shaw-tham'*; a prim. root; to *unveil* (fig.):—be open.

8366. שָׁתַן shâthan, *shaw-than'*; a prim. root; (caus.) to *make water*, i.e. *urinate:*—piss.

8367. שָׁתַק shâthaq, *shaw-thak'*; a prim. root; to *subside:*—be calm, cease, be quiet.

8368. שָׂתַר sâthar, *saw-thar'*; a prim. root; to *break* out (as an eruption):—have in [one's] secret parts.

8369. שֵׁתָר Shêthâr, *shay-thawr'*; of for. der.; *Shethar*, a Pers. satrap:—Shethar.

8370. שְׁתַר בּוֹזְנַי Shethar Bôwzenay, *sheth-ar' bo-zen-ah'ee;* of for. der.; *Shethar-Bozenai*, a Pers. officer:—Shethar-boznai.

8371. שָׁתַת shâthath, *shaw-thath'*; a prim. root; to *place*, i.e. *array;* reflex. to *lie:*—be laid, set.

ת

8372. תָּא tâ', *taw;* and (fem.)

תָּאָה tâ'âh (Ezek. 40 : 12), *taw-aw'*; from (the base of) 8376; a *room* (as *circumscribed*):—(little) chamber.

8373. תָּאַב tâ'ab, *taw-ab'*; a prim. root; to *desire:*—long.

8374. תָּאַב tâ'ab, *taw-ab'*; a prim. root [prob. rather ident. with 8373 through the idea of *puffing* disdainfully at; comp. 340]; to *loathe* (mor.):—abhor.

8375. תַּאֲבָה ta'âbâh, *tah-ab-aw'*; from 8374 [comp. 15]; *desire:*—longing.

8376. תָּאָה tâ'âh, *taw-aw'*; a prim. root; to *mark* off, i.e. (intens.) *designate:*—point out.

8377. תְּאוֹ te'ôw, *teh-o'*; and

תּוֹא tôw' (the orig. form), *toh;* from 8376; a species of *antelope* (prob. from the white *stripe* on the cheek):—wild bull (ox).

8378. תַּאֲוָה ta'âvâh, *tah-av-aw'*; from 183 (abbrev.); a *longing;* by impl. a *delight* (subj. *satisfaction*, obj. a *charm*):—dainty, desire, × exceedingly, × greedily, lust (ing), pleasant. See also 6914.

8379. תַּאֲוָה ta'âvâh, *tah-av-aw'*; from 8376; a *limit*, i.e. full extent:—utmost bound.

8380. תָּאוֹם tâ'ôwm, *taw-ome';* or

תָּאֹם tâ'ôm, *taw-ome'*; from 8382; a *twin* (in plur. only), lit. or fig.:—twins.

8381. תַּאֲלָה ta'âlâh, *tah-al-aw'*; from 422; an *imprecation:*—curse.

8382. תָּאַם tâ'am, *taw-am'*; a prim. root; to *be complete;* but used only as denom. from 8380, to *be* (caus. *make*) *twinned*, i.e. (fig.) *duplicate* or (arch.) *jointed:*—coupled (together), bear twins.

תְּאֹם tâ'ôm. See 8380.

8383. תְּאֻן te'ûn, *teh-oon'*; from 205; *naughtiness*, i.e. *toil:*—lie.

8384. תְּאֵן te'ên, *teh-ane';* or (in the sing., fem.)

תְּאֵנָה te'ênâh, *teh-ay-naw'*; perh. of for. der.; the *fig* (tree or fruit):—fig (tree).

8385. תַּאֲנָה ta'ănâh, *tah-an-aw';* or

תֹּאֲנָה tô'ănâh, *to-an-aw'*; from 579; an *opportunity* or (subj.) *purpose:*—occasion.

8386. תַּאֲנִיָּה ta'ănîyâh, *tah-an-ee-yaw'*; from 578; *lamentation:*—heaviness, mourning.

8387. תַּאֲנַת שִׁלֹה Ta'ănath Shîlôh, *tah-an-ath' shee-lo'*; from 8385 and 7887; *approach of Shiloh; Taanath-Shiloh*, a place in Pal.:—Taanath-shiloh.

8388. תָּאַר tâ'ar, *taw-ar'*; a prim. root; to *delineate;* reflex. to *extend:*—be drawn, mark out, [Rimmon-] methoar [*by union with* 7417].

8389. תֹּאַר tô'ar, *to'-ar*; from 8388; *outline*, i.e. *figure* or *appearance:*— + beautiful, × comely, countenance, + fair, × favoured, form, × goodly, × resemble, visage.

8390. תַּאֲרֵעַ Ta'ărêa', *tah-ar-ay'-ah*; perh. from 772; *Taareä*, an Isr.:—Tarea. See 8475.

8391. תְּאַשּׁוּר te'ashshûwr, *teh-ash-shoor'*; from 833; a species of *cedar* (from its *erectness*):—box (tree).

8392. תֵּבָה têbâh, *tay-baw'*; perh. of for. der.; a *box:*—ark.

8393. תְּבוּאָה tebûw'âh, *teb-oo-aw'*; from 935; *income*, i.e. *produce* (lit. or fig.):—fruit, gain, increase, revenue.

8394. תָּבוּן tâbûwn, *taw-boon';* and (fem.)

תְּבוּנָה tebûwnâh, *teb-oo-naw';* or

תּוֹבֻנָה° tôwbûnâh, *to-boo-naw'*; from 995; *intelligence;* by impl. an *argument;* by extens. *caprice:*—discretion, reason, skilfulness, understanding, wisdom.

8395. תְּבוּסָה tebûwçâh, *teb-oo-saw'*; from 947: a *treading down*, i.e. *ruin:*—destruction.

8396. תָּבוֹר Tâbôwr, *taw-bore'*; from a root corresp. to 8406; *broken* region; *Tabor*, a mountain in Pal., also a city adjacent:—Tabor.

8397. תֶּבֶל tebel, *teh'-bel*; appar. from 1101; *mixture*, i.e. *unnatural* bestiality:—confusion.

8398. תֵּבֵל têbêl, *tay-bale'*; from 2986; the *earth* (as *moist* and therefore inhabited); by extens. the *globe;* by impl. its *inhabitants;* spec. a partic. *land*, as Babylonia, Pal.:—habitable part, world.

תֻּבַל Tûbal. See 8422.

8399. תַּבְלִית tablîyth, *tab-leeth'*; from 1086; *consumption:*—destruction.

8400. תְּבַלֻּל teballûl, *teb-al-lool'*; from 1101 in the orig. sense of *flowing;* a *cataract* (in the eye):—blemish.

8401. תֶּבֶן teben, *teh'-ben*; prob. from 1129; prop. *material*, i.e. (spec.) refuse *haum* or stalks of grain (as *chopped* in threshing and used for fodder):—chaff, straw, stubble.

8402. תִּבְנִי Tibnî, *tib-nee'*; from 8401; *strawy; Tibni*, an Isr.:—Tibni.

8403. תַּבְנִית tabnîyth, *tab-neeth'*; from 1129; *structure;* by impl. a *model*, *resemblance:*—figure, form, likeness, pattern, similitude.

8404. תַּבְעֵרָה Tab'êrâh, *tab-ay-raw'*; from 1197; *burning; Taberah*, a place in the Desert:—Taberah.

8405. תֵּבֵץ Têbêts, *tay-bates'*; from the same as 948; *whiteness; Tebets*, a place in Pal.:—Thebez.

8406. תְּבַר tebar (Chald.), *teb-ar'*; corresp. to 7665; to *be fragile* (fig.):—broken.

8407. תִּגְלַת פִּלְאֶסֶר Tiglath Pil'eçer, *tig-lath' pil-eh'-ser;* or

תִּגְלַת פְּלֶסֶר Tiglath Peleçer, *tig-lath pel-eh'-ser;* or

תִּלְגַת פִּלְנְאֶסֶר Tilgath Pilne'eçer, *til-gath' pil-neh-eh'-ser;* or

תִּלְגַת פִּלְנֶסֶר Tilgath Pilneçer, *til-gath' pil-neh'-ser;* of for. der.; *Tiglath-Pileser* or *Tilgath-pilneser*, an Assyr. king:—Tiglath-pileser, Tilgath-pilneser.

8408. תַּגְמוּל **tagmûwl**, *tag-mool'*; from 1580; a *bestowment:*—benefit.

8409. תִּגְרָה **tigrâh**, *tig-raw'*; from 1624; *strife*, i.e. *infliction:*—blow.

תֹּגַרְמָה **Tôgarmâh**. See 8425.

8410. תִּדְהָר **tidhâr**, *tid-hawr'*; appar. from 1725; *enduring;* a species of hard-wood or *lasting* tree (perh. *oak*):—pine (tree).

8411. תְּדִירָא **tᵉdîyrâʼ** (Chald.), *ted-ee-raw'*; from 1753 in the orig. sense of *enduring; permanence*, i.e. (adv.) *constantly:*—continually.

8412. תַּדְמֹר **Tadmôr**, *tad-more'*; or

תַּמֹּר° **Tammôr** (1 Kings 9 : 18), *tam-more'*; appar. from 8558; *palm-city; Tadmor*, a place near Pal.:—Tadmor.

8413. תִּדְעָל **Tidʻâl**, *tid-awl'*; perh. from 1763; *fearfulness; Tidal*, a Canaanite:—Tidal.

8414. תֹּהוּ **tôhûw**, *to'-hoo*; from an unused root mean. to lie *waste;* a *desolation* (of surface), i.e. *desert;* fig. a *worthless* thing; adv. in *vain:*—confusion, empty place, without form, nothing, (thing of) nought, vain, vanity, waste, wilderness.

8415. תְּהוֹם **tᵉhôwm**, *teh-home'*; or

תְּהֹם **tᵉhôm**, *teh-home'*; (usually fem.) from 1949; an *abyss* (as a *surging* mass of water), espec. the *deep* (the *main* sea or the subterranean *water-supply*):—deep (place), depth.

8416. תְּהִלָּה **tᵉhillâh**, *teh-hil-law'*; from 1984; *laudation;* spec. (concr.) a *hymn:*—praise.

8417. תָּהֳלָה **tohŏlâh**, *to-hol-aw'*; fem. of an unused noun (appar. from 1984) mean. *bluster; braggadocio*, i.e. (by impl.) *fatuity:*—folly.

8418. תַּהֲלֻכָה **tahălûkâh**, *tah-hal-oo-kaw'*; from 1980; a *procession:*— × went.

תְּהֹם **tᵉhôm**. See 8415.

8419. תַּהְפֻּכָה **tahpûkâh**, *tah-poo-kaw'*; from 2015; a *perversity* or *fraud:*—(very) froward (-ness, thing), perverse thing.

8420. תָּו **tâv**, *tawv*; from 8427; a *mark;* by impl. a *signature:*—desire, mark.

8421. תּוּב **tûwb** (Chald.), *toob*; corresp. to 7725; to *come back;* spec. (trans. and ellip.) to *reply:*—answer, restore, return (an answer).

8422. תּוּבַל **Tûwbal**, *too-bal'*; or

תֻּבַל **Tûbal**, *too-bal'*; prob. of for. der.; *Tubal*, a postdiluvian patriarch and his posterity:—Tubal.

8423. תּוּבַל קַיִן **Tûwbal Qayin**, *too-bal' kah'-yin*; appar. from 2986 (comp. 2981) and 7014; *offspring of Cain; Tubal-Kajin*, an antediluvian patriarch:—Tubal-cain.

תּוֹבֻנָה° **tôwbûnâh**. See 8394.

8424. תּוּגָה **tûwgâh**, *too-gaw'*; from 3013; *depression* (of spirits); concr. a *grief:*—heaviness, sorrow.

8425. תּוֹגַרְמָה **Tôwgarmâh**, *to-gar-maw'*; or

תֹּגַרְמָה **Tôgarmâh**, *to-gar-maw'*; prob. of for. der.; *Togarmah*, a son of Gomer and his posterity:—Togarmah.

8426. תּוֹדָה **tôwdâh**, *to-daw'*; from 3034; prop. an *extension* of the hand, i.e. (by impl.) *avowal*, or (usually) *adoration;* spec. a *choir* of worshippers:—confession, (sacrifice of) praise, thanks (-giving, offering).

8427. תָּוָה **tâvâh**, *taw-vaw'*; a prim. root; to *mark* out, i.e. (prim.) *scratch* or (def.) *imprint:*—scrabble, set [a mark].

8428. תָּוָה **tâvâh**, *taw-vaw'*; a prim. root [or perh. ident. with 8427 through a similar idea from *scraping* to pieces]; to *grieve:*—limit [*by confusion with* 8427].

8429. תְּוַהּ **tᵉvahh** (Chald.), *tev-ah'*; corresp. to 8539 or perh. to 7582 through the idea of *sweeping* to ruin [comp. 8428]; to *amaze*, i.e. (reflex. by impl.) *take alarm:*—be astonied.

8430. תּוֹחַ **Tôwach**, *to'-akh*; from an unused root mean. to *depress; humble; Toäch*, an Isr.:—Toah.

8431. תּוֹחֶלֶת **tôwcheleth**, *to-kheh'-leth*; from 3176; *expectation:*—hope.

תּוֹךְ **tôwk**. See 8496.

8432. תָּוֶךְ **tâvek**, *taw'-vek*; from an unused root mean. to *sever;* a *bisection*, i.e. (by impl.) the *centre:*—among (-st), × between, half, × (there-, where-) in (-to), middle, mid [-night], midst (among), × out (of), × through, × with (-in).

8433. תּוֹכֵחָה **tôwkêchâh**, *to-kay-khaw'*; and

תּוֹכַחַת **tôwkachath**, *to-kakh'-ath*; from 3198; *chastisement;* fig. (by words) *correction, refutation, proof* (even in defence):—argument, × chastened, correction, reasoning, rebuke, reproof, × be (often) reproved.

תֻּכִּי **tûwkkîy**. See 8500.

8434. תּוֹלָד **Tôwlâd**, *to-lawd'*; from 3205; *posterity; Tolad*, a place in Pal.:—Tolad. Comp. 513.

8435. תּוֹלְדָה **tôwlᵉdâh**, *to-led-aw'*; or

תֹּלְדָה **tôlᵉdâh**, *to-led-aw'*; from 3205; (plur. only) *descent*, i.e. *family;* (fig.) *history:*—birth, generations.

8436. תּוּלוֹן° **Tûwlôn**, *too-lone'*; from 8524; *suspension; Tulon*, an Isr.:—Tilon [*from the marg.*].

8437. תּוֹלָל **tôwlâl**, *to-lawl'*; from 3213; *causing to howl*, i.e. an *oppressor:*—that wasted.

8438. תּוֹלָע **tôwlâʻ**, *to-law'*; and (fem.)

תּוֹלֵעָה **tôwlêʻâh**, *to-lay-aw'*; or

תּוֹלַעַת **tôwlaʻath**, *to-lah'-ath*; or

תֹּלַעַת **tôlaʻath**, *to-lah'-ath*; from 3216; a *maggot* (as *voracious*); spec. (often with ellips. of 8144) the crimson-*grub*, but used only (in this connection) of the color from it, and cloths dyed therewith:—crimson, scarlet, worm.

8439. תּוֹלָע **Tôwlâʻ**, *to-law'*; the same as 8438; *worm; Tola*, the name of two Isr.:—Tola.

8440. תּוֹלָעִי **Tôwlâʻîy**, *to-law-ee'*; patron. from 8439; a *Tolaïte* (collect.) or desc. of Tola:—Tolaites.

8441. תּוֹעֵבָה **tôwʻêbâh**, *to-ay-baw'*; or

תֹּעֵבָה **tôʻêbâh**, *to-ay-baw'*; fem. act. part. of 8581; prop. something *disgusting* (mor.), i.e. (as noun) an *abhorrence;* espec. *idolatry* or (concr.) an *idol:*—abominable (custom, thing), abomination.

8442. תּוֹעָה **tôwʻâh**, *to-aw'*; fem. act. part. of 8582; *mistake*, i.e. (mor.) *impiety*, or (political) *injury:*—error, hinder.

8443. תּוֹעָפָה **tôwʻâphâh**, *to-aw-faw'*; from 3286; (only in plur. collect.) *weariness*, i.e. (by impl.) *toil* (*treasure* so obtained) or *speed:*—plenty, strength.

8444. תּוֹצָאָה **tôwtsâʼâh**, *to-tsaw-aw'*; or

תֹּצָאָה **tôtsâʼâh**, *to-tsaw-aw'*; from 3318; (only in plur. collect.) *exit*, i.e. (geographical) *boundary*, or (fig.) *deliverance*, (act.) *source:*—border (-s), going (-s) forth (out), issues, outgoings.

8445. תּוֹקְהַת° **Tôwqahath**, *to-kah'-ath*; from the same as 3349; *obedience; Tokahath*, an Isr.:—Tikvath [*by correction for* 8616].

8446. תּוּר **tûwr**, *toor*; a prim. root; to *meander* (caus. *guide*) about, espec. for trade or reconnoitring:—chap [-man], sent to descry, be excellent, merchant [-man], search (out), seek, (e-) spy (out).

8447. תּוֹר **tôwr**, *tore*; or

תֹּר **tôr**, *tore*; from 8446; a *succession*, i.e. a *string* or (abstr.) *order:*—border, row, turn.

8448. תּוֹר **tôwr**, *tore*; prob. the same as 8447; a *manner* (as a sort of *turn*):—estate.

8449. תּוֹר **tôwr**, *tore*; or

תֹּר **tôr**, *tore*; prob. the same as 8447; a *ring-dove*, often (fig.) as a term of endearment:—(turtle) dove.

8450. תּוֹר **tôwr** (Chald.), *tore*; corresp. (by perm.) to 7794; a *bull:*—bullock, ox.

8451. תּוֹרָה **tôwrâh**, *to-raw'*; or

תֹּרָה **tôrâh**, *to-raw'*; from 3384; a *precept* or *statute*, espec. the *Decalogue* or *Pentateuch:*—law.

8452. תּוֹרָה **tôwrâh**, *to-raw'*; prob. fem. of 8448; a *custom:*—manner.

8453. תּוֹשָׁב **tôwshâb**, *to-shawb'*; or

תֹּשָׁב **tôshâb** (1 Kings 17 : 1), *to-shawb'*; from 3427; a *dweller* (but not outlandish [5237]); espec. (as distinguished from a native citizen [act. part. of 3427] and a temporary inmate [1616] or mere lodger [3885]) resident *alien:*—foreigner, inhabitant, sojourner, stranger.

8454. תּוּשִׁיָּה **tûwshîyâh**, *too-shee-yaw'*; or

תֻּשִׁיָּה **tûshîyâh**, *too-shee-yaw'*; from an unused root prob. mean. to *substantiate; support* or (by impl.) *ability*, i.e. (direct) *help*, (in purpose) an *undertaking*, (intellectual) *understanding:*—enterprise, that which (thing as it) is, substance, (sound) wisdom, working.

8455. תּוֹתָח **tôwthâch**, *to-thawkh'*; from an unused root mean. to *smite;* a *club:*—darts.

8456. תָּזַז **tâzaz**, *taw-zaz'*; a prim. root; to *lop* off:—cut down.

8457. תַּזְנוּת **taznûwth**, *taz-nooth'*; or

תַּזְנֻת **taznûth**, *taz-nooth'*; from 2181; *harlotry*, i.e. (fig.) *idolatry:*—fornication, whoredom.

8458. תַּחְבֻּלָה **tachbûlâh**, *takh-boo-law'*; or

תַּחְבּוּלָה **tachbûwlâh**, *takh-boo-law'*; from 2254 as denom. from 2256; (only in plur.) prop. *steerage* (as a management of *ropes*), i.e. (fig.) *guidance* or (by impl.) a *plan:*—good advice, (wise) counsels.

8459. תֹּחוּ **Tôchûw**, *to'-khoo*; from an unused root mean. to *depress; abasement, Tochu*, an Isr.:—Tohu.

8460. תְּחוֹת **tᵉchôwth** (Chald.), *tekh-ōth'*; or

תְּחֹת **tᵉchôth** (Chald.), *tekh-ōth'*; corresp. to 8478; *beneath:*—under.

8461. תַּחְכְּמֹנִי **Tachkᵉmônîy**, *takh-kem-o-nee'*; prob. for 2453; *sagacious; Tachkemoni*, an Isr.:—Tachmonite.

8462. תְּחִלָּה **tᵉchillâh**, *tekh-il-law'*; from 2490 in the sense of *opening;* a *commencement;* rel. *original* (adv. *-ly*):—begin (-ning), first (time).

8463. תַּחֲלוּא **tachălûwʼ**, *takh-al-oo'*; or

תַּחֲלֻא **tachălûʼ**, *takh-al-oo'*; from 2456; a *malady:*—disease, × grievous, (that are) sick (-ness).

8464. תַּחְמָס **tachmâç**, *takh-mawce'*; from 2554; a species of unclean bird (from its *violence*), perh. an *owl:*—night hawk.

8465. תַּחַן **Tachan**, *takh'-an*; prob. from 2583; *station; Tachan*, the name of two Isr.:—Tahan.

8466. תַּחֲנָה **tachănâh**, *takh-an-aw'*; from 2583; (only plur. coll.) an *encampment:*—camp.

8467. תְּחִנָּה **tᵉchinnâh**, *tekh-in-naw'*; from 2603; *graciousness;* caus. *entreaty:*—favour, grace, supplication.

8468. תְּחִנָּה **Tᵉchinnâh**, *tekh-in-naw'*; the same as 8467; *Techinnah*, an Isr.:—Tehinnah.

8469. תַּחֲנוּן **tachănûwn**, *takh-an-oon'*; or (fem.)

תַּחֲנוּנָה **tachănûwnâh**, *takh-an-oo-naw'*; from 2603; earnest *prayer:*—intreaty, supplication.

8470. תַּחֲנִי **Tachănîy**, *takh-an-ee'*; patron. from 8465; a *Tachanite* (collect.) or desc. of Tachan:—Tahanites.

8471. תַּחְפַּנְחֵס **Tachpanchêç**, *takh-pan-khace';* or

תְּחַפְנְחֵס **Tᵉchaphnᵉchêç** (Ezek. 30 : 18), *tekh-af-nekh-ace';* or

תַּחְפְּנֵס **Tachpᵉnêç** (Jer. 2 : 16), *takh-pen-ace';* of Eg. der.; *Tachpanches, Techaphneches* or *Tachpenes*, a place in Egypt:—Tahapanes, Tahpanhes, Tehaphnehes.

8472. תַּחְפְּנֵיס **Tachpᵉnêyç**, *takh-pen-ace';* of Eg. der.; *Tachpenes*, an Eg. woman:—Tahpenes.

8473. תַּחֲרָא **tachărâʼ**, *takh-ar-aw';* from 2734 in the orig. sense of 2352 or 2353; a linen *corslet* (as *white* or *hollow*):—habergeon.

8474. תַּחָרָה **tachârâh**, *takh-aw-raw';* a factitious root from 2734 through the idea of the *heat* of jealousy; to *vie* with a rival:—close, contend.

8475. תַּחְרֵעַ **Tachrêaʻ**, *takh-ray'-ah;* for 8390; *Tachreä*, an Isr.:—Tahrea.

8476. תַּחַשׁ **tachash**, *takh'-ash;* prob. of for. der.; a (clean) animal with fur, prob. a species of *antelope:*—badger.

8477. תַּחַשׁ **Tachash**, *takh'-ash;* the same as 8476; *Tachash*, a relative of Abraham:—Thahash.

8478. תַּחַת **tachath**, *takh'-ath;* from the same as 8430; the *bottom* (as *depressed*); only adv. *below* (often with prep. pref. *underneath*), in *lieu of*, etc.:—as, beneath, × flat, in (-stead), (same) place (where . . . is), room, for . . . sake, stead of, under, × unto, × when . . . was mine, whereas, [where-] fore, with.

8479. תַּחַת **tachath** (Chald.), *takh'-ath;* corresp. to 8478:—under.

8480. תַּחַת **Tachath**, *takh'-ath;* the same as 8478; *Tachath*, the name of a place in the Desert, also of three Isr.:—Tahath.

תְּחוֹת **tᵉchôth**. See 8460.

8481. תַּחְתּוֹן **tachtôwn**, *takh-tone';* or

תַּחְתֹּן **tachtôn**, *takh-tone';* from 8478; *bottommost:*—lower (-est), nether (-most).

8482. תַּחְתִּי **tachtîy**, *takh-tee';* from 8478; *lowermost;* as noun (fem. plur.) the *depths* (fig. a *pit*, the *womb*):—low (parts, -er, -er parts, -est), nether (part).

8483. תַּחְתִּים חָדְשִׁי **Tachtîym Chodshîy**, *takh-teem' khod-shee';* appar. from the plur. masc. of 8482 or 8478 and 2320; *lower* (ones) *monthly; Tachtim-Chodshi*, a place in Pal.:—Tahtim-hodshi.

8484. תִּיכוֹן **tîykôwn**, *tee-kone';* or

תִּיכֹן **tîykôn**, *tee-kone';* from 8432; *central:*—middle (-most), midst.

8485. תֵּימָא **Têymâʼ**, *tay-maw';* or

תֵּמָא **Têmâʼ**, *tay-maw';* prob. of for. der.; *Tema*, a son of Ishmael, and the region settled by him:—Tema.

8486. תֵּימָן **têymân**, *tay-mawn';* or

תֵּמָן **têmân**, *tay-mawn';* denom. from 3225; the *south* (as being on the *right* hand of a person facing the east):—south (side, -ward, wind).

8487. תֵּימָן **Têymân**, *tay-mawn';* or

תֵּמָן **Têmân**, *tay-mawn';* the same as 8486; *Teman*, the name of two Edomites, and of the region and desc. of one of them:—south, Teman.

8488. תֵּימְנִי **Têymᵉnîy**, *tay-men-ee';* prob. for 8489; *Temeni*, an Isr.:—Temeni.

8489. תֵּימָנִי **Têymânîy**, *tay-maw-nee';* patron. from 8487; a *Temanite* or desc. of Teman:—Temani, Temanite.

8490. תִּימָרָה **tîymârâh**, *tee-maw-raw';* or

תִּמָרָה **tîmârâh**, *tee-maw-raw';* from the same as 8558; a *column*, i.e. cloud:—pillar.

8491. תִּיצִי **Tîytsîy**, *tee-tsee';* patrial or patron. from an unused noun of uncert. mean.; a *Titsite* or desc. or inhab. of an unknown Tits:—Tizite.

8492. תִּירוֹשׁ **tîyrôwsh**, *tee-roshe';* or

תִּירֹשׁ **tîyrôsh**, *tee-roshe';* from 3423 in the sense of *expulsion; must* or fresh grape-juice (as just *squeezed* out); by impl. (rarely) fermented *wine:*—(new, sweet) wine.

8493. תִּירְיָא **Tîyrᵉyâʼ**, *tee-reh-yaw';* prob. from 3372; *fearful; Tirja*, an Isr.:—Tiria.

8494. תִּירָס **Tîyrâç**, *tee-rawce';* prob. of for. der.; *Tiras*, a son of Japheth:—Tiras.

תִּירֹשׁ **tîyrôsh**. See 8492.

8495. תַּיִשׁ **tayish**, *tah'-yeesh;* from an unused root mean. to *butt;* a *buck* or he-goat (as given to *butting*):—he goat.

8496. תֹּךְ **tôk**, *toke;* or

תּוֹךְ **tôwk** (Psa. 72 : 14), *toke;* from the same base as 8432 (in the sense of *cutting* to pieces); *oppression:*—deceit, fraud.

8497. תָּכָה **tâkâh**, *taw-kaw';* a prim. root; to *strew*, i.e. *encamp:*—sit down.

8498. תְּכוּנָה **tᵉkûwnâh**, *tek-oo-naw';* fem. pass. part. of 8505; *adjustment*, i.e. *structure;* by impl. *equipage:*—fashion, store.

8499. תְּכוּנָה **tᵉkûwnâh**, *tek-oo-naw';* from 3559; or prob. ident. with 8498; something *arranged* or *fixed*, i.e. a *place:*—seat.

8500. תֻּכִּי **tukkîy**, *took-kee';* or

תּוּכִּי **tûwkkîy**, *took-kee';* prob. of for. der.; some imported creature, prob. a *peacock:*—peacock.

8501. תָּכָךְ **tâkâk**, *taw-kawk';* from an unused root mean. to *dissever*, i.e. *crush:*—deceitful.

8502. תִּכְלָה **tiklâh**, *tik-law';* from 3615; *completeness:*—perfection.

8503. תַּכְלִית **taklîyth**, *tak-leeth';* from 3615; *completion;* by impl. an *extremity:*—end, perfect (-ion).

8504. תְּכֵלֶת **tᵉkêleth**, *tek-ay'-leth;* prob. for 7827; the cerulean *mussel*, i.e. the color (*violet*) obtained therefrom or stuff dyed therewith:—blue.

8505. תָּכַן **tâkan**, *taw-kan';* a prim. root; to *balance*, i.e. *measure* out (by weight or dimension); fig. to *arrange, equalize*, through the idea of *levelling* (ment. *estimate, test*):—bear up, direct, be ([un-]) equal, mete, ponder, tell, weigh.

8506. תֹּכֶן **tôken**, *to'-ken;* from 8505; a fixed *quantity:*—measure, tale.

8507. תֹּכֶן **Tôken**, *to'-ken;* the same as 8506; *Token*, a place in Pal.:—Tochen.

8508. תָּכְנִית **toknîyth**, *tok-neeth';* from 8506; *admeasurement*, i.e. *consummation:*—pattern, sum.

8509. תַּכְרִיךְ **takrîyk**, *tak-reek';* appar. from an unused root mean. to *encompass;* a *wrapper* or robe:—garment.

8510. תֵּל **têl**, *tale;* by contr. from 8524; a *mound:*—heap, × strength.

8511. תָּלָא **tâlâʼ**, *taw-law';* a prim. root; to *suspend;* fig. (through *hesitation*) to *be uncertain;* by impl. (of ment. *dependence*) to *habituate:*—be bent, hang (in doubt).

8512. תֵּל אָבִיב **Têl ʼÂbîyb**, *tale aw-beeb';* from 8510 and 24; *mound* of *green* growth; *Tel-Abib*, a place in Chaldæa:—Tel-abib.

8513. תְּלָאָה **tᵉlâʼâh**, *tel-aw-aw';* from 3811; *distress:*—travail, travel, trouble.

8514. תַּלְאוּבָה **talʼûwbâh**, *tal-oo-baw';* from 3851; *desiccation:*—great drought.

8515. תְּלַאשָּׂר **Tᵉlaʼssar**, *tel-as-sar';* or

תְּלַשָּׂר **Tᵉlassar**, *tel-as-sar';* of for. der.; *Telassar*, a region of Assyria:—Telassar.

8516. תַּלְבֹּשֶׁת **talbôsheth**, *tal-bo'-sheth;* from 3847; a *garment:*—clothing.

8517. תְּלַג **tᵉlag** (Chald.), *tel-ag';* corresp. to 7950; *snow:*—snow.

תִּלְגַת **Tilgath**. See 8407.

תֹּלְדָה **tôlᵉdâh**. See 8435.

8518. תָּלָה **tâlâh**, *taw-law';* a prim. root; to *suspend* (espec. to *gibbet*):—hang (up).

8519. תְּלוּנָה **tᵉlûwnâh**, *tel-oo-naw';* or

תְּלֻנָּה **tᵉlunnâh**, *tel-oon-naw';* from 3885 in the sense of *obstinacy;* a *grumbling:*—murmuring.

8520. תֶּלַח **Telach**, *teh'-lakh;* prob. from an unused root mean. to *dissever; breach; Telach*, an Isr.:—Telah.

8521. תֵּל חַרְשָׁא **Têl Charshâʼ**, *tale kharshaw';* from 8510 and the fem. of 2798; *mound of workmanship; Tel-Charsha*, a place in Bab.:—Tel-haresha, Tel-harsa.

8522. תְּלִי **tᵉlîy**, *tel-ee';* prob. from 8518; a *quiver* (as *slung*):—quiver.

8523. תְּלִיתַי **tᵉlîythay** (Chald.), *tel-ee-thah'ee;* or

תַּלְתִּי **taltîy** (Chald.), *tal-tee';* ordinal from 8532; *third:*—third.

8524. תָּלַל **tâlal**, *taw-lal';* a prim. root; to *pile* up, i.e. *elevate:*—eminent. Comp. 2048.

8525. תֶּלֶם **telem**, *teh'-lem;* from an unused root mean. to *accumulate;* a *bank* or *terrace:*—furrow, ridge.

8526. תַּלְמַי **Talmay**, *tal-mah'ee;* from 8525; *ridged; Talmai*, the name of a Canaanite and a Syrian:—Talmai.

8527. תַּלְמִיד **talmîyd**, *tal-meed';* from 3925; a *pupil:*—scholar.

8528. תֵּל מֶלַח **Têl Melach**, *tale meh'-lakh;* from 8510 and 4417; *mound of salt; Tel-Melach*, a place in Bab.:—Tel-melah.

תְּלֻנָּה **tᵉlunnâh**. See 8519.

8529. תָּלַע **tâlaʻ**, *taw-law';* a denom. from 8438; to *crimson*, i.e. dye that color:—× scarlet.

תֹּלַעַת **tôlaʻath**. See 8438.

8530. תַּלְפִּיָּה **talpîyâh**, *tal-pee-yaw';* fem. from an unused root mean. to *tower;* something *tall*, i.e. (plur. collect.) *slenderness:*—armoury.

תְּלַשָּׂר **Tᵉlassar**. See 8515.

8531. תְּלַת **tᵉlath** (Chald.), *tel-ath';* from 8532; a *tertiary* rank:—third.

8532. תְּלָת **tᵉlâth** (Chald.), *tel-awth';* masc.

תְּלָתָה **tᵉlâthâh** (Chald.), *tel-aw-thaw';* or

תְּלָתָא **tᵉlâthâʼ** (Chald.), *tel-aw-thaw';* corresp. to 7969; *three* or *third:*—third, three.

תַּלְתִּי **tally**. See 8523.

8533. תְּלָתִין **tᵉlâthîyn** (Chald.), *tel-aw-theen';* mult. of 8532; *ten times three:*—thirty.

8534. תַּלְתַּל **taltal**, *tal-tal';* by redupl. from 8524 through the idea of *vibration;* a trailing *bough* (as *pendulous*):—bushy.

8535. תָּם **tâm**, *tawm;* from 8552; *complete;* usually (mor.) *pious;* spec. *gentle, dear:*—coupled together, perfect, plain, undefiled, upright.

8536. תָּם **tâm** (Chald.), *tawm;* corresp. to 8033; *there:*—× thence, there, × where.

8537. תֹּם **tôm**, *tome;* from 8552; *completeness;* fig. *prosperity;* usually (mor.) *innocence:*—full, integrity, perfect (-ion), simplicity, upright (-ly, -ness), at a venture. See 8550.

תֵּמָא **Têmâʼ**. See 8485.

8538. תֻּמָּה **tummâh**, *toom-maw';* fem. of 8537; *innocence:*—integrity.

8539. תָּמַהּ **tâmahh**, *taw-mah';* a prim. root; to *be in consternation:*—be amazed, be astonished, marvel (-lously), wonder.

8540. תְּמַהּ **tᵉmahh** (Chald.), *tem-ah';* from a root corresp. to 8539; a *miracle:*—wonder.

8541. תִּמָּהוֹן **timmâhôwn**, *tim-maw-hone';* from 8539; *consternation:*—astonishment.

8542. תַּמּוּז **Tammûwz**, *tam-mooz'*; of uncert. der.; *Tammuz*, a Phœnician deity:—Tammus.

8543. תְּמוֹל **temôwl**, *tem-ole'*; or

תְּמֹל **temôl**, *tem-ole'*; prob. for 865; prop. *ago*, i.e. a (short or long) *time since;* espec. *yesterday*, or (with 8032) *day before yesterday*:— + before (-time), + these [three] days, + heretofore, + time past, yesterday.

8544. תְּמוּנָה **temûwnâh**, *tem-oo-naw'*; or

תְּמֻנָה **temûnâh**, *tem-oo-naw'*; from 4327; *something portioned* (i.e. *fashioned*) out, as a *shape*, i.e. (indef.) *phantom*, or (spec.) *embodiment*, or (fig.) *manifestation* (of favor):—image, likeness, similitude.

8545. תְּמוּרָה **temûwrâh**, *tem-oo-raw'*; from 4171; *barter, compensation:*— (ex-) change (-ing), recompense, restitution.

8546. תְּמוּתָה **temûwthâh**, *tem-oo-thaw'*; from 4191; *execution* (as a doom):—death, die.

8547. תֶּמַח **Temach**, *teh'-makh*; of uncert. der.; *Temach*, one of the Nethinim:—Tamah, Thamah.

8548. תָּמִיד **tâmîyd**, *taw-meed'*; from an unused root mean. to *stretch;* prop. *continuance* (as indef. *extension*); but used only (attributively as adj.) *constant* (or adv. *constantly*); ellipt. the *regular* (daily) sacrifice:—alway (-s), continual (employment, -ly), daily, ([n-]) ever (-more), perpetual.

8549. תָּמִים **tâmîym**, *taw-meem'*; from 8552; *entire* (lit., fig. or mor.); also (as noun) *integrity, truth:*—without blemish, complete, full, perfect, sincerely (-ity), sound, without spot, undefiled, upright (-ly), whole.

8550. תֻּמִּים **Tummîym**, *toom-meem'*; plur. of 8537; *perfections*, i.e. (techn.) one of the epithets of the objects in the high-priest's breastplate as an emblem of *complete* Truth:—Thummim.

8551. תָּמַךְ **tâmak**, *taw-mak'*; a prim. root; to *sustain;* by impl. to *obtain, keep fast;* fig. to *help, follow close:*—(take, up-) hold (up), maintain, retain, stay (up).

תְּמֹל **temôl**. See 8543.

8552. תָּמַם **tâmam**, *taw-mam'*; a prim. root; to *complete*, in a good or a bad sense, lit. or fig., trans. or intrans. (as follows):—accomplish, cease, be clean [pass-] ed, consume, have done, (come to an, have an, make an) end, fail, come to the full, be all gone, × be all here, be (make) perfect, be spent, sum, be (shew self) upright, be wasted, whole.

תֵּמָן **têmân, Têmân**. See 8486, 8487.

8553. תִּמְנָה **Timnâh**, *tim-naw'*; from 4487; a *portion* assigned; *Timnah*, the name of two places in Pal.:—Timnah, Timnath, Thimnathah.

תְּמֻנָה **temûnâh**. See 8544.

8554. תִּמְנִי **Timnîy**, *tim-nee'*; patrial from 8553; a *Timnite* or inhab. of Timnah:—Timnite.

8555. תִּמְנָע **Timnâ'**, *tim-naw'*; from 4513; *restraint; Timna*, the name of two Edomites:—Timna, Timnah.

8556. תִּמְנַת חֶרֶס **Timnath Chereç**, *tim-nath kheh'-res*; or

תִּמְנַת סֶרַח **Timnath Çerach**, *tim-nath seh'-rakh*; from 8553 and 2775; *portion of* (the) *sun; Timnath-Cheres*, a place in Pal.:—Timnath-heres, Timnath-serah.

8557. תֶּמֶס **temeç**, *teh'-mes*; from 4529; *liquefaction*, i.e. *disappearance:*—melt.

8558. תָּמָר **tâmâr**, *taw-mawr'*; from an unused root mean. to *be erect;* a *palm* tree:—palm (tree).

8559. תָּמָר **Tâmâr**, *taw-mawr'*; the same as 8558; *Tamar*, the name of three women and a place:—Tamar.

8560. תֹּמֶר **tômer**, *to'-mer*; from the same root as 8558; a *palm* trunk:—palm tree.

8561. תִּמֹּר **timmôr** (plur. only), *tim-more'*; or (fem.)

תִּמֹּרָה **timmôrâh** (sing. and plur.), *tim-mo-raw'*; from the same root as 8558; (arch.) a *palm*-like pilaster (i.e. umbellate):—palm tree.

תַּמֹּר **Tammôr**. See 8412.

תִּמָרָה **tîmârâh**. See 8490.

8562. תַּמְרוּק **tamrûwq**, *tam-rook'*; or

תַּמְרֻק **tamrûq**, *tam-rook'*; or

תַּמְרִיק **tamrîyq**, *tam-reek'*; from 4838; prop. a *scouring*, i.e. *soap* or *perfumery* for the bath; fig. a *detergent:*—× cleanse, (thing for) purification (-fying).

8563. תַּמְרוּר **tamrûwr**, *tam-roor'*; from 4843; *bitterness* (plur. as collect.):—× most bitter (-ly).

תַּמְרֻק **tamrûq**, and

תַּמְרִיק **tamrîyq**. See 8562.

8564. תַּמְרוּר **tamrûwr**, *tam-roor'*; from the same root as 8558; an *erection*, i.e. *pillar* (prob. for a guide-board):—high heap.

8565. תַּן **tan**, *tan*; from an unused root prob. mean. to *elongate;* a *monster* (as preternaturally formed), i.e. a *sea-serpent* (or other huge marine animal); also a *jackal* (or other hideous land animal):—dragon, whale. Comp. 8577.

8566. תָּנָה **tânâh**, *taw-naw'*; a prim. root; to *present* (a mercenary inducement), i.e. *bargain* with (a harlot):—hire.

8567. תָּנָה **tânâh**, *taw-naw'*; a prim. root [rather ident. with 8566 through the idea of *attributing* honor]; to *ascribe* (praise), i.e. *celebrate, commemorate:*—lament, rehearse.

8568. תַּנָּה **tannâh**, *tan-naw'*; prob. fem. of 8565; a female *jackal:*—dragon.

8569. תְּנוּאָה **tenûw'âh**, *ten-oo-aw'*; from 5106; *alienation;* by impl. *enmity:*—breach of promise, occasion.

8570. תְּנוּבָה **tenûwbâh**, *ten-oo-baw'*; from 5107; *produce:*—fruit, increase.

8571. תְּנוּךְ **tenûwk**, *ten-ook'*; perh. from the same as 594 through the idea of *protraction;* a *pinnacle*, i.e. *extremity:*—tip.

8572. תְּנוּמָה **tenûwmâh**, *ten-oo-maw'*; from 5123; *drowsiness*, i.e. *sleep:*—slumber (-ing).

8573. תְּנוּפָה **tenûwphâh**, *ten-oo-faw'*; from 5130; a *brandishing* (in threat); by impl. *tumult;* spec. the official *undulation* of sacrificial offerings:—offering, shaking, wave (offering).

8574. תַּנּוּר **tannûwr**, *tan-noor'*; from 5216; a *fire-pot:*—furnace, oven.

8575. תַּנְחוּם **tanchûwm**, *tan-khoom'*; or

תַּנְחֻם **tanchûm**, *tan-khoom'*; and (fem.)

תַּנְחוּמָה **tanchûwmâh**, *tan-khoo-maw'*; from 5162; *compassion, solace:*—comfort, consolation.

8576. תַּנְחֻמֶת **Tanchûmeth**, *tan-khoo'-meth*; for 8575 (fem.); *Tanchumeth*, an Isr.:—Tanhumeth.

8577. תַּנִּין **tannîyn**, *tan-neen'*; or

תַּנִּים **tannîym** (Ezek. 29 : 3), *tan-neem'*; intens. from the same as 8565; a marine or land *monster*, i.e. *sea-serpent* or *jackal:*—dragon, sea-monster, serpent, whale.

8578. תִּנְיָן **tinyân** (Chald.), *tin-yawn'*; corresp. to 8147; *second:*—second.

8579. תִּנְיָנוּת **tinyânûwth** (Chald.), *tin-yaw-nooth'*; from 8578; a *second time:*—again.

8580. תִּנְשֶׁמֶת **tanshemeth**, *tan-sheh'-meth*; from 5395; prop. a hard *breather*, i.e. the name of two unclean creatures, a lizard and a bird (both perh. from changing color through their *irascibility*), prob. the *tree-toad* and the *water-hen:*—mole, swan.

8581. תָּעַב **tâ'ab**, *taw-ab'*; a prim. root; to *loathe*, i.e. (mor.) *detest:*—(make to be) abhor (-red), (be, commit more, do) abominable (-y), × utterly.

תֹּעֵבָה **tô'êbâh**. See 8441.

8582. תָּעָה **tâ'âh**, *taw-aw'*; a prim. root; to *vacillate*, i.e. *reel* or *stray* (lit. or fig.); also caus. of both:—(cause to) go astray, deceive, dissemble, (cause to, make to) err, pant, seduce, (make to) stagger, (cause to) wander, be out of the way.

8583. תֹּעוּ **Tô'ûw**, *to'-oo*; or

תֹּעִי **Tô'îy**, *to'-ee*; from 8582; *error; Toü* or *Toï*, a Syrian king:—Toi, Tou.

8584. תְּעוּדָה **te'ûwdâh**, *teh-oo-daw'*; from 5749; *attestation*, i.e. a *precept, usage:*—testimony.

8585. תְּעָלָה **te'âlâh**, *teh-aw-law'*; from 5927; a *channel* (into which water is *raised* for irrigation); also a *bandage* or *plaster* (as placed *upon* a wound):—conduit, cured, healing, little river, trench, watercourse.

8586. תַּעֲלוּל **ta'ălûwl**, *tah-al-ool'*; from 5953; *caprice* (as a fit *coming on*), i.e. *vexation;* concr. a *tyrant:*—babe, delusion.

8587. תַּעֲלֻמָּה **ta'ălummâh**, *tah-al-oom-maw'*; from 5956; a *secret:*—thing that is hid, secret.

8588. תַּעֲנוּג **ta'ănûwg**, *tah-an-oog'*; or

תַּעֲנֻג **ta'ănûg**, *tah-an-oog'*; and (fem.)

תַּעֲנֻגָה **ta'ănûgâh**, *tah-an-oog-aw'*; from 6026; *luxury:*—delicate, delight, pleasant.

8589. תַּעֲנִית **ta'ănîyth**, *tah-an-eeth'*; from 6031; *affliction* (of self), i.e. *fasting:*—heaviness.

8590. תַּעֲנָךְ **Ta'ănâk**, *tah-an-awk'*; or

תַּעְנָךְ **Ta'nâk**, *tah-nawk'*; of uncert. der.; *Taanak* or *Tanak*, a place in Pal.:—Taanach, Tanach.

8591. תָּעַע **tâ'a'**, *taw-ah'*; a prim. root; to *cheat;* by anal. to *maltreat:*—deceive, misuse.

8592. תַּעֲצֻמָה **ta'ătsûmâh**, *tah-ats-oo-maw'*; from 6105; *might* (plur. collect.):—power.

8593. תַּעַר **ta'ar**, *tah'-ar*; from 6168; a *knife* or *razor* (as *making* bare); also a *scabbard* (as *being bare*, i.e. empty):—[pen-] knife, rasor, scabbard, shave, sheath.

8594. תַּעֲרֻבָה **ta'ărûbâh**, *tah-ar-oo-baw'*; from 6148; *suretyship*, i.e. (concr.) a *pledge:*— + hostage.

8595. תַּעְתֻּעַ **ta'tûa'**, *tah-too'-ah*; from 8591; a *fraud:*—error.

8596. תֹּף **tôph**, *tofe*; from 8608 contr.; a *tambourine:*—tabret, timbrel.

8597. תִּפְאָרָה **tiph'ârâh**, *tif-aw-raw'*; or

תִּפְאֶרֶת **tiph'ereth**, *tif-eh'-reth*; from 6286; *ornament* (abstr. or concr., lit. or fig.):—beauty (-iful), bravery, comely, fair, glory (-ious), honour, majesty.

8598. תַּפּוּחַ **tappûwach**, *tap-poo'-akh*; from 5301; an *apple* (from its *fragrance*), i.e. the fruit or the tree (prob. includ. others of the *pome* order, as the quince, the orange, etc.):—apple (tree). See also 1054.

8599. תַּפּוּחַ **Tappûwach**, *tap-poo'-akh*; the same as 8598; *Tappüach*, the name of two places in Pal., also of an Isr.:—Tappuah.

8600. תְּפוֹצָה **tephôwtsâh**, *tef-o-tsaw'*; from 6327; a *dispersal:*—dispersion.

8601. תֻּפִין **tûphîyn**, *too-feen'*; from 644; *cookery*, i.e. (concr.) a *cake:*—baked piece.

8602. תָּפֵל **tâphêl**, *taw-fale'*; from an unused root mean. to *smear; plaster* (as *gummy*) or *slime;* (fig.) *frivolity:*—foolish things, unsavoury, untempered.

8603. תֹּפֶל **Tôphel**, *to'-fel*; from the same as 8602; *quagmire; Tophel*, a place near the Desert:—Tophel.

8604. תִּפְלָה **tiphlâh**, *tif-law'*; from the same as 8602; *frivolity:*—folly, foolishly.

8605. תְּפִלָּה **tᵉphillâh**, *tef-il-law';* from 6419; *intercession, supplication;* by impl. a *hymn:*—prayer.

8606. תִּפְלֶצֶת **tiphletseth**, *tif-leh'-tseth;* from 6426; *fearfulness:*—terrible.

8607. תִּפְסַח **Tiphçach**, *tif-sakh';* from 6452; *ford; Tiphsach,* a place in Mesopotamia:—Tipsah.

8608. תָּפַף **tâphaph**, *taw-faf';* a prim. root; to *drum,* i.e. play (as) on the tambourine:—taber, play with timbrels.

8609. תָּפַר **tâphar**, *taw-far';* a prim. root; to *sew:*—(women that) sew (together).

8610. תָּפַשׂ **tâphas**, *taw-fas';* a prim. root; to *manipulate,* i.e. *seize;* chiefly to *capture, wield;* spec. to *overlay;* fig. to *use* unwarrantably:—catch, handle, (lay, take) hold (on, over), stop, × surely, surprise, take.

8611. תֹּפֶת **tôpheth**, *to'-feth;* from the base of 8608; a *smiting,* i.e. (fig.) *contempt:*—tabret.

8612. תֹּפֶת **Tôpheth**, *to'-feth;* the same as 8611; *Topheth,* a place near Jerus.:—Tophet, Topheth.

8613. תָּפְתֶּה **Tophteh**, *tof-teh';* prob. a form of 8612; *Tophteh,* a place of cremation:—Tophet.

8614. תִּפְתַּי **tiphtay** (Chald.), *tif-tah'ee;* perh. from 8199; *judicial,* i.e. a *lawyer:*—sheriff.

תֹּצָאָה **tôtsâ'âh**. See 8444.

8615. תִּקְוָה **tiqvâh**, *tik-vaw';* from 6960; lit. a *cord* (as an *attachment* [comp. 6961]); fig. *expectancy:*—expectation ([-ted]), hope, live, thing that I long for.

8616. תִּקְוָה **Tiqvâh**, *tik-vaw';* the same as 8615; *Tikvah,* the name of two Isr.:—Tikvah.

8617. תְּקוּמָה **tᵉqûwmâh**, *tek-oo-maw';* from 6965; *resistfulness:*—power to stand.

8618. תְּקוֹמֵם **tᵉqôwmêm**, *tek-o-mame';* from 6965; an *opponent:*—rise up against.

8619. תָּקוֹעַ **tâqôwaʻ**, *taw-ko'-ah;* from 8628 (in the musical sense); a *trumpet:*—trumpet.

8620. תְּקוֹעַ **Tᵉqôwaʻ**, *tek-o'-ah;* a form of 8619; *Tekoä,* a place in Pal.:—Tekoa, Tekoah.

8621. תְּקוֹעִי **Tᵉqôwʻîy**, *tek-o-ee';* or

תְּקֹעִי **Tᵉqôʻîy**, *tek-o-ee';* patron. from 8620; a *Tekoïte* or inhab. of Tekoah:—Tekoite.

8622. תְּקוּפָה **tᵉqûwphâh**, *tek-oo-faw';* or

תְּקֻפָה **tᵉqûphâh**, *tek-oo-faw';* from 5362; a *revolution,* i.e. (of the sun) *course,* (of time) *lapse:*—circuit, come about, end.

8623. תַּקִּיף **taqqîyph**, *tak-keef';* from 8630; *powerful:*—mightier.

8624. תַּקִּיף **taqqîyph** (Chald.), *tak-keef';* corresp. to 8623:—mighty, strong.

8625. תְּקַל **tᵉqal** (Chald.), *tek-al';* corresp. to 8254; to *balance:*—Tekel, be weighed.

8626. תָּקַן **tâqan**, *taw-kan';* a prim. root; to *equalize,* i.e. *straighten* (intrans. or trans.); fig. to *compose:*—set in order, make straight.

8627. תְּקַן **tᵉqan** (Chald.), *tek-an';* corresp. to 8626; to *straighten* up, i.e. *confirm:*—establish.

8628. תָּקַע **tâqaʻ**, *taw-kah';* a prim. root; to *clatter,* i.e. *slap* (the hands together), *clang* (an instrument); by anal. to *drive* (a nail or tent-pin, a dart, etc.); by impl. to *become bondsman* (by handclasping):—blow ([a trumpet]), cast, clap, fasten, pitch [tent], smite, sound, strike, × suretiship, thrust.

8629. תֵּקַע **têqaʻ**, *tay-kah';* from 8628; a *blast* of a trumpet:—sound.

תְּקֹעִי **Tᵉqôʻîy**. See 8621.

8630. תָּקַף **tâqaph**, *taw-kaf';* a prim. root; to *overpower:*—prevail (against).

8631. תְּקֵף **tᵉqêph** (Chald.), *tek-afe';* corresp. to 8630; to *become* (caus. *make*) *mighty* or (fig.) *obstinate:*—make firm, harden, be (-come) strong.

8632. תְּקֹף **tᵉqôph** (Chald.), *tek-ofe';* corresp. to 8633; *power:*—might, strength.

8633 תֹּקֶף **tôqeph**, *to'-kef;* from 8630; *might* or (fig.) *positiveness:*—authority, power, strength.

תְּקֻפָה **tᵉqûphâh**. See 8622.

תֹּר **tôr**. See 8447, 8449.

8634. תַּרְאֲלָה **Tar'ălâh**, *tar-al-aw';* prob. for 8653; a *reeling; Taralah,* a place in Pal.:—Taralah.

8635. תַּרְבּוּת **tarbûwth**, *tar-booth';* from 7235; *multiplication,* i.e. *progeny:*—increase.

8636. תַּרְבִּית **tarbîyth**, *tar-beeth';* from 7235; *multiplication,* i.e. *percentage* or *bonus* in addition to principal:—increase, unjust gain.

8637. תִּרְגַּל **tirgal**, *teer-gal';* a denom. from 7270; to *cause to walk:*—teach to go.

8638. תִּרְגַּם **tirgam**, *teer-gam';* a denom. from 7275 in the sense of *throwing* over; to *transfer,* i.e. *translate:*—interpret.

תֹּרָה **tôrâh**. See 8451.

8639. תַּרְדֵּמָה **tardêmâh**, *tar-day-maw';* from 7290; a *lethargy* or (by impl.) *trance:*—deep sleep.

8640. תִּרְהָקָה **Tirhâqâh**, *teer-haw'-kaw;* of for. der.; *Tirhakah,* a king of Kush:—Tirhakah.

8641. תְּרוּמָה **tᵉrûwmâh**, *ter-oo-maw';* or

תְּרֻמָה **tᵉrûmâh** (Deut. 12 : 11), *ter-oo-maw';* from 7311; a *present* (as offered *up*), espec. in *sacrifice* or as *tribute:*—gift, heave offering ([shoulder]), oblation, offered (-ing).

8642. תְּרוּמִיָּה **tᵉrûwmîyâh**, *ter-oo-mee-yaw';* formed as 8641; a sacrificial *offering:*—oblation.

8643. תְּרוּעָה **tᵉrûwʻâh**, *ter-oo-aw';* from 7321; *clamor,* i.e. *acclamation* of joy or a *battle-cry;* espec. *clangor* of trumpets, as an *alarum:*—alarm, blow (-ing) (of, the) (trumpets), joy, jubile, loud noise, rejoicing, shout (-ing), (high, joyful) sound (-ing).

8644. תְּרוּפָה **tᵉrûwphâh**, *ter-oo-faw';* from 7322 in the sense of its congener 7495; a *remedy:*—medicine.

8645. תִּרְזָה **tirzâh**, *teer-zaw';* prob. from 7329; a species of tree (appar. from its *slenderness*), perh. the *cypress:*—cypress.

8646. תֶּרַח **Terach**, *teh'-rakh;* of uncert. der.; *Terach,* the father of Abraham; also a place in the Desert:—Tarah, Terah.

8647. תִּרְחֲנָה **Tirchănâh**, *teer-khan-aw';* of uncert. der.; *Tirchanah,* an Isr.:—Tirhanah.

8648. תְּרֵין **tᵉrêyn** (Chald.), *ter-ane';* fem.

תַּרְתֵּין **tartêyn**, *tar-tane';* corresp. to 8147; *two:*—second, + twelve, two.

8649. תָּרְמָה **tormâh**, *tor-maw';* and

תַּרְמוּת° **tarmûwth**, *tar-mooth';* or

תַּרְמִית **tarmîyth**, *tar-meeth';* from 7411; *fraud:*—deceit (-ful), privily.

תְּרֻמָה **tᵉrûmâh**. See 8641.

8650. תֹּרֶן **tôren**, *to'-ren;* prob. for 766; a *pole* (as a mast or flag-staff):—beacon, mast.

8651. תְּרַע **tᵉraʻ** (Chald.), *ter-ah';* corresp. to 8179; a *door;* by impl. a *palace:*—gate mouth.

8652. תָּרָע **târâʻ** (Chald.), *taw-raw';* from 8651; a *doorkeeper:*—porter.

8653. תַּרְעֵלָה **tarʻêlâh**, *tar-ay-law';* from 7477; *reeling:*—astonishment, trembling.

8654. תִּרְעָתִי **Tirʻâthîy**, *teer-aw-thee';* patrial from an unused name mean. *gate;* a *Tirathite* or inhab. of an unknown Tirah:—Tirathite.

8655. תְּרָפִים **tᵉrâphîym**, *ter-aw-feme';* plur. per. from 7495; a *healer; Teraphim* (sing. or plur.) a family idol:—idols (-atry), images, teraphim.

8656. תִּרְצָה **Tirtsâh**, *teer-tsaw';* from 7521; *delightsomeness; Tirtsah,* a place in Pal.; also an Israelitess:—Tirzah.

8657. תֶּרֶשׁ **Teresh**, *teh'-resh;* of for. der.; *Teresh,* a eunuch of Xerxes:—Teresh.

8658. תַּרְשִׁישׁ **tarshîysh**, *tar-sheesh';* prob. of for. der. [comp. 8659]; a gem, perh. the *topaz:*—beryl.

8659. תַּרְשִׁישׁ **Tarshîysh**, *tar-sheesh';* prob. the same as 8658 (as the region of the stone, or the reverse); *Tarshish,* a place on the Mediterranean, hence the epithet of a *merchant* vessel (as if for or from that port); also the name of a Persian and of an Isr.:—Tarshish, Tharshish.

8660. תִּרְשָׁתָא **Tirshâthâ'**, *teer-shaw-thaw';* of for. der.; the title of a Pers. deputy or *governor:*—Tirshatha.

תַּרְתֵּין **tartêyn**. See 8648.

8661. תַּרְתָּן **Tartân**, *tar-tawn';* of for. der.; *Tartan,* an Assyrian:—Tartan.

8662. תַּרְתָּק **Tartâq**, *tar-tawk';* of for. der.; *Tartak,* a deity of the Avvites:—Tartak.

8663. תְּשֻׁאָה **tᵉshûʼâh**, *tesh-oo-aw';* from 7722; a *crashing* or loud *clamor:*—crying, noise, shouting, stir.

תֹּשָׁב **tôshâb**. See 8453.

8664. תִּשְׁבִּי **Tishbîy**, *tish-bee';* patrial from an unused name mean. *recourse;* a *Tishbite* or inhab. of Tishbeh (in Gilead):—Tishbite.

8665. תַּשְׁבֵּץ **tashbêts**, *tash-bates';* from 7660; *checkered* stuff (as *reticulated*):—broidered.

8666. תְּשׁוּבָה **tᵉshûwbâh**, *tesh-oo-baw';* or

תְּשֻׁבָה **tᵉshûbâh**, *tesh-oo-baw';* from 7725; a *recurrence* (of time or place); a *reply* (as *returned*):—answer, be expired, return.

8667. תְּשׂוּמֶת **tᵉsûwmeth**, *tes-oo-meth';* from 7760; a *deposit,* i.e. *pledging:*—+ fellowship.

8668. תְּשׁוּעָה **tᵉshûwʻâh**, *tesh-oo-aw';* or

תְּשֻׁעָה **tᵉshûʻâh**, *tesh-oo-aw';* from 7768 in the sense of 3467; *rescue* (lit. or fig., pers., national or spir.):—deliverance, help, safety, salvation, victory.

8669. תְּשׁוּקָה **tᵉshûwqâh**, *tesh-oo-kaw';* from 7783 in the orig. sense of *stretching* out after; a *longing:*—desire.

8670. תְּשׁוּרָה **tᵉshûwrâh**, *tesh-oo-raw';* from 7788 in the sense of *arrival;* a *gift:*—present.

תַּשְׁחֵת **tashchêth**. See 516.

תֻּשִׁיָּה **tûshîyâh**. See 8454.

8671. תְּשִׁיעִי **tᵉshîyʻîy**, *tesh-ee-ee';* ord. from 8672; *ninth:*—ninth.

תְּשֻׁעָה **tᵉshûʻâh**. See 8668.

8672. תֵּשַׁע **têshaʻ**, *tay'-shah;* or (masc.)

תִּשְׁעָה **tishʻâh**, *tish-aw';* perh. from 8159 through the idea of a *turn* to the next or full number ten; *nine* or (ord.) *ninth:*—nine (+ -teen, + -teenth, -th).

8673. תִּשְׁעִים **tishʻîym**, *tish-eem';* multiple from 8672; *ninety:*—ninety.

8674. תַּתְּנַי **Tattᵉnay**, *tat-ten-ah'ee;* of for. der.; *Tattenai,* a Persian:—Tatnai.

PLACES WHERE THE HEBREW AND THE ENGLISH BIBLES DIFFER IN THE DIVISION OF CHAPTERS AND VERSES.

	English.	*Hebrew.*
Genesis	31:55	32: 1
	32: 1-32	2-33
Exodus	8: 1-4	7:26-29
	5-32	8: 1-28
	22: 1	21:37
	2-31	22: 1-30
Leviticus	6: 1-7	5:20-26
	8-30	6: 1-23
Numbers	16:36-50	17: 1-15
	17: 1-13	16-28
	26: 1 (first clause)	25:19
	29:40	30: 1
	30: 1-16	2-17
Deuteronomy	5:18-33	5:17-30
	12:32	13: 1
	13: 1-18	2-19
	22:30	23: 1
	23: 1-25	2-26
	29: 1	28:69
	2-29	29: 1-28
Joshua	21:36, 37	(not in most copies)
	38-45	21:36-43
1 Samuel	19: 2 (first clause)	19: 1
	20:42	21: 1
	21: 1-15	2-16
	23:29	24: 1
	24: 1-22	2-23
2 Samuel	17:28 (first word)	29 (middle)
	18:33	19: 1
	19: 1-43	2-44
1 Kings	4:21-34	5: 1-14
	5: 1-18	15-32
	18:33 (l. half)	(first half)18:34
	20: 2 (l. half)	(first half)20: 3
	22:22 (f. clause)	(l. cl.)22:21
	43 (last half)	44
	44-53	45-54
2 Kings	11:21	12: 1
	12: 1-21	2-22
1 Chronicles	6: 1-15	5:27-41
	16-81	6: 1-66
2 Chronicles	2: 1	1:18
	2-18	2: 1-17
	14: 1	13:23
	2-15	14: 1-14
Nehemiah	4: 1-6	3:33-38
	7-23	4: 1-17
	9:38	10: 1
	10: 1-39	2-40
Job	41: 1-8	40:25-32
	9-34	41: 1-26
Psalms	3:*title*	3: 1
	1-8	3-9
	4:*title*	4: 1
	1-8	2-9
	5:*title*	5: 1
	1-12	2-13
	6:*title*	6: 1
	1-10	2-11
	7:*title*	7: 1
	1-17	2-18
	8:*title*	8: 1
	1-9	2-10
	9:*title*	9: 1
	1-20	2-21
	11:*title* (first clause)	11: 1
	12:*title*	12: 1
	1-8	2-9
	13:*title*	13: 1
	1-5	2-6
	6 (last half)	6
	14:*title* (first clause)	14: 1
	15:*title* (first clause)	15: 1
	16:*title* (first clause)	16: 1
	17:*title* (first clause)	17: 1
	18:*title*	18:1&(f.c.)2
	1-50	2-51
	19:*title*	19: 1
	1-14	2-15

	English.	*Hebrew.*
Psalms	20:*title*	20: 1
	1-9	2-10
	21:*title*	21: 1
	1-13	2-14
	22:*title*	22: 1
	1-31	2-32
	23:*title* (first clause)	23: 1
	24-28:*title* (first clause)	24-28: 1
	29:*title* (first clause)	29: 1
	30:*title*	30: 1
	1-12	2-13
	31:*title*	31: 1
	1-24	2-25
	32:*title* (first clause)	32: 1
	34:*title*	34: 1
	1-22	2-23
	35&37:*title* (first word)	35&37: 1
	36:*title*	36: 1
	1-12	2-13
	38:*title*	38: 1
	1-22	2-23
	39:*title*	39: 1
	1-13	2-14
	40:*title*	40: 1
	1-17	2-18
	41:*title*	41: 1
	1:13	2-14
	42:*title*	42: 1
	1-11	2-12
	44:*title*	44: 1
	1-26	2-27
	45:*title*	45: 1
	1-17	2-18
	46:*title*	46: 1
	1-11	2-12
	47:*title*	47: 1
	1-9	2-10
	48:*title*	48: 1
	1-14	2-15
	49:*title*	49: 1
	1-20	2-21
	50:*title* (first clause)	50: 1
	51:*title*	51: 1&2
	1-19	2-21
	52:*title* (first clause)	52: 1 & 2
	1-9	2-11
	53:*title*	53: 1
	1-6	2-7
	54:*title*	54: 1 & 2
	1-7	2-9
	55:*title*	55: 1
	1-23	2-24
	56:*title*	56: 1
	1-23	2-24
	57:*title*	57: 1
	1-11	2-12
	58:*title*	58: 1
	1-11	2-12
	59:*title*	59: 1
	1-17	2-18
	60:*title*	60: 1 &2
	1-12	3-14
	61:*title*	61: 1
	1-8	2-9
	62:*title*	62: 1
	1-12	2-13
	63:*title*	63: 1
	1-11	2-12
	64:*title*	64: 1
	1-10	2-11
	65:*title*	65: 1
	1-13	2-14
	66:*title* (first clause)	66: 1
	67:*title*	67: 1
	1-7	2-8
	68:*title*	68: 1
	1-35	2-36
	69:*title*	69: 1
	1-36	2-37

	English.	*Hebrew.*
Psalms	70:*title*	70: 1
	1-5	2-6
	72:*title* (first word)	72: 1
	73:*title* (first clause)	73: 1
	74:*title* (first clause)	74: 1
	1-10	2-11
	76:*title*	76: 1
	1-12	2-13
	77:*title*	77: 1
	1-20	2-21
	78 & 79:*title* (f. clause)	78&79: 1
	80:*title*	80: 1
	1-19	2-20
	81:*title*	81: 1
	1-16	2-17
	82:*title* (first clause)	82: 1
	83:*title*	83: 1
	1-18	2-19
	84:*title*	84: 1
	1-12	2-13
	85:*title*	85: 1
	1-13	2-14
	86 & 87:*title* (first cl.)	86&87: 1
	88:*title*	88: 1
	1-18	2-19
	89:*title*	89: 1
	1-52	2-53
	90:*title* (first clause)	90: 1
	92:*title*	92: 1
	11-5	2-16
	98:*title* (first word)	98: 1
	100&101:*title* (1st cl.)	100&101: 1
	102:*title*	102: 1
	1-28	2-29
	103:*title* (first word)	103: 1
	108:*title*	108: 1
	1-13	2-14
	109, 110, 120-134, 138 and 139:*title* (first cl.) same	1
	140:*title*	140: 1
	1-13	2-14
	141:*title* (first clause)	141: 1
	142:*title*	142: 1
	1-6	2-7
	143:*title* (first clause)	143: 1
	144:*title* (first word)	144: 1
	145:*title* (first clause)	145: 1
Ecclesiastes	5: 1	4:17
	2-20	5: 1-19
Canticles	6:13	7: 1
	7: 1-13	2-14
Isaiah	9: 1	8:23
	2-21	9: 1-20
	64: 1	63:19
	2-12	64: 1-11
Jeremiah	9: 1	8:23
	2-26	9: 1-25
Ezekiel	20:45-49	21: 1-5
	21: 1-32	6-37
Daniel	4: 1-3	3:31-33
	4-37	4: 1-34
	5:31	6: 1
	6: 1-28	2-29
Hosea	1:10, 11	2: 1, 2
	2: 1-23	3-25
	11:12	12: 1
	12: 1-14	2-15
	13:16	14: 1
	14: 1-9	2-10
Joel	2:28-32	3: 1-5
	3: 1-21	4: 1-21
Jonah	1:17	2: 1
	2: 1-10	2-11
Micah	5: 1	4:14
	2-15	5: 1-14
Nahum	1:15	2: 1
	2: 1-13	2-14
Zechariah	1:18	2: 1-4
	2: 1-13	2-17
Malachi	4: 1-6	3:19-24

DICTIONARY

OF THE

GREEK TESTAMENT.

PLAN OF THE BOOK.

1. All the original words are treated in their alphabetical Greek order, and are numbered regularly from the first to the last, each being known throughout by its appropriate number. This renders reference easy without recourse to the Greek characters.

2. Immediately after each word is given its exact equivalent in English letters, according to the system of transliteration laid down in the scheme here following, which is substantially that adopted in the Common English Version, only more consistently and uniformly carried out; so that the word could readily be turned back again into Greek from the form thus given it.

3. Next follows the precise pronunciation, according to the usual English mode of sounding syllables, so plainly indicated that none can fail to apprehend and apply it. The most approved sounds are adopted, as laid down in the annexed scheme of articulation, and in such a way that any good Græcist would immediately recognise the word if so pronounced, notwithstanding the minor variations current among scholars in this respect.

4. Then ensues a tracing of the etymology, radical meaning, and applied significations of the word, justly but tersely analyzed and expressed, with any other important peculiarities in this regard.

5. In the case of proper names, the same method is pursued, and at this point the regular mode of Anglicizing it, after the general style of the Common English Version, is given, and a few words of explanation are added to identify it.

6. Finally (after the punctuation-mark :—) are given all the different renderings of the word in the Authorized English Version, arranged in the alphabetical order of the leading terms, and conveniently condensed according to the explanations given below.

By searching out these various renderings in the Main Concordance, to which this Dictionary is designed as a companion, and noting the passages to which the same number corresponding to that of any given Greek word is attached in the marginal column, the reader, whether acquainted with the original language or not, will obtain a complete *Greek Concordance* also, expressed in the words of the Common English Version. This is an advantage which no other Concordance or Lexicon affords.

GREEK ARTICULATION.

The following explanations are sufficient to show the mode of writing and pronouncing Greek words in English adopted in this *Dictionary*.

1. The *Alphabet* is as follows:

No.	Form.		Name.	Transliteration and Power.
1.	Α	α	Alpha (*al'-fah*)	a, as in *arm* or
2.	Β	β	Bēta (*bay'-tah*)	b [*man**
3.	Γ	γ	Gamma (*gam'-mah*)	g hard †
4.	Δ	δ	Dĕlta (*del'-tah*)	d
5.	Ε	ε	Ĕpsilŏn (*ep'-see-lon*)	ĕ, as in *met*
6.	Ζ	ζ	Zēta (*dzay'-tah*)	z, as in *adze*‡
7.	Η	η	Ēta (*ay'-tah*)	ē, as in *they*
8.	Θ	θ or ϑ	Thēta (*thay'-tah*)	th, as in *thin*§
9.	Ι	ι	Iōta (*ee-o'-tah*)	i, as in *ma-*
10.	Κ	κ or ϰ	Kappa (*cap'-pah*)	k [*chine*‖
11.	Λ	λ	Lambda (*lamb'-dah*)	l
12.	Μ	μ	Mu (*moo*)	m
13.	Ν	ν	Nu (*noo*)	n
14.	Ξ	ξ	Xi (*ksee*)	x = *ks*
15.	Ο	ο	Omikrŏn (*om'-e-cron*)	ŏ, as in *not*
16.	Π	π	Pi (*pee*)	p
17.	Ρ	ρ	Rhō (*hro*)	r
18.	Σ	σ, final ς	Sigma (*sig'-mah*)	s sharp
19.	Τ	τ	Tau (*tŏw*)	t¶
20.	Υ	υ	Upsilŏn (*u'-pse-lon*)	u, as in *full*
21.	Φ	φ	Phi (*fee*)	ph = *f*
22.	Χ	χ	Chi (*khee*)	German ch *
23.	Ψ	ψ	Psi (*psee*)	ps
24.	Ω	ω	Omĕga (*o'-meg-ah*)	ō, as in *no*.

* α, when *final*, or before ρ final or followed by any *other* consonant, is sounded like *a* in *arm*; elsewhere like *a* in *man*.

† γ, when followed by γ, κ, χ, or ξ, is sounded like *ng* in *king*.

‡ ζ is always sounded like *dz*.

§ θ never has the guttural sound, like *th* in *this*.

‖ ι has the sound of *ee* when it *ends* an *accented* syllable; in other situations a more obscure sound, like *i* in *amiable* or *imbecile*.

¶ τ never has a sibilant sound, like *t* in *nation*, *nature*.

2. The mark ʽ, placed over the *initial* vowel of a word, is called the *Rough Breathing*, and is equivalent to the English *h*, by which we have accordingly represented it. Its *absence* over an initial vowel is indicated by the mark ʼ, called the *Smooth Breathing*, which is unappreciable or silent, and is therefore not represented in our method of transliteration.†

3. The following are the Greek *diphthongs*, properly so called :‡

Form.	Transliteration and Power.	Form.	Transliteration and Power.
αι	ai (*ah'ee*) [ă + ĕ]	αυ	ow, as in *now*
ει	ei, as in *height*	ευ	eu, as in *feud*
οι	oi, as in *oil*	ου	ou, as in *through*.
υι	we, as in *sweet*		

* From the difficulty of producing the true sound of χ, it is generally sounded like *k*.

† These signs are placed over the *second* vowel of a *diphthong*. The same is true of the accents.

The *Rough* Breathing always belongs to υ initial.

The Rough Breathing is always used with ρ, when it begins a word. If this letter be doubled in the middle of a word, the first takes the Smooth, and the second the Rough, Breathing.

As these signs cannot conveniently be written over the first letter of a word, when a *capital*, they are in such cases placed *before* it. This observation applies also to the *accents*. The aspiration *always* begins the syllable.

Occasionally, in consequence of a contraction (*crasis*), the Smooth Breathing is made to stand in the middle of a word, and is then called *Coro'nis*.

‡ The above are combinations of two *short* vowels, and are pronounced like their respective elements, but in more rapid succession than otherwise. Thus αι is midway between *i* in *high*, and *ay* in *say*.

Besides these, there are what are called *improper* diphthongs, in which the former is a *long* vowel. In these,

ᾳ sounds like α	ηυ sounds like η + υ
ῃ " " η	ωυ " " ω + υ.
ῳ " " ω	

the second vowel, when ι, is written *under* the first (unless that be a capital), and is *silent;* when υ, it is sounded separately. When the initial is a capital, the ι is placed after it, but does not take the breathing nor accent.

The sign ¨, called *diær'esis*, placed over the *latter* of two vowels, indicates that they do *not* form a diphthong.

4. The *accent* (stress of voice) falls on the syllable where it is written.* It is of three forms: the *acute* (ʹ), which is the only true accent; the *grave* (ˋ) which is its substitute; and the *circumflex* (ˆ or ˜), which is the union of the two. The acute may stand on any one of the last *three* syllables, and in case it occurs on the final syllable, before another word in the same sentence, it is written as a grave. The grave is understood (but never written as such) on every other syllable. The circumflex is written on any syllable (necessarily the last or next to the last one of a word), formed by the contraction of two syllables, of which the *first* would properly have the acute.

5. The following *punctuation*-marks are used: the comma (,), the semicolon (·), the colon or period (.), the interrogation-point (;), and by some editors, also the exclamation-point, parentheses and quotation-marks.

* Every word (except a few monosyllables, called *Aton'ics*) must have one accent; several small words (called *Enclit'ics*) throw their accent (always as an acute) on the last syllable of the preceding word (in addition to its own accent, which still has the principal stress), where this is possible.

ABBREVIATIONS EMPLOYED.

abst. = abstract (-ly)
acc. = accusative (case)
adv. = adverb (-ial) (-ly)
aff. = affinity
alt. = alternate (-ly)
anal. = analogy
app. = apparent (-ly)
caus. = causative (-ly)
cer. = { ceremony / ceremonial (-ly) }
Chald. = Chaldee
Chr. = Christian
coll. = collective (-ly)
comp. = { comparative / comparatively / compare / compound (-s) }
concr. = concrete (-ly)
corr. = corresponding
dat. = dative (case)
der. = { derivation / derivative / derived }
dim. = diminutive
dir. = direct (-ly)
E. = East
eccl. = ecclesiastical (-ly)
Eg. = Egypt (-ian)
ell. = { ellipsis / elliptical (-ly) }
eq. = equivalent
esp. = especially
euph. = { euphemism / euphemistic / euphemistically }
ext. = extension
fem. = feminine
fig. = figurative (-ly)
for. = foreign
gen. = genitive (case)
Gr. = Greek
Heb. = { Hebraism / Hebrew }
i.e. = { *id est* / that is }
imper. = imperative
imperf. = imperfect
impers. = impersonal (-ly)
impl. = { implication / implied }
incl. = including
ind. = indicative (-ly)
indiv. = individual (-ly)
inf. = infinitive
inh. = inhabitant (-s)
intens. = intensive (-ly)
intr. = intransitive (-ly)
invol. = { involuntary / involuntarily }
irr. = irregular (-ly)
Isr. = { Israelite (-s) / Israelitish }
Jer. = Jerusalem
Lat. = Latin
lit. = literal (-ly)
mean. = meaning
ment. = mental (-ly)
mid. = middle (voice)
mor. = moral (-ly)
mult. = multiplicative
nat. = natural (-ly)
neg. = negative (-ly)
neut. = neuter
obj. = objective (-ly)
obs. = obsolete
or. = origin (-al) (-ly)
Pal. = Palestine
part. = participle
pass. = passive (-ly)
perh. = perhaps
pers. = person (-al) (-ly)
phys. = physical (-ly)
pl. = plural
pref. = prefix (-ed)
pos. = positive (-ly)
prim. = primary
prob. = probably
prol. = { prolongation / prolonged }
pron. = { pronominal (-ly) / pronoun }
prop. = properly
redupl. = { reduplicated / reduplication }
refl. = reflexive (-ly)
rel. = relative (-ly)
Rom. = Roman
sing. = singular
spec. = special (-ly)
subj. = subjective (-ly)
sup. = superlative (-ly)
tech. = technical (-ly)
term. = termination
trans. = transitive (-ly)
transp. = { transposed / transposition }
typ. = typical (-ly)
unc. = uncertain
var. = { variation / various }
voc. = vocative
vol. = { voluntarily / voluntary }

SIGNS EMPLOYED.

+ (*addition*) denotes a rendering in the A. V. of one or more Gr. words in connection with the one under consideration.

× (*multiplication*) denotes a rendering in the A. V. that results from an idiom peculiar to the Gr.

( ) (*parenthesis*), in the renderings from the A. V., denotes a word or syllable sometimes given in connection with the principal word to which it is annexed.

[ ] (*bracket*), in the rendering from the A. V., denotes the inclusion of an additional word in the Gr.

Italics, at the end of a rendering from the A. V., denote an explanation of the variations from the usual form.

NOTE.

Owing to changes in the enumeration while in progress, there were no words left for Nos. *2717* and *3203–3302*, which were therefore silently dropped out of the vocabulary and references as redundant. This will occasion no practical mistake or inconvenience.

GREEK DICTIONARY OF THE NEW TESTAMENT.

A.

N. B.—The numbers *not in italics* refer to the words in the *Hebrew Dictionary*. Significations within quotation-marks are derivative representatives of the Greek.

1. Α α, *al'-fah;* of Heb. or.; the first letter of the alphabet; fig. only (from its use as a numeral) the *first:*—Alpha. Often used (usually ἀν **an**, before a vowel) also in composition (as a contraction from *427*) in the sense of *privation;* so in many words beginning with this letter; occasionally in the sense of *union* (as a contraction of *260*).

2. Ἀαρών **Aarōn**, *ah-ar-ohn';* of Heb. or. [175]; *Aaron*, the brother of Moses:—Aaron.

3. Ἀβαδδών **Abaddōn** *ab-ad-dohn';* of Heb. or. [11]; a destroying *angel:*—Abaddon.

4. ἀβαρής **abarēs**, *ab-ar-ace';* from *1* (as a neg. particle) and *922; weightless*, i.e. (fig.) *not burdensome:*—from being burdensome.

5. Ἀββᾶ **Abba**, *ab-bah';* of Chald. or. [2]; *father* (as a voc.):—Abba.

6. Ἄβελ **Abĕl**, *ab'-el;* of Heb. or. [1893]; *Abel*, the son of Adam:—Abel.

7. Ἀβιά **Abia**, *ab-ee-ah';* of Heb. or. [29]; *Abijah*, the name of two Isr.:—Abia.

8. Ἀβιάθαρ **Abiathar**, *ab-ee-ath'-ar;* of Heb. or. [54]; *Abiathar*, an Isr.:—Abiathar.

9. Ἀβιληνή **Abilēnē**, *ab-ee-lay-nay';* of for. or. [comp. 58]; *Abilene*, a region of Syria:—Abilene.

10. Ἀβιούδ **Abiŏud**, *ab-ee-ood';* of Heb. or. [31]; *Abihud*, an Isr.:—Abiud.

11. Ἀβραάμ **Abraam**, *ab-rah-am';* of Heb. or. [85]; *Abraham*, the Heb. patriarch:—Abraham. [In Acts 7 : 16 the text should prob. read *Jacob*.]

12. ἄβυσσος **abussŏs**, *ab'-us-sos;* from *1* (as a neg. particle) and a var. of *1037; depthless*, i.e. (spec.) (infernal) "*abyss*":—deep, (bottomless) pit.

13. Ἄγαβος **Agabŏs**, *ag'-ab-os;* of Heb. or. [comp. 2285]; *Agabus*, an Isr.:—Agabus.

14. ἀγαθοεργέω **agathŏĕrgĕō**, *ag-ath-er-gheh'-o;* from *18* and *2041;* to *work good:*—do good.

15. ἀγαθοποιέω **agathŏpŏiĕō**, *ag-ath-op-oy-eh'-o;* from *17;* to *be a well-doer* (as a favor or a duty):—(when) do good (well).

16. ἀγαθοποιΐα **agathŏpŏiïa**, *ag-ath-op-oy-ee'-ah;* from *17; well-doing*, i.e. *virtue:*—well-doing.

17. ἀγαθοποιός **agathŏpŏiŏs**, *ag-ath-op-oy-os';* from *18* and *4160;* a *well-doer*, i.e. *virtuous:*—them that do well.

18. ἀγαθός **agathŏs**, *ag-ath-os';* a prim. word; "*good*" (in any sense, often as noun):—benefit, good (-s, things), well. Comp. *2570*.

19. ἀγαθωσύνη **agathōsunē**, *ag-ath-o-soo'-nay;* from *18; goodness*, i.e. *virtue* or *beneficence:*—goodness.

20. ἀγαλλίασις **agalliasis**, *ag-al-lee'-as-is;* from *21; exultation;* spec. *welcome:*—gladness, (exceeding) joy.

21. ἀγαλλιάω **agalliaō**, *ag-al-lee-ah'-o;* from ἄγαν **agan** (*much*) and *242;* prop. to *jump for joy*, i.e. *exult:*—be (exceeding) glad, with exceeding joy, rejoice (greatly).

22. ἄγαμος **agamŏs**, *ag'-am-os;* from *1* (as a neg. particle) and *1062; unmarried:*—unmarried.

23. ἀγανακτέω **aganaktĕō**, *ag-an-ak-teh'-o;* from ἄγαν **agan** (*much*) and ἄχθος **achthŏs** (*grief;* akin to the base of *43*); to *be greatly afflicted*, i.e. (fig.) *indignant:*—be much (sore) displeased, have (be moved with, with) indignation.

24. ἀγανάκτησις **aganaktēsis**, *ag-an-ak'-tay-sis;* from *23; indignation:*—indignation.

25. ἀγαπάω **agapaō**, *ag-ap-ah'-o;* perh. from ἄγαν **agan** (*much*) [or comp. 5689]; to *love* (in a social or moral sense):—(be-) love (-ed). Comp. *5368*.

26. ἀγάπη **agapē**, *ag-ah'-pay;* from *25; love*, i.e. *affection* or *benevolence;* spec. (plur.) a *love-feast:*—(feast of) charity ([-ably]), dear, love.

27. ἀγαπητός **agapētŏs**, *ag-ap-ay-tos';* from *25; beloved:*—(dearly, well) beloved, dear.

28. Ἄγαρ **Agar**, *ag'-ar;* of Heb. or. [1904]; *Hagar*, the concubine of Abraham:—Hagar.

29. ἀγγαρεύω **aggarĕuō**, *ang-ar-yew'-o;* of for. or. [comp. 104]; prop. to *be a courier*, i.e., (by impl.) to *press* into public service:—compel (to go).

30. ἀγγεῖον **aggĕiŏn**, *ang-eye'-on;* from ἄγγος **aggŏs** (a *pail*, perh. as *bent;* comp. the base of *43*); a *receptacle:*—vessel.

31. ἀγγελία **aggĕlia**, *ang-el-ee'-ah;* from *32;* an *announcement*, i.e. (by impl.) *precept:*—message.

32. ἄγγελος **aggĕlŏs**, *ang'-el-os;* from ἀγγέλλω **aggĕllō** [prob. der. from *71;* comp. *34*] (to *bring tidings*); a *messenger;* esp. an "*angel*"; by impl. a *pastor:*—angel, messenger.

33. ἄγε **agĕ**, *ag'-eh;* imper. of *71;* prop. *lead*, i.e. *come on:*—go to.

34. ἀγέλη **agĕlē**, *ag-el'-ay;* from *71* [comp. *32*]; a *drove:*—herd.

35. ἀγενεαλόγητος **agĕnĕalŏgētŏs**, *ag-en-eh-al-og'-ay-tos;* from *1* (as neg. particle) and *1075; unregistered* as to birth:—without descent.

36. ἀγενής **agĕnēs**, *ag-en-ace';* from *1* (as neg. particle) and *1085;* prop. *without kin*, i.e. (of unknown descent, and by impl.) *ignoble:*—base things.

37. ἁγιάζω **hagiazō**, *hag-ee-ad'-zo;* from *40;* to *make holy*, i.e. (cer.) *purify* or *consecrate;* (mentally) to *venerate:*—hallow, be holy, sanctify.

38. ἁγιασμός **hagiasmŏs**, *hag-ee-as-mos';* from *37;* prop. *purification*, i.e. (the state) *purity;* concr. (by Hebr.) a *purifier:*—holiness, sanctification.

39. ἅγιον **hagiŏn**, *hag'-ee-on;* neut. of *40;* a *sacred* thing (i.e. spot):—holiest (of all), holy place, sanctuary.

40. ἅγιος **hagiŏs**, *hag'-ee-os;* from ἅγος **hagŏs** (an *awful* thing) [comp. *53*, 2282]; *sacred* (phys. *pure*, mor. *blameless* or *religious*, cer. *consecrated*):—(most) holy (one, thing), saint.

41. ἁγιότης **hagiŏtēs**, *hag-ee-ot'-ace;* from *40; sanctity* (i.e. prop. the state):—holiness.

42. ἁγιωσύνη **hagiōsunē**, *hag-ee-o-soo'-nay;* from *40; sacredness* (i.e. prop. the quality):—holiness.

43. ἀγκάλη **agkalē**, *ang-kal'-ay;* from ἄγκος **agkŏs** (a *bend*, "*ache*"); an *arm* (as *curved*):—arm.

44. ἄγκιστρον **agkistrŏn**, *ang'-kis-tron;* from the same as *43;* a *hook* (as *bent*):—hook.

45. ἄγκυρα **agkura**, *ang'-koo-rah;* from the same as *43;* an "*anchor*" (as *crooked*):—anchor.

46. ἄγναφος **agnaphŏs**, *ag'-naf-os;* from *1* (as a neg. particle) and the same as *1102;* prop. *unfulled*, i.e. (by impl.) *new* (cloth):—new.

47. ἁγνεία **hagnĕia**, *hag-ni'-ah;* from *53; cleanliness* (the quality), i.e. (spec.) *chastity:*—purity.

48. ἁγνίζω **hagnizō**, *hag-nid'-zo;* from *53;* to *make clean*, i.e. (fig.) *sanctify* (cer. or mor.):—purify (self).

49. ἁγνισμός **hagnismŏs**, *hag-nis-mos';* from *48;* a *cleansing* (the act), i.e. (cer.) *lustration:*—purification.

50. ἀγνοέω **agnŏĕō**, *ag-no-eh'-o;* from *1* (as a neg. particle) and *3539; not to know* (through lack of information or intelligence); by impl. to *ignore* (through disinclination):—(be) ignorant (-ly), not know, not understand, unknown.

51. ἀγνόημα **agnŏēma**, *ag-no'-ay-mah;* from *50;* a thing *ignored*, i.e. *shortcoming:*—error.

52. ἄγνοια **agnŏia**, *ag'-noy-ah;* from *50; ignorance* (prop. the quality):—ignorance.

53. ἁγνός **hagnŏs**, *hag-nos';* from the same as *40;* prop. *clean*, i.e. (fig.) *innocent, modest, perfect:*—chaste, clean, pure.

54. ἁγνότης **hagnŏtēs**, *hag-not'-ace;* from *53; cleanness* (the state), i.e. (fig.) *blamelessness:*—pureness.

55. ἁγνῶς **hagnōs**, *hag-noce';* adv. from *53; purely*, i.e. *honestly:*—sincerely.

56. ἀγνωσία **agnōsia**, *ag-no-see'-ah;* from *1* (as neg. particle) and *1108; ignorance* (prop. the state):—ignorance, not the knowledge.

57. ἄγνωστος **agnōstŏs**, *ag'-noce-tos;* from *1* (as neg. particle) and *1110; unknown:*—unknown.

58. ἀγορά **agŏra**, *ag-or-ah';* from ἀγείρω **agĕirō** (to *gather;* prob. akin to *1453*); prop. the *town-square* (as a place of public resort); by impl. a *market* or *thoroughfare:*—market (-place), street.

59. ἀγοράζω **agŏrazō**, *ag-or-ad'-zo;* from *58;* prop. to *go to market*, i.e. (by impl.) to *purchase;* spec. to *redeem:*—buy, redeem.

60. ἀγοραῖος **agŏraiŏs**, *ag-or-ah'-yos;* from *58; relating to the market-place*, i.e. *forensic* (times); by impl. *vulgar:*—baser sort, low.

61. ἄγρα **agra**, *ag'-rah;* from *71;* (abstr.) a *catching* (of fish); also (concr.) a *haul* (of fish):—draught.

62. ἀγράμματος **agrammatŏs**, *ag-ram-mat-os;* from *1* (as neg. particle) and *1121; unlettered*, i.e. *illiterate:*—unlearned.

63. ἀγραυλέω **agraulĕō**, *ag-row-leh'-o;* from *68* and *832* (in the sense of *833*); to *camp out:*—abide in the field.

64. ἀγρεύω **agrĕuō**, *ag-rew'-o;* from *61;* to *hunt*, i.e. (fig.) to *entrap:*—catch.

65. ἀγριέλαιος **agriĕlaiŏs**, *ag-ree-el'-ah-yos;* from *66* and *1636;* an *oleaster:*—olive tree (which is) wild.

66. ἄγριος **agriŏs**, *ag'-ree-os;* from *68; wild* (as pertaining to the *country*), lit. (*natural*) or fig. (*fierce*):—wild, raging.

67. Ἀγρίππας **Agrippas**, *ag-rip'-pas;* appar. from *66* and *2462; wild-horse* tamer; *Agrippas*, one of the Herods:—Agrippa.

68. ἀγρός **agrŏs**, *ag-ros';* from *71;* a *field* (as a *drive* for cattle); gen. the *country;* spec. a *farm*, i.e. *hamlet:*—country, farm, piece of ground, land.

69. ἀγρυπνέω **agrupnĕō**, *ag-roop-neh'-o;* ultimately from *1* (as neg. particle) and *5258;* to *be sleepless*, i.e. *keep awake:*—watch.

70. ἀγρυπνία **agrupnia**, *ag-roop-nee'-ah;* from *69; sleeplessness*, i.e. a *keeping awake:*—watch.

71. ἄγω **agō**, *ag'-o;* a prim. verb; prop. to *lead;* by impl. to *bring, drive*, (reflex.) *go*, (spec.) *pass* (time), or (fig.) *induce:*—be, bring (forth), carry, (let) go, keep, lead away, be open.

72. ἀγωγή **agōgē**, *ag-o-gay';* redupl. from *71;* a *bringing up*, i.e. *mode of living:*—manner of life.

73. ἀγών **agōn**, *ag-one'*; from *71*; prop. a place of *assembly* (as if *led*), i.e. (by impl.) a *contest* (held there); fig. an *effort* or *anxiety*:—conflict, contention, fight, race.

74. ἀγωνία **agōnia**, *ag-o-nee'-ah*; from *73*; a *struggle* (prop. the state), i.e. (fig.) *anguish*:—agony.

75. ἀγωνίζομαι **agōnizŏmai**, *ag-o-nid'-zom-ahee*; from *73*; to *struggle*, lit. (to *compete* for a prize), fig. (to *contend* with an adversary), or gen. (to *endeavor* to accomplish something):—fight, labor fervently, strive.

76. Ἀδάμ **Adam**, *ad-am'*; of Heb. or. [121]; *Adam*, the first man; typ. (of Jesus) *man* (as his representative):—Adam.

77. ἀδάπανος **adapanŏs**, *ad-ap'-an-os*; from *1* (as neg. particle) and *1160*; *costless*, i.e. *gratuitous*:—without expense.

78. Ἀδδί **Addi**, *ad-dee'*; prob. of Heb. or. [comp. 5716]; *Addi*, an Isr.:—Addi.

79. ἀδελφή **adĕlphē**, *ad-el-fay'*; fem. of *80*; a *sister* (nat. or eccles.):—sister.

80. ἀδελφός **adĕlphŏs**, *ad-el-fos'*; from *1* (as a connective particle) and δελφύς **dĕlphus** (the *womb*); a *brother* (lit. or fig.) near or remote [much like 1]:—brother.

81. ἀδελφότης **adĕlphŏtēs**, *ad-el-fot'-ace*; from *80*; *brotherhood* (prop. the feeling of *brotherliness*), i.e. the (Christian) *fraternity*:—brethren, brotherhood.

82. ἄδηλος **adēlŏs**, *ad'-ay-los*; from *1* (as a neg. particle) and *1212*; *hidden*, fig. *indistinct*:—appear not, uncertain.

83. ἀδηλότης **adēlŏtēs**, *ad-ay-lot'-ace*; from *82*; *uncertainty*:— × uncertain.

84. ἀδήλως **adēlōs**, *ad-ay'-loce*; adv. from *82*; *uncertainly*:—uncertainly.

85. ἀδημονέω **adēmŏnĕō**, *ad-ay-mon-eh'-o*: from a der. of ἀδέω **adĕō**, (to be *sated* to loathing); to *be in distress* (of mind):—be full of heaviness, be very heavy.

86. ᾅδης **hadēs**, *hah'-dace*; from *1* (as a neg. particle) and *1492*; prop. *unseen*, i.e. "*Hades*" or the place (state) of departed souls:—grave, hell.

87. ἀδιάκριτος **adiakritŏs**, *ad-ee-ak'-ree-tos*; from *1* (as a neg. particle) and a der. of *1252*; prop. *undistinguished*, i.e. (act.) *impartial*:—without partiality.

88. ἀδιάλειπτος **adialĕiptŏs**, *ad-ee-al'-ipe-tos*; from *1* (as a neg. particle) and a der. of a compound of *1223* and *3007*; *unintermitted*, i.e. *permanent*:—without ceasing, continual.

89. ἀδιαλείπτως **adialĕiptōs**, *ad-ee-al-ipe'-toce*; adv. from *88*; *uninterruptedly*, i.e. *without omission* (on an appropriate occasion):—without ceasing.

90. ἀδιαφθορία **adiaphthŏria**, *ad-ee-af-thor-ee'-ah*; from a der. of a compound of *1* (as a neg. particle) and a der. of *1311*; *incorruptibleness*, i.e. (fig.) *purity* (of doctrine):—uncorruptness.

91. ἀδικέω **adikĕō**, *ad-ee-keh'-o*; from *94*; to *be unjust*, i.e. (act.) *do wrong* (mor., socially or phys.):—hurt, injure, be an offender, be unjust, (do, suffer, take) wrong.

92. ἀδίκημα **adikēma**, *ad-eek'-ay-mah*; from *91*; a *wrong* done:—evil doing, iniquity, matter of wrong.

93. ἀδικία **adikia**, *ad-ee-kee'-ah*; from *94*; (legal) *injustice* (prop. the quality, by impl. the act); mor. *wrongfulness* (of character, life or act):—iniquity, unjust, unrighteousness, wrong.

94. ἄδικος **adikŏs**, *ad'-ee-kos*; from *1* (as a neg. particle) and *1349*; *unjust*; by extens. *wicked*; by impl. *treacherous*; spec. *heathen*:—unjust, unrighteous.

95. ἀδίκως **adikōs**, *ad-ee'-koce*; adv. from *94*; *unjustly*:—wrongfully.

96. ἀδόκιμος **adŏkimŏs**, *ad-ok'-ee-mos*; from *1* (as a neg. particle) and *1384*; *unapproved*, i.e. *rejected*; by impl. *worthless* (lit. or mor.):—castaway, rejected, reprobate.

97. ἄδολος **adŏlŏs**, *ad'-ol-os*; from *1* (as a neg. particle) and *1388*; *undeceitful*, i.e. (fig.) *unadulterated*:—sincere.

98. Ἀδραμυττηνός **Adramuttēnŏs**, *ad-ram-oot-tay-nos'*; from Ἀδραμύττειον **Adramuttĕiŏn** (a place in Asia Minor); *Adramyttene* or belonging to Adramyttium:—of Adramyttium.

99. Ἀδρίας **Adrias**, *ad-ree'-as*; from Ἀδρία **Adria** (a place near its shore); the *Adriatic* sea (including the Ionian):—Adria.

100. ἁδρότης **hadrŏtēs**, *had-rot'-ace*; from ἁδρός **hadrŏs** (*stout*); *plumpness*, i.e. (fig.) *liberality*:—abundance.

101. ἀδυνατέω **adunatĕō**, *ad-oo-nat-eh'-o*; from *102*; to *be unable*, i.e. (pass.) *impossible*:—be impossible.

102. ἀδύνατος **adunatŏs**, *ad-oo'-nat-os*; from *1* (as a neg. particle) and *1415*; *unable*, i.e. *weak* (lit. or fig.); pass. *impossible*:—could not do, impossible, impotent, not possible, weak.

103. ᾄδω **aidō**, *ad'-o*; a prim. verb; to *sing*:—sing.

104. ἀεί **aĕi**, *ah-eye'*; from an obs. prim. noun (appar. mean. continued *duration*); "*ever*;" by qualification *regularly*; by impl. *earnestly*:—always, ever.

105. ἀετός **aĕtŏs**, *ah-et-os'*; from the same as *109*; an *eagle* (from its *wind*-like flight):—eagle.

106. ἄζυμος **azumŏs**, *ad'-zoo-mos*; from *1* (as a neg. particle) and *2219*; *unleavened*, i.e. (fig.) *uncorrupted*; (in the neut. plur.) spec. (by impl.) the *Passover* week:—unleavened (bread).

107. Ἀζώρ **Azōr**, *ad-zore'*; of Heb. or. [comp. 5809]; *Azor*, an Isr.:—Azor.

108. Ἄζωτος **Azōtŏs**, *ad'-zo-tos*; of Heb. or. [795]; *Azotus* (i.e. Ashdod), a place in Pal.:—Azotus.

109. ἀήρ **aēr**, *ah-ayr'*; from ἄημι **aēmi** (to *breathe* unconsciously, i.e. *respire*; by anal. to *blow*); "*air*" (as naturally *circumambient*):—air. Comp. *5594*.

ἀθά **atha**. See *3134*.

110. ἀθανασία **athanasia**, *ath-an-as-ee'-ah*; from a compound of *1* (as a neg. particle) and *2288*; *deathlessness*:—immortality.

111. ἀθέμιτος **athĕmitŏs**, *ath-em'-ee-tos*; from *1* (as a neg. particle) and a der. of θέμις **thĕmis** (*statute*; from the base of *5087*); *illegal*; by impl. *flagitious*:—abominable, unlawful thing.

112. ἄθεος **athĕŏs**, *ath'-eh-os*; from *1* (as a neg. particle) and *2316*; *godless*:—without God.

113. ἄθεσμος **athĕsmŏs**, *ath'-es-mos*; from *1* (as a neg. particle) and a der. of *5087* (in the sense of *enacting*); *lawless*, i.e. (by impl.) *criminal*:—wicked.

114. ἀθετέω **athĕtĕō**, *ath-et-eh'-o*; from a compound of *1* (as a neg. particle) and a der. of *5087*; to *set aside*, i.e. (by impl.) to *disesteem*, *neutralize* or *violate*:—cast off, despise, disannul, frustrate, bring to nought, reject.

115. ἀθέτησις **athĕtēsis**, *ath-et'-ay-sis*; from *114*; *cancellation* (lit. or fig.):—disannulling, put away.

116. Ἀθῆναι **Athēnai**, *ath-ay'-nahee*; plur. of Ἀθήνη **Athēnē** (the goddess of wisdom, who was reputed to have founded the city); *Athenæ*, the capital of Greece:—Athens.

117. Ἀθηναῖος **Athēnaiŏs**, *ath-ay-nah'-yos*; from *116*; an *Athenæan* or inhab. of Athenæ:—Athenian.

118. ἀθλέω **athlĕō**, *ath-leh'-o*; from ἄθλος **athlŏs** (a *contest* in the public lists); to *contend* in the competitive games:—strive.

119. ἄθλησις **athlēsis**, *ath'-lay-sis*; from *118*; a *struggle* (fig.):—fight.

120. ἀθυμέω **athumĕō**, *ath-oo-meh'-o*; from a comp. of *1* (as a neg. particle) and *2372*; to *be spiritless*, i.e. *disheartened*:—be dismayed.

121. ἄθωος **athōŏs**, *ath'-o-os*; from *1* (as a neg. particle) and a prob. der. of *5087* (mean. a *penalty*); *not guilty*:—innocent.

122. αἴγειος **aigĕŏs**, *ah'-ee-ghi-os*; from αἴξ **aix**, (a *goat*); belonging to a *goat*:—goat.

123. αἰγιαλός **aigialŏs**, *ahee-ghee-al-os'*; from ἀΐσσω **aissō** (to *rush*) and *251* (in the sense of the *sea*); a *beach* (on which the *waves dash*):—shore.

124. Αἰγύπτιος **Aiguptiŏs**, *ahee-goop'-tee-os*; from *125*; an *Ægyptian* or inhab. of Ægyptus:—Egyptian.

125. Αἴγυπτος **Aiguptŏs**, *ah'ee-goop-tos*; of uncert. der.; *Ægyptus*, the land of the Nile:—Egypt.

126. ἀΐδιος **aïdiŏs**, *ah-id'-ee-os*; from *104*; *everduring* (forward and backward, or forward only):—eternal, everlasting.

127. αἰδώς **aidōs**, *ahee-doce'*; perh. from *1* (as a neg. particle) and *1492* (through the idea of *downcast* eyes); *bashfulness*, i.e. (towards men), *modesty* or (towards God) *awe*:—reverence, shamefacedness.

128. Αἰθίοψ **Aithiŏps**, *ahee-thee'-ops*; from αἴθω **aithō** (to *scorch*) and ὤψ **ōps** (the *face*, from *3700*); an *Æthiopian* (as a *blackamoor*):—Ethiopian.

129. αἷμα **haima**, *hah'ee-mah*; of uncert. der.; *blood*, lit. (of men or animals), fig. (the *juice* of grapes) or spec. (the atoning *blood* of Christ); by impl. *bloodshed*, also *kindred*:—blood.

130. αἱματεκχυσία **haimatĕkchusia**, *hahee-mat-ek-khoo-see'-ah*; from *129* and a der. of *1632*; an *effusion of blood*:—shedding of blood.

131. αἱμοῤῥέω **haimŏrrhĕō**, *hahee-mor-hreh'-o*; from *129* and *4482*; to *flow blood*, i.e. *have a hæmorrhage*:—diseased with an issue of blood.

132. Αἰνέας **Ainĕas**, *ahee-neh'-as*; of uncert. der.; *Ænĕas*, an Isr.:—Æneas.

133. αἴνεσις **ainĕsis**, *ah'ee-nes-is*; from *134*; a *praising* (the act), i.e. (spec.) a *thank* (-offering):—praise.

134. αἰνέω **ainĕō**, *ahee-neh'-o*, from *136*; to *praise* (God):—praise.

135. αἴνιγμα **ainigma**, *ah'ee-nig-ma*; from a der. of *136* (in its prim. sense); an *obscure* saying ("enigma"), i.e. (abstr.) *obscureness*:— × darkly.

136. αἶνος **ainŏs**, *ah'ee-nos*; appar. a prim. word; prop. a *story*, but used in the sense of *1868*; *praise* (of God):—praise.

137. Αἰνών **Ainōn**, *ahee-nohn'*; of Hebr. or. [a der. of 5869, *place of springs*]; *Ænon*, a place in Pal.:—Ænon.

138. αἱρέομαι **hairĕŏmai**, *hahee-reh'-om-ahee*; prob. akin to *142*; to *take for oneself*, i.e. to *prefer*:—choose. Some of the forms are borrowed from a cognate ἕλλομαι **hellŏmai**, *hel'-lom-ahee*; which is otherwise obsolete.

139. αἵρεσις **hairĕsis**, *hah'ee-res-is*; from *138*; prop. a *choice*, i.e. (spec.) a *party* or (abstr.) *disunion*:—heresy [*which is the Gr. word itself*], sect.

140. αἱρετίζω **hairĕtizō**, *hahee-ret-id'-zo*; from a der. of *138*; to *make a choice*:—choose.

141. αἱρετικός **hairĕtikŏs**, *hahee-ret-ee-kos'*; from the same as *140*; a *schismatic*:—heretic [*the Gr. word itself*].

142. αἴρω **airō**, *ah'ee-ro*; a prim. verb; to *lift*; by impl. to *take up* or *away*; fig. to *raise* (the voice), *keep in suspense* (the mind); spec. to *sail* away (i.e. *weigh anchor*); by Heb. [comp. 5375] to *expiate* sin:—away with, bear (up), carry, lift up, loose, make to doubt, put away, remove, take (away, up).

143. αἰσθάνομαι **aisthanŏmai**, *ahee-sthan'-om-ahee*; of uncert. der.; to *apprehend* (prop. by the senses):—perceive.

144. αἴσθησις **aisthēsis**, *ah'ee-sthay-sis*; from *143*; *perception*, i.e. (fig.) *discernment*:—judgment.

145. αἰσθητήριον **aisthētēriŏn**, *ahee-sthay-tay'-ree-on*; from a der. of *143*; prop. an *organ of perception*, i.e. (fig.) *judgment*:—senses.

146. αἰσχροκερδής **aischrŏkĕrdēs**, *ahee-skhrok-er-dace'*; from *150* and κέρδος **kerdos** (*gain*); *sordid*:—given to (greedy of) filthy lucre.

147. αἰσχροκερδῶς **aischrŏkĕrdōs**, *ahee-skhrok-er-doce'*; adv. from *146*; *sordidly*:—for filthy lucre's sake.

148. αἰσχρολογία **aischrŏlŏgia**, *ahee-skhrol-og-ee'-ah*; from *150* and *3056*; *vile conversation*:—filthy communication.

149. αἰσχρόν **aischrŏn**, *ahee-skhron'*; neut. of *150*; a *shameful* thing, i.e. *indecorum*:—shame.

150. **αἰσχρός aischrŏs**, *ahee-skhros';* from the same as *153; shameful,* i.e. *base* (spec. *venal*):—filthy.

151. **αἰσχρότης aischrŏtēs**, *ahee-skhrot'-ace;* from *150; shamefulness,* i.e. *obscenity:*—filthiness.

152. **αἰσχύνη aischunē**, *ahee-skhoo'-nay;* from *153; shame* or *disgrace* (abstr. or concr.):—dishonesty, shame.

153. **αἰσχύνομαι aischunŏmai**, *ahee-skhoo'-nom-ahee;* from **αἶσχος aischŏs** (*disfigurement,* i.e. *disgrace*); to *feel shame* (for oneself):—be ashamed.

154. **αἰτέω aitĕō**, *ahee-teh'-o;* of uncert. der.; to *ask* (in gen.):—ask, beg, call for, crave, desire, require. Comp. *4441.*

155. **αἴτημα aitēma**, *ah'ee-tay-mah;* from *154;* a *thing asked* or (abstr.) an *asking:*—petition, request, required.

156. **αἰτία aitia**, *ahee-tee'-a;* from the same as *154;* a *cause* (as if *asked* for), i.e. (logical) *reason* (motive, matter), (legal) *crime* (alleged or proved):—accusation, case, cause, crime, fault, [wh-]ere [-fore].

157. **αἰτίαμα aitiama**, *ahee-tee'-am-ah;* from a der. of *156;* a *thing charged:*—complaint.

158. **αἴτιον aitiŏn**, *ah'ee-tee-on;* neut. of *159;* a *reason* or *crime* [like *156*]:—cause, fault.

159. **αἴτιος aitiŏs**, *ah'ee-tee-os;* from the same as *154; causative,* i.e. (concr.) a *causer:*—author.

160. **αἰφνίδιος aiphnidiŏs**, *aheef-nid'-ee-os;* from a comp. of *1* (as a neg. particle) and *5316* [comp. *1810*] (mean. *non-apparent*); *unexpected,* i.e. (adv.) *suddenly:*—sudden, unawares.

161. **αἰχμαλωσία aichmalōsia**, *aheekh-mal-o-see'-ah;* from *164; captivity:*—captivity.

162. **αἰχμαλωτεύω aichmalōtĕuō**, *aheekh-mal-o-tew'-o;* from *164;* to *capture* [like *163*]:—lead captive.

163. **αἰχμαλωτίζω aichmalōtizō**, *aheekh-mal-o-tid'-zo;* from *164:* to *make captive:*—lead away captive, bring into captivity.

164. **αἰχμαλωτός aichmalōtŏs**, *aheekh-mal-o-tos';* from **αἰχμή aichmē** (a *spear*) and a der. of the same as *259;* prop. a *prisoner of war,* i.e. (gen.) a *captive:*—captive.

165. **αἰών aiōn**, *ahee-ohn';* from the same as *104;* prop. an *age;* by extens. *perpetuity* (also past); by impl. the *world;* spec. (Jewish) a Messianic period (present or future):—age, course, eternal, (for) ever (-more), [n-]ever, (beginning of the, while the) world (began, without end). Comp. *5550.*

166. **αἰώνιος aiōniŏs**, *ahee-o'-nee-os;* from *165; perpetual* (also used of past time, or past and future as well):—eternal, for ever, everlasting, world (began).

167. **ἀκαθαρσία akatharsia**, *ak-ath-ar-see'-ah;* from *169; impurity* (the quality), phys. or mor.:—uncleanness.

168. **ἀκαθάρτης akathartēs**, *ak-ath-ar'-tace;* from *169; impurity* (the state), mor.:—filthiness.

169. **ἀκάθαρτος akathartŏs**, *ak-ath'-ar-tos;* from *1* (as a neg. particle) and a presumed der. of *2508* (mean. *cleansed*); *impure* (cer., mor. [*lewd*] or spec. [*dæmonic*]):—foul, unclean.

170. **ἀκαιρέομαι akairĕŏmai**, *ak-ahee-reh'-om-ahee;* from a comp. of *1* (as a neg. particle) and *2540* (mean. *unseasonable*); to *be inopportune* (for oneself), i.e. to *fail of a proper occasion:*—lack opportunity.

171. **ἀκαίρως akairōs**, *ak-ah'ee-roce;* adv. from the same as *170; inopportunely:*—out of season.

172. **ἄκακος akakŏs**, *ak'-ak-os;* from *1* (as a neg. particle) and *2556; not bad,* i.e. (obj.) *innocent* or (subj.) *unsuspecting:*—harmless, simple.

173. **ἄκανθα akantha**, *ak'-an-thah;* prob. from the same as *188;* a *thorn:*—thorn.

174. **ἀκάνθινος akanthinŏs**, *ak-an'-thee-nos;* from *173; thorny:*—of thorns.

175. **ἄκαρπος akarpŏs**, *ak'-ar-pos;* from *1* (as a neg. particle) and *2590; barren* (lit. or fig.):—without fruit, unfruitful.

176. **ἀκατάγνωστος akatagnōstŏs**, *ak-at-ag'-noce-tos;* from *1* (as a neg. particle) and a der. of *2607; unblamable:*—that cannot be condemned.

177. **ἀκατακάλυπτος akatakaluptŏs**, *ak-at-ak-al'-oop-tos;* from *1* (as a neg. particle) and a der. of a comp. of *2596* and *2572; unveiled:*—uncovered.

178. **ἀκατάκριτος akatakritŏs**, *ak-at-ak'-ree-tos;* from *1* (as a neg. particle) and a der. of *2632; without* (legal) *trial:*—uncondemned.

179. **ἀκατάλυτος akatalutŏs**, *ak-at-al'-oo-tos;* from *1* (as a neg. particle) and a der. of *2647; indissoluble,* i.e. (fig.) *permanent:*—endless.

180. **ἀκατάπαυστος akatapaustŏs**, *ak-at-ap'-ow-stos;* from *1* (as a neg. particle) and a der. of *2664; unrefraining:*—that cannot cease.

181. **ἀκαταστασία akatastasia**, *ak-at-as-tah-see'-ah;* from *182; instability,* i.e. *disorder:*—commotion, confusion, tumult.

182. **ἀκατάστατος akatastatŏs**, *ak-at-as'-tat-os;* from *1* (as a neg. particle) and a der. of *2525; inconstant:*—unstable.

183. **ἀκατάσχετος akataschĕtŏs**, *ak-at-as'-khet-os;* from *1* (as a neg. particle) and a der. of *2722; unrestrainable:*—unruly.

184. **Ἀκελδαμά Akeldama**, *ak-el-dam-ah';* of Chald. or. [mean. *field of blood;* corresp. to 2506 and 1818]; *Akeldama,* a place near Jerus.:—Aceldama.

185. **ἀκέραιος akĕraiŏs**, *ak-er'-ah-yos;* from *1* (as a neg. particle) and a presumed der. of *2767: unmixed,* i.e. (fig.) *innocent:*—harmless, simple.

186. **ἀκλινής aklinēs**, *ak-lee-nace';* from *1* (as a neg. particle) and *2827; not leaning,* i.e. (fig.) *firm:*—without wavering.

187. **ἀκμάζω akmazō**, *ak-mad'-zo;* from the same as *188;* to *make a point,* i.e. (fig.) *mature:*—be fully ripe.

188. **ἀκμήν akmēn**, *ak-mane';* accus. of a noun ("*acme*") akin to **ἀκή akē** (a *point*) and mean. the same; adv. *just* now, i.e. *still:*—yet.

189. **ἀκοή akŏē**, *ak-ŏ-ay';* from *191; hearing* (the act, the sense or the thing heard):—audience, ear, fame, which ye heard, hearing, preached, report, rumor.

190. **ἀκολουθέω akŏlŏuthĕō**, *ak-ol-oo-theh'-o;* from *1* (as a particle of union) and **κέλευθος kĕlĕuthŏs** (a *road*); prop. to *be in the same way with,* i.e. to *accompany* (spec. as a disciple):—follow, reach.

191. **ἀκούω akŏuō**, *ak-oo'-o;* a prim. verb; to *hear* (in various senses):—give (in the) audience (of), come (to the ears), ([shall]) hear (-er, -ken), be noised, be reported, understand.

192. **ἀκρασία akrasia**, *ak-ras-ee'-a;* from *193; want of self-restraint:*—excess, incontinency.

193. **ἀκράτης akratēs**, *ak-rat'-ace;* from *1* (as a neg. particle) and *2904; powerless,* i.e. *without self-control:*—incontinent.

194. **ἄκρατος akratŏs**, *ak'-rat-os;* from *1* (as a neg. particle) and a presumed der. of *2767; undiluted:*—without mixture.

195. **ἀκρίβεια akribĕia**, *ak-ree'-bi-ah;* from the same as *196; exactness:*—perfect manner.

196. **ἀκριβέστατος akribĕstatŏs**, *ak-ree-bes'-ta-tos;* superlative of **ἀκρίβης akribēs** (a der. of the same as *206*); *most exact:*—most straitest.

197. **ἀκριβέστερον akribĕstĕrŏn**, *ak-ree-bes'-ter-on;* neut. of the comparative of the same as *196;* (adv.) *more exactly:*—more perfect (-ly).

198. **ἀκριβόω akribŏō**, *ak-ree-bŏ'-o;* from the same as *196;* to *be exact,* i.e. *ascertain:*—enquire diligently.

199. **ἀκριβῶς akribōs**, *ak-ree-boce';* adv. from the same as *196; exactly:*—circumspectly, diligently, perfect (-ly).

200. **ἀκρίς akris**, *ak-rece';* appar. from the same as *206;* a *locust* (as *pointed,* or as *lighting* on the *top* of vegetation):—locust.

201. **ἀκροατήριον akrŏatēriŏn**, *ak-rŏ-at-ay'-ree-on;* from *202;* an *audience-room:*—place of hearing.

202. **ἀκροατής akrŏatēs**, *ak-rŏ-at-ace';* from **ἀκροάομαι akrŏaŏmai** (to *listen;* appar. an intens. of *191*); a *hearer* (merely):—hearer.

203. **ἀκροβυστία akrŏbustia**, *ak-rob-oos-tee'-ah;* from *206* and prob. a modified form of **πόσθη pŏsthē** (the *penis* or *male* sexual organ); the *prepuce;* by impl. an *uncircumcised* (i.e. *gentile,* fig. *unregenerate*) *state* or *person:*—not circumcised, uncircumcised [*with 2192*], uncircumcision.

204. **ἀκρογωνιαῖος akrŏgōniaiŏs**, *ak-rog-o-nee-ah'-yos;* from *206* and *1137;* belonging to the extreme *corner:*—chief corner.

205. **ἀκροθίνιον akrŏthiniŏn**, *ak-roth-in'-ee-on;* from *206* and **θίς this** (a *heap*); prop. (in the plur.) the *top of the heap,* i.e. (by impl.) *best of the booty:*—spoils.

206. **ἄκρον akrŏn**, *ak'-ron;* neut. of an adj. prob. akin to the base of *188;* the *extremity:*—one end . . . other, tip, top, uttermost part.

207. **Ἀκύλας Akulas**, *ak-oo'-las;* prob. for Lat. *aquila* (an *eagle*); *Akulas,* an Isr.:—Aquila.

208. **ἀκυρόω akurŏō**, *ak-oo-rŏ'-o;* from *1* (as a neg. particle) and *2964;* to *invalidate:*—disannul, make of none effect.

209. **ἀκωλύτως akōlutōs**, *ak-o-loo'-toce;* adv. from a compound of *1* (as a neg. particle) and a der. of *2967;* in *an unhindered manner,* i.e. *freely:*—no man forbidding him.

210. **ἄκων akōn**, *ak'-ohn;* from *1* (as a neg. particle) and *1635; unwilling:*—against the will.

211. **ἀλάβαστρον alabastrŏn**, *al-ab'-as-tron;* neut. of **ἀλάβαστρος alabastrŏs** (of uncert. der.), the name of a stone; prop. an "*alabaster*" box, i.e. (by extens.) a perfume *vase* (of any material):—(alabaster) box.

212. **ἀλαζονεία alazŏnĕia**, *al-ad-zon-i'-a;* from *213; braggadocio,* i.e. (by impl.) *self-confidence:*—boasting, pride.

213. **ἀλαζών alazōn**, *al-ad-zone';* from **ἄλη alē** (*vagrancy*); *braggart:*—boaster.

214. **ἀλαλάζω alalazō**, *al-al-ad'-zo;* from **ἀλαλή alalē** (a *shout,* "*halloo*"); to *vociferate,* i.e. (by impl.) to *wail;* fig. to *clang:*—tinkle, wail.

215. **ἀλάλητος alalētŏs**, *al-al'-ay-tos;* from *1* (as a neg. particle) and a der. of *2980; unspeakable:*—unutterable, which cannot be uttered.

216. **ἄλαλος alalŏs**, *al'-al-os;* from *1* (as a neg. particle) and *2980; mute:*—dumb.

217. **ἅλας halas**, *hal'-as;* from *251; salt;* fig. *prudence:*—salt.

218. **ἀλείφω alĕiphō**, *al-i'-fo;* from *1* (as particle of union) and the base of *3045;* to *oil* (with perfume):—anoint.

219. **ἀλεκτοροφωνία alektŏrŏphōnia**, *al-ek-tor-of-o-nee'-ah;* from *220* and *5456; cock-crow,* i.e. the third night-watch:—cockcrowing.

220. **ἀλέκτωρ alĕktōr**, *al-ek'-tore;* from **ἀλέκω** (to *ward* off); a *cock* or male fowl:—cock.

221. **Ἀλεξανδρεύς Alĕxandrĕus**, *al-ex-and-reuce';* from **Ἀλεξάνδρεια** (the city so called); an *Alexandreian* or inhab. of Alexandria:—of Alexandria, Alexandrian.

222. **Ἀλεξανδρῖνος Alĕxandrinŏs**, *al-ex-an-dree'-nos;* from the same as 221; *Alexandrine,* or belonging to Alexandria:—of Alexandria.

223. **Ἀλέξανδρος Alĕxandrŏs**, *al-ex'-an-dros;* from the same as (the first part of) *220* and *435; man-defender; Alexander,* the name of three Isr. and one other man:—Alexander.

224. **ἄλευρον alĕurŏn**, *al'-yoo-ron;* from **ἀλέω alĕō** (to *grind*); *flour:*—meal.

225. **ἀλήθεια alēthĕia**, *al-ay'-thi-a;* from *227; truth:*—true, × truly, truth, verity.

226. **ἀληθεύω alēthĕuō**, *al-ayth-yoo'-o;* from *227;* to *be true* (in doctrine and profession):—speak (tell) the truth.

227. **ἀληθής alēthēs**, *al-ay-thace';* from *1* (as a neg. particle) and *2990; true* (as *not concealing*):—true, truly, truth.

228. ἀληθινός **alēthinŏs**, *al-ay-thee-nos'*; from *227*; *truthful*:—true.

229. ἀλήθω **alēthō**, *al-ay'-tho*; from the same as *224*; to *grind*:—grind.

230. ἀληθῶς **alēthōs**, *al-ay-thoce'*; adv. from *227*; *truly*:—indeed, surely, of a surety, truly, of a (in) truth, verily, very

231. ἁλιεύς **haliĕus**, *hal-ee-yoos'*; from *251*; a *sailor* (as engaged on the *salt* water), i.e. (by impl.) a *fisher*:—fisher (-man).

232. ἁλιεύω **haliĕuō**, *hal-ee-yoo'-o*; from *231*; to *be a fisher*, i.e. (by impl.) to *fish*:—go a-fishing.

233. ἁλίζω **halizō**, *hal-id'-zo*; from *251*; to *salt*:—salt.

234. ἀλίσγεμα **alisgĕma**, *al-is'-ghem-ah*; from ἀλισγέω **alisgĕō** (to *soil*); (cer.) *defilement*:—pollution.

235. ἀλλά **alla**, *al-lah'*; neut. plur. of *243*; prop. *other* things, i.e. (adv.) *contrariwise* (in many relations):—and, but (even), howbeit, indeed, nay, nevertheless, no, notwithstanding, save, therefore, yea, yet.

236. ἀλλάσσω **allassō**, *al-las'-so*; from *243*; to *make different*:—change.

237. ἀλλαχόθεν **allachŏthĕn**, *al-lakh-oth'-en*; from *243*; *from elsewhere*:—some other way.

238. ἀλληγορέω **allēgŏrĕō**, *al-lay-gor-eh'-o*; from *243* and ἀγορέω **agŏrĕō** (to *harangue* [comp. *58*]); to *allegorize*:—be an allegory [*the Gr. word itself*].

239. ἀλληλουΐα **allēlŏuïa**, *al-lay-loo'-ee-ah*; of Heb. or. [imper. of 1984 and 3050]; *praise ye Jah!*, an adoring exclamation:—alleluiah.

240. ἀλλήλων **allēlōn**, *al-lay'-lone*; Gen. plur. from *243* redupl.; *one another*:—each other, mutual, one another, (the other), (them-, your-) selves, (selves) together [*sometimes with 3326 or 4314*].

241. ἀλλογενής **allŏgĕnēs**, *al-log-en-ace'*; from *243* and *1085*; *foreign*, i.e. not a Jew:—stranger.

242. ἅλλομαι **hallŏmai**, *hal'-lom-ahee*; mid. of appar. a prim. verb; to *jump*; fig. to *gush*:—leap, spring up.

243. ἄλλος **allŏs**, *al'-los*; a prim. word; "*else*," i.e. *different* (in many applications):—more, one (another), (an-, some an-) other (-s, -wise).

244. ἀλλοτριεπίσκοπος **allotriĕpiskŏpŏs**, *al-lot-ree-ep-is'-kop-os*; from *245* and *1985*; *overseeing others'* affairs, i.e. a *meddler* (spec. in Gentile customs):—busybody in other men's matters.

245. ἀλλότριος **allŏtriŏs**, *al-lot'-ree-os*; from *243*; *another's*, i.e. not one's own; by extens. *foreign*, *not akin*, *hostile*:—alien, (an-) other (man's, men's), strange (-r).

246. ἀλλόφυλος **allŏphulŏs**, *al-lof'-oo-los*; from *243* and *5443*; *foreign*, i.e. (spec.) *Gentile*:—one of another nation.

247. ἄλλως **allōs**, *al'-loce*; adv. from *243*; *differently*:—otherwise.

248. ἀλοάω **alŏaō**, *al-o-ah'-o*; from the same as *257*; to *tread* out grain:—thresh, tread out the corn.

249. ἄλογος **alŏgŏs**, *al'-og-os*; from *1* (as a neg. particle) and *3056*; *irrational*:—brute, unreasonable.

250. ἀλοή **alŏē**, *al-ŏ-ay'*; of for. or. [comp. 174]; *aloes* (the gum):—aloes.

251. ἅλς **hals**, *halce*; a prim. word; "*salt*":—salt.

252. ἁλυκός **halukŏs**, *hal-oo-kos'*; from *251*; *briny*:—salt.

253. ἀλυπότερος **alupŏtĕrŏs**, *al-oo-pot'-er-os*; compar. of a comp. of *1* (as a neg. particle) and *3077*; *more without grief*:—less sorrowful.

254. ἅλυσις **halusis**, *hal'-oo-sis*; of uncert. der.; a *fetter* or *manacle*:—bonds, chain.

255. ἀλυσιτελής **alusitĕlēs**, *al-oo-sit-el-ace'*; from *1* (as a neg. particle) and the base of *3081*; *gainless*, i.e. (by impl.) *pernicious*:—unprofitable.

256. Ἀλφαῖος **Alphaiŏs**, *al-fah'-yos*; of Heb. or. [comp. 2501]; *Alphœus*, an Isr.:—Alpheus.

257. ἅλων **halōn**, *hal'-ohn*; prob. from the base of *1507*; a threshing-*floor* (as *rolled* hard), i.e. (fig.) the *grain* (and chaff, as just threshed):—floor.

258. ἀλώπηξ **alōpĕx**, *al-o'-pakes*; of uncert. der.; a *fox*, i.e. (fig.) a *cunning* person:—fox.

259. ἅλωσις **halōsis**, *hal'-o-sis*; from a collateral form of *138*; *capture*:—be taken.

260. ἅμα **hama**, *ham'-ah*; a prim. particle; prop. *at the* "*same*" *time*, but freely used as a prep. or adv. denoting close association:—also, and, together, with (-al).

261. ἀμαθής **amathēs**, *am-ath-ace'*; from *1* (as a neg. particle) and *3129*; *ignorant*:—unlearned.

262. ἀμαράντινος **amarantinŏs**, *am-ar-an'-tee-nos*; from *263*; "*amaranthine*", i.e. (by impl.) *fadeless*:—that fadeth not away.

263. ἀμάραντος **amarantŏs**, *am-ar'-an-tos*; from *1* (as a neg. particle) and a presumed der. of *3133*; *unfading*, i.e. (by impl.) *perpetual*:—that fadeth not away.

264. ἁμαρτάνω **hamartanō**, *ham-ar-tan'-o*; perh. from *1* (as a neg. particle) and the base of *3313*; prop. to *miss* the mark (and so *not share* in the prize), i.e. (fig.) to *err*, esp. (mor.) to *sin*.—for your faults, offend, sin, trespass.

265. ἁμάρτημα **hamartēma**, *ham-ar'-tay-mah*; from *264*; a *sin* (prop. concr.):—sin.

266. ἁμαρτία **hamartia**, *ham-ar-tee'-ah*; from *264*; *sin* (prop. abstr.):—offence, sin (-ful).

267. ἀμάρτυρος **amarturŏs**, *am-ar'-too-ros*; from *1* (as a neg. particle) and a form of *3144*; *unattested*:—without witness.

268. ἁμαρτωλός **hamartōlŏs**, *ham-ar-to-los'*; from *264*; *sinful*, i.e. a *sinner*:—sinful, sinner.

269. ἄμαχος **amachŏs**, *am'-akh-os*; from *1* (as a neg. particle) and *3163*; *peaceable*:—not a brawler.

270. ἀμάω **amaō**, *am-ah'-o*; from *260*; prop. to *collect*, i.e. (by impl.) *reap*:—reap down.

271. ἀμέθυστος **amĕthustŏs**, *am-eth'-oos-tos*; from *1* (as a neg. particle) and a der. of *3184*; the "*amethyst*" (supposed to *prevent intoxication*):—amethyst.

272. ἀμελέω **amĕlĕō**, *am-el-eh'-o*; from *1* (as a neg. particle) and *3199*; to *be careless* of:—make light of, neglect, be negligent, not regard.

273. ἄμεμπτος **amĕmptŏs**, *am'-emp-tos*; from *1* (as a neg. particle) and a der. of *3201*; *irreproachable*:—blameless, faultless, unblamable.

274. ἀμέμπτως **amĕmptōs**, *am-emp'-toce*; adv. from *273*; *faultlessly*:—blameless, unblamably.

275. ἀμέριμνος **amĕrimnŏs**, *am-er'-im-nos*; from *1* (as a neg. particle) and *3308*; *not anxious*:—without care (-fulness), secure.

276. ἀμετάθετος **amĕtathĕtŏs**, *am-et-ath'-et-os*; from *1* (as a neg. particle) and a der. of *3346*; *unchangeable*, or (neut. as abstr.) *unchangeability*:—immutable (-ility).

277. ἀμετακίνητος **amĕtakinētŏs**, *am-et-ak-in'-ay-tos*; from *1* (as a neg. particle) and a der. of *3334*; *immovable*:—unmovable.

278. ἀμεταμέλητος **amĕtamĕlētŏs**, *am-et-am-el'-ay-tos*; from *1* (as a neg. particle) and a presumed der. of *3338*; *irrevocable*:—without repentance, not to be repented of.

279. ἀμετανόητος **amĕtanŏētŏs**, *am-et-an-ŏ'-ay-tos*; from *1* (as a neg. particle) and a presumed der. of *3340*; *unrepentant*:—impenitent.

280. ἄμετρος **amĕtrŏs**, *am'-et-ros*; from *1* (as a neg. particle) and *3358*; *immoderate*:—(thing) without measure.

281. ἀμήν **amēn**, *am-ane'*; of Heb. or. [543]; prop. *firm*, i.e. (fig.) *trustworthy*; adv. *surely* (often as interj. *so be it*):—amen, verily.

282. ἀμήτωρ **amētōr**, *am-ay'-tore*; from *1* (as a neg. particle) and *3384*; *motherless*, i.e. *of unknown maternity*:—without mother.

283. ἀμίαντος **amiantŏs**, *am-ee'-an-tos*; from *1* (as a neg. particle) and a der. of *3392*; *unsoiled*, i.e. (fig.) *pure*:—undefiled.

284. Ἀμιναδάβ **Aminadab**, *am-ee-nad-ab'*; of Heb. or. [5992]; *Aminadab*, an Isr.:—Aminadab.

285. ἄμμος **ammŏs**, *am'-mos*; perh. from *260*; *sand* (as *heaped* on the beach):—sand.

286. ἀμνός **amnŏs**, *am-nos'*; appar. a prim. word; a *lamb*:—lamb.

287. ἀμοιβή **amŏibē**, *am-oy-bay'*; from ἀμείβω **amĕibō** (to *exchange*); *requital*:—requite.

288. ἄμπελος **ampĕlŏs**, *am'-pel-os*; prob. from the base of *297* and that of *257*; a *vine* (as *coiling about* a support):—vine.

289. ἀμπελουργός **ampĕlŏurgŏs**, *am-pel-oor-gos'*; from *288* and *2041*; a *vine-worker*, i.e. *pruner*:—vine-dresser.

290. ἀμπελών **ampĕlōn**, *am-pel-ohn'*; from *288*; a *vineyard*:—vineyard.

291. Ἀμπλίας **Amplias**, *am-plee'-as*; contr. for Lat. *ampliatus* [*enlarged*]; *Amplias*, a Rom. Chr.:—Amplias.

292. ἀμύνομαι **amunŏmai**, *am-oo'-nom-ahee*; mid. of a prim. verb; to *ward off* (for oneself), i.e. *protect*:—defend.

293. ἀμφίβληστρον **amphiblēstrŏn**, *am-fib'-lace-tron*; from a comp. of the base of *297* and *906*; a (fishing) *net* (as *thrown about* the fish):—net.

294. ἀμφιέννυμι **amphiĕnnumi**, *am-fee-en'-noo-mee*; from the base of *297* and ἕννυμι **hĕnnumi** (to *invest*); to *enrobe*:—clothe.

295. Ἀμφίπολις **Amphipŏlis**, *am-fip'-ol-is*; from the base of *297* and *4172*; a *city surrounded* by a river; *Amphipolis*, a place in Macedonia:—Amphipolis.

296. ἄμφοδον **amphŏdŏn**, *am'-fod-on*; from the base of *297* and *3598*; a *fork* in the road:—where two ways meet.

297. ἀμφότερος **amphŏtĕrŏs**, *am-fot'-er-os*; compar. of ἀμφί **amphi** (*around*); (in plur.) *both*:—both.

298. ἀμώμητος **amōmētŏs**, *am-o'-may-tos*; from *1* (as a neg. particle) and a der. of *3469*; *unblameable*:—blameless.

299. ἄμωμος **amōmŏs**, *am'-o-mos*; from *1* (as a neg. particle) and *3470*; *unblemished* (lit. or fig.):—without blame (blemish, fault, spot), faultless, unblameable.

300. Ἀμών **Amōn**, *am-one'*; of Heb. or. [526]; *Amon*, an Isr.:—Amon.

301. Ἀμώς **Amōs**, *am-oce'*; of Heb. or. [531]; *Amos*, an Isr.:—Amos.

302. ἄν **an**, *an*; a prim. particle, denoting a *supposition*, *wish*, *possibility* or *uncertainty*:—[what-, where-, whither-, who-]soever. Usually unexpressed except by the subjunctive or potential mood. Also contr. for *1437*.

303. ἀνά **ana**, *an-ah'*; a prim. prep. and adv.; prop. *up*; but (by extens.) used (distributively) *severally*, or (locally) *at* (etc.):—and, apiece, by, each, every (man), in, through. In compounds (as a prefix) it often means (by impl.) *repetition*, *intensity*, *reversal*, etc.

304. ἀναβαθμός **anabathmŏs**, *an-ab-ath-mos'*; from *305* [comp. *898*]; a *stairway*:—stairs.

305. ἀναβαίνω **anabainō**, *an-ab-ah'ee-no*; from *303* and the base of *939*; to *go up* (lit. or fig.):—arise, ascend (up), climb (go, grow, rise, spring) up, come (up).

306. ἀναβάλλομαι **anaballŏmai**, *an-ab-al'-lom-ahee*; mid. from *303* and *906*; to *put off* (for oneself):—defer.

307. ἀναβιβάζω **anabibazō**, *an-ab-ee-bad'-zo*; from *303* and a der. of the base of *939*; *to cause to go up*, i.e. *haul* (a net):—draw.

308. ἀναβλέπω **anablĕpō**, *an-ab-lep'-o*; from *303* and *991*: to *look up*; by impl. to *recover sight*:—look (up), see, receive sight.

309. ἀνάβλεψις **anablĕpsis**, *an-ab'-lep-sis*; from *308*; *restoration of sight*:—recovering of sight.

310. ἀναβοάω **anabŏaō**, *an-ab-o-ah'-o*; from *303* and *994*; to *halloo*:—cry (aloud, out).

311. ἀναβολή **anabŏlē**, *an-ab-ol-ay'*; from *306*; a *putting off*:—delay.

312. ἀναγγέλλω **anaggĕllō**, *an-ang-el'-lo;* from 303 and the base of 32; to *announce* (in detail):—declare, rehearse, report, show, speak, tell.

313. ἀναγεννάω **anagĕnnaō**, *an-ag-en-nah'-o;* from 303 and 1080; to *beget* or (by extens.) *bear* (again):—beget, (bear) × again.

314. ἀναγινώσκω **anaginōskō**, *an-ag-in-oce'-ko;* from 303 and 1097; to *know again*, i. e. (by extens.) to *read:*—read.

315. ἀναγκάζω **anagkazō**, *an-ang-kad'-zo;* from 318; to *necessitate;*—compel, constrain.

316. ἀναγκαῖος **anagkaiŏs**, *an-ang-kah'-yos;* from 318; *necessary;* by impl. *close* (of kin):—near, necessary, necessity, needful.

317. ἀναγκαστῶς **anagkastŏs**, *an-ang-kas-toce';* adv. from a der. of 315; *compulsorily:*—by constraint.

318. ἀναγκή **anagkē**, *an-ang-kay';* from 303 and the base of 43; *constraint* (lit. or fig.); by impl. *distress:*—distress, must needs, (of) necessity (-sary), needeth, needful.

319. ἀναγνωρίζομαι **anagnōrizŏmai**, *an-ag-no-rid'-zom-ahee;* mid. from 303 and 1107; to *make* (oneself) *known:*—be made known.

320. ἀνάγνωσις **anagnōsis**, *an-ag'-no-sis;* from 314; (the act of) *reading:*—reading.

321. ἀνάγω **anagō**, *an-ag'-o;* from 303 and 71; to *lead up;* by extens. to *bring out;* spec. to *sail away:*—bring (again, forth, up again), depart, launch (forth), lead (up), loose, offer, sail, set forth, take up.

322. ἀναδείκνυμι **anadĕiknumi**, *an-ad-ike'-noo-mee;* from 303 and 1166; to *exhibit*, i.e. (by impl.) to *indicate, appoint:*—appoint, shew.

323. ἀνάδειξις **anadĕixis**, *an-ad'-ike-sis;* from 322; (the act of) *exhibition:*—shewing.

324. ἀναδέχομαι **anadĕchŏmai**, *an-ad-ekh'-om-ahee;* from 303 and 1209; to *entertain* (as a guest):—receive.

325. ἀναδίδωμι **anadidōmi**, *an-ad-eed'-om-ee;* from 303 and 1325; to *hand over:*—deliver.

326. ἀναζάω **anazaō**, *an-ad-zah'-o;* from 303 and 2198; to *recover life* (lit. or fig.):—(be a-) live again, revive.

327. ἀναζητέω **anazētĕō**, *an-ad-zay-teh'-o;* from 303 and 2212; to *search* out:—seek.

328. ἀναζώννυμι **anazōnnumi**, *an-ad-zone'-noo-mee;* from 303 and 2224; to *gird afresh:*—gird up.

329. ἀναζωπυρέω **anazōpurĕō**, *an-ad-zo-poor-eh'-o;* from 303 and a comp. of the base of 2226 and 4442; to *re-enkindle:*—stir up.

330. ἀναθάλλω **anathallō**, *an-ath-al'-lo;* from 303 and θάλλω **thallō** (to *flourish*); to *revive:*—flourish again.

331. ἀνάθεμα **anathĕma**, *an-ath'-em-ah;* from 394; a (religious) *ban* or (concr.) *excommunicated* (thing or person):—accursed, anathema, curse, × great.

332. ἀναθεματίζω **anathĕmatizō**, *an-ath-em-at-id'-zo;* from 331; to *declare* or *vow* under penalty of execration:—(bind under a) curse, bind with an oath.

333. ἀναθεωρέω **anathĕōrĕō**, *an-ath-eh-o-reh'-o;* from 303 and 2334; to *look again* (i.e. *attentively*) at (lit. or fig.):—behold, consider.

334. ἀνάθημα **anathēma**, *an-ath'-ay-mah;* from 394 [like 331, but in a good sense]; a *votive* offering:—gift.

335. ἀναίδεια **anaidĕia**, *an-ah'-ee-die-ah';* from a comp. of 1 (as a neg. particle [comp. 427]) and 127; *impudence*, i.e. (by impl.) *importunity:*—importunity.

336. ἀναίρεσις **anairĕsis**, *an-ah'-ee-res-is;* from 337; (the act of) *killing:*—death.

337. ἀναιρέω **anairĕō**, *an-ahee-reh'-o;* from 303 and (the act. of) 138; to *take up*, i.e. *adopt;* by impl. to *take away* (violently), i.e. *abolish, murder:*—put to death, kill, slay, take away, take up.

338. ἀναίτιος **anaitiŏs**, *an-ah'-ee-tee-os;* from 1 (as a neg. particle) and 159 (in the sense of 156); *innocent:*—blameless, guiltless.

339. ἀνακαθίζω **anakathizō**, *an-ak-ath-id'-zo;* from 303 and 2523; prop. to *set up*, i.e. (reflex.) to *sit up:*—sit up.

340. ἀνακαινίζω **anakainizō**, *an-ak-ahee-nid'-zo;* from 303 and a der. of 2537; to *restore:*—renew.

341. ἀνακαινόω **anakainŏō**, *an-ak-ahee-nŏ'-o;* from 303 and a der. of 2537; to *renovate:*—renew.

342. ἀνακαίνωσις **anakainōsis**, *an-ak-ah'ee-no-sis;* from 341; *renovation:*—renewing.

343. ἀνακαλύπτω **anakaluptō**, *an-ak-al-oop'-to;* from 303 (in the sense of *reversal*) and 2572; to *unveil:*—open, ([un-]) taken away.

344. ἀνακάμπτω **anakamptō**, *an-ak-amp'-to;* from 303 and 2578; to *turn back:*—(re-) turn.

345. ἀνακεῖμαι **anakĕimai**, *an-ak-i'-mahee;* from 303 and 2749; to *recline* (as a corpse or at a meal):—guest, lean, lie, sit (down, at meat), at the table.

346. ἀνακεφαλαιόμαι **anakĕphalaiŏmai**, *an-ak-ef-al-ah'ee-om-ahee;* from 303 and 2775 (in its or. sense); to *sum up:*—briefly comprehend, gather together in one.

347. ἀνακλίνω **anaklinō**, *an-ak-lee'-no;* from 303 and 2827; to *lean back:*—lay, (make) sit down.

348. ἀνακόπτω **anakŏptō**, *an-ak-op'-to;* from 303 and 2875; to *beat back*, i.e. *check:*—hinder.

349. ἀνακράζω **anakrazō**, *an-ak-rad'-zo;* from 303 and 2896; to *scream up* (aloud):—cry out.

350. ἀνακρίνω **anakrinō**, *an-ak-ree'-no;* from 303 and 2919; prop. to *scrutinize*, i.e. (by impl.) *investigate, interrogate, determine:*—ask, question, discern, examine, judge, search.

351. ἀνάκρισις **anakrisis**, *an-ak'-ree-sis;* from 350; a (judicial) *investigation:*—examination.

352. ἀνακύπτω **anakuptō**, *an-ak-oop'-to;* from 303 (in the sense of *reversal*) and 2955; to *unbend*, i.e. *rise;* fig. *be elated:*—lift up, look up.

353. ἀναλαμβάνω **analambanō**, *an-al-am-ban'-o;* from 303 and 2983; to *take up:*—receive up, take (in, unto, up).

354. ἀνάληψις **analēpsis**, *an-al'-ape-sis;* from 353; *ascension:*—taking up.

355. ἀναλίσκω **analiskō**, *an-al-is'-ko;* from 303 and a form of the alternate of 138; prop. to *use up*, i.e. *destroy:*—consume.

356. ἀναλογία **analŏgia**, *an-al-og-ee'-ah;* from a comp. of 303 and 3056; *proportion:*—proportion.

357. ἀναλογίζομαι **analŏgizŏmai**, *an-al-og-id'-zom-ahee;* mid. from 356; to *estimate*, i.e. (fig.) *contemplate:*—consider.

358. ἄναλος **analŏs**, *an'-al-os;* from 1 (as a neg. particle) and 251; *saltless*, i.e. *insipid:*— × lose saltness.

359. ἀνάλυσις **analusis**, *an-al'-oo-sis;* from 360; *departure:*—departure.

360. ἀναλύω **analuō**, *an-al-oo'-o;* from 303 and 3089; to *break up*, i.e. *depart* (lit. or fig.):—depart, return.

361. ἀναμάρτητος **anamartētŏs**, *an-am-ar'-tay-tos;* from 1 (as a neg. particle) and a presumed der. of 264; *sinless:*—that is without sin.

362. ἀναμένω **anemĕnō**, *an-am-en'-o;* from 303 and 3306; to *await:*—wait for.

363. ἀναμιμνήσκω **anamimnēskō**, *an-am-im-nace'-ko;* from 303 and 3403; to *remind;* reflex. to *recollect:*—call to mind, (bring to, call to, put in), remember (-brance).

364. ἀνάμνησις **anamnēsis**, *an-am'-nay-sis;* from 363; *recollection:*—remembrance (again).

365. ἀνανεόω **ananĕŏō**, *an-an-neh-ŏ'-o;* from 303 and a der. of 3501; to *renovate*, i.e. *reform:*—renew.

366. ἀνανήφω **ananēphō**, *an-an-ay'-fo;* from 303 and 3525; to become *sober again*, i.e. (fig.) *regain* (one's) *senses:*—recover self.

367. Ἀνανίας **Ananias**, *an-an-ee'-as;* of Heb. or. [2608]; *Ananias*, the name of three Isr.:—Ananias.

368. ἀναντίρρητος **anantirrhētŏs**, *an-an-tir'-hray-tos;* from 1 (as a neg. particle) and a presumed der. of a comp. of 473 and 4483; *indisputable:*—cannot be spoken against.

369. ἀναντιρρήτως **anantirrhētōs**, *an-an-tir-hray'-toce;* adv. from 368; *promptly:*—without gainsaying.

370. ἀνάξιος **anaxiŏs**, *an-ax'-ee-os;* from 1 (as a neg. particle) and 514; *unfit:*—unworthy.

371. ἀναξίως **anaxiōs**, *an-ax-ee'-oce;* adv. from 370; *irreverently:*—unworthily.

372. ἀνάπαυσις **anapausis**, *an-ap'-ŏw-sis;* from 373; *intermission;* by impl. *recreation:*—rest.

373. ἀναπαύω **anapauō**, *an-up-ŏw'-o;* from 303 and 3973; (reflex.) to *repose* (lit. or fig. [*be exempt*], *remain*); by impl. to *refresh:*—take ease, refresh, (give, take) rest.

374. ἀναπείθω **anapĕithō**, *an-ap-i'-tho;* from 303 and 3982; to *incite;*—persuade.

375. ἀναπέμπω **anapĕmpō**, *an-ap-em'-po;* from 303 and 3992; to *send up* or *back:*—send (again).

376. ἀνάπηρος **anapĕrŏs**, *an-ap'-ay-ros;* from 303 (in the sense of *intensity*) and πῆρος **pērŏs** (*maimed*); *crippled:*—maimed.

377. ἀναπίπτω **anapipto**, *an-ap-ip'-to;* from 303 and 4098; to *fall back*, i.e. *lie down, lean back:*—lean, sit down (to meat).

378. ἀναπληρόω **anaplērŏō**, *an-ap-lay-rŏ'-o;* from 303 and 4137; to *complete;* by impl. to *occupy, supply;* fig. to *accomplish* (by coincidence or obedience):—fill up, fulfil, occupy, supply.

379. ἀναπολόγητος **anapŏlŏgētŏs**, *an-ap-ol-og'-ay-tos;* from 1 (as a neg. particle) and a presumed der. of 626; *indefensible:*—without excuse, inexcusable.

380. ἀναπτύσσω **anaptussō**, *an-ap-toos'-so;* from 303 (in the sense of *reversal*) and 4428; to *unroll* (a scroll or volume):—open.

381. ἀνάπτω **anaptō**, *an-ap'-to;* from 303 and 681; to *enkindle:*—kindle, light.

382. ἀναρίθμητος **anarithmētŏs**, *an-ar-ith'-may-tos;* from 1 (as a neg. particle) and a der. of 705; *unnumbered*, i.e. *without number:*—innumerable.

383. ἀνασείω **anasĕiō**, *an-as-i'-o;* from 303 and 4579; fig. to *excite:*—move, stir up.

384. ἀνασκευάζω **anaskĕuazō**, *an-ask-yoo-ad'-zo;* from 303 (in the sense of *reversal*) and a der. of 4632; prop. to *pack up* (baggage), i.e. (by impl. and fig.) to *upset:*—subvert.

385. ἀνασπάω **anaspaō**, *an-as-pah'-o;* from 303 and 4685; to *take up* or *extricate:*—draw up, pull out.

386. ἀνάστασις **anastasis**, *an-as'-tas-is;* from 450; a *standing up* again, i.e. (lit.) a *resurrection* from death (individual, gen. or by impl. [its author]), or (fig.) a (moral) *recovery* (of spiritual truth):—raised to life again, resurrection, rise from the dead, that should rise, rising again.

387. ἀναστατόω **anastatŏō**, *an-as-tat-ŏ'-o;* from a der. of 450 (in the sense of *removal*); prop. to *drive out* of home, i.e. (by impl.) to *disturb* (lit. or fig.):—trouble, turn upside down, make an uproar.

388. ἀνασταυρόω **anastaurŏō**, *an-as-tŏw-rŏ'-o;* from 303 and 4717; to *recrucify* (fig.):—crucify afresh.

389. ἀναστενάζω **anastĕnazō**, *an-as-ten-ad'-zo;* from 303 and 4727; to *sigh deeply:*—sigh deeply.

390. ἀναστρέφω **anastrĕphō**, *an-as-tref'-o;* from 303 and 4762; to *overturn;* also to *return;* by impl. to *busy* oneself, i.e. *remain, live:*—abide, behave self, have conversation, live, overthrow, pass, return, be used.

391. ἀναστροφή **anastrŏphē**, *an-as-trof-ay';* from 390; *behavior:*—conversation.

392. ἀνατάσσομαι **anatassŏmai**, *an-at-as'-som-ahee;* from 303 and the mid. of 5021; to *arrange:*—set in order.

393. ἀνατέλλω **anatĕllō**, *an-at-el'-lo;* from 303 and the base of 5056; to (*cause to*) *arise:*—(a-, make to) rise, at the rising of, spring (up), be up.

394. ἀνατίθεμαι **anatithĕmai**, *an-at-ith'-em-ahee;* from 303 and the mid. of 5087; to *set forth* (for oneself), i.e. *propound:*—communicate, declare.

395. **ἀνατολή anatŏlē**, *an-at-ol-ay'*; from *393*; a *rising* of light, i.e. *dawn* (fig.); by impl. the *east* (also in plur.):—dayspring, east, rising.

396. **ἀνατρέπω anatrĕpō**, *an-at-rep'-o*; from *303* and the base of *5157*; to *overturn* (fig.):—overthrow, subvert.

397. **ἀνατρέφω anatrĕphō**, *an-at-ref'-o*; from *303* and *5142*; to *rear* (phys. or ment.):—bring up, nourish (up).

398. **ἀναφαίνω anaphainō**, *an-af-ah'ee-no*; from *303* and *5316*; to *show*, i.e. (reflex.) *appear*, or (pass.) *have pointed* out:—(should) appear, discover.

399. **ἀναφέρω anaphĕrō**, *an-af-er'-o*; from *303* and *5342*; to *take up* (lit. or fig.):—bear, bring (carry, lead) up, offer (up).

400. **ἀναφωνέω anaphōnĕō**, *an-af-o-neh'-o*; from *303* and *5455*; to *exclaim*:—speak out.

401. **ἀνάχυσις anachusis**, *an-akh'-oo-sis*; from a comp. of *303* and **χέω chĕō** (to *pour*); prop. *effusion*, i.e. (fig.) *license*:—excess.

402. **ἀναχωρέω anachōrĕō**, *an-akh-o-reh'-o*; from *303* and *5562*; to *retire*:—depart, give place, go (turn) aside, withdraw self.

403. **ἀνάψυξις anapsuxis**, *an-aps'-ook-sis*; from *404*; prop. a *recovery of breath*, i.e. (fig.) *revival*:—revival.

404. **ἀναψύχω anapsuchō**, *an-aps-oo'-kho*; from *303* and *5594*; prop. to *cool off*, i.e. (fig.) *relieve*:—refresh.

405. **ἀνδραποδιστής andrapŏdistēs**, *an-drap-od-is-tace'*; from a der. of a comp. of *435* and *4228*; an *enslaver* (as bringing *men* to his *feet*):—menstealer.

406. **Ἀνδρέας Andrĕas**, *an-dreh'-as*; from *435*; *manly*; *Andreas*, an Isr.:—Andrew.

407. **ἀνδρίζομαι andrizŏmai**, *an-drid'-zom-ahee*; mid. from *435*; to *act manly*:—quit like men.

408. **Ἀνδρόνικος Andrŏnikŏs**, *an-dron'-ee-kos*; from *435* and *3534*; *man of victory*; *Andronicos*, an Isr.:—Andronicus.

409. **ἀνδροφόνος andrŏphŏnŏs**, *an-drof-on'-os*; from *435* and *5408*; a *murderer*:—manslayer.

410. **ἀνέγκλητος anĕgklētŏs**, *an-eng'-klay-tos*; from *1* (as a neg. particle) and a der. of *1458*; *unaccused*, i.e. (by impl.) *irreproachable*:—blameless.

411. **ἀνεκδιήγητος anĕkdiēgētŏs**, *an-ek-dee-ay'-gay-tos*; from *1* (as a neg. particle) and a presumed der. of *1555*; *not expounded* in full, i.e. *indescribable*:—unspeakable.

412. **ἀνεκλάλητος anĕklalētŏs**, *an-ek-lal'-ay-tos*; from *1* (as a neg. particle) and a presumed der. of *1583*; *not spoken out*, i.e. (by impl.) *unutterable*:—unspeakable.

413. **ἀνέκλειπτος anĕklĕiptŏs**, *an-ek'-lipe-tos*; from *1* (as a neg. particle) and a presumed der. of *1587*; *not left out*, i.e. (by impl.) *inexhaustible*:—that faileth not.

414. **ἀνεκτότερος anĕktŏtĕrŏs**, *an-ek-tot'-er-os*; compar. of a der. of *430*; *more endurable*:—more tolerable.

415. **ἀνελεήμων anĕlĕēmōn**, *an-eleh-ay'-mone*; from *1* (as a neg. particle) and *1655*; *merciless*:—unmerciful.

416. **ἀνεμίζω anemizō**, *an-em-id'-zo*; from *417*; to *toss with the wind*:—drive with the wind.

417. **ἄνεμος anĕmŏs**, *an'-em-os*; from the base of *109*; *wind*; (plur.) by impl. (the four) *quarters* (of the earth):—wind.

418. **ἀνένδεκτος anĕndĕktŏs**, *an-en'-dek-tos*; from *1* (as a neg. particle) and a der. of the same as *1735*; *unadmitted*, i.e. (by impl.) *not supposable*:—impossible.

419. **ἀνεξερεύνητος anĕxĕrĕunētŏs**, *an-ex-er-yoo'-nay-tos*; from *1* (as a neg. particle) and a presumed der. of *1830*; *not searched out*, i.e. (by impl.) *inscrutable*:—unsearchable.

420. **ἀνεξίκακος anĕxikakŏs**, *an-ex-ik'-ak-os*; from *430* and *2556*; *enduring of ill*, i.e. *forbearing*:—patient.

421. **ἀνεξιχνίαστος anĕxichniastŏs**, *an-ex-ikh-nee'-as-tos*; from *1* (as a neg. particle) and a presumed der. of a comp. of *1537* and a der. of *2487*; *not tracked out*, i.e. (by impl.) *untraceable*:—past finding out, unsearchable.

422. **ἀνεπαίσχυντος anĕpaischuntŏs**, *an-ep-ah'ee-skhoon-tos*; from *1* (as a neg. particle) and a presumed der. of a comp. of *1909* and *153*; *not ashamed*, i.e. (by impl.) *irreprehensible*:—that needeth not to be ashamed.

423. **ἀνεπίληπτος anĕpilēptŏs**, *an-ep-eel'-ape-tos*; from *1* (as a neg. particle) and a der. of *1949*; *not arrested*, i.e. (by impl.) *inculpable*:—blameless, unrebukeable.

424. **ἀνέρχομαι anĕrchŏmai**, *an-erkh'-om-ahee*; from *303* and *2064*; to *ascend*:—go up.

425. **ἄνεσις anĕsis**, *an'-es-is*; from *447*; *relaxation* or (fig.) *relief*:—eased, liberty, rest.

426. **ἀνετάζω anĕtazō**, *an-et-ad'-zo*; from *303* and **ἐτάζω ĕtazō** (to *test*); to *investigate* (judicially):—(should have) examine (-d).

427. **ἄνευ anĕu**, *an'-yoo*; a prim. particle; *without*:—without. Comp. *1*.

428. **ἀνεύθετος anĕuthĕtŏs**, *an-yoo'-the-tos*; from *1* (as a neg. particle) and *2111*; *not well set*, i.e. *inconvenient*:—not commodious.

429. **ἀνευρίσκω anĕuriskō**, *an-yoo-ris'-ko*; from *303* and *2147*; to *find out*:—find.

430. **ἀνέχομαι anĕchŏmai**, *an-ekh'-om-ahee*; mid. from *303* and *2192*; to *hold oneself up* against, i.e. (fig.) *put up* with:—bear with, endure, forbear, suffer.

431. **ἀνέψιος anĕpsiŏs**, *an-eps'-ee-os*; from *1* (as a particle of union) and an obsolete **νέπος nĕpŏs** (a *brood*); prop. *akin*, i.e. (spec.) a *cousin*:—sister's son.

432. **ἄνηθον anēthŏn**, *an'-ay-thon*; prob. of for. or.; *dill*:—anise.

433. **ἀνήκω anēkō**, *an-ay'-ko*; from *303* and *2240*; to *attain to*, i.e. (fig.) *be proper*:—convenient, be fit.

434. **ἀνήμερος anēmĕrŏs**, *an-ay'-mer-os*; from *1* (as a neg. particle) and **ἥμερος hēmĕrŏs** (*lame*); *savage*:—fierce.

435. **ἀνήρ anēr**, *an'-ayr*; a prim. word [comp. *444*]; a *man* (prop. as an individual male):—fellow, husband, man, sir.

436. **ἀνθίστημι anthistēmi**, *anth-is'-tay-mee*; from *473* and *2476*; to *stand against*, i.e. *oppose*:—resist, withstand.

437. **ἀνθομολογέομαι anthŏmŏlŏgĕŏmai**, *anth-om-ol-og-eh'-om-ahee*; from *473* and the mid. of *3670*; to *confess in turn*, i.e. *respond* in praise:—give thanks.

438. **ἄνθος anthŏs**, *anth'-os*; a prim. word; a *blossom*:—flower.

439. **ἀνθρακιά anthrakia**, *anth-rak-ee-ah'*; from *440*; a bed of burning *coals*:—fire of coals.

440. **ἄνθραξ anthrax**, *anth'-rax*; of uncert. der.; a live *coal*:—coal of fire.

441. **ἀνθρωπάρεσκος anthrōparĕskŏs**, *anth-ro-par'-es-kos*; from *444* and *700*; *man-courting*, i.e. *fawning*:—men-pleaser.

442. **ἀνθρώπινος anthrōpinŏs**, *anth-ro'-pee-nos*; from *444*; *human*:—human, common to man, man[-kind], [man-]kind, men's, after the manner of men.

443. **ἀνθρωποκτόνος anthrōpŏktŏnŏs**, *anth-ro-pok-ton'-os*; from *444* and **κτείνω ktĕinō** (to *kill*); a *manslayer*:—murderer. Comp. *5406*.

444. **ἄνθρωπος anthrōpŏs**, *anth'-ro-pos*; from *435* and **ὤψ ōps** (the *countenance*; from *3700*); *man-faced*, i.e. a *human* being:—certain, man.

445. **ἀνθυπατεύω anthupatĕuō**, *anth-oo-pat-yoo'-o*; from *446*; to *act as proconsul*:—be the deputy.

446. **ἀνθύπατος anthupatŏs**, *anth-oo'-pat-os*; from *473* and a superlative of *5228*; *instead* of the *highest* officer, i.e. (spec.) a Roman *proconsul*:—deputy.

447. **ἀνίημι aniēmi**, *an-ee'-ay-mee*; from *303* and **ἵημι hiēmi** (to *send*); to *let up*, i.e. (lit.) *slacken*, or (fig.) *desert*, *desist* from:—forbear, leave, loose.

448. **ἀνίλεως anilĕōs**, *an-ee'-leh-oce*; from *1* (as a neg. particle) and *2436*; *inexorable*:—without mercy.

449. **ἄνιπτος aniptŏs**, *an'-ip-tos*; from *1* (as a neg. particle) and a presumed der. of *3538*; *without ablution*:—unwashen.

450. **ἀνίστημι anistēmi**, *an-is'-tay-mee*; from *303* and *2476*; to *stand up* (lit. or fig., trans. or intrans.):—arise, lift up, raise up (again), rise (again), stand up (-right).

451. **Ἄννα Anna**, *an'-nah*; of Heb. or. [2584]; *Anna*, an Israelitess:—Anna.

452. **Ἄννας Annas**, *an'-nas*; of Heb. or. [2608]; *Annas* (i.e. *367*), an Isr.:—Annas.

453. **ἀνόητος anŏētŏs**, *an-ŏ'-ay-tos*; from *1* (as a neg. particle) and a der. of *3539*; *unintelligent*; by impl. *sensual*:—fool (-ish), unwise.

454. **ἄνοια anŏia**, *an'-oy-ah*; from a comp. of *1* (as a neg. particle) and *3563*; *stupidity*; by impl. *rage*:—folly, madness.

455. **ἀνοίγω anŏigō**, *an-oy'-go*; from *303* and **οἴγω ŏigō** (to *open*); to *open up* (lit. or fig., in various applications):—open.

456. **ἀνοικοδομέω anŏikŏdŏmĕō**, *an-oy-kod-om-eh'-o*; from *303* and *3618*; to *rebuild*:—build again.

457. **ἄνοιξις anŏixis**, *an'-oix-is*; from *455*; *opening* (throat):—× open.

458. **ἀνομία anŏmia**, *an-om-ee'-ah*; from *459*; *illegality*, i.e. *violation of law* or (gen.) *wickedness*:—iniquity, × transgress (-ion of) the law, unrighteousness.

459. **ἄνομος anŏmŏs**, *an'-om-os*; from *1* (as a neg. particle) and *3551*; *lawless*, i.e. (neg.) *not subject to* (the Jewish) *law*; (by impl. a *Gentile*), or (pos.) *wicked*:—without law, lawless, transgressor, unlawful, wicked.

460. **ἀνόμως anŏmōs**, *an-om'-oce*; adv. from *459*; *lawlessly*, i.e. (spec.) *not amenable to* (the Jewish) *law*:—without law.

461. **ἀνορθόω anŏrthŏō**, *an-orth-ŏ'-o*; from *303* and a der. of the base of *3717*; to *straighten up*:—lift (set) up, make straight.

462. **ἀνόσιος anŏsiŏs**, *an-os'-ee-os*; from *1* (as a neg. particle) and *3741*; *wicked*:—unholy.

463. **ἀνοχή anŏchē**, *an-okh-ay'*; from *430*; *self-restraint*, i.e. *tolerance*:—forbearance.

464. **ἀνταγωνίζομαι antagōnizŏmai**, *an-tag-o-nid'-zom-ahee*; from *473* and *75*; to *struggle against* (fig.) ["antagonize"]:—strive against.

465. **ἀντάλλαγμα antallagma**, *an-tal'-ag-mah*; from a comp. of *473* and *236*; an *equivalent* or *ransom*:—in exchange.

466. **ἀνταναπληρόω antanaplērŏō**, *an-tan-ap-lay-rŏ'-o*; from *473* and *378*; to *supplement*:—fill up.

467. **ἀνταποδίδωμι antapŏdidōmi**, *an-tap-od-ee'-do-mee*; from *473* and *591*; to *requite* (good or evil):—recompense, render, repay.

468. **ἀνταπόδομα antapŏdŏma**, *an-tap-od'-om-ah*; from *467*; a *requital* (prop. the thing):—recompense.

469. **ἀνταπόδοσις antapŏdŏsis**, *an-tap-od'-os-is*; from *467*; *requital* (prop. the act):—reward.

470. **ἀνταποκρίνομαι antapŏkrinŏmai**, *an-tap-ok-ree'-nom-ahee*; from *473* and *611*; to *contradict* or *dispute*:—answer again, reply against.

471. **ἀντέπω antĕpō**, *an-tep'-o*; from *473* and *2036*; to *refute* or *deny*:—gainsay, say against.

472. **ἀντέχομαι antĕchŏmai**, *an-tekh'-om-ahee*; from *473* and the mid. of *2192*; to *hold* oneself *opposite* to, i.e. (by impl.) *adhere to*; by extens. to *care for*:—hold fast, hold to, support.

473. **ἀντί anti**, *an-tee'*; a prim. particle; *opposite*, i.e. *instead* or *because* of (rarely *in addition* to):—for, in the room of. Often used in composition to denote *contrast*, *requital*, *substitution*, *correspondence*, etc.

474. ἀντιβάλλω **antiballō**, *an-tee-bal'-lo;* from 473 and 906; *to bandy:*—have.

475. ἀντιδιατίθεμαι **antidiatithĕmai**, *an-tee-dee-at-eeth'-em-ahee;* from 473 and 1303; *to set oneself opposite,* i.e. *be disputatious:*—that oppose themselves.

476. ἀντίδικος **antidikŏs**, *an-tid'-ee-kos;* from 473 and 1349; an *opponent* (in a lawsuit); spec. *Satan* (as the arch-enemy):—adversary.

477. ἀντίθεσις **antithĕsis**, *an-tith'-es-is;* from a comp. of 473 and 5087; *opposition,* i.e. a *conflict* (of theories):—opposition.

478. ἀντικαθίστημι **antikathistēmi**, *an-tee-kath-is'-tay-mee;* from 473 and 2525; *to set down* (troops) *against,* i.e. *withstand:*—resist.

479. ἀντικαλέω **antikalĕō**, *an-tee-kal-eh'-o;* from 473 and 2564; *to invite in return:*—bid again.

480. ἀντίκειμαι **antikĕimai**, *an-tik'-i-mahee;* from 473 and 2749; *to lie opposite,* i.e. *be adverse* (fig. *repugnant*) to:—adversary, be contrary, oppose.

481. ἀντικρύ **antikru**, *an-tee-kroo';* prol. from 473; *opposite:*—over against.

482. ἀντιλαμβάνομαι **antilambanŏmai**, *an-tee-lam-ban'-om-ahee;* from 473 and the mid. of 2983; *to take* hold of *in turn,* i.e. *succor;* also to *participate:*—help, partaker, support.

483. ἀντίλεγω **antilĕgō**, *an-til'-eg-o;* from 473 and 3004; *to dispute, refuse:*—answer again, contradict, deny, gainsay (-er), speak against.

484. ἀντίληψις **antilēpsis**, *an-til'-ape-sis;* from 482; *relief:*—help.

485. ἀντιλογία **antilŏgia**, *an-tee-log-ee'-ah;* from a der. of 483; *dispute, disobedience:*—contradiction, gainsaying, strife.

486. ἀντιλοιδορέω **antilŏidŏrĕō**, *an-tee-loy-dor-eh'-o;* from 473 and 3058; *to rail in reply:*—revile again.

487. ἀντίλυτρον **antilutrŏn**, *an-til'-oo-tron;* from 473 and 3083; a *redemption-price:*—ransom.

488. ἀντιμετρέω **antimĕtrĕō**, *an-tee-met-reh'-o;* from 473 and 3354; *to mete in return:*—measure again.

489. ἀντιμισθία **antimisthia**, *an-tee-mis-thee'-ah;* from a comp. of 473 and 3408; *requital, correspondence:*—recompense.

490. Ἀντιόχεια **Antiŏchĕia**, *an-tee-okh'-i-ah;* from Ἀντίοχος **Antiŏchus** (a Syrian king); *Antiochia,* a place in Syria:—Antioch.

491. Ἀντιοχεύς **Antiŏchĕus**, *an-tee-okh-yoos';* from 490; an *Antiochian* or inhab. of Antiochia:—of Antioch.

492. ἀντιπαρέρχομαι **antiparĕrchŏmai**, *an-tee-par-er'-khom-ahee;* from 473 and 3928; *to go along opposite:*—pass by on the other side.

493. Ἀντίπας **Antipas**, *an-tee'-pas;* contr. for a comp. of 473 and a der. of 3962; *Antipas,* a Chr.:—Antipas.

494. Ἀντιπατρίς **Antipatris**, *an-tip-at-rece';* from the same as 493; *Antipatris,* a place in Pal.:—Antipatris.

495. ἀντιπέραν **antipĕran**, *an-tee-per'-an;* from 473 and 4008; *on the opposite side:*—over against.

496. ἀντιπίπτω **antipiptō**, *an-tee-pip'-to;* from 473 and 4098 (includ. its alt.); *to oppose:*—resist.

497. ἀντιστρατεύομαι **antistratĕuŏmai**, *an-tee-strat-yoo'-om-ahee;* from 473 and 4754; (fig.) *to attack,* i.e. (by impl.) *destroy:*—war against.

498. ἀντιτάσσομαι **antitassŏmai**, *an-tee-tas'-som-ahee;* from 473 and the mid. of 5021; *to range oneself against,* i.e. *oppose:*—oppose themselves, resist.

499. ἀντίτυπον **antitupŏn**, *an-teet'-oo-pon;* neut. of a comp. of 473 and 5179; *corresponding* ["antitype"], i.e. a *representative, counterpart:*—(like) figure (whereunto).

500. ἀντίχριστος **antichristŏs**, *an-tee'-khris-tos:* from 473 and 5547; an *opponent of the Messiah:*—antichrist.

501. ἀντλέω **antlĕō**, *ant-leh-o;* from ἄντλος **antlŏs** (the *hold* of a ship); *to bale* up (prop. bilge water), i.e. *dip* water (with a bucket, pitcher, etc.):—draw (out).

502. ἄντλημα **antlēma**, *ant'-lay-mah;* from 501; a *baling-vessel:*—thing to draw with.

503. ἀντοφθαλμέω **antŏphthalmĕō**, *ant-of-thal-meh'-o;* from a comp. of 473 and 3788; *to face:*—bear up into.

504. ἄνυδρος **anudrŏs**, *an'-oo-dros;* from 1 (as a neg. particle) and 5204; *waterless,* i.e. *dry:*—dry, without water.

505. ἀνυπόκριτος **anupŏkritŏs**, *an-oo-pok'-ree-tos;* from 1 (as a neg. particle) and a presumed der. of 5271; *undissembled,* i.e. *sincere:*—without dissimulation (hypocrisy), unfeigned.

506. ἀνυπότακτος **anupŏtaktŏs**, *an-oo-pot'-ak-tos;* from 1 (as a neg. particle) and a presumed der. of 5293; *unsubdued,* i.e. *insubordinate* (in fact or temper):—disobedient, that is not put under, unruly.

507. ἄνω **anō**, *an'-o;* adv. from 473; *upward* or *on the top:*—above, brim, high, up.

508. ἀνώγεον **anōgĕŏn**, *an-ogue'-eh-on;* from 507 and 1093; *above the ground,* i.e. (prop.) the *second floor* of a building; used for a *dome* or a *balcony* on the upper story:—upper room.

509. ἄνωθεν **anōthĕn**, *an'-o-then;* from 507; *from above;* by anal. *from the first;* by impl. *anew:*—from above, again, from the beginning (very first), the top.

510. ἀνωτερικός **anōtĕrikŏs**, *an-o-ter-ee-kos';* from 511; *superior,* i.e. (locally) *more remote:*—upper.

511. ἀνώτερος **anōtĕrŏs**, *an-o'-ter-os;* comp. degree of 507; *upper,* i.e. (neut. as adv.) to a *more conspicuous* place, in a *former* part of the book:—above, higher.

512. ἀνωφελές **anōphĕlĕs**, *an-o-fel'-ace;* from 1 (as a neg. particle) and the base of 5624; *useless* or (neut.) *inutility:*—unprofitable (-ness).

513. ἀξίνη **axinē**, *ax-ee'-nay;* prob. from ἄγνυμι **agnumi** (to *break;* comp. 4486); an *axe:*—axe.

514. ἄξιος **axiŏs**, *ax'-ee-os;* prob. from 71; *deserving, comparable* or *suitable* (as if *drawing* praise):—due reward, meet, [un-] worthy.

515. ἀξιόω **axiŏō**, *ax-ee-ŏ'-o;* from 514; *to deem entitled* or *fit:*—desire, think good, count (think) worthy.

516. ἀξίως **axiōs**, *ax-ee'-oce;* adv. from 514; *appropriately:*—as becometh, after a godly sort, worthily (-thy).

517. ἀόρατος **aŏratŏs**, *ah-or'-at-os;* from 1 (as a neg. particle) and 3707; *invisible:*—invisible (thing).

518. ἀπαγγέλλω **apaggĕllō**, *ap-ang-el'-lo;* from 575 and the base of 32; *to announce:*—bring word (again), declare, report, shew (again), tell.

519. ἀπάγχομαι **apagchŏmai**, *ap-ang'-khom-ahee;* from 575 and ἄγχω **agchō** (to *choke;* akin to the base of 43); *to strangle oneself off* (i.e. to death):—hang himself.

520. ἀπάγω **apagō**, *ap-ag'-o;* from 575 and 71; *to take off* (in various senses):—bring, carry away, lead (away), put to death, take away.

521. ἀπαίδευτος **apaidĕutŏs**, *ap-ah'ee-dyoo-tos;* from 1 (as a neg. particle) and a der. of 3811; *uninstructed,* i.e. (fig.) *stupid:*—unlearned.

522. ἀπαίρω **apairō**, *ap-ah'ee-ro;* from 575 and 142; *to lift off,* i.e. *remove:*—take (away).

523. ἀπαιτέω **apaitĕō**, *ap-ah'ee-teh-o;* from 575 and 154; *to demand back:*—ask again, require.

524. ἀπαλγέω **apalgĕō**, *ap-alg-eh'-o;* from 575 and ἀλγέω **algĕō** (to *smart*); *to grieve out,* i.e. *become apathetic:*—be past feeling.

525. ἀπαλλάσσω **apallassō**, *ap-al-las'-so;* from 575 and 236; *to change away,* i.e. *release,* (reflex.) *remove:*—deliver, depart.

526. ἀπαλλοτριόω **apallŏtriŏō**, *ap-al-lot-ree-ŏ'-o;* from 575 and a der. of 245; *to estrange away,* i.e. (pass. and fig.) to *be non-participant:*—alienate, be alien.

527. ἁπαλός **apalŏs**, *ap-al-os';* of uncert. der.; *soft:*—tender.

528. ἀπαντάω **apantaō**, *ap-an-tah'-o;* from 575 and a der. of 473; *to meet away,* i.e. *encounter:*—meet.

529. ἀπάντησις **apantēsis**, *ap-an'-tay-sis;* from 528; a (friendly) *encounter:*—meet.

530. ἅπαξ **hapax**, *hap'-ax;* prob. from 537; *one* (or a *single*) *time* (numerically or conclusively):—once.

531. ἀπαράβατος **aparabatŏs**, *ap-ar-ab'-at-os;* from 1 (as a neg. particle) and a der. of 3845; *not passing away,* i.e. *untransferable* (perpetual):—unchangeable.

532. ἀπαρασκεύαστος **aparaskĕuastŏs**, *ap-ar-ask-yoo'-as-tos;* from 1 (as a neg. particle) and a der. of 3903; *unready:*—unprepared.

533. ἀπαρνέομαι **aparnĕŏmai**, *ap-ar-neh'-om-ahee;* from 575 and 720; *to deny utterly,* i.e. *disown, abstain:*—deny.

534. ἀπάρτι **aparti**, *ap-ar'-tee;* from 575 and 737; *from now,* i.e. *henceforth* (*already*):—from henceforth.

535. ἀπαρτισμός **apartismŏs**, *ap-ar-tis-mos';* from a der. of 534; *completion:*—finishing.

536. ἀπαρχή **aparchē**, *ap-ar-khay';* from a comp. of 575 and 756; a *beginning* of sacrifice, i.e. the (Jewish) *first-fruit* (fig.):—first-fruits.

537. ἅπας **hapas**, *hap'-as;* from 1 (as a particle of union) and 3956; absolutely *all* or (sing.) *every* one:—all (things), every (one), whole.

538. ἀπατάω **apataō**, *ap-at-ah'-o;* of uncert. der.; *to cheat,* i.e. *delude:*—deceive.

539. ἀπάτη **apatē**, *ap-at'-ay;* from 538; *delusion:*—deceit (-ful, -fulness), deceivableness (-ving).

540. ἀπάτωρ **apatōr**, *ap-at'-ore;* from 1 (as a neg. particle) and 3962; *fatherless,* i.e. *of unrecorded paternity:*—without father.

541. ἀπαύγασμα **apaugasma**, *ap-ŏw'-gas-mah;* from a comp. of 575 and 826; an *off-flash,* i.e. *effulgence:*—brightness.

542. ἀπείδω **apĕidō**, *ap-i'-do;* from 575 and the same as 1492; *to see* fully:—see.

543. ἀπείθεια **apĕithĕia**, *ap-i'-thi-ah;* from 545; *disbelief* (obstinate and rebellious):—disobedience, unbelief.

544. ἀπειθέω **apĕithĕō**, *ap-i-theh'-o;* from 545; *to disbelieve* (wilfully and perversely):—not believe, disobedient, obey not, unbelieving.

545. ἀπειθής **apĕithēs**, *ap-i-thace';* from 1 (as a neg. particle) and 3982; *unpersuadable,* i.e. *contumacious:*—disobedient.

546. ἀπειλέω **apĕilĕō**, *ap-i-leh'-o;* of uncert. der.; *to menace;* by impl. *to forbid:*—threaten.

547. ἀπειλή **apĕilē**, *ap-i-lay';* from 546; a *menace:*— × straitly, threatening.

548. ἄπειμι **apĕimi**, *ap'-i-mee;* from 575 and 1510; *to be away:*—be absent. Comp. 549.

549. ἄπειμι **apĕimi**, *ap'-i-mee;* from 575 and εἶμι **ĕimi** (to *go*); *to go away:*—go. Comp. 548.

550. ἀπειπόμην **apĕipŏmēn**, *ap-i-pom'-ane;* reflex. past of a comp. of 575 and 2036; *to say off* for oneself, i.e. *disown:*—renounce.

551. ἀπείραστος **apĕirastŏs**, *ap-i'-ras-tos;* from 1 (as a neg. particle) and a presumed der. of 3987; *untried,* i.e. *not temptable:*—not to be tempted.

552. ἄπειρος **apĕirŏs**, *ap'-i-ros;* from 1 (as a neg. particle) and 3984; *inexperienced,* i.e. *ignorant:*—unskilful.

553. ἀπεκδέχομαι **apĕkdĕchŏmai**, *ap-ek-dekh'-om-ahee;* from 575 and 1551; *to expect fully:*—look (wait) for.

554. ἀπεκδύομαι **apĕkduŏmai**, *ap-ek-doo'-om-ahee;* mid. from 575 and 1562; *to divest wholly* oneself, or (for oneself) *despoil:*—put off, spoil.

555. ἀπέκδυσις **apĕkdusis**, *ap-ek'-doo-sis;* from 554; *divestment:*—putting off.

556. ἀπελαύνω **apĕlaunō**, *ap-el-ŏw'-no;* from 575 and 1643; *to dismiss:*—drive.

557. **ἀπελεγμός apĕlĕgmŏs**, *ap-el-eg-mos'*; from a comp. of 575 and 1651; *refutation*, i.e. (by impl.) *contempt*:—nought.

558. **ἀπελεύθερος apĕlĕuthĕrŏs**, *ap-el-yoo'-ther-os*; from 575 and 1658; one *freed away*, i.e. a *freedman*:—freeman.

559. **Ἀπελλῆς Apĕllēs**, *ap-el-lace'*; of Lat. or.; *Apelles*, a Chr.:—Apelles.

560. **ἀπελπίζω apĕlpizō**, *ap-el-pid'-zo*; from 575 and 1679; to *hope out*, i.e. *fully expect*:—hope for again.

561. **ἀπέναντι apĕnanti**, *ap-en'-an-tee*; from 575 and 1725; *from in front*, i.e. *opposite*, *before* or *against*:—before, contrary, over against, in the presence of.

ἀπέπω apĕpō. See 550.

562. **ἀπέραντος apĕrantŏs**, *ap-er'-an-tos*; from 1 (as a neg. particle) and a secondary der. of 4008; *unfinished*, i.e. (by impl.) *interminable*:—endless.

563. **ἀπερισπάστως apĕrispastōs**, *ap-er-is-pas-toce'*; adv. from a comp. of 1 (as a neg. particle) and a presumed der. of 4049; *undistractedly*, i.e. *free from* (domestic) *solicitude*:—without distraction.

564. **ἀπερίτμητος apĕritmētŏs**, *ap-er-eet'-may-tos*; from 1 (as a neg. particle) and a presumed der. of 4059; *uncircumcised* (fig.):—uncircumcised.

565. **ἀπέρχομαι apĕrchŏmai**, *ap-erkh'-om-ahee*; from 575 and 2064; to *go off* (i.e. *depart*), *aside* (i.e. *apart*) or *behind* (i.e. *follow*), lit. or fig.:—come, depart, go (aside, away, back, out, . . . ways), pass away, be past.

566. **ἀπέχει apĕchĕi**, *ap-ekh'-i*; 3d pers. sing. pres. indic. act. of 568 used impers.; *it is sufficient*:—it is enough.

567. **ἀπέχομαι apĕchŏmai**, *ap-ekh'-om-ahee*; mid. (reflex.) of 568; to *hold oneself off*, i.e. *refrain*:—abstain.

568. **ἀπέχω apĕchō**, *ap-ekh'-o*; from 575 and 2192; (act.) to *have out*, i.e. *receive in full*; (intrans.) to *keep* (oneself) *away*, i.e. *be distant* (lit. or fig.):—be, have, receive.

569. **ἀπιστέω apistĕō**, *ap-is-teh'-o*; from 571; to *be unbelieving*, i.e. (trans.) *disbelieve*, or (by impl.) *disobey*:—believe not.

570. **ἀπιστία apistia**, *ap-is-tee'-ah*; from 571; *faithlessness*, i.e. (neg.) *disbelief* (*want of* Chr. *faith*), or (pos.) *unfaithfulness* (*disobedience*):—unbelief.

571. **ἄπιστος apistŏs**, *ap'-is-tos*; from 1 (as a neg. particle) and 4103; (act.) *disbelieving*, i.e. *without* Chr. *faith* (spec. a *heathen*); (pass.) *untrustworthy* (person), or *incredible* (thing):—that believeth not, faithless, incredible thing, infidel, unbeliever (-ing).

572. **ἁπλότης haplŏtēs**, *hap-lot'-ace*; from 573; *singleness*, i.e. (subj.) *sincerity* (*without dissimulation* or *self-seeking*), or (obj.) *generosity* (*copious bestowal*):—bountifulness, liberal (-ity), simplicity, singleness.

573. **ἁπλοῦς haplŏus**, *hap-looce'*; prob. from 1 (as a particle of union) and the base of 4120; prop. *folded together*, i.e. *single* (fig. *clear*):—single.

574. **ἁπλῶς haplōs**, *hap-loce'*; adv. from 573 (in the obj. sense of 572); *bountifully*:—liberally.

575. **ἀπό apŏ**, *apŏ'*; a prim. particle; "*off*," i.e. *away* (from something near), in various senses (of place, time, or relation; lit. or fig.):—(× here-) after, ago, at, because of, before, by (the space of), for (-th), from, in, (out) of, off, (up-) on (-ce), since, with. In composition (as a prefix) it usually denotes *separation, departure, cessation, completion, reversal*, etc.

576. **ἀποβαίνω apŏbainō**, *ap-ob-ah'ee-no*; from 575 and the base of 939; lit. to *disembark*; fig. to *eventuate*:—become, go out, turn.

577. **ἀποβάλλω apŏballō**, *ap-ob-al'-lo*; from 575 and 906; to *throw off*; fig. to *lose*:—cast away.

578. **ἀποβλέπω apŏblĕpō**, *ap-ob-lep'-o*; from 575 and 991; to *look away* from everything else, i.e. (fig.) intently *regard*:—have respect.

579. **ἀπόβλητος apŏblētŏs**, *ap-ob'-lay-tos*; from 577; *cast off*, i.e. (fig.) such as to *be rejected*:—be refused.

580. **ἀποβολή apŏbŏlē**, *ap-ob-ol-ay'*; from 577; *rejection*; fig. *loss*:—casting away, loss.

581. **ἀπογενόμενος apŏgĕnŏmĕnŏs**, *ap-og-en-om'-en-os*; past part. of a comp. of 575 and 1096; *absent*, i.e. *deceased* (fig. *renounced*):—being dead.

582. **ἀπογραφή apŏgraphē**, *ap-og-raf-ay'*; from 583; an *enrollment*; by impl. an *assessment*:—taxing.

583. **ἀπογράφω apŏgraphō**, *ap-og-raf'-o*; from 575 and 1125; to *write off* (a copy or list), i.e. *enrol*:—tax, write.

584. **ἀποδείκνυμι apŏdĕiknumi**, *ap-od-ike'-noo-mee*; from 575 and 1166; to *show off*, i.e. *exhibit*; fig. to *demonstrate*, i.e. *accredit*:—(ap-) prove, set forth, shew.

585. **ἀπόδειξις apŏdĕixis**, *ap-od'-ike-sis*; from 584; *manifestation*:—demonstration.

586. **ἀποδεκατόω apŏdĕkatŏō**, *ap-od-ek-at-ŏ'-o*; from 575 and 1183; to *tithe* (as debtor or creditor):—(give, pay, take) tithe.

587. **ἀπόδεκτος apŏdĕktŏs**, *ap-od'-ek-tos*; from 588; *accepted*, i.e. *agreeable*:—acceptable.

588. **ἀποδέχομαι apŏdĕchŏmai**, *ap-od-ekh'-om-ahee*; from 575 and 1209; to *take fully*, i.e. *welcome* (persons), *approve* (things):—accept, receive (gladly).

589. **ἀποδημέω apŏdēmĕō**, *ap-od-ay-meh'-o*; from 590; to *go abroad*, i.e. *visit a foreign land*:—go (travel) into a far country, journey.

590. **ἀπόδημος apŏdēmŏs**, *ap-od'-ay-mos*; from 575 and 1218; *absent from* one's own *people*, i.e. a *foreign traveller*:—taking a far journey.

591. **ἀποδίδωμι apŏdidōmi**, *ap-od-eed'-o-mee*; from 575 and 1325; to *give away*, i.e. *up*, *over*, *back*, etc. (in various applications):—deliver (again), give (again), (re-) pay (-ment be made), perform, recompense, render, requite, restore, reward, sell, yield.

592. **ἀποδιορίζω apŏdiŏrizō**, *ap-od-ee-or-id'-zo*; from 575 and a comp. of 1223 and 3724; to *disjoin* (by a boundary, fig. a party):—separate.

593. **ἀποδοκιμάζω apŏdŏkimazō**, *ap-od-ok-ee-mad'-zo*; from 575 and 1381; to *disapprove*, i.e. (by impl.) to *repudiate*:—disallow, reject.

594. **ἀποδοχή apŏdŏchē**, *ap-od-okh-ay'*; from 588; *acceptance*:—acceptation.

595. **ἀπόθεσις apŏthĕsis**, *ap-oth'-es-is*; from 659; a *laying aside* (lit. or fig.):—putting away (off).

596. **ἀποθήκη apŏthēkē**, *ap-oth-ay'-kay*; from 659; a *repository*, i.e. *granary*:—barn, garner.

597. **ἀποθησαυρίζω apŏthēsaurizō**, *ap-oth-ay-sŏw-rid'-zo*; from 575 and 2343; to *treasure away*:—lay up in store.

598. **ἀποθλίβω apŏthlibō**, *ap-oth-lee'-bo*; from 575 and 2346; to *crowd* from (every side):—press.

599. **ἀποθνήσκω apŏthnēskō**, *ap-oth-nace'-ko*; from 575 and 2348; to *die off* (lit. or fig.):—be dead, death, die, lie a-dying, be slain (× with).

600. **ἀποκαθίστημι apŏkathistēmi**, *ap-ok-ath-is'-tay-mee*; from 575 and 2525; to *reconstitute* (in health, home or organization):—restore (again).

601. **ἀποκαλύπτω apŏkaluptō**, *ap-ok-al-oop'-to*; from 575 and 2572; to take *off the cover*, i.e. *disclose*:—reveal.

602. **ἀποκάλυψις apŏkalupsis**, *ap-ok-al'-oop-sis*; from 601; *disclosure*:—appearing, coming, lighten, manifestation, be revealed, revelation.

603. **ἀποκαραδοκία apŏkaradŏkia**, *ap-ok-ar-ad-ok-ee'-ah*; from a comp. of 575 and a comp. of **κάρα kara** (the *head*) and 1380 (in the sense of *watching*); *intense anticipation*:—earnest expectation.

604. **ἀποκαταλλάσσω apŏkatallassō**, *ap-ok-at-al-las'-so*; from 575 and 2644; to *reconcile fully*:—reconcile.

605. **ἀποκατάστασις apŏkatastasis**, *ap-ok-at-as'-tas-is*; from 600; *reconstitution*:—restitution.

606. **ἀπόκειμαι apŏkĕimai**, *ap-ok'-i-mahee*; from 575 and 2749; to *be reserved*; fig. to *await*:—be appointed, (be) laid up.

607. **ἀποκεφαλίζω apŏkĕphalizō**, *ap-ok-ef-al-id'-zo*; from 575 and 2776; to *decapitate*:—behead.

608. **ἀποκλείω apŏklĕiō**, *ap-ok-li'-o*; from 575 and 2808; to *close fully*:—shut up.

609. **ἀποκόπτω apŏkŏptō**, *ap-ok-op'-to*; from 575 and 2875; to *amputate*; reflex. (by irony) to *mutilate* (the privy parts):—cut off. Comp. 2699.

610. **ἀπόκριμα apŏkrima**, *ap-ok'-ree-mah*; from 611 (in its orig. sense of *judging*); a judicial *decision*:—sentence.

611. **ἀποκρίνομαι apŏkrinŏmai**, *ap-ok-ree'-nom-ahee*; from 575 and **κρίνω krino**; to *conclude for oneself*, i.e. (by impl.) to *respond*; by Hebr. [comp. 6030] to *begin to speak* (where an address is expected):—answer.

612. **ἀπόκρισις apŏkrisis**, *ap-ok'-ree-sis*; from 611; a *response*:—answer.

613. **ἀποκρύπτω apŏkruptō**, *ap-ok-roop'-to*; from 575 and 2928; to *conceal away* (i.e. *fully*); fig. to *keep secret*:—hide.

614. **ἀπόκρυφος apŏkruphŏs**, *ap-ok'-roo-fos*; from 613; *secret*; by impl. *treasured*:—hid, kept secret.

615. **ἀποκτείνω apŏktĕinō**, *ap-ok-ti'-no*; from 575 and **κτείνω ktĕinō** (to *slay*); to *kill* outright; fig. to *destroy*:—put to death, kill, slay.

616. **ἀποκυέω apŏkuĕō**, *ap-ok-oo-eh'o*; from 575 and the base of 2949; to *breed forth*, i.e. (by transf.) to *generate* (fig.):—beget, bring forth.

617. **ἀποκυλίω apŏkuliō**, *ap-ok-oo-lee'-o*; from 575 and 2947; to *roll away*:—roll away (back).

618. **ἀπολαμβάνω apŏlambanō**, *ap-ol-am-ban'-o*; from 575 and 2983; to *receive* (spec. in *full*, or as a host); also to *take aside*:—receive, take.

619. **ἀπόλαυσις apŏlausis**, *ap-ol'-ŏw-sis*; from a comp. of 575 and **λαύω lauō** (to *enjoy*); full *enjoyment*:—enjoy (-ment).

620. **ἀπολείπω apŏlĕipō**, *ap-ol-ipe'-o*; from 575 and 3007; to *leave* behind (pass. *remain*); by impl. to *forsake*:—leave, remain.

621. **ἀπολείχω apŏlĕichō**, *ap-ol-ī'-kho*; from 575 and **λείχω lĕichō** (to "*lick*"); to *lick* clean:—lick.

622. **ἀπόλλυμι apŏllumi**, *ap-ol'-loo-mee*; from 575 and the base of 3639; to *destroy* fully (reflex. to *perish*, or *lose*), lit. or fig.:—destroy, die, lose, mar, perish.

623. **Ἀπολλύων Apŏlluōn**, *ap-ol-loo'-ohn*; act. part. of 622; a *destroyer* (i.e. *Satan*);—Apollyon.

624. **Ἀπολλωνία Apŏllōnia**, *ap-ol-lo-nee'-ah*; from the pagan deity **Ἀπόλλων Apŏllōn** (i.e. the *sun*; from 622); *Apollonia*, a place in Macedonia:—Apollonia.

625. **Ἀπολλώς Apŏllōs**, *ap-ol-loce'*; prob. from the same as 624; *Apollos*, an Isr.:—Apollos.

626. **ἀπολογέομαι apŏlŏgĕŏmai**, *ap-ol-og-eh'-om-ahee*: mid. from a comp. of 575 and 3056; to *give an account* (legal *plea*) of oneself, i.e. *exculpate* (self):—answer (for self), make defence, excuse (self), speak for self.

627. **ἀπολογία apŏlŏgia**, *ap-ol-og-ee'-ah*; from the same as 626; a *plea* ("apology"):—answer (for self), clearing of self, defence.

628. **ἀπολούω apŏlŏuō**, *ap-ol-oo'-o*; from 575 and 3068; to *wash* fully, i.e. (fig.) *have remitted* (reflex.):—wash (away).

629. **ἀπολύτρωσις apŏlutrōsis**, *ap-ol-oo'-tro-sis*; from a comp. of 575 and 3083; (the act) *ransom* in full, i.e. (fig.) *riddance*, or (spec.) Chr. *salvation*:—deliverance, redemption.

630. **ἀπολύω apŏluō**, *ap-ol-oo'-o*; from 575 and 3089; to *free* fully, i.e. (lit.) *relieve, release, dismiss* (reflex. *depart*), or (fig.) *let die, pardon*, or (spec.) *divorce*:—(let) depart, dismiss, divorce, forgive, let go, loose, put (send) away, release, set at liberty.

631. **ἀπομάσσομαι apŏmassŏmai**, *ap-om-as'-som-ahee*; mid. from 575 and **μάσσω massō** (to *squeeze, knead, smear*); to *scrape away*:—wipe off.

632. **ἀπονέμω apŏnĕmō**, *ap-on-em'-o*; from 575 and the base of 3551; to *apportion*, i.e. *bestow*:—give.

633. **ἀπονίπτω apŏniptō**, *ap-on-ip'-to;* from *575* and *3538;* to *wash off* (reflex. one's own hands symbolically):—wash.

634. **ἀποπίπτω apŏpiptō**, *ap-op-ip'-to;* from *575* and *4098;* to *fall off:*—fall.

635. **ἀποπλανάω apŏplanaō**, *ap-op-lan-ah'-o;* from *575* and *4105;* to *lead astray* (fig.); pass. to *stray* (from truth):—err, seduce.

636. **ἀποπλέω apŏplĕō**, *ap-op-leh'-o;* from *575* and *4126;* to *set sail:*—sail away.

637. **ἀποπλύνω apŏplunō**, *ap-op-loo'-no;* from *575* and *4150;* to *rinse off:*—wash.

638. **ἀποπνίγω apŏpnigō**, *ap-op-nee'-go;* from *575* and *4155;* to *stifle* (by drowning or overgrowth):—choke.

639. **ἀπορέω apŏrĕō**, *ap-or-eh'-o;* from a comp. of *1* (as a neg. particle) and the base of *4198;* to *have no way* out, i.e. *be at a loss* (mentally):—(stand in) doubt, be perplexed.

640. **ἀπορία apŏria**, *ap-or-ee'-a;* from the same as *639;* a (state of) *quandary:*—perplexity.

641. **ἀποῤῥίπτω apŏrrhiptō**, *ap-or-hrip'-to;* from *575* and *4496;* to *hurl off*, i.e. *precipitate* (oneself):—cast.

642. **ἀπορφανίζω apŏrphanizō**, *ap-or-fan-id'-zo;* from *575* and a der. of *3737;* to *bereave wholly*, i.e. (fig.) *separate* (from intercourse):—take.

643. **ἀποσκευάζω apŏskĕuazō**, *ap-osk-yoo-ad'-zo;* from *575* and a der. of *4632;* to *pack up* (one's) *baggage:*—take up . . . carriages.

644. **ἀποσκίασμα apŏskiasma**, *ap-os-kee'-as-mah;* from a comp. of *575* and a der. of *4639;* a *shading off*, i.e. *obscuration:*—shadow.

645. **ἀποσπάω apŏspaō**, *ap-os-pah'-o;* from *575* and *4685;* to *drag forth*, i.e. (lit.) *unsheathe* (a sword), or rel. (with a degree of force implied) *retire* (pers. or factiously):—(with-) draw (away), after we were gotten from.

646. **ἀποστασία apŏstasia**, *ap-os-tas-ee'-ah;* fem. of the same as *647;* *defection* from truth (prop. the state) ["apostasy"]:—falling away, forsake.

647 **ἀποστάσιον apŏstasiŏn**, *ap-os-tas'-ee-on;* neut. of a (presumed) adj. from a der. of *868;* prop. something *separative*, i.e. (spec.) *divorce:*—(writing of) divorcement.

648. **ἀποστεγάζω apŏstĕgazō**, *ap-os-teg-ad'-zo;* from *575* and a der. of *4721;* to *unroof:*—uncover.

649. **ἀποστέλλω apŏstĕllō**, *ap-os-tel'-lo;* from *575* and *4724;* *set apart*, i.e. (by impl.) to *send out* (prop. on a mission) lit. or fig.:—put in, send (away, forth, out), set [at liberty].

650. **ἀποστερέω apŏstĕrĕō**, *ap-os-ter-eh'-o;* from *575* and **στερέω stĕrĕō** (to *deprive*); to *despoil:*—defraud, destitute, kept back by fraud.

651. **ἀποστολή apŏstŏlē**, *ap-os-tol-ay';* from *649*, *commission*, i.e. (spec.) *apostolate:*—apostleship.

652. **ἀπόστολος apŏstŏlŏs**, *ap-os'-tol-os;* from *649;* a *delegate;* spec. an *ambassador* of the Gospel; officially a *commissioner* of Christ ["*apostle*"] (with miraculous powers):—apostle, messenger, he that is sent.

653. **ἀποστοματίζω apŏstŏmatizō**, *ap-os-tom-at-id'-zo;* from *575* and a (presumed) der. of *4750;* to *speak off-hand* (prop. *dictate*), i.e. to *catechize* (in an invidious manner):—provoke to speak.

654. **ἀποστρέφω apŏstrĕphō**, *ap-os-tref'-o;* from *575* and *4762;* to *turn away* or *back* (lit. or fig.):—bring again, pervert, turn away (from).

655. **ἀποστυγέω apŏstugĕō**, *ap-os-toog-eh'-o;* from *575* and the base of *4767;* to *detest* utterly:—abhor.

656. **ἀποσυνάγωγος apŏsunagōgŏs**, *ap-os-oon-ag'-o-gos;* from *575* and *4864;* *excommunicated:*—(put) out of the synagogue (-s).

657. **ἀποτάσσομαι apŏtassŏmai**, *ap-ot-as'-som-ahee;* mid. from *575* and *5021;* lit. to *say adieu* (by departing or dismissing); fig. to *renounce:*—bid farewell, forsake, take leave, send away.

658. **ἀποτελέω apŏtĕlĕō**, *ap-ot-el-eh'-o;* from *575* and *5055;* to *complete entirely*, i.e. *consummate:*—finish.

659. **ἀποτίθημι apŏtithēmi**, *ap-ot-eeth'-ay-mee;* from *575* and *5087;* to *put away* (lit. or fig.):—cast off, lay apart (aside, down), put away (off).

660. **ἀποτινάσσω apŏtinassō**, *ap-ot-in-as'-so;* from *575* and **τινάσσω tinassō** (to *jostle*); to *brush off:*—shake off.

661. **ἀποτίνω apŏtinō**, *ap-ot-ee'-no;* from *575* and *5099;* to *pay* in full:—repay.

662. **ἀποτολμάω apŏtŏlmaō**, *ap-ot-ol-mah'-o;* from *575* and *5111;* to *venture* plainly:—be very bold.

663. **ἀποτομία apŏtŏmia**, *ap-ot-om-ee'-ah;* from the base of *664;* (fig.) *decisiveness*, i.e. *rigor:*—severity.

664. **ἀποτόμως apŏtŏmōs**, *ap-ot-om'-oce;* adv. from a der. of a comp. of *575* and **τέμνω tĕmnō** (to *cut*); *abruptly*, i.e. *peremptorily:*—sharply (-ness).

665. **ἀποτρέπω apŏtrĕpō**, *ap-ot-rep'-o;* from *575* and the base of *5157;* to *deflect*, i.e. (reflex.) *avoid:*—turn away.

666. **ἀπουσία apŏusia**, *ap-oo-see'-ah;* from the part. of *548;* a *being away:*—absence.

667. **ἀποφέρω appŏhĕrō**, *ap-of-er'-o;* from *575* and *5342;* to *bear off* (lit. or rel.):—bring, carry (away).

668. **ἀποφεύγω apŏphĕugō**, *ap-of-yoo'-go;* from *575* and *5343;* (fig.) to *escape:*—escape.

669. **ἀποφθέγγομαι apŏphthĕggŏmai**, *ap-of-theng'-om-ahee;* from *575* and *5350;* to *enunciate* plainly, i.e. *declare:*—say, speak forth, utterance.

670. **ἀποφορτίζομαι apŏphŏrtizŏmai**, *ap-of-or-tid'-zom-ahee;* from *575* and the mid. of *5412;* to *unload:*—unlade.

671. **ἀπόχρησις apŏchrēsis**, *ap-okh'-ray-sis;* from a comp. of *575* and *5530;* the act of *using up*, i.e. *consumption:*—using.

672. **ἀποχωρέω apŏchōrĕō**, *ap-okh-o-reh'-o;* from *575* and *5562;* to *go away:*—depart.

673. **ἀποχωρίζω apŏchōrizō**, *ap-okh-o-rid'-zo;* from *575* and *5563;* to *rend apart;* reflex. to *separate:*—depart (asunder).

674. **ἀποψύχω apŏpsuchō**, *ap-ops-oo'-kho;* from *575* and *5594;* to *breathe out*, i.e. *faint:*—hearts failing.

675. **Ἄππιος 'Appiŏs**, *ap'-pee-os:* of Lat. or.; (in the genitive, i.e. possessive case) *of Appius*, the name of a Roman:—Appii.

676. **ἀπρόσιτος aprŏsitŏs**, *ap-ros'-ee-tos;* from *1* (as a neg. particle) and a der. of a comp. of *4314* and **εἶμι ĕimi** (to *go*); *inaccessible:*—which no man can approach.

677. **ἀπρόσκοπος aprŏskŏpŏs**, *ap-ros'-kop-os;* from *1* (as a neg. particle) and a presumed der. of *4350;* act. *inoffensive*, i.e. *not leading into sin;* pass. *faultless*, i.e. *not led into sin:*—none (void of, without) offence.

678. **ἀπροσωπολήπτως aprŏsōpŏlēptōs**, *ap-ros-o-pol-ape'-toce;* adv. from a comp. of *1* (as a neg. particle) and a presumed der. of a presumed comp. of *4383* and *2983* [comp. *4381*]; in a way *not accepting* the *person*, i.e. *impartially:*—without respect of persons.

679. **ἄπταιστος aptaistŏs**, *ap-tah'-ee-stos;* from *1* (as a neg. particle) and a der. of *4417;* *not stumbling*, i.e. (fig.) *without sin:*—from falling.

680. **ἅπτομαι haptŏmai**, *hap'-tom-ahee;* reflex. of *681;* prop. to *attach* oneself to, i.e. to *touch* (in many implied relations):—touch.

681. **ἅπτω haptō**, *hap'-to;* a prim. verb; prop. to *fasten* to, i.e. (spec.) to *set* on fire:—kindle, light.

682. **Ἀπφία Apphia**, *ap-fee'-a;* prob. of for. or.; *Apphia*, a woman of Colossæ:—Apphia.

683. **ἀπωθέομαι apōthĕŏmai**, *ap-o-theh'-om-ahee;* or **ἀπώθομαι apōthŏmai**, *ap-o'-thom-ahee;* from *575* and the mid. of **ὠθέω ōthĕō** or **ὤθω ōthō** (to *shove*); to *push off*, fig. to *reject:*—cast away, put away (from), thrust away (from).

684. **ἀπώλεια apōlĕia**, *ap-o'-li-a;* from a presumed der. of *622;* *ruin* or *loss* (phys., spiritual or eternal):—damnable (-nation), destruction, die, perdition, × perish, pernicious ways, waste.

685. **ἀρά ara**, *ar-ah';* prob. from *142;* prop. *prayer* (as *lifted* to Heaven), i.e. (by impl.) *imprecation:*—curse.

686. **ἄρα ara**, *ar'-ah;* prob. from *142* (through the idea of *drawing* a conclusion); a particle denoting an *inference* more or less decisive (as follows):—haply, (what) manner (of man), no doubt, perhaps, so be, then, therefore, truly, wherefore. Often used in connection with other particles, especially *1065* or *3767* (after) or *1487* (before). Comp. also *687*.

687. **ἆρα ara**, *ar'-ah;* a form of *686*, denoting an *interrogation* to which a negative answer is presumed:—therefore.

688. **Ἀραβία Arabia**, *ar-ab-ee'-ah;* of Heb. or. [6152]; *Arabia*, a region of Asia:—Arabia.

ἄραγε aragĕ. See *686* and *1065*.

689. **Ἀράμ Aram**, *ar-am';* of Heb. or. [7410]; *Aram* (i.e. *Ram*), an Isr.:—Aram.

690. **Ἄραψ 'Araps**, *ar'-aps;* from *688;* an *Arab* or native of Arabia:—Arabian.

691. **ἀργέω argĕō**, *arg-eh'-o;* from *692;* to *be idle*, i.e. (fig.) to *delay:*—linger.

692. **ἀργός argŏs**, *ar-gos';* from *1* (as a neg. particle) and *2041;* *inactive*, i.e. *unemployed;* (by impl.) *lazy, useless:*—barren, idle, slow.

693. **ἀργύρεος argurĕŏs**, *ar-goo'-reh-os;* from *696;* made *of silver:*—(of) silver.

694. **ἀργύριον arguriŏn**, *ar-goo'-ree-on;* neut. of a presumed der. of *696;* *silvery*, i.e. (by impl.) *cash;* spec. a *silverling* (i.e. *drachma* or *shekel*):—money, (piece of) silver (piece).

695. **ἀργυροκόπος argurŏkŏpŏs**, *ar-goo-rok-op'-os;* from *696* and *2875;* a *beater* (i.e. *worker*) *of silver:*—silversmith.

696. **ἄργυρος argurŏs**, *ar'-goo-ros;* from **ἀργός argŏs** (*shining*); *silver* (the metal, in the articles or coin):—silver.

697. **Ἄρειος Πάγος Arĕiŏs Pagŏs**, *ar'-i-os pag'-os;* from **Ἄρης Arēs** (the name of the Greek deity of war) and a der. of *4078;* *rock of Ares*, a place in Athens:—Areopagus, Mars' Hill.

698. **Ἀρεοπαγίτης Arĕŏpagitēs**, *ar-eh-op-ag-ee'-tace;* from *697;* an *Areopagite* or member of the court held on Mars' Hill:—Areopagite.

699. **ἀρέσκεια arĕskĕia**, *ar-es'-ki-ah;* from a der. of *700;* *complaisance:*—pleasing.

700. **ἀρέσκω arĕskō**, *ar-es'-ko;* prob. from *142* (through the idea of *exciting* emotion); to *be agreeable* (or by impl. to seek to be so):—please.

701. **ἀρεστός arĕstŏs**, *ar-es-tos';* from *700;* *agreeable;* by impl. *fit:*—(things that) please (-ing), reason.

702. **Ἀρέτας Arĕtas**, *ar-et'-as;* of for. or.; *Aretas*, an Arabian:—Aretas.

703. **ἀρέτη arĕtē**, *ar-et'-ay;* from the same as *730;* prop. *manliness* (*valor*), i.e. *excellence* (intrinsic or attributed):—praise, virtue.

704. **ἀρήν arēn**, *ar-ane';* perh. the same as *730;* a *lamb* (as a *male*):—lamb.

705. **ἀριθμέω arithmĕō**, *ar-ith-meh'-o;* from *706;* to *enumerate* or *count:*—number.

706. **ἀριθμός arithmŏs**, *ar-ith-mos';* from *142;* a *number* (as reckoned *up*):—number.

707. **Ἀριμαθαία Arimathaia**, *ar-ee-math-ah'ee-ah;* of Heb. or. [7414]; *Arimathæa* (or *Ramah*), a place in Pal.:—Arimathæa.

708. **Ἀρίσταρχος Aristarchŏs**, *ar-is'-tar-khos;* from the same as *712* and *757;* *best ruling; Aristarchus*, a Macedonian:—Aristarchus.

709. **ἀριστάω aristaō**, *ar-is-tah'-o;* from *712;* to *take the principal meal:*—dine.

710. **ἀριστερός aristĕrŏs**, *ar-is-ter-os';* appar. a comp. of the same as *712;* the *left* hand (as *second-best*):—left [hand].

711. **Ἀριστόβουλος Aristŏbŏulŏs**, *ar-is-tob'-oo-los;* from the same as *712* and *1012; best counselling; Aristoboulus*, a Chr.:—Aristobulus.

712. **ἄριστον aristŏn**, *ar'-is-ton;* appar. neut. of a superlative from the same as *730;* the *best* meal [or *breakfast;* perh. from **ἦρι ēri** ("*early*")], i.e. *luncheon:*—dinner.

713. **ἀρκετός arkĕtŏs**, *ar-ket-os';* from *714; satisfactory:*—enough, suffice (-ient).

714. **ἀρκέω arkĕō**, *ar-keh'-o;* appar. a prim. verb [but prob. akin to *142* through the idea of *raising* a barrier]; prop. to *ward off*, i.e. (by impl.) to *avail* (fig. *be satisfactory*):—be content, be enough, suffice, be sufficient.

715. **ἄρκτος arktŏs**, *ark'-tos;* prob. from *714;* a *bear* (as *obstructing* by ferocity):—bear.

716. **ἅρμα harma**, *har'-mah;* prob. from *142* [perh. with *1* (as a particle of union) prefixed]; a *chariot* (as *raised* or fitted *together* [comp. *719*]):—chariot.

717. **Ἀρμαγεδδών Armagĕddōn**, *ar-mag-ed-dohn';* of Heb. or. [2022 and 4023]; *Armageddon* (or *Har-Megiddon*), a symbol. name:—Armageddon.

718. **ἁρμόζω harmŏzō**, *har-mod'-zo;* from *719;* to *joint*, i.e. (fig.) to *woo* (reflex. to *betroth*):—espouse.

719. **ἁρμός harmŏs**, *har-mos';* from the same as *716;* an *articulation* (of the body):—joint.

720. **ἀρνέομαι arnĕŏmai**, *ar-neh'-om-ahee;* perh. from *1* (as a neg. particle) and the mid. of *4483;* to *contradict*, i.e. *disavow, reject, abnegate:*—deny, refuse.

721. **ἀρνίον arniŏn**, *ar-nee'-on;* diminutive from *704;* a *lambkin:*—lamb.

722. **ἀροτριόω arŏtriŏō**, *ar-ot-ree-ŏ'-o;* from *723;* to *plough:*—plow.

723. **ἄροτρον arŏtrŏn**, *ar'-ot-ron;* from **ἀρόω arŏō** (to *till*); a *plough:*—plow.

724. **ἁρπαγή harpagē**, *har-pag-ay';* from *726; pillage* (prop. abstr.):—extortion, ravening, spoiling.

725. **ἁρπαγμός harpagmŏs**, *har-pag-mos';* from *726; plunder* (prop. concr.):—robbery.

726. **ἁρπάζω harpazō**, *har-pad'-zo;* from a der. of *138;* to *seize* (in various applications):—catch (away, up), pluck, pull, take (by force).

727. **ἅρπαξ harpax**, *har'-pax;* from *726; rapacious:*—extortion, ravening.

728. **ἀρραβών arrhabōn**, *ar-hrab-ohn';* of Heb. or. [6162]; a *pledge*, i.e. part of the purchase-money or property given in advance as *security* for the rest:—earnest.

729. **ἄρραφος arrhaphŏs**, *ar'-hhraf-os;* from *1* (as a neg. particle) and a presumed der. of the same as *4476; unsewed*, i.e. of a single piece:—without seam.

730. **ἄρρην arrhēn**, *ar'-hrane;* or
ἄρσην arsēn, *ar'-sane;* prob. from *142; male* (as stronger for *lifting*):—male, man.

731. **ἄρρητος arrhētŏs**, *ar'-hray-tos;* from *1* (as a neg. particle) and the same as *4490; unsaid*, i.e. (by impl.) *inexpressible:*—unspeakable.

732. **ἄρρωστος arrhōstŏs**, *ar'-hroce-tos;* from *1* (as a neg. particle) and a presumed der. of *4517; infirm:*—sick (folk, -ly).

733. **ἀρσενοκοίτης arsĕnŏkŏitēs**, *ar-sen-ok-oy'-tace;* from *730* and *2845;* a *sodomite:*—abuser of (that defile) self with mankind.

734. **Ἀρτεμᾶς Artĕmas**, *ar-tem-as';* contr. from a comp. of *735* and *1435; gift of Artemis; Artemas* (or *Artemidorus*), a Chr.:—Artemas.

735. **Ἄρτεμις Artĕmis**, *ar'-tem-is;* prob. from the same as *736; prompt; Artemis*, the name of a Grecian goddess borrowed by the Asiatics for one of their deities:—Diana.

736. **ἀρτέμων artĕmōn**, *ar-tem'-ohn;* from a der. of *737:* prop. something *ready* [or else more remotely from *142* (comp. *740*); something *hung* up], i.e. (spec.) the *topsail* (rather *foresail* or *jib*) of a vessel:—mainsail.

737. **ἄρτι arti**, *ar'-tee;* adv. from a der. of *142* (comp. *740*) through the idea of *suspension;* just *now:*—this day (hour), hence [-forth], here [-after], hither [-to], (even) now, (this) present.

738. **ἀρτιγέννητος artigĕnnētŏs**, *ar-teeg-en'-nay-tos;* from *737* and *1084; just born*, i.e. (fig.) a *young convert:*—new born.

739. **ἄρτιος artiŏs**, *ar'-tee-os;* from *737; fresh*, i.e. (by impl.) *complete:*—perfect.

740. **ἄρτος artos**, *ar'-tos;* from *142; bread* (as *raised*) or a *loaf:*—(shew-) bread, loaf.

741. **ἀρτύω artuō**, *ar-too'-o;* from a presumed der. of *142;* to *prepare*, i.e. *spice* (with *stimulating* condiments):—season.

742. **Ἀρφαξάδ Arphaxad**, *ar-fax-ad';* of Heb. or. [775]; *Arphaxad*, a post-diluvian patriarch:—Arphaxad.

743. **ἀρχάγγελος archaggĕlŏs**, *ar-khang'-el-os;* from *757* and *32;* a *chief angel:*—archangel.

744. **ἀρχαῖος archaiŏs**, *ar-khah'-yos;* from *746; original* or *primeval:*—(them of) old (time).

745. **Ἀρχέλαος Archĕlaŏs**, *ar-khel'-ah-os;* from *757* and *2994; people-ruling; Archelaus*, a Jewish king:—Archelaus.

746. **ἀρχή archē**, *ar-khay';* from *756;* (prop. abstr.) a *commencement*, or (concr.) *chief* (in various applications of order, time, place or rank):—beginning, corner, (at the, the) first (estate), magistrate, power, principality, principle, rule.

747. **ἀρχηγός archēgŏs**, *ar-khay-gos';* from *746* and *71;* a *chief leader:*—author, captain, prince.

748. **ἀρχιερατικός archiĕratikŏs**, *ar-khee-er-at-ee-kos';* from *746* and a der. of *2413; high-priestly:*—of the high-priest.

749. **ἀρχιερεύς archiĕrĕus**, *ar-khee-er-yuce';* from *746* and *2409;* the *high-priest* (lit. of the Jews, typ. Christ); by extens. a *chief priest:*—chief (high) priest, chief of the priests.

750. **ἀρχιποίμην archipŏimēn**, *ar-khee-poy'-mane;* from *746* and *4166;* a *head shepherd:*—chief shepherd.

751. **Ἄρχιππος Archippŏs**, *ar'-khip-pos;* from *746* and *2462; horse-ruler; Archippus*, a Chr.:—Archippus.

752. **ἀρχισυνάγωγος archisunagōgŏs**, *ar-khee-soon-ag'-o-gos;* from *746* and *4864; director of the synagogue* services:—(chief) ruler of the synagogue.

753. **ἀρχιτέκτων architĕktōn**, *ar-khee-tek'-tone;* from *746* and *5045;* a *chief constructor*, i.e. "*architect*":—masterbuilder.

754. **ἀρχιτελώνης architĕlōnēs**, *ar-khee-tel-o'-nace;* from *746* and *5057;* a *principal tax-gatherer:*—chief among the publicans.

755. **ἀρχιτρίκλινος architriklinŏs**, *ar-khee-tree'-klee-nos;* from *746* and a comp. of *5140* and *2827* (a *dinner-bed*, because composed of three couches); *director of* the *entertainment:*—governor (ruler) of the feast.

756. **ἄρχομαι archŏmai**, *ar'-khom-ahee;* mid. of *757* (through the impl. of *precedence*); to *commence* (in order of time):—(rehearse from the) begin (-ning).

757. **ἄρχω archō**, *ar'-kho;* a prim. verb; to be *first* (in political rank or power):—reign (rule) over.

758. **ἄρχων archōn**, *ar'-khone;* pres. part. of *757;* a *first* (in rank or power):—chief (ruler), magistrate, prince, ruler.

759. **ἄρωμα "arōma,"** *ar'-o-mah;* from *142* (in the sense of *sending* off scent); an *aromatic:*—(sweet) spice.

760. **Ἀσά Asa**, *as-ah';* of Heb. or. [609]; *Asa*, an Isr.:—Asa.

761. **ἀσάλευτος asalĕutŏs**, *as-al'-yoo-tos;* from *1* (as a neg. particle) and a der. of *4531; unshaken*, i.e. (by impl.) *immovable* (fig.):—which cannot be moved, unmovable.

762. **ἄσβεστος asbĕstŏs**, *as'-bes-tos;* from *1* (as a neg. particle) and a der. of *4570; not extinguished*, i.e. (by impl.) *perpetual:*—not to be quenched, unquenchable.

763. **ἀσέβεια asĕbĕia**, *as-eb'-i-ah;* from *765; impiety*, i.e. (by impl.) *wickedness:*—ungodly (-liness).

764. **ἀσεβέω asĕbĕō**, *as-eb-eh'-o;* from *765;* to *be* (by impl. *act*) *impious* or *wicked:*—commit (live, that after should live) ungodly.

765. **ἀσεβής asĕbēs**, *as-eb-ace';* from *1* (as a neg. particle) and a presumed der. of *4576; irreverent*, i.e. (by extens.) *impious* or *wicked:*—ungodly (man).

766. **ἀσέλγεια asĕlgĕia**, *as-elg'-i-a;* from a comp. of *1* (as a neg. particle) and a presumed **σελγής sĕlgēs** (of uncert. der., but appar. mean. *continent*); *licentiousness* (sometimes including other vices):—filthy, lasciviousness, wantonness.

767. **ἄσημος asēmŏs**, *as'-ay-mos;* from *1* (as a neg. particle) and the base of *4591; unmarked*, i.e. (fig.) *ignoble:*—mean.

768. **Ἀσήρ Asēr**, *as-ayr';* of Heb. or. [836]; *Aser* (i.e. *Asher*), an Isr. tribe:—Aser.

769. **ἀσθένεια asthĕnĕia**, *as-then'-i-ah;* from *772; feebleness* (of body or mind); by impl. *malady;* mor. *frailty:*—disease, infirmity, sickness, weakness.

770. **ἀσθενέω asthĕnĕō**, *as-then-eh'-o;* from *772;* to *be feeble* (in any sense):—be diseased, impotent folk (man), (be) sick, (be, be made) weak.

771. **ἀσθένημα asthĕnēma**, *as-then'-ay-mah;* from *770;* a *scruple* of conscience:—infirmity.

772. **ἀσθενής asthĕnēs**, *as-then-ace';* from *1* (as a neg. particle) and the base of *4599; strengthless* (in various applications, lit., fig. and mor.):—more feeble, impotent, sick, without strength, weak (-er, -ness, thing).

773. **Ἀσία Asia**, *as-ee'-ah;* of uncert. der.; *Asia*, i.e. *Asia Minor*, or (usually) only its western shore:—Asia.

774. **Ἀσιανός Asianŏs**, *as-ee-an-os';* from *773;* an *Asian* (i.e. *Asiatic*) or inhab. of Asia:—of Asia.

775. **Ἀσιάρχης Asiarchēs**, *as-ee ar'-khace;* from *773* and *746;* an *Asiarch* or president of the public festivities in a city of Asia Minor:—chief of Asia.

776. **ἀσιτία asitia**, *as-ee-tee'-ah;* from *777; fasting* (the state):—abstinence.

777. **ἄσιτος asitŏs**, *as'-ee-tos;* from *1* (as a neg. particle) and *4621; without* (taking) *food:*—fasting.

778. **ἀσκέω askĕō**, *as-keh'-o;* prob. from the same as *4632;* to *elaborate*, i.e. (fig.) *train* (by impl. *strive*):—exercise.

779. **ἀσκός askŏs**, *as-kos';* from the same as *778;* a leathern (or skin) *bag* used as a bottle:—bottle.

780. **ἀσμένως asmĕnōs**, *as-men'-oce;* adv. from a der. of the base of *2237; with pleasure:*—gladly.

781. **ἄσοφος asŏphŏs**, *as'-of-os;* from *1* (as a neg. particle) and *4680; unwise:*—fool.

782. **ἀσπάζομαι aspazŏmai**, *as-pad'-zom-ahee;* from *1* (as a particle of union) and a presumed form of *4685;* to *enfold* in the arms, i.e. (by impl.) to *salute*, (fig.) to *welcome:*—embrace, greet, salute, take leave.

783. **ἀσπασμός aspasmŏs**, *as-pas-mos';* from *782;* a *greeting* (in person or by letter):—greeting, salutation.

784. **ἄσπιλος aspilŏs**, *as'-pee-los;* from *1* (as a neg. particle) and *4695; unblemished* (phys. or mor.):—without spot, unspotted.

785. **ἀσπίς aspis**, *as-pece';* of uncert. der.; a *buckler* (or *round* shield); used of a serpent (as *coiling* itself), prob. the "*asp*":—asp.

786. **ἄσπονδος aspŏndŏs**, *as'-pon-dos;* from *1* (as a neg. particle) and a der. of *4689;* lit. *without libation* (which usually accompanied a treaty), i.e. (by impl.) *truceless:*—implacable, truce-breaker.

787. **ἀσσάριον assariŏn**, *as-sar'-ee-on;* of Lat. or.; an *assarius* or *as*, a Roman coin:—farthing.

788. **ἆσσον assŏn**, *as'-son;* neut. comparative of the base of *1451; more nearly*, i.e. *very near:*—close.

789. **Ἄσσος Assŏs**, *as'-sos;* prob. of for. or.; *Assus*, a city of Asia Minor:—Assos.

790. **ἀστατέω astatĕō**, *as-tat-eh'-o;* from *1* (as a neg. particle) and a der. of *2476;* to *be non-stationary*, i.e. (fig.) *homeless:*—have no certain dwelling-place.

791. **ἀστεῖος astĕiŏs**, *as-ti'-os;* from **ἄστυ astu** (a *city*); *urbane*, i.e. (by impl.) *handsome:*—fair.

792. **ἀστήρ astēr**, *as-tare';* prob. from the base of *4766;* a *star* (as *strown* over the sky), lit. or fig.:—star.

793. **ἀστήρικτος astēriktŏs**, *as-tay'-rik-tos;* from *1* (as a neg. particle) and a presumed der. of *4741;* *unfixed*, i.e. (fig.) *vacillating:*—unstable.

794. **ἄστοργος astŏrgŏs**, *as'-tor-gos;* from *1* (as a neg. particle) and a presumed der. of **στέργω stĕrgō** (to *cherish* affectionately); *hard-hearted* towards kindred:—without natural affection.

795. **ἀστοχέω astŏchĕō**, *as-tokh-eh'-o;* from a comp. of *1* (as a neg. particle) and **στόιχος stŏichŏs** (an *aim*); to *miss* the mark, i.e. (fig.) *deviate* from truth:—err, swerve.

796. **ἀστραπή astrapē**, *as-trap-ay';* from *797;* *lightning;* by anal. *glare:*—lightning, bright shining.

797. **ἀστράπτω astraptō**, *as-trap'-to;* prob. from *792;* to *flash* as lightning:—lighten, shine.

798. **ἄστρον astrŏn**, *as'-tron;* neut. from *792;* prop. a *constellation;* put for a single *star* (nat. or artificial):—star.

799. **Ἀσύγκριτος Asugkritŏs**, *as-oong'-kree-tos;* from *1* (as a neg. particle) and a der. of *4793;* *incomparable; Asyncritus*, a Chr.:—Asyncritus.

800. **ἀσύμφωνος asumphōnŏs**, *as-oom'-fo-nos;* from *1* (as a neg. particle) and *4859;* *inharmonious* (fig.):—agree not.

801. **ἀσύνετος asunĕtŏs**, *as-oon'-ay-tos;* from *1* (as a neg. particle) and *4908;* *unintelligent;* by impl. *wicked:*—foolish, without understanding.

802. **ἀσύνθετος asunthĕtŏs**, *as-oon'-thet-os;* from *1* (as a neg. particle) and a der. of *4934;* prop. *not agreed*, i.e. *treacherous* to compacts:—covenant-breaker.

803. **ἀσφάλεια asphalĕia**, *as-fal'-i-ah;* from *804;* *security* (lit. or fig.):—certainty, safety.

804. **ἀσφαλής asphalēs**, *as-fal-ace';* from *1* (as a neg. particle) and **σφάλλω sphallō** (to "*fail*"); *secure* (lit. or fig.):—certain (-ty), safe, sure.

805. **ἀσφαλίζω asphalizō**, *as-fal-id'-zo;* from *804;* to *render secure:*—make fast (sure).

806. **ἀσφαλῶς asphalōs**, *as-fal-oce';* adv. from *804;* *securely* (lit. or fig.):—assuredly, safely.

807. **ἀσχημονέω aschēmŏnĕō**, *as-kay-mon-eh'-o;* from *809;* to *be* (i.e. *act*) *unbecoming:*—behave self uncomely (unseemly).

808. **ἀσχημοσύνη aschēmŏsunē**, *as-kay-mos-oo'-nay;* from *809;* an *indecency;* by impl. the *pudenda:*—shame, that which is unseemly.

809. **ἀσχήμων askēmōn**, *as-kay'-mone;* from *1* (as a neg. particle) and a presumed der. of *2192* (in the sense of its congener *4976*); prop. *shapeless*, i.e. (fig.) *inelegant:*—uncomely.

810. **ἀσωτία asōtia**, *as-o-tee'-ah;* from a comp. of *1* (as a neg. particle) and a presumed der. of *4982;* prop. *unsavedness*, i.e. (by impl.) *profligacy:*—excess, riot.

811. **ἀσώτως asōtōs**, *as-o'-toce;* adv. from the same as *810;* *dissolutely:*—riotous.

812. **ἀτακτέω ataktĕō**, *at-ak-teh'-o;* from *813;* to *be* (i.e. *act*) *irregular:*—behave self disorderly.

813. **ἄτακτος ataktŏs**, *at'-ak-tos;* from *1* (as a neg. particle) and a der. of *5021;* *unarranged*, i.e. (by impl.) *insubordinate* (religiously):—unruly.

814. **ἀτάκτως ataktōs**, *at-ak'-toce;* adv. from *813;* *irregularly* (mor.):—disorderly.

815. **ἄτεκνος atĕknŏs**, *at'-ek-nos;* from *1* (as a neg. particle) and *5043;* *childless:*—childless, without children.

816. **ἀτενίζω atĕnizō**, *at-en-id'-zo;* from a comp. of *1* (as a particle of union) and **τείνω tĕinō** (to *stretch*); to *gaze* intently:—behold earnestly (stedfastly), fasten (eyes), look (earnestly, stedfastly, up stedfastly), set eyes.

817. **ἄτερ atĕr**, *at'-er;* a particle prob. akin to *427;* *aloof*, i.e. *apart* from (lit. or fig.):—in the absence of, without.

818. **ἀτιμάζω atimazō**, *at-im-ad'-zo;* from *820;* to *render infamous*, i.e. (by impl.) *contemn* or *maltreat:*—despise, dishonour, suffer shame, entreat shamefully.

819. **ἀτιμία atimia**, *at-ee-mee'-ah;* from *820;* *infamy*, i.e. (subj.) comparative *indignity*, (obj.) *disgrace:*—dishonour, reproach, shame, vile.

820. **ἄτιμος atimŏs**, *at'-ee-mos;* from *1* (as a neg. particle) and *5092;* (neg.) *unhonoured* or (pos.) *dishonoured:*—despised, without honour, less honourable [*comparative degree*].

821. **ἀτιμόω atimŏō**, *at-ee-mŏ'-o;* from *820;* used like *818*, to *maltreat:*—handle shamefully.

822. **ἀτμίς atmis**, *at-mece';* from the same as *109;* *mist:*—vapour.

823. **ἄτομος atŏmŏs**, *at'-om-os;* from *1* (as a neg. particle) and the base of *5114;* *uncut*, i.e. (by impl.) *indivisible* [an "*atom*" of time]:—moment.

824. **ἄτοπος atŏpŏs**, *at'-op-os;* from *1* (as a neg. particle) and *5117;* *out of place*, i e. (fig.) *improper, injurious, wicked:*—amiss, harm, unreasonable.

825. **Ἀττάλεια Attalĕia**, *at-tal'-i-ah;* from **Ἄτταλος Attalŏs** (a king of Pergamus); *Attaleia*, a place in Pamphylia:—Attalia.

826. **αὐγάζω augazō**, *ŏw-gad'-zo;* from *827;* to *beam* forth (fig.):—shine.

827. **αὐγή augē**, *ŏwg'-ay;* of uncert. der.; a *ray* of light, i.e. (by impl.) *radiance, dawn:*—break of day.

828. **Αὔγουστος Augŏustŏs**, *ŏw'-goos-tos;* from Lat. ["august"]; *Augustus*, a title of the Rom. emperor:—Augustus.

829. **αὐθάδης authadēs**, *ŏw-thad'-ace;* from *846* and the base of *2237;* *self-pleasing*, i.e. *arrogant:*—self-willed.

830. **αὐθαίρετος authairĕtŏs**, *ŏw-thah'ee-ret-os;* from *846* and the same as *140;* *self-chosen*, i.e. (by impl.) *voluntary:*—of own accord, willing of self.

831. **αὐθεντέω authĕntĕō**, *ŏw-then-teh'-o;* from a comp. of *846* and an obsol. **ἕντης hĕntēs** (a *worker*); to *act of oneself*, i.e. (fig.) *dominate:*—usurp authority over.

832. **αὐλέω aulĕō**, *ŏw-leh'-o;* from *836;* to play the *flute:*—pipe.

833. **αὐλή aulē**, *ŏw-lay';* from the same as *109;* a *yard* (as open to the *wind*); by impl. a *mansion:*—court, ([sheep-]) fold, hall, palace.

834. **αὐλητής aulētēs**, *ŏw-lay-tace';* from *832;* a *flute-player:*—minstrel, piper.

835. **αὐλίζομαι aulizŏmai**, *ŏw-lid'-zom-ahee;* mid. from *833;* to *pass the night* (prop. in the open air):—abide, lodge.

836. **αὐλός aulŏs**, *ŏw-los';* from the same as *109*, a *flute* (as *blown*):—pipe.

837. **αὐξάνω auxanō**, *ŏwx-an'-o;* a prolonged form of a prim. verb; to *grow* ("*wax*"), i.e. *enlarge* (lit. or fig., act. or pass.):—grow (up), (give the) increase.

838. **αὔξησις auxēsis**, *ŏwx'-ay-sis;* from *837;* *growth:*—increase.

839. **αὔριον auriŏn**, *ŏw'-ree-on;* from a der. of the same as *109* (mean. a *breeze*, i.e. the morning *air*); prop. *fresh*, i.e. (adv. with ellipsis of *2250*) *to-morrow:*—(to-) morrow, next day.

840. **αὐστηρός austērŏs**, *ŏw-stay-ros';* from a (presumed) der. of the same as *109* (mean. *blown*); *rough* (prop. as a *gale*), i.e. (fig.) *severe:*—austere.

841. **αὐτάρκεια autarkeia**, *ŏw-tar'-ki-ah;* from *842;* *self-satisfaction*, i.e. (abstr.) *contentedness*, or (concr.) a *competence:*—contentment, sufficiency.

842. **αὐτάρκης autarkēs**, *ŏw-tar'-kace;* from *846* and *714;* *self-complacent*, i.e. *contented:*—content.

843. **αὐτοκατάκριτος autŏkatakritŏs**, *ŏw-tok-at-ak'-ree-tos;* from *846* and a der. of *2632;* *self-condemned:*—condemned of self.

844. **αὐτόματος autŏmatŏs**, *ŏw-tom'-at-os;* from *846* and the same as *3155;* *self-moved* ["automatic"], i.e. *spontaneous:*—of own accord, of self.

845. **αὐτόπτης autŏptēs**, *ŏw-top'-tace;* from *846* and *3700;* *self-seeing*, i.e. an *eye-witness:*—eye-witness.

846. **αὐτός autŏs**, *ŏw-tos';* from the particle **αὖ au** [perh. akin to the base of *109* through the idea of a *baffling* wind] (*backward*); the reflex. pron. *self*, used (alone or in the comp. *1438*) of the third pers., and (with the prop. pers. pron.) of the other persons:—her, it (-self), one, the other, (mine) own, said, ([self-], the) same, ([him-, my-, thy-]) self, [your-] selves, she, that, their (-s), them ([-selves]), there [-at, -by, -in, -into, -of, -on, -with], they, (these) things, this (man), those, together, very, which. Comp. *848*.

847. **αὐτοῦ autŏu**, *ŏw-too';* genitive (i.e. possessive) of *846*, used as an adv. of location; prop. belonging to the *same* spot, i.e. *in this* (or *that*) *place:*—(t-) here.

848. **αὑτοῦ hautŏu**, *how-too';* contr. for *1438;* *self* (in some oblique case or reflex. relation):—her (own), (of) him (-self), his (own), of it, thee, their (own), them (-selves), they.

849. **αὐτόχειρ autŏchĕir**, *ŏw-tokh'-ire;* from *846* and *5495;* *self-handed*, i.e. doing *personally:*—with . . . own hands.

850. **αὐχμηρός auchmērŏs**, *ŏwkh-may-ros';* from **αὐχμός auchmŏs** [prob. from a base akin to that of *109*] (*dust*, as *dried* by wind); prop. *dirty*, i.e. (by impl.) *obscure:*—dark.

851. **ἀφαιρέω aphairĕō**, *af-ahee-reh'-o;* from *575* and *138;* to *remove* (lit. or fig.):—cut (smite) off, take away.

852. **ἀφανής aphanēs**, *af-an-ace';* from *1* (as a neg. particle) and *5316;* *non-apparent:*—that is not manifest.

853. **ἀφανίζω aphanizō**, *af-an-id'-zo;* from *852;* to *render unapparent*, i.e. (act.) *consume* (*becloud*), or (pass.) *disappear* (*be destroyed*):—corrupt, disfigure, perish, vanish away.

854. **ἀφανισμός aphanismŏs**, *af-an-is-mos';* from *853;* *disappearance*, i.e. (fig.) *abrogation:*—vanish away.

855. **ἄφαντος aphantŏs**, *af'-an-tŏs;* from *1* (as a neg. particle) and a der. of *5316;* *non-manifested*, i.e. *invisible:*—vanished out of sight.

856. **ἀφεδρών aphĕdrōn**, *af-ed-rone';* from a comp. of *575* and the base of *1476;* a place of *sitting apart*, i.e. a *privy:*—draught.

857. **ἀφειδία aphĕidia**, *af-i-dee'-ah;* from a comp. of *1* (as a neg. particle) and *5339;* *unsparingness*, i.e. *austerity* (*ascetism*):—neglecting.

858. **ἀφελότης aphĕlŏtēs**, *af-el-ot'-ace;* from a comp. of *1* (as a neg. particle) and **φέλλος phĕllŏs** (in the sense of a *stone* as *stubbing* the foot); *smoothness*, i.e. (fig.) *simplicity:*—singleness.

859. **ἄφεσις aphĕsis**, *af'-es-is;* from *863;* *freedom;* (fig.) *pardon:*—deliverance, forgiveness, liberty, remission.

860. **ἁφή haphē**, *haf-ay';* from *680;* prob. a *ligament* (as *fastening*):—joint.

861. **ἀφθαρσία aphtharsia**, *af-thar-see'-ah;* from *862;* *incorruptibility;* gen. *unending existence;* (fig.) *genuineness:*—immortality, incorruption, sincerity.

862. **ἄφθαρτος aphthartŏs**, *af'-thar-tos;* from *1* (as a neg. particle) and a der. of *5351;* *undecaying* (in essence or continuance):—not (in-, un-) corruptible, immortal.

863. **ἀφίημι aphiēmi**, *af-ee'-ay-mee;* from *575* and **ἵημι hiemi** (to *send;* an intens. form of **εἶμι ĕimi**, to *go*); to *send forth*, in various applications (as follow):—cry, forgive, forsake, lay aside, leave, let (alone, be, go, have), omit, put (send) away, remit, suffer, yield up.

864. **ἀφικνέομαι aphiknĕŏmai**, *af-ik-neh'-om-ahee;* from *575* and the base of *2425;* to *go* (i.e. *spread*) *forth* (by rumor):—come abroad.

865. **ἀφιλάγαθος aphilagathŏs**, *af-il-ag'-ath-os;* from *1* (as a neg. particle) and *5358;* *hostile to virtue:*—despiser of those that are good.

866. **ἀφιλάργυρος aphilargurŏs**, *af-il-ar'-goo-ros;* from *1* (as a neg. particle) and *5366;* *unavaricious:*—without covetousness, not greedy of filthy lucre.

867. **ἄφιξις aphixis**, *af'-ix-is;* from *864;* prop. *arrival*, i.e. (by impl.) *departure:*—departing.

868. **ἀφίστημι aphistēmi**, *af-is'-tay-mee;* from *575* and *2476;* to *remove*, i.e. (act.) *instigate* to revolt;

usually (reflex.) to *desist, desert,* etc.:—depart, draw (fall) away, refrain, withdraw self.

869. ἄφνω **aphnō**, *af'-no;* adv. from *852* (contr.); *unawares,* i.e. *unexpectedly:*—suddenly.

870. ἀφόβως **aphŏbōs**, *af-ob'-oce;* adv. from a comp. of *1* (as a neg. particle) and *5401; fearlessly:*—without fear.

871. ἀφομοιόω **aphŏmŏiŏō**, *af-om-oy-ŏ'-o;* from *575* and *3666;* to *assimilate* closely:—make like.

872. ἀφοράω **aphŏraō**, *af-or-ah'-o;* from *575* and *3708;* to *consider* attentively:—look.

873. ἀφορίζω **aphŏrizō**, *af-or-id'-zo;* from *575* and *3724;* to *set off* by boundary, i.e. (fig.) *limit, exclude, appoint,* etc.:—divide, separate, sever.

874. ἀφορμή **aphŏrmē**, *af-or-may';* from a comp. of *575* and *3729;* a *starting*-point, i.e. (fig.) an *opportunity:*—occasion.

875. ἀφρίζω **aphrizō**, *af-rid'-zo;* from *876;* to *froth* at the mouth (in epilepsy):—foam.

876. ἀφρός **aphrŏs**, *af-ros';* appar. a prim. word; *froth,* i.e. *slaver:*—foaming.

877. ἀφροσύνη **aphrŏsunē**, *af-ros-oo'-nay;* from *878; senselessness,* i.e. (euphem.) *egotism;* (mor.) *recklessness:*—folly, foolishly (-ness).

878. ἄφρων **aphrōn**, *af'-rone;* from *1* (as a neg. particle) and *5424;* prop. *mindless,* i.e. *stupid,* (by impl.) *ignorant,* (spec.) *egotistic,* (practically) *rash,* or (mor.) *unbelieving:*—fool (-ish), unwise.

879. ἀφυπνόω **aphupnŏō**, *af-oop-nŏ'-o;* from a comp. of *575* and *5258;* prop. to *become awake,* i.e. (by impl.) to *drop* (off) in slumber:—fall asleep.

880. ἄφωνος **aphōnŏs**, *af'-o-nos;* from *1* (as a neg. particle) and *5456; voiceless,* i.e. *mute* (by nature or choice); fig. *unmeaning:*—dumb, without signification.

881. Ἀχάζ **Achaz**, *akh-adz';* of Heb. or. [271]; *Achaz,* an Isr.:—Achaz.

882. Ἀχαΐα **Achaïa**, *ach-ah-ee'-ah;* of uncert. der.; *Achaïa* (i.e. *Greece*), a country of Europe:—Achaia.

883. Ἀχαϊκός **Achaïkŏs**, *ach-ah-ee-kos';* from *882;* an *Achaïan; Achaïcus,* a Chr.:—Achaicus.

884. ἀχάριστος **acharistŏs**, *ach-ar'-is-tos;* from *1* (as a neg. particle) and a presumed der. of *5483; thankless,* i.e. *ungrateful:*—unthankful.

885. Ἀχείμ **Achĕim**, *akh-ime';* prob. of Heb. or. [comp. 3137]; *Achim,* an Isr.:—Achim.

886. ἀχειροποίητος **achĕirŏpŏiētŏs**, *akh-i-ropoy'-ay-tos;* from *1* (as a neg. particle) and *5499; unmanufactured,* i.e. *inartificial:*—made without (not made with) hands.

887. ἀχλύς **achlus**, *akh-looce';* of uncert. der.; *dimness* of sight, i.e. (prob.) a *cataract:*—mist.

888. ἀχρεῖος **achrĕiŏs**, *akh-ri'-os;* from *1* (as a neg. particle) and a der. of *5534* [comp. *5532*]; *useless,* i.e. (euphem.) *unmeritorious:*—unprofitable.

889. ἀχρειόω **achrĕiŏō**, *akh-ri-ŏ'-o;* from *888;* to *render useless,* i.e. *spoil:*—become unprofitable.

890. ἄχρηστος **achrēstŏs**, *akh'-race-tos;* from *1* (as a neg. particle) and *5543; inefficient,* i.e. (by impl.) *detrimental:*—unprofitable.

891. ἄχρι **achri**, *akh'-ree;* or ἄχρις **achris**, *akh'-rece;* akin to *206* (through the idea of a *terminus*); (of time) *until* or (of place) *up to:*—as far as, for, in (-to), till, (even, un-) to, until, while. Comp. *3360.*

892. ἄχυρον **achurŏn**, *akh'-oo-ron;* perh. remotely from χέω **chĕō** (to *shed* forth); *chaff* (as *diffusive*):—chaff.

893. ἀψευδής **apsĕudēs**, *aps-yoo-dace';* from *1* (as a neg. particle) and *5579; veracious:*—that cannot lie.

894. ἄψινθος **apsinthŏs**, *ap'-sin-thos;* of uncert. der.; *wormwood* (as a type of *bitterness,* i.e. [fig.] *calamity*):—wormwood.

895. ἄψυχος **apsuchŏs**, *ap'-soo-khos;* from *1* (as a neg. particle) and *5590; lifeless,* i.e. *inanimate* (mechanical):—without life.

B

896. Βάαλ **Baal**, *bah'-al;* of Heb. or. [1168]; *Baal,* a Phœnician deity (used as a symbol of idolatry):—Baal.

897. Βαβυλών **Babulōn**, *bab-oo-lone';* of Heb. or. [894]; *Babylon,* the capital of Chaldæa (lit. or fig. [as a type of tyranny]):—Babylon.

898. βαθμός **bathmŏs**, *bath-mos';* from the same as *899;* a *step,* i.e. (fig.) *grade* (of dignity):—degree.

899. βάθος **bathŏs**, *bath'-os;* from the same as *901; profundity,* i.e. (by impl.) *extent;* (fig.) *mystery:*—deep (-ness, things), depth.

900. βαθύνω **bathunō**, *bath-oo'-no;* from *901;* to *deepen:*—deep.

901. βαθύς **bathus**, *bath-oos';* from the base of *939; profound* (as *going* down), lit. or fig.:—deep, very early.

902. βαΐον **baïŏn**, *bah-ee'-on;* a diminutive of a der. prob. of the base of *939;* a palm *twig* (as *going* out far):—branch.

903. Βαλαάμ **Balaam**, *bal-ah-am';* of Heb. or. [1109]; *Balaam,* a Mesopotamian (symb. of a false teacher):—Balaam.

904. Βαλάκ **Balak**, *bal-ak';* of Heb. or. [1111]; *Balak,* a Moabite:—Balac.

905. βαλάντιον **balantiŏn**, *bal-an'-tee-on;* prob. remotely from *906* (as a *depository*); a *pouch* (for money):—bag, purse.

906. βάλλω **ballō**, *bal'-lo;* a prim. verb; to *throw* (in various applications, more or less violent or intense):—arise, cast (out), × dung, lay, lie, pour, put (up), send, strike, throw (down), thrust. Comp. *4496.*

907. βαπτίζω **baptizō**, *bap-tid'-zo;* from a der. of *911;* to *make whelmed* (i.e. *fully wet*); used only (in the N. T.) of ceremonial *ablution,* espec. (techn.) of the ordinance of Chr. *baptism:*—baptist, baptize, wash.

908. βάπτισμα **baptisma**, *bap'-tis-mah;* from *907; baptism* (techn. or fig.):—baptism.

909. βαπτισμός **baptismŏs**, *bap-tis-mos';* from *907; ablution* (cerem. or Chr.):—baptism, washing.

910. Βαπτιστής **Baptistēs**, *bap-tis-tace';* from *907;* a *baptizer,* as an epithet of Christ's forerunner:—Baptist.

911. βάπτω **baptō**, *bap'-to;* a prim. verb; to *whelm,* i.e. cover wholly with a fluid; in the N. T. only in a qualified or spec. sense, i.e. (lit.) to *moisten* (a part of one's person), or (by impl.) to *stain* (as with dye):—dip.

912. Βαραββᾶς **Barabbas**, *bar-ab-bas';* of Chald. or. [1247 and *5*]; *son of Abba; Bar-abbas,* an Isr.:—Barabbas.

913. Βαράκ **Barak**, *bar-ak';* of Heb. or. [1301]; *Barak,* an Isr.:—Barak.

914. Βαραχίας **Barachias**, *bar-akh-ee'-as;* of Heb. or. [1296]; *Barachias* (i.e. *Berechijah*), an Isr.:—Barachias.

915. βάρβαρος **barbarŏs**, *bar'-bar-os;* of uncert. der.; a *foreigner* (i.e. *non-Greek*):—barbarian (-rous).

916. βαρέω **barĕō**, *bar-eh'-o;* from *926;* to *weigh* down (fig.):—burden, charge, heavy, press.

917. βαρέως **barĕōs**, *bar-eh'-oce;* adv. from *926; heavily* (fig.):—dull.

918. Βαρθολομαῖος **Barthŏlŏmaiŏs**, *bar-thol-om-ah'-yos;* of Chald. or. [1247 and 8526]; *son of Tolmai; Bar-tholomæus,* a Chr. apostle:—Bartholomeus.

919. Βαριησοῦς **Bariēsŏus**, *bar-ee-ay-sooce';* of Chald. or. [1247 and 3091]; *son of Jesus* (or *Joshua*); *Bar-jesus,* an Isr.:—Barjesus.

920. Βαριωνᾶς **Bariōnas**, *bar-ee-oo-nas';* of Chald. or. [1247 and 3124]; *son of Jonas* (or *Jonah*); *Bar-jonas,* an Isr.:—Bar-jona.

921. Βαρνάβας **Barnabas**, *bar-nab'-as;* of Chald. or. [1247 and 5029]; *son of Nabas* (i.e. *prophecy*); *Barnabas,* an Isr.:—Barnabas.

922. βάρος **barŏs**, *bar'-os;* prob. from the same as *939* (through the notion of *going* down; comp. *899*); *weight;* in the N. T. only fig. a *load, abundance, authority:*—burden (-some), weight.

923. Βαρσαβᾶς **Barsabas**, *bar-sab-as';* of Chald. or. [1247 and prob. 6634]; *son of Sabas* (or *Tsaba*); *Bar-sabas,* the name of two Isr.:—Barsabas.

924. Βαρτιμαῖος **Bartimaiŏs**, *bar-tim-ah'-yos;* of Chald. or. [1247 and 2931]; *son of Timæus* (or the *unclean*); *Bar-timæus,* an Isr.:—Bartimæus.

925. βαρύνω **barunō**, *bar-oo'-no;* from *926;* to *burden* (fig.):—overcharge.

926. βαρύς **barus**, *bar-ooce';* from the same as *922; weighty,* i.e. (fig.) *burdensome, grave:*—grievous, heavy, weightier.

927. βαρύτιμος **barutimŏs**, *bar-oo'-tim-os;* from *926* and *5092;* highly *valuable:*—very precious.

928. βασανίζω **basanizō**, *bas-an-id'-zo;* from *931;* to *torture:*—pain, toil, torment, toss, vex.

929. βασανισμός **basanismŏs**, *bas-an-is-mos';* from *928; torture:*—torment.

930. βασανιστής **basanistēs**, *bas-an-is-tace';* from *928;* a *torturer:*—tormentor.

931. βάσανος **basanŏs**, *bas'-an-os;* perh. remotely from the same as *939* (through the notion of *going* to the bottom); a *touch-stone,* i.e. (by anal.) *torture:*—torment.

932. βασιλεία **basilĕia**, *bas-il-i'-ah;* from *935;* prop. *royalty,* i.e. (abstr.) *rule,* or (concr.) a *realm* (lit. or fig.):—kingdom, + reign.

933. βασίλειον **basilĕiŏn**, *bas-il'-i-on;* neut. of *934;* a *palace:*—king's court.

934. βασίλειος **basilĕiŏs**, *bas-il'-i-os;* from *935; kingly* (in nature):—royal.

935. βασιλεύς **basilĕus**, *bas-il-yooce';* prob. from *939* (through the notion of a *foundation* of power); a *sovereign* (abs., rel. or fig.):—king.

936. βασιλεύω **basilĕuō**, *bas-il-yoo'-o;* from *935;* to *rule* (lit. or fig.):—king, reign.

937. βασιλικός **basilikŏs**, *bas-il-ee-kos';* from *935; regal* (in relation), i.e. (lit.) belonging to (or befitting) the sovereign (as land, dress, or a *courtier*), or (fig.) *preeminent:*—king's, nobleman, royal.

938. βασίλισσα **basilissa**, *bas-il'-is-sah;* fem. from *936;* a *queen:*—queen.

939. βάσις **basis**, *bas'-ece;* from βαίνω **bainō** (to *walk*); a *pace* ("base"), i.e. (by impl.) the *foot:*—foot.

940. βασκαίνω **baskainō**, *bas-kah'ee-no;* akin to *5335;* to *malign,* i.e. (by extens.) to *fascinate* (by false representations):—bewitch.

941. βαστάζω **bastazō**, *bas-tad'-zo;* perh. remotely der. from the base of *939* (through the idea of *removal*); to *lift,* lit. or fig. (*endure, declare, sustain, receive,* etc.):—bear, carry, take up.

942. βάτος **batŏs**, *bat'-os;* of uncert. der.; a *brier* shrub:—bramble, bush.

943. βάτος **batŏs**, *bat'-os;* of Heb. or. [1324]; a *bath,* or measure for liquids:—measure.

944. βάτραχος **batrachŏs**, *bat'-rakh-os;* of uncert. der.; a *frog:*—frog.

945. βαττολογέω **battŏlŏgĕō**, *bat-tol-og-eh'-o;* from Βάττος **Battŏs** (a proverbial stammerer) and *3056;* to *stutter,* i.e. (by impl.) to *prate* tediously:—use vain repetitions.

946. βδέλυγμα **bdĕlugma**, *bdel'-oog-mah;* from *948;* a *detestation,* i.e. (spec.) *idolatry:*—abomination.

947. βδελυκτός **bdĕluktŏs**, *bdel-ook-tos';* from *948; detestable,* i.e. (spec.) *idolatrous:*—abominable.

948. βδελύσσω **bdĕlussō**, *bdel-oos'-so;* from a (presumed) der. of βδέω **bdĕō** (to *stink*); to *be disgusted,* i.e. (by impl.) *detest* (espec. of idolatry):—abhor, abominable.

949. βέβαιος **bĕbaiŏs**, *beb'-ah-yos;* from the base of *939* (through the idea of *basality*); *stable* (lit. or fig.):—firm, of force, stedfast, sure.

950. βεβαιόω **bĕbaiŏō**, *beb-ah-yŏ'-o;* from *949;* to *stabilitate* (fig.):—confirm, (e-) stablish.

951. βεβαίωσις **bĕbaiōsis**, *beb-ah'-yo-sis;* from *950; stabiliment:*—confirmation.

952. βέβηλος **bĕbēlŏs**, *beb'-ay-los;* from the base of *939* and βηλός **bēlŏs** (a *threshold*); *accessible* (as by *crossing the door-way*), i.e. (by impl. of Jewish notions) *heathenish, wicked*:—profane (person).

953. βεβηλόω **bĕbēlŏō**, *beb-ay-lŏ'-o;* from *952;* to *desecrate*:—profane.

954. Βεελζεβούλ **Bĕĕlzĕbŏul**, *beh-el-zeb-ool';* of Chald. or. [by parody upon 1176]; *dung-god; Beelzebul,* a name of Satan:—Beelzebub.

955. Βελίαλ **Bĕlial**, *bel-ee'-al;* of Heb. or. [1100]; *worthlessness; Belial,* as an epithet of Satan:—Belial.

956. βέλος **bĕlŏs**, *bel'-os;* from *906;* a *missile,* i.e. *spear* or *arrow*:—dart.

957. βελτίον **bĕltiŏn**, *bel-tee'-on;* neut. of a comp. of a der. of *906* (used for the comp. of *18*); *better*:—very well.

958. Βενιαμίν **Bĕniamin**, *ben-ee-am-een';* of Heb. or. [1144]; *Benjamin,* an Isr.:—Benjamin.

959. Βερνίκη **Bĕrnikē**, *ber-nee'-kay;* from a provincial form of *5342* and *3529; victorious; Bernicè,* a member of the Herodian family:—Bernice.

960. Βέροια **Bĕrŏia**, *ber'-oy-ah;* perh. a provincial from a der. of *4008* [*Peræa,* i.e. the region *beyond* the coast-line]; *Berœa,* a place in Macedonia:—Berea.

961. Βεροιαῖος **Bĕrŏiaiŏs**, *ber-oy-ah'-yos;* from *960;* a *Berœæan* or native of Berœa:—of Berea.

962. Βηθαβαρά **Bēthabara**, *bay-thab-ar-ah';* of Heb. or. [1004 and 5679]; *ferry-house; Bethabara* (i.e. *Bethabarah*), a place on the Jordan:—Bethabara.

963. Βηθανία **Bēthania**, *bay-than-ee'-ah;* of Chald. or.; *date-house; Beth-any,* a place in Pal.:—Bethany.

964. Βηθεσδά **Bēthĕsda**, *bay-thes-dah';* of Chald. or. [comp. 1004 and 2617]; *house of kindness; Beth-esda,* a pool in Jerus.:—Bethesda.

965. Βηθλεέμ **Bēthlĕĕm**, *bayth-leh-em';* of Heb. or. [1036]; *Bethleem* (i.e. *Beth-lechem*), a place in Pal.:—Bethlehem.

966. Βηθσαϊδά **Bēthsaïda**, *bayth-sahee-dah';* of Chald. or. [comp. 1004 and 6719]; *fishing-house; Beth-saïda,* a place in Pal.:—Bethsaida.

967. Βηθφαγή **Bēthphagē**, *bayth-fag-ay';* of Chald. or. [comp. 1004 and 6291]; *fig-house; Beth-phagè,* a place in Pal.:—Bethphage.

968. βῆμα **bēma**, *bay'-ma;* from the base of *939;* a *step,* i.e. *foot-breath;* by impl. a **rostrum**, i.e. *tribunal*:—judgment-seat, set [foot] on, throne.

969. βήρυλλος **bērullŏs**, *bay'-rool-los;* of uncert. der.; a "*beryl*":—beryl.

970. βία **bia**, *bee'-ah;* prob. akin to *979* (through the idea of *vital* activity); *force*:—violence.

971. βιάζω **biazō**, *bee-ad'-zo;* from *970;* to *force,* i.e. (reflex.) to *crowd oneself* (into), or (pass.) to *be seized*:—press, suffer violence.

972. βίαιος **biaiŏs**, *bee'-ah-yos;* from *970; violent*:—mighty.

973. βιαστής **biastēs**, *bee-as-tace';* from *971;* a *forcer,* i.e. (fig.) *energetic*:—violent.

974. βιβλιαρίδιον **bibliaridiŏn**, *bib-lee-ar-id'-ee-on;* a dimin. of *975;* a *booklet*:—little book.

975. βιβλίον **bibliŏn**, *bib-lee'-on;* a dimin. of *976;* a *roll*:—bill, book, scroll, writing.

976. βίβλος **biblŏs**, *bib'-los;* prop. the inner *bark* of the papyrus plant, i.e. (by impl.) a *sheet* or *scroll* of writing:—book.

977. βιβρώσκω **bibrōskō**, *bib-ro'-sko;* a reduplicated and prolonged form of an obsol. prim. verb [perh. causative of *1006*]; to *eat*:—eat.

978. Βιθυνία **Bithunia**, *bee-thoo-nee'-ah;* of uncert. der.; *Bithynia,* a region of Asia:—Bithynia.

979. βίος **biŏs**, *bee'-os;* a prim. word; *life,* i.e. (lit.) the present state of existence; by impl. the means of *livelihood*:—good, life, living.

980. βιόω **biŏō**, *bee-ŏ'-o;* from *979;* to *spend existence*:—live.

981. βίωσις **biōsis**, *bee'-o-sis;* from *980; living* (prop. the act, by impl. the mode):—manner of life.

982. βιωτικός **biōtikŏs**, *bee-o-tee-kos';* from a der. of *980; relating to* the present *existence*:—of (pertaining to, things that pertain to) this life.

983. βλαβερός **blabĕrŏs**, *blab-er-os';* from *984; injurious*:—hurtful.

984. βλάπτω **blaptō**, *blap'-to;* a prim. verb; prop. to *hinder,* i.e. (by impl.) to *injure*:—hurt.

985. βλαστάνω **blastanō**, *blas-tan'-o;* from βλαστός **blastŏs** (a *sprout*); to *germinate;* by impl. to *yield* fruit:—bring forth, bud, spring (up).

986. Βλάστος **Blastŏs**, *blas'-tos;* perh. the same as the base of *985; Blastus,* an officer of Herod Agrippa:—Blastus.

987. βλασφημέω **blasphēmĕō**, *blas-fay-meh'-o;* from *989;* to *vilify;* spec. to *speak impiously*:—(speak) blaspheme (-er, -mously, -my), defame, rail on, revile, speak evil.

988. βλασφημία **blasphēmia**, *blas-fay-me'-ah;* from *989; vilification* (espec. against God):—blasphemy, evil speaking, railing.

989. βλάσφημος **blasphēmŏs**, *blas'-fay-mos;* from a der. of *984* and *5345; scurrilous,* i.e. *calumnious* (against man), or (spec.) *impious* (against God):—blasphemer (-mous), railing.

990. βλέμμα **blemma**, *blem'-mah;* from *991; vision* (prop. concr.; by impl. abstr.):—seeing.

991. βλέπω **blĕpō**, *blep'-o;* a prim. verb; to *look* at (lit. or fig.):—behold, beware, lie, look (on, to), perceive, regard, see, sight, take heed. Comp. *3700.*

992. βλητέος **blētĕŏs**, *blay-teh'-os;* from *906;* fit *to be cast* (i.e. *applied*):—must be put.

993. Βοανεργές **Bŏanĕrgĕs**, *bŏ-an-erg-es';* of Chald. or. [1123 and 7266]; *sons of commotion; Boänerges,* an epithet of two of the Apostles:—Boanerges.

994. βοάω **bŏaō**, *bŏ-ah'-o;* appar. a prol. form of a prim. verb; to *halloo,* i.e. *shout* (for help or in a tumultuous way):—cry.

995. βοή **bŏē**, *bŏ-ay';* from *994;* a *halloo,* i.e. *call* (for aid, etc.):—cry.

996. βοήθεια **bŏēthĕia**, *bŏ-ay'-thi-ah;* from *998; aid;* spec. a rope or chain for *frapping* a vessel:—help.

997. βοηθέω **bŏēthĕō**, *bŏ-ay-theh'-o;* from *998;* to *aid* or *relieve*:—help, succour.

998. βοηθός **bŏēthŏs**, *bŏ-ay-thos';* from *995* and θέω **thĕō** (to *run*); a *succorer*:—helper.

999. βόθυνος **bŏthunŏs**, *both'-oo-nos;* akin to *900;* a *hole* (in the ground); spec. a *cistern*:—ditch, pit.

1000. βολή **bŏlē**, *bol-ay';* from *906;* a *throw* (as a measure of distance):—cast.

1001. βολίζω **bŏlizō**, *bol-id'-zo;* from *1002;* to *heave* the lead:—sound.

1002. βολίς **bŏlis**, *bol-ece';* from *906;* a *missile,* i.e. *javelin*:—dart.

1003. Βοόζ **Bŏŏz**, *bŏ-oz';* of Heb. or. [1162]; *Boöz,* (i.e. *Boäz*), an Isr.:—Booz.

1004. βόρβορος **bŏrbŏrŏs**, *bor'-bor-os;* of uncert. der.; *mud*:—mire.

1005. βορρᾶς **borrhas**, *bor-hras';* of uncert. der.; the *north* (prop. wind):—north.

1006. βόσκω **bŏskō**, *bos'-ko;* a prol. form of a prim. verb [comp. *977, 1016*]; to *pasture;* by extens. to *fodder;* reflex. to *graze*:—feed, keep.

1007. Βοσόρ **Bŏsŏr**, *bos-or';* of Heb. or. [1160]; *Bosor* (i.e. *Beör*), a Moabite:—Bosor.

1008. βοτάνη **bŏtanē**, *bot-an'-ay;* from *1006; herbage* (as if for *grazing*):—herb.

1009. βότρυς **bŏtrus**, *bot'-rooce;* of uncert. der.; a *bunch* (of grapes):—(vine) cluster (of the vine).

1010. βουλευτής **bŏulĕutēs**, *bool-yoo-tace';* from *1011;* an *adviser,* i.e. (spec.) a *councillor* or member of the Jewish Sanhedrim:—counsellor.

1011. βουλεύω **bŏulĕuō**, *bool-yoo'-o;* from *1012;* to *advise,* i.e. (reflex.) *deliberate,* or (by impl.) *resolve*:—consult, take counsel, determine, be minded, purpose.

1012. βουλή **bŏulē**, *boo-lay';* from *1014; volition,* i.e. (obj.) *advice,* or (by impl.) *purpose*:— + advise, counsel, will.

1013. βούλημα **bŏulēma**, *boo'-lay-mah;* from *1014;* a *resolve*:—purpose, will.

1014. βούλομαι **bŏulŏmai**, *boo'-lom-ahee;* mid. of a prim. verb; to "*will*," i.e. (reflex.) *be willing*:—be disposed, minded, intend, list, (be, of own) will (-ing). Comp. *2309.*

1015. βουνός **bŏunŏs**, *boo-nos';* prob. of for. or.; a *hillock*:—hill.

1016. βοῦς **bŏus**, *booce;* prob. from the base of *1006;* an *ox* (as *grazing*), i.e. an animal of that species ("beef"):—ox.

1017. βραβεῖον **brabĕiŏn**, *brab-i'-on;* from βραβεύς **brabĕus** (an *umpire;* of uncert. der.); an *award* (of arbitration), i.e. (spec.) a *prize* in the public games:—prize.

1018. βραβεύω **brabĕuō**, *brab-yoo'-o;* from the same as *1017;* to *arbitrate,* i.e. (gen.) to *govern* (fig. *prevail*):—rule.

1019. βραδύνω **bradunō**, *brad-oo'-no;* from *1021;* to *delay*:—be slack, tarry.

1020. βραδυπλοέω **braduplŏĕō**, *brad-oo-plŏ-eh'-o;* from *1021* and a prol. form of *4126;* to *sail slowly*:—sail slowly.

1021. βραδύς **bradus**, *brad-ooce';* of uncert. affin.; *slow;* fig. *dull*:—slow.

1022. βραδύτης **bradutēs**, *brad-oo'-tace;* from *1021; tardiness*:—slackness.

1023. βραχίων **brachiōn**, *brakh-ee'-own;* prop. comp. of *1024,* but appar. in the sense of βράσσω **brassō** (to *wield*); the *arm,* i.e. (fig.) *strength*:—arm.

1024. βραχύς **brachus**, *brakh-ooce';* of uncert. affin.; *short* (of time, place, quantity, or number):—few words, little (space, while).

1025. βρέφος **brĕphŏs**, *bref'-os;* of uncert. affin.; an *infant* (prop. unborn) lit. or fig.:—babe, (young) child, infant.

1026. βρέχω **brĕchō**, *brekh'-o;* a prim. verb; to *moisten* (espec. by a shower):—(send) rain, wash.

1027. βροντή **brŏntē**, *bron-tay';* akin to βρέμω **brĕmō** (to *roar*); *thunder*:—thunder (-ing).

1028. βροχή **brŏchē**, *brokh-ay';* from 1026; *rain*:—rain.

1029. βρόχος **brŏchŏs**, *brokh'-os;* of uncert. der.; a *noose*:—snare.

1030. βρυγμός **brugmŏs**, *broog-mos';* from *1031;* a *grating* (of the teeth):—gnashing.

1031. βρύχω **bruchō**, *broo'-kho;* a prim. verb; to *grate* the teeth (in pain or rage):—gnash.

1032. βρύω **bruō**, *broo'-o;* a prim. verb; to *swell* out, i.e. (by impl.) to *gush*:—send forth.

1033. βρῶμα **brōma**, *bro'-mah;* from the base of *977; food* (lit. or fig.), espec. (cer.) articles allowed or forbidden by the Jewish law:—meat, victuals.

1034. βρώσιμος **brōsimŏs**, *bro'-sim-os;* from *1035; eatable*:—meat.

1035. βρῶσις **brōsis**, *bro'-sis;* from the base of *977;* (abstr.) *eating* (lit. or fig.); by extens. (concr.) *food* (lit. or fig.):—eating, food, meat.

1036. βυθίζω **buthizō**, *boo-thid'-zo;* from *1037;* to *sink;* by impl. to *drown*:—begin to sink, drown.

1037. βυθός **buthŏs**, *boo-thos';* a var. of *899; depth,* i.e. (by impl.) the *sea*:—deep.

1038. βυρσεύς **bursĕus**, *boorce-yooce';* from βύρσα **bursa** (a *hide*); a *tanner*:—tanner.

1039. βύσσινος **bussinŏs**, *boos'-see-nos;* from *1040;* made of *linen* (neut. a linen *cloth*):—fine linen.

1040. βύσσος **bussŏs**, *boos'-sos;* of Heb. or. [948]; white *linen*:—fine linen.

1041. βῶμος **bōmŏs**, *bo'-mos;* from the base of *939;* prop. a *stand,* i.e. (spec.) an *altar*:—altar.

Γ

1042. γαββαθά **gabbatha**, *gab-bath-ah';* of Chald. or. [comp. 1355]; *the knoll; gabbatha,* a vernacular term for the Roman tribunal in Jerus.:—Gabbatha.

1043. **Γαβριήλ Gabriēl**, *gab-ree-ale'*; of Heb. or. [1403]; *Gabriel*, an archangel:—Gabriel.

1044. **γάγγραινα gaggraina**, *gang'-grahee-nah;* from **γραίνω grainō** (to *gnaw*); an *ulcer* ("gangrene"):—canker.

1045. **Γάδ Gad**, *gad;* of Heb. or. [1410]; *Gad*, a tribe of Isr.:—Gad.

1046. **Γαδαρηνός Gadarēnŏs**, *gad-ar-ay-nos';* from **Γαδαρά** (a town E. of the Jordan); a *Gadarene* or inhab. of Gadara:—Gadarene.

1047. **γάζα gaza**, *gad'-zah;* of for. or.; a *treasure:*—treasure.

1048. **Γάζα Gaza**, *gad'-zah;* of Heb. or. [5804]; *Gazah* (i.e. *'Azzah*), a place in Pal.:—Gaza.

1049. **γαζοφυλάκιον gazŏphulakiŏn**, *gad-zof-oo-lak'-ee-on;* from *1047* and *5438*; a *treasure-house*, i.e. a court in the temple for the collection-boxes:—treasury.

1050. **Γάϊος Gaïŏs**, *gah'-ee-os;* of Lat. or.; *Gaïus* (i.e. *Caius*), a Chr.:—Gaius.

1051. **γάλα gala**, *gal'-ah;* of uncert. affin.; *milk* (fig.):—milk.

1052. **Γαλάτης Galatēs**, *gal-at'-ace;* from *1053*; a *Galatian* or inhab. of Galatia:—Galatian.

1053. **Γαλατία Galatia**, *gal-at-ee'-ah;* of for. or.; *Galatia*, a region of Asia:—Galatia.

1054. **Γαλατικός Galatikŏs**, *gal-at-ee-kos';* from *1053; Galatic* or relating to Galatia:—of Galatia.

1055. **γαλήνη galēnē**, *gal-ay'-nay;* of uncert. der.; *tranquillity:*—calm.

1056. **Γαλιλαία Galilaia**, *gal-il-ah'-yah;* of Heb. or. [1551]; *Galilæa* (i.e. the heathen *circle*), a region of Pal.:—Galilee.

1057. **Γαλιλαῖος Galilaiŏs**, *gal-ee-lah'-yos;* from *1056; Galilæan* or belonging to Galilæa:—Galilæan, of Galilee.

1058. **Γαλλίων Galliōn**, *gal-lee'-own;* of Lat. or.; *Gallion* (i.e. *Gallio*), a Roman officer:—Gallio.

1059. **Γαμαλιήλ Gamaliēl**, *gam-al-ee-ale';* of Heb. or. [1583]; *Gamaliel* (i.e. *Gamliel*), an Isr.:—Gamaliel.

1060. **γαμέω gamĕō**, *gam-eh'-o;* from *1062*; to *wed* (of either sex):—marry (a wife).

1061. **γαμίσκω gamiskō**, *gam-is'-ko;* from *1062*; to *espouse* (a daughter to a husband):—give in marriage.

1062. **γάμος gamŏs**, *gam'-os;* of uncert. affin.; *nuptials:*—marriage, wedding.

1063. **γάρ gar**, *gar;* a prim. particle; prop. assigning a *reason* (used in argument, explanation or intensification; often with other particles):—and, as, because (that), but, even, for, indeed, no doubt, seeing, then, therefore, verily, what, why, yet.

1064. **γαστήρ gastēr**, *gas-tare';* of uncert. der.; the *stomach;* by anal. the *matrix;* fig. a *gourmand:*—belly, + with child, womb.

1065. **γέ gĕ**, *gheh;* a prim. particle of *emphasis* or *qualification* (often used with other particles prefixed):—and besides, doubtless, at least, yet.

1066. **Γεδεών Gĕdĕōn**, *ghed-eh-own';* of Heb. or. [1439]; *Gedeon* (i.e. *Gid[e]on*), an Isr.:—Gedeon.

1067. **γέεννα gĕĕnna**, *gheh'-en-nah;* of Heb. or [1516 and 2011]; *valley of* (the son of) *Hinnom; gehenna* (or *Ge-Hinnom*), a valley of Jerus., used (fig.) as a name for the place (or state) of everlasting punishment:—hell.

1068. **Γεθσημανῆ Gĕthsēmanē**, *gheth-say-man-ay';* of Chald. or. [comp. 1660 and 8081]; *oil-press; Gethsemane*, a garden near Jerus.:—Gethsemane.

1069. **γείτων gĕitōn**, *ghi'-tone;* from *1093*; a *neighbor* (as adjoining one's *ground*); by impl. a *friend:*—neighbour.

1070. **γελάω gĕlaō**, *ghel-ah'-o;* of uncert. affin.; to *laugh* (as a sign of joy or satisfaction):—laugh.

1071. **γέλως gĕlōs**, *ghel'-oce;* from *1070*; *laughter* (as a mark of gratification):—laughter.

1072. **γεμίζω gĕmizō**, *ghem-id'-zo;* trans. from *1073*. to *fill* entirely:—fill (be) full.

1073. **γέμω gĕmō**, *ghem'-o;* a prim. verb; to *swell* out, i.e. *be full:*—be full.

1074. **γενεά gĕnĕa**, *ghen-eh-ah';* from (a presumed der. of) *1085*; a *generation;* by impl. an *age* (the period or the persons):—age, generation, nation, time.

1075. **γενεαλογέω gĕnĕalŏgĕō**, *ghen-eh-al-og-eh'-o;* from *1074* and *3056*; to *reckon by generations*, i.e. *trace in genealogy:*—count by descent.

1076. **γενεαλογία gĕnĕalŏgia**, *ghen-eh-al-og-ee'-ah;* from the same as *1075*; *tracing by generations*, i.e. "*genealogy*":—genealogy.

1077. **γενέσια gĕnĕsia**, *ghen-es'-ee-ah;* neut. plur. of a der. of *1078*; *birthday* ceremonies:—birthday.

1078. **γένεσις gĕnĕsis**, *ghen'-es-is;* from the same as *1074*; *nativity;* fig. *nature:*—generation, nature (-ral).

1079. **γενετή gĕnĕtē**, *ghen-et-ay';* fem. of a presumed der. of the base of *1074*; *birth:*—birth.

1080. **γεννάω gĕnnaō**, *ghen-nah'-o;* from a var. of *1085*; to *procreate* (prop. of the father, but by extens. of the mother); fig. to *regenerate:*—bear, beget, be born, bring forth, conceive, be delivered of, gender, make, spring.

1081. **γέννημα gĕnnēma**, *ghen'-nay-mah;* from *1080*; *offspring;* by anal. *produce* (lit. or fig.):—fruit, generation.

1082. **Γεννησαρέτ Gĕnnēsarĕt**, *ghen-nay-sar-et';* of Heb. or. [comp. 3672]; *Gennesaret* (i.e. *Kinnereth*), a lake and plain in Pal.:—Gennesaret.

1083. **γέννησις gĕnnēsis**, *ghen'-nay-sis;* from *1080*; *nativity:*—birth.

1084. **γεννητός gĕnnētŏs**, *ghen-nay-tos';* from *1080*; *born:*—they that are born.

1085. **γένος gĕnŏs**, *ghen'-os;* from *1096*; "*kin*" (abstr. or concr., lit. or fig., indiv. or coll.):—born, country (-man), diversity, generation, kind (-red), nation, offspring, stock.

1086. **Γεργεσηνός Gĕrgĕsēnŏs**, *gher-ghes-ay-nos';* of Heb. or. [1622]; a *Gergesene* (i.e. *Girgashite*) or one of the aborigines of Pal.:—Gergesene.

1087. **γερουσία gĕrŏusia**, *gher-oo-see'-ah;* from *1088*; the *eldership*, i.e. (collect.) the Jewish *Sanhedrim:*—senate.

1088. **γέρων gĕrōn**, *gher'-own;* of uncert. affin. [comp. *1094*]; *aged:*—old.

1089. **γεύομαι gĕuŏmai**, *ghyoo'-om-ahee;* a prim. verb; to *taste;* by impl. to *eat;* fig. to *experience* (good or ill):—eat, taste.

1090. **γεωργέω gĕōrgĕō**, *gheh-ore-gheh'-o;* from *1092*; to *till* (the soil):—dress.

1091. **γεώργιον gĕōrgiŏn**, *gheh-ore'-ghee-on;* neut. of a (presumed) der. of *1092*; *cultivable*, i.e. a *farm:*—husbandry.

1092. **γεωργός gĕōrgŏs**, *gheh-ore-gos';* from *1093* and the base of *2041*; a *land-worker*, i.e. *farmer:*—husbandman.

1093. **γῆ gē**, *ghay;* contr. from a prim. word; *soil;* by extens. a *region*, or the solid part or the whole of the *terrene* globe (includ. the occupants in each application):—country, earth (-ly), ground, land, world.

1094. **γῆρας gēras**, *ghay'-ras;* akin to *1088*; *senility:*—old age.

1095. **γηράσκω gēraskō**, *ghay-ras'-ko;* from *1094*; to *be senescent:*—be (wax) old.

1096. **γίνομαι ginŏmai**, *ghin'-om-ahee;* a prol. and mid. form of a prim. verb; to *cause to be* ("*gen*"-*erate*), i.e. (reflex.) to *become* (*come into being*), used with great latitude (lit., fig., intens., etc.):—arise, be assembled, be (come, -fall, -have self), be brought (to pass), (be) come (to pass), continue, be divided, be done, draw, be ended, fall, be finished, follow, be found, be fulfilled, + God forbid, grow, happen, have, be kept, be made, be married, be ordained to be, partake, pass, be performed, be published, require, seem, be showed, × soon as it was, sound, be taken, be turned, use, wax, will, would, be wrought.

1097. **γινώσκω ginōskō**, *ghin-oce'-ko;* a prol. form of a prim. verb; to "*know*" (absol.), in a great variety of applications and with many impl. (as follow, with others not thus clearly expressed):—allow, be aware (of), feel, (have) know (-ledge), perceive, be resolved, can speak, be sure, understand.

1098. **γλεῦκος glĕukŏs**, *glyoo'-kos;* akin to *1099*; *sweet* wine, i.e. (prop.) *must* (fresh juice), but used of the more saccharine (and therefore highly inebriating) fermented *wine:*—new wine.

1099. **γλυκύς glukus**, *gloo-koos';* of uncert. affin.; *sweet* (i.e. not bitter nor salt):—sweet, fresh.

1100. **γλῶσσα glōssa**, *gloce-sah';* of uncert. affin.; the *tongue;* by impl. a *language* (spec. one naturally unacquired):—tongue.

1101. **γλωσσόκομον glōssŏkŏmŏn**, *gloce-sok'-om-on;* from *1100* and the base of *2889*; prop. a *case* (to keep mouthpieces of wind-instruments in), i.e. (by extens.) a *casket* or (spec.) *purse:*—bag.

1102. **γναφεύς gnaphĕus**, *gnaf-yuce';* by var. for a der. from **κνάπτω knaptō** (to *tease* cloth); a cloth-*dresser:*—fuller.

1103. **γνήσιος gnēsiŏs**, *gnay'-see-os;* from the same as *1077*; *legitimate* (of birth), i.e. *genuine:*—own, sincerity, true.

1104. **γνησίως gnēsiōs**, *gnay-see'-oce;* adv. from *1103*; *genuinely*, i.e. *really:*—naturally.

1105. **γνόφος gnŏphŏs**, *gnof'-os;* akin to *3509*; *gloom* (as of a storm):—blackness.

1106. **γνώμη gnōmē**, *gno'-may;* from *1097*; *cognition*, i.e. (subj.) *opinion*, or (obj.) *resolve* (*counsel*, *consent*, etc.):—advice, + agree, judgment, mind, purpose, will.

1107. **γνωρίζω gnōrizō**, *gno-rid'-zo;* from a der. of *1097*; to *make known;* subj. to *know:*—certify, declare, make known, give to understand, do to wit, wot.

1108. **γνῶσις gnōsis**, *gno'-sis;* from *1097*; *knowing* (the act), i.e. (by impl.) *knowledge:*—knowledge, science.

1109. **γνώστης gnōstēs**, *gnoce'-tace;* from *1097*; a *knower:*—expert.

1110. **γνωστός gnōstŏs**, *gnoce-tos';* from *1097*; well *known:*—acquaintance, (which may be) known, notable.

1111. **γογγύζω gŏgguzō**, *gong-good'-zo;* of uncert. der.; to *grumble:*—murmur.

1112. **γογγυσμός gŏggusmŏs**, *gong-goos-mos';* from *1111*; a *grumbling:*—grudging, murmuring.

1113. **γογγυστής gŏggustēs**, *gong-goos-tace';* from *1111*; a *grumbler:*—murmurer.

1114. **γόης gŏēs**, *gŏ'-ace;* from **γοάω gŏaō** (to *wail*); prop. a *wizard* (as *muttering* spells), i.e. (by impl.) an *impostor:*—seducer.

1115. **Γολγοθᾶ Golgŏtha**, *gol-goth-ah';* of Chald. or. [comp. 1538]; *the skull; Golgotha*, a knoll near Jerus.:—Golgotha.

1116. **Γόμορρα Gŏmŏrrha**, *gom'-or-hrah;* of Heb. or. [6017]; *Gomorrha* (i.e. *'Amorah*), a place near the Dead Sea:—Gomorrha.

1117. **γόμος gŏmŏs**, *gom'-os;* from *1073*; a *load* (as *filling*), i.e. (spec.) a *cargo*, or (by extens.) *wares:*—burden, merchandise.

1118. **γονεύς gŏnĕus**, *gon-yooce';* from the base of *1096*; a *parent:*—parent.

1119. **γονύ gŏnu**, *gon-oo';* of uncert. affin.; the "*knee*":—knee (× -l).

1120. **γονυπετέω gŏnupĕtĕō**, *gon-oo-pet-eh'-o;* from a comp. of *1119* and the alt of *4098*; to *fall* on the *knee:*—bow the knee, kneel down.

1121. **γράμμα gramma**, *gram'-mah;* from *1125*; a *writing*, i.e. a *letter*, *note*, *epistle*, *book*, etc.; plur. *learning:*—bill, learning, letter, scripture, writing, written.

1122. **γραμματεύς grammatĕus**, *gram-mat-yooce';* from *1121*; a *writer*, i.e. (professionally) *scribe* or *secretary:*—scribe, town-clerk.

1123. **γραπτός graptŏs**, *grap-tos';* from *1125*; *inscribed* (fig.):—written.

1124. **γραφή graphē**, *graf-ay';* from *1125*; a *document*, i.e. holy *Writ* (or its contents or a statement in it):—scripture.

1125. γράφω **graphō**, *graf'-o;* a prim. verb; to "*grave*", espec. to *write;* fig. to *describe:*—describe, write (-ing, -ten).

1126. γραώδης **graōdēs**, *grah-o'-dace;* from γραῦς **graus** (an *old woman*) and *1491; crone-like,* i.e. *silly:*—old wives'.

1127. γρηγορεύω **grēgŏrĕuō**, *gray-gor-yoo'-o;* from *1453;* to *keep awake,* i.e. *watch* (lit. or fig.):—be vigilant, wake, (be) watch (-ful).

1128. γυμνάζω **gumnazō**, *goom-nad'-zo;* from *1131;* to *practise naked* (in the games), i.e. *train* (fig.):—exercise.

1129. γυμνασία **gumnasia**, *goom-nas-ee'-ah;* from *1128; training,* i.e. (fig.) *asceticism:*—exercise.

1130. γυμνητεύω **gumnētĕuō**, *goom-nayt-yoo'-o;* from a der. of *1131;* to *strip,* i.e. (reflex.) *go poorly clad:*—be naked.

1131. γυμνός **gumnŏs**, *goom-nos';* of uncert. affin.; *nude* (absol. or rel., lit. or fig.):—naked.

1132. γυμνότης **gumnŏtēs**, *goom-not'-ace;* from *1131; nudity* (absol. or comp.):—nakedness.

1133. γυναικάριον **gunaikariŏn**, *goo-nahee-kar'-ee-on;* a dimin. from *1135;* a *little* (i.e. *foolish*) *woman:*—silly woman.

1134. γυναικεῖος **gunaikĕiŏs**, *goo-nahee-ki'-os;* from *1135; feminine:*—wife.

1135. γυνή **gunē**, *goo-nay';* prob. from the base of *1096;* a *woman;* spec. a *wife:*—wife, woman.

1136. Γώγ **Gōg**, *gogue;* of Heb. or. [1463]; *Gog,* a symb. name for some future Antichrist:—Gog.

1137. γωνία **gōnia**, *go-nee'-ah;* prob. akin to *1119;* an *angle:*—corner, quarter.

Δ

1138. Δαβίδ **Dabid**, *dab-eed';* of Heb. or. [1732]; *Dabid* (i.e. *David*), the Isr. king:—David.

1139. δαιμονίζομαι **daimŏnizŏmai**, *dahee-mon-id'-zom-ahee;* mid. from *1142;* to *be exercised by a dæmon:*—have a (be vexed with, be possessed with) devil (-s).

1140. δαιμόνιον **daimŏniŏn**, *dahee-mon'-ee-on;* neut. of a der. of *1142;* a *dæmonic being;* by extens. a *deity:*—devil, god.

1141. δαιμονιώδης **daimŏniōdēs**, *dahee-mon-ee-o'-dace;* from *1140* and *1142; dæmon-like:*—devilish.

1142. δαίμων **daimōn**, *dah'ee-mown;* from δαίω **daiō** (to *distribute* fortunes); a *dæmon* or supernatural spirit (of a bad nature):—devil.

1143. δάκνω **daknō**, *dak'-no;* a prol. form of a prim. root: to *bite,* i.e. (fig.) *thwart:*—bite.

1144. δάκρυ **dakru**, *dak'-roo;* or

δάκρυον **dakruŏn**, *dak'-roo-on;* of uncert. affin.; a *tear:*—tear.

1145. δακρύω **dakruō**, *dak-roo'-o;* from 1144; to *shed tears:*—weep. Comp. *2799.*

1146. δακτύλιος **daktuliŏs**, *dak-too'-lee-os;* from *1147;* a *finger*-ring:—ring.

1147. δάκτυλος **daktulŏs**, *dak'-too-los;* prob. from *1176;* a *finger:*—finger.

1148. Δαλμανουθά **Dalmanŏutha**, *dal-man-oo-thah';* prob. of Chald. or.; *Dalmanûtha,* a place in Pal.:—Dalmanutha.

1149. Δαλματία **Dalmatia**, *dal-mat-ee'-ah;* prob. of for. der.; *Dalmatia,* a region of Europe:—Dalmatia.

1150. δαμάζω **damazō**, *dam-ad'-zo;* a var. of an obs. prim. of the same mean.; to *tame:*—tame.

1151. δάμαλις **damalis**, *dam'-al-is;* prob. from the base of *1150;* a *heifer* (as *tame*):—heifer.

1152. Δάμαρις **Damaris**, *dam'-ar-is;* prob. from the base of *1150;* perh. *gentle; Damaris,* an Athenian woman:—Damaris.

1153. Δαμασκηνός **Damaskēnŏs**, *dam-as-kay-nos';* from *1154;* a *Damascene* or inhab. of Damascus:—Damascene.

1154. Δαμασκός **Damaskŏs**, *dam-as-kos';* of Heb. or. [1834]; *Damascus,* a city of Syria:—Damascus.

1155. δανείζω **danĕizō**, *dan-ide'-zo;* from *1156;* to *loan* on interest; reflex. to *borrow:*—borrow, lend.

1156. δάνειον **danĕiŏn**, *dan'-i-on;* from δάνος **danŏs** (a *gift*); prob. akin to the base of *1325;* a *loan:*—debt.

1157. δανειστής **danĕistēs**, *dan-ice-tace';* from *1155;* a *lender:*—creditor.

1158. Δανιήλ **Daniēl**, *dan-ee-ale';* of Heb. or. [1840]; *Daniel,* an Isr.:—Daniel.

1159. δαπανάω **dapanaō**, *dap-an-ah'-o;* from *1160;* to *expend,* i.e. (in a good sense) to *incur cost,* or (in a bad one) to *waste:*—be at charges, consume, spend.

1160. δαπάνη **dapanē**, *dap-an'-ay;* from δάπτω **daptō** (to *devour*); *expense* (as *consuming*):—cost.

1161. δέ **dĕ**, *deh;* a prim. particle (adversative or continuative); *but, and,* etc.:—also, and, but, moreover, now [*often unexpressed in English*].

1162. δέησις **dĕēsis**, *deh'-ay-sis;* from *1189;* a *petition:*—prayer, request, supplication.

1163. δεῖ **dĕi**, *die;* 3d pers. sing. act. pres. of *1210;* also δεόν **dĕŏn**, *deh-on';* neut. act. part. of the same; both used impers.; *it is* (*was,* etc.) *necessary* (as *binding*):—behoved, be meet, must (needs), (be) need (-ful), ought, should.

1164. δεῖγμα **dĕigma**, *digh'-mah;* from the base of *1166;* a *specimen* (as *shown*):—example.

1165. δειγματίζω **dĕigmatizō**, *digh-mat-id'-zo;* from *1164;* to *exhibit:*—make a shew.

1166. δεικνύω **dĕiknuō**, *dike-noo'-o;* a prol. form of an obs. prim. of the same mean.; to *show* (lit. or fig.):—shew.

1167. δειλία **dĕilia**, *di-lee'-ah;* from *1169; timidity:*—fear.

1168. δειλιάω **dĕiliaō**, *di-lee-ah'-o;* from *1167;* to *be timid:*—be afraid.

1169. δειλός **dĕilŏs**, *di-los';* from δέος **dĕŏs** (*dread*); *timid,* i.e. (by impl.) *faithless:*—fearful.

1170. δεῖνα **dĕina**, *di'-nah;* prob. from the same as *1171* (through the idea of forgetting the name as *fearful,* i.e. *strange*); *so and so* (when the person is not specified):—such a man.

1171. δεινῶς **dĕinōs**, *di-noce';* adv. from a der. of the same as *1169; terribly,* i.e. *excessively:*—grievously, vehemently.

1172. δειπνέω **dĕipnĕō**, *dipe-neh'-o;* from *1173;* to *dine,* i.e. take the principal (or evening) meal:—sup (× -per).

1173. δεῖπνον **dĕipnŏn**, *dipe'-non;* from the same as *1160; dinner,* i.e. the chief meal (usually in the evening):—feast, supper.

1174. δεισιδαιμονέστερος **dĕisidaimŏnĕstĕrŏs**, *dice-ee-dahee-mon-es'-ter-os;* the comp. of a der. of the base of *1169* and *1142; more religious* than others:—too superstitious.

1175. δεισιδαιμονία **dĕisidaimŏnia**, *dice-ee-dahee-mon-ee'-ah;* from the same as *1174; religion:*—superstition.

1176. δέκα **dĕka**, *dek'-ah;* a prim. number; *ten:*—[eight-] een, ten.

1177. δεκαδύο **dĕkaduŏ**, *dek-ad-oo'-ŏ;* from *1176* and *1417; two* and *ten,* i.e. *twelve:*—twelve.

1178. δεκαπέντε **dĕkapĕntĕ**, *dek-ap-en'-teh;* from *1176* and *4002; ten* and *five,* i.e. *fifteen:*—fifteen.

1179. Δεκάπολις **Dĕkapŏlis**, *dek-ap'-ol-is;* from *1176* and *4172;* the *ten-city* region; the *Decapolis,* a district in Syria:—Decapolis.

1180. δεκατέσσαρες **dĕkatĕssarĕs**, *dek-at-es'-sar-es;* from *1176* and *5064; ten* and *four,* i.e. *fourteen:*—fourteen.

1181. δεκάτη **dĕkatē**, *dek-at'-ay;* fem. of *1182;* a *tenth,* i.e. as a percentage or (tech.) *tithe:*—tenth (part), tithe.

1182. δέκατος **dĕkatŏs**, *dek'-at-os;* ordinal from *1176; tenth:*—tenth.

1183. δεκατόω **dĕkatŏō**, *dek-at-ŏ'-o;* from *1181;* to *tithe,* i.e. to *give* or *take a tenth:*—pay (receive) tithes.

1184. δεκτός **dĕktŏs**, *dek-tos';* from *1209; approved;* (fig.) *propitious:*—accepted (-table).

1185. δελεάζω **dĕlĕazō**, *del-eh-ad'-zo;* from the base of *1388;* to *entrap,* i.e. (fig.) *delude:*—allure, beguile, entice.

1186. δένδρον **dĕndrŏn**, *den'-dron;* prob. from δρύς **drus** (an *oak*); a *tree:*—tree.

1187. δεξιολάβος **dĕxiŏlabŏs**, *dex-ee-ol-ab'-os;* from *1188* and *2983;* a *guardsman* (as if *taking the right*) or light-armed soldier:—spearman.

1188. δεξιός **dĕxiŏs**, *dex-ee-os';* from *1209;* the *right* side or (fem.) hand (as that which usually *takes*):—right (hand, side).

1189. δέομαι **dĕŏmai**, *deh'-om-ahee;* mid. of *1210;* to *beg* (as *binding oneself*), i.e. *petition:*—beseech, pray (to), make request. Comp. 4441.

δεόν **dĕŏn**. See *1163.*

1190. Δερβαῖος **Dĕrbaiŏs**, *der-bah'-ee-os;* from *1191;* a *Derbæan* or inhab. of Derbe:—of Derbe.

1191. Δέρβη **Dĕrbē**, *der'-bay;* of for. or.; *Derbè,* a place in Asia Minor:—Derbe.

1192. δέρμα **dĕrma**, *der'-mah;* from 1194; a *hide:*—skin.

1193. δερμάτινος **dĕrmatinŏs**, *der-mat'-ee-nos;* from *1192;* made of *hide:*—leathern, of a skin.

1194. δέρω **dĕrō**, *der'-o;* a prim. verb; prop. to *flay,* i.e. (by impl.) to *scourge,* or (by anal.) to *thrash:*—beat, smite.

1195. δεσμεύω **dĕsmĕuō**, *des-myoo'-o;* from a (presumed) der. of *1196;* to *be a binder* (*captor*), i.e. to *enchain* (a prisoner), to *tie on* (a load):—bind.

1196. δεσμέω **dĕsmĕō**, *des-meh'-o;* from *1199;* to *tie,* i.e. *shackle:*—bind.

1197. δεσμή **dĕsmē**, *des-may';* from *1196;* a *bundle:*—bundle.

1198. δέσμιος **dĕsmiŏs**, *des'-mee-os;* from *1199;* a *captive* (as *bound*):—in bonds, prisoner.

1199. δεσμόν **dĕsmŏn**, *des-mon';* or

δεσμός **dĕsmŏs**, *des-mos';* neut. and masc. respectively from *1210;* a *band,* i.e. *ligament* (of the body) or *shackle* (of a prisoner); fig. an *impediment* or *disability:*—band, bond, chain, string.

1200. δεσμοφύλαξ **dĕsmŏphulax**, *des-mof-oo'-lax;* from *1199* and *5441;* a *jailer* (as *guarding* the *prisoners*):—jailor, keeper of the prison.

1201. δεσμωτήριον **dĕsmōtēriŏn**, *des-mo-tay'-ree-on;* from a der. of *1199* (equiv. to *1196*); a *place of bondage,* i.e. a *dungeon:*—prison.

1202. δεσμώτης **dĕsmōtēs**, *des-mo'-tace;* from the same as *1201;* (pass.) a *captive:*—prisoner.

1203. δεσπότης **dĕspŏtēs**, *des-pot'-ace;* perh. from *1210* and πόσις **pŏsis** (a *husband*); an absolute *ruler* ("despot"):—Lord, master.

1204. δεῦρο **dĕurŏ**, *dyoo'-rŏ;* of uncert. affin.; *here;* used also imper. *hither!;* and of time, *hitherto:*—come (hither), hither [-to].

1205. δεῦτε **dĕutĕ**, *dyoo'-teh;* from *1204* and an imper. form of εἶμι **ĕimi** (to *go*); *come hither!:*—come, × follow.

1206. δευτεραῖος **dĕutĕraiŏs**, *dyoo-ter-ah'-yos;* from *1208; secondary,* i.e. (spec.) on the *second* day:—next day.

1207. δευτερόπρωτος **dĕutĕrŏprōtŏs**, *dyoo-ter-op'-ro-tos;* from *1208* and *4413; second-first,* i.e. (spec.) a designation of the Sabbath immediately after the Paschal week (being the *second* after Passover day, and the *first* of the seven Sabbaths intervening before Pentecost):—second . . . after the first.

1208. δεύτερος **dĕutĕrŏs**, *dyoo'-ter-os;* as the comp. of *1417;* (ordinal) *second* (in time, place or rank; also adv.):—afterward, again, second (-arily, time).

1209. δέχομαι **dĕchŏmai**, *dekh'-om-ahee;* mid. of a prim. verb; to *receive* (in various applications, lit. or fig.):—accept, receive, take. Comp. *2983.*

1210. δέω **dĕō**, *deh'-o;* a prim. verb; to *bind* (in various applications, lit. or fig.):—bind, be in bonds, knit, tie, wind. See also *1163, 1189.*

1211. δή **dē**, *day;* prob. akin to *1161;* a particle of emphasis or explicitness; *now, then,* etc.:—also, and, doubtless, now, therefore.

1212. δῆλος **dēlŏs**, *day'-los;* of uncert. der.; *clear:*— + bewray, certain, evident, manifest.

1213. δηλόω **dēlŏō**, *day-lŏ'-o;* from *1212;* to *make plain* (by words):—declare, shew, signify.

1214. Δημᾶς **Dēmas**, *day-mas';* prob. for *1216; Demas,* a Chr.:—Demas.

1215. δημηγορέω **dēmēgŏrĕō**, *day-may-gor-eh'-o;* from a comp. of *1218* and *58;* to *be a people-gatherer,* i.e. to *address* a public assembly:—make an oration.

1216. Δημήτριος **Dēmētriŏs**, *day-may'-tree-os;* from Δημήτηρ **Dēmētēr** (*Ceres*); *Demetrius,* the name of an Ephesian and of a Chr.:—Demetrius.

1217. δημιουργός **dēmiŏurgŏs**, *day-me-oor-gos';* from *1218* and *2041;* a *worker* for the *people,* i.e. *mechanic* (spoken of the *Creator*):—maker.

1218. δῆμος **dēmŏs**, *day'-mos;* from *1210;* the *public* (as *bound* together socially):—people.

1219. δημόσιος **dēmŏsiŏs**, *day-mos'-ee-os;* from *1218; public;* (fem. sing. dat. as adv.) *in public:*—common, openly, publickly.

1220. δηνάριον **dēnariŏn**, *day-nar'-ee-on;* of Lat. or.; a *denarius* (or *ten asses*):—pence, penny [-worth].

1221. δήποτε **dēpŏtĕ**, *day'-pot-eh;* from *1211* and *4218;* a particle of generalization; *indeed, at any time:*—(what-) soever.

1222. δήπου **dēpŏu**, *day'-poo;* from *1211* and *4225;* a particle of asseveration; *indeed doubtless:*—verily.

1223. διά **dia**, *dee-ah';* a prim. prep. denoting the *channel* of an act; *through* (in very wide applications, local, causal or occasional):—after, always, among, at, to avoid, because of (that), briefly, by, for (cause) . . . fore, from, in, by occasion of, of, by reason of, for sake, that, thereby, therefore, × though, through (-out), to, wherefore, with (-in). In composition it retains the same general import.

Δία **Dia**. See *2203*.

1224. διαβαίνω **diabainō**, *dee-ab-ah'ee-no;* from *1223* and the base of *939;* to *cross:*—come over, pass (through).

1225. διαβάλλω **diaballō**, *dee-ab-al'-lo;* from *1223* and *906;* (fig.) to *traduce:*—accuse.

1226. διαβεβαιόομαι **diabĕbaiŏŏmai**, *dee-ab-eb-ahee-ŏ'-om-ahee;* mid. of a comp. of *1223* and *950;* to *confirm thoroughly* (by words), i.e. *asseverate:*—affirm constantly.

1227. διαβλέπω **diablĕpō**, *dee-ab-lep'-o;* from *1223* and *991;* to *look through,* i.e. *recover full vision:*—see clearly.

1228. διάβολος **diabŏlŏs**, *dee-ab'-ol-os;* from *1225;* a *traducer;* spec. *Satan* [comp. 7854]:—false accuser, devil, slanderer.

1229. διαγγέλλω **diaggĕllō**, *de-ang-gel'-lo;* from *1223* and the base of *32;* to *herald thoroughly:*—declare, preach, signify.

1230. διαγίνομαι **diaginŏmai**, *dee-ag-in'-om-ahee;* from *1223* and *1096;* to *elapse meanwhile:*— × after, be past, be spent.

1231. διαγινώσκω **diaginōskō**, *dee-ag-in-o'-sko;* from *1223* and *1097;* to *know thoroughly,* i.e. *ascertain exactly:*—(would) enquire, know the uttermost.

1232. διαγνωρίζω **diagnōrizō**, *dee-ag-no-rid'-zo;* from *1123* and *1107;* to *tell abroad:*—make known.

1233. διάγνωσις **diagnōsis**, *dee-ag'-no-sis;* from *1231;* (magisterial) *examination* ("diagnosis"):—hearing.

1234. διαγογγύζω **diagŏgguzō**, *dee-ag-ong-good'-zo;* from *1223* and *1111;* to *complain throughout* a crowd:—murmur.

1235. διαγρηγορέω **diagrēgŏrĕō**, *dee-ag-ray-gor-eh'-o;* from *1223* and *1127;* to *waken thoroughly:*—be awake.

1236. διάγω **diagō**, *dee-ag'-o:* from *1223* and *71;* to *pass* time or life:—lead life, living.

1237. διαδέχομαι **diadĕchŏmai**, *dee-ad-ekh'-om-ahee;* from *1223* and *1209;* to *receive in turn,* i.e. (fig.) *succeed to:*—come after.

1238. διάδημα **diadēma**, *dee-ad'-ay-mah;* from a comp. of *1223* and *1210;* a "*diadem*" (as *bound about* the head):—crown. Comp. *4735*.

1239. διαδίδωμι **diadidōmi**, *dee-ad-id'-o-mee;* from *1223* and *1325;* to *give throughout* a crowd, i.e. *deal out;* also to *deliver* over (as to a successor):—(make) distribute (-ion), divide, give.

1240. διάδοχος **diadŏchŏs**, *dee-ad'-okh-os;* from *1237;* a *successor* in office:—room.

1241. διαζώννυμι **diazōnnumi**, *dee-az-own'-noo-mee;* from *1223* and *2224;* to *gird tightly:*—gird.

1242. διαθήκη **diathēkē**, *dee-ath-ay'-kay;* from *1303;* prop. a *disposition,* i.e. (spec.) a *contract* (espec. a devisory *will*):—covenant, testament.

1243. διαίρεσις **diairĕsis**, *dee-ah'ee-res-is;* from *1244;* a *distinction* or (concr.) *variety:*—difference, diversity.

1244. διαιρέω **diairĕō**, *dee-ahee-reh'-o;* from *1223* and *138;* to *separate,* i.e. *distribute:*—divide.

1245. διακαθαρίζω **diakatharizō**, *dee-ak-ath-ar-id'-zo;* from *1223* and *2511;* to *cleanse perfectly,* i.e. (spec.) *winnow:*—throughly purge.

1246. διακατελέγχομαι **diakatĕlĕgchŏmai**, *dee-ak-at-el-eng'-khom-ahee;* mid. from *1223* and a comp. of *2596* and *1651;* to *prove downright,* i.e. *confute:*—convince.

1247. διακονέω **diakŏnĕō**, *dee-ak-on-eh'-o;* from *1249;* to *be an attendant,* i.e. *wait upon* (menially or as a host, friend or [fig.] teacher); techn. to *act as a* Chr. *deacon:*—(ad-) minister (unto), serve, use the office of a deacon.

1248. διακονία **diakŏnia**, *dee-ak-on-ee'-ah;* from *1249; attendance* (as a servant, etc.); fig. (eleemosynary) *aid,* (official) *service* (espec. of the Chr. teacher, or techn. of the *diaconate*):—(ad-) minister (-ing, -tration, -try), office, relief, service (-ing).

1249. διάκονος **diakŏnŏs**, *dee-ak'-on-os;* prob. from an obs. διάκω **diakō** (to *run* on errands; comp. *1377*); an *attendant,* i.e. (gen.) a *waiter* (at table or in other menial duties); spec. a Chr. *teacher* and *pastor* (techn. a *deacon* or *deaconess*):—deacon, minister, servant.

1250. διακόσιοι **diakŏsiŏi**, *dee-ak-os'-ee-oy;* from *1364* and *1540; two hundred:*—two hundred.

1251. διακούομαι **diakŏuŏmai**, *dee-ak-oo'-om-ahee;* mid. from *1223* and *191;* to *hear throughout,* i.e. *patiently listen* (to a prisoner's plea):—hear.

1252. διακρίνω **diakrinō**, *dee-ak-ree'-no;* from *1223* and *2919;* to *separate thoroughly,* i.e. (lit. and reflex.) to *withdraw* from, or (by impl.) *oppose;* fig. to *discriminate* (by impl. *decide*), or (reflex.) *hesitate:*—contend, make (to) differ (-ence), discern, doubt, judge, be partial, stagger, waver.

1253. διάκρισις **diakrisis**, *dee-ak'-ree-sis;* from *1252;* judicial *estimation:*—discern (-ing), disputation.

1254. διακωλύω **diakōluō**, *dee-ak-o-loo'-o;* from *1223* and *2967;* to *hinder altogether,* i.e. *utterly prohibit:*—forbid.

1255. διαλαλέω **dialalĕō**, *dee-al-al-eh'-o;* from *1223* and *2980;* to *talk throughout* a company, i.e. *converse* or (gen.) *publish:*—commune, noise abroad.

1256. διαλέγομαι **dialĕgŏmai**, *dee-al-eg'-om-ahee;* mid. from *1223* and *3004;* to *say thoroughly,* i.e. *discuss* (in argument or exhortation):—dispute, preach (unto), reason (with), speak.

1257. διαλείπω **dialĕipō**, *dee-al-i'-po;* from *1223* and *3007;* to *leave off in the middle,* i.e. *intermit:*—cease.

1258. διάλεκτος **dialĕktŏs**, *dee-al'-ek-tos;* from *1256;* a (mode of) *discourse,* i.e. "*dialect*":—language, tongue.

1259. διαλλάσσω **diallassō**, *dee-al-las'-so;* from *1223* and *236;* to *change thoroughly,* i.e. (ment.) to *conciliate:*—reconcile.

1260. διαλογίζομαι **dialŏgizŏmai**, *dee-al-og-id'-zom-ahee;* from *1223* and *3049;* to *reckon thoroughly,* i.e. (gen.) to *deliberate* (by reflection or discussion):—cast in mind, consider, dispute, muse, reason, think.

1261. διαλογισμός **dialŏgismŏs**, *dee-al-og-is-mos';* from *1260; discussion,* i.e. (internal) *consideration* (by impl. *purpose*), or (external) *debate:*—dispute, doubtful (-ing), imagination, reasoning, thought.

1262. διαλύω **dialuō**, *dee-al-oo'-o;* from *1223* and *3089;* to *dissolve utterly:*—scatter.

1263. διαμαρτύρομαι **diamarturŏmai**, *dee-am ar-too'-rom-ahee;* from *1223* and *3140;* to *attest* or *protest earnestly,* or (by impl.) *hortatively:*—charge, testify (unto), witness.

1264. διαμάχομαι **diamachŏmai**, *dee-am-akh'-om-ahee;* from *1223* and *3164;* to *fight fiercely* (in altercation):—strive.

1265. διαμένω **diamĕnō**, *dee-am-en'-o;* from *1223* and *3306;* to *stay constantly* (in being or relation):—continue, remain.

1266. διαμερίζω **diamĕrizō**, *dee-am-er-id'-zo;* from *1223* and *3307;* to *partition thoroughly* (lit. in distribution, fig. in dissension):—cloven, divide, part.

1267. διαμερισμός **diamĕrismŏs**, *dee-am-er-is-mos';* from *1266; disunion* (of opinion and conduct):—division.

1268. διανέμω **dianĕmō**, *dee-an-em'-o;* from *1223* and the base of *3551;* to *distribute,* i.e. (of information) to *disseminate:*—spread.

1269. διανεύω **dianĕuō**, *dee-an-yoo'-o;* from *1223* and *3506;* to *nod* (or *express* by signs) *across* an intervening space:—beckon.

1270. διανόημα **dianŏēma**, *dee-an-ŏ'-ay-mah;* from a comp. of *1223* and *3539;* something *thought through,* i.e. a *sentiment:*—thought.

1271. διάνοια **dianŏia**, *dee-an'-oy-ah;* from *1223* and *3563; deep thought,* prop. the faculty (*mind* or its *disposition*), by impl. its exercise:—imagination, mind, understanding.

1272. διανοίγω **dianŏigō**, *dee-an-oy'-go;* from *1223* and *455;* to *open thoroughly,* lit. (as a first-born) or fig. (to *expound*):—open.

1273. διανυκτερεύω **dianuktĕrĕuō**, *dee-an-ook-ter-yoo'-o;* from *1223* and a der. of *3571;* to *sit up the whole night:*—continue all night.

1274. διανύω **dianuō**, *dee-an-oo'-o;* from *1223* and ἀνύω **anuō** (to *effect*); to *accomplish thoroughly:*—finish.

1275. διαπαντός **diapantŏs**, *dee-ap-an-tos';* from *1223* and the genit. of *3956; through all* time, i.e. (adv.) *constantly:*—alway (-s), continually.

1276. διαπεράω **diapĕraō**, *dee-ap-er-ah'-o;* from *1223* and a der. of the base of *4008;* to *cross entirely:*—go over, pass (over), sail over.

1277. διαπλέω **diaplĕō**, *dee-ap-leh'-o;* from *1223* and *4126;* to *sail through:*—sail over.

1278. διαπονέω **diapŏnĕō**, *dee-ap-on-eh'-o;* from *1223* and a der. of *4192;* to *toil through,* i.e. (pass.) *be worried:*—be grieved.

1279. διαπορεύομαι **diapŏrĕuŏmai**, *dee-ap-or-yoo'-om-ahee;* from *1223* and *4198;* to *travel through:*—go through, journey in, pass by.

1280. διαπορέω **diapŏrĕō**, *dee-ap-or-eh'-o;* from *1223* and *639;* to *be thoroughly nonplussed:*—(be in) doubt, be (much) perplexed.

1281. διαπραγματεύομαι **diapragmatĕuŏmai**, *dee-ap-rag-mat-yoo'-om-ahee;* from *1223* and *4231;* to *thoroughly occupy oneself,* i.e. (trans. and by impl.) to *earn* in business:—gain by trading.

1282. διαπρίω **diapriō**, *dee-ap-ree'-o;* from *1223* and the base of *4249;* to *saw asunder,* i.e. (fig.) to *exasperate:*—cut (to the heart).

1283. διαρπάζω **diarpazō**, *dee-ar-pad'-zo;* from *1223* and *726;* to *seize asunder,* i.e. *plunder:*—spoil.

1284. διαῤῥήσσω **diarrhēssō**, *dee-ar-hrayce'-so;* from *1223* and *4486;* to *tear asunder:*—break, rend.

1285. διασαφέω **diasaphĕō**, *dee-as-af-eh'-o;* from *1223* and σαφής **saphēs** (*clear*); to *clear thoroughly,* i.e. (fig.) *declare:*—tell unto.

1286. διασείω **diasĕiō**, *dee-as-i'-o;* from *1223* and *4579;* to *shake thoroughly,* i.e. (fig.) to *intimidate:*—do violence to.

1287. διασκορπίζω **diaskŏrpizō**, *dee-as-kor-pid'-zo;* from *1223* and *4650;* to *dissipate,* i.e. (gen.) to *rout* or *separate;* spec. to *winnow;* fig. to *squander:*—disperse, scatter (abroad), strew, waste.

1288. διασπάω **diaspaō**, *dee-as-pah'-o;* from *1223* and *4685;* to *draw apart,* i.e. *sever* or *dismember:*—pluck asunder, pull in pieces.

1289. διασπείρω **diaspĕirō**, *dee-as-pi'-ro;* from *1223* and *4687;* to *sow throughout,* i.e. (fig.) *distribute* in foreign lands:—scatter abroad.

1290. διασπορά **diaspŏra**, *dee-as-por-ah';* from *1289; dispersion,* i.e. (spec. and concr.) the (converted) Isr. *resident* in Gentile countries:—(which are) scattered (abroad).

1291. διαστέλλομαι **diastĕllŏmai**, *dee-as-tel'-lom-ahee;* mid. from *1223* and *4724;* to *set* (oneself) *apart* (fig. *distinguish*), i.e. (by impl.) to *enjoin:*—charge, that which was (give) commanded (-ment).

1292. διάστημα **diastēma**, *dee-as'-tay-mah;* from *1339;* an *interval:*—space.

1293. διαστολή **diastŏlē**, *dee-as-tol-ay';* from *1291;* a *variation:*—difference, distinction.

1294. διαστρέφω **diastrĕphō**, *dee-as-tref'-o;* from *1223* and *4762;* to *distort,* i.e. (fig.) *misinterpret,* or (mor.) *corrupt:*—perverse (-rt), turn away.

1295. διασώζω **diasōzō**, *dee-as-odze'-o;* from *1223* and *4982;* to *save thoroughly,* i.e. (by impl. or anal.) to *cure, preserve, rescue,* etc.:—bring safe, escape (safe), heal, make perfectly whole, save.

1296. διαταγή **diatagē**, *dee-at-ag-ay';* from *1299; arrangement,* i.e. *institution:*—instrumentality.

1297. διάταγμα **diatagma**, *dee-at'-ag-mah;* from *1299;* an *arrangement,* i.e. (authoritative) *edict:*—commandment.

1298. διαταράσσω **diatarassō**, *dee-at-ar-as'-so;* from *1223* and *5015;* to *disturb wholly,* i.e. *agitate* (with alarm):—trouble.

1299. διατάσσω **diatassō**, *dee-at-as'-so;* from *1223* and *5021;* to *arrange thoroughly,* i.e. (spec.) *institute, prescribe,* etc.:—appoint, command, give, (set in) order, ordain.

1300. διατελέω **diatĕlĕō**, *dee-at-el-eh'-o;* from *1223* and *5055;* to *accomplish thoroughly,* i.e. (subj.) to *persist:*—continue.

1301. διατηρέω **diatērĕō**, *dee-at-ay-reh'-o;* from *1223* and *5083;* to *watch thoroughly,* i.e. (pos. and trans.) to *observe* strictly, or (neg. and reflex.) to *avoid* wholly:—keep.

1302. διατί **diati**, *dee-at-ee';* from *1223* and *5101; through what* cause ?, i.e. *why?:*—wherefore, why.

1303. διατίθεμαι **diatithĕmai**, *dee-at-ith'-em-ahee;* mid. from *1223* and *5087;* to *put apart,* i.e. (fig.) *dispose* (by assignment, compact or bequest):—appoint, make, testator.

1304. διατρίβω **diatribō**, *dee-at-ree'-bo;* from *1223* and the base of *5147;* to *wear through* (time), i.e. *remain:*—abide, be, continue, tarry.

1305. διατροφή **diatrŏphē**, *dee-at-rof-ay';* from a comp. of *1223* and *5142; nourishment:*—food.

1306. διαυγάζω **diaugazō**, *dee-ŏw-gad'-zo;* from *1223* and *826;* to *glimmer through,* i.e. *break* (as day):—dawn.

1307. διαφανής **diaphanēs**, *dee-af-an-ace';* from *1223* and *5316; appearing through,* i.e. "*diaphanous*":—transparent.

1308. διαφέρω **diaphĕrō**, *dee-af-er'-o;* from *1223* and *5342;* to *bear through,* i.e. (lit.) *transport;* usually to *bear apart,* i.e. (obj.) to *toss about* (fig. *report*); subj. to "*differ,*" or (by impl.) *surpass:*—be better, carry, differ from, drive up and down, be (more) excellent, make matter, publish, be of more value.

1309. διαφεύγω **diaphĕugō**, *dee-af-yoo'-go;* from *1223* and *5343;* to *flee through,* i.e. *escape:*—escape.

1310. διαφημίζω **diaphēmizō**, *dee-af-ay-mid'-zo;* from *1223* and a der. of *5345;* to *report thoroughly,* i.e. *divulgate:*—blaze abroad, commonly report, spread abroad, fame.

1311. διαφθείρω **diaphthĕirō**, *dee-af-thi'-ro;* from *1225* and *5351;* to *rot thoroughly,* i.e. (by impl.) to *ruin* (pass. *decay* utterly, fig. *pervert*):—corrupt, destroy, perish.

1312. διαφθορά **diaphthŏra**, *dee-af-thor-ah';* from *1311; decay:*—corruption.

1313. διάφορος **diaphŏrŏs**, *dee-af'-or-os;* from *1308; varying;* also *surpassing:*—differing, divers, more excellent.

1314. διαφυλάσσω **diaphulassō**, *dee-af-oo-las'-so;* from *1223* and *5442;* to *guard thoroughly,* i.e. *protect:*—keep.

1315. διαχειρίζομαι **diachĕirizŏmai**, *dee-akh-i-rid'-zom-ahee;* from *1223* and a der. of *5495;* to *handle thoroughly,* i.e. *lay* violent *hands* upon:—kill, slay.

1316. διαχωρίζομαι **diachōrizŏmai**, *dee-akh-o-rid'-zom-ahee;* from *1223* and the mid. of *5563;* to *remove* (oneself) *wholly,* i.e. *retire:*—depart.

1317. διδακτικός **didaktikŏs**, *did-ak-tik-os';* from *1318; instructive* ("didactic"):—apt to teach.

1318. διδακτός **didaktŏs**, *did-ak-tos';* from *1321;* (subj.) *instructed* or (obj.) *communicated* by teaching:—taught, which . . . teacheth.

1319. διδασκαλία **didaskalia**, *did-as-kal-ee'-ah;* from *1320; instruction* (the function or the information):—doctrine, learning, teaching.

1320. διδάσκαλος **didaskalŏs**, *did-as'-kal-os;* from *1321;* an *instructor* (gen. or spec.):—doctor, master, teacher.

1321. διδάσκω **didaskō**, *did-as'-ko;* a prol. (caus.) form of a prim. verb δάω **daō** (to *learn*); to *teach* (in the same broad application):—teach.

1322. διδαχή **didachē**, *did-akh-ay';* from *1321; instruction* (the act or the matter):—doctrine, hath been taught.

1323. δίδραχμον **didrachmŏn**, *did'-rakh-mon;* from *1364* and *1406;* a *double drachma* (*didrachm*):—tribute.

1324. Δίδυμος **Didumŏs**, *did'-oo-mos;* prol. from *1364; double,* i.e. *twin; Didymus,* a Chr.:—Didymus.

1325. δίδωμι **didōmi**, *did'-o-mee;* a prol. form of a prim. verb (which is used as an altern. in most of the tenses); to *give* (used in a very wide application, prop. or by impl., lit. or fig.; greatly modified by the connection):—adventure, bestow, bring forth, commit, deliver (up), give, grant, hinder, make, minister, number, offer, have power, put, receive, set, shew, smite (+ with the hand), strike (+ with the palm of the hand), suffer, take, utter, yield.

1326. διεγείρω **diĕgĕirō**, *dee-eg-i'-ro;* from *1223* and *1453;* to *wake fully,* i.e. *arouse* (lit. or fig.):—arise, awake, raise, stir up.

1327. διέξοδος **diĕxŏdŏs**, *dee-ex'-od-os;* from *1223* and *1841;* an *outlet through,* i.e. prob. an open *square* (from which roads diverge):—highway

1328. διερμηνευτής **diĕrmēnĕutēs**, *dee-er-main-yoo-tace';* from *1329;* an *explainer:*—interpreter.

1329. διερμηνεύω **diĕrmēnĕuō**, *dee-er-main-yoo'-o;* from *1223* and *2059;* to *explain thoroughly;* by impl. to *translate:*—expound, interpret (-ation).

1330. διέρχομαι **diĕrchŏmai**, *dee-er'-khom-ahee;* from *1223* and *2064;* to *traverse* (lit.):—come, depart, go (about, abroad, every where, over, through, throughout), pass (by, over, through, throughout), pierce through, travel, walk through.

1331. διερωτάω **diĕrōtaō**, *dee-er-o-tah'-o;* from *1223* and *2065;* to *question throughout,* i.e. *ascertain* by interrogation:—make enquiry for.

1332. διετής **diĕtēs**, *dee-et-ace';* from *1364* and *2094; of two years* (in age):—two years old.

1333. διετία **diĕtia**, *dee-et-ee'-a;* from *1332;* a space of *two years* (*biennium*):—two years.

1334. διηγέομαι **diēgĕŏmai**, *dee-ayg-eh'-om-ahee;* from *1223* and *2233;* to *relate fully:*—declare, shew, tell.

1335. διήγεσις **diēgĕsis**, *dee-ayg'-es-is;* from *1334;* a *recital:*—declaration.

1336. διηνεκές **diēnĕkĕs**, *dee-ay-nek-es';* neut. of a comp. of *1223* and a der. of an alt. of *5342; carried through,* i.e. (adv. with *1519* and *3588* pref.) *perpetually:*—+ continually, for ever.

1337. διθάλασσος **dithalassŏs**, *dee-thal'-as-sos;* from *1364* and *2281; having two seas,* i.e. a *sound* with a double outlet:—where two seas met.

1338. διϊκνέομαι **diiknĕŏmai**, *dee-ik-neh'-om-ahee;* from *1223* and the base of *2425;* to *reach through,* i.e. *penetrate:*—pierce.

1339. διΐστημι **diistēmi**, *dee-is'-tay-mee;* from *1223* and *2476;* to *stand apart,* i.e. (reflex.) to *remove, intervene:*—go further, be parted, after the space of.

1340. διϊσχυρίζομαι **diischurizŏmai**, *dee-is-khoo-rid'-zom-ahee;* from *1223* and a der. of *2478;* to *stout* it *through,* i.e. *asseverate:*—confidently (constantly) affirm.

1341. δικαιοκρισία **dikaiŏkrisia**, *dik-ah-yok-ris-ee'-ah;* from *1342* and *2920;* a *just sentence:*—righteous judgment.

1342. δίκαιος **dikaiŏs**, *dik'-ah-yos;* from *1349; equitable* (in character or act); by impl. *innocent, holy* (absol. or rel.):—just, meet, right (-eous).

1343. δικαιοσύνη **dikaiŏsunē**, *dik-ah-yos-oo'-nay;* from *1342; equity* (of character or act); spec. (Chr.) *justification:*—righteousness.

1344. δικαιόω **dikaiŏō**, *dik-ah-yŏ'-o;* from *1342;* to *render* (i.e. *show* or *regard* as) *just* or *innocent:*—free, justify (-ier), be righteous.

1345. δικαίωμα **dikaiōma**, *dik-ah'-yo-mah;* from *1344;* an *equitable deed;* by impl. a *statute* or *decision:*—judgment, justification, ordinance, righteousness.

1346. δικαίως **dikaiōs**, *dik-ah'-yoce;* adv. from *1342; equitably:*—justly, (to) righteously (-ness).

1347. δικαίωσις **dikaiōsis**, *dik-ah'-yo-sis;* from *1344; acquittal* (for Christ's sake):—justification.

1348. δικαστής **dikastēs**, *dik-as-tace';* from a der. of *1349;* a *judger:*—judge.

1349. δίκη **dikē**, *dee'-kay;* prob. from *1166; right* (as self-*evident*), i.e. *justice* (the principle, a decision, or its execution):—judgment, punish, vengeance.

1350. δίκτυον **diktuŏn**, *dik'-too-on;* prob. from a prim. verb δίκω **dikō** (to *cast*); a *seine* (for fishing):—net.

1351. δίλογος **dilŏgŏs**, *dil'-og-os;* from *1364* and *3056; equivocal,* i.e. telling a different story:—double tongued.

1352. διό **diŏ**, *dee-ŏ';* from *1223* and *3739; through which* thing, i.e. *consequently:*—for which cause, therefore, wherefore.

1353. διοδεύω **diŏdĕuō**, *dee-od-yoo'-o;* from *1223* and *3593;* to *travel through:*—go throughout, pass through.

1354. Διονύσιος **Diŏnusiŏs**, *dee-on-oo'-see-os;* from Διόνυσος **Diŏnusŏs** (*Bacchus*); *reveller; Dionysius,* an Athenian:—Dionysius.

1355. διόπερ **diŏpĕr**, *dee-op'-er;* from *1352* and *4007; on which very account:*—wherefore.

1356. διοπετής **diŏpĕtēs**, *dee-op-et'-ace;* from the alt. of *2203* and the alt. of *4098; sky-fallen* (i.e. an *aerolite*):—which fell down from Jupiter.

1357. διόρθωσις **diŏrthōsis**, *dee-or'-tho-sis;* from a comp. of *1223* and a der. of *3717,* mean. to *straighten thoroughly; rectification,* i.e. (spec.) the Messianic *restauration:*—reformation.

1358. διορύσσω **diŏrussō**, *dee-or-oos'-so;* from *1223* and *3736;* to *penetrate* burglariously:—break through (up).

Διός **Diŏs**. See *2203*.

1359. Διόσκουροι **Diŏskŏurŏi**, *dee-os'-koo-roy;* from the alt. of *2203* and a form of the base of *2877; sons of Jupiter,* i.e. the twins *Dioscuri:*—Castor and Pollux.

1360. διότι **diŏti**, *dee-ot'-ee;* from *1223* and *3754; on the very account that,* or *inasmuch as:*—because (that), for, therefore.

1361. Διοτρεφής **Diŏtrĕphēs**, *dee-ot-ref-ace';* from the alt. of *2203* and *5142; Jove-nourished; Diotrephes,* an opponent of Christianity:—Diotrephes.

1362. διπλοῦς **diplŏus**, *dip-looce';* from *1364* and (prob.) the base of *4119; two-fold:*—double, two-fold more.

1363. διπλόω **diplŏō**, *dip-lŏ'-o;* from *1362;* to *render two-fold:*—double.

1364. δίς **dis**, *dece;* adv. from *1417;* *twice:*—again, twice.

Δίς **Dis**. See *2203*.

1365. διστάζω **distazō**, *dis-tad'-zo;* from *1364;* prop. to *duplicate*, i.e. (ment.) to *waver* (in opinion):—doubt.

1366. δίστομος **distŏmŏs**, *dis'-tom-os;* from *1364* and *4750;* *double-edged:*—with two edges, two-edged.

1367. δισχίλιοι **dischiliŏi**, *dis-khil'-ee-oy;* from *1364* and *5507:* *two thousand:*—two thousand.

1368. διϋλίζω **diulizō**, *dee-oo-lid'-zo;* from *1223* and ὑλίζω **hulizō**, *hoo-lid'-zo* (to *filter*); to *strain out:*—strain at [*prob. by misprint*].

1369. διχάζω **dichazō**, *dee-khad'-zo;* from a der. of *1364;* to *make apart*, i.e. *sunder* (fig. *alienate*):—set at variance.

1370. διχοστασία **dichŏstasia**, *dee-khos-tas-ee'-ah;* from a der. of *1364* and *4714;* *disunion*, i.e. (fig.) *dissension:*—division, sedition.

1371. διχοτομέω **dichŏtŏmĕō**, *dee-khot-om-eh'-o;* from a comp. of a der. of *1364* and a der. of τέμνω **tĕmnō** (to *cut*); to *bisect*, i.e. (by extens.) to *flog* severely:—cut asunder (in sunder).

1372. διψάω **dipsaō**, *dip-sah'-o;* from a var. of *1373;* to *thirst* for (lit. or fig.):—(be, be a-) thirst (-y).

1373. δίψος **dipsŏs**, *dip'-sos;* of uncert. affin.; *thirst:*—thirst.

1374. δίψυχος **dipsuchŏs**, *dip'-soo-khos;* from *1364* and *5590;* *two-spirited*, i.e. *vacillating* (in opinion or purpose):—double minded.

1375. διωγμός **diōgmŏs**, *dee-ogue-mos';* from *1377;* *persecution:*—persecution.

1376. διώκτης **diōktēs**, *dee-oke'-tace;* from *1377;* a *persecutor:*—persecutor.

1377. διώκω **diōkō**, *dee-o'-ko;* a prol. (and caus.) form of a prim. verb δίω **diō** (to *flee;* comp. the base of *1169* and *1249*); to *pursue* (lit. or fig.); by impl. to *persecute:*—ensue, follow (after), given to, (suffer) persecute (-ion), press toward.

1378. δόγμα **dŏgma**, *dog'-mah;* from the base of *1380;* a *law* (civil, cer. or eccl.):—decree, ordinance.

1379. δογματίζω **dŏgmatizō**, *dog-mat-id'-zo;* from *1378;* to *prescribe* by statute, i.e. (reflex.) to *submit to* cer. *rule:*—be subject to ordinances.

1380. δοκέω **dŏkĕō**, *dok-eh'-o;* a prol. form of a prim. verb δόκω **dŏkō**, *dok'-o* (used only as an alt. in certain tenses; comp. the base of *1166*) of the same mean.; to *think;* by impl. to *seem* (truthfully or uncertainly):—be accounted, (of own) please (-ure), be of reputation, seem (good), suppose, think, trow.

1381. δοκιμάζω **dŏkimazō**, *dok-im-ad'-zo;* from *1384;* to *test* (lit. or fig.); by impl. to *approve:*—allow, discern, examine, × like, (ap-) prove, try.

1382. δοκιμή **dŏkimē**, *dok-ee-may';* from the same as *1384;* *test* (abstr. or concr.); by impl. *trustiness:*—experience (-riment), proof, trial.

1383. δοκίμιον **dŏkimiŏn**, *dok-im'-ee-on;* neut. of a presumed der. of *1382;* a *testing;* by impl. *trustworthiness:*—trial, trying.

1384. δόκιμος **dŏkimŏs**, *dok'-ee-mos;* from *1380;* prop. *acceptable* (*current* after assayal), i.e. *approved:*—approved, tried.

1385. δοκός **dŏkŏs**, *dok-os';* from *1209* (through the idea of *holding* up); a *stick* of timber:—beam.

δόκω **dŏkō**. See *1380*.

1386. δόλιος **dŏliŏs**, *dol'-ee-os;* from *1388;* *guileful:*—deceitful.

1387. δολιόω **dŏliŏō**, *dol-ee-ŏ'-o;* from *1386;* to *be guileful:*—use deceit.

1388. δόλος **dŏlŏs**, *dol'-os;* from an obs. prim. δέλλω **dĕllō** (prob. mean. to *decoy;* comp. *1185*); a *trick* (*bait*), i.e. (fig.) *wile:*—craft, deceit, guile, subtilty.

1389. δολόω **dŏlŏō**, *dol-ŏ'-o;* from *1388;* to *ensnare*, i.e. (fig.) *adulterate:*—handle deceitfully.

1390. δόμα **dŏma**, *dom'-ah;* from the base of *1325;* a *present:*—gift.

1391. δόξα **dŏxa**, *dox'-ah;* from the base of *1380;* *glory* (as very *apparent*), in a wide application (lit. or fig., obj. or subj.):—dignity, glory (-ious), honour, praise, worship.

1392. δοξάζω **dŏxazō**, *dox-ad'-zo;* from *1391;* to *render* (or *esteem*) *glorious* (in a wide application):—(make) glorify (-ious), full of (have) glory, honour, magnify.

1393. Δορκάς **Dŏrkas**, *dor-kas';* *gazelle; Dorcas*, a Chr. woman:—Dorcas.

1394. δόσις **dŏsis**, *dos'-is;* from the base of *1325;* a *giving;* by impl. (concr.) a *gift:*—gift, giving.

1395. δότης **dŏtēs**, *dot'-ace;* from the base of *1325;* a *giver:*—giver.

1396. δουλαγωγέω **dŏulagōgĕō**, *doo-lag-ogue-eh'-o;* from a presumed comp. of *1401* and *71;* to *be a slave-driver*, i.e. to *enslave* (fig. *subdue*):—bring into subjection.

1397. δουλεία **dŏulĕia**, *doo-li'-ah;* from *1398;* *slavery* (cer. or fig.):—bondage.

1398. δουλεύω **dŏulĕuō**, *dool-yoo'-o;* from *1401;* to *be a slave* to (lit. or fig., invol. or vol.):—be in bondage, (do) serve (-ice).

1399. δούλη **dŏulē**, *doo'-lay;* fem. of *1401;* a *female slave* (invol. or vol.):—handmaid (-en).

1400. δοῦλον **dŏulŏn**, *doo'-lon;* neut. of *1401;* *subservient:*—servant.

1401. δοῦλος **dŏulŏs**, *doo'-los;* from *1210;* a *slave* (lit. or fig., invol. or vol.; frequently therefore in a qualified sense of *subjection* or *subserviency*):—bond (-man), servant.

1402. δουλόω **dŏulŏō**, *doo-lŏ'-o;* from *1401;* to *enslave* (lit. or fig.):—bring into (be under) bondage, × given, become (make) servant.

1403. δοχή **dŏchē**, *dokh-ay';* from *1209;* a *reception*, i.e. convivial *entertainment:*—feast.

1404. δράκων **drakōn**, *drak'-own;* prob. from an alt. form of δέρκομαι **dĕrkŏmai** (to *look*); a fabulous kind of *serpent* (perh. as supposed to *fascinate*):—dragon.

1405. δράσσομαι **drassŏmai**, *dras'-som-ahee;* perh. akin to the base of *1404* (through the idea of *capturing*); to *grasp*, i.e. (fig.) *entrap:*—take.

1406. δραχμή **drachmē**, *drakh-may';* from *1405;* a *drachma* or (silver) coin (as *handled*):—piece (of silver).

δρέμω **drĕmō**. See *5143*.

1407. δρέπανον **drĕpanŏn**, *drep'-an-on;* from δρέπω **drĕpō** (to *pluck*); a gathering *hook* (espec. for harvesting):—sickle.

1408. δρόμος **drŏmŏs**, *drom'-os;* from the alt. of *5143;* a *race*, i.e. (fig.) *career:*—course.

1409. Δρούσιλλα **Drŏusilla**, *droo'-sil-lah;* a fem. dimin. of *Drusus* (a Rom. name); *Drusilla*, a member of the Herodian family:—Drusilla.

δῦμι **dumi**. See *1416*.

1410. δύναμαι **dunamai**, *doo'-nam-ahee;* of uncert. affin.; to *be able* or *possible:*—be able, can (do, + -not), could, may, might, be possible, be of power.

1411. δύναμις **dunamis**, *doo'-nam-is;* from *1410;* *force* (lit. or fig.); spec miraculous *power* (usually by impl. a *miracle* itself):—ability, abundance, meaning, might (-ily, -y, -y deed), (worker of) miracle (-s), power, strength, violence, mighty (wonderful) work.

1412. δυναμόω **dunamŏō**, *doo-nam-ŏ'-o;* from *1411;* to *enable:*—strengthen.

1413. δυνάστης **dunastēs**, *doo-nas'-tace;* from *1410;* a *ruler* or *officer:*—of great authority, mighty, potentate.

1414. δυνατέω **dunatĕō**, *doo-nat-eh'-o;* from *1415;* to *be efficient* (fig.):—be mighty.

1415. δυνατός **dunatŏs**, *doo-nat-os';* from *1410;* *powerful* or *capable* (lit. or fig.); neut. *possible:*—able, could, (that is) mighty (man), possible, power, strong.

1416. δύνω **dunō**, *doo'-no;* or

δῦμι **dumi**, *doo'-mee;* prol. forms of an obs. prim. δύω **duō**, *doo'-o* (to *sink*); to *go 'down'':*—set.

1417. δύο **duŏ**, *doo'-ŏ;* a prim. numeral; "*two*":—both, twain, two.

1418. δυσ- **dus-**, *doos;* a prim. inseparable particle of uncert. der.; used only in composition as a pref.; *hard*, i.e. *with difficulty:*— + hard, + grievous, *etc.*

1419. δυσβάστακτος **dusbastaktŏs**, *doos-bas'-tak-tos;* from *1418* and a der. of *941;* *oppressive:*—grievous to be borne.

1420. δυσεντερία **dusĕntĕria**, *doos-en-ter-ee'-ah;* from *1418* and a comp. of *1787* (mean. a *bowel*); a "*dysentery*":—bloody flux.

1421. δυσερμήνευτος **dusĕrmēnĕutŏs**, *doos-er-mane'-yoo-tos;* from *1418* and a presumed der. of *2050;* *difficult of explanation:*—hard to be uttered.

1422. δύσκολος **duskŏlŏs**, *doos'-kol-os;* from *1418* and κόλον **kŏlŏn** (*food*); prop. *fastidious about eating* (*peevish*), i.e. (gen.) *impracticable:*—hard.

1423. δυσκόλως **duskŏlōs**, *doos-kol'-oce;* adv. from *1422;* *impracticably:*—hardly.

1424. δυσμή **dusmē**, *doos-may';* from *1416;* the sun-*set*, i.e. (by impl.) the *western* region:—west.

1425. δυσνόητος **dusnŏētŏs**, *doos-nŏ'-ay-tos;* from *1418* and a der. of *3539;* *difficult of perception:*—hard to be understood.

1426. δυσφημία **dusphēmia**, *doos-fay-mee'-ah;* from a comp. of *1418* and *5345;* *defamation:*—evil report.

δύω **duō**. See *1416*.

1427. δώδεκα **dōdĕka**, *do'-dek-ah;* from *1417* and *1176;* *two* and *ten*, i.e. a *dozen:*—twelve.

1428. δωδέκατος **dōdĕkatŏs**, *do-dek'-at-os;* from *1427;* *twelfth:*—twelfth.

1429. δωδεκάφυλον **dōdĕkaphulŏn**, *do-dek-af'-oo-lon;* from *1427* and *5443;* the *commonwealth* of Israel:—twelve tribes.

1430. δῶμα **dōma**, *do'-mah;* from δέμω **dĕmō** (to *build*); prop. an *edifice*, i.e. (spec.) a *roof:*—housetop.

1431. δωρεά **dōrĕa**, *do-reh-ah';* from *1435;* a *gratuity:*—gift.

1432. δωρεάν **dōrĕan**, *do-reh-an';* acc. of *1431* as adv.; *gratuitously* (lit. or fig.):—without a cause, freely, for naught, in vain.

1433. δωρέομαι **dōrĕŏmai**, *do-reh'-om-ahee;* mid. from *1435;* to *bestow* gratuitously:—give.

1434. δώρημα **dōrēma**, *do'-ray-mah;* from *1433;* a *bestowment:*—gift.

1435. δῶρον **dōrŏn**, *do'-ron;* a *present;* spec. a *sacrifice:*—gift, offering.

E

1436. ἔα **ĕa**, *eh'-ah;* appar. imper. of *1439;* prop. *let it be*, i.e. (as interj.) *aha!:*—let alone.

1437. ἐάν **ĕan**, *eh-an';* from *1487* and *302;* a *conditional* particle; *in case* that, *provided*, etc.; often used in connection with other particles to denote *indefiniteness* or *uncertainty:*—before, but, except, (and) if, (if) so, (what-, whither-) soever, though, when (-soever), whether (or), to whom, [who-] so (-ever). See *3361*.

ἐάν μή **ĕan mē**. See *3361*.

1438. ἑαυτοῦ **hĕautŏu**, *heh-ŏw-too'* (incl. all the other cases); from a reflex. pron. otherwise obsol. and the gen. (dat. or acc.) of *846;* *him-* (*her-*, *it-*, *them-*, also [in conjunction with the pers. pron. of the other persons] *my-*, *thy-*, *our-*, *your-*) *self* (*selves*), etc.:—alone, her (own, -self), (he) himself, his (own), itself, one (to) another, our (thine) own (-selves), + that she had, their (own, own selves), (of) them (-selves), they, thyself, you, your (own, own conceits, own selves, -selves).

1439. ἐάω **ĕaō**, *eh-ah'-o;* of uncert. affin.; to *let be*, i.e. *permit* or *leave* alone:—commit, leave, let (alone), suffer. See also *1436*.

1440. ἑβδομήκοντα **hĕbdŏmēkŏnta**, *heb-dom-ay'-kon-tah;* from *1442* and a modified form of *1176*, *seventy:*—seventy, three score and ten.

1441. ἑβδομηκοντακίς **hĕbdŏmēkŏntakis**, *heb-dom-ay-kon-tak-is';* multiple adv. from *1440;* *seventy times:*—seventy times.

1442. ἕβδομος **hĕbdŏmŏs**, *heb'-dom-os;* ordinal from 2033; *seventh:*—seventh.

1443. Ἐβέρ **Ĕbĕr**, *eb-er';* of Heb. or. [5677]; *Eber,* a patriarch:—Eber.

1444. Ἑβραϊκός **Hĕbraïkŏs**, *heb-rah-ee-kos';* from 1443; *Hebraïc* or the *Jewish* language:—Hebrew.

1445. Ἑβραῖος **Hĕbraiŏs**, *heb-rah'-yos;* from 1443; a *Hebræan* (i.e. Hebrew) or *Jew:*—Hebrew.

1446. Ἑβραΐς **Hĕbraïs**, *heb-rah-is';* from 1443; the *Hebraistic* (i.e. *Hebrew*) or *Jewish* (*Chaldee*) language:—Hebrew.

1447. Ἑβραϊστί **Hĕbraïsti**, *heb-rah-is-tee';* adv. from 1446; *Hebraistically* or in the Jewish (Chaldee) language:—in (the) Hebrew (tongue).

1448. ἐγγίζω **ĕggizō**, *eng-id'-zo;* from 1451; to make *near,* i.e. (reflex.) *approach:*—approach, be at hand, come (draw) near, be (come, draw) nigh.

1449. ἐγγράφω **ĕggraphō**, *eng-graf'-o;* from 1722 and 1125; to "*engrave*", i.e. *inscribe:*—write (in).

1450. ἔγγυος **ĕgguŏs**, *eng'-goo-os;* from 1722 and γυῖον **guiŏn** (a *limb*); *pledged* (as if *articulated* by a member), i.e. a *bondsman:*—surety.

1451. ἐγγύς **ĕggus**, *eng-goos';* from a prim. verb ἄγχω **agchō** (to *squeeze* or *throttle;* akin to the base of 43); *near* (lit. or fig., of place or time):—from, at hand, near, nigh (at hand, unto), ready.

1452. ἐγγύτερον **ĕggutĕrŏn**, *eng-goo'-ter-on;* neut. of the comp. of 1451; *nearer:*—nearer.

1453. ἐγείρω **ĕgĕirō**, *eg-i'-ro;* prob. akin to the base of 58 (through the idea of *collecting* one's faculties); to *waken* (trans. or intrans.), i.e. *rouse* (lit. from sleep, from sitting or lying, from disease, from death; or fig. from obscurity, inactivity, ruins, nonexistence):—awake, lift (up), raise (again, up), rear up, (a-) rise (again, up), stand, take up.

1454. ἔγερσις **ĕgĕrsis**, *eg'-er-sis;* from 1453; a *resurgence* (from death):—resurrection.

1455. ἐγκάθετος **ĕgkathĕtŏs**, *eng-kath'-et-os;* from 1722 and a der. of 2524; *subinduced,* i.e. surreptitiously *suborned* as a lier-in-wait:—spy.

1456. ἐγκαίνια **ĕgkainia**, *eng-kah'ee-nee-ah;* neut. plur. of a presumed comp. from 1722 and 2537; *innovatives,* i.e. (spec.) *renewal* (of religious services after the Antiochian interruption):—dedication.

1457. ἐγκαινίζω **ĕgkainizō**, *eng-kahee-nid'-zo;* from 1456; to *renew,* i.e. *inaugurate:*—consecrate, dedicate.

1458. ἐγκαλέω **ĕgkalĕō**, *eng-kal-eh'-o;* from 1722 and 2564; to *call in* (as a debt or demand), i.e. *bring to account* (*charge, criminate,* etc.):—accuse, call in question, implead, lay to the charge.

1459. ἐγκαταλείπω **ĕgkatalĕipō**, *eng-kat-al-i'-po;* from 1722 and 2641; to *leave behind in* some place, i.e. (in a good sense) *let remain over,* or (in a bad one) to *desert:*—forsake, leave.

1460. ἐγκατοικέω **ĕgkatŏikĕō**, *eng-kat-oy-keh'-o;* from 1722 and 2730; to *settle down in* a place, i.e. *reside:*—dwell among.

1461. ἐγκεντρίζω **ĕgkĕntrizō**, *eng-ken-trid'-zo;* from 1722 and a der. of 2759; to *prick in,* i.e. *ingraft:*—graff in (-to).

1462. ἔγκλημα **ĕgklēma**, *eng'-klay-mah;* from 1458; an *accusation,* i.e. *offence* alleged:—crime laid against, laid to charge.

1463. ἐγκομβόομαι **ĕgkŏmbŏŏmai**, *eng-kom-bŏ'-om-ahee;* mid. from 1722 and κομβόω **kŏmbŏō** (to *gird*); to *engirdle* oneself (for labor), i.e. fig. (the apron being a badge of servitude) to *wear* (in token of mutual deference):—be clothed with.

1464. ἐγκοπή **ĕgkŏpē**, *eng-kop-ay';* from 1465; a *hindrance:*— × hinder.

1465. ἐγκόπτω **ĕgkŏptō**, *eng-kop'-to;* from 1722 and 2875; to *cut into,* i.e. (fig.) *impede, detain:*—hinder, be tedious unto.

1466. ἐγκράτεια **ĕgkratĕia**, *eng-krat'-i-ah;* from 1468; *self-control* (espec. *continence*):—temperance.

1467. ἐγκρατεύομαι **ĕgkratĕuŏmai**, *eng-krat-yoo'-om-ahee;* mid. from 1468; to *exercise self-restraint* (in diet and chastity):—can ([-not]) contain, be temperate.

1468. ἐγκρατής **ĕgkratēs**, *eng-krat-ace';* from 1722 and 2904; *strong in* a thing (*masterful*), i.e. (fig. and reflex.) *self-controlled* (in appetite, etc.):—temperate.

1469. ἐγκρίνω **ĕgkrinō**, *eng-kree'-no;* from 1722 and 2919; to *judge in,* i.e. *count* among:—make of the number.

1470. ἐγκρύπτω **ĕkgruptō**, *eng-kroop'-to;* from 1722 and 2928; to *conceal in,* i.e. *incorporate with:*—hid in

1471. ἔγκυος **ĕgkuŏs**, *eng'-koo-os;* from 1722 and the base of 2949; *swelling inside,* i.e. *pregnant:*—great with child.

1472. ἐγχρίω **ĕgchriō**, *eng-khree'-o;* from 1722 and 5548; to *rub in* (oil), i.e. *besmear:*—anoint.

1473. ἐγώ **ĕgō**, *eg-o';* a prim. pron. of the first pers. *I* (only expressed when emphatic):—I, me. For the other cases and the plur. see 1691, 1698, 1700, 2248, 2249, 2254, 2257, etc.

1474. ἐδαφίζω **ĕdaphizō**, *ed-af-id'-zo;* from 1475; to *raze:*—lay even with the ground.

1475. ἔδαφος **ĕdaphŏs**, *ed'-af-os;* from the base of 1476; a *basis* (*bottom*), i.e. the *soil:*—ground.

1476. ἑδραῖος **hĕdraiŏs**, *hed-rah'-yos;* from a der. of ἕζομαι **hĕzŏmai** (to *sit*); *sedentary,* i.e. (by impl.) *immovable:*—settled, stedfast.

1477. ἑδραίωμα **hĕdraiōma**, *hed-rah'-yo-mah;* from a der. of 1476; a *support,* i.e. (fig.) *basis:*—ground.

1478. Ἐζεκίας **Ĕzĕkias**, *ed-zek-ee'-as;* of Heb. or. [2396]; *Ezekias* (i.e. *Hezekiah*), an Isr.:—Ezekias.

1479. ἐθελοθρησκεία **ĕthĕlŏthrēskĕia**, *eth-el-oth-race-ki'-ah;* from 2309 and 2356; *voluntary* (*arbitrary* and *unwarranted*) *piety,* i.e. *sanctimony:*—will worship.

ἐθέλω **ĕthĕlō**. See 2309.

1480. ἐθίζω **ĕthizō**, *eth-id'-zo;* from 1485; to *accustom,* i.e. (neut. pass. part.) *customary:*—custom.

1481. ἐθνάρχης **ĕthnarchēs**, *eth-nar'-khace;* from 1484 and 746; the *governor* [not king] *of a district:*—ethnarch.

1482. ἐθνικός **ĕthnikŏs**, *eth-nee-kos';* from 1484; *national* ("*ethnic*"), i.e. (spec.) a *Gentile:*—heathen (man).

1483. ἐθνικῶς **ĕthnikōs**, *eth-nee-koce';* adv. from 1482; *as a Gentile:*—after the manner of Gentiles.

1484. ἔθνος **ĕthnŏs**, *eth'-nos;* prob. from 1486; a *race* (as of the same *habit*), i.e. a *tribe;* spec. a *foreign* (*non-Jewish*) one (usually by impl. *pagan*):—Gentile, heathen, nation, people.

1485. ἔθος **ĕthŏs**, *eth'-os;* from 1486; a *usage* (prescribed by habit or law):—custom, manner, be wont.

1486. ἔθω **ĕthō**, *eth'-o;* a prim. verb; to *be used* (by habit or conventionality); neut. perf. part. *usage:*—be custom (manner, wont).

1487. εἰ **ĕi**, *i;* a prim. particle of conditionality; *if, whether, that,* etc.:—forasmuch as, if, that, ([al-]) though, whether. Often used in connection or composition with other particles, espec. as in 1489, 1490, 1499, 1508, 1509, 1512, 1513, 1536, 1537. See also 1437.

1488. εἶ **ĕi**, *i;* second pers. sing. pres. of 1510; thou *art:*—art, be.

1489. εἴγε **ĕigĕ**, *i'-gheh;* from 1487 and 1065; *if indeed, seeing that, unless,* (with neg.) *otherwise:*—if (so be that, yet).

1490. εἰ δὲ μή(γε) **ĕi dĕ mē(gĕ)**, *i deh may'-(gheh);* from 1487, 1161 and 3361 (sometimes with 1065 added); *but if not:*—(or) else, if (not, otherwise), otherwise.

1491. εἶδος **ĕidŏs**, *i'-dos,* from 1492; a *view,* i.e. *form* (lit. or fig.):—appearance, fashion, shape, sight.

1492. εἴδω **ĕidō**, *i'-do;* a prim. verb; used only in certain past tenses, the others being borrowed from the equiv. 3700 and 3708; prop. to *see* (lit. or fig.); by impl. (in the perf. only) to *know:*—be aware, behold, × can (+ not tell), consider, (have) know (-ledge), look (on), perceive, see, be sure, tell, understand, wist, wot. Comp. 3700.

1493. εἰδωλεῖον **ĕidōlĕiŏn**, *i-do-li'-on;* neut. of a presumed der. of 1497; an *image-fane:*—idol's temple.

1494. εἰδωλόθυτον **ĕidōlŏthutŏn**, *i-do-loth'-oo-ton;* neut. of a comp. of 1497 and a presumed der. of 2380; an *image-sacrifice,* i.e. part of an *idolatrous offering:*—(meat, thing that is) offered (in sacrifice, sacrificed) to (unto) idols.

1495. εἰδωλολατρεία **ĕidōlŏlatrĕia**, *i-do-lol-at-ri'-ah;* from 1497 and 2999; *image-worship* (lit. or fig.):—idolatry.

1496. εἰδωλολάτρης **ĕidōlŏlatrēs**, *i-do-lol-at'-race;* from 1497 and the base of 3000; an *image-* (*servant* or) *worshipper* (lit. or fig.):—idolater.

1497. εἴδωλον **ĕidōlŏn**, *i'-do-lon;* from 1491; an *image* (i.e. for worship); by impl. a heathen *god,* or (plur.) the *worship* of such:—idol.

1498. εἴην **ĕiēn**, *i'-ane;* optative (i.e. Eng. subjunctive) pres. of 1510 (includ. the other pers.); *might* (*could, would* or *should*) *be:*—mean, + perish, should be, was, were.

1499. εἰ καί **ĕi kai**, *i kahee;* from 1487 and 2532; *if also* (or *even*):—if (that), though.

1500. εἰκῆ **ĕikē**, *i-kay';* prob. from 1502 (through the idea of *failure*); *idly,* i.e. *without reason* (or *effect*):—without a cause, (in) vain (-ly).

1501. εἴκοσι **ĕikŏsi**, *i'-kos-ee;* of uncert. affin.; a *score:*—twenty.

1502. εἴκω **ĕikō**, *i'-ko;* appar. a prim. verb; prop. to *be weak,* i.e. *yield:*—give place.

1503. εἴκω **ĕikō**, *i'-ko;* appar. a prim. verb [perh. akin to 1502 through the idea of *faintness* as a copy]; to *resemble:*—be like.

1504. εἰκών **ĕikōn**, *i-kone';* from 1503; a *likeness,* i.e. (lit.) *statue, profile,* or (fig.) *representation, resemblance:*—image.

1505. εἰλικρίνεια **ĕilikrinĕia**, *i-lik-ree'-ni-ah;* from 1506; *clearness,* i.e. (by impl.) *purity* (fig.):—sincerity.

1506. εἰλικρινής **ĕilikrinēs**, *i-lik-ree-nace';* from εἵλη **hĕilē** (the sun's *ray*) and 2919; *judged by sunlight,* i.e. tested as *genuine* (fig.):—pure, sincere.

1507. εἱλίσσω **hĕilissō**, *hi-lis'-so;* a prol. form of a prim. but defective verb εἵλω **hĕilō** (of the same mean.); to *coil* or *wrap:*—roll together. See also 1667.

1508. εἰ μή **ĕi mē**, *i may;* from 1487 and 3361; *if not:*—but, except (that), if not, more than, save (only) that, saving, till.

1509. εἰ μή τι **ĕi mē ti**, *i may tee;* from 1508 and the neut. of 5100; *if not somewhat:*—except.

1510. εἰμί **ĕimi**, *i-mee';* first pers. sing. pres. indic.; a prol. form of a prim. and defective verb; I *exist* (used only when emphatic):—am, have been, × it is I, was. See also 1488, 1498, 1511, 1527, 2258, 2071, 2070, 2075, 2076, 2771, 2468, 5600.

1511. εἶναι **ĕinai**, *i'-nahee;* pres. infin. from 1510; *to exist:*—am, are, come, is, × lust after, × please well, there is, to be, was.

εἵνεκεν **hĕinĕkĕn**. See 1752.

1512. εἴ περ **ĕi pĕr**, *i per;* from 1487 and 4007; *if perhaps:*—if so be (that), seeing, though.

1513. εἴ πως **ĕi pōs**. *i poce;* from 1487 and 4458; *if somehow:*—if by any means.

1514. εἰρηνεύω **ĕirēnĕuō**, *i-rane-yoo'-o;* from 1515; *to be* (*act*) *peaceful:*—be at (have, live in) peace, live peaceably.

1515. εἰρήνη **ĕirēnē**, *i-ray'-nay;* prob. from a prim. verb εἴρω **ĕirō** (to *join*); *peace* (lit. or fig.); by impl. *prosperity:*—one, peace, quietness, rest, + set at one again.

1516. εἰρηνικός **ĕirēnikŏs**, *i-ray-nee-kos';* from 1515; *pacific;* by impl. *salutary:*—peaceable.

1517. εἰρηνοποιέω **ĕirēnŏpŏiĕō**, *i-ray-nop-oy-eh'-o;* from 1518; *to be a peace-maker,* i.e. (fig.) to *harmonize:*—make peace.

1518. εἰρηνοποιός **ĕirēnŏpŏiŏs**, *i-ray-nop-oy-os';* from 1515 and 4160; *pacificatory,* i.e. (subj.) *peaceable:*—peacemaker.

εἴρω **ĕirō**. See 1515, 4483, 5346.

1519. **εἰς ĕis**, *ice;* a prim. prep.; *to* or *into* (indicating the point reached or entered), of place, time, or (fig.) purpose (result, etc.); also in adv. phrases:—[abundant-] ly, against, among, as, at, [back-] ward, before, by, concerning, + continual, + far more exceeding, for [intent, purpose], fore, + forth, in (among, at, unto, -so much that, -to), to the intent that, + of one mind, + never, of, (up-) on, + perish, + set at one again, (so) that, therefore (-unto), throughout, till, to (be, the end, -ward), (here-) until (-to), . . . ward, [where-] fore, with. Often used in composition with the same general import, but only with verbs (etc.) expressing motion (lit. or fig.).

1520. **εἷς hĕis**, *hice;* (includ. the neut. [etc.] **ἕν hĕn**); a prim. numeral; *one:*—a (-n, -ny, certain), + abundantly, man, one (another), only, other, some. See also *1527, 3367, 3391, 3762.*

1521. **εἰσάγω ĕisagō**, *ice-ag'-o;* from *1519* and *71;* to *introduce* (lit. or fig.):—bring in (-to), (+ was to) lead into.

1522. **εἰσακούω ĕisakŏuō**, *ice-ak-oo'-o;* from *1519* and *191;* to *listen* to:—hear.

1523. **εἰσδέχομαι ĕisdĕchŏmai**, *ice-dekh'-om-ahee;* from *1519* and *1209;* to *take into* one's favor:—receive.

1524. **εἴσειμι ĕisĕimi**, *ice'-i-mee;* from *1519* and **εἶμι ĕimi** (to *go*); to *enter:*—enter (go) into.

1525. **εἰσέρχομαι ĕisĕrchŏmai**, *ice-er'-khom-ahee;* from *1519* and *2064;* to *enter* (lit. or fig.):—× arise, come (in, into), enter in (-to), go in (through).

1526. **εἰσί ĕisi**, *i-see';* 3d pers. plur. pres. indic. of *1510;* they *are:*—agree, are, be, dure, × is, were.

1527. **εἷς καθ' εἷς hĕis kath' hĕis**, *hice kath hice;* from *1520* repeated with *2596* inserted; *severally:*—one by one.

1528. **εἰσκαλέω ĕiskalĕō**, *ice-kal-eh'-o;* from *1519* and *2564;* to *invite* in:—call in.

1529. **εἴσοδος ĕisŏdŏs**, *ice'-od-os;* from *1519* and *3598;* an *entrance* (lit. or fig.):—coming, enter (-ing) in (to).

1530. **εἰσπηδάω ĕispēdaō**, *ice-pay-dah'-o;* from *1519* and **πηδάω pēdaō** (to *leap*); to *rush in:*—run (spring) in.

1531. **εἰσπορεύομαι ĕispŏrĕuŏmai**, *ice-por-yoo'-om-ahee;* from *1519* and *4198;* to *enter* (lit. or fig.):—come (enter) in, go into.

1532. **εἰστρέχω ĕistrĕchō**, *ice-trekh'-o;* from *1519* and *5143;* to *hasten inward:*—run in.

1533. **εἰσφέρω ĕisphĕrō**, *ice-fer'-o;* from *1519* and *5342;* to *carry inward* (lit. or fig.):—bring (in), lead into.

1534. **εἶτα ĕita**, *i'-tah;* of uncert. affin.; a particle of *succession* (in time or logical enumeration), *then, moreover:*—after that (-ward), furthermore, then. See also *1899.*

1535. **εἴτε ĕitĕ**, *i'-teh;* from *1487* and *5037;* *if too:*—if, or, whether.

1536. **εἴ τις ĕi tis**, *i tis;* from *1487* and *5100;* *if any:*—he that, if a (-ny) man ('s, thing, from any, ought), whether any, whosoever.

1537. **ἐκ ĕk**, *ek;* or

ἐξ ĕx, *ex;* a prim. prep. denoting *origin* (the point *whence* motion or action proceeds), *from, out* (of place, time or cause; lit. or fig.; direct or remote):—after, among, × are, at, betwixt (-yond), by (the means of), exceedingly, (+ abundantly above), for (-th), from (among, forth, up), + grudgingly, + heartily, × heavenly, × hereby, + very highly, in, . . . ly, (because, by reason) of, off (from), on, out among (from, of), over, since, × thenceforth, through, × unto, × vehemently, with (-out). Often used in composition, with the same general import; often of *completion.*

1538. **ἕκαστος hĕkastŏs**, *hek'-as-tos;* as if a superlative of **ἕκας hĕkas** (*afar*); *each* or *every:*—any, both, each (one), every (man, one, woman), particularly.

1539. **ἑκάστοτε hĕkastŏtĕ**, *hek-as'-tot-eh;* as if from *1538* and *5119;* at *every time:*—always.

1540. **ἑκατόν hĕkatŏn**, *hek-at-on';* of uncert. affin.; a *hundred:*—hundred.

1541. **ἑκατονταέτης hĕkatŏntaĕtēs**, *hek-at-on-tah-et'-ace;* from *1540* and *2094;* *centenarian:*—hundred years old.

1542. **ἑκατονταπλασίων hĕkatŏntaplasiōn**, *hek-at-on-ta-plah-see'-own;* from *1540* and a presumed der. of *4111;* a *hundred times:*—hundredfold.

1543. **ἑκατοντάρχης hĕkatŏntarchēs**, *hek-at-on-tar'-khace;* or

ἑκατόνταρχος hĕkatŏntarchŏs, *hek-at-on'-tar-khos;* from *1540* and *757;* the *captain of one hundred men:*—centurion.

1544. **ἐκβάλλω ĕkballō**, *ek-bal'-lo;* from *1537* and *906;* to *eject* (lit. or fig.):—bring forth, cast (forth, out), drive (out), expel, leave, pluck (pull, take, thrust) out, put forth (out), send away (forth, out).

1545. **ἔκβασις ĕkbasis**, *ek'-bas-is;* from a comp. of *1537* and the base of *939* (mean. to *go out*); an *exit* (lit. or fig.):—end, way to escape.

1546. **ἐκβολή ĕkbŏlē**, *ek-bol-ay';* from *1544;* *ejection,* i.e. (spec.) a *throwing overboard* of the cargo:—+ lighten the ship.

1547. **ἐκγαμίζω ĕkgamizō**, *ek-gam-id'-zo;* from *1537* and a form of *1061* [comp. *1548*]; to *marry off* a daughter:—give in marriage.

1548. **ἐκγαμίσκω ĕkgamiskō**, *ek-gam-is'-ko;* from *1537* and *1061;* the same as *1547:*—give in marriage.

1549. **ἔκγονον ĕkgŏnŏn**, *ek'-gon-on;* neut. of a der. of a comp. of *1537* and *1096;* a *descendant,* i.e. (spec.) *grandchild:*—nephew.

1550. **ἐκδαπανάω ĕkdapanaō**, *ek-dap-an-ah'-o;* from *1537* and *1159;* to *expend* (wholly), i.e. (fig.) *exhaust:*—spend.

1551. **ἐκδέχομαι ĕkdĕchŏmai**, *ek-dekh'-om-ahee;* from *1537* and *1209;* to *accept from* some source, i.e. (by impl.) to *await:*—expect, look (tarry) for, wait (for).

1552. **ἔκδηλος ĕkdēlŏs**, *ek'-day-los;* from *1537* and *1212;* *wholly evident:*—manifest.

1553. **ἐκδημέω ĕkdēmĕō**, *ek-day-meh'-o;* from a comp. of *1537* and *1218;* to *emigrate,* i.e. (fig.) *vacate* or *quit:*—be absent.

1554. **ἐκδίδωμι ĕkdidōmi**, *ek-did-o'-mee;* from *1537* and *1325;* to *give forth,* i.e. (spec.) to *lease:*—let forth (out).

1555. **ἐκδιηγέομαι ĕkdiēgĕŏmai**, *ek-dee-ayg-eh'-om-ahee;* from *1537* and a comp. of *1223* and *2233;* to *narrate* through wholly:—declare.

1556. **ἐκδικέω ĕkdikĕō**, *ek-dik-eh'-o;* from *1558;* to *vindicate, retaliate, punish:*—a (re-) venge.

1557. **ἐκδίκησις ĕkdikēsis**, *ek-dik'-ay-sis;* from *1556;* *vindication, retribution:*—(a-, re-) venge (-ance), punishment.

1558. **ἔκδικος ĕkdikŏs**, *ek'-dik-os;* from *1537* and *1349;* carrying *justice out,* i.e. a *punisher:*—a (re-) venger.

1559. **ἐκδιώκω ĕkdiōkō**, *ek-dee-o'-ko;* from *1537* and *1377;* to *pursue out,* i.e. *expel* or *persecute* implacably:—persecute.

1560. **ἔκδοτος ĕkdŏtŏs**, *ek'-dot-os;* from *1537* and a der. of *1325;* *given out* or *over,* i.e. *surrendered:*—delivered.

1561. **ἐκδοχή ĕkdŏchē**, *ek-dokh-ay';* from *1551;* *expectation:*—looking for.

1562. **ἐκδύω ĕkduō**, *ek-doo'-o;* from *1537* and the base of *1416;* to cause to *sink out* of, i.e. (spec. as of clothing) to *divest:*—strip, take off from, unclothe.

1563. **ἐκεῖ ĕkĕi**, *ek-i';* of uncert. affin.; *there;* by extens. *thither:*—there, thither (-ward), (to) yonder (place).

1564. **ἐκεῖθεν ĕkĕithĕn**, *ek-i'-then;* from *1563;* *thence:*—from that place, (from) thence, there.

1565. **ἐκεῖνος ĕkĕinŏs**, *ek-i'-nos;* from *1563;* *that* one (or [neut.] thing); often intensified by the art. prefixed:—he, it, the other (same), selfsame, that (same, very), × their, × them, they, this, those. See also *3778.*

1566. **ἐκεῖσε ĕkĕisĕ**, *ek-i'-seh;* from *1563;* *thither:*—there.

1567. **ἐκζητέω ĕkzētĕō**, *ek-zay-teh'-o;* from *1537* and *2212;* to *search out,* i.e. (fig.) *investigate, crave, demand,* (by Hebr.) *worship:*—en- (re-) quire, seek after (carefully, diligently).

1568. **ἐκθαμβέω ĕkthambĕō**, *ek-tham-beh'-o;* from *1569;* to *astonish* utterly:—affright, greatly (sore) amaze.

1569. **ἔκθαμβος ĕkthambŏs**, *ek'-tham-bos;* from *1537* and *2285;* *utterly astounded:*—greatly wondering.

1570. **ἔκθετος ĕkthĕtŏs**, *ek'-thet-os;* from *1537* and a der. of *5087;* *put out,* i.e. *exposed* to perish:—cast out.

1571. **ἐκκαθαίρω ĕkkathairō**, *ek-kath-ah'ee-ro;* from *1537* and *2508;* to *cleanse thoroughly:*—purge (out).

1572. **ἐκκαίω ĕkkaiō**, *ek-kah'-yo;* from *1537* and *2545;* to *inflame* deeply:—burn.

1573. **ἐκκακέω ĕkkakĕō**, *ek-kak-eh'-o;* from *1537* and *2556;* to *be* (*bad* or) *weak,* i.e. (by impl.) to *fail* (in heart):—faint, be weary.

1574. **ἐκκεντέω ĕkkĕntĕō**, *ek-ken-teh'-o;* from *1537* and the base of *2759;* to *transfix:*—pierce.

1575. **ἐκκλάω ĕkklaō**, *ek-klah'-o;* from *1537* and *2806;* to *exscind:*—break off.

1576. **ἐκκλείω ĕkklĕiō**, *ek-kli'-o;* from *1537* and *2808;* to *shut out* (lit. or fig.):—exclude.

1577. **ἐκκλησία ĕkklēsia**, *ek-klay-see'-ah;* from a comp. of *1537* and a der. of *2564;* a *calling out,* i.e. (concr.) a popular *meeting,* espec. a religious *congregation* (Jewish *synagogue,* or Chr. community of members on earth or saints in heaven or both):—assembly, church.

1578. **ἐκκλίνω ĕkklinō**, *ek-klee'-no;* from *1537* and *2827;* to *deviate,* i.e. (absol.) to *shun* (lit. or fig.), or (rel.) to *decline* (from piety):—avoid, eschew, go out of the way.

1579. **ἐκκολυμβάω ĕkkŏlumbaō**, *ek-kol-oom-bah'-o;* from *1537* and *2860;* to *escape by swimming:*—swim out.

1580. **ἐκκομίζω ĕkkŏmizō**, *ek-kom-id'-zo;* from *1537* and *2865;* to *bear forth* (to burial):—carry out.

1581. **ἐκκόπτω ĕkkŏptō**, *ek-kop'-to;* from *1537* and *2875;* to *exscind;* fig. to *frustrate:*—cut down (off, out), hew down, hinder.

1582. **ἐκκρέμαμαι ĕkkrĕmamai**, *ek-krem'-am-ahee;* mid. from *1537* and *2910;* to *hang upon* the lips of a speaker, i.e. *listen closely:*—be very attentive.

1583. **ἐκλαλέω ĕklalĕō**, *ek-lal-eh'-o;* from *1537* and *2980;* to *divulge:*—tell.

1584. **ἐκλάμπω ĕklampō**, *ek-lam'-po;* from *1537* and *2989;* to *be resplendent:*—shine forth.

1585. **ἐκλανθάνομαι ĕklanthanŏmai**, *ek-lan-than'-om-ahee;* mid. from *1537* and *2990;* to *be utterly oblivious* of:—forget.

1586. **ἐκλέγομαι ĕklĕgŏmai**, *ek-leg'-om-ahee;* mid. from *1537* and *3004* (in its prim. sense); to *select:*—make choice, choose (out), chosen.

1587. **ἐκλείπω ĕklĕipō**, *ek-li'-po;* from *1537* and *3007;* to *omit,* i.e. (by impl.) *cease* (*die*):—fail.

1588. **ἐκλεκτός ĕklĕktŏs**, *ek-lek-tos';* from *1586;* *select;* by impl. *favorite:*—chosen, elect.

1589. **ἐκλογή ĕklŏgē**, *ek-log-ay';* from *1586;* (divine) *selection* (abstr. or concr.):—chosen, election.

1590. **ἐκλύω ĕkluō**, *ek-loo'-o;* from *1537* and *3089;* to *relax* (lit. or fig.):—faint.

1591. **ἐκμάσσω ĕkmassō**, *ek-mas'-so;* from *1537* and the base of *3145;* to *knead out,* i.e. (by anal.) to *wipe dry:*—wipe.

1592. **ἐκμυκτερίζω ĕkmuktĕrizō**, *ek-mook-ter-id'-zo;* from *1537* and *3456;* to *sneer* outright at:—deride.

1593. **ἐκνεύω ĕknĕuō**, *ek-nyoo'-o;* from *1537* and *3506;* (by anal.) to *slip off,* i.e. quietly *withdraw:*—convey self away.

1594. **ἐκνήφω ĕknēphō**, *ek-nay'-fo;* from *1537* and *3525;* (fig.) to *rouse* (oneself) *out* of stupor:—awake.

1595. **ἑκούσιον hĕkŏusiŏn**, *hek-oo'-see-on;* neut. of a der. from *1635;* *voluntariness:*—willingly.

1596. ἑκουσίως **hěkŏusiōs**, *hek-oo-see'-oce;* adv. from the same as *1595*; *voluntarily:*—wilfully, willingly.

1597. ἔκπαλαι **ěkpalai**, *ek'-pal-ahee;* from *1537* and *3819*; *long ago, for a long while:*—of a long time, of old.

1598. ἐκπειράζω **ěkpěirazō**, *ek-pi-rad'-zo;* from *1537* and *3985*; to *test thoroughly:*—tempt.

1599. ἐκπέμπω **ěkpěmpō**, *ek-pem'-po;* from *1537* and *3992*; to *despatch:*—send away (forth).

ἐκπερισσοῦ **ěkpěirissŏu**. See *1537* and *4053*.

1600. ἐκπετάννυμι **ěkpětannumi**, *ek-pet-an'-noo-mee;* from *1537* and a form of *4072*; to *fly out*, i.e. (by anal.) *extend:*—stretch forth.

1601. ἐκπίπτω **ěkpiptō**, *ek-pip'-to;* from *1537* and *4098*; to *drop away;* spec. *be driven out* of one's course; fig. to *lose, become inefficient:*—be cast, fail, fall (away, off), take none effect.

1602. ἐκπλέω **ěkplěō**, *ek-pleh'-o;* from *1537* and *4126*; to *depart* by ship:—sail (away, thence).

1603. ἐκπληρόω **ěkplērŏō**, *ek-play-rŏ'-o;* from *1537* and *4137*; to *accomplish* entirely:—fulfill.

1604. ἐκπλήρωσις **ěkplērōsis**, *ek-play'-ro-sis;* from *1603*; *completion:*—accomplishment.

1605. ἐκπλήσσω **ěkplēssō**, *ek-place'-so;* from *1537* and *4141*; to *strike* with astonishment:—amaze, astonish.

1606. ἐκπνέω **ěkpněō**, *ek-pneh'-o;* from *1537* and *4154*; to *expire:*—give up the ghost.

1607. ἐκπορεύομαι **ěkpŏrěuŏmai**, *ek-por-yoo'-om-ahee;* from *1537* and *4198*; to *depart, be discharged, proceed, project:*—come (forth, out of), depart, go (forth, out), issue, proceed (out of).

1608. ἐκπορνεύω **ěkpŏrněuō**, *ek-porn-yoo'-o;* from *1537* and *4203*; to *be utterly unchaste:*—give self over to fornication.

1609. ἐκπτύω **ěkptuō**, *ek-ptoo'-o;* from *1537* and *4429*; to *spit out*, i.e. (fig.) *spurn:*—reject.

1610. ἐκριζόω **ěkrizŏō**, *ek-rid-zŏ'-o;* from *1537* and *4492*; to *uproot:*—pluck up by the root, root up.

1611. ἔκστασις **ěkstasis**, *ek'-stas-is;* from *1839*; a *displacement* of the mind, i.e. *bewilderment*, "*ecstasy*":— + be amazed, amazement, astonishment, trance.

1612. ἐκστρέφω **ěkstrěphō**, *ek-stref'-o;* from *1537* and *4762*; to *pervert* (fig.):—subvert.

1613. ἐκταράσσω **ěktarassō**, *ek-tar-as'-so;* from *1537* and *5015*; to *disturb wholly:*—exceedingly trouble.

1614. ἐκτείνω **ěktěinō**, *ek-ti'-no;* from *1537* and τείνω **těinō** (to *stretch*); to *extend:*—cast, put forth, stretch forth (out).

1615. ἐκτελέω **ěktělěō**, *ek-tel-eh'-o;* from *1537* and *5055*; to *complete* fully:—finish.

1616. ἐκτένεια **ěktěněia**, *ek-ten'-i-ah;* from *1618*; *intentness:*— × instantly.

1617. ἐκτενέστερον **ěktěněstěrŏn**, *ek-ten-es'-ter-on;* neut. of the comp. of *1618*; *more intently:*—more earnestly.

1618. ἐκτενής **ěktěnēs**, *ek-ten-ace';* from *1614*; *intent:*—without ceasing, fervent.

1619. ἐκτενῶς **ěktěnōs**, *ek-ten-oce';* adv. from *1618*; *intently:*—fervently.

1620. ἐκτίθημι **ěktithēmi**, *ek-tith'-ay-mee;* from *1537* and *5087*; to *expose;* fig. to *declare:*—cast out, expound.

1621. ἐκτινάσσω **ěktinassō**, *ek-tin-as'-so;* from *1537* and τινάσσω **tinassō** (to *swing*); to *shake* violently:—shake (off).

1622. ἐκτός **ěktŏs**, *ek-tos';* from *1537*; the *exterior;* fig. (as a prep.) *aside from, besides:*—but, except (-ed), other than, out of, outside, unless, without.

1623. ἕκτος **hěktŏs**, *hek'-tos;* ordinal from *1803*; *sixth:*—sixth.

1624. ἐκτρέπω **ěktrěpō**, *ek-trep'-o;* from *1537* and the base of *5157*; to *deflect*, i.e. *turn away* (lit. or fig.):—avoid, turn (aside, out of the way).

1625. ἐκτρέφω **ěktrěphō**, *ek-tref'-o;* from *1537* and *5142*; to *rear up* to maturity, i.e. (gen.) to *cherish* or *train:*—bring up, nourish.

1626. ἔκτρωμα **ěktrōma**, *ek'-tro-mah;* from a comp. of *1537* and τιτρώσκω **titrōskō** (to *wound*); a *miscarriage* (*abortion*), i.e. (by anal.) *untimely birth:*—born out of due time.

1627. ἐκφέρω **ěkphěrō**, *ek-fer'-o;* from *1537* and *5342*; to *bear out* (lit. or fig.):—bear, bring forth, carry forth (out).

1628. ἐκφεύγω **ěkphěugō**, *ek-fyoo'-go;* from *1537* and *5343*; to *flee out:*—escape, flee.

1629. ἐκφοβέω **ěkphŏběō**, *ek-fob-eh'-o;* from *1537* and *5399*; to *frighten utterly:*—terrify.

1630. ἔκφοβος **ěkphŏbŏs**, *ek'-fob-os;* from *1537* and *5401*; *frightened out* of one's wits:—sore afraid, exceedingly fear.

1631. ἐκφύω **ěkphuō**, *ek-foo'-o;* from *1537* and *5453*; to *sprout up:*—put forth.

1632. ἐκχέω **ěkchěō**, *ek-kheh'-o;* or (by var.) ἐκχύνω **ěkchunō**, *ek-khoo'-no;* from *1537* and χέω **chěō** (to *pour*); to *pour forth;* fig. to *bestow:*—gush (pour) out, run greedily (out), shed (abroad, forth), spill.

1633. ἐκχωρέω **ěkchōrěō**, *ek-kho-reh'-o;* from *1537* and *5562*; to *depart:*—depart out.

1634. ἐκψύχω **ěkpsuchō**, *ek-psoo'-kho;* from *1537* and *5594*; to *expire:*—give (yield) up the ghost.

1635. ἑκών **hěkōn**, *hek-own';* of uncert. affin.; *voluntary:*—willingly.

1636. ἐλαία **ělaia**, *el-ah'-yah;* fem. of a presumed der. from an obsol. prim.; an *olive* (the tree or the fruit):—olive (berry, tree).

1637. ἔλαιον **ělaiŏn**, *el'-ah-yon;* neut. of the same as *1636*; olive *oil:*—oil.

1638. ἐλαιών **ělaiōn**, *el-ah-yone';* from *1636*; an *olive-orchard*, i.e. (spec.) the *Mt. of Olives:*—Olivet.

1639. Ἐλαμίτης **Ělamitēs**, *el-am-ee'-tace;* of Heb. or. [5867]; an *Elamite* or Persian:—Elamite.

1640. ἐλάσσων **ělassōn**, *el-as'-sone;* or ἐλάττων **ělattōn**, *el-at-tone';* comp. of the same as *1646*; *smaller* (in size, quantity, age or quality):—less, under, worse, younger.

1641. ἐλαττονέω **ělattŏněō**, *el-at-ton-eh-o;* from *1640*; to *diminish*, i.e. *fall short:*—have lack.

1642. ἐλαττόω **ělattŏō**, *el-at-tŏ'-o;* from *1640*; to *lessen* (in rank or influence):—decrease, make lower.

1643. ἐλαύνω **ělaunō**, *el-ŏw'-no;* a prol. form of a prim. verb (obsol. except in certain tenses as an altern. of this) of uncert. affin.; to *push* (as wind, oars or dæmoniacal power):—carry, drive, row.

1644. ἐλαφρία **ělaphria**, *el-af-ree'-ah;* from *1645*; *levity* (fig.), i.e. *fickleness:*—lightness.

1645. ἐλαφρός **ělaphrŏs**, *el-af-ros';* prob. akin to *1643* and the base of *1640*; *light*, i.e. *easy:*—light.

1646. ἐλάχιστος **ělachistŏs**, *el-akh'-is-tos;* superl. of ἔλαχυς **ělachus** (*short*); used as equiv. to *3398*; *least* (in size, amount, dignity, etc.):—least, very little (small), smallest.

1647. ἐλαχιστότερος **ělachistŏtěrŏs**, *el-akh-is-tot'-er-os;* comp. of *1646*; *far less:*—less than the least.

1648. Ἐλεάζαρ **Ělěazar**, *el-eh-ad'-zar;* of Heb. or. [499]; *Eleazar*, an Isr.:—Eleazar.

1649. ἔλεγξις **ělěgxis**, *el'-eng-xis;* from *1651*; *refutation*, i.e. *reproof:*—rebuke.

1650. ἔλεγχος **ělěgchŏs**, *el'-eng-khos;* from *1651*; *proof, conviction:*—evidence, reproof.

1651. ἐλέγχω **ělěgchō**, *el-eng'-kho;* of uncert. affin.; to *confute, admonish:*—convict, convince, tell a fault, rebuke, reprove.

1652. ἐλεεινός **ělěěinŏs**, *el-eh-i-nos';* from *1656*; *pitiable:*—miserable.

1653. ἐλεέω **ělěěō**, *el-eh-eh'-o;* from *1656*; to *compassionate* (by word or deed, spec. by divine grace):—have compassion (pity on), have (obtain, receive, shew) mercy (on).

1654. ἐλεημοσύνη **ělěēmŏsunē**, *el-eh-ay-mos-oo'-nay;* from *1656*; *compassionateness*, i.e. (as exercised towards the poor) *beneficence*, or (concr.) a *benefaction:*—alms (-deeds).

1655. ἐλεήμων **ělěēmōn**, *el-eh-ay'-mone;* from *1653*; *compassionate* (actively):—merciful.

1656. ἔλεος **ělěŏs**, *el'-eh-os;* of uncert. affin.; *compassion* (human or divine, espec. active):— (+ tender) mercy.

1657. ἐλευθερία **ělěuthěria**, *el-yoo-ther-ee'-ah;* from *1658*; *freedom* (legitimate or licentious, chiefly mor. or cer.):—liberty.

1658. ἐλεύθερος **ělěuthěrŏs**, *el-yoo'-ther-os;* prob. from the alt. of *2064*; *unrestrained* (to *go* at pleasure), i.e. (as a citizen) *not a slave* (whether *freeborn* or *manumitted*), or (gen.) *exempt* (from obligation or liability):—free (man, woman), at liberty.

1659. ἐλευθερόω **ělěuthěrŏō**, *el-yoo-ther-ŏ'-o;* from *1658*; to *liberate*, i.e. (fig.) to *exempt* (from mor., cer. or mortal liability):—deliver, make free.

ἐλεύθω **ělěuthō**. See *2064*.

1660. ἔλευσις **ělěusis**, *el'-yoo-sis;* from the alt. of *2064*; an *advent:*—coming.

1661. ἐλεφάντινος **ělěphantinŏs**, *el-ef-an'-tee-nos;* from ἔλεφας **ělěphas** (an "*elephant*"); *elephantine*, i.e. (by impl.) composed of *ivory:*—of ivory.

1662. Ἐλιακείμ **Ěliakěim**, *el-ee-ak-ime';* of Heb. or. [471]; *Eliakim*, an Isr.:—Eliakim.

1663. Ἐλιέζερ **Ěliězěr**, *el-ee-ed'-zer;* of Heb. or. [461]; *Eliezer*, an Isr.:—Eliezer.

1664. Ἐλιούδ **Ěliŏud**, *el-ee-ood';* of Heb. or. [410 and 1935]; *God of majesty; Eliud*, an Isr.:—Eliud.

1665. Ἐλισάβετ **Ělisabět**, *el-ee-sab'-et;* of Heb. or. [472]; *Elisabet*, an Israelitess:—Elisabeth.

1666. Ἐλισσαῖος **Ělissaiŏs**, *el-is-sah'-yos;* of Heb. or. [477]; *Elissæus*, an Isr.:—Elissæus.

1667. ἑλίσσω **hělissō**, *hel-is'-so;* a form of *1507*; to *coil* or *wrap:*—fold up.

1668. ἕλκος **hělkŏs**, *hel'-kos;* prob. from *1670*; an *ulcer* (as if drawn together):—sore.

1669. ἑλκόω **hělkŏō**, *hel-kŏ'-o;* from *1668*; to *cause to ulcerate*, i.e. (pass.) *be ulcerous:*—full of sores.

1670. ἑλκύω **hělkuō**, *hel-koo'-o;* or ἕλκω **hělkō**, *hel'-ko;* prob. akin to *138*; to *drag* (lit. or fig.):—draw. Comp. *1667*.

1671. Ἑλλάς **Hěllas**, *hel-las';* of uncert. affin.; *Hellas* (or *Greece*), a country of Europe:—Greece.

1672. Ἕλλην **Hěllēn**, *hel'-lane;* from *1671*; a *Hellen* (*Grecian*) or inhab. of Hellas; by extens. a *Greek-speaking* person, espec. a *non-Jew:*—Gentile, Greek.

1673. Ἑλληνικός **Hěllēnikŏs**, *hel-lay-nee-kos';* from *1672*; *Hellenic*, i.e. *Grecian* (in language):—Greek.

1674. Ἑλληνίς **Hěllēnis**, *hel-lay-nis';* fem. of *1672*; a *Grecian* (i.e. *non-Jewish*) woman:—Greek.

1675. Ἑλληνιστής **Hěllēnistēs**, *hel-lay-nis-tace';* from a der. of *1672*; a *Hellenist* or Greek-speaking Jew:—Grecian.

1676. Ἑλληνιστί **Hěllēnisti**, *hel-lay-nis-tee';* adv. from the same as *1675*; *Hellenistically*, i.e. in the Grecian language:—Greek.

1677. ἐλλογέω **ěllŏgěō**, *el-log-eh'-o;* from *1722* and *3056* (in the sense of *account*); to *reckon in*, i.e. *attribute:*—impute, put on account.

ἔλλομαι **hěllŏmai**. See *138*.

1678. Ἐλμωδάμ **Ělmōdam**, *el-mo-dam';* of Heb. or. [perh. for 486]; *Elmodam*, an Isr.:—Elmodam.

1679. ἐλπίζω **ělpizō**, *el-pid'-zo;* from *1680*; to *expect* or *confide:*—(have, thing) hope (-d) (for), trust.

1680. ἐλπίς **ělpis**, *el-pece';* from a prim. ἔλπω **ělpō** (to *anticipate*, usually with pleasure); *expectation* (abstr. or concr.) or *confidence:*—faith, hope.

1681. Ἐλύμας **Ělumas**, *el-oo'-mas;* of for. or.; *Elymas*, a wizard:—Elymas.

1682. ἐλοΐ **ělŏï**, *el-o-ee';* of Chald. or. [426 with pron. suff.]; *my God:*—Eloi.

1683. ἐμαυτοῦ **ĕmautŏu**, *em-ŏw-too'*; gen. comp. of 1700 and 846; *of myself* (so likewise the dat.

ἐμαυτῷ **ĕmautōi**, *em-ow-tō'*; and acc.

ἐμαυτόν **ĕmautŏn**, *em-ow-ton'*):—me, mine own (self), myself.

1684. ἐμβαίνω **ĕmbainō**, *em-ba'hee-no;* from 1722 and the base of 939; to *walk on*, i.e. *embark* (aboard a vessel), *reach* (a pool):—come (get) into, enter (into), go (up) into, step in, take ship.

1685. ἐμβάλλω **ĕmballō**, *em-bal'-lo;* from 1722 and 906; to *throw on*, i.e. (fig.) *subject to* (eternal punishment):—cast into.

1686. ἐμβάπτω **ĕmbaptō**, *em-bap'-to;* from 1722 and 911; to *whelm on*, i.e. *wet* (a part of the person, etc.) by contact with a fluid:—dip.

1687. ἐμβατεύω **ĕmbatĕuō**, *em-bat-yoo'-o;* from 1722 and a presumed der. of the base of 939; equiv. to 1684; to *intrude on* (fig.):—intrude into.

1688. ἐμβιβάζω **ĕmbibazō**, *em-bib-ad'-zo;* from 1722 and βιβάζω **bibazō** (to *mount*; causat. of 1684); to *place on*, i.e. *transfer* (aboard a vessel):—put in.

1689. ἐμβλέπω **ĕmblĕpō**, *em-blep'-o;* from 1722 and 991; to *look on*, i.e. (rel.) to *observe* fixedly, or (absol.) to *discern* clearly:—behold, gaze up, look upon, (could) see.

1690. ἐμβριμάομαι **ĕmbrimaŏmai**, *em-brim-ah'-om-ahee;* from 1722 and βριμάομαι **brimaŏmai** (to *snort* with anger); to have *indignation on*, i.e. (trans.) to *blame*, (intrans.) to *sigh* with chagrin, (spec.) to sternly *enjoin:*—straitly charge, groan, murmur against.

1691. ἐμέ **ĕmĕ**, *em-eh';* a prol. form of 3165; *me:*—I, me, my (-self).

1692. ἐμέω **ĕmĕō**, *em-eh'-o;* of uncert. affin.; to *vomit:*—(will) spue.

1693. ἐμμαίνομαι **ĕmmainŏmai**, *em-mah'ee-nom-ahee;* from 1722 and 3105; to *rave on*, i.e. *rage at:*—be mad against.

1694. Ἐμμανουήλ **Ĕmmanŏuēl**, *em-man-oo-ale';* of Heb. or. [6005]; *God with us; Emmanuel*, a name of Christ:—Emmanuel.

1695. Ἐμμαούς **Ĕmmaŏus**, *em-mah-ooce';* prob. of Heb. or. [comp. 3222]; *Emmaüs*, a place in Pal.:—Emmaus.

1696. ἐμμένω **ĕmmĕnō**, *em-men'-o;* from 1722 and 3306; to *stay in* the same place, i.e. (fig.) to *persevere:*—continue.

1697. Ἐμμόρ **Ĕmmŏr**, *em-mor';* of Heb. or. [2544]; *Emmor* (i.e. *Chamor*), a Canaanite:—Emmor.

1698. ἐμοί **ĕmŏi**, *em-oy';* a prol. form of 3427; *to me:*—I, me, mine, my.

1699. ἐμός **ĕmŏs**, *em-os';* from the oblique cases of 1473 (1698, 1700, 1691); *my:*—of me, mine (own), my.

1700. ἐμοῦ **ĕmŏu**, *em-oo';* a prol. form of 3450; *of me:*—me, mine, my.

1701. ἐμπαιγμός **ĕmpaigmŏs**, *emp-aheeg-mos';* from 1702; *derision:*—mocking.

1702. ἐμπαίζω **ĕmpaizō**, *emp-aheed'-zo;* from 1722 and 3815; to *jeer at*, i.e. *deride:*—mock.

1703. ἐμπαίκτης **ĕmpaiktēs**, *emp-aheek-tace';* from 1702; a *derider*, i.e. (by impl.) a *false teacher:*—mocker, scoffer.

1704. ἐμπεριπατέω **ĕmpĕripatĕō**, *em-per-ee-pat-eh'-o;* from 1722 and 4043; to *perambulate on* a place, i.e. (fig.) to *be occupied among* persons:—walk in.

1705. ἐμπίπλημι **ĕmpiplēmi**, *em-pip'-lay-mee;* or

ἐμπλήθω **ĕmplēthō**, *em-play'-tho;* from 1722 and the base of 4118; to *fill in* (up), i.e. (by impl.) to *satisfy* (lit. or fig.):—fill.

1706. ἐμπίπτω **ĕmpiptō**, *em-pip'-to;* from 1722 and 4098; to *fall on*, i.e. (lit.) *be entrapped by*, or (fig.) *be overwhelmed with:*—fall among (into).

1707. ἐμπλέκω **ĕmplĕkō**, *em-plek'-o;* from 1722 and 4120; to *entwine*, i.e. (fig.) *involve* with:—entangle (in, self with).

ἐμπλήθω **ĕmplēthō**. See 1705.

1708. ἐμπλοκή **ĕmplŏkē**, *em-plok-ay';* from 1707; elaborate *braiding* of the hair:—plaiting.

1709. ἐμπνέω **ĕmpnĕō**, *emp-neh'-o;* from 1722 and 4154; to *inhale*, i.e. (fig.) to *be animated by* (*bent upon*):—breathe.

1710. ἐμπορεύομαι **ĕmpŏrĕuŏmai**, *em-por-yoo'-om-ahee;* from 1722 and 4198; to *travel in* (a country as a pedlar), i.e. (by impl.) to *trade:*—buy and sell, make merchandise.

1711. ἐμπορία **ĕmpŏria**, *em-por-ee'-ah;* fem. from 1713; *traffic:*—merchandise.

1712. ἐμπόριον **ĕmpŏriŏn**, *em-por'-ee-on;* neut. from 1713; a *mart* ("*emporium*"):—merchandise.

1713. ἔμπορος **ĕmpŏrŏs**, *em'-por-os;* from 1722 and the base of 4198; a (wholesale) *tradesman:*—merchant.

1714. ἐμπρήθω **ĕmprēthō**, *em-pray'-tho;* from 1722 and πρήθω **prēthō** (to *blow* a flame): to *enkindle*, i.e. *set on fire:*—burn up.

1715. ἔμπροσθεν **ĕmprŏsthĕn**, *em'-pros-then;* from 1722 and 4314; *in front of* (in place [lit. or fig.] or time):—against, at, before, (in presence, sight) of.

1716. ἐμπτύω **ĕmptuō**, *emp-too'-o;* from 1722 and 4429; to *spit at* or *on:*—spit (upon).

1717. ἐμφανής **ĕmphanēs**, *em-fan-ace';* from a comp. of 1722 and 5316; *apparent in* self:—manifest, openly.

1718. ἐμφανίζω **ĕmphanizō**, *em-fan-id'-zo;* from 1717; to *exhibit* (in person) or *disclose* (by words):—appear, declare (plainly), inform, (will) manifest, shew, signify.

1719. ἔμφοβος **ĕmphŏbŏs**, *em'-fob-os;* from 1722 and 5401; *in fear*, i.e. *alarmed:*—affrighted, afraid, tremble.

1720. ἐμφυσάω **ĕmphusaō**, *em-foo-sah'-o;* from 1722 and φυσάω **phusaō** (to *puff*) [comp. 5453]; to *blow at* or *on:*—breathe on.

1721. ἔμφυτος **ĕmphutŏs**, *em'-foo-tos;* from 1722 and a der. of 5453; *implanted* (fig.):—engrafted.

1722. ἐν **ĕn**, *en;* a prim. prep. denoting (fixed) *position* (in place, time or state), and (by impl.) *instrumentality* (medially or constructively), i.e. a relation of *rest* (intermediate between 1519 and 1537); "*in*," *at*, (up-) *on*, *by*, etc.:—about, after, against, + almost, × altogether, among, × as, at, before, between, (here-) by (+ all means), for (. . . sake of), + give self wholly to, (here-) in (-to, -wardly), × mightily, (because) of, (up-) on, [open-] ly, × outwardly, one, × quickly, × shortly, [speedi-] ly, × that, × there (-in, -on), through (-out), (un-) to (-ward), under, when, where (-with), while, with (-in). Often used in compounds, with substantially the same import: rarely with verbs of motion, and then not to indicate direction, except (elliptically) by a separate (and different) prep.

1723. ἐναγκαλίζομαι **ĕnagkalizŏmai**, *en-ang-kal-id'-zom-ahee;* from 1722 and a der. of 43; to *take in* one's *arms*, i.e. *embrace:*—take up in arms.

1724. ἐνάλιος **ĕnaliŏs**, *en-al'-ee-os;* from 1722 and 251; *in the sea*, i.e. *marine:*—thing in the sea.

1725. ἔναντι **ĕnanti**, *en'-an-tee;* from 1722 and 473; *in front* (i.e. fig. *presence*) *of:*—before.

1726. ἐναντίον **ĕnantiŏn**, *en-an-tee'-on;* neut. of 1727; (adv.) *in the presence* (*view*) *of:*—before, in the presence of.

1727. ἐναντίος **ĕnantiŏs**, *en-an-tee'-os;* from 1725; *opposite;* fig. *antagonistic:*—(over) against, contrary.

1728. ἐνάρχομαι **ĕnarchŏmai**, *en-ar'-khom-ahee;* from 1722 and 756; to *commence on:*—rule [*by mistake for* 757].

1729. ἐνδεής **ĕndĕēs**, *en-deh-ace';* from a comp. of 1722 and 1210 (in the sense of *lacking*); *deficient in:*—lacking.

1730. ἔνδειγμα **ĕndĕigma**, *en'-dighe-mah;* from 1731; an *indication* (concr.):—manifest token.

1731. ἐνδείκνυμι **ĕndĕiknumi**, *en-dike'-noo-mee;* from 1722 and 1166; to *indicate* (by word or act):—do, show (forth).

1732. ἔνδειξις **ĕndĕixis**, *en'-dike-sis;* from 1731; *indication* (abstr.):—declare, evident token, proof.

1733. ἕνδεκα **hĕndĕka**, *hen'-dek-ah;* from (the neut. of) 1520 and 1176; *one and ten*, i.e. *eleven:*—eleven.

1734. ἑνδέκατος **hĕndĕkatŏs**, *hen-dek'-at-os.* ord. from 1733; *eleventh:*—eleventh.

1735. ἐνδέχεται **ĕndĕchĕtai**, *en-dekh'-et-ahee;* third pers. sing. pres. of a comp. of 1722 and 1209; (impers.) *it is accepted in*, i.e. *admitted* (*possible*):—can (+ not) be.

1736. ἐνδημέω **ĕndēmĕō**, *en-day-meh'-o;* from a comp. of 1722 and 1218; to *be in* one's own *country*, i.e. *home* (fig.):—be at home (present).

1737. ἐνδιδύσκω **ĕndiduskō**, *en-did-oos'-ko;* a prol. form of 1746; to *invest* (with a garment):—clothe in, wear.

1738. ἔνδικος **ĕndikŏs**, *en'-dee-kos;* from 1722 and 1349; *in the right*, i.e. *equitable:*—just.

1739. ἐνδόμησις **ĕndŏmēsis**, *en-dom'-ay-sis;* from a comp. of 1722 and a der. of the base of 1218; a *housing in* (*residence*), i.e. *structure:*—building.

1740. ἐνδοξάζω **ĕndŏxazō**, *en-dox-ad'-zo;* from 1741; to *glorify:*—glorify.

1741. ἔνδοξος **ĕndŏxŏs**, *en'-dox-os;* from 1722 and 1391; *in glory*, i.e. *splendid*, (fig.) *noble:*—glorious, gorgeous [-ly], honourable.

1742. ἔνδυμα **ĕnduma**, *en'-doo-mah;* from 1746; *apparel* (espec. the outer *robe*):—clothing, garment, raiment.

1743. ἐνδυναμόω **ĕndunamŏō**, *en-doo-nam-ŏ'-o;* from 1722 and 1412; to *empower:*—enable, (increase in) strength (-en), be (make) strong.

1744. ἐνδύνω **ĕndunō**, *en-doo'-no;* from 1772 and 1416; to *sink* (by impl. *wrap* [comp. 1746]) *on*, i.e. (fig.) *sneak:*—creep.

1745. ἔνδυσις **ĕndusis**, *en'-doo-sis;* from 1746; *investment* with clothing:—putting on.

1746. ἐνδύω **ĕnduō**, *en-doo'-o;* from 1722 and 1416 (in the sense of *sinking* into a garment); to *invest* with clothing (lit. or fig.):—array, clothe (with), endue, have (put) on.

ἐνέγκω **ĕnĕgkō**. See 5342.

1747. ἐνέδρα **ĕnĕdra**, *en-ed'-rah;* fem. from 1722 and the base of 1476; an *ambuscade*, i.e. (fig.) *murderous purpose:*—lay wait. See also 1749.

1748. ἐνεδρεύω **ĕnĕdrĕuō**, *en-ed-ryoo'-o;* from 1747; to *lurk*, i.e. (fig.) *plot* assassination:—lay wait for.

1749. ἔνεδρον **ĕnĕdrŏn**, *en'-ed-ron;* neut. of the same as 1747; an *ambush*, i.e. (fig.) *murderous design:*—lying in wait.

1750. ἐνειλέω **ĕnĕilĕō**, *en-i-leh'-o;* from 1772 and the base of 1507; to *enwrap:*—wrap in.

1751. ἔνειμι **ĕnĕimi**, *en'-i-mee;* from 1772 and 1510; to *be within* (neut. part. plur.):—such things as . . . have. See also 1762.

1752. ἕνεκα **hĕnĕka**, *hen'-ek-ah;* or

ἕνεκεν **hĕnĕkĕn**, *hen'-ek-en;* or

εἵνεκεν **hĕinĕkĕn**, *hi'-nek-en;* of uncert. affin.; *on account of:*—because, for (cause, sake), (where-) fore, by reason of, that.

1753. ἐνέργεια **ĕnĕrgĕia**, *en-erg'-i-ah;* from 1756; *efficiency* ("*energy*"):—operation, strong, (effectual) working.

1754. ἐνεργέω **ĕnĕrgĕō**, *en-erg-eh'-o;* from 1756; to *be active, efficient:*—do, (be) effectual (fervent), be mighty in, shew forth self, work (effectually in)

1755. **ἐνέργημα ĕnĕrgēma**, *en-erg'-ay-mah;* from *1754*: an *effect*:—operation, working.

1756. **ἐνεργής ĕnĕrgēs**, *en-er-gace';* from *1722* and *2041*: *active, operative*:—effectual, powerful.

1757. **ἐνευλογέω ĕnĕulŏgĕō**, *en-yoo-log-eh'-o;* from *1722* and *2127*; to *confer a benefit on*:—bless.

1758. **ἐνέχω ĕnĕchō**, *en-ekh'-o;* from *1722* and *2192*; to *hold in* or *upon*, i.e. *ensnare;* by impl. to *keep a grudge*:—entangle with, have a quarrel against, urge.

1759. **ἐνθάδε ĕnthadĕ**, *en-thad'-eh;* from a prol. form of *1722*; prop. *within*, i.e. (of place) *here, hither*:—(t-) here, hither.

1760. **ἐνθυμέομαι ĕnthumĕŏmai**, *en-thoo-meh'-om-ahee;* from a comp. of *1722* and *2372*; to *be inspirited*, i.e. *ponder*:—think.

1761. **ἐνθύμησις ĕnthumēsis**, *en-thoo'-may-sis;* from *1760*; *deliberation*:—device, thought.

1762. **ἔνι ĕni**, *en'-ee;* contr. for third pers. sing. pres. indic. of *1751*; impers. *there is* in or among:—be, (there) is.

1763. **ἐνιαυτός ĕniautŏs**, *en-ee-ow-tos';* prol. from a prim. **ἔνος ĕnŏs** (a *year*); a *year*:—year.

1764. **ἐνίστημι ĕnistēmi**, *en-is'-tay-mee;* from *1722* and *2476*; to *place on* hand, i.e. (reflex.) *impend*, (part.) be *instant*:—come, be at hand, present.

1765. **ἐνισχύω ĕnischuō**, *en-is-khoo'-o;* from *1722* and *2480*; to *invigorate* (trans. or reflex.):—strengthen.

1766. **ἔννατος ĕnnatŏs**, *en'-nat-os;* ord. from *1767*: *ninth*:—ninth.

1767. **ἐννέα ĕnnĕa**, *en-neh'-ah;* a prim. number; *nine*:—nine.

1768. **ἐννενηκονταεννέα ĕnnĕnēkŏntaĕnnĕa**, *en-nen-ay-kon-tah-en-neh'-ah;* from a (tenth) multiple of *1767* and *1767* itself; *ninety-nine*:—ninety and nine.

1769. **ἐννεός ĕnnĕŏs**, *en-neh-os';* from *1770*; *dumb* (as *making signs*), i.e. *silent* from astonishment:—speechless.

1770. **ἐννεύω ĕnnĕuō**, *en-nyoo'-o;* from *1722* and *3506*; to *nod at*, i.e. *beckon* or *communicate by gesture*:—make signs.

1771. **ἔννοια ĕnnŏia**, *en'-noy-ah;* from a comp. of *1722* and *3563*; *thoughtfulness*, i.e. moral *understanding*:—intent, mind.

1772. **ἔννομος ĕnnŏmŏs**, *en'-nom-os;* from *1722* and *3551*; (subj.) *legal*, or (obj.) *subject* to:—lawful, under law.

1773. **ἔννυχον ĕnnuchŏn**, *en'-noo-khon;* neut. of a comp. of *1722* and *3571*; (adv.) *by night*:—before day.

1774. **ἐνοικέω ĕnŏikĕō**, *en-oy-keh'-o;* from *1722* and *3611*; to *inhabit* (fig.):—dwell in.

1775. **ἑνότης hĕnŏtēs**, *hen-ot'-ace;* from *1520*; *oneness*, i.e. (fig.) *unanimity*:—unity.

1776. **ἐνοχλέω ĕnŏchlĕō**, *en-okh-leh'-o;* from *1722* and *3791*; to *crowd in*, i.e. (fig.) to *annoy*:—trouble.

1777. **ἔνοχος ĕnŏchŏs**, *en'-okh-os;* from *1758*; *liable* to (a condition, penalty or imputation):—in danger of, guilty of, subject to.

1778. **ἔνταλμα ĕntalma**, *en'-tal-mah;* from *1781*; an *injunction*, i.e. religious *precept*:—commandment.

1779. **ἐνταφιάζω ĕntaphiazō**, *en-taf-ee-ad'-zo;* from a comp. of *1722* and *5028*; to *inswathe* with cerements for interment:—bury.

1780. **ἐνταφιασμός ĕntaphiasmŏs**, *en-taf-ee-as-mos';* from *1779*; *preparation* for interment:—burying.

1781. **ἐντέλλομαι ĕntĕllŏmai**, *en-tel'-lom-ahee;* from *1722* and the base of *5056*; to *enjoin*:—(give) charge, (give) command (-ments), injoin.

1782. **ἐντεῦθεν ĕntĕuthĕn**, *ent-yoo'-then;* from the same as *1759*; *hence* (lit. or fig.); (repeated) *on both sides*:—(from) hence, on either side.

1783. **ἔντευξις ĕntĕuxis**, *ent'-yook-sis;* from *1793*; an *interview*, i.e. (spec.) *supplication*:—intercession, prayer.

1784. **ἔντιμος ĕntimŏs**, *en'-tee-mos;* from *1722* and *5092*; *valued* (fig.):—dear, more honourable, precious, in reputation.

1785. **ἐντολή ĕntŏlē**, *en-tol-ay';* from *1781*; *injunction*, i.e. an authoritative *prescription*:—commandment, precept.

1786. **ἐντόπιος ĕntŏpiŏs**, *en-top'-ee-os;* from *1722* and *5117*; a *resident*:—of that place.

1787. **ἐντός ĕntŏs**, *en-tos';* from *1722*; *inside* (adv. or noun):—within.

1788. **ἐντρέπω ĕntrĕpō**, *en-trep'-o;* from *1722* and the base of *5157*; to *invert*, i.e. (fig. and reflex.) in a good sense, to *respect;* or in a bad one, to *confound*:—regard, (give) reverence, shame.

1789. **ἐντρέφω ĕntrĕphō**, *en-tref'-o;* from *1722* and *5142*; (fig.) to *educate*:—nourish up in.

1790. **ἔντρομος ĕntrŏmŏs**, *en'-trom-os;* from *1722* and *5156*; *terrified*:—× quake, × trembled.

1791. **ἐντροπή ĕntrŏpē**, *en-trop-ay';* from *1788*; *confusion*:—shame.

1792. **ἐντρυφάω ĕntruphaō**, *en-troo-fah'-o;* from *1722* and *5171*; to *revel in*:—sporting selves.

1793. **ἐντυγχάνω ĕntugchanō**, *en-toong-khan'-o;* from *1722* and *5177*; to *chance upon*, i.e. (by impl.) *confer with;* by extens. to *entreat* (in favor or against):—deal with, make intercession.

1794. **ἐντυλίσσω ĕntulissō**, *en-too-lis'-so;* from *1722* and **τυλίσσω tulissō** (to *twist;* prob. akin to *1507*); to *entwine*, i.e. *wind* up in:—wrap in (together).

1795. **ἐντυπόω ĕntupŏō**, *en-too-pŏ'-o;* from *1722* and a der. of *5179*; to *enstamp*, i.e. *engrave*:—engrave.

1796. **ἐνυβρίζω ĕnubrizō**, *en-oo-brid'-zo;* from *1722* and *5195*; to *insult*:—do despite unto.

1797. **ἐνυπνιάζομαι ĕnupniazŏmai**, *en-oop-nee-ad'-zom-ahee;* mid. from *1798*; to *dream*:—dream (-er).

1798. **ἐνύπνιον ĕnupniŏn**, *en-oop'-nee-on;* from *1722* and *5258*; something seen *in sleep*, i.e. a *dream* (*vision* in a dream):—dream.

1799. **ἐνώπιον ĕnōpiŏn**, *en-o'-pee-on;* neut. of a comp. of *1722* and a der. of *3700*; *in* the *face* of (lit. or fig.):—before, in the presence (sight) of, to.

1800. **Ἐνώς Ĕnōs**, *en-oce';* of Heb. or. [583]; *Enos* (i.e. *Enosh*), a patriarch:—Enos.

1801. **ἐνωτίζομαι ĕnōtizŏmai**, *en-o-tid'-zom-ahee;* mid. from a comp. of *1722* and *3775*; to take *in one's ear*, i.e. to *listen*:—hearken.

1802. **Ἐνώχ Ĕnōk**, *en-oke';* of Heb. or. [2585]; *Enoch* (i.e. *Chanok*), an antediluvian:—Enoch.

ἐξ ĕx. See *1537*.

1803. **ἕξ hĕx**, *hex;* a prim. numeral; *six*:—six.

1804. **ἐξαγγέλλω ĕxaggĕllō**, *ex-ang-el'-lo;* from *1537* and the base of *32*; to *publish*, i.e. *celebrate*:—shew forth.

1805. **ἐξαγοράζω ĕxagŏrazō**, *ex-ag-or-ad'-zo;* from *1537* and *59*; to *buy up*, i.e. *ransom;* fig. to *rescue* from loss (*improve* opportunity):—redeem.

1806. **ἐξάγω ĕxagō**, *ex-ag'-o;* from *1537* and *71*; to *lead forth*:—bring forth (out), fetch (lead) out.

1807. **ἐξαιρέω ĕxairĕō**, *ex-ahee-reh'-o;* from *1537* and *138*; act. to *tear out;* mid. to *select;* fig. to *release*:—deliver, pluck out, rescue.

1808. **ἐξαίρω ĕxairō**, *ex-ah'ee-ro;* from *1537* and *142*; to *remove*:—put (take) away.

1809. **ἐξαιτέομαι ĕxaitĕŏmai**, *ex-ahee-teh'-om-ahee;* mid. from *1537* and *154*; to *demand* (for trial):—desire.

1810. **ἐξαίφνης ĕxaiphnēs**, *ex-ah'eef-nace;* from *1537* and the base of *160*; *of a sudden* (*unexpectedly*):—suddenly. Comp. *1819*.

1811. **ἐξακολουθέω ĕxakŏlŏuthĕō**, *ex-ak-ol-oo-theh'-o;* from *1537* and *190*; to *follow out*, i.e. (fig.) to *imitate, obey*, yield to:—follow.

1812. **ἑξακόσιοι hĕxakŏsiŏi**, *hex-ak-os'-ee-oy;* plur. ordinal from *1803* and *1540*; *six hundred*:—six hundred.

1813. **ἐξαλείφω ĕxalĕiphō**, *ex-al-i'-fo;* from *1537* and *218*; to *smear out*, i.e. *obliterate* (*erase* tears, fig. *pardon* sin):—blot out, wipe away.

1814. **ἐξάλλομαι ĕxallŏmai**, *ex-al'-lom-ahee;* from *1537* and *242*; to *spring forth*:—leap up.

1815. **ἐξανάστασις ĕxanastasis**, *ex-an-as'-tas-is;* from *1817*; a *rising from* death:—resurrection.

1816. **ἐξανατέλλω ĕxanatĕllō**, *ex-an-at-el'-lo;* from *1537* and *393*; to *start up out of* the ground, i.e. *germinate*:—spring up.

1817. **ἐξανίστημι ĕxanistēmi**, *ex-an-is'-tay-mee;* from *1537* and *450*; obj. to *produce*, i.e. (fig.) *beget;* subj. to *arise*, i.e. (fig.) *object*:—raise (rise) up.

1818. **ἐξαπατάω ĕxapataō**, *ex-ap-at-ah'-o;* from *1537* and *538*; to *seduce wholly*:—beguile, deceive.

1819. **ἐξάπινα ĕxapina**, *ex-ap'-ee-nah;* from *1537* and a der. of the same as *160*; *of a sudden*, i.e. *unexpectedly*:—suddenly. Comp. *1810*.

1820. **ἐξαπορέομαι ĕxapŏrĕŏmai**, *ex-ap-or-eh'-om-ahee;* mid. from *1537* and *639*; to *be utterly at a loss*, i.e. *despond*:—(in) despair.

1821. **ἐξαποστέλλω ĕxapŏstĕllō**, *ex-ap-os-tel'-lo;* from *1537* and *649*; to *send away forth*, i.e. (on a mission) to *despatch*, or (peremptorily) to *dismiss*:—send (away, forth, out).

1822. **ἐξαρτίζω ĕxartizō**, *ex-ar-tid'-zo;* from *1537* and a der. of *739*; to *finish out* (time); fig. to *equip fully* (a teacher):—accomplish, thoroughly furnish.

1823. **ἐξαστράπτω ĕxastraptō**, *ex-as-trap'-to;* from *1537* and *797*; to *lighten forth*, i.e. (fig.) to *be radiant* (of very white garments):—glistening.

1824. **ἐξαύτης ĕxautēs**, *ex-ow'-tace;* from *1537* and the gen. sing. fem. of *846* (*5610* being understood); *from that* hour, i.e. *instantly*:—by and by, immediately, presently, straightway.

1825. **ἐξεγείρω ĕxĕgĕirō**, *ex-eg-i'-ro;* from *1537* and *1453*; to *rouse fully*, i.e. (fig.) to *resuscitate* (from death), *release* (from infliction):—raise up.

1826. **ἔξειμι ĕxĕimi**, *ex'-i-mee;* from *1537* and **εἶμι ĕimi** (to *go*); to *issue*, i.e. *leave* (a place), *escape* (to the shore):—depart, get [*to land*], go out.

1827. **ἐξελέγχω ĕxĕlĕgchō**, *ex-el-eng'-kho;* from *1537* and *1651*; to *convict fully*, i.e. (by impl.) to *punish*:—convince.

1828. **ἐξέλκω ĕxĕlkō**, *ex-el'-ko;* from *1537* and *1670*; to *drag forth*, i.e. (fig.) to *entice* (to sin):—draw away.

1829. **ἐξέραμα ĕxĕrama**, *ex-er'-am-ah;* from a comp. of *1537* and a presumed **ἐράω ĕraō** (to *spue*); *vomit*, i.e. *food disgorged*:—vomit.

1830. **ἐξερευνάω ĕxĕrĕunaō**, *ex-er-yoo-nah'-o;* from *1537* and *2045*; to *explore* (fig.):—search diligently.

1831. **ἐξέρχομαι ĕxĕrchŏmai**, *ex-er'-khom-ahee;* from *1537* and *2064*; to *issue* (lit. or fig.):—come-(forth, out), depart (out of), escape, get out, go (abroad, away, forth, out, thence), proceed (forth), spread abroad.

1832. **ἔξεστι ĕxĕsti**, *ex'-es-tee;* third pers. sing. pres. indic. of a comp. of *1537* and *1510*; so also **ἐξόν ĕxŏn**, *ex-on';* neut. pres. part. of the same (with or without some form of *1510* expressed); impers. *it is right* (through the fig. idea of *being out* in public):—be lawful, let, × may (-est).

1833. **ἐξετάζω ĕxĕtazō**, *ex-et-ad'-zo;* from *1537* and **ἐτάζω ĕtazō** (to *examine*); to *test thoroughly* (by questions), i.e. *ascertain* or *interrogate*:—ask, enquire, search.

1834. **ἐξηγέομαι ĕxēgĕŏmai**, *ex-ayg-eh'-om-ahee;* from *1537* and *2233*; to *consider out* (aloud), i.e. *rehearse, unfold*.—declare, tell.

1835. **ἑξήκοντα hĕxēkŏnta**, *hex-ay'-kon-tah;* the tenth multiple of *1803; sixty:*—sixty [-fold], threescore.

1836. **ἑξῆς hĕxēs**, *hex-ace';* from *2192* (in the sense of *taking hold* of, i.e. *adjoining*); *successive:*—after, following, × morrow, next.

1837. **ἐξηχέομαι ĕxēchĕŏmai**, *ex-ay-kheh'-om-ahee;* mid. from *1537* and *2278;* to "*echo*" *forth*, i.e. *resound* (be generally *reported*):—sound forth.

1838. **ἕξις hĕxis**, *hex'-is;* from *2192; habit*, i.e. (by impl.) *practice:*—use.

1839. **ἐξίστημι ĕxistēmi**, *ex-is'-tay-mee;* from *1537* and *2476;* to *put* (*stand*) *out* of wits, i.e. *astound*, or (reflex.) *become astounded, insane:*—amaze, be (make) astonished, be beside self (selves), bewitch, wonder.

1840. **ἐξισχύω ĕxischuō**, *ex-is-khoo'-o;* from *1537* and *2480;* to *have full strength*, i.e. *be entirely competent:*—be able.

1841. **ἔξοδος ĕxŏdŏs**, *ex'-od-os;* from *1537* and *3598;* an *exit*, i.e. (fig.) *death:*—decease, departing.

1842. **ἐξολοθρεύω ĕxŏlŏthrĕuō**, *ex-ol-oth-ryoo'-o;* from *1537* and *3645;* to *extirpate:*—destroy.

1843. **ἐξομολογέω ĕxŏmŏlŏgĕō**, *ex-om-ol-og-eh'-o;* from *1537* and *3670;* to *acknowledge* or (by impl. of *assent*) *agree fully:*—confess, profess, promise.

ἐξόν ĕxŏn. See *1832*.

1844. **ἐξορκίζω ĕxŏrkizō**, *ex-or-kid'-zo;* from *1537* and *3726;* to *exact an oath*, i.e. *conjure:*—adjure.

1845. **ἐξορκιστής ĕxŏrkistēs**, *ex-or-kis-tace';* from *1844;* one *that binds by an oath* (or *spell*), i.e. (by impl.) an "*exorcist*" (*conjurer*):—exorcist.

1846. **ἐξορύσσω ĕxŏrussō**, *ex-or-oos'-so;* from *1537* and *3736;* to *dig out*, i.e. (by extens.) to *extract* (an eye), *remove* (a roofing):—break up, pluck out.

1847. **ἐξουδενόω ĕxŏudĕnŏō**, *ex-oo-den-ŏ'-o;* from *1537* and a der. of the neut. of *3762;* to *make utterly nothing of*, i.e. *despise:*—set at nought. See also *1848*.

1848. **ἐξουθενέω ĕxŏuthĕnĕō**, *ex-oo-then-eh'-o;* a var. of *1847* and mean. the same:—contemptible, despise, least esteemed, set at nought.

1849. **ἐξουσία ĕxŏusia**, *ex-oo-see'-ah;* from *1832* (in the sense of *ability*); *privilege*, i.e. (subj.) *force, capacity, competency, freedom*, or (obj.) *mastery* (concr. *magistrate, superhuman, potentate, token of control*), delegated *influence:*—authority, jurisdiction, liberty, power, right, strength.

1850. **ἐξουσιάζω ĕxŏusiazō**, *ex-oo-see-ad'-zo;* from *1849;* to *control:*—exercise authority upon, bring under the (have) power of.

1851. **ἐξοχή ĕxŏchē**, *ex-okh-ay';* from a comp. of *1537* and *2192* (mean. to *stand out*); *prominence* (fig.):—principal.

1852. **ἐξυπνίζω ĕxupnizō**, *ex-oop-nid'-zo;* from *1853;* to *waken:*—awake out of sleep.

1853. **ἔξυπνος ĕxupnŏs**, *ex'-oop-nos;* from *1537* and *5258; awake:*— × out of sleep.

1854. **ἔξω ĕxō**, *ex'-o;* adv. from *1537; out* (*-side, of doors*), lit. or fig.:—away, forth, (with-) out (of, -ward), strange.

1855. **ἔξωθεν ĕxōthĕn**, *ex'-o-then;* from *1854; external* (*-ly*):—out (-side -ward, -wardly), (from) without.

1856. **ἐξωθέω ĕxōthĕō**, *ex-o-theh'-o;* or

ἐξώθω ĕxōthō, *ex-o'-tho;* from *1537* and **ὠθέω ōthĕō** (to *push*); to *expel;* by impl. to *propel:*—drive out, thrust in.

1857. **ἐξώτερος ĕxōtĕrŏs**, *ex-o'-ter-os;* comp. of *1854; exterior:*—outer.

1858. **ἑορτάζω hĕŏrtazō**, *heh-or-tad'-zo;* from *1859;* to *observe a festival:*—keep the feast.

1859. **ἑορτή hĕŏrtē**, *heh-or-tay';* of uncert. affin.; a *festival:*—feast, holyday.

1860. **ἐπαγγελία ĕpaggĕlia**, *ep-ang-el-ee'-ah;* from *1861;* an *announcement* (for information, assent or pledge; espec. a divine *assurance* of good):—message, promise.

1861. **ἐπαγγέλλω ĕpaggĕllō**, *ep-ang-el'-lo;* from *1909* and the base of *32;* to *announce upon* (reflex.), i.e. (by impl.) to *engage* to do something, to *assert* something respecting oneself:—profess, (make) promise.

1862. **ἐπάγγελμα ĕpaggĕlma**, *ep-ang'-el-mah;* from *1861;* a *self-committal* (by *assurance* of conferring some good):—promise.

1863. **ἐπάγω ĕpagō**, *ep-ag'-o;* from *1909* and *71;* to *superinduce*, i.e. *inflict* (an evil), *charge* (a crime):—bring upon.

1864. **ἐπαγωνίζομαι ĕpagōnizŏmai**, *ep-ag-o-nid'-zom-ahee;* from *1909* and *75;* to *struggle for:*—earnestly contend for.

1865. **ἐπαθροίζω ĕpathrŏizō**, *ep-ath-roid'-zo;* from *1909* and **ἀθροίζω athrŏizō** (to *assemble*); to *accumulate:*—gather thick together.

1866. **Ἐπαίνετος Ĕpainĕtŏs**, *ep-a'hee-net-os;* from *1867; praised; Epænetus*, a Chr.:—Epenetus.

1867. **ἐπαινέω ĕpainĕō**, *ep-ahee-neh'-o;* from *1909* and *134;* to *applaud:*—commend, laud, praise.

1868. **ἔπαινος ĕpainŏs**, *ep'-ahee-nos;* from *1909* and the base of *134; laudation;* concr. a *commendable* thing:—praise.

1869. **ἐπαίρω ĕpairō**, *ep-ahee'-ro;* from *1909* and *142;* to *raise up* (lit. or fig.):—exalt self, poise (lift, take) up.

1870. **ἐπαισχύνομαι ĕpaischunŏmai**, *ep-ahee-skhoo'-nom-ahee;* from *1909* and *153;* to *feel shame for* something:—be ashamed.

1871. **ἐπαιτέω ĕpaitĕō**, *ep-ahee-teh'-o;* from *1909* and *154;* to *ask for:*—beg.

1872. **ἐπακολουθέω ĕpakŏlŏuthĕō**, *ep-ak-ol-oo-theh'-o;* from *1909* and *190;* to *accompany:*—follow (after).

1873. **ἐπακούω ĕpakŏuō**, *ep-ak-oo'-o;* from *1909* and *191;* to *hearken* (favorably) *to:*—hear.

1874. **ἐπακροάομαι ĕpakrŏaŏmai**, *ep-ak-rŏ-ah'-om-ahee;* from *1909* and the base of *202;* to *listen* (intently) *to:*—hear.

1875. **ἐπάν ĕpan**, *ep-an';* from *1909* and *302;* a particle of indef. contemporaneousness; *whenever, as soon as:*—when.

1876. **ἐπάναγκες ĕpanagkĕs**, *ep-an'-ang-kes;* neut. of a presumed comp. of *1909* and *318;* (adv.) *on necessity*, i.e. *necessarily:*—necessary.

1877. **ἐπανάγω ĕpanagō**, *ep-an-ag'-o;* from *1909* and *321;* to *lead up on*, i.e. (techn.) to *put out* (to sea); (intrans.) to *return:*—launch (thrust) out, return.

1878. **ἐπαναμιμνήσκω ĕpanamimnēskō**, *ep-an-ah-mim-nace'-ko;* from *1909* and *363;* to *remind of:*—put in mind.

1879. **ἐπαναπαύομαι ĕpanapauŏmai**, *ep-an-ah-pŏw'-om-ahee;* mid. from *1909* and *373;* to *settle on;* lit. (*remain*) or fig. (*rely*):—rest in (upon).

1880. **ἐπανέρχομαι ĕpanĕrchŏmai**, *ep-an er'-khom-ahee;* from *1909* and *424;* to *come up on*, i.e. *return:*—come again, return.

1881. **ἐπανίσταμαι ĕpanistamai**, *ep-an-is'-tam-ahee;* mid. from *1909* and *450;* to *stand up on*, i.e. (fig.) to *attack:*—rise up against.

1882. **ἐπανόρθωσις ĕpanŏrthōsis**, *ep-an-or'-tho-sis;* from a comp. of *1909* and *461;* a *straightening up again*, i.e. (fig.) *rectification* (*reformation*):—correction.

1883. **ἐπάνω ĕpanō**, *ep-an'-o;* from *1909* and *507; up above*, i.e. *over* or *on* (of place, amount, rank, etc.):—above, more than, (up-) on, over.

1884. **ἐπαρκέω ĕparkĕō**, *ep-ar-keh'-o;* from *1909* and *714;* to *avail for*, i.e. *help:*—relieve.

1885. **ἐπαρχία ĕparchia**, *ep-ar-khee'-ah;* from a comp. of *1909* and *757* (mean. a *governor* of a district, "eparch"); a special *region* of government, i.e. a Roman *præfecture:*—province.

1886. **ἔπαυλις ĕpaulis**, *ep'-ŏw-lis;* from *1909* and an equiv. of *833;* a *hut over* the head, i.e. a *dwelling*.

1887. **ἐπαύριον ĕpauriŏn**, *ep-ow'-ree-on;* from *1909* and *839;* occurring *on the succeeding* day, i.e. (*2250* being implied) *to-morrow:*—day following, morrow, next day (after).

1888. **ἐπαυτοφώρῳ ĕpautŏphōrōi**, *ep-ow-tof-o'-ro;* from *1909* and *846* and (the dat. sing. of) a der. of **φώρ phōr** (a *thief*); *in theft itself*, i.e. (by anal.) *in actual crime:*—in the very act.

1889. **Ἐπαφρᾶς Ĕpaphras**, *ep-af-ras';* contr. from *1891; Epaphras*, a Chr.:—Epaphras.

1890. **ἐπαφρίζω ĕpaphrizō**, *ep-af-rid'-zo;* from *1909* and *875;* to *foam upon*, i.e. (fig.) to *exhibit* (a vile passion):—foam out.

1891. **Ἐπαφρόδιτος Ĕpaphrŏditŏs**, *ep-af-rod'-ee-tos;* from *1909* (in the sense of *devoted* to) and **Ἀφροδίτη Aphrŏditē** (*Venus*); *Epaphroditus*, a Chr.:—Epaphroditus. Comp. *1889*.

1892. **ἐπεγείρω ĕpĕgĕirō**, *ep-eg-i'-ro;* from *1909* and *1453;* to *rouse upon*, i.e. (fig.) to *excite* against:—raise, stir up.

1893. **ἐπεί ĕpĕi**, *ep-i';* from *1909* and *1487; thereupon*, i.e. *since* (of time or cause):—because, else, for that (then, -asmuch as), otherwise, seeing that, since, when,

1894. **ἐπειδή ĕpĕidē**, *ep-i-day';* from *1893* and *1211; since now*, i.e. (of time) *when*, or (of cause) *whereas:*—after that, because, for (that, -asmuch as), seeing, since.

1895. **ἐπειδήπερ ĕpĕidēpĕr**, *ep-i-day'-per;* from *1894* and *4007; since indeed* (of cause):—forasmuch.

1896. **ἐπεῖδον ĕpĕidŏn**, *ep-i'-don;* and other moods and persons of the same tense; from *1909* and *1492;* to *regard* (favorably or otherwise):—behold, look upon.

1897. **ἐπείπερ ĕpĕipĕr**, *ep-i'-per;* from *1893* and *4007; since* indeed (of cause):—seeing.

1898. **ἐπεισαγωγή ĕpĕisagōgē**, *ep-ice-ag-o-gay';* from a comp. of *1909* and *1521;* a *superintroduction:*—bringing in.

1899. **ἔπειτα ĕpĕita**, *ep'-i-tah;* from *1909* and *1534; thereafter:*—after that (-ward), then.

1900. **ἐπέκεινα ĕpĕkĕina**, *ep-ek'-i-nah;* from *1909* and (the acc. plur. neut. of) *1565; upon those* parts of, i.e. *on the further side of:*—beyond.

1901. **ἐπεκτείνομαι ĕpĕktĕinŏmai**, *ep-ek-ti'-nom-ahee;* mid. from *1909* and *1614;* to *stretch* (oneself) forward *upon:*—reach forth.

1902. **ἐπενδύομαι ĕpĕnduŏmai**, *ep-en-doo'-om-ahee;* mid. from *1909* and *1746;* to *invest upon* oneself:—be clothed upon.

1903. **ἐπενδύτης ĕpĕndutēs**, *ep-en-doo'-tace;* from *1902;* a *wrapper*, i.e. outer garment:—fisher's coat.

1904. **ἐπέρχομαι ĕpĕrchŏmai**, *ep-er'-khom-ahee;* from *1909* and *2064;* to *supervene*, i.e. *arrive, occur, impend, attack*, (fig.) *influence:*—come (in, upon).

1905. **ἐπερωτάω ĕpĕrōtaō**, *ep-er-o-tah'-o;* from *1909* and *2065;* to *ask for*, i.e. *inquire, seek:*—ask (after, questions), demand, desire, question.

1906. **ἐπερώτημα ĕpĕrōtēma**, *ep-er-o'-tay-mah;* from *1905;* an *inquiry:*—answer.

1907. **ἐπέχω ĕpĕchō**, *ep-ekh'-o;* from *1909* and *2192;* to *hold upon*, i.e. (by impl.) to *retain;* (by extens.) to *detain;* (with impl. of *3563*) to *pay attention to:*—give (take) heed unto, hold forth, mark, stay.

1908. **ἐπηρεάζω ĕpērĕazō**, *ep-ay-reh-ad'-zo;* from a comp. of *1909* and (prob.) **ἀρειά arĕia** (*threats*); to *insult, slander:*—use despitefully, falsely accuse.

1909. **ἐπί ĕpi**, *ep-ee';* a prim. prep. prop. mean. *superimposition* (of time, place, order, etc.), as a relation of *distribution* [with the gen.], i.e. *over, upon*, etc.; of *rest* (with the dat.) *at, on*, etc.; of *direction* (with the acc.) *towards, upon*, etc.:—about (the times), above, after, against, among, as long as (touching), at, beside, × have charge of, (be-, [where-]) fore, in (a place, as much as, the time of, -to), (because) of, (up-) on (behalf of), over, (by, for) the space of, through (-out), (un-) to (-ward), with. In compounds it retains essentially the same import, *at, upon*, etc. (lit. or fig.).

1910. **ἐπιβαίνω ĕpibainō**, *ep-ee-bah'ee-no;* from *1909* and the base of *939;* to *walk upon*, i.e. *mount, ascend, embark, arrive:*—come (into), enter into, go abroad, sit upon, take ship.

1911. **ἐπιβάλλω ĕpiballō**, *ep-ee-bal'-lo;* from *1909* and *906;* to *throw upon* (lit. or fig., trans. or reflex.; usually with more or less force); spec. (with *1438* implied) to *reflect;* impers. to *belong to:*—beat into, cast (up-) on, fall, lay (on), put (unto), stretch forth, think on.

1912. **ἐπιβαρέω ĕpibarĕō**, *ep-ee-bar-eh'-o;* from *1909* and *916;* to *be heavy upon,* i.e. (pecuniarily) to *be expensive to;* fig. to *be severe towards:*—be chargeable to, overcharge.

1913. **ἐπιβιβάζω ĕpibibazō**, *ep-ee-bee-bad'-zo;* from *1909* and a redupl. deriv. of the base of *939* [comp. *307*]; to *cause to mount* (an animal):—set on.

1914. **ἐπιβλέπω ĕpiblĕpō**, *ep-ee-blep'-o;* from *1909* and *991;* to *gaze at* (with favor, pity or partiality):—look upon, regard, have respect to.

1915. **ἐπίβλημα ĕpiblēma**, *ep-ib'-lay-mah;* from *1911;* a *patch:*—piece.

1916. **ἐπιβοάω ĕpibŏaō**, *ep-ee-bo-ah'-o;* from *1909* and *994;* to *exclaim against:*—cry.

1917. **ἐπιβουλή ĕpibŏulē**, *ep-ee-boo-lay';* from a presumed comp. of *1909* and *1014;* a *plan against* someone, i.e. a *plot:*—laying (lying) in wait.

1918. **ἐπιγαμβρεύω ĕpigambrĕuō**, *ep-ee-gam-bryoo'-o;* from *1909* and a der. of *1062;* to *form affinity with,* i.e. (spec.) in a levirate way:—marry.

1919. **ἐπίγειος ĕpigĕiŏs**, *ep-ig'-i-os;* from *1909* and *1093;* *worldly* (phys. or mor.):—earthly, in earth, terrestrial.

1920. **ἐπιγίνομαι ĕpiginŏmai**, *ep-ig-in'-om-ahee;* from *1909* and *1096;* to *arrive upon,* i.e. *spring up* (as a wind):—blow.

1921. **ἐπιγινώσκω ĕpiginōskō**, *ep-ig-in-oce'-ko;* from *1909* and *1097;* to *know upon* some mark, i.e. *recognise;* by impl. to *become fully acquainted with,* to *acknowledge:*—(ac-, have, take) know (-ledge, well), perceive.

1922. **ἐπίγνωσις epignōsis**, *ep-ig'-no-sis;* from *1921;* *recognition,* i.e. (by impl.) full *discernment, acknowledgment:*—(ac-) knowledge (-ing, -ment).

1923. **ἐπιγραφή ĕpigraphē**, *ep-ig-raf-ay';* from *1924;* an *inscription:*—superscription.

1924. **ἐπιγράφω ĕpigraphō**, *ep-ee-graf'-o;* from *1909* and *1125;* to *inscribe* (phys. or ment.):—inscription, write in (over, thereon).

1925. **ἐπιδείκνυμι ĕpidĕiknumi**, *ep-ee-dike'-noo-mee;* from *1909* and *1166;* to *exhibit* (phys. or ment.):—shew.

1926. **ἐπιδέχομαι ĕpidĕchŏmai**, *ep-ee-dekh'-om-ahee;* from *1909* and *1209;* to *admit* (as a guest or [fig.] teacher):—receive.

1927. **ἐπιδημέω ĕpidēmĕō**, *ep-ee-day-meh'-o;* from a comp. of *1909* and *1218;* to *make oneself at home,* i.e. (by extens.) to *reside* (in a foreign country):—[be] dwelling (which were) there, stranger.

1928. **ἐπιδιατάσσομαι ĕpidiatassŏmai**, *ep-ee-dee-ah-tas'-som-ahee;* mid. from *1909* and *1299;* to *appoint besides,* i.e. *supplement* (as a codicil):—add to.

1929. **ἐπιδίδωμι ĕpididōmi**, *ep-ee-did'-o-mee;* from *1909* and *1325;* to *give over* (by hand or surrender):—deliver unto, give, let (+ [her drive]), offer.

1930. **ἐπιδιορθόω ĕpidiŏrthŏō**, *ep-ee-dee-or-thŏ'-o;* from *1909* and a der. of *3717;* to *straighten further,* i.e. (fig.) *arrange additionally:*—set in order.

1931. **ἐπιδύω ĕpiduō**, *ep-ee-doo'-o;* from *1909* and *1416;* to *set* fully (as the sun):—go down.

1932. **ἐπιείκεια ĕpiĕikĕia**, *ep-ee-i'-ki-ah;* from *1933;* *suitableness,* i.e. (by impl.) *equity, mildness:*—clemency, gentleness.

1933. **ἐπιεικής ĕpiĕikēs**, *ep-ee-i-kace';* from *1909* and *1503;* *appropriate,* i.e. (by impl.) *mild:*—gentle, moderation, patient.

1934. **ἐπιζητέω ĕpizētĕō**, *ep-eed-zay-teh'-o;* from *1909* and *2212;* to *search* (*inquire*) *for;* intens to *demand,* to *crave:*—desire, enquire, seek (after, for).

1935. **ἐπιθανάτιος ĕpithanatiŏs**, *ep-ee-than-at'-ee-os;* from *1909* and *2288;* doomed *to death:*—appointed to death.

1936. **ἐπίθεσις ĕpithĕsis**, *ep-ith'-es-is;* from *2007;* an *imposition* (of hands officially):—laying (putting) on.

1937. **ἐπιθυμέω ĕpithumĕō**, *ep-ee-thoo-meh'-o;* from *1909* and *2372;* to set the *heart upon,* i.e. *long* for (rightfully or otherwise):—covet, desire, would fain, lust (after).

1938. **ἐπιθυμητής ĕpithumētēs**, *ep-ee-thoo-may-tace';* from *1937;* a *craver:*— + lust after.

1939. **ἐπιθυμία ĕpithumia**, *ep-ee-thoo-mee'-ah;* from *1937;* a *longing* (espec. for what is forbidden):—concupiscence, desire, lust (after).

1940. **ἐπικαθίζω ĕpikathizō**, *ep-ee-kath-id'-zo;* from *1909* and *2523;* to *seat upon:*—set on.

1941. **ἐπικαλέομαι ĕpikalĕŏmai**, *ep-ee-kal-eh'-om-ahee;* mid. from *1909* and *2564;* to *entitle;* by impl. to *invoke* (for aid, worship, testimony, decision, etc.):—appeal (unto), call (on, upon), surname.

1942. **ἐπικάλυμα ĕpikaluma**, *ep-ee-kal'-oo-mah;* from *1943;* a *covering,* i.e. (fig.) *pretext:*—cloke.

1943. **ἐπικαλύπτω ĕpikaluptō**, *ep-ee-kal-oop'-to;* from *1909* and *2572;* to *conceal,* i.e. (fig.) *forgive:*—cover.

1944. **ἐπικατάρατος ĕpikataratŏs**, *ep-ee-kat-ar'-at-os;* from *1909* and a der. of *2672;* *imprecated,* i.e. *execrable:*—accursed.

1945. **ἐπίκειμαι ĕpikĕimai**, *ep-ik'-i-mahee;* from *1909* and *2749;* to *rest upon* (lit. or fig.):—impose, be instant, (be) laid (there-, up-) on, (when) lay (on), lie (on), press upon.

1946. **Ἐπικούρειος Ĕpikŏurĕiŏs**, *ep-ee-koo'-ri-os;* from **Ἐπίκουρος Ĕpikŏurŏs** [comp. *1947*] (a noted philosopher); an *Epicurean* or follower of Epicurus:—Epicurean.

1947. **ἐπικουρία ĕpikŏuria**, *ep-ee-koo-ree'-ah;* from a comp. of *1909* and a (prol.) form of the base of *2877* (in the sense of *servant*); *assistance:*—help.

1948. **ἐπικρίνω ĕpikrinō**, *ep-ee-kree'-no;* from *1909* and *2919;* to *adjudge:*—give sentence.

1949. **ἐπιλαμβάνομαι ĕpilambanŏmai**, *ep-ee-lam-ban'-om-ahee;* mid. from *1909* and *2983;* to *seize* (for help, injury, attainment or any other purpose; lit. or fig.):—catch, lay hold (up-) on, take (by, hold of, on).

1950. **ἐπιλανθάνομαι ĕpilanthanŏmai**, *ep-ee-lan-than'-om-ahee;* mid. from *1909* and *2990;* to *lose out* of mind; by impl. to *neglect:*—(be) forget (-ful of).

1951. **ἐπιλέγομαι ĕpilĕgŏmai**, *ep-ee-leg'-om-ahee;* mid. from *1909* and *3004;* to *surname, select:*—call, choose.

1952. **ἐπιλείπω ĕpilĕipō**, *ep-ee-li'-po;* from *1909* and *3007;* to *leave upon,* i.e. (fig.) to *be insufficient for:*—fail.

1953. **ἐπιλησμονή ĕpilēsmŏnē**, *ep-ee-lace-mon-ay';* from a der. of *1950;* *negligence:*— × forgetful.

1954. **ἐπίλοιπος ĕpilŏipŏs**, *ep-il'-oy-pos;* from *1909* and *3062;* *left over,* i.e. *remaining:*—rest.

1955. **ἐπίλυσις ĕpilusis**, *ep-il'-oo-sis;* from *1956;* *explanation,* i.e. *application:*—interpretation.

1956. **ἐπιλύω ĕpiluō**, *ep-ee-loo'-o;* from *1909* and *3089;* to *solve further,* i.e. (fig.) to *explain, decide:*—determine, expound.

1957. **ἐπιμαρτυρέω ĕpimarturĕō**, *ep-ee-mar-too-reh'-o;* from *1909* and *3140;* to *attest further,* i.e. *corroborate:*—testify.

1958. **ἐπιμέλεια ĕpimĕlĕia**, *ep-ee-mel'-i-ah;* from *1959;* *carefulness,* i.e. kind *attention* (*hospitality*):— + refresh self.

1959. **ἐπιμελέομαι ĕpimĕlĕŏmai**, *ep-ee-mel-eh'-om-ahee;* mid. from *1909* and the same as *3199;* to *care for* (phys. or otherwise):—take care of.

1960. **ἐπιμελῶς ĕpimĕlōs**, *ep-ee-mel-oce';* adv. from a der. of *1959;* *carefully:*—diligently.

1961. **ἐπιμένω ĕpimĕnō**, *ep-ee-men'-o;* from *1909* and *3306;* to *stay over,* i.e. *remain* (fig. *persevere*):—abide (in), continue (in), tarry.

1962. **ἐπινεύω ĕpinĕuō**, *ep-een-yoo'-o;* from *1909* and *3506;* to *nod at,* i.e. (by impl.) to *assent:*—consent.

1963. **ἐπίνοια ĕpinŏia**, *ep-in'-oy-ah;* from *1909* and *3563;* *attention* of the mind, i.e. (by impl.) *purpose:*—thought.

1964. **ἐπιορκέω ĕpiŏrkĕō**, *ep-ee-or-keh'-o;* from *1965;* to *commit perjury:*—forswear self.

1965. **ἐπίορκος ĕpiŏrkŏs**, *ep-ee'-or-kos;* from *1909* and *3727;* *on oath,* i.e. (falsely) a *forswearer:*—perjured person.

1966. **ἐπιοῦσα ĕpiŏusa**, *ep-ee-oo'-sah;* fem. sing. part. of a comp. of *1909* and **εἶμι hĕimi** (to *go*); *supervening,* i.e. (*2250* or *3571* being expressed or implied) the *ensuing* day or night:—following, next.

1967. **ἐπιούσιος ĕpiŏusiŏs**, *ep-ee-oo'-see-os;* perh. from the same as *1966;* *to-morrow's;* but more prob. from *1909* and a der. of the pres. part. fem. of *1510;* *for subsistence,* i.e. *needful:*—daily.

1968. **ἐπιπίπτω ĕpipiptō**, *ep-ee-pip'-to;* from *1909* and *4098;* to *embrace* (with affection) or *seize* (with more or less violence; lit. or fig.):—fall into (on, upon), lie on, press upon.

1969. **ἐπιπλήσσω ĕpiplēssō**, *ep-ee-place'-so;* from *1909* and *4141;* to *chastise,* i.e. (with words) to *upbraid:*—rebuke.

1970. **ἐπιπνίγω ĕpipnigō**, *ep-ee-pnee'-go;* from *1909* and *4155;* to *throttle upon,* i.e. (fig.) *overgrow:*—choke.

1971. **ἐπιποθέω ĕpipŏthĕō**, *ep-ee-poth-eh'-o;* from *1909* and **ποθέω pŏthĕō** (to *yearn*); to *dote upon,* i.e. *intensely crave* possession (lawfully or wrongfully):—(earnestly) desire (greatly), (greatly) long (after), lust.

1972. **ἐπιπόθησις ĕpipŏthēsis**, *ep-ee-poth'-ay-sis;* from *1971;* a *longing for:*—earnest (vehement) desire.

1973. **ἐπιπόθητος ĕpipŏthētŏs**, *ep-ee-poth'-ay-tos;* from *1909* and a der. of the latter part of *1971;* *yearned upon,* i.e. *greatly loved:*—longed for.

1974. **ἐπιποθία ĕpipŏthia**, *ep-ee-poth-ee'-ah;* from *1971;* *intense longing:*—great desire.

1975. **ἐπιπορεύομαι ĕpipŏrĕuŏmai**, *ep-ee-por-yoo'-om-ahee;* from *1909* and *4198;* to *journey further,* i.e. *travel on* (*reach*):—come.

1976. **ἐπιῤῥάπτω ĕpirrhaptō**, *ep-ir-hrap'-to;* from *1909* and the base of *4476;* to *stitch upon,* i.e. *fasten* with the needle:—sew on.

1977. **ἐπιῤῥίπτω ĕpirrhiptō**, *ep-ir-hrip'-to;* from *1909* and *4496;* to *throw upon* (lit. or fig.):—cast upon.

1978. **ἐπίσημος ĕpisēmŏs**, *ep-is'-ay-mos;* from *1909* and some form of the base of *4591;* *remarkable,* i.e. (fig.) *eminent:*—notable, of note.

1979. **ἐπισιτισμός ĕpisitismŏs**, *ep-ee-sit-is-mos';* from a comp. of *1909* and a der. of *4621;* a *provisioning,* i.e. (concr.) *food:*—victuals.

1980. **ἐπισκέπτομαι ĕpiskĕptŏmai**, *ep-ee-skep'-tom-ahee;* mid. from *1909* and the base of *4649;* to *inspect,* i.e. (by impl.) to *select;* by extens. to *go to see, relieve:*—look out, visit.

1981. **ἐπισκηνόω ĕpiskēnŏō**, *ep-ee-skay-nŏ'-o;* from *1909* and *4637;* to *tent upon,* i.e. (fig.) *abide with:*—rest upon.

1982. **ἐπισκιάζω ĕpiskiazō**, *ep-ee-skee-ad'-zo;* from *1909* and a der. of *4639;* to *cast a shade upon,* i.e. (by anal.) to *envelop* in a haze of brilliancy; fig. to *invest* with preternatural influence:—overshadow.

1983. **ἐπισκοπέω ĕpiskŏpĕō**, *ep-ee-skop-eh'-o;* from *1909* and *4648;* to *oversee;* by impl. to *beware:*—look diligently, take the oversight.

1984. **ἐπισκοπή ĕpiskŏpē**, *ep-is-kop-ay';* from *1980;* *inspection* (for relief); by impl. *superintendence;* spec. the Chr. "*episcopate*":—the office of a "bishop", bishoprick, visitation.

1985. **ἐπίσκοπος ĕpiskŏpŏs**, *ep-is'-kop-os;* from *1909* and *4649* (in the sense of *1983*); a *superintendent,* i.e. Chr. officer in gen. charge of a (or the) church (lit. or fig.):—bishop, overseer.

1986. **ἐπισπάομαι ĕpispaŏmai**, *ep-ee-spah'-om-ahee;* from *1909* and *4685;* to *draw over,* i.e. (with *203* implied) *efface* the mark of *circumcision* (by recovering with the foreskin):—become uncircumcised.

1987. **ἐπίσταμαι ĕpistamai**, *ep-is'-tam-ahee;* appar. a mid. of *2186* (with *3563* implied); to *put the* mind *upon,* i.e. *comprehend,* or *be acquainted with:*—know, understand.

1988. **ἐπιστάτης ĕpistatēs**, *ep-is-tat'-ace;* from *1909* and a presumed der. of *2476;* an *appointee over,* i.e. *commander* (*teacher*):—master.

1989. **ἐπιστέλλω ĕpistĕllō**, *ep-ee-stel'-lo;* from *1909* and *4724;* to *enjoin* (by writing), i.e. (gen.) to *communicate by letter* (for any purpose):—write (a letter, unto).

1990. **ἐπιστήμων ĕpistēmōn**, *ep-ee-stay'-mone;* from *1987;* *intelligent:*—endued with knowledge.

1991. **ἐπιστηρίζω ĕpistērizō**, *ep-ee-stay-rid'-zo;* from *1909* and *4741;* to *support further,* i.e. *reëstablish:*—confirm, strengthen.

1992. **ἐπιστολή ĕpistŏlē**, *ep-is-tol-ay';* from *1989;* a *written message:*—"epistle", letter.

1993. **ἐπιστομίζω ĕpistŏmizō**, *ep-ee-stom-id'-zo;* from *1909* and *4750;* to put something *over* the *mouth,* i.e. (fig.) to *silence:*—stop mouths.

1994. **ἐπιστρέφω ĕpistrĕphō**, *ep-ee-stref'-o;* from *1909* and *4762;* to *revert* (lit., fig. or mor.):—come (go) again, convert, (re-) turn (about, again).

1995. **ἐπιστροφή ĕpistrŏphē**, *ep-is-trof-ay';* from *1994;* *reversion,* i.e. mor. *revolution:*—conversion.

1996. **ἐπισυνάγω ĕpisunagō**, *ep-ee-soon-ag'-o;* from *1909* and *4863;* to *collect upon* the same place:—gather (together).

1997. **ἐπισυναγωγή ĕpisunagōgē**, *ep-ee-soon-ag-o-gay';* from *1996;* a complete *collection;* spec. a Chr. *meeting* (for worship):—assembling (gathering) together.

1998. **ἐπισυντρέχω ĕpisuntrĕchō**, *ep-ee-soon-trekh'-o;* from *1909* and *4936;* to *hasten together upon* one place (or a partic. occasion):—come running together.

1999. **ἐπισύστασις ĕpisustasis**, *ep-ee-soo'-stas-is;* from the mid. of a comp. of *1909* and *4921;* a *conspiracy,* i.e. *concourse* (riotous or friendly):—that which cometh upon, + raising up.

2000. **ἐπισφαλής ĕpisphalēs**, *ep-ee-sfal-ace';* from a comp. of *1909* and **σφάλλω sphallō** (to *trip*); fig. *insecure:*—dangerous.

2001. **ἐπισχύω ĕpischuō**, *ep-is-khoo'-o;* from *1909* and *2480;* to *avail further,* i.e. (fig.) *insist stoutly:*—be the more fierce.

2002. **ἐπισωρεύω ĕpisōrĕuō**, *ep-ee-so-ryoo'-o;* from *1909* and *4987;* to *accumulate further,* i.e. (fig.) *seek* additionally:—heap.

2003. **ἐπιταγή ĕpitagē**, *ep-ee-tag-ay';* from *2004;* an *injunction* or *decree;* by impl. *authoritativeness:*—authority, commandment.

2004. **ἐπιτάσσω ĕpitassō**, *ep-ee-tas'-so;* from *1909* and *5021;* to *arrange upon,* i.e. *order:*—charge, command, injoin.

2005. **ἐπιτελέω ĕpitĕlĕō**, *ep-ee-tel-eh'-o;* from *1909* and *5055;* to *fulfill further* (or *completely*), i.e. *execute;* by impl. to *terminate, undergo:*—accomplish, do, finish, (make) (perfect), perform (× -ance).

2006. **ἐπιτήδειος ĕpitēdĕiŏs**, *ep-ee-tay'-di-os;* from **ἐπιτηδές ĕpitēdĕs** (*enough*); *serviceable,* i.e. (by impl.) *requisite:*—things which are needful.

2007. **ἐπιτίθημι ĕpitithēmi**, *ep-ee-tith'-ay-mee;* from *1909* and *5087;* to *impose* (in a friendly or hostile sense):—add unto, lade, lay upon, put (up) on, set on (up), + surname, × wound.

2008. **ἐπιτιμάω ĕpitimaō**, *ep-ee-tee-mah'-o;* from *1909* and *5091;* to *tax upon,* i.e. *censure* or *admonish;* by impl. *forbid:*—(straitly) charge, rebuke.

2009. **ἐπιτιμία ĕpitimia**, *ep-ee-tee-mee'-ah;* from a comp. of *1909* and *5092;* prop. *esteem,* i.e. *citizenship;* used (in the sense of *2008*) of a *penalty:*—punishment.

2010. **ἐπιτρέπω ĕpitrĕpō**, *ep-ee-trep'-o;* from *1909* and the base of *5157;* to *turn over* (*transfer*), i.e. *allow:*—give leave (liberty, license), let, permit, suffer.

2011. **ἐπιτροπή ĕpitrŏpē**, *ep-ee-trop-ay';* from *2010;* *permission,* i.e. (by impl.) full *power:*—commission.

2012. **ἐπίτροπος ĕpitrŏpŏs**, *ep-it'-rop-os;* from *1909* and *5158* (in the sense of *2011*); a *commissioner,* i.e. domestic *manager, guardian:*—steward, tutor.

2013. **ἐπιτυγχάνω ĕpitugchanō**, *ep-ee-toong-khan'-o;* from *1909* and *5177;* to *chance upon,* i.e. (by impl.) *attain:*—obtain.

2014. **ἐπιφαίνω ĕpiphainō**, *ep-ee-fah'ee-no;* from *1909* and *5316;* to *shine upon,* i.e. *become* (lit.) *visible* or (fig.) *known:*—appear, give light.

2015. **ἐπιφάνεια ĕpiphanĕia**, *ep-if-an'-i-ah;* from *2016;* a *manifestation,* i.e. (spec.) the *advent* of Christ (past or fut.):—appearing, brightness.

2016. **ἐπιφανής ĕpiphanēs**, *ep-if-an-ace';* from *2014;* *conspicuous,* i.e. (fig.) *memorable:*—notable.

2017. **ἐπιφαύω ĕpiphauō**, *ep-ee-fōw'-o;* a form of *2014;* to *illuminate* (fig.):—give light.

2018. **ἐπιφέρω ĕpiphĕrō**, *ep-ee-fer'-o;* from *1909* and *5342;* to *bear upon* (or *further*), i.e. *adduce* (pers. or judicially [*accuse, inflict*]), *superinduce:*—add, bring (against), take.

2019. **ἐπιφωνέω ĕpiphōnĕō**, *ep-ee-fo-neh'-o;* from *1909* and *5455;* to *call at* something, i.e. *exclaim:*—cry (against), give a shout.

2020. **ἐπιφώσκω ĕpiphōskō**, *ep-ee-foce'-ko;* a form of *2017;* to begin to *grow light:*—begin to dawn, × draw on.

2021. **ἐπιχειρέω ĕpichĕirĕō**, *ep-ee-khi-reh'-o;* from *1909* and *5495;* to put the *hand upon,* i.e. *undertake:*—go about, take in hand (upon).

2022. **ἐπιχέω ĕpichĕō**, *ep-ee-kheh'-o;* from *1909* and **χέω chĕō** (to *pour*); to *pour upon:*—pour in.

2023. **ἐπιχορηγέω ĕpichŏrēgĕō**, *ep-ee-khor-ayg-eh'-o;* from *1909* and *5524;* to *furnish besides,* i.e. fully *supply,* (fig.) *aid* or *contribute:*—add, minister (nourishment, unto).

2024. **ἐπιχορηγία ĕpichŏrēgia**, *ep-ee-khor-ayg-ee'-ah;* from *2023;* *contribution:*—supply.

2025. **ἐπιχρίω ĕpichriō**, *ep-ee-khree'-o;* from *1909* and *5548;* to *smear over:*—anoint.

2026. **ἐποικοδομέω ĕpŏikŏdŏmĕō**, *ep-oy-kod-om-eh'-o;* from *1909* and *3618;* to *build upon,* i.e. (fig.) to *rear up:*—build thereon (thereupon, on, upon).

2027. **ἐποκέλλω ĕpŏkĕllō**, *ep-ok-el'-lo;* from *1909* and **ὀκέλλω ŏkĕllō** (to *urge*); to *drive upon* the shore, i.e. to *beach* a vessel:—run aground.

2028. **ἐπονομάζω ĕpŏnŏmazō**, *ep-on-om-ad'-zo;* from *1909* and *3687;* to *name further,* i.e. *denominate:*—call.

2029. **ἐποπτεύω ĕpŏptĕuō**, *ep-opt-yoo'-o;* from *1909* and a der. of *3700;* to *inspect,* i.e. *watch:*—behold.

2030. **ἐπόπτης ĕpŏptēs**, *ep-op'-tace;* from *1909* and a presumed der. of *3700;* a *looker-on:*—eye-witness.

2031. **ἔπος ĕpŏs**, *ep'-os;* from *2036;* a *word:*—× say.

2032. **ἐπουράνιος ĕpŏuraniŏs**, *ep-oo-ran'-ee-os;* from *1909* and *3772;* *above the sky:*—celestial, (in) heaven (-ly), high.

2033. **ἑπτά hĕpta**, *hep-tah';* a prim. number; *seven:*—seven.

2034. **ἑπτάκις hĕptakis**, *hep-tak-is';* adv. from *2033;* *seven times:*—seven times.

2035. **ἑπτακισχίλιοι hĕptakischiliŏi**, *hep-tak-is-khil'-ee-oy;* from *2034* and *5507;* *seven times a thousand:*—seven thousand.

2036. **ἔπω ĕpō**, *ep'-o;* a prim. verb (used only in the def. past tense, the others being borrowed from *2046, 4483* and *5346*); to *speak* or *say* (by word or writing):—answer, bid, bring word, call, command, grant, say (on), speak, tell. Comp. *3004*.

2037. **Ἔραστος Ĕrastŏs**, *er'-as-tos;* from **ἐράω ĕraō** (to *love*); *beloved; Erastus,* a Chr.:—Erastus.

2038. **ἐργάζομαι ĕrgazŏmai**, *er-gad'-zom-ahee;* mid. from *2041;* to *toil* (as a task, occupation, etc.), (by impl.) *effect, be engaged in* or *with,* etc.:—commit, do, labor for, minister about, trade (by), work.

2039. **ἐργασία ĕrgasia**, *er-gas-ee'-ah;* from *2040;* *occupation;* by impl. *profit, pains:*—craft, diligence, gain, work.

2040. **ἐργάτης ĕrgatēs**, *er-gat'-ace;* from *2041;* a *toiler;* fig. a *teacher:*—labourer, worker (-men).

2041. **ἔργον ĕrgŏn**, *er'-gon;* from a prim. (but obsol.) **ἔργω ĕrgō** (to *work*); *toil* (as an effort or occupation); by impl. an *act:*—deed, doing, labour, work.

2042. **ἐρεθίζω ĕrĕthizō**, *er-eth-id'-zo;* from a presumed prol. form of *2054;* to *stimulate* (espec. to anger):—provoke.

2043. **ἐρείδω ĕrĕidō**, *er-i'-do;* of obscure affin.; to *prop,* i.e. (reflex.) *get fast:*—stick fast.

2044. **ἐρεύγομαι ĕrĕugŏmai**, *er-yoog'-om-ahee;* of uncert. affin.; to *belch,* i.e. (fig.) to *speak out:*—utter.

2045. **ἐρευνάω ĕrĕunaō**, *er-yoo-nah'-o;* appar. from *2046* (through the idea of *inquiry*); to *seek,* i.e. (fig.) to *investigate:*—search.

2046. **ἐρέω ĕrĕō**, *er-eh'-o;* prob. a fuller form of *4483;* an alt. for *2036* in cert. tenses; to *utter,* i.e. *speak* or *say:*—call, say, speak (of), tell.

2047. **ἐρημία ĕrēmia**, *er-ay-mee'-ah;* from *2048;* *solitude* (concr.):—desert, wilderness.

2048. **ἔρημος ĕrēmŏs**, *er'-ay-mos;* of uncert. affin.; *lonesome,* i.e. (by impl.) *waste* (usually as a noun, *5561* being implied):—desert, desolate, solitary, wilderness.

2049. **ἐρημόω ĕrēmŏō**, *er-ay-mŏ'-o;* from *2048;* to *lay waste* (lit. or fig.):—(bring to, make) desolate (-ion), come to nought.

2050. **ἐρήμωσις ĕrēmōsis**, *er-ay'-mo-sis;* from *2049;* *despoliation:*—desolation.

2051. **ἐρίζω ĕrizō**, *er-id'-zo;* from *2054;* to *wrangle:*—strive.

2052. **ἐριθεία ĕrithĕia**, *er-ith-i'-ah;* perh. from the same as *2042;* prop. *intrigue,* i.e. (by impl.) *faction:*—contention (-ious), strife.

2053. **ἔριον ĕriŏn**, *er'-ee-on;* of obscure affin.; *wool:*—wool.

2054. **ἔρις ĕris**, *er'-is;* of uncert. affin.; a *quarrel,* i.e. (by impl.) *wrangling:*—contention, debate, strife, variance.

2055. **ἐρίφιον ĕriphiŏn**, *er-if'-ee-on;* from *2056;* a *kidling,* i.e. (gen.) *goat* (symbol. *wicked* person):—goat.

2056. **ἔριφος ĕriphŏs**, *er'-if-os;* perh. from the same as *2053* (through the idea of *hairiness*); a *kid* or (gen.) *goat:*—goat, kid.

2057. **Ἑρμᾶς Hĕrmas**, *her-mas';* prob. from *2060;* *Hermas,* a Chr.:—Hermas.

2058. **ἑρμηνεία hĕrmēnĕia**, *her-may-ni'-ah;* from the same as *2059;* *translation:*—interpretation.

2059. **ἑρμηνεύω hĕrmēnĕuō**, *her-mayn-yoo'-o;* from a presumed der. of *2060* (as the god of language); to *translate:*—interpret.

2060. **Ἑρμῆς Hĕrmēs**, *her-mace';* perh. from *2046;* *Hermes,* the name of the messenger of the Gr. deities; also of a Chr.:—Hermes, Mercury.

2061. **Ἑρμογένης Hĕrmŏgĕnēs**, *her-mog-en'-ace;* from *2060* and *1096;* *born of Hermes; Hermogenes,* an apostate Chr.:—Hermogenes.

2062. **ἑρπετόν hĕrpĕtŏn**, *her-pet-on';* neut. of a der. of **ἕρπω hĕrpō** (to *creep*); a *reptile,* i.e. (by Hebr. [comp. 7431]) a small *animal:*—creeping thing, serpent.

2063. **ἐρυθρός ĕruthrŏs**, *er-oo-thros';* of uncert. affin.; *red,* i.e. (with *2281*) the *Red* Sea:—red.

2064. **ἔρχομαι ĕrchŏmai**, *er'-khom-ahee;* mid. of a prim. verb (used only in the pres. and imperf. tenses, the others being supplied by a kindred [mid.] **ἐλεύθομαι ĕlĕuthŏmai**, *el-yoo'-thom-ahee;* or [act.] **ἔλθω ĕlthō**, *el'-tho;* which do not otherwise occur); to *come* or *go* (in a great variety of applications, lit. and fig.):—accompany, appear, bring, come enter, fall out, go, grow, × light, × next, pass, resort, be set.

2065. **ἐρωτάω ĕrōtaō**, *er-o-tah'-o;* appar. from *2046* [comp. *2045*]; to *interrogate;* by impl. to *request:*—ask, beseech, desire, intreat, pray. Comp. *4441*.

2066. ἐσθής **ĕsthēs**, *es-thace'*; from ἕννυμι **hĕnnumi** (to *clothe*); *dress*:—apparel, clothing, raiment, robe.

2067. ἔσθησις **ĕsthēsis**, *es'-thay-sis*; from a der. of *2066*; *clothing* (concr.):—garment.

2068. ἐσθίω **ĕsthiō**, *es-thee'-o*; strengthened for a prim. ἔδω **ĕdō** (*to eat*); used only in certain tenses, the rest being supplied by *5315*; *to eat* (usually lit.):—devour, eat, live.

2069. Ἐσλί **Ĕsli**, *es-lee'*; of Heb. or. [prob. for 454]; *Esli*, an Isr.:—Esli.

2070. ἐσμέν **ĕsmĕn**, *es-men'*; first pers. plur. indic. of *1510*; we *are*:—are, be, have our being, × have hope, + [the gospel] was [preached unto] us.

2071. ἔσομαι **ĕsŏmai**, *es'-om-ahee*; fut. of *1510*; *will be*:—shall (should) be (have), (shall) come (to pass), × may have, × fail, what would follow, × live long, × sojourn.

2072. ἔσοπτρον **ĕsŏptrŏn**, *es'-op-tron*; from *1519* and a presumed der. of *3700*; a *mirror* (for *looking into*):—glass. Comp. *2734*.

2073. ἑσπέρα **hĕspĕra**, *hes-per'-ah*; fem. of an adj. ἑσπερός **hĕspĕrŏs** (*evening*); the *eve* (*5610* being impl.):—evening (-tide).

2074. Ἐσρώμ **Ĕsrōm**, *es-rome'*; of Heb. or. [2696]; *Esrom* (i.e. *Chetsron*), an Isr.:—Esrom.

2075. ἐστέ **ĕstĕ**, *es-teh'*; second pers. plur. pres. indic. of *1510*; ye *are*:—be, have been, belong.

2076. ἐστί **ĕsti**, *es-tee'*; third pers. sing. pres. indic. of *1510*; he (she or it) *is*; also (with neut. plur.) they *are*:—are, be (-long), call, × can [-not], come, consisteth, × dure for awhile, + follow, × have, (that) is (to say), make, meaneth, × must needs, + profit, + remaineth, + wrestle.

2077. ἔστω **ĕstō**, *es'-to*; second pers. sing. pres. imper. of *1510*; *be* thou; also

ἔστωσαν **ĕstōsan**, *es'-to-san*; third pers. of the same; *let* them *be*:—be.

2078. ἔσχατος **ĕschatŏs**, *es'-khat-os*; a superl. prob. from *2192* (in the sense of *contiguity*); *farthest*, *final* (of place or time):—ends of, last, latter end, lowest, uttermost.

2079. ἐσχάτως **ĕschatōs**, *es-khat'-oce*; adv. from *2078*; *finally*, i.e. (with *2192*) *at the extremity* of life:—point of death.

2080. ἔσω **ĕsō**, *es'-o*; from *1519*; *inside* (as prep. or adj.):—(with-) in (-ner, -to, -ward).

2081. ἔσωθεν **ĕsōthĕn**, *es'-o-then*; from *2080*; *from inside*; also used as equiv to *2080* (*inside*):—inward (-ly), (from) within, without.

2082. ἐσώτερος **ĕsōtĕrŏs**, *es-o'-ter-os*; compar. of *2080*; *interior*:—inner, within.

2083. ἑταῖρος **hĕtairŏs**, *het-ah'ee-ros*; from ἔτης **ĕtēs** (a *clansman*); a *comrade*:—fellow, friend.

2084. ἑτερόγλωσσος **hĕtĕrŏglōssŏs**, *het-er-og'-loce-sos*; from *2087* and *1100*; *other-tongued*, i.e. a *foreigner*:—man of other tongue.

2085. ἑτεροδιδασκαλέω **hĕtĕrŏdidaskalĕō**, *het-er-od-id-as-kal-eh'-o*; from *2087* and *1320*; *to instruct differently*:—teach other doctrine (-wise).

2086. ἑτεροζυγέω **hĕtĕrŏzugĕō**, *het-er-od-zoog-eh'-o*; from a comp. of *2087* and *2218*; *to yoke up differently*, i.e. (fig.) to *associate discordantly*:—unequally yoke together with.

2087. ἕτερος **hĕtĕrŏs**, *het'-er-os*; of uncert. affin.; (an-, the) *other* or *different*:—altered, else, next (day), one, (an-) other, some, strange.

2088. ἑτέρως **hĕtĕrōs**, *het-er'-oce*; adv. from *2087*; *differently*:—otherwise.

2089. ἔτι **ĕti**, *et'-ee*; perh. akin to *2094*; "*yet*," *still* (of time or degree):—after that, also, ever, (any) further, (t-) henceforth (more), hereafter, (any) longer, (any) more (-one), now, still, yet.

2090. ἑτοιμάζω **hĕtŏimazō**, *het-oy-mad'-zo*; from *2092*; *to prepare*:—prepare, provide, make ready. Comp. *2680*.

2091. ἑτοιμασία **hĕtŏimasia**, *het-oy-mas-ee'-ah*; from *2090*; *preparation*:—preparation.

2092. ἕτοιμος **hĕtŏimŏs**, *het-oy'-mos*; from an old noun ἔτεος **hĕtĕŏs** (*fitness*); *adjusted*, i.e. *ready*:—prepared, (made) ready (-iness, to our hand).

2093. ἑτοίμως **hĕtŏimōs**, *het'-oy-moce*; adv. from *2092*; *in readiness*:—ready.

2094. ἔτος **ĕtŏs**, *et'-os*; appar. a prim. word; a *year*:—year.

2095. εὖ **ĕu**, *yoo*; neut. of a prim. εὖς **ĕus** (*good*); (adv.) *well*:—good, well (done).

2096. Εὔα **Ĕua**, *yoo'-ah*; of Heb. or. [2332]; *Eua* (or *Eva*, i.e. *Chavvah*), the first woman:—Eve.

2097. εὐαγγελίζω **ĕuaggĕlizō**, *yoo-ang-ghel-id'-zo*; from *2095* and *32*; to *announce good* news ("evangelize") espec. the gospel:—declare, bring (declare, show) glad (good) tidings, preach (the gospel).

2098. εὐαγγέλιον **ĕuaggĕliŏn**, *yoo-ang-ghel'-ee-on*; from the same as *2097*; a *good message*, i.e. the *gospel*:—gospel.

2099. εὐαγγελιστής **ĕuaggĕlistēs**, *yoo-ang-ghel-is-tace'*; from *2097*; a *preacher* of the gospel:—evangelist.

2100. εὐαρεστέω **ĕuarĕstĕō**, *yoo-ar-es-teh'-o*; from *2101*; to *gratify entirely*:—please (well).

2101. εὐάρεστος **ĕuarĕstŏs**, *yoo-ar'-es-tos*; from *2095* and *701*; *fully agreeable*:—acceptable (-ted), wellpleasing.

2102. εὐαρέστως **ĕuarĕstōs**, *yoo-ar-es'-toce*; adv. from *2101*; *quite agreeably*:—acceptably, + please well.

2103. Εὔβουλος **Ĕubŏulŏs**, *yoo'-boo-los*; from *2095* and *1014*; *good-willer*; *Eubulus*, a Chr.:—Eubulus.

2104. εὐγένης **ĕugĕnēs**, *yoog-en'-ace*; from *2095* and *1096*; *well born*, i.e. (lit.) *high* in rank, or (fig.) *generous*:—more noble, nobleman.

2105. εὐδία **ĕudia**, *yoo-dee'-ah*; fem. from *2095* and the alt. of *2203* (as the god of the weather); a *clear sky*, i.e. *fine weather*:—fair weather.

2106. εὐδοκέω **ĕudŏkĕō**, *yoo-dok-eh'-o*; from *2095* and *1380*; to *think well* of, i.e. *approve* (an act); spec. to *approbate* (a person or thing):—think good, (be well) please (-d), be the good (have, take) pleasure, be willing.

2107. εὐδοκία **ĕudŏkia**, *yoo-dok-ee'-ah*; from a presumed comp. of *2095* and the base of *1380*; *satisfaction*, i.e. (subj.) *delight*, or (obj.) *kindness*, *wish*, *purpose*:—desire, good pleasure (will), × seem good.

2108. εὐεργεσία **ĕuĕrgĕsia**, *yoo-erg-es-ee'-ah*; from *2110*; *beneficence* (gen. or spec.):—benefit, good deed done.

2109. εὐεργετέω **ĕuĕrgĕtĕō**, *yoo-erg-et-eh'-o*; from *2110*; to *be philanthropic*:—do good.

2110. εὐεργέτης **ĕuĕrgĕtēs**, *yoo-erg-et'-ace*; from *2095* and the base of *2041*; a *worker of good*, i.e. (spec.) a *philanthropist*:—benefactor.

2111. εὔθετος **ĕuthĕtŏs**, *yoo'-thet-os*; from *2095* and a der. of *5087*; *well placed*, i.e. (fig.) *appropriate*:—fit, meet.

2112. εὐθέως **ĕuthĕōs**, *yoo-theh'-oce*; adv. from *2117*; *directly*, i.e. *at once* or *soon*:—anon, as soon as, forthwith, immediately, shortly, straightway.

2113. εὐθυδρομέω **ĕuthudrŏmĕō**, *yoo-thoo-drom-eh'-o*; from *2117* and *1408*; to *lay a straight course*, i.e. *sail direct*:—(come) with a straight course.

2114. εὐθυμέω **ĕuthumĕō**, *yoo-thoo-meh'-o*; from *2115*; to *cheer up*, i.e. (intrans.) *be cheerful*; neut. comp. (adv.) *more cheerfully*:—be of good cheer (merry).

2115. εὔθυμος **ĕuthumŏs**, *yoo'-thoo-mos*; from *2095* and *2372*; in *fine spirits*, i.e. *cheerful*:—of good cheer, the more cheerfully.

2116. εὐθύνω **ĕuthunō**, *yoo-thoo'-no*; from *2117*; to *straighten* (*level*); tech. to *steer*:—governor, make straight.

2117. εὐθύς **ĕuthus**, *yoo-thoos'*; perh. from *2095* and *5087*; *straight*, i.e. (lit.) *level*, or (fig.) *true*; adv. (of time) *at once*:—anon, by and by, forthwith, immediately, straightway.

2118. εὐθύτης **ĕuthutēs**, *yoo-thoo'-tace*; from *2117*; *rectitude*:—righteousness.

2119. εὐκαιρέω **ĕukairĕō**, *yoo-kahee-reh'-o*; from *2121*; to *have good time*, i.e. *opportunity* or *leisure*:—have leisure (convenient time), spend time.

2120. εὐκαιρία **ĕukairia**, *yoo-kahee-ree'-ah*; from *2121*; a favorable *occasion*:—opportunity.

2121. εὔκαιρος **ĕukairŏs**, *yoo'-kahee-ros*; from *2095* and *2540*; *well-timed*, i.e. *opportune*:—convenient, in time of need.

2122. εὐκαίρως **ĕukairōs**, *yoo-kah'ee-roce*; adv. from *2121*; *opportunely*:—conveniently, in season.

2123. εὐκοπώτερος **ĕukŏpōtĕrŏs**, *yoo-kop-o'-ter-os*; comp. of a comp. of *2095* and *2873*; *better for toil*, i.e. *more facile*:—easier.

2124. εὐλάβεια **ĕulabĕia**, *yoo-lab'-i-ah*; from *2126*; prop. *caution*, i.e. (religiously) *reverence* (*piety*); by impl. *dread* (concr.):—fear (-ed).

2125. εὐλαβέομαι **ĕulabĕŏmai**, *yoo-lab-eh'-om-ahee*; mid. from *2126*; to *be circumspect*, i.e. (by impl.) to *be apprehensive*; religiously, to *reverence*:—(moved with) fear.

2126. εὐλαβής **ĕulabēs**, *yoo-lab-ace'*; from *2095* and *2983*; *taking well* (*carefully*), i.e. *circumspect* (religiously, *pious*):—devout.

2127. εὐλογέω **ĕulŏgĕō**, *yoo-log-eh'-o*; from a comp. of *2095* and *3056*; to *speak well of*, i.e. (religiously) to *bless* (*thank* or *invoke a benediction upon*, *prosper*):—bless, praise.

2128. εὐλογητός **ĕulŏgētŏs**, *yoo-log-ay-tos'*; from *2127*; *adorable*:—blessed.

2129. εὐλογία **ĕulŏgia**, *yoo-log-ee'-ah*; from the same as *2127*; *fine speaking*, i.e. *elegance of language*; *commendation* ("*eulogy*"), i.e. (reverentially) *adoration*; religiously, *benediction*; by impl. *consecration*; by extens. *benefit* or *largess*:—blessing (a matter of) bounty (× -tifully), fair speech.

2130. εὐμετάδοτος **ĕumĕtadŏtŏs**, *yoo-met-ad'-ot-os*; from *2095* and a presumed der. of *3330*; *good at imparting*, i.e. *liberal*:—ready to distribute.

2131. Εὐνίκη **Ĕunikē**, *yoo-nee'-kay*; from *2095* and *3529*; *victorious*; *Eunice*, a Jewess:—Eunice.

2132. εὐνοέω **ĕunŏĕō**, *yoo-nŏ-eh'-o*; from a comp. of *2095* and *3563*; to *be well-minded*, i.e. *reconcile*:—agree.

2133. εὔνοια **ĕunŏia**, *yoo'-noy-ah*; from the same as *2132*; *kindness*; euphem. *conjugal duty*:—benevolence, good will.

2134. εὐνουχίζω **ĕunŏuchizō**, *yoo-noo-khid'-zo*, from *2135*; to *castrate* (fig. *live unmarried*):—make . . . eunuch.

2135. εὐνοῦχος **ĕunŏuchŏs**, *yoo-noo'-khos*; from εὐνή **ĕunē** (a *bed*) and *2192*; a *castrated* person (such being employed in Oriental bed-chambers); by extens. an *impotent* or *unmarried* man; by impl. a *chamberlain* (*state-officer*):—eunuch.

2136. Εὐοδία **Ĕuŏdia**, *yoo-od-ee'-ah*; from the same as *2137*; *fine travelling*; *Euodia*, a Chr. woman:—Euodias.

2137. εὐοδόω **ĕuŏdŏō**, *yoo-od-ŏ'-o*; from a comp. of *2095* and *3598*; to *help on the road*, i.e. (pass.) *succeed in reaching*; fig. to *succeed* in business affairs:—(have a) prosper (-ous journey).

2138. εὐπειθής **ĕupĕithēs**, *yoo-pi-thace'*; from *2095* and *3982*; *good* for *persuasion*, i.e. (intrans.) *compliant*:—easy to be intreated.

2139. εὐπερίστατος **ĕupĕristatŏs**, *yoo-per-is'-tat-os*; from *2095* and a der. of a presumed comp. of *4012* and *2476*; *well standing around*, i.e. (a *competitor*) *thwarting* (a racer) in every direction (fig. of sin in gen.):—which doth so easily beset.

2140. εὐποιΐα **ĕupŏiia**, *yoo-poy-ee'-ah*; from a comp. of *2095* and *4160*; *well doing*, i.e. *beneficence*:—to do good.

2141. εὐπορέω **ĕupŏrĕō**, *yoo-por-eh'-o*; from a comp. of *2090* and the base of *4107*; (intrans.) to *be good* for *passing* through, i.e. (fig.) *have* pecuniary *means*:—ability.

2142. εὐπορία **ĕupŏria**, *yoo-por-ee'-ah*; from the same as *2141*; pecuniary *resources*:—wealth.

2143. **εὐπρέπεια ĕuprĕpĕia**, *yoo-prep'-i-ah;* from a comp. of *2095* and *4241;* *good suitableness*, i.e. *gracefulness:*—grace.

2144. **εὐπρόσδεκτος ĕuprŏsdĕktŏs**, *yoo-pros'-dek-tos;* from *2095* and a der. of *4327;* *well-received*, i.e. *approved, favorable:*—acceptable (-ted).

2145. **εὐπρόσεδρος ĕuprŏsĕdrŏs**, *yoo-pros'-ed-ros;* from *2095* and the same as *4332;* *sitting well towards*, i.e. (fig.) *assiduous* (neut. *diligent service*):—× attend upon.

2146. **εὐπροσωπέω ĕuprŏsōpĕō**, *yoo-pros-o-peh'-o;* from a comp. of *2095* and *4383;* to *be of good countenance*, i.e. (fig.) to *make a display:*—make a fair show.

2147. **εὑρίσκω hĕuriskō**, *hyoo-ris'-ko;* a prol. form of a prim.

εὕρω hĕurō, *hyoo'-ro;* which (together with another cognate form

εὑρέω hĕurĕō, *hyoo-reh'-o*) is used for it in all the tenses except the pres. and imperf.; to *find* (lit. or fig.):—find, get, obtain, perceive, see.

2148. **Εὐροκλύδων Ĕurŏkludōn**, *yoo-rok-loo'-dohn;* from **Εὖρος Ĕurŏs** (the *east* wind) and *2830;* a *storm from the East* (or S.E.), i.e. (in modern phrase) a *Levanter:*—Euroklydon.

2149. **εὐρύχωρος ĕuruchōrŏs**, *yoo-roo'-kho-ros;* from **εὐρύς ĕurus** (*wide*) and *5561;* *spacious:*—broad.

2150. **εὐσέβεια ĕusĕbĕia**, *yoo-seb'-i-ah;* from *2152;* *piety;* spec. the *gospel* scheme:—godliness, holiness.

2151. **εὐσεβέω ĕusĕbĕō**, *yoo-seb-eh'-o;* from *2152;* to *be pious*, i.e. (towards God) to *worship*, or (towards parents) to *respect* (*support*):—show piety, worship.

2152. **εὐσεβής ĕusĕbēs**, *yoo-seb-ace';* from *2095* and *4576;* *well-reverent*, i.e. *pious:*—devout, godly.

2153. **εὐσεβῶς ĕusĕbōs**, *yoo-seb-oce';* adv. from *2152;* *piously:*—godly.

2154. **εὔσημος ĕusēmŏs**, *yoo'-say-mos;* from *2095* and the base of *4591;* *well indicated*, i.e. (fig.) *significant:*—easy to be understood.

2155. **εὔσπλαγχνος ĕusplagchnŏs**, *yoo'-splangkh-nos;* from *2095* and *4698;* *well compassioned*, i.e. *sympathetic:*—pitiful, tender-hearted.

2156. **εὐσχημόνως ĕuschēmŏnōs**, *yoo-skhay-mon'-oce;* adv. from *2158;* *decorously:*—decently, honestly.

2157. **εὐσχημοσύνη ĕuschēmŏsunē**, *yoo-skhay-mos-oo'-nay;* from *2158;* *decorousness:*—comeliness.

2158. **εὐσχήμων ĕuschēmōn**, *yoo-skhay'-mone;* from *2095* and *4976;* *well-formed*, i.e. (fig.) *decorous*, *noble* (in rank):—comely, honourable.

2159. **εὐτόνως ĕutŏnōs**, *yoo-ton'-oce;* adv. from a comp. of *2095* and a der. of **τείνω tĕinō** (to *stretch*); *in a well-strung manner*, i.e. (fig.) *intensely* (in a good sense, *cogently;* in a bad one, *fiercely*):—mightily, vehemently.

2160. **εὐτραπελία ĕutrapĕlia**, *yoo-trap-el-ee'-ah;* from a comp. of *2095* and a der. of the base of *5157* (mean. *well-turned*, i.e. *ready at repartee, jocose*); *witticism*, i.e. (in a vulgar sense) *ribaldry:*—jesting.

2161. **Εὔτυχος Ĕutuchŏs**, *yoo'-too-khos;* from *2095* and a der. of *5177;* *well-fated*, i.e. *fortunate; Eutychus*, a young man:—Eutychus.

2162. **εὐφημία ĕuphēmia**, *yoo-fay-mee'-ah;* from *2163;* *good language* ("*euphemy*"), i.e. *praise* (*repute*):—good report.

2163. **εὔφημος ĕuphēmŏs**, *yoo'-fay-mos;* from *2095* and *5345;* *well spoken of*, i.e. *reputable:*—of good report.

2164. **εὐφορέω ĕuphŏrĕō**, *yoo-for-eh'-o;* from *2095* and *5409;* to *bear well*, i.e. *be fertile:*—bring forth abundantly.

2165. **εὐφραίνω ĕuphrainō**, *yoo-frah'ee-no;* from *2095* and *5424;* to *put* (mid. or pass. *be*) *in a good frame of mind*, i.e. *rejoice:*—fare, make glad, be (make) merry, rejoice.

2166. **Εὐφράτης Ĕuphratēs**, *yoo-frat'-ace;* of for. or. [comp. 6578]; *Euphrates*, a river of Asia:—Euphrates.

2167. **εὐφροσύνη ĕuphrŏsunē**, *yoo-fros-oo'-nay;* from the same as *2165;* *joyfulness:*—gladness, joy.

2168. **εὐχαριστέω ĕucharistĕō**, *yoo-khar-is-teh'-o;* from *2170;* to *be grateful*, i.e. (act.) to *express gratitude* (towards); spec. to *say grace* at a meal:—(give) thank (-ful, -s).

2169. **εὐχαριστία ĕucharistia**, *yoo-khar-is-tee'-ah;* from *2170;* *gratitude;* act. *grateful language* (to God, as an act of worship):—thankfulness, (giving of) thanks (-giving).

2170. **εὐχάριστος ĕucharistŏs**, *yoo-khar'-is-tos;* from *2095* and a der. of *5483;* *well favored*, i.e. (by impl.) *grateful:*—thankful.

2171. **εὐχή ĕuchē**, *yoo-khay';* from *2172;* prop. a *wish*, expressed as a *petition* to God, or in *votive* obligation:—prayer, vow.

2172. **εὔχομαι ĕuchŏmai**, *yoo'-khom-ahee;* mid. of a prim. verb; to *wish;* by impl. to *pray* to God:—pray, will, wish.

2173. **εὔχρηστος ĕuchrēstŏs**, *yoo'-khrays-tos;* from *2095* and *5543;* *easily used*, i.e. *useful:*—profitable, meet for use.

2174. **εὐψυχέω ĕupsuchĕō**, *yoo-psoo-kheh'-o;* from a comp. of *2095* and *5590;* to *be in good spirits*, i.e. *feel encouraged:*—be of good comfort.

2175. **εὐωδία ĕuōdia**, *yoo-o-dee'-ah;* from a comp. of *2095* and a der. of *3605;* *good-scentedness*, i.e. *fragrance:*—sweet savour (smell, -smelling).

2176. **εὐώνυμος ĕuōnumŏs**, *yoo-o'-noo-mos;* from *2095* and *3686;* prop. *well-named* (*good-omened*), i.e. the *left* (which was the *lucky* side among the pagan Greeks); neut. as adv. *at the left* hand:—(on the) left.

2177. **ἐφάλλομαι ĕphallŏmai**, *ef-al'-lom-ahee;* from *1909* and *242;* to *spring upon:*—leap on.

2178. **ἐφάπαξ ĕphapax**, *ef-ap'-ax;* from *1909* and *530;* *upon one occasion* (only):—(at) once (for all).

2179. **Ἐφεσῖνος Ĕphĕsinŏs**, *ef-es-ee'-nos;* from *2181;* *Ephesine*, or situated at Ephesus:—of Ephesus.

2180. **Ἐφέσιος Ĕphĕsiŏs**, *ef-es'-ee-os;* from *2181;* an *Ephesian* or inhab. of Ephesus:—Ephesian, of Ephesus.

2181. **Ἔφεσος Ĕphĕsŏs**, *ef'-es-os;* prob. of for. or.; *Ephesus*, a city of Asia Minor:—Ephesus.

2182. **ἐφευρέτης ĕphĕurĕtēs**, *ef-yoo-ret'-ace;* from a comp. of *1909* and *2147;* a *discoverer*, i.e. *contriver:*—inventor.

2183. **ἐφημερία ĕphēmĕria**, *ef-ay-mer-ee'-ah;* from *2184;* *diurnality*, i.e. (spec.) the quotidian *rotation* or *class* of the Jewish priests' service at the Temple, as distributed by families:—course.

2184. **ἐφήμερος ĕphēmĕrŏs**, *ef-ay'-mer-os;* from *1909* and *2250;* *for a day* ("ephemeral"), i.e. *diurnal:*—daily.

2185. **ἐφικνέομαι ĕphiknĕŏmai**, *ef-ik-neh'-om-ahee;* from *1909* and a cognate of *2240;* to *arrive upon*, i.e. *extend to:*—reach.

2186. **ἐφίστημι ĕphistēmi**, *ef-is'-tay-mee;* from *1909* and *2476;* to *stand upon*, i.e. *be present* (in various applications, friendly or otherwise, usually lit.):—assault, come (in, to, unto, upon), be at hand (instant), present, stand (before, by, over).

2187. **Ἐφραΐμ Ĕphraïm**, *ef-rah-im';* of Heb. or. [669 or better 6085]; *Ephraïm*, a place in Pal.:—Ephraim.

2188. **ἐφφαθά ĕphphatha**, *ef-fath-ah';* of Chald. or. [6606]; *be opened!:*—Ephphatha.

2189. **ἔχθρα ĕchthra**, *ekh'-thrah;* fem. of *2190;* *hostility;* by impl. a reason for *opposition:*—enmity, hatred.

2190. **ἐχθρός ĕchthrŏs**, *ekh-thros';* from a prim. **ἔχθω ĕchthō** (to *hate*); *hateful* (pass. *odious*, or act. *hostile*); usually as a noun, an *adversary* (espec. *Satan*):—enemy, foe.

2191. **ἔχιδνα ĕchidna**, *ekh'-id-nah;* of uncert. or.; an *adder* or other poisonous snake (lit. or fig.):—viper.

2192. **ἔχω ĕchō**, *ekh'-o* (includ. an alt. form **σχέω schĕō**, *skheh'-o;* used in certain tenses only); a prim. verb; to *hold* (used in very various applications, lit. or fig., direct or remote; such as *possession, ability, contiguity, relation* or *condition*):—be (able, × hold, possessed with), accompany, + begin to amend, can (+ -not), × conceive, count, diseased, do, + eat, + enjoy, + fear, following, have, hold, keep, + lack, + go to law, lie, + must needs, + of necessity, + need, next, + recover, + reign, + rest, return, × sick, take for, + tremble, + uncircumcised, use.

2193. **ἕως hĕōs**, *heh'-oce;* of uncert. affin.; a conj., prep. and adv. of continuance, *until* (of time and place):—even (until, unto), (as) far (as), how long, (un-) til (-l), (hither-, un-, up) to, while (-s).

Z

2194. **Ζαβουλών Zabŏulōn**, *dzab-oo-lone';* of Heb. or. [2074]; *Zabulon* (i.e. *Zebulon*), a region of Pal.:—Zabulon.

2195. **Ζακχαῖος Zakchaiŏs**, *dzak-chah'ee-yos;* of Heb. or. [comp. 2140]; *Zacchæus*, an Isr.:—Zacchæus.

2196. **Ζαρά Zara**, *dzar-ah';* of Heb. or. [2226]; *Zara* (i.e. *Zerach*), an Isr.:—Zara.

2197. **Ζαχαρίας Zacharias**, *dzakh-ar-ee'-as;* of Heb. or. [2148]; *Zacharias* (i.e. *Zechariah*), the name of two Isr.:—Zacharias.

2198. **ζάω zaō**, *dzah'-o;* a prim. verb; to *live* (lit. or fig.):—life (-time), (a-) live (-ly), quick.

2199. **Ζεβεδαῖος Zĕbĕdaiŏs**, *dzeb-ed-ah'-yos;* of Heb. or. [comp. 2067]; *Zebedæus*, an Isr.:—Zebedee.

2200. **ζεστός zĕstŏs**, *dzes-tos';* from *2204;* *boiled*, i.e. (by impl.) *calid* (fig. *fervent*):—hot.

2201. **ζεῦγος zĕugŏs**, *dzyoo'-gos;* from the same as *2218;* a *couple*, i.e. a *team* (of oxen yoked together) or *brace* (of birds tied together):—yoke, pair.

2202. **ζευκτηρία zĕuktēria**, *dzyook-tay-ree'-ah*, fem. of a der. (at the second stage) from the same as *2218;* a *fastening* (*tiller-rope*):—band.

2203. **Ζεύς Zĕus**, *dzyooce;* of uncert. affin.; in the oblique cases there is used instead of it a (prob. cognate) name

Δίς Dis, *deece*, which is otherwise obsolete; *Zeus* or *Dis* (among the Latins *Jupiter* or *Jove*), the supreme deity of the Greeks:—Jupiter.

2204. **ζέω zĕō**, *dzeh'-o;* a prim. verb; to *be hot* (*boil*, of liquids; or *glow*, of solids), i.e. (fig.) *be fervid* (*earnest*):—be fervent.

2205. **ζῆλος zēlŏs**, *dzay'-los;* from *2204;* prop. *heat*, i.e. (fig.) "*zeal*" (in a favorable sense, *ardor;* in an unfavorable one, *jealousy*, as of a husband [fig. of God], or an enemy, *malice*):—emulation, envy (-ing), fervent mind, indignation, jealousy, zeal.

2206. **ζηλόω zēlŏō**, *dzay-lŏ'-o;* from *2205;* to *have warmth* of feeling for or against:—affect, covet (earnestly), (have) desire, (move with) envy, be jealous over, (be) zealous (-ly affect).

2207. **ζηλωτής zēlōtēs**, *dzay-lo-tace';* from *2206;* a "*zealot*":—zealous.

2208. **Ζηλωτής Zēlōtēs**, *dzay-lo-tace';* the same as *2207;* a *Zealot*, i.e. (spec.) *partisan* for Jewish political independence:—Zelotes.

2209. **ζημία zēmia**, *dzay-mee'-ah;* prob. akin to the base of *1150* (through the idea of *violence*); *detriment:*—damage, loss.

2210. **ζημιόω zēmiŏō**, *dzay-mee-ŏ'-o;* from *2209;* to *injure*, i.e. (reflex. or pass.) to *experience detriment:*—be cast away, receive damage, lose, suffer loss.

2211. **Ζηνᾶς Zēnas**, *dzay-nas';* prob. contr. from a poetic form of *2203* and *1435;* *Jove-given; Zenas*, a Chr.:—Zenas.

2212. **ζητέω zētĕō**, *dzay-teh'-o;* of uncert. affin.; to *seek* (lit. or fig.); spec. (by Heb.) to *worship* (God), or (in a bad sense) to *plot* (against life):—be (go) about, desire, endeavour, enquire (for), require, (× will) seek (after, for, means). Comp. *4441*.

2213. ζήτημα **zētēma**, *dzay'-tay-mah;* from *2212;* a *search* (prop. concr.), i.e. (in words) a *debate:*—question.

2214. ζήτησις **zētēsis**, *dzay'-tay-sis;* from *2212;* a *searching* (prop. the act), i.e. a *dispute* or its *theme:*—question.

2215. ζιζάνιον **zizaniŏn**, *dziz-an'-ee-on;* of uncert. or.; *darnel* or false grain:—tares.

2216. Ζοροβάβελ **Zŏrŏbabĕl**, *dzor-ob-ab'-el;* of Heb. or. [2216]; *Zorobabel* (i.e. *Zerubbabel*), an Isr.:—Zorobabel.

2217. ζόφος **zŏphŏs**, *dzof'-os;* akin to the base of *3509; gloom* (as shrouding like a *cloud*).—blackness, darkness, mist.

2218. ζυγός **zugŏs**, *dzoo-gos';* from the root of ζεύγνυμι **zĕugnumi** (to *join* espec. by a "yoke"); a *coupling*, i.e. (fig.) *servitude a law* or *obligation*); also (lit.) the *beam* of the balance (as *connecting* the scales).—pair of balances, yoke.

2219. ζύμη **zumē**, *dzoo'-may;* prob. from *2204; ferment* (as if *boiling* up):—leaven.

2220. ζυμόω **zumŏō**, *dzoo-mŏ'-o;* from *2219;* to *cause to ferment:*—leaven.

2221. ζωγρέω **zōgrĕō**, *dzogue-reh'-o;* from the same as *2226* and *64;* to *take alive* (*make a prisoner of war*), i.e. (fig.) to *capture* or *ensnare:*—take captive, catch.

2222. ζωή **zōē**, *dzo-ay';* from *2198; life* (lit. or fig.):—life (-time). Comp. *5590*.

2223. ζώνη **zōnē**, *dzo'-nay;* prob. akin to the base of *2218;* a *belt;* by impl. a *pocket:*—girdle, purse.

2224. ζώννυμι **zōnnumi**, *dzone'-noo-mi;* from *2223;* to *bind about* (espec. with a belt):—gird.

2225. ζωογονέω **zōŏgŏnĕō**, *dzo-og-on-eh'-o;* from the same as *2226* and a der. of *1096;* to *engender alive* i.e. (by anal.) to *rescue* (pass. *be saved*) from death:—live, preserve.

2226. ζῶον **zōŏn**, *dzo'-on;* neut. of a der. of *2198;* a *live* thing, i.e. an *animal:*—beast.

2227. ζωοποιέω **zōŏpŏiĕō**, *dzo-op-oy-eh'-o;* from the same as *2226* and *4160;* to (*re-*) *vitalize* (lit. or fig.):—make alive, give life, quicken.

Η

2228. ἤ **ē**, *ay;* a prim. particle of distinction between two connected terms; disjunctive, *or;* comparative, *than:*—and, but (either), (n-) either, except it be, (n-) or (else), rather, save, than, that, what, yea. Often used in connection with other particles. Comp. especially *2235, 2260, 2273*.

2229. ἦ **ē**, *ay;* an adv. of *confirmation;* perh. intens. of *2228;* used only (in the N. T.) before *3303; assuredly:*—surely.

ἧ **hē**. See *3588*.

ᾗ **hē**. See *3739*.

ᾖ **ē**. See *5600*.

2230. ἡγεμονεύω **hēgĕmŏnĕuō**, *hayg-em-on-yoo'-o;* from *2232;* to *act as ruler:*—be governor.

2231. ἡγεμονία **hēgĕmŏnia**, *hayg-em-on-ee'-ah;* from *2232; government*, i.e. (in time) official *term:*—reign.

2232. ἡγεμών **hēgĕmōn**, *hayg-em-ohn';* from *2233;* a *leader*, i.e. *chief* person (or fig. place) of a province:—governor, prince, ruler.

2233. ἡγέομαι **hēgĕŏmai**, *hayg-eh'-om-ahee;* mid. of a (presumed) strengthened form of *71;* to *lead*, i.e. *command* (with official authority); fig. to *deem*, i.e. *consider:*—account, (be) chief, count, esteem, governor, judge, have the rule over, suppose, think.

2234. ἡδέως **hēdĕōs**, *hay-deh'-oce;* adv. from a der. of the base of *2237; sweetly*, i.e. (fig.) *with pleasure:*—gladly.

2235. ἤδη **ēdē**, *ay'-day;* appar. from *2228* (or possibly *2229*) and *1211; even now:*—already, (even) now (already), by this time.

2236. ἥδιστα **hēdista**, *hay'-dis-tah;* neut. plur. of the superl. of the same as *2234; with great pleasure:*—most (very) gladly.

2237. ἡδονή **hēdŏnē**, *hay-don-ay';* from ἀνδάνω **handanō** (to *please*); sensual *delight;* by impl. *desire:*—lust, pleasure.

2238. ἡδύοσμον **hēduŏsmŏn**, *hay-doo'-os-mon;* neut. of a comp. of the same as *2234* and *3744;* a *sweet-scented* plant, i.e. *mint:*—mint.

2239. ἦθος **ēthŏs**, *ay'-thos;* a strengthened form of *1485; usage*, i.e. (plur.) moral *habits:*—manners.

2240. ἥκω **hēkō**, *hay'-ko;* a prim. verb; to *arrive*, i.e. *be present* (lit. or fig.):—come.

2241. ἠλί **ēli**, *ay-lee';* of Heb. or. [410 with pron. suffix]; *my God:*—Eli.

2242. Ἡλί **Hēli**, *hay-lee';* of Heb. or. [5941]; *Heli* (i.e. *Eli*), an Isr.:—Heli.

2243. Ἡλίας **Hēlias**, *hay-lee'-as;* of Heb. or. [452]; *Helias* (i.e. *Elijah*), an Isr.:—Elias.

2244. ἡλικία **hēlikia**, *hay-lik-ee'-ah;* from the same as *2245; maturity* (in years or size):—age, stature.

2245. ἡλίκος **hēlikŏs**, *hay-lee'-kos;* from ἧλιξ **hēlix** (a *comrade*, i.e. one of the same age); *as big as*, i.e. (interjectively) *how much:*—how (what) great.

2246. ἥλιος **hēliŏs**, *hay'-lee-os;* from ἕλη **hēlē** (a *ray;* perh. akin to the alt. of *138*); the *sun;* by impl. *light:*— + east, sun.

2247. ἧλος **hēlŏs**, *hay'-los;* of uncert. affin.; a *stud*, i.e. *spike:*—nail.

2248. ἡμᾶς **hēmas**, *hay-mas';* acc. plur. of *1473; us:*—our, us, we.

2249. ἡμεῖς **hēmĕis**, *hay-mice';* nom. plur. of *1473; we* (only used when emphatic):—us, we (ourselves).

2250. ἡμέρα **hēmĕra**, *hay-mer'-ah;* fem. (with *5610* implied) of a der. of ἧμαι **hēmai** (to *sit;* akin to the base of *1476*) mean. *tame*, i.e. *gentle; day*, i.e. (lit.) the time space between dawn and dark, or the whole 24 hours (but several days were usually reckoned by the Jews as inclusive of the parts of both extremes); fig. a *period* (always defined more or less clearly by the context):—age, + alway, (mid-) day (by day, [-ly]), + for ever, judgment, (day) time, while, years.

2251. ἡμέτερος **hēmĕtĕrŏs**, *hay-met'-er-os;* from *2349; our:*—our, your [*by a different reading*].

2252. ἤμην **ēmēn**, *ay'-mane;* a prol. form of *2358;* I *was:*—be, was. [*Sometimes unexpressed*.]

2253. ἡμιθανής **hēmithanēs**, *hay-mee-than-ace';* from a presumed comp. of the base of *2255* and *2348; half dead*, i.e. *entirely exhausted:*—half dead.

2254. ἡμῖν **hēmin**, *hay-meen';* dat. plur. of *1473;* to (or *for, with, by*) *us:*—our, (for) us, we.

2255. ἥμισυ **hēmisu**, *hay'-mee-soo;* neut. of a der. from an inseparable pref. akin to *260* (through the idea of *partition* involved in *connection*) and mean. *semi-;* (as noun) *half:*—half.

2256. ἡμιώριον **hēmiōriŏn**, *hay-mee-o'-ree-on;* from the base of *2255* and *5610;* a *half-hour:*—half an hour.

2257. ἡμῶν **hēmōn**, *hay-mone';* gen. plur. of *1473; of* (or *from*) *us:*—our (company), us, we.

2258. ἦν **ēn**, *ane;* imperf. of *1510; I* (*thou*, etc.) *was* (*wast* or *were*):— + agree, be, × have (+ charge of), hold, use, was (-t), were.

2259. ἡνίκα **hēnika**, *hay-nee'-kah;* of uncert. affin.; *at which time:*—when.

2260. ἤπερ **ēpĕr**, *ay'-per;* from *2228* and *4007; than at all* (or *than perhaps, than indeed*):—than.

2261. ἤπιος **ēpiŏs**, *ay'-pee-os;* prob. from *2031;* prop. *affable*, i.e. *mild* or *kind:*—gentle.

2262. Ἤρ **Ēr**, *ayr;* of Heb. or. [6147]; *Er*, an Isr.:—Er.

2263. ἤρεμος **ērĕmŏs**, *ay'-rem-os;* perh. by transposition from *2048* (through the idea of *stillness*); *tranquil:*—quiet.

2264. Ἡρώδης **Hērōdēs**, *hay-ro'-dace;* comp. of ἥρως **hērōs** (a "*hero*") and *1491; heroic; Herodes*, the name of four Jewish kings:—Herod.

2265. Ἡρωδιανοί **Hērōdianŏi**, *hay-ro-dee-an oy';* plur. of a der. of *2264; Herodians*, i.e. partisans of Herodes:—Herodians.

2266. Ἡρωδιάς **Hērōdias**, *hay-ro-dee-as';* from *2264; Herodias*, a woman of the Herodian family:—Herodias.

2267. Ἡρωδίων **Hērōdiōn**, *hay-ro-dee'-ohn;* from *2264; Herodion*, a Chr.:—Herodion.

2268. Ἡσαΐας **Hēsaïas**, *hay-sah-ee'-as;* of Heb. or. [3470]; *Hesaias* (i.e. *Jeshajah*), an Isr.:—Esaias.

2269. Ἠσαῦ **Ēsau**, *ay-sŏw';* of Heb. or. [6215]; *Esau*, an Edomite:—Esau.

2270. ἡσυχάζω **hēsuchazō**, *hay-soo-khad'-zo;* from the same as *2272;* to *keep still* (intrans.), i.e. *refrain* from labor, meddlesomeness or speech:—cease, hold peace, be quiet, rest.

2271. ἡσυχία **hēsuchia**, *hay-soo-khee'-ah;* fem. of *2272;* (as noun) *stillness*, i.e. desistance from bustle or language:—quietness, silence.

2272. ἡσύχιος **hēsuchiŏs**, *hay-soo'-khee-os;* a prol. form of a comp. prob. of a der. of the base of *1476* and perh. *2192;* prop. *keeping* one's *seat* (*sedentary*), i.e. (by impl.) *still* (*undisturbed, undisturbing*):—peaceable, quiet.

2273. ἤτοι **ētŏi**, *ay'-toy;* from *2228* and *5104; either indeed:*—whether.

2274. ἡττάω **hēttaō**, *hayt-tah'-o;* from the same as *2276;* to *make worse*, i.e. *vanquish* (lit. or fig.); by impl. to *rate lower:*—be inferior, overcome.

2275. ἥττημα **hēttēma**, *hayt'-tay-mah;* from *2274;* a *deterioration*, i.e. (obj.) *failure* or (subj.) *loss:*—diminishing, fault.

2276. ἧττον **hēttŏn**, *hate'-ton;* neut. of comp. of ἧκα **hēka** (*slightly*) used for that of *2556; worse* (as noun); by impl. *less* (as adv.):—less, worse.

2277. ἤτω **ētō**, *ay'-to;* third pers. sing. imperative of *1510; let him* (or *it*) *be:*—let . . . be.

2278. ἠχέω **ēchĕō**, *ay-kheh'-o;* from *2279;* to *make* a loud *noise*, i.e. *reverberate:*—roar, sound.

2279. ἦχος **ēchŏs**, *ay'-khos;* of uncert. affin.; a loud or confused *noise* ("*echo*"), i.e. *roar;* fig. a *rumor:*—fame, sound.

Θ

2280. Θαδδαῖος **Thaddaiŏs**, *thad-dah'-yos;* of uncert. or.; *Thaddæus*, one of the Apostles:—Thaddæus.

2281. θάλασσα **thalassa**, *thal'-as-sah;* prob. prol. from *251;* the *sea* (gen. or spec.):—sea.

2282. θάλπω **thalpō**, *thal'-po;* prob. akin to θάλλω **thallō** (to *warm*); to *brood*, i.e. (fig.) to *foster:*—cherish.

2283. Θάμαρ **Thamar**, *tham'-ar;* of Heb. or. [8559]; *Thamar* (i.e. *Tamar*), an Israelitess:—Thamar.

2284. θαμβέω **thambĕō**, *tham-beh'-o;* from *2285;* to *stupefy* (with surprise), i.e. *astound:*—amaze, astonish.

2285. θάμβος **thambŏs**, *tham'-bos;* akin to an obsol. τάφω **taphō** (to *dumbfound*); *stupefaction* (by surprise), i.e. *astonishment:*— × amazed, + astonished, wonder.

2286. θανάσιμος **thanasimŏs**, *than-as'-ee-mos;* from *2288; fatal*, i.e. *poisonous:*—deadly.

2287. θανατήφορος **thanatēphŏrŏs**, *than-at-ay'-for-os;* from (the fem. form of) *2288* and *5342; death-bearing*, i.e. *fatal:*—deadly.

2288. θάνατος **thanatŏs**, *than'-at-os;* from *2348;* (prop. an adj. used as a noun) *death* (lit. or fig.):— × deadly, (be . . .) death.

2289. θανατόω **thanatŏō**, *than-at-ŏ'-o;* from *2288;* to *kill* (lit. or fig.):—become **dead**, (cause to be) put to death, kill, mortify.

θάνω **thanō**. See *2348*.

2290. θάπτω **thaptō**, *thap'-to;* a prim. verb; to *celebrate funeral rites*, i.e. *inter:*—bury.

2291. Θάρα **Thara**, *thar'-ah;* of Heb. or. [8646]; *Thara* (i.e. *Terach*), the father of Abraham:—Thara.

2292. θαῤῥέω **tharrhĕō**, *thar-hreh'-o;* another form for *2293;* to *exercise courage:*—be bold, × boldly, have confidence, be confident. Comp. *5111.*

2293. θαρσέω **tharsĕō**, *thar-seh'-o;* from *2294;* to *have courage:*—be of good cheer (comfort). Comp. *2292.*

2294. θάρσος **tharsŏs**, *thar'-sos;* akin (by transp.) to θράσος **thrasŏs** (*daring*); *boldness* (subj.):—courage.

2295. θαῦμα **thauma**, *thŏw'-mah;* appar. from a form of *2300;* *wonder* (prop. concr.; but by impl. abstr.):—admiration.

2296. θαυμάζω **thaumazō**, *thŏw-mad'-zo;* from *2295;* to *wonder;* by impl. to *admire:*—admire, have in admiration, marvel, wonder.

2297. θαυμάσιος **thaumasiŏs**, *thŏw-mas'-ee-os;* from *2295;* *wondrous*, i.e. (neut. as noun) a *miracle:*—wonderful thing.

2298. θαυμαστός **thaumastŏs**, *thŏw-mas-tos';* from *2296;* *wondered* at, i.e. (by impl.) *wonderful:*—marvel (-lous).

2299. θεά **thĕa**, *theh-ah';* fem. of *2316;* a female *deity:*—goddess.

2300. θεάομαι **thĕaŏmai**, *theh-ah'-om-ahee;* a prol. form of a prim. verb; to *look* closely at, i.e. (by impl.) to *perceive* (lit. or fig.); by extens. to *visit:*—behold, look (upon), see. Comp. *3700.*

2301. θεατρίζω **thĕatrizō**, *theh-at-rid'-zo;* from *2302;* to *expose as a spectacle:*—make a gazing stock.

2302. θέατρον **thĕatrŏn**, *theh'-at-ron;* from *2300;* a *place for public show* ("theatre"), i.e. general *audience-room;* by impl. a *show* itself (fig.):—spectacle, theatre.

2303. θεῖον **thĕiŏn**, *thi'-on;* prob. neut. of *2304* (in its or. sense of *flashing*); *sulphur:*—brimstone.

2304. θεῖος **thĕiŏs**, *thi'-os;* from *2316;* *godlike* (neut. as noun, *divinity*):—divine, godhead.

2305. θειότης **thĕiŏtēs**, *thi-ot'-ace;* from *2304;* *divinity* (abstr.):—godhead.

2306. θειώδης **thĕiōdēs**, *thi-o'-dace;* from *2303* and *1491;* *sulphur-like*, i.e. *sulphurous:*—brimstone.

θελέω **thĕlĕō**. See *2309.*

2307. θέλημα **thĕlēma**, *thel'-ay-mah;* from the prol. form of *2309;* a *determination* (prop. the thing), i.e. (act.) *choice* (spec. *purpose, decree;* abstr. *volition*) or (pass.) *inclination:*—desire, pleasure, will.

2308. θέλησις **thĕlēsis**, *thel'-ay-sis;* from *2309;* *determination* (prop. the act), i.e. *option:*—will.

2309. θέλω **thĕlō**, *thel'-o;* or ἐθέλω **ĕthĕlō**, *eth-el'-o;* in certain tenses θελέω **thĕlĕō**, *thel-eh'-o;* and ἐθελέω **ĕthĕlĕō**, *eth-el-eh'-o*, which are otherwise obsol.; appar. strengthened from the alt. form of *138;* to *determine* (as an act. *option* from subj. impulse; whereas *1014* prop. denotes rather a pass. *acquiescence* in obj. considerations), i.e., *choose* or *prefer* (lit. or fig.); by impl. to *wish*, i.e. *be inclined* to (sometimes adv. *gladly*); impers. for the fut. tense, to *be about to;* by Heb. to *delight in:*—desire, be disposed (forward), intend, list, love, mean, please, have rather, (be) will (have, -ling, -ling [ly]).

2310. θεμέλιος **thĕmĕliŏs**, *them-el'-ee-os;* from a der. of *5087;* something *put down*, i.e. a *substruction* (of a building, etc.), (lit. or fig.):—foundation.

2311. θεμελιόω **thĕmĕliŏō**, *them-el-ee-ŏ'-o;* from *2310;* to *lay a basis* for, i.e. (lit.) *erect*, or (fig.) *consolidate:*—(lay the) found (-ation), ground, settle.

2312. θεοδίδακτος **thĕŏdidaktŏs**, *theh-od-id'-ak-tos;* from *2316* and *1321;* *divinely instructed:*—taught of God.

2312'. θεολόγος **thĕŏlŏgŏs**, *theh-ol-og'-os;* from *2316* and *3004;* a "*theologian*":—divine.

2313. θεομαχέω **thĕŏmachĕō**, *theh-o-makh-eh'-o;* from *2314;* to *resist deity:*—fight against God.

2314. θεόμαχος **thĕŏmachŏs**, *theh-om'-akh-os;* from *2316* and *3164;* an *opponent of deity:*—to fight against God.

2315. θεόπνευστος **thĕŏpnĕustŏs**, *theh-op'-nyoo-stos;* from *2316* and a presumed der. of *4154;* *divinely breathed* in:—given by inspiration of God.

2316. θεός **thĕŏs**, *theh'-os;* of uncert. affin.; a *deity*, espec. (with *3588*) *the* supreme *Divinity;* fig. a *magistrate;* by Heb. *very:*— × exceeding, God, god [-ly, -ward].

2317. θεοσέβεια **thĕŏsĕbĕia**, *theh-os-eb'-i-ah;* from *2318;* *devoutness*, i.e. *piety:*—godliness.

2318. θεοσεβής **thĕŏsĕbēs**, *theh-os-eb-ace';* from *2316* and *4576;* *reverent of God*, i.e. *pious:*—worshipper of God.

2319. θεοστυγής **thĕŏstugēs**, *theh-os-too-gace';* from *2316* and the base of *4767;* *hateful to God*, i.e. *impious:*—hater of God.

2320. θεότης **thĕŏtēs**, *theh-ot'-ace;* from *2316;* *divinity* (abstr.):—godhead.

2321. Θεόφιλος **Thĕŏphilŏs**, *theh-of'-il-os;* from *2316* and *5384;* *friend of God;* *Theophilus*, a Chr.:—Theophilus.

2322. θεραπεία **thĕrapĕia**, *ther-ap-i'-ah;* from *2323;* *attendance* (spec. medical, i.e. *cure*); fig. and collec. *domestics:*—healing, household.

2323. θεραπεύω **thĕrapĕuō**, *ther-ap-yoo'-o;* from the same as *2324;* to *wait upon* menially, i.e. (fig.) to *adore* (God), or (spec.) to *relieve* (of disease):—cure, heal, worship.

2324. θεράπων **thĕrapōn**, *ther-ap'-ohn;* appar. a part. from an otherwise obsol. der. of the base of *2330;* a menial *attendant* (as if *cherishing*):—servant.

2325. θερίζω **thĕrizō**, *ther-id'-zo;* from *2330* (in the sense of the *crop*); to *harvest:*—reap.

2326. θερισμός **thĕrismŏs**, *ther-is-mos';* from *2325;* *reaping*, i.e. the *crop:*—harvest.

2327. θεριστής **thĕristēs**, *ther-is-tace';* from *2325;* a *harvester:*—reaper.

2328. θερμαίνω **thĕrmainō**, *ther-mah'-ee-no;* from *2329;* to *heat* (oneself):—(be) warm (-ed, self).

2329. θέρμη **thĕrmē**, *ther'-may;* from the base of *2330;* *warmth:*—heat.

2330. θέρος **thĕrŏs**, *ther'-os;* from a prim. θέρω **thĕrō** (to *heat*); prop. *heat*, i.e. *summer:*—summer.

2331. Θεσσαλονικεύς **Thĕssalŏnikĕus**, *thes-sal-on-ik-yoos';* from *2332;* a *Thessalonican*, i.e. inhab. of Thessalonice:—Thessalonian.

2332. Θεσσαλονίκη **Thĕssalŏnikē**, *thes-sal-on-ee'-kay;* from Θεσσαλός **Thĕssalŏs** (a *Thessalian*) and *3529;* *Thessalonice*, a place in Asia Minor:—Thessalonica.

2333. Θευδᾶς **Thĕudas**, *thyoo-das';* of uncert. or.; *Theudas*, an Isr.:—Theudas.

θέω **thĕō**. See *5087.*

2334. θεωρέω **thĕōrĕō**, *theh-o-reh'-o;* from a der. of *2300* (perh. by add. of *3708*); to *be a spectator* of, i.e. *discern*, (lit., fig. [*experience*] or intens. [*acknowledge*]):—behold, consider, look on, perceive, see. Comp. *3700.*

2335. θεωρία **thĕōria**, *theh-o-ree'-ah;* from the same as *2334;* *spectatorship*, i.e. (concr.) a *spectacle:*—sight.

2336. θήκη **thēkē**, *thay'-kay;* from *5087;* a *receptacle*, i.e. *scabbard:*—sheath.

2337. θηλάζω **thēlazō**, *thay-lad'-zo;* from θηλή **thēlē** (the *nipple*); to *suckle;* by impl. to *suck:*—(give) suck (-ling).

2338. θῆλυς **thēlus**, *thay'-loos;* from the same as *2337;* *female:*—female, woman.

2339. θήρα **thēra**, *thay'-rah;* from θήρ **thēr** (a wild *animal*, as *game*); *hunting*, i.e. (fig.) *destruction:*—trap.

2340. θηρεύω **thērĕuō**, *thay-ryoo'-o;* from *2339;* to *hunt* (an animal), i.e. (fig.) to *carp at:*—catch.

2341. θηριομαχέω **thēriŏmachĕō**, *thay-ree-om-akh-eh'-o;* from a comp. of *2342* and *3164;* to *be a beast-fighter* (in the gladiatorial show), i.e. (fig.) to *encounter* (furious men):—fight with wild beasts.

2342. θηρίον **thēriŏn**, *thay-ree'-on;* dimin. from the same as *2339;* a *dangerous animal:*—(venomous, wild) beast.

2343. θησαυρίζω **thēsaurizō**, *thay-sŏw-rid'-zo;* from *2344;* to *amass* or *reserve* (lit. or fig.):—lay up (treasure), (keep) in store, (heap) treasure (together, up).

2344. θησαυρός **thēsaurŏs**, *thay-sow-ros';* from *5087;* a *deposit*, i.e. *wealth* (lit. or fig.):—treasure.

2345. θιγγάνω **thigganō**, *thing-gan'-o;* a prol. form of an obsol. prim. θίγω **thigō** (to *finger*); to *manipulate*, i.e. *have to do with;* by impl. to *injure:*—handle, touch.

2346. θλίβω **thlibō**, *thlee'-bo;* akin to the base of *5147;* to *crowd* (lit. or fig.):—afflict, narrow, throng, suffer tribulation, trouble.

2347. θλῖψις **thlipsis**, *thlip'-sis;* from *2346;* *pressure* (lit. or fig.):—afflicted (-tion), anguish, burdened, persecution, tribulation, trouble.

2348. θνήσκω **thnēskō**, *thnay'-sko;* a strengthened form of a simpler prim. θάνω **thanō**, *than'-o* (which is used for it only in certain tenses); to *die* (lit. or fig.):—be dead, die.

2349. θνητός **thnētŏs**, *thnay-tos';* from *2348;* *liable to die:*—mortal (-ity).

2350. θορυβέω **thŏrubĕō**, *thor-oo-beh'-o;* from *2351;* to *be in tumult*, i.e. *disturb, clamor:*—make ado (a noise), trouble self, set on an uproar.

2351. θόρυβος **thŏrubŏs**, *thor'-oo-bos;* from the base of *2360;* a *disturbance:*—tumult, uproar.

2352. θραύω **thrauō**, *thrŏw'-o;* a prim. verb; to *crush:*—bruise. Comp. *4486.*

2353. θρέμμα **thrĕmma**, *threm'-mah;* from *5142;* *stock* (as *raised* on a farm):—cattle.

2354. θρηνέω **thrēnĕō**, *thray-neh'-o;* from *2355;* to *bewail:*—lament, mourn.

2355. θρῆνος **thrēnŏs**, *thray'-nos;* from the base of *2360;* *wailing:*—lamentation.

2356. θρησκεία **thrēskĕia**, *thrace-ki'-ah;* from a der. of *2357;* ceremonial *observance:*—religion, worshipping.

2357. θρῆσκος **thrēskŏs**, *thrace'-kos;* prob. from the base of *2360;* *ceremonious* in worship (as *demonstrative*), i.e. *pious:*—religious.

2358. θριαμβεύω **thriambĕuō**, *three-am-byoo'-o;* from a prol. comp. of the base of *2360* and a der. of *680* (mean. a *noisy iambus*, sung in honor of Bacchus); to *make an acclamatory procession*, i.e. (fig.) to *conquer* or (by Hebr.) to *give victory:*—(cause) to triumph (over).

2359. θρίξ **thrix**, *threeks;* gen. τριχός **trichŏs**, etc.; of uncert. der.; *hair:*—hair. Comp. *2864.*

2360. θροέω **thrŏĕō**, *thrŏ-eh'-o;* from θρέομαι **thrĕŏmai** (to *wail*); to *clamor*, i.e. (by impl.) to *frighten:*—trouble.

2361. θρόμβος **thrŏmbŏs**, *throm'-bos;* perh. from *5142* (in the sense of *thickening*); a *clot:*—great drop.

2362. θρόνος **thrŏnŏs**, *thron'-os;* from θράω **thraō** (to *sit*); a stately *seat* ("*throne*"); by impl. *power* or (concr.) a *potentate:*—seat, throne.

2363. Θυάτειρα **Thuatĕira**, *thoo-at'-i-rah;* of uncert. der.; *Thyatira*, a place in Asia Minor:—Thyatira.

2364. θυγάτηρ **thugatēr**, *thoo-gat'-air;* appar. a prim. word [comp. "daughter"]; a *female child*, or (by Hebr.) *descendant* (or *inhabitant*):—daughter.

2365. θυγάτριον **thugatriŏn**, *thoo-gat'-ree-on;* from *2364;* a *daughterling:*—little (young) daughter.

2366. θύελλα **thuĕlla**, *thoo'-el-lah;* from *2380* (in the sense of *blowing*) a storm:—tempest.

2367. θύϊνος **thuinŏs**, *thoo'-ee-nos;* from a der. of *2380* (in the sense of *blowing;* denoting a certain *fragrant* tree); made of *citron*-wood:—thyine.

2368. θυμίαμα **thumiama**, *thoo-mee'-am-ah;* from *2370;* an *aroma*, i.e. fragrant *powder* burnt in religious service; by impl. the *burning* itself:—incense, odour.

2369. θυμιαστήριον **thumiastēriŏn**, *thoo-mee-as-tay'-ree-on;* from a der. of *2370;* a *place of fumigation*, i.e. the *altar of incense* (in the Temple):—censer.

2370. θυμιάω **thumiaō**, *thoo-mee-ah'-o;* from a der. of *2380* (in the sense of *smoking*); to *fumigate*, i.e. *offer* aromatic *fumes:*—burn incense.

2371. θυμομαχέω **thumŏmachĕō**, *thoo-mom-akh-eh'-o;* from a presumed comp. of *2372* and *3164;* to *be in a furious fight*, i.e. (fig.) to *be exasperated:*—be highly displeased.

2372. θυμός **thumŏs**, *thoo-mos';* from *2380; passion* (as if *breathing* hard):—fierceness, indignation, wrath. Comp. *5590*.

2373. θυμόω **thumŏō**, *thoo-mŏ'-o;* from *2372;* to *put in a passion*, i.e. *enrage:*—be wroth.

2374. θύρα **thura**, *thoo'-rah;* appar. a prim. word [comp. "door"]; a *portal* or entrance (the opening or the closure, lit. or fig.):—door, gate.

2375. θυρεός **thurĕŏs**, *thoo-reh-os';* from *2374;* a large *shield* (as *door*-shaped):—shield.

2376. θυρίς **thuris**, *thoo-rece';* from *2374;* an *aperture*, i.e. *window:*—window.

2377. θυρωρός **thurōrŏs**, *thoo-ro-ros';* from *2374* and οὖρος **ŏurŏs** (a *watcher*); a *gate-warden:*—that kept the door, porter.

2378. θυσία **thusia**, *thoo-see'-ah;* from *2380; sacrifice* (the act or the victim, lit. or fig.):—sacrifice.

2379. θυσιαστήριον **thusiastēriŏn**, *thoo-see-as-tay'-ree-on;* from a der. of *2378;* a *place of sacrifice*, i.e. an *altar* (spec. or gen., lit. or fig.):—altar.

2380. θύω **thuō**, *thoo'-o;* a prim. verb; prop. to *rush* (*breathe* hard, *blow*, *smoke*), i.e. (by impl.) to *sacrifice* (prop. by fire, but gen.); by extens. to *immolate* (*slaughter* for any purpose):—kill, (do) sacrifice, slay.

2381. Θωμᾶς **Thōmas**, *tho-mas';* of Chald. or. [comp. 8380]; *the twin; Thomas*, a Chr.:—Thomas.

2382. θώραξ **thōrax**, *tho'-rax;* of uncert. affin.; the *chest* ("*thorax*"), i.e. (by impl.) a *corslet:*—breastplate.

I

2383. Ἰάειρος **Iaĕirŏs**, *ee-ah'-i-ros;* of Heb. or. [2971]; *Jäirus* (i.e. *Jair*), an Isr.:—Jairus.

2384. Ἰακώβ **Iakōb**, *ee-ak-obe';* of Heb. or. [3290]; *Jacob* (i.e. *Ja'akob*), the progenitor of the Isr.; also an Isr.:—Jacob.

2385. Ἰάκωβος **Iakōbŏs**, *ee-ak'-o-bos;* the same as *2384* Græcized; *Jacobus*, the name of three Isr.:—James.

2386. ἴαμα **iama**, *ee'-am-ah;* from *2390;* a *cure* (the effect):—healing.

2387. Ἰαμβρῆς **Iambrēs**, *ee-am-brace';* of Eg. or.; *Jambres*, an Eg.:—Jambres.

2388. Ἰαννά **Ianna**, *ee-an-nah';* prob. of Heb. or. [comp. 3238]; *Janna*, an Isr.:—Janna.

2389. Ἰαννῆς **Iannēs**, *ee-an-nace';* of Eg. or.; *Jannes*, an Eg.:—Jannes.

2390. ἰάομαι **iaŏmai**, *ee-ah'-om-ahee;* mid. of appar. a prim. verb; to *cure* (lit. or fig.):—heal, make whole.

2391. Ἰάρεδ **Iarĕd**, *ee-ar'-ed;* of Heb. or. [3382]; *Jared* (i.e. *Jered*), an antediluvian:—Jared.

2392. ἴασις **iasis**, *ee'-as-is;* from *2390; curing* (the act):—cure, heal (-ing).

2393. ἴασπις **iaspis**, *ee'-as-pis;* prob. of for. or. [see 3471]; "*jasper*", a gem:—jasper.

2394. Ἰάσων **Iasōn**, *ee-as'-oan;* fut. act. part. masc. of *2390; about to cure; Jason*, a Chr.:—Jason.

2395. ἰατρός **iatrŏs**, *ee-at-ros';* from *2390;* a *physician:*—physician.

2396. ἴδε **idĕ**, *id'-eh;* second pers. sing. imper. act. of *1492;* used as interj. to denote *surprise; lo!:*—behold, lo, see.

2397. ἰδέα **idĕa**, *id-eh'-ah;* from *1492;* a *sight* [comp. fig. "idea"], i.e. *aspect:*—countenance.

2398. ἴδιος **idiŏs**, *id'-ee-os;* of uncert. affin.; *pertaining to self*, i.e. one's *own;* by impl. *private* or *separate:*— × his acquaintance, when they were alone, apart, aside, due, his (own, proper, several), home, (her, our, thine, your) own (business), private (-ly), proper, severally, their (own).

2399. ἰδιώτης **idiōtēs**, *id-ee-o'-tace;* from *2398;* a *private* person, i.e. (by impl.) an *ignoramus* (comp. "idiot"):—ignorant, rude, unlearned.

2400. ἰδού **idŏu**, *id-oo';* second pers. sing. imper. mid. of *1492;* used as imper. *lo!:*—behold, lo, see.

2401. Ἰδουμαία **Idŏumaia**, *id-oo-mah'-yah;* of Heb. or. [123]; *Idumæa* (i.e. *Edom*), a region E. (and S.) of Pal.:—Idumæa.

2402. ἱδρώς **hidrōs**, *hid-roce';* a strengthened form of a prim. ἴδος **idŏs** (*sweat*); *perspiration:*—sweat.

2403. Ἰεζαβήλ **Iĕzabēl**, *ee-ed-zab-ale';* of Heb. or. [348]; *Jezabel* (i.e. *Jezebel*), a Tyrian woman (used as a synonym of a termagant or false teacher):—Jezabel.

2404. Ἱεράπολις **Hiĕrapŏlis**, *hee-er-ap'-ol-is;* from *2413* and *4172; holy city; Hierapolis*, a place in Asia Minor:—Hierapolis.

2405. ἱερατεία **hiĕratĕia**, *hee-er-at-i'-ah;* from *2407; priestliness*, i.e. the *sacerdotal function:*—office of the priesthood, priest's office.

2406. ἱεράτευμα **hiĕratĕuma**, *hee-er-at'-yoo-mah;* from *2407;* the *priestly fraternity*, i.e. a *sacerdotal order* (fig.):—priesthood.

2407. ἱερατεύω **hiĕratĕuō**, *hee-er-at-yoo'-o;* prol. from *2409;* to *be a priest*, i.e. *perform his functions:*—execute the priest's office.

2408. Ἱερεμίας **Hiĕrĕmias**, *hee-er-em-ee'-as;* of Heb. or. [3414]; *Hieremias* (i.e. *Jermijah*), an Isr.:—Jeremiah.

2409. ἱερεύς **hiĕrĕus**, *hee-er-yooce';* from *2413;* a *priest* (lit. or fig.):—(high) priest.

2410. Ἱεριχώ **Hiĕrichō**, *hee-er-ee-kho';* of Heb. or. [3405]; *Jericho*, a place in Pal.:—Jericho.

2411. ἱερόν **hiĕrŏn**, *hee-er-on';* neut. of *2413;* a *sacred* place, i.e. the entire precincts (whereas *3485* denotes the central *sanctuary* itself) of the *Temple* (at Jerus. or elsewhere):—temple.

2412. ἱεροπρεπής **hiĕrŏprĕpēs**, *hee-er-op-rep-ace';* from *2413* and the same as *4241; reverent:*—as becometh holiness.

2413. ἱερός **hiĕrŏs**, *hee-er-os';* of uncert. affin.; *sacred:*—holy.

2414. Ἱεροσόλυμα **Hiĕrŏsŏluma**, *hee-er-os-ol'-oo-mah;* of Heb. or. [3389]; *Hierosolyma* (i.e. *Jerushalaïm*), the capital of Pal.:—Jerusalem. Comp. *2419*.

2415. Ἱεροσολυμίτης **Hiĕrŏsŏlumitēs**, *hee-er-os-ol-oo-mee'-tace;* from *2414;* a *Hierosolymite*, i.e. inhab. of Hierosolyma:—of Jerusalem.

2416. ἱεροσυλέω **hiĕrŏsulĕō**, *hee-er-os-ool-eh'-o;* from *2417;* to *be a temple-robber* (fig.):—commit sacrilege.

2417. ἱερόσυλος **hiĕrŏsulŏs**, *hee-er-os'-oo-los;* from *2411* and *4813;* a *temple-despoiler:*—robber of churches.

2418. ἱερουργέω **hiĕrŏurgĕō**, *hee-er-oorg-eh'-o;* from a comp. of *2411* and the base of *2041;* to *be a temple-worker*, i.e. *officiate as a priest* (fig.):—minister.

2419. Ἱερουσαλήμ **Hiĕrŏusalēm**, *hee-er-oo-sal-ame';* of Heb. or. [3389]; *Hierusalem* (i.e. *Jerushalem*), the capital of Pal.:—Jerusalem. Comp. *2414*.

2420. ἱερωσύνη **hiĕrōsunē**, *hee-er-o-soo'-nay;* from *2413; sacredness*, i.e. (by impl.) the *priestly office:*—priesthood.

2421. Ἰεσσαί **Iĕssai**, *es-es-sah'ee;* of Heb. or. [3448]; *Jessæ* (i.e. *Jishai*), an Irs.:—Jesse.

2422. Ἰεφθάε **Iĕphthaĕ**, *ee-ef-thah'-eh;* of Heb. or. [3316]; *Jephthaē* (i.e. *Jiphtach*), an Isr.:—Jephthah.

2423. Ἰεχονίας **Iĕchŏnias**, *ee-ekh-on-ee'-as;* of Heb. or. [3204]; *Jechonias* (i.e. *Jekonjah*), an Isr.:—Jechonias.

2424. Ἰησοῦς **Iēsŏus**, *ee-ay-sooce';* of Heb. or. [3091]; *Jesus* (i.e. *Jehoshua*), the name of our Lord and two (three) other Isr.:—Jesus.

2425. ἱκανός **hikanŏs**, *hik-an-os';* from ἵκω **hikō** [ἱκάνω or ἱκνέομαι, akin to *2240*] (to *arrive*): *competent* (as if *coming* in season), i.e. *ample* (in amount) or *fit* (in character):—able, + content, enough, good, great, large, long (while), many, meet, much, security, sore, sufficient, worthy.

2426. ἱκανότης **hikanŏtēs**, *hik-an-ot'-ace;* from *2425; ability:*—sufficiency.

2427. ἱκανόω **hikanŏō**, *hik-an-ŏ'-o;* from *2425;* to *enable*, i.e. *qualify:*—make able (meet).

2428. ἱκετηρία **hikĕtēria**, *hik-et-ay-ree'-ah;* from a der. of the base of *2425* (through the idea of *approaching* for a favor); *intreaty:*—supplication.

2429. ἰκμάς **hikmas**, *hik-mas';* of uncert. affin.; *dampness:*—moisture.

2430. Ἰκόνιον **Ikŏniŏn**, *ee-kon'-ee-on;* perh. from *1504; image-like; Iconium*, a place in Asia Minor:—Iconium.

2431. ἱλαρός **hilarŏs**, *hil-ar-os';* from the same as *2436; propitious* or *merry* ("*hilarious*"), i.e. *prompt* or *willing:*—cheerful.

2432. ἱλαρότης **hilarŏtēs**, *hil-ar-ot'-ace;* from *2431; alacrity:*—cheerfulness.

2433. ἱλάσκομαι **hilaskŏmai**, *hil-as'-kom-ahee;* mid. from the same as *2436;* to *conciliate*, i.e. (trans.) to *atone* for (sin), or (intrans.) *be propitious:*—be merciful, make reconciliation for.

2434. ἱλασμός **hilasmŏs**, *hil-as-mos'; atonement*, i.e. (concr.) an *expiator:*—propitiation.

2435. ἱλαστήριον **hilastēriŏn**, *hil-as-tay'-ree-on;* neut. of a der. of *2433;* an *expiatory* (place or thing), i.e. (concr.) an atoning *victim*, or (spec.) the *lid* of the Ark (in the Temple):—mercyseat, propitiation.

2436. ἵλεως **hilĕōs**, *hil'-eh-oce;* perh. from the alt. form of *138; cheerful* (as *attractive*), i.e. *propitious;* adv. (by Hebr.) God be *gracious!*, i.e. (in averting some calamity) *far* be it:—be it far, merciful.

2437. Ἰλλυρικόν **Illurikŏn**, *il-loo-ree-kon';* neut. of an adj. from a name of uncert. der.; (the) *Illyrican* (shore), i.e. (as a name itself) *Illyricum*, a region of Europe:—Illyricum.

2438. ἱμάς **himas**, *hee-mas';* perh. from the same as *260;* a *strap*, i.e. (spec.) the *tie* (of a sandal) or the *lash* (of a scourge):—latchet, thong.

2439. ἱματίζω **himatizō**, *him-at-id'-zo;* from *2440;* to *dress:*—clothe.

2440. ἱμάτιον **himatiŏn**, *him-at'-ee-on;* neut. of a presumed der. of ἕννυμι **ĕnnumi** (to *put on*); a *dress* (inner or outer):—apparel, cloke, clothes, garment, raiment, robe, vesture.

2441. ἱματισμός **himatismŏs**, *him-at-is-mos';* from *2439; clothing:*—apparel (× -led), array, raiment, vesture.

2442. ἱμείρομαι **himĕirŏmai**, *him-i'-rom-ahee;* mid. from ἵμερος **himĕrŏs** (a *yearning;* of uncert. affin); to *long for:*—be affectionately desirous.

2443. ἵνα **hina**, *hin'-ah;* prob. from the same as the former part of *1438* (through the *demonstrative* idea; comp. *3588*); in order *that* (denoting the *purpose* or the *result*):—albeit, because, to the intent (that), lest, so as, (so) that, (for) to. Comp. *3363*.

ἵνα μή **hina mē**. See *3363*.

2444. ἱνατί **hinati**, *hin-at-ee';* from *2443* and *5101; for what* reason ?, i.e. *why?:*—wherefore, why.

2445. Ἰόππη **Iŏppē**, *ee-op'-pay;* of Heb. or. [3305]; *Joppe* (i.e. *Japho*), a place in Pal.:—Joppa.

2446. Ἰορδάνης **Iŏrdanēs**, *ee-or-dan'-ace;* of Heb. or. [3383]; the *Jordanes* (i.e. *Jarden*), a river of Pal.:—Jordan.

2447. ἰός **iŏs**, *ee-os';* perh. from εἶμι **ĕimi** (to *go*) or ἵημι **hiēmi** (to *send*); *rust* (as if *emitted* by metals); also *venom* (as *emitted* by serpents):—poison, rust.

2448. Ἰουδά **Iŏuda**, *ee-oo-dah';* of Heb. or. [3063 or perh. 3194]; *Judah* (i.e. *Jehudah* or *Juttah*), a part of (or place in) Pal.:—Judah.

2449. Ἰουδαία **Iŏudaia**, *ee-oo-dah'-yah;* fem. of 2453 (with 1093 impl.); the *Judæan* land (i.e. *Judæa*), a region of Pal.:—Judæa.

2450. Ἰουδαΐζω **Iŏudaïzō**, *ee-oo-dah-id'-zo;* from 2453; to *become a Judæan*, i.e. "*Judaize*":—live as the Jews.

2451. Ἰουδαϊκός **Iŏudaïkŏs**, *ee-oo-dah-ee-kos';* from 2453; *Judaïc*, i.e. *resembling a Judæan:*—Jewish.

2452. Ἰουδαϊκῶς **Iŏudaïkōs**, *ee-oo-dah-ee-koce';* adv. from 2451; *Judaïcally* or *in a manner resembling a Judæan:*—as do the Jews.

2453. Ἰουδαῖος **Iŏudaiŏs**, *ee-oo-dah'-yos;* from 2448 (in the sense of 2455 as a country); *Judæan*, i.e. belonging to *Jehudah:*—Jew (-ess), of Judæa.

2454. Ἰουδαϊσμός **Iŏudaïsmŏs**, *ee-oo-dah-is-mos';* from 2450; "*Judaïsm*", i.e. the *Jewish faith* and usages:—Jews' religion.

2455. Ἰουδάς **Iŏudas**, *ee-oo-das';* of Heb. or. [3063]; *Judas* (i.e. *Jehudah*), the name of ten Isr.; also of the posterity of one of them and its region:—Juda (-h, -s); Jude.

2456. Ἰουλία **Iŏulia**, *ee-oo-lee'-ah;* fem. of the same as 2457; *Julia*, a Chr. woman:—Julia.

2457. Ἰούλιος **Iŏuliŏs**, *ee-oo'-lee-os;* of Lat. or.; *Julius*, a centurion:—Julius.

2458. Ἰουνίας **Iŏunias**, *ee-oo-nee'-as;* of Lat. or.; *Junias*, a Chr.:—Junias.

2459. Ἰοῦστος **Iŏustŏs**, *ee-ooce'-tos;* of Lat. or. ("*just*"); *Justus*, the name of three Chr.:—Justus.

2460. ἱππεύς **hippĕus**, *hip-yooce';* from 2462; an *equestrian*, i.e. member of a *cavalry* corps:—horseman.

2461. ἱππικόν **hippikŏn**, *hip-pee-kon';* neut. of a der. of 2462; the *cavalry* force:—horse [-men].

2462. ἵππος **hippŏs**, *hip'-pos;* of uncert. affin.; a *horse:*—horse.

2463. ἶρις **iris**, *ee'-ris;* perh. from 2046 (as a symb. of the female *messenger* of the pagan deities); a *rainbow* ("*iris*"):—rainbow.

2464. Ἰσαάκ **Isaak**, *ee-sah-ak';* of Heb. or. [3327]; *Isaac* (i.e. *Jitschak*), the son of Abraham:—Isaac.

2465. ἰσάγγελος **isaggĕlŏs**, *ee-sang'-el-los;* from 2470 and 32; *like an angel*, i.e. *angelic:*—equal unto the angels.

2466. Ἰσαχάρ **Isachar**, *ee-sakh-ar';* of Heb. or. [3485]; *Isachar* (i.e. *Jissaskar*), a son of Jacob (fig. his desc.):—Issachar.

2467. ἴσημι **isēmi**, *is'-ay-mee;* assumed by some as the base of cert. irreg. forms of 1492; to *know:*—know.

2468. ἴσθι **isthi**, *is'-thee;* sec. pers. imper. pres. of 1510; *be thou:*— + agree, be, × give thyself wholly to.

2469. Ἰσκαριώτης **Iskariōtēs**, *is-kar-ee-o'-tace;* of Heb. or. [prob. 377 and 7149]; *inhab. of Kerioth; Iscariotes* (i.e. *Keriothite*), an epithet of Judas the traitor:—Iscariot.

2470. ἴσος **isŏs**, *ee'-sos;* prob. from 1492 (through the idea of *seeming*); *similar* (in amount or kind):— + agree, as much, equal, like.

2471. ἰσότης **isŏtēs**, *ee-sot'-ace;* *likeness* (in condition or proportion); by impl. *equity:*—equal (-ity).

2472. ἰσότιμος **isŏtimŏs**, *ee-sot'-ee-mos;* from 2470 and 5092; *of equal value* or *honor:*—like precious.

2473. ἰσόψυχος **isŏpsuchŏs**, *ee-sop'-soo-khos;* from 2470 and 5590; *of similar spirit:*—likeminded.

2474. Ἰσραήλ **Israēl**, *is-rah-ale';* of Heb. or. [3478]; *Israel* (i.e. *Jisrael*), the adopted name of Jacob, includ. his desc. (lit. or fig.):—Israel.

2475. Ἰσραηλίτης **Israēlitēs**, *is-rah-ale-ee'-tace;* from 2474; an "*Israelite*", i.e. desc. of Israel (lit. or fig.):—Israelite.

2476. ἵστημι **histēmi**, *his'-tay-mee;* a prol. form of a prim. στάω **staō**, *stah'-o* (of the same mean., and used for it in certain tenses); to *stand* (trans. or intrans.), used in various applications (lit. or fig.):—abide, appoint, bring, continue, covenant, establish, hold up, lay, present, set (up), stanch, stand (by, forth, still, up). Comp. 5087.

2477. ἱστορέω **histŏrĕō**, *his-tor-eh'-o;* from a der. of 1492; to *be knowing* (*learned*), i.e. (by impl.) to *visit* for information (*interview*):—see.

2478. ἰσχυρός **ischurŏs**, *is-khoo-ros';* from 2479; *forcible* (lit. or fig.):—boisterous, mighty (-ier), powerful, strong (-er, man), valiant.

2479. ἰσχύς **ischus**, *is-khoos';* from a der. of ἰς **is** (*force;* comp. ἔσχον **ĕschŏn**, a form of 2192); *forcefulness* (lit. or fig.):—ability, might ([-ily]), power, strength.

2480. ἰσχύω **ischuō**, *is-khoo'-o;* from 2479; to *have* (or *exercise*) *force* (lit. or fig.):—be able, avail, can do ([-not]), could, be good, might, prevail, be of strength, be whole, + much work.

2481. ἴσως **isōs**, *ee'-soce;* adv. from 2470; *likely*, i.e. *perhaps:*—it may be.

2482. Ἰταλία **Italia**, *ee-tal-ee'-ah;* prob. of for. or.; *Italia*, a region of Europe:—Italy.

2483. Ἰταλικός **Italikŏs**, *ee-tal-ee-kos';* from 2482; *Italic*, i.e. belonging to Italia:—Italian.

2484. Ἰτουραία **Itŏuraia**, *ee-too-rah'-yah;* of Heb. or. [3195]; *Ituræa* (i.e. *Jetur*), a region of Pal.:—Ituræa.

2485. ἰχθύδιον **ichthudiŏn**, *ikh-thoo'-dee-on;* dimin. from 2486; a *petty fish:*—little (small) fish.

2486. ἰχθύς **ichthus**, *ikh-thoos';* of uncert. affin.; a *fish:*—fish.

2487. ἴχνος **ichnŏs**, *ikh'-nos;* from ἰκνέομαι **iknĕŏmai** (to *arrive;* comp. 2240); a *track* (fig.):—step.

2488. Ἰωάθαμ **Iōatham**, *ee-o-ath'-am;* of Heb. or. [3147]; *Joatham* (i.e. *Jotham*), an Isr.:—Joatham.

2489. Ἰωάννα **Iōanna**, *ee-o-an'-nah;* fem. of the same as 2491; *Joanna*, a Chr.:—Joanna.

2490. Ἰωαννᾶς **Iōannas**, *ee-o-an-nas';* a form of 2491; *Joannas*, an Isr.:—Joannas.

2491. Ἰωάννης **Iōannēs**, *ee-o-an'-nace;* of Heb. or. [3110]; *Joannes* (i.e. *Jochanan*), the name of four Isr.:—John.

2492. Ἰώβ **Iōb**, *ee-obe';* of Heb. or. [347]; *Job* (i.e. *Ijob*), a patriarch:—Job.

2493. Ἰωήλ **Iōēl**, *ee-o-ale';* of Heb. or. [3100]; *Joel*, an Isr.:—Joel.

2494. Ἰωνάν **Iōnan**, *ee-o-nan';* prob. for 2491 or 2495; *Jonan*, an Isr.:—Jonan.

2495. Ἰωνᾶς **Iōnas**, *ee-o-nas';* of Heb. or. [3124]; *Jonas* (i.e. *Jonah*), the name of two Isr.:—Jonas.

2496. Ἰωράμ **Iōram**, *ee-o-ram';* of Heb. or. [3141]; *Joram*, an Isr.:—Joram.

2497. Ἰωρείμ **Iōrĕim**, *ee-o-rime';* perh. for 2496; *Jorim*, an Isr.:—Jorim.

2498. Ἰωσαφάτ **Iōsaphat**, *ee-o-saf-at';* of Heb. or. [3092]; *Josaphat* (i.e. *Jehoshaphat*), an Isr.:—Josaphat.

2499. Ἰωσή **Iōsē**, *ee-o-say';* gen. of 2500; *Jose*, an Isr.:—Jose.

2500. Ἰωσῆς **Iōsēs**, *ee-o-sace';* perh. for 2501; *Joses*, the name of two Isr.:—Joses. Comp. 2499.

2501. Ἰωσήφ **Iōsēph**, *ee-o-safe';* of Heb. or. [3130]; *Joseph*, the name of seven Isr.:—Joseph.

2502. Ἰωσίας **Iōsias**, *ee-o-see'-as;* of Heb. or. [2977]; *Josias* (i.e. *Joshiah*), an Isr.:—Josias.

2503. ἰῶτα **iōta**, *ee-o'-tah;* of Heb. or. [the tenth letter of the Heb. alphabet]; "*iota*", the name of the ninth letter of the Gr. alphabet, put (fig.) for a very small part of anything:—jot.

K

2504. κἀγώ **kagō**, *kag-o';* from 2532 and 1473 (so also the dat.

κἀμοί **kamŏi**, *kam-oy';* and acc.

κἀμέ **kamĕ**, *kam-eh';* *and* (or *also*, *even*, etc.) *I*, (*to*) *me:*—(and, even, even so, so) I (also, in like wise), both me, me also.

2505. καθά **katha**, *kath-ah';* from 2596 and the neut. plur. of 3739; *according to which* things, i.e. *just as:*—as.

2506. καθαίρεσις **kathairĕsis**, *kath-ah'ee-res-is;* from 2507; *demolition;* fig. *extinction:*—destruction, pulling down.

2507. καθαιρέω **kathairĕō**, *kath-ahee-reh'-o;* from 2596 and 138 (includ. its alt.); to *lower* (or with violence) *demolish* (lit. or fig.):—cast (pull, put, take) down, destroy.

2508. καθαίρω **kathairō**, *kath-ah'ee-ro;* from 2513; to *cleanse*, i.e. (spec.) to *prune;* fig. to *expiate:*—purge.

2509. καθάπερ **kathapĕr**, *kath-ap'-er;* from 2505 and 4007; *exactly as:*—(even, as well) as.

2510. καθάπτω **kathaptō**, *kath-ap'-to;* from 2596 and 680; to *seize upon:*—fasten on.

2511. καθαρίζω **katharizō**, *kath-ar-id'-zo;* from 2513; to *cleanse* (lit. or fig.):—(make) clean (-se), purge, purify.

2512. καθαρισμός **katharismŏs**, *kath-ar-is-mos';* from 2511; a *washing* off, i.e. (cer.) *ablution*, (mor.) *expiation:*—cleansing, + purge, purification, (-fying).

2513. καθαρός **katharŏs**, *kath-ar-os';* of uncert. affin.; *clean* (lit. or fig.):—clean, clear, pure.

2514. καθαρότης **katharŏtēs**, *kath-ar-ot'-ace;* from 2513; *cleanness* (cer.):—purification.

2515. καθέδρα **kathĕdra**, *kath-ed'-rah;* from 2596 and the same as 1476; a *bench* (lit. or fig.):—seat.

2516. καθέζομαι **kathĕzŏmai**, *kath-ed'-zom-ahee;* from 2596 and the base of 1476; to *sit down:*—sit.

2517. καθεξῆς **kathĕxēs**, *kath-ex-ace';* from 2596 and 1836; *thereafter*, i.e. *consecutively;* as a noun (by ell. of noun) a *subsequent* person or time:—after (-ward), by (in) order.

2518. καθεύδω **kathĕudō**, *kath-yoo'-do;* from 2596 and εὕδω **hĕudō** (to *sleep*); to lie *down to rest*, i.e. (by impl.) to *fall asleep* (lit. or fig.):—(be a-) sleep.

2519. καθηγητής **kathēgētēs**, *kath-ayg-ay-tace';* from a comp. of 2596 and 2233; a *guide*, i.e. (fig.) a *teacher:*—master.

2520. καθήκω **kathēkō**, *kath-ay'-ko;* from 2596 and 2240; to *reach to*, i.e. (neut. of pres. act. part., fig. as adj.) *becoming:*—convenient, fit.

2521. κάθημαι **kathēmai**, *kath'-ay-mahee;* from 2596 and ἧμαι **hēmai** (to *sit;* akin to the base of 1476); to *sit down;* fig. to *remain*, *reside:*—dwell, sit (by, down).

2522. καθημερινός **kathēmĕrinŏs**, *kath-ay-mer-ee-nos';* from 2596 and 2250; *quotidian:*—daily.

2523. καθίζω **kathizō**, *kath-id'-zo;* another (act.) form for 2516; to *seat down*, i.e. *set* (fig. *appoint*); intrans. to *sit* (down); fig. to *settle* (*hover*, *dwell*):—continue, set, sit (down), tarry.

2524. καθίημι **kathiēmi**, *kath-ee'-ay-mee;* from 2596 and ἵημι **hiēmi** (to *send*); to *lower:*—let down.

2525. καθίστημι **kathistēmi**, *kath-is'-tay-mee;* from 2596 and 2476; to *place down* (permanently), i.e. (fig.) to *designate*, *constitute*, *convoy:*—appoint, be, conduct, make, ordain, set.

2526. καθό **kathŏ**, *kath-o';* from 2596 and 3739; *according to which* thing, i.e. *precisely as*, *in proportion as:*—according to that, (inasmuch) as.

2526'. καθολικός, **kathŏlikŏs**, *kath-ol-ee-kos';* from 2527; *universal:*—general.

2527. καθόλου, **kathŏlŏu**, *kath-ol'-oo;* from 2596 and 3650; *on the whole*, i.e. *entirely:*—at all.

2528. καθοπλίζω **kathŏplizō**, *kath-op-lid'-zo;* from 2596 and 3695; to *equip fully* with armor:—arm.

2529. καθοράω **kathŏraō**, *kath-or-ah'-o;* from 2596 and 3708; to *behold fully*, i.e. (fig.) *distinctly apprehend:*—clearly see.

2530. καθότι **kathŏti**, *kath-ot'-ee;* from 2596 and 3739 and 5100; *according to which certain* thing, i.e. *as far* (or *inasmuch*) *as:*—(according, forasmuch) as, because (that).

2531. **καθώς kathōs**, *kath-oce'*; from 2596 and 5613; *just* (or *inasmuch*) *as, that*:—according to, (according, even) as, how, when.

2532. **καί kai**, *kahee*; appar. a prim. particle, having a *copulative* and sometimes also a *cumulative* force; *and, also, even, so, then, too*, etc.; often used in connection (or composition) with other particles or small words:—and, also, both, but, even, for, if, indeed, likewise, moreover, or, so, that, then, therefore, when, yea, yet.

2533. **Καϊάφας Kaïaphas**, *kah-ee-af'-as*; of Chald. or.; *the dell*; *Caïapha*? (i.e. *Cajepha*), an Isr.:—Caiaphas.

2534. **καίγε kaigĕ**, *ka'hee-gheh*; from 2532 and 1065; *and at least* (or *even, indeed*):—and, at least.

2535. **Κάϊν Kaïn**, *kah'-in*; of Heb. or. [7014]; *Caïn* (i.e. *Cajin*), the son of Adam:—Cain.

2536. **Καϊνάν Kaïnan**, *kah-ee-nan'*; of Heb. or. [7018]; *Caïnan* (i.e. *Kenan*), the name of two patriarchs:—Cainan.

2537. **καινός kainŏs**, *kahee-nos'*; of uncert. affin.; *new* (espec. in *freshness*; while 3501 is prop. so with respect to *age*):—new.

2538. **καινότης kainŏtēs**, *kahee-not'-ace*; from 2537; *renewal* (fig.):—newness.

2539. **καίπερ kaipĕr**, *kah'ee-per*; from 2532 and 4007; *and indeed*, i.e. *nevertheless* or *notwithstanding*:—and yet, although.

2540. **καιρός kairŏs**, *kahee-ros'*; of uncert. affin.; an *occasion*, i.e. *set* or *proper* time:— × always, opportunity, (convenient, due) season, (due, short, while) time, a while. Comp. 5550.

2541. **Καῖσαρ Kaisar**, *kah'ee-sar*; of Lat. or.; *Cæsar*, a title of the Rom. emperor:—Cæsar.

2542. **Καισάρεια Kaisarĕia**, *kahee-sar'-i-a*; from 2541; *Cæsaria*, the name of two places in Pal.:—Cæsarea.

2543. **καίτοι kaitŏi**, *kah'ee-toy*; from 2532 and 5104; *and yet*, i.e. *nevertheless*:—although.

2544. **καίτοιγε kaitŏigĕ**, *kah'ee-toyg-eh*; from 2543 and 1065; *and yet indeed*, i.e. *although really*:—nevertheless, though.

2545. **καίω kaiō**, *kah'-yo*; appar. a prim. verb; to *set on fire*, i.e. *kindle* or (by impl.) *consume*:—burn, light.

2546. **κἀκεῖ kakĕi**, *kak-i'*; from 2532 and 1563; *likewise in that place*:—and there, there (thither) also.

2547. **κἀκεῖθεν kakĕithĕn**, *kak-i'-then*; from 2532 and 1564; *likewise from that place* (or *time*):—and afterward (from) (thence), thence also.

2548. **κἀκεῖνος kakĕinŏs**, *kak-i'-nos*; from 2532 and 1565; *likewise that* (or *those*):—and him (other, them), even he, him also, them (also), (and) they.

2549. **κακία kakia**, *kak-ee'-ah*; from 2556; *badness*, i.e. (subj.) *depravity*, or (act.) *malignity*, or (pass.) *trouble*:—evil, malice (-iousness), naughtiness, wickedness.

2550. **κακοήθεια kakŏēthĕia**, *kak-ŏ-ay'-thi-ah*; from a comp. of 2556 and 2239; *bad character*, i.e. (spec.) *mischievousness*:—malignity.

2551. **κακολογέω kakŏlŏgĕō**, *kak-ol-og-eh'-o*; from a comp. of 2556 and 3056; to *revile*:—curse, speak evil of.

2552. **κακοπάθεια kakŏpathĕia**, *kak-op-ath'-i-ah*; from a comp. of 2556 and 3806; *hardship*:—suffering affliction.

2553. **κακοπαθέω kakŏpathĕō**, *kak-op-ath-eh'-o*; from the same as 2552; to *undergo hardship*:—be afflicted, endure afflictions (hardness), suffer trouble.

2554. **κακοποιέω kakŏpŏiĕō**, *kak-op-oy-eh'-o*; from 2555; *to be a bad-doer*, i.e. (obj.) to *injure*, or (gen.) to *sin*:—do (-ing) evil.

2555. **κακοποιός kakŏpŏiŏs**, *kak-op-oy-os'*; from 2556 and 4160; a *bad-doer*; (spec.) a *criminal*:—evil-doer, malefactor.

2556. **κακός kakŏs**, *kak-os'*; appar. a prim. word; *worthless* (*intrinsically* such; whereas 4190 prop. refers to *effects*), i.e. (subj.) *depraved*, or (obj.) *injurious*:—bad, evil, harm, ill, noisome, wicked.

2557. **κακοῦργος kakŏurgŏs**, *kak-oor'-gos*; from 2556 and the base of 2041; a *wrong-doer*, i.e. *criminal*:—evil-doer, malefactor.

2558. **κακουχέω kakŏuchĕō**, *kak-oo-kheh'-o*; from a presumed comp. of 2556 and 2192; to *maltreat*:—which suffer adversity, torment.

2559. **κακόω kakŏō**, *kak-ŏ'-o*; from 2556; to *injure*; fig. to *exasperate*:—make evil affected, entreat evil, harm, hurt, vex.

2560. **κακῶς kakōs**, *kak-oce'*; adv. from 2556; *badly* (phys. or mor.):—amiss, diseased, evil, grievously, miserably, sick, sore.

2561. **κάκωσις kakōsis**, *kak'-o-sis*; from 2559; *maltreatment*:—affliction.

2562. **καλάμη kalamē**, *kal-am'-ay*; fem. of 2563; a *stalk* of grain, i.e. (collect.) *stubble*:—stubble.

2563. **κάλαμος kalamŏs**, *kal'-am-os*; of uncert. affin.; a *reed* (the plant or its stem, or that of a similar plant); by impl. a *pen*:—pen, reed.

2564. **καλέω kalĕō**, *kal-eh'-o*; akin to the base of 2753; to "*call*" (prop. aloud, but used in a variety of applications, dir. or otherwise):—bid, call (forth), (whose, whose sur-) name (was [called]).

2565. **καλλιέλαιος kalliĕlaiŏs**, *kal-le-el'-ah-yos*; from the base of 2566 and 1636; a *cultivated olive* tree, i.e. a *domesticated* or *improved* one:—good olive tree.

2566. **καλλίον kalliŏn**, *kal-lee'-on*; neut. of the (irreg.) comp. of 2570; (adv.) *better* than many:—very well.

2567. **καλοδιδάσκαλος kalŏdidaskalŏs**, *kal-od-id-as'-kal-os*; from 2570 and 1320; a *teacher of* the *right*:—teacher of good things.

2568. **Καλοὶ Λιμένες Kalŏi Limĕnĕs**, *kal-oy' lee-men'-es*; plur. of 2570 and 3040; *Good Harbors*, i.e. *Fairhaven*, a bay of Crete:—fair havens.

2569. **καλοποιέω kalŏpŏiĕō**, *kal-op-oy-eh'-o*; from 2570 and 4160; to *do well*, i.e. live virtuously:—well doing.

2570. **καλός kalŏs**, *kal-os'*; of uncert. affin.; prop. *beautiful*, but chiefly (fig.) *good* (lit. or mor.), i.e. *valuable* or *virtuous* (for *appearance* or *use*, and thus distinguished from 18, which is prop. *intrinsic*):— × better, fair, good (-ly), honest, meet, well, worthy.

2571. **κάλυμα kaluma**, *kal'-oo-mah*; from 2572; a *cover*, i.e. *veil*:—vail.

2572. **καλύπτω kaluptō**, *kal-oop'-to*; akin to 2813 and 2928; to *cover* up (lit. or fig.):—cover, hide.

2573. **καλῶς kalōs**, *kal-oce'*; adv. from 2570; *well* (usually mor.):—(in a) good (place), honestly, + recover, (full) well.

2574. **κάμηλος kamēlŏs**, *kam'-ay-los*; of Heb. or. [1581]; a "*camel*":—camel.

2575. **κάμινος kaminŏs**, *kam'-ee-nos*; prob. from 2545; a *furnace*:—furnace.

2576. **καμμύω kammuō**, *kam-moo'-o*; for a comp. of 2596 and the base of 3466; to *shut down*, i.e. *close* the eyes:—close.

2577. **κάμνω kamnō**, *kam'-no*; appar. a prim. verb; prop. to *toil*, i.e. (by impl.) to *tire* (fig. *faint, sicken*):—faint, sicken, be wearied.

2578. **κάμπτω kamptō**, *kamp'-to*; appar. a prim. verb; to *bend*:—bow.

2579. **κἄν kan**, *kan*; from 2532 and 1437; *and* (or *even*) *if*:—and (also) if (so much as), if but, at the least, though, yet.

2580. **Κανᾶ Kana**, *kan-ah'*; of Heb. or. [comp. 7071]; *Cana*, a place in Pal.:—Cana.

2581. **Κανανίτης Kananitēs**, *kan-an-ee'-tace*; of Chald. or. [comp. 7067]; *zealous*; *Cananitès*, an epithet:—Canaanite [*by mistake for a der. from 5477*].

2582. **Κανδάκη Kandakē**, *kan-dak'-ay*; of for. or.; *Candacè*, an Eg. queen:—Candace.

2583. **κανών kanōn**, *kan-ohn'*; from **κάνη kanē** (a straight *reed*, i.e. *rod*); a *rule* ("*canon*"), i.e. (fig.) a *standard* (of faith and practice); by impl. a *boundary*, i.e. (fig.) a *sphere* (of activity):—line, rule.

2584. **Καπερναούμ Kapĕrnaŏum**, *cap-er-nah-oom'*; of Heb. or. [prob. 3723 and 5151]; *Capernaüm* (i.e. *Caphanachum*), a place in Pal.:—Capernaum.

2585. **καπηλεύω kapēlĕuō**, *kap-ale-yoo'-o*; from **κάπηλος kapēlŏs** (a *huckster*); to *retail*, i.e. (by impl.) to *adulterate* (fig.):—corrupt.

2586. **καπνός kapnŏs**, *kap-nos'*; of uncert. affin.; *smoke*:—smoke.

2587. **Καππαδοκία Kappadŏkia**, *kap-pad-ok-ee'-ah*; of for. or.; *Cappadocia*, a region of Asia Minor:—Cappadocia.

2588. **καρδία kardia**, *kar-dee'-ah*; prol. from a prim. **κάρ kar** (Lat. *cor*, "*heart*"); the *heart*, i.e. (fig.) the *thoughts* or *feelings* (*mind*); also (by anal.) the *middle*:—(+ broken-) heart (-ed).

2589. **καρδιογνώστης kardiŏgnōstēs**, *kar-dee-og-noce'-tace*; from 2588 and 1097; a *heart-knower*:—which knowest the hearts.

2590. **καρπός karpŏs**, *kar-pos'*; prob. from the base of 726; *fruit* (as *plucked*), lit. or fig.:—fruit.

2591. **Κάρπος Karpŏs**, *kar'-pos*; perh. for 2590; *Carpus*, prob. a Chr.:—Carpus.

2592. **καρποφορέω karpŏphŏrĕō**, *kar-pof-or-eh'-o*; from 2593; to *be fertile* (lit. or fig.):—be (bear, bring forth) fruit (-ful).

2593. **καρποφόρος karpŏphŏrŏs**, *kar-pof-or'-os*; from 2590 and 5342; *fruitbearing* (fig.):—fruitful.

2594. **καρτερέω kartĕrĕō**, *kar-ter-eh'-o*; from a der. of 2904 (transp.); to *be strong*, i.e. (fig.) *steadfast* (*patient*):—endure.

2595. **κάρφος karphŏs**, *kar'-fos*; from **κάρφω karphō** (to *wither*); a dry *twig* or *straw*:—mote.

2596. **κατά kata**, *kat-ah'*; a prim. particle; (prep.) *down* (in place or time), in varied relations (according to the case [gen., dat. or acc.] with which it is joined):—about, according as (to), after, against, (when they were) × alone, among, and, × apart, (even, like) as (concerning, pertaining to, touching), × aside, at, before, beyond, by, to the charge of, [charita-] bly, concerning, + covered, [dai-] ly, down, every, (+ far more) exceeding, × more excellent, for, from . . . to, godly, in (-asmuch, divers, every, -to, respect of), . . . by, after the manner of, + by any means, beyond (out of) measure, × mightily, more, × natural, of (up-) on (× part), out (of every), over against, (+ your) × own, + particularly, so, through (-oughout, -oughout every), thus, (un-) to (-gether, -ward), × uttermost, where (-by), with. In composition it retains many of these applications, and frequently denotes *opposition, distribution* or *intensity*.

2597. **καταβαίνω katabainō**, *kat-ab-ah'ee-no*; from 2596 and the base of 939; to *descend* (lit. or fig.):—come (get, go, step) down, descend, fall (down).

2598. **καταβάλλω kataballō**, *kat-ab-al'-lo*; from 2596 and 906; to *throw down*:—cast down, descend, fall (down).

2599. **καταβαρέω katabarĕō**, *kat-ab-ar-eh'-o*; from 2596 and 916; to *impose upon*:—burden.

2600. **κατάβασις katabasis**, *kat-ab'-as-is*; from 2597; a *declivity*:—descent.

2601. **καταβιβάζω katabibazō**, *kat-ab-ib-ad'-zo*; from 2596 and a der. of the base of 939; to *cause to go down*, i.e. *precipitate*:—bring (thrust) down.

2602. **καταβολή katabŏlē**, *kat-ab-ol-ay'*; from 2598; a *deposition*, i.e. *founding*; fig. *conception*:—conceive, foundation.

2603. **καταβραβεύω katabrabĕuō**, *kat-ab-rab-yoo'-o*; from 2596 and 1018 (in its orig. sense); to *award* the price *against*, i.e. (fig.) to *defraud* (of salvation):—beguile of reward.

2604. **καταγγελεύς kataggĕlĕus**, *kat-ang-gel-yooce'*; from 2605; a *proclaimer*:—setter forth.

2605. **καταγγέλλω kataggĕllō**, *kat-ang-gel'-lo*; from 2596 and the base of 32; to *proclaim, promulgate*:—declare, preach, shew, speak of, teach.

2606. **καταγελάω katagĕlaō**, *kat-ag-el-ah'-o*; to *laugh down*, i.e. *deride*:—laugh to scorn.

2607. **καταγινώσκω kataginōskō**, *kat-ag-in-o'-sko*; from 2596 and 1097; to *note against*, i.e. *find fault with*:—blame, condemn.

2608. **κατάγνυμι katagnumi**, *kat-ag'-noo-mee*; from 2596 and the base of 4486; to *rend in pieces*, i.e. *crack apart*:—break.

2609. κατάγω katagō, *kat-ag'-o;* from *2596* and *71;* to *lead down;* spec. to *moor* a vessel:—bring (down, forth), (bring to) land, touch.

2610. καταγωνίζομαι katagōnizŏmai, *kat-ag-o-nid'-zom-ahee;* from *2596* and *75;* to *struggle against*, i.e. (by impl.) to *overcome:*—subdue.

2611. καταδέω katadĕō, *kat-ad-eh'-o;* from *2596* and *1210;* to *tie down*, i.e. *bandage* (a wound):—bind up.

2612. κατάδηλος katadēlŏs, *kat-ad'-ay-los;* from *2596* intens. and *1212; manifest:*—far more evident.

2613. καταδικάζω katadikazō, *kat-ad-ik-ad'-zo;* from *2596* and a der. of *1349;* to *adjudge against*, i.e. *pronounce guilty:*—condemn.

2614. καταδιώκω katadiōkō, *kat-ad-ee-o'-ko;* from *2596* and *1377;* to *hunt down*, i.e. *search for:*—follow after.

2615. καταδουλόω katadŏulŏō, *kat-ad-oo-lŏ'-o;* from *2596* and *1402;* to *enslave utterly:*—bring into bondage.

2616. καταδυναστεύω katadunastĕuō, *kat-ad-oo-nas-tyoo'-o;* from *2596* and a der. of *1413;* to *exercise dominion against*, i.e. *oppress:*—oppress.

2617. καταισχύνω kataischunō, *kat-ahee-skhoo'-no;* from *2596* and *153;* to *shame down*, i.e. *disgrace* or (by impl.) *put to the blush:*—confound, dishonour, (be a-, make a-) shame (-d).

2618. κατακαίω katakaiō, *kat-ak-ah'ee-o;* from *2596* and *2545;* to *burn down* (to the ground), i.e. *consume wholly:*—burn (up, utterly).

2619. κατακαλύπτω katakaluptō, *kat-ak-al-oop'-to;* from *2596* and *2572;* to *cover wholly*, i.e. *veil:*—cover, hide.

2620. κατακαυχάομαι katakauchaŏmai, *kat-ak-ŏw-khah'-om-ahee;* from *2596* and *2744;* to *exult against* (i.e. *over*):—boast (against), glory, rejoice against.

2621. κατάκειμαι katakĕimai, *kat-ak'-i-mahee;* from *2596* and *2749;* to *lie down*, i.e. (by impl.) *be sick;* spec. to *recline* at a meal:—keep, lie, sit at meat (down).

2622. κατακλάω kataklaō, *kat-ak-lah'-o;* from *2596* and *2806;* to *break down*, i.e. *divide:*—break.

2623. κατακλείω kataklĕiō, *kat-ak-li'-o;* from *2596* and *2808;* to *shut down* (in a dungeon), i.e. *incarcerate:*—shut up.

2624. κατακληροδοτέω kataklērŏdŏtĕō, *kat-ak-lay-rod-ot-eh'-o;* from *2596* and a der. of a comp. of *2819* and *1325;* to *be a giver of lots to each*, i.e. (by impl.) to *apportion an estate:*—divide by lot.

2625. κατακλίνω kataklinō, *kat-ak-lee'-no;* from *2596* and *2827;* to *recline down*, i.e. (spec.) to *take a place* at table:—(make) sit down (at meat).

2626. κατακλύζω katakluzō, *kat-ak-lood'-zo;* from *2596* and the base of *2830;* to *dash* (*wash*) *down*, i.e. (by impl.) to *deluge:*—overflow.

2627. κατακλυσμός kataklusmŏs, *kat-ak-looce-mos';* from *2626;* an *inundation:*—flood.

2628. κατακολουθέω katakŏlŏuthĕō, *kat-ak-ol-oo-theh'-o;* from *2596* and *190;* to *accompany closely:*—follow (after).

2629. κατακόπτω katakŏptō, *kat-ak-op'-to;* from *2596* and *2875;* to *chop down*, i.e. *mangle:*—cut.

2630. κατακρημνίζω katakrēmnizō, *kat-ak-rame-nid'-zo;* from *2596* and a der. of *2911;* to *precipitate down:*—cast down headlong.

2631. κατάκριμα katakrima, *kat-ak'-ree-mah;* from *2632;* an *adverse sentence* (the verdict):—condemnation.

2632. κατακρίνω katakrinō, *kat-ak-ree'-no;* from *2596* and *2919;* to *judge against*, i.e. *sentence:*—condemn, damn.

2633. κατάκρισις katakrisis, *kat-ak'-ree-sis;* from *2632; sentencing adversely* (the act):—condemn (-ation).

2634. κατακυριεύω katakuriĕuō, *kat-ak-oo-ree-yoo'-o;* from *2596* and *2961;* to *lord against*, i.e. *control, subjugate:*—exercise dominion over (lordship), be lord over, overcome.

2635. καταλαλέω katalalĕō, *kat-al-al-eh'-o;* from *2637;* to *be a traducer*, i.e. to *slander:*—speak against (evil of).

2636. καταλαλιά katalalia, *kat-al-al-ee'-ah;* from *2637; defamation:*—backbiting, evil speaking.

2637 κατάλαλος katalalŏs, *kat-al'-al-os;* from *2596* and the base of *2980; talkative against*, i.e. a *slanderer:*—backbiter.

2638. καταλαμβάνω katalambanō, *kat-al-am-ban'-o;* from *2596* and *2983;* to *take eagerly*, i.e. *seize, possess*, etc. (lit. or fig.):—apprehend, attain, come upon, comprehend, find, obtain, perceive, (over-) take.

2639. καταλέγω katalĕgō, *kat-al-eg'-o;* from *2596* and *3004* (in its orig. mean.); to *lay down*, i.e. (fig.) to *enrol:*—take into the number.

2640. κατάλειμμα katalĕimma, *kat-al'-ime-mah;* from *2641;* a *remainder*, i.e. (by impl.) a *few:*—remnant.

2641. καταλείπω katalĕipō, *kat-al-i'-po;* from *2596* and *3007;* to *leave down*, i.e. *behind;* by impl. to *abandon, have remaining:*—forsake, leave, reserve.

2642. καταλιθάζω katalithazō, *kat-al-ith-ad'-zo;* from *2596* and *3034;* to *stone down*, i.e. *to death:*—stone.

2643. καταλλαγή katallagē, *kat-al-lag-ay';* from *2644; exchange* (fig. *adjustment*), i.e. *restoration* to (the divine) favor:—atonement, reconciliation (-ing).

2644. καταλλάσσω katallassō, *kat-al-las'-so;* from *2596* and *236;* to *change mutually*, i.e. (fig.) to *compound* a difference:—reconcile.

2645. κατάλοιπος katalŏipŏs, *kat-al'-oy-pos;* from *2596* and *3062; left down* (*behind*), i.e. *remaining* (plur. the *rest*):—residue.

2646. κατάλυμα kataluma, *kat-al'-oo-mah;* from *2647;* prop. a *dissolution* (breaking up of a journey), i.e. (by impl.) a *lodging-place:*—guestchamber, inn.

2647. καταλύω kataluō, *kat-al-oo'-o;* from *2596* and *3089;* to *loosen down* (*disintegrate*), i.e. (by impl.) to *demolish* (lit. or fig.); spec. [comp. *2646*] to *halt* for the night:—destroy, dissolve, be guest, lodge, come to nought, overthrow, throw down.

2648. καταμανθάνω katamanthanō, *kat-am-an-than'-o;* from *2596* and *3129;* to *learn thoroughly*, i.e. (by impl.) to *note carefully:*—consider.

2649. καταμαρτυρέω katamarturĕō, *kat-am-ar-too-reh'-o;* from *2596* and *3140;* to *testify against:*—witness against.

2650. καταμένω katamĕnō, *kat-am-en'-o;* from *2596* and *3306;* to *stay fully*, i.e. *reside:*—abide.

2651. καταμόνας katamŏnas, *kat-am-on'-as;* from *2596* and acc. plur. fem. of *3441* (with *5561* impl.); *according to sole* places, i.e. (adv.) *separately:*—alone.

2652. κατανάθεμα katanathĕma, *kat-an-ath'-em-ah;* from *2596* (intens.) and *331;* an *imprecation:*—curse.

2653. καταναθεματίζω katanathĕmatizō, *kat-an-ath-em-at-id'-zo;* from *2596* (intens.) and *332;* to *imprecate:*—curse.

2654. καταναλίσκω katanaliskō, *kat-an-al-is'-ko;* from *2596* and *355;* to *consume utterly:*—consume.

2655. καταναρκάω katanarkaō, *kat-an-ar-kah'-o;* from *2596* and **ναρκάω narkaō** (to *be numb*); to *grow utterly torpid*, i.e. (by impl.) *slothful* (fig. *expensive*):—be burdensome (chargeable).

2656. κατανεύω katanĕuō, *kat-an-yoo'-o;* from *2596* and *3506;* to *nod down* (*towards*), i.e. (by anal.) to *make signs* to:—beckon.

2657. κατανοέω katanŏĕō, *kat-an-o-eh'-o;* from *2596* and *3539;* to *observe fully:*—behold, consider, discover, perceive.

2658. καταντάω katantaō, *kat-an-tah'-o;* from *2596* and a der. of *473;* to *meet against*, i.e. *arrive* at (lit. or fig.):—attain, come.

2659. κατάνυξις katanuxis, *kat-an'-oox-is;* from *2660;* a *prickling* (sensation, as of the limbs asleep), i.e. (by impl. [perh. by some confusion with *3506* or even with *3571*]) *stupor* (*lethargy*):—slumber.

2660. κατανύσσω katanussō, *kat-an-oos'-so;* from *2596* and *3572;* to *pierce thoroughly*, i.e. (fig.) to *agitate* violently ("sting to the quick"):—prick.

2661. καταξιόω kataxiŏō, *kat-ax-ee-ŏ'-o;* from *2596* and *515;* to *deem entirely deserving:*—(ac-) count worthy.

2662. καταπατέω katapatĕō, *kat-ap-at-eh'-o;* from *2596* and *3961;* to *trample down;* fig. to *reject* with disdain:—trample, tread (down, underfoot).

2663. κατάπαυσις katapausis, *kat-ap'-ŏw-sis;* from *2664; reposing down*, i.e. (by Hebr.) *abode:*—rest.

2664. καταπαύω katapauō, *kat-ap-ŏw'-o;* from *2596* and *3973;* to *settle down*, i.e. (lit.) to *colonize*, or (fig.) to (*cause to*) *desist:*—cease, (give) rest (-rain).

2665. καταπέτασμα katapĕtasma, *kat-ap-et'-as-mah;* from a comp. of *2596* and a congener of *4072;* something *spread thoroughly*, i.e. (spec.) the door *screen* (to the Most Holy Place) in the Jewish Temple:—vail.

2666. καταπίνω katapinō, *kat-ap-ee'-no;* from *2596* and *4095;* to *drink down*, i.e. *gulp entire* (lit. or fig.):—devour, drown, swallow (up).

2667. καταπίπτω katapiptō, *kat-ap-ip'-to;* from *2596* and *4098;* to *fall down:*—fall (down).

2668. καταπλέω kataplĕō, *kat-ap-leh'-o;* from *2596* and *4126;* to *sail down* upon a place, i.e. to *land* at:—arrive.

2669. καταπονέω katapŏnĕō, *kat-ap-on-eh'-o;* from *2596* and a der. of *4192;* to *labor down*, i.e. *wear with toil* (fig. *harass*):—oppress, vex.

2670. καταποντίζω katapŏntizō, *kat-ap-on-tid'-zo;* from *2596* and a der. of the same as *4195;* to *plunge down*, i.e. *submerge:*—drown, sink.

2671. κατάρα katara, *kat-ar'-ah;* from *2596* (intens.) and *685; imprecation, execration:*—curse (-d, -ing).

2672. καταράομαι kataraŏmai, *kat-ar-ah'-om-ahee;* mid. from *2671;* to *execrate;* by anal. to *doom:*—curse.

2673. καταργέω katargĕō, *kat-arg-eh'-o;* from *2596* and *691;* to *be* (*render*) *entirely idle* (*useless*), lit. or fig.:—abolish, cease, cumber, deliver, destroy, do away, become (make) of no (none, without) effect, fail, loose, bring (come) to nought, put away (down), vanish away, make void.

2674. καταριθμέω katarithmĕō, *kat-ar-ith-meh'-o;* from *2596* and *705;* to *reckon among:*—number with.

2675. καταρτίζω katartizō, *kat-ar-tid'-zo;* from *2596* and a der. of *739;* to *complete thoroughly*, i.e. *repair* (lit. or fig.) or *adjust:*—fit, frame, mend, (make) perfect (-ly join together), prepare, restore.

2676. κατάρτισις katartisis, *kat-ar'-tis-is;* from *2675; thorough equipment* (subj.):—perfection.

2677. καταρτισμός katartismŏs, *kat-ar-tis-mos';* from *2675; complete furnishing* (obj.):—perfecting.

2678. κατασείω katasĕiō, *kat-as-i'-o;* from *2596* and *4579;* to *sway downward*, i.e. *make a signal:*—beckon.

2679. κατασκάπτω kataskaptō, *kat-as-kap'-to;* from *2596* and *4626;* to *undermine*, i.e. (by impl.) *destroy:*—dig down, ruin.

2680. κατασκευάζω kataskĕuazō, *kat-ask-yoo-ad'-zo;* from *2596* and a der. of *4632;* to *prepare thoroughly* (prop. by external *equipment;* whereas *2090* refers rather to internal *fitness*); by impl. to *construct, create:*—build, make, ordain, prepare.

2681. κατασκηνόω kataskēnŏō, *kat-as-kay-nŏ'-o;* from *2596* and *4637;* to *camp down*, i.e. *haunt;* fig. to *remain:*—lodge, rest.

2682. κατασκήνωσις kataskēnōsis, *kat-as-kay'-no-sis;* from *2681;* an *encamping*, i.e. (fig.) a *perch:*—nest.

2683. κατασκιάζω kataskiazō, *kat-as-kee-ad'-zo;* from *2596* and a der. of *4639;* to *overshade*, i.e. *cover:*—shadow.

684. κατασκοπέω **kataskŏpĕō**, *kat-as-kop-*'-o; from 2685; to *be a sentinel*, i.e. to *inspect in-*diously:—spy out.

685. κατάσκοπος **kataskŏpŏs**, *kat-as'-kop-os;* om 2596 (intens.) and 4649 (in the sense of a *atcher*); a *reconnoiterer:*—spy.

686. κατασοφίζομαι **katasŏphizŏmai**, *kat-*-*of-id'-zom-ahee;* mid. from 2596 and 4679; to *be* *afty against*, i.e. *circumvent:*—deal subtilly with.

687. καταστέλλω **katastĕllō**, *kat-as-tel'-lo;* om 2596 and 4724; to *put down*, i.e. *quell:*—appease, uiet.

688. κατάστημα **katastēma**, *kat-as'-tay-mah;* om 2525; prop. a *position* or *condition*, i.e. (subj.) *emeanor:*—behaviour.

689. καταστολή **katastŏlē**, *kat-as-tol-ay';* om 2687; a *deposit*, i.e. (spec.) *costume:*—apparel.

690. καταστρέφω **katastrĕphō**, *kat-as-tref'-o;* om 2596 and 4762; to *turn* upside *down*, i.e. *upset:*—verthrow.

691. καταστρηνιάω **katastrēniaō**, *kat-as-*-*ay-nee-ah'-o;* from 2596 and 4763; to *become volup-*ious against:—begin to wax wanton against.

692. καταστροφή **katastrŏphē**, *kat-as-trof-*y'; from 2690; an *overturn* ("*catastrophe*"), i.e. emolition; fig. *apostasy:*—overthrow, subverting.

693. καταστρώννυμι **katastrōnnumi**, *kat-as-*-*one'-noo-mee;* from 2596 and 4766; to *strew down*, e. (by impl.) to *prostrate* (*slay*):—overthrow.

694. κατασύρω **katasurō**, *kat-as-oo'-ro;* from 596 and 4951; to *drag down*, i.e. *arrest* judicially:—ale.

695. κατασφάττω **katasphattō**, *kat-as-fat'-to;* om 2596 and 4969; to *kill down*, i.e. *slaughter:*—slay.

696. κατασφραγίζω **katasphragizō**, *kat-as-*-*ag-id'-zo;* from 2596 and 4972; to *seal closely:*—seal.

697. κατάσχεσις **kataschĕsis**, *kat-as'-khes-is;* om 2722; a *holding down*, i.e. *occupancy:*—posses-ion.

698. κατατίθημι **katatithēmi**, *kat-at-ith'-ay-*iee; from 2596 and 5087; to *place down*, i.e. *deposit* lit. or fig.):—do, lay, shew.

699. κατατομή **katatŏmē**, *kat-at-om-ay';* from comp. of 2596 and τέμνω **tĕmnō** (to *cut*); a *cut-*ing down (*off*), i.e. *mutilation* (ironically):—conci-ion. Comp. 609.

700. κατατοξεύω **katatŏxĕuō**, *kat-at-ox-yoo'-o;* om 2596 and a der. of 5115; to *shoot down* with an rrow or other missile:—thrust through.

701. κατατρέχω **katatrĕchō**, *kat-at-rekh'-o;* om 2596 and 5143; to *run down*, i.e. *hasten* from a ower:—run down.

καταφάγω **kataphagō**. See 2719.

702. καταφέρω **kataphĕrō**, *kat-af-er'-o;* from 596 and 5342 (includ. its alt.); to *bear down*, i.e. (fig.) *vercome* (with drowsiness); spec. to *cast* a vote:—ll, give, sink down.

703. καταφεύγω **kataphĕugō**, *kat-af-yoo'-go;* om 2596 and 5343; to *flee down* (*away*):—flee.

704. καταφθείρω **kataphthĕirō**, *kat-af-thi'-*o; from 2596 and 5351; to *spoil entirely*, i.e. (lit.) to *estroy;* or (fig.) to *deprave:*—corrupt, utterly perish.

705. καταφιλέω **kataphilĕō**, *kat-af-ee-leh'-o;* om 2596 and 5368; to *kiss earnestly:*—kiss.

706. καταφρονέω **kataphrŏnĕō**, *kat-af-ron-*o; from 2596 and 5426; to *think against*, i.e. *dis-steem:*—despise.

707. καταφρονητής **kataphrŏntēs**, *kat-af-ron-*ice'; from 2706; a *contemner:*—despiser.

708. καταχέω **katachĕō**, *kat-akh-eh'-o;* from 596 and χέω **chĕō** (to *pour*); to *pour down* (*out*):—our.

709. καταχθόνιος **katachthŏniŏs**, *kat-akh-*hon'-ee-os; from 2596 and χθών **chthōn** (the round); *subterranean*, i.e. *infernal* (belonging to he world of departed spirits):—under the earth.

710. καταχράομαι **katachraŏmai**, *kat-akh-*ah'-om-ahee; from 2596 and 5530; to *overuse*, i.e. *isuse:*—abuse.

2711. καταψύχω **katapsuchō**, *kat-ap-soo'-kho;* from 2596 and 5594; to *cool down* (*off*), i.e. *refresh:*—cool.

2712. κατείδωλος **katĕidōlŏs**, *kat-i'-do-los;* from 2596 (intens.) and 1497; *utterly idolatrous:*—wholly given to idolatry.

κατελεύθω **katĕlĕuthō**. See 2718.

2713. κατέναντι **katĕnanti**, *kat-en'-an-tee;* from 2596 and 1725; *directly opposite:*—before, over against.

κατενέγκω **katĕnĕgkō**. See 2702.

2714. κατενώπιον **katĕnōpiŏn**, *kat-en-o'-pee-on;* from 2596 and 1799; *directly in front of:*—before (the presence of), in the sight of.

2715. κατεξουσιάζω **katĕxŏusiazō**, *kat-ex-oo-see-ad'-zo;* from 2596 and 1850; to *have* (*wield*) *full privilege over:*—exercise authority.

2716. κατεργάζομαι **katĕrgazŏmai**, *kat-er-gad'-zom-ahee;* from 2596 and 2038; to *work fully*, i.e. *accomplish;* by impl. to *finish*, *fashion:*—cause, do (deed), perform, work (out).

2718. κατέρχομαι **katĕrchŏmai**, *kat-er'-khom-ahee;* from 2596 and 2064 (includ. its alt.); to *come* (or *go*) *down* (lit. or fig.):—come (down), depart, descend, go down, land.

2719. κατεσθίω **katĕsthiō**, *kat-es-thee'-o;* from 2596 and 2068 (includ. its alt.); to *eat down*, i.e. *devour* (lit. or fig.):—devour.

2720. κατευθύνω **katĕuthunō**, *kat-yoo-thoo'-no;* from 2596 and 2116; to *straighten fully*, i.e. (fig.) *direct:*—guide, direct.

2721. κατεφίστημι **katĕphistēmi**, *kat-ef-is'-tay-mee;* from 2596 and 2186; to *stand over against*, i.e. *rush upon* (*assault*):—make insurrection against.

2722. κατέχω **katĕchō**, *kat-ekh'-o;* from 2596 and 2192; to *hold down* (*fast*), in various applications (lit. or fig.):—have, hold (fast), keep (in memory), let, × make toward, possess, retain, seize on, stay, take, withhold.

2723. κατηγορέω **katēgŏrĕō**, *kat-ay-gor-eh'-o;* from 2725; to *be a plaintiff*, i.e. to *charge* with some offence:—accuse, object.

2724. κατηγορία **katēgŏria**, *kat-ay-gor-ee'-ah;* from 2725; a *complaint* ("category"), i.e. criminal *charge:*—accusation (× -ed).

2725. κατήγορος **katēgŏrŏs**, *kat-ay'-gor-os;* from 2596 and 58; *against* one in the *assembly*, i.e. a *complainant* at law; spec. *Satan:*—accuser.

2726. κατήφεια **katēphĕia**, *kat-ay'-fi-ah;* from a comp. of 2596 and perh. a der. of the base of 5316 (mean. *downcast* in look); *demureness*, i.e. (by impl.) *sadness:*—heaviness.

2727. κατηχέω **katēchĕō**, *kat-ay-kheh'-o;* from 2596 and 2279; to *sound down* into the ears, i.e. (by impl.) to *indoctrinate* ("catechize") or (gen.) to *apprise* of:—inform, instruct, teach.

2728. κατιόω **katiŏō**, *kat-ee-ŏ'-o;* from 2596 and a der. of 2447; to *rust down*, i.e. *corrode:*—canker.

2729. κατισχύω **katischuō**, *kat-is-khoo'-o;* from 2596 and 2480; to *overpower:*—prevail (against).

2730. κατοικέω **katŏikĕō**, *kat-oy-keh'-o;* from 2596 and 3611; to *house permanently*, i.e. *reside* (lit. or fig.):—dwell (-er), inhabitant (-ter).

2731. κατοίκησις **katŏikēsis**, *kat-oy'-kay-sis;* from 2730; *residence* (prop. the act; but by impl. concr. the mansion):—dwelling.

2732. κατοικητήριον **katŏikētēriŏn**, *kat-oy-kay-tay'-ree-on;* from a der. of 2730; a *dwelling-place:*—habitation.

2733. κατοικία **katŏikia**, *kat-oy-kee'-ah;* *residence* (prop. the condition; but by impl. the abode itself):—habitation.

2734. κατοπτρίζομαι **katŏptrizŏmai**, *kat-op-trid'-zom-ahee;* mid. from a comp. of 2596 and a der. of 3700 [comp. 2072]; to *mirror oneself*, i.e. to *see reflected* (fig.):—behold as in a glass.

2735. κατόρθωμα **katŏrthōma**, *kat-or'-tho-mah;* from a comp. of 2596 and a der. of 3717 [comp. 1357]; something *made fully upright*, i.e. (fig.) *rectification* (spec. *good* public *administration*):—very worthy deed.

2736. κάτω **katō**, *kat'-o;* also (comp.)

κατωτέρω **katōtĕrō**, *kat-o-ter'-o* [comp. 2737]; adv. from 2596; *downwards:*—beneath, bottom, down, under.

2737. κατώτερος **katōtĕrŏs**, *kat-o'-ter-os;* comp. from 2736; *inferior* (locally, of Hades):—lower.

2738. καῦμα **kauma**, *kŏw'-mah;* from 2545; prop. a *burn* (concr.), but used (abstr.) of a *glow:*—heat.

2739. καυματίζω **kaumatizō**, *kŏw-mat-id'-zo;* from 2738; to *burn:*—scorch.

2740. καῦσις **kausis**, *kŏw'-sis;* from 2545; *burning* (the act):—be burned.

2741. καυσόω **kausŏō**, *kŏw-sŏ'-o;* from 2740; to *set on fire:*—with fervent heat.

2742. καύσων **kausōn**, *kŏw'-sone;* from 2741; a *glare:*—(burning) heat.

2743. καυτηριάζω **kautēriazō**, *kŏw-tay-ree-ad'-zo;* from a der. of 2545; to *brand* ("*cauterize*"), i.e. (by impl.) to *render unsensitive* (fig.):—sear with a hot iron.

2744. καυχάομαι **kauchaŏmai**, *kŏw-khah'-om-ahee;* from some (obsol.) base akin to that of αὐχέω **auchĕō** (to *boast*) and 2172; to *vaunt* (in a good or a bad sense):—(make) boast, glory, joy, rejoice.

2745. καύχημα **kauchēma**, *kŏw'-khay-mah;* from 2744; a *boast* (prop. the object; by impl. the act) in a good or a bad sense:—boasting, (whereof) to glory (of), glorying, rejoice (-ing).

2746. καύχησις **kauchēsis**, *kŏw'-khay-sis;* from 2744; *boasting* (prop. the act; by impl. the object), in a good or a bad sense:—boasting, whereof I may glory, glorying, rejoicing.

2747. Κεγχρεαί **Kĕgchrĕai**, *keng-khreh-a'hee;* prob. from κέγχρος **kĕgchrŏs** (*millet*); *Cenchreæ*, a port of Corinth:—Cenchrea.

2748. Κεδρών **Kĕdrōn**, *ked-rone';* of Heb. or. [6939]; *Cedron* (i.e. *Kidron*), a brook near Jerus.:—Cedron.

2749. κεῖμαι **kĕimai**, *ki'-mahee;* mid. of a prim. verb; to *lie* outstretched (lit. or fig.):—be (appointed, laid up, made, set), lay, lie. Comp. 5087.

2750. κειρία **kĕiria**, *ki-ree'-ah;* of uncert. affin.; a *swathe*, i.e. *winding-sheet:*—graveclothes.

2751. κείρω **kĕirō**, *ki'-ro;* a prim. verb; to *shear:*—shear (-er).

2752. κέλευμα **kĕlĕuma**, *kel'-yoo-mah;* from 2753; a *cry* of incitement:—shout.

2753. κελεύω **kĕlĕuō**, *kel-yoo'-o;* from a prim. κέλλω **kĕllō** (to *urge* on); "hail"; to *incite* by word, i.e. *order:*—bid, (at, give) command (-ment).

2754. κενοδοξία **kĕnŏdŏxia**, *ken-od-ox-ee'-ah;* from 2755; *empty glorying*, i.e. *self-conceit:*—vain-glory.

2755. κενόδοξος **kĕnŏdŏxŏs**, *ken-od'-ox-os;* from 2756 and 1391; *vainly glorifying*, i.e. *self-conceited:*—desirous of vain-glory.

2756. κενός **kĕnŏs**, *ken-os';* appar. a prim. word; *empty* (lit. or fig.):—empty, (in) vain.

2757. κενοφωνία **kĕnŏphōnia**, *ken-of-o-nee'-ah;* from a presumed comp. of 2756 and 5456; *empty sounding*, i.e. *fruitless discussion:*—vain.

2758. κενόω **kĕnŏō**, *ken-ŏ'-o;* from 2756; to *make empty*, i.e. (fig.) to *abase*, *neutralize*, *falsify:*—make (of none effect, of no reputation, void), be in vain.

2759. κέντρον **kĕntrŏn**, *ken'-tron;* from κεντέω **kĕntĕō** (to *prick*); a *point* ("centre"), i.e. a *sting* (fig. *poison*) or *goad* (fig. divine *impulse*):—prick, sting.

2760. κεντυρίων **kĕnturiōn**, *ken-too-ree'-ohn;* of Lat. or.; a *centurion*, i.e. *captain* of one hundred soldiers:—centurion.

2761. κενῶς **kĕnōs**, *ken-oce';* adv. from 2756; *vainly*, i.e. *to no purpose:*—in vain.

2762. κεραία **kĕraia**, *ker-ah'-yah;* fem. of a presumed der. of the base of 2768; something *horn-like*, i.e. (spec.) the *apex* of a Heb. letter (fig. the least *particle*):—tittle.

2763. κεραμεύς **kĕramĕus**, *ker-am-yooce';* from 2766; a *potter:*—potter.

2764. κεραμικός kĕramikŏs, *ker-am-ik-os';* from *2766; made of clay,* i.e. *earthen:*—of a potter.

2765. κεράμιον kĕramiŏn, *ker-am'-ee-on;* neut. of a presumed der. of *2766;* an *earthenware* vessel, i.e. *jar:*—pitcher.

2766. κέραμος kĕramŏs, *ker'-am-os;* prob. from the base of *2767* (through the idea of *mixing* clay and water); *earthenware,* i.e. a *tile* (by anal. a thin *roof* or *awning*):—tiling.

2767. κεράννυμι kĕrannumi, *ker-an'-noo-mee;* a prol. form of a more prim. κεράω kĕraō, *ker-ah'-o* (which is used in certain tenses); to *mingle,* i.e. (by impl.) to *pour* out (for drinking):—fill, pour out. Comp. *3396.*

2768. κέρας kĕras, *ker'-as;* from a prim. κάρ kar (the *hair* of the head); a *horn* (lit. or fig.):—horn.

2769. κεράτιον kĕratiŏn, *ker-at'-ee-on;* neut of a presumed der. of *2768;* something *horned,* i.e. (spec.) the *pod* of the carob-tree:—husk.

κεράω kĕraō. See *2767.*

2770. κερδαίνω kĕrdainō, *ker-dah'-ee-no,* from *2771;* to *gain* (lit. or fig.):—(get) gain, wi

2771. κέρδος kĕrdŏs, *ker'-dos;* of uncert affin.; *gain* (pecuniary or gen.):—gain, lucre.

2772. κέρμα kĕrma, *ker'-mah;* from *2751,* a *clipping* (*bit*), i.e. (spec.) a *coin:*—money

2773. κερματιστής kĕrmatistēs, *ker-mat-is-tace';* from a der. of *2772;* a *handler of coins,* i.e. *money-broker:*—changer of money.

2774. κεφάλαιον kĕphalaiŏn, *kef-al'-ah-yon;* neut. of a der. of *2776;* a *principal* thing, i.e. *main point;* spec. an *amount* (of money):—sum.

2775. κεφαλαιόω kĕphalaiŏō, *kef-al-ahee-ŏ'-o;* from the same as *2774;* (spec.) to *strike on the head:*—wound in the head.

2776. κεφαλή kĕphalē, *kef-al-ay';* prob. from the prim. κάπτω kaptō (in the sense of *seizing*); the *head* (as the part most readily *taken* hold of), lit. or fig.:—head.

2777. κεφαλίς kĕphalis, *kef-al-is';* from *2776;* prop. a *knob,* i.e. (by impl.) a *roll* (by extens. from the *end* of a stick on which the MS. was rolled):—volume.

2778. κῆνσος kēnsŏs, *kane'-sos;* of Lat. or.; prop. an *enrolment* ("*census*"), i.e. (by impl.) a *tax:*—tribute.

2779. κῆπος kēpŏs, *kay'-pos;* of uncert. affin.; a *garden:*—garden.

2780. κηπουρός kēpŏurŏs, *kay-poo-ros';* from *2779* and οὖρος ŏurŏs (a *warden*); a *garden-keeper,* i.e. *gardener:*—gardener.

2781. κηρίον kēriŏn, *kay-ree'-on;* dimin. from κηός kēŏs (*wax*); a *cell* for honey, i.e. (collect.) the *comb:*—[honey-] comb.

2782. κήρυγμα kērugma, *kay'-roog-mah;* from *2784;* a *proclamation* (espec. of the gospel; by impl. the *gospel* itself):—preaching.

2783. κήρυξ kērux, *kay'-roox;* from *2784;* a *herald,* i.e. of divine truth (espec. of the gospel):—preacher.

2784. κηρύσσω kērussō, *kay-roos'-so;* of uncert. affin.; to *herald* (as a public *crier*), espec. divine truth (the gospel):—preach (-er), proclaim, publish.

2785. κῆτος kētŏs, *kay'-tos;* prob. from the base of *5490;* a huge *fish* (as *gaping* for prey):—whale.

2786. Κηφᾶς Kēphas, *kay-fas';* of Chald. or. [comp. 3710]; *the Rock; Cephas* (i.e. *Kepha*), a surname of Peter:—Cephas.

2787. κιβωτός kibōtŏs, *kib-o-tos';* of uncert. der.; a *box,* i.e. the sacred *ark* and that of Noah:—ark.

2788. κιθάρα kithara, *kith-ar'-ah;* of uncert. affin.; a *lyre:*—harp.

2789. κιθαρίζω kitharizō, *kith-ar-id'-zo;* from *2788;* to *play on a lyre:*—harp.

2790. κιθαρῳδός kitharōidŏs, *kith-ar-o'-dos;* from *2788* and a der. of the same as *5603;* a *lyre-singer (-player),* i.e. *harpist:*—harper.

2791. Κιλικία Kilikia, *kil-ik-ee'-ah;* prob. of for. or., *Cilicia,* a region of Asia Minor:—Cilicia.

2792. κινάμωμον kinamōmon, *kin-am'-o-mon;* of for. or. [comp. 7076]; *cinnamon:*—cinnamon.

2793. κινδυνεύω kindunĕuō, *kin-doon-yoo'-o;* from *2794;* to *undergo peril:*—be in danger, be (stand) in jeopardy.

2794. κίνδυνος kindunŏs, *kin'-doo-nos;* of uncert. der.; *danger:*—peril.

2795. κινέω kinĕō, *kin-eh'-o;* from κίω kiō (poetic for εἶμι ĕimi, to *go*); to *stir* (trans.), lit. or fig.:—(re-) move (-r), wag.

2796. κίνησις kinēsis, *kin'-ay-sis;* from *2795;* a *stirring:*—moving.

2797. Κίς Kis, *kis;* of Heb. or. [7027]; *Cis* (i.e. *Kish*), an Isr.:—Cis.

κίχρημι kichrēmi. See *5531.*

2798. κλάδος kladŏs, *klad'-os;* from *2806;* a *twig* or *bough* (as if broken off):—branch.

2799. κλαίω klaiō, *klah'-yo;* of uncert. affin.; to *sob,* i.e. *wail* aloud (whereas *1145* is rather to *cry* silently):—bewail, weep.

2800. κλάσις klasis, *klas'-is;* from *2806; fracture* (the act):—breaking.

2801. κλάσμα klasma, *klas'-mah;* from *2806;* a *piece* (*bit*):—broken, fragment.

2802. Κλαύδη Klaudē, *klŏw'-day;* of uncert. der.; *Claude,* an island near Crete:—Clauda.

2803. Κλαυδία Klaudia, *klŏw-dee'-ah;* fem. of *2804; Claudia,* a Chr. woman:—Claudia.

2804. Κλαύδιος Klaudiŏs, *klŏw'-dee-os;* of Lat. or.; *Claudius,* the name of two Romans:—Claudius.

2805. κλαυθμός klauthmŏs, *klŏwth-mos';* from *2799; lamentation:*—wailing, weeping, × wept.

2806. κλάω klaō, *klah'-o;* a prim. verb; to *break* (spec. of bread):—break.

2807. κλείς klĕis, *klice;* from *2808;* a *key* (as *shutting* a lock), lit. or fig.:—key.

2808. κλείω klĕiō, *kli'-o;* a prim. verb; to *close* (lit. or fig.):—shut (up).

2809. κλέμμα klĕmma, *klem'-mah;* from *2813; stealing* (prop. the thing stolen, but used of the act):—theft.

2810. Κλεόπας Klĕŏpas, *kleh-op'-as;* prob. contr. from Κλεόπατρος Klĕŏpatrŏs (comp. of *2811* and *3962*); *Cleopas,* a Chr.:—Cleopas.

2811. κλέος klĕŏs, *kleh'-os;* from a shorter form of *2564; renown* (as if *being called*):—glory.

2812. κλέπτης klĕptēs, *klep'-tace;* from *2813;* a *stealer* (lit. or fig.):—thief. Comp. *3027.*

2813. κλέπτω klĕptō, *klep'-to;* a prim. verb; to *filch:*—steal.

2814. κλῆμα klēma, *klay'-mah;* from *2806;* a *limb* or *shoot* (as if *broken* off):—branch.

2815. Κλήμης Klēmēs, *klay'-mace;* of Lat. or.; *merciful; Clemes* (i.e. *Clemens*), a Chr.:—Clement.

2816. κληρονομέω klērŏnŏmĕō, *klay-ron-om-eh'-o;* from *2818;* to *be an heir* to (lit. or fig.):—be heir, (obtain by) inherit (-ance).

2817. κληρονομία klērŏnŏmia, *klay-ron-om-ee'-ah;* from *2818; heirship,* i.e. (concr.) a *patrimony* or (gen.) a *possession:*—inheritance.

2818. κληρονόμος klērŏnŏmŏs, *klay-ron-om'-os;* from *2819* and the base of *3551* (in its orig. sense of *partitioning,* i.e. [reflex.] *getting* by apportionment); a *sharer by lot,* i.e. an *inheritor* (lit. or fig.); by impl. a *possessor:*—heir.

2819. κλῆρος klērŏs, *klay'-ros;* prob. from *2806* (through the idea of using *bits* of wood, etc., for the purpose); a *die* (for drawing chances); by impl. a *portion* (as if so secured); by extens. an *acquisition* (espec. a *patrimony,* fig.):—heritage, inheritance, lot, part.

2820. κληρόω klērŏō, *klay-rŏ'-o;* from *2819;* to *allot,* i.e. (fig.) to *assign* (a privilege):—obtain an inheritance.

2821. κλῆσις klēsis, *klay'-sis;* from a shorter form of 2564; an *invitation* (fig.):—calling, vocation.

2822. κλητός klētŏs, *klay-tos';* from the same *2821; invited,* i.e. *appointed,* or (spec.) a *saint* called.

2823. κλίβανος klibanŏs, *klib'-an-os;* of unce der.; an earthen *pot* used for baking in:—oven.

2824. κλίμα klima, *klee'-mah;* from *2827;* a *slo* i.e. (spec.) a "*clime*" or *tract* of country:—pa region.

2825. κλίνη klinē, *klee'-nay;* from *2827;* a *cou* (for sleep, sickness, sitting or eating):—bed, table.

2826. κλινίδιον klinidiŏn, *klin-id'-ee-on;* ne of a presumed der. of *2825;* a *pallet* or *little couch.* bed.

2827. κλίνω klinō, *klee'-no;* a prim. verb; *slant* or *slope,* i.e. *incline* or *recline* (lit. or fig.):—b (down), be far spent, lay, turn to flight, wear away

2828. κλισία klisia, *klee-see'-ah;* from a der. *2827;* prop. *reclination,* i.e. (concr. and spec.) a *pa* at a meal:—company.

2829. κλοπή klŏpē, *klop-ay';* from *2813; ste ing:*—theft.

2830. κλύδων kludōn, *kloo'-dohn;* from κλ kluzō (to *billow* or *dash* over); a *surge* of the s (lit. or fig.):—raging, wave.

2831. κλυδωνίζομαι kludōnizŏmai, *kloo-nid'-zom-ahee;* mid. from *2830;* to *surge,* i.e. (fig.) *fluctuate:*—toss to and fro.

2832. Κλωπᾶς Klōpas, *klo-pas';* of Chald. (corresp. to *256*); *Clopas,* an Isr.:—Clopas.

2833. κνήθω knēthō, *knay'-tho;* from a pri κνάω knaō (to *scrape*); to *scratch,* i.e. (by im to *tickle:*— × itching.

2834. Κνίδος Knidŏs, *knee'-dos;* prob. of f or.; *Cnidus,* a place in Asia Minor:—Cnidus.

2835. κοδράντης kŏdrantēs, *kod-ran'-tace;* Lat. or.; a *quadrans,* i.e. the fourth part of an as farthing.

2836. κοιλία kŏilia, *koy-lee'-ah;* from κοῖλ kŏilŏs ("*hollow*"); a *cavity,* i.e. (spec.) the *ab men;* by impl. the *matrix;* fig. the *heart:*—bel womb.

2837. κοιμάω kŏimaō, *koy-mah'-o;* from 27 to *put to sleep,* i.e. (pass. or reflex.) to *slumber;* f to *decease:*—(be a-, fall a-, fall on) sleep, be dead.

2838. κοίμησις kŏimēsis, *koy'-may-sis;* fr *2837; sleeping,* i.e. (by impl.) *repose:*—taking of res

2839. κοινός kŏinŏs, *koy-nos';* prob. from *48 common,* i.e. (lit.) shared by all or several, or (ce *profane:*—common, defiled, unclean, unholy.

2840. κοινόω kŏinŏō, *koy-nŏ'-o;* from *2839;* make (or *consider*) *profane* (cer.):—call common, d file, pollute, unclean.

2841. κοινωνέω kŏinōnĕō, *koy-no-neh'-o;* fr *2844;* to *share* with others (obj. or subj.):—commu cate, distribute, be partaker.

2842. κοινωνία kŏinōnia, *koy-nohn-ee'-ah;* fr *2844; partnership,* i.e. (lit.) *participation,* or (soci *intercourse,* or (pecuniary) *benefaction:*—(to) co municate (-ation), communion, (contri-) distributio fellowship.

2843. κοινωνικός kŏinōnikŏs, *koy-no-nee-ko* from *2844; communicative,* i.e. (pecuniarily) *liberal:* willing to communicate.

2844. κοινωνός kŏinōnŏs, *koy-no-nos';* fro *2839;* a *sharer,* i.e. *associate:*—companion, × fello ship, partaker, partner.

2845. κοίτη kŏitē, *koy'-tay;* from *2749;* a *couc* by extens. *cohabitation;* by impl. the male *sperm:* bed, chambering, × conceive.

2846. κοιτών kŏitōn, *koy-tone';* from *2845;* a *be room:*—+ chamberlain.

2847. κόκκινος kŏkkinŏs, *kok'-kee-nos;* fro *2848* (from the *kernel*-shape of the insect); *crimso* colored:—scarlet (colour, coloured).

2848. κόκκος kŏkkŏs, *kok'-kos;* appar. a pri word; a *kernel* of seed:—corn, grain.

2849. κολάζω kŏlazō, *kol-ad'-zo;* from κόλ kŏlos (*dwarf*); prop. to *curtail,* i.e. (fig.) to *chasti* (or *reserve* for infliction).—punish.

2850. κολακεία kŏlakĕia, *kol-ak-i'-ah;* from a der. of κόλαξ kŏlax (a *fawner*); *flattery:*— × flattering.

2851. κόλασις kŏlasis, *kol'-as-is;* from *2849;* penal *infliction:*—punishment, torment.

2852. κολαφίζω kŏlaphizō, *kol-af-id'-zo;* from a der. of the base of *2849;* to *rap* with the fist:—buffet.

2853. κολλάω kŏllaō, *kol-lah'-o;* from κόλλα kŏlla ("*glue*"); to *glue,* i.e. (pass. or reflex.) to *stick* (fig.):—cleave, join (self), keep company.

2854. κολλούριον kŏllŏuriŏn, *kol-loo'-ree-on;* neut. of a presumed der. of κολλύρα kŏllura (a *cake;* prob. akin to the base of *2853*); prop. a *poultice* (as made of or in the form of *crackers*), i.e. (by anal.) a *plaster:*—eyesalve.

2855. κολλυβιστής kŏllubistēs, *kol-loo-bis-tace';* from a presumed der. of κόλλυβος kŏllubŏs (a small *coin;* prob. akin to *2854*); a *coin-dealer:*—(money-) changer.

2856. κολοβόω kŏlŏbŏō, *kol-ob-ŏ'-o;* from a der. of the base of *2849;* to *dock,* i.e. (fig.) *abridge:*—shorten.

2857. Κολοσσαί Kŏlŏssai, *kol-os-sah'ee;* appar. fem. plur. of κολοσσός kŏlŏssŏs ("*colossal*"); *Colossæ,* a place in Asia Minor:—Colosse.

2858. Κολοσσαεύς Kŏlŏssaĕus, *kol-os-sayoos';* fr. *2857;* a *Colossæan,* i.e. inh. of Colossæ:—Colossian.

2859. κόλπος kŏlpŏs, *kol'-pos;* appar. a prim. word; the *bosom;* by anal. a *bay:*—bosom, creek.

2860. κολυμβάω kŏlumbaō, *kol-oom-bah'-o;* from κόλυμβος kŏlumbŏs (a *diver*); to *plunge* into water:—swim.

2861. κολυμβήθρα kŏlumbēthra, *kol-oom-bay'-thrah;* from *2860;* a *diving-place,* i.e. *pond* for bathing (or swimming):—pool.

2862. κολωνία kŏlōnia, *kol-o-nee'-ah;* of Lat. or.; a Roman "*colony*" for veterans:—colony.

2863. κομάω kŏmaō, *kom-ah'-o;* from *2864;* to *wear tresses* of hair:—have long hair.

2864. κόμη kŏmē, *kom'-ay;* appar. from the same as *2865;* the *hair* of the head (*locks,* as *ornamental,* and thus differing from *2359,* which prop. denotes merely the *scalp*):—hair.

2865. κομίζω kŏmizō, *kom-id'-zo;* from a prim. κομέω kŏmĕō (to *tend,* i.e. take care of); prop. to *provide* for, i.e. (by impl.) to *carry* off (as if from harm; gen. *obtain*):—bring, receive.

2866. κομψότερον kŏmpsŏtĕrŏn, *komp-sot'-er-on;* neut. compar. of a der. of the base of *2865* (mean. prop. *well dressed,* i.e. *nice*); fig. *convalescent:*—+ began to amend.

2867. κονιάω kŏniaō, *kon-ee-ah'-o;* from κονία kŏnia (*dust;* by anal. *lime*); to *whitewash:*—whiten.

2868. κονιορτός kŏniŏrtŏs, *kon-ee-or-tos';* from the base of *2867* and ὄρνυμι ŏrnumi (to "*rouse*"); *pulverulence* (as *blown* about):—dust.

2869. κοπάζω kŏpazō, *kop-ad'-zo;* from *2873;* to *tire,* i.e. (fig.) to *relax:*—cease.

2870. κοπετός kŏpĕtŏs, *kop-et-os';* from *2875;* *mourning* (prop. by *beating* the breast):—lamentation.

2871. κοπή kŏpē, *kop-ay';* from *2875;* *cutting,* i.e. *carnage:*—slaughter.

2872. κοπιάω kŏpiaō, *kop-ee-ah'-o;* from a der. of *2873;* to *feel fatigue;* by impl. to *work hard:*—(bestow) labour, toil, be wearied.

2873. κόπος kŏpŏs, *kop'-os;* from *2875;* a *cut,* i.e. (by anal.) *toil* (as *reducing* the strength), lit. or fig.; by impl. *pains:*—labour, + trouble, weariness.

2874. κοπρία kŏpria, *kop-ree'-ah;* from κόπρος kŏprŏs (*ordure;* perh. akin to *2875*); *manure:*—dung (-hill).

2875. κόπτω kŏptō, *kop'-to;* a prim. verb; to "*chop*"; spec. to *beat* the breast in grief:—cut down, lament, mourn, (be-) wail. Comp. the base of *5114.*

2876. κόραξ kŏrax, *kor'-ax;* perh. from *2880;* a *crow* (from its *voracity*):—raven.

2877. κοράσιον kŏrasiŏn, *kor-as'-ee-on,* neut. of a presumed der. of κόρη kŏrē (a *maiden*); a (little) *girl:*—damsel, maid.

2878. κορβᾶν kŏrban, *kor-ban';* and κορβανᾶς kŏrbanas, *kor-ban-as';* of Heb. and Chald. or. respectively [7133]; a votive *offering* and *the offering;* a *consecrated present* (to the Temple fund); by extens. (the latter term) the *Treasury* itself, i.e. the room where the contribution boxes stood:—Corban, treasury.

2879. Κορέ Kŏrĕ, *kor-eh';* of Heb. or. [7141]; *Corè* (i.e. *Korach*), an Isr.:—Core.

2880. κορέννυμι kŏrĕnnumi, *kor-en'-noo-mee;* a prim. verb; to *cram,* i.e. *glut* or *sate:*—eat enough, full.

2881. Κορίνθιος Kŏrinthiŏs, *kor-in'-thee-os;* from *2882;* a *Corinthian,* i.e. inhab. of Corinth:—Corinthian.

2882. Κόρινθος Kŏrinthŏs, *kor'-in-thos;* of uncert. der.; *Corinthus,* a city of Greece:—Corinth.

2883. Κορνήλιος Kŏrnēliŏs, *kor-nay'-lee-os;* of Lat. or.; *Cornelius,* a Roman:—Cornelius.

2884. κόρος kŏrŏs, *kor'-os;* of Heb. or. [3734]; a *cor,* i.e. a specific measure:—measure.

2885. κοσμέω kŏsmĕō, *kos-meh'-o;* from *2889;* to *put in* proper *order,* i.e. *decorate* (lit. or fig.); spec. to *snuff* (a wick):—adorn, garnish, trim.

2886. κοσμικός kŏsmikŏs, *kos-mee-kos';* from *2889* (in its secondary sense); *terrene* ("*cosmic*"), lit. (*mundane*) or fig. (*corrupt*):—worldly.

2887. κόσμιος kŏsmiŏs, *kos'-mee-os;* from *2889* (in its prim. sense); *orderly,* i.e. *decorous:*—of good behaviour, modest.

2888. κοσμοκράτωρ kŏsmŏkratōr, *kos-mok-rat'-ore;* from *2889* and *2902;* a *world-ruler,* an epithet of Satan:—ruler.

2889. κόσμος kŏsmŏs, *kos'-mos;* prob. from the base of *2865;* orderly *arrangement,* i.e. *decoration;* by impl. the *world* (in a wide or narrow sense, includ. its inhab., lit. or fig. [mor.]):—adorning, world.

2890. Κούαρτος Kŏuartŏs, *koo'-ar-tos;* of Lat. or. (*fourth*); *Quartus,* a Chr.:—Quartus.

2891. κοῦμι kŏumi, *koo'-mee;* of Chald. or. [6966]; *cumi* (i.e. *rise!*):—cumi.

2892. κουστωδία kŏustōdia, *koos-to-dee'-ah;* of Lat. or.; "*custody*", i.e. a Roman *sentry:*—watch.

2893. κουφίζω kŏuphizō, *koo-fid'-zo;* from κοῦφος kŏuphŏs (*light* in weight); to *unload:*—lighten.

2894. κόφινος kŏphinŏs, *kof'-ee-nos;* of uncert. der.; a (small) *basket:*—basket.

2895. κράββατος krabbatŏs, *krab'-bat-os;* prob. of for. or.; a *mattress:*—bed.

2896. κράζω krazō, *krad'-zo;* a prim. verb; prop. to "*croak*" (as a raven) or *scream,* i.e. (gen.) to *call* aloud (*shriek, exclaim, intreat*):—cry (out).

2897. κραιπάλη kraipalē, *krahee-pal'-ay;* prob. from the same as *726;* prop. a *headache* (as a *seizure* of pain) from drunkenness, i.e. (by impl.) a *debauch* (by anal. a *glut*):—surfeiting.

2898. κρανίον kraniŏn, *kran-ee'-on;* dimin. of a der. of the base of *2768;* a *skull* ("*cranium*"):—Calvary, skull.

2899. κράσπεδον kraspĕdŏn, *kras'-ped-on;* of uncert. der.; a *margin,* i.e. (spec.) a *fringe* or *tassel:*—border, hem.

2900. κραταιός krataiŏs, *krat-ah-yos';* from *2904;* *powerful:*—mighty.

2901. κραταιόω krataiŏō, *krat-ah-yŏ'-o;* from *2900;* to *empower,* i.e. (pass.) *increase in vigor:*—be strenghtened, be (wax) strong.

2902. κρατέω kratĕō, *krat-eh'-o;* from *2904;* to *use strength,* i.e. *seize* or *retain* (lit. or fig.):—hold (by, fast), keep, lay hand (hold) on, obtain, retain, take (by).

2903. κράτιστος kratistŏs, *krat'-is-tos;* superl. of a der. of *2904;* *strongest,* i.e. (in dignity) *very honorable:*—most excellent (noble).

2904. κράτος kratŏs, *krat'-os;* perh. a prim. word; *vigor* ["great"] (lit. or fig.):—dominion, might [-ily], power, strength.

2905. κραυγάζω kraugazō, *krŏw-gad'-zo;* from *2906;* to *clamor:*—cry out.

2906. κραυγή kraugē, *krŏw-gay';* from *2896;* an *outcry* (in notification, tumult or grief):—clamour, cry (-ing).

2907. κρέας krĕas, *kreh'-as;* perh. a prim. word; (butcher's) *meat:*—flesh.

2908. κρεῖσσον krĕissŏn, *krice'-son;* neut. of an alt. form of *2909;* (as noun) *better,* i.e. *greater advantage:*—better.

2909. κρείττων krĕittōn, *krite'-tohn;* compar. of a der. of *2904;* *stronger,* i.e. (fig.) *better,* i.e. *nobler:*—best, better.

2910. κρεμάννυμι krĕmannumi, *krem-an'-noo-mee;* a prol. form of a prim. verb; to *hang:*—hang.

2911. κρημνός krēmnŏs, *krame-nos';* from *2910;* *overhanging,* i.e. a *precipice:*—steep place.

2912. Κρής Krēs, *krace;* from *2914;* a *Cretan,* i.e. inhab. of Crete:—Crete, Cretian.

2913. Κρήσκης Krēskēs, *krace'-kace;* of Lat. or.; *growing; Cresces* (i.e. *Crescens*), a Chr.:—Crescens.

2914. Κρήτη Krētē, *kray'-tay;* of uncert. der.; *Cretè,* an island in the Mediterranean:—Crete.

2915. κριθή krithē, *kree-thay';* of uncert. der.; *barley:*—barley.

2916. κρίθινος krithinŏs, *kree'-thee-nos;* from *2915;* consisting *of barley:*—barley.

2917. κρίμα krima, *kree'-mah;* from *2919;* a *decision* (the function or the effect, for or against ["crime"]):—avenge, condemned, condemnation, damnation, + go to law, judgment.

2918. κρίνον krinŏn, *kree'-non;* perh. a prim. word; a *lily:*—lily.

2919. κρίνω krinō, *kree'-no;* prop. to *distinguish,* i.e. *decide* (mentally or judicially); by impl. to *try, condemn, punish:*—avenge, conclude, condemn, damn, decree, determine, esteem, judge, go to (sue at the) law, ordain, call in question, sentence to, think.

2920. κρίσις krisis, *kree'-sis;* *decision* (subj. or obj., for or against); by extens. a *tribunal;* by impl. *justice* (spec. divine *law*):—accusation, condemnation, damnation, judgment.

2921. Κρίσπος Krispŏs, *kris'-pos;* of Lat. or.; "*crisp*"; *Crispus,* a Corinthian:—Crispus.

2922. κριτήριον kritēriŏn, *kree-tay'-ree-on;* neut. of a presumed der. of *2923;* a *rule* of judging ("*criterion*"), i.e. (by impl.) a *tribunal:*—to judge, judgment (seat).

2923. κριτής kritēs, *kree-tace';* from *2919;* a *judge* (gen. or spec.):—judge.

2924. κριτικός kritikŏs, *krit-ee-kos';* from *2923;* *decisive* ("*critical*"), i.e. *discriminative:*—discerner.

2925. κρούω krŏuō, *kroo'-o;* appar. a prim. verb; to *rap:*—knock.

2926. κρυπτή kruptē, *kroop-tay';* fem. of *2927;* a *hidden* place, i.e. *cellar* ("*crypt*"):—secret.

2927. κρυπτός kruptŏs, *kroop-tos';* from *2928;* *concealed,* i.e. *private:*—hid (-den), inward [-ly], secret.

2928. κρύπτω kruptō, *kroop'-to;* a prim. verb; to *conceal* (prop. by *covering*):—hide (self), keep secret, secret [-ly].

2929. κρυσταλλίζω krustallizō, *kroos-tal-lid'-zo;* from *2930;* to *make* (i.e. intrans. *resemble*) *ice* ("crystallize"):—be clear as crystal.

2930. κρύσταλλος krustallŏs, *kroos'-tal-los;* from a der. of κρύος kruŏs (*frost*); *ice,* i.e. (by anal.) rock "*crystal*":—crystal.

2931. κρυφῆ kruphē, *kroo-fay';* adv. from *2928;* *privately:*—in secret.

2932. κτάομαι ktaŏmai, *ktah'-om-ahee;* a prim. verb; to *get,* i.e. *acquire* (by any means; *own*):—obtain, possess, provide, purchase.

2933. **κτῆμα ktēma**, *ktay'-mah;* from *2932;* an *acquirement*, i.e. *estate:*—possession.

2934. **κτῆνος ktēnŏs**, *ktay'-nos;* from *2932; property*, i.e. (spec.) a domestic *animal:*—beast.

2935. **κτήτωρ ktētōr**, *ktay'-tore;* from *2932;* an *owner:*—possessor.

2936. **κτίζω ktizō**, *ktid'-zo;* prob. akin to *2932* (through the idea of the *proprietorship* of the *manufacturer*); to *fabricate*, i.e. *found* (*form* originally):—create, Creator, make.

2937. **κτίσις ktisis**, *ktis'-is;* from *2936;* original *formation* (prop. the act; by impl. the thing, lit. or fig.):—building, creation, creature, ordinance.

2938. **κτίσμα ktisma**, *ktis'-mah;* from *2936;* an original *formation* (concr.), i.e. *product* (created thing):—creature.

2939. **κτιστής ktistēs**, *ktis-tace';* from *2936;* a *founder*, i.e. *God* (as author of all things):—Creator.

2940. **κυβεία kubĕia**, *koo-bi'-ah;* from **κύβος kubŏs** (a "*cube*", i.e. *die* for playing); *gambling*, i.e. (fig.) *artifice* or *fraud:*—sleight.

2941. **κυβέρνησις kubĕrnēsis**, *koo-ber'-nay-sis;* from **κυβερνάω kubĕrnaō** (of Lat. or., to *steer*); *pilotage*, i.e. (fig.) *directorship* (in the church):—government.

2942. **κυβερνήτης kubĕrnētēs**, *koo-ber-nay'-tace;* from the same as *2941; helmsman*, i.e. (by impl.) *captain:*—(ship) master.

2943. **κυκλόθεν kuklŏthĕn**, *koo-kloth'-en;* adv. from the same as *2945; from the circle*, i.e. *all around:*—(round) about.

κυκλός kuklŏs. See *2945*.

2944. **κυκλόω kuklŏō**, *koo-klŏ'-o;* from the same as *2945;* to *encircle*, i.e. *surround:*—compass (about), come (stand) round about.

2945. **κύκλῳ kuklōi**, *koo'-klo;* as if dat. of **κύκλος kuklŏs** (a *ring*, "*cycle*"; akin to *2947*); i.e. *in a circle* (by impl. of *1722*), i.e. (adv.) *all around:*—round about.

2946. **κύλισμα kulisma**, *koo'-lis-mah;* from *2947;* a *wallow* (the effect of *rolling*), i.e. *filth:*—wallowing.

2947. **κυλιόω kuliŏō**, *koo-lee-ŏ'-o;* from the base of *2949* (through the idea of *circularity;* comp. *2945*, *1507*); to *roll* about:—wallow.

2948. **κυλλός kullŏs**, *kool-los';* from the same as *2947; rocking* about, i.e. *crippled* (*maimed*, in feet or hands):—maimed.

2949. **κῦμα kuma**, *koo'-mah;* from **κύω kuō** (to *swell* [with young], i.e. *bend, curve*); a *billow* (as *bursting* or *toppling*):—wave.

2950. **κύμβαλον kumbalŏn**, *koom'-bal-on;* from a der. of the base of *2949;* a "*cymbal*" (as *hollow*):—cymbal.

2951. **κύμινον kuminŏn**, *koo'-min-on;* of for. or. [comp. 3646]; *dill* or *fennel* ("cummin"):—cummin.

2952. **κυνάριον kunariŏn**, *koo-nar'-ee-on;* neut. of a presumed der. of *2965;* a *puppy:*—dog.

2953. **Κύπριος Kupriŏs**, *koo'-pree-os;* from *2954;* a *Cyprian* (*Cypriot*), i.e. inhab. of Cyprus:—of Cyprus.

2954. **Κύπρος Kuprŏs**, *koo'-pros;* of uncert. or.; *Cyprus*, an island in the Mediterranean:—Cyprus.

2955. **κύπτω kuptō**, *koop'-to;* prob. from the base of *2949;* to *bend* forward:—stoop (down).

2956. **Κυρηναῖος Kurēnaiŏs**, *koo-ray-nah'-yos;* from *2957;* a *Cyrenæan*, i.e. inhab. of Cyrene:—of Cyrene, Cyrenian.

2957. **Κυρήνη Kurēnē**, *koo-ray'-nay;* of uncert. der.; *Cyrenè*, a region of Africa:—Cyrene.

2958. **Κυρήνιος Kurēniŏs**, *koo-ray'-nee-os;* of Lat. or.; *Cyrenius* (i.e. *Quirinus*), a Roman:—Cyrenius.

2959. **Κυρία Kuria**, *koo-ree'-ah;* fem. of *2962; Cyria*, a Chr. woman:—lady.

2960. **κυριακός kuriakŏs**, *koo-ree-ak-os';* from *2962; belonging to* the *Lord* (Jehovah or Jesus):—Lord's.

2961. **κυριεύω kuriĕuō**, *koo-ree-yoo'-o;* from *2962;* to *rule:*—have dominion over, lord, be lord of, exercise lordship over.

2962. **κύριος kuriŏs**, *koo'-ree-os;* from **κῦρος kurŏs** (*supremacy*); *supreme* in authority, i.e. (as noun) *controller;* by impl. *Mr.* (as a respectful title):—God, Lord, master, Sir.

2963. **κυριότης kuriŏtēs**, *koo-ree-ot'-ace;* from *2962; mastery*, i.e. (concr. and coll.) *rulers:*—dominion, government.

2964. **κυρόω kurŏō**, *koo-rŏ'-o;* from the same as *2962;* to *make authoritative*, i.e. *ratify:*—confirm.

2965. **κύων kuōn**, *koo'-ohn;* a prim. word; a *dog* ["*hound*"] (lit. or fig.):—dog.

2966. **κῶλον kōlŏn**, *ko'-lon;* from the base of *2849;* a *limb* of the body (as if *lopped*):—carcase.

2967. **κωλύω kōluō**, *ko-loo'-o;* from the base of *2849;* to *estop*, i.e. *prevent* (by word or act):—forbid, hinder, keep from, let, not suffer, withstand.

2968. **κώμη kōmē**, *ko'-may;* from *2749;* a *hamlet* (as if *laid* down):—town, village.

2969. **κωμόπολις kōmŏpŏlis**, *ko-mop'-ol-is;* from *2968* and *4172;* an unwalled *city:*—town.

2970. **κῶμος kōmŏs**, *ko'-mos;* from *2749;* a *carousal* (as if a *letting loose*):—revelling, rioting.

2971. **κώνωψ kōnōps**, *ko'-nopes;* appar. from a der. of the base of *2759* and a der. of *3700;* a *mosquito* (from its *stinging proboscis*):—gnat.

2972. **Κῶς Kōs**, *koce;* of uncert. or.; *Cos*, an island in the Mediterranean:—Cos.

2973. **Κωσάμ Kōsam**, *ko-sam';* of Heb. or. [comp. 7081]; *Cosam* (i.e. *Kosam*), an Isr.:—Cosam.

2974. **κωφός kōphŏs**, *ko-fos';* from *2875; blunted*, i.e. (fig.) of hearing (*deaf*) or speech (*dumb*):—deaf, dumb, speechless.

Λ

2975. **λαγχάνω lagchanō**, *lang-khan'-o;* a prol. form of a prim. verb, which is only used as an alt. in certain tenses; to *lot*, i.e. *determine* (by impl. *receive*) espec. by lot:—his lot be, cast lots, obtain.

2976. **Λάζαρος Lazarŏs**, *lad'-zar-os;* prob. of Heb. or. [499]; *Lazarus* (i.e. *Elazar*), the name of two Isr. (one imaginary):—Lazarus.

2977. **λάθρα lathra**, *lath'-rah;* adv. from *2990; privately:*—privily, secretly.

2978. **λαῖλαψ lailaps**, *lah'ee-laps;* of uncert. der.: a *whirlwind* (*squall*):—storm, tempest.

2979. **λακτίζω laktizō**, *lak-tid'-zo;* from adv. **λάξ lax** (*heelwise*); to *recalcitrate:*—kick.

2980. **λαλέω lalĕō**, *lal-eh'-o;* a prol. form of an otherwise obsol. verb; to *talk*, i.e. *utter* words:—preach, say, speak (after), talk, tell, utter. Comp. *3004*.

2981. **λαλιά lalia**, *lal-ee-ah';* from *2980; talk:*—saying, speech.

2982. **λαμά lama**, *lam-ah';* or

λαμμᾶ lamma, *lam-mah';* of Heb. or. [4100 with prep. pref.]; *lama* (i.e. *why*):—lama.

2983. **λαμβάνω lambanō**, *lam-ban'-o;* a prol. form of a prim. verb, which is used only as an alt. in certain tenses; to *take* (in very many applications, lit. and fig. [prop. obj. or act., to *get hold of;* whereas *1209* is rather subj. or pass., to *have offered* to one; while *138* is more violent, to *seize* or *remove*]):—accept, + be amazed, assay, attain, bring, × when I call, catch, come on (× unto), + forget, have, hold, obtain, receive (× after), take (away, up).

2984. **Λάμεχ Lamĕch**, *lam'-ekh;* of Heb. or. [3929]; *Lamech* (i.e. *Lemek*), a patriarch:—Lamech.

λαμμᾶ lamma. See *2982*.

2985. **λαμπάς lampas**, *lam-pas';* from *2989;* a "*lamp*" or *flambeau:*—lamp, light, torch.

2986. **λαμπρός lamprŏs**, *lam-pros';* from the same as *2985; radiant;* by anal. *limpid;* fig. *magnificent* or *sumptuous* (in appearance):—bright, clear, gay, goodly, gorgeous, white.

2987. **λαμπρότης lamprŏtēs**, *lam-prot'-ace;* from *2896; brilliancy:*—brightness.

2988. **λαμπρῶς lamprōs**, *lam-proce';* adv. from *2986; brilliantly*, i.e. (fig.) *luxuriously:*—sumptuously.

2989. **λάμπω lampō**, *lam'-po;* a prim. verb; to *beam*, i.e. *radiate* brilliancy (lit. or fig.):—give light, shine.

2990. **λανθάνω lanthanō**, *lan-than'-o;* a prol. form of a prim. verb, which is used only as an alt. in certain tenses; to *lie hid* (lit. or fig.); often used adv. *unwittingly:*—be hid, be ignorant of, unawares.

2991. **λαξευτός laxĕutŏs**, *lax-yoo-tos';* from a comp. of **λᾶς las** (a *stone*) and the base of *3584* (in its orig. sense of *scraping*); *rock-quarried:*—hewn in stone.

2992. **λαός laŏs**, *lah-os';* appar. a prim. word; a *people* (in gen.; thus differing from *1218*, which denotes one's *own* populace):—people.

2993. **Λαοδίκεια Laŏdikĕia**, *lah-od-ik'-i-ah;* from a comp. of *2992* and *1349; Laodicia*, a place in Asia Minor:—Laodicea.

2994. **Λαοδικεύς Laŏdikĕus**, *lah-od-ik-yooce';* from *2993;* a *Laodicean*, i.e. inhab. of Laodicia:—Laodicean.

2995. **λάρυγξ larugx**, *lar'-oongks;* of uncert. der.; the *throat* ("*larynx*"):—throat.

2996. **Λασαία Lasaia**, *las-ah'-yah;* of uncert. or.; *Lasæa*, a place in Crete:—Lasea.

2997. **λάσχω laschō**, *las'-kho;* a strengthened form of a prim. verb, which only occurs in this and another prol. form as alt. in certain tenses; to *crack* open (from a fall):—burst asunder.

2998. **λατομέω latŏmĕō**, *lat-om-eh'-o;* from the same as the first part of *2991* and the base of *5114;* to *quarry:*—hew.

2999. **λατρεία latrĕia**, *lat-ri'-ah;* from *3000; ministration* of God, i.e. *worship:*—(divine) service.

3000. **λατρεύω latrĕuō**, *lat-ryoo'-o;* from **λάτρις latris** (a hired *menial*); to *minister* (to God), i.e. *render* religious *homage:*—serve, do the service, worship (-per).

3001. **λάχανον lachanŏn**, *lakh'-an-on;* from **λαχαίνω lachainō** (to *dig*); a *vegetable:*—herb.

3002. **Λεββαῖος Lĕbbaiŏs**, *leb-bah'-yos;* of uncert. or.; *Lebbæus*, a Chr.:—Lebbæus.

3003. **λεγεών lĕgĕōn**, *leg-eh-ohn';* of Lat. or.; a "*legion*", i.e. Rom. *regiment* (fig.):—legion.

3004. **λέγω lĕgō**, *leg'-o;* a prim. verb; prop. to "*lay*" forth, i.e. (fig.) *relate* (in words [usually of systematic or set *discourse;* whereas *2036* and *5346* generally refer to an *individual* expression or speech respectively; while *4483* is prop. to *break silence* merely, and *2980* means an *extended* or random harangue]); by impl. to *mean:*—ask, bid, boast, call, describe, give out, name, put forth, say (-ing, on), shew, speak, tell, utter.

3005. **λεῖμμα lĕimma**, *lime'-mah;* from *3007;* a *remainder:*—remnant.

3006. **λεῖος lĕiŏs**, *li'-os;* appar. a prim. word; *smooth*, i.e. "*level*":—smooth.

3007. **λείπω lĕipō**, *li'-po;* a prim. verb; to *leave*, i.e. (intrans. or pass.) to *fail* or *be absent:*—be destitute (wanting), lack.

3008. **λειτουργέω lĕitŏurgĕō**, *li-toorg-eh'-o;* from *3011;* to be a *public servant*, i.e. (by anal.) to *perform* religious or charitable *functions* (*worship, obey, relieve*):—minister.

3009. **λειτουργία lĕitŏurgia**, *li-toorg-ee'-ah;* from *3008; public function* (as priest ["*liturgy*"] or almsgiver):—ministration (-try), service.

3010. **λειτουργικός lĕitŏurgikŏs**, *li-toorg-ik-os';* from the same as *3008; functional publicly* ("*liturgic*"), i.e. *beneficent:*—ministering.

3011. **λειτουργός lĕitŏurgŏs**, *li-toorg-os';* from a der. of *2992* and *2041;* a *public servant*, i.e. a *functionary* in the Temple or Gospel, or (gen.) a *worshipper* (of God) or *benefactor* (of man):—minister (-ed).

3012. **λέντιον lĕntiŏn**, *len'-tee-on;* of Lat. or.; a "*linen*" cloth, i.e. *apron:*—towel.

3013. **λεπίς lĕpis**, *lep-is';* from **λέπω lĕpō** (to *peel*); a *flake:*—scale.

3014. λέπρα **lĕpra**, *lep'-rah;* from the same as 3013; *scaliness*, i.e. "*leprosy*":—leprosy.

3015. λεπρός **lĕprŏs**, *lep-ros';* from the same as 3014; *scaly*, i.e. *leprous* (a *leper*):—leper.

3016. λεπτόν **lĕptŏn**, *lep-ton';* neut. of a der. of the same as 3013; something *scaled* (*light*), i.e. a small *coin:*—mite.

3017. Λευΐ **Lĕui**, *lyoo-ee';* of Heb. or. [3878]; *Levi*, the name of three Isr.:—Levi. Comp. 3018.

3018. Λευΐς **Lĕuis**, *lyoo-is';* a form of 3017; *Lewis* (i.e. *Levi*), a Chr.:—Levi.

3019. Λευΐτης **Lĕuitēs**, *lyoo-ee'-tace;* from 3017; a *Levite*, i.e. desc. of Levi:—Levite.

3020. Λευϊτικός **Lĕuitikŏs**, *lyoo-it'-ee-kos;* from 3019; *Levitic*, i.e. relating to the Levites:—Levitical.

3021. λευκαίνω **lĕukainō**, *lyoo-kah'ee-no;* from 3022; to *whiten:*—make white, whiten.

3022. λευκός **lĕukŏs**, *lyoo-kos';* from λύκη **lukē** ("*light*"); *white:*—white.

3023. λεών **lĕōn**, *leh-ohn';* a prim. word; a "*lion*":—lion.

3024. λήθη **lēthē**, *lay'-thay;* from 2990; *forgetfulness:*— + forget.

3025. ληνός **lēnŏs**, *lay-nos';* appar. a prim. word; a *trough*, i.e. *wine-vat:*—winepress.

3026. λῆρος **lērŏs**, *lay'-ros;* appar. a prim. word; *twaddle*, i.e. an *incredible story:*—idle tale.

3027. λῃστής **lēistēs**, *lace-tace';* from ληΐζομαι **lēizŏmai** (to *plunder*); a *brigand:*—robber, thief.

3028. λῆψις **lēpsis**, *lape'-sis;* from 2983; *receipt* (the act):—receiving.

3029. λίαν **lian**, *lee'-an;* of uncert. affin.; *much* (adv.):—exceeding, great (-ly), sore, very (+ chiefest).

3030. λίβανος **libanŏs**, *lib'-an-os;* of for. or. [3828]; the *incense-tree*, i.e. (by impl.) *incense* itself:—frankincense.

3031. λιβανωτός **libanōtŏs**, *lib-an-o-tos';* from 3030; *frankincense*, i.e. (by extens.) a *censer* for burning it:—censer.

3032. Λιβερτῖνος **Libĕrtinŏs**, *lib-er-tee'-nos;* of Lat. or.; a Rom. *freedman:*—Libertine.

3033. Λιβύη **Libuē**, *lib-oo'-ay;* prob. from 3047; *Libye*, a region of Africa:—Libya.

3034. λιθάζω **lithazō**, *lith-ad'-zo;* from 3037; to *lapidate:*—stone.

3035. λίθινος **lithinŏs**, *lith'-ee-nos;* from 3037; *stony*, i.e. made of *stone:*—of stone.

3036. λιθοβολέω **lithŏbŏlĕō**, *lith-ob-ol-eh'-o;* from a comp. of 3037 and 906; to *throw stones*, i.e. *lapidate:*—stone, cast stones.

3037. λίθος **lithŏs**, *lee'-thos;* appar. a prim. word; a *stone* (lit. or fig.):—(mill-, stumbling-) stone.

3038. λιθόστρωτος **lithŏstrōtŏs**, *lith-os'-tro-tos;* from 3037 and a der. of 4766; *stone-strewed*, i.e. a tessellated *mosaic* on which the Rom. tribunal was placed:—Pavement.

3039. λικμάω **likmaō**, *lik-mah'-o;* from λικμός **likmŏs**, the equiv. of λίκνον **liknŏn** (a winnowing *fan* or basket); to *winnow*, i.e. (by anal.) to *triturate:*—grind to powder.

3040. λιμήν **limēn**, *lee-mane';* appar. a prim. word; a *harbor:*—haven. Comp. 2568.

3041. λίμνη **limnē**, *lim'-nay;* prob. from 3040 (through the idea of the nearness of shore); a *pond* (large or small):—lake.

3042. λιμός **limŏs**, *lee-mos';* prob. from 3007 (through the idea of *destitution*); a *scarcity* of food:—dearth, famine, hunger.

3043. λίνον **linŏn**, *lee'-non;* prob. a prim. word; *flax*, i.e. (by impl.) "*linen*":—linen.

3044. Λῖνος **Linŏs**, *lee'-nos;* perh. from 3043; *Linus*, a Chr.:—Linus.

3045. λιπαρός **liparŏs**, *lip-ar-os';* from λίπος **lipŏs** (*grease*); *fat*, i.e. (fig.) *sumptuous:*—dainty.

3046. λίτρα **litra**, *lee'-trah;* of Lat. or. [*libra*]; a *pound* in weight:—pound.

3047. λίψ **lips**, *leeps;* prob. from λείβω **lĕibō** (to *pour* a "libation"); the *south* (-west) wind (as bringing rain, i.e. (by extens.) the *south* quarter:—southwest.

3048. λογία **lŏgia**, *log-ee'-ah;* from 3056 (in the commercial sense); a *contribution:*—collection, gathering.

3049. λογίζομαι **lŏgizŏmai**, *log-id'-zom-ahee;* mid. from 3056; to *take an inventory*, i.e. *estimate* (lit. or fig.):—conclude, (ac-) count (of), + despise, esteem, impute, lay, number, reason, reckon, suppose, think (on).

3050. λογικός **lŏgikŏs**, *log-ik-os';* from 3056; *rational* ("*logical*"):—reasonable, of the word.

3051. λόγιον **lŏgiŏn**, *log'-ee-on;* neut. of 3052; an *utterance* (of God):—oracle.

3052. λόγιος **lŏgiŏs**, *log'-ee-os;* from 3056; *fluent*, i.e. an *orator:*—eloquent.

3053. λογισμός **lŏgismŏs**, *log-is-mos';* from 3049; *computation*, i.e. (fig.) *reasoning* (*conscience*, *conceit*):—imagination, thought.

3054. λογομαχέω **lŏgŏmachĕō**, *log-om-akh-eh'-o;* from a comp. of 3056 and 3164; to *be disputatious* (on trifles):—strive about words.

3055. λογομαχία **lŏgŏmachia**, *log-om-akh-ee'-ah;* from the same as 3054; *disputation* about trifles ("*logomachy*"):—strife of words.

3056. λόγος **lŏgŏs**, *log'-os;* from 3004; something *said* (including the *thought*); by impl. a *topic* (subject of discourse), also *reasoning* (the mental faculty) or *motive;* by extens. a *computation;* spec. (with the art. in John) the Divine *Expression* (i.e. *Christ*):—account, cause, communication, × concerning, doctrine, fame, × have to do, intent, matter, mouth, preaching, question, reason, + reckon, remove, say (-ing), shew, × speaker, speech, talk, thing, + none of these things move me, tidings, treatise, utterance, word, work.

3057. λόγχη **lŏgchē**, *long'-khay;* perh. a prim. word; a "*lance*":—spear.

3058. λοιδορέω **lŏidŏrĕō**, *loy-dor-eh'-o;* from 3060; to *reproach*, i.e. *vilify:*—revile.

3059. λοιδορία **lŏidŏria**, *loy-dor-ee'-ah;* from 3060; *slander* or *vituperation:*—railing, reproach [-fully].

3060. λοίδορος **lŏidŏrŏs**, *loy'-dor-os;* from λοιδός **lŏidŏs** (*mischief*); *abusive*, i.e. a *blackguard:*—railer, reviler.

3061. λοιμός **lŏimŏs**, *loy-mos';* of uncert. affin.; a *plague* (lit. the *disease*, or fig. a *pest*):—pestilence (-t).

3062. λοιποί **lŏipŏy**, *loy-poy';* masc. plur. of a der. of 3007; *remaining* ones:—other, which remain, remnant, residue, rest.

3063. λοιπόν **lŏipŏn**, *loy-pon';* neut. sing. of the same as 3062; something *remaining* (adv.):—besides, finally, furthermore, (from) henceforth, moreover, now, + it remaineth, then.

3064. λοιποῦ **lŏipŏu**, *loy-poo';* gen. sing. of the same as 3062; *remaining* time:—from henceforth.

3065. Λουκᾶς **Lŏukas**, *loo-kas';* contr. from Lat. *Lucanus; Lucas*, a Chr.:—Lucas, Luke.

3066. Λούκιος **Lŏukiŏs**, *loo'-kee-os;* of Lat. or.; *illuminative; Lucius*, a Chr.:—Lucius.

3067. λουτρόν **lŏutrŏn**, *loo-tron';* from 3068; a *bath*, i.e. (fig.) *baptism:*—washing.

3068. λούω **lŏuō**, *loo'-o;* a prim. verb; to *bathe* (the *whole* person; whereas 3538 means to wet a *part* only, and 4150 to wash, cleanse *garments* exclusively):—wash.

3069. Λύδδα **Ludda**, *lud'-dah;* of Heb. or. [3850]; *Lydda* (i.e. *Lod*), a place in Pal.:—Lydda.

3070. Λυδία **Ludia**, *loo-dee'-ah;* prop. fem. of Λύδιος **Ludiŏs** [of for. or.] (a *Lydian*, in Asia Minor); *Lydia*, a Chr. woman:—Lydia.

3071. Λυκαονία **Lukaŏnia**, *loo-kah-on-ee'-ah;* perh. remotely from 3074; *Lycaonia*, a region of Asia Minor:—Lycaonia.

3072. Λυκαονιστί **Lukaŏnisti**, *loo-kah-on-is-tee';* adv. from a der. of 3071; *Lycaonistically*, i.e. in the language of the Lycaonians:—in the speech of Lycaonia.

3073. Λυκία **Lukia**, *loo-kee'-ah;* prob. remotely from 3074; *Lycia*, a province of Asia Minor:—Lycia.

3074. λύκος **lukŏs**, *loo'-kos;* perh. akin to the base of 3022 (from the *whitish* hair); a *wolf:*—wolf.

3075. λυμαίνομαι **lumainŏmai**, *loo-mah'ee-nom-ahee;* mid. from a prob. der. of 3089 (mean. *filth*); prop. to *soil*, i.e. (fig.) *insult* (*maltreat*):—make havock of.

3076. λυπέω **lupĕō**, *loo-peh'-o;* from 3077; to *distress;* reflex. or pass. to *be sad:*—cause grief, grieve, be in heaviness, (be) sorrow (-ful), be (make) sorry.

3077. λύπη **lupē**, *loo'-pay;* appar. a prim. word; *sadness:*—grief, grievous, + grudgingly, heaviness, sorrow.

3078. Λυσανίας **Lusanias**, *loo-san-ee'-as;* from 3080 and ἀνία **ania** (*trouble*); *grief-dispelling; Lysanias*, a governor of Abilene:—Lysanias.

3079. Λυσίας **Lusias**, *loo-see'-as;* of uncert. affin.; *Lysias*, a Rom.:—Lysias.

3080. λύσις **lusis**, *loo'-sis;* from 3089; a *loosening*, i.e. (spec.) *divorce:*—to be loosed.

3081. λυσιτελεῖ **lusitĕlĕi**, *loo-sit-el-i';* third pers. sing. pres. indic. act. of a der. of a comp. of 3080 and 5056; impers. it *answers* the *purpose*, i.e. *is advantageous:*—it is better.

3082. Λύστρα **Lustra**, *loos'-trah;* of uncert. or.; *Lystra*, a place in Asia Minor:—Lystra.

3083. λύτρον **lutrŏn**, *loo'-tron;* from 3089; something to *loosen* with, i.e. a redemption *price* (fig. *atonement*):—ransom.

3084. λυτρόω **lutrŏō**, *loo-trŏ'-o;* from 3083; to *ransom* (lit. or fig.):—redeem.

3085. λύτρωσις **lutrōsis**, *loo'-tro-sis;* from 3084; a *ransoming* (fig.):— + redeemed, redemption.

3086. λυτρωτής **lutrōtēs**, *loo-tro-tace';* from 3084; a *redeemer* (fig.):—deliverer.

3087. λυχνία **luchnia**, *lookh-nee'-ah;* from 3088; a *lamp-stand* (lit. or fig.):—candlestick.

3088. λύχνος **luchnŏs**, *lookh'-nos;* from the base of 3022; a portable *lamp* or other *illuminator* (lit. or fig.):—candle, light.

3089. λύω **luō**, *loo'-o;* a prim. verb; to "*loosen*" (lit. or fig.):—break (up), destroy, dissolve, (un-) loose, melt, put off. Comp. 4486.

3090. Λωΐς **Lōis**, *lo-ece';* of uncert. or.; *Loïs*, a Chr. woman:—Lois.

3091. Λώτ **Lōt**, *lote;* of Heb. or. [3876]; *Lot*, a patriarch:—Lot.

M

3092. Μαάθ **Maath**, *mah-ath';* prob. of Heb. or.; *Maath*, an Isr.:—Maath.

3093. Μαγδαλά **Magdala**, *mag-dal-ah';* of Chald. or. [comp. 4026]; *the tower; Magdala* (i.e *Migdala*), a place in Pal.:—Magdala.

3094. Μαγδαληνή **Magdalēnē**, *mag-dal-ay-nay';* fem. of a der. of 3093; a female *Magdalene*, i.e. inhab. of Magdala:—Magdalene.

3095. μαγεία **magĕia**, *mag-i'-ah;* from 3096; "*magic*":—sorcery.

3096. μαγεύω **magĕuō**, *mag-yoo'-o;* from 3097; to *practice magic:*—use sorcery.

3097. μάγος **magŏs**, *mag'-os;* of for. or. [7248]; a *Magian*, i.e. Oriental *scientist;* by impl. a *magician:*—sorcerer, wise man.

3098. Μαγώγ **Magōg**, *mag-ogue';* of Heb. or. [4031]; *Magog*, a for. nation, i.e. (fig.) an Antichristian party:—Magog.

3099. Μαδιάν **Madian**, *mad-ee-an';* of Heb. or. [4080]; *Madian* (i.e. *Midian*), a region of Arabia:—Madian.

3100. μαθητεύω **mathētĕuō**, *math-ayt-yoo'-o;* from 3101; intrans. to *become a pupil;* trans. to *disciple*, i.e. enrol as scholar:—be disciple, instruct, teach.

3101. μαθητής **mathētēs**, *math-ay-tes';* from 3129; a *learner*, i.e. *pupil:*—disciple.

3102. μαθήτρια **mathētria**, *math-ay'-tree-ah;* fem. from 3101; a female *pupil:*—disciple.

3103. Μαθουσάλα **Mathŏusala**, *math-oo-sal'-ah;* of Heb. or. [4968]; *Mathusala* (i.e. *Methushelach*), an antediluvian:—Mathusala.

3104. Μαϊνάν **Maïnan**, *mahee-nan';* prob. of Heb. or.; *Maïnan*, an Isr.:—Mainan.

3105. μαίνομαι **mainŏmai**, *mah'ee-nom-ahee;* mid. from a prim. μάω **maō** (to *long* for; through the idea of insensate *craving*); to *rave* as a "maniac":—be beside self (mad).

3106. μακαρίζω **makarizō**, *mak-ar-id'-zo;* from *3107;* to *beatify*, i.e. *pronounce* (or *esteem*) *fortunate:*—call blessed, count happy.

3107. μακάριος **makariŏs**, *mak-ar'-ee-os;* a prol. form of the poetical μάκαρ **makar** (mean. the same); supremely *blest;* by extens. *fortunate, well off:*—blessed, happy (× -ier).

3108. μακαρισμός **makarismŏs**, *mak-ar-is-mos';* from *3106;* *beatification*, i.e. *attribution of good fortune:*—blessedness.

3109. Μακεδονία **Makĕdŏnia**, *mak-ed-on-ee'-ah;* from *3110;* *Macedonia*, a region of Greece:—Macedonia.

3110. Μακεδών **Makĕdōn**, *mak-ed'-ohn;* of uncert. der.; a *Macedon* (*Macedonian*), i.e. inhab. of Macedonia:—of Macedonia, Macedonian.

3111. μάκελλον **makĕllŏn**, *mak'-el-lon;* of Lat. or. [*macellum*]; a *butcher's stall, meat market* or *provision-shop:*—shambles.

3112. μακράν **makran**, *mak-ran';* fem. acc. sing. of *3117* (*3598* being implied); *at a distance* (lit. or fig.):—(a-) far (off), good (great) way off.

3113. μακρόθεν **makrŏthĕn**, *mak-roth'-en;* adv. from *3117;* *from a distance* or *afar:*—afar off, from far.

3114. μακροθυμέω **makrŏthumĕō**, *mak-roth-oo-meh'-o;* from the same as *3116;* *to be long-spirited*, i.e. (obj.) *forbearing* or (subj.) *patient:*—bear (suffer) long, be longsuffering, have (long) patience, be patient, patiently endure.

3115. μακροθυμία **makrŏthumia**, *mak-roth-oo-mee'-ah;* from the same as *3116;* *longanimity*, i.e. (obj.) *forbearance* or (subj.) *fortitude:*—longsuffering, patience.

3116. μακροθυμώς **makrŏthumōs**, *mak-roth-oo-moce';* adv. of a comp. of *3117* and *2372;* *with long* (*enduring*) *temper*, i.e. *leniently:*—patiently.

3117. μακρός **makrŏs**, *mak-ros';* from *3372;* *long* (in place [*distant*] or time [neut. plur.]):—far, long.

3118. μακροχρόνιος **makrŏchrŏniŏs**, *mak-rokh-ron'-ee-os;* from *3117* and *5550;* *long-timed*, i.e. *long-lived:*—live long.

3119. μαλακία **malakia**, *mal-ak-ee'-ah;* from *3120;* *softness*, i.e. *enervation* (*debility*):—disease.

3120. μαλακός **malakŏs**, *mal-ak-os';* of uncert. affin.; *soft*, i.e. *fine* (clothing); fig. a *catamite:*—effeminate, soft.

3121. Μαλελεήλ **Malĕlĕēl**, *mal-el-eh-ale';* of Heb. or [4111]; *Maleleël* (i.e. *Mahalalel*), an antediluvian:—Maleleel.

3122. μάλιστα **malista**, *mal'-is-tah;* neut. plur. of the superl. of an appar. prim. adv. μάλα **mala** (*very*); (adv.) *most* (*in the greatest degree*) or *particularly:*—chiefly, most of all, (e-) specially.

3123. μᾶλλον **mallŏn**, *mal'-lon;* neut. of the compar. of the same as *3122;* (adv.) *more* (*in a greater degree*) or *rather:*— + better, × far, (the) more (and more), (so) much (the more), rather.

3124. Μάλχος **Malchŏs**, *mal'-khos;* of Heb. or. [4429]; *Malchus*, an Isr.:—Malchus.

3125. μάμμη **mammē**, *mam'-may;* of nat. or. ["mammy"]; a *grandmother:*—grandmother.

3126. μαμμωνᾶς **mammōnas**, *mam-mo-nas';* of Chald. or. (*confidence*, i.e. fig. *wealth*, personified); *mammonas*, i.e. *avarice* (deified):—mammon.

3127. Μαναήν **Manaēn**, *man-ah-ane';* of uncert. or.; *Manaën*, a Chr.:—Manaen.

3128. Μανασσῆς **Manassēs**, *man-as-sace';* of Heb. or. [4519]; *Manasses* (i.e. *Menashsheh*), an Isr.:—Manasses.

3129. μανθάνω **manthanō**, *man-than'-o;* prol. from a prim. verb, another form of which, μαθέω **mathĕō**, is used as an alt. in cert. tenses; *to learn* (in any way):—learn, understand.

3130. μανία **mania**, *man-ee'-ah;* from *3105;* *craziness:*—[+ make] × mad.

3131. μάννα **manna**, *man'-nah;* of Heb. or. [4478]; *manna* (i.e. *man*), an edible gum:—manna.

3132. μαντεύομαι **mantĕuŏmai**, *mant-yoo'-om-ahee;* from a der. of *3105* (mean. a *prophet*, as supposed to *rave* through *inspiration*); *to divine*, i.e. *utter spells* (under pretence of foretelling):—by soothsaying.

3133. μαραίνω **marainō**, *mar-ah'ee-no;* of uncert. affin.; *to extinguish* (as fire), i.e. (fig. and pass.) *to pass away:*—fade away.

3134. μαρὰν ἀθά **maran atha**, *mar'-an ath'-ah;* of Chald. or. (mean. *our Lord has come*); *maranatha*, i.e. an exclamation of the approaching *divine judgment:*—Maran-atha.

3135. μαργαρίτης **margaritēs**, *mar-gar-ee'-tace;* from μάργαρος **margarŏs** (a pearl-*oyster*); a *pearl:*—pearl.

3136. Μάρθα **Martha**, *mar'-thah;* prob. of Chald. or. (mean. *mistress*); *Martha*, a Chr. woman:—Martha.

3137. Μαρία **Maria**, *mar-ee'-ah;* or

Μαριάμ **Mariam**, *mar-ee-am';* of Heb. or. [4813]; *Maria* or *Mariam* (i.e. *Mirjam*), the name of six Chr. females:—Mary.

3138. Μάρκος **Markŏs**, *mar'-kos;* of Lat. or.; *Marcus*, a Chr.:—Marcus, Mark.

3139. μάρμαρος **marmarŏs**, *mar'-mar-os;* from μαρμαίρω **marmairō** (to *glisten*); *marble* (as sparkling *white*):—marble.

μάρτυρ **martur**. See *3144*.

3140. μαρτυρέω **marturĕō**, *mar-too-reh'-o;* from *3144;* *to be a witness*, i.e. *testify* (lit. or fig.):—charge, give [*evidence*], bear record, have (obtain, of) good (honest) report, be well reported of, testify, give (have) testimony, (be, bear, give, obtain) witness.

3141. μαρτυρία **marturia**, *mar-too-ree'-ah;* from *3144;* *evidence* given (judicially or gen.):—record, report, testimony, witness.

3142. μαρτύριον **marturiŏn**, *mar-too'-ree-on;* neut. of a presumed der. of *3144;* something *evidential*, i.e. (gen.) *evidence* given or (spec.) the *Decalogue* (in the sacred Tabernacle):—to be testified, testimony, witness.

3143. μαρτύρομαι **marturŏmai**, *mar-too'-rom-ahee;* mid. from *3144;* *to be adduced as a witness*, i.e. (fig.) *to obtest* (in affirmation or exhortation):—take to record, testify.

3144. μάρτυς **martus**, *mar'-toos;* of uncert. affin.; a *witness* (lit. [judicially] or fig. [gen.]); by anal. a "*martyr*":—martyr, record, witness.

3145. μασσάομαι **massaŏmai**, *mas-sah'-om-ahee;* from a prim. μάσσω **massō** (to *handle* or *squeeze*); to *chew:*—gnaw.

3146. μαστιγόω **mastigŏō**, *mas-tig-ŏ'-o;* from *3148;* to *flog* (lit. or fig.):—scourge.

3147. μαστίζω **mastizō**, *mas-tid'-zo;* from *3149;* to *whip* (lit.):—scourge.

3148. μάστιξ **mastix**, *mas'-tix;* prob. from the base of *3145* (through the idea of *contact*); a *whip* (lit. the Roman *flagellum* for criminals; fig. a *disease*):—plague, scourging.

3149. μαστός **mastŏs**, *mas-tos';* from the base of *3145;* a (prop. female) *breast* (as if *kneaded* up):—pap.

3150. ματαιολογία **mataiŏlŏgia**, *mat-ah-yol-og-ee'-ah;* from *3151;* *random talk*, i.e. *babble:*—vain jangling.

3151. ματαιολόγος **mataiŏlŏgŏs**, *mat-ah-yol-og'-os;* from *3152* and *3004;* an *idle* (i.e. *senseless* or *mischievous*) *talker*, i.e. a *wrangler:*—vain talker.

3152. μάταιος **mataiŏs**, *mat'-ah-yos;* from the base of *3155;* *empty*, i.e. (lit.) *profitless*, or (spec.) an *idol:*—vain, vanity.

3153. ματαιότης **mataiŏtēs**, *mat-ah-yot'-ace;* from *3152;* *inutility;* fig. *transientness;* mor. *depravity:*—vanity.

3154. ματαιόω **mataiŏō**, *mat-ah-yŏ'-o;* from *3152;* to *render* (pass. *become*) *foolish*, i.e. (mor.) *wicked* or (spec.) *idolatrous:*—become vain.

3155. μάτην **matēn**, *mat'-ane;* accus. of a der. of the base of *3145* (through the idea of tentative *manipulation*, i.e. unsuccessful *search*, or else of *punishment*); *folly*, i.e. (adv.) *to no purpose:*—in vain.

3156. Ματθαῖος **Matthaiŏs**, *mat-thah'-yos;* a shorter form of *3161;* *Matthæus* (i.e. *Matthitjah*), an Isr. and Chr.:—Matthew.

3157. Ματθάν **Matthan**, *mat-than';* of Heb. or. [4977]; *Matthan* (i.e. *Mattan*), an Isr.:—Matthan.

3158. Ματθάτ **Matthat**, *mat-that';* prob. a shortened form of *3161;* *Matthat* (i.e. *Mattithjah*), the name of two Isr.:—Mathat.

3159. Ματθίας **Matthias**, *mat-thee'-as;* appar. a shortened form of *3161;* *Matthias* (i.e. *Mattithjah*), an Isr.:—Matthias.

3160. Ματταθά **Mattatha**, *mat-tath-ah';* prob. a shortened form of *3161* [comp. 4992]; *Mattatha* (i.e. *Mattithjah*), an Isr.:—Mattatha.

3161. Ματταθίας **Mattathias**, *mat-tath-ee'-as;* of Heb. or. [4993]; *Mattathias* (i.e. *Mattithjah*), an Isr. and Chr.:—Mattathias.

3162. μάχαιρα **machaira**, *makh'-ahee-rah;* prob. fem. of a presumed der. of *3163;* a *knife*, i.e. *dirk;* fig. *war*, judicial *punishment:*—sword.

3163. μάχη **machē**, *makh'-ay;* from *3164;* a *battle*, i.e. (fig.) *controversy:*—fighting, strive, striving.

3164. μάχομαι **machŏmai**, *makh'-om-ahee;* mid. of an appar. prim. verb; to *war*, i.e. (fig.) to *quarrel, dispute:*—fight, strive.

3165. μέ **mĕ**, *meh;* a shorter (and prob. orig.) form of *1691;* *me:*—I, me, my.

3166. μεγαλαυχέω **mĕgalauchĕō**, *meg-al-ŏw-kheh'-o;* from a comp. of *3173* and αὐχέω **auchĕō** (to *boast;* akin to *837* and *2744*); to *talk big*, i.e. *be grandiloquent* (*arrogant, egotistic*):—boast great things.

3167. μεγαλεῖος **mĕgalĕiŏs**, *meg-al-i'-os;* from *3173;* *magnificent*, i.e. (neut. plur. as noun) a conspicuous *favor*, or (subj.) *perfection:*—great things, wonderful works.

3168. μεγαλειότης **mĕgalĕiŏtēs**, *meg-al-i-ot'-ace;* from *3167;* *superbness*, i.e. *glory* or *splendor:*—magnificence, majesty, mighty power.

3169. μεγαλοπρεπής **mĕgalŏprĕpēs**, *meg-al-op-rep-ace';* from *3173* and *4241;* *befitting greatness* or *magnificence* (*majestic*):—excellent.

3170. μεγαλύνω **mĕgalunō**, *meg-al-oo'-no;* from *3173;* to *make* (or *declare*) *great*, i.e. *increase* or (fig.) *extol:*—enlarge, magnify, shew great.

3171. μεγάλως **mĕgalōs**, *meg-al'-oce;* adv. from *3173;* *much:*—greatly.

3172. μεγαλωσύνη **mĕgalōsunē**, *meg-al-o-soo'-nay;* from *3173;* *greatness*, i.e. (fig.) *divinity* (often *God* himself):—majesty.

3173. μέγας **mĕgas**, *meg'-as* [includ. the prol. forms, fem. μεγάλη **mĕgalē**, plur. μεγάλοι **mĕgalŏi**, etc.; comp. also *3176*, *3187*]; *big* (lit. or fig., in a very wide application):—(+ fear) exceedingly, great (-est), high, large, loud, mighty, + (be) sore (afraid), strong, × to years.

3174. μέγεθος **mĕgĕthŏs**, *meg'-eth-os;* from *3173;* *magnitude* (fig.):—greatness.

3175. μεγιστᾶνες **mĕgistanĕs**, *meg-is-tan'-es;* plur. from *3176;* *grandees:*—great men, lords.

3176. μέγιστος **mĕgistŏs**, *meg'-is-tos;* superl. of *3173;* *greatest* or *very great:*—exceeding great.

3177. μεθερμηνεύω **mĕthĕrmēnĕuō**, *meth-er-mane-yoo'-o;* from *3326* and *2059;* to *explain over*, i.e. *translate:*—(by) interpret (-ation).

3178. μέθη **mĕthē**, *meth'-ay;* appar. a prim. word; an *intoxicant*, i.e. (by impl.) *intoxication:*—drunkenness.

3179. μεθίστημι **mĕthistēmi**, *meth-is'-tay-mee;* or (1 Cor. 13 : 2)

μεθιστάνω **mĕthistanō**, *meth-is-tan'-o;* from *3326* and *2476;* to *transfer*, i.e. *carry away, depose* or (fig.) *exchange, seduce:*—put out, remove, translate, turn away.

3180. μεθοδεία **mĕthŏdĕia**, *meth-od-i'-ah;* from a comp. of *3326* and *3593* [comp. "method"]; *travelling over*, i.e. *travesty* (*trickery*):—wile, lie in wait.

3181. μεθόριος **mĕthŏriŏs**, *meth-or'-ee-os;* from *3326* and *3725; bounded alongside*, i.e. *contiguous* (neut. plur. as noun, *frontier*):—border.

3182. μεθύσκω **mĕthuskō**, *meth-oos'-ko;* a prol. (trans.) form of *3184;* to *intoxicate:*—be drunk (-en).

3183. μέθυσος **mĕthusŏs**, *meth'-oo-sos;* from *3184; tipsy*, i.e. (as noun) a *sot:*—drunkard.

3184. μεθύω **mĕthuō**, *meth-oo'-o;* from another form of *3178;* to *drink* to *intoxication*, i.e. *get drunk:*—drink well, make (be) drunk (-en).

3185. μεῖζον **mĕizŏn**, *mide'-zon;* neut. of *3187;* (adv.) in a *greater* degree:—the more.

3186. μειζότερος **mĕizŏtĕrŏs**, *mide-zot'-er-os;* continued compar. of *3187; still larger* (fig.):—greater.

3187. μείζων **mĕizōn**, *mide'-zone;* irreg. compar. of *3173; larger* (lit. or fig., spec. in age):—elder, greater (-est), more.

3188. μέλαν **mĕlan**, *mel'-an;* neut. of *3189* as noun; *ink:*—ink.

3189. μέλας **mĕlas**, *mel'-as;* appar. a prim. word; *black:*—black.

3190. Μελεᾶς **Mĕlĕas**, *mel-eh-as';* of uncert. or.; *Meleas*, an Isr.:—Meleas.

μέλει **mĕlĕi**. See *3199*.

3191. μελετάω **mĕlĕtaō**, *mel-et-ah'-o;* from a presumed der. of *3199;* to *take care of*, i.e. (by impl.) *revolve* in the mind:—imagine, (pre-) meditate.

3192. μέλι **mĕli**, *mel'-ee;* appar. a prim. word; *honey:*—honey.

3193. μελίσσιος **mĕlissiŏs**, *mel-is'-see-os;* from *3192; relating to honey*, i.e. *bee* (comb):—honeycomb.

3194. Μελίτη **Mĕlitē**, *mel-ee'-tay;* of uncert. or.; *Melita*, an island in the Mediterranean:—Melita.

3195. μέλλω **mĕllō**, *mel'-lo;* a strengthened form of *3199* (through the idea of *expectation*); to *intend*, i.e. *be about* to be, do, or suffer something (of persons or things, espec. events; in the sense of *purpose, duty, necessity, probability, possibility*, or *hesitation*):—about, after that, be (almost), (that which is, things, + which was for) to come, intend, was to (be), mean, mind, be at the point, (be) ready, + return, shall (begin), (which, that) should (after, afterwards, hereafter) tarry, which was for, will, would, be yet.

3196. μέλος **mĕlŏs**, *mel'-os;* of uncert. affin.; a *limb* or *part* of the body:—member.

3197. Μελχί **Mĕlchi**, *mel-khee';* of Heb. or. [4428 with pron. suf., *my king*]; *Melchi* (i.e. *Malki*), the name of two Isr.:—Melchi.

3198. Μελχισεδέκ **Mĕlchisĕdĕk**, *mel-khis-ed-ek';* of Heb. or. [4442]; *Melchisedek* (i.e. *Malkitsedek*), a patriarch:—Melchisedec.

3199. μέλω **mĕlō**, *mel'-o;* a prim. verb; to *be of interest* to, i.e. to *concern* (only third pers. sing. pres. indic. used impers. *it matters*):—(take) care.

3200. μεμβράνα **mĕmbrana**, *mem-bran'-ah;* of Lat. or. ("*membrane*"); a (written) sheep-*skin:*—parchment.

3201. μέμφομαι **mĕmphŏmai**, *mem'-fom-ahee;* mid. of an appar. prim. verb; to *blame:*—find fault.

3202. μεμψίμοιρος **mĕmpsimŏirŏs**, *mem-psim'-oy-ros;* from a presumed der. of *3201* and μοῖρα **mŏira** (*fate;* akin to the base of *3313*); *blaming fate*, i.e. *querulous* (*discontented*):—complainer.

3303. μέν **mĕn**, *men;* a prim. particle; prop. indic. of *affirmation* or *concession* (*in fact*); usually followed by a *contrasted* clause with *1161* (*this* one, the *former*, etc.):—even, indeed, so, some, truly, verily. Often compounded with other particles in an *intensive* or *asseverative* sense.

3304. μενοῦνγε **mĕnŏungĕ**, *men-oon'-geh;* from *3303* and *3767* and *1065; so then at least:*—nay but, yea doubtless (rather, verily).

3305. μέντοι **mĕntŏi**, *men'-toy;* from *3303* and *5104; indeed though*, i.e. *however:*—also, but, howbeit, nevertheless, yet.

3306. μένω **mĕnō**, *men'-o;* a prim. verb; to *stay* (in a given place, state, relation or expectancy):—abide, continue, dwell, endure, be present, remain, stand, tarry (for), × thine own.

3307. μερίζω **mĕrizō**, *mer-id'-zo;* from *3313;* to *part*, i.e. (lit.) to *apportion, bestow, share*, or (fig.) to *disunite, differ:*—deal, be difference between, distribute, divide, give part.

3308. μέριμνα **mĕrimna**, *mer'-im-nah;* from *3307* (through the idea of *distraction*); *solicitude:*—care.

3309. μεριμνάω **mĕrimnaō**, *mer-im-nah'-o;* from *3308;* to *be anxious* about:—(be, have) care (-ful), take thought.

3310. μερίς **mĕris**, *mer-ece';* fem. of *3313;* a *portion*, i.e. *province, share* or (abstr.) *participation:*—part (× -akers).

3311. μερισμός **mĕrismŏs**, *mer-is-mos';* from *3307;* a *separation* or *distribution:*—dividing asunder, gift.

3312. μεριστής **mĕristēs**, *mer-is-tace';* from *3307;* an *apportioner* (*administrator*):—divider.

3313. μέρος **mĕrŏs**, *mer'-os;* from an obsol. but more prim. form of μείρομαι **mĕirŏmai** (to *get* as a *section* or *allotment*); a *division* or *share* (lit. or fig., in a wide application):—behalf, coast, course, craft, particular (+ -ly), part (+ -ly), piece, portion, respect, side, some sort (-what).

3314. μεσημβρία **mĕsēmbria**, *mes-ame-bree'-ah;* from *3319* and *2250; midday;* by impl. the *south:*—noon, south.

3315. μεσιτεύω **mĕsitĕuō**, *mes-it-yoo'-o;* from *3316;* to *interpose* (as arbiter), i.e. (by impl.) to *ratify* (as surety):—confirm.

3316. μεσίτης **mĕsitēs**, *mes-ee'-tace;* from *3319;* a *go-between*, i.e. (simply) an *internunciator*, or (by impl.) a *reconciler* (*intercessor*):—mediator.

3317. μεσονύκτιον **mĕsŏnuktiŏn**, *mes-on-ook'-tee-on;* neut. of a comp. of *3319* and *3571; midnight* (espec. as a watch):—midnight.

3318. Μεσοποταμία **Mĕsŏpŏtamia**, *mes-op-ot-am-ee'-ah;* from *3319* and *4215; Mesopotamia* (as lying between the Euphrates and the Tigris; comp. 763), a region of Asia:—Mesopotamia.

3319. μέσος **mĕsŏs**, *mes'-os;* from *3326; middle* (as adj. or [neut.] noun):—among, × before them, between, + forth, mid [-day, -night], midst, way.

3320. μεσότοιχον **mĕsŏtŏichŏn**, *mes-ot'-oy-khon;* from *3319* and *5109;* a *partition* (fig.):—middle wall.

3321. μεσουράνημα **mĕsŏuranēma**, *mes-oo-ran'-ay-mah;* from a presumed comp. of *3319* and *3772; mid-sky:*—midst of heaven.

3322. μεσόω **mĕsŏō**, *mes-ŏ'-o;* from *3319;* to *form* the *middle*, i.e. (in point of time), to *be half-way* over:—be about the midst.

3323. Μεσσίας **Mĕssias**, *mes-see'-as;* of Heb. or. [4899]; the *Messias* (i.e. *Mashiach*), or Christ:—Messias.

3324. μεστός **mĕstŏs**, *mes-tos';* of uncert. der.; *replete* (lit. or fig.):—full.

3325. μεστόω **mĕstŏō**, *mes-tŏ'-o;* from *3324;* to *replenish*, i.e. (by impl.) to *intoxicate:*—fill.

3326. μετά **mĕta**, *met-ah';* a prim. prep. (often used adv.); prop. denoting *accompaniment;* "*amid*" (local or causal); modified variously according to the case (gen. *association*, or acc. *succession*) with which it is joined; occupying an intermediate position between *575* or *1537* and *1519* or *4314;* less intimate than *1722*, and less close than *4862*):—after (-ward), × that he again, against, among, × and, + follow, hence, hereafter, in, of, (up-) on, + our, × and setting, since, (un-) to, + together, when, with (+ -out). Often used in composition, in substantially the same relations of *participation* or *proximity*, and *transfer* or *sequence*.

3327. μεταβαίνω **mĕtabainō**, *met-ab-ah'ee-no;* from *3326* and the base of *939;* to *change place:*—depart, go, pass, remove.

3328. μεταβάλλω **mĕtaballō**, *met-ab-al'-lo;* from *3326* and *906;* to *throw over*, i.e. (mid. fig.) to *turn about* in opinion:—change mind.

3329. μετάγω **mĕtagō**, *met-ag'-o;* from *3326* and *71;* to *lead over*, i.e. *transfer* (*direct*):—turn about.

3330. μεταδίδωμι **mĕtadidōmi**, *met-ad-id'-o-mee;* from *3326* and *1325;* to *give over*, i.e. *share:*—give, impart.

3331. μετάθεσις **mĕtathĕsis**, *met-ath'-es-is;* from *3346; transposition*, i.e. *transferral* (to heaven), *disestablishment* (of a law):—change, removing, translation.

3332. μεταίρω **mĕtairō**, *met-ah'ee-ro;* from *3326* and *142;* to *betake* oneself, i.e. *remove* (locally):—depart.

3333. μετακαλέω **mĕtakalĕō**, *met-ak-al-eh'-o;* from *3326* and *2564;* to *call elsewhere*, i.e. *summon:*—call (for, hither).

3334. μετακινέω **mĕtakinĕō**, *met-ak-ee-neh'-o;* from *3326* and *2795;* to *stir* to a place *elsewhere*, i.e. *remove* (fig.):—move away.

3335. μεταλαμβάνω **mĕtalambanō**, *met-al-am-ban'-o;* from *3326* and *2983;* to *participate;* gen. to *accept* (and use):—eat, have, be partaker, receive, take.

3336. μετάληψις **mĕtalēpsis**, *met-al'-ape-sis;* from *3335; participation:*—taking.

3337. μεταλλάσσω **mĕtallassō**, *met-al-las'-so;* from *3326* and *236;* to *exchange:*—change.

3338. μεταμέλλομαι **mĕtamĕllŏmai**, *met-am-el'-lom-ahee;* from *3326* and the mid. of *3199;* to *care afterwards*, i.e. *regret:*—repent (self).

3339. μεταμορφόω **mĕtamŏrphŏō**, *met-am-or-fŏ'-o;* from *3326* and *3445;* to *transform* (lit. or fig. "metamorphose"):—change, transfigure, transform.

3340. μετανοέω **mĕtanŏĕō**, *met-an-ŏ-eh'-o;* from *3326* and *3539;* to *think differently* or *afterwards*, i.e. *reconsider* (mor. *feel compunction*):—repent.

3341. μετάνοια **mĕtanŏia**, *met-an'-oy-ah;* from *3340;* (subj.) *compunction* (for guilt, includ. *reformation*); by impl. *reversal* (of [another's] decision):—repentance.

3342. μεταξύ **mĕtaxu**, *met-ax-oo';* from *3326* and a form of *4862; betwixt* (of place or person); (of time) as adj. *intervening*, or (by impl.) *adjoining:*—between, mean while, next.

3343. μεταπέμπω **mĕtapĕmpō**, *met-ap-emp'-o;* from *3326* and *3992;* to *send* from *elsewhere*, i.e. (mid.) to *summon* or *invite:*—call (send) for.

3344. μεταστρέφω **mĕtastrĕphō**, *met-as-tref'-o;* from *3326* and *4762;* to *turn across*, i.e. *transmute* or (fig.) *corrupt:*—pervert, turn.

3345. μετασχηματίζω **mĕtaschēmatizō**, *met-askh-ay-mat-id'-zo;* from *3326* and a der. of *4976;* to *transfigure* or *disguise;* fig. to *apply* (by accommodation) :—transfer, transform (self) ; to *change*.

3346. μετατίθημι **mĕtatithēmi**, *met-at-ith'-ay-mee;* from *3326* and *5087;* to *transfer*, i.e. (lit.) *transport*, (by impl.) *exchange*, (reflex.) *change sides*, or (fig.) *pervert:*—carry over, change, remove, translate, turn.

3347. μετέπειτα **mĕtĕpĕita**, *met-ep'-i-tah;* from *3326* and *1899; thereafter:*—afterward.

3348. μετέχω **mĕtĕchō**, *met-ekh'-o;* from *3326* and *2192;* to *share* or *participate;* by impl. *belong* to, *eat* (or *drink*):—be partaker, pertain, take part, use.

3349. μετεωρίζω **mĕtĕōrizō**, *met-eh-o-rid'-zo;* from a comp. of *3326* and a collat. form of *142* or perh. rather of *109* (comp. "meteor"); to *raise in mid-air*, i.e. (fig.) *suspend* (pass. *fluctuate* or *be anxious*):—be of doubtful mind.

3350. μετοικεσία **mĕtŏikĕsia**, *met-oy-kes-ee'-ah;* from a der. of a comp. of *3326* and *3624;* a *change of abode*, i.e. (spec.) *expatriation:*— × brought, carried (-ying) away (in-) to.

3351. μετοικίζω **mĕtŏikizō**, *met-oy-kid'-zo;* from the same as 3350; to *transfer* as a *settler* or *captive*, i.e. *colonize* or *exile*:—carry away, remove into.

3352. μετοχή **mĕtŏchē**, *met-okh-ay';* from 3348; *participation*, i.e. *intercourse*:—fellowship.

3353. μέτοχος **mĕtŏchŏs**, *met'-okh-os;* from 3348; *participant*, i.e. (as noun) a *sharer*; by impl. an *associate*:—fellow, partaker, partner.

3354. μετρέω **mĕtrĕō**, *met-reh'-o;* from 3358; to *measure* (i.e. ascertain in size by a fixed standard); by impl. to *admeasure* (i.e. allot by rule); fig. to *estimate*:—measure, mete.

3355. μετρητής **mĕtrētēs** *met-ray-tace';* from 3354; a *measurer*, i.e. (spec.) a certain standard *measure* of capacity for liquids:—firkin.

3356. μετριοπαθέω **mĕtriŏpathĕō**, *met-ree-op-ath-eh'-o;* from a comp. of the base of 3357 and 3806; to *be moderate in passion*, i.e. *gentle* (to *treat indulgently*):—have compassion.

3357. μετρίως **mĕtriōs**, *met-ree'-oce;* adv. from a der. of 3358; *moderately*, i.e. *slightly*:—a little.

3358. μέτρον **mĕtrŏn**, *met'-ron;* an appar. prim. word; a *measure* ("metre"), lit. or fig.; by impl. a limited *portion* (*degree*):—measure.

3359. μέτωπον **mĕtōpŏn**, *met'-o-pon;* from 3326 and ὤψ **ōps** (the *face*); the *forehead* (as *opposite* the *countenance*):—forehead.

3360. μέχρι **mĕchri**, *mekh'-ree;* or

μεχρίς **mĕchris**, *mekh-ris';* from 3372; *as far as*, i.e. *up to* a certain point (as prep. of extent [denoting the *terminus*, whereas 891 refers espec. to the *space* of time or place intervening] or conj.):—till, (un-) to, until.

3361. μή **mē**, *may;* a prim. particle of qualified *negation* (whereas 3756 expresses an absolute denial); (adv.) *not*, (conj.) *lest*; also (as interrog. implying a *neg.* answer [whereas 3756 expects an *affirm.* one]) *whether*:—any, but (that), × forbear, + God forbid, + lack, lest, neither, never, no (× wise in), none, nor, [can-] not, nothing, that not, un [-taken], without. Often used in compounds in substantially the same relations. See also 3362, 3363, 3364, 3372, 3373, 3375, 3378.

3362. ἐὰν μή **ĕan mē**, *eh-an' may;* i.e. 1437 and 3361; *if not*, i.e. *unless*:— × before, but, except, if no, (if, + whosoever) not.

3363. ἵνα μή **hina mē**, *hin'-ah may;* i.e. 2443 and 3361; *in order* (or *so*) *that not*:—albeit not, lest, that no (-t, [-thing]).

3364. οὐ μή **ŏu mē**, *oo may;* i.e. 3756 and 3361; a double neg. strengthening the denial; *not at all*:—any more, at all, by any (no) means, neither, never, no (at all), in no case (wise), nor ever, not (at all, in any wise). Comp. 3378.

3365. μηδαμῶς **mēdamōs**, *may-dam-oce';* adv. from a comp. of 3361 and ἀμός **amŏs** (*somebody*); *by no means*:—not so.

3366. μηδέ **mēdĕ**, *may-deh';* from 3361 and 1161; *but not, not even*; in a continued negation, *nor*:—neither, nor (yet), (no) not (once, so much as).

3367. μηδείς **mēdĕis**, *may-dice';* includ. the irreg. fem. μηδεμία **mēdĕmia**, *may-dem-ee'-ah*, and the neut. μηδέν **mēdĕn**, *may-den';* from 3361 and 1520; *not even one* (man, woman, thing):—any (man, thing), no (man), none, not (at all, any man, a whit), nothing, + without delay.

3368. μηδέποτε **mēdĕpŏtĕ**, *may-dep'-ot-eh;* from 3366 and 4218; *not even ever*:—never.

3369. μηδέπω **mēdĕpō**, *may-dep'-o;* from 3366 and 4452; *not even yet*:—not yet.

3370. Μῆδος **Mēdŏs**, *may'-dos;* of for. or. [comp. 4074]; a *Median*, or inhab. of Media:—Mede.

3371. μηκέτι **mēkĕti**, *may-ket'-ee;* from 3361 and 2089; *no further*:—any longer, (not) henceforth, hereafter, no henceforward (longer, more, soon), not any more.

3372. μῆκος **mēkŏs**, *may'-kos;* prob. akin to 3173; *length* (lit. or fig.):—length.

3373. μηκύνω **mēkunō**, *may-koo'-no;* from 3372; to *lengthen*, i.e. (mid.) to *enlarge*:—grow up.

3374. μηλωτή **mēlōtē**, *may-lo-tay';* from μῆλον **mēlŏn** (a *sheep*); a *sheep-skin*:—sheepskin.

3375. μήν **mēn**, *mane;* a stronger form of 3303; a particle of affirmation (only with 2229); *assuredly*:— + surely.

3376. μήν **mēn**, *mane;* a prim. word; a *month*:—month.

3377. μηνύω **mēnuō**, *may-noo'-o;* prob. from the same base as 3145 and 3415 (i.e. μάω **maō**, to *strive*); to *disclose* (through the idea of mental *effort* and thus calling to *mind*), i.e. *report, declare, intimate*:—shew, tell.

3378. μὴ οὐκ **mē ŏuk**, *may ook;* i.e. 3361 and 3756; as interrog. and neg. *is it not that?*:—neither (followed by *no*), + never, not. Comp. 3364.

3379. μήποτε **mēpŏtĕ**, *may'-pot-eh;* or

μή ποτε **mē pŏtĕ**, *may pot'-eh;* from 3361 and 4218; *not ever*; also *if* (or *lest*) *ever* (or *perhaps*):—if peradventure, lest (at any time, haply), not at all, whether or not.

3380. μήπω **mēpō**, *may'-po;* from 3361 and 4452; *not yet*:—not yet.

3381. μήπως **mēpōs**, *may'-poce;* or

μή πως **mē pōs**, *may poce;* from 3361 and 4458; *lest somehow*:—lest (by any means, by some means, haply, perhaps).

3382. μηρός **mērŏs**, *may-ros';* perh. a prim. word; a *thigh*:—thigh.

3383. μήτε **mētĕ**, *may'-teh;* from 3361 and 5037; *not too*, i.e. (in continued negation) *neither* or *nor*; also, *not even*:—neither, (n-) or, so much as.

3384. μήτηρ **mētēr**, *may'-tare;* appar. a prim. word; a "*mother*" (lit. or fig., immed. or remote):—mother.

3385. μήτι **mēti**, *may'-tee;* from 3361 and the neut. of 5100; *whether at all*:—not [*the particle usually not expressed, except by the form of the question*].

3386. μήτιγε **mētigĕ**, *may'-tig-eh;* from 3385 and 1065; *not at all then*, i.e. *not to say* (*the rather still*):—how much more.

3387. μήτις **mētis**, *may'-tis;* or

μή τις **mē tis**, *may tis;* from 3361 and 5100; *whether any*:—any [*sometimes unexpressed except by the simple interrogative form of the sentence*].

3388. μήτρα **mētra**, *may'-trah;* from 3384; the *matrix*:—womb.

3389. μητραλῴας **mētralōˌas**, *may-tral-o'-as;* from 3384 and the base of 257; a *mother-thresher*, i.e. *matricide*:—murderer of mothers.

3390. μητρόπολις **mētrŏpŏlis**, *may-trop'-ol-is;* from 3384 and 4172; a *mother city*, i.e. "*metropolis*":—chiefest city.

3391. μία **mia**, *mee'-ah;* irreg. fem. of 1520; *one* or *first*:—a (certain), + agree, first, one, × other.

3392. μιαίνω **miainō**, *me-ah'ee-no;* perh. a prim. verb; to *sully* or *taint*, i.e. *contaminate* (cer. or mor.):—defile.

3393. μίασμα **miasma**, *mee'-as-mah;* from 3392 ("*miasma*"); (mor.) *foulness* (prop. the effect):—pollution.

3394. μιασμός **miasmŏs**, *mee-as-mos';* from 3392; (mor.) *contamination* (prop. the act):—uncleanness.

3395. μίγμα **migma**, *mig'-mah;* from 3396; a *compound*:—mixture.

3396. μίγνυμι **mignumi**, *mig'-noo-mee;* a prim. verb; to *mix*:—mingle.

3397. μικρόν **mikrŏn**, *mik-ron';* masc. or neut. sing. of 3398 (as noun); a *small* space of *time* or *degree*:—a (little) (while).

3398. μικρός **mikrŏs**, *mik-ros';* includ. the comp.

μικρότερος **mikrŏtĕrŏs**, *mik-rot'-er-os;* appar. a prim. word; *small* (in size, quantity, number or (fig.) dignity):—least, less, little, small.

3399. Μίλητος **Milētŏs**, *mil'-ay-tos;* of uncert. or.; *Miletus*, a city of Asia Minor:—Miletus.

3400. μίλιον **miliŏn**, *mil'-ee-on;* of Lat. or.; a *thousand* paces, i.e. a "*mile*":—mile.

3401. μιμέομαι **mimĕŏmai**, *mim-eh'-om-ahee;* mid. from μῖμος **mimŏs** (a "*mimic*"); to *imitate*:—follow.

3402. μιμητής **mimētēs**, *mim-ay-tace';* from 3401; an *imitator*:—follower.

3403. μιμνήσκω **mimnēskō**, *mim-nace'-ko;* a prol. form of 3415 (from which some of the tenses are borrowed); to *remind*, i.e. (mid.) to *recall to mind*:—be mindful, remember.

3404. μισέω **misĕō**, *mis-eh'-o;* from a prim. μῖσος **misŏs** (*hatred*); to *detest* (espec. to *persecute*); by extens. to *love less*:—hate (-ful).

3405. μισθαποδοσία **misthapŏdŏsia**, *mis-thap-od-os-ee'-ah;* from 3406; *requital* (good or bad):—recompence of reward.

3406. μισθαποδότης **misthapŏdŏtēs**, *mis-thap-od-ot'-ace;* from 3409 and 591; a *remunerator*:—rewarder.

3407. μίσθιος **misthiŏs**, *mis'-thee-os;* from 3408; a *wage-earner*:—hired servant.

3408. μισθός **misthŏs**, *mis-thos';* appar. a prim. word; *pay* for service (lit. or fig.), good or bad:—hire, reward, wages.

3409. μισθόω **misthŏō**, *mis-tho'-o;* from 3408; to *let out for wages*, i.e. (mid.) to *hire*:—hire.

3410. μίσθωμα **misthōma**, *mis'-tho-mah;* from 3409; a *rented* building:—hired house.

3411. μισθωτός **misthōtŏs**, *mis-tho-tos';* from 3409; a *wage-worker* (good or bad):—hired servant, hireling.

3412. Μιτυλήνη **Mitulēnē**, *mit-oo-lay'-nay;* for μυτιλήνη **mutilēnē** (*abounding in shell-fish*); *Mitylene* (or *Mytilene*), a town in the island Lesbos:—Mitylene.

3413. Μιχαήλ **Michaēl**, *mikh-ah-ale';* of Heb. or. [4317]; *Michaël*, an archangel:—Michael.

3414. μνᾶ **mna**, *mnah;* of Lat. or.; a *mna* (i.e. *mina*), a certain *weight*:—pound.

3415. μνάομαι **mnaŏmai**, *mnah'-om-ahee;* mid. of a der. of 3306 or perh. of the base of 3145 (through the idea of *fixture* in the mind or of mental *grasp*); to *bear in mind*, i.e. *recollect*; by impl. to *reward* or *punish*:—be mindful, remember, come (have) in remembrance. Comp. 3403.

3416. Μνάσων **Mnasōn**, *mnah'-sohn;* of uncert. or.; *Mnason*, a Chr.:—Mnason.

3417. μνεία **mnĕia**, *mni'-ah;* from 3415 or 3403; *recollection*; by impl. *recital*:—mention, remembrance.

3418. μνῆμα **mnēma**, *mnay'-mah;* from 3415; a *memorial*, i.e. sepulchral *monument* (*burial-place*):—grave, sepulchre, tomb.

3419. μνημεῖον **mnēmĕiŏn**, *mnay-mi'-on;* from 3420; a *remembrance*, i.e. *cenotaph* (*place of interment*):—grave, sepulchre, tomb.

3420. μνήμη **mnēmē**, *mnay'-may;* from 3403; *memory*:—remembrance.

3421. μνημονεύω **mnēmŏnĕuō**, *mnay-mon-yoo'-o;* from a der. of 3420; to *exercise memory*, i.e. *recollect*; by impl. to *punish*; also to *rehearse*:—make mention, be mindful, remember.

3422. μνημόσυνον **mnēmŏsunŏn**, *mnay-mos'-oo-non;* from 3421; a *reminder* (*memorandum*), i.e. *record*:—memorial.

3423. μνηστεύω **mnēstĕuō**, *mnace-tyoo'-o;* from a der. of 3415; to *give a souvenir* (engagement present), i.e. *betroth*:—espouse.

3424. μογιλάλος **mŏgilalŏs**, *mog-il-al'-os;* from 3425 and 2980; *hardly talking*, i.e. *dumb* (*tongue-tied*):—having an impediment in his speech.

3425. μόγις **mŏgis**, *mog'-is;* adv. from a prim. μόγος **mŏgŏs** (*toil*); *with difficulty*:—hardly.

3426. μόδιος **mŏdiŏs**, *mod'-ee-os;* of Lat. or.; a *modius*, i.e. certain measure for things dry (the quantity or the utensil):—bushel.

3427. μοί **mŏi**, *moy;* the simpler form of 1698; to *me*:—I, me, mine, my.

3428. μοιχαλίς **mŏichalis**, *moy-khal-is'*; a prol. form of the fem. of 3432; an *adulteress* (lit. or fig.):—adulteress (-ous, -y).

3429. μοιχάω **mŏichaō**, *moy-khah'-o*; from 3432; (mid.) to *commit adultery*:—commit adultery.

3430. μοιχεία **mŏichĕia**, *moy-khi'-ah*; from 3431; *adultery*:—adultery.

3431. μοιχεύω **mŏichĕuō**, *moy-khyoo'-o*; from 3432; to *commit adultery*:—commit adultery.

3432. μοιχός **mŏichŏs**, *moy-khos'*; perh. a prim. word; a (male) *paramour*; fig. *apostate*:—adulterer.

3433. μόλις **mŏlis**, *mol'-is*; prob. by var. for 3425; *with difficulty*:—hardly, scarce (-ly), + with much work.

3434. Μολόχ **Mŏlŏch**, *mol-okh'*; of Heb. or. [4432]; *Moloch* (i.e. *Molek*), an idol:—Moloch.

3435. μολύνω **mŏlunō**, *mol-oo'-no*; prob. from 3180; to *soil* (fig.):—defile.

3436. μολυσμός **mŏlusmŏs**, *mol-oos-mos'*; from 3435; a *stain*, i.e. (fig.) *immorality*:—filthiness.

3437. μομφή **mŏmphē**, *mom-fay'*; from 3201; *blame*, i.e. (by impl.) a *fault*:—quarrel.

3438. μονή **mŏnē**, *mon-ay'*; from 3306; a *staying*, i.e. *residence* (the act or the place):—abode, mansion.

3439. μονογενής **mŏnŏgĕnēs**, *mon-og-en-ace'*; from 3441 and 1096; *only-born*, i.e. *sole*:—only (begotten, child).

3440. μόνον **mŏnŏn**, *mon'-on*; neut. of 3441 as adv.; *merely*:—alone, but, only.

3441. μόνος **mŏnŏs**, *mon'-os*; prob. from 3306; *remaining*, i.e. *sole* or *single*; by impl. *mere*:—alone, only, by themselves.

3442. μονόφθαλμος **mŏnŏphthalmŏs**, *mon-of'-thal-mos*; from 3441 and 3788; *one-eyed*:—with one eye.

3443. μονόω **mŏnŏō**, *mon-ŏ'-o*; from 3441; to *isolate*, i.e. *bereave*:—be desolate.

3444. μορφή **mŏrphē**, *mor-fay'*; perh. from the base of 3313 (through the idea of *adjustment* of parts); *shape*; fig. *nature*:—form.

3445. μορφόω **mŏrphŏō**, *mor-fŏ'-o*; from the same as 3444; to *fashion* (fig.):—form.

3446. μόρφωσις **mŏrphōsis**, *mor'-fo-sis*; from 3445; *formation*, i.e. (by impl.) *appearance* (*semblance* or [concr.] *formula*):—form.

3447. μοσχοποιέω **mŏschŏpŏiĕō**, *mos-khop-oy-eh'-o*; from 3448 and 4160; to *fabricate* the image of a *bullock*:—make a calf.

3448. μόσχος **mŏschŏs**, *mos'-khos*; prob. strengthened for ὄσχος **ŏschŏs** (a *shoot*); a young *bullock*:—calf.

3449. μόχθος **mŏchthŏs**, *mokh'-thos*; from the base of 3425; *toil*, i.e. (by impl.) *sadness*:—painfulness, travail.

3450. μοῦ **mŏu**, *moo*; the simpler form of 1700; *of me*:—I, me, mine (own), my.

3451. μουσικός **mŏusikŏs**, *moo-sik-os'*; from Μοῦσα **Mŏusa** (a *Muse*); "*musical*", i.e. (as noun) a *minstrel*:—musician.

3452. μυελός **muĕlŏs**, *moo-el-os'*; perh. a prim. word; the *marrow*:—marrow.

3453. μυέω **muĕō**, *moo-eh'-o*; from the base of 3466; to *initiate*, i.e. (by impl.) to *teach*:—instruct.

3454. μῦθος **muthŏs**, *moo'-thos*; perh. from the same as 3453 (through the idea of *tuition*); a *tale*, i.e. *fiction* ("*myth*"):—fable.

3455. μυκάομαι **mukaŏmai**, *moo-kah'-om-ahee*; from a presumed der. of μύζω **muzō** (to "*moo*"); to *bellow* (*roar*):—roar.

3456. μυκτηρίζω **muktērizō**, *mook-tay-rid'-zo*; from a der. of the base of 3455 (mean. *snout*, as that whence *lowing* proceeds); to *make mouths* at, i.e. *ridicule*:—mock.

3457. μυλικός **mulikŏs**, *moo-lee-kos'*; from 3458; *belonging to a mill*:—mill [-stone].

3458. μύλος **mulŏs**, *moo'-los*; prob. ultimately from the base of 3433 (through the idea of *hardship*); a "*mill*", i.e. (by impl.) a *grinder* (*millstone*):—millstone.

3459. μύλων **mulōn**, *moo'-lone*; from 3458; a *mill-house*:—mill.

3460. Μύρα **Mura**, *moo'-rah*; of uncert. der.; *Myra*, a place in Asia Minor:—Myra.

3461. μυριάς **murias**, *moo-ree'-as*; from 3463; a *ten-thousand*; by extens. a "*myriad*" or indefinite number:—ten thousand.

3462. μυρίζω **murizō**, *moo-rid'-zo*; from 3464; to *apply* (perfumed) *unguent* to:—anoint.

3463. μύριοι **muriŏi**, *moo'-ree-oi*; plur. of an appar. prim. word (prop. mean. *very many*); *ten thousand*; by extens. *innumerably* many:—ten thousand.

3464. μύρον **murŏn**, *moo'-ron*; prob. of for. or. [comp. 4753, 4666]; "*myrrh*", i.e. (by impl.) *perfumed oil*:—ointment.

3465. Μυσία **Musia**, *moo-see'-ah*; of uncert. or.; *Mysia*, a region of Asia Minor:—Mysia.

3466. μυστήριον **mustēriŏn**, *moos-tay'-ree-on*; from a der. of μύω **muō** (to *shut* the mouth); a *secret* or "*mystery*" (through the idea of *silence* imposed by *initiation* into religious rites):—mystery.

3467. μυωπάζω **muōpazō**, *moo-ope-ad'-zo*; from a comp. of the base of 3466 and ὤψ **ōps** (the *face*: from 3700); to *shut* the *eyes*, i.e. *blink* (*see indistinctly*):—cannot see afar off.

3468. μώλωψ **mōlōps**, *mo'-lopes*; from μῶλος **mōlŏs** ("*moil*"; prob. akin to the base of 3433) and prob. ὤψ **ōps** (the *face*; from 3700); a *mole* ("black eye") or *blow-mark*:—stripe.

3469. μωμάομαι **mōmaŏmai**, *mo-mah'-om-ahee*; from 3470; to *carp* at, i.e. *censure* (*discredit*):—blame.

3470. μῶμος **mōmŏs**, *mo'-mos*; perh. from 3201; a *flaw* or *blot*, i.e. (fig.) *disgraceful* person:—blemish.

3471. μωραίνω **mōrainō**, *mo-rah'ee-no*; from 3474; to *become insipid*; fig. to *make* (pass. *act*) as a *simpleton*:—become fool, make foolish, lose savour.

3472. μωρία **mōria**, *mo-ree'-ah*; from 3474; *silliness*, i.e. *absurdity*:—foolishness.

3473. μωρολογία **mōrŏlŏgia**, *mo-rol-og-ee'-ah*; from a comp. of 3474 and 3004; *silly talk*, i.e. *buffoonery*:—foolish talking.

3474. μωρός **mōrŏs**, *mo-ros'*; prob. from the base of 3466; *dull* or *stupid* (as if *shut* up), i.e. *heedless*, (mor.) *blockhead*, (appar.) *absurd*:—fool (-ish, × -ishness).

3475. Μωσεύς **Mōsĕus**, *moce-yoos'*; or
Μωσῆς **Mōsēs**, *mo-sace'*; or
Μωϋσῆς **Mōüsēs**, *mo-oo-sace'*; of Heb. or.; [4872]; *Moseus*, *Moses* or *Moüses* (i.e. *Mosheh*), the Heb. lawgiver:—Moses.

N

3476. Ναασσών **Naassōn**, *nah-as-sone'*; of Heb. or. [5177]; *Naasson* (i.e. *Nachshon*), an Isr.:—Naasson.

3477. Ναγγαί **Naggai**, *nang-gah'ee*; prob. of Heb. or. [comp. 5052]; *Nangæ* (i.e. perh. *Nogach*), an Isr.:—Nagge.

3478. Ναζαρέθ **Nazarĕth**, *nad-zar-eth'*; or
Ναζαρέτ **Nazarĕt**, *nad-zar-et'*; of uncert. der.; *Nazareth* or *Nazaret*, a place in Pal.:—Nazareth.

3479. Ναζαρηνός **Nazarēnŏs**, *nad-zar-ay-nos'*; from 3478; a *Nazarene*, i.e. inhab. of Nazareth:—of Nazareth.

3480. Ναζωραῖος **Nazōraiŏs**, *nad-zo-rah'-yos*; from 3478; a *Nazoræan*, i.e. inhab. of Nazareth; by extens. a *Christian*:—Nazarene, of Nazareth.

3481. Ναθάν **Nathan**, *nath-an'*, of Heb. or. [5416]; *Nathan*, an Isr.:—Nathan.

3482. Ναθαναήλ **Nathanaēl**, *nath-an-ah-ale'*; of Heb. or. [5417]; *Nathanaël* (i.e. *Nathanel*), an Isr. and Chr.:—Nathanael.

3483. ναί **nai**, *nahee*; a prim. particle of strong affirmation; *yes*:—even so, surely, truth, verily, yea, yes.

3484. Ναΐν **Naïn**, *nah-in'*; prob. of Heb. or. [comp. 4999]; *Naïn*, a place in Pal.:—Nain.

3485. ναός **naŏs**, *nah-os'*; from a prim. ναίω **naiō** (to *dwell*); a *fane*, *shrine*, *temple*:—shrine, temple. Comp. 2411.

3486. Ναούμ **Naŏum**, *nah-oom'*; of Heb. or. [5151]; *Naüm* (i.e. *Nachum*), an Isr.:—Naum.

3487. νάρδος **nardŏs**, *nar'-dos*; of for. or. [comp. 5373]; "*nard*":—[spike-] nard.

3488. Νάρκισσος **Narkissŏs**, *nar'-kis-sos*; a flower of the same name, from ναρκη **narkē** (*stupefaction*, as a "narcotic"); *Narcissus*, a Roman:—Narcissus.

3489. ναυαγέω **nauagĕō**, *nŏw-ag-eh'-o*; from a comp. of 3491 and 71; to *be shipwrecked* (*stranded*, "navigate"), lit. or fig.:—make (suffer) shipwreck.

3490. ναύκληρος **nauklērŏs**, *nŏw'-klay-ros*; from 3491 and 2819 ("clerk"); a *captain*:—owner of a ship.

3491. ναῦς **naus**, *nŏwce*; from νάω **naō** or νέω **nĕō** (to *float*); a *boat* (of any size):—ship.

3492. ναύτης **nautēs**, *now'-tace*; from 3491; a *boatman*, i.e. *seaman*:—sailor, shipman.

3493. Ναχώρ **Nachōr**, *nakh-ore'*; of Heb. or. [5152]; *Nachor*, the grandfather of Abraham:—Nachor.

3494. νεανίας **nĕanias**, *neh-an-ee'-as*; from a der. of 3501; a *youth* (up to about forty years):—young man.

3495. νεανίσκος **nĕaniskŏs**, *neh-an-is'-kos*; from the same as 3494; a *youth* (under forty):—young man.

3496. Νεάπολις **Nĕapŏlis**, *neh-ap'-ol-is*; from 3501 and 4172; *new town*; *Neäpolis*, a place in Macedonia:—Neapolis.

3497. Νεεμάν **Nĕĕman**, *neh-eh-man'*; of Heb. or. [5283]; *Neëman* (i.e. *Naaman*), a Syrian:—Naaman.

3498. νεκρός **nĕkrŏs**, *nek-ros'*; from an appar. prim. νέκυς **nĕkus** (a *corpse*); *dead* (lit. or fig.; also as noun):—dead.

3499. νεκρόω **nĕkrŏō**, *nek-rŏ'-o*; from 3498; to *deaden*, i.e. (fig.) to *subdue*:—be dead, mortify.

3500. νέκρωσις **nĕkrōsis**, *nek'-ro-sis*; from 3499; *decease*; fig. *impotency*:—deadness, dying.

3501. νέος **nĕŏs**, *neh'-os*; includ. the comp.
νεώτερος **nĕōtĕrŏs**, *neh-o'-ter-os*; a prim. word; "*new*", i.e. (of persons) *youthful*, or (of things) *fresh*; fig. *regenerate*:—new, young.

3502. νεοσσός **nĕŏssŏs**, *neh-os-sos'*; from 3501; a *youngling* (*nestling*):—young.

3503. νεότης **nĕŏtēs**, *neh-ot'-ace*; from 3501; *newness*, i.e. *youthfulness*:—youth.

3504. νεόφυτος **nĕŏphutŏs**, *neh-of'-oo-tos*; from 3501 and a der. of 5453; *newly planted*, i.e. (fig.) a *young convert* ("*neophyte*"):—novice.

3505. Νέρων **Nĕrōn**, *ner'-ohn*; of Lat. or.; *Neron* (i.e. *Nero*), a Rom. emperor:—Nero.

3506. νεύω **nĕuō**, *nyoo'-o*; appar. a prim. verb; to "*nod*", i.e. (by anal.) to *signal*:—beckon.

3507. νεφέλη **nĕphĕlē**, *nef-el'-ay*; from 3509; prop. *cloudiness*, i.e. (concr.) a *cloud*:—cloud.

3508. Νεφθαλείμ **Nĕphthalĕim**, *nef-thal-ime'*; of Heb. or. [5321]; *Nephthaleim* (i.e. *Naphthali*), a tribe in Pal.:—Nephthalim.

3509. νέφος **nĕphŏs**, *nef'-os*; appar. a prim. word; a *cloud*:—cloud.

3510. νεφρός **nĕphrŏs**, *nef-ros'*; of uncert. affin.; a *kidney* (plur.), i.e. (fig.) the inmost *mind*:—reins.

3511. νεωκόρος **nĕōkŏrŏs**, *neh-o-kor'-os*; from a form of 3485 and κορέω **kŏrĕō** (to *sweep*); a *temple-servant*, i.e. (by impl.) a *votary*:—worshipper.

3512. νεωτερικός **nĕōtĕrikŏs**, *neh-o-ter'-ik-os*; from the comp. of 3501; *appertaining to younger* persons, i.e. *juvenile*:—youthful.

νεώτερος **nĕōtĕrŏs**. See 3501.

3513. νή **nē**, *nay*; prob. an intens. form of 3483; a particle of attestation (accompanied by the object invoked or appealed to in confirmation); *as sure as*:—I protest by.

3514. νήθω **nēthō**, *nay'-tho*; from νέω **nĕō** (of like mean.); to *spin*:—spin.

3515. **νηπιάζω nēpiazō**, *nay-pee-ad'-zo;* from *3516;* to *act* as a *babe*, i.e. (fig.) *innocently:*—be a child.

3516. **νήπιος nēpiŏs**, *nay'-pee-os;* from an obsol. particle **νη- nē-** (implying *negation*) and *2031;* *not speaking*, i.e. an *infant* (*minor*); fig. a *simple-minded* person, an *immature* Christian:—babe, child (+ -ish).

3517. **Νηρεύς Nērĕus**, *nare-yoos';* appar. from a der. of the base of *3491* (mean. *wet*); *Nereus*, a Chr.:—Nereus.

3518. **Νηρί Nēri**, *nay-ree';* of Heb. or. [5374]; *Neri* (i.e. *Nerijah*), an Isr.:—Neri.

3519. **νησίον nēsiŏn**, *nay-see'-on;* dimin. of *3520;* an *islet:*—island.

3520. **νῆσος nēsŏs**, *nay'-sos;* prob. from the base of *3491;* an *island:*—island, isle.

3521. **νηστεία nēstĕia**, *nace-ti'-ah;* from *3522;* *abstinence* (from lack of food, or voluntary and religious); spec. the *fast* of the Day of Atonement:—fast (-ing.)

3522. **νηστεύω nēstĕuō**, *nace-tyoo'-o;* from *3523;* to *abstain* from food (religiously):—fast.

3523. **νῆστις nēstis**, *nace'-tis;* from the insep. neg. particle **νη- nē-** (*not*) and *2068;* *not eating*, i.e. *abstinent* from food (religiously):—fasting.

3524. **νηφάλεος nēphalĕŏs**, *nay-fal'-eh-os;* or

νηφάλιος nēphaliŏs, *nay-fal'-ee-os;* from *3525;* *sober*, i.e. (fig.) *circumspect* —sober, vigilant.

3525. **νήφω nēphō**, *nay'-fo;* of uncert. affin.; to *abstain* from wine (*keep sober*), i.e. (fig.) *be discreet:*—be sober, watch.

3526. **Νίγερ Nigĕr**, *neeg'-er;* of Lat. or.; *black; Niger*, a Chr.:—Niger.

3527. **Νικάνωρ Nikanōr**, *nik-an'-ore;* prob. from *3528;* *victorious; Nicanor*, a Chr.:—Nicanor.

3528. **νικάω nikaō**, *nik-ah'-o;* from *3529;* to *subdue* (lit. or fig.):—conquer, overcome, prevail, get the victory.

3529. **νίκη nikē**, *nee'-kay;* appar. a prim. word; *conquest* (abstr.), i.e. (fig.) the *means of success:*—victory.

3530. **Νικόδημος Nikŏdēmŏs**, *nik-od'-ay-mos;* from *3534* and *1218;* *victorious* among his *people; Nicodemus*, an Isr.:—Nicodemus.

3531. **Νικολαΐτης Nikŏlaïtēs**, *nik-ol-ah-ee'-tace;* from *3532;* a *Nicolaïte*, i.e. adherent of *Nicolaüs:*—Nicolaitane.

3532. **Νικόλαος Nikŏlaŏs**, *nik-ol'-ah-os;* from *3534* and *2992;* *victorious* over the *people; Nicolaüs*, a heretic:—Nicolaus.

3533. **Νικόπολις Nikŏpŏlis**, *nik-op'-ol-is;* from *3534* and *4172;* *victorious city; Nicopolis*, a place in Macedonia:—Nicopolis.

3534. **νῖκος nikŏs**, *nee'-kos;* from *3529;* a *conquest* (concr.), i.e. (by impl.) *triumph:*—victory.

3535. **Νινευΐ Ninĕuï**, *nin-yoo-ee';* of Heb. or. [5210]; *Ninevi* (i.e. *Nineveh*), the capital of Assyria:—Nineve.

3536. **Νινευΐτης Ninĕuïtēs**, *nin-yoo-ee'-tace;* from *3535;* a *Ninevite*, i.e. inhab. of Nineveh:—of Nineve, Ninevite.

3537. **νιπτήρ niptēr**, *nip-tare';* from *3538;* a *ewer:*—bason.

3538. **νίπτω niptō**, *nip'-to;* to *cleanse* (espec. the hands or the feet or the face); cer. to *perform ablution:*—wash. Comp. *3068*.

3539. **νοιέω nŏiĕō**, *noy-eh'-o;* from *3563;* to *exercise* the *mind* (*observe*), i.e. (fig.) to *comprehend, heed:*—consider, perceive, think, understand.

3540. **νόημα nŏēma**, *nŏ'-ay-mah;* from *3539;* a *perception*, i.e. *purpose*, or (by impl.) the *intellect, disposition*, itself:—device, mind, thought.

3541. **νόθος nŏthŏs**, *noth'-os;* of uncert. affin.; a *spurious* or *illegitimate* son:—bastard.

3542. **νομή nŏmē**, *nom-ay';* fem. from the same as *3551;* *pasture*, i.e. (the act) *feeding* (fig. *spreading* of a gangrene), or (the food) *pasturage:*— × eat, pasture.

3543. **νομίζω nŏmizō**, *nom-id'-zo;* from *3551;* prop. to *do* by *law* (*usage*), i.e. to *accustom* (pass. *be usual*); by extens. to *deem* or *regard:*—suppose, think, be wont.

3544. **νομικός nŏmikŏs**, *nom-ik-os';* from *3551;* *according* (or *pertaining*) *to law*, i.e. *legal* (cer.); as noun, an *expert in* the (Mosaic) *law:*—about the law, lawyer.

3545. **νομίμως nŏmimŏs**, *nom-im'-oce;* adv. from a der. of *3551;* *legitimately* (spec. agreeably to the rules of the lists):—lawfully.

3546. **νόμισμα nŏmisma**, *nom'-is-mah;* from *3543;* *what is reckoned* as of value (after the Lat. *numisma*), i.e. current *coin:*—money.

3547. **νομοδιδάσκαλος nŏmŏdidaskalŏs**, *nom-od-id-as'-kal-os;* from *3551* and *1320;* an *expounder of* the (Jewish) *law*, i.e. a *Rabbi:*—doctor (teacher) of the law.

3548. **νομοθεσία nŏmŏthĕsia**, *nom-oth-es-ee'-ah;* from *3550;* *legislation* (spec. the *institution of* the Mosaic *code*):—giving of the law.

3549. **νομοθετέω nŏmŏthĕtĕō**, *nom-oth-et-eh'-o;* from *3550;* to *legislate*, i.e. (pass.) to *have* (the Mosaic) *enactments* injoined, *be sanctioned* (by them):—establish, receive the law.

3550. **νομοθέτης nŏmŏthĕtēs**, *nom-oth-et'-ace;* from *3551* and a der. of *5087;* a *legislator:*—lawgiver.

3551. **νόμος nŏmŏs**, *nom'-os;* from a prim. **νέμω nĕmō** (to *parcel* out, espec. *food* or *grazing* to animals); *law* (through the idea of prescriptive *usage*), gen. (*regulation*), spec. (of Moses [includ. the volume]; also of the Gospel), or fig. (a *principle*):—law.

3552. **νοσέω nŏsĕō**, *nos-eh'-o;* from *3554;* to *be sick*, i.e. (by impl. of a diseased appetite) to *hanker* after (fig. to *harp* upon):—dote.

3553. **νόσημα nŏsēma**, *nos'-ay-ma;* from *3552;* an *ailment:*—disease.

3554. **νόσος nŏsŏs**, *nos'-os;* of uncert. affin.; a *malady* (rarely fig. of mor. *disability*):—disease, infirmity, sickness.

3555. **νοσσιά nŏssia**, *nos-see-ah';* from *3502;* a *brood* (of chickens):—brood.

3556. **νοσσίον nŏssiŏn**, *nos-see'-on;* dimin. of *3502;* a *birdling:*—chicken.

3557. **νοσφίζομαι nŏsphizŏmai**, *nos-fid'-zom-ahee;* mid. from **νοσφί nŏsphi** (*apart* or *clandestinely*); to *sequestrate* for oneself, i.e. *embezzle:*—keep back, purloin.

3558. **νότος nŏtŏs**, *not'-os;* of uncert. affin.; the *south* (*-west*) *wind;* by extens. the *southern quarter* itself:—south (wind).

3559. **νουθεσία nŏuthĕsia**, *noo-thes-ee'-ah;* from *3563* and a der. of *5087;* calling *attention* to, i.e. (by impl.) mild *rebuke* or *warning:*—admonition.

3560. **νουθετέω nŏuthĕtĕō**, *noo-thet-eh'-o;* from the same as *3559;* to *put in mind*, i.e. (by impl.) to *caution* or *reprove* gently:—admonish, warn.

3561. **νουμηνία nŏumēnia**, *noo-may-nee'-ah;* fem. of a comp. of *3501* and *3376* (as noun by impl. of *2250*); the festival of *new moon:*—new moon.

3562. **νουνεχῶς nŏunĕchōs**, *noon-ekh-oce';* adv. from a comp. of the acc. of *3563* and *2192;* in a *mind-having* way, i.e. *prudently:*—discreetly.

3563. **νοῦς nŏus**, *nooce;* prob. from the base of *1097;* the *intellect*, i.e. *mind* (divine or human; in thought, feeling, or will); by impl. *meaning:*—mind, understanding. Comp. *5590*.

3564. **Νυμφᾶς Numphas**, *noom-fas';* prob. contr. for a comp. of *3565* and *1435;* *nymph-given* (i.e. *-born*); *Nymphas*, a Chr.:—Nymphas.

3565. **νύμφη numphē**, *noom-fay';* from. a prim. but obsol. verb **νύπτω nuptō** (to *veil* as a bride; comp. Lat. "*nupto*," to *marry*); a young *married* woman (as *veiled*), includ. a *betrothed* girl; by impl. a *son's wife:*—bride, daughter in law.

3566. **νυμφίος numphiŏs**, *noom-fee'-os;* from *3565;* a *bride-groom* (lit. or fig.):—bridegroom.

3567. **νυμφών numphōn**, *noom-fohn';* from *3565;* the *bridal* room:—bridechamber.

3568. **νῦν nun**, *noon;* a prim. particle of present time; "*now*" (as adv. of date, a transition or emphasis); also as noun or adj. *present* or *immediate:*—henceforth, + hereafter, of late, soon, present, this (time). See also *3569*, *3570*.

3569. **τανῦν tanun**, *tan-oon';* or

τὰ νῦν ta nun, *tah noon;* from neut. plur. of *3588* and *3568;* *the* things *now*, i.e. (adv.) *at present:*—(but) now.

3570. **νυνί nuni**, *noo-nee';* a prol. form of *3568* for emphasis; *just now:*—now.

3571. **νύξ nux**, *noox;* a prim. word; "*night*" (lit. or fig.):—(mid-) night.

3572. **νύσσω nussō**, *noos'-so;* appar. a prim. word; to *prick* ("nudge"):—pierce.

3573. **νυστάζω nustazō**, *noos-tad'-zo;* from a presumed der. of *3506;* to *nod*, i.e. (by impl.) to *fall asleep;* fig. to *delay:*—slumber.

3574. **νυχθήμερον nuchthēmĕrŏn**, *nookh-thay'-mer-on;* from *3571* and *2250;* a *day-and-night*, i.e. full *day* of twenty-four hours:—night and day.

3575. **Νῶε Nōĕ**, *no'-eh;* of Heb. or. [5146]; *Noë*, (i.e. *Noäch*), a patriarch:—Noe.

3576. **νωθρός nōthrŏs**, *no-thros';* from a der. of *3541;* *sluggish*, i.e. (lit.) *lazy*, or (fig.) *stupid:*—dull, slothful.

3577. **νῶτος nōtŏs**, *no'-tos;* of uncert. affin.; the *back:*—back.

Ξ

3578. **ξενία xĕnia**, *xen-ee'-ah;* from *3581;* *hospitality*, i.e. (by impl.) a *place of entertainment:*—lodging.

3579. **ξενίζω xĕnizō**, *xen-id'-zo;* from *3581;* to be *a host* (pass. a *guest*); by impl. *be* (*make, appear*) *strange:*—entertain, lodge, (think it) strange.

3580. **ξενοδοχέω xĕnŏdŏchĕō**, *xen-od-okh-eh'-o;* from a comp. of *3581* and *1209;* to *be hospitable:*—lodge strangers.

3581. **ξένος xĕnŏs**, *xen'-os;* appar. a prim. word; *foreign* (lit. *alien*, or fig. *novel*); by impl. a *guest* or (vice-versa) *entertainer:*—host, strange (-r).

3582. **ξέστης xĕstēs**, *xes'-tace;* as if from **ξέω xĕō** (prop. to *smooth;* by impl. [of *friction*] to *boil* or *heat*); a *vessel* (as *fashioned* or for *cooking*) [or perh. by corruption from the Lat. *sextarius*, the *sixth* of a modius, i.e. about a *pint*], i.e. (spec.) a *measure* for liquids or solids, (by anal. a *pitcher*):—pot.

3583. **ξηραίνω xērainō**, *xay-rah'ee-no;* from *3584;* to *desiccate;* by impl. to *shrivel*, to *mature:*—dry up, pine away, be ripe, wither (away).

3584. **ξηρός xērŏs**, *xay-ros';* from the base of *3582* (through the idea of *scorching*); *arid;* by impl. *shrunken, earth* (as opposed to water):—dry, land, withered.

3585. **ξύλινος xulinŏs**, *xoo'-lin-os;* from *3586;* *wooden:*—of wood.

3586. **ξύλον xulŏn**, *xoo'-lon;* from another form of the base of *3582;* *timber* (as fuel or material); by impl. a *stick, club* or *tree* or other wooden article or substance:—staff, stocks, tree, wood.

3587. **ξυράω xuraō**, *xoo-rah'-o;* from a der. of the same as *3586* (mean. a *razor*); to *shave* or "*shear*" the hair:—shave.

O

3588. **ὁ hŏ**, *hŏ;* includ. the fem.

ἡ hē, *hay;* and the neut.

τό tŏ, *tŏ*, in all their inflections; the def. article; *the* (sometimes to be supplied, at others omitted in English idiom):—the, this, that, one, he, she, it, etc.

ὅ hŏ. See *3739*.

3589. **ὀγδοήκοντα ŏgdŏēkŏnta**, *og-dŏ-ay'-kon-tah;* from *3590;* *ten times eight:*—fourscore.

3590. **ὄγδοος ŏgdŏŏs**, *og'-dŏ-os;* from *3638;* the *eighth:*—eighth.

3591. **ὄγκος ŏgkŏs**, *ong'-kos;* prob. from the same as *43;* a *mass* (as *bending* or *bulging* by its load), i.e. *burden* (*hindrance*):—weight.

3592. **ὅδε hŏdĕ**, *hod'-eh;* includ. the fem.
ἥδε hēdĕ, *hay'-deh;* and the neut.
τόδε tŏdĕ, *tod'-e;* from *3588* and *1161;* the *same,* i.e. *this* or *that* one (plur. *these* or *those*); often used as pers. pron.:—he, she, such, these, thus.

3593. **ὁδεύω hŏdĕuō**, *hod-yoo'-o;* from *3598;* to *travel:*—journey.

3594. **ὁδηγέω hŏdēgĕō**, *hod-ayg-eh'-o;* from *3595;* to *show* the *way* (lit. or fig. [*teach*]):—guide, lead.

3595. **ὁδηγός hŏdēgŏs**, *hod-ayg-os';* from *3598* and *2233;* a *conductor* (lit. or fig. [*teacher*]):—guide, leader.

3596. **ὁδοιπορέω hŏdŏipŏrĕō**, *hod-oy-por-eh'-o;* from a comp. of *3598* and *4198;* to *be a wayfarer,* i.e. *travel:*—go on a journey.

3597. **ὁδοιπορία hŏdŏipŏria**, *hod-oy-por-ee'-ah;* from the same as *3596; travel:*—journey (-ing).

3598. **ὁδός hŏdŏs**, *hod-os';* appar. a prim. word; a *road;* by impl. a *progress* (the route, act or distance); fig. a *mode* or *means:*—journey, (high-) way.

3599. **ὀδούς ŏdŏus**, *od-ooce ;* perh. from the base of *2068;* a "*tooth*":—tooth.

3600. **ὀδυνάω ŏdunaō**, *od-oo-nah'-o;* from *3601;* to *grieve:*—sorrow, torment.

3601. **ὀδύνη ŏdunē**, *od-oo'-nay;* from *1416; grief* (as *dejecting*):—sorrow.

3602. **ὀδυρμός ŏdurmŏs**, *od-oor-mos';* from a der. of the base of *1416; moaning,* i.e. *lamentation:*—mourning.

3603. **ὅ ἐστι hŏ esti**, *hŏ es-tee';* from the neut. of *3739* and the third pers. sing. pres. ind. of *1510; which is:*—called, which is (make), that is (to say).

3604. **Ὀζίας Ŏzias**, *od-zee'-as;* of Heb. or. [5818]; *Ozias* (i.e. *Uzzijah*), an Isr.:—Ozias.

3605. **ὄζω ŏzō**, *od'-zo;* a prim. verb (in a strengthened form); to *scent* (usually an ill "odor"):—stink.

3606. **ὅθεν hŏthĕn**, *hoth'-en;* from *3739* with the directive enclitic of source; *from which* place or source or cause (adv. or conj.):—from thence, (from) whence, where (-by, -fore, -upon).

3607. **ὀθόνη ŏthŏnē**, *oth-on'-ay;* of uncert. affin.; a *linen* cloth, i.e. (espec.) a *sail:*—sheet.

3608. **ὀθόνιον ŏthŏniŏn**, *oth-on'-ee-on;* neut. of a presumed der. of *3607;* a linen *bandage:*—linen clothes.

3609. **οἰκεῖος ŏikĕiŏs**, *oy-ki'-os;* from *3624; domestic,* i.e. (as noun), a *relative, adherent:*—(those) of the (his own) house (-hold).

3610. **οἰκέτης ŏikĕtēs**, *oy-ket'-ace;* from *3611;* a fellow *resident,* i.e. menial *domestic:*—(household) servant.

3611. **οἰκέω ŏikĕō**, *oy-keh'-o;* from *3624;* to *occupy a house,* i.e. *reside* (fig. *inhabit, remain, inhere*); by impl. to *cohabit:*—dwell. See also *3625.*

3612. **οἴκημα ŏikēma**, *oy'-kay-mah;* from *3611;* a *tenement,* i.e. (spec.) a *jail:*—prison.

3613. **οἰκητήριον ŏikētēriŏn**, *oy-kay-tay'-ree-on;* neut. of a presumed der. of *3611* (equiv. to *3612*); a *residence* (lit. or fig.):—habitation, house.

3614. **οἰκία ŏikia**, *oy-kee'-ah;* from *3624;* prop. *residence* (abstr.), but usually (concr.) an *abode* (lit. or fig.); by impl. a *family* (espec. *domestics*):—home, house (-hold).

3615. **οἰκιακός ŏikiakŏs**, *oy-kee-ak-os';* from *3614; familiar,* i.e. (as noun) *relatives:*—they (them) of (his own) household.

3616. **οἰκοδεσποτέω ŏikŏdĕspŏtĕō**, *oy-kod-es-pot-eh'-o;* from *3617;* to *be the head of* (i.e. *rule*) a *family:*—guide the house.

3617. **οἰκοδεσπότης ŏikŏdĕspŏtēs**, *oy-kod-es-pot'-ace;* from *3624* and *1203; the head of a family:*—goodman (of the house), householder, master of the house.

3618. **οἰκοδομέω ŏikŏdŏmĕō**, *oy-kod-om-eh'-o;* from the same as *3619;* to *be a house-builder,* i.e. *construct* or (fig.) *confirm:*—(be in) build (-er, -ing, up), edify, embolden.

3619. **οἰκοδομή ŏikŏdŏmē**, *oy-kod-om-ay';* fem. (abstr.) of a comp. of *3624* and the base of *1430; architecture,* i.e. (concr.) a *structure;* fig. *confirmation:*—building, edify (-ication, -ing).

3620. **οἰκοδομία ŏikŏdŏmia**, *oy-kod-om-ee'-ah;* from the same as *3619; confirmation:*—edifying.

3621. **οἰκονομέω ŏikŏnŏmĕō**, *oy-kon-om-eh'-o;* from *3623;* to *manage* (a house, i.e. an estate):—be steward.

3622. **οἰκονομία ŏikŏnŏmia**, *oy-kon-om-ee'-ah;* from *3623; administration* (of a household or estate); spec. a (religious) "*economy*":—dispensation, stewardship.

3623. **οἰκονόμος ŏikŏnŏmŏs**, *oy-kon-om'-os;* from *3624* and the base of *3551;* a *house-distributor* (i.e. *manager*), or *overseer,* i.e. an employee in that capacity; by extens. a fiscal *agent* (*treasurer*); fig. a *preacher* (of the Gospel):—chamberlain, governor, steward.

3624. **οἶκος ŏikŏs**, *oy'-kos;* of uncert. affin.; a *dwelling* (more or less extensive, lit. or fig.); by impl. a *family* (more or less related, lit. or fig.):—home, house (-hold), temple.

3625. **οἰκουμένη ŏikŏumĕnē**, *oy-kou-men'-ay;* fem. part. pres. pass. of *3611* (as noun, by impl. of *1093*); *land,* i.e. the (terrene part of the) *globe;* spec. the Roman *empire:*—earth, world.

3626. **οἰκουρός ŏikŏurŏs**, *oy-koo-ros';* from *3624* and **οὖρος ŏurŏs** (a *guard;* be "ware"); a *stayer at home,* i.e. *domestically inclined* (a "good housekeeper"):—keeper at home.

3627. **οἰκτείρω ŏiktĕirō**, *oyk-ti'-ro;* also (in certain tenses) prol.
οἰκτερέω ŏiktĕrĕō, *oyk-ter-eh'-o;* from **οἶκτος ŏiktŏs** (*pity*); to *exercise pity:*—have compassion on.

3628. **οἰκτιρμός ŏiktirmŏs**, *oyk-tir-mos';* from *3627; pity:*—mercy.

3629. **οἰκτίρμων ŏiktirmōn**, *oyk-tir'-mone;* from *3627; compassionate:*—merciful, of tender mercy.
οἶμαι ŏimai. See *3633.*

3630. **οἰνοπότης ŏinŏpŏtēs**, *oy-nop-ot'-ace;* from *3631* and a der. of the alt. of *4095;* a *tippler:*—winebibber.

3631. **οἶνος ŏinŏs**, *oy'-nos;* a prim. word (or perh. of Heb. or. [3196]); "*wine*" (lit. or fig.):—wine.

3632. **οἰνοφλυγία ŏinŏphlugia**, *oy-nof-loog-ee'-ah;* from *3631* and a form of the base of *5397;* an *overflow* (or surplus) of *wine,* i.e. *vinolency* (*drunkenness*):—excess of wine.

3633. **οἴομαι ŏiŏmai**, *oy'-om-ahee;* or (shorter)
οἶμαι ŏimai, *oy'-mahee;* mid. appar. from *3634;* to *make like* (oneself), i.e. *imagine* (*be of the opinion*):—suppose, think.

3634. **οἷος hŏiŏs**, *hoy'-os;* prob. akin to *3588, 3739,* and *3745; such* or *what sort* of (as a correl. or exclamation); espec. the neut. (adv.) with neg. not *so:*—so (as), such as, what (manner of), which.
οἴω ŏiō. See *5342.*

3635. **ὀκνέω ŏknĕō**, *ok-neh'-o;* from **ὄκνος ŏknŏs** (*hesitation*); to *be slow* (fig. *loath*):—delay.

3636. **ὀκνηρός ŏknērŏs**, *ok-nay-ros';* from *3635; tardy,* i.e. *indolent;* (fig.) *irksome:*—grievous, slothful.

3637. **ὀκταήμερος ŏktaēmĕrŏs**, *ok-tah-ay'-mer-os;* from *3638* and *2250;* an *eight-day* old person or act:—the eighth day.

3638. **ὀκτώ ŏktō**, *ok-to';* a prim. numeral; "*eight*":—eight.

3639. **ὄλεθρος ŏlĕthrŏs**, *ol'-eth-ros;* from a prim. **ὄλλυμι ŏllumi** (to *destroy;* a prol. form); *ruin,* i.e. *death, punishment:*—destruction.

3640. **ὀλιγόπιστος ŏligŏpistŏs**, *ol-ig-op'-is-tos;* from *3641* and *4102; incredulous,* i.e. *lacking confidence* (in Christ):—of little faith.

3641. **ὀλίγος ŏligŏs**, *ol-ee'-gos;* of uncert. affin.; *puny* (in extent, degree, number, duration or value); espec. neut. (adv.) *somewhat:*— + almost, brief [-ly], few, (a) little, + long, a season, short, small, a while.

3642. **ὀλιγόψυχος ŏligŏpsuchŏs**, *ol-ig-op'-soo-khos;* from *3641* and *5590; little-spirited,* i.e. *faint-hearted:*—feebleminded.

3643. **ὀλιγωρέω ŏligōrĕō**, *ol-ig-o-reh'-o;* from a comp. of *3641* and **ὥρα ōra** ("*care*"); to *have little regard* for, i.e. to *disesteem:*—despise.

3644. **ὀλοθρευτής ŏlŏthrĕutēs**, *ol-oth-ryoo-tace';* from *3645;* a *ruiner,* i.e. (spec.) a venomous *serpent:*—destroyer.

3645. **ὀλοθρεύω ŏlŏthrĕuō**, *ol-oth-ryoo'-o;* from *3639;* to *spoil,* i.e. *slay:*—destroy.

3646. **ὁλοκαύτωμα hŏlŏkautōma**, *hol-ok-ow'-to-mah;* from a der. of a comp. of *3650* and a der. of *2545;* a *wholly-consumed* sacrifice ("holocaust"):—(whole) burnt offering.

3647. **ὁλοκληρία hŏlŏklēria**, *hol-ok-lay-ree'-ah;* from *3648; integrity,* i.e. physical *wholeness:*—perfect soundness.

3648. **ὁλόκληρος hŏlŏklērŏs**, *hol-ok'-lay-ros;* from *3650* and *2819; complete* in every *part,* i.e. perfectly *sound* (in body):—entire, whole.

3649. **ὀλολύζω ŏlŏluzō**, *ol-ol-ood'-zo;* a redupl. prim. verb; to "*howl*" or "*halloo*", i.e. *shriek:*—howl.

3650. **ὅλος hŏlŏs**, *hol'-os;* a prim. word; "*whole*" or "*all*", i.e. *complete* (in extent, amount, time or degree), espec. (neut.) as noun or adv.:—all, altogether, every whit, + throughout, whole.

3651. **ὁλοτελής hŏlŏtĕlēs**, *hol-ot-el-ace';* from *3650* and *5056; complete* to the *end,* i.e. *absolutely perfect:*—wholly.

3652. **Ὀλυμπᾶς Olumpas**, *ol-oom-pas';* prob. a contr. from **Ὀλυμπιόδωρος Olumpiŏdōrŏs** (*Olympian-bestowed,* i.e. *heaven-descended*); *Olympas,* a Chr.:—Olympas.

3653. **ὄλυνθος ŏlunthŏs**, *ol'-oon-thos;* of uncert. der.; an *unripe* (because out of season) *fig:*—untimely fig.

3654. **ὅλως hŏlōs**, *hol'-oce;* adv. from *3650; completely,* i.e. *altogether;* (by anal.) *everywhere;* (neg.) not *by any means:*—at all, commonly, utterly.

3655. **ὄμβρος ŏmbrŏs**, *om'-bros;* of uncert. affin.; a thunder *storm:*—shower.

3656. **ὁμιλέω hŏmilĕō**, *hom-il-eh'-o;* from *3658;* to *be in company* with, i.e. (by impl.) to *converse:*—commune, talk.

3657. **ὁμιλία hŏmilia**, *hom-il-ee'-ah;* from *3658; companionship* ("homily"), i.e. (by impl.) *intercourse:*—communication.

3658. **ὅμιλος hŏmilŏs**, *hom'-il-os;* from the base of *3674* and a der. of the alt. of *138* (mean. a *crowd*); *association together,* i.e. a *multitude:*—company.

3659. **ὄμμα ŏmma**, *om'-mah;* from *3700;* a *sight,* i.e. (by impl.) the *eye:*—eye.

3660. **ὀμνύω ŏmnuō**, *om-noo'-o;* a prol. form of a prim. but obsol. **ὄμω ŏmō**, for which another prol. form (**ὀμόω ŏmŏō**, *om-ŏ'-o*) is used in certain tenses; to *swear,* i.e. *take* (or *declare on*) *oath:*—swear.

3661. **ὁμοθυμαδόν hŏmŏthumadŏn**, *hom-oth-oo-mad-on';* adv. from a comp. of the base of *3674* and *2372; unanimously:*—with one accord (mind).

3662. **ὁμοιάζω hŏmŏiazō**, *hom-oy-ad'-zo;* from *3664;* to *resemble:*—agree.

3663. **ὁμοιοπαθής hŏmŏiŏpathēs**, *hom-oy-op-ath-ace';* from *3664* and the alt. of *3958; similarly affected:*—of (subject to) like passions.

3664. **ὅμοιος hŏmŏiŏs**, *hom'-oy-os;* from the base of *3674; similar* (in appearance or character):—like, + manner.

3665. **ὁμοιότης hŏmŏiŏtēs**, *hom-oy-ot'-ace;* from *3664; resemblance:*—like as, similitude.

3666. **ὁμοιόω hŏmŏiŏō**, *hom-oy-ŏ'-o;* from *3664;* to *assimilate,* i.e. *compare;* pass. to *become similar:*—be (make) like, (in the) liken (-ess), resemble.

3667. **ὁμοίωμα hŏmŏiōma**, *hom-oy'-o-mah;* from *3666;* a *form;* abstr. *resemblance:*—made like to, likeness, shape, similitude.

3668. ὁμοίως **hŏmŏiōs**, *hom-oy'-oce;* adv. from *3664; similarly:*—likewise, so.

3669. ὁμοίωσις **hŏmŏiōsis**, *hom-oy'-o-sis;* from *3666; assimilation,* i.e. *resemblance:*—similitude.

3670. ὁμολογέω **hŏmŏlŏgĕō**, *hom-ol-og-eh'-o;* from a comp. of the base of *3674* and *3056;* to *assent,* i.e. *covenant, acknowledge:*—con- (pro-) fess, confession is made, give thanks, promise.

3671. ὁμολογία **hŏmŏlŏgia**, *hom-ol-og-ee'-ah;* from the same as *3670; acknowledgment:*—con- (pro-) fession, professed.

3672. ὁμολογουμένως **hŏmŏlŏgŏumĕnōs**, *hom-ol-og-ow-men'-oce;* adv. of pres. pass. part. of *3670; confessedly:*—without controversy.

3673. ὁμότεχνος **hŏmŏtĕchnŏs**, *hom-ot'-ekh-nos;* from the base of *3674* and *5078;* a *fellow-artificer:*—of the same craft.

3674. ὁμοῦ **hŏmŏu**, *hom-oo';* gen. of ὁμός **hŏmŏs** (the *same;* akin to *260*) as adv.; *at the same* place or time:—together.

3675. ὁμόφρων **hŏmŏphrōn**, *hom-of'-rone;* from the base of *3674* and *5424; like-minded,* i.e. *harmonious:*—of one mind.

ὁμόω **ŏmŏō**. See *3660.*

3676. ὅμως **hŏmōs**, *hom'-oce;* adv. from the base of *3674; at* the *same* time, i.e. (conj.) *notwithstanding, yet still:*—and even, nevertheless, though but.

3677. ὄναρ **ŏnar**, *on'-ar;* of uncert. der.; a *dream:*—dream.

3678. ὀνάριον **ŏnariŏn**, *on-ar'-ee-on;* neut. of a presumed der. of *3688;* a *little ass:*—young ass.

ὀνάω **ŏnaō**. See *3685.*

3679. ὀνειδίζω **ŏnĕidizō**, *on-i-did'-zo;* from *3681;* to *defame,* i.e. *rail at, chide, taunt:*—cast in teeth, (suffer) reproach, revile, upbraid.

3680. ὀνειδισμός **ŏnĕidismŏs**, *on-i-dis-mos';* from *3679; contumely:*—reproach.

3681. ὄνειδος **ŏnĕidŏs**, *on'-i-dos;* prob. akin to the base of *3686; notoriety,* i.e. a *taunt* (*disgrace*):—reproach.

3682. Ὀνήσιμος **Ŏnēsimŏs**, *on-ay'-sim-os;* from *3685; profitable; Onesimus,* a Chr.:—Onesimus.

3683. Ὀνησίφορος **Ŏnēsiphŏrŏs**, *on-ay-sif'-or-os;* from a der. of *3685* and *5411; profit-bearer; Onesiphorus,* a Chr.:—Onesiphorus.

3684. ὀνικός **ŏnikŏs**, *on-ik-os';* from *3688; belonging to an ass,* i.e. *large* (so as to be turned by an ass):—millstone.

3685. ὀνίνημι **ŏninēmi**, *on-in'-ay-mee;* a prol. form of an appar. prim. verb

(ὄνομαι **ŏnŏmai**, to *slur*); for which another prol. form (ὀνάω **ŏnaō**) is used as an alt. in some tenses [unless indeed it be identical with the base of *3686* through the idea of *notoriety*]; to *gratify,* i.e. (mid.) to *derive pleasure* or *advantage* from:—have joy.

3686. ὄνομα **ŏnŏma**, *on'-om-ah;* from a presumed der. of the base of *1097* (comp. *3685*); a "*name*" (lit. or fig.) [*authority, character*]:—called, (+ sur-) name (-d).

3687. ὀνομάζω **ŏnŏmazō**, *on-om-ad'-zo;* from *3686;* to *name,* i.e. *assign an appellation;* by extens. to *utter, mention, profess:*—call, name.

3688. ὄνος **ŏnŏs**, *on'-os;* appar. a prim. word; a *donkey:*—ass.

3689. ὄντως **ŏntōs**, *on'-toce;* adv. of the oblique cases of *5607; really:*—certainly, clean, indeed, of a truth, verily.

3690. ὄξος **ŏxŏs**, *ox'-os;* from *3691; vinegar,* i.e. *sour* wine:—vinegar.

3691. ὀξύς **ŏxus**, *ox-oos';* prob. akin to the base of *188* ["*acid*"]; *keen;* by anal. *rapid:*—sharp, swift.

3692. ὀπή **ŏpē**, *op-ay';* prob. from *3700;* a *hole* (as if for light), i.e. *cavern;* by anal. a *spring* (of water):—cave, place.

3693. ὄπισθεν **ŏpisthĕn**, *op'-is-then;* from ὄπις **ŏpis** (*regard;* from *3700*) with enclitic of source; *from the rear* (as a secure *aspect*), i.e. *at the back* (adv. and prep. of place or time):—after, backside, behind.

3694. ὀπίσω **ŏpisō**, *op-is'-o;* from the same as *3693* with enclitic of direction; *to the back,* i.e. *aback* (as adv. or prep. of time or place; or as noun):—after, back (-ward), (+ get) behind, + follow.

3695. ὁπλίζω **hŏplizō**, *hop-lid'-zo;* from *3696;* to *equip* (with weapons [mid. and fig.]):—arm self.

3696. ὅπλον **hŏplŏn**, *hop'-lon;* prob. from a prim. ἕπω **hĕpō** (to be *busy* about); an *implement* or *utensil* or *tool* (lit. or fig., espec. offensive for war):—armour, instrument, weapon.

3697. ὁποῖος **hŏpŏiŏs**, *hop-oy'-os;* from *3739* and *4169;* of *what* kind *that,* i.e. *how* (*as*) *great* (*excellent*) (spec. as indef. correl. to anteced. def. *5108* of quality):—what manner (sort) of, such as, whatsoever.

3698. ὁπότε **hŏpŏtĕ**, *hop-ot'-eh;* from *3739* and *4218; what* (-ever) *then,* i.e. (of time) *as soon as:*—when.

3699. ὅπου **hŏpŏu**, *hop'-oo;* from *3739* and *4225; what* (-ever) *where,* i.e. *at whichever* spot:—in what place, where (-as, -soever), whither (+ soever).

3700. ὀπτάνομαι **ŏptanŏmai**, *op-tan'-om-ahee;* a (mid.) prol. form of the prim. (mid.)

ὄπτομαι **ŏptŏmai**, *op'-tom-ahee,* which is used for it in certain tenses; and both as alt. of *3708;* to *gaze* (i.e. with wide-open eyes, as at something remarkable; and thus differing from *991,* which denotes simply *voluntary* observation; and from *1492,* which expresses merely mechanical, passive or casual vision; while *2300,* and still more emphatically its intens. *2334,* signifies an earnest but more continued *inspection;* and *4648* a watching *from a distance*):—appear, look, see, shew self.

3701. ὀπτασία **ŏptasia**, *op-tas-ee'-ah;* from a presumed der. of *3700; visuality,* i.e. (concr.) an *apparition:*—vision.

ὄπτομαι **ŏptŏmai**. See *3700.*

3702. ὀπτός **ŏptŏs**, *op-tos';* from an obsol. verb akin to ἕψω **hĕpsō** (to "*steep*"); *cooked,* i.e. *roasted:*—broiled.

3703. ὀπώρα **ŏpōra**, *op-o'-rah;* appar. from the base of *3796* and *5610;* prop. *even-tide* of the (summer) season (*dog-days*), i.e. (by impl.) *ripe* fruit:—fruit.

3704. ὅπως **hŏpōs**, *hop'-oce;* from *3739* and *4459; what* (-ever) *how,* i.e. *in the manner that* (as adv. or conj. of coincidence, intentional or actual):—because, how, (so) that, to, when.

3705. ὅραμα **hŏrama**, *hor'-am-ah;* from *3708; something gazed at,* i.e. a *spectacle* (espec. supernat.):—sight, vision.

3706. ὅρασις **hŏrasis**, *hor'-as-is;* from *3708;* the act of *gazing,* i.e. (external) an *aspect* or (intern.) an inspired *appearance:*—sight, vision.

3707. ὁρατός **hŏratŏs**, *hor-at-os';* from *3708; gazed at,* i.e. (by impl.) *capable of being seen:*—visible.

3708. ὁράω **hŏraō**, *hor-ah'-o;* prop. to *stare* at [comp. *3700*], i.e. (by impl.) to *discern* clearly (phys. or ment.); by extens. to *attend* to; by Hebr. to *experience;* pass. to *appear:*—behold, perceive, see, take heed.

3709. ὀργή **ŏrgē**, *or-gay';* from *3713;* prop. *desire* (as a *reaching* forth or *excitement* of the mind), i.e. (by anal.) violent *passion* (*ire,* or [justifiable] *abhorrence*); by impl. *punishment:*—anger, indignation, vengeance, wrath.

3710. ὀργίζω **ŏrgizō**, *or-gid'-zo;* from *3709;* to *provoke* or *enrage,* i.e. (pass.) *become exasperated:*—be angry (wroth).

3711. ὀργίλος **ŏrgilŏs**, *org-ee'-los;* from *3709; irascible:*—soon angry.

3712. ὀργυιά **ŏrguia**, *org-wee-ah';* from *3713;* a *stretch* of the arms, i.e. a *fathom:*—fathom.

3713. ὀρέγομαι **ŏrĕgŏmai**, *or-eg'-om-ahee;* mid. of appar. a prol. form of an obsol. prim. [comp. *3735*]; to *stretch* oneself, i.e. *reach* out after (*long* for):—covet after, desire.

3714. ὀρεινός **ŏrĕinŏs**, *or-i-nos';* from *3735; mountainous,* i.e. (fem. by impl. of *5561*) the *Highlands* (of Judæa):—hill country.

3715. ὄρεξις **ŏrĕxis**, *or'-ex-is;* from *3713; excitement* of the mind, i.e. *longing* after:—lust.

3716. ὀρθοποδέω **ŏrthŏpŏdĕō**, *or-thop-od-eh'-o;* from a comp. of *3717* and *4228;* to *be straight-footed,* i.e. (fig.) to *go directly* forward:—walk uprightly.

3717. ὀρθός **ŏrthŏs**, *or-thos';* prob. from the base of *3735; right* (as *rising*), i.e. (perpendicularly) *erect* (fig. *honest*), or (horizontally) *level* or *direct:*—straight, upright.

3718. ὀρθοτομέω **ŏrthŏtŏmĕō**, *or-thot-om-eh'-o;* from a comp. of *3717* and the base of *5114;* to *make a straight cut,* i.e. (fig.) to *dissect* (*expound*) *correctly* (the divine message):—rightly divide.

3719. ὀρθρίζω **ŏrthrizō**, *or-thrid'-zo;* from *3722,* to *use* the *dawn,* i.e. (by impl.) to *repair betimes:*—come early in the morning.

3720. ὀρθρινός **ŏrthrinŏs**, *or-thrin-os';* from *3722; relating to the dawn,* i.e. *matutinal* (as an epithet of Venus, espec. brilliant in the early day):—morning.

3721. ὄρθριος **ŏrthriŏs**, *or'-three-os;* from *3722; in the dawn,* i.e. up *at day-break:*—early.

3722. ὄρθρος **ŏrthrŏs**, *or'-thros;* from the same as *3735; dawn* (as *sun-rise, rising* of light); by extens. *morn:*—early in the morning.

3723. ὀρθῶς **ŏrthōs**, *or-thoce';* adv. from *3717; in a straight* manner, i.e. (fig.) *correctly* (also mor.):—plain, right (-ly).

3724. ὁρίζω **hŏrizō**, *hor-id'-zo;* from *3725;* to *mark* out or *bound* ("horizon"), i.e. (fig.) to *appoint, decree, specify:*—declare, determine, limit, ordain.

3725. ὅριον **hŏriŏn**, *hor'-ee-on;* neut. of a der. of an appar. prim. ὅρος **hŏrŏs** (a *bound* or *limit*); a *boundary*-line, i.e. (by impl.) a *frontier* (*region*):—border, coast.

3726. ὁρκίζω **hŏrkizō**, *hor-kid'-zo;* from *3727;* to *put on oath,* i.e. *make swear;* by anal. to solemnly *enjoin:*—adjure, charge.

3727. ὅρκος **hŏrkŏs**, *hor'-kos;* from ἕρκος **hĕrkŏs** (a *fence;* perh. akin to *3725*); a *limit,* i.e. (sacred) *restraint* (spec. *oath*):—oath.

3728. ὁρκωμοσία **hŏrkōmŏsia**, *hor-ko-mos-ee'-ah;* from a comp. of *3727* and a der. of *3660; asseveration on oath:*—oath.

3729. ὁρμάω **hŏrmaō**, *hor-mah'-o;* from *3730;* to *start, spur* or *urge* on, i.e. (reflex.) to *dash* or *plunge:*—run (violently), rush.

3730. ὁρμή **hŏrmē**, *hor-may';* of uncert. affin.; a violent *impulse,* i.e. *onset:*—assault.

3731. ὅρμημα **hŏrmēma**, *hor'-may-mah;* from *3730;* an *attack,* i.e. (abstr.) *precipitancy:*—violence.

3732. ὄρνεον **ŏrnĕŏn**, *or'-neh-on;* neut. of a presumed der. of *3733;* a *birdling:*—bird, fowl.

3733. ὄρνις **ŏrnis**, *or'-nis;* prob. from a prol. form of the base of *3735;* a *bird* (as *rising* in the air), i.e. (spec.) a *hen* (or female domestic fowl):—hen.

3734. ὁροθεσία **hŏrŏthĕsia**, *hor-oth-es-ee'-ah;* from a comp. of the base of *3725* and a der. of *5087;* a *limit-placing,* i.e. (concr.) *boundary-line:*—bound.

3735. ὄρος **ŏrŏs**, *or'-os;* prob. from an obsol. ὄρω **ŏrō** (to *rise* or "*rear*"; perh. akin to *142;* comp. *3733*); a *mountain* (as *lifting* itself above the plain):—hill, mount (-ain).

3736. ὀρύσσω **ŏrussō**, *or-oos'-so;* appar. a prim. verb; to "*burrow*" in the ground, i.e. *dig:*—dig.

3737. ὀρφανός **ŏrphanŏs**, *or-fan-os';* of uncert. affin.; *bereaved* ("*orphan*"), i.e. *parentless:*—comfortless, fatherless.

3738. ὀρχέομαι **ŏrchĕŏmai**, *or-kheh'-om-ahee;* mid. from ὄρχος **ŏrchŏs** (a *row* or *ring*); to *dance* (from the *ranklike* or *regular* motion):—dance.

3739. ὅς **hŏs**, *hos;* includ. fem.

ἥ **hē**, *hay;* and neut.

ὅ **hŏ**, *hŏ;* prob. a prim. word (or perh. a form of the art. *3588*); the rel. (sometimes demonstrative) pron., *who, which, what, that:*—one, (an-, the) other, some, that, what, which, who (-m, -se), etc. See also *3757.*

3740. **ὁσάκις hŏsakis**, *hos-ak'-is;* multiple adv. from *3739;* *how* (i.e. with *302*, *so*) *many times* as:—as oft (-en) as.

3741. **ὅσιος hŏsiŏs**, *hos'-ee-os;* of uncert. affin.; prop. *right* (by intrinsic or divine character; thus distinguished from *1342*, which refers rather to *human* statutes and relations; from *2413*, which denotes formal *consecration;* and from *40*, which relates to *purity* from defilement), i.e. *hallowed* (*pious, sacred, sure*):—holy, mercy, shalt be.

3742. **ὁσιότης hŏsiŏtēs**, *hos-ee-ot'-ace;* from *3741;* *piety:*—holiness.

3743. **ὁσίως hŏsiōs**, *hos-ee-oce';* adv. from *3741;* *piously:*—holily.

3744. **ὀσμή ŏsmē**, *os-may';* from *3605;* *fragrance* (lit. or fig.):—odour, savour.

3745. **ὅσος hŏsŏs**, *hos'-os;* by redupl. from *3739;* *as* (*much, great, long*, etc.) *as:*—all (that), as (long, many, much) (as), how great (many, much), [in-] asmuch as, so many as, that (ever), the more, those things, what (great, -soever), wheresoever, wherewithsoever, which, × while, who (-soever).

3746. **ὅσπερ hŏspĕr**, *hos'-per;* from *3739* and *4007;* *who especially:*—whomsoever.

3747. **ὀστέον ŏstĕŏn**, *os-teh'-on;* or contr.

ὀστοῦν ŏstŏun, *os-toon';* of uncert. affin.; a *bone:*—bone.

3748. **ὅστις hŏstis**, *hos'-tis;* includ. the fem.

ἥτις hētis, *hay'-tis;* and the neut.

ὅ,τι hŏ,ti, *hot'-ee;* from *3739* and *5100;* *which some*, i.e. *any that;* also (def.) *which same:*—× and (they), (such) as, (they) that, in that they, what (-soever), whereas ye, (they) which, who (-soever). Comp. *3754*.

3749. **ὀστράκινος ŏstrakinŏs**, *os-tra'-kin-os;* from **ὄστρακον ŏstrakŏn** ["oyster"] (a *tile*, i.e. *terra cotta*); *earthen*-ware, i.e. *clayey;* by impl. *frail:*—of earth, earthen.

3750. **ὄσφρησις ŏsphrēsis**, *os'-fray-sis;* from a der. of *3605;* *smell* (the sense):—smelling.

3751. **ὀσφύς ŏsphus**, *os-foos';* of uncert. affin.; the *loin* (extern.), i.e. the *hip;* intern. (by extens.) *procreative power:*—loin.

3752. **ὅταν hŏtan**, *hot'-an;* from *3753* and *302;* *whenever* (implying *hypothesis* or more or less *uncertainty*); also caus. (conj.) *inasmuch as:*—as long (soon) as, that, + till, when (-soever), while.

3753. **ὅτε hŏtĕ**, *hot'-eh;* from *3739* and *5037;* at *which* (thing) *too*, i.e. *when:*—after (that), as soon as, that, when, while.

ὅ,τε hŏ,tĕ, *hŏ,t'-eh;* also fem.

ἥ,τε hē,tĕ, *hay'-teh;* and neut.

τό,τε tŏ,tĕ, *tot'-eh;* simply the art. *3588* followed by *5037;* so written (in some editions) to distinguish them from *3752* and *5119*.

3754. **ὅτι hŏti**, *hot'-ee;* neut. of *3748* as conj.; demonst. *that* (sometimes redundant); caus. *because:*—as concerning that, as though, because (that), for (that), how (that), (in) that, though, why.

3755. **ὅτου hŏtŏu**, *hot'-oo;* for the gen. of *3748* (as adv.); during *which same* time, i.e. *whilst:*—whiles.

3756. **οὐ ŏu**, *oo;* also (before a vowel)

οὐκ ŏuk, *ook;* and (before an aspirate)

οὐχ ŏuch, *ookh;* a prim. word; the absol. neg. [comp. *3361*] adv.; *no* or *not:*—+ long, nay, neither, never, no (× man), none, [can-] not, + nothing, + special, un ([-worthy]), when, + without, + yet but. See also *3364*, *3372*.

3757. **οὗ hŏu**, *hoo;* gen. of *3739* as adv.; at *which* place, i.e. *where:*—where (-in), whither ([-soever]).

3758. **οὐά ŏua**, *oo-ah';* a prim. exclamation of surprise; "*ah*":—ah.

3759. **οὐαί ŏuai**, *oo-ah'ee;* a prim. exclamation of grief: "*woe*":—alas, woe.

3760. **οὐδαμῶς ŏudamōs**, *oo-dam-oce';* adv. from (the fem.) of *3762;* *by no means:*—not.

3761. **οὐδέ ŏudĕ**, *oo-deh';* from *3756* and *1161;* *not however*, i.e. *neither, nor, not even:*—neither (indeed), never, no (more, nor, not), nor (yet), (also, even, then) not (even, so much as), + nothing, so much as.

3762. **οὐδείς ŏudĕis**, *oo-dice';* includ. fem.

οὐδεμία ŏudĕmia, *oo-dem-ee'-ah;* and neut.

οὐδέν ŏudĕn, *oo-den';* from *3761* and *1520;* *not even one* (man, woman or thing), i.e. *none, nobody, nothing:*—any (man), aught, man, neither any (thing), never (man), no (man), none (+ of these things), not (any, at all, -thing), nought.

3763. **οὐδέποτε ŏudĕpŏtĕ**, *oo-dep'-ot-eh;* from *3761* and *4218;* *not even at any time*, i.e. *never at all:*—neither at any time, never, nothing at any time.

3764. **οὐδέπω ŏudĕpō**, *oo-dep'-o;* from *3761* and *4452;* *not even yet:*—as yet not, never before (yet), (not) yet.

3765. **οὐκέτι ŏukĕti**, *ook-et'-ee;* also (separately)

οὐκ ἔτι ŏuk ĕti, *ook et'-ee;* from *3756* and *2089;* *not yet, no longer:*—after that (not), (not) any more, henceforth (hereafter) not, no longer (more), not as yet (now), now no more (not), yet (not).

3766. **οὐκοῦν ŏukŏun**, *ook-oon';* from *3756* and *3767;* is it *not therefore* that, i.e. (affirm.) *hence* or *so:*—then.

3767. **οὖν ŏun**, *oon;* appar. a prim. word; (adv.) *certainly*, or (conj.) *accordingly:*—and (so, truly), but, now (then), so (likewise then), then, therefore, verily, wherefore.

3768. **οὔπω ŏupō**, *oo'-po;* from *3756* and *4452;* *not yet:*—hitherto not, (no . . .) as yet, not yet.

3769. **οὐρά ŏura**, *oo-rah';* appar. a prim. word; a *tail:*—tail.

3770. **οὐράνιος ŏuraniŏs**, *oo-ran'-ee-os;* from *3772;* *celestial*, i.e. *belonging to* or *coming from* the *sky:*—heavenly.

3771. **οὐρανόθεν ŏuranŏthĕn**, *oo-ran-oth'-en;* from *3772* and the enclitic of source; *from the sky:*—from heaven.

3772. **οὐρανός ŏuranŏs**, *oo-ran-os';* perh. from the same as *3735* (through the idea of *elevation*); the *sky;* by extens. *heaven* (as the abode of God); by impl. *happiness, power, eternity;* spec. the *Gospel* (*Christianity*):—air, heaven ([-ly]), sky.

3773. **Οὐρβανός Ŏurbanŏs**, *oor-ban-os';* of Lat. or.; *Urbanus* (*of the city*, "*urbane*"), a Chr.:—Urbanus.

3774. **Οὐρίας Ŏurias**, *oo-ree'-as;* of Heb. or. [223]; *Urias* (i.e. *Urijah*), a Hittite:—Urias.

3775. **οὖς ŏus**, *ooce;* appar. a prim. word; the *ear* (phys. or ment.):—ear.

3776. **οὐσία ŏusia**, *oo-see'-ah;* from the fem. of *5607;* *substance*, i.e. *property* (*possessions*):—goods, substance.

3777. **οὔτε ŏutĕ**, *oo'-teh;* from *3756* and *5037;* *not too*, i.e. *neither* or *nor;* by anal. *not even:*—neither, none, nor (yet), (no, yet) not, nothing.

3778. **οὗτος hŏutŏs**, *hoo'-tos;* includ. nom. masc. plur.

οὗτοι hŏutŏi, *hoo'-toy;* nom. fem. sing.

αὕτη hautē, *hŏw'-tay;* and nom. fem. plur.

αὗται hautai, *hŏw'-tahee;* from the art. *3588* and *846;* *the he* (*she* or it), i.e. *this* or *that* (often with art. repeated):—he (it was that), hereof, it, she, such as, the same, these, they, this (man, same, woman), which, who.

3779. **οὕτω hŏutō**, *hoo'-to;* or (before a vowel)

οὕτως hŏutōs, *hoo'-toce;* adv. from *3778;* *in this way* (referring to what precedes or follows):—after that, after (in) this manner, as, even (so), for all that, like (-wise), no more, on this fashion (-wise), so (in like manner), thus, what.

3780. **οὐχί ŏuchi**, *oo-khee';* intens. of *3756;* *not indeed:*—nay, not.

3781. **ὀφειλέτης ŏphĕilĕtēs**, *of-i-let'-ace;* from *3784;* an *ower*, i.e. person *indebted;* fig. a *delinquent;* mor. a *transgressor* (against God):—debtor, which owed, sinner.

3782. **ὀφειλή ŏphĕilē**, *of-i-lay';* from *3784;* *indebtedness*, i.e. (concr.) a *sum* owed; fig. *obligation*, i.e. (conjugal) *duty:*—debt, due.

3783. **ὀφείλημα ŏphĕilēma**, *of-i'-lay-mah;* from (the alt. of) *3784;* *something owed*, i.e. (fig.) a *due;* mor. a *fault:*—debt.

3784. **ὀφείλω ŏphĕilō**, *of-i'-lo;* or (in cert. tenses) its prol. form

ὀφειλέω ŏphĕilĕō, *of-i-leh'-o;* prob. from the base of *3786* (through the idea of *accruing*); to *owe* (pecuniarily); fig. to *be under obligation* (*ought, must, should*); mor. to *fail* in duty:—behove, be bound, (be) debt (-or), (be) due (-ty), be guilty (indebted), (must) need (-s), ought, owe, should. See also *3785*.

3785. **ὄφελον ŏphĕlŏn**, *of'-el-on;* first pers. sing. of a past tense of *3784;* *I ought* (*wish*), i.e. (interj.) *oh that!:*—would (to God.)

3786. **ὄφελος ŏphĕlŏs**, *of'-el-os;* from **ὀφέλλω ŏphĕllō** (to *heap* up, i.e. *accumulate* or *benefit*); *gain:*—advantageth, profit.

3787. **ὀφθαλμοδουλεία ŏphthalmŏdŏulĕia**, *of-thal-mod-oo-li'-ah;* from *3788* and *1397;* *sight-labor*, i.e. that needs watching (*remissness*):—eye-service.

3788. **ὀφθαλμός ŏphthalmŏs**, *of-thal-mos';* from *3700;* the *eye* (lit. or fig.); by impl. *vision;* fig. *envy* (from the jealous side-glance):—eye, sight.

3789. **ὄφις ŏphis**, *of'-is;* prob. from *3700* (through the idea of *sharpness* of vision); a *snake*, fig. (as a type of sly cunning) an artful *malicious* person, espec. *Satan:*—serpent.

3790. **ὀφρύς ŏphrus**, *of-roos';* perh. from *3700* (through the idea of the shading or proximity to the organ of *vision*); the eye-"*brow*" or *forehead*, i.e. (fig.) the *brink* of a precipice:—brow.

3791. **ὀχλέω ŏchlĕō**, *okh-leh'-o;* from *3793;* to *mob*, i.e. (by impl.) to *harass:*—vex.

3792. **ὀχλοποιέω ŏchlŏpŏiĕō**, *okh-lop-oy-eh'-o;* from *3793* and *4160;* to *make a crowd*, i.e. *raise a public disturbance:*—gather a company.

3793. **ὄχλος ŏchlŏs**, *okh'-los;* from a der. of *2192* (mean. a *vehicle*); a *throng* (as *borne* along); by impl. the *rabble;* by extens. a *class* of people; fig. a *riot:*—company, multitude, number (of people), people, press.

3794. **ὀχύρωμα ŏchurōma**, *okh-oo'-ro-mah;* from a remote der. of *2192* (mean. to *fortify*, through the idea of *holding* safely); a *castle* (fig. *argument*):—stronghold.

3795. **ὀψάριον ŏpsariŏn**, *op-sar'-ee-on;* neut. of a presumed der. of the base of *3702;* a *relish* to other food (as if cooked *sauce*), i.e. (spec.) *fish* (presumably salted and dried as a condiment):—fish.

3796. **ὀψέ ŏpsĕ**, *op-seh';* from the same as *3694* (through the idea of *backwardness*); (adv.) *late* in the day; by extens. *after the close* of the *day:*—(at) even, in the end.

3797. **ὄψιμος ŏpsimŏs**, *op'-sim-os;* from *3796;* *later*, i.e. *vernal* (showering):—latter.

3798. **ὄψιος ŏpsiŏs**, *op'-see-os;* from *3796;* *late;* fem. (as noun) *afternoon* (early eve) or *nightfall* (later eve):—even (-ing, [-tide]).

3799. **ὄψις ŏpsis**, *op'-sis;* from *3700;* prop. *sight* (the act), i.e. (by impl.) the *visage*, an external *show:*—appearance, countenance, face.

3800. **ὀψώνιον ŏpsōniŏn**, *op-so'-nee-on;* neut. of a presumed der. of the same as *3795;* *rations* for a soldier, i.e. (by extens.) his *stipend* or *pay:*—wages.

3801. **ὁ ὢν καὶ ὁ ἦν καὶ ὁ ἐρχόμενος hŏ ōn kai hŏ ēn kai hŏ ĕrchŏmĕnŏs**, *hŏ own kahee hŏ ane kahee hŏ er-khom'-en-os;* a phrase combining *3588* with the pres. part. and imperf. of *1510* and the pres. part. of *2064* by means of *2532;* *the one being and the* one that *was and the* one *coming*, i.e. *the Eternal*, as a divine epithet of Christ:—which art (is, was), and (which) wast (is, was), and art (is) to come (shalt be).

Π

3802. **παγιδεύω pagidĕuō**, *pag-id-yoo'-o;* from *3803;* to *ensnare* (fig.):—entangle.

3803. **παγίς pagis**, *pag-ece';* from *4078;* a *trap*

(as *fastened* by a noose or notch); **fig.** a *trick* or *stratagem* (*temptation*):—snare.

Πάγος Pagŏs. See *697*.

3804. **πάθημα pathēma**, *path'-ay-mah;* from a presumed der. of *3806;* something *undergone*, i.e. *hardship* or *pain;* subj. an *emotion* or *influence:*—affection, affliction, motion, suffering.

3805. **παθητός pathētŏs**, *path-ay-tos';* from the same as *3804;* *liable* (i.e. *doomed*) *to experience pain:*—suffer.

3806. **πάθος pathŏs**, *path'-os;* from the alt. of *3958;* prop. *suffering* ("*pathos*"), i.e. (subj.) a *passion* (espec. *concupiscence*):—(inordinate) affection, lust.

πάθω pathō. See *3958*.

3807. **παιδαγωγός paidagōgŏs**, *pahee-dag-o-gos';* from *3816* and a redupl. form of *71;* a *boy-leader*, i.e. a servant whose office it was to take the children to school; (by impl. [fig.] a *tutor* ["*pædagogue*"]):—instructor, schoolmaster.

3808. **παιδάριον paidariŏn**, *pahee-dar'-ee-on;* neut. of a presumed der. of *3816;* a *little boy:*—child, lad.

3809. **παιδεία paidĕia**, *pahee-di'-ah;* from *3811;* *tutorage*, i.e. *education* or *training;* by impl. disciplinary *correction:*—chastening, chastisement, instruction, nurture.

3810. **παιδευτής paidĕutēs**, *pahee-dyoo-tace';* from *3811;* a *trainer*, i.e. *teacher* or (by impl.) *discipliner:*—which corrected, instructor.

3811. **παιδεύω paidĕuō**, *pahee-dyoo'-o;* from *3816;* to *train* up a child, i.e. *educate*, or (by impl.) *discipline* (by punishment):—chasten (-ise), instruct, learn, teach.

3812. **παιδιόθεν paidiŏthĕn**, *pahee-dee-oth'-en;* adv. (of *source*) from *3813;* *from infancy:*—of a child.

3813. **παιδίον paidiŏn**, *pahee-dee'-on;* neut. dimin. of *3816;* a *childling* (of either sex), i.e. (prop.) an infant, or (by extens.) a half-grown *boy* or girl; fig. an *immature* Christian:—(little, young) child, damsel.

3814. **παιδίσκη paidiskē**, *pahee-dis'-kay;* fem. dimin. of *3816;* a *girl*, i.e. (spec.) a *female slave* or *servant:*—bondmaid (-woman), damsel, maid (-en).

3815. **παίζω paizō**, *paheed'-zo;* from *3816;* to *sport* (as a boy):—play.

3816. **παῖς pais**, *paheece;* perh. from *3817;* a *boy* (as often *beaten* with impunity), or (by anal.) a *girl*, and (gen.) a *child;* spec. a *slave* or *servant* (espec. a *minister* to a king; and by eminence to God):—child, maid (-en), (man) servant, son, young man.

3817. **παίω paiō**, *pah'-yo;* a prim. verb; to *hit* (as if by a single blow and less violently than *5180*); spec. to *sting* (as a scorpion):—smite, strike.

3818. **Πακατιανή Pakatianē**, *pak-at-ee-an-ay';* fem. of an adj. of uncert. der.; *Pacatianian*, a section of Phrygia:—Pacatiana.

3819. **πάλαι palai**, *pal'-ahee;* prob. another form for *3825* (through the idea of *retrocession*); (adv.) *formerly*, or (by rel.) *sometime since;* (ellipt. as adj.) *ancient:*—any while, a great while ago, (of) old, in time past.

3820. **παλαιός palaiŏs**, *pal-ah-yos';* from *3819;* *antique*, i.e. *not recent, worn out:*—old.

3821. **παλαιότης palaiŏtēs**, *pal-ah-yot'-ace;* from *3820;* *antiquatedness:*—oldness.

3822. **παλαιόω palaiŏō**, *pal-ah-yŏ'-o;* from *3820;* to *make* (pass. *become*) *worn out*, or *declare obsolete:*—decay, make (wax) old.

3823. **πάλη palē**, *pal'-ay;* from **πάλλω pallō** (to *vibrate;* another form for *906*); *wrestling:*—+ wrestle.

3824. **παλιγγενεσία paliggĕnĕsia**, *pal-ing-ghen-es-ee'-ah;* from *3825* and *1078;* (spiritual) *rebirth* (the state or the act), i.e. (fig.) spiritual *renovation;* spec. Messianic *restoration:*—regeneration.

3825. **πάλιν palin**, *pal'-in;* prob. from the same as *3823* (through the idea of *oscillatory* repetition); (adv.) *anew*, i.e. (of place) *back*, (of time) *once more*, or (conj.) *furthermore* or *on the other hand:*—again.

3826. **παμπληθεί pamplēthĕi**, *pam-play-thi';* dat. (adv.) of a comp. of *3956* and *4128;* *in full multitude*, i.e. *concertedly* or *simultaneously:*—all at once.

3827. **πάμπολυς pampŏlus**, *pam -pol-ooce;* from *3956* and *4183;* *full many*, i.e. *immense:*—very great.

3828. **Παμφυλία Pamphulia**, *pam-fool-ee'-ah;* from a comp. of *3956* and *5443;* *every-tribal*, i.e. *heterogeneous* (*5561* being impl.); *Pamphylia*, a region of Asia Minor:—Pamphylia.

3829. **πανδοχεῖον pandŏchĕiŏn**, *pan-dokh-i'-on;* neut. of a presumed comp. of *3956* and a der. of *1209;* *all-receptive*, i.e. a public *lodging*-place (*caravanserai* or *khan*):—inn.

3830. **πανδοχεύς pandŏchĕus**, *pan-dokh-yoos';* from the same as *3829;* an *innkeeper* (*warden of a caravanserai*):—host.

3831. **πανήγυρις panēguris**, *pan-ay'-goo-ris;* from *3956* and a der. of *58;* a *mass-meeting*, i.e. (fig.) *universal companionship:*—general assembly.

3832. **πανοικί panŏiki**, *pan-oy-kee';* adv. from *3956* and *3624;* *with* the *whole family:*—with all his house.

3833. **πανοπλία panŏplia**, *pan-op-lee'-ah;* from a comp. of *3956* and *3696;* *full armor* ("*panoply*"):—all (whole) armour.

3834. **πανουργία panŏurgia**, *pan-oorg-ee'-ah;* from *3835;* *adroitness*, i.e. (in a bad sense) *trickery* or *sophistry:*—(cunning) craftiness, subtilty.

3835. **πανοῦργος panŏurgŏs**, *pan-oor'-gos;* from *3956* and *2041;* *all-working*, i.e. *adroit* (*shrewd*):—crafty.

3836. **πανταχόθεν pantachŏthĕn**, *pan-takh-oth'-en;* adv. (of *source*) from *3837;* *from all* directions:—from every quarter.

3837. **πανταχοῦ pantachŏu**, *pan-takh-oo';* gen. (as adv. of *place*) of a presumed der. of *3956;* *universally:*—in all places, everywhere.

3838. **παντελής pantĕlēs**, *pan-tel-ace';* from *3956* and *5056;* *full-ended*, i.e. *entire* (neut. as noun, *completion*):—+ in [no] wise, uttermost.

3839. **πάντη pantē**, *pan'-tay;* adv. (of *manner*) from *3956;* *wholly:*—always.

3840. **πάντοθεν pantŏthĕn**, *pan-toth'-en;* adv. (of *source*) from *3956;* *from* (i.e. *on*) *all* sides:—on every side, round about.

3841. **παντοκράτωρ pantŏkratōr**, *pan-tok-rat'-ore;* from *3956* and *2904;* the *all-ruling*, i.e. *God* (as absolute and universal *sovereign*):—Almighty, Omnipotent.

3842. **πάντοτε pantŏtĕ**, *pan'-tot-eh;* from *3956* and *3753;* *every when*, i.e. *at all* times:—alway (-s), ever (-more).

3843. **πάντως pantōs**, *pan'-toce;* adv. from *3956;* *entirely;* spec. *at all events*, (with neg. following) *in* no *event:*—by all means, altogether, at all, needs, no doubt, in [no] wise, surely.

3844. **παρά para**, *par-ah';* a prim. prep.; prop. *near*, i.e. (with gen.) *from beside* (lit. or fig.), (with dat.) *at* (or *in*) the *vicinity* of (obj. or subj.), (with acc.) to the *proximity* with (local [espec. *beyond* or *opposed* to] or causal [*on account* of]):—above, against, among, at, before, by, contrary to, × friend, from, + give [such things as they], + that [she] had, × his, in, more than, nigh unto, (out) of, past, save, side . . . by, in the sight of, than, [there-] fore, with. In compounds it retains the same variety of application.

3845. **παραβαίνω parabainō**, *par-ab-ah'ee-no;* from *3844* and the base of *939;* to *go contrary to*, i.e. *violate* a command:—(by) transgress (-ion).

3846. **παραβάλλω paraballō**, *par-ab-al'-lo;* from *3844* and *906;* to *throw alongside*, i.e. (reflex.) to *reach* a place, or (fig.) to *liken:*—arrive, compare.

3847. **παράβασις parabasis**, *par-ab'-as-is;* from *3845;* *violation:*—breaking, transgression.

3848. **παραβάτης parabatēs**, *par-ab-at'-ace;* from *3845;* a *violator:*—breaker, transgress (-or).

3849. **παραβιάζομαι parabiazŏmai**, *par-ab-ee-ad'-zom-ahee;* from *3844* and the mid. of *971;* to *force contrary* to (nature), i.e. *compel* (by entreaty):—constrain.

3850. **παραβολή parabŏlē**, *par-ab-ol-ay';* from *3846;* a *similitude* ("*parable*"), i.e. (symbol.) *fictitious narrative* (of common life conveying a moral), *apothegm* or *adage:*—comparison, figure, parable, proverb.

3851. **παραβουλεύομαι parabŏulĕuŏmai**, *par-ab-ool-yoo'-om-ahee;* from *3844* and the mid. of *1011;* to *misconsult*, i.e. *disregard:*—not (to) regard (-ing).

3852. **παραγγελία paraggĕlia**, *par-ang-gel-ee'-ah;* from *3853;* a *mandate:*—charge, command.

3853. **παραγγέλλω paraggĕllō**, *par-ang-gel'-lo;* from *3844* and the base of *32;* to *transmit a message*, i.e. (by impl.) to *enjoin:*—(give in) charge, (give) command (-ment), declare.

3854. **παραγίνομαι paraginŏmai**, *par-ag-in'-om-ahee;* from *3844* and *1096;* to *become near*, i.e. *approach* (*have arrived*); by impl. to *appear* publicly:—come, go, be present.

3855. **παράγω paragō**, *par-ag'-o;* from *3844* and *71;* to *lead near*, i.e. (reflex. or intrans.) to *go along* or *away:*—depart, pass (away, by, forth).

3856. **παραδειγματίζω paradĕigmatizō**, *par-ad-igue-mat-id'-zo;* from *3844* and *1165;* to *show alongside* (the public), i.e. *expose to infamy:*—make a public example, put to an open shame.

3857. **παράδεισος paradĕisŏs**, *par-ad'-i-sos;* of Oriental or. [comp. 6508]; a *park*, i.e. (spec.) an *Eden* (place of future happiness, "*paradise*"):—paradise.

3858. **παραδέχομαι paradĕchŏmai**, *par-ad-ekh'-om-ahee;* from *3844* and *1209;* to *accept near*, i.e. *admit* or (by impl.) *delight* in:—receive.

3859. **παραδιατριβή paradiatribē**, *par-ad-ee-at-ree-bay';* from a comp. of *3844* and *1304;* *misemployment*, i.e. *meddlesomeness:*—perverse disputing.

3860. **παραδίδωμι paradidōmi**, *par-ad-id'-o-mee;* from *3844* and *1325;* to *surrender*, i.e. *yield up, intrust, transmit:*—betray, bring forth, cast, commit, deliver (up), give (over, up), hazard, put in prison, recommend.

3861. **παράδοξος paradŏxŏs**, *par-ad'-ox-os;* from *3844* and *1391* (in the sense of *seeming*); *contrary to expectation*, i.e. *extraordinary* ("*paradox*"):—strange.

3862. **παράδοσις paradŏsis**, *par-ad'-os-is;* from *3860;* *transmission*, i.e. (concr.) a *precept;* spec. the Jewish *traditionary law:*—ordinance, tradition.

3863. **παραζηλόω parazēlŏō**, *par-ad-zay-lŏ'-o;* from *3844* and *2206;* to *stimulate alongside*, i.e. *excite to rivalry:*—provoke to emulation (jealousy).

3864. **παραθαλάσσιος parathalassiŏs**, *par-ath-al-as'-see-os;* from *3844* and *2281;* *along* the *sea*, i.e. *maritime* (*lacustrine*):—upon the sea coast.

3865. **παραθεωρέω parathĕōrĕō**, *par-ath-eh-o reh'-o;* from *3844* and *2334;* to *overlook* or *disregard:*—neglect.

3866. **παραθήκη parathēkē**, *par-ath-ay'-kay;* from *3908;* a *deposit*, i.e. (fig.) *trust:*—committed unto.

3867. **παραινέω parainĕō**, *par-ahee-neh'-o;* from *3844* and *134;* to *mispraise*, i.e. *recommend* or *advise* (a different course):—admonish, exhort.

3868. **παραιτέομαι paraitĕŏmai**, *par-ahee-teh'-om-ahee;* from *3844* and the mid. of *154;* to *beg off*, i.e. *deprecate, decline, shun:*—avoid, (make) excuse, intreat, refuse, reject.

3869. **παρακαθίζω parakathizō**, *par-ak-ath-id'-zo;* from *3844* and *2523;* to *sit down near:*—sit.

3870. **παρακαλέω parakalĕō**, *par-ak-al-eh'-o;* from *3844* and *2564;* to *call near*, i.e. *invite, invoke* (by *imploration, hortation* or *consolation*):—beseech, call for, (be of good) comfort, desire, (give) exhort (-ation), intreat, pray.

3871. **παρακαλύπτω parakaluptō**, *par-ak-al-oop'-to;* from *3844* and *2572;* to *cover alongside*, i.e. *veil* (fig.):—hide.

3872. **παρακαταθήκη parakatathēkē**, *par-ak-at-ath-ay'-kay;* from a comp. of *3844* and *2698;* something *put down alongside*, i.e. a *deposit* (sacred *trust*):—that (thing) which is committed (un-) to (trust).

3873. **παράκειμαι parakĕimai**, *par-ak'-i-mahee;* from 3844 and 2749; to *lie near*, i.e. *be at hand* (fig. *be prompt* or *easy*):—be present.

3874. **παράκλησις paraklēsis**, *par-ak'-lay-sis;* from 3870; *imploration, hortation, solace:*—comfort, consolation, exhortation, intreaty.

3875. **παράκλητος paraklētŏs**, *par-ak'-lay-tos;* an *intercessor, consoler:*—advocate, comforter.

3876. **παρακοή parakŏē**, *par-ak-ŏ-ay';* from 3878; *inattention*, i.e. (by impl.) *disobedience:*—disobedience.

3877. **παρακολουθέω parakŏlŏuthĕō**, *par-ak-ol-oo-theh'-o;* from 3844 and 190; to *follow near*, i.e. (fig.) *attend* (as a result), *trace out, conform* to:—attain, follow, fully know, have understanding.

3878. **παρακούω parakŏuō**, *par-ak-oo'-o;* from 3844 and 191; to *mishear*, i.e. (by impl.) to *disobey:*—neglect to hear.

3879. **παρακύπτω parakuptō**, *par-ak-oop'-to;* from 3844 and 2955; to *bend beside*, i.e. *lean over* (so as to *peer within*):—look (into), stoop down.

3880. **παραλαμβάνω paralambanō**, *par-al-am-ban'-o;* from 3844 and 2983; to *receive near*, i.e. *associate with* oneself (in any familiar or intimate act or relation); by anal. to *assume* an office; fig. to *learn:*—receive, take (unto, with).

3881. **παραλέγομαι paralĕgŏmai**, *par-al-eg'-om-ahee;* from 3844 and the mid. of 3004 (in its orig. sense); (spec.) to *lay* one's course *near*, i.e. *sail past:*—pass, sail by.

3882. **παράλιος paraliŏs**, *par-al'-ee-os;* from 3844 and 251; *beside* the *salt* (sea), i.e. *maritime:*—sea coast.

3883. **παραλλαγή parallagē**, *par-al-lag-ay';* from a comp. of 3844 and 236; *transmutation* (of phase or orbit), i.e. (fig.) *fickleness:*—variableness.

3884. **παραλογίζομαι paralŏgizŏmai**, *par-al-og-id'-zom-ahee;* from 3844 and 3049; to *misreckon*, i.e. *delude:*—beguile, deceive.

3885. **παραλυτικός paralutikŏs**, *par-al-oo-tee-kos';* from a der. of 3886; as if *dissolved*, i.e. "*paralytic*":—that had (sick of) the palsy.

3886. **παραλύω paraluō**, *par-al-oo'-o;* from 3844 and 3089; to *loosen beside*, i.e. *relax* (perf. pas. part. *paralyzed* or *enfeebled*):—feeble, sick of the (taken with) palsy.

3887. **παραμένω paramĕnō**, *par-am-en'-o;* from 3844 and 3306; to *stay near*, i.e. *remain* (lit. *tarry;* or fig. *be permanent, persevere*):—abide, continue.

3888. **παραμυθέομαι paramuthĕŏmai**, *par-am-oo-theh'-om-ahee;* from 3844 and the mid. of a der. of 3454; to *relate near*, i.e. (by impl.) *encourage, console:*—comfort.

3889. **παραμυθία paramuthia**, *par-am-oo-thee'-ah;* from 3888; *consolation* (prop. abstr.):—comfort.

3890. **παραμύθιον paramuthiŏn**, *par-am-oo'-thee-on;* neut. of 3889; *consolation* (prop. concr.):—comfort.

3891. **παρανομέω paranŏmĕō**, *par-an-om-eh'-o;* from a comp. of 3844 and 3551; to *be opposed to law*, i.e. to *transgress:*—contrary to law.

3892. **παρανομία paranŏmia**, *par-an-om-ee'-ah;* from the same as 3891; *transgression:*—iniquity.

3893. **παραπικραίνω parapikrainō**, *par-ap-ik-rah'ee-no;* from 3844 and 4087; to *embitter alongside*, i.e. (fig.) to *exasperate:*—provoke.

3894. **παραπικρασμός parapikrasmŏs**, *par-ap-ik-ras-mos';* from 3893; *irritation:*—provocation.

3895. **παραπίπτω parapiptō**, *par-ap-ip'-to;* from 3844 and 4098; to *fall aside*, i.e. (fig.) to *apostatize:*—fall away.

3896. **παραπλέω paraplĕō**, *par-ap-leh'-o;* from 3844 and 4126; to *sail near:*—sail by.

3897. **παραπλήσιον paraplēsiŏn**, *par-ap-lay'-see-on;* neut. of a comp. of 3844 and the base of 4139 (as adv.); *close by*, i.e. (fig.) *almost:*—nigh unto.

3898. **παραπλησίως paraplēsiōs**, *par-ap-lay-see'-oce;* adv. from the same as 3897; *in a manner near by*, i.e. (fig.) *similarly:*—likewise.

3899. **παραπορεύομαι parapŏrĕuŏmai**, *par-ap-or-yoo'-om-ahee;* from 3844 and 4198; to *travel near:*—go, pass (by).

3900. **παράπτωμα paraptōma**, *par-ap'-to-mah;* from 3895; a *side-slip* (*lapse* or *deviation*), i.e. (unintentional) *error* or (wilful) *transgression:*—fall, fault, offence, sin, trespass.

3901. **παραῤῥυέω pararrhuĕō**, *par-ar-hroo-eh'-o;* from 3844 and the alt. of 4482; to *flow by*, i.e. (fig.) carelessly *pass* (*miss*):—let slip.

3902. **παράσημος parasēmŏs**, *par-as'-ay-mos;* from 3844 and the base of 4591; *side-marked*, i.e. *labelled* (with a *badge* [*figure-head*] of a ship):—sign.

3903. **παρασκευάζω paraskĕuazō**, *par-ask-yoo-ad'-zo;* from 3844 and a der. of 4632; to *furnish aside*, i.e. *get ready:*—prepare self, be (make) ready.

3904. **παρασκευή paraskĕuē**, *par-ask-yoo-ay';* as if from 3903; *readiness:*—preparation.

3905. **παρατείνω paratĕinō**, *par-at-i'-no;* from 3844 and **τείνω tĕinō** (to *stretch*); to *extend along*, i.e. *prolong* (in point of time):—continue.

3906. **παρατηρέω paratērĕō**, *par-at-ay-reh'-o;* from 3844 and 5083; to *inspect alongside*, i.e. *note insidiously* or *scrupulously:*—observe, watch.

3907. **παρατήρησις paratērēsis**, *par-at-ay'-ray-sis;* from 3906; *inspection*, i.e. *ocular evidence:*—observation

3908. **παρατίθημι paratithēmi**, *par-at-ith'-ay-mee;* from 3844 and 5087; to *place alongside*, i.e. *present* (food, truth); by impl. to *deposit* (as a trust or for protection):—allege, commend, commit (the keeping of), put forth, set before.

3909. **παρατυγχάνω paratugchanō**, *par-at-oong-khan'-o;* from 3844 and 5177; to *chance near*, i.e. *fall in with:*—meet with.

3910. **παραυτίκα parautika**, *par-ŏw-tee'-kah;* from 3844 and a der. of 846; *at the very* instant, i.e. *momentary:*—but for a moment.

3911. **παραφέρω paraphĕrō**, *par-af-er'-o;* from 3844 and 5342 (includ. its alt. forms); to *bear along* or *aside*, i.e. *carry off* (lit. or fig.); by impl. to *avert:*—remove, take away.

3912. **παραφρονέω paraphrŏnĕō**, *par-af-ron-eh'-o;* from 3844 and 5426; to *misthink*, i.e. *be insane* (*silly*):—as a fool.

3913. **παραφρονία paraphrŏnia**, *par-af-ron-ee'-ah;* from 3912; *insanity*, i.e. *foolhardiness:*—madness.

3914. **παραχειμάζω parachĕimazō**, *par-akh-i-mad'-zo;* from 3844 and 5492; to *winter near*, i.e. *stay* with over the *rainy* season:—winter.

3915. **παραχειμασία parachĕimasia**, *par-akh-i-mas-ee'-ah;* from 3914; a *wintering* over:—winter in.

3916. **παραχρῆμα parachrēma**, *par-akh-ray'-mah;* from 3844 and 5536 (in its orig. sense); *at the thing* itself, i.e. *instantly:*—forthwith, immediately, presently, straightway, soon.

3917. **πάρδαλις pardalis**, *par'-dal-is;* fem. of **πάρδος pardŏs** (a *panther*); a *leopard:*—leopard.

3918. **πάρειμι parĕimi**, *par'-i-mee;* from 3844 and 1510 (includ. its various forms); to *be near*, i.e. *at hand;* neut. pres. part. (sing.) *time being*, or (plur.) *property:*—come, × have, be here, + lack, (be here) present.

3919. **παρεισάγω parĕisagō**, *par-ice-ag'-o;* from 3844 and 1521; to *lead in aside*, i.e. *introduce surreptitiously:*—privily bring in.

3920. **παρείσακτος parĕisaktŏs**, *par-ice'-ak-tos;* from 3919; *smuggled in:*—unawares brought in.

3921. **παρεισδύνω parĕisdunō**, *par-ice-doo'-no;* from 3844 and a comp. of 1519 and 1416; to *settle in alongside*, i.e. *lodge stealthily:*—creep in unawares.

3922. **παρεισέρχομαι parĕisĕrchŏmai**, *par-ice-er'-khom-ahee;* from 3844 and 1525; to *come in alongside*, i.e. *supervene additionally* or *stealthily:*—come in privily, enter.

3923. **παρεισφέρω parĕisphĕrō**, *par-ice-fer'-o;* from 3844 and 1533; to *bear in alongside*, i.e. *introduce simultaneously:*—give.

3924. **παρεκτός parĕktŏs**, *par-ek-tos';* from 3844 and 1622; *near outside*, i.e. *besides:*—except, saving, without.

3925. **παρεμβολή parĕmbŏlē**, *par-em-bol-ay';* from a comp. of 3844 and 1685; a *throwing in beside* (*juxtaposition*), i.e. (spec.) *battle-array, encampment* or *barracks* (tower Antonia):—army, camp, castle.

3926. **παρενοχλέω parĕnŏchlĕō**, *par-en-okh-leh'-o;* from 3844 and 1776; to *harass further*, i.e. *annoy:*—trouble.

3927. **παρεπίδημος parĕpidēmŏs**, *par-ep-id'-ay-mos;* from 3844 and the base of 1927; an *alien alongside*, i.e. a *resident foreigner:*—pilgrim, stranger.

3928. **παρέρχομαι parĕrchŏmai**, *par-er'-khom-ahee;* from 3844 and 2064; to *come near* or *aside*, i.e. to *approach* (*arrive*), *go by* (or *away*), (fig.) *perish* or *neglect*, (caus.) *avert:*—come (forth), go, pass (away, by, over), past, transgress.

3929. **πάρεσις parĕsis**, *par'-es-is;* from 3935; *prætermission*, i.e. *toleration:*—remission.

3930. **παρέχω parĕchō**, *par-ekh'-o;* from 3844 and 2192; to *hold near*, i.e. *present, afford, exhibit, furnish occasion:*—bring, do, give, keep, minister, offer, shew, + trouble.

3931. **παρηγορία parēgŏria**, *par-ay-gor-ee'-ah;* from a comp of 3844 and a der. of 58 (mean. to *harangue* an assembly); an *address alongside*, i.e. (spec.) *consolation:*—comfort.

3932. **παρθενία parthĕnia**, *par-then-ee'-ah;* from 3933; *maidenhood:*—virginity.

3933. **παρθένος parthĕnŏs**, *par-then'-os;* of unknown or.; a *maiden;* by impl. an unmarried *daughter:*—virgin.

3934. **Πάρθος Parthŏs**, *par'-thos;* prob. of for. or.; a *Parthian*, i.e. inhab. of Parthia:—Parthian.

3935. **παρίημι pariēmi**, *par-ee'-ay-mi;* from 3844 and **ἵημι hiēmi** (to *send*); to *let by*, i.e. *relax:*—hang down.

3936. **παρίστημι paristēmi**, *par-is'-tay-mee;* or prol. **παριστάνω paristanō**, *par-is-tan'-o;* from 3844 and 2476; to *stand beside*, i.e. (trans.) to *exhibit, proffer*, (spec.) *recommend*, (fig.) *substantiate;* or (intrans.) to *be at hand* (or *ready*), *aid:*—assist, bring before, command, commend, give presently, present, prove, provide, shew, stand (before, by, here, up, with), yield.

3937. **Παρμενᾶς Parmĕnas**, *par-men-as';* prob. by contr. for **Παρμενίδης Parmĕnidēs** (a der. of a comp. of 3844 and 3306); *constant; Parmenas*, a Chr.:—Parmenas.

3938. **πάροδος parŏdŏs**, *par'-od-os;* from 3844 and 3598; a *by-road*, i.e. (act.) a *route:*—way.

3939. **παροικέω parŏikĕō**, *par-oy-keh'-o;* from 3844 and 3611; to *dwell near*, i.e. *reside* as a *foreigner:*—sojourn in, be a stranger.

3940. **παροικία parŏikia**, *par-oy-kee'-ah;* from 3941; *foreign residence:*—sojourning, × as strangers.

3941. **πάροικος parŏikŏs**, *par'-oy-kos;* from 3844 and 3624; having a *home near*, i.e. (as noun) a *by-dweller* (*alien resident*):—foreigner, sojourn, stranger.

3942. **παροιμία parŏimia**, *par-oy-mee'-ah;* from a comp. of 3844 and perh. a der. of 3633; appar. a state *alongside of supposition*, i.e. (concr.) an *adage;*

spec. an enigmatical or fictitious *illustration*:—parable, proverb.

3943. πάροινος parŏinŏs, *par'-oy-nos;* from 3844 and 3631; staying *near wine*, i.e. *tippling* (a *toper*):—given to wine.

3944. παροίχομαι parŏichŏmai, *par-oy'-khom-ahee;* from 3844 and οἴχομαι **ŏichŏmai** (to *depart*); to *escape along*, i.e. *be gone*:—past.

3945. παρομοιάζω parŏmŏiazō, *par-om-oy-ad'-zo;* from 3946; to *resemble*:—be like unto.

3946. παρόμοιος parŏmŏiŏs, *par-om'-oy-os;* from 3844 and 3664; *alike nearly*, i.e. *similar*:—like.

3947. παροξύνω parŏxunō, *par-ox-oo'-no;* from 3844 and a der. of 3691; to *sharpen alongside*, i.e. (fig.) to *exasperate*:—easily provoke, stir.

3948. παροξυσμός parŏxusmŏs, *par-ox-oos-mos';* from 3947 ("*paroxysm*"); *incitement* (to good), or *dispute* (in anger):—contention, provoke unto.

3949. παροργίζω parŏrgizō, *par-org-id'-zo;* from 3844 and 3710; to *anger alongside*, i.e. *enrage*:—anger, provoke to wrath.

3950. παροργισμός parŏrgismŏs, *par-org-is-mos';* from 3949; *rage*:—wrath.

3951. παροτρύνω parŏtrunō, *par-ot-roo'-no;* from 3844 and ὀτρύνω **ŏtrunō** (to *spur*); to *urge along*, i.e. *stimulate* (to hostility):—stir up.

3952. παρουσία parŏusia, *par-oo-see'-ah;* from the pres. part. of 3918; a *being near*, i.e. *advent* (often, *return*; spec. of Christ to punish Jerusalem, or finally the wicked); (by impl.) phys. *aspect*:—coming, presence.

3953. παροψίς parŏpsis, *par-op-sis';* from 3844 and the base of 3795; a *side-dish* (the receptacle):—platter.

3954. παῤῥησία parrhēsia, *par-rhay-see'-ah;* from 3956 and a der. of 4483; *all out-spokenness*, i.e. *frankness, bluntness, publicity;* by impl. *assurance*:—bold (× -ly, -ness, -ness of speech), confidence, × freely, × openly, × plainly (-ness).

3955. παῤῥησιάζομαι parrhēsiazŏmai, *par-hray-see-ad'-zom-ahee;* mid. from 3954; to *be frank* in utterance, or *confident* in spirit and demeanor:—be (wax) bold, (preach, speak) boldly.

3956. πᾶς pas, *pas;* includ. all the forms of declension; appar. a prim. word; *all, any, every,* the *whole*:—all (manner of, means), alway (-s), any (one), × daily, + ever, every (one, way), as many as, + no (-thing), × throughly, whatsoever, whole, whosoever.

3957. πάσχα pascha, *pas'-khah;* of Chald. or. [comp. 6453]; the *Passover* (the meal, the day, the festival or the special sacrifices connected with it):—Easter, Passover.

3958. πάσχω paschō, *pas'-kho;* includ. the forms πάθω (**pathō**, *path'-o*) and πένθω (**pĕnthō**, *pen'-tho*), used only in certain tenses for it; appar. a prim. verb; to *experience* a sensation or impression (usually painful):—feel, passion, suffer, vex.

3959. Πάταρα Patara, *pat'-ar-ah;* prob. of for. or.; *Patara*, a place in Asia Minor:—Patara.

3960. πατάσσω patassō, *pat-as'-so;* prob. prol. from 3817; to *knock* (gently or with a weapon or fatally):—smite, strike. Comp. 5180.

3961. πατέω patĕō, *pat-eh'-o;* from a der. prob. of 3817 (mean. a "*path*"); to *trample* (lit. or fig.):—tread (down, under foot).

3962. πατήρ patēr, *pat-ayr';* appar. a prim. word; a "*father*" (lit. or fig., near or more remote):—father, parent.

3963. Πάτμος Patmŏs, *pat'-mos;* of uncert. der.; *Patmus*, an islet in the Mediterranean:—Patmos.

3964. πατραλῴας patralōias, *pat-ral-o'-as;* from 3962 and the same as the latter part of 3389; a *parricide*:—murderer of fathers.

3965. πατριά patria, *pat-ree-ah';* as if fem. of a der. of 3962; paternal *descent*, i.e. (concr.) a *group* of families or a whole *race* (*nation*):—family, kindred, lineage.

3966. πατριάρχης patriarchēs, *pat-ree-arkh'-ace;* from 3965 and 757; a *progenitor* ("patriarch"):—patriarch.

3967. πατρικός patrikŏs, *pat-ree-kos';* from 3962; *paternal*, i.e. *ancestral*:—of fathers.

3968. πατρίς patris, *pat-rece';* from 3962; a *father-land*, i.e. *native town;* (fig.) heavenly *home*:—(own) country.

3969. Πατρόβας Patrŏbas, *pat-rob'-as;* perh. contr. for Πατρόβιος **Patrŏbiŏs** (a comp. of 3962 and 979); *father's life; Patrobas*, a Chr.:—Patrobas.

3970. πατροπαράδοτος patrŏparadŏtŏs, *pat-rop-ar-ad'-ot-os;* from 3962 and a der. of 3860 (in the sense of *handing over* or *down*); *traditionary*:—received by tradition from fathers.

3971. πατρῷος patrōiŏs, *pat-ro'-os;* from 3962; *paternal*, i.e. *hereditary*:—of fathers.

3972. Παῦλος Paulŏs, *pŏw'-los;* of Lat. or.; (*little;* but remotely from a der. of 3973, mean. the same); *Paulus*, the name of a Rom. and of an apostle:—Paul, Paulus.

3973. παύω pauō, *pŏw'-o;* a prim. verb ("*pause*"); to *stop* (trans. or intrans.), i.e. *restrain, quit, desist, come to an end*:—cease, leave, refrain.

3974. Πάφος Paphŏs, *paf'-os;* of uncert. der.; *Paphus*, a place in Cyprus:—Paphos.

3975. παχύνω pachunō, *pakh-oo'-no;* from a der. of 4078 (mean. *thick*); to *thicken*, i.e. (by impl.) to *fatten* (fig. *stupefy* or *render callous*):—wax gross.

3976. πέδη pĕdē, *ped'-ay;* ultimately from 4228; a *shackle* for the feet:—fetter.

3977. πεδινός pĕdinŏs, *ped-ee-nos';* from a der. of 4228 (mean. the *ground*); *level* (as easy for the *feet*):—plain.

3978. πεζεύω pĕzĕuō, *ped-zyoo'-o;* from the same as 3979; to *foot* a journey, i.e. *travel* by land:—go afoot.

3979. πεζῇ pĕzēi, *ped-zay';* dat. fem. of a der. of 4228 (as adv.); *foot-wise*, i.e. by *walking*:—a- (on) foot.

3980. πειθαρχέω pĕitharchĕō, *pi-tharkh-eh'-o;* from a comp. of 3982 and 757; to *be persuaded* by a *ruler*, i.e. (gen.) to *submit* to authority; by anal. to *conform* to advice:—hearken, obey (magistrates).

3981. πειθός pĕithŏs, *pi-thos';* from 3982; *persuasive*:—enticing.

3982. πείθω pĕithō, *pi'-tho;* a prim. verb; to *convince* (by argument, true or false); by anal. to *pacify* or *conciliate* (by other fair means); reflex. or pass. to *assent* (to evidence or authority), to *rely* (by inward certainty):—agree, assure, believe, have confidence, be (wax) conflent, make friend, obey, persuade, trust, yield.

3983. πεινάω pĕinaō, *pi-nah'-o;* from the same as 3993 (through the idea of pinching *toil;* "*pine*"); to *famish* (absol. or comparatively); fig. to *crave*:—be an hungered.

3984. πεῖρα pĕira, *pi'-rah;* from the base of 4008 (through the idea of *piercing*); a *test*, i.e. *attempt, experience*:—assaying, trial.

3985. πειράζω pĕirazō, *pi-rad'-zo;* from 3984; to *test* (obj.), i.e. *endeavor, scrutinize, entice, discipline*:—assay, examine, go about, prove, tempt (-er), try.

3986. πειρασμός pĕirasmŏs, *pi-ras-mos';* from 3985; a putting to *proof* (by experiment [of good], *experience* [of evil], solicitation, discipline or provocation); by impl. *adversity*:—temptation, × try.

3987. πειράω pĕiraō, *pi-rah'-o;* from 3984; to *test* (subj.), i.e. (reflex.) to *attempt*:—assay.

3988. πεισμονή pĕismŏnē, *pice-mon-ay';* from a presumed der. of 3982; *persuadableness*, i.e. *credulity*:—persuasion.

3989. πέλαγος pĕlagŏs, *pel'-ag-os;* of uncert. affin.; deep or open *sea*, i.e. the *main*:—depth, sea.

3990. πελεκίζω pĕlĕkizō, *pel-ek-id'-zo;* from a der. of 4141 (mean. an *axe*); to *chop* off (the head), i.e. *truncate*:—behead.

3991. πέμπτος pĕmptŏs, *pemp'-tos;* from 4002; *fifth*:—fifth.

3992. πέμπω pĕmpō, *pem'-po;* appar. a prim. verb; to *dispatch* (from the subj. view or point of *departure*, whereas ἵημι **hiēmi** [as a stronger form of εἶμι **ĕimi**] refers rather to the obj. point or *terminus ad quem*, and 4724 denotes prop. the *orderly* motion involved), espec. on a temporary errand; also to *transmit, bestow*, or *wield*:—send, thrust in.

3993. πένης pĕnēs, *pen'-ace;* from a prim. πένω **pĕnō** (to *toil* for daily subsistence); *starving*, i.e. *indigent*:—poor. Comp. 4434.

3994. πενθερά pĕnthĕra, *pen-ther-ah';* fem. of 3995; a *wife's mother*:—mother in law, wife's mother.

3995. πενθερός pĕnthĕrŏs, *pen-ther-os';* of uncert. affin.; a *wife's father*:—father in law.

3996. πενθέω pĕnthĕō, *pen-theh'-o;* from 3997; to *grieve* (the feeling or the act):—mourn, (be-) wail.

3997. πένθος pĕnthŏs, *pen'-thos;* strengthened from the alt. of 3958; *grief*:—mourning, sorrow.

3998. πεντιχρός pĕntichrŏs, *pen-tikh-ros';* prol. from the base of 3993; *necessitous*:—poor.

3999. πεντακίς pĕntakis, *pen-tak-ece';* mult. adv. from 4002; *five times*:—five times.

4000. πεντακισχίλιοι pĕntakischiliŏi, *pen-tak-is-khil'-ee-oy;* from 3999 and 5507; *five times a thousand*:—five thousand.

4001. πεντακόσιοι pĕntakŏsiŏi, *pen-tak-os'-ee-oy;* from 4002 and 1540; *five hundred*:—five hundred.

4002. πέντε pĕntĕ, *pen'-teh;* a prim. number; "*five*":—five.

4003. πεντεκαιδέκατος pĕntĕkaidĕkatŏs, *pen-tek-ahee-dek'-at-os;* from 4002 and 2532 and 1182; *five and tenth*:—fifteenth.

4004. πεντήκοντα pĕntēkŏnta, *pen-tay'-kon-tah;* mult. of 4002; *fifty*:—fifty.

4005. πεντηκοστή pĕntēkŏstē, *pen-tay-kos-tay';* fem. of the ord. of 4004; *fiftieth* (2250 being implied) from Passover, i.e. the festival of "*Pentecost*":—Pentecost.

4006. πεποίθησις pĕpŏithēsis, *pep-oy'-thay-sis;* from the perf. of the alt. of 3958; *reliance*:—confidence, trust.

4007. περ pĕr, *per;* from the base of 4008; an enclitic particle significant of *abundance* (*thoroughness*), i.e. *emphasis; much, very* or *ever*:—[whom-] soever.

4008. πέραν pĕran, *per'-an;* appar. acc. of an obsol. der. of πείρω **pĕirō** (to "*pierce*"); *through* (as adv. or prep.), i.e. *across*:—beyond, farther (other) side, over.

4009. πέρας pĕras, *per'-as;* from the same as 4008; an *extremity*:—end, ut- (ter-) most part.

4010. Πέργαμος Pĕrgamŏs, *per'-gam-os;* from 4444; *fortified; Pergamus*, a place in Asia Minor:—Pergamos.

4011. Πέργη Pĕrgē, *perg'-ay;* prob. from the same as 4010; a *tower; Perga*, a place in Asia Minor:—Perga.

4012. περί pĕri, *per-ee';* from the base of 4008; prop. *through* (all over), i.e. *around;* fig. *with respect* to; used in various applications, of place, cause or time (with the gen. denoting the *subject* or *occasion* or *superlative* point; with the acc. the *locality, circuit, matter, circumstance* or general *period*):—(there-) about, above, against, at, on behalf of, × and his company, which concern, (as) concerning, for, × how it will go with, ([there-, where-]) of, on, over, pertaining (to), for sake, × (e-) state, (as) touching, [where-] by (in), with. In comp. it retains substantially the same mean. of circuit (*around*), excess (*beyond*), or completeness (*through*).

4013. **περιάγω pĕriagō**, *per-ee-ag'-o;* from *4012* and *71;* to *take around* (as a companion); reflex. to *walk around:*—compass, go (round) about, lead about.

4014. **περιαιρέω pĕriairĕō**, *per-ee-ahee-reh'-o;* from *4012* and *138* (incl. its alt.); to *remove* all *around,* i.e. *unveil, cast off* (anchor); fig. to *expiate:*—take away (up).

4015. **περιαστράπτω pĕriastraptō**, *per-ee-as-trap'-to;* from *4012* and *797;* to *flash* all *around,* i.e. *envelop in light:*—shine round (about).

4016. **περιβάλλω pĕriballō**, *per-ee-bal'-lo;* from *4012* and *906;* to *throw* all *around,* i.e. *invest* (with a palisade or with clothing):—array, cast about, clothe (-d me), put on.

4017. **περιβλέπω pĕriblĕpō**, *per-ee-blep'-o;* from *4012* and *991;* to *look* all *around:*—look (round) about (on).

4018. **περιβόλαιον pĕribŏlaiŏn**, *per-ib-ol'-ah-yon;* neut. of a presumed der. of *4016;* something *thrown around* one, i.e. a *mantle, veil:*—covering, vesture.

4019. **περιδέω pĕridĕō**, *per-ee-deh'-o;* from *4012* and *1210;* to *bind around* one, i.e. *enwrap:*—bind about.

περιδρέμω pĕridrĕmō. See *4063*.

περιέλλω pĕriĕllō. See *4014*.

περιέλθω pĕriĕlthō. See *4022*.

4020. **περιεργάζομαι pĕriĕrgazŏmai**, *per-ee-er-gad'-zom-ahee;* from *4012* and *2038;* to *work* all *around,* i.e. *bustle about* (*meddle*):—be a busybody.

4021. **περίεργος pĕriĕrgŏs**, *per-ee'-er-gos;* from *4012* and *2041;* *working all around,* i.e. *officious* (*meddlesome,* neut. plur. *magic*):—busybody, curious arts.

4022. **περιέρχομαι pĕriĕrchŏmai**, *per-ee-er'-khom-ahee;* from *4012* and *2064* (includ. its alt.); to *come* all *around,* i.e. *stroll, vacillate, veer:*—fetch a compass, vagabond, wandering about.

4023. **περιέχω pĕriĕchō**, *per-ee-ekh'-o;* from *4012* and *2192;* to *hold* all *around,* i.e. *include, clasp* (fig.):— + astonished, contain, after [this manner].

4024. **περιζώννυμι pĕrizōnnumi**, *per-id-zone'-noo-mee;* from *4012* and *2224;* to *gird* all *around,* i.e. (mid. or pass.) to *fasten on one's belt* (lit. or fig.):—gird (about, self).

4025. **περίθεσις pĕrithĕsis**, *per-ith'-es-is;* from *4060;* a *putting* all *around,* i.e. *decorating* oneself with:—wearing.

4026. **περιΐστημι pĕriistēmi**, *per-ee-is'-tay-mee;* from *4012* and *2476;* to *stand* all *around,* i.e. (near) to *be a bystander,* or (aloof) to *keep away* from:—avoid, shun, stand by (round about).

4027. **περικάθαρμα pĕrikatharma**, *per-ee-kath'-ar-mah;* from a comp. of *4012* and *2508;* something *cleaned off* all *around,* i.e. *refuse* (fig.):—filth.

4028. **περικαλύπτω pĕrikaluptō**, *per-ee-kal-oop'-to;* from *4012* and *2572;* to *cover* all *around,* i.e. *entirely* (the face, a surface):—blindfold, cover, overlay.

4029. **περίκειμαι pĕrikĕimai**, *per-ik'-i-mahee;* from *4012* and *2749;* to *lie* all *around,* i.e. *inclose, encircle, hamper* (lit. or fig.):—be bound (compassed) with, hang about.

4030. **περικεφαλαία pĕrikĕphalaia**, *per-ee-kef-al-ah'-yah;* fem. of a comp. of *4012* and *2776;* *encirclement of* the *head,* i.e. a *helmet:*—helmet.

4031. **περικρατής pĕrikratēs**, *per-ee-krat-ace';* from *4012* and *2904;* *strong* all *around,* i.e. a *master* (*manager*):— + come by.

4032. **περικρύπτω pĕrikruptō**, *per-ee-kroop'-to;* from *4012* and *2928;* to *conceal* all *around,* i.e. *entirely:*—hide.

4033. **περικυκλόω pĕrikuklŏō**, *per-ee-koo-klŏ'-o;* from *4012* and *2944;* to *encircle* all *around,* i.e. *blockade completely:*—compass round.

4034. **περιλάμπω pĕrilampō**, *per-ee-lam'-po;* from *4012* and *2989;* to *illuminate* all *around,* i.e. *invest with a halo:*—shine round about.

4035. **περιλείπω pĕrilĕipō**, *per-ee-li'-po;* from *4012* and *3007;* to *leave* all *around,* i.e. (pass.) *survive:*—remain.

4036. **περίλυπος pĕrilupŏs**, *per-il'-oo-pos;* from *4012* and *3077;* *grieved* all *around,* i.e. *intensely sad:*—exceeding (very) sorry (-owful).

4037. **περιμένω pĕrimĕnō**, *per-ee-men'-o;* from *4012* and *3306;* to *stay around,* i.e. *await:*—wait for.

4038. **πέριξ pĕrix**, *per'-ix;* adv. from *4012;* all *around,* i.e. (as adj.) *circumjacent:*—round about.

4039. **περιοικέω pĕriŏikĕō**, *per-ee-oy-keh'-o;* from *4012* and *3611;* to *reside around,* i.e. *be a neighbor:*—dwell round about.

4040. **περίοικος pĕriŏikŏs**, *per-ee'-oy-kos;* from *4012* and *3624;* *housed around,* i.e. *neighboring* (ellipt. as noun):—neighbour.

4041. **περιούσιος pĕriŏusiŏs**, *per-ee-oo'-see-os;* from the pres. part. fem. of a comp. of *4012* and *1510;* *being beyond* usual, i.e. *special* (one's *own*):—peculiar.

4042. **περιοχή pĕriŏchē**, *per-ee-okh-ay';* from *4023;* a *being held around,* i.e. (concr.) a *passage* (of Scripture, as *circumscribed*):—place.

4043. **περιπατέω pĕripatĕō**, *per-ee-pat-eh'-o;* from *4012* and *3961;* to *tread* all *around,* i.e. *walk* at large (espec. as proof of ability); fig. to *live, deport oneself, follow* (as a companion or votary):—go, be occupied with, walk (about).

4044. **περιπείρω pĕripĕirō**, *per-ee-pi'-ro;* from *4012* and the base of *4008;* to *penetrate entirely,* i.e. *transfix* (fig.):—pierce through.

4045. **περιπίπτω pĕripiptō**, *per-ee-pip'-to;* from *4012* and *4098;* to *fall* into something that is all *around,* i.e. *light among* or *upon, be surrounded with:*—fall among (into).

4046. **περιποιέομαι pĕripŏiĕŏmai**, *per-ee-poy-eh'-om-ahee;* mid. from *4012* and *4160;* to *make around oneself,* i.e. *acquire* (*buy*):—purchase.

4047. **περιποίησις pĕripŏiēsis**, *per-ee-poy'-ay-sis;* from *4046;* *acquisition* (the act or the thing); by extens. *preservation:*—obtain (-ing), peculiar, purchased, possession, saving.

4048. **περιῤῥήγνυμι pĕrirrhēgnumi**, *per-ir-hrayg'-noo-mee;* from *4012* and *4486;* to *tear* all *around,* i.e. *completely away:*—rend off.

4049. **περισπάω pĕrispaō**, *per-ee-spah'-o;* from *4012* and *4685;* to *drag* all *around,* i.e. (fig.) to *distract* (with care):—cumber.

4050. **περισσεία pĕrissĕia**, *per-is-si'-ah;* from *4052;* *surplusage,* i.e. *superabundance:*—abundance (-ant, [-ly]), superfluity.

4051. **περίσσευμα pĕrissĕuma**, *per-is'-syoo-mah;* from *4052;* a *surplus,* or *superabundance:*—abundance, that was left, over and above.

4052. **περισσεύω pĕrissĕuō**, *per-is-syoo'-o;* from *4053;* to *superabound* (in quantity or quality), *be in excess, be superfluous;* also (trans.) to *cause to superabound* or *excel:*—(make, more) abound, (have, have more) abundance, (be more) abundant, be the better, enough and to spare, exceed, excel, increase, be left, redound, remain (over and above).

4053. **περισσός pĕrissŏs**, *per-is-sos';* from *4012* (in the sense of *beyond*); *superabundant* (in quantity) or *superior* (in quality); by impl. *excessive;* adv. (with *1537*) *violently;* neut. (as noun) *preeminence:*—exceeding abundantly above, more abundantly, advantage, exceedingly, very highly, beyond measure, more, superfluous, vehement [-ly].

4054. **περισσότερον pĕrissŏtĕrŏn**, *per-is-sot'-er-on;* neut. of *4055* (as adv.); in a *more superabundant* way:—more abundantly, a great deal, far more.

4055. **περισσότερος pĕrissŏtĕrŏs**, *per-is-sot'-er-os;* comp. of *4053;* *more superabundant* (in number, degree or character):—more abundant, greater (much) more, overmuch.

4056. **περισσοτέρως pĕrissŏtĕrōs**, *per-is-sot-er'-oce;* adv. from *4055;* *more superabundantly:*—more abundant (-ly), × the more earnest, (more) exceedingly, more frequent, much more, the rather.

4057. **περισσῶς pĕrissōs**, *per-is-soce';* adv. from *4053;* *superabundantly:*—exceedingly, out of measure, the more.

4058. **περιστερά pĕristĕra**, *per-is-ter-ah';* of uncert. der.; a *pigeon:*—dove, pigeon.

4059. **περιτέμνω pĕritĕmnō**, *per-ee-tem'-no;* from *4012* and the base of *5114;* to *cut around,* i.e. (spec.) to *circumcise:*—circumcise.

4060. **περιτίθημι pĕritithēmi**, *per-ee-tith'-ay-mee;* from *4012* and *5087;* to *place around;* by impl. to *present:*—bestow upon, hedge round about, put about (on, upon), set about.

4061. **περιτομή pĕritŏmē**, *per-it-om-ay';* from *4059;* *circumcision* (the rite, the condition or the people, lit. or fig.):— × circumcised, circumcision.

4062. **περιτρέπω pĕritrĕpō**, *per-ee-trep'-o;* from *4012* and the base of *5157;* to *turn around,* i.e. (ment.) to *craze:*— + make mad.

4063. **περιτρέχω pĕritrĕchō**, *per-ee-trekh'-o;* from *4012* and *5143* (includ. its alt.); to *run around,* i.e. *traverse:*—run through.

4064. **περιφέρω pĕriphĕrō**, *per-ee-fer'-o;* from *4012* and *5342;* to *convey around,* i.e. *transport hither and thither:*—bear (carry) about.

4065. **περιφρονέω pĕriphrŏnĕō**, *per-ee-fron-eh'-o;* from *4012* and *5426;* to *think beyond,* i.e. *depreciate* (*contemn*):—despise.

4066. **περίχωρος pĕrichōrŏs**, *per-ikh'-o-ros;* from *4012* and *5561;* *around* the *region,* i.e. *circumjacent* (as noun, with *1093* impl. *vicinity*):—country (round) about, region (that lieth) round about.

4067. **περίψωμα pĕripsōma**, *per-ip'-so-mah;* from a comp. of *4012* and **ψάω psaō** (to *rub*); something *brushed* all *around,* i.e. *off-scrapings* (fig. *scum*):—offscouring.

4068. **περπερεύομαι pĕrpĕrĕuŏmai**, *per-per-yoo'-om-ahee;* mid. from **πέρπερος pĕrpĕrŏs** (*braggart;* perh. by redupl. of the base of *4008*); to *boast:*—vaunt itself.

4069. **Περσίς Pĕrsis**, *per-sece';* a *Persian* woman; *Persis,* a Chr. female:—Persis.

4070. **πέρυσι pĕrusi**, *per'-oo-si;* adv. from *4009;* the *by-gone,* i.e. (as noun) *last year:*— + a year ago.

πετάομαι pĕtaŏmai. See *4072*.

4071. **πετεινόν pĕtĕinŏn**, *pet-i-non';* neut. of a der. of *4072;* a *flying* animal, i.e. *bird:*—bird, fowl.

4072. **πέτομαι pĕtŏmai**, *pet'-om-ahee;* or prol. **πετάομαι pĕtaŏmai**, *pet-ah'-om-ahee;* or contr. **πτάομαι ptaŏmai**, *ptah'-om-ahee;* mid. of a prim. verb; to *fly:*—fly (-ing).

4073. **πέτρα pĕtra**, *pet'-ra;* fem. of the same as *4074;* a (mass of) *rock* (lit. or fig.):—rock.

4074. **Πέτρος Pĕtrŏs**, *pet'-ros;* appar. a prim. word; a (piece of) *rock* (larger than *3037*); as a name, *Petrus,* an apostle:—Peter, rock. Comp. *2786*.

4075. **πετρώδης pĕtrōdēs**, *pet-ro'-dace;* from *4073* and *1491;* *rock-like,* i.e. *rocky:*—stony.

4076. **πήγανον pēganŏn**, *pay'-gan-on;* from *4078;* *rue* (from its *thick* or *fleshy* leaves):—rue.

4077. **πηγή pēgē**, *pay-gay';* prob. from *4078* (through the idea of *gushing* plumply); a *fount* (lit. or fig.), i.e. *source* or *supply* (of water, blood, enjoyment) (not necessarily the original spring):—fountain, well.

4078. **πήγνυμι pēgnumi**, *payg'-noo-mee;* a prol. form of a prim. verb (which in its simpler form occurs only as an alt. in certain tenses); to *fix* ("*peg*"), i.e. (spec.) to *set up* (a tent):—pitch.

4079. **πηδάλιον pēdaliŏn**, *pay-dal'-ee-on;* neut. of a (presumed) der. of **πηδόν pēdŏn** (the *blade* of an oar; from the same as *3976*); a "*pedal*", i.e. *helm:*—rudder.

4080. **πηλίκος pēlikŏs**, *pay-lee'-kos;* a quantitative form (the fem.) of the base of *4225;* *how much* (as indef.), i.e. in size or (fig.) dignity:—how great (large).

4081. **πηλός pēlŏs**, *pay-los';* perh. a prim. word; *clay:*—clay.

4082. πήρα **pēra**, *pay'-rah;* of uncert. affin.; a *wallet* or leather *pouch* for food:—scrip.

4083. πῆχυς **pēchus**, *pay'-khoos;* of uncert. affin.; the *fore-arm*, i.e. (as a measure) a *cubit:*—cubit.

4084. πιάζω **piazō**, *pee-ad'-zo;* prob. another form of *971;* to *squeeze*, i.e. *seize* (gently by the hand [*press*], or officially [*arrest*], or in hunting [*capture*]):—apprehend, catch, lay hand on, take. Comp. *4085.*

4085. πιέζω **piĕzō**, *pee-ed'-zo;* another form for *4084;* to *pack:*—press down.

4086. πιθανολογία **pithanŏlŏgia**, *pith-an-ol-og-ee'-ah;* from a comp. of a der. of *3982* and *3056;* *persuasive language:*—enticing words.

4087. πικραίνω **pikrainō**, *pik-rah'ee-no;* from *4089;* to *embitter* (lit. or fig.):—be (make) bitter.

4088. πικρία **pikria**, *pik-ree'-ah;* from *4089;* *acridity* (espec. *poison*), lit. or fig.:—bitterness.

4089. πικρός **pikrŏs**, *pik-ros';* perh. from *4078* (through the idea of *piercing*); *sharp* (*pungent*), i.e. *acrid* (lit. or fig.):—bitter.

4090. πικρῶς **pikrōs**, *pik-roce';* adv. from *4089;* *bitterly*, i.e. (fig.) *violently:*—bitterly.

4091. Πιλάτος **Pilatŏs**, *pil-at'-os;* of Lat. or.; *close-pressed*, i.e. *firm; Pilatus*, a Rom.:—Pilate.

πίμπλημι **pimplēmi**. See *4130.*

4092. πίμπρημι **pimprēmi**, *pim'-pray-mee;* a redupl. and prol. form of a prim.

πρέω **prĕō**, *preh'-o* (which occurs only as an alt. in certain tenses); to *fire*, i.e. *burn* (fig. and pass. *become inflamed* with fever):—be (× should have) swollen.

4093. πινακίδιον **pinakidiŏn**, *pin-ak-id'-ee-on;* dimin. of *4094;* a *tablet* (for writing on):—writing table.

4094. πίναξ **pinax**, *pin'-ax;* appar. a form of *4109;* a *plate:*—charger, platter.

4095. πίνω **pinō**, *pee'-no;* a prol. form of

πίω **piō**, *pee'-o*, which (together with another form πόω **pŏō**, *pŏ'-o*) occurs only as an alt. in cert. tenses; to *imbibe* (lit. or fig.):—drink.

4096. πιότης **piŏtēs**, *pee-ot'-ace;* from πίων **piōn** (*fat;* perh. akin to the alt. of *4095* through the idea of *repletion*); *plumpness*, i.e. (by impl.) *richness* (*oiliness*):—fatness.

4097. πιπράσκω **piprasko**, *pip-ras'-ko;* a redupl. and prol. form of

πράω **praō**, *prah'-o* (which occurs only as an alt. in cert. tenses); contr. from περάω **pĕraō** (to *traverse;* from the base of *4008*); to *traffic* (by *travelling*), i.e. *dispose* of as merchandise or into slavery (lit. or fig.):—sell.

4098. πίπτω **piptō**, *pip'-to;* a redupl. and contr. form of πέτω **pĕtō**, *pet'-o* (which occurs only as an alt. in cert. tenses); prob. akin to *4072* through the idea of *alighting;* to *fall* (lit or fig.):—fail, fall (down), light on.

4099. Πισιδία **Pisidia**, *pis-id-ee'-ah;* prob. of for. or.; *Pisidia*, a region of Asia Minor:—Pisidia.

4100. πιστεύω **pistĕuō**, *pist-yoo'-o;* from *4102;* to *have faith* (in, upon, or with respect to, a person or thing), i.e. *credit;* by impl. to *entrust* (espec. one's spiritual well-being to Christ):—believe (-r), commit (to trust), put in trust with.

4101. πιστικός **pistikŏs**, *pis-tik-os';* from *4102;* *trustworthy*, i.e. *genuine* (*unadulterated*):—spike-[nard].

4102. πίστις **pistis**, *pis'-tis;* from *3982;* *persuasion*, i.e. *credence;* mor. *conviction* (of religious truth, or the truthfulness of God or a religious teacher), espec. *reliance* upon Christ for salvation; abstr. *constancy* in such profession; by extens. the system of religious (Gospel) *truth* itself:—assurance, belief, believe, faith, fidelity.

4103. πιστός **pistŏs**, *pis-tos';* from *3982;* obj. *trustworthy;* subj. *trustful:*—believe (-ing, -r), faithful (-ly), sure, true.

4104. πιστόω **pistŏō**, *pis-tŏ'-o;* from *4103;* to *assure:*—assure of.

4105. πλανάω **planaō**, *plan-ah'-o;* from *4106;* to (prop. *cause* to) *roam* (from safety, truth, or virtue):—go astray, deceive, err, seduce, wander, be out of the way.

4106. πλάνη **planē**, *plan'-ay;* fem. of *4108* (as abstr.); obj. *fraudulence;* subj. a *straying* from orthodoxy or piety:—deceit, to deceive, delusion, error.

4107. πλανήτης **planētēs**, *plan-ay'-tace;* from *4108;* a *rover* ("planet"), i.e. (fig.) an *erratic* teacher:—wandering.

4108. πλάνος **planŏs**, *plan'-os;* of uncert. affin.; *roving* (as a *tramp*), i.e. (by impl.) an *impostor* or *misleader:*—deceiver, seducing.

4109. πλάξ **plax**, *plax;* from *4111;* a *moulding-board*, i.e. *flat* surface ("*plate*", or *tablet*, lit. or fig.):—table.

4110. πλάσμα **plasma**, *plas'-mah;* from *4111;* something *moulded:*—thing formed.

4111. πλάσσω **plassō**, *plas'-so;* a prim. verb; to *mould*, i.e. *shape* or *fabricate:*—form.

4112. πλαστός **plastŏs**, *plas-tos';* from *4111;* *moulded*, i.e. (by impl.) *artificial* or (fig.) *fictitious* (*false*):—feigned.

4113. πλατεῖα **platĕia**, *plat-i'-ah;* fem. of *4116;* a *wide* "*plat*" or "*place*", i.e. open *square:*—street.

4114. πλάτος **platŏs**, *plat'-os;* from *4116;* *width:*—breadth.

4115. πλατύνω **platunō**, *plat-oo'-no;* from *4116;* to *widen* (lit. or fig.):—make broad, enlarge.

4116. πλατύς **platus**, *plat-oos';* from *4111;* spread out "*flat*" ("plot"), i.e. *broad:*—wide.

4117. πλέγμα **plĕgma**, *pleg'-mah;* from *4120;* a *plait* (of hair):—broidered hair.

πλεῖον **plĕiŏn**. See *4119.*

4118. πλεῖστος **plĕistŏs**, *plice'-tos;* irreg. superl. of *4183;* the *largest number* or *very large:*—very great, most.

4119. πλείων **plĕiōn**, *pli'-own;* neut.

πλεῖον **plĕiŏn**, *pli'-on;* or

πλέον **plĕŏn**, *pleh'-on;* compar. of *4183;* *more* in quantity, number, or quality; also (in plur.) the *major portion:*— × above, + exceed, more excellent, further, (very) great (-er), long (-er), (very) many, greater (more) part, + yet but.

4120. πλέκω **plĕkō**, *plek'-o;* a prim. word; to *twine* or *braid:*—plait.

πλέον **plĕŏn**. See 4119.

4121. πλεονάζω **plĕŏnazō**, *pleh-on-ad'-zo;* from *4119;* to *do*, *make* or *be more*, i.e. *increase* (trans. or intrans.); by extens. to *superabound:*—abound, abundant, make to increase, have over.

4122. πλεονεκτέω **plĕŏnĕktĕō**, *pleh-on-ek-teh'-o;* from *4123;* to *be covetous*, i.e. (by impl.) to *over-reach:*—get an advantage, defraud, make a gain.

4123. πλεονέκτης **plĕŏnĕktēs**, *pleh-on-ek'-tace;* from *4119* and *2192;* *holding* (*desiring*) *more*, i.e. *eager for gain* (*avaricious*, hence a *defrauder*):—covetous.

4124. πλεονεξία **plĕŏnĕxia**, *pleh-on-ex-ee'-ah;* from *4123;* *avarice*, i.e. (by impl.) *fraudulency*, *extortion:*—covetous (-ness) practices, greediness.

4125. πλευρά **plĕura**, *plyoo-rah';* of uncert. affin.; a *rib*, i.e. (by extens.) *side:*—side.

4126. πλέω **plĕō**, *pleh'-o;* another form for

πλεύω **plĕuō**, *plyoo'-o*, which is used as an alt. in certain tenses; prob. a form of *4150* (through the idea of *plunging* through the water); to *pass* in a vessel:—sail. See also *4130.*

4127. πληγή **plēgē**, *play-gay';* from *4141;* a *stroke;* by impl. a *wound;* fig. a *calamity:*—plague, stripe, wound (-ed).

4128. πλῆθος **plēthŏs**, *play'-thos;* from *4130;* a *fulness*, i.e. a *large number, throng, populace:*—bundle, company, multitude.

4129. πληθύνω **plēthunō**, *play-thoo'-no;* from another form of *4128;* to *increase* (trans. or intrans.):—abound, multiply.

4130. πλήθω **plēthō**, *play'-tho;* a prol. form of a prim. πλέω **plĕō**, *pleh'-o* (which appears only as an alt. in certain tenses and in the redupl. form πίμπλημι **pimplēmi**); to "*fill*" (lit. or fig. [*imbue, influence, supply*]); spec. to *fulfil* (time):—accomplish, full (. . . come), furnish.

4131. πλήκτης **plēktēs**, *plake'-tace;* from *4141;* a *smiter*, i.e. *pugnacious* (*quarrelsome*):—striker.

4132. πλήμμυρα **plēmmura**, *plame-moo'-rah;* prol. from *4130;* *flood-tide*, i.e. (by anal.) a *freshet:*—flood.

4133. πλήν **plēn**, *plane;* from *4119;* *moreover* (*besides*), i.e. *albeit, save that, rather, yet:*—but (rather), except, nevertheless, notwithstanding, save, than.

4134. πλήρης **plērēs**, *play'-race;* from *4130;* *replete*, or *covered* over; by anal. *complete:*—full.

4135. πληροφορέω **plērŏphŏrĕō**, *play-rof-or-eh'-o;* from *4134* and *5409;* to *carry* out *fully* (in evidence), i.e. *completely assure* (or *convince*), *entirely accomplish:*—most surely believe, fully know (persuade), make full proof of.

4136. πληροφορία **plērŏphŏria**, *play-rof-or-ee'-ah;* from *4135;* *entire confidence:*—(full) assurance.

4137. πληρόω **plērŏō**, *play-rŏ'-o;* from *4134;* to *make replete*, i.e. (lit.) to *cram* (a net), *level* up (a hollow), or (fig.) to *furnish* (or *imbue, diffuse, influence*), *satisfy, execute* (an office), *finish* (a period or task), *verify* (or *coincide* with a prediction), etc.:—accomplish, × after, (be) complete, end, expire, fill (up), fulfil, (be, make) full (come), fully preach, perfect, supply.

4138. πλήρωμα **plērōma**, *play'-ro-mah;* from *4137;* *repletion* or *completion*, i.e. (subj.) what *fills* (as contents, supplement, copiousness, multitude), or (obj.) what is *filled* (as container, performance, period):—which is put in to fill up, piece that filled up, fulfilling, full, fulness.

4139. πλησίον **plēsiŏn**, *play-see'-on;* neut. of a der. of πέλας **pĕlas** (*near*); (adv.) *close* by; as noun, a *neighbor*, i.e. *fellow* (as man, countryman, Chr. or friend):—near, neighbour.

4140. πλησμονή **plēsmŏnē**, *place-mon-ay';* from a presumed der. of *4130;* a *filling* up, i.e. (fig.) *gratification:*—satisfying.

4141. πλήσσω **plēssō**, *place'-so;* appar. another form of *4111* (through the idea of *flattening* out); to *pound*, i.e. (fig.) to *inflict* with (calamity):—smite. Comp. *5180.*

4142. πλοιάριον **plŏiariŏn**, *ploy-ar'-ee-on;* neut. of a presumed der. of *4143;* a *boat:*—boat, little (small) ship.

4143. πλοῖον **plŏiŏn**, *ploy'-on;* from *4126;* a *sailer*, i.e. *vessel:*—ship (-ping).

4144. πλόος **plŏŏs**, *plŏ'-os;* from *4126;* a *sail*, i.e. *navigation:*—course, sailing, voyage.

4145. πλούσιος **plŏusiŏs**, *ploo'-see-os;* from *4149;* *wealthy;* fig. *abounding* with:—rich.

4146. πλουσίως **plŏusiōs**, *ploo-see'-oce;* adv. from *4145;* *copiously:*—abundantly, richly.

4147. πλουτέω **plŏutĕō**, *ploo-teh'-o;* from *4148;* to *be* (or *become*) *wealthy* (lit. or fig.):—be increased with goods, (be made, wax) rich.

4148. πλουτίζω **plŏutizō**, *ploo-tid'-zo;* from *4149;* to *make wealthy* (fig.):—en- (make) rich.

4149. πλοῦτος **plŏutŏs**, *ploo'-tos;* from the base of *4130;* *wealth* (as *fulness*), i.e. (lit.) *money, possessions*, or (fig.) *abundance, richness*, (spec.) valuable *bestowment:*—riches.

4150. πλύνω **plunō**, *ploo'-no;* a prol. form of an obsol. πλύω **pluō** (to "*flow*"); to "*plunge*", i.e. *launder* clothing:—wash. Comp. *3068, 3538.*

4151. πνεῦμα **pnĕuma**, *pnyoo'-mah;* from *4154;* a *current* of air, i.e. *breath* (*blast*) or a *breeze;* by anal. or fig. a *spirit*, i.e. (human) the rational *soul*, (by impl.) *vital principle*, mental *disposition*, etc., or (superhuman) an *angel, dæmon*, or (divine) *God*, Christ's *spirit*, the Holy *Spirit:*—ghost, life, spirit (-ual, -ually), mind. Comp. *5590.*

4152. πνευματικός **pnĕumatikŏs**, *pnyoo-mat-ik-os'*; from *4151*; *non-carnal*, i.e. (humanly) *ethereal* (as opposed to gross), or (dæmoniacally) a *spirit* (concr.), or (divinely) *supernatural*, *regenerate*, *religious*:—spiritual. Comp. *5591*.

4153. πνευματικῶς **pnĕumatikōs**, *pnyoo-mat-ik-oce'*; adv. from *4152*; *non-physically*, i.e. *divinely*, *figuratively*:—spiritually.

4154. πνέω **pnĕō**, *pneh'-o*; a prim. word; to *breathe* hard, i.e. *breeze*:—blow. Comp. *5594*.

4155. πνίγω **pnigō**, *pnee'-go*; strengthened from *4154*; to *wheeze*, i.e. (caus. by impl.) to *throttle* or *strangle* (*drown*):—choke, take by the throat.

4156. πνικτός **pniktŏs**, *pnik-tos'*; from *4155*; *throttled*, i.e. (neut. concr.) an animal *choked* to death (*not bled*):—strangled.

4157. πνοή **pnŏē**, *pno-ay'*; from *4154*; *respiration*, a *breeze*:—breath, wind.

4158. ποδήρης **pŏdērēs**, *pod-ay'-race*; from *4228* and another element of uncert. affin.; a *dress* (*2066* implied) *reaching* the *ankles*:—garment down to the foot.

4159. πόθεν **pŏthĕn**, *poth'-en*; from the base of *4213* with enclitic adv. of origin; *from which* (as interrog.) or *what* (as rel.) place, state, source or cause:—whence.

4160. ποιέω **pŏiĕō**, *poy-eh'-o*; appar. a prol. form of an obsol. prim.; to *make* or *do* (in a very wide application, more or less direct):—abide, + agree, appoint, × avenge, + band together, be, bear, + bewray, bring (forth), cast out, cause, commit, + content, continue, deal, + without any delay, (would) do (-ing), execute, exercise, fulfil, gain, give, have, hold, × journeying, keep, + lay wait, + lighten the ship, make, × mean, + none of these things move me, observe, ordain, perform, provide, + have purged, purpose, put, + raising up, × secure, shew, × shoot out, spend, take, tarry, + transgress the law, work, yield. Comp. *4238*.

4161. ποίημα **pŏiēma**, *poy'-ay-mah*; from *4160*; a *product*, i.e. *fabric* (lit. or fig.):—thing that is made, workmanship.

4162. ποίησις **pŏiēsis**, *poy'-ay-sis*; from *4160*; *action*, i.e. *performance* (of the law):—deed.

4163. ποιητής **pŏiētēs**, *poy-ay-tace'*; from *4160*; a *performer*; spec. a "*poet*";—doer, poet.

4164. ποικίλος **pŏikilŏs**, *poy-kee'-los*; of uncert. der.; *motley*, i.e. *various* in character:—divers, manifold.

4165. ποιμαίνω **pŏimainō**, *poy-mah'-ee-no*; from *4166*; to *tend* as a shepherd (or fig. *superviser*):—feed (cattle), rule.

4166. ποιμήν **pŏimēn**, *poy-mane'*; of uncert. affin.; a *shepherd* (lit. or fig.):—shepherd, pastor.

4167. ποίμνη **pŏimnē**, *poym'-nay*; contr. from *4165*; a *flock* (lit. or fig.):—flock, fold.

4168. ποίμνιον **pŏimniŏn**, *poym'-nee-on*; neut. of a presumed der. of *4167*; a *flock*, i.e. (fig.) *group* (of believers):—flock.

4169. ποῖος **pŏiŏs**, *poy'-os*; from the base of *4226* and *3634*; individualizing interrog. (of character) *what* sort of, or (of number) *which* one:—what (manner of), which.

4170. πολεμέω **pŏlĕmĕō**, *pol-em-eh'-o*; from *4171*; to *be* (engaged) in *warfare*, i.e. to *battle* (lit. or fig.):—fight, (make) war.

4171. πόλεμος **pŏlĕmŏs**, *pol'-em-os*; from πέλομαι **pĕlŏmai** (to *bustle*); *warfare* (lit. or fig.; a single encounter or a series):—battle, fight, war.

4172. πόλις **pŏlis**, *pol'-is*; prob. from the same as *4171*, or perh. from *4183*; a *town* (prop. with walls, of greater or less size):—city.

4173. πολιτάρχης **pŏlitarchēs**, *pol-it-ar'-khace*; from *4172* and *757*; a *town-officer*, i.e. *magistrate*:—ruler of the city.

4174. πολιτεία **pŏlitĕia**, *pol-ee-ti'-ah*; from *4177* ("*polity*"); *citizenship*; concr. a *community*:—commonwealth, freedom.

4175. πολίτευμα **pŏlitĕuma**, *pol-it'-yoo-mah*; from *4176*; a *community*, i.e. (abstr.) *citizenship* (fig.):—conversation.

4176. πολιτεύομαι **pŏlitĕuŏmai**, *pol-it-yoo'-om-ahee*; mid. of a der. of *4177*; to *behave* as a citizen (fig.):—let conversation be, live.

4177. πολίτης **pŏlitēs**, *pol-ee'-tace*; from *4172*; a *townsman*:—citizen.

4178. πολλάκις **pŏllakis**, *pol-lak'-is*; mult. adv. from *4183*; *many times*, i.e. *frequently*:—oft (-en, -entimes, -times).

4179. πολλαπλασίων **pŏllaplasiōn**, *pol-lap-las-ee'-ohn*; from *4183* and prob. a der. of *4120*; *manifold*, i.e. (neut. as noun) *very much more*:—manifold more.

4180. πολυλογία **pŏlulŏgia**, *pol-oo-log-ee'-ah*; from a comp. of *4183* and *3056*; *loquacity*, i.e. *prolixity*:—much speaking.

4181. πολυμέρως **pŏlumĕrōs**, *pol-oo-mer'-oce*; adv. from a comp. of *4183* and *3313*; *in many portions*, i.e. *variously* as to time and agency (*piecemeal*):—at sundry times.

4182. πολυποίκιλος **pŏlupŏikilŏs**, *pol-oo-poy'-kil-os*; from *4183* and *4164*; *much variegated*, i.e. *multifarious*:—manifold.

4183. πολύς **pŏlus**, *pol-oos'*; includ. the forms from the alt. πολλός **pŏllŏs**; (sing.) *much* (in any respect) or (plur.) *many*; neut. (sing.) as adv. *largely*; neut. (plur.) as adv. or noun *often*, *mostly*, *largely*:—abundant, + altogether, common, + far (passed, spent), (+ be of a) great (age, deal, -ly, while), long, many, much, oft (-en [-times]), plenteous, sore, straitly. Comp. *4118*, *4119*.

4184. πολύσπλαγχνος **pŏlusplagchnŏs**, *pol-oo'-splankh-nos*; from *4183* and *4698* (fig.); *extremely compassionate*:—very pitiful.

4185. πολυτελής **pŏlutĕlēs**, *pol-oo-tel-ace'*; from *4183* and *5056*; *extremely expensive*:—costly, very precious, of great price.

4186. πολύτιμος **pŏlutimŏs**, *pol-oot'-ee-mos*; from *4183* and *5092*; *extremely valuable*:—very costly, of great price.

4187. πολυτρόπως **pŏlutrŏpōs**, *pol-oot-rop'-oce*; adv. from a comp. of *4183* and *5158*; *in many ways*, i.e. *variously* as to method or form:—in divers manners.

4188. πόμα **pŏma**, *pom'-ah*; from the alt. of *4095*; a *beverage*:—drink.

4189. πονηρία **pŏnēria**, *pon-ay-ree'-ah*; from *4190*; *depravity*, i.e. (spec.) *malice*; plur. (concr.) *plots*, *sins*:—iniquity, wickedness.

4190. πονηρός **pŏnērŏs**, *pon-ay-ros'*; from a der. of *4192*; *hurtful*, i.e. *evil* (prop. in effect or influence, and thus differing from *2556*, which refers rather to *essential* character, as well as from *4550*, which indicates *degeneracy* from original virtue); fig. *calamitous*; also (pass.) *ill*, i.e. *diseased*; but espec. (mor.) *culpable*, i.e. *derelict*, *vicious*, *facinorous*; neut. (sing.) *mischief*, *malice*, or (plur.) *guilt*; masc. (sing.) the *devil*, or (plur.) *sinners*:—bad, evil, grievous, harm, lewd, malicious, wicked (-ness). See also *4191*.

4191. πονηρότερος **pŏnērŏtĕrŏs**, *pon-ay-rot'-er-os*; compar. of *4190*; *more evil*:—more wicked.

4192. πόνος **pŏnŏs**, *pon'-os*; from the base of *3993*; *toil*, i.e. (by impl.) *anguish*:—pain.

4193. Ποντικός **Pŏntikŏs**, *pon-tik-os'*; from *4195*; a *Pontican*, i.e. native of Pontus:—born in Pontus.

4194. Πόντιος **Pŏntiŏs**, *pon'-tee-os*; of Lat. or.; appar. *bridged*; *Pontius*, a Rom.:—Pontius.

4195. Πόντος **Pŏntŏs**, *pon'-tos*; a *sea*; *Pontus*, a region of Asia Minor:—Pontus.

4196. Πόπλιος **Pŏpliŏs**, *pop'-lee-os*; of Lat. or.; appar. "*popular*"; *Poplius* (i.e. *Publius*), a Rom.:—Publius.

4197. πορεία **pŏrĕia**, *por-i'-ah*; from *4198*; *travel* (by land); fig. (plur.) *proceedings*, i.e. *career*:—journey [-ing], ways.

4198. πορεύομαι **pŏrĕuŏmai**, *por-yoo'-om-ahee*; mid. from a der. of the same as *3984*; to *traverse*, i.e. *travel* (lit. or fig.; espec. to *remove* [fig. *die*], live, etc.);—depart, go (away, forth, one's way, up), (make a, take a) journey, walk.

4199. πορθέω **pŏrthĕō**, *por-theh'-o*; prol. from πέρθω **pĕrthō** (to *sack*); to *ravage* (fig.):—destroy, waste.

4200. πορισμός **pŏrismŏs**, *por-is-mos'*; from a der. of πόρος **pŏrŏs** (a *way*, i.e. *means*); *furnishing* (*procuring*), i.e. (by impl.) *money-getting* (*acquisition*):—gain.

4201. Πόρκιος **Pŏrkiŏs**, *por'-kee-os*; of Lat. or.; appar. *swinish*; *Porcius*, a Rom.:—Porcius.

4202. πορνεία **pŏrnĕia**, *por-ni'-ah*; from *4203*; *harlotry* (includ. *adultery* and *incest*); fig. *idolatry*:—fornication.

4203. πορνεύω **pŏrnĕuō**, *porn-yoo'-o*; from *4204*; to *act* the *harlot*, i.e. (lit.) *indulge* unlawful *lust* (of either sex), or (fig.) *practise idolatry*:—commit (fornication).

4204. πόρνη **pŏrnē**, *por'-nay*; fem. of *4205*; a *strumpet*; fig. an *idolater*:—harlot, whore.

4205. πόρνος **pŏrnŏs**, *por'-nos*; from πέρνημι **pĕrnēmi** (to *sell*; akin to the base of *4097*); a (male) *prostitute* (as *venal*), i.e. (by anal.) a *debauchee* (*libertine*):—fornicator, whoremonger.

4206. πόῤῥω **pŏrrhō**, *por'-rho*; adv. from *4253*; *forwards*, i.e. *at a distance*;—far, a great way off. See also *4207*.

4207. πόῤῥωθεν **pŏrrhōthĕn**, *por'-rho-then*; from *4206* with adv. enclitic of source; *from far*, or (by impl.) *at a distance*, i.e. *distantly*:—afar off.

4208. ποῤῥωτέρω **pŏrrhōtĕrō**, *por-rho-ter'-o*; adv. compar. of *4206*; *farther*, i.e. *a greater distance*:—further.

4209. πορφύρα **pŏrphura**, *por-foo'-rah*; of Lat. or.; the "*purple*" mussel, i.e. (by impl.) the *red-blue* color itself, and finally a garment dyed with it:—purple.

4210. πορφυροῦς **pŏrphurŏus**, *por-foo-rooce'*; from *4209*; *purpureal*, i.e. *bluish red*:—purple.

4211. πορφυρόπωλις **pŏrphurŏpōlis**, *por-foo-rop'-o-lis*; fem. of a comp. of *4209* and *4453*; a *female trader in purple* cloth:—seller of purple.

4212. ποσάκις **pŏsakis**, *pos-ak'-is*; mult. from *4214*; *how many times*:—how oft (-en).

4213. πόσις **pŏsis**, *pos'-is*; from the alt. of *4095*; a *drinking* (the act), i.e. (concr.) a *draught*:—drink.

4214. πόσος **pŏsŏs**, *pos'-os*; from an obsol. πός **pŏs** (*who*, *what*) and *3739*; interrog. pron. (of amount) *how much* (*large*, *long* or [plur.] *many*):—how great (long, many), what.

4215. ποταμός **pŏtamŏs**, *pot-am-os'*; prob. from a der. of the alt. of *4095* (comp. *4224*); a *current*, *brook* or *freshet* (as *drinkable*), i.e. *running water*:—flood, river, stream, water.

4216. ποταμοφόρητος **pŏtamŏphŏrētŏs**, *pot-am-of-or'-ay-tos*; from *4215* and a der. of *5409*; *river-borne*, i.e. *overwhelmed by a stream*:—carried away of the flood.

4217. ποταπός **pŏtapŏs**, *pot-ap-os'*; appar. from *4219* and the base of *4226*; interrog. *whatever*, i.e. of *what possible* sort:—what (manner of).

4218. ποτέ **pŏtĕ**, *pot-eh'*; from the base of *4225* and *5037*; indef. adv., at *some time*, *ever*:—afore- (any, some-) time (-s), at length (the last), (+ n-) ever, in the old time, in time past, once, when.

4219. πότε **pŏtĕ**, *pot'-eh*; from the base of *4226* and *5037*; interrog. adv., at *what time*:— + how long, when.

4220. πότερον **pŏtĕrŏn**, *pot'-er-on*; neut. of a compar. of the base of *4226*; interrog. as adv., *which* (of two), i.e. *is it* this or that:—whether.

4221. ποτήριον **pŏtēriŏn**, *pot-ay'-ree-on*; neut. of a der. of the alt. of *4095*; a *drinking-vessel*; by extens. the contents thereof, i.e. a *cupful* (*draught*); fig. a *lot* or *fate*:—cup.

4222. ποτίζω **pŏtizō**, *pot-id'-zo*; from a der. of the alt. of *4095*; to *furnish drink*, *irrigate*:—give (make) to drink, feed, water.

4223. Ποτίολοι **Pŏtiŏlŏi**, *pot-ee'-ol-oy;* of Lat. or.; *little wells*, i.e. *mineral springs; Potioli* (i.e. *Puteoli*), a place in Italy:—Puteoli.

4224. πότος **pŏtŏs**, *pot'-os;* from the alt. of 4095; a *drinking-bout* or *carousal:*—banqueting.

4225. πού **pŏu**, *poo;* gen. of an indef. pron. πός **pŏs** (*some*) otherwise obsol. (comp. 4214); as adv. of place, *somewhere*, i.e. *nearly:*—about, a certain place.

4226. ποῦ **pŏu**, *poo;* gen. of an interrog. pron. πός **pŏs** (*what*) otherwise obsol. (perh. the same as 4225 used with the rising slide of inquiry); as adv. of place; *at* (by impl. *to*) *what* locality:—where, whither.

4227. Πούδης **Pŏudēs**, *poo'-dace;* of Lat. or.; *modest; Pudes* (i.e. *Pudens*), a Chr.:—Pudens.

4228. πούς **pŏus**, *pooce;* a prim word; a "*foot*" (fig. or lit.):—foot (-stool).

4229. πρᾶγμα **pragma**, *prag'-mah;* from 4238; a *deed;* by impl. an *affair;* by extens. an *object* (material):—business, matter, thing, work.

4230. πραγματεία **pragmatĕia**, *prag-mat-i'-ah;* from 4231; a *transaction*, i.e. *negotiation:*—affair.

4231. πραγματεύομαι **pragmatĕuŏmai**, *prag-mat-yoo'-om-ahee;* from 4229; to *busy oneself* with, i.e. to *trade:*—occupy.

4232. πραιτώριον **praitōriŏn**, *prahee-to'-ree-on;* of Lat. or.; the *prætorium* or governor's *court-room* (sometimes includ. the whole *edifice* and *camp*):—(common, judgment) hall (of judgment), palace, prætorium.

4233. πράκτωρ **praktōr**, *prak'-tore;* from a der. of 4238; a *practiser*, i.e. (spec.) an official *collector:*—officer.

4234. πρᾶξις **praxis**, *prax'-is;* from 4238; *practice*, i.e. (concr.) an *act;* by extens. a *function:*—deed, office, work.

4235. πρᾷος **pra₁ŏs**, *prah'-os;* a form of 4239, used in cert. parts; *gentle*, i.e. *humble:*—meek.

4236. πρᾳότης **pra₁ŏtēs**, *prah-ot'-ace;* from 4235; *gentleness;* by impl. *humility:*—meekness.

4237. πρασιά **prasia**, *pras-ee-ah';* perh. from πράσον **prasŏn** (a *leek*, and so an *onion-patch*); a garden-*plot*, i.e. (by impl. of regular *beds*) a *row* (repeated in plur. by Hebr. to indicate an arrangement):—in ranks.

4238. πράσσω **prassō**, *pras'-so;* a prim. verb; to "*practise*", i.e. *perform repeatedly* or *habitually* (thus differing from 4160, which prop. refers to a *single* act); by impl. to *execute, accomplish*, etc.; spec. to *collect* (dues), *fare* (personally):—commit, deeds, do, exact, keep, require, use arts.

4239. πραΰς **praüs**, *prah-ooce';* appar. a prim. word; *mild*, i.e. (by impl.) *humble:*—meek. See also 4235.

4240. πραΰτης **praütēs**, *prah-oo'-tace;* from 4239; *mildness*, i.e. (by impl.) *humility:*—meekness.

4241. πρέπω **prĕpō**, *prep'-o;* appar. a prim. verb; to *tower* up (*be conspicuous*), i.e. (by impl.) to *be suitable* or *proper* (third pers. sing. pres. indic. often used impers., it is *fit* or *right*):—become, comely.

4242. πρεσβεία **prĕsbĕia**, *pres-bi'-ah;* from 4243; *seniority* (*eldership*), i.e. (by impl.) an *embassy* (concr. *ambassadors*):—ambassage, message.

4243. πρεσβεύω **prĕsbĕuō**, *pres-byoo'-o;* from the base of 4245; to be a *senior*, i.e. (by impl.) *act as a representative* (fig. *preacher*):—be an ambassador.

4244. πρεσβυτέριον **prĕsbutĕriŏn**, *pres-boo-ter'-ee-on;* neut. of a presumed der. of 4245; the *order of elders*, i.e. (spec.) Isr. *Sanhedrim* or Chr. "*presbytery*":—(estate of) elder (-s), presbytery.

4245. πρεσβύτερος **prĕsbutĕrŏs**, *pres-boo'-ter-os;* compar. of πρέσβυς **prĕsbus** (*elderly*); *older;* as noun, a *senior;* spec. an Isr. *Sanhedrist* (also fig. member of the celestial council) or Chr. "*presbyter*":—elder (-est), old.

4246. πρεσβύτης **prĕsbutēs**, *pres-boo'-tace;* from the same as 4245; an *old man:*—aged (man), old man.

4247. πρεσβῦτις **prĕsbutis**, *pres-boo'-tis;* fem. of 4246; an *old woman:*—aged woman.

πρήθω **prēthō**. See 4092.

4248. πρηνής **prēnēs**, *pray-nace';* from 4253; *leaning* (*falling*) *forward* ("*prone*"), i.e. *head foremost:*—headlong.

4249. πρίζω **prizō**, *prid'-zo;* a strengthened form of a prim. πρίω **priō** (to *saw*); to *saw* in two:—saw asunder.

4250. πρίν **prin**, *prin;* adv. from 4253; *prior, sooner:*—before (that), ere.

4251. Πρίσκα **Priska**, *pris'-kah;* of Lat. or.; fem. of *Priscus, ancient; Priska*, a Chr. woman:—Prisca. See also 4252.

4252. Πρίσκιλλα **Priscilla**, *pris'-cil-lah;* dimin. of 4251; *Priscilla* (i.e. *little Prisca*), a Chr. woman:—Priscilla.

4253. πρό **prŏ**, *prŏ;* a prim. prep.; "*fore*", i.e. *in front of, prior* (fig. *superior*) *to:*—above, ago, before, or ever. In comp. it retains the same significations.

4254. προάγω **prŏagō**, *prŏ-ag'-o;* from 4253 and 71; to *lead forward* (magisterially); intrans. to *precede* (in place or time [part. *previous*]):—bring (forth, out), go before.

4255. προαιρέομαι **prŏairĕŏmai**, *prŏ-ahee-reh'-om-ahee;* from 4253 and 138; to *choose* for oneself *before* another thing (*prefer*), i.e. (by impl.) to *propose* (*intend*):—purpose.

4256. προαιτιάομαι **prŏaitiaŏmai**, *prŏ-ahee-tee-ah'-om-ahee;* from 4253 and a der. of 156; to *accuse already*, i.e. *previously charge:*—prove before.

4257. προακούω **prŏakŏuō**, *prŏ-ak-oo'-o;* from 4253 and 191; to *hear already*, i.e. *anticipate:*—hear before.

4258. προαμαρτάνω **prŏamartanō**, *prŏ-am-ar-tan'-o;* from 4253 and 264; to *sin previously* (to conversion):—sin already, heretofore sin.

4259. προαύλιον **prŏauliŏn**, *prŏ-ŏw'-lee-on;* neut. of a presumed comp. of 4253 and 833; a *fore-court*, i.e. *vestibule* (*alley-way*):—porch.

4260. προβαίνω **prŏbainō**, *prob-ah'ee-no;* from 4253 and the base of 939; to *walk forward*, i.e. *advance* (lit. or in years):— + be of a great age, go farther (on), be well stricken.

4261. προβάλλω **prŏballō**, *prob-al'-lo;* from 4253 and 906; to *throw forward*, i.e. *push to the front, germinate:*—put forward, shoot forth.

4262. προβατικός **prŏbatikŏs**, *prob-at-ik-os';* from 4263; *relating to sheep*, i.e. (a *gate*) through which they were led into Jerusalem:—sheep (market).

4263. πρόβατον **prŏbatŏn**, *prob'-at-on;* prop. neut. of a presumed der. of 4260; *something that walks forward* (a *quadruped*), i.e. (spec.) a *sheep* (lit. or fig.):—sheep ([-fold]).

4264. προβιβάζω **prŏbibazō**, *prob-ib-ad'-zo;* from 4253 and a redupl. form of 971; to *force forward*, i.e. *bring to the front, instigate:*—draw, before instruct.

4265. προβλέπω **prŏblĕpō**, *prob-lep'-o;* from 4253 and 991; to *look out beforehand*, i.e. *furnish in advance:*—provide.

4266. προγίνομαι **prŏginŏmai**, *prog-in'-om-ahee;* from 4253 and 1096; to *be already*, i.e. *have previously transpired:*—be past.

4267. προγινώσκω **prŏginōskō**, *prog-in-oce'-ko;* from 4253 and 1097; to *know beforehand*, i.e. *foresee:*—foreknow (ordain), know (before).

4268. πρόγνωσις **prŏgnōsis**, *prog'-no-sis;* from 4267; *forethought:*—foreknowledge.

4269. πρόγονος **prŏgŏnŏs**, *prog'-on-os;* from 4266; an *ancestor*, (*grand-*) *parent:*—forefather, parent.

4270. προγράφω **prŏgraphō**, *prog-raf'-o;* from 4253 and 1125; to *write previously;* fig. to *announce, prescribe:*—before ordain, evidently set forth, write (afore, aforetime).

4271. πρόδηλος **prŏdēlŏs**, *prod'-ay-los;* from 4253 and 1212; *plain before* all men, i.e. *obvious:*—evident, manifest (open) beforehand.

4272. προδίδωμι **prŏdidōmi**, *prod-id'-o-mee;* from 4253 and 1325; to *give before* the other party has given:—first give.

4273. προδότης **prŏdŏtēs**, *prod-ot'-ace;* from 4272 (in the sense of *giving forward* into another's [the enemy's] hands); a *surrender:*—betrayer, traitor.

προδρέμω **prŏdrĕmō**. See 4390.

4274. πρόδρομος **prŏdrŏmŏs**, *prod'-rom-os;* from the alt. of 4390; a *runner ahead*, i.e. *scout* (fig. *precursor*):—forerunner.

4275. προείδω **prŏĕidō**, *pro-i'-do;* from 4253 and 1492; *foresee:*—foresee, saw before.

προειρέω **prŏĕirĕō**. See 4280.

4276. προελπίζω **prŏĕlpizō**, *prŏ-el-pid'-zo;* from 4253 and 1679; to *hope in advance* of other confirmation:—first trust.

4277. προέπω **prŏĕpō**, *prŏ-ep'-o;* from 4253 and 2036; to *say already*, to *predict:*—forewarn, say (speak, tell) before. Comp. 4280.

4278. προενάρχομαι **prŏĕnarchŏmai**, *prŏ-en-ar'-khom-ahee;* from 4253 and 1728; to *commence already:*—begin (before).

4279. προεπαγγέλλομαι **prŏĕpaggĕllŏmai**, *prŏ-ep-ang-ghel'-lom-ahee;* mid. from 4253 and 1861; to *promise of old:*—promise before.

4280. προερέω **prŏĕrĕō**, *prŏ-er-eh'-o;* from 4253 and 2046; used as alt. of 4277; to *say already, predict:*—foretell, say (speak, tell) before.

4281. προέρχομαι **prŏĕrchŏmai**, *prŏ-er'-khom-ahee;* from 4253 and 2064 (includ. its alt.); to *go onward, precede* (in place or time):—go before (farther, forward), outgo, pass on.

4282. προετοιμάζω **prŏĕtŏimazō**, *prŏ-et-oy-mad'-zo;* from 4253 and 2090; to *fit up in advance* (lit. or fig.):—ordain before, prepare afore.

4283. προευαγγελίζομαι **prŏĕuaggĕlizŏmai**, *prŏ-yoo-ang-ghel-id'-zom-ahee;* mid. from 4253 and 2097; to *announce* glad news *in advance:*—preach before the gospel.

4284. προέχομαι **prŏĕchŏmai**, *prŏ-ekh-om-ahee;* mid. from 4253 and 2192; to *hold* oneself *before* others, i.e. (fig.) to *excel:*—be better.

4285. προηγέομαι **prŏēgĕŏmai**, *prŏ-ay-geh'-om-ahee;* from 4253 and 2233; to *lead the way* for others, i.e. *show deference:*—prefer.

4286. πρόθεσις **prŏthĕsis**, *proth'-es-is;* from 4388; a *setting forth*, i.e. (fig.) *proposal* (*intention*); spec. the *show*-bread (in the Temple) as *exposed* before God:—purpose, shew [-bread].

4287. προθέσμιος **prŏthĕsmiŏs**, *proth-es'-mee-os;* from 4253 and a der. of 5087; *fixed beforehand*, i.e. (fem. with 2250 impl.) a *designated* day:—time appointed.

4288. προθυμία **prŏthumia**, *proth-oo-mee'-ah;* from 4289; *predisposition*, i.e. *alacrity:*—forwardness of mind, readiness (of mind), ready (willing) mind.

4289. πρόθυμος **prŏthumŏs**, *proth'-oo-mos;* from 4253 and 2372; *forward* in spirit, i.e. *predisposed;* neut. (as noun) *alacrity:*—ready, willing.

4290. προθύμως **prŏthumōs**, *proth-oo'-moce;* adv. from 4289; *with alacrity:*—willingly.

4291. προΐστημι **prŏïstēmi**, *prŏ-is'-tay-mee;* from 4253 and 2476; to *stand before*, i.e. (in rank) to *preside*, or (by impl.) to *practise:*—maintain, be over, rule.

4292. προκαλέομαι **prŏkalĕŏmai**, *prok-al-eh'-om-ahee;* mid. from 4253 and 2564; to *call forth to oneself* (*challenge*), i.e. (by impl.) to *irritate:*—provoke.

4293. προκαταγγέλλω **prŏkataggĕllō**, *prok-at-ang-ghel'-lo;* from 4253 and 2605; to *announce beforehand*, i.e. *predict, promise:*—foretell, have notice (shew) before.

4294. προκαταρτίζω **prŏkatartizō**, *prok-at-ar-tid'-zo;* from 4253 and 2675; to *prepare in advance:*—make up beforehand.

4295. πρόκειμαι **prŏkĕimai**, *prok'-i-mahee;* from 4253 and 2749; to *lie before* the view, i.e. (fig.) to *be present* (to the mind), to *stand forth* (as an example or reward):—be first, set before (forth).

4296. προκηρύσσω **prŏkērussō**, *prok-ay-rooce'-so;* from 4253 and 2784; to *herald* (i.e. *proclaim*) *in advance:*—before (first) preach.

4297. προκοπή **prŏkŏpē**, *prok-op-ay';* from 4298; *progress*, i.e. *advancement* (subj. or obj.):—furtherance, profit.

4298. προκόπτω **prŏkŏptō**, *prok-op'-to;* from 4253 and 2875; to *drive forward* (as if by beating), i.e. (fig. and intrans.) to *advance* (in amount, to *grow;* in time, to *be well along*):—increase, proceed, profit, be far spent, wax.

4299. πρόκριμα **prŏkrima**, *prok'-ree-mah;* from a comp. of 4253 and 2919; a *prejudgment* (*prejudice*), i.e. *prepossession:*—prefer one before another.

4300. προκυρόω **prŏkurŏō**, *prok-oo-rŏ'-o;* from 4253 and 2964; to *ratify previously:*—confirm before.

4301. προλαμβάνω **prŏlambanō**, *prol-am-ban'-o;* from 4253 and 2983; to *take in advance*, i.e. (lit.) *eat before* others have an opportunity; (fig.) to *anticipate*, *surprise:*—come aforehand, overtake, take before.

4302. προλέγω **prŏlĕgō**, *prol-eg'-o;* from 4253 and 3004; to *say beforehand*, i.e. *predict*, *forewarn:*—foretell, tell before.

4303. προμαρτύρομαι **prŏmarturŏmai**, *prom-ar-too'-rom-ahee;* from 4253 and 3143; to *be a witness in advance*, i.e. *predict:*—testify beforehand.

4304. προμελετάω **prŏmĕlĕtaō**, *prom-el-et-ah'-o;* from 4253 and 3191; to *premeditate:*—meditate before.

4305. προμεριμνάω **prŏmĕrimnaō**, *prom-er-im-nah'-o;* from 4253 and 3309; to *care* (anxiously) *in advance:*—take thought beforehand.

4306. προνοέω **prŏnŏĕō**, *pron-ŏ-eh'-o;* from 4253 and 3539; to *consider in advance*, i.e. *look* out for *beforehand* (act. by way of *maintenance* for others; mid. by way of *circumspection* for oneself):—provide (for).

4307. πρόνοια **prŏnŏia**, *pron'-oy-ah;* from 4306; *forethought*, i.e. provident *care* or *supply:*—providence, provision.

4308. προοράω **prŏŏraō**, *prŏ-or-ah'-o;* from 4253 and 3708; to *behold in advance*, i.e. (act.) to *notice* (another) *previously*, or (mid.) to *keep in* (one's own) *view:*—foresee, see before.

4309. προορίζω **prŏŏrizō**, *prŏ-or-id'-zo;* from 4253 and 3724; to *limit in advance*, i.e. (fig.) *predetermine:*—determine before, ordain, predestinate.

4310. προπάσχω **prŏpaschō**, *prop-as'-kho;* from 4253 and 3958; to *undergo* hardship *previously:*—suffer before.

4311. προπέμπω **prŏpĕmpō**, *prop-em'-po;* from 4253 and 3992; to *send forward*, i.e. *escort* or *aid* in travel:—accompany, bring (forward) on journey (way), conduct forth.

4312. προπετής **prŏpĕtēs**, *prop-et-ace';* from a comp. of 4253 and 4098; *falling forward*, i.e. *headlong* (fig. *precipitate*):—heady, rash [-ly].

4313. προπορεύομαι **prŏpŏrĕuŏmai**, *prop-or-yoo'-om-ahee;* from 4253 and 4198; to *precede* (as guide or herald):—go before.

4314. πρός **prŏs**, *pros;* a strengthened form of 4253; a prep. of direction; *forward to*, i.e. *toward* (with the genit. *the side* of, i.e. *pertaining to;* with the dat. *by the side of*, i.e. *near to;* usually with the accus. the place, time, occasion, or respect, which is the *destination* of the relation, i.e. *whither* or *for* which it is predicated):—about, according to, against, among, at, because of, before, between, ([where-]) by, for, × at thy house, in, for intent, nigh unto, of, which pertain to, that, to (the end that), + together, to ([you]) -ward, unto, with (-in). In comp. it denotes essentially the same applications, namely, motion *towards*, accession *to*, or nearness *at*.

4315. προσάββατον **prŏsabbatŏn**, *pros-ab'-bat-on;* from 4253 and 4521; a *fore-sabbath*, i.e. the *Sabbath-eve:*—day before the sabbath. Comp. 3904.

4316. προσαγορεύω **prŏsagŏrĕuō**, *pros-ag-or-yoo'-o;* from 4314 and a der. of 58 (mean. to *harangue*); to *address*, i.e. salute by *name:*—call.

4317. προσάγω **prŏsagō**, *pros-ag'-o;* from 4314 and 71; to *lead towards*, i.e. (trans.) to *conduct near* (*summon*, *present*), or (intrans.) to *approach:*—bring, draw near.

4318. προσαγωγή **prŏsagōgē**, *pros-ag-ogue-ay';* from 4317 (comp. 72); *admission:*—access.

4319. προσαιτέω **prŏsaitĕō** *pros-ahee-teh'-o;* from 4314 and 154; to *ask repeatedly* (*importune*), i.e. *solicit:*—beg.

4320. προσαναβαίνω **prŏsanabainō**, *pros-an-ab-ah'ee-no;* from 4314 and 305; to *ascend farther*, i.e. *be promoted* (*take an upper* [*more honorable*] *seat*):—go up.

4321. προσαναλίσκω **prŏsanaliskō**, *pros-an-al-is'-ko;* from 4314 and 355; to *expend further:*—spend.

4322. προσαναπληρόω **prŏsanaplērŏō**, *pros-an-ap-lay-rŏ'-o;* from 4314 and 378; to *fill up further*, i.e. *furnish fully:*—supply.

4323. προσανατίθημι **prŏsanatithēmi**, *pros-an-at-ith'-ay-mee;* from 4314 and 394; to *lay up in addition*, i.e. (mid. and fig.) to *impart* or (by impl.) to *consult:*—in conference add, confer.

4324. προσαπειλέω **prŏsapĕilĕō**, *pros-ap-i-leh'-o;* from 4314 and 546; to *menace additionally:*—threaten further.

4325. προσδαπανάω **prŏsdapanaō**, *pros-dap-an-ah'-o;* from 4314 and 1159; to *expend additionally:*—spend more.

4326. προσδέομαι **prŏsdĕŏmai**, *pros-deh'-om-ahee;* from 4314 and 1189; to *require additionally*, i.e. *want further:*—need.

4327. προσδέχομαι **prŏsdĕchŏmai**, *pros-dekh'-om-ahee;* from 4314 and 1209; to *admit* (to intercourse, hospitality, credence or [fig.] endurance); by impl. to *await* (with confidence or patience):—accept, allow, look (wait) for, take.

4328. προσδοκάω **prŏsdŏkaō**, *pros-dok-ah'-o;* from 4314 and δοκεύω **dŏkĕuō** (to *watch*); to *anticipate* (in thought, hope or fear); by impl. to *await:*—(be in) expect (-ation), look (for), when looked, tarry, wait for.

4329. προσδοκία **prŏsdŏkia**, *pros-dok-ee'-ah;* from 4328; *apprehension* (of evil); by impl. *infliction* anticipated:—expectation, looking after.

προσδρέμω **prŏsdrĕmō**. See 4370.

4330. προσεάω **prŏsĕaō**, *pros-eh-ah'-o;* from 4314 and 1439; to *permit further* progress:—suffer.

4331. προσεγγίζω **prŏsĕggizō**, *pros-eng-ghid'-zo;* from 4314 and 1448; to *approach near:*—come nigh.

4332. προσεδρεύω **prŏsĕdrĕuō**, *pros-ed-ryoo'-o;* from a comp. of 4314 and the base of 1476; to *sit near*, i.e. *attend* as a servant:—wait at.

4333. προσεργάζομαι **prŏsĕrgazŏmai**, *pros-er-gad'-zom-ahee;* from 4314 and 2038; to *work additionally*, i.e. (by impl.) *acquire besides:*—gain.

4334. προσέρχομαι **prŏsĕrchŏmai**, *pros-er'-khom-ahee;* from 4314 and 2064 (includ. its alt.); to *approach*, i.e. (lit.) *come near*, *visit*, or (fig.) *worship*, *assent to:*—(as soon as he) come (unto), come thereunto, consent, draw near, go (near, to, unto).

4335. προσευχή **prŏsĕuchē**, *pros-yoo-khay';* from 4336; *prayer* (*worship*); by impl. an *oratory* (*chapel*):— × pray earnestly, prayer.

4336. προσεύχομαι **prŏsĕuchŏmai**, *pros-yoo'-khom-ahee;* from 4314 and 2172; to *pray to* God, i.e. *supplicate*, *worship:*—pray (× earnestly, for), make prayer.

4337. προσέχω **prŏsĕchō**, *pros-ekh'-o;* from 4314 and 2192; (fig.) to *hold* the mind (3563 impl.) *towards*, i.e. *pay attention to*, *be cautious about*, *apply oneself* to, *adhere to:*—(give) attend (-ance, -ance at, -ance to, unto), beware, be given to, give (take) heed (to, unto) have regard.

4338. προσηλόω **prŏsēlŏō**, *pros-ay-lŏ'-o;* from 4314 and a der. of 2247; to *peg to*, i.e. *spike* fast:—nail to.

4339. προσήλυτος **prŏsēlutŏs**, *pros-ay'-loo-tos;* from the alt. of 4334; an *arriver* from a foreign region, i.e. (spec.) an *acceder* (*convert*) to Judaism ("*proselyte*"):—proselyte.

4340. πρόσκαιρος **prŏskairŏs**, *pros'-kahee-ros;* from 4314 and 2540; *for* the *occasion* only, i.e. *temporary:*—dur- [eth] for awhile, endure for a time, for a season, temporal.

4341. προσκαλέομαι **prŏskalĕŏmai**, *pros-kal-eh'-om-ahee;* mid. from 4314 and 2564; to *call toward oneself*, i.e. *summon*, *invite:*—call (for, to, unto).

4342. προσκαρτερέω **prŏskartĕrĕō**, *pros-kar-ter-eh'-o;* from 4314 and 2594; to *be earnest towards*, i.e. (to a thing) to *persevere*, *be constantly* diligent, or (in a place) to *attend* assiduously all the exercises, or (to a person) to *adhere* closely *to* (as a servitor):—attend (give self) continually (upon), continue (in, instant in, with), wait on (continually).

4343. προσκαρτέρησις **prŏskartĕrēsis**, *pros-kar-ter'-ay-sis;* from 4342; *persistency:*—perseverance.

4344. προσκεφάλαιον **prŏskĕphalaiŏn**, *pros-kef-al'-ahee-on;* neut. of a presumed comp. of 4314 and 2776; something *for* the *head*, i.e. a *cushion:*—pillow.

4345. προσκληρόω **prŏsklērŏō**, *pros-klay-rŏ'-o;* from 4314 and 2820; to *give a common lot to*, i.e. (fig.) to *associate with:*—consort with.

4346. πρόσκλισις **prŏsklisis**, *pros'-klis-is;* from a comp. of 4314 and 2827; a *leaning towards*, i.e. (fig.) *proclivity* (*favoritism*):—partiality.

4347. προσκολλάω **prŏskŏllaō**, *pros-kol-lah'-o;* from 4314 and 2853; to *glue to*, i.e. (fig.) to *adhere:*—cleave, join (self).

4348. πρόσκομμα **prŏskŏmma**, *pros'-kom-mah;* from 4350; a *stub*, i.e. (fig.) *occasion of apostasy:*—offence, stumbling (-block, [-stone]).

4349. προσκοπή **prŏskŏpē**, *pros-kop-ay';* from 4350; a *stumbling*, i.e. (fig. and concr.) *occasion of sin:*—offence.

4350. προσκόπτω **prŏskŏptō**, *pros-kop'-to;* from 4314 and 2875; to *strike at*, i.e. *surge against* (as water); spec. to *stub on*, i.e. *trip up* (lit. or fig.):—beat upon, dash, stumble (at).

4351. προσκυλίω **prŏskuliō**, *pros-koo-lee'-o;* from 4314 and 2947; to *roll towards*, i.e. *block against:*—roll (to).

4352. προσκυνέω **prŏskunĕō**, *pros-koo-neh'-o;* from 4314 and a prob. der. of 2965 (mean. to *kiss*, like a dog *licking* his master's hand); to *fawn* or *crouch to*, i.e. (lit. or fig.) *prostrate* oneself in homage (*do reverence to*, *adore*):—worship.

4353. προσκυνητής **prŏskunētēs**, *pros-koo-nay-tace';* from 4352; an *adorer:*—worshipper.

4354. προσλαλέω **prŏslalĕō**, *pros-lal-eh'-o;* from 4314 and 2980; to *talk to*, i.e. *converse with:*—speak to (with).

4355. προσλαμβάνω **prŏslambanō**, *pros-lam-ban'-o;* from 4314 and 2983; to *take to* oneself, i.e. *use* (food), *lead* (aside), *admit* (to friendship or hospitality):—receive, take (unto).

4356. πρόσληψις **prŏslēpsis**, *pros'-lape-sis;* from 4355; *admission:*—receiving.

4357. προσμένω **prŏsmĕnō**, *pros-men'-o;* from 4314 and 3306; to *stay further*, i.e. *remain* in a place, with a person; fig. to *adhere* to, *persevere* in:—abide still, be with, cleave unto, continue in (with).

4358. προσορμίζω **prŏsŏrmizō**, *pros-or-mid'-zo;* from 4314 and a der. of the same as 3730 (mean. to *tie* [*anchor*] or *lull*); to *moor to*, i.e. (by impl.) *land at:*—draw to the shore.

4359. προσοφείλω **prŏsŏphĕilō**, *pros-of-i'-lo;* from 4314 and 3784; to *be indebted additionally:*—over besides.

4360. προσοχθίζω **prŏsŏchthizō**, *pros-okh-thid'-zo;* from 4314 and a form of ὀχθέω **ŏchthĕō** (to be *vexed* with something irksome); to *feel indignant at:*—be grieved with.

4361. πρόσπεινος **prŏspĕinŏs**, *pros'-pi-nos;* from 4314 and the same as 3983; *hungering further*, i.e. *intensely hungry:*—very hungry.

4362. **προσπήγνυμι prŏspēgnumi**, *pros-payg'-noo-mee*; from 4314 and 4078; to *fasten to*, i.e. (spec.) to *impale* (on a cross):—crucify.

4363. **προσπίπτω prŏspiptō**, *pros-pip'-to*; from 4314 and 4098; to *fall towards*, i.e. (gently) *prostrate* oneself (in supplication or homage), or (violently) to *rush* upon (in storm):—beat upon, fall (down) at (before).

4364. **προσποιέομαι prŏspŏiĕŏmai**, *pros-poy-eh'-om-ahee*; mid. from 4314 and 4160; to *do forward for oneself*, i.e. *pretend* (as if about to do a thing):—make as though.

4365. **προσπορεύομαι prŏspŏrĕuŏmai**, *pros-por-yoo'-om-ahee*; from 4314 and 4198; to *journey towards*, i.e. *approach* [not the same as 4313]:—go before.

4366. **προσρήγνυμι prŏsrēgnumi**, *pros-rayg'-noo-mee*; from 4314 and 4486; to *tear towards*, i.e. *burst upon* (as a tempest or flood):—beat vehemently against (upon).

4367. **προστάσσω prŏstassō**, *pros-tas'-so*; from 4314 and 5021; to *arrange towards*, i.e. (fig.) *enjoin*:—bid, command.

4368. **προστάτις prŏstatis**, *pros-tat'-is*; fem. of a der. of 4291; a *patroness*, i.e. *assistant*:—succourer.

4369. **προστίθημι prŏstithēmi**, *pros-tith'-ay-mee*; from 4314 and 5087; to *place additionally*, i.e. *lay beside*, *annex*, *repeat*:—add, again, give more, increase, lay unto, proceed further, speak to any more.

4370. **προστρέχω prŏstrĕchō**, *pros-trekh'-o*; from 4314 and 5143 (includ. its alt.); to *run towards*, i.e. *hasten* to meet or join:—run (thither to, to).

4371. **προσφάγιον prŏsphagiŏn**, *pros-fag'-ee-on*; neut. of a presumed der. of a comp. of 4314 and 5315; something *eaten in addition* to bread, i.e. a *relish* (spec. *fish*; comp. 3795):—meat.

4372. **πρόσφατος prŏsphatŏs**, *pros'-fat-os*; from 4253 and a der. of 4969; *previously* (*recently*) *slain* (*fresh*), i.e. (fig.) *lately made*:—new.

4373. **προσφάτως prŏsphatōs**, *pros-fat'-oce*; adv. from 4372; *recently*:—lately.

4374. **προσφέρω prŏsphĕrō**, *pros-fer'-o*; from 4314 and 5342 (includ. its alt.); to *bear towards*, i.e. *lead to*, *tender* (espec. to God), *treat*:—bring (to, unto), deal with, do, offer (unto, up), present unto, put to.

4375. **προσφιλής prŏsphilēs**, *pros-fee-lace'*; from a presumed comp. of 4314 and 5368; *friendly towards*, i.e. *acceptable*:—lovely.

4376. **προσφορά prŏsphŏra**, *pros-for-ah'*; from 4374; *presentation*; concr. an *oblation* (bloodless) or *sacrifice*:—offering (up).

4377. **προσφωνέω prŏsphōnĕō**, *pros-fo-neh'-o*; from 4314 and 5455; to *sound towards*, i.e. *address*, *exclaim*, *summon*:—call unto, speak (un-) to.

4378. **πρόσχυσις prŏschusis**, *pros'-khoo-sis*; from a comp. of 4314 and **χέω chĕō** (to *pour*); a *shedding forth*, i.e. *affusion*:—sprinkling.

4379. **προσψαύω prŏspsauō**, *pros-psow'-o*; from 4314 and **ψαύω psauō** (to *touch*); to *impinge*, i.e. *lay a finger on* (in order to relieve):—touch.

4380. **προσωποληπτέω prŏsōpŏlēptĕō**, *pros-o-pol-ape-teh'-o*; from 4381; to *favor an individual*, i.e. *show partiality*:—have respect to persons.

4381. **προσωπολήπτης prŏsōpŏlēptēs**, *pros-o-pol-ape'-tace*; from 4383 and 2983; an *accepter of a face* (*individual*), i.e. (spec.) one *exhibiting partiality*:—respecter of persons.

4382. **προσωποληψία prŏsōpŏlēpsia**, *pros-o-pol-ape-see'-ah*; from 4381; *partiality*, i.e. *favoritism*:—respect of persons.

4383. **πρόσωπον prŏsōpŏn**, *pros'-o-pon*; from 4314 and **ὤψ ōps** (the *visage*; from 3700); the *front* (as being *towards view*), i.e. the *countenance*, *aspect*, *appearance*, *surface*; by impl. *presence*, *person*:—(outward) appearance, × before, countenance, face, fashion, (men's) person, presence.

4384. **προτάσσω prŏtassō**, *prot-as'-so*; from 4253 and 5021; to *pre-arrange*, i.e. *prescribe*:—before appoint.

4385. **προτείνω prŏtĕinō**, *prot-i'-no*; from 4253 and **τείνω tĕinō** (to *stretch*); to *protend*, i.e. *tie prostrate* (for scourging):—bind.

4386. **πρότερον prŏtĕrŏn**, *prot'-er-on*; neut. of 4387 as adv. (with or without the art.); *previously*:—before, (at the) first, former.

4387. **πρότερος prŏtĕrŏs**, *prot'-er-os*; compar. of 4253; *prior* or *previous*:—former.

4388. **προτίθεμαι prŏtithĕmai**, *prot-ith'-em-ahee*; mid. from 4253 and 5087; to *place before*, i.e. (for oneself) to *exhibit*; (to oneself) to *propose* (*determine*):—purpose, set forth.

4389. **προτρέπομαι prŏtrĕpŏmai**, *prot-rep'-om-ahee*; mid. from 4253 and the base of 5157; to *turn forward* for oneself, i.e. *encourage*:—exhort.

4390. **προτρέχω prŏtrĕchō**, *prot-rekh'-o*; from 4253 and 5143 (includ. its alt.); to *run forward*, i.e. *outstrip*, *precede*:—outrun, run before.

4391. **προϋπάρχω prŏüparchō**, *prŏ-oop-ar'-kho*; from 4253 and 5225; to *exist before*, i.e. (adv.) to *be* or *do* something *previously*:— + be before (-time).

4392. **πρόφασις prŏphasis**, *prof'-as-is*; from a comp. of 4253 and 5316; an *outward showing*, i.e. *pretext*:—cloke, colour, pretence, show.

4393. **προφέρω prŏphĕrō**, *prof-er'-o*; from 4253 and 5342; to *bear forward*, i.e. *produce*:—bring forth.

4394. **προφητεία prŏphētĕia**, *prof-ay-ti'-ah*; from 4396 ("*prophecy*"); *prediction* (scriptural or other):—prophecy, prophesying.

4395. **προφητεύω prŏphētĕuō**, *prof-ate-yoo'-o*; from 4396; to *foretell* events, *divine*, *speak* under *inspiration*, *exercise* the prophetic *office*:—prophesy.

4396. **προφήτης prŏphētēs**, *prof-ay'-tace*; from a comp. of 4253 and 5346; a *foreteller* ("*prophet*"); by anal. an *inspired speaker*; by extens. a *poet*:—prophet.

4397. **προφητικός prŏphētikŏs**, *prof-ay-tik-os'*; from 4396; *pertaining to a foreteller* ("*prophetic*"):—of prophecy, of the prophets.

4398. **προφῆτις prŏphētis**, *prof-ay'-tis*; fem. of 4396; a *female foreteller* or an *inspired woman*:—prophetess.

4399. **προφθάνω prŏphthanō**, *prof-than'-o*; from 4253 and 5348; to *get an earlier start of*, i.e. *anticipate*:—prevent.

4400. **προχειρίζομαι prŏchĕirizŏmai**, *prokh-i-rid'-zom-ahee*; mid. from 4253 and a der. of 5495; to *handle* for oneself *in advance*, i.e. (fig.) to *purpose*:—choose, make.

4401. **προχειροτονέω prŏchĕirŏtŏnĕō**, *prokh-i-rot-on-eh'-o*; from 4253 and 5500; to *elect in advance*:—choose before.

4402. **Πρόχορος Prŏchŏrŏs**, *prokh'-or-os*; from 4253 and 5525; *before the dance*; *Prochorus*, a Chr.:—Prochorus.

4403. **πρύμνα prumna**, *proom'-nah*; fem. of **πρυμνύς prumnus** (*hindmost*); the *stern* of a ship:—hinder part, stern.

4404. **πρωΐ prōi**, *pro-ee'*; adv. from 4253; at *dawn*; by impl. the *day-break* watch:—early (in the morning), (in the) morning.

4405. **πρωΐα prōïa**, *pro-ee'-ah*; fem. of a der. of 4404 as noun; *day-dawn*:—early, morning.

4406. **πρώϊμος prōïmŏs**, *pro'-ee-mos*; from 4404; *dawning*, i.e. (by anal.) *autumnal* (showering, the first of the rainy season):—early.

4407. **πρωϊνός prōïnŏs**, *pro-ee-nos'*; from 4404; pertaining to the *dawn*, i.e. *matutinal*:—morning.

4408. **πρώρα prōra**, *pro'-ra*; fem. of a presumed der. of 4253 as noun; the *prow*, i.e. forward part of a vessel:—forepart (-ship).

4409. **πρωτεύω prōtĕuō**, *prote-yoo'-o*; from 4413; to *be first* (in rank or influence):—have the preeminence.

4410. **πρωτοκαθεδρία prōtŏkathĕdria**, *pro-tok-ath-ed-ree'-ah*; from 4413 and 2515; a *sitting first* (in the front row), i.e. *preeminence* in council:—chief (highest, uppermost) seat.

4411. **πρωτοκλισία prōtŏklisia**, *pro-tok-lis-ee'-ah*; from 4413 and 2828; a *reclining first* (in the place of honor) at the dinner-bed, i.e. *preeminence* at meals:—chief (highest, uppermost) room.

4412. **πρῶτον prōtŏn**, *pro'-ton*; neut. of 4413 as adv. (with or without 3588); *firstly* (in time, place, order, or importance):—before, at the beginning, chiefly, (at, at the) first (of all).

4413. **πρῶτος prōtŏs**, *pro'-tos*; contr. superl. of 4253; *foremost* (in time, place, order or importance):—before, beginning, best, chief (-est), first (of all), former.

4414. **πρωτοστάτης prōtŏstatēs**, *pro-tos-tat'-ace*; from 4413 and 2476; one *standing first* in the ranks, i.e. a *captain* (*champion*):—ringleader.

4415. **πρωτοτόκια prōtŏtŏkia**, *pro-tot-ok'-ee-ah*; from 4416; *primogeniture* (as a privilege):—birthright.

4416. **πρωτοτόκος prōtŏtŏkŏs**, *pro-tot-ok'-os*; from 4413 and the alt. of 5088; *first-born* (usually as noun, lit. or fig.):—firstbegotten (-born).

4417. **πταίω ptaiō**, *ptah'-yo*; a form of 4098; to *trip*, i.e. (fig.) to *err*, *sin*, *fail* (of salvation):—fall, offend, stumble.

4418. **πτέρνα ptĕrna**, *pter'-nah*; of uncert. der.; the *heel* (fig.):—heel.

4419. **πτερύγιον ptĕrugiŏn**, *pter-oog'-ee-on*; neut. of a presumed der. of 4420; a *winglet*, i.e. (fig.) *extremity* (top corner):—pinnacle.

4420. **πτέρυξ ptĕrux**, *pter'-oox*; from a der. of 4072 (mean. a *feather*); a *wing*:—wing.

4421. **πτηνόν ptēnŏn**, *ptay-non'*; contr. for 4071; a *bird*:—bird.

4422. **πτοέω ptŏĕō**, *ptŏ-eh'-o*; prob. akin to the alt. of 4098 (through the idea of causing to *fall*) or to 4072 (through that of causing to *fly* away); to *scare*:—frighten.

4423. **πτόησις ptŏēsis**, *ptŏ'-ay-sis*; from 4422; *alarm*:—amazement.

4424. **Πτολεμαΐς Ptŏlĕmaïs**, *ptol-em-ah-is'*; from **Πτολεμαῖος Ptŏlĕmaiŏs** (*Ptolemy*, after whom it was named); *Ptolemaïs*, a place in Pal.:—Ptolemais.

4425. **πτύον ptuŏn**, *ptoo'-on*; from 4429; a *winnowing-fork* (as *scattering* like spittle):—fan.

4426. **πτύρω pturō**, *ptoo'-ro*; from a presumed der. of 4429 (and thus akin to 4422); to *frighten*:—terrify.

4427. **πτύσμα ptusma**, *ptoos'-mah*; from 4429; *saliva*:—spittle.

4428. **πτύσσω ptussō**, *ptoos'-so*; prob. akin to **πετάννυμι pĕtannumi** (to *spread*; and thus appar. allied to 4072 through the idea of *expansion*, and to 4429 through that of *flattening*; comp. 3961); to *fold*, i.e. *furl* a scroll:—close.

4429. **πτύω ptuō**, *ptoo'-o*; a prim. verb (comp. 4428); to *spit*:—spit.

4430. **πτῶμα ptōma**, *pto'-mah*; from the alt. of 4098; a *ruin*, i.e. (spec.) lifeless *body* (*corpse*, *carrion*):—dead body, carcase, corpse.

4431. **πτῶσις ptōsis**, *pto'-sis*; from the alt. of 4098; a *crash*, i.e. *downfall* (lit. or fig.):—fall.

4432. **πτωχεία ptōchĕia**, *pto-khi'-ah*; from 4433; *beggary*, i.e. *indigence* (lit. or fig.):—poverty.

4433. **πτωχεύω ptōchĕuō**, *pto-khyoo'-o*; from 4434; *to be a beggar*, i.e. (by impl.) to *become indigent* (fig.):—become poor.

4434. **πτωχός ptōchŏs**, *pto-khos'*; from **πτώσσω ptōssō** (to *crouch*; akin to 4422 and the alt. of 4098); a *beggar* (as *cringing*), i.e. *pauper* (strictly denoting absolute or public *mendicancy*, although also used in a qualified or relative sense; whereas 3993 prop. means only *straitened* circumstances in private), lit. (often as noun) or fig. (*distressed*):—beggar (-ly), poor.

4435. **πυγμή pugmē**, *poog-may'*; from a prim. **πύξ pux** (the *fist* as a weapon); the clenched *hand*, i.e. (only in dat. as adv.) *with* the *fist* (hard *scrubbing*):—oft.

4436. **Πύθων Puthōn**, *poo'-thone;* from **Πυθώ Puthō** (the name of the region where Delphi, the seat of the famous *oracle*, was located); a *Python*, i.e. (by anal. with the supposed *diviner* there) *inspiration* (*soothsaying*):—divination.

4437. **πυκνός puknŏs**, *pook-nos';* from the same as *4635;* *clasped* (*thick*), i.e. (fig.) *frequent;* neut. plur. (as adv.) *frequently:*—often (-er).

4438. **πυκτέω puktĕō**, *pook-teh'-o;* from a der. of the same as *4435;* to *box* (with the fist), i.e. *contend* (as a boxer) at the games (fig.):—fight.

4439. **πύλη pulē**, *poo'-lay;* appar. a prim. word; a *gate*, i.e. the leaf or wing of a folding *entrance* (lit. or fig.):—gate.

4440. **πυλών pulōn**, *poo-lone';* from *4439;* a *gateway*, *door-way* of a building or city; by impl. a *portal* or *vestibule:*—gate, porch.

4441. **πυνθάνομαι punthanŏmai**, *poon-than'-om-ahee;* mid. prol. from a prim. **πύθω puthō** (which occurs only as an alt. in certain tenses); to *question*, i.e. *ascertain* by inquiry (as a matter of *information* merely; and thus differing from *2065*, which prop. means a *request* as a favor; and from *154*, which is strictly a *demand* of something due; as well as from *2212*, which implies a *search* for something hidden; and from *1180*, which involves the idea of urgent *need*); by impl. to *learn* (by casual intelligence):—ask, demand, enquire, understand.

4442. **πῦρ pur**, *poor;* a prim. word; "*fire*" (lit. or fig., spec. *lightning*):—fiery, fire.

4443. **πυρά pura**, *poo-rah';* from *4442;* a *fire* (concr.):—fire.

4444. **πύργος purgŏs**, *poor'-gos;* appar. a prim. word ("*burgh*"); a *tower* or *castle:*—tower.

4445. **πυρέσσω purĕssō**, *poo-res'-so;* from *4443;* to *be on fire*, i.e. (spec.) to *have a fever:*—be sick of a fever.

4446. **πυρετός purĕtŏs**, *poo-ret-os';* from *4445;* *inflamed*, i.e. (by impl.) *feverish* (as noun, *fever*):—fever.

4447. **πύρινος purinŏs**, *poo'-ree-nos;* from *4443;* *fiery*, i.e. (by impl.) *flaming:*—of fire.

4448. **πυρόω purŏō**, *poo-rŏ'-o;* from *4442;* to *kindle*, i.e. (pass.) to *be ignited*, *glow* (lit.), *be refined* (by impl.), or (fig.) to *be inflamed* (with anger, grief, lust):—burn, fiery, be on fire, try.

4449. **πυῤῥάζω purrhazō**, *poor-hrad'-zo;* from *4450;* to *redden* (intrans.):—be red.

4450. **πυῤῥός purrhŏs**, *poor-hros';* from *4442;* *fire-like*, i.e. (spec.) *flame-colored:*—red.

4451. **πύρωσις purōsis**, *poo'-ro-sis;* from *4448;* *ignition*, i.e. (spec.) *smelting* (fig. *conflagration*, *calamity* as a *test*):—burning, trial.

4452. **-πω -pō**, *po;* another form of the base of *4458;* an enclitic particle of indefiniteness; *yet*, *even;* used only in comp. See *3369*, *3380*, *3764*, *3768*, *4455*.

4453. **πωλέω pōlĕō**, *po-leh'-o;* prob. ultimately from **πέλομαι pĕlŏmai** (to *be busy*, to *trade*); to *barter* (as a *pedlar*), i.e. to *sell:*—sell, whatever is sold.

4454. **πῶλος pōlŏs**, *po'-los;* appar. a prim. word; a "*foal*" or "*filly*", i.e. (spec.) a *young ass:*—colt.

4455. **πώποτε pōpŏtĕ**, *po'-pot-e;* from *4452* and *4218;* *at any time*, i.e. (with neg. particle) *at no time:*—at any time, + never (. . . to any man), + yet never man.

4456. **πωρόω pōrŏō**, *po-rŏ'-o;* appar. from **πῶρος pōrŏs** (a kind of *stone*); to *petrify*, i.e (fig.) to *indurate* (*render stupid* or *callous*):—blind, harden.

4457. **πώρωσις pōrōsis**, *po'-ro-sis;* from *4456;* *stupidity* or *callousness:*—blindness, hardness.

4458. **-πώς -pōs**, *poce;* adv. from the base of *4225;* an enclitic particle of indefiniteness of manner; *somehow* or *anyhow;* used only in comp.:—haply, by any (some) means, perhaps. See *1513*, *3381*. Comp. *4459*.

4459. **πῶς pōs**, *poce;* adv. from the base of *4226;* an interrog. particle of manner; *in what way?* (sometimes the question is indirect, *how?*); also as exclamation, *how* much!:—how, after (by) what manner (means), that. [*Occasionally unexpressed in English.*]

P

4460. **Ῥαάβ Rhaab**, *hrah-ab';* of Heb. or. [7343]; *Raab* (i.e. *Rachab*), a Canaanitess:—Rahab. See also *4477*.

4461. **ῥαββί rhabbi**, *hrab-bee';* of Heb. or. [7227 with pron. suffix]; *my master*, i.e. *Rabbi*, as an official title of honor:—Master, Rabbi.

4462. **ῥαββονί rhabbŏni**, *hrab-bon-ee';* or

ῥαββουνί rhabbŏuni, *hrab-boo-nee';* of Chald. or.; corresp. to *4461:*—Lord, Rabboni.

4463. **ῥαβδίζω rhabdizō**, *hrab-did'-zo;* from *4464;* to *strike with a stick*, i.e. *bastinado:*—beat (with rods).

4464. **ῥάβδος rhabdŏs**, *hrab'-dos;* from the base of *4474;* a *stick* or *wand* (as a *cudgel*, a *cane* or a *baton* of royalty):—rod, sceptre, staff.

4465. **ῥαβδοῦχος rhabdŏuchŏs**, *hrab-doo'-khos;* from *4464* and *2192;* a *rod-* (the Lat. *fasces*) *holder*, i.e. a Rom. *lictor* (*constable* or *executioner*):—serjeant.

4466. **Ῥαγαῦ Rhagau**, *hrag-ŏw';* of Heb. or. [7466]; *Ragau* (i.e. *Reü*), a patriarch:—Ragau.

4467. **ῥᾳδιούργημα rhaidiŏurgēma**, *hrad-ee-oorg'-ay-mah;* from a comp. of **ῥᾴδιος rhaidiŏs** (*easy*, i.e. *reckless*) and *2041;* *easy-going behavior*, i.e. (by extens.) a *crime:*—lewdness.

4468. **ῥᾳδιουργία rhaidiŏurgia**, *hrad-ee-oorg-ee'-a;* from the same as *4467;* *recklessness*, i.e. (by extens.) *malignity:*—mischief.

4469. **ῥακά rhaka**, *rhak-ah';* of Chald. or. [comp. 7386]; O *empty* one, i.e. thou *worthless* (as a term of utter vilification):—Raca.

4470. **ῥάκος rhăkŏs**, *hrak'-os;* from *4486;* a "*rag*," i.e. *piece* of cloth:—cloth.

4471. **Ῥαμᾶ Rhama**, *hram-ah';* of Heb. or. [7414]; *Rama* (i.e. *Ramah*), a place in Pal.:—Rama.

4472. **ῥαντίζω rhantizō**, *hran-tid'-zo;* from a der. of **ῥαίνω rhainō** (to *sprinkle*); to *render besprinkled*, i.e. *asperse* (cer. or fig.):—sprinkle.

4473. **ῥαντισμός rhantismŏs**, *hran-tis-mos';* from *4472;* *aspersion* (cer. or fig.):—sprinkling.

4474. **ῥαπίζω rhapizō**, *hrap-id'-zo;* from a der. of a prim. **ῥέπω rhĕpō** (to *let fall*, "*rap*"); to *slap:*—smite (with the palm of the hand). Comp. *5180*.

4475. **ῥάπισμα rhapisma**, *hrap'-is-mah;* from *4474;* a *slap:*—(+ strike with the) palm of the hand, smite with the hand.

4476. **ῥαφίς rhaphis**, *hraf-ece';* from a prim. **ῥάπτω rhaptō** (to *sew;* perh. rather akin to the base of *4474* through the idea of *puncturing*); a *needle:*—needle.

4477. **Ῥαχάβ Rhachab**, *hrakh-ab';* from the same as *4460;* *Rachab*, a Canaanitess:—Rachab.

4478. **Ῥαχήλ Rhachēl**, *hrakh-ale';* of Heb. or. [7354]; *Rachel*, the wife of Jacob:—Rachel.

4479. **Ῥεβέκκα Rhĕbĕkka**, *hreb-bek'-kah;* of Heb. or. [7259]; *Rebecca* (i.e. *Ribkah*), the wife of Isaac:—Rebecca.

4480. **ῥέδα rhĕda**, *hred'-ah;* of Lat. or.; a *rheda*, i.e. four-wheeled *carriage* (*wagon* for riding):—chariot.

4481. **Ῥεμφάν Rhĕmphan**, *hrem-fan';* by incorrect transliteration for a word of Heb. or. [3594]; *Remphan* (i.e. *Kijun*), an Eg. idol:—Remphan.

4482. **ῥέω rhĕō**, *hreh'-o;* a prim. verb; for some tenses of which a prol. form

ῥεύω rhĕuō, *hryoo'-o*, is used; to *flow* ("*run*", as water):—flow.

4483. **ῥέω rhĕō**, *hreh'-o;* for certain tenses of which a prol. form

ἐρέω ĕrĕō, *er-eh'-o*, is used; and both as alt. for *2036;* perh. akin (or ident.) with *4482* (through the idea of *pouring* forth); to *utter*, i.e. *speak* or *say:*—command, make, say, speak (of). Comp. *3004*.

4484. **Ῥήγιον Rhēgiŏn**, *hrayg'-ee-on;* of Lat. or.; *Rhegium*, a place in Italy:—Rhegium.

4485. **ῥῆγμα rhēgma**, *hrayg'-mah;* from *4486;* something *torn*, i.e. a *fragment* (by impl. and abstr. a *fall*):—ruin.

4486. **ῥήγνυμι rhēgnumi**, *hrayg'-noo-mee;* or

ῥήσσω rhēssō, *hrace'-so;* both prol. forms of **ῥήκω rhēkō** (which appears only in certain forms, and is itself prob. a strengthened form of **ἄγνυμι agnumi** [see in *2608*]); to "*break*", "*wreck*" or "*crack*", i.e. (espec.) to *sunder* (by *separation* of the parts; *2608* being its intensive [with the prep. in comp.], and *2352* a *shattering* to minute fragments; but not a *reduction* to the constituent particles, like *3089*) or *disrupt*, *lacerate;* by impl. to *convulse* (with *spasms*); fig. to *give vent* to joyful emotions:—break (forth), burst, rend, tear.

4487. **ῥῆμα rhēma**, *hray'-mah;* from *4483;* an *utterance* (individ., collect. or spec.); by impl. a *matter* or *topic* (espec. of narration, command or dispute); with a neg. *naught* whatever:— + evil, + nothing, saying, word.

4488. **Ῥησά Rhēsa**, *hray-sah';* prob. of Heb. or. [appar. for 7509]; *Resa* (i.e. *Rephajah*), an Isr.:—Rhesa.

4489. **ῥήτωρ rhētōr**, *hray'-tore;* from *4483;* a *speaker*, i.e. (by impl.) a forensic *advocate:*—orator.

4490. **ῥητῶς rhētōs**, *hray-toce';* adv. from a der. of *4483;* out-*spokenly*, i.e. *distinctly:*—expressly.

4491. **ῥίζα rhiza**, *hrid'-zah;* appar. a prim. word; a "*root*" (lit. or fig.):—root.

4492. **ῥιζόω rhizŏō**, *rhid-zŏ'-o;* from *4491;* to *root* (fig. *become stable*):—root.

4493. **ῥιπή rhipē**, *hree-pay';* from *4496;* a *jerk* (of the eye, i.e. [by anal.] an *instant*):—twinkling.

4494. **ῥιπίζω rhipizō**, *hrip-id'-zo;* from a der. of *4496* (mean. a *fan* or *bellows*); to *breeze up*, i.e. (by anal.) to *agitate* (into waves):—toss.

4495. **ῥιπτέω rhiptĕō**, *hrip-teh'-o;* from a der. of *4496;* to *toss* up:—cast off.

4496. **ῥίπτω rhiptō**, *hrip'-to;* a prim. verb (perh. rather akin to the base of *4474*, through the idea of sudden *motion*); to *fling* (prop. with a quick *toss*, thus differing from *906*, which denotes a *deliberate* hurl; and from **τείνω tĕinō** [see in *1614*], which indicates an *extended* projection); by qualification, to *deposit* (as if a load); by extens. to *disperse:*—cast (down, out), scatter abroad, throw.

4497. **Ῥοβοάμ Rhŏbŏam**, *hrob-ŏ-am';* of Heb. or. [7346]; *Roboäm* (i.e. *Rechabam*), an Isr.:—Roboam.

4498. **Ῥόδη Rhŏdē**, *hrod'-ay;* prob. for **ῥοδή rhŏdē** (a *rose*); *Rodè*, a servant girl:—Rhoda.

4499. **Ῥόδος Rhŏdŏs**, *hrod'-os;* prob. from **ῥόδον rhŏdŏn** (a *rose*); *Rhodus*, an island of the Mediterranean:—Rhodes.

4500. **ῥοιζηδόν rhŏizēdŏn**, *hroyd-zay-don';* adv. from a der. of **ῥοῖζος rhŏizŏs** (a *whir*); *whizzingly*, i.e. *with a crash:*—with a great noise.

4501. **ῥομφαία rhŏmphaia**, *hrom-fah'-yah;* prob. of for. or.; a *sabre*, i.e. a long and broad *cutlass* (any *weapon* of the kind, lit. or fig.):—sword.

4502. **Ῥουβήν Rhŏubēn**, *hroo-bane';* of Heb. or. [7205]; *Ruben* (i.e. *Reuben*), an Isr.:—Reuben.

4503. **Ῥούθ Rhŏuth**, *hrooth;* of Heb. or. [7327]; *Ruth*, a Moabitess:—Ruth.

4504. **Ῥοῦφος Rhŏuphŏs**, *hroo'-fos;* of Lat. or.; *red;* *Rufus*, a Chr.:—Rufus.

4505. **ῥύμη rhumē**, *hroo'-may;* prol. from *4506* in its orig. sense; an *alley* or *avenue* (as crowded):—lane, street.

4506. **ῥύομαι rhuŏmai**, *rhoo'-om-ahee;* mid. of an obsol. verb, akin to *4482* (through the idea of a *current;* comp. *4511*); to *rush* or *draw* (for oneself), i.e. *rescue:*—deliver (-er).

4507. **ῥυπαρία rhuparia**, *hroo-par-ee'-ah;* from *4508;* *dirtiness* (mor.):—filthiness.

4508. ῥυπαρός rhuparŏs, *rhoo-par-os'*; from 4509; *dirty*, i.e. (rel.) *cheap* or *shabby*; mor. *wicked*:—vile.

4509. ῥύπος rhupŏs, *hroo'-pos*; of uncert. affin.; *dirt*, i.e. (mor.) *depravity*:—filth.

4510. ῥυπόω rhupŏō, *rhoo-pŏ'-o*; from 4509; to *soil*, i.e. (intrans.) to *become dirty* (mor.):—be filthy.

4511. ῥύσις rhusis, *hroo'-sis*; from 4506 in the sense of its congener 4482; a *flux* (of blood):—issue.

4512. ῥυτίς rhutis, *hroo-tece'*; from 4506; a *fold* (as *drawing* together), i.e. a *wrinkle* (espec. on the face):—wrinkle.

4513. Ῥωμαϊκός Rhōmaïkŏs, *rho-mah-ee-kos'*; from 4514; *Romaïc*, i.e. *Latin*:—Latin.

4514. Ῥωμαῖος Rhōmaiŏs, *hro-mah'-yos*; from 4516; *Romæan*, i.e. *Roman* (as noun):—Roman, of Rome.

4515. Ῥωμαϊστί Rhōmaïsti, *hro-mah-is-tee'*; adv. from a presumed der. of 4516; *Romaïstically*, i.e. *in* the *Latin* language:—Latin.

4516. Ῥώμη Rhōmē, *hro'-may*; from the base of 4517; *strength*; *Roma*, the capital of Italy:—Rome.

4517. ῥώννυμι rhōnnumi, *hrone'-noo-mee*; prol. from **ῥώομαι rhōŏmai** (to *dart*; prob. akin to 4506); to *strengthen*, i.e. (imper. pass.) *have health* (as a parting exclamation, *good-bye*):—farewell.

Σ

4518. σαβαχθανί sabachthani, *sab-akh-than-ee'*; of Chald. or. [7662 with pron. suff.]; *thou hast left me*; *sabachthani* (i.e. *shebakthani*), a cry of distress:—sabachthani.

4519. σαβαώθ sabaōth, *sab-ah-ōwth'*; of Heb. or. [6635 in fem. plur.]; *armies*; *sabaoth* (i.e. *tsebaoth*), a military epithet of God:—sabaoth.

4520. σαββατισμός sabbatismŏs, *sab-bat-is-mos'*; from a der. of 4521; a "*sabbatism*", i.e. (fig.) the *repose* of Christianity (as a type of heaven):—rest.

4521. σάββατον sabbatŏn, *sab'-bat-on*; of Heb. or. [7676]; the *Sabbath* (i.e. *Shabbath*), or day of weekly *repose* from secular avocations (also the observance or institution itself); by extens. a *se'nnight*, i.e. the interval between two Sabbaths; likewise the plur. in all the above applications:—sabbath (day), week.

4522. σαγήνη sagēnē, *sag-ay'-nay*; from a der. of **σάττω sattō** (to *equip*) mean. *furniture*, espec. a *pack-saddle* (which in the East is merely a bag of *netted* rope); a "*seine*" for fishing:—net.

4523. Σαδδουκαῖος Saddŏukaiŏs, *sad-doo-kah'-yos*; prob. from 4524; a *Sadducæan* (i.e. *Tsadokian*), or follower of a certain heretical Isr.:—Sadducee.

4524. Σαδώκ Sadōk, *sad-oke'*; of Heb. or. [6659]; *Sadoc* (i.e. *Tsadok*), an Isr.:—Sadoc.

4525. σαίνω sainō, *sah'ee-no*; akin to 4579; to *wag* (as a dog its tail fawningly), i.e. (gen.) to *shake* (fig. *disturb*):—move.

4526. σάκκος sakkŏs, *sak'-kos*; of Heb. or. [8242]; "*sack*"-cloth, i.e. *mohair* (the material or garments made of it, worn as a sign of grief):—sackcloth.

4527. Σαλά Sala, *sal-ah'*; of Heb. or. [7974]; *Sala* (i.e. *Shelach*), a patriarch:—Sala.

4528. Σαλαθιήλ Salathiēl, *sal-ath-ee-ale'*; of Heb. or. [7597]; *Salathiël* (i.e. *Sheältiël*), an Isr.:—Salathiel.

4529. Σαλαμίς Salamis, *sal-am-ece'*; prob. from 4535 (from the *surge* on the shore); *Salamis*, a place in Cyprus:—Salamis.

4530. Σαλείμ Salĕim, *sal-ime'*; prob. from the same as 4531; *Salim*, a place in Pal.:—Salim.

4531. σαλεύω salĕuō, *sal-yoo'-o*; from 4535; to *waver*, i.e. *agitate*, *rock*, *topple* or (by impl.) *destroy*; fig. to *disturb*, *incite*:—move, shake (together), which can [-not] be shaken, stir up.

4532. Σαλήμ Salēm, *sal-ame'*; of Heb. or. [8004]; *Salem* (i.e. *Shalem*), a place in Pal.:—Salem.

4533. Σαλμών Salmōn, *sal-mone'*; of Heb. or. [8012]; *Salmon*, an Isr.:—Salmon.

4534. Σαλμώνη Salmōnē, *sal-mo'-nay*; perh. of similar or. to 4529; *Salmone*, a place in Crete:—Salmone.

4535. σάλος salŏs, *sal'-os*; prob. from the base of 4525; a *vibration*, i.e. (spec.) *billow*:—wave.

4536. σάλπιγξ salpigx, *sal'-pinx*; perh. from 4535 (through the idea of *quavering* or *reverberation*): a *trumpet*:—trump (-et).

4537. σαλπίζω salpizō, *sal-pid'-zo*; from 4536; to *trumpet*, i.e. *sound a blast* (lit. or fig.):—(which are yet to) sound (a trumpet).

4538. σαλπιστής salpistēs, *sal-pis-tace'*; from 4537; a *trumpeter*:—trumpeter.

4539. Σαλώμη Salōmē, *sal-o'-may*; prob. of Heb. or. [fem. from 7965]; *Salomè* (i.e. *Shelomah*), an Israelitess:—Salome.

4540. Σαμάρεια Samarĕia, *sam-ar'-i-ah*; of Heb. or. [8111]; *Samaria* (i.e. *Shomeron*), a city and region of Pal.:—Samaria.

4541. Σαμαρείτης Samarĕitēs, *sam-ar-i'-tace*; from 4540; a *Samarite*, i.e. inhab. of Samaria:—Samaritan.

4542. Σαμαρεῖτις Samarĕitis, *sam-ar-i'-tis*; fem. of 4541; a *Samaritess*, i.e. woman of Samaria:—of Samaria.

4543. Σαμοθρᾴκη Samŏthra$_{i}$kē, *sam-oth-rak'-ay*; from 4544 and **Θρᾴκη Thra$_{i}$kē** (*Thrace*); *Samo-thracè* (*Samos of Thrace*), an island in the Mediterranean:—Samothrace.

4544. Σάμος Samŏs, *sam'-os*; of uncert. affin.; *Samus*, an island of the Mediterranean:—Samos.

4545. Σαμουήλ Samŏuēl, *sam-oo-ale'*; of Heb. or. [8050]; *Samuel* (i.e. *Shemuel*), an Isr.:—Samuel.

4546. Σαμψών Sampsōn, *samp-sone'*; of Heb. or. [8123]; *Sampson* (i.e. *Shimshon*), an Isr.:—Samson.

4547. σανδάλιον sandaliŏn, *san-dal'-ee-on*; neut. of a der. of **σάνδαλον sandalŏn** (a "*sandal*"; of uncert. or.); a *slipper* or *sole-pad*:—sandal.

4548. σανίς sanis, *san-ece'*; of uncert. affin.; a *plank*:—board.

4549. Σαούλ Saŏul, *sah-ool'*; of Heb. or. [7586]; *Saül* (i.e. *Shaül*), the Jewish name of *Paul*:—Saul. Comp. 4569.

4550. σαπρός saprŏs, *sap-ros'*; from 4595; *rotten*, i.e. *worthless* (lit. or mor.):—bad, corrupt. Comp. 4190.

4551. Σαπφείρη Sapphĕirē, *sap-fi'-ray*; fem. of 4552; *Sapphirè*, an Israelitess:—Sapphira.

4552. σάπφειρος sapphĕirŏs, *sap'-fi-ros*; of Heb. or. [5601]; a "*sapphire*" or *lapis-lazuli* gem:—sapphire.

4553. σαργάνη sarganē, *sar-gan'-ay*; appar. of Heb. or. [8276]; a *basket* (as *interwoven* or *wicker-work*):—basket.

4554. Σάρδεις Sardĕis, *sar'-dice*; plur. of uncert. der.; *Sardis*, a place in Asia Minor:—Sardis.

4555. σάρδινος sardinŏs, *sar'-dee-nos*; from the same as 4556; *sardine* (3037 being impl.), i.e. a gem, so called:—sardine.

4556. σάρδιος sardiŏs, *sar'-dee-os*; prop. adj. from an uncert. base; *sardian* (3037 being impl.), i.e. (as noun) the gem so called:—sardius.

4557. σαρδόνυξ sardŏnux, *sar-don'-oox*; from the base of 4556 and **ὄνυξ ŏnux** (the *nail* of a finger; hence the "*onyx*" stone); a "*sardonyx*", i.e. the gem so called:—sardonyx.

4558. Σάρεπτα Sarĕpta, *sar'-ep-tah*; of Heb. or. [6886]; *Sarepta* (i.e. *Tsarephath*), a place in Pal.:—Sarepta.

4559. σαρκικός sarkikŏs, *sar-kee-kos'*; from 4561; *pertaining to flesh*, i.e. (by extens.) *bodily*, *temporal*, or (by impl.) *animal*, *unregenerate*:—carnal, fleshly.

4560. σάρκινος sarkinŏs, *sar'-kee-nos*; from 4561; *similar to flesh*, i.e. (by anal.) *soft*:—fleshly.

4561. σάρξ sarx, *sarx*; prob. from the base of 4563; *flesh* (as *stripped* of the skin), i.e. (strictly) the *meat* of an animal (as food), or (by extens.) the *body* (as opposed to the soul [or spirit], or as the symbol of what is external, or as the means of kindred), or (by impl.) *human nature* (with its frailties [phys. or mor.] and passions), or (spec.) a *human being* (as such):—carnal (-ly, + -ly minded), flesh ([-ly]).

4562. Σαρούχ Sarŏuch, *sar-ooch'*; of Heb. or. [8286]; *Saruch* (i.e. *Serug*), a patriarch:—Saruch.

4563. σαρόω sarŏō, *sar-ŏ'-o*; from a der. of **σαίρω sairō** (to *brush* off; akin to 4951) mean. a *broom*; to *sweep*:—sweep.

4564. Σάῤῥα Sarrha, *sar'-hrah*; of Heb. or. [8283]; *Sarra* (i.e. *Sarah*), the wife of Abraham:—Sara, Sarah.

4565. Σάρων Sarōn, *sar'-one*; of Heb. or. [8289]; *Saron* (i.e. *Sharon*), a district of Pal.:—Saron.

4566. Σατᾶν Satan, *sat-an'*; of Heb. or. [7854]; *Satan*, i.e. the *devil*:—Satan. Comp. 4567.

4567. Σατανᾶς Satanas, *sat-an-as'*; of Chald. or. corresp. to 4566 (with the def. affix); *the accuser*, i.e. the *devil*:—Satan.

4568. σάτον satŏn, *sat'-on*; of Heb. or. [5429]; a certain *measure* for things dry:—measure.

4569. Σαῦλος Saulŏs, *sŏw'-los*; of Heb. or., the same as 4549; *Saulus* (i.e. *Shaül*), the Jewish name of *Paul*:—Saul.

σαυτοῦ sautŏu, etc. See 4572.

4570. σβέννυμι sbĕnnumi, *sben'-noo-mee*; a prol. form of an appar. prim. verb; to *extinguish* (lit. or fig.):—go out, quench.

4571. σέ sĕ, *seh*; accus. sing. of 4771; *thee*:—thee, thou, × thy house.

4572. σεαυτοῦ sĕautŏu, *seh-ŏw-too'*; gen. from 4571 and 846; also dat. of the same, **σεαυτῷ sĕautō$_{i}$**, *seh-ŏw-to'*; and acc. **σεαυτόν sĕautŏn**, *seh-ŏw-ton'*; likewise contr. **σαυτοῦ sautŏu**, *sŏw-too'*; **σαυτῷ sautō$_{i}$**, *sŏw-to'*; and **σαυτόν sautŏn**, *sŏw-ton'*; respectively; *of* (*with*, *to*) *thyself*:—thee, thine own self, (thou) thy (-self).

4573. σεβάζομαι sĕbazŏmai, *seb-ad'-zom-ahee*; mid. from a der. of 4576; to *venerate*, i.e. *adore*:—worship.

4574. σέβασμα sĕbasma, *seb'-as-mah*; from 4573; something *adored*, i.e. an *object of worship* (god, altar, etc.):—devotion, that is worshipped.

4575. σεβαστός sĕbastŏs, *seb-as-tos'*; from 4573; *venerable* (*august*), i.e. (as noun) a title of the Rom. *Emperor*, or (as adj.) *imperial*:—Augustus (-').

4576. σέβομαι sĕbŏmai, *seb'-om-ahee*; mid. of an appar. prim. verb; to *revere*, i.e. *adore*:—devout, religious, worship.

4577. σειρά sĕira, *si-rah'*; prob. from 4951 through its congener **εἴρω ĕirō** (to *fasten*; akin to 138); a *chain* (as *binding* or *drawing*):—chain.

4578. σεισμός sĕismŏs, *sice-mos'*; from 4579; a *commotion*, i.e. (of the air) a *gale*, (of the ground) an *earthquake*:—earthquake, tempest.

4579. σείω sĕiō, *si'-o*; appar. a prim. verb; to *rock* (*vibrate*, prop. sideways or to and fro), i.e. (gen.) to *agitate* (in any direction; cause to *tremble*); fig. to throw into a *tremor* (of fear or concern):—move, quake, shake.

4580. Σεκοῦνδος Sĕkŏundŏs, *sek-oon'-dos*; of Lat. or.; "*second*"; *Secundus*, a Chr.:—Secundus.

4581. Σελεύκεια Sĕlĕukĕia, *sel-yook'-i-ah*; from **Σέλευκος Sĕlĕukŏs** (*Seleucus*, a Syrian king); *Seleucia*, a place in Syria:—Seleucia.

4582. σελήνη sĕlēnē, *sel-ay'-nay*; from **σέλας sĕlas** (*brilliancy*; prob. akin to the alt. of 138, through the idea of *attractiveness*); the *moon*:—moon.

4583. σεληνιάζομαι sĕlēniazŏmai, *sel-ay-nee-ad'-zom-ahee*; mid. or pass. from a presumed der. of 4582; to *be moon-struck*, i.e. *crazy*:—be lunatic.

4584. Σεμεΐ **Sĕmĕï**, *sem-eh-ee';* of Heb. or. [8096]; *Semeï* (i.e. *Shimi*), an Isr.:—Semei.

4585. σεμίδαλις **sĕmidalis**, *sem-id'-al-is;* prob. of for. or.; fine wheaten *flour:*—fine flour.

4586. σεμνός **sĕmnŏs**, *sem-nos';* from *4576; venerable*, i.e. *honorable:*—grave, honest.

4587. σεμνότης **sĕmnŏtēs**, *sem-not'-ace;* from *4586; venerableness*, i.e. *probity:*—gravity, honesty.

4588. Σέργιος **Sĕrgiŏs**, *serg'-ee-os;* of Lat. or.; *Sergius*, a Rom.:—Sergius.

4589. Σήθ **Sēth**, *sayth;* of Heb. or. [8352]; *Seth* (i.e. *Sheth*), a patriarch:—Seth.

4590. Σήμ **Sēm**, *same;* of Heb. or. [8035]; *Sem* (i.e. *Shem*), a patriarch:—Sem.

4591. σημαίνω **sēmainō**, *say-mah'ee-no;* from σῆμα **sēma** (a *mark;* of uncert. der.); to *indicate:*—signify.

4592. σημεῖον **sēmĕiŏn**, *say-mi'-on;* neut. of a presumed der. of the base of *4591;* an *indication*, espec. cer. or supernat.:—miracle, sign, token, wonder.

4593. σημειόω **sēmĕiŏō**, *say-mi-ŏ'-o;* from *4592;* to *distinguish*, i.e. *mark* (for avoidance):—note.

4594. σήμερον **sēmĕrŏn**, *say'-mer-on;* neut. (as adv.) of a presumed comp. of the art. *3588* (τ changed to σ) and *2250;* on *the* (i.e. *this*) *day* (or *night* current or just passed); gen. *now* (i.e. at *present, hitherto*):—this (to-) day.

4595. σήπω **sēpō**, *say'-po;* appar. a prim. verb; to *putrefy*, i.e. (fig.) *perish:*—be corrupted.

4596. σηρικός **sērikŏs**, *say-ree-kos';* from Σήρ **Sēr** (an Indian tribe from whom *silk* was procured; hence the name of the *silk-worm*); *Seric*, i.e. *silken* (neut. as noun, a *silky* fabric):—silk.

4597. σής **sēs**, *sace;* appar. of Heb. or. [5580]; a *moth:*—moth.

4598. σητόβρωτος **sētŏbrōtŏs**, *say-tob'-ro-tos;* from *4597* and a der. of *977; moth-eaten:*—motheaten.

4599. σθενόω **sthĕnŏō**, *sthen-ŏ'-o;* from σθένος **sthĕnŏs** (bodily *vigor;* prob. akin to the base of *2476*); to *strengthen*, i.e. (fig.) *confirm* (in spiritual knowledge and power):—strengthen.

4600. σιαγών **siagōn**, *see-ag-one';* of uncert. der.; the *jaw*-bone, i.e. (by impl.) the *cheek* or side of the face:—cheek.

4601. σιγάω **sigaō**, *see-gah'-o;* from *4602;* to *keep silent* (trans. or intrans.):—keep close (secret, silence), hold peace.

4602. σιγή **sigē**, *see-gay';* appar. from σίζω **sizō** (to *hiss*, i.e. *hist* or *hush*); *silence:*—silence. Comp. *4623*.

4603. σιδήρεος **sidērĕŏs**, *sid-ay'-reh-os;* from *4604;* made *of iron:*—(of) iron.

4604. σίδηρος **sidērŏs**, *sid'-ay-ros;* of uncert. der.; *iron:*—iron.

4605. Σιδών **Sidōn**, *sid-one';* of Heb. or. [6721]; *Sidon* (i.e. *Tsidon*), a place in Pal.:—Sidon.

4606. Σιδώνιος **Sidōniŏs**, *sid-o'-nee-os;* from *4605;* a *Sidonian*, i.e. inhab. of Sidon:—of Sidon.

4607. σικάριος **sikariŏs**, *sik-ar'-ee-os;* of Lat. or.; a *dagger-man* or *assassin;* a *freebooter* (Jewish *fanatic* outlawed by the Romans):—murderer. Comp. *5406*.

4608. σίκερα **sikĕra**, *sik'-er-ah;* of Heb. or. [7941]; an *intoxicant*, i.e. intensely fermented *liquor:*—strong drink.

4609. Σίλας **Silas**, *see'-las;* contr. for *4610; Silas*, a Chr.:—Silas.

4610. Σιλουανός **Silŏuanŏs**, *sil-oo-an-os';* of Lat. or.; "*silvan*"; *Silvanus*, a Chr.:—Silvanus. Comp. *4609*.

4611. Σιλωάμ **Silōam**, *sil-o-am';* of Heb. or. [7975]; *Siloäm* (i.e. *Shiloäch*), a pool of Jerus.:—Siloam.

4612. σιμικίνθιον **simikinthiŏn**, *sim-ee-kin'-thee-on;* of Lat. or.; a *semicinctium* or *half-girding*, i.e. narrow covering (*apron*):—apron.

4613. Σίμων **Simōn**, *see'-mone;* of Heb. or. [8095]; *Simon* (i.e. *Shimon*), the name of nine Isr.:—Simon. Comp. *4826*.

4614. Σινᾶ **Sina**, *see-nah';* of Heb. or. [5514]; *Sina* (i.e. *Sinai*), a mountain in Arabia:—Sina.

4615. σίναπι **sinapi**, *sin'-ap-ee;* perh. from σίνομαι **sinŏmai** (to *hurt*, i.e. *sting*); *mustard* (the plant):—mustard.

4616. σινδών **sindōn**, *sin-done';* of uncert. (perh. for.) or.; *byssos*, i.e. bleached *linen* (the cloth or a garment of it):—(fine) linen (cloth).

4617. σινιάζω **siniazō**, *sin-ee-ad'-zo;* from σινίον **siniŏn** (a *sieve*); to *riddle* (fig.):—sift.

σῖτα **sita**. See *4621*.

4618. σιτευτός **sitĕutŏs**, *sit-yoo-tos';* from a der. of *4621; grain-fed*, i.e. *fattened:*—fatted.

4619. σιτιστός **sitistŏs**, *sit-is-tos';* from a der. of *4621; grained*, i.e. *fatted:*—fatling.

4620. σιτόμετρον **sitŏmĕtrŏn**, *sit-om'-et-ron;* from *4621* and *3358;* a *grain-measure*, i.e. (by impl.) *ration* (*allowance* of food):—portion of meat.

4621. σῖτος **sitŏs**, *see'-tos;* plur. irreg. neut.

σῖτα **sita**, *see'-tah;* of uncert. der.; *grain*, espec. *wheat:*—corn, wheat.

4622. Σιών **Siōn**, *see-own';* of Heb. or. [6726]; *Sion* (i.e. *Tsijon*), a hill of Jerus.; fig. the *Church* (militant or triumphant):—Sion.

4623. σιωπάω **siōpaō**, *see-o-pah'-o;* from σιωπή **siōpē** (*silence*, i.e. a *hush;* prop. *muteness*, i.e. *involuntary* stillness, or *inability* to speak; and thus differing from *4602*, which is rather a voluntary *refusal* or *indisposition* to speak, although the terms are often used synonymously); to *be dumb* (but not *deaf* also, like *2974* prop.) fig. to *be calm* (as *quiet* water):—dumb, (hold) peace.

4624. σκανδαλίζω **skandalizō**, *skan-dal-id'-zo* ("scandalize"); from *4625;* to *entrap*, i.e. *trip* up (fig. *stumble* [trans.] or *entice* to sin, apostasy or displeasure):—(make to) offend.

4625. σκάνδαλον **skandalŏn**, *skan'-dal-on* ("scandal"); prob. from a der. of *2578;* a *trap-stick* (*bent* sapling), i.e. *snare* (fig. *cause* of displeasure or sin):—occasion to fall (of stumbling), offence, thing that offends, stumblingblock.

4626. σκάπτω **skaptō**, *skap'-to;* appar. a prim. verb; to *dig:*—dig.

4627. σκάφη **skaphē**, *skaf'-ay;* a "*skiff*" (as if *dug* out), or *yawl* (carried aboard a large vessel for landing):—boat.

4628. σκέλος **skĕlŏs**, *skel'-os;* appar. from σκέλλω **skĕllō** (to *parch;* through the idea of *leanness*); the *leg* (as *lank*):—leg.

4629. σκέπασμα **skĕpasma**, *skep'-as-mah;* from a der. of σκέπας **skĕpas** (a *covering;* perh. akin to the base of *4649* through the idea of *noticeableness*); *clothing:*—raiment.

4630. Σκευᾶς **Skĕuas**, *skyoo-as';* appar. of Lat. or.; *left-handed; Scevas* (i.e. *Scævus*), an Isr.:—Sceva.

4631. σκευή **skĕuē**, *skyoo-ay';* from *4632; furniture*, i.e. spare *tackle:*—tackling.

4632. σκεῦος **skĕuŏs**, *skyoo'-os;* of uncert. affin.; a *vessel, implement, equipment* or *apparatus* (lit. or fig. [spec. a *wife* as contributing to the usefulness of the husband]):—goods, sail, stuff, vessel.

4633. σκηνή **skēnē**, *skay-nay';* appar. akin to *4632* and *4639;* a *tent* or cloth hut (lit. or fig.):—habitation, tabernacle.

4634. σκηνοπηγία **skēnŏpēgia**, *skay-nop-ayg-ee'-ah;* from *4636* and *4078;* the *Festival of Tabernacles* (so called from the custom of erecting booths for temporary homes):—tabernacles.

4635. σκηνοποιός **skēnŏpŏiŏs**, *skay-nop-oy-os';* from *4633* and *4160;* a *manufacturer of tents:*—tentmaker.

4636. σκῆνος **skēnŏs**, *skay'-nos;* from *4633;* a *hut* or temporary residence, i.e. (fig.) the human *body* (as the abode of the spirit):—tabernacle.

4637. σκηνόω **skēnŏō**, *skay-nŏ'-o;* from *4636;* to *tent* or *encamp*, i.e. (fig.) to *occupy* (as a mansion) or (spec.) to *reside* (as God did in the Tabernacle of old, a symbol of protection and communion):—dwell.

4638. σκήνωμα **skēnōma**, *skay'-no-mah;* from *4637;* an *encampment*, i.e. (fig.) the *Temple* (as God's residence), the *body* (as a tenement for the soul):—tabernacle.

4639. σκιά **skia**, *skee'-ah;* appar. a prim. word; "*shade*" or a shadow (lit. or fig. [darkness of *error* or an *adumbration*]):—shadow.

4640. σκιρτάω **skirtaō**, *skeer-tah'-o;* akin to σκαίρω **skairō** (to *skip*); to *jump*, i.e. sympathetically *move* (as the *quickening* of a fœtus):—leap (for joy).

4641. σκληροκαρδία **sklērŏkardia**, *sklay-rok-ar-dee'-ah;* fem. of a comp. of *4642* and *2588; hard-heartedness*, i.e. (spec.) *destitution of* (spiritual) *perception:*—hardness of heart.

4642. σκληρός **sklērŏs**, *sklay-ros';* from the base of *4628; dry*, i.e. *hard* or *tough* (fig. *harsh, severe*):—fierce, hard.

4643. σκληρότης **sklērŏtēs**, *sklay-rot'-ace;* from *4642; callousness*, i.e. (fig.) *stubbornness:*—hardness.

4644. σκληροτράχηλος **sklērŏtrachēlŏs**, *sklay-rot-rakh'-ay-los;* from *4642* and *5137; hard-naped*, i.e. (fig.) *obstinate:*—stiffnecked.

4645. σκληρύνω **sklērunō**, *sklay-roo'-no;* from *4642;* to *indurate*, i.e. (fig.) *render stubborn:*—harden.

4646. σκολιός **skŏliŏs**, *skol-ee-os';* from the base of *4628; warped*, i.e. *winding;* fig. *perverse:*—crooked, froward, untoward.

4647. σκόλοψ **skŏlŏps**, *skol'-ops;* perh. from the base of *4628* and *3700; withered* at the *front*, i.e. a *point* or *prickle* (fig. a bodily *annoyance* or *disability*):—thorn.

4648. σκοπέω **skŏpĕō**, *skop-eh'-o;* from *4649;* to take *aim* at (*spy*), i.e. (fig.) *regard:*—consider, take heed, look at (on), mark. Comp. *3700*.

4649. σκοπός **skŏpŏs**, *skop-os'* ("scope"); from σκέπτομαι **skĕptŏmai** (to *peer* about ["skeptic"]; perh. akin to *4626* through the idea of *concealment;* comp. *4629*); a *watch* (*sentry* or *scout*), i.e. (by impl.) a *goal:*—mark.

4650. σκορπίζω **skŏrpizō**, *skor-pid'-zo;* appar. from the same as *4651* (through the idea of *penetrating*); to *dissipate*, i.e. (fig.) *put to flight, waste, be liberal:*—disperse abroad, scatter (abroad).

4651. σκορπίος **skŏrpiŏs**, *skor-pee'-os;* prob. from an obsol. σκέρπω **skĕrpō** (perh. strengthened from the base of *4649* and mean. to *pierce*); a "*scorpion*" (from its *sting*):—scorpion.

4652. σκοτεινός **skŏtĕinŏs**, *skot-i-nos';* from *4655; opaque*, i.e. (fig.) *benighted:*—dark, full of darkness.

4653. σκοτία **skŏtia**, *skot-ee'-ah;* from *4655; dimness, obscurity* (lit. or fig.):—dark (-ness).

4654. σκοτίζω **skŏtizō**, *skot-id -zo;* from *4655;* to *obscure* (lit. or fig.):—darken.

4655. σκότος **skŏtŏs**, *skot'-os;* from the base of *4639; shadiness*, i.e. *obscurity* (lit. or fig.):—darkness.

4656. σκοτόω **skŏtŏō**, *skot-ŏ'-o;* from *4655;* to *obscure* or *blind* (lit. or fig.):—be full of darkness.

4657. σκύβαλον **skubalŏn**, *skoo'-bal-on;* neut. of a presumed der. of *1519* and *2965* and *906;* what is *thrown to the dogs*, i.e. *refuse* (*ordure*):—dung.

4658. Σκύθης **Skuthēs**, *skoo'-thace;* prob. of for. or.; a *Scythene* or *Scythian*, i.e. (by impl.) a *savage:*—Scythian.

4659. σκυθρωπός **skuthrōpŏs**, *skoo-thro-pos';* from σκυθρός **skuthrŏs** (*sullen*) and a der. of *3700; angry-visaged*, i.e. *gloomy* or affecting a *mournful* appearance:—of a sad countenance.

4660. σκύλλω **skullō**, *skool'-lo;* appar. a prim. verb; to *flay*, i.e. (fig.) to *harass:*—trouble (self).

4661. σκῦλον **skulŏn**, *skoo'-lon;* neut. from *4660;* something *stripped* (as a *hide*), i.e. *booty:*—spoil.

4662. σκωληκόβρωτος **skōlēkŏbrōtŏs**, *sko-lay-kob'-ro-tos;* from *4663* and a der. of *977; worm-eaten*, i.e. *diseased with maggots:*—eaten of worms.

4663. σκώληξ **skōlēx**, *sko'-lakes;* of uncert. der.; a *grub, maggot* or *earth-worm:*—worm.

4664. σμαράγδινος **smaragdinŏs**, *smar-ag'-dee-nos;* from 4665; consisting *of emerald:*—emerald.

4665. σμάραγδος **smaragdŏs**, *smar'-ag-dos;* of uncert. der.; the *emerald* or green gem so called:—emerald.

4666. σμύρνα **smurna**, *smoor'-nah;* appar. strengthened for 3464; *myrrh:*—myrrh.

4667. Σμύρνα **Smurna**, *smoor'-nah;* the same as 4666; *Smyrna*, a place in Asia Minor:—Smyrna.

4668. Σμυρναῖος **Smurnaiŏs**, *smoor-nah'-yos;* from 4667; a *Smyrnæan:*—in Smyrna.

4669. σμυρνίζω **smurnizō**, *smoor-nid'-zo;* from 4667; to *tincture with myrrh*, i.e. *embitter* (as a narcotic):—mingle with myrrh.

4670. Σόδομα **Sŏdŏma**, *sod'-om-ah;* plur. of Heb. or. [5467]; *Sodoma* (i.e. *Sedom*), a place in Pal.:—Sodom.

4671. σοί **sŏi**, *soy;* dat. of 4771; *to thee:*—thee, thine own, thou, thy.

4672. Σολομών or Σολομῶν **Sŏlŏmōn**, *sol-om-one';* of Heb. or. [8010]; *Solomon* (i.e. *Shelomoh*), the son of David:—Solomon.

4673. σορός **sŏrŏs**, *sor-os';* prob. akin to the base of 4987; a *funereal receptacle* (*urn, coffin*), i.e. (by anal.) a *bier:*—bier.

4674. σός **sŏs**, *sos;* from 4771; *thine:*—thine (own), thy (friend).

4675. σοῦ **sŏu**, *soo;* gen. of 4771; *of thee, thy:*—× home, thee, thine (own), thou, thy.

4676. σουδάριον **sŏudariŏn**, *soo-dar'-ee-on;* of Lat. or.; a *sudarium* (*sweat-cloth*), i.e. *towel* (for wiping the perspiration from the face, or binding the face of a corpse):—handkerchief, napkin.

4677. Σουσάννα **Sŏusanna**, *soo-san'-nah;* of Heb. or. [7799 fem.]; *lily; Susannah* (i.e. *Shoshannah*), an Israelitess:—Susanna.

4678. σοφία **sŏphia**, *sof-ee'-ah;* from 4680; *wisdom* (higher or lower, worldly or spiritual):—wisdom.

4679. σοφίζω **sŏphizō**, *sof-id'-zo;* from 4680; to *render wise;* in a sinister acceptation, to *form "sophisms"*, i.e. *continue plausible error:*—cunningly devised, make wise.

4680. σοφός **sŏphŏs**, *sof-os';* akin to σαφής **saphēs** (*clear*); *wise* (in a most gen. application):—wise. Comp. 5429.

4681. Σπανία **Spania**, *span-ee'-ah;* prob. of for. or.; *Spania*, a region of Europe:—Spain.

4682. σπαράσσω **sparassō**, *spar-as'-so;* prol. from σπαίρω **spairō** (to *gasp;* appar. strengthened from 4685 through the idea of *spasmodic* contraction); to *mangle*, i.e. *convulse* with epilepsy:—rend, tear.

4683. σπαργανόω **sparganŏō**, *spar-gan-ŏ'-o;* from σπάργανον **sparganŏn** (a *strip;* from a der. of the base of 4682 mean. to *strap* or *wrap* with strips); to *swathe* (an infant after the Oriental custom):—wrap in swaddling clothes.

4684. σπαταλάω **spatalaō**, *spat-al-ah'-o;* from σπατάλη **spatalē** (*luxury*); to *be voluptuous:*—live in pleasure, be wanton.

4685. σπάω **spaō**, *spah'-o;* a prim. verb; to *draw:*—draw (out).

4686. σπεῖρα **spĕira**, *spi'-rah;* of immed. Lat. or., but ultimately a der. of 138 in the sense of its cogn. 1507; a *coil* (*spira*, "spire"), i.e. (fig.) a *mass* of men (a Rom. military *cohort;* also [by anal.] a *squad* of Levitical janitors):—band.

4687. σπείρω **spĕirō**, *spi'-ro;* prob. strengthened from 4685 (through the idea of *extending*); to *scatter*, i.e. *sow* (lit. or fig.):—sow (-er), receive seed.

4688. σπεκουλάτωρ **spĕkŏulatōr**, *spek-oo-lat'-ore;* of Lat. or.; a *speculator*, i.e. military *scout* (*spy* or [by extens.] *life-guardsman*):—executioner.

4689. σπένδω **spĕndō**, *spen'-do;* appar. a prim. verb; to *pour* out as a libation, i.e. (fig.) to *devote* (one's life or blood, as a sacrifice) ("*spend*"):—(be ready to) be offered.

4690. σπέρμα **spĕrma**, *sper'-mah;* from 4687; something *sown*, i.e. *seed* (includ. the male "*sperm*"); by impl. *offspring;* spec. a *remnant* (fig. as if kept over for planting):—issue, seed.

4691. σπερμολόγος **spĕrmŏlŏgŏs**, *sper-mol-og'-os;* from 4690 and 3004; a *seed-picker* (as the crow), i.e. (fig.) a *sponger, loafer* (spec. a *gossip* or *trifler* in talk):—babbler.

4692. σπεύδω **spĕudō**, *spyoo'-do;* prob. strengthened from 4228; to "*speed*" ("study"), i.e. *urge* on (diligently or earnestly); by impl. to *await* eagerly:—(make, with) haste unto.

4693. σπήλαιον **spēlaiŏn**, *spay'-lah-yon;* neut. of a presumed der. of σπέος **spĕŏs** (a *grotto*); a *cavern;* by impl. a *hiding-place* or *resort:*—cave, den.

4694. σπιλάς **spilas**, *spee-las';* of uncert. der.; a *ledge* or *reef* of rock in the sea:—spot [*by confusion with* 4696].

4695. σπιλόω **spilŏō**, *spee-lŏ'-o;* from 4696; to *stain* or *soil* (lit. or fig.):—defile, spot.

4696. σπίλος **spilŏs**, *spee'-los;* of uncert. der.; a *stain* or *blemish*, i.e. (fig.) *defect, disgrace:*—spot.

4697. σπλαγχνίζομαι **splagchnizŏmai**, *splangkh-nid'-zom-ahee;* mid. from 4698; to have the *bowels* yearn, i.e. (fig.) *feel sympathy*, to *pity:*—have (be moved with) compassion.

4698. σπλάγχνον **splagchnŏn**, *splangkh'-non;* prob. strengthened from σπλήν **splēn** (the "*spleen*"); an *intestine* (plur.); fig. *pity* or *sympathy:*—bowels, inward affection, + tender mercy.

4699. σπόγγος **spŏggŏs**, *spong'-gos;* perh. of for. or.; a "*sponge*":—spunge.

4700. σποδός **spŏdŏs**, *spod-os';* of uncert. der.; *ashes:*—ashes.

4701. σπορά **spŏra**, *spor-ah';* from 4687; a *sowing*, i.e. (by impl.) *parentage:*—seed.

4702. σπόριμος **spŏrimŏs**, *spor'-ee-mos;* from 4703; *sown*, i.e. (neut. plur.) a planted *field:*—corn (-field).

4703. σπόρος **spŏrŏs**, *spor'-os;* from 4687; a *scattering* (of seed), i.e. (concr.) *seed* (as sown):—seed (× sown).

4704. σπουδάζω **spŏudazō**, *spoo-dad'-zo;* from 4710; to *use speed*, i.e. to *make effort*, *be prompt* or *earnest:*—do (give) diligence, be diligent (forward), endeavour, labour, study.

4705. σπουδαῖος **spŏudaiŏs**, *spoo-dah'-yos;* from 4710; *prompt, energetic, earnest:*—diligent.

4706. σπουδαιότερον **spŏudaiŏtĕrŏn**, *spoo-dah-yot'-er-on;* neut. of 4707 as adv.; *more earnestly* than others), i.e. very *promptly:*—very diligently.

4707. σπουδαιότερος **spŏudaiŏtĕrŏs**, *spoo-dah-yot'-er-os;* compar. of 4705; *more prompt, more earnest:*—more diligent (forward).

4708. σπουδαιοτέρως **spŏudaiŏtĕrōs**, *spoo-dah-yot-er'-oce;* adv. from 4707; *more speedily*, i.e. *sooner* than otherwise:—more carefully.

4709. σπουδαίως **spŏudaiōs**, *spoo-dah'-yoce;* adv. from 4705; *earnestly, promptly:*—diligently, instantly.

4710. σπουδή **spŏudē**, *spoo-day';* from 4692; "*speed*", i.e. (by impl.) *despatch, eagerness, earnestness:*—business, (earnest) care (-fulness), diligence, forwardness, haste.

4711. σπυρίς **spuris**, *spoo-rece';* from 4687 (as *woven*); a *hamper* or *lunch-receptacle:*—basket.

4712. στάδιον **stadiŏn**, *stad'-ee-on;* or masc. (in plur.) στάδιος **stadiŏs**, *stad'-ee-os;* from the base of 2476 (as *fixed*); a *stade* or certain measure of distance; by impl. a *stadium* or *race-course:*—furlong, race.

4713. στάμνος **stamnŏs**, *stam'-nos;* from the base of 2476 (as *stationary*); a *jar* or earthen *tank:*—pot.

4714. στάσις **stasis**, *stas'-is;* from the base of 2476; a *standing* (prop. the act), i.e. (by anal.) *position* (*existence*); by impl. a popular *uprising;* fig. *controversy:*—dissension, insurrection, × standing, uproar.

4715. στατήρ **statēr**, *stat-air';* from the base of 2746; a *stander* (*standard* of value), i.e. (spec.) a *stater* or certain coin:—piece of money.

4716. σταυρός **staurŏs**, *stŏw-ros';* from the base of 2476; a *stake* or *post* (as *set* upright), i.e. (spec.) a *pole* or *cross* (as an instrument of capital punishment); fig. *exposure to death*, i.e. *self-denial;* by impl. the *atonement* of Christ:—cross.

4717. σταυρόω **staurŏō**, *stŏw-rŏ'-o;* from 4716; to *impale* on the cross; fig. to *extinguish* (*subdue*) passion or selfishness:—crucify.

4718. σταφυλή **staphulē**, *staf-oo-lay';* prob. from the base of 4735; a *cluster* of grapes (as if *intertwined*):—grapes.

4719. στάχυς **stachus**, *stakh'-oos;* from the base of 2476; a *head* of grain (as *standing* out from the stalk):—ear (of corn).

4720. Στάχυς **Stachus**, *stakh'-oos;* the same as 4719; *Stachys*, a Chr.:—Stachys.

4721. στέγη **stĕgē**, *steg'-ay;* strengthened from a prim. τέγος **tĕgŏs** (a "*thatch*" or "*deck*" of a building); a *roof:*—roof.

4722. στέγω **stĕgō**, *steg'-o;* from 4721; to *roof* over, i.e. (fig.) to *cover* with silence (*endure* patiently):—(for-) bear, suffer.

4723. στεῖρος **stĕirŏs**, *sti'-ros;* a contr. from 4731 (as *stiff* and *unnatural*); "*sterile*":—barren.

4724. στέλλω **stĕllō**, *stel'-lo;* prob. strengthened from the base of 2476; prop. to *set* fast ("*stall*"), i.e. (fig.) to *repress* (reflex. *abstain* from associating with):—avoid, withdraw self.

4725. στέμμα **stĕmma**, *stem'-mah;* from the base of 4735; a *wreath* for show:—garland.

4726. στεναγμός **stĕnagmŏs**, *sten-ag-mos';* from 4727; a *sigh:*—groaning.

4727. στενάζω **stĕnazō**, *sten-ad'-zo;* from 4728; to *make* (intrans. *be*) *in straits*, i.e. (by impl.) to *sigh, murmur, pray* inaudibly:—with grief, groan, grudge, sigh.

4728. στενός **stĕnŏs**, *sten-os';* prob. from the base of 2476; *narrow* (from obstacles *standing* close about):—strait.

4729. στενοχωρέω **stĕnŏchōrĕō**, *sten-okh-o-reh'-o;* from the same as 4730; to *hem* in closely, i.e. (fig.) *cramp:*—distress, straiten.

4730. στενοχωρία **stĕnŏchōria**, *sten-okh-o-ree'-ah;* from a comp. of 4728 and 5561; *narrowness of room*, i.e. (fig.) *calamity:*—anguish, distress.

4731. στερεός **stĕrĕŏs**, *ster-eh-os';* from 2476; *stiff*, i.e. *solid, stable* (lit. or fig.):—stedfast, strong, sure.

4732. στερεόω **stĕrĕŏō**, *ster-eh-ŏ'-o;* from 4731; to *solidify*, i.e. *confirm* (lit. or fig.):—establish, receive strength, make strong.

4733. στερέωμα **stĕrĕōma**, *ster-eh'-o-mah;* from 4732; something *established*, i.e. (abstr.) *confirmation* (*stability*):—stedfastness.

4734. Στεφανᾶς **Stĕphanas**, *stef-an-as';* prob. contr. for στεφανωτός **stĕphanōtŏs** (*crowned;* from 4737); *Stephanas*, a Chr.:—Stephanas.

4735. στέφανος **stĕphanŏs**, *stef'-an-os;* from an appar. prim. στέφω **stĕphō** (to *twine* or *wreathe*); a *chaplet* (as a badge of royalty, a prize in the public games or a symbol of honor gen.; but more conspicuous and elaborate than the simple *fillet*, 1238), lit. or fig.:—crown.

4736. Στέφανος **Stĕphanŏs**, *stef'-an-os;* the same as 4735; *Stephanus*, a Chr.:—Stephen.

4737. στεφανόω **stephanŏō**, *stef-an-ŏ'-o;* from 4735; to *adorn with* an honorary *wreath* (lit. or fig.):—crown.

4738. στῆθος **stēthŏs**, *stay'-thos;* from 2476 (as *standing* prominently); the (entire extern.) *bosom*, i.e. *chest:*—breast.

4739. στήκω **stēkō**, *stay'-ko;* from the perf. tense of 2476; to *be stationary*, i.e. (fig.) to *persevere:*—stand (fast).

4740. στηριγμός **stērigmŏs**, *stay-rig-mos';* from 4741; *stability* (fig.):—stedfastness.

4741. στηρίζω **stērizō**, *stay-rid'-zo;* from a presumed der. of *2476* (like *4731*); to *set fast*, i.e. (lit.) to *turn resolutely* in a certain direction, or (fig.) to *confirm:*—fix, (e-) stablish, stedfastly set, strengthen.

4742. στίγμα **stigma**, *stig'-mah;* from a prim. στίζω **stizō** (to "*stick*", i.e. *prick*); a *mark* incised or punched (for recognition of ownership), i.e. (fig.) *scar* of service:—mark.

4743. στιγμή **stigmē**, *stig-may';* fem. of *4742;* a *point* of time, i.e. an *instant:*—moment.

4744. στίλβω **stilbō**, *stil'-bo;* appar. a prim. verb; to *gleam*, i.e. *flash* intensely:—shining.

4745. στοά **stŏa**, *stŏ-ah';* prob. from *2476;* a *colonnade* or interior *piazza:*—porch.

4746. στοιβάς **stŏibas**, *stoy-bas';* from a prim. στείβω **stĕibō** (to "*step*" or "*stamp*"); a *spread* (as if *tramped* flat) of loose materials for a couch, i.e. (by impl.) a *bough* of a tree so employed:—branch.

4747. στοιχεῖον **stŏichĕiŏn**, *stoy-khi'-on;* neut. of a presumed der. of the base of *4748;* something *orderly* in arrangement, i.e. (by impl.) a *serial* (*basal, fundamental, initial*) constituent (lit.), proposition (fig.):—element, principle, rudiment.

4748. στοιχέω **stŏichĕō**, *stoy-kheh'-o;* from a der. of στείχω **stĕichō** (to *range* in regular line); to *march* in (military) rank (*keep step*), i.e. (fig.) to *conform* to virtue and piety:—walk (orderly).

4749. στολή **stŏlē**, *stol-ay';* from *4724;* *equipment*, i.e. (spec.) a "*stole*" or long-fitting *gown* (as a mark of dignity):—long clothing (garment), (long) robe.

4750. στόμα **stŏma**, *stom'-a;* prob. strengthened from a presumed der. of the base of *5114;* the *mouth* (as if a *gash* in the face); by impl. *language* (and its relations); fig. an *opening* (in the earth); spec. the *front* or *edge* (of a weapon):—edge, face, mouth.

4751. στόμαχος **stŏmachŏs**, *stom'-akh-os;* from *4750;* an *orifice* (the *gullet*), i.e. (spec.) the "*stomach*":—stomach.

4752. στρατεία **stratĕia**, *strat-i'-ah;* from *4754;* military *service*, i.e. (fig.) the apostolic *career* (as one of hardship and danger):—warfare.

4753. στράτευμα **stratĕuma**, *strat'-yoo-mah;* from *4754;* an *armament*, i.e. (by impl.) a body of *troops* (more or less extensive or systematic):—army, soldier, man of war.

4754. στρατεύομαι **stratĕuŏmai**, *strat-yoo'-om-ahee;* mid. from the base of *4756;* to *serve* in a military campaign; fig. to *execute the apostolate* (with its arduous duties and functions), to *contend* with carnal inclinations:—soldier, (go to) war (-fare).

4755. στρατηγός **stratēgŏs**, *strat-ay-gos';* from the base of *4756* and *71* or *2233;* a *general*, i.e. (by impl. or anal.) a (military) *governor* (*prætor*), the *chief* (*præfect*) of the (Levitical) temple-wardens:—captain, magistrate.

4756. στρατία **stratia**, *strat-ee'-ah;* fem. of a der. of στρατός **stratŏs** (an *army;* from the base of *4766*, as *encamped*); *camp-likeness*, i.e. an *army*, i.e. (fig.) the *angels*, the celestial *luminaries:*—host.

4757. στρατιώτης **stratiōtēs**, *strat-ee-o'-tace;* from a presumed der. of the same as *4756;* a *camper-out*, i.e. a (common) *warrior* (lit. or fig.):—soldier.

4758. στρατολογέω **stratŏlŏgĕō**, *strat-ol-og-eh'-o;* from a comp. of the base of *4756* and *3004* (in its orig. sense); to *gather* (or *select*) as a *warrior*, i.e. *enlist* in the army:—choose to be a soldier.

4759. στρατοπεδάρχης **stratŏpĕdarchēs**, *strat-op-ed-ar'-khace;* from *4760* and *757;* a *ruler of an army*, i.e. (spec.) a Prætorian *præfect:*—captain of the guard.

4760. στρατόπεδον **stratŏpĕdŏn**, *strat-op'-ed-on;* from the base of *4756* and the same as *3977;* a *camping-ground*, i.e. (by impl.) a body of *troops:*—army.

4761. στρεβλόω **strĕblŏō**, *streb-lŏ'-o;* from a der. of *4762;* to *wrench*, i.e. (spec.) to *torture* (by the rack), but only fig. to *pervert:*—wrest.

4762. στρέφω **strĕphō**, *stref'-o;* strengthened from the base of *5157;* to *twist*, i.e. *turn* quite around or *reverse* (lit. or fig.):—convert, turn (again, back again, self, self about).

4763. στρηνιάω **strēniaō**, *stray-nee-ah'-o;* from a presumed der. of *4764;* to *be luxurious:*—live deliciously.

4764. στρῆνος **strēnŏs**, *stray'-nos;* akin to *4731;* a "*straining*", "*strenuousness*" or "*strength*", i.e. (fig.) *luxury* (*voluptuousness*):—delicacy.

4765. στρουθίον **strŏuthiŏn**, *stroo-thee'-on;* dimin. of στρουθός **strŏuthŏs** (a *sparrow*); a *little sparrow:*—sparrow.

4766. στρώννυμι **strōnnumi**, *strone'-noo-mee;* or simpler

στρωννύω **strōnnuō**, *strone-noo'-o;* prol. from a still simpler

στρόω **strŏō**, *strŏ'-o* (used only as an alt. in certain tenses; prob. akin to *4731* through the idea of *positing*); to "*strew*", i.e. *spread* (as a carpet or couch):—make bed, furnish, spread, strew.

4767. στυγνητός **stugnētŏs**, *stoog-nay-tos';* from a der. of an obsol. appar. prim. στύγω **stugō** (to *hate*); *hated*, i.e. *odious:*—hateful.

4768. στυγνάζω **stugnazō**, *stoog-nad'-zo;* from the same as *4767;* to *render gloomy*, i.e. (by impl.) *glower* (*be overcast* with clouds, or *sombreness* of speech):—lower, be sad.

4769. στῦλος **stulŏs**, *stoo'-los;* from στύω **stuō** (to *stiffen;* prop. akin to the base of *2476*); a *post* ("*style*"), i.e. (fig.) *support:*—pillar.

4770. Στωϊκός **Stōikŏs**, *sto-ik-os';* from *4745;* a "*Stoic*" (as occupying a particular porch in Athens), i.e. adherent of a certain philosophy:—Stoick.

4771. σύ **su**, *soo;* the pers. pron. of the sec. pers. sing.; *thou:*—thou. See also *4571*, *4671*, *4675;* and for the plur. *5209*, *5210*, *5213*, *5216*.

4772. συγγένεια **suggĕnĕia**, *soong-ghen'-i-ah;* from *4773;* *relationship*, i.e. (concr.) *relatives:*—kindred.

4773. συγγενής **suggĕnēs**, *soong-ghen-ace';* from *4862* and *1085;* a *relative* (by blood); by extens. a fellow *countryman:*—cousin, kin (-sfolk, -sman).

4774. συγγνώμη **suggnōmē**, *soong-gno'-may;* from a comp. of *4862* and *1097;* *fellow knowledge*, i.e. *concession:*—permission.

4775. συγκάθημαι **sugkathēmai**, *soong-kath'-ay-mahee;* from *4862* and *2521;* to *seat oneself* in company *with:*—sit with.

4776. συγκαθίζω **sugkathizō**, *soong-kath-id'-zo;* from *4862* and *2523;* to *give* (or *take*) *a seat* in company *with:*—(make) sit (down) together.

4777. συγκακοπαθέω **sugkakŏpathĕō**, *soong-kak-op-ath-eh'-o;* from *4862* and *2553;* to *suffer hardship* in company *with:*—be partaker of afflictions.

4778. συγκακουχέω **sugkakŏuchĕō**, *soong-kak-oo-kheh'-o;* from *4862* and *2558;* to *maltreat* in company *with*, i.e. (pass.) *endure persecution together:*—suffer affliction with.

4779. συγκαλέω **sugkalĕō**, *soong-kal-eh'-o;* from *4862* and *2564;* to *convoke:*—call together.

4780. συγκαλύπτω **sugkaluptō**, *soong-kal-oop'-to;* from *4862* and *2572;* to *conceal altogether:*—cover.

4781. συγκάμπτω **sugkamptō**, *soong-kamp'-to;* from *4862* and *2578;* to *bend together*, i.e. (fig.) to *afflict:*—bow down.

4782. συγκαταβαίνω **sugkatabainō**, *soong-kat-ab-ah'ee-no;* from *4862* and *2597;* to *descend* in company *with:*—go down with.

4783. συγκατάθεσις **sugkatathĕsis**, *soong-kat-ath'-es-is;* from *4784;* a *deposition* (of sentiment) in company *with*, i.e. (fig.) *accord* with:—agreement.

4784. συγκατατίθεμαι **sugkatatithĕmai**, *soong-kat-at-ith'-em-ahee;* mid. from *4862* and *2698;* to *deposit* (one's vote or opinion) in company *with*, i.e. (fig.) to *accord* with:—consent.

4785. συγκαταψηφίζω **sugkatapsēphizō**, *soong-kat-aps-ay-fid'-zo;* from *4862* and a comp. of *2596* and *5585;* to *count down* in company *with*, i.e. *enroll among:*—number with.

4786. συγκεράννυμι **sugkĕrannumi**, *soong-ker-an'-noo-mee;* from *4862* and *2767;* to *commingle*, i.e. (fig.) to *combine* or *assimilate:*—mix with, temper together.

4787. συγκινέω **sugkinĕō**, *soong-kin-eh'-o;* from *4682* and *2795;* to *move together*, i.e. (spec.) to *excite* as a mass (to sedition):—stir up.

4788. συγκλείω **sugklĕiō**, *soong-kli'-o;* from *4862* and *2808;* to *shut together*, i.e. *include* or (fig.) *embrace* in a common subjection to:—conclude, inclose, shut up.

4789. συγκληρονόμος **sugklērŏnŏmŏs**, *soong-klay-ron-om'-os;* from *4862* and *2818;* a *co-heir*, i.e. (by anal.) *participant in common:*—fellow (joint) -heir, heir together, heir with.

4790. συγκοινωνέω **sugkŏinōnĕō**, *soong-koy-no-neh'-o;* from *4862* and *2841;* to *share* in company *with*, i.e. *co-participate* in:—communicate (have fellowship) with, be partaker of.

4791. συγκοινωνός **sugkŏinōnŏs**, *soong-koy-no-nos';* from *4862* and *2844;* a *co-participant:*—companion, partake (-r, -r with).

4792. συγκομίζω **sugkŏmizō**, *soong-kom-id'-zo;* from *4862* and *2865;* to *convey together*, i.e. *collect* or *bear* away in company *with* others:—carry.

4793. συγκρίνω **sugkrinō**, *soong-kree'-no;* from *4862* and *2919;* to *judge* of one thing in connection *with* another, i.e. *combine* (spiritual ideas with appropriate expressions) or *collate* (one person with another by way of contrast or resemblance):—compare among (with).

4794. συγκύπτω **sugkuptō**, *soong-koop'-to;* from *4862* and *2955;* to *stoop altogether*, i.e. *be completely overcome* by:—bow together.

4795. συγκυρία **sugkuria**, *soong-koo-ree'-ah;* from a comp. of *4862* and κυρέω **kurĕō** (to *light* or *happen;* from the base of *2962*); *concurrence*, i.e. *accident:*—chance.

4796. συγχαίρω **sugchairō**, *soong-khah'ee-ro;* from *4862* and *5463;* to *sympathize in gladness, congratulate:*—rejoice in (with).

4797. συγχέω **sugchĕō**, *soong-kheh'-o;* or

συγχύνω **sugchunō**, *soong-khoo'-no;* from *4862* and χέω **chĕō** (to *pour*) or its alt.; to *commingle* promiscuously, i.e. (fig.) to *throw* (an assembly) *into disorder*, to *perplex* (the mind):—confound, confuse, stir up, be in an uproar.

4798. συγχράομαι **sugchraŏmai**, *soong-khrah'-om-ahee;* from *4862* and *5530;* to *use jointly*, i.e. (by impl.) to *hold intercourse in common:*—have dealings with.

4799. σύγχυσις **sugchusis**, *soong'-khoo-sis;* from *4797;* *commixture*, i.e. (fig.) riotous *disturbance:*—confusion.

4800. συζάω **suzaō**, *sood-zah'-o;* from *4862* and *2198;* to continue to *live* in common *with*, i.e. *co-survive* (lit. or fig.):—live with.

4801. συζεύγνυμι **suzĕugnumi**, *sood-zyoog'-noo-mee;* from *4862* and the base of *2201;* to *yoke together*, i.e. (fig.) *conjoin* (in marriage):—join together.

4802. συζητέω **suzētĕō**, *sood-zay-teh'-o;* from *4862* and *2212;* to investigate *jointly*, i.e. *discuss, controvert, cavil:*—dispute (with), enquire, question (with), reason (together).

4803. συζήτησις **suzētēsis**, *sood-zay'-tay-sis;* from *4802;* *mutual questioning*, i.e. *discussion:*—disputation (-ting), reasoning.

4804. συζητητής **suzētētēs**, *sood-zay-tay-tace';* from *4802;* a *disputant*, i.e. *sophist:*—disputer.

4805. σύζυγος **suzugŏs**, *sood'-zoo-gos;* from *4801;* *co-yoked*, i.e. (fig.) as noun, a *colleague;* prob. rather as prop. name; *Syzygus*, a Chr.:—yokefellow.

4806. συζωοποιέω **suzōŏpŏiĕō**, *sood-zo-op-oy-eh'-o;* from *4862* and *2227;* to *reanimate conjointly* with (fig.):—quicken together with.

4807. συκάμινος **sukaminŏs**, *soo-kam'-ee-nos;* of Heb. or. [8256] in imitation of *4809;* a *sycamore-fig* tree:—sycamine tree.

4808. συκῆ **sukē**, *soo-kay';* from *4810;* a *fig-tree:*—fig tree.

4809. συκομωραία **sukŏmōraia**, *soo-kom-o-rah'-yah;* from *4810* and μόρον **mŏrŏn** (the *mul-*

berry); the "*sycamore*"-fig tree:—sycamore tree. Comp. *4807*.

4810. **σῦκον sukŏn**, *soo'-kon;* appar. a prim. word; a *fig:*—fig.

4811. **συκοφαντέω sukŏphantĕō**, *soo-kof-an-teh'-o;* from a comp. of *4810* and a der. of *5316;* to *be a fig-informer* (reporter of the law forbidding the exportation of figs from Greece), "*sycophant*", i.e. (gen. and by extens.) to *defraud* (*exact* unlawfully, *extort*):—accuse falsely, take by false accusation.

4812. **συλαγωγέω sulagōgĕō**, *soo-lag-ogue-eh'-o;* from the base of *4813* and (the redupl. form of) *71;* to *lead* away as *booty*, i.e. (fig.) *seduce:*—spoil.

4813. **συλάω sulaō**, *soo-lah'-o;* from a der. of **σύλλω sullō** (to *strip;* prob. akin to *138;* comp. *4661*); to *despoil:*—rob.

4814. **συλλαλέω sullalĕō**, *sool-lal-eh'-o;* from *4862* and *2980;* to *talk together*, i.e. *converse:*—commune (confer, talk) with, speak among.

4815. **συλλαμβάνω sullambanō**, *sool-lam-ban'-o;* from *4862* and *2983;* to *clasp*, i.e. *seize* (*arrest, capture*); spec. to *conceive* (lit. or fig.); by impl. to *aid:*—catch, conceive, help, take.

4816. **συλλέγω sullĕgō**, *sool-leg'-o;* from *4862* and *3004* in its orig. sense; to *collect:*—gather (together, up).

4817. **συλλογίζομαι sullŏgizŏmai**, *sool-log-id'-zom-ahee;* from *4862* and *3049;* to *reckon together* (with oneself), i.e. *deliberate:*—reason with.

4818. **συλλυπέω sullupĕō**, *sool-loop-eh'-o;* from *4862* and *3076;* to *afflict jointly*, i.e. (pass.) *sorrow at* (on account of) some one:—be grieved.

4819. **συμβαίνω, sumbainō**, *soom-bah'ee-no;* from *4862* and the base of *939;* to *walk* (fig. *transpire*) *together*, i.e. *concur* (*take place*):—be (-fall), happen (unto).

4820. **συμβάλλω sumballō**, *soom-bal'-lo;* from *4862* and *906;* to *combine*, i.e. (in speaking) to *converse, consult, dispute*, (mentally) to *consider*, (by impl.) to *aid*, (personally) to *join, attack:*—confer, encounter, help, make, meet with, ponder.

4821. **συμβασιλεύω sumbasilĕuō**, *soom-bas-il-yoo'-o;* from *4862* and *936;* to *be co-regent* (fig.):—reign with.

4822. **συμβιβάζω sumbibazō**, *soom-bib-ad'-zo;* from *4862* and **βιβάζω bibazō** (to *force;* caus. [by redupl.] of the base of *939*); to *drive together*, i.e. *unite* (in association or affection), (mentally) to *infer, show, teach:*—compact, assuredly gather, instruct, knit together, prove.

4823. **συμβουλεύω sumbŏulĕuō**, *soom-bool-yoo'-o;* from *4862* and *1011;* to *give* (or *take*) *advice jointly*, i.e. *recommend, deliberate* or *determine:*—consult, (give, take) counsel (together).

4824. **συμβούλιον sumbŏuliŏn**, *soom-boo'-lee-on;* neut. of a presumed der. of *4825; advisement;* spec. a *deliberative* body, i.e. the provincial *assessors* or lay-court:—consultation, counsel, council.

4825. **σύμβουλος sumbŏulŏs**, *soom'-boo-los;* from *4862* and *1012;* a *consultor*, i.e. *adviser:*—counsellor.

4826. **Συμεών Sumĕōn**, *soom-eh-one';* from the same as *4613; Symeon* (i.e. *Shimon*), the name of five Isr.:—Simeon, Simon.

4827. **συμμαθητής summathētēs**, *soom-math-ay-tace';* from a comp. of *4862* and *3129;* a *co-learner* (of Christianity):—fellowdisciple.

4828. **συμμαρτυρέω summarturĕō**, *soom-mar-too-reh'-o;* from *4862* and *3140;* to *testify jointly*, i.e. *corroborate* by (concurrent) evidence:—testify unto, (also) bear witness (with).

4829. **συμμερίζομαι summĕrizŏmai**, *soom-mer-id'-zom-ahee;* mid. from *4862* and *3307;* to *share jointly*, i.e. *participate* in:—be partaker with.

4830. **συμμέτοχος summĕtŏchŏs**, *soom-met'-okh-os;* from *4862* and *3353;* a *co-participant:*—partaker.

4831. **συμμιμητής summimētēs**, *soom-mim-ay-tace';* from a presumed comp. of *4862* and *3401;* a *co-imitator*, i.e. *fellow votary:*—follower together.

4832. **σύμμορφος summŏrphŏs**, *soom-mor-fos';* from *4862* and *3444; jointly formed*, i.e. (fig.) *similar:*—conformed to, fashioned like unto.

4833. **συμμορφόω summŏrphŏō**, *soom-mor-fŏ'-o;* from *4832;* to *render like*, i.e. (fig.) to *assimilate:*—make conformable unto.

4834. **συμπαθέω sumpathĕō**, *soom-path-eh'-o;* from *4835;* to *feel* "*sympathy*" with, i.e. (by impl.) to *commiserate:*—have compassion, be touched with a feeling of.

4835. **συμπαθής sumpathēs**, *soom-path-ace';* from *4841; having a fellow-feeling* ("*sympathetic*"), i.e. (by impl.) *mutually commiserative;*—having compassion one of another.

4836. **συμπαραγίνομαι sumparaginŏmai**, *soom-par-ag-in'-om-ahee;* from *4862* and *3854;* to *be present together*, i.e. to *convene;* by impl. to *appear in aid:*—come together, stand with.

4837. **συμπαρακαλέω sumparakalĕō**, *soom-par-ak-al-eh'-o;* from *4862* and *3870;* to *console jointly:*—comfort together.

4838. **συμπαραλαμβάνω sumparalambanō**, *soom-par-al-am-ban'-o;* from *4862* and *3880;* to *take along in company:*—take with.

4839. **συμπαραμένω sumparamĕnō**, *soom-par-am-en'-o;* from *4862* and *3887;* to *remain in company*, i.e. *still live:*—continue with.

4840. **συμπάρειμι sumparĕimi**, *soom-par'-i-mee;* from *4862* and *3918;* to *be at hand together*, i.e. *now present:*—be here present with.

4841. **συμπάσχω sumpaschō**, *soom-pas'-kho;* from *4862* and *3958* (includ. its alt.); to *experience pain jointly* or of the *same kind* (spec. *persecution;* to "*sympathize*"):—suffer with.

4842. **συμπέμπω sumpĕmpō**, *soom-pem'-po;* from *4862* and *3992;* to *despatch in company:*—send with.

4843. **συμπεριλαμβάνω sumpĕrilambanō**, *soom-per-ee-lam-ban'-o;* from *4862* and a comp. of *4012* and *2983;* to *take by inclosing altogether*, i.e. *earnestly throw the arms about one:*—embrace.

4844. **συμπίνω sumpinō**, *soom-pee'-no;* from *4862* and *4095;* to *partake a beverage in company:*—drink with.

4845. **συμπληρόω sumplērŏō**, *soom-play-rŏ'-o;* from *4862* and *4137;* to *implenish completely*, i.e. (of space) to *swamp* (a boat), or (of time) to *accomplish* (pass. be *complete*):—(fully) come, fill up.

4846. **συμπνίγω sumpnigō**, *soom-pnee'-go;* from *4862* and *4155;* to *strangle completely*, i.e. (lit.) to *drown*, or (fig.) to *crowd:*—choke, throng.

4847. **συμπολίτης sumpŏlitēs**, *soom-pol-ee'-tace;* from *4862* and *4177;* a *native of the same town*, i.e. (fig.) *co-religionist* (*fellow-Christian*):—fellow-citizen.

4848. **συμπορεύομαι sumpŏrĕuŏmai**, *soom-por-yoo'-om-ahee;* from *4862* and *4198;* to *journey together;* by impl. to *assemble:*—go with, resort.

4849. **συμπόσιον sumpŏsiŏn**, *soom-pos'-ee-on;* neut. of a der. of the alt. of *4844;* a *drinking*-party ("*symposium*"), i.e. (by extens.) a *room* of guests:—company.

4850. **συμπρεσβύτερος sumprĕsbutĕrŏs**, *soom-pres-boo'-ter-os;* from *4862* and *4245;* a *co-presbyter:*—presbyter, also an elder.

συμφάγω sumphagō. See *4906*.

4851. **συμφέρω sumphĕrō**, *soom-fer'-o;* from *4862* and *5342* (includ. its alt.); to *bear together* (*contribute*), i.e. (lit.) to *collect*, or (fig.) to *conduce;* espec. (neut. part. as noun) *advantage:*—be better for, bring together, be expedient (for), be good, (be) profit (-able for).

4852. **σύμφημι sumphēmi**, *soom'-fay-mee;* from *4862* and *5346;* to *say jointly*, i.e. *assent to:*—consent unto.

4853. **συμφυλέτης sumphulĕtēs**, *soom-foo-let'-ace;* from *4862* and a der. of *5443;* a *co-tribesman*, i.e. *native of the same country:*—countryman.

4854. **σύμφυτος sumphutŏs**, *soom'-foo-tos;* from *4862* and a der. of *5453; grown* along *with* (*connate*), i.e. (fig.) closely *united* to:—planted together.

4855. **συμφύω sumphuō**, *soom-foo'-o;* from *4862* and *5453;* pass. to *grow jointly:*—spring up with.

4856. **συμφωνέω sumphōnĕō**, *soom-fo-neh'-o;* from *4859;* to be *harmonious*, i.e. (fig.) to *accord* (*be suitable, concur*) or *stipulate* (by compact):—agree (together, with).

4857. **συμφώνησις sumphōnēsis**, *soom-fo'-nay-sis;* from *4856; accordance:*—concord.

4858. **συμφωνία sumphōnia**, *soom-fo-nee'-ah;* from *4859; unison* of sound ("*symphony*"), i.e. a *concert* of instruments (harmonious *note*):—music.

4859. **σύμφωνος sumphōnŏs**, *soom'-fo-nos;* from *4862* and *5456; sounding together* (*alike*), i.e. (fig.) *accordant* (neut. as noun, *agreement*):—consent.

4860. **συμψηφίζω sumpsēphizō**, *soom-psay-fid'-zo;* from *4862* and *5585;* to *compute jointly:*—reckon.

4861. **σύμψυχος sumpsuchŏs**, *soom'-psoo-khos;* from *4862* and *5590; co-spirited*, i.e. *similar in sentiment:*—like-minded.

4862. **σύν sun**, *soon;* a prim. prep. denoting *union; with* or *together* (but much closer than *3326* or *3844*), i.e. by association, companionship, process, resemblance, possession, instrumentality, addition etc.:—beside, with. In comp. it has similar applications, includ. *completeness*.

4863. **συνάγω sunagō**, *soon-ag'-o;* from *4862* and *71;* to *lead together*, i.e. *collect* or *convene;* spec. to *entertain* (hospitably):— + accompany, assemble (selves, together), bestow, come together, gather (selves together, up, together), lead into, resort, take in.

4864. **συναγωγή sunagōgē**, *soon-ag-o-gay';* from (the redupl. form of) *4863;* an *assemblage* of persons; spec. a Jewish "*synagogue*" (the meeting or the place); by anal. a Christian *church:*—assembly, congregation, synagogue.

4865. **συναγωνίζομαι sunagōnizŏmai**, *soon-ag-o-nid'-zom-ahee;* from *4862* and *75;* to *struggle* in company *with*, i.e. (fig.) to *be a partner* (*assistant*):—strive together with.

4866. **συναθλέω sunathlĕō**, *soon-ath-leh'-o;* from *4862* and *118;* to *wrestle* in company *with*, i.e. (fig.) to *seek jointly:*—labour with, strive together for.

4867. **συναθροίζω sunathrŏizō**, *soon-ath-royd'-zo;* from *4862* and **ἀθροίζω athrŏizō** (to *hoard*); to *convene:*—call (gather) together.

4868. **συναίρω sunairō**, *soon-ah'ee-ro;* from *4862* and *142;* to *make up together*, i.e. (fig.) to *compute* (an account):—reckon, take.

4869. **συναιχμάλωτος sunaichmalōtŏs**, *soon-aheekh-mal'-o-tos;* from *4862* and *164;* a *co-captive:*—fellowprisoner.

4870. **συνακολουθέω sunakŏlŏuthĕō**, *soon-ak-ol-oo-theh'-o;* from *4862* and *190;* to *accompany:*—follow.

4871. **συναλίζω sunalizō**, *soon-al-id'-zo;* from *4862* and **ἁλίζω halizō** (to *throng*); to *accumulate*, i.e. *convene:*—assemble together.

4872. **συναναβαίνω sunanabainō**, *soon-an-ab-ah'ee-no;* from *4862* and *305;* to *ascend* in company *with:*—come up with.

4873. **συνανάκειμαι sunanakĕimai**, *soon-an-ak'-i-mahee;* from *4862* and *345;* to *recline* in company *with* (at a meal):—sit (down, at the table, together) with (at meat).

4874. **συναναμίγνυμι sunanamignumi**, *soon-an-am-ig'-noo-mee;* from *4862* and a comp. of *303* and *3396;* to *mix up together*, i.e. (fig.) *associate with:*—(have, keep) company (with).

4875. **συναναπαύομαι sunanapauŏmai**, *soon-an-ap-ŏw'-om-ahee;* mid. from *4862* and *373;* to *recruit oneself* in company *with:*—refresh with.

4876. **συναντάω sunantaō**, *soon-an-tah'-o;* from *4862* and a der. of *473;* to *meet with;* fig. to *occur:*—befall, meet.

4877. **συνάντησις sunantēsis**, *soon-an'-tay-sis;* from *4876*; a *meeting with*:—meet.

4878. **συναντιλαμβάνομαι sunantilambanŏmai**, *soon-an-tee-lam-ban'-om-ahee;* from *4862* and *482*; to *take* hold of *opposite together*, i.e. *co-operate* (*assist*):—help.

4879. **συναπάγω sunapagō**, *soon-ap-ag'-o;* from *4862* and *520*; to *take off together*, i.e. *transport with* (*seduce*, pass. *yield*):—carry (lead) away with, condescend.

4880. **συναποθνήσκω sunapŏthnēskō**, *soon-ap-oth-nace'-ko;* from *4862* and *599*; to *decease* (lit.) in company *with*, or (fig.) similarly *to*:—be dead (die) with.

4881. **συναπόλλυμι sunapŏllumi**, *soon-ap-ol'-loo-mee;* from *4862* and *622*; to *destroy* (mid. or pass. *be slain*) in company *with*:—perish with.

4882. **συναποστέλλω sunapŏstĕllō**, *soon-ap-os-tel'-lo;* from *4862* and *649*; to *despatch* (on an errand) in company *with*:—send with.

4883. **συναρμολογέω sunarmŏlŏgĕō**, *soon-ar-mol-og-eh'-o;* from *4862* and a der. of a comp. of *719* and *3004* (in its orig. sense of *laying*); to *render close-jointed together*, i.e. *organize compactly*:—be fitly framed (joined) together.

4884. **συναρπάζω sunarpazō**, *soon-ar-pad'-zo;* from *4862* and *726*; to *snatch together*, i.e. *seize*:—catch.

4885. **συναυξάνω sunauxanō**, *soon-owx-an'-o;* from *4862* and *837*; to *increase* (*grow up*) *together*:—grow together.

4886. **σύνδεσμος sundĕsmŏs**, *soon'-des-mos;* from *4862* and *1199*; a *joint tie*, i.e. *ligament*, (fig.) *uniting principle, control*:—band, bond.

4887. **συνδέω sundĕō**, *soon-deh'-o;* from *4862* and *1210*; to *bind with*, i.e. (pass.) *be a fellow-prisoner* (fig.):—be bound with.

4888. **συνδοξάζω sundŏxazō**, *soon-dox-ad'-zo;* from *4862* and *1392*; to *exalt* to dignity in company (i.e. *similarly*) *with*:—glorify together.

4889. **σύνδουλος sundŏulŏs**, *soon'-doo-los;* from *4862* and *1401*; a *co-slave*, i.e. *servitor* or *ministrant of the same master* (human or divine):—fellowservant.

συνδρέμω sundrĕmō. See *4936*.

4890. **συνδρομή sundrŏmē**, *soon-drom-ay';* from (the alt. of) *4936*; a *running together*, i.e. (riotous) *concourse*:—run together.

4891. **συνεγείρω sunĕgĕirō**, *soon-eg-i'-ro;* from *4862* and *1453*; to *rouse* (from death) in company *with*, i.e. (fig.) to *revivify* (spiritually) in resemblance to:—raise up together, rise with.

4892. **συνέδριον sunĕdriŏn**, *soon-ed'-ree-on;* neut of a presumed der. of a comp. of *4862* and the base of *1476*; a *joint session*, i.e. (spec.) the Jewish *Sanhedrim*; by anal. a subordinate *tribunal*:—council.

4893. **συνείδησις sunĕidēsis**, *soon-i'-day-sis;* from a prol. form of *4894*; *co-perception*, i.e. moral *consciousness*:—conscience.

4894. **συνείδω sunĕidō**, *soon-i'-do;* from *4862* and *1492*; to *see completely*; used (like its prim.) only in two past tenses, respectively mean. to *understand* or *become aware*, and to *be conscious* or (clandestinely) *informed of*:—consider, know, be privy, be ware of.

4895. **σύνειμι sunĕimi**, *soon'-i-mee;* from *4862* and *1510* (includ. its various inflections); to *be* in company *with*, i.e. *present* at the time:—be with.

4896. **σύνειμι sunĕimi**, *soon'-i-mee;* from *4862* and **εἶμι ĕimi** (to *go*); to *assemble*:—gather together.

4897. **συνεισέρχομαι sunĕisĕrchŏmai**, *soon-ice-er'-khom-ahee;* from *4862* and *1525*; to *enter* in company *with*:—go in with, go with into.

4898. **συνέκδημος sunĕkdēmŏs**, *soon-ek'-day-mos;* from *4862* and the base of *1553*; a *co-absentee* from home, i.e. *fellow-traveller*:—companion in travel, travel with.

4899. **συνεκλεκτός sunĕklĕktŏs**, *soon-ek-lek-tos';* from a comp. of *4862* and *1586*; *chosen* in company *with*, i.e. *co-elect* (*fellow Christian*):—elected together with.

4900. **συνελαύνω sunĕlaunō**, *soon-el-ow'-no;* from *4862* and *1643*; to *drive together*, i.e. (fig.) *exhort* (to reconciliation):— + set at one again.

4901. **συνεπιμαρτυρέω sunĕpimarturĕō**, *soon-ep-ee-mar-too-reh'-o;* from *4862* and *1957*; to *testify further jointly*, i.e. *unite in adding evidence*:—also bear witness.

4902. **συνέπομαι sunĕpŏmai**, *soon-ep'-om-ahee;* mid. from *4862* and a prim. **ἕπω hĕpō** (to *follow*); to *attend* (*travel*) in company *with*:—accompany.

4903. **συνεργέω sunĕrgĕō**, *soon-erg-eh'-o;* from *4904*; to *be a fellow-worker*, i.e. *co-operate*:—help (work) with, work (-er) together.

4904. **συνεργός sunĕrgŏs**, *soon-er-gos';* from a presumed comp. of *4862* and the base of *2041*; a *co-laborer*, i.e. *coadjutor*:—companion in labour, (fellow-) helper (-labourer, -worker), labourer together with, workfellow.

4905. **συνέρχομαι sunĕrchŏmai**, *soon-er'-khom-ahee;* from *4862* and *2064*; to *convene*, *depart* in company *with*, *associate* with, or (spec.) *cohabit* (conjugally):—accompany, assemble (with), come (together), come (company, go) with, resort.

4906. **συνεσθίω sunĕsthiō**, *soon-es-thee'-o;* from *4862* and *2068* (includ. its alt.); to *take food* in company *with*:—eat with.

4907. **σύνεσις sunĕsis**, *soon'-es-is;* from *4920*; a mental *putting together*, i.e. *intelligence* or (concr.) the *intellect*:—knowledge, understanding.

4908. **συνετός sunĕtŏs**, *soon-et'-os;* from *4920*; mentally *put* (or *putting*) *together*, i.e. *sagacious*:—prudent. Comp. *5429*.

4909. **συνευδοκέω sunĕudŏkĕō**, *soon-yoo-dok-eh'-o;* from *4862* and *2106*; to *think well of in common*, i.e. *assent to*, *feel gratified with*:—allow, assent, be pleased, have pleasure.

4910. **συνευωχέω sunĕuōchĕō**, *soon-yoo-o-kheh'-o;* from *4862* and a der. of a presumed comp. of *2095* and a der. of *2192* (mean. to *be in good condition*, i.e. [by impl.] to *fare well*, or *feast*); to *entertain* sumptuously in company *with*, i.e. (mid. or pass.) to *revel together*:—feast with.

4911. **συνεφίστημι sunĕphistēmi**, *soon-ef-is'-tay-mee;* from *4862* and *2186*; to *stand up together*, i.e. to *resist* (or *assault*) *jointly*:—rise up together.

4912. **συνέχω sunĕchō**, *soon-ekh'-o;* from *4862* and *2192*; to *hold together*, i.e. to *compress* (the ears, with a crowd or siege) or *arrest* (a prisoner); fig. to *compel, perplex, afflict, preoccupy*:—constrain, hold, keep in, press, lie sick of, stop, be in a strait, straiten, be taken with, throng.

4913. **συνήδομαι sunēdŏmai**, *soon-ay'-dom-ahee;* mid. from *4862* and the base of *2237*; to *rejoice* in *with* oneself, i.e. *feel satisfaction* concerning:—delight.

4914. **συνήθεια sunēthĕia**, *soon-ay'-thi-ah;* from a comp. of *4862* and *2239*; *mutual habituation*, i.e. *usage*:—custom.

4915. **συνηλικιώτης sunēlikiōtēs**, *soon-ay-lik-ee-o'-tace;* from *4862* and a der. of *2244*; a *co-aged* person, i.e. *alike* in years:—equal,

4916. **συνθάπτω sunthaptō**, *soon-thap'-to;* from *4862* and *2290*; to *inter* in company *with*, i.e. (fig.) to *assimilate* spiritually (to Christ by a sepulture as to sin):—bury with.

4917. **συνθλάω sunthlaō**, *soon-thlah'-o;* from *4862* and **θλάω thlaō** (to *crush*); to *dash together*, i.e. *shatter*:—break.

4918. **συνθλίβω sunthlibō**, *soon-thlee'-bo;* from *4862* and *2346*; to *compress*, i.e. *crowd* on all sides:—throng.

4919. **συνθρύπτω sunthruptō**, *soon-throop'-to;* from *4862* and **θρύπτω thruptō** (to *crumble*); to *crush together*, i.e. (fig.) to *dispirit*:—break.

4920. **συνίημι suniēmi**, *soon-ee'-ay-mee;* from *4862* and **ἵημι hiēmi** (to *send*); to *put together*, i.e. (mentally) to *comprehend*; by impl. to *act piously*:—consider, understand, be wise.

4921. **συνιστάω sunistaō**, *soon-is-tah'-o;* or (strengthened)

συνιστάνω sunistanō, *soon-is-tan'-o;* or

συνίστημι sunistēmi, *soon-is'-tay-mee;* from *4862* and *2476* (includ. its collat. forms); to *set together*, i.e. (by impl.) to *introduce* (favorably), or (fig.) to *exhibit*; intrans. to *stand near*, or (fig.) to *constitute*:—approve, commend, consist, make, stand (with).

4922. **συνοδεύω sunŏdĕuō**, *soon-od-yoo'-o;* from *4862* and *3593*; to *travel* in company *with*:—journey with.

4923. **συνοδία sunŏdia**, *soon-od-ee'-ah;* from a comp. of *4862* and *3598* ("*synod*"); *companionship* on a journey, i.e. (by impl.) a *caravan*:—company.

4924. **συνοικέω sunŏikĕō**, *soon-oy-keh'-o;* from *4862* and *3611*; to *reside together* (as a family):—dwell together.

4925. **συνοικοδομέω sunŏikŏdŏmĕō**, *soon-oy-kod-om-eh'-o;* from *4862* and *3618*; to *construct*, i.e. (pass.) to *compose* (in company with other Christians, fig.):—build together.

4926. **συνομιλέω sunŏmilĕō**, *soon-om-il-eh'-o;* from *4862* and *3656*; to *converse* mutually:—talk with.

4927. **συνομορέω sunŏmŏrĕō**, *soon-om-or-eh'-o;* from *4862* and a der. of a comp. of the base of *3674* and the base of *3725*; to *border together*, i.e. *adjoin*:—join hard.

4928. **συνοχή sunŏchē**, *soon-okh-ay';* from *4912*; *restraint*, i.e. (fig.) *anxiety*:—anguish, distress.

4929. **συντάσσω suntassō**, *soon-tas-so;* from *4862* and *5021*; to *arrange jointly*, i.e. (fig.) to *direct*:—appoint.

4930. **συντέλεια suntĕlĕia**, *soon-tel'-i-ah;* from *4931*; *entire completion*, i.e. *consummation* (of a dispensation):—end.

4931. **συντελέω suntĕlĕō**, *soon-tel-eh'-o;* from *4862* and *5055*; to *complete entirely*; gen. to *execute* (lit. or fig.):—end, finish, fulfil, make.

4932. **συντέμνω suntĕmnō**, *soon-tem'-no;* from *4862* and the base of *5114*; to *contract* by cutting, i.e. (fig.) *do concisely* (*speedily*):—(cut) short.

4933. **συντηρέω suntērĕō**, *soon-tay-reh'-o;* from *4862* and *5083*; to *keep* closely *together*, i.e. (by impl.) to *conserve* (from ruin); ment. to *remember* (and *obey*):—keep, observe, preserve.

4934. **συντίθεμαι suntithĕmai**, *soon-tith'-em-ahee;* mid. from *4862* and *5087*; to *place jointly*, i.e. (fig.) to *consent* (*bargain, stipulate*), *concur*:—agree, assent, covenant.

4935. **συντόμως suntŏmōs**, *soon-tom'-oce;* adv. from a der. of *4932*; *concisely* (*briefly*):—a few words.

4936. **συντρέχω suntrĕchō**, *soon-trekh'-o;* from *4862* and *5143* (includ. its alt.); to *rush together* (hastily *assemble*) or *headlong* (fig.):—run (together, with).

4937. **συντρίβω suntribō**, *soon-tree'-bo;* from *4862* and the base of *5147*; to *crush completely*, i.e. to *shatter* (lit. or fig.):—break (in pieces), broken to shivers (+ -hearted), bruise.

4938. **σύντριμμα suntrimma**, *soon-trim'-mah;* from *4937*; *concussion* or utter *fracture* (prop. concr.), i.e. complete *ruin*:—destruction.

4939. **σύντροφος suntrŏphŏs**, *soon'-trof-os;* from *4862* and *5162* (in a pass. sense); a *fellow-nursling*, i.e. *comrade*:—brought up with.

4940. **συντυγχάνω suntugchanō**, *soon-toong-khan'-o;* from *4862* and *5177*; to *chance together*, i.e. *meet* with (*reach*):—come at.

4941. **Συντύχη Suntuchē**, *soon-too'-khay;* from *4940*; an *accident*; *Syntyche*, a Chr. female:—Syntyche.

4942. **συνυποκρίνομαι sunupŏkrinŏmai**, *soon-oo-pok-rin'-om-ahee;* from *4862* and *5271*; to *act hypocritically* in concert *with*:—dissemble with.

4943. **συνυπουργέω sunupŏurgĕō**, *soon-oop-oorg-eh'-o;* from *4862* and a der. of a comp. of *5259* and the base of *2041*; to *be a co-auxiliary*, i.e. *assist*:—help together.

4944. συνωδίνω sunōdinō, *soon-o-dee'-no;* from *4862* and *5605;* to *have* (parturition) *pangs* in company (concert, simultaneously) *with*, i.e. (fig.) to *sympathize* (in expectation of relief from suffering):—travail in pain together.

4945. συνωμοσία sunōmŏsia, *soon-o-mos-ee'-ah*, from a comp. of *4862* and *3660;* a *swearing together*, i.e. (by impl.) a *plot:*—conspiracy.

4946. Συράκουσαι Surakŏusai, *soo-rak'-oo-sahee;* plur. of uncert. der.; *Syracusæ*, the capital of Sicily:—Syracuse.

4947. Συρία Suria, *soo-ree'-ah;* prob. of Heb. or. [6865]; *Syria* (i.e. *Tsyria* or *Tyre*), a region of Asia:—Syria.

4948. Σύρος Surŏs, *soo'-ros;* from the same as *4947;* a *Syran* (i.e. prob. *Tyrian*), a native of Syria:—Syrian.

4949. Συροφοίνισσα Surŏphŏinissa, *soo-rof-oy'-nis-sah;* fem. of a comp. of *4948* and the same as *5403;* a *Syro-phœnician* woman, i.e. a female native of Phœnicia in Syria:—Syrophenician.

4950. σύρτις surtis, *soor'-tis;* from *4951;* a *shoal* (from the sand *drawn* thither by the waves), i.e. the *Syrtis* Major or great bay on the N. coast of Africa:—quicksands.

4951. σύρω surō, *soo'-ro;* prob. akin to *138;* to *trail:*—drag, draw, hale.

4952. συσπαράσσω susparassō, *soos-par-as'-so;* from *4862* and *4682;* to *rend completely*, i.e. (by anal.) to *convulse* violently:—throw down.

4953. σύσσημον sussēmŏn, *soos'-say-mon;* neut. of a comp. of *4862* and the base of *4591;* a *sign in common*, i.e. preconcerted *signal:*—token.

4954. σύσσωμος sussōmŏs, *soos'-so-mos;* from *4862* and *4983;* of *a joint body*, i.e. (fig.) a *fellow-member* of the Christian community:—of the same body.

4955. συστασιαστής sustasiastēs, *soos-tas-ee-as-tace';* from a comp. of *4862* and a der. of *4714;* a *fellow-insurgent:*—make insurrection with.

4956. συστατικός sustatikŏs, *soos-tat-ee-kos';* from a der. of *4921;* *introductory*, i.e. *recommendatory:*—of commendation.

4957. συσταυρόω sustaurŏō, *soos-tow-rŏ'-o;* from *4862* and *4717;* to *impale* in company *with* (lit. or fig.):—crucify with.

4958. συστέλλω sustĕllō, *soos-tel'-lo;* from *4862* and *4724;* to *send* (*draw*) *together*, i.e. *enwrap* (*enshroud* a corpse for burial), *contract* (an interval):—short, wind up.

4959. συστενάζω sustĕnazō, *soos-ten-ad'-zo;* from *4862* and *4727;* to *moan jointly*, i.e. (fig.) *experience a common calamity:*—groan together.

4960. συστοιχέω sustŏichĕō, *soos-toy-kheh'-o;* from *4862* and *4748;* to *file together* (as soldiers in ranks), i.e. (fig.) to *correspond* to:—answer to.

4961. συστρατιώτης sustratiōtēs, *soos-trat-ee-o'-tace;* from *4862* and *4757;* a *co-campaigner*, i.e. (fig.) an *associate* in Christian toil:—fellowsoldier.

4962. συστρέφω sustrĕphō, *soos-tref'-o;* from *4862* and *4762;* to *twist together*, i.e. *collect* (a bundle, a crowd):—gather.

4963. συστροφή sustrŏphē, *soos-trof-ay';* from *4962;* a *twisting together*, i.e. (fig.) a secret *coalition*, riotous *crowd:*—+ band together, concourse.

4964. συσχηματίζω suschēmatizō, *soos-khay-mat-id'-zo;* from *4862* and a der. of *4976;* to *fashion alike*, i.e. *conform* to the same pattern (fig.):—conform to, fashion self according to.

4965. Συχάρ Suchar, *soo-khar';* of Heb. or. [7941]; *Sychar* (i.e. *Shekar*), a place in Pal.:—Sychar.

4966. Συχέμ Suchĕm, *soo-khem';* of Heb. or. [7927]; *Sychem* (i.e. *Shekem*), the name of a Canaanite and of a place in Pal.:—Sychem.

4967. σφαγή sphagē, *sfag-ay';* from *4969;* *butchery* (of animals for food or sacrifice, or [fig.] of men [*destruction*]):—slaughter.

4968. σφάγιον sphagiŏn, *sfag'-ee-on;* neut. of a der. of *4967;* a *victim* (in sacrifice):—slain beast.

4969. σφάζω sphazō, *sfad'-zo;* a prim. verb; to *butcher* (espec. an animal for food or in sacrifice) or (gen.) to *slaughter*, or (spec.) to *maim* (violently):—kill, slay, wound.

4970. σφόδρα sphŏdra, *sfod'-rah;* neut. plur. of **σφοδρός sphŏdrŏs** (*violent;* of uncert. der.) as adv.; *vehemently*, i.e. in *a high degree, much:*—exceeding (-ly), greatly, sore, very.

4971. σφοδρῶς sphŏdrōs, *sfod-roce';* adv. from the same as *4970;* *very much:*—exceedingly.

4972. σφραγίζω sphragizō, *sfrag-id'-zo;* from *4973;* to *stamp* (with a signet or private mark) for security or preservation (lit. or fig.); by impl. to *keep secret*, to *attest:*—(set a, set to) seal up.

4973. σφραγίς sphragis, *sfrag-ece';* prob. strengthened from *5420;* a *signet* (as *fencing* in or protecting from misappropriation); by impl. the *stamp* impressed (as a mark of privacy, or genuineness), lit. or fig.:—seal.

4974. σφυρόν sphurŏn, *sfoo-ron';* neut. of a presumed der. prob. of the same as **σφαῖρα sphaira** (a *ball*, "*sphere*"; comp. the fem. **σφῦρα sphura**, a *hammer*); the *ankle* (as *globular*):—ancle bone.

4975. σχεδόν schĕdŏn, *skhed-on';* neut. of a presumed der. of the alt. of *2192* as adv.; *nigh*, i.e. *nearly:*—almost.

σχέω schĕō. See *2192.*

4976. σχῆμα schēma, *skhay'-mah;* from the alt. of *2192;* a *figure* (as a *mode* or *circumstance*), i.e. (by impl.) external *condition:*—fashion.

4977. σχίζω schizō, *skhid'-zo;* appar. a prim. verb; to *split* or *sever* (lit. or fig.):—break, divide, open, rend, make a rent.

4978. σχίσμα schisma, *skhis'-mah;* from *4977;* a *split* or *gap* ("*schism*"), lit. or fig.:—division, rent, schism.

4979. σχοινίον schŏiniŏn, *skhoy-nee'-on;* dimin. of **σχοῖνος schŏinŏs** (a *rush* or *flag*-plant; of uncert. der.); a *rushlet*, i.e. *grass-withe* or *tie* (gen.):—small cord, rope.

4980. σχολάζω schŏlazō, *skhol-ad'-zo;* from *4981;* to *take a holiday*, i.e. *be at leisure* for (by impl. *devote oneself* wholly to); fig. to *be vacant* (of a house):—empty, give self.

4981. σχολή schŏlē, *skhol-ay';* prob. fem. of a presumed der. of the alt. of *2192;* prop. *loitering* (as a *withholding* of oneself from work) or *leisure*, i.e. (by impl.) a "*school*" (as *vacation* from phys. employment):—school.

4982. σώζω sōzō, *sode'-zo;* from a prim. **σῶς sōs** (contr. for obsol. **σάος saŏs**, "*safe*"); to *save*, i.e. *deliver* or *protect* (lit. or fig.):—heal, preserve, save (self), do well, be (make) whole.

4983. σῶμα sōma, *so'-mah;* from *4982;* the *body* (as a *sound* whole), used in a very wide application, lit. or fig.:—bodily, body, slave.

4984. σωματικός sōmatikŏs, *so-mat-ee-kos';* from *4983;* *corporeal* or *physical:*—bodily.

4985. σωματικῶς sōmatikōs, *so-mat-ee-koce';* adv. from *4984;* *corporeally* or *physically:*—bodily.

4986. Σώπατρος Sōpatrŏs, *so'-pat-ros;* from the base of *4982* and *3962;* *of a safe father; Sopatrus*, a Chr.:—Sopater. Comp. *4989.*

4987. σωρεύω sōrĕuō, *sore-yoo'-o;* from another form of *4673;* to *pile* up (lit. or fig.):—heap, load.

4988. Σωσθένης Sōsthĕnēs, *soce-then'-ace;* from the base of *4982* and that of *4599;* *of safe strength; Sosthenes*, a Chr.:—Sosthenes.

4989. Σωσίπατρος Sōsipatrŏs, *so-sip'-at-ros;* prol. for *4986;* *Sosipatrus*, a Chr.:—Sosipater.

4990. σωτήρ sōtēr, *so-tare';* from *4982;* a *deliverer*, i.e. God or Christ:—saviour.

4991. σωτηρία sōtēria, *so-tay-ree'-ah;* fem. of a der. of *4990* as (prop. abstr.) noun; *rescue* or *safety* (phys. or mor.):—deliver, health, salvation, save, saving.

4992. σωτήριον sōtēriŏn, *so-tay'-ree-on;* neut. of the same as *4991* as (prop. concr.) noun; *defender* or (by impl.) *defence:*—salvation.

4993. σωφρονέω sōphrŏnĕō, *so-fron-eh'-o;* from *4998;* to *be of sound mind*, i.e. *sane*, (fig.) *moderate:*—be in right mind, be sober (minded), soberly.

4994. σωφρονίζω sōphrŏnizō, *so-fron-id'-zo;* from *4998;* to *make of sound mind*, i.e. (fig.) to *discipline* or *correct:*—teach to be sober.

4995. σωφρονισμός sōphrŏnismŏs, *so-fron-is-mos';* from *4994;* *discipline*, i.e. *self-control:*—sound mind.

4996. σωφρόνως sōphrŏnōs, *so-fron'-oce;* adv. from *4998;* *with sound mind*, i.e. *moderately:*—soberly.

4997. σωφροσύνη sōphrŏsunē, *so-fros-oo'-nay;* from *4998;* *soundness of mind*, i.e. (lit.) *sanity* or (fig.) *self-control:*—soberness, sobriety.

4998. σώφρων sōphrōn, *so'-frone;* from the base of *4982* and that of *5424;* *safe* (*sound*) in *mind*, i.e. *self-controlled* (*moderate* as to opinion or passion):—discreet, sober, temperate.

T

τά ta. See *3588.*

4999. Ταβέρναι Tabĕrnai, *tab-er'-nahee;* plur. of Lat. or.; *huts* or *wooden-walled* buildings; *Tabernæ:*—taverns.

5000. Ταβιθά Tabitha, *tab-ee-thah';* of Chald. or. [comp. 6646]; *the gazelle; Tabitha* (i.e. *Tabjetha*), a Chr. female:—Tabitha.

5001. τάγμα tagma, *tag'-mah;* from *5021;* something orderly in *arrangement* (a *troop*), i.e. (fig.) a *series* or *succession:*—order.

5002. τακτός taktŏs, *tak-tos';* from *5021;* *arranged*, i.e. *appointed* or *stated:*—set.

5003. ταλαιπωρέω talaipōrĕō, *tal-ahee-po-reh'-o*, from *5005;* to *be wretched*, i.e. *realize* one's own *misery:*—be afflicted.

5004. ταλαιπωρία talaipōria, *tal-ahee-po-ree'-ah;* from *5005;* *wretchedness*, i.e. *calamity:*—misery.

5005. ταλαίπωρος talaipōrŏs, *tal-ah'ee-po-ros;* from the base of *5007* and a der. of the base of *3984;* *enduring trial*, i.e. *miserable:*—wretched.

5006. ταλαντιαῖος talantiaiŏs, *tal-an-tee-ah'-yos;* from *5007;* *talent-like* in weight:—weight of a talent.

5007. τάλαντον talantŏn, *tal'-an-ton;* neut. of a presumed der. of the orig. form of **τλάω tlaō** (to *bear;* equiv. to *5342*); a *balance* (as *supporting* weights), i.e. (by impl.) a certain *weight* (and thence a *coin* or rather *sum* of money) or "*talent*":—talent.

5008. ταλιθά talitha, *tal-ee-thah';* of Chald. or. [comp. 2924]; *the fresh*, i.e. young *girl; talitha* (*O maiden*):—talitha.

5009. ταμεῖον tamĕiŏn, *tam-i'-on;* neut. contr. of a presumed der. of **ταμίας tamias** (a *dispenser* or *distributor;* akin to **τέμνω tĕmnō**, to *cut*); a *dispensary* or *magazine*, i.e. a chamber on the ground-floor or interior of an Oriental house (gen. used for *storage* or *privacy*, a spot for retirement):—secret chamber, closet, storehouse.

τανῦν tanun. See *3568.*

5010. τάξις taxis, *tax'-is;* from *5021;* regular *arrangement*, i.e. (in time) fixed *succession* (of rank or character), official *dignity:*—order.

5011. ταπεινός tapĕinŏs, *tap-i-nos';* of uncert. der.; *depressed*, i.e. (fig.) *humiliated* (in circumstances or disposition):—base, cast down, humble, of low degree (estate), lowly.

5012. ταπεινοφροσύνη tapĕinŏphrŏsunē, *tap-i-nof-ros-oo'-nay;* from a comp. of *5011* and the base of *5424;* *humiliation of mind*, i.e. *modesty:*—humbleness of mind, humility (of mind), lowliness (of mind).

5013. ταπεινόω tapĕinŏō, *tap-i-nŏ'-o;* from *5011;* to *depress;* fig. to *humiliate* (in condition or heart):—abase, bring low, humble (self).

5014. ταπείνωσις tapĕinōsis, *tap-i'-no-sis;* from *5013;* *depression* (in rank or feeling):—humiliation, be made low, low estate, vile.

5015. ταράσσω tarassō, *tar-as'-so;* of uncert. affin.; to *stir* or *agitate* (*roil* water):—trouble.

5016. **ταραχή tarachē**, *tar-akh-ay'*; fem. from 5015; *disturbance*, i.e. (of water) *roiling*, or (of a mob) *sedition*:—trouble (-ing).

5017. **τάραχος tarachŏs**, *tar'-akh-os*; masc. from 5015; a *disturbance*, i.e. (popular) *tumult*:—stir.

5018. **Ταρσεύς Tarsĕus**, *tar-syoos'*; from 5019; a *Tarsean*, i.e. native of Tarsus:—of Tarsus.

5019. **Ταρσός Tarsŏs**, *tar-sos'*; perh. the same as **ταρσός tarsŏs** (a *flat* basket); *Tarsus*, a place in Asia Minor:—Tarsus.

5020. **ταρταρόω tartarŏō**, *tar-tar-ŏ'-o*; from **Τάρταρος Tartarŏs** (the deepest *abyss* of Hades); to *incarcerate* in eternal torment:—cast down to hell.

5021. **τάσσω tassō**, *tas'-so*; a prol. form of a prim. verb (which latter appears only in certain tenses); to *arrange* in an orderly manner, i.e. *assign* or *dispose* (to a certain position or lot):—addict, appoint, determine, ordain, set.

5022. **ταῦρος taurŏs**, *tŏw'-ros*; appar. a prim. word [comp. 8450, "*steer*"]; a *bullock*:—bull, ox.

5023. **ταῦτα tauta**, *tŏw'-tah*; nom. or acc. neut. plur. of 3778; *these* things:— + afterward, follow, + hereafter, × him, the same, so, such, that, then, these, they, this, those, thus.

5024. **ταὐτά tauta**, *tow-tah'*; neut. plur. of 3588 and 846 as adv.; in *the same* way:—even thus, (manner) like, so.

5025. **ταύταις tautais**, *tŏw'-taheece*; and

ταύτας tautas, *tŏw'-tas*; dat. and acc. fem. plur. respectively of 3778; (*to* or *with* or *by*, etc.) *these*:—hence, that, then, these, those.

5026. **ταύτῃ tautē̦**, *tŏw'-tay*; and

ταύτην tautēn, *tŏw'-tane*; and

ταύτης tautēs, *tŏw'-tace*; dat., acc. and gen. respectively of the fem. sing. of 3778; (*towards* or *of*) *this*:—her, + hereof, it, that, + thereby, the (same), this (same).

5027. **ταφή taphē**, *taf-ay'*; fem. from 2290; *burial* (the act):— × bury.

5028. **τάφος taphŏs**, *taf'-os*; masc. from 2290; a *grave* (the place of interment):—sepulchre, tomb.

5029. **τάχα tacha**, *takh'-ah*; as if neut. plur. of 5036 (adv.); *shortly*, i.e. (fig.) *possibly*:—peradventure (-haps).

5030. **ταχέως tachĕōs**, *takh-eh'-oce*; adv. from 5036; *briefly*, i.e. (in time) *speedily*, or (in manner) *rapidly*:—hastily, quickly, shortly, soon, suddenly.

5031. **ταχινός tachinŏs**, *takh-ee-nos'*; from 5034; *curt*, i.e. *impending*:—shortly, swift.

5032. **τάχιον tachiŏn**, *takh'-ee-on*; neut. sing. of the compar. of 5036 (as adv.); *more swiftly*, i.e. (in manner) *more rapidly*, or (in time) *more speedily*:—out [run], quickly, shortly, sooner.

5033. **τάχιστα tachista**, *takh'-is-tah*; neut. plur. of the superl. of 5036 (as adv.); *most quickly*, i.e. (with 5613 pref.) *as soon* as possible:— + with all speed.

5034. **τάχος tachŏs**, *takh'-os*; from the same as 5036; a *brief* space (of time), i.e. (with 1722 pref.) in *haste*:— + quickly, + shortly, + speedily.

5035. **ταχύ tachu**, *takh-oo'*; neut. sing. of 5036 (as adv.); *shortly*, i.e. *without delay*, *soon*, or (by surprise) *suddenly*, or (by impl. of ease) *readily*:—lightly, quickly.

5036. **ταχύς tachus**, *takh-oos'*; of uncert. affin.; *fleet*, i.e. (fig.) *prompt* or *ready*:—swift.

5037. **τέ tĕ**, *teh*; a prim. particle (enclitic) of connection or addition; *both* or *also* (prop. as correl. of 2532):—also, and, both, even, then, whether. Often used in comp., usually as the latter part.

5038. **τεῖχος tĕichŏs**, *ti'-khos*; akin to the base of 5088; a *wall* (as *formative* of a house):—wall.

5039. **τεκμήριον tĕkmēriŏn**, *tek-may'-ree-on*; neut. of a presumed der. of **τεκμάρ tĕkmar** (a *goal* or fixed *limit*); a *token* (as *defining* a fact), i.e. *criterion* of certainty:—infallible proof.

5040. **τεκνίον tĕkniŏn**, *tek-nee'-on*; dimin. of 5043; an *infant*, i.e. (plur. fig.) *darlings* (Christian *converts*):—little children.

5041. **τεκνογονέω tĕknŏgŏnĕō**, *tek-nog-on-eh'-o*; from a comp. of 5043 and the base of 1096; *to be a child-bearer*, i.e. *parent* (*mother*):—bear children.

5042. **τεκνογονία tĕknŏgŏnia**, *tek-nog-on-ee'-ah*; from the same as 5041; *childbirth* (*parentage*), i.e. (by impl.) *maternity* (the performance of *maternal duties*):—childbearing.

5043. **τέκνον tĕknŏn**, *tek'-non*; from the base of 5088; a *child* (as *produced*):—child, daughter, son.

5044. **τεκνοτροφέω tĕknŏtrŏphĕō**, *tek-not-rof-eh'-o*; from a comp. of 5043 and 5142; *to be a child-rearer*, i.e. *fulfil* the duties of *a female parent*:—bring up children.

5045. **τέκτων tĕktōn**, *tek'-tone*; from the base of 5088; an *artificer* (as *producer* of fabrics), i.e. (spec.) a *craftsman* in wood:—carpenter.

5046. **τέλειος tĕlĕiŏs**, *tel'-i-os*; from 5056; *complete* (in various applications of labor, growth, mental and moral character, etc.); neut. (as noun, with 3588) *completeness*:—of full age, man, perfect.

5047. **τελειότης tĕlĕiŏtēs**, *tel-i-ot'-ace*; from 5046; (the state) *completeness* (ment. or mor.):—perfection (-ness).

5048. **τελειόω tĕlĕiŏō**, *tel-i-ŏ'-o*; from 5046; to *complete*, i.e. (lit.) *accomplish*, or (fig.) *consummate* (in character):—consecrate, finish, fulfil, (make) perfect.

5049. **τελείως tĕlĕiōs**, *tel-i'-oce*; adv. from 5046; *completely*, i.e. (of hope) *without wavering*:—to the end.

5050. **τελείωσις tĕlĕiōsis**, *tel-i'-o-sis*; from 5448; (the act) *completion*, i.e. (of prophecy) *verification*, or (of expiation) *absolution*:—perfection, performance.

5051. **τελειωτής tĕlĕiōtēs**, *tel-i-o-tace'*; from 5048; a *completer*, i.e. *consummater*:—finisher.

5052. **τελεσφορέω tĕlĕsphŏrĕō**, *tel-es-for-eh'-o*; from a comp. of 5056 and 5342; *to be a bearer to completion* (maturity), i.e. to *ripen* fruit (fig.):—bring fruit to perfection.

5053. **τελευτάω tĕlĕutaō**, *tel-yoo-tah'-o*; from a presumed der. of 5055; to *finish* life (by impl. of 979), i.e. *expire* (*demise*):—be dead, decease, die.

5054. **τελευτή tĕlĕutē**, *tel-yoo-tay'*; from 5053; *decease*:—death.

5055. **τελέω tĕlĕō**, *tel-eh'-o*; from 5056; to *end*, i.e. *complete*, *execute*, *conclude*, *discharge* (a debt):—accomplish, make an end, expire, fill up, finish, go over, pay, perform.

5056. **τέλος tĕlŏs**, *tel'-os*; from a prim. **τέλλω tĕllō** (to *set out* for a definite point or *goal*); prop. the point aimed at as a *limit*, i.e. (by impl.) the *conclusion* of an act or state (*termination* [lit., fig. or indef.], *result* [immed., ultimate or prophetic], *purpose*); spec. an *impost* or *levy* (as *paid*):— + continual, custom, end (-ing), finally, uttermost. Comp. 5411.

5057. **τελώνης tĕlōnēs**, *tel-o'-nace*; from 5056 and 5608; a *tax-farmer*, i.e. *collector of* public *revenue*:—publican.

5058. **τελώνιον tĕlōniŏn**, *tel-o'-nee-on*; neut. of a presumed der. of 5057; a *tax-gatherer's* place of business:—receipt of custom.

5059. **τέρας tĕras**, *ter'-as*; of uncert. affin.; a *prodigy* or *omen*:—wonder.

5060. **Τέρτιος Tĕrtiŏs**, *ter'-tee-os*; of Lat. or.; *third*; *Tertius*, a Chr.:—Tertius.

5061. **Τέρτυλλος Tĕrtullŏs**, *ter'-tool-los*; of uncert. der.; *Tertullus*, a Rom.:—Tertullus.

τέσσαρα tĕssara. See 5064.

5062. **τεσσαράκοντα tĕssarakŏnta**, *tes-sar-ak'-on-tah*; the decade of 5064; *forty*:—forty.

5063. **τεσσαρακονταετής tĕssarakŏntaĕtēs**, *tes-sar-ak-on-tah-et-ace'*; from 5062 and 2094; *of forty years* of age:—(+ full, of) forty years (old).

5064. **τέσσαρες tĕssarĕs**, *tes'-sar-es*; neut.

τέσσαρα tĕssara, *tes'-sar-ah*; a plur. number; *four*:—four.

5065. **τεσσαρεσκαιδέκατος tĕssarĕskaidĕkatŏs**, *tes-sar-es-kahee-dek'-at-os*; from 5064 and 2532 and 1182; *fourteenth*:—fourteenth.

5066. **τεταρταῖος tĕtartaiŏs**, *tet-ar-tah'-yos*; from 5064; pertaining to the *fourth* day:—four days.

5067. **τέταρτος tĕtartŏs**, *tet'-ar-tos*; ord. from 5064; *fourth*:—four (-th).

5068. **τετράγωνος tĕtragōnŏs**, *tet-rag'-o-nos*; from 5064 and 1137; *four-cornered*, i.e. *square*:—foursquare.

5069. **τετράδιον tĕtradiŏn**, *tet-rad'-ee-on*; neut. of a presumed der. of **τέτρας tĕtras** (a *tetrad*; from 5064); a *quaternion* or squad (picket) of four Rom. soldiers:—quaternion.

5070. **τετρακισχίλιοι tĕtrakischiliŏi**, *tet-rak-is-khil'-ee-oy*; from the mult. adv. of 5064 and 5507; *four times a thousand*:—four thousand.

5071. **τετρακόσιοι tĕtrakŏsiŏi**, *tet-rak-os'-ee-oy*; neut. **τετρακόσια tĕtrakŏsia**, *tet-rak-os'-ee-ah*; plur. from 5064 and 1540; *four hundred*:—four hundred.

5072. **τετράμηνον tĕtramēnŏn**, *tet-ram'-ay-non*; neut. of a comp. of 5064 and 3376; a *four months'* space:—four months.

5073. **τετραπλόος tĕtraplŏŏs**, *tet-rap-lŏ'-os*; from 5064 and a der. of the base of 4118; *quadruple*:—fourfold.

5074. **τετράπους tĕtrapŏus**, *tet-rap'-ooce*; from 5064 and 4228; a *quadruped*:—fourfooted beast.

5075. **τετραρχέω tĕtrarchĕō**, *tet-rar-khch'-o*; from 5076; *to be a tetrarch*:—(be) tetrarch.

5076. **τετράρχης tĕtrarchēs**, *tet-rar'-khace*; from 5064 and 757; the *ruler of a fourth* part of a country ("*tetrarch*"):—tetrarch.

τεύχω tĕuchō. See 5177.

5077. **τεφρόω tĕphrŏō**, *tef-rŏ'-o*; from **τέφρα tephra** (*ashes*); to *incinerate*, i.e. *consume*:—turn to ashes.

5078. **τέχνη tĕchnē**, *tekh'-nay*; from the base of 5088; *art* (as *productive*), i.e. (spec.) a *trade*, or (gen.) *skill*:—art, craft, occupation.

5079. **τεχνίτης tĕchnitēs**, *tekh-nee'-tace*; from 5078; an *artisan*; fig. a *founder* (*Creator*):—builder, craftsman.

5080. **τήκω tēkō**, *tay'-ko*; appar. a prim. verb; to *liquefy*:—melt.

5081. **τηλαυγῶς tēlaugōs**, *tay-lŏw-goce'*; adv. from a comp. of a der. of 5056 and 827; in a *far-shining* manner, i.e. *plainly*:—clearly.

5082. **τηλικοῦτος tēlikŏutŏs**, *tay-lik-oo'-tos*; fem. **τηλικαύτη tēlikautē**, *tay-lik-ŏw'-tay*; from a comp. of 3588 with 2245 and 3778; *such as this*, i.e. (in [fig.] magnitude) *so vast*:—so great, so mighty.

5083. **τηρέω tērĕō**, *tay-reh'-o*; from **τηρός tērŏs** (a *watch*; perh. akin to 2334); to *guard* (from *loss* or *injury*, prop. by keeping *the eye* upon; and thus differing from 5442, which is prop. to *prevent* escaping; and from 2892, which implies a *fortress* or full military lines of apparatus), i.e. to *note* (a prophecy; fig. to *fulfil* a command); by impl. to *detain* (in custody; fig. to *maintain*); by extens. to *withhold* (for personal ends; fig. to *keep unmarried*):—hold fast, keep (-er), (ob-, pre-, re) serve, watch.

5084. **τήρησις tērēsis**, *tay'-ray-sis*; from 5083; a *watching*, i.e. (fig.) *observance*, or (concr.) a *prison*:—hold.

τῇ tē̦, **τήν tēn**, **τῆς tēs**. See 3588.

5085. **Τιβεριάς Tibĕrias**, *tib-er-ee-as'*; from 5086; *Tiberias*, the name of a town and a lake in Pal.:—Tiberias.

5086. **Τιβέριος Tibĕriŏs**, *tib-er'-ee-os*; of Lat. or.; prob. *pertaining to the* river *Tiberis* or *Tiber*; *Tiberius*, a Rom. emperor:—Tiberius.

5087. **τίθημι tithēmi**, *tith'-ay-mee*; a prol. form of a prim.

θέω thĕō, *theh'-o* (which is used only as alt. in certain tenses); to *place* (in the widest application, lit. and fig.; prop. in a passive or horizontal posture, and thus different from 2476, which prop. denotes an upright and active position, while 2749 is prop. reflexive and utterly prostrate):— + advise, appoint, bow, commit, conceive, give, × kneel down, lay (aside, down, up), make, ordain, purpose, put, set (forth), settle, sink down.

5088. **τίκτω tiktō**, *tik'-to;* a strengthened form of a prim. **τέκω tĕkō**, *tek'-o* (which is used only as alt. in certain tenses); to *produce* (from seed, as a mother, a plant, the earth, etc.), lit. or fig.:—bear, be born, bring forth, be delivered, be in travail.

5089. **τίλλω tillō**, *til'-lo;* perh. akin to the alt. of *138*, and thus to *4951;* to *pull* off:—pluck.

5090. **Τίμαιος Timaiŏs**, *tim'-ah-yos;* prob. of Chald. or. [comp. 2931]; *Timæus* (i.e. *Timay*), an Isr.:—Timæus.

5091. **τιμάω timaō**, *tim-ah'-o;* from *5093;* to *prize*, i.e. *fix a valuation* upon; by impl. to *revere:*—honour, value.

5092. **τιμή timē**, *tee-may';* from *5099;* a *value*, i.e. *money* paid, or (concr. and collect.) *valuables;* by anal. *esteem* (espec. of the highest degree), or the *dignity* itself:—honour, precious, price, some.

5093. **τίμιος timiŏs**, *tim'-ee-os;* includ. the comp.

τιμιώτερος timiōtĕrŏs, *tim-ee-o'-ter-os;* and the superl.

τιμιώτατος timiōtatŏs, *tim-ee-o'-tat-os;* from *5092;* *valuable*, i.e. (obj.) *costly*, or (subj.) *honored*, *esteemed*, or (fig.) *beloved:*—dear, honourable, (more, most) precious, had in reputation.

5094. **τιμιότης timiŏtēs**, *tim-ee-ot'-ace;* from *5093;* *expensiveness*, i.e. (by impl.) *magnificence:*—costliness.

5095. **Τιμόθεος Timŏthĕŏs**, *tee-moth'-eh-os;* from *5092* and *2316;* *dear to God; Timotheus*, a Chr.:—Timotheus, Timothy.

5096. **Τίμων Timōn**, *tee'-mone;* from *5092;* *valuable; Timon*, a Chr.:—Timon.

5097. **τιμωρέω timōrĕō**, *tim-o-reh'-o;* from a comp. of *5092* and **οὖρος ŏurŏs** (a *guard*); prop. to *protect* one's *honor*, i.e. to *avenge* (*inflict a penalty*):—punish.

5098. **τιμωρία timōria**, *tee-mo-ree'-ah;* from *5097;* *vindication*, i.e. (by impl.) a *penalty:*—punishment.

5099. **τίνω tinō**, *tee'-no;* strengthened for a prim.

τίω tiō, *tee'-o* (which is only used as an alt. in certain tenses); to *pay* a price, i.e. as a *penalty:*—be punished with.

5100. **τὶς tis**, *tis;* an enclit. indef. pron.; *some* or *any* person or object:—a (kind of), any (man, thing, thing at all), certain (thing), divers, he (every) man, one (× thing), ought, + partly, some (man, -body, -thing, -what), (+ that no-) thing, what (-soever), × wherewith, whom [-soever], whose ([-soever]).

5101. **τίς tis**, *tis;* prob. emphat. of *5100;* an interrog. pron., *who*, *which* or *what* (in direct or indirect questions):—every man, how (much), + no (-ne, thing), what (manner, thing), where ([-by, -fore, -of, -unto, -with, -withal]), whether, which, who (-m, -se), why.

5102. **τίτλος titlŏs**, *tit'-los;* of Lat. or.; a *titulus* or "*title*" (*placard*):—title.

5103. **Τίτος Titŏs**, *tee'-tos*, of Lat. or. but uncert. signif.; *Titus*, a Chr.:—Titus.

τίω tiō. See *5099*.

τό tŏ. See *3588*.

5104. **τοί tŏi**, *toy;* prob. for the dat. of *3588;* an enclit. particle of *asseveration* by way of contrast; *in sooth:*—[*used only with other particles in comp., as 2544, 3305, 5105, 5106*, etc.]

5105. **τοιγαροῦν tŏigarŏun**, *toy-gar-oon';* from *5104* and *1063* and *3767;* *truly for then*, i.e. *consequently:*—there- (where-) fore.

τοίγε tŏigĕ. See *2544*.

5106. **τοίνυν tŏinun**, *toy'-noon;* from *5104* and *3568;* *truly now*, i.e. *accordingly:*—then, therefore.

5107. **τοιόσδε tŏiŏsdĕ**, *toy-os'-deh* (includ. the other inflections); from a der. of *5104* and *1161;* *such-like then*, i.e. *so great:*—such.

5108. **τοιοῦτος tŏiŏutŏs**, *toy-oo'-tos* (includ. the other inflections); from *5104* and *3778;* *truly this*, i.e. *of this sort* (to denote character or individuality):—like, such (an one).

5109. **τοῖχος tŏichŏs**, *toy'-khos;* another form of *5038;* a *wall:*—wall.

5110. **τόκος tŏkŏs**, *tok'-os;* from the base of *5088;* *interest* on money loaned (as a *produce*):—usury.

5111. **τολμάω tŏlmaō**, *tol-mah'-o;* from **τόλμα tŏlma** (*boldness;* prob. itself from the base of *5056* through the idea of *extreme* conduct); to *venture* (obj. or in *act;* while *2292* is rather subj. or in *feeling*); by impl. to be *courageous:*—be bold, boldly, dare, durst.

5112. **τολμηρότερον tŏlmērŏtĕrŏn**, *tol-may-rot'-er-on;* neut. of the comp. of a der. of the base of *5111* (as adv.); *more daringly*, i.e. *with greater confidence* than otherwise:—the more boldly.

5113. **τολμητής tŏlmētēs**, *tol-may-tace';* from *5111;* a *daring* (*audacious*) man:—presumptuous.

5114. **τομώτερος tŏmōtĕrŏs**, *tom-o'-ter-os;* comp. of a der. of the prim. **τέμνω tĕmnō** (to *cut;* more comprehensive or decisive than *2875*, as if by a *single* stroke; whereas that implies repeated blows, like *hacking*); *more keen:*—sharper.

5115. **τόξον tŏxŏn**, *tox'-on;* from the base of *5088;* a *bow* (appar. as the simplest fabric):—bow.

5116. **τοπάζιον tŏpaziŏn**, *top-ad'-zee-on;* neut. of a presumed der. (alt.) of **τόπαζος tŏpazŏs** (a "*topaz*"; of uncert. or.); a gem, prob. the *chrysolite:*—topaz.

5117. **τόπος tŏpŏs**, *top'-os;* appar. a prim. word; a *spot* (gen. in *space*, but limited by occupancy; whereas *5561* is a larger but partic. *locality*), i.e. *location* (as a position, home, tract, etc.); fig. *condition*, *opportunity;* spec. a *scabbard:*—coast, licence, place, × plain, quarter, + rock, room, where.

5118. **τοσοῦτος tŏsŏutŏs**, *tos-oo'-tos;* from **τόσος tŏsŏs** (*so much;* appar. from *3588* and *3739*) and *3778* (includ. its variations); *so vast as this*, i.e. *such* (in quantity, amount, number or space):—as large, so great (long, many, much), these many.

5119. **τότε tŏtĕ**, *tot'-eh;* from (the neut. of) *3588* and *3753;* *the when*, i.e. *at the time* that (of the past or future, also in consecution):—that time, then.

5120. **τοῦ tŏu**, *too;* prop. the gen. of *3588;* sometimes used for *5127;* *of this person:*—his.

5121. **τοὐναντίον tŏunantiŏn**, *too-nan-tee'-on;* contr. for the neut. of *3588* and *1726;* *on the contrary:*—contrariwise.

5122. **τοὔνομα tŏunŏma**, *too'-no-mah;* contr. for the neut. of *3588* and *3686;* *the name* (is):—named.

5123. **τουτέστι tŏutĕsti**, *toot-es'-tee;* contr. for *5124* and *2076;* *that is:*—that is (to say).

5124. **τοῦτο tŏutŏ**, *too'-to;* neut. sing. nom. or acc. of *3778;* *that* thing:—here [-unto], it, partly, self [-same], so, that (intent), the same, there [-fore, -unto], this, thus, where [-fore].

5125. **τούτοις tŏutŏis**, *too'-toice;* dat. plur. masc. or neut. of *3778;* *to* (*for*, *in*, *with* or *by*) *these* (persons or things):—such, them, there [-in, -with], these, this, those.

5126. **τοῦτον tŏutŏn**, *too'-ton;* acc. sing. masc. of *3778;* *this* (person, as obj. of verb or prep.):—him, the same, that, this.

5127. **τούτου tŏutŏu**, *too'-too;* gen. sing. masc. or neut. of *3778;* *of* (*from* or *concerning*) *this* (person or thing):—here [-by], him, it, + such manner of, that, thence [-forth], thereabout, this, thus.

5128. **τούτους tŏutŏus**, *too'-tooce;* acc. plur. masc. of *3778;* *these* (persons, as obj. of verb or prep.):—such, them, these, this.

5129. **τούτῳ tŏutōi**, *too'-to;* dat. sing. masc. or neut. of *3778;* *to* (*in*, *with* or *by*) *this* (person or thing):—here [-by, -in], him, one, the same, there [-in], this.

5130. **τούτων tŏutōn**, *too'-tone;* gen. plur. masc. or neut. of *3778;* *of* (*from* or *concerning*) *these* (persons or things):—such, their, these (things), they, this sort, those.

5131. **τράγος tragŏs**, *trag'-os;* from the base of *5176;* a *he-goat* (as a *gnawer*):—goat.

5132. **τράπεζα trapĕza**, *trap'-ed-zah;* prob. contr. from *5064* and *3979;* a *table* or *stool* (as being *four legged*), usually for food (fig. a *meal*); also a *counter* for money (fig. a broker's *office* for loans at interest):—bank, meat, table.

5133. **τραπεζίτης trapĕzitēs**, *trap-ed-zee'-tace;* from *5132;* a money-*broker* or *banker:*—exchanger.

5134. **τραῦμα trauma**, *trŏw'-mah;* from the base of **τιτρώσκω titrōskō** (to *wound;* akin to the base of *2352, 5147, 5149*, etc.); a *wound:*—wound.

5135. **τραυματίζω traumatizō**, *trŏw-mat-id'-zo;* from *5134;* to *inflict a wound:*—wound.

5136. **τραχηλίζω trachēlizō**, *trakh-ay-lid'-zo;* from *5137;* to *seize* by *the throat* or *neck*, i.e. to *expose* the *gullet* of a victim for killing (gen. to *lay bare*):—opened.

5137. **τράχηλος trachēlŏs**, *trakh'-ay-los;* prob. from *5143* (through the idea of *mobility*); the *throat* (*neck*), i.e. (fig.) *life:*—neck.

5138. **τραχύς trachus**, *trakh-oos';* perh. strengthened from the base of *4486* (as if *jagged* by rents); *uneven*, *rocky* (*reefy*):—rock, rough.

5139. **Τραχωνῖτις Trachōnitis**, *trakh-o-nee'-tis;* from a der. of *5138;* *rough* district; *Trachonitis*, a region of Syria:—Trachonitis.

5140. **τρεῖς trĕis**, *trice;* neut.

τρία tria, *tree'-ah;* a prim. (plur.) number; "*three*":—three.

5141. **τρέμω trĕmō**, *trem'-o;* strengthened from a prim. **τρέω trĕō** (to "*dread*", "*terrify*"); to "*tremble*" or *fear:*—be afraid, trembling.

5142. **τρέφω trĕphō**, *tref'-o;* a prim. verb (prop. **θρέφω thrĕphō**; but perh. strength. from the base of *5157* through the idea of *convolution*); prop. to *stiffen*, i.e. *fatten* (by impl. to *cherish* [with food, etc.], *pamper*, *rear*):—bring up, feed, nourish.

5143. **τρέχω trĕchō**, *trekh'-o;* appar. a prim. verb (prop. **θρέχω thrĕchō**; comp. *2359*); which uses **δρέμω drĕmō**, *drem'-o* (the base of *1408*) as alt. in certain tenses; to *run* or *walk hastily* (lit. or fig.):—have course, run.

5144. **τριάκοντα triakŏnta**, *tree-ak'-on-tah;* the decade of *5140;* *thirty:*—thirty.

5145. **τριακόσιοι triakŏsiŏi**, *tree-ak-os'-ee-oy;* plur. from *5140* and *1540;* *three hundred:*—three hundred.

5146. **τρίβολος tribŏlŏs**, *trib'-ol-os;* from *5140* and *956;* prop. a *crow-foot* (*three-pronged* obstruction in war), i.e. (by anal.) a *thorny plant* (*caltrop*):—brier, thistle.

5147. **τρίβος tribŏs**, *tree'-bos;* from **τρίβω tribō** (to "*rub*"; akin to **τείρω tĕirō**, **τρύω truō**, and the base of *5131, 5134*); a *rut* or worn *track:*—path.

5148. **τριετία triĕtia**, *tree-et-ee'-ah;* from a comp. of *5140* and *2094;* a *three years' period* (*triennium*):—space of three years.

5149. **τρίζω trizō**, *trid'-zo;* appar. a prim. verb; to *creak* (*squeak*), i.e. (by anal.) to *grate* the teeth (in frenzy):—gnash.

5150. **τρίμηνον trimēnŏn**, *trim'-ay-non;* neut. of a comp. of *5140* and *3376* as noun; a *three months'* space:—three months.

5151. **τρίς tris**, *trece;* adv. from *5140;* *three times:*—three times, thrice.

5152. **τρίστεγον tristĕgŏn**, *tris'-teg-on;* neut. of a comp. of *5140* and *4721* as noun; a *third roof* (*story*):—third loft.

5153. **τρισχίλιοι trischiliŏi**, *tris-khil'-ee-oy;* from *5151* and *5507;* *three times a thousand:*—three thousand.

5154. **τρίτος tritŏs**, *tree'-tos;* ord. from *5140;* *third;* neut. (as noun) a *third part*, or (as adv.) a (or the) *third* time, *thirdly:*—third (-ly).

τρίχες trichĕs, etc. See *2359*.

5155. **τρίχινος trichinŏs**, *trikh'-ee-nos;* from *2359;* *hairy*, i.e. made *of hair* (*mohair*):—of hair.

5156. τρόμος **trŏmŏs**, *trom'-os;* from 5141; a "*trembling*", i.e. quaking with *fear:*— + tremble (-ing).

5157. τροπή **tropē**, *trop-ay';* from an appar. prim. τρέπω **trĕpō** (to *turn*); a *turn* ("trope"), i.e. *revolution* (fig. *variation*):—turning.

5158. τρόπος **trŏpŏs**, *trop'-os;* from the same as 5157; a *turn*, i.e. (by impl.) *mode* or *style* (espec. with prep. or rel. pref. as adv. *like*); fig. *deportment* or *character:*—(even) as, conversation, [+ like] manner (+ by any) means, way.

5159. τροποφορέω **trŏpŏphŏrĕō**, *trop-of-or-eh'-o;* from 5158 and 5409; to *endure* one's *habits:*—suffer the manners.

5160. τροφή **trŏphē**, *trof-ay';* from 5142; *nourishment* (lit. or fig.); by impl. *rations* (*wages*):—food, meat.

5161. Τρόφιμος **Trŏphimŏs**, *trof'-ee-mos;* from 5160; *nutritive; Trophimus*, a Chr.:—Trophimus.

5162. τροφός **trŏphŏs**, *trof-os';* from 5142; a *nourisher*, i.e. *nurse:*—nurse.

5163. τροχιά **trŏchia**, *trokh-ee-ah';* from 5164; a *track* (as a wheel-*rut*), i.e. (fig.) a *course* of conduct:—path.

5164. τροχός **trŏchŏs**, *trokh-os';* from 5143; a *wheel* (as a *runner*), i.e. (fig.) a *circuit* of phys. effects:—course.

5165. τρύβλιον **trubliŏn**, *troob'-lee-on;* neut. of a presumed der. of uncert. affin.; a *bowl:*—dish.

5166. τρυγάω **trugaō**, *troo-gah'-o;* from a der. of τρύγω **trugō** (to *dry*) mean. ripe *fruit* (as if *dry*); to *collect* the vintage:—gather.

5167. τρυγών **trugōn**, *troo-gone';* from τρύζω **truzō** (to *murmur;* akin to 5149, but denoting a *duller* sound); a *turtle-dove* (as *cooing*):—turtle-dove.

5168. τρυμαλιά **trumalia**, *troo-mal-ee-ah';* from a der. of τρύω **truō** (to *wear* away; akin to the base of 5134, 5147 and 5176); an *orifice*, i.e. a needle's *eye:*—eye. Comp. 5169.

5169. τρύπημα **trupēma**, *troo'-pay-mah;* from a der. of the base of 5168; an *aperture*, i.e. a needle's *eye:*—eye.

5170. Τρύφαινα **Truphaina**, *troo'-fahee-nah;* from 5172; *luxurious; Tryphæna*, a Chr. woman:—Tryphena.

5171. τρυφάω **truphaō**, *troo-fah'-o;* from 5172; to *indulge in luxury:*—live in pleasure.

5172. τρυφή **truphē**, *troo-fay';* from θρύπτω **thruptō** (to *break* up or [fig.] *enfeeble*, espec. the mind and body by indulgence); *effeminacy*, i.e. *luxury* or *debauchery:*—delicately, riot.

5173. Τρυφῶσα **Truphōsa**, *troo-fo'-sah;* from 5172; *luxuriating; Tryphosa*, a Chr. female:—Tryphosa.

5174. Τρωάς **Trōas**, *tro-as';* from Τρός **Trŏs** (a *Trojan*); the *Troad* (or plain of Troy), i.e. *Troas*, a place in Asia Minor:—Troas.

5175. Τρωγύλλιον **Trōgulliŏn**, *tro-gool'-lee-on;* of uncert. der.; *Trogyllium*, a place in Asia Minor:—Trogyllium.

5176. τρώγω **trōgō**, *tro'-go;* prob. strength. from a collat. form of the base of 5134 and 5147 through the idea of *corrosion* or *wear;* or perh. rather of a base of 5167 and 5149 through the idea of a *craunching* sound; to *gnaw* or *chew*, i.e. (gen.) to *eat:*—eat.

5177. τυγχάνω **tugchanō**, *toong-khan'-o;* prob. for an obsol. τύχω **tuchō** (for which the mid. of another alt. τεύχω **tĕuchō** [to *make ready* or *bring to pass*] is used in cert. tenses; akin to the base of 5088 through the idea of *effecting;* prop. to *affect;* or (spec.) to *hit* or *light upon* (as a mark to be reached), i.e. (trans.) to *attain* or *secure* an object or end, or (intrans.) to *happen* (as if *meeting* with); but in the latter application only impers. (with 1487), i.e. *perchance;* or (pres. part.) as adj. *usual* (as if commonly *met with*, with 3756, *extraordinary*), neut. (as adv.) *perhaps;* or (with another verb) as adv. by *accident* (*as it were*):—be, chance, enjoy, little, obtain, × refresh . . . self, + special. Comp. 5180.

5178. τυμπανίζω **tumpanizō**, *toom-pan-id'-zo;* from a der. of 5180 (mean. a *drum*, "*tympanum*"); to stretch on an instrument of *torture* resembling a drum, and thus *beat* to death:—torture.

5179. τύπος **tupŏs**, *too'-pos;* from 5180; a *die* (as *struck*), i.e. (by impl.) a *stamp* or *scar;* by anal. a *shape*, i.e. a *statue*, (fig.) *style* or *resemblance;* spec. a *sampler* ("*type*"), i.e. a *model* (for imitation) or *instance* (for warning):—en- (ex-) ample, fashion, figure, form, manner, pattern, print.

5180. τύπτω **tuptō**, *toop'-to;* a prim. verb (in a strength. form); to "*thump*", i.e. *cudgel* or *pummel* (prop. with a stick or *bastinado*), but in any case by *repeated* blows; thus differing from 3817 and 3960, which denote a [usually single] blow with the hand or any instrument, or 4141 with the *fist* [or a *hammer*], or 4474 with the *palm;* as well as from 5177, an *accidental* collision); by impl. to *punish;* fig. to *offend* (the conscience):—beat, smite, strike, wound.

5181. Τύραννος **Turannŏs**, *too'-ran-nos;* a provincial form of the der. of the base of 2962; a "*tyrant*"; *Tyrannus*, an Ephesian:—Tyrannus.

5182. τυρβάζω **turbazō**, *toor-bad'-zo;* from τύρβη **turbē** (Lat. *turba*, a *crowd;* akin to 2351); to *make* "*turbid*", i.e. *disturb:*—trouble.

5183. Τύριος **Turiŏs**, *too'-ree-os;* from 5184; a *Tyrian*, i.e. inhab. of Tyrus:—of Tyre.

5184. Τύρος **Turŏs**, *too'-ros;* of Heb. or. [6865]: *Tyrus* (i.e. *Tsor*), a place in Pal.:—Tyre.

5185. τυφλός **tuphlŏs**, *toof-los';* from 5187; *opaque* (as if *smoky*), i.e. (by anal.) *blind* (phys. or ment.):—blind.

5186. τυφλόω **tuphlŏō**, *toof-lŏ'-o;* from 5185; to *make blind*, i.e. (fig.) to *obscure:*—blind.

5187. τυφόω **tuphŏō**, *toof-ŏ'-o;* from a der. of 5188; to envelop with *smoke*, i.e. (fig.) to *inflate* with self-conceit:—high-minded, be lifted up with pride, be proud.

5188. τυφῶ **tuphō**, *too'-fo;* appar. a prim. verb; to make a *smoke*, i.e. slowly *consume* without flame:—smoke.

5189. τυφωνικός **tuphōnikŏs**, *too-fo-nee-kos';* from a der. of 5188; *stormy* (as if *smoky*):—tempestuous.

5190. Τυχικός **Tuchikŏs**, *too-khee-kos';* from a der. of 5177; *fortuitous*, i.e. *fortunate; Tychicus*, a Chr.:—Tychicus.

Υ

5191. ὑακίνθινος **huakinthinŏs**, *hoo-ak-in'-thee-nos;* from 5192; "*hyacinthine*" or "*jacinthine*", i.e. deep *blue:*—jacinth.

5192. ὑάκινθος **huakinthŏs**, *hoo-ak'-in-thos;* of uncert. der.; the "*hyacinth*" or "*jacinth*", i.e. some gem of a deep *blue* color, prob. the *zirkon:*—jacinth.

5193. ὑάλινος **hualinŏs**, *hoo-al'-ee-nos;* from 5194; *glassy*, i.e. *transparent:*—of glass.

5194. ὕαλος **hualŏs**, *hoo'-al-os;* perh. from the same as 5205 (as being transparent like *rain*); *glass:*—glass.

5195. ὑβρίζω **hubrizō**, *hoo-brid'-zo;* from 5196; to *exercise violence*, i.e. *abuse:*—use despitefully, reproach, entreat shamefully (spitefully).

5196. ὕβρις **hubris**, *hoo'-bris;* from 5228; *insolence* (as *over-bearing*), i.e. *insult, injury:*—harm, hurt, reproach.

5197. ὑβριστής **hubristēs**, *hoo-bris-tace';* from 5195; an *insulter*, i.e. *maltreater:*—despiteful, injurious.

5198. ὑγιαίνω **hugiainō**, *hoog-ee-ah'ee-no;* from 5199; to *have* sound *health*, i.e. *be well* (in body); fig. to be *uncorrupt* (*true* in doctrine):—be in health, (be safe and) sound, (be) whole (-some).

5199. ὑγιής **hugiēs**, *hoog-ee-ace';* from the base of 837; *healthy*, i.e. *well* (in body); fig. *true* (in doctrine):—sound, whole.

5200. ὑγρός **hugrŏs**, *hoo-gros';* from the base of 5205; *wet* (as if with *rain*), i.e. (by impl.) *sappy* (*fresh*):—green.

5201. ὑδριά **hudria**, *hoo-dree-ah';* from 5204; a *water-jar*, i.e. *receptacle* for family supply:—waterpot.

5202. ὑδροποτέω **hudrŏpŏtĕō**, *hoo-drop-ot-eh'-o;* from a comp. of 5204 and a der. of 4095; to *be a water-drinker*, i.e. to *abstain from vinous beverages:*—drink water.

5203. ὑδρωπικός **hudrōpikŏs**, *hoo-dro-pik-os';* from a comp. of 5204 and a der. of 3700 (as if *looking watery*); to be "*dropsical*":—have the dropsy.

5204. ὕδωρ **hudōr**, *hoo'-dore;* gen. ὕδατος **hudatŏs**, *hoo'-dat-os*, etc.; from the base of 5205; *water* (as if *rainy*) lit. or fig.:—water.

5205. ὑετός **huĕtŏs**, *hoo-et-os';* from a prim. ὕω **huō** (to *rain*); *rain*, espec. a *shower:*—rain.

5206. υἱοθεσία **huiŏthĕsia**, *hwee-oth-es-ee'-ah;* from a presumed comp. of 5207 and a der. of 5087; the *placing* as a *son*, i.e. *adoption* (fig. Chr. *sonship* in respect to God):—adoption (of children, of sons).

5207. υἱός **huiŏs**, *hwee-os';* appar. a prim. word; a "*son*" (sometimes of animals), used very widely of immed., remote or fig. kinship:—child, foal, son.

5208. ὕλη **hulē**, *hoo-lay';* perh. akin to 3586; a *forest*, i.e. (by impl.) *fuel;*—matter.

5209. ὑμᾶς **humas**, *hoo-mas';* acc. of 5210; *you* (as the obj. of a verb or prep.):—ye, you (+ -ward), your (+ own).

5210. ὑμεῖς **humĕis**, *hoo-mice';* irreg. plur. of 4771; *you* (as subj. of verb):—ye (yourselves), you.

5211. Ὑμεναῖος **Humĕnaiŏs**, *hoo-men-ah'-yos;* from Ὑμήν **Humēn** (the god of *weddings*); "*hymenæal*"; *Hymenæus*, an opponent of Christianity:—Hymenæus.

5212. ὑμέτερος **humĕtĕrŏs**, *hoo-met'-er-os;* from 5210; *yours*, i.e. *pertaining to you:*—your (own).

5213. ὑμῖν **humin**, *hoo-min';* irreg. dat. of 5210; *to* (*with* or *by*) *you:*—ye, you, your (-selves).

5214. ὑμνέω **humnĕō**, *hoom-neh'-o;* from 5215; to *hymn*, i.e. sing a religious ode; by impl. to *celebrate* (God) in song:—sing an hymn (praise unto).

5215. ὕμνος **humnŏs**, *hoom'-nos;* appar. from a simpler (obsol.) form of ὕδέω **hudĕō** (to *celebrate;* prob. akin to 103; comp. 5567); a "*hymn*" or religious ode (one of the Psalms):—hymn.

5216. ὑμῶν **humōn**, *hoo-mone';* gen. of 5210; *of* (*from* or *concerning*) *you:*—ye, you, your (own, -selves).

5217. ὑπάγω **hupagō**, *hoop-ag'-o;* from 5259 and 71; to *lead* (oneself) *under*, i.e. *withdraw* or *retire* (as if *sinking* out of sight), lit. or fig.:—depart, get hence, go (a-) way.

5218. ὑπακοή **hupakŏē**, *hoop-ak-ŏ-ay';* from 5219; *attentive hearkening*, i.e. (by impl.) *compliance* or *submission:*—obedience, (make) obedient, obey (-ing).

5219. ὑπακούω **hupakŏuō**, *hoop-ak-oo'-o;* from 5259 and 191; to *hear under* (as a *subordinate*), i.e. to *listen attentively;* by impl. to *heed* or *conform* to a command or authority:—hearken, be obedient to, obey.

5220. ὕπανδρος **hupandrŏs**, *hoop'-an-dros;* from 5259 and 435; in subjection *under a man*, i.e. a *married* woman:—which hath an husband.

5221. ὑπαντάω **hupantaō**, *hoop-an-tah'-o;* from 5259 and a der. of 473; to *go opposite* (*meet*) *under* (*quietly*), i.e. to *encounter, fall in with:*—(go to) meet.

5222. ὑπάντησις **hupantēsis**, *hoop-an'-tay-sis;* from 5221; an *encounter* or *concurrence* (with 1519 for infin., in order to *fall in with*):—meeting.

5223. ὕπαρξις **huparxis**, *hoop'-arx-is;* from 5225; *existency* or *proprietorship*, i.e. (concr.) *property, wealth:*—goods, substance.

5224. ὑπάρχοντα **huparchŏnta**, *hoop-ar'-khon-tah;* neut. plur. of pres. part. act. of 5225 as noun; things *extant* or *in hand*, i.e. *property* or *possessions:*—goods, that which one has, things which (one) possesseth, substance, that hast.

5225. **ὑπάρχω huparchō**, *hoop-ar'-kho;* from *5259* and *756;* to *begin under* (*quietly*), i.e. *come into existence* (*be present* or *at hand*); expletively, to *exist* (as copula or subordinate to an adj., part., adv. or prep., or as auxil. to principal verb):—after, behave, live.

5226. **ὑπείκω hupĕikō**, *hoop-i'-ko;* from *5259* and **εἴκω ĕikō** (to *yield*, be "*weak*"); to *surrender:*—submit self.

5227. **ὑπεναντίος hupĕnantiŏs**, *hoop-en-an-tee'-os;* from *5259* and *1727; under* (*covertly*) *contrary* to, i.e. *opposed* or (as noun) an *opponent:*—adversary, against.

5228. **ὑπέρ hupĕr**, *hoop-er';* a prim. prep.; "*over*", i.e. (with the gen.) of place, *above, beyond, across*, or causal, *for* the sake of, *instead, regarding;* with the acc. *superior to*, more *than:*—(+ exceeding abundantly) above, in (on) behalf of, beyond, by, + very chiefest, concerning, exceeding (above, -ly), for, + very highly, more (than), of, over, on the part of, for sake of, in stead, than, to (-ward), very. In comp. it retains many of the above applications.

5229. **ὑπεραίρομαι hupĕrairŏmai**, *hoop-er-ah'ee-rom-ahee;* mid. from *5228* and *142;* to *raise* oneself *over*, i.e. (fig.) to *become haughty:*—exalt self, be exalted above measure.

5230. **ὑπέρακμος hupĕrakmŏs**, *hoop-er'-ak-mos;* from *5228* and the base of *188; beyond* the "*acme*", i.e. fig. (of a daughter) *past* the *bloom* (*prime*) of youth:— + pass the flower of (her) age.

5231. **ὑπεράνω hupĕranō**, *hoop-er-an'-o;* from *5228* and *507; above upward*, i.e. *greatly higher* (in place or rank):—far above, over.

5232. **ὑπεραυξάνω hupĕrauxanō**, *hoop-er-ŏwx-an'-o;* from *5228* and *837;* to *increase above* ordinary degree:—grow exceedingly.

5233. **ὑπερβαίνω hupĕrbainō**, *hoop-er-bah'ee-no;* from *5228* and the base of *939;* to *transcend*, i.e. (fig.) to *overreach:*—go beyond.

5234. **ὑπερβαλλόντως hupĕrballŏntōs**, *hoop-er-bal-lon'-toce;* adv. from pres. part. act. of *5235; excessively:*—beyond measure.

5235. **ὑπερβάλλω hupĕrballō**, *hoop-er-bal'-lo;* from *5228* and *906;* to *throw beyond* the usual mark, i.e. (fig.) to *surpass* (only act. part. *supereminent*):—exceeding, excel, pass.

5236. **ὑπερβολή hupĕrbŏlē**, *hoop-er-bol-ay';* from *5235;* a *throwing beyond* others, i.e. (fig.) *supereminence;* adv. (with *1519* or *2596*) *pre-eminently:*—abundance, (far more) exceeding, excellency, more excellent, beyond (out of) measure.

5237. **ὑπερείδω hupĕrĕidō**, *hoop-er-i'-do;* from *5228* and *1492;* to *overlook*, i.e. *not punish:*—wink at.

5238. **ὑπερέκεινα hupĕrĕkĕina**, *hoop-er-ek'-i-nah;* from *5228* and the neut. plur. of *1565; above those* parts, i.e. *still farther:*—beyond.

5239. **ὑπερεκτείνω hupĕrĕktĕinō**, *hoop-er-ek-ti'-no;* from *5228* and *1614;* to *extend inordinately:*—stretch beyond.

5240. **ὑπερεκχύνω hupĕrĕkchunō**, *hoop-er-ek-khoo'-no;* from *5228* and the alt. form of *1632;* to *pour out over*, i.e. (pass.) to *overflow:*—run over.

ὑπερεκπερισσοῦ hupĕrĕkpĕrissŏu. See *5228* and *1537* and *4053*.

5241. **ὑπερεντυγχάνω hupĕrĕntugchanō**, *hoop-er-en-toong-khan'-o;* from *5228* and *1793;* to *intercede in behalf of:*—make intercession for.

5242. **ὑπερέχω hupĕrĕchō**, *hoop-er-ekh'-o;* from *5228* and *2192;* to *hold* oneself *above*, i.e. (fig.) to *excel;* part. (as adj., or neut. as noun) *superior, superiority:*—better, excellency, higher, pass, supreme.

5243. **ὑπερηφανία hupĕrēphania**, *hoop-er-ay-fan-ee'-ah;* from *5244; haughtiness:*—pride.

5244. **ὑπερήφανος hupĕrēphanŏs**, *hoop-er-ay'-fan-os;* from *5228* and *5316; appearing above* others (*conspicuous*), i.e. (fig.) *haughty:*—proud.

ὑπερλίαν hupĕrlian. See *5228* and *3029*.

5245. **ὑπερνικάω hupĕrnikaō**, *hoop-er-nik-ah'-o;* from *5228* and *3528;* to *vanquish beyond*, i.e. *gain* a decisive *victory:*—more than conquer.

5246. **ὑπέρογκος hupĕrŏgkŏs**, *hoop-er'-ong-kos;* from *5228* and *3591; bulging over*, i.e. (fig.) *insolent:*—great swelling.

5247. **ὑπεροχή hupĕrŏchē**, *hoop-er-okh-ay';* from *5242; prominence*, i.e. (fig.) *superiority* (in rank or character):—authority, excellency.

5248. **ὑπερπερισσεύω hupĕrpĕrissĕuō**, *hoop-er-per-is-syoo'-o;* from *5228* and *4052;* to *superabound:*—abound much more, exceeding.

5249. **ὑπερπερισσῶς hupĕrpĕrissōs**, *hoop-er-per-is-soce';* from *5228* and *4057; superabundantly*, i.e. *exceedingly:*—beyond measure.

5250. **ὑπερπλεονάζω hupĕrplĕŏnazō**, *hoop-er-pleh-on-ad'-zo;* from *5228* and *4121;* to *superabound:*—be exceeding abundant.

5251. **ὑπερυψόω hupĕrupsŏō**, *hoop-er-oop-sŏ'-o;* from *5228* and *5312;* to *elevate above* others, i.e. *raise* to the *highest* position:—highly exalt.

5252. **ὑπερφρονέω hupĕrphrŏnĕō**, *hoop-er-fron-eh'-o;* from *5228* and *5426;* to *esteem* oneself *overmuch*, i.e. *be vain* or *arrogant:*—think more highly.

5253. **ὑπερῷον hupĕrō$_1$ŏn**, *hoop-er-o'-on;* neut. of a der. of *5228;* a *higher* part of the house, i.e. apartment in the *third story:*—upper chamber (room).

5254. **ὑπέχω hupĕchō**, *hoop-ekh'-o;* from *5259* and *2192;* to *hold* oneself *under*, i.e. *endure* with patience:—suffer.

5255. **ὑπήκοος hupēkŏŏs**, *hoop-ay'-kŏ-os;* from *5219; attentively listening*, i.e. (by impl.) *submissive:*—obedient.

5256. **ὑπηρετέω hupērĕtĕō**, *hoop-ay-ret-eh'-o;* from *5257;* to *be a subordinate*, i.e. (by impl.) *subserve:*—minister (unto), serve.

5257. **ὑπηρέτης hupērĕtēs**, *hoop-ay-ret'-ace;* from *5259* and a der. of **ἐρέσσω ĕrĕssō** (to *row*); an *under-oarsman*, i.e. (gen.) *subordinate* (*assistant, sexton, constable*):—minister, officer, servant.

5258. **ὕπνος hupnŏs**, *hoop'-nos;* from an obsol. prim. (perh. akin to *5259* through the idea of *subsilience*); *sleep*, i.e. (fig.) spiritual *torpor:*—sleep.

5259. **ὑπό hupŏ**, *hoop-ŏ';* a prim. prep.; *under*, i.e. (with the gen.) of place (*beneath*), or with verbs (the agency or means, *through*); (with the acc.) of place (whither [*underneath*] or where [*below*]) or time (when [*at*]):—among, by, from, in, of, under, with. In comp. it retains the same gen. applications, espec. of *inferior* position or condition, and spec. *covertly* or *moderately*.

5260. **ὑποβάλλω hupŏballō**, *hoop-ob-al'-lo;* from *5259* and *906;* to *throw* in *stealthily*, i.e. *introduce* by collusion:—suborn.

5261. **ὑπογραμμός hupŏgrammŏs**, *hoop-og-ram-mos';* from a comp. of *5259* and *1125;* an *underwriting*, i.e. *copy* for imitation (fig.):—example.

5262. **ὑπόδειγμα hupŏdĕigma**, *hoop-od'-igue-mah;* from *5263;* an *exhibit* for imitation or warning (fig. *specimen, adumbration*):—en- (ex-) ample, pattern.

5263. **ὑποδείκνυμι hupŏdĕiknumi**, *hoop-od-ike'-noo-mee;* from *5259* and *1166;* to *exhibit under* the eyes, i.e. (fig.) to *exemplify* (*instruct, admonish*):—show, (fore-) warn.

5264. **ὑποδέχομαι hupŏdĕchŏmai**, *hoop-od-ekh'-om-ahee;* from *5259* and *1209;* to *admit under* one's roof, i.e. *entertain* hospitably:—receive.

5265. **ὑποδέω hupŏdĕō**, *hoop-od-eh'-o;* from *5259* and *1210;* to *bind under* one's feet, i.e. *put on* shoes or sandals:—bind on, (be) shod.

5266. **ὑπόδημα hupŏdēma**, *hoop-od'-ay-mah;* from *5265;* something *bound under* the feet, i.e. a *shoe* or *sandal:*—shoe.

5267. **ὑπόδικος hupŏdikŏs**, *hoop-od'-ee-kos;* from *5259* and *1349; under sentence*, i.e. (by impl.) *condemned:*—guilty.

5268. **ὑποζύγιον hupŏzugiŏn**, *hoop-od-zoog'-ee-on;* neut. of a comp. of *5259* and *2218;* an animal *under* the *yoke* (*draught-beast*), i.e. (spec.) a *donkey:*—ass.

5269. **ὑποζώννυμι hupŏzōnnumi**, *hoop-od-zone'-noo-mee;* from *5259* and *2224;* to *gird under*, i.e. *frap* (a vessel with cables across the keel, sides and deck):—undergirt.

5270. **ὑποκάτω hupŏkatō**, *hoop-ok-at'-o;* from *5259* and *2736; down under*, i.e. *beneath:*—under.

5271. **ὑποκρίνομαι hupŏkrinŏmai**, *hoop-ok-rin'-om-ahee;* mid. from *5259* and *2919;* to *decide* (*speak* or *act*) *under* a false part, i.e. (fig.) *dissemble* (*pretend*):—feign.

5272. **ὑπόκρισις hupŏkrisis**, *hoop-ok'-ree-sis;* from *5271; acting under* a feigned part, i.e. (fig.) *deceit* ("*hypocrisy*"):—condemnation, dissimulation, hypocrisy.

5273. **ὑποκριτής hupŏkritēs**, *hoop-ok-ree-tace';* from *5271;* an *actor under* an assumed character (*stage-player*), i.e. (fig.) a *dissembler* ("*hypocrite*"):—hypocrite.

5274. **ὑπολαμβάνω hupŏlambanō**, *hoop-ol-am-ban'-o;* from *5259* and *2983;* to *take* from *below*, i.e. *carry upward;* fig. to *take up*, i.e. *continue* a discourse or topic; ment. to *assume* (*presume*):—answer, receive, suppose.

5275. **ὑπολείπω hupŏlĕipō**, *hoop-ol-i'-po;* from *5295* and *3007;* to *leave under* (*behind*), i.e. (pass.) to *remain* (*survive*):—be left.

5276. **ὑπολήνιον hupŏlēniŏn**, *hoop-ol-ay'-nee-on;* neut. of a presumed comp. of *5259* and *3025;* vessel or receptacle *under* the *press*, i.e. lower *winevat:*—winefat.

5277. **ὑπολιμπάνω hupŏlimpanō**, *hoop-ol-im-pan'-o;* a prol. form for *5275;* to *leave behind*, i.e. *bequeath:*—leave.

5278. **ὑπομένω hupŏmĕnō**, *hoop-om-en'-o;* from *5259* and *3306;* to *stay under* (*behind*), i.e. *remain;* fig. to *undergo*, i.e. *bear* (trials), *have fortitude, persevere:*—abide, endure, (take) patient (-ly), suffer, tarry behind.

5279. **ὑπομιμνήσκω hupŏmimnēskō**, *hoop-om-im-nace'-ko;* from *5259* and *3403;* to *remind quietly*, i.e. *suggest* to the (mid. one's own) memory:—put in mind, remember, bring to (put in) remembrance.

5280. **ὑπόμνησις hupŏmnēsis**, *hoop-om'-nay-sis;* from *5279;* a *reminding* or (reflex.) *recollection:*—remembrance.

5281. **ὑπομονή hupŏmŏnē**, *hoop-om-on-ay';* from *5278;* cheerful (or hopeful) *endurance, constancy:*—enduring, patience, patient continuance (waiting).

5282. **ὑπονοέω hupŏnŏĕō**, *hoop-on-ŏ-eh'-o;* from *5259* and *3539;* to *think under* (*privately*), i.e. to *surmise* or *conjecture:*—think, suppose, deem.

5283. **ὑπόνοια hupŏnŏia**, *hoop-on'-oy-ah;* from *5282; suspicion:*—surmising.

5284. **ὑποπλέω hupŏplĕō**, *hoop-op-leh'-o;* from *5259* and *4126;* to *sail under* the lee of:—sail under.

5285. **ὑποπνέω hupŏpnĕō**, *hoop-op-neh'-o;* from *5259* and *4154;* to *breathe gently*, i.e. *breeze:*—blow softly.

5286. **ὑποπόδιον hupŏpŏdiŏn**, *hoop-op-od'-ee-on;* neut. of a comp. of *5259* and *4228;* something *under* the *feet*, i.e. a *foot-rest* (fig.):—footstool.

5287. **ὑπόστασις hupŏstasis**, *hoop-os'-tas-is;* from a comp. of *5259* and *2476;* a *setting under* (*support*), i.e. (fig.) concr. *essence*, or abstr. *assurance* (obj. or subj.):—confidence, confident, person, substance.

5288. **ὑποστέλλω hupŏstĕllō**, *hoop-os-tel'-lo;* from *5259* and *4724;* to *withhold under* (*out of sight*), i.e. (reflex.) to *cower* or *shrink*, (fig.) to *conceal* (*reserve*):—draw (keep) back, shun, withdraw.

5289. **ὑποστολή hupŏstŏlē**, *hoop-os-tol-ay';* from *5288; shrinkage* (*timidity*), i.e. (by impl.) *apostasy:*—draw back.

5290. **ὑποστρέφω hupŏstrĕphō**, *hoop-os-tref'-o;* from *5259* and *4762;* to *turn under* (*behind*), i.e. to *return* (lit. or fig.):—come again, return (again, back again), turn back (again).

5291. **ὑποστρώννυμι hupŏstrōnnumi**, *hoop-os-trone'-noo-mee;* from *5259* and *4766;* to *strew underneath* (the feet as a carpet):—spread.

5292. ὑποταγή hupŏtagē, *hoop-ot-ag-ay'*; from 5293; *subordination*:—subjection.

5293. ὑποτάσσω hupŏtassō, *hoop-ot-as'-so*; from 5259 and 5021; to *subordinate*; reflex. to *obey*:—be under obedience (obedient), put under, subdue unto, (be, make) subject (to, unto), be (put) in subjection (to, under), submit self unto.

5294. ὑποτίθημι hupŏtithēmi, *hoop-ot-ith'-ay-mee*; from 5259 and 5087; to *place underneath*, i.e. (fig.) to *hazard*, (reflex.) to *suggest*:—lay down, put in remembrance.

5295. ὑποτρέχω hupŏtrĕchō, *hoop-ot-rekh'-o*; from 5259 and 5143 (includ. its alt.); to *run under*, i.e. (spec.) to *sail past*:—run under.

5296. ὑποτύπωσις hupŏtupōsis, *hoop-ot-oop'-o-sis*; from a comp. of 5259 and a der. of 5179; *typification under* (*after*), i.e. (concr.) a *sketch* (fig.) for imitation:—form, pattern.

5297. ὑποφέρω hupŏphĕrō, *hoop-of-er'-o*; from 5259 and 5342; to *bear* from *underneath*, i.e. (fig.) to *undergo* hardship:—bear, endure.

5298. ὑποχωρέω hupŏchōrĕō, *hoop-okh-o-reh'-o*; from 5259 and 5562; to *vacate down*, i.e. *retire* quietly:—go aside, withdraw self.

5299. ὑπωπιάζω hupōpiazō, *hoop-o-pee-ad'-zo*; from a comp. of 5259 and a der. of 3700; to hit *under the eye* (*buffet* or *disable* an antagonist as a pugilist), i.e. (fig.) to *tease* or *annoy* (into compliance), *subdue* (one's passions):—keep under, weary.

5300. ὗς hus, *hoos*; appar. a prim. word; a *hog* ("*swine*"):—sow.

5301. ὕσσωπος hussōpŏs, *hoos'-so-pos*; of for. or. [231]; "*hyssop*":—hyssop.

5302. ὑστερέω hustĕrĕō, *hoos-ter-eh'-o*; from 5306; to *be later*, i.e. (by impl.) to *be inferior*; gen. to *fall short* (*be deficient*):—come behind (short), be destitute, fail, lack, suffer need, (be in) want, be the worse.

5303. ὑστέρημα hustĕrēma, *hoos-ter'-ay-mah*; from 5302; a *deficit*; spec. *poverty*:—that which is behind, (that which was) lack (-ing), penury, want.

5304. ὑστέρησις hustĕrēsis, *hoos-ter'-ay-sis*; from 5302; a *falling short*, i.e. (spec.) *penury*:—want.

5305. ὕστερον hustĕrŏn, *hoos'-ter-on*; neut. of 5306 as adv.; *more lately*, i.e. *eventually*:—afterward, (at the) last (of all).

5306. ὕστερος hustĕrŏs, *hoos'-ter-os*; compar. from 5259 (in the sense of *behind*); *later*:—latter.

5307. ὑφαντός huphantŏs, *hoo-fan-tos'*; from ὑφαίνω huphainō (to *weave*); *woven*, i.e. (perh.) *knitted*:—woven.

5308. ὑψηλός hupsēlŏs, *hoop-say-los'*; from 5311; *lofty* (in place or character):—high (-er, -ly) (esteemed).

5309. ὑψηλοφρονέω hupsēlŏphrŏnĕō, *hoop-say-lo-fron-eh'-o*; from a comp. of 5308 and 5424; to *be lofty in mind*, i.e. *arrogant*:—be highminded.

5310. ὕψιστος hupsistŏs, *hoop'-sis-tos*; superl. from the base of 5311; *highest*, i.e. (masc. sing.) the *Supreme* (God), or (neut. plur.) the *heavens*:—most high, highest.

5311. ὕψος hupsŏs, *hoop'-sos*; from a der. of 5228; *elevation*, i.e. (abstr.) *altitude*, (spec.) the *sky*, or (fig.) *dignity*:—be exalted, height, (on) high.

5312. ὑψόω hupsŏō, *hoop-sŏ'-o*; from 5311; to *elevate* (lit. or fig.):—exalt, lift up.

5313. ὕψωμα hupsōma, *hoop'-so-mah*; from 5312; an *elevated* place or thing, i.e. (abstr.) *altitude*, or (by impl.) a *barrier* (fig.):—height, high thing.

Φ

5314. φάγος phagŏs, *fag'-os*; from 5315; a *glutton*:—gluttonous.

5315. φάγω phagō, *fag'-o*; a prim. verb (used as an alt. of 2068 in cert. tenses); to *eat* (lit. or fig.):—eat, meat.

5316. φαίνω phainō, *fah'ee-no*; prol. for the base of 5457; to *lighten* (*shine*), i.e. *show* (trans. or intrans., lit. or fig.):—appear, seem, be seen, shine, × think.

5317. Φάλεκ Phalĕk, *fal'-ek*; of Heb. or. [6389]; *Phalek* (i.e. *Peleg*), a patriarch:—Phalec.

5318. φανερός phanĕrŏs, *fan-er-os'*; from 5316; *shining*, i.e. *apparent* (lit. or fig.); neut. (as adv.) *publicly, externally*:—abroad, + appear, known, manifest, open [+ -ly], outward ([+ -ly]).

5319. φανερόω phanĕrŏō, *fan-er-ŏ'-o*; from 5318; to *render apparent* (lit. or fig.):—appear, manifestly declare, (make) manifest (forth), shew (self).

5320. φανερῶς phanĕrōs, *fan-er-oce'*; adv. from 5318; *plainly*, i.e. *clearly* or *publicly*:—evidently, openly.

5321. φανέρωσις phanĕrōsis, *fan-er'-o-sis*; from 5319; *exhibition*, i.e. (fig.) *expression*, (by extens.) a *bestowment*:—manifestation.

5322. φανός phanŏs, *fan-os'*; from 5316; a *lightener*, i.e. *light*; *lantern*:—lantern.

5323. Φανουήλ Phanŏuēl, *fan-oo-ale'*; of Heb. or. [6439]; *Phanuēl* (i.e. *Penuēl*), an Isr.:—Phanuel.

5324. φαντάζω phantazō, *fan-tad'-zo*; from a der. of 5316; to *make apparent*, i.e. (pass.) to *appear* (neut. part. as noun, a *spectacle*):—sight.

5325. φαντασία phantasia, *fan-tas-ee'-ah*; from a der. of 5324; (prop. abstr.) a (vain) *show* ("fantasy"):—pomp.

5326. φάντασμα phantasma, *fan'-tas-mah*; from 5324; (prop. concr.) a (mere) *show* ("phantasm"), i.e. *spectre*:—spirit.

5327. φάραγξ pharagx, *far'-anx*; prop. strength. from the base of 4008 or rather of 4486; a *gap* or *chasm*, i.e. *ravine* (*winter-torrent*):—valley.

5328. Φαραώ Pharaō, *far-ah-o'*; of for. or. [6547]; *Pharaō* (i.e. *Pharoh*), an Eg. king:—Pharaoh.

5329. Φαρές Pharĕs, *far-es'*; of Heb. or. [6557]; *Phares* (i.e. *Perets*), an Isr.:—Phares.

5330. Φαρισαῖος Pharisaiŏs, *far-is-ah'-yos*; of Heb. or. [comp. 6567]; a *separatist*, i.e. exclusively *religious*; a *Pharisæan*, i.e. Jewish sectary:—Pharisee.

5331. φαρμακεία pharmakĕia, *far-mak-i'-ah*; from 5332; *medication* ("pharmacy"), i.e. (by extens.) *magic* (lit. or fig.):—sorcery, witchcraft.

5332. φαρμακεύς pharmakĕus, *far-mak-yoos'*; from φάρμακον pharmakŏn (a *drug*, i.e. spell-giving *potion*); a *druggist* ("pharmacist") or *poisoner*, i.e. (by extens.) a *magician*:—sorcerer.

5333. φαρμακός pharmakŏs, *far-mak-os'*; the same as 5332:—sorcerer.

5334. φάσις phasis, *fas'-is*; from 5346 (not the same as "phase", which is from 5316); a *saying*, i.e. *report*:—tidings.

5335. φάσκω phaskō, *fas'-ko*; prol. from the same as 5346; to *assert*:—affirm, profess, say.

5336. φάτνη phatnē, *fat'-nay*; from πατέομαι patĕŏmai (to *eat*); a *crib* (for fodder):—manger, stall.

5337. φαῦλος phaulŏs, *fow'-los*; appar. a prim. word; "*foul*" or "*flawy*", i.e. (fig.) *wicked*:—evil.

5338. φέγγος phĕggŏs, *feng'-gos*; prob. akin to the base of 5457 [comp. 5350]; *brilliancy*:—light.

5339. φείδομαι phĕidŏmai, *fi'-dom-ahee*; of uncert. affin.; to *be chary* of, i.e. (subj.) to *abstain* or (obj.) to *treat leniently*:—forbear, spare.

5340. φειδομένως phĕidŏmĕnōs, *fi-dom-en'-oce*; adv. from part. of 5339; *abstemiously*, i.e. *stingily*:—sparingly.

5341. φελόνης phĕlŏnēs, *fel-on'-ace*; by transp. for a der. prob. of 5316 (as *showing* outside the other garments); a *mantle* (*surtout*):—cloke.

5342. φέρω phĕrō, *fer'-o*; a prim. verb (for which other and appar. not cognate ones are used in certain tenses only; namely,

οἴω ŏiō, *oy'-o*; and

ἐνέγκω ĕnĕgkō, *en-eng'-ko*); to "*bear*" or *carry* (in a very wide application, lit. and fig., as follows):—be, bear, bring (forth), carry, come, + let her drive, be driven, endure, go on, lay, lead, move, reach, rushing, uphold.

5343. φεύγω phĕugō, *fyoo'-go*; appar. a prim. verb; to *run away* (lit. or fig.); by impl. to *shun*; by anal. to *vanish*:—escape, flee (away).

5344. Φῆλιξ Phēlix, *fay'-lix*; of Lat. or.; *happy*: *Phelix* (i.e. *Felix*), a Rom.:—Felix.

5345. φήμη phēmē, *fay'-may*; from 5346; a *saying*, i.e. *rumor* ("fame"):—fame.

5346. φημί phēmi, *fay-mee'*; prop. the same as the base of 5457 and 5316; to *show* or *make known* one's thoughts, i.e. *speak* or *say*:—affirm, say. Comp. 3004.

5347. Φῆστος Phēstŏs, *face'-tos*; of Lat. der.; *festal*; *Phestus* (i.e. *Festus*), a Rom.:—Festus.

5348. φθάνω phthanō, *fthan'-o*; appar. a prim. verb; to *be beforehand*, i.e. *anticipate* or *precede*, by extens. to *have arrived* at:—(already) attain, come, prevent.

5349. φθαρτός phthartŏs, *fthar-tos'*; from 5351; *decayed*, i.e. (by impl.) *perishable*:—corruptible.

5350. φθέγγομαι phthĕggŏmai, *ftheng'-gom-ahee*; prob. akin to 5338 and thus to 5346; to *utter* a clear sound, i.e. (gen.) to *proclaim*:—speak.

5351. φθείρω phthĕirō, *fthi'-ro*; prob. strength. from φθίω phthiō (to *pine* or *waste*); prop. to *shrivel* or *wither*, i.e. to *spoil* (by any process) or (gen.) to *ruin* (espec. fig. by mor. influences, to *deprave*):—corrupt (self), defile, destroy.

5352. φθινοπωρινός phthinŏpōrinŏs, *fthin-op-o-ree-nos'*; from a der. of φθίνω phthinō (to *wane*; akin to the base of 5351) and 3703 (mean. *late autumn*); *autumnal* (as *stripped* of leaves):—whose fruit withereth.

5353. φθόγγος phthŏggŏs, *fthong'-gos*; from 5350; *utterance*, i.e. a *musical* note (vocal or instrumental):—sound.

5354. φθονέω phthŏnĕō, *fthon-eh'-o*; from 5355; to *be jealous* of:—envy.

5355. φθόνος phthŏnŏs, *fthon'-os*; prob. akin to the base of 5351; *ill-will* (as *detraction*), i.e. *jealousy* (*spite*):—envy.

5356. φθορά phthŏra, *fthor-ah'*; from 5351; *decay*, i.e. *ruin* (spontaneous or inflicted, lit. or fig.):—corruption, destroy, perish.

5357. φιάλη phialē, *fee-al'-ay*; of uncert. affin.; a broad shallow *cup* ("phial"):—vial.

5358. φιλάγαθος philagathŏs, *fil-ag'-ath-os*; from 5384 and 18; *fond to good*, i.e. a *promoter of virtue*:—love of good men.

5359. Φιλαδέλφεια Philadĕlphĕia, *fil-ad-el'-fee-ah*; from Φιλάδελφος Philadĕlphŏs (the same as 5361), a king of Pergamos; *Philadelphia*, a place in Asia Minor:—Philadelphia.

5360. φιλαδελφία philadĕlphia, *fil-ad-el-fee'-ah*; from 5361; *fraternal affection*:—brotherly love (kindness), love of the brethren.

5361. φιλάδελφος philadĕlphŏs, *fil-ad'-el-fos*; from 5384 and 80; *fond of brethren*, i.e. *fraternal*:—love as brethren.

5362. φίλανδρος philandrŏs, *fil'-an-dros*; from 5384 and 435; *fond of man*, i.e. *affectionate* as a wife:—love their husbands.

5363. φιλανθρωπία philanthrōpia, *fil-an-thro-pee'-ah*; from the same as 5364; *fondness of mankind*, i.e. *benevolence* ("*philanthropy*"):—kindness, love towards man.

5364. φιλανθρώπως philanthrōpōs, *fil-an-thro'-poce*; adv. from a comp. of 5384 and 444; *fondly to man* ("philanthropically"), i.e. *humanely*:—courteously.

5365. φιλαργυρία philarguria, *fil-ar-goo-ree'-ah*; from 5366; *avarice*:—love of money.

5366. φιλάργυρος philargurŏs, *fil-ar'-goo-ros*; from 5384 and 696; *fond of silver* (*money*), i.e. *avaricious*:—covetous.

5367. φίλαυτος philautŏs, *fil'-ow-tos*; from 5384 and 846; *fond of self*, i.e. *selfish*:—lover of own self.

5368. φιλέω philĕō, *fil-eh'-o*; from 5384; to *be a friend to* (*fond of* [an individual or an object]), i.e. *have affection* for (denoting *personal* attachment, as a matter of sentiment or feeling; while 25 is wider, embracing espec. the judgment and the *deliberate* assent of the will as a matter of principle, duty and propriety: the two thus stand related very much as 2309 and 1014, or as 2372 and 3563 respectively; the former being chiefly of the *heart* and the latter of the *head*); spec. to *kiss* (as a mark of tenderness):—kiss, love.

5369. **φιλήδονος philēdŏnŏs**, *fil-ay'-don-os;* from 5384 and 2237; *fond of pleasure*, i.e. *voluptuous:*—lover of pleasure.

5370. **φίλημα philēma**, *fil'-ay-mah;* from 5368; a *kiss:*—kiss.

5371. **Φιλήμων Philēmōn**, *fil-ay'-mone;* from 5368; *friendly; Philemon*, a Chr.:—Philemon.

5372. **Φιλητός Philētŏs**, *fil-ay-tos';* from 5368; *amiable; Philetus*, an opposer of Christianity:—Philetus.

5373. **φιλία philia**, *fil-ee'-ah;* from 5384; *fondness:*—friendship.

5374. **Φιλιππήσιος Philippēsiŏs**, *fil-ip-pay'-see-os;* from 5375; a *Philippesian* (*Philippian*), i.e. native of Philippi:—Philippian.

5375. **Φίλιπποι Philippŏi**, *fil'-ip-poy;* plur. of 5376; *Philippi*, a place in Macedonia:—Philippi.

5376. **Φίλιππος Philippŏs**, *fil'-ip-pos;* from 5384 and 2462; *fond of horses; Philippus*, the name of four Isr.:—Philip.

5377. **φιλόθεος philŏthĕŏs**, *fil-oth'-eh-os;* from 5384 and 2316; *fond of God*, i.e. *pious:*—lover of God.

5378. **Φιλόλογος Philŏlŏgŏs**, *fil-ol'-og-os;* from 5384 and 3056; *fond of words*, i.e. *talkative* (*argumentative, learned*, "*philological*"); *Philologus*, a Chr.:—Philologus.

5379. **φιλονεικία philŏnĕikia**, *fil-on-i-kee'-ah;* from 5380; *quarrelsomeness*, i.e. a *dispute:*—strife.

5380. **φιλόνεικος philŏnĕikŏs**, *fil-on'-i-kos;* from 5384 and **νεῖκος nĕikŏs** (a *quarrel;* prob. akin to 3534); *fond of strife*, i.e. *disputatious:*—contentious.

5381. **φιλονεξία philŏnĕxia**, *fil-on-ex-ee'-ah;* from 5382; *hospitableness:*—entertain strangers, hospitality.

5382. **φιλόξενος philŏxĕnŏs**, *fil-ox'-en-os;* from 5384 and 3581; *fond of guests*, i.e. *hospitable:*—given to (lover of, use) hospitality.

5383. **φιλοπρωτεύω philŏprōtĕuō**, *fil-op-rote-yoo'-o;* from a comp. of 5384 and 4413; *to be fond of being first*, i.e. *ambitious* of distinction:—love to have the preeminence.

5384. **φίλος philŏs**, *fee'-los;* prop. *dear*, i.e. a *friend;* act. *fond*, i.e. *friendly* (still as a noun, an *associate, neighbor*, etc.):—friend.

5385. **φιλοσοφία philŏsŏphia**, *fil-os-of-ee'-ah;* from 5386; "*philosophy*", i.e. (spec.) Jewish *sophistry:*—philosophy.

5386. **φιλόσοφος philŏsŏphŏs**, *fil-os'-of-os;* from 5384 and 4680; *fond of wise* things, i.e. a "*philosopher*":—philosopher.

5387. **φιλόστοργος philŏstŏrgŏs**, *fil-os'-tor-gos;* from 5384 and **στοργή stŏrgē** (*cherishing* one's kindred, espec. parents or children); *fond of* natural *relatives*, i.e. *fraternal* towards fellow Chr.:—kindly affectioned.

5388. **φιλότεκνος philŏtĕknŏs**, *fil-ot'-ek-nos;* from 5384 and 5043; *fond of* one's *children*, i.e. *maternal:*—love their children.

5389. **φιλοτιμέομαι philŏtimĕŏmai**, *fil-ot-im-eh'-om-ahee;* mid. from a comp. of 5384 and 5092; to be *fond of honor*, i.e. *emulous* (*eager* or *earnest* to do something):—labour, strive, study.

5390. **φιλοφρόνως philŏphrŏnōs**, *fil-of-ron'-oce;* adv. from 5391; *with friendliness of mind*, i.e. *kindly:*—courteously.

5391. **φιλόφρων philŏphrōn**, *fil-of'-rone;* from 5384 and 5424; *friendly of mind*, i.e. *kind:*—courteous.

5392. **φιμόω phimŏō**, *fee-mŏ'-o;* from **φιμός phimŏs** (a *muzzle*); to *muzzle:*—muzzle.

5393. **Φλέγων Phlĕgōn**, *fleg'-one;* act. part. of the base of 5395; *blazing; Phlegon*, a Chr.:—Phlegon.

5394. **φλογίζω phlŏgizō**, *flog-id'-zo;* from 5395; to *cause a blaze*, i.e. *ignite* (fig. to *inflame* with passion):—set on fire.

5395. **φλόξ phlŏx**, *flox;* from a prim. **φλέγω phlĕgō** (to "*flash*" or "*flame*"); a *blaze:*—flame (-ing).

5396. **φλυαρέω phluarĕō**, *floo-ar-eh'-o;* from 5397; to *be a babbler* or *trifler*, i.e. (by impl.) to *berate* idly or mischievously:—prate against.

5397. **φλύαρος phluarŏs**, *floo'-ar-os;* from **φλύω phluō** (to *bubble*); a *garrulous* person, i.e. *prater:*—tattler.

5398. **φοβερός phŏbĕrŏs**, *fob-er-os';* from 5401; *frightful*, i.e. (obj.) *formidable:*—fearful, terrible.

5399. **φοβέω phŏbĕō**, *fob-eh'-o;* from 5401; to *frighten*, i.e. (pass.) to *be alarmed;* by anal. to *be in awe* of, i.e. *revere:*—be (+ sore) afraid, fear (exceedingly), reverence.

5400. **φόβητρον phŏbētrŏn**, *fob'-ay-tron;* neut. of a der. of 5399; a *frightening* thing, i.e. *terrific* portent:—fearful sight.

5401. **φόβος phŏbŏs**, *fob'-os;* from a prim. **φέβομαι phĕbŏmai** (to *be* put in *fear*); *alarm* or *fright:*—be afraid, + exceedingly, fear, terror.

5402. **Φοίβη Phŏibē**, *foy'-bay;* fem. of **φοῖβος phŏibŏs** (*bright;* prob. akin to the base of 5457); *Phœbe*, a Chr. woman:—Phebe.

5403. **Φοινίκη Phŏinikē**, *foy-nee'-kay;* from 5404; *palm*-country; *Phœnice* (or *Phœnicia*), a region of Pal.:—Phenice, Phenicia.

5404. **φοῖνιξ phŏinix**, *foy'-nix;* of uncert. der.; a *palm-tree:*—palm (tree).

5405. **Φοῖνιξ Phŏinix**, *foy'-nix;* prob. the same as 5404; *Phœnix*, a place in Crete:—Phenice.

5406. **φονεύς phŏnĕus**, *fon-yooce';* from 5408; a *murderer* (always of *criminal* [or at least *intentional*] homicide; which 443 does not necessarily imply; while 4607 is a spec. term for a *public* bandit):—murderer.

5407. **φονεύω phŏnĕuō**, *fon-yoo'-o;* from 5406; to *be a murderer* (of):—kill, do murder, slay.

5408. **φόνος phŏnŏs**, *fon'-os;* from an obsol. prim. **φένω phĕnō** (to *slay*); *murder:*—murder, + be slain with, slaughter.

5409. **φορέω phŏrĕō**, *for-eh'-o;* from 5411; to *have a burden*, i.e. (by anal.) to *wear* as clothing or a constant accompaniment:—bear, wear.

5410. **Φόρον Phŏrŏn**, *for'-on;* of Lat. or.; a *forum* or market-place; only in comp. with 675; a *station* on the Appian road:—forum.

5411. **φόρος phŏrŏs**, *for'-os;* from 5342; a *load* (as *borne*), i.e. (fig.) a *tax* (prop. an individ. *assessment* on persons or property; whereas 5056 is usually a gen. *toll* on goods or travel):—tribute.

5412. **φορτίζω phŏrtizō**, *for-tid'-zo;* from 5414; to *load* up (prop. as a vessel or animal), i.e. (fig.) to *overburden* with ceremony (or spiritual anxiety):—lade, be heavy laden.

5413. **φορτίον phŏrtiŏn**, *for-tee'-on;* dimin. of 5414; an *invoice* (as part of *freight*), i.e. (fig.) a *task* or *service:*—burden.

5414. **φόρτος phŏrtŏs**, *for'-tos;* from 5342; something *carried*, i.e. the *cargo* of a ship:—lading.

5415. **Φορτουνάτος Phŏrtŏunatŏs**, *for-too-nat'-os;* of Lat. or.; "*fortunate*"; *Fortunatus*, a Chr.:—Fortunatus.

5416. **φραγέλλιον phragĕlliŏn**, *frag-el'-le-on;* neut. of a der. from the base of 5417; a *whip*, i.e. Rom. *lash* as a public punishment:—scourge.

5417. **φραγελλόω phragĕllŏō**, *frag-el-lŏ'-o;* from a presumed equiv. of the Lat. *flagellum;* to *whip*, i.e. *lash* as a public punishment:—scourge.

5418. **φραγμός phragmŏs**, *frag-mos';* from 5420; a *fence*, or inclosing *barrier* (lit. or fig.):—hedge (+ round about), partition.

5419. **φράζω phrazō**, *frad'-zo;* prob. akin to 5420 through the idea of *defining;* to *indicate* (by word or act), i.e. (spec.) to *expound:*—declare.

5420. **φράσσω phrassō**, *fras'-so;* appar. a strength. form of the base of 5424; to *fence* or inclose, i.e. (spec.) to *block* up (fig. to *silence*):—stop.

5421. **φρέαρ phrĕar**, *freh'-ar;* of uncert. der.; a *hole* in the ground (dug for obtaining or holding water or other purposes), i.e. a *cistern* or *well;* fig. an *abyss* (as a *prison*):—well, pit.

5422. **φρεναπατάω phrĕnapataō**, *fren-ap-at-ah'-o;* from 5423; to *be a mind-misleader*, i.e. *delude:*—deceive.

5423. **φρεναπάτης phrĕnapatēs**, *fren-ap-at-ace;* from 5424 and 539; a *mind-misleader*, i.e. *seducer:*—deceiver.

5424. **φρήν phrēn**, *frane;* prob. from an obsol. **φράω phraō** (to *rein* in or *curb;* comp. 5420); the *midrif* (as a *partition* of the body), i.e. (fig. and by impl. of sympathy) the *feelings* (or sensitive nature; by extens. [also in the plur.] the *mind* or cognitive faculties):—understanding.

5425. **φρίσσω phrissō**, *fris'-so;* appar. a prim. verb; to "*bristle*" or *chill*, i.e. *shudder* (*fear*):—tremble.

5426. **φρονέω phrŏnĕō**, *fron-eh'-o;* from 5424; to *exercise* the *mind*, i.e. *entertain* or *have a sentiment* or *opinion;* by impl. to *be* (mentally) *disposed* (more or less earnestly in a certain direction); intens. to *interest oneself* in (with concern or obedience):—set the affection on, (be) care (-ful), (be like-, + be of one, + be of the same, + let this) mind (-ed), regard, savour, think.

5427. **φρόνημα phrŏnēma**, *fron'-ay-mah;* from 5426; (mental) *inclination* or *purpose:*—(be, + be carnally, + be spiritually) mind (-ed).

5428. **φρόνησις phrŏnēsis**, *fron'-ay-sis;* from 5426; mental *action* or *activity*, i.e. intellectual or mor. *insight:*—prudence, wisdom.

5429. **φρόνιμος phrŏnimŏs**, *fron'-ee-mos;* from 5424; *thoughtful*, i.e. *sagacious* or *discreet* (implying a *cautious* character; while 4680 denotes *practical* skill or acumen; and 4908 indicates rather *intelligence* or mental acquirement); in a bad sense *conceited* (also in the compar.):—wise (-r).

5430. **φρονίμως phrŏnimōs**, *fron-im'-oce;* adv. from 5429; *prudently:*—wisely.

5431. **φροντίζω phrŏntizō**, *fron-tid'-zo;* from a der. of 5424; to *exercise thought*, i.e. *be anxious:*—be careful.

5432. **φρουρέω phrŏurĕō**, *froo-reh'-o;* from a comp. of 4253 and 3708; *to be a watcher in advance*, i.e. to *mount guard* as a sentinel (*post spies* at gates); fig. to *hem in, protect:*—keep (with a garrison). Comp. 5083.

5433. **φρυάσσω phruassō**, *froo-as'-so;* akin to 1032, 1031; to *snort* (as a spirited horse), i.e. (fig.) to *make a tumult:*—rage.

5434. **φρύγανον phruganŏn**, *froo'-gan-on;* neut. of a presumed der. of **φρύγω phrugō** (to *roast* or *parch;* akin to the base of 5395); something *desiccated*, i.e. a dry *twig:*—stick.

5435. **Φρυγία Phrugia**, *froog-ee'-ah;* prob. of for. or.; *Phrygia*, a region of Asia Minor:—Phrygia.

5436. **Φύγελλος Phugĕllŏs**, *foog'-el-los;* prob. from 5343; *fugitive; Phygellus*, an apostate Chr.:—Phygellus.

5437. **φυγή phugē**, *foog-ay';* from 5343; a *fleeing*, i.e. *escape:*—flight.

5438. **φυλακή phulakē**, *foo-lak-ay';* from 5442; a *guarding* or (concr. *guard*), the act, the person; fig. the place, the condition, or (spec.) the time (as a division of day or night), lit. or fig.:—cage, hold, (im-) prison (-ment), ward, watch.

5439. **φυλακίζω phulakizō**, *foo-lak-id'-zo;* from 5441; to *incarcerate:*—imprison.

5440. **φυλακτήριον phulaktēriŏn**, *foo-lak-tay'-ree-on;* neut. of a der. of 5442; a *guard-case*, i.e. "*phylactery*" for wearing slips of Scripture texts:—phylactery.

5441. **φύλαξ phulax**, *foo'-lax;* from 5442; a *watcher* or *sentry:*—keeper.

5442. **φυλάσσω phulassō**, *foo-las'-so;* prob. from 5443 through the idea of *isolation;* to *watch*, i.e.

be on guard (lit. or fig.); by impl. to *preserve, obey, avoid:*—beware, keep (self), observe, save. Comp. *5083*.

5443. **φυλή phulē**, *foo-lay';* from *5453* (comp. *5444*); an *offshoot*, i.e. *race* or *clan:*—kindred, tribe.

5444. **φύλλον phullŏn**, *fool'-lon;* from the same as *5443*; a *sprout*, i.e. *leaf:*—leaf.

5445. **φύραμα phurama**, *foo'-ram-ah;* from a prol. form of **φύρω phurō** (to *mix* a liquid with a solid; perh. akin to *5453* through the idea of *swelling* in bulk), mean to *knead;* a *mass* of dough:—lump.

5446. **φυσικός phusikŏs**, *foo-see-kos';* from *5449*; "*physical*", i.e. (by impl.) *instinctive:*—natural. Comp. *5591*.

5447. **φυσικῶς phusikōs**, *foo-see-koce';* adv. from *5446*; "*physically*", i.e. (by impl.) *instinctively:*—naturally.

5448. **φυσιόω phusiŏō**, *foo-see-ŏ'-o;* from *5449* in the prim. sense of *blowing;* to *inflate*, i.e. (fig.) *make proud* (*haughty*):—puff up.

5449. **φύσις phusis**, *foo'-sis;* from *5453; growth* (by *germination* or *expansion*), i.e. (by impl.) natural *production* (lineal *descent*); by extens. a *genus* or *sort;* fig. native *disposition, constitution* or *usage:*—([man-]) kind, nature ([-al]).

5450. **φυσίωσις phusiōsis**, *foo-see'-o-sis;* from *5448; inflation*, i.e. (fig.) *haughtiness:*—swelling.

5451. **φυτεία phutĕia**, *foo-ti'-ah;* from *5452;* trans-*planting*, i.e. (concr.) a *shrub* or *vegetable:*—plant.

5452. **φυτεύω phutĕuō**, *foot-yoo'-o;* from a der. of *5453;* to *set out* in the earth, i.e. *implant;* fig. to *instil* doctrine:—plant.

5453. **φύω phuō**, *foo'-o;* a prim. verb; prob. orig. to "*puff*" or *blow*, i.e. to *swell* up; but only used in the impl. sense, to *germinate* or *grow* (*sprout, produce*), lit. or fig.:—spring (up).

5454. **φωλεός phōlĕŏs**, *fo-leh-os';* of uncert. der.; a *burrow* or *lurking-place:*—hole.

5455. **φωνέω phōnĕō**, *fo-neh'-o;* from *5456;* to emit a *sound* (animal, human or instrumental); by impl. to *address* in words or by name, also in imitation:—call (for), crow, cry.

5456. **φωνή phōnē**, *fo-nay';* prob. akin to *5316* through the idea of *disclosure;* a *tone* (articulate, bestial or artificial); by impl. an *address* (for any purpose), *saying* or *language:*—noise, sound, voice.

5457. **φῶς phōs**, *foce;* from an obsol. **φάω phaō** (to *shine* or make *manifest*, espec. by *rays;* comp. *5316, 5346*); *luminousness* (in the widest application, nat. or artificial, abstr. or concr., lit. or fig.):—fire, light.

5458. **φωστήρ phōstēr**, *foce-tare';* from *5457:* an *illuminator*, i.e. (concr.) a *luminary*, or (abstr.) *brilliancy:*—light.

5459. **φωσφόρος phōsphŏrŏs**, *foce-for'-os;* from *5457* and *5342; light-bearing* ("phosphorus"), i.e. (spec.) the *morning-star* (fig.):—day star.

5460. **φωτεινός phōtĕinŏs**, *fo-ti-nos';* from *5457; lustrous*, i.e. *transparent* or *well-illuminated* (fig.):—bright, full of light.

5461. **φωτίζω phōtizō**, *fo-tid'-zo;* from *5457;* to *shed rays*, i.e. to *shine* or (trans.) to *brighten* up (lit. or fig.):—enlighten, illuminate, (bring to, give) light, make to see.

5462. **φωτισμός phōtismŏs**, *fo-tis-mos';* from *5461; illumination* (fig.):—light.

X

5463. **χαίρω chairō**, *khah'-ee-ro;* a prim. verb; to be "*cheer*"*ful*, i.e. calmly *happy* or well-off; impers. espec. as salutation (on meeting or parting), *be well:*—farewell, be glad, God speed, greeting, hail, joy (-fully), rejoice.

5464. **χάλαζα chalaza**, *khal'-ad-zah;* prob. from *5465; hail:*—hail.

5465. **χαλάω chalaō**, *khal-ah'-o;* from the base of *5490;* to *lower* (as into a *void*):—let down, strike.

5466. **Χαλδαῖος Chaldaiŏs**, *khal-dah'-yos;* prob. of Heb. or. [3778]; a *Chaldæan* (i.e. *Kasdi*), or native of the region of the lower Euphrates:—Chaldæan.

5467. **χαλεπός chalĕpŏs**, *khal-ep-os';* perh. from *5465* through the idea of *reducing* the strength; *difficult*, i.e. *dangerous*, or (by impl.) *furious:*—fierce, perilous.

5468. **χαλιναγωγέω chalinagōgĕō**, *khal-in-ag-ogue-eh'-o;* from a comp. of *5469* and the redupl. form of *71;* to be a *bit-leader*, i.e. to *curb* (fig.):—bridle.

5469. **χαλινός chalinŏs**, *khal-ee-nos';* from *5465;* a *curb* or *head-stall* (as *curbing* the spirit):—bit, bridle.

5470. **χάλκεος chalkĕŏs**, *khal'-keh-os;* from *5475; coppery:*—brass.

5471. **χαλκεύς chalkĕus**, *khalk-yooce';* from *5475;* a *copper-worker* or *brazier:*—coppersmith.

5472. **χαλκηδών chalkēdōn**, *khal-kay-dohn';* from *5475* and perh. *1491; copper-like*, i.e. "*chalcedony*":—chalcedony.

5473. **χαλκίον chalkiŏn**, *khal-kee'-on;* dimin. from *5475;* a *copper dish:*—brazen vessel.

5474. **χαλκολίβανον chalkŏlibanŏn**, *khal-kol-ib'-an-on;* neut. of a comp. of *5475* and *3030* (in the impl. mean. of *whiteness* or *brilliancy*); *burnished copper*, an alloy of copper (or gold) and silver having a brilliant lustre:—fine brass.

5475. **χαλκός chalkŏs**, *khal-kos';* perh. from *5465* through the idea of *hollowing* out as a vessel (this metal being chiefly used for that purpose); *copper* (the substance, or some implement or coin made of it):—brass, money.

5476. **χαμαί chamai**, *kham-ah'ee;* adv. perh. from the base of *5490* through the idea of a *fissure* in the soil; *earthward*, i.e. *prostrate:*—on (to) the ground.

5477. **Χαναάν Chanaan**, *khan-ah-an';* of Heb. or. [3667]; *Chanaan* (i.e. *Kenaan*), the early name of Pal.:—Chanaan.

5478. **Χαναναῖος Chananaiŏs**, *khan-ah-an-ah'-yos;* from *5477;* a *Chanaanæan* (i.e. *Kenaanite*), or native of gentile Pal.:—of Canaan.

5479. **χαρά chara**, *khar-ah';* from *5463; cheerfulness*, i.e. calm *delight:*—gladness, × greatly, (× be exceeding) joy (-ful, -fully, -fulness, -ous).

5480. **χάραγμα charagma**, *khar'-ag-mah;* from the same as *5482;* a *scratch* or *etching*, i.e. *stamp* (as a *badge* of servitude), or *sculptured* figure (*statue*):—graven, mark.

5481. **χαρακτήρ charaktēr**, *khar-ak-tare';* from the same as *5482;* a *graver* (the tool or the person), i.e. (by impl.) *engraving* (["*character*"], the *figure* stamped, i.e. an exact *copy* or [fig.] *representation*):—express image.

5482. **χάραξ charax**, *khar'-ax;* from **χαράσσω charassō** (to *sharpen* to a point; akin to *1125* through the idea of *scratching*); a *stake*, i.e. (by impl.) a *palisade* or *rampart* (military *mound* for circumvallation in a siege):—trench.

5483. **χαρίζομαι charizŏmai**, *khar-id'-zom-ahee;* mid. from *5485;* to grant as a *favor*, i.e. gratuitously, in kindness, pardon or rescue:—deliver, (frankly) forgive, (freely) give, grant.

5484. **χάριν charin**, *khar'-in;* acc. of *5485* as prep.; through *favor* of, i.e. *on account* of:—be-(for) cause of, for sake of, + . . . fore, × reproachfully.

5485. **χάρις charis**, *khar'-ece;* from *5463; graciousness* (as *gratifying*), of manner or act (abstr. or concr.; lit., fig. or spiritual: espec. the divine influence upon the heart, and its reflection in the life; including *gratitude*):—acceptable, benefit, favour, gift, grace (-ious), joy liberality, pleasure, thank (-s, -worthy).

5486. **χάρισμα charisma**, *khar'-is-mah;* from *5483;* a (divine) *gratuity*, i.e. *deliverance* (from danger or passion); (spec.) a (spiritual) *endowment*, i.e. (subj.) religious *qualification*, or (obj.) miraculous *faculty:*—(free) gift.

5487. **χαριτόω charitŏō**, *khar-ee-tŏ'-o;* from *5485;* to *grace*, i.e. indue with special *honor:*—make accepted. be highly favoured.

5488. **Χαῤῥάν Charrhan**, *khar-hran';* of Heb. or. [2771]; *Charrhan* (i.e. *Charan*), a place in Mesopotamia:—Charran.

5489. **χάρτης chartēs**, *khar'-tace;* from the same as *5482;* a *sheet* ("chart") of writing-material (as to be *scribbled* over):—paper.

5490. **χάσμα chasma**, *khas'-mah;* from a form of an obsol. prim. **χάω chaō** (to "*gape*" or "*yawn*"); a "*chasm*" or *vacancy* (impassable *interval*):—gulf.

5491. **χεῖλος chĕilŏs**, *khi'-los;* from a form of the same as *5490;* a *lip* (as a *pouring* place); fig. a *margin* (of water):—lip, shore.

5492. **χειμάζω chĕimazō**, *khi-mad'-zo;* from the same as *5494;* to *storm*, i.e. (pass.) to *labor under a gale:*—be tossed with tempest.

5493. **χείμαρρος chĕimarrhŏs**, *khi'-mar-hros;* from the base of *5494* and *4482;* a *storm-runlet*, i.e. *winter-torrent:*—brook.

5494. **χειμών chĕimōn**, *khi-mone';* from a der. of **χέω chĕō** (to *pour;* akin to the base of *5490* through the idea of a *channel*), mean. a *storm* (as *pouring* rain); by impl. the *rainy* season, i.e. *winter:*—tempest, foul weather, winter.

5495. **χείρ chĕir**, *khire;* perh. from the base of *5494* in the sense of its congener the base of *5490* (through the idea of *hollowness* for grasping); the *hand* (lit. or fig. [*power*]; espec. [by Heb.] a *means* or *instrument*):—hand.

5496. **χειραγωγέω chĕiragōgĕō**, *khi-rag-ogue-eh'-o;* from *5497;* to be a *hand-leader*, i.e. to *guide* (a blind person):—lead by the hand.

5497. **χειραγωγός chĕiragōgŏs**, *khi-rag-o-gos';* from *5495* and a redupl. form of *71;* a *hand-leader*, i.e. personal *conductor* (of a blind person):—some to lead by the hand.

5498. **χειρόγραφον chĕirŏgraphŏn**, *khi-rog'-raf-on;* neut. of a comp. of *5495* and *1125;* something *hand-written* ("*chirograph*"), i.e. a *manuscript* (spec. a legal *document* or *bond* [fig.]):—handwriting.

5499. **χειροποίητος chĕirŏpŏiētŏs**, *khi-rop-oy'-ay-tos;* from *5495* and a der. of *4160; manufactured*, i.e. *of human construction:*—made by (make with) hands.

5500. **χειροτονέω chĕirŏtŏnĕō**, *khi-rot-on-eh'-o;* from a comp. of *5495* and **τείνω tĕinō** (to *stretch*); to be a *hand-reacher* or *voter* (by raising the hand), i.e. (gen.) to *select* or *appoint:*—choose, ordain.

5501. **χείρων chĕirōn**, *khi'-rone;* irreg. comp. of *2556;* from an obsol. equiv. **χέρης chĕrēs** (of uncert. der.); *more evil* or *aggravated* (phys., ment. or mor.):—sorer, worse.

5502. **χερουβίμ chĕrŏubim**, *kher-oo-beem';* plur. of Heb. or. [3742]; "*cherubim*" (i.e. *cherubs* or *kerubim*):—cherubims.

5503. **χήρα chēra**, *khay'-rah;* fem. of a presumed der. appar. from the base of *5490* through the idea of *deficiency;* a *widow* (as *lacking* a husband), lit. or fig.:—widow.

5504. **χθές chthĕs**, *khthes;* of uncert. der.; "*yesterday*"; by extens. *in time past* or *hitherto:*—yesterday.

5505. **χιλιάς chilias**, *khil-ee-as';* from *5507;* one *thousand* ("*chiliad*"):—thousand.

5506. **χιλίαρχος chiliarchŏs**, *khil-ee'-ar-khos;* from *5507* and *757;* the *commander of a thousand* soldiers ("*chiliarch*"), i.e. *colonel:*—(chief, high) captain.

5507. **χίλιοι chiliŏi**, *khil'-ee-oy;* plur. of uncert. affin.; a *thousand:*—thousand.

5508. **Χίος Chiŏs**, *khee'-os;* of uncert. der.; *Chios*, an island in the Mediterranean:—Chios.

5509. **χιτών chitōn**, *khee-tone';* of for. or. [3801]; a *tunic* or *shirt:*—clothes, coat, garment.

5510. **χιών chiōn**, *khee-one';* perh. akin to the base of *5490* (*5465*) or *5494* (as *descending* or *empty*); *snow:*—snow.

5511. **χλαμύς chlamus**, *khlam-ooce';* of uncert. der.; a military *cloak:*—robe.

5512. χλευάζω **chlĕuazō**, *khlyoo-ad'-zo;* from a der. prob. of *5491;* to *throw out* the *lip*, i.e. *jeer* at:—mock.

5513. χλιαρός **chliarŏs**, *khlee-ar-os';* from χλίω **chliō** (to *warm*); *tepid:*—lukewarm.

5514. Χλόη **Chlŏē**, *khlŏ'-ay;* fem. of appar. a prim. word; "*green*"; *Chloë*, a Chr. female:—Chloe.

5515. χλωρός **chlōrŏs**, *khlo-ros';* from the same as *5514; greenish*, i.e. *verdant, dun-colored:*—green, pale.

5516. χξϛ **chi xi stigma**, *khee xee stig'-ma;* the 22d, 14th and an obsol. letter (*4742* as a *cross*) of the Greek alphabet (intermediate between the 5th and 6th), used as numbers; denoting respectively 600, 60 and 6; 666 as a numeral:—six hundred threescore and six.

5517. χοϊκός **chŏïkŏs**, *khŏ-ik-os';* from *5522; dusty* or *dirty* (*soil*-like), i.e. (by impl.) *terrene:*—earthy.

5518. χοῖνιξ **chŏinix**, *khoy'-nix;* of uncert. der.; a *chœnix* or cert. dry measure:—measure.

5519. χοῖρος **chŏirŏs**, *khoy'-ros;* of uncert. der.; a *hog:*—swine.

5520. χολάω **chŏlaō**, *khol-ah'-o;* from *5521;* to *be bilious*, i.e. (by impl.) *irritable* (*enraged*, "*choleric*"):—be angry.

5521. χολή **chŏlē**, *khol-ay';* fem. of an equiv. perh. akin to the same as *5514* (from the *greenish* hue); "*gall*" or *bile*, i.e. (by anal.) *poison* or an *anodyne* (wormwood, poppy, etc.):—gall.

5522. χόος **chŏŏs**, *khŏ'-os;* from the base of *5494;* a *heap* (as *poured* out), i.e. *rubbish;* loose *dirt:*—dust.

5523. Χοραζίν **Chŏrazin**, *khor-ad-zin';* of uncert. der.; *Chorazin*, a place in Pal.:—Chorazin.

5524. χορηγέω **chŏrēgĕō**, *khor-ayg-eh'-o;* from a comp. of *5525* and *71;* to be a *dance-leader*, i.e. (gen.) to *furnish:*—give, minister.

5525. χορός **chŏrŏs**, *khor-os';* of uncert. der.; a *ring*, i.e. round *dance* ("*choir*"):—dancing.

5526. χορτάζω **chŏrtazō**, *khor-tad'-zo;* from *5528;* to *fodder*, i.e. (gen.) to *gorge* (*supply food* in abundance):—feed, fill, satisfy.

5527. χόρτασμα **chŏrtasma**, *khor'-tas-mah;* from *5526; forage*, i.e. *food:*—sustenance.

5528. χόρτος **chŏrtŏs**, *khor'-tos;* appar. a prim. word; a "*court*" or "*garden*", i.e. (by impl. of *pasture*) *herbage* or *vegetation:*—blade, grass, hay.

5529. Χουζᾶς **Chŏuzas**, *khood-zas';* of uncert. or.; *Chuzas*, an officer of Herod:—Chuza.

5530. χράομαι **chraŏmai**, *khrah'-om-ahee;* mid. of a prim. verb (perh. rather from *5495*, to *handle*); to *furnish* what is needed; (give an *oracle*, "*graze*" [touch slightly], *light* upon, etc.), i.e. (by impl.) to *employ* or (by extens.) to *act towards* one in a *given* manner:—entreat, use. Comp. *5531, 5534*.

5531. χράω **chraō**, *khrah'-o;* prob. the same as the base of *5530;* to *loan:*—lend.

5532. χρεία **chrĕia**, *khri'-ah;* from the base of *5530* or *5534; employment*, i.e. an *affair;* also (by impl.) *occasion, demand, requirement* or *destitution:*—business, lack, necessary (-ity), need (-ful), use, want.

5533. χρεωφειλέτης **chrĕōphĕilĕtēs**, *khreh-o-fi-let'-ace;* from a der. of *5531* and *3781;* a *loan-ower*, i.e. *indebted* person:—debtor.

5534. χρή **chrē**, *khray;* third pers. sing. of the same as *5530* or *5531* used impers.; it *needs* (*must* or *should*) be:—ought.

5535. χρῄζω **chrēizō**, *khrade'-zo;* from *5532;* to *make* (i.e. *have*) *necessity*, i.e. *be in want* of:—(have) need.

5536. χρῆμα **chrēma**, *khray'-mah;* something *useful* or *needed*, i.e. *wealth, price:*—money, riches.

5537. χρηματίζω **chrēmatizō**, *khray-mat-id'-zo;* from *5536;* to *utter an oracle* (comp. the orig. sense of *5530*), i.e. divinely *intimate;* by impl. (comp. the secular sense of *5532*) to constitute a *firm* for business, i.e. (gen.) *bear* as a *title:*—be called, be admonished (warned) of God, reveal, speak.

5538. χρηματισμός **chrēmatismŏs**, *khray-mat-is-mos';* from *5537;* a divine *response* or *revelation:*—answer of God.

5539. χρήσιμος **chrēsimŏs**, *khray'-see-mos;* from *5540; serviceable:*—profit.

5540. χρῆσις **chrēsis**, *khray'-sis;* from *5530; employment*, i.e. (spec.) sexual *intercourse* (as an *occupation* of the body):—use.

5541. χρηστεύομαι **chrēstĕuŏmai**, *khraste-yoo'-om-ahee;* mid. from *5543;* to *show oneself useful*, i.e. *act benevolently:*—be kind.

5542. χρηστολογία **chrēstŏlŏgia**, *khrase-tol-og-ee'-ah;* from a comp. of *5543* and *3004; fair speech*, i.e. *plausibility:*—good words.

5543. χρηστός **chrēstŏs**, *khrase-tos';* from *5530; employed*, i.e. (by impl.) *useful* (in manner or morals):—better, easy, good (-ness), gracious, kind.

5544. χρηστότης **chrēstŏtēs**, *khray-stot'-ace;* from *5543; usefulness*, i.e. mor. *excellence* (in character or demeanor):—gentleness, good (-ness), kindness.

5545. χρίσμα **chrisma**, *khris'-mah;* from *5548;* an *unguent* or *smearing*, i.e. (fig.) the spec. *endowment* ("chrism") of the Holy Spirit:—anointing, unction.

5546. Χριστιανός **Christianŏs**, *khris-tee-an-os';* from *5547;* a *Christian*, i.e. follower of Christ:—Christian.

5547. Χριστός **Christŏs**, *khris-tos';* from *5548; anointed*, i.e. the *Messiah*, an epithet of Jesus:—Christ.

5548. χρίω **chriō**, *khree'-o;* prob. akin to *5530* through the idea of *contact;* to *smear* or *rub* with oil, i.e. (by impl.) to *consecrate* to an office or religious service:—anoint.

5549. χρονίζω **chrŏnizō**, *khron-id'-zo;* from *5550;* to *take time*, i.e. *linger:*—delay, tarry.

5550. χρόνος **chrŏnŏs**, *khron'-os;* of uncert. der.; a space of *time* (in gen., and thus prop. distinguished from *2540*, which designates a *fixed* or special occasion; and from *165*, which denotes a particular *period*) or *interval;* by extens. an individ. *opportunity;* by impl. *delay:*— + years old, season, space, (× often-) time (-s), (a) while.

5551. χρονοτριβέω **chrŏnŏtribĕō**, *khron-ot-rib-eh'-o;* from a presumed comp. of *5550* and the base of *5147;* to be a *time-wearer*, i.e. to *procrastinate* (*linger*):—spend time.

5552. χρύσεος **chrusĕŏs**, *khroo'-seh-os;* from *5557;* made *of gold:*—of gold, golden.

5553. χρυσίον **chrusiŏn**, *khroo-see'-on;* dimin. of *5557;* a *golden* article, i.e. gold plating, ornament, or coin:—gold.

5554. χρυσοδακτύλιος **chrusŏdaktuliŏs**, *khroo-sod-ak-too'-lee-os;* from *5557* and *1146; gold-ringed*, i.e. *wearing* a golden finger-ring or similar *jewelry:*—with a gold ring.

5555. χρυσόλιθος **chrusŏlithŏs**, *khroo-sol'-ee-thos;* from *5557* and *3037; gold-stone*, i.e. a *yellow gem* ("*chrysolite*"):—chrysolite.

5556. χρυσόπρασος **chrusŏprasŏs**, *khroo-sop'-ras-os;* from *5557* and πράσον **prasŏn** (a *leek*); a *greenish-yellow* gem ("*chrysoprase*"):—chrysoprase.

5557. χρυσός **chrusŏs**, *khroo-sos';* perh. from the base of *5530* (through the idea of the *utility* of the metal); *gold;* by extens. a *golden* article, as an ornament or coin:—gold.

5558. χρυσόω **chrusŏō**, *khroo-sŏ'-o;* from *5557;* to *gild*, i.e. *bespangle* with golden ornaments:—deck.

5559. χρώς **chrōs**, *khroce;* prob. akin to the base of *5530* through the idea of *handling;* the *body* (prop. its *surface* or *skin*):—body.

5560. χωλός **chōlŏs**, *kho-los';* appar. a prim. word; "*halt*", i.e. *limping:*—cripple, halt, lame.

5561. χώρα **chōra**, *kho'-rah;* fem. of a der. of the base of *5490* through the idea of *empty* expanse; *room*, i.e. a space of *territory* (more or less extensive; often includ. its inhab.):—coast, county, fields, ground, land, region. Comp. *5117*.

5562. χωρέω **chōrĕō**, *kho-reh'-o;* from *5561;* to *be in* (*give*) *space*, i.e. (intrans.) to *pass, enter*, or (trans.) to *hold, admit* (lit. or fig.):—come, contain, go, have place, (can, be room to) receive.

5563. χωρίζω **chōrizō**, *kho-rid'-zo;* from *5561;* to *place room* between, i.e. *part;* reflex. to *go away:*—depart, put asunder, separate.

5564. χωρίον **chōriŏn**, *kho-ree'-on;* dimin. of *5561;* a *spot* or *plot* of ground:—field, land, parcel of ground, place, possession.

5565. χωρίς **chōris**, *kho-rece';* adv. from *5561; at a space*, i.e. *separately* or *apart* from (often as prep.):—beside, by itself, without.

5566. χῶρος **chōrŏs**, *kho'-ros;* of Lat. or.; the *north-west* wind:—north west.

Ψ

5567. ψάλλω **psallō**, *psal'-lo;* prob. strengthened from ψάω **psaō** (to *rub* or *touch* the surface; comp. *5597*); to *twitch* or *twang*, i.e. to *play* on a stringed instrument (*celebrate* the divine worship *with music* and accompanying odes):—make melody, sing (psalms).

5568. ψαλμός **psalmŏs**, *psal-mos';* from *5567;* a set piece of *music*, i.e. a sacred *ode* (accompanied with the voice, harp or other instrument; a "*psalm*"); collect. the book of the *Psalms:*—psalm. Comp. *5603*.

5569. ψευδάδελφος **psĕudadĕlphŏs**, *psyoo-dad'-el-fos;* from *5571* and *80;* a *spurious brother*, i.e. *pretended associate:*—false brethren.

5570. ψευδαπόστολος **psĕudapŏstŏlŏs**, *psyoo-dap-os'-tol-os;* from *5571* and *652;* a *spurious apostle*, i.e. *pretended preacher:*—false teacher.

5571. ψευδής **psĕudēs**, *psyoo-dace';* from *5574; untrue*, i.e. *erroneous, deceitful, wicked:*—false, liar.

5572. ψευδοδιδάσκαλος **psĕudŏdidaskalŏs**, *psyoo-dod-id-as'-kal-os;* from *5571* and *1320;* a *spurious teacher*, i.e. *propagator* of *erroneous* Chr. *doctrine:*—false teacher.

5573. ψευδολόγος **psĕudŏlŏgŏs**, *psyoo-dol-og'-os;* from *5571* and *3004; mendacious*, i.e. *promulgating erroneous* Chr. *doctrine:*—speaking lies.

5574. ψεύδομαι **psĕudŏmai**, *psyoo'-dom-ahee;* mid. of an appar. prim. verb; to *utter an untruth* or attempt to *deceive* by falsehood:—falsely, lie.

5575. ψευδομάρτυρ **psĕudŏmartur**, *psyoo-dom-ar'-toor;* from *5571* and a kindred form of *3144;* a *spurious witness*, i.e. *bearer* of *untrue testimony:*—false witness.

5576. ψευδομαρτυρέω **psĕudŏmarturĕō**, *psyoo-dom-ar-too-reh'-o;* from *5575;* to *be an untrue testifier*, i.e. offer *falsehood in evidence:*—be a false witness.

5577. ψευδομαρτυρία **psĕudŏmarturia**, *psyoo-dom-ar-too-ree'-ah;* from *5575; untrue testimony:*—false witness.

5578. ψευδοπροφήτης **psĕudŏprŏphētēs**, *psyoo-dop-rof-ay'-tace;* from *5571* and *4396;* a *spurious prophet*, i.e. *pretended foreteller* or religious *impostor:*—false prophet.

5579. ψεῦδος **psĕudŏs**, *psyoo'-dos;* from *5574;* a *falsehood:*—lie, lying.

5580. ψευδόχριστος **psĕudŏchristŏs**, *psyoo-dokh'-ris-tos;* from *5571* and *5547;* a *spurious Messiah:*—false Christ.

5581. ψευδώνυμος **psĕudōnumŏs**, *psyoo-do'-noo-mos;* from *5571* and *3686; untruly named:*—falsely so called.

5582. ψεῦσμα **psĕusma**, *psyoos'-mah;* from *5574;* a *fabrication*, i.e. *falsehood:*—lie.

5583. ψεύστης **psĕustēs**, *psyoos-tace';* from *5574;* a *falsifier:*—liar.

5584. ψηλαφάω **psēlaphaō**, *psay-laf-ah'-o;* from the base of *5567* (comp. *5586*); to *manipulate*, i.e. *verify* by contact; fig. to *search* for:—feel after, handle, touch.

5585. ψηφίζω **psēphizō**, *psay-fid'-zo;* from *5586;* to *use pebbles* in enumeration, i.e. (gen.) to *compute:*—count.

5586. ψῆφος **psēphŏs**, *psay'-fos;* from the same as *5584;* a *pebble* (as worn smooth by *handling*), i.e.

(by impl. of use as a *counter* or *ballot*) a *verdict* (of acquittal) or *ticket* (of admission); a *vote*:—stone, voice.

5587. ψιθυρισμός **psithurismŏs**, *psith-oo-ris-mos'*; from a der. of ψίθος **psithŏs** (a *whisper*; by impl. a *slander*; prob. akin to 5574); *whispering*, i.e. secret *detraction*:—whispering.

5588. ψιθυριστής **psithuristēs**, *psith-oo-ris-tace'*; from the same as 5587; a secret *calumniator*:—whisperer.

5589. ψιχίον **psichiŏn**, *psikh-ee'-on*; dimin. from a der. of the base of 5567 (mean. a *crumb*); a *little bit* or *morsel*:—crumb.

5590. ψυχή **psuchē**, *psoo-khay'*; from 5594; *breath*, i.e. (by impl.) *spirit*, abstr. or concr. (the *animal* sentient principle only; thus distinguished on the one hand from 4151, which is the rational and immortal *soul*; and on the other from 2222, which is mere *vitality*, even of plants: these terms thus exactly correspond respectively to the Heb. 5315, 7307 and 2416):—heart (+ -ily), life, mind, soul, + us, + you.

5591. ψυχικός **psuchikŏs**, *psoo-khee-kos'*; from 5590; *sensitive*, i.e. *animate* (in distinction on the one hand from 4152, which is the higher or *renovated* nature; and on the other from 5446, which is the lower or *bestial* nature):—natural, sensual.

5592. ψύχος **psuchŏs**, *psoo'-khos*; from 5594; *coolness*:—cold.

5593. ψυχρός **psuchrŏs**, *psoo-chros'*; from 5592; *chilly* (lit. or fig.):—cold.

5594. ψύχω **psuchō**, *psoo'-kho*; a prim. verb; to *breathe* (*voluntarily* but *gently*; thus differing on the one hand from 4154, which denotes prop. a *forcible* respiration; and on the other from the base of 109, which refers prop. to an inanimate *breeze*), i.e. (by impl. of reduction of temperature by evaporation) to *chill* (fig.):—wax cold.

5595. ψωμίζω **psōmizō**, *pso-mid'-zo*; from the base of 5596; to *supply* with *bits*, i.e. (gen.) to *nourish*:—(bestow to) feed.

5596. ψωμίον **psōmiŏn**, *pso-mee'-on*; dim. from a der. of the base of 5597; a *crumb* or *morsel* (as if *rubbed* off), i.e. a *mouthful*:—sop.

5597. ψώχω **psōchō**, *pso'-kho*; prol. from the same base as 5567; to *triturate*, i.e. (by anal.) to *rub* out (kernels from husks with the fingers or hand):—rub.

Ω

5598. Ω ō, i.e. ὦμεγα **ōmĕga**, *o'-meg-ah*; the last letter of the Gr. alphabet, i.e. (fig.) the *finality*:—Omega.

5599. ὦ ō, *o*; a prim. interj.; as a sign of the voc. *O*; as a note of exclamation, *oh*:—O.

5600. ὦ ō, *o*; includ. the oblique forms, as well as ἦς **ēs**, *ace*; ἦ ē, *ay*, etc.; the subjunctive of 1510; (*may*, *might*, *can*, *could*, *would*, *should*, *must*, etc.; also with 1487 and its comp., as well as with other particles) *be*:— + appear, are, (may, might, should) be, × have, is, + pass the flower of her age, should stand, were.

5601. Ὠβήδ **Obēd**, *o-bade'*; of Heb. or. [5744]; *Obed*, an Isr.:—Obed.

5602. ὧδε **hōdĕ**, *ho'-deh*; from an adv. form of 3592; *in this* same spot, i.e. *here* or *hither*:—here, hither, (in) this place, there.

5603. ᾠδή **ōidē**, *o-day'*; from 103; a *chant* or "*ode*" (the gen. term for any words sung; while 5215 denotes espec. a *religious* metrical composition, and 5568 still more spec. a *Heb.* cantillation):—song.

5604. ὠδίν **ōdin**, *o-deen'*; akin to 3601; a *pang* or *throe*, esp. of childbirth:—pain, sorrow, travail.

5605. ὠδίνω **ōdinō**, *o-dee'-no*; from 5604; to *experience* the *pains* of parturition (lit. or fig.):—travail in (birth).

5606. ὦμος **ōmŏs**, *o'-mos*; perh. from the alt. of 5342; the *shoulder* (as that on which burdens are *borne*):—shoulder.

5607. ὤν **ōn**, *oan*; includ. the fem.

οὖσα **ŏusa**, *oo'-sah*; and the neut.

ὄν **ŏn**, *on*; pres. part. of 1510; *being*:—be, come, have.

5608. ὠνέομαι **ōnĕŏmai**, *o-neh'-om-ahee*; mid. from an appar. prim. ὦνος **ōnŏs** (a *sum* or *price*); to *purchase* (synon. with the earlier 4092):—buy.

5609. ᾠόν **ōŏn**, *o-on'*; appar. a prim. word; an "*egg*":—egg.

5610. ὥρα **hōra**, *ho'-rah*; appar. a prim. word; an "*hour*" (lit. or fig.):—day, hour, instant, season, × short, [even-] tide, (high) time.

5611. ὡραῖος **hōraiŏs**, *ho-rah'-yos*; from 5610; *belonging* to the right *hour* or *season* (*timely*), i.e. (by impl.) *flourishing* (*beauteous* [fig.]):—beautiful.

5612. ὠρύομαι **ōruŏmai**, *o-roo'-om-ahee*; mid. of an appar. prim. verb; to "*roar*":—roar.

5613. ὡς **hōs**, *hoce*; prob. adv. of comp. from 3739; *which how*, i.e. *in that manner* (very variously used, as follows):—about, after (that), (according) as (it had been, it were), as soon (as), even as (like), for, how (greatly), like (as, unto), since, so (that), that, to wit, unto, when ([-soever]), while, × with all speed.

5614. ὡσαννά **hōsanna**, *ho-san-nah'*; of Heb. or. [3467 and 4994]; *oh save!*; *hosanna* (i.e. *hoshia-na*), an exclamation of adoration:—hosanna.

5615. ὡσαύτως **hōsautōs**, *ho-sow'-toce*; from 5613 and an adv. from 846; *as thus*, i.e. *in the same way*:—even so, likewise, after the same (in like) manner.

5616. ὡσεί **hōsĕi**, *ho-si'*; from 5613 and 1487; *as if*:—about, as (it had been, it were), like (as).

5617. Ὠσηέ **Hōsēĕ**, *ho-say-eh'*; of Heb. or. [1954]; *Hoseë* (i.e. *Hosheä*), an Isr.:—Osee.

5618. ὥσπερ **hōspĕr**, *hoce'-per*; from 5613 and 4007; *just as*, i.e. *exactly like*:—(even, like) as.

5619. ὡσπερεί **hōspĕrĕi**, *hoce-per-i'*; from 5618 and 1487; *just as if*, i.e. *as it were*:—as.

5620. ὥστε **hōstĕ**, *hoce'-teh*; from 5613 and 5037; *so too*, i.e. *thus therefore* (in various relations of *consecution*, as follow):—(insomuch) as, so that (then), (insomuch) that, therefore, to, wherefore.

5621. ὠτίον **ōtiŏn**, *o-tee'-on*; dimin. of 3775; an *earlet*, i.e. *one* of the ears, or perh. the *lobe* of the ear:—ear.

5622. ὠφέλεια **ōphĕlĕia**, *o-fel'-i-ah*; from a der. of the base of 5624; *usefulness*, i.e. *benefit*:—advantage, profit.

5623. ὠφελέω **ōphĕlĕō**, *o-fel-eh'-o*; from the same as 5622; to *be useful*, i.e. to *benefit*:—advantage, better, prevail, profit.

5624. ὠφέλιμος **ōphĕlimŏs**, *o-fel'-ee-mos*; from a form of 3786; *helpful* or *serviceable*, i.e. *advantageous*:—profit (-able).

VARIATIONS

IN THE NUMBERING OF VERSES IN THE GREEK AND ENGLISH NEW TESTAMENT.

English.	*Greek.*
Mark 13: 8 (last clause)	(first clauses) 9
Luke 22: 66 (last word)	(first word) 67
John 1: 38 (all after first clause)	39
39	40
40	41
41	42
42	43
John 1: 43	44
44	45
45	46
46	47
47	48
48	49
49	50
John 1: 50	51
51	52
Acts 4: 6 (last clause)	(in) 5
13: 33 (former half)	(latter half) 32
1 Pet 2: 8 (first two clauses)	(last two clauses) 7

Notes

Notes

Notes

Notes

Notes

Notes

Notes

Notes

Notes

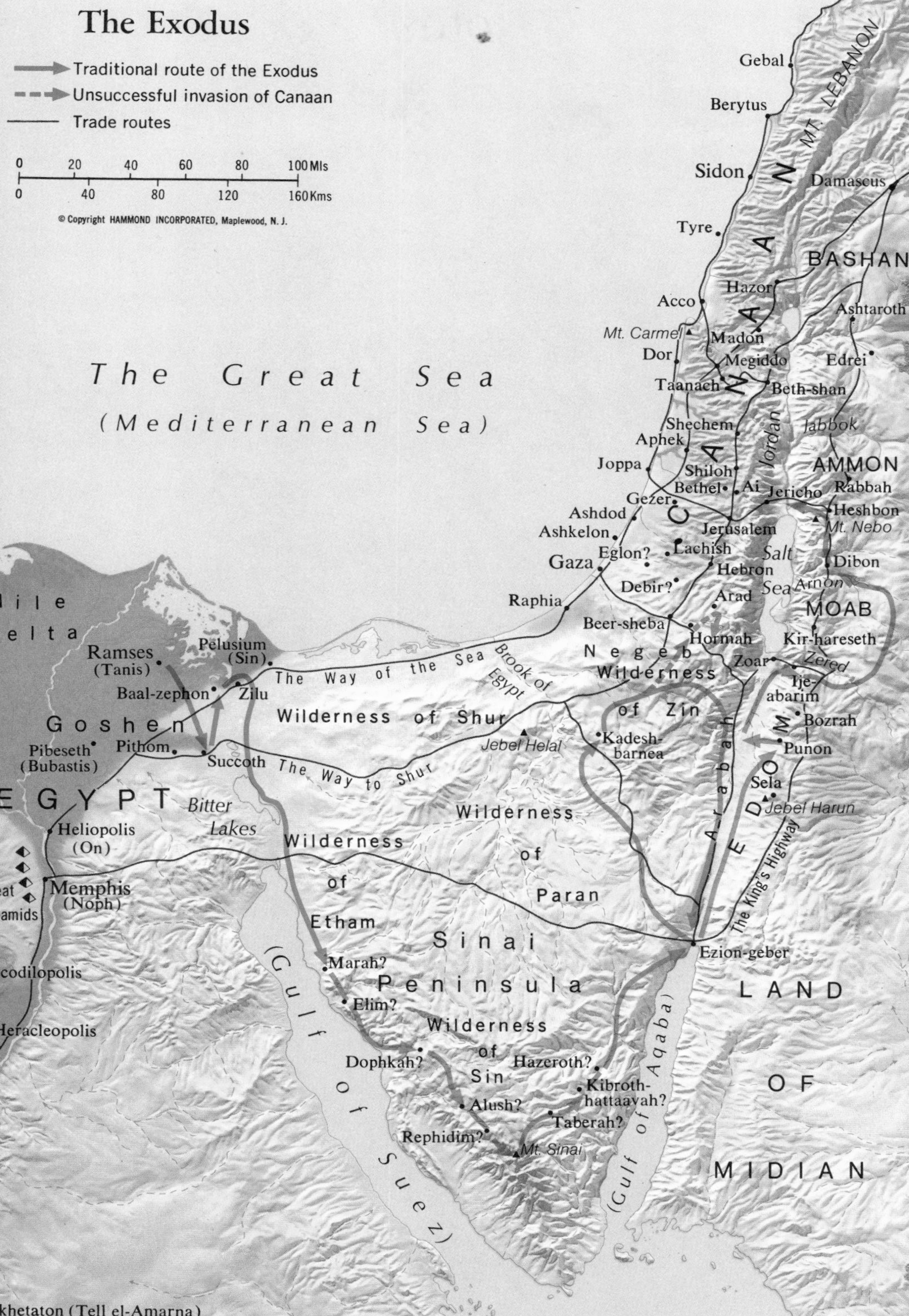

The Exodus
Traditional route of the Exodus
Unsuccessful invasion of Canaan
Trade routes
0 20 40 60 80 100 Mls
0 40 80 120 160 Kms
© Copyright HAMMOND INCORPORATED, Maplewood, N. J.
The Great Sea
(Mediterranean Sea)
Gebal
Berytus
MT. LEBANON
Sidon
Damascus
Tyre
CANAAN
BASHAN
Hazor
Acco
Ashtaroth
Mt. Carmel
Madon
Dor
Megiddo
Edrei
Taanach
Beth-shan
Shechem
Jabbok
Aphek
Jordan
Joppa
Shiloh
AMMON
Bethel
Ai
Jericho
Rabbah
Gezer
Heshbon
Ashdod
Jerusalem
Mt. Nebo
Ashkelon
Lachish
Salt Sea
Eglon?
Gaza
Hebron
Dibon
Debir?
Arnon
Raphia
Arad
MOAB
Beer-sheba
Hormah
Kir-hareseth
Pelusium (Sin)
Negeb
Zoar
Zered
Ramses (Tanis)
Brook of Egypt
Wilderness of Zin
Ije-abarim
Baal-zephon
Zilu
The Way of the Sea
Goshen
Wilderness of Shur
EDOM
Bozrah
Pibeseth (Bubastis)
Pithom
Jebel Helal
Kadesh-barnea
Punon
Succoth
The Way to Shur
Arabah
Sela
EGYPT
Bitter Lakes
Jebel Harun
Heliopolis (On)
Wilderness of Paran
The King's Highway
Wilderness of Etham
Memphis (Noph)
Sinai Peninsula
Ezion-geber
Marah?
LAND OF MIDIAN
Elim?
(Gulf of Suez)
Wilderness of Sin
Dophkah?
Hazeroth?
Kibroth-hattaavah?
Alush?
Taberah?
Rephidim?
Mt. Sinai
(Gulf of Aqaba)
Nile Delta
Heracleopolis
khetaton (Tell el-Amarna)
Red Sea

Early Israelite Settlement in Canaan
Area settled by Israelites
JUDAH Twelve Israelite tribes
Gezer Unconquered Canaanite city (according to Judges 1)
0 5 10 15 20 25 30 35 Mls
0 10 20 30 40 50 Kms
© Copyright HAMMOND INCORPORATED, Maplewood, N. J.
The Great Sea
SIDONIANS
MT. LEBANON
HIVITES
ARAMEANS
MT. HERMON
Sidon
Damascus
Ahlab
Tyre
Dan (Laish)
Beth-shemesh?
DAN
ASHER
NAPHTALI
Kedesh
Achzib
Hazor
Merom
Beth-anath?
Acco
Rehob
Aphek
Sea of Chinnereth
Bashan
ZEBULUN
Golan
Ashtaroth
Shimron
Mt. Tabor
Kishon
ISSACHAR
Edrei
Havvoth-jair
Dor
Megiddo
Jezreel
Ramoth-gilead
Taanach
Beth-shan
Ibleam
Jabesh-gilead
Plain of Sharon
Hepher
MANASSEH
Gilead
Tirzah
Mt. Ebal
Shechem
Succoth
Mt. Gerizim
Jordan
Jabbok
AMMON
Aphek
GAD
Shiloh
Joppa
EPHRAIM
Jazer
Rabbah
Bethel
Gath
Ai
Gilgal
Shaalbim
Gezer
BENJAMIN
Jericho
Gibeon
Sorek
DAN
Aijalon
Ekron
Heshbon
Bezer
Ashdod
Jerusalem
Mt. Nebo
Libnah
Beth-shemesh
Ashkelon
Adullam
REUBEN
Gath?
Beth-zur
Lachish
Salt Sea
Gaza
Eglon?
Hebron
PHILISTINES
Debir?
JUDAH
Aroer
Wilderness of Judah
Arnon
Gerar
Ziklag?
Arad
Besor
Beer-sheba
MOAB
Hormah
Kir-hareseth
SIMEON
Negeb
Zoar
Zered
Tamar
Arabah
EDOM

The Empire of David and Solomon

Boundary of the empire at its greatest extent

Territory conquered by David

Fortified places of Solomon

Copper mining centers

0 10 25 50 75 Mls

0 20 40 60 80 100 120 Kms

Hamath
Arvad
Kadesh
ARAM–
ZOBAH
Zedad
Lebo-hamath
Hazar-enan
Gebal
LEBANON
Berothai
Berytus
BETH–REHOB
PHOENICIA
Sidon
MT.
ARAM–
DAMASCUS
MT. HERMON
Damascus
Tyre
Abel
Dan
Kedesh
MAACAH
The Great Sea
(Mediterranean Sea)
Hazor
ARGOB
Acco
Cabul
Mt. Carmel
GESHUR
Ashtaroth
Dor
TOB
Edrei
Megiddo
Jezreel
Taanach
Mt. Gilboa
Beth-shan
Ramoth-gilead
Salecah
Hepher
Jordan
Shechem
Mahanaim
Succoth
Joppa
ISRAEL
Gezer
Beth-horon
Rabbah
PHILISTIA
Bethel
AMMON
Gibeah
Jericho
Ashdod
Jerusalem
Heshbon
Beth-shemesh
Ashkelon
Gath?
Medeba
JUDAH
Hebron
Gaza
Lachish
Salt Sea
PHILISTIA
Ziklag ?
Aroer
Gerar
Raphia
Beer-sheba
Arad
MOAB
Kir-hareseth
Tamar
AMALEK
Bozrah
Kadesh-barnea
Punon
River of Egypt
Arabah
EDOM
Sela
Sinai
Ezion-geber

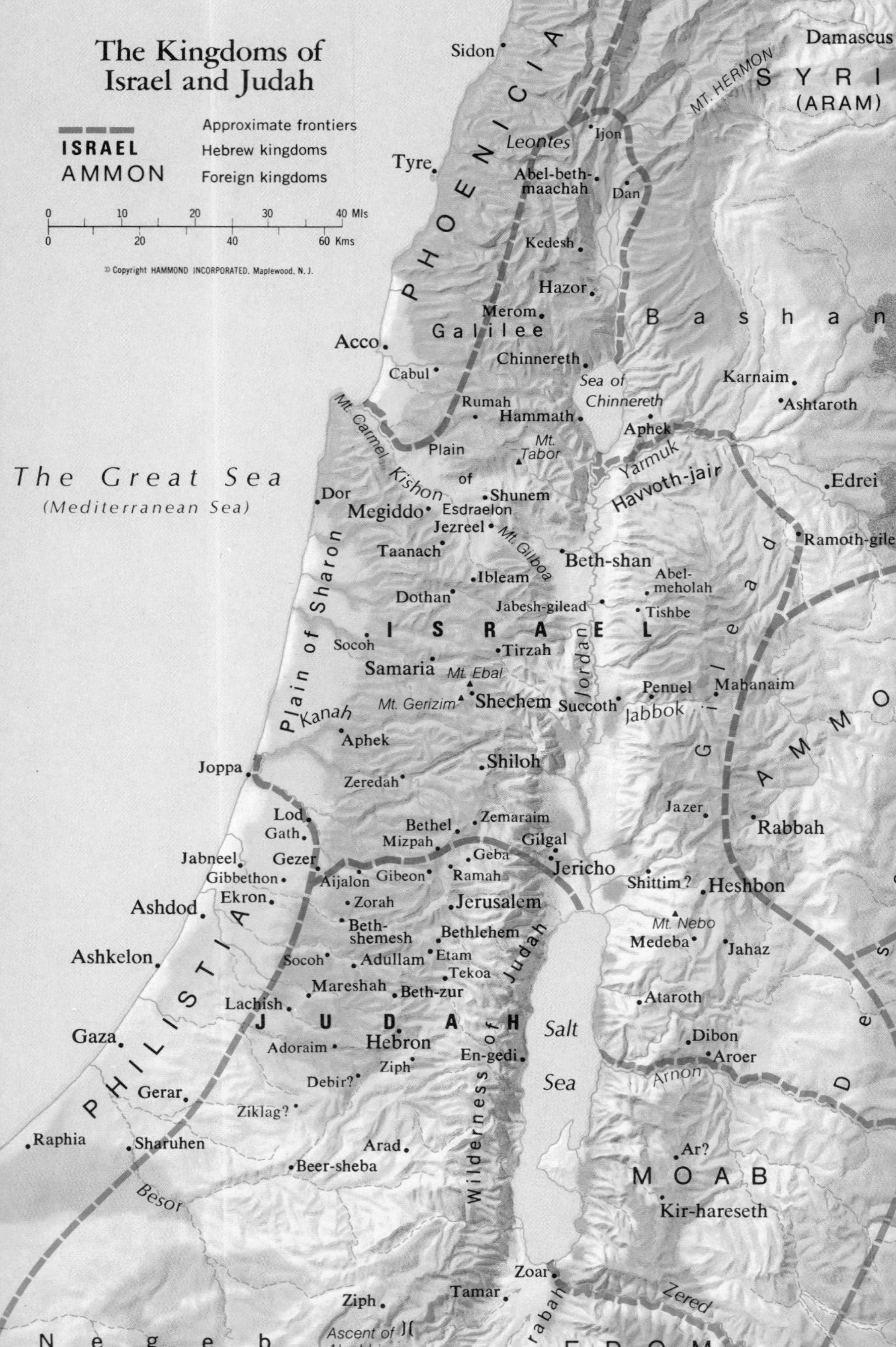

The Kingdoms of Israel and Judah
ISRAEL Hebrew kingdoms
AMMON Foreign kingdoms
Approximate frontiers
0 10 20 30 40 Mls
0 20 40 60 Kms
© Copyright HAMMOND INCORPORATED, Maplewood, N. J.
The Great Sea
(Mediterranean Sea)
Sidon
Damascus
SYRIA
(ARAM)
MT. HERMON
PHOENICIA
Leontes
Ijon
Tyre
Abel-beth-maachah
Dan
Kedesh
Hazor
Bashan
Merom
Galilee
Acco
Chinnereth
Cabul
Sea of Chinnereth
Karnaim
Ashtaroth
Rumah
Hammath
Aphek
Mt. Carmel
Plain of Esdraelon
Mt. Tabor
Yarmuk
Kishon
Havvoth-jair
Edrei
Dor
Shunem
Megiddo
Jezreel
Mt. Gilboa
Ramoth-gilea
Taanach
Beth-shan
Ibleam
Abel-meholah
Dothan
Jabesh-gilead
Tishbe
ISRAEL
Socoh
Tirzah
Samaria
Mt. Ebal
Plain of Sharon
Jordan
Gilead
Penuel
Mahanaim
Mt. Gerizim
Shechem
Succoth
Jabbok
Kanah
Aphek
AMMON
Shiloh
Joppa
Zeredah
Jazer
Rabbah
Lod
Bethel
Zemaraim
Gath
Mizpah
Gilgal
Jabneel
Gezer
Geba
Jericho
Gibbethon
Aijalon
Gibeon
Ramah
Shittim?
Heshbon
Ekron
Zorah
Jerusalem
Ashdod
Beth-shemesh
Bethlehem
Mt. Nebo
Medeba
Jahaz
Ashkelon
Socoh
Adullam
Etam
Tekoa
PHILISTIA
Mareshah
Beth-zur
Lachish
Ataroth
JUDAH
Salt Sea
Gaza
Adoraim
Hebron
Dibon
En-gedi
Aroer
Ziph
Arnon
Debir?
Gerar
Wilderness of Judah
Ziklag?
Raphia
Sharuhen
Arad
Ar?
Beer-sheba
MOAB
Besor
Kir-hareseth
Zoar
Tamar
Ziph
Zered
Ascent of Akrabbim
Arabah
Negeb
EDOM
Desert

The Roman World
Limits of direct Roman rule or political influence at the birth of Christ
Provincial or state boundaries
SYRIA Roman provinces
LYCIA Client kingdoms or states
0 100 200 300 400 500 Mls
0 200 400 600 800 Kms
© Copyright HAMMOND INCORPORATED, Maplewood, N. J.
Britannia
Atlantic Ocean
Lost to Rome in A.D. 9
(Elbe)
Rhine
Germania
Lutetia
BELGICA
Augusta Treverorum
LUGDUNENSIS
Gaul
AQUITANIA
Burdigala
Lugdunum
Danube
RAETIA
NORICUM
ALPS
ALPES
NARBONENSIS
Narbo
TARRACONENSIS
LUSITANIA
Caesarea Augusta
Hispania
Emerita Augusta
Tarraco
BAETICA
Corduba
Tingis
MAURETANIA
Caesarea
Cirta
Carthage
Mare Internum
(Mediterranean Sea)
CORSICA AND SARDINIA
Caralis
Rome
Rubicon
ITALY
Aquileia
PANNONIA
ILLYRICUM
Salonae
Sea of Adria
Tarentum
SICILIA
Syracuse
AFRICA
Leptis Magna
Sarmatia
CARPATHIANS
Dacia
Ister (Danube)
MOESIA
THRACE
MACEDONIA
Byzantium
Thessalonica
ACHAIA
Corinth
Athens
Aegean Sea
CRETA
Cyrene
CYRENAICA
BOSPORUS KDM.
Black Sea
Sinope
Trapezus
BITHYNIA & PONTUS
Ancyra
Pergamum
ASIA
Ephesus
GALATIA
LYCIA
PAMPHYLIA
CILICIA
Tarsus
CAPPADOCIA
COMMAGENE
CYPRUS
Antioch
SYRIA
KDM. OF HEROD
Jerusalem
NABATEA
Alexandria
Memphis
EGYPT
Nile
Thebes
Red Sea
Arabia
Rha (Volga)
Caspian Sea
CAUCASUS
Colchis
Iberia
Albania
Artaxata
ARMENIA
PARTHIAN EMPIRE
Tigris
Euphrates
Ctesiphon

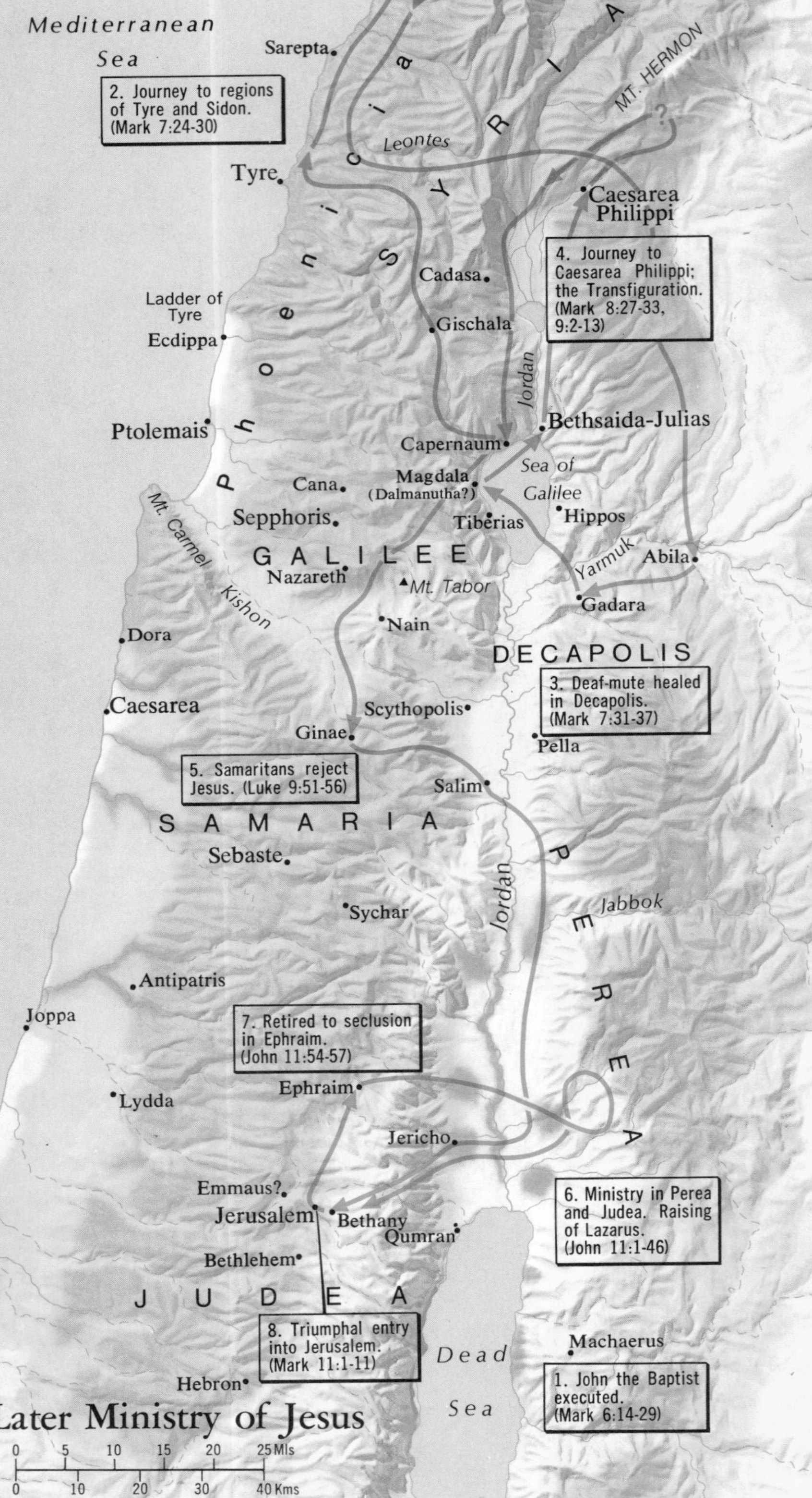
Mediterranean Sea
2. Journey to regions of Tyre and Sidon. (Mark 7:24-30)
Sarepta
Phoenicia
SYRIA
MT. HERMON
Leontes
Tyre
Caesarea Philippi
4. Journey to Caesarea Philippi; the Transfiguration. (Mark 8:27-33, 9:2-13)
Cadasa
Ladder of Tyre
Ecdippa
Gischala
Jordan
Ptolemais
Bethsaida-Julias
Capernaum
Sea of Galilee
Magdala (Dalmanutha?)
Cana
Mt. Carmel
Sepphoris
Tiberias
Hippos
GALILEE
Yarmuk
Abila
Nazareth
Mt. Tabor
Gadara
Kishon
Nain
Dora
DECAPOLIS
3. Deaf-mute healed in Decapolis. (Mark 7:31-37)
Caesarea
Scythopolis
Ginae
Pella
5. Samaritans reject Jesus. (Luke 9:51-56)
Salim
SAMARIA
Sebaste
PEREA
Jabbok
Sychar
Antipatris
Joppa
7. Retired to seclusion in Ephraim. (John 11:54-57)
Ephraim
Lydda
Jericho
Emmaus?
Jerusalem
Bethany
Qumran
6. Ministry in Perea and Judea. Raising of Lazarus. (John 11:1-46)
Bethlehem
JUDEA
8. Triumphal entry into Jerusalem. (Mark 11:1-11)
Machaerus
Dead Sea
Hebron
1. John the Baptist executed. (Mark 6:14-29)
0 5 10 15 20 25 Mls
0 10 20 30 40 Kms

Later Ministry of Jesus

Journeys of the Apostles
Philip's journeys
Saul's (Paul's) journeys
Peter's journey
Barnabas' journey
Barnabas' and Paul's journey
Barnabas' and Mark's journey
0 10 25 50 75 Mls
0 20 40 60 80 100 120 Kms
© Copyright HAMMOND INCORPORATED, Maplewood, N. J.
Tarsus
CILICIA
AMANUS MTS.
Alexandria
leucia Tracheotis
Antioch
Seleucia Pieria
Orontes
Laodicea ad Mare
Apamea
mis
CYPRUS
Epiphania
SYRIA
Ardus (Arvad)
Emesa
Mediterranean Sea
Tripolis
LEBANON
Byblos
Phoenicia
Heliopolis
Berytus
MT.
Chalcis
Leontes
Abilene
Sidon
Damascus
Tyre
Caesarea Philippi
NABATEANS
ARABIA
Ptolemais
Galilee
Sea of Galilee
Tiberias
?
Caesarea
Scythopolis
Decapolis
Bostra
Samaria
Pella
Sebaste
Jordan
Gerasa
Joppa
Lydda
Philadelphia
Azotus
Jerusalem
Jericho
Gaza
Judea
Dead Sea

Lands of the Bible in Modern Times